Who's Who in America®

1998

52nd Edition

Volume 2
L–Z

MARQUIS
Who'sWho®

121 Chanlon Road
New Providence, NJ 07974 U.S.A.

Table of Contents

Preface

"WHO'S WHO IN AMERICA *shall endeavor to list those individuals who are of current national reference interest and inquiry either because of meritorious achievement or because of the positions they hold."*

Albert Nelson Marquis
Founder, 1899

A Standard Reference Work

When the first edition of *Who's Who in America* appeared in 1899, it presented itself as a new and untried experiment in the field of American reference book publishing. It was the first publication ever issued which claimed to be, in any comprehensive degree, a general biographical directory of notable American contemporaries. During the generations that have passed, *Who's Who in America* has garnered a worldwide reputation for presenting the most accurate, current biographical data available. Quickly establishing itself as a standard reference work, it has grown steadily in public favor, and today is recognized globally as the premier reference pertaining to notable living Americans.

The 52nd Edition upholds the guiding principle set forth by A.N. Marquis in 1899: The editors of *Who's Who in America* continue to strive to identify and chronicle the achievements of men and women who have become the leaders in our society's political, cultural, and economic affairs.

One Principle Governs Selection

In 1899, Marquis Biographees numbered 8,602, or one person per 10,000 of U.S. population. In this 52nd Edition, Marquis Who's Who proudly presents the biographies of over 100,000 outstanding individuals. While our Biographees have grown in number, our selection standards remain stringent. Fewer than four in 10,000 people are included in *Who's Who in America*.

Selection is based solely on reference value. Individuals become eligible for listing by virtue of their positions and/or noteworthy achievements that have proven to be of significant value to society. An individual's desire to be listed is not sufficient reason for inclusion. Similarly, wealth or social position are not criteria. Of course, Marquis Who's Who has never charged a fee for publishing a biography, nor is purchase of the book ever a factor in the selection of Biographees.

Compiling the Most Accurate Biographical Data

Through fifty-two editions, the basic *Who's Who in America* compilation process has remained unchanged. Potential Biographees are identified by Marquis researchers and editors. Candidates are sent data forms and are invited to submit complete biographical and career information. These data are reviewed to confirm that candidates meet the stringent selection criteria. Sketches are then prepared and sent to Biographees for prepublication checking.

In some cases, Marquis staff members compile and/or verify the biographical data through independent research. Sketches compiled in this manner are denoted by asterisks. For a small number of cases, where detailed information is not available at publication, the editors have written brief sketches with current career information; these are also indicated by asterisks.

To maintain its reputation for currency, and at the same time to adhere to space limitations, *Who's Who in America* undergoes meticulous review of selection criteria with each edition. Deletion of some names is inevitable; such deletion is not arbitrary. For example, if a Biographee has retired from active participation in a career or public life, the sketch may be excluded. In large part, it is career development that determines inclusion and continuation.

Annual publication enables *Who's Who in America* to bring users more new names and update more existing entries each edition. In all, over 20,000 new names appear in the 52nd Edition.

Responding to Your Reference Needs

Who's Who in America provides a number of useful reference features. As a complement to the biographical profiles, the Geographic and Professional Indexes make *Who's Who in America* an even more productive research tool. Through these indexes, users can identify and locate individuals in any of thirty-eight categories, as well as by country, state, or city.

This edition also contains a cumulative Retiree Index of persons whose names were deleted from the 49th through 51st Editions because they have retired from active work. This index enables the user to locate the last published biographical sketch of each listee.

There is also a Necrology of Biographees whose sketches appeared in the 51st Edition and whose deaths were reported prior to the closing of this edition. The sketches have been removed from the book. (For those Biographees whose deaths were reported prior to July 1996, complete biographical information, including date of death and place of interment, can be found in Volume XI of *Who Was Who in America*.)

Finally, many of the women and men profiled in *Who's Who in America* have included in their biographies a listing of their avocations, thus providing additional insights into their personal lives and interests. Some of the sketches also end with an italicized feature, "Thoughts on My Life." The statement is written by the Biographees and reflects their own principles, goals, ideals, and values that have been guidelines for their success and achievement.

Our Challenge

Putting together a reference source as comprehensive as *Who's Who in America* is a monumental challenge. Over our long history, Marquis Who's Who researchers and editors have exercised diligent care in preparing each sketch for publication. Despite all precautions, however, errors do occasionally occur. Users of this directory are invited to notify the publisher of any such errors so that corrections can be made in a subsequent edition.

Board of Advisors

Marquis Who's Who gratefully acknowledges the following distinguished individuals who have made themselves available for review, evaluation, and general comment with regard to the publication of the 52nd Edition of *Who's Who in America*. The advisors have enhanced the reference value of this edition by the nomination of outstanding individuals for inclusion. However, the Board of Advisors, either collectively or individually, is in no way responsible for the selection of names appearing in this volume, nor does the Board of Advisors bear responsibility for the accuracy or comprehensiveness of the biographical information or other material contained herein.

Standards of Admission

The foremost consideration in determining who will be admitted to the pages of *Who's Who in America* is the extent of an individual's reference interest. Reference value is based on either of two factors: 1) the position of responsibility held or 2) the level of significant achievement attained in a career of noteworthy activity. The majority of Biographees qualify for admission on the basis of the first factor, a specific position of responsibility. Incumbency in the position makes the person someone of high reference interest. The factor of position includes the following categories:

1. High-ranking members of the executive, legislative, and judicial branches of the United States government. This group includes, for example, the President of the United States, members of Congress, cabinet secretaries, chief administrators of selected federal agencies and commissions, and justices of the federal courts.

2. Military officers on active duty with the rank of Major General or higher in the Army, Air Force, and Marine Corps, and of Rear Admiral or higher in the U.S. Navy.

3. Specified state government officials. Among these are governors, lieutenant governors, secretaries of state, attorneys general, and treasurers. Also included under this standard are presidents of state senates, state university system administrators, chief state health officers, and officials of American territories.

4. Judges of state and territorial courts of the highest appellate jurisdiction.

5. High-level officials of principal cities, based on population. These officials include mayors, police chiefs, school superintendents, and other selected positions.

6. Leading government officials of Canada and Mexico. In Canada, this group includes the prime minister, premiers of the provinces, ministers of departments of the federal government, and justices of the highest courts. Examples in the Mexican government are the president of the country and cabinet secretaries of the national government.

7. Principal officers of major national and international businesses as defined by several quantitative criteria.

8. Ranking administrative officials of major universities and colleges. Some of the officers included in this category are president, provost, dean, and selected department heads.

9. Heads of leading philanthropic, cultural, educational, professional, and scientific institutions and associations. These institutions include, for example, selected foundations, museums, symphony orchestras, libraries, and research laboratories.

10. Selected members of certain honorary and professional organizations, such as the National Academy of Sciences, the National Academy of Design, the American College of Trial Lawyers, and the Royal Society of Canada.

11. Chief ecclesiastics of the principal religious denominations.

12. Recipients of major national and international awards, such as the Nobel and Pulitzer Prizes, the Academy Awards and the Antoinette Perry, or Tony Awards. Also included are winners of important professional awards, such as the American Institute of Architecture's Gold Medal for Architecture.

Admission by the second factor—significant achievement—is based on the application of objective criteria established for each field. An artist whose works are included in major museums qualifies for admission for noteworthy accomplishment. The professor who has made important research contributions in his field is of reference interest because of his outstanding achievements. Qualitative standards determine eligibility for every field.

In many instances there is considerable overlap between the two factors used for inclusion in *Who's Who in America*. For example, the head of a major library is in the book because of position, but reaching that responsibility also signifies important achievement. Similarly, a state governor not only holds a position that warrants inclusion; attaining that post also represents significant achievement in the political world. In both cases, the reference value of the biographical sketch is significant. Whether the person has been selected because of position or as a mark of achievement, the Biographee in *Who's Who in America* has noteworthy accomplishments beyond those of the vast majority of contemporaries.

Key to Information

[1] **GIBSON, OSCAR JULIUS,** [2] physician, medical educator; [3] b. Syracuse, N.Y., Aug. 31, 1937; [4] s. Paul Oliver and Elizabeth H. (Thrun) G.; [5] m. Judith S. Gonzalez, Apr. 28, 1968; [6] children: Richard Gary, Matthew Cary, Samuel Perry. [7] BA magna cum laude, U. Pa., 1960; MD, Harvard U., 1964. [8] Diplomate Am. Bd. Internal Medicine, Am. Bd. Preventive Medicine. [9] Intern Barnes Hosp., St. Louis, 1964-65, resident, 1965-66; clin. assoc. Nat. Heart Inst., NIH, Bethesda, Md., 1966-68; chief resident medicine U. Okla. Hosps., 1968-69; asst. prof. community health Okla. Med. Ctr., 1969-70, assoc. prof., 1970-74, prof., chmn. dept., 1974-80; dean U. Okla. Coll. Medicine, 1978-82; v.p. med. staff affairs Bapt. Med. Ctr., Oklahoma City, 1982-86, exec. v.p., 1986-88, chmn., 1988-95, chmn, CEO, 1995—; [10] mem. governing bd. Ambulatory Health Care Consortium, Inc., 1979-80; mem. Okla. Bd. Medicolegal Examiners, 1985—; mem. Okla. Bd. of Medical Ethics, 1994—. [11] Contrb. articles to profl. jours. [12] Bd. dirs., v.p. Okla. Arthritis Found., 1982—; trustee North Central Mental Health Ctr., 1985—. [13] Served with U.S. Army, 1955-56. [14] Recipient R.T. Chadwick award NIH, 1968; Am. Heart Assn. grantee, 1985-86, 88, 1995-96. [15] Fellow Assn. Tchrs. Preventive Medicine; mem. Am. Fedn. Clin. Research, Assn. Med. Colls., AAAS, AMA, Masons, Shriners, Sigma Xi. [16] Republican. [17] Roman Catholic. [18] Avocations: swimming, weight lifting, travel. [19] Home: 6060 N Ridge Ave Oklahoma City OK 73126 [20] Office: Bapt Med Ctr 1986 Cuba Hwy Oklahoma City OK 73120

KEY

[1]   Name
[2]   Occupation
[3]   Vital statistics
[4]   Parents
[5]   Marriage
[6]   Children
[7]   Education
[8]   Professional certifications
[9]   Career
[10] Career-related
[11] Writings and creative works
[12] Civic and political activities
[13] Military
[14] Awards and fellowships
[15] Professional and association memberships, clubs and lodges
[16] Political affiliation
[17] Religion
[18] Avocations
[19] Home address
[20] Office address

Table of Abbreviations

The following abbreviations and symbols are frequently used in this book.

*An asterisk following a sketch indicates that it was researched by the Marquis Who's Who editorial staff and has not been verified by the Biographee.

A Associate (used with academic degrees only)

AA, A.A. Associate in Arts, Associate of Arts

AAAL American Academy of Arts and Letters

AAAS American Association for the Advancement of Science

AACD American Association for Counseling and Development

AACN American Association of Critical Care Nurses

AAHA American Academy of Health Administrators

AAHP American Association of Hospital Planners

AAHPERD American Alliance for Health, Physical Education, Recreation, and Dance

AAS Associate of Applied Science

AASL American Association of School Librarians

AASPA American Association of School Personnel Administrators

AAU Amateur Athletic Union

AAUP American Association of University Professors

AAUW American Association of University Women

AB, A.B. Arts, Bachelor of

AB Alberta

ABA American Bar Association

ABC American Broadcasting Company

AC Air Corps

acad. academy, academic

acct. accountant

acctg. accounting

ACDA Arms Control and Disarmament Agency

ACHA American College of Hospital Administrators

ACLS Advanced Cardiac Life Support

ACLU American Civil Liberties Union

ACOG American College of Ob-Gyn

ACP American College of Physicians

ACS American College of Surgeons

ADA American Dental Association

a.d.c. aide-de-camp

adj. adjunct, adjutant

adj. gen. adjutant general

adm. admiral

adminstr. administrator

adminstrn. administration

adminstrv. administrative

ADN Associate's Degree in Nursing

ADP Automatic Data Processing

adv. advocate, advisory

advt. advertising

AE, A.E. Agricultural Engineer

A.E. and P. Ambassador Extraordinary and Plenipotentiary

AEC Atomic Energy Commission

aero. aeronautical, aeronautic

aerodyn. aerodynamic

AFB Air Force Base

AFL-CIO American Federation of Labor and Congress of Industrial Organizations

AFTRA American Federation of TV and Radio Artists

AFSCME American Federation of State, County and Municipal Employees

agr. agriculture

agrl. agricultural

agt. agent

AGVA American Guild of Variety Artists

agy. agency

A&I Agricultural and Industrial

AIA American Institute of Architects

AIAA American Institute of Aeronautics and Astronautics

AIChE American Institute of Chemical Engineers

AICPA American Institute of Certified Public Accountants

AID Agency for International Development

AIDS Acquired Immune Deficiency Syndrome

AIEE American Institute of Electrical Engineers

AIM American Institute of Management

AIME American Institute of Mining, Metallurgy, and Petroleum Engineers

AK Alaska

AL Alabama

ALA American Library Association

Ala. Alabama

alt. alternate

Alta. Alberta

A&M Agricultural and Mechanical

AM, A.M. Arts, Master of

Am. American, America

AMA American Medical Association

amb. ambassador

A.M.E. African Methodist Episcopal

Amtrak National Railroad Passenger Corporation

AMVETS American Veterans of World War II, Korea, Vietnam

ANA American Nurses Association

anat. anatomical

ANCC American Nurses Credentialing Center

ann. annual

ANTA American National Theatre and Academy

anthrop. anthropological

AP Associated Press

APA American Psychological Association

APGA American Personnel Guidance Association

APHA American Public Health Association

APO Army Post Office

apptd. appointed

Apr. April

apt. apartment

AR Arkansas

ARC American Red Cross

arch. architect

archeol. archeological

archtl. architectural

Ariz. Arizona

Ark. Arkansas

ArtsD, ArtsD. Arts, Doctor of

arty. artillery

AS American Samoa

AS Associate in Science

ASCAP American Society of Composers, Authors and Publishers

ASCD Association for Supervision and Curriculum Development

ASCE American Society of Civil Engineers

ASHRAE American Society of Heating, Refrigeration, and Air Conditioning Engineers

ASME American Society of Mechanical Engineers

ASNSA American Society for Nursing Service Administrators

ASPA American Society for Public Administration

ASPCA American Society for the Prevention of Cruelty to Animals

assn. association

assoc. associate

asst. assistant

ASTD American Society for Training and Development

ASTM American Society for Testing and Materials

astron. astronomical

astrophys. astrophysical

ATLA Association of Trial Lawyers of America

ATSC Air Technical Service Command

AT&T American Telephone & Telegraph Company

atty. attorney

Aug. August

AUS Army of the United States

aux. auxiliary

Ave. Avenue

AVMA American Veterinary Medical Association

AZ Arizona

AWHONN Association of Women's Health Obstetric and Neonatal Nurses

B. Bachelor

b. born

BA, B.A. Bachelor of Arts

BAgr, B.Agr. Bachelor of Agriculture

Balt. Baltimore

Bapt. Baptist

BArch, B.Arch. Bachelor of Architecture

BAS, B.A.S. Bachelor of Agricultural Science

BBA, B.B.A. Bachelor of Business Administration

BBB Better Business Bureau

BBC British Broadcasting Corporation

BC, B.C. British Columbia
BCE, B.C.E. Bachelor of Civil Engineering
BChir, B.Chir. Bachelor of Surgery
BCL, B.C.L. Bachelor of Civil Law
BCLS Basic Cardiac Life Support
BCS, B.C.S. Bachelor of Commercial Science
BD, B.D. Bachelor of Divinity
bd. board
BE, B.E. Bachelor of Education
BEE, B.E.E. Bachelor of Electrical
   Engineering
BFA, B.F.A. Bachelor of Fine Arts
bibl. biblical
bibliog. bibliographical
biog. biographical
biol. biological
BJ, B.J. Bachelor of Journalism
Bklyn. Brooklyn
BL, B.L. Bachelor of Letters
bldg. building
BLS, B.L.S. Bachelor of Library Science
BLS Basic Life Support
Blvd. Boulevard
BMI Broadcast Music, Inc.
BMW Bavarian Motor Works (Bayerische
   Motoren Werke)
bn. battalion
B.&O.R.R. Baltimore & Ohio Railroad
bot. botanical
BPE, B.P.E. Bachelor of Physical Education
BPhil, B.Phil. Bachelor of Philosophy
br. branch
BRE, B.R.E. Bachelor of Religious
   Education
brig. gen. brigadier general
Brit. British, Brittanica
Bros. Brothers
BS, B.S. Bachelor of Science
BSA, B.S.A. Bachelor of Agricultural Science
BSBA Bachelor of Science in Business
   Administration
BSChemE Bachelor of Science in Chemical
   Engineering
BSD, B.S.D. Bachelor of Didactic Science
BSEE Bachelor of Science in Electrical
   Engineering
BSN Bachelor of Science in Nursing
BST, B.S.T. Bachelor of Sacred Theology
BTh, B.Th. Bachelor of Theology
bull. bulletin
bur. bureau
bus. business
B.W.I. British West Indies

CA California
CAA Civil Aeronautics Administration
CAB Civil Aeronautics Board
CAD-CAM Computer Aided Design–
   Computer Aided Model
Calif. California
C.Am. Central America
Can. Canada, Canadian
CAP Civil Air Patrol
capt. captain
cardiol. cardiological
cardiovasc. cardiovascular
CARE Cooperative American Relief
   Everywhere
Cath. Catholic
cav. cavalry
CBC Canadian Broadcasting Company
CBI China, Burma, India Theatre of
   Operations
CBS Columbia Broadcasting Company
C.C. Community College
CCC Commodity Credit Corporation
CCNY City College of New York

CCRN Critical Care Registered Nurse
CCU Cardiac Care Unit
CD Civil Defense
CE, C.E. Corps of Engineers, Civil Engineer
CEN Certified Emergency Nurse
CENTO Central Treaty Organization
CEO chief executive officer
CERN European Organization of Nuclear
   Research
cert. certificate, certification, certified
CETA Comprehensive Employment Training
   Act
CFA Chartered Financial Analyst
CFL Canadian Football League
CFO chief financial officer
CFP Certified Financial Planner
ch. church
ChD, Ch.D. Doctor of Chemistry
chem. chemical
ChemE, Chem.E. Chemical Engineer
ChFC Chartered Financial Consultant
Chgo. Chicago
chirurg. chirurgical
chmn. chairman
chpt. chapter
CIA Central Intelligence Agency
Cin. Cincinnati
cir. circle, circuit
CLE Continuing Legal Education
Cleve. Cleveland
climatol. climatological
clin. clinical
clk. clerk
C.L.U. Chartered Life Underwriter
CM, C.M. Master in Surgery
CM Northern Mariana Islands
CMA Certified Medical Assistant
cmty. community
CNA Certified Nurse's Aide
CNOR Certified Nurse (Operating Room)
C.&N.W.Ry. Chicago & North Western
   Railway
CO Colorado
Co. Company
COF Catholic Order of Foresters
C. of C. Chamber of Commerce
col. colonel
coll. college
Colo. Colorado
com. committee
comd. commanded
comdg. commanding
comdr. commander
comdt. commandant
comm. communications
commd. commissioned
comml. commercial
commn. commission
commr. commissioner
compt. comptroller
condr. conductor
Conf. Conference
Congl. Congregational, Congressional
Conglist. Congregationalist
Conn. Connecticut
cons. consultant, consulting
consol. consolidated
constl. constitutional
constn. constitution
constrn. construction
contbd. contributed
contbg. contributing
contbn. contribution
contbr. contributor
contr. controller
Conv. Convention
COO chief operating officer

coop. cooperative
coord. coordinator
CORDS Civil Operations and Revolutionary
   Development Support
CORE Congress of Racial Equality
corp. corporation, corporate
corr. correspondent, corresponding,
   correspondence
C.&O.Ry. Chesapeake & Ohio Railway
coun. council
CPA Certified Public Accountant
CPCU Chartered Property and Casualty
   Underwriter
CPH, C.P.H. Certificate of Public Health
cpl. corporal
CPR Cardio-Pulmonary Resuscitation
C.P.Ry. Canadian Pacific Railway
CRT Cathode Ray Terminal
C.S. Christian Science
CSB, C.S.B. Bachelor of Christian Science
C.S.C. Civil Service Commission
CT Connecticut
ct. court
ctr. center
ctrl. central
CWS Chemical Warfare Service
C.Z. Canal Zone

D. Doctor
d. daughter
DAgr, D.Agr. Doctor of Agriculture
DAR Daughters of the American Revolution
dau. daughter
DAV Disabled American Veterans
DC, D.C. District of Columbia
DCL, D.C.L. Doctor of Civil Law
DCS, D.C.S. Doctor of Commercial Science
DD, D.D. Doctor of Divinity
DDS, D.D.S. Doctor of Dental Surgery
DE Delaware
Dec. December
dec. deceased
def. defense
Del. Delaware
del. delegate, delegation
Dem. Democrat, Democratic
DEng, D.Eng. Doctor of Engineering
denom. denomination, denominational
dep. deputy
dept. department
dermatol. dermatological
desc. descendant
devel. development, developmental
DFA, D.F.A. Doctor of Fine Arts
D.F.C. Distinguished Flying Cross
DHL, D.H.L. Doctor of Hebrew Literature
dir. director
dist. district
distbg. distributing
distbn. distribution
distbr. distributor
disting. distinguished
div. division, divinity, divorce
divsn. division
DLitt, D.Litt. Doctor of Literature
DMD, D.M.D. Doctor of Dental Medicine
DMS, D.M.S. Doctor of Medical Science
DO, D.O. Doctor of Osteopathy
docs. documents
DON Director of Nursing
DPH, D.P.H. Diploma in Public Health
DPhil, D.Phil. Doctor of Philosophy
D.R. Daughters of the Revolution
Dr. Drive, Doctor
DRE, D.R.E. Doctor of Religious Education
DrPH, Dr.P.H. Doctor of Public Health,
   Doctor of Public Hygiene
D.S.C. Distinguished Service Cross

DSc, D.Sc. Doctor of Science
DSChemE Doctor of Science in Chemical Engineering
D.S.M. Distinguished Service Medal
DST, D.S.T. Doctor of Sacred Theology
DTM, D.T.M. Doctor of Tropical Medicine
DVM, D.V.M. Doctor of Veterinary Medicine
DVS, D.V.S. Doctor of Veterinary Surgery

E, E. East
ea. eastern
E. and P. Extraordinary and Plenipotentiary
Eccles. Ecclesiastical
ecol. ecological
econ. economic
ECOSOC Economic and Social Council (of the UN)
ED, E.D. Doctor of Engineering
ed. educated
EdB, Ed.B. Bachelor of Education
EdD, Ed.D. Doctor of Education
edit. edition
editl. editorial
EdM, Ed.M. Master of Education
edn. education
ednl. educational
EDP Electronic Data Processing
EdS, Ed.S. Specialist in Education
EE, E.E. Electrical Engineer
E.E. and M.P. Envoy Extraordinary and Minister Plenipotentiary
EEC European Economic Community
EEG Electroencephalogram
EEO Equal Employment Opportunity
EEOC Equal Employment Opportunity Commission
E.Ger. German Democratic Republic
EKG Electrocardiogram
elec. electrical
electrochem. electrochemical
electrophys. electrophysical
elem. elementary
EM, E.M. Engineer of Mines
EMT Emergency Medical Technician
ency. encyclopedia
Eng. England
engr. engineer
engring. engineering
entomol. entomological
environ. environmental
EPA Environmental Protection Agency
epidemiol. epidemiological
Episc. Episcopalian
ERA Equal Rights Amendment
ERDA Energy Research and Development Administration
ESEA Elementary and Secondary Education Act
ESL English as Second Language
ESPN Entertainment and Sports Programming Network
ESSA Environmental Science Services Administration
ethnol. ethnological
ETO European Theatre of Operations
Evang. Evangelical
exam. examination, examining
Exch. Exchange
exec. executive
exhbn. exhibition
expdn. expedition
expn. exposition
expt. experiment
exptl. experimental
Expy. Expressway
Ext. Extension

F.A. Field Artillery
FAA Federal Aviation Administration
FAO Food and Agriculture Organization (of the UN)
FBA Federal Bar Association
FBI Federal Bureau of Investigation
FCA Farm Credit Administration
FCC Federal Communications Commission
FCDA Federal Civil Defense Administration
FDA Food and Drug Administration
FDIA Federal Deposit Insurance Administration
FDIC Federal Deposit Insurance Corporation
FE, F.E. Forest Engineer
FEA Federal Energy Administration
Feb. February
fed. federal
fedn. federation
FERC Federal Energy Regulatory Commission
fgn. foreign
FHA Federal Housing Administration
fin. financial, finance
FL Florida
Fl. Floor
Fla. Florida
FMC Federal Maritime Commission
FNP Family Nurse Practitioner
FOA Foreign Operations Administration
found. foundation
FPC Federal Power Commission
FPO Fleet Post Office
frat. fraternity
FRS Federal Reserve System
FSA Federal Security Agency
Ft. Fort
FTC Federal Trade Commission
Fwy. Freeway

G-1 (or other number) Division of General Staff
GA, Ga. Georgia
GAO General Accounting Office
gastroent. gastroenterological
GATE Gifted and Talented Educators
GATT General Agreement on Tariffs and Trade
GE General Electric Company
gen. general
geneal. genealogical
geod. geodetic
geog. geographic, geographical
geol. geological
geophys. geophysical
geriat. geriatrics
gerontol. gerontological
G.H.Q. General Headquarters
GM General Motors Corporation
GMAC General Motors Acceptance Corporation
G.N.Ry. Great Northern Railway
gov. governor
govt. government
govtl. governmental
GPO Government Printing Office
grad. graduate, graduated
GSA General Services Administration
Gt. Great
GTE General Telephone and ElectricCompany
GU Guam
gynecol. gynecological

HBO Home Box Office
hdqs. headquarters

HEW Department of Health, Education and Welfare
HHD, H.H.D. Doctor of Humanities
HHFA Housing and Home Finance Agency
HHS Department of Health and Human Services
HI Hawaii
hist. historical, historic
HM, H.M. Master of Humanities
HMO Health Maintenance Organization
homeo. homeopathic
hon. honorary, honorable
Ho. of Dels. House of Delegates
Ho. of Reps. House of Representatives
hort. horticultural
hosp. hospital
H.S. High School
HUD Department of Housing and Urban Development
Hwy. Highway
hydrog. hydrographic

IA Iowa
IAEA International Atomic Energy Agency
IATSE International Alliance of Theatrical and Stage Employees and Moving Picture Operators of the United States and Canada
IBM International Business Machines Corporation
IBRD International Bank for Reconstruction and Development
ICA International Cooperation Administration
ICC Interstate Commerce Commission
ICCE International Council for Computers in Education
ICU Intensive Care Unit
ID Idaho
IEEE Institute of Electrical and Electronics Engineers
IFC International Finance Corporation
IGY International Geophysical Year
IL Illinois
Ill. Illinois
illus. illustrated
ILO International Labor Organization
IMF International Monetary Fund
IN Indiana
Inc. Incorporated
Ind. Indiana
ind. independent
Indpls. Indianapolis
indsl. industrial
inf. infantry
info. information
ins. insurance
insp. inspector
insp. gen. inspector general
inst. institute
instl. institutional
instn. institution
instr. instructor
instrn. instruction
instrnl. instructional
internat. international
intro. introduction
IRE Institute of Radio Engineers
IRS Internal Revenue Service
ITT International Telephone & Telegraph Corporation

JAG Judge Advocate General
JAGC Judge Advocate General Corps
Jan. January
Jaycees Junior Chamber of Commerce
JB, J.B. Jurum Baccalaureus

JCB, J.C.B. Juris Canoni Baccalaureus
JCD, J.C.D. Juris Canonici Doctor, Juris
 Civilis Doctor
JCL, J.C.L. Juris Canonici Licentiatus
JD, J.D. Juris Doctor
jg. junior grade
jour. journal
jr. junior
JSD, J.S.D. Juris Scientiae Doctor
JUD, J.U.D. Juris Utriusque Doctor
jud. judicial

Kans. Kansas
K.C. Knights of Columbus
K.P. Knights of Pythias
KS Kansas
K.T. Knight Templar
KY, Ky. Kentucky

LA, La. Louisiana
L.A. Los Angeles
lab. laboratory
L.Am. Latin America
lang. language
laryngol. laryngological
LB Labrador
LDS Latter Day Saints
LDS Church Church of Jesus Christ of Latter
 Day Saints
lectr. lecturer
legis. legislation, legislative
LHD, L.H.D. Doctor of Humane Letters
L.I. Long Island
libr. librarian, library
lic. licensed, license
L.I.R.R. Long Island Railroad
lit. literature
litig. litigation
LittB, Litt.B. Bachelor of Letters
LittD, Litt.D. Doctor of Letters
LLB, LL.B. Bachelor of Laws
LLD, L.L.D. Doctor of Laws
LLM, L.L.M. Master of Laws
Ln. Lane
L.&N.R.R. Louisville & Nashville Railroad
LPGA Ladies Professional Golf Association
LPN Licensed Practical Nurse
LS, L.S. Library Science (in degree)
lt. lieutenant
Ltd. Limited
Luth. Lutheran
LWV League of Women Voters

M. Master
m. married
MA, M.A. Master of Arts
MA Massachusetts
MADD Mothers Against Drunk Driving
mag. magazine
MAgr, M.Agr. Master of Agriculture
maj. major
Man. Manitoba
Mar. March
MArch, M.Arch. Master in Architecture
Mass. Massachusetts
math. mathematics, mathematical
MATS Military Air Transport Service
MB, M.B. Bachelor of Medicine
MB Manitoba
MBA, M.B.A. Master of Business
 Administration
MBS Mutual Broadcasting System
M.C. Medical Corps
MCE, M.C.E. Master of Civil Engineering
mcht. merchant
mcpl. municipal
MCS, M.C.S. Master of Commercial Science

MD, M.D. Doctor of Medicine
MD, Md. Maryland
MDiv Master of Divinity
MDip, M.Dip. Master in Diplomacy
mdse. merchandise
MDV, M.D.V. Doctor of Veterinary
 Medicine
ME, M.E. Mechanical Engineer
ME Maine
M.E.Ch. Methodist Episcopal Church
mech. mechanical
MEd., M.Ed. Master of Education
med. medical
MEE, M.E.E. Master of Electrical
 Engineering
mem. member
meml. memorial
merc. mercantile
met. metropolitan
metall. metallurgical
MetE, Met.E. Metallurgical Engineer
meteorol. meteorological
Meth. Methodist
Mex. Mexico
MF, M.F. Master of Forestry
MFA, M.F.A. Master of Fine Arts
mfg. manufacturing
mfr. manufacturer
mgmt. management
mgr. manager
MHA, M.H.A. Master of Hospital
 Administration
M.I. Military Intelligence
MI Michigan
Mich. Michigan
micros. microscopic, microscopical
mid. middle
mil. military
Milw. Milwaukee
Min. Minister
mineral. mineralogical
Minn. Minnesota
MIS Management Information Systems
Miss. Mississippi
MIT Massachusetts Institute of Technology
mktg. marketing
ML, M.L. Master of Laws
MLA Modern Language Association
M.L.D. Magister Legnum Diplomatic
MLitt, M.Litt. Master of Literature, Master
 of Letters
MLS, M.L.S. Master of Library Science
MME, M.M.E. Master of Mechanical
 Engineering
MN Minnesota
mng. managing
MO, Mo. Missouri
moblzn. mobilization
Mont. Montana
MP Northern Mariana Islands
M.P. Member of Parliament
MPA Master of Public Administration
MPE, M.P.E. Master of Physical Education
MPH, M.P.H. Master of Public Health
MPhil, M.Phil. Master of Philosophy
MPL, M.P.L. Master of Patent Law
Mpls. Minneapolis
MRE, M.R.E. Master of Religious Education
MRI Magnetic Resonance Imaging
MS, M.S. Master of Science
MS, Ms. Mississippi
MSc, M.Sc. Master of Science
MSChemE Master of Science in Chemical
 Engineering
MSEE Master of Science in Electrical
 Engineering

MSF, M.S.F. Master of Science of Forestry
MSN Master of Science in Nursing
MST, M.S.T. Master of Sacred Theology
MSW, M.S.W. Master of Social Work
MT Montana
Mt. Mount
MTO Mediterranean Theatre of Operation
MTV Music Television
mus. museum, musical
MusB, Mus.B. Bachelor of Music
MusD, Mus.D. Doctor of Music
MusM, Mus.M. Master of Music
mut. mutual
MVP Most Valuable Player
mycol. mycological

N. North
NAACOG Nurses Association of the
 American College of Obstetricians and
 Gynecologists
NAACP National Association for the
 Advancement of Colored People
NACA National Advisory Committee for
 Aeronautics
NACDL National Association of Criminal
 Defense Lawyers
NACU National Association of Colleges and
 Universities
NAD National Academy of Design
NAE National Academy of Engineering,
 National Association of Educators
NAESP National Association of Elementary
 School Principals
NAFE National Association of Female
 Executives
N.Am. North America
NAM National Association of Manufacturers
NAMH National Association for Mental
 Health
NAPA National Association of Performing
 Artists
NARAS National Academy of Recording
 Arts and Sciences
NAREB National Association of Real Estate
 Boards
NARS National Archives and Record Service
NAS National Academy of Sciences
NASA National Aeronautics and Space
 Administration
NASP National Association of School
 Psychologists
NASW National Association of Social
 Workers
nat. national
NATAS National Academy of Television
 Arts and Sciences
NATO North Atlantic Treaty Organization
NATOUSA North African Theatre of
 Operations, United States Army
nav. navigation
NB, N.B. New Brunswick
NBA National Basketball Association
NBC National Broadcasting Company
NC, N.C. North Carolina
NCAA National College Athletic Association
NCCJ National Conference of Christians and
 Jews
ND, N.D. North Dakota
NDEA National Defense Education Act
NE Nebraska
NE, N.E. Northeast
NEA National Education Association
Nebr. Nebraska
NEH National Endowment for Humanities
neurol. neurological
Nev. Nevada
NF Newfoundland

NFL National Football League
Nfld. Newfoundland
NG National Guard
NH, N.H. New Hampshire
NHL National Hockey League
NIH National Institutes of Health
NIMH National Institute of Mental Health
NJ, N.J. New Jersey
NLRB National Labor Relations Board
NM New Mexico
N.Mex. New Mexico
No. Northern
NOAA National Oceanographic and
    Atmospheric Administration
NORAD North America Air Defense
Nov. November
NOW National Organization for Women
N.P.Ry. Northern Pacific Railway
nr. near
NRA National Rifle Association
NRC National Research Council
NS, N.S. Nova Scotia
NSC National Security Council
NSF National Science Foundation
NSTA National Science Teachers Association
NSW New South Wales
N.T. New Testament
NT Northwest Territories
nuc. nuclear
numis. numismatic
NV Nevada
NW, N.W. Northwest
N.W.T. Northwest Territories
NY, N.Y. New York
N.Y.C. New York City
NYU New York University
N.Z. New Zealand

OAS Organization of American States
ob-gyn obstetrics-gynecology
obs. observatory
obstet. obstetrical
occupl. occupational
oceanog. oceanographic
Oct. October
OD, O.D. Doctor of Optometry
OECD Organization for Economic
    Cooperation and Development
OEEC Organization of European Economic
    Cooperation
OEO Office of Economic Opportunity
ofcl. official
OH Ohio
OK Oklahoma
Okla. Oklahoma
ON Ontario
Ont. Ontario
oper. operating
ophthal. ophthalmological
ops. operations
OR Oregon
orch. orchestra
Oreg. Oregon
orgn. organization
orgnl. organizational
ornithol. ornithological
orthop. orthopedic
OSHA Occupational Safety and Health
    Administration
OSRD Office of Scientific Research and
    Development
OSS Office of Strategic Services
osteo. osteopathic
otol. otological
otolaryn. otolaryngological

PA, Pa. Pennsylvania

P.A. Professional Association
paleontol. paleontological
path. pathological
PBS Public Broadcasting System
P.C. Professional Corporation
PE Prince Edward Island
pediat. pediatrics
P.E.I. Prince Edward Island
PEN Poets, Playwrights, Editors, Essayists
    and Novelists (international association)
penol. penological
P.E.O. women's organization (full name not
    disclosed)
pers. personnel
pfc. private first class
PGA Professional Golfers' Association of
    America
PHA Public Housing Administration
pharm. pharmaceutical
PharmD, Pharm.D. Doctor of Pharmacy
PharmM, Pharm.M. Master of Pharmacy
PhB, Ph.B. Bachelor of Philosophy
PhD, Ph.D. Doctor of Philosophy
PhDChemE Doctor of Science in Chemical
    Engineering
PhM, Ph.M. Master of Philosophy
Phila. Philadelphia
philharm. philharmonic
philol. philological
philos. philosophical
photog. photographic
phys. physical
physiol. physiological
Pitts. Pittsburgh
Pk. Park
Pky. Parkway
Pl. Place
P.&L.E.R.R. Pittsburgh & Lake Erie
    Railroad
Plz. Plaza
PNP Pediatric Nurse Practitioner
P.O. Post Office
PO Box Post Office Box
polit. political
poly. polytechnic, polytechnical
PQ Province of Quebec
PR, P.R. Puerto Rico
prep. preparatory
pres. president
Presbyn. Presbyterian
presdl. presidential
prin. principal
procs. proceedings
prod. produced (play production)
prodn. production
prodr. producer
prof. professor
profl. professional
prog. progressive
propr. proprietor
pros. atty. prosecuting attorney
pro tem. pro tempore
PSRO Professional Services Review
    Organization
psychiat. psychiatric
psychol. psychological
PTA Parent-Teachers Association
ptnr. partner
PTO Pacific Theatre of Operations, Parent
    Teacher Organization
pub. publisher, publishing, published
pub. public
publ. publication
pvt. private

quar. quarterly
qm. quartermaster

Q.M.C. Quartermaster Corps
Que. Quebec

radiol. radiological
RAF Royal Air Force
RCA Radio Corporation of America
RCAF Royal Canadian Air Force
RD Rural Delivery
Rd. Road
R&D Research & Development
REA Rural Electrification Administration
rec. recording
ref. reformed
regt. regiment
regtl. regimental
rehab. rehabilitation
rels. relations
Rep. Republican
rep. representative
Res. Reserve
ret. retired
Rev. Reverend
rev. review, revised
RFC Reconstruction Finance Corporation
RFD Rural Free Delivery
rhinol. rhinological
RI, R.I. Rhode Island
RISD Rhode Island School of Design
Rlwy. Railway
Rm. Room
RN, R.N. Registered Nurse
roentgenol. roentgenological
ROTC Reserve Officers Training Corps
RR Rural Route
R.R. Railroad
rsch. research
rschr. researcher
Rt. Route

S. South
s. son
SAC Strategic Air Command
SAG Screen Actors Guild
SALT Strategic Arms Limitation Talks
S.Am. South America
san. sanitary
SAR Sons of the American Revolution
Sask. Saskatchewan
savs. savings
SB, S.B. Bachelor of Science
SBA Small Business Administration
SC, S.C. South Carolina
SCAP Supreme Command Allies Pacific
ScB, Sc.B. Bachelor of Science
SCD, S.C.D. Doctor of Commercial Science
ScD, Sc.D. Doctor of Science
sch. school
sci. science, scientific
SCLC Southern Christian Leadership
    Conference
SCV Sons of Confederate Veterans
SD, S.D. South Dakota
SE, S.E. Southeast
SEATO Southeast Asia Treaty Organization
SEC Securities and Exchange Commission
sec. secretary
sect. section
seismol. seismological
sem. seminary
Sept. September
s.g. senior grade
sgt. sergeant
SHAEF Supreme Headquarters Allied
    Expeditionary Forces
SHAPE Supreme Headquarters Allied Powers
    in Europe
S.I. Staten Island

S.J. Society of Jesus (Jesuit)
SJD Scientiae Juridicae Doctor
SK Saskatchewan
SM, S.M. Master of Science
SNP Society of Nursing Professionals
So. Southern
soc. society
sociol. sociological
S.P.Co. Southern Pacific Company
spkr. speaker
spl. special
splty. specialty
Sq. Square
S.R. Sons of the Revolution
sr. senior
SS Steamship
SSS Selective Service System
St. Saint, Street
sta. station
stats. statistics
statis. statistical
STB, S.T.B. Bachelor of Sacred Theology
stblzn. stabilization
STD, S.T.D. Doctor of Sacred Theology
std. standard
Ste. Suite
subs. subsidiary
SUNY State University of New York
supr. supervisor
supt. superintendent
surg. surgical
svc. service
SW, S.W. Southwest
sys. system

TAPPI Technical Association of the Pulp and Paper Industry
tb. tuberculosis
tchg. teaching
tchr. teacher
tech. technical, technology
technol. technological
tel. telephone
Tel. & Tel. Telephone & Telegraph
telecom. telecommunications
temp. temporary
Tenn. Tennessee
Ter. Territory
Ter. Terrace
TESOL Teachers of English to Speakers of Other Languages
Tex. Texas
ThD, Th.D. Doctor of Theology
theol. theological

ThM, Th.M. Master of Theology
TN Tennessee
tng. training
topog. topographical
trans. transaction, transferred
transl. translation, translated
transp. transportation
treas. treasurer
TT Trust Territory
TV television
TVA Tennessee Valley Authority
TWA Trans World Airlines
twp. township
TX Texas
typog. typographical

U. University
UAW United Auto Workers
UCLA University of California at Los Angeles
UDC United Daughters of the Confederacy
U.K. United Kingdom
UN United Nations
UNESCO United Nations Educational, Scientific and Cultural Organization
UNICEF United Nations International Children's Emergency Fund
univ. university
UNRRA United Nations Relief and Rehabilitation Administration
UPI United Press International
U.P.R.R. United Pacific Railroad
urol. urological
U.S. United States
U.S.A. United States of America
USAAF United States Army Air Force
USAF United States Air Force
USAFR United States Air Force Reserve
USAR United States Army Reserve
USCG United States Coast Guard
USCGR United States Coast Guard Reserve
USES United States Employment Service
USIA United States Information Agency
USMC United States Marine Corps
USMCR United States Marine Corps Reserve
USN United States Navy
USNG United States National Guard
USNR United States Naval Reserve
USO United Service Organizations
USPHS United States Public Health Service
USS United States Ship
USSR Union of the Soviet Socialist Republics
USTA United States Tennis Association

USV United States Volunteers
UT Utah

VA Veterans Administration
VA, Va. Virginia
vet. veteran, veterinary
VFW Veterans of Foreign Wars
VI, V.I. Virgin Islands
vice pres. vice president
vis. visiting
VISTA Volunteers in Service to America
VITA Volunteers in Technical Assistance
vocat. vocational
vol. volunteer, volume
v.p. vice president
vs. versus
VT, Vt. Vermont

W, W. West
WA Washington (state)
WAC Women's Army Corps
Wash. Washington (state)
WATS Wide Area Telecommunications Service
WAVES Women's Reserve, US Naval Reserve
WCTU Women's Christian Temperance Union
we. western
W. Ger. Germany, Federal Republic of
WHO World Health Organization
WI Wisconsin
W.I. West Indies
Wis. Wisconsin
WSB Wage Stabilization Board
WV West Virginia
W.Va. West Virginia
WWI World War I
WWII World War II
WY Wyoming
Wyo. Wyoming

YK Yukon Territory
YMCA Young Men's Christian Association
YMHA Young Men's Hebrew Association
YM & YWHA Young Men's and Young Women's Hebrew Association
yr. year
YT, Y.T. Yukon Territory
YWCA Young Women's Christian Association

zool. zoological

Alphabetical Practices

Names are arranged alphabetically according to the surnames, and under identical surnames according to the first given name. If both surname and first given name are identical, names are arranged alphabetically according to the second given name.

Surnames beginning with De, Des, Du, however capitalized or spaced, are recorded with the prefix preceding the surname and arranged alphabetically under the letter D.

Surnames beginning with Mac and Mc are arranged alphabetically under M.

Surnames beginning with Saint or St. appear after names that begin Sains, and are arranged according to the second part of the name, e.g. St. Clair before Saint Dennis.

Surnames beginning with Van, Von, or von are arranged alphabetically under the letter V.

Compound surnames are arranged according to the first member of the compound.

Many hyphenated Arabic names begin Al-, El-, or al-. These names are alphabetized according to each Biographee's designation of last name. Thus Al-Bahar, Neta may be listed either under Al- or under Bahar, depending on the preference of the listee.

Also, Arabic names have a variety of possible spellings when transposed to English. Spelling of these names is always based on the practice of the Biographee. Some Biographees use a Western form of word order, while others prefer the Arabic word sequence.

Similarly, Asian names may have no comma between family and given names, but some Biographees have chosen to add the comma. In each case, punctuation follows the preference of the Biographee.

Parentheses used in connection with a name indicate which part of the full name is usually deleted in common usage. Hence Chambers, E(lizabeth) Anne indicates that the usual form of the given name is E. Anne. In such a case, the parentheses are ignored in alphabetizing and the name would be arranged as Chambers, Elizabeth Anne. However, if the name is recorded Chambers, (Elizabeth) Anne, signifying that the entire name Elizabeth is not commonly used, the alphabetizing would be arranged as though the name were Chambers, Anne. If an entire middle or last name is enclosed in parentheses, that portion of the name is used in the alphabetical arrangement. Hence Chambers, Elizabeth (Anne) would be arranged as Chambers, Elizabeth Anne.

Where more than one spelling, word order, or name of an individual is frequently encountered, the sketch has been entered under the form preferred by the Biographee, with cross-references under alternate forms.

Who'sWho in America®
Biographies L–Z

LAALY, HESHMAT OLLAH, chemist, roofing materials executive, consultant; b. Kermanshah, Iran, June 23, 1927; came to Germany, 1951, Can., 1967, U.S., 1984; s. Jacob and Saltanat (Afshani) L.; m. Parvaneh Modarai, Oct. 7, 1963; (div. 1971); children: Ramesh, Edmond S.; m. Parivash M. Farahmand, Feb. 7, 1982. BS in Chemistry, U. Stuttgart, Germany, 1955; MS in Chemistry, U. Stuttgart, Republic of Germany, 1958, PhD in Chemistry, 1962. Chief chemist Kress Sohne, Krefeld, Germany, 1963-67; analytical chemist Gulf Oil Research Ctr., Montreal, Que., Can., 1967-70; material scientist Bell-Northern Research, Ottawa, Ont., Can., 1970-71; research officer NRC of Can., Ottawa, 1972-84; pres. Roofing Materials Sci. and Tech., L.A., 1984—; Patentee in field. Author: The Science and Technology of Traditional and Modern Roofing Systems, 1992 (World Lifetime Achievement award Am. Biog. Inst. 1992); patentee bi-functional photovoltaic single ply roofing membrane. Mem. ASTM, Inst. Roofing and Waterproofing Cons., Single-Ply Roofing Inst., Assn. Profl. Engrs. Ontario, Am. Chem. Soc., Internat. Union of Testing and Rsch. Labs. for Material and Structures (tech. com. 75), Constrn. Specifications Inst., Nat. Roofing Contractors Assn., UN Indsl. Devels. Orgn., Internat. Conf. Bldg. Ofcls., Roofing Cons. Inst., Inst. for Roofing and Waterproofing Cons., Can. Standard Assn., Can. Gen. Standards Bd., The Engineered Wood Assn. Office: Roofing Materials Sci & Tech 9037 Monte Mar Dr Los Angeles CA 90035-4235

LAANANEN, DAVID HORTON, mechanical engineer, educator; b. Winchester, Mass., Nov. 11, 1942; s. Joseph and Helen Katherine (Horton) L.; m. Mary Ellen Storck, Sept. 9, 1967 (div. 1981); children: Gregg David, Robin Kaye; m. Delores Ann Talbert, May 21, 1988. BS in Mech. Engring., Worcester Poly. Inst., 1964; MS, Northeastern U., 1965, PhD, 1968. Project engr. Dynamic Sci., Phoenix, 1972-74; asst. prof. Pa. State U., State College, 1974-78; mgr. R&D Simula Inc., Phoenix, 1978-83; assoc. prof. Ariz. State U., Tempe, 1983-97, prof., 1997—, dir. aerospace rsch. ctr., 1992-93. Referee: Jour. Aircraft, Jour. Mech. Design; contbr. articles to Jour. Aircraft, Jour. Am. Helicopter Soc., Jour. Safety Rsch., Jour. Thermoplastic Composite Materials, Composites Sci. and Tech. Fellow AIAA (assoc.; design engring. tech. com.); mem. ASME, Am. Helicopter Soc., Sigma Xi, Sigma Gamma Tau, Pi Tau Sigma. Democrat. Achievements include research in aircraft crash survivability, composite structures. Office: Ariz State U Dept Mech Aerospace En Tempe AZ 85287

LAANE, JAAN, chemistry educator; b. Paide, Estonia, June 20, 1942; came to U.S., 1949.; s. Robert Freidrich and Linda (Treufeldt) L.; m. Tiiu Virkhaus, Sept. 3, 1966; children: Christina J., Lisa A. BS in Chemistry, U. Ill., 1964; PhD in Chemistry, MIT, 1967. Asst. prof. of chemistry Tufts U., Medford, Mass., 1967-68; asst. prof. of chemistry Tex. A&M U., College Station, 1968-72, assoc. prof. of chemistry, 1972-76, prof. of chemistry, 1976—, chmn. div. of physical and nuclear chemistry, 1977-87, 93-94, dir. inst. for Pacific Asia, 1987-90; assoc. dean sci., 1994—; dep. exec. dir., sr. policy advisor Tex. A&M U./Koriyama, College Station, 1990-94; editor Jour. Molecular Structure, 1994—; reviewer numerous profl. jours. and grant agys., 1968—; cons. indsl. and govt. orgns., 1970—; vis. prof. U. Bayreuth, Fed. Republic Germany, 1979-80; speaker Tex. A&M Faculty Senate, College Station, 1985-86; dir. NATO Advanced Rsch. Workshop, Ulm, Germany, 1992. Contbr. numerous articles to profl. jours.; lectr. numerous sci. presentations. Pres., founder College Station Assn. for Gifted and Talented, 1982-83. Recipient 10 rsch. grants Robert A. Welch Found., 1970-97, 9 rsch. grants NSF, 1976-97, U.S. Sr. Scientist award Alex Von Humboldt Found., Fed. Republic Germany, 1979, Disting. Tchg. award Tex. A&M Assn. Former Students; elected to Estonian Acad. Sci., 1995. Fellow Am. Inst. Chemists, Am. Phys. Soc.; mem. Am. Chem. Soc. (sect. pres. 1977-78), Soc. for Applied Spectroscopy, Coblentz Soc. (bd. dirs., treas. 1986-89), Tex. A&M Faculty Club (pres. 1987-88), Phi Beta Delta (pres. 1990-91). Achievements include research in molecular spectroscopy and vibrational potential energy functions of molecules, laser Raman spectroscopy, laser induced fluorescence spectroscopy, ft-infrared spectroscopy. Home: 1906 Comal Cir College Station TX 77840-4818 Office: Tex A&M U Chemistry Dept College Station TX 77843

LAANO, ARCHIE BIENVENIDO MAAÑO, cardiologist; b. Tayabas, Quezon, Philippines, Aug. 10, 1939; naturalized U.S. citizen; s. Francisco M. and Iluminada (Maaño) L.; m. Maria Esmeralda Eleazar, May 2, 1964; 1 child, Sylvia Marie. A.A., U. Philippines, 1958, B.S., 1959, M.D., 1963; postgrad. Command and Gen. Staff Sch., Ft. Totten, N.Y., Ft. Leavenworth, Kans., 1978-79, Oxford (Eng.) U., 1985-86, Cambridge (Eng.) U., 1986-87. Diplomate Am. Bd. Internal Medicine. Rotating intern Hosp. St. Raphael, New Haven, 1963-64; resident internal medicine, 1964-65; rotating resident pulmonary diseases Laurel Heights Hosp., Shelton, Conn., 1965; affiliated rotating resident Yale-New Haven Med. Ctr., 1965; resident internal medicine Westchester County Med. Ctr., Valhalla, N.Y., 1965-66, resident cardiology, 1966-67; resident fellow cardiology Maimonides Med. Ctr., Bklyn., 1967-68; rotating sr. resident cardiology Coney Island Hosp., Bklyn., 1967-68; fellow internal medicine Mercy Hosp., Rockville Centre, N.Y., 1968-70; med. dir. 54 Main St. Med. Ctr., Hempstead, N.Y., 1971-76, Bloomingdale's, Garden City, N.Y., 1972—, Esselte Pendaflex Corp., Garden City, 1976—; attending staff Nassau County (N.Y.) Med. Ctr., Hempstead Gen. Hosp.; practice medicine specializing in cardiology, internal medicine, Nassau County, 1971—; chief med. svcs., chief profl. svcs. U.S. Army 808th Sta. Hosp., Hempstead, N.Y., 1979—; brig. gen. 1st U.S. Army AMEDD Augmentation Detachment, Ft. Meade, Md., 1989—, M.C., chief of staff, chief profl. svcs. U.S. Army Meddac Hosp., Ft. Dix., N.J., 1990—; med. dir. Cities Svc. Oil Co. (CITGO), L.I. div., 1972— ; mem. adv. bd. Guardian Bank, Hempstead, chmn. adv. coun., 1973-89; clin. prof. medicine SUNY at Stony Brook, 1979—; professorial lectr. medicine (cardiology) U.S. Mil. Acad.-Keller Army Med. Ctr., West Point, N.Y., 1979; affiliated teaching hosp. Harvard Med. Sch, 1979; vis. prof. Harvard U., 1979—; cons. physician ICC, Citgo, Liberty Mut. Ins. Co. Boston, 1972—, U.S. Dept. Transp.; post-doctoral in medicine-cardiovasc. diseases Brasenose Coll., Oxford U., U.K., 1985-65, post-doctoral in medicine-cardiology Corpus Christi Coll., Cambridge U., U.K., 1986-87; counsel White House Commn. on Mil. Medicine, 1988—. Perpetual benefactor endowed Dr. Archie B.M. Laano Professorial Chair in Cardiology, U.P. Coll. of Medicine, U.P.-P.G.H. Med. Ctr., Manila, 1983—, Permanent Endowment Fund, U. Philippines Coll. of Medicine, Manila, 1987—, Dr. Archie B.M. Laano Scholarship Fund, U. Philippines, Diliman, Quezon City, 1987—. Decorated Silver Star, Bronze Star, Legion of Merit, Soldiers medal, Joint Svc. Command medal, Army Meritorious Svc. medal, Dept. Def. Joint Svc. Achievement award, Southwest Asia Svc. award-Desert Storm, others. Fellow Internat. Coll. Angiology, Am. Coll. Angiology, Am. Coll. Internat. Physicians, Internat. Coll. Applied Nutrition, Am. Soc. Contemporary Medicine and Surgery, Acad. Preventive Medicine, Internat. Acad. Med. Preventives, Philippine Coll. Physicians, Am. Coll. Acupuncture, N.Y. Acad. of Sci.; mem. AMA, Am. Coll. Cardiology, N.Y. Med. Soc., Nassau County Med. Soc., Am. Heart Assn., N.Y. Cardiol. Soc., World Med. Assn., Royal Soc. Medicine (overseas, London), Nassau Acad. Medicine, Am., N.Y. State, Nassau Soc. Internal Medicine, N.Y. Soc. Acupuncture for Physicians, Am. Geriatrics Soc., Nassau Physicians Guild, Res. Officers Assn. U.S., Assn. Mil. Surgeons, Assn. Philippine Physicians Am. (bd. govs. rep. N.Y. State 1984-86, v.p. 1988-89, chmn. com. nominations and election 1987-88. spl. counsel to pres. 1986-87), Philippine Med. Assn. Am. (spl. counsel 1988-89, bd. dirs, 1989-90, spl. counsel to pres, 1986—, dir. continuing med. edn. 1990—, chmn. scholarship com. 1989—), Assn. Philippine Physicians of N.Y. (founding v.p., pres. 1985-87, pres. emeritus 1988—, chmn. com. on constitution and by-laws, nominations and election, med. coord. Internat. Games for Disabled Olympics 1984), Soc. Philippine Surgeons Am. (Medallion of Honor 1991), U.S. Knights of Rizal, U. Philippines Med. Alumni Soc. (pres. class of 1963, 1981—), U. Philippines Med. Alumni Soc. Am. (chmn. bd. 1985—), Royal Soc. Medicine Club, The Oxford Club, Rolls Royce Club L.I., N.Y. Club (chmn. 1987—), West Point Officers Club, Garden City Country Club, Phi Kappa Mu (overseas coord. U. Philippines 1985—), Beta Sigma (coun. advisers Ea. U.S. 1990—, program chmn. 1975—, chmn. bd. 1978—, pres. 1978-79), Lions (Garden City program chmn. 1975—, chmn. bd. 1978—, pres. 1978-79). Republican. Roman Catholic. Home: 80 Stratford Ave Garden City NY 11530-2531 Office: 230 Hilton Ave Ste 106 Hempstead NY 11550-8116

LA ARCAND, PIERRE, radio station executive. V.p., gen. mgr. CKVL-AM, Montreal, Can. Office: CKVL-AM, 211 Gordon Ave, Montreal, PQ Canada H4G 2R2

LABA, MARVIN, management consultant; b. Newark, Mar. 17, 1928; s. Joseph Abraham and Jean Cecil (Saunders) L.; m. Sandra Seltzer, Apr. 16, 1961 (div. May 1974); children: Stuart Michael, Jonathan Todd; m. Elizabeth Luger, June 11, 1974 (div. 1979). BBA, Ind. U., 1951. Buyer Bamberger's (Macy's N.J.), Newark, 1951-67; v.p., mdse. adminstr. Macy's N.Y., 1967-73; v.p., gen. mdse. mgr. Howland/Steinback, White Plains, N.Y., 1973-75, Pomeroy's, Levittown, Pa., 1975-76; v.p., gen. mdse. mgr., sr. v.p., exec. v.p. May Co. Calif., North Hollywood, 1976-79; pres., chief exec. officer G. Fox & Co. (div. of the May dept. stores), Hartford, Conn., 1979-82; pres. Richard Theobald & Asocs., L.A., 1983; pres., chief exec. officer Marvin Laba & Assocs., L.A., 1983—. With U.S. Army, 1946-48. Avocations: coins, tennis, theatre, travel. Office: Marvin Laba & Assoc 6255 W Sunset Blvd Ste 617 Los Angeles CA 90028-7407

LABALME, PATRICIA HOCHSCHILD, educational administrator; b. N.Y.C., Feb. 26, 1927; d. Walter and Kathrin (Samstag) Hochschild; m. George Labalme, Jr., June 6, 1958; children: Jennifer R., Henry G., Lisa G., Victoria A. B.A. magna cum laude, Bryn Mawr Coll., 1948; M.A., Harvard U., 1950, Ph.D., 1958. Instr. history Wellesley Coll., Mass., 1952-57; tchr. history Brearley Sch., N.Y.C., 1957-59; lectr. Barnard Coll., N.Y.C., 1961-77; adj. assoc. prof. history Hunter Coll., N.Y.C., 1979; lectr. NYU, N.Y.C., 1980-82; adj. prof. history NYU, 1986-87; assoc. dir. Inst. for Advanced Study, Princeton, N.J., 1982-88; sec. corp. Inst. for Advanced Study, Princeton, 1982-92, asst. to dir., 1992-97; mem. adv. bd. G.K. Delmas Found., N.Y.C., 1976-79, trustee, 1979—; trustee Am. Acad. in Rome, N.Y.C., 1979—; exec. dir. Renaissance Soc. Am., N.Y.C., 1982-85, trustee, 1982-89; bd. dirs. Quantum Chem. Corp., 1990-93. Author: Bernardo Giustiniani: A Venetian of the Quattrocento, 1969; contbg. editor: Beyond Their Sex: Learned Women of the European Past, 1980, A Century Recalled: Essays in Honor of Bryn Mawr College, 1987; contbr. articles to profl. jours. and publs. Trustee Brearley Sch., 1975-83, pres., 1978-82, hon. trustee, 1983—; trustee Lawrenceville Sch., 1986-89, trustee emerita, 1996—. Recipient Caroline A. Wilby prize Radcliffe Coll., 1958. Mem. Am. Hist. Assn., Soc. for Renaissance Studies, Renaissance Soc. Am., Ateneo Veneto, Cosmopolitan Club, Harvard Club (N.Y.C.), Cream Hill Lake Assn. (West Cornwall, Conn.), Phi Beta Kappa. Office: Inst for Advanced Study Olden Ln Princeton NJ 08540-4920

LABAN, MYRON MILES, physician, administrator; b. Detroit, Mar. 9, 1936; s. Larry Max and Mary Marsha (Harris) LaB.; m. Rita Joyce Hochman, Aug. 17, 1958; children: Terry, Amy, Craig. B.A., U. Mich., Ann Arbor, 1957, M.D., 1967; M.Med. Sci., Ohio State U., Columbus, 1965. Diplomate Am. Bd. Phys. Medicine and Rehab. Intern Sinai Hosp., Detroit, 1961-62; resident Ohio State U. Hosp., 1962-65; assoc. dir. phys. medicine and rehab. Letterman Gen. Hosp., San Francisco, 1965-67; dir. phys. medicine and rehab. William Beaumont Hosp., Royal Oak, Mich., 1967—; Licht lecturer Ohio State U., 1986, clin. prof., 1993; clin. prof. Wayne State U., Detroit, 1990, clin. prof. Oakland U., Rochester, Mich., 1983, Ohio State U., Columbus, 1992; bd. dirs. Oakland County Med. Bd., Birmingham, Mich., 1982-87; rep. to Commn. on Phys. Medicine and Rehab., Mich. State Med. Soc. Contbr. chpts. in books, articles to profl. publs. Med. dir. Oakland County March of Dimes, Mich., 1969-83. Served to capt. U.S. Army, 1965-67. Fellow Am. Acad. Phys. Medicine and Rehab. (bd. dirs. 1980, pres. 1985-86, Bernard Baruch Rsch. award 1961, R. Rosenthal Rsch. award 1982, Zeiter lectureship, Disting. Clinician award 1991, "Top Doc" PM&R Detroit Monthly 1993, 96); mem. AMA, Am. Congress Rehab. Medicine, Am. Assn. Electromyography and Electrodiagnosis (program dir. 1972), Oakland County Med. Soc. (treas. 1983, pres.-elect 1987, pres. 1988-89), Mich. State Med. Soc., Mich. Acad. Phys. Med. and Rehab. (pres. 1982-84, jud. commr. 1991-95, mem. editl. bd. Jour. Phys. Med. and Rehab.). Republican. Jewish. Avocations: gardening; ship modeling. Office: LMT Rehabilitation Assocs 3535 W 13 Mile Rd Rm 703 Royal Oak MI 48073-6706

LABAREE, BENJAMIN WOODS, history educator; b. New Haven, Conn., July 21, 1927; s. Leonard Woods and Elizabeth Mary (Calkins) L.; m. Linda Carol Prichard, June 27, 1959; children: Benjamin Woods Jr., Jonathan Martin, Sarah Calkins. BA, Yale U., 1950; AM, Harvard U., 1953, PhD, 1957. Instr. history Conn. Coll., New London, 1957-58; from instr. to asst. prof. history, Allston Burr Sr. tutor Harvard U., Cambridge, Mass., 1958-63; dean Williams Coll., Williamstown, Mass., 1963-67, assoc. to prof. history, 1963-77, Ephraim Williams Prof. Am. History, 1972-77; dir. Williams Coll.-Mystic Seaport Program/Mystic Seaport Mus., Mystic, Conn., 1977-89; dir. Ctr. for Environ. Studies Williams Coll., 1989-91; prof. history and environ. studies Williams Coll., Williamstown, 1989-92; prof. emeritus, 1992—; vis. prof. Trinity Coll., Conn., 1993, Williams Coll., 1994, Clark U., 1997; dir. Munson Inst. Am. Maritime Studies, Mystic, 1974-96; mng. editor Essex Inst. Hist . Collections, Salem, Mass., 1956-60; co-dir. summer inst. Am. and the Sea NEH, 1996. Author: Patriots and Partisans, 1962, The Boston Tea Party, 1964, America's Nation-Time, 1972, Colonial Massachusetts, 1979; co-author: New England and The Sea, 1972, Empire or Independence, 1976. Mem. Mt. Greylock Regional H.S. Com., Williamstown, 1971-74; bd. dirs. Newburyport Maritime Soc., 1991—, Lowell's Boat Shop trust, 1992—. With USNR, 1945-46. Recipient Wilbur Cross award Conn. Humanities Coun., 1990, Samuel Eliot Morison award USS Constitution Mus., 1993. Mem. Am. Hist. Assn. (com. 1971-73), Am. Antiquarian Soc., Colonial Soc. Mass., Mass. Hist. Soc., Inst. for Early Am. History and Culture (coun. mem. 1983-86), others. Democrat. Unitarian-Universalist. Avocations: sailing, rowing, swimming. Home and Office: 2 Andrews Ln Amesbury MA 01913-4102

LABARGE, MARGARET WADE, medieval history educator; b. N.Y.C., July 18, 1916; arrived in Can., 1940; d. Alfred Byers and Helena (Mein) Wade; m. Raymond C. Labarge, June 20, 1940 (dec. May 1972); children: Claire Labarge Morris, Suzanne, Charles, Paul. BA, Radcliffe Coll., 1937; LittB, Oxford (Eng.) U., 1939; LittD (hon.), Carleton U., Ottawa, Ont., Can., 1976; LLD (hon.), U. Waterloo, Ont., Can., 1993. Lectr. history U. Ottawa, Carleton U., 1950-62; adj. prof. history Carleton U., Ottawa, 1983—. Author: Simon de Montfort, 1962, A Baronial Household, 1965, Gascony, 1980, A Small Sound of the Trumpet, 1987, A Medieval Miscellany, 1997, others; contbr. articles to profl. jours. Bd. dirs. St. Vincent's Hosp., Ottawa, 1969-81; chmn. 1977-79; pub. rep. bd. dirs. Can. Nurses Assn., 1980-83; bd. dirs. Carleton U., 1984-93, Coun. on Aging, 1986-93 (pres., 1989-91). Recipient Alumnae Recognition award Radcliffe Coll., 1987. Fellow Royal Soc. Can.; mem. Medieval Acad., Order of Can., Phi Beta Kappa. Roman Catholic. Avocations: traveling, reading, walking. Home and Office: 402-555 Wilbrod St, Ottawa, ON Canada K1N 5R4

LABARRE, CARL ANTHONY, retired government official; b. Sherwood, N.D., July 16, 1918; s. William Paul and Josephine K. LaB.; m. Persis Wester, Sept. 9, 1941; 1 son, William Paul, II. Student, U. Mont., 1936-40; postgrad., Naval Acad. Postgrad. Sch., 1945-46; grad., Naval War Coll., 1958-59, Advanced Mgmt. Program, Harvard U. Commd. ensign U.S. Navy, 1941, advanced through grades to capt., 1971; served in various fin., inventory control systems and purchasing assignments, to 1971; insp. gen. (Naval Supply Systems Command), to 1971; ret., 1971; dep. dir. materials mgmt. service GPO, Washington, 1971-75; dir. materials mgmt. service GPO, 1975, asst. public printer, supt. documents, 1975-82. Decorated Navy Commendation medal with V, Joint Service commendation medal, Legion of Merit with gold star; recipient Public Printers Disting. Service award, 1977, 81. Club: Harvard Bus. Sch. (Washington).

LABATH, OCTAVE AARON, mechanical engineer; b. Milw., Sept. 22, 1941; s. Octave Adrain and Bertha Jane (Johnson) LaB.; m. Carole Marion Clay, Jan. 23, 1965; children—Melissa, Michelle, Mark. B.S. in Mech. Engring., U. Cin., 1964, M.S., 1969. Registered profl. engr., Ohio. v.p. engring. Cin. Gear Co., 1972—. Contbr. articles to profl. jours. Mem. Am. Gear Mfg. Assn., ASME. Methodist. Men's Club. Home: 5105 Kenridge Dr Cincinnati OH 45242-4831 Office: Cin Gear 5657 Wooster Pike Cincinnati OH 45227-4120

LABAY, EUGENE BENEDICT, lawyer; b. El Campo, Tex., July 20, 1938; s. Ben F. and Cecelia M. (Orsak) L.; m. Katherine Sue Ermis, Dec. 29, 1962; children: Michael, Joan, John, Paul, David, Patrick, Steven. BBA, St. Mary's U., San Antonio, 1960, JD, 1965. Bar: Tex. 1965, U.S. Dist. Ct. (we. dist.) Tex. 1968, U.S. Dist. Ct. (no. dist.) Tex. 1973, U.S. Ct. Appeals (5th cir.) 1968, U.S. Ct. Appeals (11th cir.) 1981, U.S. Supreme Ct. 1980, U.S. Dist. Ct. (ea. dist.) Tex. 1986. Briefing atty. Supreme Ct. Tex., Austin, 1965-66; assoc. Cox & Smith Inc., San Antonio, 1966-71, ptnr., 1972-83, v.p., 1972-94; pvt. practice., 1994—. Served to 1st lt. U.S. Army, 1960-62. Mem. ABA, State Bar Tex. (chmn. sect. internat. law 1979-80), San Antonio Bar Assn., Fed. Bar Assn., Inter-Am. Bar Assn., Am. Judicature Soc., Catholic Lawyers Guild San Antonio, Phi Delta Phi, Roman Catholic. Clubs: Serra (San Antonio); KC (council grand knight 1982-83). Contbr. articles to legal jours. Home: 31720 Post Oak Trl Boerne TX 78015-4133 Office: 1140 Milam Bldg 115 E Travis St San Antonio TX 78205-1611

LABAYEN, LOUIE ANTHONY LOPEZ, information analyst, consultant; b. Manila, Jan. 17, 1960; came to U.S., 1976; s. Wilfredo Lizares and Rose Jocelyn Ocampo (Lopez) L.; m. Rosalinda Maglonzo Torres, June 6, 1987; children: John Gustav Torres, James Daniel Torres. BA, De La Salle U., Manila, 1981; MusM, U. No. Colo., 1986. Mgr. Network Mgmt. Corp., Kansas City, Mo., 1988-90; sr. analyst Blue Cross Blue Shield, Kansas City, Mo., 1990-94; v.p. Patriot Mortgage Co., 1994; team leader Tapestry Computing, 1994-95; sr. cons. Oracle Corp., 1995; devel. mgr. Uniband, Inc., 1995-96; prin. cons. Paladin Data Sys., Inc., 1996—; lectr. Mt. Carmel Coll., Baler, Philippines, 1982-83; project leader Blue Cross Blue Shield, 1991-94. Mem. Am. Symphony Orch. League, 1985—. Mem. IEEE, Mu Phi Epsilon, Rotary (exch. student Antwerp, Ohio 1976). Avocations: photography, gourmet cooking, sailing, golf, architecture. Home and Office: 11225 19th Ave SE Apt E104 Everett WA 98208-5139

LABBE, ARMAND JOSEPH, museum curator, anthropologist; b. Lawrence, Mass., June 13, 1944; s. Armand Henri and Gertrude Marie (Martineau) L.; m. Denise Marie Scott, Jan. 17, 1969 (div. 1972). BA in Anthropology, Univ. Mass., 1969; MA in Anthropology, Calif. State U., 1986; lifetime instr. credential in anthropology, State Calif. Curator collections Bowers Mus., Santa Ana, Calif., 1978-79, curator anthropology, 1979-86, chief curator, 1986—, dir. rsch. and collections, 1991—; instr. prof. Santa Ana Coll., 1981-86, U. Calif., Irvine, 1983, 87, 91, 93, Chapman U., 1996, Calif. State U., Fullerton, 1982, 83, 88, appt. rsch. assoc. dept. anthropology, 1997—; trustee Balboa Arts Conservation Ctr., San Diego, 1989—, Ams. Found., Greenfield, Mass., 1985-94, Quintcentenary Festival Discovery, Orange County, Calif., 1990-91, Mingei Internat. Mus., La Jolla, Calif., 1993—, treas. bd. dirs. 1996—; mem. adv. bd. Elan Internat., Newport Beach, Calif., 1992-95; inaugural guest lectr. Friends of Ethnic Art, San Francisco, 1988; hon. bd. dirs., Ethnic Arts Coun., L.A. Author: Man and Cosmos, 1982, Ban Chiang, 1985, Colombia Before Columbus, 1986 (1st prize 1987), Leigh Wiener: Portraits, 1987, Colombia Antes de Colón, 1988 (honored at Gold Mus. Bogotá, Colombia, 1988), Images of Power: Master Works of the Bowers Museum of Cultural Art, 1992; co-author Tribute to The Gods: Treasures of the Museo del Oro, Bogotá, 1992, Guardians of the Life Stream: Shamans, Art and Power In Prehispanic Central Panama, 1995. Hon. bd. dirs. Ethnic Arts Coun. L.A.; cons. Orange County Coun. on History and Art, Santa Ana, 1981-85; mem. Task Force on County Cultural Resources, Orange County, 1979; cons., interviewer TV prodn. The Human Journey, Fullerton, 1986-89; treas., bd. trustees Mingei Internat. Mus., San Diego, 1996—. With USAF, 1963-67. Recipient cert. of Recognition Orange County Bd. Suprs., 1982, award for outstanding scholarship Colombian Community, 1987; honored for authorship Friends of Libr., 1987, 88. Fellow Am. Anthrop. Assn.; mem. AAAS, Am. Assn. Mus., N.Y. Acad. Scis., S.W. Anthrop. Assn. Avocations: photography, travel. Home: 2854 Royal Palm Dr Apt C Costa Mesa CA 92626-3828

LABBE, PATRICK CHARLES, legal nursing consultant; b. Providence; s. Roland Herve and Lucille Rose (Chartier) L.; m. Linda Collette, May 8, 1979 (div. 1981); m. Pauline Rosemarie Allard Labbe, Mar. 15, 1985; children: David Richard, Christopher Micheal, Alicia Rose, Kathryn Tahirih. A in Health Sci. Nursing, Florence Darlington Tech. Coll., 1990; BS in Liberal Studies, Regents Coll., 1993; BSN, City Univ. L.A., 1993, MSN, 1994. RN, S.C.; cert. legal nursing cons., BLS. Staff nurse McLeod Regional Med. Ctr., Florence, S.C., 1990-91, 94-96; inservice coord. Correctional Med. Sys., Bennettsville, S.C., 1991-93; home health nurse Florence (S.C.) Vis. Nurses, 1993-94; staff nurse Florence Nursing Svc., 1991—; legal nurse cons. First Vision Profl. Svcs., Dillon, S.C., 1993—; health occupations instr. Dillon County Applied Tech. Ctr., 1996—. Author: Inside the Radical Poet, 1981, Disease Prevention and Health Promotion in a Correctional Setting, 1994. Fellow Grand Coll. of Rites; mem. Am. Soc. Quality Control, Am. Assn. Legal Nurse Cons., N.G. Assn., Nat. League for Nursing, Assn. N.G. Nurses, Res. Officers Assn., The Philalethes, Internat. Assn. of Forensic Nurses, Masons (Lodge Blue #142), Scottish Rite Rsch. Soc., Pee Dee Scottish Rite Club, York Rite Bodies of S.C., Knights of Pythias. Mem. Restoration Ch. of Jesus Christ LDS. Avocations: camping, travel, writing fiction and poetry, studying ancient religions. Office: Dillon County Applied Tech Ctr Main St Dillon SC 29536

LABBÉ, PAUL, export corporation executive; b. Buckingham, Que., Can., Mar. 11, 1939; s. Arthur and Dorothy Frances (Gorman) L.; m. Kathryn Grace Cameron, July 10, 1965; children: Marie-Paule, Marc, Philippe, David, Robert. BA, U. Ottawa, 1961; BCL, McGill U., 1964; student, Ecole Nationale D'Administration, Paris, 1969, Harvard Grad. Sch. Bus., 1990. Bar: Que. 1965. Comml. sec. Can. Embassy, Paris, 1966-69; exec. asst. to minister Dept. Industry, Trade & Commerce, Ottawa, Ont., 1969-73; assoc.

Interimco, Inc., 1973-75, pres., 1975-81; pres. CDN Indsl. Rev. Bd., 1981-85; commr. Fgn. Investment Rev. Agy., 1985; pres. Investment Can., Ottawa, 1985-91; pres., CEO Export Devel. Corp., Ottawa, 1991—. Gov. Can. Comprehensive Auditing Found. Mem. Rideau Club, Hunt Club. Home: 216 Clemow Ave, Ottawa, ON Canada K1S 2B6 Office: Export Development Corp, 151 O'Connor St, Ottawa, ON Canada K1A 1K3

LABBETT, JOHN EDGAR, senior financial executive; b. Chesham, Bucks, Eng., June 19, 1950; came to U.S., 1987; s. Gordon F. and Sylvia (Dalton) L.; m. Mary McGagh, Jan. 30, 1976; children: Jennifer F., Alexander T. Audit clk. White Withers and Co., Bexhill, Eng., 1966-71; auditor Peat Marwick Mitchell, London, 1971-73; chief acct. Guild S&V Ltd., London, 1973-74; from fin. analyst to contr. Roneo Vickers Ltd., London, 1974-81; fin. contr. Cambridge (Eng.) Instruments Ltd., 1981-82; fin. dir. Linfood C&C Ltd. subsid. Dee Corp., Milton Keynes, U.K., 1982-85; fin. controller Dee Corp., Milton Keines, 1985-87; exec. v.p., chief fin. officer Hermans Sporting Goods, Inc., Carteret, N.J., 1987-93; v.p., CFO The Petfood Giant, Inc., 1994-95; exec. v.p., chief fin. officer House of Fabrics, Inc., Sherman Oaks, Calif., 1995—. Fellow Inst. Chartered Accts. Eng. and Wales. Mem. Ch. Eng. Home: 5565 Canoga Ave # 302 Woodland Hills CA 91367

LABE, ROBERT BRIAN, lawyer; b. Detroit, Sept. 2, 1959; s. Benjamin Mitchell and Gloria Florence (Wright) L.; m. Mary Lou Budman, Nov. 12, 1989; 1 child, Bridget. BA with high honors, Mich. State U., 1981; JD, Wayne State U., 1984; LLM, Boston U., 1985. Bar: Mich. 1984, U.S. Dist. Ct. Mich. 1985, U.S. Tax Ct. 1985. Assoc. Weingarden & Hauer, P.C., Bingham Farms, Mich., 1988-92, shareholder, 1992-94; prin. Robert B. Labe, P.C., Southfield, Mich., 1994—; adj. prof. taxation and estate planning Walsh Coll., Troy, Mich., 1990-92; lectr. and presenter in field. Author: Research Edge-Taxation Guide, 1994, Bus. Succession Planning, 1996; mem. publ. adv. bd. Inst. Continuing Legal Edn. U. Mich., 1993—; contbr. articles to profl. jours. Avocations: tennis, spectator sports. Office: Robert B Labe P C 2000 Town Ctr Ste 1780 Southfield MI 48075-1150

LABELLE, EUGENE JEAN-MARC, airport director general; b. Montreal, Que., Can., Nov. 26, 1941; s. Paul Eugene and Pauline (Brissette) L.; m. Louise Gingras; 1 child, Anne Marie. BA in Sci. and Math., U. Montreal, 1962, BS in Applied Scis. (civil engring.), 1967; postgrad. in transp. mgmt., various colls., 1975-85. Registered profl. engr., Que.; cert. expert of Internat. Aviation Orgn., expert of World Bank. With Transport Canada, 1967—; field engr. constrn. br. Que. region, 1967-68, design engr. constrn. br., 1968-71; mgr. engring. and maintenance svcs. Dorval, 1971-75; regional mgr. airport ops. Que. Region, 1975-80; acting airport gen. mgr. Dorval, 1980-81; mgr. airport ops. & svcs. Mirabel, 1981-82; airport gen. mgr. Dorval, 1982-88; dir. gen. Montreal Airports, 1988-92; exec. v.p., COO Aeroports de Montreal, Canada, 1992-94, group v.p. planning and devel., 1994—; pres., gen. mgr. Aeroports de Montreal Svcs. Inc., group v.p., planning & devel.; mem. planning missions, aerodrome engr. and/or mgmt. cons. for Internat. Civil Aviation Orgn. and World Bank, Congo, 1981, Cameroun, 1983, Chad, 1983, 84, 85, Senegal, 1984, Kenya, 1984, Jordan, 1985, Hdqrs., Montreal, 1986, Madagascar, 1985, Sierra Leone, Qatar, 1986, Turks and Caicos Islands, program evaluation officer, Kigali, Rwanda, 1986; aerodrome mgmt. cons. study of civil aviation reorgn., Conakry, (Guinea), World Bank Mission, 1986; ICAO Program Evaluation Officer, UN Tchad, 1987; aerodrome mgmt. cons., Warsaw, Poland, 1987; aerodrome engring cons., Kuwait, 1988, St. Vincent and the Grenadines, 1989, Uruguay, 1989; lectr. Civil Aviation Acad., Leningrad, USSR, 1990; aerodrome mgmt. advisor Santo Domingo, 1990; aerodrome mgmt. and engring. advisor Trinidad and Tobago, 1991, 92; UN program evaluation officer, Mozambique, 1990; aerodrome planning engr., Lebanon, 1993; project mgr. Piarco Airport Trinidad and Tobago, 1993, UFA Airport, Bashkortostan, 1995, Macau Airport Certification Program, 1995; aerodrome gnr., project mgr. E.T. Joshua Airport, St. Vincent & Grenadines, 1995. Mem. ASCE, Chambre de Commerce de Montreal, Can. Inst.of Engrs., Am. Assn. Airport Execs., Airports Coun. Internat., Airports Conss. Coun., Can. Exporters Assn. Avocations: classical music, opera, reading, arts, golf. Home: 337 Perrault St, Rosemere, PQ Canada J7A 1C4 Office: Aeroports de Montreal, 1100 Rene-Levesque Blvd W 21st fl, Montreal, PQ Canada H3B 4X8

LABELLE, JAMES WILLIAM, pediatrician; b. Newark, Oct. 1, 1935; s. James William and Suzanne Josephine (Liebl) LaB.; m. Sara Klopfenstein, Aug. 3, 1957; children: James W., Elizabeth S., Michael E. BA, U. Ariz., 1957; MD, U. Colo., 1961. Cert. Am. Bd. Pediats. Resident L.A. Childrens Hosp., 1964-66; pvt. practice, 1970—; chief of staff Tucson Med. Ctr., 1992-94. Maj. USAF, 1962-70. Avocation: golf. Office: Catalina Pediats 5335 E Erickson Dr Tucson AZ 85712-2826

LABELLE, PATTI, singer; b. Phila., Oct. 4, 1944; d. Henry Holte; m. Armstead Edwards; children: Zuri, Stanley, Dodd. Singer Patti LaBelle and the Bluebelles, 1962-70; lead singer musical group LaBelle, 1970-76; solo performer, 1977—. Albums include Over the Rainbow, 1967, La Belle, 1971, Moon Shadows, 1972, Pressure Cookin', 1974, Chameleon, 1976, Patti LaBelle, 1977, Live at the Apollo, 1980, Gonna Take A Miracle-The Spirit's in It, 1982, I'm in Love Again, 1984, Winner in You, 1986, The Best of Patti LaBelle, Patti, Be Yourself, Burnin', 1991, Live (Apollo Theater), 1993, Gems, 1994; appeared in films A Soldier's Story, 1985, Beverly Hills Cop, 1985; appeared in TV movie Unnatural Causes, 1986, TV series A Different World, Out All Night, 1992. Recipient award of Merit, Phila. Art Alliance, 1987.Recipient Grammy award: best Rhythm & Blues vocal for "Burnin'", 1991, Grammy nomination (Best Rhythym & Blues Female Vocal, 1994) for "All Right Now". Home: 8730 W Sunset Blvd Ph W Los Angeles CA 90069-2210 Office: care MCA Records Inc 70 Universal City Plz Universal Cty CA 91608-1011*

LABELLE, THOMAS JEFFREY, academic administrator; b. Owen, Wis., Sept. 21, 1941; s. Wendell Allen and Katherine (Dolan) LaB.; m. Nancy Reik, June 16, 1966 (dec. 1981); children: Katherine Anne, Jeanette Marie. AA, Pierce Coll., Woodland Hills, Calif., 1962; BA, Calif. State U., Northridge, 1964; MA, U. N.Mex., Albuquerque, 1967, PhD, 1969. Prof. UCLA, 1969-86, asst. dean edn., 1971-79, assoc. dean grad. div., 1980-86; prof. comparative and internat. edn. U. Pitts., 1986-90, dean Sch. Edn., 1986-90; v.p. acad. programs, provost Ga. State U., Atlanta, 1990-93; provost, v.p. acad. affairs and rsch. W.Va. U., Morgantown, 1993-96; provost v.p. acad. affairs San Francisco State U., 1996—; cons. InterAm. Found., U.S. AID, Ford Found., CBS, Acad. Ednl. Devel., Juarez and Assocs. Author: Education and Development in Latin America, 1972, Nonformal Education in Latin America and the Caribbean, 1986, Stability, Reform or Revolution, 1986, Education and Intergroup Relations, 1985, Multiculturalism and Education, 1994, Ethnic Studies and Multiculturalism, 1996. Vol. Peace Corps, Colombia, 1964-66. Grantee Fulbright Found., 1983, 96, InterAm. Found., Latin America, 1984; recipient Andres Bello award 1st Class, Venezuela, 1987. Fellow Soc. Applied Anthropology; mem. Comparative and Internat. Edn. Soc. (pres. 1981), Coun. on Anthropology and Edn. (bd. dirs. 1977), Inter-Am. Found. (chmn. learning fellowship on social change), Golden Key, Omicron Delta Kappa, Phi Kappa Phi. Democrat. Office: San Francisco State U Acad Affairs 1600 Holloway Ave San Francisco CA 94132-1722

LABINS, DEBORAH LYNNE, maternal women's health nurse; b. Atlanta, Jan. 5, 1957; d. Harold Whitney and Lois Romaine (Moudy) Hampson; m. Steven Thomas Labins, Mar. 18, 1978; children: Jennifer, Christine, Eric. AA in Nursing, Pierce Coll., Woodland Hills, Calif., 1978. RN, Calif. Nurses' aide Motion Picture and TV Hosp., Woodland Hills; staff nurse labor and delivery room, postpartum, nursery Granada Hills (Calif.) Community Hosp.; nurse labor and delivery room West Hills Regional Med. Ctr. (formerly Humana Hosp.), West Hills, Calif.

LABITZKE, DALE RUSSELL, chemical processing engineer; b. St. Louis, Mo., Dec. 3, 1945; s. Ralph Edgar and Thelma Lois Labitzke; m. Norine Bardill, July 1, 1994. BSChemE, Washington U., St. Louis, 1967. Registered profl. engr. Fla. Process engr. Olin Corp., East Alton, Ill., 1967-68; project engr. Olin Corp., St. Marks, Fla., 1969-71, sr. project engr., 1977; sr. project engr. Olin Corp., Tehran, Iran, 1978; sr. process engr. Olin Corp., St. Marks, 1979-81; assoc. project engr. Olin Corp., Jacksonville, Fla., 1982; project mgr. Olin Corp., Belgrade, Yugoslavia, 1983-85; process engring. mgr. Olin Corp., St. Marks, 1986-92, tech. mgr., 1993-96; tech. mgr. Primex Techs., St. Marks, 1997—; prin. Dale R. Labitzke and Assocs., Tallahassee, Fla., 1992—. Author: Ball Powder Theory and Practice, 1982. With USN, 1971-76. Mem. Am. Def. Preparedness Assn., Fla. Engring. Soc. (bd. mem., rep.), AIChE, NSPE. Avocations: travel, gardening. Home: 1529 Chowkeebin Nene Tallahassee FL 32301-4705 Office: Olin Corp PO Box 222 Saint Marks FL 32355-0222

LA BLANC, CHARLES WESLEY, JR., financial consultant; b. Bayshore, L.I., N.Y., June 4, 1925; s. Charles Wesley and Anne (Dobson) LaB.; m. Marie Dolan, Oct. 26, 1963 (dec. Jan. 1985); children: Charles Wesley III, Gregory, Suzanne; m. Joan H. Trapp, Dec. 29, 1993. BS, Tufts Coll., 1949; MBA, NYU, 1952, PhD, 1956. Securities portfolio mgr. Manhattan Life Ins. Co., N.Y.C., 1952-57; asst. to pres. Magnavox Co., Ft. Wayne, Ind., 1957-60; security analyst C.W. LaBlanc & Assos., N.Y.C., 1960-62; treas. Macke Co., Cheverly, Md., 1962-72, dir., 1974-80; exec. v.p., sec.-treas., dir. After Six, Inc., Phila., 1972-84; pres. Bert Paley Ltd., Inc. subs., 1976-77; chmn. bd. dirs. Cymaticolor, 1983-84; CFO Std. Telecom. Sys. Inc., South Hackensack, N.J., 1983-87, also bd. dirs.; pres. Std. Profit Sharing Fund, 1987—; bd. dirs. Acad. of Vocal Arts. Pres. Queens County Young Reps., 1955-57; bd. dirs. adv. council Temple U. With AC USNR, 1943-46. Fellow N.Y. Soc. Security Analysts; mem. Washington Soc. Investment Analysts, Fin. Analysts Phila., Fin. Execs. Inst., Am. Acctg. Assn., Am. Soc. Ins. Mgmt., Pub. Rels. Soc. Am., Nat. Assn. Bus. Economists, Nat. Investor Rels. Inst., Nat. Assn. Corp. Dirs., Phila. Securities Assn. (pres. 1991, bd. dirs.), Am. Stock Exch. Club, Union League, The Bond Club. Home: 370 Aubrey Rd Wynnewood PA 19096-1819 also: Apt 1905 111 N Pompano Beach Blvd Pompano Beach FL 33062 also: 35487 Davis Wharf Rd Belle Haven VA 23306-1909 Office: The Union League of Phila 140 S Broad St Philadelphia PA 19102-3003

LA BLANC, ROBERT EDMUND, consulting company executive; b. N.Y.C., Mar. 21, 1934; s. Charles Wesley and Anne R. (Dobson) La B.; m. Elizabeth Lammers, 1962; children: Elizabeth, Robert, Jeanne Marie, Paul, Michelle. B.E.E., Manhattan Coll., 1956; M.B.A., NYU, 1962. With Bell System, 1956-69; mem. tech. staff Bell Telephone Labs., 1961-62; seminar leader AT&T Long Lines, Cooperstown, N.Y., 1965-67; mktg. supr. AT&T Hdqrs., N.Y.C., 1967-68; planning engr. N.Y. Telephone, 1968-69; mgr. Salomon Bros., N.Y.C., 1969-73; v.p. Salomon Bros., 1973-75, gen. partner, 1975-79; vice chmn. Continental Telephone Corp., N.Y.C., 1979-81; pres. Robert E. LaBlanc Assocs., Inc., 1981—; bd. dirs. Salient 3 Comm., Inc., Storage Tech. Corp., Titan Corp., Tribune Co., Prudential Europe Growth Fund, Inc., Prudential Global Genesis Fund, Inc., Prudential Instnl. Liquidity Portfolio, Inc., Prudential MoneyMart Assets, Inc., Prudential Natural Resources Fund, Inc., Prudential Pacific Growth Fund., Inc., Prudential Spl. Money Market Fund, Inc., Prudential Tax-Free Money Fund, Inc., Prudential World Fund, Inc.; trustee Command Govt. Fund, Command Money Fund and Command Tax-Free Fund. Vice chmn. bd. trustees Manhattan Coll., 1987-93, trustee, 1994—. Served to 1st lt. USAF, 1956-59. Named Wall St. Leading Analyst Instl. Investor Mag., 1973-78. Fellow Fin. Analysts Fedn.; mem. N.Y. Soc. Security Analysts (sr.), Assn. for Computing Machinery, Univ. Club, Econ. Club. Republican. Roman Catholic.

LABODA, AMY SUE, writer; b. Phila., Sept. 10, 1962; d. Gerald and Sheila Lois (Plasky) L.; m. Barry Lee Marz, Mar. 5, 1987; children: Rose Marie, Leah Ann. BA, Sarah Lawrence Coll., 1984. Airline transport pilot rating, Flight Safety Internat. Vol. U.S. Peace Corps, Togo, 1985; flight instr., pilot Redwood Aviation, Santa Rosa, Calif., 1986, Qualiflight Tng., Ft. Worth, 1987-88; depts. editor Flying mag., N.Y.C., 1988-90; free-lance writer, mktg. cons. Ft. Myers, Fla., 1990—; mem. selection com. Am. Flyers Scholarship, Pal-Walkee, Ill., 1990-96. N.Am. editl. dir. textbook series: The Pilot's Manual, 2d edit., 1993; editor: Flying Ultralights, U.S. edit., Principles of Helicopter Flight; contbr. articles to various mags. Mem. Exptl. Aircraft Assn., Aircraft Owners and Pilots Assn., Women in Aviation (internat. exec. bd. dirs.), Women's Scuba Assn., Diver's Alert Network. Avocations: scuba diving, soaring, skydiving.

LABODA, GERALD, oral and maxillofacial surgeon; b. Phila., Aug. 15, 1936; s. Lewis and Rose (Waldman) L.; m. Sheila Lois Plasky, Aug. 2, 1956; children: Amy, Michèle, Alane, Bruce. Student, Temple U., 1954-56, DMD, 1960; postgrad., U. Pa., 1960-61. Diplomate Am. Bd. Oral and Maxillofacial Surgery. Resident physician in oral and maxillofacial surgery Jefferson U. Hosp., Phila., 1961-63; pvt. practice oral and maxillofacial surgery S.W. Fla. Oral and Facial Surgery Assocs., Ft. Myers, 1965—; sr. dir. Barnett Bank of Lee County, Ft. Myers; chmn. bd. trustees S.W. Fla. Regional Med. Ctr., Ft. Myers, 1989-94, sec. bd. trustees, 1974—; med. dir. S.W. Fla. divsn. Columbia/HCA Healthcare Corp., 1994—; mem. bd. trustees East Pointe Hosp. Lehigh, Fla., Gulf Coast Hosp., Ft. Myers; v.p. Flordeco, Inc.; chmn. bd. dirs. Procraft Industries, L.L.C. Contbr. articles to profl. jours. Pres. YMCA of Lee County, 1976; pres., bd. dirs. Found. for Lee County Pub. Schs., Ft. Myers, 1991, Fla. Gulf Coast Univ. Found.; vice chmn. Downtown Redevel. Agy., Ft. Myers, 1985-93, chmn., 1993—; bd. dirs. United Way of Lee County, 1981. Fellow Am. Assn. Oral and Maxillofacial Surgeons (trustee Dist. III 1984-87, v.p. 1987-88, pres. 1989-90); mem. Fla. Soc. Oral and Maxillofacial Surgeons (pres. 1980-81), Fla. Dental Soc. of Anesthesiology (pres. 1978-79), S.W. Fla. Dental Soc. (pres. 1974), Oral and Maxillofacial Surgery Found. (bd. dirs. 1993—, vice chmn. 1997). Republican. Jewish. Avocations: flying, skiing, scuba diving, white water rafting. Office: SW Fla Oral Facial Surg Assocs Summerlin Med Park 5285 Summerlin Rd Fort Myers FL 33919-7602

LABONTE, BOBBY, professional race car driver; b. Corpus Christi, Tex., May 8, 1964; m. Donna Labonte; 1 child, Robert Tyler. Professional race car driver NASCAR Winston Cup, 1991—; winner 1991 NASCAR Busch Series, 1992, Coca-Cola 600, Charlotte, N.C., 1995. Office: c/o NASCAR PO Box 2875 Daytona Beach FL 32120-2875

LA BONTÉ, C(LARENCE) JOSEPH, weight management and lifestyle company executive; b. Salem, Mass., Sept. 23, 1939; s. Arthur and Alice La Bonté; m. Donna Marie Chiaradonna, Aug. 2, 1959; children: Linda, Joseph. BS, Northeastern U., 1966, AME, 1968; MBA with distinction (Baker scholar), Harvard U., 1969. With H.P. Hood & Sons, Boston, 1958-63; project engr., mktg. coordinator Market Forge Co., Everett, Mass., 1963-67; with ARA Services, Inc., Phila., 1969-79, exec. asst. to pres., 1969-71, v.p., 1971-72, exec. v.p., 1976-79; pres. Western Co., Los Angeles, 1972-76; pres., chief operating officer, dir. Twentieth Century-Fox Film Corp., Beverly Hills, Calif., 1979-83; chmn., chief exec. officer The Vantage Group Inc., 1983-87, 90—; pres., chief operating officer Reebok Internat. Ltd., Stoughton, Mass., 1987-90; also bd. dirs. Reebok Internat., Stoughton, Mass.; chmn., CEO, Vantage Group, Inc., Palos Verdes, Calif., 1990-94; pres., CEO, Jenny Craig, Internat., La Jolla, Calif., 1994—; also bd. dirs., mem. exec. com. Jenny Craig, Internat., Del Mar, Calif.; bd. dirs. several cos.; founder, pres. Am. Bus. Initiative for Free South Africa, 1990-95; bd. dirs. U.S.-SALEP, Washington. Founding dir. South African Free Elections Fund, 1993-94; nat. bd. dirs. Big Bros. Am., 1970-74, pres., 1986-87; bd. dirs. L.A. Philharm. Assn., 1990-94, chmn. bd. dirs., 1994—, pres.; trustee Northeastern U., 1974-95; mem. Harvard U. Bus. Sch. Fund, 1971—; trustee Orthop. Hosp., L.A., 1980-86. Mem. Harvard U. Bus. Sch. Assn., Husky Assocs. Northeastern U., Huntington Soc., Human Rights Watch (Calif. exec. com.), Phila. Country Club Down Town Club, Vesper Club, Bankers Club San Francisco, 100 of L.A. Office: Jenny Craig Internat PO Box 387910 11355 N Torrey Pines Rd La Jolla CA 92038-9748

LABONTE, TERRY, professional race car driver; b. Corpus Christi, Tex., Nov. 16, 1956; m. Kim Labonte; children: Justin, Kristy. Profl. race car driver NASCAR Winston Cup, 1978—, winner The Winston at Charlotte, 1988, IROC title, 1989, 1984 Winston Cup champion; winner First Union 400, N Wilkesboro, N.C., 1994, Miller Genuine Draft 400, Richmond, Va., 1994; winner Pontiac Excitement 400, Richmond, 1995, UAW-GM Teamwork 500, Pocono, Pa., 1995, Goody's 500, Bristol, Tenn., 1995. Office: c/o NASCAR PO Box 2875 Daytona Beach FL 32120-2875

LABOON, LAWRENCE JOSEPH, personnel consultant; b. St. Louis, Aug. 4, 1938; s. Joseph Warren and Ruth (Aab) LaB.; children: Lindsey Beth, Allison Ruth; m. Glynys M. Brown, Sept. 16, 1989; children: Lawrence Bradley, Meredith Ashley. BS magna cum laude, Tex. Wesleyan U., 1962. Cert. pers. cons. Operating mgr. Firestone Tire & Rubber Co., Akron, Ohio, 1962-66; pres. Met. Pers., Inc., Phila., 1966—, Metro Tech, Valley Forge, Pa., 1977—, Metro Temps, Valley Forge, 1978—, Transport Tng. Corp., Valley Forge, 1993—; dir. Alpha-Indian Rock Savs. and Loan Assn., chmn. compensation com., 1986-90; chmn. pvt. employment agy. adv. coun. Pa. Dept. Labor and Industry, 1973-82; guest lectr. Drexel U., 1976-91; human resources del. to USSR, Citizen Amb. Program, 1991. Mem. People to People Internat. Mission, Vietnam, Asia, 1993. With USAF, 1954-60. Mem. Nat. Employment Assn. (state certification bd. chmn. 1969-71, bd. dirs. 1972-74, chmn. bd. regents 1973), Pa. Assn. Pers. Svcs. (pres. 1971-72, Blanchet Meml. award 1973), Nat. Assn. Pers. Cons., Am. Soc. Pers. Adminstrn., Mid-Atlantic Assn. Temporary Svcs. (pres. 1983-84), TEMPNET (bd. dirs. 1986-88), Nat. Assn. Profl. Employers, Exec. Riders Ltd. (pres. 1986-88), Glenhardie Condominium Assn. (non-resident exec. bd. 1989-91), Alpha Chi. Republican. Methodist. Home: 255 Country Ln Valley Forge PA 19482 Office: 1260 Valley Forge Rd Valley Forge PA 19482-0641

LABOON, ROBERT BRUCE, lawyer; b. St. Louis, June 14, 1941; s. Joseph Warren LaBoon and Ruth (Aab) LaBoon Freling; m. Ramona Ann Hudgins, Aug. 24, 1963; children: John Andrew, Robert Steven. BSC, Tex. Christian U., 1963; LLB cum laude, So. Meth. U., 1965. Bar: Tex. 1965. Ptnr. Liddell, Sapp, Zivley, Hill & LaBoon, L.L.P., Houston, 1965-86, 88—; vice chmn. and gen. counsel Tex. Commerce Bancshares, Inc., 1986-88; dir. Tex. Commerce Bank, Gamma Biol. Inc., Tex. Med. Ctr. Bd. dirs. The Inst. Rehab. and Rsch., The Greater Houston Partnership, Houston area ARC, Greater Houston Community Found.; bd. dirs. Retina Rsch. Found.; trustee Tex. Christian U., The Kayser Found.; mem. Bd. of Visitors of the M.D. Anderson Cancer Ctr.-U. Cancer Found. Fellow Tex. Bar Found., Am. Coll. of Trust and Estate Counsel; mem. ABA, Am. Law Inst., Tex. Assn. of Bank Counsel, Houston Bar Assn., State Bar Tex.; mem. Houston Club, River Oaks Country Club. Office: Liddell Sapp Zivley Hill & LaBoon LLP 600 Travis St Ste 3500 Houston TX 77002-3004

LABORDE, ALDEN JAMES, oil company executive; b. Vinton, La., Dec. 18, 1915; s. Cliffe E. and Hilda (Moreau) L.; m. Margaret Bienueu, Mar. 11, 1943; children: Susan, J. Monroe, John P., Stephanie, Jane. Student, La. State U., 1932-34; B.S., U.S. Naval Acad., 1938; DEng (hon.), Cath. U. Am., 1991; LLD (hon.), Loyola U., 1996; LHD (hon.), Xavier U., 1996. Engr., S.W. Richardson Oil Co., 1946-48; marine supt. Kerr McGee Oil Industries, 1948-52; pres. Ocean Drilling & Exploration Co., 1953-74, chmn. bd., c.e.o., 1974-77; offshore oil industry cons., 1977-85; chmn. bd., c.e.o. Gulf Island Fabrication Co., 1985—; chmn. All Aboard Devel. Corp. Trustee Catholic U. Am.; mem. bd. liquidation city debt, New Orleans; mem. New Orleans Sewage and Water Bd.; bd. adminstrs. Tulane U., 1975-85. Served from ensign to comdr. USNR, 1938-46. Decorated knight St. Gregory the Great, Vatican; recipient Order St. Louis medal, 1976; Disting. Achievement award Offshore Tech. Conf., 1977; St. Mary's Dominican Coll. medal, 1978; Loyola U. award; named to Fortune mag. Nat. Bus. Hall of Fame, 1985. Mem. Internat. Assn. Oilwell Drilling Contractors. (pres. 1973), Midcontinent Oil and Gas Assn. (pres. 1970-71), Nat. Petroleum Council, St. Vincent de Paul Soc. Home: 63 Oriole St New Orleans LA 70124-4517

LABORDE, TERRENCE LEE, small business owner, negotiator; b. DuBois, Pa., June 20, 1947; s. Donald Leo and Anna Lee (Wise) LaB.; m. Brenda Sue Roberts, May 16, 1970 (div. 1975); 1 child, Terrence Lee II; m. Elisa Jean Meenan, Sept. 12, 1975; children: Marc Elliott, Dawn Ann. BS, Nat. Coll., 1973. Sr. auditor Def. Contract Audit Agy., State Coll., Pa., 1973-84; contract negotiator Pa. State U., State Coll., 1984-88, subcontract adminstr., 1988-91, mgr. grant & subcontract adminstrn., 1991-92; pres., CEO Keystone for Future Decisions, Inc., Pennsylvania Furnace, Pa., 1992—; owner LaBorde Enterprises, 1984—, Pennsylvania Furnace, Pa., 1991—. Sgt. USAF, 1966-70. Democrat. Lutheran. Avocations: hunting, fishing, landscaping, financial and educational consulting. Home and Office: Ramblewood 1 110 Elm Rd Pennsylvania Furnace PA 16865-9538 Branch Office: Future Decisions Inc 209 Beaver Dr DuBois PA 15801

LABOVITZ, DEBORAH ROSE RUBIN, occupational therapist, educator; b. Phila., Oct. 13, 1942; d. Samuel Frank and Clara (Blank) Rubin; m. Judah Isaiah Labovitz, June 3, 1962; children: Gail Susan Labovitz Seligman, Bruce Joel, Daniel Mark. BS in Occupational Therapy, U. Pa., 1963, Ma in Sociology, 1974, PhD in Sociology, 1979. Lic. occupl. therapist Nat. Bd. for Cert. of Occupl. Therapy. Dir. occupational therapy Mercy Douglas Hosp., Dept Psychiatry, Univ. Pa., Phila., 1963-66; adj. lectr. U. Pa., Phila., 1967-69, adj. instr., 1971-72, instr., 1972-76, asst. prof., 1976-80; prof. and chair dept. occupational therapy NYU, N.Y.C., 1980—; cons. Ea. Pa. Psychiatric Inst., 1967-69, to pres. Beaver Coll., Phila., 1980; adj. lectr. U. Pa., 1980-81; mem. NYU Faculty Senate (acad. affairs com. 1987-88, faculty coun. exec. com. 1988-89, acad. affairs com. 1989=90, mandatory retirement subcom., 1988-92, fin. affairs com., 1988-90), Faculty Resource Network, Minority Conf. Com., 1991-92; Sch. of Edn. Budget Adv. Com., 1985—, chair 1992-93; Sch. of Edn. Instl. Planning and Devel. Com., 1986—, chair 1992-93; chair Sch. of Edn. Senate and Faculty Coun.; other coms. and offices. Contbr. articles to profl. jours.; presenter at numerous profl. confs. and ednl. meetings. Alt. del. Dem. Nat. Conv., Miami Beach, Fla., 1972. Grantee: N.Y.C. Bd. Edn., 1990-93, 93-96, MCH grant project, RSA long term tng. grantee, 1984-87, 87—, AOA, 1988-90, NYU Challenge grant, 1990, and others. Fellow Am. Occupational Therapy Assn. (vice chair commn. on edn. steering com. 1991-93; reviewer conf. papers, rsch. grants, postdoctoral fellowships, various books and articles, many other coms. and com. offices, Svc. award 1986, 89, 93, Cert. of Appreciation 1991); mem. AAUP, Pa. Occupational Therapy Assn. Dist. V., World Fedn. of Occupational Therapists, N.Y. State Occupational Therapy Assn. (mem. chief's group met. N.Y. dist., Cert. Appreciation 1987). Office: NYU Dept Occup Therapy 35 W 4th St Fl 11 New York NY 10012-1120

LABRECQUE, RICHARD JOSEPH, industrial executive; b. Lawrence, Mass., Dec. 19, 1938; s. Eugene N. and Ludivine M. (Roy) L.; m. Janet Marie Michaud, July 16, 1960; children: David R., Lisa M., Susan M. BSEE, Tufts U., 1962; MS in Indsl. Adminstrn., Union U., 1971. Mgr. mfg. engring. GE Aircraft Engine Group, Lynn, Mass., 1962-68; with Colt Industries, 1969-81; pres. FM Pump div., Kansas City, Kans., 1973-78, Quincy (Ill.) Compressor div., 1979-81; with ITT Industries, Inc., Skokie, Ill., 1982—, pres. fluid handling div., 1982-95, sr. v.p., 1996—; pres., CEO ITT Fluid Tech. Corp., Midland Pk., N.J., 1996—. Campaign chmn. United Way Wyandotte County, Kansas City, 1979. Mem. Hydraulic Inst. (bd. dirs. 1976—, pres. 1979, 96, chmn. 1997—).

LABRECQUE, THEODORE JOSEPH, lawyer; b. Portland, Oreg., Mar. 8, 1903; s. Herman F. and Clara (Thibault) L.; m. Marjorie Uprichard, Jan. 31, 1931; children: Theodore J., Katherine Labrecque Skiba, Thomas G., Jeanne M. Labrecque Gagliano, Robert S., David F., Susan Labrecque Woolley, Barbara Anne Labrecque Danowitz. Ed., Manhattan Coll., 1920-21; LLB, Fordham U., 1924; LLD (hon.), Georgian Ct. Coll., 1986. Bar: N.J. 1925, ICC 1936, U.S. Tax Ct. 1943, U.S. Supreme Ct. 1957. Gen. practice law Red Bank, N.J., 1925-60; mem. Quinn, Parsons & Doremus, 1929-37, Parsons, Labrecque, Canzona & Blair, and predecessor firms, 1937-60; mem. N.J. Divsn. Tax Appeals, 1946-60, pres., 1956-60; judge N.J. Superior Ct., 1960-73; judge appellate div. Superior Ct., 1964-73; presiding judge part D appellate div. Superior Ct., 1972-73; of counsel Parsons, Cappiello & Nardelli and predecessor firms, Red Bank, N.J., 1973—. Chmn., Monmouth County Transp. Coordinating Com., 1973—; chmn. North Jersey Transit Adv. Com., 1980-87; mem. Monmouth County Hist. Commn., 1988-90. Recipient Salvation Army award, 1982, Boy Scouting's Joshua Huddy Disting. Citizen award, 1988, N.J. Gov.'s Charles A. Lindbergh Transp. award, 1992. Fellow Am. Coll. Trial Lawyers, Am. Bar Found.; mem. ABA, N.J. State Bar Assn. (pres. 1960), Essex County Bar Assn., Monmouth Bar Assn., Am. Judicature Soc., Elks, Red Bank Lions Club (pres. 1939), Phi Delta Phi (hon.). Democrat. Roman Catholic. Home: 410 Rumson Rd Little Silver NJ 07739-1659 Office: 612 River Rd Fair Haven NJ 07704-3221 also: PO Box 770 Red Bank NJ 07701-0770

LABRECQUE, THOMAS G., bank executive; b. Long Branch, N.J., Sept. 17, 1938; s. Theodore Joseph and Marjorie (Uprichard) L.; m. Sheila English Cardone, June 16, 1962; children: Thomas, Douglas, Karen, Barbara. BA, Villanova U., 1960; postgrad., Am. U., 1962-64, NYU, 1965; D (hon.), Villanova U., U. Charleston, Drexel U., Marymount Coll. Mem. special devel. program The Chase Manhattan Corp., N.Y.C., 1964-65; with corp. portfolio adv. group portfolio and investment banking dept. The Chase Manhattan Corp., 1965-66, asst. treas., 1966-67, second v.p., 1967-69, 1967-69, v.p. and mgr. correspondent bank portfolio advisory, 1969-70; assoc. sec. planning to corp. exec. office The Chase Manhattan Corp., N.Y.C., 1970-71, sr. v.p. bank portfolio group, 1971-74, exec. v.p. treasury dept. and treas., 1974-76, mem. mgmt. com., 1976-80; vice chmn., CEO The Chase Manhattan Corp. and The Chase Manhattan Bank, N.A., N.Y.C., 1980-81, responsible for comml. banking, retail banking, trust and fiduciary investment, ops. dept. and corp. systems functon, 1980-81, pres., 1981-90, chmn., CEO, 1990-1996, also bd. dirs., 1990-1996; pres., COO, bd. dirs. The Chase Manhattan Corp., 1996—; bd. dirs. Pfizer, Inc., Alumax, Inc.; rep. on team that worked out the financial arrangements associated with the release of Am. hostages from Iran, Chase Manhattan Bank, 1980. Trustee Brookings Instn., Central Park Conservancy, N.Y. Pub. Libr.; bd. dirs. Fund for N.Y.C. Pub. Edn., United Way Tri-State, United Way N.Y.C.; bd. visitors Duke U. Fuqua Sch. Bus.; mem. Coun. Fgn. Rels., Trilateral Commn., Bus.-Higher Edn. Forum, Cystic Fibrosis Rsch. Devel. Coun.; mem. exec. com. Partnerships for Quality Edn. Mem. Bus. Coun., Bus. Roundtable, N.Y. Chamber of Commerce and Industry (bd. dirs.), N.Y.C. Partnership. Office: Chase Manhattan Bank NA 1 Chase Manhattan Plz New York NY 10081-1000*

LABRIE, FERNAND, physician; b. Quebec, Que., Can., June 28, 1937; s. François-Xavier and Rose-Alma (Dubois) L.; m. Nicole Cantin; children: Claude, Pierre, Danielle, Anne, Isabelle. BA magna cum laude, Laval U., 1957, MD magna cum laude, 1962, PhD in Endocrinology summa cum laude, 1966; postgrad. of Biochemistry, Univ. Cambridge and Sussex, 1966-69. Jr. intern l'Enfant-Jésus Hosp., Québec, Qué., Can., 1961-62; resident internal medicine L'Hôtel-Dieu de Québec, 1962-63; asst. prof. dept physiology Laval U., 1966-69; tutor dept. biochemistry Cambridge (Eng.) U., 1966-67, Sussex (Eng.) U., 1967-68; assoc. prof. dept. physiology Laval U., 1969-74, dir. lab. molecular endocrinology, 1969—, prof. dept. physiology, 1974—; physician dept. medicine Le Centre Hospitalier de l'u Laval, 1972—; dir. rsch. Laval U. Hosp. Rsch. Ctr., 1982—; head dept. physiology Laval U., 1990—; dir. Med. Rsch. Coun. group in molecular endocrinology Med. Rsch. Coun., 1973—; Keith Harrison meml. lectr. Endocrine Soc. Australia, 1984; mem. med. adv. bd. Gairdner Found., Toronto, 1979-85; mem. adv. bd. Fondation de Recherche en Hormonologie, Paris, 1979-83; mem. selection panel Steacie Prize, 1982, 83; mem. mission of concertation minister for sci. and tech. Govt. Que., 1982-84; mem. steering com. Task Force on Methods for Regulation of Male Fertility, WHO, Geneva, 1982; cons. study sect. Centre for Population Rsch., Nat. Inst. Childhood Diseases, NIH, Bethesda, Md., 1976, 77, 79, 80, 83, 84; mem. Sci. Coun. Can., 1984-87; mem. sci. com. 1st Internat. Congress on Neuroendocrinology, 1985-86; mem. Nat. Adv. Bd. Sci. and Tech. Can., 1994-96; invited spkr. more than 600 symposia, confs., workshops, cong., U.S., Can., Europe, Asia, Japan, S.Am. Assoc. editor Can. Jour. Biochemistry, 1973-78, Jour. Molecular and Cellular Endocrinology, 1973-81; mem. editl. bd. Jour. Cyclic Nucleotide Rsch., 1974-80, Advances in Sex Hormone Rsch., Urban and Schwarzenberg, 1975-81, Endocrinology, 1977-81, Maturitas, 1979-83, Jour. Andrology, 1979-83, Hormones, 1982-90, Contraceptive Delivery Sys., MTP Press Ltd., 1983-90, Clin. and Investigative Medicine, 1985—, Clin. Endocrinology Monographs, 1977-85, Jour. Clin. Investigation, 1977-82, Jour. Endocrinological Investigation, 1983-87; mem. editl. com. Interface, 1984-86, mem. sci. com., 1984-88; mem. editl. sci. com. Hormones-reproduction-metabolisme, 1984—; mem. editl. bd. Jour. Steroid Biochemistry and Molecular Biology, 1987—; editor: Hypothalamus and Endocrine Functions, 1976, Clinical Neuroendocrinology, a pathophysiological approach, 1979, Prolactin and Prolactinomas, 1983, (with P. Mauvais-Jarvis and R. Sitruk-Ware) Medecine de la Réproduction, Gynécologie Endocrinienne, 1982, (with A. Bélanger and A. Dupont) LHRH and Its Analogues, Basic and Clinical Aspects, 1984, (with L. Proulx) Endocrinology, 1984, (with V. K. Wenderoth) A New Approach to the Treatment of Prostate Cancer, 1985, (with others) Early Stage Prostate Cancer: Diagnosis and Choice of Therapy, 1989, (with others) Advances in Diagnosis and Treatment of Early Stage Prostate Cancer, 1993, (with others) Localized Prostate Cancer: Recent Advances in Diagnosis and Treatment, 1996, (with others) DHEA Transformation in Target Tissues, 1996. Pres. Le Fonds de la Recherche en Santé du Qué., 1992-95, mem. coun., 1981-87, Fondation du Centre Hospitalier de U. Laval, 1981—; trustee Fondation Skibec Alpin, 1981-90, founding mem.; chmn. Skibec Alpin, 1980-85; pres. Skibec, 1980-85, Que. Ski Show, 1980, 81, hon. pres., 1982, 84; coun. mem. Que. Zone Water Ski Assn., 1979-80; founding pres. Que. Water Ski Found., 1988; pres. organizing com., race chmn. Mont Ste.-Anne World Cup, 1983, 84; mem. coun. Can. Ski Assn., 1982-87; pres. Que. Water Ski Assn., 1987-89; coun. mem. Can. Water Ski Assn., 1987-89. Decorated chevalier Ordre de Malte, Order of Que., 1991, Order of Can., 1981; recipient medal city of Nice, 1977; award Fondation de Recherche en Hormologie, 1981, award MDS Health Group, 1981, award Fideides of C. of C. of Ste.-Foy, 1984, 88, medal Coll. de France, Paris, 1984, Excel award, 1985, Gloire de l'Escolle award Laval U. Alumni, 1991; Med. Rsch. Coun. Can. fellow, 1962-68, Centennial fellow, 1968-69, scholar, 1969-73, Disting. Scientist, 1996; named Grand Québécois, Met. Que. C. of C., 1991, Most Cited Can. Sci., Inst. Sci. Info., 1973-88; numerous other awards, honors. Fellow Royal Soc. Can. (program com. 1983-84, com. for McLaughlin medal 1982-84, pres. com. for McLaughlin medal 1983-84, mem. coun. 1983-84); mem. Coll. des Médecins et Chirurgiens de la Province de Que., Royal Coll. Physicians and Surgeons Can. (assoc.), AAAS, Assn. des Médecins de Langue Française du Can. (Fondamental rsch. award 1972), Assn. Canadienne-Française pour l'Avancement des Scis. (Vincent medal 1976), Soc. Study Reproduction (rsch. award 1980), Internat. Soc. Neuroendocrinology (sec.-treas. 1984-92, v.p. 1992-96), Internat. Soc. Endocrinology (exec. com. 1984-88), Biochem. Soc. (Gt. Britain), Endocrine Soc., Can. Biochem. Soc., Can. Physiol. Soc. (Michel Sarrazin prize 1990), Club de Recherches Cliniques du Québec (Michel Sarrazin prize 1990), Am. Soc. Cell Biology, Am. Fertility Soc., Tissue Culture Assn., Can. Soc. Clin. Investigation (pres. 1981-82, pres. program com. 1982), Cans. for Health Rsch. (bd. dirs. 1983-88), Can. Soc. Endocrinology and Metabolism (chmn. liaison com. 1975-84, pres. 1978-79), Am. Soc. Andrology (coun. 1982-85), N.Y. Acad. Scis., Royal Soc. Medicine (affiliate), Soc. Argentina de Urologia (miembro correspondiente), Philippine Urol. Assn. (hon.), Société Française d'Endocrinologie (hon.), Am. Soc. Biol. Chemists, Can. Fertility and Andrology Soc., Soc. Obstetricians and Gynaecologists Can. (assoc.), Can. Investigators in Reproduction, Internat. Menopause Club, Internat. Soc. Andrology, Internat. Study Group Steroid Hormones, Am. Soc. Clin. Investigation, Société d'Andrologie de Langue Française (hon.). Home: 2989 Rue de la Promenade, Ste-Foy, PQ Canada G1W 2J5 Office: Laval U Hosp, 2705 Laurier Blvd, Quebec, PQ Canada G1V 4G2

LABRUYERE, THOMAS EDWARD, health facility administrator; b. St. Louis, Aug. 2, 1955; s. Thomas Edward and Daisy Lillian (Nussbaum) LaB.; m. Annette Sue Gusoskey, Oct. 27, 1979; children: Thomas Edward III, Christopher John, Sarah Elizabeth. AAS, Maryville Coll., 1979, BS in Mgmt. with honors, 1990; MBA, Maryville U., 1993. Registered respiratory therapist. Coord. insvc. edn. Normandy Hosp., St. Louis, 1977-79; mgr. dept. Lifemark Cardiopulmonary, Houston, 1979-81; from asst. supr. respiratory therapy to adminstrv. dir. St. Anthony's Med. Ctr., St. Louis, 1981-95, adminstrv. dir. Cardiopulmonary and Radiology, 1995—; mem. respiratory care adv. com. Forest Park C.C., St. Louis, 1993—; bd. dirs. Nalco Credit Union, vice chmn., 1995—, mem. supervisory com., 1991-93. Asst. scoutmaster Boy Scouts Am., St. Louis, 1995-96, asst. cubmaster, 1993, 94, troop com. chmn., 1996—; coach CYC Baseball, St. Louis, 1993-96, CYC Soccer, 1993-96. Mem. Am. Coll. Healthcare Execs. (assoc.), Am. Coll. Cardiovascular Adminstrs., Am. Assn. Respiratory Care. Avocations: blackbelt Tae Kwon Do, camping. Home: 3036 Armona Dr Saint Louis MO 63129-5202 Office: Saint Anthony's Med Ctr 10010 Kennerly Rd Saint Louis MO 63128-2106

LA BUDDE, KENNETH JAMES, librarian; b. Sheboygan Falls, Wis., Jan. 20, 1920; s. Arno Peter and Claire (Devoy) LaB. A.B., U. Wis., 1941, B.L.S., 1942; student, U. Chgo., 1943-44; M.A., U. Minn., 1948; Ph.D., 1954. Student asst. U. Wis. Library, 1939-42; sr. library asst. Milw. Pub. Library, 1942; librarian Sheboygan (Wis.) Press, 1944-46; instr. English Milton (Wis.) Coll., 1946-47; dir. libraries U. Mo. at Kansas City, 1950-85, asst. prof. history, 1958-61, assoc. prof., 1961, prof., 1962-85, prof. emeritus, 1985—. Contbr. articles profl. jours. Served with AUS, 1942-44. Recipient Thomas Jefferson award U. Mo., 1988. Mem. ALA, Am. Studies Assn., Bibliog. Soc. Am., Mo. Libr. Assn. (chmn. coll. and univ. divsn. 1954-55), Kansas City Posse of Westerners, Wis. Meml. Union, Mid-Continent Am. Studies Assn. (pres. 1963-64, arts editor jour. 1959-63), Orgn. Am. Historians, Soc. Archtl. Historians, Garden History soc., Decorative Arts Soc., Rockhill Tennis Club, Beta Phi Mu, Phi Kappa Phi, Phi Alpha Theta. Home: 309 Brush Creek Blvd Kansas City MO 64112-1792

LABUDDE, ROY CHRISTIAN, lawyer; b. Milw., July 21, 1921; s. Roy Lewis and Thea (Otteson) LaB.; m. Anne P. Held, June 7, 1952; children: Jack, Peter, Michael, Susan, Sarah. AB, Carleton Coll., 1943; JD, Harvard U., 1949. Bar: Wis. 1949, U.S. Dist. Ct. (ea. and we. dists.) Wis. 1950, U.S. Ct. Appeals (7th cir.) 1950, U.S. Supreme Ct. 1957. Assoc. Michael, Best & Friedrich, Milw., 1949-57, ptnr., 1958—; dir. DEC-Inter, Inc., Milw. Western Bank, Western Bancshares, Inc., Superior Die Set Corp., Aunt Nellie's Farm Kitchens, Inc. Bd. dirs. Wis. Hist. Soc. Found.; chmn., bd. dirs. Milw. div. Am. Cancer Soc. Served to lt. j.g. USNR, 1943-46. Mem. Milw. Estate Planning Coun. (past pres.), Wis. Bar Assn., Wis. State Bar Attys. (chmn. tax sch., bd. dirs. taxation sect.), Univ. Club, Milw. Club, Milw. Country Club. Republican. Episcopalian. Home: 4201 W Stonefield Rd Mequon WI 53092-2771 Office: Michael Best & Friedrich 100 E Wisconsin Ave Ste 3300 Milwaukee WI 53202-4107

LABUNSKI, STEPHEN BRONISLAW, professional society administrator; b. Jordanow, Poland, Sept. 24, 1924; came to U.S., 1928, naturalized, 1943; s. Wiktor and Wanda (Mlynarski) L.; m. Betty E. Marley, Oct. 2, 1947 (div. June 1963); children: Linda, Richard, Roger; m. Jeralyn LeBrun, Aug. 28, 1967. Student, U. Kansas City, Mo., 1946-49, George Washington U., 1950. Adminstrv. asst. to U.S. Congressman Richard W. Bolling, 1949-51; with Storz Broadcasting Co., 1954-57; v.p. ABC radio network, 1957; head broadcast div. Crowell Collier Pub. Co., 1958; v.p., gen. mgr. WMCA Radio/Straus Broadcasting Group, N.Y.C., 1958-65; pres. radio div. NBC, 1965-69; mng. dir. WMCA Radio, 1969-71; v.p., partner Chuck Blore Creative Services, 1971-75; exec. v.p. Merv Griffin Group Radio, 1975-77; exec. dir. Internat. Radio and TV Soc., N.Y.C., 1978-94, Circles Spl. Events, N.Y.C., 1994—; Bd. dirs. Radio Advt. Bur., 1965-69, Nat. Assn. Broadcasters, 1965-67. Chmn. adv. com. Voice of Am., 1987-89; Democratic candidate for Mo. Legislature, 1948. With USAAF, 1943-46. Mem. Advt. Council. Home: 30 E 37th St New York NY 10016-3019 Office: 404 Park Ave S New York NY 10016

LABUTTI, GERALD MICHAEL, company executive; b. Providence, R.I., May 15, 1945; s. Michael and Adella (Stawaris) LaB. BSEE, U. R.I., Kingston, 1967; MBA, Columbia U., N.Y.C., 1978. Pres. Aerospace Aeronomics, Inc., Bohemia, N.Y., 1988-93; group pres. F. Industries, Bohemia, 1988-93; pres. Coto Corp., Providence, 1994—. 1st Lt. U.S. Army, 1967-69. Recipient Bronze Star U.S. Army, 1969. Mem. Instrument Assn. Soc. Am., R.I. Mtg. Assn. Avocations: boating, traveling. Home: 5 Farnum Ave North Providence RI 02911 Office: Coto Corp 55 Dupont Dr Providence RI 02907-3105

LACAGNINA, MICHAEL ANTHONY, judge; b. Rochester, N.Y., July 6, 1932; s. Frank and Josephine (LoMaglio) L.; m. Mary Laura Mantle, June 8, 1952; children: John Michael, Gina Laura, Frank Anthony. B.S. in Bus. Adminstrn, U. Ariz., 1955, LL.B., 1957. Bar: Ariz. 1957. Asst. U.S. atty. Tucson, 1958-60; partner firm Bilby, Shoenhair, Warnock & Dolph, Tucson, 1960-83; of counsel Bilby, Shoenhair, Warnock & Dolph, 1983-84; judge divsn. II Ariz. Ct. Appeals, 1984-95; vice chief judge Div. II, Ariz. Ct. Appeals, 1985-87, chief judge, 1987-89. Served with USMCR, 1950-52. Fellow Am. Coll. Trial Attys., Ariz. Bar Found. (chmn. fellows 1986-87); mem. ABA, Ariz. Bar Assn., Pima County Bar Assn. (pres. 1981), Nat. Assn. R.R. Trial Attys., Am. Bd. Trial Advs. (nat. exec. com., nat. sec. 1981, nat. pres. 1983), Ariz. Judges Assn. (exec. com. 1985-95), Tucson Def. Attys. (pres.), Phi Delta Phi, Alpha Kappa Psi. Democrat. Episcopalian. Home: 7100 E River Canyon Rd Tucson AZ 85750-2110

LACAPRA, DOMINICK CHARLES, historian; b. N.Y.C., July 13, 1939; s. Joseph and Mildred (Sciascia) LaC.; m. Anne-Marie Hlasny, June 15, 1965 (div.); 1 dau., Veronique. B.A., Cornell U., 1961; Ph.D., Harvard U., 1970. Tutor Harvard U., Cambridge, Mass., 1967-69; asst. prof. history Cornell U., Ithaca, N.Y., 1969-74, assoc. prof., 1974-79, prof. history, 1979—; Goldwin Smith prof. European intellectual history Cornell U., Ithaca, 1985-92, Bryce and Edith M. Bowmar prof. humanistic studies, 1992—; assoc. dir. Sch. of Criticism and Theory Cornell U., 1997—. Author: Emile Durkheim, 1972, A Preface to Sartre, 1978, "Madame Bovary" on Trial, 1982, Rethinking Intellectual History, 1983, History and Criticism, 1985, History, Politics and the Novel, 1987, Soundings in Critical Theory, 1989, Representing the Holocaust, 1994. Fulbright fellow France, 1961-62, Woodrow Wilson fellow Harvard U., 1962-63, sr. fellow NEH, 1979, Sch. Criticism and Theory; recipient Disting. Tchg. award Coll. Arts and Scis. Cornell U., 1979. Mem. MLA, Am. Hist. Assn., Internat. Assn. Philosophy and Lit., Soc. Phenomenological and Existential Philosophy, Soc. for the Humanities (dir.). Home: 119 Terrace Pl Ithaca NY 14850-4254 Office: Cornell U History Dept McGraw Hall Ithaca NY 14853

LACER, ALFRED ANTONIO, lawyer, educator; b. Hammonton, N.J., Feb. 14, 1952; s. Vincent and Carmen (Savall) L.; m. Kathleen Visser, June 15, 1974; children: Margaret, James, Matthew. BA in Polit. Sci., Gordon Coll., 1974; JD, Cath. U. Am., 1977. Bar: Md. 1977, U.S. Dist. Ct. Md. 1980, U.S. Ct. Appeals (4th cir.) 1980. Law clk. to Honorable Joseph A. Mattingly, Jr. Cir. Ct. St. Mary's County, Leonardtown, Md., 1977-78; ptnr. Kenney, Lacer & Sparling, Lexington Park, Md., 1978—; adj. prof. bus. law Fla. Inst. Tech., Patuxent, Md., 1989-92, 95—; vis. instr. St. Mary's Coll. of Md., 1988, 91; mem. bd. edn. St. Mary's County (Md.) Pub. Schs., 1989-94, pres., 1991-92; mem. inquiry panel Atty. Grievance Commn. of Md., 1984-90. Bd. dirs. St. Mary's Hosp., Leonardtown, 1982-88, v.p., 1985-88; bd. dirs. So. Md. Community Action, Inc., Hughsville, Md., 1982-84. Mem. ABA, Md. Bar Assn. (com. on jud. appointments 1982-85), St. Mary's County Bar Assn. (v.p. 1979-80, pres. 1980-81), Md. Trial Lawyers Assn. Episcopalian. Office: Kenney Lacer & Sparling 100 Exploration Ste 2030 Lexington Park MD 20653 also: 65 Duke St Prince Frederick MD 20678

LACEY, BEATRICE CATES, psychophysiologist; b. N.Y.C., July 22, 1919; d. Louis Henry and Mollie (Libowitz) Cates; m. John I. Lacey, Apr. 16, 1938; children: Robert Arnold, Carolyn Ellen. Student, Columbia U., 1935-38; A.B. with distinction, Cornell U., 1940; M.A., Antioch Coll., 1958. Mem. staff Fels Research Inst., Yellow Springs, Ohio, 1953-82; sr. investigator Fels Research Inst., 1966-72, sr. scientist, 1972-82; instr. Antioch Coll., Yellow Springs, 1956-63, asst. prof., 1963-68, assoc. prof., 1968-73, prof., 1973-82; Fels prof. psychiatry Wright State U. Sch. Medicine, 1977-82, clin. prof. psychiatry, 1982-89, Fels prof. emeritus, 1989—; acting sci. dir. Fels Research Inst., 1979-82. Assoc. editor Psychophysiology, 1975-78; reviewer Jour. Abnormal Psychology, Psychophysiology, Biol. Psychology, Cognitive Psychology, Sci.; contbr. articles to profl. jours.; researcher, author numerous publs. in psychophysiology of the autonomic nervous system. Recipient Disting. Sci. Contbn. award, Am. Psychol. Assn., 1976, Psychol. Sci. Gold Medal award, Am. Psychol. Found., 1985. Fellow Acad. Behavioral Medicine Research, Soc. Exptl. Psychologists, Am. Psychol. Soc. (William James fellow 1989); mem. Soc. Psychophysiol. Research (dir. 1972-75, pres. 1978-79), Soc. Neurosci., Phi Kappa Phi. Achievements include rsch. and publs. in psychophysiology of the autonomic nervous system. Home: 70-260 Mottle Cir Rancho Mirage CA 92270

LACEY, CLOYD EUGENE, retired insurance company executive; b. New Lexington, Ohio, Mar. 12, 1918; s. Russell Anderson and Freda (Bahr) L.; m. Jane Linn Williams, Sept. 12, 1941; children: Thomas, Melinda Lacey Houfek, Janene Lacey Paulus. B.S. in Bus. Adminstrn., Ohio State U., 1941. Acct., asst. treas. Pioneer Mut. Causualty Co., Columbus, Ohio, 1945-51; various corp. fin. positions Nationwide Ins. Cos., Columbus, 1951-73, v.p., asst. controller, 1973-75, v.p., corp. controller, 1975-78, v.p. Office of Treas., controller, 1978-81, sr. v.p. fin., 1981-82, ret., 1982. Served with U.S. Army, 1943-45. Republican. Methodist. *I believe in God and put my trust in him. I believe in treating other people fairly and in giving them credit for accomplishments. I believe in maintaining a high degree of integrity. I believe in diligence and determination in performing a task. I believe in striving for excellence.*

LACEY, HENRY BERNARD, lawyer; b. Aurora, Colo., Nov. 30, 1963; s. Leonard Joseph and Colleen Trece (Ryan) L. BS, Ariz. State U., 1988, JD, 1991. Bar: Ariz. 1991, Oreg. 1996; U.S. Dist. Ct. Ariz. 1991, U.S. Ct. Appeals (9th cir.) 1992. Jud. law clk. to Hon. Cecil F. Poole U.S. Ct. Appeals 9th Cir., San Francisco, 1991-92; assoc. Kimball & Curry, P.C., Phoenix, 1992-93; atty. Law Office of Henry B. Lacey, Phoenix, Ariz., 1993-94, 96—; vis. fellow Natural Resources Law Inst. Northwestern Sch. Law, Lewis and Clark Coll., Portland, Oreg., 1994-95; atty. Wilenchik & Bartness, P.C., Phoenix, 1996-97; counsel/environ. group adv. bd. dirs. Coalition to Reform the Ctrl. Ariz. Project, Phoenix, 1993; vol. lawyer/Ariz. bd. dirs. Land and Water Fund of the Rockies, Boulder, Colo., 1993—; vol. lawyer Portland Audubon Soc., 1996—. Gen. counsel Maricopa County, Ariz. Dem. Party, 1992-94; counsel Carol Cure for Congress Campaign, Phoenix, 1994; vol. Ariz. for Clinton-Gore '92, 1992. Mem. ABA, Ariz. State Bar, Maricopa County Bar Assn. (environ. law com. 1993—), Environ. Law Inst., Am. Inns of Ct., Order of Coif, Phi Delta Phi. Roman Catholic. Avocations: hiking, bicycling, reading, photography. Office: 919 N 1st St Phoenix AZ 85004-1902

LACEY, HUGH MATTHEW, philosophy educator; b. Sydney, Australia, Sept. 7, 1939; came to U.S., 1972; s. Owen Charles and Margaret Jane (Devine) L.; m. Maria Ines Rocha E. Silva, Aug. 14, 1966; children: Andrew David, Daniel Carlos. BA, U. Melbourne, Australia, 1962, MA, 1964; PhD, Ind. U., 1966. Tutor in math. U. Melbourne, 1961-63; lectr. history and philosophy of sci. U. Sydney, 1966-68; prof. philosophy U. São Paulo, Brazil, 1969-72; prof. philosophy Swarthmore (Pa.) Coll., 1972, chmn. dept. philosophy, 1973-83, Eugene M. Lang Rsch. Prof. of Philosophy, 1993—; vis. prof. Temple U., Phila., spring 1983, Villanova U., fall 1984, Instituto de Teologia, São Paulo, spring 1988, fall, 1992, Ctrl. Am. U., El Salvador, summer 1991, U.Pa., fall 1995, U. Melbourne, spring 1996, U. São Paulo, fall 1996; Dyason lectr. Australasian Assn. History Philosophy and Social Studies of Sci., 1996. Author: A Linguagem Do Espaco E do Tempo, 1972; co-author: Behaviorism, Science and Human Nature, 1982; co-editor: Towards a Society That Serves Its People: The Thought of El Salvador's Murdered Jesuits, 1991; cons. editor: Jour. for Theory of Social Behavior, 1977—, Behavior and Philosophy, 1987—, Jour. for Peace and Justice Studies, 1987—. Bd. dirs. Chester-Swarthmore Coll. Cmty. Coalition, 1993—. NSF fellow, 1975, 79, 83; Fulbright grantee, 1963; Research Found. of State of São Paulo grantee, 1969, 73, 96. Mem. Philosophy of Sci. Assn., Am. Philos. Assn., Am. Psychol. Assn. (commn. on behavior modification 1974-77), Brazilian Soc. for the Advancement of Sci. Roman Catholic. Home: 4 Whittier Pl Swarthmore PA 19081-1142 Office: Dept Philosophy Swarthmore 500 College Ave Swarthmore PA 19081-1306

LACEY, JOHN IRVING, psychologist, physiologist, educator; b. Chgo., Apr. 11, 1915; s. David and Cecelia (Burnstein) L.; m. Beatrice Lucile Cates, Apr. 16, 1938; children—Robert Arnold, Carolyn Ellen. A.B., Cornell U., 1937, Ph.D., 1941. Instr. Queen's Coll., Flushing, N.Y., 1941-42; mem. faculty Antioch Coll., 1946-77, prof. psychophysiology, 1956-77; mem. staff Fels Research Inst., Yellow Springs, Ohio, 1946-82, chief sect. behavioral physiology, 1946-82; Fels prof. psychiatry Wright State U. Med. Sch., 1977-82, prof. emeritus, 1982—; cons. USPHS, 1957-82, FDA, 1977-82; mem. bd. sci. counselors Nat. Inst. Aging, NIH, 1977-80;. Cons. editor Jour. Comparative and Physiol. Psychology, 1953-69, Jour. Psychosomatic Medicine, 1962-65, Jour. Psychophysiology, 1964-69, Jour. Physiol. Psychology; contbr. articles to profl. jours. Served to capt. USAAF, 1942-46. Centennial scholar Johns Hopkins U., 1976; recipient Psychol. Sci. Gold medal Am. Psychol. Found., 1985. Fellow Am. Psychol. Soc. (William James fellow 1989); mem. Soc. Psychophysiol. Research (award for disting. contbns. 1970, pres. 1961-62, dir. 1965-68), Am. Psychosomatic Soc. (bd. dirs. 1959-62), Soc. Exptl. Psychologists, Am. Psychol. Assn. (pres. div. physiol. and comparative psychology 1969-70, mem. council 1964-68, 70-73, 78-79, bd. dirs. 1974-77, Disting. Sci. Contbn. award 1976), AAAS (chmn. sect. 1985-86), Psychonomic Soc., Soc. for Neurosci., Acad. Behavioral Medicine Rsch., Internat. Brain Rsch. Orgn., Nat. Acad. Scis. (chair com. new techs. in cognitive psychophysiology with NRC 1988), Sigma Xi, Phi Kappa Phi. Home: 70-260 Mottle Cir Rancho Mirage CA 92270

LACEY, JOHN WILLIAM CHARLES, management consultant; b. London, May 1, 1930; came to U.S., 1956; s. William J. and Florence (Farbus) L.; m. Edna Winifred Burns, July 28, 1951; children: Jonathan Charles, Erika Jane. B.A. with honors, Oxford U., 1952, M.A. with honors, 1956. Sr. sci. officer Govt. of U.K., 1952-60; U.S. liaison officer Brit. embassy, Washington, 1956-60; mgr. research and devel., spl. systems Control Data Corp., Bloomington, Minn., 1960-63, dir. ops., 1963; pres. Control Data subs. Control Corp., Bloomington, 1964-65, gen. mgr. Devel. and Standard Systems div., 1965, v.p. computer equipment group, 1966-67, v.p. corp. devel., 1967-71, v.p., sr. staff officer corp. plans and controls, 1971-73, sr. v.p. corp. plans and controls, chmn. mgmt. com., 1973-77; pres. Control Data Edn. Co., 1977-79, Control Data Info. and Edn. Systems Co., 1979-82; exec. v.p. Control Data Corp., 1982-86; cons. in field, 1986—; chmn. bd. Control Corp., Adcomp Corp., 1963-66; bd. dirs. Graco, Inc., 1973-95, Instron Corp., LSC Inc. Bd. dirs. Jr. Achievement Greater Mpls., 1966-76, Mpls. Acquatennial, 1975-82, Guthrie Theater, 1983-88; bd. dirs. Computer Mus., 1982-86, trustee, 1986-93. With Brit. Royal Navy, 1948-49.

LACH, ALMA ELIZABETH, food and cooking writer, consultant; b. Petersburg, Ill.; d. John H. and Clara E. (Boeker) Satorius; diplome de Cordon Bleu, Paris, 1956; m. Donald F. Lach, Mar. 18, 1939; 1 dau., Sandra Judith. Feature writer Children's Activities mag., 1954-55; creator, performer TV show Let's Cook, children's cooking show, 1955; hostess weekly food program on CBS, 1962-66, performer TV show Over Easy, PBS, 1977-78; food editor Chgo. Daily Sun-Times, 1957-65; pres. Alma Lach Kitchens Inc., Chgo., 1966—; dir. Alma Lach Cooking Sch., Chgo.; lectr. U. Chgo. Downtown Coll., Gourmet Inst., U. Md., 1963, Modesto (Calif.) Coll., 1978, U. Chgo., 1981; resident master Shoreland Hall, U. Chgo., 1978-81; food cons. Food Bus. Mag., 1964-66, Chgo.'s New Pump Room, Lettuce Entertain You, Bitter End Resort, Brit. V.I., Midway Airlines, Flying Food Fare, Inc., Berghoff Restaurant, Hans' Bavarian Lodge, Unocal '76, Univ. Club Chgo.; columnist Modern Packaging, 1967-68, Travel & Camera, 1969, Venture, 1970, Chicago mag., 1978, Bon Appetit, 1980, Tribune Syndicate, 1982; inventor: Curly-Dog Cutting Bd., 1995, Alma's Walker Tray, 1996. Recipient Pillsbury award, 1958; Grocery Mfrs. Am. Trophy award, 1959, certificate of Honor, 1961; Chevalier du Tastevin, 1962; Commanderie de l'Ordre des Anysetiers du Roy, 1963; Confrerie de la Chaine des Rotisseurs, 1964; Les Dames D'Escoffier, 1982, Culinary Historians of Chgo., 1993. Mem. Am. Assn. Food Editors (chmn. 1959). Clubs: Tavern, Quadrangle (Chgo.). Author: A Child's First Cookbook, 1950; The Campbell Kids Have a Party, 1953; The Campbell Kids at Home, 1953; Let's Cook, 1956; Candlelight Cookbook, 1959; Cooking a la Cordon Bleu, 1970; Alma's Almanac, 1972; Hows and Whys of French Cooking, 1974; contbr. to World Book Yearbook, 1961-75, Grolier Soc. Yearbook, 1962. Home and Office: 5750 S Kenwood Ave Chicago IL 60637-1744 *The art of cooking rests upon one's ability to taste, to reproduce taste, and to create taste. To achieve distinction the cook must taste everything, study cookbooks of all kinds, and experiment constantly in the kitchen. I stress in my writing and teaching the logic of food preparation, for the cook who possesses logic, knows how to create dishes rather than being content merely to duplicate the recipes of others.*

LACH, JOSEPH THEODORE, physicist; b. Chgo., May 12, 1934; s. Joseph and Kate (Ziemba) L.; m. Barbara Ryan, June 26, 1965; children—Michael, Elizabeth. A.B., U. Chgo., 1953, M.S., 1956; Ph.D., U. Calif.-Berkeley, 1963. Rsch. assoc. in physics Yale U., New Haven, 1963-65, asst. prof. physics, 1966-69; physicist Fermi Nat. Accelerator Lab., Batavia, Ill, 1969—, chmn. dept. physics, 1974-75; chmn. Gordon Rsch. Conf. in Elem. Particle Physics, 1975; mem. joint rsch. program with USSR and People's Republic of China. Fellow Am. Phys. Soc., Physicians for Social Responsibility, Ill. Geol. Survey (rsch. affiliate). Home: 28w364 Indian Knoll Trl West Chicago IL 60185-3013 Office: Fermilab PO Box 500 Batavia IL 60510-0500

LACHANCE, JANICE RACHEL, federal agency administrator, lawyer; b. Biddeford, Maine, June 17, 1953; d. Ralph L. and Rachel A. (Desnoyers) L. BA, Manhattanville Coll., 1974; JD, Tulane U., 1978. Bar: Maine 1978, D.C. 1982. Staff dir. subcom. on antitrust Ho. of Reps., Washington, 1982-83; adminstrv. asst. Congresswoman Katie Hall, 1983-84; asst. pres. sec.

Mondale-Ferraro Campaign, Washington, 1984; press sec. Congressman Tom Daschle, 1985; ptnr. Lachance and Assocs., Washington, 1985-87; dir. communications and polit. action Am. Fedn. Govt. Employees (AFL-CIO), Washington, 1987-93; dir. policy and communications U.S. Office Pers. Mgmt., Washington, 1993-96, chief of staff, 1996—; vis. scholar Cornell U., 1972-73. Editor newsletter Govt. Standard, 1987-93. Mem. Delta Delta Delta, Phi Alpha Delta. Democrat. Roman Catholic. Office: US Office Pers Mgmt 1900 E St NW Washington DC 20415-0001

LACHANCE, PAUL ALBERT, food science educator, clergyman; b. St. Johnsbury, Vt., June 5, 1933; s. Raymond John and Lucienne (Landry) L.; m. Therese Cecile Cote; children: Michael P., Peter A., M.-Andre, Susan A. BS, St. Michael's Coll., 1955; postgrad., U. Vt., 1955-57; PhD, U. Ottawa, 1960; cert. in pastoral counseling, N.Y. Theol. Sem., 1981; DSc (hon.), St. Michael's Coll., 1982. Ordained deacon Roman Cath. Ch., 1977. Assigned to St. Paul's Ch. Princeton, N.J.; aerospace biologist Aeromed. Research Labs., Wright-Patterson AFB, Ohio, 1960-63; lectr. dept. biology U. Dayton, Ohio, 1963; flight food and nutrition coordinator NASA Manned Spacecraft Center, Houston, 1963-67; assoc. prof. dept. food sci. Rutgers U., New Brunswick, N.J., 1967-72, dir. Sch. Feeding effectiveness research project, 1969-72, prof., 1972—, faculty rep. to bd. trustees, 1988-90, dir. grad. program food sci., 1988-91, chmn. food sci. dept., 1991—, chmn. univ. senate, 1990-93; faculty rep. to bd. govs., 1990-94; cons. Nutritional Aspects of Food Processing, Nutraceuticals; mem. nutrition adv. com. Whitehall-Robins/Lederle Consumer Divsn., 1989—; mem. sci. adv. bd. Roche chem. divsn. Hoffmann La Roche Co., 1976-88; mem. nutrition policy com. Beatrice Foods Co., 1979-86; trustee religious ministries com. Princeton Med. Ctr.; bd. dirs. J.R. Short Milling Co., 1990—. Mem. editorial adv. bd., Sch. Food Service Research Rev., 1977-82, Jour. Am. Coll. Nutrition, 1986—, Jour. Med. Consultation, 1985—, Nutrition Reports Internat., 1963-83, Profl. Nutritionist, 1977-80; contbr. articles to profl. jours. Served to capt. USAF, 1960-63. Recipient Endel Karmas award for excellence in teaching food sci., 1988, WilliamCruess award for excellence in teaching Inst. Food Technologists, 1991. Fellow Inst. Food Technologists, Am. Coll. Nutrition; mem. Am. Assn. Cereal Chemists, AAAS, Am. Inst. Nutrition, N.Y. Inst. Food Technologists (chmn. 1977-78), Am. Soc. Clin. Nutrition, N.Y. Acad. Sci., Am. Dietetic Assn., Soc. Nutrition Edn., Am. Public Health Assn., Nat. Assn. Cath. Chaplains, Sociedad Latino Americano de Nutricion, Sigma Xi, Delta Epsilon Sigma. Home: 34 Taylor Rd Princeton NJ 08540-9521 Office: Rutgers U Cook Coll Food Sci New Brunswick NJ 08903-0231

LACHAPELLE, CLEO EDWARD, real estate broker; b. West Warwick, R.I., Aug. 16, 1925; s. Wilfrid Maxim and Alice (Michaud) L.; m. Ann Wilcox, July 17, 1954; children: Linda, Susan. BA in Sociology, St. Bonaventure U., 1950. Registered social worker; cert. social worker; lic. clin. social worker, real estate broker, R.I. Probation officer R.I. Dept. Social Welfare, Cranston, 1951-53; prevention coord. R.I. Juvenile and Family Cts., Providence, 1953-63; asst. dir. Providence Youth Progress Bd., Inc., 1963-64, exec. dir., 1965-67; exec. dir. Progress for Providence, Inc., 1967-70; adminstr. Marathon House, Inc., Providence, 1970-77; dir. Washingtonian Hosp. and Ctr. for Addictions, Boston, 1977-80; state refugee coord. R.I. Office Refugee Resettlement, Cranston, 1980-85; broker, owner C.E. Lachapelle Real Estate Agy., Warwick, 1986—; social svcs. cons. VA Hosp., 1971-72, Nat. Ctr. Urban Ethnic Affairs, Washington, 1974-76, City of Providence, 1976-77, HHS, 1985, NIMH, 1985, and others; part-time detached youth worker Providence Recreation Dept., 1953-63; mem. mayor's adv. bd. City of Providence Model Cities Program, 1968-70; mem. adv. panel Nat. Inst. Drug Abuse, Rockville, Md., 1978; chair gov.'s study com. spl. needs population State of R.I., 1982-85; chair refugee policy Northeastern Regional Consultations, Boston, 1983; active U.S. Refugee Coodinators Policy Adv. Group, Washington, 1983, and others. Sgt. USAF, 1943-46, PTO. Mem. Nat. Assn. Realtors, R.I. Assn. Realtors, Kent Washington Bd. Realtors, Internat. Platform Assn., Audubon Soc., Nat. Trust for Hist. Preservation. Roman Catholic. Avocations: reading, golf, gardening, structure restoration and environment preservation. Home: 39 Winslow Ave Warwick RI 02886-4724 Office: CE Lachapelle Real Estate 2905 Post Rd Warwick RI 02886-3117

LACHEMANN, MARCEL, professional baseball manager; b. L.A., June 13, 1941. BSBA, U. So. Calif., 1962. Former player Kansas City A's (moved to Oakland); pitching coach Calif. Angels (now Anaheim Angels), 1983-92, 97—, mgr., head coach, 1994-96; pitching coach Anaheim Angels, 1996—, Fla. Marlins, 1992-94. Office: Anaheim Angels 2000 E Gene Autry Way Anaheim CA 92806-6100*

LACHENAUER, ROBERT ALVIN, retired school superintendent; b. Newark, Apr. 1, 1929; s. Alvin Frederick and Helen Louise (Bowers) L.; m. Patricia McConnell, June 14, 1952; children: Jane, Nancy, Robert. AB, Montclair State U., 1951, MA, 1956; EdS, Seton Hall U., 1983. Diplomate in sch. adminstrn., 1988; cert. sch. adminstr., N.J., sch. bus. adminstr., N.J., tchr., N.J., supr., N.J., secondary sch. prin., N.J. Tchr. Bd. Edn., Union, N.J., 1951-52, 54-57, asst. bd. sec., 1957-61; dep. supt. New Providence (N.J.) Sch. Dist., 1961-76, supt., 1976-91, vice pres. Rigorous Ednl. Assistance Deserving Youth Found., 1991-93; treas. sch. monies Morris-Union Jointure Commn., 1987-93; pres. Union County Sch. Bus. Ofcls., 1967-68, Title IV State Adv. Council, Trenton, N.J., 1976-78, Morris-Union Consortium, N.J., 1981-83, Union County Supts. Roundtable, 1983-84; adv. bd. Summit Trust Co., 1971-86. Elder treas. Presbyn. Ch., New Providence, 1958-62; treas. New Providence Hist. Soc., 1966-76; pres. United Way, New Providence, 1978; property mgr. Providence Presbyn. Ch., Hilton Head Island, 1993, elder, 1995. Served as seaman USN, 1952-54. Named Disting. Scholar of the Acad. Nat. Acad. for Sch. Execs., 1990. Mem. N.J. Assn. Sch. Adminstrs. (exec. bd. 1986-91), N.J. Assn. Sch. Bus Officials (pres. 1974-75), Assn. Sch. Bus Officials U.S. (professionalization com. 1974, membership chmn. 1976), N.J. Assn. Ednl. Secs. (adv. bd. 1976—, Outstanding Adminstr. of Yr. 1987). Lodge: Rotary (pres. 1980-81). Home: Sea Pines Plantation 84 Governors Rd Hilton Head Island SC 29928-3032

LACHEY, JAMES MICHAEL, professional football player; b. St. Henry, Ohio, June 4, 1963. BA Mktg., Ohio State Univ., 1985. With San Diego Chargers, 1985-88, L.A. Raiders, 1988; offensive tackle Washington Redskins, 1988—. Named offensive tackle The Sporting News NFL All-Pro team, 1989-91. Played in Pro Bowl, 1987, 90-91. Office: Washington Redskins Dulles Intl Airport PO Box 17247 Washington DC 20041*

LACHICA, R(EYNATO) VICTOR, microbiologist; b. Cebu, Philippines, Feb. 24, 1943; came to U.S., 1960; s. Alfredo and Lily P. (Flores) L.; m. Lois Jean Holmes, June 21, 1974. BA, Wartburg Coll., 1963; PhD, Iowa State U., 1967. Rsch. assoc. U. Wis., Madison, 1967-68; asst. rsch. microbiologist U. Calif., Davis, 1969-74; head microbiology br. WHO-Sponsored Food Control Lab., Guatemala, 1974-80; rsch. microbiologist U.S. Army Natick (Mass.) Ctr., 1984—; adj. prof. U. Ariz., Tucson, 1981-83; vis. microbiologist USDA, Phila., 1983-84; mem. edit. bd. Applied & Environ. Microbiology, 1990—, Letters in Applied Microbiology, 1990—. Editl. bd. Jour. of Food Protection, 1997—. Judge J.F. K. Jr. High Sch. Sci. Fair, Natick, 1985, 86, 87, 88, 89, 90. Mem. Am. Soc. Microbiology, AAAS, Inst. Food Techs. Achievements include patent for Identification of Pathogenic Yersinia enterocolitica; first reporting of association of plasmid-mediated surface properties of yersinia; development of methods for identification of pathogenic staphylococci, guide to salvage temperature-abused chilled/frozen foods, rapid method to detect pathogen listeria in foods. Office: US Army RDE Ctr Kansas St Natick MA 01760

LACHMAN, LAWRENCE, business consultant, former department store executive; b. N.Y.C., Jan. 9, 1916; s. Charles and Dorothy (Rubin) L.; m. Judith Lehman, Apr. 8, 1945; children: Robert Ian, Charles Scott. BS summa cum laude, NYU, 1936. Controller James McCreery & Co., N.Y.C., 1938-46; treas., dir. Citizens Utilities Co., Stamford, Conn., 1946-47; treas. Bloomingdale's, N.Y.C., 1947-53; v.p. personnel and ops. Bloomingdale's, 1953-58, exec. v.p. adminstrn. and personnel, 1958-64, pres., chief exec. officer, 1964-69, chmn. bd., chief exec. officer, 1969-78; chmn. bd., chief exec. officer Bus. Mktg. Corp., 1978-80; bd. dirs. DFS Group Ltd., ADVO, Inc. Trustee NYU, 1974-90. Served to maj. USAAF, 1942-46. Decorated Bronze Star; French Legion of Honor; recipient Madden award N.Y. U., 1969. Home: 104 E 68th St Apt 5A New York NY 10021-5905

LACHMAN, MARGUERITE LEANNE, real estate investment advisor; b. Vancouver, B.C., Can., Mar. 16, 1943; came to U.S., 1955; d. Wilfred Harry and Claire Elisha (Silverthorn) L. BA, U. So. Calif., 1964; MA, Claremont Grad. Sch., 1966. With Real Estate Rsch. Corp., 1965-87; sr. v.p. Real Estate Research Corp., 1977-79, pres., CEO, 1979-87; mng. dir. Schroder Real Estate Assocs., 1987—, Schroder Mortgage Assocs., 1992—; bd. dirs. Chgo. Title and Trust, Lincoln Nat. Corp., Liberty Property Trust; frequent lectr. seminars and profl. groups. Author: (with Al Smith and Anthony Downs) Achieving Effective Desegregation, 1973, (with Susan Olson) Tax Delinquency in the Inner City, 1976, Emerging Trends in Real Estate, 1981, 82, 83, 84, 85, 86, 87, Decade to Decade, 1988, Real Estate's Demographic Puzzle, 1995; contbr. articles to profl. jours. Trustee, exec. com. Urban Land Inst., Urban Land Found. Mem. N.Y. Women's Forum, Inc., Comml. Club Chgo. Office: Schroder Real Estate Assocs 437 Madison Ave New York NY 10022-7001

LACHMAN, MORTON, writer, theatrical director and producer; b. Seattle, Mar. 20, 1918; s. Sol and Rose (Bloom) L.; m. Elaine Lachman, June 23, 1940; children: Joanne, Dianne, Robert. B.A., U. Wash., Seattle, 1939. Exec. producer TV series One Day at a Time, All in the Family, Archie Bunker's Place, Sanford, Gimme A Break, Kate & Allie; head writer, producer, dir. The Bob Hope Show; head writer Acad. Award shows; co-writer feature films Mixed Company, Yours, Mine & Ours. With AUS, 1942-45. Recipient Emmy award for directing The Girl Who Couldn't Lose, 1975. Clubs: El Caballero, Queens, Tamerisk, Rangoon Racquet. Address: 2780 Bottlebrush Dr Los Angeles CA 90077-2010

LACHS, JOHN, philosopher, educator; b. Budapest, Hungary, July 17, 1934; s. Julius and Magda (Brod) L.; m. Shirley Marie Mellow, June 3, 1967; children: Sheila Marie, James Richard. B.A., McGill U., 1956, M.A., 1957; Ph.D., Yale, 1961. From asst. prof. to prof. philosophy Coll. William and Mary, 1959-67; prof. philosophy Vanderbilt U., 1967—, Centennial Prof., 1993—; chair Vanderbilt U. Faculty Senate, 1990-91. Author: Marxist Philosophy: A Bibliographical Guide, 1967, The Ties of Time, 1970, Intermediate Man, 1981, Mind and Philosophers, 1987, George Santayana, 1988, The Relevance of Philosophy to Life, 1995; editor: Animal Faith and Spiritual Life, 1967, Physical Order and Moral Liberty, 1969; co-editor: The Human Search, 1981; co-translator: Fichte, Science of Knowledge, 1970; contbr. numerous articles to profl. jours. Past chmn. Tenn. Com. for Humanities. Recipient Award for Advancement of Scholarship Phi Beta Kappa, 1962, Harris Harbison award for distinguished teaching Danforth Found., 1967, Chancellor's cup Vanderbilt U., 1970, Madison Sarratt prize excellence undergrad. teaching, 1972, Alumni Edn. award Vanderbilt U., 1991. Mem. Internat. Neoplatonic Soc., World Sociology Assn. (alienation rsch. com.), Am. Acad. Polit. and Social Sci., Am. Philos. Assn., Metaphys. Soc. Am. (pres.), Royal Inst. Philosophy, Soc. Advancement Am. Philosophy (past pres.), Soc. Health and Human Values, C.S. Peirce Soc. (past pres.), Va. Philos. Assn., Tenn. Philos. Assn., So. Soc. Philosophy and Psychology, Hasting Ctr. Episcopalian. Home: 1968 Edenbridge Way Nashville TN 37215-5809 Office: Vanderbilt U 2305 W End Ave Nashville TN 37203-1700

LACITIS, ERIK, journalist; b. Buenos Aires, Argentina, Dec. 10, 1949; came to U.S., 1960, naturalized, 1965; s. Erik and Irene Z. L.; m. Malorie Nelson, Aug. 30, 1976. Student, Coll. Forest Resources, U. Wash., 1967-71. Editor U. Wash. Daily, 1970; pub. New Times Jour., 1970-71; reporter, pop-music cons. Seattle Post Intelligencer, 1972—; reporter, columnist Seattle Times, 1972; v.p., treas. Malorie Nelson, Inc., 1980—. Recipient numerous awards from Wash. State chpt. Sigma Delta Chi; Nat. Headliners Club award, 1978; winner gen. interest competition Nat. Soc. Newspaper Columnists, 1987. Lutheran. Office: The Seattle Times PO Box 70 Fairview Ave N & John St Seattle WA 98111-0070

LACIVITA, MICHAEL JOHN, safety engineer; b. Youngstown, Ohio, June 26, 1924; s. John and Carmela (Cacciavillani) L.; m. Margaret Mary Savoia, May 17, 1952; children: Linda Marie Lacivita Krieger, Sandra Marie Lacivita Vicarel. BSBA, Youngstown State U., 1951. Quality control techncian, supr. Republic Rubber div. Aeroquip Corp., Youngstown, 1951-65, mgr. quality control, 1965-67, prodn. supt., 1965-71; quality control mgr. Comml. Shearing Inc., Youngstown, 1971-75, dir. corp. safety, 1975-79, dir. corp. safety and security, 1979-86. Contbr. articles to profl. jours. and newspapers; patentee in field of bicycles; one-man photography shows include Butler Inst. Am. Art, 1984, 89, 92, Apple Gallery, Youngstown, 1985, Youngstown State U. Libr., 1986, Bank One, Youngstown, 1988. With USN, 1943-46. Named to Ohio Sr. Citizens Hall of Fame, 1996. Mem. Am. Soc. Safety Engrs. (safety profl. of yr. award Ohio-Pa. chpt. 1984), Forging Industry Assn. (nat. safety and health com. 1980-83). Home: 3220 Eldora Dr Youngstown OH 44511-1252 *Personal philosophy: My staff of life has been one of a never ending yearn to learn.*

LACK, ANDREW, broadcast executive. Office: NBC News 30 Rockefeller Plz New York NY 10112*

LACK, JAMES J., state senator, lawyer; b. N.Y.C., Oct. 18, 1944; s. Harry A. and Eve (Kaufman) L.; m. Therese M. Gutleber, Jan. 19, 1969; children: Katherine Shana, Jeremy David. B.A., U. Pa., 1966; J.D., Fordham U., 1969. Bar: N.Y. 1970. Counsel to N.Y. State Consumer Protection Bd., 1970-72; prin. asst. frauds bur. dist. attys. office County of Suffolk, N.Y., 1972-73; commr. Suffolk County Dept. Consumer Affairs, Hauppauge, N.Y., 1974-77; pres. Better Bus. Bur. Met. N.Y., 1977-78; ptnr. Smyth & Lack, Huntington, N.Y., 1983—; mem. N.Y. Senate, 1979—; chmn. Senate Labor com., 1985-93, Majority Steering com., 1989-94, Senate com. on judiciary, 1994—, dep. majority whip, 1995—, Nat. Commn. Employment Policy; pres. Nat. Conf. State Legislatures, 1995-96. Republican. Office: NY State Senate State Capitol Albany NY 12247

LACK, LEON, pharmacology and biochemistry educator; b. Bklyn, Jan. 7, 1922; s. Jacob and Yetta (Wolf) L.; m. Pauline Kaplan, Feb. 14, 1948; children: Elias David, Joshua Morris, Johanna Elaine, Adina Roberta, Evonne Clara. B.A., Bklyn. Coll., 1943; M.S., Mich. Stae Coll., 1948; Ph.D., Columbia U., 1953; postgrad. (Univ. postdoctoral fellow), Duke U., 1954-55. Instr. in pharmacology and exptl. therapeutics Johns Hopkins U. Sch. Medicine, 1955-59, asst. prof. pharmacology and exptl. therapeutics, 1959-63; asst. prof. physiology and pharmacology Duke U. Med. Center, 1964-66, prof. pharmacology, 1966-92, prof. emeritus pharmacology, 1992—, chief biochemist to clin. research, 1966-70; cons. E.I. DuPont de Nemours and Co., 1990-91, Monsanto, 1992-93. Contbr. numerous articles to profl. publs. Served with USAAF, 1943-46, PTO. Grantee NIH, 1960-90, OSHA, Ctr. for Disease Control, 1991-93. Mem. Am. Soc. Biol. Chemists, Am. Soc. Pharmacology and Exptl. Therapeutics. Jewish. Rsch. in pharmacology of cholesterol and lipids, pharmacology of intestinal bile salt transport, enzyme inhibitors relevant to prostatic cancer. Home: 2936 Welcome Dr Durham NC 27705-5556 Office: Duke U Med Ctr PO Box 3185 Durham NC 27715-3185

LACKENMIER, JAMES RICHARD, college president, priest; b. Lackawanna, N.Y., May 15, 1938; s. Harold and Margaret (Murphy) L. AB, Stonehill Coll., 1961; STL, Pontifical Gregorian U., Rome, 1965; AM, U.N.C., 1968; MA, U. Chgo., 1970. Ordained priest, Roman Catholic Ch. Tchr. English Notre Dame High Sch., Bridgeport, Conn., 1965-66, St. Peter's High Sch., Gloucester, Mass., 1966-68; chaplain St. Xavier Coll., Chgo., 1969-71; dir. collegiate formation Moreau Sem., Notre Dame, Ind., 1971-73; dir. campus ministry King's Coll., Wilkes-Barre, Pa., 1974-75, dir. devel., 1975-81, pres., 1981—. Bd. regents U. Portland, 1993—; bd. trustees Mercy Hosp., 1989-95; bd. dirs. Pa. Ednl. Telecom. Exch. Network, 1994—, Com. on Econ. Growth, Earth Conservancy, 1992—, Pa. Ind. Coll. and Univ. Rsch. Ctr., 1995—, Ctr. for Agile Pa. Edn., 1994—, Greater Wilkes-Barre Partnership, Inc.; mem. United Way Campaign Cabinet, 1995—; adv. bd. Pa. Mountains coun. Boy Scouts Am., North Tier Advanced Tech. Ctr. Ben Franklin Partnership Program, 1983—, Tuition Acct. Program, Office of Gov., Commonwealth Pa., 1992-96; adv. group Higher Edn. Com., 1990-96; chmn. United Way Wyoming Valley, 1986. Mem. Wilkes-Barre C. of C., Westmoreland Club (bd. govs. local chpt. 1989-91), Mid. State Assn. Colls. and Schs. (commn. higher edn.), Pa. Assn. Colls. and Univs. (com. on acad. issues). Democrat. Lodges: Rotary Internat.; K.C. Office: King's Coll 133 N River St Wilkes Barre PA 18711-0852

LACKLAND, JOHN, lawyer; b. Parma, Idaho, Aug. 29, 1939. A.B., Stanford U., 1962; J.D., U. Wash., 1964; master gradener, Colo. State U., 1996. Bar: Wash. 1965, U.S. Dist. Ct. (we. dist.) Wash. 1965, (ea. dist.) Wash. 1973, U.S. Ct. Appeals (9th cir.) 1965, Conn. 1981, U.S. Dist. Ct. Conn. 1983, U.S. Supreme Ct. 1973, U.S. Dist. Ct. (so. dist.) N.Y. 1988. Assoc. firm Lane Powell Moss & Miller, Seattle, 1965-69; asst. atty. gen. State of Wash., Seattle, 1969-72; asst. chief State of Wash. (U. Wash. div.), 1969-72; v.p., sec., gen. counsel Western Farmers Assn., Seattle, 1972-76, Fotomat Corp., Stamford, Conn., 1976-80; ptnr. Leepson & Lackland, 1981-88, Lackland and Nalewaik, 1988-92; pvt. practices Westport, Conn., 1992-94; prin. Lackland Assocs., Grand Junction, Colo., 1994—. Bd. dirs. Mercer Island (Wash.) United Ch., 1967-70, pres. bd. dirs., 1970-72; mem. land use plan steering com. City of Mercer Island, 1970-72; bd. dirs. Mercer Island Sch. Dist., 1970-73, v.p. bd. dirs., 1972, pres. 1973; trustee Mid-Fairfield Child Guidance Ctr., 1982-84, Norfield Congl. Ch., 1982-84; bd. dirs. Grand Junction Symphony Orch., 1995—.

LACKLAND, THEODORE HOWARD, lawyer; b. Chgo., Dec. 4, 1943; s. Richard and Cora Lee (Sanders) L.; m. Dorothy Ann Gerald, Jan. 2, 1970; 1 child, Jennifer Noel. BS, Loyola U., Chgo., 1965; MA, Howard U., 1967; JD, Columbia U., 1975; grad. U.S. Army Ranger Sch., 1968. Bar: N.J. 1975, U.S. Dist. Ct. N.J. 1975, Ga. 1982, U.S. Tax Ct. 1983, U.S. Supreme Ct. 1979, U.S. Dist. Ct. (no. dist.) Ga. 1982, U.S. Dist. Ct. (mid. dist.) Ga. 1985. Assoc. Dewey, Ballantine, Bushby, Palmer & Wood, N.Y.C., 1975-78; asst. U.S. atty. Dist. N.J., Newark, 1978-81; ptnr. Arnall Golden & Gregory, Atlanta, 1981-93, Lackland & Assocs., Atlanta, 1993-95, Lackland & Heyward, 1995—; adj. prof. law Ga. State U. Law Sch., 1989—. Assoc. editor Columbia Human Rights Law Rev., 1974-75; contbr. articles to profl. jours. Adv. dir. Atlanta Bus. Devel. Ctr., Minority Bus. Devel. Council, Atlanta, 1983-91; mem. exec. com. Leadership Atlanta 1986, 1990-91. Capt. U.S. Army, 1967-71. Decorated Bronze Star with 1 oak leaf cluster, Purple Heart, Air Medal. Mem. ABA, N.J. Bar Assn., Ga. Bar Assn., Fed. Bar Assn., Gate City Bar Assn. Democrat. Roman Catholic. Home: 4400 Oak Ln Marietta GA 30062-6355 Office: Lackland & McManus 235 Peachtree St NE Ste 1700 Atlanta GA 30303-1405

LACKNER, JAMES ROBERT, aerospace medicine educator; b. Virginia, Minn., Nov. 11, 1940; s. William and Lillian Mae (Galbraith) L.; m. Ann Martin Graybiel, Aug. 26, 1970. BSc, MIT, 1966, PhD, 1970. Asst. prof. psychology Brandeis U., Waltham, Mass., 1970-74, assoc. prof. psychology, 1974-79, Riklis prof. physiology dept. psychology, 1977—, chmn. dept. psychology, 1975-83, provost, dean faculty, 1986-89, dir. Ashton Graybiel Spatial Orientation Lab., 1982—; research assoc. dept. psychology and clin. research ctr. MIT, Cambridge, 1970-80; sci. adv. bd. Space Biomed. Research Inst., Houston, 1982—, Aphasia Research Ctr. Boston U. Sch. Med., 1977-82, Eunice Kennedy Shriver Ctr. Harvard U. Med. Sch., Cambridge, 1980—; sci. adv. panel astronaut longitudinal health program Johnson Space Ctr., NASA, 1983, exec. sec. space adaptation syndrome steering com., 1982-84, pre-adaption trainer working group, 1986—, artificial gravity working group, 1987—; fabricant com. life scis. experiments for a space sta., 1982; space scis. bd. sensory motor panel NAS, 1984-86; com. on hearing, bioacoustics and biomechanics NRC, 1985-89, com. on vision, 1987-92, com. on space, biology and medicine, 1991—, mem. com. virtual reality rsch. and devel., 1992—. Mem. editorial bd. Presence, 1992—, Jour. Vestibular Rsch., Jour. Neurophysiology, 1995—, Exptl. Brain Rsch., 1997; contbr. more than 200 articles to sci. jours. Mem. Am. Soc. for Gravitational and Space Biology, Aerospace Med. Assn. (Arnold B. Tuttle award), Soc. for Neurosci., Psychonomics Soc., Internat. Brain Research Orgn., Barany Soc. (hon.), Internat. Acad. Astronautics (hon.). Achievements include research in human sensory-motor coordination and spatial orientation. Home: Boyce Farm Rd Lincoln MA 01773-4813 Office: Brandeis U Ashton Graybiel Lab PO Box 9110/415 South St Waltham MA 02154-9100

LACKNER, RUDY PAUL, cardiothoracic surgeon; b. Queens, N.Y., July 25, 1958; s. Rudolph and Dorothy (Peplinski) L.; m. Carol Ann Cudone, May 15, 1990; children: Rudi, Pearl, Timothy. BS summa cum laude, Manhattan Coll., 1980; MD, N.Y. Med. Coll., 1985. Diplomate Am. Bd. Thoracic Surgery, Am. Bd. Gen. Surgery. Resident in gen. surgery L.I. Jewish Med. Ctr., New Hyde Park, N.Y., 1985-90; rsch. fellow in cardiothoracic surgery U. Chgo., 1990-91, resident in cardiothoracic surgery, 1991-93; fellow in thoracic transplant U. N.C., Chapel Hill, 1993-94; asst. prof. surgery, dir. lung transplant program U. Nebr., Omaha, 1994—. Recipient 1st prize ACS, 1989. Mem. Am. Coll. Chest Physicians, Am. Thoracic Soc., Assn. for Acad. Surgery, Internat. Soc. Heart and Lung Transplant, Epsilon Sigma Pi, Beta Beta Beta. Avocation: diving. Office: U Nebr Div Cardiothoracic Surgery 600 S 42nd St Omaha NE 68198-1002

LACLAIR, PATRICIA MARIE, physical education director, medical technician; b. East Liverpool, Ohio, Dec. 29, 1958; d. James Herbert and Irene Marie (Ruthledge) LaC. BS in Edn., Youngstown State U. Dir. elem. phys. edn. Trinity (Tex.) Ind. Sch. Dist., 1985—; instr. CPR AHA, Bryan, Tex., 1985, instr. phys. edn., 1989—; emergency med. svcs. program instr., 1994—, emergency med. svcs. program examiner, 1994—, basic critical incident stress mgmt. trainer, 1994—; instr. Trinity Peninsula Ambulance Svc., 1994-95; sec. bd. dirs. Trinity Emergency Med. Svc., 1990-95, mgr. 1986-95; instr., trainer Primecare Emergency Med. Svc., 1996—, Jacksonville Fire Dept. Emergency Med. Svcs., 1996—. Vol. EMT, 1985-95. Home: 206 Valley Ln Crockett TX 75835

LACOSTA, COSMO JOSEPH, medical center executive; b. N.Y.C., Apr. 2, 1942; s. Vito Emanuel and Angela (Cardella) LaC.; m. Elizabeth Barrett Browning, Aug. 6, 1966; children: Lisa, Cosmo J., John, Robert. BS, Fordham U., 1963; MPA, NYU, 1973. Asst. dir. The N.Y. Hosp., N.Y.C., 1971-75, assoc. dir., 1975-82, sr. assoc. dir., 1982-83, exec. assoc. dir., 1983-89; assoc. dean ops. Cornell U., N.Y.C., 1989-91; sr. v.p. Allen Pav./Presbyn. Hosp., N.Y.C., 1991-93; exec. v.p., COO Brookdale Univ. Hosp. and Med. Ctr., Bklyn., 1993—. Tech. advisor: (film) Burn Nursing: A Very Special Challenge, 1978; prodr.: (film) When You Need It: A Burn Center for You, 1979; exec. prodr.: (film) BURNWISE, 1982. Hon. dep. fire chief N.Y.C. Fire Dept., 1985; mem. N.Y. State Hon. Fire Chiefs Assn., 1984; bd. trustees N.Y.C. Fire Mus.; mem. bd. dirs. Vols. for Elderly, N.Y.C.-Yorkville, 1984. Capt. U.S. MSC, 1964-66 (ret.). Recipient Cert. of Merit, N.Y. Uniformed Firefighters Assn., 1989, Commendation N.Y. Firefighters Burn Ctr. Fedn., 1988. Fellow Am. Coll. Healthcare Execs.; mem. HANYS (mem. tech. adv. group 1985—, mem., chmn. com. on mgmt./planning 1995-96, mem., chmn. health and human svcs. com.), Am. Hosp. Assn., Nat. Fire Protection Assn., N.Y. Soc. Health Planning, Nat. Inst. Bldg. Scis., N.Y. State Dept. Health Nursing Home (bd. examiners 1994—), Coun. on Tchg. Hosps. Roman Catholic. Office: Brookdale Univ Hosp & Med Ctr One Brookdale Plz Brooklyn NY 11212

LACOSTE, PAUL, lawyer, educator, university official; b. Montreal, Que., Can., Apr. 24, 1923; s. Emile and Juliette (Boucher) L.; m. Louise Marcil, Aug. 31, 1973 (div.); children: Helene, Paul-André, Anne-Marie. BA, U. Montreal, 1943, MA, 1944, Licenciate in Philosophy, 1946, Licenciate in Law, 1960; postgrad., U. Chgo., 1946-47; Docteur de l'Universite, U. Paris, 1948; LLD (hon.), McGill U., 1975, U. Toronto, 1978; D Univ. (hon.), Laval U., 1986. Bar: Que. 1960. Prof. philosophy U. Montreal, 1946-86, prof. law, 1960-68, 1985-87, vice rector, 1966-68, exec. vice rector, 1968-75, rector, 1975-85, prof. emeritus, 1987—; moderator, commentator CBC, 1956-63; mem. firm Lalande, Brière, Reeves, Lacoste et Paquette, Montreal, 1964-66; mem. Royal Commn. on Bilingualism and Biculturism, 1963-71, Que. Superior Coun. Edn., 1964-68, Que. Coun. Univs., 1969-77; mem. Conf. Rectors and Prins. Que. Univs., 1967-85, pres. 1977-79; chmn. Fed. Commn. and Coms. for Environ. Projects, 1991—. Author: (with others) La crise de l'enseignement au Canada Francais, 1961, Justice et Paix scolaire, 1962, A Place of Liberty, 1964, Le Canada au seuil du siecle de l'abondance, 1969, Education permanente et potentiel universitaire, 1977; contbr. articles to profl. jours. Mem. Corp. de l'Ecole des Hautes Etudes Commerciales, 1975-85, Ecole Polytechnique, 1975-85, Corp. du Coll. Marie de France; bd. dirs. Clin. Rsch. Inst. of Montreal, 1975-85; pres. Assn. des universités partiellement ou entièrement de langue française, 1978-81. Mem. Assn. Univs. and Colls. of Can. (mem. com. of pres. 1975-85, v.p. 1977, pres. 1978-79), Assn. Commonwealth Univs. (dir. 1977-80). Home: 356 Woodlea, Ville Mont Royal, PQ Canada H3P 1R5 Office: Université de Montréal, CP 6128 Pavillon 2910 bur 6, Montreal, PQ Canada H3C 3J7

LACOURSIERE, ROY BARNABY, psychiatrist; b. Windsor, Ont., Can., Aug. 9, 1937; s. Lionel and Cecile (Robinet) L.; m. Marilyn E. Marshall, Sept. 9, 1961 (div. Apr. 1974); children: Jacqueline, Joan, Colette; m. Joanna Durrance, Sept. 25, 1982; 1 stepchild, Eric. BA with honors, U. Windsor, 1962; MD, McGill U., Montreal, Can., 1966. Diplomate Am. Bd. Psychiatry and Neurology, Diplomate Am. Bd. Forensic Psychiatry; cert. in alcoholism ASAM. Intern then resident Menninger Sch. Psychiatry, Topeka, Kans., 1966-71; dir. community service office Menninger Found., Topeka, 1971-74; chief chem. problems treatment unit, extended care/ geriatric psychiatry unit VA Hosp., Topeka, 1975-97, cons. psychiatry, 1972-74; practice medicine specializing in forensic psychiatry Topeka, 1973—; vis. prof. Washburn U. Law Sch., Topeka, 1974—. Author: The Life Cycle of Groups, 1980, (with others): Patients, Psychiatrists and Lawyers: Law and the Mental Health System, 1989; contbr. articles to profl. jours. Vestry St. David's Episc. Ch., Topeka, 1985-88. Fellow Am. Psychiat. Assn., ACP, Royal Coll. Physicians and Surgeons Can.; mem. Am. Acad. Psychiatry and Law, Am. Acad. Forensic Scis. Avocations: travel, reading. Home: 28 SW Pepper Tree Ln Topeka KS 66611-2056 Office: 3600 SW Burlingame Rd Topeka KS 66611-2053

LACOVARA, PHILIP ALLEN, lawyer; b. N.Y.C., July 11, 1943; s. P. Philip and Elvira Lacovara; m. Madeline E. Papio, Oct. 14, 1961; children: Philip, Michael, Christopher, Elizabeth, Karen, Daniel, Andrew. AB magna cum laude, Georgetown U., 1963; JD summa cum laude, Columbia U., 1966. Bar: N.Y. 1967, D.C. 1974, U.S. Supreme Ct. 1970. Law clk. to presiding justice U.S. Ct. Appeals D.C. Cir., 1966-67; asst. to solicitor gen. U.S. Washington, 1967-69; assoc. Hughes Hubbard & Reed, N.Y.C., 1969-71; ptnr. Hughes Hubbard & Reed, N.Y.C. and Washington, 1974-88; v.p., sr. counsel GE, Fairfield, Conn., 1988-90; mng. dir, gen. counsel Morgen Stanley & Co., N.Y.C., 1990-93; ptnr. Mayer, Brown & Platt, N.Y.C. and Washington, 1993—; spl. counsel to N.Y.C. Police Commr., 1971-72; dep. solicitor gen. U.S. Dept. Justice, Washington, 1972-73; counsel to spl. prosecutor Watergate Spl. Prosecution Force, 1973-74; lectr. law Columbia U.; adj. prof. Georgetown U. Law Ctr.; vis. lectr. various colls., univs.; mem. Jud. Conf. D.C. Circuit, 1973—; chmn. commn. on admissions and grievances U.S. Ct. Appeals for D.C. Circuit, 1980-86; spl. counsel U.S. Ho. of Reps. Com. on Standards Ofcl. Conduct, 1976-77; chmn. bd. trustees Public Defender Service for D.C., 1976-81; sec. exec. com. bd. visitors Columbia U. Sch. Law; pres. Columbia U. Sch. Law Alumni Assn., 1986-88; bd. govs. D.C. Bar, 1981-84, gen. counsel, 1985-87, pres., 1988-89, mem. legal ethics com., 1976-81, chmn. code subcom., 1977-81. Contbr. articles to profl. jours. Co-chair, Washington Lawyers Com. for Civil Rights Under Law, 1982-84; mem. D.C. Jud. Nomination Commn., 1981-86; bd. dirs. Legal Aid Soc. of N.Y.C., 1992—. Fellow Am. Coll. Trial Lawyers; mem. ABA (ho. of dels. 1978-89, vice-chmn. sect. individual rights and responsibilities 1985-87, 89-91, chmn. 1991-92), Am. Law Inst., Practicing Law Inst. (trustee), Cath. Interracial Coun. N.Y., Lawyers Com. for Human Rights (trustee 1991—), Legal Aid Soc. N.Y.C. (bd. dirs. 1992—), 1925 F St. Club, Lotos Club, Knights of Malta. Roman Catholic. Home: 39 Mill Rd New Canaan CT 06840-4305 Office: 1675 Broadway New York NY 10019-5820

LACROIX, CHRISTIAN MARIE MARC, fashion designer; b. Arles, Bouches du Rhône, France, May 16, 1951; s. Maxime and Jeannette (Bergier) L. Grad., U. Valery, Montpelier, France, 1973. Asst. Hermes Co., Paris, 1978-79, Guy Paulin Co., Paris, 1980-81; chief designer Jean Patou Co., Paris, 1982-87; prin. Christian Lacroix Co., Paris, 1987—. Author: Pieces of a Pattern, 1992, The Diary of a Collector, 1996. Decorated chevalier des Arts et Lettres, 1992; recipient Golden Thimble award, 1986, 88, Coun. Fashion Designer Am. award, 1987, Prix Balzac, 1989, Das Goldene Spinnrad award Kreffeld, R.F.A., 1990, MoliÉre Best Costumes award, 1996. Roman Catholic. Office: Christian Lacroix, 73 Faubourg Saint-Honoré, 75008 Paris France

LACROIX, PIERRE, professional sports team professional; m. Colombe Lacroix; children: Martin, Eric. Agt. NHL; gen. mgr. Denver Avalanche, 1994—. Recipient 1996 Stanley Cup Championship, Denver Avalanche; named 1996 NHL Exec. of Yr., The Hockey News. Office: Denver Avalanche McNichols Arena/1635 Clay S Denver CO 80204

LA CROSSE, JAMES, retail executive; b. 1932. Student, Wesleyan Univ., 1954; MBA, Harvard Univ., 1956. Miller Stevenson Chemical Co., 1956-59, Amerace-Ense Co., 1960-69, Bio-Dynamics Co. Inc., 1965-59; Nat. WIne & Spirits Corp., 1970—, CEO, 1991—. Office: PO Box 1602 Indianapolis IN 46206-1602

LACY, ALEXANDER SHELTON, lawyer; b. South Boston, Va., Aug. 18, 1921; s. Cecil Baker and Lura Elizabeth (Byram) L.; m. Carol Jemison, Aug. 8, 1952; children: John Blakeway, Joan Elizabeth Chancey, Alexander Shelton. B.S. in Chemistry, U. Ala., 1943; LL.B., U. Va., 1949. Bar: Ala. 1949, U.S. Ct. Appeals (5th, 11th and D.C. cirs.) 1981, U.S. Supreme Ct. 1979. Assoc. Bradley, Arant, Rose & White, Birmingham, Ala., 1949-54; with Ala. Gas Corp., Birmingham, 1954-86; v.p., asst. sec., atty. Ala. Gas Corp./Energen Corp., 1969-86; v.p., sec., atty. Ala. Gas Corp., 1974-86; with Patrick and Lacy, Birmingham, 1986-96. Pres., chmn. bd. Birmingham Symphony Assn., 1964-67; chmn. Birmingham-Jefferson Civic Center Authority, 1965-71. Served with USN, 1943-46. Mem. ABA, Ala. Bar Assn. (chmn. energy law com. 1984-86), Birmingham Bar Assn., Am. Gas Assn. (chmn. legal sect. 1983-85), Fed. Energy Bar Assn., Fed. Bar Assn., Am. Judicature Soc., Mountain Brook Club, Phi Gamma Delta, Phi Delta Phi. Episcopalian. Home: 3730 Montrose Rd Birmingham AL 35213-3824

LACY, ANDRE BALZ, industrial executive; b. Indpls., Sept. 12, 1939; s. Howard J. II and Edna B. (Balz) L.; m. Julia Lello, Feb. 23, 1963; children: John Andre, Mark William, Peter Lello. BA Econs., Denison U.; DEng (hon.), Rose-Hulman Inst. Various mgmt. positions U.S. Corrugated, Indpls., 1961-69, exec. v.p., 1969-72; exec. v.p., chief ops. officer Lacy Diversified Industries, Indpls., 1972-78, chmn. bd. subs., 1973-78, pres., chief ops. officer, 1978-83; pres., chief exec. officer Lacy Diversified Industries, now LDI, Ltd., Indpls., 1983—, chmn., 1992; bd. dirs. Indpls. Power and Light, Indpls. IPALCO Enterprises, Inc., Indpls., Tredegar Industries, Inc., Richmond, Va., Albemarle Corp., Richmond, Herff Jones, Inc., Indpls., Patterson Dental Co., Mpls., Mid-Am. Capital Resources, Inc.; dir. Finish Master, Inc., Nat. Bank Indpls. Mem. bd. mgrs. Rose-Hulman Inst., Terre Haute, Ind.; pres. Indpls. Bd. Sch. Commn., Indpls., 1985-86; hon. mem. 500 Festival Assocs., Inc., Indpls.; chmn. United Way Greater Indpls., 1989-91; bd. dirs. Hudson Inst., Indpls. Conv. and Visitors Assn., 1996. Mem. Young Pres. Orgn., Ind. C. of C. (bd. dirs. 1989), Ind. Pres. Orgn., Kiwanis Club of Indpls., Skyline Club, Columbia Club, Meridian Hills Golf and Country Club (Indpls.), Lost Tree Club. Republican. Episcopalian. Avocation: sailing. Home: 5686 N Pennsylvania St Indianapolis IN 46220-3026 Office: LDI Ltd 54 Monument Cir Indianapolis IN 46204-2942

LACY, BILL, academic administrator; b. Madill, Okla., Apr. 16, 1933; s. Leon and Eunice L.; m. Susan Cavert Butler, Dec. 27, 1992; children: Jan, Kate, Shawn, Ross, Jessica. B.Arch., Okla. State U., 1955, M.Arch., 1958; D.F.A. (hon.), Miami U., Oxford, Ohio, 1985. Design architect Caudill, Rowlett, Scott, Houston, 1958-61; prof., assoc. chmn. dept. architecture Rice U., Houston, 1961-65; prof., dean sch. architecture U. Tenn., Knoxville, 1965-70; v.p. Omniplan, Dallas, 1970-71; dir. architecture and environ. arts Nat. Endowment Arts, Washington, 1971-77, dir. fed. design program, 1972-77; pres. Am. Acad. in Rome, N.Y.C., 1977-80, The Cooper Union, N.Y.C., 1980-88, SUNY, Purchase Coll., 1993—; archtl. cons. Fgn. Bldgs. Ops., Dept. State. Author: 100 Contemporary Architects, 1991, Angels and Franciscans, 1992; contbr. articles, designs to profl. jours. Bd. dirs. Internat. Design Conf. Aspen, 1973-92; bd. dirs. Tiffancy Found., Am. Archtl. Found.; cons. Rothschild Found., J. Paul Getty Trust; exec. dir. Pritzker Prize Jury. With U.S. Army, 1955-57. Loeb fellow Harvard U., 1973. Fellow AIA; mem. Univ. Club. Office: 735 Anderson Hill Rd Purchase NY 10577-1445

LACY, CAROLYN JEAN, elementary education educator, secondary education educator; b. Marshall, Ark., Apr. 6, 1944; d. Charles Ira Bolch and Edna Rebecca Cherry; 1 child, Kelli Jean. AA with distinction, Riverside City Coll., 1980; BA, U. Calif., Riverside, 1982, postgrad., 1983; MEd, U.S. Internat. U., 1993. Cert. social sci. tchr., Calif. Educator Perris (Calif.) Elem. Sch. Dist., 1984-89, Rialto (Calif.) Unified Sch. Dist., 1989—; instr. Developing Capable People, Riverside, Calif., 1986-89; presenter, lectr. Jurupa Unified Sch. Dist., Riverside, 1990, Rialto Unified Sch. Dist., 1990; developer peer tutor program Perris Elem. Sch. Dist., 1989; dir. chess club Dollahan Elem. Sch., 1995, computer chmn., 1995—. Editor: (newsletter) Perris Lights, 1989. Active Students in Environ. Action, Riverside, 1978; mem. Riverside County Task Force for Self-Esteem. Named Mentor Tchr. State of Calif., 1988. Mem. AAUW, NEA, Calif. Tchrs. Assn., Internat. Reading Assn., U. Calif. Alumni Assn., Phi Delta Kappa, Alpha Gamma Sigma. Democrat. Mem. LDS Ch. Avocations: painting, writing, gardening, reading, travel. Home: 4044 Wallace St Riverside CA 92509-6809

LACY, ELIZABETH BERMINGHAM, state supreme court justice; b. 1945. BA cum laude, St. Mary's Coll., Notre Dame, Ind., 1966; JD, U. Tex., 1969; LLM, U. Va., 1992. Bar: Tex. 1969, Va. 1977. Staff atty. Tex. Legis. Coun., Austin, 1969-72; atty. Office of Atty. Gen., State of Tex., Austin, 1973-76; legis. aide Va. Del. Carrington Williams, Richmond, 1976-77; dep. atty. gen. jud. affairs div. Va. Office Atty. Gen., Richmond, 1982-85; mem. Va. State Corp. Commn., Richmond, 1985-89; justice Supreme Ct. Va., Richmond, 1989—. Office: Va Supreme Ct PO Box 1315 100 N 9th St Richmond VA 23210

LACY, HERMAN EDGAR, management consultant; b. Chgo., June 21, 1935; s. Herman E. and Florence L.; m. Mary C. Lacy; children: Frederick H., Carlton E., Douglas H., Jennifer S., Victoria J., Rebecca M. BS in Indsl. Engring., Bradley U., 1957; MBA, U. Chgo., 1966. Cert. mgmt. cons. Plant mgr., indsl. engring. supr. Hammond Organ Co., Chgo., 1961-66; mgr. corp. indsl. engring. Consol. Packaging Corp., Chgo., 1966-68; mgr. mgmt. cons. Peat, Marwick, Mitchell & Co., Chgo., 1968-70; dir. ops. Wilton Enterprises, Inc., Chgo., 1970-77; v.p., gen. mgr. Intercraft Industries Corp., Chgo., 1978-79; pres. Helmco Cons. Assocs., Glenview, Ill., 1979—; instr. Roosevelt U., Oakton Coll., Harper Coll. Served to capt. USAF, 1957-61. Mem. Inst. Indsl. Engrs. (past pres., founder north suburban Ill. chpt.), Am. Mgmt. Assn., Nat. Coun. Phys. Distbn. Mgmt., Soc. Mfg. Engrs., Inst. Mgmt. Cons. Office: Helmco Cons Assocs 1920 Waukegan Rd Ste 212 Glenview IL 60025-1700

LACY, JOHN FORD, lawyer; b. Dallas, Sept. 11, 1944; s. John Alexander and Glenda Arcenia (Ford) L.; m. Cece Smith, Apr. 22, 1978. BA, Baylor U., 1965; JD, Harvard U., 1968. Bar: Tex. 1968. Assoc. atty. Akin, Gump, Strauss, Hauer & Feld L.L.P., Dallas, 1968-72, ptnr., 1973-82; pres. Ford Lacy PC (affiliated with Akin, Gump et al.), Dallas, 1982—; chmn. Normandy Capital Co., Dallas, 1978—. Contbr. articles to profl. jours. Cofounder, co-chmn. pres. rsch. coun. U. Tex. Southwestern Med. Ctr., Dallas, 1985-91; dir., Vis. Nurse Assn. Tex., 1994-97. With U.S. Army, 1968-74. Rsch. fellow Southwestern Legal Found., Dallas. Mem. ABA, Dallas Bar Assn., State Bar Tex. (coun. bus. law sect. 1992-95). Home: 3710 Shenandoah St Dallas TX 75205-2121 Office: Akin Gump Strauss et al 1700 Pacific Ave Ste 4100 Dallas TX 75201-4624

LACY, JOSEPH NEWTON, architect; b. Kansas City, Mo., Oct. 6, 1905; s. John James and Theresa (Conboy) L.; m. Mary Duncan, Oct. 6, 1927 (dec. Aug. 1978); children: Mary-Louise, John Duncan, William Duncan; m. Martha E. Sadler, Apr. 19, 1980 (dec. Feb. 1987). B.Arch., U. Pa., 1927. Assoc. several archtl. firms in Phila., 1927-45; including Paul P. Cret, 1941-43, Louis I. Kahn, 1943-45; assoc. Eliel and Eero Saarinen, Bloomfield Hills, Mich., 1945-51; ptnr. Eero Saarinen & Assos., Bloomfield Hills, 1951-66; ret. Eero Saarinen & Assos., 1966. Mem. Coll. Fellows of AIA, Hon. Order Ky. Cols. Specialized in devel. of new bldg. materials. *Association with Eliel and Eero Saarinen, two of the great architects of modern times, gave me the opportunities to participate in the carrying out of my principles and goals of architecture. I became part of a team that designed such outstanding structures as the Jefferson Memorial Arch in St. Louis.*

LACY, PAUL ESTON, pathologist; b. Trinway, Ohio, Feb. 7, 1924; s. Benjamin Lemmert and Amy Cass (Cox) L.; m. Emelyn Ellen Talbot, June 7, 1945; children: Paul E. Jr., Steven T. BA cum laude, Ohio State U., 1945, MD cum laude, MSc in Anatomy, 1948; PhD in Pathology, U. Minn.-Mayo Found., 1955; Doctor of Medicine (honoris causa), Uppsala (Sweden) U., 1977. Asst. instr. anatomy Ohio State U., Columbus, 1944-48; intern White Cross Hosp., Columbus, 1948-49; fellow in pathology Mayo Clinic, Rochester, Minn., 1951-55; postdoctoral fellow Washington U. Med. Sch., St. Louis, 1955-56, instr. pathology, 1956-57, asst. prof. pathology, 1957-61, asst. dean, 1959-61, assoc. prof. pathology, 1961, Mallinckrodt prof., chmn. dept. pathology, 1961-85, Robert L. Kroc prof. of pathology, 1985-95, prof. emeritus pathology, 1995—; pathologist-in-chief Barnes & Allied Hosps., St. Louis, 1985-95, pathologist, 1985-95, prof. emeritus pathology, 1995—. Served to capt. U.S. Army, 1949-51. Recipient Banting award Brit. Diabetes Assn., 1963, Am. Diabetes Assn., 1970, 3M Life Scis. award FASEB, 1981, Rous-Whipple award Am. Assn. Pathologists, 1984. Fellow AAAS, Am. Acad. Arts and Sci.; mem. NAS, Inst. Medicine. Avocations: horticulture, literature. Office: Washington Univ Med Sch Dept of Pathology 660 S Euclid Ave Saint Louis MO 63110-1010

LACY, ROBINSON BURRELL, lawyer; b. Boston, May 7, 1952; s. Benjamin Hammett and Jane (Burrell) L.; m. Elizabeth Coutrakon, Oct. 20, 1984. AB, U. Calif., Berkeley, 1974; JD, Harvard U., 1977. Bar: N.Y. 1978, U.S. Dist. Ct. (so. and ea. dists.) N.Y. 1979, U.S. Dist. Ct. (we. dist.) N.Y. 1992, U.S. Ct. Appeals (2d cir.) 1983, U.S. Ct. Appeals (10th cir.) 1990, U.S. Supreme Ct. 1986. Law clk. to judge U.S. Dist. Ct. (so. dist.) N.Y., N.Y.C., 1977-78; law clk. to chief justice Warren Burger U.S. Supreme Ct., Washington, 1978-79; assoc. Sullivan & Cromwell, N.Y.C., 1979-85, ptnr., 1985—. Mem. ABA, Assn. of Bar of City of N.Y., N.Y. State Bar Assn. Office: Sullivan & Cromwell 125 Broad St New York NY 10004-2400

LACY, STEVE, jazz musician; b. N.Y.C., 1934. Played soprano sax at Schillinger House, Boston; performed with Pee Wee Russell, Rex Stewart, Buck Clayton, Jimmy Rushing, Dicky Wells, Walter Page, N.Y.C., 1953-54; played with Cecil Taylor; then with Gil Evans' orch., 1957; formed quartet with Roswell Rudd, experimenting with chord-free improvisation and unusual song forms, early 1960s; formed sextet Paris, 1970; played regular duets with Mal Waldron, 1979—. Recordings include Soprano Sax (debut), 1957, Reflections: Steve Lacy Plays Thelonius Monk, 1958, Evidence (with Don Cherry), 1961, Paris Blues (with Gil Evans), Raps, 1977, Steve Lacy Three: New York Capers, 1979, The Way, 1979, Ballets, 1980, Herbe de L'Oubli & Snake Out (with Mal Waldron), 1981, Songs (with Brion Gysin), 1985, 86, Let's Call This (with Mal Waldron), Prospectus, 1986, Steve Lacy Two, Five & Six: Blinks, 1986, Steve Lacy Nine: Futurities, 1986, The Straight Horn of Steve Lacy, The Door (duos, trios, etc.), 1989, Anthem, 1990, Hot House (with Mal Waldron), 1991, Live at Sweet Basil, 1992, Steve Lacy Solo, 1993, Vespers, 1993, Spirit of Mingus (with Eric Watson), 1996; composed/played musical score Landing live for D. Dunn, 1992. Frequent winner Down Beat Mag. poll, best soprano saxist, 1992. *

LACZKO, BRIAN JOHN, theater director; b. Cleve., Aug. 7, 1952; s. Joseph John and Avonelle Dorothy (Toth) L.; m. Jill Maree Aude, Aug. 12, 1978; children: Brian John, Stefanie Dale. BA, Denison U., 1974; MA, W.Va. U., 1978. Prodn. mgr. Advent Theatre, Nashville, 1978-79; prodn. mgr. Tenn. Performing Arts Ctr., Nashville, 1980-81, dir. ops., 1981-82, asst. mng. dir., 1982-86; gen. mgr. Starwood Amphitheatre, Nashville, 1986-87; mng. dir. Tenn. Repertory Theatre, Nashville, 1987—; adjudicator Tenn. Arts Commn., Nashville, 1991—, chair adv. panel, 1992—, Met. Nashville Arts Commn., 1991—; mem. profl. cos. panel Opera-Musical Theatre Program NEA. Scenic and lighting dir. over 50 theater prodns. Mem. Am. Arts Alliance, Internat. Theatre Inst. of U.S., Theatre Communications Group, Nat. Alliance Musical Theatre Producers, Alliance Performing Arts Presenters, Tenn. Theatre Assn., Tennesseans for Arts, Nashville C. of C. Office: Tenn Repertory Theatre 427 Chestnut St Nashville TN 37203-4826

LACZKO, ROBERT MATTHIAS, cook; b. Cleve., Dec. 18, 1964; s. Robert Paul and Geraldine Louise (Quinlan) L. AA, Bucks County C.C., Newtown, Pa., 1987. From dishwasher to cook Pennswood Village, Newtown, 1981—. Founder, trustee, pres. Trenton Gay/Lesbian Civic Assn., 1995—; mem. Trenton Human Rels. Commn., 1993-95; del. Trenton Coun. Civic Assns., 1996—. Avocations: science fiction, philosophy.

LADANYI, BRANKA MARIA, chemist, educator; b. Zagreb, Croatia, Sept. 7, 1947; came to U.S., 1969; d. Branko and Nevenka (Zilic) L.; m. Marshall Fixman, Dec. 7, 1974. BSc, McGill U., Montreal, Can., 1969; M in Philosophy, Yale U., 1971, PhD, 1973. Vis. prof. of chemistry U. Ill., 1974; postdoctoral research assoc. Yale U., 1974-77, research assoc., 1977-79; asst. prof. chemistry Colo. State U., Ft. Collins, 1979-84, assoc. prof. chemistry, 1985-87, prof. chemistry, 1987—; vis. fellow Joint Inst. for Lab. Astrophysics, 1993-94. Assoc. editor Jour. Chem. Physics, 1994—; referee and contbr. articles to profl. jours. Fellow Sloan Found., 1982-84, Dreyfus Found., 1983-87; vis. fellow JILA, 1993-94; grantee NSF, NATO, 1983-89. Mem. AAAS, Am. Chem. Soc. (PRF grantee 1979-82, 1989-91, 95—), Am. Phys. Soc., Sigma Xi. Office: Colo State U Dept Chemistry Fort Collins CO 80523

LADANYI, BRANKO, civil engineer; b. Zagreb, Croatia, Dec. 14, 1922; emigrated to Can., 1962, naturalized, 1967; s. Adalbert and Zora (Kniewald) L.; m. Nevenka Zilic, Dec. 14, 1946; children: Branka, Thomas, Marc. BCE, U. Zagreb, 1947; PhD in Soil Mechanics, U. Louvain, Belgium, 1959. Design engr. Dept. Transp., Zagreb, 1947-52; teaching asst. U. Zagreb, 1952-58; research engr. Belgian Geotech. Inst., Ghent, 1958-62; asso. prof., then prof. civil engring. Laval U., Quebec, Can., 1962-67; prof. civil engring. Ecole Poly., U. Montreal, 1967-94, prof. emeritus, 1994—, dir. North Engring. Centre, 1972—. Author papers in geotech. field, chpts. in books. Recipient Que. sci. award Que. Ministry Edn., 1974, De Beer Geotech. award Belgian Geotech. Soc., 1986, Elbert F. Rice Meml. award ASCE and U. Alaska, Fairbanks, 1991, North Sci. award Govt. of Can., 1996. Fellow ASCE (amity award 1995), Royal Soc. Can., Can, Acad. Engring., Engring. Inst. Can., Can. Soc. Civil Engring.; mem. ASTM, Order Engrs. Que., Can. Geotech. Soc. (R.F. Legget geotech. award 1981, Roger J.E. Brown meml. award 1993), Can. Inst. Mining and Metallurgy. Office: Dept Civil Engring, Ecole Poly CP 6079 Succ Centre-Ville, Montreal, PQ Canada *There is no end to learning.*

LADAR, JERROLD MORTON, lawyer; b. San Francisco, Aug. 2, 1933. AB, U. Wash., 1956; LLB, U. Calif., Berkeley, 1960. Bar: Calif. 1961, U.S. Supreme Ct. 1967. Law clk. to judge U.S. Dist. Ct. (no. dist.) Calif., 1960-61; asst. U.S. atty. San Francisco, 1961-70; chief criminal div., 1968-70; mem. firm MacInnis & Donner, San Francisco, 1970-72; prof. criminal law and procedure U. San Francisco Law Sch., 1962-83; pvt. practice San Francisco., 1970-94; ptnr. Ladar & Knapp, San Francisco, 1994—; lectr. Hastings Coll. Law, Civil and Criminal Advocacy Programs, 1985—; chair pvt. defender panel U.S. Dist. Ct. (no. dist.) Calif., 1980-90; ct. apptd. chair stats. and tech. subcom. Fed. Civil Justice Reform Act Com. (no. dist.) Calif., 1990-95; ct. apptd. mem. Fed. Ct. Civil Local Rules Revision Com. (no. dist.) Calif., 1994—; chmn. Criminal Local Rules Revision Com. (no. dist.) Calif., 1991—; mem. continuing edn. of bar criminal law adv. com. U. Calif., Berkeley, 1978-83, 89—; panelist, mem. nat. planning com. ABA White Collar Crime Inst., 1995—. Author: (with others) Selected Trial Motions, California Criminal Law Procedure and Practice, 1986, (supplements to) California Criminal Law and Procedure, 1987-92, (chpts.) 2d edit., 1993, Direct Examination-Tips and Techniques, 1982, Violent Crime Control Bill of 1994, 1995, Immunity Backfire, 1996; co-author: Criminal Trial Tactics, 1985, The Turn in the Road-Collateral Effects of Convistions, 1997. Trustee Tamalpais Union High Sch. Dist., 1968-77, chmn. bd., 1973-74; mem. adv. com. Nat. PTA Assn., 1972-78; apptd. mem. criminal justice act com. U.S. Ct. Appeals (9th cir). Fellow Am. Bd. Criminal Lawyers; mem. ABA (panelist sect. taxation), San Francisco Bar Assn. (editor in Re 1974-76), State Bar Calif. (pro-tem disciplinary referee 1976-78, vice chmn. pub. interest and edn. com. criminal law sect., mem. exec. com. criminal law sect. 1980-87, editor Criminal Law Sect. News 1981-87, chmn. exec. com. 1983-84), Am. Inns. of Ct. (exec. com. 1994-97), Fed. Bar Assn. (panelist), Nat. Sentencing Inst. Office: 507 Polk St Ste 310 San Francisco CA 94102-3339

LADAU, ROBERT FRANCIS, architect, planner; b. N.Y.C., Jan. 31, 1940; s. A. Ralph and Marguerite Louise (de Valois-Vignand) L.; m. Anne Horton, May 30, 1970. A.B., Columbia U., 1961, B.Arch., M.Arch., 1965. Chmn. bd. dirs., chief exec. officer Environers Inc., N.Y.C., 1964-66, dir., 1966-73; assoc. Rogers, Butler & Burgun, Architects, N.Y.C., 1966-69; prin. Robert F. Ladau, AIA Architect/Planner, N.Y.C., 1969-70, pres., 1973—; ptnr. Metcalf & Assocs. Architects & Engrs., Washington and N.Y.C. and founder and ptnr. Sir Robert Matthew, Metcalf & Ptnrs., London and Edinburgh, 1970-73; v.p. architecture A.M. Kinney Affiliation Architects & Engrs., Cin., N.Y.C., Chgo., Denver, L.A., San Juan and Basel, Switzerland, 1975-80; sr. v.p. Welton Becket Assocs., N.Y.C., 1980-84; pres., chief exec. officer The Miller Orgn., 1984-90; pres. Emery Roth & Sons Interior Design/Facilities Mgmt., 1990—; lectr. on planning, design health facilities; mem. nat. panel Am. Arbitration Assn. Bd. fellows Frick Collection; chmn. long range planning com. bd. govs. Columbia U. Club N.Y.; mem. Bedford (N.Y.) Conservation Bd., 1975-78. Contbr. articles to profl. jours. Co-author: Color in Interior Design and Architecture, 1988; designer numerous office and comml., health, ednl., urban, recreational, residential and indsl. facilities. Recipient Group Exhibit award Rockefeller Found., 1964; design awards Rockefeller Found., 1962, N.Y. Soc. Architects, 1966, Internat. Conf. Med. Primatology, 1974, Carnegie Heroism medal, 1989; William Kinne Fellows traveling fellow, 1965; registered architect, N.Y., N.J., Del., D.C., Conn. Mem. AIA, N.Y. Soc. Architects, N.Y State Assn. Architects, Nat. Council Archtl. Registration Bds. (certified), Humane Soc. N.Y. (bd. advisors 1992-93, trustee 1993—). Clubs: Princeton, Mashomack, Quaker Hill. Home: Mooney Hill Rd Patterson NY 12563 Office: 560 Lexington Ave New York NY 10022-6828

LADD, ALAN WALBRIDGE, JR., motion picture company executive; b. L.A., Oct. 22, 1937; s. Alan Walbridge and Marjorie Jane (Harrold) L.; m. Patricia Ann Beazley, Aug. 30, 1959 (div. 1983); children: Kelliann, Tracy Elizabeth, Amanda Sue; m. Cindra Kay, July 13, 1985. Motion picture agt. Creative Mgmt., L.A., 1963-69; v.p. prodn. 20th Century-Fox Film Corp., L.A., 1973-74; sr. v.p. 20th Century-Fox Film Corp. (Worldwide Prodns. div.), Beverly Hills, Calif., 1974-76; pres. 20th Century-Fox Pictures, 1976-79, Ladd Co., Burbank, Calif., 1979-83; pres., chief oper. officer MGM/UA Entertainment Co., 1983-86; chief exec. officer MGM/UA Entertainment Co, from 1986, also chmn. bd. dirs.; chmn., chief exec. officer Metro-Goldwyn-Mayer Pictures, Inc., Culver City, Calif., until 1988; pres., chmn. Pathe Entertainment, L.A., 1989-90; co-chmn. MGM-Pathe, L.A., 1990-93, MGM, L.A., 1990-93; chmn., CEO MGM-Pathe Communications, L.A., 1991-93; pres. The Ladd Co., L.A., 1993—. Prodr.: (films) Walking Stick, 1969, A Severed Head, 1969, TamLin, 1970, Villian Zee and Co., 1971, Fear is the Key, 1973, Braveheart, 1995 (Acad. award nominee for best picture of yr. 1996); exec. prodr.: (films) Nightcomers, 1971, Vice Versa, 1988, The Brady Bunch, 1995, Braveheart, 1995. Served with USAF, 1961-63. Office: The Ladd Co care Paramount 5555 Melrose Ave Los Angeles CA 90038-3112*

LADD, CHARLES CUSHING, III, civil engineering educator; b. Bklyn., Nov. 23, 1932; s. Charles Cushing and Elizabeth (Swan) L.; m. Carol Lee Ballou, June 11, 1954; children: Melissa, Charles IV, Ruth, Matthew. AB, Bowdoin Coll., 1955; SB, MIT, 1955, SM, 1957, ScD, 1961. Asst. prof. civil engring. MIT, 1961-64, assoc. prof., 1964-70, prof., 1970-94, dir. Ctr. Sci. Excellence in Offshore Engring., 1983-94, Edmund K. Turner prof., 1994—; gen. reporter 9th Internat. Conf. Soil Mechanics and Found. Engring., Tokyo, 1977; co-gen. reporter 11th Internat. Conf. Soil Mechanics and Found. Engring., San Francisco, 1985; mem. geotech. bd. NRC, 1992-94. Contbr. articles to profl. jours. Mem. Concord (Mass.) Republican Town Com., 1968-82; commr. Concord Dept. Pub. Works, 1965-78, chmn., 1972-74. Fellow ASCE (rsch. prize 1969, Croes medal 1973, Norman medal 1976, Terzaghi lectr. 1986, exec. com. geotech. engring. divsn. 1989—, chmn. 1993-94, hon. mem. 1995, Middlebrooks award 1996); mem. NAE, ASTM (Hogentogler award 1990), NSPE, Boston Soc. Civil Engrs. (bd. govs. 1972-81, pres. 1977-78), Transp. Rsch. Bd., Internat. Soc. Soil Mechanics and Found. Engring., Am. Soc. Engring. Edn., Assn. Engring. Firms Practicing in the Geoscis., AAUW, Brit. Geotech. Soc., Can. Geotech. Soc. Home: 7 Thornton Ln Concord MA 01742-4107 Office: MIT Dept Civil & Environ Engrng Cambridge MA 02139

LADD, CHERYL (CHERYL STOPPLEMOOR), actress; b. Huron, S.D., July 12, 1951; d. Dolores Katz; m. David Alan Ladd (div. 1980); m. Brian Russell, Jan. 3, 1981; children: Jordan, Elizabeth, Lindsay. Studies with Milton Katselas. Mem. Music Shop musical group, 1968-70; Goodwill amb. to Childhelp U.S.A. (Woman of the World award 1987); spokesperson Retinitis Pigmentosa International. TV shows and movies include (animated) Josie and the Pussycats, 1970-72, The Ken Berry Wow Show, 1972, Satan's School for Girls, 1973, Charlie's Angels, 1977-81, Cheryl Ladd, 1979, Cheryl Ladd-Souvenirs, 1980, Cheryl Ladd: Scenes from a Special, 1982, Roots, Police Woman, Happy Days, Switch, When She Was Bad, 1979, Grace Kelly, 1983, Kentucky Woman, 1983, Romance on the Orient Express, 1985, A Death in California, 1985, Crossings, 1986, Blue Grass, 1988, Deadly Care, 1987, The Fulfillment of Mary Gray, 1989, Jekyll and Hyde, 1990, The Girl Who Came Between Them, 1990, Crash: The Mystery of Flight 1501, 1990, Danielle Steele's Changes, 1991, Locked Up: A Mother's Rage, 1991, Dead Before Dawn, 1992, Broken Promises, 1993, Dancing With Danger, 1994, The Lady, 1995, Kiss & Tell, 1995, (syndicated series) One West Waikiki, 1995; stage appearances include Anything Goes, 1986, Hasty Heart; films include The Treasure of Jamaica Reef, 1975, Purple Hearts, 1994, Now and Forever, 1985, Millenium, 189, Lisa, 1990, Poison Ivy, 1992, One West Waikiki, 1994; numerous TV commls.; albums include Cheryl Ladd, 1978, Dance Forever, 1979. Mem. AFTRA, SAG, AGVA. *

LADD, CULVER SPROGLE, secondary education educator; b. Bismarck, N.D., Nov. 15, 1929; s. Culver Sprogle and Eleanor (Pearson)L. BS, U. Md., 1953; MA, Am. U., 1963, PhD, 1984; postgrad., Harvard U., summer 1963, Oxford (Eng.) U., 1975-76; cert. by correspondence, Nat. Def. U., Thailand, 1972. Clk.-photographer Dept. Justice, FBI, Washington, 1946-54; intercept controller Dept. of Def., USAF, 1954-56; asst. office mgr. Covington & Burling, Lawyers, Washington, 1956-62; tchr. Internat. Sch. Bangkok, Thailand, 1964-66; lectr. U. Md., Thailand, 1966-67, 71-74; project dir. Bus. Rsch. Ltd., Thailand, 1966-67, 72-74; spl. lectr. Payap U., Chiang Mai, Thailand, 1974-75; tchr. D.C. Pub. Schs., 1978—; cons. USAID, Thailand, 1973-74; vis. scientist Brookhaven Nat. Labs., L.I., 1988; master tchr. Woodrow Wilson Fellowship Found., 1989. Capt. USAFR, 1953-72; PTO. Recipient Appreciation award Payap U. 1987. Mem. Mid-Atlantic Region Assn. for Asian Studies, Acad. Polit. Sci., Nat. Capital Area Polit. Sci. Assn., Nat. Coun. Tchrs. Math., Mid. States Coun. Social Studies, Aircraft Owners and Pilots Assn., Omicron Delta Kappa, Pi Sigma Alpha. Republican. Presbyterian. Avocations: gardening, flying. Home: PO Box 2084 Lusby MD 20657-1884 Office: POACRE Airfield PO Box 2084 845 Crystal Rock Rd Lusby MD 20657-1884

LADD, JAMES ROGER, international management consultant, accountant; b. San Diego, Mar. 5, 1943; s. Robert Dwinell and Virginia Ruth (Dole) L.; m. Sharon Patricia Smith, Aug. 22, 1964; children—Brian Andrew, Jennifer Louise, Casey James. AB, Duke U., 1964. CPA. With Deloitte Haskins & Sells, Seattle, 1964-79; mng. ptnr. Deloitte Haskins & Sells, Tokyo, 1979-84; U.S. pers. ptnr. Deloitte Haskins & Sells, N.Y.C., 1984-86; area mng. ptnr. Deloitte Haskins & Sells, Seattle, 1986-89; mng. dir. Deloitte & Touche, Seattle, 1989-92; pres. Ladd Pacific Cons., Seattle, 1992—. Pres. Seattle Children's Home, 1979; bd. dirs. Corp. Coun. for Arts, 1986-92; bd. dirs., treas. Seattle Found., 1988-97; trustee Duke U., 1991-93; chair internat. bus. adv. coun. U. Wash., 1995-97. Mem. AICPA, Japan Am. Soc. State Wash. (pres. 1996-97), Wash. Soc. CPAs, Duke Alumni Assn. (nat. pres. 1991-92), Inst. Mgmt. Cons., Rainier Club. Office: 9621 Hilltop Rd Bellevue WA 98004-4007

LADD, JOHN CURRAN, lawyer; b. Mpls., Nov. 24, 1945; s. John Greeley and Beatrice (Brand) L.; m. Karen Elizabeth Harnish, Oct. 13, 1984; children: Anne, Jessica. LLB, Yale U., 1970. Bar: Calif. 1970. Jud. law clk. to Stanley A. Weigel U.S. Dist. Ct. (no. dist.) Calif., 1970-71; from assoc. to ptnr. Steinhart & Falconer, San Francisco, 1971-82; ptnr. Morgenstein, Ladd & Jubelirer, San Francisco, 1982-86, Jackson & Ladd, San Francisco, 1988-89; pvt. practice law San Francisco, 1987, 89-90; ptnr. Ropers, Majeski, Kohn & Bentley, San Francisco, 1990—; co-chair San Francisco Lawyer's Com. for Urban Affairs, 1981-83; mem. Legal Svcs. Trust Fund Commn. of State Bar, 1982-86; lectr. Def. Rsch. Inst., Andrews Seminars Asbestos Litigation Ann. Programs, 1995-96. Active in U.S. Masters Swimming. Home: 1616 Castro St San Francisco CA 94114-3707 Office: Ropers Majeski Kohn & Bentley 670 Howard St San Francisco CA 94105-3916

LADD, JOSEPH CARROLL, retired insurance company executive; b. Chgo., Jan. 26, 1927; s. Stephen C. and Laura (McBride) L.; m. Barbara Virginia Carter, June 5, 1965; children: Carroll, Joseph Carroll, Barbara, Virginia, William. BA, Ohio Wesleyan U., 1950; CLU, Am. Coll., Bryn Mawr; D in Bus. Adminstrn. (hon.), Spring Garden Coll., 1985. Agt. Conn. Gen. Life Ins. Co., Chgo., 1950-53; staff asst. Conn. Gen. Life Ins. Co., 1953-54, mgr. Evanston (Ill.) br. office, 1954-60, dir. agys., 1960-62, mgr. Los Angeles br. office, 1963; v.p. sales Fidelity Mut. Life Ins. Co., Phila., 1964-67; sr. v.p. sales Fidelity Mut. Life Ins. Co., 1968, exec. v.p., 1969-71, pres., chief exec. officer, dir., 1971-84, chmn., chief exec. officer, dir., 1984-89, chmn., dir., 1989-91; ret.; bd. dirs. Corestates Fin., Phila. Suburban Corp., Phila. Electric Co. Trustee Bryn Mawr Hosp.; trustee United Way of S.E. Pa.; trustee Phila. United Way, also gen. chmn. 1978 campaign; bd. dirs. Phila. YMCA. Served with USNR, 1945-46. Recipient Civic Achievement award Am. Jewish Com., 1978, Achiever's award WHEELS Med. and Specialized Transp., 1978, Ohio Wesleyan U. Life Achievement award Delta Tau Delta, 1982, William Penn award, Greater Phila. C. ofC. and PENJERDEL Coun., 1988, Robert Morris Citizenship award Valley Forge Coun. Boy Scouts Am., 1988; named YMCA Man of Yr., 1979, William Penn Found. Disting. Pennsylvanian, 1980. Mem. Greater Phila. C. of C. (dir., chmn. 1979, 83-84), Phila. Country Club, Union League Club (Phila.), Summer Beach (Fla.) Country Club.

LADD, LOUISE ELIZABETH, investments company executive; b. Waco, Tex., Sept. 17, 1950; d. Ludwig Nitter and Rae Elizabeth (Skibrek) L. BA, U. Wis., 1972. CFP. Mktg. rep. Marine Bank (Banc One), Milw., 1973-74; sales specialist Xerox, Wauwatosa, Wis., 1974-78; account exec. Dean Witter, Wauwatosa, 1978-82, assoc. v.p. investments, 1982-85, v.p. investments, 1985-96; 1st v.p. investments Dean Witter, Wauwatosa, Wis., 1996—; bd. dirs. Presdl. Dimensions. Bd. dirs. Nex Door Found., Milw., 1991—. Am. Field Svc. scholar, 1967. Mem. Inst. Cert. Fin. Planner, Profl. Dimensions, Milw. Found. Womens Fund(devel. com.), Milw. Bond Club. Avocations: skiing, traveling, tennis. Office: Dean Witter 2500 N Mayfair Rd Ste 600 Wauwatosa WI 53226-1415

LADD, MARCIA LEE, medical equipment and supplies company executive; b. Bryn Mawr, Pa., July 22, 1950; d. Edward Wingate and Virginia Lee (McGinnes) Mullinix; children: Joshua Wingate, McGinnes Lee. BA, U. Pa., 1972; MEd, U. Va., 1973; MA, Emory U., 1979. Rsch. assoc. N.C. Tng. and Standards Coun., Raleigh, 1973-75; dir. counseling svc. N.C. State Youth Svcs. Agy., Raleigh, 1975-76; acad. dean Duke U., Durham, N.C., 1976-77; prin. Ladd & Assocs. Mgmt. Cons., Chapel Hill, N.C., 1979-88; v.p. adminstrn. CompuChem Corp., Research Triangle Park, N.C., 1988-91; v.p. mktg. Prentke Romich Co., Wooster, Ohio, 1991-94; v.p. ops. Exec. Staffing Svcs., Inc., Cary, N.C., 1994; pres., CEO, owner Triangle Aftercare, Durham, N.C., 1994—. Bd. dirs. Wayne County Arts Coun., Wooster, 1992, Stoneridge/Sedgefield Swim/Racquet Club, Chapel Hill, N.C., 1985-88, Oakwood Hist. Soc., Raleigh, 1981-84; mem. bd. visitors Carolina Friends Sch., Durham, 1986-89; Stephen min. Univ. Presbyn. Ch., Chapel Hill, 1994-97, youth group leader, 1995—. Decorated Order of Long Leaf Pine Gov. of N.C., 1976; named one of Impact 100 Most Influential People, Research Triangle, N.C., 1997. Presbyterian. Office: Triangle Aftercare 249 W Hwy 54 Durham NC 27713

LADDON, WARREN MILTON, lawyer; b. Washington, July 2, 1933; s. Misha and Hannah (Cooper) L.; m. Paula K. Cramer; children: Michael, Susan, Benjamin. BS, Wilson Tchrs. Coll., 1955; JD, U. Mich., 1962. Bar: Calif. 1963, D.C. 1966, Pa. 1967. Tchg. assoc. Boalt Hall U. Calif., Berkeley, 1962-63; trial and appellate atty. Dept. Labor, Washington, 1963-65; appellate atty. NLRB, Washington, 1965-67; assoc. Morgan Lewis & Bockius, Phila., 1967-71; ptnr. Morgan Lewis & Bockius, 1971-86; chief counsel CIGNA Corp., 1986—. Lt. (j.g.) USNR, 1956-59. Mem. ABA. Office: CIGNA Corp One Liberty Pl 1650 Market St Philadelphia PA 19103-7301

LADEHOFF, LEO WILLIAM, metal products manufacturing executive; b. Gladbrook, Iowa, May 4, 1932; s. Wendell Leo and Lillian A. L.; m. Beverly Joan Dreessen, Aug. 1, 1951; children: Debra K., Lance A. B.S., U. Iowa, 1957. Supt. ops. Square D Co., 1957-61; mfg. mgr. Fed. Pacific Electric Co., 1961; v.p. ops. Avis Indsl. Corp., 1961-67; pres. energy products Group Gulf & Western Industries, Inc., 1967-78; chmn. bd., pres., chief exec. officer, dir. Amcast Indsl. Corp., Ohio, 1978-95, also chmn. bd. dirs., 1995—; bd. dirs. Key Bank. With USAF, 1951-54, Korea. Mem. Soc. Automotive Engrs., U. Iowa Alumni Assn., Moraine Country Club, Forest Highlands Country Club, Ventana Canyon Country Club, Alpha Kappa Psi. Republican. Home: 7211 E Desert Moon Loop Tucson AZ 85750-0921 Office: Amcast Indsl Corp PO Box 98 Dayton OH 45401-0098 also: Elkhart Products Corp 1255 Oak St Elkhart IN 46514-2277

LADEHOFF, ROBERT LOUIS, bishop; b. Feb. 19, 1932; m. Jean Arthur Burcham (dec. Feb. 1992); 1 child, Robert Louis Jr. Grad., Duke U., 1954, Gen. Theol. Sem., 1957, Va. Theol. Sem., 1980. Ordained deacon, priest The Episcopal Ch., 1957;. Priest in charge N.C. parishes, 1957-60; rector St. Christopher's Ch., Charlotte, N.C., 1960-74, St. John's Ch., Fayetteville, 1974-85; bishop, co-adjutor of Oreg., 1985, bishop, 1986—. Office: Diocese of Oreg PO Box 467 Lake Oswego OR 97034-0467

LADEN, BEN ELLIS, economist; b. Savannah, Ga., Mar. 4, 1942; s. Bernard and Fannie Rachel (Cooper) L.; m. Susan Sherman, Aug. 16, 1964; children: Francine, Jonathan, Paul. A.B., Princeton U., 1963; Ph.D., Johns Hopkins U., 1969. Asst. prof. econs. Ohio State U., 1967-71; economist Fed. Res. Bd., 1971-74; v.p., chief economist T. Rowe Price Assocs., Balt., 1974-87; dir. fin. instns. regulation staff HUD, Washington, 1990-94; pres. Bel Assocs., Washington, 1994—. Author: Economic Trend, 1974-87; also articles. Fellow Nat. Assn. Bus. Economists (dir. 1981-87, pres. 1984-85); mem. Am. Econs. Assn. Jewish. Home: 3111 Rittenhouse St NW Washington DC 20015-1614 *Each person has to find his own unique formula for success. My greatest achievements have come from the following elements. 1. A clear concept of priorities with persistent concentration on the highest priority. 2. Building structures which will continue to payoff in the future, rather than trying for immediate results. 3. Identifying those areas where my contribution could be the greatest and could be unique. 4. Always striving for the highest quality in my work. 5. Most important, learning from the experience of others and respecting the individual ways of other people.*

LADEN, KARL, toiletries company executive; b. Bklyn., Aug. 10, 1932; s. Judah and Anna (Bernstein) L.; m. Judy Talisman, June 24, 1956; children—Ben, Ethan, Adam, Noam, Zev. B.S., U. Akron, Ohio, 1954; Ph.D., Northwestern U., 1957. Cons. Indsl. Bio-Test Labs., Northbrook, Ill., 1955-57; research chemist William Wrigley Jr. Co., Chgo., 1957-58; research mgr. Toni Co., Chgo., 1959-64; with Gillette Research Inst., Washington, 1964-76, v.p. biomed. scis., 1968-71, pres., 1971-76; v.p. research and devel. Carter Products Co., Cranbury, N.J., 1976-86; cons. tech. transfer, new product devel., 1986—. Contbg. editor, Nat. Beauty Sch. Jour., 1970-77; Contbr. articles to profl. jours. Recipient award Internat. Flavors and Fragrances, 1963, 67. Fellow Soc. Cosmetic Chemists (pres. 1977, chmn. bd. 1978, editor jour. 1967-72, Mid-West chpt. award 1964, Lit. award 1969, Merit award 1972, Medal award 1979); mem. Am. Chem. Soc. Home: 31 Yafe Nof, Haifa Israel Office: PO Box 866 Freehold NJ 07728-0866

LADEN, SUSAN, publisher, consultant; b. Washington, Aug. 3, 1942; d. Louis and Irene (Berenter) Sherman; m. Ben E. Laden, Aug. 16, 1964; children: Francine, Jonathan, Paul. AB, Vassar Coll., 1964. Caseworker Dept. Welfare, Balt., 1964-66; publ. Biblical Archaeology rev., Washington, 1976-94, Bible rev., Washington, 1984-94, Moment mag., Washington, 1987-94; pres. Laden & Assocs., 1994, Jewish Family & Life, Washington, 1996—, Rejuvenation, Inc., 1995—; bd. dirs. Portfolio Travel, Washington. Treas. Lafayette Home and Sch. Assn., Washington, 1973-75; v.p. Jewish Ednl. Ventures, Boston, 1987-94; sec. Jewish Coun. for the Aging, Rockville, Md., 1992-94, treas., 1994; sec.-treas., Bibl. Archeology Soc., 1977-94. Democrat. Home and Office: Jewish Family Life 3111 Rittenhouse St NW Washington DC 20015-1614

LADER, LAWRENCE, writer; b. N.Y.C., Aug. 6, 1919; s. Ludwig and Myrtle (Powell) L.; m. Jean MacInnis, Aug. 24, 1942 (div. Jan. 1946); m. Joan Summers, Sept. 27, 1961; 1 dau., Wendy Summers. A.B., Harvard U., 1941. With press dept. ABC, 1941-42; contbg. editor Coronet mag., 1946; feature editor Glamour mag., 1953; lectr. NYU, 1957-59, Philips Brooks Assn., Harvard, 1962—; regular contbr. Am. Heritage, Reader's Digest, N.Y. Times mags., others, 1941—; exec. dir. Hugh Moore Fund, 1966-67; fgn. corr. Arab-Israel War, 1948, other overseas assignments, 1951, 55, 57; adj. assoc. prof. journalism NYU, 1967-72. Author: Margaret Sanger, 1955, The Bold Brahmins, New England's War Against Slavery, 1961, Abortion, 1966; juvenile Margaret Sanger, 1969; Breeding Ourselves to Death, 1971, Foolproof Birth Control, 1972, Abortion II: Making the Revolution, 1973, Power on the Left: American Radical Movements since 1946, 1979, Politics, Power and the Church, 1987, Ru 486, 1991, A Private Matter, 1995. Chmn. exec. com. Nat. Abortion Rights Action League, 1969-72, chmn. bd., 1972-76; pres. Abortion Rights Mobilization, 1976—. Served to lt. AUS, 1942-46; officer-in-charge N.Y. Troop Information, Armed Forces Radio Service. Recipient Benjamin Franklin Mag. award, 1969, Cert. Distinction, NOW, 1989; named Feminist Majority Feminist of Yr., 1992. Mem. Authors Guild. Club: Harvard, Century Assn. (N.Y.C.). Home: 51 5th Ave New York NY 10003-4320

LADER, PHILIP, government official, business executive; b. Jackson Heights, N.Y., Mar. 17, 1946. BA, Duke U., 1966; MA, U. Mich., 1967, Oxford U., England, 1968; JD, Harvard U., 1972; LLD (hon.), Limestone Coll.; SJD (hon.), U. S.C.; LHD (hon.), Youngstown State U.; LLD (hon.), Lander U., Columbia Coll. Bar: Fla. 1972, D.C. 1973, S.C. 1979. Assoc. Sullivan & Cromwell, N.Y.C., 1972; law clk. to U.S. cir. judge, 1973; ptnr. Hartzog, Lader & Richards, Washington and Hilton Head Island, S.C., 1974-89; pres. Sea Pines Co., Hilton Head Island, 1979-83, Winthrop U., Rock Hill, S.C., 1983-85, GOSL Land Assets Mgmt., Hilton Head Island, S.C., 1986-88; pres./mng. dir. 1st Southern Corp., Hilton Head Island, 1989-91, 1997—; pres. Bus. Execs. for Nat. Security, Washington, 1991, Bond U., Gold Coast, Australia, 1991-93; adminstr. SBA, Washington, 1994-97; mem. President's Cabinet, Washington, 1994-97; dep. dir. for mgmt. Office Mgmt. and Budget Exec. Office Pres., 1993; dep. chief of staff White House, asst. to Pres., 1993-94; chmn. Pres.'s Coun. on Integrity and Efficiency, 1993, Pres.'s Mgmt. Coun.; chmn. policy com. Nat. Performance Rev., 1993. Candidate for gov. of S.C., 1986; chmn. bd. visitors Duke U. Sanford Inst. Pub. Policy; bd. dirs. ARC, 1996-97. Hon. fellow Pembroke Coll., Oxford U. Mem. Coun. Fgn. Rels., Chief Execs. Orgn., D.C. Met. Club, World Pres.'s Orgn., Soc. Internat. Bus. Fellows, Phi Beta Kappa. Episcopalian.

LADERMAN, EZRA, composer, educator, college dean; b. Bklyn., June 29, 1924. MA, Columbia U, 1952; studies with Stefan Wolpe, Otto Luening, D. Moore, P. Lang, Columbia U. Dir. music program Nat. Endowment for Arts, 1979-82; pres. Nat. Music Coun., 1985-89; dean Sch. Music Yale U., New Haven, 1989-95; chmn. Am. Composers Orch., 1987-90. Compositions include 8 symphonies, 9 string quartets, 7 operas, 150 compositions and 25 recordings; (dramatic operas) Jacob and the Indians, 1954, Goodbye to the Clowns, 1956, The Hunting of the Snark, 1958, Sarah, 1959, Air Raid, 1965, Shadows Among Us, 1967, Galileo Galilei, 1978, Marilyn, 1993; (orchestral) Piano Concerto, 1939, Leipzig Symphony, 1945, Piano Concerto, 1957, 8 Symphonies, 1964-84, Flute Concerto, 1968, Viola Concerto, 1975, Violin Concerto, 1978, Piano Concerto No. 1, 1978, Concert for String Quartet and Orchestra, 1981, Cello Concerto, 1984, Clarinet Concerto, 1995; (vocal) oratorio The Eagle Stirred, 1961, oratorio The Trials of Galileo, 1967, Columbus, 1975, oratorio A Mass for Cain, 1983; (chamber) Wind Octet, 1957, Clarinet Sonata, 1958, 9 String Quartets, 1959-96, Double Helix for Flute, Oboe, and String Quartet, 1968, Partita for Violin, 1982, Double String Quartet, 1983; (film scores) The Charter, 1958, The Invisible Aton, 1958, The Question Tree, 1962, Odyssey, 1964, The Eleanor Roosevelt Story, 1965, The Black Fox, 1965, Magic Prison, 1966, The Meaning of Modern Art, 1967, Confrontation, 1968, Image of Love, 1968, The Bible as Literature, 1972, Burden of Mystery, 1972; (television movie scores) Herschel, 1959, Invisible City, 1961, The Voice of the Desert, 1962, Eltanin, 1962, Grand Canyon, 1964, The Forgotten Peninsula, 1967, Our Endangered Wildlife, 1967, California the Most, 1968, Before Cortez, 1970, In the Fall of 1844, 1971, Cave People of the Philippines, 1972, Lamp Unto My Feet, 1978. Guggenheim fellow 1955, 58, 64; recipient Rome prize, 1963; Kennedy Center Friedheim Award, 2nd place, 1981. mem. Am. Acad. and Inst. of Arts and Letters, 1991. Office: Yale U Sch Music Office of Dean New Haven CT 06520

LADERMAN, GABRIEL, artist; b. Bklyn., Dec. 26, 1929; s. Isidore and Leah (Stock) L.; m. Carol Ciavati, Feb. 12, 1953; children—Raphael, Michael. B.A., Bklyn. Coll., 1952; M.F.A., Cornell U., 1957. Faculty State U. N.Y., New Paltz, 1957-59, Pratt Inst., 1959-66; faculty Queens Coll., Flushing, N.Y., 1966—; chmn. Queens Coll., 1979-83; vis. prof. La. State U., Baton Rouge, 1966-67, Yale U., 1968, 81, 83, 89, 91, Viterbo Coll., 1969, 80, Art Students League, 1972-81, Boston U., 1973, N.Y. Studio Sch., Am. U., 1994—; dir. G.-T. Mus., 1980-84, Caumsett Summer Landscape Painting Program, 1980, 81; vis. critic, lectr. Yale U., Syracuse U., Bennington Coll., Vassar Coll., Rutgers U., Princeton, Cooper-Union, Phila. Coll. Art, Mus. Fine Arts, Boston, Md. Inst. Art, Swain Sch., Boston U., Boston Mus. Sch., Ind. U., Bard Coll., Kansas City Art Inst., Fla. State U., SUNY at New Paltz, Amherst Coll., Skowhegan Sch., Yale-Norfolk Sch., New York Studio Sch., Pratt Inst., N.Y. Inst. Tech., Boston Mus., Tyler Sch. of Temple U., U. R.I., U. N.H., Artists for Environment, Iowa State U., Hobart Coll., U. Wis., 1980, Md. Art Inst., 1980, Royal Sch. Art, Bangkok, Thailand, 1976, Nat. Art Sch., Jakarta, Indonesia, 1975, Art Sch., Surabaya, Indonesia, 1975, Victorian Coll. Art, Melbourne, Australia, 1975, Coll. Art, Ballarat, Australia, 1975, Prahran Coll., Melbourne, 1975, U. Minn., 1987, Yale U., 1987, State U. Calif. Arts seminars San Luis Obispo, 1986, Stanford U., 1987, 91, U. Calif., Santa Barbara, 1987, Calif. State U., Long Beach, 1987, Pa. Acad., 1988, Chautauqua Art Program, N.Y. Acad. Art, numerous others; USIS lectr., Japan, 1975; vis. lectr., critic Long Beach State Coll., 1987, Parsons Sch., 1991, Ox Bow Sch., 1991, N.Y. Acad., 1987, 91; vis. critic Chautauqua Art Sch., 1993; critic, lectr. Stanford U. Chautauqua Art Program, Bard Coll., Pa. Acad.; Disting. vis. prof. Am. Univ., Washington, 1994. Contbr. articles to profl. jours.; one man shows at Schoelkopf Gallery, 1964, 67, 70, 72, 74, 77, 86, 90, Hobart Coll., 1968, R.I. U., 1969, Temple U., 1971, La. State U., 1967, Bennington Coll., Ithaca Coll., R.I. U., So. U., Dart Gallery, Chgo., 1977, Savage Gallery, Boston, 1976, Meade Mus., Amherst Coll., 1983, Contemporary Realists Gallery, San Francisco, 1987, 90, Jessica Darraby Gallery, Los Angeles, 1987, Peter Tattistcheff Gallery, N.Y., 1994; exhibited in group shows at Whitney Mus., 1971, Mus. Modern Art, 1974, Corcoran Gallery, 1972, 76, Boston Mus., 1974, 75, Bklyn. Mus., 1952, 57, 59, 61, Library of Congress, 1957, 59, Gallery of Modern Art, 1972, N.Y. Cultural Center, 1972, Phila. Mus., 1970, Wadsworth Atheneum, 1976, Fogg Mus., 1976, Mpls. Inst. Arts, 1976, Milw. Art Center, 1977, Ft. Worth Art Mus., 1977, High Mus., 1977, San Francisco Mus. Modern Art, 1977, Pa. Acad., 1981, traveling shows sponsored by A.F.A., Smithsonian Instn., Library of Congress, Pa. Acad. Arts; represented in permanent collections Witherspoon Mus., Cleve. Mus., Mus. Fine Arts, Boston, Brandeis U. Art Mus., Chase-Manhattan Bank, A.D. White Mus. Cornell U., Nat. Gallery Art, Muzium Negara, Kuala Lumpur, Mead Mus. Amherst Coll., Glen S. Janss Collection Boise Art Mus., FMC Corp. Chgo., Archdiocese of Baton Rouge, Fidelity Bank Collection, Phila., Sierra Club. Recipient Rsch. award CUNY, 1970-71, 75-76, 82, 86-87, 88-89, Fed. Govt. Commn., through Interior Dept. for Bicentennial, 1974, award Rockefeller Found. at Bellagio, 1989, Altman Figure Painting prize Nat. Acad. Biennial, 1995; asst. Cornell U., 1955-57; L.C. Tiffany grantee, 1959; Fulbright fellow to Italy, 1962-63; Yaddo fellow, 1960, 62; Ingram Merrill fellow, 1975-76, 84, 90; J.S. Guggenheim fellow, 1989-90; NEA sr. grantee, 1983, 87-88; juror NEA, 1984, N.Y. State Coun. on Arts, 1985; Altman prize for Figure Painting 170th Annual Exhbn. of Nat. Acad., 1995, vis. Artist U. Pa., 1997, juror Bowery Gallery Exhbn., 1996, vis. disting. prof. Am. U., 1994-95, Washington. Mem. Nat. Acad. (Proctor Portrait Prize Biennial Exhbn. 1993). Office: Queens Coll Flushing NY 11367

LADIGES, LORI JEAN, learning disabilities specialist; b. Sheboygan, Wis., Feb. 25, 1956; d. Donald William and Marion Margaret (Henning) L. BS in Edn., U. Wis., 1978; MA in Learning Disabilities, Cardinal Stritch Coll., 1984. Cert. tchr. elem. (grades 1-8), Cognitive disorders (K-12) and learning disabilities (K-12). Learning disabilities specialist Kohler (Wis.) Pub. Sch., 1978—; part-time instr. Silver Lake Coll., Manitowoc, Wis., 1984-92; tchr. Cardinal Stritch Coll., Milw., 1989, adj. asst. prof., 1996—; sch. evaluation consortium chair spl. edn. Kohler Pub. Schs., 1989—, learning disabilities specialist, rep. long-range planning com., 1992—, cheerleading advisor, 1981-84, yearbook advisor, 1985-86; reviewer Sch. Evaluation Consortium, 1995, adj. asst. prof., Cardinal Stritch Coll. Mem. Sch. to Work com., Alpha Sigma (Grace Alvord award 1978). Lutheran. Avocations: traveling, reading, fashion design/coordination. Home: 2236 N 23rd St Sheboygan WI 53083-4443

LADIN, EUGENE, communications company executive; b. N.Y.C., Oct. 26, 1927; s. Nat and Mae (Cohen) L.; m. Millicent Dolly Frankel, June 27, 1948; children: Leslie Hope, Stephanie Joy. B.B.A., Pace U., 1956; M.B.A., Air Force Inst. Tech., 1959; postgrad., George Washington U., 1966-69. Cost engr. Rand Corp., Santa Monica, Calif., 1960-62; mgr. cost and econ. analysis Northrop Corp., Hawthorne, Calif., 1962-66; dir. financial planning Communications Satellite Corp., Washington, 1966-70; treas., chief fin. and adminstrv. officer Landis & Gyr, Inc., Elmsford, N.Y., 1970-76; v.p., treas., comptroller P.R. Telephone Co., San Juan, 1976-77; v.p. fin. Comtech Telecommunications Corp., Smithtown, N.Y., 1977—; acting pres. Comtech Antenna Corp., St. Cloud, Fla., 1978-80; chmn., chief exec. officer Telephone Interconnect Enterprises/Sunshine Telephone Co., Balt., Md. and Orlando, Fla., 1980-82; pres. Ladin and Assocs., Cons. and Commodity Traders, Maitland, Fla., 1982-84; pres., chief fin. officer Braintech Inc., South Plainfield, N.J., 1984; sr. v.p. fin., chief fin. officer Teltec Savs. Communications Co., Miami, Fla., 1984-88; chief fin. officer Hurwitz Group Inc., North Miami Beach, Fla., 1988-91; cons. pvt. practice, 1991—; assoc. prof. acctg. So. Ill. U., East St. Louis, 1960; asst. prof. bus. U. Md., 1969-70; adj. prof. George Washington U., 1969-70; vis. prof. acctg. Pace U., 1970; cons. E. Ladin, Pembroke Pines, Fla., 1991—. Served to capt. USAF, 1951-60. Decorated Air Force Commendation medal; recipient Air Force Outstanding Unit award. Mem. Nat. Assn. Accts., Fin. Exec. Inst. Democrat. Jewish. Club: Flamingo Country Club. Avocations: golf, sailing. Home and Office: 13355 SW 16th Ct Apt 401E Hollywood FL 33027-2429 *An individual must have sufficient self esteem to sustain the courage of his convictions, a high degree of professional integrity, and his individual character. Society has adopted a philosophy of "walk the middle road".*

LADJEVARDI, HABIB, historian; b. Tehran, Iran, May 28, 1938; came to U.S., 1950; s. Seyed Mahmoud and Tahereh (Kashani) L.; m. Mina Nassirzadeh, Aug. 3, 1962 (div. June 1979); children: Mahmoud, Mariam, Leila. BS, Yale U., 1961; MBA, Harvard U., 1963; DPhil, Oxford U., 1981. Personnel dir. Behshahr Ind. Group, Tehran, 1963-65, mktg. dir., 1966-69; pres. Paxan Corp., Tehran, 1969-70; chmn. bd. dirs. Container Corp. of Iran, 1969-79; founder, v.p. Iran Ctr. Mgmt. Studies, Tehran, 1970-79; sr. rsch. assoc. Harvard U. Bus. Sch., Cambridge, Mass., 1980-81; rsch. assoc. Harvard U. Ctr. for Middle Eastern Studies, 1981—, assoc. dir., 1987-90, dir. Iranian oral history project, 1981—; mem. acceptance coms. Tehran Stock Exch., 1973-76; lectr. Iran Ctr. for Mgmt. Studies, 1975-79; vis. fellow Oxford (Eng.) Ctr. Mgmt. Studies, 1976-79; v.p. exec. coun. Harvard U. Bus. Sch., 1978-79; exec. sec. Soc. for Iranian Studies, Cambridge, 1982-87; chmn. Iranian Studies Harvard U. Ctr. for Middle Eastern Studies, 1990—, chmn. pubs. com., 1990—. Author: Labor Unions & Autocracy in Iran, 1985, Guide to the Iranian Oral History Collection, 1993, Memoirs of Ali Amini, 1995, Memoirs of Shapour Bakhtiar, 1996; contbr. articles to profl. jours., chpts. to books. Mem. coun. of state Adminstrv. and Employment Affairs of Iran, 1972-76; dir. devel. and investment Bank of Iran, 1972-79; mem. ctrl. coun. Pres. of Univs. and Colls. of Iran, 1971-78; pres. Tahereh Found., Lincoln, Mass., 1982—. NEH grantee, 1984-87. Mem. Am. Hist. Assn., Young Presidents Orgn., Acad. Polit. Sci., N.Y. Acad. Scis., Iranian Assn. of Boston (founder, pres. 1988-91), Yale U. Class Coun., Yale Club of N.Y., Harvard Club of Boston. Democrat. Avocations: squash, skiing, grandchildren. Office: Harvard U Ctr Mid Eastern Studies 1737 Cambridge St Cambridge MA 02138-3016

LADJEVARDI, HAMID, fund manager; b. Tehran, Iran, June 11, 1948; came to U.S., 1960; s. Ahmad and Banoo (Barzin) L.; m. Manijeh Mirdamad, July 19, 1978; children: Adella, Lilly. BA in Econs., BA in Polit. Sci., U. Calif., Berkeley, 1971; MBA, Harvard U., 1973. Dep. mng. dir. Behshahr Indsl. Group, Tehran, 1974-79; vice-chmn., fin. dir. Akam Group of Cos., Tehran, 1975-79; investment mgr., v.p. Morgan Stanley & Co., N.Y.C., 1980-92; mgr. Baltic Fund 1 LLC, N.Y., 1992—; pres. Baltic

Mgmt. LLC, N.Y., 1994; instr. Fairleigh Dickinson U., Rutherford, N.J., 1984; mem. supervisory coun. Vilnians Bank, Lithuania; chmn. Baltic Fund Hotels, Vilnius, 1996—. Mem. Fgn. Policy Assn., Carnegie Coun. on Ethics and Internat. Affairs, U.S. Senatorial Club, Harvard Club. Home: 66 Brite Ave Scarsdale NY 10583-1637 Office: Baltic Fund 1LP 123 Main St White Plains NY 10601-3104

LADLY, FREDERICK BERNARD, health services and financial services company executive; b. Toronto, Ont., Can., July 14, 1930; s. John Bernard and Olivia Montgomery (Fenimore) L.; m. Sharon Mary Davidson; children: Patricia, Elizabeth, Katherine, Martha, Sarah, Meghan. BA, U. Toronto. Gen. mgr. internat. ops. Can. Packers Inc., Toronto, 1973, v.p., 1974-78, dir., 1975-84, exec. v.p., 1978-84; pres., CEO Extendicare Health Svcs. Inc., Markham, 1984-94, Extendicare Inc. (formerly Crownx Inc.), Markham, 1992-95; chmn. United Health, Inc., Milw., 1984—; vice chmn. Crown Life Ins. Co., Regina, 1994—; CEO, dep. chmn. Extendicare Inc., 1996—; chmn. Extendicare (Can.) Inc., Extendicare (U.K.) Ltd.; bd. dirs. Extendicare Inc., Crown Life Ins. Co., Swiss Bank Corp. Trust.

LADMAN, A(ARON) J(ULIUS), anatomist, educator; b. Jamaica, N.Y., July 3, 1925; s. Thomas and Ida (Sobin) L.; m. Barbara Powers, 1948 (div. 1980); children: Susan Elizabeth, Thomas Frederick; m. Patricia A. Bergbauer, 1982; 1 child, Peter John. Student, Miami U., Oxford, Ohio, 1942-43; AB, NYU, 1947; postgrad., U. Cin., 1948-49; Ph.D., Ind. U., 1952. Teaching fellow anatomy U. Cin., 1948-49, Ind. U., 1949-52; with Harvard Med. Sch., 1952-61, assoc., 1955-61; assoc. prof. U. Tenn. Med. Units, 1961-64; vis. assoc. prof. Yale, 1964; prof., chmn. dept. anatomy U. N.Mex. Sch. Medicine, Albuquerque, 1964-81; prof. anatomy Hahnemann U., Phila., 1981-94, Med. Coll. Pa. and Hahnemann U. Sch. Medicine, Phila., 1995; adj. prof. neurobiology and anatomy Allegheny U., Phila., 1996; dean Sch. Allied Health Professions Hahnemann U., 1981-86. Assoc. editor Anat. Record, 1967-68, editor-in-chief, 1968—; contbr. articles to profl. jours. Recipient Rsch. Career Devel. award USPHS, 1962-64; rsch. fellow Am. Cancer Soc., 1952-55, spl. rsch. fellow USPHS, 1955-57, 71-72. Fellow AAAS; mem. Am. Assn. Anatomists (exec. com. 1972-76, 2d v.p. 1980-81, 1st v.p. 1981-82), Am. Soc. for Cell Biology, Nat. Inst. Gen. Med. Scis. (rsch. cancer awards com. 1967-71), Electron Microscope Soc. Am. (exec. coun. 1974-76), Coun. Biol. Editors (sec. 1977-82), Histochem. Soc. Home: 103 Arbor Way Lansdale PA 19446-6433 Office: Allegheny U Dept Neurobiol and Anat MCP Hahnemann Sch Medicine Broad and Vine St Philadelphia PA 19102-1192

LADMAN, JERRY R., economist, educator; b. Sioux City, Iowa, Dec. 30, 1935; s. Harry L. and Amy I. (Swearingen) L.; m. Carmen Aida; children—Jeffrey, James, Michael, Stephanie. B.S., Iowa State U., 1958, Ph.D., 1968. Placement officer Coll. Agr., Iowa State U., Ames, 1963-65, research asst., 1965-67; asst. prof. Ariz. State U., 1967-72, assoc. prof., 1972-78, prof. econs., 1979—, dir. Ctr. for Latin Am. Studies, 1976-90; prof. agrl. econs. Ohio State U., Columbus, 1990—; asst. dir. Ohio LEAD Program, Columbus, 1995-97, dir., 1997—; program asst. Ford Found., Mexico City, 1971-72; vis. prof. Nat. Sch. Agr., Chapingo, Mex., 1965-67, 71-72, Ohio State U., 1979; vis. scholar Stanford U., 1975; hon. prof. Cath. U. Bolivia, 1986; participant U.S.-U.S.S.R. Cultural Exchange, 1986. Author: The Development of Mexicali Regional Economy, 1975, United States-Mexican Energy Relationships: Realities and Prospects, 1981, Modern Day Bolivia: The Legacy of the Revolution and Prospects for the Future, 1982, Mexico: A Country in Crisis, 1987, Redemocratization in Bolivia: A Political Economic Analysis of the Siles Suazo Government, 1982-1985, 1990; contbr. articles to profl. jours., chpts. to books. Chmn. troop com. Boy Scouts Am., Tempe, Ariz., 1976-84; bd. dirs. Friends of Mexican Art, 1977-86. Served to capt. USAR, 1958-65. Fulbright lectr., Ecuador, 1974. Mem. Am. Econ. Assn., Am. Agrl. Econ. Assn., Latin Am. Studies Assn., Pacific Coast Council Latin Am. Studies (treas. 1977-86, v.p. 1986, pres. 1987), Rocky Mountain Council Latin Am. Studies (bd. dirs. 1976-90), Phoenix Com. Fgn. Relations, Ariz.-Mex. Commn. (bd. dirs. 1982-90), Assn. Borderlands Scholars (pres. 1983-85), PROFMEX (bd. dirs. 1983-90). Office: Ohio State U Dept Agrl Econs 2120 Fyffe Rd Columbus OH 43210-1010

LADNER, THOMAS E., lawyer; b. Vancouver, B.C., Can., Dec. 8, 1916. B.A., U. B.C., 1937; LLB, Osgoode Hall. Bar: B.C. bar 1940. Ret. partner firm Ladner Downs, Vancouver. Mem. Canadian, Vancouver bar assns., Law Soc. B.C. Office: PO Box 48600, 1200-200 Burrard St, Vancouver, BC Canada V7X 1T2

LADOW, C. STUART, consultant financial services; b. Warren, Pa., Apr. 21, 1925; s. Clyde and Glendine (Bentley) LaD.; m. Donna Elizabeth Miller, Aug. 21, 1993; 1 child, Paul Stuart. B.A., Cornell U., 1947. With Gen. Electric Co., 1947-50; mgr. N.Y. region Gen. Electric Credit Corp., N.Y.C., 1950-80; v.p. Gen. Electric Credit Corp., Stamford, Conn., 1971-80; pres. GECC Fin. Services, 1975-78, Color Tyme TV Rental div. Curtis Mathes Corp., Athens, Tex., 1980; sr. v.p. Yegen Assocs., Inc., Paramus, N.J., 1981-85; exec. v.p. Yegen Assocs., Inc., Paramus, 1985-87; pres. Yegen Equity Loan Corp., Paramus, N.J., 1987; fin. svcs. cons. Allison Park, Pa., 1988—; dir. Nat. Capital Funding, 1997—; dir. Puritan Life Ins. Co., Providence, Am. Bankers Ins. Group, Miami, Fla., 1980-81. Vice pres., bd. dirs. Jr. Achievement of Stamford, Inc., 1973-80; mem. exec. budget com., chmn. budget panel United Way of Stamford, 1973-80; chmn. Stamford chpt. Am. Cancer Soc., 1977; pres. Spring Meadow Condominium Assn., Wyckoff, N.J., 1983, trustee, 1983-88; moderator Emmanuel Bapt. Ch., Ridgewood, N.J., 1985-86; trustee North Hills Community Baptist Ch., 1988-91; dir. Hampton Twsp. Mcpl. Authority, Allison Park, Pa., 1991—, dir., treas. Baptist Homes of Western Pa., 1992—, pres. Arbors Homeowners Assn., Allison Park, 1992-93; pres. Cornell U. Class of 1947, 1992—; dir. Nat. Capital Funding, 1997—. Recipient Community Service award Gen. Electric Credit Corp., 1976. Mem. Nat. Second Mortgage Assn. (pres. 1987-88, Outstanding Service award, Meritorious Svc. award 1989), Nat. Consumer Finance Assn. (certificate of appreciation), Masons, Shriners, Cornell Club of Pitts. Republican. Baptist. Home and Office: 4211 Latour Ct Allison Park PA 15101-2968 *Ours is a great country that deserves the devotion and strong support of those who call it home. There can be few satisfactions in life greater than assisting in the moral, spiritual and career growth of those whom we have the opportunity to know and possibly influence.*

LA DU, BERT NICHOLS, JR., pharmacology educator, physician; b. Lansing, Mich., Nov. 13, 1920; s. Bert Nichols and Natalie (Kerr) La D.; m. Catherine Shilson, June 14, 1947; children: Elizabeth, Mary, Anne, Jane. B.S., Mich. State Coll., 1943; M.D., U. Mich., 1945; Ph.D. in Biochemistry, U. Calif., Berkeley, 1952. Intern Rochester (N.Y.) Gen. Hosp., 1945-46; research asso. N.Y.U. Research Service, Goldwater Meml. Hosp., N.Y.C., 1950-53; sr. asst. surgeon USPHS, Nat. Heart Inst., 1954-57; surgeon, later sr. surgeon, med. dir. Nat. Inst. Arthritis and Metabolic Disease, 1957-63; prof., chmn. dept. pharmacology N.Y.U. Med. Sch., 1963-74; prof. pharmacology U. Mich. Med. Sch., Ann Arbor, 1974-89, prof. emeritus, 1989—, chmn. dept., 1974-81. Contbr. articles to profl. jours. Served with AUS, 1943-45. Mem. AAAS, Am. Chem. Soc., N.Y. Acad. Sci. (pres.), Am. Soc. Biol. Chemistry, Am. Soc. Pharmacol. Therapeutics (pres.), Am. Soc. Human Genetics, Biochem. Soc. (Gt. Britain). Home: 817 Berkshire Rd Ann Arbor MI 48104-2630 Office: U Mich Med Sch 7422 Med Sci I Ann Arbor MI 48109-0615

LADUKE, NANCIE, lawyer, corporate executive; b. Mayfield, Ky.; m. Daniel E. LaDuke, 1978. BA, Wayne State U., 1962; JD, U. Detroit, 1976. Pvt. practice Detroit, 1976; atty. KMart, Troy, Mich., 1977-84, comml. law counsel, 1984-90, v.p., sec., 1991—. Office: KMart Corp 3100 W Big Beaver Rd Troy MI 48084-3004

LADWIG, HAROLD ALLEN, neurologist; b. Manilla, Iowa, May 11, 1922; s. Ernest and Iva Marie (Allen) L.; m. Marjorie Lois Foster, June 26, 1946; children: Stephen H., Rosemary A. BA, U. Iowa, 1952, MD, 1947. Intern St. Joseph Hosp., Sioux City, Iowa, 1947-48; resident U. Minn., 1949-50; pres. Omaha Neurol. Clinic, 1972-83. Contbr. articles to profl. jours. Bd. dirs. Boys and Girls Club, Wilson, N.C., 1995—, Salvation Army, Wilson, 1996, Country Drs. Mus., Bailey, N.C., 1995—, Mental Health Bd., Wilson, 1995—. Comdr. USNR, 1950-52. Fellow Am. Coll. Physicians, Am. Acad. Neurology; mem. AMA, Am. Assn. Electrodiagnostic Medicine, Am. Soc. Electroencephalography and Neurophysiology, Wilson County Med. Soc. (sec. 1993, v.p. 1994, pres. 1995), Wilson Meml. Hosp. Found. (pres. 1993—), Douglas County Med. Soc. (exec. bd. 1960-63), Kiwanis (pres. Wilson chpt. 1995, Kiwanian of Yr. award 1992-93), Phi Beta Kappa, Beta Beta Beta. Methodist. Avocation: computers. Home: PO Box 3049 Wilson NC 27895-3049

LAEMMLE, CHERYL MARIE VICARIO, artist; b. Mpls., 1947. BA, Humboldt State U., Arcata, N.Y., 1974; MFA, Washington State U., 1978. One-woman shows at Tex. Gallery, Houston, 1982, Barbara Toll Fine Arts, N.Y.C., 1983, Sharpe Gallery, N.Y.C., 1984, 86, Hokin/Kaufman Gallery, Chgo., 1986, GregKucera Gallery, Seattle, 1988, 90, 92, Fay Gold Gallery, Atlanta, 1989, 92, Nat. Mus. Women in Arts, Washington, 989, Rena Bransten Gallery, San Francisco, 1989, Mus. Art, Washington State U., Pullman, 1990, Terry Dintenfass, N.Y.C., 1991, Allene LaPides Gallery, Santa Fe, N.Mex., 1992, Midtown Payson Galleries, N.Y.C., 1994; exhibited in group shows at Tweed Mus. Art, U. Minn., Duluth, 1989, Greg Kucera Gallery, Seattle, 1989, Art Mus. Fla. Internat. U., Miami, 1989, Terra Mus. Am. Art, Chgo., 1989, Laumeler Sculpture Park, St. Louis, 989, Grand Rapids (Mich.) Art Mus., 989, Arnot Art Mus., Elmira, N.Y., 1989, Hudson River Mus. Westchester, Yonkers, N.Y., 1989, Pa. Acad. Fine Arts, Phila., 1989, Denver Art Mus., 1989, New Orleans Mus. Art, 1989, Cin. Art Mus., 1989, Whitney Mus. Am. Art at Equitable Ctr., N.Y.C., 1990, U. Art Gallery, Calif. State U., Chico, 1990, Terry Dintenfass, N.Y.C., 1990, Mint Mus. Art, Charlotte, N.C., 1991, Visual Art Ctr., Calif. State U., Fullerton, 1991, Midtown Payson Galleries, N.Y.C., 1992, 94, Nancy Margolis Gallery, N.Y.C., 1995, others; represented in permanent collections at Dannheisser Found., Eli Broad Family Found., L.A., Frederick Welsman Collection, L.A., Met. Mus. Art, N.Y.C., Museo Rufino Tamayo, Mexico City, Walker Art Ctr., Mpls., Edward Downe Jr. Found., Corcoran Gallery Art, Washington, High Art Mus., Atlanta, Mint Mus. Art, Charlotte, N.C. Recipient Creative Artists Pub. Svc. Program fellowship, 980, Vera G. List award, 1984, painting fellowships Nat. Endowment for Arts, 1985-86, 86-87.

LAESSIG, RONALD HAROLD, pathology educator, state official; b. Marshfield, Wis., Apr. 4, 1940; s. Harold John and Ella Louise (Gumz) L.; m. Joan Margaret Spreda, Jan. 29, 1966; 1 child, Elizabeth Susan. B.S., U. Wis.-Stevens Point, 1962; Ph.D., U. Wis.-Madison, 1965. Jr. faculty Princeton (N.J.) U., 1966; chief clin. chemistry Wis. State Lab. Hygiene, Madison, 1966-80, dir., 1980—; asst. prof. preventive medicine U. Wis.-Madison, 1966-72, assoc. prof., 1972-76, prof., 1976—, prof. pathology, 1980—; cons. Ctr. Disease Control, Atlanta; dir. Nat. Com. for Clin. Lab. Standards, Villanova, Pa., 1977-80; chmn. invitro diagnostic products adv. com. FDA, 1974-75; mem. rev. com. Nat. Bur. Standards, 1983-86. Mem. editorial bd. Med. Electronics, 1970—, Analytical Chemistry, 1970-76, Health Lab. Sci., 1970—; contbr. articles to profl. jours. Mem. State of Wis. Tech. Com. Alcohol and Traffic Safety, 1970-88. Sloan Found. grantee, 1966; recipient numerous grants. Mem. Am. Assn. Clin. Chemistry (chmn. safety com. 1984-86, bd. dirs. 1986-89, Natelson award 1989, Contbns. Svc. to Profession award 1990), Am. Pub. Health Assn. (Difco award 1974), Am. Soc. for Med. Tech., Nat. Com. Clin. Lab. Standards (pres. 1980-82, bd. dirs. 1984-87), Sigma Xi. Avocation: Woodworking. Office: State Lab Hygiene 465 Henry Mall Madison WI 53706-1501 *If you are doing something you really enjoy and it affords you the opportunity to really help your fellow man--you're really blessed (like I am).*

LAESSIG, WALTER BRUCE, publishing executive; b. Englewood, N.J., Aug. 11, 1941; s. George Bruce Laessig and Eileen May (Codling) Roma; m. Susan Lamme, June 13, 1964; children: Katherine Anne, Sarah Eileen, Matthew Lamme. AB in History, Cornell U., 1963, MBA in Fin., 1966, LLB, 1966. Bar: N.Y. 1966, D.C. 1968. Atty. Nixon, Hargrave, Devans & Doyle, Rochester, N.Y., 1966-68, Martin, Whitfield & Thaler, Washington, 1968-70; minority economist, counsel Joint Econ. Com., U.S. Congress, Washington, 1971-75; minority tax counsel Com. on Ways and Means, U.S. Ho. Reps., Washington, 1975-77; gen. counsel Nat. Assn. REITs, Washington, 1977-79; atty. Laessig, Brown, Hearn & Clohan, Washington, 1979-84; v.p. Warren, Gorham & Lamont, N.Y.C., 1984-85, exec. v.p., 1986, pres., chief exec. officer, 1987-89; exec. v.p., chief oper. officer Thomson Profl. Pub., Stamford, Conn., 1989-90; pres., chief exec. officer The Argus Group, Washington, 1990—. Republican. Presbyterian. Office: The Argus Group 1101 Vermont Ave NW Ste 400 Washington DC 20005-3521

LAETTNER, CHRISTIAN DONALD, professional basketball player; b. Angola, N.Y., Aug. 17, 1969. Student, Duke U. Basketball player Minn. Timberwolves, 1992-1995; now with Atlanta Hawks. Named Most Outstanding Player in NCAA Divsn. 1A Tournament, 1991, Sporting News Coll. Player of Yr., 1992, Sporting News All-Am. First Team, 1992, Naismith award, 1992, Wooden award, 1992; mem. Gold medal Winning Olympic Team, Barcelona, Spain, 1992. Named to NBA All-Rookie first team, 1993; mem. NCAA Divsn. I Championship Teams, 1991-92. Office: Atlanta Hawks 1 Cnn Ctr NW Atlanta GA 30303-2705*

LA FALCE, JOHN JOSEPH, congressman, lawyer; b. Buffalo, N.Y., Oct. 6, 1939; s. Dominic E. and Catherine M. (Stasio) La F.; m. Patricia Fisher, 1979. BS, Canisius Coll., 1961; JD, Villanova U., 1964; LLD (hon.), Niagara U., 1979, St. Johns U., 1989; LHD (hon.), Canisius Coll., 1990; LLD (hon.), Villanova U., 1991. Bar: N.Y. 1964. Mem. N.Y. State Legislature, 1971-74, 94th-104th Congresses from 32nd (now 29th) N.Y. dist., 1975—. Capt. adj. gen. corps AUS. Democrat. Home: 35 Danbury Ln Buffalo NY 14217-2101 Office: US Ho of Reps Rm 2310 Rayburn House Office Bldg Washington DC 20515

LA FARGE, TIMOTHY, plant geneticist; b. N.Y.C., Mar. 14, 1930; s. Louis Bancel and Hester Alida (Emmet) La F.; m. Anne Blackstone, Oct. 16, 1960 (div. Mar. 1964); m. Frances Madelyne Holst, Aug. 6, 1966 (dec. 1992); 1 child, Jason Emmet; m. Nkem R. Salako, Dec. 4, 1993. BA in Dance, Black Mountain Coll., 1952; BSc in Forestry, U. Maine, 1964; M Forestry, Yale U., 1965; PhD, Mich. State U., 1971. Forestry aid Forest Svc., Orono, Maine, 1962-64; lab. technician geology dept. Yale U., New Haven, 1965; rsch. forester USDA Forest Svc., Macon, Ga., 1965-69, plant geneticist Southea. Sta., 1970-82; plant geneticist Nat. Forest Sys. USDA Forest Svc., Atlanta, 1982—. Contbr. articles to profl. jours. Recipient Certs. of Merit, USDA Forest Svc., Atlanta, 1986, 88. Mem. AAAS, Soc. Am. Foresters. Democrat. Achievements include demonstration that backcrossing and hybridization between shortleaf pine and loblolly pine can effectively produce fast-growing back-cross hybrids that are resistant to fusiform rust; application of Best Linear Prediction to analysis of unbalanced or messy progeny test data. Home: 2679 Tritt Springs Trce Marietta GA 30062-5266 Office: USDA Forest Svc 1720 Peachtree Rd NW Atlanta GA 30309-2439

LAFAVE, HUGH GORDON JOHN, medical association executive, psychiatrist, educator, consultant; b. Montmarte, Sask., Can., Apr. 28, 1929; s. Leslie Alexander and Mary (Flaman) L.; m. Joann Sanderson, June 1956; children: Bonnie Lynn, Leslie Hugh, Maria Delee. B.A. cum laude, U. Sask., 1951; MD, Chirurgiae Magistri, McGill U., 1953. Diplomate: Am. Bd. Psychiatry and Neurology. Intern Detroit Receiving Hosp., 1953-54; gen. practice medicine Rockglen, Assiniboia, Sask., Can., 1954-56; resident Medfield State Hosp., 1956-57, 58-60, Inst. Living, Hartford, Conn., 1957-58; chief rehab. Medfield State Hosp., Harding, Mass., 1960-61; clin. dir. Sask. Hosp., Weyburn, Can., 1962-64, supt., 1964-66; assoc. commr. dept. mental hygiene State of N.Y., Albany, 1966-69; dir. Eleanor Roosevelt Devel. Services, Schenectady, 1969-76; exec. dir. psychiat. services br. Dept. Health-Sask., Can., 1976-79; exec. v.p. Can. Assn. Mentally Retarded (now Can. Assn. Community Living), Downsview, Ont., 1979-84; pvt. practice specializing in psychiatry Red Deer Regional Hosp, 1984-85; dir. rehab. programs Brockville Psychiatric Hosp, 1985-94; assoc. prof. Albany Med. Coll., N.Y., 1968-76, assoc. prof. pediatrics, 1971-76, prof.; assoc. dean, prof. N.Y. Sch. Psychiatry, Poughkeepsie, 1969-76; clin. assoc. prof. psychiatry, U. Sask. Med. Coll., 1976-83, U. Ottawa, 1985-94; pres. Wellness Can., Hugh Lafave Holdings Ltd., 1981-96; med. dir. Smokers Treatment Ctr., Ottawa, 1993-96; mem., chmn. exptl., spl. tng. rev. com. NIMH, Chevy Chase, Md., 1970-74; mem. editl. bd. Can.'s Mental Health, 1978-80; mem. rehab.-cmty. psychiatry com. U. Ottawa, 1886-92; prin. investigator Health Innovation Grant Cmty. Rehab. Program, 1990-93; pres. Cmty. Living Cons., 1994—. Author: (with others) State Hospitals—What Happens When They Close?, 1976, Is the Community Ready?; contbr. numerous articles to profl. jours. Mem. awards com. Kennedy Found., 1977-78; bd. dirs. Byrd Hoffman Found., Inc., N.Y.C., 1974-80, Family Focus, Brockville, Can., 1986-90. Recipient Outstanding Achievement Amethyst award Province of Ont. Ministry of Citizenship, 1994; selected as Health Innovator by Ont. Premier's Health Coun., 1991-93. Mem. Can. Psychiat. Assn. (bd. dirs. 1976-79), Am. Psychiat. Assn., Can. Pub. Health Assn., Workshop, Inc. (profl. adv. com. 1970-75), Nat. Inst. Mental Retardation (assoc. 1984—), Can. Mental Health Assn. (Toronto) (consumer participation task force 1986-90), Royal Coll. Psychiatrists. Home and Office: PO Box 13, Elgin, ON Canada K0G 1E0 Office: PO Box 13, Elgin, ON Canada KOG 1EO *People, all kinds of people, their rights, their health, their wellbeing, have been the focus of my career and my life, without regret.*

LAFAVE, LEANN LARSON, lawyer; b. Ramona, S.D., May 31, 1953; d. Floyd Burdette and Janice Anne (Quist) L.; m. Richard Curtis Finke, May 19, 1973 (div. Jan. 1978); 1 child, Timothy; m. Dwayne Jeffery LaFave, May 31, 1981 (div. 1992); children: Jeffrey, Allison. BS, U. S.D., 1974, JD with honors, 1977. Bar: S.D. 1977, U.S. Dist. Ct. S.D. 1977, U.S. Ct. Appeals (8th cir.) 1977, N.D. 1978, U.S. Dist. Ct. N.D. 1978. Asst. atty. gen. State of S.D., Pierre, 1977-78, 79-81; assoc. Bjella, Neff, Rathert & Wahl, Williston, N.D., 1978-79, Tobin Law Offices, P.C., Winner, S.D., 1981-83; assoc. dean, asst. prof. U. S.D. Sch. Law, Vermillion, 1983-86, dir. continuing legal edn., 1983-89, assoc. prof. law, 1986-89; ptnr. Aho & LaFave, Brookings, S.D., 1990-91; pvt. practice Brookings, 1991-92; asst. U.S. atty. U.S. Dist. S.D., 1992—; mem. S.D. Bd. Pardons and Paroles, 1987-90, chmn., 1989-90; comml. arbitrator Am. Arbitration Assn., 1985—; prof. Kilian C.C. Contbr. articles to profl. jours. Mem. planning coun. Nat. Identification Program for Advancement Women in Higher Edn. Adminstrn., Am. Coun. on Edn., S.D., 1984-90; bd. dirs. Mo. Shores Women's Resource Ctr., Pierre, 1980, W.H. Over Mus., Vermillion, 1986-87, S.D. Vol. Lawyers for Arts, 1987—, Brookings Interagy. Coun., 1990-91, Brookings Women's Ctr., 1990-94; sec. Mediation Ctr., Inc. Named S.D. Woman Atty. of Yr. Women in Law U. S.D., 1985. Mem. S.D. Bar Assn. (bd. govs. young lawyers sect. 1983-84), S.D. Mediation Assn., Epsilon Sigma Alpha (S.D. coun. sect. 1985-86). Republican. Episcopalian. Avocation: reading. Home: 1808 S Jefferson Ave Sioux Falls SD 57105-2415 Office: PO Box 5073 Sioux Falls SD 57117-5073

LAFAVORE, MICHAEL J., magazine editor; b. Portland, Maine, Apr. 28, 1952; s. Joseph T. and Marion (Brown) L.; m. Trieste A. Kennedy; children: Nico, Alec. BA in English, U. Maine, 1975. Reporter Jour. Tribune, Biddeford, Maine, 1975-79; sr. editor Organic Gardening, Emmaus, Pa., 1979-84, Practical Homeowner, Emmaus, Pa., 1984-88; exec. editor Men's Health Homeowner, Emmaus, Pa., 1988—; screening com. mem. Nat. Mag. Awards, N.Y.C., 1994. Author: The Home Gym, 1978, Radon: The Invisible Threat, 1985; editor: Men's Health Advisor, 1992, 93. Author: The Home Gym, 1978, Radon: The Invisible Threat, 1985; editor: Men's Health Advisor, 1992, 93. Recipient Mont award Photo Design Mag., 1989, Mental Health Media award Nat. Mental Health Assn., 1991, Award for Excellence, Men's Fashion Assn., 1992, 1995, Editor of the Yr. award Advertising Age, 1995, Nat. Mag. awards nomination, 1995, 96. Office: Rodale Press 33 E Minor St Emmaus PA 18098-0001

LAFEBER, WALTER FREDERICK, history educator, author; b. Walkerton, Ind., Aug. 30, 1933; s. Ralph N. and Helen (Lidecker) LaF.; m. Sandra Gould, Sept. 11, 1955; children: Scott Nichols, Suzanne Margaret. B.A., Hanover Coll., 1955; M.A., Stanford, 1956; Ph.D., U. Wis., 1959. Asst. prof. history Cornell U., 1959-63, assoc. prof., 1963-67, prof., 1967-68, Noll prof. history, 1968—, Weiss Presdl. Tchg. fellow, 1994—; Commonwealth lectr. U. London, Eng., 1973; Callander lectr. U. Aberdeen, 1987; Shaw lectr. Johns Hopkins U., 1989; Landmark prof. Am. U., 1992; Jefferson lectr. U. Calif., Berkeley, 1992; Mem. adv. com. hist. div. State Dept., 1971-75. Author: The New Empire...1860-1898, 1963, America, Russia and the Cold War, 8th edit., 1996, The Panama Canal, The Crisis in Historical Perspective, 1978, expanded edit., 1979, 2d edit., 1989, Inevitable Revolutions: The U.S. in Central America, 1983, 2d edit., 1992, The American Age...1750 to the Present, 1989, 2d edit. 1994, The American Search for Opportunity, 1865-1913, 1993, The Clash: U.S. Relations with Japan from the 1850's to the Present, 1997; co-author: The American Century, 5th edit, 1997; America in Vietnam, 1985; editor: John Quincy Adams and American Continental Empire, 1965, America in the Cold War, 1969, also others; co-editor: Behind the Throne, Essays in Honor of Fred Harvey Harrington, 1993; mem. editorial adv. bd., Polit. Sci. Quar. Recipient Gustavus Myers prize, 1985; Guggenheim fellow, 1990. Mem. Orgn. Am. Historians, Am. Hist. Assn. (Albert Beveridge prize 1962), Am. Acad. Arts and Scis. Office: Cornell U Dept History McGraw Hall Ithaca NY 14853-4601

LAFER, FRED SEYMOUR, data processing company executive; b. Passaic, N.J., Mar. 17, 1929; s. Abraham David and Pauline (Braer) L.; m. Barbara Bernstein, Apr. 4, 1954; children: Deborah, Gordon, Diana. BIE, NYU, 1950, JD, 1961; LHD (hon.), William Paterson Coll., 1987. Bar: N.J. 1961. Sec. to Justice Hayden Proector, N.J. Supreme Ct., 1961-62; partner firm Hoffman Humphreys Lafer, Wayne, N.J., 1962-67; sec., gen. counsel Automatic Data Processing, Inc., Clifton, N.J., 1967—; v.p. Automatic Data Processing, Inc., 1968-81, sr. v.p., 1981-96; pres. N.J. Nets Profl. Basketball Team, 1984; pres. Taub Found., 1996—. Chmn. United Jewish Appeal Fedn. North Jersey, 1973-74; pres. Jewish Fedn. North Jersey, 1976-77; v.p. N.J. Bd. Edn., 1967-68; bd. dirs. Chilton Meml. Hosp., Pompton Plains, N.J., 1970-72; trustee William Paterson Coll., 1974—, vice-chmn. bd., 1977, chmn. bd., 1978-80; pres. Am. Friends of Hebrew U., 1985-89; exec. com. Washington Inst. Near East Policy, sec.-treas., 1993—. Served to lt. USAF, 1951-52. Recipient honorary doctorate Hebrew U. of Jerusalem, 1995. Mem. Computer Law Assn. (pres. 1972-74), Assn. Data Processing Service Orgns. (chmn. 1983), ABA. Office: ADP Inc 1 ADP Blvd Roseland NJ 07068-1728

LAFEVER, HOWARD NELSON, plant breeder, geneticist, educator; b. Wayne County, Ind., May 13, 1938; s. Samuel L. and Flossie B. (Ellis) L.; m. Kay M. Schutz, Aug. 30, 1958; children: Julie, Jeff. BS, Purdue U., 1959, MS, 1961, PhD, 1963. Instr. Wis. State U., LaCrosse, 1963; assoc. prof. Purdue U., West Lafayette, Ind., 1963; research geneticist USDA-Agrl. Research Service, Starkville, Miss., 1963-65; plant breeder, prof. agronomy Ohio State U., Ohio Agr. Research and Devel. Ctr., Wooster, 1965-91; owner Sunbeam Extract Co., 1991—. Patentee Becker, Cardinal, Dynasty, Excel and Freedom wheats plus 14 other small grain varieties; contbr. numerous articles to profl. jours. Fellow Am. Soc. Agronomy (bd. dirs. 1982-84, assoc. editor 1982-85); mem. Assn. Ofcl. Seed Certifying Agys., Ohio Seed Improvement Assn. (dir. 1968-83, grantee 1975-91). Presbyterian. Avocations: woodworking; golf. Home: 500 Danberry Dr Wooster OH 44691-5211

LAFFERTY, BEVERLY LOU BROOKOVER, retired physician, consultant; b. Newark, Ohio, Aug. 15, 1938; d. Lawrence William and Rosie (Rey) Brookover; B.S., Ohio State U., 1959, M.D., 1963; diplomate Am. Bd. Family Practice; children—Marla Michele, William Brookover, Wesley Voris, Latour Rey. Intern Grant Hosp., Columbus, Ohio, 1963-64; practice medicine, West Union, Ohio, 1964-75, Sun City Center, Fla., 1975-79, Brandon, Fla., 1979-95; mem. staff Adams County Hosp., v.p., 1971-72, chief of staff, 1973-75; mem. staff Columbia Regional Med. Ctr., Brandon, 1977—, chmn. dept. family practice, 1984-86, hosp. trustee, 1984-92, chief of staff elect, 1986-88, chief of staff, 1988-90; physician adv. utilization mgmt. dept. South Bay Hosp., Sun City Ctr., Fla., 1995—. Mem. AMA, Fla., Hillsborough County med. assns., Am. Acad. Family Physicians, Fla. Acad. Family Physicians, Alpha Lambda Delta, Alpha Epsilon Iota, Alpha Epsilon Delta (sec. 1958-59). Home: 3913 John Moore Rd Brandon FL 33511-8020

LAFFERTY, JAMES MARTIN, physicist; b. Battle Creek, Mich., Apr. 27, 1916; s. James V. and Ida M. (Martin) L.; m. Eleanor J. Currie, June 27, 1942; children: Martin C., Ronald J., Douglas J., Lawrence E. Student, Western Mich. U., 1934-37; B.S. in Engring. Physics, U. Mich., 1939, M.S. in Physics, 1940, Ph.D. in Elec. Engring, 1946. Physicist Eastman Kodak Research Lab., Rochester, N.Y., 1939; physicist Gen. Electric Research Lab., Schenectady, 1940, 42-81; mgr. power electronics lab. Gen. Electric Research Lab., 1972-81; with Carnegie Instn., Washington, 1941-42; past pres. Internat. Union Vacuum Sci. Technique and Applications, 1980-83; People to People citizen ambassador program group leader for Vacuum Sci. and Tech. delegation to Europe, 1984, China, 1986, Australia, 1988, Soviet Union, 1990. Editor, contbg. author: Scientific Foundations of Vacuum Technique (Dushman), 1962; editor: Vacuum Arcs, Theory and Applications, 1980; asso. editor: Jour. Vacuum Sci. and Tech, 1966-69; Editorial bd.:

Internat. Jour. Electronics, 1968-89; contbr. articles to profl. jours. Mem. greater consistory Ref. Ch.; trustee Schenectady Museum, 1967-73, sec., 1971-72, pres., 1972-73. Recipient Devel. award Bur. Naval Ordnance, 1946; Distinguished Alumnus citation U. Mich., 1953; IR-100 award, 1968. Fellow AAAS, IEEE (Lamme medal 1979), Am. Phys. Soc.; mem. Nat. Acad. Engring., Am. Vacuum Soc. (hon. life mem.; dir. 1962-70, sec. 1965-67, pres. 1968-69), U.S. Power Squadrons (comdr. Lake George squadron 1975-76, comdr. Dist. 2 1981-82, nat. rear comdr. 1987-91, treas. Ednl. Fund 1992—), Sigma Xi, Phi Kappa Phi, Iota Sigma, Tau Beta Pi. Patentee in field; inventor lanthanum boride cathode, 1950, hot cathode magnetron ionization gauge, 1961, triggered vacuum gap, 1966. Home: 1202 Hedgewood Ln Niskayuna NY 12309-4605

LAFFERTY, JOYCE G. ZVONAR, retired middle school educator; b. Balt., July 9, 1931; d. George S. and Carolyn M. (Bothe) Greener; children: Barbara Z. Gunter, John G. Zvonar, David A. Zvonar. BS, Towson State, 1963; M. equivalent, Md. Inst. Coll. of Art, 1978. Cert. tchr., Md. Tchr., dept. chmn. Hampstead Hill. Jr. High Annex, Balt.; tchr. Forest Park Sr. High, Balt.; tchr., dept. chmn. Roland Park Mid. Sch., Balt. Mem. Nat. Art Edn. Assn., Internat. Soc. Artists, Balt. Tchrs. Union. Home: 1101 Gilcrest Ct Baltimore MD 21234-5924

LAFFERTY, RICHARD THOMAS, architect; b. Allentown, Pa., Dec. 12, 1932; s. Arthur M. and Emily (May) L.; m. Janece Fiore, Apr. 28, 1962; children: Alicia, Hope. BArch, Syracuse U., 1956. Registered architect, N.Y. Draftsman Sweeney-Burden, Architects, Syracuse, 1954-56, Gordon P. Schopfer, AIA, Syracuse, 1959-63; job capt. Sargent, Webster, Crenshaw & Folley, Syracuse, 1963-75, assoc., chief estimator, 1975-88; project architect V.I.P. Archtl. Assocs., Syracuse, 1988-90, assoc., 1989-90, project architect Schopfer Architects, 1990-93; architect, Richard T. Lafferty, 1993-94; architect, Fuligni-Fragola Architects, 1994—; instr. drafting Onondaga Community Coll., Syracuse, 1968-70, instr. codes, 1972-76, curriculum adviser archtl. tech., 1986—; curriculum adviser archtl. tech. SUNY, Delhi, 1984—; mem. N.Y. State Bd. Architecture, 1990—, chmn., 1995-96; sec. region II NCARB, 1995—, mem. code com., 1996—. Adv. mem. Onondaga County Plumbing Bd., Syracuse, 1978—; curriculum adviser Nat. Tech. Inst. for Deaf, Rochester, N.Y., 1984—, mem. Uniform Code Syracuse/Watertown Bd. Rev., 1984—; mem. Capitol Dist. Bd. of Rev., 1997—. Served to capt. USAF, 1956-59. Recipient, Matthew W. Del Gaudio award, 1983. Mem. AIA (energy com. 1981-85, profl. devel. com. 1981-85), Central N.Y. AIA (treas. 1978-79, pres. 1981, sec. 1989-94, editor newsletter 1978—, chmn. code com. 1983-84, 1989—), N.Y. State Assn. Architects (dir. 1980-84, mem. handicap com. 1983-84, pres. 1987, past pres. 1988, Pres. Medal 1991), N.Y. State Assns. of Professions (pres. 1991). Republican. Roman Catholic. Home and Office: Limeledge and Glover Rds Marcellus NY 13108

LAFFITTE, HECTOR MANUEL, federal judge; b. Ponce, P.R., Apr. 13, 1934; s. Miguel and Gilda (Colomer) L.; m. Nydia M. Rossy, June 13, 1958; children: Yasmin, Hector W., Bernice M., Walter M., Giselle M. BA, Interamerican U., 1955; LLB, U. P.R., 1958; LLM, Georgetown U., 1960. Bar: U.S. Dist. Ct. P.R. 1959, U.S. Ct. Appeals (1st cir.) 1959, Supreme Ct. P.R. 1959, U.S. Mil. Appeals 1960, U.S. Supreme Ct. 1976. Assoc. Hartzell, Fernandez & Novas, 1959-64; pvt. practice law, 1965-66; ptnr. Nachman, Feldstein, Laffitte, & Smith, 1966-69, Laffitte & Dominguez, 1970-83; judge U.S. Dist. Ct. P.R., 1983—. Mem. ABA, Inst. Jud. Adminstrn. Office: US Dist Ct CH-142 Fed Bldg 150 Carlos Chardon Ave Hato Rey San Juan PR 00918-1757*

LAFLAMME-ZUROWSKI, VIRGINIA M., secondary school special education educator; b. Moosup, Conn., May 3, 1946; d. Wilfred A. and Palma R. (Potvin) LaFlamme; children: Laura P., Helena M., Timothy W. BA in English, R.I. Coll., 1988, MEd in Spl. Edn., 1989. Spl. edn. tchr., homebound tchr. Burrillville (R.I.) Middle Sch., 1989-90; spl. edn. tchr. Cumberland (R.I.) High Sch., 1990—; pres. Cumberland Spl. Edn. Adv. Com.; lectr. R.I. Gov.'s Conf. on Children at Risk, 1985; guest speaker R.I. Coun. on Arts, 1990, 91; numerous leadership roles. Active Girls Scouts U.S.A., ch., numerous others; hon. mem. Cumberland Sch. Vols. Mem. ASCD, NEA, R.I. Edn. Assn., Nat. Coun. Tchrs. English. Home: 22 Ryder Ln Cumberland RI 02864-4255 Office: Cumberland High Sch 2602 Mendon Rd Cumberland RI 02864-3726

LAFLEY, ALAN FREDERICK, retired banker; b. Stamford, Conn., Aug. 26, 1922; s. Alan George and Clara (Petersen) L.; m. Kathryn Margaret Irwin, Mar. 1, 1946; children: Alan George, Nora Kathryn, Jo Anne, Mary Patricia. B.B.A., Clarkson U., Potsdam, N.Y., 1946; M.B.A., U. Mich., 1948. Asst. prof. Sch. of Bus.; placement dir. Clarkson U., 1948-50, Sch. Bus., Ind. U., Bloomington, 1950-51; with Gen. Electric Co., 1951-73; mgr. exec. personnel and compensation Gen. Electric Co., N.Y.C., 1968-73; v.p. personnel Clark Equipment Co., Buchanan, Mich., 1973-75; exec. v.p. human resources Chase Manhattan Bank, N.Y.C., 1975-84; mng. dir. Korn Ferry Internat., 1984-86; exec. in residence, vis. prof. U. Mich. Sch. Bus., Ann Arbor, 1984-85; cons., advisor, lectr,. human resources mgr. Mem. adv. coun. Sch. Bus., Clarkson U. Served to 1st lt. U.S. Army and USAAF, 1942-46. Fellow Human Resources Policy Inst., Boston U.

LA FOLLETTE, DOUGLAS J., secretary of state; b. Des Moines, June 6, 1940; s. Joseph Henry and Frances (Van der Wilt) LaF. B.S., Marietta Coll., 1963; M.S., Stanford U., 1964; Ph.D., Columbia U., 1967. Asst. prof. chemistry and ecology U. Wis.-Parkside, 1969-72; mem. Wis. Senate, 1973-75; sec. state State of Wis., Madison, 1975-79, 83—. Author: Wisconsin's Survival Handbook, 1971, The Survival Handbook, 1991. Mem. Council Econ. Priorities; mem. Lake Michigan Fed., Wis. Environ. Decade, 1971, S.E. Wis. Coalition for Clean Air, Dem. candidate for U.S. Congress, 1970, for Wis. lt. gov., 1978, for U.S. Senate, 1988. Recipient Environ. Quality EPA, 1976. Mem. Am. Fedn. Tchrs., Fedn. Am. Scientists, Phi Beta Kappa. Office: Office Sec State of Wis PO Box 7848 Madison WI 53707-7848

LAFONTAINE, PAT, professional hockey player; b. St. Louis, Feb. 22, 1965. With U.S. Olympic Hockey Team, 1984, N.Y. Islanders, 1983-91, Buffalo Sabres, 1991—; player All-Star game, 1988-91, 93. Recipient Dodge Performer Yr. award, 1989-90, Michel Briere award, 1982-83, Jean Beliveau trophy, 1982-83, Des Instructeurs trophy, 1982-83, Guy LaFleur trophy, 1982-83, Bill Masterton Meml. Trophy, 1995; named to Sporting News All-Star Team, 1989-90, Player of the Year Canadian Hockey League, 1982-83. Office: Buffalo Sabres Marine Midland Arena One Main St Buffalo NY 14202-4110*

LAFONTANT-MANKARIOUS, JEWEL (MRS. NAGUIB S. MANKARIOUS), diplomat, lawyer; b. Chgo., Apr. 28, 1922; d. Cornelius Francis Stradford and Aida Arabella Carter; m. John Rogers, 1946 (dissolved 1961); 1 child, John W. Rogers Jr.; m. H. Ernest Lafontant, 1961 (dec. 1976); m. Naguib Soby Mankarious, Dec. 17, 1989. AB in Polit. Sci., Oberlin Coll., 1943; JD, U. Chgo., 1946; LLD (hon.), Cedar Crest Coll., 1973; D Humanitarian Svc. (hon.), Providence Coll., 1973; LLD (hon.), Ea. Mich. U., 1973; LHD (hon.), Howard U., 1974; LLD (hon.), Heidelberg Coll., 1975, Lake Forest Coll., 1977, Marymount Manhattan Coll., 1978, Oberlin Coll., 1979; LHD (hon.), Governor's State U., 1980, LLD (hon.), 1980; citation for pub. svc., U. Chgo., 1980; LLD (hon.), Chgo. Med. Sch., 1982, Loyola U. of Chgo., 1982, Roosevelt U., 1990. Bar: Ill. 1947. Asst. U.S. atty., 1955-58; sr. ptnr. Lafontant, et al., Chgo., 1961-83, Vedder, Price, Kaufman & Kammholz, Chgo., 1983-89; dep. solicitor gen. U.S. Dept. State, Washington, 1972-75, amb.-at-large, U.S. coord. for refugee affairs, 1989-93; ptnr. Holleb & Coff, Chgo., 1993—; bd. dirs. Mobil Corp., Continental Bank, Foote, Cone & Belding, Equitable Life Assurance Soc. U.S., Trans World Corp., Revlon, Inc., Ariel-Capital Mgmt., Harte-Hanks Communications, Inc., Pantry Pride, Inc., Revlon Group, Howard U.; past dir. Jewel Cos., Inc., TWA, Hanes Corp.; past mem. U.S. Adv. Commn. Internat. Edn. and Cultural Affairs, Nat. Coun. Minority Bus. Enterprises, Nat. Coun. on Ednl. Rsch.; past chmn. adv. bd. Civil Rights Commn.; mem. Pres.'s Pvt. Sector Survey Cost Control; pres. Exec. Exchange; past U.S. rep. to UN. Bd. editors: Am. Bar Assn. Jour. Former trustee Lake Forest (Ill.) Coll., Oberlin Coll., Howard U., Tuskegee Inst.; bd. govs. Ronald Reagan Presdl. Found.; mem. Martin Luther King, Jr., Fed. Holiday Commn.; dir. Project Hope; chmn. Ill. adv. com. U.S. Civil Rights Commn.; mem. bd. overseers Hoover Instn.; mem. nat. adv. bd. Salvation Army. Recipient Howard B. Shepard award Protestant Found., Little Flowers Sem. Soc., Svc. award U.S. Dept. Justice, Humanitarian award Opportunities Industrialization Ctrs. of Am., Inc., Candace award Nat. Coalition of Black Women, Adlai A. Stevenson II award for svc. and support UN, Par Excellence Svc. award People United to Save Humanity, Disting. Svc. award Interracial Coun. for Bus. Opportunity, 1988, Woman of Distinction award Nat. Conf. for Coll. Women Student Leaders and Women of Achievement, 1988, Abraham Lincoln Marovitz award B'nai Brith, 1989, Disting. Svc. to Law and Soc. award Ill. Bar Found., 1989, cert. of recognition Vietnamese Community Leaders in U.S., 1990, Wiley A. Branton Issues Symposium award 1991, United Charities Legal Aid Soc. award, 1991, Spl. Recognition award Assyrian Am. Nat. Found., 1992, Chgo. Chpt. of Links, Inc. award, 1992, CARE Humanitarian award, 1994, Luminary award Girl Scouts U.S., 1995, Raoul Wallenberg award Am. Com. for Shaare Zedek Med. Ctr., Jerusalem, 1995, others; named Hon. Citizen of Abilene, Tex., 1991; named one of One Hundred Most Influential Black Ams., Ebony Mag., 1973-74, one of Crain's Chgo. bus. One Hundred Most Influential Women, 1996. Fellow Internat. Acad. Trial Lawyers; mem. NAACP (sec. Chgo. br.), ACLU (bd. dirs.), Chgo. Bar Assn. (bd. govs., Earl B. Dickerson award 1995), Comml. Club, Econs. Club (past bd. dirs.), Rotary (hon.), Cosmopolitan C. of C. (chairperson 1996 benefit).

LA FORCE, JAMES CLAYBURN, JR., economist, educator; b. San Diego, Dec. 28, 1928; s. James Clayburn and Beatrice Maureen (Boyd) La F.; m. Barbara Lea Latham, Sept. 23, 1952; children: Jessica, Allison, Joseph. BA, San Diego State Coll., 1951; MA, UCLA, 1958, PhD, 1962. Asst. prof. econs. UCLA, 1962-66, assoc. prof., 1967-70, prof., 1971-93, prof. emeritus, 1993—, chmn. dept. econs., 1969-78, dean Anderson Sch. Mgmt., 1978-93; acting dean Hong Kong U. Sci. & Tech., 1991-93; bd. dirs. Rockwell Internat., Eli Lilly & Co., Jacobs Engring. Group Inc., The Timken Co., The Black Rock Funds, Imperial Credit Industries, Inc., Payden & Rygel Investment Trust, Providence Investment Coun. Mut. Funds; chmn. adv. com. Calif. Workmen's Compensation. Author: The Development of the Spanish Textile Industry 1750-1800, 1965, (with Warren C. Scoville) The Economic Development of Western Europe, vols. 1-5, 1969-70. Bd. dirs. Nat. Bur. Econ. Rsch., 1975-88, Found. Francisco Marroquin, Lynde and Harry Bradley Found., Pacific Legal Found., 1981-86; trustee Found. for Rsch. in Econs. and Edn., 1970—, chmn., 1977—; mem. bd. overseers Hoover Inst. on War, Revolution and Peace, 1979-85, 86-93; mem. nat. coun. on humanities NEH, 1981-88; chmn. Pres.'s Task Force on Food Assistance, 1983-84. Social Sci. Research Council research tng. fellow, 1958-60; Fulbright sr. research grantee, 1965-66; Am. Philos. Soc. grantee, 1965-66. Mem. Econ. History Assn., Mont Pelerin Soc., Phi Beta Kappa. Office: UCLA Anderson Grad Sch Mgmt 405 Hilgard Ave Los Angeles CA 90095-9000

LAFORCE, WILLIAM LEONARD, JR., photojournalist; b. Albemarle County, Va., Aug. 24, 1940; s. William Leonard and Florence Alberta (Sandridge) LaF.; m. Dorothy Lee Kesler, June 8, 1963 (div. 1987); children: William Perry, Glenn Edward. Student, U. Va., 1958-60; B.S., Johns Hopkins U., 1967, M.Liberal Arts, 1972. Dir. photography Balt. Sun papers, 1962-74; chief photographer, graphics editor and editl. page columnist N.J. edit. N.Y. Daily News, 1974-79; photojournalist N.Y. staff N.Y. Daily News, N.Y.C., 1979-94; contbg. photographer N.Y. Times, AP, 1994—; scholastic journalism faculty Columbia U., 1971-75; advisor Montclair U. Student Newspaper, 1980-84; lectr. to various news and photography orgns. Judge Miss Delmarva Pageant, 1969-74; planning com. Balt. City Fair, 1971; pres. Rumsey Island Residents Assn., Joppa, Md., 1969-72, Rumsey House Restoration Found., 1968-70, Mountain Lakes (N.J.) Fire Dept., 1977-79; Democratic committeeman, Mountain Lakes, 1976-78; chmn. Wildwood Sch. Bd., 1976-77; mgr. Mountain Lakes Little League, 1981, 85-86; bd. dirs. Joppatowne Civic Assn., 1969-71, vice chmn. citizens nominating com., 1977-81; mem. Pedestrian Safety Com., 1976-80; bd. dirs. Mountain Lakes Hist. Soc., 1987—, Am. Police Hall of Fame, 1987—; Morris County disability commn., 1995—. Recipient Best Fire Photo in U.S. award Internat. Assn. Firefighters, 1967, Disting. Community Service award Jaycees, 1971, 1st Pl. Annapolis Fine Arts Festival, 1971, award for disting. community service Rumsey Island Residents Assn., 1972; Best Photo of Preakness Race award City of Balt., 1972, Page One award for best news photo in N.Y.C. Newspaper Guild, 1983, One Man Exhibition, Overseas Press Club, 1983; Best News Photo award N.Y. Press Club, 1984; 1st place Spot News award N.J. Press Assn., 1985, 91, Best PIX Story award N.Y.C. Police, 1986, 1st place Gen. News award N.J. Press Assn., 1991, nominated for Pulitzer award, 1984, 91. Mem. Nat. Press Photographers Assn. (dir. Mid-Atlantic region 1977-81, Pres.'s citation 1980, Bootstrap Leadership award 1981, chair nat. portfolio critique 1981-86), Photographic Adminstrs. N.Y. (bd. dirs. 1986—, v.p. 1988-95), N.Y. Press Photographers Club, N.J. Press Photographers, N.Y. Press Club. Home and Office: PO Box 31 Mountain Lakes NJ 07046-0031

LAFOREST, LANA JEAN, lawyer, real estate broker; b. Providence, Apr. 14, 1952; d. Harold Joseph Ecker and Nettie Jean (Starks) Page; children: Timothy Charles, Tisha DeAnne. AA in Humanities and Social Scis., Niagara County C. C., 1989; BA in English Lit. magna cum laude, Buffalo State Coll., 1990, MA in English Lit., 1992; JD, SUNY Buffalo Sch. Law, 1994; doctoral student, SUNY, Buffalo, 1994—. Lic. real estate broker. Property mgr. Personal Income Property Mgmt., Lockport, 1976—; sales assoc. John F. Collins Realty, Lockport, 1979-83, Town Crier Clark Nodine Realty, Lockport, 1983-90, McKnight, Hogan & Noonan, Lockport, 1990-91, H. Potter Realty, Lockport, 1991-93; advocate Family Court Resource Project Haven House, 1994—; advocate domestic violence clinic U. Buffalo Law Sch., 1994; pvt. practice East Amherst, N.Y., 1994—; owner, operator Custom Crafts by Lana, Lockport, 1975-79; adv. domestic violence clinic U. Buffalo Law Sch., 1994. Editor: (lit. mag.) Writer's Revue, 1989; corr. Union-Sun and Jour., summer 1989. Girl scouts coord. Niagara County Coun. Girl Scouts, Sanborn, N.Y., 1978-84; clover clan 4-H club leader Niagara County Coop. Extension, Lockport, 1984-87; with Project Dandelion, Neighborhood Legal Svcs., 1994—. Mem. ABA, MLA, N.Y. State Bar Assn., Niagara Linguistics Soc., Nat. Assn. Realtors, Univ. Buffalo Law Sch. Alumni Assn., Buffalo State Coll. Alumni Assn., Niagara County Community Coll. Alumni Assn., U. Buffalo Assn. Women Law Students, Erie County Bar Assn., Women's Bar Assn. Erie County, Phi Alpha Delt. Avocations: writing, sewing, gourmet cooking, painting. Office: 100 Garden Village Dr Cheektowaga NY 14227-3320

LAFORGE, EDWARD, state legislator; b. Nov. 22, 1935. Grad., Bronson Hosp. Sch. Nursing. Rep. Mich. State Dist. 60, 1995—; chair Human Svcs. and Children, Agr. Conservation, Environment and Recreation, Edn., Mental Health, Urban Policy and Econ. Devel. Address: PO Box 30014 Lansing MI 48909-7514

LA FOSSE, ROBERT, ballet dancer, choreographer; b. Beaumont, Tex.. Student, Marsha Woody Acad. of Dance; Studied with David Howard, Harkness House, N.Y.C., 1977. With Am. Ballet Theatre, N.Y.C., 1977-86, mem. corps de ballet, 1977-81, soloist, 1981-83, prin., 1983-86; prin. N.Y.C. Ballet, 1986—. Created roles at Am. Ballet Theatre in Cinderella, Lynne Taylor-Corbett's Great Galloping Gottschalk, John McFall's Follow the Feet, Kenneth MacMillan's The Wild Boy and Twyla Tharp's, Bach Partita; other Am. Ballet repertoire includes: La Bayadere, Billy the Kid, Clair de Lune, Don Quixote, Fancy Free, Giselle, Jardin Aux Lilas, Swan Lake Act II, The Leaves are Fading, Prodigal Son, Les Rendezvous, Symphonie Concertante, Rodeo, Other Dances, N.Y. Export: Op. Jazz, Romeo & Juliet, Dim Luster, Nutcracker, La Sonnambula & Coppelia; created roles at N.Y. City Ballet include Quiet City, Piccalo Balleto, West Side Story Suite, A Fool for You, Tea Rose, Newcomers; repertoire at N.Y. City Ballet includes Slaughter on 10th Ave., Opus 19, The Dreamer, Raymonda Variations, Who Cares?, Davidsbundlertanze, Ballo del Regina, La Baiser de la Fee, Nutcracker, Prodigal Son, Dances at a Gathering, Scotch Symphony, Agon, Vienna Waltzes, Four Seasons, La Source, Union Jack, Dances Concertant, Coppelia, Valse Triste, Western Symphony, Goldberg Variations in G Major, Donizetti Variations, Afternoon of a Faun; dancer: (Broadway) leading roles in Dancin', 1979, Jerome Robbins, 1989; Dancing Hands, Live from Off Center, 1988; (Off Broadway) Splendora; choreographer Gretry pas de deux, Rappaccini's Daughter, 1985, (for Sch. Am. Ballet) Yesterdays, 1987, Woodland Sketches, N.Y.C. Ballet, 1988, Haydn Trumpet Concerto, 1989, Puss in Boots, 1990, Waltz Trilogy, 1991, I Have My Own Room, 1992, Four for 4, 1992, Danses de Cour, 1994; TV appearances: Ray Charles and N.Y.C. Ballet, PBS, 1989; also Am. Ballet Theatre at the Met (Triad), Am. Ballet Theatre in San Francisco (Jardin Aux Lilas, Great Galloping Gottschalk), Baryishnikov Dances Tharp (Push comes to Shore), Dance in America, Western Symphony, 1990, (movie) Nutcracker, 1993; author: Nothing to Hide: A Dancer's Life. Office: NYC Ballet NY State Theatre Lincoln Ctr Plz New York NY 10023*

LAFRAMBOISE, JOAN CAROL, middle school educator; b. Bklyn., June 23, 1934; d. Anthony Peter and Nellie Eva (Zaleski) Ruggles; m. Albert George Laframboise, Aug. 5, 1961; children: Laura J., Brian A. BS in Edn., Springfield (Mass.) Coll., 1956. Cert. tchr. social sci., and mid. sch.; cert. tchr. support specialist. Tchr. Meml. Jr. H.S., Wilbraham, Mass., 1956-61, Midland Park (N.J.) Jr./Sr. H.S., 1961-63, Luke Garrett Middle Sch., Austell, Ga., 1983-93; tchr. lang. arts Pine Mountain Middle Sch., Kennesaw, Ga., 1993—. Coun. pres. Knights of Lithuania, Westfield, Mass., 1973-75, Holyoke, Mass., 1975-76, New Eng. dist. pres., 1976-77; mem. Wistariahurst Mus. Assocs., Holyoke, 1975-77. Jr. League mini-grantee, 1991. Mem. ASCD, NEA, Ga. Assn. Educators, Cobb County Assn. Educators, Nat. Coun. Tchrs. English, Nat. Coun. Social Studies. Home: 2891 Dara Dr Marietta GA 30066-4009

LAFRAMBOISE, PATRICK JOSEPH, trade association administrator; b. Yakima, Wash., June 19, 1951; s. Leon and Mary (Hardman) LaF. BA, Wash. State U., 1973. Dir. ops. Clapp & Poliak, Inc., N.Y.C., 1977-83; v.p. Graphic Arts Show Co., Reston, Va., 1983-94; pres., CEO Internat. Woodworking Fair, Norcross, Ga., 1994—. Mem. Internat. Assn. Exhbn. Mgrs., Major Am. Trade Show ORganizers (pres. 1990-91). Office: Internat Woodworking Fair 6525 The Corners Pky Ste 115 Norcross GA 30092

LAFREDO, STEPHEN CHRISTOPHER, consultant; b. Norristown, Pa., Aug. 21, 1962; s. Frank Joseph and Yuriko (Mizuo) L. BS in Microbiology, Pa. State U., 1984; AAS magna cum laude, Montgomery County C.C., 1992, AS magna cum laude, 1992. Rsch. technician Thomas Jefferson Sch. Medicine, Phila., 1984-86; rsch. assoc. Temple Sch. Medicine, Phila., 1986-88, R.W. Johnson Pharm. Rsch. Inst., Raritan, N.J., 1988-91; clin. rsch. assoc. Rhone-Poulenc Rorer Ctrl. Rsch., Collegeville, Pa., 1991-93; advanced programmer/analyst Shared Med Systems, Malvern, Pa., 1993-95; sr. cons. KPMG Peat Marwick LLP, Radnor, Pa., 1995-96; tech. designer Computer Scis. Corp., Cons. & Sys. Integration, Berwyn, Pa., 1996-97; sr. sys. analyst Merck & Co., Inc., West Point, Pa., 1997—. Contbr. articles to profl. jours. Sgt. U.S. Army N.G., 1983-89. Mem. Assn. for Computing Machinery, Fraternal Order of Police (assoc.). Avocations: bicycling, reading, stunt-kite flying, English steel tip darts. Home: 9 Traverse Dr Norristown PA 19401-2533

LAFVING, BRIAN DOUGLAS, lawyer; b. Michigan City, Ind., Mar. 31, 1953; s. Allen Herschel and Barbara Joan (Rachow) L.; m. Diane Leigh Pierce, Aug. 16, 1975; children: Bridgette, Brandon, Brittany. BA, BFA, So. Meth. U., 1974, JD, 1977. Bar: Tex. 1977, U.S. Ct. Dist. (no. dist.) Tex., 1977. Assoc. Stalcup, Johnson, Meyers & Miller, Dallas, 1977-79, Baker, Glast, Riddle, Tuttle & Elliott, Dallas, 1979-80; ptnr. Glast & Miller, Dallas, 1980-83, Jones, Day, Reavis & Pogue, Dallas, 1983—. Mem. ABA, Tex. Bar Assn. Republican. Methodist. Office: Jones Day Reavis & Pogue 2300 Trammell Crow Ctr 2001 Ross Ave Dallas TX 75201-8001

LAGALLY, MAX GUNTER, physics educator; b. Darmstadt, Germany, May 23, 1942; came to U.S., 1953, naturalized, 1960; s. Paul and Herta (Rudow) L.; m. Shelley Meserow, Feb. 15, 1969; children—Eric, Douglas, Karsten. BS in Physics, Pa. State U., 1963; MS in Physics, U. Wis.-Madison, 1965, PhD in Physics, 1968. Registered profl. engr., Wis. Instr. physics U. Wis., Madison, 1970-71, asst. prof. materials sci., 1971-74, assoc. prof., 1974-77, prof. materials sci. and physics, 1977—, dir. thin-film deposition and applications ctr., 1982-93, John Bascom Prof. materials sci., 1986—, E.W. Mueller Prof. materials sci. and physics, 1993—; Gordon Godfrey vis. prof. physics, U. New South Wales, Sydney, Australia, 1987; cons. in thin films, 1977—; vis. scientist Sandia Nat. Lab., Albuquerque, 1975. Editor: Kinetics of Ordering and Growth at Surfaces, 1990, (with others) Methods of Experimental Physics, 1985, Evolution of Surface and Thin-Film Microstructure, 1993; mem. editorial bd., also editor spl. issue Jour. Vacuum Sci. and Tech., 1978-81; prin. editor Jour. Materials Rsch., 1990-93; mem. editorial bd. Surface Sci., 1994—, Revs. Sci. Instruments, 1997—; contbr. articles to profl. jours.; patentee in field. Max Planck Gesellschaft fellow, 1968, Alfred P. Sloan Found. fellow, 1972, H.I. Romnes fellow, 1976, Humboldt Sr. Rsch. fellow, 1992; grantee fed. agys. and industry; recipient Outstanding Sci. Alumnus award Pa. State U. Fellow Am. Phys. Soc. (D. Adler award 1994, Davisson-Germer prize 1995), Australian Inst. Physics, Am. Vacuum Soc. (program and exec. coms. 1974-79, M.W. Welch prize 1991, trustee 1995-97); mem. AAAS, Am. Chem. Soc. (colloid and surface chemistry divsn.), Materials Rsch. Soc. (medal 1994). Home: 5110 Juneau Rd Madison WI 53705-4744 Office: U Wis Materials Sci & Engring 1509 University Ave Madison WI 53706-1538

LAGARDE, JACQUES YVES, metal products company executive; b. Rennes, Bretagne, France, May 2, 1938; m. Marie-Christine Cottard; children: Marion, Charlotte, Cecile, Antoine, Julie. MBA, Ecole des Hautes Etudes Commerciales, Paris, 1960; advanced mgmt. program, Harvard Bus. Sch., 1975. Advt. promotion mgr. Time Life Internat., London, N.Y.C., 1960-61; officer French Marine, Algeria, 1961-63; diverse positions Gillette France, Annecy, 1963-70; product line mgr. Braun AG, Kronberg, Germany, 1970-72; dean. Grad. Sch. Bus., Lyon, France, 1972-81; pres. Gillette France, Annecy, 1981-85, Oral-B Labs. Inc., San Francisco, 1985-89; v.p. Gillette Co., Boston, 1990-93, 1990—; chmn. bd. Mgmt. of Braun A.G., Germany; exec. v.p. Diversified Group/The Gillette Co., Boston, 1993—. Recipient Chevalier award Ordre Nat. du Merite. Office: The Gillette Co Prudential Twr Bldg Boston MA 02199

LAGARIAS, JOHN SAMUEL, engineering executive; b. Rochester, N.Y., July 4, 1921; s. Soterios Nicholas and Aspacia (Basil) L.; m. Virginia Jane Clark, June 16, 1947; children: Jeffrey, Peter, Clark. BS in Physics, Rensselaer Poly. Inst., 1948; postgrad., Oak Ridge Sch. Reactor Tech., 1955-56. Registered profl. engr., Md. Rsch. engr. Westinghouse Electric Rsch. Labs., Pitts., 1948-51; mgr. metal products rsch. Koppers Co., Inc., Pitts., 1951-63; mgr. R&D Am. Instrument Co., Silver Spring, Md., 1963-64; pres. Resources Rsch., Inc., Reston, Va., 1964-71; dir. environ. quality Kaiser Engrs., Oakland, Calif., 1971-84; pres. Lagarias Assocs., Moraga, 1984—; lectr. civil engring. dept. U. Md., 1970-71; mem. tech. adv. com. Washington Coun. Govts., 1968-70, Commonwealth of Va., 1969-71; conf. chmn. 2d Internat. Clean Air Congress, Washington, 1970; bd. mem. Calif. Air Resources Bd., 1985-96. Contbr. articles to profl. jours.; patentee electrostatic precipitators, analytical instruments and indsl. gas cleaning equipment. Planning commr. City of Moraga, Calif., 1975-82; mem. Calif. Air Resources Bd., 1986-96. With AUS, 1943-46. Fellow Air Pollution Control Assn. (hon., pres. 1968-69), Internat. Soc. Electrostatic Precipitation (bd. dirs. 1984, conf. chmn. 1st internatl conf.); mem. IEEE (sr., life), Am. Acad. Environ. Engrs. (diplomate). Office: 5954 Autumnwood Dr Apt 5C Walnut Creek CA 94595-3922

LAGASSÉ, PIERRE PHILIPPE, exercise science educator; b. Dec. 15, 1944; s. Jacques Lagassé; m. Daniele Roberge, May. 27, 1967 (div. 1982); children: Jean-Francois, Genevieve; m. Lucille Lessard, Feb. 19, 1983; 1 child, Marie-Pier. BA, U. Sherbrooke, Que., Can., 1965; B Phys. Edn., U. Ottawa, Ont., Can., 1967; MA, Pa. State U., 1970; PhD, U. Mass., 1974. Asst. prof. exercise sci. U. Sherbrooke, 1973-75; assoc. prof. U. Laval, St. Foy, Que., 1975-83, prof., 1983—, dir. Labsap, 1977-81, 87-90, dir. dept. exercise sci., 1990—; cons. Thomson-Rogers, Toronto, Ont., 1979-81, Borden and Elliot, Toronto, 1983-84, Que. Police Commn., 1985—, Que. Min. Health, 1993—. Contbr. articles to sci. jours. Fellow Am. Coll. Sports Medicine; mem. Can. Soc. Biomechanics (sec./treas. 1975-77, pres. 1977-78). Office: U Laval, 2160 PEPS, Sainte Foy, PQ Canada G1K 7P4

LAGER, ROBERT JOHN, state agency administrator; b. Fairhope, Ala., Aug. 19, 1934; s. Edward Glen and Dorothy (Niemeyer) L. AB, Syracuse U., 1957; PhD, Georgetown U., 1970. Asst. prof. Russian Georgetown U., Washington, 1965-71, chmn. dept. Russian, 1971-78; exec. asst. Gov. Fob James, Montgomery, Ala., 1978-80; dir. Ctr. for Internat. Trade, Mobile, Ala., 1980—; exec. dir. Ala. Fgn. Trade Commn., Mobile, 1983—; dir. Coun. on Internat. Edn. Exchange, N.Y.C., 1969-78; Presdl. appointment to Ala.

Export Coun.; cons. U.S. Dept. State, Voice of Am., Washington, 1969-78, Am. Coun. on Edn., Washington, 1975-78; adj. assoc. prof. Russian and Latin, U. South Ala., 1983—. Contbr. articles on Russian lang. and lit. to profl. jours. Trustee Ala. Inst. for Deaf and Blind, Talladega, 1979-86; mem. So. Growth Policies Bd.; bd. dirs. Mobile United. Served with USAF, 1956-60. Fellow Internat. Bus. Fellows; mem. Ala. World Trade Assn. (exec. dir. 1984-91), So. Ctr. for Internat. Studies (trustee 1986-95), Mobile Area C. of C. (cons. leadership program 1985, chmn. task force), Japan-U.S. Soc. Ala. (exec. com. 1989-93), Propeller Club, Phi Beta Kappa. Democrat. Roman Catholic. Avocations: sailing, tennis, reading, antique cars. Office: Ala Fgn Trade Commn 250 N Water St Ste 131 Mobile AL 36602-4021

LAGIN, NEIL, property management executive, landscape designer, consultant; b. Bronx, N.Y., Jan. 10, 1942; s. Barney and Helen (Goldberg) L.; m. Pamela Christine Lagin; children: Jenny Janette, Laurence Connor. Cert. xeriscape mgr. South Fla. Mgmt. Buyer Alexanders, N.Y.C., 1961-69; sales mgr. Halldon, Ltd., N.Y.C., 1969-79; mgr., ptnr. in concession Michele Craig, Westbury, N.Y., 1979-85; ptnr. ALW Trading, "9", N.Y.C., 1985-87; owner, operator Accent Foliage, Delray Beach, Fla., 1987-89; pres. Neil Lagin Property Mgmt., Neil's Landscape Svc., Boca Raton, Fla., 1988—. Author poetry; exhibitor photography shows, Ward Nasse Gallery-Salon, 1975-79, Timothy Blackburn Gallery, 1978, Washington Art Show and others. Notary pub., Fla., 1990; mem. nursery adv. bd. Habilitation Ctr. for the Handicapped, Boca Raton, 1991—; mem. overall adv. com. Palm Beach County Ext., 1993—, sec., chair program rev. com.; bd. dirs. Greater Palm Beach Area Alzheimers Assn., 1993; mem. Environ. Resource Landscape Team; mem. Boca Raton Postal Customer Adv. Coun., 1994-96; memb. bd. dirs. Pheasant Walk Homeowners Assoc., 1996-97; adv. ocun. Plant the Planet TV series, 1997. Named Fla. Master Gardener, Inst. Food and Agrl. Scis., U. Fla., 1989, Best Landscaper in Boca Raton, South Fla. Newspaper Network, 1991, Best Local Vol. in Boca Raton, 1994, Outstanding MAster Gardener, State of Fla., 1995. Mem. Internat. Palm Soc. (Palm Beach chpt.), Rare Fruit Coun. Internat. (Palm Beach chpt.), Boca Raton C. of C. (grad. leadership program 1991), Boca Raton Postal Customer Adv. Coun. Home and Office: 21170 White Oak Ave Boca Raton FL 33428

LAGO, MARY MCCLELLAND, English language educator, author; b. Pitts., Nov. 4, 1919; d. Clark Russell and Olive Arabella (Malone) McClelland; m. Gladwyn Vaile Lago, Mar. 4, 1944; children: Jane Hazel, Donald Russell. BA, Bucknell U., 1940; MA, U. Mo., 1965, PhD, 1969; DLitt (hon.), Bucknell U., 1981. Editorial asst. Friendship Press, N.Y.C., 1941-43, Congl. Ch. Nat. Hdqrs., N.Y.C., 1944-47; teaching asst. U. Mo., Columbia, 1964-70, lectr. English, 1971-77, assoc. prof., 1977-79, prof. English, 1979-88, Catherine Paine Middlebush prof. of English, 1988-89, prof. emeritus, 1990—; mem. dean's adv. com. Bucknell U., Lewisburg, Pa., 1979-81; hon. vis. prof. U. Manchester, 1985-86; vis. fellow St. Edmund's House, Cambridge U., 1982-83, vis. Bye-Fellow Selwyn Coll., 1991-92. Editor: Imperfect Encounter, 1972, (with K. Beckson) Max and Will, 1975, Rothenstein, Men and Memories, 1978, Burne-Jones Talking, 1980, Forster Number, Twentieth Century Literature, 1985, (with P.N. Furbank) Selected Letters of E.M. Forster, 2 vols., 1984, 85, (with Ronald Warwick) Perspectives in Time, 1989; author: Rabindranath Tagore, 1976, E.M. Forster: A Literary Life, 1996, Christiana Herringham and the Edwardian Art Scene, 1996; editl. bd. Twentieth Century Lit., 1979—; translator (with Supriya Bari) The Broken Nest (Tagore), 1971; translator (with Krishna Dutta) Tagore Selected Stories, 1991; contbr. articles and revs. to mags. Convener community adv. bd. NPR/Sta. KBIA-FM, U. Mo., Columbia, 1979-88. Recipient Disting. Faculty award, Arts and Sci. Disting. Alumna award, Curator's award for Scholarly Excellence U. Mo., 1997; rsch. grantee Am. Philos. Soc., 1966, 67, 72, NEH, 1980-83, Am. Coun. Learned Socs.; recipient summer rsch. stipend NEH, 1976. Mem. MLA, Soc. Authors (London), Univ. Women's Club (London), Phi Beta Kappa. Home: 13 Springer Dr Columbia MO 65201-5424 Office: U Mo Dept English 107 Tate Hall Columbia MO 65211

LAGOS, JAMES HARRY, lawyer; b. Springfield, Ohio, Mar. 14, 1951; s. Harry Thomas and Eugenia (Papas) L.; m. Nike Daphne Pavlatos, July 3, 1976. BA cum laude, Wittenberg U., 1970; JD, Ohio State U., 1972. Bar: U.S. Supreme Ct. 1976, U.S. Ct. Appeals (6th cir.) 1979, U.S. Dist. Ct. (so. dist.) Ohio 1973, U.S. Tax Ct. 1975, Ohio Supreme Ct. 1973. Asst. pros. atty. Clark County, Ohio, 1972-75; ptnr. Lagos & Lagos, Springfield, 1975—; mem. Springfield Small Bus. Council, past chmn., 1977—, Ohio Small Bus. Council, 1980—, past chmn., vice chmn.; past pres., v.p. Nat. Small Bus. United, 1982—; del. Small Bus. Nat. Issues Conf., 1984, Ohio Gov.'s Conf. Small Bus., 1984, resource person regulatory and licensing reform com., 1984. Bd. dirs., past pres. Greek Orthodox Ch., 1974—; mem. diocese council Greek Orthodox Diocese of Detroit, 1985-86; past chmn. Clark County Child Protection Team, 1974-82, Clark County Young Rep. Club, past pres., sec., treas., 1968-76, chmn. Ohio del. White House Conf. Small Bus., 1985-86, del. White House Conf. Small Bus., 1995, bd. dirs. Small Bus. Found. Am., 1993. Served as staff sgt. Ohio Air N.G., 1970-76. Recipient Dr. Melvin Emanuel award West Central Ohio Hearing and Speech Assn., 1983, Medal of St. Paul the Apostle Greek Orthodox Archdiocese of North and South Am., 1985; Disting. Service award Springfield-Clark County, 1977; named one of Outstanding Young Men of Am., 1978, Small Bus. Adv. Yr. U.S. Small Bus. Adminstrn., 1991. Mem. Am. Hellenic Inst. (pub. affairs com. 1979—, bd. dirs.), Am. Hellenic Ednl. Progressive Assn. (past treas), Small Bus. Found. of Am., (bd. dirs. 1993—), C. of C. (bd. dirs.), Jaycees (past chmn. several coms. 1973-89, Spoke award 1974), ABA, Ohio State Bar Assn., Springfield Bar and Law Library Assn. (past sec., exec. com. 1973—), West Cen. Ohio Hearing and Speech Assn. (bd. dirs., pres., v.p. 1973-84), Alpha Alpha Kappa, Phi Eta Sigma, Tau Pi Phi, Pi Sigma Alpha. Home: 2023 Audubon Park Dr Springfield OH 45504-1113 Office: Lagos & Lagos 1 S Limestone St Ste 1000 Springfield OH 45502-1243

LAGOWSKI, BARBARA JEAN, writer, book editor; b. Adams, Mass., Nov. 9, 1955; d. Frank Louis and Jeanette (Wanat) L.; m. Richard Dietrich Mumma III, Oct. 11, 1980; 1 child, Adam Dietrich. BA, U. South Fla., 1977; MA, Johns Hopkins U., 1978. Asst. editor Fred Jordan Books Grossett and Dunlap Pubs., N.Y.C., 1978-80; mng. editor Methuen Inc., N.Y.C., 1980-81; mng. assoc., sr. editor Bobb-Merrill Co Inc., N.Y.C., 1981-84; editor New Am. Libr., N.Y.C., 1984-85; poet-in-the-schs. Hillsborough County Arts Council, Tampa., Fla., 1976-77; poet-in-residence Cloisters Children's Mus., Balt., 1977-78. Author: Silver Skates series, 1988-89; co-author: Good Spirits, 1986, Teen Terminators, 1989, How to Get the Best Public School Education for Your Child, 1991, The Sports Curmudgeon, 1993, How to Attract Anyone, Anytime, Anyplace, 1993, Daily Negations: A Malcontent's Book of Meditations for Every Interminable Day of the Year, 1996, 101 Ways to Flirt: How to Get More Dates and Meet Your Mate, 1997. Mem. Authors Guild, Phi Kappa Phi. Home: 442 Dewey St Long Branch NJ 07740-5915

LAGOWSKI, J(OSEPH) J(OHN), chemist; b. Chgo., June 8, 1930; s. Joseph Thomas and Helen (Kasprycski) L.; m. Jeanne Wecker Mund, Feb. 13, 1954. B.S., U. Ill., 1952; M.S., U. Mich., 1954; Ph.D., Mich. State U., 1957; Ph.D. (Marshall scholar), Cambridge (Eng.) U., 1959. Asst. demonstrator and supr. in inorganic chemistry Cambridge U., 1958-59; asst. prof. chemistry U. Tex., Austin, 1959-63; asso. prof. U. Tex., 1963-67, prof. chemistry and edn., 1967—, Piper prof., 1981. Author: (with G.W. Watt and L.F. Hatch) Chemistry, 1974, Chemistry in the Laboratory, 1964, The Structure of Atoms, 1964, The Chemical Bond, 1966, Modern Inorganic Chemistry, 1973; editor: Jour. Chem. Edn, 1979-96. Recipient award Chem. Mfrs. Assn., 1981, Am. Chem. Soc. award in Chem. Edn., 1989. Fellow AAAS; mem. Am. Chem. Soc. (Union Carbide Corp. Chem. Edn. award 1989, S.W. Regional award 1996), Chem. Soc. (London), AAAS, Sigma Xi, Phi Lambda Upsilon. Office: U Tex Dept Chemistry Austin TX 78712

LAGRANGE, CLAIRE MAE, school librarian; b. Tarkio, Mo., Oct. 11, 1937; d. Floyd Gerald and Phyllis Geneva (Wilson) McElfish; m. Irving Joseph LaGrange, May 20, 1955; children: Raymond, Robert, Rhonda, Roger. BA, U. Southwestern La., 1983; MEd, Northwestern State U., 1990. Cert. English, spl. edn., K-12 mild and moderate, assessment tchr., libr. sci., La. Tchr.'s aide St. Martin Parish Sch. Bd., Cecilia, La., 1979-82; tchr. English Florien (La.) High Sch., 1984-86; tchr. Zwolle (La.) High Sch., 1986-90, Cecilia Jr. High Sch., 1990-92, Cecilia High Sch., 1992-96; libr. Teche Elem. Sch., Breaux, La., 1996—. Den mother Cub Scouts-Boy Scouts Am., Spokane, Wash., 1967-69; Sunday sch. tchr. First Friends Ch., Spokane, 1968-69. Fellow U. S.W. La Alumni Assn., Northwestern State U. Alumni Assn.; mem. NEA, ALA, Coun. Exceptional Children, Nat. English Honor Soc., Internat. Reading Assn., La. Assn. Educators, La. Ednl. Assessment Tchrs. Assn., La. Reading Assn., St. Martin Assn. Educators. Avocations: sketching, reading, writing, crossword puzzles, camping. Home: 1052 Charles Marks Rd Arnaudville LA 70512-3820

LAGRONE, ALFRED HALL, electrical engineering educator; b. DeBerry, Tex., Sept. 25, 1912; s. William Taylor and Lena Enola (Westmoreland) LaG.; m. Dixie Louise Ballard, Sept. 8, 1955; children: Carrie Sue, Howard, Tracy, Kimberly. B.S. in Elec. Enging, U. Tex., Austin, 1938, M.S., 1948, Ph.D., 1954. Distbn. engr. San Antonio Pub. Service Co., 1938-42; research engr. U. Tex., Austin, 1946-54; assoc. prof. U. Tex., 1954-60, prof., 1960-92, prof. emeritus, 1992—, dir. antennas and propagation lab., 1966—; Cons. ABC, Collins Radio Co., Honeywell, Inc., Tex. Nuclear Co.; chmn. U.S. Commn. F of Union Radio-Scientifique Internationale, 1975—. Served to capt. USNR, 1942-46. Recipient Scott Helt Meml. award I.R.E., 1960. Fellow I.E.E.E. (nat. chmn. fellow com.); mem. Sigma Xi, Eta Kappa Nu, Tau Beta Pi. Home: 3925 Sierra Dr Austin TX 78731-3911

LAGUEUX, RONALD RENE, federal judge; b. Lewiston, Maine, June 30, 1931; s. Arthur Charles and Laurette Irene (Turcotte) L.; m. Denise Rosemarie Boudreau, June 30, 1956; children: Michelle Simone, Gregory Charles, Barrett James. AB, Bowdoin Coll., 1953; LLB, Harvard U., 1956. Assoc. then ptnr. Edwards and Angell Law Firm, Providence, R.I., 1956-68; assoc. justice Superior Ct. State of R.I., Providence, 1968-86; judge U.S. Dist. Ct., Providence, 1986—; chief judge, 1992—; exec. counsel to Gov. Chafee, R.I., 1963-65. Rep. candidate for U.S. Senate, 1964; corporator R.I. Hosp., Providence, 1965—; solicitor Southeastern New Eng. Province United Way, 1957-68. Mem. ABA, Bowdoin Coll. Alumni Council (past v.p., pres.), Am.-French Geneal. Soc. Home: 90 Greenwood Ave Rumford RI 02916-1934 Office: US Dist Ct One Exchange Ter 1 Exchange Ter Providence RI 02903-1720

LAGUNOFF, DAVID, physician, educator; b. N.Y.C., Mar. 14, 1932; s. Robert and Cicele (Lipman) L.; m. Susan P. Powers, Mar. 8, 1958; children: Rachel, Liza, Michael. MD, U. Chgo., 1957. Rsch. asst. microbiology U. Miami, Coral Gables, Fla., 1951-53; intern U. Calif. San Francisco Hosp., 1957-58; postdoctoral fellow dept. pathology U. Wash., Seattle, 1958-59, trainee in pathology, 1959-60, instr. pathology, 1960-62, asst. prof., 1962-65, assoc. prof., 1965-69, prof., 1969-79; prof. dept. pathology St. Louis U., 1979—, chmn. dept. pathology, 1979-89, 91-96, asst. v.p., 1989-93; assoc. dean rsch. St. Louis U. Sch. Medicine, 1989-96. Nat. Heart Inst. fellow Carlsberg Laboratorium, Copenhagen, 1962-64, Nat. Cancer Inst. fellow Sir William Dunn Sch. Pathology, Oxford, Eng., 1970. Mem. AAAS, AAUP, Am. Soc. Cell Biology, Am. Assn. Pathologists, Am. Assn. Immunologists. Office: St Louis Univ Sch Medicine Dept Pathology 1402 S Grand Blvd Saint Louis MO 63104-1004

LAHAINE, GILBERT EUGENE, retail lumber company executive; b. Owosso, Mich., Jan. 30, 1926; s. Eric Eugene and Martha Dorothy (Wetzel) LaH.; m. Dorothy Jean Williams, July 1, 1945; children: Gilbert Eugene Jr., Susan, Karen, David, Barbara, Ruth, Marianne, Steven, Eric. BA, Mich. State U., 1949. Acct. Hazen Lumber Co., Lansing, Mich., 1949-56; pres., mgr. Gilbert Lumber Co., Lansing, 1956-94, also bd. dirs., sec., 1994—; sec. bd. dirs. Duane Bone Builder, Inc., East Lansing, Mich. Bd. dirs. Mo. Synod, Luth. Ch., St. Louis, 1987-95. With USN, 1944-46. Avocations: fishing, softball, reading, hunting. Home: 3904 SW Wolf St Lawton OK 73505-7532 Office: Gilbert Lumber Co 3501 S Pennsylvania Ave Lansing MI 48910-4734

LAHAY, DAVID GEORGE MICHAEL, ballet company director; b. Barrie, Ont., Can., July 15, 1949; s. George Anthony and Edna Alice (Silverberg) LaH. B.A., Trent U., Peterborough, Ont., 1971; B.F.A. with honors, York U., Toronto, 1973. Prin. dancer Les Grands Ballets Canadiens, Montreal, 1978-87, asst. ballet master, 1987-91; prin. dancer Atlanta Ballet, 1978; ballet master Ottawa Ballet, 1991; ballet pedagogue, choreographer The Banff (Alta.) Ctr., 1993-96. Choreographer Canadian Heritage Festival, 1989, 90, 91, The Banff Ctr., 1993-96; balletmaster Alberta Ballet. Ont. scholar, 1968; Can Council grantee, 1973, 75, 78. Office: Alberta Ballet Nat Christie Ctr, 141 18th Ave, Calgary, AB Canada T2S 0B8

LAHEY, RICHARD THOMAS, JR., nuclear engineer, fluid mechanics engineer; b. St. Petersburg, Fla., Feb. 20, 1939; married, 1961; 3 children. BS, U.S. Merchant Marine Acad., 1961; MS, Rensselaer Polytechnic Inst., 1964; ME, Columbia U., 1966; PhD in Mechanical Engring., Stanford U., 1971. Engr. Knolls Atomic Power Lab., 1961-64; rsch. assoc. Columbia U., 1964-66; mgr. core & safety devel. nuclear energy divsn. Gen. Electric, 1966-75; chmn. dept. nuclear engring. Rensselaer Poly. Inst., Troy, N.Y., 1975-87, prof. nuclear engring. and engring. physics, 1987-89, prof. dept. chem. engring., 1987-89, Edward E. Hood, Jr. prof. engring., 1989-94, dir. ctr. multiphase rsch., 1991-94; dean engring. Rensselaer Poly. Inst., Troy, 1994—; mem. sci. adv. com. EG&G Idaho, Inc., 1976—; mem. Advanced Code Rev. Group & LOFT Rev. Group U.S. Nuclear Regulatory Commn., 1976-84; commr. Engring. Manpower Commn., 1981-84; pres. R.T. Lahey, Inc., 1981-83; adj. prof. U. Pisa, Italy and Claude Bernard U., France, 1987; Alexander von Humboldt Sr. scientist fellow, 1994-95. Editor: Jour. Nuclear Engring. & Design, 1983-94. Recipient Arthur Holly Compton award, 1989, Glenn T. Seaborg medal, 1992, E. O. Lawrence Meml. award U.S. Dept. Energy, 1988; Fulbright fellow Magdalen Coll., Oxford U., 1983-84. Fellow ASME, AIChE, Am. Nuclear Soc. (Tech. Achievement award 1985), N.Y. Acad. Scis., Am. Soc. Engring. Edn. (Glen Murphy award 1985), Sigma Xi; mem. NAS, Nat. Acad. Engring., Nat. Acad. Sci. (fgn. mem. Bashkorstan, Russia). Research in two-phase flow and boiling heat transfer technology; nuclear reactor thermal-hydraulics and safety. Office: Rensselaer Poly Inst Office Dean Sch of Engring 110 8th St Troy NY 12180-3522

LAHIFF, MARILYN J., nursing administrator; b. Youngstown, Ohio; d. Jack L. and Lila J. (Webb) Mills; m. Lawrence C. Lahiff, Apr. 26, 1974. AAS, Lorain County C.C., Elyria, Ohio, 1973; student, Youngstown U., 1960-61. RN, Fla., Ohio; lic. rehab. svc. provider, Fla.; cert. rehab. nurse, cert. ins. rehab. specialist, cert. case mgr. Team leader pediatrics Lakewood (Ohio) Hosp., 1973-75; adminstr. Upjohn HealthCare Svcs., Reno, N.Y., 1977-78, 83-84; occupational health/sch. nurse Medina (Ohio) County Achievement Ctr., 1979-83; regional mgr. Beverly Enterprises, Torrance, Calif., 1984-87; program mgr. RehabCare Corp., Cleve., 1988-89; supr. med./vocat.rehab Feisco, Sarasota, Fla., 1989-92; cons., med. case mgmt. Riscorp, Sarasota, 1993-94; chief operating officer Prime Managed Care Svcs., Inc., Sarasota, 1994—. Mem. editl. bd. Directions in Rehab. Counseling, 1994. Mem. Assn. Rehab. Nurses, Fla. State Assn. Rehab. Nurses, Phi Theta Kappa. Avocations: boating, reading. Home: 18 Stonesthrow Way Englewood FL 34223-1939

LAHIRI, DEBOMOY KUMAR, molecular neurobiologist, educator; b. Varanasi, Uttar Pradesh, India, Sept. 9, 1955; came to U.S. 1983.; s. Benoy Kumar and Nilima Rani (Moitra) L.; m. Mithu Mukherjee, Dec. 15, 1991; 1 child, Niloy K. MS, Benaras Hindu U., India, 1975, PhD, 1980. Rsch. fellow Benaras Hindu U., Varanasi, 1975-79; jr. scientist Indian Coun. of Agrl. Rsch., New Delhi, India, 1979-81; postdoctoral fellow McMaster U. Sch. Medicine, Hamilton, Ont., Can., 1982; asst. rsch. scientist NYU, N.Y.C., 1983-86; rsch. assoc. N.Y. State Inst. for Basic Rsch., Staten Island, N.Y., 1987; asst. prof. Mt. Sinai Sch. Medicine, N.Y.C., 1988-90; asst. prof., chief molecular neurogenetics lab. Inst. Psychiat. Rsch. Ind. U. Sch. Medicine, Indpls., 1990—, asst. prof. med. & molecular genetics, 1994-96, assoc. prof. med. neurobiology and med. & molecular genetics, 1996—; presenter in field. Contbr. articles to profl. jours. U.P. Govt. Merit scholar, 1970-75; Univ. Grants Commn. New Delhi jr. rsch. fellow, 1975-79; grantee NIH, 1991—. Mem. AAAS, Am. Soc. Cell Biology, Am. Soc. Human Genetics, Am. Soc. for Neurochemistry, Am. Soc. Biochemistry and Molecular Biology, Genetics Soc. Am., Internat. Soc. for Neurochemistry, Soc. Biol. Psychiatry, Soc. for Neurosci., N.Y. Acad. Scis. Democrat. Hindu. Achievements include the molecular cloning and sequencing a cDNA for a major hnRNP (heterogeneous nuclear ribonucleoprotein particle) core protein; determination of the presence of beta amyloid precursor protein (APP) in different regions of human brain, and alternatively spliced APP transcripts in different tissues and various cell types; demonstration of a relationship between cholinergic agonists and the processing of APP; elucidation of the role of cholinesterase inhibitor on the processing of APP, first demonstration that tacrine can alter the secretion/metabolism of APP in cultured cells; first characterization of the beta amyloid gene promoter; and an enhancer like element in the beta amyloid gene promoter; research related to the origin and biogenesis of Alzheimer amyloid plaque and the general areas of gene regulation and genetics of Alzheimer's Disease, development of a rapid, economical, non-enzymatic and non-organic method for DNA extraction, elucidation of the genetic basis of neuropsychiatric disorders by the linkage studies using molecular genetic methods and PCR (polymerase chain reaction) based genotyping, RFLP (restriction fragment length ploymorphism) and candidate gene studies in families ascertained through the NIMH Genetics Initiative in order to confirm association between the inheritance of a molecular marker with the member of the family sharing the illness, development of a sensitive radioimmunoassay to measure melatonin in human plasma samples, bipolar patients have an increased sensitivity to the effects of light on the circadian rhythm of melatonin secretion, and the risk of mood disorder seems to be related to this hypersensitivity to light, the suppression of melatonin by light may be a trait marker for bipolar affective disorder; demonstration pineal hormone melatonin can regulate the processing of Alzheimer's amyloid precursor protein in cultured cells. Home: 5731 Arabian Run Indianapolis IN 46228-1684 Office: Inst Psychiat Rsch Ind Univ 791 Union Dr Indianapolis IN 46202-2873

LAHOOD, MARVIN JOHN, English educator; b. Auburn, N.Y., Mar. 21, 1933; s. Salem and Anna (Mahfoud) L.; m. Marjorie Braun, Aug. 22, 1959; children: John, Melissa, Mark. BS, Boston Coll., 1954; MA in English, U. Notre Dame, 1958, PhD in English, 1962. Instr. Niagara U., 1960-61, assoc. prof., 1962-64; assoc. prof. Buffalo (N.Y.) State Coll., 1964-67, prof., 1967-71, prof. ind. study, 1968-69, prof., assoc. for acad. devel., 1969-71, prof., 1978-95, Disting. tchg. prof., 1995—; prof., acad. dean Coll. Misericordia, 1971-72, Salem State Coll., 1972-75; prof., dean faculty D'Youville Coll., 1975-78; chair Burchfield Poets and Writers Com., 1985—; manuscript reviewer Prentice Hall, 1986-88; lectr. U. Dortmund, Germany, 1986, Lille U., France, Cath. U. Lille, 1991; chair SUNY Senate Ops. Com., 1994-97. Author: Conrad Richter's America, 1974, State University College at Buffalo, A History: 1946-1972, 1980; editor: Latvian Literature, 1964, Tender Is the Night: Essays in Criticism, 1969; contbr. articles to prof. jours. Pres. Mt. St. Mary Acad. Bd. Trustees, 1990-94. SUNY Faculty Rsch. fellow, 1967, 68, USOE fellow Inst. on Ednl. Media, 1967, SUNY fellow Inst. for Devel. Black Studies, 1969; SUNY Faculty Exch. scholar, 1969—; recipient SUNY Chancellor's award Excellence in Teaching, 1985. Office: Buffalo State College 1300 Elmwood Ave Buffalo NY 14222-1004

LAHOOD, RAY, congressman; b. Ill., Dec. 6, 1945; m. Kathleen (Kathy) Dunk LaHood; children: Darin, Amy, Sam, Sara. Student, Canton Jr. Coll., Ill.; BS in Edn. and Sociology, Bradley U., 1971. Tchr. Catholic and pub. jr. high schs., 1971-77; dist. administrv. asst. to congressman Tom Railsback, 1977; mem. Ill. Ho. of Reps., 1982; Chief of Staff Ho. of Reps.; mem. 104th Congress from 18th Ill. dist., 1995—; Mem. Agriculture Com., Transp. and Infrastructure Com. Bd. dirs. Economic Devel. Coun.; pres. sch. bd. Spalding and Notre Dame H.Schs., Bradley U. Nat. Alumni Bd.; svc. to Children's Hosp. Bd., Peoria Area Retarded Citizens Bd.; dir. Rock Island County Youth Svcs. Bur. Mem. ITOO Soc., Downtown Rotary Club, Holy Family Ch. (Peoria), Peoria Area C. of C. Roman Catholic. Office: US House Reps 329 Cannon Bldg Washington DC 20515-1318 Office: US Rep Ray LaHood 100 NE Monroe St Ste 100 Peoria IL 61602-1003

LAHOURCADE, JOHN BROSIUS, retired service company executive; b. San Antonio, Tex., Nov. 18, 1924; s. Frederic Eugene and Hildagarde (Brosius) L.; m. Mary Lou Williamson, Sept. 6, 1947; children: Lynne Breuer, Lee A., Lance. BBA, U. Tex., 1948. CPA, Tex. Staff acct. Stanolind Oil & Gas Co., Brownfield, Tex., 1948-51, Carneiro Chumney CPA's, San Antonio, 1951-55; ptnr. Bielstein, Lahourcade & Lewis CPA's, San Antonio, 1955-69; v.p. Luby's Cafeterias Inc., San Antonio, 1969-74, sr. v.p. fin., 1974-79, exec. v.p., 1979-82, pres., chief exec. officer, 1982-88, chmn., CEO, 1988-90, chmn. bd. dirs., 1990-96; ret., 1996. Trustee S.W. Tex. Meth. Hosp., San Antonio, 1974-83; adv. council U. Tex. Sch. Bus. Adminstrn. Found., Austin, 1986-89; bd. dirs. San Antonio Econ. Devel. Found., 1984-95. Mem. Tex. Soc. CPA's (bd. dirs. 1965-68), San Antonio CPA's (pres. 1965).

LAHR, JACK LEROY, lawyer; b. Toledo, Aug. 5, 1934; s. Clarence L. and Josephine E. (Rosenbrook) L.; m. Greta Mars, Dec. 17, 1955 (div. 1987); children: Ellen, Julie; m. Joanna Risdon Hanes, Aug. 8, 1992. BS in Mech. Engring., U. Toledo, 1956; JD with honors, George Washington U., 1963. Bar: Va. 1963, D.C. 1963. Ptnr. Arent, Fox, Kintner, Plotkin & Kahn, 1971-80; ptnr. Foley & Lardner, Washington, 1980—; adj. prof. Georgetown U. Law Ctr., Washington, 1980-83. Author: (with E. Kintner) An Intellectual Property Law Primer, 2d edit., 1982. Served with USN, 1956-59. Mem. ABA (council adminstrv. law sect. 1971-74, chmn. administrv. law judges com. 1974-80), Order of Coif. Office: Foley & Lardner 3000 K St NW Washington DC 20007-5109

LAHR, JOHN, author; b. Los Angeles, July 12, 1941; s. Bert and Mildred (Schroeder) L.; m. Anthea Mander, Aug. 12, 1965; children: Christopher, James Anthony and Nicholas Dodds (twins) (dec.). B.A., Yale, 1963, Worcester Coll., Oxford, 1965; M.A., Worcester Coll., Oxford. Drama critic Manhattan East, 1966-68, New York Free Press, 1968-70, Evergreen Rev., 1968-71, Village Voice, 1969-72, The Nation, 1981-82, British Vogue, 1986-92, The New Yorker, 1992—; contbg. editor Harper's, 1979-83; lit. adviser Tyrone Guthrie Theatre, Mpls., 1968; lit. mgr. Repertory Theatre of Lincoln Center, 1969-71. Author: Notes on a Cowardly Lion: The Biography of Bert Lahr, 1969, Up Against the Fourth Wall, 1970, The Autograph Hound, 1973, Astonish Me, 1973, (with Jonathan Price) Life-Show, 1973, Hot to Trot, 1974, Prick Up Your Ears: The Biography of Joe Orton, 1978 (Gay News lit. prize 1979), Coward: the Playwright, 1983, Automatic Vaudeville, 1984, (play) Diary of a Somebody, 1989, Dame Edna Everage and the Rise of Western Civilization: Backstage with Barry Humphries, 1991 (Roger Machell prize 1992), Light Fantastic, 1996; Editor: (with Anthea Lahr) Casebook on Harold Pinter's The Homecoming, 1969, The Complete Plays of Joe Orton, 1976, The Orton Diaries, 1987; co-producer: (film) Prick Up Your Ears, 1987. Mem. Rockefeller Theatre panel, 1969-73, Nat. Endowment for the Arts, 1969-73, Theatre Devel. Fund, 1970-73; Bd. dirs. Choreoconcerts, 1966—. Recipient George Jean Nathan award for drama criticism, 1969, 95, ASCAP-Deems Taylor award 1980-81. Mem. P.E.N. (dir.). Address: 11A Chalcot Gardens, London NW3 4YB, England

LAHRI, RAJEEVA, electronics executive; b. Kanpur, India, Sept. 12, 1955; came to U.S., 1980; s. Rajni Kant and Pushpa (Srivastava) Lehri; m. Sangeeta Srivastava, Dec. 1, 1983; children: Shephalie, Shilpika. MSc in Physics, Indian Inst. of Tech., Kanpur, 1974, MTech in Materials Sci., 1976; PhD in Elec. Engring., SUNY, Buffalo, 1982. Mem. tech. staff Hewlett Packard Co., Corvallis, Oreg., 1982-86; mgr. Bipolar/BiCMOS devel. Fairchild/Nat. Semiconductor, Puyallup, Wash., 1986-90; dir. tech. devel. Nat. Semiconductor Corp., Santa Clara, Calif., 1990-95; v.p. corp. r & d VLSI Tech., Inc., San Jose, Calif., 1995—. Co-author: BiCMOS Technology and Its Applications, 1989; patentee BJT device formation related, 1992. Home: 643 Pilgrim Loop Fremont CA 94539-6285

LAHTI, CHRISTINE, actress; b. Detroit, Apr. 5, 1950; d. Paul Theodore and Elizabeth Margaret (Tabar) L.; m. Thomas Schlamme, Sept. 4, 1983; 1 child, Wilson Lahti. BA in Speech, U. Mich., 1972; postgrad., Fla. State U., 1972-73; studies with William Esper, Uta Hagen, Herbert Berghof Studios. Actress: (stage prodns.) The Woods, 1978 (Theater World award 1979), Division Street, 1980, Loose Ends, 1981, Present Laughter, 1983, Landscape of the Body, 1984, The Country Girl, 1984, Cat on a Hot Tin Roof, 1985, Little Murders, 1987, The Heidi Chronicles, 1989, Three Hotels, 1993; regular mem. cast (TV series) Dr. Scorpion, 1978, The Harvey Korman Show, 1978, Chicago Hope, 1995—, (TV films) The Last Tenant, 1978, The Henderson Monster, 1980, The Executioner's Song, 1982, Single Bars, Single Women, 1984, Love Lives On, 1985, Amerika, 1987, No Place Like Home, 1989, Crazy from the Heart, 1991, The Fear Inside, 1992, The Good Fight, 1985, The Four Diamonds, 1995, (feature films) And Justice For All, 1979, Whose Life Is It, Anyway?, 1981, Swing Shift, 1984 (N.Y. Film Critics Circle award for best supporting actress 1985, Acad. award nominee 1985, Golden

Globe award nominee 1985), Ladies and Gentlemen: The Fabulous Stains, 1985, Just Between Friends, 1986, Housekeeping, 1987, Season of Dreams, 1987, Stacking, 1988, Running on Empty, 1988, Gross Anatomy, 1989, Miss Firecracker, 1989, Funny About Love, 1990, The Doctor, 1991, Leaving Normal, 1992, Hideaway, 1995, Pie in the Sky, 1995, A Weekend in the Country, 1996; prodr. short action film, actress: Lieberman in Love, 1995 (Acad. award nominee for best live action short film 1996). Recipient Golden Globe award for Best Actress in a Miniseries or Motion picture Made for TV. Office: ICM 8942 Wilshire Blvd Beverly Hills CA 90211-1934

LAHVIS, SYLVIA LEISTYNA, art historian, educator, curator; b. Ilion, N.Y., Dec. 6, 1936; d. Arthur Leistyna and Margareta Maresch; m. W. Frederick Lahvis, Nov. 12, 1960; children: Garet Paul, Matthew Arthur. BA, U. Rochester, 1958; MA, Oberlin Coll., 1972; PhD, U. Del., 1990. Curatorial asst. Yale U. Art Gallery, New Haven; curator New Milford (Conn.) Hist. Soc., 1975-78; co-curator Univ. Gallery U. Del., Newark, 1985; curatorial dir. The Sewell C. Biggs Mus. Am. Art, Dover, Del., 1993-95; lectr. edn. dept. Albright-Knox Art Gallery, Buffalo; lectr. art history Wykeham Rise Sch., Washington, Conn.; instr. Canterbury Sch., New Milford; adj. prof. U. Del., 1986-87, Rutgers U., Camden, 1988, 91-92, dept. art history U. Del., 1989, Coll. Human Resources, 1988-89, adj. prof. dept. art history, 1989—, Master of Arts in Liberal Studies program, 1992—, U. Del; curator Index of Am. Sculpture, 1982-86, symposium com., 1985; vis. asst. prof. Washington U., Chestertown, Md., 1989; presenter in field. Contbr. articles to art jours. Interpace and Clevepak Corp. fellow U. Del.; Henry Luce Found. grantee. Mem. Coll. Art Assn., Assn. Am. Mus., Soc. Archtl. Historians, Decorative Arts Soc., Nat. Trust for Hist. Preservation, Archives of Am. Art, Phi Kappa Phi, Phi Beta Kappa. Democrat. Mem. Unitarian Ch. Avocations: singing, designing. Home: 2309 W 18th St Wilmington DE 19806

LAI, JUEY HONG, chemical engineer; b. Taipei, Taiwan, Dec. 4, 1936; came to U.S., 1961, naturalized, 1976; s. Kwo-Wang and Chin-Fong L.; m. Li-Huey Chang, June 30, 1968; children: Eric Yo-Ping, Bruce Yo-Sheng. B.S. in Chem. Engring., Nat. Taiwan U., 1959; M.S. in Chem. Engring., U. Wash., 1963, Ph.D. in Phys. Chemistry, 1969. Rsch. specialist dept. chemistry U. Minn., 1969-73; prin. research scientist Honeywell Phys. Scis. Ctr., Honeywell, Inc., Bloomington, Minn., 1973-78, sr. prin. research scientist, 1978-83; staff scientist Honeywell Tech. Ctr., Honeywell, Inc., 1983-87; pres. Lai Labs., Inc., Burnsville, Minn., 1988—; lectr. SUNY, New Paltz, 1983. Author/editor: Polymers for Electronic Applications, 1989; contbr. articles on solid state chemistry, polymer chemistry and dental materials to tech. jours.; rschr. on polymer materials for electronics, gas removal tech., solid state chemistry and dental materials; holder 9 patents in electronic and dental materials. Bd. dirs. Chinese Am. Assn. Minn., 1977-79, Minn. Taiwanese Assn., 1995-97. Recipient H.W. Sweatt Tech. award Honeywell, Inc., 1980, Small Bus. Innovation Rsch. award Dept. Health and Human Svcs., 1990, 93, 94, 96, 97. Fellow Am. Inst. Chemists; mem. Am. Assn. Dental Rsch., Am. Chem. Soc., Sigma Xi, Phi Lambda Upsilon. Office: Lai Labs Inc 12101 16th Ave S Burnsville MN 55337-2982

LAI, WAIHANG, art educator; b. Hong Kong, Jan. 7, 1939; s. Sing and Yu-ching L.; came to U.S., 1964; BA, Chinese U. Hong Kong, 1964; MA, Claremont Grad. Sch., 1967; m. Celia Cheung, Aug. 13, 1966. Asst. prof. art Maunaolu Coll., Maui, Hawaii, 1968-70; prof. art Kauai (Hawaii) Community Coll., 1970—. Vis. prof. art Ariz. State U., Tempe, summer 1967. Recipient Excellence in Teaching award U. Hawaii, 1992, Nat. Inst. Staff and Orgnl. Devel. Excellence award U. Tex., 1993. Mem. Kauai (pres. 1974—) Watercolor Socs., Phila. Watercolor Club, Hawaii Computer Art Soc., Kauai Oriental Art Soc. (pres. 1981—), AM. Watercolor Soc. Author: The Chinese Landscape Paintings of Waihang Lai, 1966, The Watercolors of Waihang Lai, 1967; illustrator: The Tao of Practice Success, 1991, Advertisements for Acupuncturists, 1992. Home: PO Box 363 Lihue HI 96766-0363 Office: Kauai Community Coll Lihue HI 96766

LAI, W(EI) MICHAEL, mechanical engineer, educator; b. Amoy, Fukien, China, Nov. 29, 1930; naturalized U.S. citizen, 1967; s. Chia-pan and Shue-Chin (Lo) L.; m. Linda Yu-ling Chu, Dec. 21, 1963; children: David, Michelle. BSCE, Nat. Taiwan U., 1953; MS in Engring. Mech., U. Mich., 1959, PhD, 1962. Asst. prof. mechanics Renssalaer Poly. Inst., Troy, N.Y., 1961-66, assoc. prof., 1967-77, prof., 1978-87, acting dept. chmn., 1986-87; prof. mech. engring. and orthopaedic bioengring. Columbia U., N.Y.C., 1987—, acting chmn. dept. mech. engring., 1995-96, chmn. dept. mech. engring., 1996—. Author: Elements of Elasticity, 1965, Introduction to Continuum Mechanics, 1974, 3rd edit., 1993. Fellow ASME (chmn. bioengring. divsn. 1996-97, Melville medal for Best Paper 1982, Best Paper award bioengring. divsn. 1991), Am. Inst. Med. and Biol. Engring.; mem. AAAS, Am. Soc. Biomechanics, Orthopaedic Rsch. Soc. Home: 215 W 95th St Apt 9H New York NY 10025-6355 Office: Columbia U Dept Mech Engring W 120th St Mail Code 4703 New York NY 10027

LAIBINIS, PAUL EDWARD, chemical engineering educator; b. Wilkes-Barre, Pa., Dec. 8, 1963; s. Edward Bernard and Helen Jean (Draminski) L. BSChemE, BS in Chemistry, MIT, 1985; MA in Chemistry, Harvard U., 1987, PhD in Chemistry, 1991. Teaching/rsch. asst. Harvard U., Cambridge, Mass., 1985-91; postdoctoral fellow Calif. Inst. Tech., Pasadena, 1991-93; asst. prof. MIT, Cambridge, 1993-94, Texaco-Mangelsdorf asst. prof., 1994-96, Doherty asst. prof., 1996—; corr. Sci.-by-Mail, 1994-95; Beckman Fedn. young investigator, 1995—, Office of Naval Rsch. young investigator, 1996—. Recipient Predsl. Early Career award for Scientists and Engrs., 1996. Mem. AAAS, AIChE, Am. Chem. Soc. (Victor K. LaMer award divsn. colloid and surface sci. 1994). Republican. Roman Catholic. Achievements include contributions to more than 40 sci. publs., 1 patent in area of thin films and nanotechnology. Avocations: hiking, swimming, racket sports, film, theater. Home: 56 Winslow Ave Apt 1 Somerville MA 02144-2501 Office: MIT Dept Chemical Engring Cambridge MA 02139

LAIBLE, JON MORSE, retired mathematics educator, dean; b. Bloomington, Ill., July 25, 1937; s. Russell James and Margaret (Herold) L.; m. Jo Ann Ivens, June 14, 1959; children: Kathy Jo, Kenneth Russell, Jackie Ann Laible Muhs, Michael Howard. Student, Carleton Coll., 1955-57; BS, U. Ill., 1959; MA, U. Minn., 1961; PhD, U. Ill., 1967. Asst. prof. Western Ill. U., Macomb, 1962-64; asst. prof., assoc. prof. then prof. math. Ea. Ill. U., Charleston, 1964-80, dean Coll. Liberal Arts and Scis., 1980-93, dean Coll. Scis., 1993-94; ret., 1994; vis. prof. math. Millikin U., Decatur, Ill., 1994—. Chmn. citizens cons. coun. Unit #1 Pub. Schs., Charleston, 1975-78; adv. com. Sarah Bush Lincoln Health Ctr., Charleston, 1986; bd. dirs. Ea. Ill. U. Found., 1995—, v.p., 1996, 97; pres. Tarble Arts Ctr. Adv. Bd. Recipient Outstanding Faculty Merit award Ea. Ill. Univ., 1978, Univ. Svc. award, 1991. Mem. Math. Assn. Am. (bd. govs. 1977-80, chmn. com. vis. lectrs. and cons. 1980-88, Disting. Svc. award Ill. sect. 1985), Ill. Sect. Math. Assn. Am. (chmn. 1975, 94), Sigma Xi. Democrat. Avocation: photography.

LAIDIG, WILLIAM RUPERT, retired paper company executive; b. Sterling, Ill., Feb. 3, 1927; s. George and Margaret Anne (Gnewuch) L.; m. Lorraine Mae Grom, Jan. 2, 1952; children: Ann Marie, Mary Katherine, Margaret Anne, William Andrew. B.S.M.E., Marquette U., 1949. Registered profl. engr., Ga., Ala., Wis., Ark. Engr. Inland Steel Products, 1949-50; engr. Nekoosa Papers Inc., Port Edwards, Wis., 1950-62, mgr., 1962-66; mgr. Nekoosa Papers Inc., Ashdown, Ark., 1966-72; mill mgr. Nekoosa Papers Inc., Port Edwards, Wis., 1972-75; v.p., resident mgr. Gt. So. Paper Co.., Cedar Springs., Ga., 1975-80, sr. v.p., 1979-80, pres., 1980-84; exec. v.p. Gt. No. Nekoosa Corp., Stamford, Conn., 1980-84, pres., chief exec. officer, chmn., dir., 1984-90; chmn. Jaakko Pöyry (USA), Inc., Raleigh, N.C., 1991-92; ret. Pres. Village of Port Edwards, Wis., 1966-67; trustee Marquette U., Milw.; bd. dirs. Tasman Chile Ltd., 1993. Lt. USN, 1952-53. Roman Catholic. Clubs: Eagle Creek Country (Fla.). Lodges: K.C., Elks. Home: PO Box 39 Manitowish Waters WI 54545-0039

LAIDLAW, ANDREW R., lawyer; b. Durham, N.C., Aug. 28, 1946. BA, Northwestern U., 1969; JD, U. N.C., 1972. Bar: Ill. 1972. Chair exec com., mem. Seyfarth, Shaw, Fairweather & Geraldson, Chgo.; CEO Seyfarth, Shaw, Fairweather & Geraldson, Chicago. Contbr. articles to profl. jours. Mem. ABA (antitrust and securities law coms. 1982—), Barristers. Office: Seyfarth Shaw Fairweather & Geraldson Mid Continental Plz 55 E Monroe St Chicago IL 60603-5701

LAIDLAW, HARRY HYDE, JR., entomology educator; b. Houston, Apr. 12, 1907; s. Harry Hyde and Elizabeth Louisa (Quinn) L.; BS, La. State U., 1933, MS, 1934; PhD (Univ. fellow, Genetics fellow, Wis. Dormitory fellow, Wis. Alumni Rsch. Found. fellow), U. Wis., 1939; m. Ruth Grant Collins, Oct. 26, 1946; 1 child, Barbara Scott Laidlaw Murphy. Teaching asst. La. State U., 1933-34, rsch. asst., 1934-35; prof. biol. sci. Oakland City (Ind.) Coll., 1939-41; state apiarist Ala. Dept. Agr. and Industries, Montgomery, 1941-42; entomologist First Army, N.Y.C., 1946-47; asst. prof. entomology, asst. apiculturist U. Calif.-Davis, 1947-53, assoc. prof. entomology, assoc. apiculturist, 1953-59, prof. entomology, apiculturist, 1959-74, asso. dean Coll. Agr., 1960-64, chair agr. faculty, staff, 1965-66, prof. entomology emeritus, apiculturist emeritus, 1974—; coord. U. Calif.-Egypt Agrl. Devel. Program, AID, 1979-83. Rockefeller Found. grantee, Brazil, 1954-55, Sudan, 1967; honored guest Tamagawa U., Tokyo, 1980. Trustee, Yolo County (Calif.) Med. Soc. Scholarship Com., 1965-83. Served to capt. AUS, 1942-46. Recipient Cert. of Merit Am. Bee Jour., 1957, Spl. Merit award U. Calif.-Davis, 1959, Merit award Calif. Central Valley Bee Club, 1974, Merit award Western Apicultural Soc., 1980, Gold Merit award Internat. Fedn. Beekeepers' Assns., 1986; recipient Disting. Svc. award Ariz. Beekeepers Assn., 1988. Cert. of Appreciation Calif. State Beekeepers' Assn., 1987, award Alan Clemson Meml. Found., 1989: NIH grantee, 1963-66; NSF grantee, 1966-74. Fellow AAAS, Entomol. Soc. Am. (honoree spl. symposium 1990, C.W. Woodworth award Pacific br. 1981); mem. Am. Inst. Biol. Scis., Am. Soc. Naturalists, Am. Soc. Integrative Biology, Nat. Assn. Uniformed Svcs., Ret. Officers Assn. (2d v.p. Sacramento chpt. 1984-86), Scabbard and Blade, Sigma Xi (treas. Davis chpt. 1959-60, v.p. chpt. 1966-67), Alpha Gamma Rho (pres. La. chpt. 1933-34, counsellor Western Province 1960-66). Democrat. Presbyterian. Author books including Instrumental Insemination of Honey Bee Queens, 1977; Contemporary Queen Rearing, 1979, Queen Rearing and Bee Breeding, 1997; author slide set: Instrumental Insemination of Queen Honey Bees, 1976. Achievements include determination of cause of failure of attempts to artificially inseminate queen honey bees; invention of instruments and procedures to consistently accomplish same; elucidation of genetic relationships of individuals of polyandrous honey bee colonies; design of genetic procedures for behavioral study and breeding of honey bees for general and specific uses. Home: 761 Sycamore Ln Davis CA 95616-3432 Office: U Calif Dept Entomology Davis CA 95616

LAIDLAW, ROBERT RICHARD, publishing company executive; b. Berwyn, Ill., Mar. 25, 1923; s. John and Mabel Josephine (Howard) L.; m. Evangeline Rene Harrelson, Aug. 12, 1944; children—Andrew Robert, Kimberly, Lisa. Student, Dartmouth Coll., 1941-42; A.B., U. N.C., 1947, J.D., 1950. Sales rep. Laidlaw Bros. (textbook pubs.), River Forest, Ill., 1950-58; sales mgr. Laidlaw Bros. (textbook pubs.), 1958-60, exec. v.p., 1960-68, pres., 1968-85. Served with USNR, 1942-45. Congregationalist.

LAIDLER, DAVID ERNEST WILLIAM, economics educator; b. Tynemouth, Northumberland, Eng., Aug. 12, 1938; s. John Alphonse and Leonora (Gosman) L.; m. Antje Charlotte Breitwisch, Jan. 29, 1965; 1 dau., Nicole Joanna; m. Frances Joan Hutner, Aug. 1960 (div. 1964). B.Sc., London Sch. Econs., 1959; M.A., U. Syracuse, 1960; Ph.D., U. Chgo., 1964; M.A., U. Manchester, Eng., 1973. Temporary asst. lectr. London Sch. Econs., 1961-62; asst. prof. U. Calif.-Berkeley, 1963-66; lectr. econs. U. Essex, Colchester, Eng., 1966-69; prof. econs. U. Manchester, 1969-75; vis. prof. econs. Brown U., Providence, 1973; prof. econs. U. Western Ont., London, Can., 1975—; mem. econ. adv. panel to Marc Lalonde, minister fin., Ottawa, Ont., 1982-84; research coord. Macdonald Royal Commn., 1984-85; scholar in residence C.D. Howe Inst., 1990-91, adj. scholar, 1991—; mem. econs. com. Social Sci. Research Council, Gt. Britain, 1972-75; mem. program adv. com. Carnegie-Rochester Pub. Policy Conf. Series, Rochester, Pitts., 1978-79; Lister lecter. Brit. Assn. Advancement Sci., 1972. Author: The Demand for Money - Theories and Evidence, 1969, Introduction to Microeconomics, 1974, Essays on Money and Inflation, 1975, Monetarist Perspectives, 1982, Taking Money Seriously, 1990, The Golden Age of the Quantity Theory, 1991, (with W. Robson) The Great Canadian Disinflation, 1993; mem. editl. bd. Rev. Econ. Studies, 1970-75, Am. Econ. Rev., 1976-78, Can. Jour. Econs., 1977-79, Jour. Econ. Lit., 1978-91; assoc. editor: Jour. Money, Credit and Banking, 1979—. Rsch. grantee NSF, 1964-66, Social Sci. Rsch. Coun., 1971-76, Social Scis. and Humanities Rsch. Coun. Can., 1977-81, 94-99, 94—, Bradley Found., 1991-96. Fellow Royal Soc. Can.; mem. Am. Econ. Assn., Can. Econ. Assn. (exec. com. 1980-83, pres. 1987-88, Douglas Purvis Meml. prize 1994). Home: 345 Grangeover Ave, London, ON Canada N69 4K8 Office: U Western Ont, Dept Econs, London, ON Canada N6A 5C2

LAINCZ, BETSY ANN, nurse; b. Phila., Feb. 7, 1949; d. Harry Ellsworth and Betty Mary (Minton) Henderson; m. Douglas Dardaris, 1968 (div. 1975); children: Amy, Christopher; m. Fred J. Laincz, Jan. 12, 1982; children: Joshua, Emily, Michael. Student, Bucks County C.C., Newtown, 1969-87, Temple U., Phila., 1973, Upper Bucks Sch. of Nursing, Perkasie, 1983, Internat. Sch. of Shiatsu, Doylestown, 1995-96. Lic. practical nurse, Pa. Staff nurse, mental health technician Doylestown (Penn.) Hosp., 1983-85, data abstractor med. records, 1988-89; nurse, coun., asst. mgr. NutriSystem, Warrington, Penn., 1985-88; nurse Independence Court, Quakerstown, Pa., 1991; health svcs. supr. Bucks County Assn. Retarded Citizens, Quakerstown, 1992-95; nurse Penn Found. Drug and Alcohol Recovery Ctr., 1996; owner, operator Complimentary Healing Arts Agency, Perkasic, Pa., 1996—; supports and standards com. Bucks County Assn. Retarded Citizens, 1995. Mem. United Friends Sch. (fundraising co-chair 1989—; nominating com., 1995—; ann. auction com. 1990—; devel. com, 1991-92); mem. Individual's Person Centered Planning Team, 1994—; mem. Inst. of Noetic Scis., 1993—. Mem. Am. Holistic Nurses Assn., Area Healing Arts Assn., Buck Womens Investment Club (v.p. 1995), Moon Lodge, The Smithsonian Instn., Libr. of Congress Assn., Nat. Assn. of Investers Corp., Quakertown Bus. and Profl. Women's Club, Co-op Am. Republican. Mem. United Ch. Christ. Avocations: reading, writing, art, antiques. Home: 532 W Market St Perkasie PA 18944

LAINE, CLEO (CLEMENTINA DINAH DANKWORTH), singer; b. Southall, Middlesex, Eng., Oct. 28, 1927; d. Alexander and Minnie (Bullock) Campbell; m. George Langridge, 1947 (div.); m. John Philip William Dankworth, 1958; children: Stuart, Alec, Jackie. MA (hon.), Open U., 1975; MusD (hon.), Berklee Coll. Music, 1982. Vocalist Dankworth Orch., 1953-58; lead role in Seven Deadly Sins, Edinburgh, Scotland Festival and Sadlers Wells, 1961, in Showboat, 1972; acting roles Edinburgh Festival, 1966, 67, Colette, 1980; appeared in A Time to Laugh, Hedda Gabler, The Women of Troy, The Mystery of Edwin Drood, 1986 (Theatre World award nomination), Into the Woods, 1989 (L.A. Drama Critics award nomination); guest appearances symphony orchs. Eng. and abroad; numerous TV appearances and record albums; most recent albums That Old Feeling, 1985, Cleo Sings Sondheim, 1988, Woman to woman, 1989, Jazz, 1991, Nothing Without You (with Mel Torme), 1992, Smilin' Through (with Dudley Moore), 1992, Cleo at Carnegie, 1993, Born on Friday, 1993, A Beautiful Thing, 1994, Blue and Sentimental, 1994, Solitude (with John Dankworth), 1997; gold records: Feel the Warm, I'm a Song, Live at Melbourne; Platinum records: Best Friends, Sometimes When We Touch; author: Cleo, an autobiography, 1994. Decorated Order Brit. Empire, dame Order Brit. Empire; recipient Golden Feather award Los Angeles Times, 1973, Edison award, 1974, Grammy award for best female jazz vocal, 1985, Theatre World award, 1986; named Show Bus. Personality of Yr., Variety Club, 1977, Singer of Yr., TV Times, 1978; Tony nominee, 1986; recipient Theatre World award, 1986, Lifetime Achievement award N.A.R.M., 1990, Brit. Jazz award for best female vocalist, 1990. Office: care Sonoma-Hope Inc 179-9 Rte 46 W # 102 Rockaway NJ 07866 also: Gurtman and Murtha's Newsmakers 450 7th Ave Ste 603 New York NY 10123*

LAINE, ELAINE FRANCES, school system administrator; b. Huntington, Ind., July 25, 1951; d. Howard James and Frances Mary (Graft) Harold; m. Rudolph Lewis Laine, Oct. 26, 1975; 1 child, Christina Elaine. BA, Purdue U., 1973; MA, George Mason U., 1985, postgrad., 1996—; adminstrv. cert., U. Va., 1989. Cert. tchr. French, Spanish, middle and high sch. prin., Va. Foreign lang. tchr. Fairfax County Pub. Schs., Springfield, Va., 1981-85, Thomas Jefferson Sch. for Sci and Tech., Alexandria, Va., 1985-86; resource tchr. foreign langs. and ESL area IV adminstrv. offices Fairfax County Pub. Schs., Fairfax, Va., 1986-91; foreign lang. dept. chairperson Ormond Stone Sch. Fairfax County Pub. Schs., Centreville, Va., 1991-93; asst. prin. Cooper Mid. Sch. Fairfax County Pub. Schs., McLean, Va., 1993-96, Langley H.S., McLean, 1996—; mem. foreign lang. curriculum adv. bd. Fairfax Pub. Schs., Springfield, 1990-91, supt.'s adv. coun., 1991-93, chairperson foreign lang. dept. adv. coun., 1992-93, mem. fine arts curriculum adv. com., 1993-96, mem. lang. arts curriculum adv. com., 1995—; bd. Judges Columbia Scholastic Press Assn., 1992-93. Named Exemplary Tchr., Fairfax County Pub. Schs., Springfield, Va., 1988, '92, Outstanding Tchr., Fairfax County Sch. Bd., Springfield, 1992; recipient Medalist awards Columbia Scholastic Press Assn., N.Y.C., 1990, '91, Crown Nominee, 1991; invited speaker Annual Conv. Columbia Scholastic Press Assn., 1992. Mem. ASCD, Nat. Sch. Bd. Assn., Assn. Secondary Asst. Prins., Greater Washington Assn. of Tchrs. of Foreign Langs. (del. at large No. Va. 1983, '89. Disting. Educator 1985), Purdue Alumni Assn. Avocations: travel, gourmet cooking, piano, singing, hiking. Home: 12670 Still Pond Ln Herndon VA 20171-2226 Office: Fairfax County Pub Schs Langley High Sch 6520 Georgetown Pike Mc Lean VA 22101-2222

LAING, BEVERLY ANN, sports administrator; b. Newark, Mar. 13, 1959; d. Gustave Raymond Hicks and Gloria Mildred (Bellina) Hicks-Prestinari; m. James Thomas Laing Sr., Mar. 10, 1979; children: Christina Marie, James Thomas Jr. A degree, Lab. Inst. Merchandising, N.Y.C., 1979. Pension adminstr. Prudential Ins. Co., Florham Park, N.J., 1976-79; paralegal O'Donnell, Kennedy, Esqs., West Orange, N.J., 1986-90; mgr. women's adminstrn, rules and competitions dept. U.S. Golf Assn., Far Hills, N.J., 1991—; mem. steering com. Women in Golf Summits, LPGA Hdqs., Daytona Beach, Fla., 1996; mem. steering com. U.S. Women's Open, 1996—; mem. steering com. LPGA Girls' Jr. Clinic Program, 1997—. Vol. player registration Children's Miracle Network Golf Tournament, 1992. Recipient 1st pl. ribbon N.J. Ceramic Show, 1984. Mem. U.S. Golf Assn., Exec. Women's Golf League. Republican. Roman Catholic. Avocations: golf, hiking, sketching. Office: US Golf Assn Golf House Liberty Corner Rd Far Hills NJ 07931

LAING, DAVID, natural science educator; b. Hanover, N.H., Aug. 18, 1940; s. Alexander Kinnan and Dilys Anwyl (Bennett) L.; m. Lenore Jennifer Stewart, My 25, 1962 (div. 1981); children: Robin Maddox, Heather Edwards; m. Margaret Brenda Lecesne, May 4, 1986. BA, Dartmouth Coll., 1963; MA, Harvard U., 1972; postgrad., U. Ariz., 1973-76. Rsch. asst. Lab. of Tree Ring Rsch., Tucson, Ariz., 1974-76; exploration geologist Rosario Resources Corp., Tucson, 1976-77; dir. Environ. Land Surveys, Carbondale, Colo., 1978-80; asst. prof. in geology Ea. New Mex. U., Portales, 1981-83; environ. educator, ranger U.S. Forest Svc., Minturn, Colo., 1984-85; rsch. assoc. Mangrove Sys., Key Biscayne, Fla., 1985-86; asst. prof., instr. U. Maine Presque Isle, Ft. Kent, Maine, 1986-90; rsch. asst. Dartmouth Coll., Hanover, 1990-92; staff naturalist Killington Ltd., Killington, Vt., 1992—; lectr. in geomorphology Antioch NE Grad. Sch., Keene, N.H., 1996—. Author: Aspen High Country: The Geology, 1980, Pitt's Manual in Earth Science, 1982, The Earth System, 1991, The Nature of Killington, 1994. Mem. Hartford Conservation Commn., Hartford, Vt., 1993, Norwich (Vt.)Cons. Commn., 1996—. Mem. Geol. Soc. of Am., Vt. Geol. Soc. Avocations: nature, hiking, skiing, sailing, classical music, Chinese language, philosophy. Office: Killington Ltd Killington Rd Killington VT 05751

LAING, KAREL ANN, magazine publishing executive; b. Mpls., July 5, 1939; d. Edward Francis and Elizabeth Jane Karel (Templeton) Hannon; m. G. R. Cheesebrough, Dec. 19, 1959 (div. 1969); 1 child, Jennifer Read; m. Ronald Harris Laing, Jan. 6, 1973; 1 child, Christopher Harris. Grad., U. Minn., 1960. With Guthrie Symphony Opera Program, Mpls.,, 1969-71; account supr. Colle & McVoy Advt. Agy., Richfield, Minn., 1971-74; owner The Cottage, Edina, Minn., 1974-75; salespromotion rep. Robert Meyers & Assocs., St. Louis Park, Minn., 1975-76; cons. Webb Co., St. Paul, 1976-77, custom pub. dir., 1977-89; pres. K.L. Publs., Inc., Bloomington, Minn., 1989—. Contbr. articles to profl. jours. Community vol. Am. Heart Assn., Am. Cancer Soc., Edina PTA; charter sponsor Walk Around Am., St. Paul, 1985. Mem. Bank Mktg. Assn., Fin. Instn. Mktg. Assn., Advt. Fedn. Am., Am. Bankers Assn., Direct Mail Mktg. Assn., St. Andrews Soc. Republican. Presbyterian. Avocations: painting; gardening; reading; traveling. Office: KL Publs 2001 Killebrew Dr Minneapolis MN 55425-1865

LAING, PENELOPE GAMBLE, art educator; b. Dallas, July 24, 1944; d. William Oscar and Beth (Robertson) G.; m. Richard Harlow Laing, June 29, 1970; children: Scott Emerson, Lindsey Elizabeth. BA in Art, N. Tex. State U., 1966; MFA, Edinboro State Coll., 1979. Cert. tchr., Tex. (life), N.C. (Art all-level). Art cons. Lawrence (Kans.) Unified Sch. Dist., 1966-68; instr. art Ball State U., Muncie, Ind., 1969-71, Edinboro (Pa.) State U., 1976-77, Pitt C.C., Greenville, N.C., 1980-83; exec. dir. Pitt-Greenville Arts Coun., Greenville, 1983-84; free-lance designer, 1984-90; art tchr., head dept. art Pitt County Schs., 1990—; seminar participant N.C. Ctr. for Advancement of Teaching, 1993, tchr.-scholar, 1994, 95. Bd. dirs., v.p. Pitt-Greenville Arts Coun., 1979-82; mem. adv. bd. Pitt County Schs., Greenville, 1985-87; pres. PTA S. Greenville Sch., 1986-87. Tchr. Exec. Inst. fellow Pitts County Edn. Found., Greenville, 1992, N.C. Prin. fellow, 1997; grantee Pitt County Edn. Found., 1991-93. Mem. Nat. Art Edn. Assn., N.C. Art Edn. Assn. (bd. dirs., chmn. elem. divsn. 1992-94), Surface Design Assocs. (southeastern rep.), Phi Delta Kappa. Democrat. Avocations: travel, reading. Home: 204 Pineview Dr Greenville NC 27834-6434 Office: 1325 Red Banks Rd Greenville NC 27858-5315

LAINGEN, LOWELL BRUCE, diplomat; b. Odin Twp., Minn., Aug. 6, 1922; s. Palmer K. and Ida Mabel (Eng) L.; m. Penelope Babcock, June 1, 1957; children: William Bruce, Charles Winslow, James Palmer. B.A. cum laude, St. Olaf Coll., 1947; M.A. in Internat. Relations, U. Minn., 1949. Internat. rels. officer State Dept., 1949-50; joined U.S. Fgn. Svc., 1950; vice consul Hamburg, Germany, 1951-53; 3d sec. embassy Teheran, Iran, 1953-54; consul Meshed, Iran, 1954-55; asst., then officer chargé Greek affairs State Dept., 1956-60; 2d sec., then 1st sec. embassy Karachi, Pakistan, 1960-64; with Pakistan/Afghanistan affairs bur. State Dept., 1964-67; assigned Nat. War Coll., 1967-68; dep. chief mission to Afghanistan Kabul, 1968-71; country dir. Pakistan, Afghanistan and Bangladesh; country dir. State Dept., 1971-73, India, Nepal, Sri Lanka and the Maldives, 1973-74; acting dep. asst. sec. state for Near Eastern and South Asian affairs State Dept., 1974-75, dep. asst. sec. state for European affairs, 1975-76; ambassador to Malta, 1977-79; chargé d'affaires Am. Embassy, Teheran, Iran, 1979; held hostage by Iranian student militants, 1979-81; v.p. Nat. Def. U., Ft. McNair, Washington, 1981-86; exec. dir. Nat. Commn. Pub. Service, Washington, 1987-90; pres. Am. Acad. Diplomacy, 1991—. Home: 5627 Old Chester Rd Bethesda MD 20814-1035

LAIOU, ANGELIKI EVANGELOS, history educator; b. Athens, Greece, Apr. 6, 1941; came to U.S., 1959; d. Evangelos K. and Virginia I. (Apostolides) Laios; m. Stavros B. Thomadakis, July 14, 1973; 1 son, Vassili N. B.A., Brandeis U., 1961; M.A., Harvard U., 1962, Ph.D., 1966. Asst. prof. history Harvard U., Cambridge, Mass., 1969-72, Dumbarton Oaks prof. Byzantine history, 1981—; assoc. prof. Brandeis U., Waltham, 1972-75; prof. Rutgers U., New Brunswick, N.J.., 1975-79, disting. prof., 1979-81; chmn. Gennadeion com. (Am. Sch. Classical Studies), Athens, Greece, 1981-84; dir. Dumbarton Oaks, 1989—. Author: Constantinople and the Latins, 1972, Peasant Society in the Late Byzantine Empire, 1977, Mariage, amour et parenté à Byznace, XIe-XIIIe siècles, 1992, Gender, Society and Economic Life in Byzantium, 1992, Consent and Coercion to Sex and Marriage in Ancient and Medieval Societies, 1993. Guggenheim Found. fellow, 1971-72, 79-80, Dumbarton Oaks sr. fellow, 1983-88, Am. Coùn. Learned Socs. fellow, 1988-89. Fellow Am. Acad. Arts and Scis., Medieval Acad.; mem. Am. Hist. Assn., Medieval Acad. Am., Societa Ligure di Storia Patria, Greek Com. Study of South Eastern Europe. Office: Dumbarton Oaks 1703 32nd St NW Washington DC 20007-2934

LAIR, ROBERT LOUIS, catering company executive; b. Albuquerque, Aug. 13, 1921; s. Louis E. and Inez B. (Mudd) L.; m. June Marie Moran, Aug. 9, 1941 (dec. Apr. 1983); children—Christopher Louis, Catherine Ann, Cynthia Susan; m. Therese C. Kronkowski, Sept. 15, 1984. With Boeing Airplane Co., 1940-53, dir. sub-contract adminstrn. USN, 1944-46, supr. materiel, 1947-53; with Cessna Aircraft Co., Wichita, Kans., 1953-83, sr. v.p., dir., 1969-83; chmn. bd. Precision Composites, Inc., 1984-87; co-owner Tee-C's Catering, 1987—. Bd. dirs. Jr. Achievement Wichita. Mem. Falstaff

Soc., Food and Wine Soc. Wichita, Wichita Country Club, Rotary. Home: 105 N Woodlawn Ct Wichita KS 67218-1838

LAIRD, BRADLEY DUANE, social services administrator, psychotherapist; b. Oakland, Calif., Feb. 5, 1956; s. Duane Richard and Eunice Delphine (Glock) L.; m. Elizabeth Lorraine Hughson, Aug. 3, 1985; children: Cameron James, Rhiannon Elizabeth, Quinn Campbell. AA, Concordia Luth. Coll., 1976; BS in Psychology, Valparaiso (Ind.) U., 1978; MSW, Loyola U., 1986; student, Ctr. Psychoanalytic Study, Chgo., 1993—. Psychiat. technician Porter-Starke Svcs., Inc., Valparaiso, 1978-81; staff therapist II Tri-City Community Mental Health Ctr., East Chicago, Ind., 1981-83, staff therapist IV, 1983-86, program supr., 1986-88, svc. dir., 1988-90; intern U. Chgo. Hosps., 1985-86; pvt. practice psychotherapist Merrillville, Ind., 1989-91; div. dir. Habilitative Systems, Inc., Chgo., 1990-91; assoc. dir. Children's Campus Family and Children's Ctr., Mishawaka, Ind., 1991-95; exec. dir. Family Svc. Assn. LaPorte County, Inc., Michigan City, Ind., 1995—. Gen. mem. Miller and Gary Citizens Corp., 1984-91—, bd. dirs., treas., 1986-88; bd. dirs. Neighborhood Housing Svcs. of South Bend, 1993—; bd. trustees First Unitarian Ch. of South Bend, 1994-97, v.p., 1995, 96, pres. 1996-97. Mem. NASW, Nat. Fedn. Socs. for Clin. Social Work, Am. Group Psychotherapy Assn., Am. Soc. Quality Control. Avocations: hiking, camping, fishing, reading, gardening.

LAIRD, CHARLES DAVID, zoology and genetics educator, researcher; b. Portland, Oreg., May 12, 1939; s. Charles Bruce and Mary (Gray) L.; m. Judith Helen Shepherd; children: Michael, John, Andrew, Jennifer. BA, U. Oreg., 1961; postgrad., U. Zürich, Switzerland, 1961-62; PhD, Stanford U., 1966. Postdoctoral fellow in microbiology and genetics U. Wash., Seattle, 1966-68, assoc. prof. zoology, 1971-74, prof., 1975—, chmn. dept., 1985-89, adj. prof. genetics, 1975—, rsch. affiliate Child Devel. and Mental Retardation Ctr., 1988—; mem. Fred Hutchinson Cancer Rsch. Ctr., 1990—; asst. prof. zoology U. Tex., Austin, 1968-71. Contbr. articles to profl. jours. Recipient Career Devel. award NIH, 1969; fellow NSF, 1962, NIH, 1966. Fellow AAAS; mem. Genetic Soc. Am. Office: Fred Hutchinson Cancer Rsch Ctr 1124 Columbia St Seattle WA 98104-2015

LAIRD, DAVID, humanities educator emeritus; b. Marshfield, Wis., Oct. 17, 1927; s. Melvin Robert and Helen Melissa (Connor) L.; m. Helen Astrid Lauritzen, Sept. 10, 1955; 1 child, Vanessa Ann. PhB, U. Chgo., 1947; BA with highest honor, U. Wis., 1950, MA, 1951, PhD, 1955; postgrad., Courtauld Inst., 1953. Instr. to asst. prof. Oberlin Coll., 1955-58; mem. faculty Calif. State U., L.A., 1958—; chmn. dept. English Calif. State U., 1969-73, chmn. dept. Am. studies, 1977-79; Nat. Humanities Inst. fellow U. Chgo., 1978-79; sr. Fulbright lectr. U. Tunis, Tunisia, 1979-80; fellow Folger Shakespeare Libr., 1982; Fulbright lectr. Odense U. (Denmark), 1983-84; vis. prof. U. Ottawa, 1984-85; cons. to Choice. Mem. editorial bd. Jour. Forest History; contbr. articles on Shakespeare, Am. lit. and cultural history to profl. jours. Mem. Western Shakespeare Seminar, Friends of Huntington Libr. Recipient Outstanding Prof. award Calif. State U., 1987, Nat. Endowment for the Humanities Summer Seminar award Northwestern U., 1989; Uhrig Found. grantee, 1964-65; Fulbright fellow, 1953-54. Mem. MLA, Malone Soc., Am. Studies Assn., Phi Beta Kappa. Home: 208 S Cherry Ave Marshfield WI 54449-3732 Office: Humanities Dept Calif State U Los Angeles CA 90032

LAIRD, JEAN ELOUISE RYDESKI (MRS. JACK E. LAIRD), author, adult education educator; b. Wakefield, Mich., Jan. 18, 1930; d. Chester A. and Agnes A. (Petranek) Rydeski; m. Jack E. Laird, June 9, 1951; children: John E., Jayne E., Joan Ann P., Jerilyn S., Jacquelyn T. Bus. Edn. degree Duluth (Minn.) Bus. U., 1948; posgrad. U. Minn., 1949-50. Tchr. Oak Lawn (Ill.) High Sch. Adult Evening Sch., 1964-72, St. Xavier Coll., Chgo., 1974—; lectr., commencement address cir. Writer newspaper column Around The House With Jean, A Woman's Work, 1965-70, Chicagotown News column The World As I See It, 1969, hobby column Modern Maturity mag., travel column Travel/Leisure mag., beauty column Ladycom mag., Time and Money Savers column Lady's Circle mag., consumerism column Ladies' Home Jour. Mem. Canterbury Writers Club Chgo. (past. pres.), Oak Lawn Bus. and Profl. Women's Club (Woman of Yr. award 1987), St. Linus Guild, Mt. Assisi Acad., Marist, Queen of Peace parents clubs. Roman Catholic. Author: Lost in the Department Store, 1964; Around The House Like Magic, 1968; Around The Kitchen Like Magic, 1969; How To Get the Most From Your Appliances, 1967; Hundreds of Hints for Harrassed Homemakers, 1971; The Alphabet Zoo, 1972; The Plump Ballerina, 1971; The Porcupine Story Book, 1974; Fried Marbles and Other Fun Things To Do, 1975; Hundreds of Hints for Harassed Homemakers; The Homemaker's Book of Time and Money Savers, 1979; Homemaker's Book of Energy Savers, 1981; also 348 paperback booklets. Contbr. numerous articles to mags. Home: 10540 Lockwood Ave Oak Lawn IL 60453-5161 also: 1 Magnificent Mile Bldg Chicago IL 60600 also: Vista De Lago Lake Geneva WI 53147

LAIRD, JERE DON, news reporter; b. Topeka, Aug. 8, 1933; s. Gerald Howard and Vivian Gertrude (Webb) L.; m. Alexandra Berezowsky, Aug. 4, 1957; children: Lee, Jennifer, Christopher. BA in Journalism, U. Nev., 1960. Disc jockey Sta. KHBC Radio, Hilo, Hawaii, 1949-50; announcer, chief engr. Sta. KOLO Radio, Reno, Nev., 1951-58; program dir. Sta. KOLO-TV, Reno, 1958-60; news reporter Sta. KCRA Radio and TV, Sacramento, Calif., 1960-61, Sta. KRLA Radio, L.A., 1962-63; news reporter, editor Sta. KNXT-TV, L.A., 1964-68; news reporter, fin. editor Sta. KNX-CBS Radio, L.A., 1968—; fin. reporter Sta. KCBS-TV, L.A., 1990—; lectr. U. So. Calif., L.A., 1984-85; instr. Calif. State U., Northridge, 1978-79. Cpl. U.S. Army, 1953-55. Recipient Emmy award, L.A., 1964, Peabody award, U. Ga., 1984, Best Bus. News award, L.A. Press Club, 1983, 84, 86, 87, 88, 89, Martin K. Gainsburgh award, Fiscal Policy Coun., Fla., 1978. Mem. Radio TV News Assn. (bd. dirs. 1966-68, Golden Mike award 1984), Sigma Delta Chi. Avocation: sailing. Office: Sta KNX-CBS 6121 W Sunset Blvd Los Angeles CA 90028-6423

LAIRD, MARY See **WOOD, LARRY**

LAIRD, MELVIN ROBERT, former secretary of defense; b. Omaha, Sept. 1, 1922; s. Melvin R. and Helen (Connor) L.; m. Barbara Masters (dec. Jan. 1992); children: John, Alison, David; m. Carole Howard. B.A., Carleton Coll., 1942; LHD (hon.), Lincoln Coll., Ill., 1971; D Polit. Sci. (hon.), U. Pacific, 1968; HHD (hon.), St. Leo's Coll., 1969; LLD (hon.), U. Wis., 1982. Mem. Wis. Senate, 1946-52; chmn. Wis. Legis. Council; mem. 83d-91st Congresses; mem. Rep. Coordinating com. 83d-90th Congresses; sec. of def., 1969-73; dir., sr. counsellor nat. and internat. affairs Pres. Nixon, 1973-74; sr. counsellor nat. and internat. affairs Reader's Digest Assn., 1974—; bd. dirs., dirs. adv. bd. Met. Life Ins. Co.; bd. dirs. IDS Mut. Fund Group, Sci. Applications Internat., Inc., Reader's Digest, Lila Wallace-Reader's Digest Fund Bd., DeWitt Wallace-Reader's Digest Fund Bd.; bd. dirs. pub. oversight bd. SEC practice sect. AICPA. Author: A House Divided: America's Strategy Gap, 1962; Editor: The Conservative Papers, 1964, Republican Papers, 1968. Bd. dirs. World Rehab. Fund, Boys Clubs Am., George Washington U., Airlie Found., Laird Youth Leadership Found., Pres.'s Reagan Moscow Assessment Rev. Panel, 1987; trustee Kennedy Center; chmn. Nat. Election Commn., 1986; co-chmn. platform com. Rep. Nat. Conv., 1960, chmn., 1964. Decorated Order of Merit 1st class Fed. Republic Germany; comdr. Nat. Order Legion of Honor, France; recipient 15th Ann. Albert Lasker med. award; Man of Year award Am. Cancer Soc.-Nat. Assn. Mental Health; Humanitarian award John E. Fogarty Found. for Mentally Retarded, 1974; Presdl. Medal of Freedom, 1974, Harry S. Truman award, 1985. Mem. Mil. Order Purple Heart, 40 and 8, Am. Legion, VFW, DAV. Presbyterian (elder). Clubs: Burning Tree, Augusta Nat. Golf. Lodge: Masons. Office: 1730 Rhode Island Ave NW Ste 212 Washington DC 20036

LAIRD, ROBERT WINSLOW, journalist; b. Chgo., Sept. 25, 1936; s. Robert Winslow and Evelyn (Emerson) L.; m. Marsa Radbill, Dec. 1, 1962; children—Michael Winslow, Joshua Radbill. B.A., Yale U., 1959. Reporter World Telegram and Sun, N.Y.C., 1963-66; dep. press. sec. to Mayor John Lindsay N.Y.C., 1966-73; press sec. to Gov. Hugh Carey Albany, N.Y., 1974-76; opinions editor, weekly columnist Daily News, N.Y.C., 1977—. Vol. Peace Corps, Gebileh, Somalia, 1962-63; chmn. schs. com. Yale U Alumni, 1979-84. Recipient Editorial Writing award N.Y.C. Citizens Housing and Planning Coun., 1987; co-recipient Editorial Excellence award Nat. Assn. Edn. Writers, 1989. Mem. U.S. Paddle Tennis Assn. (bd. dirs. 1978-82, 87—). Avocations: tennis; paddle tennis. Home: 17 Stuyvesant Oval New York NY 10009-1920 Office: NY Daily News 450 E 33rd St Fl 3 New York NY 10016

LAIRD, ROY DEAN, political science educator; b. Blue Hill, Nebr., July 15, 1925. B.A. in Biology, Hastings Coll., 1947; M.A. in Polit. Sci, U. Nebr., 1952; postgrad., U. Glasgow, Scotland, 1952-53; Ph.D., U. Wash., 1956. Research analyst CIA, Washington, 1956-57; asst. prof. polit. sci. U. Kans., Lawrence, 1957-62; assoc. prof. U. Kans., 1962-66, prof. polit. sci. and Soviet and Eastern European area studies, 1966-90, prof. emeritus, 1990—; cons. Spl. Ops. Research Office, Washington, 1960; guest researcher Inst. for Study of USSR, Munich, W. Ger., 1963-64; founder Internat. Conf. on Soviet and East European Agriculture, 1962. Author: Collective Farming in Russia, 1958, (with Betty A. Laird) Soviet Communism and Agrarian Revolution, 1958, The Soviet Paradigm: An Experiment in Creating a Monohierarchial Polity, 1970, To Live Long Enough: The Memoirs of Naum Jasny, Scientific Analysis, 1976; editor: (with Betty A. Laird) Soviet Agricultural and Peasant Affairs, 1963, The Future of Agriculture in the Soviet Union and Eastern Europe, 1977, (with Ronald A. Francisco and Betty A. Laird) The Political Economy of Collectivized Agriculture, 1979; author: (with Ronald A. Francisco and Betty A. Laird) The Politburo: Demographic Trend, Gorbachev and the Future, 1986, A Soviet Lexicon: Important Terms Concepts and Phrases, 1988, The Soviet Legacy, 1993; contbr. chpts. to books, articles to profl. jours. Rockefeller Found. fellow, 1963-64; NSF grantee, 1966, 67-68; NDEA-Fulbright Hays fellow, 1967; NASA grantee, 1971-72. Mem. AAUP, Am. Assn. Advancement of Slavic Studies, Cen. Slavic Assn., Conf. Soviet Agrl. and Peasant Studies (founder), Am. Polit. Sic. Assn., Western Slavic Studies Assn., Western Slavic Conf. (v.p. 1975-76), Kans. Polit. Sci. Assn., Midwest Conf. Slavic Studies, Midwest Polit. Sci. Assn. Office: U Kans Dept Polit Sci Blake Hall Lawrence KS 66045

LAIRD, WALTER JONES, JR., investment professional; b. Phila., June 15, 1926; s. Walter Jones and Rebecca (Sedberry) L.; m. Antonia Valerie Bissell, Nov. 24, 1951; children: David E., William Ian, Philip L., Walter J. III, Emily B., Stephen P. BS, Princeton U., 1948; MSCE, M.I.T., 1950. Mgr. bldg. product sales E.I. duPont de Nemours, Wilmington, Del., 1951-68; exec. v.p. Laird, Bissell and Meeds, Wilmington, 1968-73; sr. v.p. Dean Witter Reynolds, Wilmington, 1973—; bd. dirs. Del. Trust Co., Wilmington, Meridian Asset Mgmt., Wentz Corp., Sinkler Corp. Trustee Winterthur Mus. and Gardens, 1969—, chmn., 1988-94, chmn. emeritus, 1994—; trustee St. Andrews Sch., Middletown, Del., 1967-92. Mem. Fin. Analysts Fedn., Wilmington Club (bd. govs. 1978—), Wilmington Country Club (v.p. 1995—), Ocean Forest Golf Club, Grand Senechal Chevaliers du Tastevin, Soc. Colonial Wars (gov. 1993—). Avocations: golf, skiing. Home: 1202 Stockford Rd Chadds Ford PA 19317-9349 Office: Dean Witter Reynolds Inc PO Box 749 Wilmington DE 19899-0749

LAIRD, WILBUR DAVID, JR., bookseller, editor; b. Kansas City, Mo., Mar. 15, 1937; s. Wilbur David and Alma Blanche (Turner) L.; children: Wendy, Cynthia, Brian Andrew, David Alexander; m. Helen M. Ingram, July 12, 1984. Student, U. Wichita, 1959-60; BA, UCLA, 1965, MLS, 1966. Reference libr. U. Calif., Davis, 1966-67; acquisitions libr. U. Utah, 1967-70, asst. dir. for tech. svcs., 1970-71, assoc. dir., 1971-72; univ. libr. U. Ariz., Tucson, 1972-90; pres. Books West S.W., Tucson, 1990—. Author: Hopi Bibliography, 1977; editor: Books of the Southwest, 1977-97. Bd. dirs. Westerners Internat., 1974-87, Tucson Civic Ballet, 1975-76, S.W. Pks. and Mon. Assn., 1993—. With USN, 1955-59. Mem. ALA, Ariz. State Libr. Assn. (pres. 1978-79), Western History Assn., Western Lit. Assn., Guild Ariz. Antiquarian Booksellers. Office: Books West Southwest Inc 14 Whitman Ct Irvine CA 92612-4056

LAIRD, WILLIAM EVERETTE, JR., economics educator, administrator; b. Hattiesburg, Miss., Feb. 4, 1934; s. William Everette and Mildred Alva (Howard) L.; m. Doris Anne Marley, Mar. 13, 1964; children: William Everette III, Andrew Marley, Glen Howard. B.S., Stetson U., 1956; M.A., George Washington U., 1958; Ph.D., U. Va., 1962. Asst. prof. Fla. State U., Tallahassee, 1960-66, assoc. prof., 1966-71, prof., 1971—; chmn. dept. econs. Fla State U., Tallahassee, 1974—. Contbr. articles to profl. jours. DuPont fellow, 1959-60; recipient awards Fla. State U. Grad. Research Council, 1965, 66, Faculty Devel. awards Fla. State U., 1971. Mem. Am. Econs. Assn., So. Econ. Assn. Methodist. Clubs: Magna Charta Barons, Jamestowne Soc., St. Andrew Soc., Order of First Families of Va. Home: 1125 Mercer Dr Tallahassee FL 32312-2833 Office: Fla State U Dept Econs Tallahassee FL 32306

LAIRES, FERNANDO, concert piano educator; b. Lisbon, Portugal, Jan. 3, 1925; came to U.S., 1956; s. Joaquim Augusto and Clementina (Belfo) L.; m. Nelita True, Dec. 24, 1971. Artist diploma, Nat. Conservatory Music, Lisbon, 1945. Prof. piano Nat. Conservatory Music, Lisbon, 1949-56; asst. prof. U. Tex., Austin, 1956-61; artist-in-residence, prof. piano Okla. Coll. Liberal Arts, Chickasha, 1961-68; artist-in-residence, chmn. piano dept. Interlochen (Mich.) Arts Acad., Interlochen, 1968-72; prof. piano Peabody Conservatory, Balt., 1972-87; adj. prof. piano Cath. U. Am., Washington, 1978-92; artist faculty Eastman Sch. Music, Rochester, N.Y., 1992-95; permanent guest prof. piano performance Shenyang (People's Republic of China) Conservatory of Music, 1989—; juror Tchaikowsky Internat. Piano Competition, Moscow, 1982, Van Cliburn Internat. Piano Competition, Ft. Worth, 1973, Gina Bachauer Internat. Piano Competition, Salt Lake City, 1978, 80, U. Md. Internat. Piano Competition, College Park, 1975, 77, 86, Franz Liszt Internat. Piano Competition, Budapest, 1996; dir. U. Md. Internat. Piano Festival, 1979-81. Performed in cycle the 32 piano sonatas of Beethoven, 1944; dir.-founder 20-record Anthology Portuguese classical music, 1972-82; co-founder Pro-Arte Concert Soc., Portugal, 1949, The Am. Liszt Soc., 1964; contbr. articles to Clavier, The Piano Quar., Am. Music Tchr. Decorated comdr. Order of Price Henry the Navigator (Portugal); recipient Beethoven medal Harriet Cohen Internat. Music Awards, London, 1956, Franz Liszt medal Liszt Soc. Hungary, Budapest, 1984, Liszt medal for excellence Am. Liszt Soc., Inc., 1985, Liszt Commemorative medal Hungarian People's Republic, 1986. Mem. European Piano Tchrs. Assn., Am. Liszt Soc., Inc. (pres. 1976-85, 89—), Music Tchrs. Nat. Assn., Am. Liszt Soc. (pres.). Avocations: travel, reading, writing. Home: 210 Devonshire Dr Rochester NY 14625-1905

LAITIN, DAVID DENNIS, political science educator; b. Bklyn., June 4, 1945; s. Daniel and Frances (Blumenkranz) L.; m. Delia Fortune; children: Marc Oliver, Anna Elizabeth. BA, Swarthmore Coll., 1967; PhD, U. Calif., Berkeley, 1974. Instr. Nat. Tchr. Edn. Ctr., Afgoy, Somalia, 1969; master Grenada Boys' Secondary Sch., West Indies, 1970-71; asst. prof. dept. polit. sci. U. Calif.-San Diego, La Jolla, 1975-79, prof., 1984-87, chmn., 1986-87; reader dept. polit. sci. U. Ife, Nigeria, 1979-80; prof. polit. sci., dir. Wilder House Ctr. for Study Politics, History and Culture U. Chgo., 1987—, William R. Kenan, Jr. prof., 1992—; expert witness fgn. affairs subcom. U.S. Ho. Reps., 1981; resident Rockefeller Found., Bellagio Ctr., Sept. 1996. Author: Politics, Language and Thought: The Somali Expeirence, 1977, Hegemony and Culture: Politics and Religious Change Among the Yoruba, 1986, Somalia: A Nation in Search of a State, 1987, Language Repertoires and State Construction in Africa, 1992. Fellow NEH, 1979-80, Howard Found., 1984-85, German Marshall Fund, 1984-85, John Simon Guggenheim Found., 1995-96; co-prin. investigator award NSF, 1993-95. Mem. Am. Polit. Sci. Assn., Am. Acad. Arts and Scis., Coun. Am. Polit. Sci. Assn. Office: U Chgo Dept Of Polit Sci Chicago IL 60637

LAITIN, JOSEPH, journalist, former government spokesman and public relations consultant; b. Bklyn., Oct. 2, 1914; s. Harry and Irene (Lubetkin) L.; m. Christine Henriette Houdayer (dec. Apr. 5, 1995), Apr. 26, 1961; children: Sigrid, Peter. Corr. United Press, Washington, 1941-45; fgn. corr. Reuters, Far East, Europe, Latin Am., 1945-50; chief corr. Research Inst. Am., Washington, 1950-52; freelance writer and broadcaster Hollywood, Calif., 1952-63; asst. to dir. Bur. of Budget, Washington, 1963-64; dep. press sec. to Pres. The White House, Washington, 1965-66; asst. to dir. for pub. affairs Office Mgmt. and Budget, Washington, 1966-74; asst. sec. pub. affairs Dept. Def., Washington, 1974-75; asst. adminstr. FAA, Washington, 1975-77; asst. sec. treasury U.S. Dept. Treasury, Washington, 1977-81; pvt. cons. govt. and pub. rels. Washington; advisor Hill & Knowlton, 1981-85; ombudsman Washington Post, 1986-88; sr. cons. Fleishman-Hillard, Inc., 1989-93; instr. Art Ctr. Sch. L.A., 1952-63, George Washington U., Washington, 1987; cons. Commn. on Selective Svc., 1966-67, Nat. Commn. on Causes and Prevention of Violence, 1968-70, Presdl. Commn. on Campus Unrest, 1970, Nat. Commn. on Exec., Legis. and Jud. Salaries, 1989, Paul Volcker Commn. on Pub. Svc., 1988-89; fellow media studies project Woodrow Wilson Ctr., 1990; mem. regional selection com. White House Fellows Program, 1994—. Recipient Calif. State Fair award for best radio documentary CBS The Changing Face of Hollywood, 1957; Disting. Public Service medal Dept. Def., 1975.

LAITONE, EDMUND VICTOR, mechanical engineer; b. San Francisco, Sept. 6, 1915; s. Victor S. L.; m. Dorothy Bishop, Sept. 1, 1951; children: Victoria, Jonathan A. BSME, U. Calif., Berkeley, 1938; PhD in Applied Mechanics, Stanford U., 1960. Aero. engr. Nat. Adv. Com. for Aeros., Langley Field, Va., 1938-45; sect. head, flight engr. Cornell Aero. Lab., Buffalo, 1945-47; prof. U. Calif., Berkeley, 1947—; cons. aero. engr. Hughes Aircraft & Douglas Aircraft, 1948-78; U.S. acad. rep. to flight mechanics AGARD/NATO, 1984-88; chmn. engring. dept. U. Calif. Extension, Berkeley, 1979-96. Author: Surface Waves, 1960; author, editor: Integrated Design of Advanced Fighter Aircraft, 1987; contbr. articles to Jour. Aero. Scis., Aircraft and Math. Jour. Named Miller Rsch. prof., 1960, U.S. Exch. prof., Moscow, 1964; vis. fellow Balliol Coll., 1968; vis. prof. Northwestern Poly. Inst., Xian, China, 1980. Fellow AIAA (San Francisco region chmn. 1960-61, assoc. fellow 1964-88); mem. Am. Math Soc., Am. Soc. for Engring. Edn. Achievements include discovery of effect of acceleration on longitudinal dynamic stability of a missile; nonlinear dynamic stability of space vehicles entering or leaving atmosphere; higher approximations to nonlinear water waves. Home: 6915 Wilson Way El Cerrito CA 94530-1853 Office: U of Calif Dept Mech Engring Berkeley CA 94720

LAJEUNESSE, MARCEL, university administrator, educator; b. Mont-Laurier, Que., Can., June 28, 1942; s. Achille and Gertrude (Grenier) L.; m. Louise Beauregard, Dec. 20, 1975; 1 child, Anne. BA, U. Laval, Que., Can., 1964; B. Bibliotheconomie, U. de Montreal, Que., Can., 1964, Licence ès Lettres, 1967, MA, 1968; PhD, U. Ottawa, Can., 1977. Prof. Coll. L'Outaouais, Hull, 1968-70, U. de Montreal, 1970—; prof., dir. Grad. Sch. Libr. and Info. Sci., 1987-94, assoc. dean for planning Faculty of Arts and Scis., 1994—; cons. Aupelf UREF, IDRC, Can. Internat. Devel. Agy., Agence de cooperation culturelle et technique, UNESCO. Author, co-author 17 books; contbr. numerous articles to profl. and scholarly jours. Mem. Conseil de la Langue Française, Que., 1987-91.—. Mem. Assn. Libr. and Info. Sci. Edn., Assn. Internat. des Écoles de Scis. de l'Information, Assn. pour l'Avancement des Scis. et des Techniques de la Documentation, Corp. des Bibliothécaires professionnels de Québec, Inst. French Am. History, Bibliog. Soc. Can. Home: 126 Dobie, Mont-Royal, PQ Canada H3P 1S4 Office: FAS-Direction, U de Montreal, CP 6128 Succ A, Montreal, PQ Canada H3C 3J7

LAJOIE, ROLAND, army officer; b. Nashua, N.H., Aug. 11, 1936; s. Ernest Joseph and Alice (Bechard) L.; m. Joann Theresa Sinibaldi, Feb. 11, 1961; children: Michelle, Christopher, Renee. BA in Govt., U. N.H., 1958; MA in History, U. Colo., 1971; diploma, Army Command & Staff Coll., 1973, U.S. Army War Coll., 1981. Commd. 2d lt. U.S. Army, 1958, advanced through grades to maj. gen., 1991; served as asst. army attache Am. Embassy, Moscow, 1973-76; commandant U.S. Army Russian Inst., Garmisch, Fed. Republic Germany, 1976-79; bn. comdr. 1st Psychol. Ops. Bn., Ft. Bragg, N.C., 1979-80; rsch. fellow U.S. Army War Coll., Carlisle, Pa., 1980-81, Harvard U., Cambridge, Mass., 1980-81; army attache Am. Embassy, Moscow, 1981-83; chief of mission U.S. Mil. Liaison Mission, Berlin, Potsdam, German Dem. Republic, 1983-86; def. and army attache Am. Embassy, Paris, 1986-88; dir. U.S. On-Site Inspection Agy., 1988-91; dep. dir. internat. negotiations J5 The Joint Staff, Washington, 1991-92; assoc. dep. dir. for ops./mil. affairs CIA, Washington, 1992-94, dep. asst. to sec. of def., 1994—. Decorated Nat. Intel Disting. Svc. medal, Def. Disting. Svc. medal, Bronze Star, Legion of Merit, Def. Meritorious Svc., Def. Superior Svc., Nat. Order Merit (France). Mem. VFW, Retired Officer Assn. Avocations: tennis, skiing. Home: 3727 Riverwood Rd Alexandria VA 22309-2724

LAKAH, JACQUELINE RABBAT, political scientist, educator; b. Cairo, Apr. 14, 1933; came to U.S., 1969, naturalized, 1975; d. Victor Boutros and Alice (Mounayer) Rabbat; m. Antoine K. Lakah, Apr. 8, 1951; children: Micheline, Mireille, Caroline. BA, Am. U. Beirut, 1968; MPh, Columbia U., 1974, cert. Mid. East Inst., 1975, PhD, 1978. Assoc. prof. polit. sci. and world affairs Fashion Inst. Tech., N.Y.C., 1978—, asst. chairperson social scis. dept., 1989-95, chairperson social scis. dept., 1995-97; asst. prof. grad. faculty polit. sci. Columbia U., N.Y.C., summer 1979, vis. scholar, 1982-83, also mem. seminar on Mid. East; guest faculty Sarah Lawrence Coll., 1981-82; cons. on Mid. East; faculty rsch. fellow SUNY, summer 1982. Fellow Columbia Faculty, 1970-73, NDEA Title IV, 1971-72; Mid. East Inst. scholar, 1976; Rockefeller Found. scholar, 1967-69. Mem. European Cmty. Studies Assn., Am. Polit. Sci. Assn., Fgn. Policy Assn., Internat. Studies Assn., Internat. Polit. Sci. Assn. Roman Catholic. Home: 41-15 94th St Flushing NY 11373-1745 Office: 7th Ave At 27th St New York NY 10001-5992

LAKATTA, EDWARD GERARD, biomedical researcher; b. Scranton, Pa., May 10, 1944; s. Edward and Pauline Ann (Lucas) L.; m. Loretta Ellen Cantwell, July 27, 1968; children: Edward A., Christiana, Lucas A. BS in Biology, U. Scranton, 1966; MD, Georgetown U., 1970. Intern Strong Meml. Hosp., Rochester, N.Y., 1970-71, asst. resident, 1971-72; clin. assoc. Gerontology Rsch. Ctr. cardiovascular sect. NIH, Nat. Inst. Child Health & Human Devel., Clin. Physiology Br., Balt., 1972-74; asst. in medicine Johns Hopkins Sch. Medicine, Balt., 1973-74; fellow in cardiology Georgetown U. Hosp., Washington, 1974-75; fellow in med. sci. Am. Coll. Physicians for 1975 dept. physiology Univ. Coll., London, 1975-76; fellow in med. sci. dept. cardiac medicine Cardiothoracic Inst., London, 1975-76; chief cardiovascular sect. clin. physiology br. Gerontology Rsch. Ctr., Nat. Inst. Aging NIH, Balt., 1976-85, chief Lab. Cardiovascular Sci., Gerontology Rsch. Ctr., Nat. Inst. Aging, 1985—, acting sci. dir. Nat. Inst. Aging, 1994-95; prof. medicine Johns Hopkins Sch. Medicine, Balt., 1983—; prof. physiology Sch. Medicine U. Md., Balt., 1985—; vis. physician Bayview Med. Ctr., Balt., Md.; mem. ad hoc study sect. on animal model for study of pathogenesis of spl. heart muscle disease NIH, 1981; mem. ad hoc grant proposal reviews and site visit coms. VA and NSF; ad hoc reviewer Am. Jour. Physiology, Can. Jour. Physiology and Pharmacology, Circulation Rsch., Jour. Molecular and Cellular Cardiology, Sci.; mem. search com. for dir. Nat. Heart, Lung and Blood Inst., 1981, Gerontology Rsch. Ctr., 1988; chmn. intramural promotions and tenure review com. Nat. Inst. Aging, 1989-91; cons. in field. Editor for clin. scis. Exptl. Aging Rsch., 1982-89; assoc. editor Jour. Molecular and Cellular Cardiology, 1987—; mem. editorial bd. Jour. Gerontology, Jour. Molecular and Cellular Cardiology, Cardiosci., Current Problems in Geriatrics, Jour. Cardiovascular Electrophysiology; contbr. numerous articles to profl. jours., chpts. to books. Med. dir. USPHS, 1976. Recipient Paul Dudley White award Assn. Mil. Surgeons of U.S., 1992, Achievement in Aging award Allied Signal, 1993; Eli Lilly Med. Sci. fellow Am. Coll. Physicians, 1975. Fellow Am. Physiol. Soc. (cardiovascular sect.), Am. Heart Assn. (coun. basic sci., Cardiovascular B rsch. study com. 1987-89, application task force Mission to Elderly 1989-90, 90-91), Am. Soc. Clin. Investigation, Am. Assn. Physicians, Internat. Soc. for Heart Rsch. (coun.), Biophys. Soc.; mem. Physiol. Soc. (London). Avocation: fine wine and food. Home: 126 Briarcliff Ln Bel Air MD 21014-5553 Office: Nat Inst Aging Lab Cardiovascular Sci Gerontology Rsch Ctr Rm 3D09 Baltimore MD 21224-2780

LAKDAWALA, SHARAD R., psychiatrist; b. Broach, India, Oct. 7, 1949; came to U.S., 1977; s. Ramprasad D. and Kailasben Lakdawala; m. Bhavna B. Khatri, Jan. 2, 1978; children: Viraj, Ravi. BJ, Med. Coll., Ahmedabad, India, 1972. Diplomate Am. Bd. Psychiatry and Neurology, Am. Bd. Geriat. Psychiatry. Intern Civil Hosp., Ahmedabad, 1972-73; resident in psychiatry B.J. Med. Coll. and Civil Hosp., Ahmedabad, 1974-75; med. officer in-charge psychiat. unit Kasama (Zambia) Gen. Hosp., 1975-77; rotating intern NYU Med. Ctr., 1977-78, Bellevue Hosp., 1977-78; resident CUNY/Mt. Sinai Svcs., 1978-81; pvt. practice, 1981—; dir. mental health svcs. Tampa Gen. Hosp., 1988-93, chmn. dept. psychiatry, 1990-93; med.

dir., svc. dir. adult psychiatry Charter Hosp. Tampa Bay; chmn. dept. psychiatry Tampa Gen. Hosp.; past pres. med. staff Charter Hosp. Tampa Bay, svc. dir. adult psychiatry; mem. St. Joseph's Hosp., U. Community Hosp., Affiliated Svcs. Tampa Gen. Hosp.; med. dir. Charter Behavioral Health Sys. Tampa Bay; cons. in field. Fellow Am. Psychiat. Assn., Fla. Psychiat. Soc., Tampa Psychiat. Assn. (v.p. 1989-90, pres. 1990-91), Fla. Med. Assn., Hillsborough County Med Assn., Am. Assn. Psychiatrist India (pres-elect Fla. chpt.). Office: 2908 W Waters Ave # 101 Tampa FL 33614-1855 also: 505 Eichenfeld Dr # 106 Brandon FL 33511-5956

LAKE, CARNELL AUGUSTINO, professional football player; b. Salt Lake City, July 15, 1967. Student, UCLA. Safety Pitts. Steelers, 1989—. Named to Coll. All-Am. 2d Team, Sporting News, 1987; selected to Pro Bowl, 1994, 96. Office: 300 Stadium Cir Pittsburgh PA 15212-5729*

LAKE, CAROL LEE, anesthesiologist, educator; b. Altoona, Pa., July 14, 1944; d. Samuel Lindsay and Edna Winifred (McMahan) L. BS, Juniata Coll., 1966; MD, Med. Coll. Pa., 1970; postgrad., U. Calif., Irvine. Intern Mercy Hosp., Pitts., 1970-71, resident in anesthesiology, 1971-73; staff anesthesiologist Pitts. Anesthesia Assocs., 1973-75; asst. prof. anesthesiology U. Va., Charlottesville, 1975-80, assoc. prof., 1980-89, prof. anesthesiology, 1989-94; prof. anesthesiology, chair U. Calif., Davis, 1994-95, prof. clin. anesthesiology, 1996; chief of staff Roudebush VA Med. Ctr., 1997—; asst. dean for vets. affairs, prof. anesthesia Ind. U., Indpls., 1997—; sr. assoc. examiner Am. Bd. Anesthesiology, 1981—. Author: Cardiovascular Anesthesia, 1985; editor: Pediatric Cardiac Anesthesia, 1988, ed edit., 1997; Clinical Monitoring, 1990, 2d edit., 1994; co-editor: Blood: Hemostasis, Transfusion and Alternatives in the Perioperative Period, 1995; editor Advances in Anesthesia, 1993—. Fellow Am. Coll. Cardiology; mem. Assn. Cardiac Anesthesiologists (pres. 1987-88), Soc. Cardiovascular Anesthesiologists (bd. dirs. 1988-92), Assn. Univ. Anesthesiologists, Alpha Omega Alpha. Presbyterian. Avocations: music, entomology, gardening. Office: Roudebush VA Med Ctr 1481 W 10th St Indianapolis IN 46202-2803

LAKE, DAVID S., publisher, lawyer; b. Youngstown, Ohio, July 17, 1938; s. Frank and Charlotte (Stahl) L.; m. Sandra J. Levin, Dec. 18, 1960 (div. Aug. 14, 1987); children: Joshua Seth, Jonathan Daniel. B.A. in Math, Youngstown State U., 1960; J.D. cum laude, Cleve. State U., 1965. Bar: Ohio 1965, D.C. 1970, U.S. Supreme Ct. 1969. Gen. counsel World Pub. Co., Cleve., 1965-68; dir. devel. Cath. U. Am., Washington, 1968-69; v.p., gen. counsel Microform Pub. Corp., Washington, 1969-70; dir. spl. projects Library Resources, Inc., Chgo., 1970-72; gen. mgr., partner Nat. Textbook Co., Skokie, Ill., 1972-76; pres. David S. Lake Pubs., Belmont, Calif., 1976-89, pres, owner, 1984-89; owner Lake Pub. Co., Belmont, 1989—. Contbr. to: Cleve. Marshall Law Rev, 1964. Served with USMC, 1960-62. Jewish. Office: Lake Pub Co 67 W Shore Rd Belvedere CA 94920-2461

LAKE, JOSEPH EDWARD, ambassador; b. Jacksonville, Tex., Oct. 18, 1941; s. Lloyd Euel and Marion Marie (Allen) L.; m. Sarah Ann Bryant (div.); children: Joseph Edward, Mary Elizabeth; m. Jo Ann Kessler, June 12, 1971; 1 child, Michael Allen. BA summa cum laude, Tex. Christian U., 1962, MA, 1967. Second sec. U.S. Embassy, Lagos, Nigeria, 1977-78; prin. officer and consul U.S. Consulate, Kaduna, Nigeria, 1978-81; with Fgn. Svc. Inst., Washington, 1981-82; first sec. U.S. Embassy, Sofia, Bulgaria, 1982-84, charge d'affaires, 1984, counselor, dep. chief mission, 1984-85; dep. dir. regional affairs , bur. East Asian and Pacific Affairs Dept. State, 1985-86; advisor U.S. delegation 41st UN Gen. Assembly, 1986; dir. ops. ctr. Dept. State, Washington, 1987-90; amb. to Rep. of Mongolia, Ulaanbaatar, 1990-93, Rep. of Albania, Tirana, 1994-96; dep. asst. sec. of state for info. mgmt. Dept. State, Washington, 1996—. Contbr. articles to profl. jours. Mem. Am. Fgn. Svc. Assn. Home: PO Box 2523 Merrifield VA 22116-2523 Office: Dept of State A/IM Washington DC 20520

LAKE, KATHLEEN C., lawyer; b. San Antonio, Jan. 11, 1955; d. Herschel Taliaferro and Virginia Mae (Hylton) Cooper; m. Randall Brent Lake, Apr. 9, 1977; 1 child, Ethan Taliaferro. AB magna cum laude in Polit. Sci. with high honors, Middlebury Coll., 1977; JD with high honors, U. Tex., 1980. Bar: Tex. 1980, U.S. Ct. Appeals (5th cir.) 1981, U.S. Ct. Appeals (D.C. and 3d cirs.) 1984. Assoc. atty. Vinson & Elkins, Houston, 1980-88; ptnr. Vinson & Elkins, LLP, Houston, 1989—. Adult leader, mem. com. Sam Houston Area Coun.-Golden Arrow dist. Boys Scouts Am., 1993— . Recipient Unit Svc. award Sam Houston Area Coun.-Golden Arrow dist. Boy Scouts Am. Fellow Tex. Bar Found., Houston Bar Found.; mem. ABA, Fed. Energy Bar Assn., State Bar Tex., Tex. Law Rev. Assn. (life), Houston Bar Assn., Middlebury Coll. Alumni Assn. (com. mem. 1980—), Phi Beta Kappa, Phi Kappa Phi, Order of the Coif. Office: Vinson & Elkins LLP 2300 First City Twr 1001 Fannin St Houston TX 77002-6706

LAKE, KEVIN BRUCE, medical association administrator; b. Seattle, Jan. 25, 1937; s. Winston Richard and Vera Emma (Davis) L.; m. Suzanne Roto, Oct. 25, 1986; children from previous marriage: Laura, Kendrick, Wesley. BS, Portland State U., 1960; MD, U. Oreg., 1964. Intern, Marion County Gen. Hosp. and Ind. Med. Center, Indpls., 1964-65; resident U. Oreg. Hosps. and Clinics, 1968-70; fellow in infectious and pulmonary diseases, 1970-71; fellow in pulmonary diseases U. So. Calif., 1971-72, instr. medicine, 1972-75, asst. clin. prof., 1975-79, assoc. clin. prof., 1979-84, clin. prof., 1986—; dir. med. edn. and research La Vina Hosp., 1972-75; dir. respiratory therapy Methodist Hosp., Arcadia, Calif., 1975—; mem. staff Los Angeles County/U. So. Calif. Med. Center, Santa Teresita Hosp., Duarte, Calif., Huntington Meml. Hosp., Pasadena, Calif.; attending physician, mem. med. adv. bd. Foothill Free Clinic, Pasadena. Mem. exec. com. Profl. Staff Assn. U. So. Calif. Sch. Medicine; 2d v.p. bd. mgmt. Palm St. br. YMCA, Pasadena, 1974, 1st v.p., 1975, chmn., 1976-78, met. bd. dirs., 1976-84; bd. dirs. Mendenhall Ministries, La Vie Holistic Ministries, Hospice of Pasadena, Hastings Found. co-pres. PTA, Allendale Grade Sch., Pasadena, 1975-76; deacon Pasadena Covenant Ch., 1976-79. Served to lt. U.S. Navy, 1965-68. NIH grantee, 1971-72. Fellow ACP, Am. Coll. Chest Physicians; mem. Am. Thoracic Soc., Calif. Thoracic Soc., Oreg. Thoracic Soc., Trudeau Soc., Am. Soc. Microbiology, N.Y. Acad. Scis., Calif. Med. Assn., Los Angeles County Med. Assn. Democrat. Contbr. articles to profl. jours. Home: 875 S Madison Ave Pasadena CA 91106-4404 Office: 50 Alesandro Pl Ste 330 Pasadena CA 91105-3149

LAKE, RICKI, talk show host, actress; b. N.Y.C., Sept. 21, 1968; m. Rob Sussman; 1 child, Milo. Syndicated talk show host Ricki Lake. Movie appearances include: Hairspray, 1988, Working Girl, 1988, Cookie, 1989, Cry-Baby, 11990, Last Exit to Brooklyn, 1989, Where the Day Takes You, 1992, Inside Monkey Zetterland, 1993, Serial Mom, 1994, Cabin Boy, 1994, Skinner, 1995, Mrs. Winterbourne, 1996; TV appearances include (series) China Beach, 1990, Kate and Allie, Fame, (spls.) A Family Again, 1988, Starting Now, 1989, Gravedale High, 1990, (movies) Babycakes, 1989, The Chase, 1991, Basedon an Untrue Story, (pilot) Starting Now; stage actress: A Girl's Guide to Chaos, 1990, (off-Broadway) The Early Show, Youngsters, 1983. Office: Entrada Prodns 401 5th Ave Fl 7 New York NY 10016-3317 also: WMA 151 El Camino Dr Beverly Hills CA 90212*

LAKE, SIMEON TIMOTHY, III, federal judge; b. Chgo., July 4, 1944; s. Simeon T. Jr. and Helen (Hupka) L.; m. Carol Illig, Dec. 30, 1970; children: Simeon Timothy IV, Justin Carl. BA, Tex. A&M, 1966; JD, U. Tex., 1969. Bar: Tex. 1969, U.S. Dist. Ct. (so. dist.) Tex. 1969, U.S. Ct. Appeals (5th cir.) 1969, U.S. Supreme Ct. 1976, U.S. Ct. Appeals (3d cir.) 1981, U.S. Dist. Ct. (no. dist.) Tex. 1983. From assoc. to ptnr. Fulbright & Jaworski, Houston, 1969-70, 72-88; judge U.S. Dist. Ct. (so. dist.) Tex., Houston, 1988—. Past editor Houston Lawyer. Served to capt. U.S. Army., 1970-71. Fellow Tex. Bar Assn., Houston Bar Assn., State Bar Tex., Am. Law Inst. Office: US Dist Ct 9535 US Courthouse 515 Rusk Ave RM 9535 Houston TX 77002*

LAKE, WESLEY WAYNE, JR., internist, allergist, educator; b. New Orleans, Oct. 11, 1937; s. Wesley Wayne and Mary McGehee (Snowden) L.; m. Abby F. Arnold, Aug. 1959 (div. 1974 children: Courtenay B., Corinne A., Jane S. AB in Chemistry, Princeton U., 1959; MD, Tulane U., 1963. Diplomate Am. Bd. Internal Medicine, Am. Bd. Allergy and Immunology. Intern Charity Hosp. of La., New Orleans, 1963-64, resident internal medicine, 1966-69; NIH fellow allergy and immunology La. State U. Med. Ctr., 1969-70; instr. dept. medicine Tulane U., New Orleans, 1967-69; fellow dept. medicine La. State U., New Orleans, 1969-70, instr. dept. medicine, 1970-73, asst. clin. prof. medicine, 1973-77; chief allergy clinic La. State U. Svc. Charity Hosp. La., New Orleans, 1970-77; assoc. clin. prof. medicine Tulane U., New Orleans, 1978—; temp. staff positions various hosps., 1963-70, including Baton Rouge Gen. Hosp., Our Lady of the Lake Hosp., Glenwood Hosp., St. Francis Hosp., Monroe, La., Lallie Kemp Charity Hosp., Independence, La., Huey P. Long Hosp., Pineville, La.; gen. med. officer outpatient clinic Hunter AFB, Savannah, Ga., 1964-65, gen. med. officer internal medicine svc., 1965-66; cons. physician Seventh Ward Gen. Hosp., Hammond, La., 1971-77, Slidell (La.) Meml. Hosp., 1971-89, St. Tammany Parish Hosp., Covington, La., 1977-85; cons. physician East Jefferson Hosp., Metairie, La., 1971-77, staff physician, 1990—; assoc. vis. physician Charity Hosp. New Orleans, 1970-75, staff physician, 1975-77, vis. phys. Tulane divsn., 1979—; assoc. physician So. Bapt. Hosp., New Orleans, 1970-75, staff physician, 1975—, chmn. dept. medicine, chmn. internal medicine com., 1982-84, chmn. pharmacy and therapeutics, 1980-82, mem. investigative rev. com., 1984-85, mem. internal medicine quality assurance com., 1989-94; staff physician Kenner (La.) Regional Med. Ctr. (formerly St. Jude Med. Ctr.), 1985—, chmn. quality assurance com., 1987-89. Author: (with others) Infiltrative Hypersensitivity Chest Diseases, 1975; contbr. articles to profl. jours. including Jour. Immunology, Internat. Archives Allergy and Applied Immunology, Jour. Allergy and Clin. Immunology; also chpts. in books concerning chest diseases. Fellow ACP, Am. Coll. Allergy, Sigma Xi; mem. New Orleans Acad. Internal Medicine, Musser-Burch Soc., S.E. Allergy Soc., La. Allergy Soc. (sec. 1975-76, v.p. 1976-77, pres. 1977-78). Republican. Episcopalian. Home: 1308 Bordeaux St New Orleans LA 70115 Office: 4224 Houma Blvd Ste 250 Metairie LA 70006-2935

LAKE, WILLIAM THOMAS, financial consultant; b. Ocean City, N.J., June 14, 1910; s. William Carson and Marie Cecelia (Kaiser) L.; m. V. Blair Torbert, Nov. 25, 1933 (div.); children: Donna Blair Lake Wright, Deborah Caren Lake Coates, Darelle Dee Lake Riabov, Carson Thomas; m. Dorothy Howell Caddelle, Mar. 1, 1968; 1 stepdau., Lynne E. Caddelle (Mrs. W. Dean Boecher). Grad., Rider Coll., Trenton, N.J., 1930. C.P.A., N.J., Pa., Mich., Calif., Colo., N.Y. Pub. acct. Lybrand Ross Bros. and Montgomery, Phila., 1932-39; controller Keystone Portland Cement Co., Phila., 1939-42; controller, treas. narrow fabric div. Burlington Mills, Allentown, Pa., 1946-48; controller Rouge plants Ford Motor Co., 1948-53; comptroller Curtiss Wright Corp., Wood Ridge, 1953-61, Gen. Dynamics Corp., 1961-68; v.p. finance aerospace and systems group Rockwell Internat., 1968-70; fin. cons., 1970—; pres. Talmud Internat. Mgmt. Co., Peripheral Engring. Inc.; treas. Talmud Internat. Ltd. Served to comdr. USNR, World War II; supply officer 4th Naval Dist., Naval Ordnance Plant York, Pa. Mem. Am. Inst. Profl. Cons. (charter), Fin. Execs. Inst. (life), AICPA (50 year hon. mem. award), N.J., Calif., Colo., Pa., Mich., N.Y. socs. CPAs, Am. Ordnance Assn., Navy League U.S. Presbyterian. Clubs: Masons (N.Y.C.) (32 deg.); Shriners; Economic (N.Y.C.), Engineers (N.Y.C.); Pinehurst Country. Home: 9 Oakwood Dr Queensbury NY 12804-1327

LAKIER, NANCY S., health care consultant; b. Ft. Madison, Iowa, Nov. 17, 1952; d. Bernard A. and Ruth Mary Mehmert; m. Richard Stephen Lakier, Nov. 12, 1983; 1 child, Andrea. BSN, Creighton U., 1975; MBA, U. Nebr., 1985. Staff and mid. mgmt. positions various orgns., 1975-83; v.p. nursing Children's Hosp., Omaha, 1983-86, Ft. Hamilton (Ohio)-Hughes, 1986-88, San Bernardino (Calif.) Community Hosp., 1988-90; assoc. adminstr. Scripps Meml. Hosp., La Jolla, Calif., 1990-96; pres. InnoVia Health, La Jolla, 1996—. Case Mgmt. and Critical Path Documentation System, 1991, CareTracs, 1991. Pres. alumni adv. bd. dirs. Creighton U., Omaha, 1984-88. Recipient One-Calif. Nursing Leadership award. Mem. Am. Orgn. Nurse Execs. (chpt. pres. 1994-96, bd. dirs. Calif. chpt.), VHA Nat. Nursing Adv. Bd. Avocations: walking, hiking, reading, gardening. Office: InnoVia Health 9834 Genesee Ave Ste 320 La Jolla CA 92037-1215

LAKIER, THELMA, child development specialist, librarian; b. Pietersburg, Transvaal, S. Africa, May 28, 1941; came to U.S., 1978; d. Abraham and Berthe (MIchelsohn) Perlmann; m. Jeffrey Lakier, Dec. 20, 1964; children: Beth, Louise. BA, U. Witaters, Johannesburg, S. Africa, 1962; Transvaal tchrs. higher diploma, Johannesburg Coll. Edn., S. Africa, 1963; postgrad., Erikson Inst., Chgo., 1988-91; MEd, Loyola U., Chgo., 1992. Cert. tchr., Mich. Tchr. Transvaal Edn. Dept., S. Africa, 1964, 66-72; libr. Libr. of Johannesburg, 1965; tchr. Hebrew Acad., San Francisco, 1972-74, Discovery Corner, Troy, Mich., 1982-88, Michael Reese Day Care, Chgo., 1988-89; child devel. specialist Luth. Gen. Children's Day Care Ctr., Des Plaines, Ill., 1989—, resource libr. for staff and parents, 1993—. Mem. Luth. Gen. Found Benefit Com., Chgo., 1989—. Mem. Nat. Assn. for Edn. of Young Children (workshop co-leader Chgo. chpt. 1992), Assn. for Childhood Edn. Internat. Avocations: music, reading, needlework. Home: 2751 The Mews Northbrook IL 60062-2617 Office: Luth Gen Children's Day Care 9375 W Church St Des Plaines IL 60016-4271

LAKIN, JAMES DENNIS, allergist, immunologist, director; b. Harvey, Ill., Oct. 4, 1945; s. Ora Austin and Annie Pitranella (Johnson) L.; m. Sally A. Stuteville, July 22, 1972; children: Margaret K., Matthew A. PhD, Northwestern U., 1968, MD, 1969; MBA in Med. Group Mgmt., U. St. Thomas, 1996. Diplomate Am. Bd. Internal Medicine, Am. Bd. Allergy and Immunology. Dir. allergy rsch. Naval Med. Rsch. Inst., Bethesda, Md., 1974-76; clin. prof. U. Okla., Oklahoma City, 1976-89; dir. lab., chmn. allergy and immunology dept. Oxboro Clinics, Bloomington, Minn., 1989—; dir. Fairview Allergy and Asthma Svcs., Bloomington, 1995—; bd. dirs. Okla. Med. Rsch. Found., Oklahoma City, 1980-89; regional cons. Diver Alert Network, Duke U., Chapel Hill, N.C., 1987—; cert. diving med. officer NOAA, 1988. Co-author: Allergic Diseases, 1971, 3d edit., 1986; contbr. articles, revs. to profl. publs. Councilperson Our Lord's Luth. Ch., Oklahoma City, 1978-88, Faith Luth. Ch., Lakeville, Minn., 1990-91. Lt. comdr. USN, 1970-76. Fellow ACP, Am. Acad. allergy and Immunology, Am. Coll. Chest Physicians; mem. Am. Assn. Immunologists, Med. Group Mgmt. Assn., Am. Coll. Physician Execs. Achievements include research in characterization of the immunoglobulin system of the rhesus monkey, alterations in allergic reactivity during immunosuppression. Office: Oxboro Clinic 600 W 98th St Bloomington MN 55420-4773

LAKIN, JOHN FRANCIS, lawyer; b. Chelsea, Mass., Nov. 21, 1960; s. Kenneth and Nancy Lakin; m. JoAnne Lanza, Oct. 6, 1990; children: Joy, Justin. AB, Boston Coll., 1983; JD, Mass. Sch. Law, Andover, 1990. Bar: Mass. 1990, U.S. Ct. Appeals (1st cir.) 1991, U.S. Dist. Ct. Mass. 1991, U.S. Supreme Ct. 1994. Adjuster Liberty Mut. Ins. Co., Boston, 1983-84; law clk. Marchese & Barnes, Revere, Mass., 1984-90, assoc., 1990—. Mem. ABA, Assn. Trial Lawyers Am., Mass. Acad. Trial Attys., Mass. Bar Assn. (mock-trial tchr. 1990-91), Mass. Criminal Def. Lawyers. Democrat. Office: Broadhurst Lakin & Lakin One Elm Sq Andover MA 01810-3714 also: 19 Beacon St Boston MA 02108-2821

LAKRITZ, ISAAC, management consultant; b. Milw., June 11, 1952; s. Jeffrey and Deborah (Margolis) L.; m. Lea Winninger, May 22, 1982; children: Eli, Jacob, Atara. BA, U. Wis., Milw., 1973, MA, 1974. Cert. secondary sch. tchr. Coordinator Jewish Student Services Hillel, Milw., 1972-74; analyst Israel Ministry Social Welfare, Jerusalem, 1975-76; exec. dir. Jewish Nat. Fund Wis., Milw., 1977; devel. dir. Milw. Jewish Home, 1977-78; asst. dir. N.Y. Assn. for New Americans, N.Y.C., 1978-81; nat. youth dir. Zionist Orgn. Am., N.Y.C., 1981-84; asst. dir. Jacksonville (Fla.) Jewish Fedn., 1984-87, exec. v.p., 1987-90; exec. dir. east cen. region Am. Soc. for Technion, Detroit, 1990-95; mgmt. cons., West Bloomfield, Mich., 1995—. Chmn. Israel com. Conf. Jewish Communal Svc., 1982-92. Recipient Top Pub. Rels. award in N.Am. Coun. Jewish Fedn. Mem. Assn. Jewish Community Orgn. Personnel, Phi Kappa Phi. Avocations: opera, stamps, computers. *Our task is to build a more just and compassionate world. With mankind's considerable technical expertise, we have shown that we can accomplish just about anything we really desire. Let us create an environment where that which is right and kind is desirable.*

LAKSHMANAN, T.R., federal agency administrator, geography and environmental engineering educator, writer; m. Lata Chatterjee; children: Srobona, Indira. Corp. v.p. CONSAD Rsch. Corp., Pitts.; sr. analyst, assoc. Alan M. Voorhees Assocs.; prof. geography and environ. engring. Johns Hopkins U., 1973-78; founder., exec. dir. Ctr. for Energy and Environ. Studies Boston U.; first dir. Bur. Transp. Statistics U.S. Dept. Transp., Washington; vis. scholar Netherlands Inst. for Adv. Studies in the Humanities and Social Scis., Internat. Inst. for Applied Systems Analysis, Austria, Cambridge U., U.K., MIT; cons. UN, The World Bank, Japan's EPA, many govts. in Europe and Asia. Author 10 books; contbr. over 60 articles to profl. jours. Recipient James Anderson medal Assn. Am. Geographers. Mem. Clare Hall Coll. Cambridge U. (elected life). Office: Dept Transp Transp Statistics Bureau 400 7th St SW Washington DC 20590-0001

LAKSHMIKANTHAM, VANGIPURAM, mathematics educator; b. Hyderabad, India, Aug. 8, 1926; came to U.S., 1960, naturalized, 1966; s. Soroja Bukkapatnam, Feb. 22, 1942; children: Sreekantham, Neerada, Nirupama. MA, Osmania U., Hyderabad, 1955, PhD, 1958. Mem. faculty UCLA, 1960-61, Math. Rsch. Ctr., U. Wis., Madison, 1961-62; mem. Rsch. Inst. Advanced Studies, Balt., 1962-63; assoc. prof. U. Alta., Calgary, Can., 1963-64; prof., chmn. dept. math. Marathwada U., Aurangabad, India, 1964-66, U. R.I., Kingston, 1966-73, U. Tex., Arlington, 1973-88; prof., dir. interdisciplinary programs Fla. Inst. Tech., Melbourne, 1989—. Author 22 books; founder, editor: Jour. Nonlinear Analysis, Nonlinear World, Nonlinear Studies, Stochastic Analysis and Applications, Mathematical Problems in Engineering; assoc. editor other jours.; contbr. over 250 rsch. articles to profl. publs. Mem. Am. Math. Soc., Indian Math. Soc., Soc. Indsl. and Aplied Math., Nat. Acad. Sci. India, Internat. Fedn. Nonlinear Analysts (founder). Office: Fla Inst Tech Dept Applied Math 150 W University Blvd Melbourne FL 32901-6982

LAKSHMINARAYANA, BUDUGUR, aerospace engineering educator; b. Shimoga, India, Feb. 15, 1935; came to U.S., 1963, naturalized, 1971; m. Saroja Lakshminarayana; children: Anita, Arvind. BME, Mysore U., India, 1958; PhD, U. Liverpool, Eng., 1963, DEng, 1981. Asst. mech. engr. Kolar (India) Gold Mining Undertakings, 1958-60; rschr. in mech. engring. U. Liverpool, 1960-63, Leverhulme fellow, 1962-63; asst. prof. aerospace engring. Pa. State U., University Park, 1963-69, assoc. prof., 1969-74, prof., 1974-85, dir. computational fluid dynamics studies, 1980-87, disting. alumni prof., 1985-86, Evan Pugh prof., 1986—, dir. Ctr. for Gas Turbines and Power, 1994—; vis. fellow scientist Cambridge U., St. John's Coll., Eng., 1971-72; vis. assoc. prof. aeros. and astronautics MIT, 1972; vis. prof. dept. mech. engring. Indian Inst. Sci., 1979; aerospace engr. computational fluid mechanics group NASA Ames Rsch. Ctr., Moffett Field, Calif., 1979; CNRS vis. prof. Laboratoire de Mecanique des Fluides at d'Acoustique, Ecole Centrale de Lyon, France, 1987-88; vis. prof. Tech. U. of Aachen, Germany, 1988; adv. prof. Inst. Thermophysics Chinese Acad. Scis., 1993, Shanghai Jiao Tong U., China, 1993; cons. Pratt & Whitney Aircraft, GE Aircraft Engine Div., Allied Signal, Allison Engine Co., Teledyne CAE, Inc.; UN, NATO/AGARD lectr.; Gen. Motors, Rolls Royce, European Space Agy.; mem. NASA adv. group on computational fluid dynamics, 1980; lectr. in field. Author: Fluid Dynamics and Heat Transfer of Turbomachinery, 1995; editor 2 books; contbr. numerous articles on fluid dynamics, turbomachinery, computational fluid dynamics, turbulence modelling and acoustics to profl. publs. Recipient Henry R. Worthington N.Am. tech. award, 1977, sr. prof. Fulbright award, 1988, Arch. T. Colwell merit award Soc. Automotive Engrs., 1992; merit scholar Mysore U., 1953-57; grantee NSF, numerous others. Fellow AIAA (chmn. Ctrl. Pa. chpt. 1970, Pendrey Lit. award 1989, Airbreathing Propulsion award 1994), ASME (Freeman Scholar award 1990, Fluids Engring. award 1996, IGTI aircraft engine tech. award 1997). Office: Pa State U Coll Engring 153 Hammond Bldg University Park PA 16802-1400

LAKSHMIVARAHAN, SIVARAMAKRISHNAN, computer science educator; b. Karaikurichi, Tamil Nadu, India, June 12, 1944; came to U.S., 1975; s. Sankaran Sivaramakrishna and Subbulakshmi (Narayanan) Iyer; m. Shantha Sitaram Varahan, Feb. 5, 1973; children: Subha, Bharathram. BSc in Physics with distinction, U. Madras, India, 1964; BE in Elec. Tech. with distinction, Indian Inst. Sci., Bangalore, 1967, ME in Applied Electronics, 1969, PhD in Learning Algorithms, 1973. Rsch. asst. dept. elec. engring. Indian Inst. Sci., Bangalore, 1969-73; project asst. Sch. Automation Indian Inst. Tech., Bangalore, 1973; lectr., asst. prof. dept. computer sci. Indian Inst. Tech., Madras, 1973-75; vis. asst. prof. div. applied math. Brown U., Providence, 1975-76; asst. prof. dept. engring. and applied sci. Yale U., New Haven, 1976-78; assoc. prof. Sch. Elec. Engring. and Computer Sci., U. Okla., Norman, 1978-84, prof., 1984-92, prof. Sch. Computer Sci., 1992—, Hallibuurton disting. lectr. Coll. Engring., 1984-86, Assocs. disting. lectr., 1986-87, George Lynn Cross rsch. prof., 1995; vis. prof. U. Bonn, 1980, 82, U. Laval, Quebec City, Can., 1982, AMOCO Prodn. Rsch. Ctr., Tulsa, summer 1983, Nat. Inst. Standards and Tech., Gaithersburg, Md., summer 1985, Tech. Inst. for Higher Studies Monterrey, Mex., 1988, 90, 93, Nat. Tsing-Huo U., Hinshu, Taiwan, 1992, Indian Inst. Sch., Bangalore, 1993; cons. AMOCO Prodn. Rsch. Ctr., Nat. Inst. Standards and Tech.; colloquium speaker in field. Author: Lectures on Automata Theory, 1974, Learning Algorithms: Theory and Application, 1982, (with S.K. Dhall) Analysis and Design of Parallel Algorithms, 1990, Parallel Prefix Computations, 1994; editor: Procs. of Workshop on Parallel Processing using Heterogeneous Element Processor, 1985, spl. issue Info. Scis.-Internat. Jour., 1987; contbr. numerous articles to sci. jours., chpts. to books. Recipient Regents award for rsch. and creative activities U. Okla., 1982, Regents award for superior teaching, 1992; grantee NSF, 1981-83, 85, 86-87, 89-93, U. Okla. Office Rsch. Adminstrn., 1981, AMOCO, summers 1983-86, 1985-85, 87-88, U. Okla. Energy Resource Inst., 1984-86, Denelcor, Inc., 1985, Okla. Gov.'s Coun. on Sci. and Tech., 1986, More Okla. Sci. and Tech. Fellow IEEE (citation for contbns. to learning algorithms, parallel computing and their applications 1993), IEEE Computer Soc. (vice chmn. Oklahoma City chpt. 1982-83, chmn. 1983-85), Assn. for Computing Machinery (editl. bd. Applied Computing Rev. 1993—, nat. lectr. selection com. 1992-93, nat. lectr. 1989-92, faculty advisor student chpt. U. Okla. 1987-89, citation for contbns. to learning and parallel algorithms). Avocation: Indian classical music. Office: U Okla Sch Computer Sci Norman OK 73019

LAL, DEVENDRA, nuclear geophysics educator; b. Varanasi, India, Feb. 14, 1929; s. Radhe Krishna and Sita Devi (Gupta) L.; m. Aruna Damany, May 17, 1955 (dec. July 1993). BS, Banaras Hindu U., Varanasi, 1947, MS, 1949, DSc (hon. causa), 1984; PhD, Bombay U., 1960. Research student Tata Inst. of Fundamental Research, Bombay, 1949-60, research fellow, fellow, assoc. prof., 1960-63, prof., 1963-70, sr. prof., 1970-72; dir. Phys. Research Lab., Ahmedabad, India, 1972-83; sr. prof. Phys. Research Lab., Ahmedabad, 1983-89; vis. prof. UCLA, 1965-66, 83-84; prof. Scripps Instn. Oceanography, La Jolla, Calif., 1967—; fellow Phys. Rsch. Lab. Ahmedabad, 1989—. Editor: Early Solar System Processes and the Present Solar System, 1980, Biogeochemistry of the Arabian Sea, 1995. Recipient K.S. Krishnan Gold medal Indian Geophys. Union, 1965, S.S. Bhatnagar award for Physics, Govt. of India, 1971, award for Excellence in Sci. and Tech., Gedn. of Indian Chamber Com., 1974, Pandit Jawaharlal Nehru award for Scis., 1986, Group Achievement award NASA, 1986, Raman Birth Centenary award, 1996, V.M. Goldschmidt medal, 1997. Fellow Royal Soc. London, Indian Nat. Sci. Acad., Indian Acad. Scis., Geol. Soc. India (hon.), Tata Inst. Fundamental Rsch.; mem. NAS U.S.A. (fgn. assoc.), Third World Acad. Scis. (founding mem.), Indian Geophys. Union, NAS India, Royal Astron. Soc. (assoc.), Internat. Acad. Aeronautics, Internat. Union of Geodesy and Geophysics (pres. 1984-87), Am. Acad. Arts and Scis. (fgn., hon. mem.), Internat. Assn. Phys. Sci. of Ocean (hon. mem., pres. 1979-83). Hindu. Avocations: chess, photography, painting, math. puzzles. Office: U Calif Scripps Inst Oceanography GRD-0220 La Jolla CA 92093-0220

LALA, DOMINICK J., manufacturing company executive; b. N.Y.C., June 2, 1928; s. Joseph and Mary (Billera) L.; m. Nancy Bosco, Nov. 30, 1957; children: John, Steven, James, Thomas, Patrice. B.S., NYU, 1951. Mem. staff BDO/Seidman (CPAs), N.Y.C., 1951-62; v.p., contr. Universal Am. Corp., N.Y.C., 1962-68; sr. v.p. finance Paramount Pictures Corp., 1968-70; exec. v.p. Gould Paper Corp., 1970—. Served with AUS, 1946-47. Mem. AICPA, N.Y. State Soc. CPAs, Fin. Execs. Inst. Home: 10 Burnham Pl Manhasset NY 11030-2709 Office: Gould Paper Corp 315 Park Ave S New York NY 10010-3607

LALA, JAYNARAYAN HOTCHAND, computer engineer; b. Hyderabad, Sind, Pakistan, Jan. 12, 1951; came to U.S., 1971; s. Hotchand Menghraj and Jamuna (Gandhi) L.; m. Michele Simone Breton, Sept. 2, 1977. SB in Aero. Engring., Indian Inst. Tech., 1971; SM in Aeros.-Astronautics, MIT, 1973, ScD in Instrumentation, 1976. Mem. tech. staff Charles Stark Draper Lab.,

Inc., Cambridge, Mass., 1976-83, chief systems architecture sect. NASA dept., 1983-85, div. leader fault tolerant systems div., 1985-91, leader advanced computer architectures group, 1991-93; prin. mem. tech. staff, 1993—; advisor USN Combat System Architecture Adv. Panel, 1985-86; session chmn. 8th Digital Avionics Systems Conf., San Jose, Calif., 1988, Workshop on Fault Tolerance in Parallel and Distributed Computing, 1987, Conf. on Dependable Computing for Critical Applications, 1989; mem. program com. 20th Internat. Symposium on Fault Tolerant Computing, 1990, 21st Internat. Symposium, 1991, tech. program chmn. 22nd Internat. Symposium, 1992; mem. program com. 2nd Conf. on Dependable Computing for Critical Applications, Tucson, 1991, program com. 3d Conf., Sicily, Italy, 1992; mem. battle mgmt. panel Strategic Def. Initiative, 1992; tech. dir. Bosnia Command and Control Augmentation Program, 1996. Producer, dir., writer tech. documentary Advanced Information Processing System, 1989; contbr. articles to profl. jours., chpts. to books; patentee fault tolerant computer designs. Recipient Best Paper award C.S. Draper Lab., 1989, 94, Best Patent award, 1990; Draper fellow, 1972-76; scholar Indian Sci. Talent Bd., 1966, Indian Inst. Tech., 1967-71. Fellow AIAA (assoc., chmn. digital avionics tech. subcom. 1987-91), IEEE; mem. Internat. Fedn. Info. Processing (working group on dependable computing and fault tolerance 1988—), Indian Inst. Tech. Soc. New Eng. (v.p. 1995-97). Hindu. Avocations: flying, chess, tennis, piano. Home: 2802 Battery Pl NW Washington DC 20016-3439 Office: Charles Stark Draper Lab Inc 555 Technology Sq Cambridge MA 02139-3539

LALA, PEEYUSH KANTI, medical scientist, educator; b. Chittagong, Bengal, India, Nov. 1, 1934; came to U.S., 1963, to Can., 1967.; s. Sudhangshu Bimal and Nani Bala (Chaudhuri) L.; m. Arati Roy-Burman, July 7, 1962 (dec.); children: Probal, Prasun; m. Shipra Bhattacareya, Nov. 6, 1992. MBBS, Calcutta (India) U., 1957, PhD in Med. Biophysics, 1962. Demonstrator pathology Calcutta Med. Coll., 1959-60, NRS Med. Coll., Calcutta, 1961-62; resident research assoc. Biol. and Med. Research div. Argonne (Ill.) Nat. Lab., 1963-64; research scientist lab radiobiology U. Calif. Med. Ctr., San Francisco, 1964-66; research scientist Biol. and Health Physics div. Chalk River (Ont., Can.) Nuclear Lab., 1967-68; from asst. prof. to assoc. prof. dept. anatomy McGill U., Montreal, Que., Can., 1968-77, prof. dept. anatomy, 1977-83; prof. dept. anatomy U. Western Ont., London, 1983—, chmn. dept. anatomy, 1983-93, prof. dept. oncology, 1990—; mem. grants panel MRC Can., Ottawa, Ont., 1983-87, 93-96, NIH U.S.A., Bethesda, Md., 1977-95, Nat. Cancer Inst. Can., Toronto, 1987-90, Cancer Rsch. Soc., Montreal, 1987-90; mem. Cannaught Com., Toronto, 1990-91; vis. prof. Walter and Eliza Hall Inst. Med. Rsch., U. Melbourne, Australia, 1977-78. Mem. editl. bd. Leukemia Rsch., 1977-86, Exptl. Hematology, 1974-77, Am. Jour. Reproductive Immunology, 1989-93, Early Pregnancy: Biology and Medicine, 1995—, Plaecenta, 1996—; assoc. editor Am. Jour. Anatomy, 1987-90; contbr. over 150 articles to profl. jours. Chmn. Bengali Cultural Ctr., Montreal, 1978-83. Grantee MRC Can., 1968—, NCI Can., 1968—, NIH, 1976-79, Cancer Rsch. Soc., 1978—, U.S. Army Med. Rsch., 1996—; Fulbright Found. fellow, 1962. Mem. Am. Assn. Cancer Research, Am. Assn. Anatomists, Can. Assn. Anatomists (chmn. awards com. 1987-89, v.p. and pres. elect 1989-90, pres. 1991-93, J.C.B. Grant award 1990), Internat. Soc. Exptl. Hematology, Soc. Leukocyte Biology, Am. Assn. Immunologists, Can. Soc. Immunologists, Internat. Soc. Reproductive Immunology (councillor 1986-89), Am. Soc. Reproductive Immunology (v.p. 1985-86). Achievements include discovery of new mode of cancer immunotherapy, resulting in a successful phase two human trial. Office: U Western Ont, Dept Anatomy, London, ON Canada N6A 5C1

LALAS, ALEXI, professional soccer player; b. Birmingham, Mich.; s. Demetrius and Anne Lalas. BA in English, Rutgers U., 1991. Mem. U.S. Olympic Soccer Team, 1992, World Cup U.S. Soccer Team, 1993-94, Football Club Padova, Italian League, 1994-95, Major League Soccer, with New England Revolution, 1995—; defender U.S. Nat. Soccer Team, Chgo., 1990—; mem. U.S. Olympic Festival Team, 1989, U.S. Pan-Am. Team, 1991. Mem. group Gypsies; rec. Woodland. Recipient Hermann trophy, 1991; named Mich. Player of Yr., 1987, Mo. Athletic Club Player of Yr., 1991, Coll. Soccer Player of Yr., 1991, U.S. Male Athlete of Yr., 1995. Avocation: acoustic guitar. Office: New England Revolution Foxboro Stadium Rt 1 Foxboro MA 02035*

LALE, CISSY STEWART (LLOYD LALE), freelance writer; b. Port Arthur, Tex., Jan. 15, 1924; d. Lloyd M. and May (Cowart) Stewart; m. Max Sims Lale, Oct. 9, 1983. BJ, U. Tex., 1945. Reporter Record-News, Wichita Falls, Tex., 1945, News-Messenger, Marshall, Tex., 1945-47; editor Times-Rev., Cleburne, Tex., 1947-49; women's editor, columnist Star-Telegram, Ft. Worth, 1949-87; freelance writer Children's Promise mag., Health-Scope mag., Ft. Worth, 1987-89. Bd. dirs. Trinity Terr. Retirement Community, 1991-94; historian, editor newsletter, mem. Jewel Charity Ball. Cissy Stewart Day proclaimed by Ft. Worth City Coun., 1987, portrayed in outdoor mural City of Ft. Worth, 1987. Mem. Women in Comm., Inc. (nat. pres. 1968-71), Tex. State Hist. Assn. (pres. 1996-97), East Tex. Hist. Assn. (pres. 1994), Tex. Heritage, Inc. (bd. dirs. Ft. Worth chpt. 1990), Womans Club Ft. Worth, Ft. Worth Garden Club (v.p. 1995-96). Episcopalian. Home: # 101 3900 White Settlement Rd Fort Worth TX 76107-7822

LALL, B. KENT, civil engineering educator; b. Feb. 4, 1939; m. Margaret Vivienne Boult, Nov. 30, 1970; 1 child, Niren Nicolaus. BS in Civil Engring., Panjab Engring. Coll., Chandigarh, India, 1961; ME in Hwy. Engring., U. Roorkee, India, 1964; PhD in Transp., U. Birmingham, Eng., 1969. Registered profl. engr. Commonwealth scholar U. Birmingham, 1966-69; lectr. Indian Inst. Tech., New Delhi, 1964-72, asst. prof., 1972-75; assoc. prof. U. Man., Winnipeg, Can., 1975-77; assoc. prof. civil engring. Portland (Oreg.) State U., 1977-84, prof., 1984—; vis. prof. U. Adelaide, South Australia, 1985; cons. Nat. Rds. Bd., Ministry of Works, Wellington, New Zealand, 1986. Editor procs., co-author: Transportation Engineering; contbr. articles to profl. jours. Vol. Meals on Wheels, Portland, 1991—. Fellow ASCE (chmn. transp. congress 1995, exec. com. urban transp. divsn. 1994-95, pub. transp. com. 1988-91, mem. high speed ground transport com.), Inst. Transp. Engrs., Transp. Rsch. Bd., Rotary (bd. dirs. S.W. Portland 1990-91, 95—, pres.-elect 1997-98), High Speed Rail/Maglev Assn., Intelligent Transp. Soc. of Am. Office: Portland State U Dept Civil Engring PO Box 751 Portland OR 97207-0751

LALLEY, FRANK EDWARD, federal government official; b. Woonsocket, R.I., Jan. 11, 1944; s. Frank Edward III and Lois Eva (Parkin) L.; m. Joyce Lynne Rynkiewicz, June 11, 1983; children: Jonathan, Robert, Adrienne, Andrea. B in Mgmt. Engring., Rensselaer Poly. Inst., 1965; MBA, So. Ill. U., 1971; postgrad., George Washington U., 1972-75. Ops. rsch. analyst U.S. Army, 1969-74; energy analyst FEA, Washington, 1974-77; dir. petroleum supply div. U.S. Dept. Energy, Washington, 1977-87; dir. Office Info., Mgmt. and Stats. U.S. Dept. Vets. Affairs, Washington, 1987-90; assoc. dep. asst. sec. Info. Resources Policies and Oversight U.S. Dept. Vets. Affairs, 1990-94, assoc. dep. asst. sec. Telecom., 1994—; co-chmn. publ. U.S. Refining Industry, Nat. Petroleum Coun., 1986, govt. liaison publ. U.S. Oil and Gas Outlook, 1987; mem. Nat. Performance Review, 1993; chmn. Interagency Com. Info. Resources Mgmt., 1994-95, chmn. Interagency Mgmt. Coun., 1997—; mem. Nat. Comm. Sys. Com. of Principals, 1996-97. Capt. USAF, 1965-69. Home: 13001 Shadwell Ct Woodbridge VA 22192-3364 Office: Dept Vets Affairs 810 Vermont Ave NW Washington DC 20420-0001

LALLI, CELE GOLDSMITH, editor; b. Scranton, Pa., Apr. 8, 1933; d. Arthur Langfeld and Viola Catherine (Wolfort) Goldsmith; m. Michael Anthony Lalli, Apr. 4, 1964; children—Francesca Ann, Erica Catherine. BA, Vassar Coll., 1955. From asst. editor to editor Amazing Sci. Fiction Stories, N.Y.C., 1955-65; mng. editor Modern Bride's Guide to Decorating Your First Home, N.Y.C., 1965-69; exec. editor Modern Bride, N.Y.C., 1969-81, editor-in-chief, v.p., 1982—. Co-author: Modern Bride Guide to Your Wedding and Marriage, 1984, Modern Bride Complete Wedding Planner, 1997; author: Modern Bride Guide to Etiquette, 1993. Bd. dirs. Conn. Assn. for Children with Learning Disabilities, 1984-93. Recipient Invisible Little Man award West Coast Sci. Fiction Orgn., 1961; named to YWCA Acad. of Women Achievers, 1986. Mem. Am. Soc. Mag. Editors, Fashion Group. Republican. Roman Catholic. Office: Modern Bride K-III Comms 249 W 17th St New York NY 10011-5300

LALLI, FRANK, magazine editor. Mng. editor Money mag., N.Y.C. Office: Money Magazine Time & Life Bldg Rockefeller Ctr 33rd fl New York NY 10020 Office: Money Magazine Time & Life Bldg 1271 Avenue Of The Americas New York NY 10020-1300*

LALLI, MARY SCHWEITZER, writer, artist; b. Newark, Ohio, June 24, 1925; d. Clemence Sylvester and Ethel Ann (Deem) Schilling; m. Francis Edward Schweitzer, Aug. 23, 1947 (div. Oct. 1974); children: Dale Francis, Darrell Charles, David Edward; m. Joseph G. Lalli, June 21, 1975. BA, Denison U., 1947. Lic. tchr. English. Tchr. English Ctrl. Jr. High, Newark, 1947-48; profl. artist Nat. Forum Profl. Artists, Phila., 1968-75; dir. art shows Phila., 1968—. Writer Doll Castle News, Doll Times, Doll Reader, Antique Doll World, Doll Collector's Price Guide, Doll World, 1983—; photojournalist Doll Times; columnist Doll Designs. Recipient 125 art awards Phila. Plastic Club, 1972, 73, 78, award of honor Inst. Pub. Edn., Drexel Hill, Pa., 1980. Mem. Nat. League Am. Pen Women (1st v.p. 1985-89), DaVinci Art Alliance (sec.), Plastic Club (pres., v.p.), Chester County Art Assn. Avocations: attending art shows, doll shows, classical music concerts, doing research.

L'ALLIER, JAMES JOSEPH, educational multimedia company executive, instructional designer; b. St. Paul, June 24, 1945; s. Charlemagne Joseph and Mildred Marie (LeVasseur) L'A.; m. Susan Kay Margulies, Apr. 28, 1973. BS magna cum laude, U. Wis., River Falls, 1969, MS, 1973; PhD, U. Minn., 1980. Instr. English River Falls Sr. High Sch., 1969-71, Stillwater (Minn.) Sr. High Sch., 1971-80; mgr. computer assisted instrn. Wilson Learning Corp., Mpls., 1980-83, dir. R&D, 1983-86; v.p. R&D Wilson Learning Interactive Tech. Group, Santa Fe, 1986-89; v.p. product devel. Nippon Wilson Learning, Tokyo, 1989-90; v.p. instructional systems Whole Systems International, Cambridge, Mass., 1990-93; v.p. product devel. Nat. Edn. Tng. Group, Naperville, Ill., 1993—; expert witness Universal Tng., Chgo., 1989-91. Author: (video prodns.) Who Shot the Terminal?, 1984, The Tenth Woman, 1987, Working Toward the Future, 1991, America's Workforce: A Vision for the Future, 1992; mem. editorial bd. Learning Age, Mpls., 1987-89; product reviewer Ednl. Tech., N.Y.C., 1981-83; assoc. editor Performance and Instrn., Washington, 1983-85. Curriculum chair Total Info. Ednl. Systems, St. Paul, 1971-76; fund raiser U. Minn. Alliance, Mpls., 1983-89; contbr. Am. Cancer Soc., Washington, 1987—; mem. pub. svc. com. Instructional Systems Assn., Sunset Beach, Calif., 1988—. U. Minn. Grad. Sch. Edn. sr. fellow, 1984; U.S. Dept. Labor grantee, 1991. Mem. U. Wis. Alumni Assn., Instructional Systems Assn. (conf. chair 1980, 84), U. Minn. Alumni Assn., Boston Computer Soc., Pres.'s Club U. Minn., Heritage Soc. U. Wis.; reviewer William H. Donner Found. Inc., N.Y.C., 1993—. Avocations: reading, photography, music, computer programming. Office: Nat Edn Tng Group 1751 W Diehl Rd Naperville IL 60563-1840

LALLY, LAURA HOLLOWAY, computer information systems educator; b. Queens Village, N.Y.. MBA in Computer Methodology, Baruch Coll., 1984; PhD in Info. Systems, NYU, 1992. Spl. asst. prof. Hofstra U., Hempstead, N.Y., 1989-92, asst. prof., 1992-95, assoc. prof., 1995—. Rsch. grantee NSF, 1994. Office: Hofstra U 134 Hofstra Hempstead NY 11550

LALLY, MICHAEL DAVID, writer, actor; b. Orange, N.J., May 25, 1942; s. James A. and Irene I. (Dempsey) L.; children: Caitlin Maeve, Miles Aaron. BA, U. Iowa, 1968, MFA, 1969. Instr. Trinity Coll., Washington, 1969-74; book reviewer Washington Post, 1974-77; editor Franklin Library div. Franklin Mint, 1976-79; editor, pub. various newspapers and presses including Iowa Defender, Some of Us Press, The Washington Review of the Arts, 1966-80, Venice mag., 1988-91, The Hollywood Rev., 1991; bd. dirs. The Print Center, Bklyn., 1972-75, Washington Film Classroom, 1970-72. Actor: (films) Last Rites, 1980, The Nesting, 1981, White Fang, 1991, Cool World, 1992, Basic Instinct, 1992, Not Again, 1996, (stage) The Heroes, 1981, Balm in Gilead, 1983, The Rhythm of Torn Stars, 1988-89, Short Eyes, 1994, (TV) Cagney and Lacey, 1984, Berrengers, 1985, Hardcastle and McCormick, 1986, L.A. Law, 1989, Father Dowling's Mysteries, 1991, Caught in the Act, 1993, Diagnosis Murder, 1994, NYPD Blue, 1995, 97; freelance writer, reviewer, actor, N.Y.C., 1975-82; screenwriter, actor, L.A., 1982—; author 20 books including Rocky Dies Yellow, 1974, German edit., 1982, Dues, 1974, Catch My Breath, 1976, 95, Just Let Me Do It, 1978, Attitude, 1982, Hollywood Magic, 1982, Can't Be Wrong, 1996; author, dir. (one-act play) Four Grown Men, N.Y.C., 1982, Hollywood Magic, L.A., 1983; co-author (play) The Rhythm of Torn Stars, 1988-89; 3 short plays, 1995; recorded poems on CD, What You Find There, 1994; contbr. articles and poetry to profl. jours., newspapers, mags. Served with USAF, 1962-66. Nat. Endowment for Arts fellow, 1974, 81; recipient Discovery award N.Y. Poetry Ctr., 1972, award Poets Found., 1974, Lit. Prize award Pacificus Found., 1996. Mem. Screen Actors Guild, Writers Guild Am., AFTRA, P.E.N. (Oakland Josephine Miles award for excellence in lit. 1996).

LALLY, NORMA ROSS, federal agency administrator, retired; b. Crawford, Nebr., Aug. 10, 1932; d. Roy Anderson and Alma Leona (Barber) Lively; m. Robert Edward Lally, Dec. 4, 1953 (div. Mar. 1986); children: Robyn Carol Murch, Jeffrey Alan, Gregory Roy. BA, Boise (Idaho) State U., 1974, MA, 1976; postgrad., Columbia Pacific U., 1988—. With grad. admissions Boise State U., 1971-74; with officer programs USN Recruiting, Boise, 1974; pub. affairs officer IRS, Boise and Las Vegas, 1975-94; ret., 1994; speaker in field, Boise and Las Vegas, 1977—. Contbr. articles to newspapers. Mem. task force Clark County Sch. Dist., Las Vegas. Staff sgt. USAF, 1950-54. Mem. NAFE, Women in Mil. Svc. Am., Mensa, Toastmasters (Las Vegas), Marine's Meml. Club (life), Am. Legion. Avocations: writing, dancing, music, golf, swimming. Home: 3013 Hawksdale Dr Las Vegas NV 89134-8967

LALLY, RICHARD FRANCIS, aviation security consultant, former association executive, former government official; b. Newark, Nov. 23, 1925; s. Francis J. and Helen (Fennesy) L.; m. Doris P. Yasko, Sept. 10, 1949; children: Barbara J. Lally-Dittler, Joan E. Lally Stalder. B.S., Upsala Coll., 1950. Spl. agt. FBI, Atlanta, Cin. and Washington, 1951-60; area dir., chief gen. investigations Dept. Labor, Newark and Washington, 1960-63; dep. dir. compliance and security FAA, Washington, 1963-65; dir. compliance and security FAA, 1965-67; dir. investigations and security Dept. Transp., Washington, 1967-70; dir. equal opportunity Dept. Transp., 1967-70, dir. civil rights, 1970-72, dir. transp. security, 1972-74; dir. civil aviation security FAA, 1974-82; v.p. security Air Transport Assn. Am., 1982-91; aviation security consultant, 1991—. Served with AC U.S. Army, 1944-46. Recipient Exceptional Svc. citation Dept. Trans., 1969, Meritorious Achievement award, 1970, Sec.'s award, 1973, Superior Achievement award, 1970, Sec.'s award, 1973, Superior Achievement award, 1973, 76, Superior Achievement in Equal Opportunity award, 1977, Disting. Alumnus award Upsala Coll., 1979, Presdl. Rank Sr. Exec. award, 1980, Extraordinary Svc. award FAA, 1991, Internat. Security Mgmt. Assn. J. Paul Breslin Recognition award, 1993. Home and Office: Bay Colony 25 Indian River Dr Dagsboro DE 19939

LALLY, VINCENT EDWARD, atmospheric scientist; b. Brookline, Mass., Oct. 13, 1922; s. Michael James and Ellen Teresa (Dolan) L.; m. Marguerite Mary Tibert, June 5, 1949; children: Dennis V., Marianne Baugh, Stephen J. BS in Meteorology, U. Chgo., 1944; BSEE, MIT, 1948, MS in Engring. Adminstrn., 1949. Engr. Bendix-Friez, Balt., 1949-51; chief metall. equip. devel. Air Force Cambridge Rsch. Labs., Bedford, Mass., 1951-58; rsch. dir. Teledynamics, Phila., 1958-61; dir. Nat. Sci. Balloon Facility Nat. Ctr. for Atmospheric Rsch., Boulder, Colo., 1961-66, sr. scientist, 1966-91, sr. scientist emeritus, 1991—. Contbr. articles to sci. jours., chpt. to handbook in field. 1st lt. USAAC, 1942-46. Fellow Am. Meteorol. Soc. (Cleveland Abbe award 1990); mem. Inst. Navigation, Sigma Xi. Achievements include 7 patents for space inflatables, superpressure balloons, rocket instruments, communications techniques; made first balloon flight around the world, longest balloon flight; pioneered technology in measurements from radiosondes, aircraft and rockets. Avocations: running, golf, application of Monte Carlo techniques to gaming. Home: 4475 Laguna Pl # 305 Boulder CO 80303 Office: Nat Ctr Atmospheric Rsch PO Box 3000 Boulder CO 80307

LALONDE, BERNARD JOSEPH, educator; b. Detroit, June 3, 1933; s. John Bernard and Fannie (Napier) LaL.; m. Barbara Elaine Eggenberger, Sept. 6, 1958; children—Lisa Renee, Michell Ann, Christopher John. A.B., U. Notre Dame, 1955; M.B.A., U. Detroit, 1957; Ph.D., Mich. State U., 1961. Asst. prof. mktg. U. Colo., Boulder, 1961-65; assoc. prof. Mich. State U., East Lansing, 1965-69; James R. Riley prof. mktg. and logistics Ohio State U., Columbus, 1969-85; Raymond E. Mason prof. transp. and logistics Ohio State U., 1985-95, prof. emeritus, 1995. Author: Physical Distribution Management, 2d edit, 1968, Customer Service: A Management Perspective, 1988; Editor: Jour. Bus. Logistics; Jour. book and monographs editor, Am. Mktg. Assn.; Contbr. articles to profl. jours. Pres. Transp. Research Found. Recipient John Drury Sheehan award, 1976; Formerly Ford scholar; Gen. Electric fellow. Mem. Am. Marketing Assn., Regional Sci. Assn., Council Logistic Mgmt., Soc. Logistics Engrs., Beta Gamma Sigma, Alpha Kappa Psi. Roman Catholic. Home: 8538 Pitlochry Ct Dublin OH 43017-9770 Office: Ohio State U Coll Bus Logistics Rsch Group 421 Hagerty Hall Columbus OH 43210

LA LONDE, LAWRENCE LEE, family practice physician; b. Bay City, Mich., Feb. 8, 1951; s. Raymond Lawrence and Bernice (Trombley) La L.; m. Laura Christine Madison, June 26, 1976; children: Lawrence Christian, Loren Michael, Lindsey David. B in Gen. Studies, U. Mich., 1973; MD, Wayne State U., 1978. Diplomate Am. Bd. of Family Practice. Resident in Family Practice Saginaw (Mich.) Coop. Hosps., Inc., 1981; physician Oscoda (Mich.) Family Physicians, 1981-85, Ctrl. Calif. Faculty Med. Group, Fresno, Calif., 10985, Saginaw (Mich.) Family Physicians, 1986-87, St. Mary's Seton Corp., Saginaw, Mich., 1987-89, pvt. practice, Saginaw, 1989—. adj. asst. dir. Family Practice Resident Program, Saginaw Coop Hosps., 1986—. Office: 5421 Colony Dr N Saginaw MI 48603-7128

LALONDE, MARC, lawyer, former Canadian government official; b. Ile Perrot, Que., Can., July 26, 1929; s. J. Albert and Nora (St-Aubin) L.; m. Claire Tetreau, Sept. 8, 1955; children: Marie, Luc, Paul, Catherine. BA, Coll. St. Laurent, Montreal, 1950; LLB, U. Montreal, 1964, LLM, 1955; MA in Econs. and Polit. Sci., Oxford (Eng.) U., 1957; PhD honoris causa, Limburg U., The Netherlands, 1989. Bar: Que. 1955, Queen's Coun. 1971, Order of Can, 1988. Prof. bus. law and econs. U. Montreal, 1957-59; spl. asst. to Minister of Justice, Ottawa, Ont., Can., 1959-60; partner firm Gelinas, Bourque, Lalonde & Benoit, Montreal, 1960-68; policy adviser to Prime Minister Lester B. Pearson, Ottawa, 1967-68; prin. sec. to Prime Minister Pierre E. Trudeau, Ottawa, 1968-72; elected to House of Commons for Montreal-Outremont, 1972, minister of nat. health and welfare, 1972-77, minister of state for fed.-provincial relations, 1977-78, minister responsible for status of women, 1975-78, minister of justice and atty. gen. Can., 1978-79, minister of energy, mines and resources, 1980-82, minister of finance, 1982-84; ptnr. Stikeman, Elliott, Montreal; bd. dirs. Orleans Resources, Inc., Citibank of Can., Camdev Corp.; advisor Internat. Coun. Presidium of Ukraine; ad hoc judge Internat. Ct. Justice, 1995—. Author: The Changing Role of the Prime Minister's Office, 1971. Decorated officer Order of Can.; recipient Dana award APHA, 1978. Mem. Internat. Coun. on Comml. Arbitration, Am. Arbitration Assn. (exec. bd. dirs.), London Ct. Internat. Arbitration. Mem. Liberal Party. Home: 5440 Legare, Montreal, PQ Canada H3T 1Z4

LALONDE, ROBERT FREDERICK, state senator, retired; b. Bay City, Mich., Dec. 1, 1922; s. Joseph and Mildred Amanda (Brimmer) LaL.; m. Betty Ellen Schwartz, Aug. 2, 1941; 1 child, Rose Marie. BGE in Bus., U. Omaha, 1965. Airport mgr. Jackson (Wyo.) Hole Airport, Jackson, Wyo., 1972-80; county commr. Teton County, Jackson, 1982-86, rental property owner, 1970-88; Wyo. state senator Jackson, 1989-95. Author: The Dangerous Trilogy, 1973. Chmn. Teton County Rep. Com., Jackson, 1975-77; del. Rep. Nat. Conv., Detroit, 1980; mem. Electoral Coll., Cheyenne, Wyo., 1980; sec. Wyo. Rep. party, 1980-82; chmn. Teton County Planning Commn., Jackson, 1973-78. Col. USAF, 1943-70. Mem. Am. Legion (comdr. 1989-94), Wyo. Airport Operators Assn. (founder, pres. 1973-75, Disting. Svc. award 1979), Jackson Hole C. of C. (pres. 1977-79, Citizen of Yr. 1975, Disting. Svc. award 1980), Rotary (pres. 1976-77). Christian Scientist. Avocations: hunting, fishing. Home: PO Box 1707 Jackson WY 83001-1707

LALOR, EDWARD DAVID DARRELL, labor and employment arbitrator, lawyer; b. Madison, Wis., Jan. 29, 1944; s. Edward Richard and Viola (Byrne) Lalor; adult adopted mother: Helen Rose (Litney) Pribble; m. Paula Sue Tompkins, Aug. 12, 1978; children. BBA, U. Wis., 1966, JD, 1969. Bar: Wis., 1969, Minn., 1980, U.S. Dist. Ct. (we. dist.) Wis., 1969, U.S. Supreme Ct., 1979. Gen. atty. NLRB, Kansas City, Mo., Kans., 1969-80; atty. advice divsn., advice br. NLRB, Washington, 1973-74; trial specialist NLRB, Kansas City, 1977-80; arbitrator labor and employment, pres. Pribble Arbitration and Mediation Svcs., Inc., Mpls., 1980-85; arbitrator, pres. Pribble Arbitration and Mediation Svcs., Inc., St. Cloud, Minn., 1985-95; CEO, pres., arbitrator Lalor Arbitration and Mediation, Inc., St. Cloud, Minn., 1995—; mcpl. judge City Countryside (Kans.), 1979-80; mem. arbitration panels Fed. Mediation and Conciliation Svc., 1982—, Am. Arbitration Assn., 1984—, Nat. Mediation Bd., 1991—, Iowa Pub. Employment Rels. Bd., 1983—; pvt. panel EDDL Case Corp. and I.A. Machinists and Aerospace Workers Local 2525, Fargo, N.D., 1985—; full-day moderator in arbitration, labor and employement law discrimination, alt. dispute resolution, evidence and family law programs Minn. Continuing Legal Edn., 1989—; labor and employment arbitrator Minn. Cts. Alt. Dispute Resolution, 1994—. Contbr. articles to profl. jours. Mem. Minn. Dem. Farm Labor State and Congl. Dist. Ctrl. Com., 1981—, Minn. State Platform Commn., Dem. Farm Labor Party, 1984-85, chmn. senate dist., 1984-85, fundraiser, initiator, co-founder Dr. Guy Stanton Ford Ednl. Found., 1964-69; co-founder Westport Free Health Clinic, Kansas City, Mo., 1970-80; active coun. Land of Lakes coun. Girl Scouts, Minn., 1985—, lifetime mem. adult leader mem.; active Leadership Coun. So. Poverty Ctr., Habitat for Humanity Internat. Ptnrs. Coun.; coach Girls Youth Basketball League, St. Cloud, 1992—; bd. dirs. St. Cloud Symphony Orch., 1992-94; chair New Voter registration Drives Senate Dist. 59, 1981-85, Stearns-Benton County Senate Dist.17, 1989-91; historian Lalor Clan for the Ams.; host family for Irish polit. prisoners children's holiday, 1996—; mem. Internat. Hearing Found. Mem. ABA (labor and employment law sects. 1978—), Fed. Bar Assn. (labor and employment law sects. 1974—), Minn. Bar Assn. (labor and employment law sects. 1980—, mock trial program judge 1989-93), Nat. Youth Sports Coaches Assn. (cert.), Wis. Bar Assn. (labor and employment law sects. 1969—), Internat. Indsl. Rels. Assn., Soc. Profls. in Dispute Resolution Internat., Indsl. Rels. Rsch. Assn., EDDL Internat., Theta Delta Chi Internat. Roman Catholic. Avocations: reading, family history, fishing, stock investing. Office: Lalor Arbitration & Mediation Inc 1220 North Thirteenth Saint Cloud MN 56303-2733

LAM, CHEUNG-WEI, electrical engineer; b. Hong Kong, Mar. 5, 1965; came to U.S., 1987; s. Yeung-Tak and Sau-Jin (Wong) L.; m. Hoi-Man Sarah Hui, May 29, 1993; 1 child, Isaac Samuel. BS, Chinese U. Hong Kong, 1987; MS, MIT, 1989, PhD, 1993. Rsch. asst. MIT, Cambridge, 1988-93; rschr. Schlumberger-Doll Rsch, Ridgefield, Conn., 1990; mem. tech. staff Quad Design Tech., Camarillo, Calif., 1993—; mem. com. Soc. Automotive Engrs./Electromagnetic Compatibility Modeling Task Force, 1994—. Contbr. articles to Jour. Superconductivity, IEEE, Jour. Electromagnetic Waves and Applications. Bank of Am. scholar, 1985, Du Pont scholar, 1986. Mem. IEEE (prize 1987), Sigma Xi. Achievements include design of efficient electromagnetic interference simulator, nonlinear models for superconducting transmission lines; research in high-speed electronic interconnection and packaging, acoustic logging in borehole structures. Home: 1395 La Culebra Cir Camarillo CA 93012-5551 Office: Quad Design Tech 1385 Del Norte Rd Camarillo CA 93010-8437

LAM, PAULINE POHA, library director; b. Hong Kong, Oct. 21, 1950; came to U.S., 1971; d. Cheung and Kam-Chun (Mo) Li; m. Frank Sung-Lun Lam, Nov. 28, 1973; children: Candace See-Win Lam, Megan See-Kay Lam. BA, U. B.C., 1977; MLS, U. Tex., 1980; cert. City Mgmt. Acad., Austin C.C., 1994. Libr. dir. City of Cedar Park (Tex.); bd. dirs. Cedar Park Pub. Libr. Found., 1994—. Mem. Work Force Literacy Com. Literacy Coun. of Williamson County, 1995; bd. dirs. ARC of Ctrl. Tex., Austin, 1995—. Mem. ALA, Tex. Libr. Assn., Tex. Mcpl. League Libr. Dir. Assn. Avocations: reading, crocheting, painting. Office: Cedar Park Pub Libr 550 Discovery Blvd Cedar Park TX 78613-2200

LAM, SIMON SHIN-SING, computer science educator; b. Macao, July 31, 1947; came to U.S., 1966; s. Chak Han and Kit Ying (Tang) L.; m. Amy Leung, Mar. 29, 1971; 1 child, Eric. B.S.E.E. with distinction, Wash. State U., 1969; M.S. in Engring., UCLA, 1970, Ph.D., 1974. Research engr. ARPA Network Measurement Ctr., UCLA, Los Angeles, 1971-74; research staff mem. IBM Watson Research Ctr, Yorktown Heights, N.Y., 1974-77; asst. prof. U. Tex.-Austin, Austin, 1977-79, assoc. prof., 1979-83, prof. computer sci., 1983—; David S. Bruton Centennial prof. U. Tex., Austin, 1985-88, anonymous prof., 1988—; chmn. dept. computer sci. U. Tex.-Austin, Austin, 1992-94. Editor-in-chief IEEE/ACM Transactions on Networking, 1995—; editor: Principles of Communication and Networking Protocols; contbr. articles to profl. jours. NSF grantee, 1978—; Chancellor's Teaching fellow UCLA, 1969-73. Fellow IEEE (Leonard G. Abraham prize 1975); mem. Assn. for Computing Machinery (program chmn. symposium 1983). Avocations: tennis, swimming, skiing, travel. Office: Univ Tex Dept Comp Sci Austin TX 78712

LAMALIE, ROBERT EUGENE, retired executive search company executive; b. Fremont, Ohio, June 3, 1931; s. Glennis and Mildred M. (Hetrick) L.; m. Dorothy M. Zilles, June 20, 1953; children: Deborah, Dawn, Elaine. BA, Capital U., Columbus, Ohio, 1954; postgrad., Case Western Res. U. Asst. dir. recruiting Xerox Corp., 1959-62; mgr. orgn. planning and profl. recruiting Glidden Co., 1962-65; search cons. Booz, Allen & Hamilton, Inc., Cleve., 1965-67; pres., chief exec. officer Lamalie Assocs., Inc., Tampa, Fla., 1967-84, chmn. bd. dirs., chief exec. officer, 1984-87, chmn. bd. dirs., 1987-88; pres. Robert Lamalie, Inc., Marco Island, Fla., 1988-90, ret., 1990. Served with U.S. Army, 1954-56, Korea.

LAMAN, JERRY THOMAS, mining company executive; b. Muskogee, Okla., Mar. 1, 1947; s. Thomas J. and Juanita J. (Pittman) L.; m. Lenora J. Laman, July 1, 1972; children: Troy T., Brian D. Silver Diploma, Colo. Sch. Mines, 1969. Refinery engr. ARCO, Torrance, Calif., 1969-71; chem. engr. Cleveland-Cliffs Iron Co., Mountain City, Nev., 1971-73, asst. mine supt., 1973-77; chief uranium metallurgist Cleveland-Cliffs Iron Co., Casper, Wyo., 1977-83; project mgr. In-Situ, Inc., Laramie, Wyo., 1983-85, v.p., 1985—; also bd. dirs. In-Situ, Inc.; pres. Solution Mining Corp., Laramie, Wyo., 1990—, also bd. dirs., 1990—. Mem. Soc. for Mining, Metallurgy and Exploration, Optimist (pres. Laramie club 1989). Avocations: golf, fishing. Home: 1085 Colina Dr Laramie WY 82070-5014

LAMANTIA, CHARLES ROBERT, management consulting company executive; b. N.Y.C., June 12, 1939; s. Joseph Ferdinand and Catherine (Perniciaro) LaM.; m. Ann Christine Carmody, Sept. 16, 1961; children: Elise, Matthew. BA, Columbia U., 1960, BS, 1961, MS, 1962, ScD, 1965; grad. advanced mgmt. program, Harvard Bus. Sch., 1979. Cons. staff Arthur D. Little, Inc., Cambridge, Mass., 1967-77, v.p., 1977-81, pres., chief oper. officer, 1987-88, pres., chief exec. officer, 1988—, also bd. dirs.; pres., chief exec. officer Koch Process Systems, Westboro, Mass., 1981-86; mem. adv. coun. Sch. Engring. Columbia U., Sch. Mgmt. Boston Coll.; bd. dirs. State St. Boston Corp., 1993—; trustee Meml. Dr. Trust, 1988—. Mem. Corp. Woods Hole Oceanog. Inst., 1996—; mem. bd. overseers Mus. Sci., Boston, 1988—, Sta. WGBH pub. broadcasting, 1991—, mem. Conf. Bd., 1989—; mem. Mass. Gov.'s Coun., Mass. Bus. Roundtable, 1992—. Lt. USN, 1965-67. NSF fellow, 1965; Sloan Found. fellow, 1962. Mem. Am. Inst. Chem. Engrs., Soc. Chem. Industries. Office: Arthur D Little Inc 25 Acorn Park Cambridge MA 02140-2301

LAMAR, HOWARD ROBERTS, educational administrator, historian; b. Tuskegee, Ala., Nov. 18, 1923; s. John Howard and Elma (Roberts) L.; m. Doris Shirley White, Sept. 3, 1959; children: Susan Kent, Sarah Howard. BA, Emory U., 1944; MA, Yale U., 1945, PhD, 1951; LHD (hon.), Emory U., 1975; LLD (hon.), Yale U., 1993; LittD (hon.), U. Nebr., 1994. Instr. U. Mass., 1945-46, Wesleyan U., Middletown, Conn., 1948-49; mem. faculty Yale U., 1949-94, prof. Am. History and history Am. West, 1964-94, W.R. Coe prof. Am. history, 1987-94, Sterling prof. history, 1987—, chmn. history dept., 1962-63, 67-70, dir. history grad. studies, 1964-67, fellow Ezra Stiles Coll., 1961-94, dean, 1979-85, pres., 1992-93, Sterling prof. history emeritus, 1994—. Author: Dakota Territory, 1861-1889, 1956, The Far Southwest, 1846-1912, A Territorial History, 1966; also articles, reviews.; Editor: (Joseph Downey) Cruise of the Portsmouth, 1958, Western Americana Series, 1961—, Reader's Encyclopedia of the American West, 1977, Gold Seeker: Adventures of A Belgian Argonaut in California, 1985; co-author, co-editor The Frontier in History: North America and Southern Africa Compared, 1981. Alderman, New Haven, 1951-53. Mem. Orgn. Am. Historians, Western History Assn. (pres. 1971-72), Am. Antiquarian Soc., Elihu Soc., Phi Beta Kappa. Democrat. Home: 1747 Hartford Tpke North Haven CT 06473-1249 Office: Yale U Dept History New Haven CT 06520

LAMAR, JAMES LEWIS, JR., chemical engineer; b. Antlers, Okla., June 13, 1959; s. James Lewis and Priscilla (Henderson) L.; m. Carol Horton, May 16, 1982; children: Joy Loree, Amanda Beth. AS, Bee County Coll., 1979; BSChemE, Tex. A&I U., 1982. Cert. quality engr., 1991, cert. quality auditor, 1992, RAB quality systems lead auditor, 1993. Prodn. engr. Union Carbide Corp., Soutn Charleston, W.Va., 1982-86; diagnostic engr. Union Carbide Chems. & Plastics, South Charleston, W.Va., 1986-90; sr. quality engr. Union Carbide Chems. & Plastics, League City, Tex., 1990-94; quality engr. UCC, Texas City, 1994—; prin. Quality Systems Svcs., 1997—; instr. Tex. Dept. Commerce, Houston, 1992. Author/programmer software, 1989-96. Mem. Pine Dr. Babt. Sch. Bd., Dickinson, Tex., 1992. Named Jaycees Outstanding Young Men Am., 1983. Mem. Am. Soc. Quality Control (sr.), Cowboys for Christ. Republican. Office: Union Carbide Bldg 2-UP PO Box 471 Texas City TX 77592-0471

LAMAR, MARTHA LEE, chaplain; b. Birmingham, Jan. 2, 1935; d. Alco L. and Anne Lee (Morris) Lee; m. William Fred Lamar, Jr., June 7, 1986; children: Barbara Gayle Martin, Owen Parker Jr. BS, Auburn U., 1955; MA, Christian Theol. Sem., Indpls., 1992. From adminstv. asst. to rsch. coord. Ala. Affiliate Am. Heart Assn., Birmingham, 1977-86; adminstrv. asst. alumni office De Pauw U., Greencastle, Ind., 1986-89; nursing home chaplain Heritage House Health and Rehab. Ctr., Greencastle, 1989—; nursing home chaplain Garfield Park Health Facility, Indpls., 1992-94, Heritage House Health and Rehab. Ctr., Martinsville, Ind., 1992-95; chaplain cons. Oakwood Corp., Indpls., 1991—. Vol. chaplain's office De Pauw U., 1986—, community work for homeless, Greencastle, 1986—, Fountain Sq. Devel. Corp., Indpls., 1992. Mem. Am. Soc. on Aging, Forum on Religion, Spirituality and Aging, Ind. Health Care Chaplains Assn. Methodist. Avocations: traveling, hiking, reading, entertaining. Office: Heritage House Health & Rehab Ctr 1601 Hospital Dr Greencastle IN 46135-2268

LAMARRE, BERNARD, engineering, contracting and manufacturing advisor; b. Chicoutimi, Que., Can., Aug. 6, 1931; s. Emile J. and Blanche M. (Gagnon) L.; m. Louise Lalonde, Aug. 30, 1952; children: Jean, Christine, Lucie, Monique, Michèle, Philippe, Mireille. BSc, Ecole Poly., Montreal, Que., Can., 1952; MSc, Imperial Coll., U. London, 1955; LLD, St. Francis Xavier U., N.S., Can., 1980; D in Engring. (hon.), U. Waterloo, Ont., 1984; LLD (hon.), U. Concordia, Montreal, 1985; D in Engring. (hon.), U. Montreal, 1985; D in Applied Sci. (hon.), U. Sherbrooke, Que., 1986; D in Bus. Adminstrn. (hon.), U. Chicoutimi, Que., 1987; D in Sci. (hon.), Queen's U., Kingston, Ont., 1987; D in Engring. (hon.), U. Ottawa, Ont., 1988, Tech. U. N.S., 1989, Royal Mil. Coll., Kingston, 1990. Structural and founds. engr. Lalonde-Valois, Montreal, 1955-60, chief engr., 1960-62; ptnr., gen. mgr., pres. Lalonde, Valois, Lamarre, Valois, Montreal, 1962-72; chmn., chief exec. officer Lavalin Group, 1972-91; sr. advisor SNC-Lavalin Inc., 1991—; chmn. Ordre des Ingenieurs du Quebec, Montreal Design Inst., Infradev Internat. Inc., Soc. du Vieux Port de Montreal, Bellechasse Santé; bd. dirs. Videotron Inc. Bd. dirs. Telesystems Inc., Concom Inc., Tembec Inc., U. of Montreal; hon. chmn. Montreal Mus. Fine Arts. Decorated officer Ordre nat. du Québec, Order of Can.; Athlone fellow, 1952. Fellow Engring. Inst. Can., Can. Soc. Civil Engring.; mem. ASCE, Order Engrs. Que., Mont-Royal Club, St. Denis Club, Laval-sur-le Lac Club. Roman Catholic. Home: 4850 Cedar Crescent, Montreal, PQ Canada H3W 2H9

LAMAS, LORENZO, actor, race car driver; b. Santa Monica, Calif., Jan. 20, 1958; s. Fernando Lamas and Arlene Dahl; children: Alvaro Joshua, Shayne Dahl, Paton Lee. Grad., Farragut Acad., Pine Beach, N.J., 1975, Jim Russel Sch. Motor Racing, 1985. Ptnr. LeConte Driving Sch., Willow Springs, Calif., 1985—; driver Phil Conte Racing, Paramount, Calif., 1985—, driver competition in Internat. Motor Sports Assn. prototypes, 1988, 89. Appeared in films, Grease, 1978, Take Down, 1978, Tilt, 1979, Body Rock, 1984, Snake Eater, 1989, The Killing Streets, 1991, Night of the Warrior, 1991, also co-prodr. Snake Eater II: The Drug Buster, 1991, Final Impact, 1992, C.I.A., Code Name Alexa, 1992, Snake Eater III: His Law, 1992, Final Round, 1993, Bounty Tracker, 1993, The Swordsman, 1993, C.I.A. II: Target Alexa, 1994 (also dir.); (TV movies) Detour to Terror, 1980, Bad Blood, 1994; appeared in TV series, California Fever, 1979, Midland Heights, 1980, Falcon Crest, 1981-90, Dancin' to the Hits, 1986, Renegade Series, 1992. Winner Toyota Grand Prix of Long Beach, 1985. Avocations: surfing; skiing; golf; motorcycles; karate. Office: No Rain Prodns Inc care L & L Bus Mgmt 3727 W Magnolia Blvd # 807 Burbank CA 91505-2818

LAMB, CHARLES F., minister; b. Maryville, Tenn., Dec. 18, 1934; s. C. Fred and Sadie Ellen (Tedder) L.; children: Elizabeth Susan, Linda Louise, Jennifer Janet; m. Betty Jane Zimmerman, Dec. 29, 1979. BA, Maryville Coll., 1956; MDiv, Grad. Sem. of Phillips U., 1961; D in Ministry, N.Y. Theol. Sem., 1990. Ordained to ministry Christian Ch., 1961. Pastor East Aurora Christian Ch., N.Y., 1961-71; assoc. regional min. Christian Ch., Disciples of Christ, Northeastern Region, Buffalo, N.Y., 1971-75; regional min. Christian Ch., Disciples of Christ, Northeastern Region, Buffalo, 1975—; mem. orgns. clergy and coun. of chs. Trustee Village of East Aurora, 1968-73; active environ. groups Conf. Mayors and Village Ofcls. N.Y., 1968-73. Author: Doc's Diary, 1996. Pres. Coll. Regional Mins., 1997-99; mem. adminstrv. com. Gen. Bd. of Christian Ch., Disciples of Christ, 1997-99. Mem. Conf. Regional Ministers and Moderators of the Disciples of Christ (pres. 1997-98). Democrat. Office: 1272 Delaware Ave Buffalo NY 14209-2401

LAMB, DARLIS CAROL, sculptor; b. Wausa, Nebr.; d. Lindor Soren and June Berniece (Skalberg) Nelson; m. James Robert Lamb; children: Sherry Lamb Sobh, Michael, Mitchell. BA in Fine Arts, Columbia Pacific U., San Rafael, Calif., 1988; MA in Fine Arts, Columbia Pacific U., 1989. Exhibited in group shows at Nat. Arts Club, N.Y.C., 1983, 85, 89, 91, 92, 93, 95, 96 (Catherine Lorillard Wolfe award sculpture 1983, C.L. Wolfe Horse's Head award 1994, Anna Hyatt Huntington cash award 1995, honorable mention 1996), N.Am. Sculpture Exhibit, Foothills Art Ctr., Golden, Colo., 1983-84, 86-87, 90-91 (Pub. Svc. Co. of Colo. sculpture award 1990), Nat. Acad. of Design, 1986, Nat. Sculpture Soc., 1985, 91, 95 (C. Percival Dietch Sculpture prize 1991), Loveland Mus. and Gallery, 1990-91, Audubon Artists, 1991, Allied Artists Am., 1992, 95, Pen and Brush, 1993, 95-96 (Roman Bronze award 1995), Colorado Springs Fine Arts Mus., 1996, others; represented in permanent collections in Nebr. Hist. Soc., Am. Lung Assn. of Colo., Benson Park Sculpture Garden, Loveland, U.S. Space Found., others. Mem. Catherine Lorillard Wolfe Art Club, N.Am. Sculpture Soc. Office: PO Box 9043 Englewood CO 80111-0301

LAMB, FREDERIC DAVIS, lawyer; b. Oak Park, Ill., Nov. 23, 1931; s. Frederic Horace and Alice Emily (Davis) L.; m. Barbara Ann Bullard, Apr. 6, 1954; children: Deborah Ann Lamb Dunn, Jeffrey Davis. BA, Wabash Coll.; JD, U. Mich. Bar: Ohio 1957, Conn. 1989. Atty. Vick Chem. Co., N.Y.C. and Cin., 1956-63; v.p., counsel Merrell div. Richardson-Merrell Inc., Cin., 1964-80; asst. gen. counsel Richardson-Vicks Inc., Wilton, Conn., 1981-83, v.p., gen. counsel, sec., 1984-92; pvt. practice, 1993—. Mayor, councilman City of Forest Park, Ohio, 1971-75; chmn. Forest Park Charter Commn., 1969-70; trustee Food Drug Law Inst., mem. scholarship com., 1985-92. Mem. Silver Spring Country Club (pres., treas., sec. 1989-97). Republican. Avocations: golf; tennis; boating. Home: 30 Keelers Ridge Rd Wilton CT 06897-1607 Office: PO Box 7414 180 Old Ridgefield Rd Wilton CT 06897

LAMB, GEORGE RICHARD, foundation executive; b. Cleve., Aug. 15, 1928; s. Harold George and Mildred (Oller) L.; m. Edith Mathews Read, June 18, 1955; children: Graham Read, George Kinsey, Gwynne Lamb Grimes. B.S., Ohio State U., 1953; M.Sc., Yale U., 1955. Mgr. Tinicum Wildlife Preserve, Phila., 1957-60; exec. sec. Pres. Task Force on Natural Beauty, Washington, 1964; fed. coord. White House Conf. Natural Beauty, Washington, 1965; program and policy staff Outdoor Recreation Resources Review Commn., Washington, 1960-61; budget examiner Bur. Budget, Exec. Office Pres., Washington, 1961-65; pres. Jackson Hole Preserve, N.Y.C., trustee, 1978—; trustee, v.p. Am. Conservation Assn., N.Y.C., 1978-94; assoc. philanthropy L.S. Rockefeller, N.Y.C., 1975-96. Photographer (film) Birds of Tinicum, 1959. Mem. Palisades Interstate Park Commn., N.Y., N.J., 1973-75; pres. Rye Conservation Soc., N.Y., 1968; dir. Federated Conservationists Westchester County, 1965-82; pres. Audobon Soc. Cen. Atlantic States, Washington, 1964-65; trustee Coun. on Environment, N.Y.C., Greenacre Found., N.Y.C., Gallman Meml. Found. With USAF, 1946-49. Fellow Internat. Council Bird Preservation, Cuba, P.R., 1956. Mem. Manursing Island Club, Campfire Club (Pleasantville, N.Y.), Tamarack Club. Office: 30 Rockefeller Plz Rm 5600 New York NY 10112

LAMB, GORDON HOWARD, music educator; b. Eldora, Iowa, Nov. 6, 1934; s. Capp and Ethel (Hayden) L; m. Nancy Ann Painter; children: Kirk, Jon, Phillip. B in Music Edn., Simpson Coll., 1956; M of Music, U. Nebr., 1962; PhD, U. Iowa, 1973. Choral dir. Iowa pub. schs., Tama/Paullina, Sac City, 1957-68; asst. prof. music U. Wis., Stevens Point, 1969-70, U. Tex., Austin, 1970-74; prof., dir. divsn. music U. Tex., San Antonio, 1974-79, prof., v.p. acad. affairs, 1979-86; pres. Northeastern Ill. U., Chgo., 1986-95, pres. emeritus, 1996—; Disting. prof. music dept. Western Ill. U., 1996—. Author: Choral Techniques, 1974, 3d edit. 1988; editor: Guide for the Beginning Choral Director; contbr. articles to scholarly and profl. jours.; composer numerous pieces choral music. Served with U.S. Army, 1957-58. Recipient Most Supportive Pres. or Chancellor award Am. Assn. Colls. for Tchr. Edn., 1992. Mem. Am. Assn. Higher Edn., Am. Assn. State Colls. and Univs., Am. Choral Dirs. Assn. (life, chmn. nat. com. 1970-72). *

LAMB, IRENE HENDRICKS, medical researcher; b. Ky., May 9, 1940; d. Daily P. and Bertha (Hendricks) Lamb; m. Edward B. Meadows. Diploma in nursing, Ky. Bapt. Hosp., Louisville; student, Berea (Ky.) Coll., Calif. State U., L.A. RN, Ky. Charge nurse, head nurse acute medicine, med. ICU, surgical ICU, emergency room various med. ctrs., 1963-67; staff nurse rsch. CCU U. So. Calif./L.A. County Med. Ctr., 1968; nurse coord. clin. rsch. ctr. U. So. Calif./Los Angeles County Med. Ctr., L.A., 1969-74; sr. rsch. nurse cardiology Stanford (Calif.) U. Sch. Medicine, 1974-85, rsch. coord. pvt. clin., 1988; dir. clin. rsch. San Diego Cardiac Ctr., 1989-92; sr. cmty. health nurse Madison County Health Dept., Berea, 1993—; clin. rsch. cons., 1988-97. Co-contbr. numerous articles to med. jours.; contbr. articles to nursing jours., chpts. to med. books. Mem. Am. Heart Assn. (cardiovasc. nursing sect.). Avocations: hand weaving, photography. Home: 107 Lorraine Ct Berea KY 40403-1317 *Choose work situations that stimulate your intellect and force learning...and when that situation becomes easy move forward to more difficult work. Along the way read, read, read.*

LAMB, JAMIE PARKER, JR., mechanical engineer, educator; b. Boligee, Ala., Sept. 21, 1933; s. Jamie Parker and Cletus (Hixson) L.; m. Nancy Catherine Flaherty, June 11, 1955; children: David Parker, Stephen Patrick. B.S., Auburn U., 1954; M.S., U. Ill., 1958, Ph.D., 1961. Asst. prof. engring. mechanics N.C. State U., Raleigh, 1961-63; mem. faculty dept. mech. engring. U. Tex., Austin, 1963—; prof. U. Tex., 1970—, chmn. dept., 1970-76, 96—, assoc. dean engring., 1976-81, prof. faculty aerospace engring., 1981-88, chmn. dept., 1981-88, Ernest Cockrell Jr. Meml. prof., 1981—; dir. engring. program U. Tex.-Pan Am., 1993-94; cons. LTV Aerospace Corp., Dallas, Marshall Space Flight Center, Huntsville, Ala., Tracor, Inc., Austin, Rocketdyne, McGregor, Tex., ARO, Inc., Tullahoma, Tenn., Tex. Gas Transport Co., Austin; spl. cons. U. São Paulo, Brazil, 1974; cons. Mobil Oil Corp., Dallas, Gilbarco, Inc., Greensboro, N.C.; mem. bd. boiler rules Tex. Dept. Labor and Standards, 1977-81; mem. rev. panel postdoctoral assoc. NRC, 1981-95, mem. U.S. nat. com. on theoretical and applied mechanics, 1985-89; chmn. 10th U.S. Nat. Congress Applied Mechanics, 1986. Assoc. tech. editor: Jour. Fluids Engring., 1976-79; contbr. articles to profl. jours. Served to 1st lt. USAF, 1955-57. Recipient Joe J. King Profl. Engring. Achievement award U. Tex. at Austin, 1984, Disting. Alumnus award U. Ill. Dept. Mech. and Indsl. Engring., 1985, Centennial Alumnus award Auburn U. Dept. Mech. Engring., 1986. Fellow ASME (chmn. fluid mechanics tech. com. 1982-84, Founder's award Central Tex. sect. 1975, Leadership award 1976, 81, Centennial award 1980); assoc. fellow AIAA; mem. Am. Soc. Engring. Edn. (chmn. summer faculty programs com. 1978-80, chmn. mech. engring. div. 1979-80, bd. dirs. Profl. Interest Council I, 1981-82), Nat. Soc. Profl. Engrs., Sigma Xi, Pi Tau Sigma, Tau Beta Pi, Sigma Gamma Tau. Baptist. Home: 2605 Pinewood Ter Austin TX 78757-2136

LAMB, JOANN ISABEL, adult nurse practitioner; b. Ottawa, Ont., Can., Oct. 18, 1939; came to U.S., 1961; d. Joseph Gordon and Amelia Marguerite (Gillis) L. BSN, SUNY, Albany, 1980; MA in Nursing Edn., Columbia U., 1980, MSN, 1987. RN, N.Y. Surg. ICU head nurse Columbia-Presbyn. Med. Ctr., N.Y.C., 1973-79, procurement coord. Organ Bank, 1979-80, cardiac transplant coord., 1980-87, nurse practitioner Cardiothoracic Transplant Program, 1987-91, mgr. Cardiothoracic Transplant Program, 1991; v.p. patient svcs. The Dobelle Inst., N.Y.C., 1991—; co-owner Carlam Consultants, Inc., N.Y.C., 1979-83; mem. com. for the devel. of critical care stds. Emergency Med. Svcs. Sys., City of N.Y., 1978-79; mem. planning task force 3d Internat. Intensive Care Nursing Meeting, Montreal, 1985-88; site visitor U. Alta. Hosps., Edmonton, 1988; mem. expert panel selecting cardiac transplant ctrs. managed care program John Hancock Ins. Co., 1990, 91; participant Partnership for Organ Donation, Inc., Washington, 1990; lectr. in the field. Author: (with others) Cardiovascular Nursing, 1986, Pediatric Cardiology, 1986, Standards for Critical Care Nursing, 3d edit., 1988, Organ & Tissue Transplantation: Nursing Care from Procurement through Rehabilitation, 1991, SCCM Textbook of Critical Care Medicine, 1995, Pocket Companion to: Textbook of Critical Care, 1996; mem. editl. bd. Heart & Lung: The Jour. of Critical Care, 1978-81, Life Support Nursing, 1981-83, Critical Care Communique, 1978-81; contbr. more than 30 articles to profl. jours. Recipient Norma J. Shoemaker award for Critical Care Nursing Excellence, Soc. of Critical Care Medicine, 1996. Fellow Am. Coll. Critical Care Medicine; mem. AACN (co-chair program com. N.Y.C. chpt. 1977-78, scholarship com. 1977-78, chair symposium com. 1979-80, bd. dirs. 1981-83, membership com. 1983-88), Soc. for Critical Care Medicine (external affairs com., 1980-81, chair nursing section, 1983, coun. mem., 1984-87, sec., 1987-89, selection panel 1988-89, co-chair mem. com., 1990-94), Columbia U. Sch. Nursing Alumni Assn., Ottawa Civic Hosp. Sch. Nursing Alumni Assn., Am. Assn. Neurosci. Nurses, Am. Assn. Physician Assts., RNs Assn. Ont. (Can.).

LAMB, KATIE A., nursing educator; b. San Saba, Tex., Dec. 9, 1940; d. Wayne C. and Mable Ruth (Mackie) Towerton; m. Edward Lee Lamb, Aug. 27, 1961; children: John Edward, Janet Lea. BS, Union Coll., 1961; MSN, U. Cen. Ark., 1982; PhD, U. Tenn., 1997. Staff nurse Porter Meml. Hosp., Denver, Washington Adventist Hosp., Takoma Park, Md.; dir. operating room Madison (Tenn.) Hosp.; dean sch. nursing So. Adventist U., Collegedale, Tenn. Mem. Am. Nurses Assn., Tenn. Nurses Assn., NLN, Sigma Theta Tau.

LAMB, PATRICK JOHN, research associate, accountant; b. Charleston, W.Va., Oct. 22, 1938; s. Charles Bernard and Grace Frances (Jackson) L.; m. Kathleen Campbell, May 5, 1962; children: Christine M., Mary K., Charles P., Michael J., Karen P. BSBA, W.Va. State Coll., 1962; MBA, W.Va. Coll. Grad. Studies, 1984. Auditor W.Va. Tax Dept., Charleston, 1961-63; acct. The Diamond, Charleston, 1963-66, W.Va. Water Co., Charleston, 1966-69; sr. rsch. assoc., acct. W.Va. Rsch. League, Charleston, 1969—. Author: The Economic Impact of the Arts in West Virginia, 1988. Mem. W.Va. Pub. Accts. Assn., KC (grand knight 1986-88, 94-96, Cath. layman 1981, dist. dep. 1988-93, state warden 1993-95, state advocate 1995-96, state treas. 1996—). Republican. Roman Catholic. Home: 1403 Jackson St Charleston WV 25301-1909

LAMB, PETER JAMES, meteorology educator, researcher, consultant; b. Nelson, New Zealand, June 21, 1947; came to U.S., 1971; s. George Swan and Dorothy Elizabeth (Smith) L.; m. Barbara Helen Harrison, Aug. 29, 1970; children: Karen Deborah, Brett Timothy. BA, U. Canterbury, Christchurch, New Zealand, 1969; MA with honours, U. Canterbury, Christ Ch., New Zealand, 1971; PhD, U. Wis., 1976. Asst. lectr. U. Canterbury, 1971; rsch. asst. U. Wis., Madison, 1971-76, rsch. assoc., 1976; lectr. U. Adelaide, Australia, 1976-79; sr. sci. Ill. State Water Survey, Champaign, 1979-91, section head, 1984-90; prof. U. Okla., Norman, 1991—; vis. rsch. assoc. U. Miami, Fla., 1978-79; adj. prof. U. Ill., Urbana, 1983-94; dir. Coop. Inst. Mesoscale Meteorol. Studies, Norman, 1991—; dir. Internat. Ctr. Disaster Rsch., 1994—; assoc. dir. Weather Ctr. Programs, Norman, 1996—; cons. Dept. State, Dept. Energy, Agy. Internat. Devel., Nat. Oceanic and Atmospheric Adminstrn., NSF, World Meteorol. Orgn., Kingdom of Morocco, U. Wis., U. Adelaide, Univs. Space Rsch. Assn., EPA, 1983—; site sci. atmospheric radiation measurement program Dept. Energy, 1992—. Co-author rsch. monographs, book chpt., numerous sci. papers. Coach Champaign Youth Soccer Orgn., 1983-91. Recipient more than 35 rsch. grants from U.S. Fed. Agys. including NSF, EPA, Dept. Energy, Nat. Atmospheric & Oceanic Adminstrn., Agy. Internat. Devel.; grantee MacArthur Found., Ins. Inst. Property Loss Reduction, Japan Marine Sci. and Tech. Ctr. Fellow Am. Meteorol. Soc. (chief editor Jour. Climate 1989-95); mem. Royal Meteorol. Soc. (Margary lectr. 1991), Am. Assn. State Climatologists, Sigma Xi. Achievements include research on heat transport by the Atlantic Ocean; investigations into the role of the ocean in causing droughts in Sahelian Africa; study of N.Am. precipitation patterns; assessment of economic value of weather and climate information. Home: 3616 Burlington Dr Norman OK 73072-3647 Office: Univ of Oklahoma CIMMS-Sarkeys Energy Ctr 100 E Boyd St Rm 1110 Norman OK 73019-1011

LAMB, ROBERT EDWARD, diplomat; b. Atlanta, Nov. 17, 1936; s. T.E. and Lois (Harris) L.; m. Lucille Trujillo, Jan. 13, 1962; children: Robert Edward, Anne Gretchen, Michael David. BA in Internat. Rels., U. Pa., 1962. Joined Fgn. Service, Dept. State, 1963; dir. fin. services Dept. State, Washington, 1975-77, dir. passport office, 1977-79; adminstrv. counsellor U.S. Embassy, Bonn, Fed. Republic Germany, 1979-83; asst. sec. of state for adminstrn. Dept. State, Washington, 1983-85; asst. sec. of state Diplomatic Security, 1985-89; U.S. Amb. to Cyprus Cyprus, 1990-93; spl. Cyprus coord., 1993-94; exec. dir Am. Philatelic Soc., State Coll., Pa., 1994—. Served with USMC, 1958-61. Mem. Am. Philatelic Soc. Home and Office: PO Box 8000 State College PA 16803-8000

LAMB, ROBERT LEWIS, electric utility executive; b. Goodland, Kans., Mar. 29, 1932; s. Perl and Josephine (Cullins) L.; m. Patricia Jean Kanuch, Sept. 6, 1953; children: Nancy Jo, David Lewis. BSEE, U. Kans., 1955. Engr. The Empire Dist. Electric Co., Joplin, Mo., 1958-67, distbn. engr., 1967-69; supt. engring. The Empire Electric Co., Joplin, 1969-74; v.p. customer services The Empire Dist. Electric Co., Joplin, 1974-78, exec. v.p., 1978-82, pres., chief exec. officer, 1982—, dir., 1978—; bd. dirs. Edison Electric Inst.; chmn. Mokan Power Pool, 1986-87, S.W. Power Pool, 1989-91. Pres. Joplin United Way, 1981, Joplin Indsl. Devel. Authority, 1992-95; v.p., dir. Joplin So. Corp., 1974-90; bd. dirs. St. John's Regional Med. Ctr., Joplin, 1981-90, 91—, chmn., 1982-84, 92-94; trustee N.Am. Electric Reliability Coun., 1989-91; bd. dirs. Mo. So. State Coll., 1993—. Capt. USAF, 1955-58. Mem. Missouri Valley Elec. Assn. (pres. 1993-94), Joplin C. of C. (pres. 1979-80), Mo. C. of C. and Industry (bd. dirs. 1983—, treas. 1990-93, chmn. 1993-95), Twin Hills Country Club (Joplin), Kansas City (Mo.) Club. Republican. Lutheran. Office: Empire Dist Electric Co 602 Joplin St PO Box 127 Joplin MO 64801

LAMB, STACIE THOMPSON, elementary school educator; b. Abilene, Tex., Nov. 9, 1965; d. George Lyman and Shirley Elizabeth (Burton) T.; m. Dennis A. Lamb; children: Lane, Logann. BS in Edn., Lubbock Christian Coll., 1986; postgrad., Tex. Tech U. Elem. Edn. grades 1-6, Tex. 1st grade tchr. Lubbock (Tex.) I.S.D. Brown Elem., 1986-87; 3rd grade tchr., chairperson Morton (Tex.) I.S.D., 1987-89; 5th grade lang. arts tchr. Whiteface (Tex.) C.I.S.D., 1990—. Mem. ASCD, Classroom Tchrs. Assn. (sec. 1988-89, elem. rep. 1991-92). Home: 2104 Tech Dr Levelland TX 79336-7035 Office: PO Box 117 Whiteface TX 79379-0117

LAMB, SYDNEY MACDONALD, linguistics and cognitive science educator; b. Denver, May 4, 1929; s. Sydney Bishop and Jean Louisa (MacDonald) L.; m. Sharon Reese Rowell, June 17, 1956 (div. 1971); children: Christina, Sarah, Nancy; m. Susan Ellen Jones, May 15, 1977. BA, Yale U., 1951; PhD, U. Calif., Berkeley, 1958. From asst. to assoc. prof.

linguistics U. Calif., Berkeley, 1958-64; from assoc. to prof. Yale U., New Haven, 1964-77; mng. ptnr. Semionics Assocs., Houston, 1977-93; prof. Rice U., Houston, 1980—; fellow Ctr. for Advanced Study in Behavioral Scis., Stanford, Calif., 1973-74. Author: Outline of Stratificational Grammar, 1966, (with others) Sprung from Some Common Source, 1991; inventor associative computer memory, 1977, 80, 4 patents; contbr. articles to profl. jours. NSF grantee, 1959-64, 66-70; Am. Council of Learned Soc. grantee, 1973-74. Mem. Linguistic Soc. Am. (exec. com. 1966-68), Linguistics Assn. of Can. and U.S. (pres. 1983-84, chmn. bd. dirs. 1995—), Houston Philos. Soc. (treas. 1985-86, v.p. 1991-92, pres. 1992-93). Avocations: singing, songwriting. Office: Rice U Dept Linguistics Houston TX 77251

LAMB, WILLIS EUGENE, JR., physicist, educator; b. L.A., July 12, 1913; s. Willis Eugene and Marie Helen (Metcalf) L.; m. Ursula Schaefer, June 5, 1939 (dec. Aug. 1996); m. Bruria Kaufman, Nov. 29, 1996. BS, U. Calif., 1934, PhD, 1938; DSc (hon.), U. Pa., 1953, Gustavus Adolphus Coll., 1975, Columbia U., 1990; MA (hon.), Oxford (Eng.) U., 1956, Yale, 1961; LHD (hon.), Yeshiva U., 1965. Mem. faculty Columbia U., 1938-52, prof. physics, 1948-52; prof. physics Stanford U., 1951-56; Wykeham prof. physics and fellow New Coll., Oxford U., 1956-62; Henry Ford 2d prof. physics Yale U., 1962-72, J. Willard Gibbs prof. physics, 1972-74; prof. physics and optical scis. U. Ariz., Tucson, 1974—, Regents prof., 1990—; Morris Loeb lectr. Harvard U., 1953-54; Gordon Shrum lectr. Simon Fraser U., 1972; cons. Philips Labs., Bell Telephone Labs., Perkin-Elmer, NASA; vis. com. Brookhaven Nat. Lab. Recipient (with P. Kusch) Nobel prize in physics, 1955, Rumford premium Am. Acad. Arts and Scis., 1953; award Rsch. Corp., 1954, Yeshiva award, 1962; Guggenheim fellow, 1960-61, sr. Alexander von Humboldt fellow, 1992-94. Fellow Am. Phys. Soc., N.Y. Acad. Scis.; hon. fellow Inst. Physics and Phys. Soc. (Guthrie lectr. 1958), Royal Soc. Edinburgh (fgn. mem.); mem. Nat. Acad. Scis., Phi Beta Kappa, Sigma Xi. Office: U Ariz Optical Scis Ctr PO Box 210094 Tucson AZ 85721-0094

LAMBERG, STANLEY LAWRENCE, medical technologist, educator; b. Bklyn., Oct. 2, 1933; s. Joseph and Ray C. (Miller) L.; m. Charlotte Frances Rothschild, June 15, 1963; children: Steven Kenneth, Eric Michael. BS, Bklyn. Coll., 1955; MA, Oberlin Coll., 1957; MS, Tufts U., 1962; PhD, NYU, 1968. Chief lab. tech. dept. biochemistry Sch. Medicine Cornell U., N.Y.C., 1957-58; Charleton rsch. and USPHS fellow dept. physiology Tufts U., Boston, 1958-61; NIDR predoctoral trainee NYU, 1961-66; lectr. dept. biology CCNY, 1966-67; instr. to asst. prof. dept. biology Bklyn. Ctr., LIU, 1967-70; part-time asst. rsch. scientist Guggenheim Inst. for Dental Rsch., NYU, 1968-69; asst. prof. dept. biology SUNY, Farmingdale, 1970-71, asst. prof. dept. med. lab. tech., 1971-73, assoc. prof., 1973-75, prof., 1975-95. Co-author various lab. manuals. Adv. chmn. Boy Scouts Am., Hauppauge, N.Y., 1982—. Recipient Chancellor's award for Excellence in Teaching SUNY, 1976; NSF fellow, 1971, others. Mem. N.Y. State Histotech. Soc., Nat. Soc. Histotech., N.Y. State Soc. Med. Tech. (treas. 1980-93, bd. dirs. 1980-93, 94—), N.Y. Acad. Scis., Sigma Xi.

LAMBERG-KARLOVSKY, CLIFFORD CHARLES, anthropologist, archaeologist; b. Prague, Czechoslovakia, Oct. 2, 1937; came to U.S., 1939; s. Carl Othmar von Lamberg and Bellina Karlovsky; m. Martha Louise Veale, Sept. 12, 1959; children: Karl Emil Othmar, Christopher William. A.B., Dartmouth Coll., 1959; M.A. (Wenner-Gren fellow), U. Pa., 1964, Ph.D., 1965; M.A. (hon.), Harvard U., 1970. Asst. prof. sociology and anthropology Franklin and Marshall Coll., 1964-65; asst. prof. anthropology Harvard U., 1965-69, prof., 1969-90, Stephen Phillips prof. archaeology, 1991—; curator Near Eastern archaeology Peabody Museum Archaeology and Ethnology, 1969—, mus. dir., 1977-90; assoc. Columbia U., 1969—; trustee Am. Inst. Iranian Studies, 1968—, Am. Inst. Yemeni Studies, 1976-77; dir. rsch. Am. Sch. Prehist. Rsch., 1974-79, 86—, Centro di Richerche Ligabue, 1984; Reckitt archaeol. surveys in Syria, 1965, excavation projects at Tepe Yahya, Iran, 1967-75, Sarazm, Tadjikistan, USSR, 1985, archaeol. surveys in Saudi Arabia, 1977-80, USSR, 1990-91; dir. survey and excavations Anau, Turkmenistan, 1992—; corr. fellow Inst. Medio and Extremo Orient, Italy; mem. UNESCO com. for sci. study of mankind, 1989—. Author: (with J. Sabloff) Ancient Civilizations: The Near East and Mesoamerica, 1979; editor: (with J. Sabloff) The Rise and Fall of Civilizations, 1973, Ancient Civilizations and Trade, 1975, Hunters, Farmers and Civilization, 1979, Archaeological Thought in America, 1988, Beyond the Tigris and Euphrates, 1996; author, gen. editor: Tepe Yahya: The Early Periods, 1986. Recipient medal Iran-Am. Soc., 1972; NSF grantee, 1966-75, 78-80, 93, Nat. Endowment for Arts grantee, 1977—, NEH grantee, 1977—. Fellow AAAS (chmn. USA/USSR archaeol. exch. program), Am. Acad. Arts and Scis., Soc. Antiquaries Gt. Britain and Ireland (sec. N.Am. chpt. 1985-93), Am. Anthrop. Assn., N.Y. Acad. Sci., USSR Acad. Sci., Soc. Am. Archaeology, Archeol. Inst. Am.; mem. German Archaeol. Inst., Danish Archaeol. Inst., Brit. Archaeol. Inst., Tavern Club (Boston). Office: Peabody Mus Archaeology & Ethnology 11 Divinity Ave Cambridge MA 02138-2019

LAMBERSON, JOHN ROGER, insurance company executive; b. Aurora, Mo., Aug. 16, 1933; s. John Oral Lamberson and Golda May (Caldwell) Tidwell; m. Virginia Lee, Aug. 10, 1957; 1 child, John Clinton. BA, U. Calif., Berkeley, 1954. Coach, tchr. Thousand Palms (Calif.) Sch., 1954-55; underwriter trainee Fireman's Fund Ins. Co., San Francisco, 1955; surety mgr. Safeco Ins. Co. (formerly Gen. Ins. Co.), San Francisco and Sacramento, Calif., 1957-61; pres., COO Willis Corroon Corp., N.Y.C., 1966-92, also bd. dirs., chmn. constrn. industry div., mem. exec. com., aquisition com.; pres., chmn., CEO Lamberson Koster & Co., San Francisco, 1992—; bd. dirs. Willis Corroon Group PLC, London, Consumers Benefit Life Ins. Co., Nova Group, Inc.; chmn., CEO Lamberson Koster and Co. Mem. Nat. Assn. Heavy Engring. Constructors (bd. dirs. 1985—, Golden Beavers award for outstanding svc. to industry), Constrn. Fin. Mgmt. Assn. (bd. dirs. 1987-91, exec. com.), Assoc. Gen. Contractors Am. (membership devel. com., past chmn. bd. dirs. nat. assoc. mems. coun.), Assoc. Gen. Contractors Calif. (bd. dirs. 1976), Nat. Assn. Surety Bond Prodrs. (past nat. pres., regional v.p.), Am. Inst. Contractors, Soc. Am. Mil. Engrs., The Moles-Heavy Engring. Constrn. Soc., Young Pres. Orgn. (sem. leader), Bankers Club, Commonwealth Club, Sharon Heights Golf and Country Club, Bermuda Dunes Country Club, Rockaway Hunting Club, Villa Taverna Club. Home: 85 Greenoaks Dr Atherton CA 94027-2160 Office: Lamberson Koster & Co 580 California St San Francisco CA 94104-1000

LAMBERT, DANIEL MICHAEL, academic administrator; b. Kansas City, Mo., Jan. 16, 1941; s. Paul McKinley and Della Mae (Rogers) L.; m. Carolyn Faye Bright, Dec. 27, 1969; children: Kristian Paige, Dennis McKinley. AB, William Jewell Coll., 1963; MA, Northwestern U., 1965; postgrad., Harvard U., 1965-66; PhD, U. Mo., Columbia, 1977. Dean student affairs William Jewell Coll., Liberty, Mo., 1970-77, exec. asst. to pres., 1977-80, v.p., 1980-85; pres. College Hill Investments Inc., Liberty, 1985-87, Baker U., Baldwin City, Kans., 1987—; bd. dirs. Ferrell Co., Liberty; dir. Kansas City Bd. of Trade, 1988-90; hon. trustee Dohto U., Japan. Bd. dirs. Nat. Assn. Intercollegiate Athletics, The Barstow Sch., Kans. Ind. Colls. Assn.; trustee Midwest Rsch. Inst. Capt. U.S. Army, 1966-70, Vietnam. Recipient Civic Leadership award Mo. Mcpl. League, 1986. Club: KC (Alvamar). Home: 505 E 8th St Baldwin City KS 66006 Office: Baker U Office of Pres PO Box 65 Pres Baldwin City KS 66006*

LAMBERT, DEBORAH KETCHUM, public relations executive; b. Greenwich, Conn., Jan. 22, 1942; d. Alton Harrington and Robyna (Neilson) Ketchum; m. Harvey R. Lambert, Nov. 23, 1963 (div. 1985); children: Harvey Richard Jr., Eric Harrington. BS, Columbia U., 1965. Researcher, writer The Nowland Orgn., Greenwich, Conn., 1964-67; model Country Fashions, Greenwich, Conn., 1964-67; freelance writer to various newspapers and mags., 1977-82; press sec. Va. Del. Gwen Cody, Annandale, Va., 1981-82; assoc. editor Campus Report, Washington, 1985—; adminstrv. asst. Accuracy in Media, Inc., Washington, 1983-84, dir. pub. affairs, 1985—; TV producer weekly program The Other Side of the Story, 1994—; bd. dirs. Accuracy in Academia, Washington; film script cons. The Seductive Illusion, 1988-89. Columnist: The Eye, The Washington Inquirer, 1984—, Squeaky Chalk, Campus Report, 1985—; contbr. articles to various mags.; producer: The Other Side of the Story, 1993—. Co-founder, mem. Va. Rep. Forum, McLean, 1983—; mem. Rep. Women's Fed. Forum. Mem. Am. Bell Assn., Pub. Rels. Soc. Am., DAR., World Media Assn., Am. Platform Assn. Republican. Presbyterian. Home: 1945 Lorraine Ave Mc Lean VA 22101-5331 Office: Accuracy in Media Inc 4455 Connecticut Ave NW Washington DC 20008-2328

LAMBERT, ETHEL GIBSON CLARK, secondary school educator; b. Atlanta, Apr. 18, 1943; d. Robert Harold and Ethel (Gibson) Clark; m. Hugh Felder Lambert, June 27, 1964 (div. Nov. 3, 1988); children: Courtney, Elizabeth, Hugh Lambert Jr. BA, Oglethorpe U., Atlanta, 1965; MEd, Kennesaw State Coll., Marietta, Ga., 1992; EdS, State U. West Ga., Carrollton, 1997. Lic. tchr. T-5, Ga. Tchr. Clayton County Bd. Edn., Jonesboro, Ga., 1965-66, Fulton County Bd. Edn., Atlanta, 1966-67; tchr. pre-sch. weekday program First Bapt. Ch., Gainesville, Ga., 1984-88; tchr. remedial edn. program Riverdale H.S./Clayton County Bd. Edn., 1990—. Author: The Impact of Geography on the Campaigns of the Civil War Fought in Georgia, 1993, The Utilization of Georgia Historical Sites as Teaching Methodology in MIddle Grades Education, 1993, (juvenile) Obnoxious Bill, 1993, Research on Academic Motivation of Elementary, Middle and Secondary School Students in America, 1993, Reading Strategies that Address the Reluctant Reader in America's Public Middle and High Schools, 1995. Den leader Cub Scouts Am., Gainesville, 1980-83; mem. Christian Businessmen's Prayer Breakfast, Atlanta, 1990-95, 96. Mem. Profl. Assn. Ga. Educators, Order Ea. Star, College Park Women's Club, College Park Hist. Soc. Baptist. Avocations: swimming, water skiing, reading, walking, genealogy. Home: 1881 Myrtle Dr SW Apt 711 Atlanta GA 30311-4919 Office: Riverdale High Sch 160 Roberts Dr Riverdale GA 30274-3302

LAMBERT, EUGENE KENT, oncologist, hematologist; b. Hinsdale, Ill., Feb. 13, 1944; s. Eugene Nelson and Dorothy Louise (Diedrichson) L.; m. Maria Natalie Gonzalez,June 19, 1971; children: Carlotta Pilar, Danielle Suzanne, Jori Marie. BA, North Ctrl. Coll., Naperville, Ill., 1966; MD, U. Ill., Chgo., 1970. Diplomate Am. Bd. Internal Medicine, Am. Bd. Hematology, Am. Bd. Med. Oncology. Fellow in hematology Michael Reese Hosp., Chgo., 1976; fellow Northwestern U., Chgo., 1979; oncologist Wichita (Kans.) Clinic, 1979-81, Dreyer Med. Clinic, Aurora, Ill., 1981-86, Fond du Lac (Wis.) Clinic, 1986—; med. dir. at large Wis. divsn. Am. Cancer Soc., 1991-96. Bd. dirs. Girl Scouts Am., Aurora, Ill., 1985-86, El Centro, Aurora, 1985-86, Fond du Lac Regional Clinic, 1992. Lt. USNR, 1971-73. Mem. AMA, ACP, Am. Soc. Hematology, Am. Soc. Clin. Oncologists. Avocations: music, volley ball, reading, cross country skiing. Office: Fond du Lac Clinic 80 Sheboygan St Fond Du Lac WI 54935-4333

LAMBERT, FREDERICK WILLIAM, lawyer, educator; b. Millburn, N.J., Feb. 12, 1943; m. Barbara E. Fogell, Aug. 13, 1965; children: Elisabeth, Mark. BA, U. Mich., 1965, JD, 1969. Bar: Ohio 1969, Fla. 1973, Calif. 1973, U.S. Supreme Ct. 1975. Law clk. to Stanley N. Barnes, U.S. Cir. Judge U.S. Cir. Ct., L.A., 1969-70; spl. asst. Office Legal Counsel U.S. Dept. Justice, Washington, 1970-71; law clk. to Justice William H. Rehnquist U.S. Supreme Ct., Washington, 1971-72; pvt. practice L.A., 1973-90; acting gen. counsel Itel Corp., San Francisco, 1981-82; ptnr. Adams, Duque & Hazeltine, L.A., 1985-90, chmn. bus. law dept., 1989-90; assoc. prof. Hastings Coll. Law, U. Calif., San Francisco, 1993—; vis. prof. U. Mich. Law Sch., Ann Arbor, 1990-91, Duke Law Sch., Durham, N.C., 1992-93. Mem. Calif. State Bar Assn. Home: 1531 Willard St San Francisco CA 94117-3708

LAMBERT, GARY ERVERY, lawyer; b. Providence, Oct. 27, 1959; s. Ervery Eldege and Melitta (Hirsch) L.; m. Lori Keller, Apr. 22, 1995; 1 child, Katherine Elizabeth. BS in Chemistry and Biology, Valparaiso (Ind.) U., 1981; JD with honors, Drake U., 1984. Bar: Iowa 1984, Mass. 1986, U.S. Ct. Mil. Appeals 1986, U.S. Dist. Ct. Mass. 1987, U.S. Ct. Appeals (1st cir.) 1987, U.S. Patent and Trademark Office 1993, U.S. Ct. Appeals (fed. cir.) 1996. Litigator Gallagher & Gallagher, P.C., Boston, 1987-89; owner Law Office of Gary Lambert, Boston, 1989-93; ptnr. Lambert & Garrison, P.C., Boston, 1993—; intellectual property judge advocate, hdqs. USMC, 1997—. Capt. USMC, 1984-87, Japan. Mem. Boston Bar Assn., Boston Patent Law Assn., Am. Intellectual Property Assn., Marine Corps Res. Officers Assn. (life), NRA (life). Republican. Lutheran. Home: 32 Columbia Ave Nashua NH 03060-1601 Office: Lambert & Garrison 92 State St Boston MA 02109-2004

LAMBERT, GEORGE ROBERT, lawyer, insurance company executive, legal consultant; b. Muncie, Ind., Feb. 21, 1933; s. George Russell and Velma Lou (Jones) L.; m. Mary Virginia Alling, June 16, 1956; children: Robert Allen, Ann Holt, James William. BS, Ind. U., Bloomington, 1955; JD, Ill. Inst. Tech. Chgo.-Kent Coll. Law, 1962. Bar: Ill. 1962, U.S. Dist. Ct. (no. dist.) Ill. 1962, Iowa 1984, Pa. 1988. V.p., gen. counsel, sec. Washington Nat. Ins. Co., Evanston, Ill., 1958-82; v.p., gen. counsel Washington Nat. Corp., Evanston, 1979-82; sr. v.p., gen. counsel Life Investors Inc., Cedar Rapids, Iowa, 1982-88; v.p., gen. counsel Provident Mut. Life Ins. Co. Phila., 1988-95; pres. Lambert Legal Consulting, Inc., Palm Beach Gardens, Fla., 1995—; realtor Gimelstob Realty Inc./Better Homes and Gardens, North Palm Beach, Fla., 1996—. Alderman, Evanston City Council, 1980-82. Served to lt. USAF, 1955-57. Mem. ABA (ho. of dels. 1987-89, chair life ins. law com. 1989-90, chair scope and correlation com. 1992-93, mem. Ill. State Bar Assn., Assn. of Life Ins. Counsel (past pres.), Am. Corporate Counsel Assn. (Del Valley chap., bd. dirs. 1992-95). Home and Office: 135 Emerald Key Ln Palm Beach Gardens FL 33418-4022 Office: 11940 Us Highway 1 No Palm Beach FL 33408-2832

LAMBERT, JEREMIAH DANIEL, lawyer; b. N.Y.C., Sept. 11, 1934; s. Noah D. and Clara (Ravage) L.; m. Vicki Anne Asher, July 25, 1959 (div.); children: Nicole Stirling, Alix Stewart, Leigh Asher; m. Sanda Kayden, Dec. 3, 1983; children: Clare Kayden, Hilary Kayden. A.B., Princeton U., 1955; LL.B., Yale U., 1959. Bar: N.Y. 1960, D.C. 1964, U.S. Ct. Appeals (5th cir.) 1964, U.S. Supreme Ct. 1964. Assoc. Cravath, Swaine & Moore, N.Y.C., 1959-63; pvt. practice law Washington, 1963-66; ptnr. Drew & Lambert, Washington, 1966-69; sr. ptnr. Peabody, Lambert & Meyers, Washington, 1969-84; ptnr. Lane & Mittendorf, Washington, 1991—; adj. prof. law Georgetown U., Washington, 1978-79; trustee Internat. Law Inst., Washington, 1983-88; mem. adv. com. on Electricity Futures Contracts, N.Y. Merc. Exch., 1994-95. Co-author: (with Lawrence White) Handbook of Modern Construction Law, 1982; author, editor: Economic and Political Incentives to Petroleum Development, 1990; contbr. articles to legal publs. 1st lt. USAR, 1963-66. Fulbright scholar U. Copenhagen, 1955-56. Mem. ABA, Am. Soc. Internat. Law, D.C Bar Assn., Bar Assn. of City of N.Y., Cosmos Club, Princeton Club, Yale Club, Chevy Chase Club. Office: Lane & Mittendorf 919 18th St NW Washington DC 20006-5503

LAMBERT, JOAN DORETY, elementary education educator; b. Trenton, N.J., Oct. 21, 1937; d. John William and Margaret (Fagan) Dorety; m. James E. Lambert Sr., June 25, 1960; children: Margi, Karen, James E., Kevin. BA, Georgian Ct. Coll., Lakewood, N.J., 1958. Cert. tchr., Pa., N.J. Tchr. 2d and 3d grades combined Washington Elem. Sch., Trenton, 1958-61; tchr. kindergarten music St. Genevieve Sch., Flourtown, Pa., 1968-78, tchr. 3d grade, 1978—; producer, dir. musical shows for St. Genevieve Sch., 1970-78; demonstration classroom for writing process on computers Chestnut Hill Coll. Mem. Jr. League of Trenton, 1960-68, Jr. League of Phila., 1968-70. Teleflex Internat. grantee, 1989-92, Anna B. Stokes Meml. scholar, 1960, Met. Opera grantee, 1958-60. Mem. NEA. Republican. Roman Catholic. Avocations: walking, theater, reading, swimming, family activities. Home: 33 Coventry Ct Blue Bell PA 19422-2528 Office: St Genevieve Sch 1237 Bethlehem Pike Flourtown PA 19031-1902

LAMBERT, JOHN BOYD, chemical engineer, consultant; b. Billings, Mont., July 5, 1929; s. Jean Arthur and Gail (Boyd) L.; m. Jean Wilson Bullard, June 20, 1953 (dec. 1958); children: William, Thomas, Patricia, Cathy, Karen; m. Ilse Crager, Sept. 20, 1980 (dec. 1995). BS in Engring., Princeton U., 1951; PhD, U. Wis., 1956. Rsch. engr. E.I. DuPont de Nemours Co., Wilmington, Del., 1956-69; sr. rsch. engr. Fansteel, Inc., Balt., 1969, mktg. mgr./plant mgr., North Chicago, Ill., 1970-73, mgr. mfg. engring., Waukegan, Ill., 1974-80, corp. tech. dir., North Chicago, 1980-86, gen. mgr. metals, 1987-90, v.p., corp. tech. dir., 1990-91; IESC vol., Brazil, 1995; ind. cons., Lake Forest, Ill., 1991—; bd. dirs. Lake Forest Grad. Sch. Mgmt., 1984-91, Delta Star, Inc., 1995—. Contbr. to profl. publs. Sec. Del. Jr. C. of C., Wilmington, 1972-74. Recipient Charles Hatchett medal Inst. Metals, London, 1986. Mem. AICE, Am. Chem. Soc., Am. Soc. Metals, Sigma Xi. Episcopalian. Achievements include patents in field of dispersion-strengthened metals, refractory metals, chemical vapor deposition, both products and processes. Home and Office: 617 Greenbriar Ln Lake Forest IL 60045-3214

LAMBERT, JOHN PHILLIP, financial executive, consultant; b. Davenport, Iowa, Aug. 17, 1944; s. Dale Edward Lambert and Phyllis Meeker; m. Carol Ann Moreira, Aug. 10, 1981; children: Dawn, Kimberly, Kim. BA, Augustana Coll., Rock Island, Ill., 1966. CPA, Ill. Sr. auditor Price Waterhouse, Chgo., 1966-71; sr. v.p. fin. Burger King Corp., Miami, Fla., 1971-82; exec. v.p., chief fin. officer W.R. Grace Restaurants, Irvine, Calif., 1983-84, Perkins Family Restaurants, L.P., Memphis, 1985-89; pvt. practice fin. cons. Sarasota, Fla., 1989—; dir. Farmers & Merchants Holding Co., Boise, Idaho, 1994—; fin. cons. to restaurant industry. Recipient All Am. Wrestler award NCAA, 1966; named one of Outstanding Young Men of Am., 1976. Mem. AICPA. Republican. Presbyterian. Avocations: reading, golf, boating, gardening. Home and Office: 3770 Prairie Dunes Dr Sarasota FL 34238-2853

LAMBERT, JOSEPH BUCKLEY, chemistry educator; b. Ft. Sheridan, Ill., July 4, 1940; s. Joseph Idus and Elizabeth Dorothy (Kirwan) L.; m. Mary Wakefield Pulliam, June 27, 1967; children: Laura Kirwan, Alice Pulliam, Joseph Cannon. BS, Yale U., 1962; Ph.D. (Woodrow Wilson fellow 1962-63, NSF fellow 1962-65), Calif. Inst. Tech., 1965. Asst. prof. chemistry Northwestern U., Evanston, Ill., 1965-69, assoc. prof., 1969-74, prof. chemistry, 1974-91, Clare Hamilton Hall prof. chemistry, 1991—; chmn. dept. Northwestern U., 1986-89, dir. integrated sci. program, 1982-85; vis. assoc. Brit. Mus., 1973, Polish Acad. Scis., 1981, Chinese Acad. Scis., 1988. Author: Organic Structural Analysis, 1976, Physical Organic Chemistry through Solved Problems, 1978, The Multinuclear Approach to NMR Spectroscopy, 1983, Archaeological Chemistry III, 1984, Introduction to Organic Spectroscopy, 1987, Recent Advances in Organic NMR Spectroscopy, 1987, Acyclic Organonitrogen Stereodynamics, 1992, Cyclic Organonitrogen Stereodynamics, 1992, Prehistoric Human Bone, 1993; audio course Intermediate NMR Spectroscopy, 1973; editor in chief Journal of Physical Organic Chemistry; editorial bd. Magnetic Resonance Chemistry, Archaeometry; contbr. articles to sci. jours. Recipient Nat. Fresenius award, 1976, James Flack Norris award, 1987, Fryxell award, 1989, Nat. Catalyst award, 1993; Alfred P. Sloan fellow, 1968-70, Guggenheim fellow, 1973, Interacad. exch. fellow (U.S.-Poland), 1985, Air Force Office sci. rsch. fellow, 1990. Fellow AAAS, Japan Soc. for Promotion of Sci., Brit. Interplanetary Soc., Ill. Acad. Sci. (life); mem. Am. Chem. Soc. (chmn. history of chemistry divsn., 1996), Royal Soc. Chemistry, Soc. Archaeol. Scis. (pres. 1986-87, assoc. editor Bull.), Phi Beta Kappa, Sigma Xi. Home: 1956 Linneman St Glenview IL 60025-4264 Office: Northwestern University Dept of Chemistry 2145 Sheridan Rd Evanston IL 60208-0834

LAMBERT, JOSEPH PARKER, dentist; b. Bronte, Tex., Oct. 6, 1921; s. Joseph P. and Mary Josephine (Robison) L.; m. Jean Molesworth, Dec. 8, 1945; children: Jean Elizabeth, Mary Catherine, Helen Patricia, Thomas Joseph, Charlotte Anne. DDS, Baylor U., 1952. Cert. Tex. State Bd. Dental Examiners, Wyo. State Bd. Dental Examiners, 1952. Instr. Baylor U. Coll. Dentistry, Dallas, 1952-56, from asst. prof. to prof., dept. chmn., 1957-86, prof. emeritus, 1986—; cons. Baylor U. Med. Ctr., Dallas, VA Hosp., Dallas, VA Hosp., Banham, Tex., VA Hosp. Big Spring, Tex. With USN, 1942-45. Fellow Am. Coll. Dentists; mem. ADA, Tex. Dental Assn., Dallas County Dental Assn., Omicron Kappa Upsilon. Republican. Methodist. Avocations: church work, gardening. Office: Private Dental Office 3707 Gaston Ave Dallas TX 75246-1540

LAMBERT, JUDITH A. UNGAR, lawyer; b. N.Y.C., Apr. 13, 1943; d. Alexander Lawrence and Helene (Rosenson) Ungar; m. Peter D. Leibowits, Aug. 22, 1965 (div. 1971); 1 child, David Gary. BS, U. Pa., 1964; JD magna cum laude, U. Miami, 1984. Bar: N.Y. 1985, Fla. 1990. Assoc. Proskauer Rose Goetz & Mendelsohn, N.Y.C., 1984-86, Taub & Fasciana, N.Y.C., 1986-87, Hoffinger Friedland Dobrish Bernfeld & Hasen, N.Y.C., 1987-88; pvt. practice N.Y.C., 1988—. Mem. ABA, N.Y. State Bar Assn., Assn. Bar of City of N.Y., N.Y. Women's Bar Assn. (family law and trusts and estates com.), N.Y. County Lawyers Assn. Avocations: travel, music, theater. Office: 245 E 54th St New York NY 10022-4707

LAMBERT, LINDA MARGARET, reading specialist; b. Livingston County, Ky., Jan. 17, 1941; d. Wiley Jackson and Florence Allie (Davidson) Stallions; m. Leland Dawson Lambert; children: Sharon Kay, Sheila Lynn, Wiley Lee. AA, Yuba Coll., 1970; BLS, Mary Washington Coll., 1980; MEd, U. Va., 1986. Cert. tchr., Va. Elem. tchr. Stafford (Va.) County Schs., 1979-91, reading specialist, 1991—; mem. com. Devel. Elem. Counselors, Stafford, 1987-89, Devel. Appropriate Assessment, Stafford, 1993-94. Sponsor Ghostwriter Mystery Club, Garrisonwoods Estates, 1993—; mem. Falmouth Bapt. Ch., Stafford Dem. Com., 1996—; del. Va. State Dem. Convention. Mem. NEA, Va. Edn. Assn., Stafford County Edn. Assn., Internat. Reading Assn., Va. State Reading Assn., Rappahanook Reading Coun., Hist. Fredericksburg Antique Automobile Club. Democrat. Avocations: swimming, reading, antiques. Home: 203 Rumford Rd Fredericksburg VA 22405-3206 Office: Hampton Oaks Elem Sch 107 Northampton Blvd Stafford VA 22554-7660

LAMBERT, LYN DEE, library media specialist, law librarian; b. Fitchburg, Mass., Jan. 5, 1954; m. Paul Frederick Lambert, Aug. 11, 1979; children: Gregory John, Emily Jayne, Nicholas James. BA in History, Fitchburg State Coll., 1976, MEd in History, 1979; JD, Franklin Pierce Law Ct., 1983; MLS, Simmons Coll., 1986. Law libr. Fitchburg Law Libr., Mass. Trial Ct., 1985-96; media specialist libr. Samoset Sch., Leominster, Mass., 1996—; instr. paralegal studies courses Fisher Coll., Fitchburg, 1989-94, Anna Maria Coll., Paxton, Mass., 1995—, Atlantic Union Coll., Lancaster, Mass., 1995—, pre-law coll. courses Fitchburg State Coll., 1995—; tech. com. City of Leominster Shc., Net Day Participant and trainer/leader, Leominster H.S., Northwest Johnny Appleseed, Fall Brook, Southeast and Samoset. Mem. Am. Legion Band, Fitchburg, 1959—, Westminster (Mass.) Town Band, 1965—; appt. to Mass. Strategic Plan Com. for delivery of libr. svcs. among multi-type librs. within the commonwealth. Recipient Community Leadership award Xi Psi chpt. Kappa Delta Pi-Fitchburg State Coll. chpt., 1993. Mem. ALA, Am. Assn. Law Librarians (copyright com. 1987-89, publs. rev. com. 1990-92, state, ct. and county law librs. spl. interest sect. publicity com. 1993—), Law Librarians New Eng. (conf. com. 1988), Mass. Libr. Assn. (edn. chair 1991-93, freedom of info. com., legislation com.), New Eng. Libr. Assn., New Eng. Microcomputer Users Group (profl. assoc.), North Cen. Mass. Libr. Alliance (newsletter editor 1990—), Spl. Libr. Assn., Beta Phi Mu, Phi Alpha Delta, Phi Delta Kappa (Montachusett chpt.). Avocations: singing, guitar, clarinet, hiking, camping. Office: Samoset Libr Media Ctr 100 DeCicco Dr Leominster MA 01453

LAMBERT, MICHAEL MALET, investment and hospitality consultant; b. Liverpool, Eng., Sept. 30, 1930; came to Can., 1956, naturalized, 1968; s. Arthur Reginald and Kathleen (Backhouse) L.; m. Sally Ann Day, May 15, 1957; children—Christopher Malet, Simon Day. Hotel gen. mgr. Western Internat. Hotels, Vancouver, B.C., Can., 1957-64; hotel gen. mgr. Calgary, Alta., 1964-68, Montreal, P.Q., Can., 1968-71, Washington, 1971-73; from v.p. to exec. v.p. Four Seasons Hotels Ltd., Toronto, Ont., Can., 1973-84; pres. Four Seasons Hotels Ltd., Singapore, 1984-85; regional v.p. Can. Pacific Hotels, 1985-95; gen. mgr. hotel, 1985-95, ret., 1995; pres. Michael Lambert and Assocs., Bowen Island, B.C., 1995—. Served to lt. Army of Gt. Britain, 1949-50. Avocations: history; antiques; tennis; gardening; bridge. Office: 1639 Old Eaglecliffe Rd, Bowen Island, BC Canada V0N 1G0

LAMBERT, NADINE MURPHY, psychologist, educator; b. Ephraim, Utah; m. Robert E. Lambert, 1956; children—Laura Allan, Jeffrey. Ph.D. in Psychology, U. So. Calif., 1965. Diplomate Am. Bd. Profl. Psychology, Am. Bd. Sch. Psychology. Sch. psychologist Los Nietos Sch. Dist., Whittier, Calif., 1952-53, Bellflower (Calif.) Unified Sch. Dist., 1953-58; research cons. Calif. Dept. Edn., Los Angeles, 1958-64; dir. sch. psychology tng. program U. Calif., Berkeley, 1964—; asst. prof. edn. U. Calif., 1964-70, asso. prof., 1970-76, prof., 1976—; assoc. dean for student svcs. U. Calif., Berkeley, 1988-94; mem. Joint Com. Mental Health of Children, 1967-68; cons. state depts. edn., Calif., Ga., Fla.; cons. Calif. Dept. Justice; mem. panel on testing handicapped people Nat. Acad. Scis., 1978-81. Author: School Version of the AAMD Adaptive Behavior Scale, 3d edit., 1993; co-author: (with Wilcox and Gleason) Educationally Retarded Child: Comprehensive Assessment and Planning for the EMR and Slow-Learning Child, 1974, (with Hartsough and Bower) Process for Assessment of Effective Functioning, 1981, (with Windmiller and Turiel) Moral Development and Socialization -- Three Perspectives, 1979; assoc. editor Am. Jour. Orthopsychiatry, 1975-81, Am. Jour. Mental Deficiency, 1977-80, others. With Hartsough and Sandoval Children's Attention and Adjustment Survey, 1990. Recipient Dorothy Hughes award for outstanding contbn. to ednl. and sch. psychology NYU, 1990, Tobacco Disease Related Rsch. award U. Calif., 1990-94, NIDA, 1994—; grantee NIMH, 1965-87, Calif. State Dept. Edn., 1-72, 76-78, NHSTE Dept. Transportation, 1995. Fellow APA (coun. reps. divsn. sch. psychologists, bd. dirs. 1984-87, mem. bd. profl. affairs 1981-83, bd. ednl. affairs 1991-94, chmn. 1992-94, exec. com. divsn. sch. psychology 1994-96, mem. commn. for recognition of specialities and professions in psychology 1993—, Disting. Svc. award 1980, award for disting. profl. contbns. 1986), Am. Orthopsychiat. Assn.; mem. NEA, Calif. Assn. Sch. Psychologists and Psychometrists (pres. 1962-63, Sandra Goff award 1985), Am. Ednl. Rsch. Assn. Office: U Calif Dept Educ Berkeley CA 94720-1670

LAMBERT, OLAF CECIL, hotel executive; b. Sherfield-on-London, Hampshire, Eng.; came to U.S., 1946; naturalized, 1958; s. Stanilas and Jeanne Claire (Helsen) Lubienski; m. Trudy Guidroz, Sept. 2, 1995. Grad., Ecole Hoteliere, Nice, France, 1937. Gen. mgr. Queensbury Hotel, Glens Falls, N.Y., 1956-57; resident mgr. Istanbul (Turkey) Hilton, 1957-58; resident mgr., asst. project mgr. Berlin Hilton, 1958-59; v.p., gen. mgr. Royal Orleans, New Orleans, 1959-65, Americana of N.Y., N.Y.C., 1965-66; gen. mgr. Chateau Louisianne, New Orleans, 1966-68; treas. So. Motor Lodge, 1964—; pres. Dauphine Orleans Hotel Corp., Olaf Lambert and Assocs. Inc., New Orleans. served to flight lt. RAF, 1939-45; prisoner of war, 1942-45. Recipient Instns. Nat. Merit award Hotel Mgmt. Rev., 1958, Golden Host Merit award, 1964. Mem. Chaine des Rotisseurs, New Orleans Hotel Assn., Hotel Sales Mgmt. Assn., Global Hoteliers Club, Am. Hotel & Motel Assn., Internat. Coun. Hotel-Motel Mgmt. Cos., Masons, Shriners. Office: 412 Dauphine St New Orleans LA 70112-3150

LAMBERT, RICHARD BOWLES, JR., national science foundation program director, oceonographer; b. Clinton, Mass., Apr. 20, 1939; s. Richard Bowles and Dorothy Elisabeth (Peck) L.; m. Sherrill Faye Smith, July 4, 1964; 1 child, Lisa Beth Lauren. AB in Physics, Lehigh U., 1961; ScM in Physics, Brown U., 1964, PhD in Physics, 1966; postgrad., Goethe Institut, Germany, 1966, NATO Internat. Sch., Germany, 1966, Max Planck Inst. for Physics & Astrophysics, Germany, 1966. Fulbright Postdoctoral fellow Institut fur Stromungsmechanik Technische Hochschule, Munich, Germany, 1966-67; asst. prof. Grad. Sch. Oceanography U. R.I., 1968-74, assoc. prof. Grad. Sch. Oceanography, 1974; program dir. physical oceanography program NSF, Washington, 1975-77; rsch. oceanographer Sci. Applications Internat. Corp., 1977-79, mgr. ocean physics divsn., 1979-83, asst. v.p., 1980-83, sr. rsch. oceanographer, 1983-84; assoc. program dir. physical oceanography program NSF, Washington, 1984-91, program dir. physical oceanography program, 1991—; adv. com. NOAA; assoc. dir. U.S. TOGA Project Office 1985-91; delegate Intergovernmental TOGA Bd.; delegation head Intergovernmental WOCE Panel; co-investigator R/V Trident Oceanographic Cruises, Feb. 1971 (21 days), Dec. 1971 (6 days), April 1974 (14 days), Nov. 1974 (19 days); chief scientist R/V Trident Oceanographic Cruises, Oct. 1971 (17 days), Nov. 1971 (8 days), April 1973 (15 days); co-investigator R/V Atlantis II Oceanographic Cruises, July 1973 (18 days). Contbr. articles to Jour. Fluid Mech. and other profl. jours. Bd. dirs. Christian Performing Artist's Fellowship, Fairfax, Va., 1993—. Mem. Am. Geophys. Union, The Oceanography Soc. (life mem.), Phi Beta Kappa, Sigma Xi. Office: NSF Phys Oceanography Program 4201 Wilson Blvd Arlington VA 22230-0001

LAMBERT, ROBERT FRANK, electrical engineer, consultant; b. Warroad, Minn., Mar. 14, 1924; s. Fred Joseph and Nutah (Gibson) L.; m. June Darlene Flatten, June 30, 1951; children—Cynthia Marie, Susan Ann, Katherine Cheryl. B.E.E., U. Minn., 1948, M.S. in Elec. Engring, 1949, Ph.D., 1953. Asst. prof. U. Minn. Inst. Tech., Mpls., 1953-54; assoc. prof. U. Minn. Inst. Tech., 1955-59, prof. elec. engring., 1959-94, prof. emeritus, 1994; dir. propagation research lab. U. Minn., 1968-87; assoc. dean U. Minn. (Inst. Tech.), 1967-68; asst. prof. Mass. Inst. Tech., 1954-55; cons. elec. engr., also in acoustics, 1953—; guest scientist Third Phys. Inst., Göttingen, Fed. Republic Germany, 1964; vis. scientist NASA, Hampton, Va., 1979; dir. Inst. Noise Control Engring., Washington, 1972-75. Contbr. numerous articles to tech. jours. Served with USNR, 1943-46. Fellow IEEE, Acoustical Soc. Am. (assoc. editor jour. 1985-93); mem. Am. Soc. Engring. Edn., Am. Soc. Engring. Sci., AAAS, Inst. Noise Control Engring. (dir., John C. Johnson Meml. award), Sigma Xi, Tau Beta Pi, Eta Kappa Nu, Gamma Alpha. Lutheran. Rsch. in acoustics, communication tech. random vibrations. Home: 2503 Snelling Curve Saint Paul MN 55113 Office: U Minn Inst Tech Dept Elec Engring Minneapolis MN 55455

LAMBERT, ROBERT LOWELL, scientific investigator; b. Mpls., Jan. 3, 1923; s. Luell E. and Amy (Schwerin) L.; m. Jean Louise Zavodney, Mar. 19, 1949; children: Thomas R., John N. Student, U. Utah, 1941-42, Tex. A&M Coll., 1943-44, Biarritz (France) Am. U., 1945; B.S., UCLA, 1947, M.B.A., 1948; grad. student, U. Minn., 1948-50; Ph.D., U. Beverly Hills, 1982. Instr. bus. adminstrn. U. Minn., 1948-50; with Budget Pack, Inc., Los Angeles, 1950-55; v.p. Budget Pack, Inc., 1954-55; with Riverside Cement Co. div. Amcord, Inc., Los Angeles, 1955-61; treas. Riverside Cement Co. div. Amcord, Inc., 1960- 61; finance dir. Amcord, Inc., 1961-72, treas., 1965-72, 75-80, v.p., 1967-72, sec., 1972-74, sr. v.p., 1972-80; pres., dir. Inst. for Bus. Edn., Newport Beach, Calif., 1981-83; ind. investigator, author in field of chronobiological epidemiology, 1984—; former dir., officer various subsidiaries Amcord, Inc. Contbr. articles to profl. jours. Vice pres. Amcord Found., 1958-80. Served with inf. AUS, World War II, ETO. Decorated Combat Inf. badge, Bronze star with oak leaf cluster, Presdl. Unit citiation, Belgian Fourragere. Mem. Tau Kappa Epsilon, Beta Gamma Sigma, Alpha Kappa Psi. Lutheran. Clubs: Big Canyon Country (Newport Beach); Palm Desert Resort Country. Home: 13 Cool Brk Irvine CA 92612-3412

LAMBERT, SAMUEL WALDRON, III, lawyer, foundation executive; b. N.Y.C., Jan. 12, 1938; s. Samuel W. and Mary (Hamill) L.; m. Louisa Garnsey, Aug. 25, 1962; children—Louisa Kelly, Samuel William, Sarah Hamill. B.A., Yale U., 1960; LL.B., Harvard U., 1963. Bar: N.J. 1964, U.S. Tax Ct. 1975. Assoc. Albridge C. Smith III, Princeton, N.J., 1964-67; ptnr. Smith, Cook, Lambert & Miller, and predecessors, Princeton, 1967-80; officer, dir. Smith, Lambert, Hicks & Miller, P.C., Princeton, 1981-87; ptnr. in charge of office Drinker, Biddle & Reath, 1988—, mng. ptnr., 1994-96; pres. The Bunbury Co., Princeton. Bd. dirs. Winslow Found., Windham Found., Curtis W. McGraw Found.; capt. Princeton Republican County Com., 1967-69. Served with USAR, 1963-69. Mem. Princeton Bar Assn. (pres. 1976-77), N.J. Bar Assn., ABA.

LAMBERT, STEPHEN R., electrical engineer, consultant; b. Oct. 30, 1946. BSEE, U. Ill., 1969, MS, 1969. Sr. cons. Power Techs., Inc. Fellow IEEE (vice-chmn., sec., tech. coun. PES, past chmn. switchgear com., past chmn. high-voltage breaker sub-com., past chmn. TRV working group). Office: Power Tech Inc PO Box 1058 Schenectady NY 12301

LAMBERT, STEVEN CHARLES, lawyer; b. Kingsport, Tenn., Aug. 22, 1947; s. M. Charles and Janet (Sultner) L.; children: Shelley Elizabeth, Charles Burnette. BA, Duke U., 1969; JD, Georgetown U., 1974. Bar: D.C. 1975, U.S. Ct. Fed. Claims, U.S. Ct. Appeals (fed. cir.), U.S. Tax Ct. Law clk. to Chief Judge Wilson Cowen, U.S. Ct. Claims, Washington, 1974-75; assoc. Wilkinson, Cragun & Barker, Washington, 1975-80; ptnr. Wilkinson, Cragun & Barker, 1980-82, Hamel & Park, Washington, 1982-88, Hopkins & Sutter, Washington, 1988—; chmn. adv. coun. U.S. Ct. Claims, 1982-86, mem. adv. coun., 1986—, chmn. bicentennial commn., 1987-91. Co-author: Tax Ideas Desk Book, 1980; contbr. articles to profl. jours. Trustee Ferrum Coll.; mem. bd. pensions United Meth. Ch. With U.S. Army, 1970-72. Fellow Am. Bar Found.; mem. ABA (sec. litigation and natural resources), Am. Arbitration Assn., Claims Ct. Bar Assn. (pres. 1990-91), Fed. Cir. Bar Assn. (bd. dirs. 1986-88), Bar Assn. D.C. (bd. dirs. 1981-83). Methodist. Avocations: boating, fishing, tennis. Office: Hopkins & Sutter 888 16th St NW Washington DC 20006-4103

LAMBERT, VICKIE ANN, dean; b. Hastings, Nebr., Oct. 28, 1943; d. Victor E. and Edna M. (Hein) Wagner; m. Clinton E. Lambert, Jr., June 30, 1974; 1 child, Alexandra. Diploma, Mary Lanning Sch. Nursing, 1964; BSN, U. Iowa, 1966; MSN, Case Western Res. U., 1973; DNSc, U. Calif., San Francisco, 1981. RN, Ga. Acting chair dept. nursing adminstrn. Med. Coll. Ga., Augusta, 1982-84, coord. doctoral program nursing, 1984-85; coord. doctoral program nursing George Mason U., Fairfax, Va., 1986-88; assoc. dean Case Western Res. U., Cleve., 1989-90; dean Sch. Nursing Med. Coll. Ga., Augusta, 1990—. Contbr. articles to profl. jours. Fellow Am. Acad. Nursing; mem. ANA, Sigma Theta Tau, Sigma Xi. Home: 1421 Waters Edge Dr Augusta GA 30801

LAMBERT, WILLIAM G., journalist, consultant; b. Langford, S.D., Feb. 2, 1920; s. William G. and Blanche (Townsend) L.; m. Jean Kenway Mead, July 7, 1945; children: Kathryn, Heather Lambert Oxberry. Nieman fellow journalism, Harvard U., 1959-60. Reporter, news editor Enterprise-Courier, Oregon City, Oreg., 1945-50; reporter The Oregonian, Portland, 1950-59; anchor, news dir. KPTV, Oreg. Television, Inc., Portland, 1961-62; corr. Time mag., 1962-63; assoc. editor, staffwriter Life mag., N.Y.C., 1963-71; staff corr. Time-Life News Service, 1971-73; free-lance journalist, 1973; staff writer, cons. Phila. Inquirer, 1974-90; freelance journalist, libel litigation cons., 1990—; cons., U.S. commr. edn. Office of Edn., Washington, 1962. Served in U.S. Army, WWII, PTO, to maj. Res., ret. Decorated bronze star. Recipient Pulitzer prize for local reporting, 1957, Heywood Broun award, 1957, award for mag. reporting Sigma Delta Chi, 1967, Worth Bingham prize for distinguished reporting, 1967, Heywood Brown award, 1969, George Polk award for mag. reporting Abe Fortas articles, Sigma Delta Chi award, Nat. Headliners Club award, Page One award, 1970, Pa. Bar Assn. award, Phila. Bar Assn. award, Phila. Sigma Delta Chi award, AP Mng. Editors award (Pa.), 1981. Home: 529 Chandler Ln Villanova PA 19085-1026

LAMBERTH, ROYCE C., federal judge; b. 1943. BA, U. Tex., 1965, LLB, 1967. With civil dir. U.S. Atty's. Office, Wasshington, 1974-77, asst. chief, 1977-78; chief U.S. Atty's. Office, 1978-87; judge U.S. Dist. Ct. (D.C. dist.), Washington, 1987—. Capt. (j.a.g.) U.S. Army, 1967-74. Mem. ABA (chmn. armed svcs. and vets. affairs com. sect. adminstrv. law 1983-83), Fed. Bar Assn. (chmn. fed. litigation sect. 1986—), Jud. Conf. D.C. Cir. (arangements com. 1985, D.C. Bar, D.C. Bar Assn. (Cert. Appreciatio 1977), State Bar Tex. Office: US Dist Ct US Courthouse Rm 4317 333 Constitution Ave NW Washington DC 20001-2802*

LAMBERTI, MARJORIE, history educator; b. New Haven, Sept. 30, 1937; d. James and Anna (Vanacore) L. B.A., Smith Coll., 1959; M.A., Yale U., 1960, Ph.D., 1965. Prof. history Middlebury Coll., Vt., 1964—, Charles A. Dana prof., 1984—. Author: Jewish Activism in Imperial Germany, 1978, State, Society and the Elementary School in Imperial Germany, 1989; edtl. bd. History of Edn. Quar., 1992-94; contbr. articles to profl. jours. Mem. exec. com. Friends of Smith Coll. Librs., 1995—. NEH fellow, 1968-69, 81-82; German Acad. Exch. Svc. rsch. grant, 1988. Fellow Inst. for Advanced Study (Princeton 1992-93), The Woodrow Wilson Ctr.; mem. Am. Hist. Assn., Conf. Group for Ctrl. European History, Leo Baeck Inst., Phi Beta Kappa. Home: 8 S Gorham Ln Middlebury VT 05753-1002 Office: Middlebury Coll Dept History Middlebury VT 05753

LAMBERT LINCOLN, BLANCHE M., former congresswoman; b. Helena, Ark., Sept. 30, 1960. BA, Randolph-Macon Woman's Coll., 1982. Sr. assoc. The Pagonis & Donnelly Group, Inc., 1989-91; elected mem. 103rd Congress from 1st Dist., 1992-96. Office: Rte 2 PO Box 19 Hughes AR 72348*

LAMBERTSEN, CHRISTIAN JAMES, environmental physiologist, physician, educator; b. Westfield, N.J., May 15, 1917; s. Christian and Ellen (Stevens) L.; m. Naomi Helen Hill, Feb. 5, 1944; children—Christian James, David Lee, Richard Hill, Bradley Stevens. BS, Rutgers U., 1939; MD, U. Pa., 1943. Prof. pharmacology and exptl. therapeutics, prof. medicine U. Pa. Sch. Medicine, 1946-87; founding dir. Inst. for Environ. Medicine, U. Pa. Med. Ctr., 1968—, disting. prof. environ. medicine, 1985—; mem. adv. panel on med. scis. Office of Asst. Sec. Defense, 1954-61; sec. basic scis. Nat. Bd. Med. Examiners, 1955-71; mem. Pres.'s Space Panel, 1967-70; mem. oceanographic adv. bd. Office of Asst. Sec. of Navy for R & D, 1968-77; mem. marine bd. Nat. Acad. Engring., 1973-77; dir. Environ. Biomedical Rsch. Data Ctr., 1992—; adviser Office of Marine Resources, NOAA, 1972-76; med. adviser Ocean Systems Inc., Houston, 1960-83; med. dir. SubSea International, 1984—; chmn. com. Man in Space; Space Sci. Bd., NAS, 1960-62; chmn. life scis. adv. bd. McDonnell-Douglas Aircraft Corp., St. Louis, 1960-67; mem. research adv. bd. Mead-Johnson Corp., Evansville, Ind., 1960-67; sr. life scis. adviser Union Carbide Corp., Buffalo, N.Y., Westinghouse Elec. Corp., Annapolis, Md., 1972-74, Air Products and Chemicals Corp., Allentown, Pa., 1983-87; pres. Ecosystems Inc., Phila., 1972—. Editor: Underwater Physiology Symposium, II, III, IV, V, 1963-76; mem. editorial bd. Marine Tech. Soc. Jour., 1977-85. Contbr. articles to med., sci. jours. Served to maj. AUS, 1944-46. Decorated Legion of Merit: recipient Lindback award for Disting. Teaching, 1967; Aerospace Med. Assn. Tuttle award, 1970; Undersea Med. Behnke award, 1970; Dept. Def. Disting. Pub. Service medal, 1972; Marine Tech. Soc. award in Ocean Sci. and Engring., 1972; Dept. Navy Commendation Adv. Service, 1972; award in environ. scis. N.Y. Acad. Scis., 1974; Disting. Pub. Service award USCG, 1976; NIH, USN, USAF, NASA, NOAA Research grantee. Fellow Aerospace Med. Assn. (v.p. 1968); mem. Am. Coll. Clin. Pharmacology and Chemotherapy, Am. Soc. Pharmacology and Exptl. Therapeutics, Am. Physiol. Soc., Am. Soc. Clin. Investigation, Assn. Am. Med. Colls., Phila. Coll. Physicians, Internat. Acad. Astronautics, Internat. Astronautic Fedn., Internat. Union Physiol. Scis., Nat. Acad. Engring., John Morgan Med. Rsch. Soc., Marine Tech. Soc., Peripatetic Med. Soc., Undersea Med. Soc. (founding pres.), Phila. County Med. Soc., Pa. Med. Soc., Phila. Maritime Mus., Phila. Physiol. Soc., Cosmos Club (Washington), Sigma Xi. Home: 3500 Westchester Pike No 129 Newtown Square PA 19073 Office: U PA Med Ctr Inst Envrion Medicine 1 John Morgan Bldg Philadelphia PA 19104-6068

LAMBETH, THOMAS WILLIS, foundation executive; b. Clayton, N.C., Jan. 8, 1935; s. Mark Thomas and Ina Henrietta (Willis) L.; m. Donna Brooks Irving, July 18, 1964; children: Donna Catherine, Mark Hunter, Thomas Richard. AB in History, U. N.C., 1957; DHL (hon.), Pfeiffer Coll., Misenheimer, N.C., 1982. Reporter Winston-Salem Jour., 1959-60; adminstrv. asst. Gov. of N.C., 1961-65; staff mem. Smith Richardson Found., Greensboro, N.C., 1965-69; adminstrv. asst. Congressman Richardson Preyer, Washington, 1969-78; exec. dir. Z. Smith Reynolds Found., Winston-Salem, 1978—; acting dir. Kennedy Assasination Investigation, Washington, 1977; dir. Coun. on Founds., Washington, 1988-94, program chmn. ann. meeting, 1988-89, ch. family founds. com.; chmn. bd. Southeastern Coun. of Founds., Atlanta, 1985-87. Trustee, chmn. bd. U. N.C., Chapel Hill, 1969-83; chmn. Tchg. Fellow Commn., 1987-91, 93—. Recipient Disting. Alumnus award U. N.C., 1988. Mem. Alumni Assn. U. N.C. (pres. 1989-90). Democrat. Methodist. Home: 700 Yorkshire Rd Winston Salem NC 27106-5518 Office: Z Smith Reynolds Found 101 Reynolda Vlg Winston Salem NC 27106-5122

LAMBETH, VICTOR NEAL, horticulturist, researcher; b. Sarcoxie, Mo., July 5, 1920; s. Odus Houston and Carrie (Woods) L.; m. Sarah Katherine Smarr, May 24, 1946; children: Victoria Kay, Debra Jean. B.S., U. Mo., 1942, M.A., 1948, Ph.D., 1950. Asst. prof. U. Mo., Columbia, 1950-51, assoc. prof., 1951-59, prof. dept. horticulture, 1959-91, prof. emeritus, 1991—; cons. horticulture to Thailand, Taiwan, Liberia; judge All-Am. Vegetable Trials, 1985-92. Inventor plant growth media, 1979; plant breeder tomato lines and cultivars; contbr. articles to profl. jours. Mem. Fin. Com. City of Columbia, Mo., 1970, mem. Bd. Zoning Adjustment, 1973-76, mem. Bd. Spl. Appeals, 1975-77. Served to lt. USN, 1943-46, PTO. Recipient Hort. award Mo. Hort. Soc., 1942; recipient Alumni Faculty award U. Mo. Alumni Assn., 1974; NSF grantee, 1982. Fellow Am. Soc. Hort. Sci. (grad. teaching award 1978); mem. Am. Soc. Plant Physiologists, Internat. Soc. Hort. Sci., Sigma Xi, Gamma Sigma Delta (pres. Mo. chpt. 1959-60). Methodist. Home: 1327 Lambeth Dr Columbia MO 65202-2466 Office: U Mo Dept Horticulture I-87 Agrl Bldg Columbia MO 65211

LAMBIRD, MONA SALYER, lawyer; b. Oklahoma City, July 19, 1938; d. B.M. Jr. and Pauline A. Salyer; m. Perry A. Lambird, July 30, 1960; children: Allison Lambird Watson, Jennifer Salyer, Elizabeth Gard, Susannah Johnson. BA, Wellesley Coll., 1960; LLB, U. Md., 1963. Bar: Okla. 1968, Md. Ct. Appeals 1963, U.S. Supreme Ct. 1967. Atty. civil div. Dept. Justice, Washington, 1963-65; sole practice law Balt. and Oklahoma City, 1965-71; mem. firm Andrews Davis Legg Bixler Milsten & Price, Inc. and predecessor firm, Oklahoma City, 1971—; minority mem. Okla. Election Bd., 1984—, vice chmn., 1990-94; mem. profl. responsibility tribunal Okla. Supreme Ct., 1984-90; Master of Bench, sec.-treas. Luther Bohanan Am. Inn of Ct., Oklahoma City, 1986—, pres., 1994—. Editor: Briefcase, Oklahoma County Bar Assn., 1976. Profl. liaison com. City Oklahoma City, 1974-80; mem. Hist. Preservation of Oklahoma City, Inc., 1970—; del. Oklahoma County and Okla. State Republican Party Conv., 1971—; Okla. City Orch. League Inc., legal advisor, 1973—, bd. dirs., 1973—; incorporator, bd. dirs. R.S.V.P. of Oklahoma County, pres., 1982-83; bd. dirs. Congregate Housing for Elderly, 1978—, Vis. Nurses Assn., 1983-86, Oklahoma County Friends of Library, 1980-91, The Support Ctrs., Inc., 1989—; bd. trustees Okla. Found. Excellence, 1997—; fellow Am. Bar Found. Mem. Okla. Women's Hall of Fame, 1995. Mem. ABA, Am. Judicature Soc. (trustee 1994—), Okla. Bar Assn. (pres. labor and employment law sect., bd. govs. 1992-94, pres. 1996), Oklahoma County Bar Assn. (bd. dirs. 1986—, pres. 1990), Oklahoma County Bar Found. (pres. 1988), Jr. League Oklahoma City (bd. dirs. 1973-76, legal advisor), Oklahoma County and State Med. Assn. Aux. (bd. dirs.), Leadership Okla., Class X, Seven Sisters Colls. Club (pres. 1972-76), Women's Econ. Club (steering com. 1981-86). Methodist. Home: 419 NW 14th St Oklahoma City OK 73103-3510 Office: 500 W Main St Oklahoma City OK 73102-2253

LAMBIRD, PERRY ALBERT, pathologist; b. Reno, Nev., Feb. 7, 1939; s. C. David and Florence (Knowlton) L.; m. Mona Sue Salyer, July 30, 1960; children: Allison Thayer Watson, Jennifer Salyer, Elizabeth Gard, Susannah Johnson. BA, Stanford U., 1958; MD, Johns Hopkins U., 1962; MBA, Okla. City U., 1973. Diplomate Am. Bd. Pathology. Fellow in internal medicine Johns Hopkins Hosp., Balt., 1962-63, resident pathologist, 1965-68, chief resident, 1968-69; med. cons. USPHS, Washington, 1963-65; pathologist Med. Arts Lab., Oklahoma City, 1969-96, Okla. Meml. Hosp., Southwest Med. Ctr., 1974—, Nat. Cancer Inst., 1974-81; chmn. PATHCOR, Inc. 1995—; propr. Lambird Mgmt. Cons. Service, Oklahoma City, 1974—; pres. Ind. Pathology Inst., Inc., 1984-88, chmn. bd. dirs., 1988—; assoc. prof. pathology and orthopedic surgery U. Okla. Coll. Medicine, 1980-90, prof., 1990—; cons. in field. Reviewer Jour. Am. Med. Assn, 1983—; contbr. articles to profl. jours. Pres. Okla. Symphony Orch., 1974-75, Ballet Okla., 1978-79; del. Republican Nat. Conv., 1976, alt. del., 1984; bd. regents Uniformed Svcs. U. Health Scis., 1983-88; mem. task force entitlements and human assistance programs U.S. Ho. of Reps., 1983-88; bd. dirs. Commn. on Office Lab. Assessment, 1988—, chmn., 1992-94. Served to lt. comdr. USPHS, 1963-65. Recipient Exec. Leadership award Oklahoma City U., 1976, Physician's Recognition award AMA, 1969-95, Outstanding Pathologist award Am. Pathology Found., 1984; named Disting. Practioner Nat. Acad. of Practice, 1990. Fellow Am. Soc. Clin. Pathologists, Coll. Am. Pathologists, (gov. 1984-92); mem. AMA (ho. of dels., coun. on med. svc.), Okla. Med. Assn. (ho. of dels., trustee, pres.), Okla. County Med. Soc. (pres.), Okla. Soc. Cytopathology (pres.), Am. Pathology Found. (pres.), Okla. Found. for Peer Rev. (dir.), Arthur Purdy Stout Soc. Surg. Pathologists, Am. Assn. Pathologists, Okla. Assn. Pathologists (pres.), So. Med. Assn., N.Y. Acad. Sci., Am. Soc. Cytology, Okla. Soc. Cytopaths (pres.), Osler Soc., Okla. City Clin. Soc., Johns Hopkins Med. and Surg. Assn., Phi Beta Kappa (Phi Beta Kappa of Yr. 1996), Alpha Omega Alpha. Republican. Methodist. Home: 419 NW 14th St Oklahoma City OK 73103-3510 Office: PATHCOR PO Box 60609 Oklahoma City OK 73146-0609

LAMBORN, LEROY LESLIE, legal educator; b. Marion, Ohio, May 12, 1937; s. LeRoy Leslie and Lola Fern (Grant) L. A.B., Oberlin Coll., 1959; LL.B., Western Res. U., 1962; LL.M., Yale U., 1963; J.S.D., Columbia U., 1973. Bar: N.Y. 1965, Mich. 1974. Asst. prof. law U. Fla., 1965-69; prof. Wayne State U., 1970-83; vis. prof. State U., Utrecht, 1981. Author: Legal Ethics and Professional Responsibility, 1963; contbr. articles on victimology to legal jours. Mem. Am. Law Inst., Nat. Orgn. Victim Assistance (bd. dirs. 1979-88, 90-91), World Soc. Victimology (exec. com. 1982-94). Office: Wayne State ULaw Sch 1300 E Lafayette St Apt 2502 Detroit MI 48207-2924

LAMBREMONT, EDWARD NELSON, JR., nuclear science educator; b. New Orleans, July 29, 1928; s. Edward Nelson and Caroline Josephine (Joachim) L.; m. Janice P. Savoy, Apr. 6, 1990; m. Mary Chris Bittle, May 30, 1981 (dec. Jan. 1987); m. Carol Jane Annis, June 16, 1951; children: Carol, Suzanne, John, Barbara. B.S., Tulane U., 1949, M.S., 1951; Ph.D., Ohio State U., 1958. Research entomologist U.S. Dept. Agr., Baton Rouge, 1958-66; assoc. prof. nuclear sci. La. State U., Baton Rouge, 1966-73, prof., 1973—, dir. Nuclear Sci. Ctr., 1974—; councilor Oak Ridge Assoc. Univs., 1971-79, bd. dirs., 1979-84, vis. scientist med. div., 1967-87; vis. scientist Internat. Atomic Energy Agy. Lab., Seibersdorf, Austria, 1988-90; cons. nuclear-related corps., 1978—. Contbr. articles to sci. jours. Served with U.S. Army, 1951-54, col. Res. (ret.). Grantee NIH, 1964-71; grantee NSF, 1971-77, U.S. Dept. Agr., 1979-83. Mem. Am. Nuclear Soc., Entomol. Soc. Am. (Deep South chpt.), Health Physics Soc. (treas.), Sigma Xi (bd. dirs. 1984-91). Home: 2913 Calanne Ave Baton Rouge LA 70820-5408 Office: La State U Nuclear Sci Ctr Baton Rouge LA 70803

LAMBRO, DONALD JOSEPH, columnist; b. Wellesley, Mass., July 24, 1940; s. Pascal and Mary (Lapery) L.; m. Jacquelyn Mae Killmon, Oct. 6, 1968; 1 son, Jason Phillip. B.S., Boston U., 1963. Reporter, Boston Traveler, 1963; freelance writer Washington, 1965-67; statehouse reporter UPI, Hartford, Conn., 1968-70; reporter UPI, Washington, 1970-80; columnist United Feature Syndicate, Washington, 1981—; commentator AP Radio Network, 1982-83, Nat. Pub. Radio, 1984-85; polit. writer The Washington Times; writer, host TV documentary Star Spangled Spenders, 1982; host, co-writer PBS TV documentary Inside the Republican Revolution, 1995; nat. editor Washington Times, 1987-88; chief polit. corr. Washington Times, 1988—. Author: The Federal Rathole, 1975; The Conscience of a Young Conservative, 1976; Fat City: How Washington Wastes Your Taxes, 1980; Washington-City of Scandals, 1984; Land of Opportunity, 1986. Recipient Warren Brookes award for Excellence in Journalism, Am. Legis. Exch. Coun., 1995. Albanian Orthodox. Office: The Washington Times 3000 New York Ave NE Washington DC 20002*

LAMBRO, PHILLIP, composer, conductor, pianist; b. Wellesley, Mass., Sept. 2, 1935; s. Pascal and Mary (Lapery) L. Student, Music Acad. West, 1955. Piano debut Pianist's Fair, Symphony Hall, Boston, 1952; composer Miraflores for String Orchestra, Dance Barbaro for Percussion, Two Pictures for Solo Percussionist and Orchestra, Four Songs for Soprano and Orchestra, Toccata for Piano, Toccata for Guitar, Parallelograms for Flute Quartet and Jazz Ensemble, Music for Wind Brass and Percussion, Obelisk for Oboist and Percussionist, Structures for String Orchestra, Fanfare and Tower Music for Brass Quintet, Night Pieces for Piano, Biospheres for 6 Percussionists, Trumpet Voluntary, Eight Little Trigams for piano; composer, condr. for films including documentaries Energy on the Move, Mineral King; compositions performed by Leopold Stokowski, Philippe Entremont, Santiago Rodriguez, Phila. Orch., Rochester (N.Y.) Philharm., Balt. Symphony, Indpls. Symphony, Okla. Symphony, Denver Symphony, Europe, S.Am., Asia, Israel; condr. debut rec. of U.S. Internat. Orch. Active in population control, protection of animals, conservation; mem. NATO Tennis team, 1958-59. With inf. and 1st Missile Command, U.S. Army. Recipient award for best music for Mineral King, Nat. Bd. Rev., 1972. Mem. ASCAP, U.S. Tennis Assn., Raelian Movement, Tau Kappa Epsilon. Office: 1888 Century Park E Ste 1900 Los Angeles CA 90067-1723

LAMBROS, LAMBROS JOHN, lawyer, petroleum company executive; b. Sharon, Pa., 1935; s. John and Niki (George) L.; m. Cynthia Ryan, 1965; children: John F., Olivia W. A.B. magna cum laude in History and Lit, Harvard U., 1957, J.D., 1960. Bar: N.Y. 1961. Assoc. White & Case, N.Y.C., 1961-64; of counsel W.R. Grace & Co., N.Y.C., 1964-74, chief internat. counsel, 1970-74; v.p., gen. counsel Amerada Hess Corp., N.Y.C., 1974-76, sr. v.p., gen. counsel, 1976-80, sr. v.p., 1980-83, exec. v.p., dir., 1983-85; chmn., pres., chief exec. officer Norfolk Holdings Inc., Houston, 1986-93, also bd. dirs.; mng. dir. J.W. Childs Assocs., L.P., Boston, 1995—;

bd. dirs. 1st Empire State Corp. Home: 131 Goshen Rd Norfolk CT 06058-1301

LAMEL, LINDA HELEN, insurance company executive, former college president, lawyer; b. N.Y.C., Sept. 10, 1943; d. Maurice and Sylvia (Abrams) Treppel; 1 child, Diana Ruth Sands. BA magna cum laude, Queens Coll., 1964; MA, NYU, 1968; JD, Bklyn. Law Sch., 1976. Bar: N.Y. 1977, U.S. Dist. Ct. (3d dist.) N.Y. 1977. Mgmt. analyst U.S. Navy, Bayonne, N.J., 1964-65; secondary sch. tchr. Farmingdale Pub. Sch., N.Y., 1965-73; curriculum specialist Yonkers Bd. Edn., N.Y., 1973-75; program dir. Office of Lt. Gov., Albany, N.Y., 1975-77; dep. supt. N.Y. State Ins. Dept., N.Y.C., 1977-83; pres., CEO Coll. of Ins., N.Y.C., 1983-88; v.p. Tchr.'s Ins. and Annuity Assn., N.Y.C., 1988-96; exec. dir. Risk and Ins. Mgmt. Soc., N.Y.C. Contbr. articles to profl. jours. Campaign mgr. lt. gov.'s primary race, N.Y. State, 1974; v.p. Spencer Ednl. Found. Mem. ABA (tort and ins. sect. com. chmn. 1985-86), N.Y. State Bar Assn. (exec. com. ins. sect. 1984-88), Assn. of Bar of City of N.Y. (chmn. med. malpractice com. 1989-91), Am. Mgmt. Assn. (ins. and risk mgmt. council), Fin. Women's Assn., Assn. Profl. Ins. Women (Woman of Yr. award 1988), Phi Beta Kappa (v.p. 1992—). *One's life develops much like a patchwork quilt: there are opportunities to add color, texture, and design; and there are missed stitches and uneven seams. Each result is unique and adds value.*

LAMENDOLA, WALTER FRANKLIN, human services, information technology consultant; b. Donora, Pa., Jan. 29, 1943. BA in English, St. Vincent Coll., 1964; MSWin Community Orgn., U. Pitts., 1966; diploma in Sociology and Social Welfare, U. Stockholm, 1970; PhD in Social Work, U. Minn., 1976. Cmty. svcs. dir. Ariz. tng. programs State Dept. Mental Retardation, Tucson, 1970-73; assoc. prof. social welfare adminstrn. Fla. State U., 1976-77; pres., CEO Minn. Rsch. and Tech., Inc., 1977-81; assoc. prof., dir. Allied Health Computer Lab. East Carolina U., 1981-84; prof., dir. info. tech. ctr. Grad. Sch. Social Work U. Denver, 1984-87; cons. info. tech., rsch. human svcs., 1987-90; v.p. rsch. Colo. Trust, Denver, 1990-93, info. tech. and rsch. cons., 1993—; cons. European Network Info. Tech. & Human Svcs.; mem. rebldg. cmtys. initiative PODER project Casey Found., 1996-97; mem. adv. bd. ctr. human svcs. U. Southampton, Brit. Rsch. Coun. Univs., Human Svc. Info. Tech. Applications, CREON Found., The Netherlands; lectr. conf., symposia, univs. U.S., Europe; mem. nat. adv. bd. Native Elder Health Resource Ctr., 1994-96; co-founder Denver Free Net, 1993—; info. tech. cons. Healthy Nations Program Robert Wood Johnson Found., 1993-96; evaluator Nat. Libr. Rsch. Program, Access Colo. grant, 1994, Nat. Info. Infrastructure grant Colo. State Libr.; cons. set up on the Internet for U.S. Cts.-Ct. for Mental Health Svcs., NIH, Frontier Mental Health Svcs. Network grant; collaborating investigator SBIR award Computerized Advance Directives, tech. plan San Mateo County and Seattle Dist. Cts.; keynote spkr. conf. Human Svc. Info. Tech. Applications, Finland, 1996. Co-author: Choices for Colorado's Future, 1993, The Integrity of Intelligence: A Bill of Rights for the Information Age, 1992, Choices for Colorado's Future: Executive Summary, 1991, Choices for Colorado's Future: Regional Summaries, 1991; co-editor: A Casebook of Computer Applications in Health and Social Services, 1989; contbr. numerous articles to profl. jours. Capt. U.S. Army, 1966-69. Recipient Innovative Computer Application award Internat. Fedn. Info. Processing Socs., 1979; Nat. Lib. Rsch. Evaluator grantee, Colo., 1994—, Nat. Info. Infrastructure grantee Dept. Edn., State Libr. and Adult Literacy, 1994-95; Funds & Couns. Tng. scholar United Way Am., 1964-66, Donaldson Fund scholar, 1965-66, NIMH scholar, 1964-66, 73-76, St. Vincent Coll. Benedictine Soc. scholar, 1963-64; vis. fellow U. Southampton. Office: 4098 Field Dr Wheat Ridge CO 80033-4358

LAMER, ANTONIO, Canadian supreme court chief justice; b. Montreal, Can., July 8, 1933; s. Antonio and Florence (Storey) L.; m. Danièle Tremblay; children: Stephane, Melanie, Jean-Frederic. BA, Licentiate in Laws, U. Montreal, 1956; LLD, U. Moncton, 1981, U. Montreal, 1991, U. Toronto, 1992, U. N.B., 1995, Dalhousie U., 1996; D Univ. (hon.), U. Ottawa, 1987. Bar: Que. 1957. Justice Superior Ct. Que., 1969-78, Que. Ct. Appeal, 1978-80, Supreme Ct. Can., 1980—; vice chmn. Nat. Law Reform Commn., 1971-75, chmn., 1975-78; prof. agrege U. Montreal, 1967—; read law with Cutler, Lamer, Bellemare & Assocs.; lectr. U. Montreal, Can. Jud. Conf.; former sr. ptnr. Cutler, Lamer, Bellemare & Assocs.; Que. Bar rep. govt. interdisciplinary com. on structures U. Que.; chmn. Can. Law Reform Commn., 1975. Served with Can. Army Res., 1952, hon. lt.-col. Decorated Knight, Order of St. John, 1993; recipient Order of Merit, U. Montreal, 1991. Mem. Privy Coun. Can., Can. Jud. Coun. (chmn.), Nat. Jud. Inst. (chmn.). Office: Supreme Ct Can, Wellington St, Ottawa, ON Canada K1A 0J1

LAMIA, THOMAS ROGER, lawyer; b. Santa Monica, Calif., May 31, 1938; s. Vincent Robert, II, and Maureen (Green) L.; m. Susan Elena Brown, Jan. 10, 1969; children: Nicholas, Katja, Jenna, Tatiana, Carlyn, Mignon. Student U. So. Calif., 1956, BS, 1961; student U. Miss., 1957-58; JD, Harvard U., 1964. Bar: Calif. 1965, U.S. Dist. Ct. (cen. dist.) Calif. 1965, D.C. 1980, U.S. Dist. Ct. D.C. 1980, U.S. Tax Ct. 1982, N.Y. 1990. Assoc. McCutchen, Black, Verleger & Shea, Los Angeles, 1964-66; lectr. in law U. Ife, Ile-Ife, Nigeria, 1966-67, U. Zambia, Lusaka, 1967-68; assoc. Paul, Hastings, Janofsky & Walker, 1968-72, ptnr., 1972—. Mem. ABA (bus., banking, fed. regulation of securities com., SEC adminstrn., budget and legislation subcom., internat. law com.), Internat. Bar Assn., Harvard Law Sch. Assn., Nat. Aquarium Soc. (bd. dirs. 1982—). Office: Paul Hastings Janofsky Walker 10th Flr 1299 Pennsylvania Ave NW Washington DC 20004-2400

LAMIRANDE, ARTHUR GORDON, editor, author, musician, actor; b. Holyoke, Mass., July 19, 1936; s. Joseph Armand Arthur and Marion Gordon (Beaton) L. AA, Holyoke Community Coll., 1956; student, Peabody Conservatory Music, 1956-57; BA, Am. Internat. Coll., 1959. Editorial asst. Merriam-Webster Dictionary, Springfield, Mass., 1959-61; instr. English dept. Chicopee (Mass.) High Sch., 1961-62; asst. editor Hawthorn Books, N.Y.C., 1962-63; editl. cons., N.Y.C., 1963-66, 73-81, 95—; assoc. editor N.Y. Acad. Scis., N.Y.C., 1966-67, Grune & Stratton Pub. Co., N.Y.C., 1967-68, H.S. Stuttman Co., N.Y.C., 1968-70; mng. editor United Pub. Co., Washington, 1970-71, Sci. and Medicine Pub. Co., N.Y.C., 1971-73; dir. editorial dept. Profl. Exam. Svc., N.Y.C., 1981-92, exec. editor, 1992-94; titular organist St. Catherine of Siena Ch., N.Y.C., 1994-95; editl. cons. N.Y.C., 1995—. Contbr. articles to The Diapason, Lyrichord Discs, PES News; rec. artist (organ) Lyrichord Discs, N.Y.C., 1975; concerts at Cathedral of St. John the Divine, Riverside Ch., Trinity Ch., N.Y., Sacred Heart Cathedral, Newark, Christ Ch. Cathedral, St. Louis, Christ Ch. Cathedral, Springfield, Mass; actor in TV and radio, 1997—. Asst. organist Christ Ch. Cathedral, Springfield, Mass., 1960-61; organist, mus. dir. Ch. of Immaculate Conception, Astoria, N.Y., 1963-66; titular organist Ch. of Holy Name of Jesus, N.Y.C., 1973-82, St. Catherine of Siena Ch., N.Y.C., 1994-95. Home and Office: 461 Fort Washington Ave New York NY 10033-4653

LAMIS, LEROY, artist, retired educator; b. Eddyville, Iowa, Sept. 27, 1925; s. Leo and Blanche (Bennett) L.; m. Esther Sackler, Aug. 13, 1954; children: Alexander, Jonas. B.A., N.Mex. Highlands U., 1953; M.A., Columbia U., 1956. mem. faculty dept. art Ind. State U., 1961—, prof., 1972-89, retired 1989; artist-in-residence Dartmouth Coll., 1970; founder PC ART, 1983. One-man sculpture exhbns. include Staempfli Gallery, N.Y.C., 1966, 69, 73, Gillman Gallery, Chgo., 1967, Tacoma Mus., 1970, Ft. Wayne Art Mus., 1968, Des Moines Art Ctr., 1970, La Jolla Mus., 1970, Ind. State U., 1976, Sheldon Swope Art Mus., Terre Haute, Ind., 1979; kinetic computer art exhbns. at Ben Shahn Gallery, William Patterson Coll., N.J., Ind. State U., 1985, Bronx Mus. Art, 1986, 55 Mercer Gallery, 1990, Indpls. Art Mus., 1992, Evansville Mus. Sci. and Art, 1994, Swope Art Mus., Terre Haute, 1996-97; represented in permanent collections Albright-Knox Mus., Des Moines Art Ctr., Whitney Mus. Am. Art, Joseph H. Hirshorn Collection, Washington, Indpls. Mus., J.B. Speed Mus., Louisville; author: (computer program) Eighty 5, 1985; creator, prodr. various computer software. Served with AUS, 1943. Recipient Award Commn. N.Y. State Coun. of the Arts, 1970. Mem. Am. Abstract Artists. Address: 332 White Oak Ln Terre Haute IN 47804-1081

LAMKA, PHILIP CHARLES, broadcasting company executive; b. El Reno, Okla., Feb. 10, 1947; s. Charles Edwin and Ardelle (Johns) L.; m. Sharman Stewart, Nov. 14, 1981; children by previous marriage—Michael Charles, Philip Glenn. Sales rep. William H. Rorer Pharms., Houston, 1970-73; acct. exec. Sta. KYOK, Houston, 1973-76, local sales mgr., 1977-80; acct. exec. Sta. KLYX, Houston, 1976-77; gen. mgr. Sta. WBOK, New Orleans, 1980-81; gen. mgr. Sta. WWWW, Detroit, 1981—. Mem. Nat. Radio Broadcasters Assn., Nat. Assn. Broadcasters, Mich. Assn. Broadcasters, Detroit Radio Broadcasting Group. Club: Detroit Yacht. Office: Sta WCXI 2930 E Jefferson Ave Detroit MI 48207-5029

LAMKIN, BILL DAN, psychologist, educator, consultant; b. Cleburne, Tex., Feb. 26, 1929; s. Walter Lee and Evelyn Agnes (Watters) L.; m. Robbie Jane Stanley, Aug. 27, 1950; children: Louella Leigh, Rebecca Elizabeth, Melissa Jay. BA, Baylor U., 1950, MA, 1955; PhD, U. Tex., 1967. Tchr. English Bangs (Tex.) High Sch., 1950-53, Waco (Tex.) Schs., 1953-59; counselor Waco High Sch., 1959-60; dir. guidance Los Alamos (N.Mex.) Schs., 1960-65; research assoc. U. Tex., Austin, 1965-67; from asst. to assoc. to prof. Baylor U., Waco, 1967-81, prof. ednl. psychology, 1993—, dean Sch. Edn., 1981-93; cons. Region XII Edn. Svc. Ctr., Waco, 1967-79, New Horizons Residential Ctr., Goldthwaite, Tex., 1974-96, Midway Home for Children, 1992-96, Esperansa Home for Children, 1993-97; teaching cons. Family Medicine Faculty Devel. Ctr., Waco, 1978-92. Contbr. articles to Jour. Med. Edn. Mem. APA, Assn. for Counseling and Devel., Am. Ednl. Rsch. Assn., Coll. of Preceptors. Democrat. Baptist. Home: 2608 Lake Oaks Rd Waco TX 76710-1616 Office: Baylor U Sch of Edn Waco TX 76798

LAMKIN, E(UGENE) HENRY, JR., internist, medical management executive; b. Owensboro, Ky., Feb. 23, 1935; s. Eugene Henry and Nancy Elizabeth (Davidson) L.; m. Martha Savannah Dampf, Aug. 24, 1968; children: Melinda Magness, Matthew Davidson. BA, DePauw U., Greencastle, Ind., 1956; MD, Ind. U., 1960. Diplomate Am. Bd. Internal Medicine. Intern Phila. Gen. Hosp., 1960-61; resident in internal medicine Ind. U. Med. Ctr., 1961-62, 64-65, fellow in endocrinology and metabolism, 1965-66; pvt. practice internal medicine Indpls., 1966-96; pres. Allied Profl. Svcs., Indpls., 1989—; founding pres. Aegis Med. Clinic, Indpls., 1990-92; mem. Ind. Ho. of Reps., 1996-82, majority leader, 1976-80; pres. Ind. Employers Healthcare Coalition, 1993—; v.p., chief med. officer Key Family of Cos., 1996—; asst. clin. prof. medicine Ind. U. Sch. Medicine, 1966—; formerly med. dir. Millennium Mgmt. Co., 1983-89, Farm Bur. Healthcare Network, Indpls., 1989-92; v.p. med. staff Meth. Hosp. of Ind., 1974-75, pres., 1976-77. Bd. dirs. Physicians Med. Alliance Ind., 1983—; mem. organizing com. Ind. Bus. Health Care Coalition, 1989-90. Capt. U.S. Army, 1962-64. Recipient Otis R. Bowen Physician Cmty. Svc. award, Ind. Optometry Assn. award, Appreciation award Ind. Acad. Family Practice, others. Fellow ACP; mem. AMA, Am. Coll. Physician Execs., Nat. Assn. Managed Care Physicians, Nat. Assn. for Health Care Quality. Avocations: theater/music, golf, tennis, gardening, cooking. Home: 4145 N Washington Blvd Indianapolis IN 46205-2616 Office: Allied Profl Svcs 8250 Haverstick Rd Ste 295 Indianapolis IN 46240-2402

LAMKIN, WILLIAM PIERCE, editor; b. Ansley, La., Oct. 17, 1919; s. John Mays and Carrie Ellen (Posey) L.; m. Irma Hazel Page, Dec. 30, 1948 (div.); children: John Page, Mary Jean, Carol Ellen; m. Jene Eagar Mills, Mar. 17, 1973. AB, U. N.C., 1948. Reporter Alexandria (La.) Daily Town Talk, 1941-43; copyreader Charlotte (N.C.) Observer, 1948-49, asst. city editor, night city editor, 1950-58, city editor, religion editor, 1958-61; news dir. Presbyn. Ch. U.S., 1961-78; editor Presbyn. Survey, Atlanta, 1978-80; editor and pub. Presbyn. Survey, 1980-83; editor Friendship mag., 1983—. With USAAF, 1943-45. Decorated D.F.C. (4), Air Medal (5). Democrat. Home: 4201 Ridgehurst Dr Smyrna GA 30080-3114 Office: 57 Forsyth St NW Ste 900 Atlanta GA 30303-2213 *The most critical issue facing humankind as we approach the 21st century is how to assure world peace. I am convinced that the best approach is through friendship and understanding. We need organized efforts to "walk in other people's shoes". It goes without saying that a world of friends is a world of peace.*

LAMM, CAROLYN BETH, lawyer; b. Buffalo, Aug. 22, 1948; d. Daniel John and Helen Barbara (Tatakis) L.; m. Peter Edward Halle, Aug. 12, 1972; children: Alexander P., Daniel E. BS, SUNY Coll. at Buffalo, 1970; JD, U. Miami (Fla.), 1973. Bar: Fla., 1973, D.C., 1976, N.Y. 1983. Trial atty. frauds sect. civil div. U.S. Dept. Justice, Washington, 1973-78, asst. chief comml. litigation sect. civil div., 1978, asst. dir., 1978-80; assoc. White & Case, Washington, 1980-84, ptnr., 1984—; mem. Sec. State's Adv. Com. Pvt. Internat. law, 1988-91; arbitrator U.S. Panel of Arbitrators, Internat. Ctr. Settlement of Investment Disputes, 1995—. Mem. bd. editors Can./U.S. Rev. Bus. Law, 1987-92; mem. editorial adv. bd. Inside Litigation; contbr. articles to legal publs. Fellow Am. Bar Found.; mem. ABA (chmn. young lawyers divsn., rules and calendar com., chmn. house membership com., chmn. assembly resolution com., sec. 1984-85, chmn. internat. litigation com. coun. 1991-94, sect. litigation, ho. dels. 1982—, nomination com. 1984-87, chair 1995-96, past D.C. Cir. mem., standing com. fed. judiciary 1992-95, chmn. com. scope and correlation of work 1996-97), Am. Arbitration Assn. (arbitrator, com. on fed. arbitration act), Fed. Bar Assn. (chmn. sect. on antitrust and trade regulation), Bar Assn. D.C. (bd. dirs., sec.), D.C. Bar (pres.-elect, bd. govs. 1987-93, steering com. litigation sect.), Am. Law Inst., Women's Bar Assn. D.C., Am. Soc. Internat. Law, Internat. Bar Assn. (bus. law sect., internat. litigation com.), Am. Indonesian C. of C. (bd. dirs.), Am. Uzbekistan C. of C. (bd. dirs., sec., gen. counsel), Am. Turkish Friendship Coun. (bd. dirs., chair dirs., sec., gen. counsel), Nat. Women's Forum, Columbia Country Club. Democrat. Home: 2801 Chesterfield Pl NW Washington DC 20008-1015 Office: White and Case 601 13th St NW Washington DC 20005-3807

LAMM, DONALD STEPHEN, publishing company executive; b. N.Y.C., May 31, 1931; s. Lawrence William and Aleen Antonia (Lassner) L.; m. Jean Stewart Nicol, Sept. 27, 1958; children: Douglas William, Robert Lawrence, Wendy Nicol. BA with honors, Yale, 1953; postgrad., Oxford (Eng.) U., 1956. With W.W. Norton & Co., Inc., N.Y.C., 1956-68; from v.p. to pres. W.W. Norton & Co., Inc., 1968-94, chmn., 1984—, also dir.; bd. dirs. W.W. Norton & Co., Ltd., London, Liveright Pub. Corp., Nat. Book Co., Scranton, Pa.; guest fellow Yale U., 1980, 85, Phi Beta Kappa lectr. 1994; Ida Beam disting. vis. prof. U. Iowa, 1987-88; guest fellow Woodrow Wilson Ctr., 1996; regents lectr. U. Calif., Berkeley, 1997—; pres. Yale U. Press; mem. bd. advisors Yale Rev., mem. bd. Control U. Calif. Press. Author: (with others) The Spread of Economic Ideas, 1989, Beyond Literacy, 1990, Book Publishing in the United States Today, 1997; mem. editl. bd. Logos. Mem. coun. Woodrow Wilson Ctr., Inst. Early Am. History and Culture, Williamsburg, Va.; bd. dirs. Roper Ctr. Pub. Opinion Rsch. With U.S. Army, 1953-55. Fellow Branford Coll., Yale U. Fellow Am. Acad. Arts and Scis.; mem. Manuscript Soc., Coun. Fgn. Rels., Century Assn., Elizabethan Club, Phi Beta Kappa (senator 1990—). Home: 741 Calle Picacho Santa Fe NM 87501 Office: WW Norton & Co Inc 500 5th Ave New York NY 10110

LAMM, HARRIET A., mathematics educator; b. Beeville, Tex., Dec. 4, 1948; d. James R. and Dorothy D. (Kendall) L. BA, Tex. Christian U., 1971; BS in Edn., S.W. Tex. State U., 1973, MEd, 1976; PhD, Tex. A&M U., 1993. Cert. secondary tchr., Tex. Instr. math. South San Antonio Ind. Sch. Dist., San Antonio, 1973-74; teaching asst. in math. S.W. Tex. State U., San Marcos, 1974-76; tchr. math. Seguin (Tex.) Ind. Sch. Dist., 1976-78, George West (Tex.) Ind. Sch. Dist., 1978-83, Lingleville (Tex.) Ind. Sch. Dist., 1983, Northside Ind. Sch. Dist., San Antonio, 1984-87, Beeville (Tex.) Ind. Sch. Dist., 1987-88; teaching asst. Tex. A&M U., College Station, 1991-92; instr. math. Bee County Coll., Beeville, 1988-91, 1992—; instr. math. Tarleton State U., Stephenville, Tex., 1983. Mem. Nat. Coun. Tchrs. Math., Tex. Coun. Tchrs. Math., Sch. Sci. and Math. Assn., Math. Assn. Am., Assn. Tex. Profl. Educators, Rsch. Coun. for Diagnostic and Prescriptive Math. Avocations: ranching, sculpture, drawing.

LAMM, MICHAEL EMANUEL, pathologist, immunologist, educator; b. Bklyn., May 19, 1934; s. Stanley S. and Rose (Lieberman) L.; m. Ruth Audrey Kumin, Dec. 16, 1961; children—Jocelyn, Margaret. Student, Amherst Coll., 1951-54; M.D., U. Rochester, 1959; M.S. in Chemistry, Western Res. U., 1962. Diplomate Am. Bd. Pathology. Intern, asst. resident in pathology Inst. Pathology Western Res. U. and Univ. Hosps. of Cleve., 1959-62; research assoc. NIMH, Bethesda, Md., 1962-64; asst. prof. pathology NYU Sch. Medicine, N.Y.C., 1964-68, assoc. prof., 1968-73, prof., 1973-81; prof. dept. pathology Case We. Res. U. Sch. Medicine, 1981—; chmn. dept. Case Western Res. U. Sch. Medicine, 1981—; vis. sci. dept. biochemistry U. Oxford, 1968; vis. prof. dept. pathology U. Geneva, 1976-77; mem. cancer spl. program adv. com. Nat. Cancer Inst., Bethesda, 1976-79, mem. bd. sci. counselors divsn. cancer biology, diagnosis and ctrs., 1993-95; mem. sci. adv. com. Damon Runyon-Walter Winchell Cancer Fund, N.Y.C., 1978-82; mem. immunol. sci. study sect. NIH, Bethesda, 1988-92; mem. immunotoxicology subcom. NRC, 1989-90; mem. toxin peer rev. panel Am. Inst. Biol. Sci., 1990—; bd. dirs. Univ. Associated for Rsch. and Edn. Pathology. Mem. editl. bd. Procs. Soc. Exptl. Biology and Medicine, 1973-82, Molecular Immunology, 1979-83, Jour. Immunol. Methods, 1980—, Jour. Immunology, 1981-85, Am. Jour. Pathology, 1982-92, Regional Immunology, 1988-95, Modern Pathology, 1989-96; contbr. articles to profl. jours. Recipient for excellence in teaching NYU Sch. Medicine, 1974; named Career Scientist Health Research Council, City of N.Y., 1966-75; NIH grantee, 1965—. Fellow N.Y. Acad. Scis.; mem. Am. Assn. Pathologists (councilor 1986-88, sec. treas. 1988-90, v.p. 1990-91, pres. 1991-92), Am. Assn. Immunologists, Am. Soc. Biochemistry and Molecular Biology, Coll. Am. Pathologists, U.S. and Can. Acad. Pathology, Soc. for Exptl. Biol. Medicine, Clin. Immunology Soc., Soc. Mucosal Immunology, Am. Soc. Clin. Pathologists, Harvey Soc., Sigma Xi, Alpha Omega Alpha. Home: 2856 Glengary Rd Cleveland OH 44120-1731

LAMM, NORMAN, academic administrator, rabbi; b. Bklyn., Dec. 19, 1927; s. Samuel and Pearl (Baumol) L.; m. Mindella Mehler, Feb. 23, 1954; children: Chaye Lamm Warburg, Joshua B., Shalom E., Sara Rebecca Lamm Dratch. B.A. summa cum laude, Yeshiva Coll., 1949; Ph.D., Bernard Revel Grad. Sch., 1966; Dr. of Hebrew Letters (hon.), Hebrew Theol. Coll., 1977. Ordained rabbi, 1951; asst. rabbi Congregation Kehilath Jeshurun, N.Y.C., 1952-53; rabbi Congregation Kodimoh, Springfield, Mass., 1954-58, Jewish Center, N.Y.C., 1958-76; Erna and Jakob Michael prof. Jewish philosophy Yeshiva U., N.Y.C., 1966—; pres. Yeshiva U., 1976—, Rabbi Isaac Elchanan Theol. Sem., N.Y.C., 1976—; vis. prof. Judaic studies Bklyn. Coll., 1974-75; dir. Union Orthodox Jewish Congregations Am. Author: A Hedge of Roses, 1966, The Royal Reach, 1970, Faith and Doubt, 1971, Torah Lishmah, 1972 (rev. English edition 1989), The Good Society, 1974; editor: Library of Jewish Law and Ethics, 1975—; co-editor: The Leo Jung Jubilee Volume, 1962, A Treasury of Tradition, 1967, The Joseph B. Soloveitchik Jubilee Vol., 1984, Halakhot ve'Halikhot (Heb.): Essays on Jewish Law, 1990, Torah Umadda: The Encounter of Religious Learning and Worldly Knowledge in the Jewish Tradition, 1990. Trustee-at-large Fedn. Jewish Philanthropies, N.Y.; mem. exec. com. Assn. for a Better N.Y.; bd. dirs. Am. Friends-Alliance Israelite Universelle; mem. Pres.'s Commn. on the Holocaust, 1978-89; chmn. N.Y. Conf. on Soviet Jewry, 1970; mem. Halakhah Commn., Rabbinical Council Am. Recipient Abramowitz Zeitlin award, 1972. Mem. Assn. Orthodox Jewish Scientists (charter; bd. govs.). Office: Yeshiva U Office of Pres 500 W 185th St New York NY 10033-3201 also: Rabbi Isaac Eichanan Theol Sem 2540 Amsterdam Ave New York NY 10033-2807

LAMMIE, JAMES L., financial planner, consultant; b. 1932. Grad., U.S. Mil. Acad., 1953. Active U.S. Corps of Engrs., 1953-75; CEO Parsons Brinckerhoff, Inc., N.Y.C., 1975-94; also bd. dirs. Office: Parsons Brinckerhoff Inc 1 Penn Plz Fl 2 New York NY 10119-0299 Office: One Penn Plaza 2nd Fl New York NY 10119*

LAMON, HARRY VINCENT, JR., lawyer; b. Macon, Ga., Sept. 29, 1932; s. Harry Vincent and Helen (Bewley) L.; m. Ada Healey Morris, June 17, 1954; children: Hollis Morris, Kathryn Gurley. BS cum laude, Davidson Coll., 1954; JD with distinction, Emory U., 1958. Bar: Ga. 1958, D.C. 1965. Of counsel Troutman Sanders LLP, Atlanta, 1995—; adj. prof. law Emory U., 1960-79. Contbr. articles to profl. jours. Mem. adv. bd. Atlanta chpt. Salvation Army, 1963—, chmn., 1975-79, 91-92, mem. nat. adv. bd., 1976-95, emeritus, 1995—, life mem., 1997; mem. Adv. Coun. on Employee Welfare and Pension Benefit Plans, U.S. Dept. Labor, 1975-79; mem. Employee Benefits Reporter adv. bd. Bur. Nat. Affairs; mem. bd. visitors Davidson Coll., 1979-89; trustee, pres. So. Fed. Tax Inst., Inc., 1965—; trustee Am. Tax Policy Inst., Inc., 1989-96, Embry-Riddle Aero U., 1989—, Cathedral of St. Philip, Atlanta, 1989-95; mem. adv. bd. Salvation Army, Atlanta, 1997. 1st lt. AUS, 1954-56. Recipient Others award Salvation Army, 1979, Centennial honoree, 1990. Fellow Am. Bar Found., Am. Coll. Trust and Estate Counsel, Am. Coll. Tax Counsel, Internat. Acad. Estate and Trust Law, Ga. Bar Found.; mem. ABA, FBA, Atlanta Bar Assn., Am. Bar Retirement Assn. (bd. dirs. 1989-96, pres. 1994-95), Am. Law Inst. (life), Am. Employee Benefits Conf., So. Employee Benefits Conf. (life, pres. 1972), State Bar Ga. (chmn. sect. taxation 1969-70, vice chmn. commn. on continuing lawyer competency 1982-89), Am. Judicature Soc., Atlanta Tax Forum, Lawyers Club Atlanta, Nat. Emory U. Law Sch. Alumni Assn. (pres. 1967), Practicing Law Inst., ALI-ABA Inst., CLUs Inst., Kiwanis Club Atlanta (pres. 1994), Peachtree Racket Club (pres. 1986-87), Atlanta Coffee House Club, Capital City Club, Peachtree Club, Cosmos Club, Univ. Club (Washington), Phi Beta Kappa, Omicron Delta Kappa, Phi Delta Phi, Phi Delta Theta (chmn. cmty. svc. day 1969-72, legal commr. 1973-76, prov. pres. 1976-79). Episcopalian. Home: 4415 Paces Battle NW Atlanta GA 30327 Office: Troutman Sanders LLP 600 Peachtree St NE Ste 5200 Atlanta GA 30308-2214

LAMON, KATHY LYNN, nursing administrator; b. Moultrie, Ga., July 24, 1961; d. James Daniel and Sammie Ruth (Fletcher) Miles; m. Thomas Eldred Lamon, Aug. 23, 1980. BSN, Valdosta State U., 1983. RN, Fla. Surg. staff nurse Putnam Cmty. Hosp., Palatka, Fla., 1983-84, surg. charge nurse, 1984-86, surg. asst. nurse mgr., 1986-87, nurse mgr. progressive care unit, 1987-90; sr. cmty. health nurse Putnam County Pub. Health Dept., Palatka, 1990; DON Palatka Health Care Ctr., 1991-94; asst. regional nurse North Fla. region Nat. Healthcare, Ocala, 1994—. Author: Pockety Buddy for Nurses PCH, 1991. Youth group leader Palatka Bapt. Temple, 1992-95. Recipient Dr. Frist Humanitarian award Hosp. Corp. of Am., 1988, Recipient of the Nat. Healthcare Patient Care award, 1994. others; named Outstanding Young Med. Profl., Jaycees, 1988. Mem. Nat. Assn. DON, Intravenous Nurses Soc., N.E. Fla. DON. Republican. Office: Nat Healthcare 3400 SW 27th Ave Ocala FL 34474-4404

LAMONE, RUDOLPH PHILIP, business educator; b. Wellsburg, W.Va., Dec. 20, 1931; s. Dominic and Maria (Branch) L.; m. Linda A. Hefler, Jan. 29, 1970. B.S., U. N.C., Chapel Hill, 1960, Ph.D., 1966. Instr. U. N.C., 1963-66; mem. faculty U. Md., College Park, 1966—, prof. mgmt. sci., 1971—, dean Coll. Bus. and Mgmt., 1973-92, prof., chair adv. bd. Michael Dingman Ctr. Entrepreneurship, 1993—; bd. dirs. Md. Ctr. Productivity and Quality of Working Life, EA Engring. Sci. and Tech. Inc.; chmn. govtl. rels. com. Am. Assembly Collegiate Schs. Bus., 1977-78; cons. Tatung Co., Taiwan; mem. adv. com. Md. Dept. Econ. and Cmty. Devel. Co-author: Linear Programming for Management Decisions, 1969, Marketing Management and the Decision Sciences, 1971, Production-Operations Management, 1972. Served with AUS, 1952-55. Mem. Acad. Mgmt., Inst. Mgmt. Scis., Am. Inst. Decision Scis., Md. C. of C. (dir.), Phi Beta Kappa, Beta Gamma Sigma. Democrat. Roman Catholic. Club: Annapolis Yacht (bd. dirs.). Office: U Md Dingman Ctr Entrepreneurship College Park MD 20742

LAMONICA, P(AUL) RAYMOND, lawyer, academic administrator, educator; b. Baton Rouge, June 10, 1944; s. Leonard and Olivia (Frank) L.; m. Dianne Davis, Aug. 23, 1971; children: Drew, Neal, Leigh. BA, La. State U., 1965, MA, 1966, JD, 1970. Bar, La. 1970. Law clk. to chief judge U.S. Dist. Ct. (we. dist.) La., 1970-71; assoc. Hebert, Moss & Graphia, Baton Rouge, 1971; judge pro tem 19th Jud. Dist. Ct., East Baton Rouge Parish, 1979; prof. La. State U. Law Sch., Baton Rouge, 1973-86; exec. counsel to La. Gov., 1983-84; U.S. atty. for mid. dist. La., 1986-94; vice chancellor, prof. law La. State U., Baton Rouge, 1994—; counsel La. Ho. of Reps., 1976-79, 80-83. Fellow Am. Bar Found.; mem. ABA, La. Bar Assn. (bd. govs. 1979). Republican. Roman Catholic. Office: La State U 210 LSU Law Ctr Baton Rouge LA 70803

LAMONSOFF, NORMAN CHARLES, psychiatrist; b. Bklyn., Sept. 16, 1936; s. Isidore and Kate (Wolfe) L.; m. Sheila R. Kaplan, Aug. 27, 1961; children: Karen M., Jacob D. BA, Cornell U., 1958; MD, SUNY, 1962. Diplomate Am. Bd. Psychiatry and Neurology. Medical internship Bklyn. Jewish Hosp., 1963; residency psychiatry Kings County Hosp., Bklyn., 1966-68; sr. supervising psychiatrist St. Vincent's Hosp. of Richmond, Staten Island, N.Y., 1968-70; cons. psychiatrist Staten Island Hosp., 1968-87; dir. psychiatry N.Y.C. Dept. Mental Health and Mental Retardation Svcs., 1970-

74; attending psychiatrist Jersey City (N.J.) Medical Ctr., 1974-76; program dir. addiction svcs. unit Jersey City Medical Ctr., 1974-76; medical dir. Somerset County Com. Mental Health Ctr., Somerville, N.J., 1976-83, Helene Fuld Crisis Ctr., Trenton, N.J., 1984-87; chmn. psychiatry Helene Fuld Med. Ctr.; medical dir. Bristol-Bensalem Human Svcs. Ctr., Newportville, Pa., 1987—; clinical supr. residency training The Trenton Psychiatric Hosp., clinical asst. prof. N.J. Coll. Medicine. Contbr. articles to profl. jours. With U.S. Army, 1966-68. Decorated Army Commendation medal; recipient Exemplary Psychiatrist award Bucks County area chpt., Nat. Alliance for the Mentally Ill., 1994. Mem. N.Y. Soc. Clinical Psychiatry, Am. Psychiatry Assn., Am. Medical Assn., Mercer County Medical Soc. Home: 121 Trappe Ln Langhorne PA 19047 Office: Bristol-Bensalem Human Svcs 340 E Maple Ave Ste 104 Langhorne PA 19047-2851 Address: PO Box L-27 Langhorne PA 19047

LAMONT, LANSING, journalist, public affairs executive, author; b. N.Y.C., Mar. 13, 1930; s. Thomas Stilwell and Elinor (Miner) L.; m. Ada Jung, Sept. 18, 1954; children: Douglas Ranlet, Elisabeth Jung Lamont Wolcott, Virginia Alden Lamont Cazedessus, Thomas Stilwell II. A.B., Harvard U., 1952; M.S. in Journalism with honors, Columbia U., 1958. Reporter, Washington Star, 1958-59; Washington corr. Worcester (Mass.) Gazette, also other New Eng. papers, 1959-60; sci. reporter Washington bur. Time mag., 1961-63, polit. reporter, 1964-68, corr., dep. chief London bur., 1969-71, chief Can. corr., chief Ottawa bur., 1971-73; chief corr. UN bur. Time mag., N.Y.C., 1973-74; v.p., mng. dir. Can. Affairs The Americas Soc., 1981-91, sr. fellow, 1991-94. Author: Day of Trinity (alt. selection Lit. Guild Am.), 1965, Campus Shock, 1979; co-editor Private Letters of John Masefield, 1979, Friends So Different: Essays on Canada and U.S. in the 1980's, 1989, Journey to the Last Empire: The Soviet Union in Transition, 1991, Breakup: The Coming End of Canada and the Stakes for America, 1994 (Notable Books of Yr., N.Y. Times), Sand and Glitter: Exploring the Ancient Middle East, 1994-95. Mem. alumni bd. dirs. Harvard U., also chmn. nominating com. for overseers; trustee Milton Acad., Am. Mus. Natural History, N.Y.C., chmn. libr. com., fellow of libr. Nat. Inst. for Music Theatre; mem. Can.-Am. Com., 1984-94, Coun. Fgn. Rels. 1985—. Served to 1st lt., inf. U.S. Army, 1954-57. William Cullen Bryant fellow Met. Mus. Art, 1984—. Mem. Century Assn. (N.Y.C.), Harvard Club (N.Y.C.). Episcopalian. Office: 133 E 80th St New York NY 10021-0305

LAMONT, LEE, music management executive; b. Queens, N.Y.; m. August Tagliamonte, Apr. 30, 1951; 1 child, Leslie Lamont. With Nat. Concerts & Artists Group, N.Y.C., 1955-58; asst. Sol Hurok Concerts, N.Y.C., 1958-67; person rep. for concerts, rec. and TV Isaac Stern, N.Y.C., 1968-76; v.p. ICM Artists Ltd., N.Y.C., 1976-85; pres. ICM Artists Ltd. and ICM Artists (London) Ltd., N.Y.C., 1985-95, chmn. bd. dirs., 1995—; Mem. adv. com. Hannover (Germany) Internat. Violin Competition. Mem. Am. Coun. on the Arts, Japan Soc., Asia Soc., Am. Symphony Orch. League (bd. dirs.), Bohemian Club. Avocations: painting, sculpture. Office: ICM Artists Ltd 40 W 57th St Fl 16 New York NY 10019-4001

LAMONT, PETER, production designer, art director. Art dir.: (films) The Seven Percent Solution, 1976, The Spy Who Loved Me, 1977 (Academy award nomination best art direction 1977), The Boys from Brazil, 1978; prodn. designer: (films) For Your Eyes Only, 1981, Octopussy, 1983, Top Secret!, 1984, A View to a Kill, 1985, Aliens, 1986 (Academy award nomination best art direction 1986), The Living Daylights, 1987, Consuming Passions, 1988, Licence to Kill, 1989, Eve of Destruction, 1991, The Taking of Beverly Hills, 1992, True Lies, 1994. Office: The Lyons/Sheldon Agency 800 S Robertson Blvd Ste 6 Los Angeles CA 90035-1606*

LAMONT, ROSETTE CLEMENTINE, Romance languages educator, theatre journalist, translator; b. Paris; came to U.S., 1941, naturalized, 1946; d. Alexandre and Loudmilla (Lamont) L.; m. Frederick Hyde Farmer, Aug. 9, 1969. B.A., Hunter Coll., 1947; M.A., Yale U., 1948, Ph.D., 1954. Tutor Romance langs. Queens Coll., CUNY, 1950-54, instr., 1954-61, asst. prof., 1961-64, assoc. prof., 1965-67, prof., 1967-96; mem. doctoral faculties, comparative lit., theatre, French and women's studies cert. program CUNY, 1968-96, prof. emeritus PhD program in theater, 1996—; State Dept. envoy Scholar Exch. Program, USSR, 1974; rsch. fellow, 1976; lectr. Alliance Francaise, Maison Francaise of NYU; vis. prof. Sorbonne, Paris, 1985-86; vis. prof. theatre Sarah Lawrence Coll., 1994, 97. Author: The Life and Works of Boris Pasternak, 1964, De Vive Voix, 1971, Ionesco, 1973, The Two Faces of Ionesco, 1978, Ionesco's Imperatives: The Politics of Culture, 1993, Women on the Verge, 1993; translator: Days and Memory, 1990, Auschwitz and After, 1995 (ALTA prize), Brazen, 1996; also contbr. to various books; author, guest editor The Metaphysical Farce issue Collages and Bricolages, 1996-97; mem. editl. bd. Western European Stages, also contbg. editor; European corr. Theatre Week: Columbia Dictionary of Modern European Literature; fgn. corr. Stages; reviewer France-Amérique-Le Figaro. Decorated chevalier, then officier des Palmes Academiques, officier des Arts et Lettres (France); named to Hunter Coll. Hall of Fame, 1991; Guggenheim fellow, 1973-74; Rockefeller Found. humanities fellow, 1983-84. Mem. PEN, MLA, Am. Soc. Theatre Research, Internat. Brecht Soc., Drama Desk (voting mem.), Internat. Assn. Theatre Critics, Phi Beta Kappa, Sigma Tau Delta, Pi Delta Phi. Club: Yale. Home: 260 W 72nd St Apt 9D New York NY 10023-2822 Office: CUNY Queens Coll Dept European Langs Flushing NY 11367 *An educator does not merely impart knowledge: he or she communicates an attitude, a way of looking at the world. So does the writer. Through each creative mind the world is born anew.*

LAMONT, SANDERS HICKEY, journalist; b. Atlanta, Nov. 9, 1940; s. Louis Earnest and Dorothy Rebecca (Strickland) LaM.; m. Patricia Jean Taylor, Aug. 5, 1966; children—Patricia Ruth, Zachary Taylor. A.A., Marion Mil. Inst., Ala., 1960; B.A. in Journalism, U. Ala., 1962; postgrad. U. Mich., 1977-78. Reporter, bur. chief Gannett News Service, various locations, 1961-74; mng. editor Ft. Myers News Press, Fla., 1974-77; exec. editor Marietta Times, Ohio, 1978-80, Modesto Bee, Calif., 1980—; chmn. AP News Execs. Council, Calif., 1984-85. NEH journalism fellow, U. Mich., 1977-78; Pulitzer prize juror, 1984-85. Served to 1st lt. U.S. Army, 1963-65. Mem. Am. Soc. Newspaper Editors, AP Mng. Editors, Soc. Profl. Journalists. Methodist. Office: The Modesto Bee PO Box 5256 Modesto CA 95352-5256

LAMONT-HAVERS, RONALD WILLIAM, physician, research administrator; b. Wymondham, Norfolk, Eng., Mar. 6, 1920; came to U.S., 1955, naturalized, 1964; s. William Fredrick L.-H.; m. Gabrielson, Oct. 16, 1965; children—Wendy, Melinda, Ian. B.A., U. B.C., 1942; M.D., U. Toronto, 1946; diploma in internal medicine, McGill U., 1953. Intern Vancouver (B.C., Can.) Gen. Hosp., 1946-48; resident in internal medicine Queen Mary Vets. Hosp., Montreal, Que., Can., 1949-51; Canadian Arthritis and Rheumatism Soc. fellow Columbia Presbyterian Hosp., Coll. Physicians and Surgeons, Columbia U., N.Y.C., 1951-53; med. dir. Canadian Arthritis and Rheumatism Soc., B.C. div., Vancouver, 1953-55, Arthritis and Rheumatism Found., N.Y.C., 1955-64; instr. in medicine Coll. Physicians and Surgeons, Columbia U., 1955-64; assoc. dir. extramural programs NIAMD, Bethesda, Md., 1964-68, dep. dir., 1972-74; assoc. dir. extramural programs NIH, Bethesda, Md., 1968-72; acting dir., dep. dir. NIH, Bethesda, Md., 1974-76, acting dir., 1975, dep. dir., 1974-76; dep. to gen. dir. for rsch. policy and adminstrn. Mass. Gen. Hosp., Boston, 1976-87, v.p. rsch. and tech. affairs, 1987-90, sr. cons. for rsch., 1990—; dep. dir. Cutaneous Biology Rsch. Ctr. Mass. Gen. Hosp. and Harvard U., 1990—; del. USSR-Arthritis Exchange Program, 1964; U.S. coordinator U.S.-USSR Coop. Program in Arthritis, 1973-75.; Served with M.C. Royal Canadian Army, 1944-46. Recipient Golden Pen award Jour. Am. Phys. Therapy Assn., 1965; Superior Service award HEW, 1973; Spl. citation Sec. HEW, 1975. Fellow Royal Coll. Physicians (Can.); mem. Am. Coll. Rheumatology (dir. Met. Washington sect. 1964-66), N.Y. Rheumatism Assn. (pres. 1960), Arthritis Found. (dir., governing mem. 1966-80, pres. Mass. chpt. 1987-89), Am. Acad. Orthopaedic Surgeons (hon.), Am. Gastroent. Assn. (affiliate), Alpha Omega Alpha. Office: Mass Gen Hosp 13th St Bldg 149 Charlestown MA 02129-2000

LA MONT-WELLS, TAWANA FAYE, camera operator, video director; b. Ft. Worth, May 12, 1948; d. Jerry James and Roberta Ann (Wilkinson) La M. AA, Antelope Coll., 1979; BA in Anthropology, UCLA, 1982. Forest technician, trail constrn. supr. Angeles Nat. Forest, Region 9 U.S. Forest Svc., Pear Blossom, Calif., 1974-79; trail constrn. supr., maintenance asst. Calif. State Parks, 1979-81; cable TV installer Sammons Comm., Glendale, Calif., 1981-83, camera operator, 1983-87; video studio and ENG remotes dir., mgr., program mgr. channel 6 Sammons Cable, Glendale, Calif., 1981-97; video studio and ENG remotes dir., mgr., program mgr. channel 21 Marcus Cable, Glendale, Calif., 1981-97; video dir., prodr. LBW & Assocs. Internat., Ltd., 1988—; pres., CEO Chamblee Found., Ltd., 1995—; mem. ednl. access channel satellite program evaluation com., Glendale and Burbank, 1990-92; mem. Foothill Cmty. TV Network, Glendale and Burbank, 1987-97. Prodr., dir. (homeless video) Bittersweet Streets, 1988; cameraperson Rockin in A Hard Place, 1988-93; dir., editor over 1000 videos. Active Glendale Hist. Soc., 1992-97; bd. dirs. Am. Heart Assn., 1992-96, comms. chair; bd. dirs. ARC, 1993—, mem. disaster svcs. team, cultural diversity chair, 1994-95; mem. mktg. com. Burbank YMCA, 1994-96; bd. dirs. Glendale Rose Float Assn., 1995—. Recipient award of appreciation LBW and Assocs. Internat., 1988, Bur. Census, 1990, USMC, 1991, Verdugo Disaster Recovery Project, 1995, ARC, 1995, ARC Spl. citation for exceptional vol. svc., 1995, award of outstanding pub. svc. Social Security Adminstrn. HHS, 1989, dedicated svc. award Am. Heart Assn., 1992, cert. of appreciation, 1994, 95. Mem. NAFE, NRA, Internat. Alliance Theatrical Stage Employees, Moving Picture Technicians, Artists and Allied Crafts, Internat. Photographer's Guild, Am. Women in Radio and TV, Am. Bus. Women Assn., UCLA Alumni Assn. (life), Wildlife Waystation, Alpha Gamma. Democrat. Avocations: photography, animals, flying, sailing, travel. Office: PO Box 142 Lake Hughes CA 93532-0142

LAMOREAUX, PHILIP ELMER, geologist, hydrogeologist, consultant; b. Chardon, Ohio, May 12, 1920; s. Elmer I. and Gladys (Rhodes) L.; m. Ura Mae Munro, Nov. 11, 1943; children: Philip E Jr., James W., Karen L. BA, Denison U., 1943, PhD (hon.), 1972; MS, U. Ala., 1949. Registered profl. geologist, Ga., N.C., S.C., Tenn., Ind., Ariz., Ark., Fla., Ky., Wyo., Pa., Mo., Ala. Geologist U.S. Geol. Survey, Tuscaloosa, Ala., 1943-45, dist. geologist Groundwater Office, 1945-57, divsn. hydrologist Water Resources Programs, 1957-59; chief Ground Water Br. U.S. Geol. Survey, Washington, 1959-61; state geologist, oil and gas supr. Ala. Geol. Survey, Tuscaloosa, 1961-76; pres. P.E. LaMoreaux & Assocs. Inc., Tuscaloosa, 1976-87, chmn. bd. dirs., 1987-90, sr. hydrologist, 1990—; lectr. Am. Geol. Inst. Coll. Program, 1969-71, Am. Geophys. Union Coll. Program, 1961—, NSF, Ala. Acad. Sci. H.S. Program, 1961—, No. Engring. and Testing, Salt Lake City, 1985, Ga. State U., Fla. State U., Vanderbilt U., Denison U., Auburn U., U. of Montpellier, France, U. Christ Church, New Zealand, University of Praetoria, South Africa; hydrogeology cons. to 30 fgn. countries. Editor in chief Jour. Environ. Geology, 1982—; editor in chief: Annotated Bibliography Carbonate Rocks, vols. 1-5; contbr. articles to profl. jours. Mem. Nat. Drinking Water Adv. Coun. EPA, 1984-88, mem. Tech. Rev. Group Oak Ridge Nat. Lab., 1984-88; trustee Denison U. Recipient Comdrs. medal C.E., 1990. Mem. NAE, ASTM, AIME, NAS (nat. rsch. coun. geotech. bd. 1990-92, water sci. and tech. bd. 1990—, bd. earth scis. and resources 1992—, earth resources com. 1995—), AAAS, Ala. Acad. Sci., Ala. Geol. Soc., Am. Assn. Petroleum Geologists (acad. liaison com., Ho. of Dels. 1970-72, com. preservation samples and cores, chmn. divsn. geosci. hydrogeology com.), Am. Geol. Inst. (chmn. com. on publs. 1968-70, pres. 1971-72, Ian Campbell award 1990, chmn. environ. geosci. adv. com. 1994—, William B. Heroy award 1995, chmn. A61 Environ. Geosciences Adv. com., bd. trustees), Am. Geophys. Union, Am. Inst. Hydrology, Am. Inst. Profl. Geologists (chmn. com. on rels. with govtl. agencies 1967-70, bd. dirs. 1969-70), Assn. Am. State Geologists (statistician 1966-69, chmn. liaison com. fed. agencies 1968-70, pres.), Geol. Soc. Am. (1st chmn. hydrogeology group 1963, chmn. O.E. Meinzer award com. 1965, cons. membership S.E. sect. 1967-68, chmn. nominating com., bd. dirs., bd. trustees, publs. com.), Geol. Soc. London, Internat. Assn. Hydrogeologists (pres. 1977-80, v.p. 1973-77, com. on water rsch. 1978-80, Karst Commn. 1961—, chmn. hydrology hazardous waste commn. 1983-91, mem. com. thermal and mineral waters 1994—, adv. to pres. 1995—), Internat. Water Resources Assn., Interstate Oil Compact Commn. (vice chmn. 1963, chmn. rsch. com.), Miss. Geol. Soc., Nat. Assn. Geology Tchrs., Nat. Rivers and Harbors Congress, Nat. Speleological Soc., Nat. Water Resources Assn., Nat. Water Well Assn., Soc. Econ. Geologists, Soc. Econ. Paleontologists and Mineralogists, Soil Conservation Soc. Am., Southeastern Geol. Soc., Ala. C. of C. (Pres.'s adv. com., Rep. of Energy 1980), Geol. Soc. Am. (chmn.); numerous others. Republican. Presbyterian. Avocations: photography, stamp collecting, coin collecting, gardening. Office: P E LaMoreaux & Assocs Inc 2610 University Blvd Tuscaloosa AL 35401-1508

LAMOREAUX, PHILLIP ADDISON, investment management company executive; b. Vallejo, Calif., May 8, 1941; s. Page Halleck and Marjorie Ruth (Nelson) L.; m. Sonia Ann Zeltin, Aug. 13, 1965 (div. 1988); children: Anne Elizabeth, Brian Brook. BA, Stanford U., 1963; MBA, Harvard U., 1967. Analyst Dean Witter & Co., San Francisco, 1963-65; portfolio mgr. Am. Express Investment Mgmt. Co., San Francisco, 1967-74; gen. ptnr. Lamoreaux, Glynn & Assocs., San Francisco, 1974-83, Lamoreaux Ptnrs., Sausalito, Calif., 1983—, Lamoreaux Ventures, San Francisco, 1983-90, New West Capital Ptnrs., San Francisco, 1990-93. Pres. Interfaith Housing Found., Mill Valley, Calif., 1970-76; bd. dirs. Marin Theatre Co., Mill Valley, 1985-91; bd. dirs., treas. Hospice Marin, San Rafael, Calif., 1978-84. Mem. Western Venture Capital Assn., Security Analysts San Francisco, Olympic Club, The Family (San Francisco), Mill Valley Tennis Club, Sausalito Yacht Club. Avocations: skiing, running, handball, tennis. Home: 1001 Bridgeway Ste 205 Sausalito CA 94965-2158 Office: 1505 Bridgeway Ste 125 Sausalito CA 94965-1967

LAMORIELLO, LOUIS ANTHONY, professional hockey team executive; b. Providence, Oct. 21, 1942; s. Nicholas Schiano and Rose (Ventura) L.; m. Patricia A. Renaldo, Aug. 9, 1970; children: Christopher, Heidi, Timothy. BA in Math. and Econs., Providence Coll., 1963. Hockey coach Providence Coll., 1968-82, athletic dir., 1982-87; pres., gen. mgr. N.J. Devils, East Rutherford, 1987—; commr. Hockey East Assn., Providence, 1984-87; mem. hockey com. U.S. Olympics 1984, 88; pres. Am. Hockey Coaches Assn., 1982-83. Named to Hall of Fame Providence Coll. Athletic Dept., 1982, I.T.L.U.-Am. Hall of Fame, 1986, R.I. Hall of Fame, 1987. Mem. Nat. Collegiate Athletic Assn. (profl. devel. com. 1984-87). Office: NJ Devils PO Box 504 East Rutherford NJ 07073-0504*

LAMOS, MARK, artistic director, administrator, actor; b. Melrose Park, Ill., Mar. 10, 1946; s. Gustav and Ruth (Oechslin) L. BS, Northwestern U., 1969; hon. doctorate, Conn. Coll., 1990, U. Hartford, 1990, Trinity Coll., 1993. Artistic dir. Ariz. Theatre Co., Tucson, 1978, Calif. Shakespearean Festival, Visalia, 1980-81, Hartford (Conn.) State Co., 1980—. Stage appearances include (stage debut) Lovers, Lake Forest, Ill., (Broadway debut) Pvt. Bowers in Love Suicide at Schofield Barracks, ANTA Theatre, 1971, Another Part of the Forest, Chgo., 1971-72, as Abel in The Creation of the World and Other Business, N.Y.C., 1972, as Christian de Neuvillette in Cyrano, N.Y.C., 1973, title role in Hamlet, San Diego, 1977, as Rex in City Sugar, N.Y.C., 1978, as Feste in Twelfth Night, Stratford, Conn., 1978, as Octavius in Man and Superman, N.Y.C., 1978, A Month in the Country, Princeton, N.J., 1978-79, title role in Anatol, Hartford, Conn., 1984, as Dr. Rank in A Doll House, Hartford Stage Co., 1986, as Jack Worthing in The Importance of Being Earnest, Hartford Stage Co., 1989, others; toured as Solomon Rothschild in The Rothschilds, 1972; theater dir. Dear Liar, Guthrie Theatre, 1976, la finta giardiniera, Glimmerglass, 1996, Washington Opera, 1996, Turn of the Screw, N.Y.C. Opera, 1996, (Ariz. Theatre Co.) The Threepenny Opera, 1978, The Seagull, 1979, Twelfth Night, 1979, (Calif. Shakespearean Festival) Romeo and Juliet, 1979, The Taming of the Shrew, 1979, Hamlet, 1980, A Midsummer Night's Dream, 1980, (Hartford Stage Co.) Mackerel, 1977, The Beaux Stratagem, 1980, Cymbeline, 1981, Undiscovered Country, 1981, Antony and Cleopatra, 1981, Kean, 1982, The Greeks, 1982, The Great Magoo, 1982, The Portage to San Cristobal of A.H., 1983, The Misanthrope, 1983, The Three Sisters, 1984, The Tempest, 1985, Twelfth Night, 1985, Distant Fires, 1986, The Gilded Age, 1986, Pericles, 1987, Morocco, 1987, Hamlet, 1987, Hedda Gabler, 1988, The School for Wives, 1988, A Midsummer Night's Dream, 1988, Peer Gynt, 1989, The Importance of Being Earnest, 1989, The Illusion, 1990, The Miser, 1990, Our Country's Good, 1990, The Master Builder, 1991, Julius Caesar, 1991, All's Well That Ends Well, 1991, Hidden Laughter, 1992, Tartuffe, 1992, Martin Guerre, 1993, Richard III, 1994, Arms and the Man, 1995 Dybbuk, 1995, Romeo and Juliet, 1995, The Rivals, 1996, Ghosts, 1996, la finta giardinera, Under Milk Wood, 1996; opera dir. Don Giovanni, St. Louis Opera, 1983, Arabella, Santa Fe Opera, 1983, The Aspern Papers, Dallas Opera, 1988, La Boheme, Glimmerglass Opera Theater, 1990, Il Re Pastore, Glimmerglass Opera Theater, 1991, 94, The Turn of the Screw, Glimmerglass Opera Theater, 1992, Cosi fan Tutte, Portland Opera, 1993, Werther, Glimmerglass Opera Theater, 1993, Merchant of Venice, Hartford Stage, 1993, I Lombardi, Met. Opera, 1994, The Turn of The Screw, Seattle Opera, 1994, False Admissions, Hartford Stage, 1994, A Scourge of Hyacinths (world premiere), Munich Biennale, Germany, Ariadne Auf Naxos, 1994, Paul Bunyan, Glimmerglass Opera, 1995 la Boheme, San Francisco Opera, 1996, la Finta Glimmerglass Opera, 1996, Turn of the Screw N.Y.C. Co., 1996; also dir. The Merchant of Venice, Stratford Festival, 1984, The Voyage of Edgar Allan Poe, Stora Teatern, Goteborg, Sweden, 1985, The School for Wives, La Jolla (Calif.) Playhouse, 1987, Desire Under the Elms, Pushkin Drama Theatre, Moscow, 1988, Measure for Measure, Lincoln Ctr., N.Y.C., 1989, Our Country's Good, Nederlander Theater, N.Y.C., 1991 (Tony nomination), The End of the Day, Playwrights Horizons, N.Y.C., 1992; TV appearance in School for Scandal, Great Performances, PBS, 1975; film appearance in Longtime Companion, Am. Playhouse Theatrical Films, 1989; author: (play) Some Other Time, 1970. Mem. Theater Comm. Group (trustee 1991—). Office: Hartford Stage Co 50 Church St Hartford CT 06103-1201

LAMOTTE, JANET ALLISON, management specialist; b. Norfolk, Va., Mar. 3, 1942; d. Charles Nelson Jr. and Geneva Elizabeth (Baird) Johnson; m. Larry LaMotte, Aug. 30, 1964 (div. Aug. 1979); children: Lisa Renee LaMotte Buchholz, Lori Louise. AA, Rose State Coll., 1982; BA, U. Ctrl. Okla., 1984; MA in Human Rels., U. Okla., 1986. Clk./typist U.S. Army, Washington, 1960, Fort Belvoir, Va., 1961, Dallas, 1961; clk./typist IRS, Dallas, 1962, Richmond, Va., 1962-63; clk./typist DLA, Alexandria, Va., 1978, IRS, Oklahoma City, 1978-79, Tinker AFB, 1979; sec. IRS, Richmond, 1963-64, Tinker AFB, 1981-82; pers. asst. State Bd. Control, Austin, Tex., 1964-65; procurement clk. FAA, Oklahoma City, 1965-66; acctg. clk. Tinker AFB, 1980-81, clk./stenographer, 1980-81, supply specialist, 1982-87, recoverable inventory mgmt. specialist, 1987—. Federally Employed Women scholar, 1984. Mem. NAFE, AAUW, Am. Bus. Women's Assn. (v.p. membership downtown reflections chpt. 1992-93), Air Force Assn. (v.p. pub. rels. Gerrity chpt. 1994, v.p. comm. 1995—, Medal of Merit 1995, exceptional svc. award 1996), Okla. Air Force Assn. (v.p. 1995-96, mem. of yr. award 1996, exec. sec. 1996—), Tinker (Okla.) Mgmt. Assn. (membership, ticket monitor 1994—, 1st place new mem. recruitment, scholar 1981, 82, 83, 84, 85), Toastmasters (area gov. 1991-92, area editor Toastmaster Area K-3 Newsletter 1992-93, pres. Tinker chpt. 1989, edn. v.p. 1988, editor Tinker Toastmasters Table Talk 1988-89). Avocations: swimming, walking, dancing, crafts, reading. Home: 9525 Ridgeview Dr Oklahoma City OK 73120

LA MOTTE, LOUIS COSSITT, JR., medical scientist, consultant; b. Clinton, S.C., Jan. 21, 1928; s. Louis Cossitt Sr. and Sarah (Hunter) La M.; m. Lila Jean Magruder, Dec. 31, 1948; children: Barbara Jones, Robert, Nancy Warren, Diane La Placa, Cynthia Love. AB, Duke U., 1948; MS in Pub. Health, U. N.C., 1951; ScD, Johns Hopkins U., 1958. Bacteriologist N.C. State Lab. Hygiene, Raleigh, 1948-51; virologist U.S. Army Chem. Corps, Ft. Detrick, Md., 1951-58; chief virus investigations unit Communicable Disease Ctr., Greeley, Colo., 1958-66, asst. chief disease ecology sect., 1965-66; chief cmty. studies br. Communicable Disease Ctr., Atlanta, 1966-69; dir. microbiology divsn. Ctr. for Disease Control, Atlanta, 1969-73, dir. tech. evaluation and assistance divsn., 1973-86; mem. dean's alumni coun. Sch. Hygiene and Pub. Health, Johns Hopkins U., Balt., 1995—; cons. Divsn. Pub. Health Ga., Atlanta, 1994; mem. recombinant adv. com. NIH, Bethesda, Md., 1970; mem. exec. com. Am. Com. on Arthropod-borne Viruses, Atlanta, 1964-66. Author: (with others) Federal Legislation & the Clinical Laboratory, 1981; contbr. articles to profl. jours. Trustee Ga. Fed. Mil. Retiree Coalition, Atlanta, 1990-93; coord. Neighborhood Watch Assn., Dunwoody, Ga., 1986—; advisor Sch. Pub. Health, Emory U., Atlanta, 1994—. Recipient Superior Svc. award USPHS, 1981. Republican. Presbyterian. Avocations: computer utilization, development of learning community in N.C. town. Home: 4820 Leeds Ct Dunwoody GA 30338

LAMOUREUX, CHARLES HARRINGTON, botanist, arboretum administrator; b. West Greenwich, R.I., Sept. 14, 1933; s. Emile and Cora May (Harrington) L.; m. Florence May Kettelle, Aug. 28, 1954; children: Mark Harrington, Anne Maile. BS in Botany, U. R.I., 1953; MS in Botany, U. Hawaii, 1955; PhD in Botany, U. Calif., Davis, 1961. From asst. to assoc. prof. botany U. Hawaii, Honolulu, 1959-71, prof., 1971—, chair dept. botany, 1962-65, 76-78, acting assoc. dean curriculum coll. arts and scis., 1976-77, 83, project coord. instrnl. assistance unit, 1977-79, assoc. dean acad. affairs coll. arts and scis., 1985-91; dir. Harold L. Lyon Arboretum, U. Hawaii, Honolulu, 1992—; rsch. assoc. botany Bernice P. Bishop Mus., Honolulu, 1963—; vis. asst. prof. botany U. B.C., Can., summer 1963; vis. colleague dept. botany Canterbury U., Christchurch, New Zealand, 1965-66; mem. sci. adv. com. Pacific Tropical Bot. Garden (name changed to Nat. Tropical Bot. Garden), 1967-94; dir. summer inst. sci. and math. tchrs. U.S. children Far East NSF, Chofu, Japan, 1968-71, reviewer, mem. various rev. panels; faculty mem. ctr. Pacific islands studies U. Hawaii, 1971—; guest sci. Nat. Biol. Inst. Indonesia, Bogor, 1972-73, 79-80; mem. adv. com. plants and animals quarantine br. Hawaii State Dept. Agr., 1973-79, 89—; study lectr./leader Smithsonian Assocs. Study Tours S.E. Asia, 1985, 86, 88-95, Melanesia, 1987; rschr. in field; bot. and ecol. cons. to various businesses and agys. including State Hawaii Dept. Bus. and Econ. Devel., UNESCO, UN Devel. Programme. Author: Trailside Plants of Hawaii's National Parks, 1976, (U.S. Nat. Pk. Svc. Dir.'s award 1977, Nat. Pks. Coop. Assn. Award of Excellence 1977-78), rev. edits., 1982, 96; bd. editors Pacific Sci., 1965—, editor-in-chief, 1985-86; mem. editorial com. Allertonia, 1977-90; manuscript reviewer for various jours. and presses; contbr. articles to profl. jours. Active Hawaii Audubon Soc., 1959—, past pres., 1st v.p., Hawaiian Bot. Gardens Found., 1959-67, 1st v.p.; life mem. Conservation Coun. Hawaii, 1959—, state bd. dirs., mem. com. flora conservation, Hawaiian Bot. Soc., 1959—, trustee endowment fund, past pres., v.p., sec., treas., newsletter editor; bd. dirs. Hawaii Mus. Assn., 1996—; bd. dirs. Friends Honolulu Bot. Garden, 1992—, trustee Nat. Ctr. for Plant Conservation, 1996—. Mem. Bot. Soc. Am., Am. Assn. Bot. Gardens and Arboreta, Hawaiian Acad. Sci. (councillor 1991-93, pres.-elect 1993, pres. 1994-95), Pacific Sci. Assn. (life, standing com. botany 1971—), Internat. Assn. Plant Taxonomists, Internat. Assn. Wood Anatomists. Avocations: photography, travel, opera. Home: 3426 Oahu Ave Honolulu HI 96822-1254 Office: Harold L Lyon Arboretum 3860 Manoa Rd Honolulu HI 96822-1180

LAMOUREUX, GLORIA KATHLEEN, nurse, air force officer; b. Billings, Mont., Nov. 2, 1947; d. Laurits Bungaard and Florence Esther (Nielsen) Nielsen; m. Kenneth Earl Lamoureux, Aug. 31, 1973 (div. Feb. 1979). BS, U. Wyo., 1970; MS, U. Md., 1984. Staff nurse, ob-gyn DePaul Hosp., Cheyenne, Wyo., 1970; enrolled USAF, 1970, advanced through grades to col.; staff nurse ob-gyn dept. 57th Tactical Hosp., Nellis AFB, Nev., 1970-71, USAF Hosp., Clark AB, Republic Philippines, 1971-73; charge nurse ob-gyn dept. USAF Regional Hosp., Sheppard AFB, Tex., 1973-75; staff nurse ob-gyn dept. USAF Regional Hosp., MacDill AFB, Fla., 1976-79; charge nurse ob-gyn dept. USAF Med. Ctr., Andrews AFB, Md., 1979-80, MCH coord., 1980-82; chief nurse USAF Clinic, Eielson AFB, Alaska, 1984-86, Air Force Systems Command Hosp., Edwards AFB, Calif., 1986-90; comdr. 7275th Air Base Group Clinic, Italy, 1990-92, 42d Med. Group, Loring AFB, Maine, 1992-94; 347th Med. Group, Moody AFB, Ga., 1994-96; chief nursing svcs. divsn. Hdqrs. Air Edn. and Tng. Command, Randolph AFB, Tex., 1996—. Mem. Assn. Women's Health, Obstetric, and Neonatal Nurses (sec.-treas. armed forces dist. 1986-88, vice-chmn. armed forces dist. 1989-91), Air Force Assn., Assn. Mil. Surgeons U.S., Bus. and Profl. Women's Assn. (pub. rels. chair Prince George's County chpt. 1981-82), Assn. Healthcare Execs., Sigma Theta Tau. Republican. Lutheran. Avocations: reading, needlework, piano, photography. Home: 13515 Thessaly Universal City TX 78148

LAMP, BENSON J., tractor company executive; b. Cardington, Ohio, Oct. 7, 1925; m. Martha Jane Motz, Aug. 21, 1948; children: Elaine, Marlene, Linda, David. BS in Agr. and B in Agrl. Engring., Ohio State U., 1949, MS in Agrl. Engring., 1952; PhD in Agrl. Engring., Mich. State U., 1960. Registered profl. engr., Ohio. Prof. agrl. engring. Ohio State U., Columbus, 1949-61, 87-91, prof. emeritus, 1991—; product mgr. Massey Ferguson Ltd., Toronto, Can., 1961-66; product planning mgr. Ford Tractor Ops. div. Ford Motor Co., Troy, Mich., 1966-71, mktg. mgr., 1971-76, bus. planning mgr.,

1978-87; v.p. mktg. and devel. Ford Aerospace div. Ford Motor Co., Dearborn, Mich., 1976-78. Author: Corn Harvesting, 1962. Served to 2d lt. USAF, 1943-45. Fellow Am. Soc. Agrl. Engrs. (pres. 1985-86, Gold medal 1993), Country Club at Muirfield Village (Dublin, Ohio). Avocations: golf, tennis, bridge. Office: BJM Company Inc 6128 Inverurie Dr E Dublin OH 43017-9472

LAMP, FREDERICK JOHN, museum curator; b. Malvern, Pa., Nov. 20, 1944; s. Clyde Herman and Grace Ebersole (Landis) L.; m. Diane Frank, May 18, 1974 (div. 1984). BS, Kent State U., 1967; MA, Ohio U., 1971; PhD, Yale U., 1982. Adminstr., lectr. Mus. African Art, Washington, 1973-77; curator Balt. Mus. Art, 1981—. Author Art of Baga, La Guinee, African Art of W Atlantic Coast. Contbr. articles to profl. jours. Nat. Mus. Act degree fellow, 1977-79; rsch. grantee Nat. Endowment Arts, 1976, 85, Social Sci. Rsch. Coun., 1979-81, 88, Smithsonian Instn., 1985, Fulbright, 1991-92, Nat. Gallery Art, 1995-96. Mem. Coll. Art Assn., African Studies Assn. (Arts Council). Democrat. Avocation: collecting African Art. Office: Balt Mus Art Art Museum Dr Baltimore MD 21218-3898

LAMP, JOHN ERNEST, lawyer; b. Spokane, Wash., Jan. 17, 1943; s. Raymond Holmes and Marie (Cunningham) L.; m. Louise Edwards, June 26, 1976; children—Amanda Catherine Marie, Victoria Louise. B.A., Wash. State U., 1965; J.D., Willamette U., 1968. Bar: Wash. 1968. Asst. atty. gen. State of Wash., Olympia, 1968-69, 71-76; sr. asst. atty. gen. chief Spokane and Eastern Wash. br. Wash. State Atty. Gen.'s Office, 1976-81; U.S. Atty. Eastern Dist. Wash. State, 1981-91; spl. atty. to U.S. Atty. Gen., 1990-92. Mem. Atty. Gen.'s adv. com. U.S. Attys., 1983-86; apptd. to White House Conf. for Drug Free Am., 1987; apptd. to bd. dirs. Drug Watch Internat., Internat. Drug Strategy Inst., 1993. Capt. U.S. Army, 1969-71, Vietnam. Decorated Bronze Star; recipient Alumni Achievement award Wash. State U., 1986; recipient Medal Commitment Greater Spokane Substance Abuse Coun., 1989, Community Svc., Community Rels. Svc. award U.S. Dept. Justice, 1991. Mem. Wash. Bar Assn. Home: 11205 S Hatch Rd Spokane WA 99224-8212 Office: Caine McLaughlin Wash Mut Fin Ctr 601 W Main Ave Ste 1015 Spokane WA 99201-0613

LAMPARELLO, PATRICK JOHN, surgeon, educator; b. Jersey City, Mar. 22, 1951; s. Patrick John and Julia Josephine (Castro) L.; m. Alexis Jane Rich, July 27, 1974; children: Patrick, Tracy, Emily, Ashley. BA magna cum laude, U. Pa., 1973; MD, Albert Einstein Coll. Medicine, 1976. Diplomate Am. Bd. Gen. and Vascular Surgery. From resident to chief resident Montefiore Med. Ctr., Bronx, 1976-80; fellow vascular surgery NYU Med. Ctr., N.Y.C., 1980-81, attending surgeon, 1981—, assoc. prof. surgery, 1991—; chief vascular surgery Manhattan VA Hosp., N.Y.C., 1985-88; dir. vascular surgery Bellevue Hosp. Ctr., N.Y.C., 1990—. Author: Current Therapy in Vascular Surgery, 1994; author book chpts. Coach Old Tappan (N.J.) Baseball Assn., 1984-93, Old Tappan Soccer League, 1986-90; team physician Northern Valley Jr. Football League, Bergen County, N.J., 1990-91. Fellow Am. Coll. Surgeons: mem. N.Y. Regional Vascular Soc. (coun. 1984—), Internat. Cardiovascular Soc., Ea. Vascular Soc., Perepheral Vascular Soc., N.Y. Cardiovascular Soc. (v.p. 1990—). Roman Catholic. Avocations: golf, tennis, skiing. Office: NYU Med Ctr 530 1st Ave # 6F New York NY 10016-6451

LAMPARTER, WILLIAM C., printing and publishing consultant, digital printing and information systems specialist; b. Bklyn., July 13, 1929; s. William C. and Nadine (Lesch) L.; m. Ann E. Martyn; children: Ellen, Susan, David. B.S., Springfield (Mass.) Coll., 1951; M.S., Boston U., 1952. V.p., gen. mgr. Mead Digital Systems, 1975-78; pres. Nat. Assn. Printers and Lithographers, Teaneck, N.J., 1978-82, PrintCom Cons. Group, 1982—; mem. adv. com. to Sch. of Printing Mgmt. and Scis., Rochester Inst. Tech., adv. to Graphic Arts Tech. and Edn. Ctr., bd. dirs. CIMSPrint, Inc.; internat. lectr. in field. Author: Forecast of Long-Term Business and Technological Trends in the Graphic Arts, 1968, transl. into Polish, Russian, 1973, The Electronic Superhighway Revolution 1994-1997-2000-2010, 1994, The Impact of the Information Superhighway on Traditional Print Media, 1995, Critical Trends Update - An Overview of Printing Industry Trends in the Year of the Digital Drupa, 1996, Management Guide to Digital Printing, 1996; prin. economist, author Printing Industry Quar. Bus. Indicator Report, 1979-85, Ann. Tech. Impact Rev., 1985, Interpretative Tech. Analysis, 1986, Printing Industry Materials Mgmt. Newsletter, 1985-86; pub., prin. editor FYI/HarbingerWatch, 1995. Served with U.S. Army. Recipient Tech. Leadership award Nat. Assn. Printers and Lithographers, 1995. Mem. Printing Industries Am. Inc., Nat. Assn. Printers and Lithographers, Tech. Assn. Graphic Arts, Rsch. and Engring. Coun. of Graphic Arts Industry Inc. (mem. exec. com.), Assn. for Graphic Arts Tng., World Future Soc., Am. Soc. Quality Control, Soderstrom Soc., Inst. of Printing (London), Nat. Printing Equip. Assn. (former bd. mem.), Sigma Delta Chi. Home and Office: 1020 Farm Creek Rd Waxhaw NC 28173-7793 *Commitment, developing people and combining their skills with the advantages of automation in a bottom-line oriented but innovative entrepreneurial atmosphere are the keys to success in today's changing business environment.*

LAMPE, FREDERICK WALTER, chemistry educator, consultant; b. Chgo., Jan. 5, 1927; s. Joseph Dell and Christine Wood (Phillips) L.; m. Eleanor Frances Coffin, Mar. 26, 1949; children: Joan Dell, Kathy Lee, Erik Steven, Beth Ann, Kristina Jean. BS, Mich. State Coll., 1950; AM, Columbia U., 1951, PhD, 1953. Research chemist Humble Oil and Refining Co., Baytown, Tex., 1953-56, sr. research chemist, 1956-59, specialist research, 1959-60; assoc. prof. Pa. State U., University Park, 1960-65, prof., 1965-92; prof. emeritus, 1992—; head dept. chemistry Pa. State U., University Park, 1983-88; Robert A. Welch Found. lectr., Tex., 1982, J.L. Franklin Meml. lectr., 1990; cons. Mobil Oil Corp., Pennington, N.J., 1961-69, Sci. Rsch. Instruments Corp., Balt., 1967-77, IBM Corp., Yorktown Heights, N.Y., 1980-85, Chemetron Corp., PPG Biomed., St. Louis, 1982-90, Polaroid Corp., Waltham, Mass., 1986-88, Marquette Electronics Corp., 1993—. bd. dirs. Vestec Corp., Houston. Author: (with H.R. Allcock) Contemporary Polymer Chemistry, 1981, 2d edit. 1990; patentee in field; contbr. 160 articles to profl. jours. Served with USN, 1944-46, ATO. NSF sr. postdoctoral fellow, 1966-67; recipient Sr. U.S. Scientist award Alexander von Humboldt Found., 1973-74, 84. Fellow Am. Physical Soc.; mem. Am. Chem. Soc., Am. Soc. for Mass Spectrometry (bd. dirs. 1981-83). Republican. Methodist. Home: 542 Ridge Ave State College PA 16803-3441 Office: Pa State U Dept of Chemistry 152 Davey Lab University Park PA 16802-6300

LAMPEN, RICHARD JAY, lawyer, investment banker; b. New Brunswick, N.J., Nov. 12, 1953; s. J. Oliver and Miriam (Walsh) L.; m. Susan Matson, June 8, 1975; children: Katharine, Caroline. BA, Johns Hopkins U., 1975; JD, Columbia U., 1978. Bar: Fla. 1978, U.S. Dist. Ct. (so. dist.) Fla. 1978. From assoc. to ptnr. Steel Hector & Davis, Miami, Fla., 1978-86, co-chmn. corp. dept., 1992-95; mng. dir. Salomon Bros. Inc., N.Y.C., 1986-92; exec. v.p., gen. counsel New Valley Corp., Miami, Fla., 1995—; bd. dirs. New Valley Corp., Roland Internat. Corp., Thinking Machines Corp., PC411 Inc. Mem. Fla. Bar Assn. (chmn. securities law com. 1985-86), City Club, Riviera Club. Office: New Valley Corp 100 SE 2nd St Fl 32 Miami FL 33131-2100

LAMPERT, ELEANOR VERNA, retired human resources specialist; b. Porterville, Calif., Mar. 23; d. Ernest Samuel and Violet Edna (Watkins) Wilson; student in bus., fin. Porterville Jr. Coll., 1977-78; grad. Anthony Real Estate Sch., 1971; student Laguna Sch. of Art, 1972, U. Calif.-Santa Cruz, 1981; m. Robert Mathew Lampert, Aug. 21, 1935; children—Sally Lu Winton, Lary Lampert, Carol R. John. Bookkeeper, Porterville (Calif.) Hosp., 1956-71; real estate sales staff Ray Realty, Porterville, 1973; sec. Employment Devel. Dept., State of Calif., Porterville, 1973-83, orientation and tng. specialist CETA employees, 1976-80. Author: Black Bloomers and Han-Ga-Ber, 1986. Sec., Employer Adv. Group, 1973-80, 81—; mem. U.S. Senatorial Bus. Adv. Bd., 1981-84; charter mem. Presdl. Republican Task Force, 1981—; mem. Rep. Nat. Congl. Com., 1982-88; pres. Sierra View Hosp. Vol. League, 1988-89 ; vol. Calif. Hosp. Assn., 1983-89, Calif. Spl. Olympics Spirit Team. Recipient Merit Cert., Gov. Pat Brown, State of Calif., 1968. Mem. Lindsay Olive Growers, Sunkist Orange Growers, Am. Kennel Club, Internat. Assn. Personnel in Employment Security, Calif. State Employees Assn. (emeritus Nat. Wildlife Fedn., NRA, Friends of Porterville Library, Heritage Found., DAR (Kaweah chpt. rec. sec. 1988—), Internat. Platform Assn. Dist. Fedn. Women's Clubs (recording sec. Calif. chpt. 1988—), Ky. Hist. Soc., Women's Club of Calif. (pres. Porterville chpt. 1988-89, dist. rec. sec. 1987-89), Mo. Rep. Women of Taney County, Internat. Sporting and Leisure Club, Ladies Aux. VFW (No. 5168 Forsyth, Mo.), Ozark Walkers League.

LAMPERT, MICHAEL ALLEN, lawyer; b. Phila., May 6, 1958; s. Arnold Leonard and Marilyn (Sternberg) L.; m. Angela Gallicchio, Dec. 6, 1987; 1 child, David Max. AB in Econs. cum laude, U. Miami, Coral Gables, Fla., 1979, postgrad., 1980; JD, Duke U., 1983; LLM in Taxation, NYU, 1984. Bar: Fla. 1983, D.C. 1984, Pa. 1984, U.S. Tax Ct. 1984, U.S. Ct. of Appeals for the Armed Forces 1995. Assoc. Cohen, Scherer, Cohn & Silverman, P.A., North Palm Beach, Fla., 1984-88; instr. div. continuing edn. Fla. Atlantic U., Boca Raton, 1988—; prin. Jacobson & Lampert, P.A., Boca Raton, 1988-91; pvt. practice West Palm Beach, 1991—. Mem. editl. bd. Southeastern Tax Alert, 1993—. Instr., trainer, chpt. vice-chair, emergency svcs. chair ARC, Palm Beach County, Fla.; bd. dirs. Jewish Fedn. Palm Beach County, 1989-91; bd. dirs. Jewish Family and Children's Svc. Palm Beach County, 1988—, treas., 1991-94, pres., 1997—; mem. nat. planned giving com. Weismann Inst., Israel. Recipient Safety award ARC, 1989, Cert. of Merit, Am. Radio Relay League, West Palm Beach Club, 1988, Cert. of Appreciation for Leadership, ARC Disaster Svcs., Palm Beach County, 1989, Disaster Svc. award, 1994, Human Resources award, 1993, Tax Law award Legal Aid Soc. of Palm Beach County and Palm Beach County Bar Assn., 1993. Mem. Palm Beach Tax Inst. (pres., bd. dirs.), Fla. Bar (exec. coun., tax sect.), Palm Beach County Bar Assn. (chair bus. and corp. continuing legal edn. com. 1989-90, chair legal assistance com. 1988-91, Tax Law award 1993), Legal Aid Soc. of Palm Beach County, Inc. Avocations: aquatics, amateur radio, running. Office: Ste 900 1655 Palm Beach Lakes Blvd West Palm Beach FL 33401-2211

LAMPERT, S. HENRY, dentist; b. Bklyn., Mar. 10, 1929; s. Joseph and Sadie (Bass) L.; m. Jacqueline Adler, Mar. 27, 1955; children: Karen Ann, Beth Robin, Judith Ellen. BA, U. Ill., 1950; DDS, NYU, 1954. Intern in dentistry Mt. Sinai Hosp., N.Y.C., 1954-55; gen. practice dentistry, Essex Junction, Vt., 1957-95, ret., 1995; dir. Temporo Mandibular Joint Program, Med. Ctr. Hosp. Vt., Burlington, 1970-76, attending staff 1957-92, peer rev. com., 1978-92; mem. staff Fanny Allen Hosp., Winooski, Vt., 1961-89 ; assoc. prof. Sch. Allied Health Scis., U. Vt., Burlington, 1963-73, clin. instr. Coll. Medicine, 1974-75, clin. instr. dept. oral surgery, 1986. Sec., Vt. Bd. Dental Examiners, 1973-76, pres., 1976-77; instr. photography Church St. Ctr. for Community Edn., U. Vt.; mem. NE Regional Bd. Dental Examiners, 1973-84, 96—; lectr. in field; CPR instr. Vt. Heart Assn. Capt. AUS, 1955-57. Fellow Internat. Coll. Dentists; mem. ADA (standard setting com. of coun. on nat. bd. exams. 1978-81), Champlain Valley (pres. 1961-62), Acad. Operative Dentistry, Am. Prosthodontic Soc., Am. Assn. Dental Examiners, 1973-84, Vt. State Dental Soc., Alpha Omega. Jewish (bd. govs. synagogue 1967-70, 72-73, chmn. bd. edn.). Lodge: Rotary, Masons. Contbr. articles to profl. jours.; photographs pub. numerous mags., jours. Home: 22 Forest Rd Essex Junction VT 05452-3819

LAMPERT, STEVEN A., lawyer; b. Chgo., Nov. 11, 1944. BS, U. Ill., 1966; JD cum laude, Northwestern U., 1969. Bar: Ill. 1969. Mem. Neal, Gerber & Eisenberg, Chgo. Mem. editorial bd. Northwestern U. Law Rev., 1968-69. Mem. ABA, Ill. State Bar Assn., Chgo. Bar Assn., Chgo. Estate Planning Coun. Office: Neal Gerber & Eisenberg 2 N La Salle St Ste 2200 Chicago IL 60602-3801

LAMPERT, WAYNE MORRIS, corporate financier; b. N.Y.C., Feb. 4, 1941; s. William B. and Fagel (Lefrak) L.; m. Sara Joyce Kirsch, Sept. 11, 1966 (div. 1978); children: Marcie Lynn, Warren Harris. BA, Syracuse U., 1962; LLD, Fordham U., 1965; MArch, U. Houston, 1992. Bar: N.Y. 1966, Fla. 1976, Tex. 1987, U.S. Customs Ct., U.S. Supreme Ct. Mgmt. intern Gen. Svcs. Adminstrn., Washington, 1965-66; atty. Legal Aid Soc., N.Y.C., 1966-67; asst. dist. atty. Kings County Dist. Atty.'s Office, Bklyn., 1967-69; pvt. practice Queens, N.Y., 1969-71, Miami, Fla., 1976-86; law sec. N.Y. State Ct. Claims, N.Y.C., 1971-73; chmn. bd. dirs. Texam Exploration Co., Inc., Houston, 1986-88; owner Vision Travel, Inc., Coral Gables, Fla., 1977—; tchr. law Charron Williams Coll., Miami, 1976-78. Bd. dirs. LeFrak Found., Queens, 1962-70, Youth Ednl. Coun., Ft. Lauderdale, Fla., 1965—; campaign mgr. Morris Kirsch for Bklyn. Borough Pres., 1973. Fellow Met. Mus. Art; mem. Lawrence Yacht Club (treas. 1972-73), Neptune Flamingo Yacht Club (chaplain 1977-78, commdr. St. Thomas U.S. power squadron 1994-96), Kappa Phi Kappa, Phi Alpha Delta, Tau Sigma Delta. Republican. Avocations: fishing, boating, gardening. Office: 2222 Ponce De Leon Blvd Coral Gables FL 33134

LAMPERTI, JOHN WILLIAMS, mathematician, educator; b. Montclair, N.J., Dec. 20, 1932; s. Frank A. and Louise (Williams) L.; m. Claudia Jane McKay, Aug. 17, 1957; children—Matthew, Steven, Aaron, Noelle. B.S., Haverford Coll., 1953; Ph.D., Calif. Inst. Tech., 1957. Instr., then asst. prof. math. Stanford, 1957-62; research asso. Rockefeller Inst., 1962-63; faculty Dartmouth, 1963—, prof. math., 1968—; Sci. exch. visitor to USSR, 1970; vis. prof. U. Aarhus, Denmark, 1972-73, Nicaraguan Nat. U., 1990; cons. Am. Friends Svc. Com., 1980, 85, 91. Author: Probability: A Survey of the Mathematical Theory, 1966, 2d edit., 1996, Stochastic Processes: A survey of the Mathematical Theory, 1977, What Are We Afraid Of? An Assessment of the "Communist Threat" in Central America, 1988. Fellow Inst. Math. Stats.; mem. ACLU, War Resisters League, Peace Action, Amnesty Internat., Fedn. Am. Scientists. Home: Upper Loveland Rd Norwich VT 05055 Office: Dartmouth Coll Dept Math Hanover NH 03755

LAMPINEN, JOHN A., newspaper editor; b. Waukegan, Ill., Nov. 26, 1951; s. Walter Valentine and Patricia Mae Irene (Pruess) L.; m. Belinda Walter, Oct. 20, 1973; children: Amanda Michelle, Heidi Elizabeth. BS in Comm., U. Ill., 1973. Staff writer Paddock Cir. Newspapers, Libertyville, Ill., 1973-75; regional editor The Jour., New Ulm, Minn., 1975-76; various positions Daily Herald, Arlington Heights, Ill., 1976-90; asst. v.p., mng. editor Daily Herald, Arlington Heights, 1990—; adj. prof. Medill Sch. Journalism, Northwestern U., Evanston, Ill., 1995—. Mem. APME, SPJ. Avocations: baseball, long-distance running, coaching girls softball. Office: Daily Herald 217 W Campbell St Arlington Heights IL 60005-1411

LAMPING, MARK, professional sports team executive; m. Cheryl Lamping; three children. BS in Acctg., Rockhurst Coll.; MBA, St. Louis U. Group dir. of sports mktg. Anheuser-Busch, 1981-94; pres. St. Louis Cardinals, 1994—; apptd. commr. Continental Basketball League, 1994. Office: St Louis Cardinals 250 Stadium Plaza Saint Louis MO 63102

LAMPL, PEGGY ANN, social services administrator; b. N.Y.C., Dec. 12, 1930; d. Joseph and Alice L. B.A., Bennington Coll., 1952. Dir. program devel. dept. mental health AMA, Chgo., 1962-66; spl. asst. NIMH, HEW, Washington, 1967-69; public relations dir. League Women Voters of U.S., Washington, 1969-73; exec. dir. League Women Voters of U.S., 1973-78; dep. asst. Sec. of State for congressional relations Dept. State, Washington, 1978-80; dep. dir. Iris Systems Devel., 1982-83; exec. dir. Children's Def. Fund, Washington, 1984-89, LWV, Washington, 1989—. Club: Federal City. Home: 2500 Q St NW Washington DC 20007-4373

LAMPORT, FELICIA (MRS. BENJAMIN KAPLAN), writer; b. N.Y.C., Jan. 4, 1916; d. Samuel C. and Miriam (Dworsky) L.; m. Benjamin Kaplan, Apr. 16, 1942; children: James, Nancy Mansbach. B.A., Vassar Coll., 1937. Reporter N.Y. Jour., N.Y.C., 1935-36; dialogue sub-title writer MGM, N.Y.C., 1937-49; instr. expository writing Harvard U., 1980-88; instr. creative writing Harvard U. Extension, 1988—. Freelance writer for various mags., newspapers including N.Y. Times, 1949—; columnist for Boston Globe, 1981—; author: Mink on Weekdays, 1950, Scrap Irony, 1961, Cultural Slag, 1966; Light Metres, 1982; Political Plumlines, 1984. Bd. dirs. MacDowell Colony, 1970-80, Am. Chess Found., 1965-80. Mem. PEN, Author's Guild, Nat. Writers Union. Home: 2 Bond St Cambridge MA 02138-2308

LAMPORT, LESLIE B., computer scientist; b. N.Y.C., Feb. 7, 1941; s. Benjamin and Hannah (Lasser) L.; m. Carol Dahl Crum, Oct. 31, 1968 (div. Feb. 1978); 1 child, Jason Christopher. BS, MIT, 1960; MA, Brandeis U., 1963, PhD, 1972. Mem. faculty Marlboro (Vt.) Coll., 1965-69; systems analyst Mass. Computer Assocs., Wakefield, 1970-77; sr. computer scientist SRI Internat., Menlo Park, Calif., 1977-85; sr. cons. engr. Digital Equipment Corp., Palo Alto, Calif., 1985—. Patentee in field. Mem. NAE. Office: Digital Equipment Corp Systems Rsch Ctr 130 Lytton Ave Palo Alto CA 94301-1044

LAMPSON, BUTLER WRIGHT, computer scientist; b. Washington, Dec. 23, 1943; s. Edward Tudor and Mary Caroline (Wright) L.; m. Lois Helen Alterman, Sept. 23, 1967; children—Michael Alterman, David Wright. A.B., Harvard U., 1964; Ph.D., U. Calif.-Berkeley, 1967; D.Sc. (hon.), Eidgenossiche Technische Hochschule, Zurich, 1986; D in Info. (hon.), U. Bologna, 1996. Asst. prof. U. Calif.-Berkeley, 1967-70, assoc. prof., 1970-71; dir. system devel. Berkeley Computer Corp., 1969-71; prin. scientist Xerox Research Ctr., Palo Alto, Calif., 1971-75, sr. research fellow, 1975-84; sr. cons. engr. Digital Equipment Corp., Palo Alto, 1984-86, corp. cons. engr., 1986-93, sr. corp. cons. engr., 1993-95; arch. Microsoft Corp., Cambridge, Mass., 1995—; adj. prof. elec. engring. and computer sci. MIT, 1987—. Contbr. articles to profl. jours. Patentee in field. Recipient IEEE Computer Pioneer award, 1996. Fellow AAAS, Assn. Computing Machinery (Software System award 1984, A.M. Turing award 1992); mem. NAE.

LAMPSON, NICK, congressman; b. Beaumont, Tex.; m. Susan Lampson; children: Hillary, Stephanie. BA, Lamar U., MA. Biology tchr. Beaumont Pub. Schs.; tax assessor-collector Jefferson County, Tex.; mem. 105th Congress from 9th Tex. dist., 1997—. Del. White Ho. Conf. Aging, 1995; dir. Area Agy. Aging; active Am. Heart Assn., Land Manor, Young Men's Bus. Assn.; chair Bishop's Faith Appeal St. Jude Cath. Ch., 1995. Named Outstanding Young Man of Beaumont Tex. Jaycees, 1978. Office: 417 Cannon HOB Washington DC 20515

LAMPTON, ROBERT DONALD, JR., chemical engineer, consultant; b. Newark, Ohio, Mar. 10, 1956; s. Robert Donald and Vera Nell (Smith) L.; m. Nancy Jane Cole, May 14, 1977; children: Robert Matthew, Amanda Kathryn, Michelle Erin. BS in Chem. Engring., Tex. A&M U., 1978; MBA in Mgmt., U. Houston, Clear Lake, Tex., 1984. Project leader Dow Chem. Co., Freeport, Tex., 1978-89; rsch. mgr. Internat. Paint Powder Coatings, Inc., Houston, 1989-93; cons. RDL Consulting, Friendswood, Tex., 1993—; cons. on epoxy coatings and coating processes USN, Port Hueneme, Calif., 1993—. Mem. ASTM (sec. com. epoxy coating task groups 1989—), Nat. Assn. Corrosion Engrs., Concrete Reinforcing Steel Inst. (sec. epoxy coating tech. com., sec. epoxy coating adv. com., sec. plant cert. com. 1989—), Beta Gamma Sigma (charter mem.). Achievements include patents for Dow Epoxy Resins for rebar coatings and pipe coatings, Dow Hardener for rebar coatings, others. Home and Office: 1402 Silverleaf Dr Friendswood TX 77546-4876

LAMSON, EVONNE VIOLA, therapist, health care administrator, consultant, pastor, Christian educator; b. Ithaca, Mich., July 8, 1946; d. Donald and Mildred (Perdew) Guild; m. James E. Lamson, Nov. 2, 1968; 1 child, Lillie D. Assoc. in Math., Washtenaw C.C., Ypsilanti, Mich., 1977; BS, Ea. Mich. U., 1989; MA in Pastoral Counseling Ashland (Ohio) Theol. Sem., 1993. Lic. profl. counselor, Mich. Data base mgr. ERIM, Ann Arbor, Mich., 1978-81; mgr. product svcs. Comshare, Ann Arbor, 1981-90, project leader, tng. course designer info. techs., 1991-93; founder, pres. G & L Consultants, Brighton, Mich., 1982—; tng. specialist Comshare, Ann Arbor, 1990-93; Assoc. Pastor, dir. Christian edn. Keystone Cmty. Ch., Saline, Mich., 1993-95; founder Living Waters Counseling, 1993—. Study leader Brighton Wesleyan Ch., 1981-93; lic. minister Weseleyan Ch. Am., 1993—; program dir. Wesleyan Womens Assn. of Brighton, 1983-91; clin. staff counselor Women's Resource Ctr., Howell, Mich., 1991-94; clin. counselor Livingston Counseling and Assessment, 1994—, clin. team leader, 1995-97, clin. supr., 1997—. Mem. AACD, NAFE, AACC, Am. Mgmt. Assn., Fairbanks Family of Am., Internat. Platform Assn. Avocations: skiing, motivational speaking, reading. Home: 6708 Calfhill Ct Brighton MI 48116-7419

LAMSON, GEORGE HERBERT, economics educator; b. Hartford, Conn., Feb. 21, 1940; s. Arroll Liscomb and Marguerite (Brechbuhler) L.; m. Susan Kathryn Lippert, Sept. 7, 1968; children: Scott, Brandon. A.B., Princeton U., 1963; M.A., Northwestern U., 1966, Ph.D., 1971. Research asst. Northwestern U. Econ. Survery of Liberia, Monrovia, 1962-63; instr. dept. econs. Loyola U., Chgo., 1967-68, U. Conn., Storrs, 1968-69; asst. prof. then assoc. prof. dept. econs. Carleton Coll., Northfield, Minn., 1969-80, Williams prof., 1981—, chmn. dept., 1978-84; cons. Minn. Higher Edn. Coordinating Com., St. Paul, 1971-72; textbook reviewer John Wiley & Sons, N.Y.C., 1979-82; reviewer NSF grad. fellowship program, 1988-90; vis. prof. U. Internat. Bus. and Econs., Beijing, China, 1994, 97; dir. Carleton Oversees seminar in econs. Cambridge, U.K., 1986, 91, 97. Intersocietal studies fellow Northwestern U., 1966-67; recipient Faculty Devel. awards 1979, 90-91. Mem. Am. Econ. Assn., Midwest Econ. Assn., Minn. Econ. Assn. (bd. dirs. 1981-83, pres. 1984). Republican. Home: 4485 Detelemark Rd Dundas MN 55019-4003 Office: Carleton Coll Dept Econs Northfield MN 55057

LAMSON, ROBERT WOODROW, retired school system administrator; b. L.A., Dec. 28, 1917; s. Ernest K. and Mabel (Mahoney) L.; m. Jeannette Juett, July 22, 1949; children: Robert Woodrow Jr., Nancy Virginia, Kathleen Patricia. BA, Occidental Coll., 1940; MA, U. So. Calif., 1955. Cert. tchr., prin., supt., Calif. Tchr. El Monte (Calif.) Sch. Dist., 1940-43; tchr. L.A. City Sch. Dist., 1945-49, prin., 1949-55, supr., 1955-57, adminstrv. asst., 1957-59, area supt., 1959-78; ret., 1978; agt. Keilholtz Realtors, La Canada, Calif.; instr. various colls. and univs. so. Calif.; a founder, v.p., bd. dirs. U.S. Acad. Decathlon, Cerritos, Calif., 1981-86. Bd. dirs. 10th Dist. PTA, L.A., 1965-70; chmn. Scout-O-Rama, Gt. Western coun. Boy Scouts Am., 1980. Lt. comdr. USNR, 1943-46, mem. Res. ret. Mem. Am. Assn. Sch. Adminstrs., Assn. Adminstrs. L.A., Alumni Occidental Coll. in Edn. (a founder, past pres., bd. dirs.), Town Hall, Nat. PTA (hon. life), Calif. PTA (hon. life, bd. dirs. 1978-80), 31st Dist. PTA (hon. life, bd. dirs. 1965-78, auditorium named in his honor 1978), Phi Beta Kappa, Alpha Tau Omega. Republican. Avocations: gardening, reading. Home: 4911 Vineta Ave La Canada Flintridge CA 91011-2624 Office: Richard Keilholtz Realtors 727 Foothill Blvd La Canada Flintridge CA 91011-3405

LAMY, MARTINE, dancer; b. Trois-Rivières, Que., Can.. Attended, Nat. Ballet Sch. Dancer Nat. Ballet Co., Can., 1983-90, prin. dancer, 1990—. Dance performances include Swan Lake, Giselle, The Sleeping Beauty, Don Quixote, La Fille Mal Gardée, The Taming of the Shrew, Coppelia, others; also appeared in work of contemporary choreographers including William Forsythe, James Kudelka, Glen Tetley, George Balanchine; appeared in fielm version of La Ronde, also documentaries Bold Steps, BBC and Making Ballet. Recipient medals Jr. Women's Divsn. Moscow Internat. Ballet Competition, 1981. Office: Nat Ballet Co Can, 470 Queens Quay W, Toronto, ON Canada M5V 3K4

LAN, DONALD PAUL, JR., lawyer; b. Orange, N.J., July 19, 1952; s. Donald Paul and Hannah Paula (Resnik) L.; m. Deborah Sue Rothenberg, Aug. 20, 1978; children: Jennifer Robyn, Adam Christopher, Eric Jacob. BS in Acctg., U. R.I., 1974; JD, Rutger U., 1977; LLM in Taxation, Georgetown U., 1982. Bar: N.J. 1977, D.C. 1978, Tex. 1983, U.S. Dist. Ct. N.J. 1977, U.S. Dist. Ct. (no. dist.) Tex. 1983, U.S. Ct. Claims 1978, U.S. Tax Ct. 1977, U.S. Ct. Appeals (fed. cir.) 1978, U.S. Ct. Appeals (5th cir.) 1984. Clk. to spl. trial judge U.S. Tax Ct., Washington, 1977-78; trial atty. tax div. U.S. Dept. Justice, Washington, 1978-82; assoc., ptnr. Shank, Irwin & Conant, Dallas, 1982-87; ptnr. Finley, Kumble Wagner et al, Dallas, 1987, Strasburger & Price, Dallas, 1988-96; shareholder Kroney Silverman, Mincey, Inc., Dallas, 1996—; adj. prof. law So. Meth. U., 1990—; lectr. on tax controversy and litigation, 1983—. Named Outstanding Atty. tax div. U.S. Dept. Justice, 1980. Mem. ABA (ct. procedures com. tax sect. 1987, stds. in tax practice com. tax sect. 1992), State Bar Tex. (chmn. ct. procedures com. tax sect.), Dallas Bar Assn., D.C. Bar Assn., Phi Kappa Phi, Beta Alpha Psi, Beta Gamma Sigma. Jewish. Avocation: all sports. Office: Kroney Silverman Mincey 12221 Merit Dr Dallas TX 75251-2216

LANAHAN, JOHN STEVENSON, management consultant; b. Pitts., June 13, 1922; s. James S. and Katharine L. (Lauck) L.; m. Rosemary Lourdes Ford, Feb. 20, 1954; children—Margaret Kayne, Brian James, Ellen Ford. BA, Duke U., 1945; MBA, Harvard U., 1949. Sales mgr. Mid-

Atlantic region Allen B. Dumont Labs., E. Paterson, N.J., 1950-53; sr. asso. Booz, Allen & Hamilton, Inc., N.Y.C., 1954-59; pres. Richmond Hotels, Inc., Va., 1959-69, Flagler System, Inc., Palm Beach, Fla., 1969-71, Carlton House Resort Inns, Inc., Richmond, 1971-73; exec. v.p. Braniff Internat. Hotels, Dallas, 1973-74; pres., chief exec. officer The Greenbrier, White Sulphur Springs, W.Va., 1974-80; sr. v.p.-comml. Chessie System, Inc., 1980-85; pres., mng. dir. Strategic Enterprises, Inc., 1986-89; dir. Figgie Internat. Inc., 1985-96. Mem. adv. bd. W.Va. Found. for Ind. Colls.; chmn. bd. Richmond Forward, 1968; mem. bd. visitors Trinity Coll. Duke U., 1988-94. Served to lt. (j.g.) USNR, World War II. Named to Hotel Industry Hall of Fame, 1971; Hotel Mgr. of Yr. Am. Hotel and Motel Assn., 1979. Mem. Va. Hotel and Motel Assn. (pres. 1965), Commonwealth Club of Richmond (bd. govs.), Rotary, Beta Theta Pi, Omicron Delta Kappa. Republican. Roman Catholic. Home: 36 E Lower Tuckahoe Rd Richmond VA 23233-6140

LANAM, LINDA LEE, lawyer; b. Ft. Lauderdale, Fla., Nov. 21, 1948; d. Carl Edward and Evelyn (Bolton) L. BS, Ind. U., 1970, JD, 1975. Bar: Ind. 1975, Pa. 1979, U.S. Dist. Ct. (no. and so. dists.) Ind. 1975, U.S. Supreme Ct. 1982, Va. 1990. Atty., asst. counsel Lincoln Nat. Life Ins. Co., Ft. Wayne, Ind., 1975-76, 76-78; atty., mng. atty. Ins. Co. of N.Am., Phila., 1978-79, 80-81; legis. liaison Pa. Ins. Dept., Harrisburg, 1981-82, dep. ins. commr., 1982-84; exec. dir., Washington rep. Blue Cross and Blue Shield Assn., Washington, 1984-86; v.p. and sr. counsel Union Fidelity Life Ins. Co., Am. Patriot Health Ins. Co., etc., Trevose, Pa., 1986-89; sr. v.p., gen. counsel, corp. sec. The Life Ins. Co. Va., Richmond, 1989—, also bd. dirs.; chmn. adv. com. health care legis. Nat. Assn. Ins. Commrs., 1985-87, chmn. long term care, 1986-87, mem. tech. resource com. on cost disclosure and genetic testing, 1993-97; mem. tech. adv. com. Health Ins. Assn. Am., 1986-89; mem. legis. com. Am. Coun. Life Ins., 1994-96, mem. market conduct com., 1997. Contbr. articles to profl. jours. Pres. Phila. Women's Network, 1980-81; chmn. city housing code bd. appeals Harrisburg, 1985-86. Mem. ABA, Richmond Bar Assn. Republican. Presbyterian. Office: The Life Ins Co Va GE Capital C 6610 W Broad St Richmond VA 23230-1702

LANCASTER, ALDEN, educational consultant; b. Balt., Feb. 25, 1956; d. Henry Carrington and Martha (Roe) L. BA magna cum laude, Duke U., 1977; MA, George Washington U., 1979. Program designer, coord. Duke U., Durham, N.C., 1977-79; mgr. profl. tng. programs Nat. Assn. Coll. and Univ. Bus. Officers, Washington, 1979-80; assoc. dir. refugee relief agy. Ch. of the Saviour, Bangkok, Thailand, 1980-81; dir. community svcs. U.S. Cath. Conf. Refugee Resettlement Agy., San Diego, 1981-82; nat. project dir. Bread for the World Ednl. Fund, Washington, 1982-83; edn. dir., exec. dir. Ptnrs. for Global Justice, Washington, 1983-85; dir. adult edn. programs, tchr. Spanish Ednl. Devel. Ctr., Washington, 1983-86; exec. dir., cons. Samaritan Ministry Greater Washington, 1985-87; career counselor, tng. cons. Rockport Inst., Washington, 1985—; dir. nat. literacy tng., ednl. cons. Assn. for Community Based Edn., Washington, 1987—; mgmt. cons. Women's Tech. Assistance Project, Ctr. Cmty. Change, Washington, 1988-89; ednl. cons. George Washington U., Washington, 1989-93; ednl. cons. Pub./Pvt. Ventures, Phila., Savannah, Ga., Ft. Lauderdale, Fla., 1990-91; ednl. cons., dir. nat. literacy projects Wider Opportunities for Women, Washington, 1991-94; ednl. cons. United Way of Am., 1992—; curriculum devel. cons. Eckerd Family Youth Alternatives, Clearwater, Fla., 1993—; evaluation and literacy staff devel. cons. Nat. Inst. Literacy, 1993—; staff devel. cons. Ramah Navajo Sch. Bd., Pine Hill, N.Mex., 1993—; adj. assoc. prof. George Washington U., 1993; cons. Utah Office Edn., 1994; contextual literacy cons. Friends of the Family, Inc., Balt., 1994, literacy staff devel. cons. State of Maine, 1994-96; contextual literacy cons. State Literacy Resource Ctr., S.C., 1995—; staff devel. cons. Centro de Estudios de Espanol Pop Wuj, Quetzaltenango, Guatemala, 1995; sr. adult literacy expert Atlantic Resources Corp., Reston, Va., 1995—; tng. cons. Neighborhoods, Inc., Battle Creek, Mich., 1995—; adult literacy advisor Inst. for Internat. Rsch., Roslyn, Va., 1996—; trainer of trainers D.C. Literacy Resource Ctr., 1996—; ednl. TV outreach cons., Mars Hill, 1996—; staff tng. and career devel. cons. McNeil Techs., 1997—. Co-author: National Institute for Literacy 1992-93 National Literacy Grants Final Report, 1995; author: An Introduction to Intergenerational Literacy, 1992; co-author: (with Thomas G. Sticht) Functional Context Education: A Primer for Program Providers, 1992; author white paper for two coms. of Congress, Nat. Inst. for Literacy, 1995; editor, primary author: Literacy for Empowerment: A Resource Handbook for Community Based Educators, 1989. Mem. nat. adv. bd. Project Lifelong Learning Pa. State U., 1992-93. Mem. Assn. Cmty. Based Edn. Democrat. Quaker. Home and Office: 6708 Poplar Ave Takoma Park MD 20912-4810

LANCASTER, B. JEANETTE, dean, nursing educator. BSN, U. Tenn.; MSN, Case Western Res. U.; PhD, U. Okla. Staff nurse U. Tenn.; nurse clinician Univ. Hosps. of Cleve.; assoc. prof. psychiat. nursing Tex. Christian U.; coord. cmty. health nursing U. Ala., Birmingham, chair master's degree program Sch. Nursing; dean, prof. Sch. Nursing Wright State U., Dayton, Ohio; now dean, prof. nursing U. Va., Charlottesville; assoc. dir. patient care svcs. U. Va. Health Scis. Ctr., Charlottesville; assoc. Va. Health Policy Rsch. Ctr.; chmn. bd. dirs. Statewide Area Health Edn. Ctr. Program; mem. study group for nurse practitioners Va. Gen. Assembly; presenter in field. Author 4 books, including Community Health Nursing: Processes and Practices for Promoting Health; editor Family and Cmty. Health; contbr. articles to profl. jours. Recipient Disting. Alumni award Frances Payne Bolton Sch. Nursing-Case Western Res. U., 1984, Outstanding Alumni award U. Tenn. Coll. Nursing, 1985. Fellow Am. Acad. Nursing; mem. Am. Assn. Colls. Nursing (bd. dirs.). Office: U Va Sch Nursing Charlottesville VA 22903

LANCASTER, CAROLYN HOHN, secondary school educator; b. Harrison/Allegheny County, Pa., July 24, 1952; d. Carl Maurice Sr. and Doris Myrtle (Gilday) Hohn; m. Walter T. Johnson, Sept. 4, 1971 (dec. Oct. 1979); 1 child, David Alan Johnson; m. Ronald Lee Lancaster, Mar. 31, 1988. AAS, Cape Fear Tech. Inst., Wilmington, N.C., 1986; BS, U. Ctrl. Fla., Orlando, 1981; MS, N.C. A&T State U., Greensboro, 1993. Cert. technology, electronics tchr., N.C. Computer technician Nat. Data Processing GE, Wilmington, 1986-88; electronics technician Applied Tech. Assn., New Bern, N.C., 1988-89; computer tchr. Onslow County Schs., Jacksonville, N.C., 1989-90; indsl. arts tchr. Person County Schs., Roxboro, N.C., 1992-93; technology tchr. Alamance County Schs., Graham, N.C., 1993—; technology advisor Technology Student Assn., Graham, N.C., 1993—; chairperson Raleigh Regional Program Area Leadership Coun. for Tech., 1996-97; vice chair Raleigh region Program Area Leadership Coun. for Tech., 1995-96. Mem. Jaycees, Orlando, 1980. With USCG Res., 1985-88. Recipient Tandy Tchr. Award cert. 1995-96; Profl. Devel. scholar N.C. Technology Educators Assn., 1993. Mem. NEA, N.C. Edn. Assn., Am. Vocat. Assn., Internat. Tech. Educators Assn., N.C. Tech. Educators Assn., Nat. Assn. Underwater Instrs. Methodist. Avocations: swimming, computers. Home: 114 Florence St Graham NC 27253-4002 Office: Graham HS 903 Trollinger Rd Graham NC 27253-1945

LANCASTER, CARROLL TOWNES, JR., business executive; b. Waco, Tex., Mar. 14, 1929; s. Carroll T. and Beatrice (Hollaman) L.; student U. Tex., 1948-51, 52-53; m. Catherine Virginia Frommel, May 29, 1954; children—Loren Thomas, Barbara, Beverly, John Tracy. Sales coordinator Union Tank div. Butler Mfg. Co., Houston, 1954-56, sales rep., New Orleans, 1956-57, br. mgr., 1957-60; asst. to exec. v.p. Maloney-Crawford Mfg. Co., Tulsa, 1960-62; mktg. cons., sr. asso. Market/Product Facts, Tulsa, 1962-63; market devel. asst. Norriseal Controls div. Dover Corp., Houston, 1963-66; area dir. Arthritis Found., Houston, 1966-69, dir. S.W. div., 1969-70; exec. dir. United Cerebral Palsy Tex. Gulf Coast, 1971-74; exec. dir. Leukemia Soc. Am., Gulf Coast, 1974-76, Lancaster & Assos., 1976—. Christian edn. tchr., 1966-70, supr., 1971, asst. youth football coach, Bellaire, 1967-68, 70-71; mem. Houston-Galveston Area Health Commn. Study Group, 1972-76, co-chmn., 1976; dir., essayist Tex. Low Vision Council, 1976-79, sec.-treas., 1978-81, pres., 1981-85; pres. Bellaire Civic Action Club, 1987-88; del. Houston Interfaith Sponsoring Com., 1979-81; bd. dirs. Council Chs. Greater Houston, 1966-68, v.p., 1968. Served with USNR, 1946-48, 51-52. Recipient award for securing free blood for indigent Harris County Hosp. Dist., 1968. Mem. Am. Mktg. Assn., Huguenot Soc., Military Order of Stars and Bars, San Marcos Acad. Ex-students Assn. (pres. 1982-84), SAR, Delta Sigma Phi. Episcopalian (vestryman 1975-78). Home: 4901 Holly St Bellaire TX 77401-5714 Office: PO Box 745 Bellaire TX 77402-0745

LANCASTER, CLAY, architecture/design educator, writer; b. Lexington, Ky., Mar. 30, 1917. Attended, Art Students League, N.Y., 1936; AB, U. Ky., 1938, MA, 1939; attended, Columbia U., 1944-50. Instr. in drawing Art Dept. U. Ky., 1938-39; staff theatre set design and constrn. Guignol Theatre, Lexington, Ky., 1939-43; asst. Avery Architecture Library Columbia U., 1944-45, ware librarian, 1946-49, lectr. dept. fine arts and archaeology, 1948-53; lectr. art dept. Vassar Coll., 1950-51; lectr. Cooper Union, 1951-53, Metropolitan Mus. Art/Columbia U., 1953; curator Prospect Park, Bklyn., 1966-67; lectr. Sch. Continuing Edn. NYU, 1968, 69; instr., lectr. Traphagen Sch., N.Y., 1956-58; adv. U.S. State Dept., 1951-53; vis. prof. Transylvania U., Lexington, 1979-81, U. Ky., 1979; Frederick Lindley Morgan prof. U. Louisville, Ky., 1983—; cons. Woodstock, Fayette COunty, Ky., Henry Clay Law Office, Sugar Hill, Woodford County, Big Spring Meeting House, Warwick, Mercer County, Liberty Hall, Franklin County, Ridgeway, Jefferson County, Peter Paul House, Fayette County, Mt. Hope, Robert Swain House, Nantucket, Mass., Eugene R. Black House, COlumbia Heights, N.Y., James W. Kennedy Residence, Mt. Eden, Cin., Ohio, Malverne, Va., Locust Grove, Stanardsville, Va. Author: (books) Back Streets and Pine Trees: The Work of John McMurtry, Nineteenth Century Architect-Builder of Kentucky, 1956, Architectural Follies in America, or Hammer Sawtooth and Nail, 1960, The Periwinkle Steamboat, 1961, Old Brooklyn Heights: New York's First Suburb, 1961, Ante Bellum Houses of the Bluegrass, 1961, The Japanese Influence in America, 1963, Nantucket in the Nineteenth Century, 1979, The American Bungalow, 1985, Antebellum Architecture of Kentucky, 1991, Holiday Island: Nantucket Hostelries and Summer Life, 1992; The Breadth and Depth of East and West: A Survey and an Assessment of Civilization Based on Universal Considerations, 1995; contbr. articles to numerous jours. Guggenheim fellow, 1953, 64; recipient Cert. of Merit Mcpl. Art Soc. N.Y., 1962, Spl. citation Pres. Borough of Bklyn. Heights, Hall of Disting Alumni award U. Ky., 1975, Merit award Ala. Hist. Commn., 1975, Preservation award Lexington-Fayette County Historic Commn., 1979, Profl. award Ky. Heritage Coun. Preservation, 1979, John Wesley Hunt award for Historic Preservation Blue Grass Trust, 1986. Home: Oregon Rd Salvisa KY 40372

LANCASTER, H(AROLD) MARTIN, former congressman, former advisor to the President; b. Patetown Community, N.C., Mar. 24, 1943; s. Harold Wright and Eva (Pate) L.; m. Alice Matheny; children: Ashley Elizabeth, Mary Martin. AB, U. N.C., 1965, JD, 1967. Asst. staff judge adv. 12th Naval Dist., San Francisco, 1968; staff judge adv. USN, USS Hancock, 1968-70; ptnr. Baddour, Lancaster, Parker, Hine & Keller P.A., Goldsboro, N.C., 1970-86; rep. N.C. Gen. Assembly, Raleigh, 1978-86; mem. 100th-103rd Congresses from 3d N.C. dist., Washington, D.C., 1987-94; mem. armed svcs. com., readiness subcom., mil. pers. subcom.; chmn. morale, welfare and recreation panel; small bus. com. Mcht. Marine and Fisheries com.; special advisor to the Pres. on chem. weapons, 1995; chmn. judiciary com. N.C. Ho. of Reps., 1983-86; chmn. hwy. safety com., 1981-83; chmn. congrl. study group on Germany, 1994, North Atlantic Assembly, 1989-94; former mem. numerous other coms. Chmn. N.C. Arts Coun., 1977-81, Goldsboro Wayne Bicentennial Commn., 1975-76; pres. Community Arts Coun., 1973-74, Wayne Community Concert Assn., 1972-73; chmn. bd. trustees Wayne County Pub. Libr., 1979-80; chmn. Wayne chpt. ARC, 1978-79; mem. adv. bd. Z. Smith Reynolds Found.; deacon First Presbyn. Ch., 1972-75, elder, 1980-86. Recipient Disting. Svc. award Goldsboro Jaycees, 1977, N.C. Crime and Justice award Gov.'s Crime Commn., 1984, Spl. award Gov.'s Adv. Coun. for Persons with Disabilities, 1985, Valand award Mental Health Assn. N.C., 1985, Outstanding Legislators awards Neuse River Coun. Govts., N.C. Assn. Sch. Counselors, Nat. Security Leadership award, 1987, 89, 90, 91, 92, Sound Dollar award, 1988, 89, 90, Spirit of Enterprise award U.S. C. of C., 1989, 92, 93, Doer of Deeds award House Leadership, 1989, Pub. Health Svc. award N.C. Primary Care Assn., 1991, Charles Dick Medal of Merit, U.S. Nat. Guard Assn., 1992, Tad Davis Meml. award, U.S. Mil. Sports Assn., 1992; named N.C. and U.S. Alumnus of Yr., 4-H, 1987. Mem. ABA, Assn. Trial Lawyers Am., N.C. Bar Assn. (bd. govs.), Eighth Jud. Dist. Bar Assn., N.C. Acad. Trial Lawyers (Outstanding Legislator award), Wayne County Hist. Soc. Lodges: Masons, Shriners, Elks. Office: 108 Army Pentagon Washington DC 20310-0108

LANCASTER, JOHN HOWARD, civil engineer; b. Bklyn., July 3, 1917; s. George York and Alice Eliot (Littlejohn) L.; m. Phyllis Elaine Metcalf, June 1, 1938; children: Judith Ann, Barbara Jean, Marylin Sharon, Kathryn Joy, Debra Elizabeth. BS, Worcester (Mass.) Poly. Inst., 1939. Registered profl. engr., N.Y., N.Mex.; lic. master mariner USCG. Engr. Austin Co., N.Y.C., 1939-40; engr. C.E., N.Y.C., 1940-42, asst. to divsn. engr., 1942-43; chief engring. and constrn. AEC, Upton, N.Y., 1946-54; chief project engr. Brookhaven Nat. Lab., Upton, 1954-72; asst. dir. Nat. Radio Astronomy Obs. and program mgr. very large array radiotelescope program, Socorro, N.Mex., 1972-81; propr. John H. Lancaster & Assos. (cons. engrs.), 1950-72; cons. NRAO/Associated Univs. Inc., 1981—; cons. in field, 1970—; bd. dirs., sec. corp. Seven Seas Cruising Assn.; cons. NSF, 1970, Cornell U., 1971, Fermi Nat. Accelerator Lab., 1980. Bd. dirs. Good Samaritan Nursing Home; treas. Socorro Pub. Libr. With USNR, 1942-46. Recipient Meritorious Service award NSF, 1976. Mem. NSPE, N.Y. Soc. Profl. Engrs., N.Mex. Soc. Profl. Engrs., N.Mex. Tech. Club, Rotary, Masons, Scottish Rite, Shriners, Ea. Star, Sigma Xi, Alpha Tau Omega.

LANCASTER, JOHN LYNCH, III, lawyer; b. Dallas, Nov. 10, 1936; s. John Lynch Jr. and Loretta Charlotte (Delaney) L.; m. Jane Frances Riddle, Sept. 5, 1959; children: Delaney, John, Jim. Student, Washington and Lee U., 1954-56; BA, U. Tex., 1958, LLB, 1960. Bar: Tex. 1960; diplomate Am. Bd. Trial Advs. Ptnr. Jackson & Walker, L.L.P., Dallas, 1962—. Mayor Town of Highland Park, Tex., 1984-86. Fellow Am. Coll. Trial Lawyers; mem. Inn of Ct. (master). Office: Jackson & Walker LLP 901 Main St Ste 6000 Dallas TX 75202-3748

LANCASTER, KELVIN JOHN, economics educator; b. Sydney, Australia, Dec. 10, 1924; s. John Kelvin and Margaret Louise (Gray) L.; m. Deborah Grunfeld, June 10, 1963; children—Clifton John, Gilead. BSc, Sydney U., 1948, BA, 1949, MA, 1953; BSc in Econs., London U., 1953, PhD, 1958. Asst. lectr., lectr. London Sch. Economics, 1954-59; reader economics U. London, 1959-62; prof. polit. economy Johns Hopkins U., 1962-66; prof. econs., 1966-78, John Bates Clark prof. econs., 1978—; John Bates Clark prof. econs. Columbia U., N.Y.C.; Ford faculty fellow, 1968-69, chmn. dept. econs., 1970-73, 89-90, Wesley Clair Mitchell research prof., 1973-74; vis. prof. U. Birmingham, Brown U., 1961-62, CUNY, 1965-66, NYU, Australian Nat. U., 1969-77, Ottawa U., 1972; fellow Inst. Advanced Studies Hebrew U., Jerusalem, 1976-77; dir. Nat. Bur. Econ. Rsch., 1971-73; trustee BT Investment Funds, 1986—. Author: Mathematical Economics, 1968, Introduction to Modern Microeconomics, 1969, Consumer Demand: A New Approach, 1971, Modern Economics: Principles and Policy, 1973, Variety, Equity and Efficiency, 1979, Modern Consumer Theory, 1991, Trade, Markets and Welfare, 1996; contbr. articles in econs. to profl. jours. Served with Royal Australian Air Force, 1943-45. Fellow Econometric Soc., Am. Acad. Arts and Scis., Am. Econ. Assn. (disting.); mem. N.Y. State Econ. Assn. (pres. 1974-75). Home: 35 Claremont Ave New York NY 10027-6823 also: 3 Overlook Ct Avon CT 06001-4526 Office: Columbia U Dept Econs New York NY 10027

LANCASTER, RALPH IVAN, JR., lawyer; b. Bangor, Maine, May 9, 1930; s. Ralph I. and Mary Brigid (Kelleher) L.; m. Mary Lou Pooler, Aug. 21, 1954; children: Mary Lancaster Miller, Anne, Elizabeth, Christopher, John, Martin. A.B., Coll. Holy Cross, 1952; LL.B., Harvard U., 1955; LLD (hon.), St. Joseph's Coll., 1991. Bar: Maine 1955, Mass. 1955. Law clk. U.S. Dist. Ct. Dist. Maine, 1957-59; ptnr. firm Pierce Atwood, Portland, Maine, 1961—; mng. ptnr. Pierce Atwood, 1993-96; condr. trial advocacy seminar Harvard U.; lectr. U. Maine; chmn. merit selection panel U.S. Magistrate for Dist. of Maine, 1982, '88; bd. visitors U. Maine Sch. Law, 1991—, chair 1991-93; spl. master by appointment U.S. Supreme Ct. in State of N.J. vs. State of Nev. et al, 1987-88; mem. 1st Ct. Adv. Com. on Rules, 1991—, legal adv. bd. Martindale Hubbell, 1990—. Mem. Diocese of Portland Bur. Edn. With U.S. Army, 1955-57. Mem. Maine Jud. Coun., Am Coll. Trial Lawyers (chmn. Maine 1974-79, bd. regents 1982-87, treas. 1985-87, pres. 1989-90), Maine Bar Assn. (pres. 1982), Cumberland County Bar Assn., Canadian Bar Assn. (hon.). Republican. Roman Catholic. Home: 162 Woodville Rd Falmouth ME 04105-1120 Office: 1 Monument Sq Portland ME 04101-4033

LANCASTER, ROBERT SAMUEL, lawyer, educator; b. Floyd, Va., July 9, 1909; s. Robert Tazwell and Rachel Elma (Barnard) L.; m. Ernestine Martha DeSporte, June 21, 1931; children: Ulysse (Mrs. Wallace Matthews), Evelyn Rachel (Mrs. David Tyrrell) (dec.); m. Elizabeth Craig, Jan. 4, 1980 (dec.). B.A., Hampden-Sydney Coll., 1929, D.Litt. (hon.), 1980; M.A., U. South, 1934, D.C.L., 1979; student, Andrew Jackson Law U., Nashville, 1937; Ph.D., U. Mich., 1952. Bar: Va. 1937. Instr. Gulf Coast Mil. Acad., Gulfport, Miss., 1929-31; instr. Sewanee (Tenn.) Mil. Acad., 1931-38, 46-49, comdt. cadets, 1941-43; pvt. practice Pulaski, Va., 1938-41; mem. faculty U. of South, 1949—, acting dir. devel., 1965-66, prof. polit. sci., 1953—, dean men, 1951-56; dean U. of South (Coll. Arts and Scis.), 1957-69; Fulbright lectr. Coll. Arts and Scis., Baghdad, Iraq, 1955-56, Coll. Arts and Scis. and Coll. of Law, Seoul (Korea) Nat. U., 1964-65. Author: The Better Parts of a Life: An Authobiograhy, 1990; co-author: An Introduction to American Government, 1954; contbr. articles to legal jours. Trustee Duck River Electric Membership Corp.; mem. acad. adv. bd. U.S. Naval Acad., 1970-75. Served to lt. (s.g.) USNR, 1943-46. Fellow Internat. Inst. Arts and Letters; mem. Va. Bar Assn., Tenn. Bar Assn., So. Polit. Sci. Assn., Phi Beta Kappa, Chi Phi, Phi Kappa Phi, Sigma Upsilon, Tau Kappa Alpha, Pi Gamma Mu, Pi Sigma Alpha, Blue Key. Republican. Episcopalian.

LANCASTER, RUTH VYSOKY, tax training manager; b. Cleve., May 28, 1937; d. John and Agnes Ann (Mehalko) Vysoky; m. William Dean Lancaster, Aug. 13, 1960; 1 child, Leslie Renée. BS in English, Carnegie Inst. Tech., 1959. Tchr. English Cleve. Bd. Edn., 1959-64; asst. editor Am. Ceramic Soc., Columbus, Ohio, 1973-77, Edutronics, Inc., Kansas City, Mo., 1978-80; programmed instrn. specialist H&R Block, Inc., Kansas City, Mo., 1980-82, tax rsch. and tng. specialist, 1982-92; mgr. tax tng. H&R Block Tax Svcs., Inc., Kansas City, Mo., 1992—. Avocations: gardening, handcrafts, music, sports. Office: H&R Block 4400 Main St Kansas City MO 64111-1812

LANCASTER, SALLY RHODUS, non-profit consultant; b. Gladewater, Tex., June 28, 1938; d. George Lee and Milly Maria (Meadows) Rhodus; m. Olin C. Lancaster Jr., Dec. 23, 1960; children: Olin C. III, George Charles, Julie Meadows. BA magna cum laude, So. Meth. U., 1960, MA, 1979; PhD, East Tex. State U. (now Tex. A&M at Commerce), 1983. Tchr. English, Tex. pub. schs., 1960-61, 78-79; sr. advisor Meadows Found., Inc., Dallas, 1979-96, also trustee and dir.; cons. to non-profit sector, 1996—. Trustee So. Meth. U., 1980-88, East Tex. State U., regent 1987-93; Tex. del. White House Conf. on Tourism, 1995; adv. dir. Los Caminos del Rio Inc.; dir. Inst. Nautical Archaeology; dir. emeritus Meadows Found.; mem. adv. bd. Communities Found. Tex. Disting. Alumni, So. Meth. U., East Tex. State U. Mem. Philos. Soc. Tex., Phi Beta Kappa. Office: 4802 Cole Ave Apt 1301 Dallas TX 75205-5511

LANCE, ALAN GEORGE, lawyer, legislator, attorney general; b. McComb, Ohio, Apr. 27, 1949; s. Cloyce Lowell and Clara Rose (Wilhelm) L.; m. Sheryl C. Holden, May 31, 1969; children: Lisa, Alan Jr., Luke. BA, S.D. State U., 1971; JD, U. Toledo, 1973. Bar: Ohio 1974, U.S. Dist. Ct. (no. dist.) Ohio 1974, U.S. Ct. Mil. Appeals 1974, Idaho 1978, U.S. Supreme Ct. 1996. Asst. pros. atty. Fulton County, Wauseon, Ohio, 1973-74; ptnr. Foley and Lance, Chartered, Meridian, Idaho, 1978-90; prin. Alan G. Lance, Meridian, Idaho, 1990-94; rep. Idaho Ho. of Reps., Boise, 1990-94, majority caucus chmn., 1992-94; atty. gen. State of Idaho, 1995—. Capt. AUS, 1974-78. Mem. ABA, Nat. Assn. Attys. Gen. (exec. com. conf. western attys. gen.), Ohio Bar Assn., Idaho Bar Assn., Idaho Trial Lawyers Assn., Meridian C. of C. (pres. 1983), Am. Legion (judge adv. 1981-90, state comdr. 1988-89, alt. nat. exec. com. 1992-94, nat. exec. com. 1994-96, chmn. nat. fgn. rels. commn. 1996—, ex-officio mem. N.H. POW/MIA com. 1996—), Elks. Republican. Avocation: fishing. Home: 1370 Eggers Pl Meridian ID 83642-6528 Office: PO Box 83720 Statehouse Rm 210 Boise ID 83720-0010

LANCE, GEORGE MILWARD, mechanical engineering educator; b. Youngstown, Ohio, Dec. 4, 1928; s. Ray Clifford and Louisa Brigetta (Emch) L.; m. Phyllis Joanne Sprague, Aug. 8, 1964; children: Kathryn, Deborah, John, Rebecca, George. B.S. in Mech. Engring, Case Inst. Tech., 1952, M.S. in Instrumentation Engring, 1954. Instr. Case Inst. Tech., Cleve., 1952-54; research engr. TRW Inc., Cleve., 1954-56; lectr. Washington U., St. Louis, 1956-60; sr. systems engr. Moog, Inc., 1960-61; asst. prof., then prof. mech. engring. U. Iowa, Iowa City, 1961-91; prof. emeritus U. Iowa, 1991—; acting chair mech. engring. U. Iowa, Iowa City, 1972-74; asso. dean engring. U. Iowa, 1974-79; cons. McDonnell Aircraft, Boeing Airplane Co., Collins Radio Co., U.S. Army Weapons Command, CADSI. Served with USN, 1946-48. Mem. ASME, Am. Soc. Engring. Edn., Sigma Xi, Tau Beta Pi, Pi Tau Sigma. Patentee in valves. Home: 609 S Summit St Iowa City IA 52240-5657 Office: Univ Iowa Coll Engring Iowa City IA 52242

LANCE, LEONARD, assemblyman; b. Easton, Pa., June 25, 1952; s. Wesley L. and Anne (Anderson) L.; m. Heidi A. Rohrbach. BA, Lehigh U., 1974; JD, Vanderbilt U., 1977; MPA, Princeton U., 1982. Law clk. to judges Warren County Ct., Belvidere, N.J., 1977-78; asst. counsel Office of N.J. Gov. Thomas H. Kean, Trenton, N.J., 1983-90; mem. N.J. Gen. Assembly, 1991—. Mem. Grandin Libr. Bd., Clinton, N.J., 1990—, N.J. Coun. for the Humanities, Trenton, 1994—; bd. trustees Newark Mus., 1995—. Mem. Princeton Club N.Y., Phi Beta Kappa. Republican. Home: PO Box 5240 Clinton NJ 08809-0240 Office: NJ Gen Assembly 119 Main St Flemington NJ 08822-1615

LANCHNER, BERTRAND MARTIN, lawyer, advertising executive; b. Boston, Oct. 3, 1929; s. Abraham Joseph and Mina (Grossman) L.; m. Nancy Nelson, Apr. 26, 1979; 1 son by previous marriage, David; 1 stepdau., Renate. B.A., Stanford U., 1951; postgrad., Columbia U. Grad. Sch. Bus., 1951-52, U. Vienna, Austria, summer 1955; J.D., Harvard U., 1955. Bar: N.Y. bar 1956. Asso. firm Sage, Gray, Todd & Sims, N.Y.C., 1955-57; atty. Warner Bros. Pictures, N.Y.C., 1957-59; asst. gen. counsel Dancer-Fitzgerald-Sample, N.Y.C., 1959-62; gen. counsel Lawrence C. Gumbinner Advt. Agy., N.Y.C., 1962-63; dir. bus. affairs and sports contract negotiations CBS-TV, N.Y.C., 1963-69; gen. counsel, exec. v.p. Videorecord Corp. Am., Westport, Conn., 1969-73; sr. v.p., sec., gen. counsel N.W. Ayer, Inc., N.Y.C., 1973—, also bd. dirs.; bd. dirs. 170 E. 79th St. Corp., Advt. Info. Services Inc., N.Y.C.; guest lectr. Yale U. Law Sch. Mem. adv. bd.: Communications and the Law. Mem. ABA, N.Y. State Bar Assn., Assn. of Bar of City of N.Y. (chmn. subcom. advt. agy. 1981-83), Copyright Soc. U.S., Am. Assn. Advt. Agys. (chmn. legal com. 1986-89, 95—), Am. Corp. Counsel Assn. (chair advt. com. 1996—), Am. Advt. Fedn. (mem. legal com.), Harvard Club N.Y.C., Bridgehampton Tennis and Surf Club, East Hampton Tennis Club, Tennisport Club. Office: N W Ayer Inc Worldwide Plz 825 8th Ave New York NY 10019-7416

LANCIONE, BERNARD GABE, lawyer; b. Bellaire, Ohio, Feb. 3, 1939; s. Americus Gabe and June (Morford) L.; m. Rosemary C., Nov. 27, 1976; children: Amy, Caitin, Gillian, Bernard Gabe II, Elizabetta Marie. BS, Ohio U., 1960; JD, Capitol U., 1965. Bar: Ohio 1965, U.S. Dist. Ct. (so. dist.) Ohio 1967, U.S. Supreme Ct., 1969, U.S. Ct. Appeals (4th cir.) 1982, U.S. Dist. Ct. (no. dist.) Ohio, 1989. Pres. Lancione Law Office, Co. L.P.A., Bellaire, Ohio, 1965-87, mng. atty. Cichon Lancione Co., L.P.A., St. Clairsville, Ohio, 1982-85, of counsel Ward, Kaps, Bainbridge, Maurer, Bloomfield and Melvin, Columbus, Ohio, 1987-88; Ohio Asst. Atty. Gen., Columbus, 1988-91; sole practice, 1991—; spl. counsel Ohio Atty. Gen's. Office, 1991-95; solicitor Bellaire City (Ohio), 1968-72; asst. prosecutor County of Belmont (Ohio), 1972-76; legal counsel Young Democrats Am., 1971-73; pack com. chmn. Pack 961, Westerville, Ohio Cub Scouts of Am., 1992-93. Mem. ABA, Ohio State Bar Assn., Assn. Trial Lawyers Am., Ohio Acad. Trial Lawyers (award of merit 1972). Democrat. Roman Catholic. Home: 1108 Acillom Dr Westerville OH 43081-1104 Office: 647 Park Meadow Rd # E Westerville OH 43081-2878

LANCLOS, RITCHIE PAUL, petroleum engineer; b. Opelousas, La., Sept. 20, 1964; s. Curley Joseph and Velma Marie (Folks) L.; m. Courtney Thereśe Brennan, Mar. 26, 1994. BS in Petroleum Engring., U. Southwestern La., 1987; MS in Petroleum Engring. cum laude, Tex. A&M U., 1990. Registered profl. engr., La. Petroleum engr. exploration and prodn. Mobil Oil Corp., New Orleans, 1987-89, Conoco, Inc., New Orleans, 1990-93; petroleum engr. property acquisitions WRT Energy Corp., The Woodlands, Tex., 1994; petroleum engr. reservoir engring. Petrobras Am., Inc., Houston, 1995—; petroleum cons. The Scotia Group, Inc., Houston, 1994—. Bd. dirs. Big Bros./Big Sisters, New Orleans, 1991-94, Boys/Girls Club, Lafayette, La., 1992-94, Vol. Instrs. Teaching Adults (VITA), Lafayette, 1991-94; loaned exec. United Way, New Orleans, 1993-94. Scholar Am. Petroleum Inst., Lafayette, 1985-86, scholar Texaco Rsch. Ctr., Texaco Inc., College Station, Tex., 1989-90; fellow Petroleum Engring., 1989-90. Mem. Soc. Petroleum Engrs., Tex. A&M U. Petroleum Engring. Alumni (v.p. 1994-95, thesis adv. com.). Republican. Roman Catholic. Achievements include developments in the field of reservoir fluid characterization. Avocations: traveling, golfing, reading. Home: 37 Fallshire Dr The Woodlands TX 77381

LAND, CECIL E., electrical engineer; b. Lebanon, Mo., Jan. 8, 1926; married; 2 chilren. BS, Okla. State U., 1949; DSc (hon.), Okla. Christian Coll., 1978. Profl. engr., electronics divsn. Westinghouse Elec. Corp., Md., 1949-56; staff mem. Sandia Nat. Labs., Albuquerque, 1956-83, disting. mem. tech. staff, 1983—. Recipient award NSPE, 1973, Frances Rice Darne Meml. award Soc. Info. Display, 1976. Fellow IEEE (chmn. ferroelectrics com. 1978-90), Am. Ceratmics Soc.; mem. Optical Soc. Am. Office: 2118 Gretta St NE Albuquerque NM 87112-3238

LAND, GEOFFREY ALLISON, science administrator; b. Jeannette, Pa., July 9, 1942; s. Albert E. Jr. and Helene (Matthews) L.; m. Maxine McCluskey, Jan. 22, 1966; children: Kevin Jeffrey, Melissa Allison, Kyle Robert. MS in Biology (Biochemistry), Tex. Christian U., 1970; PhD in Microbiology/Immunology, Tulane U., 1973. Cert. clin. lab. dir. Am. Bd. Bioanalysis. Dir. mycology Wadley Institutes Molecular Medicine, Dallas, 1974-78; dir. mycology, assc. dir. microbiology U. Cin. Med. Ctr., 1978-81; dir. microbiology/immunology Meth. Med. Ctr., Dallas, 1981—, assoc. adminstrv. dir. pathology, 1990—; dir. histocompatibility Stewart Blood Ctr., Tyler, Tex., 1987—; sci. dir. pathology and labs. Meth. Med. Ctr., Dallas, 1993—; adj. full prof. biology Tex. Christian U., Ft. Worth, 1982—. Mem. rev. bd. Jour. Clin. Microbiology, 1980—, Am. Jour. Tropical Medicne and Hygiene, 1989—; author: Pictorial Handbook of Medically Important Fungi, 1982, (with others) The Dermatophytes, 1996, Handbook of Applied Mycoses, 1991, Manual of Clinical Microbiology, 1992, Clinical Microbiology Procedures Manual, 1994. Coach Denton (Tex.) Soccer Assn., 1981—; min. Tioga (Tex.) Ch. of Christ, 1985—; chmn.-elect Region 4 histocompatibility com. United Network for Organ Sharing, 1993. Recipient Svc. Above Self award Rotary Club. Mem. Mycol. Soc. Am. (pres. 1990-93, Billy H. Cooper-Meridian award 1992), Tex. Soc. Clin. Microbiology (pres. 1977-79, 81-83), N.Y. Acad. Sci., Am. Soc. Histocompatibility and Immunogenetics (commr. region 2 1995—, author procedure manual 1996—), Am. Soc. Microbiology. Mem. Ch. of Christ. Office: Meth Med Ctr 1441 N Beckley Ave Dallas TX 75203-1201

LAND, GEORGE A., philosopher, writer, educator, consultant; b. Hot Springs, Ark., Feb. 27, 1933; s. George Thomas Lock and Mary Elizabeth Land; m. Jo A. Gunn, 1957 (dec. 1969); children—Robert E., Thomas G., Patrick A.; m. Beth Smith Jarman, 1987. Student, Millsaps Coll., 1952-54, U. Veracruz, Mexico, 1957-59; numerous hon. degrees U.S. and abroad. Program dir. Woodall TV Stas. of Ga., Columbus, 1951-52; ops. mgr. Lamar Broadcasting, Jackson, Miss., 1952-54; anthrop. research Cora, Huichole and Yaqui tribes, Latin Am. Mexico, 1955-60; dir. gen. Television del Norte (NBC), Mexico, 1960-62; v.p. Roman Corp., St. Louis, 1962-64; chmn. Transolve Inc., Cambridge, Mass., and St. Petersburg, Fla., 1964-68; chief exec., chmn. Innotek Corp., N.Y.C.; also pres. Hal Roach Studios, Los Angeles and N.Y.C., 1969-71; chmn. emeritus Turtle Bay Inst., N.Y.C., 1971-80; vice chmn. Wilson Learning Corp., Mpls., 1980-86; pres. Leadership 2000, Phoenix, 1986—, Inst. Transformational Research, Honolulu and Buffalo, 1980—; prof. Mankato State U., 1973-74; sr. fellow U. Minn., 1982—; cons.-in-residence Synplex Inc., N.Y.C., AT&T, Forest Hosp., Des Plaines, Social Systems Inc., Chapel Hill, N.C., Children's Hosp., Nat. Med. Ctr., Washington, Herman Miller, Inc., Arthur Anderson & Co., Intermedics Orthopedics; Mem. Nat. Action Com. on Drug Edn., 1974-75; co-chmn. Syncon Conf., So. Ill. U., 1972-74; keynoter Emerging Trends in Edn. Conf., Minn., 1974, 75, Bicentennial Conf. on Limits to Growth, So. Ill. U., 1976, No. States Power Conf., 1975, U.S. Office of Edn., Nat. Conf. Improvements in Edn., 1979, World Conf. on Gifted, 1977, S.W. Conf. on Arts, 1977, World Symposium on Humanity, 1979, Internat. Conf. Internal Auditors, 1977, Four Corners Conf. on Arts, 1977, Chautaugua Inst., 1977, 78, Conf. Am. Art Tchrs. Assn., 1979, Internat. Conf. on Gifted, 1982, Japan Mgmt. Assn., Nat. Conf. of Art Curators, Chgo, 1985, others; keynoter, Nat. Conf. on Econ. Devel., Mex., 1988, Credit Union Roundtable, Tampa, Fla., 1988, Internat. Bihai Conf., Princeton, N.J., 1982, co-chmn. com. on society World Conf. Peace and Poverty, St. Joseph's U., Phila., 1968, Internat. Bahai Conf. Princeton U., 1987, Gov.'s Trade Corridor Conf., Phoenix, 1994, Cath. Hosp. Assn., Phila., 1994, Am. Assn. Adminstrs., 1994, Inst. Pub. Execs., 1994, Fed. Conf. Quality, Washington, 1994, MAC IS Nat. Conf., Ont., 1994, Innovative Thinking Conf., 1994, Ventaua Groupware Conf., 1994, Young Pres.' Orgn., Cannes, 1993, Assn. Convn. and Visitors Bureau, Phenix, 1993, Profession Conv. Mgmt. Assn., Atlanta, Internat. Assn. Law Enforcement, 1995, Cath. Health Assn., 1995, Excellence in Govt. Fellows, 1996, and many others; mem. Nat. Security Seminar, U.S. Dept. Def., 1975; cons., keynoter corp. policy strategic seminars The Bell System, AT&T, 1978—; mem. faculty Edison Electric Grad. Mgmt. Inst., 1972-78; lectr., seminarian in transformation theory, strategic planning and interdisciplinary research Menninger Found., U. Ga., Emory U., Waterloo (Can.) U., Office of Sec. HEW, Jamestown (N.Y.) Coll., Hofstra U., U.S. Office Edn., Calif. Dept. Edn., St. Louis U., Coll. William and Mary, Webster Coll., St. Louis, Wash. State Dept. Edn., U. Ky., So. Ill. U., St. John's U., Harvard U., U. South Fla., MIT, U. Veracruz, Children's Hosp. D.C., Gov.'s Sch. N.C., Scottsdale (Ariz.) Ctr. Arts, Humbolt U., East Berlin, AAAS, others; advanced faculty Creative Problem Solving Inst., SUNY, 1965—, S. Conn. Coll.; disting. lectr. Northwestern State U., La., State U. Coll. N.Y., Coll. of the Lakes, Ill.; cons. govt., industry and instns. in U.S. and abroad, including AT&T, IBM, Dow Chem., Dow Corning, DuPont, Hughes, TRW, 3M, OAS, Fed. Quality Inst., U.S. Dept. Commerce, Office Patent & Trademarks, U.S. Gen. Svc. Adminstrn., Gen. Mills, Gen. Motors, Moore Corp., Branch Corp., Credit Union Nat. Assn., others. Author: Innovation Systems, 1967, Innovation Technology, 1968, Four Faces of Poverty, 1968, (as George T.L. Land) Grow or Die: The Unifying Principle of Transformation, 1973, Creative Alternatives and Decision Making, 1974, The Opportunity Book, 1980, (with Vaune E. Ainsworth), Breakpoint and Beyond, 1994, New Paradigm in Business, 1994, Community Building in Business, 1995, Forward to Basics; contbr. to profl. jours. and gen. mags. Fellow N.Y. Acad. Scis., World Bus. Acad.; mem. AAAS, Soc. Gen. Systems Rsch., Soc. Study Gen. Process (founding dir.), Am. Soc. Cybernetics (past v.p.), Creative Edn. Found. (trustee, Lifetime Achievement award 1993, New Paradigm in Bus. award 1994, colleague), Soc. Am. Value Engrs. (past dir.), World Future Soc., Com. for Future (colleague), Authors Guild, Authors League Am. Achievements include research on interdisciplinary unification, orginated transformation theory. Inventor computer-assisted group creative thinking processes, "The Innovator," "CoNexus," "TeamWare" and others. Home: 7470 E San Miguel Ave Scottsdale AZ 85250 Office: Leadership 2000 3333 N 44th St Phoenix AZ 85018-6461 *I was fortunate enough in my youth to experience and learn what has been the most important idea and principle in my life, the natural law of enrichment through diversity. This concept means that change and growth come about more by combining differentnesses than by adding likenesses. As in the biological world, where such behavior produces the vitality of hybrids, and as in chemistry, where the co-valent bonds of carbon make life possible, in human life we can also benefit immeasurably from using our differences as a creative way to grow anew. Thus, we can evolve beyond polarizations such as nationalism, racism, sexism, institutionalism and other obstacles that separate us and stunt our ability to realize the full community of Man.*

LAND, KENNETH CARL, sociology educator, demographer, statistician, consultant; b. Llano, Tex., Aug. 19, 1942; s. Otto Carl and Tillie (Lindemann) L.; m. Jacqueline Yvette Apere, Mar. 22, 1969; 1 child, Kristoffer Carl. B.A., Tex. Luth. Coll., 1964; M.A., U. Tex., 1966, Ph.D., 1969. Staff assoc. Russell Sage Found., N.Y.C., 1969-73; lectr. Columbia U., N.Y.C., 1970-73; assoc. prof. U. Ill.-Urbana, 1973-76, prof., 1976-81; prof. sociology U. Tex.-Austin, 1981-86; prof., chmn. dept. sociology Duke U., Durham, N.C., 1986-97, John Franklin Crowell prof. sociology, 1990—. Editor: Social Indicator Models, 1975; Social Accounting Systems, 1981; Multidimensional Mathematical Demography, 1982; Forecasting in the Social and Natural Sciences, 1987; contbr. articles to profl. jours. Fellow Am. Statis. Assn., Am. Assn. for the Advancement of Sci.; mem. Sociol. Research Assn., Am. Sociol. Assn., Population Assn. Am., Am. Soc. Criminology. Lutheran. Office: Duke U Dept Sociology Durham NC 27708-0088

LAND, REBEKAH RUTH, marriage and family therapist; b. Columbus, Ga., Feb. 5, 1946; d. Roland Irving and Thelma Rebekah (Gibbins) Van Hooser; m. Richard Dale Land, Sr., May 29, 1971; children: Jennifer Rebekah, Richard Dale Jr., Rachel Elisabeth. AB, Samford U., 1967; M in Religious Edn., New Orleans Bapt. Theol. Sem., 1970; MSW, Tulane U., 1971; PhD, Tex. Woman's U., 1988. Lic. profl. counselor; lic. marital and family therapist; lic. clin. social worker; diplomate Am. Bd. Sexology. Sch. social worker Chattanooga Pub. Schs., 1967-68; edn. and youth dir. Trinity Bapt. Ch., New Orleans, 1968-69; caseworker Youth Study Ctr., New Orleans, 1972; adj. prof. Criswell Coll., Dallas, 1976-89; counselor First Bapt. Ch., Dallas, 1982-85; psychotherapist Minirth-Meier Clinic, Richardson, Tex., 1985-87; asst. dir. counseling Dallas Theol. Sem., 1987-89; pvt. practice Nashville, 1989—; coord. Trilogy Program Parthenon Pavilion Psychiat. Hosp., Nashville, 1990-94. Mem. ACA, Am. Assn. Marriage and Family Therapy (clin.), Am. Assn. Sex Educators (cert. sex therapist), Counselors and Therapists, Assn. for Religious Values in Counseling. Republican. Baptist. Avocations: crafts, sewing. Office: Parkview Towers 210 25th Ave N Ste 1010 Nashville TN 37203-1611

LAND, REGINALD BRIAN, library administrator; b. Niagara Falls, Ont., Can., July 29, 1927; s. Allan Reginald and Beatrice Beryl (Boyle) L.; m. Edith Wyndham Eddis, Aug. 29, 1953; children—Mary Beatrice, John Robert Eddis. BA, U. Toronto, Ont., Can., 1949, BLS, 1953, MLS, 1956, MA, 1963. Catalogue copy editor T. Eaton Co. Ltd., Toronto, 1950-51; reference librarian Toronto Pub. Library, 1953-55; cataloguer U. Toronto Library, 1955-56, asst. librarian, 1959-63, assoc. librarian, 1963; head div. bus. and industry Windsor Pub. Library, Ont., Can., 1956-57; asst. editor Canadian Bus. Mag., Montreal, Que., Can., 1957-58, assoc. editor, 1958-59; exec. asst. to Minister Fin. of Can., Ottawa, Ont., 1963-64; prof. library sci. U. Toronto, 1964-78, part-time prof., 1978-93, prof. emeritus, 1993—, dean Faculty Library Sci., 1964-72; exec. dir. Ont. Legis. Library,, Toronto, 1978-93. Author: Sources of Information for Canadian Business, 1962, 4th rev. edit., 1985, Eglinton: The Election Study of a Federal Constituency, 1965; founder, gen. editor: Directory of Associations in Canada, 1974, 17th rev. edit., 1996. Mem., Canadian Radio-TV and Telecommunications Commn., 1973-78. Decorated Knight Hospitaller Order of St. John of Jerusalem; recipient Kenneth R. Wilson Meml. award Bus. Newspapers Assn. Can., 1959, Disting. Achievement award Ont. Library Trustees Assn., 1968, Queen Elizabeth IIs Silver Jubilee medal, 1977, Spl. Librarianship award Can. Assn. for Spl. Librs. and Info. Svcs., 1991, 125th Anniversary Confederation Can. medal, 1992, Alumni Jubilee award U. Toronto Libr. & Info. Sci. Alumni Assn., 1994. Mem. ALA (chmn. com. on accreditation 1973-74), Assn. Parliamentary Librs. in Can. (pres. 1982-84), Can. Libr. Assn. (pres. 1975-76), Ont. Libr. Assn. (1st v.p. 1962-63), Ont. Govt. Librs. Coun. (chmn. 1984-85), Assn. for Libr. and Info. Sci. Edn. (pres. 1973-74), Bibliog. Soc. Can., Can. Assn. for Grad. Edn. in Libr. Archival and Info. Studies (pres. 1966-67), Can. Assn. Univ. Tchrs., Can. Coun. Libr. Schs. (chmn. 1971-72), Ex Libris Assn. (bd. dirs. 1994—, v.p. 1996-97), Inst. Profl. Librs. Ont. (pres. 1961-62), Ont. Coun. Libr. Schs. (chmn. 1968-72), Spl. Librs. Assn. (Mem. of Yr. award Toronto chpt. 1986), Ont. Geneal. Soc., Ont. Coll. and Univ. Librs. Assn. (merit award 1962). Mem. Anglican Ch. Home: 9 Wild Rose Court, Guelph, ON Canada N1G 4X7

LANDA, HOWARD MARTIN, lawyer, business executive; b. Bklyn., Oct. 12, 1943; s. George and Lilli (Skolnik) L.; m. Nori Neinstein, Mar. 14, 1971; children—Alyson, David. B.A. (N.Y. State Regents scholar), Bklyn. Coll., 1964; J.D. (tuition scholar), U. Chgo., 1967. Bar: N.Y. 1968. Sole practice N.Y.C., 1968-69; assoc. Garfield, Solomon & Mainzer, N.Y.C., 1969-70, Szold, Brandwen, Meyers & Altman, N.Y.C., 1970-74; v.p., sec., gen. counsel IPCO Corp., White Plains, N.Y., 1974-90, also bd. dirs.; pres., mng. dir. Martin Hand Assocs., Inc., Greenwich, Conn., 1990-92, also bd. dirs.; owner Law Offices of Howard M. Landa, N.Y.C., 1990-94; counsel Rand Rosenzweig Smith Gordon & Burstein LLP, N.Y.C., 1994—; lectr. Dental Lab. Conf., 1977. Contbr. articles to profl. jours. Mem. Mayor N.Y.C. Panel to Study Dept. Gen. Services' Div. Mcpl. Supplies, 1978-79; vice chmn. So. N.Y. chpt. Nat. Multiple Sclerosis Soc., 1988—. Mem. ABA, N.Y. County Lawyers Assn., Corp. Bar Assn., Rockland Bus. Assn., Bus. Network Internat. Office: 605 3rd Ave New York NY 10158

LANDA, WILLIAM ROBERT, foundation executive; b. Jersey City, Dec. 4, 1919; s. G.B. and Henrietta (Elder) L.; m. Anne E. Longley, June 24, 1939; children: Susanne (Mrs. J.B. Moliere), Stephen R., Scott W., Richard W. Student, Ohio U., 1937-39. Salesman Sterling Drug, Inc., 1942-44; asst. export mgr. Taylor, Pinkham & Co., Inc., 1944-52; export mgr. Bates Fabrics, Inc., 1952-55; pres. Burlington Export Co., N.Y.C., 1955-62; v.p. Burlington Mills Corp., 1957-62, Burlington Industries, Inc., Greensboro, N.C., 1959-62, Warner Bros. Co., Bridgeport, Conn., 1962-66; pres. Warner Bros. Co. (Warner Bros. Internat.), 1962-66; exec. v.p. Turner Jones & Co., 1966-67, pres., 1967-68; group v.p. internat. Genesco, Inc., N.Y.C., 1968-70; v.p. Farah Mfg. Co., 1970-74; pres., dir. Holguin & Assos. Inc., El Paso, Tex., 1978-81; pres. Western Mktg. Corp., El Paso, 1981-85; spl. asst. to pres. Free/Congress Research and Edn. Found. Inc., Washington, 1986-89; dir. Affiliated Mfrs., Inc., North Branch, N.J., AMI-PRESCO; hon. consul of Belgium for West Tex. and State of N.Mex., 1981-86; Mem. Gen. Arbitration Council Textile Industry; mem. Nat. Export Council, 1965-66; cons. Internat. Mktg., 1988—. Decorated chevalier Order of Crown (Belgium). Mem. Commerce and Industry Assn. N.Y., Internat. Execs. Assn., U.S. C. of C. (spl. adv. com. on internat. trade), Am. Arbitration Assn., Beta Theta Pi. Presbyterian. Home: 2032 Birch Dr Culpeper VA 22701-4063

LANDAHL, HERBERT DANIEL, biophysicist, mathematical biologist, researcher, consultant; b. Fancheng, China, Apr. 23, 1913; (parents Am. citizens); s. Carl W. and Alice (Holmberg) L.; m. Evelyn Christine Blomberg, Aug. 23, 1940; children: Carl David, Carol Ann Landahl Kubai, Linda C. Landahl Shidner. Student, U. Minn., 1931-32; AB, St. Olaf Coll., Northfield, Minn., 1934; SM, U. Chgo., 1936, PhD, 1941. Rsch. asst. psychometric lab. U. Chgo., 1937-39, rsch. asst. math. biophysics, 1938-41, instr., 1942-45, asst. prof. com. on math. biology, 1945-48, assoc. prof., 1949-56, prof., 1956-68, acting. chmn., 1965-67; prof. biophysics and math. U. Calif., San Francisco, 1968-80, prof. emeritus, 1980—; cons. Respiratory Project, U. Chgo., 1944-46, toxicity lab. U. Chgo., 1947-51, USAF radiation lab., U. Chgo., 1951-67, dept. biomath. U. Tex., Houston, 1968-89; mem. NIH com. on epidemiology and biometry, Bethesda, Md., 1960-64. Co-author: Mathematical Biophysics of Central Nervous System, 1945; contbr. approximately 190 sci. papers to various jours.; chief editor Bull. Math. Biophysics, 1973-80; mem. editorial bd. Computers in Biology and Medicine, 1971-90. Recipient Career Devel. award NIH, 1962-67, Career Achievement award Soc. Toxicology, 1987; grantee NIH, 1963-67. Fellow AAAS; mem. Biophys. Soc., Biometric Soc. (charter), Bioengring. Soc. (charter), Latin Am. Biomath. Soc. (charter), Soc. for Math. Biology (founding, pres. 1981-83). Home: 472 Lansdale Ave San Francisco CA 94127-1617 Office: U Calif-San Francisco PO Box 970 San Francisco CA 94143-0001

LANDAN, HENRY SINCLAIR, lawyer, business consultant; b. Chgo., Aug. 4, 1943. BS, DePaul U., 1965, JD, 1969; LLM in Taxation, NYU, 1970. Bar: Ill. 1969, N.Y. 1971, U.S. Supreme Ct. 1976. Assoc. Altman, Kurlander & Weiss, Chgo., 1969-70, Roberts & Holland, N.Y.C., 1970-72; sr. ptnr. Kamensky & Landan and predecessor, Chgo., 1972-84, Henry S. Landan, Chgo, 1984-88; of counsel Keck, Mahin & Cate, Chgo., 1988-90, ptnr., 1990-96; counsel Caribbean Hotel Assn., Santurce, P.R., 1975-83. Contbg. author: Tax Planning for Professionals; contbr. articles to profl. jours. Mem. exec. com., bd. dirs. Jewish Coun. for Youth Svcs., 1972-77; mem. exec. com., bd. dirs. Men's Coun., Mus. Contemporary Art, Chgo., 1977-84, pres., 1980-82; bd. dirs. Little City, Chgo., 1977-82; bd. dirs., mem. exec. com. Renaissance Soc. U. Chgo., 1984-96, v.p., 1988-95; mem. Soc. Contemporary Art, Art Inst. Chgo., 1982-95; mem. Contemporary Arts Coun., Chgo., 1994-96; mem. bd. mgrs. Henry Horner Boys and Girls Club, 1992-95, James Jordan Boys and Girls Club, 1995-96; bd. dirs., mem. exec. com. Randolph St. Gallery, Chgo., 1983-88, mem. adv. bd., 1988-96. Named Life Dir., Young Men's Jewish Coun., 1980, Man of Yr., 1985. Mem. ABA, N.Y. Bar Assn. Home: PO Box 4228 Wheaton IL 60189-4228

LANDAU, BERNARD ROBERT, biochemistry educator, physician; b. Newark, N.J., June 24, 1926; s. Morris Harry and Estelle (Kirsch) L.; m. Lucille Slosberg, Jan. 11, 1956; children: Steven Brian, Deborah Louise (dec.), Rodger Martin. S.B., MIT, 1947; Ph.D., Harvard U., 1950, M.D., 1954; MD (hon.), Karolinska Inst., 1993. Diplomate: Am. Bd. Internal Medicine. Intern Peter Bent Brigham Hosp., Boston, 1954-55; clin. assoc. Nat. Cancer Inst., Bethesda, Md., 1955-57; fellow in biochemistry Harvard U., 1957-58; sr. resident Peter Bent Brigham Hosp., 1958-59; asst. prof. medicine Case Western Res. U., 1959-62, assoc. prof., 1962-67, prof., 1969—, prof. biochemistry, 1979—, physician Univ. Hosps., 1969—; dir. dept. biochemistry Merck and Co., Rahway, N.J., 1967-69. Contbr. articles to profl. jours. Fellow Commonwealth fund, 1965-66, Fogarty Sr. Internat. fellow 1986-87, 93-94; grantee Am. Heart Assn., 1959-64; recipient William B. Peck Postgrad. Research award, 1961. Fellow AAAS; mem. Am. Fedn. Clin. Research, Am. Soc. Clin. Investigation, Assn. Am. Physicians, Am. soc. Biol. Chemists, Am. Physiol. Soc., Endocrine Soc., Central Soc. Clin. Research, Am. Diabetes Assn., Am. Thyroid Assn., Sigma Xi, Alpha Omega Alpha. Home: 19501 S Woodland Rd Cleveland OH 44122-2834 Office: University Hosps Cleveland 11100 Euclid Ave Cleveland OH 44106-1736

LANDAU, DAVID PAUL, physics educator; b. St. Louis, June 22, 1941; s. Bernard Israel and Selma (Goldstein) L.; m. Heidi Humpert, Aug. 28, 1966; children: Ladina Aviva, Anya Karina. BA, Princeton U., 1963; MS, Yale U., 1965, PhD, 1967. Chargé de recherche CNRS, Grenoble, France, 1967-68; lectr. Yale U., New Haven, 1968-69; asst. prof. physics U. Ga., Athens, 1969-73, assoc. prof., 1973-78, prof., 1978-84, rsch. prof., 1984—, dir. Ctr. for Simulational Physics, 1986—. Editor books; author more than 200 sci. publs. Recipient Creative Rsch. medal U. Ga., 1981, sr. U.S. scientist prize Alexander von Humboldt Found., 1988. Fellow Am. Phys. Soc. (Jesse Beams award 1987). Jewish. Office: U Ga Ctr Simulational Physics Athens GA 30602

LANDAU, DOROTHY, psychotherapist, consultant; b. N.Y.C., Jan. 16, 1944; d. John Charles Sobczak and Evelyn (Schurstedt) Koritor; m. Sal Napolitano, May 4, 1963 (div. Sept. 1982); children: Debra, Drew; m. Jay Arthur Landau, Jan. 6, 1989. AAS, SUNY, Farmingdale, 1977; BSN, SUNY, Stony Brook, 1983, MS, 1992. Cert. clin. nurse specialist; cert. addictions RN; cert. nurse pratitioner in psychiatry. Staff nurse Suffolk Devel. Ctr., Melville, N.Y., 1978; head nurse/asst. supr. Brunswick House, Amityville, N.Y., 1978-80; nurse adminstr. C.K. Post Alcoholism Treatment Ctr., Brentwood, N.Y., 1981-89; asst. DON Kings Park (N.Y.) Psychiat. Ctr., 1989-93; dir. partial hospitalization program and inpatient mental health and substances abuse svcs. Mercy Med. Ctr., Rockville Centre, N.Y., 1993-94; psychotherapist Commack, N.Y., 1992—; pvt. cons. Smithtown, N.Y., 1994—; mem. adv. bd. Sch. Nursing, SUNY, Farmingdale, 1990—. Rschr. in field of substance abuse. Mem. N.Y. State Coalition of Nurse Practitioners, Soc. for Edn. and Rsch. in Psychiatric Nursing, Network of Clin. Specialists in Psychiatric Nursing, Nassau-Suffolk Coordinating Coun. (bd. dirs. 1990-93), Sigma Theta Tau. Avocation: sailing. Home: 41 Valley Ave Smithtown NY 11787-1114 Office: 283 Commack Rd Commack NY 11725-3400

LANDAU, ELLIS, gaming company executive; b. Phila., Feb. 24, 1944; s. Manfred and Ruth (Fischer) L.; m. Kathy Suzanne Thomas, May 19, 1968 (div.); children: Rachel, David; m. Yvette Ehr Cohen, Nov. 1, 1992. BA in Econs., Brandeis U., 1965; MBA, Columbia U., 1967. Fin. analyst SEC, Washington, 1968-69; asst. treas. U-Haul Internat., Phoenix, 1969-71; v.p., treas. Ramada, Inc., Phoenix, 1971-90; CFO Boyd Gaming Corp., Las Vegas, Nev., 1990—. Home: 7571 Silver Meadow Ct Las Vegas NV 89117 Office: Boyd Gaming Corp 2950 S Industrial Rd Las Vegas NV 89109-1100

LANDAU, EMANUEL, epidemiologist; b. N.Y.C., Nov. 28, 1919; s. Meyer and Annie (Heller) L.; B.A., CCNY, 1939; Ph.D., Am. U., 1966; m. Davetta Goldberg, Sept. 4, 1948; children: Melanie (dec.), Elizabeth. Supervisory analytical statistician Calif. Dept. Public Health, 1957-59, chief biometry sect., div. air pollution, 1959-62; head lab. and clin. trials sect. Nat. Cancer Inst., 1962-65; statis. adviser Nat. Air Pollution Control Adminstrn., 1965-69; epidemiologist Environ. Health Service, 1969-71, chief epidemiologic studies br. Bur. Radiol. Health, 1971-74; project dir., sci. cons. Am. Pub. Health Assn., 1975—; cons., adv. in field. Vol. White House Health Care Reform Corr. With AUS, 1942-46. Decorated Belgian Fourragere; recipient Superior Service award HEW, 1963. Fellow Am. Pub. Health Assn., Royal Soc. Health; mem. Soc. Epidemiologic Research, Am. Statis. Assn. (chmn. com. on stats. and environ.). Democrat. Jewish. Club: Cosmos (Washington). Author, editor articles, reports in field. Home: 4601 N Park Ave Apt 208 Chevy Chase MD 20815-4520 Office: Am Pub Health Assn 1015 15th St NW Washington DC 20005-2605

LANDAU, HENRY GROH, geoenvironmental consulting engineer; b. N.Y.C., Mar. 1, 1943; s. Henry G. and Ann Marie (Skvarich) L.; m. Joyce Kathryn Van de Merlen, July 27, 1965; children: Greg, Amy, Michael. BS in Civil Engring., CCNY, 1965; MS in Geotech. Engring., Purdue U., 1966, PhD in Engring., 1973. Profl. engr., Wash., N.Y., Alaska. Civil engr. Geotechnica, Sao Paulo, Brazil, 1966-67; officer U.S. Army C.E., South Vietnam, 1967-70; sr. engr. Dames & Moore, Seattle, 1973-82; pres., CEO Landau Assocs., Inc., Edmonds, Wash., 1982—; vis. prof. Fed. U., Paraiba, Brazil, 1978-79; mem. Gov.'s Sci. Adv. Bd., Olympia, Wash., 1987-90, chmn., 1990—. Contbr. articles to profl. jours. Tutor math. and sci. Edmonds Sch. Dist., 1990—; scout leader Boy Scouts Am., Edmonds, 1986-90. 1st lt., U .S. Army, 1967-70, Vietnam. Mem. ASCE, Soc. Am. Mil. Engrs., Assn. Groundwater Scientists & Engrs. Avocations: bicycling, sailing, nature study, water sports. Office: Landau Assocs Inc 23107 100th Ave W Edmonds WA 98020-5017

LANDAU, JACOB, artist; b. Phila., Dec. 17, 1917; s. Samuel and Deana (Kitaynick) L.; m. Frances Paul, May 5, 1949; children: Stephan Paul, Jonas Michael. Student, Phila. Coll. Art, 1936-39, New Sch., N.Y.C., 1948-49, 52-53, Acad. de la Grande Chaumiere, Paris, France, 1950-52; DFA (hon.), Monmouth U., N.J., 1996. Prof. graphic art Pratt Inst., Bklyn., now prof. emeritus; founder, formerly learning coordinator integrative studies program; vis. scholar Memphis Acad. Arts, 1969, U. Notre Dame, Ind., 1969; graphic arts panelist N.J. Arts Council, 1969-73; vis. artist Skidmore Coll., Saratoga Springs, N.Y., 1971, Brookdale Coll., Lincroft, N.J., 1976, U. No. Mich., 1981, Ea. and Western Carolina Univs., Greenville and Cullowhee, N.C., 1982; panelist N.J. State Mus., Trenton, 1973, NYU, 1974, Rutgers U., New Brunswick, N.J., 1976; artist-in-residence U. No. Iowa, 1977; resident artist Pima Community Coll., Univ. Ariz., Tucson, 1984; tchr. Artist/Tchr. Inst., N.J. State Council on Arts, 1978-89; academician Nat. Acad. Design, N.Y.; cons. N.J. Dept. Higher Edn., 1974. One-man shows include Galerie LeBar, Paris, 1952, Art Alliance, Phila., 1954, 75, Art Ctr., New Brunswick, N.J., 1957, Samuel Fleisher Meml. Gallery, Phila., 1959, Assoc. Am. Artists Gallery, N.Y.C., 1960, 70, U. Maine, 1961, 71, Cober Gallery, N.Y.C., 1961, 63, Zora Gallery, L.A., 1964, Original Prints Gallery, San Francisco, 1965, Gallery 100, Princeton, N.J., 1966, Art Gallery, U. Notre Dame, 1969, A.A.A. Gallery N.Y., 1970, Print Club, Phila., 1970, Giraffe Gallery, L.A., 1970, Van Straaten Gallery, Chgo., 1970, Lunn Gallery, Washington, 1970, Jorgensen Auditorium, U. Conn. at Storrs, 1971, Bloomfield (N.J.) Coll., 1971, 72, Orpheus Ascending Gallery, Stockbridge, Mass., 1972, Galeria Pecanins, Mexico City, 1972, Imprint Gallery, San Francisco, 1973, Congregation Keneseth Israel, Elkins Park, Pa., 1974, ACA Galleries, N.Y.C., 1976, Woodbridge (N.J.) Cultural Arts Commn., Schneider-Sato Gallery, Karlsruhe, Germany, 1977, N.J. Mus., 1981, U. Ga., 1982, Phila. Mus. Judaica, 1983, Phila. Coll. Art, 1985, Galerie Neuheisel, Saarbrucken, Fed. Republic Germany, Galerie Michael Hagen, Offenburg, Fed. Republic Germany, 1985, Martin Sumers Graphics, N.Y., 1988, Rider Coll., Lawrenceville, N.J., 1988, The Mariboe Gallery, Peddie Sch., Hightstown, N.J., 1992, Judah L. Magnes Mus., 1993, N.J. State Mus., 1994, Kennseth Israel, Elkins Park, Pa., 1995, Brandywine workshop, Phila., 1996, (with Bernarda Shahn) Printmaking Coun. N.J., North Branch Stattion, N.J., 1996, Monmouth U., N.J., 1997; numerous group shows, 1955—, latest include Four Painters, Art Alliance Phila., 1961, New Humanism, Nat. Sch. Plastics Arts, U. Mexico, 1963, regional exhbn., Pa. Acad. Fine Arts, 1964, N.J. and the Artist, N.J. State Mus., Trenton, 1965, Drawing Soc. Eastern Cen. Region, Phila. Mus. Art, 1965, N.J. Tercentenary Show, 1965, Contemporary N.J. Art, Newark Mus., 1965, Prize-Winning Am. Prints, circulating show, N.Y. State Council on Arts, 1967, Drawings U.S.A, St. Paul Art Ctr., 1968, Am. Prints Today,

Mus. Art, Munson-Williams-Proctor Inst., Utica, N.Y., 1968, Selections from 50th Ann. Soc. Am. Graphic Artists, USIA Nr. East Traveling Show, 1970, Tamarind: A Renaissance of Lithography, circulating show, Internat. Exhbns. Found., 1971, SUNY Coll. at Brockport, 1972, Iowa State U., 1972, N.J. Arts Council, 1972, Art. Mus., Sao Paulo, Brazil, 1972, Am. Acad. Arts and Letters, 1973, 74, NAD, 1974, Washington Club, 1976, Soc. Am. Graphic Artists Show, 1976, 77, Am. Color Print Soc. 35th Exhbn., Phila., 1976, 1st Biennial N.J. Artists, 1977, State U., Potsdam, N.Y., 1978, Portsmouth Arts Ctr., Portsmouth, Va., 1979, Carnegie Mellon U., Pitts., 1980, Minn. Mus. Art, St. Paul, 1980, Worcester Art Mus., Worcester, Mass., 1981, Noyes Mus., Oceanville, N.J., 1983, 1991, Purdue U., W. Lafayette, Ind., 1986, Middlesex County Mus., Piscataway, N.J., 1987, Fellowship Exhbn, The Monmouth Mus., 1988, Guild Hall Mus., East Hampton, N.Y., 1990, Rubelle and Norman Schafler Gallery, Pratt Inst. 1990-91, Mercer County (N.J.) Communtiy Coll., 1991, Printmaking Coun., Sommerville, N.J., 1991, Ellarslie Mus., Trenton, N.J., 1992; numerous nat. and internat. shows, 1953—, latest include woodcut annuals, Print Club Phila., 1955, 59, 92d, 95th, 97th Am. Watercolor Soc. anns., NAD, 1954, 62, 64, 12th-17th print biennials, Bklyn. Mus., 1960, 62, 64, 66, 68, 70, Xylon Internats., 1962, 65, Recent Paintings, U.S.A-The Figure, Mus. Modern Art, 1962, nominee exhbn., Nat. Inst. Arts and Letters, 1962, 65, 156th, 158th, 160th, 162d anns., Pa. Acad. Fine Arts, 1961, 63, 65, 67, graphics U.S.A., USIA traveling exhbn., 1963—, 19th, 20th print exhbns., Library of Congress, 1963, 66, 30th ann., Butler Art Inst., Youngstown, Ohio, 1965, Smithsonian invitational exhbn., White House, 1966, Nat. Drawing Exhbn., Rutgers U., 1975, Hawaii Nat. Print Exhbn, Honolulu Acad. Arts, 1975, Nat. Coll. Fine Arts, Miami Graphics, Biennial Met. Mus., Coral Gables, Fla., Boston Printmakers, De Cordova Mus., Lincoln, Mass., Hunterdon (N.J.) Art Center, 1977; also exhibited at Mus. Modern Art, N.Y.C., 1969, Whitney Mus., N.Y.C., 1969, Mus. Art, Phila., 1970, NAD 157th Ann., Ohio State U., 1982, Utopian Visions in Modern Art, Hirshhorn Mus. and Sculpture Garden, Washington, 1984, Third Internat. Biennial Print Exhbn., Hangzhou, People's Republic of China, 1989; represented in permanent collections Whitney Mus. Am. Art, Mus. Modern Art, Met. Mus., Pa. Acad. Fine Arts, art museums in Balt., Atlanta, New Orleans, Phila., Bklyn., Norfolk, Va., San Antonio, Tucson, Ariz., Malmo, Sweden, Nuremberg, Fed. Republic Germany, Slater Mus., Norwich, Conn., Library of Congress, Joseph J. Hirschhorn collection, also univs. Princeton, Rutgers, Maine, Minn., Syracuse, Yale, Ky., U. Calif. at Berkeley, U. Mass., U. South Fla., Columbia, Butler Inst., Youngstown, Ohio, M.H. DeYoung Mus., San Francisco, N.J. State Mus., Trenton, Bibliotheque Nationale, Paris, Lessing Rosenwald Collection, also pvt. collections, commns. include sketches of participants at Pacem In Terris II, 1967; print of Peace, Internat. Art Program, Nat. Collection Fine Arts, Smithsonian Instn., 1967; cycle of ten stained glass windows The Prophetic Quest, Keneseth Israel Congregation, Elkins Park, 1970; lithograph, Behold Jewish Ctr., Trenton, 1973, But if the Cause, Roten Galleries, Balt., 1976; etching, Einstein, Washington Print Club, 1982; lithograph, Thirty-Fourth Psalm, Jewish Family Svc. of Del. Valley, Trenton, N.J., 1988. Trustee N.J. Sch. Arts, 1981-85, Nat. Guild of Community Schs. of Arts; mem. nat. com. U. of Arts, Phila. Recipient Lessing Rosenwald Purchase award Print Club Phila., 1955, 59; recipient Woodcut prize Print Fair of Phila. Free library, 1960, Louis Comfort Tiffany award, 1962; recipinet hon. mention Am. Water Color Soc., 1962; recipient Paul F. Norton and Asso. Am. Artists awards Soc. Am. Graphic Artists, 1962, hon. mention Audubon Artists, 1965; named One of New Jersey's Five Finest Com. Curators and Critics, 1962; recipient Phila. Watercolor prize Pa. Acad. Fine Arts, 1963; First award N.J. Tercentenary Art Festival, 1963; fellow Tamarind Lithography Workshop, Los Angeles, 1965; Edna Pennypacker Stauffer prize Soc. Am. Graphic Artists, 1965; purchase awards Asso. Am. Artists, 1967; purchase awards Dulin Gallery Art, Knoxville, Tenn.; purchase awards Drawing U.S.A. '68, St. Paul Art Center; purchase awards Contemporary Graphic Art on Contemporary Law and Justice, Assn. Bar City N.Y.; Vera List purchase prize Soc. Am. Graphic Artists, 1972; Childe Hassam purchase award Am. Acad. Arts and Letters, 1973-74; purchase prize Nat. Drawing Exhbn., Rutgers U., 1975; Purchase prize Nat. Print Exhbn., Hunterdon; Purchase prize AAA Gallery, N.Y.C., 1977; Ann. award YM-YWHA, Union, N.J., 1984; Alumni Silver Star award Phila. Colls. Art, 1985; Grantee Nat. Arts Council, 1966; Grantee N.J. State Arts Council, 1974; Grantee Ford Found., 1975; Guggenheim Found. fellow, 1968-69; recipient N.J. State Arts Coun. fellowship, 1988, Gov.'s award for disting. svc. in arts and edn., 1989. Mem. Soc. Am. Graphic Artists. Home and Studio: 30 Lake Dr PO Box 328 Roosevelt NJ 08555-0328 *For me, art is more than formal exploration or exploitation. Without it, we are an endangered and endangering species.*

LANDAU, LAURI BETH, accountant, tax consultant; b. Bklyn., July 21, 1952; d. Jack and Audrey Carolyn (Zuckernick) L. BA, Skidmore Coll., 1973; postgrad., Pace. U., 1977-79. CPA, N.Y., Oreg. Mem. staff Audrey Z. Landau, CPA, Suffern, N.Y., 1976-78; mem. staff Ernst & Whinney, N.Y.C., 1979-80, mem. sr. staff, 1980-82, supr., 1982-84; mgr. Arthur Young & Co., N.Y.C., 1984-87, prin., 1987-89; sr. mgr. Ernst & Young, N.Y.C., 1989-92; ptnr. Landau & Landau, Pomona, N.Y., 1992—; ptnr. Audrey Z. Landau & Co., Wilmington, Vt., 1995—; spkr. World Trade Inst., N.Y.C., 1987—, Nat. Fgn. Trade Coun., N.Y.C., 1989—. Composer songs. Career counselor Skidmore Coll., Saratoga Springs, N.Y., 1977—; mem. leadership com. Class of 1973, 83-85, pres., 1985-93, fund chmn., 1987-88, mem. planned gift com., 1989—; mem. Rockland Bus. Assn. N.Y. State Regents scholar, 1970. Mem. Nat. Conf. CPA Practitioners, N.Y. State Soc. CPAs, Rockland Bus. Assn., Skidmore Coll. Alumni Assn. (mem. nominating com. 1989-92). Skidmore Alumni Club. Democrat. Avocations: music, ballet, photography, sports. Office: 26 Firemans Memorial Dr Pomona NY 10970-3569

LANDAU, MARTIN, actor; b. Bklyn., June 20, 1934; m. Barbara Bain (div.); children: Susie, Juliet. Student, Art Students League, Actors Studio. Staff artist, cartoonist N.Y. Daily News. Star TV series Mission: Impossible, 1966-69 (Golden Globe award 1967), Space 1999, 1974-77, others; TV appearances include Omnibus, Playhouse 90, G.E. Theatre, Gunsmoke, Twilight Zone; also TV movies Welcome Home, Johnny Bristol, 1972, Savage, 1973, The Death of Ocean View Park, 1979, The Harlem Globetrotters on Gilligan's Island, 1981, The Fall of the House of Usher, 1982, The Neon Empire, 1989, By Dawn's Early Light, 1990, Something to Live For: The Alison Gertz Story, 1992, Legacy of Lies, 1992 (Ace award), 12:01, 1993, miniseries Joseph, 1995; films include Pork Chop Hill, North by Northwest, 1959, Stagecoach to Dancer's Rock, 1961, Cleopatra, 1962, Hallelujah Trail, 1964, The Greatest Story Ever Told, 1965, Nevada Smith, 1966, They Call Me Mr. Tibbs, 1970, Operation SNAFU, 1970, A Town Called Hell, 1971, Johnny Bristol, 1971, Black Gunn, 1972, Strange Shadows in an Empty Room, 1977, Meteor, 1979, The Last Word, 1979, Without Warning, 1980, Operation Moonbase Alpha, 1980, Earthright, 1980, Beauty and the Beast, 1981, Alone in the Dark, 1982, Trial by Terror, 1983, Tucker: The Man and His Dreams, 1988 (Acad. Award nominee 1988), Crimes and Misdemeanors, 1989, (Golden Globe award 1989, Acad. award nominee 1989) Paint It Black, 1990, Real Bullets, 1990, Firehead, 1991, Eye of the Widow, 1991, Mistress, 1992, Sliver, 1993, Intersection, 1994, Ed Wood, 1994 (Best Supporting Actor Acad. award 1994, Golden Globe award 1994, SAG award 1994, Am. Comedy award 1994, N.Y. Film Critics award 1994, L.A. Film Critics award 1994, Chgo. Film Critics award 1994, Nat. Soc. Film Critics award 1994, Boston Film Critics award 1994, Tex. Film Critics award 1994, Lifetime Achievement award Houston Film Festival 1994, Lifetime Achievement award Charleston Film Festival 1994), City Hall, 1995, The Legend of Pinocchio, 1996, B.A.P.S (Black Am. Princesses), 1997; stage appearances include Middle of the Night, Uncle Vanya, Stalag 17, Wedding Breakfast, First Love, The Goat Song, Dracula. Emmy nominee. Mem. Acad. Motion Picture Arts and Scis., Actors Studio (W. Coast dir.). Office: 23717 Long Valley Rd Calabasas CA 91302-2409

LANDAU, MARTIN, political science educator; b. N.Y.C., July 12, 1921; s. User Noah and Clara (Markowitz) L.; m. Bernice Feldman, July 11, 1943; children—Madeline, Claudia. A.B., Bklyn. Coll., 1947; M.A. in Pub. Adminstrn, N.Y. U., 1948; Ph.D., 1952; Docteur Honoris Causa, U. Paris, Dauphine, 1993. Vis. research prof. U. Calif. at Berkeley, 1969-71, prof. polit. sci., 1972—; Distinguished prof. City U. N.Y., Bklyn., 1970-72; lectr. orgn. and decision theory Fgn. Service Inst., U.S. Dept. State, Washington, 1969-72; cons. in field; chancellor Grad. Sch. Pub. Adminstrn., U. P.R., San Juan, 1970-71; Berkeley Exch. prof., Peking U., 1985; Phi Beta Kappa Nat. Lectr., 1984; dir. Berkeley-Hong Kong Project, 1984—. Author: Political Theory and Political Science; Studies in the Methodology of Political Inquiry, 1972; Chmn. editorial bd.: Polit. Sci, 1971—; mem. editorial bd.: Jour. Comparative Adminstrv. Studies, 1969—, Comparative Politics, 1970—, Jour. Theoretical Politics, 1988—, Jour. Behavioral Decision Making, 1988—. Served with Signal Corps AUS, 1941-45. Recipient Distinguished Teaching award Bklyn. Coll., 1963, E. Harris Harbison award gifted teaching Danforth Found., 1969-70, William E. Mosher award distinguished scholarship Soc. Pub. Adminstrn., 1970, 79; John Simon Guggenheim fellow, 1976-77; fellow Center Advanced Study in Behavioral Sci., 1976-77. Fellow Nat. Acad. Public Adminstrn.; mem. Am. Polit. Sci. Assn., Philosophy of Sci. Assn. Home: 1410 Summit Rd Berkeley CA 94708-2215 Office: U Calif Dept Polit Sci Berkeley CA 94720

LANDAU, MASON STEPHEN, business broker, insurance professional; b. N.Y.C., Oct. 31, 1948; s. Milton Harold and Charlotte Helen (Perlburg) L.; m. Susanne Marie Drown, May 7, 1983; children: Elizabeth, Joshua. AAS in Agr., SUNY, Farmingdale, 1968; BS in Psychology, Kans. State U., 1972, MS in Bus., 1973. Div. mgr. Sears & Roebuck, Manhattan, Kans., 1972-73; sales agt. Family Life Ins. Co., Overland Park, Kans., 1974-76; bus. mgr. Metcalf Datsun, Overland Park, 1976-79; pres. Continental Benefit Industries, Inc., Mission, Kans., 1979-84; pres., chmn. Corp. Adminstrv. Svcs., Inc., Lenexa, Kans., 1984—, RM corp., Inc., Lenexa, 1984—, Continuous Svc. Care, Inc., Lenexa, 1984—, Continental Casualty and Indemnity, Turks and Caicos Islands, Brit. W.I., 1984—; chmn. Citation Am. Group, Inc., Lenexa, 1991—; cons. in field; bd. dirs. Continental Casualty and Indemnity, RM Corp., N.Y.C. Active Johnson County Civil Def., 1970—; asst. cubmaster Boy Scouts Am. Mem. Profl. Ins. Assn., Mo-Kan Coun. Amateur Radio Clubs (past pres., com. mem.). Avocations: amateur radio, horses, skiing. Office: Cir Citation America Group 12400 W 62nd Ter Shawnee Mission KS 66216-1810

LANDAU, PETER EDWARD, editor; b. N.Y.C., July 16, 1933; s. Edward and Charlotte (Schmidt) L. A.B., Duke, 1955; M.S. in Econs, Columbia, 1959. Editorial asst. Newsweek mag., N.Y.C., 1955-57, asst. editor, 1958-61, assoc. editor, 1962-67; v.p. Tiderock Corp., 1967; sr. editor Instl. Investor, N.Y.C., 1968, mng. editor, 1968-70, editor, 1971-91, editor-at-large, 1991—. Co-author: Presidential Lies: The Illustrated History of White House Golf, 1996. Home: 300 E 51st St New York NY 10022-7806 Office: Instl Investor 488 Madison Ave New York NY 10022-5702

LANDAU, RICHARD L., physician, educator; b. St. Louis, Aug. 8, 1916; s. Milton S. and Amelia (Rich) L.; m. Claire Schmuckel, Dec. 4, 1943; children—James, Susan, Kay. B.S., M.D., Washington U., St. Louis, 1940. Intern U. Chgo. Clinics, 1940-41, resident, 1941-42; mem. faculty U. Chgo. Sch. Medicine, 1946—, prof. medicine, 1959-88, prof. medicine emeritus, 1988—; head sect. endocrinology, 1967-78. Editor: Perspectives in Biology and Medicine, 1973—; mem. editorial bd.: Jour. Lab. and Clin. Medicine, 1957-62, Ann. Rev. Medicine, 1959-68, Jour. AMA, 1981-89. Served to capt. M.C. AUS, 1943-46. Decorated Bronze Star. Mem. Endocrine Soc. (council 1962-65), Central Soc. Clin. Research, Am. Soc. Clin. Investigation, A.M.A., Chgo. Soc. Internal Medicine (pres. 1968). Spl. rsch. in endocrinologic aspects of reprodn., metabolic influence of progesterone. Home: 5732 S Kenwood Ave Chicago IL 60637-1719

LANDAU, SIDNEY I., publishing executive, lexicographer; b. N.Y.C., Apr. 11, 1933; s. Emanuel and Sadie Mildred (Halpern) L.; m. Sarah Gaston Bradford, June 19, 1959; children: Paul, Amy. BA in English, Queens Coll., 1954; MFA in Creative Writing, U. Iowa, 1959. Instr. English Miami U., Oxford, Ohio, 1959-61; editor, then editor in chief dictionaries Funk & Wagnalls, N.Y.C., 1961-70; editor in chief Doubleday Dictionary, Doubleday Roget's Thesaurus Doubleday & Co., N.Y.C., 1975-77; editor in chief Internat. Dictionary of Medicine and Biology, John Wiley & Sons, N.Y.C., 1977-88, mgr. med. jours., 1982-84, exec. editor medicine, 1985-87, pub. chemistry and life scis. sci.-tech. div., 1987-88; dir. reference, editor-in-chief Cambridge Dictionary of Am. English, N.Y.C., 1988—. Author: Dictionaries: The Art and Craft of Lexicography, 1984, paperback edit., 1989; contbr. numerous articles to profl. jours. With U.S. Army, 1954-56. Mem. Am. Dialect Soc., Dictionary Soc. N.Am. (pres. 1993-95), Am. Coun. Learned Socs. (del. 1994—). Home: 50 W 96th St Apt 2A New York NY 10025-6527 Office: Cambridge U Press 40 W 20th St New York NY 10011-4211

LANDAU, WALTER LOEBER, lawyer; b. New Orleans, Sept. 9, 1931; s. Walter Loeber and Mae (Wilzin) L.; m. Barbara Jane Gordon, June 23, 1954; children: Donna Hardiman, Blair Trippe, Gordon Loeber. BA, Princeton U., 1953; LLB, Harvard U., 1956. Bar: N.Y. 1956, U.S. Dist. Ct. (so. dist.) N.Y. 1962, U.S. Supreme Ct. 1971. Assoc. firm Sullivan & Cromwell, N.Y.C., 1959-65; ptnr. Sullivan & Cromwell, 1966—; bd. dirs. Alumax, Inc., U.S. Life Ins. Co., N.Y.C. Trustee Reece Sch., N.Y.C.; mem. Met. Opera Assn.; bd. dirs. Opera Orch. N.Y., N.Y.C. Opera, treas.; bd. dirs., sec. Manhattan Theater Club. Fellow Am. Bar Found.; mem. ABA, N.Y. State Bar Assn., Assn. Bar City N.Y., Am. Law Inst. Republican. Office: Sullivan & Cromwell 125 Broad St New York NY 10004-2400

LANDAUER, ROLF WILLIAM, physicist; b. Stuttgart, Germany, Feb. 4, 1927; came to U.S., 1938, naturalized, 1944; s. Karl and Anna Landauer; m. Muriel Jussim, Feb. 26, 1950; children—Karen, Carl, Thomas. SB, Harvard U., 1945, AM, 1947, PhD, 1950; DSc (hon.), Technion, 1991. Solid state physicist Lewis Lab., NACA (now NASA), Cleve., 1950-52; with IBM Research (and antecedent groups), 1952—; asst. dir. research IBM Research (T. J. Watson Research Center), Yorktown Heights, N.Y., 1966-69, IBM fellow, 1969—. Contbr. articles on solid state theory, computing devices, statis. mechanics of computational process to profl. jours. Served with USNR, 1945-46. Recipient Stewart Ballantine medal Franklin Inst., 1992, Centennial medal Harvard U., 1993, sci. for art prize Moet Hennessy Luis Vuitton, Inc., 1997. Fellow IEEE, AAAS, Am. Phys. Soc. (Buckley prize 1995); mem. NAE, NAS, European Acad. Scis. and Arts, Am. Acad. Arts and Scis. Achievements include initiating IBM programs leading to injection laser, large scale integration. Office: IBM Rsch Ct PO Box 218 Yorktown Heights NY 10598-0218

LANDAW, STEPHEN ARTHUR, physician, educator; b. Paterson, N.J., June 20, 1936; s. Louis and Ida (Machowsky) L.; children: Jared Lawrence, Nicole Renee. B.S., U. Wis., 1955; M.D., George Washington U., 1959; Ph.D., U. Calif., Berkeley, 1969. Cert. rsch. adminstr. Intern Mt. Sinai Hosp., N.Y.C., 1959-60; resident in internal medicine Mt. Sinai Hosp., 1960-61; fellow in hematology Med. Coll. Va., 1962-63; fellow in nuclear medicine Donner Lab., U. Calif., 1963-69, asst. physician, 1970-73; chief isotope lab. Highland-Alameda County Hosp., Oakland, Calif., 1970-73; asso. prof. SUNY, Syracuse, 1973-78; prof. SUNY, 1978—; asso. chief staff research and devel. VA Med. Center, Syracuse, 1973-94; vis. prof. Rockefeller U., N.Y.C., 1988; vis. physician Rockefeller U. Hosp., N.Y.C., 1988; pres. Ctrl. N.Y. Rsch. Corp., 1989-94. Contbr. in field. Served with U.S. Army, 1961-62. VA grantee, 1973-93; NASA grantee, 1976-82; recipient NASA Kosmos Achievement awards, 1975, 77. Fellow ACP; mem. Am. Soc. Hematology, Am. Fedn. Clin. Rsch., Soc. Pediat. Rsch., Soc. Exptl. Biology and Medicine, N.Y. Acad. Sci., Sigma Xi, Alpha Omega Alpha. Jewish. Home: 3159 Burrwood Dr Baldwinsville NY 13027-1708 Office: VA Med Ctr 800 Irving Ave Syracuse NY 13210-2716

LANDBERG, GEORGE GUSTAF, mechanical engineer; b. Seneca Falls, N.Y., Sept. 25, 1939; s. Erik Gustaf and Darthea Elizabeth (Wilgus) L.; m. Melody Anne Moore, Oct. 21, 1961; children: Peter (dec.), Cynthia, Jennifer. BS in Mech. Engring., U. Rochester, 1961, MS in Aerospace Sci., 1964. Registered profl. engr., N.Y. Devel. engr. Allis Chalmers Mfg. Co., Cin., 1961-63; teaching asst. U. Rochester, N.Y., 1963-65; v.p. Lightnin A Unit Gen. Signal Corp., Rochester, 1965-82; pres. Aerocleve-Pentech Divsn. Clevepak Corp., Fall River, Mass., 1982-83; v.p., gen. mgr. process sealing divsn. EG&G Sealol, Cranston, R.I., 1983-84; pres. Warren (Mass.) Pumps Inc., 1984-90; pres., CEO, Valcor Engring. Corp., Springfield, N.J., 1990-96; pres., CEO Drexel Industries, Inc., Horsham, Pa., 1996—; bd. dirs. JMS Industries, Englewood, N.J. Recipient Nat. Design award James F. Lincoln Arc Welding Found., Cleve., 1963, Commendation Bd. Edn., Fall River, Mass., 1983, Disting. Alumni award U. Rochester, 1986. Mem. ASME, Rochester Engring. Soc. (pres. 1979-80). Episcopalian. Achievements include patents for fan-cooled electric motor, draft tube arrangement for starting in settled solids, impeller for mixing liquids or the like; recognized authority in design of high specific speed axial flow impellers. Office: 331 Maple Ave Horsham PA 19044-2139

LANDE, JAMES AVRA, lawyer, contracts manager; b. Chgo., Oct. 2, 1930; s. S. Theodore and Helen C. (Hamburger) L.; m. Ann Mari Gustavsson, Feb. 21, 1959; children: Rebecca Susanne, Sylvia Diane. BA, Swarthmore Coll., 1952; JD, Columbia U., 1955; Bar: N.Y. 1958, Calif. 1967. Assoc. Rein, Mound & Cotton, N.Y.C., 1957-59; atty. VA, Seattle, 1959-61, Weyerhaeuser Co., Tacoma, 1961-63, Lande Assoc., San Francisco, 1963-67; atty. NASA, Ames Research Center, Moffett Field, Calif., 1967-70; house counsel Syntex Corp., Palo Alto, Calif., 1970-73; dir. contracts dept. Electric Power Research Inst., Palo Alto, Calif., 1973-81; corp. atty., dir contracts Lurgi Corp., Belmont, Calif., 1981-82; contracts mgr. Bechtel Corp., San Francisco, 1982-92, sr. contract mgr. Bay Area Rapid Transit Dist., Oakland, Calif., 1992—; adj. prof. U. San Francisco Sch. Law, 1972-73; lectr. law U. Santa Clara Sch. Law, 1968-82. Pres. Syntex Fed. Credit Union, 1971-72. Served with U.S. Army, 1955-57. Mem. Calif. Bar Assn., Nat. Contract Mgmt. Assn. (past pres., dir. Golden Gate chpt.), Lawyers Club of San Francisco. Home: 1330 33rd Ave San Francisco CA 94122-1305 Office: Bay Area Rapid Transit Dist 979 Broadway Millbrae CA 94030-1912

LANDE, KENNETH, physicist, astronomer, educator; b. Vienna, Austria, June 5, 1932; came to U.S., 1939; s. Bernard and Frieda (Kavaler) L.; m. Gabriella Rosner, June 9, 1963; children—David, Elia, Leah. A.B., Columbia U., 1953, M.A., 1955, Ph.D., 1958. Instr. physics U. Pa., Phila., 1957-59, asst. prof., 1959-63, assoc. prof., 1963-74, prof., 1974—, chmn. astronomy and astrophysics, 1984-94; guest scientist Brookhaven Nat. Lab., Upton, N.Y., 1973-84. Contbr. articles to profl. jours. Mem. Am. Physical Soc., Am. Astron. Soc., Internat. Astron. Union, Sigma Xi. Office: David Rittenhouse Lab 209 S 33rd St Philadelphia PA 19104

LANDEGGER, CARL CLEMENT, machinery and pulp manufacturing executive; b. Vienna, Austria, Sept. 20, 1930; came to U.S., 1937, naturalized, 1947; s. Karl F. and Helena (Berger) L. BS in Social Sci., Georgetown U., 1951; children: Christine, Carl, Claudia, Cary, Celia, Gregory. Vice chmn., Parsons and Whittermore, Inc., N.Y.C., 1953—; with Black Clawson Co., N.Y.C., 1956—, exec. v.p., 1959-65, pres., 1965—, chmn., 1967—; chmn. St. Anne Nackawic Pulp & Paper Co.; vice chmn. Ala. River Pulp Co., Monroeville, Ala.; geno ptnr., Hagerstown Fiber Ltd. Partnership; bd. dirs. Georgetown U., Gregorian U. Found. 1st lt. USAF, 1951-53. Mem. Explorers Club, Road Runners Club (bd. dirs.). Office: Black Clawson Co 405 Lexington Ave Fl 61 New York NY 10174-6199

LANDEGGER, GEORGE F., engineering executive; b. 1937. BS, Georgetown U., 1958. With Parsons & Whittemore Inc., Port Chester, N.Y., 1960—, now CEO. Office: Parsons & Whittemore 4 International Dr Rye Brook NY 10573-1065*

LANDEL, ROBERT FRANKLIN, physical chemist, rheologist; b. Pendleton, N.Y., Oct. 10, 1925; s. Carlisle Oscar and Grace Elisabeth (McEachren) L.; m. Aurora Mamauag; children: Carlisle P., Grace P., Hans F., Robert F. Jr., Kevin L., Matthew N. BA, U. Buffalo, 1949, MA, 1950; PhD, U. Wis., 1954. Rsch. assoc. U. Wis., Madison, 1954-55; sr. rsch. engr. Jet Propulsion Lab. Calif. Inst. Tech., Pasadena, 1955-59, sect. mgr., 1959-85, sr. rsch. fellow CIT, 1966-69, sr. rsch. scientist Jet Propulsion Lab., 1980-92; cons., 1992—; rsch. affiliate Rancho Los Amigos Hosp., Downey, 1976—; vis. prof. Ecole Poly Fed., Lausanne, Switzerland, 1984, U. Philippines, Manila, 1993-94; cons. Sandia Nat. Labs., Albuquerque, 1983; mem. NASA Aircraft Fire Safety Tech. Panel, 1973-80; mem. U.S.-U.K. Working Group on Antimisting Aircraft Fuels, 1978-82, Joint Dept. Def./NASA Working Group on Mech. Properties of Solid Propellants, 1957-78, 85-92, 97; cons. in field. Mem. editorial bd. various polymers jours.; contbr. over 90 articles to profl. jours. and 2 books; patentee in field. Mem., officer YMCA Indian Guides, Altadena, Calif., 1960-74. With U.S. Army combat infantry, 1943-45, ETO. French Govt. fellow Sadron Inst., Strasbourg, 1972, Sr. Fulbright fellow U. Naples, Italy, 1971-72; recipient Exceptional Sci. Achievement award, NASA, 1976, Exceptional Svc. medal, 1989, Humboldt Sr. Rsch. Scientist award, 1990. Fellow Am. Phys. Soc. (exec. com. high polymer physics div.); mem. Soc. Rheology (v.p. 1983-85, pres. 1985-87), Am. Chem. Soc., Sigma Xi (sec.-treas. Caltech chpt. 1974-75, v.p. 1975-76, pres. 1976-77). Avocations: backpacking, camping, photography, hiking.

LANDEN, ROBERT GERAN, historian, university administrator; b. Boston, July 13, 1930; s. Harry James and Evelyn Gertrude (Geran) L.; m. Patricia Kizzia, July 19, 1958; children—Michael Geran, Robert Kizzia, Jill Arnett, Amy Patricia. A.B., Coll. of William and Mary, 1952; M.A., U. Mich., 1953; A.M., Princeton U., 1958, Ph.D. (Ford Found. fellow), 1961. Asst. prof. social sci. Ball State U., Muncie, Ind., 1959-60; asst. prof. near eastern studies U. Mich., Ann Arbor, 1960-61; asst. prof. history Dartmouth, Hanover, N.H., 1961-66; asst. dean of freshmen Dartmouth, 1963-64, asso. prof. history, 1966-67; prof., head dept. history Va. Poly. Inst. and State U., Blacksburg, 1967-69; prof. history U. S.C., Columbia, 1969-75; asso. vice provost U. S.C., 1971-72, asso. provost, 1972-73; dean U. S.C. (Coll. of Social and Behavioral Scis.), 1972-75; prof. history U. Tex. at Arlington, 1975-77; dean U. Tex. at Arlington (Coll. Liberal Arts), 1975-77; prof. history U. Tenn., Knoxville, 1977-86; dean Coll. Liberal Arts, 1977-85; prof. history, v.p. acad. affairs, provost U. Montevallo, 1986-88; prof. history and humanities, dir. programs in the humanities Va. Poly Inst. and State U., Blacksburg, 1988—. Author: Oman Since 1856, 1967, The Emergence of the Modern Middle East, 1970, (with Abid Al-Marayati) The Middle East, Its Governments and Politics, 1972; contbr. articles to profl. jours. and book revs. to hist. publs. Served with AUS, 1953-55. Am. Coun. Learned Socs. fellow, 1965-66, Comparative Studies Ctr. Faculty fellow, 1965-66, Malone fellow, 1988. Fellow Middle East Studies Assn. of N. Am.; mem. Theta Delta Chi, Phi Kappa Phi. Roman Catholic. Home: 108 Edgewood Ln Williamsburg VA 23185-3213 Office: Va Poly Inst Ctr for Interdisciplinary Studies Office of Dir Programs Humanities Lane Hall Blacksburg VA 24061

LANDER, DAVID ALLAN, lawyer; b. St. Louis, Oct. 2, 1944; s. Louis and Edna (Schramm) L.; m. Carole Weissman Aug. 12, 1965; children—Brad, Rachel. B.A. cum laude, Bowdoin Coll., 1966; J.D., U. Chgo, 1969. Bar: Mo. 1969, U.S. Dist. Ct. (ea. dist.) Mo. 1969, U.S. Ct. Appeals (8th cir.) 1970. Atty., exec. dir. Legal Aid Soc St. Louis City-County, 1975-80; asst. prof. law, St. Louis U., 1973-75, instr., 1980—; ptnr. Thompson and Mitchell, St. Louis, 1981—; lectr. numerous programs on secured lending, bus. bankruptcy and workouts. Exec. com. mem. Consumer Counseling Credit Service, St. Louis; dir. Legal Services Eastern Mo. Mem. ABA (chmn. com. on agrl. and agri-bus. fin.), Am. Coll. Bankruptcy, Am. Coll. Comml. Finance Attys., Am. Law Inst. (study com. on article 9 uniform comml. code), Mo. Bar Assn., Bar Assn. Met. St. Louis. Contbr. articles to profl. jours. Office: Thompson & Mitchell 1 Mercantile Ctr Ste 3300 Saint Louis MO 63101-1643

LANDER, HOWARD, entertainment newspaper publisher; b. N.Y.C., Oct. 25, 1950; s. Leo T. and Doris (Davis) L.; m. Gail Melanie Ravitz, Sept. 6, 1976; children: Aimee, Jared. BA, Rutgers U., Newark, 1972. Sportswriter Buffalo Courier-Express, 1973; reporter Amusement Bus., N.Y.C., 1973-76, sales rep., 1976-79; advt. mgr. Residential Interiors mag., N.Y.C., 1980; pub. Amusement Bus., Nashville, 1981-88; v.p., group pub. BPI Communications, 1988-90; pub. Billboard Mag., N.Y.C., 1990-91; sr. v.p. BPI Comms., 1991-92, exec. v.p., 1993—; pres. Billboard Music Group, 1994—. Mem. Country Music Assn., Internat. Assn. Auditorium Mgrs., Internat. Assn. Amusement Parks and Attractions, Assn. Bus. Pubs. Lodge: B'nai Brith. Avocations: raquetball, tennis, music.

LANDER, JAMES ALBERT, retired military officer, state senator; b. Abbeville, S.C., Apr. 9, 1930; s. William Jones and Annie (Cheatham) L.; m. Jolene Patricia Smith, June 8, 1952; children: Theresa, Britt, Leslie, Victoria (dec.), Gail, Jean, David. BS, Lander Coll., 1986. Technician S.C. Nat. Guard, Abbeville, 1952-53; life ins. salesman Gulf Life Pilot, Met., Anderson, S.C., 1953-66; maj. U.S. Army, 1966-71; plans and ops. officer, chief of staff S.C. Army N.G., Columbia, 1971-85, maj. gen. mil., 1988-91; mem. S.C. Senate, Columbia, 1993—. Chmn. RSVP Adv. Com., 1991—, Newberry County Literacy Assn., 1991-93; deacon Newberry 1st Bapt. Ch., 1981; past chmn. Boy Scouts Am., Newberry. Decorated Bronze Star,

Legion of Merit; recipient Order of Palmetto State of S.C., 1985, Palmetto Cross, 1991, Silver Beaver award Boy Scouts Am., 1990. Mem. Assn. U.S. Army, C. of C. Newberry, Exch. Club (pres.), Rotary, Masons. Democrat. Baptist. Avocations: reading, gardening. Home: 2029 Main St Newberry SC 29108-3521 Office: SC Senate 601 Gressette Bldg Columbia SC 29202

LANDER, JOYCE ANN, nursing educator, medical/surgical nurse; b. Benton Harbor, Mich., July 27, 1942; d. James E. and Anna Mae (Versaw) Remus. LPN, Kalamazoo Practical Nursing, Ctr., 1967; AAS, Kalamazoo Valley C.C., 1981, Grad. Massage Therapy Program, 1995. LPN-RN Bronson Meth. Hosp., Kalamazoo, 1972-82; RN med./surg. unit Borgess Med. Ctr., Kalamazoo, 1982-84; RN pediatrics Upjohn Home Health Care, Kalamazoo, 1984-88; supr. nursing lab Kalamazoo Valley Community Coll., 1982—; with Business Kneading Peace Therapeutic Massage, Kalamazoo, 1995—; nursing asst., instr. State of Mich. Observer, 1996—. Author: What Is A Nurse, 1980. Address: 3834 Greenleaf Cir Kalamazoo MI 49008-2509

LANDER, RUTH A., medical group and association administrator; b. Fitchburg, Mass., Dec. 13, 1948; d. H. Allison and Violet K. (Erickson) Linné; m. C. Stephen Lander, June 28, 1968; children: Timothy, Mary. BA, Ohio State U., 1978; postgrad., Kennedy-We. U., 1995—. Dir. fin. Luth. Svc. Assn. of New Eng., Natick, Mass., 1973-76; gen. mgr. Logos, Columbus, 1976-87; practice adminstr. Columbus Oncology Assocs., Inc., 1987—; sec., treas. Adminstrs. in Oncology Hematology Assembly, Englewood, Colo., 1994-95, legis. liaison, 1994-95, pres.-elect, 1995-96, pres., 1996-97. Editor: Adminstrs. in Oncology Hematology Assembly News, 1994-95; contbr. articles to profl. jours. Tchr. Vineyard Christian Fellowship, Westerville, Ohio, 1995—; grass roots legislative group Ohio Med. Group Mgmt. Assn., Columbus, 1994—. Fellow Med. Group Mgmt. Assn., Am. Coll. Med. Practice Execs.; mem. Am. Acad. Med. Adminstr., Leading Edge Alliance-Womenin Healthcare Leadership, Mid-Ohio Med. Group Mgmt. Assn. (pres. 1993-94, sec. 1992-93, program dir. 1991-92, exec. com. 1990-97), Assn. Cmty. Cancer Ctr., Ohio Med. Group Mgmt. Assn. (exec. com. 1994—, sec. 1995-96, pres.-elect 1996-97). Republican. Avocations: reading, computers, crafts, knitting, Bible study. Office: Columbus Oncology Assocs 500 Thomas Ln Ste 3A Columbus OH 43214-1419

LANDERS, ANDY, head coach women's basketball; b. Oct. 8, 1952; m. Pam McClellan; children: Andrea Lauren, Andrew Joseph. BS in Phys. Edn., Tenn. Tech., 1974, MS, 1975. Women's basketball coach Roane State Cmty. Coll., Harriman, Tenn., 1975-79, U. Ga., 1979—; head coach North Squad, U.S. Olympic Festival, 1991. Named Nat. Coach of Yr., 1986, 87, 96, SEC Coach of Yr., 1984, 91, 96. Office: U Ga PO Box 1472 Athens GA 30603-1472

LANDERS, ANN (MRS. ESTHER P. LEDERER), columnist; b. Sioux City, Iowa, July 4, 1918; d. Abraham B. and Rebecca (Rushall) Friedman; m. Jules W. Lederer, July 2, 1939 (div. 1975); 1 dau., Margo Lederer Howard. Student, Morningside Coll., 1936-39, LHD (hon.), 1964; hon. degree, Wilberforce (Ohio) Coll., 1972, Am. Coll. Greece, 1979, Meharry Med. Coll., 1981, Jacksonville U., 1983, St. Leo Coll., 1984, Fla. Internat. U., 1984, Med. Coll. Pa., 1985, New Eng. Coll., 1985, U. Wis., 1985, Lincoln Coll., 1986, Nat. Coll. Edn., 1986, Southwestern Adventist Coll., 1987, Duke U., 1987, Rosary Coll., 1989, U. Hartford, 1989, L.I. U., 1989, Med. Coll. Ohio, 1989, Roosevelt U., 1991, Ind. U., 1991, Howard U., 1991, Bellevue U., 1992, DePaul U., 1992, Ursinus Coll., 1992, Hillsdale Coll., 1993, St. Xavier U., 1993, Chgo. Theol. Sem., 1993, Barry U., 1993, Northwestern U., 1994, Columbia Coll., 1995. Syndicated columnist Chgo., 1955—; pres. Eppie Co., Inc., Chgo. Author: Since You Asked Me, 1962, Ann Landers Talks to Teen-agers about Sex, 1964, Truth is Stranger, 1968, Ann Landers Speaks Out, 1975, The Ann Landers Encyclopedia, 1978, Wake Up and Smell the Coffee, 1996; also pub. svc. booklets and numerous mag. articles; syndicated columnist Los Angeles Times-Creators Syndicates. Chmn. Eau Claire (Wis.) Gray-Lady Corps, ARC, 1947-53; chmn. Minn.-Wis. council Anti-Defamation League, 1945-49; asst. Wis. chmn. Nat. Found. Infantile Paralysis, 1951-53; hon. nat. chmn. 1963 Tb Christmas Seal Campaign; bd. sponsors Mayo Clinic, 1970; mem. sponsors com. Mayo Found.; nat. adv. bd. Dialogue for the Blind, 1972; adv. com. on better health services AMA; county chmn. Democratic Party Eau Claire; bd. dirs. Rehab. Inst. Chgo.; nat. bd. dirs. Am. Cancer Soc., Nat. Cancer Inst.; vis. com. bd. overseers Harvard Med. Sch.; mem. Pres.'s Commn. Drunk Driving; trustee Menninger Found., Nat. Dermatology Found., Am. Coll. Greece, Deree-Pierce Coll., Athens, Meharry Med. Sch., Hereditary Disease Found.; dirs. adv. bd. Yale Comprehensive Cancer Ctr. Recipient award Nat. Family Service Assn., 1965, Adolf Meyer award Assn. Mental Health N.Y., 1965, Pres.'s Citation and nat. award Nat. Council on Alcoholism, 1966, 2d nat. award, 1975, Golden Stethoscope award Ill. Med. Soc., 1967, Humanitarianism award Internat. Lions Club, 1967; plaque of honor Am. Friends of Hebrew U., 1968, Gold Plate award Acad. Achievement, 1969; Nat. Service award Am. Cancer Soc., 1971, Robert T. Morse award Am. Psychiat. Assn., 1972; plaque recognizing establishment of chair in chem. immunology Weizmann Inst., 1974, Jane Addams Public Service award Hull House, 1977, Health Achievement award Nat. Kidney Found., 1978, Nat. award Epilepsy Found. Am., 1978, James Ewing Layman's award Soc. Surg. Oncologists, 1979, citation for disting. service AMA, 1979, Thomas More medal Thomas More Assn., 1979, NEA award, 1979, Margaret Sanger award, 1979, Stanley G. Kay medal Am. Cancer Soc., 1983, 1st William C. Menninger medal for achievement in mental health, 1984, Albert Lasker pub. service award, 1985, Edwin C. Whitehead award, 1988, City of Medicine award for Disting. Achievement to Medicine, Duke U., 1988, Community Svc. award Gateway Found.'s Citizen's Coun., 1989, Pub. Svc. award NIMH, 1989, award for outstanding pub. edn. Nat. Alliance for the Mentally Ill, 1990, Oustanding Pub. Svc. to Sci. award Nat. Assn. for Biomed. Rsch., 1990, World of Children award UNICEF, 1993, Auxiliary Pub. Spirit award Am. Legion, 1995, Chgo. Journalism Hall of Fame, 1996, Ctrs. for Disease Control Champion of Prevention award, 1996. Fellow Chgo. Gynecol. Soc. (citizen hon.); mem. LWV (pres. 1948), Brandeis U. Women (pres. 1960), Chgo. Econs. Club (dir. 1975), Harvard Club (Award 1994), Sigma Delta Chi. Clubs: Chgo. Econs. (dir. 1975), Harvard, Sigma Delta Chi. Office: Chgo Tribune 435 N Michigan Ave Chicago IL 60611 *Trouble is the great equalizer. It doesn't make any difference who you are, or what you have, when you and your neighbor share the same problem you become brothers and sisters under the skin.*

LANDERS, JAMES MICHAEL (JIM LANDERS), news editor, bureau chief; b. San Francisco, Calif., Feb. 11, 1951; s. William Edward and Loretta Mae (Fouts) L.; m. Susan Ann Moran, Dec. 26, 1981; children: Amy Foster, Noelle Christine, Jessica Elizabeth. BA in English with honors, Va. Poly. Inst. and State U., 1974. Staff writer The Washington Post, 1971-74; freelance journalist Belfast, Northern Ireland, 1974; staff writer The Richmond (Va.) Mercury, 1975, The Trenton (N.J.) Times, 1975-77; features editor Arab News, Jeddah, Saudi Arabia, 1978-79; sr. editor Saudi Bus. & Arab Econ. Report, Jeddah, 1979-80; Washington corr. The Dallas Morning News, Washington, 1981-88; internat. editor The Dallas Morning News, Dallas, 1988-94, internat. affairs corr. Washington bur., 1994—, Washington news editor, dep. bur. chief. U.S. del. French-Am. Found., Taormina Young Leaders Conf., 1989. Named Outstanding Washington corr. Nat. Press Club, 1985, Finalist Pulitzer prize for Explanatory Journalism, N.Y.C., 1990; recipient World Hunger Media award World Hunger Yr., N.Y.C., 1990, Pulitzer prize for Internat. Reporting, 1994. Mem. Coun. Fgn. Rels., Am. Coun. on Germany, Dallas Com. Fgn. Rels. Roman Catholic. Avocations: running, camping, home renovation, model railroading. Home: 5208 Knoughton Way Centreville VA 22020-3336 Office: The Dallas Morning News 1325 G St NW Ste 250 Washington DC 20005-3104

LANDERS, RENÉE MARIE, lawyer; b. Springfield, Ill., July 25, 1955; d. Robert Edward and Marvel Margaret (Neal) L.; m. Thomas L. Barrette, Jr., Aug. 2, 1980; 1 child, Nelson Landers Barrette. AB, Harvard U.-Radcliffe Coll., 1977; JD, Boston Coll., 1985. Bar: Mass. 1985, U.S. Dist. Ct. Mass. 1986, U.S. Ct. Appeals (1st cir.) 1986, U.S. Supreme Ct. 1996. Program devel. specialist Office Mass. Sec. State, Boston, 1978-79, chief adminstrv. asst. to sec., 1979-80, dep. sec. state for pub. records, acting supr. pub. records, 1980, dep. sec. state Comml. Bur., 1980-82; law clk. to chief justice Mass. Supreme Jud. Ct., Boston, 1985-86; assoc. Ropes & Gray, Boston, 1986-88; asst. prof. law Boston Coll. Law Sch., Newton, Mass., 1988-93; dep. asst. atty. gen. Office of Policy Devel. U.S. Dept. Justice, 1993-96; dep. gen. counsel HHS, Washington, 1996—; mem., subcom. co-chmn. gender bias study Mass. Supreme Jud. Ct., 1986-89, mem. racial and ethnic bias study, 1990-94. Mem. editl. bd. Mass. Law Rev., 1987-93, Am. Jour. Law and Medicine, 1989-93. Mem. bd. overseers Harvard U., 1991-97, pres. 1996-97; mem. Watertown (Mass.) Dem. Town Com., 1981-93, vice chmn., 1986-93; trustee Radcliffe Coll., 1987-89; bd. dirs., v.p. Hist. Mass., Inc., 1989-91, Big Sister Assn. Greater Boston, 1990-93; bd. dirs. Mass. Eye and Ear Infirmary, 1993-96. Mem. Boston Bar Assn. (coun. 1988-91, chmn. com. on gender and justice 1989-93), Harvard U. Alumni Assn. (nominating com. for dirs. and overseers 1981-84, bd. dirs. 1990-92), Radcliffe Coll. Alumnae Assn. (pres. 1987-89, nominating com. 1983-84). Avocations: choral singing, jogging, tennis, reading. Office: HHS 200 Independence Ave SW Rm 707F Washington DC 20201-0004

LANDERS, STEVEN E., lawyer; b. N.Y.C., May 23, 1947. BA, Antioch Coll., 1969; JD, Harvard U., 1973. Gen. counsel N.Y. State Exec. adv. com. Sentencing, 1978-79; sec. N.Y. State adv. commn. Adminstrn. Justice, 1981-83; ptnr. Paul, Weiss, Rifkind, Wharton & Garrison, N.Y.C. and Paris. Mem. Internat. Bar Assn., Assn. Bar City N.Y., D.C. Bar, Am. C. of C. in France (chmn. pres.'s coun. 1995-97). Office: Paul Weiss et al, 62 rue d Faubourg St Honore, 75008 Paris France

LANDERS, TERESA PRICE, librarian; b. N.Y.C., Dec. 28, 1954; d. Stanley and June Ethel (Novick) Price; m. Gary David Landers, Sept. 2, 1979; children: Joshua Price, Alisha Rose. BA in History cum laude, Williams Coll., 1976; MA in LS, U. Denver, 1978; postgrad., Ctrl. Wash. U., 1980. Libr., asst. analyst Earl Combs, Inc., Mercer Island, Wash., 1979; reference libr. Yakima (Wash.) Valley Regional Libr., 1981-83, coord. youth svcs., 1983-84; libr. Tempe (Ariz.) Pub. Libr., 1984-85; supervisory libr. Mesa (Ariz.) Pub. Libr., 1985-90; head telephone reference Phoenix Pub. Libr., 1990-91, head bus. and scis., 1991-95; info. svcs. mgr., 1995—; cons. Fed. Dept. Corrections, Phoenix, 1993. Mem. Ariz. Right To Choose, Phoenix, 1992—. Mem. ALA, Ariz. Libr. Assn., Phoenix C. of C. (libr. rep. 1993—), Nat. Wildlife Fedn. (life), Beta Phi Mu. Democrat. Unitarian. Avocations: cooking, camping. Office: Phoenix Libr Info Svcs Dept 1221 N Central Ave Phoenix AZ 85004-1820

LANDERS, VERNETTE TROSPER, writer, educator, association executive; b. Lawton, Okla., May 3, 1912; d. Fred Gilbert and LaVerne Hamilton (Stevens) Trosper; m. Paul Albert Lum, Aug. 29, 1952 (dec. May 1955); 1 child, William Tappan; m. 2d, Newlin Landers, May 2, 1959 (dec. Apr. 1990); children: Lawrence, Marlin. AB with honors, UCLA, 1933, MA, 1935, EdD, 1953; Cultural doctorate (hon.) Lit. World U., Tucson, 1985. Tchr. secondary schs., Montebello, Calif., 1935-45, 48-50, 51-59; prof. Long Beach City Coll., 1946-47; asst. prof. Los Angeles State Coll., 1950; dean girls Twenty Nine Palms (Calif.) High Sch., 1960-65; dist. counselor Morongo (Calif.) Unified Sch. Dist., 1965-72, coordinator adult edn., 1965-67, guidance project dir., 1967; clk.-in-charge Landers (Calif.) Post Office, 1962-82; ret., 1982. V.p., sec. Landers Assn., 1965—; sec. Landers Vol. Fire Dept., 1972—; life mem. Hi-Desert Playhouse Guild, Hi-Desert Meml. Hosp. Guild; bd. friends Copper Mountain Coll., 1990-91; bd. dirs., sec. Desert Emergency Radio Service; mem. Rep. Senatorial Inner Circle, 1990-92, Regent Nat. Fedn. Rep. Women, 1990-92, Nat. Rep. Congl. Com., 1990-91, Presdl. Task Force, 1990-92; lifetime mem. Girl Scouts U.S., 1991. Recipient internat. diploma of honor for community service, 1973; Creativity award Internat. Personnel Research Assn., 1972, award Goat Mt. Grange No. 818, 1987; cert. of merit for disting. svc. to edn., 1973; Order of Rose, 1978, Order of Pearl, 1989, Alpha Xi Delta; poet laureate Center of Internat. Studies and Exchanges, 1981; diploma of merit in letters U. Arts, Parma, Italy, 1982; Golden Yr. Bruin UCLA, 1983; World Culture prize Nat. Ctr. for Studies and Research, Italian Acad., 1984; Golden Palm Diploma of Honor in poetry Leonardo Da Vinci Acad., 1984; Diploma of Merit and titular mem. internat. com. Internat. Ctr. Studies and Exchanges, Rome, 1984; Recognition award San Gorgonio council Girl Scouts U.S., 1984—; Cert. of appreciation Morongo Unified Sch. Dist., 1984, 89; plaque for contribution to postal service and community U.S. Postal Service, 1984; Biographee of Yr. award for outstanding achievement in the field of edn. and service to community Hist. Preservations of Am.; named Princess of Poetry of Internat. Ctr. Cultural Studies and Exchange, Italy, 1985; community dinner held in her honor for achievement and service to Community, 1984; Star of Contemporary Poetry Masters of Contemporary Poetry, Internat. Ctr. Cultural Studies and Exchanges, Italy, 1984; named to honor list of leaders of contemporary art and lit. and apptd. titular mem. of Internat. High Com. for World Culture & Arts Leonardo Da Vinci Acad., 1987; named to honor list Foremost Women 20th Century for Outstanding Contbn. to Rsch., IBC, 1987; Presdl. Order of Merit Pres. George Bush-Exec. Coun. of Nat. Rep. Senatorial Com., Congl. cert. of Appreciation U.S. Ho. of Reps.; other awards and certs. Life fellow Internat. Acad. Poets, World Lit. Acad.; mem. Am. Personnel and Guidance Assn., Internat. Platform Assn., Nat. Ret. Tchrs. Assn., Calif. and Nat. Assn. for Counseling and Devel., Am. Assn. for Counseling and Devel. (25 yr. membership pin 1991), Nat. Assn. Women Deans and Adminstrs., Montebello Bus. and Profl. Women's Club (pres.), Nat. League Am. Pen Women (sec. 1985-86), Leonardo Da Vinci Acad. Internat. Winged Glory diploma of honor in letters 1982), Landers Area C. of C. (sec. 1985-86, Presdl. award for outstanding service, Internat. Honors Cup 1992-93), Desert Nature Mus., Phi Beta Kappa, Pi Lambda Theta (Mortar Bd., Prytanean UCLA, UCLA Golden Yr. Bruin 1983), Sigma Delta Pi, Pi Delta Phi. Clubs: Whittier Toastmistress (Calif.) (pres. 1957); Homestead Valley Women's (Landers). Lodge: Soroptimists (sec. 29 Palms chpt. 1962, life mem. 1983, Soroptimist of Yr. local chpt. 1967, Woman of Distinction local chpt. 1987-88). Author: Impy, 1974, Talkie, 1975, Impy's Children, 1975; Nineteen O Four, 1976, Little Brown Bat, 1976; Slo-Go, 1977; Owls Who and Who Who, 1978; Sandy, The Coydog, 1979; The Kit Fox and the Walking Stick, 1980; contbr. articles to profl. jours., poems to anthologies. Guest of honor ground breaking ceremony Landers Elem. Sch., 1989, dedication ceremony, 1991. Home: 632 N Landers Ln PO Box 3839 Landers CA 92285

LANDES, GEORGE MILLER, biblical studies educator; b. Kansas City, Mo., Aug. 2, 1928; s. George Y. and Margaret B. (Fizzell) L.; m. Carol Marie Dee, Aug. 30, 1953; children: George Miller Jr., Margaret Dee, John Christopher. A.B., U. Mo., 1949; M.Div., McCormick Theol. Sem., 1952; Ph.D., Johns Hopkins U., 1956. Minister to youth Second Presbyn. Ch., Balt., 1952-53, Govans Presbyn. Ch., Balt., 1953-56; instr. Old Testament Union Theol. Sem., N.Y.C., 1956-58, asst. prof. Old Testament, 1958-62, assoc. prof., 1962-70, prof., 1970-95; prof. emeritus Union Theol. Sem, N.Y.C., 1995—; ann. prof. Am. Sch. Oriental Research, Jersusalem, Israel, 1967-68. Author: A Student's Vocabulary of Biblical Hebrew, 1961; editor, author: Report on Archaeological Work, 1975. Nettie F. McCormick fellow, 1952-54; Am. Council Learned Socs. fellow, 1967-68. Mem. Soc. Bibl. Lit., Amman Ctr. Archaeol. Rsch. (v.p. 1969-79), Am. Schs. Oriental Rsch. (sec. 1972-94), Phi Beta Kappa.

LANDES, WILLIAM M., law educator; b. 1939. AB, Columbia U., 1960, PhD in Econs., 1966. Asst. prof. econs. Stanford U., 1965-66; asst. prof. U. Chgo., 1966-69; asst. prof. Columbia U., 1969-72; assoc. prof. Grad. Ctr., CUNY, 1972-73; now prof. U. Chgo. Law Sch.; founder, chmn. Lexecon Inc.,1977—; mem. bd. examiners GRE in Econs., ETS, 1967-74. Mem. Am. Econ. Assn., Am. Law and Econ. Assn. (v.p. 1991-92, pres. 1992-93), Mont Pelerin Soc. Author: (with Richard Posner) The Economic Structure of Tort Law, 1987; editor: (with Gary Becker) Essays in the Economics of Crime and Punishment, 1974; editor Jour. Law and Econs., 1975-91, Jour. Legal Studies, 1991—. Office: U Chgo Sch Law 1111 E 60th St Chicago IL 60637-2702 also: Lexecon Inc 332 S Michigan Ave Chicago IL 60604-4301

LANDESMAN, FREDRIC ROCCO, theatre executive; b. St. Louis, July 20, 1947; s. Alfred and Paula (Berwald) L.; m. Heidi Prentice Ettinger, June 18, 1977; children: North, Nash, Dodge. BA, U. Wis., 1969; MFA, Yale U., 1972, DFA, 1976. Asst. prof. Sch. Drama, Yale U., New Haven, 1972-77; pres. Jujamcyn Theatres, N.Y.C., 1987—; bd. dirs. Municipal Arts Soc., 1989—; owner, mgr. The Cardinal Fund A Pvt. Hedge Fund, 1977-90; bd. dirs. Actor's Fund, N.Y.C., 1990—. Editor Yale/Theater mag., 1972-77; contbr. articles, revs. to profl. jours.; producer Broadway mus. Big River, Into the Woods, The Secret Garden. Bd. dirs. Ednl. Found. Am., Westport, Conn., 1980-87, Ettinger Found., N.Y.C., 1984—. Recipient Tony award Am. Theater Wing, 1985. Mem. League Am. Theaters and Producers (exec. bd. 1987—). Democrat. Jewish. Avocations: baseball, horse racing, country music, reading.

LANDESS, FRED S., lawyer; b. Memphis, Jan. 27, 1933; s. Sterling Stone and Beulah Elizabeth (Melton) L.; m. Catherine Sue Lee, Dec. 27, 1953; children—Susan Elinor, Charles Barton, Catherine Elizabeth. Student, Wake Forest Coll., 1951-53; A.B., George Washington U., 1955; LL.B., U. Va., 1958. Bar: Va. 1958. Enforcement atty. NLRB, Washington, 1958-60; assoc., then ptnr. McGuire, Woods, Battle & Boothe, Charlottesville, VA., 1960—. Sec. Bd. Zoning Appeals, City of Charlottesville, Va., 1967-69; bd. dirs. YMCA, Charlottesville, 1975, Westminister Child Care Ctr., Charlottesville, 1978. Fellow Am. Coll. Real Estate Lawyers; mem. Charlottesville-Albemarle Bar Assn. (pres. 1983-84), Va. Bar Assn. (real estate com.), Va. State Bar (7th dist. disciplinary com. 1986-88, sec. 1987, chmn. 1987-88), Charlottesville-Albemarle Bd. Realtors (assoc.), Blue Ridge Homebuilders Assn. (assoc.). Democrat. Presbyterian. Clubs: Boar's Head Sports (Charlottesville). Avocations: tennis, sailing, gardening. Home: 515 Wiley Dr Charlottesville VA 22903-4650

LANDESS, MIKE (MALCOLM LEE LANDESS, III), television news anchorman; b. Houston, June 20, 1946; s. Malcolm Lee Jr. Landess and Joyce Ardis (Halley) Quitter; children: Kristen and Jennifer. Grad., Robert E. Lee H.S., Tyler, Tex. Radio reporter WFAA-AM, Dallas, 1969-70; TV reporter WFAA-TV, Dallas, 70-72, KTRK-TV, Houston, 1972-73; noon anchor, reporter KYW-TV, Phila., 1973-74; NBC news anchor WKYC-TV, Cleve., 1974-77; news anchor KUSA-TV, Denver, 1977-93; Gannett anchor WXIA-TV, Atlanta, 1993—. anchor, reporter, producer: (TV documentary) Wednesday's Child, 1978, Fight of His Life, 1982; anchor, reporter (TV spl.) Say "NO" to Strangers, 1979. Bd. dirs. Am. Cancer Soc., Denver, 1982-86, Colo. Head Injury Assn., Denver, 1990-93, Brain Injury Assn Ga., Atlanta, 1994—. Recipient numerous Emmy awards: Outstanding Achievement Anchor, 1988, 91, Outstanding Achievement Children's Programming, 1983, TV Programming Excellence, 1995, Outstanding Achievement award Luth. Social Svcs., Am. Cancer Soc. Mem. NATAS, Radio & TV News Dir. Assn., Atlanta Press Club, Sigma Delta Chi. Baptist. Avocations: vintage guitars, motorsports. Office: WXIA-TV 1611 W Peachtree St NE Atlanta GA 30309-2641

LANDETA, SEAN, professional football player; b. Balt., Jan. 6, 1962. Student, Towson State U. With Phila. Stars, U.S. Football League, 1983-84, Balt. Stars, U.S. Football League, 1985, N.Y. Giants, NFL, 1985-93, L.A. Rams, NFL, 1993-94; punter St. Louis Rams, NFL, 1995—. Named to U.S. Football League All-Star Team, Sporting News, 1983-84, to NFL All-Pro Team, Sporting News, 1986, 89, 90, to NFL Pro Bown Team, 1986, 90; mem. N.Y. Giants Super Bowl Champion Team, 1986, 90. Office: St Louis Rams 1 Rams Way Earth City MO 63045-1523*

LANDGREBE, DAVID ALLEN, electrical engineer; b. Huntingburg, Ind., Apr. 12, 1934; s. Albert E. and Sarah A. L.; m. Margaret Ann Swank, June 7, 1959; children: James David, Carole Ann, Mary Jane. BSEE, Purdue U., 1956, MSEE, 1958, PhD, 1962. Mem. tech. staff Bell Telephone Labs., Murray Hill, N.J., 1956; electronics engr. Interstate Electronics Corp., Anaheim, Calif., 1958, 59, 62; mem. faculty Purdue U., West Lafayette, Ind., 1962—; dir. lab. for applications of remote sensing Purdue U., 1969-81, prof. elec. engring., 1970—, assoc. dean engring., 1981-84; acting head sch. elec. and computer engring. Purdue U., West Lafayette, 1995-96; rsch. scientist Douglas Aircraft Co., Newport Beach, Calif., 1964; dir. Univ. Space Rsch. Assn., 1975-78. Author: (with others) Remote Sensing: The Quantitative Approach, 1978. Recipient medal for exceptional sci. achievement NASA, 1973, William T. Pecora award NASA/U.S. Dept. Interior, 1990. Fellow IEEE (pres. Geosci. and Remote Sensing Soc. 1986-87, Sci. Achievement award 1992), Am. Soc. Photogrammetry and Remote Sensing; mem. Am. Soc. for Engring. Edn., Sigma Xi, Tau Beta Pi, Eta Kappa Nu. Office: Purdue U Dept Elec Engring West Lafayette IN 47907-1285

LANDGREBE, JOHN ALLAN, chemistry educator; b. San Francisco, May 6, 1937; s. Herbert Frederick and Janet Miller (Allan) L.; m. Carolyn Jean Thomson, Dec. 23, 1961; children—Carolyn Janet, John Frederick. B.S., U. Calif.-Berkeley, 1959; Ph.D., U. Ill., 1962. Asst. prof. U. Kans., Lawrence, 1962-67, assoc. prof., 1967-71, prof., 1971—, dept. chmn., 1970-80; vis. prof. U. Calif.-Berkeley, 1974. Author: Theory and Practice in the Organic Laboratory, 1973, 4th edit., 1993. NSF fellow, 1960-62; E. Watkins Faculty fellow U. Kans., 1963. Mem. Am. Chem. Soc., Royal Soc. of Chemistry, Phi Lambda Upsilon. Republican. Lutheran. Avocations: metal enameling; painting; camping; hiking. Home: 1125 Highland Dr Lawrence KS 66044-4523 Office: U Kansas Dept Chemistry Lawrence KS 66045

LANDGREN, CRAIG RANDALL, academic administrator; b. St. Paul, Dec. 20, 1947; s. C. Robert and Alice Elizabeth (Ryder) L.; m. Susan Carina Gatwood, July 23, 1983. BA summa cum laude, Albion Coll., 1969; MA in Biology, Harvard U., 1970, PhD, 1974. Asst. prof. George Mason U., Fairfax, Va., 1974-77; vis. asst. prof. U. Oreg., Eugene, 1976-77; asst. prof. Middlebury Coll., Vt., 1977-82, assoc. prof., 1982-89, prof., 1989—, chmn. dept. biology, 1982-88, 92, 93-96, dir. No. Studies program, 1984-87, chmn. natural scis. div., 1985-88; dir. SCIENS minority program, 1987-90, 92; dir. Reaccreditation Self-Study, 1989-90; dir. Freshman Seminar Program, 1990-91, 95-96, dir. Writing Program, 1992-93; dean instrnl. resources, 1995-96, dir. acad. facilities planning; rsch. assoc. U. Oreg., 1978, 79, 80; exch. scientist U.S. Nat. Acad. Scis. program, Moscow and Kiev, 1980, vis. rsch. prof. Hoeskolan, Kalmar, Kalmar, Sweden, 1997-98. Author: The Trees of the Middlebury College Campus, 1981; contbr. articles to profl. jours. Auditor Addison N.E. Union Supervisory Dist., 1988-91, Lincoln Hist. Soc., 1989-92, Danforth Assocs. New Eng., 1989-93; devel. com., The Coll. Bd. ATP Biology Ach. Test, 1990-95, chair, 1992-95. Albion fellow, 1969. Mem. Sigma Xi, Phi Beta Kappa (pres. Beta of Vt. 1985-87), Omicron Delta Kappa, Phi Eta Sigma, Beta Beta Beta (founder George Mason U. chpt. 1976). Avocations: painting, cooking, stained glass, woodworking. Home: 16 Springside Rd Middlebury VT 05753-1229 Office: Middlebury Coll Acad Facilities Planning Middlebury VT 05753-6151

LANDGREN, GEORGE LAWRENCE, electrical engineer, consultant; b. Duluth, Minn., July 22, 1919; s. Clarence Robert and Bertha Elizabeth (Borgeson) L.; m. Anna Jean Sinamark, July 26, 1943; children: Karen J., Nancy E., Larry A., David G. B.E.E., U. Minn., 1941; M.S.E.E., Northwestern U., 1955. Registered profl. engr., Ill. Elec. engr. Commonwealth Edison Co., Chgo., 1941-85. Served to capt. U.S. Army, 1942-46, PTO. Fellow IEEE (life, Best Paper 1973). Republican. Presbyterian.

LANDI, DALE MICHAEL, industrial engineer, academic administrator; b. Cleve., July 8, 1938; s. Lawrence Roy and Lillian (Caramell) L.; m. Mary Margaret Lipke, Mar. 23, 1974; children: Michael Kenneth, Kristin Marie. BS, Northwestern U., 1960, MS, 1963, PhD, 1965. Systems analyst Gen. Electric Corp., Chgo., 1960-61; research specialist Rand Corp., Santa Monica, Calif., 1965-68, assoc. dept. head, 1968-70, program dir., 1973-78, v.p., 1978-87; asst. budget dir. N.Y.C., 1970-71; asst. police commr. N.Y.C., 1971-73; v.p. SUNY, Buffalo, 1987—. Home: 238 Brantwood Rd Buffalo NY 14226-4306 Office: SUNY at Buffalo 516 Capen Blvd Buffalo NY 14226-2822

LANDING, BENJAMIN HARRISON, pathologist, educator; b. Buffalo, Sept. 11, 1920; s. Benjamin Harrison Sr. and Margaret Catherine (Crohen) L.; m. Dorothy Jean Hallas; children: Benjamin H., Susan L. Phillips, William M., David A. AB, Harvard U., 1942, MD, 1945. Diplomate Am. Bd. Pathology (anatomic pathology and pediatric pathology). Intern pathology Children's Hosp., Boston, 1945-46, asst. resident, then resident pathology, 1948-49; resident pathology Boston Lying-in Hosp., 1949, Free Hosp. for Women, Brookline, Mass., 1949; pathologist Children's Med. Ctr., Boston, 1950-53, Cin., 1953-61; pathologist-in-chief Children's Hosp., L.A., 1961-88, rsch. pathologist, 1988—; asst. pathologist Harvard U. Med. Sch., Boston, 1950-53; from asst. prof. to assoc. prof. U. Cin. Coll. Medicine, 1953-61; prof. pathology and pediatrics U. So. Calif. Sch. Medicine, L.A., 1961-91, prof. emeritus, 1991—. Author: Butterfly Color/Behavior Patterns, 1984; author chpts. in books; contbr. articles to profl. jours. Chmn. Pacific S.W. Dist. Unitarian-Universalist Assn., 1968-70; pres. Burbank (Calif.) Unitarian Fellowship, 1964-66. Capt. Med. Corps AUS, 1946-48. Mem. Soc. for Pediatric Pathology (pres. 1973-74), Internat. Pediatric Pathology Soc. (pres.

1980). Democrat. Unitarian-Universalist. Home: 4513 Deanwood Dr Woodland Hills CA 91364-5622 Office: Childrens Hosp LA Box 103 4650 W Sunset Blvd Los Angeles CA 90027-6062

LANDINI, RICHARD GEORGE, university president, emeritus English educator; b. Pitts., June 4, 1929; s. George R. and Alice (Hoy) L.; m. Phyllis Lesnick, Nov. 26, 1952 (dec. Mar. 1992); children: Richard, Gregory, Matthew, Cynthia, Vincent; m. Barbara Lee Shockley, Oct. 5, 1997. A.B., U. Miami, 1954, M.A., 1956; Ph.D., U. Fla., 1959; D.Civil Law, Quincy Coll., 1985; LLD, U. Miami, 1980, Baiko Jo Gakuin Coll., Japan, 1987, Ind. State U., 1996. From asst. prof. to prof. English Ariz. State U., 1959-70, dean, 1968-70; prof. English, acad. v.p. U. Mont., 1970-75; pres. Ind. State U., 1975-92, prof. English, 1975—. Contbr. articles on lit. and higher edn. to profl. jours. Served with U.S. Army, 1948-51. Decorated knight of the Holy Sepulchre Jerusalem, 1996. Mem. Phi Beta Kappa, Phi Delta Kappa, Phi Alpha Theta, Phi Kappa Phi, Sigma Tau Delta. Roman Catholic. Office: Ind State Univ Dept English Root Hall # A-288 Terre Haute IN 47809

LANDIS, DAVID MORRISON, state legislator; b. Lincoln, Nebr., June 10, 1948; m. Melodee Ann McPherson, June 6, 1969; children: Matthew, Melissa. BA U. Nebr., 1970, JD, 1971, M in Cmty. Regional Planning, 1995, MPA U. Nebr., Omaha, 1984. Bar: Nebr. 1972; practice law, Lincoln, 1972-74; mem. Nebr. Legislature, 1978—, chmn. govt. mil. and vets. affairs com., 1983-87, chmn. banking, commerce and ins., 1988—; instr. Coll. Law U. Nebr., 1990—; adj. faculty mem. dept. pub. adminstrn. U. Nebr., Omaha, 1984, adj. faculty mem. NE Wesleyan U., 1995—; adj. mem. bus. faculty Doane Coll., 1985-95. Named Doane Coll. Tchr. of Yr., 1987, 88, 92. Bd. dirs. Lower Platte S. Natural Resources Dist., 1971-78; officer PTA, 1979-80; adminstrv. law judge Dept. Labor, 1977-78; mem. Nebr. Humanities Council; mem. NE Repertory Theatre. Mem. The Innocents Soc. (hon.), Golden Key Soc. (hon., U. Nebr.). Office: Nebr State Legislature Rm 1116 State Capitol Lincoln NE 68509

LANDIS, DONNA MARIE, nursing administrator, women's health nurse; b. Lebanon, Pa., Sept. 5, 1944; d. James O.A. and Helen Joan (Fritz) Muench; m. David J. Landis, 1967 (div. 1985); children: Danielle M. Landis Farley, David J., Derek J.; m. John C. Broderick, 1990 (div. 1995). Diploma, St. Joseph's Hosp. Sch. Nursing, Reading, Pa., 1965. RN, Md.; cert. densitometry technologist. Head nurse med.-surg. unit Hosp. of U. Pa., 1965-67; nurse various hosps. and physician's offices, Md., Pa., 1965-85; clin. dir., clin. rsch. study coord., dual energy xray absorptiometry technologist Osteoporosis Diagnostic and Monitoring Ctr., Laurel, Md., 1985-95, owner, 1995—; clin. dir., clin. rsch. study coord. Osteoporosis Assessment Ctr., Wheaton, Md., 1985-95; clin. dir./owner Women's Health Rsch. Ctr., Laurel, Md., 1996—; cons. on osteoporosis and DEXA, Merck Pharm., 1995—; mem. Md. State Task Force on Osteoporosis, 1996—. With Task Force Com. on Osteoporosis State of Maryland. Mem. Balt. Bone Club, Washington Met. Bone Club (steering com. 1996—), Soc. Clin. Densitometry (steering com. 1993-96, assoc. editor SCAN 1994—, sci. adv. bd. 1996—, certification & credentialing com. technologists & physicians 1995—), Nat. Osteoporosis Found., Sandoz Women's Speakers Bur., Allied Health Profls./Arthritis Found., St. Joseph's Hosp. Alumni Assn. Office: 14201 Laurel Park Dr Ste 104 Laurel MD 20707-5203

LANDIS, EDGAR DAVID, services business company executive; b. Myerstown, Pa., Jan. 7, 1932; s. Edgar Michael and Anna Irene (Dubble) L.; m. Patrecia Ann Leininger, June 13, 1953; children—Susan Pauline, Jean Ann. B.S., Lebanon Valley Coll., 1953; M.B.A., U. Pa., 1957. C.P.A. Acct., audit supr. Peat, Marwick, Mitchell & Co., Phila., 1957-64; corp. controller, div. exec. v.p. Carlisle Corp., Pa., 1964-73; v.p., sr. v.p., now exec. v.p. CDI Corp., Phila., 1973—, also dir.; dir. affiliates in U.S. and Europe. Bd. dirs. Carlisle Sch. Dist., 1967-71, Carlisle City Airport, 1968-71, YMCA, Ardmore, Pa., 1981-87, chmn., 1984-86, YMCA, Phila., 1988—, vice chmn. 1991—. With U.S. Army, 1954-56, Japan. Mem. Lebanon Valley Coll. Alumni Assocs. (regional chmn. 1977-82). Republican. Methodist. Home: 222 Church Rd Ardmore PA 19003-3302 Office: CDI Corp 1717 Arch St Philadelphia PA 19103-2713

LANDIS, ELWOOD WINTON, retired newspaper editor; b. Wichita, Kans., June 14, 1928; s. Jacob Harrison and Christina (Fry) L.; m. Nancy Gauss, Nov. 22, 1961; children: Frederic, Laura. B.A., Friends U., Wichita, 1950; M.S. in Journalism, Northwestern U., 1953. Reporter Wichita Eagle, 1953; copy editor Omaha World-Herald, 1955-57; publicity dir. Bethany (Kans.) Coll., 1957-61; publs. dir. tchr. edn. project Central Mich. U., 1961-64; mng. editor Voice newspaper, Mich. Edn. Assn., East Lansing, Mich., 1965-93. Mem. Williamston (Mich.) City Planning Commn., 1972-75; bd. dirs. Lansing Ballet Assn., 1980-81. Served with AUS, 1953-55. Recipient awards Edn. Press Assn. Am. Mem. Sigma Delta Chi. Democrat. Home: 308 S Circle Dr Williamston MI 48895-1014

LANDIS, FRED, mechanical engineering educator; b. Munich, Mar. 21, 1923; came to U.S., 1947, naturalized, 1954; s. Julius and Elsie (Schulhoff) L.; m. Billie H. Schiff, Aug. 26, 1951 (dec. Jan. 10, 1985); children—John David, Deborah Ellen, Mark Edward. B.Eng., McGill U., 1945; S.M., MIT, 1949, Sc.D., 1950. Design engr. Canadian Vickers, Ltd., Montreal, Can., 1945-47; asst. prof. mech. engring. Stanford U., 1950-52; research engr. Northrop Aircraft, Inc., Hawthorne, Calif., 1952-53; asst. prof. NYU, 1953-56, assoc. prof., 1956-61, prof., 1961-73, chmn. dept. mech. engring., 1963-73; dean, prof. mech. engring. Poly. U., Bklyn., 1973-74; dean Coll. Engring. and Applied Sci., U. Wis., Milw., 1974-83, prof. mech. engring., 1984-94; emeritus prof. U. Wis., Milw., 1994—; staff cons. Pratt & Whitney Aircraft Co., 1957-88. Cons. editor, Macmillan Co., 1960-68; cons. editorial bd.: Funk & Wagnalls Ency., 1969—, Compton's Ency., 1984—; contbr. numerous rsch. articles to profl. jours. and encys., including Ency. Britannica. Mem. Dobbs Ferry (N.Y.) Bd. Edn., 1965-71, v.p. 1966-67, 70-71, pres., 1967-68; bd. dirs. Westchester County Sch. Bds. Assn., 1969-70, v.p., 1970, pres., 1970-71; bd. dirs. Engring. Found., 1986-94. Fellow AIAA (assoc.), ASME (hon. mem., divsn. sec. com. 1965-73, policy bd. 1973-89, v.p. 1985-89, 92-95, bd. govs. 1989-91), Am. Soc. Engring. Edn.; mem. Sigma Tau, Tau Beta Pi, Pi Tau Sigma. Home: 2420 W Acacia Rd Milwaukee WI 53209-3306

LANDIS, GEOFFREY ALAN, physicist, writer; b. Detroit, May 28, 1955; s. John Lloyd and Patricia (Sheridan) L. BS and BEE, MIT, 1980; MS, MEE, PhD, Brown U., 1988. Staff scientist Spire Corp., Bedford, Mass., 1977-82; rsch. assoc. Solar Energy Rsch. Inst., Golden, Colo., 1986-87, NASA Lewis Rsch. Ctr., Cleve., 1988-90; physicist Sverdup Tech., Brook Park, Ohio, 1990-93; sr. engr. NYMA, Inc., Brook Park, 1994-95; adj. prof. Ohio Aerospace Inst., Brook Park, 1990-92; sr. rsch. assoc. Ohio Aerospace Inst., 1995—; trustee Nat. Assn. Rocketry, Pa., 1978-81; mem. U.S. team Spacemodeling World Championships, Jambol, Bulgaria, 1978; tech. chmn. Vision 21 Conf., Cleve., 1990, 93. Editor: (procs.) Vision 21: Space Travel for the Next Millenium, 1991, Vision 21: Interdisciplinary Science and Engineering, 1993; author: (short story collection) Author's Choice Monthly, 1991 (Hugo award for best sci.-fiction short story 1992); author over 50 pub. sci.-fiction short stories; contbr. over 150 articles to profl. jours. Mem. Am. Phys. Soc., Sic. Fiction Writers Am. (Nebula award 1990), Artemis Soc. Achievements include 4 patents; participation with MIT human-powered flight team for Chrysalis and Monarch aircraft; membership in Mars Pathfinder science team; research in semiconductor physics, solar energy and astronautics. Office: NASA Lewis Rsch Ctr 302-1 21000 Brookpark Rd Cleveland OH 44135-3127

LANDIS, JAMES DAVID, publishing company executive, retired, author; b. Springfield, Mass., June 30, 1942; s. Edward and Eve (Saltman) L.; m. Patricia Lawrence Straus, Aug. 15, 1964 (div.); children: Sara Cass; m. Denise Evelyn Tillar, July 20, 1983; children: Jacob Dean, Benjamin Nicholas. B.A. magna cum laude, Yale Coll., 1964. Asst. editor Abelard Schuman, N.Y.C., 1966-67; editor-sr. editor William Morrow & Co., N.Y.C., 1967-80, editorial dir., sr. v.p., pub. Quill trade paperbacks, 1980-85; sr. v.p. William Morrow & Co., 1985-91, pub., editor-in-chief, 1988-91; pub., editor-in-chief Beech Tree Books, 1985-87. Author: The Sisters Impossible, 1979, Daddy's Girl, 1984, Love's Detective, 1984, Joey and the Girls, 1987, The Band Never Dances, 1989, Looks Aren't Everything, 1990, Lying in Bed, 1995. Recipient Roger Klein award for editing, 1973, Advocate Humanitarian award, 1977, Morton Dauwen Zabel award for fiction Am. Acad. Arts and Letters, 1996. Mem. Phi Beta Kappa.

LANDIS, JOHN DAVID, film director, writer; b. Chgo., Aug. 3, 1950; s. Marshall David and Shirley (Magaziner) L.; m. Deborah Nadoolman, July 27, 1980; 2 children. Mem. crew MGM film Kelly's Heroes; stuntman, writer-dir. Schlock, 1971, An American Werewolf in London, 1981; dir. Kentucky Fried Movie, 1977, National Lampoon's Animal House, 1978, Trading Places, 1983, Into the Night, 1985, Spies Like Us, 1985, Three Amigos, 1986, Coming to America, 1988, Oscar, 1991, Innocent Blood, 1992, Michael Jackson's Black or White, 1992, Beverly Hills Cop III, 1994, The Stupids, 1995; co-writer, dir. The Blues Brothers, 1980, Michael Jackson's Thriller; writer, dir., producer The Twilight Zone, 1983; frequent dir., exec. prodr. TV series Dream On, 1991— (ACE awards); exec. prodr. (TV series) Weird Science, 1994—, Sliders, 1995—, Campus Cops, 1995. Decorated chevalier dans L'Ordre des Arts et des Lettres (France), 1985; recipient numerous awards including NAACP Image awards, W.C. Handy award, People's Choice awards, internat. film festival awards. Mem. Writers Guild Am., Dirs. Guild Am., Screen Actors Guild, Acad. Motion Picture Arts and Scis. Office: William Morris Agy 151 S El Camino Dr Beverly Hills CA 90212-2704*

LANDIS, JOHN WILLIAM, engineering and construction executive, government advisor; b. Kutztown, Pa., Oct. 10, 1917; s. Edwin Charles and Estella Juliabelle (Barto) L.; m. Muriel Trayes Souders, July 5, 1941; children: Maureen Lucille, Marcia Millicent. BS in Engring. Physics summa cum laude, Lafayette Coll., Easton, Pa., 1939, ScD (hon.), 1960. Registered profl. engr., Calif. Research engr. Eastman Kodak Co., Rochester, N.Y., 1939-43; cons. Navy Dept., Washington, 1946-50; head sci. and engring. dept. Ednl. Testing Service, Princeton, N.J., 1948-50; reactor engr. AEC, Washington, 1950-53; dir. customer relations atomic energy div. Babcock & Wilcox Co., N.Y.C., 1953-55; asst. mgr. atomic energy div. Babcock & Wilcox Co., Lynchburg, Va., 1955-62, mgr. atomic energy div., 1962-65; gen. mgr. Washington ops. Babcock & Wilcox Co., 1965-68; regional v.p. Gulf Gen. Atomic Co., Washington, 1968-69; group v.p. Gulf Gen. Atomic Co., LaJolla, Calif., 1969-70, pres., dir. subs., 1970-74; pres. Power Systems Co., Gen. Atomic Partnership, LaJolla, Calif., 1974-75; sr. v.p., dir., pres. subs. Stone & Webster Engring. Corp., Boston, 1975-92, pvt. cons., 1992—; founding dir. Cen. Fidelity Banks, Inc., Richmond, Va.; founding gov. Nat. Materials Property Data Network, Inc., Phila.; chmn. adv. com. isotopes and radiation devel. and four other adv. coms. AEC, Washington, 1957-70; chmn. coms., co. rep. Atomic Indsl. Forum (now U.S. Nuclear Energy Inst.), Washington, 1953—; mem. N.Y. State Adv. Com. on Atomic Energy, 1956-59, Va. State Adv. Com. on Nuclear Energy, 1959-68; vice chmn. mgmt. com. Nat. Environ. Studies Project, Washington, 1974-89; dir., v.p., pres., chmn. bds. and coms., trustee Internat. Fund, Am. Nat. Standards Inst., N.Y.C., 1957—; vice chmn. ISO-9000 Registration Com.; dir., chmn. Fusion Power Assocs., Gaithersburg, Md., 1981—; chmn. U.S. Fusion Industry Coun., Internat. Thermonuclear Exptl. Reactor Industry Coun., 1994—; chmn. com. on energy-related atmospheric pollution World Energy Conf., London, 1984-90, N.Am. coord. global energy study, 1989-93; dir., chmn. com. on protection of environ. U.S. Energy Assn., Washington, 1981—; mem. fusion adv. panel U.S. Ho. Reps., Washington, 1979-87; charter mem. magnetic fusion adv. com. U.S. Dept. Energy, Washington, 1982-84, chmn. internat. rsch. and devel. panel, chmn. civilian nuclear power panel, vice chmn., chmn. energy rsch. advisory bd., 1984-90; mem. adv. bd. Sec. of Energy, 1990-93, fusion energy adv. com., 1994—; advisor Carnegie-Mellon U., Pitts., 1971-73, Pa. State U., State College, 1980-83, U. Calif. San Diego, 1974-82; vis. and sustaining fellow MIT, Cambridge, 1971-90; chmn. bus. adminstrn. adv. bd. U. San Diego, 1972-75; chmn. engnring. adv. com. Lafayette Coll., 1988—. Co-author: six books; contbr. articles to profl. and trade jours. Trustee, chmn. Randolph-Macon Woman's Coll., Lynchburg, Va., 1963—; trustee Lafayette Coll., Easton, Pa., 1962—, Va. Poly. Inst. and State U., Blacksburg, 1966-70; bd. dirs. Va. Poly. Inst. Ednl. Found., Blacksburg, 1968—; mem. U. Calif. Pres.'s Coun. on the Nat. Labs., 1993—; chmn. MIT Reactor Com., 1995—; mem. Sr. Rev. Group, Amarillo Nat. Resource Ctr. for Plutonium, 1994—; mem. Va. Adv. Bd. on Indsl. Devel. and Planning, Richmond, 1962-72; bd. dirs. Va. Engring. Found., Charlottesville, 1962-65; trustee Seven Hills Sch., Lynchburg, Va., 1960-65; dir. Harvard U. Ctr. for Blood Rsch., 1992—; mem. Mayor's Com. on Energy, San Diego, 1973-75; chmn., mem. six coms. Nat. Rsch. Coun., 1976—. Served to lt. USN, 1943-46, ETO. Decorated Letter of Commendation, two battle stars; recipient Gen. of Industry award State of Okla., 1971, George Washington Kidd award, Joseph E. Bell award Lafayette Coll., Lehigh Valley Favorite Son award State of Pa., 1976, Dwight D. Eisenhower Award of Honor, 1990, Winston Churchill Medal of Wisdom, 1988, Disting. Career award Fusion Power Assocs., 1991, Howard Coonley medal Am. Nat. Standards Inst., 1991, Exceptional Pub. Svc. award U.S. Dept. Energy, 1992, Henry DeWolf Smyth Nuclear States award Am. Nuclear Soc. and Nuclear Energy Inst., 1996; named Hon. Citizen City of Dallas, 1973, Alumni fellow Lafayette Coll., 1984; elected to Soc. d'Honneur Lafayette Coll., 1989; elected to Wisdom Hall of Fame, 1987. Fellow Am. Nuclear Soc. (pres. 1971-72, v.p. 1970-71, treas. 1964-68, chmn. coms. 1956—, bd. dirs. 1956-74), ASME; mem. NAE, Am. Soc. Macro-Engring. (pres. 1985-88, chancellor 1988—, charter bd. dirs. 1983—), Internat. Assn. Macro-Engring. Socs. (founding dir. 1987—, treas. 1989—), San Diego Hall Sci. (life), Phi Beta Kappa, Sigma Xi, Tau Beta Pi, Pi Delta Epsilon, Omicron Delta Kappa. Avocations: photography, landscaping, book-collecting, hiking. Home: 4 Whispering Ln Weston MA 02193-1157

LANDIS, LARRY SEABROOK, marketing and communications consultant; b. Princeton, N.J., Nov. 2, 1945; s. Donald Edward and Caroline Ann (Magalhaes) L.; m. Carol Louise Butz, Sept. 28, 1974; 1 child, Christopher Seabrook. AB cum laude, Wabash Coll., 1967; postgrad., U. N.C., 1967-68, Ind. U., 1969-70. Asst. to mayor Richard G. Lugar (now U.S. Senator, R-Ind.), Indpls., 1969-71; press sec. to Otis R. Bowen (Rep. candidate for gov., Ind.) Indpls., 1972; dir. mktg. svcs. Garrison, Jasper Rose & Co., Indpls., 1972-76; v.p. mktg. and media services Hickman & assoc., Indpls., 1976-80; v.p. corp. advt. Am. Fletcher Nat. Bank (Bank One Indpls., N.A.), Indpls., 1980-84; dir. communications PALLM, Inc., Indpls., 1984-85; v.p., dir. account planning Handley & Miller, Inc., Indpls., 1985-91; pres. Marketrends, Inc., 1991—; lectr. polit. sci. Ind. U./Purdue U., Indpls., 1969-71; bd. dirs. Event Techs., Inc., 1994-96. Co-author: How To, 1974; contbr. articles to profl. jours. Active gov.-elect Ad Hoc Com. on Ednl. Fin., Indpls., 1972-73, campaign mgr. Salin for Congress Com., Ft. Wayne, Ind., 1971-72; mem. exec. com. statewide Rep. legis. campaign Victory '90, Ind., 1989-90; mem. mktg. com. United Way Ctrl. Ind., 1992-93; mem. mktg. adv. com. Indpls. Symphony Orch., 1992—; bd. dirs. USCO Adult Edn. Program, Indpls., 1975-82, pres., 1980-82, Citizens Environ. Coun., Inc., Zionsville, Ind., 1984-86, v.p., 1986-96; rsch. dir. Ruckelshaus for U.S. Senate, 1968; mem. exec. com. Blankenbaker for Congress, 1995-96. With U.S. Army, 1968-69. Mem. Am. Mktg. Assn., Acad. Health Svcs. Mktg., Bank Mktg. Assn., Indpls. C. of C., Indpls. Advt. Club, Ind. Hist. Soc. (life, trustee 1995—, exec. com. 1996—), Indpls. Press Club, Columbia Club, Econ. Club, Indsl. Computing Soc. (founding), Ind. Software Assn., Nature Conservancy, English-Speaking Union, Pi Delta Epsilon, Delta Sigma Rho/Tau Kappa Alpha, Phi Kappa Psi. Republican. Methodist. Avocations: photography, woodworking, gardening. Home: 1126 W 77th St South Dr Indianapolis IN 46260 Office: Marketrends Inc Circle Tower Bldg 55 Monument Circle Ste 522 Indianapolis IN 46204-5911

LANDIS, LINDA KAY, music educator; b. Keyser, W. Va., May 2, 1950; d. Donald Avis L. and Uldene May Mongold Duke. BS, West Chester State U., 1972, MM in Voice, 1976. Registered music educator; cert. profl. II. Music educator Phoenixville (Pa.) Area Middle Sch., 1972—; soprano soloist St. John's Lutheran Ch., Phoenixville, Pa., 1972—. Composer: As The Daisy Fields Grow, 1984, God's Rainbow, 1985, Wedding Song, 1995. Sunday sch. tchr. St. John's Luth. Ch., Phoenixville, Pa., 1966—, mem. Christian edn. com., 1983-93, Stephen ministry leader mem., 1990—, mem. ch. coun., 1985-93. Mem. NEA, Pa. State Edn. Assn., Phoenixville Area Edn. Assn., Music Educators Nat. Conf., Pa. Music Edn. Assn., Bus. and Profl. Women (past dist. dir., Dist. Ten Woman of Yr. 1996-97), Acad. Boosters Club, Order Eastern Star (past matron), Delta Kappa Gamma. Lutheran. Avocation: Christian clowning, travel, counted cross-stitch, photography. Home: 514 W Pothouse Rd Phoenixville PA 19460-2242 Office: Phoenixvill Area Middle Sch 1330 S Main St Phoenixville PA 19460-4452

LANDIS, WAYNE G., environmental toxicologist; b. Washington, Jan. 20, 1952; s. James G. and Harriet E. L.; m. Linda S.; children: Margaret Evelyn, Eva Armstrong. BA in Biology, Wake Forest U., 1974; MA in Biology, Ind. U., 1978, PhD in Zoology, 1979. Document mgr. Franklin Rsch. Ctr., Silver Spring, Md., 1979-81; rsch. biologist U.S. Army Chem. Rsch., Devel. & Engring. Ctr., Aberdeen Proving Ground, Md., 1982-89; dir., prof. Inst. Environ. Toxicology & Chemistry, Western Wash. U., Bellingham, 1989—. Contbr. numerous articles to profl. jours. Recipient Hankins scholarship Wake Forest U., 1972-74, U.S. Army Rsch. and Devel. Achievement award, 1984, Spl. Act award, 1985, Exceptional Performance award, 1986; named to Outstanding ILIR Rsch. Program, 1983, 84. Mem. AAAS, ASTM, Soc. Environ. Toxicology and Chemistry (Pacific NW chpt.), Genetics Soc. Am., Sigma Xi. Achievements include evaluation of aquatic toxicology of smoke, riot control materials and binary system compounds; devel. theory to predict response of biol. communities to chem. insults using resource competition models, of new methods for ecosystem anal. and applications of chaos theory to chem. impacts. Office: Western Wash U Huxley Coll Dept Environ Toxicology 516 High St Bellingham WA 98225-5946

LANDO, JEROME BURTON, macromolecular science educator; b. Bklyn., May 23, 1932; s. Irving and Ruth (Schwartz) L.; m. Geula Ahroni, Dec. 2, 1962; children: Jeffrey, Daniel, Avital. A.B., Cornell U., 1953; Ph.D., Poly. Inst. Bklyn., 1963. Chemist Camille Dreyfus Lab., Research Triangle Inst., Durham, N.C., 1963-65; asst. prof. macromolecular sci. Case Western U., Cleve., 1965-68, assoc. prof., 1968-74, prof., 1974—; chmn. dept. Case Western, Cleve., 1978-85; dir. Macro-Epic (acad.-indsl. research program), 1985—; Erna and Jakob Michael vis. prof. Weizmann Inst. Sci., Rehovot, Israel, 1987; Lady Davis vis. prof. Technion, Haifa, Israel, 1992-93. Author: (with S. Maron) Fundamentals of Physical Chemistry, 1974; editorial adv. bd. Jour. Molecular Electronics, Polymers for Advanced Technologies, Jour. Materials Chemistry. Served to lt. U.S. Army, 1953-55. Named Alexander Von Humboldt Sr. Am. Scientist U. Mainz (Fed. Republic Germany), 1974, disting. alumnus Poly. U., 1990; recipient rsch. award Soc. Plastics Engrs., 1994. Fellow Am. Phys. Soc.; mem. Am. Chem. Soc., Am. Crustallographic Assn., Soc. Plastics Engrs., Sigma Xi. Jewish. Home: 21925 Byron Rd Cleveland OH 44122-2942 Office: Case Western Res U Dept Macromolecular Sci Kent Hale Smith Bldg 321 Cleveland OH 44106

LANDOLT, ARLO UDELL, astronomer, educator; b. Highland, Ill., Sept. 29, 1935; s. Arlo Melvin and Vesta (Kraus) L.; m. Eunice Jean Casper, June 8, 1966; 1 child, Jennifer; stepchildren: Lynda, Barbara, Vicky, Debra. B.A., Miami U., Oxford, Ohio, 1955; M.A., Ind. U., 1960, Ph.D., 1963. Mem. 1st wintering-over party Internat. Geophys. Year, Amundson-Scott South Pole Sta., Antarctica, 1957; asst. prof. physics and astronomy La. State U., 1962-65, asso. prof., 1965-68, prof., 1968—, dir. La. State U. Obs., 1970-88, acting chmn. dept. physics and astronomy, summers 1972-73, pres. faculty senate, 1979-80; program dir. astronomy sect. NSF, 1975-76; mem. governing bd. Am. Inst. of Physics, 1985-91, 95—; guest investigator Kitt Peak Nat. Obs., Tucson, Cerro Tololo Inter-Am. Obs.,Las Campanas Observatory, La Serena, Chile, Dyer Obs., Vanderbilt U., Goethe Link Obs., Ind. U. Rsch. grantee NSF, 1964, 66, 69, 71, 73, 75, 92-97, NASA, 1965, 92, Rsch. Corp., 1964, Air Force Office Sci., 1977-87, Space Telescope Sci. Inst., 1985-90, 92. Fellow AAAS (sec. Sect. D 1970-78); mem. AAUP, Am. Astron. Soc. (sec. 1980-89, 95—), Internat. Astron. Union (sec. U.S. nat. com. 1980-89, 96—), Royal Astron. Soc. (Eng.), Astron. Soc. Pacific, Am. Polar Soc., Am. Philatelic Soc., Sigma Xi, Pi Mu Epsilon. Office: La State U Dept Physics And Astro Baton Rouge LA 70803-4001

LANDOLT, ROBERT GEORGE, chemistry educator; b. Houston, Apr. 4, 1939; s. Robert Garland and Mary Ella (Campbell) L.; m. Margaret Ann Brown, June 8, 1962; children: Laura, Lisa, Robert. BA, Austin Coll., Sherman, Tex., 1961; PhD, U. Tex., 1965. Rsch. assoc. U. Ill., Urbana, 1965-67; asst. prof., assoc. prof. Muskingum Coll., New Concord, Ohio, 1967-80; sr. scientist Radian Corp., Austin, Tex., 1980-81; assoc. prof. chemistry Tex. Weslayan U., Ft. Worth, 1981-89, prof., 1989—; resident cons. Battelle Meml. Lab., Columbus, Ohio, 1974-75; cons. Naval Rsch. Lab., Washington, 1982-83; dir. rsch. div. Tex. Higher Edn. Coord. Bd., 1991. Contbr. articles on chemical informatics and organic chemistry to profl. jours. Mem. AAAS, AAUP, Am. Chem. Soc. (Congl. fellow 1986-87), Sigma Xi. Office: Tex Weleyan U 1201 Wesleyan St Fort Worth TX 76105-1536

LANDON, FORREST MALCOLM, retired newspaper executive; b. Pontiac, Mich., Sept. 24, 1933; s. DeWitt Dale Landon and Eleanor (Stevens) Landon Smith; m. Barbara Jean Patrick, Sept. 25, 1955; children—Jeffrey William, Tracy Alice. B in Journalism, U. Mo., 1955. Reporter Sta. WDBJ-AM-FM-TV, Roanoke, VA., 1955-59; news dir. Sta. WDBJ-AM-FM, Roanoke, VA., 1959-64; assoc. editorials editor Roanoke Times, VA., 1964-67, from editl. page editor to exec. editor, v.p., 1967-95; exec. dir. Va. Coalition for Open Govt., 1995—; host weekly program pub. TV, Roanoke, 1968-79; tchr. journalism Hollins Coll., Va., 1970-74. Pres. Roanoke Valley Council Community Services, 1973-74, Roanoke Valley Indsl. Mgmt. Council, 1961. Named to Va. Comm. Hall of Fame, 1997. Mem. Soc. Profl. Journalists (pres. Blue Ridge chpt. 1977-78, award 1988), Va. Press Assn. (pres. 1993-94, award 1974), Va. AP Newspapers (pres. 1989-90), Va. AP Broadcasters (award 1958, 60), Am. Soc. Newspaper Editors (FOI com. chmn. 1995-96), Torch Club (pres. Roanoke 1984-85). Unitarian. Home: 1603 Deyerle Rd SW Roanoke VA 24018-1313 Office: Roanoke Times PO Box 2491 201-209 W Campbell Ave Roanoke VA 24010-2491

LANDON, JAMES HENRY, lawyer; b. Atlanta, Ga., Oct. 24, 1945; s. Ralph Henry and Gertrude Leola (Rew) L. BA, Vanderbilt U., Nashville, Tenn., 1967; JD, Harvard U., Cambridge, Mass., 1970. Bar: Ga. 1971, U.S. Dist. Ct. (no. dist.) Ga. 1971, U.S. Ct. Claims 1972, U.S. Supreme Ct. 1976, U.S. Tax Ct. 1980. Assoc. Hansell & Post, Atlanta, Ga., 1971-76, ptnr., 1976-89; ptnr. Jones, Day, Reavis & Pogue, Atlanta, Ga., 1989—; Adj. prof. Emory Law School, Atlanta, Ga., 1983-84; dir. TRC Staffing Serv., Inc., Atlanta, Ga., 1987—; mem. steering com. So. Pension Conf., Atlanta, Ga., 1985-88. Co-author: Transportation Politics in Atlanta, 1970; contbr. article to profl. jour. Gen. counsel Woodruff Arts Ctr., Inc., 1993—; trustee Atlanta Symphony Orchestra, 1981-87, 89-92, The Hambidge Ctr., 1994—, Atlanta Med. Heritage, Inc., 1993—, pres. 1996-97; trustee Atlanta Hist. Soc., 1983—, Ctr. for Puppetry Arts, Inc., 1995—; mem. cmty. adv. bd. Jr. League of Atlanta, 1987-90. Mem. ABA, Ga. Bar Assoc., Atlanta Bar Assoc., Explorers Club of N.Y.C., Phi Beta Kappa. Presbyterian. Avocations: mountain climbing, hiking. Home: 1327 Peachtree St NE Apt 503 Atlanta GA 30309-3254 Office: Jones Day Reavis & Pogue 3500 One Peachtree Ctr 303 Peachtree St NE Atlanta GA 30308-3201

LANDON, JOHN CAMPBELL, medical research company executive; b. Hornell, N.Y., Jan. 3, 1937; s. Earl Shephard and Eleanor (Crane) L.; m. Nancy Ann Bachenheimer, Aug. 24, 1958; children: David Bacheheimer, Martha Susan, Katherine Ellen, Peter Crane. BA in Biology, Alfred (N.Y.) U., 1959; MS in Biology, George Washington U., Washington, 1962, PhD in Biology, 1967. Biologist Nat. Cancer Inst., NIH, Bethesda, Md., 1960-65; from virologist to dir. Litton Bionetics, Kensington, Md., 1965-75; pres., dir. EG&G Mason Rsch. Inst., Worcester, Mass., 1975-82; pres., CEO Bioqual, Inc., Rockville, Md., 1982—; founder, v.p., co-owner Brewster (Mass.) Book Store, Inc., Brewster, Mass, 1982—; pres., CEO Sema, Inc., Rockville, 1986-91; pres., CEO Diagnon Corp., Rockville, 1986—, also chmn. bd. dirs.; founder, pres., CEO Enhanced Therapeutics, Inc., Rockville, Md., 1994—; cons. EG&G, Worcester, Mass., 1982-85; reviewer ad-hoc com. NIH, Bethesda, Md., 1981—; exec. com., bd. dirs., v.p. bd. Nat. Assn. Life Sci. Industries, 1975-81; nat. coun. arts and scis. George Washington U., 1996—. Contbr. articles to profl. jours. Bd. dirs. Peirce Warwick Adoption Svc., Washington, 1970-79 (pres. 1972-75), Venture Expeditionary (pres. 1981-83), Washington, 1979-83; mem. credit com. Potomac Community Fed. Credit Union, 1982-85. Mem. AAAS, Am. Soc. Cell Biology, Am. Soc. Microbiology, N.Y. Acad. Scis., Sigma Xi. Office: Diagnon Corp 9600 Medical Center Dr Rockville MD 20850-3336 Office: Brewster Bookstore 2648 Main St Brewster MA 02631-1958

LANDON, JOHN WILLIAM, minister, social worker, educator; b. Marlette, Mich., Mar. 24, 1937; s. Norman A. and Merle Irene (Lawrason) L. BA, Taylor U., 1959; MDiv, Northwestern U., Christian Theol. Sem., 1962; MSW, Ind. U., 1966; PhD in Social Sci., Ball State U., 1972. Regional supr. Iowa Dept. Social Welfare, Des Moines, 1965-67; acting chmn. dept. sociology Marion (Ind.) Coll., 1967-69; asst. prof. sociology and social work Ball State U., Muncie, Ind., 1969-71; asst. prof. social work, coord. base courses Coll. Social Work U. Ky., Lexington, 1971-73, assoc. prof., coord. Undergrad. Program in Social Work Coll. of Social Work, 1974-85, prof., assoc. dean, 1985—; dir. social work edn. Taylor U., Upland, Ind., 1973-74. Author: From These Men, 1966; Jesse Crawford, Poet of the Organ, Wizard of the Mighty Wurlitzer, 1974; Behold the Mighty Wurlitzer, The History of the Theatre Pipe Organ, 1983; The Development of Social Welfare, 1986. Mem. AAUP, Coun. on Social Work Edn., Nat. Assn. Social Workers, Am. Guild Organists. Home: 809 Celia Ln Lexington KY 40504-2305 Office: U Ky Coll Social Work Lexington KY 40506-0027

LANDON, MICHAEL DE LAVAL, historian, educator; b. St. John, N.B., Can., Oct. 8, 1935; came to U.S., 1960; s. Arthur Henry Whittington and Elizabeth Worthington (Fair) L.; m. Doris Lee Clay, Dec. 31, 1959 (div. May 1980); children: Clay de Laval, Letitia Elizabeth; m. Carole Marie Prather, Feb. 28, 1981. BA, Oxford (Eng.) U., 1958, MA, 1961; MA, U. Wis., 1962, PhD, 1966. Asst. master Manor House Sch., Horsham, Eng., 1957, Dalhousie Sch., Ladybank, Scotland, 1958, Lakefield (Ont.) Coll. Sch., 1958-60; asst. prof. history U. Miss., Oxford, 1964-67, assoc. prof., 1967-72, prof., 1972—, acting dir. librs., 1986-87, acting chair modern langs., 1996—. Author: The Triumph of the Lawyers, 1970, The Honor and Dignity of the Profession, 1979, Erin and Britannia, 1980, The Challenge of Service, 1995. Commr. City Housing Authority, Oxford, 1983—, chmn., 1993—; lay Eucharistic minister Episcopal Ch. Am. Philos. Soc. Rsch. grantee, 1967, 74. Fellow Royal Hist. Soc. (U.K.); mem. Am. Soc. for Legal History (sec.-treas. 1988—), Phi Kappa Phi, Sigma Phi, Phi Alpha Theta. Episcopalian. Avocation: bird feeding. Home: 219 Bramlett Blvd Oxford MS 38655-3415 Office: Univ of Miss Dept of History University MS 38677

LANDON, ROBERT GRAY, retired manufacturing company executive; b. Portsmouth, Ohio, Dec. 22, 1928; s. Herman Robert and Hazel Ruth (Tener) L.; m. Sarah A. Newpher, July 2, 1954; children: Geoffrey, Suzanne. Student, Cornell U., 1947-49; BA in Econs., U. Pa., 1955; grad. advanced mgmt. program, Harvard Sch. Bus., 1978. Loan officer Nat. City Bank, Cleve., 1955-60; SEC adminstr. Smith Kline Corp., 1960-64; controller, treas. Grumman Allied Industries, Inc., Garden City, N.Y., 1964-76; v.p. Grumman Allied Industries, Inc., 1977-82; v.p. investment mgmt. Grumman Corp., Bethpage, N.Y., 1978-79; pres. Grumman Ohio Corp., Worthington, Ohio, 1979-88. Served with AC USN, 1949-53. Mem. The Oaks Club.

LANDON, ROBERT KIRKWOOD, insurance company executive; b. N.Y.C., Apr. 27, 1929; s. Kirk A. and Edith (Ungar) L.; m. Beulah Pair, Mar. 19, 1965; children: Chris, Kathleen Landon Staley, Kellyann Landon Spears. Student, U. Va., 1946-48; B.S., Ga. Inst. Tech., 1950. With Am. Bankers Life Assurance Co., Miami, Fla., 1952—; pres. Am. Bankers Life Assurance Co., 1960-74, chmn., chief exec. officer, 1974—; chmn. bd., CEO Am. Bankers Ins. Group Inc., Miami, 1980-95, chmn. bd., 1980—; pres. Landon Corp., Dover, Del., 1971—; charter mem. advisory bd. Fla. Internat. U., 1972-74. Trustee Kirk A. and Dorothy P. Landon Found., 1969—, Barry U. Served to lt. (j.g.) USNR, 1950-53. Mem. Coun. Internat. Visitors, World Bus. Coun., Scabbard and Blade, Grove Isle Club, Phi Gamma Delta. Republican. Congregationalist. Home: 2 Casuarina Concourse Coral Gables FL 33143-6502 Office: Am Bankers Ins Group Inc 11222 Quail Roost Dr Miami FL 33157-6543

LANDON, SUSAN MELINDA, petroleum geologist; b. Mattoon, Ill., July 2, 1950; d. Albert Leroy and Nancy (Wallace) L.; m. Richard D. Dietz, Jan. 24, 1993. BA, Knox Coll., 1972; MA, SUNY, Binghamton, 1975. Cert. profl. geologist; cert. petroleum geologist. Petroleum geologist Amoco Prodn. Co., Denver, 1974-87; mgr. exploration tng. Amoco, Houston, 1987-89; ind. petroleum geologist Denver, 1990—; instr. petroleum geology & exploration Bur. of Land Mgmt., U.S. Forest Svc., Nat. Park Svc., 1978-86. Editor: Interior Rift Basins, 1993. Mem., chmn. Colo. Geol. Survey Adv. Com., Denver, 1991-93; mem. Bd. on Earth Sci. and Resources-NRC, 1992—. Recipient Disting. Alumni award Knox Coll., 1986, Disting. Svc. award Rocky Mountain Assn. Geologists, 1986. Mem. Am. Assn. Petroleum Geologists (treas., Disting. Svc. award 1995), Am. Inst. Profl. Geologists (pres. Martin Van Couvering award 1991). Achievements include frontier exploration for hydrocarbons in U.S., especially in Midcontinent Rift System. Home: 790 Ballantine Rd Golden CO 80401-9503 Office: Thomasson Ptnr Assocs 1100 Stout St Ste 1400 Denver CO 80204-2070

LANDOW-ESSER, JANINE MARISE, lawyer; b. Omaha, Sept. 23, 1951; d. Erwin Landow and Beatrice (Hart) Appel; m. Jeffrey L. Esser, June 2, 1974; children: Erica, Caroline. BA, U. Wis., 1973; JD with honors, George Washington U., 1976. Bar: Va. 1976, D.C. 1977, Ill. 1985. Lawyer U.S. Dept. Energy, Washington, 1976-83, Bell, Boyd & Lloyd, Chgo., 1985-86, Seyfarth, Shaw, Fairweather & Geraldson, Chgo., 1986-88, Holleb & Coff, Chgo., 1988—; chmn. Environ. Safety and Health Practice Group, 1988—, mem. exec. com., 1994—. Contbr. articles to profl. jours. Bd. dirs. Bernard Zell Anshe Emet Day Sch. Parent-Tchr. Orgn., 1991-95. Mem. ABA, Chgo. Bar Assn. (vice chmn. environ. law com. 1990-91, chmn. 1991-92), Am. Jewish Congress Commn. on Women's Equality (bd. dirs. 1995—). Office: Holleb & Coff 55 E Monroe St Ste 4100 Chicago IL 60603-5803

LANDRIAULT, JACQUES EMILE, retired bishop; b. Alfred, Ont., Can., Sept. 23, 1921; s. Amedee and Marie-Louise (Brisebois) L. BPh, U. Ottawa; Licence in Theology, St. Paul U. Sem., Ottawa. Ordained priest Roman Cath. Ch., 1947; curate in Noranda Que.; chancellor Diocese Timmins, Ont., 1953; bishop of Cadi, titular bishop of Alexandria Ont., 1962-64, bishop of Hearst, 1964-71; adminstr. bishop of Hearst, 1971-74, bishop of Timmins, 1971-90, bishop emeritus, 1990—; mem. Can. Conf. Cath. Bishops Commn.: Liturgy, Mission; mem. Ont. Episcopal Com. on Cath. Edn.; v.p. Ont. Cath. Episcopal Conf.; mem. Cath. Conf. Ont. Address: John Paul II Residence, 1243 Kilborn Pl Apt 206, Ottawa, ON Canada K1H 6K9

LANDRIEU, MARY L., senator; b. Nov. 23, 1955; m. E. Frank Snellings. BA, La. State U., 1977. Real estate agt., La. state rep. from dist. 90, 1979-89, La. state treas., 1987-95, U.S. Senator from Louisiana, 1997—; del., Dem. Nat. Conv., 1980. Mem. LWV, Women Execs. in State Govt., Fedn. Dem. Women, Delta Gamma. Roman Catholic. Office: 825 Hart Senate Off Bldg Washington DC 20510-1802

LANDRIGAN, PHILIP JOHN, epidemiologist; b. Boston, June 14, 1942; s. John Joseph and Frances Joan (Conlin) L.; m. Mary Florence Magee, Aug. 27, 1966; children: Mary Frances, Christopher Paul, Elizabeth Marie. A.B., Boston Coll., 1963; M.D., Harvard U., 1967; M.S., London Sch. Hygiene and Tropical Medicine, 1977, D.I.H., 1977. Diplomate Am. Bd. Pediatrics, Am. Bd. Preventive Medicine, Am. Bd. Occupational Medicine, Am. Coll. Epidemiology. Intern Cleve. Met. Gen. Hosp., 1967-68; resident in pediatrics Children's Hosp. Med. Ctr., Boston, 1968-70; fellow in pediatrics Harvard U. Med. Sch., Boston, 1969-70; clin. instr. pediatrics Emory U. Sch. Medicine, Atlanta, 1970-71; epidemic intelligence service officer Ctrs. for Disease Control, Atlanta, 1970-73, dir. research and devel. smallpox eradication program, 1973-74, chief environ. hazards activity, 1974-79; dir. div. Surveillance, Hazard Evaluations and Field Studies Nat. Inst. for Occupational Safety and Health, Cin., 1979-85; prof. community medicine and pediatrics Mt. Sinai Sch. Medicine, N.Y.C., 1985—; dir. div. environ. and occupational medicine Mt. Sinai Sch. Medicine, 1985-90; prof., chmn. dept. community medicine, 1990—; mem. bd. on toxicology and environ. health hazards Nat. Acad. Sci., Washington, vice chmn., 1981-86; clin. prof. environ. health Sch. Pub. Health U. Wash., Seattle, 1983—. Contbr. numerous articles on pediatrics, pub. health, epidemiology, occupational medicine and environ. medicine to med. jours.; cons. editor: Archives of Environ. Health, 1982—, Am. Jour. Indsl. Medicine, 1979—; editor-in-chief Environ. Research, 1987—. Recipient Vol. award Dept. HEW, 1973; recipient Pub. Health Service Career Devel. award, 1975, group citation as mem. of Ctr. for Disease Control beryllium rev. panel, 1978, Meritorious Service medal USPHS, 1985. Fellow Royal Soc. Medicine; mem. Inst. of MedicineInternat. Commn. on Occupational Health, Am. Pub. Health Assn., Am. Epidemiol. Soc., Soc. for Epidemiologic Research, AAAS. Home: 915 Stuart Ave Mamaroneck NY 10543-4124 Office: Mt Sinai Sch Medicine Dept Community Medicine 1 Gustave L Levy Pl New York NY 10029-6504

LANDRON, MICHEL JOHN, lawyer; b. Santurce, P.R., June 15, 1946; s. Francis Xavier and Francisca (Carretero) Healy; m. Carol McQuade, Apr. 22, 1989; children, Michael Francis, Ryan McQuade. BA, Lehman Coll., 1968, postgrad., 1969-73; JD, Fordham U., 1977. Bar: N.Y. 1978, U.S. Dist. Ct. (so. dist.) N.Y. 1978, U.S. Dist. Ct. (ea. dist.) N.Y. 1978. asst. atty. gen. Office of Atty. Gen., N.Y. State Dept. Law, N.Y.C., 1978-80; enforcement atty. N.Y. Stock Exch., N.Y.C., 1980-81; pvt. practice, Bklyn., 1981-82, 84—; mem. Leaf, Duell, Drogin P.C., N.Y.C., 1982-84; gen. counsel Rockcom, Inc., 1985-87, adminstr. law judge City of N.Y., 1987; of counsel Berger and Paul, N.Y.C., 1984-85; assoc. area counsel Digital Equipment Corp., 1988-89; adj. instr. N.Y. Law Sch., Ramapo Coll.; arbitrator, mediator U.S. Dist. Ct. (ea. dist.) N.Y.; mediator U.S. Dist. Ct. (ea. dist.) N.Y.; guest lectr. Lehman Coll.; cons. in field; arbitrator Civil Ct. N.Y.C., No Fault Ins. Panel State of N.Y., Nat. Assn. Securities Dealers, Inc., Am. Arbitration Assn. Author: Conflicts of Law, 1992; (with others) Personal Injury: Actions, Defenses and Damages, 1992, Choice of Law; author chpts. to books; contbr. articles to profl. jours. Mem. Bklyn. Bar Assn. (past chmn. patents trademark and copyrights com., past chmn. arbitration com.), N.Y. State Bar Assn. (com. to cooperate with law revision commn.), Assn. Arbitrators City of N.Y., Am. Judges Assn., KC, Phi Alpha Delta (Disting. Svc. award 1977). Republican. Roman Catholic. Avocations: music, reading, sports. Office: 323 46th St Brooklyn NY 11220-1109

LANDRY, G. YVES, automotive company executive. Chmn., pres., CEO Chrysler Can. Ltd., Windsor, Ont., Can. Office: Chrysler Can Ltd, 2450 Chrysler Ctr, Windsor, ON Canada N8W 3X7

LANDRY, JAMES EDWARD, trade association administrator; b. Saratoga Springs, N.Y., Nov. 3, 1928; s. Philip Joseph and May Regina (Gorman) L.; m. Judith Ann Stone, Dec. 19, 1981; children: James Jr., Christopher, Jeffrey, Carla, John Gorman. BS, Union Coll., 1949; LLB, George Washington U., 1956; diploma internat. air and space law, McGill U., 1957. Bar: D.C. Air transport examiner, trial atty. Civil Aeronautics Bd., U.S.G., Washington, 1957-61; sr. atty. dir. internat. programs Air Transport Assn. of Am., Washington, 1961-66, v.p. internat., 1966-70, gen. counsel, 1970-78, sr. vp., gen. counsel, 1978-92, pres., 1992-95; aviation expert, cons., 1996—; guest lectr. McGill Inst., Georgetown U. Sch. of Law; bd. advisors McGill's Inst. of Air and Space Law; adv. coun. Concordia U./IATA Internat. Aviation MGA programme; bus. adv. com. to the Transp. Ctr., Northwestern U. Contbr. numerous articles to profl. jours. With U.S. Army, 1951-54. Mem. ABA, D.C. Bar Assn. Roman Catholic. Home and Office: 7305 Yates Ct Mc Lean VA 22101

LANDRY, JANE LORENZ, architect; b. San Antonio, Feb. 12, 1936; d. John Henry and Lulie Amanda (Sample) L.; m. Duane Eugene Landry, Sept. 8, 1956; children: Rachel, Claire, Ellyn, Jean. Student U. Tex., 1952-55, Yale U., 1955-56; BArch, U. Pa., 1957. Registered arch., Tex. Draftsman Wade, Gibson, & Martin, Corpus Christi, Tex., 1958-59; project arch. O'Neil Ford & Assoc., San Antonio, 1959-65; prin. Duane Landry, Arch., San Antonio, 1965-68, Dallas, 1968-76; ptnr. Landry & Landry, Archs. & Planners, Dallas, 1976—, Meyer, Landry & Landry, Archs. & Planners, Dallas, 1977-80; instr. San Antonio Coll., 1965. Dir. at large Interfaith Forum on Religion, Art and Architecture, 1991—; mem. Liturgical Commn. Diocese of Dallas, 1978-90. Recipient design awards Interfaith Forum on Religion, Art and Architecture, 1985, 89, 90. Fellow AIA (mem. hist. resources com., design awards Dallas chpt. 1970, 75, 76, 77, 80); mem. Tex. Soc. Architects (design award 1969, 81). Roman Catholic. Office: Landry & Landry Archs & Planners 6319 Meadow Rd Dallas TX 75230-5140

LANDRY, JOHN MARSDALE, university fundraiser, consultant; b. New London, Conn., July 2, 1962; s. Robert Normand and Elaine Ruth (Marsdale) L. BA in English Lit., Coll. of the Holy Cross, 1984; postgrad., Jesuit Novitiate of New Eng., 1984-85. Info. and referral coord. United Way of Mass. Bay, Boston, 1985-87; capital fundraising cons. Ketchum, Inc., Pitts., 1989-93; maj. gifts officer MIT, Cambridge, 1993-94, assoc. dir. resource devel., 1994—; bd. trustees Cheverus H.S., Portland, Maine, 1993—; co-chmn. devel. com. Boston Living Ctr., 1993-94; presenter Cath. Sch. Devel. Conf., Worcester, Mass., 1993, 94, Case Dist. Conf., 1996. Del. State of Maine Dem. Conv., Portland, 1988; fundraising capt. Human Rights Campaign Fund, Washington, 1993-95; mem. Fed. Adv. Network, Washington, 1994—. Mem. Nat. Soc. Fund-Raising Execs., Coun. for Advancement and Support of Edn., Cath. Sch. Devel. Assn., Planned Giving Group New Eng.. Roman Catholic. Avocations: music (guitar, piano), compose original liturgical and folk music. Office: MIT 292 Main St # E38 202 Cambridge MA 02142-1014

LANDRY, MARK EDWARD, podiatrist, researcher; b. Washington, May 24, 1950; s. John Edward and Daphne (Fay) L.; m. Mary Ann Kotey, Sept. 7, 1974; children: John Ryan, Christopher John, Jessica Marie. D in Podiatry, Ohio Coll. Podiatric Medicine, 1975; MS in Edn., U. Kans., 1982. Diplomate Am. Bd. Podiatric Surgery, Am. Bd. Podiatric Orthopedics and Primary Podiatric Medicine. Gen. practice podiatry Kansas City, Mo., 1977—, Overland Park, Kans., 1980—; clin. asst. prof. U. Health Scis., Kansas City, 1985—; clin. assoc. prof. Coll. Podiatric Medicine and Surgery U. Osteo. Medicine and Health Scis., Des Moines, 1985-92; clin. instr. Sch. Medicine U. Mo., Kansas City, 1987-95; founder, bd. dirs. Kansas City Podiatric Residency Program, Kansas City, 1982-91; adv. bd. Rockport Shoe Co.; chmn. podiatry dept. Park Lane Med. Ctr., Kansas City, Mo., 1995-97; dir. continuing edn. Kans. Podiatric Med. Assn., 1997—. Contbr. articles to profl. jours. Cons. Mid-Am. Track and Field Assn., Lenexa, Kans., 1978-88; com. chmn. Boy Scouts Am., Overland Park, Kans.; coach Johnson County Soccer League, 1987-90; head coach 6th and 7th grade girls' Cath. Youth Orgn. Basketball, 1995-96, 97; sponsor 8 & 11 Baseball League, 1987-90. 1st lt. USAF, 1975-77. Recipient Pres.'s award Ohio Sch. Podiatric Medicine, 1975; USAF scholar Armed Forces Health Professions, 1973-75. Fellow Am. Coll. Foot Surgeons, Acad. Podiatric Sports Medicine, Am. Coll. Primary Podiatric Medicine & Podiatric Orthopedics; mem. Mid-Am. Masters Field and Track Assn., Brit. Podiatry Assn. (hon.), Am. Bd. Primary Podiatric Medicine (founding dir., bd. examiner 1994—), Holy Cross Social Club (pres. 1983-84), Brookridge Country Club, Bally Club (Overland Park), Leukemia Assn. of Am. (team in tng. 1997, corp. challenge participant 1997), K.C. (4th degree 1995—). Republican. Roman Catholic. Avocations: swimming, running, weight tng. Home: 8120 W 99th St Shawnee Mission KS 66212-3444 Office: 10550 Quivira Rd Ste 260 Overland Park KS 66215-2303

LANDRY, MICHAEL GERARD, investment company executive; b. Ottawa, Ont., Can., July 20, 1946; came to U.S., 1982; s. Edmund Oscar and Clarice (St. Germain) L.; m. Barbara Trebbi, Dec. 15, 1996; children: Noel Michael, Adam Jonah. BA in Econ., Carleton U., 1969. V.p. MD Mgmt. Ltd., Ottawa, 1977-82; sr. v.p. Templeton Investment Counsel, Ft. Lauderdale, Fla., 1982-87; v.p. Templeton Galbraith Hansberger, Nassau, 1986-87; dir. Templeton Global Growth Fund Ltd., Australia, 1987; pres., CEO Mackenzie Investment Mgmt. Inc., Boca Raton, Fla., 1987—, The Mackenzie Group of Funds, Boca Raton, 1987—, The Ivy Funds, 1992—; mem. exec. com. Mackenzie Fin. Corp., Toronto, 1994—; bd. dirs. BMC Fund. Bd. dirs., chmn. fin. com. Children's Place/Connor's Nursery, 1993—. Mem. Internat. Soc. Fin. Analysts (former bd. dirs.), Assn. Can. Pension Mgmt. (bd. dirs. 1986-89), Fin. Analysts Fedn. Roman Catholic. Office: Mackenzie Investment Mgmt Inc 700 S Federal Hwy Ste 300 Boca Raton FL 33432-6139

LANDRY, PAUL LEONARD, lawyer; b. Mpls., Nov. 23, 1950; s. LeRoy Robert Landry and Alice Ruth (Swain) Stephens; m. Lisa Yvonne Yeo, Dec. 13, 1984; children: Marc, Lauren, Matthew. BA, Macalester Coll., 1974; postgrad., Georgetown U., 1976-77; JD, Boston U., 1977. Bar: Va. 1977, D.C. 1978, Minn. 1984, U.S. Dist. Ct. D.C., U.S. Dsit. Ct. Va., U.S. Dist. Ct. Minn., U.S. Ct. Appeals (D.C., 2d, 4th and 8th cirs.). Dancer Dance Theater Harlem, N.Y.C., 1970-72; prin. dancer Dance Theatre Boston, 1972-75; atty. EPA, Washington, 1976-77; assoc. Reed, Smith, Shaw & McClay, Washington, 1977-83; officer, shareholder Fredrikson & Byron, P.A., Mpls., 1984—; adj. prof. law William Mitchell Coll. Law, St. Paul, 1985-89. Bd. dirs. Ind. Sch. Dist. 284, Wayzata, Minn., 1989-96, chmn., 1992-93; bd. dirs. Walker Art Ctr., Mpls., 1992—; advisor Kevin McCary Scholarship Fund, Flyte Tyme Found. Mem. ABA (conf. of minority ptnrs. adv. com., chmn. governance com., comm. tech. in the workplace subcom.), Nat. Bar Assn., Minn. State Bar Assn., D.C. Bar, Hennepin Conty Bar Assn., Black Entertainment and Sports Lawyers Assn., Minn. Minority Lawyers Assn., Barristers. Avocations: golf, music, basketball. Office: Fredrikson & Byron PA 900 2nd Ave S Ste 1100 Minneapolis MN 55402-3328

LANDRY, ROGER, government official; b. St.-Etienne-des Grès, Que., Can., Mar. 19, 1939; s. Malcolm and Docia (DuPont) L.; m. France allard, Aug. 13, 1966; children: Marc, Peter. BA, U. Montreal, 1961, Licence in Pédagogia, 1968; Licence in Adminstrn., Laval U., 1972. Tchr. C.S.R.M., Shawinigan, Que., 1963-66; dir. C.S.V.M., Shawinigan, 1966-94; pres., dir.-gen. Regie de la Sécurite dans les Sports du Que., Trois-Rivières, Que., 1994—. Contbr. articles to newspapers. Gov. Baseball League, Mauricie, Que., 1976-80p; mayor City of St. Alexis, Que., 1986-88; pres. Scolary Dirs., Mauricie, 1992-94. Named Man of the Yr., St. Alexis, 1986. Mem. Richelieu Club (pres. 1994). Avocations: hunting, golf, reading. Office: RSSQ, 100 Laviolette, Trois-rivieres, PQ Canada G9A 5S9

LANDRY, ROGER D., publishing company executive; b. Montreal, Que., Jan. 26, 1934; s. Charle and Mabel (Desgroseillers) L.; m. Suzanne Shepherd; children—Johane, Charle, Genevieve. Student, Sir. George Williams U., Montreal, 1953, Institut des Sci. Politiques, Paris, 1956. Mgr. mktg. services Bell Can., Montreal, 1957-63; insp. Que. Provincial Police, Montreal, 1963-65; dep. dir. 1967 World Exhbn., Montreal, 1965-68, Air Can., 1968-70; pres. Beauregard, Landry, Nantel & Assocs., Montreal, 1970-75; sr. v.p., chief adminstrv. officer ITT Can., Port Cartier, 1975-77; v.p. mktg. and pub. affairs Montreal Baseball Club Ltd., 1977-80; pres., pub. La Presse Ltd., Montreal, 1980—; bd. dirs. Can. Press. Chmn. Opéra de Montreal. Named Mktg. Man of Yr., Major League Baseball, 1980. Mem. Que. Dailies Inc. (bd. dirs.), Can. Newspaper Assn. (bd. dirs.), Can. Pub. Relations Soc. (Médaille du President 1980, Médaille Edouard-Montpetit 1984), Order Can. (companion), Order Quebec (officer), Order Golden Lion, Sons of Italy, Grande Médaille de Vermeil de la Ville de Paris. Office: La Presse, 7 Rue St Jacques, Montreal, PQ Canada H2Y 1K9

LANDRY, RONALD JUDE, lawyer, state senator; b. Lutcher, La., May 30, 1943; s. Ambroise Harry and Althae (Clement) L.; BA La. State U., JD; children: Christopher Benton, Lauryn Elizabeth; m. Patricia M. Williams, 1997. Bar: La.; sole practice law, LaPlace, La., 1969—; mem. La. Senate, 1976—. Mem. St. John Assn. Retarded Citizens, La. Assn. Deaf, River Road Hist. Soc. Lodges: Kiwanis (River Region), Lions. Democrat. Roman Catholic. Address: PO Box 189 La Place LA 70069-0189

LANDRY, THOMAS HENRY, construction executive; b. Detroit, Nov. 2, 1946; s. Ernest E. and Charman A. (Iles) L.; m. Eileen K. Iannucci, June 22, 1968; children: Paul T., Christine M. BSBA, U. Dayton, 1968; MBA, Wayne State U., 1972. Project adminstr. A.J. Etkin Constrn. Co., Farmington Hills, Mich., 1971-79, exec. v.p., 1979-85, pres., chief oper. officer, 1985—; chmn. Fin., Design & Build, Inc., Birmingham, Mich., 1986—. Bd. dirs. Metro Detroit chpt. March of Dimes, 1992—, United Cerebral Palsy; mem. Leadership Oakland, Mich., 1989—, Leadership Mich., 1995. Mem. Assoc. Gen. Contractors Am. (bd. dirs. Detroit chpt. 1987—), Engring. Soc. Detroit (vice chmn. constrn. activities com. 1987—), Mich. Constrn. Users Coun., Lakeland Country Club. Roman Catholic. Office: AJ Etkin Constrn Co 30445 Northwestern Hwy Ste 250 Farmington Hills MI 48334

LANDRY, TOM (THOMAS WADE LANDRY), former professional football coach; b. Mission, Tex., Sept. 11, 1924; s. Ray and Ruth (Coffman) L.; m. Alicia Wiggs, Jan. 28, 1949; children—Thomas, Kitty, Lisa. BBA, U. Tex., 1949; BS in Indsl. Engring., U. Houston, 1952. Player N.Y. Yankees All-Am. Football Conf., 1949; player N.Y. Giants, 1950-53, player-coach, 1954-55, defensive coach, 1956-59; head coach Dallas Cowboys, 1960-89; now chmn., CEO Landry Investment Group. Author: (with Gregg Lewis) Tom Landry: An Autobiography, 1990. Trustee Nat. Fellowship Christian Athletes, chmn. bd. Dallas chpt. Served with USAAF, World War II. Named to All-Pro team, 1954, to Pro Football Hall of Fame, 1990; coached winning Super Bowl teams, 1971, 77. Methodist (bd. govs.). Office: Landry Investment Group Inc 8411 Preston Rd Ste 720-lb3 Dallas TX 75225-5523*

LANDSBERG, JERRY, management and investment consultant, optical laboratory executive; b. Dallas, June 30, 1933; s. Max and Rose (Hechtman) L.; grad. So. Meth. U., 1954; m. Gloria Zale, Sept. 2, 1956; children: Steven Jay, Jeffrey Paul, Karen Beth, Ruth Ellen. Salesman, Remington Rand div. Sperry Rand, 1955-57; salesman Zale Corp., 1957-59, asst. mgr., 1959-60, mgr., 1960-63, merchandiser, 1963-67; registered rep., security analyst Silberberg & Co., 1967-69; owner Jerry Landsberg & Assocs., 1969-72; v.p. Ross Watch Case Corp., gen. mgr. Kenfield Jewelry div., Long Island City, N.Y., 1971-75; pres., chief operating officer King Optical Corp., Dallas, 1974-75; chmn., chief exec. officer Richland Optical Labs. Inc., 1980-95; chief exec. officer The Richland Group, current; pres. Jerry Landsberg Assos., Great Neck, N.Y., 1975—; pres. N. Am. Vision Services, Inc., Freeport, N.Y., 1987—, chmn., chief exec. officer Tech-Optics Internat. Corp. Trustee, Village of Kensington, 1967-75, commr. police, 1967-69, commr. pub. works, 1969-75, dep. mayor, 1969-75, mayor, 1973; fin. v.p. Temple Emanuel, Great Neck, 1964-66, trustee, 1964-74; bd. dirs. Great Neck Symphony Soc., 1974—, pres., 1978-81, chmn. bd., 1981—; trustee North Shore Univ. Hosp., 1981—, Am. Friends of Haifa U., 1986-88; mem. adv. bd. Adelphi U. Sch. Nursing, 1981-86, chmn., 1986-93; trustee Parker Jewish Geriatric Inst., 1979—, treas., 1983-84; bd. dirs. Great Neck Community Fund, Sch. Opticianry Interboro Inst., chmn., 1990-92; v.p. Zale Found.; Great Neck chmn. Fedn. Jewish Philanthropies; active various community drives. Mem. So. Meth. U. Alumni Assn. (dir. nat. bd., pres. N.Y. club). Clubs: U.S. Power Squadron, Masons, Shriners. Office: 59 Hanse Ave Freeport NY 11520-4608

LANDSBERG, JILL WARREN, lawyer, consultant to government agencies; b. N.Y.C., Oct. 11, 1942; d. George Richard and Evelyn (Schepps) Warren; m. Lewis Landsberg, June 14, 1964; children: Alison, Judd Warren. BA, George Washington U., Washington, 1964; MAT, Yale U., 1965; JD, Boston Coll., 1976. Bar: Mass., 1977, Ill., 1991. Assoc., dir. (ptnr.) Widett, Slater & Goldman PC, Boston, 1976-90; pvt. practice Chgo., 1991-94; faculty Med. Sch. Ethics and Human Values Dept. Northwestern U., Chgo., 1991-94; exec. asst. spl. counsel for child welfare svcs. Office of the Gov., Chgo., 1994-95, acting spl. counsel for child welfare svcs., 1995-96; mem. Legis. Com. on Juvenile Justice, Chgo., 1995-96, Task Force on Violence Against Children, Chgo., 1995—, Citizens Com. on the Juvenile Ct., Chgo., 1995—. Tutor Ptnrs. in Edn., 4th Presbyn. Ch., Chgo., 1993—; mem. steering com. Ill. Ct. Improvement Program; adv. bd. Libr. Internat. Rels., Chgo., 1993-94. Mem. ABA, Chgo. Bar Assn., Women's Bar Assn., Ill. State Bar Assn., Abraham Lincoln Marovitz Inn of Ct., Phi Beta Kappa, Order of the Coif. Home: 70 E Cedar St Chicago IL 60611-1179 Office: 11 E Adams St Ste 1600 Chicago IL 60603-6304

LANDSBERG, MICHELE, journalist; b. Toronto, July 12, 1939; d. Jack and Naomi Leah Landsberg; m. Stephen Lewis, May 30, 1963; children: Ilana Naomi, Avram David, Jenny Leah. BA, U. Toronto, 1962. Reporter Globe & Mail, Toronto, 1962-65, columnist, 1985-89; freelancer, 1965-71; editor, feature writer Chatelaine, 1971-78; columnist The Toronto Star, 1978-84, 89—, Globe and Mail, Toronto, 1985-88. Author: Women & Children First, 1982, Reading for the Love of It, 1986, This is New York, Honey! A Homage to Manhattan in Love & Rage, 1989. Recipient Nat. Newspaper award (columns), 1980, (feature writing) 81; co-recipient Florence Bird award, 1997. Office: Toronto Star, 1 Yonge St, Toronto, ON Canada M5E 1E6

LANDWEHR, ARTHUR JOHN, minister; b. Northbrook, Ill., Mar. 8, 1934; s. Arthur John Sr. and Alice Eleanor (Borchardt) L.; m. Avonna Lee, Sept. 19, 1953; children: Arthur J. III, Andrea Lea Askow. BA, Drake U., 1956; BD, Garrett-Theol. Sem., 1959; DD (hon.), North Cen. Coll., 1980. Ordained to ministry Meth. Ch., 1959. Pastor Lyndon (Ill.) United Meth. Ch., 1956-59, Marseilles (Ill.) United Meth. Ch., 1959-65, Faith United Meth. Ch., Lisle, Ill., 1965-69; sr. minister First United Meth. Ch., Elmhurst, Ill., 1969-75, Evanston, Ill., 1975-88; sr. minister Grace United Meth. Ch., Naperville, Ill., 1988—; trustee Garrett-Evang. Theol. Sem., Evanston, 1976—, 1st v.p. bd. trustees, 1977-86; del. to gen. conf. United Meth. Ch., 1976, 80, 84, 88, World Meth. Conf., Nairobi, Kenya, 1986; Wilson lectr., 1987; preacher Adams Sermon Bloomington, Ind., 1991, N.Mex. Ann. Conf.,

1992, N.W. Tex. Conf., 1992, East Ohio Conf., 1997. Author: In the Third Place, 1972, Lessons on Pastoral Epistles, 1997; contbr. articles to profl. jours. Convenor Blue Ribbon Com. for Referendum on Expanded Gambling in Ill., 1994. Recipient citation for human rels. City of Lisle, 1969; study grantee World Coun. Chs., Sri Lanka, 1983, Ecumenical Inst. for Advanced Studies, Tantur, Israel, 1977. Mem. AAAS, Am. Acad. Religion, Am. Theol. Soc., Ill. Bar Assn. (interprofl. cooperation com. 1991-95), Order of St. Luke, Univ. Club (Evanston, Ill., pres. 1986-87). Home: 520 E Highland Naperville IL 60540-5423 Office: Grace United Meth Ch 300 E Gartner Rd Naperville IL 60540-7424 *It is evident to me that life is a gift surrounded in mystery. Like most mysteries, we wait for the moment of revelation in which there is a profound understanding. I've learned that without a radical lane life has no future.*

LANDY, BURTON AARON, lawyer; b. Chgo., Aug. 16, 1929; s. Louis J. and Clara (Ernstein) L.; m. Eleanor M. Simmel, Aug. 4, 1957; children: Michael Simmel, Alisa Anne. Student, Nat. U. Mex., 1948; B.S., Northwestern U., 1950; postgrad. scholar, U. Havana, 1951; J.D., U. Miami, 1952; postgrad. fellow, Inter-Am. Acad. Comparative Law, Havana, Cuba, 1955-56. Bar: Fla. 1952. Practice law in internat. field Miami, 1955—; ptnr. firm Ammerman & Landy, 1957-63, Paul, Landy, Beiley & Harper, P.A. and predecessor firm, 1964-94, Steel Hector & Davis, 1994—; lectr. Latin Am. bus. law U. Miami Sch. Law, 1972-75; also internat. law confs. in U.S. and abroad; mem. Nat. Conf. on Fgn. Aspects of U.S. Nat. Security, Washington, 1958; mem. organizing com. Miami regional conf. Com. for Internat. Econ. Growth, 1958; mem. U.S. Dept. Commerce Regional Export Expansion Council, 1969-74, mem. Dist. Export Council, 1978—; mem. U.S. Sec. State Adv. Com. on Pvt. Internat. Law; dir. Fla. Council Internat. Devel., 1977—, chmn. 1986-87; mem. U. Miami Citizens Bd., 1977—; chmn. Fla. del. S.E. U.S.-Japan Assn., 1980-82; mem. adv. com. 1st Miami Trade Fair of Ams., 1978; dir., v.p. Greater Miami Fgn. Trade Zone, Inc., 1978—; mem. organizing com., lectr. 4 Inter-Am. Aviation Law Confs.; bd. dirs. Inter-Am. Bar Legal Found.; participant Aquaculture Symposium Sci. and Man in the Ams., Mexico City, Fla. Gov's Econ. Mission to Japan and Hong Kong, 1978; mem. bd. exec. advisors Law and Econs. Ctr.; mem. vis. com. U. Miami Sch. Bus.; mem. internat. fin. council Office Comptroller of Fla.; founding chmn. Fla.-Korea Econ. Coop. Com., 1982—, Southeast U.S.-Korea Econ. Com., 1985—; chmn. Expo 500 Fla.-Columbus Soc., 1985-87; founding co-chmn. So. Fla. Roundtable-Georgetown U. Ctr. for Strategic and Internat. Studies, 1982-85; chmn. Fla. Gov.'s Conf. on World Trade, 1984—; gen. counsel Fla. Internat. Bankers Assn.; dir., former gen. counsel Fla. Internat. Ins. and Reins. Assn., chmn. Latin Am. Carribbean Bus. Promotion Adv. Counc. to U.S. Sec. of Commerce and Aid Adminstr; appointee Fla. Internat. Trade and Investment Coun.; mem. steering com. Summit of Ams., 1994—, co-chair post summit planning com. Contbg. editor Econs. Devel. Lawyers of the Ams., 1969-74; contbr. numerous articles to legal jours. in U.S. and fgn. countries. Chmn. City of Miami Internat. Trade and Devel. Com., 1984-86; chmn. internat. task force Beacon Coun. of Dade County, Fla., 1985, dir., chmn., 1991—; bd. dirs., exec. com. Internat. Comml. Dispute Resolution Ctr., Miami Internat. Arbitration and Mediation Inst.; chmn. Comml. Dispute Resolution Ctr. for the Ams., Miami, 1995—; apptd. by Gov. of Fla. to Internat. Currency and Barter Commn., 1986; ectr. U. Miami Inter-Ban course for Latin Am. bankers; steering com. Summit of the Americas, Miami, 1994, co-chair post Summit Planning Com., 1994. With JACGC, USAF, 1952-54, Korea; to maj. Res. Named Internat. Trader of Yr., Fla. Council Internat. Devel., 1980, Bus. Person of Yr., 1986; recipient Pan Am. Informatica Comunicaciones Expo award, 1983, Lawyer of Americas award U. Miami, 1984, Richard L. McLaughlin award Fla. Econ. Devel. Coun., 1993; named hon. consul gen. Republic of Korea, Miami, 1983-88, recipient Heung-in medal (Order of Diplomatic Service), 1986, Ministerial Citation, Min. of Fgn. Affairs, 1988; apptd. Hon. consul Ft. Lauderdale, Fla., 1991—. Fellow ABA Found. (chmn. com. arrangements internat. and comparative law sect. 1964-65, com. on Inter-Am. affairs of ABA 1985-87); mem. Inter-Am. Bar Assn. (asst. sec.-gen. 1957-59, treas. 11th conf. 1959, co-chmn. jr. bar sect. 1963-65, mem council 1969—, exec. com. 1975—, pres. 1982-84, Diploma de Honor 1987, William Roy Vallance award 1989), Spanish Am. Bar Assn., Fla. Bar Assn. (vice chmn. adminstrv. law com. 1965, vice chmn. internat. and comparative law com. 1967-68, chmn. aero. law com. 1968-69), Dade County Bar Assn. (chmn. fgn. laws and langs com. 1964-65), Internat. Ctr. Fla. (pres. 1981-82), World Peace Through Law Ctr., Miami Com. Fgn. Relations, Inst. Ibero Am. Derecho Aero., Am. Soc. Internat. Law, Council Internat. Visitors, Am. Fgn. Law Assn. (pres. Miami 1958), Bar of South Korea (hon. mem.), Greater Miami C. of C. (bd. govs. 1986—), Colombian-Am. C. of C. (bd. dirs. 1986—), Peruvian-Am. C. of C. (bd. dirs.), Phi Alpha Delta. Home: 605 Almeria Ave Coral Gables FL 33134-5602 Office: 200 S Biscayne Blvd Miami FL 33131-2310

LANDY, JOANNE VEIT, foreign policy analyst; b. Chgo., Oct. 15, 1941; d. Fritz and Lucille (Stearns) Veit; m. Seymour Landy, Mar., 1959 (div. 1962); m. Nelson Lichtenstein, Mar., 1972 (div. 1976). BA in History, U. Calif., Berkeley, 1968; MA in History, U. Calif., Berkeley, 1970; MPH, Columbia U., 1982. Dir. N.Y. Met. Office, U. Chgo., N.Y.C., 1977-80; pres. Campaign for Peace and Democracy, N.Y.C., 1982—; bd. dirs. Human Rights Watch, Helsinki. Editor: Peace & Democracy, 1984—. Recipient grant for rsch. and writing John D. and Catherine T. Mac Arthur Fedn., Program on Peace and Internat. Cooperation, Chgo., 1990-91. Mem. Coun. on Fgn. Rels., Phi Beta Kappa. Home: 2785 Broadway Apt 7A New York NY 10025-2850 Office: Campaign for Peace and Democracy PO Box 1640 New York NY 10025-1560

LANDY, LISA ANNE, lawyer; b. Miami, Fla., Apr. 20, 1963; d. Burton Aaron and Eleonora Maria (Simmel) L. BA, Brown U., 1985; JD cum laude, U. Miami, 1988. Bar: Fla. 1988, U.S. Dist. Ct. (so. dist.) Fla. 1988. Atty. Paul, Landy, Beiley & Harper, P.A., Miami, Fla., 1988-94; atty. Steel Hector & Davis, Miami, Fla., 1994—, ptnr., 1996—. Bd. dirs. Miami City Ballet, 1992—, pres., 1996; bd. dirs. Women in Internat. Trade, Miami, 1992—, pres., 1994; v.p. Orgn. Women in Internat. Trade, 1997. Mem. ABA, Inter-Am. Bar Assn. (sec. young lawyers divsn. 1992). Avocations: sports, arts, fluent in Spanish, French.

LANE, ALFRED THOMAS, medical educator; b. Dayton, Ohio, July 17, 1947. BS, U. Dayton, 1969; MD, Ohio State U., 1973. Diplomate Am. Bd. Pediatrics, Am. Bd. Dermatology; lic. physician, Calif. Intern, resident pediatrics Children's Hosp. L.A., 1973-76; pvt. practice Pleasant Valley Pediatric Med. Group, Camarillo, Calif., 1976-79; resident dermatology U. Colo. Sch. Medicine, Denver, 1979-82; asst. prof. dermatology and pediatrics U. Rochester (N.Y.) Med. Ctr., 1982-88; attending physician Strong Meml. Hosp., 1982-90; staff dermatologist Rochester Gen. Hosp., 1985-90; dir. Dermatology Clinic VA, Rochester, 1985-90; assoc. prof. dermatology and pediatrics U. Rochester Med. Ctr., 1988-90; staff physician in dermatology and pediatrics Stanford (Calif.) U. Med. Ctr., Stanford Children's Hosp., 1990—, dir. pediatric dermatology, 1990—; assoc. prof. dermatology and pediatrics Stanford U. Med. Ctr., 1990-96; prof. dermatology Stanford (Calif.) U. Med. Ctr., 1996—; acting chmn. dept. dermatology Stanford U. Med. Ctr., 1995-96, chmn. dermatology, 1996—; acting chief dermatology svc. Stanford U. Med. Ctr., Stanford Health Svcs., 1995—. Author: with W.L. Weston) Color Textbook of Pediatric Dermatology, 1991; (with W.L. Weston and J.G. Morelli) Color Textbook of Pediatric Dermatology, 1995; contbr. articles to profl. jours. Recipient Buswell fellowship U. Rochester, 1982-83, Clin. Investigator award NIH, 1983-88. Fellow Am. Acad. Pediatrics, Am. Acad. Dermatology (mem. task force on pediatric dermatology 1987-92, mem. adv. coun. 1988-90, mem. Presdl. Commn. on Melanoma/Skin Cancer 1988-92, mem. task force on youth edn. 1989-94); mem. Soc. Pediatric Dermatology (bd. dirs. 1986-93, pres. elect 1990-91, pres. 1991-92), Soc. Investigative Dermatology (com. on pub. rels. 1990-94, com. on govt. and pub. rels. 1992-94), Soc. Pediatric Rsch., Am. Dermatol. Assn., Am. Soc. Laser Medicine and Surgery. Office: Stanford U Med Ctr Dept Dermatology 900 Blake Wilbur Dr # W0071 Palo Alto CA 94304-2205

LANE, ALVIN HUEY, JR., management consultant; b. Dallas, May 2, 1942; s. Alvin Huey and Marianne (Halsell) L.; m. Melanie Kadane, June 21, 1963; children—Alvin Huey, III, Michael, Lance, Marianne. B.A. (Western Electric scholar, J. Venn Leeds scholar), Rice U., Houston, 1964, B.S., 1965. Mgmt. positions with Procter & Gamble Mfg. Co., 1965-68; mgmt. cons. Ernst & Young, CPA's, Dallas, 1968-69; v.p. fin., sec. Balanced Investment Dynamics Co., Dallas, 1969-72, Dr Pepper Co., Dallas, 1972-80; sr. v.p. fin., sec. Dr Pepper Co., 1980-83; pres. Lane & Assocs., Dallas, 1983—; bd. dirs. Heartland Wireless Comms., Dallas, Love Bottling Co., Muskogee, Okla., Marketplace Christian Network, Dallas. Mem. Lakewood Country Club. Home: 3415 Colgate Ave Dallas TX 75225-4830 Office: Lane and Assocs 10440 N Central Expy Ste 610 Dallas TX 75231-2227

LANE, ALVIN S., lawyer; b. Englewood, N.J., June 17, 1918; s. Martin Lane and Nettie (Gans) Daniels; m. Terese P. Lyons, Apr. 24, 1949; children: Mary-Jo, Judith Lyons. Ph.B., U. Wis., 1940; LL.B., Harvard U., 1943. Bar: N.Y. 1947. Sr. ptnr. Wien, Lane & Malkin (now Wien & Malkin), 1954-83; chmn. Rapidata, Inc., 1967-82; Mem. adv. bd. to N.Y. atty. gen. on art legis., 1966-71. Contbr. articles to art publs. and legal jours. Mem. bd. mgmt. Henry Ittleson Rsch. Ctr. Disturbed Children, Riverdale, N.Y., 1961-70; fellow Brandeis U., 1966—, nat. adv. coun. 20th Century Art Soc. High Mus. of Art, 1986-95; sec., trustee Aldrich Mus. Contemporary Art, Inc., 1969-76; trustee Lexington Sch. Deaf, 1971; v.p., trustee Soho Ctr. Visual Artists, Inc., 1974-83; dir. Creative Artists Pub. Svc. Program, Inc., 1982-84; mem. drawing com. Whitney Mus. Am Art, 1991-93; mem. The Elvehjem Mus. Art Coun., 1992—. Served as lt. USNR, 1942-46. Mem. Assn. of Bar of City of N.Y. (chmn. com. art 1963-65), N.Y. Artists Equity Assn. (dir. 1982-84). Clubs: Harvard (N.Y.C.), Riverdale Yacht. Home: 5251 Independence Ave Riverdale NY 10471-2825 Office: 35 E 38th St New York NY 10016-2529

LANE, ARTHUR ALAN, lawyer; b. N.Y.C., Dec. 2, 1945; s. George and Delys L.; m. Jane Ficocella, Dec. 30, 1972; 1 child, Eva B. BA, Yale U., 1967; JD, Columbia U., 1970, MBA, 1971. Bar: N.Y. 1971. Assoc. Webster, Sheffield, Fleischmann, Hitchcock & Brookfield, N.Y.C., 1971-72; asst. to div. counsel Liggett & Myers Inc., N.Y.C., 1973; assoc. Wickes, Riddell, Bloomer, Jacobi & McGuire, N.Y.C., 1974-78, Morgan, Lewis & Bockius, N.Y.C., 1979; ptnr. Eaton & Van Winkle, N.Y.C., 1980-94, DeForest & Duer, N.Y.C., 1994—. Mem. ABA, Assn. of Bar of City of N.Y., Soc. of Colonial Wars. Avocation: gardening. Home: 103 Brooksite Dr Smithtown NY 11787-4456 Office: DeForest & Duer 90 Broad St New York NY 10004-2205

LANE, BARBARA ANN, environmental company official, systems analyst; b. Boston, Nov. 1, 1939; d. William James and Marguerite Jean (Lawler) Ohrenberger; m. David Joseph Lane, Nov. 2, 1963; children: David Joseph Jr., William Francis. BS summa cum laude, Northeastern U., 1989. Cert. in personal protection and safety for hazardous waste site ops. OSHA. Supr. facility lab. quality assurance and control Clean Harbors Environ. Svcs. Cos., Braintree, Mass., 1988-89, facility sys. analyst, 1989-90, sys. analyst, mgr. facilty quality assurance, 1990-93, sr. mgr. nat. facilities quality assurance, 1993-94, mem. bus. process reengring. core team, 1994—. Co-author: Resource Guide to State Agencies Serving Children and Adolescents, 1983. Bd. dirs. Pro-Arte Singers, Scituate, Mass., 1979-81, Scituate Arts Assn., 1981-83; founder, bd. dirs. Prelude Internat. Concert Series, Scituate, 1981-89, Young Performers Music Guild, Scituate, 1981-83. Recipient cmty. svc. citation Mass. Ho. of Reps., 1985, outstanding cmty. svc. citation Scituate Bd. Selectmen, 1986. Mem. AAUW, N.Y. Acad. Scis., Phi Kappa Phi. Avocations: fitness training, classical music (pianist, classical guitarist). Home: 59 Creelman Dr Scituate MA 02066-2026 Office: Clear Harbors Environ Svcs Co 1501 Washington St Braintree MA 02184-7599

LANE, BARBARA MILLER (BARBARA MILLER-LANE), humanities educator; b. N.Y.C., Nov. 1, 1934; d. George Ross Rede and Gertrude Miller; m. Jonathan Lane, Jan. 28, 1956; children: Steven Gregory, Eleanor. B.A., U. Chgo., 1953, Barnard Coll., 1956; M.A., Radcliffe Coll., 1957; Ph.D., Harvard U., 1962. Tutor history and lit. Harvard U., Cambridge, Mass., 1960-61; lectr. to prof. history Bryn Mawr Coll., Bryn Mawr, Pa., 1962-75, dir. Growth and Structure of Cities Program, 1971-89, Andrew W. Mellon prof. humanities, 1981—; vis. prof. Architecture, Columbia U., 1989; cons. NEH sr. fellowships, Washington, 1971-73, Time-Life Books, N.Y.C., 1975, Bauhaus, Dessau, 1991; advisor Macmillan Ency. of Architects, N.Y.C., 1979-82; vis. examiner U. Helsinki, 1991; vis. lectr. Technische Universität, Berlin, 1991. Author: Architecture and Politics in Germany, 1968, 85, Italian and German edits., 1973, 86; co-author: Nazi Ideology Before 1933, 1978; contbg. author: Growth and Transformation of the Modern City, 1979, Macmillan Encyclopedia of Architects, 1982, Urbanisierung im 19. und 20. Jahrhundert, 1983, Perspectives in American History, 1984, The Evidence of Art: Images and Meaning in History, 1986, Art and History, 1988, Nationalism in the Visual Arts, 1991, Moderne Architektur in Deutschland: Expressionismus und Neue Sachlichkeit, 1994; contbr. editor: Urbanism Past and Present, 1980-85; mem. bd. editors Archtl. History Found., 1988—, Ctrl. European History, 1992—; contbr. articles to profl. jours. Co-founder, dir., chmn. bd. dirs. New Gulph Child Care Ctr., Bryn Mawr, 1971-75; mem. Middle Atlantic Regional Com., Mellon Fellowships in the Humanities, 1985-87; mem. vis. com. Harvard U. Dept. History, 1986-92, Berlin Stadtforum (adv. coun. to Senator for Urban Devel. and Environment), 1991-96. Recipient Lindback award for excellence in tchg., 1988, medal of honor U. Helsinki, 1996; fellow AAUW, 1959-60, Fels Found., 1961-62, Am. Council Learned Socs., 1967-68, Guggenheim Found., 1977-78, sr. fellow Ctr. for Advanced Study in Visual Arts, Nat. Gallery Art, Washington, 1983, Am. Scandinavian Found. fellow, 1989, Wissenschaftskolleg zu Berlin fellow, 1990-91; NEH grantee, summer 1989. Mem. Soc. Archtl. Historians (bd. dirs. 1977-80, Alice Davis Hitchcock award 1968, chmn. awards coms. 1976, 82, chmn. jour. com. 1982-83), Conf. Group on Central European History (bd. dirs. 1977-79, chmn. awards com. 1987, structure and planning adv. com. 1993—), Am. Hist. Assn. (mem. council 1979-82, chmn. com. on Popular Mag. of History 1982), Coll. Art Assn., Phi Beta Kappa. Office: Bryn Mawr Coll Bryn Mawr PA 19010

LANE, BERNARD BELL, furniture company executive; b. Lynchburg, Va., Nov. 23, 1928; s. Edward Hudson and Myrtle Clyde (Bell) L.; m. Minnie Matthews Bassett, June 7, 1950; children: William R., Lucy H., Douglas B., Bernard Bell. B.S., U.S. Naval Acad., 1950. With Lane Co., Altavista, Va., 1954-87; v.p., then exec. v.p. Lane Co., 1960-76, pres., chmn. exec. com., 1976-81, chmn. bd., 1981-87. Commr. Va. Pt. Authority, 1986-91; bd. dirs. Va. Poly. Inst. and State U. Ednl. Found., 1968-76, Food for the Hungry Inc., Scottsdale, Ariz., 1985-95, chmn. bd. dirs., 1990; bd. dirs. Project Concern Internat., 1995—; mem. Va. Gov.'s Adv. Bd. on Indsl. Devel., 1970-82, Va. Gov.'s Adv. Bd. on Revenue Estimates, 1977-86; chmn. com. urol. rsch., endowment and devel. Duke U. Med. Ctr., 1974-82. Mem. Va. Mfrs. Assn. (bd. dirs. 1986-87). Methodist.

LANE, BRUCE STUART, lawyer; b. New London, Conn., May 15, 1932; s. Stanley S. and Frances M. (Antis) L.; m. Ann Elizabeth Steinberg, Aug. 10, 1958; children: Sue Ellen, Charles M., Richard I. Student, Boston U., 1948-49; AB magna cum laude, Harvard U., 1952, JD, 1955. Bar: Ohio 1955, D.C. 1966, U.S. Ct. Claims 1960, U.S. Tax Ct. 1961, U.S. Supreme Ct. 1961. Assoc. Squire, Sanders & Dempsey, Cleve., 1955-59; sr. trial atty. tax div. Dept. Justice, Washington, 1959-61; tax atty. Dinsmore, Shohl, Barrett, Coates & Deupree, Cin., 1961-65; sec., asst. gen. counsel corp. and tax matters Communications Satellite Corp., Washington, 1965-69; v.p., gen. counsel Nat. Corp. Housing Partnerships, Washington, 1969-70; pres. Lane and Edson P.C., Washington, 1970-89; ptnr. Kelley Drye & Warren, Washington, 1989-93; mng. ptnr. Peabody & Brown, Washington, 1993—. Co-editor-in-chief Housing and Devel. Reporter; author publs. and articles on tax, partnership and real estate. Incorporator, bd. dirs., past pres. D.C. Inst. Mental Health; past chmn. citizens Com. sect. 5 Chevy Chase, Md.; past mem. Montgomery County Hist. Preservation Commn., Md.; mem. chmn. coun. Crow Canyon Archeol. Ctr., Cortez, Colo. Maj. JAG, USAR, 1952-68. Mem. ABA, Am. Law Inst., Am. Coll. Real Estate Lawyers (pres. 1986-87), Anglo-Am. Real Property Inst., Phi Beta Kappa. Home: 3711 Thornapple St Chevy Chase MD 20815-4111 Office: Peabody & Brown 1255 23rd St NW Ste 800 Washington DC 20037-1125

LANE, BURTON (BURTON LEVY), composer; b. N.Y.C., Feb. 2, 1912; s. Lazarus and Frances Levy; m. Marion Seaman, June 28, 1935 (div. 1961); 1 dau.; m. Lynn Daroff Kaye, Mar. 5, 1961. Student, High Sch. of Commerce; studied piano with Simon Bucharoff. Former staff composer for Remick Music Pub. Wrote music for 2 songs in Three's a Crowd, 1930; 1 song in The Third Little Show, 1931; entire score for 9th edit. Earl Carroll's Vanities, 1931; 2 songs in Singin' the Blues, 1931; 1 song in Americana, 1932; composed mus. scores for Hold on to Your Hats, 1940, Laffing Room Only (also lyricist), 1944, Finian's Rainbow, 1947, On a Clear Day You Can See Forever (Tony nomination, Grammy award with Alan Jay Lerner 1965 Carmelina, 1979 (Tony nomination); songs for motion pictures including Dancing Lady, 1933, Babes on Broadway, 1941, Royal Wedding, 1951, Give a Girl a Break, 1953, On a Clear Day You Can See Forever, 1966; animated film Heidi, 1979; composer music for Junior Miss, TV, 1958; composer songs in revue Mighty Fine Music!, off-Broadway, 1983; songs include Everything I Have is Yours, Tony's Wife, Moments Like This, There's A Great Day Coming Mañana, On a Clear Day, The Lady's In Love With You, I Hear Music, Too Late Now, When I'm Not Near The Girl I Love, I Love The Girl I'm Near, Come Back To Me, How Are Things In Glocca Morra?, Look To The Rainbow, How Could You Believe Me When I Said I Love You When You Know I've Been A Liar All My Life, Says My Heart, Stop!, You're Breaking My Heart, (I Like New York In June) How About You?, It's Time For A Love Song, In Our United State, Old Devil Moon, What Did I Have That I Don't Have, One More Walk Around The Garden. Recipient 2 Acad. Award nominations, award for Finian's Rainbow, Essex Symphony Soc. 1947, Mercer Lifetime Achievement award, Richard Rodgers Lifetime Achievement award ASCAP, 1992; inducted into Theatre Hall of Fame, 1993. Mem. ASCAP (bd. dirs.), Am. Guild Authors and Composers (pres. 1957-67, Sigmund Romberg award), Songwriters Hall of Fame (dir.).

LANE, DANIEL MCNEEL, pediatric hematologist, lipidologist; b. Ft. Sam Houston, Tex., Jan. 25, 1936; s. Samuel Hartman and Mary Maverick (McNeel) L.; m. Carolyn Ann Spruiell, Nov. 28, 1958; children: Linda Ann, Daniel M. Jr., Maury S., Oleta K. MD, U. Tex.-Dallas, 1961; MS, U. Tenn., 1967; PhD, U. Okla., 1973. Asst. prof., head pediatric hematology/oncology U. Okla. Med. Ctr., Oklahoma City, 1966-72; rsch. fellow Okla. Med. Rsch. Found., Oklahoma City, 1969-72, adj. assoc. mem., 1986-92, adj. mem., 1993—; assoc. prof., head pediatric hematology/oncology Tulane Med. Sch., New Orleans, 1972-73; head hematology/oncology Oklahoma City Clinic, 1973-79; pvt. practice, 1979—; head Okla. Lipid Consultation Group, 1993-95; dir. clin. investigation Presbyn. Meml. Hosp., Oklahoma City, 1975-77; med. monitor HELP System project B. Braun Am., 1988-93, B. Braun Melsungen AG, FRG, cons.; assoc. prof. Tex. Tech. U. Health Scis. Ctr., Odessa, 1996—; mem. editl. bd. Atherosclerosis Rsch. Alert, London; chmn., bd. dirs. Poplar Pike Realtors, Inc., Memphis, 1973-85; cons. Programa de Prevencion del Infarto en Argentina, La Plata. Fin. chmn. Dunlap for Congress, 1976; head Physicians for Gov. Nigh, 1978; Dem. candidate for Congress, 5th Dist., 1982. USPHS fellow, 1964-66; spl. rsch. fellow Nat. Heart Lung and Blood Inst., 1969-72. Mem. AMA, Am. Soc. Clin. Oncology, Am. Soc. Hematology, Am. Coll. Nutrition. Democrat. Episcopalian. Research on infant lipid nutrition, LDL-apheresis, clin. hematology; pediatrics. Home: 650 Eastridge Rd Odessa TX 79762 Office: Dept Pediat-Tex Tech U 800 W 4th St Odessa TX 79763

LANE, DAVID CHRISTOPHER, humanities educator, author, researcher; b. Burbank, Calif., Apr. 29, 1956; s. Warren Joseph and Louise Lane; m. Jaquelyn Ann Godfrey, Dec. 16, 1978. BA in Religion, Calif. State U., Northridge, 1978; MA in Religious Studies, Grad. Theol. Union, Berkeley, Calif., 1983; MA in Sociology, U. Calif., San Diego, 1988, PhD in Sociology of Knowledge, 1991. Tchr. Moreau High Sch., Hayward, Calif., 1979-81, Chaminade Prep., Canoga Park, Calif., 1981-82, San Diego U., H.S., 1982-84, U. Calif., San Diego, 1984—; prof. philosophy & sociology Mt. San Antonio Coll., Walnut, Calif.; adj. prof. Calif. Sch. Prof. Psychology, San Diego, 1987—; prof. U. for Humanistic Studies, Del Mar, Calif., 1988—; Fate Mag. book reviewer, Hyacinth, Ill., 1983—; cult analyst for various orgns., 1978—; rschr. Inst. for Study of Am. Religion, Santa Barbara, Calif.; faculty-student chmn. Moreau High Sch., 1980-81; vis. prof. philosophy U. London, 1993, 94, founder The Neural Surfer Website. Author: The Making of a Spiritual Movement, 1983, The Radhasoami Tradition, 1991, The Unknowing Sage, 1991, DA: The Strange Case of Franklin Jones, 1995, The Socratic Universe, 1995, Why I Don't Eat Faces: A Neurological Argument for Vegetarianism, 1995, Mt. San Antonio College Philosophy Series, Exposing Cults: When the Skeptical Mind Confronts the Mystical, American Philosophers, The Enchanted Land: With the Saints of North India, Spooky Action at a Distance: Einstein's Argument with Niels Bohr and the Implications of Quantum Theory; editor (jours.) Occam's Razor, Charisma, Plato's Cave, Einstein's Chalkboard, Understanding Cults Rsch. Series. Coach St. Charles, 1978, N. Hollywood, Chaminade Coll. Prep., 1981-82. Author: The Unknowing Sage, The Radhsoami Tradition, The Making of a Spiritual Movement, 1983; editor Understanding Cults Research Series, 1984, MSAC Philosophy Series, Plato's Cave; contbg. author to profl. jours. and encycs. of religion; founding editor MSAC Surf Chronicle, Myths of the World. Mem. Mt. San Antonio Coll. Surf Assn. (founder). Republican. Roman Catholic. Clubs: U. San Diego High Sch., Surf (San Diego) (pres. 1982-84), Del Mar Surf. Avocations: surfing, basketball, travel. Office: MSAC Philosophy Dept 1100 N Grand Ave Walnut CA 91789-1341

LANE, DAVID OLIVER, retired librarian; b. Flint, Mich., Oct. 17, 1931; s. Clinton Ellis and Mary Ailene (Sanders) L. B.A., U. Mich., 1958, A.M. in L.S, 1959; doctoral fellow, U. Chgo., 1968. Various library assignments, 1959-63; asst. dir. libraries Boston U., 1963-67; asst. univ. librarian U. Calif., San Diego, 1968-69; chief librarian, prof., dept. chmn. Hunter Coll., N.Y.C., 1969-90; Dir. NSF funded study of library acquisitions, 1967-68; chmn. Council Chief Librarians, City U. N.Y., 1972-75; trustee N.Y. Met. Reference Library Agy., 1978-87. Author: Study of the Decision Making Procedures for the Acquisition of Science Library Materials, 1968. Mem. A.L.A. (life), Assn. Coll. and Research Libraries, Beta Phi Mu. Home: 27D E Hill Dr Somers NY 10589

LANE, DEBRA ANN, critical care nurse; b. Palm Springs, Calif., Jan. 14, 1954; d. Orville Lee and Ima Jean (West) Ryan; m. David S. Lane, Feb. 2, 1980. BSN, Oreg. Health Scis. U., 1978. RN, Oreg. Staff nurse emergency room Cen. Oreg. Dist. Hosp., Redmond; flight medic AirLife Oreg., Bend. Recipient Nurse of Yr. award Cen. Oreg. EMT Assn., 1983, Personal Svc. award Cen. Oreg. EMT Assn., 1986. Mem. ANA, Oreg. Nurses Assn., Emergency Nurses Assn.

LANE, DOROTHY SPIEGEL, physician; b. Bklyn., Feb. 17, 1940; d. Milton Barton and Rosalie (Jacobson) Spiegel; m. Bernard Paul Lane, Aug. 5, 1962; children: Erika, Andrew, Matthew. BA, Vassar Coll., 1961; MD, Columbia U., 1965, MPH, 1968. Diplomate Am. Bd. Preventive Medicine, Am. Bd. Family Practice. Resident preventive medicine N.Y.C. Dept. Health Dist., 1966-68; project dir. children and youth project Title V, HHS N.Y.C. Dept. Health Dist., Rockaway, 1968-69; med. cons. Maternal and Child Health Svc. HHS, Rockville, Md., 1970-71; asst. prof. preventive medicine Sch. Medicine SUNY, Stony Brook, 1971-76, assoc. prof., 1976-92, prof., 1992—, assoc. dean, 1986—; chair dept. community medicine, dir. med. edn. Brookhaven Meml. Hosp. Med. Ctr., Patchogue, N.Y., 1972-86. Contbr. numerous articles to profl. jours. Mem. exec. com. L.I. divsn. Am. Cancer Soc., 1975—; mem. nat. bd. dirs. Am. Cancer Soc., 1994-96, mem. nat. assembly, 1996—; corp. mem. Nassau Suffolk Health Sys. Agy., 1977-97; bd. dirs. Cmty. Health Plan Suffolk, Hauppauge, 1986-91. Grantee HHS-USPHS, 1977-85, 83—, Nat. Cancer Inst., 1987—. Fellow APHA, Am. Coll. Preventive Medicine (regent 1988-96, sec.-treas. 1994-96), Am. Acad. Family Physicians, N.Y. Acad. Medicine, Am. Bd. Preventive Medicine (trustee 1991—), Assn. Tchrs. Preventive Medicine (pres. 1996—). Office: SUNY at Stony Brook Sch Medicine Health Scis Ctr L-4 Stony Brook NY 11794-8437

LANE, EDWARD WOOD, JR., retired banker; b. Jacksonville, Fla., Apr. 4, 1911; s. Edward Wood and Anna Virginia (Taliaferro) L.; m. Helen Spratt Murchison, Oct. 16, 1948; children: Edward Wood III, Helen Palmer, Anna Taliaferro, Charles Murchison. A.B., Princeton, 1933; LL.B., Harvard U., 1936. Bar: Fla. 1936. Partner firm McCarthy, Lane & Adams (and predecessors), Jacksonville, 1941-60; pres. Atlantic Nat. Bank, Jacksonville, 1961-74, chmn., 1974-85; chmn. First Union Nat. Bank of Fla. (formerly Atlantic Nat. Bank), Jacksonville, 1985-86, ret., 1986. Served to lt. comdr. USNR, World War II. Mem. Phi Beta Kappa. Clubs: Florida Yacht (Jacksonville), Timuquana Country (Jacksonville), River (Jacksonville), Univ. (Jacksonville); Ponte Vedra. Home and Office: 3790 Ortega Blvd Jacksonville FL 32210

LANE, FIELDING H., lawyer; b. Kansas City, Mo., May 6, 1926; s. Ralph Fielding and Nancy Lee (Greene) L.; m. Patricia Cecil Parkhurst, Jan. 25,

1980. B.S. in Bus. Adminstrn., U. Mo.-Columbia, 1948; LL.B. cum laude, Harvard U., 1951. Bar: Mo. 1951, Calif. 1956. Assoc. Watson Ess Marshall & Enggas, Kansas City, Mo., 1951-55; assoc. Thelen Marrin Johnson & Bridges, San Francisco, 1955-66, ptnr., 1967—. Served with USN, 1944-46; PTO; lt. comdr. Res. (ret.). Club: Olympic (San Francisco). Home: 165 Villa Ter San Francisco CA 94114-2213 Office: Thelen Marrin Johnson & Bridges 2 Embarcadero Ctr Ste 2200 San Francisco CA 94111-3905

LANE, FRANK JOSEPH, JR., lawyer; b. St. Louis, May 10, 1934; s. Frank Joseph and Virginia Laurette (Hausman) L.; m. Margaret Ann Dwyer, Mar. 2, 1957; children: Mary, Stephen, Thomas, Michael. BS in Commerce, St. Louis U., 1956, JD, 1956; LLM, Georgetown U., 1960; grad. Parker Sch. Internat. Law, Columbia U., 1970; cert., Coll. Fin. Planning, Denver, 1988. Bar: Mo. 1956, U.S. Dist. Ct. (ea. dist.) Mo. 1956, U.S. Ct. Appeals (8th cir.) 1960, U.S. Supreme Ct. 1959, U.S. Ct. Mil. Appeals, 1957. Ptnr. Goldenhersh, Goldenhersh, Fredericks, Newman & Lane, St. Louis, 1960-64, Lane & Leadlove, St. Louis, 1964-66, Dill & Lane, St. Louis, 1978-79; counsel Ralston Purina Co., St. Louis, 1966-78; mem. pres.'s adv. bd., 1967-69; of counsel Petrolite Corp., St. Louis, 1979-83; v.p., trust officer Gravois Bank, St. Louis, 1983-85; regional v.p., trust officer Merc Bank N.A., St. Louis, 1985-89; of counsel Dill, Wamser & Bamvakais, St. Louis, 1989—; instr. internat. law St. Louis U., 1979. Bd. dirs. Met. St. Louis Sewer Dist., 1965-73, chmn., 1968-69; mem. planned giving com. Am. Heart Assn., St. Louis, 1986-88, St. Louis Soc. for Crippled Children, 1991; bd. dirs. Braille Vols., Inc., chmn., 1995—; pres. Ozark Cmties. Coun. St. Louis County, 1964-65. Mem. Mo. Bar Assn., Met. St. Louis Bar Assn. (chmn. rels. with law schs. com. 1961-62, enrollment com. 1962-63, chmn. office practice com. 1963-64, elected admissions com. 1967), Estate Planning Coun., Rotary (bd. dirs. Crestwood, Mo. chpt. 1988-89), KC (grand knight 1964-66, adv. West County 1983-90, Webster Groves 1991—). Republican. Roman Catholic. Avocations: oil painting, golf, travel, investment analysis. Home: 520 Lering Dr Ballwin MO 63011-1588 Office: 9939 Gravois Rd Saint Louis MO 63123-4211

LANE, FREDERICK CARPENTER, investment banker; b. Boston, Aug. 28, 1949; s. Francis Robert and Edith (Lent) L.; m. Wendy Jane Evrard, June 9, 1973; children—Jesse Evrard, Eliza Evrard. A.B. cum laude, Harvard U., 1971, M.B.A. with distinction, 1973. C.P.A., Mass. Supr. Coopers & Lybrand CPAs, Boston, 1973-76; sr. v.p., prin. Donaldson, Lufkin & Jenrette, N.Y.C. and Boston, 1976-88; exec. v.p. Bessemer Securities Corp., N.Y.C., 1988-89; mng. dir. and dir. mergers and acquistions dept. Donaldson, Lufkin & Jenrette, N.Y.C., 1989—. Dir. Process Tech. Holdings, Gastonia, N.C. Racquet and Tennis Club (N.Y.C.), Harvard Club (Boston), Field Club (Greenwich, Conn.). Republican. Episcopalian. Office: Donaldson Lufkin & Jenrette Securities Corp 277 Park Ave New York NY 10172

LANE, FREDERICK STANLEY, lawyer; b. Cumberland, Md., Jan. 16, 1915; s. Clifford Warren and Edith Persis (Mott) L.; m. Barbara Bentley, Mar. 6, 1943; children: Clifford Warren, Martha Cogswell, Susan Bonney, Jeffery Calvin. A.B. magna cum laude, Amherst Coll., 1936; LL.B., Harvard U., 1939. Bar: Mass. 1939. Assoc. Nutter, McClennen & Fish, Boston, 1939-50; ptnr. Nutter, McClennen & Fish, 1951-90; ret.; past trustee, clk. Hingham Instn. for Savs. Editor: Real Estate in Mid-Century, 1973; contbr. articles to profl. jours. Former trustee Social Law Library, Boston; former vice chmn. Council of Friends of Amherst Coll. Library. Served to lt. comdr. USNR, 1942-46. Recipient Richard B. Johnson Meml. award Mass. Conveyancers Assn., 1981. Fellow Am. Bar Found.; Mem. Boston Bar Assn., ABA (chmn. sect. real property, probate and trust law 1977-78), Anglo-Am. Real Property Inst. (chmn. 1982-83), Am. Coll. Real Estate Lawyers (pres. 1979-81), Mass. Conveyancers Assn. (pres. 1968-70), Abstract Club (pres. 1981-84), Phi Beta Kappa, Theta Delta Chi. Republican. Unitarian. Clubs: Union, Harvard, Fly Casters (pres. 1978-80). Home: 18 Ship St Hingham MA 02043-1816

LANE, GLORIA JULIAN, foundation administrator; b. Chgo., Oct. 6, 1932; d. Coy Berry and Katherine (McDowell) Julian; m. William Gordon Lane (div. Oct. 1958); 1 child, Julie Kay Rosewood. BS in Edn., Cen. Mo. State U., 1958; MA, Bowling Green State U., 1959; PhD, No. Ill. U., 1972. Cert. tchr. Assoc. prof. William Jewell Coll., Liberty, Mo., 1959-60; chair forensic div. Coral Gables (Fla.) High Sch., 1960-64; assoc. prof. No. Ill. U., DeKalb, 1964-70; prof. Elgin (Ill.) Community Coll., 1970-72; owner, pub. Lane and Assocs, Inc., San Diego, 1972-78; prof. Nat. U., San Diego, 1978-90; pres., chief exec. officer Women's Internat. Ctr., San Diego, 1982—; founder, dir. Living Legacy Awards, San Diego, 1984—. Author: Project Text for Effective Communications, 1972, Project Text for Executive Communication, 1980, Positive Concepts for Success, 1983; editor Who's Who Among San Diego Women, 1984, 85, 86, 90—, Systems and Structure, 1984. Named Woman of Accomplishment, Soroptimist Internat., 1985, Pres.'s Coun. San Diego, 1986, Center City Assn., 1986, Bus. and Profl. Women, San Diego, 1991, Woman of Yr., Girls' Clubs San Diego, 1986, Woman of Vision, Women's Internat. Ctr., 1990, Wonderwoman 2000 Women's Times Newspaper, 1991; recipient Independence award Ctr. for Disabled, 1986, Founder's award Children's Hosp. Internat., Washington, 1986. Avocations: computers, painting, writing. Home and Office: 6202 Friars Rd Apt 311 San Diego CA 92108-1008

LANE, HOLLY DIANA, artist; b. Cleve., Sept. 13, 1954; d. Edwin Joseph and Ursula Anna (Neustadt) Selyem; m. L.A. Lane, Apr. 20, 1975. AA in 2-Dimensional Art, Cuesta Coll., San Luis Obispo, Calif., 1992; BFA with great distinction, San Jose State U., 1986, MFA in Pictorial Art, 1988. One-woman shows include Ivory/Kimpton Gallery, San Francisco, 1989, Rutgers Barclay Gallery, Santa Fe, 1990, Bingham Kurts Gallery, Memphis, 1992, (solo survey show with catalog) Art Mus. of S.E. Tex., Beaumont, 1995, (4 major solo shows) Schmidt Bingham Gallery, N.Y.C., 1991, 93, 95, 97; group mus. shows include Eiteljorg Mus., Indpls., 1995, Yerba Buena Ctr. for the Arts, San Francisco, 1994, Knoxville (Tenn.) Mus. Art, 1993-94, Fine Arts Ctr. U. R.I., Kingston, 1992, The Contemporary Mus., Honolulu, 1993, Boise (Idaho) Art Mus., 1994, Castle Gallery-Coll. New Rochelle, N.Y., 1996, Kennedy Mus. Am. Art, Athens, Ohio, 1996, Calif. Ctr. for the Arts Escondido Mus., 1996, Samuel P. Harn Mus., U. Fla., Gainesville, 1996, Whitney Mus. Am. Art, Champion, Conn., 1997—; represented in permanent collections in Art Mus. S.E. Tex., A.R.A. Svcs., Phila., Dow Jones & Co., N.Y.C., Detroit Zool. Gardens, Prin. Fin. Group, Des Moines, IDS, Mpls., Memphis Cancer Ctr.; works reproduced in books, mags., calendars, jours., including ARTNews, Art in America, N.Y. Times, Art Papers, Art & Antiques, New Yorker Mag., Christian Sci. Monitor, Pvt. Arts, Forensic Examiner, Women Artists calendar 1996, 97, San Raphael, Calif., The Sciences, N.Y. Acad. Scis., 1992, 93, (textbook) Artist and Audience, (London) 1996; works presented and discussed in TV documentaries, including Welcome to Nocturnia, 1993, Women in Art, Time-Warner, Manhattan Cable, N.Y.C., 1993, 94; in books accompanying TV show Bill Moyers Genesis, A Living Tradition, PBS, 1996, Healing and the Mind, 1993. Named Alumna of Yr., Cuesta Coll., 1992; pres.'s scholar San Jose State U., 1986, Johanna Rietz scholar Art Assn. of Morro Bay, Calif., 1981; recipient honorable mention Western States Arts Fedn., Santa Fe, 1994. Mem. Coll. Art Assn. (scholarship 1981). Avocations: nature walks, contemplation, reading. Home and Studio: 182 Brian Lane Santa Clara CA 95051 Address: care Schmidt Bingham Gallery 41 East 57th St 5th Fl New York NY 10022

LANE, JAMES GARLAND, JR., diversified industry executive; b. Roxobel, N.C., Jan. 15, 1934; s. James Garl and Josie (Wembrow) L.; m. Janet Benthall Miller, Oct. 8, 1954; children—Bernice, Frances, Garland, Amy. B.S., U. N.C., 1959. Mem. audit staff S.D. Leidesdorf & Co., Greenville, S.C., 1959-65; v.p. finance Computer Servicenters, Inc., Greenville, 1965-68; exec. v.p., dir. Synalloy Corp., Spartanburg, S.C., 1968-73; pres. dir. Hewitt, Coleman & Assocs. subs. Continental Group, Inc., Greenville, 1973-86; chmn. bd., chief exec. officer Synalloy Corp., Spartanburg, 1986—. Served with USMCR, 1953-56. Home: 120 Pentland Ct Greer SC 29651-9137

LANE, JAMES MCCONKEY, investment executive; b. Pitts., July 9, 1929; s. Mortimer Bliss and Mary (Knapp) L.; m. Arlyne Ruth Nelson, Dec. 16, 1950; children: James, Theodore, Thomas, Karen, David. BA, Wheaton Coll., 1952; MBA, U. Chgo., 1953; postgrad., NYU, 1956, U. Buffalo, 1960. Credit corr. John Plain & Co., Chgo., 1951; trainee Chase Manhattan Bank, N.Y.C., 1953-55, account mgr. investment adv. divsn., 1955-59, investment officer, 1959-62, 2nd v.p., 1962-64, v.p., mgr. corp. pension trust investments, 1964-66, v.p. divsn. exec. pension trust investment divsn., 1966-68, chmn. investment policy com., 1968-78, sr. v.p., investment group exec., 1968-70, exec. v.p. fiduciary investment dept., 1970-78; pres., dir. Chase Investors Mgmt. Corp., N.Y.C., 1972-78; mng. dir. Cyrus J. Lawrence Inc., N.Y.C., 1978-82; sr. v.p., chief investment officer, head trust investment divsn. NBD Bank N.A., Detroit, 1982-94, mem. sr. mgmt., 1984-94; bd. dirs. Chateau Communities, Inc., NAIC Growth Fund, Inc. Bd. dirs. Christian Camps Inc., 1978—, Baseball Chapel Inc., 1994—, William Tyndale Coll., 1985—, chmn., 1995—; trustee Wheaton Coll., 1971—. Mem. Fin. Analysts Soc. Detroit (pres. bd. dirs. 1995-96), Grosse Pointe Yacht Club. Home and Office: 24 Harbor Hill Rd Grosse Pointe MI 48236-3748

LANE, JEFFREY BRUCE, financial services company executive; b. Bklyn., June 25, 1942; s. Murray and Arlene (Avram) L.; m. Nancy Stern, June 24, 1982. BA, NYU, 1964; MBA, Columbia U., 1970. With Shearson Lehman Hutton, N.Y.C., CFO, vice chmn., 1983-84, COO, 1984-87, pres., 1987-90; pres. Primerica Holdings, N.Y., 1990-94; vice chmn. Smith Barney Harris Upham & Co. Inc., N.Y.C., 1991—; vice chmn. and dir. Smith Barney, Shearson Inc., N.Y.C.; vice chmn. Smith Barney, Shearson, Inc., N.Y.C., Travelers Group, Inc., 1996—; vice chmn. bd. of govs. Am. Stock Exchange;. Bd. dirs. Woodmere Acad., N.Y., L.I. Jewish Hosp. Served to 1st lt. U.S. Army, 1966-68. Republican. Jewish. Office: Smith Barney Shearson Inc 388 Greenwich St New York NY 10013-2375*

LANE, JERRY ROSS, alcohol and drug abuse service counselor; b. Pampa, Tex., June 3, 1944; s. Wilbur Howard and Christina Lavina (Hendrix) L.; m. Mary Lou Jetton, July 9, 1966; children: Jeffrey Ross, Tamara Noel. BS, McMurry U., 1968; MS in Counseling Psychology, Emmanuel Bapt. U., 1988, D in Counseling Psychology, 1991. Cert. and registered hypnotherapist, CHt. Tchr. Fannin Elem., Abilene, Tex., 1968-70, Tierra Blanca Elem., Hereford, Tex., 1970-72; acctg. and sales staff Lane and Co., Inc., Panhandle, Tex., 1972-74; min. music and edn. Memphis (Tex.) United Meth. Ch., 1974-75, First United Meth. Ch., McAllen, Tex., 1975-79; chaplain cancer treatment ctr. McAllen (Tex.) Br. M.D. Anderson Hosp., 1977-79; owner, counselor Snelling and Snelling Employment, Pampa, 1979-83; tchr. Travis Elem., Pampa, 1983-89; student asst. program coord. Pampa (Tex.) Ind. Sch. Dist., 1989-92; counselor, dir. drug/alcohol program Clarendon Coll. Pampa (Tex.) Ctr., 1992-96; owner dir., Hi-Plains Hypotherapy/Counseling Inst., 1997—; trainer Developing Capable People, Provo, Utah, 1990—; trainer family cmty. leadership Tex. Extension Svc., Amarillo, Tex., 1990—; parenting cons. Region XVI Edn. Svc. Ctr., Amarillo, 1991—, adv. bd. drug/alcohol, 1992—; cons. Cal Farley's Family Living Ctr., Borger, Tex., 1992—. Bd. dirs. Pampa (Tex.) Fine Arts, 1980-83, Pampa United Way, 1996; chmn. bd. Salvation Army, Pampa, 1982; bd. pres. Civic Ballet, Pampa, 1984; choir mem., bd. dirs. First United Meth. Ch.; vol. grief counselor Hospice of Panhandle. Named Family of Yr., Mormon Ch., Pampa, 1981, Top Gun, Tex. Tech. Dads and Moms Assn., Lubbock, Tex., 1990; grantee Tex. Coun. Assn. Drug/Alcohol, Pampa (Tex.) Ind. Sch. Dist., 1989-93. Mem. Am. Assn. Christian Counselor, Nat. Christian Counselor Assn., Tex. Christian Counselors Assn., Panhandle Christian Counselors Assn., Tex. Jr. Coll. Tchrs. Assn., Pampa C. of C. Avocations: interior decorating, writing, horticulture. Home: 2007 Williston St Pampa TX 79065-3632 Office: Clarendon Coll Pampa Ctr 900 N Frost St Pampa TX 79065-5456

LANE, JOAN FLETCHER, educational administrator; b. San Francisco, May 7, 1928; d. Howard French and Kathryn Elizabeth (Kraft) Fletcher; m. Melvin Bell Lane, Feb. 15, 1953; children: Whitney Lane-Miller, Julie Lane-Gay. AB, Smith Coll., 1949. Staff World Affairs Coun. No. Calif., San Francisco, 1949-51, Inst. Internat. Edn., Stanford, Calif., 1952; spl. asst., dean Sch. H&S Stanford U., 1982-93, spl. asst. bd. trustees, 1993—; bd. dirs. McClatchy Newspapers, Sacramento, The James Irvine Found., San Francisco. Trustee San Francisco Found., 1984-92; trustee Smith Coll., Northampton, Mass., 1978-85, chmn. bd. trustees, 1982-85, v.p. alumnae assn., 1975-78; bd. dirs. Internat. House, U. Calif., Berkeley, 1971-80; pres., assoc. coun. Mills Coll., Oakland, Calif., 1974-78. Recipient John M. Greene award Smith Coll., 1988. Avocations: hiking, gardening. Home: 99 Tallwood Ct Atherton CA 94027-6431

LANE, JOHN DENNIS, lawyer; b. Norwalk, Conn.; s. John J. and Theresa A. (Donnelly) L.; m. Elizabeth J. Galliher, Apr. 28, 1949; children: Elizabeth J., John Dennis, Margaret A., Robert E., Paul G. B.S., Georgetown U., 1943, J.D., 1948. Bar: D.C. 1948, Conn. 1950. Atty. Office Chief Counsel, Bur. Internal Revenue, Washington, 1948-49; exec. sec. to U.S. Senator Brien McMahon, 1949-50; adminstrv. asst., 1950-52; pvt. practice Washington and Norwalk, 1953—; ptnr. Hedrick & Lane, 1954—82, Wilkes, Artis, Hedrick & Lane, 1982—. Mem. council Adminstrv. Conf. U.S., 1961; bd. regents Georgetown U., 1979—. Served to capt. USMCR, 1943-45. Recipient Citation of Merit. Fellow Am. Bar Found.; mem. ABA (chmn. standing com. unauthorized practice of law 1971-73, chmn. standing com. nat. conf. groups 1973-75, D.C. Cir. mem. standing com. on fed. judiciary 1984-86, alt. rep. to UN 1997—, Fed. cir. mem. 1987-90), Fed. Commn. Bar Assn. (pres.-elect 1990, pres. 1991-92), Am. Law Inst., Met. Club, Army and Navy Club, Columbia Country Club (Chevy Chase, Md.). Home: 5045 Van Ness St NW Washington DC 20016-1960 Office: 1666 K St NW Washington DC 20006-2803

LANE, JOHN RODGER, art museum director; b. Evanston, Ill., Feb. 28, 1944; s. John Crandall Lane and Jeanne Marie (Rodger) L. Moritz; m. Inge-Lise Eckmann, 1992. BA, Williams Coll., 1966; MBA, U. Chgo., 1971; AM, Harvard U., 1973, PhD, 1976; DFA (hon.), San Francisco Art Inst., 1995. Asst. dir. Fogg Art Mus., Cambridge, Mass., 1974; exec. asst. to dir., adminstr. curatorial affairs, asst. dir. curatorial affairs Bklyn. Mus., N.Y.C., 1975-80; dir. Carnegie Mus. Art, Pitts., 1980-86, San Francisco Mus. Modern Art, 1987—. Author: Stuart Davis: Art and Art Theory, 1978; co-editor: Abstract Painting and Sculpture in America, 1927-1944, 1983, Carnegie International, 1985; exec. editor: The Making of a Modern Museum/SFMOMA, 1995. Served to lt. USNR, 1966-69. Nat. Endowment Arts Mus. fellow, 1974-75. Mem. Assn. Art Mus. Dirs., Am. Assn. Museums, Internat. Council Museums, Coll. Art Assn. Office: San Francisco Mus Modern Art 151 3rd St San Francisco CA 94103-3107

LANE, JOSEPH M., orthopedic surgeon, educator, oncologist; b. N.Y.C., Oct. 27, 1939; s. Frederick and Madelaine Lane; m. Barbara Greenhouse, June 23, 1963; children: Debra, Jennifer. AB in Chemistry, Columbia U., 1957; MD, Harvard U., 1965. Surg. intern Hosp. U. Pa., Phila., 1965-66, resident in gen. surgery, 1966-67, resident, 1969-72, chief resident, 1972-73, chief MBD sect., 1973-76; rsch. assoc. NIH, NIDR, Bethesda, Md., 1967-69; rsch. fellow Phila. Gen. Hosp., 1969-70; chief MBD unit Hosp. Spl. Surgery, N.Y.C., 1976-93, 96—, dir. rsch. div., 1990-93; dir. applied clin. orthopedic rsch., 1996—; dir. postgrad. edn. Hosp. Spl. Surgery, 1996—; chief orthopedic oncology Meml. Sloan-Kettering Cancer Ctr., N.Y.C., 1977-90; prof., chmn. orthopaedic surgery UCLA Med. Sch., L.A., 1993-96; prof. orthopedic surgery Cornell U. Med. Coll., 1980-93; assoc. dir. MultiPurpose Arthritis Ctr., N.Y.C., 1988-93; cons. Genetics Inst., Andover, Mass., Orquest, Mountain Side, Calif., Exogen, Piscataway, N.J.; mem. VA Merit Grant Bd. Recipient N.Y. Mayoral Proclamation, 1988. Fellow Am. Acad. Orthopaedic Surgeons (Kappa Delta award 1973); mem. Acad. Orthopaedic Surgeons, Am. Orthopaedic Assn., Am. Soc. Bone and Mineral Rsch., Med. Soc. State N.Y., Internat. Soc. Fracture Repair, Musculoskeletal Tumor Soc. (pres. 1982-83), Orthopaedic Rsch. Soc. (pres. 1984-85). Office: Hosp Spl Surgery 535 E 70th St New York NY 10021-4892

LANE, KENNETH EDWIN, retired advertising agency executive; b. Orange, N.J., Sept. 30, 1928; s. Clarence Edwin and Erma Catherine (Kinser) L.; children by previous marriage—Kenneth, Laura, Linda, Katherine; m. Susan Spafford Zimmer, Sept. 13, 1980; stepchildren—Todd and Margaret Zimmer. B.A., U. Chgo., 1947, M.A., 1950. Mgr. media Toni div. Gillette Co., 1953-63; media dir. MacParland-Aveyard Co., 1963-64; asso. media dir. Leo Burnett Co., Chgo., 1964-71; mgr. media dept. Leo Burnett Co., 1971-75, sr. v.p. media services, 1975-84. Bd. dirs. Traffic Audit Bur. Maj. USAR ret. Mem. Am. Assn. Advt. Agys., Media Dirs. Council., Phi Beta Kappa. Office: Leo Burnett Agy 35 W Wacker Dr Chicago IL 60601-1614

LANE, LAURENCE WILLIAM, JR., retired ambassador, publisher; b. Des Moines, Nov. 7, 1919; s. Laurence William and Ruth (Bell) L.; m. Donna Jean Gimbel, Apr. 16, 1955; children: Sharon Louise, Robert Laurence, Brenda Ruth. Student, Pomona Coll., 1938-40, LLD (hon.), 1976; BJ, Stanford U., 1942; DHL (hon.), Hawaii Loa Coll., 1991. Chmn. bd. Lane Pub. Co.; pub. Sunset Mag., Sunset Books and Sunset Films; U.S. amb. to Australia and Nauru, 1985-89; ret., 1990; bd. dirs. Calif. Water Svc. Co., Crown Zellerbach Corp., Pacific Gas and Electric Co.; bd. dirs. Time Inc.; bd. dirs. Oreg. Coast Aquarium, Internat. Bd. Advice, ANZ Bank; U.S. amb. and commr. Gen. Worlds Fair, Japan, 1975-76; hon. fellow Coll. Notre Dame, 1974. Former mem. adv. bd. Sec. Interior's Bd. Nat. Parks; mem. adv. coun. Grad. Sch. Bus., Stanford U., SRI; mem. Pres.'s Nat. Productivity Adv. Com.; mem. Pacific Basin Econ. Coun.; former bd. dirs. Pacific Forum, CSI, Nat. Parks Found.; vol. The Nat. Ctr.; mem. bd. overseers Hoover Instn. War, Revolution and Peace; mem. exec. com. Ctr. for Australian Studies, U. Tex., Austin. Lt. USNR, World War II, PTO. Decorated officer Order of Australia; recipient Conservation Svc. award Sec. Interior; Theodore and Conrad Wirth award NPF, 1994; Wiliam Penn Mott Jr. Conservationist of Yr. award NPCA, 1995; named hon. prof. journalism Stanford U. Mem. Newcomen Soc. N.Am., Pacific Asia Travel Assn. (life mem., chmn. 1980-81), Coun. of Am. Ambs., Los Rancheros Vistadores, Advt. Club San Francisco, No. Calif. Alumni Assn., Bohemian Club, Pacific Union, Men's Garden Club L.A., Alpha Delta Sigma. Republican. Presbyterian. Office: 3000 Sandhill Rd Ste 215 Menlo Park CA 94025-7116

LANE, LAWRENCE JUBIN, retired electrical engineer, consultant; b. Morganton, N.C., Feb. 19, 1927; s. Lawrence and Sarah Virginia (Jubin) L.; m. Gladys Verna Lee Hock, Dec. 25, 1947 (dec. 1975); children: Priscilla Gayle Lane Purks, Richard Jubin; m. 2d Helen Elizabeth Sollazzo, Dec. 19, 1975. B.E.E., N.C. State Coll., 1950; M.S.E.E., U. Va., 1972. Lic. profl. engr., Va. Engr. GE, Schenectady, N.Y., 1950-54; class supr. GE, Phila., 1954-55; devel. engr. GE, Waynesboro, Va., 1955-63, sr. devel. engr., 1963-78; sr. systems design engr. GE, Roanoke, Va., 1978-83, cons. engr., 1983-95; ret., 1995. Patentee in field. Pres. Stuarts Draft PTA, Va., 1960, 61. Served as petty officer USN, 1944-46, 50-51. Recipient Managerial award Gen. Electric Co., 1965. Fellow IEEE (chpt. chmn. 1982-83); mem. Eta Kappa Nu, Tau Beta Pi, Phi Eta Sigma, Phi Kappa Phi. Methodist. Home: 1601 Chatham Rd Waynesboro VA 22980-3203 *Since my occupational accomplishments have been judged to be noteworthy, I am indeed fortunate. I thank God and Jesus Christ for my abilities and for the opportunities for such accomplishments.*

LANE, LILLY KATHERINE, museum staff member; b. Inverness, Fla., Mar. 25, 1934; d. Robert Joseph and Edna Lee (Rooks) Lane; children: James D. Nichols, Gayle Patricia Nichols. RN, St. Luke's Hosp., Jacksonville, Fla., 1955; BFA cum laude in Ceramics, U. Fla., 1984, BA in Asian Studies, 1985, MFA in Ceramics, 1994; postgrad., Fla. State U., 1996. RN, Fla., Va., Ill., Morocco. Swimming tchr. Port Lyautey, Morocco, 1962-63; RN various, 1955-83; English tchr. South China Normal U., Guangzhou, 1987-88; Chinese Calligraphy tchr. St. Augustine, Fla., 1992-93; asst. collections Harn Mus. Art, Gainesville, Fla., 1994—. Contbr. numerous articles in Chinese and Eng. on Ancient Ceramics to profl. jours. Pres. Naval Officers Wives Club, Washington, 1973-74. Recipient Fed. Nursing traineeship, 1964, Fla. State Nursing scholarship, 1963, Winn-Lovett Nursing scholarship, 1950, Balfour award Baldwin (Fla.) H.S., 1952. Mem. AAUW, Asia Soc., Fla. Craftsmen, Asian Ceramic Rsch. Orgn., Phi Delta Kappa. Democrat.

LANE, LOUIS, musician, conductor; b. Eagle Pass, Tex., Dec. 25, 1923; s. William Bartlett and Virginia (Gardner) L. B.Mus., U. Tex., 1943; Mus.M., Eastman Sch. Music, 1947; Mus.D. (hon.), Akron U., 1973, Cleve. State U., 1974, Kent State U., 1988; Cleve. Inst. Music, 1995. adj. prof. music Akron U., 1969-82; vis. prof. music U. Cin., 1973-75, Oberlin Coll., 1995—; artistic advisor, condr. Cleve. Inst. Music, 1982—; sr. lectr. music U. Tex., 1989-91. Mem., Cleve. Orch., 1947-73, assoc. condr., 1960-70, resident condr., 1970-73, condr., Akron (Ohio) Symphony Orch., 1959-83, co-condr., Atlanta Symphony Orch., 1977-83, prin. guest condr., Atlanta Symphony Orch., 1983-88, prin. condr., SABC Symphony Orch., Johannesburg South Africa, 1984-85, prin. guest condr., Dallas Symphony Orch., 1973-78, guest condr. in, Chgo., Seattle, St. Louis, Detroit, Houston, San Antonio, Vancouver, B.C., Can., Montevideo, Uruguay, Warsaw, Poland, Johannesburg, S.Africa, Helsinki, Finland, mus. dir., Lake Erie Opera Theatre, Cleve., 1964-72; co-dir., Blossom Festival Sch. of Cleve. Orch. and Kent State U., 1969-73; rec. artist for Columbia Records, Telarc Records. Served with F.A. AUS, 1943-46. Decorated chevalier l'Ordre des Arts et des Lettres de France; Recipient Mahler medal, 1971; Ditson award Columbia, 1972; Grammy award for best orch. rec., 1989. Home: 1808 Rockridge Pl NE Atlanta GA 30324-5264

LANE, MARGARET ANNA SMITH, property manager developer; b. Aspinwall, Pa., Nov. 26, 1918; d. Max Charles and Mary Ann (Jones) Smith; m. Frank A. Lane Jr., Feb. 7, 1954; 1 child, Alan Michael. AB, UCLA, 1940; MS, U. So. Calif., 1949. Cert. secondary tchr., Calif. Demonstration and tng. tchr. UCLA and U. Calif., Northridge, 1948-74; pvt. practice Cottonwood, Ariz., 1975—; tchr. dept. chmn. L.A. City Schs., 1948-74; sec.-treas. Silver Hoof, Inc., Sedona, Stone Pine Gallery, Ltd., Sedona. Mem. Pi Gamma Mu. Avocations: Native American cultures, art. Home: PO Box I-I West Sedona AZ 86340

LANE, MARK, lawyer, educator, author; b. N.Y.C., Feb. 24, 1927; s. Harry Arnold and Elizabeth Lane; m. Patricia Ruth Erdner, 1987; children: Anne-Marie, Christina. LLB, Bklyn. Law Sch., 1951. Bar: N.Y. 1951, D.C. 1995. Pvt. practice law N.Y.C. and Washington, 1952—; founder Mid-Harlem Community Parish Narcotics Clinic, 1953, East Harlem Reform Dem. Club, 1959; prof. law Cath. U., Washington, 1975-76; sr. ptnr. Lane & Assocs., 1986—; founder and dir. Citizens Commn. Inquiry; founder Wounded Knee Legal Def.-Offense Com., 1973, The Covered Wagon, Mountain Home, Idaho, 1971. Author: (books) Rush to Judgment, 1966, A Citizen's Dissent, 1968, Chicago Eye-Witness, 1969, Arcadia, 1970, Conversations with Americans, 1970, Executive Action, 1973, (with Dick Gregory) Code Name Zorro, 1977, The Strongest Poison, 1980, Plausible Denial, 1991, Murder in Memphis, 1993; prodr. films Rush to Judgment, 1967, Two men in Dallas, 1987, 92; writer, prodr. plays Trial of James Earl Ray, 1978, Plausible Denial, 1992, Winds of Doctrine, 1994; writer, prodr. screenplays, Arcadia, 1992, Slay the Dreamer, 1992, Plausible Denial, 1993; founder publs. Citizens Quar., 1975, Helping Hand, 1971. Mem. N.Y. State Assembly, 1960-62. With AUS, 1945-47. Home and Office: 105 2nd St NE Washington DC 20002-7303 *I do not believe that our fate is pre-ordained. I do believe that women and men, working together, can determine their own destiny and that the people write their own history. What moves me most directly into action is the fact that I hate bullies. What concerns me the most in contemporary America is the influence of the police and spy organizations with the national news media. Together these are bullies to contemplate and oppose.*

LANE, MARK, museum director. BA in Visual Design, Auburn U., 1971, postgrad., 1980. Graphic designer, sculptor Anniston, Atlanta, Ga., 1972-75; curator exhibits Anniston Mus. Natural History, 1975-79, exec. dir., 1979-81; dir. Witte Mus., San Antonio, 1981-96, dir. emeritus, 1996—; presented and facilitated numerous workshops and projects. Recipient Imagineer award in Humanities, Outstanding Contbn. to South Tex., 1982, Exhibit on Animal Senses award Tex. Hist. Commn., 1983, Un-Sch. for Edn. award, 1983. Home: 219 E Rosewood San Antonio TX 78212 Office: Witte Museum 3801 Broadway St San Antonio TX 78209-6309

LANE, MARVIN MASKALL, JR., electronics company executive; b. Oak Park, Ill., Apr. 25, 1934; s. Marvin Maskall and Lucille Ernestine (Fischer) L.; m. Joan Agar Wheeler, June 28, 1958; children—Elizabeth Agar Anderson, Marlene Celia Christensen. B.S. in Elec. Engring, U. Wis., 1956, M.B.A. in Indsl. Mgmt, 1957. With Texas Instruments Inc., Dallas, 1958—; asst. v.p. Texas Instruments Inc., 1978-80, v.p., treas., 1980-82, v.p., controller, 1982-96, ret., 1996. Trustee, chmn. Tejas Girl Scouts Found., 1988-94; bd. dirs. Dallas Area Rapid Transit, 1986-93; mem. City of Dallas Jud. Nominating Commn. Mem. Fin. Execs. Inst. Presbyterian. Office: Tex Instruments Inc PO Box 655474 Dallas TX 75265-5474

LANE, MATTHEW JAY, lawyer; b. Cin., Mar. 6, 1955; s. Joseph Alan and Adele (Stacks) L. BA, Emory U., 1977; JD, Northwestern U., 1980. Bar:

Ohio 1981, U.S. Dist. Ct. (so. dist.) Ohio 1981, U.S. Ct. Appeals (6th cir.) 1981, Fla. 1982, U.S. Ct. Appeals (11th cir.) 1982. Law clk. to chief judge U.S. Dist. Ct. (so. dist.) Ohio, Cin., 1980-82; ptnr. Lane & Guenthner Co., L.P.A., Cin., 1988-93; v.p., gen. counsel PPI, Inc., North Palm Beach, Fla., 1996—. Legal counsel Juvenile Diabetes Assn., Cin., 1984-92; legal counsel MADD, 1986-92, pres. S.W. Ohio chpt., 1988-91, pres. Palm Beach County chpt., 1993-95; mem. Cin. Bicentennial Commn., 1986-88; bd. trustees Isaac M. Wise Temple, Cin., 1987-89; mem. exec. com. leadership coun. Jewish Fedn. Cin., 1987-92, Big Bros./Big Sisters Devel. Com., 1985-88, Hamilton County Dem. Party, mem. exec. com., county, legis. and jud. selection coms., 1987-92; mem. Palm Beach County Democratic Exec. Com., 1993—; v.p., legal counsel Fetes de Jeunesse, 1984-90. Mem. ABA, Ohio Bar Assn., Fla. Bar Assn., Cin. Bar Assn. (chmn. svc. com.), Phi Beta Kappa. Home: 2840 Gettysburg Ln West Palm Beach FL 33409

LANE, MONTAGUE, physician, educator; b. N.Y.C., Aug. 28, 1929; s. George and Ida (Korn) L.; m. Chrsitine Laura; children: Laura Diane, Adam Reuben. B.A., N.Y. U., 1947; M.B., Chgo. Med. Sch., 1952, M.D., 1953; M.S., Georgetown U., 1957. Diplomate: Am. Bd. Internal Medicine (mem. subcom. on med. oncology 1974-80, cons. 1981-83). Clin. assoc. Nat. Cancer Inst., NIH, 1954-56; sr. investigator Clin. Pharmacology and Exptl. Therapeutics Service; attending physician gen. med. br. Nat. Cancer Inst., 1957-60; assoc. in medicine George Washington U., Med. Sch., 1957-60; asst. prof., assoc. prof. depts. pharmacology and medicine Baylor U. Coll. Medicine, Houston, 1960-67; prof. depts. pharm. and medicine Baylor Coll. Medicine, 1967—, head div. clin. oncology dept. pharmacology, 1969-94, head sect. med. oncology dept. medicine, 1961-92; co-dir. cancer control sci. program Meth. Hosp. and Baylor Coll. Medicine, Houston, 1981-94; mem. study sect. Nat. Cancer Inst., 1966-69, mem. cancer clin. investigations rev. com., 1972-75; chmn. new agts. com. S.W. Cancer Chemotherapy study group; cons. drug evaluations AMA; cons. Merck Manual, U.S. Pharmacopeia, 1981-83; cons. interferon program Schering Corp., 1981-82; cons. com. on orphan drugs FDA, 1986—; cons. UNOMED, 1989-91; mem. adv. bd. Cancer Info. Dissemination and Analysis Ctr., Info Ventures, Inc., 1988-93; mem. sci. adv. bd. Health Infusion, Inc., 1991-94. Assoc. editor: Cancer Research, 1970-80. External adv. bd. Howard U. Cancer Center, 1977-83. Named Disting. Alumnus Chgo. Med. Sch., 1971, Disting. Faculty Mem. Baylor Med. Alumni Assn., 1990. Fellow ACP; mem. Am. Inst. Nutrition, Am. Soc. Clin. Oncology (program chmn. 1970), Am. Soc. Clin. Pharmacology and Exptl. Therapeutics (pres. 1971-72), Am. Soc. Pharmacology and Exptl. Therapeutics, Am. Soc. Hematology, Houston Soc. Internal Medicine (v.p. 1973-74, pres. 1984-85), Am. Assn. Cancer Rsch. (program com. 1990), Harris County Med. Soc. Home: 1514 Bissonnet St Houston TX 77005-1814 Office: 6560 Fannin St Ste 1510 Houston TX 77030-2730

LANE, NANCY, editor; b. N.Y.C., Dec. 20, 1938; d. Morton and Lillian (Gelb) L. A.B. in Am. Civilization, Barnard Coll., 1960. Mem. staff N.Y. Times, 1959-61; from asst. to assoc. editor Polit. Sci. Quar. and Procs. Acad. Polit. Sci., Columbia U., N.Y.C., 1962-70; from assoc. editor to mng. editor Am. Hist. Rev. Am. Hist. Assn., 1970-74; from sr. editor to exec. editor Oxford U. Press, N.Y.C., 1974—. Mem. Am. Hist. Assn., Orgn. Am. Historians. Home: 45 W 10th St New York NY 10011-8763 Office: Oxford U Press 198 Madison Ave New York NY 10016-4308

LANE, NATHAN (JOSEPH LANE), actor; b. Jersey City, N.J., Feb. 3, 1956. Appeared in plays (off-Broadway) A Midsummer Night's Dream, (Broadway) Present Laughter, 1982-83, Merlin, N.Y.C., 1983, Love, N.Y.C., 1984, Raving, N.Y.C., 1984, She Stoops to Conquer, N.Y.C., 1984, The Common Pursuit, New Haven, 1984-85, A Backer's Audition, N.Y.C., 1985, Wind in the Willows, 1985, Measure for Measure, 1985, The Common Pursuit, 1986-87, Claptrap, N.Y.C., 1987, Broadway Bound, New Haven, L.A., Uncounted Blessings, 1988, The Film Society, 1988, The Lisbon Traviata, 1989 (Drama Desk award best actor 1989), A Pig's Valise, 1989, Some Americans Abroad, 1990, Bad Habits , 1990, Lips Together, Teeth Apart, 1991, On Borrowed Time, 1991, Guys and Dolls, 1992, Laughter on the 23rd Floor, 1993-94, Love! Valor! Compassion!, 1995, A Funny Thing Happened On The Way To The Forum, 1996 (Best Actor Tony award 1996); (TV) (miniseries) Valley of the Dolls, 1981, One of the Boys, 1982, host the 50th anniversary Tony awards show, 1996; (films) Ironweed, 1987, The Lemon Sisters, 1990, Joe Versus the Volcano, 1990, He Said, She Said, 1991, Frankie and Johnny, 1991, Life With Mikey, 1993, Addams Family Values, 1993, (voice) The Lion King, 1994, The Birdcage, 1996, Mouse Hung, 1997. Office: William Morris Agy 151 S El Camino Dr Beverly Hills CA 90212-2704

LANE, NEAL FRANCIS, university provost, physics researcher, federal administrator; b. Oklahoma City, Aug. 22, 1938; s. Walter Patrick and Harietta (Hattie) Charlotta (Hollander) L.; m. Joni Sue Williams, June 11, 1960; children: Christy Lynn Lane Saydjari, John Patrick. BS, U. Okla., 1960, MS, 1962, PhD, 1964, DHL (hon.), 1995; DSc (hon.), U. Ala., 1994, Mich. State U., 1995; DHL (hon.), Marymount U., Arlington, Va., 1995; DSc (hon.), Ohio State U., 1996. NSF postdoctoral fellow, 1964-65; asst. prof. physics Rice U., Houston, 1966-69, assoc. prof., 1969-72, prof. physics and space physics and astronomy, 1972-84, chmn. dept. physics, 1977-82; dir. divsn. physics NSF, Washington, 1979-80; chancellor U. Colo., Colorado Springs, 1984-86; provost Rice U., 1986-93; dir. NSF, Washington, 1993—; non-resident fellow Joint Inst. for Lab. Astrophysics U. Colo., Boulder, 1984-93, vis. fellow, 1965-66, 75-76; mem. commn. on phys. sci., math. and applications NRC, 1989-93; bd. overseers Superconducting Super Collider (SSC) Univs. Rsch. Assn., 1985-93; disting. Karcher lectr. U. Okla., Norman, 1983; disting. vis. scientist U. Ky., Lexington, 1980; mem. adv. com. math. and phys. sci. NSF, 1992-93. Co-author: Quantum States of Atoms, Molecules and Solids, Understanding more Quantum Physics; contbr. articles to profl. jours. Active Cath. Commn. Intellectual and Cultural Affairs, 1991. Recipient George Brown prize for superior teaching Rice U., 1973-74, 76-77, Brown Coll. Teaching award Rice U., 1972-73; Alfred P. Sloan Found. fellow, 1967-71. Fellow Am. Phys. Soc. (councilor-at-large 1981-84, chmn. panel on pub. affairs 1983, exec. com. 1981-83, chmn. divsn. electron and atomic physics 1977-78), AAAS, Am. Acad. Arts and Scis.; mem. Am. Inst. Physics (gov. bd. 1984-87), Am. Assn. Physics Tchrs., Phi Beta Kappa, Sigma Xi (pres. elect 1992, pres. 1993). Roman Catholic. Avocations: tennis; squash. Office: NSF Office of Dir 4201 Wilson Blvd Arlington VA 22203-1859

LANE, NEWTON ALEXANDER, retired lawyer; b. Boston, June 16, 1915; s. Samuel B. and Eva (Robbins) L. AB, Harvard U., 1936, JD, 1939. Bar: Mass. 1939. Ptnr. emeritus Lane Altman & Owens, Boston. Served with AUS, 1942-46. Mem. Phi Beta Kappa. Home: 704 Dedham St Newton MA 02159-2937 Office: Lane Altman & Owens 101 Federal St Boston MA 02110-1817

LANE, PATRICIA PEYTON, nursing consultant; b. Danville, Ill., Oct. 5, 1929; d. Louis Weldon Sr. and Ruth Jeanette (Meyer) Peyton; m. H.J. Lane, Dec. 23, 1950 (div.); children: Jennifer Lane-Carr, Peter Lane, Amelia Ozog. Diploma, St. Elizabeth Hosp., 1950; BA in Psychology magna cum laude, Rosary Coll., 1974; postgrad., Lakeview Coll. of Nursing, Danville, Ill., 1987-88; student, Triton Jr. Coll., River Grove, Ill., 1969-72. Staff nurse St. Elizabeth Hosp., Danville, Ill., 1950; staff nurse nursery Ill. Rsch. and Ednl. Hosp., Chgo., 1951, charge nurse tumour clinic, 1951-54; res. sch. nurse elem. schs., Oak Park, Ill., 1969-78; sta. mgr. Oak Park-River Infant Welfare, Oak Park, Ill., 1972-76; vision and hearing screener suburban elem. schs., Ill., 1980-82; sch. nurse West Subrban Assn. Spl. Edn., Cicero, 1978-80; caseworker, counselor Vermilion County Mental Health and Devel. Disabilities, Inc., Danville, 1983-86; case coord., nurse cons. Crosspoint Human Svcs., Danville, 1986-88; staff nurse psychiat. acute care unit Community Hosp. of Ottawa, Ill., 1988-89; dir. social svcs. Pleasant View Luther Home, Ottawa, 1989-93; clin. case coord. Access Svcs., Inc., Mendota, Ill., 1993-97; cmty. ombudsman LaSalle County Alternatives for the Older Adult, Peru, Ill., 1993—; cons. in field. Mem. ANA, Ill. State Nurses Assn. (cert. psychiat./mental nurse). Office: Alternatives for the Older Adult 2000 Luther Dr Peru IL 61354-1205

LANE, RICHARD ALLAN, physician, health sciences educator; b. Camp LeJuene, N.C., Feb. 5, 1956; s. Howard Allan and Elizabeth Jane (Fischer) L.; m. Cynthia Diane Gastineau, Jan. 7, 1978; children: Tiffany Marie, Laurel Christina. BS, U. Md., 1978, MD, 1982; MPH in Tropical Medicine, Tulane U., 1986. Diplomate Am. Bd. Preventive Medicine. Intern Md. Gen. Hosp., Balt., 1982-83; squadron flight surgeon, 363rd Tactical Fighter Wing USAF, Shaw AFB, 1983-85; resident in aerospace medicine USAF, Brooks AFB, 1986-87; advanced through grades to maj. USAF, 1983-87; chief aeromed. svcs. Warner Robins Air Logistics Ctr., Robins AFB, 1987-89; staff physician, microbiology instr. Liberty U., Lynchburg, Va., 1989-91, assoc. prof. health scis., 1991—; cons., spkr. Liberty Godparent Home, Lynchburg, 1989—; mem. residency adv. bd. Meharry Med. Coll., Nashville, Tenn., 1987-89; adj. faculty health sci. Internat. Health Honduras project James Madison U., Harrisonburg, Va., 1993—. Contbr. articles to profl. jours. Bd. dirs. Network for Women in Crisis, Lynchburg, 1990-91; exec. bd. Lynchburg chpt. ARC, 1991-93; founder Emmanuel Bapt. Ch., chpt. AWANA, Warner Robins, Ga., 1987-89. Fellow Am. Coll. Preventive Medicine; mem. Gideons Internat. (camp treas. 1988-89), N.Y. Acad. Scis., Am. Soc. Tropical Medicine and Hygiene, Aerospace Med. Assn. Republican. Baptist. Home: 103 Village Rd Lynchburg VA 24502-2308 Office: Liberty U Health Svc Dept Lynchburg VA 24506

LANE, ROBERT CASEY, lawyer; b. 1932. JD, Loyola U., 1960. Bar: Ill. 1960, Wash. 1969. Atty. U.S. Dept. Justice, Washington, 1960-61; assoc. Lewis, Overbeck & Furman, 1962-69; atty. Weyerhaeuser Co., Tacoma, 1969-77, asst. gen. counsel, 1977-80, v.p., gen. counsel, 1980-97; ret., 1997. Office: Weyerhaeuser Co Law Dept CH 2J28 Tacoma WA 98477

LANE, ROBERT GERHART, lawyer; b. Long Beach, Calif., Sept. 24, 1931; s. Herman G. and Adele (Steg) L.; m. Mary Ellaine Griffith, Aug. 29, 1953; children: John, Scott, David, Mary Katherine. AB, U. So. Calif., 1953, MA in Polit. Sci., 1955, LLB, 1960. Bar: Calif. 1960, U.S. Dist. Ct. (cen. dist.) Calif. 1960, U.S. Ct. Appeals (9th cir.) 1964, U.S. Supreme Ct. 1971. Assoc. Paul, Hastings, Janofsky & Walker, Los Angeles, 1960-67, ptnr., 1967-93, mng. ptnr., 1986-91; gen. counsel U. So. Calif., L.A., 1993—. Mem. Town Hall, L.A.; bd. councilors U. So. Calif., L.A.; mem. bd. alliance Natural History Mus. Los Angeles County; mem. Fellows of the Huntington Libr.; mem. law and justice com. L.A. C. of C. Served to 1st lt. USAFR, 1954-57. Mem. ABA (Robinson Patman com. antitrust sect.), Calif. Bar Assn., Los Angeles County Bar Assn., Order of Coif. Clubs: Jonathan (Los Angeles); Balboa Bay (Newport Beach, Calif.); Annandale Golf (Pasadena, Calif.). Office: U So Calif Office of Gen Counsel University Park ADM 352 Los Angeles CA 90089-5013

LANE, ROBIN, lawyer; b. Kerrville, Tex., Nov. 28 1947; d. Rowland and Gloria (Benson) Richards; m. Stanley Lane, Aug. 22, 1971 (div. 1979); m. Anthony W. Cunningham, Nov. 22, 1980; children: Joshua Lane, Alexandra Cunningham. BA with honors in Econs., U. Fla., 1969; MA, George Washington U., 1971; JD, Stetson U. Coll. Law, 1978. Bar: Fla. 1979, U.S. Ct. Appeals (11th cir.) 1981, U.S. Supreme Ct. 1986, U.S. Ct. Appeals (D.C. cir.) 1992, U.S. Ct. Appeals (3rd cir.) N.Y. 1993. Mgmt. trainee internat. banking Gulf Western Industries, N.Y.C.; internat. rsch. specialist Ryder Systems, Inc., Miami, Fla., 1973, project mgr., 1974; assoc. Wagner, Cunningham, Vaughan & McLaughlin, Tampa, Fla., 1979-85; pvt. practice law, 1985—; guest lectr. med. jurisprudence Stetson U. Coll. Law, 1982-91, also mem. exec. coun. law alumni bd. Contbr. articles to various revs. Recipient Am. Jurisprudence award-torts Lawyers Co-op. Fla., 1979; Scottish Rite fellow, 1968-69. Mem. ABA, Acad. Fla. Trial Lawyers (mem. com. 1983-84), Assn. Trial Lawyers Am., Fla. Bar Assn., Fla. Women's Alliance, Omicron Delta Epsilon. Home: 4934 Saint Croix Dr Tampa FL 33629-4831 Office: PO Box 10155 Tampa FL 33679-0155

LANE, RONALD ALAN, lawyer; b. Ames, Iowa, July 15, 1950; s. Raymond Oscar and Beverly (Burdge) L.; m. Eileen Smietana, June 17, 1972; children: Andrew, Audrey. AB, Miami U., Oxford, Ohio, 1972; JD, Northwestern U., 1975; MBA, U. Chgo., 1987. Bar: U.S. Dist. Ct. (no. dist.) Ill. 1975, U.S. Ct. Appeals (7th cir.) 1975, U.S. Supreme Ct. 1975. Atty. Atchison, Topeka & Santa Fe Ry. Co., Chgo., 1975-78; from asst. gen. atty. to gen. atty. Santa Fe So. Pacific Corp., Chgo., 1979-86, gen. corp. atty., 1986-87; asst. v.p. pers. and labor rels. Atchison, Topeka & Santa Fe Ry. Co., 1987-90; v.p., gen. counsel Ill. Cen. R.R. Co., Chgo., 1990—; mem. railroad shipper trans. adv. coun. Surface Transp. Bd., 1996—. Office: Ill Central RR Co 455 N Cityfront Plaza Dr Chicago IL 60611-5503

LANE, SARAH MARIE CLARK, elementary education educator; b. Conneaut, Ohio, July 27, 1946; d. Robert George and Julia Ellen (Sanford) Clark; m. Ralph Donaldson Lane, May 28, 1977; children: Richard, Laura. BS in Edn., Kent State U., 1977; MS in Edn., Coll. Mt. St. Joseph, 1988. Cert. tchr., Ohio. Coord. newspaper in edn. Tribune Chronicle, Warren, Ohio, 1986-89; tutor MacArthur Found. Project, Warren, Ohio, 1988-89; tchr. chpt. I Lakeview Local Schs., Cortland, Ohio, 1989—. Freelance writer newspaper Conn. News Herald, 1963-64, Tribune Chronicle, 1980-89; contbr. articles to profl. jours.; author: A Walk Through Historic Cortland, 1994. V.p. Bazetta Cortland Hist. Soc., 1983-85; chmn. com. local history project Lakeview Schs., Cortland, 1992—; mem. Trumbull County Bicentennial Commn., 1996—. George Record Found. scholar, 1964-66. Mem. Internat. Reading Assn. (Ohio coun.), Cortland Community Concert Band (pres. 1991-92),. Mem. Christian Ch. (Disciples of Christ). Avocations: writing, historical research, genealogy, reading. Home: 298 Corriedale Dr Cortland OH 44410-1622 Office: Cortland Elem Sch 264 Park Ave Cortland OH 44410-1047

LANE, SYLVIA, economist, educator; b. N.Y.C.; m. Benjamin Lane, Sept. 2, 1939; children: Leonard, Reese, Nancy. A.B., U. Calif., Berkeley, 1934, M.A., 1936; postgrad., Columbia U., 1937; Ph.D., U. So. Calif., 1957. Lectr., asst. prof. U. So. Calif., Los Angeles, 1947-60; asso. prof. econs. San Diego State U., 1961-65; assoc. prof. finance, assoc. dir. Ctr. for Econ. Edn. Calif. State U., Fullerton, 1965-69, chmn. dept. fin., 1967-69; prof. agrl. econs. U. Calif., Davis, 1969-82, prof. emerita, 1982—; prof. emerita and economist Giannini Found., U. Calif.-Berkeley, 1982—; vis. scholar Stanford U., 1975-76; cons. Calif. Adv. Commn. Tax Reform, 1963, Office Consumer Affairs, Exec. Office of Pres., 1972-77, FAO, UN, 1983. Author: (with E. Bryant Phillips) Personal Finance, 1963, rev. edit., 1979, The Insurance Tax, 1965, California's Income Tax Conformity and Withholding, 1968, (with Irma Adelman) The Balance Between Industry and Agriculture in Economic Development, 1989; editl. bd. Agrl. Econs., 1986-92; also articles, reports in field. Project economist Los Angeles County Welfare Planning Coun., 1956-59; del. White House Conf. on Food and Nutrition, 1969, Pres.'s Summit Con. on Inflation, 1974; mem. adv. com. Ctr. for Bldg. Tech., Nat. Bur. Stds., 1975-79; bd. dirs. Am. Coun. Consumer Interests, 1972-74; exec. bd. Am. Agr. Econ. Assn. 1976-79. Ford Found. fellow UCLA, 1963; Ford Found. fellow U. Chgo., 1965; fellow U. Chgo., 1968. Fellow Am. Agrl. Econ. Assn. (life, Sylvia Lane Fellowship Fund 1993); mem. Am. Econ. Assn., Am. Coun. Consumer Interests, Omicron Delta Epsilon (pres. 1973-75, trustee 1975-83, chmn. bd. trustees 1982-84). Home: 1241 Grizzly Peak Blvd Berkeley CA 94708-2127 Office: U Calif Dept Agrl & Resource Econs Berkeley CA 94720 *Select goals carefully . . .*

LANE, TED, literacy education educator; b. Albany, N.Y., June 24, 1928. BS in Elem. Edn., U. N.Mex., 1951; MS in Sch. Adminstrs. and Supervision, N.Y. State Coll. for Tchrs., 1953; EdD in Elem. Edn., NYU, 1970. 5th grade tchr. South Colonie (N.Y.) Sch. Dist., 1954-57; 5th and 6th grade tchr. Levittown (N.Y.) Sch. Dist., 1957-58; fellow NYU, N.Y.C., 1958-59; prof. literacy edn. Jersey City (N.J.) State Coll., 1959—; cons. Title I various schs., N.J., 1964—; cons. adult edn. Jersey City State Coll. Adult Resource Ctr., 1964—; cons. individualized lang. arts Weehawken (N.J.) Sch. Sys., 1965-75; cons. project read write Newark Sch. Sys., 1972-75. Mem. ASCD, Nat. Coun. Tchrs. English, Internat. Reading Assn., N.J. Reading Assn.; N.J. Edn. Assn. Office: Jersey City State Coll Dept Literacy Edn 2039 John F Kennedy Blvd Jersey City NJ 07305-1527

LANE, WALTER RONALD, JR., advertising executive, educator; b. Wilmington, N.C., Sept. 2, 1940; s. Walter Ronald and Dorothy (Holmes) L.; m. Judy Carol Smith, Nov. 14, 1963 (dec. Oct. 1992); 1 child, Sheri Lynn Lane Bevil. AB, U. Ga., 1963, MA, 1964. Promotion mgr. Ln. Labs./Mentho-Mulsion Co., Wilmington, 1961-62; advt. copywriter LSP Advt., Wilmington, 1962; account exec. Am. Lithograph/Case-Hoyt, Atlanta, 1964-67; copywriter Rhodes Advt., Atlanta, 1967; creative dir. SLRS Comms., Athens, Ga., 1967-73, pres., 1973—; prof. U. Ga., Athens, 1973—; mktg. cons. Ga. Inst. Comty. and Area Devel., 1975-81; coord. Am. Assn. Advt. Agys. Inst. Advanced Advt. Studies, Atlanta, 1981-86; advt. mgr. Jour. Advt., 1987-90; mem. accrediting coun. Accrediting Bd. Journalism Colls., 1993—; judge Addy Awards, Peabody Screening Com. Co-author: Advertising Media Problem Solving, 1968, A Perspective for Advertising/Marketing in Emerging European Countries, 1990, Kleppner's Advertising Procedure, 10th edit., 1988, 11th edit., 1990, 12th edit., 1993, 13th edit., 1996; prodr. TV videos; contbr. articles to profl. jours. Grantee Newspaper Advt. Pubs. Assn., 1990, Warning Labels design grantee Am. Cancer Soc./Ga. Med. Coll., 1990. Mem. Am. Advt. Fedn. (bd. dirs., mem. coun. govs. 1992-93, chmn. acad. divsn. 1992-93, mem. acad. divsn. exec. com. 1993-96, Hileman Outstanding Educator award 1987, Outstanding Svc. award 1986), Am. Advt. Found. (bd. dirs. 1992-95), Am. Mktg. Assn., Am. Acad. Advt., Atlanta Advt. Club, Greater Augusta Advt. Club. Presbyterian. Avocations: photography, art, writing. Home: 193 Bent Tree Dr Athens GA 30606-1945 Office: SLRS Comms Inc PO Box 5488 Athens GA 30604-5488

LANE, WILLIAM C., JR., principal. Prin. Gulf Mid. Sch., Cape Coral, Fla. Recipient Blue Ribbon Sch. award U.S. Dept. Edn., 1990-91. Office: Gulf Mid Sch 1809 SW 36th Ter Cape Coral FL 33914-5567*

LANE, WILLIAM HARRY, JR., principal; b. Camden, N.J., Apr. 12, 1951; s. William Harry Sr. and Dorothy (Critchley) L.; 1 child, Kristen Jill. AA, Wesley Coll., 1975; BS in Edn., U. Del., 1976, MEd, 1980; EdD, Widener U., 1993. Cert. tchr., adminstrn., Del. Tchr. Appoquinimink Sch. Dist., Middletown, Del., 1977-82; asst. prin. Woodbridge Jr./Sr. High Sch., Bridgeville, Del., 1982-84; adminstrv. asst. Lt. Gov. Del., Dover, 1984-85; spl. edn. tchr. Smyrna (Del.) High Sch., 1985-89; asst. prin. Delmar (Del.) Jr./Sr. High Sch., 1989-96, Lewes (Del.) Mid. Sch., 1996—. Bd. dirs. Spl. Olympics, Del., 1985-89; com. mem. Blue-Gold All-Star Football Game, Dover, 1990—, chmn. 31st Dist., Dover, 1990—; pres. Jaycees, Dover, 1989-90; bd. dirs. YMCA Resource Ctr., Wilmington, Del., 1990-95; mem. jr. bd. Kent Gen. Hosp. With USN, 1969-73. Mem. Nat. Assn. Secondary Sch. Prin., Assn. for Gifted, Del. Assn. Sch. Adminstrs., Kiwanis, Friends Old Dover, Capital Grange, Ducks Unlimited, VFW, Elks. Presbyterian. Office: Lewes Mid Sch 820 Savannah Rd Lewes DE 19958-1510

LANE, WILLIAM KENNETH, physician; b. Butte, Mont., Nov. 5, 1922; s. John Patrick and Elizabeth Marie (Murphy) L.; m. Gilda Antoinette Parision, Aug. 21, 1954; children: William S., Francine Deirdre. Student, U. Mont., 1940-41, Mt. St. Charles Coll., 1941-43; MD, Marquette U., 1946; postgrad., Med. Coll. Wis. Intern Queen of Angels Hosp., L.A., 1946-47, resident physician, 1954-56; pvt. practice internal medicine San Francisco, 1947-51; resident in urology VA Hosp., Long Beach, Calif., 1956-58; physician VA Hosp., Long Beach, Oakland and Palo Alto, Calif., 1958—; lectr. on psychology of the elderly Foothill Coll., Los Altos, 1972-74; rschr. in field. Bd. dirs., mem. No. Cheyenne Indian Sch.; mem. Josef Meier's Black Hills Theatrical Group, S.D., 1940. With U.S. Army, 1943-46, ETO, lt. USN, 1951-54, Korea. Mem. AMA, Am. Geriatrics Soc., Nat. Assn. VA Physicians, San Francisco County Med. Soc., Woodrow Wilson Ctr. (assoc.), St. Vincent de Paul Soc., Cupertino Landscape Artists (past pres.), Audubon Soc., Stanford Hist. Soc., San Jose Movie/Video Club, San Jose Camera Club, Sierra Club. Roman Catholic. Avocations: oil and watercolor painting, hiking, mountain climbing, outdoor video camcorder photography. Home: 18926 Sara Park Cir Saratoga CA 95070-4164 Office: Stanford VA Med Ctr 3801 Miranda Ave # 171 Palo Alto CA 94304-1207

LANE, WILLIAM W., electronics executive; b. Roanoke, Va., Feb. 25, 1934; s. Melvin V. and Cecile (Lane); m. Ronnie G Lane, Sept. 14, 1978; children: Jonathan D., Drew H., Craig M. B.A., Bklyn. Coll., 1956; M.B.A., Cornell U., 1958. Vice pres. Major Electronics Corp., 1959-70, chmn., dir., 1970; v.p., dir. Internat. Transistor Corp., Burbank, Calif., 1971-73; vice chmn., dir. Internat. Chia Hsin, Taipai, Taiwan, 1973-76; chmn., dir. Emerson (H.K. Ltd.), Hong Kong, from 1976; chmn., CEO, dir. Emerson Radio Corp., North Bergen, N.J., 1974-91; pres. Majorette Enterprises, from 1961; chmn. MAJ EXCO Imports Inc., 1977-85, Emerson Computer Corp., 1989-91, H.H. Scott, Inc. Cardiac Resuscitator Corp., Portland, Oreg., Emerson Italy, Emerson Spain, Atlantic Shore 400 Cons. Corp., Emerson Investment Corp., Major Realty Corp., Emteck Tech. (U.K.) Ltd.; pres. W. Lane & Assocs. Inc., 1992—. Served with AUS, 1958-59. Mem. bus. adv. bd. U.S. Senate.

LANEGRAN, DAVID ANDREW, geography educator; b. St. Paul, Nov. 27, 1941; s. Walter Bucannon and Lita Evangeline (Wilson) L.; children: Kimberley Rae, Elizabeth Ann, Erik David, Katherin Jane. BA, Macalester Coll., St. Paul, 1963; MA, U. Minn., 1966, PhD, 1970. Prof. geography Macalester Coll., 1969—; pres. Minn. Landmarks, St. Paul, 1988—, mng. dir., 1979-82; program assoc. Gen. Svc. Found., St. Paul, 1980-85; vis. prof. several univs., U.S., 1979-89; chmn. bd. dirs. Geographic Edn. Nat. Implementation Project, 1987—; coord. Minn. Alliance for Geographic Edn., St. Paul, 1987; v.p. Nat. Coun. Geographic Edn., 1995—. Author: The Saint Paul Experiment: Initiative of the Latimer Administration, 1989, St. Anthony Park: Portrait of a Community, 1987, Grand Avenue: Renaissance of an Urban Street, 1996, (with others) The Legacy of Minneapolis: Preservation Amid Change, 1983, (with Judith Martin) Where We Live: Residential Districts of the Twin Cities, 1983, (with Ernest Sandeen) The Lake District of Minneapolis: A Neighborhood History, 1979, (with P. Kane) St. Paul Omnibus, Images of the Changing City, 1979, (with Risa Palm) An Invitation to Geography, 1978, (with Patrice St. Peter) Geolinks: K-12 Geography Curriculum, 1994, (with Billine Young) Corand Avenue: Renaissance of an Urban Street, 1996. Chmn. St. Paul City Planning Commn., 1982-87; dir. Northwest Area Found., 1988-90, St. Paul Progress Housing Corp., 1984-86. Named one of ten outstanding coll. or univ. tchrs. of geography Ednl. Change Mag., 1977; recipient Award for Excellence Minn. Soc. AIA, 1978, Burlington-No. award for teaching excellence Burlington No. Found., 1988, 96, Thomas Jefferson Teaching and Cmty. Svc. award Robert McConnell Found.; named to South St. Paul Hall of Excellence, 1989. Mem. Assn. Am. Geographers (treas. 1987-89, nat. councilor 1986-89), Nat. Coun. for Geographic Edn. (joint com. for geographic edn. 1983-85, exec. com., v.p. 1995—). Democrat. Presbyterian. Home: 140 Wheeler St S Saint Paul MN 55105-1925 Office: Macalester Coll 1600 Grand Ave Saint Paul MN 55105-1801

LANER, RICHARD WARREN, lawyer; b. Chgo., July 12, 1933; s. Jack E. and Esther G. (Cohon) L.; m. Barbara Lee Shless, Aug. 15, 1954; children: Lynn, Kenneth. Student, U. Ill., 1951-54; BS, Northwestern U., 1955, LLB, 1956. Bar: Ill. 1956. Assoc. Laner, Muchin, Dombrow, Becker, Levin & Tominberg, Ltd., Chgo., 1956-62, ptnr., 1962—. Editor Northwestern Law Rev., 1954-56; contbr. articles to profl. jours. Mem. Chgo. Bar Assn. (chmn. com. labor law 1972-73), Chgo. Assn. Commerce and Industry, Order of Coif. Home: 1300 Edgewood Ln Northbrook IL 60062-4716 Office: Laner Muchin Dombrow Becker Levin & Tominberg Ltd 515 N State St Fl 28 Chicago IL 60610-4325

LANEY, JAMES THOMAS, ambassador, educator; b. Wilson, Ark., Dec. 24, 1927; s. Thomas Mann and Mary (Hughey) L.; m. Berta Joan Radford, Dec. 20, 1949; children: Berta Joan Vaughn, James T., Arthur Radford, Mary Ruth Laney Reilly, Susan Elizabeth Castle. BA, Yale U., 1950, BD, 1954, PhD, 1966; DD (hon.), Fla. So. Coll., 1977; LHD (hon.), Rhodes Coll., 1979; HHD (hon.), Mercer U., 1980; LLD (hon.), DePauw U., 1985; DD (hon.), Wofford Coll., 1986; LHD (hon.), Millsaps Coll., 1988, Austin Coll., 1990, W.Va. Wesleyan Coll., 1990, Yale U., 1993; DD (hon.), Emory U., 1994; LLD (hon.), U. St. Andrews, Scotland, 1994, Alaska Pacific U., 1994. Chaplain Choate Sch., Wallingford, Conn., 1953-55; ordained to ministry Meth. Ch., 1955; asst. lectr. Yale Div. Sch., 1954-55; pastor St. Paul Meth. Ch., Cin., 1955-58; sec. student Christian movement, prof. Yonsei U., Seoul, Korea, 1959-64; asst. prof. Christian ethics Vanderbilt U. Div. Sch., 1966-69; dean Candler Sch. Theology, Emory U., 1969-77, pres. univ., 1977-93; U.S. amb. to Republic of Korea, 1993-97; vis. prof. Harvard Div. Sch., 1974. Author: The Education of the Heart, 1994; (with J.M. Gustafson) On Being Responsible, 1968; author essays. Pres. Nashville Community Rels. Coun., 1968-69; mem. Yale Coun. Com., 1972-77; bd. dirs. Fund Theol. Edn.; chmn. United Bd. Christian Higher Edn. in Asia, 1990-93; bd. dirs. Atlanta Symphony, 1979-91; chmn. bd. overseers com. to visit Harvard Div. Sch., 1980-85; mem. Yale U. Coun. Exec. Com., 1990-93; mem. Carnegie Endowment Nat. Commn. on Am. & the New World; mem. adv. com. Atlanta Project; chmn. so. dist. Rhodes Scholarship Com., 1980-90; bd. dirs.

Atlantic Coun., 1987-93. With AUS, 1946-48. Selected for Leadership Atlanta, 1970-71; recipient Disting. Alumnus award Yale U. Div. Sch., 1979, 93, Kellogg award for leadership in higher edn., 1983, Wilbur Cross medal Yale Grad. Sch., 1996, Kangwa medal for disting. diplomatic svc., Rep. Korea, 1997, Dept. Defense medal for disting. pub. svc., U.S. Govt., 1997; D.C. Macintosh fellow Yale U., 1965-66. Mem. Am. Soc. Christian Ethics, Soc. for Values Higher Edn. (pres. 1987-91), Coun. on Fgn. Rels., Atlanta C. of C., Commerce Club, Phi Beta Kappa, Omicron Delta Kappa. Office: Emory U Pres Emeritus 1462 Clifton Rd NE Ste 302 Atlanta GA 30322-1063

LANEY, JOHN THOMAS, III, federal judge; b. Columbus, Ga., Mar. 27, 1942; s. John Thomas Jr. and Leila (Davis) L.; m. Louise Pierce, Nov. 23, 1974; children: Thomas Whitfield, Elizabeth Davis. AB, Mercer U., 1964, JD magna cum laude, 1966. Bar: Ga. 1965, U.S. Dist. Ct. (mid. dist.) Ga. 1966, U.S. Ct. Appeals (5th cir.) 1966, U.S. Ct. Mil. Appeals 1967, U.S. Ct. Appeals (11th cir.) 1981. Assoc. Swift, Pease, Davidson & Chapman, Columbus, 1970-73; ptnr. Page, Scrantom, Harris & Chapman, Columbus, 1973-86; judge mid. dist. Ga. U.S. Bankruptcy Ct., Columbus, 1986—. Co-editor-in-chief Mercer Law Rev., 1965-66; contbr. articles to profl. jours. Former pres., dir. Metro. Boys Club of Columbus. Capt. U.S. Army, 1966-70. Mem. ABA (judge adminstrv. divsn. Nat. Conf. Fed. Trial Judges), State Bar Ga. (chmn. gen. practice and trial sect. 1983-84, chmn. state disciplinary bd. 1984-85), Am. Judicature Soc., Nat. Conf. Bankruptcy Judges, Columbus Bar Assn., Inc. (pres. 1985-86), Rotary. Presbyterian. Office: US Bankruptcy Ct 1 Arsenal Pl 901 Front Ave Ste 309 Columbus GA 31901-2728

LANEY, LEROY OLAN, economist, banker; b. Atlanta, Mar. 20, 1943; s. Lee Edwin and Paula Izlar (Bishop) L.; m. Sandra Elaine Prescott, Sept. 3, 1966; children: Prescott Edwin, Lee Olan III. B Indsl. Engring., Ga. Inst. Tech., 1965; MBA in Fin., Emory U., 1967; MA in Econs., U. Colo., 1974, PhD in Econs., 1976. Budget analyst Martin-Marietta Corp., Denver, 1971-72; economist Coun. Econ. Advisers, Washington, 1974-75; internat. economist U.S. Treasury Dept., Washington, 1975-78; sr. economist Fed. Res. Bank Dallas, 1978-88; prof. econs., chmn. dept. Butler U., Indpls., 1989-90; sr. v.p. 1st Hawaiian Bank, Honolulu, 1990—; chmn. Fed. Res. Com. on Internat. Rsch., Washington, 1981-83; vis. prof. U. Tex., Arlington and Dallas, 1978-85; adj. prof. So. Meth. U., Dallas, 1982-85. Editor bank periodicals, 1975-88; contbr. articles to profl. jours. Mem. Internat. Fin. Symposium, Dallas, 1982-85; Hawaii Coun. on Revenues. Lt. USN, 1967-71. Scholar Ga. Inst. Tech., 1961; rsch. fellow Emory U., 1965-67, teaching fellow U. Colo., 1972-73; rsch. grantee Butler U., 1989-90. Mem. Am. Econ. Assn., Western Econ. Assn., Indpls. Econ. Forum, Plaza Club, Honolulu Rotary, Omicron Delta Epsilon, Lambda Alpha, Kappa Sigma. Avocations: sailing, skiing, reading, fly-fishing. Office: 1st Hawaiian Bank Rsch Dept PO Box 3200 Honolulu HI 96847-0001

LANEY, MICHAEL L., manufacturing executive; b. Los Angeles, Sept. 10, 1945; s. Roy and Wanda Laney; m. Marti Miller, Dec. 31, 1964; children: Tynna, Kristen. BS with honors, Calif. State U., Northridge, 1967; MBA, UCLA, 1969. CPA, Calif. Sr. tax acct. Haskins-Sells, Los Angeles, 1967-69; asst. prof. acctg. Calif. State U., Northridge, 1969-72; tax prin. M. Klaiman Acctg. Corp., Beverly Hills, Calif., 1972-75; pvt. practice acctg. Beverly Hills, 1975-80; v.p., controller Ducommun, Inc., Los Angeles, 1980-87; sr. v.p., fin. and adminstrn. Monarch Mirror Door Co. Inc., Chatsworth, Calif., 1987-92; v.p. ops. feature animation Walt Disney Pictures and TV (part of The Walt Disney Co.), Glendale, Calif., 1992-93; sr. v.p. ops. Warner Bros., Glendale, Calif., 1994-96; pres. Children's Wonderland, Agoura, Calif., 1996—. Mem. Fin. Execs. Inst., Tax Execs. Inst., Am. Inst. CPA's, Calif. Soc. CPA's. Office: Children's Wonderland 28310 Roadside Dr Ste 220 Agoura CA 91301-2669

LANFORD, LUKE DEAN, electronics company executive; b. Greer, S.C., Aug. 4, 1922; s. John D. and Ethel W. (Ballenger) L.; m. Donna Marie Cellar, Dec. 20, 1945 (dec. Apr. 29, 1984); 1 dau., Cynthia Lea Lanford Brown; m. Jacquelyn Sue Carr Bussell, Feb. 14, 1986. B.S.E.E., Va. Poly. Inst., 1943. With Western Electric Co., Inc., 1946-78; asst. mgr. tng. Western Electric Co., Inc., N.Y.C., 1957-60; mgr. engring. Western Electric Co., Inc., Kansas City, 1960-63; asst. works mgr. Western Electric Co., Inc., Allentown, Pa., 1963-65; plant mgr. Reading, Pa., 1965-69; gen. mgr. Indpls., 1969-78; dir. Met. Indpls. Television Assn., Inc., Sta. WFYI-TV, 1970—, pres., 1975-79. Served with U.S. Army, 1943-46. Mem. IEEE, Telephone Pioneers Am., Eta Kappa Nu, Tau Beta Pi, Phi Kappa Phi. Republican. Presbyterian. Home: 7810 Camelback Dr Indianapolis IN 46250-1840 Office: 2525 N Shadeland Ave Indianapolis IN 46219-1787

LANFORD, OSCAR ERASMUS, JR., retired university vice chancellor; b. Louisa County, Va., Dec. 19, 1914; s. Oscar E. and Ruth (Miller) L.; m. Caroline C. Sherman, Aug. 24, 1937 (dec. Jan. 1990); children—Oscar III, Caroline Aldrich (Mrs. William Eastman), Henry C. Sherman, William Armistead, Virginia Bowen (Mrs. Sedrudin Hemani); m. Esther Lund Arroe, Feb. 23, 1991. B.S., Va. Mil. Inst., 1934; A.M., Columbia, 1937, Ph.D., 1939. Research chemist Gold Dust Corp., 1934-36; instr. chemistry Columbia, 1937-40; prof. chemistry, chmn. dept. State U. N.Y. Coll., Albany, 1940-52; dean coll. State U. N.Y. Coll., 1952-61; first dir. Atmospheric Scis. Research Center, 1961; pres. Fredonia Coll., SUNY, 1961-70; dir. panel on univ. purposes and goals, gen. mgr. constrn. fund, vice chancellor SUNY, 1970-83, cons. univ. planning and mgmt., 1983—. Author textbooks, articles in sci. jours. Mem. Sigma Xi, Phi Lambda Upsilon. Club: University (Albany, N.Y.). Home and Office: 2567 Brookview Rd Castleton On Hudson NY 12033-9713

LANFORD, OSCAR ERASMUS, III, mathematics educator; b. N.Y.C., Jan. 6, 1940; s. Oscar E. and Caroline Clapp (Sherman) L.; m. Regina Victoria Krigman, Dec. 29, 1961; 1 child, Lizabeth Miller. BA, Wesleyan U., Middletown, Conn., 1960; MA, Princeton U., 1962, PhD, 1966; ScD (hon.), Wesleyan U., 1990. Asst., assoc. to prof. math. U. Calif., Berkeley, 1966-87; prof. math. Swiss Fed. Inst. Tech., Zurich, Switzerland, 1987—; prof. physics Inst. des Hautes Etudes Scientiques, Bures-sur-Yvette, France, 1982-87. Recipient award in applied math and numerical analysis, U.S. Nat. Acad. Sci., 1986. Mem. Am. Math. Soc. Office: ETH-Zentrum, Dept Math, 8092 Zurich Switzerland

LANG, CAROL MAX, veterinarian, educator; b. Paris, Ill., Dec. 29, 1937; s. Acel G. and O. Nadine (Beaver) L.; m. Sylvia Smith, Jan. 10, 1965; children: Karen E., John A., Susan C. BS, U. Ill., 1959, DVM, 1961. Diplomate Am. Coll. Lab. Animal Medicine. Capt., vet. corp. Walter Reed Army Inst. Research, Washington, 1961-63; asst. prof. Pa. State U. Coll. Medicine, Hershey, 1966-69, assoc. prof., 1969-72, prof., 1972-84, George T. Harrell Jr. prof., 1984—, asst. dean continuing edn., 1984-96. Contbr. more than 140 articles to profl. pubs. Served to capt. U.S. Army, 1961-63. Recipient Research award Am. Assn. Lab. Animal Sci., 1980-81, Charles River award Am. Vet. Med. Assn., 1987; Bowman Gray Sch. Med. postdoctoral fellow, 1963-66. Mem. Am. Vet. Med. Assn., Am. Assn. Lab. Animal Sci., Am. Coll. Lab. Animal Medicine (past pres.). Home: 472 Hilltop Rd Hummelstown PA 17036-8512 Office: Pa State U Milton S Hershey Med Ctr PO Box 850 Hershey PA 17033

LANG, CATHERINE LOU, small business owner; b. Hugo, Okla., June 12, 1946; d. John Wilburn Sr. and Velma Lou (Evans) Freeman; m. Laurence Larry Lang, Nov. 20, 1974; children: Tana Louise, Henry Nathan, Gina Elise; 1 stepchild, Michael. BA in Sociology and Econs., Northeastern State U., 1970. Co-owner C&L Jewelry, Waterford, Mich., 1980—; landlord of rental home, Novi, Mich., 1977-93. Active Northwest Child Rescue Women Jr. League, 1975—, League of Women of Detroit; mem. PTA Mercy Sch. for Girls, Farmington, Mich., 1990-94, Walled Lake Mich. Schs., 1981—; mem. Great Decisions, active in leadership, 1988; team parent Team Elan Skating Team, 1991-92; mem. Lakes Assn., Novi, 1992; mem. Covenant Bapt. Ch., 1977—, Am. Bapt. Women. Recipient (with son) Arrow of Light pin Cub Scouts. Mem. AAUW (charter, Novi-Northville br.), MADD, Internat. Fedn. Univ. Women, Nat. Assn. Investors Corp., Detroit Skating Club, Top Stock Stock Club, Lioness of Mich. Democrat. Avocations: ceramic and porcelain dolls, ice skating team supporter, nat. vol. work. Home: 1369 E Lake Dr Novi MI 48377-1442 Office: C&L Jewelry 924 W Huron St Waterford MI 48328-3726

LANG, CECIL YELVERTON, English language educator; b. Walstonburg, N.C., Sept. 18, 1920; s. Wilton Earl and Lillie (Yelverton) L.; m. Violette Noelle Guérin-Lésé, Apr. 2, 1952; 1 child, François-Michel. AB, Duke U., 1941, AM, 1942; MA, Harvard U., 1947, PhD, 1949. Instr., then asst. prof. English Yale U., New Haven, 1949-57; assoc. prof. Claremont (Calif.) Grad. Sch., 1957-59; prof. Syracuse U., N.Y., 1959-65, U. Chgo., 1965-67; prof. Ctr. for Advanced Studies U. Va., Charlottesville, 1967-70, Commonwealth prof. English, 1970-84, John Stewart Bryan prof., 1984-91, prof. emeritus, 1991—. Editor: The Swinburne Letters, 6 vols., 1959-62, New Writings of Swinburne, 1964, The pre-Raphaelites and Their Circle, 1968; co-editor: The Tennyson Letters, 3 vols., 1982-90, The Letters of Matthew Arnold, 1996-97. Served to 1st lt. USAAF, 1942-46. Guggenheim fellow, 1951-52; Fulbright fellow, 1951-52, Morse fellow, 1956-57. Fellow Brit. Acad. (corr.), Royal Soc. Lit., Arts Club (London). Home: 2401 Old Ivy Rd Apt 1507 Charlottesville VA 22903-4860 Office: Univ Va Dept Of English Charlottesville VA 22903

LANG, DANIEL S., artist; b. Tulsa, Mar. 17, 1935; s. Irving and Dorothy D. (Lauterer) L. B.F.A., Tulsa U., 1953; M.F.A., Iowa U., 1959. Asst. prof. art SUNY, Fredonia, 1959-60, Art Inst. Chgo., 1962-64, Washington U., St. Louis, 1964-65; vis. artist Ohio State U., 1968-69, U. South Fla., 1971, U. Utah, spring 1984; adj. prof. U. Utah, 1984—. One-man shows include Boston Mus. Fine Arts, 1961, Arthur Tooth & Sons, London, 1970, 74, Alexandra Monett Gallery, Brussels, Belgium, 1973, 78, Fairweather Hardin Gallery, Chgo., 1971, 77, 80, Il Gabbiano Gallery, Rome, 1975, DM Gallery, London, 1975, Gimpel & Weitzenhofer, N.Y.C., 1976, Fischbach Gallery, N.Y.C., 1977, 79, Graphik Internat. GMBH, Stuttgart, Germany, 1979, Richard Demarco Gallery, Edinburgh, Scotland, 1981, 83, Watson/Willour Gallery, Houston, 1981, David Findlay Gallery, N.Y.C., 1981, 83, Sherry French Gallery, N.Y.C., 1984, Meredith Long Gallery, Houston, 1984, Washington Gallery, Glasgow, 1986, Phillips Gallery, Salt Lake City, 1988, Gilcrease Mus., Tulsa, 1989, Am. Stock Exch., N.Y.C., 1991, Galleria Civica, Seregno, Italy, 1991, The Hokin Gallery, Palm Beach, Fla., 1991, Taylor's Contemporary Gallery, Hot Springs, Alaska, 1992, Galleria Delle Art, Cittá di Castello, Italy, 1992, William Hardie Gallery, Glasgow, Scotland, 1992, Civic Gallery, Urbino, Italy, 1992, London Art Fair, 1994, Elliot Smith Gallery, St. Louis, 1994; group shows include Am. Fedn. of Arts travelling exhbn., 1968-69, U. Pa. Inst. Contemporary Art, 1970, Moore Coll. Art, 1971, Boston U., 1972, Joslyn Art Mus., Omaha and Sheldon Meml. Art Galleries, Lincoln, Nebr., 1973-74, Sherry French Gallery, 1983, 85, 86, Ruth Siegel Gallery, N.Y.C., 1989, Antarctica 2-man show sponsored by NSF, organized by Smithsonian Instn., 1976-79, America 1976 travelling exhbn., 1976-78, including stops at Fogg Art Mus. Harvard U., Wadsworth Atheneum, Hartford, Conn. and, Corcoran Gallery Art, Washington, Watson/de Nagy Gallery of Houston travelling exhbn., 1978-79, Hirschl & Adler Gallery, N.Y.C., 1980, Gerald Peters Gallery, 1993, Landfall Press, Chgo., 1993, Cline Fine Art Gallery, Sante Fe, 1994, U. Tulsa, 1994, London Art Fair, 1997, Glasgow Art Fair, 1997, numerous others; represented in permanent collections including Bklyn. Mus. High Mus. Art, Atlanta, Denver Art Mus., Mus. Modern Art, N.Y.C., Art Inst. Chgo., Library of Congress, Boston Public Library, Calif. Palace Legion of Honor, Nelson Rockefeller Collection, N.Y.C., Victoria and Albert Mus., London, Hunterian Art Gallery, U. Glasgow, Elliot Smith Gallery, St. Louis, 1994, The Cline Fine Art Gallery, Santa Fe, 1994, R. Duane Reed, St. Louis, 1996, Galerie Hertz, Louisville, Ky., 1996, Bridgewater, Lustberg, N.Y., 1997, other pub. and pvt. collections; designer sets for Orfeo, Kent Opera Co., Eng., later filmed by BBC, 1976. Served with U.S. Army, 1954-56. Home (winter): 38 W 56th St New York NY 10019-3814 also: Montone (PG), 06014 Montone Italy

LANG, DOUGLAS STEWARD, lawyer; b. St. Louis, July 25, 1947; s. Ervin Jacob and Jacqueline Helen (Kratky) L.; m. Martha Kay Taylor, Aug. 25, 1973; children: Brian Chester and Christopher John (twins), Stewart Taylor. BS BA, Drake U., 1969; JD, U. Mo., 1972. Bar: Mo. 1972, Tex. 1973, U.S. Dist. Ct. (ea., we. and no. dists.) Tex. 1973, U.S. Ct. Appeals (5th cir.) 1977. Law clk. to Hon. Fred L. Henley Mo. Supreme Ct., St. Louis, 1972-73; assoc. Weber, Baker & Allums, Dallas, 1973-78; ptnr. Gardere, Porter & DeHay, Dallas, 1978-79, Gardere & Wynne, Dallas, 1979—; speaker continuing legal edn. seminars. Bd. dirs. Univ. Park Elem. Sch. Dads' Club, 1988-89, pres. 1990-91; chalice bearer and lay reader Ch. of Incarnation, Dallas, 1984—, mem. symposium on aging, 1990, co-chmn. annual ch. field day, 1988, 89, Sunday sch. tchr., 1982, 83, 90, vestry mem. 1990-95, Christian edn. com., 1992-95, chair bldg. com., 1993—; baseball coach gradesch. teams YMCA, Dallas, 1988-89, football coach gradesch. teams, 1987-92, soccer coach gradesch. teams, 1983-86; campaign chmn., Tex. Election Nathan L. Hecht, judge 95th dist. ct., Dallas, 1982; tribe chief Indian Guides, Dallas, 1985-87; mem. Dallas Mus. Art, 1986—; mem. Dallas County Rep. Men's Club, 1986—; bd. dirs. Girls' Adventure Trails, Inc., Dallas, 1986-92, chmn. facilities com., 1989-90, chmn. long-range planning com., 1987-88; mem. troops com. Boy Scout Troop 72, Dallas, 1989—, asst. scoutmaster, 1992—, order of arrow; v.p. Park Cities Ctrl. Dads' Club, Dallas, 1990-91; pres. Univ. Park Grade Sch. Dad's Club, 1990-91; bd. councillors U. Dallas, 1991-93. Recipient Outstanding Svc. awd. Legal Svcs. North Tex., Dallas, 1991, Alumni Achievement award, Drake U., Des Moines, Iowa, 1992, Double D award Drake U., 1993. Fellow Tex. Bar Found. (sustaining, life, trustee 1997—), Am. Bar Found., Dallas Bar Found (trustee 1991—, sec.-treas. 1994-96, vice chair 1996-97); mem. ABA (litigat. sect. 1974—, exec. com. Met. Bar Caucus 1991—, sec.-treas. 1992-93, pres.-elect 1993-94, pres. 1994-95), State Bar Tex. (coll. state bar Tex. 1992—, bd. dirs. 1992-95, exec. com. 1994-95, Outstanding Third Yr. Dir. award 1995), Dallas Bar Assn. (bd. dirs. 1976-78, 80—, pres. 1991, chmn. exec. dir. search com. 1994, v.p. adminstrv. 1979, 88, v.p. activities 1989, chmn. strategic planning com. 1982-84, mem. numerous coms.), Dallas Assn. Young Lawyers (bd. dirs. 1975, v.p. 1976, treas. 1976, pres. 1977, Outstanding Young Lawyer in Dallas 1981), Tex. Young Lawyers Assn. (bd. dirs. 1976-78), Tex. Assn. Bank Coun. (bd. dirs. 1990-93, v.p. 1994-95, pres. elect 1995-96, pres. 1996-97), Tex. Assn. Defense Counsel, Nat. Conf. Bar Pres. (ex officio, exec. coun. 1994-95, exec. counsel 1995—), Am. Inn of Ct. (membership chmn. 1991-95, exec. com. 1991—, counselor 1995, pres. 1997—), North Tex. Drake Alumni Assn. (pres. 1974-75), Salesmanship Club of Dallas. Republican. Episcopalian. Avocations: golf, hiking, rafting, camping. Office: Gardere & Wynne LLP 1601 Elm St Ste 3000 Dallas TX 75201-4757

LANG, ENID ASHER, psychiatrist; b. Los Angeles, Calif., Aug. 28, 1944; s. Alvin Melville and Inez (Silverberg) Asher; m. Norton Lang; children: Eugenie, Aaron. BA, Harvard U., 1966; MD, U. So. Calif., 1970; MPH in Pub. Health, Columbia U., N.Y.C., 1975. Intern Beth Israel Hosp., N.Y.C., 1971-72; resident in psychiatry Columbia Psychiat. Inst., N.Y.C., 1972-75; fellow Columbia Health Svc., N.Y.C., 1974-75; clin. prof. psychiatry Mt. Sianai Med. Sch., N.Y.C., 1976—; lectr. psychiatry and lit. for faculty, Mt Sinai Dept. Psychiatry, N.Y.C., 1983—. Co-author (Dr. E. Ackerman) Study of Health in Rural France, 1978; (with D. Halperin) Group Psychotherapy, 1983. Bd. govs. Harvard U., Cambridge, Mass., 1993—. Recipient Milbank fellowship, Barrio Health Care, L.A., 1970-71. Mem. Am. Psychiat. Assn., Am. Womens Med. Assn. Jewish. Avocations: literature, playing cello, judging h.s. debates. Office: 1158 5th Ave New York NY 10029-6917

LANG, ERICH KARL, physician, radiologist; b. Vienna, Austria, Dec. 7, 1929; came to U.S., 1950, naturalized, 1960; s. Johann Hans and Caecilia C. (Felkel) L.; m. Nicoli J. Miller, Apr. 21, 1956; children: Erich Christopher, Cortney Alexander Johann. Arbitur, Realgymnasium, 1947; M.S., Columbia U., 1951; M.D., U. Vienna, 1953. Intern U. Iowa Hosps., Iowa City, 1954-55; resident in internal medicine U. Iowa Hosps., 1955-56; resident in radiology Johns Hopkins U. Hosp., Balt., 1956-59; radiologist Johns Hopkins U. Hosp., 1956-61; instr. radiology Johns Hopkins U., 1956-61; radiologist, acting dir. radiology Methodist Hosp., Indpls., 1961-67; prof., chmn. dept. radiology La. State U. Med. Center, Shreveport, 1967-76, New Orleans, 1976-92; prof., chmn. dept. radiology La. State U., Tulane U. schs. medicine, 1976—; dir. radiology Charity Hosp., New Orleans, 1976-92; prof. radiology LSU, 1992—; adj. prof. urology La. State U. Med. Ctr., 1987—; guest prof. U. Vienna, 1992-93; guest/vis. prof. U. Medicine and Dentistry N.J., 1995—. Author numerous articles in field. Served as maj. M.C., U.S. Army, 1961-65. Fellow ACP, Soc. Vascular Surgeons, Am. Coll. Radiology, Billroth Med. Soc.; mem. Radiol. Soc. N. Am., Am. Roentgen Ray Soc., Soc. Nuclear Medicine, Soc. Acad.; Chmn. Radiology, Soc. U. Radiologists, La. New Orleans med. socs., Crescent City Radiol. Soc. Office: 1542 Tulane Ave New Orleans LA 70112-2825

LANG, EUGENE MICHAEL, technology development company executive; b. N.Y.C., Mar. 16, 1919; s. Daniel and Ida Lang; m. Theresa Volmar, Apr. 15, 1946; children: David A., Jane, Stephen. BA, Swarthmore Coll., 1938; MS, Columbia U., 1940; postgrad., Bklyn. Poly. Inst., 1941-42; LLD (hon.), Swarthmore Coll., 1981, St. Paul's Coll., 1987, Columbia U., 1988, SUNY, 1987, St. Michaels Coll., 1988; LHD (hon.), Coll. New Rochelle, 1986, Bank St. Coll., 1986, New Sch. Social Research, 1987, Trinity Coll., Hartford, Conn., 1988; Dr. Pub. Svc. (hon.), R.I. Coll., 1988, CUNY, 1989, Springfield Coll., Mass., 1989, Yale U., 1989, Hunter Coll., 1990, Hobart Coll., 1990, Glassboro State Coll., 1990; LHD (hon.), Bard Coll., 1991; LLD, Lawrence U., 1991, U. Mo., 1993; LHD (hon.), Whitman Coll., 1993; LHD, Goucher Coll., 1994. Works mgr. Aircraft Screw Products, Inc., N.Y.C., 1941-46; founder, pres. Clark Chem. Co., Long Island City, N.Y., 1946-48; co-founder, exec. v.p. Heli-Coil Corp. (now divsn. of Black & Decker), Danbury, Conn., 1948-52; founder, chmn. REFAC Technology Devel. Corp., N.Y.C., 1952—; chmn. Electronic Rsch. Assn., Inc., Winsted, Conn., 1978-90; bd. dirs. other U S. and fgn. cos. Patentee. Contbr. articles on internat. bus., small bus. issues, technology transfer and venture capital projects to profl. publs. Bus. chmn. Citizens for Humphrey-Muskie, N.Y., 1968; trustee, vice chmn. New Sch. Social Rsch., N.Y., 1978—; mng. dir. N.Y.C. Met. Opera Assn., 1978-93; bd. dirs. Columbia U. Grad. Sch. Bus., 1986—; adv. dir. Carnegie-Mellon Grad. Sch. Bus. Adminstrn., 1989—; dir. Mannes Coll. Music, 1989—; chmn. bd. dirs. Swarthmore Coll., Pa., 1981-88, emeritus, 1988—; chmn. Eugene M. Lang Found.; founding donor Eugene Lang Coll., New Sch. Social Rsch.; founder I Have A Dream program minority student edn.; donor Theresa Lang Children's Ambulatory Ctr. N.Y. Hosp.; guest and cultural honoree Gov. of India, 1996. Recipient George Washington award Am.-Hungarian Fedn., 1982, Community Service award Booth Meml. Med. Ctr., N.Y., 1980, Disting. Service for Trusteeship Assn. Governing Bds., Washington, 1985, Brotherhood award NCCJ, 1985, John Jay award Conf. Ind. Colls. and Univs. of N.Y. State, 1986, Booth award Vols. of Am., 1986 presdl. citations, 1979, 85, Family of Man award nat. Council of Chs., 1986, Hubert H. Humphrey Humanitarian award Nat. Urban Coalition, 1986, Jefferson award Am. Inst. Pub. Service, 1986, Martin Luther King medal of Freedom, N.Y. State, 1987, Human Rights award N.J. Ednl. Assn., 1987, Front Page award N.Y. Daily News, 1987, Leadership award Nat. Urban League, 1987, Carter Humanitarian award NAACP, 1987, Salute award U.S. C. of C., 1987, Horatio Alger award Horatio Alger Found., 1987, Pub. Service award P.R. Family Inst., 1988, Friend of Edn. award NEA, N.Y., 1988, Fisher Disting. Service to Edn. award Council for Advancement and Support of Edn., 1988, Disting. Leadership award United Negro Coll. Fund, 1988, Val-Kill award Eleanor Roosevelt Found., 1988, Finley medal CCNY Alumni Assn., 1988, Evangeline Booth award Salvation Army, 1988, CESPA award Elem. Sch. Prins. Assn., 1989, Meridian award Children's Mus. Indpls., 1989, medal of distinction Barnard Coll., 1989, Leadership award Boston Partnership in Edn., Robie award Jackie Robinson Found., 1990, Point of Light citation President George Bush, Pub. Svc. award Boston Dept. Pub. Edn., 1991, Drum Major award So. Christian Leadership Conf., 1991, Trail Blazer award Assn. Negro Bus. Women, 1991, Community Svc. award U.S. Dept. Justice, 1991, Dodge award YMCA, 1992, S. Henry Smith Pub. Svc. award Alfred U., 1992, Fgn. Trade Leadership award Charlotte World Trade Assn., 1992, Champion of Mentoring award Children's Crusade of R.I., Trustee's award Spelman Coll., 1993, Youth Svc. award Upward, Inc., Nat. Caring award, Recog. award Martin Luther King Com., Norman Vincent Peale award Norman Vincent Peale Fedn., 1994, Goodworks award Theaterworks USA, Botwinick prize Columbia U. Bus. Sch., 1995, Achievement in Edn. award McDonald's Corp., 1995, Excellence in Edn. award Pi Lambda Theta, 1995, The Presdl. Medal Freedom President Bill Clinton, 1996; torch bearer 1996 Olympic Games. Mem. Licensing Exec. Soc., Univ. Club, Century Club, Yale Club, Golden Key (hon. mem. Baruch Coll. chpt.). Home: 912 5th Ave New York NY 10021-4159 Office: REFAC Technology Devel Corp 122 E 42nd St New York NY 10168-0002

LANG, GEORGE, restaurateur; b. Székesfehérvár, Hungary, July 13, 1924; came to U.S., 1946, naturalized, 1950; s. Simon and Ilona (Lang) Deutsch; m. Jenifer Lang; children: Andrea, Brian, Simon John, Georgina Kathlyn. Student, U. Szeged, Hungary, 1945, Mozarteum, Salzburg, Austria, 1945-46, U. Stranieri, Perugia, Italy, 1950-51; LHD (hon.), Ind. Univ., 1994. Asst. banquet mgr. Waldorf-Astoria, 1953-58; v.p. sales and marketing Brass Rail Orgn., 1958-60; v.p. Restaurant Assos. Industries, 1960-71; pres. George Lang Corp., N.Y.C., 1971—; owner (with Ronald Lauder) Gundel's Restaurant, Budapest, Hungary, 1990—; co-owner Tokaj and Eger Vineyard. Author: The Cuisine of Hungary, 1971, Lang's Compendium of Culinary Nonsense and Trivia, 1980, The Cafe des Artistes Cookbook, 1984; co-author: Gundel Album, 1993; cons. editor Time-Life Book div.'s Foods of the World series, 1966-70; contbr. to Ency. Brit., 1974, also columnist mags. Pub. mem. Am. Revolution Bicentennial Commn., 1969—, mem. exec. com., chmn. Festival U.S.A. coordinating art, internat. exchange and spl. events for Bicentennial celebrations. Address: 33 W 67th St New York NY 10023-6224 *Almost anyone can be creative given enough time, budget and space, but the ones who succeed today have the common denominator of being poets of the possible.*

LANG, GEORGE EDWARD, lawyer; b. Peekskill, N.Y., Apr. 7, 1932; s. George Louis and Florence (Sheehan) L.; m. Rose Marie Corrao, June 8, 1953; children: G. Vincent Lang, Kathleen M. Lang. AB, U. Notre Dame, 1954, JD, 1955. Bar: Ky. 1955, U.S. Dist. Ct. Ky. 1956. City atty. Munfordville, Ky., 1958-85, Bonnieville, Ky., 1958-85; atty. Hart County, Munfordville, 1962-70; hearing officer Ky. Workmen's Compensation Bd., Munfordville, 1971-79; master commr. Hart Cir. Ct., Munfordville, 1984—; pres. South Ctr. Ky. Broadcasting Co., Munfordville, 1984-88; v.p. Cub Run (Ky.) Industries, 1986-90. Pres. Munfordville Indsl. Found., 1968-90; bd. dirs. Mammoth Cave (Ky.) Devel. Assn., 1972—; chmn. Hart County Dem. Party, Munfordville, 1972-78. Mem. Ctrl. Ky. Wildlife Fedn. (pres. 1962-64), Munfordville Lions Club (pres. 1966-68), Horse Cave Rotary Club (v.p. 1968-69). Roman Catholic. Home: 517 W Center St Munfordville KY 42765-8903 Office: 1 Corrao Bldg PO Box 366 Munfordville KY 42765

LANG, HANS JOACHIM, engineering company executive; b. Crailsheim, Germany, Nov. 17, 1912; came to U.S., 1920, naturalized, 1928; s. Karl Hermann and Marie (Muelberger) L.; m. Emily Ruth Crowl, Feb. 26, 1944; children—Helen Marie (Mrs. Fay Logan, Jr.), Jacqueline Ruth (Mrs. Kirk Weaver), Anne Michelle (Mrs. John Talbot), Robert Crowl. M.E., Stevens Inst. Tech., 1934; M.S., MIT, 1936. Registered profl engr., N.Y., N.J., Pa., Calif., Tex. Process engr. Standard Oil Co., N.J., 1936-41; chief process engr. Day & Zimmermann, Inc., Phila., 1942-50; project mgr. C.F. Braun & Co., Alhambra, Calif., 1950-59; mgr. European sales C.F. Braun & Co., 1959-62; v.p. N. Am. operations Lummus Co., Bloomfield, N.J., 1962-68; pres. J.F. Pritchard & Co., Kansas City, Mo., 1968-69; group pres. Internat. Systems and Controls Engring. Group of Cos., 1969-74; exec. v.p. Procon Inc., Des Plaines, Ill., 1974-75; pres. Procon Inc., 1975-77, Lang Assos. Inc., Tenafly, N.J., 1978—, The Pritchard Corp., Kansas City, Mo., 1978-84. Author books and articles in field. Mem. Am. Bar Assn., State Bar Calif., Am. Inst. Chem. Engrs., ASME, Am. Assn. Cost Engrs. (award of merit 1983). Home and Office: 136 Westervelt Ave Tenafly NJ 07670

LANG, HOWARD LAWRENCE, electrical engineer; b. St. Louis, Nov. 16, 1958; s. William and Hermine L.; m. Karen Friedman, June 26, 1988; children: Arielle Ilyssa, Emily Danielle. BS in Biophysics with high distinction, U. Ill., 1981; MSEE, Cert. Biomedical Engring., Wash. U., St. Louis, 1984; MSE in Computer and Info. Sci., U. Pa., 1990. Registered profl. engr., Pa., N.J. Biomedical engr. Midwest Rsch. Inst., Kansas City, Mo., 1983; sr. engr. AT&T Bell Labs., Holmdel, N.J., 1984—. Contbr. articles to profl. jours.; designer fiber optic comm. sys. Chmn. AT&T Magic Club, Holmdel, 1985-88, Illini Emergency Med. Svcs., Urbana, 1979-81. Mem. IEEE (sr., Service award 1984), NSPE, N.J. Soc. Profl. Engrs., Tau Beta Pi, Phi Eta Sigma. Avocations: magic, cycling. Home: PO Box 200 Holmdel NJ 07733-0200

LANG, JOHN FRANCIS, lawyer; b. Bayonne, N.J., June 8, 1915; s. Lewis F. and Pauline M. (Norwich) L.; m. Eleanor Bradford Cook, Jan. 26, 1952; children: Elaine L. Cornett, Anita L. Knowlton. BA, Georgetown U., 1937;

JD, Harvard U., 1940. Bar: N.Y. 1941, U.S. Dist. Ct. (so. dist.) N.Y., U.S. Ct. Appeals (2d cir.), U.S. Supreme Ct., 1947. Assoc. Buckley & Buckley, N.Y.C., 1940-41, Law Office of D. J. Mooney, N.Y.C., 1946-51, Nash, Ten Eyck, N.Y.C., 1951-53; ptnr. McNutt & Nash, N.Y.C., 1953-56; ptnr. Hill, Betts & Nash, LLP, N.Y.C., 1956-86, of counsel, 1986-96; bd. dirs. numerous corps.; chmn. biennial seminar in Paris on ship and aircraft fin. Co-editor: Maritime Law Handbook of the Internat. Bar Assn. Lt. comdr. USN, 1941-45. Decorated Knight Comdr. (Republic of Liberia). Mem. ABA, Internat. Bar Assn., Maritime Law Assn., Harvard Club of N.Y. Avocations: boating, skiing, travel, writing. Office: c/o Hill Betts & Nash LLP One World Trade Ctr New York NY 10048

LANG, K. D. (KATHERINE DAWN LANG), country music singer, composer; b. Consort, Alta., Can., 1961; d. Adam and Audrey L. Lang. Mem. Tex. swing fiddle band, 1982—; formed band The Reclines. Albums include A Truly Western Experience, 1984, Angel with a Lariat, 1986, Shadowland, 1988, Absolute Torch and Twang, 1990 (Can. Country Music Awards album of the yr.), Ingenue, 1992, Even Cowgirls Get the Blues (soundtrack), 1993; (with others) All You Can Eat, 1995; actress (film) Salmonberries, 1991; TV guest appearance Ellen, 1997. Recipient Can. Country Music awards, including Entertainer of Yr., 1989, Grammy award, 1990, 1993, Best Pop Female Vocal for Constant Craving, Grammy nomination Best Pop Female Vocal for Miss Chatelaine, 1994, William Harold Moon award Soc. of Composers, Authors and Music Publishers of Can., 1994. Office: Sire Records 75 Rockefeller Plz New York NY 10019-6908*

LANG, KURT, sociologist, educator, writer; b. Berlin, Jan. 25, 1924; came to U.S., 1936; s. Ernst and Ilse (Kass) L; m. Gladys Engel, June 9, 1950; children: Glenna Engel, Kevin Engel. BA, U. Chgo., 1949, MA, 1852, PhD, 1953. Rsch. analyst Office of U.S. Milit. Govt., Berlin, 1945-47; asst. prof. U. Miami, Fla., 1953-54; rsch. sociologist Can. Broadcasting Corp., Ottawa, Ont., 1954-56; from asst. to assoc. prof. Queens Coll. CUNY, Flushing, N.Y., 1956-62, assoc. prof., chair, 1963-64; prof. SUNY, Stony Brook, 1964-84, chair, 1965-68; prof. U. Wash., Seattle, 1984-93, prof. emeritus, 1993—, dir. Sch. Comm., 1984-87; vis. assoc. prof. U. Calif., Berkeley, 1962-63; vis. prof. Free U., Berlin, 1992; cons. CBS, N.Y.C., 1964-65, Nat. Adv. Commn. Civil Disorder, Washington, 1967. Author: Collective Dynamic, 1961, Television and Politics, 1968, 84, Battle for Public Opinion, 1983, Etched in Memory, 1990. U.S. Army Rsch. Inst. grantee, 1975-78, NEH fellow, 1971, Woodrow Wilson Ctr. fellow, 1978-79, Nat. Humanities Ctr. fellow, 1983-84, Sr. Fullbright fellow, 1994. Mem. Am. Polit. Sci. Assn. (Disting. Career award in polit. comm. 1994), Am. Assn. Pub. Opinion Rsch. (coun. 1975-77, Disting. Contbn. award 1989), Am. Sociol. Assn. (Edward L. Bernays award 1952), Internat. Inst. Comm. Democrat. Avocations: art study, photography, jogging. Home: 1249 20th Ave E Seattle WA 98112-3530 Office: U Washington Dept Sociology Seattle WA 98195

LANG, LENORE SCHULMAN, visual artist; b. N.Y.C., Nov. 23, 1927; d. Samuel Woolf and Rose (Horowitz) Rosenberg; m. Jerome Lewis Schulman, June 12, 1948 (div. Oct. 1973); 1 child, Ellen Frances; m. Fred Fulton Lang, Jan. 28, 1975 (dec. Nov. 1991); 1 child, Ellen Frances; m. Carl Abraham Auerbach, June 11, 1993. Student, Pratt Inst., Bklyn., 1948, Balt. Mus. Art, 1953-54, IIT Sch. Design, Chgo., 1966-67. Designer Norcross, Inc., N.Y.C., 1948-50; tchr. printmaking North Shore Art League, Winnetka, Ill., 1971-73; juror Art Inst. Chgo., 1985-87. Solo exhbns. include U. Ill. Med. Ctr., Chgo., 1971, Federal Jewish Orgn., Chgo., 1972, Mishkenot Sha'ananim, Jerusalem, 1974, Unicorn Gallery, N.Y.C., 1975, Botanic Gardens, Glencoe, Ill., 1977, Evanston (Ill.) Pub. Libr., 1982, Gruen Gallery, Chgo., 1st Ill. Ctr. bldg. lobby, Chgo., 1985, 101 N. Wacker Dr. bldg. lobby, 1986, East/West Gallery, 1988, Gallery 416, Mpls., 1995, 97; group shows include Art Inst. Chgo., 1978, 79, 87, Peace Mus., Chgo., 1981, Northwestern U., Evanston, 1982, WFMT-Chgo. Mag., 1983, Evanston Art Ctr., 1985, NAB Gallery, Chgo., 1986, Suburban Fine Arts Ctr., Highland Park, Ill., 1988, Spertus Mus., Chgo., 1988, Countryside Gallery, Arlington Heights, Ill., 1989, Chgo. Post Gallery, 1989, Evanston Art Ctr., 1989, State of Ill. Bldg., Chgo., 1989, Artemisia Gallery, Chgo., 1990, Sabbeth Gallery, Glen Cove, N.Y., 1990, Arts Club Chgo., 1991, SCAN Exhibit, Chgo., 1991, Chgo. Cultural Ctr., 1992, Riggs Gallery, La Jolla, Calif., 1992, Beacon St. Gallery, Chgo., 1994, Triangle Gallery, 1995, Ill. State Mus., Springfield, 1995, Mus. Sci. and Industry, Chgo., 1995, Athaneum Music & Art Libr., La Jolla, Calif., 1995, Loyola U., Chgo., 1995, Gallery 416, Mpls., 1995, 96, 97, Ancient Traditions Gallery, 1996, Judy A. Saslow Gallery, Chgo., 1997. Mem. Arts Club Chgo. (profl. mem.), Chgo. Artists Coalition, Cliffdweller's Club (profl. mem.). Avocations: shell, fossil and rock hunting, concerts, theatre, reading, travel. Home: 1530 Tower Rd Winnetka IL 60093-1627 Address: 939 Coast Blvd La Jolla CA 92037

LANG, MABEL LOUISE, classics educator; b. Utica, N.Y., Nov. 12, 1917; d. Louis Bernard and Katherine (Werdge) L. B.A., Cornell U., 1939; M.A., Bryn Mawr Coll., 1940, Ph.D., 1943; Litt.D., Coll. Holy Cross, 1975, Colgate U., 1978; L.H.D., Hamilton Coll. Mem. faculty Bryn Mawr Coll., 1943-91, successively instr., asst. prof., 1943-50, assoc. prof., 1950-59, prof. Greek, 1959-88, chmn. dept., 1960-88, acting dean coll. 2d semester, 1958-59, 60-61; chmn. mng. com. Am. Sch. Classical Studies, Athens, 1975-80; chmn. admissions and fellowship com. Am. Sch. Classical Studies, 1966-72; Blegen disting. rsch. prof. semester I Vassar Coll., 1976-77; Martin classical lectr. Oberlin Coll., 1982. Co-author: Athenian Agora Measures and Tokens; author: Palace of Nestor Frescoes, 1969, Athenian Agora Graffiti and Dipinti, 1976; Herodotean Narrative and Discourse, 1984, Athenian Agor Ostraka, 1990; contbr. articles profl. jours. Guggenheim fellow, 1953-54; Fulbright fellow Greece, 1959-60. Mem. Am. Philos. Soc., Am. Acad. Arts and Scis., German Archaeol. Inst., Am. Philol. Assn., Soc. Promotion Hellenic Studies (Eng.), Classical Assn. (Eng.). Home: 905 New Gulph Rd Bryn Mawr PA 19010-2941

LANG, MARGO TERZIAN, artist; b. Fresno, Calif.; d. Nishan and Araxie (Kazarosian) Terzian; m. Nov. 29, 1942; children: Sandra J. (Mrs. Ronald L. Carr), Roger Mark, Timothy Scott. Student, Fresno State U., 1939-42, Stanford U., 1948-50, Prado Mus., Madrid, 1957-59, Ariz. State U., 1960-61; workshops with, Dong Kingman, Ed Whitney, Rex Brandt, Millard Sheets, George Post. Maj. exhbns. include, Guadalajara, Mex., Brussels, N.Y.C., San Francisco, Chgo., Phoenix, Corcoran Gallery Art, Washington, internat. watercolor exhbn., Los Angeles, Bicentennial shows, Hammer Galleries, N.Y.C., spl. exhbn. aboard, S.S. France, others, over 50 paintings in various Am. embassies throughout world; represented in permanent collections, Nat. Collection Fine Arts Mus., Smithsonian Instn.; lectr., juror art shows; condr. workshops.; interviews and broadcasts on Radio Liberty, Voice of Am. Bd. dirs. Phoenix Symphony Assn., 1965-69, Phoenix Musical Theater, 1965-69. Recipient award for spl. achievements Symphony Assn., 1966, 67, 68, 72, spl. awards State of Ariz., silver medal of excellence Internat. Platform Assn., 1971; honoree U.S. Dept. State celebration of 25 yrs. of exhbn. of paintings in embassies worldwide, 1989. Mem. Internat. Platform Assn., Ariz. Watercolor Assn., Nat. Soc. Arts and Letters (nat. dir. 1971-72, nat. art chmn. 1974-76), Nat. Soc. Lit. and Arts, Phoenix Art Mus., Friends of Mexican Art, Am. Artists Profl. League, English-Speaking Union, Musical Theater Guild, Ariz. Costume Inst., Phoenix Art Mus., Scottsdale Art Ctr., Ariz. Arts Commn. (fine arts panel 1990-91), Friends of Art and Preservation in Embassies. Home: 6127 E Calle Del Paisano Scottsdale AZ 85251-4212 *As a romantic impressionist I feel a tremendous exhilaration at being able to communicate my philosophy through my paintings. I look for God's beauty and mystery in all things, and as an artist, I feel very fortunate that I can eliminate the ugliness and the negatives and concentrate on the wonders of the universe around us.*

LANG, MARVEL, urban affairs educator; b. Bay Springs, Miss., Apr. 2, 1949; s. Otha and Hattie (Denham) L.; m. Mozell Pentecost, Sept. 15, 1973; children: Martin E., Maya S. BA cum laude, Jackson State U., 1970; MA, U. Pitts., 1975; PhD in Urban/Social and Econ. Geography, Rural Settlement and Quantitative Methods/Computer Applications, Mich. State U., 1979; postgrad., St. John's Coll., Santa Fe, 1973, Miss. State U., 1979, Murray State U., 1980. Grad. teaching fellow dept. geography U. Pitts., 1970-72; instr. geography Jackson (Miss.) State U., 1972-74, asst. prof. geography, 1978-82, assoc. prof. geography, 1982-83; assoc. prof., dir. geography program Jackson (Miss.) State U. Ctr. Urban Affairs, 1983-84; grad. teaching & rsch. asst. dept. geography Mich. State U. Computer Inst. Social Sci. Rsch., East Lansing, 1974-76; grad. teaching fellow dept. geography Mich. State U., East Lansing, 1976-78; grad. asst. to dir. Mich. State U. Ctr. Urban Affairs, Coll. Urban Devel., East Lansing, 1977-78; dir. Ctr. Urban Affairs, assoc. prof. urban affairs programs Mich. State U., East Lansing, 1986-91, dir. Ctr. Urban Affairs, prof. urban affairs programs, 1991-93, prof. urban affairs programs, 1993—; profl. geographer Bureau of the Census, Washington, 1984-85, rsch. geographer, 1985-86; instr. geography Lansing C.C., 1976-78, vis. prof., 1990-91; vis. prof. grad. sch. edn. & allied professions Fairfield (Conn.) U., 1990, 91, Egeler correctional facility prison edn. program Spring Arbor Coll., Jackson, 1990, McNair summer rsch. opportunity program, Mich. State U., 1989, 90, Wilberforce U., 1991, 92; rsch. cons. Mich. State U. Ctr. Urban Studies, 1978-79; prin. investigator NASA, 1979-81, Inst. Rsch., Devel. & Engring. in Nuclear Energy, 1980-81, U.S. Dept. Energy, 1980-82; co-prin. investigator & dir. U.S. Bureau of the Census, 1988—; mem. commn. geography & Afro-Am. fellowship U. Pitts, 1970-72; mem. numerous coms. Jackson State U., Mich. State U.; commentator on various radio and television programs; conductor seminars, workshops, and presentations; cons.; speaker in field. Author: (with others) The World at Your Fingertips: A Self Instructional Geography Handbook, 1991; editor: Contemporary Urban America: Problems, Issues and Alternatives, 1991, (with C. Ford) Black Student Retention in Higher Education, 1988, Strategies for Retaining Minorities in Higher Education, 1992; author (with others) Introduction to Remote Sensing of the Environment, 1982, Black Student Retention in Higher Education, 1988, Politics and Policy in the Age of Education, 1990, International Science, Technology, and Development: Philosophy, Theory and Policy, 1990, The Second Handbook of Minority Student Services, 1990, Contemporary Urban America: Problems, Issues, and Alternatives, 1991, The Guide to College Success: For Black Students Only, 1992, numerous tech. reports; mem. editorial bd. Jour. Urban Affairs, Urban Affairs Quarterly, 1992—; referee Urban Affairs Quarterly, Jour. Urban Affairs, Social Devel. Issues Jour., Econ. Devel. Quarterly, Urban Geography Jour.; contbr. articles and reviews to profl. jours. Mem. Gov.'s Coun. Selective Svc. in the State of Miss., 1969-80; bd. dirs. Boys and Girls Clubs of Lansing, 1986-89; chair bd. program com., bd. dirs. St. Vincent Children's Home/Catholic Social Svcs. of Lansing, 1986-89; mem. com. community rels. Tri-County Coun. Aging, 1987-89; mem. adv. com. Mich. Legis. Black Caucus Found., 1987—, hon. host Ann. Black History Month Celebration, 1989-91; mem. coordinating com. Friendship Baptist Ch. Acad. Enrichment Program, 1986-89; bd. dirs. Mich. Protection & Advocacy Svcs., 1991—; faculty advisor MSU Black Grad. Student's Assn., 1989-90; active CIC Acad. Leadership Devel. Program, 1989-90; co-founder, v.p. Black Men Inc. of Greater Lansing, 1992—. Acad. and Marching Band scholar Jackson State U., 1966-70; recipient Outstanding Leadership award Friendship Bapt. Ch. Laymen's League, 1988, Meritorious Svc. award Mich. Legis. Black Caucus Found., 1988; grantee Commn. on Geography and Afro-America and the Nat. Office of Edn., 1973, Jackson State U. Grad. Sch. Rsch. and Publ. Com., 1979, NASA, 1979-80, 80-81, U.S. Dept. Energy, 1980-81, 81-82, Inst. Rsch., Devel. & Engring. Nuclear Energy, 1980-81, NSF, 1980-82, Kellogg Found., 1981-84, Miss. Coun. Humanities, 1982-83, U.S. Bureau of the Census, 1988-90, C.S. Mott Found., 1990-93. Mem. Urban Affairs Assn. (nominating com. 1987-88, membership com. 1987—, site selection com. 1988-89, governing bd. 1989—, chair membership com. 1990-91, sec., treas. 1991-92, vice chair 1992—, chair 1993—), Assn. Am. Geographers (chair com. on the status of Afro-Am. geographers 1980-83, com. affirmative action 1983—, census adv. com. 1990—), Southeast Divsn. Assn. Am. Geographers (steering com. 1980-81, com. edn. 1981-86, program com. 1982), Nat. Coun. Geog. Edn. (remote sensing com. 1981-84), Assn. Advancement of Policy, Rsch. and Devel. in the Third World (conf. program planning com. 1988-89, chair health and population sect. 1988-89), Miss. Coun. Geog. Edn. (pres., chair program com. 1979-80), Population Assn. Am., Assn. Social and Behavioral Scientists, Mich. Acad. Scis., Sigma Rho Sigma Nat. Honor Soc., Gamma Theta Upsilon Nat. Honor Soc., Alpha Kappa Mu Nat. Honor Soc., Alpha Phi Alpha Frat., Inc. Home: 3700 Colchester Rd Lansing MI 48906-3418 Office: Mich State U Ctr Urban Affairs W-104 Owen Hall East Lansing MI 48824

LANG, NICHOLAS PAUL, surgeon; b. Jonesboro, Ark., Apr. 11, 1947; s. Paul Alexandra and Lula (Cornish) L.; m. Carol Ann Holl, Aug. 1968 (div. May 1978); 1 child, Christopher; m. Helen Felecia Haley, July 25, 1979; children: Patrick, Courtney. Student, U. Ark., 1969; MD, U. Ark. Med. Scis., 1973. Diplomate Am. Bd. Surgery. Resident in surgery U. Ark. Med. Scis., Little Rock, 1973-77, assoc. prof. surgery, 1977-84, 1984-90, prof. surgery, 1990—; rsch. fellow Nat. Cancer Inst., Bethesda, Md., 1977-79; staff surgeon Little Rock VA Hosp., 1979-95, chief of surgery, 1995—. Contbr. articles to profl publs. Mem. nat. bd. Am. Cancer Soc., Atlanta, 1989-96; bd. dirs. CARTI, Little Rock, 1994—. Grantee Nat. Cancer Inst., 1995—, EPA, 1996—. Fellow ACS, Southwestern Surg. Congress (councillor 1989-95); mem. AMA, So. Surg. Assn., Assn. for Surg. Edn., Am. Assn. Cancer Rsch. Baptist. Avocations: woodworking, gardening. Home: 1323 White Rd Little Rock AR 72211 Office: Little Rock VA Hosp 4300 W 7th 112LR Little Rock AR 72205

LANG, NORMA M., dean, nursing educator; b. Wausau, Wis., Dec. 27, 1939. BSN, Alverno Coll., 1961; MSN, Marquette U., 1963, PhD, 1974. Staff nurse, asst. instr. St. Joseph's Hosp., 1961-62; instr., coord. med.-surg. nursing St. Mary's Sch. Nursing, 1964-65; instr., asst. prof. Sch. Nursing, U. Wis., Milw., 1965-69, from asst prof. to prof., 1968-92, dean, 1980-92; dean, prof. Sch. Nursing, U. Pa., Phila., 1992—; nursing coord. Wis. Regional Med. Program, 1968-73; rsch. assoc. U. Wis., Milw., 1977, ctr. sci. Urban Rsch. Ctr., 1977-79. Contbr. articles to profl. jours. Fellow Am. Acad. Nursing; mem. ANA, NAS, AAUP, APHA, Am. Heart Assn. Office: U Pa Sch Nursing 420 Guardian Dr Philadelphia PA 19104-6096*

LANG, NORTON DAVID, physicist; b. Chgo., July 5, 1940; s. Charles and Sadelle (Bilow) L.; m. Enid Asher, June 8, 1969; children: Eugenie, Aaron. A.B. summa cum laude, Harvard U., 1962, A.M., 1965, Ph.D., 1968; postgrad. (Knox fellow), London Sch. Economics, 1962-63. Asst. research physicist, lectr. U. Calif., San Diego, 1967-69; mem. staff IBM Research Center, Yorktown Heights, N.Y., 1969—; Erwin W. Mueller meml. lectr., Pa. State U., 1992. Contbr. articles on theoretical physics to profl. jours.; asso. editor: Phys. Rev. Letters, 1980-83. Fellow N.Y. Acad. Scis., Am. Phys. Soc. (chmn. fellowship com. divsn. condensed matter physics 1985-87, Davisson-Germer prize 1977, chmn. Davisson-Germer Prize com. 1990); mem. Phi Beta Kappa. Office: IBM Rsch Ctr Yorktown Heights NY 10598

LANG, OTTO E., industry executive, former Canadian cabinet minister; b. Handel, Sask., Can., May 14, 1932; s. Otto T. and Maria (Wurm) L.; m. Adrian Ann Merchant, 1963-88; children: Maria (dec.), Timothy, Gregory, Andrew, Elisabeth, Amanda, Adrian; m. Deborah McCawley, 1989; stepchildren: Andrew, Rebecca. BA, U. Sask., 1951, LLB, 1953; BCL (Rhodes scholar), Oxford (Eng.) U., 1955; LLD (hon.), U. Man., 1987. Bar: Sask. 1956, Ont., Yukon and N.W.T 1972, Man. 1988; created Queen's counsel 1972. Mem. faculty Law Sch., U. Sask., 1956-68, asso. prof. law, 1958-61, prof., dean law, 1961-68; M.P. for Sask.-Humboldt, 1968-79; Canadian minister without portfolio, 1968-69, minister for energy and water, 1969, minister of manpower and immigration, 1970-72, minister of justice, 1972-75, 78-79, minister transport, 1975-79; minister-in-charge Canadian Wheat Bd., 1969-79; exec. v.p. Pioneer Grain Co. Ltd., James Richardson & Sons Ltd., Winnipeg, Man., Can., 1979-88; chmn. Transp. Inst., U. Man., Winnipeg, 1988-93; mng. dir. Winnipeg Airports Authority, Inc., 1992-93, vice chmn., 1993—; pres., CEO Centra Gas Manitoba, Inc., Winnipeg, 1993—; mem. Queen's Privy Coun. for Can.; hon. consul gen. for Japan, 1993—; bd. dirs. Investors Group Trust Co., Winnipeg Commodity Exch.; bd. chmn. Humboldt Flour Mills, Inc. Editor: Contemporary Problems in Public Law, 1967. Vice pres. Sask. Liberal Assn., 1956-62, fed. campaign chmn., Sask., 1963-64; campaign chmn. Winnipeg United Way, 1983. Mem. St. Charles Golf Club. Roman Catholic. Office: Centra Gas, 444 St Mary Ave, Winnipeg, MB Canada R3C 3T7

LANG, PEARL, dancer, choreographer; b. Chgo., May 1922; d. Jacob and Frieda (Feder) Lack; m. Joseph Wiseman, Nov. 22, 1963. Student, Wright Jr. Coll., U. Chgo.; DFA (hon.), Juilliard Sch. Music, 1995; PhD (hon.), Juilliard Sch., 1995. Formed own co., 1953; faculty Yale, 1954-68; tchr., lectr. Juilliard, 1953-69; tchr., lectr. Jacobs Pillow, Conn. Coll., Neighborhood Playhouse, 1963-68, Israel, Sweden, Netherlands. Soloist, Martha Graham Dance Co., 1944-54; featured roles on Broadway include Carousel, 1945-47, Finian's Rainbow, 1947-48, Danced Marth Graham's roles in Appalachian Spring, 1974-76, Primitive Mysteries, 1978-79, Diversion of Angels, 1948-70, Herodiade, 1977-79; role of Solvieg opposite John Garfield Broadway include, ANTA Peer Gynt; choreographer: TV shows CBC Folio; co-dir. T.S. Eliot's Murder in the Cathedral, Stratford, Conn., Direction, 1964-66, 67, Lamp Unto Your Feet, 158, Look Up and Live TV, 1957; co-dir., choreographer: full length prodn. Dybbuk for CBC; dir. numerous Israel Bond programs; assumed roles Emily Dickinson: Letter to the World, 1970; Clytemnestra, 1973; Jocasta in: Night Journey, 1974, for Martha Graham Dance Co.; choreographer: dance works Song of Deborah, 1952, Moonsung and Windsung, 1952, Legend, 1953, Rites, 1953, And Joy Is My Witness, 1954, Nightflight, 1954, Sky Chant, 1957, Persephone, 1958, Black Marigolds, 1959, Shirah, 1960, Apasionada, 1961, Broken Dialogues, 1962, Shore Bourne, 1964, Dismembered Fable, 1965, Pray for Dark Birds, 1966, Tongues of Fire, 1967, Piece for Brass, 1969, Moonways and Dark Tides, 1970, Sharjuhm, 1971, At That Point in Place and Time, 1973, The Possessed, 1995, Prairie Steps, 1975, Bach Rondelays, 1977, I Never Saw Another Butterfly, 1977, A Seder Night, 1977, Kaddish, 1977, Icarus, 1978, Cantigas Ladino, (10 sephardic songs), 1978, Notturno, 1980, Gypsy Ballad, 1981, Hanele The Orphan, 1981, The Tailor's Megilleh, 1981, Bridal Veil, 1982, Stravinsky's opera Oedipus Rex, 1982, Song of Songs, 1983, Shiru L'adonay, 1983, Tehillim, 1983, Sephardic Romance and Tfila, 1989, Koros, 1990, Eyn Keloheynu, 1991, Schubert Quartetsatz No. 12, 1993, Schubert Quartet 15 1st Mov., 1994, Dream Voyages, 1996. Founder Pearl Lang Dance Found.; mem. Boston Symphony, Tanglewood Fest. Recipient 2 Guggenheim fellowships; recipient Goldfadden award Congress for Jewish Culture, Achievement award Artists and Writers for Peace in the Middle East, Cultural award Workmen's Circle, Queens Coll. award, 1991, Jewish Cultural achievement award Nat. Found. for Jewish Culture, 1992. Mem. Am. Guild Mus. Artists. Home: 382 Central Park W New York NY 10025-6054

LANG, PHILIP DAVID, former state legislator, insurance company executive; b. Portland, Oreg., Dec. 16, 1929; s. Henry W. and Vera (Kern) L.; m. Marcia Jean Smith, May 29, 1952 (div. Oct. 1979); 1 son, Philip David, III; m. Virginia Ann Wolf, Feb. 16, 1980. Student, Lewis and Clark Coll., 1951-53, Northwestern Coll. Law, 1956. Police officer Oreg. Dept. State Police, Salem, 1953-55; claims adjuster Glenns Falls Ins. Co., Portland, 1955-57, Oreg. Automobile Ins. Co., Portland, 1959-61; adminstrv. asst. to mayor City of Portland, 1957-58; spl. agt., underwriter North Pacific Ins. Co., Portland, 1961-63; mgr. North Pacific Ins. Co., 1963-65, asst. v.p., 1965-80, v.p., 1980-95; ret., 1995; asst. v.p. Oreg. Automobile Ins. Co., 1965-80, v.p., 1980-95; ret., 1995. Mem. Oreg. Ho. of Reps., 1960-79, speaker, 1975-79; Div. leader Multnomah County (Oreg.) Democratic Com., 1956-60, mem. precinct com., 1956—. Served with USAF, 1947-50. Mem. Oreg. Ins. Underwriters Assn., Theta Chi. Roman Catholic. Clubs: VFW, Masons, DeMolay (Legion Honor). Home: 5769 SW Huddleson St Portland OR 97219-6645 *Success is achieved through commitment to, and perserverance in, all that is undertaken; balanced with tolerance and understanding of all persons.*

LANG, RICHARD WARREN, economist; b. Mpls., Oct. 23, 1949; s. Norman George and Mildred Elizabeth (Sundheim) L.; m. Carol Jean Nelson, July 31, 1971; children—Scott, Erik. B.A., St. Olaf Coll., 1971; M.A., Ohio State U., 1973, Ph.D., 1977. From economist to sr. economist Fed. Res. Bank St. Louis, 1976-80; rsch. officer, v.p. Fed. Res. Bank Phila., 1980-84, sr. v.p., dir. rsch., 1984—; mem. faculty Ill. Bankers Sch., Carbondale, 1977-80, Pa. Bankers Sch., Lewisburg, 1981—. Contbr. articles to profl. jours. Mem. Am. Econ. Assn., Am. Fin. Assn., Nat. Assn. Bus. Economists, Phi Beta Kappa. Office: Fed Res Bank Phila 10 Independence Mall Philadelphia PA 19106

LANG, ROBERT TODD, lawyer; b. N.Y.C., July 2, 1924; s. Charles and Selma L.; m. Joann Lang, Aug. 4, 1949; children: William Gerald, James David, Nancy Adler, Carolyn Kay. BA, Yale U., 1945, LLB, 1947. Bar: N.Y., U.S. Dist. Ct. (so. dist.) N.Y. Assoc. Weil, Gotshal & Manges, N.Y.C., 1948-56; ptnr. Weil, Gotshal & Manges (P.C. since 1981), N.Y.C., 1956—. Bd. dirs. Lawyers' Com. for Human Rights. Recipient Golden Torch of Hope award City of Hope, 1971, Community Svc. award Brandeis U., 1982, Learned Hand award Am. Jewish Com., 1991. Mem. ABA (chmn. subcom. proxy solicitations/tender offers 1985-93, chmn. task force listing standards self-regulatory orgn., chmn. task force on hedge funds, chmn. ad hoc com. on instnl. investors 1991-95, mem. task force on exec. compensation 1991-94, mem. task force on rev. of fed. securities laws, mem. adv. com.), NASD (legal adv. bd.), N.Y. County Lawyers Assn. (chmn. corp. law com. 1971-76, spl. com. on legal opinions 1977-81), Am. Stock Exch. (spl. com. shareholder voting rights), Yale Club of N.Y.C., Harmonie Club, Sunningdale Country Club. Office: Weil Gotshal & Manges PC 767 5th Ave New York NY 10153-0001

LANG, THOMPSON HUGHES, publishing company executive; b. Albuquerque, Dec. 12, 1946; s. Cornelius Thompson and Margaret Miller (Hughes) L. Student, U. N.Mex., 1965-68, U. Americas, Mexico City, 1968-69. Advt. salesman Albuquerque Pub. Co., 1969-70, pres., treas., gen. mgr., dir., 1971—; pub., pres., treas., dir. Jour. Pub. Co., 1971—; pres., dir. Masthead, Internat., 1971—; pres. Magnum Systems, Inc., 1973—; pres., treas., dir. Jour. Ctr. Corp., 1979—; chmn. bd., dir. Starline Printing, Inc., 1985—; chmn. bd. dirs. Corp. Security and Investigation, Inc., 1986—; pres., bd. dirs. Eagle Systems, Inc., 1986—. Mem. HOW Orgn., Sigma Delta Chi. Home: 8643 Rio Grande Blvd NW Albuquerque NM 87114-1301 Office: Albuquerque Pub Co PO Drawer JT(87103) 7777 Jefferson St NE Albuquerque NM 87109-4343

LANG, VERA J., publishing company executive. U.S. treas. Reed Elsevier, Inc., N.Y.C. Office: Reed Elsevier Inc 200 Park Ave Fl 17 New York NY 10166

LANG, WILLIAM CHARLES, retail executive; b. Bronx, N.Y., Jan. 29, 1944; s. Harold C. and Katherine L. (Pratt) L.; m. Marilyn Warshow, June 27, 1965 (dec.); children: Kenneth William, Pamela Sue. B.S. magna cum laude, Lehigh U., 1965. C.P.A. Accounting supr. Peat, Marwick, Mitchell & Co., 1965-69; contr. Pueblo Internat., Inc., N.Y.C., 1970-72, v.p. fin., 1972-77; exec. v.p. adminstrn. and fin. Kenyon & Eckhardt, Inc., 1977-85; exec. mng. dir. Finley, Kumble, Wagner, Heine, Underberg, Manley, Myerson & Casey, 1985-88; pres., chief fin. officer Furr's Inc., Lubbock, Tex., 1989-92; sr. v.p. fin. and adminstrn., chief fin. officer Duane Reade, N.Y.C., 1993-96; sr. v.p. finance, CFO GAF Bldg. Materials Corp., Wayne, N.J., 1997—. Mem. Financial Execs. Inst., Am. Inst. C.P.A.'s, Nat. Accounting Soc., N.Y. State Soc. C.P.A.'s, Beta Gamma Sigma, Sigma Phi. Office: GAF Bldg Materials Corp 1361 Alps Rd Wayne NJ 07470-3700

LANG, WILLIAM EDWARD, mathematics educator; b. Salisbury, Md., Oct. 22, 1952; s. Woodrow Wilson and Clara T. L. BA, Carleton Coll., 1974; MS, Yale U., 1975; PhD, Harvard U., 1978. Vis. mem. Inst. for Advanced Study, Princeton, N.J., 1978-79; exch. prof. Universite de Paris, Orsay, 1980; C.L.E. Moore instr. MIT, Cambridge, 1980-82; asst. prof. U. Minn., Mpls., 1982-83, assoc. prof., 1983-89; vis. assoc. prof. Brigham Young U., Provo, Utah, 1988-89, prof., 1989—. Contbr. articles to profl. jours. Fellow NSF 1974-77, 79-80. Mem. Am. Math. Soc., Math. Assn. Am., Math. Scis. Rsch. Inst., Sigma Xi. Republican. Office: Brigham Young Univ Dept Math Provo UT 84602

LANG, WILLIAM WARNER, physicist; b. Boston, Aug. 9, 1926; s. William Warner and Lilla Gertrude (Wheeler) L.; m. Asta Ingard, Aug. 31, 1954; 1 son, Robert. B.S., Iowa State U., 1946, Ph.D., 1958; M.S., M.I.T., 1949. Acoustical engr. Bolt Beranek and Newman, Inc., Cambridge, Mass., 1949-51; instr. in physics U.S. Naval Postgrad. Sch., Monterey, Calif., 1951-55; cons. engr. E.I. du Pont de Nemours & Co., Wilmington, Del., 1955-57; mem. research staff M.I.T., 1958; physicist IBM, Poughkeepsie, N.Y., 1958-92; program mgr. acoustics tech. IBM, 1976-90, mem. sr. tech. staff, 1990-92; pres. Internat. Inst. Noise Control Engring., Poughkeepsie, 1988—. Editor: Designing for Noise Control, 1978. Pres. Noise Control Found., Poughkeepsie, 1975-92, 1994—; adj. prof. physics Vassar Coll., 1979-96; chmn. working group Internat. Orgn. Standardization, 1969—; chmn. tech. com. 29 Internat. Electrotech. Commn., 1975-84. Served with USN, 1944-47, 52. Decorated Meritorious Service medal; recipient Pro Silentio medal

Hungarian Optical, Acoustical and Film Tech. Soc., 1989. Fellow AAAS, IEEE (Audio and Electroacoustics Achievement award 1970, dir. 1970-71, Centennial medal 1984), Audio Engring. Soc., Acoustical Soc. Am. (Silver medal 1984, treas. 1994—), Inst. Acoustics (U.K.) (hon.); mem. Nat. Acad. Engring., Inst. Noise Control Engring./U.S.A. (pres. 1978), Rotary (pres. local club 1975-76). Episcopalian. Home: 29 Hornbeck Rdg Poughkeepsie NY 12603-4205 Office: Internat Inst Noise Control Engring PO Box 3067 Poughkeepsie NY 12603-3067

LANGACKER, PAUL GEORGE, physics educator; b. Evanston, Ill., July 14, 1946; s. George Rollo and Florence (Hinesley) L.; m. Irmgard Sieker, June 25, 1983. BS, MIT, 1968; PhD, U. Calif., Berkeley, 1972; MA, U. Pa., 1981. Postdoctoral assoc. Rockefeller U., N.Y.C., 1972-74; postdoctoral assoc. U. Pa., Phila., 1974-75, asst. prof. physics, 1975-81, assoc. prof. physics, 1981-85, prof. physics, 1985-93, William Smith Term prof. physics, 1993—, chair, dept. physics and astronomy, 1996—; exec. com. Divsn. Particles & Fields of Am. Phys. Soc., Washington, 1989-91; mem. editorial bd. Phys. Rev., 1986-88, 91-93; sci. dir. Theoretical Advanced Study Inst., Boulder, Colo., 1990. Editor: Testing the Standard Model, 1991, Precision Tests of the Standard Electroweak Model, 1995. Recipient Humboldt award A.V. Humboldt Soc., 1987-88. Fellow Am. Phys. Soc., AAAS. Office: U of Pa Dept of Physics 2N10 David Rittenhouse Lab Philadelphia PA 19104

LANGACKER, RONALD WAYNE, linguistics educator; b. Fond du Lac, Wis., Dec. 27, 1942; s. George Rollo and Florence (Hinesley) L.; m. Margaret G. Fullick, June 5, 1966 (dec.). A.B. in French, U. Ill., 1963, A.M. in Linguistics, 1964, Ph.D., 1966. Asst. prof. U. Calif. at San Diego, La Jolla, 1966-70; asso. prof. U. Calif. at San Diego, 1970-75, prof. linguistics, 1975—. Author: Language and its Structure, 1968, Fundamentals of Linguistic Analysis, 1972, Non-Distinct Arguments in Uto-Aztecan, 1976, An Overview of Uto-Aztecan Grammar, 1977, Foundations of Cognitive Grammar I, 1987, Concept, Image and Symbol, 1990, Foundations of Cognitive Grammar II, 1991; assoc. editor: Lang, 1971-77, Cognitive Linguistics, 1989—; contbr. articles in field to profl. jours. Guggenheim fellow, 1978. Mem. Linguistic Soc. Am., Cognitive Sci. Soc., Soc. for Study Indigenous Langs. of Ams., Internat. Cognitive Linguistics Assn., AAUP, ACLU. Home: 7381 Rue Michael La Jolla CA 92037-3915 Office: U Calif San Diego Dept Linguistics 0108 La Jolla CA 92093

LANGAN, JOHN PATRICK, philosophy educator; b. Hartford, Conn., Aug. 10, 1940; s. Eugene Edward and Sarah Cecilia (McCole) Langan. AB, Loyola U., Chgo., 1962; MA, Loyola U., 1966; BD, Woodstock Coll., N.Y.C., 1970; PhD, U. Mich., 1979. Ordained priest, Roman Cath. Ch., 1972. Instr. philosophy U. Mich., Ann Arbor, 1971-72; research fellow Woodstock Theol. Ctr., Washington, 1975-83; vis. asst. prof. social ethics Yale Div. Sch., New Haven, 1983; sr. fellow Woodstock Theol. Ctr., 1983—, acting dir., 1986-87; Rose F. Kennedy prof. Christian ethics Kennedy Inst. Ethics, Georgetown U., Washington, 1987—; bd. dirs. Georgetown U. Press, 1984—; vis. rsch. scholar Jesuit Inst. Boston Coll., 1993-94; mem. rsch. coun. Ctr. Strategic and Internat. Studies, 1993—; Wirtenberger prof. social ethics Loyola U. Chgo., 1995-97; cons. in field. Editor: The American Search for Peace, 1991, The Nuclear Dilemma and the Just War Tradition, 1986, Human Rights in the Americas: The Struggle for Consensus, 1982, Catholic Universities in Church and Society, 1993. Bd. dirs. Bon Secours Health System, 1990, Nat. Capital Presbytery, Health Care Ministries, Washington, 1989-92. Rackham Prize fellow, U. Mich., 1972-73. Mem. Am. Acad. Religion, Am. Philos. Assn., Cath. Theol. Soc. Am., Soc. Christian Ethics, Soc. Christian Philosophers, Soc. for Bus. Ethics, Internat. Studies Assn. Roman Catholic. Avocations: music, swimming. Office: Georgetown U 1437 37th St NW Washington DC 20007-2610

LANGAN, MARIE-NOELLE SUZANNE, cardiologist, educator; b. White Plains, N.Y., Aug. 4, 1960. Grad., U. Toronto, Can., 1980, MD, 1984. Diplomate Am. Bd. Internal Medicine, Am. Bd. Cardiology, Am. Bd. Clin. Electrophysiology. Intern St. Mary's Hosp./ McGill U., Montreal, Can., 1984-95; resident U. Toronto/ St. Michael's Hosp., 1985-87; cardiology fellow Phila. Heart Inst./ U. Pa. Med. Ctr., 1988-90, 1990-91; clin. instr. medicine Sch. Medicine U. Pa., 1988-89, fellow dept. medicine, 1990-91; asst. prof. medicine, dir. electrophysiology lab. George Washington U., Washington, 1991-93. Contbr. chpts. to books and articles to profl. jours. Fellow Am. Coll. Cardiology, Royal Coll. Physicians & Surgeons Can.; mem. N.Am. Soc. Pacing & Electrophysiology, Am. Heart Assn. (Clinician Scientist award 1996), Coll. Physicians & Surgeons Can.; grantee NIH. Office: Mount Sinai Med Ctr 1 Gustave L Levy Pl Box 1054 New York NY 10028

LANGBAUM, ROBERT WOODROW, English language educator, author; b. N.Y.C., Feb. 23, 1924; s. Murray and Nettie (Moskowitz) L.; m. Francesca Levi Vidale, Nov. 5, 1950; 1 child, Donata Emily. A.B., Cornell U., 1947; M.A., Columbia U., 1949, Ph.D., 1954. Instr. English Cornell U., 1950-55, asst. prof., 1955-60; assoc. prof. U. Va., Charlottesville, 1960-63; prof. English U. Va., 1963-67, James Branch Cabell prof. English and Am. lit., 1967—; vis. prof. Columbia U., summer 1960, 65-66, Harvard U., summer 1965; mem. supervising com. English Inst., 1970-71, chmn., 1972; mem. Christian Gauss Book Award Com., 1984-86; U.S. Info. Svc. lectr. Japan, Taiwan, Hong Kong, 1988. Author: The Poetry of Experience: The Dramatic Monologue in Modern Literary Tradition, 1957, The Gayety of Vision: A Study of Isak Dinesen's Art, 1964, The Modern Spirit: Essays on the Continuity of Nineteenth and Twentieth Century Literature, 1970, The Mysteries of Identity: A Theme in Modern Literature, 1977, The Word From Below: Essays on Modern Literature and Culture, 1987, Thomas Hardy in Our Time, 1995; editor: The Tempest (Shakespeare), 1964; anthology The Victorian Age: Essays in History and in Social and Literary Criticism, 1967; mem. editl. bd. Victorian Poetry, 1963—, New Lit. History, 1969—, Bull. Rsch. in Humanities, 1977—, Studies in English Lit., 1978—, So. Humanities Rev., 1979—, Studies in Browning and His Circle, 1987—, Victorian Lit. and Culture, 1991—, Symbiosis, 1995—. Served to 1st lt. M.I. AUS, 1942-46. Ford Found. fellow Center for Advanced Study, Stanford, Calif., 1961-62; Guggenheim fellow, 1969-70; sr. fellow Nat. Endowment for Humanities, 1972-73; Am. Council Learned Socs. grantee, 1961, 75-76; fellow Clare Hall, Cambridge U., Eng., 1978; U. Va. Ctr. Advanced Study fellow, 1982; resident scholar Bellagio Study and Conf. Ctr. Rockefeller Found., Italy, June 1987. Mem. MLA (del. assembly 1979-81), AAUP, PEN, Assn. Lit. Scholars and Critics, Phi Beta Kappa. Home: 223 Montvue Dr Charlottesville VA 22901-2022

LANGBEIN, JOHN HARRISS, lawyer, educator; b. Washington, Nov. 17, 1941; s. I. L. and M. V. (Harriss) L.; m. Kirsti M. Hiekka, June 24, 1973; children: Christopher, Julia, Anne. AB, Columbia U., 1964; LLB, Harvard U., 1968, Cambridge U., 1969; PhD, Cambridge U., 1971; MA (hon.), Yale U., 1990. Bar: D.C. 1969, Fla. 1970; barrister-at-law Inner Temple, Eng., 1970. Asst. prof. law U. Chgo., 1971-73, assoc. prof., 1973-74, prof., 1974-80, Max Pam prof. Am. and fgn. law, 1980-90; Chancellor Kent prof. law and legal history Yale U., New Haven, 1990—; commr. Nat. Conf. Commrs. on Uniform State Laws, 1984—; reporter Uniform Prudent Investor Act; assoc. reporter Restatement of Property (3d): Wills and Donative Transfers. Author: Prosecuting Crime in the Renaissance, 1974, Torture and the Law of Proof: Europe and England in the Ancient Regime, 1977, Comparative Criminal Procedure: Germany, 1977; (with L. Waggoner) Selected Statutes on Trusts and Estates, 1987, rev. edits., 1991, 92, 94, 95; (with B. WolK) Pension and Employee Benefit Law, 1990, 2d edit., 1995, (with R. Helmholz et al.) The Privilege Against Self-Incrimination, 1997; contbr. numerous articles on law and legal history in profl. jours. Mem. ABA, Am. Coll. Trust and Estate Counsel, Am. Law Inst., Am. Soc. Legal History, Am. Hist. Assn., Selden Soc., Gesellschaft fuer Rechtsvergleichung, Am. Acad. of Arts and Scis., Internat. Acad. Estate and Trust Law, Internat. Acad. Comparative Law. Republican. Episcopalian. Office: Yale Univ Sch Law PO Box 208215 127 Wall St New Haven CT 06520-8215

LANGBO, ARNOLD GORDON, food company executive; b. Richmond, B.C., Can., Apr. 13, 1937; s. Osbjourn and Laura Marie (Hagen) L.; m. Martha Marie Miller, May 30, 1959; children: Sharon Anne, Maureen Bernice, Susan Colleen, Roderick Arnold, Robert Wayne, Gary Thomas, Craig Peter, Keith Edward. Student, U. B.C. Retail salesman Kellogg Co., Vancouver, 1956-57; dist. mgr. Kellogg Co., Prince George, B.C., 1957-60; supermarket salesman Kellogg Co., Vancouver, 1960; dist mgr. Kellogg Co., Winnipeg, Man., 1964-65; acct. mgr. Kellog Co. of Can., Ltd., Toronto, 1965-67; sales staff asst. Kellogg Co., Battle Creek, Mich., 1967-69, adminstrv. asst. to pres., 1969; exec. v.p. Kellogg Co. of Can. Ltd., London, Ont., 1970; v.p. sales and mktg. Kellogg Salada Can. Ltd., Toronto, 1971-74, sr. v.p. sales and mktg., 1974-76, pres., chief exec. officer, 1976-78; pres. food products div. Kellogg U.S., Battle Creek, 1978-81; past exec. v.p. Kellogg Co., Battle Creek, group exec. v.p., 1983-86, exec. v.p., 1986—; pres. Kellogg Internat., Battle Creek, 1986—; pres. Mrs. Smith's Frozen Foods Co. (subs. Kellogg Co.), Battle Creek, 1983-85, chmn., chief exec. officer, 1985—; pres. Kellogg Internat., 1986—, pres., COO, internat. bd. dirs., 1990—; chmn., CEO Kellogg Co., Battle Creek, 1992—, also dir.; bd. dirs. Johnson & Johnson, Grocery Mfg. Am., Gilmore Int. Keyboard Festival. Vice-pres. Hockey Internat., Battle Creek; trustee Albion Coll.; mem. Canadian-Am. Com., B.C. Premier's Econ. Adv. Coun.; mem. adv. bd. J. L. Kellogg Grad. Sch. Mgmt., Northwestern U.; bd. dirs. Gilmore Internat. Keyboard Festival. Mem. Am. Frozen Food Inst. (bd. dirs., vice chmn. 1985), Grocery Products Mfrs. Can. (bd. dirs.), Tea Council of Can. (bd. dirs.). Office: Kellogg Co Box 3599 1 Kellogg Sq Battle Creek MI 49017-3599*

LANGBORT, POLLY, retired advertising executive; b. N.Y.C.; d. Julius and Nettie (Berman) L. BA, Adelphi U. Sec. Young & Rubicam, Inc., N.Y.C., media buyer, media planner, 1960-65, planning supr., 1965-70, v.p. group supr., 1970-75, v.p. dir. planning devel., 1975-80, sr. v.p., dir. planning, 1980-85, sr. v.p. direct mktg. and media services Wunderman, Worldwide div., 1985-86, exec. v.p. dir. mktg. & media services Wunderman, Worldwide div., 1986-90; assoc. pub. Lear's Mag., N.Y.C., 1990-91; ret., 1991. Author: DMA Factbook, 1986; contbr. articles to profl. jours. Spl. gifts chairperson Am. Cancer Soc., N.Y.C., 1985-90. Jewish. Avocations: classical music, outdoor activities. Home: 7614 La Corniche Cir Boca Raton FL 33433

LANGDALE, EMORY LAWRENCE, physician; b. Walterboro, S.C., Oct. 14, 1919; s. Clint May and Lillian Blanch (Reddish) L.; m. Maggie Lee Herndon (dec. 1971); children: Fred Emory, Betty Marlene, Thomas Wayne, Emory Lawrence, Jr.; m. Annie Newell Smith, Feb. 17, 1973. BS, Coll. Charleston, 1949; MD, Med. U. S.C., 1953. Diplomate Am. Acad. Physical Medicine and Rehab. Resident VA Hosp., Richmond, Va., 1963-66; chief rehab. medicine VA Med. Ctr., Hampton, Va., 1966-69; asst. prof. physical medicine and rehab. Med. Coll. Va., Richmond, 1969-74; med. officer Charleston (S.C.) Regional Naval Hosp., 1974-76; chief rehab. medicine VA Med. Ctr., Augusta, Ga., 1974-81; assoc. prof. Med. U. S.C., 1981-85; med. dir. Rehab. Svc. Colleton Rsch. Hosp., Walterboro, S.C., 1987-91; private practice No. Charleston, 1989—. With Coast Guard, 1942-45, ATO, PTO. Fellow Am. Acad. Physical Medicine and Rehab.; mem. AMA (physician's recognition award 1980), Med. Soc. Va., S.C. Med. Assn., So. Soc. Physical Medicine and Rehab., Charleston County Med. Soc. Republican. Baptist. Avocations: hunting, fishing. Home: 1064 Stonehenge Dr Charleston SC 29406-2417 Office: 1250 Remount Rd Charleston SC 29406-3419

LANGDALE, GEORGE WILFRED, research soil scientist; b. Walterboro, S.C., Sept. 14, 1930; s. Benjamin Hayward and Hazel Ruth (Smith) L.; m. Eugenia Miles Boatwright, Aug. 28, 1955. B.S., Clemson Univ., 1957, MS, 1961; PhD, Univ. Ga., 1969. Rsch. soil scientist USDA, Agrl. Rsch. Svc., S.C., Ga., Tex., 1957-96, ret. 1996; conservation tillage and soil erosion. Contbr. book chpts. and articles to profl. jours. Served with 27th Inf. Wolfhounds U.S. Army, 1951-53, Korea. Kellogg fellow Agr. Policy Inst., 1963-64. Fellow Soil and Water Conservation Soc. (H.H. Bennett award 1993, chpt. pres. Tex. 1970-71, Ga. 1994-95), Am. Soc. Agronomy (pres. Ga. chpt. 1986-87), Soil Sci. Soc. Am.; mem. World Assn. Soil and Water Conservation, Internat. Soil Sci. Soc., Sigma Xi. Baptist. Avocations: conservation gardening, small game hunting, genealogy. Home: 125 Orchard Knob Ln Athens GA 30605-3427

LANGDALE, JOHN WESLEY, timber executive; b. Valdosta, Ga., Feb. 8, 1917; s. Harley and Thalia (Lee) L.; m. Margaret Irene Jones, Dec. 19, 1946; children: Lee Mikuta, John Widr., Margaret Perryman. AB in Econs., U. Ga., 1939, JD, 1940; LLD (hon.), Va. State U., 1996. Mem. Ga. Ho. of Reps., Atlanta, 1949-52, Ga. State Senate, Atlanta, 1957-58; pres. The Langdale Co., Valdosta, 1976-82, vice chmn., 1983—; vice chmn. Langdale Industries Inc., 1986—; chmn. bd. dirs. Valdosta Fed. Savs. and Loan Assn., 1957—. Chmn. U. Ga. Bd. Regents, 1967-69. Served to lt. comdr. USNR, 1941-46, PTO. Decorated Bronze Star. Mem. Ga. Bar Assn. Baptist. Lodge: Rotary (pres. local chpt. 1948-49, dist. gov. 1967-68).

LANGDALE, NOAH NOEL, JR., research educator, former university president; b. Valdosta, Ga., Mar. 29, 1920; s. Noah N. and Jessie Katharine (Catledge) L.; m. Alice Elizabeth Cabaniss, Jan. 8, 1944; 1 son, Noah Michael. AB, U. Ala., 1941; LLB, Harvard U., 1948, MBA, 1950; LLD, U. Ala., 1959. Bar: Ga. bar 1951. Asst. football coach U. Ala., 1942; practiced law Valdosta, 1951-57; instr., then asst. prof. econs. and social studies, chmn. dept. accounting, econs. secretarial sci., bus. adminstrn. Valdosta State Coll., 1954-57; pres. Ga. State U., Atlanta, 1957-88, Disting. univ. rsch. prof., 1988-89, ret., 1989, pres. emeritus, disting. rsch. prof. emeritus, 1989—; dir. Guardian Life Ins. Co. Am.; past mem. U.S. Adv. Commn. Ednl. Exchange; former mem. Pres.'s Commn. NCAA. Served to lt. (s.g.) USNR, 1942-46. Recipient 1st Georgian of Year award Ga. Assn. Broadcasters, 1962; Silver Anniversary All-Am. award Sports Illustrated, 1966; Mrytle Wreath award Hadassah, 1970; Salesman of Yr. award Sales and Mktg. Execs. of Atlanta, 1975; Silver Knight of Mgmt. award Lockheed-Ga. chpt. Nat. Mgmt. Assn., 1978; Humanitarian award Nat. Jewish Hosp. and Research Center/Nat. Asthma Center, 1980, Robert T. Jones award Boy Scouts Am. Mem. ABA, Ga. Bar Assn., Ga. Bar Found. (life), Ga. Assn. Colls. (pres. 1962-63), SAR (past v.p. Ga.), Gridiron Soc., Rotary, Phi Beta Kappa, Omicron Delta Kappa, Delta Chi, Phi Kappa Phi. Methodist. Office: Library North Ga State University Atlanta GA 30303

LANGDELL, ROBERT DANA, medical educator; b. Pomona, Cal., Mar. 14, 1924; s. Walter Irving and Florence Delsa (Reichenbach) L.; m. Alice E. Pritt, June 3, 1948; children—Robert Dana, Sara Ellen. Student, Pomona Coll., 1941-43; M.D., George Washington U., 1948. Intern Henry Ford Hosp., Detroit, 1948-49; mem. faculty Sch. Medicine, U. N.C., Chapel Hill, 1949—; assoc. prof. pathology Sch. Medicine, U. N.C., 1959-61, prof., 1961—; mem. hematology study sect. USPHS, 1968-71. Editor-in-chief Transfusion, 1972-82; assoc. editor Archives of Pathology and Laboratory Medicine, 1983—. Served to capt. M.C. AUS, 1955-56. USPHS sr. research fellow, 1957-61; Career Research fellow, 1962-66. Mem. Am. Assn. Blood Banks (pres. 1972-73), Am. Soc. Clin. Pathology, AMA, Coll. Am. Pathology (gov. 1977-83), N.C. Med. Assn. Episcopalian. Rsch. in blood coagulation and hemostasis. Home: 707 Williams Cir Chapel Hill NC 27516-1527

LANGDON, FRANK CORRISTON, political science educator, researcher; b. LaGrange, Ill., June 3, 1919; s. Ernest Warren and Julia Ida (Mondeng) L.; m. Virginia Irene Osborne, Nov. 11, 1922; children: Peter John, Marc Christopher. A.B., Harvard U., 1941, A.M., 1949; Ph.D., U. Calif.-Berkeley, 1953. Japanese Lang. Sch. intelligence officer U.S. Navy, Stillwater, Okla., 1945-46; econ. analyst Hdqrs. SCAP, Fgn. Trade div., Tokyo, 1946-47; instr. polit. sci. U. Calif. Far East Program, Korea, Japan, Guam, 1953-55; sr. lectr. Canberra U. Coll., Australia, 1955-58; prof. polit. sci. U. B.C., Vancouver, 1958-84, emeritus prof., 1984—, sr. research assoc., 1984—. Author: Politics in Japan, 1967, Japan's Foreign Policy, 1973, Politics of Canadian-Japanese Economic Relations, 1952-83, 83; co-editor, co-author: Japan in the Post Hegomonic World, 1993; co-editor, contbr.: Superpower Maritime Strategy in the Pacific, 1990. Served to lt. comdr. USNR, 1941-45. Mem. Assn. for Asian Studies, Can. Polit. Sci. Assn., Can. Asian Studies Assn., Japan Studies Assn. of Can., Internat. House Japan, Am. Polit. Sci. Assn. Democrat. Presbyterian. Club: Mokuyokai (Vancouver). Home: 4736 W 4th Ave, Vancouver, BC Canada V6T 1C2 Office: U BC Inst Internat Rels, C456 1866 Main Mall, Vancouver, BC Canada V6T 1Z1

LANGDON, GLEN GEORGE, JR., electrical engineer; b. Morristown, N.J., June 30, 1936; s. Glen George and Mildred (Miller) L.; m. Marian Elizabeth Jacobsen, Aug. 10, 1963; 1 child, Karen Joan. BSEE, Wash. State U., 1957; MSEE, U. Pitts., 1963; PhD, Syracuse U., 1968. Elec. engr. Westinghouse Electric Co., East Pittsburgh, Pa., 1960-62, applications programmer, Churchill Boro, Pa., 1962-63; engr. IBM Corp., Endicott, N.Y., 1963-73, research staff mem., San Jose, Calif., 1974-87; prof. computer engring. U. Calif., Santa Cruz, Calif., 1987—; vis. prof. U. São Paulo, Brazil, 1971-72; lectr. U. Santa Clara, 1975-78, Stanford U., 1984. Author: Logic Design: A Review of Theory and Practice, 1974; (with Edson Fregni) Projecto de Computadores Digitals, 1974; Computer Design, 1982. Patentee in field. Lt. Signal Corps., U.S. Army, 1958-59. Recipient Armed Svcs. Communications award Wash. State U., 1957, outstanding innovation award IBM, 1980, 91. Fellow IEEE, Computer Soc. of IEEE (standards com. 1969-70, 74-81, sec. 1982, edn. bd. 1983-86, pub. bd. 1984-85, 87-90, bd. govs. 1984-87, v.p. edn. 1986, Compcon gen. chair 1986, Hot Chips IV Symposium gen. chair 1992); mem. Assn. Computing Machinery (vice chmn. So. Tier chpt. 1973), SPIE, SMPTE, Sigma Xi. Home: 220 Horizon Way Aptos CA 95003-2739 Office: U Calif-Santa Cruz Dept Computer Engring Santa Cruz CA 95064

LANGDON, HERSCHEL GARRETT, lawyer; b. Lowry City, Mo., Oct. 6, 1905; s. Isaac Garrett and Della (Park) L.; m. Ethel Virginia Waterson, May 26, 1931 (dec. Apr. 1979); children: Richard G., Ann Virginia (Mrs. Charles Eugene Willoughby Ward); m. Miriam Pickett, May 17, 1982. B.A., U. Iowa, 1930, J.D., 1931. Bar: Iowa 1931. Since practiced in Des Moines; mem. firm Herrick, Langdon & Langdon (and predecessors), 1935—. Fellow Am. Coll. Trial Lawyers, Am. Bar Found.; mem. Am., Iowa, Polk County bar assns., Phi Beta Kappa, Delta Sigma Rho, Phi Delta Pi. Conglist. Club: Mason. Home: 3524 Grand Ave Apt 603 Des Moines IA 50312-4344 Office: 1800 Financial Ctr 7th and Walnut Des Moines IA 50309

LANGDON, ROBERT COLIN, dermatologist, educator; b. Medford, Oreg., Oct. 29, 1954; s. Hector and Marian Louise (Green) L.; m. Beva Ann Nall, July 22, 1979. BS in Biology with honors, U. Oreg., 1976, MD, 1980. Diplomate Am. Bd. Dermatology. Intern in internal medicine Good Samaritan Hosp., Portland, Oreg., 1980-81; postdoctoral fellow in dermatology Sch. Medicine Yale U., New Haven, 1981-82, instr. in dermatology, 1984-85, asst. prof. dermatology, 1985-90, clin. asst. prof. dermatology, 1993—; resident in dermatology Yale-New Haven Hosp., 1982-84, attending physician, 1984-90, 93—; pvt. practice dermatology Westport, Conn., 1984-86, Arcadia and Covina, Calif., 1990-91, Cerritos and Glendale, Calif., 1991-92, Madison, Conn., 1992—; attending physician West Haven (Conn.) VA Med. Ctr., 1992—, Intercommunity Med. Ctr., Covina, 1990-92, Pioneer Hosp., Artesia, Calif., 1991—; founder, moderator of DERM-L, Yale U., 1994—. Reviewer Archives of Dermatology, 1989—, Jour. Clin. Investigation, 1989—, Jour. Investigative Dermatology, 1986—, Jour. Am. Acad. Dermatology, 1988—; assoc. editor Dermatology Online Jour., U. Calif., Davis, 1995—; contbr. articles to profl. publs. Maulding scholar, 1979. Fellow Am. Acad. Cosmetic Surgery; mem. AAAS, Am. Soc. Dermatologic Surgery, Am. Soc. Laser Medicine and Surgery, Am. Acad. Dermatology, Conn. State Med. Soc., Am. Soc. Liposuction Surgery, Internat. Soc. Cosmetic Laser Surgeons, New Haven County Med. Assn., Phi Beta Kappa. Home: 36 Wilkins St Hamden CT 06517-3313 Office: Shoreline Dermatology 145 Durham Rd Madison CT 06443-2674

LANGE, BILLIE CAROLA, aquatic exercise video creator and specialist; b. Cullman, Ala.; d. John George and Josephine (richard) Luyben; m. Harry E. Lange (div.); children: JoAnne Lange Graham, Linda Jean Lange Reeve; m. Melvin A. Coble (div.). Grad., Long Beach City (Calif.) Coll.; BMus, U. So. Calif. Chief piano accompanist Long Beach Civic Opera Assn.; tchr./creator aquatic exercise program U. Ala., Huntsville, 1984-87; advisor Aquatic Exercise Assn., Port Washington, Wis., 1988—; creator, prodr. aquatic video exercise tapes Billie C. Lange's Aquatics, Palm Beach, Fla., 1979—. Creator: (aquatic exercise video tapes) Slim and Trim Yoga with Billie In and Out of Pool, 1979, Slim and Trim with Billie In Pool, 1994 (televised on Today Show, NBC 1995); pianist Organ-Piano Duo and various audio tapes; instrumental, audio Tranquility, 1992. Mem. Nat. Acad. Recording Arts and Scis. Avocations: classical pianist, aquatic tapes, politics. Office: PO Box 822 Umatilla FL 32784-0822

LANGE, CARL JAMES, psychology educator; b. Seneca, Pa., June 1, 1925; s. Otto Carl and Rose Marie (Jetter) L.; m. Veronica Szelypecz, Jan. 14, 1950; children: David Carl, Veronica Jean. B.S., Duke U., 1945; M.S., U. Pitts., 1948, Ph.D., 1951. Lic. psychologist, Va. Project dir. Human Resources Research Office, George Washington U., 1953-60, dir. research, planning, 1960-69; asst. v.p. research George Washington U., 1969-75, v.p. adminstrn., research, prof. psychology, 1975-88, v.p. rsch., prof. psychology, 1988-89, prof. emeritus, 1989—; cons. NSF, Ford Found.; bd. dirs. Sch. for Contemporary Edn., Nat. Lab. Higher Edn., Eric Clearinghouse for Higher Edn., Southeastern Univs. Rsch. Assn. Contbr. articles in field to profl. jours.; bd. editors: Research in Higher Education. Served with USN, 1943-45. Fellow Am. Psychol. Assn.; mem. AAAS, Sigma Xi. Home: 7 Clarendon Ct Williamsburg VA 23188-1513

LANGE, CLIFFORD E., librarian; b. Fond du Lac, Wis., Dec. 29, 1935; s. Elmer H. and Dorothy Brick (Smithers) L.; m. Janet M. LeMieux, June 6, 1959; children: Paul, Laura, Ruth. Student, St. Norbert Coll., 1954-57; B.S., Wis. State U., 1959; M.S.L.S. (Library Services Act scholar), U. Wis., 1960, Ph.D. (Higher Edn. Act fellow), 1972. Head extension dept. Oshkosh (Wis.) Public Library, 1960-62, head reference dept., 1962-63; asst. dir. Jervis Library, Rome, N.Y., 1962; dir. Eau Claire (Wis.) Public Library, 1963-66; asst. dir. Lake County Public Library, Griffith, Ind., 1966-68; asst. prof. Sch. Library Sci., U. Iowa, 1971-73; dir. Wauwatosa (Wis.) Public Library, 1973-75; asst. prof. U. So. Calif., 1975-78; state librarian N.Mex. State Library, Santa Fe, 1978-82; dir. Carlsbad City Library, Calif., 1982—. Served with U.S. Army, 1958. Mem. ALA, Calif. Libr. Assn. Home: 3575 Ridge Rd Oceanside CA 92056-4952 Office: 1250 Carlsbad Village Dr Carlsbad CA 92008-1949

LANGE, CRYSTAL MARIE, academic administrator, nursing educator; b. Snover, Mich., Aug. 22, 1927; d. Bazil H. and Crystal S. (Hilborn) Morse; m. Elmer William Lange, June 10, 1961; children: Gregory, Frederick, Helen, Charles, G. Benson, Robert, Larry. BSN, U.Mich., 1949; MSN, Wayne State U., 1961; PhD, Mich. State U., 1972. Pvt. duty nurse, Richmond, Ind., 1949-50; asst. dir. nursing, nursing supr., instr. St. Mary's Hosp., Tucson, Ariz., 1950-58; night supr. Pima County Hosp., Tucson, 1958-59; asst. dir. Sch. Nursing, Saginaw Gen. Hosp., Mich., 1959-60; instr. to prof., chmn. div. Delta Coll., University Ctr., Mich., 1962-76; dean Sch. Nursing and Allied Health Scis., asst. to v.p. acad. affairs, prof. Saginaw Valley State Coll., University Center, 1976-96, assoc. v.p. acad. affairs, 1996—; mem. vis. com. Med. Ctr., U. Mich., 1978-81. Author: Leadership for Quality, 1966; Instructor's Guide - Nursing Skills and Techniques, 1969; The Use of the Auto-tutorial Laboratory and the Mobile Tutorial Unit in Teaching, 1969; Instructor's Guide - Nursing Skills and Techniques - Films 76-126, 1972; Instructor's Guide - Nursing Skills and Techniques - Films 127-151, 1971; Auto-Tutorial Techniques in Nursing Education, 1971; Future Education: Diagnosis Prescriptions Evaluation, 1971. Contbr. articles to profl. jours. Bd. dirs. Saginaw chpt. ARC, 1982—, Saginaw Vis. Nurse Assn., 1980—. Recipient award Mich. Acad. Sci., Arts and Letters, 1970, Monsour Found. Lectureship award Health Edn. Media Assn., 1977; NEH fellow, 1983. Fellow Am. Acad. Nursing; mem. Am. Acad. Arts and Scis., Am. Acad. Nursing (governing council, sec. 1978-80), AAUP (chpt. v.p. 1976, award citation 1970), Am. Ednl. Scis., Am. Nurses Assn., Mich. Nurses Assn., Saginaw Dist. Nurses Assn. (bd. dirs. 1976—), U. Mich. Alumnae Assn., Wayne State U. Alumnae Assn., Phi Kappa Phi, Sigma Theta Tau. Home: 4135 Kochville Rd Saginaw MI 48604-9750 Office: Saginaw Valley State U University Center MI 48710

LANGE, DAVID CHARLES, journalist; b. Natrona Hts., Pa., Oct. 14, 1949; s. Charles Manfred Lange and Helga (Hingst) Faverty; m. Linda Gaiduk, June 29, 1974; children: Erik David, Anthony Charles. BA in Journalism, Kent State U., 1975; postgrad., Akron U., 1980-83. Placement specialist Goodwill Industries Cleve., 1976-77; mng. editor, sports editor Chagrin Valley Times, Chagrin Falls, Ohio, 1977-82; editor Chagrin Valley Times/Solon Times, Chagrin Falls, 1988—; features editor, Sunday editor Lake County Telegraph, Painesville, Ohio, 1982-83; editor Geauga Times Leader, Chardon, Ohio, 1983-84; editor-in-chief Habitat, Cleve., 1984-88. Cub scout den leader, asst. leader Boy Scouts Am. Pack 102, Chagrin Falls, 1992—. With USN, 1968-71, Vietnam. Recipient Democracy in Housing award Cleve. Assn. Real Estate Brokers, 1988. Mem. Soc. Profl. Journalists (Excellence in Journalism award human interest reporting 1981), Ohio Newspaper Assn. (Hooper award for editl. writing 1991-92, 94, 96, 97, 2d place

1990, 93, Hooper award for col. writing 1993, 97), Chagrin Valley C. of C., Solon C. of C., Cleve. Press Club, Nat. Newspaper Assn., VFW, Am. Legion, Vietnam Vets. Am. (treas. Western res. chpt. 1990—). Avocations: swimming, skiing, tennis, basketball. Home: 8353 Chagrin Rd Chagrin Falls OH 44023-4757 Office: Chagrin Valley Times PO Box 150 Chagrin Falls OH 44022

LANGE, DAVID L., law educator; b. Charleston, Ill., Dec. 7, 1938; s. Charles W.S. and Mary Helen Lange; m. Teresa Tetrick, July 30, 1972; children—David, Adam, Daniel, Jennifer, William. BS, U. Ill., Urbana, 1960, JD, 1964. Bar: Ill. 1964, N.C. 1989. Pvt. practice Chgo., 1964-71; gen. counsel media task force Nat. Commn. on Violence, Washington, 1968-69; gen. ptnr. Mediamix Prodns., 1970-71; assoc. prof. law Duke U., Durham, N.C., 1971-74; prof. law Duke U., 1974—; of counsel Parker, Poe, Adams & Bernstein, Charlotte, N.C., 1987-94; cons. in intellectual property Govt. of Vietnam, 1994—; exec. dir. Ctr. for Global Info. Technologies, 1996—. Office: Duke U Sch Law Durham NC 27708

LANGE, GEORGE WILLARD, JR., trust banker, lawyer; b. West Bend, Wis., Dec. 29, 1949; s. George W. and Ruth I. (Stobbe) L.; m. Joan Elizabeth Koeln, June 26, 1971; children: Matthew Ryan, Aaron Michael. BA, Southeast Mo. State U., 1972; JD, St. Louis U., 1977; postgrad., Southwestern Sch. Banking, 1981. Bar: Mo. 1977; cert. trust and fin. advisor; accredited estate planner. Assoc. Law Office Thomas Green, St. Louis, 1977-79; trust officer Merc. Bank, N.A., St. Louis, 1979-84; sr. v.p., trust officer Mark Twain Bank, St. Louis, 1984-87; v.p., sr. trust officer Am. Pioneer Savs. Bank, Orlando, Fla., 1987-90; sr. v.p., trust officer, mgr. Bancorp Trust Co. N.A., Naples, Fla., 1990-94; pres., COO, dir. Marshall & Ilsley Trust Co. Fla., Naples, 1994—; mem. adv. dir. S.W. Fla. Bus. Hall of Fame. Bd. dirs. Mental Health Assn. of Collier County, 1990-95, treas., 1992, v.p., 1993, prs., 1994; bd. dirs. Mental Health Assn. St. Louis, 1980-82, treas., 1981; bd. dirs. Mental Health Assn. Mo., 1981-82, United Arts Coun. Collier County, 1991—, v.p., 1991-92, pres., 1992-95; mem. Friends of Eldison Collier Men, chair, 1996—; trustee Bonita Springs Firefighter's Retirement Fund. Lt. col. N.G., 1971-94. Mem. ABA (com. adminstrn. and distbn. of trusts, chmn. com. fiduciary issues of holding closely held bus. in trust), Mo. Bar Assn., Soc. Am. Mil. Engrs., Res. Officers Assn., Corp. Fiduciaries Assn. S.W. Fla., Rotary (Paul Harris fellow), Estate Planning of Naples, Collier Athletic Club, Naples Area C. of C. (pres. club, chair edn. com. 1991-93), Leadership Collier, Leadership S.W. Fla., Leadership Lee County), Fla. Bankers Assn. (trust div., vice chmn. legis. com. 1994-95, chair 1995-97, exec. com., mem. state govtl. rels. com.), S.W. Fla. C. of C. (trustee rep. 1992—), Atty. for Closing-Held Enterprises, Res. Officer Assn., De Beough Soc. St. Louis U. (hon. v.p.), Fla. Bank Pac (bd. dirs.), Phi Alpha Delta, Sigma Tau Gamma. Home: 3770 Catbrier Ct Bonita Springs FL 34134-7929 Office: Marshall & Isley Trust Co 800 Laurel Oak Dr Ste 101 Naples FL 34108-2713

LANGE, JAMES BRAXTON, chemical company executive; b. Amory, Miss., Feb. 17, 1937; s. Oliver John and Sarah Nell (Gravlee) L.; m. Margaret Terry Terrell, Aug. 9, 1969. B.S. in Psychology, Millsaps Coll., 1960; B.S. in Bus, Miss. Coll., 1970, M.B.A., 1973; postgrad., Harvard U., 1979. Indsl. rep. Miss. CD, 1971-73; sec., treas. 1st Miss. Corp., Jackson, 1973-88; dir. investor rels. and corp. affaris Himont, Inc., Wilmington, Del., 1988-90; pres., chief exec. officer Columbia Gas Found., Wilmington, Del., 1990-94; sec. Columbia Gas System Svc. Corp., Wilmington, 1990-94; v.p. corp. fin. svcs. PNC Bank, Wilmington, 1994—; bd. dirs. Primex, Inc. Charter mem. Community Action Coun., 1972-74; group leader United Way campaign, 1970-73; mem. exec. com. YMCA; mem. com. on free enterprise Miss. Econ. Coun.; trustee Grand Opera House, 1990-93. With USN, 1960-63. Mem. Am. Soc. Corp. Secs., Am. Soc. Corp. Treas., Nat. Investor Rels. Inst., Am. Soc. Pers. Adminstrn., Miss. Mfrs. Assn., Jackson C. of C., Nat. Assn. Corp. Dirs., Naval Res. Assn. (pres.), Res. Officers Assn. (past v.p.), Navy League Jackson, Lions. Republican. Home: 4 Normandy Dr Chadds Ford PA 19317-9274 Office: PNC Bank 222 Delaware Ave Wilmington DE 19801

LANGE, LESTER HENRY, mathematics educator; b. Concordia, Mo., Jan. 2, 1924; s. Harry William Christopher and Ella Martha (Alewel) L.; m. Anne Marie Pelikan, Aug. 17, 1947 (div. Oct. 1960); children: Christopher, Nicholas, Philip, Alexander; m. Beverly Jane Brown, Feb. 4, 1962; 1 son, Andrew. Student, U. Calif., Berkeley, 1943-44; B.A. in Math, Valparaiso U., 1948; M.S. in Math, Stanford, 1950; Ph.D. in Math, U. Notre Dame, 1960. Instr., then asst. prof. math. Valparaiso U., 1950-56; instr. math. U. Notre Dame, 1956-57, 59-60; mem. faculty San Jose State U., Calif., 1960—, prof. math., head dept., 1961-70, dean Sch. Natural Scis. and Math., 1970—, dean Sch. Sci., 1972-88, emeritus prof. math., emeritus dean, 1988—; founder Soc. Archimedes at San Jose State U., 1982; now spl. asst. to dir. Moss Landing (Calif.) Marine Labs. Author text on linear algebra; sr. editor Calif. Math. 1981-84; contbr. to profl. jours. Served with inf. AUS, 1943-46, ETO. Danforth fellow, 1957-58; NSF faculty fellow, 1958-59. Fellow Calif. Acad. Scis.; mem. Math. Assn. Am. (bd. govs., L.R. Ford Sr. award 1972, George Polya award 1993), Calif. Math. Coun., London Math. Soc., Fibonacci Assn. (bd. dirs. 1987-97), Nat. Coun. Tchrs. Home: 308 Escalona Dr Capitola CA 95010-3419 Office: Moss Landing Marine Labs Moss Landing CA 95039

LANGE, MARILYN, social worker; b. Milw., Dec. 6, 1936; d. Edward F. and Erna E. (Karstaedt) L.; divorced; children: Lara McKelvie, Gregory Cash. B of Social Work, U. Wis., Milw., 1962, MSW, 1974. Cert. ind. clin. social worker. Recreation specialist Dept. Army, Europe, 1962-63; social worker Family Svc. Milw., 1967-75, dir. homecare divsn., 1975-85; nat. field rep. Alzheimers Assn., Chgo., 1986-90; exec. dir. Village Adult Svcs., Milw., 1991—. Mem. Nat. Coun. Aging, Wis. Adult Daycare Assn. (pres.), Dementia Care Network, Older Adult Svc. Providers Consortium, West Allis Bus. & Profl. Women, U. Wis.-Milw. Alumni Assn. Home: 5727 W Fillmore Dr Milwaukee WI 53219-2219 Office: Village Adult Svcs 130 E Juneau Ave Milwaukee WI 53202-2552

LANGE, MARVIN ROBERT, lawyer; b. Bronx, Mar. 25, 1948; s. Arthur A. and Beatrice L. Lange; m. Ellen Metzger, Apr. 20, 1986; 1 child, Rebecca Hillary. BA, Queens Coll., 1968; JD, Harvard U., 1971. Bar: N.Y. 1972, U.S. Dist. Ct. (ea. and so. dists.) N.Y. 1975, U.S. Ct. Appeals (2d cir.) 1975, U.S. Supreme Ct. 1980, U.S. Ct. Appeals (6th cir.) 1986. Law clk. U.S. Dist. Ct., Phila., 1971-72; atty. FTC, Washington, 1972-75; assoc. Rosenman & Colin, N.Y.C., 1975-81, ptnr., 1981-93; pvt. practice law, 1993—. Editor Harvard Law Rev., 1969-71. Mem. ABA. Jewish. Office: 777 3rd Ave Fl 19 New York NY 10017-1302

LANGE, NICHOLAS THEODORE, biostatistician; b. Valparaiso, Ind., Mar. 18, 1952; s. Lester Henry and Beverley Jane (Brown) L.; m. Dorothy Cresswell, Sept. 6, 1976 (div. 1982); children: Sarah Elisabeth, Nicholas Cresswell; m. Louise Marie Ryan, Dec. 15, 1984. ScB, Northeastern U., 1976; ScM, U. Mass., 1981; ScD, Harvard U., 1986. Instr. applied math. MIT, Cambridge, Mass., 1986-87; asst. prof. med. statistics Brown U., Providence, 1987-93; specialist in neuroimaging NIH, Bethesda, Md., 1993-96; assoc. prof. psychiatry, biostats. Harvard U., Cambridge, 1996—; chief biostatistician McLean Hosp., 1996—; cons. radiology Mass. Gen. Hosp., Charlestown, 1994-96, Nat. Inst. Aging; expert witness McGovern, Noel & Benik Providence, 1991-93, 97, M. Scherzer, N.Y.C., 1993. Editor: Case Studies in Biometry, 1991-94; assoc. editor: Jour. Am. Statis. Assn. Revs., 1993—; guest editor: Statistics in Medicine, 1992; mem. editl. bd. Human Brain Mapping. Grantee Am. Cancer Soc., 1991-93, Human Brain Project (co-investigator), 1995—, NIH, 1996—; recipient Robert Reed prize Harvard U., 1986. Mem. AAAS, Am. Statis. Assn., Biometric Soc., Bernoulli Soc., Soc. Optical Engring. (hon.). Home: 243 Concord Ave Apt 11 Cambridge MA 02138-1360 Office: Brain Imaging Ctr McLean Hosp 115 Mill St Belmont MA 02178-1041

LANGE, NIELS ERIK KREBS, biotechnology company executive; b. Soenderborg, Denmark, July 20, 1948; s. Erik Krebs and Estrid (Jensen) L. MSc in Engring., Denmarks Tech. U., Copenhagen, 1973. Cert. chem. engr. Rsch. scientist Denmarks Tech. U., 1974-75; rsch. chemist Novo Nordisk A/S, Bagsvaerd, Denmark, 1976-86, mgr. product devel. and process rsch., 1986-93, mgr. enzyme product devel., 1993-95; staff scientist Novo Nordisk Biochemicals, Inc., Franklinton, N.C., 1995—. Contbr. articles to profl. jours. Mem. AAAS, Am. Assn. Textile Chemists and Colorists (sr.), IEA Bioenergy Network. Avocations: golfing, badminton, amateur theatre. Home: 7212 Stonecliff Dr #5 Raleigh NC 27615 Office: Novo Nordisk Biochemicals Inc PO Box 576 Franklinton NC 27525

LANGE, PHIL C., retired education educator; b. North Freedom, Wis., Feb. 26, 1914; s. Richard Samuel and Martha (Grosinske) L.; m. Irene Oyen, June 8, 1940; children—Dena Rae, Richard (dec.). B.A., U. Wis., 1934, M.A., 1936, Ph.D., 1941. Tchr. Reeseville (Wis.) Pub. Sch., 1935-37; chmn. English dept. Wayland Jr. Coll. and Acad., Beaver Dam, Wis., 1937-39; instr. English, student teaching supr. Beloit (Wis.) High Sch., 1939-40; asst. instr. U. Wis., Madison, 1940-41, summers 1938, 39; chmn. psychology dept., dean men. Ariz. State Coll., Flagstaff, 1941-42; chmn. edn. dept. SUNY, Fredonia, 1942-50; prof. edn., coordinator student teaching Tchrs. Coll., Columbia U., 1950—; cons., expert for Dept. State, UNESCO, AID. Author, editor curriculum materials. Served with USNR, 1943-46. Recipient Filmstrip award Graphic Arts, 1966; Communication award Nat. Soc. Programmed Instrn., 1968; award Ednl. Press Assn. Am., 1969. Home: 727 Fox Hills Dr Sun City Center FL 33573-5127 Office: Tchrs Coll Columbia Univ New York NY 10027

LANGE, ROBERT DALE, internist, educator, medical researcher; b. Redwood Falls, Minn., Jan. 24, 1920; s. John Christian and Bertha Semelia (Eggen) L.; m. Mary Jane Adams, Sept. 16, 1944; children: Ruth Ann Lange Rehm, John Carl. B.A., Macalester Coll., 1941; M.D., Washington U., 1944. Diplomate: Am. Bd. Internal Medicine. Intern Barnes Hosp., St. Louis, 1944-45; asst. resident medicine U. Minn. Hosps., Mpls., 1945-46; fellow and instr. medicine div. hematology Washington U. Sch. Medicine, St. Louis, 1948-51; practice medicine specializing in internal medicine St. Louis, 1956-62, Knoxville, Tenn., 1964—; scientist Atomic Bomb Casualty Commn., Hiroshima and Nagasaki, Japan, 1951-53; rsch. assoc. VA Hosp., Mpls., 1953-54; mem. staff Eitel Hosp., Mpls., 1953-54; chief hematology Rsch. Lab. VA Hosp., St. Louis, 1956-62; asst. prof. medicine Washington U. Sch. Medicine, St. Louis, 1956-62; assoc. prof. medicine Med. Coll. Ga., Augusta, 1962-64; mem. staff Talmadge Hosp., Augusta, 1962-65, U. Hosp., Augusta, 1964-65, U. Tenn. Meml. Hosp., Knoxville, 1965; research prof. U. Tenn. Meml. Research Center, Knoxville, 1964-78; asst. dir. research U. Tenn. Meml. Research Center, 1966-76, dir. research, 1977-81; prof. medicine U. Tenn. Center for Health Services, Knoxville, 1970—; prof. U. Tenn. Meml. Research Ctr., 1978-85, prof. emeritus, 1985—; chmn. dept. med. biology, 1978-81; cons. to Oak Ridge Associated Univs., 1969-93, Abbott Labs Rev. Bd., 1974. Contbr. chpts. in hematology to med. books; contbr. numerous articles on research in hematology and exptl. medicine to profl. jours.; reviewer various med. jours., 1960—; editorial bd.: Exptl. Hematology, 1974-77. Served to maj., M.C. U.S. Army, 1954-56. Jackson Johnson scholar, 1941-44; recipient Cert. St. Paul Jr. Assn. of Commerce, 1941. Fellow A.C.P., Internat. Soc. Hematology; mem. Am. Soc. Hematology, Internat. Soc. Exptl. Hematology, Soc. of Research Adminstrs., Soc. Exptl. Biology and Medicine, Central Soc. Clin. Research, So. Soc. Clin. Investigation, Knoxville Soc. Internal Medicine, AMA (Cert. of Merit 1954), Tenn. Med. Assn., Knoxville Acad. Medicine, AAAS, AAUP, Sigma Xi, Alpha Omega Alpha, Pi Phi Epsilon. Methodist. Home: 8116 Bennington Dr Knoxville TN 37909-2301 Office: U Tenn Med Ctr 1924 Alcoa Hwy Knoxville TN 37920-1511

LANGE, ROBERT JOHN (MUTT LANGE), producer. Composer: (film score) Don Juan DeMarco, 1995 (Acad. award nomination 1995), The Mirror Has Two Faces, 1996 (Acad. award nomination 1996); co- author (albums with Bryan Adams) Waking Up the Neighbours, 18 Til I Die; co-composer (singles with Bryan Adams) (Everything I Do) I Do It For You (Acad. award nomination), Have You Ever Really Loved a Woman? (Acad. award nomination), Star, I Finally Found Someone (Acad. award nomination). Recipient Best Prodr. Country Album Grammy award, 1996. Office: PO Box 269 Saint Regis Falls NY 12980-0269*

LANGEL, ROBERT ALLAN, III, geophysicist; b. Pitts., May 25, 1937; s. Robert Allan II and Fay Mildred (Harvey) L.; m. Carolyn May Wills, June 13, 1959; children: Kathleen Carol, Susan Lynn, Joy Christine. AB, Wheaton Coll., 1959; MS, U. Md., 1971, PhD, 1973. Physicist U.S. Naval Rsch. Lab., 1959-62; physicist microwave antennas Goddard Space Flight Ctr., Greenbelt, Md., 1963-64, magnetospheric physicist, 1964-74, geophysicist magnetic fields satellite project, 1974-97; vis. scholar Bullard Labs., Cambridge (Eng.) U., 1983-84, Purdue U., 1992-93, Copenhagen U., 1994; mem. exec. com. Nat. Geomagnetic Workshop, 1992. Spl. editor: (issue) Physics of the Earth and Planetary Interiors, 1976, Geophys. Rsch. Letters, 1982, Jour. Geophys. Rsch., 1985, Jour. Geomagnetic Geoelectricity, 1992; assoc. editor Jour. Geophys. Rsch., 1991-95; contbr. articles to sci. publs., chpts. to books. Dir. youth Grace Brethren Ch., Temple Hills, Md., 1965-68; dir. coll.-career Berwyn Bapt. Ch., College Park, Md., 1975-89, dir. singles, 1989-91. Recipient Spl. Achievement award Goddard Space Flight Ctr., 1980, 96, Group Achievement award, 1980, Exceptional Performance award, 1981, Medal for exceptional sci. achievement NASA, 1982. Fellow Am. Geophys. Union; mem. Internat. Assn. Geomagnetism and Aeronomy (vice chair Divsn. I 1983-87, chair working group on main field and secular variation 1987-91). Republican. Baptist. Home: 1008 Oak Pointe Ct Blacksburg VA 24060 Office: Goddard Space Flight Ctr Code 921 Greenbelt MD 20771 *My driving goal is to please God, which governs the things to which I commit myself and that I strive for integrity and faithfulness in what I do.*

LANGELLA, FRANK, actor; b. Bayonne, N.J., Jan. 1, 1940; m. Ruth Weil, Nov. 1977. Student, Syracuse U.; studies with Seymour Falk. Apprenticed Pocono Playhouse, Mountain Home, Pa., appeared Erie (Pa.) Playhouse, 1960, mem. original, Lincoln Center repertory tng. co., 1963; off-Broadway debut in The Immoralist, 1963; other stage appearances include: Benito Cereno, 1964, The Old Glory, 1964-65 (Obie award), Good Day, 1965-66 (Obie award), The White Devil, 1965-66 (Obie award), Long Day's Journey Into Night, The Skin of Our Teeth, The Cretan Woman, Yerma, all 1966, The Devils, Dracula, Iphigenia at Aulis, all 1967, A Cry of Players, 1968, Cyrano de Bergerac, 1971, A Midsummer Night's Dream, 1972, The Relapse, The Tooth of Crime, 1972, The Taming of the Shrew, 1973, The Seagull, 1974, Ring Round the Moon, 1975, Passion, 1983, Design for Living, 1984, After the Fall, 1984, Hurlyburly, 1985, Sherlock's Last Case, 1987, Booth, 1994, The Prince of Hamburg, Cleve. Playhouse Co., 1967-68, L.I. Festival repertory, 1968, Les Liaisons Dangereuses; Broadway debut in Seascape, 1974-75 (Drama Desk and Tony awards); stage directing debut in John and Abigail, 1969; performed in films Diary of a Mad Housewife, 1970 (Nat. Soc. Film Critics award), The Twelve Chairs, 1970, The Deadly Trap, 1972, The Wrath of God, 1972, Dracula, 1979, Those Lips Those Eyes, 1980, Sphinx, 1981, The Men's Club, 1986, Masters of the Universe, 1987, And God Created Woman, 1988, True Identity, 1991, 1492: Conquest of Paradise, 1992, Dave, 1993, Body of Evidence, 1993, Brainscan, 1994, Junior, 1994, Bad Company, 1995, Eddie, 1996, Lolita, 1997; TV appearances include: Benito Cereno, 1965, Good Day, 1967, The Mark of Zorro, 1974, The Ambassador, 1974, The Seagull, 1975, The American Woman: Portraits of Courage, 1976, Eccentricities of a Nightingale, 1976, Sherlock Holmes, Liberty, The Doomsday Gun, 1994, Moses, 1996. Bd. dirs. Berkshire Festival. Mem. Actors Equity, Screen Actors Guild. Office: Special Artists Agency 345 N Maple Dr Ste 302 Beverly Hills CA 90210-3860*

LANGENBERG, DONALD NEWTON, academic administrator, physicist; b. Devils Lake, N.D., Mar. 17, 1932; s. Ernest George and Fern (Newton) L.; m. Patricia Ann Warrington, June 20, 1953; children: Karen Kaye, Julia Ann, John Newton, Amy Paris. B.S., Iowa State U., 1953; M.S., UCLA, 1955; Ph.D. (NSF fellow), U. Calif. at Berkeley, 1959; D.Sc. (hon.), U. Pa., 1985, MA (hon.), 1971. Electronics engr. Hughes Research Labs., Culver City, Calif., 1953-55; acting instr. U. Calif. at Berkeley, 1958-59; mem. faculty U. Pa., Phila., 1960-83; prof. U. Pa., 1967-83; dir. Lab. for Research on Structure of Matter, 1972-74; vice provost for grad. studies and research, 1974-79; chancellor U. Ill.-Chgo., 1983-90, U. Md. System, Adelphi, 1990—; maitre de conference associe Ecole Normale Superieure, Paris, France, 1966-67; vis. prof. Calif. Inst. Tech., Pasadena, 1971; guest researcher Zentralinstitut für Tieftemperaturforschung der Bayerische Akademie der Wissenschaften and Technische Universität München, 1974; dep. dir. Nat. Sci. Found., 1980-82. Rschr., contbr. to publs. on solid state and low temperature physics including electronic band structure in metals and semiconductors, quantum phase coherence and nonequilibrium effects in superconductors, sci. and edn. policy and rsch. adminstrn. Recipient John Price Wetherill medal Franklin Inst., 1975, Disting. Contribution to Research Adminstrn. award Soc. Research Adminstrs., 1983, Disting. Achievement Citation, Iowa State Alumni Assn., 1984, Significant Sig award Sigma Chi, 1985; fellow NSF, 1959-60, Alfred P. Sloan Found., 1962-64; Guggenheim Found., 1966-67. Fellow AAAS (pres. 1990), Am. Phys. Soc. (pres. 1993), Sigma Xi. Office: U Md System 3300 Metzerott Rd Adelphi MD 20783-1600

LANGENBERG, FREDERICK CHARLES, business executive; b. N.Y.C., July 1, 1927; s. Frederick C. and Margaret (McLaughlin) L.; m. Jane Anderson Bartholomew, May 16, 1953; children: Frederick C., Susan Jane; m. Marguerite Cardone, Apr. 13, 1996. BS, Lehigh U., 1950, MS, 1951; PhD, Pa. State U., 1955; postgrad. execs. program, Carnegie-Mellon U., 1962. With U.S. Steel Corp., 1951-53; vis. fellow MIT, 1955-56; with Crucible Steel Corp., Pitts., 1956-68, v.p. research and engring., 1966-68; pres. Trent Tube div. Colt Industries, Milw., 1968-70; exec. v.p. Jessop Steel Co., Washington, Pa., 1970, pres., 1970-75; pres., bd. dirs. Am. Iron and Steel Inst., Washington, 1975-78; pres. Interlake Corp., Oak Brook, Ill., 1979-81, pres., chmn, chief exec. officer, 1981-91, also bd. dirs.; chmn. Langand Corp., Pitts., 1991—; bd. dirs. Carpenter Tech., Reading, Pa., The Interlake Corp., Chgo., Peoples Energy Corp., Chgo.,. Contbr. articles to tech. jours.; patentee in field. Trustee Piedmont Coll., Demorest, Ga. Served with USNR, 1944-45. Named Oak Brook Bus. Leader of the Yr., 1986, Disting. Bus. Leader, DuPage County, 1988; Alumni fellow Pa. State U., 1977; recipient Disting. Alumni award, Pa. State U., 1989, Lehigh U., 1990. Fellow Am. Soc. Metals (disting. life mem. 1982, trustee, Pitts. Nite lectr. 1970, Andrew Carnegie lectr. 1976; David Ford McFarland award Penn State chpt. 1973); mem. AIME, Am. Soc. Metals, Metals Powder Industry Fedn., Phi Beta Kappa, Sigma Xi, Tau Beta Pi. Clubs: Duquesne, St. Clair Country (Pitts.), Congl., Burning Tree, Chgo. Golf, Chgo., Commercial (Chgo.), Laurel Valley, Rolling Rock (Ligonier, Pa.), Belleair County Club (Fla.), Carefree (Ariz.), Desert Mountain (Ariz.). Office: Langand Corp 2535 Washington Rd Ste 1131 Pittsburgh PA 15241-2592

LANGENDERFER, HAROLD QUENTIN, accountant, educator; b. Swanton, Ohio, July 21, 1925; s. Omer Quintan and Minnie (Buckenmyer) L.; m. Joan Marie Etzrodt, June 17, 1950; children: Thomas, Amy, Jeffry, Chris. B.S. in Bus, Miami U., Oxford, Ohio, 1949; M.B.A., Northwestern U., 1950; D.B.A., Ind. U., 1954. C.P.A., Ind., N.C. Prof. intermediate acctg. Ind. U., Bloomington, 1952-53; KPMG Peat, Marwick prof. profl. acctg. U. N.C., Chapel Hill, 1953-93, prof. emeritus, 1993—; cons. mgmt. devel. to Ford Found., Cairo, 1961-63; tax cons. Co-author: C.P.A. Examination - A Comprehensive Review, 3d edit., 1979, Principles of Accounting, 1981, 4th edit., 1993, Income Tax Procedure, 1994; contbr. articles to acctg. jours. Served with U.S. Army, 1943-46. Named Acctg. Educator of Yr., Beta Alpha Psi, 1980. Mem. AICPAs (Acctg. Educator of Yr. 1988), N.C. Assn. CPAs (pres. 1985-86, Acctg. Educator of Yr. 1986, Outstanding Svc. award 1989), Nat. Assn. Accts., Am. Acctg. Assn. (pres. 1983-84, chmn. com. on professionalism and ethics 1987-89, internat. lectr. 1992, Outstanding Acctg. Educator award 1995, Acctg. Exemplar award 1996), Fin. Execs. Inst., Kiwanis (pres. Chapel Hill lodge 1966). Roman Catholic. Home: 1074 Canterbury Ln Chapel Hill NC 27514-5612 Office: UNC CB 3490 Carroll Hall Chapel Hill NC 27599

LANGENDOEN, DONALD TERENCE, linguistics educator; b. Paterson, N.J., June 7, 1939; s. Gerrit and Wilhelmina (Van Dyk) L.; m. Sally Wicklund, Aug. 16, 1964 (div. Mar. 1982); 1 child, David; m. Nancy Susan Kelly, July 28, 1984. BS, MIT, 1961, PhD, 1964. Asst. prof. Ohio State U., Columbus, 1964-68; vis. assoc. prof. Rockefeller U., N.Y.C., 1968-69; prof. Bklyn. C. and Grad. Ctr., CUNY, N.Y.C., 1969-88, U. Ariz., Tucson, 1988—; exec. officer grad. linguistics program, CUNY, N.Y.C., 1971-78; head dept. linguistics, U. Ariz., Tucson, 1988-97; vis. scientist IBM T.J. Watson Research Ctr., Yorktown Heights, N.Y., 1986-87; sr. lectr. Fulbright, Utrecht, Holland, 1977. Author: The London School of Linguistics, 1968; co-author: The Vastness of Natural Languages, 1984; editor: Linguistics Abstracts, 1997—; co-editor: Optimality Theory: An Overview, 1997. Fellow N.Y. Acad. of Scis., N.Y.C., 1977; named Ptnr. in Edn., Bd. of Edn., N.Y.C., 1982. Mem. AAAS, Linguistic Soc. of Am. (sec., treas. 1984-88, v.p., pres. elect. 1997-98), Assn. for Computational Linguistics, Assn. for Linguistic and Literary Computing. Office: U Ariz Dept Linguistics Box 210028 Tucson AZ 85721-0028

LANGENEGGER, ARMIN, radiation physicist; b. Mainburg, Bavaria, Germany, Oct. 12, 1953; came to U.S., 1990; s. Kurt Andreas and Anne Maria (Sommerer) L.; m. Patricia Gail Cross, Feb. 28, 1982; children: Michael, Thomas, Elyse Beth; m. Lisa Marie Nelesen, Oct. 12, 1991; children: Nicholas Kurt, Matthew John. Diploma, Gordon Inst. Tech., Geelong, Victoria, Australia, 1975; BSc, Deakin U., Geelong, 1982; M Biomed. Engring., U. NSW, Sydney, Australia, 1988. Physics technologist Prince of Wales Hosp., Sydney, 1976-79, physicist, 1979-82; sr. physicist Royal Prince Alfred Hosp., Sydney, 1982-87, dep. chief physicist, 1987-88; chief physicist Royal North Shore Hosp., Sydney, 1988-90; physicist Waukesha (Wis.) Meml. Hosp., 1990-92, chief physicist, 1992-93; physicist St. Marys Med. Ctr., Racine, Wis., 1993—; dir., cons. Ralode Pty Ltd., Sydney, 1982-88; cons. Biotel Pty. Ltd., Sydney, 1990-91, Radiation Physics Svcs., Milw., 1990—; invited participant Russian trip on radiation protection. Capt. Neighborhood Watch, Sydney, 1988-89. Mem. Am. Assn. Physicists in Medicine, Australasian Coll. Phys. Scientists and Engrs. in Medicine (sec. 1988-89). Anglican. Achievements include patent procs. couch mounted stereotactic head frame holder; creator inexpensive stereotactic radiosurgery package, dosimetry intercomparison group. Home: 3633 Canada Goose Xing Racine WI 53403-4504 Office: Southea Wis Regional Cancer Ctr All Saints Healthcare Sys 3809 Spring St Racine WI 53405-1667

LANGENFELD, MARY LUCILLE, healthcare facility administrator; b. St. Peter, Minn., Nov. 14, 1946; d. Leo John and Lucille (Meyer) Scully; m. Gerald W. Langenfeld, Apr. 19, 1969; children: Richard, David, Deborah, Amy Jo. Diploma, St. Mary Sch. Nursing, Rochester, Minn., 1967; BS, Bemidji State U., 1977; MS, U. Minn., 1980; MBA, Boise State U., 1989. RN, Minn., S.D., Idaho, Calif., Ohi, Wash. Staff nurse Northwestern Hosp., Mpls., 1967-68; charge nurse Meml. Hosp., Watertown, S.D., 1968-69, So. Hills Gen. Hosp., Hot Springs, S.D., 1969-70; supr., charge nurse Dakota Midland Hosp., Aberdeen, S.D., 1970-72; dir. nursing Community Mercy Hosp., Onamia, Minn., 1972-75, Madison (Minn.) Hosp. Assn., 1975-77; dir. patient care svcs. St. Ann's Hosp., Watertown, 1977-83; v.p. ops. Mercy Med. Ctr., Nampa, Idaho, 1983-89; v.p. St. Joseph Hosp. and Health Ctr., Lorain, Ohio, 1989-92, Olol Hosp., Pasco, Wash., 1992-93; CEO Life's Doors Hospice, Boise, 1994—; adj. prof. dept. nursing U. Akron, Ohio, 1991-92. Contbr. to profl. publs. Exec. bd. Lorainchpt. Arthritis Found., 1991-92. Fellow Am. Orgn. Nurse Execs.; mem. Am. Coll. Healthcare Execs., Ohio Orgn. Nurse Execs. (bd. dirs. 1992-94), Lorain C. of C., Sigma Theta Tau. Avocations: golf, music, tennis, running, reading. Office: Life's Doors Hospice 1111 S Orchard St Ste 400 Boise ID 83705-1966

LANGENHEIM, JEAN HARMON, biology educator; b. Homer, La., Sept. 5, 1925; d. Vergil Wilson and Jeanette (Smith) H.; m. Ralph Louis Langenheim, Dec. 1946 (div. Mar. 1961). BS, U. Tulsa, 1946; MS, U. Minn., 1949, PhD, 1953. Rsch. assoc. botany U. Calif., Berkeley, 1954-59, U. Ill., Urbana, 1959-61; rsch. fellow biology Harvard U., Cambridge, Mass., 1962-66; asst. prof. biology U. Calif., Santa Cruz, 1966-68, assoc. prof. biology, 1968-73, prof. biology, 1973—; academic v.p. Orgn. Tropical Studies, San Jose, Costa Rica, 1975-78; mem. sci.adv. bd. EPA, Washington, 1977-81; chmn. com. on humid tropics U.S. Nat. Acad. Nat. Research Council, 1975-77; mem. com. floral inventory Amazon NSF, Washington, 1975-87. Author: Botany-Plant Biology in Relation to Human Affairs.; Contbr. articles to profl. jours. Grantee NSF, 1966-88; recipient Disting. Alumni award U. Tulsa, 1979. Fellow AAAS, AAUW, Calif. Acad. Scis., Bunting Inst.; mem. Bot. Soc. Am., Ecol. Soc. Am. (pres. 1986-87), Internat. Soc. Chem. Ecology (pres. 1986-87), Assn. for Tropical Biology (pres. 1985-86), Soc. for Econ. Botany (pres. 1993-94). Home: 191 Palo Verde Ter Santa Cruz CA 95060-3214 Office: U Calif Sinsheimer Labs Dept Biol Santa Cruz CA 95064

LANGENHEIM, RALPH LOUIS, JR., geology educator; b. Cin., May 26, 1922; s. Ralph Louis and Myrtle (Helmers) L.; m. Jean C. Harmon, Dec. 23, 1946; m. Virginia A.M. Knobloch, June 5, 1963; children: Victoria Elizabeth, Ralph Louis III; m. Shirley B. Ate, May 1, 1970; stepchildren: Judy Grigg,

Lynn Ate, Kathleen Majack; m. Casey Diana, Mar. 6, 1993; stepchildren: Eric Steckler, Matthew Diana. B.S., U. Tulsa, 1943; M.S., U. Colo., 1947; Ph.D., U. Minn., 1951. Registered profl. geologist, Wyo. Teaching asst. U. Tulsa, 1941-43, U. Colo., 1947; fellow U. Minn., 1947-48, teaching asst., 1948-50; asst. prof. Coe Coll., 1950-52; asst. prof. paleontology U. Calif., Berkeley, 1952-59, curator Paleozoic and early Mesozoic fossil invertebrates, 1952-59; asst. prof. geology U. Ill., Urbana, 1959-62; asso. prof. U. Ill., 1962-67, prof., 1967-92, prof. emeritus, 1993—; also curator fossil invertebrates Mus. Nat. History, 1988-92, curator emeritus, 1993—; with Instituto Geologico Nacional de Colombia, summer 1953; Geol. Survey Can., summer 1958, Geol. Survey Iran, fall 1973, Geol. Survey Republic of China, fall 1981; ptnr. Lanman Assocs., Cons. Geologists, 1974—; cons., mem. faculty geology and mining depts. Poly. U., Albania, fall 1992; vis. disting. prof. U. Nev., Las Vegas, 1994; book rev. editor Jour. Geol. Edn., 1990—. Assoc. editor Jour. Paleontology, 1995-96. Served with USNR, 1943-46; lt. comdr. Res., ret. ecipient Rudolph Eric Raspe medal Inst. Geometaphysik Neue Schwanstein, 1973. Mem. AAAS, Nev. Petroleum Soc., Wyo. Geol. Assn., Paleontol. Soc. (sec. 1962-70), Geol. Soc. Am., Soc. Econ. Paleontologists and Mineralogists, Am. Assn. Petroleum Geologists, Ill. Geol. Soc. (sec. 1978, v.p. 1979, pres. 1980), Internat. Assn. Cnidaria Specialists (treas. 1977-79), Nat. Assn. Geology Tchrs., Ill. Acad. Sci., Rocky Mountain Biol. Lab., Explorers Club, Sigma Xi. Rsch. and publs. in stratigraphy and paleontology. Home: 401 W Vermont Ave Urbana IL 61801-4928 Office: Univ Ill Dept Geology 245NHB 1301 W Green St # 245nhb Urbana IL 61801-2919

LANGENWALTER, GARY ALLAN, manufacturing and management consulting company executive; b. Pendleton, Oreg., Jan. 11, 1946; s. Allan Charles and Florine Ruth (Brace) L.; m. Janet Ann Case, Aug. 5, 1972; children: Karl Case, Keith Allan. Diploma, NOIB, Breukelen, The Netherlands, 1966; BA in Mgmt., U. Oreg., 1967; MBA in Mgmt., Mich. State U., 1969. Cert. fellow in prodn. and inventory mgmt.; cert. in integrated resources mgmt. Programmer, analyst Arthur Andersen & Co., Detroit, 1969-72; project mgr. Burroughs Corp., Detroit and Radnor, Pa., 1972-78; mgr. MIS, Faultless Caster, Evansville, Ind., 1978-82; mgr. trading ops. Christopher Funk & Co., Lafayette, Ind., 1982-83; mgr. mfg. cons. Peat Marwick Main, Cin. and N.Y.C., 1983-87, Coopers & Lybrand, Boston, 1988; founder, pres. Langenwalter & Assocs., Stow, Mass., 1988-95; founder, pres. Mfg. Cons. Ptnrs., Inc., 1995—; adj. instr. Nichols Coll., Dudley, Mass., 1989-91; seminar leader U. Seminar Ctr., Boston, 1990-91; guest lectr. Bryant Coll., 1991-92, Assumption Coll., 1993, Worcester State Coll., 1993, Suffolk U., 1993, Clark U., 1997—. Co-author: The Handbook of Materials and Capacity Requirements Planning, 1993. Mem. adminstrv. coun. St. Matthew's United Meth. Ch., Acton, Mass., 1989-90, 93-95; capt. Stow Minutemen, 1990-95; founder Stow Civic Leadership Coun.; pres. Stow Bus. Assn., 1992-94, dir., 1995—; treas. Troop 1 Boy Scouts Am., 1990-93; mem. Stow Econ. Devel. Coun., 1996—; mem. So. New Eng. Emmaus Cmty., 1993—. With U.S. Army, 1969-71. Fellow Am. Prodn. and Inventory Control Soc. (bd. dirs., nat. rep. mfg. specific industry group 1993—, pres. Detroit chpt. 1975-76, spkr. internat. conf. 1994-96, spkr. regional chpt. meetings 1979—, ant. instr. Repetitive Mgmt. 1995—, spkr. regional meeting 1995, spkr. seminar 1996); mem. Assn. Mfg. Excellence, Orgn. Transformation Network, Assn. Quality & Participation, Beta Gamma Sigma. Home and Office: 22 Seven Star Ln Stow MA 01775-1449

LANGER, BERNHARD, professional golfer; b. Anhausen, Germany, Aug. 27, 1957; m. Vikki Langer; children: Jackie Carol, Stefan Bernhard, Christina Joy. Profl. golfer, 1972—; mem. European Ryder Cup Team, 1981, 83, 85, 87, 89, 91, World Cup Team, 1976, 77, 78, 79, 80, 90, 91, 93; capt. Nissan Cup Team, 1985, 86, Kirin Cup Team, 1987, Four Tours World Championship Team, 1989. Winner 7 German Nat. Opens and 2 German Nat. PGAs, over 30 internat. tournaments including Dunlop Masters, 1980, Colombian Open, 1980, German Open, 1981, 82, 85, 86, Bob Hope Brit. Classic, 1981, Italian Open, 1983, Glasgow Classic, 1983, Johnnie Walker Tournament, 1983, Caslo World, 1983, Irish Open, 1984, 87, Dutch Open, 1984, French Open, 1984, Spanish Open, 1984, Australian Masters, 1985, European Open, 1985, Sun City Challenge, 1985, PGA Championship Eng., 1987, Belgian Classic, 1987, European Epson Match Play, 1988, Peugeot Spanish Open, 1989, German Masters, 1989, Madrid Open, 1990, Benson & Hedges Open, 1991, Heineken Dutch Open, 1992, Honda Open, 1992, Volvo PGA Championship, 1993; co-winner Lancome Trophy; leader European Order of Merit, 1981, 84; tour victories include Masters, 1985, 93, Sea Pines Heritage Classic, 1985. Avocations: skiing, soccer. Office: care PGA 100 Avenue Of Champions Palm Beach Gardens FL 33418

LANGER, EDWARD L., trade association administrator; b. Cleve., May 8, 1936; s. Edward L. and Evelyn (Palmer) L.; m. Sheila Mary Fitzpatrick, Nov. 5, 1957 (div. Sept. 1976); children—Dennis, Edward, Michael, Thomas, Michele; m. Carol E. Stower, Aug. 4, 1979; children—Tamara, Troy. B.S., John Carroll U., 1958, M.A., 1964; postgrad., Ohio U., 1962, 63, Cleve. State U., 1967-68. Asst. dean admissions and records John Carroll U., University Heights, Ohio, 1964-65; head guidance Wickliffe City Schs., Ohio, 1965-67; successively dir. mem. relations, mktg., planning, asst. mng. dir. Am. Soc. for Metals, Materials Park, Ohio, 1967-84, mng. dir., 1984-96; prin. IBIS Assocs., Chardon, Ohio, 1996—; bd. dirs. Kolene Corp. Author: Solid State Structures and Reactions, 1968. Bd. dirs., vice chmn. Cleve. Conv. Bur., 1984—. Mem. Am. Soc. Assn. Execs. (bd. dirs., vice chmn. 1988-92), Coun. Engring. and Sci. Soc. Execs. (bd. dirs. 1987-93, pres. 1992), numerous other engring. and sci. socs. Avocations: fishing; farming; golf; horses. Office: IBIS Assocs 10880 Mitchells Mill Rd Chardon OH 44024-9652

LANGER, ELLEN JANE, psychologist, educator, writer; b. N.Y.C., Mar. 25, 1947; d. Norman and Sylvia (Tobias) L. BA, NYU, 1970; PhD, Yale U., 1974. Cert. clin. psychologist. Asst. prof. psychology The Grad. Ctr. CUNY, 1974-77; assoc. prof. psychology Harvard U., Cambridge, Mass., 1977-81; prof. Harvard U., 1981—; cons. NAS, 1979-81, NASA; mem. div. on aging Harvard U. Med. Sch., 1979—, mem. psychiat. epidemiology steering com., 1982-90; chair social psychology program Harvard U., 1982-94, chair Faculty Arts and Scis. Com. of Women, 1984-88. Author: Personal Politics, 1973, Psychology of Control, 1983, Mindfulness, 1989, The Power of Mindful Learning, 1997; editor: (with Charles Alexander) Higher Stages of Human Development, 1990, (with Roger Schank) Beliefs, Reasoning and Decision-Making, 1994; contbr. articles to profl. and scholarly jours. Guggenheim fellow; grantee NIMH, NSF, Soc. for Psychol. Study of Social Issues, Milton Fund, Sloan Found., 1982; recipient Disting. Contbn. of Basic to Applied Psychology award APS, 1995. Fellow Computers and Soc. Inst., Am. Psychol. Assn. (Disting. Contributions to Psychology in Public Interest award 1988, Disting. Contributions of Basic Sci. to Applied Psychology 1995); mem. Soc. Exptl. Social Psychology, Phi Beta Kappa, Sigma Xi. Democrat. Jewish. Avocations: theater, horseback riding, tennis. Office: Harvard U Dept Psychology 33 Kirkland St Cambridge MA 02138-2044

LANGER, JAMES STEPHEN, physicist, educator; b. Pitts., Sept. 21, 1934; s. Bernard F. and Liviette (Roth) L.; m. Elinor Goldmark Aaron, Dec. 21, 1958; children: Ruth, Stephen, David. B.S., Carnegie Inst. Tech., 1955; Ph.D., U. Birmingham, Eng., 1958. Prof. physics Carnegie-Mellon U., Pitts., 1958-82, assoc. dean, 1971-74; prof. physics U. Calif., Santa Barbara, 1982—, dir. Inst. for Theoretical Physics, 1989-95. Contbr. articles to profl. jours. Guggenheim fellow, 1974-75; Marshall scholar, 1955-57. Fellow AAAS, Am. Acad. Arts and Scis., Am. Phys. Soc. (chair divsn. condensed matter physics); mem. NAS, N.Y. Acad. Scis. Democrat. Jewish. Home: 1130 Las Canoas Ln Santa Barbara CA 93105-2331 Office: U Calif Dept Physics Santa Barbara CA 93106

LANGER, LAWRENCE LEE, English educator, writer; b. N.Y.C., June 20, 1929; s. Irving and Esther (Strauss) L.; m. Sondra Weinstein, Feb. 21, 1951; children: Andrew, Ellen. BA, CCNY, 1951; AM, Harvard U., 1952, PhD, 1961. Teaching fellow Harvard U., Cambridge, Mass., 1954-57; instr. English U. Conn., Storrs, 1957-58; instr. English Simmons Coll., Boston, 1958-61, asst. prof., 1961-66, assoc. prof., 1966-72, prof., 1972-76, Alumnae prof., 1976-92, Alumnae prof. emeritus, 1992—; Fulbright prof. Am. Lit. U. Graz, Austria, 1963-64. Author: The Holocaust and The Literary Imagination, 1975, The Age of Atrocity, 1978, Versions of Survival, 1982, Holocaust Testimonies, 1991 (Nat. Book Critics Cr. award for Criticism 1991), Art From the Ashes: A Holocaust Anthology, 1995, Admitting the Holocaust: Collected Essays, 1995. Sr. rsch. fellow NEH, 1978-79, 89-90, Koerner fellow for study of the Holocaust, Ctr. for Hebrew and Jewish Studies, Oxford, Eng., 1997; Shariro Sr. scholar-in-residence Rsch. Inst. U.S. Holocaust Meml. Mus., 1996. Mem. MLA, PEN. Office: Simmons Coll Dept English 300 Fenway Boston MA 02115-5820 also: care Yale Univ Press Authors Mail 92A Yale Ave New Haven CT 06515-2251

LANGER, LEONARD O., JR., radiologist, educator; b. Mpls., Oct. 16, 1928; s. Leonard Otto and Louise (Buro) L.; m. Rollie Helen Segal, Sept. 13, 1952; children: Maren, Sara, Elizabeth, Kristen. BA summa cum laude, U. Minn., 1950, BS, 1951, MD, 1953. Diplomate Am. Bd. Radiology. Intern Salt Lake County Hosp., Salt Lake City, 1953-54; resident in radiology U. Mich. Hosp., 1956-59; instr. radiology U. Pitts. Med. Sch., 1959-60; from instr. to assoc. prof. radiology U. Minn. Med. Sch., Mpls., 1961-66; radiologist Suburban Radiologie Cons., Mpls., 1966-78, 84-89; prof. U. Wis. Med. Sch., Madison, 1978-84; clin. assoc. prof. radiology U. Minn. Med. Sch., Mpls., 1966-78; clin. prof. U. Minn., 1984—; cons. clin. genetics divsn. U. Wis. Med. Sch., 1984—, skeletal dysplasia program, U. Minn. Med. Sch., 1984—; mem. com. Internat. Nomenclature of Constl. Diseases of Bone, Paris, 1969—. Author: Bone Dysplasias, 1974; contbr. over 100 articles to profl. med. jours. Served to capt. USAF, 1953-56. Fellow Am. Coll. Radiology; mem. Internat. Skeletal Soc. (cons. editor Skeletal Radiology 1976-89), Soc. Pediatric Radiology, Radiological Soc. N.Am., Bone Dysplasia Soc., Little People Am. (hon. life, med. adv. bd., 1966—). Democrat. Avocations: swimming, skiing, tennis. Home: 1235 Yale Pl Apt 710 Minneapolis MN 55403-1945

LANGER, RALPH ERNEST, journalist, newspaper executive and editor; b. Benton Harbor, Mich., July 30, 1937; s. Ralph L. and Mary (Skuda) L.; m. Katherine B. McGuire, June 25, 1960; children: Terri B., Tammi L. Student, Central Mich. U., 1955-57; B.A. in Journalism, U. Mich., 1957-59. Telegraph editor, reporter Grand Haven (Mich.) Daily Tribune, 1959-60; mng. editor Port Angeles (Wash.) Evening News, 1962-66; copy desk Detroit Free Press, 1966-68; asst. mng. editor Dayton Jour. Herald, 1968, mng. editor, 1968-75; editor Everett (Wash.) Herald, 1975-81; mng. editor Dallas Morning News, 1981-83, exec. editor, 1983-86, v.p., 1986-91, sr. v.p., exec. editor, 1991-96, exec. v.p., editor, 1997—. Pres. Freedom of Info. Found. Tex., 1985-89, Nat. Freedom of Info. Coalition, 1992-93, Coun. of Presidents, 1991-92.. 1st lt. U.S. Army, 1960-62. Mem. Am. Soc. Newspaper Editors, Press Club Dallas (pres. 1985-86), A.P. Mng. Editors Assn. (bd. dirs. 1980—, sec. 1989, v.p. 1990, pres. 1990-91), Coun. of Pres.'s (founding pres. 1992-93), AP Mng. Editors Assn. Found. (pres. 1991-92), Scabbard and Blade, Alpha Phi Gamma, Sigma Phi Epsilon. Office: Dallas Morning News Comm Ctr PO Box 655237 Dallas TX 75261

LANGER, RICHARD J., lawyer; b. Rockford, Ill., June 10, 1944; s. John W. and Dorothy E. (Brunn) Langrehr; m. Audrey A. Russo, Jan. 28, 1967; children: Kathleen M., Michael R. BS, U. Ill., 1967; JD, U. Wis., 1974. Bar: Wis. 1974, U.S. Dist. Ct. (we. dist.) Wis. 1974. Assoc. Ela, Esch, Hart & Clark, Madison, Wis., 1974-76; ptnr. Stolper, Koritzinsky, Brewster & Neider, Madison, 1976-91, Michael, Best & Friedrich, Madison, 1991—. Author: Guide to Property Classification, 1986, Workbook For Wisconsin Estate Planners, 1991, Family Estate Planning in Wisconsin, 1996, also articles. Sec. Combat Blindness Found., Madison, 1988—. Fellow Am. Coll. Trust and Estate Coun.; mem. ABA, State Bar Wis., Madison Estate Coun. Avocations: scuba diving, traveling, bicycling. Home: 1502 Windfield Way Madison WI 53562-3808 Office: Michael Best & Friedrich 1 S Pinckney St Madison WI 53703-2808

LANGER, ROBERT MARTIN, retired chemical engineering company executive, consultant; b. Boston, May 29, 1925; s. Samuel Morton and Ethel (Shlivek) L. B.Engring., Yale U., 1945, D.Engring., 1952; S.M., MIT, 1948. Sales mgr. The Badger Co., Inc., Cambridge, Mass., 1968-70; dep. mng. dir. Badger B.V., The Hague, The Netherlands, 1970-74, mng. dir., 1974-78; v.p., project adminstrn. The Badger Co., Inc., Cambridge, 1978-80; sr. v.p. Badger Am., Inc., Cambridge, 1981-83; v.p., treas. The Badger Co., Inc., Cambridge, 1983-87. Served to lt. j.g. USNR, 1945-46. Mem. AIChE. Home: 280 Commonwealth Ave Boston MA 02116-2422

LANGER, ROBERT SAMUEL, chemical, biomedical engineering educator; b. Albany, N.Y., Aug. 29, 1948; s. Robert Samuel Sr. and Mary (Swartz) L.; m. Laura Feigenbaum, July 31, 1988; children: Michael David, Susan Katherine, Samuel Alexander. BS, Cornell U., 1970; ScD, MIT, 1974; PhD (hon.), ETH, Switzerland, 1996, Technion U., Israel, 1997. Rsch. assoc. Children's Hosp. Med. Ctr., Boston, 1974—; asst. prof. chem. and biomed. engring. MIT, Cambridge, Mass., 1978-81; assoc. prof. MIT, Cambridge, 1981-85, prof., 1985-89, Germeshausen prof., 1989—; bd. dirs. Alkermes, Cambridge, Acusphere, Cambridge, Focal, Lexington; tchr. Group Sch., Cambridge, 1971-73; endowed lectr. U. P.R., 1983, Case Western Res. U., 1986, U. Mich., 1987, U. Wash., 1988, U. Kans., 1989, U. Calif., San Francisco, 1991, U. Wis., 1991, Ga. Inst. Tech., 1991, Ohio State U., 1991, U. Pitts., 1992, Purdue U., 1992, U. Del., 1993, Pa. State U., 1993, Beth Israel Hosp., 1994, Cornell U., 1994, Calif. Inst. Tech., 1995, Ill. Inst. Tech., 1995, Ohio State Med. Sch., 1995, U. Calif., 1996, U. Tenn., 1996, U. N.C., 1997; cons. to numerous cos., including Genentech, San Francisco, 1981—, Merck Sharpe and Dohme, 1981-85; sci. advisor Cygnus, Redwood City, Calif., 1987—, Opta Foods, Bedford, Mass., 1991—; mem. FDA Sci. Bd., 1995—. Author: (with D. Cincotta and K. Cole) Group School Chemistry Curriculum, 1972, (with W. Thilly) Laboratory in Applied Biology, 1978, Analaytical Practices in Biochemistry, 1979, (with W. Hrusheysky and F. Theeuwes) Temporal Control of Drug Delivery, 1991; editor: (with M. Chasin) Biodegradable Polymers in Drug Deliveryy, 1990, (with D. Wise) Medical Applications on Control Release, Vols. I and II, 1984, (with R. Steiner and P. Weisz) Angiogenesis, 1992; contbr. over 700 articles to sci. jours.; patentee in field. Recipient John W. Hyatt Svc. to Mankind award Soc. Plastics Engrs., 1995, Internat. award, 1996, Ebert Prize, Am. Pharm. Assn., 1995, 96, Rsch. award Am. Diabetes Assn., 1996, internat. award Gairdner Found., 1996; Union Oil fellow, 1970-71, Chevron fellow, 1971-72; cited for Outstanding Patent in Mass., Intellectual Property Owners Inc., 1989. Fellow Soc. Biomaterials (Clemson award 1990), Am. Assn. Pharm. Scis. (Disting. Pharm Sci. award 1993); mem. NAS, AIChE (Food, Pharm. and Bioengring. award 1986, Profl. Progress award 1990, Charles M. Stine Materials Sci. and Engring. award 1991, William Walker award 1996), Nat. Acad. Engring., Inst. Medicine of NAS, Am. Inst. Med. and Biol. Engrs. (founding fellow), Am. Acad. Arts and Scis., Am. Chem. Soc. (Creative Polymer award 1989, Phillips Applied Polymer Sci. award 1992, Pearlman Meml. Lectr. award 1992), Internat. Soc. Artificial Internal Organs (Organon-Teknika award 1991), Biomed. Engring. Soc. (bd. dirs. 1991-94, Whitaker lectr. 1994), Controlled Release Soc. (bd. govs. 1981-85, chmn. regulatory affairs com. 1985-89, pres. 1991-92, Founders award 1989, Outstanding Pharm. Paper award 1990, 92), Am. Soc. Artificial Internal Organs (mem. program com. 1984-87), Internat. Soc. Artificial Internal Organs. Avocations: magic, jogging. Office: MIT Dept Chem Engring 77 Massachusetts Ave Cambridge MA 02139-4301

LANGER, STEVEN, consultant human resources management and industrial psychology; b. N.Y.C., June 4, 1926; s. Israel and Anna (Glaisner) L.; BA in Psychology, Calif. State U., Sacramento, 1950; MS in Pers. Svc., U. Colo., 1958; PhD, Walden U., 1970; Lic. psychologist, Ill.; m. M. Jacquline White, Oct. 11, 1954 (dec. Dec. 1969); children: Bruce, Diana, Geoffrey; m. Elaine Catherine Brewer, Dec. 29, 1979 (dec. Feb. 1992). Asst. to pers. dir. City and County of Denver, 1956-59; pers. dir. City of Pueblo (Colo.) 1959-60; pers. cons. J.L. Jacobs & Co., Chgo., 1961-64, adminstrv. mgr., 1966-67; sales selection mgr. Reuben H. Donnelly Corp., Chgo., 1964-66; pres. Abbott, Langer & Assocs., Crete, Ill., 1967—; vis. prof. mgmt. Loyola U., Chgo., 1969-71; community prof. behavioral scis. Purdue U., Calumet campus, Hammond, Ind., 1973-75. Mem. Ill. Psychol. Assn. (chmn. sect. indsl. psychologists 1971-72), Chgo. Psychol. Assn. (pres. 1974-75, 94-95), Chgo. Indsl./Orgnl. Psychologists, Soc. Human Resources Mgmt. (accredited, chmn. research award com. 1966-69), Am. Compensation Assn., Chgo. Compensation Assn. (sec. 1976-77), Mensa (pres. Chgo. chpt. 1972-74). Unitarian. Contbr. numerous reports and articles on indsl. psychology and human resources mgmt. to profl. publs. Home: 309 Herndon St Park Forest IL 60466-1132 Office: Abbott Langer & Assoc 548 1st St Crete IL 60417-2142

LANGERAK, ESLEY OREN, retired research chemist; b. Pella, Iowa, Oct. 28, 1920; s. William Henry and Grace Dena (Vander Linden) L.; m. Elizabeth Jane Rhodes (dec.), Nov. 18, 1944; children—Kristin, Lisbeth, Peter. B.S. in Chemistry, Central Coll., Iowa, 1941; M.S., U. Del., 1947, Ph.D. in Organic Chemistry, 1949. High sch. tchr. Garden Grove Consol. Sch., Iowa, 1941-42; research chemist, supr., lab mgr. DuPont Co., Wilmington, Del., 1949-81; compensation mgr. chems. and pigments dept. DuPont Co., 1981-85; ret., 1985. Contbr. articles to profl. jours. Served with Ordnance, U.S. Army, 1942-46, PTO. Republican. Presbyterian. Club: Du-Pont Country. Patentee in field (3).

LANGERMANN, JOHN W. R., institutional equity salesperson; b. N.Y.C., Aug. 14, 1943; m. Karen Elizabeth Stives, Jan. 14, 1995. BA with highest honors, Lehigh U., 1965. Ptnr., sales mgr. L.F. Rothschild, Unterberg, Towbin, Boston, 1977-87; sr. v.p. County Nat. West Securities, Boston, 1987-90; v.p. Piper, Jaffray & Hopwood, Boston, 1990-92; sr. v.p. Needham & Co., Inc., Boston, 1993-94; mng. dir. instl. sales Ladenburg, Thalmann & Co., Inc., Boston, 1994-96; mgr. Brown Bros. Harriman & Co., Boston, 1996—. Mem. Internat. Soc. Security Analysts, Kansas City Soc. Fin. Analysts. Avocations: vintage sports car racing, curling, sculling. Home: Stonehenge Farm Dover MA 02030 Office: Brown Brothers Harriman & Co 40 Water St Boston MA 02109-3604

LANGEVIN, EDGAR LOUIS, retired humanities educator; b. Hanover, N.H., Dec. 8, 1929. BS, Worcester State Coll., 1952, MEd, 1955; MA, Assumption Coll., 1960; MBA, Anna Maria Coll., 1979; adv. grad. study cert. (CAGS), U. Mass., 1989; paralegal cert., Anna Maria Coll., 1993. Substitute tchr. Worcester (Mass.) Pub. Schs., 1953-57, tchr., 1957-63; tchr. Burncoat High, Worcester, 1963-69; assoc. prof. Framingham (Mass.) State Coll., 1969-96; ret., 1996; chair Career Day Fgn. Lang. Majors, Framingham State Coll., 1975; prof. emeritus Framingham State Coll., 1996. Active Worcester Dem. City Com., 1992—. Mem. Elks. Home: 39 Carlisle St Worcester MA 01602-3323

LANGEVIN, JAMES R., state official; b. Providence, Apr. 22, 1964; s. Richard Raymond and June Katherine (Barrett) L. B Arts and Scis., R.I. Coll., 1990; MPA, Harvard U., 1994. State rep. City of Warwick, R.I., 1988-94; sec. of state Office of the Sec. of State, Providence, R.I., 1995—. Bd. mem. United Cerebral Palsey, Pawtucket, R.I., 1993—, Tech Access, Providence, 1995, R.I. State House Restoration Com., 1995. Mem. Save the Bay R.I., K.C. Democrat. Roman Catholic. Avocations: reading, public speaking, community involvement. Office: Rm 218 RI State House Providence RI 02903

LANGEVIN, LOUIS-DE-GONZAQUE, bishop; b. Oka, Can, Oct. 31, 1921. BA, Seminaire de Philosophie de Montreal, 1944; postgrad. in theology, Scolasticat des Peres Blancs, Ottawa, 1946-50; Lic. in Theology, Gregorian U., Rome, 1957; Lic. in Holy Scripture, Sainte a l'Institut Biblique, Rome, 1957. Ordained priest Roman Catholic Ch. Provincial priest Blancs d'Afrique, Montreal, Que., Can; aux. bishop Diocese de St Hyacinthe, 1974-79, titular bishop, 1979—; pres. Episcopal Commn. on Social Communications Conf. Cath. Bishops Can.; mem. Comm. for the Lay Apostate Conf. Bishops of Que. Decorated chevalier de l'Ordre du Saint-Sepulcre de Jerusalem lieutenance du Can., a Montreal, 1975, chevalier de Colomb du 4e Degre Assemblee Antoine Girouard de Saint-Hyacinthe Province de Que., Can. Home and Office: Eveche de Saint Hyacinthe, 1900 rue Girouard ouest CP 190, Saint Hyacinthe, PQ Canada J2S 7B4*

LANGEVIN, THOMAS HARVEY, higher education consultant; b. St. Paul, Mar. 20, 1922; s. Thomas E. and Myrtle (Damsgard) L.; m. Pearl E. Mattfeld, Aug. 29, 1942; children: Dennis, Timothy. B.S., Concordia Tchrs. Coll., Seward, Neb., 1947; M.A., U. Neb., 1949, Ph.D., 1951. Quarantine insp. USPHS, 1943-45; grad. asst., asst. instr. U. Neb., 1947-51; prof. Concordia Tchrs. Coll., 1951-63, dean coll., 1961-63, acting pres., 1961-63; dir. long-range planning project Luth. Ch.-Mo. Synod, 1964-65; also cons. Bd. Higher Edn.; acad. v.p. Pacific Luth. U., 1965-69; pres. Capital U., Columbus, Ohio, 1969-79; pres. emeritus Capital U., 1979—; pres. Thomas H. Langevin Assoc., LadyLake, Fla., 1979—; prin. Registry for Interim Coll. and Univ. Pres., 1992—; chmn. Luth. Edn. Conf. N.Am., 1980-87; cons. Battelle Inst., 1979-87; cons., vis. fellow Battelle Seattle Rsch. Ctr., 1976. Co-chmn. Tacoma Area Urban Coalition Edn. Task Force, 1967-69; mem., past chmn. Ohio Com. Pub. Programs in Humanities; former exec. com. Fedn. Pub. Programs in Humanities; former mem. Ohio Higher Edn. Facilities Commn.; former mem. Commn. on Future Lutheran Edn., Luth Edn. Conf. N.Am., pres., 1977-78; bd. dirs. Nat. Urban League, 1979-80; Mem. Columbus Urban League; Former mem. Met. Columbus Sch. Com.; bd. dirs. Tacoma Citizens Com. Pub. TV, 1967-69, Design for Progress Tacoma, 1969, Tacoma Area Urban Coalition, 1967-69; bd. rev. Air U.; former adv. com. Center Sci. and Industry, Columbus; asso. in urban affairs Nat. Inst. Pub. Affairs; bd. control Concordia Coll., Portland, Oreg., 1965-69; bd. overseers Acad. Contemporary Problems, Columbus, 1972-75; trustee Columbus Symphony Orch., pres., 1979-81; past trustee Columbus Sch. Girls, Columbus Met. Area Community Action; hon. trustee Internat. Council of Mid-Ohio; past bd. govs. Goodwill Industries Central Ohio, Salesian Inner City Boys' Club; past bd. dirs., pres. Blue Cross Central Ohio; bd. dirs. Options, Learning Connections, Franklin County Heart Br., Columbus Area Mental Health Center; bd. dirs. Battelle Meml. Inst. Found., chmn., 1977-78; mem. bd. dirs. Nationwide Corp. Served with USCGR, 1943-45. Recipient Carnegie grant, postdoctoral fellow Center for Study Higher Edn., U. Mich., 1963-64. Mem. Assn. Ind. Colls. and Univs. Ohio (chmn. 1971-74), Orgn. Am. Historians, Nebr., Ohio hist. socs., Am. Assn. Higher Edn., Newcomen Soc. N.Am., Navy League U.S. (past dir. Columbus council), Columbus Area C. of C. (dir. 1971-74). Lutheran. Club: Columbus Rotary (dir.). Home: 441 San Pedro Dr Lady Lake FL 32159-8664

LANGFIELD, HELEN ELION, artist, radio commentator; b. New London, Conn., July 6, 1924; d. Harry Robert and Ida Fannie Elion; m. Raymond Lee Langfield, Oct. 6, 1952; 1 child, Joanna Langfield Rose. BA in English, Ohio State U., 1946; MA in Studio Art, Conn. Coll., 1972. Interviewer, commentator Sta. WNLC/WTYD, Waterford, Conn., 1971-88; instr. Lyman Allyn Mus., New London, Conn., 1984-86; chmn., art instr. Conn. Coll. Summer Program in Humanities, New London, 1968-72; TV interviewer, New London, 1970. Columnist New London Day, 1972; exhibited in one-woman and group shows at Wadsworth Atheneum, Hartford, 1974, Aldrich Mus. of Art, Ridgefield, Conn., 1976, 55 Mercer, N.Y.C., 1977, Whitney Counterweight, N.Y.C., 1981, Pastel Soc. Am., N.Y.C., 1982, Adam Gimbel Gallery, N.Y.C., 1982, 83, Cummings Art Ctr., New London, 1979, 83, 85, Brouhaha Gallery, Providence, 1986, Vangarde Gallery, New London, 1986, 87, 88, NOHO Gallery, N.Y.C., 1981, 85, 88, Conn. Commn. on Arts Showplace, Hartford, 1987, Lyman Allyn Mus., New London, Conn., 1988, 92, Conn. Coll., New London, 1988, MS Gallery, Hartford, 1988, Mark Humphrey Gallery, Southhampton, N.Y., 1991, Boca Raton (Fla.) Mus. Art, 1992, Hoxie Gallery, Westerly, R.I., 1994, Habitat Gallery, West Palm Beach, Fla., 1996; represented in permanent collections Michael DeSantis, Inc., N.Y.C., Radisson Hotel, New London, 1st Nat. Bank Danbury, Conn., Conn. Savings Bank, New Haven, Suisman, Shapiro, Wool, Brennan, Gray and Faulkner, P.C., New London, Citicorp, Boston, Otis Elevator, Hartford, State Ct. House, New London, pvt. collections. Commr. Conn. Commn. on the Arts, Hartford, 1983-85. Jewish. Avocations: tennis, bridge. Home: 23362 Torre Cir Boca Raton FL 33433-7026

LANGFORD, CHARLES DOUGLAS, state legislator, lawyer; b. Montgomery, Ala., Dec. 9, 1922; s. Nathan G. and Lucy B. (Brown) L. BS, Tenn. State U., Nashville, 1948; LLB, Cath. U. of Am., 1952, JD, 1967. Bar: Ala. 1953, U.S. Dist. Ct. (mid. dist.) Ala. 1954, U.S. Ct. Appeals (5th cir.) 1969, U.S. Supreme Ct. 1976, U.S. Ct. Appeals (11th cir.) 1982. Ptnr. Gray, Langford, Sapp, McGowan, Gray & Nathanson, Montgomery, Ala., 1968—; mem. Ala. State Senate, Montgomery, 1983—. Officer St. John A.M.E. Ch. With U.S. Army, 1943-46. Mem. Elks (past exalter ruler So. Pride lodge), Alpha Phi Alpha. Democrat. Home: 918 Grove St Montgomery AL 36104-4738 Office: 400 S Union St Ste 205 Montgomery AL 36104-4316

LANGFORD, DEAN TED, lighting and precision materials company executive; b. Princeton, Ill., June 19, 1939; s. Claude Robert and Dorothy Alene (Tuckerman) L.; m. Nancy Hirsch; children: Douglas T., John P. B.S.

in Math. and Aero. Engring., U. Ill., 1962, LHD, Salem State Coll., 1990. Regional sales mgr. IBM-N.E. Region, Westport, Conn., 1980-81, corp. dir. mgmt. devel., Armonk, N.Y., 1981-82, group dir., communications, Ryebrook, N.Y., 1982-83; v.p. mktg. GTE Communications Systems, Stamford, Conn., 1983-84; pres. GTE Elec. Products, Danvers, Mass., 1984-93, Osram Sylvania Inc., Danvers, Mass., 1993—. Mem. bd. advisers Sch. Engring., U. Ill.-Chgo., 1984-92; mem. adv. bd. Northeastern U., 1984—; trustee Civic Edn. Found. Lincoln-Filene Ctr., Tufts U.; mem. corp. bd. Mass. Gen. Hosp. Mem. U. Ill. Alumni Assn. (bd. dirs.), Alliance to Save Energy (bd. dirs.), Nat. Assn. of Mfg. (bd. dirs.), Nat. Elec. Mfg. Assn. (bd. dirs.), Phys. Sci. Inc. (bd. dirs.), Salem Country Club. Avocations: biking, golf, skiing. Home: 345 Beacon St Boston MA 02116-1102 Office: Osram Sylvania Inc 100 Endicott St Danvers MA 01923-3623

LANGFORD, JACK DANIEL, elementary school educator; b. Cookeville, Tenn., Jan. 15, 1960; s. Sam Harley and Mary Delma (Carr) L.; m. Marilyn Patricia Poteet. BS in Secondary Edn., Tenn. Tech. U., 1983, MA in Edn. Adminstrn. and Supervision, 1987, MA, 1993. Lic. tchr., 17 tchg. endorsements. Bus. tchr. Dekalb County H.S., Smithville, Tenn., 1984; social studies tchr. White County Mid. Sch., Sparta, Tenn., 1985-92; 1st-6th grade title I tchr. Findlay Elem. Sch., Sparta, Tenn., 1992—; chmn. Findlay Improvement Team, Sparta, 1993—. Vice-pres. White County Natural Resource Conservation Svc.; mem. Nat. Arbor Day Found. Recipient Career Ladder II State of Tenn., 1995. Mem. ASCD, NEA, Tenn. Edn. Assn., Internat. Reading Assn., Nat. Geog. Soc., White County Edn. Assn., Tenn. Cattlemen's Assn., White-Van Buren Cattlemen's Assn., White County Farm Bur., Nat. Arbor soc., Phi Delta Kappa. Avocations: reading, movies, sight seeing, conversing with friends, visiting. Home: 1404 Lawrence Hudgens Rd Sparta TN 38583

LANGFORD, JAMES JERRY, lawyer; b. Birmingham, Ala., May 19, 1933; S. N.B. and Margaret Elizabeth (Fuller) L.; m. Mary Elizabeth Fryant, Mar. 21, 1958; children: Jan Carol Langford Hammett, Joel Fryant L. BS, U. So. Miss., 1955; JD, U. Miss., 1970. Bar: Miss. 1970, U.S. Dist. Ct. (no. and so. dists.) Miss. 1970, U.S. Ct. Appeals (5th cir.) 1971, U.S. Ct. Appeals (11th cir.). Agt. Met. Life Ins. Co., Jackson, Miss., 1957-58; sales rep. Employers Mut. of Wausau, Jackson, 1958-64; v.p. Reid-McGee Ins. Co., Jackson, 1964-67; assoc. Wells Marble & Hurst, Jackson, 1970-73, ptnr., 1973-90, sr. ptnr., mng. ptnr., 1990—. Editor-in-chief Miss. Law Jour., 1969-70. Mem. U.S. Naval Inst., Annapolis, Md. 1st lt. U.S. Army, 1955-57. Mem. ABA, Fed. Bar Assn. (pres. Miss. chpt. 1981-82), Fedn. Ins. and Corp. Counsel, Nat. Assn. RR Trial Counsel, Miss. Bar Found., Miss. Bar Assn., Miss. Def. Lawyers Assn. (pres. 1992-93), Def. Rsch. Inst., Country Club Jackson, Phi Delta Phi, Omicron Delta Kappa, Pi Kappa Alpha. Presbyterian. Avocations: military history, baseball. Home: 12 Plum Tree Ln Madison MS 39110-9620 Office: Wells Marble & Hurst PO Box 131 Jackson MS 39205-0131 *People respect honesty, trustworthiness, hard work and sincerity. Do what you truly want to do for your vocation, for that is the secret of happiness in a business career.*

LANGFORD, JAMES ROULEAU, university press administrator; b. South Bend, Ind., June 12, 1937; s. Walter McCarty and Alice M. (Joubert) L.; m. Margaret Marie Hammerot, Aug. 30, 1968 (div. 1980); children: Jeremy, Joshua; m. Jill Ann Justice, July 16, 1981; children: Trevor J., Emily A. Ph.B., Aquinas Inst., 1960, M.A. in Philosophy, 1961, M.A. in Theology, 1964, S.T.L., 1965. Instr. theology St. Thomas Coll., St. Paul, 1965-67; editor Doubleday & Co., N.Y.C., 1967-69; exec. editor U. Mich. Press, Ann Arbor, 1969-74; dir. U. Notre Dame Press, Ind., 1974—; bd. dirs. Assn. Am. Univ. Presses, 1981-83. Author: Galileo, Science and the Church, 1966, rev., 1971, 3d edit., 1992, The Game Is Never Over, 1980, rev., 1982, The Cub Fan's Guide to Life, 1984, Runs, Hits and Errors, 1987, Rookie: The Story of a Seaon, 1990, Happy Are They: Living the Beatitudes in America, 1997. Pres. There Are Children Here, 1994—. Democrat. Roman Catholic. Home: 21550 New Rd Lakeville IN 46536-9342 Office: U Notre Dame Press Notre Dame IN 46556 *My life as a scholar, publisher and writer has brought me into contact with many of the most intelligent, creative and important people of our time. Those I admire most are the ones of whom it can be said "They never lost their sense of humor.".*

LANGFORD, KAREN SOLTIS, counselor, family therapist; b. Amarillo, Tex., Jan. 18, 1955; d. Raymond John and Gladys Gloria (Ross) Soltis; m. Earl Louis Gardner, June 23, 1973 (div. Aug. 1976); 1 child, Kristina Marie; m. John Stephen Langford, Nov. 5, 1982; children: Stephen Joshua, Thomas Gregory. BS, West Tex. State U., 1980; MEd, West Tex. A&M U., 1993. Tchr., coach Amarillo (Tex.) Ind. Sch. Dist., 1980-91; owner Raindancer Lawn Sprinkler Sys., Amarillo and Hereford, Tex., 1985—; sch. counselor Hereford Ind. Sch. Dist., 1992-96; therapist Quest Hosp., Amarillo, 1992—; juvenile probation counselor Deaf Smith County, Hereford, 1996—; deaf Smith Cmty. Resource Coord. group, Deaf Smith County Planning Bd., Hereford Indp. Sch. Dist. Health adv. bd.; presenter in field. Vol. counselor O'Brien House Cath. Family Svcs., Amarillo, 1993-94; vol. family counselor Child Protective Svcs., Hereford, 1994-95; vol. Cub Scout leader Boy Scouts Am., Hereford, 1995—, Hereford Health Care Alliance; rape crisis/domestic violence adv. bd. Deaf Smith County. Mem. ACA, Am. Assn. Christian Counselors, Tex. Counseling Assn., High Plains Counseling Assn., Whiteface Kiwanis, Kappa Delta Pi, Delta Psi Kappa. Republican. Methodist. Avocations: cartooning, golf, gardening, fishing, woodcarving. Home: 305 Hickory Hereford TX 79045 Office: Deaf Smith County Juvenile Probation 126 E 3rd St Hereford TX 79045-5514

LANGFORD, LAURA SUE, ratings analyst; b. Evansville, Ind., Sept. 28, 1961; d. Lee Denmar Miller and Susan E. (Morton) Reitz; m. John E. Langford, May 15, 1992; 1 child, Rowan Diane. BFA in Drama, U. So. Calif., L.A., 1983; MBA in Fin. & Pub./Non-Profit, Columbia U., 1992. Credit mgr. Super-Freeze Co., Inc., Burbank, Calif., 1984-86; asst. Salomon Bros. Inc., L.A., 1986-87; rsch. analyst Bank of Calif., N.A., L.A., 1987, pub. fin. officer, 1988-90; intern Citizens Budget Commn., N.Y.C., 1991; analyst Standard & Poor's Ratings Group, N.Y.C., 1992-93, assoc., 1993-94, assoc. dir., 1994-95, dir., 1996—. Contbr. to periodical Standard & Poor's Credit Week, 1993—; founding mem., editor GAA Gazette, 1985—. Pres.'s scholar U. Evansville, 1979-81; Divsn. Rsch. Assn. student officer fellow Columbia U., 1991-92. Avocations: skiing, science fiction, roller coasters. Office: Standard & Poor's Ratings 25 Broadway Fl 13 New York NY 10004-1010

LANGFORD, ROLAND EVERETT, military officer, environmental scientist, author; b. Owensboro, Ky., Apr. 11, 1945; s. John Roland and Mary Helen (Cockriel) L.; m. Son-Hee Shin, Dec. 18, 1971; children: John Everett, Lee Shin. AA, Armstrong State Coll., 1965; BS, Ga. So. Coll., 1967; MS, U. Ga., 1971, PhD, 1974; PhD, U. N.C., 1996; grad., U.S. Army Command and Gen. Staff Coll., 1985; PhD, U. N.C., 1996. Cert. indsl. hygienist; registered hazardous substances profl., sanitarian, Ariz.; diplomate Am. Acad. Sanitarians. Instr. Savannah (Ga.) Sci. Mus., 1971-72, Bainbridge (Ga.) Jr. Coll., 1973-74; asst. prof. chemistry Ga. Mil. Coll., Milledgeville, 1975-77; asst. prof. Ga. So. Coll., Statesboro, 1977-78; commd. capt. U.S. Army, 1978, advanced through grades to lt. col., 1992; chief chemistry sect. U.S. Army Acad. Health Scis., Ft. Sam Houston, Tex., 1978-79; sanitary engr. U.S. Army Environ. Hygiene Agy., Aberdeen Proving Ground, Md., 1979-81; comdr. environ. sanitation detachment Taegu, Republic of Korea, 1981-83; environ. sci. officer Ft. Huachuca, Ariz., 1984-88; chief occupational health rsch. U.S. Army Biomed. R&D Lab., Ft. Detrick, Md., 1991-92; comdr. med. rsch. detachment Walter Reed Army Inst. Rsch., Wright-Patterson AFB, Ohio, 1992—; preventive medicine officer NATO, Zagreb, Croatia, Sarajevo, Bosnia-Herzegovina, 1996—; panel mem. Comprehensive Assistance to Undergrad. Sci. Edn., NSF, 1975-77; judge Internat. Sci. Fair, San Antonio, 1979; mem. sci. rev. panel NIH, 1986—; adj. faculty St. Leo's Coll., San Antonio, 1978-79, U. Md., Taegu and Pusan, Korea, 1981-83, AFIT, 1993—, Purdue U., 1995—. Co-author: Hazardous Materials Training Program for International Union of Operating Engineers, 1988, Fundamentals of Hazardous Materials Incidents, 1990, Substance Abuse in the Workplace, 1994; contbr. articles to profl. jours. Active Boy Scouts Am., Ft. Sam Houston, 1978-79; mem. parish coun., lay minister Holy Family Parish, Ft. Huachuca, 1985-88, 95-96, lay min., lector 1992-96; advisor Med. Explorer Post, Ft. Huachuca, 1986-88; lay minister St. Thomas More Ch., 1988-91. Fellow Am. Inst. Chemists; mem. Am. Acad. Indsl. Hygiene (cert.), Am. Chem. Soc., Nat. Environ. Health Assn. (cert. hazardous materials profl.), Korean Chem. Soc., Royal Asiatic Soc. (bd. dirs. 1982-83), Assn. Mil. Surgeons U.S., Am. Acad. Sanitarians (cert.), Health Physics Soc., Am. Water Works Assn., Am. Indsl. Hygiene Assn., Am. Acad. Health Physics (assoc.). Republican. Roman Catholic. Avocations: ham radio, oriental studies, photography. Home: 509 Phelps Cir Dayton OH 45433-1324 Office: US Army Med Rsch Detachment Wright Patterson AFB Dayton OH 45433

LANGFORD, THOMAS ANDERSON, retired theology educator, academic administrator; b. Winston-Salem, N.C., Feb. 22, 1929; s. Thomas Anderson and Louie Mae (Hughes) L.; m. Ann Marie Daniel, Dec. 27, 1951; children: Thomas A. III, James Howard, Timothy Daniel, Stephen Hughes. AB, Davidson Coll., 1951, DD, 1975; BD, Duke U., 1954, PhD, 1958. Ordained to ministry Meth. Ch., 1952; from instr. to prof. religion Duke U., Durham, N.C., 1956—, prof. systematic theology, 1971—, William Kellon Quick Disting. prof. theology and Meth. studies, chmn. dept. religion, 1965-71, dean Div. Sch., 1971-81, vice provost for acad. affairs, 1984—, interim provost, 1990, provost, 1991-94, trustee Duke endowment, 1992-97, ret., 1997; vis. prof. U. N.C., 1962. Author: In Search of Foundations: English Theology 1900-1920, 1969, Introduction to Western Philosophy: Pre-Socratics to Mill, 1970; Editor: (with G.L. Abernathy) Philosophy of Religion, 1962, 2d edit., 1968, History of Philosophy, 1965, (with W.H. Poteat) Intellect and Hope, Essays in the Thought of Michael Polanyi, 1968, Christian Wholeness, 1979, The Harvest of the Spirit, 1981, Practical Divinity: Theology in the Wesleyan Tradition, 1983; Contbr. articles to profl. jours. World Meth. Council rep. in theol. discussions with Roman Catholic Ch. and Luth. World Fedn., 1975—, Reformed World Alliance, 1987; del. Gen. Conf. United Meth. Ch., 1976, 80, 84, 88; Southeastern Jurisdictional Conf., 1972, 76, 80, 84, 88; chmn. Duke self-study coordinating com. So. Assn. Colls. and Univs., 1975-76; trustee Bennett Coll., Greensboro; exec. com. World Meth. Council, 1976-81. Gurney Harris Kearns fellow, 1956-57; Dempster fellow, 1957; Am. Council Learned Socs. fellow, 1965-66; Soc. Religion in Higher Edn. fellow, 1969; named outstanding tchr. Duke, 1965; recipient E. Harris Harbison award Danforth Found., 1965-66. Mem. Am. Theol. Soc., Phi Beta Kappa. Office: Duke U Divinity Sch Box 90967 Durham NC 27708

LANGFORD, WALTER MARTIN, retired greeting card and gift wrap manufacturing executive; b. Steubenville, Ohio, Jan. 2, 1931; s. Martin and Ola Belle (Stiff) L.; m. Winifred Claire Major, Mar. 14, 1953; children: Martin B., Janet R., Steven M. BS in Acctg., U. Kans., 1952; JD, Ill. Inst. Tech., 1971. With Am. Can. Co., 1956-66; internal audit mgr. All-Steel, Inc., Aurora, Ill., 1966-68, div. controller, 1968-71, dir. corp. services, 1971-77; v.p. adminstrn. Gibson Greetings, Inc., Cin., 1977-79; sr. v.p. ops. Cleo Wrap Corp. div. Gibson Greetings, Inc., Memphis, 1979-87, exec. v.p., gen. mgr., 1987-90; bd. dirs., corp. sec., v.p. Gibson Greetings, Inc., Cin., 1978-91. Mem. adv. bd. State Tech. Inst., Memphis, 1986-91; bd. dirs. Jr. Achievement of Memphis, 1985-91, Theatre Memphis, 1994—; bd. trustees LeMoyne-Owen Coll., 1991—, chmn., 1994—; adv. bd. Rhodes Coll., 1995—. Lt. (j.g.) USNR, 1952-56, Korea. Mem. Ill. Bar Assn. Lodge: Rotary. Avocation: book collecting.

LANGHAM, MICHAEL, theatrical director; b. Somerset, Eng., Aug. 22, 1919; s. Seymour and Muriel (Andrews Speed) L.; m. Helen Burns, July 8, 1948 (div. 1972); 1 son, Christopher; m. Ellin Gorky, 1972. Student, Radley Coll., Abingdon, Eng., 1933-37, London U., 1937-39; D.Litt. (hon.), McMaster U., 1962, St. Scholastica Coll., 1973; LL.D., U. Toronto, 1966. Engaged in theatrical profession, 1946—; dir. prodns. Arts Council Midland Theatre Co., 1946-48, Sir Barry Jackson's Birmingham Repertory Theatre, 1948-50, Glasgow Citizens' Theatre, 1953-54; artistic dir. Guthrie Theater, Mpls., 1971-79, including direction of Relapse, 1972, Oedipus the King, 1972, 73, The Government Inspector, 1973, The Merchant of Venice, 1973, King Lear, 1974, Love's Labor's Lost, 1974, The School for Scandal, 1974, Private Lives, Measure For Measure, 1975, The Matchmaker, 1976, Winter's Tale, 1977; dir. Theatre Center, The Juilliard Sch., N.Y.C., 1980—, Julius Caesar, Stratford-upon-Avon, 1950, Stratford, Ont., 1955, The Gay Invalid, London, 1950, Pygmalion, London, 1951, The Other Heart, London, 1951, Old Vic Co., prodn., Othello at Berlin Festival, also London, 1951; Brit. Council lectr., Australia, 1952; dir. Richard III, Belgian Nat. Theatre, 1952, The Merry Wives of Windsor, The Hague, 1953, artistic dir., Stratford (Ont.) Shakespearean Festival, 1955-67, including direction of Hamlet, 1957, Henry IV, Part I, 1958, Much Ado About Nothing, 1958, Romeo and Juliet, 1960, Coriolanus, 1961, Love's Labour's Lost, 1961, Taming of the Shrew, 1962, Cyrano de Bergerac, 1962, Troilus and Cressida, 1963, Timon of Athens, 1963, King Lear, 1964, The Country Wife, 1964; also prodns. Love's Labour's Lost and Timon of Athens at Festival Theatre, Chichester, Eng., 1964; dir. prodns. Hamlet, Stratford-upon-Avon, 1956, Merchant of Venice, 1960, Much Ado About Nothing, 1961, Henry V, Edinburgh Festival, 1956, Two Gentlemen of Verona, London, 1957, A Midsummer Night's Dream, London, 1960, Andorra, N.Y.C., 1963, Twelfth Night, Am. Place Theatre, 1982; compiler, dir. univ. tour prodns., Can. and U.S. on Shakespearean comedy, 1962; author, dir. prodns. The Affliction of Love for TV, 1963; Artistic cons. prodns., LaJolla (Cal.) Theater Project, 1965. Served with Brit. Army, 1939-45. Home: 20 Beechman Pl Apt 8B New York NY 10022*

LANGHAM, NORMA, playwright, educator, poet, composer, inventor; b. California, Pa.; d. Alfred Scrivener and Mary Edith (Carter) L. BS, Ohio State U., 1942; B in Theatre Arts, Pasadena Playhouse Coll. Theatre Arts, 1944; MA, Stanford U., 1956; postgrad., Summer Radio-TV Inst., 1960, Pasadena Inst. Radio, 1944-45. Tchr. sci. California High Sch., 1942-43; asst. office pub. info. Denison U., Granville, Ohio, 1955; instr. speech dept. Westminster Coll., New Wilmington, Pa., 1957-58; instr. theatre. California U., Pa., 1959, asst. prof., 1960-62, assoc. prof., 1962-79, prof. emeritus, 1979—, co-founder, sponsor, dir. Children's Theatre, 1962-79; founder, producer, dir. Food Bank Players, 1985, Patriot Players, 1986, Noel Prodns., 1993. Writer: (plays) Magic in the Sky, 1963, Founding Daughters (Pa., Nat. DAR awards 1991), Women Whisky Rebels (Pa. Nat. DAR awards 1992), John Dough (Freedoms Found. award 1968), Who Am I?, Hippocrates Oath, Gandhi, Clementine of '49, Soul Force, Dutch Painting, Purim, Music in Freedom, The Day the Moon Fell, Norma Langham's Job Johnson; composer, lyricist (plays) Why Me, Lord?, (text) Public Speaking; co-inventor (computer game) Highway Champion. Recipient Exceptional Acad. Svc. award Pa. Dept. Edn., 1975, Appreciation award Bicentennial Commn. Pa., 1976, Gregg award Calif. U. of Pa. Alumni Assn., 1992; Henry C. Frick Ednl. Commn. grantee. Mem. AAUW (co-founder Calif. br., 1st v.p. 1971-72, pres. 1972-73, Outstanding Woman of Yr. 1986, 97), DAR, Theatre Assn. Pa., Internat. Platform Assn. (Poetry award 1993-94, Monologue award 1995), Calif. U. Pa. Assn. Women Faculty (founder, pres. 1972-73), Calif. Cmty. Choir, Calif. Hist. Soc., Washington County Hist. Soc., Dramatists Guild, Ctr. in Woods, Mensa, Alpha Psi Omega, Omicron Nu. Presbyterian (elder). Home: PO Box 459 California PA 15419-0459

LANGHANS, EDWARD ALLEN, drama and theater educator; b. Warren, Pa., Mar. 11, 1923; s. Allen Milton and Frances Allen L. BA, U. Rochester, 1948, MA in English, 1949; M.A. in Theatre, U. Hawaii, 1951; Ph.D. in Theatre, Yale U., 1955. Asst. prof. drama U. Tex., Austin, 1955-57; asst. prof. drama and theatre U. Hawaii, Honolulu, 1957-64; assoc. U. Hawaii, 1964-71, prof., chmn. dept., 1971-85, assoc. dean arts and humanities, 1987, prof. emeritus, 1988—; vis. prof. Tufts U., 1967-68; rsch. prof. George Washington U., 1975-76. Author: (with Philip Highfill and Kalman Burnim) A Biographical Dictionary of Actors, Actresses, Musicians, Dancers, Managers and Other Stage Personnel in London 1660-1800, 16 vols., 1973-93, Five Restoration Theatrical Adaptations, 1980, Restoration Promptbooks, 1981, Eighteenth-Century British and Irish Promptbooks, 1987; co-author: An International Dictionary of Theater Language, 1985; contbr. articles to The New Grove Dictionary of Opera, 4 vols., 1992, International Dictionary of Theatre: Actors, Directors and Designers, 1996; dir., designer numerous plays. Bd. dirs. Honolulu Theatre for Youth, 1958-63, Hawaii Theatre Council, 1965-70, Hawaii Theatre Festival, 1978-82. Served with USAAF, 1942-47. Decorated Air medal, D.F.C.; Nat. Endowment for Humanities grantee, 1975-76, 85-86; Folger Shakespeare Library fellow, 1970-73. Mem. Am. Assn for Theatre in Higher Edn., Soc. Theatre Research, Am. Soc. Theatre Research. Home: 1212 Punahou St Apt 3402 Honolulu HI 96826-1026

LANGHENRY, JOHN GODFRED, JR., lawyer; b. Chgo., Feb. 10, 1933; s. John Godfred and Julia Margaret (Hoffman) L.; m. Eleanor L., Dec. 1, 1956; children: Barbara, John, Mark, Mary Patricia, Paul, Thomas, Matthew. BS, Loyola U., Chgo., 1954, JD, 1956. Bar: Ill. 1956, U.S. Dist. Ct. (no. dist.) Ill. 1959, U.S. Supreme Ct. 1971. Assoc. Hinshaw & Culbertson, Chgo., 1959-64, ptnr., 1965—; lectr. med. malpractice, hosp. law, civil practice and procedure Ill. Inst. Continuing Legal Edn.; lectr. med. loss prevention Ill. State Med. Soc.; faculty mem. trial advocacy workshop for practicing attys. Loyola U. Chgo. Sch. Law. Contbr. articles to profl. jours. Bus. chmn. Crusade of Mercy, Arlington Heights, Ill., 1966-67; chmn. safety commn. Village of Arlington Heights, 1967-69, mem. planning commn., 1969-72; trustee lay adv. bd. Sacred Heart of Mary High Sch., Rolling Meadows, Ill., 1972-76, 1st pres., 1972-73; mem. fin. com. Our Lady of the Wayside Ch., Arlington Heights, 1972-82, chmn., 1981-82; Loyola U. Sch. Law Alumni Assn., pres. 1973-74, Ill. Right to Life Com., chmn. 1975-76; chmn. fund raising St. Viator High Sch., Arlington Heights, mem. lay adv. bd., 1983-84, v.p. 1985-86. Served to 1st lt. USAF, 1956-59. Fellow Am. Coll. Trial Lawyers; mem. ABA, Ill. Bar Assn., Chgo. Bar Assn., Am. Soc. Hosp. Attys., Am. Bd. Trial Advs. (charter Ill. br., treas. 1988), Def. Rsch. Inst., Fedn. Ins. Counsel (chmn. med. malpractice com. 1979-80), Soc. Trial Lawyers Ill. (treas. 1986, sec. 1987, v.p. 1988, pres. 1989), Ill. Def. Counsel (pres. 1973-74), Trial Lawyers Club Chgo. (pres. 1970-71), Big Foot Country Club (Fontana, Wis.). Roman Catholic. Office: Hinshaw Culbertson 222 N La Salle St Ste 300 Chicago IL 60601-1013

LANGHOLZ, ROBERT WAYNE, lawyer, investor; b. Sioux City, Iowa, Jan. 17, 1930; s. Harry H. and Alvina (Bockhop) L.; m. Patricia Wilson Wheeler, Mar. 6, 1994; children: Robert Wayne, Laurence Henry, Kristofer Page. B.S. with distinction, U. Iowa, 1951, J.D., 1956. Bar: Iowa 1956, Okla. 1957. Research asst. to prof. Frank R. Kennedy, U. Iowa Coll. Law, 1955-56; trainee Gulf Oil Corp., 1956; mem. firm Carlson, Lupardus, Matthews, Holliman & Huffman, Tulsa, 1956-67; stockholder Holliman, Langholz, Runnels, Holden, Forsman & Sellers, Tulsa, 1967—; chmn. bd., chief exec. officer Skinner Bros. Co. Inc., Geophys. Research Corp., Indel-Davis Inc.; bd. dirs. F&M Bank & Trust Co. Trustee Herbert Hoover Presdl. Libr. Assn., West Branch, Iowa; nat. trustee Nat. Jewish Ctr. for Immunology and Respiratory Medicine, Denver. Served with USAF, 1951-53. Mem. ABA, Iowa Bar Assn., Okla. Bar Assn., Young Pres. Orgn., World Pres. Orgn., Summit Club, So. Hills Country Club (Tulsa), Eldorado Country Club (Indian Wells, Calif.). Methodist. Home: 4033 S Yorktown Pl Tulsa OK 74105-3412 Office: Holarud Bldg 10 E 3rd St Ste 400 Tulsa OK 74103-3621

LANGHOUT-NIX, NELLEKE, artist; b. Utrecht, The Netherlands, Mar. 27, 1939; came to U.S., 1968, naturalized, 1978; d. Louis Wilhelm Frederick and Geertruida Nix; m. Ernst Langhout, July 26, 1958; 1 child, Klaas-Jan Marnix. MFA, The Hague, 1958. Head art dept. Bush Sch., Seattle, 1969-71; dir. creative projects Project Reach, Seattle, 1971-72; artist-in-residence Fairhaven Coll., Bellingham, Wash., 1974, Jefferson Cmty. Ctr., Seattle, 1978-82, Lennox Sch., N.Y.C., 1982; dir. NN Gallery, Seattle, 1970—; guest curator Holland-U.S.A. Bicentennial show U. Wash., 1982; project dir. Women in Art Today, Wash., 1989, Wash. State Centennial Celebration; Washington to Washington traveling exhibition, 1989. Executed wall hanging for King County Courthouse, Seattle, 1974; one-woman shows include: Nat. Art Center, N.Y.C., 1980, Gail Chase Gallery, Bellevue, Wash., 1979, 80, 83, 84, Original Graphics Gallery, Seattle, 1981, Bon Nat. Gallery, Seattle, 1981, Kathleen Ewing Gallery, Washington, 1986, Ina Broerse Laren, Holland, 1992, Charlotte Daneel Gallery, Holland, 1992, Christopher Gallery, Tucson, 1992, Mercer Island Cmty. Arts Ctr., 1992, Lisa Harris Gallery, Seattle, 1994, Jacques Marchais Mus. Tibetan, S.I., N.Y., 1995, 4th World Conf. on Women, China, 1995, Global Focus, Beijing, 1995, Elite Gallery, Moscow, 1995; group shows include: Cheney Cowles Mus., Spokane, 1977, Bellevue Art Mus., 1978, 86, Renwick Gallery, Washington, 1978, Kleinert Gallery, Woodstock, N.Y., 1979, Artcore Meltdown, Sydney, Australia, 1979, Tacoma Art Mus., 1979, 83, 86, 87, Ill. State Mus., Springfield, 1979, Plener Sandomierz, Poland, 1980, Plener Kielce, Poland, 1980, Western Assn. Art Museums traveling show, 1979-80, Madison Square Garden, N.Y.C., 1981, Exhbn. Space, N.Y.C., 1982, Lisa Harris Gallery, 1985, 87, 88, Wash. State Centennial, Tacoma, 1989, Nordic Heritage Mus., Seattle, 1994, Soho 20, N.Y.C., 1997; represented in permanent collections Plener Collection, Sandomierz, Poland, Bell Telephone Co. Collection, Seattle, Wash. U., Seattle, Children's Orthopedic Hosp., Seattle, Nat. Mus. Women in Arts, Washington; installations Tacoma Art Mus. Bd. dirs. Wing Luke Mus., Seattle, 1978-81, Wash. State Trust Hist. Preservation, 1990-93; v.p. Denny Regrade Cmty. Coun., 1978-79; mem. Seattle Planning Commn., 1978-84. Author (with others) Step Inside the Sacred Circle, 1989, An Artist's Book 1940-45 Remembered, 1991; author: Tsoek: Earthy Writings by a Fourpaw, 1996; designer, editor Papua New Guinea-Where She Invented Bow and Arow, 1996. Recipient Wallhanging award City of Edmonds (Wash.), 1974; Renton 83 merit award, 1984; Merit award Internat. Platform Assn. Art Exhibit, 1984, Silver medal 1st place, 1985, 87, Gold medal, Internat. Platform Assn., 1989. Mem. Denny Regrade Arts Coun. (co-founder), Internat. Platform Assn., Women in Arts N.Y.C., Nat. Mus. Women in Arts (founding mem., Libr. fellow, chairperson Wash. State com. 1988-89, mem. nat. adv. bd. 1993—), Internat. Platform Assn., Seattle-King County Cmty. Arts Network (bd. dirs. 1983-85, chmn. 1984-85), Nat. Artist Equity Assn. Address: PO Box 375 Mercer Island WA 98040-0375

LANGILL, GEORGE FRANCIS, hospital administrator, educator; b. Ottawa, Ont., Can., Dec. 31, 1946; s. Roy Joseph and Margaret (O'Hara) L.; m. Lorraine Diane Bavazeau, Aug. 10, 1947; children: Norman, Barbara Ann, Kendra. BSc with honors, Ottawa U., 1971, MHA, 1973. Adminstrv. coordinator N.S. Dept. Health, 1973-74; asst. exec. dir. Royal Ottawa Hosp., 1974-79; assoc. exec. dir. Rehab. Ctr., Ottawa, 1979-83; chief exec. officer Royal Ottawa Health Care Group, 1983—; adj. prof., part-time lectr. Faculty Adminstrn., Ottawa U., 1979—; mem. faculty health care adminstrn. WHO, Montreal, 1983—; bd. dirs., mem. exec. com. Can. council Rehab. of Disabled, Toronto, 1985—. Contbr. articles to profl. jours. Mem. Ottawa Bd. Trade, 1986. Fellow Can. Coll. Health Service Execs., Am. Coll. Health Execs.; mem. Am. Assn. Mental Health Adminstrs. Avocations: skiing, hockey, golf. Office: Royal Ottawa Health Care Group, 1145 Carling Ave, Ottawa, ON Canada K1Z 7K4

LANGLAND, JOSEPH THOMAS, author, emeritus educator; b. Spring Grove, Minn., Feb. 16, 1917; s. Charles M. and Clara Elizabeth (Hille) L.; m. Judith Gail Wood, June 26, 1943; children—Joseph Thomas, Elizabeth Langland, Paul. BA, U. Iowa, 1940; MA, 1941; DLitt (hon.), Luther Coll., 1974. Instr. in English Dana Coll., Blair, Nebr., 1941-42; part-time instr. U. Iowa, 1946-48; asst. prof., then asso. prof. U. Wyo., 1948-59; mem. faculty U. Mass., Amherst, 1959-79; prof. English U. Mass., 1964-79, prof. emeritus, 1979—; dir. program for MFA in writing, 1964-70, 78-79; vis. lectr. U. B.C., U. Wash., Seattle, San Francisco State U.; guest reader, Republic of Madedonia, 1995. Author: poems For Harold, 1945, The Green Town, 1956, The Wheel of Summer, 1963, 2d edit., 1966, An Interview and Fourteen Poems, 1973, The Sacrifice Poems, 1975, Any Body's Song (Nat. Poetry Series), 1980, (poem with etchings) A Dream of Love, 1986, Twelve: Preludes & Postludes, 1988, Selected Poems, 1991, 2d edit., 1992; co-editor: poems Poet's Choice, 1962, 83, The Short Story, 1956; co-translator: poems Poetry From the Russian Underground, 1973. Served to capt., inf. AUS, 1942-46, ETO. Ford fellow in humanities Harvard-Columbia U. 1953-54; Amy Lowell Poetry fellow, 1955-56; Arts and Humanities fellow in poetry, 1966-67; recipient Melville Cane prize poetry Poetry Soc. Am., 1964; named Living Art Treasure in Lit., New Eng. Arts Biennial, 1985. Democrat. Home: 16 Morgan Cir Amherst MA 01002-1131

LANGLANDS, ROBERT PHELAN, mathematician; b. New Westminster, Can., Oct. 6, 1936; came to U.S., 1960; s. Robert and Kathleen (Phelan) L.; m. Charlotte Lorraine Cheverie, Aug. 13, 1956; children: William, Sarah, Robert, Thomasin. BA, U. B.C., 1957, MA, 1958, DS honoris causa, 1985; PhD, Yale U., 1960; DSc (hon.), McMaster U., 1985, CUNY, 1985; D in Math. (hon.), U. Waterloo, 1988; DSc (hon.), U. Paris, 1989, McGill U., 1991, Toronto U., 1993. From instr. to asso. prof. Princeton (N.J.) U., 1960-67; prof. math. Yale U., New Haven, 1968-72, Inst. Advanced Study, Princeton, 1972—. Author: Euler Products, 1971, (with H. Jacquet) Automorphic Forms on GL (2), 1970, On the Functional Equations Satisfied by Eisenstein Series, 1976, Base Change for GL (2), 1980, Les Débuts d'une Formule des Traces Stable, 1983. Recipient Wilbur Lucius Cross medal Yale

U., 1975, Common Wealth award Sigma Xi, 1984, Mathematics award Nat. Acad. Sci., 1988, Wolf prize in math. Wolf Found., 1995-96. Fellow Royal Soc. London, Royal Soc. Can.; mem. NAS, Am. Math Soc. (Cole prize 1982), Can. Math. Soc. Office: Inst Advanced Study Sch Math Olden Ln Princeton NJ 08540

LANGLEBEN, MANUEL PHILLIP, physics educator; b. Poland, Apr. 9, 1924; emigrated to Can., 1929, naturalized, 1935; s. David and Charna Molly (Shabason) L.; m. Rose Cohen, May 25, 1948; children—Adrian, David, Louise. B.Sc., McGill U., Can., 1949, M.Sc., 1950, Ph.D., 1953. Postdoctoral fellow Meterol. Office, Dunstable, Eng., 1953-54; research asso. McGill U., Montreal, Que., 1954—; asst. prof. physics McGill U., 1960-62, assoc. prof., 1962-68, prof., 1968-90, prof. emeritus, 1990—, dir. Centre for No. Studies and Rsch., 1977-80; mem. sub-com. snow and ice, asso. com. geotech. research Nat. Research Council Can., 1968-74; mem. working group on ice reconnaissance and glaciology Canadian Adv. Com. on Remote Sensing, 1971-75; mem. panel on ice, subcom. Arctic oceanography Canadian Com. on Oceanography, 1973-84; mem. adv. bd. Ea. Arctic Marine Environ. Studies, 1977-83; mem. Working Group on Arctic Regions and Atmospheric Interactions, Can. Global Change Program, Internat. Geosphere-Biosphere Programme, 1988—. Contbr. articles sci. jours. Served with Royal Can. Navy, 1941-45. Fellow Royal Soc. Can.; mem. Canadian Assn. Physicists, Royal Meteorol. Soc., Internat. Glaciological Soc., Am. Geophys. Union, Sigma Xi. Home: 4753 Grosvenor, Montreal, PQ Canada H3W 2L9

LANGLEY, GEORGE ROSS, medical educator; b. Sydney, N.S., Can., Oct. 6, 1931; s. John Goerge Elmer and Freda Catherine (Ross) L.; m. Jean Marie Ballantyne, June 22, 1957; children: Joanne Marie, Mark Ross, Richard Graham. B.A., Mt. Allison U., 1952; M.D., Dalhousie U., 1957. Intern Victoria Gen. Hosp., Halifax, N.S., 71957; resident Victoria Gen. Hosp., 1958, Toronto (Ont.) Gen. Hosp., 1960, U. Melbourne, Australia, 1961, U. Rochester, N.Y., 1962; John and Mary Markle scholar in acad. medicine Dalhousie U., Halifax, 1963-68; from lectr. to prof. medicine Dalhousie U., 1963-69, prof., chmn. dept. medicine, 1974-82; chief of service medicine Camp Hill Hosp., Halifax, 1969-74; head dept. medicine Victoria Gen. Hosp., 1974-82; chmn. clin. investigation grants com. Med. Research Council, 1976-78; chmn. clin. and epidemiol. research adv. com., bd. dirs. Nat. Cancer Inst. Can., 1978-86. Contbr. articles to sci. jours. Decorated Queen's Jubilee medal, 1977. Fellow Internat. Soc. Hematology, Royal Coll. Physicians and Surgeons (v.p., coun., Wightman vis. prof. 1990), ACP (bd. govs. 1973-78, laureate Atlantic region 1996), Royal Coll. Physicians (Edinburgh); mem. Can. Hematology Soc. (pres. 1976-78), Can. Soc. Clin. Investigation, Am. Soc. Hematology, Can. Soc. Oncology, Alpha Omega Alpha. Mem. United Ch. Can. Home: 6025 Oakland Rd, Halifax, NS Canada B3H 1N9 Office: Victoria Gen Hosp Ste 8-024, Halifax, NS Canada B3H 2Y9

LANGLEY, JOELLEN S., music educator; b. Rocky Mt., N.C., Mar. 12, 1950; d. John Sidney Jr. and Josephine Smith; m. John B. Langley; 1 child, Jillian Joelle Cleghorn. BA in Music Edn., Temple U., 1975. Cert. K-12 music tchr., N.J., Pa. Music dir. Runnemede (N.J.) Pub. Schs., 1978—; co-owner children's music prodn. co. JJ Creations; spkr. in field. Composer, singer, tchr., adult and children's music; performer Phila. Civic Ctr., 1988; publ. children's music. U.S. rep. to Venezuela by spl. invitation of consul gen. Venezuela and min. fgn. affairs, 1995. Recipient Tchr. of Yr. award Gov. Tom Keane, N.J., 1988.

LANGLEY, LYNNE SPENCER, newspaper editor, columnist; b. West Palm Beach, Fla., June 4, 1947; d. George Hosmer and Elwa June (Harries) Spencer; m. William A. Langley, Oct. 10, 1970. student, Glasgow U., Scotland, 1967-68; BA with honors, Coll. of Wooster, 1969. Feature writer, asst. women's editor Palm Beach Times, West Palm Beach, 1969-70; asst. editor Brunswick (Maine) Times Record, 1971; investigative reporter Maine Times, Topsham, 1971-75; asst. mng. editor York County Coast Star, Kennebunk, Maine, 1976-78; environ. and med. editor, nature columnist Charleston (S.C.) Post and Courier Newspapers, 1979—; editor Maine Audubon Soc. News, 1975-76; stringer Newsweek mag., 1971-75; speaker in field; freelance writer. Author: Nature Watch, 1987. Recipient Media award S.C. Assn. Mentally Retarded, 1985. Mem. Charleston Mus., S.C. chpt. Nature Conservancy. Recipient Media awards Charleston County Parks and Recreation Commn., 1985, Am. Diabetes Assn. S.C. chpt., 1989, Communicator of Yr. award S.C. Wildlife Fedn., 1983, Writing awards S.C. Press Assn., 1987. Mem. Am. Hort. Soc., Nat. Audubon Soc., Charleston Natural History Soc. (Media award 1985), Garden Writers Assn. Am., PEO (sec. chpt. D Maine 1975-76, corr. sec. chpt. J S.C. 1986-88), Sigma Delta Chi. Home: PO Box 97 Adams Run SC 29426-0097 Office: 134 Columbus St Charleston SC 29403-4809

LANGLEY, PATRICIA COFFROTH, psychiatric social worker; b. Pitts., Mar. 1, 1924; d. John Kimmel and Anna (McDonald) Coffroth; m. George J. Langley, May 1, 1946; children: George Julius III, Mary Patricia, Kelly Joan; stepchildren: Robin Spencer, Veronica Bell. BA, Empire State Coll., 1976; MSW, Hunter Coll., 1980. Diplomate Clin. Social Worker; lic. social worker, Conn.; cert. Conn. Psychiat. rehab. worker. Credentialed alcoholism treatment counselor, supervisor, Bronx Mcpl. Hosp. Center, Albert Einstein Med. Coll., 1970-74, case worker, comprehensive alcoholism treatment center, dept. psychiatry, 1974-80; asst. coordinator outpatient psychiat. alcoholism Meridian Ctr., Stamford, Conn., 1980-83; dir. family treatment Meridian Ctr.; pvt. practice and consultation. Vol., DuBois Day Clinic, Stamford, 1966-67, Greenwich Hosp., 1966-67. Mem. NASW, Conn. Soc. for Clin. Social Workers. Home and Office: 50 Lafayette Pl Greenwich CT 06830-5405

LANGLEY, RICKY LEE, occupational medicine physician; b. Fountain, N.C., Aug. 31, 1957; s. Ernest Lee and Janie Ruth (Fulford) L.; m. Sandra Jane Ward, June 7, 1980; children: Patrick, Nicholas, Megan. BS magna cum laude, N.C. State U., 1979; MD, Bowman Grey Sch. Medicine, 1983; MPH, U. N.C., 1988. Diplomate Am. Bd. Internal Medicine, Am. Bd. Preventive Medicine. Intern East Carolina Sch. Medicine, Greenville, N.C., 1983-84, resident, 1984-86; asst. prof. dept. preventive medicine and health policy East Carolina U., Greenville, N.C., 1989-91, adj. asst. prof. dept. family medicine, 1989-91, adj. asst. prof. dept. environ. health, 1989—, asst. prof. dept. internal medicine, 1991; fellow Sch. Medicine Duke U., Durham, N.C., 1986-88, asst. cons. prof. in occupational medicine, 1989-90, asst. clin. prof. dept. community and family medicine, 1991-96; pvt. practice occupational medicine Health and Hygiene, Inc., Greensboro, N.C., 1988-89; med. dir. Mebane (N.C.) Med. Ctr., 1996—; adj. asst. prof. dept. biol. and agrl. engrng. N.C. State U., 1995—; cons. in field; mem. planning com. on agrl. safety N.C. State Fair, 1991; mem. Task Force on Agri-Bus. for Gov.'s Commn. on Reduction of infant Mortality, 1992; mem. N.C. State Task Force on Blood-Borne Pathogens, N.C. Occupl. Health and Safety Adminstrn. 1991-92; presenter in field; mem. Nat. Park Producers Coun. Task Force on Worker Health and Safety, 1995; occupl. medicine residency program evaluator for NIOSH, 1992—, mem. spl. emphasis panel, 1996—; mem. agrl. safety and health coun. N.C. Dept. Labor, 1996—. Editor: (textbook) Safety and Health in Agriculture, Forestry and Fisheries, 1997; guest editor N.C. Med. Jour., 1992, 93, 95; contbr. articles to profl. jours. Vol. Greenville Cmty. Shelter, 1990, Health Hotline, WITN, 1990, 91, State Employee Wellness Day 1989, Adopt-A-Hwy. Project, 1989; Doctor of the Day, N.C. State Legislature, 1991; doctor on call blood dr. ARC, Greensboro, 1989; vol. Freemont Peoples Clinic, 1993; pub. affairs officer Coast Guard Aux., 1996—, flotilla 18-11, 1995—; hunting safety educator, N.C., 1996—. Lloyd T. Weeks scholar, 1978, Benjamin Elloit Ibie and Benjamin Elliot Ibie Jr. Meml. scholar, 1976. Fellow ACP, Am. Coll. Occupl. and Environ. Medicine, Am. Coll. Preventive Medicine; mem. AMA, N.C. Med. Soc. (environ. health subcom. 1991—), Am. Occupl. Med. Assn. (mem. med. ctr. occupl. health com. 1990—), Carolinas Occupl. Med. Assn. (sec.-treas. 1991-92, pres-elect 1992-93, pres. 1993-94, del. 1995—), Am. Coll. Occupation and Environ. Medicine (del. 1995-96), Am. Biol., Safety Assn., Am. Conf. Govt. Indsl. Hygienists, Am. Indsl. Hygiene Assn., Tarheel Archaeology Soc. (program chair 1996), Sigma Xi, Phi Kappa Phi, Phi Eta Sigma, Gamma Sigma Delta, Alpha Epsilon Delta. Avocations: astronomy, archeology. Home: 1506 Miles Chapel Rd Mebane NC 27302-9008 Office: Mebane Med Clinic Mebane NC 27302

LANGLEY, ROLLAND AMENT, JR., engineering technology company executive; b. San Francisco, Aug. 22, 1931; s. Rolland Ament and Kathryn Lee (Beals) L.; m. Pamela Winston, May, 15, 1954 (div. 1978); children: Owen C., Cynthia, James R.; m. Chiara Bini-Sexton, Apr. 12, 1978. BS in Engring., Physics, U. Calif., Berkeley, 1953; MME, U. Pitts., 1961; MBA, Golden Gate U., 1973. Engr. Bettis Atomic Power Lab. of Westinghouse Electric Corp., Pitts., 1957-62; with Bechtel Corp., San Francisco, 1962-71; mgr. refinery and chem. nuclear fuel ops. Bechtel Inc., San Francisco, 1977-78; mgr. projects nuclear fuel ops. Bechtel Nat. Inc., San Francisco, 1979-80, mgr. decontamination and restoration nuclear fuel ops., 1980-81; v.p., mgr. nuclear fuels ops. Bechtel Nat. Inc., Oak Ridge, Tenn., 1981-84; sr. v.p., mgr. div. ops., research and devel. ops. Bechtel Nat. Inc., San Francisco, 1985-89; dep. mgr. Uranium Enrichment Assocs., San Francisco, 1972-76; v.p. Uranium Enrichment Tech. Inc., San Francisco, 1976-77; pres., dir. Bechtel Systems Mgmt. Inc., 1988-90; pres., CEO BNFL Inc., 1990—, also bd. dirs., 1994—; bd. dirs. No. Ireland Partnership-U.S.A.; trustee, pres. World Mem. Fund-U.S.A., 1993—; chmn., Pajarito Scientific Corp., 1995—, also bd. dirs. Contbr. numerous articles to profl. jours. Trustee Environ. Sci. and Tech. Inst., 1995—. Capt. USNR. Recipient Bausch and Lomb Sci. award, 1948. Mem. Naval Res Assn. (past pres. Golden Gate chpt.). Achievements include patents in nuclear fuel and reactor systems design; research on uranium enrichment, nuclear waste disposal, fast breeder reactors, and engineering management. Home: PO Box 208 Middleburg VA 20118 Office: BNFL Inc 9302 Lee Hwy Ste 950 Fairfax VA 22031-1214

LANGLINAIS, JOSEPH WILLIS, educator, chaplain; b. San Antonio, Aug. 12, 1922; s. Joseph Willis and Marie Nellie (St. Julien) L. B.S. in Edn, U. Dayton, 1943; S.T.D., U. Fribourg, Switzerland, 1954. Joined Soc. Mary, 1940; ordained priest Roman Cath. Ch., 1952; tchr. high schs. in Mo., Ill. and Man., Can., 1943-48; dir. admissions Chaminade Coll. Prep. Sch., St. Louis, 1957-59; dir. Archdiocesan High Sch. Sodality Union St. Louis, 1958-59, Marianist Novitiate, Galesville, Wis., 1959-63; mem. faculty St. Mary's U., San Antonio, 1963—, dean Sch. Arts and Scis., 1964-75, acad. v.p., 1975-81, dir. instnl. self-study, 1970-72, 82-84, chmn. theology dept., 1981-83, dean Sch. Humanities and Social Scis., 1986, chaplain Sch. of Bus., 1988—, Univ. Prof., 1993—; pres. Cen. Cath. Marianist High Sch., San Antonio, 1987-91; dir. semester in Puebla, Mex. St. Mary's U., 1994; pres. Holy Rosary Sch. Bd., 1995—; archdiocesan ecumenical rep., 1996—. Contbr.: Cath. Ency. Am., Encyclopedic Dictionary of Religion. Mem. AAUP, Cath. Theol. Soc. Am., Mariological Soc. Am., Archaeol. Soc. Am., Torch Internat., Rotary. Home: 1 Camino Santa Maria St San Antonio TX 78228-8518

LANG-MIERS, ELIZABETH ANN, lawyer; b. Mpls., Nov. 26, 1950. BA, U. Mo., 1972, JD, 1975. Bar: Mo. 1975, Tex. 1977, U.S. Ct. Appeals (5th cir.), U.S. Supreme Ct. Law clk. to presiding justice Mo. Supreme Ct., Jefferson City, 1975-76; ptnr. Locke, Purnell, Rain, Harrell, Dallas, 1976—. Mem. editorial bd. Mo. Law Review. Mem. Dallas County Med. Soc. Aux., bd. dirs. Met. YWCA; bd. dors., chairperson adv. bd. Women's Resource Ctr. Leadership Dallas, Leadership Tex., Leadership Am. Recipient Am. Jurisprudence awards 1973, 74. Mem. ABA, Tex. Bar Assn., Dallas Bar Assn. (v.p. adminstrn., v.p. activities, chmn. media rels com. 1985, chair lawyer referral svc., v.p., sec.-treas., bd. dirs., exec. com. 1987—, chmn. bd. dirs., vice-chair, pres.-elect), Tex. Young lawyers Assn. (com. chair), Dallas Assn. Young Lawyers (com. chair), State Bar (com. chair, Presdl. citation). Office: Locke Purnell Rain Harrell 2200 Ross Ave Ste 2200 Dallas TX 75201-2748

LANGMUIR, CHARLES HERBERT, geology educator; b. Chalk River, Ont., Can., Nov. 24, 1950; came to U.S., 1954; s. David Bulkeley and Marianna (Lawrence) L.; m. Diane Marie Langmuir, Sept. 22, 1973; 1 child, Molly Kathryn. BA, Harvard U., 1973; MS, SUNY, Stony Brook, 1978, PhD, 1980. From asst. to assoc. prof. Lamont-Doherty Geol. Observatory Columbia U., Palisades, N.Y., 1981-88, prof., 1988—, Arthur D. Storke Meml. prof., 1989—; vis. scientist Inst. de Physique du Globe, Paris, 1989-90; mem. adv. com. on ocean scis. NSF, 1990-93; mem. lithosphere panel Joint Oceanographic Instns. for Deep Earth Sampling, 1984-87; chmn. Conf. on Sci. Ocean Drilling II, Work Group on Mantle-Crust Interactions, 1986-87; mem. steering com. Ridge Interdisciplinary Global Experiments, 1990-93; chmn. coord. com. Project French-Am.-Ridge Atlantic, 1989—; mem. steering com. Inter Ridge, 1992—. Editor: Earth and Planetary Sci. Letters, 1989—; mem. editorial bd. Chem. Geology, 1985—; contbr. over 50 articles to profl. jours. Alfred Sloan Rsch. fellow, 1983-85, Henry Shaw fellow Harvard U., 1974. Fellow Am. Geophys. Union (fellows com. 1995—, Bowen award 1996); mem. Geol. Soc. Am. Office: RFD 1 Box 86 Palisades NY 10964

LANGRAN, ROBERT WILLIAMS, political science educator; b. N.Y.C., Feb. 15, 1935; s. Robert Joseph and Leona Gertrude (Williams) L.; m. Eleanor Victoria Groh, Dec. 26, 1959; children—Irene, Elizabeth, Thomas. B.S. with honors, Loyola U., Chgo., 1956; M.A., Fordham U., 1959; Ph.D., Bryn Mawr Coll., 1965. Prof. polit. sci. Villanova U., Pa., 1959—. Author: (book) The United States Supreme Court: An Historical and Political Analysis, 1989, 2d edit. 1992, 3d edit. 1995; contbr. articles to profl. publs. Served to 1st lt. U.S. Army, 1956-58. Mem. Am. Polit. Sci. Assn., Supreme Ct. Hist. Soc. Office: Villanova Univ Political Sci Dept Villanova PA 19085

LANGROCK, KARL FREDERICK, former academic administrator; b. Toeterville, Iowa, Jan. 26, 1927; s. Lee Henry and Alice Dora (Grube) L.; m. Rose Marie Meyer, June 4, 1950; children: Laura Sue, Charles Alan. BA, U. No. Iowa, 1949; MA, U. Iowa, 1951; MDiv, Luth. Sch. Theology, Chgo., 1955; LittD (hon.), Grand View Coll., 1989. Pastor Lake Park Luth. Ch., Milw., 1955-57, Resurrection Luth. Ch., Franklin Park, Ill., 1957-62, Luth. Ch. of the Holy Spirit, Deerfield, Ill., 1962-69; asst. to pres. Berea (Ky.) Coll., 1969-72; pres. Grand View Coll., Des Moines, 1972-88; free-lance writer, 1988—. Mem. Iowa Coll. Aid Commn., Des Moines, 1980-84, Luth. Social Services of Ill., Chgo., 1962-70, pres., 1968-70. Served in USN, 1945-46. Mem. Iowa Assn. Independent Colls. and Univs. (bd. dirs. 1972-87, chmn. 1986-87), Council of Luth. Ch. in Am. Colls. (pres. 1978), Phi Eta Sigma. Address: 2234 NE Douglas St Newport OR 97365-1837

LANGROCK, PETER FORBES, lawyer; b. N.Y.C., Feb. 2, 1938; s. Frank Langrock; m. Joann Murphy, July 4, 1960; children: Frank, Catherine, Eric. BA, U. Chgo., 1958, JD, 1960. Bar: Vt. 1964, U.S. Supreme Ct. 1966. State's atty. Addison County, Vt., 1960-65; sr. ptnr. Landrock Sperry Life & Wool, Middlebury, Vt., 1965—; commr. Nat. Conf. Commrs. on Uniform State Laws. Chmn. Vt. Breeders Stake Bd., 1984-90. Mem. ABA (chmn. individual rights and responsibilities sect. 1980-81, del. 1982-83, ho. of dels. 1984-96, bd. govs. 1993-96), Am. Law Inst. Avocations: horse breeding and racing, fishing, hunting. Home: Rd Lower Plains Rd Salisbury VT 05769 Office: 15 S Pleasant St PO Box 351 Middlebury VT 05753-0351

LANGSAM, IDA S., press agent, consultant; b. N.Y.C., Apr. 5, 1951; d. Sydney and Mary (Goldberg) L. AAS in Photography, Fashion Inst. Tech., 1971; BA in Mass Communications, Queens Coll., 1973. Publicity dir. Mike's Artist Mgmt., N.Y.C., 1978-79; sr. account exec. Howard Bloom Orgn., N.Y.C., 1979-81; publicity dir. Aucoin Mgmt., N.Y.C., 1981-82; pres. Pub. I Publicity Svcs., N.Y.C., 1982-91; exec. v.p. music divsn. Middleberg & Assocs., N.Y.C., 1991-95; pres. ISL Pub. Rels., N.Y.C., 1995—; guest panelist New Music Seminar, N.Y.C., 1985-88, CMJ/MM Seminar, N.Y.C., 1987-88, Founds. Forum, L.A., 1989, Platinum Seminar, Hoboken, N.J., 1990; instr. Discovery Ctr., N.Y.C., 1988-90; adj. profl mus. bus. profls. program grad. level NYU, 1995, music bus. professions program NYU, N.Y.C. Avocations: creative writing, painting, photography, fashion, Jewish studies. Office: ISL 333 W 52 St Ste 1003 New York NY 10019

LANGSLEY, DONALD GENE, psychiatrist, medical board executive; b. Topeka, Oct. 5, 1925; s. Morris J. and Ruth (Pressman) L.; m. Pauline R. Langsley, Sept. 9, 1955; children: Karen Jean, Dorothy Ruth, Susan Louise. B.A., SUNY, Albany, 1949; M.D., U. Rochester, 1953. Diplomate: Am. Bd. Psychiatry and Neurology (dir. 1976-80), Nat. Bd. Med. Examiners. Intern USPHS Hosp., San Francisco, 1953-54; resident psychiatry U. Calif., San Francisco, 1954-59; NIMH career tchr. in psychiatry U. Calif., 1959-61; candidate San Francisco and Chgo. insts. for psychoanalysis, 1958-67; asst. prof., assoc. prof. psychiatry U. Colo. Sch. Medicine, 1961-68; prof., chmn. dept. psychiatry U. Calif., Davis, 1968-77, U. Cin., 1977-81; prof. dept. psychiatry Northwestern U. Sch. Medicine, Chgo., 1981—; mem. psychiatry edn. com. NIMH, 1969-75; exec. v.p. Am. Bd. Med. Spltys., 1981-91; trustee Ednl. Commn. for Fgn. Med. Graduates, 1983-91; mem. adv. com. on Grad. Med. Edn. Dept. Def., 1986-87; bd. govs. EcuMed, 1983-85; bd. dirs. Nat. Resident Matching Program, 1982, sec. 1984-87, 89-91, pres. 1987-89. Author: The Treatment of Families in Crisis, 1968, Mental Health Education in the New Medical Schools, 1973, Peer Review Manual for Psychiatry, 1976, Handbook of Community Mental Health, 1981, Evaluating the Skills of Medical Specialists, 1983, Legal Aspects of Certification & Accreditation, 1983, Trends in Specialization, 1985, Hospital Privileges & Specialty Medicine, 1986, 2d edit., 1991, How To Evaluate Residents, 1986, How to Select Residents, 1988, Health Policy Issues in Graduate Medicine Education, 1992; contbr. articles to med. jours. Served with AUS, 1943-46; med. officer USPHS, 1953-54. Recipient Spl. awards Colo. Assn. for Mental Health, 1968, Spl. awards Sacramento Area Mental Health Assn., 1973. Fellow Am. Psychiat. Assn. (Hofheimer award 1971, pres. 1980-81, chmn. peer rev. com. 1975-77, Kiewit lectr. 1990, Adminstrv. Psychiatry award 1993), Am. Coll. Psychiatrists; mem. Ctrl. Calif. Psychiat. Soc. (pres. 1973-74), Colo. Psychiat. Soc. (pres.-elect 1967-68), Soc. Med. Adminstrs. Home and Office: 9445 Monticello Ave Evanston IL 60203-1117

LANGSLEY, PAULINE ROYAL, psychiatrist; b. Lincoln, Nebr., July 2, 1927; d. Paul Ambrose and Dorothy (Sibley) Royal; m. Donald G. Langsley, Sept. 9, 1955; children: Karen Jean, Dorothy Ruth Langsley Runman, Susan Louise. BA, Mills Coll., 1949; MD, U. Nebr., 1953. Cert. psychiatrist, Am. Bd. Psychiatry and Neurology. Intern Mt. Zion Hosp., San Francisco, 1954; resident U. Calif., San Francisco, 1954-57; student health psychiatrist U. Calif., Berkeley, 1957-61, U. Colo., Boulder, 1961-68; assoc. clin. prof. psychiatry U. Calif. Med. Sch., Davis, 1968-76; student health psychiatrist U. Calif., Davis, 1968-76; assoc. clin. prof. psychiatry U. Cin., 1976-82; pvt. practice psychiatry Cin., 1976-82; cons. psychiatrist Federated States of Micronesia, Pohnpei, 1984-87; resident in geriatric psychiatry Rush-Presbyn./St. Luke Hosp., Chgo., 1989-91; mem. accreditation rev. com. Accreditation Coun. for Continuing Med. Edn. Trustee Mills Coll., Oakland, 1974-78; bd. dirs. Evanston Women's Club. Fellow Am. Psychiat. Assn. (chair continuing med. edn. 1990-96); mem. AMA, Am. Med. Womens Assn., Acad. Medicine Cin., Ohio State Med. Assn., Ill. Psychiat. Assn. (sec. 1993-95, pres.-elect 1995-96, pres. 1996-97, accreditation coun. 1996—). Home and Office: 9445 Monticello Ave Evanston IL 60203-1117

LANGSNER, ALAN MICHAEL, pediatrician; b. N.Y.C., Dec. 21, 1948; s. Herman and Celeste (Prince) L.; m. Hilary Schmidt, Dec. 19, 1971. BA in Psychology, Fairleigh Dickinson U., 1970; MD, U. Autonomia Guadalajara, Jalisco, Mex., 1977; postgrad., NYU, 1977-78. Resident in pediatrics N.Y. Med. Coll./Met. Hosp. Ctr., N.Y.C., 1978-79, resident in pediatrics-primary care tng. program, 1979-80, chief resident in pediatrics-primary care tng. program, 1980-81; pvt. practice pediatric cardiology N.Y.C., 1983—; attending pediatrics, sr. cons. pediatric cardiology St. Barnabas Med. Ctr., Livingston, N.J., 1983—; assoc. cons. pediatric cardiology St. Vincent's Med. Ctr., S.I., N.Y., 1983—; cons. pediatric cardiology, clin. asst. prof. pediatrics NYU Sch. Medicine, N.Y.C., 1983—, S.I. U. Hosp., 1985—; mem. perinatal rev. com., med. bd. St. Barnabas Med. Ctr.; presenter in field. Contbr. articles to profl. jours. Mem. AMA, Essex County Med. Soc. Office: 405 Northfield Ave West Orange NJ 07052-3003

LANGSTAFF, DAVID HAMILTON, aerospace industry executive; b. Paris, June 12, 1954; s. E. Kennedy and Percy (Lee) L.; m. Cynthia Shauer, Aug. 26, 1978; children: Meredith Avery, Christopher Maxim, Thomas Stoddard, William Hamilton. BA cum laude, Harvard U., 1977, MBA, 1981. Assoc. First Boston Internat., Athens, Greece, 1977-78, Blyth Eastman Dillon & Co., Athens, 1978-79; prin. Langstaff Design & Mgmt., Cambridge, Mass., 1980-81; assoc. Inverness Group, Houston, 1981-82, v.p. corp. fin., 1982-83, v.p. corp. fin., mgr. mergers and acquisitions, 1983-84; sr. v.p., CFO, sec., treas. Space Industries Inc., Houston, 1984—; pres., CEO Calspan SRL Corp., Washington. Bd. dirs. Revels Houston, Washington Revels; bd. dirs., past pres. Houston Symphony Orch., Houston Grand Opera. Avocations: music, athletics, counseling. Office: Calspan SRL Corp 800 Connecticut Ave NW Ste 1111 Washington DC 20006-2709

LANGSTAFF, GARY LEE, marketing executive; b. Cherry Point, N.C., Aug. 21, 1948; s. Harold A. and Ruth (Means) L.; m. Claudia Gramps, Jan. 8, 1977; children: Danielle, Brett Allyn. BA in History, Polit. Sci., U. Calif., Santa Barbara, 1970; BS in Internat. mgmt., Thunderbird Grad. Sch. Bus., 1971, M in Internat. Mgmt., 1972. Account exec. Benton & Bowles, N.Y.C., 1972-77, v.p. account supr., 1977-79; sr. v.p., mgmt. supr. Benton & Bowles, N.Y.C. and Chgo., 1979-81; pres. Envision Systems, Inc., Westport, Conn., 1981-85; exec. v.p. Triparte Corp., Fresno, Calif., 1983-85; also bd. dirs. Triparte Corp., Fresno; gen. mgr. Wieden & Kennedy, Inc., Los Angeles, 1985; sr. v.p. mktg. Hardee's Food Systems, Rocky Mount, N.C., 1985-86, exec. v.p. mktg., 1986-89; exec. v.p. mktg. Burger King Corp., Miami, Fla., 1989-91; prin. Retail Resolve, Inc., Steamboat Springs, Colo., 1991—; prin., co=owner Lightbulb, Inc., 1996—, 9-1-1, Inc., 1997—. Bd. Dirs. Rocky Mount Acad., 1987-88. Republican. Office: Retail Resolve Inc 29950 Emerald Meadows Ln Steamboat Springs CO 80487 also: Lightbulb Inc PO Box 774258 Steamboat Springs CO 80477 also: 9-1-1 Inc 2639 N Southport Chicago IL 60614

LANGSTAFF, GEORGE QUIGLEY, JR., retired footwear company executive; b. Paducah, Ky., July 28, 1925; s. George Quigley and Katherine Elizabeth (Irion) L.; m. Maureen Black, Dec. 27, 1946; children: Patricia (Mrs. Charles Poole), Lynne (Mrs. Steve Frederick), Katherine (Mrs. George Stockman). B.A., U. of South, 1948; grad., Advanced Mgmt. Program, Harvard U., 1978. Mfg. mgr. Genesco, Inc., Nashville, 1948-59; mktg. mgr. Genesco, Inc., 1959-70, group pres., 1970-73, v.p., chief operating officer, 1974-78, exec. v.p., 1978-80; pres., chief exec. officer Footwear Industries Am., Inc., Phila., 1981-85. Pres. Nashville Mental Health Assn., 1970, Episcopal Churchmen of Tenn., 1966; trustee, alumni v.p. U. of the South; mem. Rep. State Exec. Com., 1952-53; bd. dirs. United Fund, Jr. Achievement; vestry St. George's Episcopal Ch., sr. warden, 1966, 89, 90. With USNR, 1943-46. Home: 6001 Andover Dr Nashville TN 37215-5731

LANGSTAFF, JOHN MEREDITH, musician; b. Bklyn., Dec. 24, 1920; s. Bridgewater Meredith and Esther Knox (Boardman) L.; m. Diane Guggenheim; 1 child, Carol; m. Nancy Graydon Woodbridge, Apr. 3, 1948; children—John Elliot, Peter Gerry, Deborah Graydon. Student, Curtis Inst. Music, Juilliard Sch. Music, Columbia U. Author (books) Frog Went a-Courtin', 1955 (Caldecott prize 1955), Over in the Meadow, 1957, On Christmas Day in the Morning, 1959, The Swapping Boy, 1960, Ol' Dan Tucker, 1963, Hi! Ho! The Rattlin' Bog, 1969, Jim Along, Josie, 1970, Gather My Gold Together, 1971, The Golden Vanity, 1971, Soldier, Soldier, Won't You Marry Me?, 1972, The Two Magicians, 1973, Shimmy, Shimmy Coke-a-pop!, 1973, St. George and the Dragon, 1973, A-Hunting We will Go, 1974, A Season for Singing, 1974, Sweetly Sings the Donkey, 1976, Hot Cross Buns, 1978, The Christmas Revels Songbook, 1985, Sally Go Round The Moon, 1986, What A Morning!, 1987, Climbing Jacob's Ladder, 1991, I Have A Song To Sing-O, 1994, A Revels Garland of Song, 1996, Old Christians, 1996; recitals, U.S., Can., Eng., Iceland, Europe, rec. for, Odeon-Capital, Jupiter, RCA-Victor, Nixa, Renaissance, Tradition, HMV, Desto, Weston Woods, Revels Records, Minstrel Records; soloist with, Cantata Singers, N.Y. Philharmonic, Nat. Symphony, Montreal Symphony Orch., Little Orch. Soc., N.Y. Oratorio Soc., Collegium Musicum, Stratford Shakespeare Festival, Eng., Mpls. Symphony Orch., radio, TV in U.S., Europe, Can., BBC, Eng.; dir. music dept., Potomac Sch., Washington, 1953-58, Shady Hill Sch., Cambridge, Mass., 1969-72, faculty, Simmons Coll., Boston, 1970-86 , Wheelock Coll., Boston, 1974-79, Mass. Coll. Art, 1977, Boston Coll., 1979, U. Conn., 1977-79, Lesley Coll., 1978—, artistic dir., Young Audiences Mass., 1972-81, adv. bd., 1981—, artist-lectr., Assn. Am. Colls. Served as 1st lt., inf. AUS, World War II. Recipient Hope S. Dean Meml. award Found. for Children's Books, 1991, citation Boston Theater, 1996. Mem. Actors Equity, Country Dance and Song Soc. Am., Internat. Folk Music Council, English Folk Song Soc. (founder and dir. Christmas Revels 1956, 57, 66, 70—, Spring Revels 1972—, Sea Revels 1983—). Office: Revels Inc One Kendall Sq Bldg 600 Cambridge MA 02139

LANGSTON, MARK EDWARD, professional baseball player; b. San Diego, Aug. 20, 1960; m. Michelle Langston; 1 child, Katie. Student, San

Jose State U. Baseball player Seattle Mariners, 1981-89, Montreal Expos, 1989, California Angels (now Anaheim Angels), 1990. Named AL Rookie Pitcher of Yr. 1984 by the Sporting News, Am. League All-Star Team, 1987, 91-93; recipient AL Gold Glove, 1987-88, 1991-94. Office: Anaheim Angels Anaheim Stadium 2000 Gene Autry Way Anaheim CA 92806*

LANGSTON, PAUL T., music educator, university dean, composer; b. Marianna, Fla., Sept. 15, 1928; s. Howard McGhee and Rosa (Jeffries) L.; m. Esther Howard, Aug. 12, 1950; children: Claire Beth, Erin, Howard. Pvt. study with, Nadia Boulanger, 1962, 63; diploma, Conservatoire Americaine, France; BA, U. Fla., 1950; MS in Music, So. Bapt. Theol. Sem., 1953; SMD, Union Theol. Sem., 1963; DMus (hon.), Stetson U., 1985. Organist-choirmaster St. John's Bapt. Ch., Charlotte, N.C., 1953-60; instr. music theory Davidson Coll., 1959-60; mem. faculty Stetson U., De Land, Fla., 1960-93; dean Sch. Music, Stetson U., 1985-93, William Kenan Jr. prof. music, 1986-93, prof. and dean music emeritus, 1993—; asso. condr. Charlotte Oratorio Singers, 1954-60; dir. Fla. Internat. Music Festival, Fla. Internat. Music Festival Inst.; research fellow Inst. Sacred Music, Yale U., 1985. Composer organ, choral works.; oratorio Petros (premier Nov. 1983). Recipient Hand award for outstanding rsch., 1993. Mem. Am. Guild Organists, Hymn Soc., Coll. Music Soc., Music Tchrs. Nat. Assn., Nat. Assn. Schs. of Music (undergrad. commn., McEniry award teaching excellence), Assn. Anglican Musicians, Soc. Composers, Omicron Delta Kappa, Pi Kappa Lambda, Delta Tau Delta. Home: 313 N Salisbury Ave Deland FL 32720-4054

LANGSTON, ROY A., insurance company consultant; b. Dallas, Feb. 13, 1912; s. Lamar Q. and Gertrude (McDaniel) L.; m. Edna Earle Scott, 1936; 1 dau., Peggy Langston Schieffer. With Trinity Universal Ins. Co., 1929-33; with Traders & Gen. Ins. Co., 1933-73, dir., 1949-73, exec. v.p., 1953-56, pres., chief exec. officer, 1956-73; founder Traders Indemnity Co., 1962; past pres. Tex. Assn. Fire & Casualty Cos. Mem. Mason (32 degree, Shriner), Oak Cliff Shrine Club (pres.). Methodist. Home: 2032 W Five Mile Pky Dallas TX 75224-3608

LANGTON, CLEVE SWANSON, advertising executive; b. N.Y.C., Sept. 1, 1950; s. Raymond Benedict and Viola (Swanson) L.; m. Patricia Scott, July 16, 1976; children: Elizabeth Renwick, Cleve, Jr. B.A., NYU, 1972; M.B.A., Columbia U., 1974. Product mgr. Gen. Foods Corp., White Plains, N.Y., 1974-76; sr. account exec. Dancer Fitzgerald Sample, N.Y.C., 1976-79; v.p., account supr. D'Arcy MacManus Masius, N.Y.C., 1979-83, corp. v.p. bus. devel. worldwide, DMB&B, N.Y.C., 1983-89; corp. sr. v.p. DDB Needham Worldwide, 1990-92; corp. exec. v.p. multinat. nat. client devel., 1993—. Bd. dirs. Columbia U. Grad. Sch. Bus., St. Bartholomew Sch. Club: Metropolitan (N.Y.C.). Office: DDB Needham Worldwide Inc 437 Madison Ave New York NY 10022-7001

LANGWIG, JOHN EDWARD, retired wood science educator; b. Albany, N.Y., Mar. 5, 1924; s. Frank Irving and Arlene Stone (Dugan) L.; m. Margaret Jacquelyn Kirk, Aug. 31, 1946; 1 dau., Nancy Ann Langwig Davis. B.S., U. Mich., 1948; M.S., Coll. of Forestry, SUNY, Syracuse, 1968, Ph.D., 1971. Asst. to supt. Widdicomb Furniture Co., Grand Rapids, Mich., 1948-50; salesman John B. Hauf Furniture, Inc., Albany, N.Y., 1950-51; asst. mgr. furniture dept. Montgomery Ward Co., Menands, N.Y., 1951-52; office mgr. U.S. Plywood Corp., Syracuse, 1952-65; instr. wood products engrng. SUNY Coll. Forestry, Syracuse, 1969-70; asst. prof. wood sci. Okla. State U., Stillwater, 1971-74; prof., head dept. forestry Okla. State U., 1974-81, prof. wood sci., wood products extension specialist, 1982-86, mem. faculty council, 1983-86; mem. Gov.'s Com. on Forest Practices, 1975-77. Contbr. articles to profl. jours. Served with AUS, 1943-45. NSF fellow, 1966-68. Mem. Soc. Am. Foresters, TAPPI, Forest Products Research Soc. (regional bd. dirs. 1983-89, regional rep. to nat. exec. bd. 1983-86), Soc. Wood Sci. and Tech., Okla. Acad. Sci., Okla. Forestry Assn. (bd. dirs. 1982-83), Council Forestry Sch. Execs., Sigma Xi, Xi Sigma Pi., Gamma Sigma Delta, Alpha Zeta, Phi Kappa Phi. Episcopalian. Home: 33 Liberty Cir Stillwater OK 74075-2015 Office: Okla State U Dept Forestry Stillwater OK 74078 *My graduate education began after a seventeen year career in the forest products industry. This additional education broadened my life, and opened up a rich new world of experience beyond my greatest expectations. I commend to all young people the pursuit of a maximum education, as one of life's most worthy efforts.*

LANGWORTHY, AUDREY HANSEN, state legislator; b. Grand Forks, N.D., Apr. 1, 1938; d. Edward H. and Arla (Kuhlman) Hansen; m. Asher C. Langworthy Jr., Sept. 8, 1962; children: Kristin H., Julia H. BS, U. Kans., 1960, MS, 1962; postgrad., Harvard U., 1989. Tchr. jr. high sch. Shawnee Mission Sch. Dist., Johnson County, Kans., 1963-65; councilperson City of Prairie Village, Kans., 1981-85; mem. Kans. State Senate, 1985—; alt. del. Nat. Conf. State Legislatures, 1985-87, del., 1987—, nominating com., 1990-92, vice chair fed. budget and taxation com., 1994, chair fed. budget and taxation com., 1995-96, vice chair assembly on federal issues, 1996-97; del. Midwestern Conf. State Legislatures, 1989. City co-chmn. Kassebaum for U.S. Senate, Prairie Village, 1978; pres. Jr. League Kansas City, Mo., 1977, Kansas City Eye Bank, 1980-82, chmn., 1983-85, bd. mem., 1977—; mem. bd. Greater Kansas City ARC, 1975—, pres., 1984, chmn. midwestern adv. coun., 1985-86, nat. bd. govs., 1987-93; mem. Johnson County C.C. Found., 1989—; mem. Leadership Kans., Germany Today Program, 1991; bd. dirs. Kans. Wildlife & Parks Fund; trustee Found. on Aging, 1992—; mem. nat. adv. panel Child Care Action Campaign, 1988—; mem. adv. com. Coro Found., 1989—; mem. adv. bd. Kans. Alliance for Mentally Ill., 1994—; hon. chair Fund Raiser for Health Partnership of Johnson County, 1995. Recipient Outstanding Vol. award Cmty. Svcs. Award Found., 1983, Confidence in Edn. award Friends of Edn., 1984, Pub. Svc. award as Kans. Legislator of Yr., Hallmark Polit. Action Com., 1991, Clara Barton Honor award Greater Kans. City ARC, Intergovtl. Leadership award League Kans. Mcpls., 1994, Disting. Pub. Svc. award United Cmty. Svcs. of Johnson County, 1995, Outstanding Achievement in Hist. Preservation award Alexander Majors Hist. House, 1995, Kansas City Spirit award, 1996, disting. pub. svc. award Prairie Village, 1995. Mem. LWV, Women's Pub. Svc. Network, U. Kans. Alumni Assn. Episcopalian. Avocations: hunting, running, family. Home: 6324 Ash St Prairie Village KS 66208-1369

LANGWORTHY, EVERETT WALTER, association executive, natural gas exploration company executive; b. West Springfield, Mass., Aug. 17, 1918; s. Walter Carr and Lucy Anne (Laurent) L.; m. Mary Jane Mateer, Nov. 30, 1946 (dec. Oct. 1966); children: John Alan, Jo Ann Langworthy Sears, Robert Carr; m. Joan E. Scott, Feb. 27, 1982; stepchildren: Russell, Michael, Gregory. B.A., U. Mass., 1940; M.A., George Washington U., 1964; grad., Nat. War Coll., 1964. Commd. 2d lt. U.S. Army, 1943; commd. capt. U.S. Air Force, 1947; advanced through grades to col., 1963, ret., 1972; v.p. ops. Meteor Aero Inc., Gaithersburg, Md., 1972-76; sec. contest and record bd. Nat. Aero. Assn., Washington, 1976-80; exec. v.p. Nat. Aero. Assn., 1980—; v.p. LABCO Inc., Martinsburg, W.Va., 1974—; gen. ptnr. M&E Assocs., Gaithersburg, 1976—; dir. Acad. Model Aeronautics, Reston, Va.; cons. FBI, 1992—; cons. FBI. Contbr. articles and columns on aerospace activities to profl. pubs. U.S. rep. Fedn. Aeronautique Internat., Paris, 1980—. Decorated DFC, Air medal African Campaign award, Berlin Air Life medal; recipient Paul Tissandier diploma Fedn. Aeronautique Internationale, 1987. Mem. Nat. Aviation Club (elder statesman aviation 1990), Aero Club Washington, Air Force Assn., Ret. Officers Assn., Soaring Soc. Am. (bd. dirs. 1980—), U.S. Hang Gliding Assn. (bd. dirs. 1980—), VFW. Republican. Club: Lakewood Country (Rockville, Md.). Avocations: golf; writing. Home: 13701 Charity Ct Germantown MD 20874-2965 Office: Nat Aeronautic Assn 1815 Ft Myer Dr Arlington VA 22209-1805

LANGWORTHY, ROBERT BURTON, lawyer; b. Kansas City, Mo., Dec. 24, 1918; s. Herman Moore and Minnie (Leach) L.; m. Elizabeth Ann Miles, Jan. 2, 1942; children: David Robert, Joan Elizabeth Langworthy Tomek, Mark Burton. AB, Princeton U., 1940; JD, Harvard U., 1943. Bar: Mo. 1943, U.S. Supreme Ct 1960. Practiced in Kansas City, 1943—; assoc., then mem. and v.p. Linde, Thomson, Langworthy, Kohn & Van Dyke, P.C., 1943-91; pres., mng. shareholder Blackwood, Langworthy & Schmelzer, P.C., Kansas City, Mo., 1991-96; mng. mem. Blackwood & Langworthy, LC, Kansas City, Mo., 1996—; lectr. on probate, law sch. CLE courses U. Mo., Kansas City. Mem. bd. editors Harvard Law Rev., 1941-43; contbr. chpts. to Guardian Desk Book of Mo. Bar. Mem. edn. appeal bd. U.S. Dept. Edn., 1982-86; commr. Housing Authority Kansas City, 1963-71, chmn., 1969-71; chmn. Bd. Election Commrs. Kansas City, 1973-77; chmn. bd. West Ctrl. area YMCA, 1969—; mem. bd. Mid-Am. region YMCA, 1970-83, vice chmn., 1970-73, chmn., 1973-78; pres. Met. Bd. Kansas City (Mo.) YMCA (now YMCA of Greater Kansas City), 1965, bd. dirs., 1965—, mem. nat. bd. 1971-78, 79-83; bd. dirs. YMCA of the Rockies, 1974—, bd. sec., 1994—; chmn. bd. trustees Sioux Indian YMCAs, 1983—; bd. dirs. Armed Svcs. YMCA, 1984-85; pres. Met. Area Citizens Edn., 1969-72; chmn. Citizens Assn. Kansas City (Mo.), 1967, bd. dirs., 1995-96; bd. dirs. Project Equality Kans.-Mo., 1967-80, pres., 1970-72, treas., 1972-73, sec., 1973-76; 1st v.p. Human Resources Corp. Kansas City, 1969-71, 72-73, bd. dirs., 1965-73; hon. v.p. Am. Sunday Sch. Union (now Am. Missionary Fellowship), 1965—; vice chmn. bd. trustees Kemper Mil. Sch., 1966-73; U.S. del. YMCA World Coun., Buenos Aires, 1977, Estes Park, Colo., 1981, Nyborg, Denmark, 1985; bd. dirs. Mo. Rep. Club, 1960—; del., mem. platform com. Rep. Nat. Conv., 1960; Rep. nominee for U.S. Congress, 1964; mem. gen. assembly Com. on Representation Presbyn., 1991-97, moderator, 1993-94; commr. to gen. assembly Presbyn. Ch., 1984; moderator Heartland Presbyn., 1984. Lt. (j.g.) USNR, 1943-46; now capt. Res. ret. Mem. ABA, Kansas City Bar Assn. (chmn. probate law com. 1988-90, living will com. 1989-91), Mo. State Bar (chmn. probate and trust com. 1983-85, chmn. sr. lawyers com. 1991-93), Lawyers Assn. Kansas City, Harvard Law Sch. Assn. Mo. (v.p. 1973-74, pres. 1974-75, 85-87), Univ. Club (Kansas City), Leawood (Kans.) Country Club. Presbyterian (elder). Home: 616 W 69th St Kansas City MO 64113-1937 Office: 1220 Washington St Ste 300 Kansas City MO 64105-1439

LANGWORTHY, THOMAS ALLAN, microbiologist, educator; b. Oak Park, Ill., Aug. 7, 1943; s. Thomas Earl and Jean Carolyn (Hruby) L.; m. Pamela Joyce Tanis, May 15, 1965 (div. 1985); children; Jocelyn Ann, Jennifer Elise; m. Jane Rae Heckenlively, Sept. 15, 1988. AB, Grinnell Coll., 1965; PhD, U. Kans., 1971. Asst. prof. U. S.D., Vermillion, 1973-78, assoc. prof., 1978-82, prof., 1982-91, prof., chair, 1991-95, prof., 1995—; Alexander von Humboldt preistrager and guest prof. U. Regensburg, Germany, 1984-85; cons. EG&G Idaho, Idaho Falls, 1984—. Contbr. articles to profl. jours. and chpts. to books; mem. editl. bd. Applied and Environ. Microbiology, 1987-96. Fellow Am. Acad. Microbiology; mem. Am. Soc. for Microbiology, AAAS, Internat. Orgn. for Mycoplasmology, Sigma Xi. Office: U SD Sch Medicine 414 E Clark St Vermillion SD 57069-2307

LANGWORTHY, WILLIAM CLAYTON, college official; b. Watertown, N.Y., Sept. 3, 1936; s. Harold Greene and Carolyn (Peach) L.; m. Margaret Joan Amos, Sept. 6, 1958; children: Kenneth, Geneva. B.S. magna cum laude, Tufts U., 1958; Ph.D., U. Calif.-Berkeley, 1962. Asst. prof. Alaska Meth. U., Anchorage, 1962-65; asst. prof. chemistry Calif. State U.-Fullerton, 1965-67, assoc. prof., 1967-72, prof., 1972-73, assoc. dean Sch. Letters Arts and Scis., 1970-73; prof. chemistry Calif. Poly. State U., San Luis Obispo, 1973-76, head dept. chemistry, 1973-76; dean Sch. Sci. and Math Calif. Poly State U., San Luis Obispo, 1976-83; v.p. acad. affairs Ft. Lewis Coll., Durango, Colo., 1983-95, prof., 1995—. Author: monograph Environmental Education, 1971; contbr. articles to profl. jours. Treas. Coun. Concerned Citizens, Inc., Arroyo Grande, Calif., 1976-83; mem. Clean Air Coalition, San Luis Obispo, 1978-83; active Mozart Festival, 1981-82; bd. dirs. Durango Choral Soc., 1984-93; bd. dirs. San Juan Symphony League, pres., 1997—; bd. dirs. Durango Repertory Theatre Co., 1990-96, pres., 1992-94. Mem. AAAS, AAHE, Am. Chem. Soc., Coun. Colls. Arts and Scis. (bd. dirs. 1982), Sierra Club, Phi Beta Kappa, Sigma Xi, Kappa Mu Epsilon, Phi Kappa Phi.

LANHAM, BETTY BAILEY, anthropologist, educator; b. Statesville, N.C., Aug. 12, 1922; d. Clyde B. and Naomi (Bailey) L. B.S., U. Va., 1944, M.A., 1947; Ph.D., Syracuse U., 1962. Mem. faculty River Falls State Tchrs. Coll., 1948-49, U. Md., 1949-50, Wakayama U., Japan, 1951-52, Randolph Macon Women's Coll., 1954-55, Oswego State Tchrs. Coll., 1956-58, Hamilton Coll., 1961-62, Ind. U., 1962-65, Western Mich. U., 1965-67, Albany Med. Coll., 1967-70, U.Guyana, 1969-70; prof. anthropology Indiana U. of Pa., 1970-88, prof. emeritus, 1988—. Contbr. articles to jours. Wenner-Gren Found. for Anthrop. Rsch. predoctoral fellow, 1951-52, AAUW predoctoral rsch. fellow, 1959-60. Mem. Am. Anthrop. Assn., Assn. Asian Studies, Soc. for Psychol. Anthropology, Caribbean Studies Assn. Democrat. Home: 2529 Willard Dr Charlottesville VA 22903-4225

LANHAM, URLESS NORTON, curator; b. Grainfield, Kans., Oct. 17, 1918; s. Urless R. and Frankie V. (Norton) L.; m. Caroline Jane Combs, Sept. 1, 1945; children: Robert, Margaret, Carl. B.A. cum laude, U. Colo., 1940; Ph.D., U. Calif., Berkeley, 1948; postgrad., UCLA, La Jolla, 1940-42, U. Chgo., 1945-46. Asst. prof., research asso. U. Mich., Ann Arbor, 1948-62; asso. prof. Monteith Coll., Wayne State U., 1959-62; vis. curator, asso. curator entomology U. Colo. Mus., Boulder, 1962-73, curator, 1973-89, prof. natural history, 1973-89, prof. emeritus, 89—, mem. Tunisian expdn., 1976; asst. prof. biophysics U. Colo. Med. Center, Denver, 1968-71; vis. lectr. Arctic-Alpine Inst., Dept. Devel. Biology, 1966-67; vis. investigator Carnegie Mus. Pitts., 1982; editor biol. sci. curriculum studies Am. Inst. Biol. Scis., 1963-66; cons. Smithsonian Instn., Washington, 1967. Author: The Fishes, 1962, The Insects, 1964, Origins of Modern Biology, 1968, German transl., 1972; The Bone Hunters, 1973, 91, The Enchanted Mesa, 1974, The Sapphire Planet, 1978, transl. into Arabic and Spanish; also tech. papers; adv. editor, Columbia U. Press, 1964-72. Served to capt. USAAF, 1942-46, PTO. Mem. Phi Beta Kappa, Sigma Xi. Home: 2670 Stephens Rd Boulder CO 80303-5762 Office: U Colo Museum Campus Box 218 Boulder CO 80309

LANICCA, ELLEN, public relations executive. Sr. v.p. Patrice Tanaka & Co., N.Y.C., 1990-94, pres., 1994—. Office: Patrice Tanaka & Co Inc 320 W 13th St Fl 7 New York NY 10014-1200

LANIER, ANITA SUZANNE, musician, piano educator; b. Talladega, Ala., May 21, 1946; d. Luther Dwight and Elva (Hornsby) L. BS in Music Edn., Jacksonville (Ala.) State U., 1969. Elem. music tchr. Talladega City Schs., 1969-81; librarian, elem. music tchr. Talladega Acad., 1981-84; tchr. piano and organ Talladega, 1981—. Organist Trinity United Meth. Ch., Talladega, 1981—. Recipient Commemorative Honor medallion, 1990, World Decoration of Excellence medallion, 1990; named Woman of the Yr., 1990, Rsch. Adv. of Yr., 1990, ABI, 1990. Mem. NAFE, AAUW, Am. Pianists Assn., Pilot Club (sec. 1977-78), World Inst. Achievement, Women's Inner Circle Achievement, Internat. Platform Assn., Delta Omicron. Home: 601 North St E Talladega AL 35160-2525

LANIER, BOB, former professional sports team executive, former basketball player; b. Buffalo, Sept. 10, 1948. Student, St. Bonaventure U., 1966-70. Basketball player Detroit Pistons, 1970-79, Milw. Bucks, 1980-84; actor various commls., 1984—; asst. basketball coach Golden State Warriors, 1994—; now owner Bob Lanier Enterprises, Milw. Mem. NBA All-Star Team, 1972-79, 82; named Most Valuable Player NBA All-Star Team, 1974. Office: Bob Lanier Enterprises 8316 N Steven Rd Milwaukee WI 53223-3355*

LANIER, BOB, mayor; b. Baytown, Tex.. Chmn. Tex. Hwy. and Pub. Transp. Commn., 1983-87, Met. Transit Authority, Houston, 1987-89; mayor City of Houston, 1992—. Recipient V.P. Al Gore's Hammer award in recognition of efforts to streamline govt., Outstanding Tex. Leader award John Ben Shepherd Pub. leadership Found. Office: City of Houston PO Box 1562 Houston TX 77251

LANIER, GEORGE H., lawyer; b. LaGrange, Ga., Feb. 20, 1944. AB cum laude, Harvard Coll., 1966; LLB, Columbia U., 1970. Bar: Ga. 1971. Ptnr. King & Spalding, Atlanta. Mem. ABA, State Bar Ga., Atlanta Bar Assn. Office: King & Spalding 191 Peachtree St NE Atlanta GA 30303-1740

LANIER, JACQUELINE RUTH, curator, artist; b. Boston, Dec. 15, 1947; d. John Stanley and Mary Elizabeth (Porter) L.; 1 child, Raymond Rashad Lanier. BS in Edn., Morgan State U., 1976. Drama specialist Day in Arts Boston Symphony, 1971; drama specialist Balt. City Cultural Arts & Urban Svcs., 1974-78; prodr. Sta. WEAA-FM, 1985-90; with ACTION, 1987-89; R & D implementer Abell Found., 1988-89; developer, curator Lanier Mus. African-Am. History, 1983—; seminar staff developer dept. edn. Balt. Cith Sch., 1988; lectr., presenter IRS, 1988; R & D implementer Lady Md. Found., 1989; lectr. D.C. Pub. Libr., 1990; asst. devel. coord., collections mgr. Heritage Mus. Art, 1990—, Lanier Enterprises Internat., 1997—; lectr. in field. Prodr. Call of the Ancestor, 1992; exhbts. include Counciling Ctr., 1992, Internat. Black Women Congress, 1992, Morgan State U., 1992, Busterizing, Inc., Md. Commn. African Am. History & Culture, 1992, City Life Mus., 1992, Encore Theatre Co., 1992, Social Security Adminstrn., 1992, New Shiloh Bapt. Ch., 1992, Enon Bapt. Ch., 1992, St. Peter Clavers Ch., 1992, Immaculate Conception Ch., 1994, Martin Luther King Ch., 1994, Heritage Mus. Art, 1994, Chesapeake Coll., 1994, 97, Native Am. Mus., 1994, Nat. Assn. Black Vets., 1994, Dept. Equal Employment Devel., 1994, Perry Point Vets. Hosp., 1994, UN, 1995, D.C. Country Club, 1995, Howard County C.C., 1995, Cambridge Coll., 1995, Johns Hopkins Rsch. Inst., 1995, Hist. Sharp. St. Ch., 1995, Balt. Aquarium, 1996, Chesapeake Coll., 1996, Allaganey County Arts Coun., 1996, Heritage Mus., 1996, Md. Humanities Coun., 1996, Nat. Aquarium Balt. 1996. Mem. exec. com. Broadway East Cmty. Assn.; bd. dirs., 2d dist. rep. Citizen Planning & Housing Assn.; chmn. East Balt. Coun. Neighborhoods, Inc.; mem. Empowerment Zone Devel. Bd.; gen. ptnr. Gay St. Housing Partnership Ltd.; bd. dirs., pres. Housing Assistance Corp.; v.p. Mid. East Cmty. Devel. Corp.; vol. Balt. City Commn. Women, Urban Svcs. Agy., Balt. City Youth Fair, WAVR Radio; com. mem. Democratic State Ctrl. Com.; mem. substance abuse prevention coun. Mayor's Coordinating Coun. Criminal Justice, Voices of Electorate; mem. Black Single Parents; mem., pres. Ira Aldridge Players; adv. com. minority bus. tourism Md. Dept. Econ. Employment Devel. Office Tourism; mem. Sankofa exhb. adv. com. Md. Hist. Soc., bd. dirs. Seventh Sons Prodn. Co. Recipient Outstanding Svc. award Campfire, Inc., Fifteen Yr. Svc. award, 100 Hours Vol. Svc. award VA, Outstanding Svc. award Md. House Dels., Citation City of Balt. Citizens, Svcs. Agy. & Citizens Balt. award Urban Svcs. Agy., Svc. to Jazz Cmty. award Gemini Prodns., Inc., Outstanding Cmty. Svc. award African Am. Women's Expo, Outstanding Leadership award AFRAM, 1995; inducted into Black Collectors Hall of Fame, 1992, Wall of Fame, 1994, Health Care Fin. Adminstrn., 1997. Mem. Nat. Assn. Fundraising Execs., Nat. Assn. Black Collectors & Dealers, New Gay St. Improvement Assn. (pres.), Black Ethnic Collectibles Mag. (adv. bd.), Transitional Housing Program (adv. com.). Democrat. Lutheran. Avocations: collecting, synchronized swimming, writing, reading, storytelling. Home: 3817 Clifton Ave Baltimore MD 21216

LANIER, JAMES ALFRED, III, aquarium administrator; b. Norfolk, Va., Sept. 28, 1941; s. James Alfred and Mary Elizabeth (Baughan) L.; m. Hope Baldwin, Aug. 1, 1964; children: Hope Baldwin (Holly), David Ludwell, Andrew Lee. BA, U. Va., 1963; MA, William and Mary Coll., 1972, PhD, 1981. Commd. ensign USNR, 1963, advanced through grades to comdr., 1983; edn. program dir. Va. Inst. Marine Sci., Gloucester Pt., Va., 1971-80; dir. edn1. programs N.J. Marine Sci. Consortium, Princeton, N.J., 1980-82; dir. N.C. Aquarium Ft. Fisher, Kure Beach, N.C., 1982—; pres. Friends Pub. Radio, Wilmington, N.C., 1990-91, Greater Wilmington C. of C. Contbr. articles to profl. jours. Recipient Gov's. award, Governor N.C., Raleigh, 1990, Pres. award Nat. Marine Educators Assn., 1989. Mem. Wilmington Rotary Club. Democrat. Episcopalian. Avocations: aquariums, bonsai, gardening. Home: 140 Edgewater Ln Wilmington NC 28403-3748 Office: North Carolina Aquarium Box 1 2201 Ft Fisher Blvd S Kure Beach NC 28449-3724

LANIER, ROBERT C. (BOB LANIER), mayor; b. Baytown, Tex., 1931. Student, Lee Coll., Univ. N.Mex.; grad. in law with hons., U. Tex. Former reporter The Baytown Sun and The Austin Am.-Statesman.; law assoc. Baker & Botts; then pvt. practice; mayor Houston, 1992—. Chmn. Tex. Highway and Pub. Transp. Commn., Houston Met. Transit Authority; founder Houston Community Coll.; founder, chmn. Bd. Hope Ctr. Wilderness Camp. Office: Office of the Mayor PO Box 1562 Houston TX 77251-1562*

LANIER, THOMAS, chemical and export company executive; b. Cienfuegos, Cuba, Sept. 18, 1923; came to U.S., 1938; s. Joseph and Irene (Medina) L.; divorced; children: Margie, Robert, George, Thomas Emil; m. Julie Gonzalez, May 1, 1980. Student, Bowens Bus. Coll., 1939-40, Latin Am. Inst., 1940-41; BBA, Havana U., 1948; postgrad., St. Mary's U., San Antonio, 1955. Mgr. sales Joskes of Tex., San Antonio, 1949-51; mgr. office investment corp. San Antonio, 1951-55; v.p. internat. sales Sun-X Internat. Export Corp., San Antonio, 1955-59; pres. Sun-X Internat. Ltd., Houston, 1963-66; pres., mgr. Tri-X Internat. Co., North Bergen, 1963—; pres., chief exec. officer Lanier Shipping Co., Inc., North Bergen, N.J., 1966-87; internat. trade cons. Falor Assocs. Inc., North Bergen, 1987—, Factory Assocs. & Exporters, East Hanover, N.J., 1987—. Served with USAF, 1943-45. Recipient E award U.S. Govt., 1963. Mem. Am. Soc. Internat. Execs., C. of C. of Shipping (pres. North Bergen 1982-88), Bogota (N.J.) Tenants Assn., Am. Radio Relay League. Democrat. Roman Catholic. Avocations: amateur radion, stamp collecting, lecturing. Office: Tri-X Internat Co 7500 Bergenline Ave North Bergen NJ 07047-5401

LANIER, WILLIAM JOSEPH, college program director; b. Great Falls, Mont., Dec. 20, 1963; s. Bolder Lanue and Nancy Jo (Kiszczak) L. AS, No. Mont. Coll., 1985, B Tech., 1987, MEd, 1989. Drafting intern Columbus Hosp., Great Falls, 1985-87; grad. asst. No. Mont. Coll., Havre, 1987-89; dir. student life Mont. State U. -No. (formerly No. Mont. Coll.), Havre, 1989-95, 1995—. Bd. dirs. Havre Encourages Long Range Prevention, 1992—, Hill County Crimestoppers, 1991-93; adv. bd. No. Ctrl. Mont. Upward Bound, Harlem, 1992—; mem. Nat. Eagle Scout Assn., Irving, Tex., 1991—. Recipient Golden N award student senate No. Mont. Coll., 1992. Mem. Am. Counseling Assn., Am. Coll. Pers. Assn., Nat. Assn. Student Pers. Adminstrs., No. Mont. Coll. Alumni Assn. (bd. dirs 1990—). Avocations: reading, collecting baseball cards. Home: MacKenzie Hall Havre MT 59501 Office: Mont State U Box 7751 Havre MT 59501

LANING, J. HALCOMBE, retired computer scientist; b. Kansas City, Mo., Feb. 14, 1920; s. J. Halcombe and Mary Alice (Knox) L.; m. Betty Arleen Kolb, June 27, 1943; children: Christine, James, Susan, Linda. Student, Kansas City Jr. Coll., 1936-38; SBChemE, MIT, 1940, postgrad., 1941, PhD in Applied Math., 1947; postgrad., Brown U., 1941-42. Engr. Watertown (Mass.) Arsenal Govt. U.S., 1942-45; group leader instrumentation lab. MIT, Cambridge, 1945-73; head dept. C.S. Draper Lab., Cambridge, 1973-88, sr. tech. advisor, 1988-89. Author: Random Processes in Automatic Control, 1956; creator computer programs; patentee in field. C.S. Draper fellow, 1982-85. Mem. NAE, Assn. Computing Machinery, Am. Math. Soc., Soc. for Indsl. and Applied Math., AIAA, IEEE, Inst. Mgmt. Scis.

LANING, RICHARD BOYER, naval officer, writer, retired; b. Washington, Jan. 1, 1918; s. Richard Henry and Marguerite (Boyer) L., m. Ruth Richmond, Sept. 5, 1942; children: Christine, Lucille. BSEE, U.S. Naval Acad., 1940; MS in Biophysics & Nuclear Physics, U. Calif., Berkeley, 1950; postgrad., U.S. Nat. War Coll., 1960. Officer USS Yorktown, 1940-41, USS Hornet Doolittle Raid, Tokyo, Battle of Midway, 1941-42; exec. officer USS Salmon Pacific Fleet, 1942-44; nuclear weapons planner OPNAV, Washington, 1953-54; commdg. officer 5 subs. including commg. 2d nuclear sub. USS Seawolf, 1956; first Polaris tender USS Proteus USN, Scotland, 1960-62; asst. chief of staff Submarines Pacific USN, Pearl Harbor, Hawaii, 1962-63; ret. USN, 1963; corp. planner, mgr. biotech. programs United Aircraft Corp., Hartford, Conn., 1963-73; life ins. underwriter Equitable of Iowa, Orlando, Fla., 1973-77; writer Orlando, Fla., 1977—; cons. in field. Contbr. articles to profl. jours. Mem. U.S. Naval Inst., Naval Acad. Alumni, Fleet Res. Assn., Navy League, Adm. Nimitz Fedn., U. Calif. Alumni, Futurist Soc., Greater Orlando C. of C., Nat. Space Soc., Navy Submarine League, Univ. Club Winter Park, Mil. Order of World Wars, Ret. Officers Assn., Smithsonian Assocs., N.Y. Acad. Scis., Am. Entrepreneurs Assn. Avocations: swimming, racquetball, computer art. Home and Office: 5955 Turnbull Dr Orlando FL 32822-1740

LANING, ROBERT COMEGYS, retired physician, former naval officer; b. Haiti, Sept. 20, 1922; s. Richard Henry and Marguerite C. (Boyer) L.; m. Alice Teresa Lech, Sept. 9, 1961; 1 dau., Maria Laning LeBerre. BA, U. Va.; MA, Ohio State U.; MD, Jefferson Med. Coll., 1948; PhD in Edn., Geo. Mason U., 1997. Diplomate: Nat. Bd. Med. Examiners, Am. Bd. Surgery. Intern Jefferson Hosp., Phila., 1948-50; enlisted USN, 1950, advanced through grades to rear adm., 1973, mem. astronaut recovery teams, 1960-66;

chief of surgery Naval Hosp., San Diego, 1967-71; med. dir. Naval Hosp., Yokosuka, Japan, 1972-73; med. officer Pacific Fleet, 1973-75; asst. chief Bur. Medicine and Surgery for Operational Med. Support, Washington, 1975-77; dep. dir. surg. service Cen. Office, VA, Washington, 1977-79, dir. surg. service, 1979-87. Fellow ACS (gov. 1984-87); mem. AMA, Am. Assn. Mil. Surgeons, Soc. Med. Cons. to ArmedForces (pres. 1988-89, bd. dirs.), Ret. Officers Assn. Roman Catholic. Home: 6532 Sunny Hill Ct Mc Lean VA 22101-1639

LANITIS, TONY ANDREW, market researcher; b. Port Said, Egypt, May 29, 1926; came to U.S., 1929; s. Christopher and Helen (Joanides) L.; m. Anne Mortimer, Feb. 4, 1947 (div. 1951); 1 son, Philip; m. Gertrude Lettese, June 14, 1959; 1 dau., Melissa. BS in Econs., NYU, 1950, MA, 1951. Assoc. research dir. Morey, Humm & Warwick, N.Y.C., 1954-55; sr. group supr. Colgate-Palmolive Co., N.Y.C., 1955-60; sr. v.p. SSC & B: Lintas Worldwide, Inc., N.Y.C., 1960-89, dir. rsch., 1960-87, dir. market planning and rsch., 1987-89; market planning and rsch. cons. N.Y.C., 1989—; instr. Ulster County C.C., 1993—; guest lectr. NYU, 1970-72, Pace Coll., 1970-73, L.I. U., 1968-70; lectr. in field. Cons. editor Psychology and Mktg. Jour., 1983—; contbr. articles to profl. jours. Bd. dirs. Port Chester (N.Y.) Coun. Arts, 1981-89, Unison Art and Learning Ctr., New Paltz, N.Y., 1990-92. Served with U.S. Army, 1944-46. Named Marketer of Month Kansas City, Am. Mktg. Assn, 1972. Mem. Am. Mktg. Assn., Advt. Research Found., Advt. Agy. Research Dirs. Council, Am. Psychol. Assn., Inst. Mgmt. Sci., Market Research Council, Communications Research Council. Club: Commerce. Home: 59 Lake Hill Rd Kingston NY 12401-8440

LANK, EDITH HANDLEMAN, columnist, educator; b. Boston, Feb. 27, 1926; m. Norman Lank; children: Avrum, David, Anna. BA magna cum laude, Syracuse U., 1947. Columnist L.A. Times Syndicate, 1976—; TV host Sta. WOKR-TV, Rochester, N.Y., 1983-84; radio host Sta. WBBF-AM, Rochester, 1984-85; lectr. St. John Fisher Coll., Rochester, 1977-89; commentator Sta. WXXI-FM, Rochester, 1977—; guest Pub. Radio Internat., St. Paul, 1987—; speaker in field. Author: Home Buying, 1981, Selling Your Home, 1982, Modern Real Estate Practice in New York, 1983, rev. 6th edit. 1997, The Home Seller's Kit, 1988, rev. 4th edit. 1997, The Complete Home Buyer's Kit, 1989, rev. 4th edit., 1997, Dear Edith, 1990, Essentials of New Jersey Real Estate, 201 Questions Every Homebuyer and Seller Must Ask, 1996; co-author: Your Home as a Tax Shelter, 1993; contbr. articles to Time, New Yorker, McCall's, Real Estate Today, Persuasions, Modern Maturity, others. Recipient media award Bar Assn. Monroe County, 1982, Matrix award Women in Ommunications, 1984, Woman of Distinction award Gov. Mario Cumo, N.Y., 1985; named Communicator of Yr., SUNY, Brockport, 1986. Mem. Real Estate Educators Assn. (bd. dirs., Consumer Edn. award 1982, 83, 86, 96, Real Estate Educator of Yr. 1984), Nat. Assn. Real Estate Editors (bd. dirs), Jane Austen Soc. N.Am. (dir.), Phi Beta Kappa. Avocations: scuba diving. Home and Office: 240 Hemingway Dr Rochester NY 14620-3316

LANKFORD, DUANE GAIL, investment banker, mountaineer; b. Ft. Collins, Colo., July 18, 1932; s. William Oliver and Mary Martha (Lago) L.; m. Eleanor Polly, June 18, 1955 (div. 1983); children: Scott, Kurt Edwin, Rebecca Ann; m. Jariyaporn Ekkanasing, Nov. 8, 1991. Student, Colo. State Coll. of Edn., 1950-51, Denver U., 1952-55. Lic. stockbroker over 40 states security commns. and all U.S. exchs. Mgr. Dial Fin., Denver, 1953-59; mgr. investment banking Peters Writer & Christianson, Denver, 1959-60, E.I. DuPont De Nemours, Denver, 1960; mgr. mcpl. investment banking Bache & Co., Denver, L.A., N.Y.C., 1961-68; v.p. sales Fin. Programs, Inc., San Francisco, 1968-69; fin. advisor Lankford & Co., Denver, 1969; mgr. muni bonds W.E. Hutton & Co., Denver, 1969-71; owner/operator Lankford & Co., Denver, 1972—, The Wilderness Inst./Lankford Mountain Guides, Denver, 1978—; chmn. Denver Lenders Exch., 1957-58; cons. advisor numerous cities, towns, states and corps.; expert witness in investment banking and mountaineering; cons. numerous legal firms; cons./advisor numerous fed. agys. Contbr. articles to profl. jours. Worldwide mountaineer numerous maj. peaks. Mem. Am. Alpine Club, Pioneers. Republican. Avocations: internat. mountaineering, internat. travel, philosophy, opera, classical music.

LANKFORD, FRANCIS GREENFIELD, JR., education educator emeritus; b. Morattico, Va., Feb. 14, 1906; s. Francis Greenfield and Alma (Coulbourne) L.; m. Florence Fleet, June 4, 1935; children: William Fleet, Francis Greenfield III. B.S., Randolph-Macon Coll., 1928, LL.D., 1959; M.A., U. Va., 1932, Ph.D., 1938. High sch. prin., 1928-31; from instr. to prof. edn. U. Va., Charlottesville, 1932-55; dir. research Richmond Pub. Schs., 1943-44; pres. Longwood Coll., Farmville, Va., 1955-65; prof. edn., dir. office instl. analysis U. Va., 1965-72, sesquicentennial scholar, 1971-72, Commonwealth prof., 1972, prof. edn. emeritus, 1972—; ednl. adviser Ford Found.-U. Chgo. Pakistan Edn. Project, 1962-63; Dir. study high sch. edn. Va. C. of C., 1942-43; dir. div. ednl. research U. Va., 1951-55; mem. Charlottesville (Va.) Sch. Bd., 1952-55. Co-author: Mathematics for the Consumer, 1947, 2d edit., 1953, Basic Ideas of Mathematics, 1953, Algebra One and Algebra Two, 1955, Essential Mathematics, 1961, 2d edit., 1967, 3d edit., 1975, Contemporary Algebra I, 1962, Contemporary Algebra II, 1963, Algebra One, 1969, 72, Algebra Two, 1969, 72, 77, Numbers and Operations, 1970, Consumer Mathematics, 1971, 2d edit., 1974, author, 1981, also articles.; Departmental editor: Math. Tchr, 1953-57. Campaign chmn. Prince Edward Community Chest, 1958. Recipient Disting. Alumnus award U. Va. Sch. Edn., 1977; Gen. Edn. Bd. fellow U. Mich., 1939-40. Mem. Nat. Council Tchrs. Math. (v.p. 1955-57), Raven Soc., Phi Beta Kappa, Omicron Delta Kappa, Phi Delta Kappa (distinguished service award U. Va. chpt. 1944). Democrat. Home: 2600 Barracks Rd Apt 396 Charlottesville VA 22901-2196

LANKFORD, OLGA JUANITA, gifted and talented and elementary educator; b. Baytown, Tex., July 9, 1937; d. Archie Houston and Leona Elizabeth McClain; m. Charles Melvin Lankford, May 22, 1955; children: Joni Elizabeth Carney, Cari Juanita Walters. Diploma, Lee Jr. Coll., Baytown, 1957; BS, Lamar U., 1985. Cert. elem. edn. Substitute tchr. Galena Park (Tex.) Ind. Sch. Dist., 1963-69; tchr. Lankford Pvt. Sch., Houston, 1970-81, Sycamore Pvt. Sch., Nederland, Tex., 1982-85, Travis Elem. Sch., Port Arthur, Tex., 1987-88, North Shore Elem. Sch., Houston, 1988—; presenter writer's workshop North Shore Elem. Sch., 1993-94. Tchr. adult Bible class Market St. Baptist Ch., Houston, 1987—; pres. Galena Park Classroom Tchrs. Assn., 1994-95. Fellow Harris County Dept. Edn.; mem. Tex. Assn. Improvement in Reading (presenter 1994-95), Galena Park Classroom Tchrs. Assn. (tchr. of yr. 1992-93), Beta Sigma Phi (pres. North Channel area 1995-96, Woman of Yr. North Shore chpt. 1980-81, 93-94, Port Arthur chpt. 1986-87). Avocations: teaching, reading, traveling, camping, oil painting. Office: North Shore Elem Sch 14310 Duncannon Dr Houston TX 77015-2514

LANKFORD, RAYMOND LEWIS, professional baseball player; b. Modesto, Calif., June 5, 1967. Student, Modesto Jr. Coll. Selected 3d round free-agt. draft Chgo. Cubs, 1986, St. Louis Cardinals, 1987; outfielder Appalachian League, 1987, Midwest League, 1988, St. Louis Cardinals, 1990—. Office: c/o St Louis Cardinals 250 Stadium Plz Saint Louis MO 63102

LANKHOF, FREDERIK JAN, publishing executive; b. Mar. 4, 1949; came to U.S., 1983; s. Adriaan Pieter and Janny (Baas) L.; m. Joyce Ganimian, May 31, 1983; children: Lauren, Nora. Attended, U. Amsterdam. Editorial asst. Meulenhoff Pub. Co., Amsterdam, The Netherlands, 1968-72; free-lance copy editor, proofreader, translator The Netherlands, 1972-83; bookseller, libr. asst. N.Y.C., 1983-86; pres., owner i.b.d., Ltd., Kinderhook, N.Y., 1989—; pres. E.J. Brill Acad. Publ., Inc., Kinderhook, 1986—, Nedbook New York, Inc., Kinderhook, 1990—, Internat. Bur. Fiscal Documentation, Kinderhook, 1993-96. Trustee Kinderhook Meml. Libr., 1994—. Avocations: reading, writing, translations, publishing. Home: 24 Hudson St Kinderhook NY 12106-2004 Office: E J Brill USA Inc 24 Hudson St Box 467 Kinderhook NY 12106*

LANKTON, STEPHEN RYAN, family therapist, management consultant; b. Lansing, Mich., May 29, 1947; s. Stanley R. and Mary Lou (Cook) L.; children: Stephen, Shawn Michael, Alicia Michelle. Student, Lansing Community Coll., 1966-68; BA, Mich. State U., 1972; MSW (scholar), U. Mich., 1974. Diplomate Am. Bd. Examiners in Clin. Social Work, NASW, Am. Hypnosis Bd. for Clin. Social Work; lic. marriage and family therapist, Fla. Youth outreach YMCA, Lansing, 1969-70; residential youth treatment Camp Highfields, Inc., Onondaga, Mich., 1970-73; instr. psychology Jackson (Mich.) Community Coll., 1974-78; clin. social worker Family Services of Jackson, 1974-78; mem. tng. staff. Huron Valley Inst., Dexter, Mich., 1978-79; pvt. practice psychology Gulf Breeze, Fla., 1980—; adj. instr. psychology U. West Fla., 1980—. Author: Practical Magic: The Clinical Application of Neuro Linguistic Programming, 1980; editor Ericksonian Mongraphs, 1984—; author: The Answer Within: A Clinical Framework of Ericksonian Hypnotherapy, 1983, Enchantment and Intervention in Family Therapy: Training in Ericksonian Approaches, 1986, Tales of Enchantment: A Collection of Goal Directed Metaphors for Adults and Children in Therapy, 1989, The Blammo-Surprise!: A Story to Help Children Overcome Fear, 1988. Recipient Lifetime Achievement award for outstanding contbns. to the field of psychotherapy, 1994. Fellow Am. Acad. Pain Mgmt., Am. Assn. Marriage and Family Therapy (approved supr., clin. mem.); mem. Internat. Transactional Analysis Assn., Acad. Cert. Social Workers, Soc. Clin. and Exptl. Hypnosis, Am. Acad. Phychotherapists, Internat. Soc. Hypnosis, Fla. Soc. Clin. Hypnosis, Am. Soc. Clin. Hypnosis (approved cons.), Am. Family Therapy Assn. (clin. tchg. mem.). Avocation: scuba diving. Office: PO Box 958 Gulf Breeze FL 32562-0958

LANMON, DWIGHT PIERSON, museum director; b. Pueblo, Colo., July 28, 1938; s. Ira Dwight and Elaine Glea Pierson (Curtis) L.; m. Ann Lorraine Welling, Jan. 10, 1970. Student, Knox Coll., 1956-58; B.A., U. Colo., 1960; postgrad., UCLA, 1961-66; M.A., U. Del., 1968. Asst. curator, assoc. curator, and in charge of conservation Winterthur Mus., Del., 1968-73; dep. dir. Corning Mus. Glass, N.Y., 1973-81, dir., 1981-92; CEO, dir., trustee Winterthur (Del.) Mus., 1992—; trustee Rockwell Mus., Corning, 1983-92, pres., 1988-92, chmn. exec. com., 1988-92, acting dir., 1986-88; trustee Corning Mus. Glass, 1981-95. Author: (with Arlene Palmer) John Frederick Amelung, 1976, 2d edit., 1981, (with Paul Hollister) Paperweights, 1978, (with David B. Whitehouse) Glass in the Robert Lehman Collection, 1993 (Urban Glass award for best. hist./acad. publ. 1995). Winterthur fellow, 1966-68. Fellow Soc. Antiquaries of London; mem. Internat. Assn. History of Glass (sec.-gen. 1981-85), Internat. Coun. Mus., Assn. Art Mus. Dirs., Am. Assn. Mus., Census of Stained Glass (dir. 1980-92), Paperweight Collectors Assn. (bd. dirs. 1991-92), Walpole Soc., Blair House Fine Arts Com., Chevaliers de Tastevin. Office: Henry Francis Du Pont Winterthur Mus RR 52 Winterthur DE 19735

LANNAMANN, RICHARD STUART, executive recruiting consultant; b. Cin., Sept. 4, 1947; s. Frank E. and Grace I. (Tomlinson) L. AB in Econs., Yale U., 1969; MBA, Harvard U., 1973; divorced; children: Thomas Cleveland, Edward Payne, John Stewart. Investment analyst U.S. Trust Co. N.Y., N.Y.C., 1969-71; rsch. analyst Smith, Barney & Co., N.Y.C., 1973-75, 2d v.p., 1975-77, v.p. successor firm rsch. div. Smith Barney Harris Upham & Co., 1977-78; v.p. Russell Reynolds Assocs., Inc., N.Y.C., 1978-83, mng. dir. 1983-86, 87—; sr. v.p. Mgmt. Asset Corp., Westport, Conn., 1986-87. Dir. Boy's Choir Harlem. Mem. N.Y. Soc. Security Analysts, Internat. Soc. of Fin. Analysts, Assn. for Investment Mgmt. and Rsch., Inst. Chartered Fin. Analysts, Riverside Yacht Club, Yale Club of N.Y., Links Club. Home: 21 Willowmere Cir Riverside CT 06878-2503 Office: 200 Park Ave New York NY 10166-0005

LANNER, MICHAEL, research administrator, consultant; b. Montreal, Sept. 14, 1943; came to U.S., 1969; s. Hyman Alter and Anne P. (Rasnikopf) L.; m. Bluma Pauline Weiskopf, Dec. 27, 1946; children: Brian, Jennifer, Lisa. BS, Loyola U., Montreal, Que., Can., 1968. Cert. rsch. adminstr. Sr. rsch. technician McGill U., Montreal, 1964-69; sr. rsch. assoc. Beth Israel Hosp., Boston, 1969-80, rsch. mgr., 1980-84, deputy dir. rsch., 1984-88, dir. rsch. adminstrn., 1988—; pvt. practice Boston, 1987—; instr. in medicine Harvard Med. Sch., 1992—. Contbr. articles to Biochemistry, Diabetes, Nature. Active Stoughton (Mass.) Town Meeting, 1985—, Stoughton Youth Commn., 1988—; chmn. Stoughton Sch. Com., 1989—. Grantee NIH, 1980—, 1990. mem. Soc. Rsch. Adminstrs. (bd. dirs., sec. 1990-91), Mass. Soc. Med. Rsch. (mem. policy bd. 1989—). Achievements include patents for Convertible Animal Cage, Insert for Animal Cage. Office: Beth Israel Hosp 330 Brookline Ave Boston MA 02215-5400

LANNERT, ROBERT CORNELIUS, manufacturing company executive; b. Chgo., Mar. 14, 1940; s. Robert Carl and Anna Martha (Cornelius) L.; m. Kathleen A. O'Toole, July 10, 1965; children: Jacqueline, Krista, Kevin, Meredith. B.S. in Indsl. Mgmt., Purdue U., 1963; M.B.A., Northwestern U., 1967; grad. Advanced Mgmt. Program, Harvard U., 1978. With Navistar Internat. Transp. Corp. (formerly Internat. Harvester), Chgo., 1963—, staff asst. overseas fin., 1967-70; asst. mgr., treas. and contr. IH Finanz AG, Zurich, Switzerland, 1970-72; mgr. overseas fin. corp. hdqrs. Navistar Internat. Transp. Corp., Chgo., 1972-76, asst. treas., 1976-79; v.p., treas. Navistar Internat. Corp., Chgo., 1979-90, exec. v.p., chief fin. officer, 1990—, also bd. dirs.; bd. dirs. NITC, Harbour Assurance Co., Bermuda, Navistar Fin. Corp., Chgo. Mem. adv. bd. to dean Krannert Sch. Purdue U. Mem. Fin. Execs. Inst. Home: 130 N Grant St Hinsdale IL 60521-3334 Office: Navistar Internat Corp 455 N Cityfront Plaza Dr Chicago IL 60611-5503

LANNES, WILLIAM JOSEPH, III, electrical engineer; b. New Orleans, Oct. 12, 1937; s. William Joseph Jr., and Rhea Helen (Simon) L.; m. Patricia Anne Didier, Jan. 17, 1961: children: David Mark, Kenneth John, Jennifer Anne. BEE, Tulane U., 1959; MEE, U.S. Naval Postgrad. Sch., 1966; registered profl. engr. Commd. 2d lt. U.S. Marine Corps, 1959, advanced through grades to maj., 1967, served as electronics officer, ops. officer, until 1970; substation engr. La. Power & Light, New Orleans, 1970-71, utility engr., 1971-76, system relay engr., 1976-77, system substation engr., 1977-79, engring. supr. for substations, 1979-83, substation engring. mgr., 1983-86, dir. systems engring., 1986—, v.p. systems engring., 1986-88, with cen. engring., 1988-89; sr. v.p. Energy Supply Fossil, 1989-91; v.p. svc. and support Entergy Corp., 1991-92; assoc. dean rsch. & grad. studies Coll. Engring., U. New Orleans, 1992—; dir. U. New Orleans EPRI Community Initiative Ctr., 1993-95; assoc. dir. Ctr. Energy Resources Mgmt., 1993-96, dir. Ctr. Energy Resources Mgmt., 1996—, dir. Engring. Mgmt. Program, 1995—; instr. Delgado Jr. Coll., 1973-74; instr. elec. engring. U. New Orleans, 1979-80; dir. 5th Dist. Savs. and Loan, 1982—; speaker profl. confs. Contbr. articles to profl. jours. Committeeman New Orleans Area Coun., Boy Scouts Am., 1972-76; vol., United Way 1975, 76, 81; treas., PTA 1971; vol. tchr. Confraternity of Christian Doctrine, 1972; mem. bus. adv. coun. Our Lady of Holy Cross Coll., 1981-86; chmn. engring. adv. coun. U. New Orleans; bd. dirs. New Life in La.; vol. coach New Orleans Recreation Dept., 1973; mem. La. Employees Com. on Polit. Action, Tulane Univ. Engring. Coun., New Orleans Archiocesan Pastoral Coun., 1988-91; mem. adv. bd. Bridge House, 1992-95. Decorated Bronze Star; Cross of Gallantry Republic S. Vietnam; recipient cert. of merit, Mayor New Orleans, 1964; registered profl. engr., La. Fellow IEEE (profl. mem., 1996, Outstanding Svc. award 1976, chmn. New Orleans sect. 1981-82, Edward Freitag award 1988, Region 3 Outstanding Engr. award 1991); mem. Electric Power Rsch. Inst. (industry advisor), Edison Electric Inst. (systems and equipment com.), Soc. Power Rsch. and Implementation (chmn. 1987—), Southeastern Electric Exchange (substation com. 1977-85), Power Engring. Soc. (Prize Paper award 1988), Sigma Xi, Eta Kappa Nu. Republican. Roman Catholic. Office: Coll Engring U New Orleans New Orleans LA 70148

LANO, CHARLES JACK, retired financial executive; b. Port Clinton, Ohio, Apr. 17, 1922; s. Charles Herbin and Antoinette (Schmitt) L.; m. Beatrice Irene Spees, June 16, 1946 (dec. 1995); children: Douglas Cloyd, Charles Lewis. B.S. in Bus. Adminstrn. summa cum laude, Ohio State U., 1949. C.P.A., Okla. With U.S. Gypsum Co., 1941-46, Ottawa Paper Stock Co., 1946-47; accountant Arthur Young & Co. (C.P.A.'s), Tulsa, 1949-51; controller Lima div. Ex-Cell-O Corp., 1951-59, electronics div. AVCO Corp., 1959-61, Servomation Corp., 1961; asst. comptroller Scovill Mfg. Co., Waterbury, Conn., 1961-62, comptroller, 1962-67; controller CF&I Steel Corp., Denver, 1967-69; v.p., controller CF&I Steel Corp., 1969-70; controller Pacific Lighting Corp., 1970-76; exec. v.p. Arts-Way Mfg. Co., Armstrong, Iowa, 1976-85; mgmt. auditor City of Anaheim, Calif., 1985-96; ret., 1996. Served with USMCR, 1942-45. Mem. Am. Inst. C.P.A.'s, Calif. Soc. C.P.A.'s, Inst. Internal Auditors. Home: 6274 E Calle Jaime Anaheim CA 92807-4005

LANOIS, DANIEL, record producer, musician, popular; b. Hull, Que., Can., 1951; s. Guy and Jill Lanois. Founder, prodr. Grant Ave. Studio, Ont., Can., 1980-85; indep. prodr., 1981—. Solo albums include Arcadie, 1989, For the Beauty of Wynona, 1993; prodr. albums by Martha and the Muffins, Brian Eno, U2 (Grammy award The Joshua Tree 1987), Peter Gabriel, Robbie Robertson, Bob Dylan, The Neville Brothers. Grammy award, Best Producer (with Brian Eno for U2's Achtung Baby),1993. Office: Warner Bros 3300 Warner Blvd Burbank CA 91505-4632*

LANOU, ROBERT EUGENE, JR., physicist, educator; b. Colchester, Vt., Feb. 13, 1928; s. Robert E. and Flora G. (Goyette) L.; m. Cornelia Rockwell Wheeler, May 14, 1960; children: Katharine, Gregory, Elizabeth, Steven. BS, Worcester Poly. Inst., 1952; PhD, Yale U., 1957. Physicist Lawrence Berkeley (Calif.) Lab., 1956-59; asst. prof. physicist Brown U., Providence, 1960-63, assoc. prof., 1963-67, prof., 1967—, chair dept. physics, 1986-92; cons. Brookhaven Nat. Lab., Upton, N.Y., Los Alamos (N.Mex.) Nat. Lab.; sci. advisor Gov. State of R.I., Providence, 1986-88. Contbr. articles to profl. jours. With USN, 1946-48, ETO. Grantee Dept. Energy, 1960—, NSF, 1995—. Fellow AAAS, Am. Phys. Soc.; mem. Sigma Xi, Tau Beta Pi. Achievements include research in experimental particle physics and astrophysics. Home: 90 Keene St Providence RI 02906-1508 Office: Brown U Dept Physics Providence RI 02906

LA NOUE, TERENCE DAVID, artist, educator; b. Hammond, Ind., Dec. 4, 1941; s. George David and Lois (Lish) L.; m. Ann Marcus, Oct. 15, 1977; children: Daniel, Alexandra. BFA, Ohio Wesleyan U., 1964; Fulbright meister student, Hochschule fur Bildenden Kunste, West Berlin, 1964-65; MFA, Cornell U., 1967; DFA, Ohio Wesleyan U., 1994. Prof. Trinity Coll., Hartford, Conn., 1967-72, CUNY, N.Y.C., 1972-85, NYU, 1987. Works represented in various museums, including Whitney Mus., Guggenheim Mus., Bklyn. Mus., Albright-Knox Mus., Corcoran Gallery Art, Carnegie Inst., Power Inst. Fine Arts, Sydney, Australia, Musé d'Art et Archeologie, Toulon, France, Musée de Strasbourg, France, Mus. Contemporary Art, Teheran, Iran, Mus. Modern Art, N.Y.C.; monograph, Terence La Noue, Ashton Dore, 1992. Grantee Fulbright Found., Berlin, 1964-65, NEA, 1972-73, 83-84, Guggenheim Found., 1982-83. Office: 714 Broadway New York NY 10003-9506

LANOUETTE, WILLIAM JOHN, writer, public policy analyst; b. New Haven, Sept. 14, 1940; s. Joseph Francis and Gertrude Veronica (Thiede) L.; m. JoAnne Marie Sheldon, Apr. 12, 1969; children: Nicole Marie, Kathryn Ann. Student, USCG Acad., 1958-59; A.B., Fordham Coll., 1963; M.Sc., London Sch. Econs. and Polit. Sci., U. London, 1966, Ph.D., 1973. Researcher, reporter Newsweek, N.Y.C., 1961-64; news editor Radio Sta. WVOX AM-FM, New Rochelle, N.Y., 1964; Am. lectr. Hansard Soc. for Parliamentary Govt., London, 1965-67, 70-71; profl. staff mem., rsch. and tech. programs subcom. Govt. Ops. Com. Ho. of Reps., Washington, 1967; legis. asst. to U.S. Rep. John S. Monagan, Washington, 1967-68; staff writer Nat. Observer, Washington, 1969-70, 72-77; staff corr. Nat. Jour., Washington, 1977-82, contbg. editor, 1982-83; communications dir. World Resources Inst., Washington, 1983-85, sr. assoc., 1985; Washington corr. Bull. Atomic Scientists, 1989-90; sr. evaluator energy and science issues U.S. Gen. Acctg. Office, Washington, 1991—; pres. Internat. Soc. Panetics. Author: Genius in the Shadows, a Biography of Leo Szilard, 1993. Recipient Forum award, 1974; fellow John F. Kennedy Sch. Govt., Harvard U., 1988-89; guest scholar Wilson Ctr., Smithsonian Instn., 1989. Democrat. Club: Potomac Boat (Washington). Home: 326 5th St SE Washington DC 20003-2048

LANSAW, CHARLES RAY, sales industry executive; b. Middletown, Ohio, Mar. 5, 1927; s. Edward Curtis and Lura (Tyra) L.; m. Joan Betty Kalbaugh, July 4, 1949; children: Charles E., Gail D., Leslie J., Kristi L. Student, Miami U., Oxford, Ohio, 1947-48; student engring., U. Cin., 1949-51. Chief engr., sales mgr. Dupps Co., Germantown, Ohio, 1950-85; pres. C.R. Lansaw, Inc., Germantown, 1985—. Past mem. Germantown Planing Commn.; bd. dirs. Germantown Pub. libr., 1991—; served with VOCA at Saratov and Volgograd, Russia, 1996, Internat. Exec. Svc. Corps, Alexandria, Egypt, 1993. With USNR, 1944-46. Mem. U.S. Power Squadron (past officer Dayton), Rotary (pres. Germantown 1987-88). Avocations: sailing, woodworking, tennis. Home: 73 Sue Dr Germantown OH 45327-1628 Office: 45 N Main St Germantown OH 45327-1349

LANSBURY, ANGELA BRIGID, actress; b. London, Oct. 16, 1925; came to U.S., 1940; d. Edgar and Moyna (Macgill) L.; m. Peter Shaw, Aug. 12, 1949; children: Anthony, Deirdre. Student, Webber-Douglas Sch. Drama, London, 1939-40, Feagin Sch. Drama, N.Y.C., 1940-42; LHD (hon.), Boston U., 1990. Host 41st, 42d and 43d Ann. Tony Awards, 45th Ann. Emmy Awards. Actress with Metro-Goldwyn-Mayer, 1943-50; films include: Gaslight, 1944 (Acad. award nomination), National Velvet, 1944, The Picture of Dorian Gray, 1944 (Golden Globe award, Acad. award nomination), The Harvey Girls, 1946, The Hoodlum Saint, 1946, Till the Clouds Roll By, 1946, The Private Affairs of Bel Ami, 1947, If Winter Comes, 1948, Tenth Avenue Angel, 1948, State of the Union, 1948, The Three Musketeers, 1948, The Red Danube, 1949, Samson and Delilah, 1949, Kind Lady, 1951, Mutiny, 1952, Remains to be Seen, 1953, A Life at Stake, 1955, The Purple Mask, 1955, A Lawless Street, 1956, Please Murder Me, 1956, The Court Jester, 1956, The Long Hot Summer, 1958, Reluctant Debutante, 1958, A Breath of Scandal, 1960, Dark at the Top of the Stairs, 1960, Season of Passion, 1961, Blue Hawaii, 1961, All Fall Down, 1962, Manchurian Candidate, 1962 (Golden Globe award, Acad. award nomination), In the Cool of the Day, 1963, Dear Heart, 1964, The World of Henry Orient, 1964, The Greatest Story Ever Told, 1965, Harlow, 1965, The Amorous Adventures of Moll Flanders, 1965, Mister Buddwing, 1966, Something for Everyone, 1970, Bedknobs and Broomsticks, 1971, Death on the Nile, 1978, The Lady Vanishes, 1980, The Mirror Crack'd, 1980, The Pirates of Penzance, 1982, The Company of Wolves, 1983, Beauty and the Beast, 1991; star TV series Murder She Wrote, 1984-96 (Golden Globe awards 1984, 86, 91, 92, 12 Emmy nominations, Lead Actress - Drama); appeared in TV mini-series Little Gloria, Happy at Last, 1982, Lace, 1984, Rage of Angels, part II, 1986; other TV movies include: The First Olympics-Athens 1896, A Talent for Murder, Gift of Love, 1982, Shootdown, 1988, The Shell Seekers, 1989, The Love She Sought, 1990, Mrs. 'Arris Goes to Paris, 1992, (musical) Mrs. Santa Claus, 1996; appeared in plays Hotel Paradiso, 1957, A Taste of Honey, 1960, Anyone Can Whistle, 1964, Mame (on Broadway), 1966, 83 (Tony award for Best Mus. Actress 1966), Dear World, 1968 (Tony award for Best Mus. Actress 1969), All Over (London Royal Shakespeare Co.), 1971, Prettybelle, 1971, Gypsy, 1974 (Tony award for Best Mus. Actress 1975, Sarah Siddons award), The King and I, 1978, Sweeney Todd, 1979 (Tony award for Best Mus. Actress 1979, Sarah Siddons award), Hamlet, Nat. Theatre, London, 1976, A Little Family Business, 1983. Named Woman of Yr., Harvard Hasty Pudding Theatricals, 1968, Comdr. of British Empire by Queen Elizabeth II, 1994; inducted Theatre Hall of Fame, 1982, TV Hall of Fame, 1996; recipient British Acad. award, 1991, Lifetime Achievement award, Screen Actors' Guild, Hollywood, 1997. Office: 100 Universal City Plz Bldg 426 Universal City CA 91608-1002

LANSBURY, EDGAR GEORGE, theatrical producer; b. London, Jan. 12, 1930; came to U.S., 1941, naturalized, 1953; s. Edgar Isaac and Charlotte Lillian (McIldowie) L.; m. Rose Anthony Kean, Aug. 12, 1955; children: James, Michael, David, George, Brian, Kate. Ed., UCLA. Designer stock and off-Broadway prodns., 1953-55; art dir. ABC-TV, 1955, CBS-TV, 1955-62, Channel 13, N.Y.C., 1962-63; motion picture art dir., 1963-64; formed Edgar Lansbury Prodns. Inc., for ind. prodn. in theatre and films, 1964—; chmn. The Acting Co.; bd. dirs. drama dept. Story Line Press; chair Russian Mus. Arts Soc. Am. Producer Broadway plays: First One Asleep Whistle, 1966, The Subject Was Roses, 1964, That Summer-That Fall, 1967, The Only Game in Town, 1968, Promenade, 1970, Look to the Lilies, 1970, Engagement Baby, 1971, Godspell, 1971, Elizabeth I, 1972, The Night That Made America Famous, 1974, The Magic Show, 1974, Gypsy, 1975, American Buffalo, 1977, Broadway Follies, 1981, O, Pioneer!, 1989, Club XII, 1990, Amphigorey, 1992, Any Given Day, 1993, Curtains, Grace and Glorie, 1996, In Circles, 1997; films The Subject was Roses, 1968, Godspell, 1973, The Wild Party, 1974, Squirm, 1976, Blue Sunshine, 1978, He Knows You're Alone, 1980, The Clairvoyant, 1982, Summer Girl, 1983, A Stranger Waits, 1986; dir. Without Apologies, 1989, All the Queen's Men, 1989, Advice from a Caterpillar, 1990, The Country Club, 1992. Pres. Agni Yoga Soc.; pres.

Nicholas Roerich Museum, N.Y.C.; bd. govs. League N.Y. Theatres and Producers. Served with U.S. Army, 1951-53. Recipient N.Y. Art Dirs. award for best comml. film, 1963; N.Y. Outer Critics Circle award, 1965; N.Y. Critics Circle award, 1965; Antoinette Perry award for best produced play, 1965; nomination for Antoinette Perry award for best mus. play, 1977; N.Y. Critics Circle award for best drama, 1977. Office: Edgar Lansbury Prodns 450 W 42nd St Ste 2C New York NY 10036-6805

LANSDOWNE, KAREN MYRTLE, retired English language and literature educator; b. Twin Falls, Idaho, Aug. 11, 1926; d. George and Effie Myrtle (Ayotte) Martin; BA in English with honors, U. Oreg., 1948, MEd, 1958, MA with honors, 1960; m. Paul L. Lansdowne, Sept. 12, 1948; children: Michele Lynn, Larry Alan. Tchr., Newfield (N.Y.) H.S., 1948-50, S. Eugene (Oreg.) H.S., 1952; mem. faculty U. Oreg., Eugene, 1958-65; asst. prof. English, Lane C.C., Eugene, 1965-82, ret., 1982; cons. Oreg. Curriculum Study Center. Rep., Cal Young Neighborhood Assn., 1978—; mem. scholarship com. First Congl. Ch., 1950-70. Mem. MLA, Pacific N.W. Regional Conf. C.C.s, Nat. Council Tchrs. English, U. Oreg. Women, AAUW (sec.), Jaycettes, Pi Lambda Theta (pres.), Phi Beta Patronesses (pres.), Delta Kappa Gamma. Co-author: The Oregon Curriculum: Language/Rhetoric, I, II, III and IV, 1970. Home: 2056 Lincoln St Eugene OR 97405-3604

LANSING, SHERRY LEE, motion picture production executive; b. Chgo., July 31, 1944; d. Norton and Margo L.; m. William Friedkin. BS summa cum laude in Theatre, Northwestern U., 1966. Tchr. math. public high schs. Los Angeles, 1966-69; model TV commls. Max Factor Co., 1969-70, Alberto-Culver Co., 1969-70; story editor Wagner Internat. Prodn. Co., 1972-74, dir. west coast devel., 1974-75; story editor MGM, 1975-77, v.p. creative affairs, 1977; v.p. prodn. Columbia Pictures, 1977-80; pres. 20th Century Fox Prodns., 1980-82; founder Jaffee-Lansing Prodns., 1982—; chmn. Paramount Motion Pictures Group, L.A.; chmn. Paramount Pictures' Motion Picture Group, 1992—. Appeared in movies Loving, 1970, Rio Lobo, 1970; exec. story editor movies, Wagner Internat., 1970-73; v.p. prodn., Heyday Prodns., Universal City, Calif., 1973-75; exec. story editor, then v.p. creative affairs, MGM Studios, Culver City, Calif., 1975-77; sr. v.p. prodn., Columbia Pictures, Burbank, Calif., 1977-80, pres., 20th Century-Fox Prodns., Beverly Hills, Calif., 1980-83; ind. producer., Jaffe-Lansing Prodns., Los Angeles, 1983-91; producer Racing With the Moon, 1984,Firstborn, 1984, Fatal Attraction, 1987, The Accused, 1988, Black Rain, 1989, School Ties, 1992, Indecent Proposal, 1993; TV exec. producer When the Time Comes,1987, Mistress, 1992. Office: Paramount Pictures Corp 5555 Melrose Ave Los Angeles CA 90038-3112*

LANSNER, KERMIT IRVIN, editor, consultant; b. N.Y.C., May 9, 1922; s. David and Anna (Gordon) L.; m. Fay Gross, Sept. 10, 1948; children: Gabrielle, Erica. B.A., Columbia U., 1942; postgrad., Harvard U., 1947, Columbia U., 1948; Fulbright scholar, Sorbonne, Paris, 1950. Asst. prof. philosophy Kenyon Coll., 1948-50; asso. editor Art News mag., 1953-54; mem. staff Newsweek mag., 1954-73, sr. editor, 1959-61, exec. editor, 1961-65, mng. editor, 1965-69, editor, 1969-72, contbg. editor, columnist, 1972-74; editor-in-chief Newsweek Books, 1972-73; cons. Louis Harris & Assocs., 1973-76, sr. v.p., 1976-82; editor-in-chief Fin. World mag., 1983-89, editl. dir., columnist, 1989-96. Columnist; contbr. New Republic, Kenyon Rev., Art News. Served to lt. USNR, 1942-46. Mem. Council Fgn. Relations, Century Assn., Phi Beta Kappa. Home and Office: 317 W 80th St New York NY 10024-5701

LANTAY, GEORGE CHARLES (WAGNER), school psychologist, psychotherapist, environmental consultant; b. N.Y.C., Aug. 1, 1942; s. George Sylvester and Geraldine LeMae (Ogline) L.; children by previous marriage: Scott Christopher, Christina, Susan Kimberly, Erica; m. Susannah Hewson, Dec. 31, 1992; 1 child, George Mason; BA, Hope (Mich.) Coll., 1965; MA, U. Ill., 1968; postgrad. in phys. therapy NYU, 1971-72; postgrad. in phys. and recreation therapy L.I. U., 1978-79; student physician asst. program Touro Coll., 1982-83; postgrad. in U.S. customs and law World Trade Inst., 1989—; postgrad. in E. Asian and African Studies St. John's U., 1993—; postgrad in electronics engring. tech. Tech. Career Inst., N.Y.C., 1993; universal HVAC cert. Mainstream Engring. Corp., 1994; postgrad. residential and comml. air conditioning Bergen County Tech. Schs., 1994-96; cert. programs air conditioning and refrigeration York Internat. Corp., 1996. Asst. prof. psychology Westminster Coll., Princeton, N.J., 1969-70; behavioral scientist, dir. Wagner Assocs., Princeton, 1969—; mgmt. tng. assoc. Western Elec. Co., N.Y.C., 1970; phys. therapist asst. Jewish Meml. Hosp., N.Y.C., 1970-72; sch. psychologist St. Agnes Cathedral High Sch., Rockville Centre, 1976—; ednl. cons. Test Preparation Centers, Riverdale, N.Y., 1975-79; intern psychologist N.Y. State Dept. Mental Hygiene, 1973-75; psychologist Odyssey House Parents Program, Wards Island, N.Y., 1973; adj. prof. behavioral scis. N.Y. Inst. Tech., Old Westbury, L.I., 1974-75; bd. dirs. div. field services N.Y. Testing and Guidance Center, Flushing, 1976—; with Adult Edn. Program Bergen County Tech. Schs., 1994-95. bd. dir. Shangri-La Day Camps, N.Y.C., 1976—; seminar instr. Nat. Traffic Safety Inst., N.Y.C., 1988—; asst. dir. aftersch. program Pub. Sch. 234, N.Y.C., 1988; founder Separation Encounter; contbr. U.S. Postal Svc., Cit. Stamp Adv. Coun., 1975-80, Pres.'s Commn. Mental Health, 1977-78; cons. Eastern Regional Inst. Edn., N.Y.U. Med. Sch. Dept. Psychiatry, Newark Council Social Agys., N.Y.C. Bd. Edn., Astor Program Intellectually Gifted Children, N.Y.C. Bd. Edn., Evaluation and Placement Unit, 1977-78, N.Y.C. Bd. Edn. Spl. Edn. Div., Queens Region, 1983, Office Contracted Services, 1983-86, Camp Northwood for Learning Disabilities, summer 1977, Esperanza Day Treatment Center, N.Y.C., 1981-82; psychologist United Cerebral Palsy of N.Y. State, 1986; field ops. supr. N.Y. regional office U.S. Census Bur., 1990; presch. sch. psychologist and outreach coord. St. Mark's Inst. for Community Mental Health, N.Y.C., 1990—; preschool psychologist Karen Horney Clinic Therapeutic Nursery Program, N.Y.C., 1992—; contbr. Commrs. Adv. Council on Vocat. Rehab., N.Y. State Edn. Dept., 1978-79; asst. dir. after school program P.S. 234, N.Y.C., 1988; registrar Ind. Order of Forresters USA, 1991; sales coord. NSA wings program, Northeast Region, USA; environ. cons., instnl. vendor Icekleen Machines, Biotrace, Everpure, Hoshizaki, Ice-O-Matic, Manitowoc and Scotsman Icemaking Machines/Diagnostic and Purification Equipment, 1996—. Named an Outstanding Young Man of Am., 1975; cert. sch. psychologist, cert. emergency med. technician, N.Y. State; qualified mental retardation profl., N.Y. State. Mem. APA (life), AAUP, Am. Ednl. Research Assn., Am. Assn. Sex Educators, Counselors and Therapists, Am. Phys. Therapy Assn. Am. Acad. Physicians Assts., Air Pollution Control Assn., Am. Soc. Heating, Refrigerating and Air Conditioning Engrs. Clubs: St. Bartholomew's Community, Downtown Glee (N.Y.C.). Author: Activities for Learning Disabled Children, 1980, Radon in Homes & What You Can Do to Protect Your Family's Health, 1987, A Nation Bored of Education, 1996; contbr. articles to Ch. Herald mag.; research on underachievement and masculine identification. Home and Office: 28 Greenwich Ave New York NY 10011-8362

LANTHIER, RONALD ROSS, retired manufacturing company executive; b. Montreal, Que., Can., May 2, 1926; s. Emile Edgar and Edith (Martin) L.; m. Jacqueline Barbara Dyment; children: April Carolyn, Bonnie Alice, Ronald Dyment, Andrea Elizabeth, John Elliott. Chartered Accountant, McGill U., 1952. Pub. accountant, 1944-51; chief accountant St. Lawrence Flour Co., 1951-52; controller Canadian Underwriters Assn., 1952-54; div. controller Canadian Aviation Electronics Co., 1954-56; treas. Webb & Knapp, Can., 1956-62; dir. adminstrn., mem. exec. com. Greenshields, Inc. (investment dealers), 1962-67; v.p. finance, treas., mem. exec. com. Canadian Marconi Co., 1967-72; v.p. finance, dir., mem. exec. com. Macdonald Tobacco, Inc., 1972-75; pres. Lanco Mgmt. Ltd., 1975—; v.p. finance MacDonald Stewart Textiles, 1976-77; v.p. fin., mem. exec. com. Electrolux Can., 1978-79; pres. Robert R. Bramhall & Assos. (Can.) Ltd., 1980-81; sr. v.p. Camflo Mines Ltd., 1981-84; v.p. fin. Starnav Corp., 1984-86; v.p. VR Fin. Svcs., 1987-95. Mem. Inst. Chartered Accts. Que. and Ont., Phi Kappa Pi. Anglican. Home: 100 Westview Dr, Aurora, ON Canada L4G 7C9

LANTIERI, MICHAEL, special effects expert. Films include Heartbeeps, 1981, The Last Starfighter, 1984, Fright Night, 1985, My Science Project, 1985, Back to School, 1986, Poltergeist, 1986, Star Trek IV: The Voyage Home, 1986, The Witches of Eastwick, 1987, Moving, 1988, Who Framed Roger Rabbit?, 1988, Twins, 1988, Back to the Future II, 1989 (Acad. award nominee for best visual effects 1989), Caddyshack II, 1989, Indiana Jones and the Last Crusade, 1989, Nothing But Trouble, 1991, Hook, 1991 (Acad. award nominee 1991), Death Becomes Her, 1992, Jurassic Park, 1993 (Acad. award 1993). Office: IATSE Local 44 11500 Burbank Blvd North Hollywood CA 91601-2308*

LANTOS, THOMAS PETER, congressman; b. Budapest, Hungary, Feb. 1, 1928; m. Annette Tillemann; children: Annette, Katrina. B.A., U. Washington, 1949, M.A., 1950; Ph.D., U. Calif.-Berkeley, 1953. Mem. faculty U. Wash., San Francisco State U., 1950-83; TV news analyst, commentator, sr. econ. and fgn. policy adviser to several U.S. senators; mem. Presdl. Task Force on Def. and Fgn. Policy, 97th-105th Congresses from 11th (now 12th) Calif dist., 1981—; ranking minority mem., internat. rels. subcom. on internat. ops. and human rels., internat. rels. subcom. on western hemisphere, mem. gov. reform and oversight com.; founder study abroad program Calif. State U. and Coll. System. Mem. Millbrae Bd. Edn., 1950-66. Democrat. Office: US Ho of Reps 2217 Rayburn HOB Washington DC 20515-0512*

LANTZ, GEORGE BENJAMIN, JR., business executive, college executive, consultant; b. Buckhannon, W.Va., Feb. 6, 1936; s. George Benjamin and Georgia Myrtle (Bodkin) L.; m. Mary Sue Powell, Feb. 25, 1957; children—Mary Lynne, Marsha, Kimberly, Rebecca, Todd. AB with honors, W.Va. Wesleyan Coll., 1960; LLD, W.Va. Wesleyan Coll., 1993; STB with honors, Boston U., 1964, PhD, 1971. Minister United Meth. Pastorates, W.Va. and Mass., 1956-75; mem. faculty W.Va. Wesleyan Coll., Buckhannon, 1967-73, chmn. div. humanities, prof. humanities and religion, 1974-75; asst. to pres., ACE fellow Ohio Wesleyan U., Delaware, 1973-74; dean coll. Mount Union Coll., Alliance, Ohio, 1975-80, pres., 1980-85; v.p. adminstrn. and devel. Nesco, Inc., Hudson, Ohio, 1985-88; pres. U. Indpls., 1988—; cons. Coun. Ind. Colls., Washington, 1982—; bd. dirs. The Nat. Bank Indpls. Trustee W.Va. Wesleyan Coll., 1986-88; bd. dirs. Dollars for Scholars Program, Ind., bd. dirs. Ind. Coll. of Ind., Salvation Army Adv. Bd. Mem., Ind. State chpt. Nat. Multiple Sclerosis Soc., Ind. Higher Edn. Telecomm. Sys., Meridian Mut. Inst.; bd. dirs. Greater Indpls. Progress Com.; bd. dirs. Internat. Fedn. for Bus. Edn.; mem. United Way Ctrl. Ind., Indpls. Downtown Inc., Japan-Am. Soc. of Ind., Inc., English Speaking Union, Ind. Soc. of Chgo.; bd. adv. Greater Johnson County Cmty. Found.; mem. Ind. Colls. Blue Ribbon panel Indpls. Bus. Jour., Mayor's Global Initiative Task Force, Mayor's Operation Respect Network Com., Ind., Ind. Bus./Higher Edn. Forum; bd. dirs. Indpls. Conv. and Visitors Assn.; trustee Cypress Am. Archeol. Rsch. Inst.; elder South Ind. Conf. United Meth. Ch. With U.S. Army, 1954-56. Recipient Cokesbury Grad. award Meth. Bd. Higher Edn. Fellow Am. Coun. Edn.; mem. AAUP, Nat. Assn. Ind. Colls. and Univs. (commn. on financing higher edn.), Am. Assn. Higher Edn., Nat. Assn. Schs. and Colls. of United Meth. Ch. (pres. 1993, mem. com. on internat. edn.), Internat. Assn. Univ. Pres., Soc. Bibl. Lit., North Ctrl. Assn. Colls. and Schs. (commr. 1978-85, cons., evaluator), Indpls. C. of C., Economic Club, Columbia Club, Skyline Club, Kiwanis. Home: 4051 Otterbein Ave Indianapolis IN 46227-3618 Office: U Indpls Office Pres 1400 E Hanna Ave Indianapolis IN 46227-3630

LANTZ, JOANNE BALDWIN, academic administrator emeritus; b. Defiance, Ohio, Jan. 26, 1932; d. Hiram J. and Ethel A. (Smith) Baldwin; m. Wayne E. Lantz. BS in Physics and Math., U. Indpls., 1953; MS in Counseling and Guidance, Ind. U., 1957; PhD in Counseling and Psychology, Mich. State U., 1969; LittD (hon.), U. Indpls., 1985; LHD (hon.), Purdue U., 1994; LLD (hon.), Manchester Coll., 1994. Tchr. physics and math. Arcola (Ind.) High Sch., 1953-57; guidance dir. New Haven (Ind.) Sr. High Sch., 1957-65; with Ind. U.-Purdue U., Fort Wayne, 1965—, interim chancellor, 1988-89, chancellor, 1989-94, chancellor emeritus, 1994—; bd. dirs. Ft. Wayne Nat. Corp., Foellinger Found. Contbr. articles to profl. jours. Mem. Ft. Wayne Econ. Devel. Adv. Bd. and Task Force, 1988-91, Corp. Coun., 1988-94; bd. advisors Leadership Ft. Wayne, 1988-94; mem. adv. bd. Ind. Sml. Bus. Devel. Ctr., 1988-90; trustee Ancilla System, Inc., 1984-89, chmn. human resources com., 1985-89, exec. com., 1985-89; trustee St. Joseph's Med. Ctr., 1983-84, pers. adv. com. to bd. dirs., 1978-84, chmn., 1980-84; bd. dirs. United Way Allen County, sec., 1979-80; bd. dirs. Anthony Wayne Vocat. Rehab. Ctr., 1969-75, Delta Kappa Gamma Edn. Found. Mem. APA, AAUW (internat. fellowship com. 1986-88, program com. 1981-83, Am. women fellowship com. 1978-83, chmn. 1981-83, trust rsch. grantee 1980), Southeastern Psychol. Assn. (referee conv. papers 1987, 88), Ft. Wayne Ind.-Purdue Alumni Soc. (hon. mem. 1987), Ind. Sch. Women's Club (v.p. program chair 1979-81), Pi Lambda Theta, Sigma Xi, Delta Kappa Gamma (editl. bd. 1986-88, gen. chair conv. 1985-86, dir. N.E. region 1982-84, adminstrv. bd., exec. bd. 1982-84, leadership devel. com. 1994-96, bd. trustees ednl. found. 1996-2000). Avocations: swimming, reading, knitting, boating.

LANTZ, KENNETH EUGENE, consulting firm executive; b. Altoona, Pa., Mar. 9, 1934; s. William Martin and Alice Lucretia (Glass) L.; m. D. Arlene Yocum, Nov. 28, 1959; children—Antonia Marie, Theresa Antoinette. B.S. cum laude, Fordham U., 1956. Cons. Sutherland Co., 1960-62; spl. rep. IBM, Los Angeles, 1962-67; dir. info. services Loyola-Marymount U., Los Angeles, 1967-70; pres. CBIS, Los Angeles, 1970-72, Kenneth Lantz Assocs., Los Angeles, 1977-82; mgr. fin. systems Occidental Life Ins. Los Angeles, 1973-77; dir. systems Sayre & Toso, Los Angeles, 1982-83; prin. Atwater, Lantz, Hunter & Co., Los Angeles, 1983—; lectr. computing topics Technology Transfer Inst., 1987-88. Author: The Prototyping Methodology, 1984. Contbr. articles to profl. jours. Served to 1st lt. USAF, 1957-60. Mem. Future of Automation Roundtable (dir. 1983—), Ins. Acctg. and Systems Assn. (Nat. Merit award 1984). Republican. Roman Catholic.

LANTZ, NORMAN FOSTER, electrical engineer; b. Pekin, Ill., June 8, 1937; s. Norman Gough and Lenore (Elsbury) L.; m. Donnis Maureen Ballinger, Sept. 7, 1958 (div. Aug. 1991); children: Katherine, Deborah, Norman Daniel; m. Judith Eliane Peach, Dec. 7, 1991. BSEE, Purdue U., 1959, MSEE, 1961. System engr. GE Co., Phila., 1961-72; mem. tech. staff The Aerospace Corp., El Segundo, Calif., 1972-75, mgr., 1975-79, dir., 1979-83, prin. dir., 1983-90, sr. project engr., 1991—; dir. Internat. Found. for Telemetering, Woodland Hills, Calif., 1985—. 2d lt. U.S. Army, 1960-61. Mem. AIAA (sr.), IEEE, Am. Mgmt. Assn. Office: The Aerospace Corp Sr Project Engineer El Segundo CA 90245-4691

LANTZ, PHILLIP EDWARD, corporate executive, consultant; b. Laramie, Wyo., Sept. 21, 1938; s. Everett Delmer and Elizabeth Mary (Stratton) L.; m. Paula Bogel, June 16, 1962; children: Kirk Edward, Eric William. BA in Math., U. Colo., 1960; MA in Math., U. Wyo., 1966; MS in Ops. Rsch., Johns Hopkins U., 1972. Grad. teaching asst. U. Wyo., Laramie, 1964-65; sr. engr. Applied Physics Lab. Johns Hopkins U., Silver Spring, Md., 1965-70; v.p. Ops. Rsch. Inc., Silver Spring, Md., 1970-72; dir. Tetra Tech. Inc., Arlington, Va., 1972-74; pres., chief exec. officer Systems Planning and Analysis, Inc., Alexandria, Va., 1974—, also bd. dirs.; bd. dirs. Bryce Resort, Basye, Va. Lt. USN, 1960-64. Home: 2911 Eddington Ter Alexandria VA 22302-3503 Office: Systems Planning and Analysis Inc Ste 400 2000 N Beauregard St Alexandria VA 22311-1712

LANYI, JANOS KAROLY, biochemist, educator; b. Budapest, Hungary, June 5, 1937; came to U.S., 1957, naturalized, 1962; s. Istvan and Klara (Rosthy) L.; m. Carol Ann Giblin, Sept. 15, 1962 (div. Dec., 1984); children: Clara Aileen, Sean Renton, Gabriella; m. Brigitte Schobert, Mar. 27, 1988. Student, Eotvos Lorand U. Scis., Budapest, 1955-56; B.S., Stanford U., 1959; M.A., Harvard U., 1961, Ph.D., 1963. Postdoctoral fellow Stanford U. Sch. Medicine, 1963-65; Nat. Acad. Scis. resident assoc. NASA-Ames Research Ctr., 1965-66; sr. scientist NASA-Ames Research Ctr., Moffett Field, Calif., 1966-80; prof. physiology and biophysics U. Calif.-Irvine, 1980—, chair dept. physiology and biophysics, 1995—; vis. fellow Cornell U., 1976. Recipient NASA medal for exceptional sci. achievement, 1977; recipient H. Julian Allen award for best sci. paper Ames Research Ctr., 1978, Alexander von Humboldt award for Sr. U.S. Scientists W.Ger., 1979-80. Mem. Am. Soc. Biol. Chemists, Biophys. Soc., Am. Soc. Microbiology, Hungarian Acad. Scis. (fgn.), Phi Beta Kappa, Sigma Xi. Office: U Calif Dept Physiology Biophy Irvine CA 92697

LANYON, ELLEN (MRS. ROLAND GINZEL), artist, educator; b. Chgo., Dec. 21, 1926; d. Howard Wesley and Ellen (Aspinwall) L.; m. Roland Ginzel, Sept. 4, 1948; children: Andrew, Lisa. BFA, Art Inst. Chgo., 1948; MFA, U. Iowa, 1950; Fulbright fellow, Courtauld Inst., U. London, 1950-51. Tchr. jr. sch. Art Inst. Chgo., 1952-54; past tchr. day sch., tchr. Rockford Coll., summer 1953, Oxbow Summer Sch. Painting, Saugatuck, Mich., 1961-62, 67-70, 71-72, 78, 88, 94, U. Ill., Chgo., 1970, U. Wis. Extension, 1971-72, Pa. State U., 1974, U. Calif., 1974, Sacramento State U., 1974, Stanford U., 1974, Boston U., 1975, Kans. State U., 1976, U. Mo., 1976, U. Houston, 1977; assoc. prof. Cooper Union, N.Y.C., 1980-93; ret., 1993; founder, sec.-treas. Chgo. Graphic Workshop, 1952-55; participant Yaddo, 1973, 75, 76, Ossobow Island Project, 1976; adj. vis. prof. So. Ill. U., 1978, No. Ill. U., 1978, SUNY, Purchase, 1978, Cooper Union, N.Y.C., 1978-79, Parsons Sch. Design, N.Y.C., 1979; disting. vis. prof. U. S.D., 1980, U. Calif. Davis, 1980, Sch. Visual Arts, N.Y.C., 1980-83; vis. artist U. N.Mex., 1981, So. Ill. U., 1984, Sch. Art Inst., Chgo., 1985, U. Tenn., Md. Inst., Northwestern Grad. Sch., 1988, U. Pa., U. Iowa, 1991, 92; instr. workshops Anderson Ranch Workshop, Snow Mass, Colo., 1994, 96, Aspen Design Conf., 1994; vis. prof. U. Iowa, 1991-92; bd. dirs. Oxbow Summer Sch. Painting, 1972-82, emeritus, 1982—, instr., 1960, 72-82, 88, 94; vis. artist, instr. workshops Vt. Studio Sch., 1995, U. Costa Rica, San Pedro and San Ramon, 1995; instr. Interlaken Sch. of Art, 1996. One woman shows, Superior St. Gallery, Chgo., 1960, Stewart Richart Gallery, San Antonio, 1962, 65, Fairweather Hardin Gallery, Chgo., 1962, Zabriskie Gallery, N.Y.C., 1962, 64, 69, 72, B.C. Holland Gallery, Chgo., 1965, 68, Ft. Wayne Art Mus., 1967, Richard Gray Gallery, Chgo., 1970, 73, 76, 79, 82, 85, Madison Art Center, 1972, Nat. Collection at Smithsonian Instn., 1972, Odyssia Gallery, Rome, 1975, Krannert Performing Arts Center, 1976, Oshkosh Pub. Mus., 1976, U. Mo., 1976, Harcus Krakow, Boston, 1977—, Fendrick Gallery, Washington, 1978, Ky. State U., 1979, Ill. Wesleyan U., 1979, U. Calif., Davis, 1980, Odyssia Gallery, N.Y., 1980, Landfall Press, 1980, Alverno Coll., Milw., 1981, Susan Caldwell, Inc., N.Y.C., 1983, N.A.M.E. Gallery, Chgo., 1983, Printworks, Ltd., Chgo., 1989, 93 Pretto Berland Hall, N.Y.C., 1989, Struve Gallery, Chgo., 1990, 93, Berland Hall Gallery, N.Y.C., 1992, Sioux City Art Mus., Iowa, 1992, U. Iowa Mus. Art, 1994, Andre Zarre Gallery, N.Y.C., 1994-96, TBA, Chgo., 1996, Centrocultural Costarricense Norteamericano, San Jose, Costa Rica, 1997, Jean Albano Gallery, 1997; retrospective exhibitions, Krannert Art Mus., McNay Art Mus., Chgo. Cultural Ctr., Stamford Mus., U. Tenn.; exhibited group shows, 1946—, including numerous traveling exhbns., Am. Fedn. Arts, 1946-48, 50, 53, 57, 65, 66, 69; Art Inst. Chgo., 1946-47, 51-53, 55, 57-58, 60-62, 64, 66-69, 71, 73, Corcoran Gallery Art, 1961, 76, Denver Art Mus., 1950, 52, Exhbn. Momentum, Chgo., 1948, 50, 52, 54, 56, Libr. Congress, 1950, 52, Met. Mus. Art, 1952, Mus. Modern Art, 1953, 62, Phila. Mus. Art, 1946, 47, 50, 54, San Francisco Mus. Art, 1946, 50, U. Ill., 1953, 54, 57, Drawing Soc., 1965-66, Mus. Contemporary Art, Chgo., 1969, Graham Gallery, N.Y.C., 1969-71; Ill. Arts Council, 1968-71; HMH Pubs. Europe, 1971, Chgo. Imagists, 1972, Chgo. Sch, 1972, Am. Women, 1972, Artists Books, 1973; Downtown Whitney, N.Y.C., 1978—, Queens Mus., 1978, Dayton Art Inst., 1978, Odyssia Gallery, N.Y.C., 1979, Chgo. Cultural Center, 1979, Aldrich Mus. Contemporary Art, 1980, Bklyn. Mus., 1980, Walker Art Ctr., 1981, also Lisbon, Venice biennales, Voorhees Mus. Rutgers U., Mus. Contemporary Art, Chgo., Milw. Art. Mus., Berkeley Art Mus., 1987, Cooper Union, 1989, Randall Gallery, St. Louis, 1991, Printworks Ltd., Chgo., 1989-96, Berland Hall, N.Y.C., 1991, The Cultural Ctr., Chgo., 1992, Matnan Locks Gallery, Phila., 1992, Art Inst. Chgo., 1992, Nat. Mus. Women in Arts, Washington, 1994-97, Wadsworth Atheneum, Hartford, Conn., 1996, Mus. Contemporary Art, 1996, Block Gallery, Northwestern U., 1996, Rockford Art Mus., Ill. State Mus., 1997; represented in permanent collections Art Inst. Chgo., Denver Art Mus., Libr. Congress, Inst. Internat. Edn., London, Finch Coll., N.Y., Krannert Mus., U. Ill., U. Mass., N.J. State Mus., Ill. State Mus., Bklyn. Mus., Mus. Contemporary Art, Chgo., Nat. Coll. Fine Arts, Walker Art Ctr., Mpls., Boston Pub. Libr., Des Moines Art Ctr., Albion Coll., Met. Mus., McNay Art Inst., Albion Coll., Kans. State U., U. Dallas, U. Houston, Cornell U., CUNY, 1997, also numerous pvt. collections.; mural paintings: Working Men's Coop. Bank Boston, 1979, State of Ill. Bldg., Chgo., 1985, State Capitol, Springfield, Ill., 1989, City of Miami Beach, Art in Public Places project, Police and Court Facility, 1993; published: Wonder Production Vol. I, 1971, Jataka Tales, 1975, Transformations, 1976, Transformations II (Endangered), 1983 ; editorial bd.: Coll. Art Jour., 1982-92; illustrator: The Wandering Tattler, 1975, Perishible Press, 1976—, Red Ozier Press, 1980—. Recipient Armstrong prize Art Inst. Chgo., 1946, 55, 77, Town and Country purchase prize, 1947, Blair prize, 1958, Palmer prize, 1962, 64, Chan prize, 1961, Vielehr prize, 1967, Logan prize, 1981; purchase prize Denver Art Mus., 1950; purchase prize Library of Congress, 1950; Cassandra Found. award, 1970; NEA grantee, 1974, 87; Herewood Lester Cook Found. grantee, 1981. Mem. Coll. Art Assn. (dir., exec. com. 1977-80), Delta Phi Delta. Address: 138 Prince St New York NY 10012-3135 also: PO Box 1045 Stockbridge MA 01262-1045

LANYON, WESLEY EDWIN, retired museum curator, ornithologist; b. Norwalk, Conn., June 10, 1926; s. William J. and Frances A. (Merrill) L.; m. Vernia E. Hall, Jan. 29, 1951; children: Cynthia Hall, Scott Merrill. A.B. in Zoology, Cornell U., 1950; Ph.D., U. Wis., 1955. Interpretive specialist Nat. Park Service, summers 1947-51; instr. zoology U. Ariz., 1955-56; asst. prof. Miami U., Oxford, Ohio, 1956-57; asst. curator birds Am. Mus. Natural History, N.Y.C., 1957-63, assoc. curator, 1963-67, curator, 1967-88; resident dir. Kalbfleisch Field Research Sta., 1958-74; adj. prof. biology City U. N.Y., 1968-87; expdns. for mus. to, C.Am. and Mexico, 1959, 60, 63, West Indies, 1960, 65, 66, S. Am., 1967-80. Contbr. articles to profl. jours. Fellow Am. Ornithologists Union (Brewster award 1968, pres. 1976-78); mem. Cooper, Wilson ornithol. socs., Eastern Bird Banding Assn., Ecol. Soc. Am., Soc. Study Evolution, Soc. Systematic Zoology, Linnaean Soc. N.Y., Sigma Xi. Home: 2398 N Lakeshore Dr Louisa VA 23093-9405

LANZA, DONALD CHARLES, otolaryngologist, rhinologist; b. Yonkers, N.Y., Jan. 16, 1959; s. Donald Charles and Lenore Angela (Boccia) L.; m. Suzanne Terse Moons, Jan. 7, 1989; children: Douglas Reid, Andrew Joseph. BS in Biology, Fordham U., 1975-79; MS in Physiology, Georgetown U., 1979-80, student, 1980-81; MD, SUNY, Bklyn., 1981-85. Diplomate Am. Bds. Otolaryngology, Med. Examiners; lic. Pa., Md., N.Y. General surgery intern Albany (N.Y.) Med. Ctr. Hosp., 1987-90, gen. surgery resident, 1986-87, otolaryngology resident, 1987-90; fellow rhinology and endoscopic sinus surgery U. Pa., Phila., 1991, Johns Hopkins Med. Instns., Balt., 1990-91; instr. surgery Albany Med. Coll., 1989-90; instr. otolaryngology Johns Hopkins Med. Instns., Balt., 1990-91; lectr. U. Pa., Phila., 1991, asst. prof., 1991-96; assoc. prof. U. Pa., 1996—; mem. numerous coms. U. Pa., 1992—, dept. otorhinolaryngology Hops. U. Pa., 1991—; guest faculty Shadyside Hosp., Pitts., 1993, Health Comms., Inc., Princeton, N.J., 1993, Albany Med. Ctr., 1990-91; course dir. U. Pa., 1991-92; instr. Med. Coll. Ga., Boca Raton, Fla., 1991, Lahey Clinic, Boston, 1990, Tulane U., New Orleans, 1990, U. Mich., Ann Arbor, 1990; advanced pediatric life support Children's Hops. Albany Med. Ctr., 1990; lectr. in field 1989—. Peer reviewer: Jour. Allergy and Clin. Immunology, 1992—, Am. Jour. Rhinology, 1991—; contbr. articles to profl. jours., chpts. to books. Recipient Otolaryngology Resident Rsch. award Albany Med. Ctr., 1988, 89. Mem. AMA, Am. Acad. Otolaryngology, Am. Acad. Otolaryngic Allergy (assoc.), Am. Rhinology Soc. (cons. to bd. dirs. 1993—), Am. Sleep Disorders Assn., Assn. Chemoreception Scis., Pa. Med. Soc., Pa. Acad. Otolaryngology, Phila. County Med. Soc., Soc. Univ. Otolaryngologists. Office: Hosp U Pa Head & Neck Surg Silverstein 5 3400 Spruce St Philadelphia PA 19104

LANZA, KENNETH ANTHONY, foreign service officer; b. Bklyn., Dec. 29, 1953; s. Anthony Robert and Carmela L.; m. Sheri Ross, May 22, 1981; children: Kelsey Anastasia, Jessica Kimberly. AB, Colgate U., 1977; MBA, U. Miami, 1979; MA, Duke U., 1994. Gen. mgr. O.H.S. Ltd., London, 1977-78; adminstrv. and fin. mgr. Burroughs Corp., Miami, Fla., 1979-80; mktg. coord. C.B.S. Internat., Miami, 1980-84; chief, pvt. sector U.S. Fgn. Svc., A.I.D., Washington, 1984—; fgn svc. officer, consular officer, sec. Diplomatic Svc. U.S.A., 1989—; dep. dir. global bur. Office of Econ. and Instnl. Reform., Office of Emerging Markets, 1996—. Contbr. articles to profl. jours., monographs. Recipient Meritorious awards U.S. Govt., 1988, 90, 91. Avocations: sculpting, photography. Office: Dept State USAID Rm 500 SA-2 Washington DC 20523

LANZA, ROBERT PAUL, medical scientist; b. Boston, Feb. 11, 1956; s. Samuel and Barbara (Corbett) L. BA, U. Pa., 1978, MD, 1983. Sr. scientist Biohybrid Techs., Shrewsbury, Mass., 1990-93, dir. transplantation biology, 1993—; clin. assoc. prof. surgery Tufts U., 1994-95; assoc. surgery Harvard Med. Sch., 1991-93. Editor: Heart Transplantation, 1984, Medical Science and the Advancement of World Health, 1985, Procurement of Pancreatic Islets I, 1994, Immunomodulation of Pancreatic Islets II, 1994, Immunoisolation of Pancreatic Islets III, 1994, One World, 1996, Tissue Engineering/Cellular Medicine Series, 1995—, Yearbook of Cell and Tissue Transplantation, 1996—, Principles of Tissue Engineering, 1997; contbr. articles to profl. jours. Prof. Howe Buck scholar, 1974-75, Benjamin Franklin scholar, 1975-78, Univ. scholar, 1976-83, Fulbright scholar, 1978-79; Hon. Christiaan Barnard fellow, 1982-84, Mry K. Iacocca Transplantion fellow, 1988-90. Home: South Meadow Pond Island 35 S Meadow Rd Clinton MA 01510-4327 Office: BioHybrid Techs 910 Boston Tpke Shrewsbury MA 01545-3396

LANZANO, RALPH EUGENE, civil engineer; b. N.Y.C., Dec. 26, 1926; s. Ralph and Frances (Giuliano) L. BCE, NYU, 1959. Registered profl. engr., N.Y. Engring. aide Seelye, Stevenson, Value & Knecht, N.Y.C., 1957-58; jr. civil engr. N.Y.C. Dept. Water Resources (formerly N.Y.C. Dept. Pub. Works), 1960-63, asst. civil engr., 1963-68; civil engr. N.Y.C. Dept. Water Resources, 1968-71; sr. san. engr. Parsons, Brinckerhoff, Quade & Douglas, N.Y.C., 1971-72; civil engr. N.Y.C. Dept. Water Resources, N.Y. Dept. Environ. Protection, 1978-90; pvt. practice profl. engr. Huntington Station, N.Y., 1990—. Mem. NRA (life), ASCE (life), ASTM, NSPE, APHA (life), N.Y. Soc. Profl. Engrs., Water Environ. Fedn., Am. Water Works Fedn., Am. Fedn. Arts, U.S. Inst. Theatre Tech., Met. Mus. Art, NYU Alumni Assn., Lincoln Ctr. for Performing Arts, Film Soc. Lincoln Ctr., N.Y.C. Ballet Guild, Asia Soc., Nat. Fire Protection Assn., N.Y. Pub. Libr., Sta. WNET-TV, U.S. Lawn Tennis Assn. (life), Nat. Wildlife Fedn., Internat. Wildlife Fedn., Bible-a-Month Club, Nat. Pks. and Conservation Assn., Nat. Geog. Soc., Nat. Audubon Soc., Am. Automobile Assn., Bklyn. Bot. Garden, Am. Mus. Natural History, Paralyzed Vets. Am., Am. Soc. Prevention Cruelty to Animals, Chi Epsilon. Avocations: books, art, music, dance, theatre. Home and Office: 17 Cottage Ct Huntington Station NY 11746

LANZEROTTI, LOUIS JOHN, physicist; b. Carlinville, Ill., Apr. 16, 1938; s. Emanuel Louis and Mary Pauline (Orienti) L.; m. Mary Yvonne DeWolf, June 19, 1965; children: Mary Yvonne, Louis DeWolf. BS, U. Ill., 1960; MA, Harvard U., 1963, PhD, 1965. Postdoctoral fellow Lucent Technologies Bell Labs., Murray Hill, N.J., 1965-67; mem. tech. staff AT&T Bell Labs., Murray Hill, N.J., 1967-82, Disting. mem. tech. staff, 1982—; adj. prof. U. Fla., Gainesville, 1978—; mem. polar rsch. bd. NRC, Washington, 1982-91, mem. space sci. bd., 1980-84, chmn. space studies bd., 1988-94, mem. ocean studies bd., 1995—, chmn. bd. rev. Army Rsch. Lab., 1996—; mem. phys. sci. com. NASA, Washington, 1975-79, chmn. space and earth adv. commn., 1984-88, mem. adv. coun., 1984-94; mem. adv. com. on future U.S. space program, 1990, mem. v.p.'s space policy adv. bd., 1992-93, v.p. blue ribbon adv. com. on redesign of space sta., 1993-94; mem. corp. Woods Hole Oceanographic Instn., 1993—; mem. governing bd. Am. Inst. Physics, 1997—. Co-author: Particle Diffusion in Rad. Belts, 1974; co-editor 2 books related to space physics, 1977, 79; contbr. over 400 tech. papers to profl. jours. V.p. Harding Twp. (N.J.) Sch. Bd., 1982-90, com., 1993—. Recipient Antarctic Svc. medal U.S., 1979, Disting. Pub. Svc. award NASA, 1988, 94, Achievement award Blackburn Coll. Alumni Assn., 1993; mountain named in his honor in Antarctica; minor planet 5504 named in his honor. Fellow Am. Phys. Soc., Am. Geophys. Union, AAAS; mem. NAE, Internat. Acad. Astronautics, Woods Hole Oceanographic Instn. Office: Bell Labs Lucent Technologies 700 Mountain Ave New Providence NJ 07974-1208

LANZILLOTTI, ROBERT FRANKLIN, economist, educator; b. Washington, June 19, 1921; s. Vincent and Gilda S. (Incutti) L.; m. Patricia Joy Jackson, Oct. 27, 1945; children—Robert J. (dec.), Donna J. Student, Dartmouth Coll., 1943; B.A., Am. U., 1946, M.A., 1947; Ph.D., U. Calif., Berkeley, 1953; D.D.L. (hon.), Tampa U., 1979; D.D.S. (hon.), Fla. Inst. Tech., 1979. Teaching fellow U. Calif. at Berkeley, 1947-49; mem. faculty Wash. State U., 1949-61, prof. econs., 1959-61; research assoc. Brookings Instn., 1956-57, 1974-75; prof. econs., chmn. dept. Mich. State U., 1961-69; prof. econs., dean Coll. Bus. Adminstrn., U. Fla., Gainesville, 1969-86, Eminent Scholar chair in Am. econ. instns., 1986-96, dir. Pub. Policy Rsch. Ctr., 1986—; mem. U.S. Price Commn., 1971-72; bd. dirs. Jim Walter Corp., Citizens and So. Bank Corp., Am. Birthright Corp., Fla. Power Corp., Bank of Ormond Beach, Fla., Talquin Corp., Bottom-Line Assoc., Fla. Progress Corp.; chmn. Econ. Adv. Bd. to Gov. Fla., 1973—; cons. Mich. Bankers Assn., attys. gen. Calif., Wis., Minn., Ill., Fla., Mich., Oreg., Washington; attys. gen. also Fed. Trade Commn., U.S. Dept. Justice, U.S. Govt. Acctg. Office, U.S. Comptroller of the Currency, U.S. Census Bur. Author: Hard-Surface Floor Covering Industry, 1955, Pricing, Production & Marketing Policies of Small Manufacturers, 1964, Banking Structure in Michigan, 1945-63, 1966; co-author: Pricing in Big Business, 1959, Phase II in Review: The Price Commission Experience, 1975, Economic Effects of Government Mandated Costs, 1979; editor: The Conglomerate Corporation, 1981; co-editor: Management Under Government Intervention: The View from Mt. Scopus, 1984; contbr. articles to profl. jours. Served to lt. (j.g.) USNR, 1943-45; lt. comdr. Res. Decorated Bronze Star (2); NATO fellow, 1964. Mem. Am. Econ. Assn., So. Econ. Assn. (1st v.p. 1972-73), Fla. Coun. of 100, Phi Beta Kappa (hon.), Beta Gamma Sigma, Omicron Delta Kappa.

LANZINGER, KLAUS, language educator; b. Woergl, Tyrol, Austria, Feb. 16, 1928; came to U.S., 1971, naturalized, 1979; m. Aida Schuessl, June, 1954; children—Franz, Christine. B.A., Bowdoin Coll., 1951; Ph.D., U. Innsbruck (Austria), 1952. Research asst. U. Innsbruck, 1957-67; assoc. prof. modern langs. U. Notre Dame (Ind.), 1967-77, prof., 1977-97, prof. emeritus, 1997—, resident dir. fgn. study program, Innsbruck, 1969-71, 76-78, 82-85; acting chmn. dept. Modern and Classical Languages, U. Notre Dame, fall 1987, chmn. dept. German and Russian, 1989-96. Author: Epik im amerikanischen Roman, 1965, Jason's Voyage: The Search for the Old World in American Literature, 1989. Editor: Americana-Austriaca, 5 vols., 1966-83. Contbr. numerous articles to profl. jours. Bowdoin Coll. fgn. student scholar, 1950-51; Fulbright research grantee U. Pa., 1961; U. Notre Dame summer research grantee Houghton Library, Harvard U., 1975, 81. Mem. MLA, Deutsche Gesellschaft für Amerikastudien, Thomas Wolfe Soc. Home: 52703 Helvie Dr South Bend IN 46635-1215 Office: Dept German Russian Langs & Lits U Notre Dame Notre Dame IN 46556

LANZKRON, ROLF WOLFGANG, manufacturing company executive; b. Hamburg, Fed. Republic of Germany, Dec. 9, 1929; came to U.S., 1951, naturalized, 1961; s. Aron Artur and Hanna (Farbstein) L. m. Amy Virginia Yarri, Mar. 5, 1961; children: Paul Joshua, Sophie Miriam, Lisa Rachel. BS, Milw. Sch. Engring., 1953; MS, U. Wis., 1955, PhD, 1956. Registered profl. engr. Calif. Computer designer Univac Sperry Rand, St. Paul, 1956-58; guidance and control systems integrations staff Martin Marietta, Orlando, Fla., 1958-61; systems engr. Martin Marietta, Balt., 1961-68; became chief command and svc. module flight project div. NASA Manned Spacecraft Ctr., Apollo Program, Houston, 1963; graphic ops. mgr. Raytheon Co., Marlborough, Mass., 1968-82, dep. dir. air traffic control, 1982-92, dir. air traffic control, 1992-95; pres. RWL Assocs. Conss., 1995; Registered profl. engr., Calif. With Israeli Army, 1948-51. Recipient NASA Outstanding Achievement award, 1964, Spl. Svc. award, 1966. Mem. AIAA, Am. Math. Soc., IEEE, Am. Mgmt. Assn., Sigma Xi. Home: 2 Mallard Way Gloucester MA 01930-3248 Office: RWL Assoc 2 Mallard Way Gloucester MA 01930-3248

LANZL, LAWRENCE HERMAN, medical physicist; b. Chgo., Apr. 8, 1921; s. Hans and Elsa (Seitz) L.; m. Elisabeth Farber, Sept. 18, 1947; children: Eric Lawrence, Barbara Jane. B.S., Northwestern U., 1943; M.S., U. Ill., 1947, Ph.D., 1951. Diplomate: Am. Bd. Health Physics (dir. 1969-73), Am. Bd. Radiology (mem. physics exam. com. 1977-83). Asst. dept. astronomy Dearborn Obs.; interim instr. dept. physics Northwestern U., Evanston, Ill., 1941-43; jr. physicist Metall. Lab., Manhattan Project, U. Chgo., 1944, Los Alamos (N.Mex.) Sci. Lab., Manhattan Project, U. Calif., 1944-45; research asst. dept. physics U. Ill., Urbana, 1946-50; asso. physicist naval reactor div. Argonne (Ill.) Nat. Lab., 1951; sr. physicist U. Chgo., Argonne Cancer Research Hosp., 1951-55, research asso., 1955-56; asst. prof. U. Chgo., 1956-59, asso. prof., 1959-68, prof. dept. radiology and Franklin McLean Meml. Research Inst.,, 1968-80, prof. emeritus, 1980—; prof. Rush Med. Coll., Chgo., 1980—; prof., chmn. dept. med. physics Coll. Health Scis. and Grad. Coll., Rush U., Chgo., 1982—; 1st officer divsn. life scis. IAEA, Vienna, Austria, 1967-68; cons. Pan Am. Health Orgn., 1993, Internat. Atomic Energy Agy., 1994; radiation hazard control expert Ill. Bd. Radiation Physics, 1960; mem. Radiation Protection Adv. Coun. State Ill., 1966—, chmn., 1971—; mem. Med. Use Adv. Bd. State Ill., 1974—; Failla meml. lectr., N.Y.C., 1996. Author: (with others) Moving Field Radiation Therapy, 1962, Radiation Accidents and Emergencies in Medicine, Research and Industry, 1965, Atlas of Radiation Dose Distributions, 1972; editor: Recent Developments in Digital Imaging, 1985, Clinical Radiotherapy Physics, Vol. 1 & 2, 1996; contbr. (with others) articles to profl. jours. Mem. DBM Adv. Panel for Californium Program AEC, 1969-73; cons. Nat. Cancer Inst., 1968-88; cons. therapeutic radiology service, sect. radiation physics Hines (Ill.) VA Hosp., 1969-87, chmn. adv. panel on radiation safety and protection, 1973-80; mem. coun. Marie Sklodowska-Curie Meml. Found., Warsaw, Poland, 1989—. Recipient Commendation VA, Washington, 1975, Alumni Honor award for disting. svc. U. Ill., 1984, Landauer award Midwest chpt. Am. Assn. Physicists in Medicine/Health Physics Soc., 1989, Disting. Svc. award Chgo. Rediological Soc., 1997; Evans scholar Northwestern U., 1940-43; Lawrence H. Lanzl Inst. of Med. Physics named in his honor. Fellow Am. Coll. Radiology (mem. commn. human resources 1976-88), Health Physics Soc. (editor assn. jour. 1979-83), Am. Assn. Physicists in Medicine (pres. 1966-67, chmn. Commn. on Accreditation 1981-89, Spl. Recognition award Midwest chpt. 1977, chmn. local arrangements 1969-86, mem. com. on tng. med. physicists 1976-90, William D. Coolidge award 1978, Farrington Daniels award 1984, Landauer Meml. award 1989, establisher Laurence H. Lanzl lecture); mem. AAAS, Am. Phys. Soc., Am. Assn. Physicists in Medicine (pres. 1990), Internat. Orgn. Med. Physics (U.S. del. 1973-85, v.p. 1982-85, pres. 1985-89, editor Med. Physics World 1982-85), Radiol. Soc. N.Am. (mem. assoc. sci. com. 1972-82), Nat. Coun. Radiation Protection and Measurements (mem. sci. coms. 1967-92), Radiation Rsch. Soc., Am. Nuclear Soc. (Midwest), Hosp. Physicists' Assn. (U.K.), Internat. Radiation Protection Assn., Assn. Med. Physicists India, Chinese Soc. Med. Physics (hon.), Internat. Union Phys. and Engring. Scis. in Medicine (coun. 1985-94, pres. 1988-91, past pres. 1991-94), Sigma Xi (Disting. Scientist Mem. award 1989, J.M. Paul Meml. award 1992). Unitarian. Club: Quadrangle. Office: Rush-Presbyn-St Luke's Med Ctr Dept Med Physics 1653 W Chicago IL 60612

LAO, LANG LI, nuclear fusion research physicist; b. Hai Duong, Vietnam, Jan. 28, 1954; came to U.S., 1972; s. Thich Cuong and Boi Phan (Loi) L.; m. Ngan Hua, Dec. 22, 1979; children: Bert J., Brian J. BS, MS, Calif. Inst. Tech., 1976; MS, U. Wis., 1977, PhD, 1979. Staff scientist Oak Ridge (Tenn.) Nat. Lab., 1979-81, TRW, Redondo Beach, Calif., 1981-82; prin. scientist Gen. Atomics, San Diego, 1982—. Contbr. articles to sci. jours. Recipient award for Excellence in Plasma Physics Research Am. Physical Society, 1994. Fellow Am. Phys. Soc. (co-recipient excellence in plasma physics rsch. award 1994). Achievements include being world leader in equilibrium analysis of magnetic fusion plasma physics experiments; developed a widely used computer code essential for successful operation and interpretation of tokamak fusion experiments. Office: General Atomics 3550 General Atomics Ct San Diego CA 92121-1122

LAPALOMBARA, JOSEPH, political science educator; b. Chgo., May 18, 1925; s. Louis and Helen (Teutonico) LaP.; m. Lyda Mae Ecke, June 22, 1947 (div.); children—Richard, David, Susan; m. Constance Ada Bezer, June, 1971. A.B., U. Ill., 1947, A.M., 1950; A.M. (Charlotte Elizabeth Proctor fellow, Class of 1883 fellow), Princeton U., 1952, Ph.D., 1954; student, U. Rome (Italy), 1952-53; M.A. (hon.), Yale U., 1964. Instr., then asst. prof. polit. sci. Oreg. State Coll., 1947-50; instr. politics Princeton U., 1952; mem. faculty Mich. State U., 1953-64, prof. polit. sci., 1958-64, head dept., 1958-63; prof. polit. sci. Yale U., 1964—; Arnold Wolfers prof., 1969—, chmn. dept. polit. sci., 1974-78, 82-85; prof. Sch. of Orgn. and Mgmt., 1979-84, 97—; dir. Instn. for Social and Policy Studies, 1987-92; chmn. Council Comparative and European Studies, 1966-71; cultural attache, first sec. U.S. embassy, Rome, 1980-81; vis. prof. U. Florence, Italy, 1957-58, U. Calif.-Berkeley, 1962, Columbia U., 1966-67, U. Turin, 1974, U. Catania, 1974; cons. FCDA, 1956, Carnegie Corp., 1959, Brookings Instn., 1962, Ford Found., 1965-76, Twentieth Century Fund, 1965-69, AID, 1967-68, Fgn. Svc. Inst., 1968-72, 74-76, Ednl. Testing Svc., 1970-75, Alcoa, 1978-80, Rohm & Haas, 1975-76, GE, 1978-80, Union Carbide, 1981-92, Montedison, 1984-85, Ente Nazionale Idrocarburi, 1983-93, Guardian Industries, 1990-93, Praxair, 1992—, Swiss Bank Corp., 1994—, Athena, 1994-95, Richard Medley Assocs., 1995—, Telecom Italia, 1996—; sr. rsch. assoc. Conf. Bd. N.Y., 1976-81; pres. Italian-Am. Multimedia Corp. N.Y., 1988—; bd. dirs. Transparency Internat.-U.S.A., 1994—. Author: The Initiative and Referendum in Oregon, 1950, The Italian Labor Movement: Problems and Prospects, 1957, Guide to Michigan Politics, rev. edit, 1960, (with Alberto Spreafico) Elezioni e Comportamento Politico in Italia, 1963, Bureaucracy and Political Development, 1963, Interest Groups in Italian Politics, 1964, Italy: The Politics of Planning, 1966, (with Myron Weiner) Political Parties and Political Development, 1966, Clientela e Parentela, 1967, Burocracia y desarrolo politico, 1970, Crises and Sequences of Political Development, (with others), 1972, Politics Within Nations, 1974, (with Stephen Blank) Multinational Corporations and National Elites: A Study in Tensions, 1975, Multinational Corporations in Comparative Perspective, 1976, Multinational Corporations and Developing Countries, 1979, A Politica nos Interior das Nações, 1982, Democracy, Italian Style, 1987, Democrazia all'italiana, 1988, Die Italiener: oder Demokratie als Lebenskunst, 1988, Democratie à l'italienne, 1990; bd. editors Midwest Jour. Polit. Sci, 1956-57, Yale U. Press, 1965-72, 73-76, ABC-CL10, 1976—, Global Perspectives, 1983—; mem. editorial bd. Comparative Politics, 1968—, Jour. Comparative and European Studies, 1969—, Am. Jour. Polit. Sci, 1976-80, Italian Jour., 1988, Yale Rev., 1993—; editor series comparative politics Prentice-Hall Co., 1971-85; mem. editorial adv. bd. Jour. Comparative Adminstrn, 1970-74, Adminstrn. and Soc, 1974—; adv. bd. ABC Polit. Sci; N.Am. editor: Mediterranean Observer, 1981-86; editor in chief Italy, Italy, 1988—; contbr. articles to profl. jours. Mem. exec. com. Inter Univ. Consortium Polit. Rsch., 1966-70; mem. staff Social Sci. Rsch. Coun., 1966-73; chmn. West European fgn. area fellowship program Social Sci. Rsch. Coun.-Am. Coun. Learned Socs., 1972-74; bd. dirs. Mich. Citizenship Clearing House, 1955; trustee, mem. internat. coun. Ctr. for Strategic and Internat. Studies, 1990—. Decorated knight comdr. Order of Merit, Republic of Italy, Fulbright scholar, 1952-53, 57-58, Penfield scholar U. Pa., 1953; fellow Social Sci. Rsch. Coun., 1952-53, Ctr. Advanced Study Behavioral Scis., 1961-62, Rockefeller Found., 1963-64, Ford Found., 1969, Guggenheim Found., 1971-72, European U. Inst., 1996, Wissenschaftszentrum Berlin, 1996; recipient Guido Dorso prize, Italy, 1984, Medal of Honor, Italian Constitutional Ct., 1993, Presidency of Italian Republic, 1993. Mem. Am. Acad. Arts and Scis., Conn. Acad. Arts and Scis., Am. Acad. in Rome (trustee 1984-90), Social Sci. Research Council (com. comparative politics 1958-72), Am. Polit. Sci. Assn. (exec. coun. 1963-65, exec. com. 1967-68, v.p. 1979-80, mem. conf. group on Italian politics and soc. 1978, conf. pres. 1984-85), Am. Acad. Polit. and Social Sci., Soc. for Italian Hist. Studies, Societá Italiana di Studi Elettorali, Consiglio Italiano di Scienze Sociali, Phi Beta Kappa, Phi Kappa Phi, Phi Eta Sigma. Clubs: Yale of N.Y., Elizabethan, Morys Assn. Home: 50 Huntington St New Haven CT 06511-1333

LAPE, ROBERT CABLE, broadcast journalist; b. Akron, Ohio; s. C. Robert and Mary Elizabeth (Cable) L.; m. Marcia Giesy, (div. Dec. 1969); children: Debra, Robert S., Alida, Douglas; m. Eve Bergman, Feb. 14, 1982. BS in Journalism and Radio Speech, Kent State U., 1955. Reporter, asst. news dir. WCUE Radio, Akron, 1954-56; news dir. WICE Radio, Providence, 1956-61; corr., news dir. WBZ Radio, Boston, 1961-68, WABC-TV, N.Y.C., 1968-82; critic, writer on food and travel, lectr. WABC, WCBS, Crain's N.Y. Bus., N.Y. Law Jour., N.Y. Post, N.Y.C., 1983—; LaCucina Italiana; bd. dirs. Internat. Food Media Conf., N.Am., 1986—. Author: Epicurean Rendezvous, 1990-96, Bob Lape's Restaurant Index, 1987-91. Nat. judge food March of Dimes, 1991—; spkr., M.C. Crohn's & Colitis Found., N.Y., Nat. Cancer Soc.; judge James Beard Found. Awards. Recipient Emmy award for TV News Coverage, 1980. Mem. SAG, AFTRA, Assn. Italian Sommeliers, Wine Media Guild, Commanderie de Cordon Bleu de France, Compagnons de Beaujolais, Friars Club. Avocations: travel, reading. Office: Bob Lape Prodns 1055 River Rd Edgewater NJ 07020-1364

LA PETINA, GARY MICHAEL, lawyer; b. Chgo., Apr. 25, 1955; s. Nicholas J. and Mildred E. (Roth) La P.; m. Donna M. Kulisz, Oct. 9, 1982; children: Patrick James, Nicole Elizabeth. BS, Loyola U., Chgo., 1977; JD, John Marshall Law Sch., Chgo., 1980. Bar: Ill. 1980. Staff atty. Internat. Assn. Lions Clubs, Oak Brook, Ill., 1982-87, gen. counsel, 1987—. Mem. ABA, Lions. Roman Catholic. Avocations: collectibles, sporting events, reading. Home: 2 S 30th Bristol Ln Warrenville IL 60555 Office: Internat Assn Lions Clubs 300 W 22nd St Oak Brook IL 60521-8815

LAPHAM, LEWIS HENRY, editor, author, television host; b. San Francisco, Jan. 8, 1935; s. Lewis Abbot and Jane (Foster) L.; m. Joan Brooke Reeves, Aug. 10, 1972; children: Lewis Andrew, Elizabeth Delphina, Winston Peale. Grad., Hotchkiss Sch., 1952; BA, Yale U., 1956; postgrad., Cambridge U., 1956-57; LLD, Hampden-Sydney Coll., Va. Reporter San Francisco Examiner, 1957-60, N.Y. Herald Tribune, 1960-62; author, editor USA-1, N.Y.C., 1962, Saturday Evening Post, N.Y.C., 1963-67; writer Life mag., Harper's, N.Y.C., 1968-70; mng. editor Harper's, N.Y.C., 1971-75; editor Harper's, 1975-81, 83—; TV host weekly series Bookmark, PBS, also host, author documentary series America's Century. Author: (essays) Fortune's Child, 1980, Money and Class in America, 1988, Imperial Masquerade, 1989, The Wish for Kings, 1993, Hotel America, 1995. Mem. Coun. on Fgn. Rels., Century Assn. Office: Harper's Mag 666 Broadway New York NY 10012-2317

LAPIDUS, ARNOLD, mathematician; b. Bklyn., Nov. 6, 1933; s. Morris and Mollie L. m. Nancy Beatrice Latner, Aug. 9, 1952. BS, Bklyn. Coll., 1956; MS, PhD, N.Y. U., 1967. Research scientist Courant Inst., N.Y.C., 1956-68; computer application math. analyst Goddard Inst. for Space Studies, N.Y.C., 1968-70, math. analyst programming methods, 1970-71, sr. mem. tech. staff computer scis., 1971-73; assoc. prof. quantitative analysis Fairleigh Dickinson U., Teaneck, N.J., 1973-83, prof., chair dept. computer and decision systems, 1983-85; sr. engr. Singer Electronic Systems Corp., Little Falls, N.J., 1986-87; owner Advanced Math. Co., Englewood, N.J., 1987—; pvt. practice Englewood, 1987—; vol. mathematician UMDNJ, Newark. Contbr. articles to profl. publs. Mem. AAAS, AAUP, Math. Assn. Am., Am. Math. Soc., Soc. Indsl. and Applied Math. Home and Office: 160 Rockwood Pl Englewood NJ 07631-5028

LAPIDUS, HERBERT, medical products executive; b. N.Y.C., Aug. 10, 1931; s. Harry and Fanny L. (Bagdenofsky) L.; m. Iris Belle Felber, Dec. 21, 1952; children: William Scott, Helane Ruth. BS, Columbia U., 1953, MS, 1955; PhD, Rutgers U., 1967. Instr. Columbia U., N.Y.C.; project leader Julius Schmid Co., N.Y.C., 1957-60; group leader Bristol-Myers Co., Hillside, N.J., 1960-63, dept. head, 1963-67, prin. rsch. investigator, 1967-70; tech. dir. Combe, Inc., White Plains, N.Y, 1970-77, v.p. rsch. devel., 1977—. With U.S. Army, 1956-57. Mem. Am. Chem. Soc., Am. Soc. Clin. Pharmacology & Therapeutics, Am. Assn. Pharm. Scientists, Soc. Cosmetic Chemists, N.Y. Acad. Sci., N.Y. Acad. Medicine. Achievements include over 30 patents in field. Office: Combe Inc 1101 Westchester Ave White Plains NY 10604-3503

LAPIDUS, JULES BENJAMIN, educational association administrator; b. Chgo., May 1, 1931; s. Leo R. and Lillian D. (Davidson) LaP.; m. Anne Marie Liebman, June 8, 1970; children: Steven, Amy, Mark, Marilyn. B.S., U. Ill., 1954; M.S., U. Wis., 1957, Ph.D., 1958. Prof. medicinal and pharm. chemistry Ohio State U., 1958-84; assoc. dean Grad. Sch., 1972-74, dean Grad. Sch., 1974-84, vice provost for research, 1974-82; pres. Council Grad. Schs., 1984—; Mem. pharmacology and toxicology tng. com. NIH, 1965-67, pharmacology program com., 1971-74; mem. Grad. Record Examination Bd., 1982—. Mem. AAAS, Am. Chem. Soc. Office: Coun Grad Schs 1 Dupont Cir NW Ste 430 Washington DC 20036-1136

LAPIDUS, MORRIS, retired architect, interior designer; b. Odessa, Russia, Nov. 25, 1902; came to U.S., 1903, naturalized, 1914; s. Leon and Eva (Sherman) L.; m. Beatrice Perlman, Feb. 22, 1929 (dec. 1992); children: Richard L., Alan H. Student, NYU, 1921-23; B. Arch., Columbia, 1927. With Warren & Wetmore, N.Y.C., 1926-28, Arthur Weisner, N.Y.C., 1928-30; asso. architect Ross-Frankel, Inc., N.Y.C., 1930-42; prin. Morris Lapidus Assos., 1942-86; keynote speaker Conv. Preserving the Recent Past, U.S. Dept. Interiors, 1995. Author: Too Much Is Never Enough, 1996. Mem. Miami Beach Devel. Commn., 1966-67. Winner nat. competition S.W. Urban Renewal Program in Wash., internat. competition for trade ctr. on The Portal Site in Washington; recipinet Justin P. Allman award Wallcovering Wholesaler's Assn., 1963; Outstanding Specifications award Gypsum Drywall Contractors Internat., 1968; cert. merit N.Y. Soc. Architects, 1971;, NYU Alumni Achievement award, 1955. Mem. Miami Beach C. of C. (gov.), Kiwanis. Achievements include initial use of modern in merchandising field; areas of work include housing, hosps., hotels, shopping ctrs., office bldgs., religious instns. Home: 3 Island Ave Miami FL 33139-1363

LAPIDUS, NORMAN ISRAEL, food broker; b. N.Y.C., July 20, 1930; s. Rueben and Laurette (Goldsmith) L.;m. Myrna Sue Cohen, Nov. 20, 1960; children: Robin Anne, Jody Beth. BBA, CCNY, 1952; postgrad. internat. Relations, CCNY, NYU, 1957-60. Salesman Rueben Lapidus Co., N.Y.C., 1954-56, pres., 1960—; sales trainee Cohn-Hall-Marx, N.Y.C., 1955; salesman to v.p. Julius Levy Co., Millburn, N.J., 1964-66, pres., 1966—; salesman Harry W. Freedman Co., Millburn, N.J., 1975-76, v.p., treas., 1976-84, pres., 1984—; pres. Julius Levy/Rueben Lapidus and Harry W. Freedman Cos. div. Pezrow Corp., Millburn, N.J., 1985-86, L&H Food Brokers, Millburn, N.J., 1986-87. Mem. Maplewood (N.J.) Bd. Adjustment, 1975-82, Bedminster (N.J.) Bd. Adjustment, 1996—; gen. chmn. Maplewood Citizens Budget Adv. Com., 1977-79; chmn. Maplewood United Jewish Appeal Drive, 1975-76, 83-84; vice-chmn. Maplewood 1st Aid Squad Bldg. Fund Dr., 1978-79; co-founder Citizens for Charter Change in Essex County, N.J., 1974, mem. exec. bd., 1974—, treas., 1983-84; founder, chmn. Music Theatre of Maplewood; pres. Maplewood Civic Assn., 1983-85; mem. bd. mgrs. Essex County unit Am. Cancer Soc., v.p., 1984-87, chmn. 1991—; mem. adv. bd. Essex County Coll., West Essex, N.J., chairperson bd., 1991—; mem., sec., bd. dirs. Knollcrest Neighborhood Assn., 1994—, pres., 1991-96, 96—; committeeman Bedminster Twp. Com., 1997; active local theatricals; commr. Suburban Mcpl. Joint Ins. Fund, 1997. Recipient Leadership Medallion United Jewish Appeal, 1970, 84. Mem. Nat. Food Brokers Assn. (regional dir., Cert. Exceptionally Meritorious Svc.), Nat. Food Svc. Sales Com., Met. Food Brokers Assn. (chmn. 1982-90), Assn. Food Industries (bd. dirs.), Nat. Food Processors Assn., Young Guard Soc., Old Guard Soc., CCNY Alumni Assn., U.S. Navy Inst., Acad. Polit. Sci., Archaeol. Inst. Am., Nat. Trust for Historic Preservation, Assn. Food Distbrs., Knollcrest Homeowners Assn. (bd. trustees), LWV, Am. Legion, Lions (bd. dirs.), B'nai Brith. Republican. Jewish. Club: Maplewood Glee. Home: 9 Lockhaven Ct Bedminster NJ 07921-1728 Office: 2204 Morris Ave Ste 310 Union NJ 07083-5914

LAPIERRE, DOMINIQUE, writer, historian, philanthropist; b. Chatelaillon, France, July 30, 1931; s. Jean and Luce (Andreota) L.; m. Dominique Conchon, Apr. 5, 1980. Student (Fulbright Exchange scholar), U. Polit. Sci., Paris, 1950-51; B.A., Lafayette Coll., Easton, Pa., 1952, LittD (hon.), 1982. Editor Paris Match News mag., 1955-67. Author: The City of Joy, 1985 (Christopher award 1986), Beyond Love, 1991; co-author: Is Paris Burning?, 1964, ...Or I'll Dress You in Mourning, 1967, O Jerusalem, 1971, Freedom at Midnight, 1975, The Fifth Horseman, 1980. Founder, pres. Action Aid for Lepers' Children of Calcutta. Decorated comdr. Order of Tastevin; recipient Gold medal of the City of Calcutta for humanitarian action, 1987. Home: 26 Ave Kleber, 75116 Paris France Office: care Morton Janklow Lit Agy 598 Madison Ave New York NY 10022-1614

LAPIN, HARVEY I., lawyer; b. St. Louis, Nov. 23, 1937; s. Lazarus L. and Lillie L.; m. Cheryl A. Lapin; children: Jeffrey, Gregg. BS, Northwestern U., 1960, JD, 1963; LLB in Taxation, Georgetown U., 1967. Bar: Ill. 1963, Fla. 1980, Wis. 1985. Cert. tax lawyer, Fla. Bar. Atty., Office Chief Counsel, IRS, Washington, 1963-65; trial atty. Office Regional Csl., IRS, Washington, 1965-68; assoc., then ptnr. Fiffer & D'Angelo, Chgo., 1968-75; pres. Harvey I. Lapin, P.C., Chgo., 1975-83; mng. ptnr. Lapin, Hoff, Spangler & Greenberg, 1983-88, Lapin, Hoff, Slaw & Laffey, 1989-91, ptnr. Gottlieb and Schwartz, Chgo., 1992-93; prin. Harvey I. Lapin & Assocs., P.C., Northbrook, Ill., 1993—; instr. John Marshall Law Sch., 1969—; facility adv. lawyers asst. program Roosevelt U., Chgo.; mem. cemetery adv. bd. Ill. Comptroller, 1974-96. C.P.A., Ill. Mem. Chgo. Bar Assn. (chmn. tax exempt orgns. subcom., sect. taxation, 1988-90), Ill. Bar Assn., ABA, Fla. Bar Assn. (Fla. cert. tax specialist), Wis. Bar Assn. Jewish. Asst. editor Fed. Bar Jour., 1965-67; contbg. editor Cemetery Business and Legal Guide and Funeral

Service Business and Legal Guide; contbr. articles to trade assn. jours. Office: Harvey I Lapin & Assocs PC PO Box 1327 Northbrook IL 60065

LAPINE, JAMES ELLIOT, playwright, director; b. Mansfield, Ohio, Jan. 10, 1949; s. David Sanford and Lillian (Feld) L.; m. Sarah Marshall Kernochan, Feb. 24, 1985; 1 child, Phoebe. BA, Franklin and Marshall Coll., Lancaster, Pa.; hon. degree, Franklin and Marshall Coll., 1994; MFA, Calif. Inst. of Arts, Valencia. Author, dir.: (plays) Photograph, 1977 (Obie award 1977), Table Settings, 1980 (George Oppenheimer/Newsday award), Twelve Dreams, 1983, Sunday in the Park with George, 1984 (N.Y. Drama Critics' Circle award 1984, Pulitzer prize for drama 1984), Into the Woods, 1987 (Tony award 1988, N.Y. Drama Critics' Circle award 1988, Drama Desk award 1988), Falsettoland, 1990 (2 Tony awards 1992), Luck, Pluck and Virtue (La Jolla Playhouse), 1993, Passion, 1994 (Tony award 1994); dir.: March of the Falsettos, 1982, Merrily We Roll Along (La Jolla Playhouse), A Midsummer Night's Dream, A Winter's Tale, 1988, Golden Child, (films) Impromptu, Passion, 1990, Life with Mikey, 1993. Recipient 4 Drama Desk awards, Outer Critics Circle award, Evening Standard award, Olivier award; Guggenheim fellow. Mem. Dramatists Guild. Office: c/o Shubert Orgn 225 W 44th St New York NY 10023

LAPINSKI, FRANCES CONSTANCE, data processing systems executive; b. Flushing, N.Y., Sept. 19, 1950; d. Frank Stanley and Frances A. (Gaziano) L. BS in Edn., SUNY, Oswego, 1972, MS in Edn., 1974; postgrad. in program edn., adminstrn., Syracuse U., 1976; MBA, NYU, 1990. Tchr. Mexico (N.Y.) Boces, 1971-72; chancellor's intern SUNY, Oswego, 1972-74; coordinator housing Lemoyne Coll., Syracuse, 1974-76; project coordinator Am. Assn. State Colls. and Univs., Washington, 1976-79; project mgr. Robt Bell & Co., Balt., 1979-81; asst. treas. Chase Manhattan Bank, N.Y., 1981-84; dir. internet svcs. Depository Trust Co., N.Y., 1984—; mem. computer security del. to People to People Citizen Amb. Program, China, 1994; mem. corp. adv. bd. Infoworld, 1995—, Tech. Mgrs. Forum, 1996—. Vol. Spl. Olympics, N.J., N.Y., 1984—, Habitat for Humanity, Newark, 1995—; chmn. Outreach Program, St. Andrew and Holy Communion Ch., South Orange, N.J., 1991-93. Mem. Microcomputer Mgrs. Assn. (vendor liaison 1986-90, bd. dirs. 1991-93, nat. award for excellence 1992, pres. N.Y. chpt. 1994). Avocations: camping, cross country skiing. Home: 11 S Kingman Rd South Orange NJ 07079-2611

LAPINSKI, TADEUSZ ANDREW, artist, educator; b. Rawamazowiecka, Poland, June 20, 1928; s. Tadeusz Alexander and Valentina (Kwiatkowska) L. MFA, Acad. Fine Arts, Warsaw, Poland, 1955. Prof. U. Md., College Park, 1973—. One-man shows include Mus. Modern Art, N.Y.C., also mus. in Washington, São Paulo and Rio de Janeiro, Brazil, Turin, Italy, Belgrade, Yugoslavia and Vienna, Austria, Regional Mus. of Torun, Poland, 1992, Plock Mus. and Libr., Poland, 1993, Regional Mus. of Zyrardow, Poland, 1994, Sci. Soc. Plock, 1993, Dist. Mus. City of Zyrardow, Poland, 1994, Zyrardow Mus. of Art, Poland, 1994; group shows include Nat. Royal Acad., London, biennial exhbns. in Venice, Italy, Paris, Buenos Aires, Argentina, John Guggenheim Gallery Exhibition, Coral Gables, Fla., 1988, numerous others; retrospective exhibition Nat. Mus. Torun, Poland, 1956-92; represented in permanent collections Mus. Modern Art, N.Y.C., Libr. of Congress, Washington, Nat. Mus. Am. Art, Washington, mus. in São Paulo, Warsaw and Cracow, Poland, others. Recipient Gold medal Print Festival, Vienna, 1979, Silver medal World Print '80, Paris, medal City of Zamosc, Poland, 1980, UNESCO prize Paris, Statue of Victory 85 World prize, Italy, Achievement award Prince George's County, 1989, Cultural Achievement award Am. Polish Art award U. Md., 1991, Am. Polish Arts Assn. award, 1991, Medal Am. Inst. Polish Culture, 1996; T. Lapinski day proclaimed by mayor of Washington, 1981; named Man of Yr. Md. Perspectives Mag., 1984, Internat. Man of Yr. Intern., Art award City Plock, Poland, 1994. Mem. Soc. Graphic Art, Painters and Sculptors Soc. N.J. Office: U Md Dept Art College Park MD 20742

LA PLATA, GEORGE, federal judge; b. 1924; m. Frances Hoyt; children: Anita J. La Plata Rard, Marshall. AB, Wayne State U., 1951; LLB, Detroit Coll. Law, 1956. Pvt. practice law, 1956-79; judge Oakland County (Mich.) Cir. Ct., Pontiac, 1979-85, U.S. Dist. Ct. (ea. dist.) Mich., Ann Arbor, 1985—; pres. & owner Allan Miller, P.C., Mich., 1996—; prof. Detroit Coll. Law, 1985-86. Trustee William Beaumont Hosp., 1979—, United Found., 1983—. Served to col. USMC, 1943-46, 52-54. Mem. ABA, Oakland County Bar Assn., Hispanic Bar Assn. Lodge: Optimists. Office: Allan Miller PC 370 E Maple 4th Flr Birmingham MI 48009*

LAPOE, WAYNE GILPIN, retired business executive; b. Waynesburg, Pa., July 13, 1924; s. James Lindsay and Mary (Gilpin) LaP.; m. Margaret Louise Clark, Feb. 21, 1953; children: Deborah Jean, Marqui Lynne. B.A., Pa. State U., 1947. With personnel and sales depts. Armstrong Cork Co., Lancaster, Pa., 1947-53, Chgo., 1947-53, San Francisco, 1947-53; personnel dir. Safeco Ins. Group., 1953-63, v.p., 1963-86; v.p. Safeco Corp., Seattle, 1976-80, sr. v.p., 1980-86; v.p. Gen. Ins. Co. Am., 1963-86, Safeco Ins. Co. Am., 1963-86, Safeco Life Ins. Co., 1963-86, First Nat. Ins. Co. Am., Seattle, 1963-86, Safeco Nat. Ins. Co., St. Louis, 1972-86. Mem. White House Conf. Children and Youth, 1960; bd. dirs. Ind. Colls. Washington. Capt. USAAF, 1943-46, USAF, 1951-52. Decorated D.F.C.; decorated Air medal with three oak leaf clusters. Mem. Mus. Flight Seattle, Ocean Liner Mus. N.Y., Am. Polit. Items Collectors (past pres.), Am. Aviation Hist. Soc., SS Hist. Soc. Am., Assn. Des Amis Des Paquebots, Nat. Trust Hist. Preservation, Phi Kappa Tau. Republican. Home: 11986 Lakeside Pl NE Seattle WA 98125-5955

LAPOINTE, LUCIE, government agency executive; b. Valleyfield, Que., Can., Dec. 23, 1954; d. Paul and Jeannette (Gagné) L.; m. Clive Willis, Apr. 13, 1996; 1 child, Lauren Lapointe-Shaw. BSc in Biol. Scis., McGill U., 1977; MBA, U. Ottawa, Ont., Can., 1982. Tech. officer divsn. biol. scis. NRC, Ottawa, 1977-80, program officer program svcs. secretariat, 1982-84, exec. mgr. pub. rels. and info. svcs., 1984-87, dir. mgmt. svcs. br., 1987-89, sec. gen. exec. offices, 1989—. Office: Nat Rsch Coun Can, Montreal Rd Bldg M-58, Ottawa, ON Canada K1A 0R6

LAPOINTE-PETERSON, KITTIE VADIS, choreographer, ballet school director, educator; b. Chgo., June 4, 1915; d. Samuel Joseph and Katie (Parbst) Andrew; m. Arthur Joseph LaPointe, Dec. 17, 1938 (dec. Apr. 1985); children: Janice Deane, Suzanne Meta; m. Ray Burt Peterson, Feb. 2, 1992 (dec. Nov. 1995). Studies with, Marie Zvolanek, Chgo., 1921-28, Laurent Novikoff, Chgo., 1928-35, Edward Caton, Chgo., 1928-35; student, Royal Danish Ballet, Copenhagen, 1926. Dancer Chgo. Civic Opera, 1929-32, Century of Progress, Chgo., 1933-34, Stone-Camryn Ballet, Chgo., 1934-35, Mary Vandas Dancers, Chgo., 1935-38, Balaban-Katz Theaters, Chgo., 1935-36; tchr., choreographer Studio of Dance Arts, Chgo., 1952-68, Herrstrom Sch., Chgo., 1968-72; dir. Le Ballet Petit Sch., Chgo., 1972-92. Soloist in Michael Fokine's Co., 1935. Mem. Danish Brotherhood and Sisterhood (pres. 1962-65, 72-75, Midwest dist. pres. 1972-74), Chgo. Outdoor Art League (sec. 1975-79, Manor Garden Club. Avocations: cooking, writing, gardening. Home: 5843 W Peterson Ave Chicago IL 60646-3907

LAPONCE, JEAN ANTOINE, political scientist; b. Decize, France, Nov. 1925; s. Fernand and Fernande (Ramond) L.; m. Joyce Price, July, 1950; children: Jean-Antoine, Marc, Patrice; m. Iza Fiszhaut, Apr. 10, 1972; 1 child, Danielle. Diploma, Institut d'études politiques, Paris, 1947; Ph.D., UCLA, 1955. Instr. U. Santa Clara, 1956; asst. prof. polit. sci. U. B.C., Can., Vancouver, 1956-61; assoc. prof. U. B.C., 1961-66, prof., 1966—; dir. Inst. Interethnic Rels. U. Ottawa, 1993—; mem. grad. faculty Aichi Shukutoku U., 1994-97. Author: The Protection of Minorities, 1961, The government of France under the Fifth Republic, 1962, People vs Politics, 1970, Left and Right, 1981, Langue et territoire, 1984, Languages and Their Territories, 1987. Fellow Royal Soc. Can. (pres. Acad. Humanities and Social Scis. 1988-91); mem. Can. Polit. Sci. Assn. (pres. 1972-73), Am. Polit. Sci. Assn., French Polit. Sci. Assn., Internat. Polit. Sci. Assn. (pres. 1973-76). Office: U BC Dept Polit Sci, Vancouver, BC Canada V6T 1Z1

LAPORTE, CLOYD, JR., retired manufacturing executive, lawyer; b. N.Y.C., June 8, 1925; s. Cloyd and Marguerite (Raeder) L.; m. Caroline E. Berry, Jan. 22, 1949; children—Elizabeth, Marguerite, Cloyd III. AB, Harvard U., 1946, JD, 1949. Bar: N.Y. 1949. Assoc. mem. firm Cravath, Swaine & Moore, N.Y.C., 1949-56; dir. adminstrn. Metals div. Olin Corp., N.Y.C., 1957-66; legal counsel Dover Corp., N.Y.C., 1966-93, sec., 1971-93. 2d lt. A.C. AUS, WWII. Mem. Harvard Club (N.Y.C.). Home: Gipsy Trail Club Carmel NY 10512

LAPORTE, GERALD JOSEPH SYLVESTRE, lawyer; b. Windsor, Ont., Can., Oct. 16, 1946; came to U.S., 1948, naturalized, 1954; s. Rosaire Joseph and Catherine Rose (Sylvestre) L. BA, Sacred Heart Sem. Coll., 1968; STB, St. Paul U., Ottawa, Ont., 1971; BTh, U. Ottawa, 1971; MA, Georgetown U., 1974; JD, George Washington U., 1976. Bar: Mich. 1976, D.C. 1977. Legis. asst. to U.S. Congressman William J. Randall, Washington, 1971-75; law clk. to U.S. Dist. Judge, Washington, 1976-77; assoc. Wilmer, Cutler & Pickering, Washington, 1977-82, Nutter, McClennen & Fish, Washington, 1987; sr. spl. counsel, Office Gen. Counsel, SEC, Washington, 1982-85; counsel to SEC Commr., 1985-87; ptnr. Patton Boggs, L.L.P., Washington, 1988-96; counsel Hogan & Hartson L.L.P., Washington, 1996—; mem. steering com. sect. corp., fin. and securities law D.C. Bar. Mng. editor George Washington Law Rev., 1975-76. Mem. ABA (sect. on bus. law, fed. regulation of securities com., subcom. SEC adminstrn., budget and legis.), Nat. Assn. Bond Lawyers (vice chmn. securities law and disclosure com. 1994-96). Democrat. Roman Catholic. Home: 3154 Key Blvd Arlington VA 22201-5037 Office: Hogan & Hartson LLP 555 13th St NW Washington DC 20004-1109

LAPORTE, LEO FREDERIC, earth sciences educator; b. Englewood, N.J., July 30, 1933; s. Leo Frederic and Edea (Giacobbe) L.; married, 1956 (div. 1983); children: Leo G., Eva R.; m. Margaret Liniecki, 1985; 1 child, Noel A. Student, Fordham Coll., 1951-53; A.B., Columbia U., 1956, Ph.D., 1960. From instr. to prof. dept. geol. scis. Brown U., Providence, 1959-71; prof. dept. earth scis. U. Calif.-Santa Cruz, 1971-94, prof. emeritus, 1994, chmn., 1972-75, dean div. natural scis., 1975-76, provost Crown Coll., 1993—, assoc. vice chancellor for undergrad. edn., 1994—; vis. prof., Yale U., 1964; geologist N.Y. State Geol. Survey, 1962-64; petroleum research cons.; mem. com. geol. scis. Nat. Acad. Sci.-NRC, 1970-72; sec. U.S. Nat. Com. Hist. Geology, 1991-93, chair, 1994-96. Author: Ancient Environments, 1968, 79, 89, Encounter with the Earth, 1975; prin. author: The Earth and Human Affairs, 1972; editor: Reefs in Time and Space, 1974, Evolution and the Fossil Record, 1978, Simple Curiosity: Family Letters of George G. Simpson, 1987, Establishment of a Geologic Framework for Paleoanthropology, 1990; contbr. articles to profl. jours. Recipient President's award Am. Assn. Petroleum Geologists, 1969; U. Calif. Santa Cruz Alumni Disting. Teaching award, 1980. Fellow AAAS, Geol. Soc. Am., Calif. Acad. Sci.; mem. History of Earth Scis. Soc. (pres. 1994), Soc. Econ. Mineralogists and Paleontologists (chmn. rsch. com., paleontology councilor, editor PALAIOS 1984-89, pres. 1995-96). Office: U Calif Crown Coll Santa Cruz CA 95064-1017

LAPOSATA, JOSEPH SAMUEL, army officer; b. Johnstown, Pa., Oct. 3, 1938; s. Joseph Thomas and Mary Marie (Coco) L.; m. Anita Louise Sabo, Aug. 12, 1961; children: Joseph S. Jr., David G., Matthew M. BS, Indiana U. Pa., 1960; MS, Cornell U., 1968; grad., Command and Gen. Staff Coll., Leavenworth, Kans., 1971, Indsl. Coll. Armed Forces, Washington, 1980. Commd. 2d lt. U.S. Army, 1960, advanced through grades to lt. gen., 1991; asst. chief of staff for logistics 5th Inf. Div., Ft. Polk, La., 1978-79; chief war res. div. Office Dep. Chief of Staff for Logistics, Hdqrs. Dept. Army, Washington, 1980-81; comdr. 8th Support Group, U.S. Army So. European Task Force, Livorno, Italy, 1981-84; dep. comdr., chief of staff U.S. Army So. European Task Force, Vicenza, Italy, 1984; exec. to dep. chief of staff for logistics Hdqrs. Dept. Army, Washington, 1984-86, dir. plans and ops., dep. chief of staff for logistics, 1986-88; comdg. gen. U.S. Army Material Command-Europe, Heidelberg, Fed. Republic Germany, 1988-89; dep. chief of staff for logistics U.S. Army Europe and 7th Army, Heidelberg, 1989-91; chief of staff Allied Forces So. Europe, Naples, Italy, 1991-93; Presdl. appointee as sec. Am. Battle Monuments Commn., Washington, 1994-95; ret.; apptd. dep. gen. mgr. and dir. Logistics Ops. and Programs, NATO Supply and Maintenance Agy., Luxembourg. Decorated Def. DDSM, DSM (1), Legion of Merit (3), Bronze Star (2); knight comdr. Republic of Italy; recipient Man of Yr. award Interclub Coun., Johnstown, Pa., 1990, Disting. Alumnus award Ind. U. of Pa., 1992; inducted into Quartermaster Hall of Fame, 1994. Mem. Assn. U.S. Army (pres. European dept. 1989-91), Quartermaster Found. (bd. dirs.), Rotary, Phi Kappa Phi. Roman Catholic. Avocation: golf. Address: 1 Rue De La Solidarite, L-8020 Strassen Luxembourg

LAPP, CHARLES WARREN, internal medicine physician, pediatrician; b. Bklyn., June 10, 1947; s. Warren Anthony and Katherine Emma (Beard) L.; m. Darie Eleanor Conners, Aug. 28, 1971; children: Lauren Michelle, Warren Rutherford. BS, Rensselaer Poly. Inst., 1969, MBME, 1970; MD, Albany Coll. Medicine, 1974. Diplomate Am. Bd. Internal Medicine, Am. Bd. Pediatrics. Intern U. N.C., Chapel Hill, 1974-75, resident, 1975-78; med. dir. Hill Haven and Blue Ridge Nursing, Raleigh, N.C., 1978-91; assoc. clin. prof. U. N.C., Chapel Hill, 1978-91, Duke. U. Med. Ctr., 1982—; founder and pres. Piedmont Med. Assn., Raleigh, N.C., 1978—; med. dir. Cheney Clinic, Charlotte, N.C., 1991-95; pres. Hunter-Holkins Ctr., P.A., Charlotte, 1995—; cons. TASA Tech. Adviser, Phoenix, 1979—; adv. bd. Raleigh Employee Assistance Plan, 1987-89, Health Plus, 1987-89; med. cons. CFIDS Assn. of Am., Charlotte, 1991—. Contbr. articles to profl. jours. including Jour. AMA and Lancet; presenter exhibits to sci. assemblies. Pres. Muscular Dystrophy Assn., 1982-84. Named Richard T. Beebe Scholar in Medicine, Albany (N.Y.) Med. Coll.) 1974; Man of the Yr., Jaycees, Raleigh, N.C., 1983. Fellow Am. Acad. Family Physicians, Am. Acad. Pediatrics, Am. Assn. Disability Evaluating Physicians; mem. AMA, N.C. Med. Soc., Am. Assn. for Chronic Fatigue Syndrome, Am. Pain Soc. Presbyterian. Avocations: boating, hiking, travel. Office: 10724 Park Rd Ste 105 Charlotte NC 28210-8469

LAPP, JAMES MERRILL, clergyman, marriage and family therapist; b. Lansdale, Pa., July 20, 1937; s. John E. and Edith (Nice) L.; m. Nancy Swartzentruber, Mar. 1, 1936; children: Cynthia Ann, J. Michael. B.A., Eastern Mennonite Coll., 1960; B.D., Goshen Bibl. Sem., 1963; D.Min., Drew U., 1981. Ordained to ministry Mennonite Ch., 1963. Pastor Belmont Mennonite Ch., Elkhart, Ind., 1961-63; tchr. Christopher Dock Mennonite High Sch., Lansdale, Pa., 1963-70; paster Perkasie Mennonite Ch., Pa., 1963-72, Albany Mennonite Ch., Oreg., 1972-81; dir. campus ministries Goshen Coll., Ind., 1981-87; gen. sec., gen. bd. Mennonite Ch., Elkhart, 1987-95; conf. pastor Fraconia Mennonite Conf., Souderton, Pa., 1996—; moderator Pacific Coast Conf. on Mennonite Ch., Oreg., 1977-79, Mennonite Gen. Assembly, Lombard, Ill., 1985-87. Contbr. articles to Mennonite Ch. publs. Democrat. Avocations: gardening, baking, walking. Home: 61 W Park Ave Sellersville PA 18960 Office: Franconia Mennonite Conf PO Box 116 Souderton PA 18964

LAPP, JOHN ALLEN, retired religious organization administrator; b. Lansdale, Pa., Mar. 15, 1933; s. John E. and Edith Ruth (Nyce) L.; m. Alice Weber, Aug. 20, 1955; children: John Franklin, Jennifer Lapp Lerch, Jessica. BA, Ea. Mennonite Coll., 1954; MA, Case Western Res. U., 1958; PhD, U. Pa., 1968. From instr. to prof. history Ea. Mennonite Coll., Harrisonburg, Va., 1958-69; exec. sec. peace sect. Mennonite Ctrl. Com., Akron, Pa., 1969-72, exec. sec., 1985-96, exec. sec. emeritus, 1996—; prof. history, dean Goshen (Ind.) Coll., 1972-79, prof. history, provost, 1979-84; rep. Ch. World Svc. and Witness, N.Y.C., 1985-96; observer World Coun. Chs., Canberra, Australia, 1991; vis. prof. history Bishop's Coll., Calcutta, India, 1996—. Author: Mennonite Church in India 1897-1962, 1972, The View from East Jerusalem, 1980; editor: Peacemaking in a Broken World, 1970; columnist Christian Living mag., 1963-80; mem. editorial bd. Mennonite Quar. Rev., 1972—; contbr. articles to profl. jours. Visitor N. Cen. Assn. Schs. and Colls., Chgo., 1976-84; pres. Rockingham Coun. on Human Rels, Harrisonburg, 1962-65; v.p. Va. Coun. on Human Rights, Richmond, 1965-69. Mem. Conf. on Faith and History, Mennonite Hist. Soc. (pres. 1972-84). Home: 13 Knollwood Dr Akron PA 17501-1113

LAPP, SUSAN BOLSTER, learning disability educator; b. Washington, Nov. 23, 1945; d. Robert Fay and Nona (Peifly) Bolster; m. Richard Gordon Lapp, Apr. 22, 1967. BS in Edn., Miami U., Oxford, Ohio, 1967; MEd, Xavier U., Cin., 1977. Cert. tchr. English; cert. in learning disabilities and behavior disorders K-12. Sec. Penta Tech. Coll., Perrysburg, Ohio, 1965-67; tchr. 3d grade Toledo Pub. Schs., 1966-67; thcr. 7th and 8th grades Fairfield (Ohio) City Schs., 1967-78, 6th, 7th and 8th grade learning disabilities tchr., 1978—, spl. svcs. coordinator, 1984—, career edn. coordinator, 1987—; career edn. coordinator Butler County Joint Vocat. Sch., Hamilton, Ohio, 1987—; student vol. dir. Fairfield Middle Sch., 1990—. Vice chair S.W. Ohio Profl. Devel. Ctr., 1993-94, co-sec., 1994. Named Spl. Edn. Tchr. of Yr., S.W. Ohio Spl. Edn. Regional Resource Ctr., 1989, Ohio Career Educator of Yr., Career Edn. Assn., 1991, Outstanding Sch. Vol.-Ptnr. award, 1991, Ohio Mid. Sch. Career Planning Team of Yr., 1994. Mem. NEA, S.W. Ohio Edn. Assn., Fairfield Classroom Tchrs. Assn., Ohio Mid. Sch. Assn., Nat. Assn. for Career Edn., Career Edn. Assn. (Ohio Career Planning Team of Yr. 1994), Orton Soc. Avocations: beach activities, reading, antiquing. Home: 900 Harrison Ave Hamilton OH 45013-3511 Office: Fairfield Middle Sch 255 Donald Dr Fairfield OH 45014-3006

LAPPAS, SPERO THOMAS, lawyer; b. Danbury, Conn., Oct. 20, 1952; s. Tom John and Alexandria (Manolakes) L.; m. Josephine Wahrendorf, Nov. 8, 1981 (div. 1986); 1 child, Thom Spero; m. Julie Marie Waugh, July 12, 1986 (div. 1995); 1 child, Alexandria Julia. BA cum laude, Allegheny Coll., Meadville, Pa., 1974; JD cum laude, Dickinson Sch. Law, Carlisle, Pa., 1977. Bar: Pa. 1977, U.S. Dist. Ct. (mid. dist.) Pa. 1977, U.S. Ct. Appeals (3rd cir.) 1980, U.S. Supreme Ct. 1991. Assoc. Law Office of Arthur Kusic, Harrisburg, Pa., 1977-79; atty. Kusic & Lappas, P.C., Harrisburg, 1979-84; pvt. practice Harrisburg, 1984-85; ptnr. Stefanon & Lappas, Harrisburg, 1985-88; prin. Law Offices Spero T. Lappas, Harrisburg, 1988—. Mem. Pa. Bar Assn., Dauphin County Bar Assn., Assn. Trial Lawyers Am., Nat. Assn. Criminal Def. Lawyers, Pa. Assn. Criminal Def. Lawyers, Mensa, Am. Hellenic Ednl. and Progressive Assn. Office: 205 State St Harrisburg PA 17101-1130

LAPPEN, CHESTER I., lawyer; b. Des Moines, May 4, 1919; s. Robert C. and Anna (Sideman) L.; m. Jon Tyroler Irmas, June 29, 1941; children—Jonathan Bailey, Timothy, Andrea L., Sally Morris. A.B. with highest honors in Econs, U. Calif., 1940; LL.B. magna cum laude (Faye diploma), Harvard, 1943. Bar: Calif. bar 1943. Practice in Los Angeles, 1946—; sr. partner firm Mitchell, Silberberg & Knupp, 1949—; advisory bd. Bank Am., 1962-65; chmn. bd., dir. Zenith Nat. Ins. Corp., 1975-77; bd. dirs. Arden Group, Inc. (chmn. exec. com. 1978), 1963-91, Data Products Corp. (chmn. fin. com.), 1965-93, City Nat. Bank Corp., 1967-92; trustee, pres. Citinat, Devel. Trust; bd. dirs., chmn. bd. Pacific Rim Holding Corp., 1987-94. Editor-in-chief: Harvard Law Rev, 1942-43. Chmn. bd. trustees Immaculate Heart Coll., 1981-88; trustee UCLA Found.; v.p., dir. Ctr. for Childhood. Served as spl. agt. CIA AUS, 1943-46. Mem. ABA, Los Angeles Bar Assn. (dir. 1953), Los Angeles Jr. Bar Assn. (pres. 1953), Beverly Hills (Calif.) Bar Assn., Harvard Law Sch. Alumni Assn. So. Calif. (pres. 1973-82), Artus (hon.). Republican. Office: Mitchell Silberberg & Knupp 11377 W Olympic Blvd Los Angeles CA 90064-1625

LAPPIN, RICHARD C., corporate executive; b. Detroit, Dec. 16, 1944; s. Thomas Gerald and Helen Marie (Manor) L.; m. Mary Ann Hopkinson; children: Sean, Reid; children from previous marriage: Jill, Richard, Nicole. BA in Mgmt., Econs. and Psychology, U. Detroit, 1968. Corp. mgr. indsl. engring. AMC Corp., Southfield, Mich., 1972-75, corp. mgr. fin., 1975-77; internat. ops. exec. Chrysler Corp., Highland Park, Mich., 1977-79; v.p. ops. Distbn. and Controls divsn. Gould Inc., Rolling Meadows, Ill., 1979-80; gen. mgr. ball and roller divsn. Hoover Uniroyal, Ann Arbor, Mich., 1980-82; asst. to pres. Northop Def. Systems, Rolling Meadows, 1982-86; group v.p. electronics, corp. v.p. bus. devel. RTE Corp., Brookfield, Wis., 1986-88; pres. N.Am. Automotive Products Champion Spark Plug, Toledo, Ohio, 1988—; pres., chief exec. officer Doehler-Jarvis/Farley Inc., Toledo, 1989—; chief exec. officer So. Fastner/Farley Inc., Statesville, N.C., 1989—; pres., chief oper. officer Farley Industries, Chgo., 1991—; vice-chmn., pres., chief operating officer Fruit of the Loom, Inc., Chgo. Office: Fruit of the Loom Inc 233 S Wacker Dr Chicago IL 60606-6306

LAPRADE, CARTER, lawyer; b. Richmond, Va., Nov. 21, 1942; s. Edmund Moseley and Page (Walker) LaP.; m. Suzanne Williams, June 7, 1967; children: Suzanne, Carter, Burch. BA, Yale U., 1965; LLB, Columbia U., 1968. Bar: N.Y. 1968, Conn. 1973, U.S. Dist. Ct. Conn. 1974, U.S. Ct. Appeals (2d cir.) 1974. Asst. U.S. atty. So. Dist. N.Y., 1971-73, Dist. of Vt., Rutland, 1973; ptnr. Thompson, Weir & Barclay, New Haven, 1973-82, Tyler, Cooper & Alcorn, New Haven, 1982-94; retired, 1994. Chmn. bd. Gaylord Hosp., Wallingford, Conn., 1985-87; pres. Conn. Soc. to Prevent Blindness, Madison, 1982-84; trustee Quinnipiac Coll., Hamden, Conn., 1987-97. Capt. USMC, 1968-71. Fellow Am. Bar Found.; mem. ABA (Profl. Merit award 1969), Conn. Bar Assn., New Haven County Bar Assn. (pres. 1988), Lawyer-Pilots Bar Assn., Yale Club New Haven (pres. 1989-91). Avocations: scuba diving, running. Home: 4618 Black Stump Rd Weems VA 22576

LAPSLEY, JAMES NORVELL, JR., minister, pastoral theology educator; b. Clarksville, Tenn., Mar. 16, 1930; s. James Norvell and Evangeline (Winn) L.; m. Brenda Ann Weakley, June 4, 1953 (dec. May 1989); children: Joseph William, Jacqueline Evangeline; m. Helen Joan Winter, Feb. 24, 1990. BA, Rhodes Coll., 1952; BD, Union Theol. Sem., 1955; PhD (Div. Sch. fellow, Rockefeller fellow), U. Chgo., 1961. Ordained to ministry Presbyn. Ch., 1955; asst. min. Gentilly Presbyn. Ch., New Orleans, 1955-57; instr. Princeton (N.J.) Theol. Sem., 1961-63, asst. prof., 1963-67, assoc. prof., 1967-76, prof. pastoral theology, 1976-80, Carl and Helen Egner prof. pastoral theology, 1980-92, acad. dean, 1984-89, prof. emeritus, 1992—; mem. editl. bd. Jour. Pastoral Care, 1966-69, 91—; bd. dirs. N.W. Maricopa UN Assn., 1994—, v.p., 1995-96, pres., 1997; pres. Critical Issues Coun. of Sun Cities, 1996-97. Editor: The Concept of Willing, 1967, Salvation and Health, 1972, Renewal in Late Life Through Pastoral Counseling, 1992; editor: (with B.H. Childs, D.W. Waanders), Festschrift: The Treasure of Earthen Vessels, 1994; chmn. editl. bd. Pastoral Psychology Jour., 1975-84. Bd. dirs. Westminster Found., Princeton U., 1970-76. Danforth fellow Menninger Found., 1960-61. Mem. Am. Acad. Religion, Phi Beta Kappa. Presbyterian. Home: 16610 N Meadow Park Dr Sun City AZ 85351-1758

LAQUEUR, MARIA, educational association administrator; b. San Francisco, Sept. 25, 1942; d. Gert Ludwig and Mary Alice (Murphy) L.; m. William Gerald Hamm, Feb. 12, 1983. BA German, Am. Univ., 1965, MA German/Linguistics, 1968; MPA, U. of No. Colo., 1978. German lang. cataloger Libr. of Congress, Washington, 1965-70, assoc. catalog editor, 1970-76, asst. dir. NUC proj., 1976-81; assoc. pub. Bemrose UK, Ltd., London, 1981-85; exec. dir. Assoc. of Part-time Profls., Falls Church, Va., 1988—. Author: Flexible Work Options: A Selected Bibliography, 1990; co-author: Breaking Out of 9 to 5, 1994.. Fellow U.S. Office Edn., 1967. Home: PO Box 2173 Ct NE Kilmarnock VA 22482-2173 Office: Assn of Part Time Profls Crescent Plaza 7700 Leesburg Pike Ste 216 Falls Church VA 22043-2615

LAQUEUR, WALTER, history educator; b. Breslau, Germany, May 26, 1921; s. Fritz and Else (Berliner) L.; m. Barbara Koch, May 29, 1941; children: Sylvia, Shlomit. Grad., Johannesgymnasium, Breslau, 1938; student, Hebrew (Jerusalem) U., 1938-39; HHD (hon.), Hebrew Union Coll., 1988, Adelphi U., 1993, Brandeis U., 1994. Agrl. worker Palestine, 1940-44; newspaper corr., free-lance author, 1944-55; founder, editor Survey, London, Eng., 1955-67; vis. prof. Johns Hopkins, 1957, U. Chgo., 1958, Harvard, 1977; dir. Inst. Contemporary History, Wiener Library, London, 1964-92; prof. history ideas and politics Brandeis U., Waltham, Mass., 1967-72; prof. history U. Tel Aviv, 1970-80; chmn. internat. research council Ctr. Strategic and Internat. Studies, Washington, 1973—; univ. prof. govt. Ctr. Strategic and Internat. Studies Georgetown U., Washington, 1977-91. Author: Communism and Nationalism in the Middle East, 1956, The Soviet Union and the Middle East, 1959, Young Germany, 1962, Russia and Germany, 1966, The Fate of the Revolution, 1967, The Road to War, 1967, The Struggle for the Middle East, 1969, Europe Since Hitler, 1970, Out of the Ruins of Europe, 1971, Confrontation: The Middle East and World Politics, 1974, A History of Zionism, 1972, Weimar, 1975, Guerrilla, 1976, Terrorism, 1977, Guerrilla Reader, 1977, Terrorism Reader, 1978, A Continent Astray, 1979, The Missing Years, 1980, Political Psychology of Appeasement, 1980, Farewell to Europe, 1981, The Terrible Secret, 1981, America, Europe, and the Soviet Union, 1983, Germany Today, 1985, A World of Secrets, 1985, The Age of Terrorism, 1987, The Long Road to Freedom: Russia and Glasnost, 1989, Stalin, 1991, Thursday's Child Has Far to Go, 1992, Black

Hundred, 1993, The Dream That Failed, 1994; co-editor, founder: Jour. Contemporary History, 1966—; founder Washington Papers, 1972—. Recipient 1st Distinguished Writer's award Center Strategic and Internat. Studies, 1969, Inter Nationes award, 1985, Grand Cross of Merit German Fed. Republic, 1987. Office: Ctr Strategic and Internat Studies 1800 K St NW Washington DC 20006-2202

LARA, ADAIR, columnist, writer; b. San Francisco, Jan. 3, 1952; d. Eugene Thomas and Lee Louise (Hanley) Daly; m. James Lee Heig, June 18, 1976 (div. 1989); children: Morgan, Patrick; m. William Murdock LeBlond, Nov. 2, 1991. BA in English, San Francisco State U., 1976. Reader Coll. of Marin, Kentfield, Calif., 1976-83; freelance editor, 1983-86; mng. editor San Francisco Focus mag., 1986-89; exec. editor San Francisco mag., 1988-89; columnist San Francisco Chronicle, 1989—. Author: History of Petaluma: A California River Town, 1982, Welcome to Earth, Mom, 1992, Slowing Down in a Speeded-up World, 1994, At Adair's House, More Columns by America's Funniest Formerly Single Man, 1995; contbr. articles to profl. publs. Recipient Best Calif. Columnist award AP, 1990. Democrat. Avocations: reading, photography, travel, softball, biking. Office: San Francisco Chronicle 901 Mission St San Francisco CA 94103-2905

LARAGH, JOHN HENRY, physician, scientist, educator; b. Yonkers, N.Y., Nov. 18, 1924; s. Harry Joseph and Grace Catherine (Coyne) L.; m. Adonia Kennedy, Apr. 28, 1949; children: John Henry, Peter Christian, Robert Sealey; m. Jean E. Sealey, Sept. 22, 1974. MD, Cornell U., 1948. Diplomate Am. Bd. Internal Medicine. Intern medicine Presbyn. Hosp., N.Y.C., 1948-49; asst. resident Presbyn. Hosp., 1949-50; cardiology trainee Nat. Heart Inst., 1950-51; rsch. fellow N.Y. Heart Assn., 1951-52; asst. physician Presbyn. Hosp., 1950-55, asst. attending, 1954-61, assoc. attending, 1961-69, attending physician, 1969-75, pres. elect med. bd., 1972-74; mem. faculty Coll. Physicians and Surgeons Columbia U., 1950-75, prof. clin. medicine, 1967-75, spokesman exec. com. faculty coun., 1971-73; vice chmn. bd. trustees for profl. and sci. affairs Presbyn. Hosp., 1974-75; dir. Hypertension Ctr., chief nephrology div. Columbia-Presbyn. Med. Ctr., 1971-75; Hilda Altschul Master prof. medicine, dir. Hypertension and Cardiovascular Ctr., N.Y. Hosp.-Cornell Med. Ctr., 1975—, chief cardiology div., 1975-95; cons. USPHS, 1964—. Editor-in-chief Am. Jour. Hypertension, Cardiovascular Reviews and Reports; Editor: Hypertension Manual, 1974, Topics in Hypertension, 1980, Frontiers in Hypertension Rsch., 1981; editor Hypertension: Pathophysiology, Diagnosis, and Management, 1990, 1995; editorial bd.: Am. Jour. Medicine, Am. Jour. Cardiology, Kidney Internat., Jour. Clin. Endocrinology and Metabolism, Hypertension, Jour. Hypertension, Circulation, Am. Heart Jour., Procs. of Soc. Exptl. Biology and Medicine, Heart and Vessels. Mem. policy adv. bd. hypertension detection and follow-up program Nat. Heart and Lung Inst., 1971, bd. sci. counselor, 1974-79; chmn. U.S.A.-USSR Joint Program in Hypertension, 1977-93. With U.S. Army, 1943-46. Recipient Stouffer prize Med. Rsch., 1969, J.K. Lattimer award Am. Urol. Assn., 1989, Robert Tigerstedt award Am. Soc. Hypertension, 1990, John P. Peters award Am. Soc. Nephrology, 1990. Lifetime Achievement in Medicine award N.Y. Acad. Medicine, 1993, Disting. Alumnus award Cornell U. Med. Coll., 1993, Squibb award for disting. achievement cardiovalcular rsch., Bristol Myers, 1996; subject of Time Mag. cover story, 1975; Most Frequently Cited Scientist: Top Ten Advances in Cardiopulmonary Medicine, 1946-75. Fellow Am. Coll. Cardiology; mem. ACP (Master), Am. Heart Assn. (chmn. med. adv. bd. coun. high blood pressure rsch. 1968-72), Am. Soc. Clin. Investigation, Assn. Am. Physicians, Assn. Univ. Cardiologists, Endocrine Soc., Am. Soc. Nephrology, Am. Soc. Hypertension (founder, 1st pres. 1986-88), Internat. Soc. Hypertension (pres. 1986-88), Harvey Soc., Kappa Sigma, Nu Sigma Nu, Alpha Omega Alpha, Winged Foot Golf Club (Mamaroneck, N.Y.), Shinnecock Hills Golf Club (Southampton, N.Y.). Achievements include research on hormones and electrolyte metabolism and renal physiology, mechanisms of edema formation and on causes and treatments of high blood pressure. Home: 27 Overlook Dr Southampton NY 11968-3206 also: 5 Sandpiper Dr Village Of Golf FL 33436-5299 Office: NY Hosp-Cornell Med Ctr 525 E 68th St # 4 New York NY 10021-4873 *In my research, a key resource has been the ability to look at everyday clinical phenomena differently, to recognize and develop new ideas and principles about human physiology. These perceptions enable hypotheses and experiments for creation and synthesis of new knowledge that redirects medical thinking.*

LARASON, TIMOTHY MANUEL, lawyer; b. Shattuck, Okla., Nov. 28, 1939; s. Albert Ray and Mary Margaret (Manuel) L.; m. Linda Jane Hinshaw, Dec. 28, 196; children: John Todd, Amber Dawn. BBA, U. Okla., 1962; postgrad., Northwestern U., 1962; JD, Oklahoma City U., 1968. Bar: Okla. 1968, U.S. Tax Ct. 1971; CPA, Okla. Acct. Arthur Young & Co., Oklahoma City, 1963-70; mem. firm Andrews, Davis, Legg, Bixler, Milstein & Price, Oklahoma City, 1970—. Treas. First Unitarian Ch., Oklahoma City, 1969-74; pres. Legal Aid of Western Okla., Oklahoma City, 1985. Avocation: computers. Office: Andrews Davis Legg Bixler Milstein & Price 500 W Main St Oklahoma City OK 73102-2253

LARAYA-CUASAY, LOURDES REDUBLO, pediatric pulmonologist, educator; b. Baguio, Philippines, Dec. 8, 1941; came to U.S., 1966; d. Jose Marquez and Lolita (Redublo) Laraya; m. Ramon Serrano Cuasay, Aug. 7, 1965; children: Raymond Peter, Catherine Anne, Margaret Rose, Joseph Paul. AA, U. Santo Tomas, Manila, Philippines, 1958, MD cum laude, 1963. Diplomate Am. Bd. Pediatrics. Resident in pediatrics U. Santo Tomas Hosp., 1963-65, Children's Hosp. Louisville, 1966-67, Charity Hosp. New Orleans-Tulane U., 1967-68; fellow child growth and devel. Children's Hosp. Phila., 1968-69; fellow pediatric pulmonary and cystic fibrosis programs St. Christopher's Hosp. for Children, Phila., 1969-71, rsch. assoc., 1971-72; clin. instr. Tulane U., New Orleans, 1967-68; asst. prof. pediatrics Temple Health Scis. Ctr., Phila., 1972-77; assoc. prof. pediatrics Thomas Jefferson Med. Sch., Phila., 1977-79; assoc. prof. pediatrics U. Medicine & Dentistry N. J., Robert Wood Johnson Med. Sch., New Brunswick, 1980-85, prof. clin. pediatrics, 1985—; dir. pediatric pulmonary and cystic fibrosis program U. Medicine and Dentistry, Robert Wood Johnson Med. Sch., New Brunswick, 1981—. Co-editor: Interstitial Lung Diseases in Children, 1988. Recipient Pediatric Rsch. award Mead Johnson Pharm. Co., Manila, 1965. Fellow Am. Coll. Chest Physicians (steering com., chmn. cardiopulmonary diseases in children 1976—), Am. Acad. Pediatrics (tobacco free generation rep. 1986-92); mem. Am. Ambulatory Pediatric Soc., Am. Thoracic Soc., Am. Sleep Disorder Assn., N.J. Thoracic Soc. (chmn. pediatric pulmonary com. 1986-91, governing coun. mem. 1981-94), Am. Coll. Physician Execs., European Respiratory Soc., Lung Club. Avocation: pianist. Home: 100 Mercer Ave Spring Lake NJ 07762-1208 Office: UMDNJ Robert Wood Johnson Med Sch CN19 New Brunswick NJ 08903

LARBERG, JOHN FREDERICK, wine consultant, educator; b. Kansas City, Mo., Jan. 21, 1930; s. Herman Alvin and Ann (Sabrowsky) L. AA, Kansas City Jr. Coll., 1948; AB cum laude, U. Mo., 1950, postgrad., 1955-56; MSW, Bryn Mawr Coll., 1961. Cert. social worker. With Westinghouse Electric Corp., 1953-56; dir. House of Industry Settlement House, Phila., 1957-61; asst. to exec. dir. Health and Welfare Coun., Inc., Phila., 1961-66; sr. staff cons., 1966-73, dir. Washington office, 1971-72, Nat. Assembly for Social Policy and Devel., Inc., N.Y.C.; nat. dir. community and patient services Nat. Multiple Sclerosis Soc., N.Y.C., 1974-81, nat. dir. spl. projects, 1981-82; adminstrv. v.p. Fedn. Protestant Welfare Agys. N.Y., 1982-86; sr. advisor, 1986-87; exec. dir. Am. Assn. State Social Work Bds., 1987-89; cons. The Wine Aficionado, N.Y., 1990—. Cons. exec. com. Commn. on Vol. Svc. and Action, 1967-76, cons. Met. N.Y. Project Equality, 1968-73, Encampment for Citizenship, 1973-74, Symphony for UN, 1974-77, Lower Eastside Fam. Union, 1984—, Wielenga Psych. Svc., 1993—, Malignant Hyperthermia Assn. U.S., 1994—, Internat. Fedn. Multiple Sclerosis Socs., 1995—, Nat. Multiple Sclerosis Soc., 1997—; bd. dirs. Health Systems Agy. of N.Y., 1984-86; trustee The Riverside Ch., N.Y.C., 1985-89, worship commn., 1992-94, ordination com., 1993—, chmn., 1996—; bd. dirs., mem. exec. com. Metro Assn. United Ch. of Christ, N.Y., 1993—, dir. N.Y. state conf., 1995—, nat. del. Gen. Synod, 1997; mem. Disciples of Christ/United Ch. of Christ N.Y. State Joint Task Force, 1996—; nat. dir. Coun. Soc. Wk. Edn., 1985-86. Served with AUS, 1951-53. Mem. Acad. Cert. Social Workers (charter), Nat. Assn. Social Workers (chpt. legis. com. 1968-70, nat. publs. com. 1968-71, nat. legal regulation com. 1987-89), Internat. Coun. Social Welfare (internat. com. of reps. 1980-84, U.S. com. for Internat. Coun. Social Welfare, bd. dirs. 1983-90, exec. com. 1983-90), Internat. Fedn. Multiple Sclerosis Socs. (vice chmn. patient services com. 1976-81, chmn. 1981-84, mem. individual and family services com. 1984—, non-govtl. rep. to UN, 1990-96, rep. to Rehab. Internat. Med. Commn. 1976-81), Nat. Conf. Social Welfare (program com. 1966-73, chmn. combined assoc. groups 1969-70, nat. dir. 1971-73, 83-87), Fedn. of Assns. Regulatory Bds. (nat. dir. 1988-89), Malignant Hyperthermia Assn. U.S. (nat. dir. 1984-93, nat. pres. 1985-89, rep. 10th Quad. World Congr. Anesth. Hague 1992), Am. Acad. Polit. and Social Sci., Nat. Urban League (nat. trustee-at-large 1968), Hawk Mountain Sanctuary Assn., Bryn Mawr Social Work Alumni Assn. (pres. 1963-65), Am. Mus. Natural History, N.Y.C. Citizen Union, N.Y. Mcpl. Art Soc., Phi Beta Kappa Assn. N.Y. (pres. 1980-82), Omicron Delta Kappa, QEBH, Alpha Phi Omega, Alpha Pi Zeta, Pi Sigma Alpha, Alpha Kappa Psi. Home and Office: 400 E 58th St 2F New York NY 10022 Office: 2F 400 E 58th St New York NY 10022

LARCH, SARA MARGARET, medical administrator; b. Des Moines, Iowa, Feb. 14, 1956; d. William Arthur and Beverly Frances (Klanjac) L. BA in Pub. Adminstrn., Miami U., Oxford, Ohio, 1978; M in Health Scis. Adminstrn., Med. Coll. Va., 1992. Personnel clk. City Nat. Bank, Detroit, 1978-79; econ. anlyst asst. Cargill, Inc., Mpls., 1979-81; adminstrv. asst. Ind. U. Med. Ctr., Indpls., 1981-82, ob-gyn. adminstr., 1982-88; adminstr. Georgetown U. Med. Ctr., Washington, 1988-94, dir. qualith and capitation sys., 1995; COO Univ. Physicians, Inc. Univ. Md., Balt., 1995—; mem. planning com. Parent Care Conf., Indpls., 1985-86. assoc. editor Ob-Gyn Newsletter, Indpls., 1984-86. Vol. Indpls. Mus. Art, 1982-83, White River Park Commn., Indpls., 1984, Indpls. Zoo, 1987-88. Mem. Assn. Mgrs. Gynecology and Obstetricians (pres. 1986-87), Med. Group Mgmt. Assn. (bd. dirs. 1995-96), Acad. Practice Assembly (pres. 1994-95). Avocations: piano, reading, traveling, skiing. Office: Univ Physicians Inc 419 W Redwood Ste 220 Baltimore MD 21201

LARCHE, JAMES CLIFFORD, II, state agency administrator; b. Mobile, Ala., Nov. 27, 1946; s. James Clifford and Alma (Dunn) L.; m. Mary Cecilia Whelchel, June 6, 1969 (div. 1972); m. Jan Pirkle, May 7, 1994. A.B., Ga. State U., 1974. Claims examiner Employees' Retirement System, Atlanta, 1969-73, div. dir., 1973-84, dep. dir., 1985—; with Nat. Conf. State Social Security Adminstrs., Atlanta, 1973—, regional v.p., 1978-80, sec., 1980-82, first v.p., 1982-83, pres., 1983-84, chmn. fed.-state procedures com., 1984-85; mem. CSPA, 1989—, chair, 1993-94. Served with N.G., 1968-74. Roman Catholic. Home: PO Box 38056 Atlanta GA 30334-0056 Office: State Social Security Adminstrs 2 Northside Ste 300 Atlanta GA 30318-7778

LARDNER, GEORGE, JR., journalist, author; b. N.Y.C., Aug. 10, 1934; s. George Edmund and Rosetta (Russo) L.; m. Rosemary Schalk, July 6, 1957; children: Helen, Edmund, Richard, Charles, Kristin (dec.). AB summa cum laude in Journalism, Marquette U., 1956, MA, 1962. Reporter The Worcester (Mass.) Telegram, 1957-59, The Miami (Fla.) Herald, 1959-63; reporter The Washington Post, 1963-64, 66—, columnist, 1964-66; bd. dirs. Fund for Investigative Journalism, Washington. Author: The Stalking of Kristin, 1995. Recipient Byline award Marquette U., 1967, Front-page Nat. News award Washington-Balt. Newspaper Guild, 1984, 86, Pulitzer Prize for feature writing, 1993. Mem. Congl. Press Gallery. Roman Catholic. Home: 5604 32nd St NW Washington DC 20015-1623 Office: Washington Post 1150 15th St NW Washington DC 20071-0001

LARDNER, HENRY PETERSEN (PETER LARDNER), insurance company executive; b. Davenport, Iowa, Apr. 5, 1932; s. James Francis and Mary Catharine (Decker) L.; m. Marion Cleaveland White, Dec. 28, 1954; children: Elisabeth, Emily Decker, David, Peter, Sarah (dec.). B.S.E. (Indsl. Engring.), U. Mich., 1954; M.A., Augustana Coll., 1982. C.P.C.U. Indsl. engr. Cutler-Hammer, Milw., 1954; Agt. H.H. Cleaveland Agy., Rock Island, Ill., 1956-60; with Bituminous Ins. Cos., Rock Island, 1960—; exec. v.p. Bituminous Ins. Cos., 1968-72, pres., 1972-95, chmn. and CEO, 1984—; pres. Bitco Corp., 1973-95, chmn., bd. dirs., 1973—; bd. dirs. Old Republic Internat., 1985—. Bd. govs. State Colls. and Univs., 1971-80; trustee Black Hawk Coll., 1964-72; mem. Ill. Bd. Higher Edn., 1976-77; chmn. Ill. State Scholarship, 1982-85. Served with AUS, 1954-56. Home: 3227 29th Ave Rock Island IL 61201-5568 Office: Bitco Corp 320 18th St Rock Island IL 61201-8716

LARDNER, RING WILMER, JR., author; b. Chgo., Aug. 19, 1915; s. Ring Wilmer and Ellis (Abbott) L.; m. Silvia Schulman, Feb. 19, 1937 (div. 1945); children: Peter, Ann; m. Frances Chaney, Sept. 28, 1946; 1 child, James; stepchildren: Katharine, Joseph. Student, Princeton, 1932-34. Reporter N.Y. Daily Mirror, 1935; press agt. Selznick Internat. Pictures, Culver City, Calif., 1935-37; screenwriter various cos., 1937-82; freelance writer, 1982—. Screenwriter: (with Michael Kanin) Woman of the Year, 1942 (Acad. award 1942), (with Leopold Atlas) Tomorrow the World, 1944, (with Albert Maltz) Cloak and Dagger, 1946, (with Philip Dunne) Forever Amber, 1947, (with Terry Southern) The Cincinnati Kid, 1965, M*A*S*H, 1970 (Acad. award 1970), The Greatest, 1977; author: (novels) The Ecstasy of Owen Muir, 1955, All for Love, 1985, The Lardners: My Family Remembered, 1976; also TV and movie pieces; collaborator Broadway mus. Foxy, 1964. Mem. Writers Guild Am. (Screen Laurel award 1989, Ian McLellan Hunter Meml. award for lifetime achievement 1992).

LARDY, HENRY A(RNOLD), biochemistry educator; b. Roslyn, S.D., Aug. 19, 1917; s. Nicholas and Elizabeth (Gebetsreiter) L.; m. Annrita Dresselhuys, Jan. 21, 1943; children: Nicholas, Diana, Jeffrey, Michael. BS, S.D. State U., 1939, DSc (hon.), 1979; MS, U. Wis., 1941, PhD, 1943. Asst. prof. U. Wis., Madison, 1945-47, assoc. prof., 1947-50, prof., 1950-88, Vilas prof. biol. sci., 1966-88, prof. emeritus, 1988—; Henry Lardy annual lectr. S.D. State U., Brookings, 1985. Edtl. bd. Archives Biochemistry and Biophysics, 1957-60, Jour. Biol. Chemistry, 1958-64, 80-85, Biochem. Preparations, Methods of Biochem. Analysis, Biochemistry; contbr. over 430 articles to profl. jours. Pres. Citizens vs McCarthy, Wis., 1950. Recipient Neuberg medal Am. Soc. European Chemists, 1956, Wolf Found. award in Agr., 1981, Nat. award Agrl. Excellence, 1982. Fellow Wis. Acad. Arts and Scis.; mem. Am. Chem. Soc. (chmn. biol. divsn. 1958, Paul-Lewis Labs. award 1949), Am. Soc. Biol. Chemists (pres. 1964, William Rose award 1988), Am. Acad. Arts and Scis. (Amory prize 1984), Am. Philos. Soc., Am. Diabetes Assn., Nat. Acad. Scis., Biochem. Soc. Great Britain, Harvey Soc., Soc. for Study of Reprodn. (Carl Hartman award 1984), Japanese Biochem. Soc. (hon.), Golden Retriever Club Am. (pres. 1964). Democrat. Achievements include patents for steroid compounds and lab. apparatus. Home: 1829 Thorstrand Rd Madison WI 53705-1052 Office: U Wis 1710 University Ave Madison WI 53705-4087

LARDY, NICHOLAS RICHARD, economics educator; b. Madison, Wis., Apr. 8, 1946; s. Henry Arnold and Annrita (Dresselhuys) L.; m. Barbara Jean Dawe, Aug. 29, 1970; children: Elizabeth Brooke, Lillian Henry. BA, U. Wis., 1968; MA, U. Mich., 1972, PhD, 1975. Asst. prof. Yale U., New Haven, 1975-79, assoc. prof., 1979-83, asst. dir. econ. growth ctr., 1979-82; assoc. prof. U. Wash., Seattle, 1983-85, chair China program, 1984-89, prof., 1985-95, dir. The Henry M. Jackson Sch. Internat. Studies, 1991-95; sr. fellow The Brookings Instn., Washington, 1995—; Frederick Frank adj. prof. in internat. trade and fin. Yale U. Sch. Mgmt., New Haven, 1997—; bd. dirs. Nat. Com. on U.S.-China Rels., N.Y.C., Comm. in Internat. Rels. Studies with China, 1989-92, Program for Internat. Studies in Asia, 1993-95; chmn. Com. on Advanced Study in China; vice chmn. com. on scholarly comm. with China NAS, Washington, 1991-95; mem. bd. mgrs. The Blakemore Found., 1993-95; founding mem. Pacific Coun. on Internat. Policy, 1995—; mem. Coun. on Fgn. Rels. Author: Economic Growth and Distibution in China, 1978, Agriculture in China's Modern Economic Development, 1983, Foreign Trade and Economic Reform in China, 1978-90, 1992, China in the World Economy, 1994, (policy study) Economic Policy Toward China in the Post-Reagan Era, 1989; mem. editl. bd. The China Quar. (London), China Econ. Rev., Jour. Asian Bus., Problems of Post-Communism. Rsch. fellow Am. Coun. Learned Socs., 1976, 78-79, 89-90, Henry Luce Found., Inc., 1980-82; faculty rsch. grantee Yale U., 1976, 78. Mem. Am. Econ. Assn., Assn. for Asian Studies (nominating com. 1986-87), Assn. for Comparative Econ. Studies (exec. com. 1986-88). Avocations: skiing, squash, tennis, sailing. Home: 2811 Albemarle St NW Washington DC 20008 Office: The Brookings Instn 1775 Massachusetts Ave NW Washington DC 20036-2188

LARDY, SISTER SUSAN MARIE, academic administrator; b. Sentinel Butte, N.D., Nov. 9, 1937; d. Peter Aloysius and Elizabeth Julia (Dietz) L. BS in Edn., U. Mary, Bismarck, N.D., 1965; MEd, U. N.D., 1972. Entered Order of St. Benedict, Bismarck, 1957. Elem. tchr. Cathedral Grade Sch., Bismarck, 1958-67, Christ the King Sch., Mandan, N.D., 1967-68, 70-72, St. Joseph's Sch., Mandan, 1968-70; asst. prof. edn. U. Mary, Bismarck, 1972-80; adminstr., asst. prioress Annunciation Priory, Bismarck, 1980-84, prioress, major superior, 1984-96; dir. U. Mary-Fargo (N.D.) Ctr., 1997—; dir. Fargo Ctr. U. Mary, 1997—. Chair Health Commn. of Diocese of Bismarck, 1991. Mem. Delta Kappa Gamma. Home: 1101 32d Ave S Fargo ND 58103 Office: U Mary Fargo Ctr 3001 25th St S Fargo ND 58103-5055

LAREAU, RICHARD GEORGE, lawyer; b. Woonsocket, R.I., June 11, 1928; s. Hector R. and Agnes P. (Valley) L.; m. Thelma Johnson, Aug. 11, 1970; 1 son, Alan Hartland; 1 son by previous marriage, William Wheeler Mohn. BA, St. Michael's Coll., Winooski Park, Vt., 1949; JD, U. Minn., 1952. Bar: Minn. 1952. Ptnr. Oppenheimer, Wolff & Donnelly, St. Paul, Mpls., 1956—; bd. dirs. Ceridan, Bloomington, Minn., Nash Finch Co., Mpls., Merrill Corp., St.Paul, No. Techs. Internat. Corp., Lino Lakes; trustee Mesabi Trust, N.Y.C.; sec. AVECOR Cardiovascular Inc., Plymouth, Minn. Sec., bd. dir. Minn. Cooperation Office for Small Bus. and Job Creation, Mpls.; bd. dirs. Minn. Project on Corp. Responsibility, Mpls. 1st lt. USAF, 1952-56. Mem. ABA, Minn. Bar Assn., Hennepin County Bar Assn., Mpls. Club. Avocation: fishing. Home: 20750 Linwood Rd Excelsior MN 55331-9386 Office: Oppenheimer Wolff & Donnelly 3400 Plz VII 45 S 7th St Minneapolis MN 55402-1614

LARESE, EDWARD JOHN, company executive; b. Kimball, W.Va., Mar. 7, 1935; s. Innocente and Velia (Pais) L.; m. Julianne Falotico, Aug. 15, 1964. Student, U. Ky., 1953-54; AB in Acctg., Duke, 1957. CPA, N.C., N.Y. Acct. Price Waterhouse & Co., N.Y.C., 1957-65; mgr.-fin. acctg. Ea. Air Lines, Inc., N.Y.C., 1965-67, asst. to sr. v.p. fin. and adminstrn., 1968-70, asst. contr. fin. planning and analysis, 1970-72; v.p., contr. Eastern Air Lines, Inc., 1972-76; v.p. planning and control IU Internat., Inc., Phila., 1976-79; CEO, pres. Altair Airlines, Inc., 1979-81; mgmt. cons. Berwyn, Pa., 1981-84; exec. v.p., CFO Finalco Group, Inc., McLean, Va., 1984-89; mgmt. cons. Warrenton, Va., 1989-91; v.p. fin. and adminstrn., CFO Star Techs., Inc., Sterling, Va., 1992-94; pres., CEO Scala, Inc., Herndon, Va., 1994—. Loaned exec. Dade County (Fla.) United Fund, 1965, corp. chmn., 1975-76. With USAFR, 1958-64. Mem. AICPA, Air Transp. Assn. (vice chmn. corp. acctg. com.), N.Y. Soc. CPAs, N.C. Assn. CPAs, Fin. Execs. Inst., Duke U. Alumni Assn., Bath Club (Miami Beach, Fla.), Radnor Hunt Club (Berwyn, Pa.), Warrenton Hunt Club, Ashland Bassetts Club, Springs Club, Fauquier Club, Sigma Nu. Republican. Episcopalian. Home: 8372 Elway Ln Warrenton VA 20186-9730 Office: Scala Inc 2323 Horse Pen Rd Ste 300 Herndon VA 20171-3405

LARGE, G. GORDON M., computer software company executive; b. Phila., Apr. 4, 1940; s. James M. and Sarah Morris (Ellison) L.; m. Janet G. Leith, 1964 (div. 1978); children: Christopher M., Allison G.; m. Theresa A. M. Misiorek, Nov. 30, 1978. BA, Princeton U., 1962; MBA, U. Pa., 1963. V.p. Smith, Barney & Co., Inc., N.Y.C., 1964-73; adminstr. N.J. State Energy Office, Trenton, 1974-75; exec. dir. N.J. Cabinet Energy Com., Trenton, 1974-75; v.p. Mathematica, Inc., Princeton, N.J., 1975-81, Mathematica Products Group, Inc., Princeton, 1981-84, Martin Marietta Data Systems, Greenbelt, Md., 1984-86; sr. v.p., chief fin. officer Palladian Software, Inc., Cambridge, Mass., 1986-88, Pansophic Systems, Inc., Lisle, Ill., 1988-91; sr. v.p., fin. and adminstrn. CFO Systems Ctr. Inc., Reston, Va., 1992-93; exec. v.p., CFO Card Establishment Svcs., Inc., Melville, N.Y., 1993-95; exec. v.p., CFO Interleaf Inc., Waltham, Mass., 1995—, also dir. Mem. Fin. Execs. Inst. Avocations: running, tennis, photography, music. Office: Interleaf Inc Prospect Pl 62 4th Ave Waltham MA 02154-7507

LARGE, JOHN ANDREW, library and information service educator; b. Mexborough, Yorkshire, Eng., Mar. 27, 1947; arrived in Can., 1989; s. Gordon and Winifred Mary (Tompkins) L.; m. Valerie Merle Wilson, Aug. 30, 1972; children: Amanda Fiona, Kirsty Jane. BSc in Econs., London U., 1968, diploma in libr., 1973; PhD, Glasgow U., Scotland, 1973. Asst. libr. Glasgow U. Libr., 1973-74; libr. Inst. Soviet and East European Studies, Glasgow U., 1974-78; prin. lectr. Coll. Librarianship Wales, Aberystwyth, 1978-89; prof., dir. Grad. Sch. Libr. and Info. Studies McGill U., Montreal, Que., Can., 1989—; vice chmn. U.K. Online User Group, London, 1987-89; chmn. Can. Coun. Libr. Schs., 1991-93; external examiner U. W.I., 1991—, U. Ibadan, Nigeria, 1992-95. Author: The Foreign-Language Barrier, 1983, The Artificial Language Movement, 1985, Japanese edit., 1995, A Modular Curriculum for Information Studies, 1987; co-author: Online Searching: Principles and Practice, 1990; editor: Manual of Online Search Strategies, 1988, 2d edit., 1992, CD-ROM Information Products: An Evaluative Guide vol. 1, 1990, vol. 2, 1991, vol. 3, 1992; mem. editl. adv. bd. Jour. Librarianship and Info. Sci., 1992—; editor jour. Edn. for Info., 1983—, CD-ROM Info. Products, 1993. Rsch. grantee Brit. Libr. R&D Dept., 1981-82, 85-86, European Space Agy., 1983-85; IBM Acad. Info. Exch. fellow, 1991-92, Social Sci. and Humanities Rsch. Coun. fellow, 1991-94, 96—; recipient Commemorative medal for 125th Anniversary of the Confedn. of Can., 1992. Mem. ALA, Am. Soc. for Info. Sci., Can. Libr. Assn., Assn. Libr. and Info. Sci. Edn., Que. Libr. Assn. Avocation: music listening and playing. Office: McGill U Grad Sch Libr and Info, Studies 3459 McTavish, Montreal, PQ Canada H3A 1Y1

LARGEN, JOSEPH, retailer, furniture manufacturer, book wholesaler; b. Union, N.J., June 13, 1940; s. Fred and Wilma Largen; children: Lori, Lisa. B.S. in Econs, U. Mo., 1963. Mgmt. trainee R.R. Donnelly Corp., Chgo., 1964-67; distbn. mgr., material control and distbn. Warwick Electronic Co., Niles, Ill., 1967-69; with Brodart, Inc., 1969—; v.p. prodn. Brodart, Inc., Williamsport, Pa., 1973-75; exec. v.p. Brodart, Inc., 1975-78, pres., 1978—. Served with USCG, 1963-64. Home: 2000 1st Ave Apt 2602 Seattle WA 98121-2172 Office: Brodart Co 500 Arch St Williamsport PA 17701-7809

LARGENT, STEVE, congressman, former professional football player; b. Tulsa, Sept. 28, 1954; m. Terry Largent; children: Kyle, Kelly, Kramer, Casie. BS in biology, U. Tulsa, 1976. Wide receiver Seattle Seahawks, NFL, Kirkland, Wash., 1976-89; player Pro Bowl, 1979, 80, 82, 85-88; mktg. cons. Sara Lee Corp., 1991-94; mem. 103rd-105th Congresses from 1st Okla. dist., Washington, DC, 1995—; mem. budget com., mem. health care task force, mem. sci. com., mem. energy & environ. and space & aeronautics subcoms., mem. commerce com. Holder NFL record for passes caught in consecutive games, also for career receiving yardage, receptions; named to NFL Hall of Fame, 1995. Office: US House Reps 426 Cannon Bldg Ofc Bldg Washington DC 20515-4318*

LARIC, MICHAEL VICTOR, academic administrator; b. Split, Yugoslavia, Feb. 8, 1945; came to U.S., 1971; s. Joseph and Ljubica (Abraham) L.; m. Roberta Kine; children: Shai Samuel, Pnina Leora, Ari Nathaniel. BA in Econs. and Polit. Sci., Hebrew U. of Jerusalem, 1968, MA in Bus., 1971; PhD, CUNY, 1976. Economist Israel Hotel & Motel Owners, Tel Aviv, 1968-69; gen. mgr. Galia Laundries, Jerusalem, 1969-71; economist Risk Analysis Corp., Alpine, N.J., 1971-72; lectr. CUNY, N.Y.C., 1972-73; asst. prof. Rutgers U., State U. N.J., Newark, 1974-75, U. Conn., Storrs, 1975-81; prof. mktg. U. Balt., 1981—, acad. assoc. dean, 1992-95; course dir. Data Tech. Inst., Clifton, N.Y., 1986-92, Frost & Sullivan, N.Y.C. and Eng., 1990—; cons. Ecomares Internat., Ellicott City, Md., 1981—. Author: Marketing Management: Analysis Using Spreedsheets, 1988, Lotus Exercises for Principles of Marketing, 1986, 14 other books; contbr. numerous articles, monographs and cases to profl. jours. Named Outstanding Young Man of The Yr. Jaycees, 1979, 80. Mem. Am. Mktg. Assn. (bd. mem. Balt. chpt. 1976-82, Outstanding Contbr. of Conn. 1978), Product Devel. and Mgmt. (bd. mem. 1981, 82), Am. Econs. Assn., Beta Gamma Sigma. Home: 4609 Morning Ride Ct Ellicott City MD 21042-5927 Office: U Balt 1420 N Charles St Baltimore MD 21201-5720

LARISON, BRENDA IRENE, law librarian; b. Springfield, Ill., Apr. 3, 1949; d. Richard Wayne and Corabell Marie (Bea) L.; 1 child, Alyce Sherbenou. BA, U. Ill., 1971; MA, Sangamon State U., Springfield, 1977; MLS, U. Mich., 1980. Corp. libr. ADP Network Svcs., Ann Arbor, Mich., 1978-86; legis. rsch. law libr. State of Ill., Springfield, 1986-91; libr. Supreme Ct. Ill., Springfield, 1992—; del. White House Conf. on Librs., 1990; midwest coord. Nat. Conf. State Legislatures, Denver, 1987-91; mem. state agy. libr. bd. State of Ill. Libr., Springfield, 1988-90. Literacy vol. Lincoln Land C.C., Springfield, 1992-95; vol. coord. Lincoln Meml. Gardens, Springfield, 1993-94. Mem. Am. Assn. Law Librs., Chgo. Assn. Law Librs., Spl. Librs. Assn. (bd. dirs. Ill. chpt. 1989-90). Avocations: gardening, birding, cycling. Office: Supreme Ct Ill Supreme Ct Bldg Springfield IL 62701

LARIVÉE, JACQUES, conservationist. Co-author: (with A. Cyr) Atlas saisonnier des oiseaux du Québec, 1995. Recipient Snowy Owl Conservation award Québec Zoological Gardens, 1993. Home: 194 Ouellet, Rimouski, PQ Canada G5L 4R5

LARIVIERE, RICHARD WILFRED, Asian studies educator, consultant; b. Chgo., Jan. 27, 1950; s. Wilfred Francis and Esther Irene (Kallestad) L.; m. Janis Anne Worcester, June 5, 1971; 1 child, Anne Elizabeth. BA, U. Iowa, 1972; PhD, U. Pa., 1978. Lectr. U. Pa., Phila., 1978-79; asst. prof. U. Iowa, Iowa City, 1980-82; prof. U. Tex., Austin, 1982—, Ralph B. Thomas Regents prof. Asian studies, 1993—; assoc. v.p. U. Tex., 1995—; dir. Sinha & Lariviere Ltd., Austin, 1994—; dir. Ctr. for Asian Studies, Nat. Resource Ctr. for South Asia; founder Doing Bus. in India seminar; cons. Perot Sys. Corp., Dallas, 1993—; bd. dirs. HCL/Perot Sys., Amsterdam, Coun. Am. Overseas Rsch. Ctrs., Washington. Author: Ordeals in Hindu Law, 1981, Narada Smrti, 1989; gen. editor Studies in South Asia. Fellow NEH, 1979-83. Fellow Royal Asiatic Soc.; mem. Am. Oriental Soc., Am. Inst. Indian Studies (sr.fellow 1989, 95, v.p. 1990), Assn. Asian Studies. Lutheran. Office: U Tex Asian Studies Mail Code G9300 Austin TX 78727

LARIZADEH, M(OHAMMED) R(EZA), business educator; b. Tehran, Iran, Apr. 14, 1947; came to U.S., 1966; s. Hassan and Nosrat (Saremi) L.; m. Dianne Ellen Pincus, Mar. 25, 1973; children: Dariush, Darya Anna. BA in Econs., Bus., UCLA, 1972, cert. in acctg., 1974. Cert. colls. teaching credential, Calif. (life); lic. real estate agent, Calif. Auditor Peat, Marwick & Mitchell, Los Angeles, 1972-74; controller Petromain Constrn. Co., Tehran, 1975-77; v.p. fin. Pilary Marine Shipping Co., Tehran, 1977-79; prof. Iranian Inst. Banking, Tehran, 1975-78; pres. Audicount Acctg. and Auditing Group, L.A., 1984—; prof. bus. and acctg. East L.A. Coll., 1980-87, vice-chmn. dept. bus. and acctg., 1987—, chmn. dept. bus. adminstrn., 1988—; prof. acctg. Santa Monica (Calif.) Coll., 1987—; mgmt. cons. L.P. Assocs. Mfg. Co., Los Angeles, 1981—; mng. dir. Barrington Enterprises, Los Angeles; prof. Santa Monica (Calif.) Coll., 1987. Author/translator: Accounting/Auditing, 1975. Mem. NEA, Internat. Fedn. Bus. Edn., Am. Mgmt. Assn., Am. Acctg. Assn., Faculty Assn. Calif. C.C.s, Am. Fedn. Tchrs., Calif. Tchrs. Assn., Am. Entrepreneur Assn., Nat. Assn. Realtors, Am. Assn. Pub. Accts., Calif. Assn. Bus. Educators, Calif. Assn. Realtors, Nat. Soc. Pub. Accts., Calif. Bus. Edn. Assn., Internat. Fedn. Bus. Edn., Inst. Mgmt. Accts., UCLA Alumni Assn. (life), Alpha Kappa Psi.

LARK, M. ANN, management consultant, strategic planner, naturalist; b. Denver, Feb. 28, 1952; d. Carl Eugene and Arlena Elizabeth (Bashor) Epperson; m. Larry S. Lark, Apr. 1, 1972 (div. 1979). Asst. corp. sec., savs. dir. Imperial Corp. dba Silver State Savs. & Loan, Denver, 1972-75; client svcs. mgr. 1st Fin. Mgmt. Corp., Englewood, Colo., 1977-81; regional account mgr. Ericsson Info. Systems, Chatsworth, Calif., 1981-82; ind. cons. Denver, 1982-84; regional account mgr. InnerLine/Am. Banker, Chgo., 1984-85; chief info. officer Security Pacific Credit Corp., San Diego, 1985-88; prin. The Genessee Group, Thousand Oaks, Calif., 1988—. Avocations: tennis, gardening, hiking, bicycling, writing, sketching. Home and Office: 1144 El Monte Dr Thousand Oaks CA 91362-2117

LARK, RAYMOND, artist, art scholar; b. Phila., June 16, 1939; s. Thomas and Bertha (Lark) Crawford. Student, Phila. Mus. Sch. Art, 1948-51, Los Angeles Trade Tech. Coll., 1961-62; B.S., Temple U., 1961; L.H.D., U. Colo., 1985. Ednl. dir. Victor Bus. Sch., Los Angeles, 1969-71; public relations exec. Western States Service Co., Los Angeles, 1968-70; owner, mgr. Raymond Lark's House of Fine Foods, Los Angeles, 1962-67; exec. sec. to v.p. Physicians Drug and Supply Co., Phila., 1957-61; lectr. L.A. Trade Tech. Coll., 1973, Compton (Calif.) Coll., 1972, Nat. Secs. Assn., Hollywood, Calif., UCLA, U. Utah, Salt Lake City, 1993, numerous others. One-man shows include, Dalzell Hatfield Galleries, Los Angeles, 1970-86, Arthur's Gallery Masterpieces and Jewels, Beverly Hills, Calif., 1971, Dorothy Chandler Pavillion Music Center, L.A., 1974, Honolulu Acad. Arts, 1975, UCLA, 1983, U. Colo. Mus., 1984, Albany State Coll. Art Gallery, Albany, Ga., 1988, Utah Mus. Fine Arts, Salt Lake City, 1989, Mind's Art Gallery, Dickinson U., Dickinson, N.D., 1989, Trinton Mus. Art, Santa Clara, Calif., Greenville (N.C.) Mus. of Art, 1993, Springfield (Mo.) Art Mus., 1995, Washington County Museum of Fine Arts, Hagerstown, Md., 1996; The Peninisula Fine Arts Center, Newport News, Va. others; group exhbns. include, Smithsonian Instn., 1971, N.J. State Mus., Trenton, 1971, Guggenheim Mus., N.Y.C., 1975, Met. Mus. Art, 1976, La Galerie Mauffe, Paris, 1977, Portsmouth (Va.) Mus., 1979, Ava Dorog Galleries, Munich, W. Ger., 1979, Accademia Italia, Parma, 1980, Ames Art Galleries and Auctioneers, Beverly Hills, 1980, Le Salon des Nations at Centre International d'Art Contemporain, Paris, 1983; represented in permanent collections, Library of Congress, Ont. Coll. Art, Toronto, Mus. African and African Am. Art and Antiquities, Buffalo, Carnegie Inst., numerous others; art commns. for TV and film studios include, All in the Family, Carol Burnett Show, Maude, The Young and the Restless, Universal City Studios, Palace of the Living Arts, Movie Land Wax Mus.; author works in field; author and contbr. more than 50 scholarly treatises on art, edn. and the hist. devel. of Black Ams., chpts. to encyclopedias and textbooks, articles to jours., introductions to mus. exhbn. catalogues. Recipient gold medal Acad. Italia, 1980, also numerous gold medals and best of show awards, 3 presdl. proclamations; award Internat. Platform Assn.; Dr. Raymond Lark Day proclaimed by State of Md., 1994; grantee Nat. Endowment Arts, ARCO Found., Colo. Humanities Program, Adolph Coors Beer Found. Mem. Art West Assn. (pres. 1968-70). Address: PO Box 76169 Los Angeles CA 90076-0169 *I was telling people that I was Black, proud, and beautiful long before it became fashionable to be very dark. I never felt, "I am the greatest." However, I never had an inferiority complex. I always knew that I had God-given talent, character, and good common sense. In addition, I have always had great confidence in God and in myself. While I am not a soothsayer and never will be a braggart, I knew my art would be recognized. For whatever recognition I have received, I have worked extremely hard and have paid my dues.*

LARKAM, PETER HOWARD, electric utility executive, entrepreneur; b. Austin, Tex., Jan. 27, 1962; s. Charles Wilbur and Beverley Jane (McCosham) L.; m. Sandra Kay Freund, Dec. 27, 1991; children: William Charles, Matthew Alexander. BSChemE, U. Tex., 1986; BA in Mgmt. Engring., Claremont McKenna Coll., 1987; MBA, U. Tex., 1995. Registered profl. engr., Tex. Mgr. customer engring. svcs. Lower Colo. River Authority, Austin, Tex., 1986—; distributor Success Motivation Inst., Austin, 1990—; owner Achievement Concepts Engring. Scis., Austin, 1990—; dealer Achievement Rsch. and Verification Systems, Inc., Albuquerque, 1992—. Alumnus Leadership Austin, 1990-91, John Ben Shepperd Pub. Leadership Forum, Austin, 1989; steering com. Austin Adopt-a-Sch. Employers Support Parenting, Austin, 1991; co-chair edn. com. Teen Leadership Austin, 1995—, Austin Symphony Orch. Vol. Ushers, 1973—. Named Outstanding Young Men of Am., 1987-90, Outstanding Vol., Lower Colo. River Authority, 1989. Mem. NSPE, Internat. Platform Assn., Jaycees (pres. Austin chpt. 1989-90), Toastmasters (pres. West Austin II chpt. 1992, mentor Lake Austin chpt. 1993—), Project Mgmt. Inst. Avocations: pilot, scuba diving, triathlons, reading. Home: PO Box 50062 Austin TX 78763-0062

LARKIN, ALFRED SINNOTT, JR., newspaper editor; b. Boston, May 13, 1947; s. Alfred Sinnott and Lillian Louise (Brunswick) L.; children: Kristin, Jessica, Hannah, Matthew. Reporter Boston Herald, 1968-72; reporter Boston Globe, 1972-74, asst. met. editor, 1974-76, reporter, 1977-81, Sunday mag. editor, 1981-82, asst. mng. editor local news, 1982-86, dep. mng. editor, 1986-88, mng. editor Sunday edition, 1988-90, mng. editor adminstrn., 1990—. Nieman fellow Harvard U., 1977. Office: Boston Globe 135 Morrissey Blvd Boston MA 02107

LARKIN, BARBARA MILLS, federal agency administrator; b. Dubuque, Iowa. BA magna cum ladue, Clarke Coll., 1973; JD with distinctions, U. Iowa, 1977. Bar: Iowa, N.C., D.C. Coord. Blouin for Congress Com., 1974; ptnr. Sanford, Adams, McCullough and Beard, Raleigh, N.C.; cons., press sec. to the Mondale-Ferraro campaign, 1984, advisor to Senator Terry Sanford, 1986, chief counsel, fgn. policy advisor to Senator Terry Sanford, 1986-92; dep. asst. sec. legis. affairs U.S. Dept. State, Washington, 1993-96, asst. sec. for legis. affairs, 1996—. Legis. asst. Dem. rep. Michael T. Blouin, Iowa, 1974-75, coord. Blouin for Congress com., 1974; advisor Senator Sanford, 1986; cons., press sec. Mondale-Ferraro campaign, N.C. Democrat. Office: Legis Affairs 2201 C St NW Washington DC 20520*

LARKIN, BARRY LOUIS, professional baseball player; b. Cin., Apr. 28, 1964; m. Lisa Davis. Student, U. Mich., 1982-85. Baseball player Cincinnati Reds, 1985—. First baseball player twice named MVP of Big Ten Athletic Conf.; two-time All-Am. honors; named MVP of National League, 1995, Rookie of Yr. and to All-Star team, 1988-95, to Topps' Triple-A All-Star team, 1986, All-Star teams by Sporting News, 1988-92, 94-95, AP, 1990, UPI, 1990, Maj. League Baseball, 1988-91, 93, to N.L. Silver Slugger team Sporting News, 1988-92, 95; recipient Gold Glove award, 1994-96. Achievements include mem. U.S. Olympic Baseball Team, 1984, World Series Team, 1990. Office: Cin Reds Cinergy Field Cincinnati OH 45202-3590*

LARKIN, DONALD WAYNE, clinical psychologist; b. Kingsport, Tenn., June 23, 1947; s. Clarence K. and Frankie E. (Fields) L.; m. Sharon Sue Marsh, Oct. 21, 1966 (div. Mar. 1989); 1 child, Doni Suzanne. BS in Psychology and Math., East Tenn. State U., 1980; MS in Clin. Psychology, Nova U., Ft. Lauderdale, Fla., 1982, PhD, 1987. Lic. clin. psychologist, Tenn. Psychology intern Miami VA, 1983-84; electrician, computer technician Tenn. Eastman Co., Kingsport, 1965-80; therapist Clin. Psychology Inst., Ft. Lauderdale, 1984-86; instr. Nova U., 1982-86; clin. psychologist Johnson City (Tenn.) Med. Ctr. Optifast Program, 1989-90; assoc. staff psychologist Woodridge Psychiat. Hosp., Johnson, 1987-93; clin. psychologist Fairview Assocs., Johnson, 1987—, clin. dir., 1989-93; clin. dir. Woodridge Psychiat. Hosp., Johnson City, 1993—; clin. asst. prof. Quillen Coll. Medicine, Johnson City, 1988—; adj. faculty East Tenn. State U., Johnson City, 1987—. Mem. Hawkins County Bd. Edn., Rogersville, Tenn., 1978-80. Mem. Am. Psychol. Assn., Tenn. Psychol. Assn., Inter-Mountain Psychol. Assn., Psi Chi, Kappa Mu Epsilon. Avocations: running, jazz, hiking. Office: Woodridge Hosp 403 N State Of Franklin Rd Johnson City TN 37604-6034

LARKIN, EDWARD COLBY, securities analyst, financial services company executive; b. Evanston, Ill., Jan. 6, 1951; s. Edward Tyrus and Ethel (Colby) L.; m. Teresa Mary Berger, Apr. 21, 1978; children: Sean, Brian, Trent. BS, U. Colo., 1973; MBA, U. Denver, 1974. Fin. analyst, supr. Nat. Assn. Securities Dealers, Denver, 1975-80; v.p. corp. fin. Wall Street West, Englewood, Colo., 1980-86, Richard Christman Lavigne, Inc., Seattle, 1986-87; exec. v.p., dir. rsch., chief fin. officer Cohig & Assocs., Denver, 1987—, pres., 1995—. Office: Cohig & Assocs 6300 S Syracuse Way Ste 430 Englewood CO 80111-6724

LARKIN, EUGENE DAVID, artist, educator; b. Mpls., June 27, 1921; s. John Peter and Martha Lavinia (Vandevere) L.; m. Audrey Jean Krueger, Jan. 29, 1947; children: Andrew, Alan. BA, U. Minn., 1946, MA, 1949. Mem. faculty dept. art Kans. State Coll., Pittsburg, 1949-54; head printmaking dept., chmn. divsn. fine arts Mpls. Sch. Art, 1954-69; prof. design dept. U. Minn., St. Paul, 1969—, prof. emeritus design, housing and apparel, 1991—. One man exhbns. include, Mpls. Inst. Arts, 1957, 60, 68, Syracuse U., 1962, Walker Art Center, Mpls., 1967, New Forms Gallery, Athens, Greece, 1967, U. Kans., 1972, Macalester Coll., 1974, U. Minn., St. Paul, 1973, 78, 87, 91; group exhbns. include, Phila. Printmakers Club, 1966, 20 American Artists, Geneva, Switzerland, 1964, Big Prints, N.Y. U., 1968, Midwestern Printmakers, Walker Art Center, 1973, Cabo Frio Internat. Print Biennial, Brazil, 1983, Nat. Works on Paper, Minot State Coll., 1986, 17th Annual Works on Paper SW State U., San Marcos, Tex., 4th Annual North Coast Coll. Soc. Exhbn., Hiram Coll., Hudson, Ohio, 1988, 20th Annual Works on Paper Dulin Nat. Knoxville, Knoxville Mus. Art, 1988, Paepcke Meml. Bldg. Gallery, 1993, Aspen Inst. and Music Assoc. of Aspen, 1993; represented in permanent collections, Mus. Modern Art, N.Y.C., Nat. Mus. S.Africa, Capetown, Library Congress, Chgo. Art Inst., Mpls. Inst. Arts, U. Minn. Gallery, Des Moines Art Center, U. Tenn., Kans. State Tchrs. Coll., Minn. Mus. Art, Nat. Collection Fine Arts, Smithsonian Instn; author: Design: The Search for Unity, 1988. Recipient juror's award Rockford Internat. Print and Drawing Biennale, 1983. Mem. Coll. Art Assn. Am. Home: 64 Groveland Ter Minneapolis MN 55403-1103

LARKIN, JOAN, poet, English educator; b. Boston, Apr. 16, 1939; d. George Joseph and Celia Gertrude (Rosenberg) Moffitt; m. James A. Larkin, Dec. 23, 1966 (div. 1969); 1 child, Kate. BA, Swarthmore Coll., 1960; MA, U. Ariz., 1969. Asst. prof. English CUNY-Bklyn. Coll., 1969-94, ret., 1994, adj. faculty MFA program, 1997—; assoc. faculty MFA program Goddard Coll., 1994-96; mem. guest faculty poetry writing Sarah Lawrence Coll., Bronxville, N.Y., 1984-86, fall 1988, spring 1997; vis. instr. Manhattan Theatre Club, Oneonta, Gainesville, Tenants Harbor and Cummington workshops; poet-in-residence Writers Community, Manhattan, West Side YMCA. Author: (poems) Housework, 1975, A Long Sound, 1986, Cold River, 1997, (rec. poetry reading) A Sign I Was Not Alone, 1980; co-editor: Gay and Lesbian Poetry in Our Time: An Anthology, 1988 (Lambda Lit. award 1988), Amazon Poetry, 1975, Lesbian Poetry, 1981; editor: The Women Writers Calendar, 1982, 83, 84; contbr. poems to periodicals including Am. Poetry Rev., Conditions, Ms., Paris Rev., Sinister Wisdom, The Village Voice, Aphra, Endymion, The Lamp in the Spine, Global City Rev., Am. Rev., Genesis West, Sojourner. NEA fellow in poetry, 1987-88, 96, N.Y. Found. for Arts fellow in poetry, 1987-88; Creative Artists Pub. Svc. Program grantee N.Y. State Coun. Arts, 1976, 80; Mass. Cultural Coun. grantee in playwriting, 1995.

LARKIN, LEE ROY, lawyer; b. Oklahoma City, Aug. 11, 1928; s. William Patrick and Agnes (Matthis) L.; m. Mary Jane Langston, Apr. 17, 1965; children—James William, John Patrick (dec.). BS, Oklahoma A&M U., Stillwater, 1950; MA, Vanderbilt U., 1952; LLB, William Mitchell U., St. Paul, 1959. Bar: Minn. 1959, Tex. 1963, D.C. 1963. Economist U.S. Dept. Agr., Washington, 1953; economist, lawyer Pillsbury, Mpls., 1953-62; ptnr. Harris & Larkin, Houston, 1963-65; sr. ptnr. Andrews & Kurth, Houston, 1966-94; retired, 1994; speaker Continuing Legal Edn. Officer Sharpstown Civic Assn., Houston, 1966-95; elder St. Philip Presbyn. Ch., Houston; moderator Presbytery of New Covenant, Houston, 1980. Served to capt. USAR, 1951-58. Fellow Tex. Bar Found., Houston Bar Found.; mem. ABA, State Bar Tex., Houston Bar Assn., Am. Intellectual Property Assn., Houston Intellectual Property Assn., Riverbend Country Club, Houston Club, Rotary (pres. 1978-79), Delta Theta Phi. Avocations: golf; tennis; ranching. Home: 3725 Wickersham Ln Houston TX 77027-4013

LARKIN, LEO PAUL, JR., lawyer; b. Ithaca, N.Y., June 19, 1925; s. Leo Paul and Juanita (Wade) L. AB, Cornell U., 1948, LLB, 1950. Bar: N.Y. 1950, U.S. Dist. Ct. (so. dist.) N.Y. 1951, U.S. Supreme Ct. 1967. Assoc., ptnr., sr. counsel Rogers & Wells and predecessor firms, N.Y.C., 1950—. Served with U.S. Army, 1943-45. Mem. ABA, Fed. Bar Coun., Univ. Club, Sky Club, Delta Phi, Phi Beta Kappa, Phi Kappa Phi, Theta Delta Phi. Home: 200 E 66th St Apt B-1804 New York NY 10021-6728 Office: Rogers & Wells 200 Park Ave Ste 5200 New York NY 10166-0005

LARKIN, MICHAEL JOHN, newspaper editor, journalist; b. Boston, Sept. 27, 1950; s. Alfred Sinnott and Lillian Louise (Brunswick) L.; m. Sarah Jane Wood, July 6, 1970 (div. 1985); children—Jonathan Michael, Joshua Stuart; m. Alison Rose Biggs, June 1, 1986. B.A. in English, U. Mass., 1973. News copy editor Boston Globe, 1974-76, sports copy editor, 1976-80, asst. bus. editor, 1980-82, Sunday editor, 1982, mag. editor, 1982-85, living/arts editor, 1985-89, sr. asst. met. editor zoned editions, 1989-92, Sunday editor, 1992-95; asst. mng. editor, 1995—. Office: Boston Globe PO Box 2378 Boston MA 02107-2378

LARKIN, MOSCELYNE, retired artistic director, dancer; b. Miami, Okla., Jan. 14, 1925; d. Reuben Frances and Eva (Matlogova) L.; m. Roman Jasinski, Dec. 24, 1943 (dec. 1991); 1 child, Roman. Studied with Serge Grigorieff, Lubov Tchernicheva, Mikhail Mordkin, Anatole Vilzak, Vincenzo Celli; hon. doctorate of Fine Arts, U. of Tulsa, 1991. With Ballet Russe, 1941-47, Ballet Russe de Monte Carlo, 1948-52; prima ballerina Radio City Music Hall, N.Y.C., 1951-52; with Alexandra's Danilova's Great Moments of Ballet touring co., 1952-54; established Tulsa Sch. Ballet, from 1956; artistic dir. Tulsa Civic Ballet, 1956-76; artistic dir. Tulsa Ballet Theatre, 1976-91, artistic dir. emerita, 1991—. Dance performances include Mikhail Forkine's Paganini and Les Sylphides; Leonid Massine's Le Beau Danube, Symphonie Fantastique, Les Presages; George Balanchine's Concerto Barocco, Night Shadow, Cotillion; Agnes De Mille's Rodeo; David Lichine's Graduation Ball; Michael Maule's The Carib Peddler. Recipient Dance Mag. award, 1988, Gov. Arts award, 1988, Rogers State Coll. Lynn Riggs award, 1989, award of Am.,1992; named to Tulsa Press Clubb Headliner award, Okla. Hall of Fame, 1979, Tulsa Hall of Fame, 1988, Okla. Womens Hall of Fame, 1993, and numerous others. Mem. Southwestern Regional Ballet Assn. (exec. v.p. 1963-76), Nat. Assn. Regional Ballet. Home: 5414 S Gillette Ave Tulsa OK 74105-6434 Office: Tulsa Ballet Theatre 4512 S Peoria Ave Tulsa OK 74105-4563

LARKIN, WILLIAM VINCENT, JR., service company executive; b. N.Y.C., July 19, 1953; s. William Vincent and Gloria Ann (Stone) L.; m. Margaret Catherine Gunn, Nov. 12, 1988; children: William Vincent III, Jeremy Stone. AB cum laude, Harvard U., 1976; M Pub. and Pvt. Mgmt., Yale U., 1980. Intern White House, 1975; staff acct. Price Waterhouse & Co., N.Y.C., 1976-78; mktg. asst. AMF Ben Hogan Co., Ft. Worth, 1980-81; asst. to pres. AMF Biol. & Diagnostic Co., Seguin, Tex., 1981-82; mktg. mgr. AMF Tuboscope, Houston, 1982-83, mgr. mill divsn., 1983-84; v.p. Tuboscope Inc., Houston, 1984-91; pres., COO Tuboscope Vetco Internat., Houston, 1991-93, pres., CEO, 1993-96; pres., COO Galtney Group, Inc., Houston, 1996—. Bd. dirs. Family Svc. Ctr. Mem. Young Pres.'s Orgn., Petroleum Equipment Suppliers Assn., Nomads, Yale Sch. Mgmt. Alumni Assn. (chmn. nominating com. 1980-82), A.D. Club (Cambridge, Mass.), Harvard Club (N.Y.C.), Yale Club (Houston). Republican. Episcopalian. Avocations: woodworking, golf, tennis. Home: 360 Westminster Dr Houston TX 77024-5608 Office: Galtney Group Inc 820 Gessner Rd Houston TX 77024

LARKS, JACK, forensic engineer, consultant; b. Chgo., Nov. 16, 1926; s. Israel David and Freida Rebecca (Morgenstern) L.; m. Norma Jean Colwell, Dec. 24, 1957; children: Terri Lynn, Kevin Jon. BSCE, MIT, 1952, MSCE, 1953; MEd, U. Houston, 1980. Registered profl. engr. Commd. 2d lt. U.S. Army, 1944, advanced through grades to lt. col., 1974, retired, 1975; supr. facilities STL/TRW, Cape Canaveral, Fla., 1957-66; assoc. prof. U. Houston, 1971-81; sr. design engr. Gulf Interstate Engring., Houston, 1981; supr. profl. devel. Hydril Co., Houston, 1982-83; constrn. mgr. Eastern Indemity Co. of Md., Houston, 1983-84; engring. designer Houston-Decco, Houston, 1985; safety cons. Larks Engring./Cons., Houston, 1985—; mem. Ansi Z359 Com., Houston, N.Y.C., 1988—. Contbr. articles to profl. jours. Fellow Nat. Acad. Forensic Engrs.; mem. Nat. Safety Engrs., World Safety Orgn. (bd. dirs. Tex. chpt. 1988-91, cert. safety exec.), Human Factors 2nd Ergonomics Soc., Scaffold Industry Assn., Am. Concrete Inst., Nat. Fire Protection Soc., Am. Welding Soc., Vets. of Safety, ASTM (various coms.), ANSI (fall protection coms.). Office: Larks Engring Cons 4762 Kingfisher Dr Houston TX 77035-4920

LARMORE, CATHERINE CHRISTINE, university official; b. West Chester, Pa., Apr. 8, 1947; d. Ashby Morton and Catherine (Burns) L.; m. Thomas Henry Beddall, May 2, 1994. BA, Earlham Coll., 1969. Tchr. Westtown (Pa.) Sch., 1969-75, asst. dean girls, 1971-73, dean girls, 1973-75; sec. U. Pa., Kennett Square, 1976-78; media coord. New Bolton Ctr U. Pa. Sch. Vet. Medicine, Kennett Square, 1978-83, dir. external affairs, 1983-88, dir. devel., 1988—. Mem. London Grove (Pa.) Twp. Planning Commn., 1990—, Chester County (Pa.) Women's Task Force, 1992-93, Chester County Women's Commn., 1994-95; sec. White Clay Watershed Assn., Landenburg, Pa., 1994-95; mem. White Clay Creek bi-state preserve adv. coun. Commonwealth of Pa., 1996—; chmn. steering com. for Ad Hoc Task Force on White Clay Creek, 1990. Recipient Take Pride in Pa. award Commonwealth of Pa., 1991. Mem. Nat. Soc. Fund Raising Execs., So. Chester County C. of C. (bd. dirs. 1989-91), Am. Horse Coun., Nat. Steeplechase and Hunt Assn., Thoroughbred Owners and Breeders Assn., Chester-Delaware County Farm Bur. Avocations: gardening and horticulture, equine carriage driving, environment and open space. Office: U Pa New Bolton Ctr 382 West Street Rd Kennett Square PA 19348

LARMORE, JENNIFER, mezzo-soprano; b. Atlanta, 1958. Debuted in La Clemenza di Tito, France; repertoire includes Rossini's Rosina, Cenerentola, Isabella, Handel's Giulio Cesare, Rinaldo, Monteverdi's Ottavia, Bellini'e Romeo, Bizet's Carmen; singer 5 solo CD's, 26 opera recordings. Office: ICM Foster Div/Caroline Woodfld 40 W 57th St New York NY 10019-4001

LARO, DAVID, judge; b. Flint, Mich., Mar. 3, 1942; s. Samuel and Florence (Chereton) L.; m. Nancy Lynn Wolf, June 18, 1967; children: Rachel Lynn, Marlene Ellen. BA, U. Mich., 1964; JD, U. Ill., 1967; LLM, NYU, 1970. Bar: Mich. 1968, U.S. Dist. Ct. (ea. dist.) Mich. 1968, U.S. Tax Ct. 1971. Ptnr., Winegarden Booth Shedd and Laro, Flint, Mich., 1970-75; sr. ptnr. Laro and Borgerson, Flint, Mich., 1975-86; prin. David Laro, P.C., Flint, 1986-92; apptd. judge U.S. Tax Ct., Washington, 1992—; of counsel Dykema Gossett, Ann Arbor, Mich., 1989-90; pres., chief exec. officer Durakon Industries, Inc., Ann Arbor, 1989-91, chmn., Lapeer, Mich., 1991—; chmn. Republic Bank, 1986—, vice chmn. Republic Bancorp, Inc., Flint, 1986—. Regent U. Mich., Ann Arbor, 1975-81; mem. Mich. State Bd. Edn., 1982-83; chmn. Mich. State Tenure Commn., 1972-75; commr. Civil Svc. Commn., Flint, Mich., 1984—. Mem. State Bar Mich., Phi Delta Phi. Republican. Office: US Tax Ct 400 2nd St NW Rm 217 Washington DC 20217-0001

LA ROCCA, ISABELLA, artist, educator; b. El Paso, Apr. 14, 1960; d. Remo and Alicia Estela (Gonzalez) La R. BA, U. Pa., 1984; MFA, Ind. U., 1993. Freelance photographer N.Y.C., 1986-90; assoc. instr. Ind. U., Bloomington, 1991-93; instr. Herron Sch. Art, Indpls., 1992; vis. asst. prof. Ind. U., 1994—; asst. prof. DePauw U., Greencastle, Omd/, 1994-95; vis. asst. prof. Bloomsburg (Pa.) U., 1995—. One-woman shows include Haas Gallery, Bloomsburg, Pa., 1996, Ctr. Photography Woodstock, N.Y., Moore Coll., Pa., 1994, Emison Art Ctr., Greencastle, Ind., 1996; exhibited in group shows at Bellevue Gallery, 1992, 494 Gallery, N.Y.C., 1993. Ind. U. CIC Minority fellow, 1990-91; Jewish Found. Edn. Women scholar, 1990; recipient Friends Photography Ferguson award, 1993.

LA ROCCA, RENATO V., oncologist, researcher; b. Cin., June 16, 1957; m. Margaret Carolyn Cauthron, Sept. 5, 1987; children: Alessandra, Marcello, Victoria, Chae. MS, Liceo Sci. Statale, Turin, Italy, 1976; postgrad., U. Padua, Italy, 1976-80; MD, Cornell U., 1982. Diplomate Nat. Bd. Med. Examiners, Am. Bd. Internal Medicine, Am. Bd. Oncology. Resident in internal medicine N.Y. Hosp.-Cornell Med. Ctr., N.Y.C., 1982-85; med. oncology fellow medicine br. Nat. Cancer Inst., Bethesda, Md., 1985-88, sr. investigator medicine br., 1988-90; pvt. practice Kentuckiana Med. Oncology Assocs., PSC, Louisville, 1990—; clin. assoc. prof. medicine U. Louisville Sch. Medicine and U. Ky. Coll. Medicine; cons. Jansen Rsch. Found.; guest rschr. med. br. Nat. Cancer Inst., NIH, Bethesda; mem. steering com. Ky. Cancer Pain Initiative; chmn. cancer com. Jewish Hosp., Louisville. Author: (chpts. in books) Molecular and Cellular Biology of Prostate Cancer, Molecular Foundations Oncology; contbr. articles to profl. jours.; patentee in field. Recipient USPHS Commendation medal, 1990, Leadership award Am. Cancer Soc., 1995. Fellow ACP; mem. Am. Soc. Clin. Oncology, Am. Assn. Cancer Rsch., Am. Cancer Soc. (v.p. Ky. divsn.), Am. Coll. Physician Inventors, Am. Pain Soc., Jefferson County Med. Soc., Ky. Oncology Soc., Ky. Med. Assn., Ind. Med. Assn., Alpha Omega Alpha. Avocations: sailing, computers, astronomy, skiing, political science. Office: Lara USA LLC 13707 Rutland Rd Goshen KY 40026-9771

LAROCCO, ELIZABETH ANNE, management information systems professional; b. Bethpage, N.Y., Feb. 15, 1957; d. Alfred Joseph and Teresa Lucille (Scalzo) Bott; m. Michael Gerard LaRocco, May 17, 1980. BBA, Hofstra U., 1979, postgrad., 1992. Programmer Computerland, Westbury, N.Y., 1980-82; software cons., propr. E.A. LaRocco, Ronkonkoma, N.Y., 1982-85; from bus. programmer to mgr. mgmt. info. sys. corp. applications NEC America, Inc., Melville, N.Y., 1984—. Mem. Huntington Twp. Art League. Mem. IEEE, NAFE, Assn. Computing Machinery. Roman

Catholic. Avocations: tennis, skiing, watercolor painting. Office: NEC Am Inc/MIS Div 8 Corporate Center Dr Melville NY 11747-3148

LAROCHE, ROGER RENAN, psychiatrist; b. St. Paul, July 12, 1960; s. Gerard Auguste and Carolyn Mae (Seese) L.; m. Elizabeth Ann Tollerud, June 25, 1988; children: Austin, Hope, Cordon. BA, Bethel Coll., St. Paul, 1982; MD, U. Minn., 1987. Diplomate Nat. Bd. Med. Examiners, Am. Bd. Psychiatry and Neurology, Am. Soc. Addiction Medicine, Geriatric Psychiatry, Addiction Psychiatry. Med. intern Hennepin County Med. Ctr., Mpls., 1987-88; resident dept. psychiatry Mayo Clinic Grad. Sch. Medicine, Rochester, Minn., 1988-91; fellowship addiction medicine dept. psychiatry Mayo Clinic Grad. Sch. Medicine, Rochester, 1991-92; med. dir. dept. psychiatry Bradford (Pa.) Regional Med. Ctr., 1992—; rotating med. student educator Mayo Med. Sch., 1987-92; contract forensic psychiatrist U.S. Bur. Prisons, Fed. Med. Ctr., Rochester, 19890-91; prin. investigator for carbamazepine in smoking cessation Mayo Clinic, Rochester, 1991-92, psychiatric rsch. com. cons., 1991-92; pvt. and consulting psychiatrist, Bradford, Pa., 1992—; staff sec.-treas. Bradford Regional Med. Ctr., 1995—, med. staff v.p., 1996. Contbr. articles to profl. jours. County del. Rep. Party Conv., Rochester, 1990. Recipient Medtronic Corp.'s Med. Fellow scholarship of excellence in leadership and acads., 1983, Acad. Writing Excellence award Mayo Clinic, 1991; Mayo Clinic Grad. Sch. Medicine grantee, 1991-92. Mem. AMA (resident physician sect. nat. del. 1990, 91), Am. Psychiat. Assn., Am. Soc. Addiction Medicine, Minn. Med. Assn. (del. ho. of dels. 1990, 91, resident physician sect. state governing officer 1990, 91), Pa. Med. Assn., Pa. Psychiat. Soc., Pa. Soc. Addiction Medicine, McKean County Med. Soc. Avocations: violist, vocal soloist, oil painting, weight training, distance biking. Home: 46 Stone Ave Bradford PA 16701-1050 Office: Med Arts Bldg 199 Pleasant St Bradford PA 16701-1098

LA ROCHELLE, PIERRE-LOUIS, civil engineering educator; b. Quebec, Que., Can., Aug. 20, 1928; s. Emile Joseph and Juliette Marie (Coulombe) LaR.; m. Rachel Grатia Bedard, July 11, 1958 (dec. Aug. 1991); children—Judith, Sophie, Anne. B.A., Seminaire De Quebec, Can., 1950; B.Sc. in Civil Engring., U. Laval, Quebec, 1954, M.Sc., 1956; Ph.D., U. London, 1960. Registered profl. engineer, Que. Asst. prof. engring. U. Laval, Quebec, 1960-63, head dept. civil engring., 1963-67, prof. engring., 1968-96, dir. grad. studies civil engring., 1992-94, prof. emeritus, 1997—; adj. prof. U. Laval, 1996-97; pres. Les Cons. PLR Inc.; cons. in geotech. engring., dam design and constrn. Hydro-Quebec, SNC, Golder, others, Can. Contbr. articles to profl. jours. Recipient Can. Geotech. Soc. Prize, 1975, R.F. Leggett award, 1977, Queen Elizabeth Jubilee's medal Can. Govt., 1978. Fellow Engring. Inst. Can.; mem. ASCE, ASTM (Hogentogler award 1985), Royal Soc. Can., Can. Acad. Engring., Internat. Com. on Landslides (pres. 1981-89), Yacht Club (Sillery, Que.; comdr. 1982). Avocations: sailing, skiing, golfing, music. Home and Office: 2528 Des Hospitalieres, Sillery, PQ Canada G1T 1V7

LAROCHELLE, RICHARD CLEMENT, tanning company executive; b. Lewiston, Maine, July 21, 1945; s. Paul H. and Jeannette D. (Jean) L.; children—Anne Marie, Paul, Christie, Marc, Peter. B.A., U. Maine, 1971; M.B.A., Northeastern U., 1976. Cert. mgmt. acct. V.p., treas. Nat. Tanning and Trading Corp., Peabody, 1976-79; exec. v.p. Hermann Loewenstein Inc., Johnstown, N.Y., 1980-82; pres. Irving Tanning Co., Hartland, Maine, 1982—, CEO, 1992—; bd. dirs. Fugua Enterprises, Inc., Hussey Seating Corp. Com. chmn. Boy Scouts Am., Johnstown, N.Y., 1981-82; trustee YMCA, Johnstown, 1982; treas. Boys/Girls Club, Waterville, Maine, 1985; co-chmn. Maine Govs. Internat. Adv. Bd., 1995—; bd. dirs. Mid-State Econ. Devel. Corp., 1995—, Maine Internat. Trade tr.; chmn. Colby Leadership Inst.; bd. advisors U. Maine Sch. Bus., 1995—. Served with USN, 1965-69. Mem. Leather Industries Am. (chmn. 1984-86, exec. com. 1982—), Footwear Industries Am. (bd. dirs. 1996—). Avocations: personal investing, personal computing. Home: PO Box 369 Hartland ME 04943-0369 Office: Irving Tanning Co Main St Hartland ME 04943

LAROCK, BRUCE EDWARD, civil engineering educator; b. Berkeley, Calif., Dec. 24, 1940; s. Ralph W. and Hazel M. L.; m. Susan E. Gardner, June 17, 1968; children: Lynne M., Jean E. BS in Civil Engring., Stanford U., 1962, MS in Civil Engring., 1963, PhD, 1966. Registered profl. engr., Calif. Asst. prof. U. Calif., Davis, 1966-72, assoc. prof., 1972-79, prof., 1979—; sr. vis. fellow U. Wales, Swansea, 1972-73; U.S. sr. scientist Tech. U., Aachen, Germany, 1986-87. Author: (with D. Newnan) Engineer-in-Training Examination Review, 3d edit., 1991; contbr. over 75 tech. articles to profl. jours. Mem. ASCE, Sigma Xi, Tau Beta Pi. Lutheran. Avocation: duplicate bridge. Office: U Calif Davis Dept Civil & Environ Engring Davis CA 95616-5294

LAROCK, TERRANCE EDMOND, health facility administrator; b. Detroit, Aug. 29, 1952; s. Wendell and Donna Jean (Elliott) LaR.; m. Bonnie Jo Campbell, July 21, 1979; 1 child, Andrew Thomas. A.A., Ohlone Jr. Coll., 1972; postgrad. Calif. State U.-Hayward, 1976, U. N.Y., 1984; B. Polit. Sci., San Jose State U., 1974. Project planner Gould Inc., Santa Clara, Calif., 1977-79; materials mgr. Stanford Assocs., Menlo Park, Calif., 1979, Delta Assocs., Milpitas, Calif., 1979-81, Masstor Systems, Sunnyvale, Calif., 1981-84; purchasing/planning mgr. Fairchild ATS, San Jose, Calif., 1984—; v.p. ops. REDIFAB, San Jose, 1984-86, v.p. USA ops. Prodstar America, 1986-89, San Jose Med. Ctr., 1990—; group v.p. purchasing Berlex Labs, Inc., Richmond, Calif., 1994—; mgr. Tandy Corp., San Jose, 1976-78; city mgr. Thrifty Rent-A-Car, San Francisco, 1975-76, Softbank Expos, 1996—. Author: Manufacturing Terms and Definition, 1978. Recipient Region 7 & 10 Excellent award, Am. Prodn. & Inventory Control, 1983, Edn. award, 1980, Membership award, 1979. Mem. Am. Prodn. and Inventory Control Soc. (region 10 edn., pres. 1980-81, v.p. bd. dirs. 1986-88), Purchasing Mgmt. Assn. Republican. Lutheran.

LA ROCQUE, EUGENE PHILIPPE, bishop; b. Windsor, Ont., Can., Mar. 27, 1927; s. Eugene Joseph and Angeline Marie (Monforton) LaR. BA, U. Western Ont., 1948; MA, Laval U., 1956. Ordained priest Roman Catholic Ch., 1952, consecrated bishop, 1974; asst. parish priest Ste. Therese Ch., Windsor, 1952-54; registrar, then dean men, lectr. Christ The King Coll., U. Western Ont., 1956-64; asst. spiritual dir. St. Peter's Sem., 1964-65; prin., dean King's Coll., 1965-68; pastor St. Joseph's Ch., Rivière-aux-Canards, Ont., 1968-70, Ste. Anne's Ch., Tecumseh, 1970-74; bishop of Alexandria-Cornwall, Ont., 1974—; dean Essex County, 1970-73; trustee Essex County Roman Cath. Separate Sch. Bd., 1972-74; 1st chmn. liaison com. Can. Jewish Congress Can. Coun. Chs. and Can. Cath. Conf. Bishops, 1977-84, mem. pro-life com., 1992-94; pres. Ont. Conf. Cath. Bishops, 1992-96; pres. Fedn. Couns. Priests of Can., 1973-74. Mem. KC (3d degree, chaplain Ont. 1977-87). Address: 200 Montreal Rd, Box 1388, Cornwall, ON Canada K6H 5V4 *Belief in God, who creates my unique human life and has a loving plan and concern for each of his children, sustains me amidst the strains, challenges and turmoils of life.*

LA ROCQUE, GENE ROBERT, retired naval officer, government official, author; b. Kankakee, Ill., June 29, 1918; s. Edward and Lucile (Eddy) La R.; m. Sarah Madeline Fox, Apr. 17, 1945 (dec. Apr. 1978); children: John C., James C., Annette D.; m. Lillian Anna Kerekes Danchik, Nov. 16, 1979 (dec. Apr. 1994); stepchildren: Howard Alan Danchik, Roger Lewis Danchik. Student, U. Ill., 1936-40; B.A., George Washington U., 1958; hon. doctorate, Hanyang U., Seoul, Korea, 1975, Haverford Coll., 1987. Commd. ensign U.S. Navy, 1941, advanced through grades to rear adm., 1965, comdr. Task Group in 6th Fleet Mediterranean Sea, 1965-66, mem. faculty Naval War Coll., 1951-53; dir. Inter-Am. Def. Coll. U.S. Navy, Washington, 1969-72; ret. U.S. Navy, 1972; pres. Ctr. Def. Info., Washington, 1972—. Decorated Bronze Star with combat V, Legion of Merit; Abdon Calderon 1st Class (Ecuador); Order Naval Merit (Brazil); Mil. Order Gt. Star (Chile). Mem. Naval Inst. Clubs: New York Yacht, Cosmos (Washington). Home: 3140 Davenport St NW Washington DC 20008-2244 Office: Center For Defense Info 1500 Massachusetts Ave NW Washington DC 20005-1821*

LAROCQUE, JUDITH ANNE, federal official; b. Hawkesbury, Ont., Can., Sept. 27, 1956; d. Jean Olier Edouard and Elizabeth Robina (Murray) LaR.; m. Andre Roland Lavoie, Mar. 15, 1991. BA with honours, Carleton U., Ottawa, Ont., 1979, MA, 1992. Notary Pub., Ont. Adminstrv. asst. Internal Audit Directorate, Pub. Svc. Commn., Ottawa, 1979; writer, researcher Prime Min.'s Office, Ottawa, 1979; spl. asst. Office Leader of Opposition, Ottawa, 1980-82; com. clk. coms. and pvt. legis. br. Can. Ho. of Commons, Ottawa, 1982-84, legis. asst. to Govt. House leader, 1984-85, head of House Bus. Office of Govt. House Leader, 1985-86; pres. Queen's Privy Coun. for Can. and min. responsible for regulatory affairs, Ottawa, 1985-86; exec. asst. to min. justice and atty. gen. Can., Ottawa, 1986-89; chief staff Office Leader Govt. in Senate and min. responsible for fed.-provincial rels., Ottawa, 1989-90; sec. to gov. gen. and herald chancellor Govt. House, Ottawa, 1990—; sec. Gen. Order Can., Order Mil. Merit. Fellow Heraldry Soc. Can. (hon.). Office: Govt House, 1 Sussex Dr, Ottawa, ON Canada K1A 0A1

LAROCQUE, MARILYN ROSS ONDERDONK, writer, public relations consultant; b. Weehawken, N.J., Oct. 14, 1934; d. Chester Douglas and Marion (Ross) Onderdonk; B.A. cum laude, Mt. Holyoke Coll., 1956; postgrad. N.Y. U., 1956-57; M. Journalism, U. Calif. at Berkeley, 1965; m. Bernard Dean Benz, Oct. 5, 1957 (div. Sept. 1971); children: Mark Douglas, Dean Griffith; m. 2d, Rodney C. LaRocque, Feb. 10, 1973. Jr. exec. Bonwit Teller, N.Y.C., 1956; personnel asst. Warner-Lambert Pharm. Co., Morris Plains, N.J., 1957; editorial asst. Silver Burdett Co., Morristown, 1958; self-employed as pub. rels. cons., Moraga, Calif., 1963-71, 73-77; pub. rels. mgr. Shaklee Corp., Hayward, 1971-73; pub. rels. dir. Fidelity Savs., 1977-78; exec. dir. No. Calif. chpt. Nat. Multiple Sclerosis Soc., 1978-80; v.p. pub. rels. Cambridge Plan Internat., Monterey, Calif., 1980-81; sr. account exec. Hoefer-Amidei Assocs., San Francisco, 1981-82; dir. corp. comms., dir. spl. projects, asst. to chmn. Cambridge Plan Internat., Monterey, Calif., 1982-84; dir. comms. Buena Vista Winery, Sonoma, Calif., 1984-86, asst. v.p. comms. and market support, 1986-87; dir. comms. Rutherford Hill Winery, St. Helena, Calif., 1987-88; pres. LaRocque Pub. Rels. and Pub. Affairs, Napa, Calif., 1988-91; pres. LaRocque Profl. Svcs., Inc., 1991-95; writer, pub. rels. cons., 1996—; instr. pub. rels. U. Calif. Extension, San Francisco, 1977-79. Mem. exec. bd., rep-at-large Oakland (Calif.) Symphony Guild, 1968-69, Napa County Landmarks, Inc.; co-chmn. pub. rels. com. Oakland Mus. Assn., 1974-75; cabinet mem. Lincoln Child Ctr., Oakland, 1967-71, pres. membership cabinet, 1970-71, 2d v.p. bd. dirs., 1970-71; bd. dirs. Calif. Spring Garden and Home Show, 1971-77, 1st Agrl. Dist., 1971-77, Dunsmuir House and Gardens, 1976-77; mem. Calif. State Rep. Cen. Com., 1964-66; v.p. Piedmont coun. Boy Scouts Am., 1977. Mem. U. Calif. Alumni Assn., Pub. Rels. Soc. Am. (chpt. dir. 1980-82; accredited), Sonoma Valley Vintners Assn. (dir. 1984-87), Internat. Wine and Food Soc. (Marin chpt.), San Francisco Mus. Soc., Smithsonian Assocs., Sonoma Valley C. of C. (bd. dirs. 1984-87), Napa County Landmarks Inc. (bd. dirs. 1993-94, mem. di Rosa Preserve vol. coun. 1997—), Am. Assn. Univ. Women (Napa Valley chpt.), Napa Valley Republican Women, Knights of the Vine (master lady 1985-90), Mount Holyoke Coll. Alumnae Club, Silverado Country Club, DAR (vineyard trails chpt.). Office: LaRocque Profl Svcs Inc 1800 Soscol Ave Napa CA 94559-1345

LAROSA, GIANNI, aerospace industry administrator; b. S. Biagio Platani, Italy, Jan. 22, 1937; came to U.S., 1954; s. Alfonso and Santa (Marino) LaR.; m. Maria Cappello, Jan. 6, 1958; children: Alfonso, Sandra, Claudio, Julio. Student, Cass Tech., 1962; diploma in art, Musée de Art Modern, Tonneins, France, 1993. Owner indsl./comml. food svc. equipment mfg. business Detroit, 1970-74; supr. aerospace industry, 1985—; presenter in field. Exhbns. include San Bernardino County (Calif.) Mus., 1992, San Clemente (Calif.) Art Fest, 1992, Paris City Hall, 1993, Modern Art Mus. Unet, Tonneins, France, 1993, Soho Internat. Art Competition, N.Y.C., 1993, Wirtz Gallery, Miami, 1993, Bower Mus., Orange County, Calif., 1995; represented in permanent collection at Modern Art du Unet, Bordeaux, France; discovery and write theory on the illusion of color perception. Recipient award Fine Arts Inst., 1992, award Soho Internat. Competition, 1993, award Mayor of Paris, Internat. Art Competition, 1993, Gold medal Musee Des D'Beux Arts D'Unet, France, 1996; named Disting. Vis., Mayor of Miami, Fla., 1994. Home: 26641 Domingo Dr Mission Viejo CA 92692-4114

LAROSE, LAWRENCE ALFRED, lawyer; b. Lowell, Mass., Oct. 26, 1958; s. Alfred M. and Rita B. (Plunkett) L.; m. Janet G. Yedwab, Aug. 12, 1984. BA summa cum laude, Tufts U., 1980; JD magna cum laude, Georgetown U., 1983. Bar: N.Y. 1984. Assoc. Sullivan & Cromwell, N.Y.C., 1983-85, 87-90, Melbourne, Australia, 1985-87; assoc. Cadwalader, Wickersham & Taft, N.Y.C., 1990-92, ptnr., 1993—; vis. fellow Faculty of Law, U. Melbourne, 1986-87. Contbr. articles to profl. publs. Bd. dirs. Soho 20 Art Gallery. Mem. ABA, N.Y. State Bar Assn., N.Y. County Lawyers Assn., Assn. Bar City N.Y., Am. Soc. Internat. Law, Georgetown U. Nat. Law Alumni Bd. (exec. com., sec.), Down Town Assn. in City of N.Y., Phi Beta Kappa. Avocations: art collecting, art history. Office: Cadwalader Wickersham & Taft 100 Maiden Ln New York NY 10038-4818

LAROSE, ROGER, former pharmaceutical company executive, former university administrator; b. Montreal, Que., Can., July 28, 1910; s. Alfred and Anna (Contant) L.; m. Rita Dagenais, Aug. 10, 1936 (dec. Oct. 1960); 1 child, Louise Larose Cuddihy; m. Julienne Begin, Aug. 4, 1961. B.A., U. Montreal, 1929, B.Sc. in Pharmacy, 1932; Licentiate in Social, Polit., and Econ. Scis, 1934. Asst. prof. pharmacy U. Montreal, 1934; dean Faculty Pharmacy, 1960-65, vice rector, 1969-79; with Ciba Co. Ltd., Montreal, 1936-71; v.p. Ciba Co. Ltd., 1958-68, pres., 1968-71, dir., 1958-71; pres. Ciba-Geigy Can. Ltd., 1971-73, dep. chmn. bd., 1973-78, chmn. bd., 1978-82; vice chmn. bd., mem. exec. com. Bank Canadian Nat., 1969-80; mem. Sci. Council Can., 1966-71; pres. com. Sci. Council on Health Scis., 1969-73. Bd. dirs. Institute recherches cliniques de Montreal, 1968-95, pres. of found. 1995-96; bd. dirs. Hotel-Dieu de Montreal, 1969-79; pres. Hopital St. -Luc de Montreal, 1978-88; bd. govs. Can. Bankers Inst., 1973-80; pres. Montreal Symphony Orch., 1978-79, pres. and mng. dir., 1979-81; pres. Chamber Orch. I Musici de Montreal, 1984-88; bd. dirs. Que. Hosp. Assn. Decorated officer Order Can. Mem. Acad. Pharmacy (France) (hon.), Pharm. Soc. Gt. Britain (hon.), Can. Hosp. Assn. (bd. dirs. 1985-89, George Findlay Stephen award 1990), St.-Denis Club (Montreal). Home: 404-205 Côte Ste, Catherine Rd, Outremont, PQ Canada H2V 2A9

LA ROSSA, JAMES M(ICHAEL), lawyer; b. Bklyn., Dec. 4, 1931; s. James Vincent and Marie Antoinette (Tronolone) La R.; m. Gayle Marino, Sept. 20, 1958; children—James M., Thomas, Nancy, Susan. B.S., Fordham U., 1953, J.D., 1958. Bar: N.Y. 1958, U.S. Dist. Ct. N.Y. 1961, U.S. Supreme Ct. 1969. Pvt. practice law N.Y.C., 1958-62, 67-74, 76—; asst. U.S. atty. Eastern Dist. N.Y., Bklyn., 1962-65; ptnr. firm Lefkowitz & Brownstien, N.Y.C., 1965-67, La Rossa, Shargel & Fishetti, N.Y.C., 1974-76, La Rossa, Brownstein & Mitchell, N.Y.C., 1980-82, La Rossa, Axenfeld & Mitchell, N.Y.C., 1982-84, La Rossa, Cooper, Axenfeld, Mitchell & Bergman, N.Y.C., 1984-85; now ptnr. La Rossa, Mitchell & Ross, N.Y.C.; participant Debate on Legal Ethics Criminal Cts. Bar Assn. Queens County, N.Y., 1978, Criminal Trial Advocacy Workshop, Harvard U. Law Sch., 1978. Author: White Collar Crimes: Defense Strategies, 1977, Federal Rules of Evidence in Criminal Matters, 1977, White Collar Crimes, 1978. Served to 1st lt. USMC, 1953-55. Recipient Guardian of Freedom award B'nai B'rith, 1979, Career Achievement awardN.Y. Coun. Def. Lawyers, 1996. Mem. ABA, N.Y. State Bar Assn. (Criminal Law Practitioner of Yr. 1990), Fed. Bar Counsel, Assn. Bar City N.Y. Office: LaRossa Mitchell & Ross 41 Madison Ave New York NY 10010-2202

LAROUNIS, GEORGE PHILIP, manufacturing company executive; b. Bklyn., Mar. 19, 1928; s. Philip John and Helen (Cormentelou) L.; m. Mary G. Efthymiatou, Jan. 13, 1958; 1 child, Daphne H. B.E.E., U. Mich., 1950, postgrad. in Law; J.D., N.Y. U., 1954. Electronics engr. in research and devel. Columbia U. Electronics Research Lab., 1952-54; assoc. firm Pennie, Edmonds, Morton, Barrows & Taylor, N.Y.C., 1954-58; fgn. patent atty. Western Electric Co., N.Y.C., 1958-60; asst. dir. Bendix Internat., Paris, 1960; dir. licensing and indsl. property rights Bendix Internat., to 1974; v.p. staff ops. Bendix Europe, 1974-77; v.p. Bendix Internat. Fin. Corp.; v.p. Europe, Middle East and Africa Bendix Corp., Paris, 1977-82; pres. Bendix Internat. Cons. Corp., 1974-86; v.p., group exec. Allied Automotive, 1982-85; pres. Allied-Signal Fibers Europe S.A.; v.p. Allied-Signal Internat., 1985-93; dir. CopyTele, Inc., Delphi Soc., Am. Farm Sch., Greece. Served with U.S. Army, 1946-47. Chevalier French Legion of Honor. Mem. N.Y. Patent Bar Assn., Fed. Patent Bar Assn., Licensing Execs. Soc., Am. C. of C. in France and Greece (dir., pres., exec. com. European Coun.), Polo Club de Paris, Papagou Tennis Club (Athens), Tau Beta Pi, Eta Kappa Nu. Home: 15-17 A Tsoha St, Athens 11521, Greece

LAROUSSI, MOUNIR, electrical engineer; b. Sfax, Tunisia, Aug. 9, 1955; came to U.S., 1981; s. Habib and Manana (Jeloul) L.; m. Nicole Christine Mache, Aug. 28, 1986; children: Alexander Habib, Alyssa Jehan. BS in Elec. Engring., Tech. Faculty Sfax, 1979; MS in Elec. Engring., Nat. Sch. Radio and Elec., Bordeaux, France, 1981; PhD in Elec. and Computer Engring., U. Tenn., 1988. Grad. teaching asst. dept. elec. and computer engring. U. Tenn., Knoxville, 1983-85, rsch. asst. plasma sci. lab., 1984-88; asst. prof. Nat. Sch. Engring., Sfax, 1988-89; assoc. prof. Faculty Scis., Sfax, 1989-90; rsch. assoc. Plasma Sci. Lab. U. Tenn., Knoxville, 1990—. Asst. editor Physics Essays; contbr. articles to profl. jours. Recipient award Air Force Office Sci. Rsch., Washington, 1991, Advanced Tech. award Inventors Clubs of Am., 1996. Mem. IEEE (Cir. and Systems Soc., Nuclear and Plasma Scis. Soc., Antennas and Propagation Soc.), Sigma Xi (rsch. award 1987). Achievements include new method to heat plasmas with magnetic pumping; invention of new type of microwave tunable filters; co-invention of an atmospheric pressure glow discharge apparatus used to change the surface properties of fabrics and polymers; invention of apparatus that uses plasmas at atmospheric pressure to sterilize contaminated media; contbn. to new technique to hide aerospace objects from radar detection using plasma cloaking. Office: U Tenn Dept Elec Engring Knoxville TN 37996

LARPENTEUR, JAMES ALBERT, JR., lawyer; b. Seattle, Aug. 6, 1935; s. James Albert and Mary Louise (Coffey) L.; m. Hazel Marie Arntson, Apr. 23, 1965 (div. 1983); children: Eric James, Jason Clifford; 1 adopted child, Brenda Mon Fong; m. Katherine Annette Bingham, Nov. 8, 1986. BS in Bus., U. Oreg., 1957, LLB, 1961. Bar: Oreg. 1961, U.S. Dist. Ct. Oreg. 1961, U.S. Tax Ct. 1962, U.S. Ct. Appeals (9th cir.) 1962, U.S. Supreme Ct. 1965. Assoc. Schwabe Williamson & Wyatt, Portland, Oreg., 1961-69, ptnr., 1969-82, sr. ptnr., 1982—, mem. exec. com., 1989-92. Dir. exec. com. Portland Rose Festival Assn., 1975—, pres., 1987; ex-officio dir. Portland Visitors Assn., 1981—; bd. dirs., mem. exec. com. Providence Child Ctr. Found., 1983-94, chmn. exec. com., 1986-87; bd. dirs. Willamette Light Brigade, 1987—, Cath. Charities Portland, 1989-92; bd. dirs. Albertina Kerr Ctrs., 1996—. Mem. Oreg. Bar Assn. (editor, writer, speaker numerous continuing legal edn. programs, chmn. bus. law sect. 1986-87, real estate, estate planning, securities regulation sects.), Multnomah Athletic Club (pres. 1984), Univ. Club Portland, Waverley Country Club, Arlington Club, City Club of Portland. Avocation: golf. Home: 324 NW Lomita Ter Portland OR 97210-3321 Office: Schwabe Williamson & Wyatt 1211 SW 5th Ave Portland OR 97204-3713

LARR, PETER, banker; b. Indpls., Jan. 17, 1939; s. David and Marjorie Kathleen (Hearne) L.; m. Rosamond Holmes Woodfield, July 7, 1962; children—Alexia Aisha, Diana Kirsten, David Hearne. B.A., Princeton U., 1960. Asst. mgr. London and Beirut brs. Chase Manhattan Bank, 1961-67, v.p., div. exec. land transp., 1976-78, v.p., group exec. credit tng. and devel., 1978-80, v.p., div. exec. commodity fin., 1980-83; sr. v.p., bus. exec. nat. corr. banking Chase Manhattan Bank, N.Y.C., 1983-85; sr. v.p., exec. domestic instl. banking Chase Manhattan Bank, 1985-90, sr. v.p., risk asset rev. exec., 1990-97; sr. v.p. sr. credit and porfolio mgmt. exec. Asia Chase Manhattan Bank, Hong Kong, 1997—; mgr. dir. group credit officer Global Bank, 1997—. Assoc. vestry Christ Ch., Rye, N.Y., 1983-85; planning commr., City of Rye, 1992-95. Mem. Assn. Res. City Bankers (assoc., bank pay sys. com. 1984-90), Am. Bankers Assn. (chmn. corp. banking divsn. 1988-94), Robert Morris Assn. N.Y. (pres. 1994), Am. Yacht Club, Apawamis Club. Avocations: tennis, golf, genealogical rsch. Office: Chase Manhattan Bank, Chase Manhattan Tower, Sha Tin Hong Kong

LARRABEE, BARBARA PRINCELAU, retired intelligence officer; b. Oakland, Calif., Sept. 21, 1923; d. Paul and Mary Emilie (Rueger) Princelau; m. John Joseph Boyle, Oct. 21, 1950 (dec.); m. Donald Richard Larrabee, Nov. 2, 1996. BA, U. Calif., Berkeley, 1948. Intelligence officer CIA, Langley, Va., 1954-82. Bd. dirs. The Thift Shop, Washington, 1988-92; mem. Women's Bd. Columbia Hosp. for Women Med. Ctr., Washington, 1986—, mem. exec. com., 1989-91, 96—; mem. com. Washington Antiques Show, 1989—; active Rep. Womens Fed. Forum, Washington, League of Rep. Women of D.C., Inc. Recipient Cert. of Distinction CIA, 1982. Mem. Ctrl. Intelligence Retiree Assn., Assn. Former Intelligence Officers (bd. dirs. 1993—, v.p. 1997—), Nat. Press Club, Sulgrave Club, U. Calif. Berkeley Alumni Club of Washington (rec. sec. 1976-77, v.p. 1984-86), Sigma Kappa (v.p. No. Va. alumnae 1992-95, devel. com. Sigma Kappa Found., Inc., 1993-95). Episcopalian. Avocations: aerobics, needlework, travel. Home: 4956 Sentinel Dr #304 Bethesda MD 20816-3562

LARRABEE, DONALD RICHARD, publishing company executive; b. Portland, Maine, Aug. 8, 1923; s. Henry Carpenter and Marion (Clapp) L.; m. Mary Elizabeth Rolfs, Oct. 9, 1948 (dec. Feb. 1996); children—Donna Louise, Robert Rolfs; m. Barbara Princelau Boyle, Nov. 2, 1996. Student, Syracuse U., 1941-43. Reporter Portland Press Herald, 1941-43, Syracuse Post Standard, 1943; reporter Griffin-Larrabee News Bur., Washington, 1946-54; mng. editor Griffin-Larrabee News Bur., 1954-67, bur. chief, 1967-69, owner, 1969-78; dir. Washington office, State of Maine, 1978-89; dir. Nat. Press Bldg. Corp., 1973-85. Bd. dirs. Nat. Press Found., 1978—. Served with USAAF, 1943-45. Mem. Me. Soc. Washington (pres. 1950-53), Corrs. for Congl. Press Galleries (standing com. 1959-60), White House Corrs. Assn., Gridiron Club (Washington), Nat. Press Club (Washington) (sec. 1953-54, treas. 1966-67, chmn. bd. 1969, pres. 1973), Chevy Chase Club. Episcopalian. Home and Office: 4956 Sentinel Dr #304 Bethesda MD 20816-3562

LARRABEE, MARTIN GLOVER, biophysics educator; b. Boston, Jan. 25, 1910; s. Ralph Clinton and Ada Perkins Miller L.; m. Sylvia Kimball, Sept. 10, 1932 (div. 1944); 1 son, Benjamin Larrabee Scherer; m. Barbara Belcher, Mar. 25, 1944; 1 son, David Belcher Larrabee. B.A., Harvard, 1932; Ph.D., U. Pa., 1937; M.D. (hon.), U. Lausanne, Switzerland, 1974. Research asst., fellow U. Pa., Phila., 1934-40; assoc. to assoc. prof. U. Pa., 1941-49; asst. prof. physiology Cornell U. Med. Coll., N.Y.C., 1940-41; assoc. prof. Johns Hopkins U., Balt., 1949-63, prof. biophysics, 1963—. Contbr. articles to scientific jours. Mem. Am. Physiol. Soc., Biophys. Soc., Am. Soc. Neurochemistry, Internat. Neurochem. Soc., Nat. Acad. Scis., Soc. for Neurosci. (treas. 1970-75), Physiol. Soc. (asso., Eng.), Phi Beta Kappa. Clubs: Appalachian Mountain, Sierra, Mountain of Md. Rsch. on circulatory, respiratory and nervous systems of animals, especially on synaptic and metabolic mechanisms in sympathetic ganglia, 1934—; wartime research on oxygen lack, decompression sickness, nerve injury, infrared viewing devices, 1941-45. Home: Glen Meadows 11630 Glen Arm Rd Unit U46 Glen Arm MD 21057-9403 Office: Johns Hopkins U Biophysics Dept Baltimore MD 21218

LARREY, INGE HARRIETTE, jazz and blues freelance photographer; b. Freiburg, Germany, Jan. 21, 1934; came to U.S., 1983; d. Friedrich W. and Claerle I. (Mueller) Luger; m. Toni Halter, Aug. 5, 1967 (div. 1977); m. Louis A. Larrey, June 13, 1981. Student, N.Y. Inst. Photography, Saudi Arabia, 1983. Au Pair, Finland, 1952; Various assignments Federal Republic of Germany in Turkey, Spain, Belgium, England, 1956-82; audit student in journalism, photography U. Houston, 1984; substitute employee with consulate gen. Federal Republic of Germany, Houston, 1985; mem. visitors' rels. dept. Sueba USA Corp., German real estate co., Houston, 1985—. Works shown in more than a dozen exhbns., 1986-91; photographs in pvt. collections, in various publs., on cassette, record covers. Vol. Houston FotoFest, Women's Caucus for Art. Mem. Nat. Mus. of Women in the Arts (charter), Am. Image News Svc., Cultural Arts Coun. of Houston, Friends of Photography, Houston Ctr. for Photography, Jazz Heritage Soc. Tex., Milt Larkin Jazz Soc. (founding). Office: Sueba USA Corp 1800 West Loop S Ste 1323 Houston TX 77027-3211

LARRIMORE, RANDALL WALTER, manufacturing company executive; b. Lewes, Del., Apr. 27, 1947; s. Randall A. and Irene (Faucett) L.; m. Judith Cutright, Aug. 29, 1970; children: Jacob, Alex. BS, Swarthmore (Pa.) Coll., 1969; MBA, Harvard U., 1971. Product mgr. Richardson-Vick, Wilton, Conn., 1971-75; sr. engagement mgr. McKinsey & Co., N.Y.C., 1975-80; pres. Pepsi-Cola Italia, Rome, 1980-83, Beatrice Home Specialties, Inc. (name changed to Twentieth Century Cos., Inc.), Skokie, Ill., 1983-87;

pres., chief exec. officer MasterBrand Industries, Inc., 1988—; v.p. Am. Brands, Inc., 1988-95; chmn. Moen Inc., 1990—, chief exec. officer, 1990-94; chmn., chief exec. officer Master Lock Co., 1996—; adv. bd. Nat. Home Ctr. Show, 1990-93. Bd. dirs. Winnetka Congl. Ch., 1989-90; mem. hardware/home improvement coun. City of Hope, 1991—, pres. 1991-93; mem. adv. bd. Nat. Home Ctr. Show, 1990-93; commr. Landmark Preservation Coun., Winnetka, 1992—; bd. dirs. Hardware Group Assn., 1996—, Evanston Hosp. Corp., 1996—. Mem. Plumbing Mfg. Inst. (bd. dirs. 1991-93). Home: 830 Sheridan Rd Winnetka IL 60093-1929 Office: MasterBrand Industries Inc 510 Lake Cook Rd Deerfield IL 60015-5610 also: Am Brands Inc 1700 E Putnam Ave Box 819 Old Greenwich CT 06870

LARROCA, RAYMOND G., lawyer; b. San Juan, P.R., Jan. 5, 1930; s. Raymond Gil and Elsa Maria (Morales) L.; m. Barbara Jean Strand, June 21, 1952 (div. 1974); children—Denise Anne Sheehan, Gail Ellen, Raymond Gil, Mark Talbot, Jeffrey William. B.S.S., Georgetown U., 1952, J.D., 1957. Bar: D.C. 1957, U.S. Supreme Ct. 1960. Assoc., Kirkland, Fleming, Green, Martin & Ellis, Washington, 1957-64; ptnr. Kirkland, Ellis, Hodson, Chaffetz & Masters, Washington, 1964-67, Miller, Cassidy, Larroca & Lewin, Washington, 1967—. Served with arty. U.S. Army, 1948-49, to 1st lt., inf., 1952-54. Mem. ABA, D.C. Bar, Bar Assn. D.C., The Barristers. Republican. Roman Catholic. Clubs: Congl. Country (Potomac, Md.); University (Washington). Office: 2555 M St NW Ste 500 Washington DC 20037-1302

LARRY, R. HEATH, lawyer; b. Huntingdon, Pa., Feb. 24, 1914; s. Ralph E. and Mabel (Heath) L.; m. Eleanor Ketler, Sept. 10, 1938; children: David Heath, Dennis Ketler, Thomas Richard. A.B., Grove City Coll., 1934, LL.D., 1964; J.D., U. Pitts., 1937. Bar: Pa. 1937, D.C. 1937. Pvt. practice, 1937-38; atty. Nat. Tube Co., 1938-44, sec., dir., 1944-48; gen. atty. U.S. Steel Corp., Pitts., 1948-52; asst. gen. solicitor U.S. Steel Corp., 1952-58, adminstrv. v.p. labor relations, 1958-66, exec. v.p., asst. to chmn., 1966-69, vice chmn. bd., 1969-77; pres. N.A.M., 1977-80; of counsel Reed Smith Shaw & McClay, Washington, 1980—; dir. emeritus Textron, Inc. Bd. visitors U. Pitts. Sch. Law; trustee Grove City Coll.; former trustee Conf. Bd. Mem. Am. Iron and Steel Inst. Presbyn. Clubs: Met. (Washington); Economic (N.Y.C.); Gulf Stream Golf, Delray Beach Yacht, Gulf Stream Bath and Tennis, Little; Bermuda Run Country Club. Home: 4333 N Ocean Blvd Apt A53 Delray Beach FL 33483 also (summer): Bermuda Vlg # 3107 Advance NC 27006-9477

LARRY, WENDY, head coach women's basketball. Head coach Va. Wesleyan Coll., 1978-79, Arizonia, 1985-86, Cape Henry Collegiate H.S., Virginia Beach, 1987—; spkr. in field. Bd. dirs. Hampton Roads Habitat for Humanity. Mem. Kodak All-Am. Com. Office: Old Dominion U Athletic Admin Bldg Rm 124 Norfolk VA 23529

LARSEN, EDWIN MERRITT, retired chemist, educator; b. Milw., July 12, 1915; s. Howard Reynolds and Ella (Tees) L.; m. Kathryn Marie Behm, Aug. 17, 1946; children—Robert, Lynn, Richard. B.S., U. Wis., 1937; Ph.D., Ohio State U., 1942. Chemist Rohm & Haas, Phila., 1937-38; teaching asst. Ohio State U., 1938-42; group leader Manhattan Dist. polonium project Monsanto Chem. Co., 1943-46; mem. faculty dept. chemistry U. Wis.-Madison, 1942-43, 46-86, prof., 1958-86, assoc. chmn. dept., 1977-86; mem. Wis. Fusion Tech. Inst.; vis. prof. U. Fla., 1958; Fulbright lectr. Technische Hochschule, Vienna, Anorganische Institut, 1966-67. Author: Transitional Elements, 1965; contbr. articles to profl. jours. on synthesis in liquid aluminum trihalides and on role of chemistry in development of fusion energy. Fellow AAAS; mem. Am. Chem. Soc. (chmn. Wis. sect.), Am. Nuclear Soc., Wis. Acad. Scis., Arts and Letters, Sigma Xi (chmn. Wis. chpt.), Phi Lambda Upsilon. Home: 109 Standish Ct Madison WI 53705-5131

LARSEN, ELIZABETH B. (LIBBY LARSEN), composer; b. Wilmington, Del., Dec. 24, 1950; m. James Reece, Sept. 6, 1975; 1 child. BA, U. Minn., 1971, MA, 1975, PhD, 1978. co-founder Minn. Composers Forum. Composer operas Silver Fox, 1979, Tumbledown Dick, 1980, Clair de Lune, 1984, Frankenstein, The Modern Prometheus, 1990, A Wrinkle in Time, 1992, Mrs. Dalloway, 1993; orchestral and chamber works Symphony: Water Music, 1985, Four on the Floor, 1983, Overture: Parachute Dancing, 1983, Symphony No. 3, 1992, Ring of Fire, 1995, Blue Fiddler, 1995; choral and solo vocal works: Coming Forth into Day, 1986, Missa Gaia, 1992. RecipientDisting. Alumni award U. Minn., 1987, Catherine Steward award, 1991, Grammy award, 1994; named Exxon/Rockefeller composer in residence, Minn. Orch., 1983-87. Address: 2205 Kenwood Pky Minneapolis MN 55405-2329

LARSEN, ERIK, art history educator; b. Vienna, Austria, Oct. 10, 1911; came to U.S., 1947, naturalized, 1953; s. Richard and Adrienne (Schapringer de Csepreg) L.; m. Lucy Roman, Oct. 4, 1932 (dec. 1981); children: Sigurd-Yves, Annik-Eve., Erik-Claude (dec.); m. Anna Gallup Moses, May 8, 1982 (div. Sept. 1986); m. Katharina Ehling, Oct. 21, 1989. Candidate, Institut Superieur d'Histoire de l'Art et d'Archéologie, Brussels, 1931; Licentiate, Louvain (Belgium) U., 1941; Docteur en Archéologie et Histoire de l'Art, 1959; D. honoris causa, Janus Pannonius U., Pécs, Hungary, 1992. Dir., editor-in-chief on semi-ofcl. cultural mission for Belgian Govt. Pictura, art. mag., Brussels, Rio de Janeiro, Brazil, 1946-47; research prof. art Manhattanville Coll. of Sacred Heart, 1947-55; instr. CCNY, 1948-55; lectr, then vis. prof. Georgetown U., 1955-58, assoc. prof. fine arts, 1958-63, prof., 1963-67, head dept. fine arts, 1960-67; prof. history of art U. Kans., 1967-80, prof. emeritus, 1980—; dir. Center for Flemish Art and Culture, 1970-80; cons. old masters' paintings, guest-prof. U. Salzburg, Austria, 1988. Author: books, the most recent being La Vie, Les Ouvrages et Les Eleves de Van Dyck, 1975, Calvinistic Economy and 17th Century Dutch Art, 1979, Anton van Dyck, 1980, Rembrandt, Peintre de Paysages: Une Vision Nouvelle, 1983, Japanese edit., 1992; Seventeenth Century Flemish Painting, 1985, The Paintings of Anthony van Dyck, 2 vols., 1988, Jan Vermeer. Catalogo completo, 1996; contbr. numerous articles, revs. to profl. publs., newspapers. Mem. Kans. Cultural Arts Commn., 1971-73; mem. Kans. Cultural Arts Adv. Council, 1973-79. Served with Belgian Underground, 1942-45. Decorated knight's cross Order Leopold, knight's cross Order of Crown, officer Order Leopold (Belgium); officer Order of Rio Branco (Brazil); recipient prix Thorlet, laureate Inst. France, Académie des sciences morales et politiques, 1962; Internat. Hon. Citizen, New Orleans, 1989; named hon. Ky. col., 1977. Fellow Soc. Antiquaries of Scotland; mem. Appraisers Assn. Am., Association des Diplomés en Histoire de l'Art et Archéologie de L'Université Catholique de Louvain, Académie d'Aix-en Provence (France) (corr.), Académie de Mâcon (France) (asso.), Académie d'Alsace (France) (titular), Comité Cultural Argentino (hon.), Schweizerisches Institut fuer Kunstwissenschaft (Zurich, Switzerland), Academia di Belle Arti Pietro Vanucci (Perugia, Italy) (hon.), Royal Soc. Arts (London) (Benjamin Franklin fellow); correspondent-academician Real Academia de Bellas Artes de San Telmo (Malága, Spain), Real Academia de Bellas Artes de San Jorge (Barcelona, Spain), Accademia Tiberina (Rome), Académie Royale D'Archéologie de Belgique (fgn. assoc.). Home: 511 S Washington St Beverly Hills FL 34465-4312

LARSEN, GARY LOY, physician, researcher; b. Wahoo, Nebr., Jan. 10, 1945; s. Allan Edward and Dorothy Mae (Hengen) L.; m. Letitia Leah Hoyt, Dec. 22, 1967; children: Kari Lyn, Amy Marie. BS, U. Nebr., 1967; MD, Columbia U., 1971. Diplomate Am. Bd. Pediatrics, Am. Bd. Pediatric Pulmonology (chmn. 1990-92)/. Pediatric pulmonologist Nat. Jewish Ctr. for Immunology & Respiratory Medicine, Denver, 1978—; mem. faculty U. Colo. Sch. Medicine, Denver, 1978—, dir. sect. of pediatric pulmonary medicine, 1987—, prof. pediatrics, 1990—. Contbr. articles to prof. jours. Major M.C., U.S. Army, 1974-76. NIH med. rsch. grantee NIH, 1981—. Mem. AM. Thoracic Soc. (chmn. pediatric assembly 1987-88), Soc. Pediatric Rsch., Phi Beta Kappa, Alpha Omega Alpha, N.Y. Acad. Scis. Lutheran. Office: Nat Jewish Ctr Immun & Resp Med 1400 Jackson St Denver CO 80206-2761

LARSEN, GWYNNE E., computer information systems educator; b. Omaha, Sept. 10, 1934; d. Melvin and Vernetta (Allen) Bannister; m. John M. Larsen, June 8, 1958; children: Bradley Allen, Blair Kevin, Randall Lawrence. A in Bus. Adminstrn., Denver U., 1956, MBA, 1975, PhD, 1979; BS, Met. State Coll., 1971. Instr. Met. State Coll. Denver, 1979-81, asst. prof., 1981-85, assoc. prof., 1985-88, prof., 1989—, acting chair computer dept., 1991-92; book reviewer McGraw Hill, 1991, Harcourt Brace Jovanovich, 1991, Macmillan Pub. Co., 1993, Southwestern Pub. Co., 1993; presenter Mountain Plains Mgmt. conf., Denver, 1982, Rocky Mountain Bus. Expo, Denver, 1982, Red Rocks C.C., 1984, Colo.-Wyo. Acad. Sci. conf., 1985, Boulder, 1986, Colorado Springs, 1987; local coord. John Wiley & Sons, Denver, 1982, 83; panel chmn. on office automation Assn. for Computing Machinery, Denver, 1985; spkr. ASTD, 1986, Am. Pub. Works Assn., 1986; participant numerous presentations and confs. Author: (with others) Computerized Business Information Systems Workbook, 1983, Collegiate Microcomputer, 1992, (with Verlene Leeberg) Word Processing: Using WordPerfect 5.0, 1989, Word Processing: Using WordPerfect 5.1, 1991, First Look at WordPerfect 5.1, 1991, First Look at DOS, 1991, First Look at NetWare, 1992, Using WordPerfect for Windows, 1993, (with Marold and Shaw) Using Microsoft Works: An Introduction to Computing, 1993, Using Microsoft Works, An Introduction to Computing, 1993, First Look at WordPerfect 6.0 for Windows, 1994, Using WordPerfect 6.0 for Windows, 1994, Using Microsoft Works for Windows, An Introduction to Computing, 1996, Beyond the Internet, 1996, (with Marold) Using Microsoft Works 4.0, 1997; apptd. editl. bd. Jour. Mgmt. Sys., 1988, Jour. Microcomputer Sys. Mgmt., 1989, Info. Resources Mgmt. Jour., 1991; mem. editl. rev. bd. Jour. Info. Resources Mgmt. Sys., 1985—, Jour. Mgmt. Info. Sys., 1986—, Jour. Database Mgmt. Sys., Jour. Database Mgmt. Sys., 1987—, Jour. End User Computing, 1990—; contbr. articles to profl. jours. Mem. Info. Resources Mgmt. Assn., Colo.-Wyo. Acad. Scis., Office Automation Soc. Internat., Internat. Acad. for Info. Mgmt., panel part., 1995. Avocations: walking, aerobics, reading detective stories. Home: 8083 S Adams Way Littleton CO 80122 Office: Met State Coll Denver Campus Box 45 PO Box 173362 Denver CO 80217-3362

LARSEN, JONATHAN ZERBE, journalist; b. N.Y.C., Jan. 6, 1940; s. Roy Edward and Margaret (Zerbe) L.; m. Katharine Wilder, May 28, 1966; m. Jane Amsterdam, Aug. 31, 1985; 1 child, Edward Roy. B.A., Harvard U., 1961, M.A.T., 1963. Contbg. editor Time mag., N.Y.C., 1965-66; corr. Time mag., Chgo., 1966-68, Los Angeles, 1968-70; bur. chief Time mag., Saigon, Vietnam, 1970-71; asso. editor Time mag., 1972-73; editor New Times mag., N.Y.C., 1974-79; Nieman fellow Harvard U., 1979-80; news editor Life mag., 1980-81, sr. editor, 1981-82; free-lance writer, 1982-88; editor-in-chief The Village Voice, N.Y.C., 1989-94. Trustee Natural Resources Def. Council., Cambridge Coll.; bd. dirs. Larsen Fund. Recipient Clarion award, 1986. Home: Finch Farm Vail Ln North Salem NY 10560

LARSEN, LAWRENCE BERNARD, JR., priest, pastoral psychotherapist; b. Yonkers, N.Y., Jan. 24, 1937; s. Lawrence Bernard and Astrid Charlotte (Bjorkgren) L.; m. Marion Davidson Hines, Nov. 29, 1968; children: Lawrence Bernard III, Hannah Hines, Sarah Astrid. BA, Trinity Coll., 1958; MDiv, The Gen. Theol. Sem., N.Y.C., 1961; diploma candidate, C.G. Jung Inst., Zurich, Switzerland, 1975; MSW, U. Tenn., 1989. Ordained priest Episcopal Ch., 1961; cert. social worker. Curate Christ Episcopal Ch., Poughkeepsie, N.Y., 1961-63; vicar All Saints Episcopal Ch., East Hartford, Conn., 1963-66; asst. to rector Trinity Ch., Southport, Conn., 1966-69; chaplain Chatham (Va.) Hall Sch., 1969-72, tchr. bible and religion, 1969-72; Jungian psychotherapist pvt. practice Lookout Mountain, Tenn., 1975-89; interim rector Episcopal Ch. Nativity, Ft. Oglethorpe, Ga., 1985-86; priest-in-charge St. Barnabas Episcopal Ch., Trion, Ga., 1987-89; staff psychotherapist Mid Hudson Consultation Ctr., Wappingers Falls, N.Y., 1989-96; pastoral psychotherapist Northeast Counseling Ctr., Katonah, N.Y., 1989-96; pastoral care coord. Hospice of No. Westchester, Mt. Kisco, N.Y., 1995; interim rector Christ Ch. Tarrytown, N.Y., 1996-97; asst. Episcopal chaplain Vassar Coll., Poughkeepsie, 1961-63. Mem. War on Poverty com. U.S. Office Econ. Opportunity, Hartford, Conn., 1965-66. Republican. Avocations: reading, crossword puzzles, politics. Home: The Meadows 17 Briar Ct Cross River NY 10518

LARSEN, PAUL EDWARD, lawyer; b. Rock Springs, Wyo., Jan. 5, 1964; s. Otto E. and Linda K. (Wright) L.; m. Dawn Jannette Griffin, June 25, 1986; 1 child, Quinne Caitlin. BA, U. Oreg., 1986, JD, 1989. Bar: Nev. 1989, U.S. Dist. Ct. Nev. 1989, U.S. Ct. Appeals (9th cir.) 1994. Atty. Lionel, Sawyer & Collins, Las Vegas, Nev., 1989—, chmn. land use and planning divsn., 1995—; gen. counsel Nev. State Democrats, 1996, corp. for solar tech. and renewable resources, 1995-96. Author, editor: Nevada Environmental Law Handbook, 1991, 1st edit., 2d edit., 3rd edit.; contbg. author: Nevada Gaming Law, 2d edit., 1995; contbr. articles to profl. jours. Pres., dir. Desert Creek Homeowners Assn., Las Vegas, 1994-95; atty. Clark County Pro-Bono Project, Las Vegas, 1989-95, Nev. Dem. Party, Las Vegas, 1994. Mem. ABA (vice chair com. natural resources pub. lands sect. 1993-95, bd. dirs. young lawyers divsn. natural resources com. 1992-95, atty. young lawyers divsn. program 1989-90), Nev.-Am. Inns of Ct., Nev. Assn. Gaming Attys., Internat. Assn. Gaming Attys. Avocations: scuba diving, golf, fishing. Office: Lionel Sawyer and Collins 300 S 4th St Ste 1700 Las Vegas NV 89101-6000

LARSEN, PAUL EMANUEL, religious organization administrator; b. Mpls., Oct. 5, 1933; s. David Paul and Myrtle (Grunnet) L.; m. Elizabeth Helen Taylor, Mar. 19, 1966; children: Kristin, Kathleen (dec.). BA, Stanford U., 1955; MDiv, Fuller Theol. Sem., 1958; STD, San Francisco Theol. Sem., 1978. Ordained to ministry Evang. Ch., 1963. Asst. pastor Evang. Ch., Eagle Rock, Calif., 1958-59; pastor Pasadena, Calif., 1963-70, Peninsula Covenant Ch., Redwood City, Calif., 1971-86; pres. Evang. Covenant Chs., Chgo., 1986—; chmn. meeting U.S. ch. leaders, 1992—. Author: Wise Up and Live, Mission of a Covenant. Home: 24 Landmark Northfield IL 60093-3452 Office: Evang Covenant Ch 5101 N Francisco Ave Chicago IL 60625-3611

LARSEN, PETER N., leisure products manufacturing executive. Chmn., CEO Brunswick Corp., Lake Forest, Ill. Office: Brunswick Corp 1 N Field Ct Lake Forest IL 60045-4810*

LARSEN, PHILLIP NELSON, electrical engineer; b. Montrose, Colo., Feb. 27, 1929; s. Virgil Clair and Katherine (Alarid) L.; m. Patricia June Swayze, Aug. 30, 1951; children: James Phillip, Lynn Katherine Larsen Johnston. BSEE, Colo. A&M Coll., 1950; MSEE, U. Ill., 1953, PhDEE, 1956; MSBA, George Washington U., 1967. Registered profl. engr., Colo. Commd. lt. USAF, 1950, advanced through grades to brig. gen., 1973; assoc. prof. elec. engring. USAF Acad., Colo., 1961-66; comdr. OLAA 12th Spl Ops Squadron, Vietnam, 1967-69; spl. asst. to dir. and to prin. dir. def. rsch. and engring. Office Sec. Def., Washington, 1969-72; comdr. Rome (N.Y.) Air Devel. Ctr., 1972-73; vice comdr. Electronic Systems Div. Hanscom AFB, Md., 1973-75; dep. chief staff/systems Hdqrs. Air Force System Command, Andrews AFB, Md., 1975-77; ret. USAF, 1977; v.p. Western Union Telegraph Co., McLean, Va., 1977-80, Systems & Applied Scis. Corp., Riverdale, Md., 1980-81; sr. mem. exec. staff Computer Scis. Corp., Falls Church, Va., 1981-90. Decorated D.S.M., Silver Star, Legion of Merit with 1 oak leaf cluster, D.F.C., Meritorious Svc. medal, Air medal with 11 oak leaf clusters, Air Force Commendation medal, Vietnamese Cross of Gallantry with Gold Star, Vietnamese Cross of Gallantry with Palm. Fellow IEEE, AAAS; mem. Air Force Assn., Armed Forces Communications & Electronics Assn., Masons. Republican. Lutheran. Avocations: fishing, leathercraft. Home: 10719 Oak Pl Fairfax VA 22030-2817

LARSEN, POUL STEEN, library educator; b. Copenhagen, Jan. 30, 1940; s. Kaj Poul and Inger Elise (Seligmann) L.; m. Marianne Pugdahl, July 27, 1963; children: Maria, Anne. Exam.Phil., U. Copenhagen, 1961. Lectr. Copenhagen Coll. Engring., 1961-73; lectr. Royal Sch. Librarianship, Denmark, 1971-73, libr., 1972, asst. dept. head, assoc. prof., 1973-76, head dept. info. media, prof., 1976—, chmn. faculty, 1992—; chmn. Danish Best Books of Yr. Com., 1982-89, Danish Standards Com. Phys. Characteristics of Media, 1988—; vice chmn. ISO com. Terminology of Info. and Documentation, 1993—; convenor ISO Expert Group Standardization of Graphic Materials, 1991—; vis. prof. UCLA, 1983. Author: Contemporary Danish Book Art, 1986, 2d edit., 1989; co-author: Informationsordbogen (Danish Standards Dictionary of Information Terms), 1991, 2d. edit., 1996; contbg. author: Danish Dictionary of National Biography, 1978-85, Danish Handbook of Cultural History, 1991, Danish National Ency., 1993—; contbr. articles to profl. jours.; editor, book designer, designer typefaces for digital typesetting: LIBER, 1993. Yale U. fellow, 1984. Home: Vasevej 85, DK-3460 Birkerod Denmark Office: Royal Sch Librarianship, DK-2300 Birketinget 6, Denmark

LARSEN, RALPH IRVING, environmental research engineer; b. Corvallis, Oreg., Nov. 26, 1928; s. Walter Winfred and Nellie Lyle (Gellatly) L.; BS in Civil Engring., Oreg. State U., 1950; MS, Harvard U., 1955, PhD in Air Pollution and Indsl. Hygiene, 1957; m. Betty Lois Garner, Oct. 14, 1950 (dec. Feb. 1989); children: Karen Larsen Cleeton, Eric, Kristine Larsen Burns, Jan Alan; m. Anne Harmon King, Aug. 3, 1991; children: Vikki King Ball, Terri King Readling, Cindi King King. San. engr. div. water pollution control USPHS, Washington, 1950-54; chief tech. service state and cmty. svc. sect. Nat. Air Pollution Control Adminstrn., Cin., 1957-61; with EPA and Nat. Air Pollution Control Adminstrn., 1961—, environ. rsch. engr. Nat. Exposure Rsch. Lab., Rsch. Triangle Park, N.C., 1971—; air pollution cons. to Poland, 1973, 75, Brazil, 1978; condr. seminars for air pollution researchers, Paris, Vienna and Milan, 1975; adj. lectr. Inst. Air Pollution Tng., 1969—; Falls of Neuse cmty. rep. City of Raleigh (N.C.), 1974—. Recipient Commendation medal USPHS, 1979. Mem. Air and Waste Mgmt. Assn. (mem. editorial bd. jour. 1971-88), Conf. Fed. Environ. Engrs., USPHS Commd. Officers Assn. (past br. pres.), Sigma Xi. Republican. Mem. Christian and Missionary Alliance Ch. (elder). Contbr. over 55 articles to profl. jours. Home: 4012 Colby Dr Raleigh NC 27609-6045 Office: Md # 56 Epa Research Triangle Park NC 27711 *God issued me a 1928-model body. It works best, for others and me, as I read a chapter of the Owner's Manual (The Holy Bible) first thing each morning.*

LARSEN, RALPH S(TANLEY), health care company executive; b. Bklyn., Nov. 19, 1938; s. Andrew and Gurine (Henningsen) L.; m. Dorothy M. Zeitfuss, Aug. 19, 1961; children: Karen, Kristen, Garret. BBA, Hofstra U., 1962. Mfg. trainee, then supr. prodn. and dir. mfg. Johnson & Johnson, New Brunswick, N.J., 1962-77; v.p. ops., v.p. mktg. McNeil Consumer Products Co. div. Johnson & Johnson, Ft. Washington, Pa., 1977-81; pres. Becton Dickenson Consumer Products, Paramus, N.J., 1981-83; pres. Chicopee div. Johnson & Johnson, New Brunswick, 1983-85; co. group chmn. Johnson & Johnson, New Brunswick, N.J., 1985-86, vice chmn., exec. com., bd. dirs., 1986-89, chmn. bd., pres., CEO, 1989—, also bd. dirs., mem. exec. com.; bd. dirs. N.Y. Stock Exch., Xerox Corp., AT&T Corp. Mem. Bus. Coun., Bus. Roundtable (policy com.). Republican. Avocations: skiing, boating, art. Office: Johnson & Johnson 1 Johnson And Johnson Plz New Brunswick NJ 08933-0001

LARSEN, RICHARD GARY, accounting firm executive; b. Tampa, Fla., Nov. 28, 1948; s. Dagfinn T. Larsen and Elizabeth M. (Koch) Thompson; m. Harriet Taylor Jones, Dec. 19, 1970; children—Jonathan Daniel, Alice Taylor. BBA in Acctg., George Washington U., 1971, JD, 1974; postgrad., Columbia U., 1985. Bar: Va. 1974; CPA, D.C., Va. Mem. staff U.S. Senate, Washington, 1967-73; ptnr. Ernst & Young, Washington, 1973—; adj. prof. U. Md., College Park, 1976-78, Am. U., Washington, 1977-78. Mem. ABA, Va. Bar Assn., AICPAs, Md. Soc. CPAs, Univ. Club (Washington), Coral Beach and Tennis Club (Bermuda), Chatham Beach and Tennis Club, Eastward Ho Country Club (Chatham), Columbia Country Club (Chevy Chase), Belle Haven Country Club, Capitol Hill Club. Home: 319 S St Asaph St Alexandria VA 22314 Office: Ernst & Young 1225 Connecticut Ave NW Washington DC 20036-2604

LARSEN, RICHARD LEE, former mayor and city manager, business, municipal and labor relations consultant, arbitrator; b. Jackson, Miss., Apr. 16, 1934; s. Homer Thorsten and Mae Cordelia (Amidon) L.; m. Virginia Fay Alley, June 25, 1955; children: Karla, Daniel, Thomas (dec.), Krista, Lisa. B.S. in Econs. and Bus. Adminstrn, Westminster Coll., Fulton, Mo., 1959; postgrad., U. Kans., 1959-61. Fin. dir. Village of Northbrook, Ill., 1961-63; city mgr. Munising, Mich., 1963-66, Sault Ste. Marie, Mich., 1966-72, Ogden, Utah, 1972-77, Billings, Mont., 1977-79; mcpl. cons., 1979—, pub./pvt. sector labor relations cons., arbitrator, 1979—; mayor City of Billings, Mont., 1990-95; dep. gen. chmn. Greater Mich. Found., 1968. Bd. dirs. Central Weber Sewer Dist., 1972-77; chmn. labor com. Utah League Cities and Towns, 1973-77, Mont. League Cities and Towns, 1977-79; bd. dirs., coach Ogden Hockey Assn., 1972-77, Weber Sheltered Workshop, 1974-77, Billings YMCA, 1980-86, Rimrock Found., 1980-86; chmn. community relations council Weber Basin Job Corps Center, 1973-77. Served with USCG, 1953-57. Recipient Cmty. Devel. Disting. Achievement awards Munising, 1964, Cmty. Devel. Disting. Achievement awards Sault Ste. Marie, 1966-70, Citizen award Dept. of Interior, 1977, Alumni Achievement award Westminster Coll., 1990, Dist. award of merit Boy Scouts Am., 1993, Silver Beaver award Boy Scouts Am., 1994; named Utah Adminstr. of Yr., 1976. Mem. Internat. City Mgmt. Assn. (L.P. Cookingham career devel. award 1974, Clarence Ridley in-service tng. award 1979), Utah City Mgrs. Assn. (pres. 1972-74), Greater Ogden C. of C. (dir.), Rotary (pres. Billings 1997-98), Phi Gamma Delta. Mem. LDS Ch. Club: Rotary. Home and Office: 1733 Parkhill Dr Billings MT 59102-2358

LARSEN, ROBERT DHU, lawyer; b. Stoughton, Wis., Oct. 20, 1922; s. Hans Christian and Helen Charlotte (Sobye) L.; m. Mary Lee Matheson, May 5, 1959 (div. 1973); children: Brooke, Christopher Dhu. AB, U. Wis., 1947; JD with honors, U. N.C., 1950. Bar: N.C. 1950, D.C. 1952, U.S. Supreme Ct. 1957, N.Y. 1959. Law clk. to presiding judge U.S. Ct. Appeals (4th cir.), Charlotte, N.C., 1950-51; from assoc. to ptnr. Rogers & Wells (and predecessors), N.Y.C., 1951-90; retired, 1990. Editor-in-chief U. N.C. Law Rev., 1950. Chmn. bd. trustees Pine Manor Coll., Chestnut Hill, Mass., 1981-84. Served to capt. inf. U.S. Army, 1943-46. Mem. Order of Coif. Democrat. Episcopalian. Home: 40 E 88th St New York NY 10128-1176

LARSEN, ROBERT EMMETT, federal judge; b. Queens, N.Y., Sept. 9, 1946; s. Robert Ludwig and Elizabeth Catherine (Colgan) L.; m. Roberta Barclay, Sept. 22, 1973; children: Matthew Robert, Thomas Barclay, Paige Barclay. BA, Rockhurst Coll., 1969; JD, U. Mo., Kansas City, 1973. Bar: Mo. 1973, U.S. Dist. Ct. (we. dist.) Mo. 1973, U.S. Ct. Appeals (D.C. cir.) 1974, U.S. Ct. Appeals (8th cir.) 1977, U.S. Supreme Ct. 1977. Staff atty. criminal div. U.S. Dept. Justice, Washington, 1974-76; asst. atty. U.S. Atty.'s Office, Kansas City, 1976-81, chief criminal div., 1981-83, atty.-in-charge organized crime drug enforcement task force, 1983-88, 1st asst. U.S. atty., 1988-90, sr. litigation counsel, 1990-91; U.S. magistrate judge U.S. Cts., Kansas City, 1991—; commr. Mental Health Commn., Mo., 1990—; chmn. Metro. Kansas City Task Force on Alcohol and Drug Abuse, 1986-90; chmn., adv. bd. Mo. Fedn. of Parents for Drug Free Youth, Springfield, Mo., 1987-88; bd. trustees Nat. Coun. Alcoholism for Drug Free Youth, Kansas City, 1988-90; bd. dirs. YouthNet, Good Samaritan Project, Kansas City Consensus, Della Lamb Community Svcs.; bd. regents Rockhurst Coll. Regents, 1994—; mem. adv. bd. drug awareness Park Hill Sch. Dist., 1988-90; mem. steering com. Coalition for Positive Family Relationships, 1992—; mem. divsn. alcohol and drug abuse States Adv. Coun., 1987-88. Author: Pretrial Preparation, 1985; contbr.: 8th Circuit Criminal Institute, 1992. Co-chmn. Harmony in World of Difference, Kansas City, 1989—; mem., bd. dirs. Life Edn. Ctr., Kansas City, 1990—, Genesis, Kansas City, 1992; active Northland Citizen's Crusade Coun., Inc., 1989—, Ad Hoc Group Against Crime, 1986—. Recipient Community Svc. award Nat. Coun. Alcohol and Drug Abuse, 1988, Cert. Appreciation, 1988, Pub. Adv. award Dept. Mental Health, State of Mo., 1988, Law Enforcement award Ad Hoc Group Against Crime, 1989, GEICO Pub. Svc. award, 1990. Mem. ABA, Mo. Bar Assn., D.C. Bar Assn., Kansas City, Mo. Bar Assn. Roman Catholic. Home: 420 NW Briarcliff Pky Kansas City MO 64116-1670 Office: US Dist Ct 231 US Courthouse 811 Grand Blvd Kansas City MO 64106-1909

LARSEN, ROBERT LEROY, artistic director; b. Walnut, Iowa, Nov. 28, 1934; s. George Dewey and Maine M. (Mickel) L. MusB, Simpson Coll., Indianola, Iowa, 1956; MusM, U. Mich., 1958; MusD, Ind. U., 1972. Music prof. Simpson Coll., 1957—, chmn. music dept., 1965—; founder, artistic dir. Des Moines Met. Opera, 1973—. Mus. coach Tanglewood, Lenox, Mass., 1963, Oglebay Pk. (W.Va.) Opera, 1965, Chgo., N.Y. studios; condr., stage dir. Simpson Coll., Des Moines Met. Opera, Miss. Opera, U. Ariz.; solo pianist, accompanismt numerous recitals; adjudicator Met. auditions and competitions, Mpls., Chgo., Kansas City, Mo., Tulsa, San Antonio; stage dir., condr. operas, Simpson Coll., Des Moines Met. Opera, 1973—; editor Opera Anthologies by G. Schirmer; piano rec. artist for G. Schirner Lib. Recipient Gov's. award State of Iowa, 1974. Mem. Am. Choral Dir. Assn., Nat. Opera Assn., Music Tchrs. Nat. Assn., Pi Kappa Lambda, Phi Kappa

Phi, Phi Mu Alpha Sinfonia (faculty advisor). Presbyterian. Avocations: reading, theatre, coaching students. Office: Des Moines Metro Opera 106 W Boston Ave Indianola IA 50125-1836

LARSEN, SAMUEL HARRY, minister, educator; b. Sterling, Kans., Feb. 3, 1947; s. Harold Julius and Edna Marguerite (Wasson) L.; m. Natalie Louise Mahlow, June 21, 1969; children: Samuel Eric, Kristen Joy, Hans Joseph. BS, U.S. Naval Acad., 1969; MDiv, Covenant Theol. Sem., 1979; D of Ministry, Reformed Theol. Sem., 1989; postgrad., Trinity Internat. U., 1996—. Ordained to ministry Presbyn. Ch., 1981. Various assignments USN, Norfolk, Va., 1969-72; instr. U.S. Naval Acad., Annapolis, Md., 1972-75; pastoral intern Community Presbyn. Ch., Nairobi, Kenya, Africa, 1977-78; officer-in-charge Naval Res. Shipboard Simulator Lab. and Sch., New Orleans, 1979-81; church planter Mission to the World, Brisbane, Australia, 1982-84; team coord. Mission to the World, Queensland, Australia, 1984-86; regional dir. Mission to the World, Australia, 1986-89; squadron chaplain Destroyer Squadron Five, San Diego, 1989-92; chaplain Naval Air Sta. Whidbey Island, Oak Harbor, Wash., 1992-95; acad. mentor Chesapeake Theol. Sem., Linthicum Heights, Md., 1996; dean Westminster Theol. Coll., Brisbane, 1986-88; del. La. Congress on World Evangelism, Manila, 1989. Pres. Covenant Sem. Student Assn., St. Louis, 1976-77; chaplain Chs. Soccer Assn., Sunshine Coast, Australia, 1984-86; tutor Logan Elem. Sch., San Diego, 1991-92; mem. adv. bd. YMCA, Oak Harbor, 1992-95. Recipient Meritorious Svc. medal Sec. of Navy, 1981, 96. Avocations: chess, astronomy, history, anthropology. Office: Trinity Internat U D578 2065 Half Day Rd Deerfield IL 60015-1241

LARSEN, STEVEN, orchestra conductor; b. Oak Park, Ill., Feb. 10, 1951; s. Edwin Earnest and Sylvia Nila Larsen; divorced; children: Vanessa, Krista; m. Martha Jane Bein, Mar. 21, 1993. MusB, Am. Conservatory Music, Chgo., 1975; MusM, Northwestern U., 1976. Cert. Nederlandse Dirigenten Kursus. Instr. music theory, chair instrumental dept Am. Conservatory Music, Chgo., 1976-82, orch. dir., 1978; music dir. Opera Theatre of San Antonio, 1987-90; orch. dir. Rockford (Ill.) Symphony Orch., 1991—; music dir., acting artistic dir. Chgo. Opera Theater, 1981-92; interim artistic dir. Dayton (Ohio) Opera, 1996; music dir. Champaign-Urbana (Ill.) Symphony, 1996—; lectr. opera performance Chgo. Mus. Coll., 1989-96. Mem. Rockford Downtown Rotary. Office: Rockford Symphony Orch 711 N Main St Rockford IL 61103-6999

LARSEN, TERRANCE A., bank holding company executive. BA, U. Dallas, 1968; PhD, Tex. A&M U., 1971. With Phila. Nat. Bank, from 1977, sr. v.p., 1980-83, exec. v.p., from 1983; exec. v.p. Corestates Fin. Corp. (parent), Phila., 1983-86, pres., 1986—, COO, 1986-87, chmn., CEO, 1988—, also bd. dirs. Office: Core States Fin Corp Centre Square West 1500 Market St 39th Fl Philadelphia PA 19102*

LARSEN, WILLIAM LAWRENCE, materials science and engineering educator; b. Crookston, Minn., July 16, 1926; s. Clarence M. and Luverne (Carlisle) L.; m. Gracie Lee Richey, June 19, 1954; children—Eric W., Thomas R. B.M.E., Marquette U., 1948; M.S., Ohio State U., 1950, Ph.D., 1956; postgrad., U. Chgo., 1950-51. Registered profl. engr., Iowa. Research assoc. Ohio State U., Columbus, 1951-56; research metallurgist E. I. duPont de Nemours & Co., Wilmington, Del., 1956-58; metallurgist Ames Lab., AEC, Iowa, 1958-73; assoc. prof. Iowa State U., Ames, 1958-73, prof. materials sci. and engring., 1973-93; prof. emeritus, 1993—; cons. metallurgical engring., 1960—. Contbr. articles to profl. jours. Served with USN, 1944-46. Mem. ASM Internat., ASTM, Am. Soc. Engring. Edn., NACE Internat. (cert.), Nat. Soc. Profl. Engrs., Nat. Collegiate Honors Coun. Home: 335 N Franklin Ave Ames IA 50014-3424 Office: Iowa State U Dept Engring/Materials Sci Ames IA 50011

LARSEN-BASSE, JORN, mechanical and materials engineering educator, researcher, consultant; b. Maribo, Denmark, Oct. 14, 1934; came to U.S., 1962; s. Asger Bernhard Bjerregaard and Ragnhild Sofie (Jorgensen) Larsen Badse; m. Margarita Simpson, Mar. 31, 1959; 1 child, Kai Erik. MSME, Royal Danish Tech. U., Copenhagen, 1958, PhD in Metallurgy, 1961. Registered mech. engr., Denmark; cert. corrosion specialist, U.S. Rsch. metallurgist Soderfors Bruk, Soderfors, Sweden, 1961-62; rsch. assoc. Stanford (Calif.) U., 1963-64; prof. mech. engring. U. Hawaii, Honolulu, 1964-86; chmn. dept. U. Hawaii, 1976-81, 82-85; prof. mech. engring. Ga. Inst. Tech., Atlanta, 1986-91; program dir. NSF, Washington, 1988—; cons. Honolulu, 1964-86; vis. prof. U. NSW, Sydney, Australia, 1978, Tsinghua U., Beijing, 1983; vis. researcher in tribophysics Commonwealth Sci. and Indsl. Rsch. Orgn., Melbourne, Australia, 1979. Assoc. editor Jour. Tribology, 1989-91; contbr. numerous articles to profl. jours. Mem. ASME, Metall. Soc. of AIME, Am. Soc. for Metals, Am. Soc. for Engring. Edn., Nat. Assn. Corrosion Engrs., Sigma Xi. Home: 6200 Perthshire Ct Bethesda MD 20817-3348 Office: NSF 4201 Wilson Blvd Arlington VA 22230-0001

LARSON, ALAN PHILIP, federal official; b. Osage, Iowa, July 19, 1949; s. Philip Harold and Marilyn (Lack) L.; m. Nancy Ruth Naden, June 3, 1972; children: NAthan Christopher, Lara Marie, Philip Gardner. BA, U. Iowa, 1971, MA, 1978, PhD, 1982. Econ. officer U.S. Embassy Dept. of State, Kinshasa, Zaire, 1975-77; dep. dir. Dept. of State, Washington, 1978-82; counselor for econ. and comml. affairs U.S. Embassy Dept. of State, Kingston, Jamaica, 1982-84; exec. asst. to undersec. Dept. of State, Washington, 1984-86, dep. asst. sec. for internat. energy, 1986-87, prin. dep. asst. sec. for econs. and bus., 1987-90; U.S. amb. to OECD Paris, 1990-94; dep. asst. sec. for internat. fin. and devel. Washington, 1994-96; asst. sec. economics & business affairs Dept. of State, Washington, 1996—. Office: Dept State 2201 C St NW Washington DC 20520*

LARSON, ALLAN LOUIS, political scientist, educator, lay church worker; b. Chetek, Wis., Mar. 31, 1932; s. Leonard Andrew and Mabel (Marek) L. BA magna cum laude, U. Wis., Eau Claire, 1954; PhD, Northwestern U., 1964. Instr. Evanston Twp. (Ill.) High Sch., 1958-61; asst. prof. polit. sci. U. Wis., 1963-64; asst. prof. Loyola U., Chgo., 1964-68, assoc. prof., 1968-74, prof., 1974—. Author: Comparative Political Analysis, 1980, (essay) The Human Triad: An Introductory Essay on Politics, Society, and Culture, 1988; (with others) Progress and the Crisis of Man, 1976; contbr. articles to profl. jours. Assoc. mem. Paul Galvin Chapel, Evanston, Ill. Norman Wait Harris fellow in polit. sci. Northwestern U., 1954-56. Mem. AAAS, ASPCA, AAUP, Humane Soc. U.S., Northwestern U. Alumni Assn., Am. Polit. Sci. Assn., Am. Acad. Polit. and Social Sci., Acad. Polit. Sci., Midwest Polit. Sci. Assn., Spiritual Life Inst., Anti-Cruelty Soc., Nat. Wildlife Fedn., N.Am. Butterfly Assn., Policy Studies Orgn., Noetic Scis. Inst., Humane Soc. U.S., Kappa Delta Pi, Pi Sigma Epsilon. Roman Catholic. Home: 2015 Orrington Ave Evanston IL 60201-2911 Office: Loyola U 6525 N Sheridan Rd Damen Hall Rm 915 Chicago IL 60626 *We are each of us mysteries to ourselves. We are on a life-long search for meaning: questions about where we have come from, what we are doing and where we are going. The deepest desires of a person embody the spiritual quest. The Kingdom of God tells us where to place our priorities. Life is short. No one is untouched by tragedy. We are reminded every day of our finiteness. We care because it is our nature to care. Christianity teaches a reverence for life that urges us to transcend narcissism and selfishness.*

LARSON, APRIL ULRING, bishop. Pastor; bishop Southeastern Minn. Synod, Evang. Luth. Ch. in Am., 1992—, La Crosse (Wis.) Area, Evang. Luth. Ch. in Am. Office: Evang Luth Ch in Am 3462 Losey Blvd S La Crosse WI 54601-7217*

LARSON, ARVID GUNNAR, electrical engineer; b. Chgo., July 26, 1937; s. Arvid G. and Marion Edith (Parker) L.; m. Gladys Lorraine Anderson, June 6, 1959 (dec. 1987); 1 son, Gregory Monte; m. Nicole Sours, Aug. 26, 1989. B.S. in Elec. Engring., Ill. Inst. Tech., Chgo., 1959; M.S. in Elec. Engring., Stanford (Calif.) U., 1966, Ph.D. in Elec. Engring., 1973. Registered profl. engr., Calif., Va. Research engr. Stanford Research Inst., Menlo Park, Calif., 1964-74; mgr. advanced research Planning Research Corp., McLean, Va., 1974-78; project mgr. System Planning Corp., Arlington, Va., 1978-80; mgr. Washington div. Advanced Research and Applications Corp., Vienna, Va., 1980-85; v.p. Analytical Disciplines Inc., Vienna, 1985-86; prin. Booz, Allen and Hamilton, Inc., 1986-90; sr. v.p. JJH Inc., Arlington, 1990-91; chmn. Nicole Larson Assocs., McLean, 1991—; rsch. prof. George Mason U., Fairfax, Va., 1991-93; chmn. bd. dirs. Electronics and Aerospace Systems Conf., 1982-84; bd. dirs. Research Inst. in Info. Scis and Engring., 1978—; bd. advisers George Mason U., Fairfax, Va., 1980-86; chmn. 3d NATO Advanced Study Inst. in Info. Scis., 1978. Served to lt. USN, 1959-63. Fellow IEEE (chmn. def. research and devel. com. 1985-86, chmn. No. Va. sect. 1986-87, vice-chmn. tech. activities com. 1986-87, chmn. new tech. issues com. 1987-89, chmn. fed. govt. activities 1989-90, gen. chmn. U.S. Tech. Policy Conf. 1988, 89, inst. editorial bd. 1986-88, editorial bd. jour. Spectrum 1988-91, Centennial medal 1984, Profl. Achievement award 1987, chmn. U.S. activities 1992, v.p. 1992, bd. dirs. 1992, chmn. govt. fellows com. 1997); mem. Am. Assn. Engring. Socs. (chmn. R&D task force 1993—), Armed Forces Communications and Electronics Assn., Sigma Xi. Club: Cosmos (chmn. fin. com. 1993-96, treas. 1997—), Shady Oaks Yacht (commodore 1991-93). Author: Information Science in Action: System Design, 1983; contbr. numerous elec. engring. articles to profl. publs. Home: 6921 Espey Ln Mc Lean VA 22101-5455 Office: Booz Allen & Hamilton Inc 502 Fillmore St Herndon VA 20170-3312

LARSON, BENNETT CHARLES, solid state physicist, researcher; b. Buffalo, N.D., Oct. 9, 1941; s. Floyd Everet and Gladys May (Hogen) L.; m. Piola Anne Taliaferro, June 6, 1969; children—Christopher Charles, Andrea Kay. B.A. in Physics, Concordia Coll., Moorhead, Minn., 1963; M.S. in Physics, U. N.D., 1965; Ph.D. in Physics, U. Mo., 1970. Rsch. physicist, group leader x-ray diffraction, sect. head thin films and microstructures solid state div. Oak Ridge Nat. Lab., Tenn., 1969—. Contbr. numerous articles to profl. jours. Recipient Sidhu award Pitts. Diffraction Soc., 1974. Fellow Am. Phys. Soc.; mem. Am. Crystallographic Assn. (Bertram E. Warren Diffraction Physics award 1985), Materials Research Soc. Office: Oak Ridge Nat Lab Solid State Dv Oak Ridge TN 37831

LARSON, BRENT T., broadcasting executive; b. Ogden, Utah, Sept. 23, 1942; s. George Theodore and Doris (Peterson) L.; m. Tracy Ann Taylor; children: Michelle, Brent Todd, Lindsey. Student, pub. schs., Los Angeles; diploma in radio operational engring., Burbank, Calif., 1962. Owner, mgr. Sta. KAIN, Boise, Idaho, 1969-77; owner, operator Sta. KXA Radio, Seattle, 1975-83, Sta. KYYX Radio, Seattle, 1980-83, Sta. KGA Radio, Spokane, Wash., 1978-84, Sta. KUUZ Radio, Boise, 1976-82, Sta. KOOS Radio, North Bend, Oreg., 1980-81, Sta. KODL Radio, The Dalles, Oreg., 1974-80, Sta. KKWZ Radio, Richfield, Utah, 1980-94, Sta. KSVC Radio, Richfield, 1980-94; v.p. Casey Larson Fast Food Co., Oreg. and Idaho, 1976-94, Imperial Broadcasting Corp., Idaho, 1970—, KSOS Am & KLZX FM, 1983—; pres. First Nat. Broadcasting Corp., 1970—; v.p. Larson-Wynn Corp., 1974—, Brentwood Properties, Ogden, 1977—; pres. Sta. KSIT Broadcasting, Rock Springs, Wyo., 1980-90, Gold Coast Communications Corp., Oreg., 1980-81, Sevier Valley Broadcasting Co., Inc., Utah, 1980-94, Brent Larson Group Stas., Western U.S., 1969—; v.p. mktg. Internat. Foods Corp., Boise, 1969-81; ptnr. Larson Tours and Travel, Burley, Idaho, 1977-87; v.p. Harrison Square Inc., 1995—; bd. dirs. Casey-Larson Foods Co., La Grande, Oreg., Studio City Entertainment (Nev. L.C.), 1996—. Bd. dirs. Met. Sch., 1981-93, Children's Aid Soc., 1991-94; chmn. bd. ZLX Limited Libility Co., 1995—. Mem. Am. Advt. Fedn., Nat. Assn. Broadcasters, Nat. Radio Broadcasters Assn., Wash. Broadcasters Assn., Oreg. Broadcasters Assn., Idaho Broadcasters Assn., Utah Broadcasters Assn., Citizens for Responsible Broadcasting (bd. dirs.). Republican. Mem. LDS Ch. Home: 2613 Seashore Dr Las Vegas NV 89128 Office: First Nat Broadcasting Corp 4455 S 5500 W Ogden UT 84315-9650

LARSON, BRIAN FOIX, architect; b. Eau Claire, Wis., July 6, 1935; s. Albert Foix and Dorothy Jean (Thompson) L.; m. Mildred Anne Nightswander, Feb. 13, 1961; children: Urban Alexander, Soren Federick. BArch, U. Ill., 1959. Registered architect, Wis., Minn., Colo., Mass., N.H., Fla. Architect-in-tng. Geometrics, Inc., Cambridge, Mass., 1959-60, Bastille Halsey Assoc., Boston, 1960-62; ptnr. Larson, Playter, Smith, Eau Claire, 1962-72; v.p. Larson, Hestekins, Smith, Ltd., Eau Claire, 1962-80, Ayres Assocs., Eau Claire, 1980—; sec. Wis. Bd. Archtl. Examiners, 1985-88, chmn., 1988-89; master juror Nat. Coun. Archtl. Rev. Bd. Bldg. Design Exam, 1987—. Prin. works include One Mill Plaza, Laconia, N.H. (Honor award New Eng. Regional Council AIA 1974), Eau Claire County Courthouse, Wis., (Honor award Wis. Soc. Architects 1978), St. Croix County Courthouse, Wis. Mem. Hist. Bldg. Code Adv. Com., Wis., 1985. Mem. AIA (bd. dirs. 1996—), Wis. Soc. Architects (pres. 1983), Wis. Architects Found. (bd. dirs.), Soc. Archtl. Historians. Home: 215 Roosevelt Ave Eau Claire WI 54701-4065 Office: Ayres Assocs PO Box 1590 Eau Claire WI 54702-1590

LARSON, CHARLES FRED, trade association executive; b. Gary, Ind., Nov. 27, 1936; s. Charles F. and Margaret J. (Taylor) L.; m. Joan Ruth Grupe, Aug. 22, 1959; children: Gregory Paul, Laura Ann. BSME, Purdue U., 1958; MBA summa cum laude, Fairleigh Dickinson U., 1973. Registered profl. engr., N.J. Project engr. Combustion Engring., Inc., East Chicago, Ind., 1958-60; sec. Welding Rsch. Council, N.Y.C., 1960-70, asst. dir., 1970-75; exec. dir. Indsl. Rsch. Inst., Inc., N.Y.C., 1975—; mem. mech. engring. adv. bd. Purdue U. Assoc. editor Jour. Pressure Vessel Tech., 1973-75; mem. bd. advisors Who's Who in Am. Mem. Wyckoff (N.J.) Bd. Edn., 1973-78, pres., 1976-77; reader In Touch Networks, Inc., N.Y.C., 1979-89; chmn. 43d Nat. Conf. on Advancement Rsch. Fellow AAAS; mem. ASME, NSPE, Am. Soc. Assn. Execs., Coun. Engring. and Sci. Soc. Execs., Univ. Club, Kenwood Club. Republican. Methodist. Office: Indsl Rsch Inst Inc 1550 M St NW Washington DC 20005-1708

LARSON, CHARLES ROBERT, naval officer; b. Sioux Falls, S.D., Nov. 20, 1936; s. Eldred Charles and Gertrude Edythe (Jensen) L.; m. Sarah Elizabeth Craig, Aug. 19, 1961; children: Sigrid Anne, Erica Lynn, Kirsten Elizabeth. BS in Marine Engring., U.S. Naval Acad., 1958. Commd. ensign USN, 1958, advanced through grades to adm., 1990; naval aviator, attack pilot, 1958-63, nuclear power, submarine tng., 1963-64, assigned nuclear subs., 1964-76, naval aide to the Pres., 1969-71, comdg. officer USS Halibut, 1973-76, comdr. submarine devel. group one, head operational deep submergence program, 1976-78, chief naval ops. staff Strategic Submarine Programs, 1978-79; dir. long range planning group Washington, 1978-82; comdr. submarines Mediterranean, 1982-83; supt. U.S. Naval Acad. Annapolis, Md., 1983-86; comdr. 2d Fleet, 1986-88; dir. plans, policies and ops. DCNO, 1988-90; comdr. U.S. Pacific Fleet, 1990-91, U.S. Pacific Command, Hawaii, 1991-94; supt. U.S. Naval Acad., 1994—; v.p. U.S. Naval Inst., 1994—. Mem. USO Coun., Honolulu, 1990-92; mem. Honolulu area coun. Boy Scouts Am., 1990-94. Decorated Def. Navy D.S.M. (6), Legion of Merit (3), Bronze Star, others; White House fellow, 1968-69. Mem. Coun. on Fgn. Rels. Home: 1 Buchanan Rd Annapolis MD 21402 Office: 121 Blake Rd Annapolis MD 21402-1300

LARSON, CLARENCE EDWARD, foundation administrator; b. Cloquet, Minn., Sept. 20, 1909; s. Louis Ludwig and Caroline Hilda (Ullman) L.; m. Gertrude Ellen Ruben, May 17, 1934 (dec. June 1952); 1 child, Robert Edward; m. Jane Ritchie Warren, Apr. 20, 1957; children—Lawrence Ernest, Lance Stafford (dec.). B.S., U. Minn., 1932; Ph.D., U. Calif.-Berkeley, 1937. Chmn. chemistry dept. Coll. of Pacific, Stockton, Calif., 1937-42; project dir., mgr. Union Carbide Corp., Oak Ridge, 1942-50; mgr. corp. research Union Carbide Corp., N.Y.C., 1955-61; pres. nuclear div. Union Carbide Corp., Oak Ridge, 1961-69; dir. Oak Ridge Nat. Lab., 1950-55; commr. AEC, Washington, 1969-74; pres. Pioneers Sci. and Tech. Hist. Assn., Washington, 1982—; chmn. Nat. Battery Adv. Commn., Washington, 1975-81. Patentee separation process for uranium. Recipient Disting. Achievement award Am. Soc. for Advancement Mgmt., 1963. Fellow Am. Nuclear Soc., Am. Inst. Chemists; mem. NAE, Am. Chem. Soc., Cosmos Club (Disting. Svc. award 1991), Knights of Malta, Rotary, Sigma Xi, Tau Beta Pi. Republican. Avocations: amateur radio; computers; scuba diving; photography; golf. Home: 6514 Bradley Blvd Bethesda MD 20817-3248

LARSON, DANIEL JOHN, physics educator; b. Mpls., Nov. 8, 1944; s. Edwin Wildridge and Verva May (Johnson) L.; m. Tanya Helen Furman, June 5, 1994. BA in Physics and Math. summa cum laude, St. Olaf Coll., 1966; MA in Phyics, Harvard U., 1967, PhD in Physics, 1971. Asst. prof. physics Harvard U., Cambridge, Mass., 1970-75; assoc. prof. physics Harvard U., Cambridge, 1975-78; assoc. prof. physics U. Va., Charlottesville, 1978-87, prof. of physics, 1987-96, assoc. dean, 1989-91, chmn. dept. physics, 1991-97, Maxine S. and Jesse W. Beams prof. physics, 1996—; mem. panel on current trends in atomic spectroscopy NRC, 1982, mem. com. of atomic, molecular and optical scis., 1987-95, vice-chmn., 1991-92, chmn., 1992-94, past chmn., 1994-95, mem. panel on future opportunities in atomic, molecular and optical scis., 1991-93, mem. AMO Scis. Assessment Panel, Commn. on Phys. Scis., Math. & Applications, 1993, Workshop on Quantitative Assessment of Health of Phys. and Math. Scis., 1993; mem. program com. Gordon Conf. on Atomic Physics, 1983, 89, 91; mem. precision measurements grants outside adv. com. Nat. Bur. Standards, 1986-90; vis. scientist Nat. Bur. Standards, Boulder, Colo., 1985-86, Lab. Aimé Cotton, Orsay, France, 1991; vis. prof. Chalmers U., Gothenburg, Sweden, 1986; chmn. Com. on Atomic, Molecular and Optical Scis, NRC, Washington, 1992-94; mem. Dept. Energy rev. com. for atomic physics program Argonne Nat. Lab., 1988, Kans. State U., 1989, Oak Ridge Nat. Lab., 1990; external reviewer dept. physics Washington and Lee U., 1988; mem. acad. program rev. dept. physics and astronomy U. Nebr., 1994; mem. rev. com. dept. physics and astronomy U. Ky., 1995; mem. ad hom com. for rsch. univs. Rsch. Corp., 1993, mem. AMO faculty early career devel. program panel NSF, 1995; cons. James Madison U., 1995, 96; mem. rev. com. dept. physics Tex. Christian U., 1995; mem. rev. panel atomic, molecular, optical and plasma physics program NSF, 1996; mem. task force on physics State Coun. Higher Edn. Va., 1995-96. Contbr. articles to profl. jours.; cons. editor Am. Inst. Physics Press, 1993-96. Rsch. grantee Office of Naval Rsch. NSF, 1978-97; Woodrow Wilson fellow, 1966, NSF grad. fellow, 1966-70. Fellow Am. Phys. Soc. (nominating com. divsn. atomic, molecular and optical physics 1986-87, 91-94, divsn. councillor 1991-94, exec. com. divsn. atomic, molecular and optical physics 1991-95, audit com. 1992, nominating com. laser sci. topical group 1991-92, chmn. 1992, com. on minorities 1992-94, com. on coms. 1993-94, chmn. 1994, nominating com. topical group on precision measurement and fundamental constants 1993-94, chmn. task force on forums 1995, Davisson-Germer prize com. 1995-96, exec. bd. 1993-94); mem. Optical Soc. Am., Phi Beta Kappa, Sigma Xi, Sigma Pi Sigma. Achievements include extensive contributions to the understanding of the interaction of light with atomic systems, especially negative ions. Home: 3265 Waverly Dr Charlottesville VA 22901 Office: U Va Dept Physics McCormick Rd Charlottesville VA 22903

LARSON, DAVID BRUCE, research epidemiologist; b. Glen Ridge, N.J., Mar. 13, 1947; s. John Owen and Peggy June (Asbury) L.; m. Susan Joan Slingerland, Dec. 20, 1975; children: David Chad, Kristen Joan. BS, Drexel U., 1969; MD, Temple U., 1973; MS in Pub. Health, U. N.C., 1983. Diplomate Nat. Bd. Med. Examiners, Am. Bd. Psychiatry. Intern MacNeal Meml. Hosp., Berwyn, Ill., 1973-74; resident in psychiatry Duke U. Med. Ctr., Durham, N.C., 1974-77, psychosomatics teaching fellow, 1975-77, fellow in behavioral scis., 1976-78; chief resident psychiatry Duke U. Med. Ctr. and Durham County Gen. Hosp., 1977-79; fellow in geropsychiatry Duke U. Med. Ctr., Durham, N.C., 1979-81; epidemiology fellow U. N.C., Chapel Hill, 1982-83; epidemiology fellow NIMH, Rockville, Md., 1983-85, rsch. psychiatrist, 1985-91; sr. policy researcher Office of the Sec., HHS, Washington, 1991-93; sr. analyst office of dir. NIH, 1993-94; pres. Nat. Inst. Healthcare Rsch., 1994—. Contbr. chpts. to books, articles to profl. jours. Mem. AAAS, AMA, So. Med. Assn., Christian Med. Soc., Am. Psychiat. Assn., So. Psychiat. Assn., Christian Assn. Psychol. Studies, Am. Assn. Marital and Family Therapy, Soc. for Sci. Study of Religion, Sigma Xi. Episcopalian. Avocations: reading, running, exercising.

LARSON, DAVID LEE, surgeon; b. Kansas City, Mo., Dec. 9, 1943; s. Leonard Nathanial and Mary Elizabeth (Stuck) L.; m. Sherrill Ankli, Apr. 16, 1977; children: Jeffrey David, Dawn Elizabeth, Bradley Jessee. BS, Bowling Green State U., 1965; JD, La. State U., 1969. Diplomate Am. Bd. Plastic Surgery (bd. dirs. 1996—). Surgeon M.D. Anderson Cancer Ctr., Houston, 1978-85; prof., chmn. dept. plastic and reconstructive surgery Med. Coll Wis., Milw., 1986—; Alano J. Ballantyne prof. in head and neck surgery, 1985. Editor: Cancer in the Neck, 1987, Essentials of Head and Neck Oncology, 1997. Capt. USNR, 1991—. Mem. Am. Assn. Plastic Surgeons, Nat. Inst. Healthcare Rsch. (chmn. bd. dirs. 1995—), Plastic Surgery Ednl. Found. (bd. dirs. 1997—). Avocations: reading, exercise. Home: 13510 Braemar Dr Elm Grove WI 53122 Office: Med Coll Wis 9200 W Wisconsin Ave Milwaukee WI 53226-3522

LARSON, DAYL ANDREW, architect; b. Denver, Aug. 13, 1930; s. Andrew and Esther (Freiberg) L.; m. Kay W. Larson; children: Linda, Lesli, Lucy. BS in Architecture, BSBA, U. Colo., 1953. Pres. Haller & Larson Architects, Denver, 1962-92. Served to capt. C.E., U.S. Army, 1953-55. Fellow AIA (pres. Denver chpt. 1978, pres-elect 1986-87); mem. Colo. AIA (pres.). Home: 2153 S Beeler Way Denver CO 80231-3409 Office: Haller & Larson 1621 18th St Ste 110 Denver CO 80202-5905*

LARSON, DONALD CLAYTON, physics educator, consultant; b. Wadena, Minn., Jan. 29, 1934; s. Clyde Melvin and Selma (Wilson) L.; m. Susan Dunnet, July 17, 1960; children: Tor Frederick, Jun Dunnet (dec.), Erika Rose. BS, U. Wash., 1956; SM, Harvard U., 1957, PhD, 1962. Asst. prof. U. Va., Charlottesville, 1962-67; assoc. prof. Drexel U., Phila., 1967-83, full prof., 1983—; vis. prof. Univ. Chile, Santiago, 1969, 73, Tel-Aviv (Israel) U., 1984, 92; vis. scientist Naval Air Devel., Warminster, Pa., summers 1981-91; cons. NIST, Gaithersburg, Md., 1984-95. Author: Physics of Thin Films, vol. VI, 1971, Experimental Methods in Preparation and Measurement of Thin Films, vol. II, 1974. Mem. Optical Soc. Am., Phi Beta Kappa, Tau Beta Pi, Sigma Xi. Home: 409 Drew Ave Swarthmore PA 19081-2407 Office: Drexel U Physics Atmospheric Sci Dept Philadelphia PA 19104

LARSON, DOYLE EUGENE, retired air force officer, consultant; b. Madelia, Minn., Oct. 2, 1930; s. Edgar Louis and Gyneth Mae (Weldy) L.; m. Lois James, May 29, 1953; children: James, Nancy, Mary, Mark. Student, Macalester Coll., 1948-51; BA, Hardin-Simmons U., 1962; postgrad., Armed Forces Staff Coll., 1965, Air War Coll., 1971; MS in Polit. Sci., Auburn U., 1971. Enlisted USAF, 1951, commd. 2d lt., 1953, advanced through grades to maj. gen., 1977; sr. mil. rep. Nat. Security Agy., Pentagon, 1971-72; asst. for joint matters, asst. chief staff for intelligence Hdqrs. USAF, 1972-73, dir. policy and resource mgmt., dep. chief staff for intelligence, 1973-74; dir. intelligence Hdqrs. Pacific Command, Camp H.M. Smith, Hawaii, 1974-77; dep. chief staff for intelligence Hdqrs. SAC, Offutt AFB, Omaha, 1977-79; comdg. gen. Security Svc., 1979-83; comdr. Electronic Security Command, San Antonio, 1979-83; dir. Joint Electronic Warfare Ctr., San Antonio, 1980-83; ret., 1983. trustee Macalester Coll. Decorated DSM, Legion of Merit with 2 oak leaf clusters, Air medal with 3 oak leaf clusters; named to Order of the Sword. Mem. Air Force Assn. (pres.). Lutheran. Home: 13509 York Ave S Burnsville MN 55337-1844

LARSON, EARL RICHARD, federal judge; b. Mpls., Dec. 18, 1911; s. Axel R. and Hannah (Johnson) L.; m. Cecill Frances Carlgren, Dec. 30, 1939; children: Jane, Earl R. BA, U. Minn., 1933, LLB, 1935. Bar: Minn. 1935. Judge U.S. Dist. Ct. Minn., Mpls., 1961-77, sr. judge, 1977—. Lt. USNR, 1943-46. Recipient Outstanding Achievement award U. Minn., 1978. Office: US Dist Ct 661 US Courthouse 110 S 4th St Minneapolis MN 55401-2244

LARSON, GARY, cartoonist; b. Tacoma, Wash., Aug. 14, 1950; s. Vern and Doris Larson; married. BA in Communications, Wash. State U., 1972. Jazz musician, 1973-76; with music store, Seattle, 1976-77, Humane Soc., Seattle, 1978-80; cartoonist Seattle Times, 1978-79; syndicated cartoonist The Far Side Chronicle Features Syndicate, San Francisco, 1979-84, Universal Press Syndicate, Kansas City, Mo., 1984-94; prodr. books and calendars. Exhbns. include The Far Side of Sci. (exhibited at Calif. Acad. Scis., 1987, Smithsonian Instn., 1987, Denver Mus. Natural History, L.A. County Mus., Shedd Aquarium, Chgo., other mus.), The Far Side of the Zoo, Wash. Pk. Zoo, Portland, Oreg., 1987; author: (cartoon collections) The Far Side, 1982, Beyond the Far side, 1983, In Search of the Far Side, 1984, Bride of the Far Side, 1985, Valley of the Far Side, 1985, It Came from the Far Side, 1986, The Far Side Observer, 1987, Hound of the Far Side, 1987, Night of the Crash-Test Dummies, 1988, Wildlife Preserves, 1989, The Prehistory of the Far Side: A 10th Anniversary Exhibit, 1989, Weiner Dog Art, 1990, Unnatural Selections, 1991, Cows of Our Planet, 1992, The Chickens are Restless, 1993, The Curse of Madame "C", 1994, Last Chapter and Worse, 1996, (cartoon anthologies) The Far Side Gallery, 1984, The Far Side Gallery II, 1986, The Far Side Gallery III, 1988, The Far Side Gallery IV, 1993, The Far Side Gallery V, 1995; television animation Gary Larson's Tales from the Far Side, 1994 (Grand prix Annecy Film Festival, 1995), 2d animated film

Gary Lason's Tales from the Far Side II, 1997. Recipient award for Best Humor Panel, Nat. Cartoonists Soc., 1986, Reuben award for Outstanding Cartoonist of Yr. Nat. Cartoonists Soc., 1991, 94, Max and Moritz prize for best internat. comic strip panel Internat. Comics Salon, 1993, other awards. Avocation: jazz music. Office: Universal Press Syndicate 4520 Main St Kansas City MO 64111-1816

LARSON, GEORGE CHARLES, magazine editor, writer; b. Mar. 31, 1942; s. George Lester and Mildred Caroline (Frehner) L.; m. Valarie Ann Thompson, Aug. 20, 1946; children: Evan Richard; Alice Lynn and Keely Mae (twins). BA, Harvard U., 1964. Staff writer Scholastic Mag., N.Y.C., 1971; regional editor, mng. editor Flying Mag., N.Y.C., 1972-78; tech. editor Bus. & Comml. Aviation Mag., White Plains, N.Y., 1980-85; editor Air & Space/Smithsonian Mag., Washington, 1985—. Author: Fly on Instruments, The Blimp Book. Served with U.S. Army, 1966-70, Vietnam. Office: Air & Space Mag 901 D St SW Washington DC 20024-2169

LARSON, GERALD LEE, auditor; b. Billings, Mont., Apr. 18, 1937; s. Phillip Antone and Eunice (LaPoint) L. Student, U. Nev., 1955-59; AS, Western Nev. U., 1975. Mil. pers. mgr. Nev. Air NG, Reno, 1973-81; mgr. employee rels. Nev. Mil. Dept., Carson City, 1981-82, mil. pers. mgr., 1982-88; auditor Nev. State Indsl. Ins., Reno, 1989-92; sr. auditor Nev. State Indsl. Ins., Carson City, 1992—. State pres. Nev. Enlisted NG Assn., Carson City, 1983-87; nat. conf. chmn. Enlisted Assn. NG U.S., Reno, 1989; project chmn. 40th ann. book Nev. Air NG, 1988. CM Sgt. Nev. Air NG, USAF, 1955-88. Named Outstanding Sr. Non-Commissioned Officer of Yr., Nev. Air NG, 1979. Avocations: travel, gardening. Office: State Indsl Ins System 515 E Musser St Carson City NV 89701-4262

LARSON, HARRY THOMAS, electronics engineer, executive, consultant; b. Berkeley, Calif., Oct. 16, 1921; s. Harry Homer and Edna Clara (Petersen) L.; m. Merry Evelyn Otteson, Dec. 26, 1956 (div. Dec. 1975); children: Kristin Eve Beltz, Margit Merry Mills, Megan Marie Hoyt. BSEE summa cum laude, U. Calif., Berkeley, 1947; MSEE, UCLA, 1954. Computer engr. Inst. for Numerical Analysis Nat. Bur. Standards, L.A., 1949-51; mem. tech. staff Advanced Electronics Lab. Hughes Aircraft Co., Culver City, Calif., 1951-54; dept. mgr. bus. applications of computers Ramo-Wooldridge Co., Inglewood, Calif., 1954-56; asst. divsn. dir. command and control systems Aero. divsn. Philco-Ford Co., Newport Beach, Calif., 1956-68; asst. div. dir. software and computing ctr. TRW Systems, Redondo Beach, Calif., 1968-69; dir. planning Calif. Computer Products, Anaheim, 1969-74; sr. scientist Hughes Aircraft, Fullerton, Calif., 1978-87; pres. Larbridge Enterprises Cons., Laguna Hills, Calif., 1970—; mem. Army Sci. Bd., Washington, 1988-92; contbd. to NASA's Mission Control Ctr. in Houston for Gemini, Apollo, Skylab and shuttle missions, Field Army tactical command and control system, first random access computer memory, early airborne digital computer, first keyboard and cathode ray tube data entry device (terminal), first-of-a-kind applications of computers in banks, factories, pension trust funds, payroll, acctg., truck scheduling, R.R. car routing, car body design and manufacture, automobile assembly plant inventory control, electrical power distbn. network, steel hot roll mill, computer programming methodologies (modularization, report generator, table-driven software), founds. for display tech. and large screen displays; lectr. workshops, conf. sessions, 1954-74. Editor Proc. Inst. Radio Engrs., 1961; editor, pub. The Labridge Letter, 1973-76; co-editor Handbook of Automation, Computation and Control, 1959; contbr. articles to profl. jours., computer publs.; patentee in field. 1st lt. USAF, 1942-45. Fellow IEEE (life; Centennial medal); mem. IEEE Computer Soc. (co-fouder, nat. chmn. 1954-55, chmn. Social Implications of Computers, 1956-70), Soc. for Info. Display, Am. Fedn. Info. Processing Soc. (bd. govs. 1956-60), Sigma Xi, Tau Beta Pi, Eta Kappa Nu. Avocations: writing, photography. Home and Office: Larbridge Enterprises 236 Calle Aragon Apt A Laguna Hills CA 92653-3492

LARSON, JANICE TALLEY, computer science educator; b. Houston, Sept. 29, 1948; d. Hiram Peak Talley and Jennie Edna (Forbes) Donahoo; m. Harold Vernon Larson, Apr. 8, 1977; children: Randall Neil, Christopher Lee. AA in Computer Sci., San Jacinto Coll., 1981; BA in Computer Info. Systems, U. Houston, Clear Lake, 1984, MA in Computer Info. Systems, 1988; postgrad. in instructional tech., U. Houston, 1994—. Programmer Control Applications, Houston, 1985-86, Tex. Eastern Pipeline, Houston, 1988-90; instr. computer sci. San Jacinto Coll., Houston, 1990-94; sponsor Computer Sci. Club, Houston, 1992-94. Mem. IEEE, U. Houston Alumni Assn., Phi Delta Kappa, Kappa Delta Pi.

LARSON, JERRY L., state supreme court justice; b. Harlan, Iowa, May 17, 1936; s. Gerald L. and Mary Eleanor (Patterson) L.; m. Debra L. Christensen, July 17, 1993; children: Rebecca, Jeffrey, Susan, David. BA, State U. Iowa, 1958, JD, 1960. Bar: Iowa. Partner firm Larson & Larson, 1961-75; dist. judge 4th Jud. Dist. Ct. of Iowa, 1975-78; justice Iowa Supreme Ct., 1978—. Office: Supreme Ct Iowa State Capital Bldg Des Moines IA 50319

LARSON, JOHN DAVID, life insurance company executive, lawyer; b. Madison, Wis., July 6, 1941; s. Lawrence John and Anna Mathilda (Furseth) L.; m. Evelyn Vie Smith, Jan. 22, 1966 (div. Apr. 1980); children: Eric John, Karen Annette; m. Nancy Jay With, Nov. 29, 1980; stepchildren: Andrew Zachary, Anne Elizabeth, Christopher Allen. BBA, U. Wis., 1964, JD, 1965, MBA, 1966. Bar: Wis. 1965, U.S. Ct. Mil. Appeals 1966; CPA, Wis.; CLU, chartered fin. cons. With Nat. Guardian Life Ins. Co., Madison, 1969—; exec. v.p., treas. Nat. Guardian Life Ins. Co., 1973, pres., dir., 1974—, pres., chief exec. officer, 1989—; dir. Firstar Bank Wis., TV Wis., Inc., Madison, KELAB, Inc., Madison. Chmn. Madison chpt. ARC, 1974-75; pres. United Way Dane County, 1975; pres. Wis. Nat. Guard Assn., 1992-96. With U.S. Army, 1966-69, brig. gen. Wis. Army N.G. Recipient Know Your Madisonian award Wis. State Jour., 1973; named Disting. Alumnus U. Wis.-Madison, 1996. Mem. ABA, State Bar Wis., Am. Soc. CLUs, Am. Soc. Chartered Fin. Cons., Madison C. of C. (dir. 1976-80), U. Wis. Bus. Alumni (bd. dirs. 1986-90). Lutheran. Clubs: Maple Bluff (dir. 1974-80), Rotary. Home: 401 New Castle Way Madison WI 53704-6070 Office: PO Box 1191 Madison WI 53701-1191

LARSON, JOHN HYDE, retired utilities executive; b. Phila., Sept. 15, 1930; s. Roy Frank and Olive (Alden) L.; m. Priscilla Hibbs Beane; children: Michael Alden, Christopher Hibbs, Cynthia Ann. BA, Trinity Coll., 1953; M City Planning, MIT, 1955. Vice-pres. The Potomac Edison Co., Hagerstown, Md., 1969-72; treas. Allegheny Power System, Inc., N.Y.C., 1973-79; v.p. fin. Conn. Energy Corp., Bridgeport, Conn., 1980-85, pres., chief exec. officer, 1985-89; exec. v.p., chief operating officer So. Conn. Gas. Co., Bridgeport, Conn., 1981-85; pres., chief exec. officer So. Conn. Gas. Co., Bridgeport, 1985-89; acting dir. fin. City of Bridgeport, 1989-90; chmn. mgmt. adv. com. City of Bridgeport, Conn., 1990-93; chmn. selectman's com. on ops. improvement Westport, Conn., 1991; bd. dirs. Bay State Gas Co., Westborough, Mass., Bolt Tech., Inc., Norwalk Conn. Vice chmn. Bridgeport Hosp., 1991-93; chmn. Nova Med. Corp., 1991-95; hon. chmn. capital funds drive Family Svcs. Woodfield, 1988. Lt. (SC) USNR. Recipient Corp. Leadership award MIT, 1987, Century Svc. award Bridgeport Boys and Girls Club, 1991, Richard P. Bodine Community Leadership award, 1993. Mem. New Eng. Gas Assn. (chmn. 1988-89). Home: Mount Hunger Rd Barnard VT 05031

LARSON, JOHN WILLIAM, lawyer; b. Detroit, June 24, 1935; s. William and Sara Eleanor (Yeatman) L.; m. Pamela Jane Wren, Sept. 16, 1959; 1 dau., Jennifer Wren. BA with distinction, honors in Economics, Stanford, 1957; LLB, Stanford U., 1962. Bar: Calif. 1962. Assoc. Brobeck, Phleger & Harrison, San Francisco, 1962-68, ptnr., 1968-71, 73—, CEO, mng. ptnr., 1988-92, chmn. of firm, CEO, 1993-96; asst. sec. Dept. Interior, Washington, 1971-73; exec. dir. Natural Resources Com., Washington, 1973; counsellor to chmn. Cost of Living Coun., Washington, 1973; faculty Practising Law Inst.; bd. dirs. Measurex Corp. Mem. 1st U.S.-USSR Joint Com. on Environment; mem. bd. visitors Stanford U. Law Sch., 1974-77, 85-87, 95—; pres. bd. trustees The Katherine Branson Sch., 1980-83. With AUS, 1957-59. Mem. ABA, Calif. Bar Assn., San Francisco C. of C. (Bay Area coun. chmn. bd. dirs.), Order of Coif, Pacific Union Club, Burlingame Country Club, Bohemian Club. Home: PO Box 349 Ross CA 94957-0349 Office: Brobeck Phleger & Harrison Spear St Tower 1 Market Plz San Francisco CA 94105

LARSON, JOSEPH STANLEY, environmentalist, educator, researcher; b. Stoneham, Mass., June 23, 1933; s. Gustave Adolph and Marian (Kelly) L.; m. Wendy Nichols, Nov. 23, 1958; children: Marion Elizabeth, Sandra Frances. BS, U. Mass., 1956, MS, 1958; PhD, Va. Poly. Inst., 1966. Registered profl. forester, Maine. Exec. sec. Wildlife Conservation, Inc., Boston, 1958-59; state ornithologist Mass. Div. Fisheries and Wildlife, Boston, 1959-60; head conservation edn. div. Natural Resources Inst., U. Md., Annapolis, 1960-62, rsch. asst. prof., LaVale, 1965-67; wildlife rsch. biologist U.S. Fish and Wildlife Svc., Amherst, Mass., 1967-69; prof., dir. The Environ. Inst., U. Mass., Amherst, 1969—; cons. in field. Contbr. articles to profl. jours. Recipient Chevron Conservation award, 1990; grantee in field. Mem. AAUP (pres. Mass. chpt. 1976-77), AAAS, Wildlife Soc. (cert. wildlife biologist), Ecol. Soc. Am. (cert. sr. ecologist), Am. Assn. Mammalogists, Nat. Wetlands Tech. Coun. (exec. chmn.), Soc. Wetland Scientists (profl. wetland scientist), Mass. Audubon Soc. (bd. dirs.), Internat. Union for Conservation of Nature and Natural Resources (commn. on ecosystem mgmt.) (Switzerland), Faculty Univ. Club, Cosmos Club, Sigma Xi, Xi Sigma Pi, Phi Sigma. Congregationalist. Home: 27 Arnold Rd Pelham MA 01002-9757 Office: U Mass Environ Inst Blaisdell House Box 30820 Amherst MA 01003-0820

LARSON, KARIN LOUISE, financial analyst; b. Mpls., Aug. 8, 1938; d. Walter Carl and Clara Margaret (Nelson) L. BA, U. Minn., 1960; MBA, U. So. Calif., 1971. With Capital Group, Los Angeles, 1961—; rsch. assoc. Capital Rsch. Co., Los Angeles, 1966-68, fin. analyst, 1968-71, v.p., 1971-80, v.p., dir., 1980-88, sr. v.p., 1987-88; exec. v.p., dir. rsch. Capital Guardian Rsch. Co., L.A., 1988-89, pres., 1990—; pres. Capital Rsch. Internat., L.A., 1994—; dir. Capital Group Cos., 1995—; v.p. Investment Co. Am., L.A., 1980-88. Baptist. Office: Capital Guardian Research Co 333 S Hope St Fl 52 Los Angeles CA 90071-1406

LARSON, KERMIT DEAN, accounting educator; b. Algona, Iowa, Apr. 7, 1939; s. Loren L. and Hansena Laurena (Andersen) L.; m. Nancy Lynne Weber, June 17, 1961; children: Julie Renee, Timothy Dean, Cynthia Lynne. A.A., Ft. Dodge Jr. Coll., 1960; B.B.A., U. Iowa, 1962, M.B.A., 1963; D.B.A., U. Colo., 1966. C.P.A., Tex. Mem. faculty U. Tex., Austin, 1966—; Arthur Andersen & Co. Alumni prof. emeritus U. Tex., 1975—, chmn. dept. accounting, 1971-75; vis. asso. prof. Tulane U., New Orleans, 1970-71; cons. sales tax audit litigation, pvt. anti-trust litigation, expropriation ins. arbitration. Author: Fundamental Accounting Principles, 1978, 14th edit., 1996, Financial Accounting, 7th edit., 1997, (with Charlene Spoede and Paul Miller) Fundamentals of Financial and Managerial Accounting, 1994; contbr. articles to profl. jours. Mem. AICPA, Am. Acctg. Assn. (v.p. 1978-79), Tex. Soc. CPAs, Beta Gamma Sigma, Beta Alpha Psi. Baptist. Home: 1310 Falcon Ledge Dr Austin TX 78746-5120

LARSON, KIRK DAVID, pomologist and extension specialist; b. Pasadena, Calif., July 1, 1953; s. David and Martha Louise (Munn) L.; m. Katherine Ann Whitson, June 29, 1985; children: Kyle Galen, Kaelyn Ann. BS with high honors, U. Calif., Davis, 1980, MS, 1984; PhD, U. Fla., 1991. Horticulturist Aponte Farms, Peñuelas, P.R., 1971-75; vol. horticulturist Guatemalan Agrl. Project, San Juan Comalapa, Guatemala, 1977-78; agronomist IRI Rsch. Inst., Tinaco, Venezuela, 1980; orchard prodn. mgr. Pike Mt. Apples, North San Juan, Calif., 1981; rsch., teaching asst. Dept. of Pomology U. Calif., Davis, 1982-84; fruit crops ext. agt. Dade County Coop. Ext. Svc., Homestead, Fla., 1985-86; orchard prodn. mgr. J. R. Brooks & Son, Inc., Homestead, Fla., 1986-88; rsch. and teaching asst. Dept. Fruit Crops U. Fla., Gainesville, 1988-91; pomologist, ext. specialist U. Calif., Davis, 1991—; horticultural cons. U.S. Agrl. Svc., Miami, Fla., 1989-91, Agridec, Inc., Miami, 1990, U. Malaga, Andalucia, Spain, 1995, Spanish Strawberry Nursery Industry, Seville, 1995, El Monte, Caja de Huelva y Sevilla, Huelva, Spain, 1995. Contbr. articles to profl. jours. and chpt. to book. Recipient citation for Outstanding Achievement in Internat. Agrl. Devel., U. Calif. Davis, 1979; grantee Calif. Strawberry Commn., 1992—, USDA, 1994—. Mem. Am. Soc. for Horticultural Sci., N.Am. Strawberry Growers Assn., Fla. State Horticultural Soc., Phi Kappa Phi, Gamma Sigma Delta. Avocations: horticulture, fgn. langs. Office: U Calif South Coast Rsch Ctr 7601 Irvine Blvd Irvine CA 92618-1201

LARSON, KURT PAUL, fire chief; b. Arlington, Va., Jan. 6, 1958; s. Leonard Paul and June Audrey (Kruck) L.; m. Linda Kay Black, Sept. 21, 1991. BS, U. Colo., 1980; MEd, U. Ariz., 1988; exec. fire officer, Nat. Fire Acad., 1996. Firefighter Wheat Ridge (Colo.) Fire Dept., 1986-89, fire marshal, 1989-90, lt., 1989-90, dep. fire chief, 1991—; performer Up With People Internat., Broomfield, Colo., 1987—; fire investigator Castlewood Fire Dept., Englewood, Colo., 1990-91; fire chief Colo. Divsn. Fire Safety, Denver, 1993—; fire svc. lectr., instr., author, Wheat Ridge, 1989—; bd. dirs. Wheat Ridge Fire Dept.; cons. Wheat Ridge, 1989—. Mem. Nat. Youth Com., Muscular Dystrophy Assn., 1979; chmn. Easter Seal Soc. Youth Program, 1980,. Named Legion of Honor Am. Legion, Denver, 1968, Chevalier Internat. Order of DeMolay, Denver, 1990, Hon. Fire Chief SW Colo. Firefighters Assn., Durango, 1992. Mem. Internat. Assn. Arson Investigators, Internat. Assn. Fire Chiefs, Colo. Fire Chiefs Assn., Nat. Fire Protection Assn., Scottish Rite of Freemasonry (officer 1982—), York Rite of Masonry, Wheat Ridge Masons (presiding officer 1982—, past master 1992), Fire Safety Educators (treas. 1988—), Fire Marshals Assn. Colo., Up With People. Republican. Home: 3565 Miller St Wheat Ridge CO 80033-5658 Office: Wheat Ridge Fire Dist 3880 Upham St Wheat Ridge CO 80033-4825

LARSON, LARRY, librarian; b. El Dorado, Ark., July 18, 1940; s. Willie Lee and Myrtle Elizabeth (McMaster) L.; m. Dorothy Ann Bing, Apr 23, 1966; 1 child, Larisa Ann. BS, Ouachita Baptist U., 1962; MLS, George Peabody Coll., 1967. Asst. librarian, media specialist Hall High Sch., Little Rock, 1962-65; asst. librarian, circulation Ark. Tech. U., Russellville, 1965-67; asst librarian reference Hendrix Coll., Conway, Ark., 1967-73; head librarian U. Ark., Monticello, 1973-75; librarian, dir. N. Ark. Regional Library, Harrison, 1975-85, Ft. Smith (Ark.) Pub. Library, 1985—. Bd. dirs. Ft. Smith Hist. Soc., 1986-90; treas. bd. dirs. Pub. Awareness Com., Ft. Smith, Ark., 1986—. Mem. ALA, Ark. Libr. Assn. (vice chair membership com. 1968, Disting. Svc. award 1985, chair pub. libr. divsn., 1993), Ark. Libr. Devel. Dist. (chair 1985-87), Ark. Adminstrs. Pub. Librs. (chair 1988-89, del. Ark. govs.' conf. on librs. 1990), Noon Exchange Club. Democrat. Baptist. Avocations: gardening, woodworking. Home: 3114 S Enid St Fort Smith AR 72903-4445 Office: Ft Smith Pub Libr 61 S 8th St Fort Smith AR 72901-2415

LARSON, MARK ALLAN, financial executive; b. Milw., June 24, 1948; s. Owen Earl and Alice May (Ulmen) L.; m. Linda Rosalie Wohlschlaeger, Jan. 3, 1970; children: Craig Allan, Emily Lin. BA, Ripon Coll., 1970; postgrad., Washington U., St. Louis, 1971-74; postgrad. in bus., St. Louis U., 1974-76. Personnel supr. Barnes Hosp., St. Louis, 1970-71; various fin. and mgmt. positions Bank Bldg. Corp., St. Louis, 1971-76, G.D. Searle & Co., Skokie, Ill., Geneva, Switzerland, 1976-85; sr. v.p., chief fin. and admistrv. officer Leaf Inc., Bannockburn, Ill., 1985-89; v.p. internat. devel. and adminstrn. Carlson Cos., Inc., Mpls., 1990-91; exec. v.p. fin. and adminstrn., travel and mktg. groups, 1992-93, exec. v.p. ops. and internat., mktg. groups, 1993-95; sr. v.p. fin. Internat. Distillers & Vintners N.Am., Hartford, Conn., 1995-96; pres. IDV Wines, San Mateo, Calif., 1997—. Home: 12 Colton Ct Redwood City CA 94062

LARSON, MARK EDWARD, JR., lawyer, educator, financial advisor; b. Oak Park, Ill., Dec. 16, 1947; s. Mark Edward and Lois Vivian (Benson) L.; m. Patricia Jo Jekerle, Apr. 14, 1973; children: Adam Douglas, Peter Joseph, Alex Edward, Gretchen Elizabeth. BS in Acctg., U. Ill., 1969; JD, Northwestern U., 1972; LLM in Taxation, NYU, 1977. Bar: Ill. 1973, U.S. Dist. Ct. (no. dist.) Ill. 1973, N.Y. 1975, U.S. Dist. Ct. (so. dist.) N.Y. 1975, U.S. Ct. Appeals (2d cir.) 1975, D.C. 1976, U.S. Ct. Appeals (7th cir.) 1976, U.S. Tax Ct. 1976, U.S. Supreme Ct. 1976, U.S. Dist. Ct. D.C. 1977, U.S. Ct. Appeals (D.C. cir.) 1977, U.S. Dist. Ct. Minn. 1982, U.S. Ct. Appeals (8th cir.) 1982, Minn. 1982, Tex. 1984; CPA, Ill. Acct. Deloitte & Touche (formerly Haskins & Sells), N.Y.C., 1973-75, Chgo., 1978-81; atty., ptnr. Larson, Perry & Ward and former firms, Chgo., 1981—; prin. Winfield Fin. Svcs. and affiliates, Chgo., 1986—; adj. prof. U. Minn., Mpls., 1982-83, Aurora (Ill.) U., 1990—; acad. chair CFPBS program Loyola U., Chgo., 1996—. Contbr. articles to profl. publs. Mem. AICPA, ABA, Am. Assn. Atty.-CPAs. Office: 1212 S Naper Blvd Ste 119 Naperville IL 60540

LARSON, MARY BEA, elementary education educator; b. Brookings, S.D., Apr. 19, 1946; d. Theodore Orville and Doris Rose (Conway) Larson; children: Christie DiRé, Corey DiRe. BA, Wash. State U., 1968, Portland State U., 1973; MA, U. Guam, 1975; postgrad., Seattle Pacific U., 1980-85, Western Wash. U., Oxford U. Cert. tchr., Wash. Tchr. early childhood and creativity Chemeketa C. C., Salem, Oreg., 1971-73; tchr. kindergarten-1st grade Govt. Guam, Agana, 1973-75; tchr. kindergarten, 3rd grade Canal Zone Govt., Balboa, Panama, 1975-78; tchr. kindergarten, 2d and 3d grades, elem. art specialist Marysville (Wash.) Sch. Dist., 1978-96; mem. profl. adv. bd. coll. edn. Western Wash. U., 1989-96. Active Snohomish County Arts Coun. Mem. NEA (del. to Nat. Rep. Assembly, Washington 1992, San Francisco 1993), Wash. Edn. Assn., Marysville Edn. Assn. (pres. 1990-92), Nat. Mus. Women in Arts (founder), Seattle Art Mus. (landmark), Alpha Delta Kappa (state sgt.-at-arms 1990-92, state chaplain 1992-94, state v.p. 1994-96). Home: 15605 N Spring Tree Ct SE Mill Creek WA 98012-5825

LARSON, MAURICE ALLEN, chemical engineer, educator; b. Missouri Valley, Iowa, July 19, 1927; s. Albert Juluis and Grace Elizabeth (Chambers) L.; m. Ruth Elizabeth Gugeler, Dec. 5, 1953; children: Richard Alan (dec.), Janet Ann, John Albert. BS, Iowa State U., 1951, PhD, 1958. Chem. engr. Dow Corning Corp., Midland, Mich., 1951-54; teaching asst. Iowa State U., 1954-55, instr. dept. chem. engring., 1955-58, asst. prof., 1958-61, assoc. prof., 1961-64, prof., 1964—, Anson Marston Disting. prof., 1977—, chmn. dept. chem. engring., 1978-83; cons. AID, Kharagpur, India, 1968, USIA, Amman, Jordan, 1983, 84, 85; Shell vis. prof. Univ. Coll., London, 1971-72; sci. exchange visitor, Czechoslovakia and Poland, 1974; vis. prof. U. Queensland, Australia, summer 1981, U. Manchester Inst. Sci. and Tech., Eng., 1984-85; guest prof. Tianjin U., Peoples Republic of China, 1982; hon. lectr. Mid. Am. State U. Assn., 1986-87; Dow Corning Australia Bicentennial lectr., Sydney, 1988. Author: (with A.D. Randolph) Theory of Particulate Processes, 1971, 2d edit., 1988; contbr. (with others) articles to profl. jours. With U.S. Army, 1946-47. Recipient H.A. Webber Teaching award Iowa State U., 1967, Western Electric Fund award Am. Soc. Engring. Edn., 1970, Faculty citation Iowa State U. Alumni, 1972, Gov.'s Sci. medal State of Iowa, 1990, D.R. Boylan Eminent Faculty award Iowa State U., 1990; NSF fellow, 1965-66. Fellow Am. Inst. Chem. Engrs. (pres. Iowa 1970-71); Mem. Am. Chem. Soc. (chmn. div. fertilizer and soil chemistry 1975), Am. Soc. Engring. Edn., Lions (pres. Ames club 1979-80), Sigma Xi, Tau Beta Pi, Phi Lambda Upsilon, Phi Kappa Phi. Democrat. Methodist. Home: 2710 Thompson Dr Ames IA 50010-4759

LARSON, MICHAEL LEN, newspaper editor; b. St. James, Minn., Feb. 3, 1944; s. Leonard O. and Lois O. (Holte) L.; m. Kay M. Monahan, June 18, 1966; children: Christopher, David, Molly. BA, U. Minn., 1966; MBA, Mankato State U., 1986. Mng. editor Paddock Circle Inc., Libertyville, Ill., 1972-74, New Ulm (Minn.) Journal, 1974-76, Republican-Eagle, Red Wing, Minn., 1976-79; mng. editor Mankato (Minn.) Free Press, 1979-84, editor, 1984-95, editor of editl. page, 1995-97; editor Minot (N.D.) Daily News, 1997—. Bd. dirs. Valley Indsl. Devel. Corp., Mankato, 1985-95, also treas.; mem. adv. bd. minn. State U. Bus. Sch. Served with U.S. Army, 1966-68, Vietnam. Recipient five First Place awards for investigative reporting Minn. Newspaper Assn., 1969, 71, 72, 76, 78, First Place award for feature writing, Suburban Newspapers Am., 1974. Mem. Minn. AP (pres. 1988—), Kiwanis. Roman Catholic. Avocation: bicycling. Home: 35 University Ct Mankato MN 56001-4182 Office: Minot Daily News 301 4th St SE Minot SD 58702

LARSON, NANCY CELESTE, computer systems manager; b. Chgo., July 17, 1951; d. Melvin Ellsworth and Ruth Margaret (Carlson) L. BS in Music Ed., U. Ill., 1973, MS in Music Edn., 1976; postgrad., Purdue Univ., 1982-86. Vocal music educator Consol. Sch. Dist., Gilman, Ill., 1975-77; elem. vocal music tchr. Sch. Dist. 161, Flossmoor, Ill., 1977-87; instr. Vander Cook Coll., Chgo., 1980-88; systems programmer analyst Sears, Roebuck & Co., Chgo., 1987-92, tech. instr., 1989-90, project leader, 1990-91, sr. systems analyst, 1991-92; sr. systems analyst Trans Union Corp., Chgo., 1992-94, project mgr., 1994, mgr., 1994—; tchr. adult computer edn. Homewood-Flossmoor High Sch., 1986-90. Chmn. Faith Luth. Ch., 1982-87, pres. bd., 1988-91, vocal soloist and voice-over performer. Mem. Ill. Music Educators Assn., Music Educators Nat. Conf., Ill. Educators Assn., Nat. Educators Assn., Am. ORFF Schulwerk Assn., Flossmoor Edn. Assn. (negotiator 1983-86). Republican. Lutheran. Avocations: swimming, skiing, reading, antique hunting. Home: 1960 N Lincoln Park W Apt 908 Chicago IL 60614-5440 Office: Trans Union Corp 555 W Adams St Chicago IL 60661-3601

LARSON, PAUL WILLIAM, public relations executive; b. Wilmington, N.C., May 28, 1956; s. Robert WIlliam and Helen Joyce (Hillen) L. BA, U. Calif., Berkeley, 1981; MS in Journalism Medill Sch. of Journalism, Northwestern U., Evanston, Ill., 1991. Reporter Turlock (Calif.) Daily Jour., 1982-84; writer, editor Paul Larson Commns., Modesto, Calif., 1984-90; dir. external affairs and publs. Medill Sch. Journalism, Northwestern U., Evanston, Ill., 1991-96; mgr. strategic comms. AMA, Chgo., 1996—; adj. lectr. Medill Sch. Journalism, Evanston, 1991—; assoc. master Commns. Residential Coll., Northwestern U., Evanston, 1993-96; judge Parenting Publs. of America Contest, Evanston, 1993—. mem. bd. dirs. Housing Options for the Mentally Ill, Evanston, 1993—, Rotary Club of Evanston, Ill., 1994—; docent Evanston Hist. Soc., 1992-95; chair comms. com. Evanston C. of C., 1995—. Recipient Rotary Group Study Exchg. award Rotary Internat., 1986, Rotary Found. Dist. Svc. award, 1995, Leadership Evanston Evanston Cmty. Rels., 1995-96, Vol. of the Yr. award Evanston McGaw YMCA, 1995. Office: AMA 515 N State St Chicago IL 60610-4325

LARSON, PETER L., legal assistant, investigator; b. Chgo., June 24, 1941; s. Allan M. and Harriet G. (Lans) L.; m. Carole J. Dierking, Feb. 4, 1961; children: Lori, Lance, Lynn, Lee. Assoc. Bus. Adminstrn., Muskegon Bus. U., 1961. Bar: Tex. (legal assts. divsn.) 1992; cert. in civil trial law, personal injury trial law Tex. Bd. Legal Specialization (L.A. divsn. stds.). South Tex. area mgr. So. Detectives, Inc., Houston, 1976-78; pres. Confidential Investigation Agy., Houston, 1978-85; sr. legal asst. Leger, Coplen & Jefferson, PC, Houston, 1985—; pres. Tex. Inc. Citizens' Property Rights Org., Houston. Chmn. Tri-County Foster Parents, Muskegon, 1974; committeeman Boy Scouts Am., Ravenna, Mich., 1972. Staff sgt. USAF, 1961-64. Mem. ATLA (paralegal affiliate), Nat. Assn. Legal Assts. (cert.), Nat. Assn. Legal Investigators (cert., Editor/Pubs. award 1994). Avocations: photography/videography, stamps, antique woodworking tools, target pistols, art. Home: 10135 Prospect Hill Dr Houston TX 77064-5439 Office: Tex Citizen Property Rights Org 5847 San Felipe Ste 2440 Houston TX 77057

LARSON, REED EUGENE, foundation administrator; b. Smith County, Kans., Sept. 27, 1922; s. George Christian and Edith Hazel (Whitney) L.; m. Marjorie Jeanne Hess, Aug. 31, 1947; children: Patricia Kay Larson Sween, Barbara Ann Larson Finnegan, Marcia Lynn Larson Craig. Student, Kans. Wesleyan U., 1940-41, Ohio State U., 1943-44; B.S. in E.E, Kans. State U., 1947. Design engr. Stein Labs., Atchison, Kans., 1947-48; processing engr. Coleman Co., Wichita, Kans., 1948-54; exec. v.p. Kansans for the Right to Work, Wichita, 1954-58; exec. v.p. Nat. Right-to-Work Com., Washington, 1959-76, pres., 1976—; exec. v.p. Nat. Right-to-Work Legal Def. Found., Washington, 1968-73, pres., 1973—; chmn. Hallmark Bank & Trust, 1984-96; vice chmn. F&M Bank-No. Va., 1996—. Served with AUS, 1943-46. Recipient Seldon Waldo award U.S. Jaycees, 1956; Silver Anvil award Public Relations Soc. Am., 1966; James J. Kilpatrick award Internat. Platform Assn., 1980; Awarded Doctor of Laws Campbell U., 1988. Mem. Mont Pelerin Soc., Phila. Soc., Eta Kappa Nu, Tau Beta Pi. Baptist. Clubs: Kansas Jaycees (pres. 1953-54), Rotary, Am. Legion. Home: 7803 Antiopi St Annandale VA 22003-1405 Office: 8001 Braddock Rd Springfield VA 22151-2110

LARSON, RICHARD SMITH, pathologist, researcher; b. Ithaca, N.Y., Aug. 27, 1962; s. Richard Ingwald and Judith Ann (Larsen) L.; m. Blaire Martin, June 4, 1989. AB in Chemistry summa cum laude, U. N.C., 1984; MD, Harvard U., 1990, PhD, 1990. Cert. anatomic and clin. pathologist Am. Bd. Pathology. Pathologist, resident Barnes Hosp., St. Louis, 1990-93; hematopathology fellow Vanderbilt U., Nashville, 1993-96; asst. prof., dir. clin. hematology lab. U. N.Mex., 1996—. Contbr. articles to profl. jours. including Jour. Biol. Chemistry, Procs. NAS, European Molecular Biology Orgn. Jour., Jour. Exptl. Medicine, Jour. Virology, Jour. Cell Biology, Advances in Immunology, Leukocyte Adhesion Molecules, Procs. Cold Spring Harbor Symposia on Quant. Biology, Leukocyte Typing IV, Cell

Regulation, Immunol. Revs., Cardiac Pathology, Diagnostic Molecular Pathology, Am. Jour. Clin. Pathology, Blood, Pediatric Nephrology, Human Path. Cancer Rsch. Recipient Nat. Rsch. Sci. award, 1986-90, 92-93. Mem. Am. Soc. Clin. Pathologists, Coll. Am. Pathologists (chmn. future tech. com.), Am. Soc. Hematology, Assn. Molecular Pathologists, Southwest Oncology Group. Phi Beta Kappa. Achievements include several patents including cDNA clone of LFA-1 alpha subunit and anti-inflamatory drugs.

LARSON, ROLAND ELMER, health care executive; b. Chgo., Jan. 21, 1939; s. Elmer Gustav and Anna (Alphida) L.; m. Noel Kathleen Brennan, June 28, 1969; children: Eric R., Jennifer L., Melissa K. BA, Augustana Coll., 1961; MHA, U. Iowa, 1963; postgrad., Harvard U., 1978. Adminstrv. asst. U. Vt. Med. Ctr., Burlington, 1962-64; assoc. adminstr. Roger Williams Hosp., Providence, 1964-73; v.p. adminstrn. Norwalk (Conn.) Hosp., 1973-81; pres., chief exec. officer Nashoba Community Hosp., Ayer, Mass., 1981-88; v.p. Charles River Assn., Boston, 1988-90; cons. Charles River Assocs., Boston, 1990-93; ind. healthcare cons. Harvard, Mass., 1990—. Chmn. Harvard (Mass.) Coalition Against Drugs and Alcohol, Opportunities, Inc., Providence, 1966-68, Greater Norwalk Community Coun., 1980; bd. dirs. Nat. Arthritis Found., N.Y.C., 1967-71, Am. Cancer Soc., Stamford, Conn., 1978-81. Fellow Am. Coll. Healthcare Execs.; mem. Cen. Mass. Hosp. Coun. (chmn. 1987-88), Rotary. Avocations: sailing, bicycling, golf, squash, woodworking. Home and Office: Larson & Assocs 28 Candleberry Ln Harvard MA 01451-1641

LARSON, ROY, journalist, publisher; b. Moline, Ill., July 27, 1929; s. Roy W. and Jane (Beall) L.; m. Dorothy Jennisch, June 7, 1950; children: Mark, Bruce, Jodie, Bradley. A.B., Augustana Coll., Rock Island, Ill., 1951; M.Div., Garrett Theol. Sem., 1955. Ordained to ministry Methodist Ch., 1956; min. Covenant United Meth. Ch., Evanston, Ill., 1963-68, First United Meth. Ch., Elmhurst, Ill., 1968-69; religion editor Chgo. Sun-Times, 1969-85; pub. The Chgo. Reporter, 1985-94; exec. dir. Garrett-Medill Ctr. for Religion and News Media, Evanston, Ill., 1995—. Home: 1508 Hinman Ave Evanston IL 60201-4664 Office: Garrett-Medill Ctr 2121 Sheridan Rd Evanston IL 60201-2926

LARSON, RUSSELL EDWARD, university provost emeritus, consultant agriculture research and development; b. Mpls., Jan. 2, 1917; s. Karl Sam and Belle (Wing) L.; m. Margaret Agnes Johnson, Aug. 19, 1939; children: Gayle Margaret, Beverly Jean, Russell Troy. BS, U. Minn., 1939, MS, 1940, PhD, 1942; DSc (hon.), Delaware Valley Coll. Sci. and Agr., 1966. Asst. prof. U. R.I., Kingston, 1941-44; asst. prof. Pa. State U., University Park, 1944-45, assoc. prof., 1945-47, prof., 1947—, head dept. horticulture, 1952-62, dean Coll. Agriculture, 1963-72, provost, 1972-77; sci. advisor Am. Cocoa Rsch. Inst., McLean, Va., 1975-87; cons. Agriculture R & D, State Coll. Pa., 1977—. Contbr. 46 tech. articles on plant sci. to profl. jours. Recipient Outstanding Alumnus award U. Minn., 1961. Fellow AAAS, Am. Soc. Hort. Sci. (pres. 1963-64, L.H. Vaughan award 1948); mem. Am. Genetic Assn., Am. Inst. Biol. Sci., Sigma Xi. Republican. Lutheran. Avocations: gardening, golf, fishing. Home: 608 Elmwood St State College PA 16801-7053 Office: Pa State U 6 Tyson Bldg University Park PA 16802-4202

LARSON, RUSSELL GEORGE, magazine and book publisher; b. Waukesha, Wis., May 4, 1942; s. George Arthur and Dorothy Edna (Hanneman) L.; m. Barbara Kay Krsek, Aug. 1, 1964; children—Eric, Craig, Denise. A.A.S., Milw. Sch. Engring., 1962. Tech. writer various publs., 1962-69; assoc. editor Model Railroader Mag., Milw., 1969-75, mng. editor, 1975-77, editor, 1977-93, v.p. editorial, 1989-93, sr. v.p. editorial, 1993—; pub. Model Railroader Mag., Trains Mag., Classic Toy Trains Mag., Collecting Toys Mag., Astronomy Mag., Earth Mag., Birder's World Mag., Garden Railways Mag., Kalmbach Books, Greenberg Books, Milw. Author: N Scale Primer, 1973, Beginner's Guide to N Scale Model Railroading, 1990, Beginner's Guide to Large Scale Model Railroading, 1994. Mem. Soc. Tech. Communication. Lutheran. Avocations: golf, model railroading, reading, travel. Office: Kalmbach Pub Co PO box 1612 21027 Crossroads Cir Waukesha WI 53186-4055

LARSON, SANDRA MAE, nursing educator; b. Chgo., Apr. 21, 1944; d. Richard Milward and Eldred Gertrude (Piehl) Blackburn; m. Eric Richard Larson, Nov. 25, 1967; children—Sarah, Keith. B.S., No. Ill. U., 1966, M.S., 1978. R.N., Ill. Nursing educator Lutheran Hosp., Moline, Ill., 1968-70; charge nurse ICU, Peninsula Hosp., Burlingame, Calif., 1970-72; staff nurse Illini Hosp., Silvis, Ill., 1972-76; nursing educator Black Hawk Coll., Moline, 1976—; interviewer Am. Cancer Soc., Moline, 1982, 84, 86. Co-author Anatomy and Physiology Testbank, 1994, 97. Mem. Am. Nurses Assn., Ill. Nurses Assn. (bd. dirs. 5th dist. 1979-82, treas., 1982-84, pres. 1984-86, 1st v.p. 1986-87, pres. 1988-92, 2nd v.p., 1993-95), Sigma Theta Tau. Democrat. Roman Catholic. Avocations: camping; reading. Home: 3009 29th St Moline IL 61265-6950 Office: Black Hawk Coll 6600 34th Ave Moline IL 61265-5870

LARSON, SIDNEY, art educator, artist, writer, painting conservator; b. Sterling, Colo., June 16, 1923; s. Harry and Ann Levin; m. George Ann Madden, Aug. 30, 1947; children: Sara Catherine, Nancy Louise. BA, U. Mo., 1949, MA in Art, 1950. Prof. art Columbia Coll., Mo., 1951—; art curator State Hist. Soc. Mo., 1962—; painting conservator, Columbia, 1960—. Exhibited paintings and drawings in group shows in Midwest, Washington, N.Y. and Japan; executed murals Daily News, Rolla, Mo., Shelter Ins., Columbia, Mo., Guitar Bldg., Columbia, Mcpl. Bldg., Jefferson City, Mo., Centerre Bank, Columbia, chs. in Okla. and Ark. Adv. Mo. State Council on Arts, 1960, Boone County Courthouse, Columbia. Served with USN, 1943-46, PTO. Fellow Huntington Hartford Found., 1962; rRecipient Commendation award Senate of State of Mo., 1977, 87, Nat. Prof. of Yr. award, Bronze medalist, Mo. State Prof. of Yr. award Coun. for Advancement and Support Edn., 1987, Disting. Svc. award State Hist. Soc. Mo., Mo. State Arts Coun. award, 1991. Mem. Am. Inst. Conservation of Hist. and Artistic Works (assoc. mem.), Nat. Assn. Mural Painters. Avocations: world travel, reading. Home: 1408 Whitburn Dr Columbia MO 65203-5172 Office: Columbia Coll Dept Art Columbia MO 65216

LARSON, WARD JEROME, lawyer, retired banker; b. Mpls., Mar. 3, 1924; s. Philip Jerome and Inez (Sandstrom) L.; m. Phyllis Jean Lindahl, June 18, 1949; children—Eric, Peter, David, Barbara. BA, North Central Coll., Naperville, Ill., 1948; LLB, Harvard U., 1951. Bar: Ill. 1951. Atty. First Nat. Bank Chgo., 1951-56; asst. trust officer, v.p. DuPage Trust Co., Glen Ellyn, Ill., 1956-62; with Fed. Res. Bank Chgo., 1962-80, v.p., gen. counsel, sec., 1968, sr. v.p., gen. counsel, sec., 1970-80; sole practice law Glen Ellyn, 1980—; Chmn. ins. com. Fed. Res. Banks, 1968-80; mem. adminstrv. bd. Fed. Res. Employee Benefits System, 1970-74, vice chmn., 1973-74. Mem. bd. edn. Sch. Dist. 41, Glen Ellyn, Ill., 1961-67, pres., 1964-67; chmn. estate planning com. North Ctrl. Coll., 1962-68, trustee, 1980-81, planned giving officer, 1987-90; chmn. trustees 1st United Meth. Ch., Glen Ellyn, 1968-69, chmn. coun. ministries, 1969-71, chmn. membership commn., 1973-75, chmn. social concerns com., 1977, membership sec., 1985-90, lay leader, 1979, 90-93, 97—; lay mem. ann. conf. United Meth. Ch. No. Ill., 1992—, mem. conf. coun. fin. and adminstrn.; bd. dirs., v.p. B.R. Ryall YMCA, Glen Ellyn, 1968-70; bd. dirs. United Meth. Found.-North Ill. Conf., 1973-76; mem. exec. com. Chgo. chpt. March of Dimes, 1978-80; mem. Coun. Laity Garrett-Evang. Theol. Sem., 1984-90; planned giving cons. Ctrl. DuPage Hosp., 1992-95. 1st lt., infantry, AUS, 1943-46. Mem. ABA, Alumni Assn. North Central Coll. (dir. 1976—, sec. 1977-78, pres. 1980-81, nat. chmn. ann. fund 1983-92, Outstanding Alumnus award 1986). Home and Office: 822 Saddlewood Dr Glen Ellyn IL 60137-3202

LARSON, WILFRED JOSEPH, chemical company executive; b. N.Y.C., July 12, 1927; s. Fred Wilfred and Mabel Louise (Messier) L.; m. Joan Jesslyn Tilford, Sept. 4, 1949; children: Linda Sue, Robert Wilfred. B.S. in Econs., U. Pa., 1951; postgrad., U. Chgo., 1958-59, Seton Hall U., 1960-61, U. Cin., 1964-65. With Ward Foods, N.Y.C., 1953-63; contr., chief fin. officer Ward Foods, 1961-63; with Drackett Co., Cin., 1963-79; fin. v.p. Drackett Co., 1966-67, adminstrv. v.p., 1967-68, exec. v.p., 1969-79; pres. Bristol-Myers Products Can., 1977-79; v.p. Bristol-Myers Squibb Co., 1981-92; pres. Westwood Squibb Pharms., Inc., 1979-92; past chmn. Western N.Y. Tech. Devel. Ctr.; bd. dirs. First Empire State Corp., MT&T Bank, Bryant & Stratton, Horus Therapeutics Inc.;. Pres., trustee Cin. Adolescent Clinic, Inc., 1968-80; trustee, past chmn. Women's & Children's Rsch. Found., Children's Hosp.; past chmn., bd dirs. Greater Buffalo YMCA; trustee, past treas. Studio Arena Theatre; chmn. SUNY-Buffalo Sch. Pharmacy Centennial, 1986; past trustee Calspan/UB Rsch. Ctr.; past vice chmn., bd. dirs. Buffalo Children's Hosp.; chmn. bd. dirs. Buffalo Philharm. Orch. Soc., Inc., 1986-91; vice chmn. bd. dirs. Greater Buffalo Devel. Found., 1987-92; bd. dirs. Buffalo Fine Arts Acad., 1988-91, Am. Symphony Orch. League, 1989-91, U. at Buffalo Found., 1990-94; mem. cmty. coun. Roswell Park Meml. Inst., 1988-94. With USNR, 1945-47, AUS, 1951-53. Named Buffalo/Niagara Sales and Mktg. Exec. of Yr., 1985, Disting. Citizen of Yr. Boy Scouts Am., 1987, Ann. Alumni award Niagara Frontier Exec. of Yr., U. Buffalo Sch. Mgmt., 1987; recipient Disting. Pub. Svc. award SUNY Buffalo Alumni Assn., 1986, Outstanding Citizens award Buffalo News, 1987, Man of Yr. award West Side Bus. and Taxpayers Assn., 1989, Bus. Exec. of Yr. award Nat. Assn. Accts. Buffalo chpt., 1989. Mem. Fin. Execs. Inst. (treas., sec. 1965-68), Greater Buffalo C. of C. (bd. dirs. 1989-92, We. New Yorker of Yr. award 1992, Patron of Arts award 1993), Leland (Mich.) Country Club, Moorings Country Club (Naples, Fla.), Commonwealth Club Cin., Buffalo Club, Royal Poinciana Golf Club (Naples). Republican. Episcopalian (vestryman, treas. 1966-69). Home: 88 Oakland Pl Buffalo NY 14222-2030 Office: 100 Forest Ave Buffalo NY 14213-1032

LA RUE, CARL FORMAN, lawyer; b. Ann Arbor, Mich., Aug. 4, 1929; s. Carl D. and Evelina F. La R.; children: Steven, Edward; m. Ann Williams Lindbloom, June 28, 1971; stepchildren: Eric, Sarah Relyea. A.B., Harvard U., 1952; LL.B., U. Mich., 1957. Bar: Ohio 1957, Ill. 1964, Calif. 1969. Assoc. firm Fuller & Henry, Toledo, 1957-59; asst. U.S. atty. for Northwestern Ohio, Dept. Justice, 1959-61; staff atty. Trinova Corp. (then Libbey-Owens-Ford Co.), Toledo, 1961-64; v.p., gen. counsel, sec. Trinova Corp., Toledo, 1978-87; of counsel Marshall & Melhorn, Toledo, 1988-96; sr. atty. Armour and Co., Chgo., 1964-68; asst. gen. counsel Rockwell Internat., Los Angeles, 1968-78. With U.S. Army, 1952-54. Mem. Toledo Club, Toledo Tennis Club, Westowne Tennis Club. Home: 3553 Brookside Rd Toledo OH 43606-2610

LA RUE, HENRY ALDRED, consultant, former oil company executive; b. Denver, Aug. 13, 1927; s. Robert Hughes and Leona Spencer (Wood) La R.; m. Marion Hardin Klein, Aug. 22, 1954. B.S. in Bus. Adminstrn., U. Kans., 1951. Pres. Pacific Gulf Oil Co., Tokyo, 1973-74; exec. v.p. Gulf Oil Middle East Co., Pitts., 1974-75, Gulf Sci. and Tech. Co., Pitts., 1975-82; pres. Gulf Research and Devel. Co., Pitts., 1975-82, Pitts. Applied Rsch. Corp., U. Pitts. Applied Rsch. Ctr., 1986-88; vice chmn. Pitts. Applied Rsch. Ctr., 1988-92; chief exec. officer Alle-Kiski Revitalization Corp., 1989-90; cons. in field. Bd. dirs. Gulf Oil Corp. Found., Pitts., 1976-82, Franklin Rsch. Ctr., Phila., 1981-86, Colo. Sch. Mines Rsch. Inst., Golden, 1981-87; v.p., dir. Bio Rsch. Ctr. Co., Tokyo, 1973-84; mem. adv. bd. Mellon Inst., Pitts., 1977-83;. sec. Salvation Army Greater Pitts., 1980—; mem. Bell Acres Borough Coun., 1992, vice chmn., 1994. Recipient achievement award indsl. research Slippery Rock U. Mem. Am. Petroleum Inst., Am. C. of C. (pres. Seoul, Korea 1970-71, 1st v.p. Taipei, Taiwan 1972-73), Duquesne Club, Edgeworth Club, Sewickley Heights Golf Club, Beta Theta Pi, Delta Sigma Pi. Republican. Episcopalian. Home: 129 Woodcock Drive Rd Sewickley PA 15143-8356 Office: Pitts Applied Research Corp 100 William Pitt Way Pittsburgh PA 15238-1327

LA RUE, (ADRIAN) JAN (PIETERS), musicologist, educator, author; b. Kisaran, Sumatra, Indonesia, July 31, 1918; s. Carl Downey and Evelina Brown (Forman) LaR.; m. Helen Claire Robison, Aug. 21, 1940; children: Charlotte (Mrs. Jonathan L. Isaacs), Christine (Mrs. Dan Honig). SB, Harvard, 1940, PhD, 1952; M.F.A., Princeton, 1942. Instr. music Wellesley Coll., 1942-43, 46-48, asst. prof., 1948-50, asso. prof., 1950-57, chmn. dept. music, 1950-57; prof. NYU, 1957-88; prof. emeritus N.Y. U., 1988—, exec. dean arts and sci., 1962-63, chmn. dept. music, 1970-73, dir. grad. studies in music, 1973-80; vis. prof. UCLA, 1947, U. Mich., 1962, Bar Ilan U., Israel, 1980, Queens U., Ont., 1996; first musicologist-in-residence Mozart Festival, The Kennedy Ctr., Washington, 1975. Author: Guidelines for Style Analysis, 1970, 2d edit., 1992, A Catalogue of 18th Century Symphonies, 1988, Vol. 1, Thematic Identifier; co-author: (with M. Ohmiya) Methods and Models for Comprehensive Style Analysis, 1988; contbg. author: Die Musik in Geschichte und Gegenwart, 1968, Grove's Dictionary of Music and Musicians, 1980, Festschriften Hans Albrecht, 1976, Karl Vötterle, 1977, Charles Cudworth, 1978, Eileen Southern, 1988, Leonard Ratner, 1990, Alan Tyson, 1997; editor: Congress Report of the Internat. Musicol. Soc., 2 vols., 1961, Festschrift Otto Erich Deutsch, 1963, Festschrift Gustave Reese: Aspects of Medieval and Renaissance Music, 1966; contbr. numerous articles on 18th century symphony and concerto, mus. analysis, watermarks, music manuscripts and computer applications to profl. jours. Mem. coun. Smithsonian Instn., 1967-73; mem. Zentralinstitut für Mozartforschung, Salzburg (Austria) Mozarteum, 1969—. lst lt. Transp. Corps, AUS, 1943-46. Fellow Ford Found., 1954, Fulbright Found., 1954-56, Am. Coun. Learned Socs., 1964, Guggenheim Found., 1965; grantee NEH, 1978, 80-84; honored with publ. of Studies in Musical Sources and Style: Essays in Honor of Jan LaRue, 1990. Mem. Music Library Assn., Soc. Ethnomusicology, Am. Musicological Soc. (pres. 1966-68), Am. Soc. Eighteenth-Century Studies (exec. bd. 1978-80), Mozart Soc. Am., Phi Beta Kappa. Home: 103 Woods End Rd New Canaan CT 06840 Office: New York Univ Dept Music New York NY 10003-6757

LARUE, PAUL HUBERT, lawyer; b. Somerville, Mass., Nov. 16, 1922; s. Lucien H. and Germaine (Choquet) LaR.; m. Helen Finnegan, July 20, 1946; children: Paul Hubert, Patricia Seward,, Mary Hogan. PhB, U. Wis., 1947, JD, 1949. Bar: Ill. 1955, Wis. 1949, U.S. Supreme Ct. 1972. Instr. polit. sci. dept. U. Wis., 1947-48; mem. staff Wis. Atty. Gen., 1949-50; trial atty., legal adviser to commr. FTC, 1950-55; pvt. practice, Chgo.; mem. Chadwell & Kayser, Ltd., 1955-90; ptnr. Vedder, Price, Kaufman & Kammholz, 1990-93, of counsel, 1993—; speaker profl. meetings. Mem. Com. Modern Cts. in Ill., 1964; mem. Ill. Com. Constl. Conv., 1968, Better Govt. Assn., 1966-70, Lawyers com. Met. Crusade of Mercy, 1967-68, lawyers' com. United Settlement Appeal, 1966-68; apptd. pub. mem. Ill. Conflict of Interest Laws Commn., 1965-67. Served with AUS, 1943-45, ETO; as capt JAGC, USAFR, 1950-55. Fellow Ill. Bar Found. (life); mem. ABA (mem. council sect. antitrust law 1980-83, chmn. Robinson-Patman Act com. 1975-78), Ill. State Bar Assn., Chgo. Bar Assn. (chmn. antitrust com. 1970-71), Wis. State Bar. Roman Catholic. Contbr. articles to profl. jours. Home: 250 Cuttriss Pl Park Ridge IL 60068 Office: Vedder Price Kaufman & Kammholz 222 N La Salle St Chicago IL 60601-1002

LARUSSA, JOSEPH ANTHONY, optical company executive; b. N.Y.C., May 10, 1925; s. Ignacio and Jennie (Bellone) LaR.; m. Stella M.A. Braconnier, July 2, 1946; children—Joseph, Raymond Paul, Debra Marie. BME, CCNY, 1949; M.S., Columbia U., 1955, postgrad. math., mechanics, 1955-59; postgrad. math., physics, NYU, 1959-62; diploma in Infrared Tech., U. Mich. Registered profl. engr., N.Y. V.p.. charge advanced engring. Farrand Optical Co., Inc., Valhalla, N.Y., 1952, sr. v.p., tech. dir., 1952-88; pres., chief oper. officer Tech. Innovation Group Inc, Pleasantville, N.Y., 1988-90, Electro Visual Engring. Inc., Yorktown Heights, N.Y., 1991—. Designed Mercury, Gemini, Apollo LM visual spaceflight simulators for NASA; designed space shuttle Aft and Ohd visual simulators for NASA, others for USAF. Patentee in field; contbr. articles profl. publs. Served with inf. AUS, World War II, ETO. Mem. AIAA (DeFlorez award 1968), Tau Beta Pi, Pi Tau Sigma. Home: 451 Rutledge Dr Yorktown Heights NY 10598-5011

LA RUSSA, TONY, JR. (ANTHONY LA RUSSA, JR.), professional baseball manager; b. Tampa, Fla., Oct. 4, 1944; m. Elaine Coker, Dec. 31, 1973; 2 daus.: Bianca, Devon. Student, U. Tampa; BA, U. So. Fla., 1969; LLB, Fla. State U., 1978. Bar: Fla., 1979. Player numerous major league and minor league baseball teams, 1962-77; coach St. Louis Cardinals orgn., 1977; mgr. minor league team Knoxville, 1978, Iowa, 1979; coach Chgo. White Sox, 1978, mgr., 1979-86; mgr. Oakland A's, 1986-95, St. Louis Cardinals, 1996—; mgr. A.L. champion Oakland A's, 1988, 89, 90, World champions, 1989; mgr. All-Star team, 1988, coach, 1984, 87. Named Am. League Mgr. of Yr. Baseball Writers' Assn. Am., 1983, 88, 92, AP, 1983, Sporting News, 1983, Am. League Mgr. of Yr., 1988, 92. Office: St Louis Cardinals Busch Stadium 250 Stadium Plz Saint Louis MO 63102-1722*

LARUSSO, NICHOLAS F., gastroenterologist, educator, scientist. Prof., chmn. divsn. gastroenterology Mayo Med. Sch. Clin. & Found., Rochester, Minn., 1977—, dir. Ctr. Basic Rsch. Digestive Disorders, 1977—. Office: Mayo Clinic Ctr Basic Rsch Digestive Disease Guggenheim 17 Rochester MN 55905

LARWOOD, LAURIE, psychologist; b. N.Y., 1941; PhD, Tulane U., 1974. Pres., Davis Instruments Corp., San Leandro, Calif., 1966-71, cons., 1969—; asst. prof. orgnl. behavior SUNY, Binghamton, 1974-76; assoc. prof. psychology, chairperson dept., assoc. prof. bus. adminstrn. Claremont (Calif.) McKenna Coll., 1976-83, Claremont Grad. Sch., 1976-85; prof., head dept. mgmt. U. Ill.-Chgo., 1983-87; dean sch. bus. SUNY, Albany, 1987-90; dean Coll. Bus. Adminstrn., U. Nev., Reno, 1990-92; dir. Inst. Strategic Bus. Issues, 1992—; mem. western regional advisory coun. SBA, 1976-81; dir. The Mgmt. Team; pres. Mystic Games, Inc. Mem. Acad. Mgmt. (editl. rev. bd. Rev. 1977-82, past chmn. women in mgmt. div., managerial consultation divsn., tech. and innovation mgmt. divsn.), Am. Psychol. Assn., Assn. Women in Psychology. Author: (with M.M. Wood) Women in Management, 1977; Organizational Behavior and Management, 1984, Women's Career Development, 1987, Strategies-Successes-Senior Executives Speak Out, 1988, Women's Careers, 1988, Managing Technological Development, 1988; mem. editl. bd. Sex Roles, 1979—, Consultation, 1986-91, Jour. Orgnl. Behavior, 1987—, Group and Orgn. Mgmt., 1982-84, editor, 1986—; founding editor Women and Work, 1983, Jour. Mgmt. Case Studies, 1983-87; contbr. numerous articles, papers to profl. jours. Home: 2855 Saggitarius Dr Reno NV 89509-3885 Office: U Nev Coll Bus Adminstrn Reno NV 89557

LARY, BANNING KENT, video producer, publisher; b. Chgo., Aug. 27, 1949; s. Banning Gray and Katherine Lee (Tedrow) L.; m. Janice Ann, Dec. 22, 1974 (div. Aug. 1977); 1 child, Venus Ayn Katherine; m. Valerie Maria Dalli, Dec. 28, 1987; children: Alexandra Lee, Kristin Gray. BJ, U. Tex., 1970. Mng. editor Beach & Town, Miami, Fla., 1976-77; gen. contractor Larydome Inc., Miami, 1977-80; exec. dir. Legal Devel. Resources, Austin, 1989—; pres. Promedion, Inc., Austin, 1990—, Am. Multimedia Pubs., Austin, 1996—; dir., 1985—; freelance writer, 1970—; creative troubleshooter, writer, editor various orgns.; video pub., 1987—. Author: Twist of Faith, 1996; writer, prodr., dir. Robbery! The Aftermath, 1988, Ten Commandments of Avoiding Legal Malpractice, 1989, Ten. Procedures for Avoiding Medical Malpractice, 1990, The Belli Tapes: Winning at Trial, 1991, Childproof: Home Safety Checklist, 1991; video prodr. Bad Paper, 1987, Extortion Set, 1988; prodr. The Sexual Harassment Prevention Kit, 1992 and many others; prodr. numerous TV comml.s.; contrb. articles to mags.; author: Twist of Faith, 1996; editor: How to Win Your Case in Court, 1996; pub. Do What You Want to Do, 1996, Gold Medal Performance Without Dangerous Steroids, 1997; editor: Dangerous Steroids (Gold medal); inventor roller washer II, golf swing muscle articulator. Mem. bd. Alpha Nu House Corp., Austin. Recipient Gold award for video prodn., 1987, silver award, 1988, 91, Prize Stories Anthology award, 1989, O'Henry awards, Best of Austin award Internat. Assn. Bus. Communicators, 1986, 93, Disting. Achievement award Am. Soc. Ind. Security-Video, 1987, 1st pl. U.S.A. Hometown Video Festival, 1991, award of excellence ACTV, 1992, Bronze award Charleston Internat. Film Festival, 1993, Bronze award Worldfest, 1995. Mem. Am. Acad. Poets, Tex. Writers League, Austin Writers League, Amnesty Internat., Sigma Chi. Avocations: photography, painting, philosophy, securities analysis, films. Office: Am Visionary Artists PO Box 3551 Austin TX 78764-3551

LASAGNA, LOUIS CESARE, medical educator; b. N.Y.C., Feb. 22, 1923; s. Joseph and Carmen (Boccignone) L.; m. Helen Chester Gersten; children: Nina, David, Maria, Kristin, Lisa, Peter, Christopher. BS, Rutgers U., 1943; MD, Columbia U., 1947; DSc (hon.), Hahnemann U., 1980, Rutgers U., 1983. Asst. prof. medicine Johns Hopkins U., Balt., 1954-57, asst. prof. pharmacology, 1954-59, assoc. prof. medicine, 1957-70, assoc. prof. pharmacology, 1959-70; prof. pharmacology and toxicology U. Rochester, 1970-86, prof. medicine, 1970-86; dean Sackler Sch. Tufts U., 1984—, prof. pharmacology and psychiatry, 1984—. Author: The Doctors' Dilemmas, 1962, Life, Death and the Doctor, 1968, Phenylpropanolamine, A Review, 1988; editor: Controversies in Therapeutics, 1980,. Sr. asst. surgeon USPHS, 1952-54. Recipient Oscar B. Hunter award Am. Soc. Clin. Pharmacology, 1975, ASPET award Am. Soc. Pharmacology and Exptl. Therapeutics, 1976, Lilly prize Brit. Pharmacological Soc., 1985, Rutgers U. award, 1993, J. Allyn Taylor Internat. prize in Medicine, 1993; named Disting. prof. Tufts U., 1994. Mem. Inst. Medicine of NAS, Am. Coll. Neuropsychopharmacology (pres. 1979-80). Republican. Roman Catholic. Home: 256 Woodland Rd Auburndale MA 02166-2707 Office: Tufts U Sackler Sch Grad Biomed Sci 136 Harrison Ave Boston MA 02111-1817

LASALA, KENNETH PAUL, engineer, consultant; b. Bronx, N.Y., Sept. 21, 1945; s. Accursio and Agnes (Caputo) LaS.; m. Rebecca Anne Whelan, Nov. 29, 1969; children: Kenneth P. Jr., Gregory T. BS in Physics, Rensselaer Polytech. Inst., 1967; MS in Physics, Brown U., 1971; PhD in Reliability Engring., U. Md., 1993. Engr. Dept. Navy, Washington, 1968-84; chief engring. divsn. Dept. Army, Alexandria, Va., 1984-86; chief reliability engring. divsn. Dept. Air Force, Washington, 1986-91; chief maintenance br. Def. Mapping Agy., Merrifield, Va., 1991-93; staff engr. sys. engring. NOAA Dept. Commerce, Silver Spring, Md., 1993—; instr., rsch. advisor U. Md., College Park, 1984, 95—. Co-author: Handbook of Reliability Engineering and Management, 1988; contbr. articles to profl. jours. Recipient Field award Reliability & Maintainability Soc. Logistics Engrs., San Jose, Calif., 1989, Washington Chpt. Reliability & Maintainability award, 1989; Reliability Divsn. scholar Am. Soc. Quality Control, 1992. Mem. IEEE (chpt. chmn., ADCOM mem.). Avocations: tennis, painting, model building. Home: 703 Cannon Rd Silver Spring MD 20904

LA SALLE, ARTHUR EDWARD, historic foundation executive; b. New Orleans, Aug. 9, 1930; s. Rene Charles and Jeanne Matilda (Senac) La S.; divorced; children—Carl Alan, Adam David, Jeanne Ambre Victoria. Student Holy Name of Jesus Coll. Founder, pres. Am. R.R. Equipment Assn., Asheville, N.C., 1960—; founder Trains of Yesterday Mus., Hilliard, Fla., 1964-73; owner, restorer Brush Hill mansion, Irwin, Pa., 1973-77; lessee, restorer Springfield mansion, Fayette, Miss., 1977—; founder, pres. Hist. Springfield Found., Fayette, 1977—; cons. Smithsonian Instn., 1959, 75, Japanese Nat. Rys., Tokyo, 1968, Henry Ford Mus., 1975 City of Natchez, Miss., 1985, Old South Soc., Church Hill, Miss., 1985—; cons. in field; lectr. in field. Author: The Marriage of Andrew Jackson at Springfield Plantation; contbr. articles to profl. jours. Mem. Ry. and Locomotive Hist. Soc., Nat. Trust for Historic Preservation, Natchez Hist. Soc., U.S. Naval Inst. Avocations: historical preservation and study; writing; painting. Home and Office: Springfield Plantation RR 1 Box 201 Fayette MS 39069-9527

LASAROW, WILLIAM JULIUS, retired federal judge; b. Jacksonville, Fla., June 30, 1922; s. David Herman and Mary (Hollins) L.; m. Marilyn Doris Powell, Feb. 4, 1951; children: Richard M., Elisabeth H. BA, U. Fla., 1943; JD, Stanford U., 1950. Bar: Calif. 1951. Counsel judiciary com. Calif. Assembly, Sacramento, 1951-52; dep. dist. atty. Stanislaus County, Modesto, Calif., 1952-53; pvt. practice law L.A., 1953-73; bankruptcy judge U.S. Cts., L.A., 1973-94; chief judge U.S. Bankruptcy Ct., Central dist., Calif., 1978-90; judge Bankruptcy Appellate Panel 9th Fed. Cir., 1980-82; fed. judge U.S. Bankruptcy Ct., L.A., 1973; faculty Fed. Jud. Ctr. Bankruptcy Seminars, Washington, 1977-82. Contbg. author, editor legal publs.; staff: Stanford U. Law Review, 1949. Mem. ABA, Am. Coll. Bankruptcy, Am. Bankruptcy Inst., L.A. County Bar Assn., Wilshire Bar Assn., Blue Key, Phi Beta Kappa, Phi Kappa Phi. Home: 11623 Canton Pl Studio City CA 91604-4164

LASCH, PAT, artist, educator; b. N.Y.C., Nov. 20, 1944; d. Fred and Helen Veronica L.; 1 child, Melinda. BA, Queens Coll., 1970; FAAR, Am. Acad. in Rome, 1983; MFA, Ga. State U., Atlanta, 1990. Mem. found. faculty Parsons Sch. of Design, N.Y.C., 1979-88; asst. prof. R.I. Sch. of Design, Providence, 1988-89; assoc. prof. U. Mass., Amherst, 1990-97, prof., 1997—. Artist: solo exhibits include A.I.R. Gallery, N.Y.C., 1973, 77, 79, 80, 94, Zabriskie Gallery, N.Y.C., 1975, Galleriet, Lund, Sweden, 1980, Galerie Ahlner, Stockholm, 1980, Kathryn Markel Gallery, N.Y.C., 1981, 84, 85, Albright Knox Gallery, Members' Gallery, Buffalo, 1977-84, Thomas Segal Gallery, Boston, 1988, Sculpture Ctr., N.Y.C., 1993, Herter Gallery, U. Mass., Amherst, 1993; group shows inclde Inst. Contemporary Art, Phila.,

Street Scenes, 1981, Malmo (Sweden) Konsthall, Food, 1984, San Francisco Internat. Airport, The Right Foot Show, 1987, Thomas Segal Gallery, The Raw and the Cooked, Boston, The New Mus., N.Y.C., Bad Girls, 1994; spl. exhibition The Mus. of Modern Art (50th Anniversary), Homage 1929-79; represented in permanent collections Met. Mus. Art, N.Y.C., Mus. Modern Art, N.Y.C., Nat. Acad. Design, N.Y.C., Woman's Mus., Washington, Oberlin Mus., Queen's Coll. Recipient Yaddo, 1978, 80, 94, Rome prize, 1982-83, Lilly fellowship, 1993-94, NEA-MCC fellowship, 1995-96; grantee: C.A.P.S., 1980, NEA, 1980-81, N.Y. State Coun. for the Arts, 1984-85, Ariana Found., 1987-88, Pollock-Krasner, 1987-88. Fellow Soc. of Fellows Am. Acad. in Rome; mem. Nat. Acad. Design (life). Democrat. Roman Catholic. Home: 463 West St Apt 228 G New York NY 10014-2030 Office: Univ Mass Fine Arts Ctr Amherst MA 01002

LASCH, ROBERT, former journalist; b. Lincoln, Neb., Mar. 26, 1907; s. Theodore Walter and Myrtle (Nelson) L.; m. Zora Schaupp, Aug. 22, 1931 (dec. 1982); children: Christopher (dec. 1994), Catherine; m. Iris C. Anderson, Sept. 14, 1986. A.B., U. Nebr., 1928; postgrad. (Rhodes scholar), Oxford, 1928-31; Nieman fellow, Harvard, 1941-42. Reporter, state editor, editorial writer Omaha World-Herald, 1931-41; editorial writer, then chief editorial writer Chgo. Sun and Sun-Times, 1942-50; editorial writer St. Louis Post-Dispatch, 1950-57, editor editorial page, 1957-71, ret. Contbr. to: Newsmen's Holiday, 1942; Author: For a Free Press, 1944 (Atlantic Monthly prize), Breaking The Building Blockade, 1946. Recipient; St. Louis Civil Liberties award, 1966; Pulitzer prize for distinguished editorial writing, 1966. Home: 685 S La Posada Cir # 703 Green Valley AZ 85614-5118

LASCHER, ALAN ALFRED, lawyer; b. N.Y.C., Dec. 8, 1941; s. Morris Julius and Sadie Lillian (Chassen) L.; m. C. Amy Weingarten, July 12, 1969; children: David, Lauren, Alexandra, Carlyn. BS, Union Coll., 1963; LLB, Bklyn. Law Sch., 1967. Bar: N.Y. 1967. Assoc. Kramer, Leven et al, N.Y.C., 1969-75; ptnr. real estate dept. Weil, Gotshal & Manges, N.Y.C., 1975—; mem. law com. N.Y. Real Estate Bd., N.Y.C., 1981—; bd. advisors Chgo. Title Ins. Co., 1995—. Served to sgt. USAF, 1968-69. Named Real Estate Lawyer of Yr. Am. Lawyer, 1982. Mem. Am. Coll. Real Estate Lawyers (mem. Resolution Trust Corp. and Bankruptcy coms.). Office: Weil Gotshal & Manges 767 5th Ave New York NY 10153-0001

LASCHUK, ROY BOGDAN, lawyer; b. Saskatoon, Sask., Can., Aug. 13, 1932; s. Nicholas and Agatha (Schyhol) L.; m. Tairroyn Riley, Aug. 21, 1964; children: Tonia Jane, Stephen Clare, Graham Christopher. BA, U. Sask., 1953, LLB, 1955. Bar: Sask.; created Queen's counsel 1978. Assoc. firm Balfour, Moss, Milliken, Laschuk & Kyle (and predecessors), Regina, Sask., 1956-61; ptnr. Balfour Moss and predecessor firms, Regina, Sask., 1961-94, of counsel, 1994—; mem. Crown Investment Rev. Commn., vice chmn. 1983-84. Bd. dirs. Regina Housing Authority, 1973—; chmn. 1987-94. Mem. Law Soc. Sask., Can. Bar Assn. (council), Regina Bar Assn. (life, dir. 1975—, v.p. 1977-78, pres. 1978, chmn. health law sect. 1990-93), Canadian Petroleum Assn. (chmn. legal com. Sask. 1972-78), Can. Assn. Occupational Therapists (hon. exec. mem. 1970-75), Royal United Svcs. Inst., Sask. Track and Field Assn. (dir. 1983-85), Assiniboia Club, Rotary (pres. 1967-68). Baptist. Home: 9443 Wascana Mews, Regina, SK Canada S4V 2V6 Office: 700-2103 11th Ave, Regina, SK Canada S4P 4G1

LASH, JAMES WILLIAM (JAY LASH), embryology educator; b. Chgo., Oct. 24, 1929; s. Joseph and Alice (Smith) L.; m. Natalie Novak, Sept. 10, 1954; 1 child, Rebecca. Phd, U. Chgo., 1954; MS (hon.), U. Pa., 1981. Postdoctoral fellow NIH, Phila., 1955-57; sr. rsch. fellow NIH, London, 1986; from asst. prof. to prof. U. Pa., Phila., 1957-95, prof. emeritus, 1995—; Helen Hay Whitney fellow Helen Hay Whitney Found., Phila., 1958-61, Helen Hay Whitney Established Investigator, 1961-66; cons. NSF, Washington, 1967-70; mem. adv. bd., cons. NIH, 1970-83. Co-editor 6 books in field. Fellow Lalor Found., 1957, Paulo Found., 1969, NIH, 1986; recipient rsch. award Wellcome Found., 1960, Lindback award for disting. tchg. Avocations: watercolors, nature, reading, music, birding. Office: RR 2 Box 716 Woodstock VT 05091-9401

LASH, MYLES PERRY, hospital administrator, consultant; b. Detroit, May 31, 1946; s. Irving and Rose (Simkovitz) L.; m. Linda Pauline Borger, June 19, 1968; children: Alissa Beth, David Howard. B.S., Wayne State U., 1968; M.Hosp. Adminstrn., U. Mich., 1970. Asst. to exec. dir. Peoples Community Hosp. Authority, Wayne, Mich., 1970-72; asst. prof. Grad. Program Hosp. Adminstrn., Ohio State U., Columbus, 1970-72; adminstr. Ohio State U. Hosps., Columbus, 1973-79; exec. dir. Med. Coll. Va., Richmond, 1979-85; nat. dir. health care Arthur Young Co., Washington, 1985-86; pres. Lash Group-Health Care Cons., Washington, 1986—. Contbr. articles to profl. jours. Bd. dirs. Univ. Hosp. Consortium, 1980-85, pres., 1985. Mem. U. Mich. Hosp. Adminstrn. Alumni Assn. (pres.), Am. Hosp. Assn., Am. Coll. Hosp. Adminstrs. (Robert S. Hudgens Meml. award 1982). Home: 6708 Bonaventure Ct Bethesda MD 20817-4026 Office: 555 13th St NW Washington DC 20004-1109

LASH, STEPHEN SYCLE, auction company executive; b. Boston, Feb. 10, 1940; s. Samuel George and Carolyn Virginia (Sycle) L.; m. Wendy Lehman, Oct. 29, 1967; children: Abigail Sycle, William Lehman. BA, Yale U., 1962; MBA, Columbia U., 1966. V.p. Bali Footwear, Inc., Marlborough, Mass., 1962-64, 66-68, S.G. Warburg and Co., London, N.Y.C., 1968-76; v.p. Christies, N.Y.C., 1976-80, sr. v.p., 1980-84, exec. v.p., 1984-93, vice chmn., 1993—; also bd. dirs. Christies Internat. PLC. Founder, pres. Ocean Liner Mus., N.Y.C., 1983-88, co-chmn., 1988-96; commr. N.Y.C. Landmarks Preservation Commn., 1973-76; bd. dirs. N.Y. Landmarks Conservancy, N.Y.C., 1975-97, chmn., 1992-95; bd. dirs. Preservation League N.Y., Albany, 1986—. With USCGR, 1962-67. Pan Am. Union fellow, 1965. Mem. Yale U. Alumni Assn. Metro N.Y. (pres. 1987-90), River Club, Mill Reef Club, Century Assn., Wadawanuck Club (Stonington, Conn.). Home: 151 E 79th St New York NY 10021-0421 Office: Christie Manson & Woods Internat Inc 502 Park Ave New York NY 10022-1108

LASH, TERRY R., federal agency administrator; b. Portland, Oreg., Nov. 22, 1942; m. Elizabeth M. Vogt; children: Benjamin, Lara. BA in Physics, Reed Coll., Portland, Oreg., 1965; MPh in Molecular Biophysics, Yale U., 1967, PhD, 1971. With numerous pub. interest orgns., 1972-84; dir. Ill. Dept. Nuclear Safety, 1984-90; spl. asst. to sec. of energy U.S. Dept. Energy; dir. office nuclear energy, sci. and tech. U.S. Dept. Energy, Washington, 1994—; cons. in field. Office: US Dept Energy 1000 Independence Ave SW Washington DC 20585-0001

LASHBROOKE, ELVIN CARROLL, JR., law educator, consultant; b. Dec. 14, 1939; s. Elvin Carroll Sr. and Lois Lenora (Weger) L.; m. Margaret Ann Jones, Dec. 19, 1964; children: Michelle Ann, David C. BA, U. Tex., 1967, MA, 1968, JD, 1972, LLM, 1977; PhD, Mich. State U., 1993. Bar: Tex. 1972, Fla. 1973. Legis. counsel Tex. Legis. Coun., Austin, 1972-75; pvt. practice law Austin, 1975-77; asst. prof. coll. of law DePaul U., Chgo., 1977-79, Stetson U., St. Petersburg, Fla., 1979-80; assoc. prof. sch. law Notre Dame, Ind., 1981-85; prof., chmn. bus. law dept. Mich. State U., East Lansing, 1985-95; assoc. dean adminstrn. Eli Broad Coll. Bus., East Lansing, 1993-97; pvt. practice cons. East Lansing, 1986-97; dean Coll. Bus. U. Nev., Las Vegas, 1997—; instr. St. Edward's U., Austin, 1975-76. Author: Tax Exempt Organizations, 1985, The Legal Handbook of Business Transactions, 1987; contbr. articles to profl. jours. Mem. ABA, Tex. Bar Assn., Fla. Bar Assn. Avocation: computers. Home: 6435 Island Lake Dr East Lansing MI 48823-9735 Office: U Nev-Las Vegas Coll Bus Las Vegas NV 89154-6001

LASHELLE, CHARLES STANTON, lawyer, insurance company executive; b. Colorado Springs, Colo., June 25, 1947; s. Stanton Duane and Glenna (Bloom) LaS.; m. Pamela Montross, Aug. 24, 1968; children: Rebecca, Karen. BA, U. No. Colo., 1969; JD, Creighton U., 1972. Bar: Nebr. 1972, U.S. Dist. Ct. Nebr. 1972, U.S. Tax Ct. 1980, U.S Ct. Appeals (8th cir.) 1980, U.S. Supreme Ct. 1980; CLU. Mktg. rep. Teton Nat. Life Ins. Co., Greeley, Colo., 1968-69; v.p., asst. gen. counsel Mut. Protective & Medico Life, Omaha, 1973-83; sr. v.p. adminstrn. Am. Founders Life Ins. Co., Austin, Tex., 1983-87; exec. v.p. adminstrn. Nat. Western Life Ins. Co., Austin, 1987-92; pres., CEO Tex. Life and Health Ins. Guaranty Assn., Austin, 1992—; pres. Comml. Adjusters Inc., Austin, 1988-92. Bd. dirs. Variety Club, Omaha, 1983, Nat. Orgn. Life & Health Guaranty Assns., 1993—, chair confederation life task force, 1994—; vice chmn. Mayor's Task Force on Drugs and Drug Abuse, 1990-91. Capt. USAR, 1972-76. Mem. ABA, Nebr. Bar Assn., Am. Soc. CLUs, Am. Coun. Life Ins., Greater Austin C. of C. (legis. com.), Sertoma Club (Round Rock, Tex.). Republican. Methodist. Avocations: golf, reading. Home: 1821 Possum Trot St Round Rock TX 78681-1710

LASHER, ESTHER LU, minister; b. Denver, June 1, 1923; d. Lindley Aubrey and Irma Jane (Rust) Pim; m. Donald T. Lasher, Apr. 9, 1950 (dec. Mar. 1982); children: Patricia Sue Becker, Donald T., Keith Alan, Jennifer Luanne Oliver. Assoc. Fine Arts, Colo. Women's Coll., 1943; BA, Denver U., 1945; MA Religious Edn., Ea. Bapt. Sem., 1948; MA, Denver U., 1967. Ordained to ministry Bapt. Ch., 1988. Christian edn. dir. 1st Bapt., Evansville, Ind., 1948-52; min. Perrysburg Bapt. Ch., Macy, Ind., 1988-95; min.-at-large Am. Baptist Conv./USA, 1996—; libr. Peru (Ind.) Pub. Schs., 1990-91; sec. Ind. Ministerial Coun., Indpls., 1990-92; chairperson Women in Ministry, Indpls., 1988-93; chmn. Fellowship Mission Circle, Rochester, Ind., 1988-93; mem. Partnership in Ministry, Indpls., 1990-94; bd. mgrs. Am. Bapts./Ind., 1991-93; asst. dir. Greenwood Pub. Library, 1978-84; dir. Fulton County Pub. Library, 1984-90. Ae./ Evansville Symphonic Orch., 1948-55, Denver Civic Orch., 1955-65; pres. Toastmasters, Rochester, 1984-90, 95, edn. v.p., 1992-93; asst. dir. Greenwood Pub. Libr., 1977-85; dir. Fulton County Pub. Libr., 1985-90; bd. dirs. Manitau Tng. Ctr., Rochester, 1988-90; v.p. Mental Health Ctr., Rochester, 1987-90; founder Fulton County Literacy Coalition, Rochester, 1989-90; tutor/trainer Peru Literacy Coalition of Peru Pub. Libr., 1994-95; sec. Northwest Area ABC/IN, 1994-95; sec.-treas. North Miami County Mins. Fellowship, 1993-95; bd. dirs. Peru Civic Ctr., 1995; active CASA Lincoln County, 1995—; chmn. Christian Edn. Bd. and ch. planter, Denver, 1953-59, Colorado Springs, 1959-68; prayer advisor Christian Women's Club, 1997—; pres. Women's Mission Cir., Damariscotta Bapt. Ch., 1997—; chaplain vol. Miles Hosp., 1997—. Named Outstanding Libr., Biog. Inst., 1989. Mem. Leadership Acad. (bd. dir., sec.), Bus. and Profl. Women (pres. Greenwood, Ind. chpt. 1984-86), Rochester Women's Club (pres. 1989-92), Fulton County Mins. Assn. (treas. 1993-95), Logansport Assn. Bapt. Women, Peru Lit. Club (v.p.-elect 1995), Christian Women's Club (hostess chair 1995—), CASA Miami County, Rotary, Sigma Alpha Iota (adv.), Christian Edn. (chmn. 1996—). Republican. Home and Office: 2063 State Rt 129 South Bristol ME 04568-9322 *Wisdom is a powerful tool, without knowledge, it can entice or terrify an individual, all depending on how it is used with much forethought.*

LASHLEY, CURTIS DALE, lawyer; b. Urbana, Ill., Nov. 3, 1956; s. Jack Dale and Janice Elaine (Holman) L.; m. Tamara Dawn Yahnig, June 14, 1986. BA, U. Mo., Kansas City, 1978, JD, 1981. Bar: Mo. 1981, U.S. Dist. Ct. (we. dist.) Mo. 1981, U.S. Tax Ct. 1982, U.S. Ct. Appeals (8th cir.) 1992. Assoc. Melvin Heller, Inc., Creve Coeur, Mo., 1982; ptnr. Domjan & Lashley, Harrisonville, Mo., 1983-86; asst. gen. counsel Mo. Dept. Revenue, Independence, 1986-89, assoc. gen. counsel, 1989-92, sr. counsel, 1992—, adminstrv. hearing officer, 1995—; spl asst. atty. gen., 1986—; spl. asst. prosecutor Jackson County, Mo., 1990—; city atty., Adrian and Strasburg, Mo., 1985-86. V.p. Cass County Young Reps., Harrisonville, 1985. Mem. ABA, Kiwanis (treas. Harrisonville chpt. 1985-86, Harrisonville Disting. Svc. award 1985), NRA, Phi Alpha Delta. Republican. Presbyterian. Office: Mo Dept Revenue 16647 E 23rd St S Independence MO 64055-1922

LASHLEY, LENORE CLARISSE, lawyer; b. N.Y.C., June 3, 1934; d. Leonard Livingston and Una Ophelia (Laurie) L.; children: Donna Bee-Gates, Michele Bee, Maria Bee. BA, CUNY, 1956; MSW, U. Calif., Berkeley, 1970, MPH, 1975; JD, U. Calif., San Francisco, 1981. Bar: Calif. 1981. Atty. W.O.M.A.N., Inc., San Francisco, 1982-84; pvt. practice San Francisco Law Office, 1984-87; dep. dist. atty. Monterey Dist. Atty., Salinas, Calif., 1987-89; trial atty. State Bar of Calif., L.A., 1989; dep. dist. atty. L.A. Dist. Atty., 1989; city atty., dep. City Atty. L.A., 1989—; chair, bd. dirs. St. Anthony's Dining Room, San Francisco, 1986-87; sec., bd. dirs. NAAC, Monterey, 1987-88; bd. dirs. Childrens Home Soc., Oakland, Calif., 1966-68. Recipient Cert. of Merit, Nat. Assn. Naval Officers, 1987. Mem. L.A. County Bar Assn. (del. to state bar 1992, 93). Roman Catholic. Avocations: running, reading, animal welfare. Office: City Atty LA 200 N Main St Ste 1700 Los Angeles CA 90012-4110

LASHLEY, VIRGINIA STEPHENSON HUGHES, retired computer science educator; b. Wichita, Kans., Nov. 12, 1924; d. Herman H. and Edith M. (Wayland) Stephenson; m. Kenneth W. Hughes, June 4, 1946 (dec.); children: Kenneth W. Jr., Linda Hughes Tindall; m. Richard H. Lashley, Aug. 19, 1954; children: Robert H., Lisa Lashley Van Amberg, Diane Lashley Tan. BA, U. Kans., 1945; MA, Occidental Coll., 1966; PhD, U. So. Calif., 1983. Cert. info. processor, tchr. secondary and community coll., Calif. Tchr. math. La Canada (Calif.) High Sch., 1966-69; from instr. to prof. Glendale (Calif.) Coll., 1970-92, chmn. bus. div., 1977-81, coord. instructional computing, 1974-92, prof. emeritus, 1992—; sec., treas., dir. Victory Montessori Schs., Inc., Pasadena, Calif., 1980—; pres. The Computer Sch., Pasadena, 1983-92; pres. San Gabriel Valley Data Processing Mgmt. Assn., 1977-79, San Gabriel Valley Assn. for Systems Mgmt., 1979-80; chmn. Western Ednl. Computing Conf., 1980, 84. Editor Jour. Calif. Ednl. Computing, 1980. Mem. DAR. NSF grantee, 1967-69, EDUCARE scholar U. So. Calif., 1980-82; John Randolph and Dora Haynes fellow, Occidental Coll., 1964-66; student computer ctr. renamed Dr. Virginia S. Lashley Ctr., 1992. Mem. AAUP, AAUW, DAR, Calif. Edn. Computing Consortium (bd. dirs. 1979—, v.p. 1983-84, pres. 1985-87), Orgn. Am. Historians, San Marino Women's Club, Colonial Dames, XVII Century, Town Hall, World Affairs Coun., Phi Beta Kappa, Pi Mu Epsilon, Phi Alpha Theta, Phi Delta Kappa, Delta Phi Upsilon, Gamma Phi Beta. Republican. Congregationalist. Home: 1240 S San Marino Ave San Marino CA 91108-1227

LASHLEY, WILLIAM BARTHOLOMEW, county official; b. Dayton, Ohio, Jan. 2, 1952; s. William Bartholomew and Retta Carolyn (Reicken) L.; m. Loukia Simopoulos, June 30, 1973; children: Nichole E., Felicite D. BA in Econs., Wright State U., 1976; opthomol. sci. degree, Regis U., 1982. Asst. mgr. First Nat. Bank, Dayton, Ohio, 1973-77; mgr. store Kroger Co., Dayton, 1977-80; cashier Frontier Bank, Denver, 1980-82; asst. v.p. Empire Savs., Denver, 1982-85; mgr. investor acctg. Security Pacific Mortgage Corp., Denver, 1985-88; corp. acct. investors Crossland Mortgage Corp., Salt Lake City, 1988-89; fiscal officer Montgomery County Cts., Dayton, 1989—; mem. Montgomery County Fiscal Task Force, Dayton, 1990—. Mem. ABA (assoc.), Am. Bankers Assn., Govt. Fin. Officers Assn., Mortgage Bankers Assn., Ohio State Bar Assn. (assoc.). Home: 3307 Waltham Ave Kettering OH 45429-3529 Office: Montgomery County Cts 41 N Perry St Dayton OH 45402-1431

LASHMAN, SHELLEY BORTIN, judge; b. Camden, N.J., Aug. 18, 1917; s. William Mitchell and Anna (Bortin) L.; m. Ruth Horn, Jan. 3, 1959; children—Karen E. Lashman Hall, Gail A. McBride, Mitchell A., Christopher R. B.S., William and Mary Coll., 1938; postgrad. Columbia U., 1938, 39; J.D., U. Mich., 1946. Bar: N.Y. 1947, N.J. 1968. Judge N.J. Workers Compensation, 1981—. With USNR, 1940-70. Mem. Atlantic County Bar Assn., Amden County Bar Assn., Am. Judges Assn., Atlantic County Hist. Soc., Am. Judicature Soc., Ret. Officers Assn., U.S. Navy League, Fleet Res. Assn., USS Yorktown CV-5 Club, Mil. Order World Wars, Atlantic City Country Club, Greater Atlantic City Yacht Club. Republican. Home: 1209 Old Zion Rd Egg Harbor Township NJ 08234-7667 Office: Workers Compensation Ct 1 Port Ctr 2 Riverside Dr Camden NJ 08102

LASHOF, JOYCE COHEN, public health educator; b. Phila.; d. Harry and Rose (Brodsky) Cohen; m. Richard K. Lashof, June 11, 1950; children: Judith, Carol, Dan. AB, Duke U., 1946; MD, Women's Med. Coll., 1950; DSc (hon.), Med. Coll. Pa., 1983. Dir. Ill. State Dept. Pub. Health, 1973-77; dep. asst. sec. for health programs and population affairs Dept. Health, Edn., and Welfare, Washington, 1977-78; sr. scholar in residence IOM, Washington, 1978; asst. dir. office of tech. assessment U.S. Congress, Washington, 1978-81; dean sch. pub. health U. Calif., Berkeley, 1981-91, prof. pub. health Sch. Pub. Health, 1981-94, prof. emerita, 1994—; co-chair Commn. on Am. after Roe vs. Wade, 1991-92; mem. Sec.'s Coun. Health Promotion and Disease Prevention, 1988-91; pres. APHA, 1992; chair Pres.'s Adv. Com. on Gulf War Vets. Illnesses, 1995-97. Vice chairperson editl. bd. Wellness Letter, 1983—; mem. editl. com. Ann. Rev. of Pub. Health, 1987-90. Recipient Alumni Achievement award Med. Coll. Pa., 1975, Sedgewick Meml. medal APHA, 1995. Avocation: hiking. Home: 601 Euclid Ave Berkeley CA 94708-1331 Office: U Calif-Berkeley Sch Pub Health 140 Earl Warren Hall Berkeley CA 94720

LASHUTKA, GREGORY S., mayor, lawyer; b. N.Y.C., 1944; m. Catherine Adams; children: Stephanie, Michael, Nicholas, Lara. BS, Ohio State U., 1967; JD, Capital U., 1974. Bar: Ohio, 1974, Fla., D.C., 1975. Former ptnr. Squire, Sanders & Dempsey, Columbus, Ohio; elected mayor City of Columbus, 1991—; former Columbus City Atty. Past chmn. Columbus-Area Sports Devel. Corp.; 1st v.p. Nat. League of Cities; comentator of the Ohio State U. Football Color, 1983-90; active civic and charitable orgns. including Charity Newsies Assocs., Nat. Football Found., Ohio State U. Varsity "O". Served to lt., USN. Named Mcpl. Leader of the Yr., Am. City and County mag., 1993. Office: Office of the Mayor City Hall Room 247 90 W Broad St Columbus OH 43215-9000*

LASICH, VIVIAN ESTHER LAYNE, secondary education educator; b. Hopewell Twp., Pa., Dec. 17, 1935; d. Charles McClung and Harriette Law (George) Layne; m. William G. Lasich, Apr. 10, 1958; children: C. Laurence, Celeste M., Michelle R. AB, Geneva Coll., 1956; MA in Edn., No. Mich. U., 1970, postgrad. Secondary tchr. Freedom (Pa.) High Sch., 1956-57; elem. educator Gilbert Elem. Sch., Gwinn, Mich., 1967-69; lang. arts educator Gwinn Mid. Sch., 1970—; adb. bd. panel Mich. Dept. Edn./Arts, 1976-79; mem. sch. improvement team, 1989-91, 93-94, co-chair, 1995—; mid sch. concept team, 1992—, mid sch. at-risk coord. dist. curriculum coord. coun., 1995—; dist. curriculum strategy action team, 1993-94; dist. profl. devel. strategy action team, 1993-94; mem. sounding bd. Mid. Sch., 1994—, dist. sch. improvement team, 1994—; rep. Gwinn Edn. Assn. Mid. Sch., 1995—. Author: Prophets Without Honor: Teachers, Students, & Trust, 1991. V.p. Marquette (Mich.) Community Theatre, 1962-63 bd. dirs. 1963-74, mem. 1961-92; pres. Marquette Arts Coun. 1973-74, v.p. 1972-73, bd. dirs. 1970-78, mem. 1970-84; pres. Upper Peninsula Arts Coordinating Bd. 1976-78, v.p. 1974-76, bd. dirs. 1978-84; bd. dirs. Mich. Community Theatre Assn. 1972-73; bd. dirs. Mich Community Arts Agys., 1976-79. Recipient Committment to Excellence award Marquette Community Theatre, 1965. Devotion to Arts Development award Upper Peninsula (Mich.) Arts Coord. Bd. 1979. Mem. ASCD, NEA, AAUW, Mich. Edn. Assn., Phi Delta Kappa. Presbyterian. Avocations: rsch., writing, theatrical direction and performance, vocal music. Home: 508 Pine St Marquette MI 49855-3838 Office: Gwinn Area Community Schs Gwinn MI 49841

LASKAWY, PHILIP A., accounting and management consulting firm executive; b. 1941. With S. D. Leidesdorf & Co., 1961-78, ptnr., 1971-78; ptnr. Ernst & Whinney (acquired S. D. Leidesdorf 1978), 1978-85, vice chmn., mng. ptnr. N.Y. region, 1983-93; chmn., CEO Ernst & Young (merger of Ernst & Whinney and Arthur Young 1993), 1993—, also bd. dirs. Office: Ernst & Young 787 7th Ave New York NY 10019-6018*

LASKER, DAVID RAYMOND, newspaper editor, musician; b. N.Y.C., Apr. 21, 1950; arrived in Can., 1974; s. Joseph Leon and Mildred (Jaspen) L. BA in History of Art cum laude, Yale U., 1972, MMus, 1974. Double-bassist Winnipeg (Man., Can.) Symphony Orch., 1974-84; freelance archtl. journalist, Toronto, Ont., Can., 1984-89; editor Contract mag., Toronto, 1989-91; editor fashion and design The Globe and Mail, Toronto, 1991-96, editor arch. and classical music, 1996—; prin. double-bassist North York Symphony Orch. Author: (children's book) The Boy Who Loved Music, 1979 (ALA Notable Book award). Avocations: collecting classical vinyl records, high-end audio, bodybuilding. Home: 533 Logan Ave, Toronto, ON Canada M4K 3B3 Office: The Globe and Mail, 444 Front St W, Toronto, ON Canada M5V 2S9

LASKER, GABRIEL WARD, anthropologist, educator; b. York, Eng., Apr. 29, 1912; s. Bruno and Margaret Naomi (Ward) L.; m. Bernice Kaplan, July 31, 1949; children: Robert Alexander, Edward Meyer, Ann Titania. Student, U. Wis., 1928-30; A.B., U. Mich., 1934; A.M., Harvard U., 1940, Ph.D., 1945. Instr. English Chiao T'ung U., Peking, China, 1936-37; teaching fellow in anatomy Harvard Med. Sch., 1941-42; mem. faculty dept. anatomy Wayne State U. Sch. Medicine, Detroit, 1946—, asst. prof., 1947-55; assoc. prof., 1955-64; prof. emeritus Wayne U. Sch. Medicine, 1982—; fellow commoner Churchill Coll. Cambridge U., 1983-84; conducted Wayne U.-Viking Fund field trip to Mexico to study effects of migration on phys. characteristics of Mexicans, 1948. Author: Physical Anthropology, The Evolution of Man, Surnames and Genetic Structure; editor: Yearbook of Phys. Anthropology, 1945-51, Human Biology, 1953-87, Research Strategies in Human Biology: Field and Survey Studies, 1993; contbr. articles to profl. jours. Fellow Am. Anthrop. Assn., AAAS (v.p. (1968); mem. Am. Assn. Phys. Anthropologists (sec.-treas. 1947-51, v.p. 1960-62, pres. 1963-65, Charles Darwin award 1993), Am. Assn. Anatomists, Human Biology Assn., (pres. 1982-84, First Franz Boas Prize, 1996), Soc. Study Human Biology (U.K.), Asociación Mexicana de Antropología Biológica, Sigma Xi. Office: 540 E Canfield St Detroit MI 48201-1928

LASKER, JONATHAN LEWIS, artist; b. Jersey City, July 30, 1948; s. Lester and Henrietta Selma (Gross) L. Student, Sch. Visual Arts, N.Y.C., 1975-77, Calif. Inst. Arts, 1977. One-man exhbns. include Landmark Gallery, N.Y., Gunnar Kaldewey, Dusseldorf, Fed. Republic Germany, 1981, Annette Gmeiner, Kirchzarten, Fed. Republic Germany, 1984, Tibor de Nagy, N.Y.C., 1984, 86, Michael Werner, Cologne, Fed. Republic Germany, 1986, 87, 90, Massimo Audiello, N.Y.C., 1986, 88, 89, Anders Tornberg, Lund, Sweden, 1987, 90, Gian Enzo Sperone, Rome, 1988, 91, Sperone Westwater Gallery, N.Y.C., 1991, 93, 96, Lars Bohman, Stockholm, 1991, 94, Inst. Contemporary ArtU. Pa., Phila., 1992, Thaddaeus Ropac Gallery, Paris, 1992, Witte de With Ctr. Contemporary Art, Rotterdam, 1993, Rhona Hoffman Gallery, Chgo., 1993, Soledad Lorenzo, Madrid, 1995, L.A. Louver Gallery, 1995, numerous others; selected group exhbns. include Mus. Ludwig, Cologne, Wacoal Art Ctr., Tokyo, 1985, Rose Art Mus. Brandeis U., Waltham, Mass., 1986, Corcoran Gallery Art, Washington, 1987, Aldrich Mus. Contemporary Art, Ridgefield, Conn., 1987, Roos Mus., Malmo, Sweden, U. N. Tex., Denton, J.B. Speed Mus., Louisville, Alta. Coll. Art., Edmonton, Can., Contemporary Arts Ctr., Cin., Santa Fe Community Coll., Gainesville, Fla., Met. Mus. Art, N.Y.C., 1988, Stedelijk Mus., Amsterdam, The Netherlands, 1989, Marc Richards Gallery, L.A., Scott Hansen Gallery, N.Y.C., 1990, Pace Gallery, N.Y.C., 1990, Sperone Westwater Gallery, N.Y.C., 1991, 94, Gallery Modern Art, Bologna, Italy, 1991, Hirshhorn Mus. and Sculpture Garden, Washington, 1991, Mus. Contemporary Art of Dayton Art Inst., 1992, Documenta IX, Kassell, Germany, Gallerie Nächst Sankt Stefan, Vienna, 1992, Thaddaeus Ropac, Paris, 1992, Ruth Bloom Gallery, L.A., 1993, Hayward Gallery, London, 1994, Ctr. for the Fine Arts, Miami, 1994, Va. Mus. Fine Arts, Richmond, 1995, Mus. Contemporary Art, Helsinki, Folkwang Mus., Essen, Germany, 1995, Mus. Reina Sofia, Madrid, 1996, Kunsthalle Zurich, Switzerland, 1996, numerous others; in pub. collections Corcoran Gallery, Hirshhorn Mus. and Sculpture Garden, Washington, Mus. Ludwig, Cologne, Wacoal Art Ctr., Tokyo, Whitney Mus. Am. Art, N.Y.C., Moderna Museet, Stockholm, Fond Nat. d'Art Contemporain, Paris, High Mus., Atlanta, Museo De Arte Contemporaneo, Seville, Spain, La Fundacion Caja De Pensiones, Madrid; critiqued numerous art books, catalogs, mags. including Beyond Boundaries: New York's New Art (Jerry Saltz), N.Y. Art Now, The Saatchi Collection (Dan Cameron), The Silent Baroque (Christian Leigh editor), Interpreting Contemporary Art (Rainer Crone and David Moos), Art at the End of the Social (Collins and Milazzo), Art Since Mid-Century: 1945 to the Present (Daniel Wheeler), Jonathan Lasker, Telling The Tales of Painting (Rainer Crone and David Moos), The 20th Century Art Book (Tony Godfrey, Melissa Larner, et al), Art News (Feb. 1990, Apr. 1992), Le Monde (June 1992). NEA fellow, 1987, 89. Office: care Sperone Westwater Gallery 142 Greene St New York NY 10012-3236

LASKER, MORRIS E., judge; Fed. judge, U.S. Dist. Ct. (so. dist.) N.Y.; fed. judge, U.S. Dist. Ct., Boston, Mass., 1994—. Office: US Dist Ct 90 Devonshire St Boston MA 02109-4501

LASKER, RICHARD S., lawyer; b. Boston, June 12, 1947. AB, Tufts U., 1969; JD, Columbia U., 1972. Bar: N.Y. 1973. Sr. atty. Cravath Swaine & Moore, N.Y.C. Mem. ABA, N.Y. State Bar Assn. Office: Cravath Swaine & Moore Worldwide Plz 825 8th Ave New York NY 10019-7416

LASKEY, RICHARD ANTHONY, biomedical device executive; b. N.Y.C., Oct. 24, 1936; s. Charles Lewis and Gertrude Ann (Stolzenthaler) L.; m. Frances M. Pollack, June 29, 1975; children: Victoria Ann, Deborah Lea. Student CCNY; BS in Chemistry, Ohio, MS in Organic Chemistry; PhD in Organic Chemistry, Sussex (Eng.) U., 1970; LLB, U. Chgo., 1972; MD (hon.), Med. Coll. S.A., 1975, fellow, Psychiatry 1976; postgrad. in ob-gyn, U. Pa., 1989-96. Diplomate Am. Bd. Examiners in Psychotherapy. Head sec. med. products, lab. mgr. Hydron Labs., North Brunswick, N.J., 1967-73; v.p. biomed. rsch. Datascope Corp., Paramus, N.J., 1973-82; pres. rsch. Millbrook Labs., Inc., Rochelle Park, N.J., 1982—; cons. in field. Recipient Doctor's award Chgo. Med. Coll., 1975; fellow Am. Acad. Behavioral Sci., 1976. Fellow Am. Inst. Chemist; mem. NRA, AAAS, Md. Med. Soc., Idaho Med. Soc., Nat. Med. Soc., Internat. Coll. Physicians and Surgeons, Am. Inst. Chemist, Am. Psychotherapy Assn., Nat. Psychol. Assn., Assn. Advancement Med. Instrumentation, Soc. Rsch. Adminstrs. Biomed. inventor, patentee. Home: PO Box 133 Washington NJ 07882-0133 Office: PO Box 125 Rochelle Park NJ 07662-0125

LASKIN, BARBARA VIRGINIA, legal association administrator; b. Chgo., July 2, 1939; d. Cyril Krieps and Gertrude Katherine (Kujawa) Szymanski; children: Dawn Katherine Doherty, Amy Lynn Anderson. BA, U. Ill., Chgo., 1967; MA, Am. U. Beirut, 1978, Georgetown U., 1985. Asst. buyer Carson, Pirie, Scott & Co., Chgo., 1967-69; fgn. svc. officer Dept. State, Washington, 1969-79; mgr. gift shops Marriott Hotels, Washington, 1979-81; office mgr. Robt Schwinn & Assoc., Bethesda, Md., 1983-85; exec. dir. Internat. Acad. Trial Lawyers, San Jose, Calif., 1985—. Fellow Rotary Club San Jose; mem. AAUW (v.p. 1987), Am. Soc. Assn. Execs., Meeting Planners Internat., Internat. Spl. Events Soc. (v.p. membership 1996), Internat. Spl. Events Found. (dir.), Profl. Conservation Mgrs. Assn. Roman Catholic. Office: Internat Acad Trial Lawyers 4 N 2nd St Ste 175 San Jose CA 95113-1306

LASKIN, DANIEL M., oral and maxillofacial surgeon, educator; b. Ellenville, N.Y., Sept. 3, 1924; s. Nathan and Flora (Kaplan) L.; m. Eve Pauline Mohel, Aug. 25, 1945; children: Jeffrey, Gary, Marla. Student, NYU, 1941-42; BS, Ind. U., 1947; MS, U. Ill., 1951. Diplomate Am. Bd. Oral and Maxillofacial Surgery. Mem. faculty U. Ill., Chgo., 1949-84, prof. dept. oral and maxillofacial surgery, 1960-84, head dept., 1973-84, clin. prof. surgery, 1961-84, dir. temporomandibular joint and facial pain research center, 1963-84; prof., chmn. dept. oral and maxillofacial surgery Med. Coll. Va., Richmond, 1984—; dir. temporomandibular joint and facial pain rsch. ctr. MCV, Richmond, 1984—; head dept. dentistry MCV Hosp., Richmond, 1986—; former attending oral surgeon Edgewater, Swedish Covenant, Ill. Masonic, Skokie Valley Community hosps., all Chgo.; former chmn. dept. oral surgery Cook County Hosp., Chgo.; cons. oral surgery to Surgeon Gen. Navy, 1977—; dental products panel FDA, 1988-92, cons., 1993—; Francis J. Reichmann Lectr., 1971, Cordwainer lectr., London, 1980. Author: Oral and Maxillofacial Surgery, Vol. I, 1980, Vol. II, 1985; contbr. articles to profl. jours.; editor-in-chief: Jour. Oral and Maxillofacial Surgery, 1972—; mem. editorial bd. Internat. Jour. Oral and Maxillofacial Surgery, 1978-88, Topics in Pain Mgmt., Densat, Internat. Jour. Oral and Maxillofacial Implants, Quintessence Internat., Revista Latino America Cirugia Traumatologia Maxilofacial, Virginia Dental Jour., Jour. Dental Rsch.; mem. internat. editorial bd. Headache Quar. Nat. hon. chmn. peer campaign A.A.O.M.S. Edn. and Rsch. Found., 1990. Recipient Disting. Alumni Svc. award Ind. U., 1975, William J. Gies editl. award hon. mention, 1975-77, 80, 88, 90, 91, 93, 95, 1st prize, 1978-79, 84, 87, 89, 92, 95, Simon P. Hullihen Meml. award, 1976, Arnold K. Maislen Meml. award, 1977, Thomas P. Hinman medallion, 1980, W. Harry Archer Achievement award for rsch., 1981, Heidbrink award, 1983, Disting. Alumnus award Ind. U. Sch. Dentistry, 1984, Rene Lefort medal, 1985, Semmelweis medallion Semmelweis Med. U., 1985, Golden Scroll award Internat. Coll. Dentists, 1986, Internat. award Friends Sch. Dental Medicine, U. Conn. Health Ctr., Donald B. Osborn award, 1991, Achievement medal Alpha Omega, 1992, Norton M. Ross Excellence in Clin. Rsch. award, 1993, Va. Commonwealth U. Faculty award of excellence, 1994; named Zendium Lectr., 1989, Edward C. Hinds Lectr., 1990, Disting. Practitioner Nat. Acads. Practice, 1992, Hon. Diplomate, Am. Soc. Osseointegration, 1992; fellow in gen. anesthesia Am. Dental Soc. Anesthesiology, fellow in dental surgery Royal Coll. Surgeons Eng., Glasgow Royal Coll. Physicians (hon.). Fellow AAAS, Am. Coll. Dentists, Internat. Coll. Dentists, Am. Acad. Implant Prosthodontists (academia), Acad. Internat. Dental Studies (hon.), Internat. Assn. Oral and Maxillofacial Surgeons (hon., exec. com. 1980—, pres. 1983-86, sec. gen. 1989-95, exec. dir. 1995—); mem. Ill. Splty. Bd. Oral Surgery, ADA (adv. com. advanced edn. in oral surgery 1968-75, cons. Coun. on Dental Edn. 1968-82, mem. Commn. on Accreditation 1975-76), Am. Assn. Oral and Maxillofacial Surgeons (editor Forum 1965-96, AAOMS Today 1996—, disting. svc. award 1972, pres. 1976-77, rsch. recognition award 1978, William J. Gies award 1979, dedication 73d ann. meeting and sci. sessions 1991), Internat. Assn. Dental Rsch., Am. Dental Soc. Anesthesiology (pres. 1976-78), Am. Soc. Exptl. Pathology, Am. Assn. Dental Editors, Royal Soc. Medicine, Brazilian Coll. Oral and Maxillofacial Surgery and Traumatology (hon.), Chilean Soc. Oral and Maxillofacial Surgery (hon.), Hellenic Assn. Oral Surgery (hon.), Sadi Fontaine Acad. (hon.), Internat. Congress Oral Implantologists (hon.), Soc. Maxillofacial and Oral Surgeons South Africa (hon., assoc. life), Am. Dental Bd. Anesthesiology (pres. 1983-92), Nat. Chronic Pain Outreach Assn. (adv. bd.), Japanese Soc. for Temporomandibular Joint (hon.), Am. Soc. Laser in Dentistry (hon. life), Internat. Study Group for the Advancement of TMJ Arthroscopy (hon.), William F. Harrigan Soc., Odontographic Soc., Can. Assn. Oral and Maxillofacial Surgeons (hon.), Soc. Oral and Maxillofacial Surgeons (hon.), Jungarian Dental Assn. (hon.), Israel Soc. Oral and Maxillofacial Surgeons (hon.), Sigma Xi, Omicron Kappa Upsilon. Rsch. and publs. on connective tissue physiology and pathology, particularly cartilage and bone metabolism, craniofacial growth, oral maxillofacial surgery, and pathology of temporomandibular joint. Office: Med Coll Va Dept Oral/Maxillofac Surg PO Box 980566 Richmond VA 23298-0566

LASKIN, LEE B., lawyer, state senator; b. Atlantic City, June 30, 1936; student Am. U., Temple U.; Rutgers U., 1960; m. Andrea Solomon; 1 dau., Shari. Bar: N.J.; asst. atty. City of Camden (N.J.), from 1962; asst. U.S. atty. N.J., 1964-68; mem. N.J. Gen. Assembly, 1968-70; mem. Camden County Bd. Chosen Freeholders, 1970-73; mem. N.J. Senate, 1977-92; judge N.J. Superior Ct., 1994—; mcpl. atty. Audubon, Berlin Borough, Berlin Twp., Clementon, Laurel Springs, Mt. Ephraim and Waterford, N.J., and Winslow Twp.; counsel Bellmawr Bd. Edn., Berlin Zoning Bd., Camden County Welfare Bd., Non-Resident Taxpayers Assn., Animal Welfare Assn., Brith Sholom Fed. Credit Union, Camden Hebrew Fed. Credit Union, Union Fed. Savs. and Loan Assn., Div. 880 Amalgamated Transit Union, Local 18 of Am. Fed. Tech. Engrs., Camden Fire Officers Assn., Am. Postal Workers Union, Fuel Mchts. Assn., Glendale Nat. Bank; field counsel Fed. Nat. Mortgage Assn.; founder, 1st chmn. Glendale Nat. Bank; del. Rep. Nat. Conv., 1984; mem. Shamong Twp. Bd. Edn., Cherry Hill Zoning Bd. Served with USMCR. Office: Camden County Hall Justice 5th & Mickle Blvd Camden NJ 08003-2090

LASKO, JOEL, company executive; b. N.Y.C., Nov. 1, 1932; s. Max Lasko and Charlotte Parker; m. Mary Anne Thune, Dec. 19, 1973; children: Elizabeth, Andrew. BS in Mktg., Syracuse U., 1955; MBA in Mktg. Mgmt., CCNY, 1957. Br. mgr. Olivetti Corp., Washington, 1958-70; pres. Washington Photocopy, Washington, 1970—. Recipient Mktg. medal Am. Mktg. Assn., 1957. Avocations: tennis, skiing. Office: Washington Photocopy 4380 Macarthur Blvd NW Washington DC 20007-2500

LASKO, WARREN ANTHONY, mortgage banker, economist; b. Bklyn., June 29, 1940; s. Albert Anthony and Mildred (Hoyer) L.; m. Lorraine Gevertz; children: Karen, Erika. AB in Econs., Columbia U., 1962, MA in Econs., 1969. V.p. mortgage backed securities Govt. Nat. Mortgage Assn., Washington, 1977-81, 81-82, exec. v.p., 1982-85; v.p. strategic planning Fed. Nat. Mortgage Assn., Washington, 1981; exec. v.p. Mortgage Bankers Assn. Am., Washington, 1985—. Bd. dirs. Boys & Girls Homes Montgomery County, Chevy Chase, Md.; mem. Greater Washington Research Ctr., Washington, Chesapeake Bay Found., The Nature Conservancy, Chevy Chase. Recipient Cert. of Merit, U.S. Dept. Housing and Urban Devel., 1979, Disting. Svc. award U.S. Govt., 1982. Mem. Columbia Club. Home: 3211 Leland St Bethesda MD 20815-4009 Office: Mortgage Bankers Assn of Am 1125 15th St NW Washington DC 20005-2707

LASKOWSKI, EDWARD JOHN, chemist; b. Milw., Dec. 24, 1950; s. Ervin Joseph and Florence Margaret Laskowski; m. Mary Ann Rizzo, July 16, 1988. BS with honors in Chemistry, U. Wis., 1972; PhD in Inorganic Chemistry, U. Ill., 1976. Postdoctoral rsch. asst. Stanford U., Palo Alto, Calif., 1976-78; mem. tech. staff Lucent Techs. Bell Labs., Murray Hill, N.J., 1978—. Contbr. articles to profl. jours. Mem. Environ. Def. Fund, 1990—, Humane Soc. U.S., 1990—; leader Boy Scouts Am., 1981-88. Mem. Am. Chem. Soc., Alpha Chi Sigma. Roman Catholic. Achievements include patents relating to etching of compound semiconductors, patent for fabrication of an electro-optic sampling probe, patents for fabrication of optical waveguides. Avocations: golf, nature study, minerology, gardening, wildlife protection. Office: Lucent Techs Bell Labs 600 Mountain Ave Murray Hill NJ 07974-2008

LASKOWSKI, LEONARD FRANCIS, JR., microbiologist; b. Milw., Nov. 16, 1919; s. Leonard Francis and Frances (Cyborowski) L.; m. Frances Bielinski, June 1, 1946; children—Leonard Francis III, James, Thomas. B.S., Marquette U., 1941, M.S., 1948; Ph.D., St. Louis U., 1951. Diplomate: Am. Bd. Microbiology. Instr. bacteriology Marquette U., 1946-48; mem. faculty St. Louis U., 1951—, prof. pathology and internal medicine, Div. Infectious Diseases, 1969-90, prof. emeritus, 1990—, assoc. prof. in internal medicine, 1977-90—; dir. clin. microbiology sect. St. Louis U. Hosps. Labs., 1965—; cons. clin microbiology Firmin Desloge Hosp., St. Louis U. Group Hosps., St. Marys Group Hosps.; cons. bacteriology VA Hosp.; asst. dept. chief Pub. Health Lab., St. Louis Civil Def., 1958—; cons. St. Elizabeths Hosp., St. Louis County Hosp., St. Francis Hosp. Contbr. articles to profl. jours. Health and tech. tng. coordinator for Latin Am. projects Peace Corps, 1962-66. Served with M.C. AUS, 1942-46. Fellow Am. Acad. Microbiology; mem. Soc. Am. Bacteriologists, N.Y. Acad. Scis., Am., Mo. pub. health assns., AAUP, Med. Mycol. Soc. Am., Alpha Omega Alpha. Home: 6229 Robertsville Rd Villa Ridge MO 63089-2617 Office: 1402 S Grand Blvd Saint Louis MO 63104-1004

LASKOWSKI, MICHAEL, JR., chemist, educator; b. Warsaw, Poland, Mar. 13, 1930; came to U.S., 1947, naturalized, 1955; s. Michael and Maria (Dabrowska) L.; m. Joan Claire Heyer, Nov. 29, 1957; children: Michael Christopher, Marta Joan. B.S. magna cum laude, Lawrence Coll., 1950; Ph.D. (NIH fellow), Cornell U., 1954, postgrad., 1954-55; postgrad., Yale U., 1955-56. Research asst. Marquette U., 1949-50; instr. Cornell U., 1956-57; asst. prof. chemistry Purdue U., 1957-61, asso. prof., 1961-65, prof., 1965—; chmn. Gordon Rsch. Conf. Physics and Phys. Chemistry Biopolymers, 1966, Proteolytic Enzymes and Their Inhibitors, 1982; mem. study sect. NIH, 1967-71, NSF, 1989, sci. adv. bd. Receptor, Inc., 1993-94, Khepri Pharms., Inc., 1993-95. Mem. editorial bd. Archives Biochemistry and Biophysics, 1972-90, Biochemistry, 1973-78, Jour. Protein Chemistry, 1981—, Jour. Biol. Chemistry, 1983-88; contbr. articles to profl. jours. Recipient McCoy award Purdue U., 1975; co-recipient award in biol. scis. Alfred Jurzykowski Found., 1977. Mem. Am. Chem. Soc. (chmn. sect. 1968-69, treas. div. biol. chemistry 1981-84, councillor 1985-88), Am. Soc. Biol. Chemists, Biophys. Soc., Protein Soc., AAAS, AAUP, Polish Acad. Arts, Sci. Am., ACLU, Sigma Xi. Home: 222 E Navajo St West Lafayette IN 47906-2155 Office: Purdue U Dept Chemistry West Lafayette IN 47907 *A scientist who claims a small subfield of science as his personal fief should strive to leave it simpler and more coherent than he originally found it.*

LASKY, DAVID, lawyer, corporate executive; b. N.Y.C., Nov. 12, 1932; s. Benjamin and Rebecca (Malumed) L.; m. Phyllis Beryl Sumper, Apr. 14, 1957; children—Jennifer Lee, Robert Barry. BA, Bklyn. Coll., 1954; LLB, Columbia U., 1957. Bar: N.Y. 1957. Atty. N.Y.C. R.R. Co., 1957-62; with Curtiss-Wright Corp., N.Y.C., 1962—, corp. counsel, 1966-67, gen. counsel, 1967-93, v.p., 1972-80, sr. v.p., 1980-93, sec., 1989-93, pres., 1993—, chmn., 1995—; bd. dirs. Primex Technologies, Inc. Chmn. zoning bd. appeals, Ramapo, N.Y., 1968-72; dir., v.p. Oak Trail Homeowners Assn., 1987-90. Mem. ABA (chmn. com. corp. gen. counsel 1992-93), N.Y. Bar Assn., Phi Beta Kappa. Office: 1200 Wall St W Ste 501 Lyndhurst NJ 07071-3616

LASKY, MOSES, lawyer; b. Denver, Nov. 2, 1907; s. Juda Eisen and Ida (Grossman) L.; m. Ruth Helen Abraham, July 6, 1933; children: Morelle, Marshall. A.B. magna cum laude, U. Colo., 1926, J.D., 1928; LHD (hon.), 1996; LL.M., Harvard U., 1929. Bar: Calif. 1930, U.S. Supreme Ct 1947. Asst. dept. econs. U. Colo., 1925-26; salesman, local sales mgr. R.C. Barnum Co., Cleve., 1927-28; asso. Brobeck, Phleger & Harrison, San Francisco, 1929-41; partner Brobeck, Phleger & Harrison, 1941-79, Lasky, Haas, Cohler & Munter, San Francisco, 1979-94; Lasky, Haas & Cohler, San Francisco, 1994—; instr. Golden Gate Law Sch., 1934-35; sr. adv. bd. U.S. Ct. Appeals (9th cir.), 1984-90, chmn., 1989-90; vis. prof. law as disting. practitioner in residence Sch. Law, U. Colo., 1995. Contbr. articles in legal field and on Jewish life to jours. and mags. Pres. bd. dirs. San Francisco Mus. Modern Art, 1963, 64, now life trustee; pres. Regional Arts Coun. San Francisco, 1963-64; v.p. bd. dirs. San Francisco Art Inst., 1964; trustee War Meml. San Francisco, 1969-75; co-chmn. San Francisco Crime Com., 1968-71; bd. dirs. The Exploratorium, San Francisco, 1979-96, dir. emeritus, 1996—; bd. overseers L.A. br. Hebrew Union Coll.; nat. exec. com. Am. Jewish Com., 1947-55. Recipient Disting. Alumnus award U. Colo. Law Sch., 1977, U. Colo. medal, 1983, 50 Yr. award Am. Bar Found., 1989. Fellow Am. Coll. Trial Lawyers; mem. ABA, Phi Beta Kappa, Delta Sigma Rho. Home: 10 Mountain Spring Ave San Francisco CA 94114-2118 Office: 505 Sansome St Fl 12 San Francisco CA 94111

LASLEY, CHARLES HADEN, cardiovascular surgeon, health and fitness consultant; b. Lewisburg, Ky., Dec. 16, 1921; s. Marion Grinter and Helen May (Murray) L.; m. Mary Brown, June 14, 1946 (div. 1966); children: Mary Ann, Charles H., Jr., Robert Murray, David Marion; m. Janet Elizabeth Evans, Jan. 28, 1967; children: Tiffany Jean, Phillip Evans. BS in chemistry, biology, U. Fla., 1939-43; MD, Harvard Med. Sch., 1944-47. Diplomate Am. Bd. Thoracic Surgery, Am. Bd. Surgery. Intern in surgery Grady Hosp., Atlanta, 1947-48; asst. resident in surgery Grady Hosp., 1948-49; resident in surgery Gorgas Hosp., Ancon, Canal Zone, 1950; sr., chief resident surgery Gorgas Hosp., 1951, staff surgeon, chief gen. surgery, 1952-53; asst. chief orthopedic surgery USAH Ft. Carson, Colorado Springs, Colo., 1953-54; resident in cardiac surgery City of Hope Med. Ctr., L.A., 1954-55; resident in thoracic, cardiovascular surgery VAH Oteen, Asheville, N.C., 1955-56; pvt. practice thoracic, cardiovascular surgery Morton Plant Hosp., Clearwater, Fla., 1956-79; chief of surgery Morton Plant Hosp., 1971-72, chief thoracic, cardiovascular surgery, 1977-78; med. dir. Longevity Clin., Clearwater, 1977-78; med. cons. Wellness Ctr. Morton Plant Hosp., 1996—. Author: Veritas, 1996. Jazz drummer Red Suspenders Jazz Band, 1991—. With US Army, 1949-54. Mem. Am. Assn. for Thoracic Surgery, Am. Coll. of Sports Medicine, Soc. of Thoracic Surgeons, So. Thoracic Surgery Assn., Fla. Soc. of Thoracic and Cardiovascular Surgeons (president 1972), Suncoast Dixieland Jazz Society. Republican. Mem. First Christian Ch. Avocations: distance running (17 marathons), triathlons, handball, dixieland jazz. Home: Unit 4 Pelican Pl 672 Poinsettia Rd Belleair FL 33756

LASORDA, THOMAS CHARLES (TOMMY LASORDA), professional baseball team manager; b. Norristown, Pa., Sept. 22, 1927; s. Sam and Carmella (Covatto) L.; m. Joan Miller, Apr. 14, 1950; children: Laura, Tom Charles. Student pub. schs., Norristown. Pitcher Bklyn. Dodgers, 1954-55, Kansas City A's, 1956; with L.A. Dodgers, 1956—; mgr. minor league clubs L.A. Dodgers, Pocatello, Idaho, Ogden, Utah, Spokane, Albuquerque, 1965-73; coach L.A. Dodgers, 1973-76, mgr., 1976-96, v.p. fin., 1996—. Author: (with David Fisher) autobiography The Artful Dodger, 1985. Served with U.S. Army, 1945-47. Named Pitcher of Yr. Internat. League, 1958; L.A. Dodgers winner Nat. League pennant, 1977, 78, 81, 88, winner World Championship, 1981, 88; 2d Nat. League mgr. to win pennant first two yrs. as mgr.; named Nat. League Mgr. Yr. UPI, 1977, AP, 1977, 81, Baseball Writers' Assn. Am., 1988, Sporting News, 1988, Baseball Writers Assn. Am., 1983, 88; recipient Milton Richman Meml. award Assn. Profl. Baseball Players Am.; coach Nat. League All-Star team, 1977, 83-84, 86, 93; elected to the Baseball Hall of Fame, 1997. Mem. Profl. Baseball Players Am. Roman Catholic. Club: Variety of Calif. (v.p.). Office: care Los Angeles Dodgers 1000 Elysian Park Ave Los Angeles CA 90012-1112*

LASPINA, PETER JOSEPH, computer resource educator; b. Bay Shore, N.Y., June 28, 1951; s. Peter Celestine and Barbara Elizabeth (Rodee) L.; m. Julia Mary Gunther, July 10, 1982; 1 child; Joseph Peter. BMus with high honors, N.Y. State Coll., Potsdam, 1973, Performer's Cert. on Piano, 1973; MS in Music Edn., L.I. U., 1978; MS in Tech. Sys. Mgmt., SUNY, Stony Brook, 1987; postgrad., Nova Southeastern U., 1995—. Tchr. music E. Meadow (N.Y.) pub. schs., 1974-75, Northport-East Northport pub. schs., 1975-86; computer resource tchr. Northport-East Northport Pub. Schs., 1986—; adj. faculty SUNY, Stony Brook, 1991—; writer master trainer N.Y. State Edn. Dept., Albany, 1987—; cons. ednl. tech., Smithtown, N.Y., 1987—; invited del. U.S./China Joint Conf. on Edn., Beijing, 1992, 95-96, and conf. presenter. Contbr. articles to profl. jours. Mem. Am. Fedn. Tchrs., N.Y. State United Tchrs., Suffolk County Music Educators Assn., Nat. Assn. Sci., Tech. and Soc., N.Y. State Assn. Computers and Techs. (mem. conf. com. 1994), Internat. Soc. for Tech. in Edn., Computer Profls. for Social Responsibility, Assn. Ednl. Comm. and Tech., HTML Writers Guild. Presbyterian. Avocations: reading, oenology, home repair, travel. Home: 749 Meadow Rd Smithtown NY 11787-1621 Office: SUNY Dept Tech and Soc Stony Brook NY 11794

LASRY, JEAN-MICHEL, mathematics educator; b. Paris, Oct. 29, 1947; m. Elisabeth du Boucher; children: Laura, Romain, Julien. M in Econs., U. Paris-Assas, 1970; these d'etat in math., U. Paris IX, 1975. Rsch. fellow Ctr. Nat. Recherche Scientifique, Paris, 1973-78; prof. Paris-Dauphine U., 1978—, chmn. math. dept., 1980-83; cons. Compagnie Bancaire, Paris, 1988-91; mem. exec. bd. Caisse des Depots, 1991-94; CEO Caisse Autonome de Refinancement, 1994-96; global head fixed income rsch. Bank Paribas, 1997. Contbr. articles to profl. jours. Mem. Am. Math. Soc., Soc. Mathematiques apliquees et industrielles (bd. dirs.), Soc. Mathematique de France, Assn. Francaise de Finance, Ecole de la Cause Freudienne.

LASSEN, ROBERT MAURIE, graphic artist, photographer, editor; b. N.Y.C., June 7, 1935; s. Ben and Beatrice (Barmak) L.; m. Olivia Veronia Cheatham, 1957 (dec. Mar. 1985). BA, CCNY, 1959, postgrad., 1965-68; cert., Germain Sch. Photography, N.Y.C., 1978. Graphic artist Ben Lassen Studio, N.Y.C., 1950-68; prin. Lassen Advt., N.Y.C., 1968-80; owner, CEO, creative dir. Graphic Art Resource Assocs., N.Y.C., 1980—; gen. ptnr., CEO, creative dir. Lopat Graphics, 1995—. Editor, designer, photographer, graphic comms. cons., pub. numerous books for acad. instns.; rep. photographic group shows Gallery on the Green, Canton, Conn. and the Salmagundi Club, N.Y.C. Community activist Hudson Towers Tenant Assn., N.Y.C., 1970-89. Recipient Am. Graphic Design award, 1995. Mem. Profl. Photographers Am., Archs., Designers & Planners Social Responsibility. Avocations: chess, theoretical cosmology, Civil War history, crossword puzzles, photographic excursions. Home and Office: 257 W 10th St # 5E New York NY 10014-2508

LASSER, HOWARD GILBERT, chemical engineer, consultant; b. N.Y.C., Nov. 24, 1926; s. Milton and Tessie (Rosenthal) L.; m. Barbara Ann Katz, Aug. 24, 1950; children: Cathy, Ellen Lasser-LeVee, Alan. BSChemE, Lehigh U., 1950; postgrad., Columbia U., 1951; Dr.Ing., Darmstadt Tech. Inst., Germany, 1956. Registered profl. engr., D.C., Va., Calif. Chem. engr. Belvoir Rsch. Engring. & Devel. Ctr., Ft. Belvoir, Va., 1951-55, 58-72; materials engr. Naval Sea Systems Command, Washington, 1956-57, chem. engr., 1955-56; materials engr. Naval Facilities Engring. Command, Alexandria, Va., 1972-82; chem. engr. Materials Rsch. Cons., Alexandria & Springfield, Va., 1982—. Author: Design of Electroplating Facilities, 1990; contbr. articles to profl. jours. Fellow AAAS, Oil and Colour and Surface Finishers Chemists Assn., Am. Inst. Chemists; mem. Am. Electroplaters Soc., AIChE, NACE Internat. (cert.), ASM Internat., SSPC Coatings Soc., Am. Watch Makers Soc., Nat. Watch and Clock Collectors Assn., Tau Beta Pi, Sigma Xi, Alpha Chi Sigma, Pi Delta Epsilon. Achievements include 6 patents in electroplating and metal finishing; description of thermodynamic properties of carbon dioxide; development of thermotropic dyes for aluminum oxides; development of dyes to match laser wavelengths to enhance etching of substrates used in the electronics industry and medicine; over 500 publs. in materials and chemical engineering. Home: 5912 Camberly Ave Springfield VA 22150-2438 Office: Materials Rsch Cons 1121 King St Alexandria VA 22314-2924

LASSER, JOSEPH ROBERT, investment company executive; b. N.Y.C., Sept. 25, 1923; s. Milton and Tessie (Rosenthal) L.; m. Nell Jean Pollak, May 4, 1925; children: James, Carol Lasser Kornblith, Jean. BS, Lehigh U., 1946; MBA, NYU, 1951. Sr. analyst Lewisohn and Co., N.Y.C., 1946-51; dir. research Walston and Co., N.Y.C., 1951-55, Wertheim and Co., N.Y.C., 1956-67; ptnr. Shufro, Rose, Ehrman and Stanley Marks, Lasser & Co., N.Y.C., 1967-75; sr. portfolio mgr. C.J. Lawrence, N.Y.C., 1975-76; prin., sr. portfolio mgr. Neuberger & Berman, N.Y.C., 1977—. Treas. Bronx House, N.Y., 1978-95; past trusteee United Jewish Appeal/Fedn. Jewish Philanthropies, mem. bd. overseers. 1st lt. USAF, 1943-45. Decorated Air medal with three bronze oak leaf clusters, one silver oak leaf cluster; recipient 1st Lit. award Soc. Paper Money, 1976. Mem. Am. Numismatic Soc. (councillor 1990-93), N.Y. Soc. Security Analysts, Chartered Fin. Analysts Assn., N.Y. Stock Exchange (allied), Phi Beta Kappa, Princeton Club (N.Y.C.), Quaker Ridge (Scarsdale N.Y.). Home: 119 Cushman Rd Scarsdale NY 10583-3405 Office: Neuberger & Berman 605 3rd Ave New York NY 10158

LASSERS, WILLARD J., judge; b. Kankakee, Ill., Aug. 24, 1919; s. Henry and Sylvia (Oppenheim) L.; m. Elisabeth Stern, June 30, 1946; 1 dau., Deborah. A.B., U. Chgo., 1940, J.D., 1942. Bar: D.C. 1941, Ill. 1942, U.S. Supreme Ct. 1965. Practiced in Chgo., 1946-78; practice with Alex Elson, Chgo., 1946-48, Elson and Cotton, 1948-49; atty. RFC, Chgo., 1950-51, Office Price Stablzn., Chgo., 1951-53; individual practice law Chgo., 1953-60; partner Elson, Lassers and Wolff, Chgo., 1960-78; judge Circuit Ct. Cook County, Chgo., 1978—; lectr. taxation U. Chgo., 1954-55. Author: (with Alex Elson and Aaron S. Wolff) Civil Practice Forms Annotated, Illinois and Federal, 1952, 65, Scapegoat Justice: Lloyd Miller and the Failure of the Legal System, 1973; reviser: Fletcher Corporation Forms, 5 vols, 1957-60. Mem. Gov.'s Com. to Study Consumer Credit Laws, 1962-63; chmn. Com. Ill. Govt., 1962-63; Bd. dirs. Ill. div. ACLU, to 1978. Served with AUS, 1943-46. Mem. Ill., Chgo. bar assns., Am. Arbitration Assn. (mem. panel labor arbitrators 1965-78). Home: 1509 E 56th St Chicago IL 60637-1910 Office: Richard J Daley Ctr Chicago IL 60602

LASSETER, EARLE FORREST, lawyer; b. Gadsden, Ala., Dec. 26, 1933; s. Thomas Hobart and Mildred (Williamson) L.; m. Sally Elizabeth Bork, Sept. 2, 1961; children: Sally Fernald, David Forrest. BS, Auburn U., 1957; LLB, U. Ala., 1966. Bar: Ala. 1966, Ala. Supreme Ct. 1966, U.S. Ct. Military Appeals 1970, U.S. Dist. Ct. D.C. 1971, U.S. Ct. Internat. Trade 1971, D.C. 1972, U.S. Supreme Ct. 1972, Ga. 1987, Ga. Supreme Ct. 1988, U.S. Ct. Appeals Ga. 1988, U.S. Dist. Ct. (no. and mid. dists.) Ga. 1988, U.S. Ct. Vet. Appeals 1992. Commd. U.S. Army, 1958, advanced through grades to col., 1987; dep. staff judge adv. Hdqs. 1st Cav. Div., Republic of Vietnam, 1968-69; exec. officer Hdqs. U.S. Army Europe, Heidelberg, Germany, 1969-70; dep. staff judge adv. U.S. Army, Berlin, 1970-72; student Command and Gen. Staff Coll., Ft. Leavenworth, Kans., 1972; staff judge adv. 82d Airborne Div., Ft. Bragg, N.C., 1972-75; legal advisor Mil. Assistance Command and Am. Embassy, Taipei, Taiwan, 1975-77; staff judge adv. U.S. Army Mil. Police Sch., Ft. McClellan, Ala., 1977-79, U.S. Army Inf. Ctr., Ft. Benning, Ga., 1979-83; student U.S. Army War Coll., Carlisle Barracks, Pa., 1983; staff judge adv. U.S. Army Forces Command, Ft. McPherson, Ga., 1983-87; ret., 1987; ptnr. Pope, McGlamry, Kilpatrick & Morrison, Atlanta, Columbus, Ga., 1988—. Contbr. articles to profl. jours. Pres. Ft. Benning Sch. Bd., 1980-82. Served to 2d lt. U.S. Army. Decorated Purple Heart, Bronze Star with Oak Leaf Cluster, Legion of Merit, Meritorious Svc. medal with two Oak Leaf Clusters; recipient Joint Svcs. Commendation medal, Air medal, Army commendation medal, Master Parachutists Wings, Taiwan. Mem. ABA (chmn. 1991-92, bd. govs. 1996—), Ga. State Bar (bd. govs. 1995—), Ala. State Bar, Ala. Trial Lawyers Assn. (bd. govs. 1989—), Ga. Trial Lawyers Assn., Army-Navy Country Club (Arlington, Va.), Army-Navy Club (Washington), Green Island Country Club. Avocations: golf, tennis, running. Home: 6855 Ranch Forest Dr Columbus GA 31904-2428

LASSETER, KENNETH CARLYLE, pharmacologist; b. Jacksonville Fla., Aug. 12, 1942; s. James and Retta (Shad) L.; BS, Stetson U., 1963; MD, U. Fla., 1967; m. Kathy G. Marks, Aug. 6, 1977; children: Kenneth C. III, Susan, Frank L. Diplomate Am. Bd. Clin. Pharmacology. Intern, resident in medicine U. Ky. Med. Ctr., 1967-71; asst. prof., assoc. prof. pharmacology and medicine U. Miami Med. Sch., 1971-81, clin. assoc. prof., 1981—; adj. assoc. prof. pharmacology, Barry U., 1986—; v.p., dir. Clin. Pharmacology Assos., Inc., Miami, 1981—. Served with USAR, 1971-76. Recipient William B. Peck Sci. Rsch. award Interstate Postgrad. Med. Assn., 1976, rsch. award Alpha Omega Alpha, 1967. Fellow Am. Coll. Clin. Pharmacology; mem. ACP, Am. Soc. Pharmacology and Exptl. Therapeutics, Am. Soc. Clin. Pharmacology and Therapeutics, Sigma Xi. Republican. Contbr. articles to profl. jours. Home: 552 Ocean Dr Key Largo FL 33037-4345 Office: Clin Pharmacol Assocs 2060 NW 22nd Ave Miami FL 33142-7338

LASSETER, ROBERT HAYGOOD, electrical engineering educator, consultant; b. Miami, Fla., Apr. 4, 1938; s. J. Haygood and Elsiemae (Davis) L.; m. Lucy Taylor, Sept. 2, 1979; children: Courtney M., Malahn P., Robert M., Lauren L. BS in Physics, N.C. State U., 1963, MS in Physics, 1967; PhD in Physics, U. Pa., 1971. Postdoctoral work U. Pa., Phila., 1971-73; cons. engr. GE Co., Phila., 1973-80; from asst. prof. to assoc. prof. U. Wis., Madison, 1980-85, assoc. chmn., 1984-85, prof., 1985—; dir. power sys. Engring. Rsch. Ctr.- Wis., 1994—; cons. engr. Siemens AG, Germany, 1985-86; cons. L.A. Power and Water, 1982-86, Formas Centrais, Brazil, 1986-88, GE, N.Y. and Pa., 1982—, Elec. Power Rsch. Inst., Palo Alto, Calif., 1990—, others; expert advisor Conf. Internat. des Grands Réseaux Electriques, 1982—. Contbr. numerous papers to profl. socs. Fellow IEEE. Achievements include pioneering work in application of digital methods to the design of high voltage direct current power systems; basic development of analytical methods for design and study of power electronic controllers in power systems. Office: Univ Wisconsin Electrical & Computer Engineering 1415 Engineering Dr Madison WI 53706-1607

LASSITER, CHARLES WHITFIELD, construction executive; b. Unice, N.Mex., Aug. 16, 1952; s. James Edward and Lollie (Barber) L.; m. Donna Jean Young, Mar. 1, 1979; children: Belinda Dawn Watts, Kimberly Renee Watts, Charlene Michelle. BS in Mech. Engring., Kensington U., 1982; postgrad., U. Tex., 1982, Pa. State U., 1990. Welder, pipefitter, supt. Modern Welding, Plano, Tex., 1970-73; welder, pipefitter, owner C&J Svcs., Garland, Tex., 1973-75, C.W. Lassiter Constrn. Svcs., Garland, 1975-81; supt., estimator, engr. F.P. Ross Inc., Houston, 1981-82; owner, welder, pipefitter C.W. Lassiter Svcs., Arlington, Tex., 1982-83; v.p., project mgr., estimator RECC, Crowley, Tex., 1984-85; project mgr., engr. Gallagher Engring., Houston, 1985-88; project mgr., v.p. fabrication and constrn. Petrofac Inc., Tyler, Tex., 1989-92; project mgr., v.p., owner Engring. Procurement and Constrn., Inc., Tyler, 1992—; mem. adv. bd. ASHRAE, N.Y.C., 1991-92. Mem. adv. bd. Indsl. Coop. Tng. program Plano H.S., 1972-73. Mem. ASME, Am. Welding Soc. Avocations: snow skiing, motorcycling, sailing, family activities. Office: EPC Inc 11182 Us Highway 69 N Tyler TX 75706-5827

LASSITER, KATRINA ANN, medical/surgical nurse; b. N.Y.C., Dec. 6, 1958; d. James Thomas and Wilhelmina (Belfield) L. BS, Hampton (Va.) U., 1982; MS, Hunter Coll., 1990. Staff nurse NYU Med. Ctr., N.Y.C., 1983-84; staff nurse Mary Immaculate Hosp., Jamaica, N.Y., 1984-85, charge nurse, 1985-88, clin. nurse mgr., 1988-90, nursing unit dir., 1990-96, nursing informatics specialist, 1996—. Bd. dirs. Am. Heart Assn., N.Y.C., 1992-95; mem. NAACP; Cadette leader Girl Scouts U.S., 1983-95; mem. nurses unit Calvary Bapt. Ch., 1983-96—. Named Outstanding Vol. Mentor, N.Y. Mentoring, 1990. Mem. Nat. Black Nurses Assn., Progressive Women Inc. (sec. 1990-91), Sigma Theta Tau, Delta Sigma Theta, Chi Eta Phi. Avocations: travel, needlepoint, reading. Home: 727 Beech St Baldwin NY 11510-2724 Office: Cath Med Ctr 88-25 153d St Jamaica NY 11432

LASSITER, KENNETH T., photography educator, consultant; b. Richmond, Va., Jan. 2, 1935; s. B. Taylor and Euzelia (Duke) L.; m. Carol Lester, Apr. 9, 1960; children: Karen, Keith. BS, Va. Poly. Inst. and State U., 1957; MS (hon.), Brooks Inst. Photography, 1992. Engr. Eastman Kodak Co., Rochester, N.Y., 1957-60, tech. editor, 1960-69, dir. publs., 1970-84, dir. photo trade rels., 1984-93, mgr. photo edn., 1986-93; retired, 1993; mng. dir. Palm Beach (Fla.) Photo Workshops, 1993-94; mem. pres.'s coun. Internat. Ctr. Photography, N.Y.C., 1985-93; dir. Photographic Art & Sci. Found., Oklahoma City, 1984-95. Author: Executive Producer: Techniques of the Masters Videoconference Series; author or editor numerous Kodak publs. Mem. Soc. for Imaging Sci. and Tech. (sr., bd. dirs. 1965-90), Friends of Photography, Nat. Press Photographers Assn., Soc. for Photographic Edn., Photo Imaging Edn. Assn. Republican. Presbyterian. Avocations: boating, photography, music, computers.

LASSITER, ROY, soccer player; b. Raleigh, N.C., Mar. 9, 1969; m. Wendy Lassiter; 1 child, Ariel Daniel. Student, N.C. State U. Past mem. Costa Rican 1st Divsn., Carmelita F.C., Turrialba; mem. Tampa Bay (Fla.) Mutiny, 1996—. Named Fgn. Player of Yr., Costa Rica, 1995, Eastern Conf. All-Star, 1996, Budweiser Scoring Champion, 1996, mem. AT&T First Eleven, Major League Soccer, 1996. Office: Tampa Bay Mutiny Ste 104 1408 N Westshore Blvd Tampa FL 33607

LASSLO, ANDREW, medicinal chemist, educator; b. Mukacevo, Czechoslovakia, Aug. 24, 1922; came to U.S., 1946, naturalized, 1951; s. Vojtech Laszlo and Terezie (Herskovicova) L.; m. Wilma Ellen Reynolds, July 9, 1955; 1 child, Millicent Andrea. MS, U. Ill., 1948, PhD, 1952, MLS, 1961. Rsch. chemist organic chems. div. Monsanto Chem. Co., St. Louis, 1952-54; asst. prof. pharmacology, divsn. basic health scis. Emory U., 1954-60; prof. and chmn. dept. med. chemistry Coll. Pharmacy, U. Tenn. Health Sci. Ctr., 1960-90, Alumni Disting. Svc. prof. and chmn., dept. medicinal chemistry, 1989-90, professor emeritus, 1990—; cons. Geschickter Fund for Med. Research Inc., 1961-62; rsch. contractor U.S. Army Med. R & D Command, 1964-67; dir. postgrad. tng. program sci. librarians USPHS, 1966-72; chmn. edn. com. Drug Info. Assn., 1966-68, bd. dirs., 1968-69; dir. postgrad. tng. program organic medicinal chemistry for chemists FDA, 1971; exec. com. adv. council S.E. Regional Med. Library Program, Nat. Library of Medicine, 1969-71; chmn. regional med. library programs com. Med. Library Assn., 1971-72; mem. pres.'s faculty adv. council U. Tenn. System, 1970-72; chmn. energy authority U. Tenn. Center for Health Scis., 1975-77, chmn. council departmental chmn., 1977, 81; chmn. Internat. Symposium on Contemporary Trends in Tng. Pharmacologists, Helsinki, 1975. Producer, moderator (TV and radio series) Health Care Perspective, 1976-78; editor: Surface Chemistry and Dental Integuments, 1973, Blood Platelet Function and Medicinal Chemistry, 1984; contbr. numerous articles in sci. and profl. jours.; mem. editorial bd. Jour. Medicinal and Pharm. Chemistry, 1961, U. Tenn. Press, 1974-77; composer (work for piano) Synthesis in C Minor, 1968; patentee in field. Trustee 1st Bohemian Meth. Ch., Chgo., 1951-52, mem. bd. stewards, 1950-52; mem. ofcl. bd. Grace Meth. Ch., Atlanta, 1955-60; mem. adminstrv. bd. Christ United Meth. Ch., Memphis, 1964-72, 73-75, 77-79, 81-83, 88-90, chmn. commn. on edn., 1965-67, chmn. bd. Day Sch., 1967-68. 1st lt. USAR, 1953-57, capt., 1957-62. Recipient Research prize U. Ill. Med. Ctr. chpt. Sigma Xi, 1949, Honor Scroll Tenn. Inst. Chemists, 1976, Americanism medal DAR, 1976; U. Ill. fellow, 1950-51; Geschickter Fund Med. Research grantee, 1959-65, USPHS Research and Tng. grantee, 1958-64, 66-72, 82-89, NSF research grantee, 1964-66, Pfeiffer Research Found. grantee, 1981-87. Fellow AAAS, Am. Assn. Pharm. Scientists, Am. Inst. Chemists (nat. councilor for Tenn. 1969-70), Acad. Pharm. Rsch. and Sci.; mem. ALA (life), Am. Chem. Soc. (sr.), Am. Pharm. Assn., Am. Soc. Pharmacology and Exptl. Therapeutics (chmn. subcom. pre and postdoctoral tng. 1974-78, exec. com. edn. and profl. affairs 1974-78), Sigma Xi (pres. elect U. Tenn. Ctr. for Health Sci. chpt. 1975-76, pres. 1976-77, Excellence in Rsch. award 1989), Beta Phi Mu, Phi Lambda Sigma, Rho Chi. Methodist. Achievements include 7 U.S. and 11 foreign patents in field; identification of platelet aggregation-inhibitory specific functions in synthetic organic molecules; design and synthesis of novel human blood platelet aggregation inhibitors, novel compound for mild stimulation of central nervous system activity; research on relationships between structural features of synthetic organic entities, their physicochemical properties and their effects on biologic activity. Home and Office: 5479 Timmons Ave Memphis TN 38119-6932 *Of all the pleasures a human being can savor, none exceeds the satisfaction of a genuine sense of accomplishment. It undergirds all elements of creative living and surmounts vicissitudes exceeding conventional human endurance.*

LASSNER, FRANZ GEORGE, educator; b. Leipzig, Germany, May 6, 1926; s. Oscar and Marga (Treskow) L.; m. Marguerite Sansone, Aug. 18, 1961; children: Alexander Nicholas, John Paul. A.B. in History, Rutgers U., 1947; M.A. in History, Georgetown U., 1951, Ph.D. in Govt., 1960. With various research projects Georgetown U., Washington, 1951-62; research supt. Russian Studies Project, Washington, 1956-57; research assoc., curator spl. collections Hoover Inst., Stanford, Calif., 1962-63; dir. Herbert Hoover Presdl. Libr., West Branch, Iowa, 1963-67; dir. archives Hoover Inst., Stanford, 1969-74, spl. rep., 1974—; dir. devel. Phila. Coll. Textiles and Sci., 1974-76; sr. v.p. programs Freedoms Found., Valley Forge, 1977-91; adj. prof. history Temple U., Phila., 1992-93, Atlantic C.C., N.J., 1992-95. Mem. adv. bd. Internat. Telecommunications Inst., Houston, 1984-89; bd. dirs. St. Lawrence Inst., Montreal, 1985-89. Mem. World Affairs Coun. Greater Valley Forge (bd. dirs. 1991-93), Lambda Chi Alpha, Delta Phi Alpha. Roman Catholic. Home: 1069 Michigan Ave Cape May NJ 08204-2541

LASSWELL, MARCIA LEE, psychologist, educator; b. Oklahoma City, July 13, 1927; d. Lee and Stella (Blackard) Eck; m. Thomas Lasswell, May 29, 1950; children: Marcia Jane, Thomas Ely, Julia Lee. B.A., U. Calif., Berkeley, 1949; M.A., U. So. Calif., 1952; postgrad., U. Calif., Riverside, U. So. Calif., U. N.C. Individual practice psychotherapy, marriage/family therapy Claremont, Calif.; asst. prof. Pepperdine Coll., Los Angeles, 1959-60; asst. prof. psychology behavioral sci. dept. Calif. State U., Pomona, 1960-64; asso. prof. Calif. State U., 1965-69, prof., 1970—, chmn. dept., 1964-69; asso. clin. dir. Human Relations Center, U. So. Calif., 1975—; vis. assoc. prof. Scripps Coll., 1968-69, U. So. Calif., 1969-70, Occidental Coll., 1971-72; lectr. various Calif. univs.; mem. staff spl. project alcoholics and narcotics offenders Calif. Prison System, 1970-73; mem. Calif. Accreditation Com. Secondary Schs. and Colls., 1965—; mem. commn. accreditation for marriage and family tng. U.S. Dept. Edn., 1981-87. Author: College Teaching of General Psychology, 1967, Love, Marriage and Family, 1973, No-Fault Marriage, 1976, Styles of Loving, 1980, Marriage and Family, 1982, rev. edit., 1987, 91, Equal Time, 1983. Recipient Outstanding Tchrs. award Calif. State U., 1971, Outstanding Contbn. to Marriage and Family Therapy, 1991, Disting. Clin. Mem. award Calif. Assn. Marriage and Family Therapists, 1995. Fellow Am. Assn. Marital and Family Therapy (bd. dirs. 1970-72, 87-91, pres. elect 1993-95, pres. 1995-97, past pres. 1997-98); mem. AAAS, Nat. Coun. Family Rels. (exec. com. 1978-80), Am. Acad. Family Therapy, So. Calif. Assn. Marital and Family Therapy (pres. 1972-73), Alpha Kappa Delta, Phi Delta Gamma, Pi Gamma Mu. Home: 800 W 1st St #2908 Los Angeles CA 90012

LAST, MICHAEL P., lawyer; b. Chgo., July 31, 1946; s. Jules Hilbert and Muriel Esther (Ruekberg) L.; m. Yong-Hee Chyun, Dec. 1970 (div.); m. Jane Antoinette Nooy Bunnell, May 29, 1983. BA magna cum laude, Lawrence U., 1968; JD cum laude, Harvard U., 1971. Bar: Mass. 1971. Ptnr., head Real Estate, Environ. Law Dept. Warner & Stackpole, Boston, 1972-84; ptnr., head Environ. Law Dept. Gaston & Snow, Boston, 1984-91; ptnr., co-chair Environ. Law sect. Mintz, Levin, Cohn, Ferris, Glovsky and Popeo P.C., Boston, 1991—; mng. dir. ML Strategies, Inc., Boston, 1991—; bd. dirs. Newell Enterprises Inc., 1983-87; co-chair Am. Law Inst./ABA Ann. Course Study Minimizing Liability for Hazardous Waste Mgmt.; lectr. in field. Contbr. articles to profl. jours. Chair wetlands regulation rev. bd. Mass. Dept. Environ. Quality Engring., 1983-85, Town Wellesley Wetlands Protection Com., 1980-82; mem. Town Wellesley Planning Bd., 1983-88; rep. Town Meeting, Wellesley; mem. rev. bd. Mass. Dept. Environ. Protection, 1991-92; mem. bd. environ. mgmt. Mass. Dept. Environ. Mgmt., 1991—, chmn., 1994—; founder, pres. Santa Fe Coun. Environ. Excellence, 1991—; founder, pres. Berkshire Inst., Inc.; mem. corp. gifts com. Boston Mus. Fine Arts Capital Fund Dr., 1979; vice chair open space plan implementation com. Town Wellesley, 1978-79; trustee, bd. govs. New Eng. Aquarium, 1995—, Mass. Eye and Ear Infirmary, 1990—; trustee, bd. govs., exec. com. Newton-Wellesley Hosp., 1987-94, chmn. joint trustee staff com., 1992-93. 1st lt. USAF, 1971-72. Warren Hurst Stevens scholar Lawrence U., 1964. Mem. ABA (standing com. environ. law 1989-91, natural resources sect., corp., banking, bus. law sect., real property, probate, trust law sect.), Boston Bar Assn. (bd. dirs. 1984-87, chair environment com. 1979-81, chair urban affairs sect. 1983-87, co-chair mcpl. planning process com. 1983-87), Greater Boston C. of C. (real estate devel. com. 1979-80, co-chair Boston 2000 project review com. 1982-90, Boston 2000 steering com. 1983-90, co-chair adv. com. Devel. Design Guideline Study Downtown Boston 1983-92), Phi Beta Kappa. Avocations: canoeing, cross country skiing, camping. Office: Mintz Levin Cohn Ferris Glovsky & Popeo PC One Financial Center Boston MA 02111

LAST, SUSAN WALKER, training developer; b. Waterbury, Conn., Sept. 26, 1962; d. Harold Alfred and Mary (Alferie) Hull; m. Michael Allen Walker, Feb. 11, 1984 (div. July 1988); 1 child, Cassandra Mary; m. Robert Lee Last, Sept. 26, 1992. BS, Ind. U., 1983. Ctr. dir. Sylvan Learning Corp., Arlington, Tex., 1984-88, franchise cons., 1988-89, dist. mgr., 1989-90; coord. of program devel. Sylvan Learning Systems, Arlington, 1991-96; dir. tng. devel. Am. Fastsigns, Inc., Carrollton, Tex., 1996—; trainer, cons. Charles R. Hobbs Corp., Salt Lake City, 1989-96; cons. Highpointe, Arlington, 1988-94. Author: (curriculum) Study Skills Program, 1990, Study Power Video, 1991, Basic Math Program (K-8), 1994, Adult Reading Program, 1993, ESL program, 1995. Mem., speaker Parents Without Ptnrs., Arlington, 1991. Mem. ASCD, ASTD, Children and Adults with Attention Deficient Disorder, Nat. Coun. Tchrs. of Math., Nat. Coun. Tchrs. of English. Avocations: reading, writing, gardening, swimming. Home: 1316 Willowwood Dr Carrollton TX 75010 Office: Am Fastsigns Inc 2550 Midway Rd Ste 150 Carrollton TX 75006-2366

LASTER, DANNY BRUCE, animal scientist; b. Scotts Hill, Tenn., Nov. 29, 1942; married 1960; 2 children. BS, U. Tenn., 1963; MS, U. Ky., 1964; PhD in Animal Breeding, Okla. State U., 1970. Rsch. specialist U. Ky., Lexington, 1965-68; asst. prof. endocrinology Iowa State U., 1970-71; rsch. leader reproduction rsch. unit, Clay ctr., agr. rsch. svc. USDA, Nebr., 1971-78; nat. program leader, assoc. dep. adminstr. beef and sheep USDA, 1981-88; dir. Roman L. Hruska U.S. Meat Animal Rsch. Ctr. Clay Ctr., Nebr., 1988—. Mem. Am. Soc. Animal Sci. Office: USDA Roman L Hruska US Meat Animal Rsch Ctr (MARC) PO Box 166 Clay Center NE 68933-0166

LASTER, LEONARD, physician, consultant, author; b. N.Y.C., Aug. 24, 1928; s. Isaac and Mary (Ehrenreich) L.; m. Ruth Ann Leventhal, Dec. 16, 1956; children: Judith Eve, Susan Beth, Stephen Jay. AB, Harvard U., 1949, MD, 1950. Diplomate Nat. Bd. Med. Examiners, Am. Bd. Internal Medicine (gastroenterology). From intern to resident in medicine Mass. Gen. Hosp., Boston, 1950-53; fellow gastroenterology Mass. Meml. Hosp., 1958-59; vis. investigator Pub. Health Rsch. Inst., N.Y.C., 1953-54; lt. commd. USPHS, 1954, advanced through grades to asst. surgeon gen. (rear adm.), 1971; mem. staff Nat. Inst. Arthritis, Metabolic and Digestive Diseases, NIH, Bethesda, Md., 1954-73, chief digestive and hereditary diseases br., 1969-73; from spl. asst. to asst. dir. human resources President's Office Sci. and Tech., 1969-73; exec. dir. Assembly Life Scis., also div. med. scis. NAS-NRC, 1973-74; ret. USPHS, 1973; v.p. acad. affairs and clin. affairs Med. Ctr., also dean Coll. Medicine, prof. medicine Downstate Med. Ctr., SUNY, Bklyn., 1974-78; pres. Oreg. Health Scis. U., Portland, 1978-87, prof. medicine, 1978-87; chancellor U. Mass. Med. Ctr., Worcester, 1987-90, disting. univ. prof. medicine and health policy, 1990—, chancellor emeritus, 1990—; bd. dirs. Thermo Cardiosystems, Inc., Woburn, Mass.; cons. mgmt. and productivity of R & D programs for numerous pharm. corps., R & D strategic planning, orgn. corp. health care programs for multinat. paper corp. and pvt. rsch. found.; lab. investigator Marine Biol. Lab., Woods Hole, Mass., summers, 1962-69, chmn. organizer symposia on nat. policy and biomed. scis., summers, 1971-72, libr. reader, summers, 1973-76, chmn. steering com. Falmouth Forum, 1994—. Author: Life After Medical School, 32 Doctors Describe How They Shaped Their Medical Careers, 1996; contbr. articles on gastrointestinal disease, inborn errors of metabolism, devel. biology to profl. jours.; contbr. op-ed column and other pieces to Washington Post, essays to Hosp. Practice and MD Mag. Active Found. Advanced Edn. Scis., Bethesda, 1965-69, Bedford Stuyvesant Family Health Ctr., Bklyn., 1975-78, Med. Rsch. Found., Oreg., 1979-87, Oreg. Symphony, 1979-85, Oreg. Contemporary Theatre, 1981-83; pres. Burning Tree Elem. Sch. PTA, Bethesda, 1972-73; bd. dirs. Internat. Artists Series, Worcester, 1988-91, Mass. Biotech. Ctrs. for Excellence, Boston, 1988-96, Mass. Biotech. Rsch. Inst., Worcester, 1988-90, Worcester Bus. Devel. Corp., 1988-91; co-chmn. United Way Ctrl. Mass., COMEC Campaign, 1989; mem. exec. com. Worcester Econ. Club, 1988-91; mem. citizen gov. bd. Worcester Fights Back, 1990-95; chmn. corp. liaison com. Marine Biol. Lab., 1991-92; mem. Worcester Com. Fgn. Rels. (affiliated with Coun. Fgn. Rels.), 1992-96. Fellow ACP; mem. Am. Fedn. Clin. Rsch., Am. Gastroenterol. Assn., Am. Soc. Biol. Chemists, Am. Soc. Clin. Investigation (emeritus), Marine Biol. Lab. Corp., Portland C. of C. (dir. 1980-84), Mass. Med. Soc. (pub. rels. com.), Worcester Dist. Med. Soc., Worcester Club, Cosmos Club (Washington), Harvard Club (N.Y.C.), Univ. Club (Portland, Oreg.), Phi Beta Kappa, Sigma Xi. Home: 8 Lawrence Farm Rd Woods Hole MA 02543 Office: U Mass Med Ctr 120 Front St Ste 800 Worcester MA 01608-1404 *Education is nurturing excellence in others and facilitating its spread as an infectious disease.*

LASTER, RICHARD, biotechnology executive, consultant; b. Vienna, Austria, Nov. 10, 1923; came to U.S., 1940; naturalized, 1944; s. Alan and Caroline (Harband) L.; m. Liselotte Schneider, Oct. 17, 1948; children: Susan Laster Rubenstein, Thomas. Student U. Wash., 1941-42; BChE cum laude, Poly. Inst. Bklyn., 1943; postgrad. Stevens Inst. Tech., 1945-47. With Gen. Foods Corp., 1944-82, corp. rsch. and devel., Hoboken, N.J., 1944-58, ops. mgr. Franklin Baker divsn., Hoboken, N.J., Atlantic Gelatin divsn., Woburn, Mass., 1958-64, mgr. rsch. devel. Jell-O divsn., White Plains, N.Y., 1958-64, corp. mgr. quality assurance, White Plains, 1964-67, ops. mgr. Maxwell House divsn., White Plains, 1967-68, exec. v.p. Maxwell House divsn., 1968-69, pres. Maxwell House divsn., 1969-71, corp. group v.p., White Plains, 1971-73, exec. v.p. Gen. Foods Corp., 1974-82, also dir., rsch., devel. and food-away-from-home, 1975-82; bd. dirs. DNA Plant Tech. Corp., 1982-94, chmn., 1988-94, CEO, 1982-92, pres. 1982-91; mgmt. cons., 1994—; bd. dirs. RiceTec; mem. sch. bd. Chappaqua, N.Y., 1971-74, pres., 1973-74; chmn., mem. bd., 1st v.p. United Way of Westchester, 1978; chmn. adv. com. Poly. Inst. Westchester, 1977; trustee Poly. Inst. N.Y.,1978—; mem. coll. coun. SUNY, Purchase, Purchase Coll. Found, 1986—; mem. corp. N.Y. Botanical Garden; mem. subcom. Export Adminstrn. Pres.'s Export Coun., 1995; chmn. Westchester Edn. Coalition, 1992—; dir. Westchester Holocaust Commn., 1994; chmn. Am. Soc. of Plant Physiologists Edn. Found., 1995; mem. New Castle Town Bd. Recipient Disting. Alumnus award, Dist. Svc. award Nat. Conf. Christians and Jews. Fellow Poly. Inst. N.Y., Disting. Svc. award Nat. Conf. Christians and Jews. Mem. AAAS, N.Y. Acad. Scis., AIChE (Food and Bioengring. award 1972), Am. Chem. Soc., Am. Inst. Chemists, Tau Beta Pi, Phi Lambda Upsilon. Contbr. articles on food sci. to profl. publs. Patentee in field. Home: 23 Round Hill Rd Chappaqua NY 10514-1622 Office: Richard Laster 103 S Bedford Rd Mount Kisco NY 10549-3440

LASTMAN, MELVIN D., mayor; b. Toronto, Ont., Can., Mar. 9, 1933; s. Louis and Rose L.; m. Marilyn Lastman, Nov. 15, 1953; children—Dale, Blayne. LLD (hon.), York U. Pres. Bad Boy Furniture & Appliances, Toronto, 1955-76; mayor North York, Ont., 1972—; bd. govs. North York Gen. Hosp.; commr. York-Finch Gen. Hosp. Found. With Pride of Israel Synagogue, Sunnybrook Med. Ctr., Ont. Men's ORT, Can. ORT Orgn., Parents Against Drugs, North York YMCA, Vol. Ctr. Met. Toronto, North York Mental Health Coun., North York Srs. Ctr., North York Hydro Commn., North York chpt. Heart and Stroke Found. Ont., Can. Found. for Ileitis and Colitis, Ont., March of Dimes, Shalom Food Project, Can. Assn. for Riding for the Disabled, St. John Ambulance Canine Therapy Program, Metro Toronto; patron Kidney Found. Can.; hon. chmn. Children's Wish Found. Ont., Drug and Alcohol Network North York, Bloorview MacMillan Ctr., Leukemia Rsch. Fund, St. John's Rehab. Hosp.; with Chi-Ping Dance Group, North York Singers. Recipient Ursaki award Can. Sales and Mktg. Execs., C. of C. Lifetime Achievement award, 1995; named Temple Sinai Brotherhood Humanitarian of Yr., 1995. Mem. North York C. of C., Older Adult Ctrs. Assn., B'nai Brith Can., Juvenile Diabetes Found. Can., Can. Cancer Soc. (Willowdale Unit), Caritas Project, Can. Soc. Yad Vashem (bd. dirs.), Assn. Children with Learning Disabilities, North York Symphony, Kiwanis Club of North York, Kinsmen Club, North York Civitan Club, Rotary. Home: 19 Wideford Pl, North York, ON Canada M2M 4H3 Office: City of North York, 5100 Yonge St, North York, ON Canada M2N 5V7

LASTOWKA, JAMES ANTHONY, former federal agency executive, lawyer; b. Chester, Pa., Oct. 1, 1951; s. Joseph Edward and Mary A. (O'Malley) L.; m. Sandra L. Pugh, Apr. 28, 1979; children: Conor David, Carey Anna, Austin Tucker. BA in Econs. cum laude, Syracuse U., 1973; JD, Georgetown U., 1976. Bar: Pa. 1976, D.C. 1990, U.S. Ct. Appeals (a4th, 5th, 9th, 10th, 11th, D.C. cirs.) 1981. Staff atty. U.S. Occupational Safety and Health Rev. Commn., Washington, 1976-78, asst. gen. counsel, 1979-80; supervisory atty. Fed. Mine Safety and Health Rev. Commn., Washington, 1978-79, dep. gen. counsel, 1980-81, gen. counsel, 1981-84, commr., 1984-90; with Jones, Day, Reavis & Pogue, Washington, 1990-92, McDermott, Will & Emery, Washington, 1992—. Contbr. editor Occupational Hazards Mag. Mem. ABA (mem. labor law sect., com. occupational safety and health law, com. natural resources, energy and environ. law). Office: McDermott Will & Emery 1850 K St NW Washington DC 20006-2213

LATAIF, LAWRENCE P., lawyer; b. Fall River, Mass., Nov. 1, 1943; s. Louis and Linda Adele (Salwan) L.; m. Noha Nader, Dec. 29, 1979; children: Nicole, Lawrence Jr., Diana. BA, Brown U., 1965; JD, Georgetown U., 1968, LLM, 1970. Bar: D.C. 1969, U.S. Ct. Appeals (D.C. cir.) 1969, U.S. Ct. Mil. Appeals 1969, U.S. Supreme Ct. 1973, Va. 1974, U.S. Tax Ct. 1979. Asst. U.S. atty. U.S. Dept. Justice, Washington, 1970-73; pvt. practice Arlington, Va., 1974-75; ptnr. Lataif & Bernșen, Arlington, 1976-77; pvt. practice Fairfax, Va., 1978-85; of counsel Jones, Day, Reavis & Pogue, Washington, 1986-88, ptnr., 1989-91; ptnr. McDermott, Will & Emery, Miami, Fla., 1991-95; prin. Lawrence P. Lataif, P.A., Ft. Lauderdale, Fla., 1995—. Bd. advisors: Corp. Counsel's Guide to Business-Related Immigration, 1989-95; contbr. articles to Wall St. Jour. and profl. jours. Mem. bd. overseers Children's Hosp., Boston, 1993; bd. dirs. Symphony of the Americas, 1995-96. Prettyman fellow Georgetown U. Law Sch., 1968. Mem. Am. Immigration Lawyers Assn. Office: 5100 N Federal Hwy Ste 202 Fort Lauderdale FL 33308-3842

LATANÉ, BIBB, social psychologist; b. N.Y.C., July 19, 1937; s. Henry Allen and Felicite Gillman (Bibb) L.; m. Deborah Ruth Richardson; children by previous marriage: Julia Gillman, Claire Augusta, Henry Arbiter. B.A., Yale U., 1958; Ph.D., U. Minn., 1963. Mem. faculty dept. social psychology Columbia U., N.Y.C., 1962-68; prof. psychology, dir. behavioral scis. lab. Ohio State U., Columbus, 1968-82; prof. psychology, dir. Inst. Research Social Sci. U.N.C.-Chapel Hill, 1982-90; prof. psychology Fla. Atlantic U., Boca Raton, 1990—. Contbr. articles to profl. jours. Guggenheim fellow, 1974-75; James McKeen Cattell fellow, 1981-82; NSF, Office of Naval Research grantee. Mem. Am. Psychol. Assn. (council rep. 1971-75), Soc. Personality and Social Psychology (pres. 1976-79, Campbell award 1986), Midwestern Psychol. Assn. (pres. 1981-84), Acad. Mgmt., AAAS (Socio-Psychol. prize 1968, 80), Am. Sociol. Assn., Animal Behavior Soc., Internat. Assn. Applied Psychology. Home: 4521 S Ocean Blvd Boca Raton FL 33487-4235 *We know so much, yet have so much to learn about each other that the science of behavior will continue to vitalize and be vital.*

LATANISION, RONALD MICHAEL, materials science and engineering educator, consultant; b. Richmondale, Pa., July 2, 1942; s. Stephen and Mary (Kopach) L.; m. Carolyn Marie Domenig, June 27, 1964; children: Ivan, Sara. BS, Pa. State U., 1964; PhD in Metall. Engring., Ohio State U., 1968. Postdoctoral fellow Nat. Bur. Standards, Washington, 1968-69; research scientist Martin Marietta, Balt., 1969-73, acting head materials sci., 1973-74; dir. H.H. Uhlig Corrosion Lab. MIT, Cambridge, 1975—, Shell Disting. prof. materials sci. and engring., 1983-88, dir. Materials Processing Ctr., 1984-91; co-founder ALTRAN Materials Engring. Corp., Boston, 1992—; mem. tech. adv. bd. Modell Devel. Corp., Framingham, Mass., 1987-94; sci. advisor com. on sci. and tech. U.S. Ho. of Reps., 1982-83; chmn. ad hoc com. Mass. Advanced Materials Ctr., Boston, 1985—; mem. adv. bd. Mass. Office Sci. and Tech.; co-PI, NSF/SSI project PALMS; chmn. MIT Coun. on Primary and Secondary Edn. Editor: Surface Effects in Crystal Plasticity, 1977, Atomistics of Fracture, 1983, Chemistry and Physics of Fracture, 1987, Advances in Mechanics and Physics of Fracture, 1981, 83, 86; contbr. articles to profl. jours. Recipient sr. scientist award Humboldt Found., 1974-75, David Ford McFarland award Pa. State U., 1986; named Henry Krumb lectr. AIME, 1984, Disting. Alumnus, Ohio State U. Coll. Engring., 1991, hon. alumnus MIT, 1992; Centennial fellow Coll. Earth and Mineral Scis., Pa. State U., 1996. Fellow Am. Soc. Metals Internat. (govt. and pub. affairs com. 1984), Nat. Assn. Corrosion Engrs. (A.B. Campbell award 1971, Willis

R. Whitney award 1994); mem. New Eng. Sci. Tchrs. (founder, co-chmn.), Nat. Acad. Engring., Am. Acad. Arts and Scis., Nat. Materials Adv. Bd. Roman Catholic. Office: MIT Materials Sci & Engring 77 Massachusetts Ave Rm 8202 Cambridge MA 02139-4301

LATCHUM, JAMES LEVIN, federal judge; b. Milford, Del., Dec. 23, 1918; s. James H. and Ida Mae (Robbins) L.; m. Elizabeth Murray McArthur, June 16, 1943; children: Su-Allan, Elizabeth M. A.B. cum laude, Princeton U., 1940; J.D., U. Va., 1946. Bar: Va. 1942, Del. 1947. Assoc. Berl, Potter & Anderson, Wilmington, 1946-53; partner Berl, Potter & Anderson, 1953-68; judge U.S. Dist. Ct. Del., Wilmington, 1968-73; chief judge U.S. Dist. Ct. Del., 1973-83, sr. judge, 1983—; New Castle County atty. Del. Hwy. Dept., 1948-50; asst. U.S. atty., 1950-53; atty. Del. Interstate Hwy. Div., 1955-62, Delaware River and Bay Authority, 1962-68. Chmn. New Castle County Democratic Com., 1953-56, Wilmington City Com., 1959-63. Served to maj. Insp. Gen. Corps AUS, 1942-46, PTO. Mem. ABA, Del. Bar Assn., Va. Bar Assn., Order of Coif, Sigma Nu Phi. Presbyn. Clubs: Wilmington, Univ. Office: US Dist Ct 844 N King St # 34 Wilmington DE 19801-3519

LATHAM, ALLEN, JR., manufacturing company consultant; b. Norwich, Conn., May 23, 1908; s. Allen and Caroline (Walker) L.; m. Ruth Nichols, Nov. 11, 1933 (dec. 1992); children: W. Nichols, Harriet Latham Robinson, David W., Thomas W.; m. Charlotte T. Goldsmith, July 4, 1992. B.S. in Mech. Engring, MIT, 1930, Sloan fellow, 1936. Devel. engr. E.I. duPont, Belle, W.Va., 1930-35; engr., treas. Polaroid Corp., Cambridge, Mass., 1936-41; engr., v.p. Arthur D. Little, Cambridge, 1941-66; pres. Cryogenic Tech., Waltham, Mass., 1966-71; founder Haemonetics, Braintree, Mass., 1971—. Recipient New Eng. Inventor award, 1987, Morton Grove-Rasmussen award Am. Assn. Blood Banks, 1989; named Engr. of Yr. Socs. New Eng. Engring., 1970. Mem. AAAS, ASME (hon.), AIChE, Instrument Soc. Am., Nat. Acad. Engring. Club: Country (Brookline, Mass.). Patentee in blood processing equipment and processes. Home: 143 Whitcomb Ave Jamaica Plain MA 02130-3436 Office: Haemonetics 400 Wood Rd Braintree MA 02184-2412

LATHAM, ELEANOR RUTH EARTHROWL, neuropsychology therapist; b. Enfield, Conn., Jan. 12, 1924; d. Francis Henry and Ruth Mary (Harris) Earthrowl; m.Vaughan Milton Latham, July 20, 1946; children: Rebecca Ann, Carol Joan, Jennifer Howe, Vaughan Milton Jr. BA, Vassar Coll., 1945; MA, Smith Coll., 1947, Clark U., Worcester, Mass., 1974; EdD, Clark U., Worcester, Mass., 1979. Lic. psychologist, Mass. Guidance counselor Worcester Pub. Schs., 1967-74, sch. psychologist, 1975-80; pvt. practice neuropsychology Worcester, 1981—; postdoctoral trainee Children's Hosp.-Harvard Med. Sch., Boston, 1980-81; mem. staff The Med. Ctr. of Ctrl. Mass. Meml.-Hahnemann, Worcester, St. Vincent Hosp., Worcester; assoc. in pediats. U. Mass. Med. Ctr. and Med. Sch., Worcester, 1982—. Author: Neuropsychological Impairment in Duchene Muscular Dystrophy, 1985, Motor Coordination and Visual-Motor Development in Duchenne Muscular Dystrophy, 1991, Developmental Considerations in Educational Planning for Boys with Duchenne Muscular Dystrophy; contbr. chpt.: Children and Death, 1987. Mem. Internat. Neuropsychology Soc., Am. Psychol. Assn. Republican. Unitarian. Avocations: chamber music, piano, travel, swimming, gardening. Home: 59 Berwick St Worcester MA 01602-1442 Office: Vernon Med Ctr 10 Winthrop St Worcester MA 01604-4435

LATHAM, JAMES DAVID, lawyer; b. Lowell, Mass., Apr. 18, 1942; s. Ernest Hargreaves and Anne Crowdis (MacIvor) L.; m. Pauline Page, Apr. 14, 1972; children: James Benjamin, Timothy David. AB, Dartmouth Coll., 1964; LLB, Boston U., 1967. Bar: Mass. 1967, U.S. Dist. Ct. Mass. 1968. Assoc. Goldman & Curtis, Lowell, 1967-72; ptnr. Goldman, Curtis, Leahey & Latham, Lowell and Boston, 1972-74; assoc. counsel ITT Sheraton Corp., Boston, 1974-78, sr. counsel, 1978-80, asst. gen. counsel, 1982-84, v.p., 1984-92, sr. v.p., sec., gen. counsel, 1992—; gen. counsel Sheraton Mgmt. Corp., London, 1980-84. Chmn. Lowell Rep. City Com., 1972. Mem. Vesper Country Club, The Internat. Club. Episcopalian. Office: ITT Sheraton Corp 60 State St Boston MA 02109-1800

LATHAM, JAMES RICHARD, research scientist; b. Pomona, Calif., July 1, 1946; s. James Richard and Norma Elizabeth (Mills) L.; m. Pamela June Staley Latham, Aug. 31, 1968, 1 child, Joan Elizabeth Latham. Student, U. Calif., Berkeley, 1964-65, Chabot Coll., Hayward, Calif., 1965-72. Technician Coast Mfg./Hexel Co., Livermore, Calif., 1966-69, Crown Zellerbach Co., San Leandro, Calif., 1969-70; sr. rsch. technician Kaiser Aluminum & Chem. Corp., Pleasanton, Calif., 1970-82; sr. technician Clorox Tech. Ctr., Pleasanton, Calif., 1982—. Patentee in field. Named Merit Scholarship Finalist; recipient NROTC scholarship. Mem. Am. Chemical Soc., Div. Chemical Technicians (treas. 1993-94), Livermore Amateur Radio Klub (sec.). Mem. LDS Ch. Avocations: sailing, amateur radio (KE6QJV).

LATHAM, JOSEPH AL, JR., lawyer; b. Kinston, N.C., Sept. 16, 1951; s. Joseph Al and Margaret Lee (Tyson) L.; m. Elaine Frances Kramer, Dec. 19, 1981; 1 child, Aaron Joshua. BA, Yale U., 1973; JD, Vanderbilt U., 1976. Bar: Calif. 1976, U.S. Dist. Ct. (cen. dist.) Calif. 1977, U.S. Ct. Appeals (9th cir.) 1977, U.S. Dist. Ct. (no. and so. dists.) Calif. 1978, Ga. 1980, U.S. Dist. Ct. (no. dist.) Ga. 1981, U.S. Ct. Appeals (5th and 11th cirs.) 1981, U.S. Dist. Ct. (mid. dist.) Ga. 1982, D.C. 1984. Assoc. Paul, Hastings, Janofsky & Walker, Orange County and L.A., 1976-80, Atlanta, 1980-83; ptnr. Paul, Hastings, Janofsky & Walker, Orange County and L.A., 1987—; chief counsel to bd. mem. NLRB, Washington, 1983-85; staff dir. U.S. Commn. on Civil Rights, Washington, 1985-86; instr. advanced profl. program U. So. Calif. Law Ctr., 1988, lectr. law, 1989—. Articles editor Vanderbilt Law Rev., 1975-76; editorial asst. Employment Discrimination Law, 2d edit., 1983; contbr. articles to Barron's, ABA Jour., Litigation, Employee Rels. Law Jour. Mem. ABA (labor and employment law sect.), Calif. Bar Assn., Ga. Bar Assn., D.C. Bar Assn., Order of Coif. Republican. Episcopalian. Office: Paul Hastings Janofsky & Walker 555 S Flower St Fl 23 Los Angeles CA 90071-2300

LATHAM, LARRY LEE, state administrator, psychologist; b. Dallas, June 27, 1945; s. James L. Latham and Sara B. (MacClaine) Dulaney; m. Helen Marie Bumpass, Dec. 19, 1966; children: Wade Lee, Ryan Justin. BS in Psychology, U. North Tex., 1966, MS in Psychology, 1967; PhD in Psychology, U. Ala., 1977. Lic. psychologist, Ala. Psychologist Outwood State Sch., Dawson Springs, Ky., 1967-69; psychologist, unit coord. Denton (Tex.) State Sch., 1969-72; dir. habilitation W.D. Partlow Devel. Ctr., Tuscaloosa, Ala., 1972-77; dir. applied rsch. Ala. Dept. Mental Health and Mental Retardation, Tuscaloosa, 1977-81; dir. L.B. Wallace Devel. Ctr. Ala. Dept. Mental Health and Mental Retardation, Decatur, 1981-84; assoc. commr. for mental retardation Ala. Dept. Mental Health and Mental Retardation, Montgomery, 1984-91; dir. Bur. Orgnl. Devel., Montgomery, 1991—; dir. Greil Psychiat. Hosp./ Ala. Dept. Mental Health and Mental Retardation, 1993—; cons. Latham & Assocs., 1969-72, Tex. Dept. Mental Health and Mental Retardation, 1987; pres. Human Svcs. Pers. Specialist, Inc. Bd. dirs. Foster Grandparents Ky., 1967-69, Ala. Spl. Olympics, 1984-91, Ala. Devel. Disabilities Coun., 1984-91. Fellow Am. Assn. Mental Retardation (pres. Ala. chpt. 1988-89). Avocations: woodworking, golf. Office: Greil Meml Psychiat Hosp 2140 Upper Wetumpka Rd Montgomery AL 36107-1342 *In this age it is best to remember that just because your values are not valued does not mean that you are wrong.*

LATHAM, LAVONNE MARLYS, physical education educator; b. Garrison, Iowa, Mar. 17, 1942; d. Harry August and Vona Irene (Loveless) Hilmer; m. Robert Allen Latham Jr., July 21, 1979. BA, U. Iowa, 1964; postgrad., No. Ill. U., 1985, Western Ill. U., 1970-88, Bemidji State U., 1979. Cert. tchr., Ill. Tchr. phys. edn., elem. computer coord. Erie (Ill.) Community Unit 1, 1964—; head counselor Camp Lenore Owaissa, Hinsdale, Mass., 1964-78. Mem. NEA, AAHPER, Ill. Assn. Health, Phys. Edn. and Recreation, U. Iowa Alumni Assn., Ill. Edn. Assn., Erie Tchrs. Assn. (pres. 1982-83), Nat. Audubon Soc., Nature Conservancy, Delta Kappa Gamma. Baptist. Avocations: violin, computers, photography, travel, outdoor activities. Home: 1002 6th St Erie IL 61250 Office: Erie Community Unit 1 605 6th Ave Erie IL 61250-9452

LATHAM, PATRICIA HORAN, lawyer; b. Hoboken, N.J., Sept. 5, 1941; d. Patrick John and Rosemary (Moller) Horan; m. Peter Samuel Latham, June 12, 1965; children: John Horan, Kerry Patricia. BA, Swarthmore Coll., 1963; JD, U. Chgo., 1966. Bar: D.C. 1967, U.S. Dist. Ct. D.C. 1967, U.S. Ct. Appeals 1967, U.S. Supreme Ct. 1970, Va. 1989, U.S. Dist. Ct. (ea. dist.) Va. 1989, U.S. Dist. Ct. Md. 1991. Assoc. Fried Frank Harris Shriver & Kampelman, Washington, 1966-69; atty. Office of Gen. Counsel, SEC, Washington, 1969-71; assoc. Martin & Smith, Washington, 1971—, ptnr., 1974-85; ptnr. Latham & Latham, Washington, 1986—; lectr. Columbus Sch. Law, Cath. U. Am., Washington, 1978-92; mem. panel of arbitrators N.Y. Stock Exch., 1985—; co-founder, co-dir. Nat. Ctr. Law and Learning Disabilities, 1992—. Co-author: Attention Deficit Disorder and the Law, 1992, Learning Disabilities and the Law, 1993, Succeeding in the Workplace, 1994, Higher Education Services for Students with Learning Disabilities and Attention Deficit Disorder: A Legal Guide, 1994, Documentation and the Law, 1996; contbg. author: ADD and the College Student, 1993, A Comprehensive Guide to ADD in Adults, 1995, Managing Attention and Learning Disorders om Late Adolescence and Adulthood, 1996, Textbook of Pediatric Neuropsychiatry, 1997. Co-founder, trustee Beacon Coll., 1989-93, chmn. bd. trustees, 1990-92; mem. nat. profl. adv. bd. Children and Adults with Attention Deficit Disorders. Mem. ABA, D.C. Bar, Am. Arbitration Assn. (panel arbitrators and mediators 1982—), Nat. Attention Deficit Disorders Assn. (bd. dirs.), Learning Disabilities Assn. Am. (nat. adv. bd. mem. 1996—), City Tavern Club. Roman Catholic. Home: 7000 Loch Edin Ct Potomac MD 20854-4844

LATHAM, PETER SAMUEL, lawyer; b. Boston, July 23, 1940; s. Earl Gansen and Margaret (Perrier) L.; m. Patricia Ann Horan, Sept. 5, 1941; children: John Horan, Kerry Patricia. BA with honors, Swarthmore Coll., 1962; LLB, U. Pa., 1965. Bar: D.C. 1966, U.S. Ct. Appeals (D.C. cir.) 1982, U.S. Dist. Ct. Md. 1991. Atty. SEC, Washington, 1965-66; assoc. firm Vom Baur, Coburn, Simmons & Turtle, Washington, 1969-71; mem. firm Wachtel, Ross and Matzkin, Washington, 1971-80; ptnr. Latham & Latham and predecessor firms, Washington, 1980—; arbitrator Am. Arbitration Assn., 1978—. Author: Government Contract Disputes, 1981, 86; co-author: Attention Deficit Disorder and the Law: A Guide for Advocates, 1992, Learning Disabilities and the Law, 1993, Succeeding in the Workplace, 1994, Higher Education Services for Students with Learning Disabilities and Attention Deficit Disorder: A Legal Guide, 1994, Documentation and the Law, 1996; contbg. author ADD and the College Student, 1993, A Comprehensive Guide to ADD in Adults, 1995, Managing Attention and Learning Disorders in Late Adolescence and Adulthood, 1996, Textbook of Pediatric Neuropsychiatry, 1997; producer, dir. The ABC's of ADD, other videos on legal topics. Co-founder, trustee Beacon Coll., 1989-93; co-founder, co-dir. Nat. Ctr. for Law and Learning Disabilities. Lt. USN, 1966-69. Decorated Navy Achievement medal with combat V. Mem. ABA, Nat. Attention Deficit Disorders Assn. (bd. dirs.), DC Procurement Reform Taskforce (mem. Alternate Dispute Resolution subcom. 1995—), City Tavern Club. Republican. Roman Catholic. Avocations: tennis, swimming. Home: 7000 Loch Edin Ct Potomac MD 20854-4844 Office: Latham and Latham PO Box 40157 Washington DC 20016

LATHAM, TOM, congressman; b. Hampton, Iowa, July 14, 1948; s. Willard and Evelyn L.; m. Kathy Swinson, 1975; children: Justin, Jennifer, Jill. Student, Watrburg Coll., Iowa State U. Bank teller, bookkeeper Brush, Colo., 1970-72; ind. ins. agent Fort Lupton, Colo., 1972-74; mktg. rep. Hartford Ins. Co., Des Moines, 1974-76; with Latham Seed Co., Alexander, Iowa, 1976—; now v.p., co-owner Latham Seed Co.; mem. 104th Congress from 6th Iowa dist., 1995—; Mem. congressman Fred Grandy's agriculture com.; sec. Republican Party of Iowa; rep. 5th dist. Republican State Ctrl. com.; co-chair Francklin County Republican Ctrl. com.; whip Iowa del. Republican Nat. Conv., 1992. Past chair Franklin County Extension Coun.; mem. Nazareth Lutheran Ch., past pres.; citizens adv. coun. Iowa State U. Mem. Am. Soybean Assn., Am. Seed Trade Assn., Iowa Farm Bur. Fedn., Iowa Soybean Assn., Iowa Corn Growers Assn., Iowa Seed Assn., Agribusiness Assn. of Iowa. Lutheran. Office: US House Reps 516 Cannon Bldg Ofc Bldg Washington DC 20515-1505

LATHAM, WELDON HURD, lawyer; b. Bklyn., Jan. 2, 1947; s. Aubrey Geddes and Avril (Hurd) L.; m. Constantia Beecher, Aug. 8, 1948; children—Nicole Marie, Brett Weldon. BA, Howard U., 1968; JD, Georgetown U., 1971; postgrad. George Washington U., 1975-76. Bar: D.C. 1972, U.S. Ct. Appeals (D.C. cir.) 1972, U.S. Ct. Mil. Appeals 1974, U.S. Ct. Claims 1975, U.S. Supreme Ct. 1975, Va. 1981, U.S. Ct. Appeals (fed. cir.) 1988. Mgmt. cons. Checchi & Co., Washington, 1968-71; atty. Covington & Burling, Washington, 1971-73; sr. atty. Fed. Energy Adminstrn., Washington, 1974; asst. gen. counsel Exec. Office Pres., Office Mgmt. and Budget The White House, 1974-76; atty. Hogan & Hartson, Washington, 1976-79; gen. dep. asst. sec. HUD, 1979-81; v.p., gen. counsel Sterling Systems, Inc. (subs. PRC), exec. asst., counsel to chmn., CEO, and assoc. gen. counsel Planning Rsch. Corp., McLean, Va., 1981-86; mng. ptnr. Reed Smith Shaw & McClay, McLean, Va., 1986-91; sr. ptnr. Shaw, Pittman, Potts & Trowbridge, Washington, 1992—; adj. prof. Howard U. Law Sch., Washington, 1972-82; guest prof. U. Va., Charlottesville, 1976-90; mem. Va. Gov.'s Bus. and Industry Adv. Com. on Crime Prevention, 1983-85, Va. Gov.'s Regulatory Reform Adv. Bd., 1982-84; chmn. task force SBA, 1982; legal counsel Md. Mondale for Pres. Campaign, 1984. Columnist Minority Bus. Entrepreneur (MBE) Mag., 1991—; gen. counsel Nat. Coalition Minority Bus., 1993—. Mem. Washington steering com. NAACP Legal Def. Fund, 1975-95, Fairfax County Airports Adv. com., 1987-88; bd. dirs., gen. counsel Northern Va. Minority Bus. and Profl. Assn., 1985-92; trustee Va. Commonwealth U., Richmond, 1986-90; bd. dirs. Washington Urban League, 1986-90, U. D.C. Found., 1982-87, Washington Coun. Lawyers, 1973, bd. dirs. Profl. Svcs. Coun., 1983-88; bd. dirs. Minority Bus. Enterprise Legal Def. and Edn. Fund, 1989-91, Wash. Hosp. Ctr. Found., 1996—; appointee Greater Washington Bd. Trade, Blue Ribbon Task Force on Home Rule, 1985-86, bd. dirs., exec. com., chmn. regional affairs com., corp. sec. Greater Wash. Bd. Trade, 1990-95; trustee George Mason U., Fairfax, Va., 1990-94; mem. adv. bd. First Union Nat. Bank, 1995—; civilian aide Sec. of Dept. of Army, 1995—; mem. Clinton Small Bus. Adminstrn. Nat. Adv. Coun., 1993—, Burger King Corp. Diversity Action Coun., 1996—, Md. Econ. Devel. Commn., 1996—; prin. coun. for Excellence in Govt., 1989—; mayor D.C. Internat. Ins. Adv. Commn., 1994-95; chair D.C. Mayor's bus. adv. coun., 1994—; vice chmn. Dem. Bus. Coun. DNC, 1994—; co-chair UNCF Sportsfest Fundraiser, 1994; mem. Gov. Md. Transition Team, 1995, Dem. Nat. Com., 1996, Platform Drafting Com., 1996; hon. vice chmn. Clinton-Gore Campaign, 1996; gen. counsel's Honors Program Office of Sec. Capt. USAF, 1973-74. Recipient SES Effective Mgr. award HUD, 1980, Nat. Assn. for Equal Achievement Opportunity in Higher Edn. award, 1987. Mem. ABA (vice-chmn. subcom. pub. contract law sect. 1988-93), Fed. Bar Assn., Nat. Bar Assn., D.C. C. of C. (gen. counsel 1979), State Va. Bar Assn., Washington Bar Assn., Bar Assn. D.C., Nat. Contract Mgmt. Assn. Mem. editorial adv. bd. Washington Bus. Jour., 1985-87. Home: 7004 Natelli Woods Ln Bethesda MD 20817-3924 Office: Shaw Pittman Potts & Trowbridge 2300 N St NW Washington DC 20037-1122

LATHAM, WILLIAM PETERS, composer, former educator; b. Shreveport, La., Jan. 4, 1917; s. Lawrence L. and Eugenia (Peters) L.; m. Joan Seyler, Apr. 18, 1946; children: Leslie Virginia, William Peters, Carol Jean. Student, Asbury Coll., Wilmore, Ky., 1933-35, Cin. Conservatory Music, 1936-38; BSc in Music Edn, U. Cin., 1938; BMus, Coll. Music Cin., 1940, MusM, 1941; PhD, Eastman Sch. Music, 1951; pupil composition with, Eugene Goossens, Howard Hanson, Herbert Elwell. Mem. faculty N. Tex. State Tchrs. Coll., 1938-39, Eastern Ill. State Tchrs. Coll., 1946; mem. faculty State Coll. Iowa, 1946-65, prof. music, 1959-65; prof. composition Sch. Music, U. N. Tex., Denton, 1965-84; dir. grad. studies Sch. Music, U. N. Tex., 1969-84, disting. prof., 1978-84, prof. emeritus, 1984—. Composer numerous works, 1938—, including works for orch., band, chorus, chamber groups, soloists, one opera and one ballet; compositions since 1980 include (chorus) Gaudeamus Academe, 1981, Bitter Land, 1985, My Heart Sings, 1988, Missa Novella, 1989, Only in Texas!, 1994; (chamber music) Ion, The Rhapsode for clarinet and piano, 1985, Metaphors, three songs for soprano, 1988, A Green Voice, cantata for soprano and tenor, 1989, (three songs for high voice) Requiem for My Love, 1994, (orch.) The Sacred Flame, 1990, Cantata for Baritone and Orch., 1990, Excelsior K-2 for Orch., 1994, (band) Suite Summertime, three movements for band, 1995. Served to 2d lt. AUS, 1942-46. Scholar in composition Cin. Coll. Music, 1939-41; recipient numerous awards and commns. Mem. ASCAP (ann. awards 1962—), Coll. Mus. Soc., Phi Mu Alpha, Pi Kappa Lambda. Home: PO Box 50373 Denton TX 76206-0373

LATHI, BHAGAWANDAS PANNALAL, electrical engineering educator; b. Bhokar, Maharashtr, India, Dec. 3, 1933; came to U.S., 1956; s. Pannalal Rupchand and Tapi Pannalal (Indani) L.; m. Rajani Damodardas Mundada, July 27, 1962; children: Anjali, Shishir. BEEE, Poona U., 1955; MSEE, U. Ill., 1957; PhD in Elec. Engring., Stanford U., 1961. Research asst. U. Ill., Urbana, 1956-57, Stanford (Calif.) U., 1957-60; research engr. Gen. Electric Co., Syracuse, N.Y., 1960-61; cons. to semicondr. industry India, 1961-62; assoc. prof. elec. engring. Bradley U., Peoria, Ill., 1962-69, U.S. Naval Acad., Annapolis, Md., 1969-72; prof. elec. engring. Campinas (Brazil) State U., 1972-78, Calif. State U., Sacramento, 1979—; vis. prof. U. Iowa, Owa City, 1979. Author: Signals, Systems and Communication, 1965, Communication Systems, 1968 (transl. into Japanese 1977), Random Signals and Communication Theory, 1968, Teoria Signalow I Ukladow Telekomunikacyjnych, 1970, Sistemy Telekomunikacyjne, 1972, Signals, Systems and Controls, 1974, Sistemas de Comunicacion, 1974, 86, Sistemas de Comunicacao, 1978, Modern Digital and Analog Communication Systems, 1983, 89 (transl. into Japanese 1986, 90), Signals and Systems, 1987, Linear Systems and Signals, 1992, Signal Processing and Linear Systems, 1997; contbr. articles to profl. jours. Fellow IEEE. Office: Calif State U 6000 J St Sacramento CA 95819-2605

LATHLAEN, ROBERT FRANK, retired construction company executive; b. Phila., May 25, 1925; s. Clarence Delcamp and Anna Marie (Schwab) L.; m. Nancy Nichols, May 1948 (div. July 1983); children: Margaret, Gail, Carol Sue; m. Margot von Harten, May 4, 1985. BSCE, Drexel U., 1945; SMCE, MIT, 1946. Registered profl. engr., N.Y. With W.J. Barney Corp., N.Y.C., 1946-94, pres., 1972-91, chmn. bd., 1991-94; vis. prof. Ea. Carolina U., 1993; adj. assoc. prof. NYU, 1984-91. Trustee St. Vincent's Hosp. and Med. Ctr., N.Y.C., 1986-90. Mem. ASCE (life), Assoc. Gen. Contractors (bd. dirs., chmn. various coms. 1976—, chmn. bldg. divsn. 1991), Gen. Bldg. Contractors N.Y. State (pres. 1975-76), N.Y. Bldg. Congress (bd. dirs. 1975-80), Am. Arbitration Asssn. (dir. 1986-94, exec. com. 1987-93, chmn. nat. constrn. industry arbitration com. 1989-90). Mem. United Ch. of Christ. Avocations: writing fiction; bicycle riding; swimming; bird watching.

LATHROP, ANN, librarian, educator; b. L.A., Nov. 30, 1935; d. Paul Ray and Margaret (Redfield) W.; divorced; children: Richard Harold, John Randolph, Rodney Grant. BA in History summa cum laude, Ea. N.Mex. U., 1957; MLS, Rutgers U., 1964; PhD, U. Oreg., 1988. Cert. elem. tchr., Calif.; cert. libr., Calif; adminstrv. credential, Calif. Elem. sch. tchr. Chalfont (Pa.) Boro Sch., 1960-61, Livingston Elem. Sch., New Brunswick, N.J., 1961-63, Rosedale Elem. Sch., Chico, Calif., 1964-65; libr. Chico (Calif.) H.S., 1965-72, Princeton (Calif.) H.S., 1972-73, Santa Maria (Calif.) H.S., 1973-77; libr. coord. San Mateo County Office Edn., Redwood City, Calif., 1977-89; assoc. prof. Calif. State U., Long Beach, 1989-92, prof., 1993—; dir. Calif. Software Clearinghouse, Calif. State U., Long Beach. Author: Online Information Retrieval as a Research Tool in Secondary School Libraries, 1988; co-author: Courseware in the Classroom, 1983; editor: Online and CD-ROM Databases in School Libraries, 1989, The 1988-89 Educational Software Preview Guide, 1988, Technology in the Curriculum Resource Guides, 1988; editor, founder: (jours.) The Digest of Software Reviews: Education, 1983-86, Software Reviews on File, 1985-86; editor: (database) California Online Resources in Education, 1989-94, Technology in the Curriculum Online, 1995—; contbr. chpts. to books, articles to profl. jours. Mem. ALA, NEA, Am. Assn. Sch. Librs., Assn. State Tech. Using Tchr. Educators, Calif. Faculty Assn., Calif. Sch. Libr. Assn., Computer Using Educators, Internat. Soc. for Tech. in Edn. Avocations: traveling, camping. Office: Calif State U 1250 N Bellflower Blvd Long Beach CA 90840-0006

LATHROP, GERTRUDE ADAMS, chemist, consultant; b. Norwich, Conn., Apr. 28, 1921; d. Williams Barrows and Lena (Adams) L. B.S., U. Conn., 1944; M.A., Tex. Woman's U., 1953, Ph.D., 1955. Devel. chemist on textiles/Alexander Smith & Sons Carpet Co. Yonkers, N.Y., 1944-52; research assoc. textiles Tex. Woman's U., 1952-56; chief chemist Glasgo Finishing Plant div. United Mchts. & Mfrs., Inc., Conn., 1956-57; chief chemist Old Fort Finishing Plant div. United Mchts. & Mfrs., Inc., N.C., 1957-63; research chemist United Mchts. Research Ctr., Langley, S.C., 1963-64; lab. mgr. automotive div. Collins & Aikman Corp., Albemarle, N.C., 1964-78; chief chemist, lab. mgr. Old Fort Finishing Plant div. United Mchts., 1979-82. Treas. 1st Congl. Ch., Asheville, N.C., 1985-87, bd. deacons, 1990-93; tax-aide counselor to elderly IRS, 1984—, Am. Assn. Ret. Person, Widowed Person Svcs., Asheville-Buncombe County, Inc., 1990-91, pres. Widowed Persons Svcs., 1992—; active RSVP Land of Sky, 1989-92; pub. Rels. com. Swannanoa Valley, N.C., Am. Assn. Ret. Persons, 1984-92, v.p., 1992, treas., 1993-94. Recipient Nat. Cmty. Svc. award Am. Assn. Ret. Persons, 1989, 96, Widowed Person's Outstanding Individual Achievement award, 1994, Disting. Alumni award U. Conn. Sch. Family Studies, 1980-81, Woman of Yr. award, 1979, Bus. and Profl. Women's Club, Albemarle, Woman of Yr. award Bus. and Profl. Women's Club Asheville, 1980, Paul M. Limbert award Buncombe County Coun. on Aging, Inc., 1996, Golden Clover award New London County 4-H Found., Inc., 1996. Mem. ASTM (chmn. transp. fabrics on flammability com. 1973-75), Am. Chem. Soc. (emeritus), Am. Assn. Textile Chemists and Colorists (emeritus sec., rsch. chmn., treas., vice chmn. 1962-64, chmn. edn. com. Piedmont sect. 1977-78), Bus. and Profl. Women's Club (chpt. pres. 1974-76), Iota Sigma Pi (emeritus mem.-at-large). Home and Office: PO Box 1166 Black Mountain NC 28711-1166

LATHROP, IRVIN TUNIS, retired academic dean, educator; b. Platteville, Wis., Sept. 23, 1927; s. Irvin J. and Marian (Johnson) L.; m. Eleanor M. Kolar, Aug. 18, 1951; 1 son, James I. B.S., Stout State Coll., 1950; M.S., Iowa State U., 1954, Ph.D., 1958. Tchr. Ottumwa (Iowa) High Sch., 1950-55; mem. faculty Iowa State U., 1957-58, Western Mich. U., 1958-59; mem. faculty Calif. State Coll., 1959-88, prof. indsl. arts, 1966-88, chmn. dept. indsl. edn., 1969-88, assoc. dean extended edn., 1978-88, prof. emeritus, 1988—; cons. Naval Ordnance Lab., Corona, Calif., 1961-63. Author: (with Marshall La Cour) Photo Technology, 1966, rev. edit., 1977, Photography, 1979, rev. edit., 1992, The Basic Book of Photography, 1979, Laboratory Manual for Photo Technology, 1973, (with John Lindbeck) General Industry, 1969, rev. edit., 1977, 86, (with Robert Kunst) Photo-Offset, 1979; Editorial cons.: (with Robert Kunst) Am. Tech. Soc; Contbr. (with Robert Kunst) articles to profl. jours. Mem. adv. com. El Camino and Orange Coast Coll.; mem. Orange County Grand Jury, 1989-90, Orange County Juvenile Justice Commn., 1991—. Mem. Nat. Soc. for Study Edn., Am. Council Indsl. Arts Tchr. Edn., Am. Vocat. Assn., Nat. Assn. Indsl. and Tech. Tchrs., Internat. Tech. Assn., Am. Ednl. Research Assn., Epsilon Pi Tau, Psi Chi, Phi Delta Kappa, Phi Kappa Phi. Home: PO Box 3430 Laguna Hills CA 92654-3430 Office: 1250 N Bellflower Blvd Long Beach CA 90840-0006

LATHROP, KAYE DON, nuclear scientist, educator; b. Bryan, Ohio, Oct. 8, 1932; s. Arthur Quay and Helen Venita (Hoos) L.; m. Judith Marie Green, June 11, 1957; children: Braxton Landess, Scottfield Michael. BS, U.S. Mil. Acad., 1955; MS, Calif. Inst. Tech., 1959, PhD, 1962. Staff mem. Los Alamos Sci. Lab., 1962-67; group leader methods devel. Gen. Atomic Co., San Diego, 1967-68; with Los Alamos Sci. Lab., 1968-84, assoc. div. leader reactor safeguards and reactor safety and tech. div., 1975-77, alt. div. leader energy div., 1977-78, div. leader computer sci. and svcs. div., 1978-79, assoc. dir. for engring. scis., 1979-84; assoc. lab dir., prof. applied rsch. Stanford Linear Accelerator Ctr. Stanford U., 1984-94, prof. emeritus, 1994—; vis. prof. U. N.Mex., 1964-65, adj. prof., 1966-67; guest lectr. IAEA, 1969; mem. adv. com. reactor physics ERDA, 1973-77; mem. reactor physics vis. com. Argonne Nat. Lab., 1978-83; mem. mgmt. adv. com. y-12 divsn. Union Carbide Corp., 1979-82; mem. engring. nat. adv. com. U. Mich., 1983-92; mem. steering com. Joint MIT-Idaho Nat. Engring. Lab. Rsch. Program, 1985-89; mem. external adv. com. Nuclear Tech. and Engring. divsn. Los Alamos Sci. Lab., 1988-91, 92-93; mem. com. on material control and acctg. for spl. nuclear materials NRC, 1988-89; mem. energy rsch. adv. bd. panel on new prodn. reactor tech. assessment Dept. of Energy, 1988; mem. electric power/energy sys. engring. com. NAE, 1992-94, chair, 1994, mem. com. on membership, 1994—, mem. presdl. nominating com., 1996-97, mem. membership policy com., 1997—; chair divsn. rev. com. tech. and safety assessment divsn. Los Alamos Nat. Lab., 1994—; mem. U. Calif. Pres.'s Coun. on Nat. Labs., 1995—, mem. sci. and tech. panel, 1993—, coun., 1995—, mem. nat. sec. panel, 1996—. Author reports, papers, chpts. to books; mem. editorial adv. bd. Progress in Nuclear Energy, 1983-85. Served to 1st lt. C.E. U.S. Army, 1955-58. Spl. fellow AEC, 1958-61; R.C. Baker Found. fellow, 1961-62; recipient E.O. Lawrence Meml. award ERDA, 1976; Disting. Svc. award Los Alamos Nat. Lab., 1984. Fellow Am. Nuclear Soc. (chmn. math. and computation div. 1970-71, nat. dir. 1973-76, 79-82, treas. 1977-79, Outstanding Performance award 1980); mem. Am. Phys. Soc., Nat. Acad. Engring. Republican. Episcopalian. Home: 190 Cedar Ln E Ridgway CO 81432-9452

LATHROP, MITCHELL LEE, lawyer; b. L.A., Dec. 15, 1937; s. Alfred Lee and Barbara (Mitchell) L.; m. Denice Annette Davis; children: Christin Lorraine Newlon, Alexander Mitchell, Timothy Trewin Mitchell. B.Sc., U.S. Naval Acad., 1959; J.D., U. So. Calif., 1966. Bar: D.C. 1966, Calif. 1966, U.S. Supreme Ct. 1969, N.Y. 1981; registered environ. assessor, Calif. Dep. counsel Los Angeles County, Calif., 1966-68; with firm Brill, Hunt, DeBuys and Burby, L.A., 1968-71; ptnr. Macdonald, Halsted & Laybourne, L.A. and San Diego, 1971-80; sr. ptnr. Rogers & Wells, N.Y.C., San Diego, 1980-86; sr. ptnr. Adams, Duque & Hazeltine, L.A., San Francisco, N.Y.C., San Diego, 1986-94, exec. com., 1986-94, firm chmn., 1992-94; sr. ptnr. Luce, Forward, Hamilton & Scripps, San Diego, N.Y.C., San Francisco, L.A., Chgo., 1994—; presiding referee Calif. Bar Ct., 1984-86, mem. exec. com., 1981-88; lectr. law Calif. Judges Assn., Practicing Law Inst. N.Y., Continuing Edn. of Bar, State Bar Calif., ABA, others. Author: State Hazardous Waste Regulation, 1991, Environmental Insurance Coverage, 1991, Insurance Coverage for Environmental Claims, 1992. Western Regional chmn. Met. Opera Nat. Coun., 1971-81, v.p., mem. exec. com., 1971—, now chmn.; trustee Honnold Libr. at Claremont Colls., 1972-80; bd. dirs. Music Ctr. Opera Assn., L.A., sec., 1974-80; bd. dirs. San Diego Opera Assn., 1980—, v.p., 1985-89, pres.-elect, 1993, pres., 1994-96; bd. dirs. Met. Opera Assn., N.Y.C.; mem. nat. steering coun. Nat. Actors Theatre, N.Y. Mem. ABA, N.Y. Bar Assn., Fed. Bar Assn., Fed. Bar Council, Calif. Bar Assn., D.C. Bar Assn., San Diego County Bar Assn. (chmn. ethics com. 1980-82, bd. dirs. 1982-85, v.p. 1985), Assn. Bus. Trial Lawyers, Assn. So. Calif. Def. Counsel, Los Angeles Opera Assos. (pres. 1970-72), Soc. Colonial Wars in Calif. (gov. 1970-72), Order St. Lazarus of Jerusalem, Friends of Claremont Coll. (dir. 1975-81, pres. 1978-79), Am. Bd. Trial Advocates, Judge Advocates Assn. (dir. Los Angeles chpt. 1974-80, pres. So. Calif. chpt. 1977-78), Internat. Assn. Def. Counsel, Brit. United Services Club (dir. Los Angeles 1973-75), Mensa Internat., Calif. Soc., S.R. (pres. 1977-79), Calif. Club (Los Angeles), Valley Hunt Club (Pasadena, Calif.), Met. Club (N.Y.C.), The Naval Club (London), Phi Delta Phi. Republican. Home: 455 Silvergate Ave San Diego CA 92106-3327 Office: Luce Forward Hamilton and Scripps 600 W Broadway Fl 26 San Diego CA 92101-3311 also: Citicorp Ctr 153 E 53rd St Frnt 26 New York NY 10022-4611

LATHROPE, DANIEL JOHN, law educator. BSBA, U. Denver, 1973; JD, Northwestern U., 1977; LLM, NYU, 1979. Bar: Ariz. 1977, Calif. 1978. Assoc. Evans, Kitchel & Jenckes, Phoenix, 1977-78; instr. law NYU, 1979-80; assoc. prof. U. Calif. Hastings Coll. Law, San Francisco, 1980-86, prof., 1986—; assoc. acad. dean U. Calif. Hastings Coll. Law, San Francisco, 1986-87, acting dean, 1987-88, acad. dean, 1988-90; prof., assoc. dean, dir. grad. tax program U. Fla. Coll. Law, Gainesville, 1995-96. Co-author: (with Lind, Schwarz and Rosenberg) Fundamentals of Corporate Taxation, 4th edit., 1997, (with Lind, Schwarz and Rosenberg) Fundamentals of Partnership Taxation, 4th edit., 1994, (with Schwarz) Black Letter on Federal Taxation of Corporations and Partnerships, 2d edit., 1994; author: The Alternative Minimum Tax-Compliance and Planning with Analysis, 1994. Mem. Order of Coif, Beta Gamma Sigma. Office: U Calif Hastings Coll of Law San Francisco CA 94102

LATIES, VICTOR GREGORY, psychology educator; b. Racine, Wis., Feb. 2, 1926; s. Simon Gregory and Rima (Kapnik) L.; m. Martha Ann Fisher, July 29, 1956; children: Nancy, Andrew, Claire. A.B., Tufts U., 1949; Ph.D., U. Rochester, N.Y., 1954. Ford Found. teaching intern Brown U., 1954-55; instr., asst. prof. dept. pharmacology Johns Hopkins U. Sch. Medicine, 1955-65; asso. prof. U. Rochester Sch. Medicine and Dentistry, 1965-71, prof. dept. biophysics, psychology, pharmacology, 1971-93, dir. toxicology tng. program, 1978-91, 95-96, dir. environ. studies program, prof. dept. environ. medicine, 1992—; mem. preclinical psychopharmacology research rev. com. NIMH, 1967-71; mem. bd. on toxicology and environ. health hazards Nat. Acad. Sci.-NRC, 1977-80, mem. toxicology info. program com., 1981-85; mem. sci. rev. com. for health research EPA, 1981-89. Editor: Jour. Exptl. Analysis of Behavior, 1972-76, exec. editor, 1966-72, 76—; editor: (with B. Weiss) Behavioral Toxicology, 1975, Behavioral Pharmacology, 1976; mem. editorial bd.: Jour. Pharmacology and Exptl. Therapeutics, 1965-71, Psychopharmacology, 1968-78, 81-89, The Behavior Analyst, 1980-82, Experimental and Clinical Psychopharmacology, 1993—; contbr. articles to profl. jours. Served with USN, 1944-46. Fellow Am. Psychol. Assn. (pres. div. psychopharmacology 1968-69, div. exptl. analysis of behavior 1979-82, bd. sci. affairs 1983-85), Behavioral Pharmacology Soc. (pres. 1966-68), Am. Soc. Pharmacology and Exptl. Therapeutics, Assn. for Behavior Analysis, Soc. Toxicology, Am. Psychol. Soc., Soc. for Exptl. Analysis of Behavior (sec.-treas. 1966—). Home: 55 Dale Rd E Rochester NY 14625-2137 Office: U Rochester Medical Ctr Dept Environ Medicine Box EHSC Rochester NY 14642

LATIMER, ALLIE B., retired lawyer; b. Coraopolis, Pa.; d. Lawnye S. and Bennie Latimer. BS, Hampton Inst., 1947; JD, Howard U., 1953, MDiv, 1986, DMin, 1988; LLM, Cath. U., 1958; postgrad., Am. U., 1960-61. Bar: N.C. bar 1955, D.C. bar 1960. Vol. in projects Am. Friends Service Com., N.J. and, Europe, 1948-49; correctional officer Fed. Reformatory for Women, Alderson, W.Va., 1949-51; personnel clk. NIH, Bethesda, 1953-55; realty officer Mitchell AFB, N.Y., 1955-56; with Office Gen. Counsel, GSA, Washington, 1957-76; chief counsel Office Gen. Counsel, GSA, after 1966, asst. gen. counsel, 1971-76, gen. counsel, 1977-87; asst. gen. counsel NASA, 1976-77; spl. counsel Gen. Svcs. Adminstrn., Washington, 1987-96; past chmn. central office com. Fed. Women's Program, GSA; mem. membership and budget com. Health and Welfare Council, 1967-72. Bd. dirs. D.C. Mental Health Assn., pres., 1977-79; bd. dirs. Friendship House, Washington; elder Presbyn. Ch.; pres. Interacial Council, 1964-75; chmn. Presbyn. Econ. Devel. Corp., 1975-81; mem. governing bd. Nat. Council Chs. of Christ in U.S.A. Recipient GSA Sustained Superior Service award, 1959, Meritorious Service award, 1964, Commendable Service award, 1964, Pub. Service award, 1971, Outstanding Performance award, 1971, Presdl. Rank award, 1983, Disting. Service award, 1984. Mem. ABA, Nat. Bar Assn. (sec. 1966-74), Fed. Bar Assn., Washington Bar Assn., N.C. Bar Assn., Nat. Bar Found. (dir. 1970-71, pres. 1974-75), Hampton Alumni Assn. (pres. Washington chpt. 1970-71), Howard Law Alumni Assn. (v.p. 1962-63) alumni assns), Links (pres. Washington chpt. 1971-74, nat. v.p. 1976-80), Federally Employed Women (founder, 1st pres.). Home: 1721 S St NW Washington DC 20009-6117

LATIMER, BEN WILLIAM, healthcare executive; b. Lawrenceville, Ga., Aug. 3, 1940; married. BA, Ga. Tech, 1962, MA, 1965. Dir. mgmt. sys. Meth. Hosp., Memphis, 1965-69; various positions to CEO Carolinas Hosp., Charlotte, N.C., 1969-81; pres., CEO SunHealth Corp. (merger Am. Hosp. Sys. and Premier), Charlotte, 1982-96; vice chmn. Premier, Inc., Charlotte, 1996—. Contbr. articles to profl. jours. Mem. AHA (del. 1980-87), HIMSS (pres. 1973). Office: Premier Inc Box 668800 Charlotte NC 28266-8800

LATIMER, HELEN, information resource manager, writer, researcher; b. Elizabeth, N.J.; d. Raymond O. and Minna A. Mercner; divorced; children: Alexander, Victoria. AB, Duke U.; MS in Journalism, Columbia U.; cert. in bus. adminstrn., Harvard-Radcliffe; MBA in Mktg., Am. U.; attended, U. Calif., Berkeley, Rutgers U.; MBA upgrade, Syracuse U., 1995. Instr. mktg. Am. U., Washington; mgr. info. resources Burdeshaw Assocs., Ltd., Bethesda, Md., 1985-94, assoc., 1994—; commr. Mayor's Commn. on Violence Against Women, Washington, 1996—; initiated publ. specialists program George Washington U., Washington; officer alumni bds. Harvard-Radcliffe Program in Adminstrn., Am. U.; comm., info. resource mgmt. cons., tech. editor MIT Servomechanisms Lab.; AA to editor Reinhold Pub. (former subs. McGraw-Hill); facilitator, subgroup on mktg. The White House Conf. on Libr. and Info. Svcs., 1991. Contbr. articles to newspapers and mags. Past leader Troop 1907, Girl Scouts Am.; mem. Troop 100 com. Boy Scouts Am. Named to D.C. Commn. for Women, 1996. Mem. Spl. Librs. Assn., Harvard Bus. Sch. Club D.C. (initiated admission of women, v.p., bd. dirs.).

LATIMER, KENNETH ALAN, lawyer; b. Chgo., Oct. 26, 1943; s. Edward and Mary (Schiller) L.; m. Carole Ross, June 23, 1968; children: Cary, Darren, Wendy. BS, U. Wis., 1966; JD with honors, George Washington U., 1969. Bar: D.C. 1969, Ill. 1970. Atty. U.S. Office of Comptroller, Washington, 1969-70; assoc. Berger, Newmark & Fenchel, Chgo., 1970-74, ptnr., 1975-86; ptnr. Holleb & Coff, Chgo., 1986—; guest speaker Ill. Inst. for Continuing Legal Edn., Chgo., 1975-87. Pres. North Suburban Jewish Cmty. Ctr., Highland Park, Ill., 1985; bd. dirs. Jewish Cmty. Ctrs. Chgo., 1985-95. Mem. Ill. Bar Assn. (chmn. sect. coun. on comml. banking and bankruptcy 1990-91), ABA (com. on banking and comml. finance), Chgo. Bar Assn. (com. on fin. instns.), Comml. Fin. Assn. Ednl. Found. (governing bd.), Assn. Comml. Fin. Attys., Am Coll. Comml. Fin Attys., Standard Club. Avocations: jogging, travel, tennis. Office: Holleb & Coff 55 E Monroe St Ste 4100 Chicago IL 60603-5803

LATIMER, PAUL JERRY, non-destructive testing engineer; b. Springfield, Tenn., July 21, 1943; s. Paul Daniel and Juanita Inez (Richey) L.; m. Sylvia Susan Cole, June 6, 1966; children: Zachary Nathaniel, Matthew Jason. BS in Physics with honors, U. Tenn., 1966, MS in Physics, 1979, PhD in Physics, 1983. Devel. engr. Oak Ridge (Tenn.) Nat. Lab., 1980-81; faculty rsch. assoc. Ohio State U., Columbus, 1981; rsch. asst. U. Tenn., Knoxville, 1981-83; sr. rsch. engr. Babcock and Wilcox, Lynchburg, Va., 1983—. Contbr. articles to profl. jours.; patentee in field. Co-leader cub pack Lynchburg Area coun. Boy Scouts Am., 1983-84; vol. United Way, 1994; mem. Pacer Club for United Way Support, 1993-97. Mem. Am. Soc. Nondestructive Testing (cert. Level III untrasonic methods), Am. Welding Soc., Sigma Pi Sigma. Avocations: martial arts, hiking, lapidary, mineral collecting. Home: 303 Juniper Dr Lynchburg VA 24502-5661 Office: Babcock and Wilcox Lynchburg Rsch Ctr Lynchburg VA 24506 *Senior research engineer with twenty years of experience in the academic community, national labs, and industry. Present field of work involves the research and development of nondestructive techniques to inspection problems in industry. These ultrasonic applications include the use of both conventional ultrasonic methods and electromagnetic acoustic transducers (EMATs). Active in innovation, as inventor or coinventor with 10 patents in the field of nondestructive testing. Also, author/coauthor of numerous presentations and professional publications. Applications in areas of aerospace, manufacturing, and fossil utilities.*

LATIMER, ROY TRUETT, museum executive; b. Albany, Tex., Aug. 23, 1928; s. Charles Lee and Zora Neil (Brock) L.; m. Judith Gail Johnson, Nov. 26, 1955 (div. 1975); children: Jeff, Laura, Tiffany; m. Harriet Calvin, Nov. 20, 1976. BA, Hardin-Simmons U., 1951, LLD, 1996. Owner Gen. Ins. Agy., Abilene, Tex., 1951-55; alumni dir. Hardin-Simmons U., Abilene, 1955-62; dir. pub. relations Tex. Assn. of Realtors, Austin, 1962-65; exec. dir. Tex. Hist. Commn., Austin, 1965-81, Tex. Hist. Found., Austin, 1972-81; v.p. pub. relations and mktg. Spaw Glass, Inc., Houston, 1981-85; pres. Houston Mus. Natural Sci., Houston, 1986—; pres. Nat. Conf. State Hist. Preservation Officers, 1974-75; bd. advisors Nat. Trust for Hist. Preservation, Washington, 1981-88; bd. dirs. Houston Conv. and Tourist Bur. Mem. Tex. Ho. Reps., Austin, 1952-62; bd. devel. Hardin-Simmons U., 1974—; bd. dirs. Downtown Houston Assn., 1983—, past pres.; bd. dirs. Rice Design Alliance, Houston, 1983-87; chmn. S. Main Ctr. Assn., 1991-93. Mem. South Main Ctr. Assn. (bd. dirs. 1988—, past pres.), Internat. Space Theatre Consortium (treas. 1995-96). Presbyterian. Avocations: running, canoeing, backpacking, travel. Home: 2807A Midlane St Houston TX 77027-4909 Office: Houston Mus Natural Sci 1 Hermann Circle Dr Houston TX 77030-1749

LATINI, ANTHONY A., financial services company executive; b. Chester, Pa., June 8, 1942; s. Angelo and Mildred (Gardner) L.; m. M. Katherine Kraft; children: Anthony A., Diane Marie. B.S., St. Joseph U., 1964. Tax mgr. Price Waterhouse & Co., Phila., 1971; dir. taxes Colonial Penn Group, Phila., 1971-76, treas., 1976-79, sr. v.p., treas., 1979-86, exec. v.p. fin. ops., 1987; chief fin. officer Pa. Conv. Authority, 1988; v.p., asst. comptr. Prudential Ins. Co. Am., South Plainfield, N.J., 1988-91, v.p. investment ops., systems and reporting, 1991—. Bd. mgrs. Children's Hosp. of Phila., 1985—, mem., chmn. long. range planning com. Mem. Fin. Execs. Inst., Tax Execs. Inst., Soc. Ins. Accts., Nat. Assn. Corp. Treas., Internat. Assn. Fin. Planners, Am. Inst. C.P.A.s, Pa. Inst. C.P.A.s. Avocations: skiing; boating; tennis. Office: Three Gateway Ctr 12th Fl Prudential Ins Co Am 100 Mulberry St Newark NJ 07102-4004

LATNO, ARTHUR CLEMENT, JR., telephone company executive; b. Ross, Calif., May 14, 1929; s. Arthur Clement and Marie (Carlin) L.; m. Dorothy Sheldon Guess, June 27, 1953; children—Jeannine Marie, Michele Claire, Arthur Clement III, Mary Suzanne, Patrice Anne. B.S., Santa Clara U., 1951. With Pacific Tel. & Tel. Co., San Francisco, 1952-92; v.p. Pacific Tel. & Tel. Co., 1972-78, exec. v.p., 1978-92; former amb. accorded by Ronald Reagan, 1988; chmn. U.S. Delegation to World Telecom. Conf., Australia; bd. dirs. WestAm. Bank, WestAm. Bancorp. Bd. dirs. Marin Gen. Hosp.; bd. dirs., former chmn. Calif. Inst. Fed. Policy Rsch.; chmn. adv. bd. Berkeley program in bus. and social policy U. Calif.; trustee St. Mary's Coll. Calif. Mem. Meadow Club, Knights of Malta, Alpha Sigma Nu. Home: 67 Convent Ct San Rafael CA 94901-1333

LATORRE, L. DONALD, chemical company executive; b. Amsterdam, N.Y., Sept. 19, 1937; s. Matthew Albert and Nancy (Donato) LaT.; m. Gloria Jean Lojpersberger, Nov. 5, 1940; children: L. Donald Jr., David S., Craig M., Amy E. BS, Lowell Tech. Inst., 1960; MS, Union Coll., 1967. Tech. sales rep. Ritter Chem. Corp., Amsterdam, 1960-66; market research, planning mgr. Diamond Shamrock, Cleve., 1967-69; market mgr. Diamond Shamrock Splty. Chems. Div., Cleve., 1969-73; comml. devel. mgr. BASF Wyandotte (Mich.) Corp., 1973-74; mktg. mgr. BASF Wyandotte Corp. Urethanes Div., 1974-79; div. mgr. BASF Wyandotte Corp. Styropor Div., Parsippany, N.J., 1980-82; exec. v.p., bd. dirs. Velcro, U.S.A., Manchester, N.H., 1982-84; sr. v.p., gen. mgr. splty. chems. div. Engelhard Corp., Iselin, N.J., 1984-88, v.p., pres. pigments and additives div., 1988-90; sr. v.p., COO Engelhard Corp., Menlo Park, N.J., 1990-95, pres., COO, 1995—, also bd. dirs.; bd. dirs. N.E. Chemcat Corp. Officer Jr. C. of C., Amsterdam, 1962; bd. dirs. Manchester C. of C., 1982-84; sd. dirs. engring. adv. bd. Mercer U., Macon, Ga., 1987—, chmn., 1995—;strustee Ind. Coll. Fund N.J., 1991—, Bloomfield Coll., 1996—. Mem. Nat. Assn. Corp. Dirs., Mfrs.' Alliance for Productivity and Innovation. Office: Engelhard Corp 101 Wood Ave Iselin NJ 08830-2703

LATORRE, ROBERT GEORGE, naval architecture and engineering educator; b. Toledo, Jan. 9, 1949; s. Robert James and Madge Violette (Roy) L. BS in Naval Architecture and Marine Engring. with honors, U. Mich., 1971, MS in Engring., 1972; MSE in Naval Architecture, U. Tokyo, 1975, PhD. in Naval Architecture, 1978. Asst. prof. U. Mich., Ann Arbor, 1979-83; assoc. prof. U. New Orleans, 1984-87, prof. naval architecture and marine engring., 1987—, prof., 1989-95, chmn. dept., 1989-95; assoc. prof. mech. engring., U. Tokyo, 1986-87; rsch. scientist, David Taylor Naval R & D Lab., Bethesda, Md., 1980, 81, Bassin d'Essais des Carenes, Paris, 1983; cons. in field. Contbr. to profl. publs. Mem. Soc. Naval Architects, Royal Inst. Naval Archtects Gt. Britain, ASME, Soc. NAval Architects Japan, Am. Soc. engring. Edn. (program chmn. ocean engring. divsn. 1989-90, Japan Club New Orleans. Roman Catholic. Home: 300 Lake Marina Dr New Orleans LA 70124-1676 Office: U New Orleans 911 Engring Bldg New Orleans LA 70148

LA TOURETTE, JOHN ERNEST, academic administrator; b. Perth Amboy, N.J., Nov. 5, 1932; s. John Crater and Charlotte Ruth (Jones) LaT.; m. Lillie M. Drum, Aug. 10, 1957; children—Marc Andrew, Yanique Renee. B.A., Rutgers U., 1954, M.A., 1955, Ph.D., 1962. From asst. prof. to prof. Rutgers U., New Brunswick, N.J., 1960-61, SUNY, Binghamton, 1961-76; chair dept. econs. SUNY, 1967-75, provost grad. studies, 1975-76; dean grad. sch., vice provost grad. studies Bowling Green (Ohio) State U., 1976-79; v.p., provost No. Ill. U., DeKalb, 1979-86; acting pres. No. Ill. U., 1984-85, pres., 1986—; vis. prof. Karlsruhe (W. Ger.) U., 1974; research prof. Brookings Inst., 1966-67; vis. scholar Ariz. State U., 1969, 70; lectr. Econs. Inst., U. Colo., 1966; dir. NSF Departmental Sci. Devel. Grant, 1970-75, First Am. Bank, DeKalb, 1985—, Higher Edn. Stategic Planning Inst., Washington, 1984-88; cons. North Cen. Assn., 1983—. Contbr. articles to profl. jours. Served to capt. USAF, 1955-58. Ford Found. grantee, 1963; SUNY Found. grantee, 1963, 65, 70. Mem. Am. Econ. Assn., Can. Econ. Assn. (fin. acctg. adv. standards coun. 1991-94). Office: No Ill U Office of Pres De Kalb IL 60115

LATOURETTE, STEVEN C., congressman; b. Cleve., July 22, 1954; m. Susan LaTourette; 4 children. BA in Hist., U. Mich., 1976; JD, Cleve. State U., 1979. Asst. pub. defender Lake County Pub. Defender's Office, 1980-83; assoc. Cannon, Stern, Aveni & Krivok, Painesville, 1983-86; with Baker, Hackenberg & Collins, Painesville, 1986-88; prosecuting atty. Lake County Prosecutor Office, 1988-93; mem. U.S. Ho. of Reps., Washington, 1994—; mem. Com. on Transp. & Infrastructure, subcom. pub. bldgs. & econ. devel., surface transp., & water resources and environ. U.S. Ho. of Reps., also vice-chmn. investigations and oversight subcom., mem. com. Reform and Oversight, mem. com. banking comm., mem. U.S. Holocaust Meml. Coun., 1995—. Office: US House Reps 1239 Longworth Bldg Washington DC 20515-3519

LATOURRETTE, JAMES THOMAS, retired electrical engineering and computer science educator; b. Miami, Ariz., Dec. 26, 1931; s. Emery Everest and Carrie D. (Hoffman) LaT.; m. Muriel Ashe, Aug. 28, 1955; children: Mary Beth, John Emery, James Thomas, Joanne. B.S., Calif. Inst. Tech., 1953; M.A. (Gen. Communication Co. fellow), Harvard U., 1954, Ph.D. (NSF fellow), 1958. Research assoc., lectr. physics Harvard U., 1957-59; physicist Gen. Electric Research Lab., Schenectady, 1960-62; sr. supervisory scientist TRG, Inc., Melville, N.Y., 1962-66; sect. head TRG div. Control Data Corp., Melville, 1966-67; prof. elec. engring. and computer sci. Poly. U. (formerly Poly. Inst. Bklyn. and Poly. Inst. N.Y.), Farmingdale, N.Y., 1967-93, prof. emeritus, 1993; assoc. dir. Weber Rsch. Inst., Poly. U., 1987-90. Contbr. articles to profl. jours. NSF postdoctoral fellow Physikalisches Institut der U. Bonn, Germany, 1959-60. Mem. AAAS, IEEE, IEEE Computer Soc., N.Y. Acad. Sci., Assn. for Computer Machinery, Sigma Xi, Tau Beta Pi. Home: 2 Candlewood Ct Huntington NY 11743-1827 Office: Poly Univ Rt 110 Farmingdale NY 11735

LATSCHAR, JOHN A., historic site administrator. Supt. Gettysburg (Pa.) Nat. Mil. Park. Office: Gettysburg Nat Mil Park 97 Taneytown Rd Gettysburg PA 17325-2804*

LATT, PAMELA YVONNE, school system administrator; b. Mineola, N.Y., Mar. 24, 1952; d. Michael and Irene (Pearlman) Vuicich; m. James Michael Latt, Aug. 31, 1974; 1 child, Jeremy Jacob. BA in Secondary Edn./English, SUNY, Fredonia, 1973, MA in English, 1974. Lectr. Adam Mickiewicz U., Poznan, Poland, 1972-74; English/reading specialist Halifax County (Va.) Pub. Schs., 1974-76; ESL tchr., grades K-6 Fairfax County (Va.) Pub. Schs., Baileys X-Roads, 1976-79; ESL tchr., grades 7-8 Fairfax County (Va.) Pub. Schs., Vienna, 1979-80; coord. of cen. registration Fairfax County (Va.) Pub. Schs., Falls Church, 1980-89, dir. of student svcs., 1989-92; subsch. prin./Lake Braddock Secondary Fairfax County (Va.) Pub. Schs., Burke, Va., 1992-93; prin. Centreville H.S., Clifton, Va., 1993—; spl. adjunct to U. Va., Falls Church, 1979-85; cons. State Dept., Arlington, Va., 1990—; mem. adv. bd. Am. Overseas Sch.; cons. Coll. Bd., Washington and N.Y., 1989—. Author/editor: School Health Care Emergencies, 1990, Handbook for School Health Risks, 1990; contbg. author/cons. Cross-Cultural Learning in K-12 Schools: Foreign Students as Resources, 1982. Cons., focus group Human Svcs./Fairfax County, 1988—. Adam Mickiewicz U. scholar, Poznan, 1970-72; named one of Outstanding Young Women of Am., 1979, Super Boss of Yr., Fairfax Assn. Ednl. Office Pers., 1989. Mem. ASCD, Nat. Assn. Sch. Prins. Secondary Schs., Nat. Assn. Fgn. Student Affairs (region 8 rep. 1987-89). Democrat. Roman Catholic. Avocations: sculpting, golf, reading and writing poetry. Office: Centreville High Sch 6001 Union Mill Rd Clifton VA 20124-1128

LATTA, GEORGE HAWORTH, III, neonatologist; b. Chattanooga, Sept. 4, 1960; s. George Haworth Jr. and Charlotte (Major) L. BS in Physics, Ga. Inst. Tech., 1982; MD in Medicine, East Tenn. State U., 1986. Cert. in pediats., neonatology. Intern, resident in pediats. Dartmouth (N.H.) U., 1986-88; resident in pediats. Stanford (Calif.) U., 1988-89; fellow in neonatology Vanderbilt U., Nashville, 1989-90, U. Tenn., Memphis, 1990-92; attending neonatologist Rose Med. Ctr., Denver, 1992-94, Forrest Gen. Hosp., Hattiesburg, Miss., 1994-95, Meth. Hosps., Memphis, 1995—. NIH pulmonary trainee grantee Vanderbilt U., 1989; March of Dimes scholar East Tenn. State U., 1984, Johnny J. Jones scholar, 1981. Fellow Am. Acad. Pediats.; mem. Memphis Med. Soc., Shelby County Med. Soc., Phi Eta Sigma. Roman Catholic. Avocations: snow skiing, camping, jazz music, aquariums, scuba diving. Home: 409 Greenfield Rd Memphis TN 38117 Office: Meth Hosps of Memphis 1265 Union Ave Memphis TN 38104-3415

LATTANZIO, STEPHEN PAUL, astronomy educator; b. Yonkers, N.Y., June 29, 1949; s. Anthony Raymond and Anella Lattanzio; m. Barbara Regina Knisely, Aug. 14, 1976; children: Gregory Paul, Timothy Paul. BA in Astronomy, U. Calif., Berkeley, 1971; MA in Astronomy, UCLA, 1973, postgrad., 1973-75. Planetarium lectr. Griffith Obs., Los Angeles, 1973-75; instr. astronomy El Camino Coll., Torrance, Calif., 1974-75; planetarium lectr. Valley Coll., Los Angeles, 1975; prof. astronomy Orange Coast Coll., Costa Mesa, Calif., 1975—, planetarium dir., 1975—; mem. adv. commn. Natural History Found. Orange County, Calif., 1988-91; scientific advisor instructional TV series Universe: The Infinite Frontier, 1992—. Co-author: Study Guide for Project: Universe, 1978, 2d rev. edition 1981; textbook reviewer, 1978—; co-screenwriter Project: Universe instructional TV series episode, 1979; contbr. articles to profl. jours. Mem. Astron. Soc. Pacific, The Planetary Soc., Sigma Xi (assoc.), Phi Beta Kappa. Avocation: astronautics. Office: Orange Coast Coll 2701 Fairview Rd Costa Mesa CA 92626-5563

LATTES, RAFFAELE, physician, educator; b. Torino, Italy, May 22, 1910; came to U.S., 1940, naturalized, 1947; s. Attilio Marco and Dolce (Noemi) L.; m. Eva H. Hahn, 1936; children—Conrad George (dec.), Robert George. M.D., U. Torino, 1933; D.M.S., Columbia, 1946. Diplomate: Am. Bd. Pathology. Tng. surgery, surg. pathology U. Torino Med. Sch., 1934-38; instr. pathology Woman's Med. Coll. Pa., Phila., 1941-43; asst. prof. pathology N.Y. Postgrad. Hosp. and Med. Sch., 1946-48; instr. surg. pathology Coll. Phys. and Surg., Columbia, 1943-46, asst. prof., 1948-49, asso. prof. surgery, surg. pathology, 1949-51, prof. surgery, surg. pathology, 1950-78, prof. emeritus, 1978—, spl. lectr. in surgery, 1978, dir. lab. surg. pathology, 1951-78. Fellow AMA, Coll. Am. Pathologists, N.Y. Acad. Medicine, Internat. Acad. Pathology; mem. AAAS, N.Y. Path. Soc., Am. Assn. Pathologists and Bacteriologists, Am. Assn. Cancer Rsch., Am. Soc. Clin. Pathologists, Arthur Purdy Stout Soc. Surg. Pathologists. Home: 597 Rutland Ave Teaneck NJ 07666-2947 Office: Coll Physicians and Surgeons 630 W 168th St New York NY 10032-3702

LATTIMER, GARY LEE, physician; b. Nanticoke, Pa., Dec. 4, 1939; s. Paul Floyd and Gene Elizabeth L.; m. Patricia Sara Weise, June 14, 1958; children: Toni Jo, Gregory Weise. M.D., Temple U., 1966; postgrad., Jefferson Med. Coll., 1970-72. Intern Allentown (Pa.) Hosp.; resident Presbyn.-Univ. Hosp., Phila., 1969-70; resident Jefferson Med. Coll. Hosp., Phila., 1970-71, chief med. resident, 1971-72; chief infectious diseases Allentown-Sacred Heart Hosp. Center, 1972-80; assoc. prof. medicine U. N.D., 1980-81, chief infectious diseases, 1980-81; chief infectious diseases New Britain (Conn.) Gen. Hosp., 1981—; assoc. prof. medicine U. Conn., 1981-83; dir. infectious diseases Williamsport Hosp., Divine Providence Hosp., 1983—. Author: Legionnaires' Disease, 1981; contbr. articles to profl. jours. Served with M.C. U.S. Army, 1967-69. Decorated Bronze Star; recipient Disting. Service award Pa. chpt. Am. Legion. Fellow ACP; mem. Am. Soc. Microbiology, AAAS, Nat. Found. Infectious Diseases, Am. Legion. Office: 904 Campbell St Williamsport PA 17701-3166

LATTIMORE, JOY POWELL, preschool administrator; b. Goldsboro, N.C., Jan. 18, 1954; d. Albert and Zudora (Baldwin) P.; m. Vergel L. Lattimore, Dec. 16, 1978; children: V. Alston, Adam V., Alia Joy. BS in Early Child Edn., Barber-Scotia Coll., 1976; MEd in Early and Mid. Child Edn., The Ohio State U., 1977. Dir. alumni affairs Barber-Scotia Coll.,

Concord, N.C., 1977-79; tchra. Concord Mid. Sch., 1979-80; asst. dir. admissions Kendall Coll., Evanston, Ill., 1980-83; dir. pre-K program Dunbar Ctr. United Way Agy., Syracuse, N.Y., 1987-89; tchr. Hughes Magnet Sch., Syracuse, 1989-90; dir. Busy Bee Day Care, Westerville, Ohio, 1991—. Mem. race adv. com. United Way, 1995-96; vol. benefit com. Columbus Works. Mem. Nat. Assn. Edn. of Young Children, AAUW, NAFE, Internat. Reading Assn., Phi Delta Kappa. Methodist. Avocations: reading, volleyball, tennis, science fiction, coin collecting. Home: 610 Olde N Church Dr Westerville OH 43081 Office: Busy Bee Day Care 610 Olde N Church Dr Westerville OH 43081

LATTIN, ALBERT FLOYD, banker; b. Everett, Wash., May 23, 1950; s. Albert S. and Erma Victoria (Hunt) L. Student, U. Nairobi, Kenya, 1970-71, Am. U. Cairo, Egypt, 1972; BA, Antioch U., 1973; MA, NYU, 1979; MBA, Columbia U., 1984. Asst. curator The Bklyn. Mus., 1973-76, assoc., 1976-79; sec. of the mus. Solomon R. Guggenheim Mus., N.Y.C., 1979-80, cons. in arts, 1980-83; banker Bankers Trust Co., N.Y.C., 1984-93; v.p. CS 1st Boston, N.Y.C., 1993-95, Credit Suisse First Boston Corp., N.Y.C., 1995—; bd. dirs., chief investment officer Praedrem Recovery Fund, N.Y.C., 1994—. Editor, researcher book and catalogue Africa in Antiquity: The Arts of Ancient Nubia and the Sudan, 1978; organizer exhibition/movie The Heritage of Islam, 1982. Dir., trustee Mus. Holography, N.Y.C., 1980-87; mem. bd. advisors Gallery Assn. N.Y. Stte, 1988—; treas. Theban Found., 1991—; mem. Bklyn. Hist. Soc., Brooklyn Heights Assn., 1986—. Mem. Am. Banking Assn., Urban Land Inst., Internat. Council of Mus., Am. Assn. Mus., Internat. Assn. Egyptologists, Roundout Valley Country Club, Columbia Club. Home: 242 Henry St Brooklyn NY 11201-4662 Office: Credit Suisse First Boston Corp 11 Madison Ave New York NY 10010-3629

LATTIS, RICHARD LYNN, zoo director; b. Louisville, May 31, 1945; s. Albert Francis and Jean Elizabeth (Baker) L.; m. Sharon Louise Elkins, June 22, 1968; children Michael David, Robert Brian, Theodore James. BS in Biol., U. Louisville, 1967, MS in Ecol., 1970. Asst. curator edn. Bronx (N.Y.) Zoo, 1974-75, curator edn., 1975-78; chmn. edn. The Wildlife Conservation Soc., 1978-80; dir. city zoos N.Y. Zoological Soc., 1980-93, v.p. and dir. conservation ctrs., 1993—; lectr., cons. zoos, aquariums, nature ctrs.; past cons. Time-Life Wild Wild World Animals film series; appeared Who's Who in the Zoo WNBC-TV, N.Y.C. Sgt. USAR, 1970-76. Mem. AAAS, Am. Assn. Zool. Parks and Aquariums (bd. dirs., bd. regents, govt. affairs. com.), Nat. Hist. Soc., Soc. Conservation Biol., Zoo Biol., Sigma Xi. Avocations: fishing, photography, golf, gardening, bird watching. Home: 1650 Maxwell Dr Yorktown Heights NY 10598-4802 Office: Wildlife Conservation Soc The Bronx Zoo Bronx NY 10460

LATTMAN, LAURENCE HAROLD, retired academic administrator; b. N.Y.C., Nov. 30, 1923; s. Jacob and Yetta (Schwartz) L.; m. Hanna Renate Cohn, Apr. 12, 1946; children—Martin Jacob, Barbara Diane. BSChemE, Coll. City N.Y., 1948; MS in Geology, U. Cin., 1951, PhD, 1953. Instr. U. Mich., 1952-53; asst. head photogeology sect. Gulf Oil Corp., Pitts., 1953-57; asst. prof. to prof. geomorphology Pa. State U., 1957-70; prof., head dept. geology U. Cin., 1970-75; dean Coll. of Mines U. Utah, 1975-83, dean Coll. Engring., 1978-83; pres. N.Mex. Tech., Socorro, 1983-93, pres. emeritus, 1993—; bd. dirs. Pub. Svc. Co. of N.Mex.; cons. U.S. Army Engrs., Vicksburg, Miss., 1965-69, also major oil cos. Author: (with R.G. Ray) Aerial Photographs in Field Geology, 1965, (with D. Zillman) Energy Law; Contbr. articles to profl. jours. Environ. improvement bd. NMex., 1996—. Served with AUS, 1943-46. Fenneman fellow U. Cin., 1953. Fellow Geol. Soc. Am.; mem. Am. Assn. Petroleum Geologists, Am. Soc. Photogrammetry (Ford Bartlett award 1968), Soc. Econ. Paleontologists and Mineralogists, AIME (Disting. mem. 1981, Mineral Industries Edn., award 1986—), Assn. Western Univs. (chmn. bd. dirs. 1986-87), Sigma Xi. Home: 11509 Penfield Ln NE Albuquerque NM 87111-6506

LATTO, LEWIS M., JR., broadcasting company executive; b. Duluth, Minn., Jan. 21, 1940; s. Lewis M. and Ethel S. L.; divorced; children: Aaron, Caroline. B.A., U. Minn., 1963. Owner, mgr. Sta. KXTP, Duluth, 1965-94, Sta. WAKX-FM, 1974-94; owner Sta. WEVE AM-FM, Eveleth, Minn., 1978—, Sta. KGPZ-FM, Grand Rapids, Minn., 1995—. Mem. Duluth City Council, 1969-75, pres., 1974. Mem. Nat. Radio Broadcasters Assn. (dir.), Minn. Broadcasters Assn. (pres. 1992-93). Republican. Methodist. Office: Northland Radio Stas 5732 Eagle View Dr Duluth MN 55803-9498

LATZ, G. IRVING, II, manufacturing company executive; b. Ft. Wayne, Ind., Feb. 12, 1920; s. G. Irving and Carrie (Stiefel) L.; m. Janet Horwitz Simon, Oct. 16, 1949; children: Sara Rose, G. Irving III. BS in Econs., U. Pa., 1941; MBA, U. Chgo., 1971. Trainee F.R. Lazarus Co., Columbus, Ohio, 1941; with Wolf & Dessauer Co., Ft. Wayne, 1946-66, treas., 1947-66, pres., 1957-66; dir. Model Cities, Columbus, 1967-68; cons. urban affairs Michael Reese Hosp. and Med. Ctr., Chgo., 1973-74; cons. econ. urban affairs, 1974-80; prin. Latz Assocs., Ft. Wayne, 1974-80; pres. Sci-Agra, Inc., Ft. Wayne, 1980—; exec. dir. Ft. Wayne Future, Inc., 1980-84; hon. bd. dirs. Ft. Wayne Nat. Bank. Gen. chmn. Ft. Wayne Fine Arts Found., 1958-67, pres., 1967-69; gen. chmn. Ft. Wayne United Fund; pres. Ind. Retail Coun., 1965-66; bd. dirs. Ft. Wayne Jewish Fedn., United Community Svcs. With AUS, 1941-46. Mem. Ft. Wayne C. of C., Ft. Wayne Country Club. Home: 6801 Covington Creek Trl Fort Wayne IN 46804-2871

LATZA, BEVERLY ANN, accountant; b. Pompton Plains, N.J., June 10, 1960; d. George and Helen Mae (Ryan) L. BA in Acctg., Bus. Adminstrn., Thiel Coll., 1982. Internal auditor Monroe Systems for Bus., Morris Plains, N.J., 1983-85; acct. Am. Airlines, Tulsa, 1985-86, Accountemps, Tulsa, 1986-87; credit investigator Denrich Leasing, Inc., Kansas City, Mo., 1987-89; with accounts receivable dept. Coca Cola Bottling Co. Am., Lenexa, Kans., 1989; tax examining asst. IRS, Kansas City, Mo., 1989—; with acctg. and accounts payable depts. Wolferman's Fine Breads, Lenexa, 1992-93. Vol., disaster action team mem. ARC, 1996—. Lutheran. Avocations: singing, counted cross-stitch. movies. Home: 13148 W 88th Ct Apt 141 Lenexa KS 66215-4923 Office: IRS 2306 E Bannister Rd Kansas City MO 64131-3011

LATZEL, LYNN MARINA, college administrator; b. Chgo., June 15, 1955; d. Frank William and Ruth Wyatt (Sieber) L. AA, Coll. DuPage, 1986; BA, Elmhurst Coll., 1988. Asst. dir. adult and transfer admissions Elmhurst (Ill.) Coll., 1993—, coord. internat. admissions, 1993—. Mem. ACLU, Assn. Internat. Educators, Ill. Assn. Coll. Registrars and Admission Counselors, Ill. Assn. Coll. Admission Counselors, U.S. Holocaust Meml. Mus. (founding mem.), Chgo. Geneal. Soc., Jewish Geneal. Soc., Mensa, Psi Chi, Phi Theta Kappa. Avocations: reading, films, dining out, geneal. rsch., baking. Office: Elmhurst Coll 190 Prospect Ave Elmhurst IL 60126-3271

LATZER, RICHARD NEAL, investment company executive; b. N.Y.C., Jan. 6, 1937; s. Paul John and Alyce A. Latzer; B.A., U. Pa., 1959, M.A., 1961; m. Ellen Weston, Sept. 5, 1965; children—Steven, David. Security analyst Mut. Benefit Life Ins. Co., Newark, 1963-66; portfolio mgr. Equitable Life Ins., Washington, 1966-68; securities analyst Investors Diversified Services, Mpls., 1968-69, dir. cert. and ins. investments, 1969-77, v.p. cert. and ins. investments, 1977-84; v.p. cert. and ins. investments IDS Fin. Services, Inc., 1984-86, IDS Fin. Corp., 1987-88; v.p. investments, IDS Reins. Co., 1986-88; asst. treas. Investors Syndicate Life Ins. & Annuity Co., Mpls., 1969-72; v.p. IDS Life Ins. Co., Mpls., 1973-80, v.p. investments, 1980-88; v.p. Investors Syndicate of Am., 1973-77, v.p. investments, 1977-84; v.p. Investors Syndicate Title & Guaranty Co., 1977-83, investment officer IDS Life Ins. Co. of N.Y., 1977-88; v.p. investments IDS Life Capital Resource Fund I, Inc., 1981-88 , IDS Spl. Income Fund, Inc., 1981-88, Am Enterprise Life Ins. Co., 1986-88, Reinsurance Co. 1986-88; IDS Life Series Fund, 1986-88; IDS Life Managed Fund, Inc., 1986-88, IDS Property Casualty, 1987-88; v.p. IDS Realty Corp., 1987-88; pres., chmn. bd., bd. dirs. Real Estate Svcs. Co., 1986-88; IDS Life Moneyshare Fund, Inc., 1981-88 ; IDS Cert. Co., 1984-88 ; chmn. bd., dir. IDS Real Estate Services Co., 1983-86; v.p. Fireman's Fund Am. Life Ins. Co., 1985-86; dir. Investors Syndicate Devel. Corp., Mpls., 1970-88 , Nuveen Realty Corp., Mpls., 1976-80; sr. v.p., chief investment officer Transamerica Corp., San Francisco, 1988—, pres., CEO Transamerica Investment Svcs., Inc., San Francisco, 1988—; dir., chief investment officer, chmn. investment com. Transamerica Occidental Life Ins. Co., L.A., 1989—, Transamerica Life Ins. and Annuity Co., L.A., 1989—; dir., chief investment officer, mem. investment com. Transamerica Ins. Group, Woodland Hills, 1988-93; bd. dirs., mem. exec. com. Transamerica Realty Svcs., Inc., San Francisco, 1988—, pres., CEO, 1996—; dir. Transamerica Realty Investment Corp., San Francisco, 1988—; chmn. pension investment com. Transamerica Corp., San Francisco, 1988—, dir. Transamerica Cash Res. Inc., L.A., 1989-90, Transamerica Income Shares, 1989—; dir., mem. investment com. Transamerica Life Ins. Co. Can., Toronto, 1991—; chief investment officer, mem. operating com. ARC Reinsurance Corp., Honolulu, 1993—. Served to lt., USN, 1960-63. Chartered fin. analyst. Mem. Security Analysts San Francisco, Chartered Fin. Analysts. Office: 600 Montgomery St San Francisco CA 94111

LAU, ALBERT MAN-FAI, physicist; b. Hong Kong, Aug. 22, 1947; came to U.S., 1966; s. Kwong Ming and Bik Wah Lau; m. Winnie Kwok-Yee Siu, June 16, 1971; children: Scott Bokhay, Winita Vinkay. BS summa cum laude, Yale U., 1970; MA, U. Calif., Berkeley, 1972, PhD, 1975. Postdoctoral physicist SRI Internat., Menlo Park, Calif., 1975-77; staff physicst Exxon Rsch. and Engring. Co., Linden, N.J., 1977-82; sr. mem. tech. staff Sandia Nat. Labs., Livermore, Calif., 1983—; vis. physicist NYU, N.Y.C., 1983, Princeton (N.J.) U., 1983; prof. invité U. Paris VI, 1979; assoc. prof. U. Paris-S., Orsay, France, 1980, U. Orleans, France, 1982. Contbr. articles to profl. jours., chpts. to books. Bd. dirs. Castro Valley Ednl. Found., 1995. Mem. Am. Phys. Soc., Laser Inst. of Am., Phi Beta Kappa. Achievements include pioneering research in laser-induced collisions and reactions, laser-induced predissociation; theoretical prediction and analyses of the photon-as-catalyst effect in laser-matter interaction. Office: Sandia Nat Labs PO Box 969 Livermore CA 94551-0969

LAU, CHARLES KWOK-CHIU, architect, architectural firm executive; b. Hong Kong, Oct. 19, 1954; came to U.S., 1973; s. Oi-Ting and Wai-Han L. BFA in Environ. Design, U. Hawaii Manoa, Honolulu, 1977. Registered architect, Hawaii. Designer CJS Group Architects, Honolulu, 1977-78, Fox Hawaii, Honolulu, 1978-80, Wimberly Allison Tong & Goo, Honolulu, 1980-82, Architects Hawaii, Honolulu, 1982-84; assoc., designer Stringer & Assocs., Honolulu, 1984-85; pres. AM Ptrns., Inc., Honolulu, 1985—; instr. U. Hawaii, Honolulu, 1987. Principal works include Crystal Fantasy, Hyatt Regency Hotel, Honolulu, 1988 (Merit award Hawaii chpt. AIA 1988), Dole Cannery Sq., Honolulu, 1989 (Merit award Hawaii Renaissance 1989), Danelle Christie's, Ala Moana Hotel, Honolulu, 1989 (Hawaii Region award Illuminating Engring. Soc. N.Am. 1989, Grand and Nat. Grand awards Hawaii Renaissance 1989, Tiger Restaurant, Lahaina, Hawaii, 1990 (Gold Key Excellence in Interior Design award Am. Hotel and Motel Assn. 1990, Nat. and Merit awards Hawaii Renaissance 1990), La Pierre du Roi, ANA Kalakaua Ctr., Honolulu, 1990 (Grand and Nat. Grand awards 1990), Crazy Shirts, Honolulu, 1991 (Grand and Overall awards Hawaii Renaissance 1991), Grand Hyatt Wailea, Maui, Hawaii, 1992 (Merit award Hawaii chpt. AIA 1992), Carrera y Carrera, Ala Moana Ctr., Honolulu, 1992 (Merit award Hawaii chpt. AIA 1992), Danelle Christie's, Outrigger Waikiki Hotel, Honolulu, 1992 (Merit award Hawaii Renaissance 1992), Exec. Ctr. Hotel, Honolulu, 1992 (Merit award Hawaii Renaissance 1992), Centre Ct. Restaurant, Honolulu, 1993 (Merit award Hawaii Renaissance 1993), Lani Huli, Kailua, 1993 (Spl. Recognition award Parade of Homes 1993), 218 Plantation Club Dr., Kapalua, Maui, 1993 (Interior Design award Am. Soc. Interior Design 1993), Royal Garden Restaurant, Alamoana Hotel, Honolulu, 1994 (Brand and Overall award Hawaii Renaissance, 1994, Lani Huli, Kailua, Hawaii (Project of Yr., City and County of Honolulu 1994). Recipient 1994 Best in Am. Living award Profl. Builders, Kapalua Residence in Maui. Mem. AIA (mem. design award jury selection com. Honolulu chpt. 1990), C. of C. Hawaii, Chinese C. of C. Hawaii, Pacific Club. Office: AM Partners Inc 1164 Bishop St Ste 1000 Honolulu HI 96813-2810

LAU, CLIFFORD, electrical engineer, researcher; b. Nov. 6, 1942. BS, U. Calif., Berkeley, 1966; MS, U. Calif., 1967; PhD, U. Calif., Santa Barbara, 1978. Electronic engr. Office of Naval Rsch. Fellow IEEE (assoc. editor IEEE Control Sys. Mag. 1985-88, publicity chmn. NIPS conf. 1988, treas. NIPS conf. 1989, tech. assoc. editor IEEE Transactions on Cirs. and Sys. 1989-90, tech. assoc. editor IEEE Transactions on Neural Networks 1991-92, editl. bd. mem. Procs. of the IEEE 1991—, mem. bd. govs. Cirs. and Sys. Soc. 1991—, gen. chmn. IJCNN 1992). Office: Office of Naval Rsch Code 311/800 N Quincy St Arlington VA 22217

LAU, HENRY, mechanical engineer, consultant; b. Hong Kong, Feb. 4, 1941; s. Mo Ngok and Julia (Seto) L.; m. Bing Sin, June 6, 1970; 1 child, Ryan. BS, U. Tenn., 1966; MS, Duke U., Durham, N.C., 1969, PhD, 1973. Rsch. assoc. Duke U., Durham, 1973-74; mech. engr. Ayres & Hayakawa Energy Mgrs., L.A., 1974-77; tech. dir. Ayres Assocs., L.A., 1977-85; prin. and tech. dir. Ayres, Ezer, Lau Inc., L.A., 1985-92; sr. engr. So. Calif. Edison, San Dimas, 1992—; cons. Lawrence Berkeley (Calif.) Lab., 1978-84, Calif. Energy Commn., Sacramento, 1978-82, Martin Marietta, L.A., 1981. Contbr. articles to profl. jours. Grantee Dow Chem., 1965, ASHRAE, 1974, U.S. Army Rsch., 1969. Mem. ASHRAE, ASME, Sigma Xi. Roman Catholic. Achievements include research in building energy systems, computer energy simulations, energy efficiency standards, indoor air quality, energy conservation, solar energy, thermal storage systems, load management. Home: PO Box 67641 Los Angeles CA 90067-0641 Office: Southern Calif Edison Co 300 N Lone Hill Ave San Dimas CA 91773-1741

LAU, IAN VAN, safety research engineer, biomechanics expert; b. Macao, Apr. 4, 1950; came to U.S., 1969; s. Wai-Hung L.; m. Helen Ting, Jan. 5, 1973; 1 child, Lisa Alison. BS, U. Mass. at Lowell, 1973; PhD, Johns Hopkins U., 1977. Rsch. engr. GM Rsch. Labs., Warren, Mich., 1978-86, sr. staff engr., 1986—; head dept. automotive safety and health GM, 1993—; mgr. USCAR safety consortium for Gen. Motors, Ford and Chrysler. Contbr. articles on injury prevention in car crashes (Caldwell award 1988, 89, 91); discoverer viscous injury index (Hwy. Safety award 1988); inventor safety steering wheel (McCuen award 1989), side impact dummy. Mem. Soc. Automotive Engrs. (Isbrandt Safety Engring. award 1986, 87, 91), Biomed. Engring. Soc. Republican. Roman Catholic. Avocation: racquetball. Office: GM Rsch Labs Automotive Safety & Health Warren MI 48090

LAU, JOHN HON SHING, business executive; b. China, June 17, 1946; came to U.S., 1973; s. Shui Hong and Mary Au L.; m. Teresa Yu, Sept. 2, 1972; 1 child, Judy M. B.S. in Civil Engring., Nat. Taiwan U., 1970; M.A.Sc. in Structural Engring., U. B.C., 1973; M.S. in Engring. Mechanics, U. Wis., 1974; Ph.D. in Theoretical and Applied Mechanics, U. Ill., 1977; M.S. in Mgmt., Fairleigh Dickinson U., 1981. Registered profl. engr., N.Y., Calif. Research engr. Exxon Prodn. and Research Co., Houston, 1977; structural specialist Control Data Corp., Sunnyvale, Calif., 1977-78; research assoc. Internat. Paper Co., Tuxedo Park, N.Y., 1978-79; sr. engr. Ebasco Services Inc., N.Y.C., 1979-81; sr. engr. Bechtel Power Corp., San Francisco, 1981-83; MTS, Sandia Nat. Lab., N.Mex., 1983-84, Hewlett-Packard Labs., 1984-95; pres. Express Packaging Sys., Inc., Palo Alto, Calif., 1995—. Contbr. articles to profl. jours. and 9 tech. books; assoc. editor for ASME Transactions Jour. Elec. Packaging. Fellow IEEE; mem. ASM Internat., AAAS, N.Y. Acad. Scis., Sigma Xi. Roman Catholic. Home: 961 Newell Rd Palo Alto CA 94303-2929 Office: EPS Inc 1137 San Antonio Rd Palo Alto CA 94303-4310

LAU, LAWRENCE JUEN-YEE, economics educator, consultant; b. Guizhou, China, Dec. 12, 1944; came to U.S., 1961, naturalized, 1974; s. Shai-Tat and Chi-Hing (Yu) Liu; m. Tamara K. Jablonski, June 23, 1984. BA with great distinction, Stanford U., 1964; MA, U. Calif.-Berkeley, 1966, PhD, 1969. Acting asst. prof. econs. Stanford U., Palo Alto, Calif., 1966-67, asst. prof., 1967-73, assoc. prof., 1973-76, prof., 1976—, Kwoh-Ting Li prof. econ. devel., 1992—; co-dir. Asia/Pacific Rsch. Ctr., 1992-96; cons. The World Bank, Washington, 1976—; vice chmn. Bank of Canton of Calif. Bldg. Corp., San Francisco, 1981-85; dir. Bank of Canton of Calif., San Francisco, 1979-85; dir. Property Resources Equity Trust, Los Gatos, 1987-88; vice-chmn. Complete Computer Co. Far Eat Ltd., Hong Kong, 1981-89. Co-author: (with D.T. Jamison) Farmer Education and Farm Efficiency, 1982, Models of Devlopment: A Comparative Study of Economic Growth in South Korea and Taiwan, 1986, rev. edit., 1990; contbr. articles to profl. jours. Adv. bd. Self-Help for Elderly, San Francisco, 1982—; bd. dirs. Chiang Ching-Kuo Found. for Internat. Scholarly Exch., 1989—; govs. coun. econ. policy advisors State of Calif., 1993—. John Simon Guggenheim Meml. fellow, 1973; fellow Ctr. for Advanced Study in Behavioral Scis., 1982; Overseas fellow Churchill Coll., Cambridge U., Eng., 1984. Fellow Econometric Soc.; mem. Academia Sinica, Conf. Research in Income and Wealth. Republican. Episcopalian. Office: Stanford U Dept Econs Stanford CA 94305

LAU, MICHELE DENISE, advertising consultant, sales trainer, television personality; b. St. Paul, Dec. 6, 1960; d. Dwyane Udell and Patricia Ann (Yri) L. Student, U. Minn., 1979-82. Pub. rels. coord. Stillwater (Minn.) C. of C., 1977-79; asst. mgr. Salkin & Linoff, Mpls., 1982, store merchandiser, sales trainer, 1982-83; rental agt. Sentinel Mgmt. Co., St. Paul, 1983-84; account exec. Community Svc. Publs., Mpls., 1984-85, frwy. news supr., 1985, asst. sales mgr., 1985-86; asst. sales mgr. St. Paul Pioneer Press Dispatch, 1986-91; pres. Promotional Ptnrs., Eden Prairie, Minn., 1991-96; on-air show host Home Shopping Network, Eden Prairie, 1996—; on-air personality Sta. WCCO II Cable TV Mpls., 1988-89, co-host Afternoon Midwest, 1989-93; co-host Home Shopping Show, host Minn. Voices, Fox 29, 1995; cons. U. Minn. Alumni mag., 1986-89. Author mechandising and sales tng. manuals. Fund-raiser sustaining program YMCA, Mpls., 1986, Jr. Achievement, St. Paul, 1988; cons. Muscular Dystrophy Assn., St. Paul, 1988-89; bd. dirs. St. Paul Jaycees. Mem. NAFE, Nat. Assn. Home Builders, Mpls. Builder Assn. (amb.), Metro-East Profl. Builders Assn. (spl. events com.), Advt. Fedn., The Newspaper Guild, Internat. Platform Assn., Speakeasy Club. Lutheran. Avocations: tennis, golf, aerobics. Home: 4961 Bacopa Ln S #102 Saint Petersburg FL 33715

LAUB, ALAN JOHN, engineering educator; b. Edmonton, Alta., Can., Aug. 6, 1948; came to U.S., 1970; naturalized, 1984; BSc with honors, U. B.C., 1969; MS, U. Minn., 1972, PhD, 1974. Asst. prof. Case Western Res. U., Cleve., 1974-75; vis. asst. prof. U. Toronto, Can., 1975-77; rsch. scientist MIT, Cambridge, Mass., 1977-79; assoc. prof. U. So. Calif., L.A., 1979-83; prof. U. Calif., Santa Barbara, 1983-96, chmn. dept. elec. and computer engring., 1989-92; dean Coll. of Engring. U. Calif. Davis, 1996—. Contbr. articles to profl. jours. Fellow IEEE; mem. IEEE Control Systems Soc. (pres. 1991, Disting. mem. award 1991, Control Systems Tech. award 1993), Soc. Indsl. Applied Math., Assn. Computing Machinery. Avocations: bridge, tennis. Office: U Calif Davis Office of Dean Coll of Engring Davis CA 95616-5294

LAUB, WILLIAM MURRAY, retired utility executive; b. Ft. Mills, Corregidor, Philippines, July 20, 1924; s. Harold Goodspeed and Marjorie M. (Murray) L.; m. Mary McDonald, July 26, 1947; children: William, Andrew, Mary, David, John. BSBA, U. Calif., Berkeley, 1947, LLB, 1950. Bar: Calif. 1951. Practice law Los Angeles, 1951-55; with Southwest Gas Corp., Las Vegas, Nev., 1948-88; v.p., gen. counsel Southwest Gas Corp., 1958-60, exec. v.p., 1960-64, pres., chief exec. officer, 1964-82, chmn., chief exec. officer, 1982-88. Pres. Boulder Dam Area council Boy Scouts Am., 1967-69, So. Nev. Indsl. Found., 1967-68, So. Nev. Meth. Found., 1967-74; chmn. Nev. Equal Rights Commn., 1966-68; Chmn. Clark County Republican Central Com., 1964-66; nat. committeeman Nev. Rep. Com., 1968-80; trustee Sch. Theology at Claremont, Calif., 1977—; trustee Inst. Gas Tech., 1983-89; nat. bd. advisors, coll. bus. and pub. adminstrn. The U. Ariz., 1985-89; bd. dirs. Alliance for Acid Rain Control, 1985-89. Served to lt. (j.g.) USNR, 1941-45. Mem. ABA, Am. Gas Assn. (bd. dirs., chmn. 1986-87), Pacific Coast Gas Assn. (chmn. 1983), Calif. Bar Assn., Nat. Coal Coun., Jonathan Club, Pauma Valley Country Club, Spanish Trail Golf and Country Club, Las Vegas Country Club. Office: 2810 W Charleston Blvd Ste 53 Las Vegas NV 89102-1906

LAUBACH, ROGER ALVIN, accountant; b. Riegelsville, N.J., July 3, 1922; s. Harry and Daisy (Cyphers) L.; diploma in bus. adminstrn. Churchman Bus. Coll., Easton, Pa., 1941; BS cum laude in Acctg., Rider U., 1949. CPA, N.Y., N.J. Acct., Coopers & Lybrand, C.P.A.s, N.Y.C., 1949-60; asst. to treas. Coca-Cola Bottling Co. N.Y., N.Y.C., 1960-63; mgr. audits and systems Atlantic Research Corp., Alexandria, Va., 1964-65; controller Ely-Cruikshank Co., Inc., realtors, N.Y.C., 1965-71, asst. treas., 1966-67, treas., dir., 1967-71; dir. N.Y. Federal Savings & Loan Assn., 1970-71; dir. Phila. Acctg. Center, Ogden Food Service Corp., 1971-72, treas., 1972-77; dir. corp. auditing Ogden Corp., N.Y.C., 1977-79; contr. Burlington County Cmty. Action Program, Burlington, N.J., 1981-84. Served with U.S. Army, 1942-46; ETO. Decorated Bronze Star. Mem. AICPA, Am. Red Cross (vol. bloodmobile 1986—), Inst. Internal Auditors, N.Y. State, N.J. Socs. CPAs, Real Estate Bd. N.Y., SAR (registrar, geneal., 1995—), VFW, Am. Legion, 100th Inf. Div. Assn., Soc. Colonial Wars, Laubach Family Assn. (book com. 1989-93), Nat. Trust for Hist. Preservation, Delta Sigma Pi (pres. 1948). Lutheran (treas., council). Home: 39 Southgate Rd Mount Laurel NJ 08054-2932

LAUBE, ROGER GUSTAV, retired trust officer, financial consultant; b. Chgo., Aug. 11, 1921; s. William C. and Elsie (Drews) L.; m. Irene Mary Chadbourne, Mar. 30, 1946; children: David Roger, Philip Russell, Steven Richard. BA, Roosevelt U., 1942; postgrad., John Marshall Law Sch., 1942, 48-50; LLB, Northwestern U., 1960; postgrad., U. Wash., 1962-64. Cert. fin. cons. With Chgo. Title & Trust Co., Chgo., 1938-42, 48-50, Nat. Bank Alaska, Anchorage, 1950-72; mgr. mortgage dept. Nat. Bank Alaska, 1950-56, v.p., trust officer, mgr. trust dept., 1956-72; v.p., trust officer, mktg. dir., mgr. estate and fin. planning div. Bishop Trust Co., Ltd., Honolulu, 1972-82; instr. estate planning U. Hawaii, Honolulu, 1978-82; exec. v.p. Design Capital Planning Group, Inc., Tucson, 1982-83; pres., sr. trust officer, registered investment adviser Advanced Capital Advisory, Inc. of Ariz., Tucson, 1983-89; registered rep., pres. Advanced Capital Investments, Inc. of Ariz., Prescott, 1983-89; pres., chief exec. officer Advanced Capital Devel., Inc. of Ariz., Prescott, 1983-89; mng. exec. Integrated Resources Equity Corp., Prescott, 1983-89; pres. Anchorage Estate Planning Coun., 1960-62, Charter mem., 1960-72, Hawaii Estate Planning Coun., 1972-82, v.p., 1979, pres., 1980, bd. dirs., 1981-82; charter mem. Prescott Estate Planning Coun., 1986-90, pres. 1988. Charter mem. Anchorage Community Chorus, 1946, pres., 1950-53, bd. dirs., 1953-72, Alaska Festival of Music, 1960-72; mem. Anchorage camp Gideons Internat., 1946-72, Honolulu camp, 1972-82, mem. Cen. camp, Tucson, 1982-85, Prescott, 1985-90, Port Angeles-Sequim Camp, 1990—; mem. adv. bd. Faith Hosp., Glenallen, Alaska, 1960—, Cen. Alaska Mission of Far Ea. Gospel Crusade, 1960—; sec., treas. Alaska Bapt. Found., 1955-72; bd. dirs. Anchorage Symphony, 1965-72; bd. dirs. Bapt. Found. of Ariz., 1985-90; bd. dirs., mem. investment com. N.W. Bapt. Found., 1991—; mem. mainland adv. coun. Hawaii Bapt. Acad., Honolulu, 1982—; pres. Sabinovista Townhouse Assn., 1983-85; bd. advisers Salvation Army, Alaska , 1961-72, chmn., Anchorage, 1969-72, bd. advisers, Honolulu, 1972-82, chmn. bd. advisers, 1976-78; asst. staff judge adv. Alaskan Command, 1946-48; exec. com. Alaska Conv., 1959-61, dir. music Chgo., 1938-42, 48-50, Alaska, 1950-72, Hawaii, 1972-82, Tucson, 1982-85, 1st So. Bapt. Ch., Prescott Valley, Ariz., 1985-90; 1st Bapt. of Sequim, Wash., 1990—; chmn. bd. trustees Hawaii, 1972-81, Prescott Valley, 1986-89, Sequim, Wash., 1991—; worship leader Waikiki Ch., 1979-82. 1st lt., JAGD, U.S. Army, 1942-48. Recipient Others award Salvation Army, 1972. Mem. Am. Inst. Banking (instr. trust div. 1961-72), Am. Bankers Assn. (legis. com., trust div. 1960-72), Nat. Assn. Life Underwriters (nat. com. for Ariz.), Yavapai County-Prescott Life Underwriters Assn. (charter), Anchorage C. of C. (awards com. 1969-71), Internat. Assn. Fin. Planners (treas. Anchorage chpt. 1969-72, exec. com. Honolulu chpt. 1972-82, Ariz. chpt. 1982-90, del. to World Congress Australia and New Zealand 1987), Am. Assn. Handbell Ringers. Baptist. Home: Sunland Country Club 212 Sunset Pl Sequim WA 98382-8515

LAUBENSTEIN, VERNON ALFRED, state agency administrator; b. Fredonia, Wisc., Mar. 17, 1933; s. Edwin R. and MArtha (Parlow) L.; m. Barbara Jean Swanson, Oct. 15, 1960; children: Jeffrey, Elizabeth, Katherine, Scott, Suzanne. BA, Ripon (Wisc.) Coll., 1954; MBA, Ind. U., 1955. Contracts and compliance mgr. Kemper Group, Long Grove, Ill., 1957-88; mgmt. ops. analyst State Of Ill., Chgo., 1988—; township supr. Schaumburg Twp., Hoffman Estates, Ill., 1969—. Pres. Twinbrook YMCA, Schaumburg, 1970-71, Twp. Suprs. of Ill., Astoria, 1988-89, Rep. Orgn. of Schaumburg, 1967-68; bd. dirs. Suburban Cook-DuPage Health Sys. Agy., Oak Park, Ill., 1976-81, Twp. Suprs. of Ill., Astoria, 1981—. 1st lt. MSC U.S. Army, 1955-57. Recipient Twinbrook award Twinbrook YMCA, 1975, Friend of Elk Grove-Schaumburg Twp. Mental Health Ctr. award, 1983. Republican. Lutheran. Avocations: fishing, camping, politics. Home: 125 Westover Ln Schaumburg IL 60193-1154 Office: Schaumburg Twp 25 Illinois Blvd Hoffman Estates IL 60194

LAUBER, JOHN K., research psychologist; b. Archbold, Ohio, Dec. 13, 1942; s. Kenneth Floyd and Fern Elizabeth (Rupp) L.; m. Susan Elizabeth Myers, Sept. 16, 1967; 1 stepchild, Sarah H. BS, Ohio State U., 1965, MS, 1967, PhD, 1969. Rsch. psychologist U.S. Naval Tng. Equipment Ctr., Orlando, Fla., 1969-73; chief aero. human factors office NASA Ames Rsch. Ctr., Moffett Field, Calif., 1973-85; mem. Nat. Transp. Safety Bd., Washington, 1985-95; v.p. corporate safety and compliance Delta Air Lines, Atlanta, 1995—; mem. Rsch., Engring. and Devel. adv. com. FAA, 1995—; mem. aero. adv. com. NASA, 1987—, USAF Studies Bd., NAS, Washington, 1987-89; bd. govs. Flight Safety found., 1995—. Contbr. articles to profl. jours. Recipient Industry Svc. award Air Transport World, N.Y.C., Disting. Svc. award Flight Safety Found., Tokyo, 1987, Joseph T. Nall Meml. award Nat. Air Traffic Contrs. Assn., 1992, Paul T. Hansen Lectureship award, 1993, Forrest & Dominique Bird award Civil Aviation Med. Assn., 1994. Fellow Aerospace Med. Assn. (chmn. aviation safety com. 1978-82, R. F. Longacre award 1990).; mem. Human Factors Soc. Democrat. Avocations: sailing, flying, amateur radio, cooking.

LAUBER, PATRICIA GRACE, writer; b. N.Y.C., Feb. 5, 1924; d. Hubert Crow and Florence (Walker) L.; m. Russell Frost III, Apr. 11, 1981. BA, Wellesley Coll., 1945. Rsch., writer Look Mag. Book Dept., N.Y.C., 1945-46; staff writer Scholastic Mags., N.Y.C., 1946-48, editor, 1948-54, freelance editor, 1954-56; freelance editor Challenge Books, Coward-McCann, N.Y.C., 1955-59; founding editor, editor-in-chief Science World, Street & Smith, N.Y.C., 1956-59; chief editor Science and Mathematics, The New Book of Knowledge, Grolier, N.Y.C., 1961-67; freelance editor Good Earth Books, Garrard, Scarsdale, N.Y., 1973-79; cons. editor Sci. Am. Books, N.Y.C., 1977-80; cons. Nat. Sci. Resources Ctr., NAS-Smithsonian Instn., 1992-94. Author numerous children's books including Volcano: The Eruption and Healing of Mount St. Helens, 1986 (Newbery honor Book 1987, N.Y. Acad. Scis. Hon. Mention 1987), From Flower to Flower: Animals and Pollination, 1986 (N.Y. Acad. Scis. Hon. Mention 1988), Dinosaurs Walked Here and Other Stories Fossils Tell, 1987, Snakes Are Hunters, 1988, Lost Star, the Story of Amelia Earhart, 1988, Yellowstone, 1988, Meteors and Meteorites: Voyagers from Space, 1989, The News About Dinosaurs, 1989 (N.Y. Acad. Scis. Hon. Mention 1990), Living with Dinosaurs, 1989 (Orbis Pictus hon. mention Nat. Coun. Tchrs. English 1990), Seeing Earth from Space, 1990 (Orbis Pictus hon. mention Nat. Coun. Tchrs. English 1991), Summer of Fire, 1991, Great Whales-The Gentle Giants, 1991, Fur, Feathers, and Flippers, 1994, What Do You See?, 1994, How Dinosaurs Came To Be, 1996, Hurricanes, 1996, Flood: Wrestling with the Mississippi, 1996, others. Recipient award for Overall Contbn. to Children's Lit., Washington Post/Children's Book Guild, 1983, Eva L. Gordon award Am. Nature Study Soc., 1988, Lit. award Cen. Mo. State U., 1989, Lifetime Achievement commendation Nat. Forum on Children's Sci. Books, Carnegie-Mellon U., 1992. Mem. PEN, The Authors Guild, Soc. Children's Book Writers. Democrat. Congregationalist. Avocations: reading, music, hiking, travel, sailing. Office: care Scholastic Press 555 Broadway New York NY 10012-3919

LAUBSCHER, LEEANN, medical and surgical nurse; b. Monticello, N.Y., Apr. 24, 1962; d. Lee Gregory Baumgardt and Carole Ann (Blume) Nicolis; m. Robert Francis Laubscher, Aug. 16, 1986. BS in Nursing, Mt. St. Mary Coll., Newburgh, N.Y., 1984; MS in Nursing, SUNY, New Paltz, 1996. RN, N.Y.; cert. med.-surg. nurse. Staff nurse Westchester County Med. Ctr., Valhalla, N.Y., 1984-90; staff nurse Castle Point (N.Y.) VA Med. Ctr., 1990—, nurse mgr. ICU, 1992, women vets. coord., 1995—; breast cancer detection awareness educator Am. Cancer Soc., N.Y., 1995—; cmty. educator LENS (Linking Edn., Nursing and Seniors) Project. Mem. N.Y. State Nurses Assn. (Dist. 12). Avocations: reading, needlework, travel. Office: Castle Point VA Med Ctr Castle Point NY 12511

LAUBSCHER, ROBERT JAMES, consumer products company executive; b. Tucson, Mar. 20, 1961; s. James Albert and Geri Lee (Bird) L.; m. Deborah Elaine Fuggles, Apr. 14, 1984; children: Stephanie Claire, Samuel Robert, Jonathan Daniel. BA in Econs., Calif. State U., Northridge, 1985; AS in Fire Tech., Oxnard Coll., 1986; cert. in ind. tax prep., Coll. for Fin. Planning, Denver, 1989. Acctg. mgr. Morning Star Labs., Inc., Moorpark, Calif., 1985-89; acctg. and credit mgr. Am. Tombow, Inc., Westlake Village, Calif., 1989-92; v.p. ops. Am. Tombow, Inc., Norcross, Ga., 1992—; owner Gold Coast Acctg. Svcs., Camarillo, Calif., 1989-92. With USMCR, 1981-87. Mem. Am. Inst. Profl. Bookkeepers, Bus. Products Credit Assn., Nat. Eagle Scout Assn. Republican. Mem. Full Gospel Ch. Avocation: running. Home: 6704 Vic Ar Rd Atlanta GA 30360-1317

LAUCHENGCO, JOSE YUJUICO, JR., lawyer; b. Manila, Philippines, Dec. 6, 1936; came to U.S., 1962; s. José Celis Sr. Lauchengco and Angeles (Yujuico) Sapota; m. Elisabeth Schindler, Feb. 22, 1968; children: Birthe, Martina, Duane, Lance. AB, U. Philippines, Quezon City, 1959; MBA, U. So. Calif., 1964; JD, Loyola U., L.A., 1971. Bar: Calif. 1972, U.S. Dist. Ct. (cen. dist.) Calif. 1972, U.S. Ct. Appeals (9th cir.) 1972, U.S. Supreme Ct. 1975. Banker First Western Bank/United Calif. Bank, L.A., 1964-71; assoc. Demler, Perona, Langer & Bergkvist, Long Beach, Calif., 1972-73; ptnr. Demler, Perona, Langer, Bergkvist, Lauchengco & Manzella, Long Beach, 1973-77; sole practice Long Beach and L.A., 1977-83; ptnr. Lauchengco & Mendoza, L.A., 1983-92; pvt. practice L.A., 1993—; mem. commn. on jud. procedures County of L.A., 1979; tchr. Confraternity of Christian Doctrine, 1972-79; counsel Philippine Presdl. Commn. on Good Govt., L.A., 1986. Chmn. Filipino-Am. Bi-Partisan Polit. Action Group, L.A., 1978. Recipient Degree of Distinction, Nat. Forensic League, 1955. Mem. Nat. Assn. Criminal Def. Lawyers, Criminal Cts. Bar Assn., Calif. Attys. Criminal Justice, Calif. Pub. Defenders Assn., Philippine-Am. Bar Assn. (bd. dirs.), U. Philippines Vanguard Assn. (life), Beta Sigma. Roman Catholic. Lodge: K.C. Avocations: classical music, opera, romantic paintings and sculpture, camping, shooting. Office: 3545 Wilshire Blvd Ste 247 Los Angeles CA 90010-2305

LAUCK, A. VICTORIA, small business owner, volunteer; b. Cin., Aug. 31, 1955; d. William Louis and Virginia Elizabeth (Hart) Pohl; m. John William Lauck, Nov. 27, 1982; 1 child, Christina Maria. BA in English, Trinity Coll., Washington D.C., 1977; MEd in Public Relations, Xavier U., Cin., 1978; attended, Mount Saint Joseph Coll., Cin., 1984. Public relations, advtg. mgr. Eagle Savings Assn., Cin., 1978-83; owner, ptnr. Make A Statement, Cin., 1991-93; owner V.P. Typesetting, 1988—; mem. bd. dirs. ProKids, Cin., 1990-93, 94-95, Jr. League of Cin., 1992-93, exec. bd. mem. 1994-96. Editor: (book) Cincinnati For Kids, 1990. Vol. catalogue writer Cin. Hist. Soc., 1984-86; printing coord. Cmty. Chest, Cin., 1985. Recipient Honor award Assn. of Jr. Leagues, Internat., 1994. Home: 7000 Graves Rd Cincinnati OH 45243-3853

LAUCK, ANTHONY JOSEPH, artist, retired art educator, priest; b. Indpls., Dec. 30, 1908; s. Anthony Peter and Marie Elizabeth (Habig) L. Diploma in fine arts, John Herron Art Sch., 1936; AB, U. Notre Dame, 1942, DFA (hon.), 1980; cert. in carving, painting, Corcoran Sch. Art, 1948. Entered Congregation of Holy Cross, 1937; ordained priest Roman Catholic Ch., 1946; priest aux. St. Martin's Ch., Washington, 1946-48, Holy Cross Ch., N.Y.C., 1948-49; priest aux. univ. ch. U. Notre Dame, Ind., 1950, mem. faculty dept. art univ. ch., 1950-82, assoc. prof. sculpture univ. ch., 1958-70, prof. sculpture, 1970-72, emeritus prof., 1973—, head dept. art, 1960-67, dir. Univ. Art Gallery, 1962-74, dir. emeritus, 1974—; chmn. art jury Nat. Sacred Heart Drawing Competition, Xavier U., 1956. Exhibited, John Herron Art Inst., Ind. State Fair, Indpls., Corcoran Gallery Art, Nat. Mus. Art, Washington, N.A.D., Audubon Artists, N.Y.C., Pa. Acad. Fine Arts, Phila., Conn. Acad. Fine Art, Hartford, Provincetown (Mass.) Art Assn., Newport (R.I.) Art Assn., sculpture retrospective, U. Notre Dame, 1980-81, Snite Mus.Art, 1993; represented permanent collections, Phila. Mus. Art, Corcoran Gallery Art, Pa. Acad. Fine Arts, Norfolk Mus. Art, South Bend Art Ctr., Indpls. Mus. Art, Snite Mus. Art, Notre Dame U., Ind. State Museum, Indpls., Grand Rapids Art Mus., Evansville Mus. Arts and Sci., Ball State U. Art Mus., Gary Art Center, Hartwick Coll., Krasl Art Ctr., Midwest Mus. of Am. Art, Ind., St. Joseph, Mich., Midwest Mus. of American Art, Elkhart, Ind. also pvt. collections.; contbr. articles on sacred art to jours. and mags. Recipient Fairmount Park purchase prize Third Sculpture Internat., 1949, George D. Widener Gold medal for sculpture Am. art exhbn. Pa. Acad. Art, 1953, John Herron Art Inst. citation, 1957, 1st prize for sculpture Newport Art Assn., Peterson Sculpture Purchase award, 1991, Sculpture Purchase prize Midwest Mus. Am. Art, 1992; inducted medalist Ind. Acad., 1973. Mem. Audubon Artists, St. Joseph Valley Watercolor Soc., No. Ind. Artist, Ind. Artists Club, Nat. Sculpture Soc. N.Y. Home: Moreau Seminary Notre Dame IN 46556 Office: U Notre Dame Snite Mus Art Notre Dame IN 46556 *My work does not enter vitally into the main currents of American life, this busy, mechanized, space-oriented, scientific world of the late 20th century. What interest can such a world have in these silent little sacred images? It's up to them, nevertheless, to exercise some aesthetic attraction upon those who can see what I've tried to reveal. I do hope, of course, that these images may implant a warm, deep reminder into a few hearts and minds.*

LAUDA, DONALD PAUL, university dean; b. Leigh, Nebr., Aug. 7, 1937; s. Joe and Libbie L.; m. Sheila H. Henderson, Dec. 28, 1966; children: Daren M., Tanya R. B.S., Wayne State Coll., 1963, M.S., 1964; Ph.D., Iowa State U., 1966. Assoc. dir. Communications Center U. Hawaii, 1966-67; assoc. prof. indsl. arts St. Cloud (Minn.) State Coll., 1967-69; asst. dean Ind. State U., 1970-73; chmn. tech. edn. W.Va. U., 1973-75; dean Sch. Tech., Eastern Ill. U., Charleston, 1975-83, Calif. State U., Long Beach, 1983—; cons. in field. Author: Advancing Technology: Its Impact on Society, 1971, Technology, Change and Society, 1978, 2d edit., 1985; contbr. articles to profl. jours. Pres. Council on Tech. Tchr. Edn.; dir. Charleston 2000 Futures Project, 1978-81. Served with USAR, 1957-59. EPDA research fellow, 1969-70; Eastern Ill. U. faculty research grantee, 1971. Mem. Future Soc. Internat. Tech. Edn. Assn., Coun. Tech. Tchr. Educators (pres., Tchr. of Yr. award 1978), World Future Soc., Internat. Tech. Edn. Assn. (pres. 1990), World Coun. Assn. Tech. Edn., Am. Vocat. Assn., Phi Kappa Phi (pres. 1993), Epsilon Pi Tau (Laureate citation 1982), Long Beach C. of C. (bd. dirs. 1995—), Japan Am. Soc. (adv. bd.). Office: Calif State U Coll Health & Human Svcs Long Beach CA 90840 *Jobs and careers come through a great deal of effort, education, but, most importantly, through the help of others. It is this input that helps one clarify goals, gain new insights, and synthesize information. The process is reciprocal in that one helps others grow. Reflecting on the past always brings to mind people rather than degrees, positions, salaries, etc. When one loses sight of this, he/she is missing the greatest achievement of life.*

LAUDER, ESTÉE, cosmetics company executive; b. N.Y.C.; m. Joseph Lauder (dec.); children: Leonard, Ronald. LLD (hon.), U. Pa., 1986. Chmn. bd. Estée Lauder Inc., 1946—. Author: Estée: A Success Story, 1985. Named One of 100 Women of Achievement Harpers Bazaar, 1967, Top Ten Outstanding Women in Business, 1970; recipient Neiman-Marcus Fashion award, 1962; Spirit of Achievement award Albert Einstein Coll. Medicine, 1968; Kaufmann's Fashion Fortnight award, 1969; Bamberger's Designer's award, 1969; Gimbel's Fashion Forum award, 1969; Internat. Achievement award Frost Bros., 1971; Pogue's Ann. Fashion award, 1975, Golda Meir 90th Anniversary Tribute award, 1988; decorated chevalier Legion of Honor France, 1978; medaille de Vermeil de la Ville de Paris, 9, 1979; 4th Ann. award for Humanitarian Service Girls' Club N.Y., 1979; 25th Anniversary award Greater N.Y. council Boy Scouts Am., 1979; L.S. Ayres award, 1981; Achievement award Girl Scouts U.S.A., 1983; Outstanding Mother award, 1984; Athena award, 1985; Pres. award Cosmetic Exec. Women, 1989, Neiman-Marcus Fashion award, 1992; honored Lincoln Ctr., World of Style, 1986; 1988 Laureate Nat. Bus. Hall of Fame. Office: Estée Lauder Cosmetics 767 5th Ave New York NY 10153-0001

LAUDER, LEONARD ALAN, cosmetic and fragrance company executive; b. N.Y.C., Mar. 19, 1933; s. Joseph H. and Estée (Mentzer) L.; m. Evelyn Hausner, July 5, 1959; children: William Phillip, Gary Mark. BS, Wharton Sch., U. Pa., 1954. With Estée Lauder, Inc., N.Y.C., 1958—, exec. v.p., 1962-72, pres., 1972-82, pres., chief exec. officer, 1982—; vice chmn. bd. CFTA, N.Y.C., 1976-79. Trustee Aspen Inst. for Humanistic Studies, 1978—, U. Pa., Phila., 1977—; pres. Whitney Mus. Am. Art, 1977—; bd. dirs. Adv. Commn. on Trade Negotiations, Washington, 1983-87; bd. govs. Joseph H. Lauder Inst. Mgmt. and Internat. Studies, 1983—. Lt. USNR, 1955-58. Mem. Chief Execs. Orgn., French-Am. C. of C. in U.S. (coun. frn. relations). Office: Estée Lauder Cosmetics 767 5th Ave New York NY 10153-0001*

LAUDER, RONALD STEPHEN, investor; b. N.Y.C., Feb. 26, 1944; s. Joseph H. and Estee (Josephine) (Mentzer) L.; m. Jo Carole Knopf, July 8, 1967; children: Aerin Rebecca, Jane Alexandra. Degree in French lit., U. Paris, 1964; B.S. in Internat. Bus., U. Pa., 1965. With Estee Lauder Inc., Brussels, Paris, N.Y.C., 1965-83, also bd. dirs.; chmn. Estee Lauder International, Inc., 1980-83; dep. asst. Sec. of Def., Washington, 1983-85; ambassador to Austria Vienna, 1986-87; chmn., pres. Lauder Investments, Inc.; pvt. investor Ea. and Cen. Europe; founder, chmn. Cen. European Devel. Corp.; chmn. bd. trustees Mus. Modern Art., 1995—. Author: Fighting Violent Crime in America, 1985. Mem. N.Y. State Econ. Devel. Bd., 1972-78; fin. chmn. N.Y. State Republican Com., 1979-82; chmn. 500 Club of N.Y. Rep. Com., 1979-83; trustee Mus. Modern Art, 1975—, Mt. Sinai Med. Ctr., 1981—; Rep. candidate, Conservative nominee for Mayor of N.Y.C., 1989. Recipient Ordre De Merit, France, 1985, Disting. Pub. Svc. medal award Dept. Def., 1986; decorated Great Cross of the Order of Aeronautical Merit with White Ribbon, Spain, 1985; Ronald S. Lauder Drawing Gallery at Mus. Modern Art named in his honor, 1984. Office: Lauder Investments Inc 767 5th Ave Ste 4200 New York NY 10153-0001

LAUDER, VALARIE ANNE, editor, educator; b. Detroit, Mar. 1; d. William J. and Murza Valerie (Mann) L. AA, Stephens Coll., Columbia, Mo., 1944; postgrad. Northwestern U. With Chgo. Daily News, 1944-52, columnist, 1946-52; lectr. Sch. Assembly Svc., also Redpath lectr., 1952-55; freelance writer for mags. and newspapers including N.Y. Times, Yankee, Ford Times, Travel & Leisure, Am. Heritage, 1955—; editor-in-chief Scholastic Roto, 1962; editor U. N.C., 1975-80, lectr. Sch. Journalism, 1980—; gen. sec. World Assn. for Pub. Opinion Rsch., 1988-95; nat. chmn. student writing project Ford Times, 1981-86; pub. rels. dir. Am. Dance Festival, Duke U., 1982-83, lectr., instr. continuing edn. program, 1984; contbg. editor So. Accents mag., 1982-86. Mem. nat. fund raising bd. Kennedy Ctr., 1962-63; bd. dirs. Chapel Hill Mus., Inc., 1996—. Recipient 1st place award Nat. Fedn. Press Women, 1981; 1st place awards Ill. Women's Press Assn., 1950, 1951. Mem. Pub. Rels. Soc. Am. (treas. N.C. chpt. 1982, sec. 1983, v.p. 1984, pres.-elect 1985, pres. 1986, chmn. council of past pres., chmn. 25th Ann. event 1987, del. Nat. Assembly 1988-94, S.E. dist. officer, nat. nominating com. 1991, 1st Pres.'s award 1993), Women in Communications (v.p. matrix N.C. Triangle chpt. 1984-85), N.C. Pub. Rels. Hall of Fame Com., DAR, Soc. Mayflower Desc. (bd. dir. Ill. Soc. 1946-52), Chapel Hill Hist. Soc. (bd. dir. 1981-85, 94—, chmn. publs. com. 1980-85, pres. 1996—), Chapel Hill Preservation Soc. (bd. trustees 1993-96, nominating com. 1994), N.C. Press Club (3d v.p. 1981-83, 2d v.p. 1983-85, pres. 1985, 1st pl. awards 1981, 82, 83, 84), Univ. Woman's Club (2d v.p. 1988), The Carolina Club, The Nat. Press Club. Office: U NC Sch Journalism and Mass Comm CB 3365 Chapel Hill NC 27599-3365

LAUDERDALE, KATHERINE SUE, lawyer; b. Wright-Patterson AFB, Ohio, May 30, 1954; d. Azo and Helen Ceola (Davis) L. BS in Polit. Sci., Ohio State U., 1975; JD, NYU, 1978. Bar: Ill. 1978, U.S. Dist. Ct. (no. dist.) Ill. 1978, Calif. 1987. Assoc. Schiff, Hardin & Waite, Chgo., 1978-82; dir. bus. and legal affairs Sta. WTTW-TV, Chgo., 1982-83, gen. counsel, 1983—, also v.p., sr. v.p., gen. counsel legal and bus. affairs, 1993—; acting sr. v.p. Prodn. Ctr., 1994; sr. v.p. New Ventures, 1995—. Mem. Lawyers Com. for Harold Washington, Chgo. 1983; bd. dirs. Midwest Women's Ctr., Chgo., 1985-94; active Chgo. Coun. Fgn. REls., 1981—, mem. fgn. affairs com., 1985—. mem. ABA, Chgo. Bar Assn. (bd. dirs. TV Prodns., Inc. 1986—), Lawyers for Creative Arts (bd. dir. 1984—), ACLU (bd. dirs. 1987-94), Nat. Acad. TV Arts and Scis., NYU Law Alumni Assn. Midwest (mem. exec. bd. 1982—), The Ohio State U. Pres.'s Nat. Adv. Coun. on Pub. Affairs (Chgo. com., 1994—), The U. Chicago Women's Bd., 1996—. Democrat. Office: Sta WTTW-TV 5400 N Saint Louis Ave Chicago IL 60625-4623

LAUDISE, ROBERT ALFRED, research chemist; b. Amsterdam, N.Y., Sept. 2, 1930; s. Anthony Thomas and Harriette Elizabeth (O'Neil) L.; m. Joyce Elizabeth DeSilvia, Aug. 24, 1957; children: Thomas Michael, Margaret Joyce, John David, Mary Elizabeth, Edward Robert. B.S. in Chemistry, Union Coll., Schenectady, N.Y., 1952; Ph.D. in Chemistry (A.D. Little fellow), M.I.T., 1956. Mem. Tech. staff Bell Telephone Labs., Murray Hill, N.J., 1956-60; head crystal chemistry rsch. dept. Bell Telephone Labs., 1960-72, asst. dir. materials research lab., 1972-74, dir. materials research lab., 1974-77, dir. phys. and inorganic chemistry research lab., 1977-87, dir. materials chemistry rsch. lab., 1988-90, dir. materials and processing rsch. lab., 1990-92, adj. dir. chem. rsch., 1994—; vis. prof. U. Aix, Marseilles, France, 1971, Hebrew U., Jerusalem, 1972, Shandong U., China, 1980; cons. Pres.'s Sci. com., 1960-64; adv. com. Nat. Bur. Standards, 1970-78; solid state scis. com. NRC, 1977-81; adv. com. NASA, 1977-82; chair Nat. Math. Adv. Bd., 1996—; adj. prof. MIT, 1988—, Rutgers U., 1991—. Author: The Growth of Single Crystals, 1970; editor: Jour. Crystal Growth, 1978-94, Jour. Materials Rsch., 1994—; contbr. articles to sci. jours. Recipient Sawyer award, 1974, Eiler award U. Toledo, 1996. Fellow AAAS, Am. Mineral Soc., Am. Ceramic Soc. (Orton award lectr. 1994); mem. NAS, NAE, Internat. Orgn. Crystal Growth (pres. award 1981), Am. Assn. Crystal Growth (pres. 1971-77), Am. Chem. soc. (Materials Chemistry prize 1990), electrochem. Soc., Am. Crystal Soc., Fedn. Math. Soc. (pres. 1995—). Roman Catholic. Patentee in field. Home: 65 Lenape Ln Berkeley Heights NJ 07922-2333 Office: Bell Lucent Tech 700 Mountain Ave New Providence NJ 07974-1208

LAUDONE, ANITA HELENE, lawyer; b. Boston, Sept. 14, 1948; d. Vincent A. and Wanda L.; m. Colin E. Harley, May 20, 1978; children: Clayton Thomas, Victoria Spencer. A.B., Conn. Coll., 1970; J.D., Columbia U., 1973. Bar: N.Y. 1974. Law clk. to judge Fed. Dist. Ct., N.Y.C., 1973-74; asso. Davis Polk & Wardwell, N.Y.C., 1974-78; assoc. Shearman & Sterling, N.Y.C., 1978-79; with Phelps Dodge Corp., N.Y.C., 1979-85; corp. sec. Phelps Dodge Corp., 1980-85, v.p., corp. sec., 1984-85. Editor: Columbia Law Rev., 1973. Home: 510 North St Greenwich CT 06830-3439

LAUENSTEIN, MILTON CHARLES, management consultant; b. Webster Groves, Mo., Feb. 16, 1926; s. Milton Charles and Helen (Scholz) L.; m. Helen Smith, Feb. 5, 1949; children: Paul C., Kurt, Maria, Fritz. BS, Purdue U., 1945; MBA, U. Chgo., 1960. Tech. svc. engr. Norton Co., Worcester, Mass., 1948-51; with silicone products dept. GE Co., Waterford, N.Y., Cleve. and Chgo., 1951-57; cons. mktg. and corp. planning A.T. Kearney & Co., Chgo., 1957-60; dir. long range planning Bell & Howell Co., Chgo., 1960-62; pres. Ventron Corp., Beverly, Mass., 1962-76, Lauenstein & Assoc., Inc. (mgmt. cons.), Wenham, Mass., 1977-91, Telequip Corp., Littleton, Mass., 1979-80; chmn. Telequip Corp., Nashua, N.H., 1989—; bd. dirs. Helix Tech. Corp., Waltham, Mass., Tech/Ops. Sevcon Corp., Boston; sr. lectr. bus. U. Chgo., 1961-62, 79-80; adj. prof. mgmt., 1983-85; exec.-in-residence Coll. Bus. Adminstrn., Northeastern U., Boston, 1980-83. Author: What's Your Game Plan?, 1986; contbns. editor Jour. Bus. Strategy. Trustee, treas. Vt. Studio Ctr., Johnson; chm., Wenham Dem. Town Com., 1967-72. With USNR, 1943-46. Fellow emeritus Am. Inst. Chemists. Avocations: painting, sailing. Home and Office: 90 Hesperus Ave Gloucester MA 01930-5273

LAUER, CLINTON DILLMAN, automotive executive; b. Joliet, Ill., Dec. 8, 1926; s. Thomas Ayscough and Francis (Dillman) L.; m. Lea Merrill, Dec. 9, 1950; children: Joanne L. Gunderson, John C. BS, U. Ill., 1948; MBA, U. Pa., 1950. Supply mgr. automotive assembly div. Ford Motor Co., Dearborn, Mich., 1971-76, dir. body and assembly purchasing N.Am. automotive ops., 1976-83, exec. dir. N.Am. Automotive Ops. prodn. purchasing, 1983-87, v.p. purchasing and supply, 1987-92; pres. Lauer and Assocs., Inc., Bloomfield Hills, Mich., 1992—; bd. dirs. Top Source Techs., Inc., Mexican Industries. Mem. exec. bd. Detroit Area coun. Boy Scouts Am., pres., 1990-92; past bd. dirs. nat. and S.E. Mich. Jr. Achievement, Boys and Girls Club of S.E. Mich. With U.S. Army, 1944-46, 50-52. Mem. Oakland Hills Country Club, Bear Creek Golf Club, Sea Pines Country Club. Republican. Episcopalian. Avocation: golf. Home: 4053 Hidden Woods Dr Bloomfield Hills MI 48301-3130 also: 26 Marsh View Rd Hilton Head SC 29928

LAUER, ELIOT, lawyer; b. N.Y.C., Aug. 17, 1949; s. George and Doris (Trenk) L.; m. Marilyn Steinberg, June 5, 1977; children: Tamar Rachel, Ilana Jennifer, Michael Jonathan, Samuel Geoffrey. BA, Yeshiva U., 1971; JD cum laude, Fordham U., 1974. Bar: D.C. 1975, N.Y. 1975, U.S. Dist. Ct. (so. and ea. dists.) N.Y. 1975, U.S. Ct. Appeals (2d cir.) 1975, U.S. Supreme Ct. 1984. Assoc. Curtis, Mallet-Prevost, Colt & Mosle, N.Y.C., 1974-82, ptnr., 1982—. Counsel Keren-Or Inc., N.Y.C., 1985—; bd. dirs. Hebrew Acad. Long Beach, N.Y., 1985—, Young Israel Lawrence, Cedarhurst, N.Y., 1984—. Mem. ABA, N.Y. State Bar Assn., Assn. of Bar of City of N.Y., Fed. Bar Council, Am. Arbitration Assn. (arbitrator 1979—), Nat. Futures Assn. (arbitrator 1983—). Republican. Office: Curtis Mallet-Prevost Colt & Mosle 101 Park Ave New York NY 10178

LAUER, JAMES LOTHAR, physicist, educator; b. Vienna, Austria, Aug. 2, 1920; came to U.S., 1938, naturalized, 1943; s. Max and Friederike (Rappaport) L.; m. Stefanie Dorothea Blank, Sept. 5, 1955; children: Michael, Ruth. A.B., Temple U., 1942, M.A., 1944; Ph.D., U. Pa., 1948; postgrad., U. Calif., San Diego, 1964-65. Scientist Sun Oil Co., Marcus Hook, Pa., 1944-52; spectroscopist Sun Oil Co., 1952-64, sr. scientist, 1965-77; asst. prof. U. Pa., 1952-55; lectr. U. Del., 1952-58; research fellow mech. engring. U. Calif., San Diego, 1964-65; research prof. mech. engring. Rensselaer Poly. Inst., Troy, N.Y., 1978-85; prof. mech. engring. Rensselaer Poly. Inst., 1985-93, prof. mech. engring. emeritus, 1993—; rsch. sci. Ctr. Magnetic Recording Rsch. U. Calif., San Diego, 1993-95, vis. scholar applied mechanics and engring. sci., 1995—; sr. faculty summer rsch. fellow NASA-Lewis Rsch. Ctr., 1986, 87; vis. prof. Ctr. for Magnetic Rec. Rsch., U. Calif., San Diego, 1991; cons. Digital Equipment Corp., 1992—, NASA-Lewis Rsch. Ctr., 1993—. Author: Infrared Fourier Spectroscopy—Chemical Applications, 1978; author numerous tech. papers. Active Penn Wynne Civic Assn., 1959-77, Country Knolls Civic Assn., 1978-93. Sun Oil Co. fellow, 1964-65, Air Force Office Sci. Rsch. grantee, 1974-86, NASA Lewis Rsch. Ctr. grantee, 1974-86, Office Naval Rsch. grantee, 1979-82, Army Rsch. Office grantee, 1985-89, NSF grantee, 1987-95, Innovative Rsch. award Soc. Mech. Engrs., 1991, Discovery awards NASA, 1993, 96. Mem. Am. Chem. Soc. (emeritus), Am. Phys. Soc., Soc. Applied Spectroscopy, Materials Rsch. Soc., Optical Soc. Am. (emeritus), Sigma Xi. Jewish. Patentee in field. Home: 7622 Palmilla Dr Apt 78 San Diego CA 92122-5049 Office: U Calif San Diego La Jolla CA 92093 *My advice to those contemplating a career in experimental research is to give much thought to these points: (1) interest, enthusiasm, willingness to work are only basics, (2) a loving and understanding wife is essential, and (3) the knowledge that one can create one's own success at any time is the driving force.*

LAUER, JEANETTE CAROL, college dean, history educator, author; b. St. Louis, July 14, 1935; d. Clinton Jones and Blanche Aldine (Gideon) Pentecost; m. Robert Harold Lauer, July 2, 1954; children: Jon, Julie, Jeffrey. BS, U. Mo., St. Louis, 1970; MA, Washington U., St. Louis, 1973, PhD, 1975. Assoc. prof. history St. Louis C.C., 1974-82; assoc. prof. history U.S. Internat. U., San Diego, 1982-90, prof., 1990-94, dean Coll. Arts and Scis., 1990-94. Author: Fashion Power, 1981, The Spirit and the Flesh, 1983, Til Death Do Us Part, 1986, Watersheds, 1988, The Quest for Intimacy, 1996, 3d edit., 1993, No Secrets, 1993, The Joy Ride, 1993, For Better of Better, 1995, True Intimacy, 1996, Intimacy on the Run, 1996, How to Build a Happy Marriage, 1996. Woodrow Wilson fellow, 1970, Washington U. fellow, 1971-75. Mem. Am. Hist. Assn., Orgn. Am. Historians. Democrat. Presbyterian. Home: 18147 Sun Maiden Ct San Diego CA 92127-3102

LAUER, MATT, broadcast journalist; b. Dec. 30, 1957. Ed., U. Ohio. Producer WOWK-TV, Huntington, W.Va., 1979-80; program host various locations, 1980-88; substitute host Day's End, ABC-TV, 1989, Esquire Show, King Prodns./Lifetime, 1988-89, 9 Broadcast Plaza, WWOR-TV, N.Y.C., 1989-91; with WNBC, N.Y.C., 1992-96; co-anchor News 4/Live at Five, N.Y.C., 1993-96, NBC News' Today Show, 1997—; news anchor NBC News' Today Show, N.Y.C., 1994-97; co-anchor News 4/Live at Five, N.Y.C., 1993-96. Office: NBC News 30 Rockefeller Plz Rm 1420 New York NY 10112

LAUER, MICHAEL THOMAS, software company executive; b. Lehighton, Pa., Feb. 13, 1955; s. Thomas Lee and Dorothy Ruth (Rehrig) L.; children from previous marriage: Michael T. Jr., Matthew T.; m. Donna Marie Baker, May 19, 1990; 1 stepchild, J. David Beales. Cert. computer analyst.

Programmer/analyst Informatics, Linthicum, Md., 1977-78; systems analyst Nat. Security Agy., Annapolis Junction, Md., 1978-79; mgr. Compuware Corp., Landover, Md., 1979-82; exec. v.p., owner Lamarian Systems, Inc., Greenbelt, Md., 1982-90; exec. v.p. Nynex World Trade, Landover, Md., 1990-92; cons. The Harmic Group, Budapest, Hungary, 1993-94; div. mgr. AT&T Global Tech. Platforms, Silver Spring, Md., 1995—; cons. MCI Telecomm., Arlington, Va., 1982-85, U.S. Dept. Transp. Maritime Adminstrn., Washington, 1986-91, Jacksonville (Fla.) Port Authority, 1987-88, Hungarian Customs & Fin. Guard, Budapest, 1992-94. Author rsch. reports in field. Sgt. USAF, 1973-77. Republican. Home: 2503 Prospect Grn Mitchellville MD 20721-2527

LAUER, RONALD MARTIN, pediatric cardiologist, researcher; b. Winnipeg, Man., Can., Feb. 18, 1930; m. Eileen Pearson, Jan. 12, 1959; children: Geoffrey, Judith Lauer. BS, U. Man., 1953, MD, 1954. Diplomate Am. Bd. Pediatrics. Asst. prof. pediatrics U. Pitts., 1960-61; asst. prof. pediatrics U. Kans., 1961-67, assoc. prof. pediatrics, 1967-68; prof. pediatrics, dir. pediatrics cardiology U. Iowa, 1968—, vice chmn. pediatrics, 1974-82, prof. pediatrics and preventive medicine 1980—. Home: RR 6 Iowa City IA 52240-9806 Office: U Iowa Coll Medicine Div Pediatric Cardiology Iowa City IA 52242*

LAUERSEN, NIELS HELTH, physician, educator; b. Denmark, Sept. 10, 1939; came to U.S., 1967, naturalized, 1977; s. Bernhard and Maria L. M.D. cum laude, U. Copenhagen, 1967, Cornell U., 1968. Diplomate: Am. Bd. Ob-Gyn. Intern, then resident in ob-gyn N.Y. Hosp.-Cornell U. Med. Center, 1968-72, assoc. prof., 1972-79; assoc. prof. ob-gyn Mt. Sinai Sch. Medicine, N.Y.C., 1979-83; prof. ob-gyn N.Y. Med. Coll., 1983—. Author: It's Your Body, A Woman's Guide to Gynecology, 1978, new version, 1993, Clinical Perinatal Biochemical Monitoring, 1981, Principles of Microsurgical Techniques in Infertility, 1982, Listen to your Body, 1982, Childbirth With Love, 1983, Modern Management of High-Risk Pregnancy, 1983, PMS: Premenstrual Syndrome and You, 1984, It's Your Pregnancy, 1987, The Endometriosis Answer Book, 1988, A Woman's Body, 1989, Getting Pregnant, 1990, You're in Charge, 1993, The Complete Book of Breast Care, 1996; also numerous articles. Served with Danish Air Force, 1958-60. Recipient Profl. Service award AMA, 1979, 80, 82, 84, 86, 88, 92. Fellow Am. Coll. Obstetricians and Gynecologists (award 1977), Soc. Gynecol. Investigation, Am. Fertility Soc., N.Y. Obstet. Soc., N.Y. Gynecol. Soc., Soc. of Perinatal Medicine; mem. AFTRA, N.Y. Gynecol. Soc., N.Y. Soc. Reproductive Medicine, Author's Guild Am. Home: 750 Park Ave New York NY 10021-4252 Office: 784 Park Ave New York NY 10021-3553 *Through helping others, you will help yourself.*

LAUFER, BEATRICE, composer; b. N.Y.C.; d. Samuel and Fanny (Silverman) L.; m. Theodore Lassoff, Oct. 2, 1940 (dec. 1955); 1 child, Samuel; m. Seymour H. Rinzler, Oct. 19, 1969 (dec. 1970). Student Julliard Sch. Music, 1944. Composer: Symphony No. 1 (performed by Eastman-Rochester Symphony Orch., 1945-46, performance Germany and Japan under auspices of State Dept., 1948, performed by Nat. Gallery Orch., Washington, 1982), Dance Festival (performed by Eastman-Rochester Symphony, 1946-47); choral compositions include: Under the Pines, Spring Thunder performed Tanglewood, 1949, Song of the Fountain, inter-racial chorus, UN Freedom celebration, 1952; Small Concerto for Chamber Orch. performed McMillan Theatre, Columbia, 1949-50; Ile, opera, world premiere Royal Opera Co., Stockholm, Sweden, 1958, recorded by Yale U. Orch. 1978, Broadcast Nat. Pub. Radio, 1980, 87, performed in Chinese at Nanjing U. World Conf. on O'Neill, Shanghai Opera House, June 1988; Second Symphony performed by Oklahoma City Orch., 1961; premiere concerto at Donnell Library Ctr., 1962; premiere performance Prelude and Fugue for Orch., Brevard Music Ctr., N.C., 1964, Cry! orchestral prelude, Orch. of Am., Town Hall, 1966, Lyric string trio, 1991, Bowdoin Coll. Contemporary Music Festival, 1966, performed with Eastman-Rochester Symphony, 1968, Shreveport Symphony Orch., 1978, Berkshire Symphony Orch., 1981; In the Throes performed Shreveport Symphony, 1980, New Orleans Symphony Orch., 1982, Berkshire Symphony Orch., 1985; Conn. Found. of Arts grantee for performance And Thomas Jefferson Said (symphonic version performed by S.W. Floridan Symphony Orch., 1987), Norwalk Symphony Orch., 1976, 3 excerpts performed by USAF Chamber Players, Washington, 1985, premiere version for concert band baritone solo performed by The Goldman Meml. Band, 1986, also at the Aspen (Colo.) Music Festival, 1987, orchestral performance We Hold These Truths, S.W. Fla. Symphony, Nov. 1987; master ceremonies Young Am. Artists, radio sta. WNYC; hostess The Conductor Speaks series sta. WNYC. Mem. ASCAP, Am. Symphony Orch. League, Am. Music Ctr. Address: PO Box 3 Lenox Hill Sta New York NY 10021

LAUFER, HANS, developmental biologist, educator; b. Germany, Oct. 18, 1929; s. Sol and Margarete (Freundlich) L.; m. Evelyn Green, Oct. 31, 1953; children: Jessica, Marc, Leonard. B.S., CCNY, 1952; M.A., Bklyn. Coll., 1953; Ph.D. (James fellow), Cornell U., Ithaca, N.Y., 1957. Research and teaching asst. Cornell U., 1953-57; NRC fellow Carnegie Instn. of Washington, 1957-59; asst. prof. biology Johns Hopkins U., 1959-65; assoc. prof. U. Conn., Storrs, 1965-72; prof. U. Conn., 1972—; vis. prof. Karolinska Inst., Stockholm, 1972, Charles U., Prague, 1974, Yale U., 1980, Harvard U., 1987-89; participant Nat. Acad. Scis.-Czechoslovak Acad. exchange program, 1974, 77; ad hoc mem. study sect. tropical medicine NIH, 1981, mem., 1982-85; Conklin Meml. fellow Marine Biology Lab., Woods Hole, Mass., 1956, Lalor fellow, 1962, 63, mem. staff, embryology course, 1968-72, mem. corp., 1962—, corp. trustee, 1978-82, mem. exec. com., 1979-80; vis. scholar Case Western Res. U., 1962; mem. NSF-NATO Fellowship Rev. Panel, 1974, 76. Contbg. author numerous books; assoc. editor Jour. Exptl. Zoology, 1969-73, 90-93, archives Insect Physiology and Biochemistry, 1983-95, Invertebrate Reprodn. and Devel., 1984-86, mng. editor, 1991—; contbr. numerous articles to profl. jours. Recipient Rsch. Svc. award NIH, 1989, Marcus Singer medal for rsch., 1986, 95; NATO sr. fellow, 1973, fellow Lady David Trust, Hebrew U., 1988; Japan Soc. Promotion of Sci. fellow, 1980; Rosenstiel scholar Brandeis U., 1973; Dozor vis. prof., Ben Gurion U., 1997. Fellow AAAS (chmn. sect. biology 1975), Royal Entomology Soc. London (fgn. fellow, elected); mem. Internat. Soc. Devel. Biology, Assn. Rsch. Couns. (nat. bd. on grad. edn. of conf. bd. 1971-75), Am. Soc. Zoology (chmn. divsn. developmental biology 1981-82), Soc. Devel. Biology, Am. Soc. Cell Biology, European Soc. Comparative Endocrinology, Am. Assn. Advancement Aging Rsch., Internat. Soc. Differentiation, Tissue Culture Assn. (coun. 1979-82), World Aquaculture Soc. Home: 57 Davis Rd Storrs Mansfield CT 06268-2525 Office: U Conn Dept Molecular & Cell Biology U-125 Storrs Mansfield CT 06268

LAUFER, IRA JEROME, physician; b. N.Y.C., Mar. 29, 1928; s. Irving and Evelyn (Weisman) L.; m. Barbara Alfandari, July 10, 1955; children: Tina, David. BA, NYU, 1948; MD, NYU Sch. Medicine, 1953. Diplomate Am. Bd. Internal Medicine. Instr. clin. medicine NYU Sch. Medicine, N.Y.C., 1959-69, asst. prof. clin. medicine, 1969-83, clin. assoc. prof. medicine, 1983—; dir. diabetes svc. Cabrini Med. Ctr., N.Y.C., 1966-89; dir. medicine N.Y. Eye and Ear Infirmary, N.Y.C., 1978-91; med. dir. Diabetes Treatment Ctr., N.Y.C., 1985-92; physician-in-charge Diabetes Treatment Program, N.Y.C., 1992—; attending physician Cabrini Med. Ctr., N.Y.C., 1989—; assoc. attending physician NYU Med. Ctr., 1983—; lectr. and cons. in field. Co-author: Diabetes Explained, 1976. Capt. USAF, 1955-57, Korea. Recipient Svc. award Am. Diabetes Assn., 1990. Fellow Am. Coll. Clin. Pharmacology, Am. Coll. Endocrinology; mem. ACP. Avocations: tennis. sailing. Office: 247 3rd Ave New York NY 10010-7457

LAUFER, NATHAN, cardiologist; b. Montreal, Mar. 12, 1953; came to U.S., 1981; s. Jack and Pearl (Brachfeld) L.; m. Judy Franceska Egett, Sept. 2, 1986; 1 child, Andrew. DCS, McGill U., 1972, MD, 1977. Diplomate Nat. Bd. Med. Examiners, Am. Bd. Internal Medicine; cert. Profl. Corp. Physicians Que. Intern, resident U. Toronto, Can., 1977-81; fellow cardiology U. Mich., Ann Arbor, 1981-83, faculty dept. cardiology, 1983-84; cardiologist Affiliated Cardiologists, Phoenix, 1984—; dir. coronary care Good Samaritan Hosp., Phoenix, 1986-92; clin. asst. prof. medicine, U. Ariz., Tucson, 1986—; pres. Cardiovascular Soc., Phoenix, 1986—; vis. prof. Chigasaki Tokushu-kai Med. Ctr., Kanagawa-ken, Japan, 1988, Leningrad Postgrad. Med. Inst., St. Petersburg, Russia, 1991; mem. dirs. Integrated Cardiovasc. Group, 1996—. Contbr. articles to profl. jours. Fellow ACP, Am. Coll. Cardiology, Am. Coll. Chest Physicians, Royal Coll. Physicians and Surgeons Can.; mem. AMA, N.Am. Soc. Pacing and Electrophysiology, Soc. Cardiac Angiography and Intervention, Am. Assn. Nuclear Cardiology, Am. Heart Assn. (pres.-elect Ariz. affiliate), Ariz. Med. Assn., Can. Cardiovascular Soc., Maricopa County Med. Assn., Cardiovascular Soc. Ariz. (founder, pres.). Avocations: skiing, tennis, computers, music, films. Home: 9100 N 55th St Paradise Valley AZ 85253 Office: Affiliated Cardiologists 370 E Virginia Phoenix AZ 85004

LAUFF, GEORGE HOWARD, biologist; b. Milan, Mich., Mar. 23, 1927; s. George John and Mary Anna (Klein) L. B.S., Mich. State U., 1949, M.S., 1951; postgrad., U. Mont., 1951, U. Wash., 1952; Ph.D., Cornell U., 1953. Fisheries research technician Mich. Dept. Conservation, 1950; teaching asst. Cornell U., 1952-53; instr. U. Mich., 1953-57, asst. prof., 1957-61, asso. prof., 1961-62; research asso. Gt. Lakes Research Inst., U. Mich., 1954-59; dir. U. Ga. Marine Inst., 1960-62; asso. prof. U. Ga., 1960-62; research coord. Sapelo Island Research Found., 1962-64; dir. Kellogg Biol. Sta., 1964-90; prof. dept. fisheries and wildlife and zoology Mich. State U., East Lansing, 1964-91, prof. emeritus, 1991—; mem. cons. and rev. panels for Smithsonian Inst., Nat. Water Commn., NSF, Nat. Acad. Sci., Am. Inst. Biol. Sci., U.S. AEC, Inst. Ecology, others. Editor: Estuaries, 1967, Experimental Ecological Reserves, 1977. Served with inf. U.S. Army, 1944-46. Office of Naval Research grantee; U.S. Dept. Interior grantee; NSF grantee; others. Fellow AAAS; mem. Am. Inst. Biol. Sci., Am. Soc. Limnology and Oceanography (pres. 1972-73), Ecol. Soc. Am., Freshwater Biology Assn., INTECOL, Societas Internationalis Limnologiae, Orgn. Biol. Field Stas., Sigma Xi, Phi Kappa Phi. Home: 3818 Heights Dr Hickory Corners MI 49060-9504 Office: 3700 E Gull Lake Dr Hickory Corners MI 49060-9505

LAUFMAN, HAROLD, surgeon; b. Milw., Jan. 6, 1912; s. Jacob and Sophia (Peters) L.; m. Marilyn Joselit, 1940 (dec. 1963); children: Dionne Joselit Weigert, Laurien Laufman Kogut; m. June Friend Moses, 1980. BS, U. Chgo., 1932; MD, Rush Med. Coll., 1937; MS in Surgery, Northwestern U., Chgo., 1946, PhD, 1948. Diplomate: Am. Bd. Surgery. Intern Michael Reese Hosp., Chgo., 1936-39; resident in gen. surgery St. Marks Hosp., London, Northwestern U. Med. Sch., Cook County Hosp., Hines VA Hosp., 1939-46; mem. faculty Northwestern U., 1941-65; from clin. asst. to prof., attending surgeon Passavant Meml. Hosp., Chgo., 1953-65; prof. surgery, history of medicine Albert Einstein Coll. Medicine, N.Y.C., 1965-82, prof. emeritus, 1982—; dir. Inst. Surg. Studies, Montefiore Hosp. and Med. Center, Bronx, N.Y., 1965-81; pvt. practice gen. and vascular surgery Chgo., 1941-65, N.Y.C., 1965-81; ret. professorial lectr. surgery Mt. Sinai Sch. Medicine, N.Y.C., 1979-83, emeritus, 1983—; attending surgeon Mt. Sinai Hosp., N.Y.C., 1979-83; cons., lectr. in field; chmn. FDA Classification Panel Gen. and Plastic Surgery Devices, 1975-78; pres. Harold Laufman Assocs., Inc., 1977—, sr. ptnr., 1988—; pres. HLA Systems. Author: (with S.W. Banks) Surgical Exposures of the Extremities, 1953, 2d edit., 1986, (with R.B. Erichson) Hematologic Problems in Surgery, 1970, Hospital Special Care Facilities, 1981, The Veins, 1986; chmn. editorial bd.: Diagnostica, 1974-79; mem. editorial bd.: Surgery, Gynecology and Obstetrics, 1974-92, Infection Control, 1980-88, Med. Instrumentation, 1972-83, Med. Rsch. Engring., 1972-79; contbr. articles to sci. publs. Chmn. bd. dirs. N.Y. Chamber Soloists, 1974-80, Chamber Music Conf. and Composers Forum of the East, 1975-91. Maj. AUS, 1942-46. Named Disting. Alumnus Rush Med. Coll., 1993. Fellow ACS; mem. Assn. Advancement Med. Instrumentation (pres. 1974-75, chmn. bd. 1976-77), Am. Assn. Hosp. Cons., Am. Med. Writers Assn. (pres. 1968-69), Am. Surg. Assn., Société Internationale de Chirurgie, Western Surg. Assn., Cen. Surg. Assn., N.Y. Surg. Soc., Soc. Vascular Surgery, Internat. Cardiovascular Soc., Soc. Surgery Alimentary Tract, Surg. Infection Soc. (councillor 1980-84), Sigma Xi, Alpha Omega Alpha, Phi Sigma Delta, Zeta Beta Tau. Jewish. Clubs: Harmonie (N.Y.C.); Willow Ridge Country (Harrison, N.Y.). Home and Office: 31 E 72nd St New York NY 10021-4146

LAUFMAN, LESLIE RODGERS, hematologist, oncologist; b. Pitts., Dec. 13, 1946; d. Marshall Charles and Ruth Rodgers; m. Harry B. Laufman, Apr. 25, 1970 (div. Apr. 1984); children: Hal, Holly; m. Rodger Mitchell, Oct. 9, 1987. BA in Chemistry, Ohio Wesleyan U., 1968; MD, U. Pitts., 1972. Diplomate Am. Bd. Internal Medicine and Hematology. Intern Montefiore Hosp., Pitts., 1972-73, resident in internal medicine, 1973-74; fellow in hemotology and oncology Ohio State Hosp., Columbus, 1974-76; dir. med. oncology Grant Med. Ctr., Columbus, 1977-92; practice medicine specializing in hematology and oncology Columbus, 1977—; bd. dirs. Columbus Cancer Clinic; prin. investigator Columbus Cmty. Clin. Oncology Program, 1989—. Contbr. articles to profl. jours. Mem. AMA, Am. Women Med. Assn. (sec./treas. 1985-86, pres. 1986-87), Am. Soc. Clin. Oncology, Southwest Oncology Group, Nat. Surg. Adjuvant Project for Breast and Bowel Cancers. Avocations: tennis, piano, sailing, hiking, travel. Office: 393 E Town St # 109 Columbus OH 43215-4741 also: 8100 Ravines Edge Ct Columbus OH 43235-5426

LAUGHLIN, CHARLES WILLIAM, agriculture educator, research administrator; b. Iowa City, Iowa, Dec. 9, 1939; s. Ralph Minard and Geraldine (O'Neill) L.; m. Barbara Waln, Dec. 17, 1966; children: Shannon Morris, Charles Tudor. BS, Iowa State U., 1963; MS, U. Md., 1966; PhD, Va. Tech., 1969. Asst. extension nematologist U. Fla., Gainesville, 1968-69; asst. prof., extension nematologist Mich. State U., East Lansing, 1969-73, assoc. prof., asst. dir. acad. and student affairs, 1973-78, prof., asst. dean, dir. acad. and student affairs, 1978-80; prof., dept. head plant pathology and weed sci. Miss. State U., Starkville, 1980-83; prof., assoc. dir. Ga. Agrl. Expt. Sta. U. Ga., Athens, 1983-92; dir. co., Agrl. Expt. Sta. Colo. State U., Ft. Collins, 1992-96; dean coll. tropical agriculture and human resources U. Hawaii, Honolulu, 1996—; cons. Brazilian Ministry of Edn. and Culture, Brasilia, Brazil, 1975-77, Brazilian Nat. Agrl. Rsch. Agy., 1978, W.K. Kellogg Found., Battle Creek, Mich., 1983—, Latin Am. Inst. of Creativity, São Paulo, Brazil, 1991. Recipient Colleague award Creative Edn. Found., 1988. Mem. Soc. Nematologists, Am. Phytopathological Soc., Brazilian Soc. Nematologists. Avocations: creative problem solving, outdoors recreation. Address: 3050 Maile Way Gilmore 202 Honolulu HI 96821

LAUGHLIN, DAVID EUGENE, materials science educator, metallurgical consultant; b. Phila., July 15, 1947; s. Eugene L. and Myrtle M. (Kramer) L.; m. Diane Rae Seamans, June 13, 1970; children—Jonathan, Elizabeth, Andrew, Daniel. B.Sc., Drexel U., 1969; Ph.D., MIT, 1973. Asst. prof. materials sci. Carnegie-Mellon U., Pitts., 1974-78, assoc. prof., 1978-82, prof., 1982—; rsch. scientist Oxford (Eng.) U., 1985; vis. scientist Alcoa Tech. Ctr., Pa., 1996—. Editor: Solid-Solid Phase Transformations, 1982; category editor of copper: Am. Soc. Metals-Nat. Bur. Stds. Phase Diagram Program, 1981-94; assoc. editor: Metall. Trans., 1982-87, editor, 1987—; contbr. more than 200 articles to profl. jours. Mem. sch. bd. Trinity Christian Sch., Pitts., 1976-85, 87-95, pres., 1978-83, sec., 1988-91, pres., 1991-94; ruling elder Covenant Presbyn. Ch., Pitts., 1982-96; foster parent Children's Home of Pitts., 1984-90; bd. dirs. Christian Schs. Internat., 1991—. Recipient Ladd Teaching award Carnegie-Mellon U., 1975; postdoctoral fellow Nat. Acad. Scis., 1974. Fellow Am. Soc. Metals; mem. Metallurgical Soc. of AIME, Am. Sci. Affiliation, Materials Rsch. Soc. Episcopalian. Avocations: sports; books. Home: 2357 Mcnary Blvd Pittsburgh PA 15235-2779 Office: Carnegie-Mellon U Dept Materials Sci Eng Pittsburgh PA 15213

LAUGHLIN, FELIX B., lawyer; b. New Orleans, Dec. 4, 1942; m. Betty Gayle Laughlin. BS with honors, U. Tenn., 1967, JD with honors, 1967; LLM, Georgetown U., 1971. Bar: Tenn. 1967, D.C. 1972, U.S. Ct. Claims 1969, U.S. Tax Ct. 1968, U.S. Dist. Ct. D.C. 1972, U.S. Ct. Appeals (D.C. cir.) 1988, U.S. Ct. Appeals (fed. cir.) 1992, U.S. Supreme Ct. 1970. With interpretation divsn. Office Chief Counsel IRS, 1967-71; assoc. Dewey Ballantine, Washington, 1972—, mem., 1975—. Dir. Friends of U.S. Nat. Arboretum, Nat. Bonsai Found. Mem. ABA (tax sect.), Fed. Bar Assn. (chmn. tax sect. 1989), Met. Club (Washington), George Town Club (Washington), Order of Coif, Sigma Alpha Epsilon, Phi Eta Sigma, Phi Kappa Phi, Phi Delta Phi. Office: Dewey Ballantine 1775 Pennsylvania Ave NW Washington DC 20006-4605

LAUGHLIN, GREGORY H. (GREG LAUGHLIN), congressman; b. Bay City, Tex., Jan. 21, 1942. BA, Tex. A&M U.; LLB, U. Tex. Asst. dist. atty. Harris County, Tex., 1970-74; pvt. practice Tex.; mem. 101st-104th Congresses from 14th Tex. dist., Washington, D.C., 1989-97; of counsel Patton Boggs, LLP, Washington, 1997—. With AUS; col. USAR. Office: Patton Boggs LLP 2550 M St NW Washington DC 20037-1301

LAUGHLIN, HENRY PRATHER, physician, psychiatrist, educator, author, editor; b. Hagerstown, Md., June 25, 1916; s. John Royer and Myrtle Frances (Binkley) L.; m. Marion Page Durkee, June 2, 1941; children: Constance Ann Kuhn, John Royer II, Robert Scott, Barbara Hilton Galant, Deborah Page Mayer. Student, Johns Hopkins U, 1936,1938; BS, Ursinus Coll., 1937, ScD, 1976; MD, Temple U., 1941; D Social Sci., U. Louisville, 1978; LittD, Albright Coll., 1994; PSD, Washington Coll., 1995. Diplomate Am. Bd. Psychiatry and Neurology, Nat. Bd. Med. Examiners. Pvt. practice Md., 1947-92; faculty psychiatry George Washington U, 1947-83; clin. prof. psychiatry George Washington U., 1948-83; disting. vis. prof. U. Louisville, 1974-89, adj. prof. emeritus, 1989; vis. prof. 60 med. ctrs. around the world, 1950-93; pres. Nat. Psychiat. Endowment Fund, Washington, Frederick, Md.,1957-91; pres. Med. Coun. of the Washington Met. area, 1959-1961; exec. dir. Nat. Inst. of Emerging Tech., Frederick, 1989-92, mem.; bd. dirs. Ursinus Coll., Collegeville, Pa., 1967-77, life mem. 1985; cons. 14 U.S. agys., Washington, 1974-79; asst. or assoc. examiner Am. Bd. Psychiatry and Neurology, 1948-82; cons. editor in psychoanalysis Psychosomatics, N.Y., 1977-87; cons. Walter Reed Army Med. Ctr., 1949-57, Nat. Naval Med. Ctr., 1972-79; co-founder, bd. dirs. Robert R. Luce Inc. Pubs., Washington, 1957-62; owner Montgomery House, Bethesda, Md. 1959-84, owner Kings Park Plz., Hyattsville, Md., 1965—; co-developer So. Manor Country Club, Boca Raton, Fla., 1970-73; dir., sec., 1982-84, dir., 1987-94, Galaxy Cos., Frederick, Md.; bd. dirs. Frederick Trading Co., 1991—, Capital Investment Co., Washington, 1959-62; co-founder, v.p., treas. Alaska-N.Am. Investment Co., Washington, 1958-62; chief psychiatry and neurology, 1954-64, attending staff, cons. to 1977, emeritus med. staff 1977—, Suburban Hosp., Bethesda, Md.; cons., emeritus staff Frederick Meml. Hosp., 1976-94, mem. hon. staff, 1994—; hon. mem. med. staff The Sheppard Pratt Health Sys., Balt., 1997. Author: The Neuroses in Clinical Practice, 1956, Mental Mechanisms, 1963, The Neuroses, 1967, 70, The Ego and Its Defenses, 1970, 79, 17 other books; assoc. editor Md. Med. Jour., 1988—; assoc. editor Physician's Practice Digest, 1989-92, editor, 1992-94, editor emeritus, 1994—; contbr. more than 148 articles and revs. to profl. jours., reports, chpts. to books. 2d pres. Linganore H.S. PTA, Frederick County, 1964-66; pres. CAMPER, U.S. Park Svc., Catoctin Mountain Park, 1987-90, bd. dirs., 1980-94, Md. Sheriffs Youth Ranch, Frederick County, 1989-90, bd. dirs., 1989-96; grand marshal Nat. Independence Day parade, Washington, 1988, 89, Grand Marshal emeritus, 1989—; capt. USN Admiral's Team, Lander, Wyo., One Shot Unit, 1991; bd. assocs. Hood Coll., 1988—; trustee, Francis Scott Key Meml. Found., 1988—; pres. Dr. Henry P. and M. Page Durkee Laughlin Found., 1991—. With MC, USN, 1941-47. Decorated six medals with four battle stars; recipient Disting. Alumni award Ursinus Coll., 1966, the Laughlin prize established in his hon., Royal Coll. Physiciatrists of Great Britain, 1979—, Laughlin Profl./Ursinus Coll. faculty achievement award established in his honor, 1988, three Salute to Excellence awards, 1990-92, 6 gov.'s citations State of Md., from 1969, hon. citizenship/comms. various states, 1st Internat. Patriot's award OAS, 1993, Pres. Spl. Achievement award Md. Sheriffs Youth Ranch, 1993, Spl. Recognition plaque Md. Sheriff's Youth Ranch, 1996, others; co-recipient Benefactor award Frederick County Mental Health Assn., 1996; Five Ann. awards at Am. Banquets in Balt. named for Dr. Henry P. Laughlin and Mrs. M. Page Duvree Laughlin. Fellow Am. Psychiat. Assn. (life), Am. Soc. of Physician Analysts (founder, hon. lifetime pres. 1982), Royal Coll. Psychiatrists (hon.), Am. Coll. of Psychiatrists (founder, pres. 1963-65), hon. mem. National Accreditation Assn. in psychoanalysis, 1978—, Am. Coll. of Psychoanalysts (founder, 1st and 8th pres., hon. life pres. 1979, established Laughlin Fellowship program, 1994—, Laughlin fellow, 1977, Gold medals 1965, 76, plaque for significant contbns. as hon. life pres. 1994), USN Psychiatrists (commodore 1978-80, hon. life commodore 1980), USN Admirals Team (capt. 1991), Med. and Chirurg. Faculty of Medicine Md. (mem. coun. 1962-73, 88-92), emeritus fellow Am. Soc. Psychoanalytic pysicians, 1987—, Montgomery County Med. Soc. (pres. 1959-60, emeritus mem. 1985), hon. mem Titus Harris Psychiatric Soc. of Tex., Frederick County Med. Soc. emeritus (pres. 1991, 92, 93), SAR (MD soc. pres. 1987-88, Md. surgeon 1994-95, v.p. gen. nat. soc. 1988, surgeon gen. 1990-91, various nat. coms. 1986—, numerous awards), Nat. Congress of Patriotic Orgns. (co-founder, inaugural pres. emeritus 1991), Am. Legion, U.K. Soc. SAR (trustee 1989-91, inaugural pres. coun. of pres. Md. Soc. 1992-94, inaugural pres. emeritus, 1994—), Gov. Md. Sons and Dau. of the Pilgrims (hon. gov. 1995), Gen. Soc. War of 1812, Pan Am. Bldg. Orgn. Am. States (1st Internat. Patriots award 1993), Rotary (Nat. Marksmanship award with Sterling Silver Cup 1996). Avocations: philately, geneology, philanthropy, big game hunting, marksmanship. Home: Freehold Park 7977 Timmons Rd Union Bridge MD 21791-7699

LAUGHLIN, JAMES, publishing company executive, writer, lecturer; b. Pitts., Oct. 30, 1914; s. Henry Hughart and Marjory (Rea) L.; m. Margaret Keyser, Mar. 13, 1942 (div. 1952); children: Paul, Leila; m. Ann Clark Resor, May 19, 1956 (dec. Nov. 1987); children: Robert (dec.), Henry; m. Gertrude Huston, Dec. 5, 1991. A.B., Harvard U., 1939; Litt.D. (hon.), Hamilton Coll., 1969, Colgate U., 1978; H.H.D. (hon.), Duquesne U., 1980; L.H.D., Yale U., 1982, Brown U., 1984, Bellarmine Coll., 1987, St. Joseph's Coll., Hartford, 1993. Founder New Directions (now New Directions Pub. Corp.), N.Y.C., 1936; pres. New Directions (now New Directions Pub. Corp.), 1964—, Intercultural Publs., Inc; pub. Perspectives, USA and Perspectives supplements The Atlantic Monthly Jour.; cons. Indian So. Langs. Book Trust, Madras, 1955; vis. Regents prof. U. Calif., San Diego, 1974; Ida Bean vis. prof. U. Iowa, 1981; chmn. creative writing panel Inst. Internat. Edn. Conf. on Arts Exchange, 1956—; adj. prof. English, Brown U., 1983, 85. Author: Some Natural Things, 1945, A Small Book of Poems, 1948, The Wild Anemone and Other Poems, 1957, Selected Poems, 1960, The Pig, 1970, Thomas Merton and James Laughlin: Selected Letters, 1977; In Another Country, 1978, Stolen and Contaminated Poems, 1984, The House of Light, 1986, Selected Poems, 1986, The Owl of Minerva, 1987, Pound as Wuz, 1987, William Carlos Williams and James Laughlin: Selected Letters, 1989, The Bird of Endless Time, 1990, Kenneth Rexroth and James Laughlin: Selected Letters, 1991, Random Essays, Random Stories, 1991, The Man in the Wall, 1993, Delmore Schwartz and James Laughlin: Selected Letters, 1993, Collected Poems, 1994, Ezra Pound and James Laughlin: Selected Letters, 1994, (novella) Angelica, 1993, Collected Poems, 1994, Phantoms, 1995, The Country Road, 1995, Heart Island, 1996, The Secret Room, 1997; profiled in New Yorker; contbr. mags. and books; collector lit. mags. (little mag. type); active prodn. documentary films on modern poets, 1983—. Bd. dirs. Goethe Bi-Centennial Found., 1949, Aspen (Colo.) Inst. Humanities, 1950; mem. Nat. Citizens Commn. for Internat. Cooperation, U.S. Nat. Commn. for UNESCO, 1960-63, Nat. Commn. for Internat. Coop. year, 1966; past trustee Allen-Chase Found.; mem. vis. com. German Princeton U.; mem. vis. com. dept. Romance langs. Harvard U.; co-trustee Merton Legacy Trust, 1969—; trustee Rosenbach Found., Phila., to 1981. Decorated chevalier Legion of Honor; hon. fellow Coll. Five, U. Calif., Santa Cruz, 1972—; recipient Disting. Svc. award Am. Acad. Arts and Letters, 1977, award for pub. PEN, 1979, Carey-Thomas citation Pubs. Weekly, 1978, Conn. Arts Comn. award, 1986, Nat. Book Found. medal for Disting. Contbn. to Am. Letters, 1992. Mem. AAAL (elected), Am. Acad. Arts and Scis., Alta Ski Lifts Co. (formerly Salt Lake City Winter Sports Assn.; dir. 1939—, v.p. 1958), Alta Lodge Co. (v.p. 1948-58, pres. 1958-59), PEN, Asia Soc. (chmn. publs. com. 1959-67), Century Assn. (N.Y.C.), Harvard Club of N.Y.C. Office: New Directions Pub Corp 80 8th Ave New York NY 10011-5126

LAUGHLIN, JOHN SETH, physicist, educator; b. Canton, Mo., Jan. 26, 1918; s. Sceva Bright and Catherine (Goodall) L.; m. Barbara Kester, June 14, 1943; children—Catherine Ann, Frances Elizabeth, Janet Judd; m. Eunice Chapin Beyersdorf, June 23, 1979. A.B., Willamette U., 1940, D.Sc., 1968; M.S., Haverford Coll., 1942; Ph.D., U. Ill., 1947. Diplomate: Am. Bd. Radiology. Research physicist OSRD, 1944-45; asst. prof. dept. physics U. Ill., 1946-48, assoc. prof. radiology, 1951-52; attending physicist Meml. Hosp., chmn. dept. med. physics, 1952-89; chief div. biophysics Sloan-Kettering Inst., N.Y.C., 1952-89; v.p. Sloan-Kettering Inst., 1966-72; prof. biophysics Sloan Kettering div. Cornell U. Grad. Sch., 1955-96; prof. radiology Cornell U. Med. Coll., 1970-96, emeritus prof., 1996—; dir. N.E. Center for Radiol. Physics, 1974-85; emeritus Meml. Sloan-Kettering Cancer Ctr., 1996—; chmn. med. radiation adv. com. Bur. Radiol. Health, 1976-79; John Wiley Jones lectr. Rochester Inst. Tech., 1977. Author: Physical Aspects of Betatron Therapy, 1954; editor: Medical Physics, 1988-97. Recipient Distinguished Service Alumni award U. Ill. Coll. Engring., 1972; Alumni citation Willamette U., 1964; Disting. Service award Health Physics Soc., 1982. Fellow Am. Phys. Soc., Am. Coll. Radiology (Gold medalist), N.Y. Acad. Scis., Am. Inst. Med. and BIol. Engring, Sigma Xi; mem. AAAS, Am. Soc. Therapeutic Radiology and Oncology (Gold medal 1993), Health Physics Soc. (pres. 1960-61), Assn. Tchrs. Physics, Radiol. Soc. N.Am., Soc. Nuclear Medicine (dir., Aebersold award 1984), Am. Radium Soc. (Gold medal 1986), Internat. Orgn. Med. Physics (v.p. 1965-69, pres. 1969-72), Radiation Research Soc. (pres. 1970-71), Am. Assn. Physicists in Medicine (pres. 1964-65, chmn. sci. com. 1968-75, Coolidge award 1974), Am. Coll. Med. Physicists (Williams award 1992). Mem. Soc. of Friends. Home: 48 Graham Rd Scarsdale NY 10583-7256 Office: 1275 York Ave New York NY 10021-6007

LAUGHLIN, LOUIS GENE, economic analyst, consultant; b. Santa Barbara, Calif., Sept. 20, 1937; s. Eston A. and Cornelia Helen (Snively) L.; student Pomona Coll., 1955-58; BA, U. Calif., Santa Barbara, 1960; post-grad. Claremont Grad. Sch., 1966-70, 85-86, Sch. Bank Mktg., U. Colo., 1974-75, Grad. Sch. Mgmt., U. Calif.-Irvine, 1983. Mgr., Wheeldex-L.A. Co., 1961-62; v.p. Warner/Walker Assocs., Inc., L.A., 1962; cons. Spectra-Sound Corp., L.A., 1964-65; rep. A.C. Nielsen Co., Chgo., 1962-64; rsch. analyst Security Pacific Nat. Bank, L.A., 1964-67, asst. rsch. mgr., 1967-68, asst. v.p., 1968-72, v.p., mgr. market info. and rsch. div., 1972-76, v.p. rsch. adminstrn., pub. affairs/rsch. dept., 1976-82, v.p. govt. rels. dept., 1982-85; dir. R & D Applied Mgmt. Systems, South Pasadena, Calif., 1986; pres. L.G. Laughlin & Assoc., Houston, 1987—; prin. Courtyard Holdings, Houston, 1988—; pres. CEO, Mastodon Capital Corp., Houston, 1988-89, 94—; corp. sec. Kestco Co. Inc., Laguna Beach, Calif.; mem. Nat. Conf. on Fin. Svcs., 1982-84, mem. policy coun., 1983-84; mem. policy coun. Nat. Conf. on Competition in Banking, 1978-79, 81. Sec. econs. Town Hall of Calif., 1966. Mem. Am. Econs. Assn., Western Econ. Assn., Nat. Assn. Bus. Economists, L.A. C. of C. (food and agr. adv. com. 1981).

LAUGHLIN, NANCY, newspaper editor. Nation/world editor Detroit Free Press. Office: Detroit Free Press Inc 321 W Lafayette Blvd Detroit MI 48226

LAUGHLIN, WILLIAM EUGENE, electric power industry executive; b. Sheffield, Ala., May 4, 1936; s. Rawlie Wayne and Nina Louise (Campbell) L.; m. Donna Lynn Blackburn, Jan. 3, 1958; children: Kevin McGregor, Christopher Scott, Laura Shannon, Alison Paige. BS, Auburn U., 1961. Registered profl. and electrical engr., Ala., Tenn., Miss. Elec. engr. Dept. Power, Water and Gas, City of Sheffield, 1961-66; chief engr., asst. mgr. Electric Plant Bd., Bowling Green, Ky., 1966-76; systems mgr. Bowling Green Mcpl. Utilities, 1975-77; gen. mgr. Fayetteville (Tenn.) Electric Systems, 1977-81, Talquin Electric Coop. Inc., Quincy, Fla., 1981—; bd. dirs., v.p. Seminole Electric Coop., Inc., Tampa, Fla.; pres. Fla. Rural Electric Coop. Assn., Tallahassee. Pres. Boys Club, Bowling Green, 1972; v.p. Bowling Green C. of C., 1975, Fayetteville C. of C., 1979; dist. chmn. Boy Scouts Am., Bowling Green, 1972, Fayetteville, 1978; pres. Fayetteville United Way, 1980. Mem. Nat. Rural Elec. Coop. Assn. (mem. regional com., nat. water task force 1995), Am. Water Works Assn., Rotary (bd. dirs. 1986-87, pres. Quincy club 1996-97), Fayetteville 1978-79), Kiwanis (dir. Bowling Green club 1973-74). Democrat. Mem. Ch. of Christ. Home: 2110 Ellicott Dr Tallahassee FL 32312-3118 Office: Talquin Electric Coop Inc PO Box 1679 Quincy FL 32353-1679

LAUGHREN, TERRY, marketing executive; b. Trenton, N.J., July 6, 1940; s. Donald Dunn and Hazel Melinda (Rogers) L.; children: Laurie Margot, B. Kenneth, Brandon Keith. BSBA with honors, Boston U., 1961. Brand mgr. Procter & Gamble Co., Cin., 1963-70; dir. mktg. Internat. Playtex Corp., N.Y.C., 1970-71; dir. corp. mktg. Mattel Inc., Hawthorne, Calif., 1971-72; pres., CEO Metaframe Corp. (subs. of Mattel), Elmwood Park, N.J., 1972-75; exec. v.p. J. Walter Thompson, Detroit and N.Y.C., 1976-80; pres. FTTL Media Co., 1981—; pres., mng. ptnr. Screenvision Cinema Network, N.Y.C., 1981-89, chmn., 1990. 1st lt. U.S. Army, 1961-63. Mem. Young Pres.'s Orgn., Nat. Alumni Coun. Boston U. (chmn.), Econ. Club Detroit, Adcraft Club, Friar's Club, Beta Gamma Sigma. Republican. Office: FTTL Media Co Inc Ste 302 311 W 43d St New York NY 10036-6413

LAUGHTER, BENNIE M., corporate lawyer. AB with honors, U. N.C., 1973; JD, Georgetown U., 1976. Bar: N.C. 1976, D.C. 1977, Ill. 1979, Ga. 1987. V.p., gen. counsel, corp. sec. Shaw Industries, Dalton, Ga., 1986—. Office: Shaw Industries Inc 616 E Walnut Ave PO Drawer 2128 Dalton GA 30722-2128

LAULICHT, MURRAY JACK, lawyer; b. Bklyn., May 12, 1940; s. Philip and Ernestine (Greenfield) L.; m. Linda Kushner, Apr. 4, 1965; children: Laurie Hasten, Pamela Hirt, Shellie Davis, Abigail Herschmann. BA, Yeshiva U., 1961; LLB summa cum laude, Columbia U., 1964. Bar: N.Y. 1965, N.J. 1968, U.S. Supreme Ct. 1976. Mem. legal staff Warren Commn., Washington, 1964; assoc. Kaye, Scholer, Fierman, Hays & Handler, N.Y.C., 1965-68; ptnr. Lowenstein, Sandler, Brochin, Kohl & Fisher, Newark, N.J., 1968-79, Pitney, Hardin, Kipp & Szuch, Florham Park, N.J., 1979—. Mem. N.J. Consumer Affairs Adv. Com., 1991-93; chmn. N.J. Commn. on Holocaust Edn., 1992-95; pres. Jewish Edn. Assn., 1981-84, Jewish Fedn. Metro West, 1996—; chmn. Cmty. Rels. Com., 1988-91; mem. exec. comm. Coun. of Jewish Fedn., 1996—. Recipient Julius Cohn Young Leadership award Jewish Fedn. Metrowest, 1976. Mem. ABA, N.J. State Bar Assn. (dist. X ethics com. 1986-89, bd. editors N.J. Law Jour. 1986-93), N.J. Lawyer Mag. (chmn. 1993-95). Democrat. Avocations: computers, communal activities. Home: 18 Crestwood Dr West Orange NJ 07052-2004 Office: Pitney Hardin Kipp & Szuch PO Box 1945 200 Campus Dr Florham Park NJ 07932-1012

LAUMAN, RICHARD H., JR., nuclear energy executive; b. Rockville Center, N.Y., Aug. 12, 1956; s. Richard H. and Joane M. (Albright) L.; m. Laura H. Cady, Aug. 28, 1982; 1 child, Richard H., III. B in Mech. Engring., Villanova U., 1978; MBA, Pace U., 1994. Field engr. Gen. Electric Co., Phila., 1979-81; mech. engr. Ebasco Svcs., Inc., N.Y.C., 1981-82; engr. nuc. ops. and maintenance N.Y. Power Authority, White Plains, 1982-86, sr. engr., 1986-88, dir. nuc. ops. and maintenance, 1988-92, dir. nuc. bus. ops., 1992—. Mem. ASME, Am. Mgmt. Assn., Planning Forum. Avocations: skiing, windsurfing, sailing. Home: 9 Serendipity Ln Wilton CT 06897-1314 Office: NY Power Authority 123 Main St White Plains NY 10601-3104

LAUMANN, ANNE ELIZABETH, dermatologist; b. Beaconsfield, Bucks, Eng., Jan. 31, 1946; came to U.S. 1976; d. Richard M. and Suzanne Marie (Weisman) Solomon; m. Edward Otto Laumann, June 21, 1980; children: Christopher Richard, Timothy Otto. MB, ChB, Birmingham Med. Sch., Eng., 1968. Diplomate Am. Bd. Dermatology. Resident in dermatology U. Chgo., 1977-79; asst. prof. dermatology U. Ill., Chgo., 1980-85; clin. asst. prof. U. Chgo., 1987-90; clin. practice dermatology Group Practice South Side Chgo., 1979—, Michael Reese Hosp. Health Plan now Humana HMO, 1986—; clin. asst. prof. dermatology U. Ill., Chgo., 1990—; interim divsn. dir. dermatology Michael Reese Hosp., Chgo., 1995—; mem. various coms. Michael Reese Hosp., Humana HMO. Fellow Am. Acad. Dermatology; mem. Royal Coll. Physicians, Brit. Assn. Dermatology, Am. Women's Dermatology Assn., Chgo. Dermatology Soc., Ill. Dermatology Soc., Am. Soc. of Psychocutaneous Medicine. Episcopalian. Avocations: hiking, cooking, children. Home: 6754 S Euclid Ave Chicago IL 60649-1028 Office: Michael Reese Hosp 2816 S Ellis Ave Chicago IL 60616-2907

LAUMANN, EDWARD OTTO, sociology educator; b. Youngstown, Ohio, Aug. 31, 1938; m. Anne Elizabeth Solomon, June 21, 1980; children: Christopher, Timothy; children by previous marriage: Eric, Lisa. AB summa cum laude, Oberlin Coll., 1960; MA, Harvard U., 1962, PhD, 1964. Asst. prof. sociology U. Mich., Ann Arbor, 1964-69, assoc. prof., 1969-72; prof. sociology U. Chgo., 1973—, George Herbert Mead Disting. Service prof., 1985—, chmn. dept., 1981-84, 97—, dean div. of social scis., 1984-92, provost, 1992-93; bd. govs. Argonne Nat. Lab., 1992-93. Author: Prestige and Associations in an Urban Community, 1966, Bonds of Pluralism, 1973, (with Franz U. Pappi) Networks of Collective Action, 1976, (with John P. Heinz) Chicago Lawyers, 1982, (with David Knoke) The Organizational State, 1987, (with John P. Heinz, Robert Nelson and Robert Salisbury) The Hollow Core, 1993, (with John Gagnon, Robert Michael, Stuart Michaels) The Social Organization of Sexuality, 1994, (with Robert Michael, John Gagnon, Gina Kolata) Sex in America, 1994; editor Am. Jour. Sociology, 1978-84, 95—. Mem. sociology panel NSF, Washington, 1972-74; commr. CBASSE, NRC, 1986-91; v.p., trustee NORC; trustee U. Chgo. Hosps., 1992-93. Fellow AAAS; mem. Sociol. Rsch. Assn., Am. Sociol. Assn., Population Assn. Am. Office: U Chgo 5848 S University Ave Chicago IL 60637-1515

LAUN, LOUIS FREDERICK, government official; b. Battle Creek, Mich., May 19, 1920; s. Louis Frederick and Roena (Graves) L.; m. Margaret West, Jan. 25, 1947; children: Nancy, Kathryn Webb, Margaret. B.A., Yale U., 1942. Asst. advt. mgr. Bates Fabrics, Inc., N.Y.C., 1946-48; asst. to pres., indsl. and public relations Bates Mfg. Co., Lewiston, Maine, 1948-55; advt. dir., out-of-town sales mgr. Burlington Industries, N.Y.C., 1955-57; gen. merchandising mgr. Celanese Fibers Co., N.Y.C., 1957-60; v.p., dir. mktg. Celanese Fibers Co., 1960-63, exec. v.p. mktg., 1963-64; pres. Celanese Fibers Mktg. Co. div. Celanese Corp., 1964-71, also v.p. corp., 1964-71; asso. adminstr. ops. SBA, Washington, 1971; dep. adminstr. SBA, 1973-77; pres. Am. Paper Inst., N.Y.C., 1977-86; asst. Sec. Commerce for Internat. Econ. Policy Dept. of Commerce, Washington, 1986-89, exec. br. commr., Commn. on Security and Cooperation in Europe, 1988-89; cons. Nat. Exec Svc. Corp, 1989—; U.S. pulp and paper rep. food and agrl. orgns. UN; bd. dirs. Overseas Pvt. Investment Corp., Noranda Aluminum, Inc.; exec. br. mem. Commn. on Security and Cooperation in Europe (Helsinki Commn.). Bd. dirs. N.Y. Bd. Trade, Better Bus. Bur. N.Y., Alliance to Save Energy, Bus. Adv. Com. on Fed. Reports, Citizens Against Govt. Waste; indsl. asst. to chmn. Opportunities Industrialization Centers Am.; nat. adv. council SBA; chmn. Republican Industry Workshop program; field dir. Com. for Re-election of Pres., 1972; trustee Taft Sch.; mem. exec. com. President's Pvt. Sector Survey on Cost Control. Served with USMCR, 1942-46. Decorated Bronze Star; recipient Human Rights award Anti-Defamation League, 1968; Achievement award Textile Vets. Assn., 1970; named Young Man of Yr. Lewiston-Auburn C. of C., 1953, Man of Yr. Textile Salesman Assn., 1970, Man of Yr. Fabric Salesmen's Guild, 1971; Gold medal for disting. service SBA, Citation Merit Taft Sch., 1988. Mem. Color Assn. U.S. (sec.), Man-Made Fiber Producers Assn. (chmn. 1967-69), Yale Club (N.Y.C.), Sleepy Hollow Country Club (Scarborough, N.Y.), Met. Club (Washington), Mid-Ocean Club (Bermuda). Home: 25 Spring Ln Chappaqua NY 10514-2607

LAUNDER, YOLANDA MARIE, graphic design director; b. Columbus, Ohio, Mar. 21, 1957; d. Wilbur Winfield and Julia Mary (Moretti) Reifein; m. David Paul Launder, Oct. 14, 1989; 1 child, Jonathan David. BFA in Design Comm., Tex. Tech. U., 1979. Graphic designer Perception, Inc., Chgo., 1980-81; graphic designer Source, Inc., Chgo., 1982-83, assoc. design mgr., 1983-84; sr. graphic designer Oscar Mayer Foods Corp., Madison, Wis., 1984-85, design mgr., 1986-88, group design mgr., 1989-95; assoc. dir., 1995—; lectr. Wis. Dept. Agr., Madison, 1988, Design Mgmt. Inst., Martha's Vineyard, Mass., 1991, Oscar Mayer Foods Corp., Women Career Devel., Madison, 1993-94, Philip Morris Packaging Roundtable, 1995. Co-inventor in field of Oscar Mayer Lunchables Packaging, 1989—. Sunday sch. tchr. St. Bernard's Ch., Dallas, 1973-75; evaluated high sch. portfolios Tex. Tech. U., Chgo., 1982-83; poll watcher David Patt Alderman campaign, Chgo., 1982; graphic design vol. Mental Health Assn. Dane County, 1986, United Way of Wis., Madison, 1992. Recipient Snack Food Package of the Yr. award Food & Drug Packaging Mag., 1989, Sial D'or award Salon International de L'alimentation, Paris, 1990, Bronze award for Excellence in Packaging for Oscar Mayer Lunchables, The Nat. Paperboard Packaging Coun., 1990, Mktg. Creativity award Kraft U.S.A., 1992, 93. Mem. Women in Design/Chgo. (program dir. 1982-83, membership dir. 1983-84, pres. 1984-85), Madison Advt. Fedn. (Addy awards com. 1985, voluntary action com. 1986), Design Madison (programs com. 1989-92), Package Designers Coun. Internat., Design Mgmt. Inst. Avocations: travel, theater, reading, art galleries, exercising. Office: Oscar Mayer Foods Corp 910 Mayer Ave Madison WI 53704-4256

LAUNER, DALE MARK, screenwriter; b. Cleve., May 19, 1952; s. Sol John and Estelle Launer. Student, Calif. State U., Northridge. Ind. screenwriter Calif., 1986—. Screenwriter: (films) Ruthless People, 1986, Blind Date, 1987; screenwriter, exec. prodr.: (films) Dirty Rotten Scoundrels, 1988; screenwriter, dir., prodr.: (films) Love Potion #9, 1991; screenwriter, prodr.: (films) My Cousin Vinny, 1992. Democrat. Jewish. Home: 639 Adelaide Dr Santa Monica CA 90402-1351

LAUNEY, GEORGE VOLNEY, III, economics educator; b. Ft. Worth, Feb. 8, 1942; s. George Volney and Harriet Louise (Pitts) L.; m. Sondra Ann Schwarz, May 29, 1965; children: George Volney IV, David Vincent. BBA, U. N. Tex., Denton, 1965, MBA, 1966; PhD, U. Ark., 1970. Asst. prof. econs. N.E. La. U., Monroe, 1968-70; asst. prof., assoc. prof. econs. Franklin (Ind.) Coll., 1970-83, chmn. econs. and bus. dept., 1971-81, prof. econs., Joyce and E. Don Tull prof. bus. and econs., 1983—, chmn. social sci. div., 1983—; pres. Econ. Evaluation, Inc., Franklin, 1985—; cons. Von Durpin, Div. Ingersol Rand, Bargersville (Ind.) State Bank, Ind. Dept. Ins., Med. Malpractice Bd., Indpls. Contbr. articles to profl. jours. Recipient Branigin award for teaching excellence Franklin Coll. Bd. Trustees, 1979. Mem. Am. Econ. Assn., Am. Assn. Forensic Economists, Am. Acad. Fin. and Econ. Experts (bd. editors 1988—). Avocation: coin collecting. Home: 1875 Hillside Dr Franklin IN 46131-8542 Office: Franklin Coll Dept Econs Franklin IN 46131

LAUPER, CYNDI, musician; b. Queens, N.Y., June 20, 1953. Studied with Katie Agresta, N.Y., 1974. Toured with Doc West's Disco Band Flyer; mem. musical group Blue Angel, N.Y.C., 1980. Featured in German TV music program; rec. artist: (album) She's So Unusual, 1983, A Night To Remember, 1989, Hat Full of Stars, 1993, Twelve Deadly Cyns...and Then Some, 1995, Sisters of Avalon, 1997; co-writer: (songs) Girls Just Want to Have Fun, She Bop, Money Changes Everything, Time After Time, Goonies R Good Enough, 1985, True Colors, 1986, A Night to Remember, 1989; contbr. A Very Special Christmas, 1992, vol. 2, 1993; star: (videos) Girls Just Want to Have Fun, Time After Time, others; appearance (film) Vibes, 1988, Off and Running, 1991, Life with Mikey, 1993; (TV movie) Mother Goose Rock n' Rhyme, 1990; TV appearances include The Tonight Show, The David Letterman Show, Mad About You (Emmy award, Guest Actress - Comedy Series, 1995); concert tours in Japan, Australia, Hawaii and Eng. Named one of Women of Yr., 1984, Best Female Video Performer, MTV Video Music Awards, 1984, Best Female Performer, Am. Video Awards, 1985; recipient 6 Grammy awards, 1985, 2 Am. Video awards, 1985. Office: Epic Records care Sony Music Entertainment 550 Madison Ave New York NY 10022-3211*

LAUPUS, WILLIAM EDWARD, physician, educator; b. Seymour, Ind., May 25, 1921; s. John George and Laura Kathryne (Hancock) L.; m. Evelyn Estelle Fike, Mar. 6, 1948; children: Patricia, John Richard, Laura (dec.), William Edward. B.S., Yale, 1943, M.D., 1945. Diplomate Am. Bd. Pediatrics (ofcl. examiner 1966-90, mem. exec. bd. 1972-77, pres. 1976-77). Intern N.Y. Hosp.-Cornell Med. Center, 1945-46; resident, 1948-51; instr. pediatrics Cornell U. Sch. Medicine, 1950-52; asst. prof., then asso. prof., prof. pediatrics Med. Coll. Ga., 1959-63; prof. pediatrics, chmn. dept. Med. Coll. Va., Va. Commonwealth U., Richmond, 1963-75; pediatrician-in-chief Med. Coll. Va. Hosps.; prof. pediatrics Sch. of Medicine East Carolina U., 1975-89, dean Sch. Medicine, 1975-82, dean Sch. Medicine, vice chancellor divsn. Health Scis., 1982-89, dean emeritus, 1989—; prof. preventive medicine and pediatrics East Carolina U. Sch. Medicine, 1989-91; pres. Am. Bd. Med. Specialists, 1984-86. Contbr. to: Nelson's Textbook of Pediatrics, 1964, 69, 75, Kendig's Respiratory Diseases in Children, 1969, 72, 77, Gellis and Kagen's Current Therapy, 1969-77. Pres. Richmond Area Community Council, 1973-75. Served with AUS, 1946-48. Mem. Am. Acad. Pediatrics (past pres. Va. chpt.), Am. Pediatric Soc., AMA, N.C. Med. Soc., Pitt County Med. Soc., Alpha Omega Alpha, Phi Kappa Phi. Office: Welco Consulting PO Box 20007 Greenville NC 27858-0007

LAUR, WILLIAM EDWARD, retired dermatologist; b. Saginaw, Mich., Nov. 17, 1919; s. Vertner Linton and Ruth Gae (Eyre) L.; m. Mary Elizabeth Kirby, Dec. 31, 1943; children: Eric, Edward, John, J. Michael. BS, Mercer U., Macon, Ga., 1941; MD, U. Mich., 1943; MS in Medicine, Wayne State U., Detroit, 1949. Diplomate Am. Bd. Dermatology. Intern John Sealy Hosp., Galveston, Tex., 1943; resident Wayne State U., Detroit, 1946-49; pvt. practice Amarillo, Tex., 1949-70; pres. High Plains Dermatology Ctr., P.A., Amarillo, 1975-90; ret.; cons. VA, USAF, 1952-90; assoc. prof. Tex. Tech. Health Sci. Ctr., Amarillo, 1965-90. Contbr. articles to profl. jours. including Archives of Dermatology, Internat. Jour. Dermatology, Cutis, So. Med. Jour., Jour. Am. Acad. Dermatology, Panhandle Med. Soc. Bull., Urologic and Cutaneous Rev. Dir. Moon Watch, NASA, Amarillo, 1956. Capt. U.S. Army, 1944-46, ETO. Fellow Am. Acad. Dermatology; mem. AMA, Tex. Med. Assn., Noah Worcester Dermatol. Soc., Potter Randall County Med. Soc. (pres. 1964). Avocations: cooking, duplicate bridge, computer activities. Home: 1607 S Fannin St Amarillo TX 79102-2412

LAURA, ANTHONY JOSEPH, lawyer; b. Bklyn., July 15, 1961; s. Andrew J. and Edda V. (DePaola) L.; m. Rosemary B. Marino, Sept. 21, 1986; children: Diana Marie, Amanda Rose. BA, Yale U., 1983; JD, Fordham U., 1986. Bar: N.J. 1986, U.S. Dist. Ct. N.J. 1986, N.Y. 1987, U.S. Dist. Ct. (so. dist.) N.Y. 1987, U.S. Ct. Appeals (3rd cir.) 1993. Assoc. atty. Kelley Drye and Warren, N.Y.C., 1986-87, Morristown, N.J., 1987-89, Parsippany, N.J., 1989-97; counsel Reed, Smith, Shaw & McClay, Newark, 1997—; bd. trustee Cmtys. on Cable, Summit, N.J., 1994—, United Way Summit, New Providence, N.J., 1995—. Township committeeman Rep. Com. Union County, Berkeley Hts., N.J., 1994—; trustee Runnells Specialized Hosp. Found., 1996—. Mem. The Mory's Assn., Park Ave Club (membership com. 1994—), Yale Club Ctrl. N.J. Avocation: golf. Office: Reed Smith Shaw & McClay 1 Riverfront Plz Newark NJ 07102-5401

LAURANCE, LEONARD CLARK, marketing researcher, educator and consultant; b. Perth, Australia, Aug. 20, 1932; came to U.S., 1963; s. Thomas Clark and Lorna Ruby (Spencer) L.; m. Lorraine Joan Harwood, June 10, 1954 (div. 1960); 1 child, Beverley Lorraine; m. Judith Ellen Krickan, Sept. 8, 1962; children: Cynthia Ellen, Amanda Lee. Gen. mgr. Ketchikan & No. Terminal Co. Inc., Ketchikan, Alaska, 1963-65; regional mgr. Alaska Steamship Co., Ketchikan, 1965-68; pres. Alaska World Travel Inc., Ketchikan, 1968-72, Leisure Corp., Ketchikan, 1972-85, AlaskaBound, Inc., Ketchikan, 1985-88, Mariner Inc., Ketchikan, 1988—; faculty mem. U. Alaska SE, Ketchikan, 1987—, Juneau, 1995; dir. mktg. Taquan Air, Ketchikan, 1991—; bd. dirs. Hist. Ketchikan, Inc.; mem. Alaska Tourism mktg. commn., 1995—. Mem. Alaska Mktg. Coun., Juneau, 1979-84, chair, 1982-84; mem. S.E. Alaska Tourism Coun., Juneau, 1982-86, 96—, chair., 1982-83; mem. mgmt. com. Sheffield Hotels, Anchorage, 1980-85; chair Alaska Marine Hwy. Task Force, Juneau, 1983-84, UAS Coll. Coun., 1982-83; mem. Ketchikan Gen. Hosp. Adv. Bd., 1973-84, chair, 1979; assemblyperson Ketchikan Gateway Borough, 1976-82. Recipient North Star award Alaska Visitors Assn., 1977, Gov.'s award State of Alaska, 1984, Presdl. award Ketchikan C. of C., 1970. Mem. Alaska Visitors Assn. (bd. dirs. 1969-93, advisor to bd. 1994—, pres. 1972-73, hon. life 1994), Ketchikan Visitors Bur. (bd. dirs. 1980—, chair 1983-84), UAS Visitor Ind. Program (adv. bd. 1986—). Republican. Episcopalian. Avocations: sportfishing, swimming, community service, tourism research. Office: Mariner Inc 5716 S Tongass PO Box 8800 Ketchikan AK 99901-3800

LAURANCE, MARK RODNEY, applications engineer, entrepreneur; b. Seattle, Nov. 27, 1959; s. Sidney Laurance and Patricia Louise Sadlier; m. Brendalynn Legarda. BS in Astronomy, U. Wash., 1984, BS in Physics, 1984, MS in Astronomy, 1992. Computer ops. programmer Seattle Police Dept., Seattle, 1980-85; researcher U. Wash., Seattle, 1984-90; lighting engr. Korry Electronics Co., Seattle, 1990-92; optical engr. Can.-France-Hawaii Telescope Corp., Kamuela, Hawaii, 1992-96; pres. Digitek Hawai'i, Inc., Kamuela, Hawaii, 1995-96; applications engr. Tech. Instrument Co., Sunnyvale, Calif., 1996—; owner Laurance Design Group, San Francisco, 1996—. Contbr. articles to profl. jours. Mem. chpt. mgmt. program mgr., exec. bd. dirs. Hawaii State Jaycees, 1995; exec. v.p. Kona Jaycees, 1994, comty. fundraising dir., 1993; cert. prime trainer Jr. Chamber Internat., 1994; mem. nat. nominations com. Outstanding Young Men of Am., 1997, Outstanding Young Women of Am., 1997. Recipient C. William Brownfield Meml. award for outstanding first yr. jaycee Kona Jaycees, 1994, Presdl. Excellence award Hawaii State Jaycees, 1995, First Place Speak-Up Competition award Hawaii State Jaycees, 1995; named to Outstanding Young Men of Am., 1989, Outstanding Exec. V.P. of Quar., Hawaii Jaycees, 1995, Finalist Three Outstanding Young Persons of Hawaii Jaycees, 1995, Outstanding Young Men of Am., 1997, Outstanding Young Ams. Nat. Nominating Com., 1997. Mem. SPIE Internat. Soc. Optical Engring. Avocations: bicycling, photography, guitar playing, dance choreography, hiking. Office: 650 N Mary Ave Sunnyvale CA 94086-2906

LAUREN, RALPH, fashion designer; b. Bronx, N.Y., Oct. 14, 1939; s. Frank and Frieda Lifshitz; m. Ricky Low Beer, Dec. 30, 1964; children: Andrew, David, Dylan. Student, CCNY; DFA (hon.), Pratt U., 1988. Salesperson Brooks Bros., N.Y.C.; asst. buyer Allied Stores, N.Y.C.; rep. Rivetz Necktie Mfrs., N.Y.C.; neckwear designer Polo divsn. Beau Brummel, N.Y.C., 1967-69; founder Polo Fashions, Inc., N.Y.C., 1968—; established Polo Men's Wear Co., N.Y.C., 1968—, Ralph Lauren Womenswear, N.Y.C., 1971—, Polo Leathergoods, 1978—, Polo/Ralph Lauren for Boys, 1978—, Polo/Ralph Lauren Luggage, 1982—, Ralph Lauren Home Collection, 1983—; launched fragrances Polo for Men, Lauren for Women, 1979—; chmn. Polo Ralph Lauren Corp. (flagship store N.Y.C., 65 other stores in U.S. and 140 stores worldwide); launched Safari fragrance for women, 1990, Safari for men, 1992, Polo Sport, 1994. Served in U.S. Army. Recipient Coty Am. Fashion awards, 1970, 73, 74, 76, 77, 81, 84, also Coty Hall of Fame award for Menswear and Womenswear, Tommy award Am. Printed Fabrics Coun., 1971, Neiman Marcus Disting. Svc. award, 1973, Am. Fashion award, 1975, award Coun. Fashion Designers Am., 1981, CFDA Lifetime Achievement award, 1992. Office: Polo Ralph Lauren Corp 650 Madison Ave New York NY 10022-1029*

LAURENCE, DAN H., author, literary and dramatic specialist; b. N.Y.C., Mar. 28, 1920. BA, Hofstra U., 1946; MA, NYU, 1950. Performed in profl. theatre, 1932-41; writer, performer Armed Forces Radio, 1942-45; writer for radio, TV U.S. and Australia, 1946-48; grad. asst. NYU, 1950-52, assoc. prof. English, 1962-67, prof., 1967-70; instr. Hofstra U., 1953-58; editor Readex Microprint Corp., 1959-60; lit. and dramatic adv. Estate of George Bernard Shaw, London, 1973-90; vis. prof. Ind. U., 1969, U. Tex., 1974-75; vis. fellow Inst. Arts and Humanistic Studies, Pa. State U., 1976; spl. cons. Humanities rsch. Ctr., U. Tex., Austin, 1975-77; Andrew W. Mellon prof. humanities Tulane U., New Orleans, 1981; Montgomery fellow Dartmouth Coll., 1982; disting. vis. prof. humanities Guelph U. (Ont., Can.), 1983, U. B.C. (Can.), 1984; adj. prof. drama Guelph U., 1986-91; literary advisor, mem. acting ensemble of Shaw Festival, Ont., 1982-90, assoc. dir., 1987—; co-founder Offstage, Inc., San Antonio, 1972. Author: (with Leon Edel) Henry James: A Bibliography, 3d edit., 1981, Robert Nathan: A Bibliography, 1960, Bernard Shaw: A Bibliography, 1983; playwright: The Black Girl in Search of God, 1977; editor: Uncollected Writing of Bernard Shaw: How to Become a Musical Critic, 1961, Platform and Pulpit, 1961, (with David H. Greene) The Matter with Ireland, 1962, Selected Non-Dramatic Writings of Shaw, 1965, Collected Letters of Bernard Shaw, 1965-88, Bernard Shaw's Collected Plays with Their Prefaces, 7 vols., 1970-74, (with Daniel J. Leary) Flyleaves, 1977, Shaw's Music, 1981, (with James Rambeau) Agitations, 1985, (with Martin Quinn) Shaw on Dickens, 1985, (with Nicholas Grene) Bernard Shaw, Lady Gregory, and the Abbey, 1993, (with Daniel J. Leary) Shaw: Complete Prefaces, 3 vols. 1993-97, Theatrics, 1995, (with Margot Peters) Unpublished Shaw, 1996. Served with USAAF, 1942-45, PTO. John Simon Guggenheim Meml. fellow, 1960, 61, 72, Pres.'s medal Hofstra U., 1990. Mem. Royal Acad. Dramatic Art (assoc.), Phi Beta Kappa, Phi Alpha Theta, Alpha Psi Omega, Phi Gamma Delta. Home: 9001 Wurzbach Rd San Antonio TX 78240-1057

LAURENCE, JEFFREY CONRAD, immunologist; b. N.Y.C., Oct. 21, 1952; s. Harry and Stephanie (Maderic) L.; m. Linda Dusenbury, July 4, 1987; children: Auden, Galen. BA summa cum laude, Columbia U., 1972; MD, U. Chgo., 1976. Diplomate Am. Bd. Internal Medicine. Rsch. assoc. Inst. for Cancer Rsch., Osaka, Japan, 1974-75; intern, resident, then hematology fellow N.Y.C. Hosp.-Cornell, 1976-82; assoc. physician The Rockefeller U., N.Y.C., 1980-84; asst. prof. Cornell U. Med. Coll., N.Y.C., 1982-87, assoc. prof., 1988-91, assoc. prof with tenure, 1991—; dir. Lab. AIDS Rsch. Cornell Med. Coll., N.Y.C., 1986—; sr. dir. Immune Tech., Inc., N.Y.C., 1986-95; sr. scientist Am. Found. AIDS Rsch., N.Y.C. and Beverly Hills, Calif., 1986—. Author: (play) Many Happy Returns, 1982;

editor-in-chief The AIDS Reader, 1991—; editor AIDS Targeted Info. Newsletter, 1987-92; assoc. editor AIDS Rsch. and Human Retroviruses, AIDS, 1987-95; editor-in-chief AIDS Patient Care and STDs, 1996—; cons. editor Infections in Medicine, 1987—; patentee in field. Recipient Clinician-Scientist award Am. Heart Assn., 1980-85; William S. Paley Found. fellow, 1982-84; Henry Luce Found. scholar, 1974, Rhodes scholar-elect, 1973. Mem. NIH (mem. study sect.), AMA, Am. Fedn. Clin. Rsch., Am. Soc. Microbiology, Am. Soc. Clin. Investigation, Phi Beta Kappa. Episcopalian. Avocations: collecting ancient med. books and sci. instruments, contemporary art. Home: 86 Brookside Dr Greenwich CT 06831-5345 Office: The NY Hosp-Cornell Med Ctr Dept Medicine Lab AIDS Rsch 411 E 69th St New York NY 10021-5603

LAURENCE, MICHAEL MARSHALL, magazine publisher, writer; b. N.Y.C., May 22, 1940; s. Frank Marshall and Edna Ann (Roeder) L.; m. Patricia Ann McDonald, Mar. 1, 1969; children—Elizabeth Sarah, John Marshall. A.B. cum laude, Harvard U., 1963. Sr. editor Playboy mag., Chgo., 1967-69, contbg. editor, 1969-72, asst. pub., 1977-82; mng. editor Oui mag., Chgo., 1973-77; editor/pub. Linn's Stamp News, Sidney, Ohio, 1982—, also columnist Editor's Choice; co-founder, dir. U.S. 1869 Pictorial Research Assocs., 1975-82. Author: Playboy's Investment Guide, 1971; also articles. Editor: U.S. Mail and Post Office Assistant, 1975. Recipient G.M. Loeb award for disting. mag. writing U. Conn., 1968; named to Writers Hall of Fame, Am. Philatelic Soc., 1994. Mem. Internat. Soc. Philatelic Journalists, U.S. Philatelic Classics Soc. (Elliott Perry award 1975; bd. dirs. 1975-81), Harvard Club (N.Y.C.), Collectors Club Chgo. (bd. dirs. 1978-82), Collectors Club N.Y.C. Avocations: stamp collecting; gardening. Office: Linn's Stamp News 911 S Vandemark Rd Sidney OH 45365-8974

LAURENCE, ROBERT LIONEL, chemical engineering educator; b. West Warwick, R.I., July 13, 1936; s. Lionel Gerard and Gertrude Sara (Lefebvre) L.; m. Carol Leah Jolicoeur, Sept. 7, 1959; children: Jonathan, Lisa, Andrew. BSChemE, MIT, 1957; MSChemE, U. R.I., 1960; PhDChemE, Northwestern U., 1966; DSc (honoris causa), Inst. Nat. Poly., 1989. Rsch. engr. Gen. Dynamics, Groton, Conn., 1957-59, E. I. du Pont de Nemours, Wilmington, Del., 1960-61; field svc. engr. E. I. du Pont de Nemours, Beaumont, Tex., 1961-63; asst. prof. chem. engring. Johns Hopkins U., Balt., 1965-68; rsch. engr. Monsanto Co., Springfield, Mass., 1968; assoc. prof. U. Mass., Amherst, 1968-73, head dept. chem. engring., 1982-89, prof., 1973—; vis. prof. Imperial Coll., London, 1974-75, Coll. de France, Paris, 1982-83; invited prof. ENSIGC, Toulouse, France, 1990; vis. rsch. fellow GE, Schenectady, 1989; vis. prof. Rijks U. Gent, 1996; cons. UN Devel. Program, Argentina, 1978, 80, Beijing, 1982; mem. Conseil Technologique Groupe Rhone-Poulenc, Paris, 1988—. Fellow Am. Inst. Chem. Engrs., Am. Inst. Chemists; mem. Am. Chem. Soc., Soc. Plastics Engrs., Am. Soc. Engring. Edn., Tau Beta Pi. Roman Catholic. Avocation: rugby. Office: U Mass Dept Chem Engring Amherst MA 01003

LAURENDI, NAT, criminal investigator; b. Sant'Eufemia d'Aspromonte, Reggio Calabria, Italy, Aug. 7, 1923; s. Domenick and Grace (Crea) L.; grad. RCA Insts., 1951; A.A.S., Coll. City N.Y., 1969; m. Laura Autelitanto, Mar. 28, 1946; children: Domenick, Susan (dec.), Adrienne, Loretta, Diana, Robert. With N.Y. Police Dept., 1951-75, N.Y. Dist. Atty's Office, 1952-75, criminal investigator, 1951-75, polygraph expert, 1962-75; pres. Certified Lie Detection, N.Y.C., 1975—, Nat. Laurendi, 1975—; mem. Frank S. Hogan Assocs., Hogan-Morgenthat Assocs.; author, lectr. on polygraph. Served with CIC, AUS, 1943-46. Decorated Bronze Star medal; recipient Excellent Police Duty award N.Y. Police Dept., 1954, 62, also Meritorious Police Duty awards. Fellow Acad. Certified Polygraphists; mem. ABA (criminal justice assoc.), AAAS, Am. Bd. Forensic Examiners, Am. Soc. Criminology, Internat. Narcotic Officers Assn., Internat. Police Assn., N.Y.C. CIC Assn. (pres. 1956), N.Y. State Polygraphists (chmn. membership com., 1964—), Am. Polygraph Assn., N.Y. State Assn. Criminal Def. Lawyers, N.Y. Acad. Scis., N.Y. State Defenders Assn., Am. Assn. Police Polygraphists, Detectives Endowment Assn., N.Y. Police Dept. Patrolmens Benevolent Assn., N.Y. Police Dept. Ret. Detectives, Ret. Patrolmen N.Y. Police Dept., Am. Soc. for Indsl. Security, Nat. Law Enforcement Assos., N.Y. Vet. Police Assn., N.Y.C. Ret. Employees Assn., Soc. Profl. Investigators, Fraternal Order Police, Superior Officers Assn. Retired N.Y.C. Police Dept., Assn. Legal, Med. and Investigative Experts. Roman Catholic. Home: 108 Village Rd S Brooklyn NY 11223-5237 Office: Certified Lie Detection 299 Broadway New York NY 10007-1901

LAURENSON, ROBERT MARK, mechanical engineer; b. Pitts., Oct. 25, 1938; s. Robert Mark and Mildred Othelia (Frandsen) L.; m. Alice Ann Scroggins, Aug. 26, 1961; children: Susan Elizabeth Laurenson Matchael, Shari Lynn, Laurenson Lawson. Student, Drury Coll., 1956-58; BS in Mech. Engring., Mo. Sch. Mines, 1961; MS in Mech. Engring., U. Mich., 1962; PhD in Mech. Engring. (NASA tng. grantee), Ga. Inst. Tech., 1968. Registered profl. engr., Mo. Dynamics engr. McDonnell Douglas Corp., St. Louis, 1962-64, sr. dynamics engr., 1968-71, group engr., 1971-74, staff engr., 1974-75, tech. specialist, 1975-78, sr. tech. specialist, 1978-81, sect. chief, 1981-85, prin. tech. specialist, 1985-87, br. chief, 1987-89, prin. mgr. engring., 1989-92; prin. tech. specialist, systems engring. mgr. McDonnell Douglas Aerospace, Seabrook, Md., 1992-93, sr. mgr., 1993-95; asst. dir. engring., 1995—; participant 14th Midwestern Mechanics Conf., 1975; lectr. engring. mechanics St. Louis U., part-time 1969-71; adj. assoc. prof. U. Mo.-Rolla Grad. Engring. Ctr., St. Louis, 1980-88; lectr. mech. engring. Johns Hopkins U., 1996—; participant Symposium on Dynamics and Control of Large Flexible Spacecraft, Blackburg, Va., 1977, In-Space Tech. Experiments Workshop NASA, 1988, Damping, '89 Conf., 1989; mem. panel Am. Astronauticla Soc. Symposium on Dynamics and Control of Nonridig Spacecraft, UCLA, 1974. Contbr. articles to profl. jours.; reviewer profl. jours.; author tech. papers Jour. Engring. for Industry, 1972,, Jour. Spacecraft and Rockets, 1973, AIAA Jour., 1976, 78, 80, 85; numerous papers presented at tech. confs. Vestryman Episcopal Ch., 1972-76, sr. warden, 1976, uscher chmn., 1978-80, Sunday sch. tchr., 1980-84, chmn. every mem. canvas, 1983, mem. steering com., 1983-88, chmn. steering com., 1987-88, mem. search com., 1984-85, mem. exec. com., 1991-92, warden, 1991-92; mem. Commn. on Ministry, Diocese of Mo., 1985-91, chmn., 1989-91; mem. standing com. Diocese of Mo., 1990-92; trustee Corp. of Episcopal Diocese of Mo., 1990-92; mem. seminarian com., 1993-97, chair, 1994-97, engring. mentor Holy Trinity Episcopal Day Sch. Fellow ASME (structures materials com. aerospace divsn. 1975-84, com. chmn. 1979-81, session organizer, chmn. ann. meeting 1975, participant ann. meeting 1986, 89, mem. exec. com. aerospace divsn. 1980-85, sec.-treas. 1981-82, vice-chmn. 1982-83, chmn. 1983-84, Flag award aerospace divsn. 1990, mem. Guggenheim medal bd. 1989-92, mem. conf. organizing com., session chmn. Structures, Structural Dynamics and Materials Conf., 1977, chmn. tech. program 1978, gen. co-chmn. 1979, gen. chmn. 1981, mem. SDM planning com. 1978-82, chmn. 1981-82, session chmn. 1985, 88, adv. com. 1978-82, participant 1979, 83, 86, 90, mech. engring. evaluator Accreditation Bd. Engring. and Tech. 1985-91, organizer symposium on microgravity fluid mechanics 1986, mem. planning com. edn. conf. 1986, editor Advances in Aerospace Structures 1982, Procs. of 1986 Edn. Conf. The Decade Ahead, bd. engring. edn. K thru 12 task force 1992-93, bd. pre-coll. edn. 1992-95, 1st alt. nat. nominating com. 1993-94, engring. accreditation com. 1993—, exec. com. 1993—, sec. 1995-96, vice chair 1996-97, rep. on Am. Assn. Engring. Soc.'s Precoll. Edn. Coun. 1993-95, exec. com. 1993-95, Dedicated Svc. award 1995); mem. AIAA (sr., gen. chmn. dynamics specialist conf. 1981, session chmn. 1987), Edison Electric Inst. (adv. com. power engring. edn. forgivable loan program 1993-94), Sigma Xi, Pi Tau Sigma, Tau Beta Pi, Phi Kappa Phi, Sigma Phi Epsilon. Home: 1104 Jasper Ct Crofton MD 21114-1658 Office: McDonnell Douglas Aerospace 7404 Executive Pl Lanham Seabrook MD 20706-2268

LAURENT, J(ERRY) SUZANNA, technical communications specialist; b. Oklahoma City, Okla., Dec. 28, 1942; d. Harry Austin and M. LaVerne (Barker) Minick; m. Leroy E. Laurent, July 2, 1960; children: Steven, Sandra, David, Debra. AS in Engr. Tech., Okla. State U., 1986. From staff to retail bus. mgr. Technically Write, Mustang, Okla., 1960-87, owner, CEO, 1989-95; sr. tech. comms. specialist Applied Intelligence Group, Edmond, Okla., 1995—. Named One of The Top Ten Business Women in Nation Am. Bus. Women's Assn., 1997. Mem. Soc. Tech. Comm. (Superscript editor 1985, feature editor 1986, v.p., 1985, student chpt. pres. 1986, program coord. Okla. chpt. 1992-93, sec. 1993-94, v.p. 1994-95, state pres. 1995-96, Disting. Chpt. Svc. award 1997, other honors), Am. Bus. Women's Assn. (Dist. III v.p. 1988-89, conf. gen. chair 1992, editor Smoke Signals 1993-95, chmn. bd. dirs. Help Us Grow Spiritually 1993-95, Bull. award 1977, 81, 83-84, 93, 95, 97, Woman of Yr. 1977, 96, One of Top Ten Women of Yr. 1997, Bus. Assoc. of Yr. 1983-84). Democrat. Baptist. Avocations: reading, public speaking, motivating people, volunteer activities. Home: 347 W Forest Dr Mustang OK 73064-3430

LAURENT, LAWRENCE BELL, communications executive, former journalist; b. Monroe, La., Mar. 9, 1925; s. Lewis Emeal and John Ethel (Dawkins) L.; m. Margaret F. Goodwillie, Nov. 1, 1949; children—Richard Sandford, Arthur Halliday, Margaret Funsten, Elizabeth MacLean. Student, U. Va., 1946-49; pvt. study with, Dr. W.Y. Elliott, 1954-56, Dr. Franklin Dunham, 1957-58. With Bluefield (W.Va.) Daily Telegraph, 1949-50, Charlottesville (Va.) Daily Progress, 1950-51; with Washington Post, 1951-82, radio-TV editor, 1953-82, radio-TV editor emeritus, 1982—; cons. Assn. Ind. TV Stas., 1982-85, dir. communication, 1985-86, v.p. communication, 1986-91; congl. cons., 1991—; editor-in-residence Broadcast Pioneers Library, 1985-96; adj. prof. communications Am. U., Washington, 1963-85; chmn. editorial bd. TV Quar., 1963-74, bd. dirs., 1974—; guest prof. Syracuse U., 1965; vis. prof. U. Detroit, 1967, George Washington U., 1982—; formerly judge Alfred I. duPont awards, Saturday Rev. Lit. TV awards, Sigma Delta Chi pub. service TV awards, Humanitas awards. Editor, author: (with Newton N. Minow) Equal Time, 1964; Contbr. to books, mags. Trustee Human Family Edn. and Cultural Inst.; bd. dirs. Pioneers Edn. Fund, Inc., 1984-94, trustee, 1995—. With USNR, 1943-46. Recipient Front Page award Am. Newspaper Guild, 1964, Disting. Tchr. award Am. U., 1978, TV Acad.'s Silver Circle award, 1988; named to Broadcast Pioneers' Hall of Fame, 1984; du Pont Journalism scholar U. Va. Mem. AAUP, NATAS (life), VFW (life), DAV (life), 593rd Joint Assault Signal Co. Assn., USS Belle Grave Historic Assn., Nat. Press Club, White House Corrs. Assn., Washington Post E-Streeters, Am. Legion (life), Sigma Delta Chi, Pi Delta Epsilon, Theta Chi. Episcopalian. Home: 215 Jefferson St Alexandria VA 22314-4323

LAURENT, PIERRE-HENRI, history educator; b. Fall River, Mass., May 15, 1933; s. Henri and Harriet (Moriarty) L.; m. Virginia Brayton, 1958; children: Paul-Henri, Bradford Webb, Nicole, Alexa. A.B., Colgate U., 1956; A.M., Boston U., 1960, Ph.D., 1964. Instr. polit. economy Boston U., 1961-64; asst. prof. history Sweet Briar Coll., 1964-66; vis. asst. prof. history U. Wis., Madison, 1966-67; asst. prof. history Tulane U., New Orleans, 1967-68, assoc. prof., 1968-70; assoc. prof. history Tufts U., Medford, Mass., 1970-75, prof., 1975—, chmn. dept., 1987-89, adj. prof. diplomatic history/Fletcher Sch. Law and Diplomacy, 1977, 84, chmn. Exptl. Coll., 1973-75, acting dir. internat. relations program, 1979, dir. internat. relations program, 1984-88; co-dir. Internat. Relations Inst. Tufts U., France, 1979-80; acad. dir. Tufts European Ctr., France, 1994—; mem. history devel. bd. Ednl. Testing Svc. of Princeton, 1979-82; instr. JFK Inst. Polit., Harvard U., Cambridge, 1989; mem. nat. screening com. Fulbright-Hays program Inst. Internat. Edn., 1988-91; rsch. assoc. Ctr. for Internat. Affairs, Harvard U. Mem. editorial bd. Jour. Social History, 1966-74; sect. editor Am. Hist. Rev., 1967-77; contbr. chpts. to books, articles to profl. jours., mags., encys. Served with USAF, 1956-58. NATO fellow, 1967, NEH fellow, 1969, Paul-Henri Spaak Found. fellow, 1976-77; Sweet Briar Faculty rsch. grantee, 1965, Tufts Faculty rsch. grantee, 1972, Inst. European Studies-Exxon Ednl. Fund grantee, 1983; Fulbright Rsch. scholar, 1992-93. Fellow Inst. des Rels. Internationales, Acad. Assoc. Atlantic Coun.; mem. AAUP (exec. com. Mass. State Conf. 1974-76, pres. Tufts U. chpt. 1982-84), European Cmty. Studies Assn. (exec. com. 1988-92, 95—, chmn. 1991-92), Belgian-Am. Edn. Found. (bd. govs. 1986-90). Office: Tufts Univ Dept Of History Medford MA 02155

LAURENTS, ARTHUR, playwright; b. N.Y.C., July 14, 1917; s. Irving and Ada (Robbins) L. BA, Cornell U., Ithaca, N.Y., 1937. Radio script writer, 1939-40. Author: (novels) The Way We Were, 1972, The Turning Point, 1977 (screen plays) The Snake Pit, 1948, Rope, 1948, Caught, 1948, Anna Lucasta, 1949, Anastasia, 1956, Bonjour Tristesse, 1958, The Way We Were, 1973, The Turning Point, 1977 (Writer Guild Am. award), (plays) Home of the Brave, 1946, The Bird Cage, 1950, The Time of the Cuckoo, 1952, A Clearing in the Woods, 1956, Invitation to a March, 1960, The Enclave, 1973, Scream, Houston, 1978, The Hunting Season (Jolson Sings Again), 1995, The Radical Mystique, 1995, My Good Name, 1997, (mus. plays) West Side Story, 1957, Gypsy, 1959, Do I Hear A Waltz?, 1964, Hallelujah, Baby, 1967 (Tony award), Nick and Nora, 1991; screenwriter, co-producer (film) The Turning Point, 1977 (Golden Glove award, Nat. Bd. Rev. award); co-author, dir.: (dramatic prodns.) My Mother was a Fortune Teller, 1978 (Drama Desk award), The Madwoman of Central Park West, (radio plays in anthologies) Radio Drama in Action, 1945, Best One Act Plays of 1944-45, 1945-46, dir.: (Broadway prodns.) Invitation to a March, 1960, I Can Get It For You Wholesale, 1962, La Cage aux Folles (Tony award for Best Dir. 1984); writer, dir.: (Broadway prodns.) Invitation to the March, 1960, Anyone Can Whistle, 1964, The Enclave, 1973, (one-act play) A Loss of Memory (Best Short Plays of 1983); dir. (London prodn.) Gypsy, 1973, N.Y. revival, 1974 (Drama Desk award), La Cage aux Folles, 1983, Australian prodn. (Best Dir's. award 1985, London prodn. 1986), Birds of Paradise, 1987, Gypsy, revival, 1989, Nick and Nora, 1991. Served with AUS, 1941-45. Recipient Variety Radio award, 1945, Am. Acad. Arts and Letters award; co-recipient Sidney Howard award, 1946. Mem. Dramatists Guild Council, P.E.N., Authors League, Screenwriters Guild, Acad. Motion Picture Arts and Scis., Theatre Hall of Fame. Address: Peter Franklin care William Morris Agency 1325 Ave of the Americas New York NY 10019

LAURENZO, VINCENT DENNIS, industrial management company executive; b. Des Moines, May 31, 1939; s. Vincent C. and B.J. (Garver) L.; m. Sherrill S. Mullen, Sept. 10, 1960; children: Lisa, David, Susan, Nancy, James. B.B.A., U. Notre Dame, 1961; M.B.A., U. Mich., 1964. With Ford Motor Co., Dearborn, Mich., 1961-66; plant controller Massey Ferguson Inc., 1967-70; with parent co. Massey Ferguson Ltd., Toronto, Ont., Can., 1971—, dir. fin. Am. div., 1977-78, v.p., comptr. Massey Ferguson Ltd., 1978-80, sr. v.p. planning and adminstrn., 1980—; pres. Varity Corp. (formerly Massey Ferguson Ltd.), Toronto, 1981-88; vice chmn. bd. Varity Corp. (formerly Massey Ferguson Ltd.), Buffalo, 1988—, vice chmn., pres., 1988-94; ret., 1994, vice chair bd. dirs. Roman Catholic.

LAURET, CURTIS BERNARD, JR., international marketing professional; b. Vicksburg, Miss., Mar. 17, 1945; s. Curtis Bernard and Ora Belle (Scott) L.; m. Mary Lorraine Fontenot, Sept. 12, 1964; children: Curtis B. III, Charles E., Christopher S., Craig T. Student, La. State U., 1963—. CLU. Dist. mgr. Nat. Life & Accident Co., Baton Rouge, 1967-74; cons. Life Ins. Mktg. Rsch. Assn., Hartford, Conn., 1974-77; asst. dir., then dir. ednl. svcs. Life Ins. Mktg. Rsch. Assn., 1977-81, dir. co. rels., 1981-83; v.p. co. rels. Life Underwriter Tng. Coun., Washington, 1983-85, v.p. mktg., 1985-87, sr. v.p. mktg., 1987-94, sr. v.p. internat., 1994—; mem. faculty Life Underwriter Tng. Coun., Washington, 1970-74. Contbr. articles to profl. publs. Mem. parish coun. St. Catherine Ch., Simsbury, Conn., 1975-81; counselor Boy Scouts Am., Conn. and Md., 1975-86; mem. Intercounty Connector Task Force, Rockville, Md., 1985-87. Fellow Life Underwriter Tng. Coun., Limra Leadership Inst.; mem. Nat. Assn. Life Underwriters, Gen. Agts. and Mgrs. Assn., Internat. Ins. Soc., K.C., La. Soc. Washington, Choral Ministry of St. Patrick's, Worldwide Marriage Encounter. Democrat. Avocations: reading, computers, tennis, bicycling. Office: Life Underwriter Tng Coun 7625 Wisconsin Ave Bethesda MD 20814-3519

LAURIE, JAMES ANDREW, journalist, broadcaster; b. Eustis, Fla., June 16, 1947; s. Andrew Louis and Geneva Lavina (Pryor) L. B.A. in History, Am. U., Washington, 1970; postgrad., George Washington U. Free-lance writer Washington, 1969, 73-74, Phnom Penh, Cambodia and Saigon, Vietnam, 1970-71; reporter NBC News, Saigon, 1971-73, 75, Tokyo, 1976-78; with ABC News, 1978—, corr., bur. chief, Hong Kong, 1978-81, opened 1st Am. radio-TV bur. in Peking, 1981, bur. chief, Peking, 1981-82, chief Asia corr., Tokyo, 1983-88, corr., bur. chief Moscow, 1989-91; sr. corr. ABC News, London, 1991-96, China, 1996—; bur. chief ABC News, Hong Kong, 1996—. Writer, narrator: (ABC Closeup documentaries) Japan: Myths behind the Miracle, 1981, The Unruly Dragon: China's Yellow River, 1988, Soviet segment ABC Spl. "Beyond the Cold War", 1989; covered Mikhail Gorbachev in Cuba, East Germany, Rome, Malta, 1989, Tien An Men Crushing of Democrats Movement, 1989, Gorbachev summit in U.S., 1990, Bush-Gorbachev summit, Moscow, 1991, coup d'etat Moscow, 1991, Somalia Famine, 1992, Iraq Crisis, 1993, Bosnia Crises, 1993, Israeli-Palestinian Negotiations, 1993, Russian Crisis October, 1993, South African elections, 1994, U.S. operation in Haiti, 1994. Recipient George Foster Peabody Broadcasting award for reporting fall of Saigon, 1976; Columbia-Dupont award for ABC Closeup documentary Cambodia: This Shattered Land, 1981; award for radio news coverage of assassination of Philippine leader Benigno Aquino, Overseas Press Club, 1983; Emmy award, 1987. Office: ABC News Citibank Plz, 2307 Asia Pacific Fin Tower, Hong Kong China

LAURIE, MARILYN, communications company executive; b. N.Y.C.; d. Abraham and Irene Gold; m. Robert Laurie; children: Amy, Lisa. BA in English, Barnard Coll., 1959; MBA, Pace U., 1975. Responsible for environ. programs AT&T, N.Y.C., 1971-75, established electronic media program, 1975-78, exec. speeches, policy statements, 1978-79, advt. mgr., 1979-80; exec. dir. AT&T Bell Labs., 1980-83; v.p. AT&T Bell Labs., N.J., 1983-84, AT&T, N.J., 1984-85; group v.p. AT&T, 1986-87; exec. v.p. pub. rels. info. AT&T, Basking Ridge, N.J., 1987-97, exec. v.p. brand strategy and mktg. comms., 1997—; chmn. AT&T Found., 1987-97. Author articles on environ. issues. Co-founder Environ. Action Coalition, 1970; co-originator Earth Day, 1970; bd. dirs. N.Y.C. Ballet, New Visions for Pub. Schs.; trustee Columbia U.; exec. com. N.Y.C. Partnership. Recipient Gold Key award Pub. Rels. News, WEAL award Women's Equity Action League, 1985, Women in Comm. Matrix award, 1988, Human Rels. award Am. Jewish Com., 1995; named to YWCA Acad. Women Achievers, 1984; named Pub. Rels. All Star, Inside Pub. Rels. Mag., 1993. Mem. Pub. Rels. Seminar (chair), Arthur Page Soc. (bd. officer), Women's Forum. Avocations: reading, tennis. Office: AT&T 295 N Maple Ave Rm 4342i3 Basking Ridge NJ 07920-1002

LAURIE, ROBIN GARRETT, lawyer; b. Mobile, Ala., June 10, 1956; s. George and Margaret Eloise (Garrett) L.; m. Deborah Dockery; children: Elizabeth Anne, Robin Garrett. AA, Marion (Ala.) Mil. Inst., 1976; BS in Bus., U. Ala., Tuscaloosa, 1978; JD, U.Ala., Tuscaloosa, 1988. Bar: Ala. 1988, U.S. Dist. Ct. (no., mid. and so. dists.) Ala. 1988, U.S. Ct. Appeals (11th cir.) 1988. Lawyer, ptnr. Balch & Bingham, Montgomery, Ala., 1988—. Lead articles editor Ala. Law Rev., 1986-88. Recipient Outstanding Svc. award Ala. Law Rev., 1988. Mem. ABA, Ala. State Bar, Montgomery County Bar Assn., Montgomery Rotary Club, Order of the Coif. Methodist. Avocations: flying small airplanes, fishing, hunting. Office: Balch & Bingham 2 Dexter Ave Montgomery AL 36104-3515

LAURIE, RONALD SHELDON, lawyer; b. San Francisco, June 30, 1942; s. Charles M. and Mimosa (Ezaoui) L.; m. Mina Heshmati, June 1, 1986. BS in Indsl. Engring., U. Calif., 1964; JD, U. San Francisco, 1968. Bar: Calif. 1969, U.S. Ct. Appeals (9th cir.) 1969, U.S. Patent Office 1969, U.S. Supreme Ct. 1971, U.S. Ct. Appeals (fed. cir.) 1972. Programmer, sys. engr. Lockheed Missiles & Space Co., Sunnyvale, Calif., 1960-64; patent atty. Kaiser Aluminum & Chem. Co., Oakland, Calif., 1968-70; ptnr. Townsend and Townsend, San Francisco, 1970-88, Irell & Manella, Menlo Park, Calif., 1988-91, Weil, Gotshal & Manges, Menlo Park, 1991-94, McCutchen, Doyle, Brown & Emersen, San Francisco, 1994—; chmn. McCutchen Computers and Software Industry Group, 1995—; lectr. computer law Stanford U. Law Sch., 1993—; advisor NAS, U.S. Copyright Office and U.S. Patent and Trademark Office, Washington, Office Tech. Assessment, U.S. Congress, World Intellectual Property Orgn., Geneva. Co-editor: International Intellectual Property, 1992; contbr. articles to profl. jours. Mem. Internat. Intellectual Property Assn. (exec. com.), State Bar Calif. (past mem. exec. com. intellectual property sect.), Computer Law Assn. (bd. dirs.). Avocation: vintage auto racing. Home: 107 Acacia Ave Belvedere CA 94920-2309 Office: McCutchen Doyle et al Three Embarcadero Ctr San Francisco CA 94111

LAURIN, PIERRE, finance company executive; b. Charlemagne, Que., Can., Aug. 11, 1939. MBA, U. Montreal, 1963; D in Bus. Adminstrn., Harvard U., 1969; PhD (hon.), U. Montreal, 1983. Dean bus. sch. U. Montreal, 1975-82; v.p. planning and adminstrn. Alcan Co. of Can., 1982-87; vice chmn., dir. gen. Merrill Lynch Can. Inc., Montreal, 1987—. Author mgmt. textbook. Named officer Order Can. Office: Merrill Lynch Can Inc, 1800 McGill College Ave Ste 2500, Montreal, PQ Canada H3A 3J6

LAURITZEN, PETER OWEN, electrical engineering educator; b. Valparaiso, Ind., Feb. 14, 1935; s. Carl W. and Edna B. (Seebach) L.; m. Helen M. Janzen, Apr. 6, 1963; children: Beth K., Margo S. B.S., Calif. Inst. Tech., 1956; M.S., Stanford U., 1958, Ph.D., 1961. Asso. evaluation engr. Honeywell Aero. Div., Mpls., 1956-57; mem. tech. staff Fairchild Semiconductor Div., Palo Alto, Calif., 1961-65; asst. prof. elec. engring. U. Wash., Seattle, 1965-68; asso. prof. U. Wash., 1968-73, prof., 1973—, adj. prof. social mgmt. of tech., 1977-83; engring. mgr. Avtech Corp., Seattle, 1979-80; cons. x-ray div. Chgo. Bridge & Iron Works, 1967-71, 78, Eldec Corp., 1982-91, Energy Internat., 1986-88; conf. chair IEEE Power Electronics Specialist Conf., 1993; co-dir. NSF industry/univ. rsch. ctr., 1995—. Pres. Coalition for Safe Energy, Wash. Citizens Group, 1975-76. Danforth asso., 1966-78; NASA-Am. Soc. Engring. Edn. summer faculty fellow, 1974. Mem. IEEE, Am. Soc. Engring. Edn., AAAS. Home: 7328 58th Ave NE Seattle WA 98115-6257 Office: U Wash Elec Engring Dept PO Box 352500 Seattle WA 98195-2500

LAURSEN, PAUL HERBERT, retired university educator; b. Ord, Nebr., Mar. 28, 1929; s. Ejvind L. and Jacobine E. (Jorgensen) L.; m. Marcia Gail Thompson, Aug. 23, 1959; children: Brett Paul, Scott Warren. B.A. cum laude, Dana Coll., Blair, Nebr., 1954; Ph.D. (duPont teaching fellow 1958-59), Oreg. State U., 1961; NSF vis. fellow, UCLA, 1967-68. Mem. faculty Nebr. Wesleyan U., Lincoln, 1959-93; prof. chemistry Nebr. Wesleyan U., 1964-93, head dept., 1961-76, chmn. div. natural scis. and math., 1966-67, 68-71, chmn. faculty, 1973-76, acad. dean, 1976-78, provost, 1978-87, trustee, bd. govs., 1973-76; dir. student sci. tng. projects NSF, 1971-75; dir. Nebr. State Sci. Talent Search, 1974-80; lectr. U. Md. Munich campus, 1987-88. Active local Boy Scouts Am., 1970-75, Habitat for Humanity, 1993—; treas. Citizens Environ. Improvement, 1971-73; co-chair Trnsition Team, Nebr. Synod of the New Luth. Ch., 1986-87; mem. com. appeals Evang. Luth. Ch. Am., 1987-93, mem. discipline com., 1993—; mem. Bd. Regents Dana Coll., 1990—, sec. 1995—. With AUS, 1951-53. Recipient Honor Faculty award Nebr. Wesleyan U. Trustees, 1969, Disting. Alumnus award Dana Coll., 1975. Mem. Am. Chem. Soc. (sec. Nebr. sect. 1989), AAAS, Nebr. Acad. Scis. (pres. 1970-71), Sigma Xi, Phi Lambda Upsilon, Sigma Pi Sigma, Phi Kappa Phi. Club: Polemic. Address: 3148 N 75th Street Ct Lincoln NE 68507-2139

LAURUS (LAURUS SKURLA), archbishop; b. Ladomirova, Czechoslovakia, Jan. 1, 1928; s. Michael Ivan and Helen Michael (Martinik) Skurla. BTh, Holy Trinity Sem., 1954. joined Holy Trinity Monastery, 1946; ordained deacon Russian Orthodox Ch. Abroad, 1950, ordained priest, 1957, consecrated bishop, 1967, elevated to archbishop, 1981. Instr. Old Testament Holy Trinity Sem., Jordanville, N.Y., 1960-65, instr. patristics, 1959-93, instr. moral theology, 1973-76, insp., 1958-67, dean, 1973-76, abbot, 1976—, rector, chmn. bd., 1976—; bishop Diocese of Manhattan, 1967-76; bishop, then archbishop Diocese of Syracuse, 1976—; sec. Synod of Bishops, 1967-77, 1986—; pres. St. John of Kronstadt Meml. Fund, 1976—. Editor Calendar, 1976—, Orthodox Life, 1991—, Orthodox Russia, 1991—; contbr. articles to ch. publs. and periodicals. Mem. Orthodox Palestine Soc., 1986—. Home: Holy Trinity Monastery Jordanville NY 13361 Office: Synod of Bishops 75 E 93rd St New York NY 10128-1331*

LAUSE, MICHAEL FRANCIS, lawyer; b. Washington, Mo., Aug. 3, 1948; s. Walter Francis and Junilla Rose (Marquart) L.; m. Ann G. Hellman, Aug. 29, 1981; children: Andrew Edward, Scott Michael. BA, St. Benedict's Coll., 1970; JD, U. Ill., 1973. Bar: Mo. 1973. Ptnr. Thompson Coburn, St. Louis, 1973—; mem. mgmt. com. Thompson Coburn, St. Louis, 1988-90, co-chmn. corp. dept., 1990—. Gen. counsel Mo. Health and Ednl. Facilities Authority, 1986—, St. Louis Zoo, 1992—. Mem. ABA, Mo. Bar Assn., St. Louis Bar Assn., Nat. Assn. Bond Lawyers, Bellerive Country Club. Roman Catholic. Home: 9822 Old Warson Rd Saint Louis MO 63124-1066 Office: Thompson Coburn One Mercantile Ctr Ste 3400 Saint Louis MO 63101

LAUTENBACH, TERRY ROBERT, information systems and communications executive; b. Cin., Aug. 10, 1938; s. Robert C. and Frances M.

(Herbert) L.; m. Carole Wuest; children: Jennifer, Susan, Julie, Martha, Mary, Anne. B in Physics, Xavier U., 1959, LLD (hon.), 1977. Pres. data processing div. IBM Corp., White Plains, N.Y., 1976-78; pres. World Trade Ams., Far East Corp. Mt. Pleasant, N.Y., 1978-83; v.p. mktg. Purchase, N.Y., 1984-85; pres. communication products div. White Plains, 1985-86, group exec., info. systems and communications group, 1986-88; sr. v.p. worldwide mfg. and devel., N.Am. mktg. and svc. IBM, 1988-92, mem. mgmt. com., 1988-92; bd. dirs. Air Products and Chem., Inc., Varian Assocs., Inc., CVS Corp., Footstar Inc.; trustee Loomis Sayles Mutual Funds. Pres. Darien Library, Conn., 1988. Mem. Sanctuary Golf Club, Wee Burn Country Club. Home: 1312 Sea Spray Ln Sanibel FL 33957-2619

LAUTENBACHER, CONRAD CHARLES, JR., naval officer; b. Phila., June 26, 1942; s. Conrad Charles and Dorthea Henrietta (Jensen) L.; m. Susan Elizabeth Scheihing, June 20, 1964; children: Elizabeth Lautenbacher Katz, Conrad John. BS, U.S. Naval Acad., 1964; MS, Harvard U., 1965, PhD, 1968. Commd. ensign USN, 1964, advanced through grades to vice adm., 1994; aide to Vice Chief Naval Ops., Chief Naval Ops. USN, Washington, 1974-75; exec. officer USS Benjamin Stoddert USN, Pearl Harbor, Hawaii, 1975-77; program analyst Chief Naval Ops. USN, Washington, 1977-80; comdg. officer USS Hewitt USN, San Diego, 1980-82; dir. program planning Chief Naval Ops. USN, Washington, 1982-86; comdg. officer Naval Sta., Norfolk USN, Va., 1986-88; insp. gen. U.S. Pacific Fleet Hdqrs. USN, Pearl Harbor, 1988-90; comdr. Cruiser-Destroyer Group 5 San Diego, 1990-91; dir. force structure, resources and assessment J-8, Joint Staff, Washington, 1991-94; spl. asst. to asst. sec. navy USN, 1994; commdr. U.S. Third Fleet, 1994-96, dir. office of program appraisal, 1996—. Decorated D.S.M. (2), Legion of Merit with 3 gold stars, Meritorious Svc. medal with 2 gold stars, Navy Commendation medal, Navy Achievement medal. Mem. U.S. Naval Inst.. Lutheran. *Life is about people and relationships. True happiness begins with sensitivity and responsiveness to the needs of others.*

LAUTENBERG, FRANK R., senator; b. Paterson, N.J., Jan. 23, 1924; s. Samuel and Mollie L.; children: Ellen, Nan, Lisa, Joshua. BS, Columbia U., 1949; DHL, Hebrew Union Coll., Cin. and N.Y.C., 1977; PhD (hon.), Hebrew U., Jerusalem, 1978. Founder Automatic Data Processing, Inc., Clifton, N.J., 1952-55; exec. v.p. adminstrn. Automatic Data Processing, Inc., 1955-69, pres., 1969-75, chief exec. officer, 1975-82, chmn. bd.; mem. U.S. Senate from N.J., 1982—. Commr. Port Authority N.Y. and N.J., 1978-82, N.J. econ. devel. coun.; trustee Sch. Bus., Columbia U.; nat. pres. Am. Friends Hebrew U., 1973-74; former gen. chmn., pres. Nat. United Jewish Appeal, 1975-77; mem. bd. overseers N.J. Symphony Orch.; mem. Pres.'s Coun. on the Holocaust; founder Lautenberg Center for Gen. and Tumor Immunology, Med. Sch., Hebrew U., Jerusalem, 1971; mem. fin. council Nat. Democratic Com. Served with Armed Forces, 1943-46, ETO; bd. mem. Montclair Art Mus., mem. adv. bd. Interfaith Hunger Appeal; trustees Tri-County Scholarship fund. Recipient Torch of Learning award Am. Friends Hebrew U., 1971, Scopus award, 1975. Mem. Nat. Assn. Data Processing Service Orgns. (pres. 1968-69, dir. from 1974), Patrons Soc. Met. Opera. Office: US Senate 506 Hart Senate Ofc Bldg Washington DC 20510-0004

LAUTENSCHLAGER, PEGGY ANN, prosecutor; b. Fond du Lac, Wis., Nov. 22, 1955; d. Milton A. and Patsy R. (Oleson) L.; m. Rajiv M. Kaul, Dec. 29, 1979 (div. Dec. 1986); children: Joshua Lautenschlager Kaul, Ryan Lautenschlager Kaul; m. William P. Rippl, May 26, 1989; 1 child, Rebecca Lautenschlager Rippl. BA, Lake Forest Coll., 1977; JD, U. Wis., 1980. Bar: Wis., U.S. Dist. Ct. (we. dist.). Pvt. practice atty. Oshkosh, Wis., 1981-85; dist. atty. Winnebago County Wis., Oshkosh, 1985-88; rep. Wis. Assembly, Fond du Lac, 1988-92; U.S. atty. U.S. Dept. of Justice, Madison, Wis., 1992—; apptd. mem. Govs. Coun. on Domestic Violence, Madison, State Elections Bd., Madison; bd. dirs. Blandine House, Inc. Active Dem. Nat. Com., Washington, 1992-93; com. Wis., 1989-92. Named Legislator of Yr., Wis. Sch. Counselors, 1992, Legislator of Yr., Wis. Corrections Coalition, 1992. Mem. Wis. Bar Assn., Dane County Bar Assn., Western Dist. Bar Assn., Fond du lac County Bar Assn., Phi Beta Kappa. Avocations: gardening, house renovation, sports, cooking, needlecrafts. Home: 1 Langdon St Apt 211 Madison WI 53703-1314

LAUTER, JAMES DONALD, retired stockbroker; b. L.A., Sept. 3, 1931; s. Richard Leo and Helen M. (Stern) L.; BS, UCLA, 1956; m. Neima Zwieli, Feb. 24, 1973; children: Walter James (dec.), Gary. Market rsch. mgr. Germain's Inc., L.A., 61; sr. v.p. investments, former branch mgr. Dean Witter Reynolds, Inc., Pasadena, Calif., 1961-96, ret., 1996. With Armed Forces, 1954-56. Recipient Sammy award L.A. Sales Execs. Club, 1961. Mem. AARP, UCLA Alumni Assn., UCLA Chancellors Assocs., Pasadena Bond Club (pres. 1995-96), Bruin Athletic Club. Home: 17237 Sunburst St Northridge CA 91325-2922

LAUTER, M. DAVID, family physician; b. Wilmington, Del., Jan. 7, 1951; s. Aaron Mordecai and Anne Marguerite (Scondin) L.; m. Diane R. Lauter, Oct. 11, 1980; children: Michael, Sara. BS, Johns Hopkins U., 1973, Ma, 1974; MD, Jefferson Med. Coll., 1978. Diplomate Am. Bd. Family Physicians. Resident family practice Ctrl. Maine Med. Ctr., Lewiston, 1978-81; clin. dir. U.S. Pub. Health Svc. Indian Hosp., Red Lake, Minn., 1981-84; pvt. practice as family doctor York, Maine, 1984—. With Pub. Health Svc., 1981-84. Office: 12 Hospital Dr York ME 03909-1030

LAUTERBACH, CHRISTINE, radio producer; b. Chgo., July 8, 1951; d. William Edward and Alberta Gertrude (Johnson) L.; m. Matthew Forest Simon, July 6, 1995. BA, Pomona Coll., 1974. Pub. affairs prodr. KSPC, Claremont, Calif., 1975-76; intern KPFK, L.A., 1976-78, news and pub. affairs prodr., 1978-79; news and pub. affairs dir. KNTF, Ontario, Calif., 1979-82; freelance news and feature reporter Calif. Pub. Radio/Nat. Pub. Radio, 1978-82; exec. producer The Broadcast Group, Washington, 1982—. Exec. prodr. In Depth Mag., 1982-84, Face-Off, 1984—, A Day's Work, Hosted by Studs Terkel, 1986, Worldtalk, 1988, Leonard Maltin on Video, 1989—, Secrets of Great Sex: The Guide to Transforming Your Intimate Relationship, 1993-94. Vol. CASA de Md., Takoma Park, 1990—. Mem. Soc. of Friends.

LAUTERBACH, EDWARD CHARLES, psychiatric educator; b. Chgo., Mar. 21, 1955; s. Edward G. and Virginia C. (Pochelski) L. AB cum laude, Augustana Coll., Rock Island, Ill., 1977; MD, Wake Forest U., 1982. Lic. psychiatrist, Mo., Pa., N.J., N.C., Ga.; diplomate Nat. Bd. Med. Examiners, Am. Bd. Psychiatry and Neurology. Intern Washington U. Sch. Medicine/Barnes Hosp., St. Louis, 1982-83, resident in psychiatry, 1983-86; clin. asst. Washington U. Sch. Medicine/Barnes Hosp., 1982-86, U. Medicine and Dentistry of N.J., New Brunswick, 1986-87, Mercer U. Sch. Medicine, Macon, Ga., 1988; chief div. adult and geriatric psychiatry, dept. psychiatry and behavioral scis. Mercer U. Sch. Medicine, Macon, 1988—, coord. grand rounds dept. psychiatry and behavioral scis., 1989—; coord. grand rounds dept. psychiatry and behavioral scis. Mercer U. Sch. Medicine, Macon, N.C., 1989—; asst prof. psychiatry Mercer U. Sch. Medicine, Macon, 1988-92, assoc. prof., 1992-96, prof., 1996—, prof. internal medicine, 1996—; pvt. practice Charlotte, N.C., 1987-88; chair free comm. IVth World Congress Biol. Psychiatry, Phila., 1985; mem. neurology staff Lyons VA Hosp., 1986; active staff privileges in neurology Mercy Hosp., Charlotte, 1987, cons., 1987; active privileges in psychiatry Med. Ctr. Ctrl. Ga., 1994—, Coliseum Psychiat. Hosp., 1994—, dir. med. staff continuing edn., 1994-96. Editorial reviewer Neuropsychiatry, Neuropsychology, and Behavioral Neurology, 1990—, Jour. Neuropsychiatry and Clin. Neuroscis., Biological Psychiatry, Movement Disorders, others; contbr. articles to profl. jours. Rock Sleyster scholar Wake Forest U., 1981. Mem. AMA (panelist DATTA coun. of sci. affairs 1990—), Am. Acad. Neurology, Am. Psychiat. Assn. (course dir. 1990-92, 94-95, symposium chairwoman 1995-96), Am. Neuropsychiat. Assn. (rsch. com.), Ga. Psychiat. Physicians Assn. (state com. on continuing med. edn.), Bibb County Med. Soc., N.C. Psychiat. Assn., Mecklenburg County Med. Soc., Med. Assn. Ga., Movement Disorder Soc., Charlotte Psychiat. Soc.

LAUTERBACH, ROBERT EMIL, steel company executive; b. Erie, Pa., May 31, 1918; s. Emil and Inez (Ricci) L.; m. Jane Stonerod; children: Jeffrey R., Marsha J., Mark S. BBA, Westminster Coll., 1939; postgrad., U. Pitts., 1939-41; LLD (hon.), Wheeling Coll., 1975. With Wheeling-Pitts. Steel Corp. and subs., 1939-78; treas. Johnson Steel & Wire Co., 1947-50, asst. sec. parent firm, 1950-52, sec., 1952-58, v.p., 1958-68; exec. v.p. Wheeling Pitts. Steel Corp., 1968-70, pres., 1970—, chmn., 1973-78, also bd. dirs.; bd. dirs. H.H. Robertson Co., Covenant Life Ins. Co. Bd. dirs. United Way of All County, Boy Scouts Am.; treas. local br. Am. Cancer Soc., 1953-62; pres. Mt. Lebanon Libr. Bd., 1962-73; pres. bd. trustees Westminster Coll., 1970-85. With AUS, 1943-46. Recipient George Washington Honor medal Freedoms Found. at Valley Forge. Mem. Am. Petroleum Inst., Am. Iron and Steel Inst., Duquesne Club, Laurel Valley Golf Club, Rolling Rock Club, Fox Chapel Golf Club. Home: 115 Forest Dr Pittsburgh PA 15238-2103

LAUTERBORN, ROBERT F., advertising educator, consultant; b. Albany, N.Y., Apr. 3, 1936; s. Ferdinand Raymond and Julia Marie (O'Brien) L.; m. Sylvia Ann Stebbings, Sept. 28, 1963; children: Michael Alan, David Ian. BA in English, Columbia U., 1956; postgrad., Syracuse U., 1957. Advt. sales rep. Syracuse (N.Y.) Herald Jour., 1957-60; mgr. creative programs Gen. Electric, Schenectady, N.Y., 1960-76; dir. mktg. communications, corp. advt. Internat. Paper, N.Y.C., 1976-86; James L. Knight prof. advertising U. N.C., Chapel Hill, 1986—; bd. dirs. Sawyer Riley Compton, Atlanta; prin. Morgan, Anderson & Co., N.Y.C., 1990—. Co-author: Integrated Marketing Communications, 1992; columnist (mag.) Advt. Age; radio commentator Sta. WUNC; contbr. articles to profl. jours. Mem. Bus. Mktg. Assn. (chmn. 1994-95), Advt. Rsch. Found., Am. Advt. Fedn., Assn. Nat. Advertisers (vice-chmn. 1985-86), Am. Acad. Advt., Mktg. Sci. Inst., Nat. Advt. Rev. Bd., Sigma Alpha Epsilon. Republican. Roman Catholic. Home: 1403 Graybluff Trl Chapel Hill NC 27514-9126

LAUTERBUR, PAUL C(HRISTIAN), chemistry educator; b. Sidney, Ohio, May 6, 1929. BS, Case Inst. Tech., 1951; PhD, U. Pitts., 1962; PhD (hon.), U. Liege, Belgium, 1984; DSc (hon.), Carnegie Mellon U., 1987; DEng (hon.), Corpernicus Med. Acad., Cracow, Poland, 1988; DSc (hon.), Wesleyan U., 1989, SUNY, Stony Brook, 1990; DEng (hon.), Rennselaer Poly. Inst., 1991, U. Mons., Hainaut, Belgium, 1996. Rsch. asst. and assoc. Mellon Inst., Pitts., 1951-53, fellow, 1955-63; assoc. prof. chemistry SUNY, Stony Brook, 1963-69, prof. chemistry, 1969-84, with, 1963-85, rsch. prof. radiology, 1978-85, univ. prof., 1984-85; prof. (4) depts. U. Ill., Urbana, 1985—; Disting. Univ. prof. Coll. Medicine U. Ill., Chgo., 1990—. Contbr. articles to profl. jours.; mem. editorial bds.; mem. sci. couns. Cpl. U.S. Army, 1953-55. Recipient Clin. Rsch. award Lasker Found., 1984, Nat. Medal of Sci., U.S.A., 1987, Fiuggi Internat. prize Fondazione Fiuggi, 1987, Roentgen medal, 1987, Gold medal Radiol. Soc. N.Am., 1987, Nat. Medal of Tech., 1988, Gold medal Soc. Computed Body Tomography, 1989, The Amsterdam (Alfred Heineken) prize in medicine, 1989, Laufman-Greatbatch award Assn. for Advancement Med. Intrumentation, 1989, Leadership Tech. award Nat. Elec. Mfr. Assn., 1990, Bower award and prize for achievement in sci. Benjamin Franklin Nat. Meml. Commn. of the Franklin Inst., 1990, Internat. Soc. Magnetic Resonance award, 1992, Kyoto prize, Inamori Foundation, 1994. Fellow AAAS, Am. Phys. Soc. (Biol. Physics prize 1983), Am. Inst. Med. and Biol. Engring.; mem. IEEE (sr.), NAS, Am. Chem. Soc., Internat. Soc. Magnetic Resonance in Medicine (Gold medal 1982). Office: U Ill 1307 W Park St Urbana IL 61801-2332

LAUTERSTEIN, JOSEPH, cardiologist; b. Vienna, Austria, Dec. 1, 1934; came to U.S., 1940; s. Bernard and Hajnalka (Stern) L.; m. Erika Stein, Jan. 24, 1964 (dec. Aug. 1990); children: Deborah Ann, Brenda Rose; m. Elisabeth Spiegl Lazaroff, Nov. 27, 1994. BA, Syracuse U., 1955; MD, U. Vienna, 1964. Lic. physician, N.Y. Intern, then resident in internal medicine The Bklyn. Cumberland Med. Ctr., 1964-66, 68-69, fellow in cardiology, 1969-70; attending physician, cons. internal medicine and cardiology Hamilton Ave. Hosp., Monticello, N.Y., 1970-78; attending physician, cons. internal medicine and cardiology Community Gen. Hosp. Sullivan County, Harris, N.Y., 1970—, chief cardiology, 1971—, chief of staff, 1981-82; mem. courtesy staff dept. internal medicine and cardiology The Bklyn. Hosp. Ctr., 1971-95; clin. asst. dept. internal medicine and cardiology St. Vincent's Hosp. and Med. Ctr. N.Y., 1974-80, asst. attending physician, 1981-86, assoc. attending physician, 1987-94, attending physician, 1995—; with Sullivan Internal Medicine Group, P.C., Monticello, 1970—; dir. ICU Community Gen. Hosp. Sullivan County, 1971-79, dir. CCU, 1978—, dir. spl. diagnostics, 1984—, pres. med. bd., 1981-82; mem. pacemaker task force Empire State Med. Sci. and Ednl. Found., 1985-89; med. dir. Sullivan County EMT-D Program, 1989—; police surgeon Village of Monticello, 1974—, Sullivan County, 1972—; med. advisor Monticello Vol. Ambulance Corps, 1970-80, 89—; mem. Sullivan County Emergency Svcs. Coun., 1990, 91. Co-contbr. articles to Jour. Cardiovascular Surgery, Annals of Thoracic Surgery, Angiology, Chest. Trustee Cmty. Gen. Hosp. Sullivan County, 1981-82, Cmty. Gen. Hosp. Found., 1990—; mem. Nat. Ski Patrol, 1979—, med. advisor So. N.Y. region, 1989-94, 97—, med. advisor So. Catskill sect., 1994-97; patroller Holiday Mountain Ski Patrol, 1979—. Capt. M.C., USAF, 1966-68. Named Citizen of Yr., SYDA Found. Sullivan County, 1991. Fellow Am. Coll. Cardiology (N.Y. State chpt., del. to N.Y. Med. Soc. Ho. Dels. 1991—, councilor 1991—, com. mem. 1990—), Am. Coll. Chest Physicians (assoc.), Am. Coll. Angiology, Internat. Coll. Angiology, N.Y. Cardiological Soc. (exec. bd. dirs. 1982—, mem. various coms.), N.Y. Acad. Medicine; mem. AMA, Am. Geriatrics Soc., Am. Soc. Internal Medicine, Soc. for Critical Care Medicine, N.Y. Acad. Scis., N.Am. Soc. for Pacing and Electrophysiology, Med. Soc. State of N.Y., others. Office: Sullivan Internal Medicine Group PC 370 Broadway Monticello NY 12701-1104

LAUTZ, LINDSAY ALLAN, retained executive search consultant; b. San Bernardino, Calif., Dec. 24, 1947; s. Carl Ernest and Carole Mae (Lindsay) L.; m. Laurie Ann Morgan, June 20, 1970; children—Christopher, Kathryn, Amy. BS, U. So. Calif., 1971, postgrad., 1971. Adminstrv. mgr. Associated Freight Lines, Los Angeles, 1969-73; with Fromm & Sichel, Inc., San Francisco, 1973-81; treas. and fin. officer Fromm & Sichel, Inc., 1977-81; co-founder, pres., CEO Positive Video, Ltd., 1981-88; founder, chmn. Morgan Board Works, Inc., San Francisco, 1989-90; prin. Korn/Ferry Internat., San Francisco, 1990-92; ptnr. Wilkinson and Ives, San Francisco, 1992-97, Lautz, Grotte, Engler, San Francisco, 1997—. Exec. producer Makaha Skate Classic, spl. interest home video; inventor skate bd. product Instant Ollie. Founder Havens Dads Club, Piedmont, Calif. With USAR, 1971-77. Mem. Commerce Assocs. (pres.), Pi Kappa, Alpha. Republican. Home: 411 Camino Sobrante Orinda CA 94563 Office: Lautz Grotte Engler One Bush St Ste 550 San Francisco CA 94104

LAUTZENHEISER, MARVIN WENDELL, computer software engineer; b. Maximo, Ohio, Feb. 19, 1929; s. Milton Leander and Mary Lucetta (Keim) L.; m. Jean Bethene Baker, Oct. 26, 1946 (div. Nov. 1986); children: Constance Kay, Thomas Edward, Jan Stephen; m. Paula Ann Keane, Mar. 10, 1990. BS in Math., Mt. Union Coll., 1953. Spl. agt. FBI, Washington, 1953-59; computer analyst Tech. Ops., Washington, 1959-64; pres. Anagram Corp., Springfield, Va., 1964-83; computer analyst Onyx Corp., McLean, Va., 1983, Inmark, Springfield, 1983-84, Memory Scis., McLean, 1984-85; software scientist Zitel Corp., San Jose, Calif., 1985—. Inventor, designer in field. Mem. Mensa, Am. Iris Soc. Avocations: theatre pipe organ, hybrid iris gardening. Home: 7216 Neuman St Springfield VA 22150-4421 Office: Zitel Corp 47211 Bayside Pky Fremont CA 94538-6517

LAUVEN, PETER MICHAEL, anesthesiologist; b. Leverkusen, Fed. Republic Germany, May 13, 1948; s. Peter Aloysius and Katharina (Oedekoven) L.; m. Anne-Kareen Wetje, Nov. 7, 1970; children: Anne-Laureen, Lars-Peter. Diploma in Chem., U. Bonn, Fed. Republic of Germany, 1970, Dr. rer. nat., 1974, Dr. med., 1979, priv.-dozent, 1985. Teaching asst. Inst. Organic Chem. U. Bonn, Fed. Republic of Germany, 1970-76, scientist Inst. Anaesthesiology, 1976-79, physician, 1979—, anaesthesiologist, 1983—, asst. dir., 1983-85, vice-chmn., 1985-92, prof. of anaesthesia, 1986—, chmn. dept. Anaesthesiology & Surg. ICU, 1993—; mem. German Fed. Drug Admission Com., 1987—. Author, co-editor: Das Zentralanticholinergische Syndrom, 1985, Klinische Pharmakologie und rationale Arzneimitteltherapie, 1992; author, editor: Anasthesie und der Geriatrische Patient, 1989, Postoperative Schmerztherapie, 1991. Recipient scholarship Stipendien Fonds der Chemischen Inst., Frankfurt, 1970, Paul Martini award, Paul Martini Found., Bonn, 1988. Mem. Gesellschaft Deutscher Chemiker, Deutsche Gesellschaft für Anaesthesiologie und Intensiv Medizin, Deutsche Gesellschaft fur experimentelle und klinische Pharmakologie und Toxikologie, Am. Soc. Anaesthesiology (affiliate), Am. Soc. Regional Anaesthesia, European Acad. Anaesthesiology, European Soc. Regional Anaesthesia, European Soc. Intensive Care Medicine, European Soc. Anaesthesiology, N.Y. Acad. of Scis. Home: Haendelstr 22, D-33604 Bielefeld Germany Office: Clin Anes and Intensive Care, Teutoburger Str 50, D-33604 Bielefeld Germany

LAUVER, EDITH BARBOUR, nonprofit organization administrator; b. Tarrytown, N.Y., Mar. 2, 1933; d. John Alan and Adelaide Cora (Marden) Barbour; m. Robert Mitchell Lauver, Dec. 16, 1961; children: Alan Jackson, Donald Marden, Robert Barbour. BSN, Skidmore Coll., 1954; MA, Columbia U., 1957; postgrad., U. Ariz., 1980-95. Sch. nurse, tchr. Pub. Schs. of Tarrytowns, North Tarrytown, N.Y., 1956-60; instr. St. Mary's Hosp. Sch. Nursing, Tucson, 1960-62; asst. prof. Coll. Nursing U. Ariz., Tucson, 1969-73, grad. teaching, rsch. assoc., 1980-85; asst. dir. nursing for pediatrics U. Ariz. Med. Ctr., Tucson, 1973-74; asst. adminstr. patient care Pima County/Kino Community Hosp., Tucson, 1974-77; asst. dir. nursing for staff devel. U. Ariz. Health Scis. Ctr., Tucson, 1978-80; dir. Interfaith Coalition for Homeless, Tucson, 1987—; mem. staff Thomas-Davis Clinic, Tucson, 1963-64; staff nurse surg. unit St. Joseph's Hosp., Tucson, 1964-65; adminstrv. asst. Tucson Ecumenical Coun., 1987; weekend relief staff nurse Handmaker Jewish Geriatric Ctr., Tucson, 1988-89. Active Accord Interfaith Soc. Action Group, 1983-94, St. Mark's Prebyn. Presch. and Kindergarten, 1965-87, St. Mark's Presbyn. Ch., 1986—, elder, 1986-92; bd. dirs. Ariz. Coalition for Human Svcs., 1987—; Mobile Meals Tucson, Inc., 1976-87, sec. 1981-83; bd. dirs. Interfaith Coalition for Homeless 1987—; participant Ariz. Women's Town Hall, 1986, 87; mem. adv. bd. Tucson Met. Ministry's Cmty. Closet, 1988-92; bd. dirs. Tucson Met. Ministry, 1989-92; active various other civic activities. Mem. ANA, Ariz. Nurses' Assn. (fin. com. 1985-87, ANA del. 1986-87, dist. bd. dirs. 1982-84, pres.-elect, pres. dist. 1985-87, various coms.), Soc. Southwestern Authors, Skidmore Coll. Alumni Assn., Sigma Theta Tau (mem. nat. fin. com. 1981-83, treas. local chpt. 1978-81, fin. com. 1974-88, pres.-elect 1990—, pres. 1988-92), Pi Lambda Theta, Phi Delta Kappa, Kappa delta Pi. Home and Office: 445 S Craycroft Rd Tucson AZ 85711-4549

LAUX, JAMES MICHAEL, historian, educator; b. La Crosse, Wis., Nov. 4, 1927; s. William M. and Clara (Smelser) L.; m. Barbara I. Robertson, 1952; children: Robert James, Stephen Andrew, Frederick Lawrence. Student, Wis. State U., 1946-48; BS, U. Wis., 1950; MA, U. Conn., 1952; PhD, Northwestern U., 1957. Instr. history Wis. State U., La Crosse, 1955-57; asst. prof. U. Cin., 1957-65, assoc. prof., 1965-69, prof., 1969-89, prof. emeritus, 1989—; vis. prof. Northwestern U., Evanston, Ill. 1966-67. Author: In First Gear, 1976, The European Automobile Industry, 1992; co-author: Revolution Automobile, 1977; co-editor: French Revolution, 1968; translator Right Wing in France, 1966; co-editor French Hist. Studies, 1985-92, Napoleon, 1989. With USN, 1945-46. Fulbright scholar, France, 1954-55; recipient Rieveschl award, U. Cin., 1981. Mem. Soc. French Hist. Studies, Soc. Automotive Historians, Amis Fondation Automobile Marius Berliet. Home: 100 S Tremain Apt G-4 Mount Dora FL 32757

LAVALLE, IRVING HOWARD, decision analysis educator; b. Hancock, N.Y., Apr. 24, 1939; s. Irving Howard and Louise Hartshorne (Wood) LaV. A.B., Trinity Coll., Conn., 1960; M.B.A., Harvard U., 1963, D.B.A., 1966. Asst. prof. A.B. Freeman Sch. Bus., Tulane U., New Orleans, 1965-68; assoc. prof. A.B. Freeman Sch. Bus., Tulane U., 1968-71; prof. A.B. Freeman Sch. Bus., Tulane U., New Orleans, 1971-93; Francis Martin prof., 1993—; chmn. Decision Analysis SIG, Balt., 1980-82, So. Cons. Group, Inc., New Orleans, 1981—. Author: Introduction to Probability, Decision and Inference, 1970; Fundamentals of Decision Analysis, 1978; also articles; editor various profl. jours. Ford Found. fellow, 1964, Frank P. Ramsey medal, 1996. Mem. Royal Statis. Soc., Inst. Mgmt. Scis., Ops. Research Soc. Am., Inst. Math. Stats., Econometric Soc. Episcopalian. Avocations: music; photography; woodworking. Home: 726 Foucher St New Orleans LA 70115-1311 Office: Tulane U Freeman Sch Bus St Charles Ave New Orleans LA 70118-5669

LAVALLEE, H.-CLAUDE, chemical engineer, researcher; b. Cap-Santé, Que., Can., July 28, 1938; s. Henri Lavallée and Yvonne Lavallée-Légaré; m. Ginette Morissette, June 25, 1966. BScA, Univ. Laval, Que., 1964, MScA, 1965, DSc, 1970. Rschr. Def. Rsch. Establishment of Valcartier Govt. of Can., Que., 1965-67; prof. chem. engring. U. Que. at Trois-Rivières, 1970-74; sr. engr. pulp & paper industry Ministry of Environment-Govt. of Que., Quebec City, 1974-87, head pulp & paper industry, 1980-87; dir. Pulp & Paper Rsch. Ctr. U. Que. at Trois-Rivières, 1987-96, dir. pulp & paper grad. studies, 1996—; pres. H.C. Lavallée Inc., Donnacona, Que., 1989—; cons. Roche Ltée, Québec City, 1988-96; adminstr. John Meunier Inc., Montréal, 1991—, Centre des technologies du gaz naturel, Montréal, 1992—. Contbr. articles to profl. jours., chpts. to books. Recipient prize Raimbeault de Montigny Conf. Technologique, Point-au-Pic, 1990, 95, prize of excellence SNC-Lavalin Assn. Que. Technique de l'eau, 1993, Best Rev. award Can. Jour. Chem. Engring., 1995-96. Mem. TAPPI, Can. Pulp and Paper Assn. (John S. Bates award 1995), Ordre des Ingénieurs du Que. Roman Catholic. Office: Ctr Rsch Pulp & Paper, 3351 Blvd des Forges, Trois Rivieres, PQ Canada G9A 5H7

LAVATELLI, LEO SILVIO, retired physicist, educator; b. Mackinac Island, Mich., Aug. 15, 1917; s. Silvio E. and Zella (Cunningham) L.; m. Anna Craig Henderson, June 14, 1941 (dec. Sept. 1966); children: Nancy Jack, Mark Leo; m. Celia Burns, Jan. 23, 1967 (dec. May 1976); 1 stepchild, Faith Stendler (dec.); m. Barbara Gow, Nov. 22, 1976 (div. Jan. 1979; dec. Mar. 1995); stepchildren: Ann Deemer, Lindsay Deemer; m. Olwen Thomas, Mar. 4, 1982; stepchildren: Alice Ann Williamson (Mrs. Michael W. Cone), Caroline Hill Williamson, Thomas Holman Williamson, Hugh Stuart Williamson. BS, Calif. Inst. Tech., 1939; MA, Princeton U., 1943, Harvard U., 1949; PhD, Harvard U., 1951. Instr. physics, chemistry, algebra, calculus, symbolic logic Deep Springs (Calif.) Jr. Coll., 1939-41; instr. Princeton (N.J.) U., 1941; rsch. asst. Manhattan Dist. Office Sci. R&D, Nat. Def. Rsch. Coun., Princeton, 1942-43; jr. staff mem. Los Alamos (N.Mex.) Nat. Lab. (formerly Manhattan Dist. Site Y), 1943-46; rsch. asst. Harvard U., Cambridge, Mass., 1946-50; asst. prof. physics, staff mem. Control Systems Lab. U. Ill., Urbana, 1950-55, assoc. prof., 1955-58, prof., 1958-79, prof. emeritus, 1979—; mem. measuring groups and witness for Trinity, the Alamogordo Atomic Bomb Test, 1945; mem. design team orbit plotting/control circuit logic FM new cyclotron project Harvard U., 1946; observer air/ground exercises U.S. Dept. Def., Waco, Tex., 1952; observer joint air exercises NATO, Fed. Republic Germany, 1955; mem. project quick-fix Control Sys. Lab., 1953; cons. Ill. group Phys. Sci. Study Com., 1956-57, Sci. Teaching Ctr., MIT, 1966, Teheran Rsch. unit U. Ill., 1970; participant info. theory in biology conf. U. Ill., 1952. Producer silent film cassettes on orbit graphing U. Ill., 1964; co-interviewee video tape Logical Thinking in Children and Science Education, Nat. Japanese TV, Tokyo, 1970; phys. sci. cons. The Macmillan Science Series, 1970 edit., The Macmillan Co., N.Y.C., 1967-70; contbr. articles and revs. to profl. publs. Co-moderator discussion Fedn. Atomic Scientists, 1945, 1947. Recipient U. Ill. Undergrad Teaching award U. St. Andrews, Scotland, summer 1965; John Simon Guggenheim Meml. fellow U. Bologna, Italy, 1957. Fellow Am. Phys. Soc.; mem. Harvard Faculty Club (non-resident). Avocations: music, painting, art history, books, movies. Home: 10181 Seven Paths Rd Spring Hope NC 27882-9543

LAVE, CHARLES ARTHUR, economics educator; b. Phila., May 18, 1938; s. Israel and Esther (Axlerod) L.; 1 child, Rebecca. BA, Reed Coll., 1960; PhD, Stanford U., 1968. Mem. faculty U. Calif., Irvine, 1966—, prof. econs., chmn. dept. econs., 1978-85, 89-92; vis. prof., vis. scholar Hampshire Coll., 1972, Stanford U., 1974, MIT, 1982, Harvard U., 1982, U. Calif., Berkeley, 1988, 94. Author: (with James March) An Introduction to Models in the Social Sciences, 1975, Energy and Auto Type Choice, 1981, Urban Transit, 1985, others. Trustee Reed Coll., Portland, Oreg., 1978-82; bd. dirs. Nat. Bur. Econ. Rsch., Cambridge, 1991—; chmn. bd. Irvine Campus Housing Authority, Inc., 1982-96, asst. to chancellor, 1996—. With USAF, 1957. Recipient Pyke Johnson award Transp. Rsch. Bd., 1987, Extraordinarius award U. Calif., 1993. Fellow Soc. Applied Anthropology; mem. Am. Econ. Assn., AAAS, Transp. Research Bd. Office: U Calif Dept Econs Irvine CA 92717

LAVE, JUDITH RICE, economics educator; came to U.S., 1961; d. J.H. Melville and G.A. Pauline (Lister) Rice; m. Lester Bernard Lave, June 21, 1965; children: Tamara Rice, Jonathan Melville. BA in Econs., Queen's U., Kingston, Ont., Can., 1957-61; MA in Econs., Harvard U., 1964, PhD, 1967; LLD, Queen's U., 1994. Lectr., asst. prof. econs. Carnegie Mellon U., Pitts., 1966-73, assoc. prof., 1973-78; dir. econ. analysis Office of Sec., Dep. of Asst. Sec. Planning and Evaluation, Washington, 1978-79; dir. office of rsch. Health Care Fin. Adminstrn., Washington, 1980-82; prof. health econs. U. Pitts., 1982—, co-dir. Ctr. for Rsch. on Health Care, 1996—; cons. Nat. Study Internal Medicine Manpower, Chgo., 1976, Wash. State Hosp. Assn., 1984, Horty, Springer & Mattern, Pitts., 1984, Hogan and Hartson, Washington, 1989, Ont. Hosp. Assn., Conn. Hosp. Assn., 1991; cons. various agys. U.S. HHS (formerly U.S. HEW), 1971-89; mem. adv. panel Robert Wood Johnson Found., Princeton, N.J., 1983-84, 96—, Leonard Davis Inst., Phila., 1984, U.S. Congress, 1977, 82, 83—; com. mem. Inst. Medicine Coms., Washington, 1975-91, Project 2000 Commn. on Future of Podiatry, Washington, 1985-86. Editl. bd. Wiley Series in Health Svcs., 1989-90, Health Svcs. Rsch., 1970-74, Inquiry, 1979-82, AUPHA Press, 1986, Jour. of Health Policy Politics and Law; co-author: Hospital Construction Act - An Evaluation of the Hill Burton Program, 1948-73, 74, Health Status, Medical Care Utilization and Outcome: A Bibliography of Empirical Studies (4 vols.) 1989, Providing Hospital Services, 1989; contbr. numerous articles to profl. jours. Mem. Prospective Payment Assessment Commn., 1993—, planning com. ARC, Pitts., 1986—; mem. rev. com. United Way, Pitts., 1988-90; bd. dirs. Craig Ho., Pitts., 1976-77. Woodrow Wilson fellow, 1961-62. Fellow Assn. Health Svcs. Rsch. (disting., pres. 1977-88, bd. dirs. 1983-93); mem. Found. for Health Svcs. Rsch. (pres. 1988-89, bd. dirs. 1983—), Am. Pub. Health Soc., Am. Econ. Soc. (com. mem.), Inst. Medicine, Nat. Acad. Social Ins., Robert wood Johnson Found. (coun. on econ. impact of health sys. change 1996—). Democrat. Home: 1008 Devonshire Rd Pittsburgh PA 15213-2914 Office: U Pitts A649 Pub Health Pittsburgh PA 15213

LAVE, LESTER BERNARD, economist, educator, researcher; b. Phila., Aug. 5, 1939; s. Israel and Esther (Axelrod) L.; m. Judith Rice, June 21, 1965; children: Tamara Rice, Jonathan Melville. B.A., Reed Coll., 1960; postgrad., MIT, 1960-61; Ph.D., Harvard U., 1963. Prof. Carnegie-Mellon U., Pitts., 1963—, James H. Higgins prof. econs., 1984, univ prof., 1992—; vis. prof. Northwestern U., Evanston, Ill., 1965-66; sr. fellow Brookings Instn., Washington, 1978-82; cons. Rand Corp., Santa Monica, Calif., 1960-74, GM Rsch. Labs., Warren, Mich., 1971-87; cons. Dept. Transp., Dept. Def., Dept. Justice, Dept. Labor, Nuclear Regulatory Commn. Author: Air Pollution and Human Health, 1977, Strategy of Social Regulation, 1981, Annual Review of Public Health, 1990, Quantitative Risk Assessment, 1983, (with A. Upton) Toxic Chemicals, Health and the Environment, 1987. Mem. Gov.'s Health Task Force, Pa., 1970-74. NIH grantee, 1967-78; Nat. Safety Council grantee, 1967-68; NSF grantee, 1978-84, 87-90, 88-90, 90—; R.K. Mellon Charitable Trusts grantee, 1970-72; Sloan Found. grantee, 1980-83. Mem. Am. Am. Econ. Assn., Soc. Risk Analysis (pres. 1985-86), Am. Pub. Health Assn., Inst. of Medicine, Phi Beta Kappa, Sigma Xi. Home: 1008 Devonshire Rd Pittsburgh PA 15213-2914 Office: Carnegie-Mellon U Grad Sch Indsl Adminstrn Pittsburgh PA 15213

LAVECK, GERALD DELOSS, physician, educator; b. Seattle, Apr. 19, 1927; s. DeLoss Francis and Helen Marie (Keller) LaV.; m. Beverly Beers Vander Veer, July 22, 1976; children: Gerald DeLoss, Roxanne M., Julie B., Amy B., Jill M. B.S., U. Wash., 1948, M.D., 1951. Clin. dir. Rainier Sch., Buckley, Wash., 1958-62; head crippled children's service Wash. Health Dept., 1962-63; dir. Nat. Inst. Child Health and Human Devel., Bethesda, 1966-73; clin. prof. pediatrics Georgetown U., Washington, 1966-73; clin. prof. U. Wash., Seattle, 1973—; dir. research Bur. Community Health Services, USPHS, Rockville, Md., 1976-77; med. cons. Region X, USPHS, Seattle, 1977-85. With USPHS, 1953-55, 72-85, ret., 1985. Recipient Superior Service award HEW, 1966. Fellow Am. Acad. Pediatrics, Am. Pub. Health Assn., Assn. Mental Deficiency. Home: 6633 NE Windermere Rd Seattle WA 98115-7942

LAVELLE, ARTHUR, anatomy educator; b. Fargo, N.D., Nov. 29, 1921; s. Frank and Lillie (Hanson) LaV.; m. Faith Evelyn Wilson, 1947; 1 dau., Audrey Anne. B.S., U. Wash., 1946; M.A., Johns Hopkins, 1948; Ph.D., U. Pa., 1951. USPHS postdoctoral fellow U. Pa., Phila., 1951-52; mem. faculty dept. anatomy U. Ill. Coll. Medicine, Chgo., 1952—; assoc. prof. U. Ill. Coll. Medicine, 1958-65, prof., 1965-87, prof. emeritus, 1987—; vis. prof. UCLA, 1968-69; cons. Galesburg (Ill.) State Rsch. Hosp., 1965-68; mem. Biol. Stain Commn., 1953-93, trustee, 1978-93, pres., 1981-86, v.p., 1991-92. Mem. editorial bd. Biotechnic and Histochemistry, 1989-93; contbr. articles to profl. jours. USPHS research grantee, 1953-70; Cerebral Palsy Found. grantee, 1964-68; Guggenheim fellow, 1968-69. Mem. Am. Assn. Anatomists, Am. Soc. Cell Biology, Soc. Developmental Biology, AAAS, Soc. Neurosci., Sigma Xi. Office: 1853 W Polk St Chicago IL 60612-4316

LAVELLE, BRIAN FRANCIS DAVID, lawyer; b. Cleve., Aug. 16, 1941; s. Gerald John and Mary Josephine (O'Callaghan) L.; m. Sara Hill, Sept. 10, 1966; children: S. Elizabeth, B. Francis D., Catherine H. BA, U. Va., 1963; JD, Vanderbilt U., 1966; LLM in Taxation, N.Y.U., 1969. Bar: N.C. 1966, Ohio 1968. Assoc. VanWinkle Buck, Wall, Starnes & Davis, Asheville, N.C., 1968-74, ptnr., 1974—; lectr. continuing edn. N.C. Bar Found., Wake Forest U. Estate Planning Inst., Hartford Tax Inst., Duke U. Estate Planning Inst. Contbr. articles on law to profl. jours. Trustee Carolina Day Sch., 1981-92, sec., 1982-85; vice-chmn. Buncombe County Indsl. Facilities and Pollution Control Authority, 1976-82; bd. dirs. Geodetic Internat., Inc. U.S. divsn., The Salvation Army, Western N.C. Community Found., 1986— (sec. 1987-90); mem. Asheville Tax Study Group, 1981—, chmn., 1984; bd. advs. U.N.C. Annual Tax Inst., 1981—. Capt. JAG USAF, 1966-67. Mem. ABA, N.C. Bar Assn. (bd. govs. 1979-82, councillor tax sect. 1979-83, councillor estate planning law sect. 1982-85), Am. Coll. Trust and Estate Counsel (state chmn. 1982-85, regent 1984-90, lectr. continuing edn.), N.C. State Bar (splty. exam. com. on estate planning and probate law 1984-90, chmn. 1990-91, cert. 1987). Episcopalian (clk. vestry All Souls Ch.). Clubs: Biltmore Forest Country. Lodge: Rotary (Asheville). Home: 45 Brookside Rd Asheville NC 28803-3015 Office: 11 N Market St PO Box 7376 Asheville NC 28802

LAVELLE, CHARLES JOSEPH, lawyer; b. Louisville, Aug. 31, 1950; s. James Ronald and Mary Elizabeth (Logan) L.; m. Donna Kay Mulligan, Jan. 21, 1978. BS with high honors, U. Notre Dame, 1972; JD, U. Ky., 1975; LLM in Taxation, NYU, 1977. Bar: Ky. 1975, U.S. Dist. Ct. (wes. dist.) Ky. 1977, U.S. Tax Ct. 1977, U.S. Claims Ct. 1986, U.S. Ct. Appeals (6th and Fed. cirs.) 1986, U.S. Supreme Ct. 1989. Assoc. Greenebaum Doll & McDonald PLLC, Louisville, 1977-82, mem., 1982—; chmn. bar liaison cen. region IRS, Cin., 1989, sec., 1997; mem. Regional Counsel Adv. Group, Cin., 1988-89. Contbr. articles to profl. jours. Bd. dirs. Ky. Ctr. Pub. Issues, 1992-94; mem. steering com. Ky. Coalition for Edn., 1993-94; mem. Ky. Ltd. Liability Co. Legislation Drafting Com., 1993-94; mem. planning com. Ky. Conclave on Legal Edn., 1995. Secondary Sci. Tng. grant NSF, U. Ga., 1967, rcsh. grantee NSF, U. Notre Dame, 1969. Mem. ABA (tax sect.), Ky. Bar Assn. (chmn. tax sect. 1992-93), Louisville Bar Assn. (chmn. tax com. 1983-84, vice chmn., treas. tax com. 1980-82), U. Ky. Law Alumni Assn. (bd. dirs. 1986—, pres. 1989-90, treas. 1987-90, 90—), Ky. C. of C. (bd. dirs. 1991—, exec. com. 1997—, tax. com.), Rotary (bd. dirs. 1991-93, 95-97, treas. 1995-97, dist. conf. chair 1994), Notre Dame Club (pres. 1984-86, chmn. 1986-88, Ky. Man of Yr. 1990), Leadership Ky. (vice chmn. membership svcs. 1995-97, alumni bd. dirs. 1992-92, pres. alumni 1993-94, bd. dirs. 1993-97, exec. com. 1995-97). Office: Greenebaum Doll & McDonald 3300 National City Tower Louisville KY 40202

LAVELLE, PAUL MICHAEL, lawyer; b. Scranton, Pa., July 19, 1956; s. James Gregory and Helen Delores (Borys) L.; m. Sue Swan, May 24, 1980. BS, U. Scranton, 1978; JD, Loyola U., New Orleans, 1981. Bar: La. 1981, U.S. Dist. Ct. (ea., mid. dists.) La., U.S. Dist. Ct. (we. dist.) La. 1985, U.S. Ct. Appeals (5th cir.) 1981. Assoc. Montgomery, Barnett, Brown & Read, New Orleans, 1981-86, ptnr., 1986-90; ptnr. Guste, Barnett & Shushan, New Orleans, 1991—; chair Nat. H.S. Mock Trial Championship, Inc., 1991-92; mem. adv. bd. La. Ctr. for Law and Civic Edn. Mem. ABA (assembly del. young lawyers divsn. 1987-88), La. Bar Assn. (chmn. h.s. mock trial 1988, rep. exec. coun. young lawyers sect. 1988), Def. Rsch. Inst., Internat. Assn. Def. Counsel, Assn. Transp. Practitioners, Order Ky. Cols. (hon.), La. Assn. Def. Counsel. Democrat. Roman Catholic. Avocations: camping, hiking, coach LaFreniere Soccer Assn. Office: Guste Barnett & Shushan 639 Loyola Ave Ste 2500 New Orleans LA 70113-7103

LAVENAS, SUZANNE, writer, editor, consultant; b. Buenos Aires, Dec. 17, 1942; came to U.S., 1955; d. Carlos Fernando and Mary (Sharp) Lavenas; m. Wesley First, Jan. 9, 1982. Student, Antioch Coll., 1960-64, 65-66. Computer programmer N.Y. Telephone, N.Y.C., 1966-68; prodn. editor, then copy editor Travel Weekly, N.Y.C., 1968-76, chief copy editor, 1976-79; mng. editor Indsl. Chem. News, N.Y.C., 1981-82; editor, writer, cons. N.Y.C., 1986—. Author numerous articles. Mem. Overseas Press Club, Soc. Silurians. Republican. Episcopalian. Avocations: reading, cooking, computer hacking, walking, cinema. Home: 236 Edgemere St Montauk NY 11954-5249

LAVENBERG, STEPHEN S., electrical engineer, researcher; b. Mar. 22, 1943. BS in Elec. Engring., Rensselaer Poly. Inst., 1963; MS in Elec. Engring., Calif. Inst. Tech., 1964, PhD in Elec. Engring., 1968. Rsch. staff mem., sr. mgr. IBM Corp. Rsch., Thomas J. Watson Rsch. Ctr. Fellow IEEE (Meritorious Svc. award 1984, Koji Kobayashi Computers and Comm. award 1991). Office: IBM Corp Rsch Thomas J Watson Rsch Ctr Yorktown Heights NY 10598*

LAVENDER, ROBERT EUGENE, state supreme court justice; b. Muskogee, Okla., July 19, 1926; s. Harold James and Vergene Irene (Martin) L.; m. Maxine Knight, Dec. 22, 1945; children—Linda (Mrs. Dean Courter), Robert K., Debra (Mrs. Thomas Merrill), William J. LL.B., U. Tulsa, 1953; grad., Appellate Judges Seminar, 1967, Nat. Coll. State Trial Judges, 1970. Bar: Okla. bar 1953. With Mass. Bonding & Ins. Co., Tulsa, 1951-53, U.S. Fidelity & Guaranty Co., Tulsa, 1953-54; asst. city atty. Tulsa, 1954-55, practice, 1955-60; practice Claremore, Okla., 1960-65; justice Okla. Supreme Ct., 1965—, chief justice, 1979-80; guest lectr. Okla. U., Oklahoma City U., Tulsa U. law schs. Republican committeeman, Rogers County, 1961-62. Served with USNR, 1944-46. Recipient Disting. Alumnus award U. Tulsa, 1993. Mem. ABA, Okla. Bar Assn., Rogers County Bar Assn., Am. Judicature Soc., Okla. Jud. Conf., Phi Alpha Delta (hon.). Methodist (adminstrv. bd.). Club: Mason (32 deg.). Home: 2910 Kerry Ln Oklahoma City OK 73120-2507 Office: US Supreme Ct Okla Rm 1 State Capitol Oklahoma City OK 73105

LAVENGOOD, LAWRENCE GENE, management educator, historian; b. Tulsa, June 30, 1924; s. Lawrence Wilbur and Elizabeth (Gardner) L.; m. Gloria M. deLeon, Aug. 27, 1947; children: Jessica, Abigail, Timothy, Rachel. M.A., U. Chgo., 1947, Ph.D., 1953. Asst. prof. bus. history Northwestern U., Evanston, Ill., 1953-59, assoc. prof., 1959-69, chmn. dept. policy and environ., 1980-82, prof. bus. history and policy and environ., 1970-94, prof. emeritus, 1994—; mem. Com. on Ethics in Bus. Edn., 1977-79; cons. on mgmt. devel. edn. U.S. and European corps.; U.S. faculty coord. Sasin Grad. Inst. Bus. Arminstrn., Chulalongkorn U., Bangkok, 1983-95; chmn. bd. dirs. ctr. for ethics Garrett-Evang. Theol. Sem., Evanston, 1995—. Editor, contbr.: Moral Man and Economic Enterprise, 1967. Mem. Bd. Edn. Ill. elem. dist. 65, Evanston, 1967-72, 75-78; bd. dirs. Evanston Comm. Found., 1996—. Recipient Ann. Kellogg Alumni Choice award, 1992. Mem. Bus. History Conf. Democrat. Presbyterian. Office: Kellog Grad Sch Mgmt Northwestern U Evanston IL 60201

LAVENSON, JAMES H., hotel industry executive; b. Phila., 1919. Grad., Williams Coll., 1941. Chmn. CEO SYR Corp., 1976-88; pres. Lavenson Mgmt. Enterprises, Inc., N.Y.C., 1976—, Plaza Hotel, N.Y.C., 1972-75, Sunwear, Inc.; chmn. Doxsee Food Co.; pres. Lavenson Bur. Advt., Inc., 1950-64; dir. Sonesta Hotels, TLC Corp.; chmn. Pine Tree Computers, Camden, Maine, 1992-94; bd. dirs. Am. Field Svc., Chief Exec. Forum. Author: Selling Made Simple, Sensuous Animal, Think Strawberries, How to Earn a MBWA Degree. Trustee Thomas Coll., 1993-94. Office: 12 Norumbega Dr Camden ME 04843-1746

LAVENSON, SUSAN BARKER, hotel corporate executive, consultant; b. L.A., July 26, 1936; d. Percy Morton and Rosalie Laura (Donner) Barker; m. James H. Lavenson, Apr. 22, 1973; 1 child, Ellen Ruth Stanclift. BA, Stanford U., 1958, MA, 1959; PhD (hon.), Thomas Coll., 1994. Cert. gen. secondary credential tchr., Calif. Tchr. Benjamin Franklin Jr. High Sch., San Francisco, 1960; tchr. French dept. Lowell High Sch., San Francisco, 1960-61; v.p. Monogram Co., San Francisco, 1961-62; creative dir. Monogram Co., N.Y.C., 1973-86; pres. SYR Corp., Santa Barbara, Calif., 1976-89; ptnr. Lavenson Ptnrs., Camden, Maine, 1989—; mem. commn. on co-edn. Wheaton Coll., Norton, Mass., 1985-87; mem. Relais et Chateaux, Paris, 1978-89; cons. World Bank Recruit Divsn., 1993. Author: Greening of San Ysidro, 1977 (Conf. award 1977). Trustee Camden Pub. Libr., 1989-95, v.p. 1991-93; vice chair bd. trustees Thomas Coll., Waterville, Maine; trustee Atlantic Ave. Trust; founding pres. Maine chpt. Internat. Women's Forum, 1991—; mem. Coun. of Advisors Coll. of the Atlantic. Bar Harbor, Maine, 1996—. Mem. Advice Inc., Camden Yacht Club, Stanford Alumni Assn., Com. of 200 (treas. 1985-86), Phi Delta Kappa. Home and Office: 12 Norumbega Dr Camden ME 04843-1746 *Three rules to remember: 1) Never take anything personally. 2) Never lose your sense of humor. 3) Keep your eye on the objective - I also like the Apocryphal writers' words: "I am not made or unmade by things that happen to me, but by my reactions to them."*

LAVENTHOL, DAVID ABRAM, newspaper editor; b. Phila., July 15, 1933; s. Jesse and Clare (Horwald) L.; m. Esther Coons, Mar. 8, 1958; children: Peter, Sarah. BA, Yale U., 1957; MA, U. Minn., 1960; LittD (hon.), Dowling Coll., 1979; LLD (hon.), Hofstra U., 1986. Reporter, news editor St. Petersburg (Fla.) Times, 1957-62; asst. editor, city editor N.Y. Herald-Tribune, 1963-66; asst. mng. editor Washington Post, 1966-69; assoc. editor Newsday, L.I., N.Y., 1969, exec. editor, 1969, editor, 1970-78, pub., chief exec. officer, 1978-86; group v.p. newspapers Times Mirror Co., L.A., 1981-86, sr. v.p., 1987-93, pres., 1987-93; pub., chief exec. officer L.A. Times, 1989-93; editor-at-large Times Mirror Co., L.A., 1994—; mem. Pulitzer Prize Bd., 1982-91, chmn., 1988-89; vice chmn. Internat. Press Inst., 1985-93, chmn., 1993-95; dir. Am. Press Inst., 1988—. Bd. dirs. United Negro Coll. Fund, 1988, Mus. Contemporary Art, L.A., 1989—, chmn., 1993—; bd. dirs. Associated Press, 1993-96, Columbia Journalism Sch., 1995—, Nat. Parkinson Found., 1995—, Saratoga Performing Arts Ctr., 1993-96. With Signal Corps AUS, 1953-55. Recipient Columbia Journalism award for Disting. Svc., 1994. Mem. Am. Soc. Newspaper Editors (chmn. writing awards bd. 1980-83), Council Fgn. Relations. Clubs: Century (N.Y.C.), Regency (L.A.). Office: LA Times Times Mirror Sq Los Angeles CA 90053-3816

LAVENTHOL, HENRY L(EE) (HANK LAVENTHOL), artist, etcher; b. Phila., Dec. 22, 1927; s. Lewis Jacob and Sadye Aileen (Horwitz) L.; m. Josephine P. Weitjens, Mar. 26, 1965. B.A., Yale U., 1947; postgrad., Columbia U., 1948-51, New Sch. Social Research, 1952-53, Academia di Bell Arte, Florence, Italy, 1961-62. Sr. acct. Laventhol Horwath & Co., N.Y.C., 1948-51; v.p. Wings Shirt Co., Inc., N.Y.C., 1951-61; guest lectr. N.Y. U., 1955, Pratt Graphic Center, N.Y.C., 1974. One-man shows include John Whibley Gallery, London, 1963-69, Galerie Goldoni, Florence, 1962, Galerie de la Madeleine, Brussels, 1962, Die Brucke, Dusseldorf, Fed. Republic Germany, 1964, Galerie Ganzoni, Geneva, 1964, Galerie de Sfinx, Amsterdam, The Netherlands, 1967, Bodley Gallery, N.Y.C., 1968-71, Mickelson Gallery, Washington, 1973, Frank Fedele Fine Arts, N.Y.C., 1980, 81, 82, Werner Gallery, N.Y.C., 1989; exhibited in group shows at Phila. Mus. Art, 1969, Print Club Phila, 1969-86, Bibliotheque Nationale Paris, 1979, Associated Am. Artists, 1968-86, Shippee Gallery, N.Y.C, 1987; represented in permanent collections, Nat. Gallery Art, Washington, IBM Corp., Armonk, N.Y., N.Y. Public Library, N.Y.C., Yale U. Art Gallery, Cigna Corp., Hartford, Conn., Forbes Coll., Pepsico, Purchase, N.Y., Lowe Mus. Art, Miami, Fla., Duke U. Mus. Art, Reuben A. Donnelley, White Plains, N.Y., Free Library Phila., Citicorp Collection, N.Y.C., Erbamont N.A., White Plains, Bibliotheque Nationale, Paris, Evansville Mus., Ind., Warnaco, Bridgeport, Conn., E.M. Warburg Pincus & Co., N.Y.C., NYNEX Corp., White Plains, N.Y.; contbr. etchings to books Le Miroir Aux Alouettes, 1973, Eyedeas, 1980, Crises, 1980. Mem. Artists Equity Assn. Home: 805 Hanover St Yorktown Heights NY 10598-5904

LAVERDIERE, CLAUDETTE MARIE, sister, head religious order. BS in Edn., Mary Rogers Coll., Maryknoll, N.Y., 1967; M Theol. Studies, Cath. Theol. Union, Chgo., 1986. Joined Maryknoll Sisters Congregation, 1956. Tchr. Nganza Secondary Sch. for Girls, Mwanza, Tanzania, 1967-71; with devel. dept. Maryknoll Sisters Congregation, 1972-74; tchr. religious edn. dept. secondary schs. Nakuru, Kenya, 1974-76; cathechetical dir. Nakuru Diocese, Kenya, 1976-79; team mem. devel. edn. program Mombasa Diocese, Kenya, 1980-84; registrar, tchr. Theol. Centre Religious, Nairobi, Kenya, 1987-90; pres. Maryknoll Sisters Congregation, 1991-97. Office: Maryknoll Sisters PO Box 311 Maryknoll NY 10545-0311

LAVERGE, JAN, tobacco company executive; b. Amsterdam, Netherlands, Nov. 17, 1909; came to U.S., 1934, naturalized, 1942; s. Hendrik Johannes and Margaretha (Van Gelder) L.; m. Henriette Amelia Boelen, May 21, 1935; children—Bart Jan, Eva S., Charlotte M. M.E., Higher Tech. Sch., Amsterdam, 1930. With Am. Tobacco Co., Amsterdam, 1930-34; with Universal Leaf Tobacco Co., Inc., Richmond, Va., 1934—; asst. v.p. Universal Leaf Tobacco Co., Inc., 1946-51, v.p., 1951-66, sr. v.p., 1966-78, dir., 1953—, chmn. exec. com., 1974-78, cons., 1978-81, dir. emeritus, 1981—. Served to maj. AUS, 1943-46. Decorated U.S. Legion of Merit, Croix de Guerre France; Netherlands Order Orange Nassau. Home: Apt 169 2300 Cedarfield Pkwy Richmond VA 23233 Office: Universal Bldg Broad and Hamilton Richmond VA 23230

LAVERTY, BRUCE, curator; b. Phila., Nov. 20, 1958; s. John Patterson and Barbara Shirley (McKee) L.; m. Wendy S. Emrich, Sept. 14, 1985; children: Allison B., Susan L. BA, La Salle Coll., 1979. Asst. dir. N.W. Phila. Hist. Site Survey, 1979-80; manuscripts libr. Hist. Soc. Pa., Phila., 1980-83; archivist Athenaeum of Phila., 1983-88, curator of architecture, 1988—; lectr. history dept. Rutgers U., Camden, 1995—; juror Charles E. Peterson Prize Hist. Am. Bldgs. Survey, Washington, 1984—; cons. Phila. Archdiocese Hist. Resource Ctr., Phila., 1994—. Bd. dirs. Old York Rd. Christian Endeavor, Phila., 1975-93, Whosoever Gospel Mission & Rescue Home, Phila., 1992—. Grantee NEA, 1993. Mem. Soc. Am. Archivists, Mid-Atlantic Regional Archivists Conf., Soc. of Archtl. Historians, Assn. of Preservation Tech. Democrat. Avocations: reading, travel, racquetball. Office: Athenaeum Phila 219 S 6th St Philadelphia PA 19106-3719

LAVERY, DANIEL P., management consultant; b. N.Y.C., June 28, 1932; B.S. with honors, Manhattan Coll., 1954; M.B.A., Rutgers U., 1963; m. Doris E. Guenther, Oct. 23, 1954; children—Daniel, Brian, Kevin, Michael. Mem. prodn. mgmt. staff, photo products dept. E.I. DuPont de Nemours & Co., Inc., 1954-65; div. mgr. Anken Industries, Williamstown, Mass., 1965-71; gen. mgr. Dymo Industries, N.Y.C., 1971-73; dir. cons. studies Quantum Sci. Corp., N.Y.C., 1973-79; mgr. strategic mktg. ITT, N.Y.C., 1979-80; sr. dir. market research Western Union, 1980-82; v.p. Pactel, Inc., mgmt. cons., N.Y.C., 1982-83; ptnr. Palo Alto Mgmt. Group, Wyckoff, N.J., 1983—. Served as capt. USAF, 1955-57. Mem. Inst. Mgmt. Cons. (cert. mgmt. cons.), Am. Arbitration Assn. (panel mem. 1985—). Office: Palo Alto Management Group Inc 458 Sicomac Ave Wyckoff NJ 07481-1120

LAVEY, STEWART EVAN, lawyer; b. Newark, July 24, 1945; m. Suzanne Laurence, July 9, 1972. AB, Syracuse U., 1967; JD, Fordham U., 1970. Bar: N.Y. 1971, N.J. 1987, Pa. 1988, D.C. 1988. Assoc. Kelley Drye & Warren, N.Y.C., 1970-71, Emil, Kobrin, Klein & Garbus, N.Y.C., 1971-72, Zimet Haines Moss & Goodkind, N.Y.C., 1972-75; asst. sec., asst. gen. counsel Norlin Corp., N.Y.C., 1975-78; sec., asst. gen. counsel Norlin Corp., 1978-85; of counsel Shanley & Fisher, P.C., Morristown, N.J., 1985-87, ptnr., 1987—; adj. assoc. prof. law Fordham U., N.Y.C., 1976-79, adj. prof., 1980—, lectr. Fordham U. Continuing Legal Edn., 1991-93. Mem. Fordham Law Rev., 1968-70. Trustee Pingry Sch., Martinsville, N.J., 1996—. Recipient Bene Merenti medal Fordham U. Mem. Am. Bar Assn., N.Y. State Bar Assn., Assn. of Bar of City of N.Y., N.J. Bar Assn. (securities law com.), Pa. Bar Assn., D.C. Bar Assn., Pingry Sch. Alumni Assn. (pres. 1996—). Office: Shanley & Fisher PC 131 Madison Ave Morristown NJ 07960-6086

LAVEZZI, JOHN CHARLES, art history educator, archaeologist; b. Chgo., July 7, 1940; s. Francis M. and Dorothy M. (Kopal) L. AB magna cum laude, Cath. U. Am., 1962; MA, U. Cin., 1965; postgrad., Am. Sch. Classical Studies, Athens, Greece, 1967-70; PhD, U. Chgo., 1973. Sec. Am. Sch. Classical Studies at Athens, 1968-70; asst. prof. Sch. Art Bowling Green (Ohio) State U., 1973-80, assoc. prof., 1980—; sr. assoc. mem. Am. Sch. Classical Studies at Athens, 1972—, rsch. assoc. Corinth Excavations, 1972—. Contbr. articles to profl. jours. Mem. Toledo Mus. Art. Recipient CUA Stratemeier award, 1962, Medici Circle teaching awards, 1986, 94; grantee Am. Philos. Soc., 1973. Mem. Archeol. Inst. Am., Midwest Art History Soc., Soc. for Preservation of Greek Heritage, Nat. Geog. Soc., Smithsonian Instn. Friends, Cyprus Am. Archeol. Rsch. Inst., Phi Beta Kappa (pres. chpt. 1992), Phi Alpha Theta, Blue Key, Delta Epsilon Sigma, Phi Eta Sigma. Roman Catholic. Office: Bowling Green State U Sch Art Bowling Green OH 43403

LA VIA, MARIANO FRANCIS, physician, pathology and laboratory medicine educator; b. Rome, Jan. 29, 1926; came to U.S., 1952; s. Vincenzo and Carmela (Carbone) La V.; m. Martha Ann Tillson, Dec. 26, 1959 (div. 1972); children: William, Maria, Charles, Jacqueline, Susan, Christopher, Thomas; m. June F.S. Bailey, Oct. 19, 1991. MD, U. Messina, Italy, 1949. Internship, residency A.M. Billings Meml. Hosp., U. Chgo., 1952-57; pathology fellow U. Rome, Italy, 1949-52; rsch. asst. pathology U. Chgo., 1952-57; resident in pathology A.M. Billings Hosp., U. Chgo., 1952-57; instr. anatomy U. Chgo., 1957-60; asst. prof. pathology U. Colo. Med. Ctr., Denver, 1960-67, assoc. prof. pathology, 1967-68; prof. pathology and lab. medicine Bowman Gray Sch. Medicine, Wake Forest U., Winston-Salem, N.C., 1968-71, Sch. Medicine, Emory U., Atlanta, 1971-79, Med. U. S.C., Charleston, 1979-95; prof. emeritus med. U. S.C., Charleston, 1996—. Contbr. numerous articles to profl. jours. Pres. Advocacy Coun. for Persons with Disabilities, 1994. Recipient NIH Rsch. Career Devel. award, 1962-68. Fellow AAAS; mem. Am. Soc. Investigative Pathology, Clin. Cytometry Soc. (past pres.), Am. Assn. Immunologists, Clin. Immunology Soc., others. Avocations: photography, pipe collecting. Office: Med U SC 171 Ashley Ave Charleston SC 29425-0001

LAVIDGE, ROBERT JAMES, marketing research executive; b. Chgo., Dec. 27, 1921; s. Arthur Wills and Mary Beatrice (James) L.; m. Margaret Mary Zwigard, June 8, 1946; children: Margaret, Kathleen, William, Lynn Elizabeth. AB, DePauw U., 1943; MBA, U. Chgo., 1947. Analyst Pepsodent div. Lever Bros., Chgo., 1947-48, new products mktg. rsch. mgr. Pepsodent div., 1948-49; asst. dir. mktg. Am. Meat Inst., Chgo., 1950-51; ptnr. Elrick, Lavidge and Co., Chgo., 1951-56; pres. Elrick and Lavidge, Inc., Chgo., 1956-86; pres. emeritus Elrick and Lavidge, Scottsdale, Ariz., 1987—; lectr. mktg. research, sales adminstrn. Northwestern U., 1950-80; mem. Nat. Mktg. Adv. Com., 1967-71, also exec. com. Trustee Village Western Springs, Ill., 1957-61, pres., 1973-77; trustee McCormick Theol. Sem., 1981-90, 92-96; mem. adv. council U. Chgo. Grad. Sch. Bus. Mem. Am. Mktg. Assn. (v.p. 1963-64, pres. 1966-67, trustee found. 1992—, chmn.), Internat. Rels. Soc. (chmn. 1961-65), Internat. Trademark Assn., Econ. Club Phoenix, De Pauw U. Alumni Assn. (pres. 1967-68), Klinger Lake Club (Mich.), Paradise Valley Country Club, Phi Beta Kappa, Beta Gamma Sigma, Sigma Delta Chi, Pi. Presbyterian.

LAVIGNE, LAWRENCE NEIL, lawyer; b. Newark, June 30, 1957; s. Daniel S. and Alice M. (Melon) L.; m. Benjie Panesh, Oct. 12, 1980; children: Gabriel A., Derek N. BA, Franklin & Marshall Coll., 1979; JD, Seton Hall U., 1982. Bar: N.J. 1982, U.S. Dist. Ct. N.J. 1982, U.S. Ct. Appeals (3d cir.) 1986, U.S. Supreme Ct. 1986, N.Y. 1989. Assoc. Shanley & Fisher, P.C., Newark, 1982-83; ptnr. Hanlon, Lavigne, Topchik, Edison, N.J., 1983—; instr. Am. Inst. Paralegal Studies, Mahwah, N.J., 1985-88. Mem. ABA (litigation sect.), N.J. Bar Assn. (product liability com.), Middlesex County Bar Assn., Trial Attys. N.J., N.J. Def. Assn., Assn. Trial Lawyers Am., Somerset Bar Assn., Worrall F. Mountain Inn of Court (barrister 1991-93). Republican. Jewish. Avocations: tennis, music, computers. Office: Hanlon Lavigne Et Al 10 Parsonage Rd Ste 200 Edison NJ 08837-2429

LAVIGNE, PETER MARSHALL, environmentalist, lawyer, consultant; b. Laconia, N.H., Mar. 25, 1957; s. Richard Byrd and D. Jacquiline (Cobleigh) L.; m. Nancy Gaile Parent, Sept. 20, 1979. BA, Oberlin Coll., 1980; MSL cum laude, Vt. Law Sch., 1983, JD, 1985. Bar: Mass. 1987. History tchr. Cushing Acad., Ashburnham, Mass., 1983-84; rsch. writer Environ. Law Ctr., Vt., 1985; lobbyist Vt. Natural Resources Coun., Montpelier, 1985; exec. dir. Westport (Mass.) River Watershed Alliance, 1986-88, Merrimack River Watershed Coun., West Newbury, 1988-89; environ. cons. Mass., N.H., Vt., and Oreg., 1990—; N.E. coord. Am. Rivers, Washington, 1990-92; dir. river leadership program River Network, Portland, Oreg., 1992-95; dir. spl. programs River Network, Portland, 1995-96; dep. dir. For the Sake of the Salmon, Portland, 1996-97; adj. prof. Antioch New Eng. Grad. Sch., Keene, N.H., 1991-92, Portland State U., 1997—; chair adv. bd. Cascadia Times, Portland, 1995—, Amigos Bravos, Taos, N.Mex., 1993—; trustee Rivers Coun. Washington, Seattle, 1993—; bd. mem. Alaska Clean Water Alliance, 1995—, Watershed adv. group Natural Resources Law Ctr. U. Colo., 1995—; coastal resources adv. bd. Commonwealth of Mass., Boston, 1987-91; adj. assoc. prof. Portland State U., 1997—. Co-author: Vermont Townscape, 1987; contbr. articles to profl. jours. Dir. Mass. League of Environ. Voters, Boston, 1988-92; mem. steering com. N.H. Rivers Campaign, 1988-92; co-founder, co-chair New England Coastal Campaign, 1988-92; EMT South Royalton (Vt.) Vol. Rescue Squad, 1982-86; dir., chairperson Vt. Emergency Med. Svcs. Dist. 8, Randolph, 1984-86; co-founder, v.p. Coalition for Buzzards Bay, Bourne, Mass., 1987; housing renewal commn. City of Oberlin, Ohio, 1980-81; mem. properties com. First Unitarian Ch., 1995. Recipient Environ. Achievement award Coalition for Buzzards Bay, 1988; land use rsch. fellow Environ. Law Ctr., Vt. Law Sch., 1984-85; Mellon found. rsch. grantee Oberlin Coll., 1980. Mem. Natural Resources Def. Coun., Oreg. Natural Resources Coun., Pacific Rivers Coun., League of Conservation Voters, Sierra Club. Democrat. Unitarian-Universalist. Avocations: sea kayaking, mountaineering, woodwork, reading, photography. Home: 3714 SE 11th Ave Portland OR 97202-3724 Office: For the Sake of the Salmon 45 82nd Dr Ste 100 Gladstone OR 97027-2522

LAVIN, CHARLES BLAISE, JR., association executive; b. Balt., Aug. 13, 1940; s. Charles Blaise and Dorothy (Sturla) L.; m. Eileen Donohue, Sept. 3, 1966; children—Charles, Michael, Kristine, Philip. Student, U. Balt., 1958-62, U.S. Army Sch. Mil. Intelligence, 1962. Exec. dir. New Eng. chpt. Associated Builders and Contractors, Waltham, Mass., 1968-78; exec. v.p. Am. Subcontractors Assn., Washington, 1978-81; exec. asst. to dep. sec. for housing HUD, Washington, 1981-82; exec. v.p. Nat. Assn. Plumbing, Heating and Cooling Contractors, Washington, 1982-87; exec. dir. and lobbyist Nat. Burglar and Fire Alarm Assn., Washington, and Cen. Sta. Alarm Assn., Bethesda, Md., 1987-90; realtor Prudential Preferred Properties, Laurel, Md., 1990-95; exec. dir. Nat. Duckpin Bowling Congress, Balt., 1995—; trustee Assoc. Splty. Contractors, Constrn. Jurisdictional Dispute Bd., 1983-85; chmn. County Real Estate Bd., 1993-95. Vice chmn. bd. dirs., chmn. fin. com. Laurel-Beltsville Gen. Hosp. (Md.), 1982-84; mem. Budget Com. Hopkinton, Mass., 1975-77, Planning Commn., 1977-78; bd. dirs. Young Republicans Balt., 1966. Served with CIC U.S. Army, 1962-65. Mem. New Eng. Soc. Assn. Execs. (pres.), Greater Washington Soc. Assn. Execs. (dir.), Am. Soc. Assn. Execs., Am. Legion (Post 60 comdr. 1994-95), U.S. C. of C., D.C. Basketball Ofcls. Assn., Internat. Assn. Basketball Ofcls., Washington Dist. Football Ofcls. Assn., Nat. Duckpin Bowling Congress (nat. dir.), Sons of Italy, KC, Loyal Order of Moose, West Laurel Recreational Coun. (chmn. 1994—). Republican. Roman Catholic. Home: 7006 Redmiles Rd Laurel MD 20707-3244 Office: Nat Duckpin Bowling Cong 4991 Fairview Ave Linthicum Heights MD 21090-1405

LAVIN, JOHN HALLEY, editor, author; b. Queens County, N.Y., Oct. 27, 1932; s. John Joseph and Dorothy Monica (Halley) L.; m. Bernadette Manning, Mar. 2, 1957; children—John Stephen, Michael James, Eileen Mary, Monica Anne. B.A., Queens Coll., 1958; health adminstrv. devel. program, Cornell U., 1969. Editor L.I. Graphic (weekly), 1958; copy editor New Haven Register, 1958-59; newsman, state news editor A.P., Newark, 1959-65; gen. news supr. A.P., N.Y.C., 1965-66; editor-writer Med. Econs. Co., mag. pubs., Oradell, N.J., 1966-82; Atlantic bur. chief Soccer Am. Mag., 1977-78; sr. editor, news div. chief. mem. editorial bd. Med. Econs., 1968-73; editor RN, 1973-75, Nursing Opportunities, 1973-75, RN Recruiter, 1974-75, Geriatric Cons., 1982-94, Pharmacy World News, 1985-86, Contemporary Sr. Health, 1989-93, Cardiology World News, 1982—. Author: Stroke: From Crisis to Victory, 1985; contbr. articles to profl. and gen. interest publs. Publicity chmn. Glen Rock (N.J.) Cub Scouts and Boy Scouts Am., 1968-73; founder, mem., trustee Glen Rock Jr. Soccer Club, 1970-74. Served with USN, 1951-55, Korea. Recipient Jesse H. Neal award Am. Bus. Press, 1976, cert., 1976; Journalism award Am. Acad. Family Physicians, 1981. Mem. Soc. Prfol. Journalists. Roman Catholic. Home: 106 Delbrook Way Marco Island FL 34145-4605 *An editor's primary responsibility is to his reader. If he has performed his corporate duties well, endeared himself to his publisher, pleased his writers and advertisers, fed his ego among his fellow editors, but has allowed the editorial excellence of his publication to be compromised, he has not met his primary responsibility. If he loses touch with the copy or the reader, he is no longer an editor; he is a manager. And he might as well be in some other business.*

LAVIN, MATTHEW T., horticultural educator. Assoc. prof. biology dept. Mont. State U., Bozeman. Recipient N.Y. Botanical Garden award Botanical Soc. Am., 1993. Office: Montana State U Dept Biology 310 Lewis Hall Bozeman MT 59717-0002*

LAVIN, PHILIP TODD, biostatistician executive; b. Rochester, N.Y., Nov. 21, 1946; s. Albert A. and Mary (Rapkin) L.; m. Mary Ellen Saunders, Aug. 23, 1970; children: Andrew, Abby. AB, U. Rochester, 1968; PhD, Brown U., 1972. Rsch. asst. prof. Brown U., Providence, 1972-74, SUNY at Buffalo, Amherst, 1974-77; asst. prof. sch. pub. health Harvard U., Boston, 1977-83, assoc. prof. surgery, 1983—; pres. Boston Biostatistics, Inc., Framingham, Mass., 1983—, Boston Biostat Rsch. Found., Newton Upper Falls, Mass., 1988—; mem. editorial bd. Drug Info. Assn., Phila., 1986-88, Anti-microbial Agents and Chemotherapy, Boston, 1987—; cons. FDA, 1983-86, 92—. Contbr. articles to on medicine and stats. to scholarly jours. Bd. dirs. William Graves Fund, Boston, 1989—. NSF trainee, 1968-72; grantee Nat. Cancer Inst., 1976-80, 87—, Nat. Heart, Lung, Blood Inst., 1985-89. Mem. Biometric Soc., Am. Statis. Assn., Soc. Clin. Trials, Regulatory Affairs Prof. Soc., Phi Beta Kappa. Achievements include development of statistical methods for the analysis of serial biomarker data applicable to the detection of biomarker shifts and trends over time, of natural history models for colorectal cancer, gastric cancer, uveal melanoma, and ovarian cancer; organization and management of data coordinating centers for multicenter studies of cancer, hypertension, infertility, obesity, and transplantation; research in chronic disease models. Home: 3 Cahill Park Dr Framingham MA 01702-6105 Office: Biostatistics Inc 615 Concord St Framingham MA 01702-8037

LAVIN, ROXANNA MARIE, finance executive; b. San Antonio, Sept. 8, 1952; d. Teddy Harold and Cora Ann (Ames) Maddox; m. Michael Paul Lavin, July 11, 1971 (div. 1997); children: Sharon Renai, Christopher Michael, Katherine Marie. Student, Ea. Mich. U., 1985, 86, 70; BBA magna cum laude, Cleary Coll., 1992; postgrad, Ctr. Mich. U., 1993, Madonna Univ., 1994; postgrad., U. Mich., 1996. Sales clk. Children's Fashion Shop, Livonia, Mich., 1970; bookkeeping clk. Ypsilanti (Mich.) Savs. Bank, 1970-73; receptionist, acctg. clk. Maize & Blue Properties, Ann Arbor, Mich., 1986-87; acctg. clk. Sensors, Saline, Mich., 1987; office supr., fin. mgr. Great Lakes Coll. Assn., Ann Arbor, 1988-94; fin., pers. mgr. Jackson (Mich.) Libr., 1994-96, interim co-dir., 1995; support analyst Fund Balance, 1997—. Sec., treas. Old Mill Hills Assn., Pinckney, Mich., 1990-93; mem. Pinckney High and Mid. Sch. Parents, 1990-92; parent vol. Lincoln Cons. Schs., Ypsilanti, 1985-86; mem. Jackson County Literacy Coun. Recipient scholarship Ea. Mich. U., 1970. Mem. AAUW, Mich. Libr. Assn. Avocations: painting, sketching, gardening, reading.

LAVINE, ALAN, columnist, writer; b. Sharon, Pa., Feb. 17, 1948; s. Milton and Doris (Helfman) L.; m. Gail Jeanne Liberman, Dec. 20, 1991. BA, Kent State U., 1970; MA, U. Akron, 1973; MBA, Clark U., 1981. Dir. of rsch. Donoghue Orgn., Holliston, Mass., 1981-83; nat. syndicated fin. columnist, 1983—; syndicated radio commentator Bus. News Network, 1994—; columnist Am. Online, 1995; presenter papers in field ann. meeting AAAS, 1972, ann. meeting Mass. Psychol. Assn., Wellesley, 1978, ann. meeting APA, 1979, Nat. Symposium on Rsch. in Art, U. Ill., 1980; guest lectr. Cornell U., 1990, 91, 92, 93. Author: Diversify: Investor's Guide to Asset Allocation Strategies, 1990 (alt. selection Fortune Book Club), Your Life Insurance Options, 1993 (endorsed Inst. CFPs), Improving Your Credit and Reducing Your Debt, 1994 (endorsed Inst. CFPs), Getting Started in Mutual Funds, 1994, Diversify Your Way to Wealth, 1994 (alt. selection Fortune Book Club), 50 Ways to Mutual Fund Profits, 1995, The Complete Idiot's Guide to Making Money with Mutual Funds, 1996; contbr. articles to profl. jours. Mem. Nat. Writers Union, Soc. Am. Bus. Editors and Writers, Inc. Home: 3606 Alder Dr Apt H2 West Palm Beach FL 33417-1182 Office: Alan Lavine Inc 3951 Haverhill Rd N Ste 210 West Palm Beach FL 33417-8145

LAVINE, HENRY WOLFE, lawyer; b. Phila., Apr. 21, 1936; s. Samuel Phillips and Sarah Pamela (Leese) L.; m. Meta Landreth Doak, Feb. 20, 1960 (div. Feb. 1980); children: Lisa, Lindsay; m. Martha Putnam Cathcart; children: Samuel Putnam, Gwenn Cathcart. BA, U. Pa., 1957, JD, 1961. Assoc. Squire, Sanders & Dempsey L.L.P., Cleve., 1961-70; ptnr. Squire, Sanders & Dempsey L.L.P., Washington, 1970-85, mng. ptnr. Washington office, 1985-91, sr. mng. ptnr., 1991—; dir. Greater Washington Bd. of Trade. Trustee Fed. City Coun., Washington; bd. assocs. Gallaudet U.; mem. The Bretton Woods Com. Mem. Siasconset Casino Club, Met. Club. Office: Squire Sanders & Dempsey 1201 Pennsylvania Ave NW PO Box 407 Washington DC 20044

LAVINE, JOHN M., journalism educator, management educator; b. Duluth, Minn., Mar. 20, 1941; s. Max H. and Frances (Hoffman) L.; m. Meryl Ette Lipton, June 1, 1980; children: Miriam, Marc, Max. B.A., Carleton Coll., Minn., 1963; postgrad., U. Minn., 1963; LL.D. (hon.), Emerson Coll., Boston, 1975. Pub., editor Lavine Newspaper Group, Chippewa Falls, Wis., 1964-89; pub. Ind. Media Group, Profl. Publs., Inc., 1984-94; Cowles prof. media mgmt. and econs. U. Minn., Mpls., 1984-89; prof., dir. NMC, a joint program Northwestern U. Kellogg Grad. Sch. Mgmt./ Medill Sch. Journalism, Evanston, Ill., 1989—; pres. NCI, Evanston, 1993—; cons., lectr. in field, vis. prof. numerous profl. and ednl. instns.; participant numerous profl. confs. Author: China, 1980; The Constant Dollar Newspaper, 1980; Managing Media Organizations, 1988; contbr. chpts. to books, articles to profl. jours. Recipient numerous awards for excellence in mgmt. and journalism. Mem. Newspaper Assn. Am., Am. Soc. Newspapers Editors, Inter Am. Press Assn., Inland Daily Press Assn. (chmn., pres. 1984-85), Wis. Newspaper Assn. (life). Home: 335 Greenleaf St Evanston IL 60202-1365 Office: NMC 1845 Sheridan Rd Evanston IL 60208-0815

LAVINE, LAWRENCE NEAL, investment banker; b. Providence, Sept. 20, 1951; s. Avery B. and Pearl (Burbil) L.; m. Pamela Ferne Selby, Jan. 3, 1981; 1 child, Jason. BS summa cum laude, Northeastern U., 1974; MBA with highest distinction, Harvard U., 1976. V.p. Kidder, Peabody & Co. Inc., N.Y.C., 1976-87; mng. dir. Donaldson, Lufkin & Jenrette, N.Y.C., 1987—. Mem. Harvard Club of N.Y., Harvard Bus. Sch. Club of N.Y., Sunningdale Country Club, Beaver Creek Club. Avocations: running, tennis, golf, skiing. Office: Donaldson Lufkin & Jenrette Securities Corp 277 Park Ave New York NY 10172

LAVINE, STEVEN DAVID, academic administrator; b. Sparta, Wis., June 7, 1947; s. Israel Harry and Harriet Hauda (Rosen) L.; m. Janet M. Sternburg, May 29, 1988. BA, Stanford U., 1969; MA, Harvard U., 1970, PhD, 1976. Asst. prof. U. Mich., Ann Arbor, 1974-81; asst. dir. arts and humanities Rockefeller Found., N.Y.C., 1983-86, assoc. dir. arts and humanities, 1986-88; pres. Calif. Inst. Arts, Valencia, 1988—; adj. assoc. prof. NYU Grad. Sch. Bus., 1984-85; cons. Wexner Found., Columbus, Ohio, 1986-87; selection panelist Input TV Screening Conf., Montreal, Can., and Granda, Spain, 1985-86; cons., panelist Nat. Endowment for Humanities, Washington, 1981-85; faculty chair Salzburg Seminar on Mus., 1989; co-dir. Arts and Govt. Program, The Am. Assembly, 1991; mem. arch. selection jury L.A. Cathedral. Editor: The Hopwood Anthology, 1981, Exhibiting Cultures, 1991, Museums and Communities, 1992; editor spl. issue Prooftexts jour., 1984. Bd. dirs. Sta. KCRW-FM (NPR), J. Paul Getty Mus., L.A. Philharm. Assn., Endowments, Inc., Bond Portfolio for Endowments, Inc. Recipient Class of 1923 award, 1979, Faculty Recognition award, 1980 U. Mich.; Charles Dexter traveling fellow Harvard U., 1972, Ford fellow, 1969-74, vis. rsch. fellow Rockefeller Found., N.Y.C., 1981-83. Jewish. Office: Calif Inst Arts Office Pres 24700 Mcbean Pky Santa Clarita CA 91355-2340

LAVINE, THELMA ZENO, philosophy educator; b. Boston; d. Samuel Alexander and Augusta Ann (Pearlman) L.; m. Jerome J. Sachs, Mar. 31, 1944; 1 child, Margaret Vera. A.B., Radcliffe Coll., 1936; A.M., Harvard U., 1937, Ph.D., 1939. Instr. Wells Coll., 1941-43, asst. prof., 1945-46; asst. prof. philosophy Bklyn. Coll., 1946-51; asst. prof. U. Md., 1955-57, assoc. prof., 1957-62, prof., 1962-65; Elton prof. George Washington U., 1965-85, chmn. dept., 1969-77; Clarence J.Robinson Univ. prof. George Mason U., Fairfax, Va., 1985—; lectr., seminar cons. Inter-Am. Def. Coll., 1975—. Author: TV course From Plato to Sartre, 1980, From Socrates to Sartre: The Philosophic Quest, 1984; co-author: History and Anti-History Philosophy, 1989, introduction to Collected Works of John Dewey, Vol. 16, 1990, Philosophy of Paul Rincoeur, 1995, Rorty and Pragmatism, 1996; contbr. articles to profl. jours., chpts. to books. Recipient Outstanding Faculty award U. Md., 1965, Outstanding Faculty award George Washington U., 1968, Alumnae Achievement award Radcliffe Coll., 1991; NEH sr. rsch fellow, 1980; Am. Enterprise Inst. Public Policy Research fellow, 1980-81, Va. Found. Humanities fellow, 1990. Mem. Am. Philos. Assn. (5th Ann. Romanell lectr. 1991), Soc. Advancement Am. Philosophy (exec. com. 1979-82, pres. 1992—), Internat. Soc. Sociology Knowledge, Internat. Soc. Ednl., Cultural and Sci. Interchanges, Internat. Soc. Polit. Psychology, Metaphys. Soc. Am., Washington Philosophy Club (pres. 1967-68), Washington Sch. Psychiatry, Forum Psychiatry and Humanities (exec. bd.), Cosmos Club, Radcliffe Club, Harvard Club, Phi Beta Kappa (pres. chpt. 1978-80). Home: 1625 35th St NW Washington DC 20007-2316 Office: George Mason U Robinsons Profs E 207 Fairfax VA 22030

LAVINGTON, MICHAEL RICHARD, venture capital company executive; b. Purley, Surrey, Eng., Feb. 21, 1943; came to U.S., 1972; s. Richard H. and Patricia (Young) L.; m. June Watford, Aug. 13, 1966; children: Susan, Victoria. B.A., Cambridge U., 1964; M.A., Columbia U., 1965; Ph.D., Lancaster U., (Eng.), 1968. Dir. Ralli Australia, 1969-71, Bowater America, N.Y.C., 1971-74; pres. Kay Jewelers Inc., Alexandria, Va., 1974-90, Watford Investment Corp., McLean, Va., 1990—. Chmn. St. Stephen's and St. Agnes Sch., Alexandria, 1981-96; trustee Ch. Schs. in Diocese of Va., 1989-96.

LAVOIE, DENNIS JAMES, secondary education educator; b. Syracuse, N.Y., Aug. 31, 1955; s. James Jay and Mary (Gadwood) L.; m. Allegra Ann Beahan, Oct. 11, 1980. BA in Spanish, St. John Fisher Coll., 1977; MA in Spanish Lang. and Lit., Middlebury Coll., 1982. Cert. tchr. Spanish, French, N-12, N.Y.; cert. secondary sch. adminstr., sch. dist. adminstr., N.Y. Fgn. lang. educator Fairport (N.Y.) Cen. Sch., 1977—, mentor tchr., 1990-91; mem. Pacesetter Spanish spl. task force Ednl. Testing Svc., 1993-94, steering com., 1995—. Recipient N.Y. Coun. for the Humanities scholarship, Colgate U., 1991, MCES scholarship N.Y. State Edn. Dept. and the Spanish Govt., Universidad de Salamanca, 1989, NEH grant, U. Va., 1989. Mem. Fgn. Lang. Assn. of Tchrs. of the Rochester Area (pres. 1980-81, v.p. 1979-80), Am. Assn. Tchrs. of Spanish and Portuguese (pres. Rochester chpt. 1990-92, v.p. 1988-90, treas. 1984-86). Democrat. Roman Catholic. Avocations: skiing, golf, travel. Office: Fairport H S 1358 Ayrault Rd Fairport NY 14450-8939

LAVOIE, LIONEL A., physician, medical executive; b. St. Brieux, Sask., Can., Aug. 24, 1937; s. Athanase T. and Ella Marie (Mevel) L.; m. Mary Tina Luchewski, Oct. 12, 1964; children: Robert, Michelle, Nicole, Andrea. BA, Ottawa U., Ont., Can., 1958, MD, 1964. Intern, then resident Univ. Hosp., Sask.; assoc. clin. prof. family medicine U. Sask., 1978—; chief of staff Melfort (Sask.) Union Hosp., 1985-90; commr. Med. Care Ins. Commn., 1984-88. Chmn. Melfort Dist. Minor Sports, 1978-80, Melfort Pks. and Recreation, 1983-86, Sask. Summer Games 1988, 1986-88. Recipient Ramstead award Jaycees of Province Sask., 1975, Dedication award Sask. Parks, Recreation and Culture, 1988, Community Recreation award Melford C. of C., 1989, Commemorative medal 125th Anniversary Can. Confed., 1993. Mem. Can. Med. Assn. (bd. dirs. 1978-83, pres. elect 1989-90, pres. 1990-91), Sask. Med. Assn. (bd. dirs. 1971-76, v.p. 1974, pres. 1975), Can. Acad. Sports Medicine, Am. Geriatric Soc., Coll. Family Physicians Can. (sec. Sask. province 1967-70), Sask. Acad. Sports Medicine (pres. 1986-88), Coun. Med. Assn. (chmn. 1985-89), Sask. Paraplegic Assn. (bd. dirs. 1978—), Can. Cancer Soc. (adv. com. Sask. div. 1986—), Nat. Aerospace Med. Assn., KC (grand knight 1980-81), Rotary (pres. Melfort club 1987-88). Avocations: golf, curling, horticulture. Home: 402 Stovel E, Melfort, SK Canada S0E 1A0 Office: Can Med Assn, 1867 Alta Vista Dr, Ottawa, ON Canada K1G 0G8

LAVOIE, SERGE, principal dancer; b. Lachine, Que., Can., Jan. 30, 1963; s. Jean Claude and Therese (Larr) L. Student, Nat. Ballet Sch., Toronto, 1979-82. Prin. dancer Northern Ballet Theatre, Manchester, Eng., 1981, 82; dancer Nat. Ballet Can., Toronto, Ont., 1982-86, 2d soloist, 1986-87, 1st soloist, 1987-88, prin. dancer, 1988—. Appeared in Raymonda Act III, Don Quixote, La Sylphide, Onegin, Napoli, The Nutcracker, Symphony in C, Romeo and Juliet, Elite Syncopations; featured in Here We Come, Endangered Species, Reminiscence, Components; created roles in L'Ile Inconnue, Blue Snake, Pastorale, The Miraculous Mandarin, The Actress; appeared in Quartet, Khachaturian Pas de Deux, 1983; appeared with stars and soloists of Can. Ballet in Etc!, On Occasion, Pastel, Swan Lake,(Italy, 1985); debuted as Prince in Swan Lake, 1985-86; danced lead in Transfigured Night and Elite Syncopations; debuted as Solor in La Bayadere Act III, as James in La Sylphide, as guest artist with London Festival Ballet; appeared with Basel Ballet in Switzerland, 1986-87 in Coppelia and The Sleeping Beauty; performed with Berlin Opera Ballet in Theme and Variations, 1987, at La Scala in Milan in The Nutcracker, in France, Italy and the U.S. with Nureyev, at Spoleta Festival in Australia; appeared with Can. Ballet Company in Concerto Barocco, Second Movement of Barocco, Forgotten Land, Death of a Lady's Man, Song of the Earth, Symphony in C, Alice, Steptext, Diana and Acteon Pas de Deux, 1987; appeared with Boston Ballet in La Sylphide, The Nutcracker, Monotones I, Sacre du Printemps, Don Quixote, Esmeralda Pas De Deux, Coppelia, Swan Lake, 1988, 89. Recipient 1st prize Internat. Ballet Competition, Moscow, 1980, Silver medal 1st N.Y.C. Internat. Ballet, 1984. Office: National Ballet of Canada, 470 Queens Quay W, Toronto, ON Canada M5V 3K4*

LAVORATO, LOUIS A., state supreme court justice; s. Charles Lavorato; m. Janis M. Lavorato; children: Cindy, Natalie, Anthony, Dominic. BS in Bus. Adminstrn., Drake U., 1959, JD, 1962. Judge Iowa Supreme Ct., Des Moines, 1986—; sole practice Des Moines, 1962-79; judge Iowa Dist. Ct., Des Moines, 1979-86; justice Iowa Supreme Ct., Des Moines, 1986—. Office: Iowa Supreme Ct St Capitol Bldg Des Moines IA 50319

LAW, BERNARD FRANCIS CARDINAL, archbishop; b. Torreon, Mex., Nov. 4, 1931; s. Bernard A. and Helen A. (Stubblefield) L. B.A., Harvard U., 1953; postgrad., St. Joseph Sem., St. Benedict, La., 1953, Pontifical Coll. Josephinum, Worthington, Ohio, 1955. Ordained priest Roman Catholic Ch., 1961, consecrated bishop, 1973; editor Natchez-Jackson diocesan paper, Jackson, 1963-68; exec. dir. U.S. Bishops Com. for Ecumenical and Interreligious Affairs, 1968-71, chmn., from 1975; vicar gen. Diocese of Natchez-Jackson, 1971-73; bishop Diocese of Springfield-Cape Girardeau, Mo., 1973-84; archbishop Archdiocese of Boston Brighton, Mass., 1984—; created cardinal, 1985; mem. adminstrv. com. Nat. Conf. Cath. Bishops, from 1975; mem. communication com. U.S. Cath. Conf., 1974, mem. adminstrv. bd., from 1975; mem. Vatican Secretariat for Promoting Christian Unity, from 1976; consultor Vatican Commn. Religious Relations with the Jews, from 1976; chmn. bd. Pope John XXIII Med.-Moral Research and Edn. Ctr., St. Louis, 1980-82; ecclesiastical del. of Pope John Paul II for matters pertaining to former Episcopal priests, 1981. Trustee Pontifical Coll. Josephinum, 1974-85, Nat. Shrine of Immaculate Conception, from 1975; bd. regents Conception (Mo.) Sem. Coll., from 1975. Office: Cardinal's Residence 2101 Commonwealth Ave Brighton MA 02135-3101*

LAW, CLARENE ALTA, innkeeper, state legislator; b. Thornton, Idaho, July 22, 1933; d. Clarence Riley and Alta (Simmons) Webb; m. Franklin Kelso Meadows, Dec. 2, 1953 (div. July 1973); children: Teresa Meadows Jillson, Charisse Meadows Haws, Steven Riley; m. Creed Law, Aug. 18, 1973. Student, Idaho State Coll., 1953. Sec., sub. tchr. Grand County Schs., Cedar City, Utah, 1954-57; UPI rep. newspaper agy. Moab, Utah Regional Papers, Salt Lake City and Denver; auditor Wort Hotel, Jackson, Wyo., 1960-62; innkeeper, CEO Elk Country Motels, Inc., Jackson, Wyo., 1962—; rep. Wyo. Ho. of Reps., Cheyenne, 1991—, chmn. house travel com., 1993—, mem. bank bd. State of Wyo., 1991—; bd. dirs. Jackson State Bank, Snow King Resort. Chmn. sch. bd. dirs. Teton County Schs., Jackson, 1983-86. Named Citizen of Yr. Jackson C. of C., 1976, Bus. Person of Yr. Jackson Hole Realtors, 1987, Wyo. Small Bus. Person SBA, 1977. Mem. Wyo. Lodging and Restaurant Assn. (pres., chmn. bd. dirs. 1988-89, Big Wyo. award 1987), Internat. Leisure Hosts (bd. dirs. Phoenix chpt. 1991—), Soroptimists (charter), BPW (Woman of Yr. 1975). Republican. Mem. LDS Ch. Avocations: travel, study. Address: Box 575 Jackson WY 83001 Office: Elk County Motels Inc 43 W Pearl Jackson WY 83001

LAW, DAVID HILLIS, physician; b. Milw., July 24, 1927; s. David Hillis Law III and Hazel Janice (May) Young; m. Patricia Bicking Thornton, Sept. 14, 1949; children: Linda Clark, Wendy, David, Kimberly Rankin, Cassandra. BS, Cornell U., 1950, MD, 1954. Resident in internal medicine Cornell U. Med. Coll., N.Y.C., 1954-57, fellow in gastroenterology, 1957-59; dir. personnel health services N.Y. Hosp., Cornell Med. Ctr., N.Y.C., 1959-60; asst. prof. medicine, chief gastroenterology Vanderbilt U. Med. Coll., Nashville, 1960-69; prof., vice chmn. dept. medicine U. New Mex. Sch. Med., Albuquerque, 1969-85; chief med. services Vets. Adminstrn. Med. Ctr., Albuquerque, 1969-85; dir. med. services Vets. Adminstrn. Cen. Office, Washington, 1985-86, dep. asst. chief med. dir. for clin. services, 1986-89, asst. chief med. dir. clin. affairs, 1989-91, acting dep. assoc. chief med. dir. for hosp.-based svcs., 1991-95, assoc. dep. chief med. dir. for clin. program, 1993-95, acting chief patient care officer, 1995-96; assoc. chief of staff for edn. Bay Pines (Fla.) Med. Ctr., 1996—; mem. human rsch. com. Los Alamos (N.Mex.) Sci. Lab., 1972-80; sabbatical dept. clin. physiology Karolinska Inst., Stockholm, 1980; bd. dirs., officer N.Mex. Nutrition Improvement Program, 1970-75; sub-com. chmn. U.S. Pharmacopeia Commn. on Revision, 1975-80. Editor, Parenteral Nutrition; mem. editorial bd., Am. Jour. Digestive Diseases, 1968-74; rev. numerous med. jours.; contbr. articles to numerous profl. jours. Bd. dirs., officer Albuquerque Friends of Music, 1975-85; mem. Nat. Digestive Disease Adv. Bd., 1989-95; mem. Interdepartmental Digestive Disease Coordinating Com. Cpl. U.S. Army, 1945-46. Named Tchr. and Attending Physician of Yr. Dept. Medicine House Staff, 1985. Fellow ACP (gov. 1989-96); mem. AMA (lectr.), Western Assn. Physicians, Western Soc. Clin. Rsch., Am. Gastroenterol. Assn., Am. Inst. Nutrition, Alpha Omega Alpha. Republican. Presbyterian. Avocation: hot air ballooning. Office: Vets Adminstrn Med Ctr 11-B Bay Pines FL 33744

LAW, FLORA ELIZABETH (LIBBY LAW), retired community health and pediatrics nurse; b. Biddeford, Maine, Sept. 11, 1935; d. Arthur Parker and Flora Alma (Knutti) Butt; m. Robert F. Law, 1961; children : Susan E., Sarah F., Christian A., Martha F.; m. John F. Brown, Jr., 1982. BA, Davis and Elkins (W.Va.) Coll., 1957; postgrad., Cornell U.-N.Y. Hosp., N.Y.C., 1960; BSN, U. Nev., Las Vegas, 1976, MS in Counseling Edn., 1981. RN, Nev.; cert. sch. nurse. Staff nurse So. Nev. Community Hosp. (now Univ. Med. Ctr.), Las Vegas, 1975-76; relief charge nurse Valley Psychiat. Inst., Las Vegas, 1976; pub. health nurse Clark County Dist. Health Dept., Las Vegas, 1977-78; sch. nurse Clark County Sch. Dist., Las Vegas, 1978-94; ret., 1994. Chair task force on sch. nursing Nev.'s Commn. for Profl. Standards in Edn.; mem. nurse practice act revision com. Nev. State Bd. Nursing. Mem. Nat. Assn. Sch. Nurses (past state dir., sch. nurse liaison Clark County Tchrs. Assn.), NEA, Clark County Assn. Sch. Nurses (past pres.), Sigma Theta Tau. Home: 3420 Clandara Ave Las Vegas NV 89121-3701

LAW, FREDERICK MASOM, engineering educator, structural engineering firm executive; b. Newark, Mar. 8, 1934; s. Frederick T. and Evelyn (Masom) L.; m. Margaret Mary Maus, Oct. 27, 1956; children: Carolyn Jean, Frederick Masom. B.S. Engring., Princeton U., 1956; M.S., N.J. Inst. Tech., 1962; Ph.D., Rutgers U., 1965. Registered profl. engr., Mass., R.I., N.Y., N.J., Pa., Fla., S.C. Structural engr. H.N.T.& B. Engrs., N.Y.C., 1956-57, 60-61, Austin Co., Roselle, N.J., 1961-63; asst. prof. engring. Newark Coll. Engring., 1963-68; assoc. prof. Pa. State U., Middletown, 1968-70; prof., chmn. dept. civil engring. U. Mass., North Dartmouth, 1970—; prin.

Frederick M. Law, P.E., South Dartmouth, 1970—; pres. Timberspan Bridges Inc., South Dartmouth, 1983—; vice chmn. Mass. Bd. Registration Profl. Engrs. and Land Surveyors, 1977-82; mem. jury Am. Inst. Steel Constrn. Prize Bridge Competition, 1982. Served to 1st lt. AUS, 1957-60, ETO. Recipient Grand Conceptor Cons. Engrs. Council Am., 1978. Fellow ASCE; mem. Nat. Soc. Profl. Engrs., Mass. Soc. Profl. Engrs. (Outstanding Engring. Achievement 1978), Am. Soc. Engring. Edn., Soaring Soc. Am. Home: 10 Swift Rd South Dartmouth MA 02748-3717 Office: U Mass Dept Civil Engring Old Westport Rd North Dartmouth MA 02747

LAW, GORDON THEODORE, JR., library director; b. Norwood, Mass., Oct. 27, 1945; s. Gordon Theodore and Laura (Andersen) L.; m. Pam Marilyn Baxter, Sept. 29, 1990;. BA in History, SUNY, Albany, 1967, MA in Social Scis., 1968, MLS, 1972. Tchr. Mynderse Acad., Seneca Falls, N.Y., 1968-71; dir. Krannert Libr., Purdue U., West Lafayette, Ind., 1983-93; head reference and info. svcs. Catherwood Libr., Cornell U., Ithaca, N.Y., 1972-83, dir. Catherwood Libr., 1993—. Author: A Guide to Information on Closely Held Corporations, 1986; editor recent publ. feature Indsl. and Labor Rels. Rev., 1974-83. Mem. Com. Indsl. Rels. Librs., Spl. Librs. Assn., Indsl. Rels. Rsch. Assn. Office: Cornell U Martin P Catherwood Libr 237 Ives Hall Ithaca NY 14853-3901

LAW, JANET MARY, music educator; b. East Orange, N.J., Mar. 8, 1931; d. Charles and Mary Ellen (Keavy) Maitland; m. William Howard Law, Dec. 13, 1952; children: Robert Alan, Gail Ellen. Lic. Practical Nurse, St. Barnabas Sch., 1971; BA magna cum laude, Fairleigh Dickinson U., Rutherford, N.J., 1981; tchr. tng. course, Westminster Choir Coll., 1990—, Queens U., Canada, 1993. Registered Suzuki tchr., Suzuki piano tchr., traditional piano tchr. Staff nurse psychiat. unit St. Barnabas Med. Ctr., Livingston, N.J., 1972-78; office nurse, asst. to pvt. physician North Arlington, N.J., 1978-79; dir., owner B Sharp Acad., Rutherford, N.J., 1979-83; founder, tchr. piano music preparatory div. Fairleigh Dickinson U., Rutherford, 1983-89; founder, coord. piano divsn. Garden State Acad. Music, Rutherford, N.J., 1989-94; tchr. piano divsn. Garden State Acad. Music, Rutherford, 1989-95; Suzuki piano coord., tchr. Suzuki piano program, coord. Suzuki piano divsn. Montclair (N.J.) State U., 1994—. Author: Keyboard Kapers, 1983; inventor music games, 1983. Mem. Music and Performing Arts Club, Profl. Music Tchrs. Guild N.J. Inc., Suzuki Assn. of the Ams. Avocation: concerts. Home: 169 Hillcrest Dr Wayne NJ 07470-5629 also: Montclair State U Valley Rd and Normal Ave Upper Montclair NJ 07043

LAW, JOHN HAROLD, biochemistry educator; b. Cleve., Feb. 27, 1931; s. John and Katherine (Frampton) L.; m. Nancy Jean Floyd, June 8, 1956. BS, Case Inst. Tech., Cleve., 1953; PhD, U. Ill., 1957; D hon. causa, U. Sofia, 1995. Postdoctoral fellow Harvard U., Cambridge, Mass., 1958-59, from instr. to asst. prof. biochemistry, 1960-65; instr. Northwestern U., Evanston, Ill., 1959-60; prof. U. Chgo., 1965-81; prof. U. Ariz., Tucson, 1981-91, Regents prof., 1991—, chmn. dept. biochemistry, 1981-86, dir. biotech. program, 1986-92; dir. Ctr. Insect Sci., 1993; assoc. dean coll. agr. U. Ariz., Tucson, 1988-90; mem. gov. bd. Internat. Ctr. Insects, Nairobi, Kenya, 1980-87; mem. bd. trust Gordon Rsch. Conf., 1992—, chmn., 1996; mem. coun. Am. Soc. Biochem. Molecular Biology, 1993-96. Recipient Gregor Mendel medal Czech Acad. Sci., 1992, J.E. Purkinje medal Czech Acad. Sci., 1994. Fellow AAAS, ESA; mem. NAS, Am. Soc. Biochem. Molecular Biology, Am. Chem. Soc., Entomol. Soc. Am. Home: 2540 E 7th St Tucson AZ 85716-4702 Office: U Ariz Dept Biochemistry Bio Scis W 345 Tucson AZ 85721

LAW, JOHN MANNING, retired lawyer; b. Chgo., Dec. 5, 1927; s. Fred Edward and Elisabeth (Emmons) L.; m. Carol Lufkin Ritter, May 14, 1955; children: John E., Lucy L., Frederick R., Beth K. Student, U. Chgo., 1944-45, St. Ambrose Coll., 1945; BA, Colo. Coll., 1948; JD, U. Colo., 1951. Bar: Colo. 1951, Ill. 1952, U.S. Ct. Appeals (10th cir.) 1954, U.S. Supreme Ct. 1989. Atty. trust dept. Harris Bank, Chgo., 1951-52; assoc. Dickerson, Morrissey, Zarlengo & Dwyer, Denver, 1952-57; ptnr. Law, Nagel & Clark, Denver, 1958-84, Law & Knous, Denver, 1984-93; ret.; mem. law com. Colo. Bd. Law Examiners, 1971-81, Colo. Ofcls. Compensation Commn., 1985-89. Mem. Moffatt Tunnel Commn., Denver, 1966-90. Capt. USNR, 1945-77, ret. Fellow Colo. Bar Found. (charter); mem. ABA (chmn. 1975, mem. com. legal assistance to mil. pers. 1973-77), Colo. Bar Assn. (bd. govs. 1968-71), Denver Bar Assn. (trustee 1971-74), Internat. Soc. Barristers, Law Club, Denver Country Club. Republican. Presbyterian. Home: 3333 E Florida Ave Apt 35 Denver CO 80210-2541

LAW, LLOYD WILLIAM, geneticist; b. Ford City, Pa., Oct. 28, 1910; s. Craig Smith and Cora Jane (Whiteley) L.; m. Bernette Bohen, May 4, 1942; children: Lloyd William, David Bradford. B.S., U. Ill., 1931; A.M., Harvard U., 1935, Ph.D. (Austin fellow), 1937; Harvard Sheldon fellow, Stanford U., 1937-38. Tchr. high sch. Charleston, Ill., 1931-34; Finney-Howell Med. research fellow Jackson Meml. Lab., Bar Harbor, Maine, 1938-41; Commonwealth Fund fellow Jackson Meml. Lab., 1941-42, research asso., 1946, sci. dir., 1947; now trustee; geneticist Nat. Cancer Inst., Bethesda, Md., 1947-52; head leukemia studies sect. Nat. Cancer Inst., 1952—, chief lab. cell biology, 1970—, mem. sci. directorate, 1970-90; Panel mem. com. on growth NRC, 1952-56; mem. pharmacology and exptl. therapeutics study sect. NIH, 1955—; mem. screening panel cancer chemotherapy Nat. Service Center, 1955—; mem. adv. bd. Nat. Blood Research Found., 1954—; adv. bd. cancer research Am. Cancer Soc., 1965—, mem. panel on etiology of cancer, 1960—; sci. bd. Children's Cancer Fund Am., 1956—; bd. sci. advisers Roswell Park (N.Y.) Cancer Inst., 1957—; expert adv. com. cancer WHO, 1960-80; mem. U.S.A. nat. com. Internat. Union Against Cancer, 1969-78; mem. bd. sci. advs. Chemotherapy Found. N.Y., 1974—; mem. bd. sci. advisers Ludwik Cancer Found., 1980—, chmn., 1985. Author: Advances in Cancer Research Vol. II, 1954, Vol. XXXII, 1980, Leukemia Research, 1955, Origins of Resistance to Toxic Agents, 1955; other books in field; editor: Tumour Antigens; contbr. articles to profl. jours., books and pamphlets. Served as capt. 2d Air Force USAAF, 1942-46. Recipient Anne Frankel Rosenthal award AAAS, 1955; USPHS Meritorious Service award, 1965; G.H.A. Clowes Meml. award in cancer research, 1965; Allesandro Pascoli prize, 1969; Disting. Service medal USPHS, 1969; G.B. Mider lecture award NIH, 1970. Mem. Soc. Exptl. Biology and Medicine, N.Y. Acad. Sci., Am. Soc. Exptl. Pathology, Am. Assn. Cancer Rsch. (dir. 1956-59, 65—, pres. 1967-68), Italian Cancer Soc., Royal Soc. Medicine, Am. Immunology Assn., Am. Assn. Cancer Rsch. (hon. 1987), Europe Assn. Cancer Rsch. (hon. 1987), Cosmos Club (Washington), Sigma Xi. Home: 9810 Fernwood Rd Bethesda MD 20817-1512 Office: Nat Cancer Inst Pub Health Service Rockville Pike Bethesda MD 20892

LAW, MARK EDWARD, electrical engineer, educator; b. St. Paul, July 19, 1959; s. Paul Rock and Bernice Edna (Brookshaw) L.; m. Alison Leigh Retz, May 30, 1981; children: Christopher, Heather. BS CprE, Iowa State U., 1981; MSEE, Stanford U., 1982, PhD in Elec. Engring., 1988. Engr. Hewlett Packard, 1982-84; rsch. asst. Stanford (Calif.) U., 1984-87, rsch. assoc., 1988; asst. prof. elec. engring. U. Fla., Gainesville, 1988-93, assoc. prof. elec. engring., 1993—; presenter, spkr. in field; session chmn. various tech. meetings in field. Author: Floods/Floops User's Manual, 1993; contbr. articles to profl. jours., chpts. to books. Recipient Young Faculty Devel. award IBM, 1988, Tech. Excellence award Semicondr. Rsch. Corp., 1993, Outstanding Young Alumnus award Iowa State U., 1994, Profl. Progress award Iowa State U., 1994; Nat. Merit scholar, 1977-81; grantee NSF, 1992—, SRC, 1989—, 93—, IBM, 1991-93; NSF Presdl. fellow, 1992. Mem. IEEE (sr., guest editor publ. 1991, assoc. editor IEEE Transactions on Semicondr. Mfg. 1996, editor Jour. on Tech. Computer Aided Design 1996, editor Circuits and Devices Mag. 1996—), Am. Soc. Engring. Edn., Am. Phys. Soc., Electrochem. Soc., Sigma Xi, Phi Beta Pi, Phi Kappa Phi. Avocations: soccer, golf. Office: U Fla 339 Larsen Hall Gainesville FL 32611-2044

LAW, MICHAEL R., lawyer; b. Rochester, N.Y., Nov. 30, 1947; s. George Robert and Elizabeth (Stoddart) L.; m. Cheryl Heller. BS, St. John Fisher Coll., 1969; JD, U. Louisville, 1975. Bar: N.Y. 1976, U.S. Dist. Ct. (we. dist.) N.Y. 1976, U.S. Supreme Ct. 1982. Assoc., Wood, P.C., Rochester, 1976-77; pvt. practice, Rochester, 1977-78; assoc. Sullivan, Peters, et al, Rochester, 1978-80, ptnr., 1980-81; ptnr. Phillips, Lytle, Hitchcock, Blaine & Huber, Rochester, 1982—. Exec. com. Camp Good Days and Spl. Times, Rochester, 1984—. Served with USAR, 1968-74. Mem. Monroe County Bar Assn. (judiciary com. 1981-88, personal injury com. 1988—, ethics com. 1988-96, profl. responsibility com. 1996—), N.Y. State Bar Assn. (trial sect., ins. negligence com.), ABA (trial law sect., trial techniques com., editor 1986 Trial Techniques, alternate dispute resolution com. 1995—), N.Y. State Trial Lawyers (bd. dirs.), Genesee Valley Trial Lawyers Assn. (treas., 1992-93, pres.-elect 1993-95, pres. 1995—). Republican. Roman Catholic. Home: 3373 Elmwood Ave Rochester NY 14610-3425 Office: Phillips Lytle Hitchcock Blaine & Huber 1400 First Federal Plz Rochester NY 14614-1909

LAW, THOMAS HART, lawyer; b. Austin, Tex., July 6, 1918; s. Robert Adger and Elizabeth (Manigault) L.; m. Terese Tarlton, June 11, 1943 (div. Apr. 1956); m. Jo Ann Nelson, Dec. 17, 1960; children: Thomas Hart Jr., Debra Ann. AB, U. Tex., 1939, JD, 1942. Bar: Tex. 1942, U.S. Supreme Ct. 1950. Assoc. White, Taylor & Chandler, Austin, 1942; assoc. Thompson, Walker, Smith & Shannon, Ft. Worth, 1946-50; ptnr. Tilley, Hyder & Law, Ft. Worth, 1950-67, Stone, Tilley, Parker, Snakard, Law & Brown, Ft. Worth, 1967-71; pres. Law, Snakard, Brown & Gambill, P.C., Ft. Worth, 1971-84; of counsel Law, Snakard & Gambill, P.C., Ft. Worth, 1984—; bd. dirs., gen. counsel Gearhart Industries, Inc., Ft. Worth, 1960-88; gen. counsel Tarrant County Jr. Coll. Dist. Chmn. Leadership Ft. Worth, 1974-90; bd. regents U. Tex. System, 1975-81, vice chmn., 1979-81. Served to lt. USNR, 1942-46. Recipient Nat. Humanitarian award Nat. Jewish Hosp./Nat. Asthma Ctr., 1983; named Outstanding Young Man, City of Ft. Worth, 1950, Outstanding Alumnus, Coll. of Humanities, U. Tex., 1977, Outstanding Citizen, City of Ft. Worth, 1984, Bus. Exec. of Yr., City of Ft. Worth, 1987, Blackstone award for contbns. field of law Ft. Worth Bar Assn., 1990. Fellow Am. Bar Found., Tex. Bar Found., Am. Coll. Probate Counsel; mem. Ft. Worth C. of C. (pres. 1972), Mortar Bd., Phi Beta Kappa, Omicron Delta Kappa, Pi Sigma Alpha, Delta Sigma Rho, Phi Eta Sigma, Delta Tau Delta. Democrat. Presbyterian. Clubs: Ft. Worth (bd. govs. 1984-90), Century II (bd. govs. to 1985), River Crest Country, Exchange (pres. 1972), Steeplechase. Lodge: Rotary (local club pres. 1960). Avocation: numismatics. Home: 6741 Brants Ln Fort Worth TX 76116-7201 Office: Law Snakard & Gambill 3200 Bank One Tower 500 Throckmorton St Fort Worth TX 76102-3708

LAWARE, JOHN PATRICK, retired banker, federal official; b. Columbus, Wis., Feb. 20, 1928; s. John Henry and Ruth (Powles) L.; m. Margery Ann Ninabuck, Dec. 22, 1952; children: John Kevin, Margaret Ann. BA in Biology, Harvard, 1950; grad., Advanced Mgmt. Program, 1975; MA in Polit. Sci. , U. Pa., 1951; LHD (hon.), Suffolk U., D in Polit. Sci. (hon), Northeastern U. Trainee Chem. Bank & Trust Co., N.Y.C., 1953-54, with credit dept., 1954-56, asst. sec., 1957-60, asst. v.p., 1960-62, v.p., 1962-65, v.p. in charge mktg. div., 1965-68, sr. v.p., 1968-72; sr. v.p. in charge holding co. ops. Chem. N.Y. Corp., from 1972; pres., dir. Shawmut Corp., 1978-80, Shawmut Bank of Boston N.A., 1978-80, chmn., dir., 1980-88; pres., dir. Shawmut Assn., Inc., 1978-80; chmn., CEO Shawmut Bank Boston, 1980-88; mem. bd. govs. FRS, Washington, 1988-95, ret., 1995; pres., dir. Devonshire Fin. Svc. Corp., 1978-88; chmn., treas. Boston Clearing House Assn., Inc.; Shawmut Corp. subs.; mem. Internat. Fin. Conf.; chmn. Mass. Bankers Assn., 1982-83, Assn. Bank Holding Cos., 1986-87; bd. dirs. Liberty Mutual Ins. Co., 1981, 88, mem. compensation com. Trustee, vice chmn., chmn. fin. com. Northeastern U., 1981-88; trustee, mem. fin. com. Mt. Holyoke Coll., 1984-88; chmn. Children's Hosp. Med. Ctr., 1989-91; past chmn., bd. dirs. Mass. Bus. Roundtable; chmn. coordinating com. Boston Bus. Leaders Orgn.; chmn. Alliance for Commonwealth, Boston. 2d lt. USAF, 1951-53. Recipient Disting. Citizen award Minuteman Coun. Boy Scouts Am., Chief Exec. Officer of Yr. award Northeastern U. Coll. Bus., Outstanding Citizen award B'nai B'rith-Antidefamation League. Mem. Assn. Bank Holding Cos. (past chmn. and dir., adv. dir. Stewart Info. Sys. Corp. 1995—, chmn. bd. trustees Ctr. Blood Rsch., Boston, chmn. bd. dirs. Alliance Commonwealth, Boston). Office: PO Box 30083 Sea Island GA 31561-0083

LAWATSCH, FRANK EMIL, JR., lawyer; b. Avenel, N.J., May 11, 1944; s. Frank Emil and Jessie Margaret L.; m. Deanna Conover, May 25, 1969; children: Amanda, Abigail, Frank. BA, Colgate U., 1966; JD, Cornell U., 1969. Bar: N.Y. 1969, Pa. 1992, N.J. 1993. Assoc. Shearman & Sterling, N.Y.C., 1969-78; sr. v.p., gen. counsel, sec. Midlantic Corp., Edison, N.J., 1978-91; sr. v.p., gen. counsel PNC Bank Corp., Pitts., 1991-92; ptnr. Crummy, Del Deo, Dolan, Griffinger & Vecchione, Newark, 1993—. Mem. ABA, N.J. Bar Assn., Pa. Bar Assn., Assn. of Bar of City of N.Y., Am. Soc. Corp. Secs. Episcopalian. Home: 11 The Fairway Montclair NJ 07043-2533 Office: Crummy Del Deo Dolan Griffinger & Vecchione One Riverfront Plz Newark NJ 07102

LAWES, PATRICIA JEAN, art educator; b. Mathis, Tex., June 28, 1940; d. Thomas Ethan and Alma Dena (Pape) Allen; m. Elmer Thomas Lawes, Apr. 9, 1960; children: Linda Lee, Tracy Dena. BA in Art Edn., U. Wyo., 1976; MA in Curriculum and Instruction, Leslie Coll., 1988. Cert. tchr., Wyo. Elem. art tchr. Laramie County Sch. Dist. # 1, Cheyenne, Wyo., 1977—, facilitator elem. art. and gifted edn., 1979-87; ret. Laramie County Sch. Dist. #1, 1994, storyteller, 1995; owner, sec. Dundele Ltd. Liability Co., Mesa, Ariz., 1994-95; artist in the sch. Mesa, Ariz., 1994-95; ednl. cons. gifted edn. Bozman, Mont., 1995-96; judge F.W. Warren AFB Artist Craftsman Show, Cheyenne, 1988-92; adjudicator for music festival for Assn. Christian Schs. Internat., Tempe, Ariz., 1995-97; storyteller Laramie County Sch. Dist. 1, 1995-96; presenter in field; artist in the sch., Tempe; instr. Smith Driving Sys. Salt River Project, Phoenix, 1996; ednl. cons. Assn. Christian Schs. Internat., Phoenix, 1995. Author, mem. visual arts task force various curricula; Author, dir: The Apron Caper, 1989 (recognition 1990), Oh Where Oh Were Have Those Little Dawgs Gone, 1989 (recognition 1990); exhibitions include Wyoming Artists Assn., Wyo., 1977, Washington Congressional Exhibit, 1977-78. Mem. state bd. dirs. Very Spl. Arts Wyo., 1995—. Recipient Cert. of Appreciation Mayor Erickson, Cheyenne, 1986, MWR Vol. Recognition F.E. Warren Moral, Welfare, Recreation Dept., Cheyenne, 1988-93; grantee Coun. on Arts, Cheyenne, 1987-91. Mem. NEA, Am. Fedn. Tchrs., Nat. art Edn. Assn., Wyo. Assn. Gifted Edn. (bd. dirs., W.E. rep. 1986—, presenter, chmn. state ass. award 1992—), Wyo. Arts Alliance for Edn. (presenter, bd. dirs. 1987—, sec. 1988-91, visual arts task force, chmn. state arts award 1990-92), Wyo. Coun. Arts (slide bank 1986—), Wyo. Odessey of Mind (bd. dirs. 1991-92), Wyo. Women's Fedn. Club (chmn. state safety 1972-75), Order of Eastern Star (presiding officer, worthy matron 1984-85, grand officer 1990-91), Daughters of Nile, Assn. of Christian Schs. Internat. Music Festival (adjudicator 1995). Avocation: art, hiking, traveling, photography, storytelling. Address: 4410 E Kiva Phoenix AZ 85044-2403

LAWHON, JOHN E., III, lawyer, former county official; b. Denton, Tex., Dec. 14, 1934; s. John E. and Gladys (Barns) L.; m. Tommie Collins, Aug. 27, 1967; 1 son, David Collins. Student, U. N.Tex., 1951-53; BBA, U. Houston, 1958, JD, 1958. Bar: Tex. 1958; cert. specialist in estate and probate law, family law. Asst. dist. and county atty. Denton County, Tex., 1958-61; dist. and county atty., 1961-77; dir. Southridge, Inc., Denton, 1962-72, Lawyers Title Agy. Denton, 1965-74; Legal adviser Denton City-County Day Nursery, 1972-80; tchr. bus. law U. North Tex. (formerly North Tex. State U.), Denton, 1969-71; mem. adv. bd. Tex. Criminal Justice Council, 1973-79; univ. atty. Tex. Woman's U., 1977-83, gen. counsel, 1983—, sec. bd. regents, 1987—. Bd. dirs. Denton County Welfare Coun., 1970-78, Denton Community Coun., 1978-79, 80-82; mem. Denton Forum; chmn. Denton County ARC, 1985-87, Denton County Probation Adv. Bd., 1985-92; mem. City of Denton Land Use Com., 1986-88. Mem. Tex. Bar Assn., Denton Bar Assn. (pres. 1968-69, bd. dirs. 1978-81), Tex. Dist. and County Attys. Assn. (bd. dirs. 1964-66), Denton Jaycees (sec. 1961), Denton C. of C., Tex. Assn. State Univ. Attys. (pres. 1983-84, Denton County crim. justice task force 1992-93, state bar coll. fellow 1995—). Baptist (deacon 1968—). Lodges: KP, Kiwanis (bd. dirs. 1981-86, pres. 1984-85). Home: 2810 Carmel St Denton TX 76205-8310 Office: Tex Woman's U Adminstrn Tower Bldg PO Box 23025 Denton TX 76204-1025

LAWHON, SUSAN HARVIN, lawyer; b. Houston, Oct. 10, 1947; d. William Charles and Ruth Helen (Beck) Harvin; m. Robert Ashton, July 25, 1970 (dec. Dec. 1992); children: Bryan Ashton, Harvin Griffith. AB, Smith Coll., Northampton, Mass., 1970; MEd, U. Tex., 1973; JD, U. Houston, 1990. Bar: Tex. 1990, U.S. Dist. Ct. (so. dist.) Tex. 1991, U.S. Ct. Appeals (5th cir.) 1993. Tchr. Nat. Cathedral Sch., Washington, 1970-71, Austin (Tex.) Ind. Sch. Dist., 1973-74, Spring Branch Ind. Sch. Dist., Houston, 1974-76; participating assoc. Fulbright & Jaworski, LLP, Houston, 1990—. Editor-in-chief: Houston Jour. Internat. Law, 1989-90. Mem. devel. coun. Tex. Children's Hosp., Houston, 1986—; mem. devel. bd. U. Tex. Health Sci. Ctr., Houston, 1984-87; sponsor Children's Fund, Inc., Houston, 1979-87; bd. dirs. Houston Child Guidance Ctr., 1977-80, Grief Ctr. Tex., 1997—, treas.; bd. dirs., treas., fin. v.p. Jr. League Houston, 1984-86; docent Bayou Bend, 1977-84. Mem. ABA, State Bar Tex., Houston Bar Assn., Houston Country Club, Smith Coll. Club (Houston) (Seven Coll fund rep. 1982-87). Episcopalian. Home: 6222 Holly Springs Dr Houston TX 77057-1137 Office: Fulbright & Jaworski LLP 1301 Mckinney St Ste 5100 Houston TX 77010-3095

LAWHON, TOMMIE COLLINS MONTGOMERY, child development and family living educator; b. Shelby County, Tex., Mar. 15; d. Marland Walker and Lillian (Tinsley) Collins; m. David Baldwin Montgomery, Mar. 31, 1962 (dec. Aug. 1964); m. John Lawhon, Aug. 27, 1967; 1 child, David Collins. B.S., Baylor U., 1954; M in Home Econs. Edn. in Home Econs., Tex. Woman's U., 1964, Ph.D., 1966. Cert. tchr., Tex., home economist, family life educator. Tchr., Victoria Pub. Schs. (Tex.), 1954-55; stewardess, supr. Am. Airlines, Dallas/Fort Worth, 1955-62; prof. home econs. Ea. Ky. U., Richmond, 1966-67, U. North Tex., Denton, 1968—; profl. presenter Profl. Devel. Inst., U. North Tex., 1981-84, mem. faculty senate 1984-90, chmn. com. on coms., 1987-88, com. status of women, 1984-87, mem. faculty salary study com., 1989-95, chmn., 1989-91, mem. tradition com., 1989-95, recorder, 1989-91; bd. dirs. Univ. union, 1985-88, mem. Status of Women Com., 1984-87, mem. Com. on Coms., 1986-89, chmn. 1987-88, vice chmn., 1988-89, mem. student mentor com., 1990-97, mem. benefits com., 1994—, vice chair, 1994-95, mem. faculty senate mentor com., 1990-96. Co-author: Children are Artists, 1971; Hidden Hazards for Children and Families, 1982; editor: What to do with Children, 1974; Field Trips for Children, 1984; contbr. articles to profl. jours. Chmn., United Way North Tex. State U., 1980-81; chmn. crusade Am. Cancer Soc., Denton County, 1982-83; chmn. nominating com. First Bapt. Ch., Denton, 1983-84, 84-85; advisor North Tex. Student Coun. on Family Rels., 1994—. Recipient Presdl. award Tex. Council on Family Rels., 1979, Fessor Graham award North Tex. State U., 1980, Svc. award Am. Cancer Soc., 1983, Outstanding Home Economists Alumni award Baylor U., 1985; named Honor Prof. North Tex. State U., 1975. Mem. Tex. Coun. on Family Rels. (pres. 1977-79, chmn. policy advisor com. 1986-88, nominating com. 1986-88, 94-96, chair 1994-96, mem. family life edn. com. 1994—, Moore-Bowman award 1994), Denton Assn. for Edn. of Young Children (pres. 1970-72, 84-85, 85-86, v.p. 1986-87), Tex. Assn. Coll. Tchrs. (nominating com. 1988-89, 89-90, v.p. 1990-92, v.p. U. North Tex. chpt. 1987-88, pres. 1988-89, 89-90), Tex. Home Econs. Assn. (chmn. FLCD nominating com. 1983-84, chmn. child devel. and family rels. sect. 1988-90, sect. rep. THEA bd. 1989-90), Nat. Coun. on Family Rels. (com. 1982-83, cert. family life continuing edn. com. 1996-97, chair elect cert. family life continuing edn. com. 1996, chair, 1996-97, cert. family life continuing edn. focus group and regional-state coord.), Nat. Assn. Early Childhood Tchr. Educators (mem. membership com. 1995—), North Tex. Home Econs. Inter-orgnl. Council (adviser 1983-85), Phi Delta Kappa (pres. local chpt. 1991-92), Alpha Iota/Phi Upsilon Omicron (advisor 1970-82, chmn. nat. com. 1984-87, nat. bd. dirs. edn. found. 1990-94, com. pubs. 1991-92, vice chair ednl. found. 1992-94). Democrat. Clubs: Tri D (v.p. Baylor U. 1953-54); Univ. Grad. (pres. Tex. Woman's U. 1965-66). Office: U North Tex Coll Edn Denton TX 76203

LAWI, DAVID STEVEN, energy, agriservice and thermoplastic resins industries executive; b. Baghdad, Iraq, Aug. 3, 1935; came to U.S., 1946, naturalized, 1952; s. Steven David and Marcelle (Masry) L.; m. Anne Shamash, June 9, 1968; children—Nicole, Neil. A.A. in Sci, N.Y. State Coll., 1955. Registered rep. Bear, Stearns & Co., N.Y.C., 1956-62; dir. Adobe Brick & Supply, West Palm Beach, Fla., 1962-64; v.p. Molly Corp., Reading, Pa., 1962-64; gen. mgr. United Shoe Machinery Corp., Reading, 1964-65; a founder, sec., treas., mem. exec. com., dir. Unimax Group Inc. (formerly Riker-Maxson Corp.), N.Y.C., 1966-80; also dir. all subs., v.p., treas. Telepictures Corp., N.Y.C., 1980-81, chmn. fin. com., sec., 1980-86; exec. v.p., sec. Helm Resources, Inc., Greenwich, Conn., 1980—, also bd. dirs.; bd. dirs., sec. Teletrak Advanced Tech. Sys., Inc., 1983—, Continuing Care Assocs., 1982—; sec., bd. dirs., chmn. exec. com. Seitel Inc. (formerly Seismic Enterprises, Inc.), 1982-84, now bd. dirs.; advisor Lorimar-Telepictures (acquired by Warner Comm., Inc. 1989), 1986, now Time-Warner, 1990—; bd. dirs., chmn. exec. com. Intersys., Inc. (formerly Bamberger Polymers, Inc.), Unipix Entertainment, Inc. (formerly Majestic Entertainment, Inc.); chmn. exec. com., bd. dirs. Cliff Engle Ltd. Served with AUS, 1968. Home: Ramapo Trail Harrison NY 10528 Office: Helm Resources Inc 537 Steamboat Rd Greenwich CT 06830-7153

LAWIT, JOHN WALTER, lawyer; b. Phila., Aug. 13, 1950; s. Alfred and Marilyn Jane (Balis) L.; m. Susan Stein, July 15, 1984; children: Andrew Alejandro, Samuel Martin, Ivan Luis (twins). Student, U. Bridgeport, 1968-70; B of Univ. Studies, U. N.Mex., 1972; JD, Franklin Pierce Law Ctr., Concord, N.H., 1977. Bar: Pa. 1978, N.Mex. 1980, Tex. 1992, U.S. Dist. Ct. (ea. dist.) Pa. 1978, U.S. Dist. Ct. N.Mex. 1980. Investigator Franklin Pierce Law Ctr., 1976-77; social researcher Commun. Svc. Coun., Concord, 1977-78; sole practitioner N.Y.C., 1978-79; atty., assoc. McCallister, Fairfield, Query, Strotz & Stribling, Albuquerque, 1979-80; sole practitioner Albuquerque, 1980—; adj. prof. immigration law U. N.Mex. Sch. Law, 1983, 84, 88; spl. immigration counsel U. N.Mex., Albuquerque, 1987—; U.S. immigration judge US. Dept. Justice, 1985; apptd. mem. N.Mex. Internat. Trade/Investment Coun., 1984-87, N.Mex. Border Commn., 1982-86; hon. cons. atty. Ministry Fgn. Affairs Republic of Mex., 1983; lobbyist, author, drafter N.Mex. Immigration & Nationality Law Practice Act. Presenter in field. Founder, profl. cons. Jewish Family Svcs. of Albuquerque, 1988—; bd. dirs., pres. Rainbow House Internat. Adoption, Belen, N.Mex., 1987—; v.p. N.Mex. Refugee Assn., Albuquerque, 1979-84; bd. dirs. N.Mex. Civil Liberties Union, 1988-90; mem. adv. bd. Healing the Children, Albuquerque, 1989—; bd. dirs. Inst. for Spanish Arts, 1994—. Recipient Disting. Svcs. award Cath. Social Svcs., 1988. Mem. N.Mex. State Bar (chair internat. and immigration lawyers sect. 1990-91, bd. dirs. 1988-90), Albuquerque Bar Assn., Am. Immigration Lawyers Assn. (nat. chair 1988-89), El Paso Assn. Immigration and Nationality Lawyers. Avocations: family activities, whitewater rafting, hiking, cross-country skiing. Office: 900 Gold Ave SW Albuquerque NM 87102-3043 also: 869 Agua Fria Santa Fe NM 87501-2010 also: L&A Law Firm Tian Mi Li Mansion 4th Fl, 8 Hua Yuan Don Lu, Beijing 100083, China

LAWLER, ALICE BONZI (MRS. OSCAR T. LAWLER), retired college administrator, civic worker; b. Milan, Italy, Dec. 25, 1914; came to U.S. 1920, naturalized 1925; d. Ercole and Alice (Spalding) Bonzi; m. Morris Warner Mothershead, Sept. 15, 1935 (dec.); children: Warner Bonzi, Maria (Mrs. Andrei Rogers); m. Oscar Thom Lawler, May 1989 (dec.). Pvt. pupil music and art; student Pasadena City Coll., 1958-60. Ptnr. Float Toy Co., Pasadena, Calif., 1942-44; community adv. Fgn. Student Program, Pasadena City Coll., from 1952, past dir. Community Liaison Ctr. Chmn. Am. Field Service Internat. Scholarships, Pasadena, 1953-55; mem. West Coast adv. bd. Inst. Internat. Edn., San Francisco, 1957-70; v.p. San Rafael Sch. PTA, Pasadena, 1945-46; active Community Chest, ARC, Pasadena; chmn. Greater Los Angeles Com. Internat. Student and Visitor Services, 1962; mem. Woman's Civic League Pasadena, chmn. city affairs com., 1985, pres., 1986-87; bd. dirs. Fine Arts Club of Pasadena, 1983-85, Pasadena City Coll. Found., 1983-85; commr. City of Pasadena Cultural Heritage Commn., 1984-89; active Caltech Y. Bd., 1993—, Caltech Assocs., 1993—. Decorated knight Govt. of Italy, 1975; recipient citation City of L.A., 1992; named Woman of Yr., Federated Italians City of L.A., County of L.A., State of Calif., 1992. Fellow Nat. History Mus., L.A.; mem. Assn. Internat. Educators (life, chmn. community sect. and v.p. 1964-65, chmn. U.S. study abroad com. 1969-70), Am. Assn. UN (chpt. 2d v.p. 1964), Soc. Women Geographers, Am. Friends Middle East, Zonta Internat. (hon. mem.), Am. Women for Internat. Understanding, Pasadena City Coll. Retirees Assn. (bd. dirs. 1991), Omicron Mu Delta. Club: International (Pasadena). Author: Social Customs and Manners in the United States, 1957; Dining Customs Around the World, 1982; co-author: 15 Years of the Foreign Student Program at Pasadena City College, 1965. Editor: Students to People to Future, 1971. Home: 480 S Orange Grove Blvd Apt 12 Pasadena CA 91105-1721

LAWLER, JAMES EDWARD, physics educator; b. St. Louis, June 29, 1951; s. James Austin and Dolores Catherine Lawler; m. Katherine Ann Moffatt, July 21, 1973; children: Emily Christine, Katie Marie. BS in Physics summa cum laude, U. Mo., Rolla, 1973; MS in Physics, U. Wis., 1974, PhD in Physics, 1978. Rsch. assoc. Stanford (Calif.) U., 1978-80; asst. prof. U. Wis., Madison, 1980-85, assoc. prof., 1985-89, prof., 1989—; product devel. cons. Nat. Rsch. Group, Inc., Madison, 1977-78; cons. GE, Schenectady, N.Y., 1985—, Teltech, Inc., 1990—; exec. com. Gaseous Electronics Conf., 1987-89, treas., 1992-94, DAMOP program com., 1993-95. Editor: (with R.S. Stewart) Optogalvanic Spectroscopy, 1991; contbr. articles to profl. jours. Recipient Penning award Internat. Conf. on Phenomena in Ionized Gases, 1995; Schumberger scholar U. Mo., 1971-72; grad. fellow U. Wis. Alumni Rsch. Found., 1973-74, NSF, 1974-76, H.I. Romnes faculty fellow U. Wis., 1987. Fellow Am. Phys. Soc. (Will Allis prize 1992), Optical Soc. Am.; mem. Sigma Xi. Achievements include patent for Echelle Sine Bar for dye laser cavity; development of laser diagnostics for glow discharge plasmas, of methods for measuring accurate atomic transition probabilities and radiative lifetimes. Office: U Wis Dept Physics 1150 University Ave Madison WI 53706-1302

LAWLER, JAMES RONALD, French language educator; b. Melbourne, Australia, Aug. 15, 1929; married, 1954; 2 children. BA, U. Melbourne, 1950, MA, 1952; DUniv., U. Paris, 1954. Lectr. French U. Queensland, Australia, 1955-56; sr. lectr. U. Melbourne, 1957-62; prof., head dept. U. Western Australia, 1963-71; prof., chmn. dept. UCLA, 1971-74; McCulloch prof. Dalhousie U., Halifax, N.S., Can., 1974-79; prof. French U. Chgo., 1979—, Edward Carson Waller Disting. Svc. prof., 1983—; vis. prof. Coll. de France, 1985, Tokyo, 1996; chmn. vis. com. Romance Langs. and Lits. Harvard U., 1991-94. Author: Form and Meaning in Valery's Le Cimetiere Marin, 1959, Lecture de Valery: Une Etude de Charmes, 1963, The Language of French Symbolism, 1969, The Poet as Analyst, 1974, Rene Char: The Myth and the Poem, 1978, Edgar Poe et les Poetes Francais, 1989, Rimbaud's Theatre of the Self, 1992, Poetry and Moral Dialectic: Baudelaire's Secret Architecture, 1997; co-author: Paul Valery; Poems, 1971, Paul Valery: Leonardo, Poe, Mallarme, 1972; editor: An Anthology of French Poetry, 1960, Paul Valery: An Anthology, 1977, Paul Valery, 1991; founding editor Essays in French Literature, 1966, Dalhousie French Studies. Decorated officier Palmes Academiques; Brit. Coun. interchange scholar, 1967; Australian Acad. Humanities fellow, 1970, Guggenheim Found. fellow, 1974, NEH fellow, 1985. Mem. MLA, Am. Assn. Tchrs. French, Internat. Assn. French Studies (v.p. 1974—). Rsch. in modern French poetry, poetics, 20th century novel. Office: U Chgo Dept Romance Langs & Lit 1050 E 59th St Chicago IL 60637-1512

LAWLER, SUSAN GEORGE, elementary education educator; b. Evergreen Park, Ill., Jan. 20, 1940; d. Louis Lawrence and Elsie Marie (Velk) George; m. Jerome Charles Lawler, Feb. 23, 1963; children: Susan Elizabeth, Kathleen Marie. BS in Edn., Mt. Mary Coll., 1961; MEd, Nat. Louis U., Evanston, Ill., 1991. Tchr. Oak Lawn (Ill.) Sch. Dist. 123, 1961-65, Palos Community Sch. Dist. 118, Palos Park, Ill., 1975—; pres. Parent-Faculty Orgn. Sch. Dist. 230, Orland Park, Ill., 1982-85. Sec. Ishnala Homeowners Assn., Palos Heights, Ill., 1972-75; active Neighborhood Watch, City of Palos Heights, 1988—. Mem. AAUW (chair hist. 1975-77), Internat. Reading Assn., Nat. Coun. Tchrs. English, Ill. Reading Assn., Palas Edn. Assn. (pres. 1992—), Mt. Mary Coll. Alumni Assn. (co-chair Chgo. chpt. 1992—), Phi Delta Kappa. Avocations: reading, bridge, taking classes, golf, walking. Home: 12932 S Comanche Dr Palos Heights IL 60463-2618 Office: Palos Community Sch Dist 118 8800 W 119th St Palos Park IL 60464-1004

LAWLESS, JAMES L., editor, columnist; b. Des Moines, Mar. 26, 1932; s. James L. and Mary O. (Gray) L.; m. Mary Belle McPherson; children: Kathleen, Maureen, Michael, Martha, Kerry, Dan. BA, Drake U., 1954. Editor, columist Des Moines Register, Des Moines, 1956—; columnist Gannett News Svc. Alexandria, Va., 1986—. Chmn. Clive (Iowa) Planning & Zoning, 1970-80; mem. bd. adjustment, Clive, 1980-90. Lt. (j.g.) USNR, 1954-56. Nat. Press Found. fellow, 1986. Republican. Roman Catholic. Avocations: tennis, travel, swimming. Home: 6137 Pleasant Dr Des Moines IA 50312-1217 Office: The Des Moines Register 715 Locust St Des Moines IA 50309-3703

LAWLESS, MICHAEL RHODES, pediatrics educator; b. Baytown, Tex., Oct. 13, 1942; s. Wallace Ervin and Amy Ruth (Broussard) L.; m. E. Sandra Johnson, Aug. 27, 1967; children: Melanie Lawless York, Stephanie Lawless Setzer. BA in Zoology, U. Tex., 1964, MD, 1968. Intern City Memphis Hosp., 1968-69; resident in pediatrics U. Tex. Med. Br., Galveston, 1969-71; instr. U. Rochester (N.Y.), Sch. Medicine, 1971-72; staff pediatrician Portsmouth (Va.) Naval Hosp., 1972-74; asst. prof. pediatrics Wake Forest U., Bowman Gray Sch. Medicine., Winston-Salem, N.C., 1974-80; assoc. prof. pediatrics Wake Forest U., Bowman Gray Sch. Medicine, Winston-Salem, 1980—, deputy assoc. dean student affairs, 1988-96. Lt. comdr. USNR, 1972-74. Fellow U. Rochester, 1971-72. Fellow Am. Acad. Pediatrics (legis. liaison 1980—); mem. Am. Bd. Pediatrics, Am. Profl. Soc. on Abuse of Children, N.C. Pediatric Soc. (child advocate 1974—), Coun. Med. Student Edn. in Pediatrics (pres. elect), Ambulatory Pediatric Assn. Avocations: tennis, hiking. Office: Wake Forest U Bowman Gray Sch Medicine Med Ctr Blvd Winston Salem NC 27157

LAWLESS, ROBERT WILLIAM, academic administrator; b. Baytown, Tex., Feb. 13, 1937; s. James Milton and Belva Ambaline (Mode) L.; m. Marcella Jane Emmert; children: Christopher, Cheryl, Diana. BS, U. Houston, 1964; PhD, Tex. A&M U., 1968. Instr., asst. prof. Tex. A&M U., College Station, 1967-69; prof., sr. vice chancellor U. Houston, 1969-82; v.p., CFO S.W. Airlines, Dallas, 1982-85, exec. v.p., COO, 1985-89; cons. Tex. Hosp. Assn., Austin, 1966-82, banks, savs. and loans, 1970-72, NASA, 1970; pres. Tex. Tech U. and Tex. Tech. U. Health Scis. Ctr., Lubbock, 1989-96, Univ. Tulsa, Okla., 1996—; ind. dir. Salomon Bros. Asset Mgmt. Co., 1991—, Cen. and S.W. Corp., 1991—; chmn. Coun. of Pub. Univ. Pres. and Chancellors, Tex. higher edn. sys., 1993-95, mem. NCAA Pres.'s Commn., 1994—. Contbr. articles to profl. jours. Mem. formula adv. com. Tex. State Coordinating Bd., Austin, 1977-89; chmn. bd. dirs. Coll. Football Assn., 1990-92; mem. Citizens Commn. on the Tex. Jud. System, 1991-93. Recipient Teaching Excellence award U. Houston, 1972, Disting. Faculty award Coll. Bus. Alumni, 1971, Disting. Alumni award Lee Coll., 1984, U. Houston, 1990. Office: Univ of Tulsa 600 S College Ave Tulsa OK 74104-3126

LAWLEY, ALAN, materials engineering educator; b. Birmingham, Eng., Aug. 29, 1933; s. Archibald and Millicent A. (Olorenshaw) L.; m. Nancy A. Kressler, Mar. 26, 1960; children—Carolyn Ann, Elizabeth Ann, Jennifer Ann. B.Sc., U. Birmingham, 1955, Ph.D., 1958. Research asso. U. Pa., 1958-61; mgr. research labs. Franklin Inst. Labs., 1961-66; A.W. Grosvenor prof. materials engring. Drexel U., Phila., 1969—; head dept. Drexel U., 1969-79, 94—; cons. to govt., industry. Editor in chief Internat. Jour. Powder Metallurgy; contbr. chpts. to books, articles to profl. jours. Recipient Disting. Svc. award Metal Powder Industries Fedn., 1991. Fellow Am. Soc. Metals (gold medal recipient); mem. AIME (pres. 1987), Minerals, Metals and Materials Soc. (pres. 1982), Am. Soc. Engring. Edn., Inst. Materials, Microscopy Soc. Am., APMI Internat., Sigma Xi, Phi Kappa Phi, Tau Beta Pi, Alpha Sigma Mu. Home: 336 Hathaway Ln Wynnewood PA 19096-1925 Office: Drexel Univ Dept Materials Engring Philadelphia PA 19104

LAWNER, RON, advertising executive. Vice chmn. Chief creative officer Arnold Comm., Inc., Boston. Office: Arnold Comm Inc 101 Arch St Boston MA 02110-1130

LAWNICZAK, JAMES MICHAEL, lawyer; b. Toledo, Sept. 11, 1951; m. Christine Nielsen, Dec. 31, 1979; children: Mara Katharine, Rachel Anne, Amy Elizabeth. BA, U. Mich., 1974, JD, 1977. Bar: Mich. 1977, Ill. 1979, Ohio 1989. Law clk. to the Honorable Robert E. DeMascio U.S. Dist. Ct. (ea. dist.) Mich., Detroit, 1977-79; assoc. Levy and Erens, Chgo., 1979-83; assoc. then ptnr. Mayer, Brown & Platt, Chgo., 1983-88; ptnr. Calfee, Halter & Griswold, Cleve., 1988—. Contbg. author: Collier on Bankruptcy. Mem. Chgo. Bar Assn. (subcom. on bankruptcy 1983-88), Cleve. Bar Assn. (bankruptcy com.). Home: 14039 Fox Hollow Dr Novelty OH 44072-9773 Office: Calfee Halter & Griswold 800 Superior Ave E Ste 1400 Cleveland OH 44114-2601

LAWRANCE, CHARLES HOLWAY, civil and sanitary engineer; b. Augusta, Maine, Dec. 25, 1920; s. Charles William and Lois Lyford (Holway) L.; m. Mary Jane Hungerford, Nov. 22, 1947; children: Kenneth A., Lois R., Robert J. BS in Pub. Health Engring., MIT, 1942; MPH, Yale U., 1952. Registered profl. engr., Calif. Sr. san. engr. Conn. State Dept. Health, Hartford, 1946-53; assoc. san. engr. Calif. Dept. Pub. Health, L.A., 1953-55; chief san. engr. Koebig & Koebig, Inc., Cons. Engrs., L.A., 1955-75; engr., mgr. Santa Barbara County Water Agy., Santa Barbara, Calif., 1975-79; prin. engr. James M. Montgomery Cons. Engrs., Pasadena, Calif., 1979-83; v.p. Lawrance, Fisk & McFarland, Inc., Santa Barbara, 1983-96; cons. engr., Santa Barbara, 1996—. Author: The Death of the Dam, 1972; co-author: Ocean Outfall Design, 1958; contbr. articles to profl. jours. Bd. dirs. Pacific Unitarian Ch., Palos Verdes Peninsula, Calif., 1956-60, chmn. bd. 1st lt. USMCR, 1942-46, PTO. Fellow ASCE (life, Norman medal 1966); mem. Am. Water Works Assn. (life), Am. Acad. Environ. Engrs. (life diplomate), Water Environment Fedn. (life). Republican. Unitarian. Home and Office: 1340 Kenwood Rd Santa Barbara CA 93109-1224

LAWRENCE, ALBERT WEAVER, insurance company executive; b. Newburgh, N.Y., Aug. 4, 1928; s. Claude D. and Janet (Weaver) L.; m. Barbara Corell, June 28, 1950; children: David, Janet, Elizabeth. BSAE in Engring., Cornell U., 1950; grad. advanced mgmt. program, Rensselaer Poly. Inst., 1975. Ins. agt., exec., 1953—; founder, chmn. A.W. Lawrence and Co. Inc., Schenectady and Albany, N.Y., 1954-82; chmn. bd. dirs. Lawrence Agy. Corp., Albany, 1982—, Lawrence Ins. Group Inc., Albany, 1986—, Lawrence Group Inc., Schenectady, 1986—; mem. Cornell Engring. Adv. Coun.; bd. dirs. Capital Dist. Ctr. for Econ. Devel.; chmn., majority owner "River Rats" Am. Hockey League team, Albany. Trustee Russell Sage Coll., Troy, N.Y., Rensselaer Poly. Inst., Sunnyview Hosp. and Rehab. Ctr.; past pres. Schenectady Girls Club, Family and Child Svc. Schenectady; bd. dirs. Ind. Living for Physically Disabled, St. Clare's Hosp., Proctor's Theatre, N.Y. State Olympic Regional Devel. Authority, 1989; co-founder Lawrence Inst. for Physically Disabled Rsch.; past chmn. Schenectady United Fund Drive, Jr. Achievement Capital Dist. With U.S. Army, 1946-47. Recipient Sca-Nec-Ta-De Civic award, 1967. Mem. Schenectady C. of C. (past pres.), Schenectady Hist. Soc. (past bd. dirs.), Mohawk Golf Club, Cornell Club (N.Y.C.), N.Y. Athletic Club, N.Y. Yacht Club, No. Lake George Yacht Club (past commodore), U. Club Albany, Ft. Orange Club Albany, Rotary Club (past pres.). Republican. Mem. First Dutch Reformed Ch. Home: 708 Riverview Rd Rexford NY 12148-1433 Office: Lawrence Group Inc 430 State St Schenectady NY 12305-2304

LAWRENCE, ALICE LAUFFER, artist, educator; b. Cleve., Mar. 2, 1916; d. Erwin Otis and Florence Mary (Menough) Lauffer; m. Walter Ernest Lawrence, Sept. 27, 1941; 1 child, Phillip Lauffer. Diploma in art, Cleve. Inst. Art, 1938; BS in Art Edn., Case Western Res. U., 1938. Grad. asst. in art edn. Kent (Ohio) State U., 1939-40; art tchr. Akron (Ohio) and Cleve. Pub. Schs.; comml. artist B.F. Goodrich Co., Akron, 1942-44; sub. art tchr. Akron Pub. Schs.; sketch artist numerous events Akron, 1945-91. Author numerous poems. Mem. Cuyahoga Valley Art Ctr., Women's Art Mus., Akron Art Mus., 1963-94. Recipient 1st pl., 2d pl. in drawing, Butler Mus. Am. Arts, 1940-41, Cleve. Mus. Art, 1944. Mem. Woman's Art League Akron (sec. 1962), Ohio Watercolor Soc., Internat. Soc. Poets (life). Republican. Avocation: writing poetry. Home: 861 Clearview Ave Akron OH 44314-2969

LAWRENCE, BRYAN HUNT, investment banking executive; b. N.Y.C., July 26, 1942; s. Bryan and Suzanne (Walbridge) L.; m. Elizabeth D. Lawrence, Sept. 25, 1965; children: Bryan R., E. Corey. BA, Hamilton Coll., 1964; MBA, Columbia U., 1966. Assoc. Dillon, Read & Co. Inc., N.Y.C., 1966-70, v.p., 1971-74, sr. v.p., 1975-81, mng. dir., 1982—; bd. dirs. Vintage Petroleum, Tulsa, Meenan Oil, Inc., Syosset, N.Y., D & K Wholesale Drug, St. Louis, Transmontaigne Oil Co., Denver, Fintube, L.P., Tulsa, Willbros Group Inc., Panama, Interenergy Corp., Denver, Benson Petroleum, Calgary, Alta. Cavell Energy, Calgary, PetroSantander Inc., Houston, Hallador Petroleum, Denver, Strega Energy, Calgary, Savoy Energy L.P., Traverse City, Mich. Trustee Hamilton Coll., Clinton, N.Y., 1991-94. Republican. Home: 116 E 63rd St New York NY 10021-7303 Office: Dillon Read & Co Inc 535 Madison Ave New York NY 10022-4212

LAWRENCE, CALEB JAMES, bishop; b. Lattie's Brook, N.S., Can., May 26, 1941; s. James Otis and Mildred Viola (Burton) L.; m. Maureen Patricia Cuddy, July 18, 1966; children: Fiona, Karen, Sean. B.A., Dalhousie U., Halifax, N.S., 1962; B.S.T., U. of King's Coll., Halifax, 1964, D.Div. (hon.), 1980. Ordained priest Anglican Ch. of Canada, 1965. Missionary priest St. Edmund's Anglican Parish, Gt. Whale River, Que., Can., 1965-74, rector, 1974-79; canon St. Jude's Cathedral, Frobisher Bay, N.W.T., Can., 1974-75; archdeacon of Arctic Que. Diocese of the Arctic, Toronto, Ont., Can., 1975-79; bishop Diocese of Moosonee, Schumacher, Ont., 1980—; mem. coun. of north Anglican Ch. Can., 1979—, mem. gen. synod, 1980—; mem. Anglican Coun. N.Am. and Caribbean, 1983-86. Translator liturgical services, hymns into Cree, 1970-80. Canon W.H. Morris travelling scholar U. of King's Coll., 1964. Home: PO Box 830, Schumacher, ON Canada P0N 1G0 Office: Anglican Ch of Can, Diocese of Moosonee, PO Box 841, Schumacher, ON Canada P0N 1GO*

LAWRENCE, CHRISTOPHER, engineering executive. Pres. Lawrence Engring., Inc., Jacksonville, Fla. Office: Lawrence Engring Inc 2000 Corporate Square Blvd Jacksonville FL 32216-1918

LAWRENCE, DAVID, JR., newspaper editor, publisher; b. N.Y.C., Mar. 5, 1942; s. David Sr. and Nancy Wemple (Bissell) L.; m. Roberta Phyllis Fleischman, Dec. 21, 1963; children: David III, Jennifer Beth, Amanda Katherine, John Benjamin, Dana Victoria. BS, U. Fla., 1963; postgrad. advanced mgmt. program, Harvard U., 1983; LHD (hon.), Siena Heights Coll., Adrian, Mich., 1985; HHD (hon.), Lawrence Inst. Tech., Detroit, 1986; LHD (hon.), No. Mich. U., 1987; LD (hon.), Barry U., 1991, Fla. Meml. U., 1992, Northwood U., 1993, U. Fla., 1993, Nova Southeastern U., 1997. Reporter, news editor St. Petersburg (Fla.) Times, 1963-67; news editor Style/Washington Post, 1967-69; mng. editor Palm Beach (Fla.) Post, 1969-71, Phila. Daily News, 1971-75; exec. editor Charlotte (N.C.) Observer, 1975-76, editor, 1976-78; exec. editor Detroit Free Press, 1978-85, pub., chmn., 1985-89; pub., chmn. The Miami Herald, 1989—. Bd. dirs. U. Fla. Found., Gov.'s commn. on Edn., Fla. Coun. of 100; chmn. United Way of Dade County; chmn. Miami Art Mus. Named Disting. Alumnus, U. Fla., 1982; recipient Nat. Human Rights award Am. Jewish Com., 1986, First Amendment Freedoms award Anti-Defamation League, 1988, Ida Wells Nat. award for advancement of minorities Nat. Assn. Black Journalists and Nat. Conf. of Edit. Writers, 1988, John S. Knight Gold medal Knight-Ridder, 1988, Silver Medallion award NCCJ, 1992, Disting. Svc. award Nat. Assn. Schs. Journalism and Mass Comm., 1992, Scripps Howard First Amendment award, 1993, Nat. Assn. of Minority Media Execs. lifetime achievement award. Mem. Am. Soc. Newspaper Editors (pres. 1991-92), Inter Am. Press Assn. (pres. 1995-96). Office: The Miami Herald 1 Herald Plz Miami FL 33132-1609

LAWRENCE, DAVID M., health facility administrator; b. 1940. BA, Amherst (N.Y.) Coll., 1962, DSc (hon.), 1994; MD, U. Ky., 1966; MPH, U. Wash., 1973; LittD (hon.), Colgate U., 1995. Cert. gen. preventive medicine. Intern in internal medicine, pediat.; health officer, dir. Multnomah County, Oreg.; v.p., area med. dir. N.W. Permanente Kaiser Found. Health Plan and Hosps., Portland, Maine, 1981-85; v.p., reg. mgr. Kaiser Found. Health Plan and Hosps., Colo., 1985-88; sr. v.p., reg. mgr. Kaiser Found. Health Plan and Hosps., N.C., 1988-89; CEO Kaiser Found. Health Plan and Hosps., Oakland, Calif., 1992—, also vice chmn. bd. dirs., 1990-91, also chmn bd. dirs.; mem. various professorships, directorships and fellowships with U. Wash., Johns Hopkins U., U. Ky.; bd. dirs. Pacific Gas and Electric Co., Hewlett Packard, Healthcare Forum, Bay Area Coun., Calif. Coll. Arts and Crafts, Colby Coll. Named Outstanding Alumnus of the Sch. Pub. Health and Cmty. Medicine U. Washington, 1980, Outstanding Alumnus of the Coll. Medicine U. Ky., 1995. Mem. APHA, Am. Hosp. Assn., Am. Coll. Preventive Medicine, Calif. Assn. Hosps. and Healty Sys., Group Health Assn. Am., Western Consortium for Pub. Health, Calif. Bus. Roundtable, The Conf. Bd. (bd. dirs.), Inst. Medicine/NAS (bd. dirs.), Alpha Omega. Office: Kaiser Found Health Plan & Hosp 1 Kaiser Plz Oakland CA 94612-3610

LAWRENCE, DAVID MICHAEL, lawyer, educator; b. Portland, Oreg., Dec. 26, 1943; s. Robert A. and Maude (Davis) L.; m. Alice Oviatt, June 18, 1966. A.B., Princeton U., 1965; J.D., Harvard U., 1968. Asst. prof. Inst. Govt.; U. N.C., Chapel Hill, 1968-71, assoc. prof., 1971-76, prof. pub. law and govt., 1976-94; Kenan prof. pub. law and govt. U. N.C., Chapel Hill, 1994—; counsel N.C. Local Govt. Study Commn., 1972-73, N.C. Open Meetings Study Commn., 1978-79. Author: Local Government Finance in North Carolina, 2d edit., 1991 (award for excellence Rsch. and Publs. Govt. Fin. Officers Assn. U.S. and Can. 1991); contbr. law articles to profl. jours. Chmn. Durham (N.C.) Hist. Dist. Commn., 1985-89. Recipient Herald prize Princeton U., 1965. Mem. N.C. State Bar, Campus Princeton U. Club. Democrat. Office: University of NC Knapp Bldg Clb # 3330 Chapel Hill NC 27599

LAWRENCE, DEAN GRAYSON, retired lawyer; b. Oakland, Calif.; d. Henry C. and Myrtle (Grayson) Schmidt; A.B., U. Calif.-Berkeley, 1934, J.D., 1939. Admitted to Calif. bar, 1943, U.S. Dist. Ct., 1944, U.S. Ct. Appeals, 1944, Tax Ct. U.S., 1945, U.S. Treasury Dept., 1945, U.S. Supreme Ct., 1967; asso. Pillsbury, Madison & Sutro, San Francisco, 1944, 45; gen. practice Oakland, 1946-50, San Jose, 1952-60, Grass Valley, 1960-63, 66—; county counsel Nevada County, 1964-65. Nevada County Bd. Suprs., 1969-73, chmn., 1971. Vol. animal welfare movement; sec. Nev. County Humane Animal Shelter Bd., 1966-86; state humane officer, 1966-82; pres. Nev. County Humane Soc., 1974-86, mem. Humane Soc. U.S., Fund for Animals; pres. Humane Information Svc., 1992—; bd. dirs. Nevada County Health Planning Council, Golden Empire Areawide Health Planning Council, 1974, 75; trustee Grass Valley Pub. Libr., 1962-64; pres. St. Francis Animal Haven. Mem. People for Ethical Treatment of Animals, Doris Day Animal League, Farm Animal Reform Movement, Performing Animal Welfare Soc., Pet Adoption League, Bus. and Profl. Women's Club, AAUW, Animal Protection Inst. Am. (Humanitarian of Yr. 1986), Animal Legal Defense Fund, Golden Empire Human Soc. (Lifetime Achievement award 1990), League Unbiased Women, Phi Beta Kappa, Sigma Xi, Kappa Beta Pi, Pi Mu Epsilon, Pi Lambda Theta. Episcopalian. Office: PO Box 66 Grass Valley CA 95945-0066

LAWRENCE, DEIRDRE ELIZABETH, librarian, coordinator research services; b. Lawton, Okla., Mar. 15, 1952; d. Herbert Thomas and Joan Roberta (McDonald) L. BA in Art History, Richmond Coll., 1974; MLS, Pratt Inst., 1979; postgrad., Harvard U., 1981-82. Prin. libr. mus. librs. and archives, coord. rsch. svcs. Bklyn. Mus., 1983—; head cataloging and tech. scvs. Mus. Fine Arts, Boston, 1980-83; mem. Rsch Libr. Group, bd. nominating com., 1994, adv. com. Getty Projects, 1996—, Met. Reference and Rsch. Libr. Agy, conservation preservation adv. coun., 1988-92, bd. trustees, 1995; grant reviewer fed. and state agys.; cons. in field. Author: New York and Hollywood Fashion, 1986, Dressing the Part: Costume Sket, 1989, Modern Art--The Production, 1989, Guide to the CUlin Archival Collection, 1996, Formation of an Islamic art library collection in an Am. museum, 1996, Culin: Collector and Documentor of the World He Saw, Fashion and How It Was Influenced by Ethnographic Collections in Museums, Native American Art and Culture: Documentory Resources, Access to Visual Images-Past and Present; contbr. articles to profl. jours.; lectr. at internat. and nat. libr. confs. Recipient Samuel H. Kress Travel grant, 1993, 95. Mem. Art Librs. Soc. N.Am., Spl. Librs. Assn., Native Am. Art Studies Assn., Internat. Fedn. Libr. Assns. Office: Brooklyn Mus 200 Eastern Pky Brooklyn NY 11238-6052

LAWRENCE, EDMUND P., JR., neurosurgeon; b. Buffalo, Sept. 18, 1946; s. Edmund P. and Ruth (Jones) L.; m. Morgan A. Lapat, July 11, 1972; 1 child, Max P. BS in Chemistry, Washington and Lee U., 1968; MD, Vanderbilt U., 1972. Diplomate Am. Bd. Neurol. Surgery. Intern, then resident in neurosurgery Northwestern U., Chgo., 1974-79; chmn. dept. neurol. surgery St. Vincent's Hosp. and Med. Ctr., Toledo, 1984—; practice medicine specializing in neurosurgery Toledo, 1987—; bd. dirs. neurol. ICU, St. Vincent's Hosp., Toledo, Ohio; pres. Neurol. Network, 1997. Contbr. numerous articles and research papers to profl. jours; exhibited in permanent collections and several one-man shows. Mem. founders soc. Detroit Inst. Art, Toledo Mus. Art, 1979—; donor Toledo Mus. Art. Recipient Eleanor Clarke Rsch. award Northwestern U. Sch. Medicine, 1975. Mem. AMA, Ohio State Med. Assn., Ohio Neurosurg. Soc., Toledo Acad. Medicine, Internat. Coll. Surgeons, Am. Assn. Neurol. Surgeons. Episcopalian. Avocation: painting, martial arts instruction. Office: Neurosurgical Network 2409 Cherry St Ste 10 Mob Toledo OH 43608-2625

LAWRENCE, FRANCIS LEO, language educator, educational administrator; b. Woonsocket, R.I., Aug. 25, 1937. B.S., St. Louis U., 1959; Ph.D. in French and Italian, Tulane U., 1962. Mem. faculty Tulane U., New Orleans, 1962-90, chmn. dept. French and Italian, 1969-76, acting dean Newcomb Coll., 1976-78, dep. provost, 1978-81, acting provost, grad. dean, 1981-82, prof. French, from 1971, acad. v.p., provost, 1982-90; pres. Rutgers, New Brunswick, N.J., 1990—. Author numerous publs. on French 17th century lit. Contbr. articles, revs. and essays to profl. publs. Decorated chevalier, Palmes Academiques, 1977. Mem. Am. Assn. Tchrs. French, N.Am. Soc. 17th Century French Lit., MLA. Office: Rutgers U Office of Pres New Brunswick NJ 08903*

LAWRENCE, GEORGE DURWOOD, JR., lawyer, corporate executive; b. Eatonton, Ga., Nov. 22, 1950; s. George Durwood Sr. and Louise (Ledbetter) L.; m. Barbara Ann Lawrence, Nov., 1995; children: George Durwood III, Sarah Grace, Scott Dickerson. Student, MIT, 1968-70; BS, U. Ga., 1972, JD, 1975. Bar: Ga. 1975, U.S. Dist. Ct. (mid. dist.) Ga. 1975, U.S. Ct. Appeals (5th and 11th cirs.) 1975. Ptnr. Lawrence, Rice & Lawrence, Eatonton, 1975-80; trial atty. U.S. Dept. Justice, Washington, 1980-82, asst. chief. environ. enforcement, 1982-85; dep. gen. counsel Tex. Internat. Co., Oklahoma City, 1985-86, gen. counsel, v.p., 1986-89, chief fin. officer, 1988-89; CEO The Phoenix Resource Cos., Inc., Oklahoma City, 1990-96; dir. Apache Corp., 1996—. Hughes Spalding scholar U. Ga. Sch. Law, 1972-75; recipient Spl. Achievement award U.S. Dept. Justice, 1983-84, Younger Fed. Lawyer award Fed. Bar Assn., 1984. Mem. ABA, Ga. Bar Assn. Home: 4225 Escondito Cir Sarasota FL 34238

LAWRENCE, GERALD, JR., lawyer; b. Phila., Jan. 10, 1968; s. Gerald and Rita Katherine (Duffy) L.; m. Andrea Stewart, Jan. 8, 1994. BSBA, Georgetown U., 1990; JD, Villanova U., 1993. Bar: Pa. 1993, U.S. Dist. Ct. Pa. 1994, U.S. Ct. Appeals (3d cir.) 1994. Assoc. Elliott Reihner Siedzikowski & Egan, Blue Bell, Harrisburg, Scranton, Pa. and Woodbury, N.J., 1992—; counsel Del. County Dem. Party, 1996—; Del. County counsel to Pa. Dem. Party Victory, 1996. Interviewer Georgetown Alumni Admission Program, 1992—; bd. dirs. James A. Finnegan Found., 1995—; v.p. Georgetown Club Phila., 1996—. Mem. ABA, ATLA, Pa. Bar Assn. (mem. judicial selection and adminstrn. com., mem. commn. to rev. and evaluate jud. campaign advt. guidelines 1996), Phila. Bar Assn. Home: 349 Oak Terr Wayne PA 19087 Office: Elliot Reihner Siedzikowski & Egan Union Meeting Corp Ctr IV 925 Harvest Dr PO Box 3010 Blue Bell PA 19422

LAWRENCE, GERALD GRAHAM, management consultant; b. U.K., June 21, 1947; came to U.S., 1962, naturalized, 1967; s. Raymond Joseph and Barbara Virginia Lawrence; 1 child, Ian Andrew; m. Julie Ann Quiram. BA in Math., Northeastern U., 1970, MA in Econs., 1973; MBA, U. Pa., 1975. Optics rsch. technologist Polaroid Corp., Cambridge, Mass., 1968-70; intern Corning Glass Works, Inc., N.Y.C., 1974; asst. brand mgr. Procter and Gamble, Cin., 1975-76; assoc. Theodore Barry & Assocs., N.Y.C., 1976-79; dir. performance improvement systems Stone & Webster Mgmt. Cons., N.Y.C., 1979-84; mgr. utility MAS Deloitte Haskins & Sells, N.Y.C., 1984-86; pres. PMC Mgmt. Cons., Inc., Three Bridges, N.J., 1986—; advisor Commerce & Econ. Devel. Dept. State of N.J.; speaker in field. Designer: auditor system nuclear power plant constrn; innovator; quality assurance for profl. cons. svcs; contbr. articles to profl. jours. Econs. fellow Northeastern U., 1973, adminstrv. fellow Wharton Sch. U. Pa., 1975. Home: 11 Thistle Ln Flemington NJ 08822-7067 Office: PMC Mgmt Cons PO Box 332 Three Bridges NJ 08887-0332

LAWRENCE, GLENN ROBERT, arbitrator, mediator; b. N.Y.C., Nov. 8, 1930; m. Nina M. Scaturro; children: David P., Eric A. JD, Bklyn. Law Sch., 1954; BA, U. Louisville, 1968; MA in Psychology, Cath. U., 1977; PhD, Am. U., 1980. Bar: N.Y. 1955, D.C. 1973, U.S. Supreme Ct. 1976. Atty. N.Y.C. Legal Aid, 1955-57; ptnr. Lawrence & Lawrence, N.Y.C., 1957-64; agt. N.Y. State, Babylon, N.Y., 1964-66; atty. U.S. Army Engrs., Washington, 1966-69; assoc. chief trial atty. U.S. Dept. Navy, Washington, 1969-78; judge adminstrv. law HEW, Camden, N.J., 1978-79, U.S. Dept. Labor, Washington, 1979-93, SEC, Washington, 1993-96; mem. bd. contract appeals U.S. Dept. Labor, Washington, 1981-93; arbitrator Nat. Assn. Securities Dealers, Inc., Washington, 1996—, Superior Ct., Washington, 1996—; adj. prof. law George Mason U., Fairfax, Va., 1980-83, Ctrl. Mich. U., Washington, 1981-95, Nat. Jud. Coll. U. Nev., Reno, 1984-88; lectr. Banares Hindu U., Varanasi, India, 1988, Law Coll., Ernakulum, Cochin, India, 1989, Washington Lee U., Lexington, Va., 1990; mem. adv. com. Georgetown U. State Cts. and Toxic Torts, 1991; advisor Judiciary Leadership Devel. Coun. Inc., 1990—; bd. dirs. Fed. Bar Found., 1994—. Author: Condemnation Law, 1969. Bd. dirs. Democracy Devel. Initiative. Mem. ABA (chmn. nat. conf. adminstrv. law judges edn. com. 1985-90, chmn. internat. conf. jud. edn. London 1985, pres. fed. adminstrv. law judge conf. 1984-85, chmn. edn. jud. adminstrn. divsn. 1987-91, chmn. confs., chmn. jud. edn. standards program 1991-95, vice chmn. govt. lawyers com. sr. lawyers divsn. 1991-95), Fed Bar Assn. (chmn. adminstrv. judiciary com. 1984-88, continuing edn. bd. 1988-91, chmn. judiciary sect. 1989-91, sect. coord. exec. com. 1992-94, editor Fed. Jurist 1991-96, chair pub. rels. com. 1993-96, chair profl. ethics com. 1996—), ATLA (pres. 1979-80).

LAWRENCE, HENRY SHERWOOD, physician, educator; b. N.Y.C., Sept. 22, 1916; s. Victor John and Agnes (Whalen) L.; m. Dorothea Wetherbee, Nov. 13, 1943; children: Dorothea, Victor, Geoffrey. AB, NYU, 1938, MD, 1943. Diplomate Am. Bd. Internal Medicine. Mem. faculty NYU, N.Y.C., 1947—; John Wyckoff fellow in medicine NYU, 1948-49, dir. student health, 1950-57, head infectious disease and immunology div., 1959—, prof. medicine, 1961-79, Jeffrey Bergstein prof. medicine, 1979—, co-dir. med. svcs., 1964—, dir. Cancer Ctr., 1974-79; dir. Ctr. for AIDS Rsch., 1989-94; vis. physician Tisch Hosp., Bellevue Hosp., 1964—; cons. medicine Manhattan VA Hosp., 1964—; infectious disease program com. VA Rsch. Svc., 1960-63; cons. allergy and immunology study sect. USPHS, 1960-63, chmn., 1963-65; assoc. mem. commn. on streptococcal and staphylococcal diseases Armed Forces Epidemiol. Bd., Dept. Def., 1956-74; mem. coms. Nat. Acad. Scis.-NRC, 1957-65, chmn. com. transplantation, 1963-65; mem. NRC, 1970-72; mem. allergy and infectious disease panel Health Rsch. Coun., N.Y.C., 1962-75, co-chmn., 1968-75; mem. sci. adv. council Am. Cancer Soc., 1973-75. Editor: Medical Clinics of North America, 1957, Cellular and Humoral Aspects of Hypersensitive States, 1959, (with M. Landy) Mediators of Cellular Immunity, 1969, (with Kirkpatrick and Burger) Immunobiology of Transfer Factor, 1983; mem. editorial bd. Transplantation, Ann. of Internal Medicine; mem. editl. adv. bd. Transplantation Procs.; founder, editor in chief Celluar Immunology, 1970-96. Served to lt. M.C. USNR, World War II. Commonwealth Fund fellow Univ. Coll., London, 1959; recipient Research Career Devel. award USPHS, 1960-65, prize Alpha Omega Alpha, 1943; Meritorious Sci. Achievement award NYU Alumni Assn., 1970, von Pirquet Gold medal Ann. Forum on Allergy, 1972, Award for Disting. Achievement in Sci. of Medicine ACP, 1973, Sci. Achievement award Am. Coll. Allergists, 1974, Sci. medal N.Y. Acad. Medicine, 1974, Bristol Sci. award Infectious Diseases Soc. Am., 1974, Charles V. Chapin medal, 1975, Lila Gruber honor award Am. Acad. Dermatology, 1975, Alumni Achievement award NYU Washington Sq. Coll., 1979. Fellow ACP (Bronze medal 1973), Am. Acad. Allergy (hon.), Royal Coll. Physicians and Surgeons Glasgow (hon.); mem. Nat. Acad. Scis., Assn. Am. Physicians, Am. Soc. for Clin. Investigation, Am. Assn. Immunologists, Soc. for Exptl. Biology and Medicine (editorial bd. procs.), Interurban Clin. Club, Harvey Soc. (sec. 1957-60, lectr. 1973—, councillor 1974-77), Peripatetic Clin. Soc., Infectious Diseases Soc. (charter, councillor 1970-72, Bristol Sci. award 1974), Royal Soc. Medicine (affiliate) (Eng.), Internat. Transplantation Soc. (chmn. constn. com., councillor), Société Française d'Allergie (corr.), Alpha Omega Alpha. Achievements include discovery of Transfer Factor - a product of lymphocytes (T-cells) which confers and/or augments immunity to mycobacterial, viral and fungal infections when administered to non-immune individuals; research on mechanisms tissue damage and homograft rejection in man. Home: 343 E 30th St New York NY 10016-6417

LAWRENCE, JACOB, artist, educator; b. Atlantic City, Sept. 7, 1917; s. Jacob and Rose Lee (Armstead) L.; m. Gwendolyn Knight, July 24, 1941. Student, Harlem Art Workshop, N.Y.C., 1932-39; scholar, Am. Artists Sch., N.Y.C., 1938-39; DFA (hon.), Denison U., 1970, Pratt Inst., 1972, Colby Coll., 1976, Md. Inst. Coll. Art, 1979, Carnegie-Mellon U., 1981, Yale U., 1986, Spelman Coll., 1987, Rutgers U., 1988, Parsons Sch. Design, N.Y.C., 1988; LHD (hon.), Howard U., 1985, Tulane U., 1989. Artist Yaddo Found., Saratoga, 1955-56; instr. Pratt Inst. Art Sch., N.Y.C., 1955-70, Art Students League, N.Y.C., 1967-69, New Sch. Social Rsch., N.Y.C., 1966-69; artist in residence Brandeis U., 1965; coord. of the arts Pratt Inst., 1970—, prof. art, 1970; prof. art U. Wash., Seattle, 1971-83, prof. emeritus, 1983—; Disting. Faculty lectr. U. Wash., 1978. Exhibits include John Brown Series, under auspices Am. Fedn. Art, 1945, 30 paintings on history U.S., Alan Gallery, 1957; one-man shows include Migration Series, Mus. Modern Art, 1944, Downtown Gallery, N.Y.C., 1941, 43, 45, 47, 50, 53, M'Bari Artists and Writers Club, Nigeria, 1962, Terry Dintenfass Gallery, N.Y.C., 1963, Francine Seders Gallery, Seattle, 1985; works included Johnson Wax Co. World tour group exhbn., 1963, U.S. State Dept. group exhbn. in, Pakistan, 1963, retrospective exhbn., Whitney Mus. Am. Art, 1974, traveling retrospective Exhbn., Seattle Art Mus., 1986-87; commd. for graphic impressions 1977 Inauguration, Washington, mural commd., Kingdome Stadium, Seattle, 1979, Mural Howard U., 1980, 85, U. Wash., 1985, others; represented in, Met. Mus. Art, Mus. Modern Art, Whitney Mus., Phillips Meml. Collection, Washington, Portland (Oreg.) Mus., Worcester (Mass.) Mus., Balt. Mus. Art, Wichita Art Mus., Albright-Knox Art Gallery, Buffalo, AAAL, N.Y.C., Mus. Modern Art, Sao Paulo, Brazil, R.I. Sch. Design, Va. Mus. Fine Arts, Bklyn. Mus., IBM Corp., Container Corp. Am., various univs.; Author: Harriet and the Promised Land, 1968; illustrator: Aesop's Fables, 1970; (book catalogue for retrospective exhbn.: Jacob Lawrence-American Painter, 1986; executed mural Theatre, 1985; executed, instated mural Orlando Fla. Internat. Airport, 1988, GSA, Jamaica, N.Y. Mem. bd. govs. Skowhegan Sch. Painting and Sculpture; mem. Fulbright Art Com., 1966-67, Wash. State Arts Commn., 1976—; elector Hall of Fame for Gt. Americans, 1976—. Rosenwald fellow, 1940-42, Guggenheim fellow, 1946; recipient purchase prize Artists for Victory, 1942, purchase prize Atlanta U., 1948, Opportunity mag. award, 1948; Norman Wait Harris medal Art Inst. Chgo., 1948; Acad. Arts and Letters grantee, 1953; Chapelbrook Found. grantee, 1955; recipient 1st prize in mural competition for UN Bldg. Nat. Council U.S. Art, Inc., 1955, Retrospective Exhbn. with Definitive Catalogue Ford Found., 1960, Retrospective Exhbn. with Definitive Catalogue Whitney Mus. Modern Art, 1974; works selected as part of exchange exhibit with Soviet Union, 1959; Spingarn medal NAACP, 1970; ann. citation Nat. Assn. Schs. Art, 1973; recipient U.S. Gen. Svcs. Adminstrn. Design award, 1990, Nat. Medal of Arts award Pres. of U.S., 1990, Gold medal Nat. Arts Club N.Y., 1993. Mem. Artist Equity Assn. (past. sec., pres. N.Y. chpt. 1957), Nat. Endowment for Arts, Nat. Inst. Arts and Letters, Nat. Coun. Arts. Address: Horizon House 900 University St # 16 Abc Seattle WA 98101-2789 also: Francine Seders Gallery 6701 Greenwood Ave N Seattle WA 98103-5255 *As an artist, I hope to contribute something of value to life in general and to my fellowman in particular. I hope that when my life ends... I would have added a little beauty, perception and quality for those who follow. During my lifetime also...I hope to learn and add further motivation, insight and dimension as to my own thinking.**

LAWRENCE, JAMES BLAND, marketing executive; b. Houston, July 22, 1947; s. Harding Luther and Jimmie Georgia (Bland) L.; m. Marie Therese Heckethorn, Feb. 7, 1976 (div. 1981); m. Pamela Douglas Moffat, Sept. 7, 1985. BA in Psychology, U. So. Calif., 1970, MA in Comm./Cinema, 1975. Account exec. KTVV TV, Austin, Tex., 1974, KXAS TV, Dallas, 1975-77; v.p. pub. affairs Braniff Internat., Dallas, 1977-78; v.p. Pacific & Asia Braniff Internat., Hong Kong, 1978-80; v.p. govt. and internat. affairs Braniff Internat., Dallas, 1980-81; v.p. Wells, Rich, Greene, Inc., N.Y.C., 1981-82; sr. v.p., mng. dir. Wells, Rich, Greene, Inc., Detroit, 1983-88, exec. v.p., mng. dir., 1988-90; exec. v.p. Wells, Rich, Greene, Inc., N.Y.C., 1990—. Dir., producer documentary film: Honky Tonk Heros, 1975. Active Foster Parents Plan, Warwick, R.I., 1988—; mem. Met. Affairs Corp., Detroit, 1989. Mem. Detroit Inst. Arts, Am. Assn. Advt. Agencies, Wilderness Soc., Nat. Wildlife Fedn., Greenfield Village/Henry Ford Mus., Adcraft Club, Fairlane Country Club, Waccabuc Country Club (N.Y.). Avocations: tennis, sailing. Office: Wells Rich Greene Inc 9 W 57th St New York NY 10019

LAWRENCE, JAMES KAUFMAN LEBENSBURGER, lawyer; b. New Rochelle, N.Y., Oct. 8, 1940; s. Michael Monet and Edna (Billings) L.; m. George-Ann Adams, Apr. 5, 1969; children: David Michael, Catherine Robin. AB, Ohio State U., 1962, JD, 1965. Bar: Ohio. 1965, U.S. Dist. Ct. (so. dist.) Ohio 1971, U.S. Ct. Appeals (6th cir.) 1971, U.S. Ct. Appeals (4th cir.) 1978. Field atty. NLRB, Cin., 1965-70; ptnr. Frost & Jacobs LLP, Cin., 1970—; adj. prof. econs. dept. and Coll. Law, U. Cin., 1975—, Ohio State U. Coll. Law, 1995—, Xavier U., 1995—, McGregor Sch., Antioch U., 1993—; master Potter Sewart Inn of Ct., Cin., 1987—, treas., 1988-90; tchg. fellow Harvard Negotiation Project, 1991; chmn. adv. panel on appointment of magistrate judges U.S. Dist. Ct. for So. Dist. Ohio, 1993—. Contbr. articles to profl. jours. Mem. nat. coun. Ohio State U. Coll. Law, 1974—; mem. steering com. Leadership Cin., 1985-89; mem. Seven Hills Neighborhood Houses, Cin., 1973-95, pres., 1992-94; bd. dirs. Beechwood Home, Cin., 1983-86; mem. adv. bd. Emerson Behavioral Health Svcs., 1990-95, chmn., 1995; chmn. Labor Dept., 1978-89, Providence Hosp. Devel. Coun., 1995—, chmn., 1996—; trustee Ctr. for Resolution of Disputes, Inc., 1988-91, treas., 1990-91; mem. Ohio Gov.'s Ops. Improvement Task Force, 1991. Mem. ABA, Cin. Bar Assn. (chmn. labor law com. 1979-82, comm. adv. com. 1994—), Ohio Bar Assn. (vice chmn. labor and employment law sect. 1987-90, chmn. 1990-92), Indsl. Rels. Rsch. Assn. (bd. govs. 1977-80), Alumni Assn. Coll. Law Ohio State U. (pres. 1984-85), Cincinnatus Assn. (pres. 1985-86), Univ. Club. Avocations: collecting movie posters, biking. Home: 3300 Columbia Pkwy Cincinnati OH 45226 Office: Frost & Jacobs LLP 2500 PNC Ctr 201 E 5th St Cincinnati OH 45202-4117

LAWRENCE, JEROME, playwright, director, educator; b. Cleve., July 14, 1915; s. Samuel and Sarah (Rogen) L. BA, Ohio State U., 1937, LHD (hon.), 1963; DLitt, Fairleigh Dickinson U., 1968; DFA (hon.), Villanova U., 1969; LittD, Coll. Wooster, 1983. Dir. various summer theaters Pa. and Mass., 1934-37; reporter, telegraph editor Wilmington (Ohio) News Jour., 1937; editor Lexington Daily News, Ohio, 1937; continuity editor radio Sta. KMPC, Beverly Hills, Calif., 1938-39; sr. staff writer CBS, Hollywood, Calif. and N.Y.C., 1939-42; pres., writer, dir. Lawrence & Lee, Hollywood, N.Y.C. and London, 1945—; vis. prof. Ohio State Univ., 1969, Salzburg Seminar in Am. Studies, 1972, Baylor Univ., 1978; prof. playwriting Univ. So. Calif. Grad. Sch., 1984—; co-founder, judge Margo Jones award, N.Y.C., 1958—; co-founder, pres. Am. Playwrights Theatre, Columbus, Ohio, 1970-85; bd. dirs. Am. Conservatory Theatre, San Francisco, 1970-80, Stella Adler Theatre, L.A., 1987—, Plumstead Playhouse, 1986—; keynote speaker Bicentennial of Bill of Rights, Congress Hall, Phila., 1991; hon. mem. Nat. Theatre Conf., 1993; adv. bd. Am. Theatre in Lit. Contemporary Arts Ednl. Project, 1993—. Scenario writer Paramount Studios, 1941; master playwright NYU Inst. Performing Arts, 1967-69; author-dir. for: radio and television UN Broadcasts; Army-Navy programs D-Day, VE-Day, VJ-Day; author: Railroad Hour, Hallmark Playhouse, Columbia Workshop; author: Off Mike, 1944, (biography, later made into PBS-TV spl.) Actor: Life and Times of Paul Muni, 1978 (libretto and lyrics by Lawrence and Lee, music by Billy Goldenberg); co-author, dir.: (album) One God; playwright: Live Spelled Backwards, 1969, Off Mike, (mus. with Robert E. Lee) Look, Ma, I'm Dancin', 1948 (music by Hugh Martin), Shangri-La, 1956 (music by Harry Warren, lyrics by James Hilton, Lawrence and Lee), Mame, 1966 (score by Jerry Herman), Dear World, 1969 (score by Jerry Herman), (non-mus.) Inherit the Wind (translated and performed in 34 langs., named best fgn. play of year London Critics Poll 1960), Auntie Mame, 1956, The Gang's All Here, 1959, Only in America, 1959, A Call on Kuprin, 1961, Diamond Orchid (revised as Sparks Fly Upward, 1966), 1965, The Incomparable Max, 1969, The Crocodile Smile, 1970, The Night Thoreau Spent in Jail, 1970, (play and screenplay) First Monday in October, 1978, (written for opening of Thurber Theatre, Columbus) Jabberwock: Improbablilities Lived and Imagined by James Thurber in the Fictional City of Columbus, Ohio, 1974, (with Robert E. Lee) Whisper in the Mind, 1994, The Angels Weep, 1992, (novel) A Golden Circle: A Tale of the Stage and the Screen and Music of Yesterday and Now and Tomorrow and Maybe the Day After Tomorrow, 1993; Decca Dramatic Albums, Musi-Plays., Selected Plays of Lawrence and Lee, 1996; contbg. editor Dramatics mag., mem. adv. bd., contbr. Writer's Digest; Lawrence and Lee collections at Libr. and Mus. of the Performing Arts, Lincoln Ctr., N.Y., Harvard's Widener Libr., Cambridge, Mass., Jerome Lawrence & Robert E. Lee Theatre Rsch. Inst. at Ohio State U., Columbus, est. 1986. A founder, overseas corr. Armed Forces Radio Service; mem. Am. Theatre Planning Bd.; bd. dirs. Nat. Repertory Theatre, Plumstead Playhouse; mem. adv. bd. USDAN Center for Creative and Performing Arts, East-West Players, Performing Arts Theatre of Handicapped., Inst. Outdoor Drama; mem. State Dept. Cultural Exchange Drama Panel, 1961-69; del. Chinese-Am. Writers Conf., 1982, 86, Soviet-Am. Writers Conf., 1984, 85; Am. Writers rep. to Hiroshima 40th Anniversary Commemorative, Japan, 1985; mem. U.S. Cultural Exchange visit to theatre communities of Beijing and Shanghai, 1985; adv. coun. Calif. Ednl. Theatre Assn., Calif. State U., Calif. Repertory Co., Long Beach, 1984—. Recipient N.Y. Press Club award, 1942, CCNY award, 1948, Radio-TV Life award, 1948, Mirror awards, 1952, 53, Peabody award, 1949, 52, Variety Showmanship award 1954, Variety Critics poll 1955, Outer-Circle Critics award 1955, Donaldson award, 1955, Ohioana award, 1955, Ohio Press Club award, 1959, Brit. Drama Critics award, 1960, Moss Hart Meml. award, 1967, State Dept. medal, 1968, Pegasus award, 1970, Lifetime Achievement award Am. Theatre Assn., 1979, Nat. Thespian Soc. award, 1980, Pioneer Broadcasters award, 1981, 95, Diamond Circle award Pacific Pioneer Broadcasters, 1995, Ohioana Library career medal, Master of Arts award Rocky Mountain Writers Guild, 1982, Centennial Award medal Ohio State U., 1970, William Inge award and lectureship Independence Community Coll., 1983, 86—, Disting. Contbr. award Psychologists for Social Responsibility, 1985, ann. awards San Francisco State U., Pepperdine U., Career award Southeastern Theatre Conf., 1990; named Playwright of Yr. Baldwin-Wallace Coll., 1960; named to Honorable Order of Ky. Colonels, 1965, Tenn. Colonels, 1988; named to Theater Hall of Fame, 1990. Fellow Coll. Am. Theatre, Kennedy Ctr.; mem. Nat. Theatre Conf. (hon.), Acad. Motion Picture Arts and Scis. (nominating com. best fgn. films 1997), Acad. TV Arts and Scis. (2 Emmy award 1988), Authors League (coun.), ANTA (dir., v.p.), Ohio State U. Assn. (dir.), Radio Writers' Guild (founder, pres.), Writers Guild Am. (dir., founding mem. Valentine Davies award), Dramatists Guild (coun.), ASCAP, Calif. Ednl. Theatre Assn. (Profl. Artist award 1992), Century Club N.Y., Phi Beta Kappa, Sigma Delta Chi. Avocations: traveling, photography, swimming. *I want people to leave the theatre after seeing a play I have written feeling as if they were taller human beings, as if their souls had been sandpapered. A work must have meanings many layers deep so that it illumines our lives and our times.*

LAWRENCE, JOHN KIDDER, lawyer; b. Detroit, Nov. 18, 1949; s. Luther Ernest and Mary Anna (Kidder) L.; m. Jeanine Ann DeLay, June 20, 1981. AB, U. Mich., 1971; JD, Harvard U., 1974. Bar: Mich. 1974, U.S. Supreme, 1977, D.C. 1978. Assoc. Dickinson, Wright, McKean & Cudlip, Detroit, 1973-74; staff atty. Office of Judge Adv. Gen., Washington, 1975-78; assoc. Dickinson, Wright, McKean, Cudlip & Moon, Detroit, 1978-81; ptnr. Dickinson, Wright, Moon, VanDusen & Freeman, Detroit, 1981—. Exec. sec. Detroit Com. on Fgn. Rels., 1988—; trustee Ann Arbor (Mich.) Summer Festival, Inc., 1990—; patron Founders Soc. Detroit Inst. Arts, 1979—. With USN, 1975-78. Mem. AAAS, ABA, Am. Law Inst., Fed. Bar Assn., State Bar Mich., D.C. Bar Assn., Am. Judicature Soc., Internat. Bar Assn., Am. Hist. Assn., Detroit Club, Detroit Athletic Club, Econ. Club Detroit, Phi Eta Sigma, Phi Beta Kappa. Democrat. Episcopalian. Office: Dickinson Wright Moon VanDusen & Freeman 500 Woodward Ave Ste 4000 Detroit MI 48226-3423

LAWRENCE, KEN, columnist; b. Chgo., Nov. 11, 1942; s. Lawrence Edward and Mary Ewing (Glickauf) Burg; m. Patricia Rose Bridges, Feb. 6, 1964 (div. Sept. 1980); children: Vernon H. Davis, Max E.; m. Kathleen Woodberry, Feb. 24, 1995. Student, Shimer Coll., 1959-61, Roosevelt U., 1962-63, 68. Freelance film technician Chgo. and Gary, Ind., 1959-71; corr. Southern Conf. Ednl. Fund, Jackson, Miss., 1971-75; editor Greenwood Press & Univ. Press of Miss., Jackson, 1976; columnist Covert Action Info. Bull., Washington, 1979—, Stamp Collector, Albany, Oreg., 1982-86, Linn's Stamp News, Sidney, Ohio, 1987—, Am. Philatelist, State College, Pa., 1991—; dir. Am. Friends Svc. Com., Jackson, 1977-79, Anti-Repression Resource Team, Jackson, 1979-93. Author: Linn's Plate Number Coil Handbook, 1990, (booklet) The New State Repression, 1980; editor: Mississippi Slave Narratives, 5 vols., 1976, The Philatelic Communicator, 1989-94; contbr. (book) Dirty Work 2-The CIA in Africa, 1979. Trainer United Meth. Voluntary Svc., N.Y.C., 1980-83; organizer Nat. Anti-Klan Network, Atlanta, 1980-85; bd. dirs. South African Mil. Refugee Aid Fund, N.Y.C., 1977-85. Recipient Rosebud, MORE Journalism Rev., 1975, Cert. of Merit, Miss. Hist. Soc., 1976. Mem. Am. Philatelic Soc. (dir.-at-large 1991-93, sec. 1993-95, v.p. 1995—, Rsch. medal 1988), Am. Philatelic Congress, Jackson Philatelic Soc. (v.p. 1990-91, pres. 1992-93), Bur. Issues Assn. (gov. 1989—), The Manuscript Soc. Avocations: stamp collector, traveling. Office: PO Box 8040 State College PA 16803-8040

LAWRENCE, LAUREN, psychoanalytical theorist, psychoanalyst; b. N.Y.C., June 26, 1950; d. Jack and Elaine (Gaumont) Soevier; m. D. Henry Lawrence, June 24, 1972; 1 child, Graham. MA in Psychology, New Sch. for Social Rsch., 1993. Psychoanalyst N.Y.C., 1992—. Contbr. articles to profl. jours.; columnist "Dreams" The New York Daily News. Mem. N.Y. Psychoanalytic Soc. Achievements include founding of a third person analysis, a new method of analysis in clinical practice, which provides the analysand a narrational objectivity; and the covert seduction theory, which expounds the dangers of a non-physical parental seduction. Avocations: tennis, musical composition, writing poetry, reading, studying Greek. Home: 31 E 72d St New York NY 10021

LAWRENCE, LINDA HIETT, retired school system administrator, writer; b. Phoenix, July 26, 1939; d. Lydle and Hazeldell (Sutton) Hiett; children: Pamela Lee Reardon, Annabel Virginia Urrea. BA, U. Ariz., 1961; MA, Ariz. State U., 1985, EdD, 1986. Cert. sch. supt., prin., tchr., Ariz. Prin. Washington Elem. Sch. Dist. 6, Phoenix, 1980-83; prin. Dysart Unified Sch. Dist. 89, Peoria, Ariz., 1985-87, asst. supt., 1987-88; supt. Cottonwood Ariz. Oak Creek Sch. Dist. 6, 1988-91; cons., writer, 1991—; owner Lawrence Properties and Enterprises; adj. prof. No. Ariz. U., 1990-91. Author: Adventures in Arizona, 1991; co-author: History of Jerome and Verde Valley, 1991. Trustee Marcus J. Lawrence Hosp.; pres. bd. dirs. Children's Advocacy Ctr. NSF grantee for Math; recipient USC's 100 Outstanding Supts. award. Mem. AAUW, Ariz. Hist. Soc., Ariz. Ctr. for the Book, Sacred Heart Alumni Assn., Ariz. State U. Alumni Assn. Ariz. Humanities Coun., Phoenix Zoo, Friends of Our Bros. and Sisters, Phi Delta Kappa.

LAWRENCE, MARGERY H(ULINGS), marketing consultant; b. Harmarville, Pa., June 17, 1934; d. Richard Nuttall and Alva (Burns) Hulings; student Bethany Coll., 1951-52; BS in Mktg., Carnegie-Mellon U., 1955. Asst. mdse. buyer Joseph Horne Co., Pitts., 1955-57; home econs. editor Pitts. Group Cos. Columbia Gas System, Pitts., 1957-64, dir. home econs., 1968-72; home economist Columbia Gas Pa., Jeannette, 1964-68, dist. marketing mgr., 1972-87, div. mgr., 1987-91; dir. mktg. Columbia Gas Pa. & Columbia Gas Md., 1991-96; mktg. & bus. cons. M.H. Lawrence Ltd., 1996—. Bd. dirs., vice chmn. Ohio Valley Gen. Hosp., Beaver Valley C. of C., Womens Golf Assn. of Western Pa. Mem. DAR, NAFE, AmGas Assn. (Home Svc. Achievement award 1964).

LAWRENCE, MARTIN, actor, comedian; b. Frankfurt, Germany, Apr. 16, 1965; s. John and Chlora L.; m. Patricia Southall, 1995. TV series include: What's Happening Now, 1985, HBO One Night Stand, 1989, Kid 'N' Play, 1990 (voice only), Russell Simmons' Def Comedy Jam, 1991-93 (host), Martin, 1992— (also creator and exec. prodr.); films include: Do the Right Thing, 1989, House Party, 1990, House Party 2, 1991, Talkin' Dirty after Dark, 1991, Boomerang, 1992, You So Crazy, 1994 (concert film, also exec. prodr.), Bad Boys, 1995, Nothing to Lose, 1997; exec. prodr., writer, dir., appeared in (film) A Thin Line Between Love and Hate, 1997. Office: c/o Fox Broadcasting Co 10201 W Pico Blvd Los Angeles CA 90064-2606*

LAWRENCE, MARY JOSEPHINE (JOSIE LAWRENCE), library official, artist; b. Carbondale, Pa., Mar. 9, 1932; d. Domenick Anthony and Teresa Rose (Zaccone) Gentile; m. John Paul Lawrence, Apr. 25, 1953 (dec. June 1977); children: Mary Josephine, Jane Therese, Susan Michele. BFA, Mass. Coll. Art, 1989; postgrad, Chelsea (Eng.) Sch. Art, 1989, San Pancrazio Art Sch., Tuscany, Italy, 1990, 91, 92; cert. in grad. studies, Guangzhou Acad. Fine Arts, China, 1993; postgrad., Md. Inst. Fine Art, Sorrento, Italy, 1994. Sales clk. Gorins, 5&10, Jordan Marsh, Boston, 1946-49; clk.-typist, sec. John Hancock Ins. Co., Boston, 1950-53; machine operator, quality control supr. Rust Craft Greeting Cards, Dedham, Mass., 1961-69; restaurant hostess Tony's Villa, Waltham, Mass., 1972-73; mus. sales clk., artist John F. Kennedy Libr., Boston, 1979-87, mgr. mus. store, supr., 1988—; tchr.'s asst. San Pancrazio Art Sch., 1992; guest appearance TAKE TWO cable TV, Channel 11, 1996. One woman shows include South Shore Arts Ctr., Cohasset, Mass., 1991, N. River Arts Soc., Marshfield Hills, Mass., Boston Visual Artists Union, 1996; exhibited in group shows at de Havilland Fine Art Gallery, Boston, 1997, Dr. James McDermott Gallery, Boston, 1997; works in permanent collections in U.S., Italy, Japan. Juror Quincy Art Assn., 1996, Weymouth Art Assn., 1997. Recipient Outstanding Achievement awards Nat. Archives and Rsch. Adminstrn., 1989, 94, 96, Svc. award, 1990, Hon. Mention award South Shore Arts Ctr., 1991, BEst of Show award De Havilland Fine Arts Gallery, 1992, Best of Show N. River Arts Soc., 1994, Honorium Weymouth Art Assn., 1995. Mem. William Henry Fine Art Gallery, Boston Visual Artist Union, de Havilland Fine Art Gallery, South Shore Art Ctr., North River Arts Soc., Nat. Mus. Women in Arts (charter), Weymouth Art Assn. (honorium). Democrat. Roman Catholic. Office: John F Kennedy Libr and Mus Columbia Pt Boston MA 02125

LAWRENCE, MERLE, medical educator; b. Remsen, N.Y., Dec. 26, 1915; s. George William and Alice Rutherford (Bowne) L.; m. Roberta Ashby Taylor Harper, Aug. 8, 1942; children—Linda Alice, Roberta Harper Lawrence Henderson, James Bowne. A.B., Princeton, 1938, M.A., 1940, Ph.D., 1941. NRC fellow Johns Hopkins Hosp., 1941; asst. prof. psychology Princeton, 1946-50; assoc. prof., 1950-52; assoc. research Lempert Inst. Otology, N.Y.C., 1946-52; assoc. prof. dept. otolaryngology U. Mich. Med. Sch., 1952-57, prof. otolaryngology, 1957-85, prof. emeritus, 1985—; research assoc. Inst. Indsl. Health, 1952—; prof. psychology U. Mich. Coll. Lit. Sci. and Arts, 1957—; dir. Kresge Hearing Research Inst., 1961-83; mem. sci. rev. bd. Deafness Research Found., 1960-66, 82-84; Nat. Adv. Neurol. and Communicative Disorders and Stroke Council, 1976-79; mem. communicative disorders research tng. com. Nat. Inst. Neurol. Diseases and Blindness, 1961-65; mem. communicative scis. study sect. div. research grants NIH, 1965-69, chmn., 1967-69, mem. communicative disorders rev. com., 1972-76; cons. Surgeon Gen. U.S. Army office Aviation Medicine, 1963-70. Served as naval aviator USNR, 1941-46, 50-51, PTO; Served as naval aviator USNR, Korean conflict, PTO. Decorated Purple Heart, Silver Star, Disting. Flying Cross (2), Air medal with nine gold stars; recipient Sec. Navy Commendation, Disting. Svc. award Princeton Class of 1938, Achievement award Am. Acad. Audiology, 1992. Fellow AAAS, Am. Acad. Otolaryngology-Head and Neck Surgery, Otosclerosis Study Group, Am. Laryngol., Rhinolog. and Otolaryngol. Soc.; mem. Acoustical Soc. Am., Mich. Acoustical Soc. (pres. 1956), Am. Acad. Ophthalmology and Otolaryngology (Merit award 1965), Am. Otol. Soc. (Merit award 1967, cons. bd. trustees rsch. fund, guest of honor 1986), Collegium Oto-Rhino-Laryngologicum Amicitiae Sacrum, Soc. U. Otolaryngologists, Assn. Rsch. Otolaryngology (Merit award 1979), Am. Auditory Soc. (coun. 1978-82), Walter P. Work Soc., Am. Tinnitus Assn., Quarter Century Wireless Assn. Clubs: Rotary (pres. 1978-79), Centurion, Mich. Masters Swim. Home (winter): 2743 Ocean Dr E-41 Vero Beach FL 32963-2059 Home (summer): 2029 Vinewood Blvd Ann Arbor MI 48104-3613

LAWRENCE, MERLOYD LUDINGTON, editor; b. Pasadena, Calif., Aug. 1, 1932; d. Nicholas Saltus and Mary Lloyd (Macy) Ludington; m. Seymour Lawrence, June 21, 1952 (div. 1984); children: Macy, Nicholas; m. John M. Myers, 1985. A.B., Radcliffe Coll., 1954, M.A., 1957. With Houghton Mifflin Co., 1955-57; free lance translator, 1957-65; editor, treas., v.p. Seymour Lawrence Inc., Boston, 1965-83; pres. Merloyd Lawrence, Inc., Boston, 1983—. Translator works of Flaubert and Balzac, modern French fiction, German and Swedish children's books.; contbr. articles to nat. mags.

Treas., v.p. Milford House Properties, Ltd., N.S., Can., 1975-80; trustee Milton (Mass.) Acad., 1974-82; mem. com. clin. investigations Beth Israel/ Deaconess Hosp. Mem. Am. Translators Assn., New Eng. Forestry Found. (exec. bd. officer 1989—), Mass. Audubon Soc. (dir. 1974—, exec. com. 1992—), Phi Beta Kappa. Home: 102 Chestnut St Boston MA 02108-1120 Office: 102A Chestnut St Boston MA 02108-1120

LAWRENCE, PAUL ROGER, retired organizational behavior educator; b. Rochelle, Ill., Apr. 26, 1922; s. Howard Cyrus and Clara (Luther) L.; m. Martha G. Stiles, Dec. 14, 1948; children: Anne Talcott, William Stiles. Student, Grand Rapids Jr. Coll., 1939-41; AB, Albion Coll., 1943; MBA, Harvard U., 1947, DCS, 1950. Mem. faculty Harvard U. Bus. Sch., Boston, 1947-91, asst. prof., 1951-56, assoc. prof., 1956-61, prof. organizational behavior, 1961-68, Donham prof. organizational behavior, 1968; retired, 1991. Author: (with others) Renewing American Industry, 1983, HRM, Trends and Challenges, 1985, Behind the Factory Walls, 1990. Served to lt. USNR, 1943-46. Fellow Acad. Mgmt.; mem. Am. Sociol. Assn. Home: 17 Willard St Cambridge MA 02138-4836 Office: Cumnock Hall Soldiers Field Boston MA 02163

LAWRENCE, RALPH WALDO, manufacturing company executive; b. Mineola, N.Y., Sept. 10, 1941; s. Ralph Waldo and Gertrude (Ingles) L.; m. Judith Alice Frost, June 20, 1964; children: Susan, Carolyn. BA, W.Va. Wesleyan Coll., 1963; M in Pub. Adminstrn., Western Mich. U., 1979. Pres. Lawrence Mfrs., Columbus, Ohio, 1970-85; chief automated info. systems contract svcs. Systems Automation Ctr., Columbus, 1980-87, chief plans and mgmt. div., 1987-88; chief ops. Constrn. Supply Ctr., Columbus, 1988-89; chief Info. Ctr. DLA Systems Automation Ctr., Columbus, Ohio, 1989-92, DISA Office of Tech. Integration, Columbus, 1992-93; dep. of def. integration mgr. CALS, Blacklick, Ohio, 1993-95; prin. info. engr. Boeing Info. Systems, Columbus, 1995; bus. mgr. Computer Scis. Corp., Moorestown, N.J., 1995-97; owner Lawrence Mfrs., Westerville, Ohio, 1997—; bus. mgr. Computer Scis. Corp., 1995-97. Served to capt. U.S. Army, 1963-66. Mem. Air Force Comm. and Engring. Assn. (charter Columbus chpt.), Data Processing Mgmt. Assn. (pres. Columbus chpt. 1987, program dir. Columbus chpt. 1985, bd. dirs. 1987-88), Masons. Republican. Presbyterian. Avocations: golf, sailing. Home: 10201 Covan Dr Westerville OH 43082-9293

LAWRENCE, RAY VANCE, chemist; b. Vance, Ala., July 6, 1910; s. William Monroe and Frances (Ray) L.; m. Barbara New, June 22, 1935; children: Robert Craig, Richard Vance. BS, U. Ala., Tuscaloosa, 1931; MS, U. Tenn., Knoxville, 1933. Instr. chemistry Marion (Ala.) Mil. Inst., 1932-33; chemist TVA, Muscle Shoals, Ala., 1933-38, Naval Stores Sta., Olustee, Fla., 1938-41, Naval Stores Rsch. Div., Washington, 1941-43; head rosin rsch. So. Regional Rsch. Lab., New Orleans, 1943-50; head rosin rsch. Naval Stores Rsch. Lab., Olustee, 1950-58, dir., 1958-73; cons. Naval Stores, Lake City, Fla., 1973—; lectr. terpene chemistry U. Fla., Gainesville, 1953-57; lectr. Nanjing (China) Forestry U., 1979. Columnist, assoc. editor Naval Stores Rev., 1977-90; contbr. articles to profl. jours.; patentee in field. Mem Am. Chem. Soc. (chmn. Fla. sect. 1965, Fla. award 1971), Am. Oil Chemists Soc. Presbyterian. Home and Office: 5900 Wilson Blvd Apt 453 Arlington VA 22205-1550

LAWRENCE, RICHARD WESLEY, JR., foundation executive; b. N.Y.C., Jan. 16, 1909; s. Richard Wesley and Ruth (Earle) L.; m. Marjorie Fitch, June 23, 1933 (dec. Feb. 1945); children: Ruth Earle Lawrence Wilson (dec.), Alida L. Currey; m. Elizabeth Hand Wadhams, Apr. 13, 1946 (dec. Nov. 1987); 1 child, Elizabeth Lawrence. B.S., Princeton U., 1931; LL.B., Columbia U., 1934. Bar: N.Y. 1935. Former chmn. bd. Printers Ink Pub. Co., Bankers Comml. Corp.; v.p., dir. Umont Mining, Inc. Chmn. Adirondack Park Agy., 1971-75; chmn. Commr. Edn.'s com. on Reference and Rsch. Libr. Resources; mem. Gov.'s Commn. on Future of Adirondacks, Gov.'s Commn. on Adirondacks in the 21st Century; past chmn. coun. State U. Coll., Plattsburgh; past chmn. bd. trustees North Country C.C.; pres. Crary Edn. Found. Capt. USAAF, 1942-44; lt. col. ret. Recipient North Country citation St. Lawrence U., 1969, Conservation award Garden Club Am., 1982, Disting. Svc. award Potsdam Coll., 1987, Founders award Adirondack Hist. Assn., 1991, Assn. for Protection of Adirondacks award, 1994. Hon. mem. N.Y. Library Assn. (Velma Moore award), Essex County Hist. Soc. (trustee); mem. Explorers Club, Union League, Princeton Club (N.Y.C.), Ausable Club. Office: PO Box 427 Elizabethtown NY 12932-0427

LAWRENCE, ROBERT SWAN, physician, educator, academic administrator; b. Phila., Feb. 6, 1938; s. Thomas George and Catherine (Swan) L.; m. Cynthia Starr Cole, July 1, 1960; children: Job Scott, Matthew Swan, Hannah Starr, Jin Sook, Sang Bo. AB magna cum laude, Harvard U., 1960, MD, 1964. Intern, then resident in internal medicine Mass. Gen. Hosp., 1964-66, 69-70; surgeon USPHS, 1966-69; asst. prof., then assoc. prof. medicine, chief div. community medicine Med. Sch. U. N.C., 1970-74; dir. div. primary care Med. Sch. Harvard U., 1974-91, assoc. prof. medicine Med. Sch., 1980-81, Charles S. Davidson assoc. prof. medicine Med. Sch., 1981-91; chmn. dept. medicine Cambridge (Mass.) Hosp., 1980-91; adj. prof. NYU Sch. of MEdicine, 1992-95; prof. health policy & mgmt. Johns Hopkins Sch. Hygiene & Pub. Health, 1995, prof. medicine, Johns Hopkin's Sch. Medicine, 1995—; mem. com. human rights NAS; chmn. bd. health promotion and disease prevention IOM, 1981-86, chmn. com. health and human rights, 1990-94; chmn. U.S. Preventive Svc. Task Force, HHS, 1984-89, active mem., 1990-96; fellow Ctr. for Advanced Study in Behavioral Scis., 1988-89; dir. health scis. Rockefeller Found., 1991-95; assoc. dean for profl. edn. Johns Hopkins Sch. Hygiene & Pub. Health, 1995—. Editor Am. Jour. Preventive Medicine, 1990-92; contbr. articles and chpts. in books. Bd. dirs. Physicians for Human Rights, 1986-91, Tchrs. Coll., Columbia U. Recipient Maimonides prize, 1964. Fellow ACP, Am. Coll. Preventive Medicine (Spl. Recognition award 1988); mem. Inst. Medicine, Am. Pub. Health Assn., Soc. Gen. Internal Medicine (pres. 1978-79), Soc. Tchrs. Preventive Medicine (Spl. Recognition award 1993), Phi Beta Kappa. Home: Highfield House 1112 4000 N Charles St Baltimore MD 21218-1737 Office: Johns Hopkins Sch Hygiene & Pub Health 615 N Wolfe St Baltimore MD 21205-2103

LAWRENCE, RUDDICK CARPENTER, public relations executive; b. Marquette, Mich., Jan. 5, 1912; s. Willard Carpenter and Verna (Ruddick) L.; m. Barbara Dole, June 5, 1937 (div. 1971); children: Dana Ann Lawrence Wetstone, Sara Hilary Lawrence Engelhardt, Megan Elizabeth Lawrence Cumming, Jean Hathaway Lawrence Petri, Ruddick C., Daniel Dole; m. Cherry McDonnell Swasey, Oct. 27, 1973; stepchildren: Leslie Denison Black Tawfik, Caroline McDonnell Black Blydenburgh. B.A. in Journalism cum laude, U. Wash., 1934. Dir. publicity Detroit Inst. Arts, 1934-36; assoc. dir. World Adventure Series, Detroit, 1934-36; mgr. Western div. Am. Boy mag., Chgo., 1936-39; Phila. and So. mgr. Fortune mag., Time, Inc., 1939-44, N.Y. mgr., assoc. advt. mgr., 1946-50; dir. sales devel. TV network, dir. promotion, planning, devel. radio and TV networks NBC, N.Y.C., 1950-53; v.p. N.Y. Stock Exchange, 1953-68, Conoco Inc. (now DuPont Co.), 1968-77; pres. Lawrence Assocs., 1977—. Trustee Sarah Lawrence Coll., 1954-69, chmn. bd. trustees, 1964-69; bd. mgrs. N.Y. Bot. Garden, 1968-92; hon. chmn., bd. dirs. N.Y. Bd. Trade, 1968-92, pres., chmn., 1978-80; bd. dirs. Internat. Film Found., 1956—, World Adventure Series, 1952-80, N.Y. State Festival, 1981-93; gov. Invest-in-Am. Nat. Coun. Inc., 1954-91; hon. pres. U.S.-Arab C. of C., pres., 1976-79, 82-83. Served from lt. (j.g.) to lt. USNR, 1944-46; staff requirements rev. bd. Office Sec. Navy, Chief Naval Ops. Decorated Star of Jordan, Cedars of Lebanon. Mem. Pub. Rels. Soc. N.Y., Pilgrims Soc., Explorers Club, Circumnavigators Club, Bronxville Field Club, Rockefeller Luncheon Club, Univ. Club, Econ. Club, Shelter Island Yacht Club, Phi Kappa Psi (chmn., trustee Endowment Fund Corp. 1960-88, Disting. Alumnus award 1988), Sigma Delta Chi. Episcopalian. Home: 3 Wellington Cir Bronxville NY 10708-3011 also: Menantic Rd PO Box 1052 Shelter Island NY 11964-1052 Office: Ste 1700 122 E 42nd St New York NY 10168-1799

LAWRENCE, RUTH ANDERSON, pediatrician, clinical toxicologist; b. N.Y.C.; d. Stephen Hayes and Loretta (Harvey) A.; m. Robert Marshall Lawrence, July 4, 1950; children, Robert Michael, Barbara Asselin, Timothy Lee, Kathleen Ann, David McDonald, Mary Khalil, Joan Margaret, John Charles, Stephen Harvey. BS in Biology summa cum laude, Antioch Coll., 1945; MD, U. Rochester, 1949. Internship and residency in pediatrics Yale New Haven (Conn.) Hosp., 1949-50; asst. resident in Medicine Yale New Haven (Conn.) Community Hosp., 1950-51; postdoctoral fellow Yale New Haven Hosp., 1951, chief resident newborn svc., 1951; cons. in medicine U.S. Army, Ft. Dix, N.J., 1952; from clin. instr. to sr. instr. in pediatrics U. Rochester, N.Y., 1952-64, assoc. resident, 1957-58, asst. prof., 1964-70, assoc. prof., 1970-85, prof. pediatrics, ob.-gyn., 1985—; rsch. pediatrician, Monroe County Health Dept., Rochester, 1952-58; dir. Finger Lakes Regional Poison Control Ctr., 1958—; chief nursery svc. Strong Meml. Hosp., Rochester, 1960-73, chief dept. pediatrics, The Highland Hosp., Rochester, 1960-91; adj. prof. Sch. Pub. Health, SUNY, Albany, 1996—; rsch. in field. Author: (book with others) Caring for Your Baby and Young Child, 1991, What to Expect in the First Year, 1989, Breastfeeding: A Guide for the Medical Profession, 4th edit. 1994; editor various periodicals; contbr. numerous articles to profl. publs. Recipient Gold Medal award U. Rochester Alumni Assn., 1979, William Keeler award Rochester Safety Coun., 1982, Civic Contribution citation Rochester Safety Coun., 1984, Career Achievement award Girl Scouts U.S. of Genesee Valley, 1987, Rochester Diocesan award for women, St. Bernard's Inst., 1989, Albert David Kaiser medal, 1991, Chamber Civic Health Care award, 1996, numerous svc. awards; named Woman of Yr. Girl Scouts U.S. of Monroe County, 1968; hon. fellow Am. Sch. Health Assn., 1960, rsch. fellow Jackson Meml. Rsch. Labs., 1945. Fellow Am. Pediatric Soc., Am. Acad. Clin. Toxicology (past trustee); mem. Internat. Soc. for Rsch. in Human Milk and Lactation (exec. com. 1995—), Human Milk Banking Assn. N.Am. (adv. bd.), Nat. Acad. Sci. (subcom. on nutrition during lactation), Acad. Breastfeeding Medicine (founding bd. dirs. 1994—), Safety Coun. Rochester and Monroe County (past pres.), Bd. of Life Line (past pres.), Alpha Omega Alpha. Roman Catholic. Office: U Rochester Sch Medicine 601 Elmwood Ave Rochester NY 14620-2945

LAWRENCE, SALLY CLARK, academic administrator; b. San Francisco, Dec. 29, 1930; d. George Dickson and Martha Marie Alice (Smith) Clark; m. Henry Clay Judd, July 1, 1950 (div. Dec. 1972); children: Rebecca, David, Nancy; m. John I. Lawrence, Aug. 12, 1976; stepchildren: Maia, Dylan. Docent Portland Art Mus., Oreg., 1958-68; gallery owner, dir., Sally Judd Gallery, Portland, 1968-75; art ins. appraiser, cons. Portland, 1975-81; interim dir. Mus. Art. Sch., Pacific Northwest Coll. Art, Portland, 1981, asst. dir., 1981-82, acting dir., 1982-84, dir., 1984-94, pres., 1994—; bd. dirs. Art Coll. Exch. Nat. Consortium, 1982-91, pres., 1983-84. Bd. dirs. Portland Arts Alliance, 1987—, Assn. Ind. Colls. of Art and Design, 1991—, pres., 1995-96, sec. 1996—. Mem. Nat. Assn. Schs. Art and Design (bd. dirs. 1984-91, treas. bd. dirs. 1994-96, pres. 1996—), Oreg. Ind. Coll. Assn. (bd. dirs. 1981—, exec. com. 1989-94, pres. 1992-93). Office: Pacific NW Coll of Art 1219 SW Park Ave Portland OR 97205-2430

LAWRENCE, SANFORD HULL, physician, immunochemist; b. Kokomo, Ind., July 10, 1919; s. Walter Scott and Florence Elizabeth (Hull) L. AB, Ind. U., 1941, MD, 1944. Fellow in biochemistry George Washington U., 1941; intern Rochester (N.Y.) Gen. Hosp., 1944-45; resident Halloran Hosp., Staten Island, N.Y., 1946-49; chief med. svce. Ft. Ord Regl. Hosp., 1945-46; dir. biochemistry rsch. lab. San Fernando (Calif.) VA Hosp.; asst. prof. UCLA, 1950—; cons. internal medicine and cardiology U.S. Govt., Los Angeles County; lectr. Faculte de Medicine, Paris, various colls. Eng., France, Belgium, Sweden, USSR, India, Japan; chief med. svc. Ft. Ord Regional Hosp.; chmn. Titus, Inc., 1982—. Author: Zymogram in Clinical Medicine, 1965; contbr. articles to sci. jours.; author: Threshold of Valhalla, Another Way to Fly, My Last Satyr, and other short stories; traveling editor: Relax Mag. Mem. Whitley Heights Civic Assn., 1952—; pres. Halloran Hosp. Employees Assn., 1947-48. Served to maj. U.S. Army, 1945-46. Recipient Rsch. award TB and Health Assn., 1955-58, Los Angeles County Heart Assn., 1957-59, Pres. award, Queen's Blue Book award, Am. Men of Sci. award; named one of 2000 Men of Achievement, Leaders of Am. Sci., Ky. Col., named Hon. Mayor of West Point, Ky. Mem. AAAS, AMA, N.Y. Acad. Scis., Am. Fedn. Clin. Research, Am. Assn. Clin. Investigation, Am. Assn. Clin. Pathology, Am. Assn. Clin. Chemistry, Los Angeles County Med. Assn. Republican. Methodist. Avocations: bridge, comml. pilot, pianist, organist. Home: 2014 Whitley Ave Los Angeles CA 90068-3235 also: 160 rue St Martin, 75003 Paris France

LAWRENCE, STEVE, entertainer; b. Bklyn., July 8, 1935; s. Max Leibowitz; m. Eydie Gorme, Dec. 29, 1957; children: David, Michael. Former mem. cast The Tonight Show; host Steve Lawrence Show, CBS-TV, 1965; has starred (with Eydie Gorme) in TV spls. honoring Gershwin, Porter and Berlin (7 Emmy awards); TV appearances include: Police Story, Murder She Wrote; also numerous TV guest appearances; performer night clubs; made stage debut in What Makes Sammy Run, 1964; co-starred: (with Eydie Gorme) in Golden Rainbow, N.Y.C., 1967; co-host: (TV series) Foul-Ups, Bleeps and Blunders, 1984; TV miniseries: Alice in Wonderland, 1985; albums include Through the Years, At the Movies, Together Forever, The Best of Steve and Eydie, 1990. Hon. chmn. entertainment com. Cerebral Palsy; bd. govs. Brookdale Hosp., N.Y.C. Served with AUS, 1958-60. Recipient N.Y. Drama Critics award for best male performance in mus. comedy, 1964, TV Critics Circle award for achievement in music 1976-77, Grammy for album We've Got Us (with Eydie Gorme). Club: Friars (N.Y.C.) (gov.). Office: Taragon Records PO Box 765 Deer Park NY 11729-0765*

LAWRENCE, THOMAS PATTERSON, public relations executive; b. Phila., Nov. 20, 1946; s. Granville Allen and Rebecca (Patterson) L.; m. Peggy Wilson, Nov. 1, 1986. BA in Journalism, Fla. So. Coll., 1968. Reporter Nashville Banner, 1968-70; account exec. Holder, Kennedy & Co., Nashville, 1971-78, exec. v.p., 1978-79; ptnr. Dye, Van Mol & Lawrence, Nashville, 1980—. Mem. Nat. Investor Rels. Inst., Nashville Soc. Fin. Analysts Inc., Nashville City Club, Hillwood Country Club. Republican. Presbyterian. Office: Dye Van Mol Lawrence 209 7th Ave N Nashville TN 37219-1802

LAWRENCE, VICKI SCHULTZ, singer, dancer, comedienne; b. Los Angeles, Mar. 26, 1949; d. Howard Axelrad and Ann Alene (Loyd) L.; m. Alvin Adolph Schultz, Jr., Nov. 16, 1974; children: Courtney Allison, Garrett Lawrence. Student, UCLA, 1967-70. Toured as entertainer with Johnny Grant, Vietnam, 1968. Appearances include (TV series) The Carol Burnett Show, CBS, 1967-78, Mama's Family, 1983-90, 87; hostess: (game shows) Win, Lose or Draw, 1987-89; recs. include The Night the Lights Went Out in Georgia (Gold record 1973); host Group W syndicated daytime talk show Vicki, 1992—. Recipient Emmy award for Burnett show, 1976. Republican. Lutheran. Avocations: needlepoint, sailing. *

LAWRENCE, WALTER, JR., surgeon; b. Chgo., May 31, 1925; s. Walter and Violette May (Matthews) L.; m. Susan Grayson Shryock, June 20, 1947; children: Walter Thomas, Elizabeth, William Amos, Edward Gene. Student, Dartmouth Coll., 1943-44; PhB, U. Chgo., 1944, SB, 1945, MD with honors, 1948. Diplomate Am. Bd. Surgery (examiner 1974-78, sr. mem. 1978—). Intern Johns Hopkins, 1948-49, asst. resident, 1949-51; fellow Meml. Sloan-Kettering Cancer Center, 1951-52, 54-56, research fellow, 1956, asst. mem., asst. attending surgeon, 1957-60, asso. mem., asso. attending surgeon, 1960-66; practice medicine specializing in surgery N.Y.C., 1956-66, Richmond, Va., 1966—; instr. surgery Cornell U., 1957-58, asst. profl. clin. surgery, 1958-63, clin. assoc. prof., 1963-66; vis. investigator Queen Victoria Hosp., East Grinstead, Eng., 1964-65; prof. surgery Med. Coll. Va., Richmond, 1966—, chmn. divsn. surg. oncology, 1966-90, exec. vice chmn. dept. surgery, 1966-73, acting chmn., 1973-74, Am. Cancer Soc. prof. clin. oncology, 1972-77; dir. Cancer Ctr., 1974-88, dir. emeritus, 1988—; chmn. surgery test com. Nat. Bd. Med. Examiners, 1973-77; med. dir.-at-large Va. divsn. Am. Cancer Soc., 1967—, med. v.p. Am. Cancer Soc., 1975-77, pres., 1977-79, nat. del., 1972-76, mem. nat. coun. for rsch. and clin. investigation, 1974-78, mem. profl. edn. com., 1982—, bd. dirs., 1985—, vice chmn., chmn. M&S com., 1986-88, chmn. M&S exec. com., 1989-90, pres. elect, 1990-91, nat. pres., 1991-92, past office dir., 1993—; bd. sci. counsellors Nat. Cancer Inst., 1978-82, chmn. surg. oncology rsch. devel. com.; mem. Nat. Cancer Adv. Bd., 1988-94; governing coun. Internat. Union Against Cancer, 1994—. Author: (with J.J. Terz) Cancer Management, 1977, (with J.J. Terz, J.P. Neifeld) Manual of Soft Tissue Surgery, 1983; mem. editl. bd. Va. Med., 1977-93, Jour. Surg. Oncology, 1978—, assoc. editor, 1991—; editl. bd. Jour. Cancer Edn., 1986; asst. editor Cancer, 1962-65, assoc. editor, 1991—; contbr. articles to med. jours. Served with USNR, 1942-46; Served with U.S. Army, 1952-54. Recipient Cancer Rsch. award Alfred P. Sloan Found., 1964; J. Shelton Horsley award Am. Cancer Soc., 1973; Disting. Svc. award U. Chgo., 1976; Va. Commonwealth U. Univ. Award for Excellence, 1988, Disting. Faculty award Med. Coll. Va. Alumni Assn., 1988, Va. Cultural Laureate award, 1992, OBICI award, 1992, Dean's award for Disting. Svc., 1992; named to Humera Soc. (hon.), 1992. Fellow ACS (commn. on cancer 1973-85, chmn. 1979-81), N.Y. Acad. Scis., Royal Soc. Medicine; mem. AAAS, AMA, Am. Assn. Cancer Edn., Am. Assn. Cancer Rsch., Am. Gastroenterol. Assn. (coun. on cancer 1972-76), Am. Surg. Assn., Halsted Soc. (pres. 1975), James Ewing Soc., Soc. Head and Neck Surgeons, Am. Soc. Clin. Oncology, Am. Radium Soc. (exec. coun. 1985-87), Soc. Surgery Alimentary Tract (founder), Soc. Surg. Oncology (exec. com. 1976-77, v.p. 1977-78, pres. 1979-80, chmn. exec. coun. 1980-81), Soc. Univ. Surgeons, Surg. Biol. Club III (founding mem.), Transplantation Soc., Collegium Internat. Chirurgiae Digestive, Southeastern Surg. Congress, Pan Am. Med. Assn., Societè Internationale de Chirurgie, Va. Surg. Soc. (v.p. 1973-74), Richmond Surg. Soc. (pres. 1986-87), Richmond Acad. Medicine (trustee 1986-87, 1st v.p. 1988), So. Surg. Assn., Argentine Surg. Assn. (hon.), Sigma Xi, Alpha Omega Alpha. Home: 6501 Three Chopt Rd Richmond VA 23226-3118 Office: Med Coll Va Hosps 1200 E Broad St PO Box 980011 Richmond VA 23298

LAWRENCE, WALTER THOMAS, plastic surgeon; b. Balt., Sept. 5, 1950; s. Walter Jr. and Susan (Shryock) L.; m. Marsha Blake, May 30, 1987. BS, Yale U., 1972; MPH, Harvard U., 1976; MD, U. Va., 1976. Diplomate Am. Bd. Surgery. Diplomate Am. Bd. Plastic Surgery. Intern and resident in gen. surgery U. N.C., Chapel Hill, 1976-78; resident gen. surgery Med. Coll. Va., Richmond, 1978-81; resident plastic surgery U. Chgo., 1981-83; expert NIH, Bethesda, Md., 1983-85; asst. prof. U. N.C., Chapel Hill, 1985-92, assoc. prof., div. chmn., 1992-95; prof., divsn. chmn. U. Mass. Med. Ctr., 1995—. Fellow Am. Coll. Surgeons; mem. Am. Assn. Plastic Surgeons, Am. Soc. Plastic and Reconstructive Surgeons, Plastic Surgery Rsch. Coun., Humera Soc., Wowack Soc. Avocations: skiing, sailing, tennis. Office: U Mass Med Ctr Divsn Plastic Surgery 55 Lake Ave N Worcester MA 01655-0002

LAWRENCE, WAYNE ALLEN, publisher; b. Cin., Dec. 11, 1938; s. Clarence E. and Edna M. (Newman) L.; m. Carol SueAnn Wisecup, July 28, 1959; children: Jeffrey Thomas, Jon Christopher, Jeremy Wayne. Student public schs., Seaman, Ohio. Advt. salesman Amos Press, Inc., Sidney, Ohio, 1957-61; v.p. Amos Press, Inc., 1973-83, sr. v.p., 1983-92, ret., 1992, also bd. dirs.; pub. Stamp World, Linns Stamp News, 1977-82; v.p. advt. Coin World, Sidney, 1973-78; advt. mgr. World Coins, Sidney, 1964-68, advt. dir., 1968-73, v.p., 1973-77; adv. mgr. Numis. Scrapbook, Sidney, 1967-68, advt. dir., 1968-73, v.p. advt., 1973-78; pub. Cars & Parts, Sidney, 1978-85; propr., dir. Sidney Camera, 1981-87; pres. Scott Pub. Co., 1984-92. Contbr. articles and editorials on coins, stamps and cars to Amos publs. Bd. dirs. Shelby County (Ohio) United Way, 1970-76, 1st United Meth. Ch., Sidney, 1982—; bd. dirs. Sidney-Shelby County C. of C., 1982-85, sec., 1985; mem. U.S. Assay Commn., 1975. Mem. Am. Mgmt. Assn., Am. Numis. Assn., Am. Philatelic Assn., Numis. Lit. Guild, Am. Stamp Dealers Assn., Mag. Pubs. Assn., Am. Motorcycle Assn., Soc. Automotive Historians. Home: 1444 Double D Dr Sevierville TN 37876-0247 Office: 911 S Vandemark Rd Sidney OH 45365-8974

LAWRENCE, WILLARD EARL, mathematics, statistics and computer science educator emeritus; b. Chassell, Mich., Apr. 8, 1917; s. William and Ruth Marie (Messner) L.; m. Lorayne Adalayde Williams, June 12, 1943; children—Victoria (Mrs. Joseph C. Barton), Barbara (Mrs. Timothy F. Columbia), Joan (Mrs. James A. Wilger), Willard, Mark. Student, Ripon Coll., 1947-49; B.S., Marquette U., 1951, M.S., 1953; postgrad., U. Wyo., summer 1959, Iowa State U., summer 1961; M.S., U. Wis., 1962, Ph.D., 1964. Prof. math. and statistics Marquette U., Milw., 1953-87; prof. emeritus math., statistics and computer sci. Marquette U., 1987—, chmn. dept., 1973-79; statis. cons. Author: Introduction to the Theory of Probability, 1967, Probability: An Introductory Course, 1970. Served with USAAF, 1941-45. Decorated Bronze Star medal.; NSF faculty fellow, 1961-62. Mem. Math. Assn. Am., Wis. Geol. Soc. Roman Catholic. Home: 13865 Adelaide Ln Brookfield WI 53005-4967 Office: Marquette U Katharine Reed Cudahy Hall Milwaukee WI 53233

LAWRENCE, WILLIAM, JR., elementary education educator; b. L.A., Mar. 2, 1930; s. Willie and Nellie (January) L.; m. Elizabeth Johnson, Jan. 13, 1951; children: William III, Timothy Dwight, Walter Fitzgerald. BA in Psychology, Columbia Coll., Mo., 1981; LLB, LaSalle U., 1982; MA in Edn., Claremont Coll., 1992; postgrad., Calif. Coast U., 1992—. Enlisted U.S. Army, 1947, advanced through grades to lt., 1957, commd. sgt. maj., 1965; served U.S. Army, Vietnam, 1965-70; instr. U.S. Military Acad., West Point, N.Y., 1970-73; with Berlin Brigade, U.S. Army, Berlin, Germany, 1973-76; dep. sheriff L.A., 1958-65; probation officer San Bernardino County, Calif., 1985-89; own recognizance investigator L.A. County, 1989; tchr. Pomona Unified Sch. Dist., Pomona, Calif., 1989—; sch. site technician, 1996. Decorated U.S. Army Dist. Svc. Cross for Extraordinary Heroism in Combat, Silver Star, 7 Purple Hearts. Mem. Legion of Valor, 555Th Parachute Battalion (pres.). Democrat. Roman Catholic. Avocations: photography, free fall parachuting. Home: 1456 S Lilac Ave Bloomington CA 92316-2130 Office: Pomona Unified Sch Dist 800 N Garey Ave Pomona CA 91767-4616

LAWRENCE, WILLIAM DORAN, physician; b. Tampa, Fla., Sept. 3, 1926; s. Joseph Daniel and Gladys Irene (Lamb) Lawrence; m. Mardelle Laura Wright, June 18, 1950; children: Jodi Werhanowicz, Patricia Lawrence, Susan Hunter. BA, State U. Iowa, 1948, MD, 1951. Diplomate Am. Bd. Ob-Gyn. Intern Parkland Hosp., Dallas, 1951-52; family doctor Hereford, Tex., 1952, 53, 56; resident, preceptorship Northwestern Hosp., Mpls., 1954-55, 57-61; pvt. practice Phoenix, 1957—. Contbr. articles to profl. jours. Physician World Brotherhood Exch. and So. Bapt. Mission, India, Africa, 1963-93. With USNR, 1944-46. Recipient Dr. Thomas Dooley medal Maricopa County Med. Soc., 1979. Mem. Ariz. Med. Assn. Republican. Avocations: flying, fishing, hunting. Home: 32 E Marshall Ave Phoenix AZ 85012-1318

LAWRENCE, WILLIAM JOSEPH, JR., retired corporate executive; b. Kalamazoo, Feb. 1, 1918; s. William J. and Borgia M. (Wheeler) L.; m. Doris Luella Fitzgerald, Aug. 19, 1955; children: Aaron Frances, Cleve Moren, Julie Anne, William III. A.B., Kalamazoo Coll., 1941. Engaged in personal investments; dir. emeritus, treas. Superior Pine Products Co.; chmn. bd. dir. Channel 41, Inc.; dir. LPI. Trustee emeritus, mem. fin. and adminstrn. com. Kalamazoo Found.; trustee emeritus Kalamazoo Coll., Borgess Med. Ctr. With AUS, 1942-46. Mem. Kalamazoo C. of C., Kiwanis, Com. of Twenty-Five (Palm Springs, Calif.), Gull Lake Country Club, Park Club. Roman Catholic. Home: PO Box 37 Richland MI 49083-0037 Office: 1000 Old Kent Bank Bldg Kalamazoo MI 49007

LAWRENCE-FORREST, LORI LOUISE, restaurateur; b. Brockton, Mass., Oct. 12, 1950; d. Hallett Thompson and Dorothy Mae (McElroy) L.; m. David John Forrest, 1994; 1 child, Cameron Stuart Forrest. AA, Canada Coll., Redwood City, Calif., 1970; postgrad., Chapman Coll., 1971-72, Foothill Coll., 1973-74. Owner, operator The Natural Gourmet, Palo Alto, Calif., 1974-76, Quiche Lori, Palo Alto, 1976-81, Lori's Kitchens, Palo Alto, 1982-91, The Rose & Crown, Palo Alto, 1991—; Contbr. articles to publs. Recipient award dessert category Cook Your Way to France Profl. Chef's Contest, 1990. Mem. San Francisco Profl. Food Soc. Avocations: oenology, foreign travel, sailplaning, skiing, hiking. Office: The Rose & Crown 547 Emerson St Palo Alto CA 94301-1608

LAWROSKI, HARRY, nuclear engineer; b. Dalton, Pa., Oct. 10, 1928; s. Alexander and Nancy (Lutchka) L.; m. Mary Ann DeWoody, Oct. 6, 1962. B.S. in Chem. Engring, Pa. State U., 1950, M.S., 1956, Ph.D., 1959. Research and devel. work in petroleum refining Pa. State U., 1950-58; instr., thesis advisor Argonne (Ill.) Nat. Lab., 1958-63; supt., asso. project dir. exptl. breeder reactor II power plant Idaho Nat. Engring. Lab., 1968-73; gen. mgr. quality assurance and environmental services Nuclear Services Corp., Campbell, Calif., 1973-76; asst. gen. mgr. nuclear fuel processing and waste mgmt. tech. Idaho chem. programs Allied Chem. Corp., Idaho Falls, 1976-79; cons., 1979—; lectr. Idaho Acad. Scis.; cons. in field; chmn. sci. and tech. project 1990 Idaho Centennial Celebration. Author. Named Outstanding Engring. Alumnus Pa. State U., 1981. Fellow Am. Nuclear Soc. (treas. 1973-77, dir. 1969-77, pres.-elect 1979-80, pres. 1980-81), Am. Inst. Chem.

Engrs. (chmn. nuclear engring. div. 1974), Skull and Bones, Sigma Xi, Tau Beta Pi, Sigma Tau, Phi Lambda Upsilon. Clubs: Rotary, Elks. Patentee in field. Home: PO Box 717 Wilson WY 83014-0717

LAWRY, SYLVIA (MRS. STANLEY ENGLANDER), health association administrator; b. N.Y.C.; d. Jack and Sonia (Tager) Friedman; m. Michael Lawry, Mar. 1944 (div. 1946); m. Stanley Englander, Apr. 1957 (dec. 1968); children: Franklin Miles, Steven Jon. A.B., Hunter Coll., 1936. Law practice and hearing reporter for State Arbitrator, 1937-40; sponsored by N.Y.C., 1942-43; law practice and hearing reporter for U.S. Atty.'s office, N.Y., 1943-44; asst. dir. radio prodn. Civilian Def. Reporting; founded Nat. Multiple Sclerosis Soc., N.Y.C., 1946; exec. dir. Nat. Multiple Sclerosis Soc., until 1982, now founder-dir., 1982—; sec. Internat. Fedn. Multiple Sclerosis Soc., 1967—. Mem. President's Com. on Employment of Handicapped. Recipient Disting. Svc. award Nat. Health Coun., Pres. Reagan's Volunteer Action award, 1987. Mem. APHA, Acad. Polit. Sci., Am. Judicature Soc., Rehab. Internat. Office: Nat Multiple Sclerosis Soc 733 3rd Ave New York NY 10017-3204

LAWS, KENNETH L., physics educator, author; b. Pasadena, Calif., May 30, 1935; s. Allen L. and Florence (Windsor) L.; m. Priscilla Watson, June 3, 1965; children: Kevin Allen, Virginia. BS, Calif. Inst. Tech., 1956; MS, U. Pa., 1959; PhD, Bryn Mawr Coll., 1962. Instr. physics Hobart and William Smith Colls., Geneva, N.Y., 1958-59; from asst. prof. to prof. physics Dickinson Coll., Carlisle, Pa., 1962—; assoc. dean, dir. summer sch. Dickinson Coll., Carlisle, 1971-77; adminstrv. dir. summer ballet program Ctrl. Pa. Youth Ballet, Carlisle, 1977-87; pres. bd. dirs. Ctrl. Pa. Youth Ballet, 1988-93; guest faculty Scientific Aspect of the Art of Dance, U. Washington Med. Sch. and Dance Dept., 1982; bd. reviewers Dance: Current Selected Research, 1985—. Author: The Physics of Dance, 1984; (with Cynthia Harvey) Physics, Dance and the Pas de Deux, 1994; contbr. articles on dance, physics to profl. jours. Office: Dickinson Coll Dept Physics Carlisle PA 17013

LAWS, PRISCILLA WATSON, physics educator; b. N.Y.C., Jan. 18, 1940; d. Morris Clemens and Frances (Fetterinan) Watson; m. Kenneth Lee Laws, June 3, 1965; children: Kevin Allen, Virginia. BA, Reed Coll., 1961; MA, Bryn Mawr Coll., 1963, PhD, 1966. Asst. prof. physics Dickinson Coll., Carlisle, Pa., 1965-70; assoc. prof. Dickinson Coll., Carlisle, 1970-79, prof. physics, 1979—, chmn. dept. physics and astronomy, 1982-83; cons. in field. Author: X Rays: More Harm than Good?, 1977, The X-Ray Information Book, 1983; contbr. numerous articles to profl. jours.; assoc. editor Am. Jour. Physics, 1989—. Vice-pres. Cumberland Conservancy, 1972-73, pres. 1973; bd. dirs. Pa. Alliance for Returnables, 1974-77; asst. sec., treas. Carlisle Hosp. Authority, 1973-76; pres. bd. Carlisle Day Care Ctr., 1973-74. Fellow NSF, 1963-64, grantee, 1989-95, Commonwealth of Pa., 1985-86, U.S. Dept. Edn. Fund for Improvement of Post-Secondary Edn., 1986-89, 89-93, AEC; recipient Innovation award Merck Found., 1989, Educom Incriptal award for curriculum innovation in sci. labs., 1989, award Sears Roebuck and Co., 1990, award Outstanding Software Devel. Computers in Physics Jour., 1991, Pioneering Achievement in Edn. award Dana Found., 1993. Mem. Am. Assn. Physics Tchrs. (Disting Svc. citation 1992, Robert A. Milliken award for Outstanding Contbns. to Physics Tchg., 1996), Fedn. Am. Scientist, Sigma Xi, Sigma Pi Sigma, Omicron Delta Kappa. Democrat. Home: 10 Douglas Ct Carlisle PA 17013-1714 Office: Dickinson Coll PO Box 1773 Carlisle PA 17013

LAWSON, A(BRAM) VENABLE, retired librarian; b. South Boston, Va., Jan. 9, 1922; s. Abram Venable and Vivien Strudwick (Moseley) L.; children—Janet Lee, Abram Venable, Mary Vivian. B.A., U. Ala., 1946; M.Ln., Emory U., 1950; D.L.S., Columbia U., 1969. Auditor Socony Mobil Oil Co., 1947-48; teller 1st Nat. Bank, Altavista, Va., 1948-49; library asst. Harvard Coll. Library, 1951-54; head reference dept. Atlanta Pub. Libr., 1954-56, coord. pub. svcs., 1956-60; asst. prof. Fla. State U., 1960-65; dir. div. librarianship Emory U., Atlanta, 1965-89; vis. prof. Clark Atlanta U., 1989-90. Active Friends of Atlanta Fulton Pub. Libr., 1987—; advisor Friends of Librs. USA, 1990-93; bd. dirs. Episcopal Chartities Found., Absalom Jones Student U., 1995—. With USAF, 1942-46. Recipient George Virgil Fuller award Columbia U., 1964, Nick Davies award Friends of Atlanta Fulton Pub. Libr., 1993. Mem. ALA, AAUP, Assn. Libr. and Info. Sci. Edn., Southeastern Libr. Assn., Ga. Libr. Assn. (Nix-Jones award for disting. svc. to Ga. librarianship 1989). Home: 1065 Briarcliff Rd NE Atlanta GA 30306-2619

LAWSON, BEN F., lawyer, international legal consultant; b. Marietta, Okla., Feb. 7, 1939; s. Woodrow W. and Lennie L. (McKay) l.; children: Nicole, Michael C. BBA, U. Houston, 1965, JD, 1967. Bar: Tex. 1967. Atty. Monsanto/Burmah Oil, Houston, 1967-72; mgr. internat. acquisitions Oxy (formerly Cities Svc. Co.), Houston, 1972-78; gen. atty. Damson Oil Corp., Houston, 1978-81; gen. counsel, v.p. Newmont Oil Co., Houston, 1981-86; pvt. practice internat. law Houston, 1986—; cons. internat., 1987—. Contbr. numerous articles to profl. jours. Staff sgt. USAF, 1959-65. Fellow Houston Bar Found.; mem. ABA, Am. Corp. Counsel Assn. (chmn. oil and gas com. 1986-87). Republican. Avocations: fishing, antiques. Address: 3027 Bernadette Ln Houston TX 77043-1302

LAWSON, BETH ANN REID, strategic planner; b. N.Y.C., Jan. 9, 1954; d. Raymond Theodore and Jean Elizabeth (Frinks) Reid; m. Michael Berry Lawson, Jan. 29, 1983; children: Rayna, Sydney. BA, Va. Tech., 1976; MPA, Golden Gate U., 1983. From systems analyst I to support ops. asst. City of Virginia Beach, Va., 1977-93; water conservation coord. City of Virginia Beach, 1993-94; owner Strategic Planning and Teamwork, Virginia Beach, 1993—; U.S. Army Corps. Engring. Va. Beach Cmty. Devel. Corp.; cons. Va. Beach Cmty. Devel. Corp., 1996, Lifesaving Mus. Va., 1994, Virginia Beach C.A.R.E. Com., 1995, Virginia Beach Rescue Squad, 1992—, Virginia Beach Mcpl. Employees Fed. Credit Union, 1992—, Virginia Beach Resort Area Adv. Commn., 1993, Virginia Beach Conv. and Visitors Devel. Bur., 1991-93; customer svc. trainer Virginia Beach Hotel/Motel Superhost. Sunday sch. tchr. Wycliffe Presbyn. Ch., Virginia Beach, softball coach, 1997. Mem. Virginia Beach Rescue Squad (hon.), Va. Tech. Alumni Assn. (pres. 1982-83), Rotary (Outstanding Employee award 1993). Avocations: tennis, movies, planning, writing. Home: 701 Earl Of Warwick Ct Virginia Beach VA 23454-2910 Office: Strategic Planning and Teamwork 701 Earl Of Warwick Ct Virginia Beach VA 23454-2910

LAWSON, DAVID E., architect; b. Eau Claire, Wis., Apr. 12, 1937; s. Ralph E. and Guida (Mahon) L.; m. Mary A. Gease, Dec. 29, 1984; children from previous marriage: Eric, Kent, Keith. BArch, U. Ill., 1960. Lic. architect Wis., Va., Iowa, Mich. Pa. Archtl. intern Tannenbaum & Koehnen, Milw., 1961-63; project mgr. Cashin & Goodwin, Madison, Wis., 1963-64; project architect Law Law Potter & Nystrom, Madison, 1964-66; exec. v.p. Potter Lawson Architects, Madison, 1966-95, pres., CEO, 1995—; bd. dirs. Associated Randall Bank, Madison, Downtown Madison Ptnrs. Inc. Architect: McPhee Physical Edn. Bldg., Eau Claire, Wis., 1970 (Honor award Wis. Soc. Arch.), Wis. Power and Light Control Ctr., 1977 (Honor award Wis. Soc. Arch.). Mem. City of Madison Urban Design Task Force, 1973; chmn. Archtl. Engring. Div. Dane County (Wis.) United Way, 1981; bd. dirs. Friends U. Wis. Arboretum, Madison, 1977-80. Named Dane County's Top Architectural Exec., Madison Mags. Survey of 1000 Bus. Leaders, 1994. Fellow AIA (bd. dirs. 1983-85, v.p. 1986, chmn. govt. affairs adv. bd., nat. registration law adv. task force, 1979-88, chmn. AIA design build task force 1989-91); mem. Wis. Soc. Archs. (chmn. legis. com 1974-81, v.p., pres. elect 1977, pres. 1978, recipient first Golden award for disting. svc. to profession 1985), Nat. Archtl. Accrediting Bd. (exec. com. 1987-88), Madison Club (bd. dirs. 1988-92, v.p. 1989-90, pres. 1990-91), Nakoma Country Club. Lutheran. Home: 2145 Middleton Beach Rd Middleton WI 53562-2904 Office: Potter Lawson Inc PO Box 44964 Madison WI 53744-4964

LAWSON, DAVID LEWIS, religious organization administrator, minister; b. Hoopeston, Ill., Feb. 9, 1932; s. Moses and Mildred Grace (Hofer) L.; m. Paula Jean Laird, June 4, 1954; children: Dayla Jean, Pamali Jill. BS, Anderson U., 1959; MA, Ball State U., 1963; DD, Mid-Am. Bible Coll., 1986. Ordained to ministry Ch. of God, 1960. Interim pastor Ch. of God, Watseka, Ill., 1958-59; assoc. pastor Ch. of God, New Albany, Ind., 1959-60; from promotional sec. to exec. dir. World Svc., Anderson, Ind., 1960-88; assoc. gen. sec. Leadership Coun., Anderson, 1980—. With U.S. Army, 1951-54, Korea. Mem. Kiwanis. Home: 1303 Frances Ln Anderson IN 46012-4523 Office: Leadership Coun Ch of God 1303 E 5th St Anderson IN 46012-3468

LAWSON, EDWARD EARLE, neonatologist; b. Winston-Salem, N.C., Aug. 6, 1946; s. Robert Barrett and Elsie Chatterton (Earle) L.; m. Rebecca Newhall Fitts, June 21, 1969; children: Katherine Tabor, Robert Barrett II. BA magna cum laude, Harvard U., 1968; MD, Northwestern U., 1972. Diplomate Am. Bd. Pediatrics and Neonatal/Perinatal Medicine. Intern then resident pediatrics Children's Hosp., Boston, 1972-75, fellow neonatology, 1975-78; from asst. prof. pediatrics to prof. pediatrics U. N.C., Chapel Hill, 1978—, chief div. neonatal medicine, 1987-95, interim chmn. dept. pediatrics, 1993-95; v. chmn., Dept. Pediatrics, 1995—. Assoc. editor Jour. of Pediatrics, 1985-95; contbr. numerous articles to profl. jours. Recipient Sidney Farber Meml. Rsch. award United Cerbral Palsy, 1982, Rsch. Career Devel. award NIH, 1982-87; fellow E. L. Trudeau, 1978-81, Alexander Von Humboldt, 1985-86; NIH grantee, 1979—. Fellow Am. Acad. Pediatrics; mem. Am. Lung Assn. (sci. adv. com. 1989-91), Am. Thoracic Soc. (bd. dirs. 1988-90), Am. Bd. Pediatrics, Am. Pediatric Soc., Perinatal Rsch. Soc. Achievements include research on developmental aspects of respiratory control, particularly physiology and neurobiology. Office: U NC Dept Pediatrics CB 7220 Chapel Hill NC 27599-7220

LAWSON, EVE KENNEDY, ballet mistress; b. Washington, Mar. 28, 1964; d. John and Elizabeth Lawson. Student, Sch. Am. Ballet, N.Y.C., 1972-83. Prin. dancer State Ballet Mo., Kansas City, 1983-87; dancer Miami City Ballet, Miami Beach, Fla., 1988-94, coord. edn., 1993-94, ballet mistress, 1994—. Created prin. roles in ballet Voyager (Bolender), 1984, Miniatures (Gamonet), 1990, Tango Tonto (Gamonet), 1991. Office: Miami City Ballet 905 Lincoln Rd Miami FL 33139

LAWSON, F. D., bishop. Bishop Ch. of God in Christ, Stillwater, Okla. Office: Ch of God in Christ PO Box 581 Stillwater OK 74076-0581*

LAWSON, FRANCES GORDON, child guidance specialist; b. Lexington, Ky., Oct. 20, 1949; d. George Frank and Novella (Thomas) G.; m. Frank Darryl Lawson (div. Sept. 1974); children: Alisa Lynnette, Darlene Lawson-Barber. BA, Ea. Ky. U., 1971, MA, 1979, Rank I cert., 1987. Cert. tchr., counselor, Ky. Tchr. Mary Todd Elem Sch., Fayette County Pub. Schs., Lexington, 1971-82, child guidance specialist Johnson Elem. Sch.,, 1982-92, child guidance specialist Booker T. Washington Elem., 1992—; dir. social svc. Madeline McDowell Breckridge Camp Found. Inc., Lexington, 1987—. Mem. Ky. Sch. Counselors Assn., Fayette County Guidance Assn., Phi Delta Kappa, Delta Sigma Theta. Democrat. Baptist. Home: 3909 Kilgary Cir Lexington KY 40515-5207 Office: Booker T Washington Elem 798 Georgetown St Lexington KY 40508-1023

LAWSON, FRANCIS COLIN, chemical company executive; b. Apr. 7, 1917; s. James and Alice (Gamble) L.; m. Mary Aileen Behan, Oct. 21, 1942; children: Paul, Judy, Tony, Moya, Clare, Margaret, James. From various clerical positions to asst. sales mgr. of subs. Australian Consol. Industries Ltd., Melbourne, 1932-50; sec. Gibson Chem. Industries Ltd., Melbourne, 1950-62, dep. mng. dir., 1970-75, mng. dir., 1975-83, chmn. bd., 1983—. Fellow Cert. Practising Accts., Australian Inst. Mgmt. Roman Catholic. Avocations: golf, public speaking. Home: 7 Limeburners Way, Portsea Victoria 3944, Australia Office: Gibson Chem Industries Ltd, 350 Reserve Rd-Cheltenham, Melbourne Victoria, Australia

LAWSON, FRED RAULSTON, banker; b. Sevierville, Tenn., Mar. 26, 1936; s. Arville Raulston and Ila Mary (Lowe) L.; m. Sharon Sheets, Jan. 1, 1982; children: Terry Lawson Akins, Laura Lawson Rathbone, Kristi Watson Newvine. Student, U. Tenn., 1953-59, La. State U. Sch. Banking of South, 1965-68, Harvard Inst. Fin. Mgmt., 1968. From br. mgr. to exec. v.p. Blount Nat. Bank, Maryville, Tenn., 1958-68, pres., 1968-86, also bd. dirs.; pres. Tenn. Nat. Bancshares, Inc., Maryville, 1971-86, Bank of East Tenn., Knoxville, 1986-92; pres., CEO BankFirst, Knoxville, 1993—; mem. Ft. Sanders Alliance Investment Mgrs. Rev. Subcom.; bd. dirs. Fortress Corp., BancInsure. Mem. Blount County Indsl. Devel. bd., 1969—; chancellors assoc. U. Tenn., Knoxville, 1971-78; trustee Carson-Newman Coll., Jefferson City, 1984-94, Harrison-Chilhowee Bapt. Acad., Seymour, Tenn., 1972-85, Pellissippi State Found., 1989-96; adv. bd. U. Tenn. Med. Rsch. Ctr. and Hosp.; bd. regents Mid-South Sch. banking, Memphis, 1982-90; bd. dirs. Thompson Cancer Survival Ctr., Knoxville, 1987—, The Downtown Orgn., Tenn. Resource Valley, East Tenn. Hist. Soc., Maryville Coll., 1995—. Recipient Tenn. Indsl. Devel. Vol. award, 1977. Mem. Assn. Bank Holding Cos. (bd. dirs. 1978-82), Tenn. Bankers Assn. (chmn. state legis. com. 1980, banking practice com. 1983, bd. dirs. 1990—, pres. 1994-95). Republican. Baptist. Home: 2101 Cochran Rd Maryville TN 37803-2812

LAWSON, H(ERBERT) BLAINE, JR., mathematician, educator; b. Norristown, Pa., Jan. 4, 1942; s. Herbert Blaine and Mary Louise (Corson) L.; m. Carolyn Elaine Pieroni, June 6, 1964 (div. Sept. 1977); children: Christina Corson, Heather Brooke. AB, ScB in Applied Mat. and Russian Lit., Brown U., 1964; MS in Math., Stanford U., 1966, PhD in Math., 1968. Lectr. math. U. Calif., Berkeley, 1968-70, assoc. prof., 1971-74, prof., 1974-80, asst. dean, 1975-77; Disting. prof., chmn. SUNY, Stony Brook, 1978—; vis. asst. prof. IMPA, Rio de Janeiro, 1970-71; vis. prof. Inst. des Hautes Etudes Scientifiques, Bures-sur-Yvette, France, 1977-78, Ecole Poly., Palaiseau, France, 1983-84; bd. dirs. U.S.-Brazilian Math. Exch., Stony Brook and Rio de Janeiro; trustee Math. Scis. Rsch. Inst., Berkeley; chmn. Nat. Com. Math. NAS, Washington, 1989-91; mem. Inst. Advanced Study, Princeton U., 1973-74; lectr. in minimal submanifolds, 1971. Author: The Theory of Gauge Fields in 4 Dimensions, 1985, Spin Geometry, 1989; editor Jour. Differential Geometry, Topology, The Princeton Mat. Series; contbr. articles to profl. jours. Sloan Found. fellow, 1971, Guggenheim Found. fellow, 1983, Japan Soc. Promotion Sci. fellow, 1985. Mem. Nat. Acad. of Sci., Am. Math. Soc. (coun. 1988-91, v.p. 1997—, , editor jour., Steele prize 1975). Achievements include construction of minimal surfaces in the 3-dimensional sphere, construction of foliations on higher dimensional spheres; characterization of boundaries of analytic varieties; co-creation of Calibrated Geometries; research on basic results on manifolds on non-positive curvature, on spaces of positive scalar curvature, on stability results for Yang-Mills fields, on relations between algebraic cycles and topology, and on structure of Chow Varieties. Home: 29 North Rd Stony Brook NY 11790-1009

LAWSON, JACK WAYNE, lawyer; b. Decatur, Ind., Sept. 23, 1935; s. Alva W. and Florence C. (Smitley) L.; m. Sarah J. Hibbard, Dec. 28, 1961; children: Mark, Jeff. BA in Polit. Sci., Valparaiso U., 1958, JD, 1961. Bar: Ind. 1961, U.S. Supreme Ct. 1970, U.S. Dist. Ct. (no., so. dists.) Ind. 1991, Ind. Supreme Ct., Appellate Cts. 1991. Ptnr. Dunten, Beckman & Lawson, Ft. Wayne, Ind., 1961-84; sr. ptnr. Beckman, Lawson, Sandler, Snyder & Federoff, Ft. Wayne, 1984—; seminar presenter and writer Ind. CLE Forum, Indpls., 1970—, Nat. Health Lawyers Assn., Washington, 1986. Editor-in-chief Indiana Real Estate Transactions; contbr. articles to profl. jours. Mem. Ft. Wayne C. of C., 1975—; small claims ct. judge, Allen County, Ind., 1963-67. Mem. Am. Coll. Real Estate Lawyers. Republican. Lutheran. Avocations: sailing, teaching religious seminars, antique consulting. Office: Beckman Lawson Sandler Snyder & Federoff 200 E Main St PO Box 800 Fort Wayne IN 40801-0800

LAWSON, JANE ELIZABETH, bank executive; b. Cornwall, Ont., Can.; d. Leonard J. and Margaret L. BA, LLB, U. N.B., Can., 1971. With law dept. Royal Bank Can., Montreal, Que., Can., 1974-78, sr. counsel, 1978-84; v.p., corp. sec. Royal Bank Can., Montreal, Que., 1988-92, sr. v.p., sec., 1992—. Mem. Can. Bar Assn., N.B. Bar Assn., Que. Bar Assn., Inst. Chartered Secs. and Adminstrs., Inst. Corp. Dirs., Inst. Donations and Pub. Affairs Rsch. (fin. com.), Am. Soc. Corp. Secs., Mt. Royal Tennis Club, Blvd. Club. Office: Royal Bank Can PO Box 6001, 1 Place Ville Marie, Montreal, PQ Canada H3C 3A9

LAWSON, JANICE RAE, retired elementary education educator; b. Chgo., Jan. 22, 1938; d. Ramon Joseph and Anne Joan (Seaquist) Wallenborn; m. Ralph Dreben Lawson, Jr. BEd, Beloit Coll., 1960; MEd, The George Washington U., 1966; postgrad., George Mason U., 1987-88, U. Va., 1965-85; Degree in Theol. Edn., U. of South, 1989. Cert. tchr. Va. Tchr. Quantico (Va.) Marine Base, 1960-62; elem. tchr. Pearl Harbor Elem. Sch., Honolulu, 1962-64; elem. tchr. Quantico Dependents Sch. System, 1964-95, ret., 1995. Counselor Diet Ctr., Springfield, Va., 1979-89. Mem. NEA (life), Quantico Edn. Assn. (treas. 1968-72), Va. Edn. Assn., Pi Lambda Theta (life), Kappa Alpha Theta (treas. 1979-81, pres. North Va. chpt. 1981-85, alumni dist. pres. 1989-95). Republican. Episcopalian. Avocations: sewing, crafts, cooking, yardwork, lay Eucharistic minister. Home: PO Box 427 Cobbs Creek VA 23035

LAWSON, JENNIFER, broadcast executive; b. Birmingham, Ala., June 8, 1946; d. Willie DeLeon and Velma Theresa (Foster) L.; m. Elbert Sampson, June 1, 1979 (div. Sept. 1980); m. Anthony Gittens, May 29, 1982: children: Kai, Zachary. Student, Tuskegee U., 1963-65; MFA, Columbia U., 1974; LHD (hon.), Teikyo Post U., Hartford, Conn., 1991. Assoc. producer William Greaves Prodns., N.Y.C., 1974-75; asst. prof. film studies Bklyn. Coll., 1975-77; exec. dir. The Film Fund, N.Y.C., 1977-80; TV coord. Program Fund Corp. for Pub. Broadcasting, Washington, 1980-83, assoc. dir. TV Program Fund, 1983-89, dir. TV Program Fund, 1989; exec. v.p. programming PBS, Alexandria, Va., 1989-95; broadcast cons. Md. Pub. TV, 1995—, exec. cons., 1996—; v.p. Internat. Pub. TV, Washington, 1984-88; panelist Fulbright Fellowships, Washington, 1988-90. Author, illustrator: Children of Africa, 1970; illustrator: Our Folktales, 1968, African Folktales: A Calabash of Wisdom, 1973. Coord. Nat. Coun. Negro Women, Washington, 1969. Avocations: painting, reading. Office: 1838 Ontario Pl NW Washington DC 20009-2109

LAWSON, JOHN H., university official; b. Gloucester, Mass; s. Howard Vincent and Alice Louise (Carpenter) L.; m. Helen Louise De Lotto, July 3, 1948 (dec. 1981); children—John, Paula, Jay; m. Sally W. Ward, Mar. 7, 1983. B.S., U. N.H., 1949, Ed.M., 1952; Ed.D., Boston U., 1958; postgrad., Guilford Coll., 1970; Aspen Humanities Inst., 1968, Columbia U. Supt.'s Workshop, 1963, Harvard Advanced Adminstrv. Inst., 1962-72, Northeastern U. (hon.), 1982. Tchr. sch. sci. and social studies, coach Antrim, N.H., 1949-51; supervising prin. Salisbury (Mass.) Meml. Sch., 1951-55; supt. schs. Salisbury and Newbury, Mass., 1955-57, Hamilton-Wenham, Mass., 1957-61, Hingham, Mass., 1961-65, Shaker Heights, Ohio, 1965-76, Lexington, Mass, 1976-81; commr. edn. Commonwealth Mass., Quincy, 1982-86; prof. ednl. adminstrn. U. N.H., Durham, 1986-91, officer dept. labor rels., 1991-93, assoc. v.p. for alumni affairs, 1993—; vis. lectr., adj. prof. Boston U., Northeastern U., Case Western Reserve U., Harvard U., Ind., U., Cleve. State U., U. Akron, U. Tex., U. Nebr., John Carroll U. Contbr. articles to profl. jours. Bd. dirs. Sci. Mus., Mus. Fine Arts, Bay State Skills Corp; trustee Econ. Edn. Council; mem. Boston U. Nat. Alumni Council, Cleve. Commn. on Higher Edn., N.C.A.T.E. Accreditation Com. on Sch. Adminstrn., M.I.T. Bd. Overseers, Mass. Telecommunications Commn., Bd. Library Commrs., Mass. State Consortium Com. for Gifted/Talented, Gov.'s Task Force on Edn. Job-Training Partnership Act; pres. U. N.H. Alumni Assn.; mem. state adv. com. Globe Scholastic Art Awards; founding dir. Teacher and Learning Ctr. Bd. Mem. Nat. Suburban Sch. Supts. (pres.), AASA (higher edn. com.), ASCD, Edn. Commn. of the States, Council of Chief State Sch. Officers (vice chmn. policies and priorities com.), Phi Delta Kappa. Home: 7 Bucks Hill Rd Durham NH 03824-3202 Office: U NH Elliott Alumni Ctr Durham NH 03824

LAWSON, JOHN QUINN, architect; b. Tucumcari, N.Mex., Apr. 11, 1940; s. Tom L. and Mable Marie (Hagglund) L.; m. Elizabeth Jo Waddel, June 4, 1961 (div. 1980); children: Bevan Eugene, Cary Augusta; m. Lorna Miriam Katz, Feb. 20, 1981. BA, Rice U., 1961, BSArch, 1962; MFA in Architecture, Princeton U., 1964. Registered architect, Pa., N.J. Staff architect Doxiadis Assocs., Phila., 1961, Collins, Uhl, Hoisington, Princeton, N.J., 1963, Frank Schlesinger, Doylestown, Pa., 1964, Kneedler Mirick & Zantzinger, Phila., 1964; staff architect Mitchell/Giurgola Architects, Phila., 1965-71, assoc., 1972-73, ptnr., 1974-85; ptnr. John Lawson Architects, Phila., 1986—; mem. adj. faculty Grad. Sch. Fine Arts U. Pa., 1972-87; chmn. archtl. adv. bd. Spring Garden Coll., Phila., 1986-92. Prin. works include United Way hdqrs. bldg., Phila., 1971, Lang Music Bldg. Swarthmore (Pa.) Coll., 1973, Ind. Nat. Hist. Park maintenance bldg., Phila., 1981, Columbia Ave. Sta. improvements, Phila., 1983, all recipients Pa. Soc. Architects awards, Benjamin Franklin Bridge Lighting Competition, Phila., 1986 (1st runner-up), Diamond Park Competition, Phila., 1987 (winner with Chuck Fahlen), Evancich residence, Phila., 1990 (1st prize Best Residential Renovation), Ctr. for Animal Health and Productivity, Sch. Vet. Medicine, U. Pa., 1990. V.p. Logan Sq. Neighborhood Assn., Phila., 1971-72; mem. Community Leadership Seminar Alumni, Phila., 1982-85; cons. Friends of Starr Garden, Inc., Phila., 1989. Lowell M. Palmer fellow Princeton U., 1964, NEA Mid-Career fellow Am. Acad. in Rome, 1980. Fellow AIA (mem. architecture for edn. com. 1976-85, chmn. urban design com. Phila. chpt. 1986—, steering com. Phila chpt. 1988—); mem. Pa. Soc. Architects, Soc. Hill Civic Assn., City Pks. Assn. (bd. dirs. 1988—), Awbury Arboretum Assn. (bd. dirs. 1989—), Soc. Hill Towers (coun. 1994—). Democrat. Office: John Lawson Architects 812 Chestnut St Fl 2 Philadelphia PA 19107-5104

LAWSON, JONATHAN NEVIN, academic administrator; b. Latrobe, Pa., Mar. 27, 1941; s. Lawrence Winters and Mary Eleanor (Rhea) L.; m. Leigh Farley (div.); children: Paul, Joshua, Jacob; m. Pamela Cross. AA, York Coll. Pa., 1962; BFA, Tex. Christian U., 1964, MA, 1966, PhD, 1970. Dir. composition St. Cloud (Minn.) State U., 1971-77, assoc. dean, 1977-81; asst. vice chancellor Minn. State U. System, St. Paul, 1980-81; dean liberal arts Winona (Minn.) State U., 1981-84; dean arts and scis. U. Hartford, West Hartford, Conn., 1984-86; sr. v.p., dean of faculty U. Hartford, 1986-95; v.p. acad. affairs Idaho State U., Pocatello, 1995—. Author: Robert Bloomfield, 1980; editor: Collected Works: Robert Bloomfield, 1971; contbr. articles and papers to scholarly publs; assoc. editor Rhetoric Soc. Quar., St. Cloud, 1974-79. Mem. regional adv. bd. Greater Hartford C.C., 1992-94; mem. bd. trustees Hartford Coll. for Women, 1992-94; mem. ID State bd. for edn. acad. affairs com., 1995—. Mem. Am. Coun. Edn., Coun. Fellows Alumni, Coun. Liberal Learning, Assn. Gen. and Liberal Studies, Assn. Am. Colls., N.E. Assn. Schs. and Colls. (chmn. commn. on instns. higher edn. 1992-95), Asian Studies Consortium (chmn. bd. 1991-94), Lambda Iota Tau (hon.), Alpha Chi (hon.). Episcopalian. Avocations: fishing, camping, writing. Home: 1401 Juniper Hill Dr Pocatello ID 83204 Office: Idaho State U Campus Box 8063 Pocatello ID 83209

LAWSON, KATHERINE ELAINE, minister, counselor, psychologist; b. Cleve, Feb. 8, 1950; d. Fred and Cora Belle Cole; m. Gerald Edward Lawson, Mar. 24, 1973; 1 child, Jordan Edward. BA, Bowling Green State U., 1972, MEd, 1974; EdD, Memphis State U., 1991. Cert. sch. psychologist, 1991. Intern sch. psychologist Wood County Schs., Bowling Green, Ohio, 1973-74; sch. psychologist Lucas County Schs., Toledo, Ohio, 1974-77; project psychologist Cin. Public Schs., 1978-79; psychometrist adolescent program Oak Tree Children's Ctr., Albany, Ga., 1979-81; sustitute tchr. Memphis State U. Early Childhood Sch., 1985; grad. asst. Memphis State U., 1986-91, adj. asst. prof., 1991-94; dir. counseling and support Abundant Grace Fellowship, Memphis, 1994—; cons. violence reduction program Memphis Area Neighborhood Watch, 1990, 91; organizing com., chair pers. The Shepherd's Sch., Memphis, 1991; adv. bd. The Healing Ctr., Memphis, 1992—; pastoral care adv. bd. Regional Med. Ctr. Memphis, 1993—. Coord. Adopt a Sch. Program, Abundant Grace and Fellowship, Memphis, 1990—; spkr. leadership panel Mid-South Regional Black Family Reunion, Memphis, 1991; mem. student achievement citizenship task force Memphis 2000, 1991-92, conf. spkr. W. Tenn. Br. Nat. Assn. of Social Workers, Shelby County Govt. Victims Assistance Ctr., Memphis, 1996; founder Victims to Victory, 1995, Victims of Crime Act, 1996; devel. team coord. Memphis Neighbors Who Care, 1996; conf. spkr. Neighbors Who Care, 1996. Victims of Crime Act grantee, 1996. Mem. Assn. Clin. Pastoral Edn., Am. Assn. Christian Counselors, Nat. Assn. for Edn. Young Children, Assn. for Death Edn. and Counseling. Avocations: walking, gourmet cooking, Rhodesian Ridgeback Dogs. Office: Abundant Grace Fellowship 843 W Raines Rd Memphis TN 38109-4229

LAWSON, MELANIE KAY, management administrator, early childhood consultant; b. Fort Valley, Ga., Feb. 8, 1955; d. William C. and Mamie Nell (Brown) Chapman; m. Robert Scott Lawson, Dec. 18, 1975; children: Robert Scott Jr., Joshua Cody, Ashley Jeanell. AA, Cisco Jr. Coll., 1984; BE in

Elem./Spl. Edn., Hardin-Simmons U., 1988, MEd in Reading, 1990; MEd in Sch. Adminstrn., Abilene Christian U., 1992; MEd in Higher Edn., Tex. Tech. U., 1996. Cert. reading specialist, supr., mid-mgmt. tchr. Speech pathology asst. Head Start/Abilene Ind. Sch. Dist., Abilene, Tex., 1983-84; assoc. tchr. Head Start/AISD, Abilene, Tex., 1984-88, cert. tchr., 1988-90; English as second lang. tchr. AISD-Curriculum div., Abilene, Tex., 1990-92; kindergarten tchr. AISD-Long Elem. Sch., Abilene, Tex., 1992-93; asst. dir. Child Devel. Ctr., Dyess AFB, Tex., 1993-94; tng. mgr. 7 SVS Squadron, Dyess AFB, Tex., 1994—. Mem. Youth Task Force, Abilene City Govt., 1994-95, Higher Edn. Working Group, Tex. Head Start Collaboration Project, local conf. corrd., Abilene Work/Family Planning Series Conf. Recipient Key City Reading award Reading Coun., 1988; Pres. Trust Fund scholarship TAEYC, 1996. Mem. AAUW, Internat. Reading Assn., Nat. Assn. Edn. of Young Children (Membership Affiliate grant 1994, academy mentor 1995—, validator 1993—), Tex. Assn. Edn. of Young Children (at-large, Tex. Affiliate grant, 1993, 94, exec. bd., chair accreditation, Pres.'s Trust Fund Scholarship 1996), Big Country Assn. for Edn. of Young children (membership chair 1988-90, pres. 1992-94, state repl 1992-94), Tex. Assn. for Gifted/Talented (grant 1991), Coun. Early Childhood Profl. Recognition (rep. 1993—), Golden Key Honor Soc., Kappa Delta Phi, Phi Delta Kappa. Baptist. Avocations: reading, sewing, walking, ceramics, wood crafts. Home: 1702 Yorktown Dr Abilene TX 79603-4216 Office: 7 SVS Squadron 309 5th St Dyess AFB TX 79607-1239

LAWSON, RANDALL CLAYTON, II, financial executive; b. Wabash, Ind., June 20, 1948; s. Randall Clayton and Evelyn Beatrice (Wright) L.; m. Julie Ann Severin, June 30, 1973; children: Randall Clayton III, Erin Elizabeth. BS, Butler U., 1970. CPA, Ind., Ohio. Jr. acct. Price Waterhouse, Indpls., 1970-73; sr. acct. Price Waterhouse, Indpls. and Cin., 1973-76; audit mgr. Price Waterhouse, Cin., 1976-79; unit devel. contr. Ponderosa, Inc., Dayton, Ohio, 1979-81, asst. corp. contr., 1981-82, corp. contr., 1982-84, v.p., corp. contr., 1984-85, sr. v.p., chief acctg. officer, 1985-87, sr. v.p., CFO, 1987; v.p., CFO Tad Tech. Svcs. Corp., Cambridge, Mass., 1988-89; v.p. fin. HydroLogic, Inc., Asheville, N.C., 1993; dir. mgmt. acctg. Rust Indsl. Cleaning Inc., Ashland, Ky., 1994-95; East region contr. Rust Indsl. Svcs., Inc., LaPorte, Tex., 1995, divsn. v.p., contr., 1996-97, v.p., contr., 1997—; adj. prof. Wilmington Coll., 1991; bus. cons., 1987—. Mem. agy. audit com. United Way Greater Cin., 1975; mem. fin. and resource allocation com. United Way Greater Dayton, 1985, mem. com. on agy. fins., 1986-87. Mem. AICPA, Ohio Soc. CPAs, Fin. Execs. Inst., Queen City Assn. Club (bd. dirs. 1978), Dayton Racquet Club, Elks, Phi Kappa Psi. Republican. Presbyterian. Avocations: golf, tennis, reading, antiques, crafts. Home: 1201 Enterprise Ave # 800 League City TX 77573

LAWSON, RICHARD LAVERNE, trade association executive, retired military officer; b. Fairfield, Iowa, Dec. 19, 1929; s. Vernon C. and Wilma Aletha (Rabel) L.; m. Joan Lee Graber, Aug. 28, 1949; children: Leslie D., Wendy L., Richard H., Randolph S. BSChemE, Parsons Coll., 1951, MSChemE, 1951; grad., Nat. War Coll.; MPA, George Washington U., 1964; PhD (hon.), Centenary Coll., 1980; PhD in Polit. Sci. (hon.), Boston U., 1985. Enlisted U.S. Army USA, 1946, advanced through grades to sgt. maj.; transferred to USAF and advanced through grades to gen., 1951; mil. asst. to Pres. The White House, Washington, 1973-75; dir. plans HQ USAF, Washington, 1975-77; comdr. 8th Air Force, Barksdale AFB, La., 1977-78; dir. Joint Chiefs of Staff, Washington, 1978-80; U.S. rep. to milit. com. NATA, Brussels, Belgium, 1980-81; chief of staff Supreme HQ Allied Powers Europe, Mons, Belgium, 1981-83; deputy comdr. in chief HQ U.S. European Command, Stuttgart, Germany, 1983-86; retired USAF, 1986; pres. Nat. Coal Assn., Washington, 1987-95, also bd. dirs.; pres., CEO Nat. Mining Assn., 1995—; Chmn. Internat. Com. Coal Rsch., Washington, 1987—, Trade Assn. Liaison Coun., Washington, 1992-93, Bus. Com. Atlantic Coun., Washington, 1987—; chmn. global climate com. U.S. Energy Assn., 1994—; chmn. U.S. Delegation, World Mining Congress, 1996—. Decorated Def. DSM with 1 oak leaf cluster, DSM with 1 oak leaf cluster, Legion of Merit with 1 oak leaf cluster, Soldiers medal, Bronze Star, Air medal with 1 oak leaf cluster, USAF Commendation medal with 3 oak leaf clusters, Republic of Vietnam Gallantry Cross with Palm, Joint Chiefs of Staff Identification Badge, Presdl. Svc. Badge, Armed Forces Expeditionary medal, Vietnam Svc. medal with 4 oak leaf clusters, USAF Overseas Long Tour ribbon with 1 oak leaf cluster, USAF Longevity Svc. award ribbon with 7 oak leaf clusters. Mem. U.S. Energy Assn. (bd. dirs.), Washington Inst. Fgn. Affairs, World Energy Coun., Nat. Energy Found., World Energy Congress., World Mining Congress (U.S. mem.). Home: 6910 Clifton Rd Clifton VA 20124 Office: Nat Mining Assn 1130 17th St NW Washington DC 20036-4604

LAWSON, ROBERT BERNARD, psychology educator; b. N.Y.C., June 20, 1940; s. Robert Bernard Sr. and Isabella Theresa (McPeake) L.; children: Christina Megan, Steven Robert, Jennifer Erin. BA in Psychology, Monmouth U., 1961; MA in Psychology, U. Del., 1963, PhD in Psychology, 1965. Mem. faculty U. Vt., Burlington, 1966—, assoc. prof. psychology, 1966-69, assoc. prof., 1969-74, prof., 1974—, assoc. v.p. acad. affairs, 1978, assoc. v.p. rsch., dean Grad. Coll., 1978-86, dir. gen. exptl. psychology, 1988-90, chair dept. pub. adminstrn., 1990-95; presenter, worker in China, Russia, and Italy; cons. Mgmt. Sys., 1986—; vis. scholar Stanford U., 1986-87; pres. Alliance Mgmt. Cons. Group, Burlington, 1987—, N.E. Assn. Grad. Schs., Princeton, N.J., 1983-86; bd. dirs. Grad. Record Exams-ETS, Princeton, 1984-88. Author: (with S.G. Goldstein and R.E. Musty) Principles and Methods of Psychology, 1975, (with W.L. Gulick) Human Stereopsis: A Psychophysical Approach, 1976, (with Zheng Shen) Organizational Psychology: Foundations and Applications, 1997. Mem. bd. govs. Univ. Press New England, 1978-86, bd. dirs., 1979-80. Recipient numerous grants NIH, NSF, USDA, numerous awards from Nat. Eye Inst. Mem. AAAS, APA, Psychonomic Soc., Coun. Grad. Schs., N.Y. Acad. Scis., Ea. Psychol. Assn. Avocations: international organizational psychology, leadership, motivation, decision making, and organizational culture. Office: U Vt Dept Psychology John Dewey Hall Burlington VT 05405-0134

LAWSON, ROBERT DAVIS, theoretical nuclear physicist; b. Sydney, Australia, July 14, 1926; came to U.S., 1949; s. Carl Herman and Angeline Elizabeth (Davis) L.; m. Mary Grace Lunn, Dec. 16, 1950 (div. 1976); children—Dorothy, Katherine, Victoria; m. Sarah Virginia Roney, Mar. 13, 1976 (dec. 1994). B.S., U. B.C., Can., 1948; M.S., U. B.C., 1949; Ph.D., Stanford U., 1953. Research assoc. U. Calif., Berkeley, 1953-57; research assoc. Fermi Inst. U. Chgo., 1957-59; assoc. physicist Argonne Nat. Lab., Ill., 1959-65; sr. physicist Argonne Nat. Lab., 1965—; vis. scientist U.K. Atomic Energy Authority, Harwell, Eng., 1962-63, Oxford U., Eng., 1970, 85; vis. prof. SUNY, Stony Brook, 1972-73; vis. fellow Australian Nat. U., Canberra, 1982; vis. prof. U. Groningen, 1973, U. Utrecht, 1974, Technische Hochschule, Darmstadt, 1975, 78, Free U., Amsterdam, 1976, 81, others; TRIUMF, U. B.C., Vancouver, Can., 1984. Author: Theory of the Nuclear Shell Model, 1980. Contbr. articles to sci. jours. Fellow Weizmann Inst. Sci., 1967-68, Niels Bohr Inst., 1976-77; Sir Thomas Lyle fellow U. Melbourne, Australia, 1987. Fellow Am. Phys. Soc. Home: 1590 Raven Hl Wheaton IL 60187-7109 Office: Argonne Nat Lab Bldg 203 Argonne IL 60439

LAWSON, SUSAN COLEMAN, lawyer; b. Covington, Ky., Dec. 4, 1949; d. John Clifford and Louise Carter Coleman; m. William Henry Lawson, June 6, 1980; 1 child, Philip. BA, U. Ky., 1971, JD, 1979. Bar: Ky. 1979. Ptnr. Lawson & Lawson, P.S.C., Harlan, 1995—; atty. Stoll, Keenon & Park, Lexington, Ky., 1979-80; atty., Harbert Constrn. Co., Middlesboro, Ky., 1980-81; ptnr. Buttermore, Turner, Lawson & Boggs, P.S.C., Harlan, Ky., 1981-94. Elder 1st Presbyn. Ch., Pineville, Ky., 1986—. Mem. ABA, Ky. Bar Assn., Harlan County Bar Assn. (pres. 1983), Order of Coif. Democrat. Avocations: tennis, golf. Home: 511 W Kentucky Ave Pineville KY 40977-1307 Office: PO Box 837 103 N 1st St Harlan KY 40831

LAWSON, THOMAS ELSWORTH, advertising agency executive; b. Taunton, Mass., May 30, 1937; s. Wilbur Lougheed and Margaret Mary (Walsh) L.; m. Nina Rae Dansky, Sept. 13, 1981; children: Patric Ian, James Francis, Samantha. B.A., Harvard U., 1959. Media trainee, media supr., account exec., v.p. account supr., sr. v.p., mgmt. supr. Ogilvy & Mather Inc. (advt. agy.), N.Y.C., 1961-70; pres., chief executive officer Rosenfeld, Sirowitz & Lawson Inc., N.Y.C., 1971-86; pres. Lawrence, Charles, Free & Lawson, Inc., 1986—; mng. ptnr., COO Arnold Comm., Boston. Served to 1st lt., inf. paratroops U.S. Army. Mem. Am. Assn. Advt. Agys. (dir., former chmn. Eastern region), Young Pres.'s Orgn. Clubs: Harvard, Manhattan Theatre (N.Y.C.). Home: 1010 5th Ave New York NY 10028-0130 Office: Arnold Comm Inc 101 Arch St Boston MA 02110*

LAWSON, WILLIAM, otolaryngologist, educator; b. N.Y.C., Nov. 23, 1934; s. Alexander and Sophia (Elkind) L.; m. Miriam Patkin, Nov. 7, 1965; 1 child, Vanessa Ann. BA, NYU, 1956, DDS, 1961, MD, 1965. Diplomate Am. Bd. Otolaryngology, Am. Bd. Cosmetic Surgery, Am. Bd. Facial Plastic Surgery. Intern Mt. Sinai Hosp., N.Y.C., 1965-66, rsch. fellow in otolaryngology, 1969-70, resident in otolaryngology, 1970-73; resident in gen. surgery Bronx (N.Y.) VA Hosp., 1966-67, chief otolaryngology, head and neck surgery, 1984—; prof. Mt. Sinai Sch. Medicine, N.Y.C., 1980—. Author: Paraganguonic Chemoreceptor Systems, 1982, Surgery of the Paranasal Sinuses, 1988, 2nd edit., 1992, External Ear, 1995; contbr. over 190 articles to med. jours., chpts. to books. Capt. M.C., U.S. Army, 1967-69. Fellow ACS, Am. Acad. Facial Plastic and Reconstructive Surgery (svc. awrd), Am. Soc. Head and Neck Surgery, Am. Soc. Maxillofacial Surgeons, Am. Rhilogic, Otologic and Laryngolic Soc., Am. Laryngol. Soc.; mem. Am. Acad. Otolaryngology (svc. award). Avocations: photography, art history, horology. Office: Mt Sinai Med Ctr 5 E 98th St New York NY 10029-6501

LAWSON, WILLIAM DAVID, III, retired cotton company executive; b. Jackson, Miss., Oct. 30, 1924; s. William David Jr. and Elizabeth Vaiden (Barksdale) L.; m. Elizabeth Coppridge Smith, June 9, 1948; children: Margaret Monroe, William David IV, Susan Barksdale, Thomas Nelson. BS, Davidson Coll., 1948; MBA, U. Pa., 1949. Trainee T.J. White and Co., Memphis, 1949-52; v.p. W.D. Lawson and Co., Gastonia, N.C., 1952-70, pres., 1971-81; pres. Lawson, Lewis & Peat, Gastonia, 1981-85, Lawson Cotton Co., Gastonia, 1985-95; v.p. Hohenberg Bros. Co. div. Cargill Inc., Memphis, 1988-95; ret., 1995; hon. dir. 1st Union Nat. Bank, Gastonia. Bd. dirs. Sister Cities Com., Gastonia; elder Presbyn. Ch. 1st lt. infantry, U.S. Army, WWII. Named Cotton Man of Year Cotton Digest, 1969, 76. Mem. Nat. Cotton Coun. (advisor; pres. 1975-76), Am. Cotton Shippers Assn. (pres. 1968-69), Atlantic Cotton Assn. (pres. 1957-58), Cotton Coun. Internat. (pres. 1972-73), Am. Cotton Exporters Assn. (pres. 1979-80), Newcomen Soc., Gaston County C. of C. (pres. 1972-73), Am. Legion, Gaston Country Club, Gastonia City Club, Rotary (pres. 1964-65, dist. gov. 1995-96), Kappa Sigma. Clubs: Gaston Country, Gastonia City. Avocations: scuba diving, tennis, golf, jogging. Home: 1341 Covenant Dr Gastonia NC 28054-3816

LAWSON, WILLIAM HAROLD, college dean, labor economist; b. San Jose, Calif., Nov. 2, 1934; s. Minter Bryan and Ruth Josephine (Hill) L.; m. Patricia Marguerette O'Carroll, Aug. 15, 1958 (div. Apr. 1979); children: Ronald W., Brian T., Thomas W.; m. Patricia Jeanne Prevedello, Feb. 6, 1982; children: Kathleen Ann Clark, George T., Tim J. BS in Civil Engring., San Jose State U., 1958, MBA, 1961; PhD in Labor Econs., Claremont Grad. Sch., 1969. Engr. Pacific Telephone, San Francisco, 1957-60; mgmt. intern U.S. Dept. Labor, Washington, 1961, pers. officer, 1962-64; instr. bus. San Bernardino (Calif.) Valley Coll., 1964-67, chmn. bus. dept., 1965-67; from tech. div. chmn. to asst. dean instrn. Moorpark (Calif.) Coll., 1967-72; dist. asst. supt. Ventura (Calif.) County Community Coll., 1972-83; dean vocat. edn. & econ. devel. Oxnard (Calif.) Coll., 1983-95, ret., 1995, tchr. credentialling mentor, 1995—; cons. Evaluation Tech. Corp. and Lawson Cons. Group, Ventura, Calif., 1968—, Chancellor's office Calif. Cmty. Colls., Sacramento, 1977-83, with spl. assignments Calif. State Dept. Edn., Sacramento, 1977-80. Producer TV shows U.S. Dept. Edn., San Bernardino Valley Coll., 1975. Legis. cons. Calif. Adv. Com. Vocat. Edn., Sacramento, 1974-76; joint com. chmn. Joint Community Coll. Dept. Edn. Plan for Vocat. Edn., Sacramento, 1977-78; chmn. community adv. bd. Calif. Conservation Corps, Camarillo, 1987-94. Mem. Am. Vocat. Assn., Calif. C.C. Adminstrn. Occupational Edn. (v.p. 1991-94), Oxnard Coll. Ctr. Internat. Trade Devel. (dir. 1989-95), Oxnard Coll. Workplace Learning Ctr. (dir. 1992-94), Econ. Devel. Network (co-counder 1987-94), Econ. Devel. Network Internat. (trade devel. com. chmn. 1988-91, chair resource devel. com. Calif. State U. Northridge-Ventura Campus 1993-95). Republican. Roman Catholic. Avocations: stamp collecting, racquetball, reading, computers. Home: 4496 Pomona St Ventura CA 93003-1920

LAWSON, WILLIAM HOGAN, III, electrical motor manufacturing executive; b. Lexington, Ky., Feb. 3, 1937; s. Otto Kirsky and Gladys (McWhorter) L.; div.; children: Elizabeth, Cynthia; m. Ruth Stanat, 1995. B.S. in Mech. Engring, Purdue U., 1959; M.B.A., Harvard U., 1961. Gen. mgr. service div. Toledo Scale Corp., 1964-68; exec. v.p., chief ops. officer Skyline Corp., Elkhart, Ind., 1968-85; chmn. bd. dirs., chief exec. officer Franklin Elec. Co., Inc., Bluffton, Ind., 1985—, also bd. dirs.; bd. dirs. JSJ Corp., Skyline Corp., Sentry Ins. (a Mut. Ins. Co.); chmn. bd. Oil Dynamics, Inc.; instr. U. Toledo, 1966-67. Trustee Ind. Inst. Tech., Am. Ground Water Trust. With U.S. Army, 1961-63. Mem. Harvard U. Bus. Sch. Assn., Ft. Wayne Country Club, Summit Club Ft. Wayne, Harvard Club N.Y.C. Republican. Presbyterian. Home: 7118 Blue Creek Dr Fort Wayne IN 46804-1483 Office: Franklin Electric Co Inc 400 E Spring St Bluffton IN 46714-3737

LAWSON DONADIO, CAROLINA ANNA, foreign language educator, translator; b. Naples, Italy, Mar. 11, 1920; d. Joseph and Concetta (Bartolomeo) Donadio; m. Allan Leroy Lawson, Sept. 15, 1945; 1 child, John. Laurea in European langs., lit., instns., Western Group Instituto Universitario Orientale, Naples, Italy, 1946; PhD in French and Italian, Tulane U., 1971. Lectr. overseas div. U. Md., Leghorn, Italy, 1952; tchr. Warren Easton High Sch., New Orleans, 1958-61; teaching asst. Tulane U., New Orleans, 1961-64; instr. Tex. Christian U., Ft. Worth, 1964-65; lectr. Downtown ctr., U.Chgo., 1967-73, U. Akron, Ohio, 1975-76; pvt. practice lectr., translator, ind. scholar, freelance writer Moncks Corner, S.C., 1985—; vis. prof. Kent (Ohio) State U., 1977-84; mem. S.C. Humanities Coun., 1989-93. Author: (textbook) Nuove Letture di Cultura Italiana, 1975; fgn. lang. editl. reviewer Ency. Brit. Chgo., 1971; rev. editor: Italian Culture, 1981-84; contbr. many articles and revs. in lit. criticism, art history, textbooks of fables, fairy tales and biographies to profl. and fgn. lang. publs. Recipient cert. of proficiency in Japanese lang. and culture Tokyo Coll., 1958. Mem. MLA, Am. Assn. Tchrs. of Italian, Am. Assn. Italian Studies, Am. Assn. Tchrs of French, Nat. Italian-Am. Found. Republican. Roman Catholic. Avocations: classical music, painting, sports, world travel.

LAWSON-JOHNSTON, PETER ORMAN, foundation executive; b. N.Y.C., Feb. 8, 1927; s. John R. and Barbara (Guggenheim) L.; m. Dorothy Stevenson Hammond, Sept. 30, 1950; children: Wendy, Tania, Peter, Mary. Reporter, yachting editor Balt. Sun Papers, 1951-53; exec. dir. Md. Classified Employees Assn., Balt., 1953-54; pub. info. dir. Md. Civil Def. Agy., Pikesville, 1954-56; sales mgr. Feldspar Corp. subs. Zemex Corp. (formerly Pacific Tin Consol.), N.Y.C., 1956-60, v.p. sales, 1961-66, v.p., 1966-72, chmn., 1972-81, bd. dirs., 1959—; v.p. Zemex Corp., 1966-72, vice chmn. 1972-75, pres., 1975-76, chmn., 1975—, also bd. dirs.; chmn. Anglo Energy, Inc., 1973-86; trustee Solomon R. Guggenheim Found. (operating Guggenheim Mus., N.Y.C. and Peggy Guggenheim Collection, Venice, Italy), 1964—, v.p. bus. adminstrn., 1965-69, pres., 1969-95, chmn., 1995—; dir. Harry Frank Guggenheim Found., 1968—, chmn., 1971—; ptnr. Guggenheim Bros., 1962-70, sr. ptnr., 1971—; ltd. ptnr. emeritus Alex. Brown & Sons, Inc.; pres., bd. dirs. Elgerbar Corp.; Nat. Rev. Inc., dir., UBS Private Investor Fund, Inc., Trustee The Lawrenceville Sch., pres. 1990—; bd. dirs. Coun. for U.S. and Italy. Served with AUS, 1945-47. Recipient Gertrude Vanderbilt Whitney award Skowhegan Sch. Painting and Sculpture, 1986, Ellis Island Medal of Honor, Nat. Ethnic Coalition Orgns., 1993. Mem. Pilgrims of U.S., Carolina Plantation Soc., U.S. Srs. Golf Assn., Edgartown Yacht Club, Edgartown Reading Room Club, Green Spring Valley Hunt Club, River Club, Century Assn., Links, Nassau Gun Club, Bedens Brook Club, Pretty Brook Tennis Club, Md. Club, Seminole Golf Club, Island Club, Brook Club (N.Y.C.), Yeamans Hall Club. Republican. Episcopalian. Home: 215 Carter Rd Princeton NJ 08540-2104 Office: Solomon R Guggenheim Found 527 Madison Ave New York NY 10022-4304

LAWSON-JOWETT, M. JULIET, lawyer; b. Mobile, Ala., May 26, 1959; d. William Max Lawson and Perina Juliet (Barich) Franc; m. Adam Geoffrey Jowett; 1 child, Caitlin Victoria Jowett. BA, U. Miss., 1981, JD, 1987. Bar: Miss. 1988, U.S. Dist. Ct. (no. and so. dists.) Miss. 1988. Tchr. Ocean Springs (Miss.) Sch. System, 1981-85; atty. Ronald W. Lewis & Assocs., Oxford, Miss., 1988-89; ptnr. occupl. hearing loss and hand-arm vibration syndrome Scruggs, Millette, Lawson, Bozeman & Dent, P.A., Pascagoula, Miss., 1989-97; gen. practice, civil rights and employment law Juliet Jowett, P.A., 1997—; cons. Occupational Hearing Loss, P.A., 1989-96. Contbr. articles to profl. jours. Mem. Walter Anderson Players, Ocean Springs, 1973-96. Mem. ABA, ATLA (chmn. occupational hearing loss litigation group 1990-94), Miss. Trial Lawyers Assn. (editor 1990-92), Magnolia Bar Assn. Democrat. Roman Catholic. Avocations: reading, golf, horseback riding, gardening, acting. Office: Juliet Jowett PA 906 Desoto St Ocean Springs MS 39564-3737

LAWTON, ALEXANDER ROBERT, III, immunologist, educator; b. Savannah, Ga., Nov. 8, 1938; s. Alexander Robert and Elizabeth (Holdrege) L.; m. Frances Ritchie Crockett, Nov. 25, 1960; children: Julia Beckwith, Alexander Robert IV. BA, Yale U., 1960; MD, Vanderbilt U., 1964. Diplomate Am. Bd. Pediatrics. Resident in pediatrics Vanderbilt U., Nashville, 1964-66; fellow dept. pediatrics U. Ala., Birmingham, 1969-71, from asst. prof. to prof. pediatrics and microbiology, 1971-80; prof. microbiology, Edward C. Stahlman prof. pediatric physiology and cell metabolism Vanderbilt U. Sch. Medicine, Nashville, 1980—; mem. cancer spl. programs rev. com. Nat. Cancer Inst., 1981-84; mem. allergy, immunology and transplantation rev. com. Nat. Inst. Allergy and Infectious Diseases, 1985-88. Contbr. over 150 articles, book chpts. to profl. publs. Surgeon USPHS, 1966-69. Grantee NIH, March of Dimes Birth Defects Found. Mem. Soc. Pediatric Rsch., Am. Pediatric Soc., Am. Soc. Clin. Investigation, Am. Assn. Immunologists, Am. Assn. Pathologists. Episcopalian. Office: Vanderbilt U Sch Medicine D3237 Med Ctr N Nashville TN 37232

LAWTON, CHARLES See HECKELMANN, CHARLES NEWMAN

LAWTON, DEBORAH SIMMONS, educational media specialist; b. Dover, N.J., Sept. 14, 1950; d. Coryden Jerome Simmons and Marjorie Lynd (Jewell) Weber; m. Ernest James Lawton III, July 8, 1972; children: Catherine Randall, Christopher James. BA, Lebanon Valley Coll., 1972; tchr. cert., Coll. St. Elizabeth, 1974; MLS, Rutgers-The State U., 1994. Cert. ednl. media specialist; cert. profl. libr. Confidential ratings analyst Martindale-Hubbell, Summit, N.J., 1972-74; tchr. St. Rose Sch., E. Hanover, N.J., 1975-77, St. Paul Sch., Princeton, N.J., 1977-78; libr. Mary Jacobs Libr., Rocky Hill, N.J., 1988-92, South Brunswick H.S., Monmouth Junction, N.J., 1994—; reviewer VOYA Mag., 1995—, Infolink, 1995—; presses rev. com. Assn. Am. U. Chair, Montgomery Jointure com., Montgomery Twp., N.J., 1985; coach/dir. Montgomery Girls Softball, 1988-91; v.p., exec. bd. Montgomery Twp. PTSA, 1986-90; pres., treas. Lawrenceville (N.J.) Presbyn. Coop. Nursery Sch., 1981-84; ranking chair jrs. N.J. Tennis Dist.; mem. INFOLINK Book Evaluation Criteria Com., KidsConnect. Internet grantee N.J. State Libr., 1994, Instrnl. Coun. grantee South Brunswick Instrnl. Coun., 1995; recipient Pres.'s award N.J. Tennis. Mem. ALA, Am. Assn. Sch. Librs. (assn. Am. univ. presses com. 1996—), Assn. for Libr. Svc. to Children, Young Adult Libr. Svcs. Assn., Intellectual Freedom Round Table, Ednl. Media Assn. N.J., N.J. Libr. Assn., Beta Phi Mu, Pi Gamma Mu. Avocations: water sports, quilting. Office: South Brunswick High School 195 Major Rd # 183 Monmouth Junction NJ 08852-2307

LAWTON, FLORIAN KENNETH, artist, educator; b. Cleve., June 20, 1921; s. Maximillian and Mary L.; m. Lois Mari Ondrey, June 19, 1948; children: Kenneth R., David F., Dawn M., Patricia A. Student, Cleve. Sch. Art, 1941-43, Cleve. Inst. Art, 1948-51, John Huntington Polytech. Inst., 1946-50. Instr. Cooper Sch. Art, Cleve., 1976-80, Cleve. Sch. Art, 1980-82; cons., instr. Orange Art Ctr., Pepper Pike, Ohio, 1978—; cons. in field, juror, 1968—. Exhbns. include Am. Watercolor Soc., N.Y., Cleve. Mus. Art, Butler Mus., Youngstown, Ohio, Canton (Ohio) Mus., Massillon (Ohio) Mus., Nat. Arts Club, N.Y.C., Pitts. Watercolor Soc., Audubon Artists, N.Y.C., Salmagundi Club, N.Y.C., Parkersburg (W.Va.) Art Ctr., Boston Mills Arts Festival, Peninsula, Ohio, Marietta (Ohio) Coll., Nat. Pks. Assn. Exhbn., 1996, many others; 25 yrs. retrospective exhbn. Amish paintings, Butler Inst. Am. Art, 1989; represented in collections including Am. Soc. Metals, Ctrl. Nat. Bank, Diamond-Shamrock, Diocese Cleve., Kaiser Found., Ohio Conservation Found., Nat. City Bank Ohio, TRW, Standard Oil Co., Huntington Bank, Nat. Mennonite Mus., Lancaster, Pa., Ohio Bell Telephone Co., Day-Glo Corp., Soc. Bank Corp., numerous others U.S. and internat., also pvt. collections; featured mags., calendars; Mill Pond Press; cons., artist (documentary) Amish Romance, 1979; official Coast Guard artist; artist Amish Documentary-PBS, 1996. Cons. Aurora (Ohio) Community Libr., 1990—. Cpl. USAF, 1943-46, PTO. Recipient Disting. Alumni award Garfield Hgts. (Ohio) High Sch., 1990, 1st place award Grand Invitational Exhbn., Akron, Ohio, 1996. Mem. Ohio Watercolor Soc. (signature, charter, Grand Buckeye award 1983), Am. Watercolor Soc. (signature, Strathmore award 1977), Nat. Watercolor Soc. (signature), Akron Soc. Artists, Assoc. Audubon Artists, Artists Fellowships Inc. (N.Y.), Ky. Watercolor Soc., Midwest Watercolor Soc., Pa. Watercolor Soc., Ga. Watercolor Soc., NOVA, Whiskey Painters Am., Rotary Club Chagrin Valley (Paul Harris fellow 1989). Office: 410-29 Willow Cirle Aurora OH 44202

LAWTON, JOSEPH J., JR., lawyer; b. Syracuse, N.Y., Aug. 8, 1926; m. Mary Clarke; children: Joe, Jeff, Eileen, Dan, Sara. BS, Niagara U., 1950; JD, St. John's U., 1953. Bar: N.Y. 1953, U.S. Dist. Ct (no. dist.) N.Y. 1954, U.S. Ct. Appeals (2d cir.) 1966, U.S. Supreme Ct. 1970. Atty. Schoeneck & King, Syracuse, N.Y., 1953; Arbitrator Am. Coll. Construction Arbitrators, 1982-90; adv. com. Legal Adv. Counsel Am. Subcontractors Assn., Washington, 1974-90, chmn. 1983-85; lectr. in field. Mem. ABA (forum Constrn. Industry), Am. Arbitration Assn. (constrn. adv. counsel 1983-90, panel arbitrators), Am. Subcontractors Assn. (chpt. atty. ctrl. N.Y. chpt. 1971-93), N.Y. State Bar Assn. (ins. sect. constrn. and surety com. 1961-90, chmn. 1967-71, continuing legal edn. com. 1973-74, chmn. 1975-77, legal edn. and admission to Bar 1980-81, chmn. 1982-84), Constrn. Specification Inst. (ctrl. N.Y. chpt.). Avocations: education, golf, travel, archtl. design, photography. Home: 3371 E Lake Rd Skaneateles NY 13152-9001 Office: Bond Schoeneck & King 1 Lincoln Ctr Fl 18 Syracuse NY 13202-1324

LAWTON, KIM AUDREY, freelance journalist; b. Springville, N.Y., July 21, 1963; d. David Edwin and Judith Anne (Churchill) L. BA in Communication, Messiah Coll., Grantham, Pa., 1985. Washington editor Christianity Today Mag., 1987-92; religion editor United Press Internat., 1992-94; mng. editor News Network Internat., 1994-96. Co-author: In the Lion's Den, 1996; contbg. author:, Elizabeth Dole, 1991; interviewer Pres. George Bush on religion, 1991. Mem. House and Senate Periodical Press Gallery, Nat. Press Club.

LAWTON, LOIS, health facility administrator; b. Lucedale, Miss., Sept. 2, 1934; d. Floyd Jefferson and Ernestine (Cooley) Eubanks; m. Frank Willingham Lawton, Aug. 17, 1952; children: Deaver Lamar, Wesley Maxwell, Alice Sandra Lawton Hogue, Sarah Diane. Student, Clark Coll., 1952-53, Miss. Coll., 1953-54, Desoto C.C., 1969. Cert. health unit coord. Nat. Assn. Health Unit Coords. Kindergarden supr., tchr. Union Ave. Bapt. Ch., Memphis, 1967-73; health unit coord. Meth. South Hosp., Memphis, 1973-76, Richmond (Va.) Meml. Hosp., 1976-77; coord., trainer health unit coords. Henrico Drs. Hosp., Richmond, 1978-88, health unit coord., 1990—; presenter, coord. seminars in field. Editor newsletter Regional 8 Communicates, 1985-90, Chapter Chatter, 1990-93; author: The History of NAHUC, 1988. Mem. Nat. Assn. Health Unit Coords., Inc. (lead regional rep. 1985-90, regional rep. 1985-90, bd. dirs. 1985-95, treas. capital area chpt. 1989-95, chair various coms. 1990-93, mem. ad hoc task force 1990-93, mem. fiscal affairs com. 1990-95, pres.-elect 1990-93, pres., CEO 1993-95, Disting. Svc. award 1990). Baptist. Avocations: flower and vegetable gardening. Home: 11602 Lothbury Ln Richmond VA 23233-4025 Office: NAHUC 1211 Locust St Philadelphia PA 19107-5409

LAWTON, LORILEE ANN, pipeline supply company owner, accountant; b. Morrisville, Vt., July 17, 1947; d. Philip Wyman Sr. and Margaret Elaine (Ather) Noyes; m. Lee Henry Lawton, Dec. 6, 1969; children: Deborah Ann, Jeffrey Lee. BBA, U. Vt., 1969. Sr. acct., staff asst. IBM, Essex Junction, Vt., 1969-72; owner, pres., chmn. bd. Red-Hed Supply Inc, Colchester, Vt., 1972—; owner, treas. Firetech Sprinkler Corp., Colchester, 1992—; treas. Greater Burlington Indsl. Corp.; bd. dirs. Merchants Bank, Burlington, Cynosure Corp., Burlington, Sm. Bus. Devel. Ctr. Vt. Mem. Assn. Gen.

Contractors Am., Assn. Gen. Contractors Vt., Am. Water Works Assn., Vt. Water Works Assn., New Eng. Water Works Assn., No. Vt. Homebuilders Assn., Water and Sewer Distbrs. Am., Am. Fire Sprinkler Assn., Nat. Fire Protection Assn. Republican. Avocations: reading, gardening. Home: 53 Middle Rd Colchester VT 05446-1117 Office: Firetech Sprinkler Corp 1720 Hegeman Ave Colchester VT 05446-3173

LAWTON, NANCY, artist; b. Gilroy, Calif., Feb. 28, 1950; d. Edward Henry and Marilyn Kelly (Boyd) L.; m. Richard Enemark, Aug. 4, 1984; children: Faith Lawton, Forrest Lawton. BA in Fine Art, Calif. State U., San Jose, 1971; MFA, Mass. Coll. Art, 1980. artist-in-residence Villa Montalvo Ctr. Arts, Los Gatos, Calif., 1971, Noble & Greenough Sch., Dedham, Mass., 1990. One-woman shows include The Bklyn. Mus., 1983, Victoria Munroe Gallery, N.Y.C., 1993; group shows include San Francisco Mus. Modern Art, 1973, The Bklyn. Mus., 1980, 83, Staempfli Gallery, N.Y.C., 1984, The Ark. Art Ctr. Mus., Little Rock, 1984, 88, 92, 93, Victoria Munroe Gallery, 1985, 87, 88, 92, Butler Inst. Am. Art, Ohio, 1988, Smith Coll. Mus. Art, Mass., 1988, NAD, N.Y.C., 1988, Reynolds Gallery, Richmond, 1994, Nancy Solomon Gallery, Atlanta, 1995; public collections include The Ark. Art Ctr. Mus., Art Inst. Chgo., Bklyn. Mus., Nat. Mus. Am. Art, Smithsonian Inst., Washington. Scholar Mellon Found., 1982; N.Y. State Creative Artists grantee, 1983, N.Y. State Arts Devel. Fund grantee, 1989. Home and Office: 49 Monument Rd Orleans MA 02653-3511

LAWTON, THOMAS, art gallery director; b. Somerset, Mass., Feb. 5, 1931; s. John Henry and Beatrice Alice (Miller) L. B.S., Durfee Tech. Inst., 1953; M.F.A., U. Iowa, 1959; Ph.D., Harvard U., 1970. Asst. curator Freer Gallery Art, Washington, 1967-70, curator Chinese Art, 1970-71, asst. dir., 1971-77, dir., 1977-87; concomitant dir. Arthur M. Sackler Gallery, Washington, 1982-87, sr. rsch. scholar, 1987—. Author: Chinese Figure Painting, 1973, Chinese Art of the Warring States Period, 1983, New Perspectives on Chu Culture During the Eastern Zhou Period, 1991; co-author: Freer: A Legacy of Art, 1993; editor-in-chief Artibus Asiae, 1993—. Grantee Ford Found., 1959-61; grantee JDR 3d Fund (China), 1966-67; Fulbright fellow, 1963-66; scholar Harvard U., 1961-63. Club: Cosmos (Washington). Home: 420 4th St SE Washington DC 20003-2005 Office: Arthur M Sackler Gallery 1050 Independence Ave SE Washington DC 20560-3912

LAX, MELVIN, theoretical physicist; b. Bklyn., Mar. 8, 1922; s. Morris and Rose H. L.; m. Judith Heckelman, June 26, 1949; children: R. Laurie, David A., Jonathan R., Naomi A. B.A. in Physics (Charles Hayden scholar 1938-42), NYU, 1942; M.S. in Physics; M.S. (fellow in applied math. 1942-43), MIT, 1943, Ph.D. (fellow in physics 1943-46, research asso. 1946-47), 1947. Mem. faculty Syracuse (N.Y.) U., 1947-55, Princeton U., 1961, Oxford (Eng.) U., 1961-62; mem. tech. staff AT&T Bell Labs., Murray Hill, N.J., 1955-72; head theoretical physics research dept. Bell Labs., 1962-64, cons., 1972—; Disting. prof. physics CCNY, 1971—; cons. to govt. and industry. Author books and numerous papers in field; bd. editors Phys. Rev., 1958-60, 84-86; editor: Advanced Series in Applied Physics, 1988—; mem. adv. bd. Modern Physics Letters, Internat. Jour. Modern Physics; editorial bd. Quantum Optics, 1992-94. Fellow AAAS, Am. Phys. Soc. (publs. com. 1980-83); mem. NAS (sec. applied scis., math. engring. class 1989-92, 95-98), Am. Phys. Soc.-Chinese Phys. Soc. (telecom. com. 1995-96), Optical Soc. Am. (publs. tech. com. 1991-94, optics letters rev. com. 1995-96). Jewish. Home: 12 High St Summit NJ 07901-2413 Office: CCNY 138th St and Convent Ave New York NY 10031

LAX, PETER DAVID, mathematics educator; b. Budapest, Hungary, May 1, 1926; came to U.S., 1941, naturalized, 1944; s. Henry and Klara (Kornfeld) L.; m. Anneli Cahn, 1948; children: John, James D. BA, N.Y. U., 1947, PhD, 1949; DSc (hon.), Kent State U., 1976; DSC (hon.), Brown U., 1993; Dr. honoris causa, U. Paris, 1979; D. Natural Scis. (hon.), Technische Hochschule Aachen, Germany, 1988; DSc (hon.), Herriot Walt U., 1990; D. (hon.), Leningrad State U., 1991, U. Md. Baltimore County, 1993; PhD (hon.), Tel Aviv U., 1992, Beijing U., 1993. Asst. prof. NYU, 1949-57, prof., 1957—; dir. Courant Inst. Math. Scis., 1972-80. Author: (with Ralph Phillips) Scattering Theory, 1967, Scattering Theory for Automorphic Functions, 1976, (with A. Lax and S.Z. Burstein) Calculus with applications and computing, 1976, Hyperbolic Systems of Conservation Laws and the Mathematical Theory of Shock Waves, 1973, Linear Algebra, 1997. Mem. Pres.'s Com. on Nat. Medal of Sci., 1976, Nat. Sci. Bd., 1980-86. Served with AUS, 1944-46. Recipient Semmelweis medal Semmelweis Med. Soc., 1975, Nat. Medal Sci., 1986, Wolf Prize, 1987. Mem. AAAS, NAS (applied math. and numerical analysis award 1983), Am. Math. Soc. (pres. 1979-80, Norbert Wiener prize 1973, Leroy P. Steele prize 1993), Math. Assn. Am.. (bd. govs., Chauvenet prize 1974), Soc. Indsl. and Applied Math., Acad. des Scis. (fgn. assoc.), Russian Acad. Sci. (fgn. assoc.), Acad. Sinica (hon.), Hungarian Acad. Sci. (hon.), Moscow Math. Soc. (hon.), London Math. Soc. (hon.). Office: Courant Inst Math Scis 251 Mercer St Rm 912 New York NY 10012-1110

LAX, PHILIP, land developer, space planner; b. Newark, Apr. 22, 1920; s. Nathan and Beckie (Hirschhorn) L.; m. Mildred Baras, Feb. 15, 1948; children: Corinne, Barbara. B.S., NYU, 1940, postgrad., 1941-42. With Lax & Co., Newark, 1942-77; v.p. Lax & Co., 1950-77; pres. Chathill Mgmt., Inc., 1977—; cons. World Book of Am. Heritage, 1992. Pres. B'nai Brith Ctr., Rochester, Minn., 1965-70, now hon. pres.; trustee Rutgers U. Hillel; pres. B'nai Brith Rutgers U. Hillel Found. Bldg. Corp., 1969—; chmn. United Jewish Appeal, Maplewood, N.J., 1966, 76; mem. N.J. region exec. bd. Anti-Defamation League, mem. nat. community rels. bd.; mem. Gov.'s Conf. on Edn., N.J., 1966, Mayor's Budget Com., Maplewood, 1958-59; co-chmn. N.J. Opera Ball, 1977; trustee B'nai Brith Found., Washington, 1967—(Philip Lax Gallery of B'nai Brith History and Archives named for him in Philip Klutznick Mus., Room named in his honor Stern Sch. Econs.); co-chmn. B'nai Brith Internat. Coun., 1979, chmn., 1980-85, hon. chmn., apptd. chmn. internat. coun., 1990; voting del. to Jewish Agy., Jerusalem; ECOSOC mem. UN, representing coordinated Bd. Jewish Orgns.; attended UNESCO Conf. in Mex., 1982, with Internat. Coun. B'nai Brith and U.S.; trustee, mem. exec. com. N.J. sect. NCCJ, 1981; trustee Henry Monsky Found., Washington, 1968—; trustee Leo N. Levi Hosp., Hot Springs, Ark., 1968-71, B'nai Brith World Jewish Ctr., Jerusalem, 1982, Nat. Arthrities Hosp., 1976—, N.Y. Statue of Liberty Centennial Found., Touro Synagogue, Newport, R.I., 1996—; hon. trustee Arts Coun. of Suburban Essex, N.J., 1980; mem. Econ. Devel. Commn., Twp. of Maplewood, 1979—; mem. steering com. to Restore Ellis Island, 1977—; nat. pres. Ellis Island Restoration Commn., 1978—, responsible for planning, funding and operating Family History Ctr. on Ellis Island; appointed to planning team of Statue of Liberty and Ellis Island by Nat. Park Service, Dept. of Interior; mem. Statue of Liberty/Ellis Island Centennial Commn., Statue of Liberty-Ellis Island Centennial Commn., Com. of Architecture and Restoration of Statue of Liberty-Ellis Island, past chmn.. Decorated cavaliere ufficiale Order of Merit of the Republic of Italy; recipient Found. award B'nai Brith, 1968, Humanitarian award, 1969, Pres.'s Gold medal, 1975; Pro Mundi Beneficio medal Brazilian Acad. Humanities, 1976; Philip Lax chapel at Rutgers U. Hillel named in his honor; honored by N.J. State Senate. Mem. Am. Soc. Interior Designers, Nat. Soc. Interior Designers (trustee 1970-73), Am. Arbitration Assn., Am. Jewish Hist. Com. (v.p.), Am. Jewish Hist. Soc. (trustee 1984), Am. Soc. Israel Philatelists, Masons (32 deg.), Shriners, B'nai Brith (v.p. Supreme Lodge 1968-71, internat. bd. govs. 1971—, mem. exec. com. of internat. coun.), NYU Club (founder 1956), Nat. Press Club. Room named in honor Stern Sch. Econs. Home: 35 Claremont Dr Maplewood NJ 07040-2119 Office: Chathill Mgmt 40 Main St Chatham NJ 07928-2402

LAXMINARAYANA, DAMA, geneticist, researcher, educator; b. Hyderabad, India, Apr. 20, 1953; came to U.S., 1990; s. Kishtaiah and Sathyamma; m. Dara Jayalakshmi; children: Dama Bhargavi, Dama Sriharsha. BSc, Osmania U., Hyderabad, 1974, MSc, 1976, PhD, 1982. Jr. sci. asst. dept. genetics Osmania U., 1977-78, lectr. dept. zoology, 1985-90; jr. rsch. fellow Indian Dept. Atomic Energy, 1978-81, postdoctoral fellow, 1982-83, rsch. assoc., 1983-85; postdoctoral fellow dept. medicine Case Western Res. U. Sch. Medicine, Cleve., 1990-91; rsch. assoc. dept. internal medicine Bowman Gray Sch. Medicine, Wake Forest U., Winston-Salem, N.C., 1991-94, rsch. instr., 1994—; conf. presenter in field. Contbr. articles to sci. jours., chpts. to books. Recipient internat. award Tata Meml. Trust, 1985; grantee Univ. Grants Commn. india, 1988-90, Lupus Found. Am., 1993-95, 96—. Mem. AAAS, Environ. Mutagen Soc. India, India Soc. Cell Biology, Soc. Geneticists and Cytologists India, N.Y. Acad. Scis. Home: 230 Melrose St Apt D Winston Salem NC 27103-1950 Office: Bowman Gray Sch Medicine Dept Internal Medicine Medical Center Blvd Winston Salem NC 27157

LAY, DONALD POMEROY, federal judge; b. Princeton, Ill., Aug. 24, 1926; s. Hardy W. and Ruth (Cushing) L.; m. Miriam Elaine Gustafson, Aug. 6, 1949; children: Stephen Pomeroy (dec.), Catherine Sue, Cynthia Lynn, Elizabeth Ann, Deborah Jean, Susan Elaine. Student, U.S. Naval Acad., 1945-46; BA, U. Iowa, 1948, JD, 1951; LLD (hon.), Mitchell Coll. Law, 1985. Bar: Nebr. 1951, Iowa 1951, Wis. 1953. Assoc. Kennedy, Holland, DeLacy & Svoboda, Omaha, 1951-53, Quarles, Spence & Quarles, Milw., 1953-54, Eisenstatt, Lay, Higgins & Miller, 1954-66; judge U.S. Ct. Appeals (8th cir.), 1966—, chief judge, 1980-92, senior judge, 1992—; faculty mem. on evidence Nat. Coll. Trial Judges, 1964-65, U. Minn. Law Sch., William Mitchell Law Sch.; mem. U.S. Jud. Conf., 1980-92. Mem. editorial bd.: Iowa Law Rev., 1950-51; contbr. articles to legal jours. With USNR, 1944-46. Recipient Hancher-Finkbine medal U. Iowa, 1980. Fellow Internat. Acad. Trial Lawyers; mem. ABA, Nebr. Bar Assn., Iowa Bar Assn., Wis. Bar Assn., Am. Judicature Soc., Assn. Trial Lawyers Am. (bd. govs. 1963-65, Jud. Achievement award), Order of Coif, Delta Sigma Rho (Significant Sig award 1986, Herbert Harley award 1988), Phi Delta Phi, Sigma Chi. Presbyterian. Office: US Ct Appeals 8th Cir Rm 560 316 Robert St N Ste 560 Saint Paul MN 55101-1423

LAY, ELIZABETH MARIAN, health association administrator; b. Reading, Eng., Oct. 11, 1949; d. John Hunter and Brigid Mary (Maas) L. BS in Biology, SUNY, Albany, 1976; Cert. in Exec. Devel., George Washington U., 1989. mem. adv. coun. No. Va. Mental Health Inst.; puppeteer Smithsonian Instn., 1970-71. Sec. Touche Ross & Co., Washington, 1971-73, para-cons., 1974-75, assoc. cons., 1975-82; fin. systems liason Student Loan Mktg. Assn., Washington, 1982-84, mgr. fin. systems, 1985-87, dir. fin. systems, 1988-95. Mem. Am. Assn. Suicidology, Nat. Mental Health Assn. (life, pres. 1994-95), Alexandria Mental Health Assn. (pres. 1984-86, 95-96, treas. 1993-94, exec. dir. 1996—, Disting. Svc. award 1994), Am. Mensa, Mental Health Assn. in Alexandria (exec. dir.). Democrat. Avocations: antique Worcester collecting, pen collecting, music composition, suicide intervention training.

LAY, KENNETH LEE, diversified energy company executive; b. Tyrone, Mo., Apr. 15, 1942; s. Omer and Ruth E. (Reese) L.; m. Linda Ann Phillips, July 10, 1982; children: Robyn Anne, Mark Kenneth, Todd David, Elizabeth Ayers, Robert Ray. BA, U. Mo., 1964, MA, 1965; PhD, U. Houston, 1970. Corp. economist Exxon Corp., Houston, 1965-68; asst. prof. and lectr. in econs. George Washington U., 1969-73; tech. asst. to commr. FERC, 1971-72; dep. undersec. for energy Dept. Interior, 1972-74; v.p. Fla. Gas Co. (now Continental Resources Co.), Winter Park, Fla., 1974-76, pres., 1976-79; exec. v.p. The Continental Group, 1979-81; pres., chief operating officer, dir. Transco Energy Co., Houston, 1981-84; chmn., chief exec officer Houston Natural Gas Corp., 1984-85; pres., chief exec. officer, chief operating officer, dir. HNG/InterNorth (now Enron Corp.), Omaha, 1985—, also chmn. bd. dirs., Houston; asst. prof. George Washington U.; bd. dirs. Eli Lilly & Co., Trust Co. West, Compaq Computer Corp.; past chmn. Greater Houston Partnership. Former chmn. bd. regents U. Houston; bd. trustees The H. John Heinz III Ctr. for Sci., Econs. & the Environment, The Bus. Coun., Am. Enterprise Inst.; Houston Host Com. for 1992 Rep. Nat. Conv.; co-chmn. 1990 Houston Econ. Summit Host. Com. Decorated Navy Commendation award; recipient Pvt. Sector Coun. Leadership award, 1997; N.A.M. fellow; State Farm fellow; Guggenheim fellow; named one of 25 Top Mgrs., Bus. Week. Mem. Nat. Petroleum Coun., River Oaks Country Club, Phi Beta Kappa. Republican. Methodist. Office: Enron Corp PO Box 1188 Houston TX 77251-1188

LAY, NORVIE LEE, law educator; b. Cardwell, Ky., Apr. 17, 1940; s. Arlie H. and Opha (Burns) L.; 1 dau., Lea Anne. B.S., U. Ky., 1960; J.D., U. Louisville, 1963; LL.M. (Cook fellow), U. Mich., 1964, S.J.D., 1967. Bar: Ky. 1963. Asst. prof. law U. Louisville, 1964-67, assoc. prof., 1967-70, prof., 1970—; asst. dean U. Louisville (Sch. Law), 1971-73, assoc. dean, 1973-84, acting dean, 1981-82; vis. prof. Southwestern U. Sch. Law, summer 1983, N.Y. Law Sch., 1983-84, Coll. of Law U. Iowa, summer 1989. Author: Tax and Estate Planning for Community Property and the Migrant Client, 1970; contbr. articles to profl. jours. Trustee St. Joseph's Infirmary, 1974-78, S.W. Jefferson Community Hosp., 1979-80, Suburban Hosp., 1981-84, Humana-Audubon Hosp., 1985-88, U. Louisville Law Sch. Alumni Found., from 1982-85; bd. dirs. Louisville Ballet, from 1982-88, Louisville Theatrical Assn., 1985-88, Louisville Art Gallery, 1984-87, Watertower Art Assn., 1986-89, Chamber Mus. Soc. of Louisville, 1985-88, Louisville Chorus, 1985-88, Ky. Contemporary Theatre, 1984, Ky. Country Day Sch., 1985-88, Ky. Arts Coun., 1991—; mem. Nat. Conf. Commrs. Uniform State Laws. Recipient Scholarship Key Delta Theta Phi, 1963, Outstanding Graduating Sr. award Omicron Delta Kappa, 1963. Fellow Am. Coll. of Trust and Estate Counsel (acad.), Am. Coll. Tax Counsel; mem. ABA, Ky. Bar Assn., Louisville Bar Assn., Am. Judicature Soc. Republican. Baptist. Office: U Louisville Sch Law Belknap Campus Louisville KY 40292

LAY, THORNE, geosciences educator; b. Casper, Wyo., Apr. 20, 1956; s. Johnny Gordon and Virginia Florence (Lee) L. BS, U. Rochester, 1978; MS, Calif. Inst. Tech., 1980, PhD, 1983. Rsch. assoc. Calif. Inst. Tech., Pasadena, 1983; asst. prof. geosciences U. Mich., Ann Arbor, 1984-88, assoc. prof., 1988-89; prof. U. Calif., Santa Cruz, 1989—; cons. Woodward Clyde cons., Pasadena, 1982-84; dir. Inst. Tectonics, 1990-94, chmn. earth sci. dept., 1994—. Author: Structure and Fate of Subducting Slabs, 1997; co-author: (with T.C. Wallace) Modern Global Seismology, 1995; contbr. over 130 articles to profl. jours. NSF fellow, 1978-81, Guttenberg fellow Calif. Inst. Tech., 1978, Lilly fellow Eli Lilly Found., 1984, Sloan fellow, 1985-87, Presidential Young Investigator, 1985-90. Fellow Royal Astron. Soc., Am. Geophys. Union (Macelwane medal 1991), Soc. Exploration Geophysicist, Seismol. Soc. Am., AAAS. Home: 32 Eastridge Dr Santa Cruz CA 95060-1803 Office: U Calif Santa Cruz Earth Sci Bd Santa Cruz CA 95064

LAYBOURNE, EVERETT BROADSTONE, lawyer; b. Springfield, Ohio, Oct. 26, 1911; s. Lawrence Everett and Jean (Broadstone) L.; m. Dorrise Barclay, Sept. 19, 1936 (dec. Nov. 1973); m. Ottilie Kruger, July 31, 1974. B.A., Ohio State U., 1932; J.D., Harvard, 1935. Bar: Calif. bar 1936. Mem. firms Macdonald, Schultheis & Pettit, 1936-40; mem. firms Schultheis & Laybourne, 1940-54, Schultheis, Laybourne & Dowds, 1954-68, Laybourne, Keeley & MacMahon, 1968-69; sr. partner Macdonald, Halsted & Laybourne, Los Angeles, 1969-88; of counsel Baker & McKenzie, Los Angeles, 1988-93; dir. Viking Industries, Pacific Energy Corp., McBain Instruments, Coldwater Investment Co., Brouse-Whited Packaging Co., Calif. Energy Co. Trustee Brite-Lite Corp. Calif.; Calif. chmn. UN Day, 1960; regional vice chmn. U.S. Com. for UN, 1961-64; mem. adv. council Stamp Out Smog, 1963-75; mem. spl. rev. com. Los Angeles Air Pollution Control Dist., 1964-65; Bd. dirs. Fedn. Hillside, Canyon Assos., Los Angeles, 1952-59, chmn. bd., 1957-59; bd. dirs. WAIF, Inc., 1977—, chmn. bd., 1978—; bd. dirs. UN Assn. U.S.A., 1964-65; bd. dirs. Ralph M. Parsons Found., 1977—, v.p., 1978—; trustee, sec. Beta Theta Pi Scholastic Found. So. Calif., 1947-58. Served as lt. USNR, 1944-46. Recipient Commendation Los Angeles City Council, 1957, Ohio State U. Alumni Centennial award, 1970, Alumni Citizenship award, 1988. Mem. Big Ten Univs. Club So. Calif. (pres. 1941-42, Man of Yr. 1997), L.A. Bar Assn. (exec. com. internat. law sect. 1968-74), World Affairs Coun., Selden Soc., Roscomare Valley Assn. (pres. 1952-54), Calif. Club, Bel-Air Country Club, Phi Beta Kappa. Republican. Episcopalian (sr. warden 1966-67). Office: 555 W 5th St Fl 35 Los Angeles CA 90013-1010

LAYBOURNE, GERALDINE, broadcasting executive; b. Plainfield, N.J., 1947; married; 2 children. BA, Vassar Coll., 1969; MS, U. Pa., 1971. Former high sch. tchr.; with Nickelodeon, 1980—, creator Nick at Nite, 1985—, pres.; also vice chmn. MTV Networks; now pres. Disney/ABC Cable Networks, N.Y.C. Office: 77 W 66th St New York NY 10023-6201

LAYCOCK, HAROLD DOUGLAS, law educator, writer; b. Alton, Ill., Apr. 15, 1948; s. Harold Francis and Claudia Anita (Garrette) L.; m. Teresa A. Sullivan, June 14, 1971; children: Joseph Peter, John Patrick. BA, Mich. State U., 1970; JD, U. Chgo., 1973. Bar: Ill. 1973, U.S. Dist. Ct. (no. dist.) Ill. 1973, Tex. 1974, U.S. Dist. Ct. (we. dist.) Tex. 1975, U.S. Ct. Appeals (5th and 11th cirs.) 1975, U.S. Supreme Ct. 1976, U.S. Ct. Appeals (6th cir.) 1987, U.S. Ct. Appeals (8th cir.) 1994. Law clk. to judge U.S. Ct. Appeals (7th cir.), Chgo., 1973-74; pvt. practice Austin, Tex., 1974-76; asst. prof. U. Chgo., 1976-80, prof., 1980-81; prof. U. Tex., Austin, 1980—, endowed professorships, 1983-88, assoc. dean for acad. affairs, 1985-86, endowed chair, 1988—, assoc. dean for rsch., 1991—; vis. prof. U. Mich., 1990; reporter com. on motion practice Ill. Jud. Conf., 1977-78. Author: Modern American Remedies, 1985, 2d edit., 1994, The Death of the Irreparable Injury Rule, 1991; mem. bd. advisors Religious Freedom Reporter, 1990—; contbr. articles to law revs. Mem. adv. bd. Consumer Svcs. Orgn., Chgo., 1979-80; mem. exec. bd. Ctr. for Ch./State Studies, DePaul U., Chgo., 1982-87; mem. adv. com. on religious liberty Presbyn. Ch. U.S.A., 1983-88, advisor restatement of restitution, 1984-85, 97—; v.p. St. Francis Sch., 1990-92, pres. 1992—; mem. bd. advisors J.M. Dawson Inst. Ch./State Studies, Baylor U., 1990—. Fellow AAAS, Internat. Acad. for Freedom of Religion and Belief; mem. AAUP (mem. com. on status of women in acad. profession 1982-85), Am. Law Inst., Chgo. Coun. Lawyers (v.p. 1977-78), Assn. Am. Law Schs. (chmn., sec. on remedies 1983, 94). Home: 4203 Woodway Dr Austin TX 78731-2034 Office: U Tex Law Sch 727 E 26th St Austin TX 78705-3224

LAYCRAFT, JAMES HERBERT, judge; b. Veteran, Alta., Can., Jan. 5, 1924; s. George Edward and Hattie (Cogswell) L.; m. Helen Elizabeth Bradley, May 1, 1948; children: James B., Anne L. BA, U. Alta., Edmonton, 1950; LLB, U. Alta., 1951; LLD (hon.), U. Calgary, Alta., 1986. Bar: Alta. Barrister Nolan Chambers & Co., Calgary, 1952-75; justice trial div. Supreme Ct. of Alta., Calgary, 1975-79; justice Ct. of Appeal of Alta., Calgary, 1979-85, chief justice of Alta., 1985-91, ret., 1991. Contbr. articles to law jours. Served to lt. Royal Can. Arty., 1941-46, PTO. Mem. United Ch. of Can. Avocations: amateur radio, fishing.

LAYDEN, FRANCIS PATRICK (FRANK LAYDEN), professional basketball team executive, former coach; b. Bklyn., Jan. 5, 1932; m. Barbara Layden; children: Scott, Michael, Katie. Student, Niagara U. High sch. basketball coach L.I., N.Y.; head coach, athletic dir. Adelphi-Suffolk Coll. (now Dowling Coll.); head basketball coach, athletic dir. Niagara U., Niagara Falls, N.Y., 1968-76; asst. coach Atlanta Hawks, 1976-79; gen. mgr. Utah Jazz, Salt Lake City, 1979-88, head coach, 1981-88, v.p. basketball ops., until 1988, pres., 1989—. Bd. dirs. Utah Soc. Prevention Blindness; bd. dirs. Utah chpt. Multiple Sclerosis Soc., Utah Spl. Olympics. Served to 1st lt. Signal Corps, AUS. Office: Utah Jazz Delta Ctr 301 W South Temple Salt Lake City UT 84101-1216*

LAYDEN, LYNN MCVEY, lawyer; b. Mpls., June 15, 1941; d. David Hugh and Adelyn Martha (Dvorak) McVey; m. Charles Max Layden, Jan. 28, 1967; children: David Charles, Kathleen Ann, John Michael, Daniel Joseph. LBA, Carleton Coll., Northfield, Minn., 1963; JD, Ind. u., 1967. Bar: Ind. 1967, U.S. Dist. Ct. (so. and no. dists.) 1967. Assoc. Vaughan, Vaughan & Layden, Lafayette, Ind., 1967-86; ptnr. Layden & Layden, Lafayette, Ind., 1986—; guardian ad litem Superior Ct. III-Juvenile Ct., Lafayette, 1986-96. Pres. devel. coun. Ivy Tech. State Coll., 1993—; pres. bd. trustees West Lafayette Sch. Corp., 1988-95. Mem. ABA, Ind. Bar Assn., Tippecanoe County Bar Assn., Order of Coif, Phi Beta Kappa. Home: 2826 Ashland St West Lafayette IN 47906-1510 Office: Layden & Layden Bank 1 Bldg Ste 712 Lafayette IN 47901

LAYISH, DANIEL T., internist. BA magna cum laude, Boston U., 1986, MD magna cum laude, 1990. Diplomate Am. Bd. Internal Medicine, Nat. Bd. Med. Examiners; ACLS, Advanced Trauma Life Support. Intern/resident, dept. internal medicine Barnes Hosp., St. Louis, 1990-93; pulmonary/critical care/sleep medicine fellow Duke U. Med. Ctr., Durham, N.C., 1994-97; critical care staff, assoc. med. staff Christian Hosp. Northeast, St. Louis, 1993-94; staff, Urgent Care Clinic Carolina Permanente, Raleigh, N.C., 1994-96. Contbr. articles to profl. jours. Recipient Med. Grad. award, Hewlett-Packard Co., 1990, Young Investigator and Alfred Soffer Rsch. awards, Am. Coll. Chest Physicians, 1995. Mem. AMA, ACP, Am. Thoracic Soc. (assoc.), Am. Coll. Chest Physicians (affiliate), Alpha Omega Alpha. Home: 5202-B Penrith Dr Durham NC 27713-1724 Office: Duke Univ Med Ctr Divsn Pulmonary/Crit Care Durham NC 27710

LAYMAN, DALE PIERRE, medical educator, author, researcher; b. Niles, Mich., July 3, 1948; s. Pierre Andre and Delphine Lucille (Lenke) L.; m. Kathleen Ann Jackowiak, Aug. 8, 1970; children: Andrew Michael, Alexis Kathryn, Allison Victoria, Amanda Elizabeth. AS in Life Sci., Lake Mich. Coll., 1968; BS in Anthropology and Zoology, U. Mich., 1971, MS in Physiology, 1974; EdS in Physiology and Health Sci., Ball State U., 1979; PhD in Health and Safety Studies, U. Ill., 1986. Histological technician in neuropathology Med. Sch. U. Mich., Ann Arbor, 1971-72, tchg. fellow in human physiology Med. Sch., 1972-74; instr. in human anatomy, physiology, and histology Lake Superior State U., Sault Ste. Marie, Mich., 1974-75; prof. med. terminology, human anatomy and physiology Joliet (Ill.) Jr. Coll., 1975—. Author: The Terminology of Anatomy and Physiology, 1983, The Medical Language: A Programmed Body-Systems Approach, 1995; contbr. articles to profl. jours. Mem. AAAS, Human Anatomy and Physiology Soc., Text and Acad. Authors Assn., Inc., Ill. Cmty. Coll. Faculty Assn., Phi Kappa Phi, Kappa Delta Pi. Avocations: running, swimming, reading motivational literature. Home: 509 Westridge Ln Joliet IL 60431-4883 Office: Joliet Jr Coll 1215 Houbolt Rd Joliet IL 60431-8938

LAYMAN, EMMA MCCLOY (MRS. JAMES W. LAYMAN), psychologist, educator; b. Danville, Va., Feb. 25, 1910; d. Charles Harold and Anna (Fisher) McCloy; m. James Walter Layman, Dec. 12, 1936 (dec. May 5, 1978). A.B., Oberlin Coll., 1930; M.A., NYU, 1931; Ph.D., U. Iowa, 1937; L.H.D. (hon.), Iowa Wesleyan Coll., 1981. Diplomate: Am. Bd. Examiners Profl. Psychology. Psychol. examiner Iowa Psychopathic Hosp., Iowa City, 1934-35, 37; clin. psychologist Mich. Children's Inst., Ann Arbor, 1935-36; supr. psychol. services Iowa Bd. Social Welfare, Des Moines, 1937-41; assoc. prof. psychology Woman's Coll., U. N.C., 1947-52; supervisory clin. psychologist Brooke Army Hosp., Ft. Sam Houston, 1952-54; chief psychologist Children's Hosp., Washington, 1954-60; head dept. psychology Iowa Wesleyan Coll., Mt. Pleasant, 1960-75, assoc. prof., 1960-61, prof., 1961-75, emeritus, 1975—, asst. acad. dean, 1964-65, chmn. social sci. div., 1969-75, dir. East Asian Inst., 1963-75, dir. internat. studies, 1970-75; pvt. practice clin. psychology, 1941—; lectr. U. Chattanooga, 1946-47; vis. prof. edn. Duke, summers 1948-50; adj. prof. Am. U., 1954-60; lectr. Howard U., 1956-60; cons. Walter Reed Army Hosp., 1956-60. Author: Mental Health Through Physical Education and Recreation, 1955, Airesboro Castle, 1974, Buddhism in America, 1976, also articles. Pres. Oberlin-Wellington bd. Ch. Women United; bd. dirs. Intergenerational House; v.p. class of 1930 Oberlin Coll., also mem. alumni coun.; mem. Spectrum Community Club. Lt. USNR, 1943-46. Fellow APA, Acad. Clin. Psychology, Sigma Xi; mem. AAUW, Am. Assn. Chinese Studies, Phi Beta Kappa. Episcopalian. Home: 154 Kendal Dr Oberlin OH 44074-1907

LAYMAN, LAWRENCE, naval officer; b. Laclede County, Mo., Oct. 28, 1930; s. Archibald A. and Zoe Ellen (Hoke) L.; m. Carmen Elizabeth Meyer, Oct. 5, 1953; children: Linda Carmen, Lawrence, Harry Arthur, John Robert. B.S., U.S. Naval Acad., 1952; M.S. in Internat. Affairs, George Washington U., 1972. Commd. ensign U.S. Navy, 1952, advanced through grades to rear adm., 1979; service to Korea and Vietnam; dep. comdr. Naval Telecommunications Command, 1978-79; dir. command, control and communications systems U.S. European Command, 1979-81; vice dir. Def. Communications Agy., Washington, 1981-83; dir. Naval Communications, Washington, 1983-86; dir. space command and control Office Chief Naval Ops., Washington, 1986-89, ret., 1989. Decorated D.S.M., Def. Superior Svc. medal with oak leaf cluster, Legion of Merit with Gold Star, Bronze Star with combat V, Meritorious Svc. medal. Home: 3429 Silver Maple Pl Falls Church VA 22042-3545

LAYMAN, WILLIAM ARTHUR, psychiatrist, educator; b. West New York, N.J., Feb. 8, 1929; s. Frank Kyle and Lucy Geraldine (Rooney) L.; 1 child, William Kraft. Student, NYU, 1946, 48; B.S. cum laude, St. Peter's Coll., 1951; M.D., Georgetown U., 1955. Diplomate: Am. Bd. Psychiatry and Neurology. Intern Hackensack (N.J.) Hosp., 1955-56; resident in psychiatry Lyons (N.J.) VA Hosp., 1956-57, Fairfield Hills Hosp., Newtown, Conn., 1957-58; fellow in psychiatry Yale U., 1958-59; instr. psychiatry

Seton Hall Coll. Medicine, 1959-61, asst. prof., 1961-65; assoc. prof. psychiatry N.J. Med. Sch., Newark, 1965-74; clin. prof. N.J. Med. Sch., 1974-77, prof., 1977—; practice medicine specializing in psychiatry Hackensack, NJ, 1959—; dep. chmn. ednl. services, dept. psychiatry and mental health sci. N.J. Med. Sch., 1976-83, acting chmn. dept. psychiatry and mental health sci., 1983-86; cons. Hackensack Hosp.; mem. staff Coll. Hosp. Contbr. articles to profl. jours. Served with U.S. Army, 1946-48. Fellow Am. Psychiat. Assn. (life); mem. AAUP, N.J. Med. Soc., Bergen County Med. Soc. Office: UMDNJ Univ Hosp G-Yellow #G/300 150 Bergen St Newark NJ 07103-2406

LAYNE, JAMES NATHANIEL, vertebrate biologist; b. Chgo., May 16, 1926; s. Leslie Joy and Harriet (Hausmann) L.; m. Lois Virginia Linderoth, Aug. 26, 1950; children: Linda Carrie, Kimberly, Jamie Linderoth, Susan Nell, Rachel Pratt. BA, Cornell U., 1950, PhD, 1954. Grad. teaching asst. Cornell U., Ithaca, N.Y., 1950-54; asso. prof. zoology Cornell U., 1963-67; asst. prof. zoology So. Ill. U., Carbondale, 1954-55; asst. prof., then asso. prof. biology U. Fla., 1955-63; asst. curator, then asso. curator mammals Fla. State Mus., Gainesville, 1955-63; research asso. Fla. State Mus., 1963-65; dir. research, then exec. dir. Archbold Biol. Sta.; Archbold curator mammals Am. Mus. Natural History, 1967-85; sr. rsch. biologist Archbold Biol. Sta., 1985-94, sr. rsch. biologist emeritus, 1994—; rsch. assoc. Fla. State Collection of Arthropods, Am. Mus. Natural History; vis. scientist primate ecology sect. Nat. Inst. Neurol. Diseases and Blindness, summers 1961-62. Contbr. articles and chpt. to profl. jours. and books. Hon. trustee Fla. Defenders of Environment; bd. dirs. Fla. Audubon Soc.; mem. Fla. Nongame Wildlife Adv. Council, Peace River Basin Bd., Fla. Panther Tech. Adv. Council. Served with USAAF, 1944-46. Fellow AAAS; mem. Am. Soc. Zoologists, Am. Soc. Mammalogists (pres. 1970-72, hon. mem. 1993, C. Hart Merriam award 1976), Ecol. Soc. Am., Soc. for Study of Evolution, Am. Soc. Naturalists, Wildlife Soc., Wildlife Disease Assn., Nature Conservancy (trustee Fla. chpt.), Fla. Acad. Scis. (pres. 1984-85, medalist 1995), Orgn. Biol. Field Stas. (pres. 1986-87), Phi Beta Kappa, Sigma Xi, Phi Kappa Phi, Phi Sigma. Office: Archbold Biol Sta PO Box 2057 Lake Placid FL 33862-2057

LAYSON, WILLIAM MCINTYRE, research consulting company executive; b. Lexington, Ky., Sept. 24, 1934; s. Zed Clark and Louise (McIntyre) L.; m. Robin Dale Fort, July 28, 1982. B.S., MIT, 1956, Ph.D., 1961; postgrad., U. Sydney, Australia, 1957-58. Research scientist European Ctr. Nuclear Research, Geneva, 1960-62; research scientist U. Calif.-Berkeley, 1962-64; mem. tech. staff Pan Am World Airways, Patrick AFB, Fla., 1964-67; research scientist Gen. Research Corp., Rosslyn, Va., 1967-70; dir. Sci. Applications Internat. Corp., McLean, Va., 1970—, sr. v.p., chmn. incentives com., 1975-93; coord. def. nuclear programs, 1975—, chmn. ethics com., 1994—; pres. Langley Sch., 1995-97; dir. Langley Sch., 1992-97; pres. Layson's Buffalo Trace Farms, 1976—. Fulbright scholar U. Sydney, Australia, 1957-58. Mem. Am. Def. Preparedness Assn. Democrat. Presbyterian (elder). Avocations: church activities, jogging, swimming, skiing. Home: 8301 Summerwood Dr Mc Lean VA 22102-2213 Office: Sci Applications Internat Corp 1710 Goodridge Dr Mc Lean VA 22102-3701

LAYTON, BILLY JIM, composer; b. Corsicana, Tex., Nov. 14, 1924; s. Roy William and Jimmie Vera (Franks) L.; m. Evro Zeniou, Feb. 2, 1949; children: Alexis Roy, Daphne Niobe. Mus.B., New Eng. Conservatory Music, 1948; Mus.M., Yale U., 1950; postgrad. (Alfred M. Hertz Travelling fellow), U. Calif. at Berkeley, 1954; Ph.D., Harvard U., 1960. Faculty New Eng. Conservatory Music, 1959-60, Harvard U., 1960-66; prof. State U. N.Y. at Stony Brook, 1966-92, chmn. dept. music, 1966-72, 82-85. Composer: Five Studies for Violin and Piano, 1952, An American Portrait; symphonic overture, 1953, Three Dylan Thomas Poems; mixed chorus, brass sextet, 1954-56, String Quartet in Two Movements, 1956, Three Studies for Piano, 1957, Divertmento, 1958-60, Dance Fantasy for Orchestra, 1964. Rome Prize fellow, 1954-57; grantee Nat. Inst. Arts and Letters, 1958; Guggenheim fellow, 1963; grantee Thorne Music Fund, 1968-70; Recipient Creative Arts award Brandeis U., 1961. Mem. Am. Music Center (dir. 1972-74), Am. Soc. Univ. Composers (founding), A.S.C.A.P., Am. Musicological Soc., Coll. Music Soc. (mem. council 1970-72), Internat. Soc. Contemporary Music (dir. U.S.A. sect. 1968-70), Soc. for Music Theory (founding). Home: 1105 Massachusetts Ave Ste 10A Cambridge MA 02138-5217

LAYTON, HARRY CHRISTOPHER, artist, lecturer; b. Safford, Ariz., Nov. 17, 1938; s. Christopher E. and Eurilda (Welker) L.; LHD, Sussex Coll., Eng., 1969; DFA (hon.), London Inst. Applied Research, 1972, DSc (hon), 1972; DD (hon.), St. Matthew U., Ohio, 1970, PhD (hon.), 1970; m. Karol Barbara Kendall, July 11, 1964 (div. Jan. 1989); children: Deborah, Christopher, Joseph, Elisabeth, Faith, Aaron, Gretchen, Benjamin, Justin, Matthew, Peter. Cert. clin. hypnotherapist. Pres. Poems, Art & Myths; pres., CEO Layton Studio Graphic Design; lectr. ancient art Serra Cath. High Sch., 1963-64, L.A. Dept. Parks and Recreation, summer 1962, 63, 64; interior decorator Cities of Hawthorne, Lawndale, Compton, Gardena and Torrance (Calif.), 1960-68; one-man shows paintings; Nahas Dept. Stores, 1962, 64; group shows include: Gt. Western Savs. & Loan, Lawndale, Calif., 1962, Gardena (Calif.) Adult Sch., 1965, Serra Cath. High Sch., Gardena, 1963, Salon de Nations Paris, 1983; represented in permanent collections: Sussex Coll., Eng., Gardena Masonic Lodge, Culver City-Foshey Masonic Lodge, Gt. Western Savs. & Loan; paintings include: The Fairy Princess, 1975, Nocturnal Covenant, 1963, Blindas Name, 1962, Creation, 1962. Elder Ch. of Jesus Christ of Latter-day Saints, Santa Monica, Calif., 1963—; works pub. in Our World's Favorite Gold and Silver Poems, 1991, Our World's Favorite Poems, 1993, World's Best Poems, 1993, Outstanding Poets of 1994, Best Poems of 1995, others; appt. dep. dir. gen. IBC for the Ams., Cambridge, Eng., 1990. Editor's Choice award Nat. Libr. of Poetry, 1994, 95. Mem. Am. Hypnotherapy Assn., Nat. Notary Assn., Internat. Soc. Artists, Internat. Platform Assn., Am. Security Council, Soc. for Early Historic Archaeology, Am. Councilor's Soc. of Psychol. Counselors, Le Salon Des Nation Paris Geneva, Ctr. Internat. d'Art Contemporain, Internat. Soc. Poets (disting.), Internat. Masonic Poetry Soc., Am. Legion, Masons (32 deg.), Shriners, K.T., Alpha Psi Omega. Republican. Home and Office: Layton Studio Graphic Design Inc 3654 Centinela Ave Apt 10 Los Angeles CA 90066-3147

LAYTON, JOHN C., federal agency administrator; b. East Stroudsburg, Pa., Oct. 9, 1944; s. Charles O. and Jeanne (Carlton) L.; m. Laura Bick, June 8, 1991; children: Gwen Ann, Susan Carlton. BS in Commerce, Rider Coll., 1966. Auditor Litton Industries, East Orange, N.J., 1969-72; spl. agt. FBI, Washington, 1972-80; dep. inspector gen. NASA, Washington, 1983-84; inspector gen. U.S. Dept. Treasury, Washington, 1984-86, U.S. Dept. Energy, Washington, 1986—. Served to 1st lt. U.S. Army, 1966-69. Mem. Assn. Govt. Accts. (chmn. ethics bd. 1985), Fed. Investigators Assn. (treas. 1982, bd. dirs. 1983-85), Soc. of Former Agts. of the FBI. Methodist. Office: Dept of Energy Inspector Gen 1000 Independence Ave SW Washington DC 20585-0001

LAYTON, ROBERT, lawyer; b. N.Y.C., Feb. 19, 1931; s. Benjamin and Ruth (Beck) L.; m. Joan Levy, May 17, 1967 (div. Jan. 1876); children: Elisabeth, Julie; m. Christine Lambert, Dec. 31, 1988. BA, U. Mich., 1951; LLB, Yale U., 1954. Teaching fellow Stanford Law Sch., Palo Alto, Calif., 1957-58; atty. U.S. Dept. Justice, Washington, 1958-62; assoc., ptnr. Gilbert, Segall & Young, N.Y.C., 1962-73; ptnr. Layton and Sherman, N.Y.C., 1973-84, Surrey & Morse, N.Y.C., 1984-85, Jones, Day, Reavis & Pogue, N.Y.C., 1986-93. Contbr. articles to internat. profl. jours. Mem. exec. com. Yale Law Sch. Assn., 1992-95. Served to sgt. U.S. Army, 1954-56. Fourth Am. recipient Diploma of The Hague Acad. Law, 1959. Club: Yale (N.Y.C.).

LAYTON, RODNEY EUGENE, controller, newspaper executive; b. Lusk, Wyo., Feb. 27, 1954; s. Raymond Dwight Layton and Mary Elizabeth (Miller) Spencer; m. Susan Carol Johnson, Jan. 8, 1977 (div.); children: Joshua, Elise, Caleb. Ba in Polit. Sci./Econs., Kearney State, 1977; student, U. Nebr., 1978-80. CPA, Nebr. Auditor State of Nebr., Lincoln, 1979-80; staff auditor Arthur Andersen, Houston, 1980-81; audit sr. McDermott & Miller, Grand Island, Nebr., 1981-82; internal audit sr. Norwest Bank Corp., Omaha, 1982-86; internal audit mgr. Berkshire Hathaway, Inc., Omaha, 1986-89; treas., controller Buffalo News, 1989—. Treas. Citizens Advocacy, Grand Island, 1981; treas., pres. Crippled Children's Camps, Inc., Buffalo, 1989-93; treas., bd. dirs. Cradle Beach Camp, Buffalo, 1989-94. Mem. AICPAs, Nebr. Soc. CPAs, Internat. Newspaper Fin. Execs. Avocations: tennis, golf, piano. Home: 3796 Teachers Ln #10 Orchard Park NY 14127 Office: Buffalo News 1 News Plz Buffalo NY 14203-2930

LAYTON, WILLIAM GEORGE, computer company executive, management consultant, human resources executive; b. Missouri Valley, Iowa, Sept. 11, 1931; s. George Holbert and Margaret (Wilson) L.; m. Caroline R. Tiffany, June 27, 1953; children: Kathleen Layton Medl, Sara Layton Howe, Thomas William. B.A., Coe Coll., 1953; M.A., U. Ill., 1955. Indsl. rels. trainee Procter & Gamble Co., Cin., 1955-57, pers. specialist, 1957-62; indsl. rels. mgr. Procter & Gamble Co., France, 1962-66; pers. mgr. European Tech. Ctr. Procter & Gamble Co., 1966-69, pers. mgr. internat., 1969-72; v.p. human resources Food Svc. div. Heublein, Inc., Louisville, 1972-77; sr. v.p. human resources Holiday Inns, Inc., Memphis, 1977-83; pres. The Layton Group, St. Petersburg, Fla., 1983—; sr. ptnr. Johnson-Layton Co. Mgmt. Cons., L.A. and St. Petersburg, 1985-95; pres. CompCom, Inc., 1994—. Bd. dirs., pres. Jr. Achievement of Memphis, 1981-83; mem. Tenn. Jobs Tng. Coordinating Coun., 1982-88; mem. Pvt. Industry Coun. of Memphis and Shelby County, 1982-88; mem. Pres.'s Coun., Rhodes Coll., Memphis, 1983-90. Served with USAF, 1953-55. Mem. Soc. for Human Resources Mgmt., Am. Mgmt. Assn. (human resources coun. 1981-83), Inst. Mgmt. Cons. (cert. mgmt. cons.), Coun. Mgmt. Cons. (1987—, Sr. Examiner Sterling Quality award Fla. 1994), Phi Beta Kappa. Republican. Presbyterian. Lodge: Rotary. Office: 1135 Pasadena Ave S Ste 307 Saint Petersburg FL 33707-2856

LAZAR, AUREL A., electrical engineer, educator; b. Jan. 30, 1950. Dipl.-ing., Technische Hochschule, Darmstadt, Germany, 1976; MS, Princeton U., 1977, MA, 1978, PhD, 1980. Prof. dept. elec. engring. Columbia U. Fellow IEEE (vice-chmn. computer comm. tech. com. Comm. Soc. 1987-88, chmn. 1989-91, editor IEEE Transactions on Comm. 1989-91, area editor 1991—). Office: Columbia U Dept Electrical Engineering 1312 Madison Ave New York NY 10128-1351*

LAZAR, LUDMILA, concert pianist, pedagogue; b. Celje, Slovenia; married; two children. MusB, Roosevelt U., 1963, MusM, 1964; D of Musical Arts, Northwestern U., 1987. Faculty Roosevelt U., Chgo., 1967—; prof. piano Chgo. Musical Coll. Roosevelt U., 1988—; chmn. keyboard dept. Roosevelt U., Chgo., 1983—. Roosevelt U. rsch. grantee, 1988; recipient Goethe Inst. award, 1987; named to All Star Profs. Team Chgo. Tribune, 1993. Mem. AAUP, Music Tchrs. Nat. Assn. (master tchr. cert. 1991), European Piano Tchrs. Assn., Ill. State Music Tchrs. Assn., Soc. Am. Musicians (pres., v.p.), Coll. Music Soc., Mu Phi Epsilon (pres., v.p.). Office: Roosevelt U 430 S Michigan Ave Chicago IL 60605-1301

LAZAR, RANDE HARRIS, otolaryngologist; b. N.Y.C., Feb. 27, 1951; s. Irving and Dorothy (Tartasky) L.; m. Linda Zishuk, Aug. 11, 1974; 1 child, Lauren K. BA, Bklyn. Coll., 1973; MD, U. Autonoma de Guadalajara, Mexico, 1978; postgrad., N.Y. Med. Coll., 1978-79. Diplomate Am. Bd. Otolaryngology-Head and Neck Surgery; lic. physician, N.Y., Ohio, Tenn. Gen. surgery resident Cornell-North Shore Community Hosp., Manhasset, N.Y., 1979-80; gen. surgery resident Cleve. Clinic Found., 1980-81, otolaryngology-head and neck surgery resident, 1980-84, chief resident dept. otolaryngology & communicative disorder, 1983-84; physician Otolaryngology Cons. Memphis, 1984—; fellow pathology head and neck dept. otolaryngologic pathology Armed Forces Inst. Pathology, Washington, 1983; pediatric otolaryngology fellow Le Bonheur Children's Med. Ctr., Memphis, 1984-85, dir. pediatric otolaryngology fellowship tng., 1989—, chief surgery, 1989, chief staff East Surgery Ctr.; chmn. dept. otolaryngology head and neck surgery Meth. Health Systems, 1990-91; courtesy staff Bapt. Meml. Hosp., Bapt. Meml. Hosp.-East, Eastwood Med. Ctr., Meth. Hosp., Germantown, Tenn.; chief dept. otolaryngology Les Passees Rehab. Ctr., 1988—. Contbr. articles to profl. jours. Bd. dirs. Bklyn. Tech. Found. Recipient award of honor Am. Acad. Otolaryngology-Head and Neck Surgery, 1991. Fellow Internat. Coll. Surgeons; mem. AMA, Am. Acad. Otolaryngology-Head and Neck Surgery, Am. Acad. Facial Plastic and Reconstructive Surgery, Am. Acad. Otolaryngic Allergy, Centurions Deafness Rsch. Found., Am. Auditory Soc., Nat. Hearing Assn., Soc. Ear, Nose Throat Advances in Children, Am. Soc. Laser Medicine and Surgery, So. Med. Assn., N.Y. Acad. Scis., Tenn. Med. Soc., Tenn. Acad. Otolaryngology-Head and Neck Surgery, Memphis and Shelby County Med. Soc., Memphis/Mid South Soc. Pediatrics. Office: Otolaryngology Cons Memphis 777 Washington Ave Ste 240P Memphis TN 38105-4566

LAZAR, RAYMOND MICHAEL, lawyer, educator; b. Mpls., July 16, 1939; s. Simon and Hessie (Teplin) L; m. Susan Leah Krantz, Dec. 27, 1966; children: Mark, Deborah. BBA, U. Minn., 1961, JD, 1964. Bar: Minn. 1964, U.S. Dist. Ct. Minn. 1964. Spl. asst. atty. gen. State of Minn., St. Paul, 1964-66; sole practice Mpls., 1966-72; ptnr. Lapp, Lazar, Laurie & Smith, Mpls., 1972-86; ptnr., officer Fredrikson & Byron P.A., Mpls., 1986—; lectr. various continuing edn. programs, 1972—; adj. prof. law U. Minn., Mpls., 1983—. Fellow Am. Acad. Matrimonial Lawyers; mem. ABA (chair divorce laws and procedures com. family law sect. 1993-94), Minn. Bar Assn., Hennepin County Bar Assn. (chair family law sect. 1978-79). Home: 1611 W 22nd St Minneapolis MN 55405-2402 Office: Fredrikson & Byron PA 1100 Internat Centre 900 2nd Ave S Minneapolis MN 55402-3314

LAZAR, RICHARD BECK, physician, medical administrator; b. N.Y.C., Oct. 9, 1954; s. Harold Paul and Molly (Beck) L.; m. Susan Merle Berman, Oct. 1, 1983; children: Spencer Berman, Winston Harold, Graham Henry Duke. BA in Biology cum laude, Harvard U., 1976; MD, Northwestern U., 1979. Attending physician Northwestern Meml. Hosp., Chgo., 1984-94, Rehab. Inst. Chgo., 1986-92; exec. v.p., med. dir. Schwab Rehab. Hosp., Chgo.; chair dept. phys. medicine & rehab. Mt. Sinai Hosp., Chgo., 1992—; clin. assoc. prof. surgery Pritzker Sch. Medicine U. Chgo., 1994—, program dir., chief subsect. phys. medicine & rehab., 1995—; mem. adv. com. patient mgmt. & tech. Nat. MS Soc., N.Y.C., 1992—; hon. com. Nat. Head Injury Found., Chgo., 1994; profl. adv. com. Nat. Easter Seal Soc., Chgo., 1994—. Co-author: Handbook of Neurorehabilitation, 1994, Spinal Injury: Medical Management and Rehabilitation, 1994. Fellow Am. Acad. Neurology, Am. Acad. Phys. Medicine, Assn. Acad. Physiatrists, Am. Congress Rehab. Medicine, Am. Soc. Neurorehab. (pres.-elect 1995-96, pres. 1996—, Outstanding Svc. & Leadership award 1990-94). Home: 5490 South Shore Dr 4N Chicago IL 60615 Office: Schwab Rehab Hosp & Care Network 1401 S California Blvd Chicago IL 60608-1612

LAZAR, THEODORE AARON, retired manufacturing company executive, lawyer; b. Chgo., July 16, 1920; s. Philip and Rena (Goodman) L.; m. Betty Jean Papermaster, July 6, 1952; children: Mark D., Paul A., Nancy Paula. JD, John Marshall Law Sch., Chgo., 1951. Bar: Ill. 1951, Wis. 1962, Ohio 1966. Sole practice, Chgo., 1951-62; asst. corp. counsel City of Chgo., 1956-59; atty. NLRB, Chgo. and Los Angeles, 1962-65; corp. counsel Lancaster Colony Corp., Columbus, Ohio, 1965-83, v.p. law, 1983-88, ret., 1988. Served as sgt. U.S. Army, 1942-46. Mem. Columbus Bar Assn. Home: 270 Bryant Ave Columbus OH 43085-3009

LAZARUS, ALLAN MATTHEW, retired newspaper editor; b. New Orleans, Nov. 21, 1927; s. Harry Adolph and Edna Mary (Wodiker) L.; m. Martha Elizabeth Ellis, July 26, 1946; children—Kenneth Wayne, Virginia Lynn. B.A. in History, Centenary Coll., 1951. Copy boy The Times, Shreveport, La., 1944-45, reporter, 1945-46, telegraph editor, 1947-58, news editor, 1958-69, mng. editor, 1969-90; Pulitzer Prize Juror, 1978; pres. La.-Miss. AP Assn., 1977-78. Served as cpl. USAF, 1946-47. Mem. AP Mng. Editors Assn. (bd. dirs. 1975-80), Soc. Profl. Journalists (pres. local chpt. 1971-72). Roman Catholic. Home: 7713 Tampa Way Shreveport LA 71105-5701

LAZARUS, ARNOLD ALLAN, psychologist, educator; b. Johannesburg, Republic of South Africa, Jan. 27, 1932; came to U.S., 1963; s. Benjamin and Rachel Leah (Mosselson) L.; m. Daphne Ann Kessel, June 10, 1956; children: Linda Sue, Clifford Neil. BA with honors, U. Witwatersrand, 1956; MA, U. Witwatersrand, Johannesburg, 1957, PhD, 1960. Diplomate: Am. Bd. Profl. Psychology, Am. Bd. Med. Psychotherapists (fellow), Internat. Acad. Behavioral Medicine, Counseling and Psychotherapy. Pvt. practice clin. psychology Johannesburg, 1959-63, 64-66; vis. asst. prof. dept. psychology Stanford (Calif.) U., 1963-64; prof. psychology Temple U. Med. Sch., Phila., 1967-70; dir. clin. tng. Yale U., New Haven, 1970-72; disting. prof. Rutgers U., New Brunswick, N.J., 1972—; mem. adv. bd. Psychologists for Social Responsibility, 1984—; cons. in field. Author: 15 books including Behavior Therapy and Beyond, 1971, Multimodal Behavior Therapy, 1976, The Practice of Multimodal Therapy, 1981, rev. edit., 1989, In the Mind's Eye, 1984, Marital Myths, 1985, Mind Power: Getting What You Want Through Mental Training, 1987, The Essential Arnold Lazarus, 1991, A Dialogue with Arnold Lazarus, 1991, Don't Believe It For A Minute!, 1993, Abnormal Psychology, 1995, Brief But Comprehensive Psychotherapy, 1997, The 60 Second Shrink, 1997; editl. bd. sci. jours.; contbr. articles to profl. jours. Recipient Disting. Svc. award Am. Bd. Profl. Psychology, Disting. Career Achievement award Am. Bd. Med. Psychotherapists, Outstanding Contbns. to Mental Health award Psychiat. Outpatient Ctrs. of the Americas, 1991, Disting. Profl. Contbns. award Divsn. Clin. Psychology, Am. Psychol. Assn., 1997. Fellow APA (Disting. Psychologist award divsn. of psychotherapy 1992, 1st Ann. Cummings Psyche award 1996), Am. Bd. Profl. Psychology (diplomate), Internat. Acad. Eclectic Psychotherapists, Acad. Clin. Psychology; mem. Am. Acad. Psychotherapy, Assn. for Advancement Psychotherapy, Nat. Acads. Practice in Psychology (disting.), Soc. for Exploration of Psychotherapy Integration. Home: 56 Herrontown Cir Princeton NJ 08540-2924 Office: Rutgers U PO Box 819 Piscataway NJ 08855-0819 *Whatever modicum of success I may have achieved is probably due, in large part, to my view of parity as a way of life. I am committed to the notion that there are no superior human beings —we are all different, indeed unique, but equal. While some people possess superior skills and abilities, this does not make them superior human beings. To respect others for their exceptional capacities, but never to deify them, enables one to learn from others instead of envying them and denigrating oneself. This egalitarian view transforms acquisitiveness, power, and aggression into love, intimacy, and productive activity.*

LAZARUS, ARTHUR, JR., lawyer; b. Bklyn., Aug. 30, 1926; s. Arthur and Frieda (Langer) L.; m. Gertrude Chiger, Jan. 8, 1956; children: Andrew Joseph, Edward Peter, Diana Ruth. BA with honors, Columbia U., 1946; JD, Yale U., 1949. Bar: N.Y. 1951, D.C. 1952, U.S. Supreme Ct. 1954. Assoc. Fried, Frank, Harris, Shriver & Jacobson, Washington, 1950-57, ptnr., 1957-91, mng. ptnr. Washington office, 1974-86; of counsel Sonosky, Chambers, Sachse & Endreson, Washington, 1994—; vis. lectr. Yale Law Sch., 1973-81. Trustee Arena Stage, 1987—, Georgetown Day Sch., 1963-71. Home: 3201 Fessenden St NW Washington DC 20008-2032

LAZARUS, DAVID, physicist, educator; b. Buffalo, Sept. 8, 1921; s. Barney B. and Lillian (Markel) L.; m. Betty Jane Ross, Aug. 15, 1943; children: Barbara, William, Mary Ann, Richard. B.S., U. Chgo., 1942, M.S., 1947, Ph.D., 1949. Instr. electronics U. Chgo., 1942-43, electronics engr., 1946-49, instr. physics, 1949; research assoc. radio research lab. Harvard, 1943-45; mem. physics faculty U. Ill., Urbana, 1949—, prof., 1959—; vis. prof. U. Paris, 1968-69, M.I.T., 1978-79, Harvard U., 1978-79; vis. scientist Am. Inst. Physics, N.Y.C., 1962-69; cons. Phys. Sci. Study Com., 1957-59, Hallicrafters Co., Chgo., 1957-69, Gen. Electric Co., Cin., 1960-68, Gen. Atomic, La Jolla, Calif., 1962-63, Lawrence Radiation Lab., 1967-68, Sandia Lab., 1970-72, Addison-Wesley Pub. Co., Reading, Mass., 1964-80; dir. Council on Materials Sci., U.S. Dept. Energy, 1981-85. Author: (with H. de Waard) Modern Electronics, 1966, (with R.I. Hulsizer) The World of Physics, 1972, (with M. Raether) Practical Physics: How Things Work, 1979; also articles. Guggenheim fellow, 1968-69. Fellow AAAS, Am. Phys. Soc. (coun. 1974-78, 80-91, exec. com. 1980-91, editor-in-chief 1980-91, publs. com. 1980-91, exec. com. div. contensed matter physics 1968-70, 74-78, chmn. New Materials prize com. 1976, chmn. Buckley prize com. 1979); mem. Am. Inst. Physics (governing bd. 1981-92, exec. com. 1981-89, publs. policy com. 1981-92). Home: 502 W Vermont Ave Urbana IL 61801-4931

LAZARUS, FRED, IV, college president; b. N.Y.C., Jan. 1, 1942; s. Fred and Irma (Mendelson) L.; m. Jonna Gane, Nov. 27, 1970; children: Anna Mendelson, Fred Lazarus V. B.A., Claremont McKenna Coll., 1964; M.B.A., Harvard U., 1966. Staff assoc. Nat. Council for Equal Bus. Opportunity, Washington, 1969-71; pres. Washington Council for Equal Bus. Opportunity, 1971-74; exec. asst. to chmn. Nat. Endowment for Arts, Washington, 1975-78; pres. Md. Inst. Coll. Art, Balt., 1978—; vice chmn. Md. Ind. Colls. and Univs. Assn.; vice chmn. Assn. Ind. Colls. Art and Design, 1992-96; trustee Alliance for Ind. Colls. Art, 1978-91, chmn., 1984-86, 89-91; founding chmn. Nat. Coalition for Edn. in Arts, 1988-90. Trustee St. Paul's Sch., 1988-96; trustee, chmn. Am. Coun. for Arts, sec., 1991-94; chmn., Americans for the Arts, Md. Art Place; trustee emeritus Ptnrs. for Livable Places; bd. dirs. Afro-Am. Newspapers, Balt. Artists Housing Corp.; chmn. Balt. Coun. for Equal Bus. Opportunity, Md. Art Place; mem. Thurgood Marshall Meml. Statue Commn. Recipient mayor's art award, City of Balt., 1988. Mem. Harvard Club (N.Y.C.). Office: Md Inst Coll Art 1300 W Mount Royal Ave Baltimore MD 21217-4134

LAZARUS, GEORGE MILTON, newspaper columnist; b. Worcester, Mass., June 16, 1932; s. Milton George and Urania (Costa) L.; m. Karen Jayne Sippel, Mar. 1, 1969; children: Lana Elizabeth, Tara Lisanne. BBA, Clark U., 1954; MS in Journalism, Northwestern U., 1957. Staff writer AP, Chgo., 1957-59; asst. editor Printers' Ink mag., Chgo., 1959-61; fin. news reporter Chgo. Daily News, 1961-69, mktg. news columnist, 1961-69; mktg. columnist Chgo. Today, 1969-72, Chgo. Tribune, 1972—, Adweek's Mktg. Week, 1982-90, N.Y. Daily News, 1984-90; spkr. and cons. in field; former commentator stas. WFLD-TV, WGN, WMAQ, WLAK, Chgo.; instr. advt. North Park Coll., 1957-58. Author: Marketing Immunity, 1988; contbr. articles to mags. Recipient Marshall Field award for editorial contbns., 1966-67, Nat. Headliners award, 1971, Compton Advt. award for best newspaper article on advt., 1983; inducted into Northwestern U. Medill Sch. Journalism Hall of Achievement, 1997. Mem. Merchandising Execs. Club Chgo. (pres. 1979-80, dir.), Lambda Chi Alpha, Alpha Delta Sigma, Sigma Delta Chi. Club: Flossmoor Country. Home: 1214 Western Ave Flossmoor IL 60422-1636 Office: The Chicago Tribune 435 N Michigan Ave Chicago IL 60611

LAZARUS, GERALD SYLVAN, physician, university dean; b. N.Y.C., Feb. 16, 1939; s. Joseph W. and Marion (Goldstein) L.; m. Sandra Jacob, Sept. 3, 1961 (dec. 1985); children: Mark, Elyse, Lynne, Laura; m. Audrey Fedyszyn Jakubowski, Apr. 7, 1990. B.A., Colby Coll., 1959; M.D., George Washington U., 1963. Intern, then resident U. Mich., Ann Arbor, 1963-64; resident in medicine U. Mich., 1964-65; NIH research asso. NIH, Bethesda, Md., 1965-68; resident in dermatology Harvard U., Cambridge, Mass., 1968-70; research fellow Strangeways Labs., Cambridge, Eng., 1970-72; assoc. prof. medicine, co-dir. dermatology tng. program Albert Einstein Med. Coll., N.Y.C., 1972-75; J. Lamar Callaway prof. Duke U., Durham, N.C., 1977-82; chief dermatology Duke U., 1975-82; Milton B. Hartzell prof. U. Pa. Sch. Medicine, Phila., 1982—, chmn. dept. dermatology, 1982-93; dean Sch. Medicine U. Calif., Davis, 1993—; mem. study sect. NIH, 1976-80. Author: (with L. Goldsmith) Diagnosis of Skin Disease, 1980, (with Herman Beerman) Tradition of Excellance: History of Dermatology at Univ. Pa. Sch. of Medicine; asso. editor: Jour. Investigative Dermatology, 1977-82; contbr. numerous articles to profl. jours. Served with USPHS, 1965-68. Carl Herzog fellow Am. Dermatology Assn., 1970-72; John Simon Guggenheim fellow U. Geneva, 1986; sr. investigator Arthritis Found., 1972-77; grantee NIH. Fellow ACP, Assn. Am. Physicians, Am. Soc. Clin. Investigation; mem. Am. Dermatol. Assn., Soc. Investigative Dermatology (dir., pres. 1996-97, Disting. alumnus award George Washington U. 1996), Biochem. Soc., Am. Acad. Dermatology (Sultzberger award 1986). Republican. Jewish. Office: U Calif Sch Medicine Office of Dean Davis CA 95616

LAZARUS, KENNETH ANTHONY, lawyer; b. Passaic, N.J., Mar. 10, 1942; s. John Joseph and Margaret (Di Cenzo) L.; m. Marylyn Jane Flemming, Aug. 13, 1966; children: Maggi Ann, John, Joseph. BA, U. Dayton, 1964; JD, U. Notre Dame, 1967; LLM in Taxation, George Washington U., 1971. Bar: N.J. 1967, U.S. Tax Ct. 1970, U.S. Ct. Claims 1970, U.S. Supreme Ct. 1971, D.C. 1976. Trial atty. U.S. Dept. Justice, 1967-71; assoc. counsel and chief counsel to Minority Com. on Judiciary, U.S. Senate, 1971-74; assoc. counsel to Pres. U.S., 1974-77; ptnr. Ward, Lazarus & Grow, Washington, 1977-91; of counsel Dixon & Jessup, Washington, 1991—; mem. adv. bd. Sch. Law Dayton U., 1975-85; adj. prof. Sch. Law Georgetown U., 1979—; mem. U.S. Adv. Com. on Trade Negotiations, 1983-87; chmn. Sailors and Mchts. Bank and Trust Co., Vienna, Va., 1987-89.

Mem. adv. bd. Houston Jour. Internat. Law, 1983-90; contbr. numerous articles to profl. publs. U.S. reporter to UN, 1975-77; mem. adv. coun. Rep. Nat. Com., 1977-80; mem. Presdl. transition team Office of Pres.-Elect, 1980-81; caucus mgr. George Bush Rep. Conv., 1988; bd. trustees Internat. Law Inst., pres., 1990-97. Mem. ABA, D.C. Bar Assn., Bar Assn. D.C., Fed. Bar Assn., N.J. Bar Assn., Am. Judicature Soc., Am. Law Inst. Home: Apt 716 4501 Connecticut Ave NW Washington DC 20008-3712 Office: 1850 M St NW Ste 450 Washington DC 20036-5815

LAZARUS, MARGARET LOUISE, film producer and director; b. N.Y.C., Jan. 22, 1949; d. Leon A. and Paula (Plesser) L.; children: Michael Lazarus Renner, Matthew Lazarus Renner. BA cum laude, Vassar Coll., 1969; MS in Broadcast, Film, Boston U., 1972. Researcher Westinghouse Broadcasting/Parallel Prodns., Boston, 1970-71; producer, writer Sta. WNAC-TV, Boston, 1971-72; producer, dir. Cambridge (Mass.) Documentary, 1973—, also pres., 1980-90; cons., bd. dirs. Cambridge Community TV, 1987-94. Producer, dir. (films) Taking Our Bodies Back, 1974, Rape Culture, 1976, 83, Eugene Debs and the American Movement, 1977, Killing Us Softly, 1979, Calling the Shots, 1982, Pink Triangles, 1984, The Last Empire, 1986, Still Killing Us Softly, 1987, Hazardous Inheritance, 1989, Not Just a Job, 1990, Advertising Alcohol, 1991, Life's Work, 1993, Defending Our Lives, 1993 (Academy Award, Best Documentary Short Subject); co-author: The New Our Bodies, Ourselves, 1984. Counselor, mem. Alliance Against Sexual Coercion, Cambridge, 1977-81; mem. peace commn. City of Cambridge, 1988-91. Recipient London Film Festival award, 1982, Mannheim (Fed. Republic Germany) Film Festival award, 1982, Berlin Film Festival award, 1982, Red Ribbon Am. Film Festival award, 1983, Melbourne (Australia) Film Festival award, 1983, 1st place Am. Jour. Nursing, 1984, 1st place Nat. Council on Family Relations, 1984, 93, Blue Ribbon award Am. Film Festival, 1987, 91, U.S.A. Film Festival award 1987, World Peace Film Festival award, 1987, Global Village Film Festival award, 1985, Filmosav award India, 1988, Golden Babe award Chicago Ednl. Film Festival, 1988, Silver Apple award Nat. Ednl. Film Festival, 1991, 94, Seattle Film Festival Silver Placque award, 1993, Chgo. Internat. Film Festival award, 1993, Exceptional Merit in Media award, 1993, PASS award Nat. Coun. on Crime and Delinquency, Chris award Columbus Internat. Film Festival, 1993, Outstanding Film of the Year award New England Film and Video Festival, 1994. Mem. Acad. Motion Picture Arts and Scis.

LAZARUS, MAURICE, retired retail executive; b. Columbus, Ohio, June 27, 1915; s. Fred, Jr. and Meta (Marx) L.; m. Nancy Stix, June 7, 1942 (dec. 1985); children: Carol, Jill; m. Nell P. Eurich, Nov. 25, 1988. Student, Ohio State U.; B.A., Harvard, 1937; LL.D., Am. Internat. Coll., 1969. Div. mdse. mgr. John Shillito Co., Columbus, 1937-41; head service and control Foley's, Houston, 1945-48; exec. v.p. Foley's, 1948-58; pres., treas. Filene's, Boston, 1958-64; chmn. bd. Filene's, 1964-65; vice chmn. Federated Dept. Stores, Inc., Boston, 1965-70; chmn. finance com. Federated Dept. Stores, Inc., 1971-82, also dir. Mem. adv. com. on nat. health ins. issues HEW, 1977-78; bd. dirs. Cambridge Ctr. Adult Edn., 1974-75; mem. adv. Council Pres.'s Commn. on Status of Women, 1963-68; chmn. exec. com. Public Agenda Found., 1987—; mem. div. health scis. and tech. Harvard U.-M.I.T., 1978-87, Harvard Cmty. Health Plan Found. Bd., 1984—, chmn., 1996—; mem. adv. bd. Schlesinger Library Women's Archives, Radcliffe Coll., 1972-76; mem. bd. overseers Harvard Coll., 1977-83; mem. ethics adv. bd. HEW, 1978-80; vis. com., chmn. central services, Med. Sch. and Dental Medicine, Sch. Public Health Harvard U., 1978-85, mem. governance com., 1968-71, mem. working group div. health policy research and edn.; chmn. adv. com. Joint Center Urban Studies., 1977-82; trustee Mass. Gen. Hosp., Old Sturbridge Village, 1965-78, Marine Biol. Lab., 1977-84, McLean Hosp., 1980—, Tufts U. Civic Edn. Found. of Lincoln Filene Center for Citizenship and Public Affairs, 1972-80, New Eng. Med. Center Hosp., 1960-78, Beth Israel Hosp., 1958-65, Bennington Coll., 1965-72, Combined Jewish Philanthropy Greater Boston, 1962-65; chmn. exec. com. Pub. Agenda Found., 1977—; bd. dirs. Boston chpt. ARC, 1962-64; dir. Med. Found., 1987—; chmn. Harvard Cmty. Health Plan, 1984-93; bd. overseers Boston Symphony Orch., 1971-74; bd. dirs. Salzburg Seminars in Am. Studies, Assoc. Harvard Alumni, 1966-73; pres. Assoc. Harvard Alumni, 1972-73; mem. Mass. Higher Edn. Facilities Commn., 1970-74; mem. corp. Northeastern U., Peter Bent Brigham Hosp.; bd. overseers Boston Symphony Orch., 1971-74; mem. M.I.T. Council Arts, 1972-77, Harvard Med. Center, 1977-79; mem. adv. com. hosp. initiatives in long-term care Am. Hosp. Assn.; chmn. bd. dirs. Harvard Cmty. Health Plan, dir. emeritus, 1994—; mem. adv. bd. Brandeis U. Ctr. Social Policy in Middle East, 1978-88. Fellow Am. Acad. Arts and Scis. Clubs: Bay (Boston), Harvard (Boston, N.Y.C.); Univ. (N.Y.C.); St. Botolph (Boston), Comml.-Mchts. (Boston). Home and Office: 144 Brattle St 3d Fl Cambridge MA 02138-2202

LAZARUS, MELL, cartoonist; b. N.Y.C, May 3, 1927; s. Sidney and Frances (Mushkin) L.; m. Eileen Hortense Israel, June 19, 1949; children: Marjorie, Suesan, Catherine; m. Sally Elizabeth Mitchell, May 13, 1995. Cartoonist-writer Miss Peach, 1957—, Momma, 1970—; author anthologies Miss Peach, Miss Peach, Are These Your Children?, Momma, We're Grownups Now!; novels The Boss is Crazy, Too, 1964, The Neighborhood Watch, 1986; plays Everybody into the Lake, Elliman's Fly, Lifetime Eggcreams, 1969-70; juvenile Francine, Your Face Would Stop a Clock, 1975; co-author Miss Peach TV spl. programs Turkey Day Pageant and Annual Heart Throb Ball. Trustee Internat. Mus. Cartoon Art. With USNR, 1945, USAFR, 1951-54. Mem. Nat. Cartoonists Soc. (pres. 1989-93, chmn. membership com. 1965, nat. rep., Humor Strip Cartoonist of Yr. 1973, 79, Reuben award 1981), Writers Guild Am. West, Nat. Press Club, The Century Assn., Newspaper Features Coun. (bd. dirs.), Sigma Delta Chi. Office: Creators Syndicate Inc 5777 W Century Blvd Los Angeles CA 90045-5600

LAZARUS, RICHARD STANLEY, psychology educator; b. N.Y.C., Mar. 3, 1922; s. Abe and Matilda (Marks) L.; m. Bernice H. Newman, Sept. 2, 1945; children—David Alan, Nancy Eve. A.B., City Coll. N.Y., 1942; M.S., U. Pitts., 1947, Ph.D., 1948; Dr. honoris causa, Johannes Gutenberg U., Mainz, Fed. Republic Germany, 1988, U. Haifa, Israel, 1995. Diplomate in clin. psychology Am. Bd. Examiners in Profl. Psychology. Asst. prof. Johns Hopkins, 1948-53; psychol. cons. VA, 1952—; assoc. prof. psychology, dir. clin. tng. program Clark U., Worcester, Mass., 1953-57; assoc. prof. psychology U. Calif. at Berkeley, 1957-59, prof. psychology, 1959-91, prof. emeritus, 1991—; prin. investigator Air Force contracts dealing with psychol. stress, 1951-53, USPHS grant on personality psychol. stress, 1953-70; NIA, NIDA, and NCI grantee on stress, coping and health, 1977-81, MacArthur Found. research grantee, 1981-84; USPHS spl. fellow Waseda U., Japan, 1963-64. Author 18 books, numerous publs. in profl. jours. Served to 1st lt. AUS, 1943-46. Recipient Disting. Sci. Achievement award Calif. State Psychol. Assn., 1984, Div. 38 Health Psychology, 1989; Guggenheim fellow, 1969-70; Army Rsch. Inst. rsch. grantee, 1973-75. Fellow AAAS, APA (Disting. Sci. Contbn. award 1989); mem. Western Psychol. Assn., Argentina Med. Assn. (hon.). Home: 1824 Stanley Dollar Dr Apt 3B Walnut Creek CA 94595-2833 Office: Univ Calif Dept Psychology Berkeley CA 94720

LAZARUS, ROCHELLE BRAFF, advertising executive; b. N.Y.C., Sept. 1, 1947; d. Lewis L. and Sylvia Ruth (Eisenberg) Braff; m. George M. Lazarus, Mar. 22, 1970; children: Theodore, Samantha, Benjamin. AB, Smith Coll., 1968; MBA, Columbia U., 1970. Product mgr. Clairol, N.Y.C., 1970-71; account exec. Ogilvy & Mather, N.Y.C., 1971-73, account supr., 1973-77, mgmt. supr., 1977-84, sr. v.p., 1981—, account group dir., 1984-87; gen. mgr. Ogilvy & Mather Direct, N.Y.C., 1987-88, mng. dir., 1988-89, pres., 1989-91; pres. Ogilvy & Mather, N.Y.C., 1991-94, pres. N. Am., 1991-94; pres., COO Ogilvy & Mather Worldwide, N.Y.C., 1995-96, CEO, 1996, chmn., 1997. Bd. dirs. Ann Taylor, Advt. Edn. Found., YMCA, Nat. Women's Law Ctr., World Wildlife Fund; mem. Com. of 200; mem. bus. com. Solomon R. Guggenheim Mus.; mem. bd. overseers Columbus Bus. Sch.; trustee Smith Coll., Columbia Presbyn. Hosp. Recipient YWCA Women Achievers award, 1985, Matrix award, 1995; named Businesswoman of Yr. N.Y.C. Partnership and C. of C., 1996. Mem. Am. Assn. Advt. Agys. (bd. dirs.), Advt. Women N.Y. (Woman of Yr. 1994). Home: 106 E 78th St New York NY 10021-0302 Office: Ogilvy & Mather Worldwide 309 W 49th St New York NY 10019-7316

LAZARUS, STEVEN S., management consultant, marketing consultant; b. Rochester, N.Y., June 16, 1943; s. Alfred and Ceal H. Lazarus; m. Elissa C. Lazarus, June 19, 1966; children: Michael, Stuart, Jean. BS, Cornell U., 1966; MS, Poly. U. N.Y., 1967; PhD, U. Rochester, 1974. Pres. Mgmt. Systems Analysis Corp., Denver, 1977—; dir. Sci. Application Intern Corp., Englewood, Colo., 1979-84; assoc. prof. Metro State Coll., Denver, 1983-84; sr. v.p. Pal Assocs. Inc., Denver, 1984-85; with strategic planning and mktg. McDonnell Douglas, Denver, 1985-86; mktg. cons. Clin. Reference Systems, Denver, 1986; pres. Mgmt. Sys. Analysis Corp., 1986-89, 95—; assoc. exec. dir. Ctr. Rsch. Ambulatory Health Care Adminstrn., Englewood, 1990-94; spl. cons. State of Colo., Denver, 1976-81; mktg. cons. IMX, Louisville, 1986-87; speaker Am. Hosp. Assn., Chgo., 1983—, Med. Group Mgmt. Assn., 1975—; asst. sec. Work Group for Elec. Data Interchange, 1995-96. Contbr. chpts. to books; patentee med. quality assurance. NDEA fellow U. Rochester, 1968-71. Fellow Healthcare Info. and Mgmt. Systems Soc.; mem. Inst. Indsl. Engring. (sr.), Med. GroupMgmt. Assn., Optimists (program chmn. Denver club 1976-78). Home: 7023 E Eastman Ave Denver CO 80224-2845 Office: MSA Corp 4949 S Syracuse St Ste 300 Denver CO 80237-2747

LAZAY, PAUL DUANE, telecommunications manufacturing company executive; b. Phila., June 2, 1939; s. Louis and Thea (Lindberg) L.; m. Joan Elizabeth Robinson, Sept. 2, 1961; 1 child, Thomas. BS, Trinity Coll., 1961; PhD, MIT, 1968. Supr. optic measurement Bell Labs., Murray Hill, N.J., 1969-83; v.p. engring. ITT-EOPD, Roanoke, Va., 1983-86; v.p. engring. Telco Systems Fiber Optics Div., Norwood, Mass., 1986-87, v.p. mktg., 1987-88, pres., gen. mgr., 1987-88; pres., chief exec. officer Telco System, Inc., Norwood, 1988-94; v.p., gen. mgr. ATM divsn. Cisco Systems, Inc., Chelmsford, Mass., 1995-96; cons., 1996—; bd. dirs. SpecTran Corp., Sturbridge, Mass. Contbr. articles on fiber optics to profl. jours.; patentee in field. Mem. IEEE, Am. Physics Soc., Optical Soc. Am.

LAZEAR, EDWARD PAUL, economics and industrial relations educator, researcher; b. N.Y.C., Aug. 17, 1948; s. Abe and Rose (Karp) L.; m. Victoria Ann Allen, July 2, 1977; 1 child, Julia Ann. A.B., UCLA, 1971, A.M., 1971; Ph.D., Harvard U., 1974. Asst. prof. econs. U. Chgo., 1974-78, assoc. prof. indsl. relations, 1978-81, prof. indsl. relations, 1981-85, Isidore and Gladys Brown prof. urban and labor econs., 1985-92; sr. fellow Hoover Instn. Stanford (Calif.) U., 1985—, coord. domestic studies Hoover Instn., 1987-90, prof. econs. and human resource mgmt. Grad. Sch. Bus., 1992-95; Jack Steele Parker prof. econs. and human resource mgmt. Stanford U., 1995—; econ. advisor to Romania, Czechoslovakia, Russia, Ukraine, Georgia; rsch. assoc. Nat. Bur. Econ. Rsch., Econs. Rsch. Ctr. of Nat. Opinion Rsch. Ctr.; fellow Inst. Advanced Study, Hebrew U., Jerusalem, 1977-8; lectr. Inst. Advanced Study, Vienna, 1983-84, Nat. Productivity Bd., Singapore, 1982, 85; vis. prof. Inst. des Etudes Politiques, Paris, 1987; Wicksell lectr., Stockholm, 1993. Author: (with R. Michael) Allocation of Income Within the Household, 1988; (with J.P. Gould) Microeconomic Theory, 1989, Personnel Economics, 1995; editor: Economic Transition in Eastern Europe and Russia, 1995; founding editor Jour. Labor Econs., 1982—; assoc. eidtor Jour. Econ. Perspectives, 1986-89; co-editor: Jour. Labor Abstracts, 1996—; contbr. numerous articles to scholarly jours. NSF grad. fellow, 1971-74. Fellow Econometric Soc., Soc. Labor Economists (1st v.p. 1995-96, pres. 1997-98); mem. Am. Econs. Assn. Home: 277 Old Spanish Trl Portola Valley CA 94028-8129 Office: Stanford U Grad Sch Bus Stanford CA 94305-5015 Also: Stanford Univ Hoover Inst Stanford CA 94305-6010

LAZECHKO, D. M. (MOLLY LAZECHKO), former state legislator; b. Innisfail, Alta., June 3, 1926; came to U.S., 1960; d. Archibald Donald and Violet Georgina (Adams) Manuel; m. Walter Vladmir Lazechko, Apr. 16, 1960; children: William Donald, Robert James. BA, Boise State U., 1976. Cert. elem. tchr. Tchr. Olds Sch. Dist., Stewart Sch., Alta., 1945-46, Innisfail (Alta.) Sch. Dist., 1946-50; tchr., vice prin. Calgary (Alta.) Sch. Dist., 1950-59; exchange tchr. Edinburgh, Scotland, 1954-55; math tutor mgr. Title I, Boise, Idaho, 1974-76; elem. tchr. Boise (Idaho) Sch. Dist., 1976-87; jr. high tchr. Chpt. I, Boise, 1987-88; ret., 1988-90; mem. Idaho Ho. of Reps., Boise, 1991, 92; pres. div. I Alta. Tchrs. Assn., Calgary, 1958-59, Whittier PTA, Boise, 1969-70, 73-74; pres., 3d v.p. Idaho State PTA, 1973-75; sec., elem. dir. Boise (Idaho) Edn. Assn., 1978-81. Treas. LWV, Boise, 1988-90, Ho. Dems. Campaign Com., Boise, 1991-92; precinct capt. Ada County Dems. Dist. 16, Boise, 1988-90; sec. Boise Ret. Tchrs., 1989-90, pres., 1993-94; bd. dirs. Boise Neighborhood Housing Svcs., 1990-96, Cmty. Contbn. Ctr., 1991-94, Idaho Housing Coalition, 1991-94, Epilepsy League Idaho, 1993-95; gubernatorial appointee to bd. dirs. Idaho Coun. on Domestic Violence, 1994-97; candidate Idaho Legis. Ho. Reps., 1994; chair Ada County Dems., 1995-96, 96-98; mem. AARP State Legis. Coun. and Capital City Task Force, 1995-97. Mem. NEA (life), Idaho Edn. Assn. (life), Idaho Conservation League, Idaho Women's Network, Grassroots Women's Lobby, Idaho Citizen's Network. Episcopalian. Avocations: politics, reading, swimming.

LAZENBY, FRED WIEHL, insurance company executive; b. Chattanooga, Jan. 13, 1932; s. John Wesley and Adela (Valenzuela) L.; m. Virginia Banks; children: Kathryn Wesley, Grace Woodard. BA cum laude, Vanderbilt U., 1954. CLU. With Nat. Life & Accident Ins. Co., Nashville, 1956-83, from agt. to pres., 1956-83; chmn. bd., chief exec. officer Southlife Holding Co., Nashville, 1983-94; chmn., CEO SouthCap Corp., 1994—, Premier Life Ins. Co., 1995—; past chmn. Life Insurers Conf.; bd. dirs. Nashville Bank of Commerce. Trustee Life Underwriting Tng. Coun., 1978-82; mem. bd. advisors Massey Sch.; chmn. Nashville Community Found. 1st lt. U.S. Army, 1954-56. Mem. Life Ins. Mgmt. Rsch. Assn. (bd. dirs. 1985-88, past chmn. combination cos. exec. com.), Belle Meade Country Club, Cumberland Club, Carolina Yatch Club, Rotary. Republican. Methodist. Avocations: tennis, golf, skiing. Office: SouthCap Corp 211 7th Ave N Nashville TN 37219-1823

LAZENBY, GAIL R., library director; b. Charlotte, N.C., May 6, 1947; d. James Yates and Marian Elizabeth (Church) Rogers. BA, Salem Coll., 1969; MLS, U. N.C., 1971. Cert. libr., Ga. Br. libr. Atlanta Pub. Libr., 1970-77; br. coord. Dekalb Libr. System, Decatur, Ga., 1977-82; asst. dir. West Ga. Regional Libr., Carrollton, 1982-83; asst. dir. Cobb County Pub. Libr., Marietta, Ga., 1983-90, dir., 1991—. Mem. Leadership Cobb, Cobb County, 1985-86. Mem. ALA, Ga. Libr. Assn. (2d v.p. 1987-89), Southeastern Libr. Assn. (v.p.-pres. elect. 1990-92, pres. 1992-94), Urban Librs. Coun., Kiwanis Club Marietta (bd. dirs. 1991-92, sec. 1992-93, sec.-treas. 1993-94, pres. 1995-96). Office: Cobb County Public Lib 266 Roswell St SE Marietta GA 30060-2005

LAZERSON, EARL EDWIN, academic administrator emeritus; b. Detroit, Dec. 10, 1930; s. Nathan and Ceil (Stashefsky) L.; m. Ann May Harper, June 11, 1966; children from previous marriage: Joshua, Paul. BS, Wayne State U., Detroit, 1953; postgrad., U. Leiden, Netherlands, 1957-58; MA, U. Mich., 1954, PhD, 1982. Mathematician Inst. Def. Analyses, Princeton, N.J., 1960-62; asst. prof. math. Washington U., St. Louis, 1962-65, 66-69; vis. asso. prof. Brandeis U., 1965-66; mem. faculty So. Ill. U., Edwardsville, 1969—, prof. math., 1973—, chmn. dept. math. studies, 1972-73, dean Sch. Sci. and Tech., 1973-76, univ. v.p., provost, 1977-79, pres., 1980-93; pres. emeritus, 1994—. Chmn. Southwestern Ill. Devel. Authority, City of East St. Louis Fin. Adv. Authority; active Leadership Coun. Southwestern Ill., Gateway Ctr. Met. St. Louis, Inc., St. Louis Symphony Soc.; trustee Jefferson Nat. Expansion Meml. Assn., Ill. Econ. Devel. Bd. Recipient Sr. Teaching Excellence award Standard Oil Found., 1970-71. Mem. Am. Math. Soc., Math. Assn. Am., European Math. Soc., London Math. Soc., Soc. Mathematique France, Fulbright Alumni Assn., Sigma Xi. Home: 5 Hidden Valley Ln Edwardsville IL 62025-3706

LAZERSON, JACK, pediatrician, educator; b. Bronx, Jan. 9, 1936; s. Mayer and Jennie (Gerson) L.; (div.); children: David, Deborah, Darlene, Donna; (div.); 1 child, Samuel. AB, NYU, 1957; MD, U. Chgo., 1961. Diplomate Am. Bd. Pediatrics. Rotating internship L.A. County Gen. Hosp., 1961-62; resident in pediatrics Stanford-Palo Alto (Calif.) Hosp., 1962-64; chief resident in pediatrics, instr. U. Wash. Hosp., Seattle, 1966-67; asst. prof. dept. pediatrics Sch. of Medicine Stanford U., 1969-72; from asst. to assoc. prof. dept. pediatrics U. So. Calif., L.A., 1972-76; assoc. prof. dept. pediatrics U. Wis., Milw., 1976-79; prof. dept. pediatrics Sch. of Medicine U. Calif., Davis, 1979-86, prof. dept. pathology, 1980-86; prof., chmn. dept. pediatrics Sch. of Medicine U. Nev., 1986-94, prof. dept. pediatrics Sch. Medicine, 1986—; chief hemophilia svc. Children's Hosp. Stanford U. Sch. of Medicine, 1969-72; assoc. hematologist div. hematology and oncology Children's Hosp. L.A., 1972-76. Contbr. numerous articles to profl. jours. Bd. dirs. hemostasis program Milw. Children's Hosp., 1976-79; med. dir. Great Lakes Hemophilia Found., 1976-79. Armour and Hyland Labs. grantee, 1969-72, 72-76, Med. Coll. of Wis. grantee, 1976-79, HEW grantee, 1976-79, Cutter Labs. grantee, 1981-82, 82-83; recipient Rsch. Funds award U. Calif.-Davis, 1981-82, Outstanding Alumnus award U. Chgo., 1981. Fellow Am. Acad. Pediatrics; mem. Am. Fedn. for Clin. Rsch., N.Y. Acad. Scis., Nat. Hemophilia Found., Am. Chem. Soc. (biochemistry sect., med. chemistry sect.), Hemostasis Assn. of Calif., Internat. Soc. Thrombosis and Hemostasis, Am. Heart Assn. Coun. on Thrombosis Basic Sci. Coun., Am. Soc. Hematology, Am. Soc. for Exptl. Pathology, World Fedn. Hemophilia, Am. Assn. Blood Banks, Am. Soc. Pediatric (hematology and oncology credentials and by-laws com., membership com.), Alpha Omega Alpha. Office: U Nev Sch Medicine 2040 W Charleston Blvd Ste 402 Las Vegas NV 89102-2250

LAZIO, RICK A., congressman, lawyer; b. Amityville, N.Y., Mar. 13, 1958; s. Anthony and Olive E. (Christensen) L. AB in Polit. Sci., Vassar Coll., 1980; JD, Am. U., 1983. Bar: N.Y. 1984, U.S. Dist. Ct. (ea. and so. dists.) N.Y., 1985. Asst. dist. atty. Suffolk County Rackets Bureau, Hauppauge, N.Y., 1983-88; exec. asst. dist. atty. Suffolk County, N.Y., 1987-88; village atty. Village of Lindenhurst, N.Y., 1988-93; mng. ptnr. Glass, Lazio and Glass, Esqs., Babylon, N.Y., 1988-93; mem. Suffolk County Legislature from 11th Dist., N.Y., 1989-93, 103rd-105th Congresses from 2nd N.Y. dist., Washington, 1993—; dep. majority whip 103d-104th Congresses from 2nd N.Y. dist., Washington; budget com. banking subcom.; chmn. subcom. on housing and cmty. opportunity; mem. capital markets, securities and govt. sponsored enterprises. Mem. admissions com. Vassar Coll., N.Y.; past pres. West Islip Rep. Club. Mem. Suffolk County Bar Assn. Roman Catholic. Avocations: numismatics, guitar. Office: US Ho of Reps 2444 Rayburn Washington DC 20515*

LAZO, JOHN, JR., physician; b. Passaic, N.J., Nov. 29, 1946; s. John and Mary (Beley) L.; m. Donnalynn Margaret Materna, July 22, 1972; children: Jonathan Christopher, Ashley Jude. BS, Fairleigh Dickinson U., 1974; MD, Univ. Autonoma de Guadalajara, Mexico, 1978. Diplomate Am. Bd. Emergency Medicine, Am. Bd. Forensic Examiners. Intern Akron (Ohio) City Hosp., 1980-81, resident in emergency medicine, 1981-83, chief resident in emergency medicine, 1982-83; med. dir. emergency svcs. Parma (Ohio) Comty. Gen. Hosp., 1986-93, vice-chmn. emergency dept., 1995—; dir. Paramedic Edn. Program, Parma, 1986-93; bd. dirs. Advantage Health Ptnrs. Sgt. USAF, 1966-70. Fellow Am. Coll. Emergency Physicians; mem. Northeast Ohio Soc. Emergency Medicine. Republican. Russian Orthodox. Avocations: photography, cooking. Home: 10010 Gatewood Dr Cleveland OH 44141-3615 Office: Parma Community Gen Hosp 7007 Powers Blvd Cleveland OH 44129-5437

LAZOR, PATRICIA ANN, interior designer; d. Charles A. and Grace E. (Siegrist) LaGattuta; m. E. Alexander Lazor, Aug. 22, 1959; children: Pamela A., Carolyn L., Charles L., Peter A. BA, Chestnut Hill Coll., 1957; MEd, Rutgers Coll., 1962; cert., N.Y. Sch. Interior Design, 1972. Tchr. Bridgewater (N.J.) Raritan Schs., 1958-69; designer Patricia A. Lazor Interior Design, Bernardsville, N.J., 1975-85; pres. Alexander Abry, Inc., Washington, 1985-87; owner, designer Patricia A. Lazor Interior Design Antiques, Inc., Bernardsville, 1985—. Rep. com. woman, Somerset County, N.J., 1978; chmn. Family Counseling Svc. Somerset County, 1972-78. Mem. Garden Club Morristown, Morristown Club, Kappa Delta Phi. Republican. Avocations: horseback riding, paddle tennis, oil painting, photography, golf. Home and Office: Interior Design/Antiques Inc Roebling Rd Bernardsville NJ 07924

LAZOR, THEODOSIUS (HIS BEATITUDE METROPOLITAN THEODOSIUS), archbishop; b. Canonsburg, Pa., Oct. 27, 1933; s. John and Mary (Kirr) L. AB, Washington and Jefferson Coll., 1957, DD (hon.), 1973; BD, St. Vladimir's Orthodox Theol. Sem., 1960; postgrad., Ecumenical Inst., Bossey, Switzerland, 1961; DD (hon.), St. Vladimir's Orthodox Theol. Sem., 1986; DHL (hon.), Georgetown U., 1988. Tonsured monk Orthodox Ch. in Am., 1961, ordained priest, 1961; priest Nativity of Holy Virgin Mary Ch., Madison, Ill., 1961-66; elected bishop of Washington, 1967, Sitka and, Alaska, 1967, Pitts. and, W.Va., 1972; elected primate of Orthodox Ch. in Am., Met. All Am. and Can.; archbishop of N.Y., 1977, archbishop of Washington and Met. of All Am. and Can., 1981—. Address: Orthodox Ch Am PO Box 675 Syosset NY 11791-0675

LAZOWICK, ANDREA LEE, pharmacist; b. Phila., Mar. 3, 1970; d. Ellis and Toby (Forman) L. BS in Pharmacy, Phila. Coll. Pharmacy and Sci., 1992; PharmD, Nova-Southeastern U., North Miami Beach, Fla., 1994. Lic. pharmacist, Fla., Pa.; bd. cert. psychiat. pharmacist. Pharmacist CVS Pharmacy, Phila., 1992, Truco Drugs, North Miami Beach, 1992-93, Pulmonary Prescription Providers, Hallandale, Fla., 1993; psychopharmacy splty. resident Albany (N.Y.) Coll. Pharmacy, 1994-95; asst. prof. pharmacy practice Fla. A&M U., Miami, 1995—; clin. pharmacist in psychiatry, Fla. A&M U., 1995—, VA Med. Ctr., Miami; faculty liaison Am. Soc. Health Sys. Pharmacists, Bethesda, Md., 1995—. Contbr. articles to profl. jours.; invited referee Annals of Pharmacotherapy Jour., 1995—. Mem. Broward Advocates for the Mentally Ill, Plantation, Fla., 1995—, OC Found., Miami, 1995—; participant "Healthy People 2000", Atlanta, 1995—. Mem. Am. Assn. Colls. of Pharmacy, Am. Coll. Clin. Pharmacy, Am. Soc. Health-Sys. Pharmacists, Am. Pharm. Assn., Mental Health Assn., Fla. Soc. Health-Sys. Pharmacists, Fla. Pharmacy Assn. Democrat. Jewish. Office: Florida A&M Univ 1500 NW 12th Ave Ste 1126 Miami FL 33136-1038

LAZZARO, ANTHONY DEREK, university administrator; b. Utica, N.Y., Jan. 31, 1921; s. Angelo Michael and Philomena (Vanilla) L.; m. Shirley Margaret Jones, Dec. 20, 1941; 1 child, Nancy. BS in Indsl. and Sys. Engring., U. So. Calif., 1948; LL.D. with honors, Pepperdine U., 1974. Registered profl. engr., Calif. Asst. bus. mgr. U. So. Calif., L.A., 1948-60, asst. bus. mgr., dir. campus devel., 1960-65, asso. bus. mgr., dir. campus devel., 1965-71, asso. v.p. bus. affairs, 1971-72, v.p. bus. affairs, 1972-86, sr. v.p. bus. affairs, 1986-88, univ. v.p., 1988-91, v.p. emeritus, 1991—; cons. HEW. Editorial cons. College and University Business, 1955-58. Mem. nat. adv. coun. United Student Aid Funds, N.Y.C., 1974-77, chmn., 1976-77; dir. Rep. Fed. Savs. & Loan Assn. and subs. corps., L.A., 1961-88; spl. studies cons. div. higher edn. Office Edn. HEW, 1956-59; mem. citizens com. Palos Verdes Bd. Edn., 1955-57; mem. Hoover urban renewal adv. com. Community Redevel. Agy. City of L.A., 1960-88. Lt. USNR, 1941-46. Mem. Nat. Assn. Coll. and Univ. Bus. Officers (pres. 1978-79, dir. 1972-80, chmn. goals and programs com. 1978, chmn. large inst. com. 1986-87, Disting. Bus. Officer award 1986), Western Assn. Coll. and Univ. Bus. Officers (pres. 1971-72), Soc. Coll. and Univ. Planning, Blue Key, Golden Key, Phi Kappa Phi, Tau Beta Pi. Club: Jonathan (Los Angeles). Home: 4012 Via Larga Vis Palos Verdes Estates CA 90274-1122

LE, CAN, mechanical engineer, inventor, author; b. Tam Quan, Vietnam, Dec. 14, 1949; arrived in Guam, 1975; s. Trac and Phung Thi (Nguyen) L. AD, Eastfield Coll., Mesquite, Tex., 1988. Helper dept. mech. engring. U. Tex., Arlington, 1978. Holder copyrights for multiplication and divsn. integrations, The Accurate PI, program P.V.T. Process, Labor Expansion; inventor Combodrafter, others. 1st lt. Vietnamese Army, 1969-75. Roman Catholic. Avocations: guitar, keyboard, magazines, jogging. Home: 2824 San Diego Dr Dallas TX 75228-1646

LE, DAN HOANG, data administrator, consultant; b. Saigon, Vietnam, Dec. 13, 1937; came to U.S., 1975; s. Le Dieu T. and Nhan T. (Luu) L.; m. Sophie M. Tran, 1959; children: My Hanh, My Thanh, Van, My Phuong, Suzanne. MBA, Pace U., 1982, MS in Info. Sys., 1992. Programming analyst Citibank N.A., N.Y.C., 1980-82; sr. programmer analyst Marine Midland Bank, N.Y.C., 1982-83; lead cons. Sycomm, N.Y.C., 1983-84; data adminstr., sr. data adminstr. The Depository Trust Co., N.Y.C., 1984—. Mem. IEEE Computer Soc., Assn. Computing Machinery, Data Adminstrn. Mgmt. Assn., N.Y. Acad. Sci. Home: 89 82 217th St Queens Village NY 11427

LE, KHANH TUONG, utility executive; b. Saigon, Vietnam, Feb. 25, 1936; parents Huy Bich and Thi Hop; m. Thi Thi Nguyen, Apr. 22, 1961; children:

Tuong-Khanh, Tuong-Vi, Khang, Tuong-Van. BS in Mech. Engring., U. Montreal, 1960, MS in Mech. Engring., 1961. Cert. profl. engr. Project mgr. Saigon Met. Water Project Ministry Pub. Works, Saigon, 1961-66; dep. dir. gen. Cen. Logistics Agy. Prime Min. Office, Saigon, 1966-70; asst. dir., chief auditor Nat. Water Supply Agy. Min. Pub. Works, Saigon, 1970-75; mgr. Willows Water Dist., Englewood, Colo., 1975—; dean sch. mgmt. scis., asst. chancellor acad. affairs Hoa-Hao U., Long-Xuyen, Vietnam, 1973-75; chmn. bd. dirs. Asian Pacific Devel. Ctr., 1994-96. Treas. Met. Denver Water Authority, 1989-92; mem. Arapahoe County Adv. Bd., Douglas County Water Authority, 1993—; mem. Front Range Water Forum presided over by Gov. Roy Romer, Colo., 1993—; vol. Water for People, 1994—; mem. bus. adv. com. C.C. of Denver. Recipient Merit medal Pres. Republic Vietnam, 1966, Pub. Health Svc. medal, 1972, Edn. Svc. 1st class medal, 1974, Pub. Works 1st class medal, 1972, Rural Reconstrn. 1st class medal, 1973, Svc. award Asian Edn. Adv. Coun., 1989; co-recipient Engring. Excellence award Am. Cons. Engrs Coun., 1994; named to Top Ten Pub. Works Leaders in Colo., Am. Pub. Works Assn., 1990. Mem. Am. Water Works Assn., Water Environ. Fedn., Colo. Water Congress, Asian C. of C. (bd. dirs. 1993-97), Vietnamese Profl. Engrs. Soc. (founder), Amnesty Inter nat., Friendship Bridge. Buddhist. Avocations: reading, swimming, tennis, hiking. Office: Willows Water Dist 6970 S Holly Cir Ste 200 Englewood CO 80112-1066

LE, THUY TRONG, research and development engineer, educator; b. Vietnam, Jan. 20, 1958; came to US, 1980; s. Thich Trong and Le-Phi Thi (Vuong) V.; m. Nhan Thi Le, Aug. 20, 1985; children: Thuy-Nhu Thi, Thi Trong. BS in Nuclear Engring., U. Calif., 1985, MS in Nuclear Engring., 1987, PhD in Engring., 1990. Electronic technician Aertech Industry, Sunnyvale, Calif., 1982; nuclear reactor operator, health physicist assistant Nuclear Engring. Dept. U. Calif., Berkeley, 1985-88, graduate student instr.Nuclear Engring. and Physics Dept., 1987-90; rsch. asst. physics divsn. Lawrence Berkeley Nat. Lab., 1988-89; instr. physics, calculus I, II, III Dept. Applied Art and Sci. Calif. Coll. of Alameda, 1989-90; rsch. engr. scientific computation divsn.applied physics group Westinghouse Savannah River Lab., 1990-93; sr. R & D engr. SuperComputer Group Fujitsu Am. Incorporation, Calif., 1993—; cons. engr. Sierra Nuclear Corp., Scotts Valley, Calif., 1989—; lectr. San Jose State U., 1996—, U. S.C., Aiken, 1991-93. Contbr. numerous articles to profl. jours. Mem. IEEE, Am. Nuclear Soc. (math. and computation divsn.). Achievements include authoring GRIMH3 computer code: multi dimensional reactor analysis code, WINDEX System: detailed energy residence treatment code, research in parallel algorithms and mathematical schemes for the development of scientific and engineering application software. Address: 44291 Pomace St Fremont CA 94539

LE, THUY XUAN, financial control systems developer, consultant, metaphysics scientist; b. Hanoi, Vietnam, Apr. 25, 1927; came to U.S., 1975; s. Chinh Xuan Le and Ty Thi Tran; m. Thin Thi Dang, Sept. 9, 1957; children: Phuong-Tram, Phuong-Thoa, Tung, Thach. Agrégé Internat. Acctg. Systems, 1970. Adminstrv. specialist U.S. AID, Saigon, Vietnam, 1958-67; acct., cons. Commonwealth Svcs. Inc., Saigon, 1967-70; dir. Biemet, Saigon, 1970-71; gen. mgr. UICC, Saigon, 1971-75; coll. and univ. prof. Saigon, 1971-75; acct., contr. pvt. enterprises Washington, 1975-79; systems acct. D.C. Govt., Washington, 1980-81; dir., fin. control systems MRI, Falls Church, Va., 1981-85; pres. Prajna Instl., Alexandria, Va., 1985—; writer, cons. educator in field, 1957—. Author: Kim-Van-Kieu I, English Translation and Commentaries, 1963, Principles of Advanced Bookkeeping and Accounting, 1971, How to Establish a Uniform Chart of Accounts for Business Enterprises, 1971, How to Establish a Powerful General Ledger System for a Government, 1981; also textbooks in field; translator (poems) Kim-Van-Kieu, 1992 (award of excellence Libr. of Congress 1992), The Super Revelation, 1993, The Prajnaparamita Sutra, 1993, The Soul of Poetry Inside Kim-Van-Kieu, 1995, Dawnlight, 1996. Sec. gen. Puginier Alumni, Saigon, 1971-74; comptr. Assn. Vietnamese Scientists, Saigon, 1972-75. Mem. Internat. Platform Assn., Internat. Soc. Poets (disting.). Prajnaparamita yogi. Avocations: chess, music, poetry, drawing, songwriting. Home and Office: 3701 Ft Worth Ave Alexandria VA 22304-1706

LE, YVONNE DIEMVAN, chemist; b. Vietnam, Nov. 21, 1961; d. Hien Trung and Thanh-Hoa Thi (Luu) L. BA in Chemistry, Math., San Jose State U., 1984. Chem. technician Hewlett Packard Co., Palo Alto, Calif., 1983; assoc. chemist Ampex Corp., Sunnyvale, Calif., 1984-86; chemist II Info. Memory Corp., Santa Clara, Calif., 1986-88; R&D project engr. Komag, Inc., Milpitas, Calif., 1988—. Mem. Am. Chem. Soc. Roman Catholic. Avocations: skiing, tennis, piano. Office: Komag Inc 275 S Hillview Dr Milpitas CA 95035-5417

LEA, GEORGE A., JR., retail food executive; b. Pine Bluff, Ark., Apr. 8, 1950; s. George A. and Lois (Hogg) L.; m. Martha Elizabeth Quinn Stuckey, Sept. 16, 1972 (div. 1987); children: George A. III, Robert Quinn, Lois Anne Elizabeth. BA in Econs. and Bus., Hendrix Coll., 1972. CPA, Ark. Acct. Glenn Railsback & Co., Pine Bluff, Ark., 1972-77; pres., CEO The Mad Butcher, Inc., Pine Bluff, 1977—. Elder Presbyn. Ch. Mem. AICPA, Ark. Soc. CPA, Ark. Grocers and Retail Mchts. (vice chmn. 1994). Home: 501 Carter Dr Pine Bluff AR 71602-3004 Office: The Mad Butcher Inc PO Box 1020 Pine Bluff AR 71613-1020

LEA, LORENZO BATES, lawyer; b. St. Louis, Apr. 12, 1925; s. Lorenzo Bates and Ursula Agnes (Gibson) L.; m. Marcia Gwendolyn Wood, Mar. 21, 1953; children—Victoria, Jennifer, Christopher. BS, MIT, 1946; JD, U. Mich., 1949; grad. Advanced Mgmt. Program, Harvard U., 1964. Bar: Ill. 1950. With Amoco Corp. (formerly Standard Oil Co. Ind.), Chgo., 1949—, asst. gen. counsel, 1963-71, assoc. gen. counsel, 1971-72, gen. counsel, 1972-78, v.p., gen. counsel, 1978-89. Trustee Village of Glenview (Ill.) Zoning Bd., 1961-63; bd. dirs. Chgo. Crime Commn., 1978—, Midwest Council for Internat. Econ. Policy, 1973—, Chgo. Bar Found., 1981—, Chgo. Area Found. for Legal Services, 1981—; bd. dirs. United Charities of Chgo., 1973—, chmn., 1985—. Served with USNR, 1943-46. Mem. ABA, Am. Petroleum Inst., Am. Arbitration Assn. (dir. 1980—), Ill. Bar Assn., Chgo. Bar Assn., Assn. Gen. Counsel, Order of Coif, Law Club, Econs. Club, Legal, Mid-Am. (Chgo.), Glen View, Wyndemere, Hole-In-The-Wall, Sigma Xi. Republican. Mem. United Ch. of Christ.

LEA, SCOTT CARTER, retired packaging company executive; b. New Orleans, Nov. 14, 1931; s. Leonard G. and Helen (Stoughton) L.; m. Marilyn Ruth Blair, Oct. 25, 1957; children: Scott, Nancy B., Mark S. BA, Amherst Coll., 1954; MBA, U. Pa., 1959. Sales and mktg. positions Riegel Paper, 1959-66, sales mgr. folding carton dept. southeastern div., 1966-67, gen. sales mgr., 1967-69, v.p. folding carton dept., 1969-71; v.p. bd. conversion div. Rexham Corp., Charlotte, N.C., 1971-73; v.p. packaging group Rexham Corp., 1973-74, pres., 1974-90; chmn. bd. Rexham Industries, Inc., 1990-92, Lance Inc., Charlotte, 1996—; bd. dirs. Speizman Industries, Inc. Trustee Johnson C. Smith U., Charlotte, N.C. With U.S. Army, 1954-57. Mem. Charlotte C. of C. (bd. dirs. 1977-78), Carmel Country Club, Quail Hollow Country Club, Wild Dunes Club (Isle of Palms, S.C.). Home: 3704 Stone Ct Charlotte NC 28226-7343 Office: Lance Inc 8600 South Blvd Charlotte NC 28273-6925

LEA, STANLEY E., artist, educator; b. Joplin, Mo., Apr. 5, 1930; s. Everett G. and Edna F. L.; m. Ruth Lowe, Aug. 19, 1951; children: Kristy Ruth, Kraig, Kelly B. B.F.A., Pitts. State U., 1953; M.F.A., U. Ark., 1961. Prof. art Sam Houston State U., Huntsville, 1961—, Mexican Field Sch., Puebla, Mexico, 1963-65; vis. artist prof. Mus. Fine Arts, Houston, 1968, 69, 70; prof. art study abroad program London, 1977-78. Juror various art exhibits, 1970-81; workshop demonstrator, E. Tex. State U., Commerce, 1977, 10th ann. color print symposium, Tex. Tech. U., Lubbock, 1983; one-man shows paintings and/or prints, Valley House Gallery, Dallas, 1963, Moody Gallery, Houston, 1976, Sol Del Rio, San Antonio, 1978, 89, Adelle M. Fine Arts, Dallas, 1978, Dubose Gallery, Houston, 1980, Cultural Activities Ctr., Temple, Tex., 1982, Tex. A&M U., College Station, 1986, Mus. at E. Tex., Lufkin, 1989; numerous group shows, latest being Moody Gallery, Houston, 1975, 77, Pecan Square Gallery, Austin, Tex., 1977, Waco Art Center, Waco, Tex., 1977, East Tex. State U., Commerce, 1977, Galveston (Tex.) Art Center, 1978, Twenty Five Nat. Printmaker, Lubbock, Tex., 1978, Beaumont (Tex.) Art Mus., 1978, Art League of Houston, 1978, Gates Gallery, Port Arthur, Tex., 1979, Ars Longa, Houston, 1974, Laguna Gloria Mus., Austin, 1979; represented in permanent collections, Library of Congress, Washington, Brit. Mus., London, Mus. Fine Arts, Houston, USIA, N.Y.C., N.Y. Public Library, N.Y.C., Mpls. Inst. Art, Kalamazoo Inst. Art, Boise (Idaho) Gallery of Art, Madison (Wis.) Art Center, Spiva Art Center, Joplin, Mo., Ft. Worth Art Mus., Cleve. Mus., Inst. Mexicano Norteamericana de Relationes, Mexico City, Smithsonian Inst., Washington, also corp. and pvt. collections. (Recipient numerous awards, latest being, Southwest Graphics Invitational award 1971, Dimensions IX Exhbn. award 1974, 68th Nat. Tex. Fine Arts Exhbn. 1979). Sam Houston State U. grantee, 1970, 74. Mem. Coll. Art Assn., So. Graphics Council. Home: 3324 Winter Way Huntsville TX 77340-8919 Office: Sam Houston State Univ Art Dept Huntsville TX 77341

LEAB, DANIEL JOSEPH, history educator; b. Berlin, Aug. 29, 1936; s. Leo and Herta (Marcus) L.; BA, Columbia U., 1957, MA, 1961, PhD, 1969; m. Katharine Kyes, Aug. 16, 1964; children: Abigail Elizabeth, Constance Martha, Marcus Rogers. With Columbia U., 1966-73, Seton Hall, 1974—; pub., co-editor Am. Book Prices Current; mng. editor Labor History; dir. Bancroft-Parkman. Fellow Met. Mus. Art; mem. Historians of Am. Communism (gen. sec.). Clubs: Century, Grolier. Home: PO Box 1216 Washington CT 06793-0216

LEACH, DAVE FRANCIS, editor, musician; b. Iowa City, Iowa, Nov. 12, 1945; s. Joseph Stanley and Thelma Maxine (Strubhar) L.; m. Donna Susan Schoeppner, Dec. 17, 1970 (div. Jan. 1979); children: Arlo Bernard, Cynthia Robin; m. Dorothy Darlene Barnes, Dec. 13, 1986. B Music Edn., Drake U., 1967. Band dir. Melcher (Iowa)/Dallas Schs., 1967-68, Lackland Air Force Band, 1968-70, Coon Rapids (Iowa) Schs., 1970; band instrument repairman Miller Music/Family Music Ctr., Des Moines, 1972—; editor, founder Prayer & Action News, Des Moines, 1989—; producer, host The Uncle Ed Show, 1995—; trumpet player Des Moines Mcpl. Band, 1963-78; musician Kingsway, St. Ambrose and St. Augustine Cathedrals, and Simpson United Meth. Ch., 1980-92. Author, composer: (musical comedy) Werld Klas Ejukashun, 1991; author (book) the Gifts of Governments, 1990. Dem. candidate for state rep., Iowa, 1986, Rep. candidate 1988, 90; active numerous conservative and grass roots groups; pres., edtor Fathers for Equal Rights, Des Moines chpt. 1985-87. Avocations: bible study, inventing, construction. Home and Office: 137 E Leach Ave Des Moines IA 50315-3643

LEACH, FRANKLIN ROLLIN, biochemistry educator; b. Gorman, Tex., Apr. 2, 1933; s. Frank Rollin and Jewel Laurie (Casey) L.; m. Mary Kathleen Kincaid, Jan. 26, 1956 (dec. Feb. 1969); children: Carolyn Ann, Janet Lynne, Barbara Naomi; m. Anna Belle Coke, Feb. 27, 1970; stepchildren: Alan Charles Coke, Barry Neil Coke, Carol Ann Coke. BA, Hardin-Simmons U., 1953; PhD, U. Tex., Austin, 1957. Rsch. asst. U. Tex., Austin, 1953-56, Hite rsch. fellow, 1956-57; Nat. Rsch. Coun. fellow med. sci. U. Calif., Berkeley, 1957-59; then asst. prof. to assoc. prof. Okla. State U., Stillwater, 1959-65, prof. biochemistry and molecular biology, 1966—, assoc. dept. head, 1990—; rsch. fellow Calif. Inst. Tech., Pasadena, 1965-66; cons. Kerr-McGee Co., Edmond, Okla., 1970-72, 3M Co., St. Paul, 1981-85, 95—, Idexx, 1994—, Teltech, 1994—; interim dept. head biochemistry Okla. State U., 1990. Author: Biochemical Indicators of Subsurface Pollution, 1980; editor Okla. Acad. Sci., 1990—; contbr. more than 100 articles to sci. jours. Pres.'s fellow, Soc. Am. Bacteriologists, 1960; recipient rsch. career devel. award, Nat. Cancer Inst., 1962-72. Mem. AAAS, Am. Soc. Biochemistry and Molecular Biology, Am. Soc. Microbiology, Am. Soc. Photobiology, Am. Chem. Soc., Coun. Biology Editors, Protein Soc., Int. Soc. Biolumin. Chemilumin., Stillwater Flying Club (pres. 1968-86). Avocations: hunting, reading, photography. Home: 1101 N Lincoln St Stillwater OK 74075-4033 Office: Okla State U Dept Biochem/Molecular Biol 246 NRC Stillwater OK 74078-3035

LEACH, JAMES ALBERT SMITH, congressman; b. Davenport, Iowa, Oct. 15, 1942; s. James Albert and Lois (Hill) L.; m. Elisabeth Foxley, Dec. 6, 1975; 1 child, Gallagher. BA, Princeton U., 1964; MA, Johns Hopkins U., 1966; postgrad., London Sch. Econs., 1966-68. Mem. staff Congressman Donald Rumsfeld, 1965-66; U.S. Fgn. Service officer, 1968-69, 70-73; spl. asst. to dir. OEO, 1969-70; mem. U.S. del. Geneva Disarmament Conf., 1971-72, UN Gen. Assembly, 1972, UN Natural Resources Conf., 1975; pres. Flamegas Companies Inc., Bettendorf, Iowa, 1973-76; chmn. bd. Adel Wholesalers, Inc., Bettendorf, 1973-76; mem. 95th-105th Congresses from 1st Iowa dist., 1977—; chmn. banking and fin. svcs. com., mem. internat. rels. com.; mem. U.S. Adv. Commn. Internat. Ednl. and Cultural Affairs, 1975-76. Chmn. Iowa Rep. Directions '76 Com. Episcopalian. Office: 2186 Rayburn Bldg Washington DC 20515-1501*

LEACH, JAMES GLOVER, lawyer; b. Panama City, Fla., Jan. 26, 1948; s. Milledge Glover and Thelma Louise (Hamilton) L.; m. Judith A. Leach, Feb. 26, 1972 (div. 1987); children: Allison, Arica. AS, Gulf Coast Coll., 1968; BA, Duke U., 1970; MBA, Ga. State U., 1974, MI, 1976; JD, Drake U., 1989. Bar: Iowa 1990; CPCU 1977, CLU 1978. Bank officer Bank South, Atlanta, 1972-75; asst. v.p. Johnson & Higgins, Atlanta, 1975-78; pres. Nat. Gen. Ins. Co., St. Louis, 1978-85, AOPA Svc. Corp., St. Louis, 1985-87, Kirke-Van Orsdel Specialty, Des Moines, 1987-89, Gallagher Specialty, St. Louis, 1990-92; prin., dir., counsel Pauli & Co. Inc., St. Louis, 1992-93; gen. counsel Am. Safety Ins., Atlanta, 1993—; cons. McDonnell Douglas, St. Louis, 1987; dir. Gateway Ins. Co., St. Louis, 1992; corp. assembly Blue Cross/Blue Shield, St. Louis, 1991-92. Contbr. articles to profl. jours. 1st lt. USAF, 1970-72, Korea. Avocations: pilot, golf. Home: 2931 Torreya Way Marietta GA 30067 Office: Am Safety Ins Group 1845 The Exchange SE Ste 200 Atlanta GA 30339-2019

LEACH, JOHN F., newspaper editor, journalism educator; b. Montrose, Colo., Aug. 6, 1952; s. Darrell Willis and Marian Ruth (Hester) L.; m. Deborah C. Ross, Jan. 2, 1982; children: Allison, Jason. BS in Journalism, U. Colo., 1974, MA in Journalism, 1979; MA in Am. Studies, U. Sussex, Falmer, Brighton, Eng., 1983. News reporter Boulder (Colo.) Daily Camera, 1974-79; news reporter Ariz. Republic, Phoenix, 1979-85, asst. city editor, 1985-93; news editor The Phoenix Gazette, 1993-94; asst. mng. editor Phoenix Gazette, 1994-95; asst. mng. editor, news ops. The Ariz. Republic and The Phoenix Gazette, 1995-97; sr. editor The Ariz. Republic, Phoenix, 1997—; faculty assoc. Ariz. State U., Tempe, 1990—; pres., dir. First Amendment Funding Inc., Phoenix. Bd. Regents scholar U. Colo., 1970, Rotary Found. scholar, 1982. Mem. Ariz. Press Club (treas. 1984-86, pres. 1986-87), Soc. Profl. Journalists, Reporter's Com. for Freedom of Press, Soc. Newspaper Design, Investigative Reporters and Editors. Home: 4313 E Calle Redonda Phoenix AZ 85018-3733 Office: The Ariz Republic 200 E Van Buren St Phoenix AZ 85004-2238

LEACH, KAY T., critical care nurse, administrator; b. Brazil, Ind., Oct. 11, 1953; d. David M. and Tamiko (Ishiguru) Oberholtzer; m. Ronald Leach, June 12, 1982; children: Brian, Kristen, Brittany, Ronald Ian. BSN, Ind. State U., 1975, MSN, 1989. Cert. emergency nurse, ACLS. House supr. Union Hosp., Terre Haute, Ind., ICU staff nurse, dir. emergency dept. Mem. Emergency Nurses Assn., Sigma Theta Tau, Phi Kappa Phi.

LEACH, MAURICE DERBY, JR., librarian; b. Lexington, Ky., June 23, 1923; s. Maurice Derby and Sallie Eleanor (Woods) L.; m. Virginia Stuart Baskett, Mar. 16, 1953; 1 dau., Sarah Stuart. A.B., U. Ky., 1945; B.L.S., U. Chgo., 1946. Bibliographer Dept. State, 1947-50; fgn. service officer Dept. State (USIS); vice consul, attache Dept. State (USIS), Cairo and Alexandria, U.A.R., Beirut, 1950-59; chmn. dept. library sci. U. Ky., 1959-66; regional program officer Ford Found., Beirut, 1967-68; univ. librarian, prof. Washington and Lee U., Lexington, Va., 1968-85, prof., asst. to pres., 1985-88; library adviser Nat. Library, Egypt, Lebanon and acad. libraries in Middle East. Contbr. articles to profl. jours. Served with AUS, 1948-49. Mem. English Speaking Union (pres. Lexington br. 1970-75), Va. Libr. Assn. (pres. 1976), Assn. Preservation of Va. Activities (dir. Lexington br. 1989-91), Rockbridge Hist. Soc., SAR (v.p. 1990-93). Episcopalian. Home: 1 Courtland Ctr Lexington VA 24450-1813

LEACH, MICHAEL GLEN, publisher; b. Chgo., Aug. 19, 1940; s. Glen E. and Sara Faith (Giarrizzo) L.; M.A., St. Mary of the Lake Coll., 1966; m. Vickie Louise Jacobi, Oct. 3, 1969; children—Christopher, Jeffrey. Adminstr., Cath. Charities of Chgo., Maryville Acad., 1966-68; v.p., sr. editor Seabury Press, N.Y.C., 1969-80; sr. v.p., asso. pub. The Crossroad Pub. Co., N.Y.C., 1981-83; pres. The Continuum Pub. Corp., N.Y.C., 1980-83; exec. v.p., assoc. pub. The Crossroad/Continuum Pub. Cos., N.Y.C., 1983-90; pres., pub. The Crossroad/Continuum Pub. Group, 1990-92; COO and pub. The Crossroad Pub. Co., N.Y.C., 1993—. Mem. Assn. Am. Pubs., Protestant Ch.-Owned Pubs. Assn., Religious Pubs. Group (pres. 1991-92), Nat. Book Critics Circle, Cath. Book Pubs. Assn. (pres. 1989-90), Riverside Acres Community Assn. (pres. 1988). Roman Catholic. Author: I Know It When I See It: Pornography, Violence and Public Sensitivity, 1975; The Boy Who Had Everything, 1977; Don't Call Me Orphan, 1979; contbr. articles to profl. jours. Home: 49 Long Meadow Rd Riverside CT 06878-1125 Office: 370 Lexington Ave New York NY 10017-6503

LEACH, RALPH F., banker; b. Elgin, Ill., June 24, 1917; s. Harry A. and Edith (Sanders) L.; m. Harriet C. Scheuerman, Nov. 18, 1944; children: C. David, H. Randall, Barbara E. A.B., U. Chgo., 1938. Investment analyst Harris Trust & Savs. Bank, Chgo., 1940-48, Valley Nat. Bank, Phoenix, 1948-50; chief govt. finance sect. Fed. Res. Bd., Washington, 1950-53; treas. Guaranty Trust Co., N.Y.C., 1953-59; v.p. Guaranty Trust Co., 1958-59; v.p., treas. Morgan Guaranty Trust Co., N.Y.C., 1959-62; sr. v.p., treas. Morgan Guaranty Trust Co., 1962-64, exec. v.p., treas., 1964-68, vice chmn. bd. dirs., 1968-71, chmn. exec. com., 1971-77; chmn. emeritus Energy Conversion Devices Inc. Served to capt. USMCR, 1940-45. Mem. Coral Ridge Country Club, Phi Kappa Psi. Home: 4211 NE 25th Ave Fort Lauderdale FL 33308-5706 Office: Energy Conversion Devices Inc 1675 W Maple Rd Troy MI 48084-7118

LEACH, RICHARD HEALD, political scientist, educator; b. Denver, May 30, 1922; s. Richard Edwards and Helen Caroline (Heald) L.; m. Betty Carroll, Sept. 5, 1947; 1 son, Christopher Alan. A.B., Colo. Coll., 1944; M.A., Princeton U., 1949, Ph.D, 1951. Asst. prof. Ga. Inst. Tech., Atlanta, 1949-53; staff assoc. So. Regional Edn. Bd., Atlanta, 1953-55; asst. prof to prof. emeritus Duke U., Durham, N.C., 1955—; vis. disting. prof. Citadel, Charleston, S.C., 1976; vis. scholar Australian Nat. U., 1975,83; cons. U.S. Adv. Commn. on Intergovt1. Relations, Am. Coll. Testing Program. Co-author: In Quest of Freedom, 1959, reissued, 1981, State and Local Government: The Third Century of Federalism, 1988; author: Governing the American Nation, 1967, American Federalism, 1970, Intergovernmental Relations in the 1980's, 1983. Mem. Durham City County Merger Study Commn., 1971-73; mem. Ill. Commn. of Scholars, 1973-77. Fulbright scholar U. Amsterdam, 1967-68. Mem. Am. Soc. Pub. Adminstrn. Clubs: Cosmos (Washington); Princeton (N.Y.C.). Lodge: Rotary. Home: 1313 Woodburn Rd Durham NC 27705-5740

LEACH, ROBERT ELLIS, physician, educator; b. Sanford, Maine, Nov. 25, 1931; s. Ellis and Estella (Tucker) L.; m. Laurine Seber, Aug. 20, 1955; children: Cathy, Brian, Michael, Craig, Karen, Diane. AB, Princeton U., 1953; MD, Columbia U., 1957. Diplomate Am. Bd. Orthopedic Surgery (treas. 1986-93). Resident orthopedic surgery U. Minn., 1957-62; orthopedic surgeon Lahey Clinic, Boston, 1964-68; chmn. dept. Lahey Clinic, 1968-70; prof., chmn. dept. Boston U. Med. Sch., 1970—; head physician U.S. Olympic Team, 1984; chmn. sports medicine coun. U.S. Olympic Com., 1984-93; vice chmn. sports medicine coun. U.S. Tennis Assn., 1988—. Editor-in-chief Am. J. Sports Med.; contbr. articles to profl. jours. Served to lt. comdr. USNR, 1962-64. Am., Brit., Canadian Orthopedic Travelling fellow, 1971; Sports Medicine Man of the Yr., 1988; recipient Rovere Career Tchg. award, 1995. Mem. Am. Acad. Orthopedic Surgeons, Continental Orthopedic Soc. (sec. 1966), Am. Orthopedic Assn. (pres. 1994), Am. Orthopedic Soc. Sports Medicine (pres. 1983), Longwood Cricket Club. Home: 40 Rockport Rd Weston MA 02193-1428 Office: 230 Calvary St Waltham MA 02154-8366

LEACH, ROBIN, producer, writer, television host; b. London, Aug. 29, 1941; came to U.S., 1963; s. Douglas Thomas and Violet (Phillips) L. Diploma, Nat. Union Journalists, 1961. Reporter Harrow (Eng.) Observer, 1958-61, Daily Mail, London, 1961-63; mag. pub. GO mag., N.Y.C., 1964-67; show bus. editor The Star, N.Y.C., 1964-79; show bus. reporter CNN, N.Y.C., 1979-80; entertainment reporter Entertainment Tonight, N.Y.C., 1980-83; exec. producer Leach Entertainment Enterprises, N.Y.C., 1983—. Author: The Go Rock & Roll Manual, 1966, 2d rev. edit., 1967, Lifestyles of the Rich and Famous, 1983, Healthy Lifestyles, 1995; prodr.: (TV shows) Lifestyles of the Rich and Famous, 1983-96 (Emmy nomination), Runaway with the Rich and Famous, The Rich and Famous Worlds Best, Fame, Fortune & Romance; host: KNBC-TV Year in Review, 1986 (Emmy award), Supermodel of the World, 1986, Home Videos of the Stars, 1991, Nitecap, ABC-TV, Heroes America for USA TV, 1996—, Gourmet Getaways for TVFN, 1995-97, Miracles and Wonders for Family Channel, 1997. Mem. AFTRA, Screen Actors Guild. Avocations: tennis, gourmet cooking. Office: Leach Entertainment Features 885 2nd Ave New York NY 10017-2201

LEACH, RONALD GEORGE, educational administration educator; b. Monroe, Mich., Feb. 22, 1938; s. Garnet William and Erma (Erbadine) L.; m. Joy Adeline Moore, Dec. 21, 1956; children—Ronald George, Debra Mabel, Catherine Louise, Shane John. B.S. in Secondary Edn, Central Mich. U., 1966; M.A. in L.S. (U.S. Office Edn. fellow 1968-69), U. Mich., 1969; Ph.D. in Higher Edn. Adminstrn, Mich. State U., 1980. Head libr. Ohio State U., Mansfield, 1969-70; asst. dir., then acting dir. libr. Lake Superior State Coll., Sault Ste. Marie, Mich., 1970-76; assoc. dir. librs. Central Mich. U., 1976-80; dean libr. svcs. Ind. State U., Terre Haute, 1980-93, assoc. v.p. info. svcs., dean of librs., 1994-97; prof. higher ednl. adminstrn., 1997—; prof. edn., mem. accreditation teams N. Central Assn. Author articles in field. Served with N.G., 1955-61. Mem. ALA, INFORMA (steering com. 1990—), Assn. Coll. and Rsch. Librs., Libr. Info. and Tech. Assn., Ind. Libr. Assn., Am. Soc. Info. Sci., Libr. Adminstrn. and Mgmt. Assn. (pres. 1985-86), Online Computer Libr. Ctr. User Council (exec. com. 1986, 88). Home: 4815 E Wolf Tree Ave Terre Haute IN 47805-9414 Office: Ind State U Dept Leadership Admin Found Terre Haute IN 47809

LEACH, RUSSELL, judge; b. Columbus, Ohio, Aug. 1, 1922; s. Charles Albert and Hazel Kirk (Thatcher) L.; m. Helen M. Sharpe, Feb. 17, 1945; children: Susan Sharpe Snyder, Terry Donnell, Ann Dunham Samuelson. B.A., Ohio State U., 1946, J.D., 1949. Bar: Ohio 1949. Clk. U.S. Geol. Survey, Columbus, 1948-49; reference and teaching asst. Coll. Law, Ohio State U., 1949-51; asst. city atty. City of Columbus, 1951, 53-57, city atty., 1957-63, presiding judge mcpl. ct., 1964-66; ptnr. Bricker & Eckler, 1966-88, chmn. exec. com., 1982-87; judge Ohio Ct. Claims, 1988—. Commr., Columbus Met. Housing Authority, 1968-74; chmn. Franklin County Republican Com., 1974-78. Served with AUS, 1942-46, 51-53. Named One of 10 Outstanding Young Men of Columbus, Columbus Jaycees, 1956, 57. Mem. ABA, FBA, Ohio Bar Assn. (coun. of dels. 1970-75), Columbus Bar Assn. (pres. 1973-74, Svc. medal 1993), Am. Judicature Soc., Pres.' Club Ohio State U., Am. Legion, Delta Theta Phi, Chi Phi. Presbyterian. Home: 1232 Kenbrook Hills Dr Columbus OH 43220-4968 Office: Ohio Ct Claims PO Box 1008 Columbus OH 43216-1008

LEACHMAN, ROGER MACK, librarian; b. Stillwater, Okla., June 3, 1942; s. Oakley Thaddeus and Mildred Violet (McNeff) L.; m. Nancy Jo Lordeman, Aug. 25, 1973; children—Emily Anne, James Oakley. A.B., U. Pa., 1967; M.S., U. N.C., 1973. Planner Pa. State Planning Bd., Harrisburg, 1967-68; rsch. libr. U. Va., Charlottesville, 1973-74, info. svcs. libr., 1974-76, dir. reference svcs., 1976-84, rare book bibliographer, 1984-88; coord. Southeast Libr. System, Rochester, Minn., 1988—. Contbr. articles to profl. jours. Served with U.S. Army, 1965-67. Gov's. fellow U. Va., Charlottesville, 1968-69. Mem. ALA, MEMO, MLA. Episcopalian. Avocations: bibliography; backpacking. Home: 822 4th St SW Rochester MN 55902-2914 Office: Southeast Libr System 107 W Frontage Rd N # 52 Rochester MN 55901-0343

LEA-COX, JOHN DEREK, plant physiologist; b. Bulawayo, Zimbabwe, Aug. 31, 1960; came to U.S., 1989; s. Nigel and Joyce (Adnams) Lea-C. BSc, U. Natal, South Africa, 1984; MSc, U. Natal, 1989; PhD, U. Fla., 1993. Mgr. nursery Amanzi Citrus Estate, Uitenhage, South Africa, 1984-86; rsch. assoc., lectr. U. Natal, 1987-89; grad. rsch. asst. U. Fla., Lake Alfred, 1989-93; assoc. nat. rsch. coun. NASA-Life Scis., Kennedy Space Center, Fla., 1993-95; rsch. scientist Dynamac Corp., Kennedy Space Center, 1996—; asst. prof. dept. natural resource scis. & landscape arch. U. Md.,

College Park, 1996—. Contbr. articles to Jour. Life Support and Biosphere Sci., Jour. Am. Soc. Horticulture Sci., Fla. Horticulture Soc., Annals of Botany. With Rhodesian African Rifles, 1979. A.S. Herlong scholar, 1989-93; Nat. Rsch. Coun. fellow, 1993-95; South Africa Citrus Nursery Men's Assn. grantee, 1987. Mem. Am. Soc. Plant Physiology, Am. Soc. Hort. Sci., Fla. Hort. Soc. Achievements include research in nutrient movement to groundwater, nutrient uptake by plants, adaptive control systems for nutrient delivery and pH control in plant growth modules for space research, advanced life support and controlled environment agriculture; current interests include information systems, nutrient management systems for nurseries, nutrient uptake and use-efficiency by tiparian buffer species. Office: U Md Dept Natural Resource Scis and Landscape Arch 2120 Plant Scis Bldg College Park MD 20742

LEADBETTER, MARK RENTON, JR., orthopedic surgeon; b. Phila., Nov. 7, 1944; s. Mark Renton and Ruth (Protzeller) L.; m. Letitia Ashby, July 28, 1973 (div. June 1990); m. Jan Saker, 1991. BA, Gettysburg Coll., 1967; MSc in Hygiene, U. Pitts., 1970; MD, Temple U., 1974. Surg. intern Univ. Hosps., Boston, 1974-75, resident in surgery, 1975-76; emergency room physician Sturdy Meml. Hosp., Attleboro, Mass., 1976-78; resident in orthopaedics U. Pitts., 1978-81; orthopaedic physician Rockingham Meml. Hosp., Harrisonburg, Va., 1981-82, courtesy staff, 1982—; pvt. practice, Staunton, Va., 1982—; mem. active staff King's Daus. Hosp., Staunton, 1982—; active staff Samaritan Hosp., Moses Lake, Wash.; courtesy staff Columbia Basin Hosp., Ephrata, Wash. Contbr. articles to med. jours.; patentee safety syringes, safety cannulas, designer of medecal equipment. Mem. Am. Coll. Sports Medicine, So. Med. Assn., So. Orthopaedic Assn., County Med. Soc., Nat. Futures Assn. (assoc.). Republican. Avocations: flying, skiing, raising bird dogs. Home: 246 Rainier View Ln Moses Lake WA 98837

LEAF, ALEXANDER, physician, educator; b. Yokohama, Japan, Apr. 10, 1920; came to U.S., 1922, naturalized, 1936; s. Aaron L. and Dora (Hural) L.; m. Barbara Louise Kincaid, Oct. 1943; children—Caroline Joan, Rebecca Louise, Tamara Jean. B.S., U. Wash., 1940; M.D., U. Mich., 1943; M.A., Harvard, 1961. Intern Mass. Gen. Hosp., Boston, 1943-44; mem. staff Mass. Gen. Hosp., 1949—, physician-in-chief, 1966-81; resident Mayo Found., Rochester, Minn., 1944-45; research fellow U. Mich., 1947-49; practice internal medicine Boston, 1949-90; faculty Med. Sch., Harvard, 1949—, Jackson prof. clin. medicine, 1966-81, Ridley Watts prof. preventive medicine, 1980-90, chmn. dept. preventive medicine and clin. epidemiology, 1980-90, Jackson prof. clin. medicine emeritus, 1990—; Disting. physician VA Medical Ctr. Brockton/W. Roxbury Hosps., Boston, 1992-97. Served to capt. M.C. AUS, 1945-46. Recipient Outstanding Achievement award U. Minn., 1964; vis. fellow Balliol Coll., Oxford, 1971-72; Guggenheim fellow, 1971-72. Fellow Am. Acad. Arts and Scis.; mem. NAS, ACP (master), Inst. Medicine, Am. Soc. Clin. Investigation (past pres.), Am. Physiol. Soc., Biophys. Soc., Assn. Am. Physicians (Kober medal 1995), Internat. Soc. Nephrology (A.M. Richards award 1997). Home: 1 Curtis Cir Winchester MA 01890-1703 Office: Mass Gen Hosp Boston MA 02114

LEAF, HOWARD WESTLEY, retired air force officer, military official; b. Menominee, Mich., Sept. 22, 1923; s. Joseph Conrad and Hilda Eugene (Lavoy) L.; m. Madonna Anne Ronan, May 21, 1955; children: Mary Beth, Barbara Anne, Timothy, Anne Marie, Thomas, James. B.S., Colo. Sch. Mines, 1950; M.S., St. Louis U., 1955; grad., Command and Staff Coll., 1961, Indsl. Coll. Armed Forces, 1969. Commd. 2d lt. U.S. Air Force, 1951, advanced through grades to lt. gen., 1980, ret., 1985; aviation cadet, 1950-51; jet pilot Korea, 1952-53; test pilot, 1955-60, geophysicist, 1961-64; ops. officer (49th Tactical Fighter Wing), Europe, 1965; squadron comdr. S.E. Asia, 1966; staff officer (Hdqrs. USAF), 1966-68, 69-71; wing comdr. 1st and 366th Tactical Fighter Wings, 1971-74; dep. chief staff for requirements Tactical Air Command, 1974-76; comdr. Air Force Test and Evaluation Ctr., Kirtland AFB, N.Mex., 1976-80; insp. gen. U.S. Air Force, Washington, 1980-83, asst. vice chief of staff, 1983-85; sr. v.p. BDM Internat. Corp., McLean, Va., 1984-91; dir. test and evaluation Hdqrs. USAF The Pentagon, Washington, 1992—; mem. Air Force Sci. Adv. Bd. Decorated D.S.M., Silver Star, Legion of Merit, D.F.C.; recipient Eugene M. Zuckert Mgmt. Award, 1978, Disting. Achievement award Colo. Sch. Mines, 1982. Mem. Internat. Test and Evaluation Assn. (sr. adv. bd., Allen R. Mattews Award, 1994). Presbyterian. Home: 8504 Brook Rd Mc Lean VA 22102-1505 Office: Hdqs USAF TE 4E-995 The Pentagon Washington DC 20330

LEAF, PAUL, producer, director, writer; b. N.Y.C., May 2, 1929; s. Manuel and Anna (Dardick) L.; m. Nydia Ellis, Oct. 22, 1955 (div. 1990); children: Jonathan, Alexandra, Ellen. BA in Drama with honors, CCNY, 1952. pres. Sea Gate Co. Dir., prodr.: 17 Broadway prodns., including The Subject Was Roses, 1964, films include: Judge Horton and the Scottsboro Boys, 1976 (Peabody award), Desperate Characters, 1972, Hail to the Chief, 1973, Sister Aimee, 1977, Every Man a King, 1977, Top Secret, 1979, God, Sex and Apple Pie, 1995, TV prodns. include Sgt. Matlovich vs. the U.S. Air Force, 1978; author: Comrades, 1985, Red, Right, Returning, 1987. Founder, chmn. Santa Monica Arts Commn., Santa Monica Arts Found.; founder, cons., bd. dirs. Santa Monica Coll. Art, Design and Architecture, 1990—; mem. grants panel Nat. Endowment for the Arts, 1993, Nat. Endowment for the Humanities, 1994. With U.S. Army, 1952-54. Decorated Meritorious Service medal; recipient 20 internat. festival and profl. awards, including Venice, 1967, London, 1967, 68, 69, N.Y., 1967, 68, 69, Berlin, 1972. Mem. Dirs. Guild Am., Writers Guild Am. Home: 2800 Neilson Way Santa Monica CA 90405-4025

LEAF, ROBERT JAY, dental insurance consultant; b. Mt. Vernon, N.Y., July 27, 1944; s. Jules William and Evelyn (Schneider) L.; m. Jeanette Ann Benjamin, June 17, 1973; children: Jeremy Robert, David Evan. DMD, Harvard U., 1969. Pres. Universal Profl. Ctrs., N.Y.C., 1971-74; dentist in pvt. practice N.Y.C., 1973-80; pres. Am. Dental Examiners, Inc., N.Y.C., 1978—; chmn. Better Benefits, Inc., N.Y.C., 1990—; pres., founder LeafRe Reins. Co., Ariz., 1993—; founder Dental Health Alliance, 1994, pres. 1994-96; cons. Guardian Life Ins. Co., N.Y.C., 1979, Prin. Life Ins. Co., Iowa, 1981, 93, Mass. Mut. Life Ins. Co., 1983, 94, Equitable, N.Y., 1985, Empire Blue Cross, 1986, Prudential, N.J., 1987, Gen. Mills, Minn., 1988, Aetna, Conn., 1989, Am. Airlines, Tex., 1990, Protective Life Ins. Co., Alabama, 1991, Gen. Am. Life Ins. Co., 1992, 94, Blue Cross/Blue Shield, R.I., 1993, Fortis Benefits Ins. Co., Mo., 1988, 93, Chubb Life Ins. Co. Am., N.H., 1993, Jefferson Pilot Life, 1994, Trustmark Life, 1994, Delta Dental Minn., 1994, Healthsource Provident Life Inst. Co., 1996, Delta Dental California, 1997, Shenandoah Life Ins. Co., 1997; lectr. at nat. confs. on dental ins., vol. dental ins., and managed dental care, group officers round table, 1985. Author: The Dental Logic System, 1984, The Dental Learning System, 1987; also articles; devel. vol. dental ins. plan. Bd. dirs. Jewish Community Ctr., Harrison, N.Y., 1992. Mem. ADA, Dental Soc. State of N.Y., First Dist. Dental Soc., Acad. Gen. Dentistry, Am. Assn. Dental Cons., Am. Soc. for Preventive Dentistry. Avocations: sailing, skiing, reading. Office: Am Dental Examiners Inc 370 7th Ave Ste 1206 New York NY 10001-3900

LEAF, ROBERT STEPHEN, public relations executive; b. N.Y.C., Aug. 9, 1931; s. Nathan and Anne (Feinman) L.; m. Adele Ornstein, June 8, 1958; 1 child, Stuart Nathan. B.J., U. Mo-Columbia, 1952, M.A., 1954. Account exec. Herbert Kaufman, N.Y.C., 1956-57; various positions Marsteller Orgn., N.Y.C., 1957-65; v.p., gen. mgr. Marsteller Internat., Brussels, 1965-68; v.p. Marsteller Internat., Europe, 1968-70; pres. Burson-Marsteller Internat. and Marsteller Internat., London, 1970-81; chmn. Burson-Marsteller Internat., London, 1985—; dir. Burson-Marsteller Ltd., (Eng.), Burson-Marsteller Inc. (U.S.), Burson-Marsteller, (Japan), Burson-Marsteller Intermarkets, Bahrain, Burson-Marsteller S.E.A., (Singapore), Burson-Marsteller Ltd., (Hong Kong), Burson-Marsteller Gmbh, Germany; dir. Burson-Marsteller S.A., (Belgium), (France); dir. Burson-Marsteller S.P.A., (Italy), Burson-Marsteller S.A., (Switzerland), Burson-Marsteller Pty., (Australia), Burson-Marsteller, China. Contbr. articles to profl. pubs. Mem. Public Relations Soc. Am., Inst. Pub. Relations Eng., Pub. Relations Consultancy Assn. (London), Fgn. Press Assn., Pub. Relations Soc. Am., Alpha Pi Zeta, Kappa Tau Alpha. Club: Hurlingham (London). Home: 3 Fursecroft George St, London W1, England Office: Burson Marsteller Internat, 24-28 Bloomsbury Way, London WC1A 2PX, England

LEAF, ROGER WARREN, business consultant; b. New Rochelle, N.Y., Aug. 3, 1946; s. Harold Edwin and Mabel (Erickson) L.; m. Judith Blaine Edds, Sept. 23, 1978; children: Spencer W., Andrew B. BA in Econs., Heidelberg Coll., 1968; MBA, NYU, 1978. V.p. pub. fin. Dean Witter Reynolds Inc., N.Y.C., 1974-81; prin. corp. fin. Morgan Stanley & Co., Inc., N.Y.C., 1981-84; v.p. pub. fin., The First Boston Corp, N.Y.C., 1984-87, dir. mcpl. securities, 1988-91, chief oper. officer fixed income divsn., 1991-93; pres. R.W. Leaf & Co., 1993—, CFO Beverage Mktg. Techs., Inc., 1995—. Trustee All Souls Sch., N.Y.C., 1984-90, treas. 1984-88. 1st lt. USAR, 1969-72. Office: RW Leaf & Co 100 Park Ave New York NY 10017-5516

LEAHEY, LYNN, editor-in-chief. Editor-in-chief Soap Opera Digest, N.Y.C. Office: Soap Opera Digest 45 W 25th St Fl 8 New York NY 10010-2003*

LEAHIGH, ALAN KENT, association executive; b. Chgo., Dec. 25, 1944; s. Leland Jean and Rena Matilda (Rodda) L.; m. Lorrie Lynn Johnson, Aug. 19, 1967; children: Matthew Alan, Nathan Andrew. BA, Ill. Wesleyan U., 1967; MA, U. Mo., 1971. Reporter, editor Daily Pantagraph, Bloomington, Ill., 1965-71; tchr. Joliet (Ill.) Pub. Sch. Dist., 1969-71; assoc. dir. pub. info. Am. Dental Assn., Chgo., 1971-75, dir. pub. edn., 1976-77, editor ADA News, 1978-80; v.p. Pub. Communications Inc., Chgo., 1981-83, sr. v.p., ptnr., 1983-90, exec. v.p., 1990-95; exec. v.p. Exec. Adminstrn., Inc., Arlington Heights, Ill., 1995—; exec. dir. Am. Soc. for Blood and Marrow Transplantation, 1997—; v.p. Living Learning Devel. Corp., Wheaton, Ill., 1980-89, Marian Park Inc., Wheaton, 1980-89; lectr. workshops in field. Contbr. articles to profl. jours. Mem. Wheaton Hist. Preservation Soc., 1978—; chmn. Wheaton Community TV Cmmn., 1986—. Mem. Pub. Rels. Soc. Am. (Silver anvil award 1982, 85, 86, 93), Soc. Profl. Journalists, Am. Hosp. Assn., Am. Soc. Assn. Execs., Chgo. Publicity Club, Chgo. Headline Club, Masons. Presbyterian. Office: Exec Adminstrn Inc 85 W Algonquin Rd Arlington Heights IL 60005-4422

LEAHY, MICHAEL JOSEPH, newspaper editor; b. Chgo., Feb. 24, 1939; s. Joseph Michael and Elizabeth Catherine (Keefe) L.; m. Harriet Smith Friday, Sept. 18, 1971; children—Christine Elizabeth, Thomas Joseph, Christopher Michael. AB, Georgetown U., 1961; MS in Journalism, Columbia U., 1966. From copy boy, news clk., copy editor to editor L.I. Weekly N.Y. Times, N.Y.C., 1961-77, editor Conn. Weekly, 1977-81, travel editor, 1982-86, editor arts & leisure sect., 1986-90, dep. editor The Week in Review, 1990-92, real estate editor, 1992—. Editor: (with A.M. Rosenthal, A. Gelb and N. Kerr) The Sophisticated Traveler series. Bd. advisors Georgetown Coll., 1990-96; mem. edn. com. St. David's Sch., 1991-93. 1st lt. U.S. Army, 1961-64. Pulitizer Traveling fellow Columbia U., 1967. Mem. Georgetown Libr. Assocs. (trustee 1981-94, 97—), Columbia Journalism Alumni (pres. 1981-83), Century Assn. Roman Catholic. Office: NY Times Co 229 W 43rd St New York NY 10036-3913

LEAHY, PATRICK JOSEPH, senator; b. Montpelier, Vt., Mar. 31, 1940; s. Howard and Alba (Zambon) L.; m. Marcelle Pomerleau, Aug. 25, 1962; children: Kevin, Alicia, Mark. B.A., St. Michael's Coll., Vt., 1961; J.D., Georgetown U., 1964. Bar: Vt. 1964, D.C. 1979, U.S. Ct. Appeals (2d cir.) 1966, Vt. Fed. Dist. Ct. 1965, U.S. Supreme Ct. 1968. State's atty. Chittenden County, Vt., 1966-75; U.S. senator from Vt., 1975—, ranking minority mem. com. on agrl., nutrition and forestry, subcom. on fgn. ops., jud. subcom. antitrust, bus. routes & competition, mem. judiciary com., mem. appropriations com., mem. appropriations com., vice chmn. senate intelligence com., 1985-86; mem. World Hunger bd.; bd. visitors U.S. Mil. Acad. West Point, Gallaudet Coll., Nat. Coll. Deaf, Washington; mem. Senate Dem. Steering & Coordination Com. Recipient 1st Amendment award Soc. Profl. Journalists. Mem. Nat. Dist. Attys. Assn. (v.p. 1971-74). Office: US Senate 433 Russell Senate Office Washington DC 20510*

LEAHY, T. LIAM, marketing and management consultant; b. Camp Legeunne, N.C., Apr. 15, 1952; s. Thomas James and Margaret May (Munnelly) L.; m. Shannon Kelly Brooks, Apr. 21, 1990. BS, St. Louis U., 1974, MA, 1975; postgrad., Hubbard Coll. of Adminstrn., L.A., 1989. V.p. sales Cablecom Inc., Chgo., 1978-81, Kaye Advt., N.Y.C., 1981-83; group pubr. Jour. Graphics Pub., N.Y.C., 1983-85; gen. mgr. Generation Dynamics, N.Y.C., 1985-86; pres. Leahy & Assocs., N.Y.C., 1982-86, Tarzana, Calif., 1982—; assoc. Am Coun. of Execs. Assoc., Glendale, 1991—; bd. dirs. Cons. Assn., Dental Am., Midland, Tex., Comprotech Svcs. Contbr. articles to profl. jours. Fellow Success Mgmt. Ctrs. (sr.); mem. Am. Coun. Execs. (bd. dirs. 1993-95), Turnaround Mgmt. Assn., L.A. C. of C. Avocations: music, film. Office: Leahy & Assocs 19131 Enadia Way Reseda CA 91335-3828

LEAHY, WILLIAM F., insurance company executive, lawyer; b. N.Y.C., July 28, 1913; s. William F. and Anna (Murphy) L.; m. Catherine Patricia Carlin, Oct. 19, 1940; children: William C., Michael J. Pre-law certificate, Coll. City N.Y., 1936; LL.B. cum laude, Bklyn. Law Sch., 1939, LL.M., 1940. Bar: N.Y. 1940. With Met. Life Ins. Co., N.Y.C., 1932-78; assoc. gen. counsel Met. Life Ins. Co., 1962-65, v.p. real estate financing, 1965 and after, sr. v.p., 1976-78; sr. real estate cons. Goldman Sachs Realty Co., 1979-85; adv. bd. N.Y. State Tchrs. Retirement Sys. Served to lt. col. USAAF, 1941-46. Mem. ABA. Home: 6152 N Verde Trl Apt D122 Boca Raton FL 33433-2419 also: 24 Cliff Dr Sag Harbor NY 11963-1805

LEAHY, WILLIAM P., academic administrator, educator; b. Omaha, July 16, 1948; s. Edward and Alice (McGinnis) L. Student, Wis. Province Soc. Jesus, 1967, Creighton U., 1966-67, Jesuit Coll., 1967-70; BA in Philosophy, St. Louis U., 1972, MA in U.S. History, 1975; MDiv in Theology, Jesuit Sch. Theology, Berkeley, Calif., 1978, S.T.M. in Hist. Theology, 1980; PhD in U.S. History, Stanford U., 1986. Ordained priest Roman Cath. Ch., 1978. Tchr. Campion Jesuit H.S., Prairie du Chien, Wis., 1973-75; tchg. asst. Stanford U., 1981; instr. history Marquette U., 1985-86, asst. prof., 1986-91, acting asst. chmn., 1988-90, assoc. prof. history, 1991—, exec. v.p., 1991-96; pres. Boston U., 1996—. Author: Adapting to America: Catholics, Jesuits and Higher Education in the Twentieth Century, 1991; contbr. articles to profl. jours. Bd. trustees Boston Coll., Loyola U., Chgo.; session commentator local ch. history conf. Sch. Sisters St Francis, Milw., 1985. Mem. Assn. Ind. Colls. and Univs. (Mass., mem. exec. com.), Am. Cath. Hist. Soc., History Edn. Soc., Orgns. Am. Historians. Office: Office Pres Boston Coll Chestnut Hill MA 02167*

LEAK, MARGARET ELIZABETH, insurance company executive; b. Atlanta, Sept. 9, 1946; d. William Whitehurst and Margaret Elizabeth (Whitsitt) L. BS in Psychology, Okla. State U., 1968; postgrad., U. Okla., 1968-69, Cornell U., 1976-78; grad. advanced mgmt. program, Harvard U., 1983-84. Editor communications Eastern State Bankcard Assn., N.Y.C., 1969-71; sr. edn. specialist Citibank, N.Y.C., 1971-73; adminstr. orgn. devel. NBC, N.Y.C., 1973-74; mgr. tng. and devel. Atlantic Mut. Cos., Property/Casualty Ins., N.Y.C., 1974-76, sec. human resources, 1976-78, v.p. human resources, 1978-84, v.p. human resources and corp. communications, 1984-86, sr. v.p. adminstrv. services, 1987—. Office: Atlantic Mut Cos 3 Giralda Farms Madison NJ 07940-1027

LEAK, NANCY MARIE, artist; b. Takoma Park, Md., Nov. 24, 1931; d. George Morton and Ella (Oberholtzer) Hinkson; m. Thomas Clayton Leak Jr., Dec. 30, 1950; children: Suzanne, Sharon, Stephen, Scott. Grad. high sch., Washington. Co-illustrator: The Kissing Hand, 1993; exhbns. include Olney Art Assn. Ann. Show, Internat. Exhbn. of the Miniature, Cider Painters Am. Nat. Exhbn., Hunterdon Art Ctr., N.J., Sumner Mus., Washington, Gurmukhs Gallery, Aspen Hill, Md., Nev. Miniature Art Soc., Hoffberger Gallery, Balt., Ocean City (Md.) Art League, Rockville (Md.) Art League, Md. Printmakers, Worldwide Miniature Exhbn. Recipient numerous awards for art. Mem. Nat. League Am. Pen Women, Md. Printmakers Assn., Miniature Painters, Sculptors & Gravers Soc. Washington, Miniature Art Soc. Fla., Rockville Art League, Olney Art Assn., Cider Painters Am., Miniature Artists Am. Democrat. Methodist. Avocations: crafts, reading, designing notecards, genealogy, photography.

LEAK, ROBERT E., economic development consultant; b. Charlotte, N.C., Sept. 15, 1934; s. James Pickett and Cornelia (Edwards) L.; m. Martha Councill, Aug. 25, 1956; children: Robert E., James Councill. B.S., Duke U., 1956; M.S., U. Tenn., 1957. With Pan Am. Petroleum Co., Lafayette, La., 1957-59, Allied Securities Corp., Raleigh, N.C., 1961-62, Cameron Brown Mortgage Co., Raleigh and Charlotte, 1962-64; with N.C. Dept. Natural and Econ. Resources, Raleigh, 1959-61, 64-76; dir. div. econ. devel. N.C. Dept. Natural and Econ. Resources, until 1976; dir. S.C. State Devel. Bd., Columbia, 1976-84; pres. Research Triangle Park Found., N.C., 1984-88; prin. Leak-Goforth Co., LLC, Raleigh, N.C., 1988—; mem. U.S. Dept. Commerce Small Bus. Adv. Council; also vice-chmn. Dist. Export Council; leader industry organized govt. approved trade and indsl. devel. missions to, Can., Europe, S.Am., Australia, Far East. Bd. dirs. Raleigh YMCA, S.C. Tech. and Comprehensive Edn., N.C. Symphony Fedn.; bd. dirs., mem. adv. bd. Duke Hosp.; bd. Duke Alumni Assn. Mem. Am. Indsl. Devel. Council (past pres.), Nat. Assn. State Devel. Agys. (past pres.). Episcopalian. Home: 3301 Landor Rd Raleigh NC 27609-7012 Office: Ste 1700 150 Fayetteville St Raleigh NC 27601-2919

LEAKE, DONALD LEWIS, oral and maxillofacial surgeon, oboist; b. Cleveland, Okla., Nov. 6, 1931; s. Walter Wilson and Martha Lee (Crowe) L.; m. Rosemary Dobson, Aug. 20, 1964; children: John Andrew Dobson, Elizabeth, Catherine. AB, U. So. Calif., 1953, MA, 1957; DMD, Harvard U., 1962, MD, Stanford U., 1969. Diplomate Am. Bd. Oral and Maxillofacial Surgery. Intern Mass. Gen. Hosp., Boston, 1962-63; resident Mass. Gen. Hosp., 1963-64; postdoctoral fellow Harvard U., 1964-66; practice medicine specializing in oral and maxillofacial surgery; asso. prof. oral and maxillofacial surgery Harbor-UCLA Med. Ctr., Torrance, 1970-74, dental dir., chief oral and maxillofacial surgery, 1970—, prof., 1974—; assoc. dir. UCLA Dental Rsch. Inst., 1979-82, dir., 1982-86; prof. extranjero Escuela de Graduados, Asociacion Medica Argentina, 1990—; cons. to hosps.; dental dir. coastal health services region, Los Angeles County, 1974-81; oboist Robert Shaw Chorale, 1954-55; solo oboist San Diego Symphony, 1954-59. Contbr. articles to med. jours.; rec. artist: (albums on Columbia label) The Music of Heinrich Schütz, Stockhausen, Zeitmasse for 5 Winds, Schönberg, Orchestra Variations-Opus 31; freelance musician various film studio orchs., Carmel Bach Festival, 1949, 52-53, 67-81, numerous concerts with Coleman Chamber Music, The Cantata Singers, Boston, Garden St. Chamber Players, Cambridge, Baroque Consortium, L.A., Corona Del Mar Baroque Festival, others; world premieres (oboe works) by Darius Milhaud, William Kraft, Alice Parker, Mark Volkert, Eugene Zádor, Robert Linn. Mem. Commn. on the Future of Rose-Hulman Inst. Tech., Terre Haute, Ind., 1992-93. Recipient 1st prize with greatest distinction for oboe and chamber music Brussels Royal Conservatory Music Belgium, 1956. Fellow ACS; mem. AAAS, Internat. Assn. Dental Rsch., Internat. Assn. Oral Surgeons, Soc. Biomaterials, Biomed. Engring. Soc. (sr. mem.), L.A. Surg. Soc., L.A. County Med. Assn., European Assn. Maxillofacial Surgeons, Brit. Assn. Oral and Maxillofacial Surgeons, Internat. Gesellschaft fur Kiefer-Gesichts-Chirurgie, Internat. Soc. Plastic, Aesthetic and Reconstructive Surgery, Phi Beta Kappa, Phi Kappa Phi. Clubs: Harvard (Boston and N.Y.C.). Achievements include patents for work related to bone reconstruction, 1974, 82, 90. Home: 2 Crest Rd W Rolling Hills CA 90274-5003 Office: Harbor-UCLA Med Ctr 1000 W Carson St Torrance CA 90502-2004 also: Harbor UCLA Profl Bldg 21840 Normandie Ave Ste 700 Torrance CA 90502-2047

LEAKE, PRESTON HILDEBRAND, tobacco research executive; b. Proffit, Va., Aug. 8, 1929; s. Perry Hansford and Lydia Viola (Cox) L.; m. Elizabeth Ann Kelly, Dec. 5, 1954; children: Luther Hildebrand, Lawrence Albert. BS, U. Va., 1950; MA, Duke U., 1953, PhD, 1954. Rsch. supr. Allied Chem. Corp., Hopewell, Va., 1954-60; asst. rsch. dir. Albemarle Paper Mfg. Co., Richmond, Va., 1960-65; asst. to mng. dir. The Am. Tobacco Co., Hopewell, 1965-68, asst. mng. dir., 1968-70, asst. R & D dir., 1970-87, dir. R & D, 1987-88, v.p. rsch., 1988-91, ret., 1991; adj. prof. organic chemistry Va. Commonwealth U., 1963-64; tobacco industry rep. to Coun. for Tobacco Rsch., 1977-88; chmn. bd. dirs. Tobacco Inst. Testing Lab., 1977-88; adv. bd. chem. abstracts Va. Jr. Acad. Sci., 1986-88, mem. planning com., 1991-95; mem. Congl. Study Com., 1984-88; expert witness patent suit Toronto, 1993-95. Patentee amino acid synthesis and tobacco cigarette filter; contbr. articles to profl. jours. Chmn. Providence Jr. High Sch. PTA, Midlothian, Va., 1968-70, Clover Hill High Sch. PTA, 1971-72; chmn. bd. trustees Chesterfield County (Va.) Pub. Librs., 1974-77; mem. County Sch. Adv. Com., Chesterfield, 1969-70; judge chemistry sect. Jr. Acad. Sci., 1991-92; mem. Hopewell Community and Indsl. Panel for Environ. Improvement, 1992—. Recipient Army Chem. Corp fellowship, 1950-52, Allied Chem. fellowship, 1952-54. Mem. Am. Chem. Soc. (treas. 1966, sec. 1967, vice chmn. 1968, chmn. 1970, mem. People to People Goodwill Tour to England, Norway, USSR, Czechoslovakia, East and West Germany 1971, Disting. Svc. award 1976), Am. Inst. Chemists (chmn. 1962), Va. Acad. Sci., Computer Users Group (pres. Richmond chpt. 1984-86), James River Catfish Club (keeper of keys 1978-80), Rotary (sec. Hopewell 1992), Sigma Xi, Phi Lambda Upsilon. Home: 401 Delton Ave Hopewell VA 23860-1815

LEAKE, ROSEMARY DOBSON, physician; b. Columbus, Ohio, July 14, 1937; d. Joseph Lawrence and Rosemary Elizabeth (Brockmeyer) Dobson; m. Donald Leake, Aug. 20, 1964; children: John, Elizabeth, Catherine. BA, Ohio State U., 1959, MD, 1962. Diplomate Am. Bd. Neonatal-Perinatal Medicine. Intern, pediatrics Mass. Gen. Hosp., Boston, 1962-63, resident, pediatrics, 1963-64; rsch. fellow Maternal Infant Health Collaborative Study The Boston Lying-In Hosp., Boston, 1965-67; neonatal fellow Stanford U. Hosp., Palo Alto, Calif., 1968-69; co-dir. NIH sponsored perinatal tng. program Harbor-UCLA Med. Ctr., Torrance, 1979, program dir. NIH sponsored perinatal rsch. ctr., 1980—; prof. pediatrics UCLA Sch. of Medicine, L.A., 1982—; dir. regionalized fellowship Harbor-UCLA/King-Drew Med. Ctr., Torrance, 1986-92; chair pediatrics Harbor-UCLA Med. Ctr., Torrance, 1992—; dir. perinatal crisis care program Harbor-UCLA Med. Ctr., Torrance, 1972-76, dir. neonatal ICU, 1974-81, assoc. prof. pediatrics, 1976-82, assoc. chief div. neonatology, 1976-77. Named UCLA Woman of Sci., 1985, Outstanding Woman Academician of Yr. Nat. Bd. Award of the Med. Coll. of Pa., 1989; recipient Alumni Achievement award Ohio State U. Sch. Medicine, 1987. Mem. Am. Pediatric Soc., Soc. for Pediatric Rsch. Home: 2 Crest Rd W Rolling Hills CA 90274-5003 Office: Harbor-UCLA Med Ctr 1000 W Carson St Torrance CA 90502-2004

LEAL, BARBARA JEAN PETERS, fundraising executive; b. Hartford, Ala., Oct. 24, 1948; d. Clarence Lee and Syble (Simmons) Peters; m. Michael Wayne Foster, 1966 (div.); children: Michaelle, Jonathan; m. Ramon Leal, 1991. AA, Enterprise State Jr. Coll., 1970; BA, U. South Fla., 1974; MA, Trinity U., San Antonio, 1975; postgrad. Universidad Nacional Autonoma de Mexico, 1982. Cert. fund raising exec. Instr., San Antonio Coll., 1975; planner Econ. Opportunities Devel. Corp., San Antonio, 1976, Alamo Area Council Govts., San Antonio, 1977-82; dir. planned giving Oblate Missions, San Antonio, 1982—; spkr. in field. Author: Paratransit Provider Handbook, 1978; contbg. author: Human Responses to Aging, 1976; Transportation for Elderly Handicapped Programs and Problems, 1978; contbr. articles to profl. pubs. Named one of Outstanding Young Women of Am., 1985. Founding mem. Nat. Soc. Fund Raising Execs. (past pres. San Antonio chpt.), Am. Coun. on Gift Annuities, Coun. Advancement and Support Edn., San Antonio Planned Giving Coun. Democrat. Roman Catholic. Office: Oblate Missions PO Box 96 San Antonio TX 78291-0096

LEAL, GEORGE D., engineering company executive; b. 1934. B in Civil Engring., MA, Santa Clara U., 1959. With Dames & Moore, Inc., L.A., 1959—, CEO, 1981—, now CEO, pres.; bd. dirs. BW/IP Internat. Inc. Office: Dames & Moore Inc 911 Wilshire Blvd Ste 700 Los Angeles CA 90017-3436*

LEAL, HERBERT ALLAN BORDEN, former university chancellor, former government official; b. Beloeil, Que., Can., June 15, 1917; s. Frederick William and Marie Ange (Ranger) L.; m. Muriel Isobel, Mar. 21, 1942; children: Kathleen Mary Leal Clark, Allan Ross, James Frederick. B.A. with honors in History, McMaster U., 1940; LL.M., Harvard U., 1957. Bar: Called to Ont. bar 1948. Read law with Frank Erichsen-Brown, Toronto, 1945-48; mem. firm Erichsen-Brown & Leal, Toronto, 1948-50; lectr. Osgoode Hall Law Sch., 1950-56, vice dean, prof., 1956-58, dean, prof., 1958-66; dep. atty. gen. Ont., 1977-81; chancellor McMaster U., Hamilton, Ont., 1977-86; chmn. Ont. Law Reform Commn., 1966-77, vice chmn., 1981-89; spl. lectr. Law Soc. Upper Can., 1951, 57, 60, 66, 77, Faculty of Law, U. Toronto, 1972-77; mem. council Medico-Legal Soc. Toronto, 1960, 1st v.p., 1968, pres., 1969. Contbr. articles to legal and profl. jours. Mem. exec. com.

Toronto br. Can. Red Cross Soc., 1959-64; co-chmn. spl. com. Assn. Am. Law Schs., Assn. Can. Law Tchrs. Can.-Am. Coop., 1962-66; commr. Ont. Uniform Law Conf. Can., 1963-86, pres., 1977-78; mem. adv. com. Can. Civil Liberties Assn. Ont., 1965-66; mem. faculty Can. Jud. Conf., 1969-73, dir., 1969-70; mem. Can. del. Hague Conf. on Pvt. Internat. Law, 1968, 72, 76, chief of del., 1980; chief Can. del. Internat. Diplomatic Conf. on Wills, Washington, 1973; chmn. spl. com. uniform law Conf. Internat. Conventions Pvt. Internat. Law, 1971-81. With Royan Can. Arty., 1943-45; reeve Village of Tweed, 1991-94. Decorated officer Order of Can.; recipient Gov. Gen. medal McMaster U., 1939; A. G. Alexander scholar, 1939; Rhodes scholar, 1940. Mem. Law Soc. Upper Can. (medal 1987), Toronto Arty. Officers Assn., Assn. Can. Law Tchrs. (pres. 1959-60), African Students Found. (bd. dirs.). Club: Masons.

LEAL, LESLIE GARY, chemical engineering educator; b. Bellingham, Wash., Mar. 18, 1943; s. Leslie Arthur and Esther Vivian (Jones) L.; m. Mary Ann Seelye, June 11, 1965; children: Heather Noel, Kameron Brie, Farrah Aimee. BS, U. Wash., 1965; MS, Stanford U., 1967, PhD, 1969. Asst. prof. chem. engring. Calif. Inst. Tech., Pasadena, 1970-75, assoc. prof., 1975-78, prof., 1978-89, Chevron Disting. prof., 1986-89; prof., chmn. dept. chem. engring. U. Calif., Santa Barbara, 1989—; cons. Firestone Rsch., Akron, Ohio, 1981-88, Dynamics Tech., Torrance, Calif., 1982-90, Richards of Rockford, Ill., 1975-79, Dowell-Schlumbargar, Tulsa, Okla., 1985-88, U. Okla. Fracturing Fluid Characterization Facility Project, 1991—; active U.S. Nat. Com. on Theoretical and Applied Mechanics, 1991—, chmn. 1994-96; vis. prof. U. Cambridge, 1996; mem. external affairs DFD, 1992—, exec. com., 1995—; lectr. in field. Assoc. editor Internat. Jour. Multiphase Flow, 1985—; mem. editl. bd. Experiments in Fluids, 1994—, Ann. Revs. Fluid Mechanics, 1985-90, Jour. Colloid and Interface Sci., AIChE Jour. Tchr.-scholar grantee Camille and Henry Dreyfus Found., 1975; fellow John Simon Guggenheim Found., 1976. Fellow Am. Phys. Soc.; mem. NAE (mem. membership policy com. 1994-97), AIChE (William H. Walker award 1993, Allan P. Colburn award 1978, tech. achievement award So. Calif. sect. 1978, chmn. nat. program com. in fluid mechanics 1984-89), Nat. Rsch. Coun. (mem. space studies bd. com. on microgravity rsch. 1993—), Soc. Rheology, Am. Soc. for Engring. Edn., Phi Beta Kappa, Tau Beta Pi, Phi Sigma Upsilon. Methodist. Home: 1560 Hillcrest Rd Santa Barbara CA 93103-1841 Office: U Calif Dept Chem and Nuc Engring Santa Barbara CA 93106

LEALE, OLIVIA MASON, import marketing company executive; b. Boston, May 5, 1944; d. William Mason and Jane Chapin (Prouty) Smith; m. Euan Harvie-Watt, Mar. 11, 1967 (div. Aug. 1979); children: Katrina, Jennifer; m. Douglas Marshall Leale, Aug. 29, 1980. BA, Vassar Coll., 1966. Cert. paralegal. Sec. to dir. Met. Opera Guild, N.Y.C., 1966; sec. to pres. Friesons Printers, London, 1974-75; guide, trainer Autoguide, London, 1977-79; ptnr. Inmark Internat. Mktg. Inc., Seattle, 1980—. Social case worker Inner London Ednl. Authority, 1975-76. Democrat. Presbyterian. Avocations: reading, making doll house furniture, painting, knitting. Home and Office: 5427 NE Penrith Rd Seattle WA 98105-2842

LEAMAN, DAVID MARTIN, cardiologist; b. Lancaster, Pa., Apr. 24, 1935; s. Benjamin Denlinger and Elise Mae (Martin) L.; m. Doris Jean Heisey; children: Gretchen Jane, Heidi Jean, Erika Ingrid. Student, Franklin & Marshall Coll., 1956-58; BA, Eastern Mennonite Coll., 1960; MD, Temple U., 1964. Intern Mary Hitchcock Hosp., Hanover, N.H., 1964-66; resident U. Vt., Burlington, 1968-71; asst. prof. medicine Pa. State U., Hershey, 1971-77, assoc. prof., 1977-84, prof., 1984—, chief div. of cardiology, 1984-95, asst. dean for student affairs, 1987-91, asst. dean for admissions, 1991-94. Contbr. articles to med. jours. Sch. dir. Lower Dauphin Sch. Dist., Hummelstown, Pa., 1977-83. Served with USPHS, 1966-68. Named Alumnus of Yr. Eastern Mennonite Coll., 1985. Fellow Am. Coll. Cardiology, Am. Coll. Chest Physicians, ACP, Soc. Cardiac Angiology, Am. Heart Assn. (mem. council on clin. cardiology, Service Recognition award 1981, Disting. Service award 1985, bd. dirs. Pa. affiliate 1975—), Alpha Omega Alpha. Republican. Mennonite. Avocations: reading, photography. Office: Pa State Univ Hershey Med Ctr PO Box 850 Hershey PA 17033-0850

LEAMAN, J. RICHARD, JR., paper company executive; b. Lancaster, Pa., Sept. 22, 1934; s. J. Richard and Margaret B. (Leaman); m. Helen Brown, June 15, 1957; children: Lynda B., J. Richard, III. BA, Dartmouth Coll., 1956, MBA, 1957; PhD (hon.), Widener U., 1988. With Scott Paper Co., Phila., 1960-95, v.p. comml. products, 1975-78, exec. v.p. mktg. and sales, 1978—, pres. Packaged Products div., 1983—, vice chmn., 1991-94, dir., 1986; pres. Scott Worldwide, 1986; pres., CEO, S.D. Warren Co., Boston, 1991-95; bd. dirs. Church & Dwight Co., Inc., Pep Boys, S.D. Warren Holdings, Ranpak Corp. Vice-chmn. exec. com., trustee Widener U., 1987; mem. conf. bd.'s coun. Global Bus. Mgmt., Dartmouth Alumni Coun., 1993-96. Capt. USAF, 1957-61. Recipient Disting. Performance in Mgmt. award Widener U. Mem. Conf. Bd.'s Coun. on Global Bus. Mgmt. Republican. Episcopalian. Clubs: Dartmouth (Phila.). Home: 317 Boot Rd Malvern PA 19355-3317 Office: 225 Franklin St Boston MA 02110-2804

LEAMAN, JACK ERVIN, landscape architect, community and regional planner; b. Mason City, Iowa, Jan. 24, 1932; s. Theodore R. and Dorothy M. (Schrum) L.; m. Darlene A. McNary, June 15, 1952; children: Jeffrey A., Danna J., Jay M., Duree K. B.S. in Landscape Architecture and Urban Planning, Iowa State U., 1954, M. Community and Regional Planning, 1982. Registered landscape architect, Calif., Iowa, Minn., N.Mex. Landscape architect Sam L. Huddleston Office, Denver, 1954-55, Phillips Petroleum Co., Bartlesville, Okla., 1955-58; landscape architect for Price Tower and residence with architect Frank Lloyd Wright Bartlesville, Okla., 1957-58; planning technician Santa Barbara County, Calif., 1958-60; planning cons. Engring. Planners, Santa Barbara, 1960-63; planning dir. City of Santa Barbara, 1963-66, City of Mason City, 1966-72; landscape architect, planning cons. Midwest Research Inst., Kansas City, Mo., 1972-74, Hansen, Lind, Meyer, Iowa City, Iowa, 1974-76, Sheffler, Leaman, Rova, Mason City, 1976-78, RCM Assocs., Inc., Hopkins, Minn. and Ames, Iowa, 1978-82; planning dir. City-County Planning, Albuquerque, 1982-86, City of Colorado Springs, Colo., 1986-90; adj. prof. dept. cmty. and regional planning Coll. of Design, Iowa State U., Ames, 1990—; landscape architect, pvt. practice planning cons. Mason City, Iowa, 1990-92; assoc. ptnr., landscape architect, community/regional planner Yaggy Colby Assocs., Mason City, 1992-95; pvt. cons. cmty. and regional planning, landscape architect Mason City, Iowa, 1995—. Recipient Residential Landscape Design award Calif. Landscape Contractors Assn., 1962, Design Achievement award Coll. of Design Iowa State U., 1988. Fellow Am. Soc. Landscape Architects (chpt. pres. 1967-68, 90-91, trustee Iowa 1980-82, N.Mex. 1982-86, Award of Excellence 1954); mem. Am. Inst. Cert. Planners, Am. Planning Assn. (chpt. pres. Iowa 1969-70), Urban Land Inst., Tau Sigma Delta.

LEAR, ERWIN, anesthesiologist, educator; b. Bridgeport, Conn., Jan. 1, 1924; s. Samuel Joseph and Ida (Ruth) L.; m. Arlene Joyce Alexander, Feb. 15, 1953; children—Stephanie, Samuel. MD, SUNY, 1952. Diplomate Am. Bd. Anesthesiology, Nat. Bd. Med. Examiners. Intern L.I. Coll. Hosp., Bklyn., 1952-53; asst. resident anesthesiology Jewish Hosp., Bklyn., 1953-54; sr. resident Jewish Hosp., 1955, asst., 1955-56, adj., 1956-58, assoc. anesthesiologist, 1958-64; attending anesthesiologist Bklyn. VA Hosp., 1958-64, cons., 1977—; assoc. vis. anesthesiologist Kings County Hosp. Ctr., Bklyn., 1957-80; staff anesthesiologist Kings County Hosp. Ctr., 1980-81; vis. anesthesiologist Queens Gen. Hosp. Ctr., 1955-67; dir. anesthesiology Queens Hosp. Ctr. Jamaica, 1964-67, cons., 1968—; chmn. dept. anesthesiology Catholic Med. Ctr., Queens and Bklyn., 1968-80; dir. anesthesiology Beth Israel Med. Ctr., N.Y.C., 1981—; clin. instr. SUNY Coll. Medicine, Bklyn., 1955-58; clin. asst. prof. SUNY Coll. Medicine, 1958-64, clin. assoc. prof., 1964-71, clin. prof., 1971-80, prof., vice-chmn. clin. anesthesiology, 1980-81; prof. anesthesiology Mt. Sinai Sch. Medicine, 1981-94, Albert Einstein Coll. of Medicine, 1994—. Author: Chemistry Applied Pharmacology of Tranquilizers; contbr. articles to profl. jours. Served with USNR, 1942-45. Fellow Am. Coll. Anesthesiologists, N.Y. Acad. Medicine (sec. sect. anesthesiology 1985-86, chmn. sect. anesthesiology 1986-87); mem. AMA, Am. Soc. Anesthesiologists (chmn. com. on by-laws 1982-83, dir. 1981—, ho. of dels. 1973—, editor newsletter 1984—, chmn. adminstrv. affairs com., 1987—), N.Y. State Bd. Profl. Med. Conduct, N.Y. State Soc. Anesthesiologists (chmn. pub. relations 1963-73, chmn. com. local arrangements 1968-73, dist. dir. 1972-73, v.p. 1974-75, pres. 1976, bd. dirs. 1972—, chmn. jud. com. 1977-81, assoc. editor Bulletin 1963-77, editor Sphere 1978-84), N.Y. State Med. Soc. (chmn. sect. anesthesiology 1966-67, sec. sect. 1977-81, Disting. Svc. award 1996), N.Y. County Med. Soc., SUNY Coll. Medicine Alumni Assn. (pres. 1983, trustee alumni fund 1980), Alpha Omega Alpha. Address: 3 Harriman Dr Sands Point NY 11050

LEAR, EVELYN, soprano; b. Bklyn., Jan. 8, 1930; m. Thomas Stewart; children: Jan, Bonni. Vocal student in, N.Y.C.; student, N.Y. U., Hunter Coll. Song recitals, Phillips Gallery, Washington; mem. Juilliard Sch. Music Workshop; recital, Town Hall, N.Y.C., 1955; lead in Marc Blitzstein's Reuben, Reuben; performed Strauss's Four Last Songs with London Symphony Orch., 1959; mem. Deutsche Opera, 1959, appeared in Lulu at Vienna Festival, 1962, The Marriage of Figaro at Salzburg Festival, 1962, debut, Vienna State Opera, 1964, Frankfurt Opera, 1965, Covent Garden, 1965, Kansas City (Mo.) Performing Arts Found., 1965, Chgo. Lyric Opera, 1966, La Scala Opera, 1971, also in Brussels, San Francisco, Los Angeles, Buenos Aires, debut at Met. Opera as Lavinia in Mourning Becomes Electra, 1967, mem. co., 1967—; roles include Tosca, Manon, Marshallin, Desdemona, Mimi, Dido, Donna Elvira, Marina, Tatiana: TV appearance in La Boheme, 1965; numerous solo appearances, 1960—; appeared in film Buffalo Bill, 1976; rec. artist Angel Records, Deutsche Grammophon. Recipient Concert Artists Guild award 1955, Liederabend, Salzburg Festival 1964, Grammy award for best operatic recording (Marie in Wozzeck) 1965; Fulbright scholar, 1957.

LEAR, NORMAN MILTON, producer, writer, director; b. New Haven, July 27, 1922; s. Herman and Jeanette (Seicol) L.; children: Ellen, Kate B. Lear LaPook, Maggie B.; m. Lyn Davis; children: Benjamin Davis, Brianna, Madeline. Student, Emerson Coll., 1940-42, HHD, 1968. Engaged in pub. relations, 1945-49; founder Act III Comms., 1987—. Comedy writer for TV, 1950-54; writer, dir. for TV and films, 1954-59; producer: films Come Blow Your Horn, 1963, Never Too Late, 1965; prodr., screenwriter: Divorce American Style, 1967, The Night They Raided Minsky's, 1968; writer, producer, dir.: film Cold Turkey, 1971; exec. prodr. film Start the Revolution Without Me, The Princess Bride, Breaking In, Fried Green Tomatoes; creator, dir.: TV shows TV Guide Awards Show, 1962, Henry Fonda and the Family, 1963, Andy Williams Spl., also, Andy Williams Series, 1965, Robert Young and the Family, 1970; exec. prodr., creator-developer: TV shows All in the Family, 1971 (4 Emmy awards 1970-73, Peabody award 1977), Maude, 1972; Sanford and Son, 1972, Good Times, 1974, The Jeffersons, 1975, Hot L Baltimore, 1975, Mary Hartman, Mary Hartman, 1976, One Day At a Time, 1975, All's Fair, 1976, A Year at the Top, 1977, All That Glitters, 1977, Fernwood 2 Night, 1977, The Baxters, 1979, Palmerstown, 1980, I Love Liberty, 1982, Sunday Dinner, 1991, The Powers That Be, 1992, 704 Hauser, 1994; creator a.k.a. Pablo, 1984; exec. producer Heartsounds, 1984. Pres. Am. Civil Liberties Found. So. Calif., 1973—; trustee Mus. Broadcasting; bd. dirs. People for the American Way; founder Bus. Enterprise Trust. Served with USAAF, 1942-45. Decorated Air medal with 4 oak leaf clusters; named One of Top Ten Motion Picture Producers, Motion Picture Exhibitors, 1963, 67, 68, Showman of Yr., Publicists Guild, 1971-77, Assn. Bus. Mgrs., 1972, Broadcaster of Yr., Internat. Radio and TV Soc., 1973; Man of Yr. Hollywood chpt. Nat. Acad. Television Arts and Scis., 1973; recipient Humanitarian award NCCJ, 1976, Mark Twain award Internat. Platform Assn., 1977, William O. Douglas award Pub. Counsel, 1981, 1st Amendment Lectr. Ford Hall Forum, 1981, Gold medal Internat. Radio and TV Soc., 1981. Disting. Am. award, 1984, Mass Media award Am. Jewish Com. Inst. of Human Relations, 1986, Internat. award of Yr., Nat. Assn. TV Program Execs., 1987; inducted into TV Acad. Hall of Fame, 1984. Mem. Writers Guild Am. (Valentine Davies award 1977), Dirs. Guild Am., AFTRA, Caucus Producers, Writers, and Dirs. Office: Act III Communications 1999 Avenue Of The Stars Los Angeles CA 90067-6022

LEAR, ROBERT WILLIAM, holding company executive; b. Canon City, Colo., May 10, 1917; s. Louis and Bertha (May) L.; m. Dorothy Schureman, Sept. 16, 1941; children—William S., Andrew R. B.A., U. Colo., 1938; M.B.A. with distinction, Harvard, 1940. Market research analyst U.S. Steel Corp., 1940-43; sales promotion mgr. Duff-Norton Co., 1946-47; corp. dir. marketing services Am. Standard Co., 1947-61; v.p. marketing Carborundum Co., 1961-64, group v.p., 1964-67; pres., dir. Indian Head Inc., 1967-72; pres., chief exec. officer, chmn., dir. F. & M. Schaefer Corp., N.Y.C., 1972-77; exec.-in-residence Columbia Grad. Bus. Sch., 1977—; prin. Lear, Yavitz & Assocs., LLP, 1996—; bd. dirs. Welsh, Carson, Anderson Assocs. Venture Funds, Korea Fund, Scudder, Stevens & Clark Instnl. Funds, others; ind. gen. ptnr. Equitable Capital Ptnrs. Author: How to Turn Your MBA into a CEO, 1987, Pressure Points, 1992; chmn. adv. bd. Chief Exec. Mag., 1994—. Bd. dirs. Waveny Care Center. Served as lt. USNR, 1943-46. Clubs: Harvard (N.Y.C.); New Canaan Country, Blind Brook, Mill Reef. Home: 429 Silvermine Rd New Canaan CT 06840-4320 Office: Columbia U 206 Uris Hall # F New York NY 10027

LEARD, DAVID CARL, lawyer; b. Hartford, Conn., Dec. 9, 1958. BA, Bucknell U., 1981; JD, U. Conn., 1984. Bar: Conn. 1984, U.S. Dist. Ct. Conn. 1985. Assoc. Podorowsky and Wladimer, Hartford, 1985; assoc. Manasse, Slaiby & Leard, Torrington, Conn., 1985-88, ptnr., 1989—; lectr. legal studies Northwestern Conn. Community Coll., Winsted, 1991-92. Contbr. articles to profl. jours. Dir., past pres. Winchester (Conn.) Land Trust, 1988-93; chmn. allocations com. United Way Torrington, 1989—. Mem. ABA, ATLA, Conn. Bar Assn. (workers compensation sect.), Nat. Orgn. Social Security Claimants Reps. Office: Manasse Slaiby & Leard PO Box 1104 459 Prospect St Torrington CT 06790-1104

LEARMANN, JUDITH MARILYN, secondary education educator; b. Charleston, Ill., Feb. 1, 1938; d. Charles P. and Estelle M. (DeWitt) Swan; m. Paul C. Learmann, Aug. 29, 1958 (dec.); children: Kevin L., Michael P. (dec.). BS, Wis. State Coll., Oshkosh, 1960; MA, Pacific Western U., 1994. Tchr. Monona (Wis.) Grove H.S., 1960-62, U.S. Army Coll. Program, Denver, 1967, Wood Mid. Sch., Ft. Leonard Wood, Mo., 1983-85; tchr., chmn. dept. lang. arts Waynesville (Mo.) H.S., 1985—; presenter in field; chmn. North Ctrl. Philosophy Com., Waynesville, 1987-88; reviewer textbook Adventures in English Literature Harcourt, Brace, Jovanovich, 1994; reviewer sci. curriculum, 1994-96, math. curriculum, 1995, social studies curriculum, 1996, bus. curriculum, 1997; mem. evaluation steering com. Mo. sch. improvement program, chair instrn. process com. Waynesville (Mo.) R-VI Sch. Dist., 1996-97. Named Most Influential Tchr. award U. Mo., 1991; recipient influential tchr. recognition letter Westminster Coll., 1992, 95. Mem. Nat. Coun. Tchrs. English, Mo. Tchrs. Assn., Mo. Tchrs. English (meeting chmn. dist. conv. 1989, 90), Cmty. Tchrs. Assn. (chmn. legal svcs. 1991-95, sick leave pool com. 1996—), Mo. State Tchrs. Assn., Phi Delta Kappa (tchr. awards, officer nomination, constn. revision coms.). Avocation: reading. Home: 1737 J C St Waynesville MO 65583-2450 Office: Waynesville HS Historic Rt 66 West Waynesville MO 65583

LEARN, ELMER WARNER, agricultural economics educator, retired; b. Sayre, Pa., Jan. 19, 1929; s. John Walter and Naomi Ruth (Warner) L.; m. Theresa Arlene Green, Sept. 22, 1956; children—Diane Marie, Linda Jean. B.S., Pa. State U., 1950, M.S., 1951, Ph.D., 1957; student, U. Minn., 1954-55. Grad. research asst., instr. Pa. State U., 1950-51, 53-54, 55-56; successively asst. prof., assoc. prof., prof. U. Minn., 1956-69, head dept. agrl. econs., 1963-64, asst. to pres. then exec. asst. to pres., also dir. planning, 1964-69; prof., exec. vice chancellor U. Calif.-Davis, 1969-84, prof., 1984-92; cons. 9th Dist. Fed. Res. Bank, 1962, Dept. Agr., 1962-65. Contbr. articles on agrl. policy, prices, fgn. trade policy to profl. jours. Served with AUS, 1951-53. Recipient Grad. Student award Am. Farm Econs. Assn., 1956. Mem. Am. Agrl. Econs. Assn., Phi Kappa Phi, Gamma Sigma Delta. Home: 1702 Sycamore Ln Davis CA 95616-0809

LEARN, RICHARD LELAND, corrections school principal; b. New Kensington, Pa., Nov. 29, 1955; s. Leland Leroy Learn and Gendolyn Leora (Furman) George; m. Rosamond Amelia Kautz, July 31, 1982; children: Rebecca Amelia, Benjamin Richard. BS in Music Edn., Indiana U. of Pa., 1977, MA in Adult/Community Edn., 1984; PhD in Edn., U. Pitts., 1991. Adult edn. instr. PIC of Westmoreland County, Greensburg, Pa., 1980-82; corrections edn. specialist Pa. State Correctional Instn., Greensburg, 1984-87; sch. prin. Pa. State Correctional Instn., Mercer, 1989-92, Cambridge Springs, 1992—; acad. support coord. Indiana U. of Pa., 1987-89. Chmn. bd. dirs. Young Adult Handicapped, Inc., Apollo, Pa., 1980-82. Mem. ASCD, Am. Vocat. Assn., Am. Correctional Assn., Pa. Assn. for Adult and Continuing Edn., Corrections Edn. Assn. Democrat. Presbyterian. Avocations: archery, music. Office: State Correctional Instn 451 Fullerton Ave Cambridge Springs PA 16403-1238

LEARNARD, WILLIAM EWING, marketing executive; b. Joliet, Ill., July 21, 1935; s. Roy Stevens and Clara (Ewing) L.; m. Susan Douglas-Willan, Oct. 1, 1960; children: Matthew, Roger, Vanessa. BA, Trinity Coll., 1957. With Smith, Kline & French, Phila., 1957-78, v.p. customer affairs, 1976-78; v.p. corp. affairs Smithkline Beckman, Phila., 1978-85; pres. Smithkline Consumer Products, Phila., 1985-89; vice chmn. Smithkline Beecham Consumer Brands, Phila., 1989-91; chmn. Coun. on Family Health, N.Y.C., 1989-91; bd. dirs. Nelson Comms., DiMark, Inc. Bd. dirs. Chestnut Hill Hosp., Phila., 1982-88, Morris Arboretum, U. Pa., Phila., 1982-92; chmn. Sta. WHYY TV & Radio, Phila., 1990-94. Capt. USAF, 1958-61. Mem. Nonprescription Drug Mfrs. Assn. (chmn. 1989-91), Phila. Cricket Club, George Town Club. Republican. Home: 48 Hillcrest Ave Philadelphia PA 19118-2620 Office: Trident Group Ste 230 Spring House Corp Ctr Ambler PA 19002

LEARNED, JOHN GREGORY, physicist; b. Plattsburgh, N.Y., Apr. 12, 1940; s. Fred. Maynall and Aurilla (Gregory) L.; m. J. Kathleen (div.); children: Bryan David, Alison Jennifer; m. Coleen Cory. AB, Columbia U., 1961; MS, U. Pa., 1963; PhD, U. Wash., 1968. Design engr. Gen. Dynamics, Plattsburgh, 1961-62, Boeing, Seattle, 1963-65; rsch. assoc. U. Wash., Seattle, 1965-69; asst. scientist U. Wis., Madison, 1968-76; dir. Dumand Project U. Hawaii, Honolulu, 1981-96, assoc. prof. dept. physics and astronomy, 1983-87, prof., 1988—; Contbr. over 200 articles to profl. jours. and publs. Contbr. over 200 articles to profl. jours. and publs. Achievements include research in particle astrophysics and newtrino astronomy. Avocations: mountain climbing, cooking, music. Office: Dept Physics and Astronomy U Hawaii 2505 Correa Rd Honolulu HI 96822-2219

LEARNED, VINCENT ROY, electrical engineer , educator; b. San Jose, Calif., Jan. 21, 1917; m. Bernice Evelyn Brown, June 5, 1938; children: Daryl Vincent, Dean Charles, Craig Edwin, Kent Brudeen, Bruce Roy. BSEE, U. Calif., 1938; PhD, Stanford U., 1943. Dir. rsch. and devel. microwave tubes Sperry Rand Corp., 1943-65; prof. elec. and computer engr. San Diego State U., 1968-87, prof. emeritus, 1987—. Fellow Inst. Radio Engrs. Office: 3842 Silvera Ct Paradise CA 95969-6677

LEARY, CAROL ANN, academic administrator; b. Niagara Falls, N.Y., Mar. 29, 1947; d. Angelo Andrew and Mary Josephine (Pullano) Gigliotti; m. Noel Robert Leary, Dec. 30, 1972. BA, Boston U., 1969; MS, SUNY, Albany, 1970; PhD, Am. Univ., 1988. Asst. to v.p. for student affairs, dir. women's programs Siena Coll., Loudonville, N.Y., 1970-72; asst. dir. housing Boston U., 1972-78; dir. residence Simmons Coll., Boston, 1978-84, assoc. dean, 1984-85; assoc. dir. The Washington Campus, Washington, 1985-86; adminstrv. v.p., asst. to pres. Simmons Coll., Boston, 1988-94; pres. Bay Path Coll., Longmeadow, Mass., 1995—. Bd. dirs. Bay State Med. Ctr., Carew Hill Girls Club, Colony Club, STCC Assistance Corp., 1996—. Fellow Ednl. Policy Fellowship Program, 1990-91. Mem. Am. Coun. Edn. (rep. Mass. divsn. 1991—), Greater Springfield C. of C. Avocations: classic movies, traveling overseas, hiking. Office: Bay Path Coll Office of the President 588 Longmeadow St Longmeadow MA 01106-2212

LEARY, DANIEL, artist; b. Glens Falls, N.Y., July 20, 1955; s. John Andrew and Maud Houston (Parkhurst) L. BFA, Antioch Coll., 1979; MFA, Syracuse U., 1996. One person exhbns. include Breedlove Gallery, Westark Cmty. Coll., Fort Smith, Ark., 1984, 85, Comart Gallery, Syracuse U., 1985, 87, The Printspace, U. Ark., Fayetteville, 1985, The Fort Smith Art Ctr., 1986, Printworks, Ltd., Chgo., 1988, 95, The Hyde Collection, Glens Falls, N.Y., 1990, The Blanden Meml. Art Mus., Fort Dodge, Iowa, 1992, The Bobbit Visual Art Ctr., Albion Coll., Mich., 1993, Sharon Campbell Gallery, Greenville, S.C., 1994, We. Mich. State U., Kalamazoo, 1994; group exhbns. include East Tenn. State U., Johnson City, 1985, Gallery Sixty-Eight, Belfast, Maine, 1985, The Fort Smith Arts Ctr., 1985, Syracuse U., 1985, The Ark. Arts Ctr. and the Decorative Arts Mus., Little Rock, 1985, The Soc. Am. Graphic Artists, 1986, Westminster Coll., New Wilmington, Pa., 1986, Joe Fawbush Editions, N.Y., 1986, Cazenovia (N.Y.) Coll., 1987, Jan Turner Gallery, L.A., 1987, The Greenville County Mus. Art, 1988, The Mpls. Inst. Arts., 1988, The Munson-Williams-Proctor Inst. Mus. Art, Utica, N.Y., 1989, The Statesville Arts and Scis. Mus., 1989, The Nat. Exhbn. Ctr. Can., Alma, Quebec, 1989, The Pyramid Arts Ctr., Rochester, N.Y., 1989, The Vero Beach Ctr. For the Arts, Fla., 1989, The Jane Voorhees Zimmerli Art Mus., Rutgers U., New Brunswick, N.J., 1990, Bradford Art Galleries and Mus., England, 1990, The Contemporary Arts Ctr., Cin., 1991, Northwest Art Gallery, Ind. U. Northwest, Gary, 1993; public collections include Albion (Mich.) Coll., The Ark. Arts Ctr., The Arts Ctr., Greenville, The Boston Pub. Library, The Blanden Meml. Art Mus., The Carnegie Mus. Art, Pitts., East Tenn. State U., The Hyde Collection, Glens Falls, The Library of Congress, Washington, D.C., The Metropolitan Mus. Art., N.Y., The Milw. Art Mus., The Mpls. Inst. Arts, The Munson-Williams-Proctor Inst. Mus. Art, The N.Y. Pub. Library, The Spencer Mus. Art, U. Kans., Syracuse U., The Toledo Mus. Art, U. Ariz. Mus. Art, The Walker Art Ctr., Mpls., We. Mich. U., The Williams Coll. Mus. Art, Williamstown, Mass., Wright State U., Dayton, Ohio, The Jane Voorhees Zimmerli Art Mus., Rutgers U., New Brunswick, N.J.; gallery reps. include Sharon Campbell Gallery, Greenville, Printworks Gallery, Chgo. Recipient Visual Artists Fellowship grantee NEA, 1989; fellow N.Y. Found. for the Arts, 1988. Home: PO Box 136 Hudson Falls NY 12839

LEARY, DAVID EDWARD, university dean; b. L.A., May 5, 1945; married; 3 children. BA in Philosophy, San Luis Rey Coll., 1968; MA in Psychology, San Jose State Coll., 1971; PhD in History of Sci., U. Chgo., 1977. Instr. psychology Holy Names Coll., Oakland, Calif., 1972-74, U. Calif. Extension Svcs., Berkeley, 1972-74; counseling psychologist Howard Inst., Oakland, 1972-74; instr. psychology San Jose (Calif.) State U. Extension Svcs., 1973-74, San Francisco State U. Extension Svcs., 1973-74, U. Calif. at Santa Cruz Extension Svcs., Monterey, 1973-74, U. Chgo., 1975; asst. prof. history and philosophy of psychology U. N.H., Durham, 1977-81, co-dir. grad. program in history and theory psychology, 1977-89, assoc. prof. psychology and humanities, 1981-87, chmn. dept. psychology, 1986-89, prof. psychology, history and humanities, 1987-89; prof. psychology, dean arts and scis. U. Richmond, Va., 1989—; vis. asst. prof. psychology Grad. Theol. Union, Berkeley, 1971-72; fellow Ctr. Advanced Study in Behavioral Scis., Stanford, Calif., 1982-83, co-dir. summer inst. on history of social sci. inquiry, 1986; assoc. prof. humanities Summer Program Cambridge U., Eng., 1984; presenter in field. Author: A Century of Psychology as Science, 2d rev. edit., 1992 (Assn. Am. Pub. award 1986), An Introduction to the Psychology of Guilt, 1975; editor: Metaphors in the History of Psychology, 1990; author: (with others) The Encyclopedia of Higher Education, 1992, Writing the Social Text: Poetics and Politics in Social Science Discourses, 1992, Annual Review of Psychology, 1991, Metaphors in the History of Psychology, 1990, Reflections on The Principles of Psychology: William James After a Century, 1990, Psychology in Twentieth-Century Thought and Society, 1987, Psychology in its Historical Context, 1985, Thinkers of the 20th Century, 1984, Studies in Eighteenth-Century Culture, 1984, The Problematic Science: Psychology in Nineteenth Century Thought, 1982; contbr. articles to profl. jours. Grantee NEH, 1982-83, 91-94, Social Sci. Rsch. Ctr. Faculty Support, U. N.H., 1988, Coll. Liberal Arts Faculty Rsch. Support, U. N.H., 1987-88, Ctrl. U. Rsch. Fund, U. N.H., 1979, 87, Mellon Found., 1986, NSF, 1980-82, 82-83; rsch. fellow History Psychology Found., 1980, summer fellow NEH, 1979, U. N.H., 1978, grad. fellow U. Chgo., 1975-77. Fellow Am. Psychol. Soc.; mem. AAAS, APA (centennial lectr. on history of psychology 1979-80, 91-92, fellow divsn. 24 1988—, fellow divsn. 1 1983—, pres. divsn. 26 1983-84, fellow divsn. 26 1982—, pres. divsn. 24 1994-95), Am. Assn. Higher Edn., Am. Conf. Acad. Deans (bd. dirs. 1994—), Am. Hist. Assn., Assn. Am. Colls. (grantee 1990-91), Soc. History of Sci. in Am., Cheiron: Internat. Soc. History of Behavioral and Social Scis., Forum History of Human Sci., History of Sci. Soc., Phi Beta Kappa (hon.). Office: Univ Richmond Office Dean Arts & Scis Richmond VA 23173

LEARY, MICHAEL WARREN, journalist; b. Rice Lake, Wis., Apr. 15, 1949; s. Warren Denis and Patricia (Berigan) L.; m. Janice Marie Kalmar, Sept. 5, 1970; children: Meghan, Evan, Kieran. Student, U. Innsbruck, Austria, 1968-69; AB cum laude, U. Notre Dame, 1971; MS, Columbia U.,

1972. Reporter Phila. Inquirer, 1972—, nat. corr. Houston Bur., 1983-86, asst. city editor, Phila., 1986-87, European corr., London, 1987-90, editor Book Rev. sect., 1990-93, assoc. editor, mem. editorial bd., 1993—. Recipient Silver Gavel award ABA, 1981, Gold award Best Op-Ed Page Assn. Opinion Page Editors, 1995. Home: 7153 Crittenden St Philadelphia PA 19119-1217 Office: Philadelphia Inquirer PO Box 8263 400 N Broad St Philadelphia PA 19101

LEARY, THOMAS BARRETT, lawyer; b. Orange, N.J., July 15, 1931; s. Daniel and Margaret (Barrett) L.; m. Stephanie Lynn Abbott, Dec. 18, 1954, June 3, 1991; children: Thomas A., David A., Alison Leary Estep. AB, Princeton U., 1952; JD magna cum laude, Harvard U., 1958. Bar: N.Y. 1959, Mich. 1972, D.C. 1983. Assoc. White & Case, N.Y.C., 1958-68, ptnr., 1968-71; atty.-in-charge antitrust Gen. Motors Corp., Detroit, 1971-77, asst. gen. counsel, 1977-82; ptnr. Hogan & Hartson, Washington, 1983—. Served to lt. USNR, 1952-55. Mem. ABA. Office: Hogan & Hartson Columbia Sq 555 13th St NW Washington DC 20004-1109

LEARY, WILLIAM JAMES, educational administrator; b. Boston, Oct. 1, 1931; s. John Gilbert and Josephine Marie (Kelley) L.; m. Joann Linda Parodi, June 25, 1960; children: Lorraine, Lisa, Linda. S.B., Boston Coll., 1953; M.Ed., Boston State Coll., 1954; postgrad. (Fulbright fellow), Sophia U., Tokyo, 1967; cert. advanced study, Harvard U., 1972, Ed.D., 1973; Ed.D., Boston U., 1971. Tchr. pub. schs. Boston, 1957-67; chmn. dept. social studies Dorchester High Sch., Boston, 1967-68; dir. curriculum Boston Dist. Pub. Schs., 1969-72, supt. schs., 1972-75; exec. dir. Met. Planning Project, Newton, Mass., 1975-77; supt. schs. Rockville Centre, N.Y., 1977-82, North Babylon, N.Y., 1982-84, Broward County, Ft. Lauderdale, Fla., 1984-88; supt. Gloucester (Mass.) Pub. Schs., 1989-93; assoc. prof. dept. ednl. leadership, dept. chair U. Miss., University, 1993—; assoc. prof. dept. continuing studies Boston State Coll., 1970-72; assoc. in edn. Harvard U. Grad. Sch. Edn., 1972-75; adj. prof. edn. Boston U., 1973-75, C.W. Post Ctr., L.I. U., 1979-84, Fla. Internat. U., 1984-88, Salem (Mass.) State Coll., 1990-93; prof. Suffolk U., 1975-77; mem. meml. scholarship fund com. Harvard U., 1977-82; TV commentator Channel 5, Boston, 1975-76; prodr. edn. programs New Eng. Cablevision, 1989-93; keynote spkr. Harvard U. Grad. Sch. Edn., 1976, NYU, 1980; mem. faculty senate U. Miss., 1994—, chair subcom. on athletics, 1994-95. Edn. columnist Boston Herald, 1975-78, L.I. News, 1982-84, Gloucester Times; edn. commentator New Eng. Cablevision, 1989-93; contbr. articles to profl. jours. Edn. coord. Boston chpt. United Way, 1974, Rockville Centre United Fund, 1979-80, Broward County chpt., 1985-87; trustee Mus. Fin. Arts, Boston, 1972-77; bd. dirs. Boston Youth Symphony, 1972-77, Edn. Devel. Ctr., 1972-77, Broward Com. of 100, Boys Club Broward County, 1985-88; mem. nat. alumni bd. Boston U., 1975—; mem. vis. com. Suffolk U., 1978-80; adv. bd. Harvard N.Y. Alumni Forums, 1980-84; mem. L.I. Regional Planning Bd., 1983-84, Gov.'s Task Force on Alt. Edn., Fla., 1986-88; mem. Atty. Gen.'s edn. adv. com., Mass., 1991-93. Recipient Friend of Youth award Hayden Goodwill Boys' Home, 1973, Ida M. Johnston Outstanding Alumni award Boston U. Sch. Edn., 1976, Man of Yr. award Pope's Hill Assn., 1976, Jenkins Meml. award for ednl. leadership N.Y. State Coun., PTA, 1980, Ednl. Leadership award L.I. chpt. NCCJ, 1980, Broward County Med. Aux., 1984, Lifetime Achievement award Matignon H.S. Alumni, 1995, Civil Rights award NAACP, 1996; selected as mem. Exec. Educator 100, Nat. Sch. Bd. Assn., 1987; named to Matignon H.S. Hall of Fame, 1995. Mem. ASCD (nat. commn. on supervision 1984-85), Am. Assn. Sch. Adminstrs. (del. assembly 1991, 92, 93, resolutions com. 1988-89, 93-94, 94-95, 95—), Am. Hist. Assn., Horace Mann League, Assn. for Asian Studies, Nat. Coun. Social Studies (nat. urban affairs com. 1977-80), Miss. Assn. Sch. Supts., Mass. Atty. Gen.'s Adv. Group, Harvard Club N.Y.C., Boston Coll., Varsity Club, KC, Rotary, Am. Legion, Phi Delta Kappa. Roman Catholic. Office: Grad Sch of Edn Univ of Mississippi PO Box 563 University MS 38677-0563 *A person's ability for creative and imaginative thinking is limited only by his/her fear to dream.*

LEASE, JANE ETTA, environmental science consultant, retired librarian; b. Kansas City, Kans., Apr. 10, 1924; d. Joy Alva and Emma (Jaggard) Omer; B.S. in Home Econs., U. Ariz., 1957; M.S. in Edn., Ind. U., 1962; M.S. in L.S., U. Denver, 1967; m. Richard J. Lease, Jan. 16, 1960; children—Janet (Mrs. Jacky B. Radifera), Joyce (Mrs. Robert J. Carson), Julia (Mrs. Earle D. Marvin), Cathy (Mrs. Edward F. Warren); stepchildren—Richard Jay II, William Harley. Newspaper reporter Ariz. Daily Star, Tucson, 1937-39; asst. home agt. Dept. Agr., 1957; homemaking tchr., Ft. Huachuca, Ariz., 1957-60; head tchr. Stonebelt Council Retarded Children, Bloomington, Ind., 1960-61; reference clk. Ariz. State U. Library, 1964-66; edn. and psychology librarian N.Mex. State U., 1967-71; Amway distbr., 1973—; cons. solid wastes, distressed land problems reference remedies, 1967; ecology lit. research and cons., 1966—. Ind. observer 1st World Conf. Human Environment, 1972; mem. Las Cruces Community Devel. Priorities Adv. Bd. Mem. ALA, Regional Environ. Edn. Research Info. Orgn., NAFE, P.E.O., D.A.R., Internat. Platform Assn., Las Cruces Antique Car Club, Las Cruces Story League, N.Mex. Library Assn. Methodist (lay leader). Address: 2145 Boise Dr Las Cruces NM 88001-5149

LEASE, MARTIN HARRY, JR., retired political science educator; b. Plainfield, Ind., Aug. 15, 1927; s. Martin Harry and Beatrice Irene (Krebs) L.; m. Jeanne Marie Lachance, Sept. 6, 1969; children—Deborah Eileen, Joshua Martin. B.A., Ind. U., 1953, M.A., 1955, Ph.D., 1961. Instr. polit. sci. U. Miami, Coral Gables, Fla., 1955-56; instr. U. Minn., Duluth, 1957-61, asst. prof., 1961-65, assoc. prof., 1965-70, prof., 1970-94, asst. dean grad. sch., 1968-77, acting acad. vice-provost, 1977-79, polit. sci. dept. head, 1979-83, dir. overseas program, Eng., 1983-84; ret., 1994; vis. lectr. Lakehead U., Thunder Bay, Ont., Can., 1975. Del. Democratic Nat. Conv., 1968; active local party offices including head of Duluth orgn.; election cons. local radio and TV, Duluth; mem. fed. dist. ct. com. on Celebration Bicentennial U.S. Constn. Nat. Ctr. for edn. in Politics fellow, 1962-63. Mem. Western Polit. Sci. Assn. (research group), Minn. Polit. Sci. Assn. (bd. dirs. 1966-68), Ctr. for Study of Presidency. Mem. Democratic Farm Labor Party. Avocations: fishing; gardening. Office: U Minn-Duluth Polit Sci Dept 302 B Cina Hall Duluth MN 55812

LEASE, RICHARD JAY, police science educator, former police officer; b. Cherokee, Ohio, Dec. 10, 1914; s. Harold and Mabelle (Fullerton) L.; m. Marjorie Faye Stoughton, Sept. 2, 1939 (div. Apr. 1957); children: Richard Jay II, William Harley; m. Jane Etta Omer, Jan. 16, 1960; stepchildren: Janet Radifera, Joyce Carson, Julia Marvin, Catherine Warren; adopted children: Alan Fudge, Stephen V. Graham. Student, Wittenberg U., 1932-33; BA, U. Ariz., 1937, MA, 1961; postgrad., Ind. U., 1950, 60, Ariz. State U., 1956, 63-65, 67—; grad., U. Louisville So. Police Inst., 1955. Grad. asst . U. Ariz., Tucson, 1937-38; with Tucson Police Dept., from 1938; advanced from patrolman to sgt., also served as safety officer Pima County Sheriff's Dept., Tucson, 1953, patrol supr., 1953-55, investigator, 1955-56; tchr. sci. pub. schs. Tucson, 1957-59; lectr. dept. police adminstrn. Ind. U., Bloomington, 1960-65; asst. prof. dept. police sci. N.Mex. State U., Las Cruces, 1965—; cons. law enforcement problems HEW, 1960, Indpls. Police Dept., 1962, Harrisburg Community Coll. Police Sci. Dept., 1967, Phoenix Police Dept., 1968—; advisor police tng. programs several small city police depts., Ind., 1960-63, Indpls., 1962; mem. oral bd. for selection chief in Bateville, Ind., 1962, oral bd. for selection sgts. and lts., Las Cruces Police Dept., 1966—. Author: (with Robert F. Borkenstein) Alcohol and Road Traffic: Problems of Enforcement and Prosecution, 1963, The Dreams, Hopes, Recollections and Thoughts of a Professional Good Samaritan; cons. editor Police, various rsch. publs. on chem. intoxification tests, psychol. errors of witnesses, reading disabilities, delinquency. Participant numerous FBI seminars; active youth work, philanthropy, among Am. Indians in Southwest; founder awards outstanding ROTC cadets N.Mex. State U., 1967—; founder Wiltberger ann. awards Nat. Police Combat Pistol Matches; scoutmaster Yucca council Boy Scouts Am., 1966—. Served to 1st lt. USMCR, 1942-45, PTO. Fellow Am. Acad. Forensic Scis. (sec. gen. sect.); mem. Internat. Assn. Chiefs of Police, Internat. Assn. Police Profs., Brit. Acad. Forensic Scis., Can. Soc. Forensic Sci., Am. Soc. Criminology, Ret. Officers Assn., Assn. U.S. Army (2d v.p. 1969—), NEA, N.Mex. Edn. Assn., N.Mex. Police and Sheriffs Assn., Internat. Crossroads, NRA (benefactor mem.), Marine Corps League (life), Sigma Chi. Lodges: Masons, Elks. Home and Office: 2145 Boise Dr Las Cruces NM 88001-5149

LEASE, ROBERT K., lawyer; b. Cleve., 1948. AB magna cum laude, Dartmouth Coll., 1970; JD cum laude, U. Conn., 1976. Bar: Ohio. Ptnr. Baker & Hostetler, Cleve. Mem. Phi Beta Kappa. Office: Baker & Hostetler 3200 Nat City Ctr 1900 E 9th St Cleveland OH 44114-3401

LEASE, RONALD CHARLES, financial economics educator; b. Davenport, Iowa, Feb. 3, 1940; s. Mace Duane and Mary Virginia (Marsh) L.; m. Judy Ellen Gifford, Aug. 24, 1962; 1 child, Tracy Rene. BS in Engring., Colo. Sch. Mines, 1963; MS, Purdue U., 1966, PhD, 1973. Metall. engr. Aluminum Co. Am., 1963-69; prof. U. Utah, Salt Lake City, 1973-86; prof., chmn. Tulane U., New Orleans, 1986-90, endowed prof., assoc. dean, 1988-90; endowed prof. U. Utah, Salt Lake City, 1990—; vis. assoc. prof. U. Chgo., 1978-79; vis. prof. U. Mich., Ann Arbor, 1985-86. Mem. editorial bd. Jour. Fin. Rsch., Phoenix, 1987-93, Fin. Mgmt., Tampa, 1986—, Jour. Corp. Fin., Pitts., 1993—; contbr. articles to profl. jours. Mem. Am. Fin. Assn., Western Fin. Assn., Fin. Mgmt. Assn. (editor Survey and Synthesis in Fin. 1984-90, pres. 1992-93, chmn. bd. dirs. 1996—), Phi Kappa Phi, Beta Gamma Sigma. Home: 1409 Spring Ln Salt Lake City UT 84117-6710 Office: U Utah Eccles Sch Bus Salt Lake City UT 84112

LEASK, JOHN MCPHEARSON, II, accountant, author, speaker; b. Bridgeport, Conn., Oct. 21, 1942; s. Haldane Burgess and Laura (Manchester) L.; m. Phoebe Kamelakis, Aug. 19, 1979; 1 child, John McPhearson III; stepchildren: Peter Rizos, Andy Rizos, Joanna Rizos Bogardus. Student U. Mich., 1961-68; AS in Acctg., Bryant Coll., 1973, BS in Acctg., 1974. CPA, Conn. Salesman for Conn. and R.I., Winthrop Lab., NYC, 1969-73; staff acct. Leask & Leask, P.C., Fairfield, Conn., 1973-75, v.p., 1976-80, audit prin., chmn. bd., mng. prin., 1980—, also dir.; adj. prof. Fairfield U., 1976—. Contbg. editor CPA Client Svc.; mem. editorial adv. bd. CPA Firm Profitability. Mem. Libr. Bldg. Com., Fairfield, 1981-83, allocations council United Way, Bridgeport, Conn., 1982-91; co-pres. Am. Field Service Parents Group, 1988-89; chmn. Fairfield Festival of Arts, 1983, 86-91, mem. bd., Biomation, 1996, mem. bd. Funkel Rotary Found., 1990—, v.p., 1996—; vice chmn. East Providence Town Com., 1971-73; chmn. audit com. Congregationalist Ch., 1986—. Recipient Vol. award United Way, 1983, Score Citation, SBA Citation. Fellow Conn. Soc. CPAs (mgmt. acctg. practice com. 1985-88, 90-94, mem. state taxation com. 1987-88, CPE com. 1985-86, 93-94); mem. Am. Inst. CPAs, Fairfield C. of C. (pres. 1983-84, Harold Harris Cmty. Svc. award 1991), Rotary (Citation Meritorious Svc. Found. Rotary Internat. 1993, Paul Harris Cmty. Svc. award 1988, Paul Harris fellow 1988, 95, Disting. Svc. award, Norm Parsells award 1996, Fairfield treas. 1983-87, v.p. programs 1987-88, chpt. 1st v.p., 1988-89, pres. 1989-90, dist. treas. 1988-90, various dist. offices 1990-94, gov. R.I. dist. 7980 1995-96). Republican. Congregationalist. Office: Leask & Leask PC CPAs 1100 Kings Hwy East PO Box 320235 Fairfield CT 06430-0159

LEASON, JODY JACOBS, newspaper columnist; b. Margarita, Venezuela, June 8, 1926; came to U.S., 1928; d. Jose Cruz Caceres and Graciela Rodriguez; m. Russell L. Jacobs (div.); 1 child, Jessica Jacobs Salet; m. Barney Leason, Dec. 29, 1976. BA, Hunter Coll.-CUNY, 1940's. Assoc. fashion editor Women's Wear Daily, N.Y.C., 1969-70; West Coast fashion editor Women's Wear Daily, L.A., 1957-69; London fashion editor Women's Wear Daily, 1970-72; soc. editor L.A. Times, 1972-86. Author: (novel) The Right Circles, 1988. Avocations: needlework, gardening.

LEATH, KENNETH THOMAS, research plant pathologist, educator, agricultural consultant; b. Providence, Apr. 29, 1931; s. Thomas and Elizabeth (Wootten) L.; m. Marie Andreozzi, Aug. 1955; children: Kenneth, Steven, Kevin, Maria Beth. BS, U. R.I., 1959; MS, PhD, U. Minn., 1966. Rsch. plant pathologist U.S. Regional Pasture Rsch. Lab. USDA-ARS, 1966-94; prof. Pa. State U., 1966-94; pvt. agrl. cons. Boalsburg, Pa., 1994—; advisor numerous state and nat. orgns. Contbr. numerous articles to profl. jours. and chpts. to books. With USN, 1951-55. Mem. Elks. Achievements include research on root diseases and systemic wilts of forage species.

LEATHAM, JOHN TONKIN, business executive; b. Chgo., July 4, 1936; s. Chester and Betty (Collins) L.; m. Sheila K. Andersen, Sept. 13, 1958; children: Lisa M., John A., Bronwen Gay, Douglas Q. B.A., Lawrence U., Appleton, Wis., 1958. Asst. cashier, lending officer Continental Ill. Nat. Bank & Trust Co., Chgo., 1962-68; with Reliance Group, Inc., N.Y.C., 1968-79; sr. v.p., chief financial officer Reliance Group, Inc., 1971-72, exec. v.p., chief operating and chief financial officer, 1972-79, dir., mem. exec. com., 1974-79; investment and merchant banker, 1979—; chmn., dir. Security Health Managed Care, Inc., 1994—; vice chmn., dir. CliniCorp, Inc., West Palm Beach, Fla., 1992-94; pres., CEO Clinicorp Midwest, Inc., 1992-93; CEO Security Health Providers, Inc., 1996—; bd. dirs., mng. dir. Scuul Ltd.; trustee Endowment Realty Investors Inc., 1987—; nat. dir. Reading is FUNdamental, Inc., 1975-91. Trustee Lawrence U., 1981—, chmn., 1990-92; trustee The Common Fund, 1987—, Endowment Advisers, Inc., Fairfield Ptnrs., Inc., 1990—, chmn., 1992-96. 1st lt. USAF, 1958-62. Decorated Air Force Commendation medal. Mem. Lawrence U. Alumni Assn. (v.p. 1963-70, dir. 1963-71). Home: 1925 Calvin Ct Deerfield IL 60015-1636

LEATHER, VICTORIA POTTS, college librarian; b. Chattanooga, June 12, 1947; d. James Elmer Potts and Ruby Lea (Bettis) Potts Wilmoth; m. Jack Edward Leather; children: Stephen, Sean. BA cum laude, U. Chattanooga, 1968; MSLS, U. Tenn., 1978. Libr. asst. East New Orleans Regional Libr., 1969-71; libr. Erlanger Nursing Sch., Chattanooga, 1971-75; chief libr. Erlanger Hosp., Chattanooga, 1975-77; dir. Eastgate Br. Libr., Chattanooga, 1977-81; dir. libr. svcs. Chattanooga State Tech. Community Coll., 1981-95, dean libr. svcs., 1996—. Mem. Allied Arts, Hunter Mus., High Mus. Art. Mem. ALA, Southeastern Libr. Assn., Tenn. Libr. Assn. (chair legislation com.), Chattanooga Area Libr. Assn. (pres. 1978-79), Tenn. Bd. Regents Media Consortium (chair 1994-95), Phi Delta Kappa. Episcopalian. Avocations: reading, needlework, traveling.

LEATHERBARROW, DAVID, architecture department chair. Chair architecture dept. U. Pa., Phila. Office: U Pa 210 S 34th St Philadelphia PA 19104-3804*

LEATHERDALE, DOUGLAS WEST, insurance company executive; b. Morden, Man., Can., Dec. 6, 1936; came to U.S., 1968; s. Walter West and Lena Elizabeth (Gilligan) L.; children—Mary Jo, Christopher. B.A., United Coll., Winnipeg, Man., 1957. Investment analyst, officer Gt. West Life Assurance Co., Winnipeg, 1957-68; assoc. exec. sec. Bd. Pensions, Luth. Ch., Mpls., 1968-72; exec. v.p., then v.p. St. Paul Investment Mgmt. Co., subs. St. Paul Cos., Inc., 1972-77; v.p.-fin. St. Paul Cos., Inc., 1974-81, sr. v.p.-fin., 1981-82, exec. v.p., 1982-89, also dir., pres., chief oper. officer, 1989-90, chmn., pres., chief exec. officer, 1990—; bd. dirs. St. Paul Fire and Marine Ins. Co., St. Paul Land Resources, Inc., St. Paul Real Estate of Ill., Inc., John Nuveen & Co. Inc., St. Paul Properties, Inc., St. Paul Oil and Gas Corp., St. Paul Fire & Marine Ins. Co. (U.K.) Ltd., St. Paul Mercury Ins. Co., St. Paul Guardian Ins. Co., St. Paul Surplus Lines Ins. Co., Nat. Ins. Wholesalers, Atwater McMillian, 77 Water St., Inc., Ramsey Ins. Co., St. Paul Risk Services, Inc., St. Paul Plymouth Ctr., Inc. Athena Assurance Co., St. Paul Fin. Group, Inc., Graham Resources, Inc., Carlyle Capital, L.P., United HealthCare Corp. Mem. Twin Cities Soc. Security Analysts, Fin. Execs. Inst. Club: Minnesota (St. Paul). Avocation: horses. Office: St Paul Cos Inc 385 Washington St Saint Paul MN 55102-1309*

LEATHERMAN, HUGH KENNETH, SR., state senator, business executive; b. Lincoln County, N.C., Apr. 14, 1931; s. John Bingham and Ada Annis (Gantt) L.; m. Jean Helms, Nov. 11, 1978; children: Sheila Dianne, Hugh Kenneth, Karen Ann, Joyce Lynn, Amy Jean, Sarah Ada. BS in Civil Engring., N.C. State U., 1953; HHD (hon.), Francis Marion Coll., 1987. Engr., then sec. Florence (S.C.) Concrete Products Inc., 1955-72, pres., 1972-93; sec. Hugh-Stan Inc., Myrtle Beach, 1974—; mem. S.C. Senate, 1980—; commr. S.C. Dept. Consumer Affairs. Deacon 1st Bapt. Ch. Named Legislator of Yr., 1982. Home: 1817 Pineland Ave Florence SC 29501-5419 Office: 205 Gressette Bldg Columbia SC 29202

LEAVELL, MICHAEL RAY, computer programmer, analyst; b. Port St. Joe, Fla., Sept. 28, 1955; s. Ray Carl and Willodean (Griggs) L. AS in Electronics Tech., Gulf Coast Jr. Coll., Panama City, Fla., 1975; BS in Systems Sci., U. West Fla., 1979. Engr. Sta. WDTB-TV (now WMBB-TV), Panama City, 1976; radio announcer Sta. WJOE, Port St. Joe, 1979; computer programmer III, Fla. Dept. Labor, Tallahassee, 1979-80, computer programmer, analyst II, 1980-96, systems project analyst, 1996—. Office: Fla Dept Labor 244 Howard Bldg Tallahassee FL 32399

LEAVENGOOD, VICTOR PRICE, telephone company executive; b. Ocala, Fla., June 2, 1924; s. Hansel Devane and Mildred (Price) L.; m. Elizabeth Lee Bird, Sept. 12, 1950; children: Sally (dec.), Ann, Hansel. BSBA, U. Fla., 1947; MBA, Harvard U., 1949. Bus. mgr. Ocala (Fla.) Star Banner (daily newspaper), 1952-59; circulation dir. Tampa (Fla.) Tribune, 1959-60, dir. community affairs, 1960-64; asst. v.p. Gen. Telephone Co. Fla., Tampa, 1964-70; sec., treas. Gen. Telephone Co. Fla., 1970-87; bd. dirs. Blue Cross Blue Shield Fla. Pres. Hills County Cmty. Coordination Coun., 1964-65, Tampa Econ. Opportunity Coun., 1965-66, Fla. Clergy Econ. Edn. Found., 1964-68, Fla. chpt. United Way, 1969-70; bd. dirs., treas. Fla. Aquarium, Hospice of Hillsborough, Fla.; bd. dirs. West Ctrl. Fla. Area Agy. on Aging, Japan-Am. Soc. Ctrl. Fla., Suncoast coun. Girl Scouts U.S.A.; bd. advisors U. South Fla. Contemporary Art Mus.; trustee Fla. Mental Health Inst.; chmn. Tampa Bay Internat. Super Task Force, Fla. Mcht. Assn., Tampa Commn. on Pub. Art; pres. United Fund Greater Tampa Inc., 1964-68, treas., 1970-75; mem. Fla. Coun. Mental Health Tng. and Rsch., 1967-74, President's Round Table, Eckerd Coll., St. Petersburg, Fla., 1969—; mem. president's coun. U. South Fla., 1974—, Hillsborough County Hosp. Authority; treas. U. South Fla. Found., 1957-80, pres., 1982-83. Comdr. USNR, 1942-47. Mem. Greater Tampa C. of C. (bd. dirs.), Fla. C. of C., edn. com. 1968-71), U.S. C. of C. (edn. com.), Phi Eta Sigma, Phi Delta Theta.; mem. Ye Mystic Krewe of Gasparilla. Democrat. Methodist (ofcl. bd.). Clubs: University (Tampa), Tampa, Tampa Yacht and Country (Tampa). Home: 4516 W Sylvan Ramble St Tampa FL 33609-4214

LEAVEY, THOMAS E., international organization administrator. Dir. gen. internat. bur. Universal Postal Union, Berne, 1995—. Office: Universal Postal Union, Case postale, 3000 Bern Switzerland

LEAVITT, AUDREY FAYE COX, television programming executive; b. Old Hickory, Tenn., June 1, 1932; d. James Aubrey and Bernice (Hudnall) Cox; student David Lipscomb Secondary Sch. and Coll., 1947, Tenn. Sch. Broadcasting, 1949-50, Vanderbilt U., 1948-50; children: Jack, Teresa. Woman commentator, continuity chief radio sta. WGNS, Murfreesboro, Tenn., 1949-50; announcer, continuity chief, traffic dir. Sta. KDWT, Stamford, Tex., 1950-51; sales account exec. Sta. KMAC, San Antonio, 1952; continuity chief, announcer Sta. KEYL-TV, San Antonio, 1952-54, also firm dir.; film buyer, mgr. Sta. WOAI-TV, San Antonio, 1954-68, ops. mgr. film, video-tape traffic, continuity, 1968-71; film and videotape operations mgr., film buyer Sta. KENS-TV, San Antonio, 1972-79; exec. v.p. Jim Thomas & Assocs., San Antonio, 1979-80; owner Communique Internationalé, TV programming syndication, 1981—, Faye Leavitt Advt., 1990—, Strategic Planning Services; exec. producer TV series The Lone Star Sportsman Show; writer, exec. producer and dir. TV series Weather or Not; writer, producer gourmet cooking show For Men Only, The Great Age, 1988; hostess radio series Our Turn, 1994—. Pub. rels dir., advt. dir. The Madison Retirement Community, San Antonio, 1991-95. Mem. NAFE, Nat. Pub. Rels. Soc., Internat. Platform Assn., Alamo Heights C. of C. (bd. dirs.), San Antonio Conservation Soc., San Antonio Livestock and Rodeo Exposition, San Antonio Apt. Assn. (publicity chmn.), Yellow Rose Tex., World Affairs Council. Office: PO Box 6493 San Antonio TX 78209-0493

LEAVITT, CHARLES LOYAL, English language educator, administrator; b. Randolph, Maine, Apr. 30, 1921; s. Charles Warren Franklin and Alice Mabel (Sparrow) L.; m. Emily Raymond Stewart, June 12, 1951 (dec. 1966); m. Virginia Louise Kracke, Sept. 6, 1969. Diploma in Edn., U. Maine, Farmington, 1941; BS in Edn., U. So. Maine, 1946; MA in English, Boston U., 1947; PhD in English, U. Wis., 1961; MLS, Columbia U., 1969. Cert. tchr. English and history, elem., secondary, coll. Tchr. pub. schs., Vanceboro, Maine, 1941-42; tchr., prin. pub. schs., York Village, Maine, 1945-47; Instr. English and history Endicott Jr. Coll., Beverly, Mass., 1947-48; assoc. prof. English Lyndon State Coll., Lyndon Center, Vt., 1948-53, 54-55; teaching asst. in English U. Wis., Madison, 1953-54, 55-59; instr. Wayne State U., Detroit, 1959-61; assoc. prof. Montclair (N.J.) State Coll, 1961-68; v.p., sec., dir. edn. Universal Learning Corp., N.Y.C., 1968-69; assoc. dir. admissions Sarah Lawrence Coll., Bronxville, N.Y., 1970-71; dir. continuing edn., asst. dean, prof. Bloomfield (N.J.) Coll., 1971-74; chmn. liberal arts, prof. Coll. of Ins., N.Y.C., 1975-86, prof. emeritus, 1987—; adj. prof. English Fairleigh Dickinson U., Teaneck, N.J., 1988-92. Author: Ten Lit. Study Guides, 1964-66; cons. editor Monarch Lit. Guides, N.Y.C., 1963-68; author chpt. in book. Treas. Youth Community Funds, York Village, Maine, 1946-47; asst. scoutmaster Boy Scouts Am., York Village, 1946-47; v.p. Overseas Neighbors, Montclair, 1974-75; tchr. Adult Sch. of Montclair, 1963-68. With USAAF, 1942-45. Named Most Popular Prof., Montclair State Coll., 1967, Prof. of Yr., Coll. of Ins., 1978; yearbook dedications Lyndon State Coll., 1950, Bloomfield Coll., 1974, Coll. of Ins., 1987; Nat. Audubon scholar, Garden Clubs York Village, 1947. Mem. AAUP, MLA, Coll. English Assn., Internat. Platform Assn., Princeton Club (N.Y.C.), Faculty Columbia U. Club, New Eng. Soc. N.Y.C. Club, Kiwanis (trustee Manhattan found. 1989—). Republican. Baptist. Home: 93 Stonebridge Rd Montclair NJ 07042-1632 Office: One Insurance Pla 101 Murray St New York NY 10007-2132

LEAVITT, DAVID ADAM, writer; b. Pitts., June 23, 1961; s. Harold Jack and Gloria (Rosenthal) L. BA, Yale U., 1983. Reader, editorial asst. Viking-Penguin Inc., N.Y.C., 1983-84. Author: Family Dancing, 1984 (Nat. Book Critics Cir. award nomination 1984, PEN-Faulkner award nomination 1985), The Lost Language of Cranes, 1986, Equal Affections, 1988, A Place I've Never Been, 1990, While England Sleeps, 1993; co-editor: The Penguin Book of Gay Short Fiction, 1994; contbr. to periodicals including Esquire, Harper's, New Yorker, N.Y. Times Book Rev., Village Voice, others. Recipient Willets prize for fiction Yale U., 1982, O. Henry Award, 1984; Nat. Endowment for Arts grantee, 1985; vis. fgn. writer Inst. Catalan Letters, Barcelona Spain, 1989; Guggenheim fellow, 1990. Mem. PEN. Office: 125 via Ghibellina, Firenze 50122, Italy*

LEAVITT, HAROLD JACK, management educator; b. Lynn, Mass., Jan. 14, 1922; s. Joseph and May (Lopata) L.; m. Gloria Rosenthal, Jan. 31, 1943 (dec.); children—John, Emily, David; m. Jean Lipman-Blumen. B.A., Harvard Coll., 1943; M.S., Brown U., 1944; Ph.D., Mass. Inst. Tech., 1949. Asst. prof. psychology Rensselaer Poly. Inst., 1949-50; assoc. prof. Sch. Bus., U. Chgo., 1954-58; prof. indsl. adminstrn. and psychology GSIA, Carnegie Inst. Tech., 1958-66; Walter Kenneth Kilpatrick prof. orgn. behavior and psychology Grad. Sch. Bus., Stanford U., 1966-90, prof. emeritus, 1990; vis. prof. London Grad. Sch. Bus. Studies, 1972; v.p. Nejelski & Co., 1951-53; cons. European Prod. Agy., Paris, 1956; faculty prin. Mgmt. Analysis Ctr., Inc., 1971—. Author: (with H. Bahrami) Managerial Psychology, 5th edit., 1988, (with W. Dill and H. Eyring) The Organizational World, 1973, Corporate Pathfinders, 1986; co-editor: Organizations of the Future, 1974. Served to lt. (j.g.) USNR, 1944-46. Fellow Am. Psychol. Assn. Home: 1520 E California Blvd Pasadena CA 91106-4104 Office: Stanford U Grad Sch Bus Stanford CA 94305

LEAVITT, JEFFREY STUART, lawyer; b. Cleve., July 13, 1946; s. Sol and Esther (Dolinsky) L.; m. Ellen Fern Sugerman, Dec. 21, 1968; children: Matthew Adam, Joshua Aaron. AB, Cornell U., 1968; JD, Case Western Res. U., 1973. Bar: Ohio 1973. Assoc. Jones, Day, Reavis & Pogue, Cleve., 1973-80, ptnr., 1981—. Contbr. articles to profl. jours. Trustee Bur. Jewish Edn., Cleve., 1981-93, v.p. 1985-87; trustee Fairmount Temple, Cleve., 1982—, v.p. 1985-90, pres., 1990-93; trustee Citizens League Greater Cleve., 1982-89, 92-94, pres., 1987-89; trustee Citizens League Rsch. Inst., Cleve., 1989—, Great Lakes Region of Union Am. Hebrew Congregations, 1990-93; mem. bd. gov. Case Western Res. Law Sch. Alumni Assn., 1989-92; sec. Kulas Found., 1986-88, 93—, asst. treas., 1989-92. Mem. ABA (employee benefits coms. 1976—), Nat. Assn. Pub. Pension Attys., Midwest Pension Conf. Jewish. Home: 25961 Annesley Rd Cleveland OH 44122-2437 Office: Jones Day Reavis & Pogue N Point 901 Lakeside Ave E Cleveland OH 44114-1116

LEAVITT, JEROME EDWARD, childhood educator; b. Verona, N.J., Aug. 1, 1916; s. Thomas Edward and Clara Marie (Sonn) L.; m. Florence

Elizabeth Wilkins, Aug. 23, 1963. B.S., Newark State Coll., 1938; M.A., N.Y. U., 1942; Ed.D., Northwestern U., 1952. Tchr. pub. schs. Roslyn Heights, N.Y., 1938-42; instr. Sperry Gyroscope, Bklyn., 1942-45; prin., supr. pub. schs. Los Alamos, N.Mex., 1945-49; prof. edn., exec. asst. to dean Portland (Oreg.) State U., 1952-66; prof. edn. U. Ariz., Tucson, 1966-69; prof. elem. edn., coordinator Child Abuse Project, Calif. State U., Fresno, 1969-81; pres. Jerome Leavitt, Inc., 1981—. Author: Nursery-Kindergarten Edn., 1958, Carpentry for Children, 1959, By Land, By Sea, By Air, 1969, The Beginning Kindergarten Teacher, 1971, America and Its Indians, 1971, The Battered Child, 1974, Herbert Sonn: Yosemite's Birdman, 1975, Child Abuse and Neglect: Research and Innovation, 1983, others; contbr. articles to profl. jours. Mem. ASCD (life), NEA (life), Assn. Childhood Edn. Internat. (life), Soc.Profs. Edn., Calif. Tchrs. Assn., Profs. Curriculum, Phi Delta Kappa, Kappa Delta Pi, Epsilon Pi Tau. Home and Office: Villa Campana 6653 E Carondelet Dr Apt 124 Tucson AZ 85710-2138

LEAVITT, LEWIS A., pediatrician, medical educator; b. N.Y.C., Nov. 7, 1941; s. Isidore and Sarah (Fishkowitz) L.; m. Judith E. Walzer, July 2, 1966; children—Sarah Abigail, David Isaac. B.S., U. Chgo., 1961, M.D., 1965. Diplomate Am. Bd. Pediatrics. Intern, resident Albert Einstein Coll. Medicine, Jacobi Hosp., Bronx, N.Y., 1965-68; prof. pediatrics U. Wis., Madison, 1984—, head infant devel. lab. Waisman Ctr. Mental Retardation and Human Devel., 1973—. Contbr. articles to profl. jours. Served to lt. comdr. USN, 1968-70. Mem. Soc. Research in Child Devel., Am. Acad. Pediatrics. Office: U Wis 1500 Highland Ave Madison WI 53705-2274

LEAVITT, MARTIN JACK, lawyer; b. Detroit, Mar. 30, 1940; s. Benjamin and Annette (Cohen) L.; m. Janice C. (McCreary) Leavitt; children: Michael J., Paul J., David A., Dean N., Keleigh R. LLB, Wayne State U., 1964. Bar: Mich. 1965, Fla. 1967. Assoc. Robert A. Sullivan, Detroit, 1968-70; officer, bd. dirs. Law Offices Sullivan & Leavitt, Northville, Mich., 1970—, pres., 1979—; bd. dirs. Tyrone Hills of Mich., Premiere Video, Inc., Menlo Tool Co., others. Lt. comdr., USNR, 1959-64. Detroit Edison Upper Class scholar, 1958-64. Mem. ABA, Mich. Bar Assn., Fla. Bar Assn., Transp. Lawyers Assn., ICC Practitioners, Meadowbrook Country Club, Huron River Hunting & Fishing Club (past pres.), Rolls Royce Owners Club (bd. dirs.). Jewish. Office: Sullivan and Leavitt PC PO Box 5490 Northville MI 48167-0997

LEAVITT, MARY JANICE DEIMEL, special education educator, civic worker; b. Washington, Aug. 21, 1924; d. Henry L. and Ruth (Grady) Deimel; BA, Am. U., Washington, 1946; postgrad. U. Md., 1963-65, U. Va., 1965-67, 72-73, 78-79, George Washington U., 1966-67; tchr.'s cert. spl. edn., 1968; m. Robert Walker Leavitt, Mar. 30, 1945; children: Michael Deimel, Robert Walker, Caroline Ann Leavitt Snyder. Tchr., Rothery Sch., Arlington, Va., 1947; dir. Sunnyside, Children's House, Washington, 1949; asst. dir. Coop. Sch. for Handicapped Children, Arlington, 1962, dir., Arlington, Springfield, Va., 1963-66; tchr. mentally retarded children Fairfax (Va.) County Pub. Schs., 1966-68; asst. dir. Burgundy Farm Country Day Sch., Alexandria, Va., 1968-69; tchr., substitute tchr. specific learning problem children Accotink Acad., Springfield, Va., 1970-80; substitute tchr. learning disabilities Children's Achievement Ctr., McLean, Va., 1973-82, Psychiat. Inst., Washington and Rockville, Md., 1976-82, Home-Bound and Substitute Program, Fairfax, Va., 1978-84; asst. info. specialist Ednl. Rsch. Svc., Inc., Rosslyn, Va., 1974-76; docent Sully Plantation, Fairfax County (Va.) Park Authority, 1981-87, 88-94, Childrens Learning Ctrs., vol. Honor Roll, 1987, Walney-Collections Fairfax County (Va.) Park Authority, 1989—; sec. Widowed Persons Svc., 1983-85, mem., 1985-90. Mem. edn. subcom. Va. Commn. Children and Youth, 1973-74; den mother Nat. Capital Area Cub Scouts, Boy Scouts Am., 1962; troop fund raising chmn. Nat. Capitol coun. Girl Scouts U.S.A., 1968-69; capt. amblyopia team No. Va. chpt. Delta Gamma Alumnae, 1969; vol. Prevention of Blindness, 1980—; fund raiser Martha Movement, 1977-78; mem. St. John's Mus. Art, Wilmington, N.C., 1989—, Corcoran Gallery Art, Washington, 1989-90, 94—, Brunswick County Literacy Coun., N.C., 1989—; sunday sch. tchr. St. Andrews Episc. Ch., Burke, Va., 1995—, mem. search com., 1996. Recipient award Nat. Assn. for Retarded Citizens, 1975, Sully Recognition gift, 1989, Ten Yr. recognition pin Honor Roll, 1990. Mem. AAUW (co-chmn. met. area mass media com. D.C. chpt. 1973-75, v.p. Alexandria br. 1974-76, fellowship co-chmn., historian Springfield-Annandale br. 1979-80, 89-94, 94-95, name grantee ednl. found. 1980, cultural co-chmn. 1983-84), Assn. Part-Time Profls. (co-chmn. Va. local groups, job devel. and membership asst. 1981), Older Women's League, Nat. Mus. of Women in the Arts (charter mem.), Delta Gamma (treas. No. Va. alumnae chpt. 1973-75, pres. 1977-79, found. chmn. 1979-81, Katie Hale award 1989, treas. House Corp. Am. U. Beta Epsilon chpt. 1994-97). Club: Mil. Dist. of Washington Officer's Clubs (Ft. McNair, Ft. Myer). Episcopalian. Home: 7129 Rolling Forest Ave Springfield VA 22152-3622

LEAVITT, MICHAEL OKERLUND, governor, insurance executive; b. Cedar City, Utah, Feb. 11, 1951; s. Dixie and Anne (Okerlund) L.; m. Jacalyn Smith; children: Michael Smith, Taylor Smith, Anne Marie Smith, Chase Smith, Weston Smith. BA, So. Utah U., 1978. CPCU. Sales rep. Leavitt Group, Cedar City, 1972-74, account exec., 1974-76; mgr. underwriting Salt Lake City, 1976-82; chief operating officer, 1982-84, pres., chief exec. officer, 1984—, gov., state of Utah, 1993—; bd. dirs. Pacificorp, Portland, Oreg., Utah Power and Light Co., Salt Lake City, Great Western Thrift and Loan, Salt Lake City. Utah Bd. Regents, chmn. instl. coun. So. Utah State U., Cedar City, 1985-89; campaign chmn. U.S. Sen. Orrin Hatch, 1982, 88, U.S. Sen. Jake Garn, 1980, 86; cons. campaign Gov. Norman Angerter, 1984; mem. staff Reagan-Bush '84. 2d lt. USNG, 1969-77. Named Disting. Alumni So. Utah State Coll. Sch. Bus., 1986. Mem. Chartered Property Casualty Underwriters. Republican. Mormon. Avocation: golf. Office: Office of the Governor 210 State Capitol Building Salt Lake City UT 84114-1202*

LEAVITT, MICHAEL P(AUL), arts manager, concert producer, records marketer; b. N.Y.C., Dec. 9, 1944; s. Harry and Bertha (Mandell) L.; m. Nancy J. Redden, April 2, 1964; children: Amy, Sarah. BA, Kans. Wesleyan U., 1965; MA, Queens Coll., 1967; M in Philosophy, CUNY, 1975. Adminstrv. dir. Gregg Smith Singers, N.Y.C., 1978-79; exec. dir. Horizon Concerts, N.Y.C., 1978-79; mng. dir. Allied Artists Bur., N.Y.C., 1979—, Beethoven Soc., 1979-85, Empire Music Group, Inc., N.Y.C., 1990—; mng. dir. MPL Advt. for Arts, N.Y.C., 1981—; pres. MPL Prodns. Home: 195 Steamboat Rd Great Neck NY 11024-1739 Office: Empire Music Group Inc 170 W 74th St New York NY 10023-2350

LEAVITT, THOMAS WHITTLESEY, museum director, educator; b. Boston, Jan. 8, 1930; s. Richard C. and Helen M. (Pratt) L.; m. Jane O. Ayer, June 23, 1951 (div. 1969); children: Katherine, Nancy, Hugh; m. Lloyd B. Carter, Sept. 14, 1978 (div. 1985); mem. Michele C. McDonald, Apr. 20, 1991; children: Zachary Leavitt, Collin McDonald. A.B., Middlebury (Vt.) Coll., 1951; M.A., Boston U., 1952; Ph.D., Harvard, 1958. Asst. to dir. Fogg Mus., Harvard, 1954-56; exec. dir. fine arts com. People to People Program, 1957; dir. Pasadena (Calif.) Art Mus., 1957-63, dir. Santa Barbara (Calif.) Mus. Art, 1963-68; dir. Andrew Dickson White Mus. Art, Cornell U., Ithaca, N.Y., 1968-73, Herbert F. Johnson Mus. Art, 1973-91; univ. prof. history art Cornell U., 1968-91, prof. emeritus, 1991—; interim dir. R.I. Sch. Design Mus. of Art, 1993-94, Newport Art Mus., 1994-95; Dir. mus. program Nat. Endowment for Arts, 1971-72, mem. museum panel, 1972-75; vice chmn. Council on Museums and Edn. in Visual Arts, 1972-76; trustee Gallery Assn. N.Y. State, 1972-78; mem. mus. panel N.Y. State Council Arts, 1975-78, 1980-82; chmn. art adv. com. Nat. Air and Space Mus., 1988—. Author exhbn. catalogs, articles. Trustee Am. Fedn. Arts, 1972-91, Newport Art Mus., 1995—; bd. dirs. Am. Arts Alliance, 1976-82, Ind. Sector, 1980-84; bd. govs. N.E. Mus. Conf., 1973-76; trustee Williamstown Regional Art Conservation Lab., 1979-91, pres., 1984-87. Mem. Assn. Art Mus. Dirs. (pres. 1977-78, trustee 1978-80), Am. Assn. Museums (council 1976-79, v.p. 1980-82, pres. 1982-85, Disting. Svc. to Museums award 1997). Home: 25 Waterway Rd Saunderstown RI 02874-3906

LEAVY, EDWARD, judge; m. Eileen Leavy; children: Thomas, Patrick, Mary Kay, Paul. AB, U. Portland, 1950, LLB, U. Notre Dame, 1953. Dist. judge Lane County, Eugene, Oreg., 1957-61, cir. judge, 1961-76; magistrate U.S. Dist. Ct. Oreg., Portland, 1976-84, judge, 1984-87, cir. judge U.S. Ct. Appeals (9th cir.), 1987—. Office: US Ct Appeals Pioneer Courthouse 555 SW Yamhill St Ste 216 Portland OR 97204-1323

LEAVY, HERBERT THEODORE, publisher; b. Detroit, July 10, 1927; s. Morris and Thelma (Davidson) L.; m. Patricia J. Moran, June 20, 1953; children: Karen, Kathryn, Jill, Jacqueline. B.S. in Journalism, Ohio U., 1951. Supervisory editor Fawcett Books, N.Y.C., 1951-60; v.p., editorial dir. Davis Publs., N.Y.C., 1960-69; founder, pres. Internat. Evaluations, Hauppage, N.Y., 1969-70; pub. dir. Countrywide Publs. Inc., N.Y.C., 1970-75; pres. Communications Devel. Co., N.Y.C., 1975-79; editorial dir. Watson-Guptil Publs., N.Y.C., 1979-80; pres. Books from Mags., Inc., Smithtown, N.Y., 1980—, Resumes Unltd., Smithtown, 1984—. Author: 101 Fast Track Resumes, The Pleasure, Executive Handbook, Vegetarian Times Cookbook, McCall's Houseplant and Indoor Landscaping Guide, Working Mother Cookbook, Carpentry, Shoe and Leather Repair at Home, The Complete Book of Beards and Moustaches, Air Conditioning-Repair and Maintenance, Designing and Building Beds, Lofts and Sleeping Areas, Wallcovering, Floor Stripping and Refinishing, Packing and Moving, Recreational Vehicles, Appliance Repair, Plumbing Handbook, Successful Small Farms; numerous others. Acting 1st sgt. USAF, 1945-47. Mem. Sales Exec. Club, Am. Soc. Mag. Editors, Nat. Sporting Goods Assn., Am. Mgmt. Assn., Mag. Advts. Sales Club, Electronics Press Club, U.S. Tennis Ct. and Track Builders Assn., Am. Motorcycle Assn., Am. Horse Council, Authors Guild, Motorcycle Industry Council, Nat. Indoor Tennis Assn., Bus./Profl. Advt. Assn., Sigma Delta Chi. Office: Resumes Unlimited 222 E Main St Ste 107A Smithtown NY 11787

LEB, ARTHUR STERN, lawyer; b. Cleve., June 26, 1930; s. Ernest A. and Bertha (Stern) L.; m. Lois Shafron, Oct. 21, 1932; children: Gerald P., Judith A., Robert B. AB, Columbia Coll., 1952; JD, Case Western Res. U., 1955. Bar: Ohio 1955, U.S. Supreme Ct., 1965. Ptnr. Leb & Halm, Canton, Ohio, 1961-84, Amerman, Burt & Jones, L.P.A., Canton, 1985-90, Buckingham, Doolittle & Burroughs, 1991—; founding mem., exec. com. Ohio Coun. Sch. Bd. Attys., 1976-84, pres. 1983. Served to 1st lt. JAGC, USAF, 1955-57. Recipient Merit award Ohio Legal Ctr. Inst., 1964. Fellow Ohio Bar Found.; mem. ABA, Stark County Bar Assn. (pres. 1985-86), Ohio Bar Assn.

LEBADANG, artist; b. Vietnam, 1922. Student, Sch. Fine Arts, Toulouse, France. Exhibited in group shows Cin. Art Mus., Newman Contemporary Art Gallery, Phila., Galerie Fontaine, Paris, Frost and Reed Gallery, London, Wonderbank Gallery, Frankfurt, Germany; represented in permanent collections Univ. Art Gallery, Lund, Sweden, Phoenix Art Mus., also pvt. and corp. collections. Address: care Circle Gallery 2501 San Diego Ave San Diego CA 92110-2841*

LEBANO, EDOARDO ANTONIO, foreign language educator; b. Palmanova, Italy, Jan. 17, 1934; s. Nicola and Flora (Puccioni) L.; came to U.S., 1957, naturalized, 1961; m. Mary Vangeli, 1957; children: Tito Nicola, Mario Antonio. Student Biennio, U. Florence, 1955; M.A., Catholic U. Am., 1961, Ph.D., 1966. Tchr. high sch., Florence, Italy, 1955-57; Italian lang. specialist Bur. Programs and Standards, CSC, Washington, 1958; lang. instr. Sch. Langs., Fgn. Services Inst., Dept. State, Washington, 1959-61; lectr. Italian, U. Va., Charlottesville, 1961-66; asst. prof. Italian, U. Wis.-Milw., 1966-69; assoc. prof., assoc. chmn. dept. French and Italian, 1969-71; assoc. prof. dept. French and Italian, Ind. U., Bloomington, 1971-83, prof., 1983—, dir. Scuola Italiana, Middlebury Coll., Vt., 1987-95. Author: A Look at Italy, 1976; Buon giorno a tutti, 1983; L'Insegnamento dell'italiano nei colleges e nelle universita del nordamerica, 1983. Contbr. articles to profl. jours. Recipient Uhrig award Faculty U. Wis., 1968. Decorated Cavaliere nell'ordine al Merito della Repubblica Italiana. Mem. MLA, AAUP, Am. Assn. Tchrs. Italian (sec. treas. 1980-84, pres. 1984-87, Disting. Svc. award 1994), Dante Soc. Am., Renaissance Soc. Am., Boccaccio Soc. Am., Nat. Italian Am. Found., Am. Italian Hist. Assn., Am. Assn. Italian Studies, Midwest MLA. Home: 715 N Plymouth Rd Bloomington IN 47408-3066 Office: Ind U Ctr for Italian Studies Bloomington IN 47405

LEBARON, CHARLES FREDERICK, JR., lawyer; b. Grand Rapids, Mich., Oct. 8, 1949; s. Charles Frederick and Barbara Jean (Day) LeB.; m. Elizabeth Ann Zwickert, Aug. 12, 1978; children: Ann Saunders, Katherine Clark, Eve Zwickert, John Frederick. AA, Grand Rapids Jr. Coll., 1969; AB, U. Mich., 1971, AMLS, 1973; JD summa cum laude, Ind. U., 1980. Bar: Ill. 1980, U.S. Dist. Ct. (no. dist.) Ill. 1980, U.S. Ct. Appeals (7th cir.) 1981. Dir. Georgetown Library, Jenison, Mich., 1974-77; law clk. to cir. judge U.S. Ct. Appeals (7th cir.), Chgo., 1980-82; assoc. Mayer, Brown & Platt, Chgo., 1982-84; atty. Centel Corp., Chgo., 1984-85, staff atty., 1985-86; corp. counsel Acco World Corp., Northbrook, Ill., 1986-88; assoc. Keck, Mahin & Cate, Chgo., 1988-89, ptnr., 1989-94; ptnr. Ross & Hardies, Chgo., 1994—. Trustee Clarendon Hills Pub. Library, Ill., 1985-89. Recipient Dyer-Ives Found. award, 1972. Mem. Order of Coif, Legal Club Chgo., Law Club Chgo. Republican. Episcopalian. Home: 114 S Prospect Ave Clarendon Hills IL 60514-1423 Office: Ross & Hardies 150 N Michigan Ave Ste 2500 Chicago IL 60601-7524

LEBARON, EDWARD WAYNE, JR., lawyer; b. San Rafael, Calif., Jan. 7, 1930; s. Edward Wayne and Mabel Butler (Sims) LeB.; m. Doralee M. LeBaron, June 4, 1954; children: Edward Wayne, William Bruce, Richard Wilson. BA, Coll. Pacific, 1950; LLB, George Washington U., 1959. Bar: Calif. bar 1960, Tex. bar 1960, Nev. bar 1967. Football quarterback Washington Redskins, 1952-59; with Dallas Cowboys, 1960-63; exec. v.p. Nevada Cement Co., 1964-65; mem. firm Wynne & Wynne, Dallas, 1960-63, Bible, McDonald & Carano, Reno, 1966-68, Laxalt & Berry, Carson City, Nev., 1969-70; partner firm Jones, Jones, Bell, LeBaron and Brown, Las Vegas, Nev., 1970-76; gen. mgr. Atlanta Falcons Football team, 1977-85; ptnr. Powell, Goldstein, Murphy & Frazer, 1986-89, Pillsbury, Madison & Sutro, 1989-94; ret., 1994; bd. dirs. Tom Brown, Inc.; ptnr LeBaron Ranches. Served with USMC, 1950-52. Decorated Purple Heart, Bronze Star.; named Sportsman of Year in Ga., 1978-79; named to Coll. Football Hall of Fame, 1980. Mem. ABA, Sutter Club, Northridge Country Club. Republican.

LEBARON, FRANCIS NEWTON, biochemistry educator; b. Framingham, Mass., July 26, 1922; s. Paul Burrows and Dorothy (Lamson) LeB.; m. Margaret Lenore Shaw, July 8, 1953; 1 child, Geoffrey Shaw. S.B., MIT, 1944; M.A., Boston U., 1948; Ph.D., Harvard U., 1951. Assoc. biochemist McLean Hosp., Belmont, Mass., 1957-64; asso. biol. chemist Harvard U. Med. Sch., 1959-64; asso. prof. biochemistry U. N.Mex. Med. Sch., 1964-69, prof., 1969-83, chmn. dept., 1971-78, chmn. ad hoc nutrition planning commn., 1969; vis. scholar Mass. Inst. Tech., 1974-75. Editorial bd.: Jour. Neurochemistry, 1965-74; Contbr. articles to profl. jours. Served with USNR, 1943-46. Mem. Am. Chem. Soc., Biochem. Soc. (London), Am. Soc. Biol. Chemists, AAAS, Internat. Soc. Neurochemistry, Am. Soc. Neurochemistry (pres. 1969-71), Theta Delta Chi. Home: PO Box 779 Mashpee MA 02649-0779

LE BARON, JOSEPH EVAN, diplomat; b. Nampa, Idaho, Sept. 3, 1947; s. Carlos Stannard and Truellen Ruth (Davis) McCracken; m. Elinor Rae Drake, Mar. 3, 1973; 1 child, Petra Drake. BS, Portland State U., Oreg., 1969; MA, Princeton U., 1978, PhD, 1980. Consular officer U.S. Embassy, Doha, Qatar, 1980-82; polit. officer U.S. Embassy, Amman, Jordan, 1982-83, econ./commercial officer, 1983-84; staff aide to amb. U.S. Embassy, Ankara, Turkey, 1984-85; polit. officer U.S. Consulate Gen., Istanbul, Turkey, 1985-87; desk officer for Lebanon U.S. State Dept., Washington, 1987-89; fgn. affairs advisor to majority leader U.S. Senate, Washington, 1989-90; consul gen. U.S. Consulate Gen., Dubai, United Arab Emirates, 1991-94; dep. amb. U.S. Embassy, Manama, Bahrain, 1994-96; dep. dir. office Iran and Iraq State Dept., Washington, 1996—. With USAF, 1970-74. Recipient Sinclaire award Disting. Lang. Study Am. Fgn. Svc. Assn., Washington, 1992; rsch. fellow for Sudan Social Sci. Rsch. Coun., N.Y.C., 1978-79; Nat. Defense Fgn. Lang. fellow Princeton U., 1976-78; Princeton U. fellow, 1976. Office: Dept State Washington DC 20520

LEBEAU, CHARLES PAUL, lawyer; b. Detroit, Dec. 11, 1944; s. Charles Henry Jr. and Mary Barbara (Moran) L.; m. Victoria Joy (Huchin), May 15, 1970; children: Jeffrey Kevin, Timothy Paul. AA, Macomb County Community Coll., Warren, Mich., 1967; BA, Wayne State U., 1969; JD, U. Detroit, 1972; grad. tax program, NYU Sch. Law, 1972-73. Bar: Mich. 1973, U.S. Tax Ct. 1973, Calif. 1987, U.S. Ct. Internat. Trade. 1988, U.S. Supreme Ct. 1988, U.S. Dist. Ct. (so. dist.) Calif. 1988. Tax atty. Ford Motor Co., Dearborn, Mich., 1973-75; assoc. Hoops & Huff, Detroit, 1975-76, Miller, Canfield, Paddock & Stone, Detroit, 1976-78; tax mgr. Oceaneering Internat., Santa Barbara, Calif., 1978-79; tax counsel Signal Cos. Inc., Beverly Hills and La Jolla, Calif., 1979-83; assoc. Gray, Cary, Ames & Frye, San Diego, 1983-84; of counsel James Watts Esq., La Jolla, 1985, Murfey, Griggs & Frederick, La Jolla, 1986; pvt. practice La Jolla and San Diego, 1987—; lectr. grad. tax program Golden Gate U., San Diego, 1979-87; adj. prof. law U. San Diego, 1982-85, 88-89; mem. Law Rev., U. Detroit, 1971-72; lectr. in taxation. Contbr. articles on internat. tax to profl. jours.; monthly tax case commentator Taxes Internat., London, 1981-85. Campaign coord. United Way, Santa Barbara, 1979. Mem. ABA, Mich. Bar Assn., Calif. Bar Assn., San Diego County Bar Assn., Pi Sigma Alpha. Republican. Roman Catholic. Avocations: sailing, tennis, walking. Home: 1999 Via Segovia La Jolla CA 92037-6441 Office: Law Offices Charles LeBeau Ste 1070 4660 La Jolla Village Dr San Diego CA 92122-4606 also: 400 Renaissance Ctr Ste 500 Detroit MI 48343

LEBEAU, HECTOR ALTON, JR., confectionary company executive; b. Hartford, Conn., July 2, 1931; s. Hector Alton and Gladys (Chester) LeB.; m. Joan Michaelson, May 31, 1955; children: Linda, Jane, Michael, Leslie. BS, U. Tex., 1960; postgrad., Harvard U., 1965. Mktg. dept. staff Gen. Foods, White Plains, N.Y., 1960-73; v.p., gen. mgr. Consol. Brands divsn. Gulf & Western, N.Y.C., 1973-78; sales and mktg. dept. staff Timex, Middlebury, Conn., 1978-80; from v.p. fields ops. to pres. Schweppes U.S.A., Stamford, Conn., 1980-84; pres. Rose Holland House, 1984-85, Cadbury U.S.A., 1985-88; sr. v.p. Cadbury Schweppes Inc., Stamford, Conn., 1985-88; pres. The Marcon Group, 1988—; pres., CEO Am. Candy Co., Selma, Ala., 1995—. Active Stanford Bd. Reps., 1966-69; mem. nat. com. Explorers, Boy Scouts Am., 1970-71; trustee St. Augustine Arts Assn., 1994—; pres. Marsh Creek Homeowners Assn., 1994-97. Capt. USAF, 1954-58. Elected dean Nat. Candy Wholesalers Assn., 1988. Mem. Union League Club, Cedar Point Yacht Club, Marsh Creek Country Club, Beta Gamma Sigma. Republican. Office: PO Box 879 Selma AL 36702-0879

LEBEC, ALAIN, investment banker; b. Dunkerque, Nord, France, Apr. 25, 1950; came to U.S., 1971; m. Leah M. Koncelik, June 27, 1981; children: Gabriel, Christina, Xavier. Diplome d'Ingenieur, Ecole Poly., Paris, 1971; MBA, Northwestern U., 1973. Mng. dir. A.G. Becker & Co., N.Y.C., 1973-84; vice chmn., investment banking group Merrill Lynch & Co., N.Y.C., 1984—. 2d lt. French Army, 1971. Office: Merrill Lynch & Co World Fin Ctr North Tower New York NY 10281-1330

LEBECK, WARREN WELLS, commodities consultant; b. Chgo., Mar. 13, 1921; s. Emil and Hazel (Wells) L.; m. Dorothy Lester, Feb. 1, 1943; children: Sara Beth, Kenneth, Clayton A., Frederick E. BA, North Central Coll., Naperville, Ill., 1942. With Montgomery Ward & Co., Chgo., 1941-42, 46-54; with Chgo. Bd. Trade, 1954-79, sec., then exec. v.p., 1957-73, pres., 1973-77, sr. exec. v.p., 1977-79; pvt. practice cons. Chgo., 1979—; past dir. Bank of Hinsdale, Ill.; past chmn. bd., pres. South Loop Improvement Project; mem. U.S. Agrl. Policy Adv. Com., 1976-87; trustee Nat. Agrl. Forum, 1983-86; bd. dirs., exec. com. U.S. Feed Grains Coun., 1978-90, Agrl. Coun. Am., 1980-90; bd. dirs., exec. com. Nat. Grain Trade Coun., 1968-90, chmn., 1988-89; mem. founding com., bd. dirs., exec. com. Nat. Futures Assn., 1982—. Former mem. bd. edn. Downers Grove (Ill.) Twp. High Sch. Served with USNR, 1942-45. Home and Office: 1060 Burning Tree Rd Pinehurst NC 28374-9271

LEBEDOFF, DAVID M., lawyer, author, investment advisor; b. Mpls., Apr. 29, 1938; s. Martin David and Mary Louise (Galanter) L.; m. Randy Louise Miller, Feb. 7, 1981; children: Caroline, Jonathan, Nicholas. BA magna cum laude, U. Minn., 1960; JD, Harvard U., 1963. Bar: Minn. 1963. Spl. asst. atty. gen. Atty. Gen. of Minn., St. Paul, 1963-65; spl. counsel U.S. Senator Walter F. Mondale, Washington, 1966; pvt. practice law Mpls., 1967-81; ptnr. Lindquist & Vennum, Mpls., 1981-91, Briggs & Morgan, Mpls., 1991-95; sr. v.p. Voyageur Asset Mgmt., Mpls., 1995—; of counsel Gray, Plant, Mooty, Mooty & Bennett, Mpls., 1995—; spl. master U.S. Dist. Ct., Mpls., 1974-75. Author: The 21st Ballot, 1969, Ward Number Six, 1972, The New Elite, 1981, Cleaning Up, 1997; contbr. articles to profl. jours. Bd. regents U. Minn., Mpls and St. Paul, 1977-89, chmn. bd. 1987-89; chmn. Mpls. Inst. Arts, 1989-91 bd. dirs. 1975—; bd. dirs. Blake Sch., U. Minn. Found. Recipient Outstanding Achievement award U. Minn., 1991. Mem. Mpls. Club (bd. dirs.), Minikahda Club, Phi Beta Kappa. Home: 1738 Oliver Ave S Minneapolis MN 55405-2222

LEBEDOFF, JONATHAN GALANTER, federal judge; b. Mpls., Apr. 29, 1938; s. Martin David and Mary (Galanter) L.; m. Sarah Sargent Mitchell, June 10, 1979; children: David Shevlin, Ann McNair. BA, U. Minn., 1960, LLB, 1963. Bar: Minn. 1963, U.S. Dist. Ct. Minn. 1964, U.S. Ct. Appeals (8th cir.) 1968. Pvt. practice Mpls., 1963-71; judge Hennepin County Mcpl. Ct., State Minn., Mpls., 1971-74; dist. ct. judge State of Minn., Mpls., 1974-91; U.S. magistrate judge U.S. Dist. Ct., St. Paul, 1991—; mem. Gov.'s Commn. on Crime Prevention, 1971-75; mem. State Bd. Continuing Legal Edn.; mem. Minn. Supreme Ct. Task Force for Gender Fairness in Cts., mem. implementation com. of gender fairness in cts.. Jewish. Avocations: reading (biographies, history), family, bridge. Office: 300 S 4th St Minneapolis MN 55401-2233

LEBEDOFF, RANDY MILLER, lawyer; b. Washington, Oct. 16, 1949; m. David Lebedoff; children: Caroline, Jonathan, Nicholas. BA, Smith Coll., 1971; JD magna cum laude, Ind. U., 1975. Assoc. Faegre & Benson, Mpls., 1975-82, ptnr., 1983-86; v.p., gen. counsel Star Tribune, Mpls., 1989—; asst. sec. Star Tribune Cowles Media Co., Mpls., 1990—; Bd. dirs. Milkweed Editions, 1989-96. Bd. dirs. Minn. Opera, 1986-90, YWCA, 1984-90, Planned Parenthood Minn., 1985-90, Fund for Legal Aid Soc., 1988-96—, Abbott-Northwestern Hosp., 1990-94. Mem. Newspaper Assn. Am. (legal affairs com. 1991—), Minn. Newspapers Assn. (bd. dirs. 1995—). Home: 1738 Oliver Ave S Minneapolis MN 55405-2222 Office: Star Tribune 425 Portland Ave Minneapolis MN 55415-1511

LEBEDOW, AARON LOUIS, consulting company executive; b. Chgo., Aug. 19, 1935; s. Isidor and Fannie (Perchikoff) L.; m. Madeleine Hellman; children: Ellen, Francine, Sheri, Sherri Michaels, Tracey Michaels. B.S. in Indsl. Engring, Ill. Inst. Tech., 1957; M.B.A., U. Mich., 1958. Cert. mgmt. cons. Asst. marketing mgr. Imperial-Eastman, Chgo., 1960-61; mgr. Corplan Assos., Chgo., 1961-66; chmn. bd. Technomic, Inc., Chgo., 1966-87, Technomic Consultants Internat., Deerfield, Ill., 1987-93, Global Marketactics Inc., Chgo., 1993—; Global Devel. Network, L.L.C., 1993—. Bd. dirs. Coun. for Jewish Elderly. Served to 1st lt. USAF, 1958-60. Mem. Am. Mgmt. Assn., Am. Mktg. Assn., Tau Epsilon Phi. Mem. B'nai B'rith. Office: Global Marketactics Inc 6540 N Kilbourn Ste A100 Lincolnwood IL 60646-3477

LEBEL, ROBERT, bishop; b. Trois Pistoles, Que., Can., Aug. 11, 1924; s. Wilfrid and Alexina (Belanger) L. L.Theol., St. Paul U., Ottawa, 1950; D.Theol., Athenee Angelicum, Rome, 1951. Ordained priest Roman Cath. Ch., 1950, consecrated bishop, 1974; tchr. theology Major Sem., Rimouski, Que., 1951-65; rector Major Sem., 1963-65, Minor Sem., 1965-68; tchr. domatic theology U. Rimouski, 1970-74; aux. bishop St. Jean, Que., 1974-76; bishop Valleyfield, Que., 1976—. Contbr. ch. publs. Mem. Roman Synod on the Christian Family, 1980. Mem. Assemblee de Eveques Que., Conf. Can. Cath. Bishops, Soc. Canadienne de Theologie, KC. Address: 11 de l'Eglise, Valleyfield, PQ Canada J6T1J5

LEBENZON, CHRIS, film editor. Editor: (documentary) (with Robert K. Lambert and Ian Masters) The Secret Life of Plants, 1978, (films) Demon, 1977, The Private Files of J. Edgar Hoover, 1978, (with Marshall M. Borden, Martin Bram, and Dennis Dolan) Wolfen, 1981, A Breed Apart, 1984, (with Scott Wallace and Mark Warner) Weird Science, 1985, Death of an Angel, 1985, (with Billy Weber) Top Gun, 1986 (Academy award nomination best film editing 1986), (with David Handman and Jon Poll) Weeds, 1987, (with Michael Tronick and Weber) Beverly Hills Cop II, 1987, (with Tronick and Weber) Midnight Run, 1988, Revenge, 1990, (with Weber) Days of Thunder, 1990, Batman Returns, 1992, Josh and S.A.M., 1993, Ed Wood, 1994. Office: 2312 California Ave Santa Monica CA 90403-4526*

LEBER, STEVEN EDWARD, film producer, corporate executive; b. Bklyn., Dec. 12, 1941; s. David and Selma (Teitelbaum) L.; m. Marion Susan Greiffenhagen, Feb. 6, 1966; children: Michelle, Jill, Jordan. BA in Mgmt. and Acctg., Northeastern U., 1964. Agt. William Morris Agy., N.Y.C., 1964-72; pres. Contemporary Communications Corp., N.Y.C., 1972—; producer Leber and Krebs, Inc., N.Y.C., 1972—; pres. Global Sports & Arts, Ltd., N.Y.C., 1989—; pres. Tyumen Cons. Group, Inc., cons. Tyumen region, Russia; founder Hollywood Stores; voting mem. Tony Selection Com., N.Y.C., 1977—. Producer: Jesus Christ Superstar-Touring Co., N.Y.C., 1972-78, Beatlemania-Broadway, 1977-84, 1st Pro-Skating Championships-ABC Wide World of Sports, 1981-83, Tennis Championships, 1981-83, Moscow Circus-Circus Prodn., Inc., N.Y.C., 1988— (Family Show of Yr. award Performance mag. 1989), Moscow Circus (Family Show of Yr. award Performance mag. 1990), Teenage Mutant Ninja Turtles' "Coming Out of Their Shells", 1990; producer Animated Films, Russia. Mem. H.E.L.P. (found. to aid homeless), N.Y.C., 1988—; bd. dirs. Children's Med. Ctr., Great Neck, N.Y., 1985—, Five Towns United Way; fund raiser Armenian Earthquake Fund, Washington/N.Y.C., 1988; exec. producer Concert for Bangledesh, 1971. Mem. NARAS (voting), N.Y. League Theatrical Producers, N.Y. Internat. Festival arts (bd. mem. 1989), Friars Club, Innercircle Club (Washington). Office: Circus Prodns Inc 155 E 55th St Apt 6H New York NY 10022-4040*

LE BERTHON, ADAM, lawyer; b. L.A., June 12, 1962; s. Edward Lynch and Veronica Rose (Franks) Le B.; m. Kelly Elizabeth McKee, Mar. 23, 1996. BA cum laude with dept. honors, U. San Diego, 1985; JD, U. So. Calif., L.A., 1989. Bar: Calif. 1989, U.S. Dist. Ct. (ctrl. dist.) Calif. 1989, U.S. Ct. Appeals (9th cir.) 1989, U.S. Dist. Ct. (so. dist.) Calif. 1990, (no. dist.) Calif. 1990, (ea. dist.) Calif. 1990. Assoc. White & Case, L.A., 1989-91, Straw & Gilmartin, Santa Monica, Calif., 1991—. Editor So. Calif. Law Rev., 1988-89; contbr. articles to profl. jours. Recipient Am. Jurisprudence award U. So. Calif., 1987. Mem. Calif. State Bar Assn., L.A. County Bar Assn., Order of the Coif, Phi Alpha Delta, Omicron Delta Epsilon, Kappa Gamma Pi. Home: 125 Montana Ave Apt 207 Santa Monica CA 90403-1054 Office: Straw & Gilmartin 100 Wilshire Blvd Ste 1325 Santa Monica CA 90401-1114

LEBLANC, DOMINIC ANTOINE JACQUES, lawyer; b. Ottawa, Ont., Can., Dec. 14, 1967; s. Roméo and Joslyn (Carter) L. Student, U. Paris, 1989; BA, U. Toronto, Ont., 1989; LLB, U. N.B., Fredericton, 1992. Barrister, solicitor, Can. Spl. asst. Leader of Opposition, Ottawa, 1991, 93; spl. advisor Office of Prime Min. Can., Ottawa, 1993—. Law Soc. scholar, 1991. Mem. Liberal Party Can. Roman Catholic. Avocations: skiing, tennis. Home: Box 91, Grande Digue, NB Canada E0A 1S0 Office: Prime Min Office, Langevin Block, Ottawa, ON Canada K1A 0A2

LEBLANC, HUGH LINUS, political science educator, consultant; b. Alexandria, La., Oct. 30, 1927; s. Moreland Paul and Carmen Marie (Haydel) LeB.; m. Shirley Jean Smith, Feb. 28, 1953; children: Leslie Ann, Alexander Hugh. BA, La. State U., 1948; MA, U. Tenn., 1950; PhD, U. Chgo., 1958. Asst. prof. George Washington U., Washington, 1955-58, assoc. prof., 1959-63, prof., 1964-90, prof. emeritus dept. polit. sci., 1991—, chmn. dept., 1963-65, 70-76, 82-88; v.p. Area Inc., Arlington, VA, 1961-63. Author: American Political Parties, 1982, (with D. Trudeau Allensworth) The Politics of States and Urban Communities, 1971; contbr. articles to polit. sci. jours. Served to lt. (j.g.) USNR, 1944-45, 52-55. Named Outstanding Prof. Interfraternity Council, George Washington U., 1963. Mem. Country Club of Fairfax (Va.). Home: 3403 Barger Dr Falls Church VA 22044-1202

LEBLANC, HUGUES, philosophy educator; b. Ste-Marie de Beauce, Que., Can., Mar. 19, 1924; came to U.S., 1946, naturalized, 1952; s. Edmond and Alice (Caron) L.; m. Virginia Southall Graham, June 10, 1950 (div. Apr. 1983); children—Gabrielle, Suzanne, Stephen. MA, U. Montreal, Que., 1946, hon. doctorate, 1980; PhD, Harvard U., 1948; hon. doctorate, Dalhousie U., 1982, U. Que., Montreal, 1985. Prof. philosophy Bryn Mawr (Pa.) Coll., 1948-67, Temple U., Phila., 1967-92, U. Que., Montréal, 1992—. Author: An Introduction to Deductive Logic, 1955, Statistical and Inductive Probabilities, 1962, Techniques of Deductive Inference, 1966, Deductive Logic, 1972, Truth, Syntax and Modality, 1973, Truth-Value Semantics, 1976, Existence, Truth and Probability, 1982, Essays on Epistemology and Semantics, 1983; also numerous papers on logic, philosophy of logic and probability theory. Fulbright fellow, 1953-54; Guggenheim fellow, 1965-66. Fellow Royal Soc. Can., Assn. for Symbolic Logic (exec. com. 1958-61, treas. 1979-91, 82-85), Soc. for Exact Philosophy (v.p. 1978-80, pres. 1980-82). Home: 460 Champ de Mars Apt 502, Montreal, PQ Canada H2Y 1B4 Office: U Que at Montreal, Dept Philosophy, Case Postale 8888, Montreal, PQ Canada H3C 3P8

LEBLANC, JAMES E., financial services company executive; b. 1942. BA, Providence Coll., 1964. With GE Credit Corp., Stamford, Conn., 1964-82; chief oper. officer Northwest Acceptance Corp., Portland, Oreg., 1982-85; pres. Pacificorp Credit, 1985-88; chmn., pres., chief exec. officer Whirlpool Fin. Corp., Benton Harbor, Mich., 1988—; also v.p. Whirlpool Corp., Benton Harbor; bd. dirs. Shoreline Fin. Corp., Shoreline Bank, Cornerstone Alliance. Office: Whirlpool Fin Corp 553 Benson Rd Benton Harbor MI 49022-2664

LEBLANC, JAMES LEO, business executive, consultant; b. Ottawa, Ont., Can., May 12, 1955; came to U.S., 1993; s. Leo Joseph and Ann (Curry) L.; m. Ruth Heather Faulkner, June 8, 1991. BA, Carleton U., 1982, MA in Internat. Affairs, 1984; MPA, Harvard U., 1994. Exec. asst. Amb. for Arms Control, Ottawa, Ont., Can., 1984-89; chief of staff Min. of Sci. and Technol., Ottawa, 1989-92, Min. of Foreign Affairs, Ottawa, 1992-93; pres. J. LeBlanc Internat. LLC, Alexandria, Va., 1994—; ptnr. Prospectus Assoc. Inc., Can., 1994—; prin. U.S. Tech. Internat. LLC, Washington, 1995—; bd. dirs., v.p. Can.-Am. Bus. Coun., Washington, 1995—; advisor Can. Advanced Tech. Assn., Can., 1994—. Bd. dirs. president's adv. coun., Carleton U., 1995—, Carlton U. (U.S.) Found., Washington, 1996—. Mem. Am. League of Lobbyists, Industry Adv. Coun., Harvard Club of Washington. Avocations: tennis, music, reading, golf, chess. Home: 5808 Woodlawn Green Ct Ste A Alexandria VA 22309 Office: J LeBlanc Internat LLC South Bldg 601 Pennsylvania Ave NW Ste 900 Washington DC 20004-2601

LEBLANC, L(OUIS) CHRISTIAN, architect; b. Heidelberg, Bavaria, Fed. Republic Germany, July 5, 1957; s. Louis Carroll LeBlanc and Gladys Jane Everett; m. Janet Beverly Frances Mulholland; children: Jacob Bodalski (stepchild), L. Christian Jr., Francesca Helen. BS in Design, Clemson U., 1980, MArch, 1982. Architect FJ Clark Inc., Anderson, S.C., 1982-86, Freeman & Major Architects Inc., Greenville, S.C., 1987-88, Narramore & Assocs., Inc., Greenville, 1988-89, Greene & Assocs., Inc., Greenville, 1989—. Mem. AIA. Republican. Roman Catholic. Avocations: languages, sailing. Home: 213 Oregon St Greenville SC 29605-1050 Office: Greene & Assocs Architects Inc 704 E Washington St Greenville SC 29601-3035*

LEBLANC, PIERRE GABRIEL, military officer; b. Montreal, Sept. 8, 1949; s. Gabriel and Fernande (Filiatreault) L.; m. Jane LeBlanc Townson, Aug. 13, 1980; children: Matthew, Philippe, Jean-Pierre. BS, Royal Mil. Coll. St.-Jean, Que., 1973. Commd. lt. Canadian Forces, 1967, advanced through grades to col., 1990; platoon comdr. and adjutant 1 Commando, 1973-74; peacekeeper UN Force, Cyprus, 1974; platoon comdr. Battalion 1 of Royal 22 Regiment, Lahr, Germany, 1975-78; officer Candidate Sch., Chilliwack, 1978-79; co. comdr. 3 Battalion of Royal 22 Regiment, Valcartier, 1981-82; commanding officer 1 Commando of Can. Airborne Regiment, Petawawa, 1983-85; staff officer for Chief Land Doctrine and Ops. Nat. Def. Hdqrs., Ottawa, 1985-86; sect. head Directorate of Land Requirements, 1986-87; project dir. Light Armoured Vehicle Project, 1987-88; comdr. Inf. Sch. at Combat Tng. Ctr., Gagetown, 1988; dir. mil. rev. land Nat. Def. Hdqrs., Ottawa, Can. Forces advisor to India, 1991-94, dir. gen. res. and cadets, then comdr. No. Area Hdqrs., 1994—. Decorated Can. Forces Decoration, 1979. Roman Catholic. Office: Canadian Forces Northern Area, Box 6666, Yellowknife, NT Canada X1A 2R3

LEBLANC, RICHARD PHILIP, lawyer; b. Nashua, N.H., Aug. 5, 1946; s. Ronald Arthur and Jeanette G. (Chomard) LeB.; m. Doris Julie Lavoie, May 25, 1968; children: Justin D., Renée M., Anne-Marie. AB summa cum laude, Coll. of the Holy Cross, 1968; JD cum laude, Harvard U., 1972. Bar: Maine 1972, U.S. Dist. Ct. Maine 1972. Assoc. Bernstein, Shur, Sawyer & Nelson, Portland, Maine, 1972-75, ptnr., 1976-95; ptnr. LeBlanc & Young, Portland, 1995—; mem. Probate Law Revision Commn., Augusta, Maine, 1975-80; mem. probate rules and forms adv. com. Maine Supreme Ct. Pres. United Way Greater Portland, 1982-84; trustee Cleverus H.S., Portland, 1982-88; bd. dirs. Habitat for Humanity, Portland, 1984-92, Cumberland County Affordable Housing Venture, Portland, 1987-94, Maine Spl. Olympics, 1988-94. Fellow Am. Coll. Trust and Estate Counsel; mem. ABA, Maine Bar Assn., Maine Estate Planning Coun. Democrat. Roman Catholic. Home: 142 Longfellow St Portland ME 04103-4027 Office: LeBlanc & Young PO Box 7950 Portland ME 04112-7950

LEBLANC, ROGER MAURICE, chemistry educator; b. Trois Rivières, Que., Can., Jan. 5, 1942; s. Henri and Rita (Moreau) L.; m. Micheline D. Veillette, June 26, 1965; children: Daniel, Hughes, Marie-Jose, Nancy. BSc, U. Laval, 1964, PhD, 1968. NRC postdoctoral fellow Davy Faraday Rsch. Lab. Royal Inst. Great Britain, London, 1968-70; prof. phys. chemistry U. Que., Trois-Rivières, 1970-93, chmn. dept., 1971-75, dir. Biophysics Rsch. Group, 1978-81, chmn. Photobiophysics Rsch. Ctr., 1981-91; prof., chmn. dept. chemistry U. Miami, Coral Gables, Fla., 1994—; hon. prof. Jilin U., Changchun, Cina, 1992. Recipient Barringer award Spectroscopy Soc. Can., 1983, Medaille du Merite Universitaire du Que. a Trois-Rivieres, 1987, Commemorative medal for 125th Anniversary of Confedn. Can., 1993. Fellow Chem. Inst. Can. (Noranda award 1982, John Labatt Ltd. award 1992); mem. Am. Chem. Soc., Assn. Canadienne Francaise pour l'Avancement des Sciences (Prix Vincent 1978), Am. Soc. Photobiology, Biophys. Soc., European Photochem. Assn. Roman Catholic. Home: 9335 SW 77th Ave Apt 251 Miami FL 33156-7925 Office: Univ Miami Dept Chemistry Cox Sci Bldg Rm 315 1301 Memorial Dr Coral Gables FL 33124-0431

LEBLANC, ROMÉO, Canadian government official; b. Memramcook, N.B., Can., Dec. 18, 1927; s. Philias and Lucie LeB.; m. Diana Fowler; 4 children. BA, St. Joseph U., 1948, BEd, 1951; postgrad., Paris U., 1953-55; DCL (hon.), Mount Allison U., New Brunswick, 1977; D Pub. Adminstrn. (hon.), U. de Moncton, New Brunswick, 1979; LLD (hon.), U. Sainte-Anne, Nova Scotia, 1995; DLL (hon.), Ryerson Polytechnic U., Ontario; PhD (hon.), U. Ottawa, Ontario, 1996. Tchr. Drummond High Sch., New Brunswick, Can., 1951-53; Prof., New Brunswick Tchrs. Coll., Fredericton, Can., 1955-59; journalist, correspondent Radio Can., Ottawa, 1960-62, United Kingdom, 1962-65, U.S.A., 1965-67; founding pres. CBC/Radio-Can. Correspondent's Assn., 1965; press sec. to Right Hon. Lester B. Pearson, 1967-68, Right Hon. Pierre Elliott Trudeau, 1968-71; asst. to pres. and dir. pub. rels. l'Universite de Moncton, Can., 1971-72; M.P. from Westmorland-Kent, New Brunswick dist. Ho. of Commons, Can., 1972-84; min. Ministry of Fisheries, 1974-76, Ministry of Fisheries and the Environ., 1976-79, Ministry of Fisheries and Oceans, 1980-82, Ministry of Pub. Works, 1982-84, Canada Mortgage and Housing Corp., 1982-84, Nat. Capital Commn., 1982-84; mem. Can. Senate, 1984-94, speaker, 1993-94; gov. general and commr. in chief Govt. Can., 1995—; ofcl. rep. Govt. Can. USSR, Poland, Cuba, The EEC, U.K., France, 1974-84; mem. del. UN Law of the Sea Conf., 1974-79; cabinet com. mem. External Affairs and Econ. Affairs, 1974-82, Comms. Com., 1974-84, chmn. Comms. Com., 1976-81, Priorities and Planning Com., 1975-84; Social Affairs, 1982-84; mem. senate com. Internal Econ., Budgets and Adminstrn., 1984-93, chmn., 1989-93, Fgn. Affairs, 1986-94, Sub. Com. on Security and Nat. Def., 1992-94; vis. scholar Inst. Can. Studies, Carleton U.; part-time faculty mem. Can. studies Concordia U., Montreal. Mem. Canada France Parliamentary Assn., Internat. Assn. French Speaking Parliamentarians. Office: Office of the Governor General, Rideau Hall 1 Sussex Dr, Ottawa, ON Canada K1A 0A1

LEBLANC, TINA, dancer; b. Erie, Pa.; m. Marco Jerkunica, May 1988. Trained, Carlisle, Pa. Dancer Joffrey II Dancers, N.Y.C., 1982-83, The Joffrey Ballet, N.Y.C., 1984-92; prin. dancer San Francisco Ballet, 1992—; guest tchr. Ctrl. Pa. Youth Ballet, 1992, 94—. Work includes roles in (with San Francisco Ballet) Con Brio, Bizet Pas de Deux, Swan Lake, Nanna's Lied, Handel -- A Celebration, La fille mal gardée, Rubies, Tchaikovsky Pas de Deux, Seeing Stars, The Nutcracker, La Pavane Rouge, Company B, Romeo and Juliet, Sleeping Beauty, The Dance House, Terra Firma, Lambarena, Fly by Night, In the Night, Ballo della Regina, The Lesson, The Tuning Game, Quartette; (with other companies) The Green Table, Les Presages, Le sacre du printemps, Les Noces, Light Rain, Romeo and Juliet, Runaway Train, Empyrean Dances, La Vivandière, L'air D'esprit, Corsaire Pas de deux, Don Quixote pas de deux. Recipient Princess Grace Found. award, 1988, Princess Grace Statuette award, 1995. Office: San Francisco Ballet 455 Franklin St San Francisco CA 94102-4438*

LEBLOND, CHARLES PHILIPPE, anatomy educator, researcher; b. Lille, France, Feb. 5, 1910; s. Oscar and Jeanne (Desmarchelier) L.; m. Gertrude Sternschuss, Oct. 22, 1936; children—Philippe L., Paul N., Pierre F., Marie Pascale. L.Sc., U. Lille, 1932; M.D., U. Paris, France, 1934, D. Sc., 1945; Ph.D., U. Montreal, 1942; DSc Acadia (hon.), McGill U., 1982, York U., 1985. Asst. histology U. Lille and U. Paris, France, 1934-35; Rockefeller fellow anatomy Yale, 1935-37; charge biology div. Lab. Synthese Atom, Paris, 1937-40; research fellow U. Rochester, N.Y., 1940-41; mem. faculty McGill U., Montreal, Que., Can., 1941—; prof. anatomy McGill U., 1948—, chmn. dept., 1957-75. Author: L'Acide Ascorbique dans les Tissues et sa Detection, 1936, Radioautography as a Tool in the Study of Protein Synthesis, 1965, also over 300 articles mainly on cell and tissue dynamics. Fogarty scholar NIH, 1975. Fellow Royal Soc. London, Royal Soc. Can., Am. Assn. Anatomy, Can. Assn. Anatomists, Prix. Scientifique du Que. Home: 68 Chesterfield St, Montreal, PQ Canada H3Y 2M5

LEBLOND, PAUL HENRI, oceanographer, educator; b. Que., Can., Dec. 30, 1938; s. Sylvio and Jeanne (Lacerte) LeB.; m. Josee Michaud (div. 1985); children: Michel, Philippe, Anne. BA, Laval U., Quebec, 1957; BS, McGill U., Montreal, Que., 1961; PhD, U. B.C., Vancouver, Can., 1964; DSc (hon.), Meml. U., Newfoundland, 1992. Prof. depts. oceanography and physics U. B.C., Vancouver, 1965, assoc. dean faculty of sci., 1982-85, head dept. oceanography, 1987-92, dir. program earth and ocean scis., 1992-96, prof. emeritus, 1996—; chmn. Can. nat. com. World Ocean Circulation Expt., 1987-92; program leader Ocean Prodn. Enhancement Network, Can., 1991-93. Co-author: Waves in the Oceans, 1978, Cadborosaurus, 1995; contbr. articles to profl. jours. Bd. dirs. Can. Ocean Frontiers Rsch. Initiative Found.; mem. Fisheries Resource Conservation Coun., 1993—. Fellow Royal Soc. Can.; mem. Can. Meteorol. and Oceanographic Soc. (Pres.'s prize 1981, Tully medal 1991), Am. Geophys. Union. Avocations: hiking, history.

LEBLOND, RICHARD FOARD, internist, educator; b. Seattle, July 17, 1947; s. Donald E. and Ruth Elizabeth (Foard) LeB.; m. Anita Caraig Carcia, Dec. 28, 1994; children: Sueno Emmeline, Edgardo Alan. AB, Princeton U., 1969; MD, U. Wash., 1972. Diplomate Am. Bd. Internal Medicine (bd. dirs. 1993—, sec.-treas. 1996—). Intern Harlem Hosp., N.Y.C., 1972-73; resident in medicine, clin. fellow in oncology U. Wash., Seattle, 1975-78; pvt. practice, Livingston, Mont., 1978-96; dir. Livingston Meml. Hosp., 1979-91, 93-96, chmn. bd. dirs., 1984-91; clin. asst. prof. medicine Mont. State U., Bozeman, 1979-96, U. Wash., 1991-96, U. Claif., San Francisco, 1991-92; acting instr. Makerere U., Kampala, 1991-92; prof. clin. medicine U. Iowa, Iowa City, 1996—; bd. dirs. Deaconess Rsch. Found., Billings, Mont., 1993-96. Dir. Park County Friends of the Arts, Livingston, 1981-87, Livingston Cmty. Trust, 1986-91. Named Regional Trustee of Yr., Am. Hosp. Assn., 1989; recipient med. achievement award Deaconess Found., 1995, Mont. ACP Laureate award, 1996. Fellow ACP; mem. AMA, Mont. Med. Assn., Am. Soc. for Internal Medicine, Nat. Rural Health Assn., Iowa Med. Soc. Avocations: fishing, hunting, hiking, reading, gardening. Home: 2023 Laurence Ct NE Iowa Cityn IA 52240 Office: Univ of Iowa Hosps and Clinics 200 Hawkins Dr Iowa City IA 52242-1009

LEBLOND, RICHARD KNIGHT, II, banker; b. Cin., Nov. 16, 1920; s. Harold R. and Elizabeth (Conroy) LeB.,; m. Sara Cordial Chapman, Dec. 11, 1948; children—Mary, Richard, E. Chapman, Elizabeth, David, Virginia, William, Thomas, Sara, Joseph. BA, Princeton U.; DCS (hon.), St. John's U., Jamaica, N.Y., 1978. Exec. v.p. Chem. Bank, N.Y.C., 1968-73; vice-chmn. bd. Chem. Bank, 1973-85, sr. advisor, 1985—; chmn. adv. bd. Chase Bank NA, 1988—; bd. dirs. Ingersoll Internat., Inc., Rockford, Ill., Bedford Stuyvesant D&S Corp., Bklyn. Trustee St. Patrick's Cath., N.Y.C. 1st lt. U.S. Army, 1943-46, PTO. Mem. N.Y. State Bankers Assn. (pres. 1979-80), Harvard Bus. Sch. Assn. (pres. 1975-76). Republican. Roman Catholic. Office: Chase Manhattan Bank 11 W 51st St Fl 2 New York NY 10019-6901

LEBOEUF, RAYMOND WALTER, manufacturing company executive; b. Chgo., Dec. 30, 1946; s. Raymond O'Dillon and Opal Rosalind (Powell) LeB.; m. Loralee Ann Sawyer, Jan. 24, 1968; children—Mandy, Whitney. BA, Northwestern U., 1967; MBA, U. Ill., 1970. Analyst Ford Motor Co., Detroit, 1970-73; asst. comptroller Union Bank, Los Angeles, 1973-74; mgr. banking Ford Motor Co., Detroit, 1974-80; treas. PPG Industries, Inc., Pitts., 1980-84, controller, 1984-86, v.p. purchasing, 1986-88, v.p. finance, 1988-94, exec. v.p., 1994—, pres., COO, 1995—, pres., CEO, 1997—; trustee Robert Morris Coll.; bd. dirs. PPG Industries, Inc., Magee-Women's Hosp., Praxair, Inc., Extra Mile Edn. Found., Chem. Mfrs. Assn. Office: PPG Industries Inc 1 Ppg Pl Pittsburgh PA 15272-0001

LE BON, DOUGLAS KENT, investment manager; b. Rapid City, S.D., Oct. 27, 1953; s. Stanley and Elodis (Holm) Le B.; m. Eva Marie Dyer; 1 child, Shauna. BSBA, Calif. State U., Dominguez Hills, 1976, MBA, 1979. Valuation cons. Houlihan, Lokey, Howard & Zukin, L.A., 1979-83; v.p., prin. Wilshire Assocs., Inc., Santa Monica, Calif., 1983-90; co-founder, mng. dir. Pathway Capital Mgmt., L.A., 1990—. Vice chmn., chmn. fin. com. L.A. area coun. Boy Scouts Am., 1991-96; mem. corp. bd. Sch. Mgmt., Calif. State U., Dominguez Hills, 1994-96. Avocations: scuba diving, skiing. Office: Pathway Capital Mgmt 18101 Von Karman Ave Ste 1860 Irvine CA 92612-1047

LEBOR, JOHN F(RANCIS), retired department store executive; b. Portland, Oreg., Mar. 22, 1906; s. John G. and Jettie P. (Cook) L.; m. Violette Steinmetz, Oct. 7, 1931 (dec. Feb. 11, 1983); children: Andrew Scott, John Cook (dec. Jan. 1990); m. Dorothy Patrick Burns, Sept. 22, 1984. B.B.A., U. Oreg., 1928; M.B.A., Harvard U., 1930. Investment analyst Scudder, Stevens & Clark, N.Y.C., 1930-33; financial staff Radio-Keith-Orpheum Corp., 1933-40; sec.-treas. York (Pa.) Corp., 1940-46; treas. Federated Dept. Stores, Inc., Cin., 1946-51; v.p., treas., dir. Federated Dept. Stores, Inc., 1951-57, v.p., dir., 1958-60, exec. v.p., dir., 1960-65; trustee The Gateway Trust, Cin. Mem. Phi Beta Kappa, Beta Gamma Sigma, Beta Alpha Psi, Alpha Kappa Psi. Episcopalian. Clubs: Queen City (Cin.), The Beach; Old Guard Soc. Palm Beach Golfers (Palm Beach, Fla.); Westchester Country (Rye, N.Y.). *An important guiding principle for evaluating myself and others has been dependability and a record of "mission accomplished," as opposed to offering alibis.*

LEBOUITZ, MARTIN FREDERICK, financial services industry executive, consultant; b. Phila., May 16, 1946; s. William and Sylvia (Magen) L.; m. Helene A. Pepe, Oct. 15, 1977; children: Clarke S., Jacqueline B. BS, U.S. Air Force Acad., Colorado Springs, Colo., 1971; MA, The Fletcher Sch. of Law and Diplomacy, 1972. Asst. v.p. Bankers Trust Co., N.Y.C., 1976-82; v.p. mgr. of planning Barclays Bank of N. Am., N.Y.C, 1982-85; v.p. corp. devel. Chase Manhattan Bank, N.Y.C., 1985-88; v.p. planning and devel. Paine Webber Group Inc., N.Y.C., 1988-90; prin. DRI/McGraw-Hill, N.Y.C., 1990-91; mng. dir. Fin. Svcs. Cons., N.Y.C., 1991-95; v.p., dir. strategy wholesale oper. products The Chase Manhattan Bank, N.A., Bklyn., 1995—. Bd. dirs., chmn. sch. rels. com. N.Y. chpt. Fletcher Sch. Capt. USAF, 1971-76. Mem. Strategic Leadership Forum (dir., chmn. program com. N.Y. chpt.), Assn. for Corp. Growth, Am. Mgmt. Assn., USAF Acad. Alumnae (treas. N.Y. metro area chpt.), Harvard Club, Fletcher Sch. Club N.Y. (chmn. sch. rels. com.). Office: The Chase Manhattan Bank NA 4 Chase Metrotech Ctr Fl 21 Brooklyn NY 11201-3858

LEBOUTILLIER, JANET ELA, real estate investment asset manager, writer; b. Marshfield, Mass., May 10, 1936; d. Preston Carleton and Barbara (Higgins) Ela; m. John Walter McNeill, Oct. 10, 1959 (div. 1970); children: Duncan Davis McNeill, Sarah McNeill Treffry; m. Martin LeBoutillier, May 10, 1986. AA, Briarcliff Jr. Coll., 1956; BA in English Lit., U. Colo., 1958; postgrad. Real Estate/Mortgage Banking, NYU, 1973-78. Lic. N.Y. and Conn. real estate broker; cert. property mgr. Sales, leasing agt. L.B. Kaye Assocs., Ltd., N.Y.C., 1969-74; comml. leasing agt. Kenneth D. Laub & Co., N.Y.C., 1975; dir. leasing, asst. bldg. mgr. Douglas Elliman Gibbons & Ives Co., N.Y.C., 1975-76; adminstr. REIT adv. unit Chase Manhattan Bank, N.A., N.Y.C., 1976-78; asst. dir. real estate investments Mass. Mut. Life Ins. Co., Springfield, Mass., 1978-80; dir. real estate investments Yale U., New Haven, Conn., 1980-81; ind. cons. N.Y.C., 1981-83; sr. analyst, equity mgmt., sales and devel. Aetna Realty Investors, Inc., Hartford, Conn., 1983-84; dir. pub. involvement unit Aetna Realty Investors, Inc., 1984-86; sr. asset mgr. Cigna Investments, Inc., Hartford, 1986-87; v.p. Wm. M. Hotchkiss Co., New Haven, Conn., 1987-88; pres., prin. LeBoutillier & LeBoutillier, Inc., Lyme, Conn., 1989-93. Author: Mediations on Joy, 1995. Mem. Grace Episcopal Ch., mem. pastoral care and healing commn., coord. prayer team ministry. Mem. Internat. Order of St. Luke the Physician (co-founder, convener Heart of COmpassion Conn. Shoreline, Conn. area chpt. 1993—), Soc. Mayflower Descendants, Nat. Soc. of Colonial Dames of Am. Democrat. Episcopalian. Avocations: prayer ministry, skiing, fishing, sailing, tennis. Home and Office: 8 Laurel Dr Old Lyme CT 06371-1462

LEBOVITZ, HAROLD PAUL (HAL LEBOVITZ), journalist; b. Cleve., Sept. 11, 1916; s. Isaiah and Celia (Levy) L.; m. Margie Glassman, Feb. 20, 1938; children: Neil Ross, Lynn Gail. BA, Case Western Res. U., 1938; MA, Western Res. U., 1942. Sci. tchr., coach Euclid (Ohio) High Sch., 1938-46; reporter, baseball writer, columnist Cleve. News, 1946-60; columnist Cleve. Plain Dealer, 1960-84, sports editor, 1964-84; columnist The Sporting News, 1970-92, Gannett Syndicate, 1979-82; dir. Cleve. Jewish News, 1971-89; baseball umpire, 1937-50, football ofcl., 1940-71, basketball ofcl., 1940-60; Cleve. corr. Sporting News, 1950-64. Author: Pitchin' Man, 1948; (with Phil R. Gilman) Springboards to Science, 1967; contbg. editor: Webster's New World Dictionary, 1983—; syndicated columnist several Ohio newspapers, 1984—; contbr. articles to various periodicals; inventor outdoor playground game Four Sq. Tennis. Mem. recreation com. University Heights, Ohio, 1965-75; bd. dirs. Jewish Community Ctr., Cleve., 1962-63, Alumni Assn. Adelbert Coll. Case-Western Res. U., 1969-83. Named Citizen of Yr. City of University Heights, 1964, Sportsman of Yr. B'rith Emeth Men's Club, 1964, Top Sportswriter Cortron Twelve of Atlantic Fleet, 1961, Sporting News Top Feature Writer, 1963-64; recipient ten best writing awards Cleve. Newspaper Guild, 1948-60, Greater Cleve. Football Coaches Golden Deeds award, 1987; inducted into Glenville High Sch. Hall of Fame, 1980, Ohio Baseball Hall of Fame, 1984, Greater Cleve. Softball Hall of Fame, 1989, Sport Media Assn. of Cleve. Hall of Fame, 1990, Cleve. Journalism Hall of Fame, 1991. Mem. Baseball Writers Assn. (pres. 1965-66, bd. dirs. 1966-67), Ohio Sports Editors Assn. (pres. 1965-66), Cleve. Football Ofcls. Assn., Ohio Football Ofcls. Assn., Cleve. Umpires Assn., Sigma Delta Chi (Disting. Svc. award 1981, Mel Harder Disting. Svc. award 1992). Home: 2380 Edgerton Rd Cleveland OH 44118-3726

LEBOW, BENNETT S., communications executive; b. Phila., 1938; 1 child, Geri. BEE, Drexel U.; postgrad., Princeton U. Prin. DSI Systems Inc., Rockville, Md., from 1961, B.S. LeBow Inc.; chmn. Western Union Corp., Upper Saddle River, N.J., New Valley Corp. (formerly Western Union Corp.), Upper Saddle River, 1993—, New Valley Corp., Miami, FL, 1995—. Office: Mai Basic Four Inc 14101 Myford Rd Tustin CA 92780-7020 also: New Valley Corp 100 SE 2nd St # 32 Miami FL 33131-2100*

LEBOW, IRWIN LEON, communications engineering consultant; b. Boston, Apr. 27, 1926; s. Samuel and Ruth (Tobey) L.; m. Grace H. Hackel, July 8, 1951; children: Judith, William, David. SB, MIT, 1948, PhD, 1951. Staff mem. MIT Lincoln Lab., 1951-60, assoc. leader satellite communications surface techniques group, 1960-65, leader, 1965-70, assoc. head communications divsn., 1970-72, assoc. head data systems divsn., 1972-75, mem. steering com., 1970-75; chief scientist, assoc. dir. tech. Def. Communications Agy., Washington, Dept. Def., Washington, 1975-81; v.p. engring. Am. Satellite Co., Rockville, Md., 1981-84; v.p. Systems Research and Applications Corp., Arlington, Va., 1984-87; ind. cons. Washington, 1987—. Author: (with others) Theory and Design of Digital Machines, 1962, The Digital Connection, 1990, Information Highways and Byways, 1995. With USNR, 1944-46. Awarded rank of Meritorious Sr. Exec., 1980; recipient Meritorious Civilian Service medal Dept. Def., 1981. Fellow Am. Phys. Soc., IEEE; mem. AAAS, Armed Forces Communications and Electronics Assn.,

Sigma Xi. Home and Office: 2800 Bellevue Ter NW Washington DC 20007-1366

LEBOW, JEFFREY ALBERT, manufacturing engineer; b. Evanston, Ill., Jan. 17, 1958; s. Jerry P. and Natalie (Shapiro) L.; m. Laurel Mary Lavin, May 29, 1988; children: Jeffrey Adam, Elizabeth Ward, Jeremy Philip II, Robert Brewster. BS in Indsl. Engring., U. Mich., 1980, MS in Indsl. Engring., 1981. Registered profl. engr., Ga.; cert. sys. integrator. Project engr. Weyerhaeuser Co., Tacoma, 1981-83; applications engr. Robot Systems, Inc., Norcross, Ga., 1983-85; project engr. Hayes Microcomputer Products, Inc., Norcross, 1985-86; project engring. group leader Mitsubishi Consumer Electronics Am. Inc., Braselton, Ga., 1986-94; mgr. tech. linkages office Econ. Devel. Inst. Ga. Tech., Atlanta, 1994—; mem. course faculty Logistics Inst.; speaker Uniform Code Coun., Dayton, Ohio, 1992; adv. bd. Leaders in Logistics. Designer (material handling system) Cabinet Conveyor, 1987-92. Pres. B'nai B'rith-Achim Lodge, Atlanta, 1986, bd. dirs., 1985-87. Named Most Valuable Mem. B'nai B'rith, 1987, Outstanding Young Mfg. Engr. Yr. Soc. Mfg. Engrs., 1992; recipient Productivity Achievement award for Mfg. Excellence, Modern Materials Handling mag., 1992. Mem. Inst. Indsl. Engrs. (sr., bd. dirs. Atlanta chpt. 1986-87, course faculty materials handling mgmt. course 1992), Robotics Internat. of SME (sr.), Electronic Industries Assn. (EIA retail bar code std. com. 1991-94), Tech. Transfer Soc., U. Mich. Alumni Assn. (life), Mensa, Michigamma, Vulvcans, Tau Beta Pi (life). Avocations: scuba diving, travel, stand-up comedy, home repairs, photography. Home: 3110 Brandy Sta NW Atlanta GA 30339-4406 Office: Ga Tech Econ Devel Inst 223 O'Keefe Bldg Atlanta GA 30332-0640

LEBOW, MARK DENIS, lawyer; b. Harrisburg, Pa., Apr. 2, 1940; s. Sylvan and Ruth M. (Lebowitz) L.; m. Catherine Maugee, Nov. 22, 1972 (div. 1982); m. Patricia Edith Harris, Jan. 30, 1988; children: Michael, Jeffrey, Alexandra. AB, Yale U., 1961; JD, Harvard U., 1964. Bar: N.Y. 1965, U.S. Ct. Appeals (2d cir.) 1965, U.S. Dist. Ct. (so. and ea. dists.) N.Y. 1966. Assoc. Coudert Bros., N.Y.C., 1965-71, ptnr., 1972—; chmn. N.Y.C. CSC, 1979-92. Chmn. St. Francis Friends of the Poor, Inc., 1991—. Lt. USNR, 1964-71. Home: 1067 Fifth Ave New York NY 10128-0101 Office: Coudert Bros 1114 Avenue Of The Americas New York NY 10036-7703

LEBOWITZ, ALBERT, lawyer, author; b. St. Louis, June 18, 1922; s. Jacob and Lena (Zemmel) L.; m. Naomi Gordon, Nov. 26, 1953; children—Joel Aaron, Judith Leah. A.B., Washington U., St. Louis, 1945; LL.B., Harvard U., 1948. Bar: Mo. bar 1948. Assoc. Frank E. Morris, St. Louis, 1948-55; partner firm Morris, Schneider & Lebowitz, St. Louis, 1955-58, Crowe, Schneider, Shanahan & Lebowitz, St. Louis, 1958-66; counsel firm Murphy & Roche, St. Louis, 1966-67, Murphy & Schlapprizzi, St. Louis, 1967-81; partner firm Murphy, Schlapprizzi & Lebowitz, 1981-86; editor lit. quar. Perspective, 1961-80; of counsel Donald L. Schlapprizzi, P.C., 1986—, John T. Murphy, Jr., 1986-88. Author: novel Laban's Will, 1966, The Man Who Wouldn't Say No, 1969, A Matter of Days, 1989; also short stories. Served as combat navigator USAAF, 1943-45, ETO. Decorated Air medal with 3 oak leaf clusters. Mem. ABA, Mo., St. Louis bar assns., Phi Beta Kappa. Home: 743 Yale Ave Saint Louis MO 63130-3120 Office: Gateway One On The Mall 701 Market St Ste 1550 Saint Louis MO 63101-1861

LEBOWITZ, JOEL LOUIS, mathematical physicist, educator; b. May 10, 1930; came to U.S., 1946, naturalized, 1951; m. Estelle Mandelbaum, June 21, 1953 (dec. Dec. 1996). BS, Bklyn. Coll., 1952; MS, Syracuse U., 1955, PhD, 1956; hon. doctorate, Ecole Poly. Federale, Lausanne, Switzerland, 1977. NSF postdoctoral fellow Yale U., New Haven, 1956-57; mem. faculty Stevens Inst. Tech., Hoboken, N.J., 1957-59; mem. faculty Yeshiva U., N.Y.C., 1959-77, prof. physics, 1965-77, acting chmn. Belfer Grad. Sch. Sci., 1964-67, chmn. dept., 1967-76; George William Hill prof math. and physics, dir. Ctr. for Math. Scis., Rutgers U., New Brunswick, N.J., 1977—. Co-editor: Phase Transitions and Critical Phenomena, 1980, editor Jour. Statis. Physics, 1975—, Studies in Statis. Mechanics, 1973—, Com. Math. Physics, 1973—; contbr. articles to profl. jours. Recipient Boltzmann medal Internat. Union Pure and Applied Physics, 1992, Max Planck Rsch. award, 1993, Delmar S. Fahrney medal Franklin Inst., 1995; Guggenheim fellow, 1976-77. Fellow AAAS, Am. Phys. Soc., N.Y. Acad. Scis. (pres. 1979, A. Cressy Morrison award in natural scis. 1986, Heinz R. Pagels Human Rights of Scientists award 1996); mem. NAS, AAUP, Am. Math. Soc., Phi Beta Kappa, Sigma Xi. Office: Rutgers U Ctr Math Sci Rsch Busch Campus-Hill Ctr New Brunswick NJ 08903

LEBOWITZ, MARSHALL, publishing company executive; b. Boston, Mar. 4, 1923; s. Max Nathan and Rissah (Zangwill) L.; m. Charlotte Lily Meyersohn, Aug. 7, 1949; children: Wendy Ann, Marian Kay, Mark Louis. AB, Harvard U., 1942. Statis. analyst U.S. WPB, Washington, 1942-43; periodicals mgr. J.S. Canner & Co. Inc., Needham Heights, Mass., 1946-68, gen. mgr., 1968-86, v.p., 1977-96; v.p. Plenum Pub. Corp., 1977-96. Mem. Natick (Mass.) Planning Bd., 1964-69, chmn., 1968-69; mem. Natick Town Meeting, 1954—, chmn. town by-laws revision com., 1965-67; pres. Greater Framingham Mental Health Assn., 1963-64, dir. 1954-63; mem. Greater Framingham Mental Health Area Bd., 1972-78, v.p., 1974-75, pres., 1975-77; mem. Regional Drug Rev. Bd., 1973; chmn. Natick Regional Vocat. Sch. Planning Com., 1974-77; mem. Natick Sch. Com., 1978-81, clk., 1979-81; chmn. legis. impact study commn. Town of Natick, 1980; chmn. town commn. to rev. by-laws and mcpl. charter, 1980-90; mem. trustees adv. coun. Leonard Morse Hosp., 1973-91, vice chmn., 1974-77, mem. mental health adv. com., 1972-91; chmn. Natick Land-Use Com., 1983—; mem. Mcpl. Charter Rev. Com., 1985-88, Framingham-Natick Golden Triangle Planning Com., 1988-93; trustee Morse Inst. Libr., 1989—, pres., 1996—; bd. dir. Framington-Natick Cemetery Assn., 1991—; mem. Mcpl. Facilities Planning Com., 1994—. With AUS, 1943-46. Jewish (fin. sec. temple 1954-56, treas. 1952-54, vice-chmn. bd. 1958-59). Home: 2 Abbott Rd Natick MA 01760-1913

LEBOWITZ, MICHAEL DAVID, epidemiologist; b. Bklyn., Dec. 21, 1939; s. Harry and Rachel (Dick) L.; m. Joyce Marian Schmidt, Sept. 9, 1960; children: Jon A., Kira L., Debra M. AB, U. Calif., 1961, MA, 1965; PhC, U. Wash., 1969, PhD, 1971. Resch. assoc. preventive medicine U. Wash., Seattle, 1967-70, rsch. assoc. environ. health, 1970-71; asst. prof. internal medicine U. Ariz., Tucson, 1971-75, assoc. prof. internal medicine, 1975-80, prof. medicine, 1980—, prof. preventive cmty. medicine, 1996—, asst. dir. div. respiratory sci., 1974-84, assoc. dir. Respiratory Sci. Ctr., 1985-96; chair epidemiol. grad. program Ariz. Prevention Ctr., Tucson, 1994—, dir. epidemiol. unit, 1996—; vis. fellow Postgrad. Cardiothoracic Inst., U. London, 1978-79; vis. prof. Groningen U., The Netherlands, 1993, U. Pisa, Italy, 1993; cons. NIH, Bethesda, Md., 1985—, EPA, Washington, 1969—, WHO, 1979—, Italian Nat. Rsch. Coun., 1979—, Polish Nat. Inst. Hygiene and Acad. Scis., 1981—, Hungarian Nat. Inst. Hygiene, 1989—, Pan Am. Health Orgn., 1985—, also numerous others; co-chmn. Indoor Air Pollutants Commn., NAS-NRC, Washington, 1979-81, WHO Guidelines for Studies in Environ. Epidemiology, 1983, WHO-EURO Monographs on Air Quality, 1982-94. Mem. editl. bd.: Jour. Behavioral Medicine, 1977-93, Jour. Air Pollution Control Assn., 1984-88, Pediat. Pulmonology, 1990-95, Archives Environ. Health, 1990—, Am. Jour. Respiratory Critical Care Medicine, 1993—; co-editor: WHO/Euro Biol. Contaminants, 1990, WHO Europ Priorities in Environ. Epidemiology, 1996; assoc. editor: Jour. Toxicology Indsl. Health, 1984—, Jour. Exposure Analysis Environ. Epidemiology, 1992—; contbr. numerous articles to profl. jours., chpts. to books and monographs. Chmn. Pima County Air Quality Adv. Coun., Tucson, 1975-78; cons. Ariz. State Dept. Health Svcs., 1972—, Ariz. Lung Assn., 1971—, State Dept. Environ. Quality, 1987—, Gov. of Ariz., 1987-93; senator U. Ariz. Faculty Senate, Tucson, 1976-78. Recipient Ariz. Clean Air award Ariz. Lung Assn., 1987; numerous epidemiology/disease grants and contracts, NIH, EPA, FDA, EPRI and others, 1964—. Fellow Am. Coll. Epidemiology, Am. Coll. Chest Physicians, Collegium Ramazzini, Internat. Acad. Indoor Air Sci.; mem. Am. Epidemiol. Soc., Am. Thoracic Soc., Internat. Epidemiol. Assn., European Respiratory Soc., Soc. Epidemiol. Rsch., Internat. Soc. Environ. Epidemiology, Internat. Soc. Exposure Analysis, Hungar Soc. Health (hon.). Office: U Ariz Coll Medicine Prevention Ctr 1501 N Campbell Ave Tucson AZ 85724-0001

LEBRATO, MARY THERESA, lawyer, psychologist; b. Ft. Wayne, Ind., June 13, 1950; d. Joseph James and Veronica (Adamonis) L. BA, U. Dayton, 1971; MA, U. Ala., Tuscaloosa, 1973, PhD, 1975; JD, Lincoln Law Sch., 1986. Bar: Calif. 1986; lic. psychologist, Calif. Psychologist Ala. Dept. Mental Hygiene, Tuscaloosa, 1975, Calif. Dept. Health, Eldridge, Calif., 1975-77; chief statewide evaluation devel. svcs. Calif. Dept. Health, Eldridge, 1977-79; dir. evaluation Oakland Perinatal Health Project, Calif. Dept. Health, Sacramento, 1979-81; coord. Maternal, Child and Adolescent Health, Sacramento, 1981-82; dir. sexual harassment in employment project Calif. Commn. on Status of Women, Sacramento, 1982-85; chief long range planning Calif. Dept. Devel. Svcs., Sacramento, 1985-88; staff counsel Calif. State Lottery, Sacramento, 1988-91. Co-author (with Marilyn Pearman) Sexual Harassment Investigators Guidebook, 1984; author, editor: Help Yourself: A Manual for Dealing with Sexual Harassment, 1986. Adv. bd. mem. Calif. State Pers. Bd., Appeals Div. Adv. Com., 1987-91; bd. mem. Sacramento Rape Crisis Ctr., 1988. Recipient fellowships in psychology NIMH, U. Ala., Tuscaloosa, 1971, 72, 73, teaching asst. in psychology U. Ala., Tuscaloosa, 1974-75. Mem. APA, ABA, Am. Assn. on Mental Deficiency, Calif. State Bar Assn., Calif. State Psychol. Assn., Calif. Women Lawyers, Sacramento County Bar Assn., Women Laywers Sacramento (bd. mem., chair del. com. 1989, chair scholarship 1990). Avocations: horse breeding, art. Home: 335 Del Wes Ln Rio Linda CA 95673-2031

LEBRECHT, THELMA JANE MOSSMAN, reporter; b. Indpls., Feb. 21, 1946; d. Elmore Somerville and Lois Thelma (Johnson) Mossman; m. Roger Dublon LeBrecht, May 4, 1968. BS in Journalism, U. Fla., 1968. Pub. affairs reporter WBT and WBTV, Charlotte, N.C., 1967-72; freelance reporter Toronto and N.Y.C., 1972-76; reporter KYW Newsradio, Phila., 1976-80; editor ABC Radio Network, N.Y.C., 1980-81; reporter AP Broadcast, Washington, 1981—. Bd. dirs. Washignton Press Club Found., 1995—. Mem. Radio and TV Corrs. Assn. in U.S. Capitol (chmn. 1991, AP Oliver S. Gramling Disting. Reporter award 1996). Office: AP Broadcast 1825 K St NW Washington DC 20006-1202

LEBRETON, PAUL M., government official; b. Edmundston, Canada, Mar. 3, 1948; m. Nicole Leger; children: Helene, Luc, Mathieu. BA, U. Moncton, 1968; LLB, U. New Brunswick, 1972. Ptnr. Landry, LeBreton & McIntyre, Moncton, N.B., Can., 1972-81; sec. Law Soc. New Brunswick, 1981-88; justice, dep. atty. gen. Govt. New Brunswick, 1988—; area dir. Legal Aid New Brunswick, 1975-81; lectr. Ecole de droit Univ. Moncton, 1979-81. Trustee Sch. Dist. 51, Fredericton, N.B., 1987-88; pres. New Maryland Minor Baseball, Fredericton, 1992-95. Mem. Nat. Com. Practice of Law, Can. Bar Assn., Coun. Law Soc. New Brunswick. Avocations: hockey, baseball. Office: Dept Justice, PO Box 6000 670 King St, Fredericton, NB Canada E3B 5H1

LE BUHN, ROBERT, investment executive; b. Davenport, Iowa, May 2, 1932; s. Dick and Mable (Blom) LeB.; m. Jo-Ann Fitzsimmons, June 19, 1954 (dec. Aug. 1991); children: Anne, Ellen, Robert, Richard; m. Elaine L. Woody, Nov. 25, 1995. B.S., Northwestern U., 1954; M.B.A., U. Pa., 1957. Security analyst Cyrus J. Lawrence & Sons, N.Y.C., 1957-62; v.p. Eppler & Co., Inc., Morristown, N.J., 1962-72; independent fin. cons., 1972-80; mng. dir. Rothschild, N.Y.C., 1980-84; chmn. Investor Internat. (U.S.), Inc., N.Y.C., 1984-94; bd. dirs. Cambrex, Inc., USAIR Group, Inc., Acceptance Ins. Cos., Inc., N.J. Steel, Enzon Corp.; pres. Geraldine R. Dodge Found. Served to lt. (j.g.) USNR, 1954-56. Home: PO Box 6287 86 St Andrews Ct Unit 72 Snowmass Village CO 81615

LE CAM, LUCIEN MARIE, mathematics educator; b. Croze Creuse, France, Nov. 18, 1924; came to U.S., 1950; s. François Marie and Marie Renée (Jouanno) Le C.; m. Louise E. Romig, Aug. 19, 1952; children: Denis A., Steven D., Linda M. Licence es Scis., U. Paris, 1947; grad. student, Sorbonne, Paris, 1947-48; Ph.D., U. Calif. at Berkeley, 1952. Mem. faculty U. Calif. at Berkeley, 1952—, from asst. to assoc. prof. stats., 1953-57, prof. stats., 1961-91, Miller prof., 1971-72, prof. math., 1973-91, chmn. dept., 1961-65, prof. emeritus, 1991—. Author: Asymptotic Methods in Statistical Decision Theory, 1986, (with Grace Lo Yang) Asymptotics in Statistics, 1990. Dir. Centre de Recherches Mathématiques, U. Montreal, 1972-73. Home: 101 Kensington Rd Kensington CA 94707-1011 Office: Univ Calif Math Dept Berkeley CA 94720-3860

LECAPITAINE, JOHN EDWARD, counseling psychology educator, researcher; b. Nov. 21, 1950; s. Vincent Bernard and Evelyn Lucille Le-Capitaine; m. Jessica Dale; 1 child, Katherine Briee. BS, U. Wis., 1973, MS, 1975; D, Boston U., 1980. Rsch. assoc. Dupont Psychol. Edn. Inst., Eau Claire, Wis., 1975-76; counseling and sch. psychologist Martin Luther King. Jr. Ctr., Boston, 1976-78; adj. prof. Boston U., 1980-90; rsch. cons. Dept. Mental Health, 1985-90; prof. counseling psychology U. Wis., River Falls, 1990—. Contbr. poetry, fiction, and acad. articles to profl. jours. Mem. APA, ACA, Inst. Noetic Scis., Internat. Biographical Inst., Nat. Assn. Sch. Psychologists, Internat. Coun. Psychologists, Assn. Play Therapy, Assn. Multicultural Counseling and Devel., Assn. Humanistic Devel. and Edn., Assn. Counselor Edn. and Supervision, Internat. Soc. Poets, Phi Delta Kappa. Avocation: fiction writing, poetry. Home: 731 Lumphrey Ct River Falls WI 54022-3426 Office: U Wis Ames Bldg River Falls WI 54022

LE CARRÉ, JOHN (DAVID JOHN MOORE CORNWELL), author; b. Poole, Dorset, Eng., Oct. 19, 1931; s. Ronald Thomas Archibald and Olive (Glassy) Cornwell; m. Alison Ann Sharp, Nov. 27, 1954 (div. dissolved 1972); children: Simon, Stephen, Timothy; m. Valerie Jane Eustace, 1972; 1 son, Nicholas. Student, Bern (Switzerland) U., 1948-49; BA in Modern Langs., Lincoln Coll., Oxford (Eng.) U., 1956; hon. doctorate, U. Exeter, 1990, St. Andrews U., 1996. Tutor Eton Coll., Berkshire, Eng., 1956-58; mem. Brit. Fgn. Service, 1959-64; 2d sec. embassy Brit. Fgn. Service, Bonn, Germany, 1961-63; consul Brit. Fgn. Service, Hamburg, Germany, 1963-64. Author: Call for the Dead, 1960, A Murder of Quality, 1962, The Spy Who Came in From the Cold, 1963 (Mystery Writers of Am. Novel of Yr., 1963, Brit. Crime Novel of Yr. award 1963), The Looking-Glass War, 1965, A Small Town in Germany, 1968, The Naive and Sentimental Lover, 1971, Tinker Tailor Soldier Spy, 1973, The Honourable Schoolboy, 1977 (James Tait Black Meml. prize, Crime Writers Assn. gold dagger), Smiley's People, 1980 (televised 1982), The Little Drummer Girl, 1983, A Perfect Spy, 1986, The Russia House, 1989 (Nikos Kasanzakis prize 1991), The Secret Pilgrim, 1991, The Night Manager, 1993, Our Game, 1995, The Tailor of Panama, 1996. Recipient Somerset Maugham award 1964, Edgar Allen Poe award Mystery Writers Am., 1965, Gold dagger Crime Writers Assn., 1978, Black Meml. award, 1978, Grand Master award Mystery Writers Am., 1986, Malaparte prize, 1987, Diamond Dagger award Crime Writers Assn., 1988; Lincoln Coll., Oxford hon. fellow, 1984. Office: David Higham Assocs Ltd, 5-8 Lower John St Golden Sq, London W1R 4HA, England

LECERF, OLIVIER MAURICE MARIE, construction company executive; b. Merville-Franceville, France, Aug. 2, 1929; s. Maurice and Colette (Lainé) L.; m. Annie Bazin de Jessey, Jan. 11, 1958; children: Christophe, Véronique, Nicolas, Patricia. Baccalauréat A in Philosophy, 1946; diploma Inst. Polit. Studies Paris, 1950; M. Law, U. Paris, 1950; diploma Indsl. Studies Ctr., U. Geneva, 1960. Asst. mgr. Omnium pour l'importation et l'exportation, Paris, 1951-56; asst. mgr. Ciments Lafarge, Can., 1956-57, and Brazil, 1958-59, asst. mgr. fgn. dept., 1961, adj. comml. dir., Paris, 1962-64, pres., CEO Lafarge Cement N.Am., Vancouver, B.C., Can., 1965, pres. Lafarge Can. Que., Montreal, 1968, pres. Lafarge Can. Ltd., 1969, gen. mgr. Can. Cement Lafarge, Montreal, 1970, exec. gen. mgr., Paris, 1971-73, chmn., CEO (now Lafarge), 1974—, hon. chmn., 1989—, also dir.; dir. Compagnie de St Gobain, L'Oréal, others; mem. adv. com. Morgan Stanley, dir., chmn. financière Lafarge; pres. Sicav, Saint Honoré, Marchés Emergents. With inf. French Army, 1950-51; lt. Res. Decorated officer de la Legion d'Honneur, commandeur Ordre National du Merite. Contbr. articles to profl. jours. Home: 8 rue Guy de Maupassant, 75116 Paris France Office: Lafarge, 61 rue des Belles Feuilles, 75116 Paris France

LECHAY, JAMES, artist, emeritus art educator; b. N.Y.C., July 5, 1907; s. Charles and Augusta (Wolfson) L.; m. Rose David, Mar. 26, 1934; children: Jo, Daniel. A.B., U. Ill., 1928; D.F.A. (hon.), Coe Coll., 1961. Asst. prof. art U. Iowa, 1945-49; assoc. prof. 1949-56, prof., 1956-75, prof. emeritus, 1975—; tchr. Stanford U., 1949, N.Y. U., 1953, Skowhegan (Maine) Sch. Painting and Sculpture, 1961; artist in residence Tamarind Inst., 1973; vis. artist New Asia Coll., Chinese U. of Hong Kong, 1976, Parsons Sch. Design, Provincetown, Mass., 1981—, Studio Art Sch. of Aegean, Samos, Greece, 1986, 87, 88. Exhibited in numerous one-man shows including N.Y.C., others in, Trieste, Italy, Chgo., Cedar Rapids, Iowa City, Des Moines Art Center, Louisville, Springfield, Ill., Ft. Dodge, Cedar Falls and Davenport, Iowa Wesleyan U., Sioux City, Iowa, Wellfleet, Mass., Palardy Gallery, Montreal, Que., Can., Dartmouth Coll., Hanover, N.H., SUNY, Binghamton; exhibited group shows Met. Mus. Art, N.Y.C., Pa. Acad. Fine Arts, Provincetown Art Assn., Mass., Va. Mus. Fine Arts, Bklyn. Mus., Chgo. Art Inst., Phillips Meml. Gallery, Whitney Mus. Am. Art, Corcoran Gallery Art, Carnegie Instn., Copenhagen City Gallery, Denmark, others; represented permanent collections, Nat. Collection Fine Arts Smithsonian Instn., Pa. Acad. Fine Arts, U. Ariz., U. Iowa, Bklyn. Mus., New Britain Inst., U. Nebr., Memphis Mus., Ill. Wesleyan U., Chgo Art Inst., Wichita Art Center, Philbrook Mus., Tulsa, Des Moines Art Center, Coe Coll., Joslyn Art Mus., U. No. Iowa, Springfield (Mo.) Art Mus., Rochester Meml. Gallery, others, also pvt. collections. Recipient Norman Wait Harris bronze medal, 52 ann. exhbn. Am. Painting, Art Inst. Chgo., 1941, Lambert purchase prize Pa. Acad., 1942; represented hon. mention for water color Art Inst. Chgo., 1943, prize for oil 2d Ann. Portrait of Am. Exbhn., 1945, hon. mention Denver Mus., 1946, 1st prize for oil Iowa State Fair Exhbn., 1946, 51, 53, 55, 1st prize First Biennial Walker Art Ctr., Mpls., 1947, Minn. Centennial award, 1949, Edmundson trustee prize Des Moines Art Ctr., 1950, 1st prize, 1952, 53, 1st prize Davenport Mcpl. Art Gallery, 1950, Rosenfield Collection purchase prize Des Moines Art Ctr., 1959, Childe Hassam purchase prize, 1974, Benjamin Altman prize NAD, 1977, 91, Henry Ward Ranger Fund purchase prize, 1979, 86, Edwin Palmer Meml. award, 1981, Adolph and Clara Obrig prize NAD, 1993, 95. Mem. NAD. Office: Kraushaar Galleries 724 5th Ave New York NY 10019-4106

LECHELT, EUGENE CARL, psychology educator; b. Edmonton, Alta., Can., Dec. 26, 1942; s. Adolph Carl and Natalie (Klapstein) L.; m. Sandra Dona Morris, Dec. 18, 1965; 1 child, David Patrick. B.Sc., U. Alta., 1964, M.Sc., 1966, Ph.D., 1969. Research assoc., lectr. Princeton U., N.J., 1969-72; asst. prof. dept. psychology U. Alta., Edmonton, 1972-76, assoc. prof., 1976-82, prof., 1982—, chmn., 1986—. Recipient Rutherford Teaching award, 1985, Vol. award Fed. Govt. of Can., 1994; U. Alta. dissertation fellow, 1968-69; Social Scis. Research Council Can. fellow, 1978-79. Mem. Psychonomic Soc., Can. Psychol. Assn., AAAS, N.Y. Acad. Scis., Sigma Xi. Home: 11723-91 Ave, Edmonton, AB Canada T6G 1B1 Office: U Alta, Dept Psychology, Edmonton, AB Canada T6G 2E9

LECHEVALIER, HUBERT ARTHUR, microbiology educator; b. Tours, Indre et Loire, France, May 12, 1926; came to U.S., 1948; s. Jean Gaston and Marie (Delorme) L.; m. Mary Pfeil, Apr. 10, 1950; children: Marc, Paul. L és Sci., Laval U., 1947, MS, 1948, DSc (hon.), 1983; PhD, Rutgers U., 1951. Asst. prof. Rutgers U., New Brunswick, N.J., 1951-56, assoc. prof., 1956-66, prof. microbiology, 1966-91, assoc. dir. Waksman Inst., 1980-88; prof. emeritus, 1991—; vis. scientist Acad. of Scis. USSR, Moscow, 1958-59, Pasteur Inst., Paris, 1961-62;. Author: (with others) A Guide to the Actinomycetes and Their Antibiotics, 1953, Neomycin--Its Nature and Practical Application, 1958, Antibiotics of Actinomycetes, 1962, Three Centuries of Microbiology, 1965, Hungarian transl., 1971, The Microbes, 1971, Macrophages and Cellular Immunity, 1972, Microbial Ecology, 1974, The Development of Applied Microbiology at Rutgers, 1982; contbr. numerous articles to profl. jours.; 4 patents. Trustee Am. Type Culture Collection, Rockville, Md., 1973-79. Recipient Lindback award 1976, Bergey award 1989; inducted into N.J. Inventors Hall of Fame, 1990. Mem. Soc. Française de Microbiology (hon.), Soc. for Indsl. Microbiology (Charles Thom award 1982). Home: RR 2 Box 2235 Morrisville VT 05661-9429

LECHEVALIER, MARY PFEIL, retired microbiologist, educator; b. Cleve., Jan. 27, 1928; d. Alfred Leslie Pfeil and Mary Edith Martin; m. Hubert Arthur Lechevalier, Apr. 7, 1950; children: Marc E.M., Paul R. BA in Physiology-Biochemistry, Mt. Holyoke Coll., 1949; MS in Microbiology, Rutgers U., 1951. Rsch. fellow Rutgers U., New Brunswick, N.J., 1949-51, rsch. assoc. inst. microbiology, 1962-74, from asst. to assoc. rsch. prof., 1974-85, rsch. prof. Waksman inst. microbiology, 1985-91, prof. emerita, 1991—; ind. rschr., 1955-59; microbiologist steroid preparative lab. E.R. Squibb and Sons, New Brunswick, 1960-61; vis. investigator Inst. Biology Czechoslovak Acad. Scis., Svc. de Mycologie Pasteur Inst., Prague, Paris, 1961-62; cons. in field. Contbr. over 100 chpts. to books and articles to rsch. jours.; mem. adv. com. actinomycetes Bergey's Manual of Determinative Bacteriology, 8th edit.; chair adv. com. muriform actinomycetes Bergey's Manual, 9th edit. Assoc. mem. Bergey's Trust, 1989-92. Recipient Charles Thom award Soc. Indsl. Microbiology, 1982, Waksman award Theobald Smith Soc., 1991. Mem. AAAS, Am. Soc. Microbiology (former mem. com. actinomycetales), U.S. Fedn. Culture Collections (exec. com. 1982-85, J. Roger Porter award nominating com. 1983-84, 87-88, chair 1989-90, J. Roger Porter award 1992), N.Am. Mycol. Assn., Soc. Gen. Microbiology, Sigma Xi (pres. Rutgers U. chpt. 1977-78). Achievements include patents for immunological adjuvant and process for preparing same, pharmaceutical composition and process, restriction endonuclease Fse I, antibiotic LL-14E605B and O-Methyl LL-14E605B. Home: RR 2 Box 2235 Morrisville VT 05661-9429

LECHNER, ALFRED JAMES, JR., judge; b. Elizabeth, N.J., Jan. 7, 1948; s. Alfred J. and Marie G. (McCormack) L.; m. Gayle K. Peterson, Apr. 3, 1976; children—Brendan Patrick, Coleman Thomas, Mary Kathleen. B.S., Xavier U., Cin., 1969; J.D., U. Notre Dame, 1972. Bar: N.J. 1972, N.Y. 1973; U.S. Dist. Ct. N.J. 1972, U.S. Dist. Ct. (so. and ea. dists.) N.Y. 1974, U.S. Ct. Appeals (2d cir.) 1974, U.S. Ct. Appeals (3d cir.) 1980, U.S. Supreme Ct. 1975. Assoc. Cadwalader, Wickersham & Taft, N.Y.C., 1972-75, MacKenzie, Welt & Duane, Elizabeth, N.J., 1975-76; ptnr. MacKenzie, Welt, Duane & Lechner, Elizabeth, 1976-84; judge Superior Ct. State N.J., 1984-86; judge U.S. Dist. Ct. N.J., 1986—. Mem. Union County (N.J.) adv. bd. Catholic Community Services, 1981-83, chmn., 1982. Maj. USMCR. Fellow Am. Bar Found.; mem. Assn. Fed. Bar of State N.J. Roman Catholic. Clubs: Friendly Sons of St. Patrick (pres. 1982), Union County. Note and comment editor Notre Dame Law Rev., 1972; contbr. articles to legal jours. Office: US Dist Ct Martin Luther King Jr Fed Bldg US Ct House Box 999 Newark NJ 07102

LECHNER, BERNARD JOSEPH, consulting electrical engineer; b. N.Y.C., Jan. 25, 1932; s. Barnard Joseph and Lillian Veronica (Stevens) L.; m. Joan Camp Mathewson, Nov. 21, 1953. BSEE, Columbia U., 1957; postgrad., Princeton U., 1957-60. Mem. tech. staff RCA Labs., Princeton, N.J., 1957-62, project leader, 1962-67, group head, 1967-77, lab. dir., 1977-83, staff v.p., 1983-87; cons., Princeton, 1987—; cons. expert on TV matters including high definition TV and flat-panel displays; bd. dirs. Palisades Inst., N.Y.C.; chmn. adv. commn. Mercer County Coll., Trenton, N.J., 1968-85. Contbr. articles to profl. jours.; holder 10 patents. Reader Recording for the Blind, Princeton, 1967-72. Served to cpl. U.S. Army, 1953-55. Recipient David Sarnoff Gold medal RCA Corp., 1962. Fellow Soc. for Info. Display (pres. 1978-80, other offices, Frances Rice Darne award 1971, Beatrice Winner award 1983), IEEE (chpt. chmn. 1964-66, Best Paper award Solid State Cirs. Conf. 1966), Soc. Motion Picture and TV Engrs. (David Sarnoff Gold Medal award 1996); mem. Am. Relay Radio League, Sigma Xi, Tau Beta Pi, Eta Kappa Nu. Episcopalian. Club: Princeton Sqs. (pres. 1981-87). Avocations: amateur radio, sq. dancing, philately, sailing, swimming. Address: 98 Carson Rd Princeton NJ 08540-2207

LECHNER, JON ROBERT, nursing administrator, educator; b. Detroit, Nov. 5, 1957; s. Monroe Stanley and Helen Cecelia (Schneider) L. Cert. in practical nursing, Oakland C.C., Southfield, Mich., 1983; ADN, Mercy Coll. Detroit, 1991, BSN, 1992. Cert. EMT; RN, ANCC, Mich. Coord. emergency med. svcs., paramedic William Beaumont Hosp., Royal Oak, Mich., 1979-84, lic. practical nurse, 1986-91, RN, 1991—, asst. nursing mgr., 1992—; pastoral assoc. St. Mary's Parish & Sch., Toledo, 1984-86; adj. clin. instr. Oakland C.C., Waterford, Mich., 1993—; cert. BLS instr. Am. Heart Assn., Southfield, 1986—. Vol. Project Health-O-Rama, 1992—, Wellness Networks, Inc., 1992—; voting mem. region I State of Mich. HIV Planning & Prevention Commn., Detroit, 1994—. Mem. Am. Assembly Men Nursing, Am. Assn. Neurosci. Nurses, Acad. Med. Surg. Nurses (charter), Assn. Nurses AIDS Care, Sigma Theta Tau. Democrat. Roman Catholic. Avocations: reading, hiking, walking, cycling, theatre. Home: 28450 Universal Dr Warren MI 48092-2441 Office: William Beaumont Hosp 3601 W 13 Mile Rd Royal Oak MI 48073-6712

LECHTANSKI, CHERYL LEE, chiropractor; b. Elizabeth, N.J., Dec. 27, 1961; d. Leo Joseph and Barbara Frances (Sullivan) L. BA in Biology and Journalism, NYU, 1985; DC, N.Y. Chiropractic Coll., 1989. Lic. chiropractor, N.J., N.Y., Pa., Del., Mich. Chiropractic assoc. Chiropractic Arts Ctr., Downingtown, Pa., 1990-91; pvt. practice Newark, NJ, 1992-93; with Morganville (N.J.) Family Chiropractic Office, 1993—. Mem. N.J. Chiropractic Soc., Pa. Chiropractic Soc., NOW, World Wildlife Fund, Save the Manatee Club, Ctr. for Marine Conservation, Phi Chi Omega. Unitarian. Avocations: horseback riding, tai chi, softball, ice skating, tap dancing. Home: 42 Hutchinson Dr Port Monmouth NJ 07758-1049 Office: Morganville Family Chiropractic Office 42 Hutchinstrn Dr Port Monmouth NJ 07758-1049

LECHTENBERG, VICTOR L., agricultural studies educator; b. Butte, Nebr., Apr. 14, 1945; m. Grayce Lechtenberg; 4 children. BS, U. Nebr., 1967; PhD in Agronomy, Purdue U., 1971. Prof. agronomy Purdue U., West Lafayette, Ind., 1971—, assoc. dir. Agrl. Experiment Sta., 1982-89, exec. assoc. dean agr., 1989-93, dean agr., 1994—, exec. assoc. dean of agr., 1989-94; dean agr. Purdue U., West Lafayette, 1994—, pres., 1996; mem. land grant univ. coms. advising USDA, U.S. Congress on funding for agrl. rsch., extension, teaching; chmn. adv. bd. USDA Nat. Agrl. Rsch., Ext., Edn., and Econs., 1996. Contbr. articles to profl. jours., chpts. to books. Scoutmaster Boy Scouts Am., 1983-85. Recipient Nebr. 4-H Dist. Alumni award, 1981. Fellow Am. Soc. Agronomy (Ciba-Geigy award), Crop Sci. Soc. Am. (past pres.); mem. Crop Sci. Soc. Agrnomy, Coun. Agrl. Sci. and Tech. (pres., bd. dirs.), Am. Registry of Cert. Profls. in Agronomy, Crops and Soils, USDA (mem., chmn. nat. agrl. rsch., extension, edn. and econs. adv. bd.). Sigma Xi, Alpha Zeta, Gamma Sigma Delta. Roman Catholic. Avocation: woodworking. Office: Purdue Univ 1140 Ag Adminstrn West Lafayette IN 47907

LECISTON, DAVID JOHN, computer scientist; b. Passaic, N.J., Dec. 25, 1958; s. Alex and Rose (Kozmoski) L.; m. Diane Carol Hirth, June 19, 1981 (div. Apr. 1985); 1 child, Jennifer Ann; m. Wendie Sue Orr, Feb. 3, 1987; children: David Jonathan, Mary Rose. BS in Computer Sci., Seton Hall U., 1982. Computer scientist U.S. Army Comms. Electronics Command, R&D Engring. Ctr., Fort Monmouth, N.J., 1988—. 1st lt. U.S. Army, 1983-87. Mem. IEEE (initiative on software engring. as a profession 1994—), Am. Computing Machinery, Armed Forces Comm. and Electronics Assn. (life). Avocations: fishing, camping, hiking, computers. Home: PO Box 639 Fort Monmouth NJ 07703-0639 Office: US Army Comm Electronics Command Bldg 1210 Rm 223 Rittko Ave Fort Monmouth NJ 07703-5207

LECKER, ABRAHAM, former banker; b. Rumania, Mar. 29, 1916; came to U.S., 1957; s. Schaje and Lisa (Schimmel) L.; m. Minnie Kamenetzky, Aug. 29, 1954; 1 dau., Lisa Joy. MBA, Cert. Assn. Brit. Inst. Bankers, London, 1947; LLB, Sch. Law, Tel Aviv, 1957; postgrad., Harvard Bus. Sch. With banks in Palestine, 1934-36, Barclays Bank DCO, Palestine, 1936-49; dep. treas., comptroller City of Haifa, Israel, 1949-57; with Exchange Nat. Bank, Chgo., 1957-81; sr. v.p., cashier Exchange Nat. Bank, 1966-73, exec. v.p., 1973-81, dir., 1971-75. Served with Brit. Army, World War II; Served with Israeli Army, 1948-49. Former mem. Am. Jewish Com., Brit. Inst. Bankers, Am. Inst. Bankers, Ill. Mfrs. Assn., Bankers Assn. Fgn. Trade, Internat. Bus. Coun. Chgo., Ill. C. of C., Svc. Corps Ret. Execs. (vol.), Exec. Svc. Corps., Internat. Exec. Svc. Corps., B'nai B'rith. Home: 3750 N Lake Shore Dr Chicago IL 60613-4238

LECKIE, GAVIN FREDERICK, lawyer; b. Cambridge, Eng., Dec. 31, 1958; came to U.S., 1987; s. Frederick Alexander and Alison Elizabeth (Wheelwright) L.; m. Elizabeth Anne O'Donnell, Aug. 15, 1987. BA in Law, Cambridge U., 1981, MA, 1985; LLM, U. Ill., 1988. Bar: N.Y. 1990, U.S. Tax Ct. 1992; solicitor Eng. and Wales, 1984. Articled clk. Lawrence Graham, London, 1982-84, solicitor, 1984-87; assoc. Milbank, Tweed, Hadley & McCloy, N.Y.C., 1988—. Mem. ABA, N.Y. State Bar Assn., N.Y. County Lawyers Assn. (mem. com. on fgn. and internat. law), Internat. Fiscal Assn., Law Soc. Eng. and Wales. Home: 226 Highbrook Ave Pelham NY 10803 Office: Milbank Tweed Hadley McCloy 1 Chase Manhattan Plz New York NY 10005-1401

LE CLAIR, CHARLES GEORGE, artist, retired university dean; b. Columbia, Mo., May 23, 1914; s. Carl Amie and Marie (Fess) LeC.; m. Margaret Foster, May 30, 1945 (dec. Nov. 1991). BS, MS, U. Wis., 1935; posgrad., Academie Ranson, Paris, 1937; grad. study, Columbia U., 1940-41. Instr. art U. Ala., 1935-36, asst. prof., head dept., 1937-42; asst. prof. art, head dept. Albion Coll., 1942-43; tchr. painting and design Albright Art Sch., Buffalo, 1943-46; assoc. prof., head dept. Chatham Coll., 1946-52, prof., 1952-60; dean Tyler Sch. Art, Temple U., Phila., 1960-74; dean emeritus Tyler Sch. Art, Temple U., 1981—, prof. painting, 1974-81, chmn. painting and sculpture dept., 1979-81; established Tyler Sch. Art, Rome, Italy, 1966. Author: The Art of Watercolor, 1985, rev. edit. full color, 1994, Color in Contemporary Painting, 1991; contbg. author: Everything You Ever Wanted to Know About Oil Painting, 1994; works exhibited Pa. Acad. Met. Mus. Art, Carnegie Inst., Whitney Mus., Corcoran Mus., Chgo. Art Inst., Richmond Mus., Butler Mus. Art, Am. Watercolor Soc., Bklyn. Mus.; oneman shows include Carnegie Inst., 1954, Salpeter Gallery, N.Y.C., 1956, 59, 65, Rochester Inst. Tech., 1958, Phila. Art Alliance, 1962, 73, Franklin and Marshall Coll., 1969, Galleria 89, Rome, 1970, Left Bank Gallery, Wellfleet, 1983, 87, 96, 40-yr. Retrospective, Temple U., 1978, Visual Images, Wellfleet, 1978, 79, 80, Gross-McCleaf Gallery, Phila., 1979, 81, 96, More Gallery Phila., 1983, 87, 89. Named Pitts. Artist of Yr., 1957; recipient Pennell medal Pa. Acad. Fine Arts, 1965, achievement award Am. Artist mag., 1995; fellow Fund for Advancement Edn. Ford Found., 1952-53. Subject of Elizabeth Leonard's book Painting Flowers, 1986. Home: 1810 Rittenhouse Sq Apt 812 Philadelphia PA 19103-5837

LECLAIR, JOHN CLARK, professional hockey player; b. St. Albans, Vt., July 5, 1969. Hockey player Montreal Canadiens, 1987-94, Phila. Flyers, 1995—. Named to ECAC All-Star 2d team, 1990-91, Sporting News All-Star 1st team, 1994-95, NHL All-Star 1st team, 1994-95.

LECLAIR, PETER R., state agency supervisor, mental retardation services professional; b. Southbridge, Mass., Nov. 22, 1952; s. George Samuel and Elizabeth Louise (Willett) LeC. AS, Quinsigamond C.C., 1975; BS, Annhurst Coll., 1977; MA, U. Conn., 1986. Cert. tchr., Conn. Aide Conn. State Dept. Mental Retardation, Putnam, Conn., 1976-77, instr., 1977-78, tchr., 1978-90, pupil svcs. specialist, 1990-91, coord. specialized employment program, 1991-92; coord. demonstration team Oreg. project Region 3 Conn. State Dept. Mental Retardation, Willimantic, Conn., 1990-91, supr. individual supports and planning unit, cons. Region 3, 1992-96; supr. individual resources and devel. day svcs. Conn. State Dept. Mental Retardation, Norwich, Conn., 1996—; cons. in field; participant Conn. State Dept. Mental Retardation Peace Corps/Romania Tng., March, 1991. Assoc. editors newsletter U. Conn., 1985-86. Foster parent Christian Children's Fund, Honduras, 1985—; chmn. memory book com. John N. Dempsey Regional Ctr. 25th Anniversary, Putnam, 1989; bd. dirs. ARC Quinebaug Valley, Putnam, 1988-90; mem. Dem. Nat. Com., 1993. Mem. Am. Assn. Mental Retardation (Conn. Tchr. of Yr. award 1986), Coun. for Exceptional Children, Amnesty Internat., JFK Libr. Found., Pi Lambda Theta. Democrat. Avocations: rock music, concert, painting, gardening, reading. Home: 131 Old Turnpike Rd Quinebaug CT 06262 Office: Conn State Dept Mental Retardation Eastern Region 201 W Thames St Ste 401 Norwich CT 06360-6838

LECLAIR, SUSAN JEAN, hematologist, clinical laboratory scientist, educator; b. New Bedford, Mass., Feb. 17, 1947; d. Joseph A. and Beatrice (Perry) L.; m. James T. Griffith; 1 child, Kimberly A. BS in med. tech., Stonehill Coll., 1968; postgrad., Northeastern U., Boston, 1972-74; MS in Med. Lab. Sci., U. Mass., Dartmouth, 1977. Cert. clin. lab. scientist; cert. med. technologist. Med. technologist Union Hosp., New Bedford, Mass., 1968-70; supr. hematology Morton Hosp., Taunton, Mass., 1970-72; edn. coord., program dir. Sch. Med. Tech. Miriam Hosp., Providence, 1972-79; hematology technologist R.I. Hosp., Providence, 1979-80; asst. prof. med. lab. sci. U. Mass., Dartmouth, 1980-84, assoc. prof. med. lab. sci., 1984-92, prof. med. lab. sci., 1992—; instr. hematology courses Brown U., Providence, 1978-80; cons. Bd. R.I. Schs. Med. Tech., R.I. Hosp. Div. Clin. Hematology, Cardinal Cushing Gen. Hosp., Charlton Meml. Hosp., St. Luke's Hosp., VA Med. Ctr., Providence, 1984—, Nemasket Group, Inc., 1984-87, Gateway Health Alliance, 1985-87; chair hematology/hemostasis com. Nat. Cert. Agy. for Med. Lab. Pers. Exam. Coun., 1994—. Contbr. articles to profl. jours.; contbr. articles to jours and chpts. to books; author computer software in hematology. Reviewer Nat. Commn. Clin. Lab. Scis., 1986-89; chairperson Mass. Assn. Health Planning Agys., 1986-87; bd. dirs. Southeastern Mass. Health Planning Devel. Inc., (1975-88, numerous other offices and coms.); planning subcom. AIDS Edn. (presentor Info Series). Mem. Am. Soc. Clin. Lab. Sci. (editor clin. practice sect. CLS jour.), Am. Soc. Med. Tech. Edn. and Rsch. Fund, Inc. (chairperson 1983-85), Mass. Assn. for Med. Tech. (pres. 1977-78), Southeastern Mass. Soc. Med. Tech. (pres. 1975-76), Alpha Mu Tau (pres. 1993-94). Avocations: choral singing, cooking, reading. Office: U Mass Dept Med Lab Sci Dartmouth MA 02747

LECLERC, PAUL, library director; b. Lebanon, N.H., May 28, 1941; s. Louis and M. Juliette (Trottier) LeC; m. Judith Ginsberg, Oct. 26, 1980; 1 child, Adam Louis. BS, Coll. Holy Cross, 1963; student, U. Paris, 1963-64; MA, Columbia U., 1966, PhD with distinction, 1969; LHD (hon.), L.I. U., 1994, Coll. of the Holy Cross, 1994, Hamilton Coll., 1995, Union Coll., 1997; Hunter Coll., 1997. Assoc. prof. French Union Coll., Schenectady, 1969-79, chmn. dept. modern langs. and lit., 1972-77, chmn. humanities div., 1975-77; univ. dean for acad. affairs CUNY, 1979-84; provost and acad. v.p. Baruch Coll., CUNY, 1984-88; pres. Hunter Coll., CUNY, 1988-93; pres., CEO New York Public Library, 1994—; bd. dirs. N.Y. Alliance for Pub. Schs., N.Y.C., 1981-84, El Museo del Barrio, The Feminist Press; pres. N.Y. Tchr. Edn. Conf. Bd., Albany, N.Y., 1983-84. Author: Voltaire and Crebillon Pere, 1972, Voltaire's Rome Sauvée, 1992; co-editor: Lettres d'André Moreliet, vol. I, 1991, vol. II, 1994, vol. III, 1996; contbr. articles to profl. jours. Decorated officier Palmes Académiques, chevalier Legion of Honor (France); grantee NEH, 1971, 79, Am. Coun. Learned Socs., 1973, Ford Found., 1979. Mem. MLA, Am. Soc. for 18th Century Studies. Office: NY Pub Libr Fifth Ave & 42nd St New York NY 10018

LECOCKE, SUZANNE ELIZABETH, lawyer; b. Nuremburg, Germany, Nov. 3, 1958; came to U.S., 1959; d. Frank Joseph and Carolyn Elizabeth (Partain) L. BS magna cum laude, U. Tex., 1981; JD, U. Houston, 1987. Bar: Tex. 1987, U.S. Dist. Ct. (so. and no. dists.) Tex. 1987, U.S. Ct. Appeals (5th and fed. cirs.) 1992, U.S. Dist. Ct. (no. dist.) Calif. 1993. Supr. systems support Southwestern Bell Telephone, San Antonio, 1981-82; engr. Mitre Corp., Houston, 1982-84; law clk. to judges DeAnda, Bue and Hoyt U.S. Dist. Ct. (so. dist.) Tex., Houston, 1986-89; assoc. Liddell, Sapp, Zivley, Hill & Laboon, Houston, 1989-91, Arnold, White & Durkee, Houston, 1991-96. Co-author: Patent Law Handbook, 1992-93, 93-94, 94-95, 95-96, 96-97. Mem. ABA, Am. Intellectual Property Law Assn., Tex. Bar Assn., Houston Intellectual Property Law Assn., Houston Young Lawyers Assn., Mensa Soc., Upsilon Pi Epsilon. Roman Catholic. Avocations: tennis, workouts, back-packing, outdoor activities, reading.

LECOCQ, KAREN ELIZABETH, artist; b. Santa Rosa, Calif., Nov. 4, 1949; d. Maynard Rodney and Lois May (Lessard) LeC.; m. David Lawrence Medley, Sept. 7, 1995. BA, Calif. State U., Fresno, 1971, MA, 1975; postgrad., Calif. Inst. of the Arts, L.A., 1971-72. Founding mem. Feminist Art Program, Fresno, Calif., 1971, Calif. Inst. of the Arts, L.A., 1972; One woman shows include Calif. State U. Art Gallery, Fresno, 1970, 76, Merced (Calif.) Coll., 1969, 77, 91, Calif. Inst. of the Arts, L.A., 1972, Recent Sculptures, Fresno, 1977, 78, Womanart Gallery, N.Y.C., 1980, Merced, 1987, Arts Coun. Gallery, Merced, 1989, Amos Eno Gallery, N.Y.C., 1994, 750 Gallery, Sacramento, 1995, Meridian Gallery, San Francisco, 1996, others; commissions include Absolut Vodka, 1993; vis. artist Merced County Schs., 1977-78, 79-82, 88-91; grad. instr. Calif. State U., Fresno, 1976-78, Merced Coll., 1973-76. Group shows include Womanhouse, L.A., 1972, Off Centre Centre, Calgary, Alta., Can., 1985, 86, Ryosuke Gallery, Osaka, Japan, 1986, Gallery Six Oh One, San Francisco, 1989, Fresno Art Mus., 1989, Ann Saunders Gallery, Jamestown, Calif., 1991, Pro arts Gallery, Oakland, Calif., 1991, Calif. Mus. Art, Santa Rosa, 1991, Harbs Gallery, Lexington, Va., 1992, Russell Sage Gallery, Troy, N.Y., 1992, Amos Eno Gallery, 1992-96, ARC Gallery, Chgo., 1993, 96, Lengyel Gallery, San Francisco, 1995, 750 Gallery, Sacramento, 1994-96, L.A. Mus. Contemporary Art, 1995, Armand Hammer Mus., L.A., 1996, many others. Docent Gallery Guide Art Train, Merced, 1983; artistic dir. Black and White Ball, Merced Regional Arts Coun., 1989-96. Cora T. McCord scholar; CETA grantee, Merced, 1978, Fresno, 1977; Calif. Inst. Arts scholar, 1972. Mem. Internat. Sculpture Source, No. Calif. Women's Caucus for Art, Pro Arts of Oakland, San Francisco Mus. Art. Democrat. Home and Office: PO Box 2204 Merced CA 95344-0204

LECOMPTE, ELIZABETH, theater director; b. Summit, N.J., Apr. 28, 1944. BS, Skidmore COll., 1967. Founder, dir. Wooster Group, N.Y.C., 1980—. Director: Frank Dell's The Temptation of Saint Antony, 1987, Brace Up!, 1991, Fish Story, 1993, The Emperor Jones, 1994, The Hairy Ape, 1995. Recipient Obie award for Point Judith; MacArthur fellow, 1995, NEA Disting. Artists fellow for lifetime achievement in Am. theater. Office: The Wooster Group PO Box 654 Canal St New York NY 10013*

LECOMPTE, ROGER BURTON, management consultant; b. Cin., May 22, 1942; s. Joseph Edward and Lefa May (Ayars) LeC.; m. Margaret Morgan, 1969 (div. 1971); m. Helen Lida Smits, Aug. 28, 1976; 1 child, Theodore Edward. BA, U. Cin., 1965; MBA, U. Pa., 1975. Cons. alt. delivery systems Blue Cross Assn., Chgo., 1971-73; asst. to pres. Albert Einstein Med. Ctr., Phila., 1975-77; cons. Lewin & Assocs., Washington, 1977-81; v.p. planning Middlesex Hosp., Middletown, Conn., 1981-93; prin. The Futures Group, Glastonbury, Conn., 1993-94; pres. LeCompte & Co. Healthcare Planning, 1993—; dir. network devel. Health Right, Inc., Meriden, Conn., 1995-96; bd. dirs. Aetna Health Plan of So. New Eng.; vol. US Peace Corps, Kumba, Cameroon, 1965-67; vice-chmn. Vis. Nurses of Lower Valley, Essex, Conn., 1983-86. Author/editor: Prepaid Group Practice Manual, 1973. Mem. bd. edn. Essex Elem. Sch., 1985-91, chmn. sch. bldg. com., 1987-93; vestryman St. John's Episcopal Ch., Essex, 1988-92, chmn. capital fund drive, 1996. Democrat. Home: 81 Main St Ivoryton CT 06442-1032

LE COMTE, EDWARD SEMPLE, author, educator; b. N.Y.C., May 28, 1916; s. John Radway and Mary (Semple) Le C.; m. Marie Munzer, Jan. 19, 1945; 1 son, Douglas Munzer. A.B., Columbia, 1939, A.M., 1940, Ph.D., 1943. Instr. English Columbia, 1943-45; asst. prof. English U. Calif.-Berkeley, 1945-48; asst. prof. English Columbia U., 1948-56, assoc. prof., 1956-64; prof. English SUNY-Albany, 1964-81, prof. emeritus, 1981—. Author: Endymion in England: The Literary History of a Greek Myth, 1944, Yet Once More: Verbal and Psychological Pattern in Milton, 1953, A Dictionary of Last Words, 1955, The Long Road Back, 1957, He and She, 1960, A Milton Dictionary, 1961, Grace to a Witty Sinner: A Life of Donne, 1965, The Notorious Lady Essex, 1969, The Man Who Was Afraid, 1969, Milton's Unchanging Mind, 1973, Poets' Riddles: Essays in Seventeenth-Century Explication, 1975, Sly Milton: The Meaning Lurking in the Contexts of His Quotations, 1976, Milton and Sex, 1978, The Professor and the Coed, 1979, A Dictionary of Puns in Milton's English Poetry, 1981, I, Eve, 1988, Milton Re-viewed: Ten Essays, 1991, Carnal Sin, 1994; also various articles in scholarly jours. on 17th century lit.; editor: Paradise Lost and Other Poems, 1961, Justa Edovardo King, 1978. Mem. Milton Soc. (hon. scholar), P.E.N., MLA, Phi Beta Kappa. Home: PO Box 143 North Egremont MA 01252-0143

LECOURS, MICHEL, electrical engineering educator; b. Montreal, Que., Can., Aug. 1, 1940; s. Henri and Germaine (L'Archeveque) L.; m. Almut Lange, July 14, 1966; children: Christiane, Mireille, Jean-Yves. BScA, Ecole Poly., Montreal, 1963; PhD, Imperial Coll., London, 1966. Registered profl. engr., Que. Mem. sci. staff Bell-No. Rsch., Ottawa, Ont., Can., 1971-72; prof. elec. engring. U. Laval, Quebec City, Que., 1967—, head dept., 1975-77, vice dean, 1977-85; cons. Lab-Volt (Que.) Ltd., Quebec City, 1981—; vis. researcher Nippon Tel. & Tel., Yokosuka, Japan, 1986. Contbr. numerous articles on electronics and communications to sci. jours.; patentee for short range high resolution radar. Recipient ann. merit award Ecole Poly., 1986. Fellow Can. Soc. for Elec. and Computer Engring., Engring. Inst. Can. (John B. Stirling medal 1997). Office: Laval Univ, Dept Elec Engring, Quebec, PQ Canada G1K 7 P4

LECUYER, ROBERT RAYMOND, aviation maintenance administrator; b. Syracuse, N.Y., Dec. 13, 1965; s. Raymond Jeremy and Karen Penelope (Van Ornam) P.; m. Wendy Elizabeth Barrows, Jan. 13, 1990; children: Christopher, Andrew, Robbyn. AS, City Univ., Bellevue, Wash., 1990; BS, So. Ill. U., 1993; MS, U. Ark., 1996. From aviation ordnance tech. to aviation maintenance admin. U.S. Navy, Memphis, 1984—; mem. tech. adv. bd. State Tech. Inst., Memphis, 1994—; enlisted air warfare tng. coord. USN, 1994-95. Dist. roundtable commr. Boy Scouts Am. Mem. Profl. Photographer's Soc. N.Y., Navy Memphis Ofcls. Assn., Am. Legion, Alpha Beta Gamma. Republican. Baptist. Avocations: volleyball, football, coin collecting, computers. Home: 5823 Port Haven Rd Millington TN 38053-8413 Office: Naval Support Activity 7300 3d Ave Millington TN 38054

LE DAIN, GERALD ERIC, retired Canadian Supreme Court justice; b. Montreal, Que., Can., Nov. 27, 1924; s. Eric George and Antoinette Louise (Whithard) Le D.; m. Cynthia Roy, Sept. 13, 1947; children—Jacqueline, Catherine, Barbara, Caroline, Eric, Jennifer. B.C.L., McGill U., Montreal, 1949; LLD (hon.), McGill U., 1985; Docteur del'Universite, U. Lyon, France, 1950; LL.D. (hon.), York U., Toronto, 1976, Concordia U., Montreal, 1976; D.C.L. (hon.), Acadia U., N.S., 1978. Bar: Que. 1949, Ont. 1968; created Queen's counsel 1961. Asso. prof. law McGill U., 1953-59, prof., 1966-67; dean, prof. Osgoode Hall Law Sch., York U., 1967-72, prof., 1972-75; practiced law with Walker, Martineau & Co., Montreal, 1950-53; with legal dept. CDN Internat Pap Co., Montreal, 1959-61; ptnr. Riel, LeDain & Co., Montreal, 1961-66; judge Fed. Ct. of Appeal of Can., Ottawa, Ont., 1975-84; judge Supreme Ct. Can., Ottawa, 1984-88, ret., 1988. Contbr. articles to legal jours. Chmn. Commn. of Inquiry Into Non-Med. Use of Drugs (Le Dain Commn.), 1969-73. Served with arty. Can. Army, 1943-46, France, Germany. Recipient Elizabeth Torrance Gold medal McGill U., 1949, Companion of the Order of Can., 1989, Justice Gerald LeDain award, Drug Policy Found., ,1990; MacDonald Travelling scholar, 1949-50. Club: Rideau (Ottawa).

LEDBETTER, CALVIN REVILLE, JR. (CAL LEDBETTER), political science educator, university dean, former legislator; b. Little Rock; s. Calvin Reville Sr. and Virginia Mae (Campbell) L.; m. Mary Brown Williams, July 26, 1953; children: Grainger, Jeffrey (dec.), Snow. BA, Princeton U., 1951; LLB, U. Ark., 1954; PhD, Northwestern U., 1960. Bar: Ark., 1954. Pvt. practice Little Rock, 1954; mem. faculty dept. polit. sci. U. Ark., Little Rock, 1960—, now prof., head dept., 1968-78, dean, 1978-88; cons. law enforcement program, advisor pre-law program; mem. Ark. Ho. of Reps., 1967-76; chmn. spl. legis. com., com. on legis. orgn.; vice chmn. legis. com. state agys. and govt. affairs; cons. pub. schs.; mem. Nat. Adv. Com. on Criminal Justice Goals and Standards; mem. adv. com. Nat. Inst. Law Enforcement and Criminal Justice.; election night analyst for Ark. congl. and Presdl. elections ABC, 1964-84. Co-author: Politics in Arkansas: The Constitutional Experience, 1972, The Arkansas Plan: A Case Study in Public Policy, 1979, Arkansas Becomes a State, 1985, Carpenter from Conway: George W. Donaghey as Governor of Arkansas 1909-1913, 1993; contbr. articles, book reviews to profl. jours. Mem. Ark. Adv. Coun. on Pub., Elem. and Secondary Edn.; Gov.'s rep. So. Regional Growth Policies Bd.; mem. Ark. Legis. Coun.; del. Ark. Constl. Conv., 1979, v.p., 1979-80; chmn. law enforcement and criminal justice task force Nat. Legis. Conf. Former chmn. coll. and univ. sect. United Fund; del. Dem. Nat. Conv., 1968, 84; mem. exec. com. Ark. Young Dems.; bd. dirs. Health and Welfare Coun. Pulaski County; trustee Philander Smith Coll., chmn. council community advisers; sec. bd. dirs. St. Vincent's Infirmary; bd. dirs. Ark. Humanities Coun., 1989-93, v.p., 1991-93, pres. 1993-94; bd. trustees Ark. Mus. Sci. and History. Served with JAGC AUS, 1955-57. Recipient award for outstanding contbn. to humanities Little Rock Arts and Humanities Commn., 1993; named Educator of Yr., Greater Little Rock Fedn. Women's Clubs, 1968. Mem. ABA, Ark. Bar Assn. (Writing Excellence award 1985-86), Pulaski County Bar Assn., Nat. Conf. State Legislators (exec. com.), Nat. Conf. Acad. Deans (pres. 1987-88), Am. Polit. Sci. Assn., So. Polit. Sci. Assn., Ark. Polit. Sci. Assn. (pres. 1980-81), Ark. Acad. Sci., Am. Acad. Polit. and Social Sci., Ark. Hist. Assn., Ark. Edn. Assn., Pulaski County Hist. Soc. (bd. dirs. 1988-90), Ark. Hist. Commn. (v.p. 1989—, pres. 1990—), Rotary (pres. West Little Rock chpt. 1987-88). Presbyterian. Home: 4322 I St Little Rock AR 72205-2054 Office: Univ Ark Little Rock Polit Sci Dept Little Rock AR 72204

LEDBETTER, DAVID OSCAR, lawyer; b. Santa Rosa, Calif., Mar. 16, 1950; s. Oscar Smith Ledbetter and Nova Nell (Huckaby) Kramer; m. Judith Louise Fischer, Dec. 14, 1976; children: Hannah J., Jordan B. BA, U. Redlands, 1972; JD, Hastings Coll. Law, 1977. Bar: Calif. 1977, D.C. 1986, Va. 1987. Assoc. Moran, Urich & Evans, San Francisco, 1977-79; trial atty. land and natural resource divsn. U.S. Dept. Justice, Washington, 1979-85; assoc., counsel, ptnr. Hunton & Williams, Richmond, Va., 1985—; bd. adv. Chem. Waste Litigation Reporter, Washington, 1983—. Co-author: Environmental Law Practice Guide, 1996; co-author, editor: Outline RCRA, Cercla Enforcement Issues and Holdings, 1996-97; contbr. articles to profl. jours. Bd. dirs. John Tyler C.C. Found., Chester, Va., 1992—; edn. adv. coun. Charles City (Va.) County Vocat., 1990—. Mem. ABA (vice chair spl. com. toxic and environ. torts), Va. State Bar Assn., Calif. Bar Assn., Bar Assn. D.C., Environ. Law Inst., Charles City Ruritan Club. Democrat. Methodist. Avocations: gardening, fishing. Home: 16530 The Glebe Ln Charles City VA 23030-3837 Office: Hunton & Williams 951 E Byrd St Richmond VA 23219-4040

LEDBETTER, DEIDRE LEDAY, special education educator; b. New Orleans, Oct. 16, 1959; d. Felton Clark Augusta and Frances Ada (Norman) Provost; m. Robert Leday, June 8, 1975 (dec. Aug. 1976); 1 child, Demetria Marie; m. George Dallas Ledbetter, Jr., Feb. 7, 1981. B Gen. Studies in Behavioral Scis., U. Southwestern La., 1982, BA in Spl. Edn., 1993, MEd in Guidance and Counseling, 1996. Resource tchr. Iberia Parish Sch. Bd., New Iberia, La., 1982-94, link cons., 1994—; mem. core com. Very Spl. Arts Festival, New Iberia, 1990-94. Active Coun. for Exceptional Children. Named Tchr. of Yr., Lee Street Elem. Sch., 1994. Mem. NEA, La. Assn. Educators, Iberia Assn. Educators (sec. 1989-90), Order Ea. Star, Order of Cyrene (royal Magdalene 1991—), Heroines of Jericho (vice ancient matron 1990—). Democrat. Methodist. Avocations: travel, sewing, cooking, photography. Home: 1007 Bank Ave New Iberia LA 70560 Office: Iberia Parish Spl Edn Dept PO Box 200 New Iberia LA 70560

LEDDICOTTE, GEORGE COMER, business executive, consultant; b. Oak Ridge, Tenn., May 28, 1947; s. George W. Leddicotte and Virginia (Comer) Leddicotte Stratton; m. Connie Laverne Sterrett, Jan. 25, 1969; 1 child, Matthew Sterrett. BA in Polit. Sci., U. Mo., 1970. Cert. relocation profl. Customer service supr. Crown Zellerbach, San Francisco, 1973-74; exec. recruiter Christopher & Long, St. Louis, 1974; regional ops. mgr. Curtin Matheson Scientific, Inc., Houston, 1974-80; regional mgr., mng. cons. Merrill Lynch Relocation Mgmt., White Plains, N.Y., 1980-82, regional v.p., nat. accounts, 1982-83, regional v.p. govt. svcs., 1983-84; dir. govt. svcs. Coldwell Banker Relocation Mgmt., Washington, 1984-85; dir. sales., account mgmt. Homequity, Wilton, Conn., 1985-87; v.p. nat. sales Premier Relocation Svcs., Inc., Irvine, Calif., 1987-88; v.p., sr. mng. cons. Premier Decision Mgmt., Irvine, 1988—; pres., CEO Feasiblility Relocation Mgmt. Svcs., Inc., Raleigh, N.C., 1988—; pres., COO Carolina Relocation Group, Rocky Mount, N.C., 1994. Pub. Relocation Update, 1993-95. First lt. U.S. Army, 1970-72, Korea. Mem. Am. Mktg. Assn., Am. Mgmt. Assn., Soc. for Human Resource Mgmt., Employee Relocation Coun. Avocations: sailing, golf, skiing. Home and Office: Feasibility Relocation Mgmt Svcs Inc 8000 Glenbrittle Way Raleigh NC 27615-4737

LEDDY, SUSAN, nursing educator; b. N.J., Feb. 23, 1939; d. Bert B. and Helen (Neumann) Kun; children: Deborah, Erin. BS, Skidmore Coll., 1960; MS, Boston U., 1965; PhD, NYU, 1973; cert., Harvard U., 1985. Chair dept. nursing Mercy Coll., Debbs Ferry, N.Y.; dean sch. nursing U. Wyo., Laramie, dean coll. health scis.; prof. Widener U. Sch. Nursing, Chester, Pa., 1988—, dean, 1988-93. Author: (with M. Pepper) Conceptual Bases of Professional Nursing, 1985, 3rd edit., 1993. Bd. dirs. Springfield Hosp., 1992-94. Postdoctoral fellow U. Pa., 1994-96. Mem. NLN (bd. dirs. and 1st v.p. 1985-87).

LEDE, RICHARD, investment company executive; b. N.Y.C., Mar. 9, 1946; s. Joseph Henry Lede and Anna Mae (O'Donnell) Lede Nichols; m.

Maribeth Ann Foster, Nov. 24, 1983; 1 stepchild, Lauren C. Kruta. BA, U. Tampa, 1968; student, Stetson U., 1968. Guest rels. staff Nat. Broadcasting Co., 1968-69; pres. Howle Film Prodns. Ltd., N.Y.C., 1969-73, also bd. dirs.; pres. Delmar Entertainment Corp., N.Y.C., L.A., 1973-83, also bd. dirs.; v.p. Fundamental Brokers U.K., London, 1983-86, MKI Securities Corp., London, 1986-88, Liberty Brokerage, N.Y.C., 1988-92; exec. v.p. S.E. Regional Securities, West Palm Beach, Fla., 1992-93, also bd. dirs.; exec. v.p. Hillman, Lede and Co. Inc., Wets Palm Beach, 1993—, also vice chmn. bd. dirs.; mng. dir. Seaboard Securities Inc., 1994-96; pres. Crown Fin. Assocs., Palm Beach, Fla., 1995—; 5 Crown Capital advisors, Palm Beach, 1995—. Non-lawyer mem. Fla. Bar. Griefance Com. Mem. West Palm Beach C. of C., Palm Beach Yacht Club, Mayacoo Lakes Country Club (bd. govs.), Moor Park Gold Club (London), Sigma Phi Epsilon. Avocations: golfing, shooting, big game saltwater fishing. Home: 2452 Seaford Dr Wellington FL 33414-6241 Office: Crown Fin Assocs 250 Royal Palm Way Palm Beach FL 33480-4309

LEDEBUR, LINAS VOCKROTH, JR., retired lawyer; b. New Brighton, Pa., June 18, 1925; s. Linas Vockroth and Mae (McCabe) L.; m. Conne Ryan, July 3, 1969; children: Gary W., Sally, Nancy, Sandra. Student, Geneva Coll., Beaver Falls, Pa., 1943, 45-46, Muhlenberg Coll., Allentown, Pa., 1943-44; J.D., U. Pitts., 1949. Bar: Pa. 1950. Assoc., then ptnr. Ledebur, McClain & Ledebur, New Brighton, 1950-63; trust mktg. mgr. Valley Nat. Bank Ariz., Phoenix, 1963-72; ptnr. Ledebur & Ledebur, New Brighton, 1972-76; sr. v.p., mgr. state trust div. Fla. Nat. Banks Fla., Inc., Jacksonville, 1976-81; sr. v.p. Fla. Nat. Bank, Jacksonville, 1977-81; pres. Northeastern Trust Co. Fla., N.A., Vero Beach, 1982-86; exec. v.p. PNC Trust Co. Fla., N.A., 1986-87; sole practice Beaver, Pa., 1987-96; master in divorce Beaver County, Pa., 1990-96; ret., 1996; instr. bus. law Geneva Coll., 1951-52, 88-96; past pres. Ctrl. Ariz. Estate Planning Coun. Chmn. Beaver County chpt. Nat. Found.-March of Dimes, Pa., 1950-63; chmn. com. corrections Pa. Citizens Assn., 1958-63; bd. dirs., counsel Beaver County Mental Health Assn., 1962-63; bd. dirs. Maricopa County chpt. ARC, Ariz. 1968-72. Served with USMC, 1943-45, 51-53. Mem. ABA, Pa. Bar Assn. Home: 652 Bank St Beaver PA 15009-2728

LEDEEN, ROBERT WAGNER, neurochemist, educator; b. Denver, Aug. 19, 1928; s. Hyman and Olga (Wagner) L.; m. Lydia Rosen Hailparn, July 2, 1982. B.S., U. Calif., Berkeley, 1949; Ph.D., Oreg. State U., 1953. Postdoctoral fellow in chemistry U. Chgo., 1953-54; rsch. assoc. in chemistry Mt. Sinai Hosp., N.Y.C., 1956-59; rsch. fellow Albert Einstein Coll. Medicine, Bronx, N.Y., 1959; asst. prof. Albert Einstein Coll. Medicine, 1963-69, assoc. prof., 1969-75, prof., 1975-91; prof., dir. div. neurochemistry U. Medicine and Dentistry N.J., Newark, 1991—. Contbr. articles to profl. jours.; dep. chief editor Jour. Neurochemistry. Mem. neurol. scis. study sect. NIH; mem. study sect. Nat. Multiple Sclerosis Soc. NIH grantee, 1963—; Nat. Multiple Sclerosis Soc. grantee, 1967-74; recipient Humboldt prize, Javits Neurosci. Investigator award. Mem. Internat. Soc. Neurochemistry, Am. Soc. Neurochemistry, Am. Chem. Soc., Am. Soc. Biol. Chemists, N.Y. Acad. Sci. Jewish. Achievements include discoveries in the biochemistry of brain glycolipids and myelin. Home: 8 Donald Ct Wayne NJ 07470-4608 Office: U Medicine and Dentistry NJ Dept Neuroscis 185 S Orange Ave Newark NJ 07103-2714

LEDER, MIMI, television director; b. N.Y.C., Jan. 26, 1952; d. Paul and Etyl Leder; m. Gary Werntz, Feb. 6, 1986; 1 child, Hannah. Student, Los Angeles City College, Am. Film Inst. Dir. TV movies A Little Piece of Heaven (also known as Honor Bright), 1991, Woman with a Past, 1992, Rio Shannon, 1992, Marked for Murder, 1992, There Was a Little Boy, 1993, House of Secrets, 1993, The Sandman, 1993; dir. TV series L.A. Law, 1986, Midnight Caller, 1988, A Year in the Life, 1988, Buck James, 1988, Just in Time, 1988, Crime Story, 1988; supervising prodr. China Beach, 1988-91 (Emmy nominations for outstanding drama series 1989, 90, and outstanding directing in drama series 1990, 91), Nightingales, 1989, ER, 1994— (Emmy award 1995). Mem. Dirs. Guild Am. *

LEDER, PHILIP, geneticist, educator; b. Washington, Nov. 19, 1934; married; 3 children. A.B., Harvard U., 1956, M.D., 1960. Research assoc. Nat. Heart Inst., Nat. Cancer Inst.; lab chief molecular genetics Nat. Inst. Child Health and Human Devel., NIH, 1972-80; prof. genetics Harvard U. Med. Sch., Boston, Mass., 1980—, now John Emory Andrus prof. genetics; sr. investigator Howard Hughes Med. Inst. Co-author: Molecular Basis of Blood Diseases, 1987; co-editor: Molecular Medicine, 1994. Recipient Albert Lasker Med. Rsch. award, 1987, Nat. Medal of Sci., 1989. Mem. NAS, Inst. Medicine. *

LEDER, SANDRA JUANITA, elementary school educator; b. Stuttgart, Ark., Apr. 17, 1942; d. Everett Samuel and Lorene (Payer) L. BS, U. Cen. Ark., 1963; MEd, McNeese State U., 1976, EdS, 1979; PhD, Fla. State U., 1984. Cert. tchr. grades 1-8, supr., prin., aerospace edn., supr. student tchrs., La.; cert. pvt. pilot. Elem. tchr. DeWitt (Ark.) Pub. Schs., 1963-66, Gillett (Ark.) Pub. Schs., 1966-69; math. tchr. Tulsa County, Tulsa, Okla., 1970; tchr. Calcasieu Parish, Lake Charles, La., 1971-94, Episcopal Day Sch., Lake Charles, La., 1994—; guest instr. McNeese State U., 1995, 96; condr., dir. numerous aerospace camps, 1980—; chmn., judge sci. fairs; com. mem. and chmn. self-study com. So. Assn. Colls. and Schs., 1985-86; arranger numerous tours and workshops in field. Manuscript rev. panel Sci. Scope, 1988-91, writer, 1992; TV interviews, 1991—; radio and ednl. TV appearances, Tchr. in Space applicant, 1985; contbr. Metric Curriculum Guide for La., 1978; presenter in field; contbr. articles to profl. jours. Vol. reader NEA, 1990; active outreach com. Episcopal Ch. of Good Shepherd, 1994; pres. Lake Charles Regional Airport Authority, 1991, 95, sec., 1993, v.p., 1994, pres., 1995; mem. gen. adv. coun. Sowela Tech. Inst., 1990; active Mayor's Commn. for Women, 1986-91, fall conf. chmn. resource fair, 1988; founder Lake Charles Ninety-Nines Challenger Ctr.; pres. La. Nat. Airshow Bd., 1993—, sec., 1993—; bd. dirs. Chenault Airpark Aviation Mus., 1994-96; tour organizer. Recipient S.W. Region Frank Brewer Aerospace Edn. award CAP, 1990, Excellence in Aviation Edn. Championship award S.W. region FAA, 1989, Acad. Edn. award Women's History Month, Lake Charles, Great Expectations Tchr. award Sta. KPLC-TV, 1993, Pinnacle award, 1993, NEWMAST award NASA, 1986, STEP award, 1993, Outstanding Young Astronaut Chpt. Leader award, 1993; grantee Space Acad., 1988, South Ctrl. Bell, 1991, 93, Olin Corp., 1994, 95, 96. Mem. Nat. Sci. Tchrs. Assn., Nat. Space Soc., La. Assn. Educators (del. to convs. 1977-79, 84, 86), Aircraft Owners and Pilots Assn., Delta Kappa Gamma (pres. 1992-94, legis. com. 1985-86, chair social com. 1987-89, comms. com. chair 1990, 94-95), Kappa Kappa Iota, Phi Delta Kappa. Republican. Episcopalian. Office: Episcopal Day Sch Ch of Good Shepherd 715 Kirkman St Lake Charles LA 70601-4350

LEDERBERG, JOSHUA, geneticist, educator; b. Montclair, N.J., May 23, 1925; s. Zwi Hirsch and Esther (Goldenbaum) L.; m. Marguerite S. Kirsch, Apr. 5, 1968; children: David Kirsch, Anne. BA, Columbia U., 1944; PhD, Yale U., 1947. With U. Wis., 1947-58; prof. genetics Sch. Medicine, Stanford (Calif.) U., 1959-78; pres. Rockefeller U., N.Y.C., 1978-90, univ. prof. Sackler Found. scholar, 1990—; adj. prof. Columbia U., 1990—; mem. adv. com. med. rsch. WHO, 1971; mem. bd. sci. advisors SAIC, McLean, Va., Antigenics, N.Y., Affymax N.V., Palo Alto, Aviron, Mountain View, Calif.; cons. U.S. Def. Sci. Bd., NSF, NIH, NASA, ACDA. Trustee Camille and Henry Dreyfus Found.; bd. dirs. Chem. Industry Inst. Toxicology, N.C. With USN, 1943-45. Recipient Nobel prize in physiology and medicine for rsch. in genetics of bacteria, 1958, U.S. Nat. Medal of Sci., 1989, Alan Newell award ACM, 1996. Fellow AAAS, Am. Philos. Soc., Am. Acad. Arts and Scis., N.Y. Acad. Medicine (hon.), Acad. Universelle Cultures (Paris); mem. Inst. Medicine NAS, Coun. Fgn. Rels., Royal Soc. London (fgn.), N.Y. Acad. Scis. (hon. life gov.), Ordre des Lettres et des Arts (comdr.). Office: Rockefeller U 1230 York Ave Ste 400 New York NY 10021-6307

LEDERBERG, VICTORIA, judge, former state legislator, lawyer, psychology educator; b. Providence, July 7, 1937; d. Frank and Victoria (Marzilli) Santopietro; m. Seymour Lederberg, 1959; children: Tobias, Sarah. AB, Pembroke Coll., 1959; AM, Brown U., 1961, PhD, 1966; JD, Suffolk U., 1976, LLD, 1995. Mem. R.I. Ho. of Reps., 1975-82, chmn. subcom. on edn., fin. com., 1975-82, subcom. on mental health, retardation and hosps. and health, spl. legis. commns pub. sch. funding and funding handicapped edn. programs; chmn. nat. adv. panel on financing elem. and sec. edn., Washington, 1979-82; mem. R.I. State Senate, 1985-91, chmn. fin. com. subcom. on social svcs., 1985-89, dep. majority leader, 1989-91; prof. psychology R.I. Coll., 1978-93; pvt. practice, Providence; mcpl. ct. judge, Providence, 1991-93; justice R.I. Supreme Court, Providence, 1993—, chmn. com. on judicial performance evaluation, 1993—, chmn. com. on user-friendly cts., 1994—. USPHS Fellow physiol. psychology, 1964-66. Trustee Brown U., 1983-89, Roger Williams U., 1980—, vice chmn. corp., dir. Sch. Law, Butler Hosp., 1985-93, also sec. of corp. Mem. New Eng. Psychol. Assn., ABA, R.I. Bar Assn., Am. Judicature Soc., Nat. Assn. Women Judges, Sigma Xi. Office: 250 Benefit St Providence RI 02903-2719

LEDERER, EDITH MADELON, journalist; b. N.Y.C., Mar. 27, 1943; d. Samuel B. Weiner and Frieda (Rich) Weiner Lederer; adopted d. Irving A. Lederer. B.S. with distinction, Cornell U., 1963; M.A., Stanford, 1964. With Sci. Service, Washington, 1964-65; free-lance writer, 1965-66; mem. staff AP, 1966—, South Vietnam, 1972-73; chief bur. AP, Lima, Peru, 1975; chief Caribbean services, San Juan, P.R., 1975-78; corr. Hong Kong, 1978-81, Nairobi, 1981-82, London, 1982-90, 91—; corr. Gulf War, Saudi Arabia, 1990-91. Recipient resolution Calif. Assembly, 1974, Nat. Press Club award, 1993, Nat. Headliner award, 1994, Journalism Honor medal for disting. svc. in journalism U. Mo. Sch. Journalism, 1996. Mem. Mortar Bd., Internat. Women's Media Found., Overseas Press Club, Phi Kappa Phi, Omicron Nu, Sigma Delta Chi. Address: care Asso Press 50 Rockefeller Plz New York NY 10020-1605 *Women should take more risks to live their dreams, which otherwise turn to nightmares of frustration as empty years pass. It is better to fail and touch the essence of life than to stand forever on the threshold as a gutless spectator.*

LEDERER, MRS. ESTHER P. See LANDERS, ANN

LEDERER, JEROME, aerospace safety consultant, engineer; b. N.Y.C., Sept. 26, 1902; m. Sarah Bojarsky, Nov. 1, 1935; children: Nancy, Susan. BSc in Mech. Engring., NYU, 1924, M.Engring., 1925. Registered profl. engr., N.Y. Aero engr. USAir mail svc., 1926-27; chief engr. Aero Ins. Underwriters, N.Y.C., 1929-40; dir. safety bur. CAB, Washington, 1940-42; mgr. Airlines War Tng. Inst., 1942-44, U.S. Strategic Bombing Survey, 1945; pres., Flight Safety found., 1947-67, pres. emeritus, 1967—; dir. Cornell-Guggenheim Aviation Safety Rsch. Ctr., N.Y.C., 1950-67; dir. Office Manned Space Flight Safety, NASA, Washington, 1967-70, dir. safety, 1970-72; ret., 1972; adj. prof. Inst. Safety and System Mgmt., U. So. Calif., ret.; past mem. adv. council Inst. Nuclear Power Ops., Atlanta, 1980-85; cons., Laguna Hills, Calif., 1974—. Author books and articles on aviation and space safety. Recipient NASA Exceptional Service medal, Daniel Guggenheim medal, Wright Bros. trophy, Amelia Earhart medal, Ziolkowski and Yuri Gagarin medals, Soviet Fedn. Cosmonauts, Von Baumhaüer medal Royal Dutch Aero. Soc., Laura Taber Barbour award, many others; named to Safety and Health Hall of Fame Internat., OX5 Club Hall of Fame, Internat. Space Hall of Fame. Fellow AIAA (hon., Life Achievement award 1997), Am. Astronautics Assn., Soc. Automotive Engrs., Royal Aero. Soc., Human Factors Soc.; mem. NAE, Airline Pilots Assn. (hon.), Mil. Order Daedalions (hon.), Wings Club (N.Y.). Home: 468 Calle Cadiz Laguna Hills CA 92653-3933

LEDERER, MARION IRVINE, cultural administrator; b. Brampton, Ont., Can., Feb. 10, 1920; d. Oliver Bateman and Eva Jane (MacMurdo) L.; m. Francis Lederer, July 10, 1941. Student, U. Toronto, 1938, UCLA, 1942-45. Owner Canoga Mission Gallery, Canoga Park, Calif., 1967—; cultural heritage monument Canoga Mission Gallery, 1974—; Vice pres. Screen Smart Set women's aux. Motion Picture and TV Fund, 1973—; founder sister city program Canoga Park-Taxco, Mexico, 1963; Mem. mayor's cultural task force San Fernando Valley, 1973—; mem. Los Angeles Cultural Affairs Commn., 1980-85. Mem. Los Angeles Cultural Affairs Commn., 1980-85. Recipient numerous pub. service awards from mayor, city council, C. of C. Mem. Canoga Park C. of C. (cultural chmn. 1973-75, dir. 1973-75). Presbyn. Home: PO Box 32 Canoga Park CA 91305-0032 Office: Canoga Mission Gallery 23130 Sherman Way Canoga Park CA 91307-1402

LEDERER, PETER DAVID, lawyer; b. Frankfurt, Germany, May 2, 1930; came to U.S., 1938; s. Leo and Alice (Freistadt) L.; m. Norma Jean Taylor, June, 1955 (div. 1966); 1 child, Patricia Ann; m. Midori Shimanouchi, Dec. 16, 1966. BA, U. Chgo., 1949, JD, 1957, M in Comparative Law, 1958. Bar: Ill. 1959, U.S. Supreme Ct. 1966, N.Y. 1967. Law and behavioral sci. rsch. fellow U. Chgo. Law Sch., 1958-59; ptnr. Baker & McKenzie, Zurich, Switzerland, 1960-66; ptnr. Baker & McKenzie, N.Y.C., 1966-94, of counsel, 1994—; dir. Nuc. Electric Ins. Ltd., Nuc. Mutual Ltd. Mem. vis. com. U. Miami Law Sch., Coral Gables, Fla., 1974—, U. Chgo. Law Sch., 1988-91; adv. bd. Wildlife Preservation Trust Internat., Phila.; dir. Asian-Am. Legal Def. & Edn. Fund, N.Y.C., The Midori Found.; pres. bd. trustees The Calhoun Sch., N.Y.C., 1980-83. With AUS, 1951-53. Mem. ABA, Assn. of Bar of City of N.Y. (chmn. com. on nuc. law 1978-81), Internat. Nuc. Law Assn. Office: Baker & McKenzie 805 3rd Ave Fl 29 New York NY 10022-7513

LEDERER, RICHARD HENRY, writer, educator, columnist; b. Phila., May 26, 1938; s. Howard Jules and Leah (Perry) L.; m. Rhoda Anne Spangenberg, Aug. 25, 1962 (div. 1986); m. Simone Johanna van Egeren, Nov. 29, 1991; children: Howard Henry, Anne Labarr, Katherine Lee. BA, Haverford Coll., 1959; student, Harvard U., 1959-60, M of Arts and Teaching, 1962; PhD, U. N.H., 1980. Tchr., coach St. Paul's Sch., Concord, N.H., 1962-89; lectr. in field. Author: Anguished English, 1987, Get Thee to a Punnery, 1988, Crazy English, 1989, The Play of Words, 1990, The Miracle of Language, 1991, More Anguished English, 1993, Building Bridge, 1994, Adventures of a Verbivore, 1994, Literary Trivia, 1994, Nothing Risqué, Nothing Gained, 1995, The Write Way, 1995, Pun and Games, 1996, Fractured English, 1996; weekly columnist Looking at Lang.; contbr. more than 2000 articles to mags. and jours.; broadcaster various radio stas.; numerous TV appearances. Recipient Lifetime Achievement award Columbia Scholastic Press Assn., N.Y.C., 1989; named Internat. Punster of Yr. Internat. Save the Pun Found., Toronto, Can., 1990; Paul Harris Rotary fellow. Mem. Am. Mensa, Phi Beta Kappa, Phi Delta Kappa. Avocations: tennis, cards, film. Home: 10324 Caminito Agadir San Diego CA 92131 *Whatever you hear about the closing of the American mind and cultural illiteracy, there has never been a more passionate moment in the history of the American love affair with language than right now. I'm exceedingly fortunate to have written books that embrace that passion.*

LEDERER, WILLIAM JULIUS, author; b. N.Y.C., Mar. 31, 1912; s. William J. and Paula (Franken) L.; m. Ethel Hackett, Apr. 21, 1940 (div. Jan. 1965); children: Brian, Jonathan, Bruce; m. Corinne Edwards Lewis, July 1965 (div. May 1976). B.S., U.S. Naval Acad., 1936; assoc. Nieman fellow, Harvard U., 1950-51. Enlisted USN, 1930, commd. ensign, 1936, advanced through grades to capt., 1952, ret., 1958; Far East corr. Reader's Digest, 1958-63; lectr. colls. and univs., 1949—. Author in residence, Harvard U., 1966-67; Author: All the Ship's at Sea, 1950, The Last Cruise, 1950, Spare Time Article Writing for Money, 1953, Ensign O'Toole and Me, 1957, A Nation of Sheep, 1961, Timothy's Song, 1965, Pink Jade, 1966, (with Eugene Burdick) The Ugly American, 1958, Sarkhan, 1965, Our Own Worst Enemy, 1967, (with Don D. Jackson) The Mirages of Marriage, 1968, (with Joe Pete Wilson) Complete Cross-Country Skiing and Ski Touring, 1970, (with others) Marriage for and Against, Marital Choices, A Happy Book of Happy Stories, I, Giorghos, 1984, Creating a Good Relationship, 1984. Mem. Signet Soc., Authors Guild, Acad. Orthomolecular Psychiatry, European Acad. Preventive Medicine, Internat. Acad. Preventive Medicine, Internat. Coll. Applied Nutrition, Lotos Club, Trap Door Spiders Club, Harvard Faculty Club, Sigma Delta Chi. Home (winter): 1350 Mayflower Ave Melbourne FL 32940 Home (summer): PO Box 748 Peacham VT 05862 *If one works at being joyful and physically functional, almost everything else seems to come along on its own. Put energy into the "here and now" and do not distract from it by worrying about either the past or the future.*

LEDERIS, KAROLIS PAUL (KARL LEDERIS), pharmacologist, educator, researcher; b. Noreikoniai, Lithuania, Aug. 1, 1920; arrived in Can., 1969; s. Paul Augustus and Franciska (Danisevicius) L.; m. Hildegard Gallistl, Feb. 28, 1952; children: Aldona Franciska, Edmund Paul. Diploma, Tchrs. Coll., Siauliai, Lithuania, 1939; BSc, U. Bristol, U.K., 1958, PhD, 1961, DSc, 1968. Jr. lectr., then lectr. and reader U. Bristol, 1961-69; prof. pharmacology and therapeutics U. Calgary, Alta., Can., 1969-89, prof. emeritus, 1989—; vis. prof. univs. in Fed. Republic Germany, Austria, Chile, Argentina, Sri Lanka, Switzerland, Lithuania, France, , USA, USSR, 1963-79, U. Bristol, 1979, U. Kyoto, Japan, 1980; career investigator, mem., chair grants com. Med. Rsch. Coun., Ottawa, Ont., Can., 1970-89, coun. mem., exec., 1983-90; mem. internat. com. Centres Excellence Networks, Ottawa, 1988-89. Author, editor: 5 books on hypothalamic hormones; editor in chief Jour. Exptl. and Clin. Pharmacology, 1977-89; contbr. approximately 350 book chpts. and articles to profl. jours.; patentee hormonal peptides. Recipient Upjohn award in pharmacology, 1990, various fellowships and scholarships in U.K., Fed. Republic of Germany, U.S. Fellow NAS, Royal Soc. Can.; mem. Western Pharmacological Soc. (pres. 1982-83), pharm., physiol., endocrinological, biochem. socs. U.K., Can., U.S., Lithuanian Club (London), Men's Can. Club, Cabot Yacht and Cruise Club (Bristol). Avocations: music, sailing, fishing, hunting, golf. Home: 147 Carthew St, Comox, BC Canada V9M 1T4 Office: U Calgary, Health Scis Centre, Calgary, AB Canada T2N 4N1

LEDERMAN, FRANK L., scientist, research center administrator; b. Buffalo, Aug. 19, 1949; s. Sol J. and Carol S. (Dankman) L.; m. Daphna Kaplansky, Aug. 8, 1993. BS in Math., Carnegie-Mellon U., 1971, MS in Physics, 1971; MS in Physics, U. Ill., 1972, PhD, 1975. Fellow U. Pa., Phila., 1975; physicist R & D ctr. GE Corp., Schenectady, N.Y., 1976-78, mgr. ultrasound program, 1978-80, mgr. energy systems mgmt. br., 1981-82, acting mgr. liaison ops., 1983-84, mgr. power electronics systems br., 1984-87, mgr. programs and resources, 1988; v.p., dir. rsch. Noranda Inc., Pointe Claire, Que., Can., 1988-91, sr. v.p. tech., 1992-95; v.p., chief tech. officer Aluminum Co. Am., Alcoa Center, Pa., 1995—. Contbr. articles to profl. jours.; patentee in field. Mem. IEEE, Indsl. Rsch. Inst., Am. Phys. Soc. Home: 4011 Pin Oak Ln Murrysville PA 15668 Office: Alcoa Tech Ctr 100 Technical Dr Alcoa Center PA 15069

LEDERMAN, LAWRENCE, lawyer, writer, educator; b. N.Y.C., Sept. 8, 1935; s. Herman Jack and Lillian (Rosenfeld) L.; children: Leandra, Evin. B.A., Bklyn. Coll., 1957; LL.B., N.Y.U., 1966. Bar: N.Y. 1968; Law clk. chief justice Calif. Sup. Ct., 1966-67; assoc. Cravath, Swaine & Moore, N.Y.C., 1968-74; ptnr. Wachtell, Lipton, Rosen & Katz, N.Y.C., 1975-91; ptnr., chmn. corp. practice Milbank, Tweed, Hadley & McCloy, 1991—; adj. prof. law N.Y.U. Sch. Law, 1974—; Chmn. bd. Phoenix House Devel. Corp., mem. Phoenix House Found. Author: Tombstones: A Lawyer's Tales from the Takeover Decades, 1992. Bd. dirs. One to One Partnership Inc., N.Y. Botanical Garden. Served with U.S. Army, 1957-59. Mem. ABA, N.Y. State Bar Assn., Order of the Coif . Contbr. articles to profl. jours. Office: Milbank Tweed Hadley & McCloy 1 Chase Manhattan Plz New York NY 10005-1401

LEDERMAN, LEON MAX, physicist, educator; b. N.Y.C., July 15, 1922; s. Morris and Minna (Rosenberg) L.; m. Florence Gordon, Sept. 19, 1945; children: Rena S., Jesse A., Heidi R.; m. Ellen Carr, Sept. 17, 1981. BS, CCNY, 1943, DSc (hon.), 1980; AM, Columbia U., 1948, PhD, 1951; DSc (hon.), No. Ill. U., 1984, U. Chgo., 1985, Ill. Inst. Tech., 1987. Assoc. in physics Columbia U., N.Y.C., 1951, asst. prof., 1952-54, assoc. prof., 1954-58, prof., 1958-89, Eugene Higgins prof. physics, 1972-79; Frank L. Sulzberger prof. physics U. Chgo., 1989-92; dir. Fermi Nat. Accelerator Lab., Batavia, Ill., 1979-89, dir. emeritus, 1989—; Pritzker prof. sci. Ill. Inst. Tech., Chgo., 1992—; dir. Nevis Labs., Irvington, N.Y., 1962-79; guest scientist Brookhaven Nat. Labs., 1955; cons. Nat. Accelerator Lab., European Orgn. for Nuclear Rsch. (CERN), 1970—; mem. high energy physics adv. panel AEC, 1966-70; mem. adv. com. to div. math. and phys. scis. NSF, 1970-72; sci. advisor to gov. State of Ill., 1989-93; chmn. XXIV Internat. Physics Olympiad, 1991-93. Author: Quarks to the Cosmos, 1989, The God Particle, 1993; also over 200 articles. Bd. dirs. Mus. Sci. Industry, Chgo., 1989—, Weizmann Inst. Sci., Israel, 1988—; trustee Univ. Rsch. Assocs., 1992—; mem. adv. bd. Sec. of Energy, 1991—. Recipient Nat. Medal of Sci., 1965, Townsend Harris medal CUNY, 1973, Elliot Cresson medal Franklin Inst., 1976, Wolf prize, 1982, Nobel prize in physics, 1988, Enrico Fermi prize, 1992, Rosenblith Lecturer in Science and Technology Nat. Acad. of Sciences, 1995, Pres.'s medal CCNY, 1993, 34 additional hon. degrees including univs. and acads. in Finland, Eng., Italy, Argentina, Mex., Brazil, and Peru; Guggenheim fellow, 1958-59, Ford Found. fellow European Ctr. for Nuclear Rsch., Geneva, 1958-59, fellow NSF, 1967, Presdl. fellow World Bank, 1997. Fellow AAAS (pres. 1990-91, chmn. 1991-92), Am. Phys. Soc.; mem. NAS, Italian Phys. Soc., Aspen Inst. Physics (pres. 1990-92), Ill. Math. Sci. Acad. (vice chmn. 1985—), Tchrs. Acad. for Math. and Sci. in Chgo. (co-chmn. 1990—), Coun. Advancement Sci. Writing, Bulletin Atomic Scientists (vice chmn. 1989—). Office: Ill Inst Tech Dept Physics 3300 S Federal St Chicago IL 60616-3732

LEDERMAN, MARIE JEAN, English language educator; b. Bklyn., Dec. 28, 1935; d. Samuel and Gladys (Leeshutz) Candel; m. Theodore Lederman, June 28, 1957 (div. 1963); 1 child, Mark; m. Martin Benis, 1977. B.S. magna cum laude, NYU, 1957, Ph.D., 1966; M.A., Bklyn. Coll., 1963. Tchr. English, N.Y.C. Bd. Edn., 1957-59, cons., 1975-76, 78-79; instr. NYU, 1965-66; asst. prof. N.Y.C. Community Coll., 1966-68; asst. prof. SEEK program CUNY, 1968-69, successively asst. prof., assoc. prof., prof. Baruch Coll., 1969-79, 88-91, prof. emerita, 1991—, cons. chancellor's SEEK task force, 1975, univ. dean acad. affairs, 1979-85; dean for freshman skills La Guardia Community Coll., Long Island City, 1985-87; cons. Mohawk Valley Community Coll., Utica, N.Y., 1980, Tex. A&I U., 1984, U. Toronto, 1984, Framingham State Coll., 1987, Woodrow Wilson Fellowship Found., 1985, Dept. Higher Edn. State of N.J., 1989-91; cons. U. Minn., 1989-90. Chgo. State U., 1991-92. Exhibited works at Cork Gallery/Lincoln Ctr., Lever House, Pen and Brush Club, Salamagundi Club, Pace U., N.Y. Law Sch.; mem. editl. bd. Jour. Basic Writing, 1987-94; contbr. articles to profl. jours. Bd. dirs. Jean Cocteau Repertory Theatre, v.p., 1988—. Recipient CUNY faculty research award, 1976-78; Fund for Improvement of Postsecondary Edn. grantee, 1981-87. Mem. Internat. Sculpture Ctr., Nat. Sculpture Soc., Art Students League, Burr Artists (bd. dirs.). Democrat. Jewish.

LEDERMAN, PETER (BERND), environmental services executive, consultant; b. Weimar, Germany, Nov. 16, 1931; came to U.S., 1939, naturalized, 1945; s. Ernst M. and Irmgard R. (Heilbrunn) L.; m. Susan Sturc, Aug. 25, 1957; children: Stuart M., Ellen L. BSE, U. Mich., 1953, MSE, 1957, PhD, 1961. Instr., U. Mich., 1959-61; research engr. Esso Research Labs., Baton Rouge, La., 1961-63; sr. engr. Esso Research & Engring. Co., Florham Park, N.J., 1963-66; asso. prof. chem. engring. Poly. Inst. Bklyn., 1966-72, adj. prof., 1972-75; dir. Ind. Waste Treatment Research Lab., EPA, Edison, N.J., 1972-75, dir. indsl. and extractive processes research EPA, Washington, 1975-76; v.p. Cottrell Environ. Scis. Div., Research Cottrell, Bound Brook, N.J., 1976-80; v.p. hazard/toxic materials mgmt. Roy F. Weston, Inc., Edison, N.J., 1980-92; dir. Ctr. for Environ. Engring. and Sci. NJIT, Newark, 1993—, rsch. prof. chem. engring., 1993—, exec. dir. patents & licensing, 1995—; mem. NRC-Nat. Acad. Sci. Rev. Panel, Office Recycled Tech., U.S. Bur. Standards, 1980-83, mem. com. decontamination and decommissioning nuclear gaseous diffusion plants; mem. expert panel PCBs Agy. for Toxic Substances and Disease Registry. Mem. editorial bd. Environ. Progress, Chem. Engring. Progress, Hazardous Waste Mgmt. Jour. Mem. exec. bd. Watchung Area council Boy Scouts Am., 1970-86; assoc. editor AWMA Jour., mem. affirmative action adv. com. New Providence (N.J.) Bd. Edn., 1979-83. Served with AUS, 1953-55. Recipient Silver medal EPA, 1976. Fellow Am. Inst. Chem. Engrs. (chmn. profl. devel. com., chmn. govt. rels. com., chmn. N.J. sect., chair environ. div., Larry K. Cecil award 1987, dir. AIChE Found., Gary Leach award 1995, Environ. Divsn. Svc. award 1995); mem. ASME, AAAS, Am. Chem. Soc., Am. Soc. Engring. Edn., Nat. Soc. Profl. Engrs., Am. Acad. Environ. Engrs. (diplomate, trustee, Stanley Kappe award 1993), Am. Arbitration Assn., Am. Assn. of Eng. Soc. (chair environ. comm.), U. Mich. Engring. Alumni Soc. (chair, bd. dirs., Chem. Engring. Merit award 1996), Sigma Xi, Phi Kappa Phi, Phi Lambda Upsilon. Contbr. numerous articles on environ. regulations, solid waste mgmt., hazardous waste mgmt., computer tech. to profl. jours. Home: 17 Pittsford Way New Providence NJ 07974-2428 Office: NJIT Ctr Environ Engring & Sci Newark NJ 07102

LEDERMAN, SALLY ANN, nutrition educator and researcher; b. N.Y.C., July 8, 1937; d. Joseph Edward and Leanora (Galeski) Rossi; m. Lawrence

Lederman, Jan. 26, 1958 (div. Feb. 1991); children: Leandra, Evin. BS in Chemistry, Bklyn. Coll., 1957; MS in Nutrition, Columbia U., 1976, PhD, 1980. Analytical chemist U.S. FDA, N.Y.C., 1957-62; lectr. dept. chemistry Bklyn. Coll., 1962-66, 74; postdoctoral fellow Inst. Human Nutrition Columbia U., N.Y.C., 1980-83, postdoctoral fellow obstetrics and biochemistry, 1983, asst. prof. Sch. Pub. Health, 1983-90, assoc. prof. Sch. Pub. Health, 1990-94; prof. Tchrs. Coll., 1994—. Editor: Controversial Issues in Public Health Nutrition, 1983; contbr. articles to profl. jours. Mem. APHA, AAAS, Am. Inst. Nutrition, Am. Women in Sci., N.Y. Acad. Scis. Office: Columbia U Tchrs Coll Box 137 525 W 120th St New York NY 10027-6625

LEDERMAN, STEPHANIE BRODY, artist; b. N.Y.C.; d. Maxwell and Ann (Rockett) Brody. Student, U. Mich.; BS in Design, Finch Coll.; MA in Painting, L.I. U., 1975. One-person exhbns. Franklin Furnace, N.Y.C., 1979, Kathryn Markel Fine Arts, N.Y.C., 1979, 81, 83, Katzen/Brown Gallery, N.Y.C., 1988, 89, Real Artways, Hartford, Conn., 1984, Alfred U., 1990, Hal Katzen Gallery, N.Y.C., 1992, Hillwood Art Mus., Brookville, N.Y., 1992, Casements Mus., Ormond Beach, Fla., 1994, Broward Cmty. Coll., Ft. Lauderdale, Fla., 1994, Hebrew Home for the Aged, N.Y.C., 1994-95, Galerie Caroline Corre, Paris, 1995, La. State U., Shreveport, 1995, Marc Miller Gallery, East Hampton, N.Y., 1996, Pierogi 2000, Bklyn., 1996; exhibited in numerous group shows including Newark Mus., 1983, Met. Mus. Art, N.Y.C., 1986, Queens Mus., 1989, Basel Art Fair, 1989, Caroline Corre, Paris, 1991, R.I. Mus. Art, 1991, Am. Acad. Arts & Letters, N.Y.C., 1992, Guild Hall Mus., East Hampton, N.Y., 1993, Ind. U, Terre Haute, 1993, Jewish Mus., N.Y.C., 1994, Nat. Mus. Women in Arts, Washington, 1994, Ronald Feldman Gallery, N.Y.C., 1995, Alternative Mus., N.Y.C., 1995, Eugenia Cucalon, Gallery, N.Y.C., 1995, Rotunda Gallery, Bklyn., 1995, The Museums at Stony Brook, N.Y., 1996, Espace Eiffel-Branly, Paris, 1996, Fotouhi Cramer Gallery, N.Y.C., 1996, 123 Watts Gallery, N.Y.C., 1996, Les Mureaux, France, 1996, Medietèque, Les Mureaux, France, 1996, San Francisco State U., 1997, Isis Conceptual Lab., West Branch, Iowa, 1997, Harper Collins Exhbn. Space, N.Y.C., 1997; represented in permanent collections Newark Mus., Mus. Modern Art, Prudential Ins., Bertelsmann Music Group, Guild Hall Mus., East Hampton, L.I., Chase Manhattan Bank, N.Y. Health and Hosp. Corp., Victoria & Albert Mus., London, Doubleday Books. Recipient Hassam and Speicher purchase award Am. Acad. and Inst. Arts and Letters, 1988, purchase award Arts in Hosps., Richmond, Va.; grantee Creative Artists Pub. Svc., 1977, Ariana Found. for Arts, 1985, Artists Space, 1987, E.D. Found., 1991, Lancaster Group., U.S. A. Comm. award, 1991, spl. opportunity stipend N.Y. State Coun. Arts, 1992, 94, Heuss House project Lower Manhattan Cultural Coun., 1992. Studio: 85 N 3rd St Fl 5 Brooklyn NY 11211-3923

LEDERMAN, SUSAN STURC, public administration educator; b. Bratislava, Slovakia, May 28, 1937; came to U.S., 1948; d. Ludovit and Helen (Reich) Sturc; m. Peter Bernd Lederman, Aug. 25, 1957; children: Stuart, Ellen. AB in Polit. Sci., U. Mich., 1958; MA in Polit. Sci., Rutgers U., 1970, PhD in Polit. Sci., 1978. Vis. instr. Fairleigh Dickinson U., Madison, N.J., 1973-74, Drew U., Madison, 1975-76; from asst. prof. to assoc. prof. pub. adminstrn. Kean Coll., Union, N.J., 1977-89, prof., dir. MPA program, 1989—; vis. fellow Woodrow Wilson Sch., Princeton (N.J.) U., 1988-89. Co-author: (book) Elections in America—Control and Influence in Democratic Politics, 1980, (monograph) Campaign Watch: A Report on the 1992 Campaign Watch Project, 1993; editor: (book) The SLERP Reforms and Their Impact, 1989; contbr. articles to profl. jours. Mem. nat. gov. bd. Common Cause, Washington, 1994—; bd. dirs., sec.-treas. The Jefferson Ctr., Mpls., 1992—; dir. Regional Plan Assn., N.Y.C., 1991—; pres. LWV of N.J., 1985-89, program v.p., 1983-85, sec., fiscal policy dir., 1981-83, fiscal policy dir., 1979-81, adminstrn. of justice dir., 1976-79; pres. LWV of U.S., 1990-92, chair edn. fund., 1990-92; mem. bd. trustees exec. com., sec. N.J. Future, 1993—; pub. mem. Supreme Ct. of N.J. Disciplinary Oversight Com., 1994—, Coun. of Engring. and Sci. Splty. Bds., 1996—; commr. N.J. State and Local Expenditure Revenue Policy Commn., 1985-88; pres. Northeastern Polit. Sci. Assn., 1984-85. Recipient Disting. Svc. award N.J. Polit. Sci. Assn., 1984, Pub. Svc. award Am. Soc. Pub. Adminstrs., 1993; rsch. grantee Fund for N.J., 1981, Florence and John Schumann Found., 1988-89. Mem. Phi Kappa Phi, Pi Sigma Alpha, Pi Alpha Alpha. Home: 17 Pittsford Way New Providence NJ 07974 Office: Kean Coll of NJ 1000 Morris Ave Union NJ 07083-7133

LEDFORD, GARY ALAN, real estate developer; b. San Diego, Dec. 30, 1946; s. Loren Oscar and Madge Francis (Condon) L.; m. Winifred Jess Ledford, Nov. 19, 1994; children: Kelly, Jeanne, Robert. BSCE, U.S. Army Engring. Coll., 1967. Pres. Mastercraft Contractors/Mastercraft Diversified Svcs., Inc./Masterplan, Inc., Colo. Springs, 1969-73; v.p. K.L. Redfern, Inc., Orange, Calif., 1973-75; pres. Ledford Industries, Inc./G.A. Ledford & Assocs., 1975-82, Watt Jess Ranch, Inc., Apple Valley, Calif., 1985-94; chmn. Jess Ranch, Apple Valley, 1994—, Jess Ranch Water Co., Apple Valley, 1986—; pres., ceo Jess Ranch Devel. Co., Inc., 1996—; pres. Jess Ranch Security Co., Inc., 1996—; v.p., gen. mgr. Jess Ranch Realty, 1996—; gen. ptnr. GLBT Assocs., 1978-79; chmn. Watt-Jess/Ledford, Apple Valley, 1992-94; pres. LJ&J Investments, Inc., Apple Valley, Ledford-Schaffer/Rogers, Apple Valley. Designer computer software, 1979. Past pres. Cultural Arts Found., 1991-92, Victorville, Calif; bd. trustees Apple Valley Christian Care Ctr., High Desert Questors, Victorville; past pres. Victor Valley Mus. Assn., Baldy View B.I.A. Capt. C.E., U.S. Army, 1967-69, Vietnam. Mem. Internat. Coun. Shopping Ctrs., Nat. Assn. Home Builders', Nat. Planning Assn., NRA (life), High Desert Constrn. Indsutry Assn. (past v.p.), Bldg. Industry Assn., VFW, Sr. Housing Coun. Republican. Avocations: hunting, chess, equestrian. Home: 11401 Apple Valley Rd Apple Valley CA 92308-7503 Office: Jess Ranch 11401 Apple Valley Rd Apple Valley CA 92308-7503

LEDFORD, JACK CLARENCE, retired aircraft company executive, former air force officer; b. Blairsville, Ga., Sept. 1, 1920; s. Jack Raymond and Clara Mae (Duckworth) L.; m. Pauline F. Knight, Dec. 9, 1973; children: Barbara Jan (Mrs. Russell J. Thomas), Jack Michael, Joseph Dan. B.S., Ohio State U.; M.B.A., George Washington U. Commd. 2d lt. Air Corps U.S. Army, 1941; advanced through grades to brig. gen. USAF, 1965; dep. chief staff Def. Atomic Support Agy., Washington, 1958-61; dir. spl. projects USAF, 1961-63; asst. dir. CIA, 1963-66; dir. inspection USAF, 1966-68; comdr. 12th Strategic Air Div., Tucson, 1968-70; ret., 1970; v.p. area devel. So. Ariz. Bank & Trust Co., Tucson., 1970-71; v.p. Hughes Aircraft Internat. Service Corp., 1971-85. Pres. Old Pueblo Boys Club.; bd. dirs. Tucson United Community Campaign, Catalina council Boy Scouts Am., Pima County Air Mus. Decorated D.S.C., D.S.M. (2), Legion of Merit, Air Medal, Purple Heart; Order of Flying Cloud and Banner China). Mem. Air Force Assn., Skyline Country Club (Tucson), Calif. Yacht Club (L.A.), Delta Upsilon.

LEDFORD, JANET MARIE SMALLEY, real estate appraiser, consultant; b. Willimantic, Conn., June 1, 1951; d. Harold Eugene and Elizabeth Louise (Loehr) Smalley; m. Timothy Eugene Ledford, Jan. 23, 1988. AA, Young Harris (Ga.) Coll., 1971; BS, W. Ga. Coll., 1973; MEd, U. Ga., 1978. Math. tchr. secondary schs., Atlanta and, V.I., 1973-82; assoc. appraiser Childers Assocs., Atlanta, 1985-87, Am. Realty Concepts, Atlanta, 1987-88; owner, appraiser, cons. Ledford & Assoc., Atlanta, 1988—. Avocations: travel, gardening, cooking.

LEDGER, WILLIAM JOE, physician, educator; b. Turtle Creek, Pa., 1932. B.A., Princeton U., 1954; M.D., U. Pa., 1958; M.S., Temple U., 1964. Diplomate Am. Bd. Ob-Gyn. Intern Hamot Hosp. Assn., Erie, N.Y., 1958-59; resident Temple U. Hosp., Phila., 1961-64; attending physician Women's Hosp.-Mich. Med. Ctr., 1964-72; assoc. prof. U. Mich., Ann Arbor; prof. U. So. Calif., L.A., 1972-79; Given Found. prof., chmn. ob-gyn. Cornell U. Med. Coll., N.Y.C., 1979—. Served to capt. USMC, 1959-61. Fellow ACS, Am. Coll. Ob-Gyn. Office: NY Hosp-Cornell Med Sch 525 E 68th St New York NY 10021-4873

LEDING, ANNE DIXON, artist, educator; b. Fort Smith, Ark., Jan. 29, 1947; d. Charles Victor Dixon and Elizabeth Johanna (Mitchell) Dixon Roderick; m. Larry Joseph Peters (dec), Jan. 6, 1967; m. John Thomas Leding, June 24, 1978; children: Jonathan Brian (Peters) Leding, Caroline Kristen Leding. Student, Memphis State U., Memphis, 1964-66, Westark C.C., Fort Smith, 1976-78. Art instr. Fort Smith (Ark.) Art Ctr., 1976; pvt. practice art instr. Fort Smith, 1977-78; classical guitar instr. Paul Mendy Guitar Studio, Fort Smith, 1978-79; cmty. svc. classical guitar instr. Westmark C.C., 1976. One-woman shows include Ariel Gallery, Fort Smith Art Ctr., Cafe Bliss, La Cima Club; group shows include Del Mar Coll., Ariel Gallery, N.Y.C.; featured in Ency. of Living Artists in Am., 1986-87; listed in N.Y. Art Rev., S.W. Art Rev., 1990-91; critiqued in Artspeak, N.Y., 1990. Mentor Grapevine (Tex.) Mid. Sch. Recipient 1st place Fort Smith Sch. Dist., 1955; letter of recognition Seventeen Mag., 1963; hon. mention Fort Smith Art Ctr. Bicentennial, 1976, Del Mar Coll., 1985, Trinity Arts Competition, 1992, Mid Cities Fine Artists Competition, 1994. Mem. Nat. Mus. Women in the Arts, Dallas Mus. Art, Kimbel Art Mus., Trinity Arts Guild, Ft. Smith Art Ctr., Toastmasters Internat. Republican. Anglican. Avocations: photography, music. Home: 402 Walden Tr Euless TX 76039-3870 Office: Anne Leding Illustrations 402 Walden Trl Euless TX 76039-3870

LEDLEY, ROBERT STEVEN, biophysicist; b. N.Y.C., June 28, 1928. DDS, NYU, 1948; MA, Columbia U., 1949. Rsch. physicist Columbia U. Radiation Labs., Columbia, 1948-50; instr. physics Columbia U., 1949-50; vis. scientist Nat. Bur. Standards, 1951-52; physicist, 1953-54; ops. rsch. analyst Johns Hopkins U., 1954-56; assoc. prof. elec. engring George Washington U., 1957-60; instr. pediatric. Johns Hopkins U., Sch. Medicine, 1960-63; prof. elec. engring. George Washington U., 1968-70; prof. physiology, biophysics & radiology Georgetown U., from 1970; pres., rsch. dir. Nat. Biomed. Rsch. Found., from 1960; pres. Digital Info. Sci. Corp., 1970-75. named to Nat. Inventor Hall of Fame, 1990. Mem. Soc. Math Biophys., Inst. Elec. & Electronics Engrs., Biphys. Soc., N.Y. Acad. Sci., Pattern Recognition Soc. Office: Georgetown U Nat Biomed Rsch Found 3900 Reservoir Rd NW Washington DC 20007-2195

LEDNUM, FLORENCE NASH, biological sciences educator; b. Abington, Pa., May 11, 1941; d. Charles Edgar and Jane (Gessner) N.; m. Allan Alfred Rieken, June 17, 1966 (div. Dec. 1976); children: Dawn Elizabeth, Holly Raina; m. Charles Wendell Lednum, Aug. 17, 1993. BS, Wash. Coll., 1962; MS, U. Del., 1964; EdD, U. Md., 1993. Biol. oceanographer U.S. Naval Oceanographic Office, Washington, 1964-69; anatomy, physiology and microbiology instr., recruiter Macqueen Gibbs Willis Sch. Nursing, Easton, Md., 1969-82; assoc. prof. biol. scis. WOR-WIC C.C., Salisbury, Md., 1982-92; prof. biol. scis., dept. chair Chesapeake Coll., Wye Mills, Md., 1992—, coord. sci. adv. com., 1994—. Coord., editor (cookbook) Trinity's Table, 1992-93. Recipient Excellence in Tchg. award Md. State Bd. for C.C.'s, 1990. Mem. Assn. for Advancement of County Coll. Tchg., Md. Assn. Sci. Tchrs., Soc. for Coll. Sci. Tchrs. Episcopalian. Avocations: quilting, gardening, sewing. Home: 31751 Tappers Corner Rd Cordova MD 21625-2133 Office: Chesapeake Coll PO Box 8 Wye Mills MD 21679-0008

LEDOGAR, STEPHEN J., diplomat; b. N.Y.C., Sept. 14, 1929; m. Marcia Hubert, Sept. 16, 1967; children: Lucy, Charles. BS, Fordham U., 1954, LLB, 1958. Bar: N.Y. 1959. Surety claims atty. Chubb & Son, N.Y.C., 1954-59; with Fgn. Svc., 1959—; press spokesman, U.S. del. Vietnam Peace Talks, Paris, 1967-72; with U.S. Mission to NATO, 1973-76; spl. asst. to undersec. of state, 1976-77; dir. Office of NATO Affairs, 1977-80; mem. State Dept. Senior Seminar, 1980-81; dep. chief of mission U.S. Mission to NATO, Brussels, 1981-87; amb., U.S. rep. European Conventional Stabilility Negotiations and Mutual and Balanced Force Reductions Talks, 1987-89, amb. and head U.S. Del. to Negotiations on Conventional Armed Forces in Europe, 1989, amb. and U.S. rep. Conference on Disarmament, 1989-97, prin. U.S. negotiator of chem. weapons conv., 1993, prin. Comprehensive Nuclear Test Ban Treaty, 1996. Lt. USN, 1949-52, USNR, 1954-60 (Naval Aviator). Office: US Del to Conf Disarmament, 11 Rte de Pregny, 1292 Geneva Switzerland

LEDOUX, CHRIS LEE, country musician; b. Biloxi, Miss., Oct. 2, 1948; s. Alfred Hector and Bonnie Jeanette (Gingrich) LeDoux; m. Peggy Jo Rhoades, Jan. 4, 1972; children: Clayton, Ned, Will, Cindi, Beau. AA, Sheridan (Wyo.) Coll., 1969. With rodeo, 1971-81, musician, 1972—; rancher Wyo., 1976—. Songwriter, singer 22 albums of songs with Western themes, 1972—, recent recordings include Western Underground, 1991, (with Garth Brooks) Watcha Gonna Do With a Cowboy, 1992, Under This Old Hat, 1993, (with Garth Brooks) Best of Chris LeDoux, 1994. Sculptor (Best Bronze of Show, State of Wyo. 1985, Best Art of Show, State of Nev., 1986), (with Toby Keith) Rodeo Rock & Roll Collection, 1995, Stampede, 1996. State spokesman, Wyo. State Centennial, 1990. Mem. Profl. Rodeo Cowboy Assn. (World Champion Bareback Broncs, 1976). Avocations: Wyo. rancher, give music concerts with Western Underground. Office: ACS Inc 1433 N Stine Rd Charlotte MI 48813-8886 also: Capitol Records 3322 West End Ave Nashville TN 37203*

LEDOUX, HAROLD ANTHONY, cartoonist, painter; b. Port Arthur, Tex., Nov. 7, 1926; s. Antoine Ovide and Pauline Zulma (Bernard) LeD.; m. Jeanne Labbe, 1964 (div. 1979); children: Lorraine Marthe, Noelle Pauline. Grad., Thomas Jefferson High Sch., Port Arthur, Tex., 1944; student, Chgo. Acad. Fine Arts, 1948-49. Cartoonist, illustrator N.Am. Syndicate, 1965—. Cartoonist, Famous Funnies, N.Y.C., 1950-53; asst. cartoonist: syndicated comic strip Judge Parker, 1953-65; represented in permanent collection Mus. of Gulf Coast, Port Arthur, Tex., Internat. Mus. Cartoon Art, Boca Raton, Fla. Advisor Council for Devel. of French in La. Served with U.S. Mcht. Marine, 1944-47. Recipient Atlantic War Zone Bar War Shipping Adminstrn. Mem. Nat. Cartoonists Soc., Comics Council, Southwestern Watercolor Soc. Club: Alliance Française. Address: N Am Syndicate 235 E 45th St New York NY 10017-3305

LEDOUX, WILLIAM JOHN, lawyer; b. Bklyn., June 30, 1931; s. William Desau and Elizabeth Ann (Horton) LeD.; m. Elma Lucia Giancaterino, Feb. 27, 1954; children: John F., William M., Michael J., Susan E. AB, Boston U., 1960, JD cum laude, 1963. Bar: Mass. 1963, U.S. Supreme Ct. 1969, U.S. Ct. Appeals (1st cir.) 1982, U.S. Dist. Ct. Mass. 1964. Ptnr. Christopher & LeDoux, Worcester, Mass., 1963-67, 89-95, Bowditch & Dewey, Worcester, 1967-89; pvt. practice William J. LeDoux, Worcester, 1996—; dir. Providence & Worcester Rail-Road, Worcester, 1990—; chmn. Clients' Security Bd. of Supreme Jud. Ct., Boston, 1988—. 1st lt. U.S. Army, 1948-54. 1st lt. U.S. Army, 1950-52, Korea; lt. col. AUS ret. Fellow Mass. Bar Found. (life), Worcester County Bar Found. (life); mem. Worcester County Bar Assn. (co-chair fee arbitration bd. 1990—). Avocations: swimming, reading. Home: 7 Brandon Rd Worcester MA 01606-1609 Office: William J LeDoux 446 Main St Worcester MA 01608-2302

LEDSINGER, CHARLES ALBERT, JR., hotel, gaming executive; b. Memphis, Jan. 1, 1950; s. Charles Albert Ledsinger Sr. and Betty L. (Clark) Heller; m. Anita Clarendon, May 11, 1974; children: Leila Grace, Katherine Elise. BA in English, U. Va., 1972; MBA in Fin., Memphis State U., 1977. Restaurant mgr. Boudreaux and Shoup Enterprises, Atlanta, 1972-74; comml. property mgr. Hoover Morris, Enterprises, Atlanta, 1974-75; fin. analyst Holiday Inns, Inc., Memphis, 1978-79, mgr. investor rels., 1980, exec. asst. to pres., 1980-83; v.p. fin. and adminstrn. Embassy Stes., Irving, Tex., 1983-87; v.p. project fin. Holiday Corp., Memphis, 1987-90; v.p., treas. The Promus Cos., Memphis, 1990; sr. v.p., CFO The Promus Cos., Memphis, 1990-95, Harrah's Entertainment, Memphis, 1995—; bd. dirs. The Restaurant Co., Perkins Mgmt. Co., Inc., Friendly Ice Cream Corp. Mem. exec. bd. Chickasaw coun. Boy Scouts Am., 1993—; trustee St. Mary's Episcopal Sch., 1994—; bd. dirs. Memphis Devel. Found., 1992—, TBC Corp., 1996—, Sky City Ltd., Auckland, New Zealand, 1995—. Office: Harrah's Entertainment Inc 1023 Cherry Rd Memphis TN 38117-5423

LE DUC, ALBERT LOUIS, JR., computer services director; b. Montgomery, Ala., Feb. 1, 1937; s. Albert Louis and Rachel Nancy (Wineinger) LeD. Student Duke U., 1954-55; B.A., Fla. State U., 1958, M.S., 1960; m. Ellen Heath, June 18, 1960; children: Albert Louis III, Charles Andrew. Civilian mathematician Army Rocket Guided Missile Agy., Huntsville, Ala., 1958, 59; mathematician analyst RCA Svc. Co., Patrick AFB, Fla., 1960-63, programming leader, 1963-67, project mgr., Eglin AFB, Fla., 1967-69, mktg. adminstr., Cherry Hill, N.J., 1969-71; tech. dir. Ind. U., Bloomington, 1971-77; dir. analysis programming Miami-Dade Community Coll., Miami, Fla., 1977-89, dir. computer svcs., 1989-97; prin. Athene Consultants, Inc., 1996-97; mgmt. cons., 1997—; part-time instr. Fla. State U., 1958-60, Brevard Engring. Coll., 1961-62, Ind. U., 1972-77. Bd. dirs. Coll. and Univ. Machine Records Conf., 1979-87. Recipient Frank Martin award Coll. and Univ. Machine Records Conf., 1985. Mem. Assn. Computing Machinery (Best Paper award 1973), Profl. Assn. for Computing and Info. Tech. in Higher Edn. (best paper award 1986), CAUSE (bd. dirs. 1993-96, Elite award 1993). Author: The Computer for Managers, 1972. Home: 10321 SW 107th St Miami FL 33176-3473 Office: 10321 SW 107th St Miami FL 33176-3473

LEDWIDGE, PATRICK JOSEPH, lawyer; b. Detroit, Mar. 17, 1928; s. Patrick Liam and Mary Josephine (Hooley) L.; m. Rosemary Lahey Mervenne, Aug. 3, 1974; stepchildren—Anne Marie, Mary Clare, John, David, Sara Mervenne. A.B., Coll. Holy Cross, 1949; J.D., U. Mich., 1952. Bar: Mich. 1952. Assoc. firm Dickinson, Wright, Moon, Van Dusen & Freeman, Detroit, 1956-63; ptnr. Dickinson, Wright, Moon, Van Dusen & Freeman, 1964—. Served to lt. j.g. U.S. Navy, 1952-55. Mem. Mich. Bar Assn., Detroit Bar Assn., Am. Law Inst. Roman Catholic. Clubs: Detroit, Detroit Athletic, Detroit Golf. Home: 777 N Williamsbury Rd Bloomfield Village MI 48301-2521 Office: Dickinson Wright Moon Van Dusen & Freeman 1 Detroit Ctr 500 Woodward Ave Ste 4000 Detroit MI 48226-3423

LEDWIG, DONALD EUGENE, association executive, former public broadcasting executive, former naval officer; b. Lubbock, Tex., Mar. 2, 1937; s. Paul Lawrence and Rose L.; m. Gail Wilcox, Jan. 30, 1965; children: Donald Eugene Jr., David W. BS, Tex. Tech. U., 1959; MBA, George Washington U., 1973; Disting. Grad. Naval War Coll., 1977. Commd. ensign, U.S. Navy, 1959, advanced through grades to capt., 1980, ship's officer U.S. Pacific Fleet, 1959-65, 77-79, staff Adm. H.G. Rickover, Nuclear Propulsion Program, 1966-72, dir. contract policy Naval Material Command, Washington, 1979-81, dep. comdr. Naval Electronic Systems Command, Washington, 1981-84, ret. 1984; v.p., treas. Corp. for Pub. Broadcasting, Washington, 1984-86, pres., chief exec. officer, 1987-92; exec. dir. Am. Prodn. and Inventory Control Soc., Falls Church, Va., 1992-95; pres. Am. Logistics Assn., Washington, 1995-96; COO Anchor Mental Health Assn., 1997—. Decorated Legion of Merit; recipient Barrow Meml. award Hastings Coll. Law, 1989, Nat. Captioning Inst. Award, 1990, Disting. Alumnus award Tex. Tech U., 1992. Mem. Am. Soc. Assn. Execs., Nat. Press. Club, Army and Navy Club, Army/Navy Country Club. Office: Anchor Mental Health Assn PO Box 29058 Washington DC 20017-0058

LEDWITH, JAMES ROBB, lawyer; b. Bryn Mawr, Pa., Feb. 14, 1936; s. Richard W. (dec.) and Elizabeth T. Ledwith; children: Cheryl D., James Robb Jr., Scott W.; m. Katherine Hoffman, Dec. 2, 1978. AB, Princeton U., 1958; LLB, U. Pa., 1963. Bar: Pa. 1964. Assoc. Pepper, Hamilton & Scheetz, Phila., 1963-71, ptnr., 1971—. Bd. dirs., trustee Coll. Settlement Phila.; bd. dirs., trustee, asst. sec., treas., past pres. bd. trustees Kuhn Day Camp; sec., trustee Curtis Inst. Music, Mary Louise Curtis Bok Found. Lt. USNR, 1958-60. Fellow Am. Coll. Trust and Estate Counsel (past bd. regents, past Pa. chmn.); mem. ABA (past chmn. com. on adminstrn. estates sect. real property, probate and trust law sect.), Pa. Bar Assn. (past chmn. sect. real property, probate and trust law), Pa. Bar Inst. (bd. dirs., past pres.), Phila. Bar Assn. (past chmn., exec. com. probate and trust law com.), Nat. Assn. Estate Planning Couns. (past bd. dirs., past pres.). Republican. Presbyterian. Avocations: tennis, squash, music (piano). Office: Pepper Hamilton & Scheetz 3000 Two Logan Sq 18th Arch St Philadelphia PA 19103

LEDWITH, JOHN FRANCIS, lawyer; b. Phila., Oct. 3, 1938; s. Francis Joseph and Jane Agnes (White) L.; m. Mary Evans, Aug. 28, 1965; children—Deirdre A., John E. A.B., U. Pa., 1960, J.D., 1963. Bar: Pa. 1965, U.S. Dist. Ct. (ea. dist.) Pa. 1965, U.S. Ct. Appeals (3rd cir.) 1965, U.S. Supreme Ct. 1970, N.Y. State, 1984. Assoc. Joseph R. Thompson, Phila., 1965-71; mem. Schubert, Mallon, Wallheim & deCindis, Phila., 1971-81, LaBrum & Doak, Phila., 1981-95; mem. Marshall, Denchey, Warner, Coleman & Goggins, Phila., 1995—. Author: (with others) Philadelphia CP Trial Manual, 1982. Bd. dirs. Chestnut Hill Community Assn., Pa., 1975, 76. Served to E-6 USCG, 1963-71. Mem. ABA, Phila. Bar Assn., Pa. Bar Assn., Def. Research Inst., Fedn. of Ins. Corp. Coun. Republican. Roman Catholic. Clubs: Racquet (Phila.), Phila. Cricket; Avalon Yacht (N.J.) (commodore 1982). Office: Marshall Dennehey Warner Coleman & Goggins 1845 Walnut St Philadelphia PA 19103-4708

LEDWITH, SISTER MARGARET CHRISTINE, nun, counselor; b. Longford, Ireland, Dec. 19, 1935; came to U.S., 1990; SRN, Whipps Cross Hosp., London, 1963; SCM, Dublin Nat. Maternity Hosp., Dublin, 1964; postgrad., London Hosp. and Royal Coll., 1967-69; M in Pastoral Counseling, Loyola Coll., Balt., 1991; postgrad. in urban ministry and CPE, Emmanuel Coll., 1991-92; postgrad. in Spanish, Maryknoll Inst., Bolivia, 1992—; clin. pastoral edn., Shannon Hosp., San Angelo, Tex., 1993, Meth. Hosp., Lubbock, Tex., 1994-95. Joined Missionary Sisters of the Holy Rosary, Roman Cath. Ch., 1955; cert. Coll. of Chaplains; cert. Nat. Assn. Cath. Chaplains.qq. Tutor midwifery Missionary Sisters of Holy Rosary, Nigeria, 1964, sr. ward sister, 1964-67; adminstr. pers. Missionary Sisters of Holy Rosary, Ireland, 1972-78, superior gen., 1978-89; chaplain Med. Ctr. Hosp., Odessa, Tex., 1993—; adminstr. nursing Tembisa Hosp., Johannesburg, South Africa, 1969-72; clin. pastoral edn. Shannon Hosp., San Angelo, Tex., 1993, Meth. Hosp., Lubbock, Tex., 1994-95; police chaplain Odessa Police Dept. Fellow Coll. of Chaplains; mem. Am. Assn. Pastoral Counselors. Address: Missionary Sisters of Holy Rosary 14 Marquee West 1111 W 13th St Odessa TX 79763 Office: Missionary Sisters of Holy Rosary 741 Polo Rd Bryn Mawr PA 19010-3825

LEDYARD, JOHN ODELL, economics educator, consultant; b. Detroit, Apr. 4, 1940; s. William Hendrie and Florence (Odell) L.; m. Bonnie Higginbottom, May 23, 1970; children: Stephen, J. Henry, Meg. BA, Wabash Coll., 1963; PhD, Purdue U., 1967; PhD (hon.), Purdue U./Ind. U., 1993. Asst. prof. Carnegie-Mellon U., Pitts., 1967-70; prof. Northwestern U., Evanston, Ill., 1970-85; prof. Calif. Inst. Tech., Pasadena, 1985—, exec. officer for social sci., 1989-92, chmn. div. humanities and social scis., 1992—. Contbr. articles to profl. jours. Fellow Econometric Soc.; mem. Pub. Choice Soc. (pres. 1980-82), Econ. Sci. Assn. (exec. com. 1986—). Office: Calif Inst of Tech Dept Econs Pasadena CA 91125

LEDYARD, ROBINS HEARD, lawyer; b. Nashville, Oct. 14, 1939; s. Quitman Robins and Alma Elizabeth (Stevenson) L.; m. Julia Bordeaux Gambill, Dec. 19, 1962; children: Stevenson Gambill, Quitman Robins II, Margaret Dabney. BA, Vanderbilt U., 1965, JD, 1966. Bar: Tenn. 1966, U.S. Supreme Ct. 1975. Atty. Nat. Life & Accident Ins. Co., Nashville, 1966-68; asst. counsel Nat. Life & Accident Ins. Co., 1968-69, asso. counsel, 1969-70, counsel, 1970-72, asso. gen. counsel, 1972-75, gen. counsel, 1975-80; partner Bass, Berry & Sims, 1980—; tchr. C.L.U.s, 1967-75. Asst. editor: Vanderbilt Law Rev., 1965-66; contbr. articles to profl. jours. Active United Way, Nashville, 1967—, Heart Fund, 1970-73; vice chmn. United Diocesan Givers, 1975; bd. dirs. St. Thomas Hosp., 1990—. With USMC, 1958-61. Recipient Bennett Douglas Bell Meml. prize, 1966; Marr scholar, 1965-66. Mem. ABA, Am. Coun. Life Ins. (chmn. tax com. 1978-80), Assn. Life Ins. Counsel (chmn. tax com. 1979-80), Tenn. Bar Assn., Nashville Bar Assn., Internat. Assn. Ins. Counsel, Global Leaders for the South, Order of Coif, Phi Delta Phi, Alpha Tau Omega. Democrat. Roman Catholic. Clubs: Belle Meade Country, Capitol of Nashville, KC. Home: 1215 Chickering Rd Nashville TN 37215-4519 Office: 2700 First American Ctr Nashville TN 37238

LEE, ADRIAN ISELIN, JR., journalist; b. Miami, Fla., Nov. 6, 1920; s. Adrian Iselin and Adriana Lanier (Owen) L.; m. Marie Lainé Santa Maria, Oct. 14, 1950; children: Adrian Iselin III, Catherine Taney, Thomas Sim, William Owen, Anne Marie, Louisa Carrell. BA, Spring Hill Coll., Mobile, Ala., 1943. With The Bulletin, Phila., 1948—; gen. assignment reporter The Bulletin, 1960—, editorial writer, 1967-72, columnist op-ed page, 1972-82; with Phila. Daily News, 1982-88; speech and op-ed writer U.S. Atty. Gen. Edwin Meese III, 1988-89; writer CBS Radio News, 1989—; tchr. editorial writing, dept. journalism Temple U. Active Chestnut Hill Community Assn. Lt. (j.g.) USNR, 1943-46, PTO. Decorated Navy Unit Commendation medal. Mem. Nat. Press Club, Pen and Pencil Club, Phila. Press Assn. (prize for coverage John F. Kennedy assassination 1963), Sigma Delta Chi (prize for column writing 1978). Republican. Roman Catholic. Home and Office: Penns Wood Apt F-20 20 E Haws Ln Flourtown PA 19031-2048

LEE, ALLAN WREN, clergyman; b. Yakima, Wash., June 3, 1924; s. Percy Anson and Agnes May (Wren) L.; m. Mildred Elaine Ferguson, June 16, 1946; 1 dau., Cynthia Ann. B.A., Phillips U., Enid, Okla., 1949; M.A., Peabody Coll. Tchrs., 1953; B.D., Tex. Christian U., 1955, D.D. (hon.), 1968. Ordained minister Christian Ch. (Disciples of Christ), 1949; pastor chs. in Tex. and Wash., 1955-60, 90—; gen. sec. World Conv. Chs. of Christ, Dallas, 1971-92; mem. gen. bd. Christian Ch., 1971-73; pres. Seattle Christian Ch. Missionary Union, 1964-66, Wash.-No. Idaho Conv. Christian Chs., 1966; TV panel mem. Am. Religious Town Hall, 1988—. Author: Bridges of Benevolence, 1962, Wit and Wisdom, 1963, The Burro and the Bibles, 1968, Under the Shadow of the Nine Dragons, 1969, Reflections Along the Reef, 1970, Disciple Down Under, 1971, Meet My Mexican Amigos, 1972, One Great Fellowship, 1974, Fifty Years of Faith and Fellowship, 1980, Recollections of a Dandy Little Up-to-Date Town, 1985, also articles. Bd. trustees N.W. Christian Coll., Eugene, Oreg., 1985-93; bd. dirs. Melissa Pub. Libr., 1992-94. With USNR, 1943-46. Recipient Disting. Service citation Children's Home Soc. Wash., 1967, Disting. Service award Bremerton Jaycees, 1959; Jamaica Tourist Bd. citation, 1984. Mem. Disciples of Christ Hist. Soc. (founder, life mem.), Religious Conv. Mgrs. Assn. (v.p. 1972-92), Am. Bible Soc. (nat. adv. coun. 1985-94). Home and Office: 2112 Stone Creek Dr Plano TX 75075-2936 *I make every effort to live a life patterned after the life and teachings of the Man of Nazareth, Jesus Christ—that is, to be compassionate, understanding, peaceful and loving.*

LEE, ALVIN A., literary educator, scholar, author; b. Woodville, Ont., Can., Sept. 30, 1930; s. Norman Osborne and Susanna Elizabeth (Found) L.; m. Hope Arnott, Dec. 21, 1957; children: Joanna, Monika, Fiona, Alison, Margaret. B.A., U. Toronto, Ont., Can., 1953, M.A. in English, 1958, Ph.D., 1961; M.Div., Victoria U., Toronto, 1957. Teaching fellow in English U. Toronto, 1957-59; asst. prof. English McMaster U., Hamilton, Ont., 1960-65; assoc. prof. McMaster U., 1966-70, prof., 1970-92, prof. emeritus, 1990—, asst. dean Sch. Grad. Studies, 1968-71, dean Sch. Grad. Studies, 1971-73, acad. v.p., 1974-79, pres., vice-chancellor, 1980-90, pres. emeritus, 1994—; Northrop Frye prof. literary theory U. Toronto, 1992; mem. Western Ont. coun. Conf. Bd. Can., 1983-90; mem. adv. bd. Medieval and Renaissance History, 1991—. Author: James Reaney, Twayne's World Authors Series, 49, 1968, The Guest-Hall of Eden: Four Essays on the Design of Old English Poetry, 1972; editor: (with Hope Arnott Lee) Wish and Nightmare, 1972, Circle of Stories: One, 1972, Two, 1972, The Garden and the Wilderness, 1973, The Temple and the Ruin, 1973, The Peaceable Kingdom, 1974; (with Robert D. Denham) The Legacy of Northrop Frye, 1994; gen. editor: McMaster Old English Studies and Texts, 1982-92, Collected Works of Northrop Frye, 1995—; editl. bd. English Studies in Canada, 1982-88; contbr. articles to profl. jours. Trustee, mem. exec. com. Chedoke-McMaster Hosps., 1980-90; mem. Community Edn. Coordinating Com., 1981-90; mem. Council Ont. Univs., 1980-90, vice chmn., 1981-83, chmn., 1983-85, mem. exec. com., 1981-87; mem. Health Scis. Liaison Com., 1980-90; dir. Council Ont. Univ. Holdings Ltd., 1981-90; mem. chancellors coun. Victoria U., U. Toronto, 1983—; hon. bd. dirs. Operation Lifeline, Hamilton, 1980-90; hon. Patron Opera Hamilton, 1982-90; vice chmn. bd., mem. exec. com. Royal Bot. Gardens, Hamilton, 1980-90, chmn. provincial and fed. relations com., 1981-90, vice chmn. sci. and ednl. com., 1981-90, mem. nominating com., 1981-90; vice chmn. bus. adv. conf. Regional Municipality of Hamilton-Wentworth, 1983-90; chmn. fund-raising liaison com. McMaster Hosps. Found/McMaster U., 1983-90; hon. patron Edn. Found. of Fedn. Chinese Can. Profls., Ont., 1984-90; mem., vice chair Can. Merit Scholarship Found., 1990-93; bd. dirs. Art Gallery Hamilton, 1991-94; mem. adminstrn. bd. McMaster Mus. Art. Mem. MLA, Mediaeval Acad. Am., Assn. Univs. and Colls. Can. (coun. univ. pres. 1980-90), Hamilton Assn. Advancement Lit., Sci. and Art (hon. pres. 1980-88), Can. Inst. Advanced Rsch., Internat. Assn. Anglo-Saxonists, Corporate-Higher Edn. Forum, McMaster U. Alumni Coun. (hon. pres. 1980-90), McMaster U. Letterman's Assn. (hon.), Hamilton and Dist. C. of C. (dir., mem. program com. 1982-87, Hamilton Gallery of Distinction 1996—). Office: McMaster U, 1280 Main St W, Hamilton, ON Canada L8S 4L9

LEE, ANDRÉ LAFAYETTE, hospital administrator; b. Detroit, Aug. 14, 1943; s. Clyde and Laura D. (Davis) L.; m. Katrina (div.); children—Andre, Bryan, Tracey, Robyn. B.S., Mich. State U., 1966; M.P.A., Cornell U., 1972; D.P.A., Nova U., Fort Lauderdale, 1978. Cert. med. technologist Am. Soc. Clin. Pathologists. Adminstr., Highland Park Hosp., Mich., 1972-76; adminstr. Sumby Hosp., River Rouge, Mich., 1976-78; asst. adminstr. St. Joseph Hosp., Fort Wayne, Ind., 1978-81; adminstr. Hubbard Hosp., Nashville, 1981-87; pres. Urban Health Assocs., Nashville, 1987—; asst. prof. Shaw Coll., Detroit, 1976-77; assoc. prof. Ind. U. Grad. Sch., Fort Wayne, 1978-80; adj. prof. Eastern U., Ann Arbor, Mich., 1976-78; asst. prof. Meharry Med. Coll., Nashville, 1981—; asst. prof. Tenn. State U., 1994—. CEO United Cmty. Hosp., Detroit, 1972—; owner, Friendship Hospice, Nashville, New Orleans, Natchez, Detroit. Author: Teach Your Child Healthy Habits, 1978; newspaper/cartoonist: Frost Illustrated, 1978-79. Contr. articles to profl. jours. Served to capt. U.S. Army, 1968-70. Fellow Am. Coll. Hosp. Adminstrn. (numerous coms.), Am. Acad. Med. Adminstrn. (state bd. dirs. 1981—); mem. Nat. Assn. Health Sci. Execs. (pres. 1985), NAACP. Methodist. Club: Optimist (River Rouge). Avocation: cartooning. Home: 100 Riverfront Dr Apt 606 Detroit MI 48226-4536 Office: United Cmty Hosp 2401 20th St Detroit MI 48216-1506

LEE, ANG, filmmaker; b. Taiwan, Oct. 23, 1954; m. Jane Lin; 2 children. BFA in Theater, U. Ill., 1980; MFA in Film, NYU, 1984. Dir. films Fine Line, 1985, Sense and Sensibility, 1996 (N.Y. Film Critics Circle award, Boston Film Critics award, Nat. Bd. Rev. award, Golden Bear award, Berlin Film Festival award, nominee Brit. Acad. Film and TV Arts award, nominee Dirs. Guild award, nominee Golden Globe award, all as best dir.); screenwriter (with Hui Ling Wang and James Schamus), dir. film Eat Drink Man Woman, 1994 (Best Fgn. Lang. Film award Nat. Bd. Rev., nominee Acad. award for Best Fgn. Lang. Film, nominee Golden Globe award for Best Fgn. Lang. Film, honored for Best Film and as Best Dir. Asian Pacific Film Festival, various Ind. Spirit award nominations); dir., prodr. films Pushing Hands, 1991 (several Golden Horse award nominations, Taiwan, Spl. Jury prize for Direction, Best Film honors Asian Pacific Film Festival 1992), The Wedding Banquet, 1993 (Asian Am. Media award 16th Asian Am. internat. Film Festival, Golden Bear award Berlin Film Festival, nominee Acad. award for Best Fgn. Lang. Film, nominee Golden Globe award for Best Fgn. Lang. Film, several Ind. Spirit award nominations, Golden Horse awards for Best Film and Best Dir.); The Wedding Banquet and Eat Drink Man Woman included in book: Two Films by Ang Lee, 1994. Address: care Good Machine 526 W 25th St New York NY 10001

LEE, ANGIE, basketball coach; d. John and Jean Lee. BS, U. Iowa, 1984, MS in Athletic Adminstrn., 1987. Asst. women's basketball coach U. Iowa, Iowa City, grad. asst. coach, 1985-87, asst. coach, 1989-96, head women's basketball coach, 1996—; asst. basketball coach Western Ill. U., 1987-89. Named Big Ten Conf. Coach of the Yr. 1996, Assoc. Press Nat. Coach of the Yr., 1996, Dist. IV WBCA Coach of the Yr., 1996, Coll. Sports Mag. Coach of the Yr. Mem. Women's Baksetball Coaches Assn. (rep. to dist. IV asst. coaches 1993-94). Office: University of Iowa 219 Carver Hawkeye Arena Iowa City IA 52242-1020

LEE, ARTHUR VIRGIL, III, biotechnology company executive; b. Detroit, Nov. 24, 1920; s. Arthur Virgil and Emily S. (Burry) L.; m. Elizabeth Hoppin Chafee, Dec. 8, 1945 (div.); children: Arthur C., Sherrill Ann Rosoff, William J., Henry C.; m. Jean Austin LaMothe, Dec. 30, 1967. BA, Williams Coll., 1942; Indsl. Adminstr. (World War II MBA), Harvard Bus. Sch., 1943. With McKesson & Robbins, Inc., Memphis, 1946-47; ops. mgr. Providence div. McKesson & Robbins, Inc., 1947-63, v.p., mgr. Providence div., 1954-59, with Boston div., 1959-63, with Pitts. div., 1963; asst. dean Harvard U. Bus. Sch., Cambridge, Mass., 1964-65, dir. corp. rels., 1965-72, dir. resources, 1972-73; v.p. Lesley Coll., Cambridge, 1973-77; dir. corp. rels. Tufts U., Medford, Mass., 1977-79; pres. Biotec Internat., Ltd., Williamstown, Mass., 1979-95. Bd. dirs. New Eng. Drug Exchange, 1956-63; trustee Am. Coll. Switzerland, 1978-82, Williamstown Theatre Festival, 1984-94, trustee emeritus, 1994—; mem. Weston Town Fin. Com., 1961-66; mem. adv. bd. Coll. Pharmacy, U. R.I., 1957-58. Lt. USNR, 1942-46. Mem. Taconic Golf Club, Alpha Delta Phi. Congregationalist. Home and Office: 1549 Green River Rd Williamstown MA 01267-3128

LEE, BARBARA A., retired federal magistrate judge. AB, Boston U., 1959; LLB, Harvard Law Sch., 1962. Bar: Conn. 1962, N.Y. 1966. Atty. Poletti Freidin Prashker Feldman & Gartner, 1968-74, ptnr., 1974-82; pvt. practice N.Y.C., 1983-87; U.S. magistrate judge U.S. Dist. Ct. (so. dist.), N.Y., 1988-96; ret., 1996; adj. prof. law Seton Hall U., So. Orange, N.J., 1984-87. Mem. com. on ecumenical and inter-religious affairs of Roman Cath. Archdiocese of N.Y., 1983—. Mem. Fed. Magistrate Judges Assn. (vice chmn. retired magistrate judge's com.), Assn. of Bar of City of N.Y. (adminstrv. law com. 1973-74, fed. cts. com. 1981-84, com. on state cts. of superior jurisdiction 1984-87, libr. com. 1989-92), N.Y. County Lawyers' Assn. (fed. cts. com. 1995—).

LEE, BARBARA ANNE, educator, lawyer; b. Newton, N.J., Apr. 9, 1949; d. Robert Hanna and Keren (Dalrymple) L.; m. James Paul Begin, Aug. 14, 1982; 1 child, Robert James. BA , U. Vt., 1971; MA, Ohio State U., 1972; JD, Georgetown U., 1982; PhD, Ohio State U., 1977. Bar: N.J. 1983, U.S. Dist. Ct. N.J. 1983. Instr., Franklin U., Columbus, Ohio, 1974-75; rsch. asst. Ohio State U., Columbus, 1975-77; policy analyst U.S. Dept. Edn., Washington, 1978-80; dir. data trends Carnegie Found., Princeton, N.J., 1980-82; asst. prof. Grad. Sch. Edn., Rutgers U., 1982-84; asst. prof. Inst. Mgmt. and Labor Rels., Rutgers U., New Brunswick, N.J., 1984-88, assoc. prof. 1988-94, prof. 1994—, assoc. provost 1995-96; mem. Study Group on Excellence in Higher Edn., Nat. Inst. Edn., 1983-84; project dir. Carnegie Corp., N.Y.C., 1982-84. Corse fellow U. Vt., 1971; recipient John F. Kennedy Labor Law award Georgetown U., 1982; grantee Bur. Labor-Mgmt. Rels. and Coop. Programs, 1985-86. Mem. ABA, N.J. Bar Assn. (mem. exec. com. labor and employment law sect. 1987—, women's rights sect.), Am. Ednl. Rsch. Assn., Indsl. Rels. Rsch. Assn., Acad. Mgmt., Assn. Study Higher Edn. (legal counsel 1982-88), Nat. Assn. Coll. and Univ. Attys. (vice chair editl. bd. 1986-89, chair 1995—, chair publs. com. 1988-91, bd. dirs. 1990-93) Author: Academics in Court, 1987; co-author: The Law of Higher Education, 3rd edit., 1995; contbr. numerous articles to profl. jours. Office: Rutgers U Dept Human Resource Mgmt Sch Mgmt and Labor Rels PO Box 5062 New Brunswick NJ 08903-5062

LEE, BENNY Y. C., import and export company executive; b. Taipei, Taiwan, Feb. 23, 1947; s. Ko Kwan and Hsiu Yen (Huang) L.; m. Edith Y.C. Lee, June 25, 1989; children: Jenny I.S., Elizabeth Jordan, Katherine Belinda. Student, Tatung Instn. Tech., Taipei. Staff engr. Bendix Corp., Taipei, 1969-70, Philco Ford Corp., Taipei, 1970; supr. quality control Arvin Corp., Taipei, 1970-72; staff engr. Midland Corp., Taipei, 1972-74, mgr., 1974-77; mgr. elec. dept. Amerex Corp., Taipei, 1977-79; pres., owner Mitco, Taipei, 1979—, Kansas City, Mo. Mem. World Trade Ctr., Kansas City Internat. Trade Club.

LEE, BERNARD SHING-SHU, research company executive; b. Nanking, People's Republic of China, Dec. 14, 1934; came to U.S., 1949; s. Wei-Kuo and Pei-fen (Tang) L.; m. Pauline Pan; children: Karen, Lesley, Tania. BSc, Poly. Inst. Bklyn., 1956, DSc in Chem. Engring., 1960. Registered profl. engr., N.Y., Ill. With Arthur D. Little, Inc., Cambridge, Mass., 1960-65; with Inst. Gas Tech., Chgo., 1965-78, pres., 1978—; chmn. M-C Power Corp., Burr Ridge, Ill.; bd. dirs. NUI corp., Bedminster, N.J., Nat. Fuel Gas Co., Buffalo, Peerless Mfg. Co., Dallas, Energy BioSystems Corp., The Woodlands, Tex., New Eng. Gas Assn.; chmn. SGT, Shanghai, People's Republic of China. Contbr. more than 60 articles to profl. jours. Recipient Outstanding Personal Achievement in Chem. Engring. award Chem. Engring. mag., 1978. Fellow AAAS, Am. Inst. Chem. Engrs. (33d inst. lectr. 1981); mem. AIME, Am. Chem. Soc., Am. Gas Assn. (Gas Industry Rsch. award 1984), Econ. Club Chgo. Office: Inst Gas Tech 1700 S Mount Prospect Rd Des Plaines IL 60018-1804

LEE, BEVERLY ING, educational administrator; b. Honolulu, Oct. 10, 1932; d. Tim Sheu and Helen (Heu) Ing; m. Daniel David Lee, June 21, 1962; children: Helen Ann Esq, Terence Daniel, Scott David. BA, Coll. of the Pacific, Stockton, Calif., 1954; MA, Columbia U., 1957. Policewoman Honolulu Police Dept., 1957-61; counselor Ewa Elem., Highlands Intermediate and Waipahu High Schs., 1961-69; adminstr. Dept. Edn. State of Hawaii, Honolulu, 1969-89; contr., v.p., pres. Classic Travel, Honolulu, 1988—; bd. dirs. Hawaii State Employees Credit Union, Honolulu, vice chair, 1994, chair, 1995; bd. dirs. Mahalo Airport Travel Agy.; mem. adv. bd. Travel Univ. Internat. Adv. Bd., 1994—. Mem. Gov.'s Commn. on Child Abuse, Honolulu, 1985-89; bd. dirs. Hawaii Family Stress Ctr., Honolulu, 1983—, Child and Family Svc., 1975-85; mem. Casey Family Program Adv. Com., 1986—, Parents Anonymous, 1988-92, Prevent Child Abuse Hawaii, 1975—. Mem. AAUW (life), Hawaiian Airlines Travel Agy. (adv. bd. 1991-93), Mahalo Airlines Travel Agy. (adv. bd. 1994—), Travel U. Internat. (adv. bd. 1994—), Casey Family (adv. bd. 1986—), Prevent Child Abuse Hawaii (bd. dir. 1975—), Child & Family Svcs. (bd. dir. 1975-85), Delta Kappa Gamma, Tri Delta. Avocations: travel, plants, photography. Office: Classic Travel 1413 S King St Ste 201 Honolulu HI 96814-2505

LEE, BLAINE NELSON, executive consultant, educator, author; b. Olympia, Wash., Apr. 3, 1946; s. Elwyn Earl and Thelma Marie (Woods) Reeder; m. Shawny Christian Lee; children: Blaine, Benjamin, Adam, Michal, Joseph, Joshua, Casey, Abraham, Eliza, Gabriel, Celeste. BS in Psychology, Brigham Young U., Provo, Utah, 1969, MS in Ednl. Psychology, 1972; PhD in Ednl. Psychology, U. Tex., 1982. Cert. ednl. specialist, secondary edn., ednl. adminstrn. Dir. instrnl. sys. USAF, San Antonio, 1972-75; assoc. prof. USAF Acad., Colorado Springs, Colo., 1975-78; edn. dir. Heritage Sch., Provo, Utah, 1978-81; asst. prof. Utah Valley State Coll., Orem, Utah, 1981-84; pres. Skills for Living, Salem, Utah, 1984-86; v.p. Covey Leadership Ctr., Provo, Utah, 1986—; ednl. cons. in field. Author: Affective Objectives, 1972, Personal Change, 1982, Stress Strategist, 1986, Principle Centered Leadership, 1990, Power Principle: Influence with Honor, 1997; contbr. articles to profl. jours. High councilman LDS Ch., mem. gen. bd., 1970-72; pres. Provo PTO. Named Outstanding Young Man of Am., U.S. C. of C., 1976, 84. Mem. APA, ASTD, Am. Mgmt. Assn., Nat. Spkrs. Assn., Phi Delta Kappa. Avocations: cmty. theatre, choir dir., camping, poetry, soccer coach. Home: 10435 S 600 E Salem UT 84653-9389 Office: Covey Leadership Ctr 360 W 4800 N Provo UT 84604-5675

LEE, BRANT THOMAS, lawyer, federal official, educator; b. San Francisco, Feb. 17, 1962; s. Ford and Patricia (Leong) L.; m. Marie Bernadette Curry, Sept. 20, 1991. BA in Philosophy, U. Calif., Berkeley, 1985; JD, Harvard U., 1990, M in Pub. Policy, 1994. Bar: Calif. 1992. Counsel subcom. on Constitution, U.S. Senate Judiciary Com., Washington, 1990-92; assoc. Breon, O'Donnell, Miller, Brown & Dannis, San Francisco, 1992-96; dep. staff sec., spl. asst. to Pres. (acting) The White House, Washington, 1993; vis. asst. prof. Syracuse (N.Y.) U. Coll. Law, 1996-97; asst. prof. U. Akron (Ohio) Sch. Law, 1997—; commr. San Francisco Ethics Commn., 1995-96. Trustee Chinese for Affirmative Action, San Francisco, 1992-96; bd. dirs. Conf. Asian Pacific Am. Leadership, Washington, 1990-92; staff mem. Dukakis for Pres., Boston, 1988. Mem. Bar Assn. San Francisco, Nat. Asian Pacific Am. Bar Assn., Asian Am. Bar Assn. Greater Bay Area. Office: U Akron Sch Law Akron OH 44325-2901

LEE, BRENDA (BRENDA MAE TARPLEY), singer, entertainer; b. Lithonia, Ga., Dec. 11, 1944; m. Ronnie Shacklett; children: Julie, Jolie. First appeared on Red Foley Ozark Jubilee Show, 1956; appeared in Opryland USA Show, Nashville, Music! Music! Music! Starring Brenda Lee, 1988; appeared in film Smokey and the Bandit II, 1980, in cable TV spl. Legendary Ladies, 1986, in PBS spl. Shake Rattle and Roll, 1988; recs. include Brenda Lee, 1960, Sincerely, 1961, All Alone Am I, 1962, By Request, 1964, Bye Bye Blues, 1966, 10 Golden Years, 1966, Memphis Portrait, 1970, Now, 1975, and many others; recent albums include Brenda Lee, 1991, Anthology Vols. 1 & 2, 1991, Greatest Hits Live, 1992. Recipient Gov.'s award Nat. Acad. Rec. Arts and Scis., 1984. Address: Brenda Lee Entertainments care Ronnie Shacklett PO Box 101188 Nashville TN 37210-1188*

LEE, BRIAN EDWARD, lawyer; b. Oceanside, N.Y., Feb. 29, 1952; s. Lewis H. Jr. and Jean Elinor (Andrews) L.; m. Eleanor L. Barker, June 5, 1982; children: Christopher Martin, Alison Ruth, Danielle Andrea. AB, Colgate U., 1974; JD, Valparaiso U., 1976. Bar: N.Y. 1977, U.S. Dist. Ct. (so. and ea. dists.) N.Y. 1978, U.S. Ct. Appeals (2nd cir. 1992). Assoc. Marshall, Bellofatto & Callahan, Lynbrook, N.Y., 1977-80, Morris, Duffy, Ivone & Jensen, N.Y.C., 1980-84; sr. assoc. Ivone, Devine & Jensen, Lake Success, N.Y., 1984-85, ptnr., 1985—. Pres., trustee Trinity Christian Sch. of Montville Inc., N.J., 1985—. Mem. ABA, N.Y. State Bar Assn., N.Y. County Lawyers Assn., Christian Legal Soc. Republican. Baptist. Home: 292 Jacksonville Rd Pompton Plains NJ 07444-1511 Office: Ivone Devine & Jensen 2001 Marcus Ave New Hyde Park NY 11042-1011

LEE, BRUCE, advertising executive; married; 2 children. Grad., CUNY; M in English Lit., U. Iowa. Various sr. creative positions several of the country's leading agys.; sr. ptnr., exec. creative dir. Ogilvy & Mather Direct. Office: Ogilvy & Mather Direct 309 W 49th St New York NY 10019-7316

LEE, BURNS WELLS, public relations executive; b. St. Louis, July 21, 1913; s. Channing B. and Rae (Wells) L.; m. Pauline Slocum, Apr. 10, 1939 (div.); m. Kathleen Booth Strutt, July 1, 1960. A.B., Occidental Coll., 1935. Publicity dir. Benton & Bowles, Inc., N.Y.C., Hollywood, 1939-42; sr. specialist war savs. staff Treasury Dept., Washington, 1942-43; pub. relations mgr. Rexall Drug Co., Los Angeles, 1946-49; pres. Bergen & Lee, Inc., Los Angeles, 1949—. Served as pub. relations officer USMCR, 1943-46. Mem. Pub. Rels. Soc. Am. (chmn. com. standards of profl. practice 1951, regional v.p. 1952-53, chmn. pub. rels. reference round table 1954-55, chmn. eligibility com. 1962, chmn. grievance bd. 1965-66, chmn. spl. task force on pub. rels. 1975-77, 1st ann. professionalism award L.A. chpt. 1964), Regional Plan Assn. So. Calif. (dir., chmn. pub. rels. com. 1967-70), Central City Assn. (dir. 1971-84), L.A. C. of C. (chmn. pub. rels., bus. outlook conf. 1974, mem. exec. com., internat. commerce coun. 1979-83, 85-89), GrandPeople (L.A., mem. bd. dirs. 1988-92),Exec. Svc. Corps. (cons. L.A. chpt. 1991—), Publicity Club L.A., Rotary L.A. (editor weekly publ. 1993—). Home: 870 Rome Dr Los Angeles CA 90065-3215

LEE, CARLA ANN BOUSKA, nursing educator; b. Ellsworth, Kans., Nov. 26, 1943; d. Frank J. and Christine Rose (Vopat) Bouska; m. Gordon Larry Lee, July 8, 1967. RN, Marymount Coll., Salina, Kans., 1964; BSN, U. Kans., 1967; MA, Wichita State U., 1972, EdS, 1975, M in Nursing, 1984; PhD, Kans. State U., 1988. RN; cert. family and adult nurse practitioner, advanced nurse adminstr., health edn. specialist. Staff, charge nurse Ellsworth (Kans.) County Vet. Meml. Hosp., 1964-65; critical, coronary, and surg. nurse Med. Ctr. U. Kans., Kansas City, 1966-67; Watkins Meml. Hosp. and Student Health Ctr., 1965-55; asst. dir., chief instr. sch. nursing Wesley Sch. Nursing, Wichita, Kans., 1967-74; asst prof., chairperson Nurse Clinician/Practitioner Dept. Wichita State U., 1974-84; assoc. prof., dir. nurse practitioner program Ft. Hays State U., Hays, Kans., 1992-95; assoc. prof., coord. postgrad. nursing studies Clark Coll., Omaha, 1995—; cons., v.p. devel. GRCI's CE Providership, 1994-96; lectr. Wichita State U., 1972-74, mem. grad. faculty, 1993-95; cons. Hays Med. Ctr.-Family Healthcare Ctr., 1993-96, Baker U., Northeastern U., Boston; mem. adv. coun. Kans. Newman Coll.; mem. adv. bd. Kans. Originals, Kans. Dept. Econ. Devel. Project, Wilson; mem. grad. faculty U. Kans. 1993-95; rschr. in field. Author: (with Ig & Barrett) Fluids and Electrolytes: A Basic Approach, 4th ed., 1996 (poetry) Seasons: Marks of Life, 1991 (Golden Poet award 1991), Winter Tree, 1995 (Internat. Poet of Merit award 1995), (booklet) Czechoslovakian History, 1988 (honor room Czech Mus. and Opera House, Wilson); author, editor: History of Kansas Nursing, 1987; contbr. articles to profl. jours. Co-founder Kans. Nurses Found., pres., trustee, 1978-93, vol. ARC, 1967-92, bd. dirs., 1977-90; mem. rschr. Gov.'s Commn. Health Care, Topeka, 1990; mem. State of Kans. health care agenda Kans. Pub. Health Assn., 1995; city coord. campaign Sec. State, 1986; vol., lectr. Am. Heart Assn., Am. Cancer Soc., 1967—; election judge Sedgwick County, Kans., 1989-94; chair Nat. Task Force on Care Competence of Nurse Practitioners, 1994-95; mem. Nat. Task Force on Feasibility of Care Exam. for Nurse Practitioners, 1994-95. Nurse Practitioner Tng. grantee U.S. Health and Human Svcs., 1966-67; named Outstanding Cmty. Leader, jaycees, Alumnus of Yr., Kansas U, 1979, marymount Coll., 1987, Poet of Yr., 1995; recipient Tchr. award Mentor Bd. Fellow Am. Acad. Nursing, Am. Acad. Nursing; mem. ANA (nat. and site visitor ANCC), Kans. Nurses Assn. (bd. dirs., treas.), Kans. Alliance Advanced Nurse Practitioners (founder, pres., 1986—), Gt. Plains Nurse Practitioners Soc., (founder, pres. 1993—), Internat. Soc. Poets (disting.), Alpha Eta (pres. Wichita State U. chpt.), Sigma Theta Tau Internat., Internat. Woman of Yr. Republican. Roman Catholic. Avocations: poetry, music, gardening, writing, sewing. Home: 1367 N Westlink St Wichita KS 67212-4238 Office: Clarkson Coll Dept Nursing 101 S 42nd St Omaha NE 68131-2715

LEE, CARLTON K. K., clinical pharmacist, consultant, educator; b. Honolulu, June 17, 1962; s. Hsiang Tsing and Ngan Kar (Ching) Lee; m. Joanne Evelyn Tilley, May 27, 1995. PharmD, U. of the Pacific, 1985; MPH, Johns Hopkins U., 1994. Hosp. pharmacy resident Johns Hopkins Hosp., Balt., 1985-86, clin. staff pharmacist pediatrics dept. pharmacy, 1986-88, sr. clin. pharmacist pediatrics dept. pharmacy, 1988-90, clin. coord. pediatrics dept. pharmacy, 1990—; asst. prof. Sch. Pharmacy, Howard U., Washignton, 1987-88; clin. asst. prof. Sch. Pharmacy, U. Md., Balt., 1989—; instr. pediatrics Sch. Medicine, Johns Hopkins U., Balt., 1992-95, asst. prof., 1995—; cons. Nat. Med. Care Inc., Columbia, Md., 1994, Home Intensive Care Inc., Hunt Valley, Md., 1992-93; founder, pres. Mid-Atlantic Pediatric Pharmacotherapy Specialists, 1993—. Contbg. author: Harriet Lane Handbook, 1990, 93, 96, Newborn Nursery Handbook, 1992, 97; investigational drug advisor Med. Sci. Bull., 1992—; contbr. articles to profl. jours.; author, co-author conf. papers. Mem. Am. Soc. Hosp. Pharmacists , Am. Coll. Clin. Pharmacy, Internat. Assn. Therapeutic Drug Monitoring and Clin. Toxicology. Office: Johns Hopkins Hosp Dept Pharmacy Svcs 600 N Wolfe St Baltimore MD 21205-2110

LEE, CAROL FRANCES, lawyer; b. Montreal, Que., Can., Sept. 17, 1955; came to U.S., 1966; d. Frank B. and Mary Lee; m. David John Seipp, Sept. 10, 1994. BA, Yale U., 1976, JD, 1981; BA, Oxford (Eng.) U., 1978. Bar: D.C. 1982, U.S. Ct. Appeals (D.C. cir.) 1982, U.S. Dist. Ct. D.C. 1984, U.S. Supreme Ct. 1986. Law clk. to judge U.S. Ct. Appeals (D.C. cir.), Washington, 1981-82; law clk. to justice U.S. Supreme Ct., Washington, 1982-83; assoc. Wilmer, Cutler & Pickering, Washington, 1983-88, ptnr., 1989-93; gen. counsel Export-Import Bank U.S., Washington, 1993-95; v.p., gen. counsel Internat. Fin. Corp. (World Bank Group), Washington, 1995—; lectr. law Harvard U., Cambridge, Mass., 1989-90, 92, Yale U., New Haven, Conn., 1991. Contbr. articles to profl. jours. Marshall scholar U.K., Oxford, 1976. Fellow Am. Bar Found.; mem. ABA, Am. Soc. Internat. Law, Am. Soc. Legal History, Phi Beta Kappa. Office: Internat Fin Corp 1850 I St NW Washington DC 20433-0003

LEE, CATHERINE, sculptor, painter; b. Pampa, Tex., Apr. 11, 1950; d. Paul Albert and Alice (Fleming) Porter; m. B. R. Mangham, 1967 (div. 1976); 1 child, Parker Valentine; m. Sean Scully, 1977. BA, San Jose State U., 1975. artist-in-residence Mpls. Coll. Art & Design, Minn. Inst. Art, 1982; vis. asst. prof. painting U. Tex., San Antonio, 1983; adj. asst. prof. Columbia U., N.Y.C., 1986-87. Group exhbns. include Albright-Knox Mus., Buffalo, 1987, Biennale de Sculpture, Monte Carlo, Monaco, 1991, Mus. Folkwang, Essen, Germany, 1992, Stadtische Galerie im Lenbachhaus, Munich, 1992, Neue Galerie Der Stadt Linz, Austria, 1992, Cleve. Mus. of Art, 1993, The Tate Gallery, 1994, many others. Creative Artists Pub. Svc. fellow, 1978; NEA grantee, 1989. Office: 106 Spring St New York NY 10012-3814 also: Galerie Karsten Greve, Wallrafplatz 3, 5000 Koln Germany also: Galerie Lelong 20 W 57th St New York NY 10019-3917

LEE, CHAN H., finance educator; b. South Korea, Jan. 24, 1931; came to U.S., 1954; s. Seung Nam and Sam Nei (Kim) L.; m. Soon-ki Lee, Dec. 15, 1970; children: Charlene, William, Mimi. BA, U. Nebr., 1957, MA, 1959; PhD, No. Ill. U., 1973. Chief Bur. of Rsch. and Statistics State of Nebr., Lincoln, 1962-66; rsch. analyst State of Ill., 1967-69; grad. instr. No. Ill. U., 1969-74; prof. fin. Mankato (Minn.) State U., 1982—, program dir., 1991—. Mem. Fin. Mgmt. Assn., Fin. Midwest Fin. Assn., Assn. Individual Investors, Internat. Assn. Fin. Planning (bd. dirs.). Home: 2025 Roe Crest Dr North Mankato MN 56003-3430 Office: Mankato State Univ Dept of Fin Mankato MN 56001

LEE, CHARLES, retired English language and literature educator, arts critic; b. Phila., Jan. 2, 1913; s. Benjamin and Lillian (Potash) Levy; divorced; children: Myles E., Gail M. A.B., U. Pa., 1933, M.A., 1936, Ph.D., 1955. Lit. editor Boston Herald-Traveler, 1936-40; contbg. reviewer

N.Y. Times Book Review, 1942-58; Lit. editor Phila. Record, 1940-47; contbg. reviewer Phila. Evening Bulletin, 1947-49; faculty U. Pa., 1949-65, prof. communications, 1959-65, prof. English, 1959-83, emeritus prof. English, 1983—; vice dean Annenberg Sch. Communications, 1959-65; roving critic WCAU radio, 1960-65, WCAU-TV, 1965-73; entertainments editor WCAU radio, 1974-79; roving critic WFLN-AM & FM, 1979—; creative cons. Four-Star Internat., Hollywood. Exhibited: one-man art show Janet Fleisher Gallery, Phila., 1972, Faculty Club, U. Pa., 1985, 89, Designer's Corner Gallery, 1990, Burrison Gallery, U. Pa., 1991, 93, 96; author Exile: A Book of Verse, 1936, How to Enjoy Reading, 1939, An Almanac of Reading, 1940, Weekend at the Waldorf, 1945, North East, South, West, 1945, The Twin Bedside Anthology, 1946, Snow, Ice and Penguins, 1950, I'll Be Waiting, 1958, The Hidden Public, 1958; Editor (author preface): The State of the Nation, 1963, Sevens Come Eleven, 1972, Ten Sevens, 1982, Love, Life and Laughter, 1990. Recipient 1st award for meritorious achievement in journalism U. Pa., 1944, achievement award Logan Square East, 1991, citation City of Phila., 1993. Mem. Soc. Am. Historians, A.A.U.P., Phi Beta Kappa. Office: WFLN-FM 8200 Ridge Ave Philadelphia PA 19128-2903 *Savor the sun. Study the dust. Enjoy what you can. Endure what you must.*

LEE, CHARLES ROBERT, telecommunications company executive; b. 1940; married; 5 children. BS in Metall. Engring., Cornell U., 1962; MBA, Harvard U., 1964. Mgr. bus. research U.S. Steel Co., 1964-71; sr. v.p. fin. Penn Ctrl. Corp., 1971-80, Columbia Pictures Industries, 1980-83, GTE Corp., Stamford, CT, 1983-86; sr. v.p. fin. & planning GTE Corp., 1986-89; pres., chief oper. officer GTE Corp., Stamford, CT, 1988-92, chmn., chief exec. officer, 1992—, also bd. dirs.; bd. dirs. United Techs. Corp., Proctor & Gamble Co., USX Corp.; mem. Pres.'s Nat. Security Telecoms. Adv. Com. Trustee Cornell U.; bd. dirs. Stamford Hosp. Found., New Am. Schs. Devel. Corp.; bd. dirs. of the assocs. Harvard Bus. Sch. Mem. Fin. Execs. Inst., Nat. Planning Assn. (com. on new Am. realities, trustee), Bus. Roundtable, Stanwich Club, Blind Brook Club, Thunderbird Country Club, Laurel Valley Golf Club. Office: GTE Service Corp 1 Stamford Forum Stamford CT 06901-3302*

LEE, CHARLYN YVONNE, chemical engineer; b. Washington, May 1, 1960; d. James Charles and Beverly Mae (Williams) L. BSChemE, MIT, 1982; MSChemE, Ga. Inst. Tech., 1984. Cert. environ. mgr. Engring. intern Naval Surface Weapons Ctr., Silver Spring, Md., 1977-78; engring. aid VA, Washington, 1978-81; engr. Dupont Savannah River Lab, Aiken, S.C., 1982-83, Dupont Exptl. Sta., Wilmington, Del., 1984-86; mfg. engr. Dupont Spruance Plant, Richmond, Va., 1986-89; rsch. engr. Dupont Jackson Lab., Deepwater, N.J., 1989-91; process engr. Dupont Pontchartrain Works, LaPlace, La., 1991-93; environ. protection specialist NIH, Bethesda, Md., 1995—. Bd. mem. Richmond Area Program for Minorities in Engring., 1987-89; corp. advisor Nat. Action Coun. for Minorities in Engring., Wilmington, 1991; mem. D.C. Youth Adv. Bd. for Mental Health, Washington. Recipient Merit award VA, 1981; Proctor and Gamble grantee, 1981; Gem fellow Nat. Consortium for Grad. Degrees for Minorities in Engring., Inc., 1982, Fed. Jr. fellow, 1978. Mem. AIChE, NAFE. Home: 4812 Illinois Ave NW Washington DC 20011-4578

LEE, CHESTER MAURICE, government official; b. New Derry, Pa., Apr. 6, 1919; s. Joseph and Mary L.; m. Rose McGinnis, Apr. 18, 1942; children: Suzanne D., David J., Virginia A., Nancy M. B.S., U.S. Naval Acad., 1941; postgrad., George Washington U., 1962-63, Nat. War Coll., 1962-63. Commd. ensign U.S. Navy, 1941, advanced through grades to capt., 1961; comdg. officer U.S.S. Rodman, Charleston, S.C., 1952-53; instr. Gen. Line Sch., Monterey, Calif., 1953-56; with Spl. Projects Office, Bur. Naval Weapons, Washington, 1956-58, 60-62; comdg. officer U.S.S. Gyatt, Norfolk, 1958-60; comdr. Destroyer Div. 132, Long Beach, 1963-64; with Office Sec. Def., Washington, 1964-65; ret., 1965; with NASA, Washington, 1965-87; dir. Apollo Mission NASA, 1969-72, program dir. Apollo/Soyuz Test Project, 1973-75, dir. space transp. systems utilization, 1975-81, dir. customer services, 1981-87, asst. assoc. adminstr. Office of Space Flight, from 1987; now pres. Spacehab Inc., Washington. Decorated Navy Commendation medal; recipient 2 Exceptional Service medals, 1969, 3 Distinguished Service medals, 1973, 75, 87, Distinguished Service medals NASA., Outstanding Leadership medal; Pres.' Rank of Meritorious Exec. with Sr. Exec. Service.. Fellow AIAA (assoc.), Am. Astronautic Soc. *

LEE, CHI HSIANG, electrical engineer, educator; b. Mar. 27, 1936. BS, Nat. Taiwan U., 1959; PhD, Harvard U., 1968. Prof. elec. engring. dept. elec. engring. U. Md. Fellow IEEE (chmn. 1986-89, lightwave tech. com., MTT-S, vice-chmn. LEOS Washington-No. Va. chpt. 1988-89). Office: Univ Maryland Dept of Electrical Engineering College Park MD 20742*

LEE, CHIN-TIAN, academic administrator, agricultural studies educator; b. Chiayi, Taiwan, June 22, 1940; came to U.S., 1967; s. Pau-Tong and Wu-May (Yang) L.; m. Shu-Teh Kuo, June 22, 1969; Corinna T., Frances T. BS, Nat. Taiwan U., Taipei, 1964, MS, 1967; MS, U. Wis., 1969, PhD, 1971. Rsch. asst. Nat. Taiwan U., Taipei, 1965-67; rsch. asst. U. Wis., Madison, 1967-71, biologist, 1971-74; asst. prof. U. Guam, Mangilao, 1974-80; assoc. prof. U. Guam, Manigilao, 1980-87, prof., 1987—, dean coll. agriculture, 1989—; dir. Guam Coop. Extension Svc., Mangilao, 1989—, Guam Agrl. Expt. Sta., Mangilao, 1989—; cons. South Pacific Commn., Suva, Fiji, 1978. Contbr. articles to profl. jours. Vice-chmn. bd. dirs. Chinese Sch. Guam, Harmon, 1984-88, advisor, 1989-91, chmn., 1992—. 2d lt. Taiwanese Air Force, 1965. Recipient Outstanding Prof. award 19th Guam Legislature, Faculty award for excellence in rsch. U. Guam, 1988; USDA grantee, 1974-89. Mem. Chinese Assn. Agrl. Sci., Asian Assn. Colls. and Univs. (bd. dirs. 1989—), We. Assn. Agrl. Exptl. Sta. Dirs. (exec. com. 1993), Am. Soc. Agronomy, Am. Soc. Horticultural Sci., Epsilon Sigma Phi. Avocations: reading, gardening, traveling, swimming, fishing. Home: Y-Papao Estates 156 Bengbing St Dededo GU 96912-2421 Office: U Guam Coll Agriculture Coll Agriculture UDG Sta Mangilao GU 96923

LEE, CHONG-SIK, political scientist, educator; b. Anju, Korea, July 30, 1931; came to U.S., 1954, naturalized, 1969; s. Bong-Joo and Bong-kye (Moon) L.; m. Myung-Sook Woo, Mar. 19, 1962; children—Sharon, Gina, Roger. B.A., UCLA, 1956, M.A., 1957; Ph.D., U. Calif., Berkeley, 1961. Instr. polit. sci. U. Colo., Boulder, 1960-61, Dartmouth Coll., Hanover, N.H., 1961-63; asst. prof. U. Pa., Phila., 1963-65; assoc. prof. U. Pa., 1965-73, prof., 1973—; dir. Anspach Inst. Diplomacy and Fgn. Affairs, 1980-85, chmn. grad. program internat. relations, 1980-85; chmn. joint com. on Korean Studies Social Sci. Research Council and Am. Council Learned Socs., 1970-77. Author: The Politics of Korean Nationalism, 1963, Counterinsurgency in Manchuria: The Japanese Experience, 1931-40, 1967, (with Robert A. Scalapino) Communism in Korea, 1973, The Life of Kim Kyu-sik, 1974, Materials on Korean Communism, 1945-47, 1977, The Korean Workers' Party: A Short History, 1978, Revolutionary Struggle in Manchuria: Chinese Communism and Soviet Interest, 1922-1945, 1983, Japan and Korea: The Political Dimension, 1985; (with Mike Langford) Korea: Land of Morning Calm, 1988, Recollections of Anti-Japanese Revolutionaries, 1988, Korea Briefing, 1990, 91, North Korea in Transition, 1991, In Search of a New Order in East Asia, 1991; mem. editorial bd.: Asian Survey, 1973-97, Jour. N.E. Asian Studies, 1982-97, Orbis, 1980-86. Mem. Task Force on Equal Ednl. Opportunity and Quality Edn., Pa. Higher Edn. Planning Commn., 1977. Social Sci. Rsch. Coun. grantee, 1963, 66-67, 72, 73-74, Rockefeller Found. grantee, 1965-66, Hoover Inst. grantee, 1980, Yonkang Found. grantee, 1990-93; Ford Found. faculty fellow, 1969-70. Mem. Am. Polit. Sci. Assn. (Woodrow Wilson Found. award for best book in polit. sci. 1974), Assn. Asian Studies. Home: 8 Cypress Ln Berwyn PA 19312-1005 Office: Univ Pa Dept Polit Sci Philadelphia PA 19104-6215

LEE, CHOOCHON, physics educator, researcher; b. Seoul, Korea, June 8, 1930; came to U.S., 1962.; s. Yoon Young and Soon Ye (Rhee) L.; m. Chung Sun Yun, Apr. 9, 1960; children: John Taihee, Jane Eun Kyoung, Carol Eunmee. BS in Physics, Seoul Nat. U., 1953, MS in Physics, 1957; PhD in Physics, U. Ill., 1968. From instr. to asst. prof. Seoul Nat. U., 1957-62; rsch. asoc. U. Ill., Urbana, 1968; rsch. physicist U. Montreal, Que., Can., 1968-75; assoc. prof. Korea Advanced Inst. Sci. and Tech., Seoul, Taejon, 1975-78, prof., 1978-92, Korea Telecom. Found. prof. physics, 1992—; pres. Korea Advanced Inst. Sci. and Tech., Seoul, 1980-92; vis. scholar Harvard U., Cambridge, Mass., 1982-83, 87-88. Author: Physics of Semiconductor Materials and Applications, 1986; contbr. over 180 articles to profl. jours. and internat. conf. procs. Decorated Order of Rose of Sharon Republic of Korea, 1995; recipient Presdl. Sci. prize Govt. of Republic of Korea, 1985, Inchon prize in acad. achievement, 1993. Mem. IEEE, Am. Phys. Soc., Korean Phys. Soc. (pres. 1991-93), Soc. Info. Display (bd. dirs. 1991—). Methodist. Achievements include discovery of negative staerble-wronski experiment; first to confirm mechanism of Controversial State III annealing in gold, to explain persistent photocontercivity in a-Si:H and a-Si:H/a-SiN multilayers; 1st observation of persistent photo conductivity in porous silicon. Home: 237 Kajong-dong KIT Apt 15-201, Yusongku Taejon 305-350, Republic of Korea Office: Korea Advanced Inst Sci and Tech, 373-1 Kusong-dong Yusong-ku, Taejon 305-701, Republic of Korea

LEE, CLEMENT WILLIAM KHAN, trade association administrator; b. N.Y.C., Feb. 7, 1938; s. William P. and Helen M. BTh, Concordia Coll., 1958; MDiv, Concordia Theol. Sem., 1962; MA, New Sch. for Social Research, 1976. Asst. exec. dir. Greater Detroit Luth. Ctr., 1962; editor Detroit and Suburban Luth. Newspaper, 1963; assoc. communications dir. Met. Detroit Council of Chs., 1964; dir. media ops. Am. Bible Soc., N.Y.C., 1967; dir. media relations Luth. Council U.S.A., N.Y.C., 1971-82, asst. exec. dir. communications and interpretation, 1977-82; dir. dept. telecommunications Luth. Ch. in Am., N.Y.C., 1983-87; dir. electronic media Episcopal Ch., N.Y.C., 1987-93, program dep. for communication, 1989-93, Episcopal telecomm. dir., 1993—; media cons. Luth. Ch.-Mo. Synod, Spaulding for Children, Metro News of Metro N.Y., Synod of Luth. Ch. Am., archtl. newsletter Window, Luth. Deaconess Assn., Concordia Coll., Bronxville, Physicians for Social Responsibility, Wheatridge Found., Luth. Sch. Theology, Chgo.; chmn. broadcast ops. com. Nat. Council Chs. of Christ U.S.A., 1976-80; vice chmn. bd. mgrs. Communications Commn., 1977-80; chmn. inter-faith Media Data System, 1981; mem. TV awards com. N.Y. Council Chs.; mgr. Lutherans-in-Media Conf. I and II, 1980, Luth. Audio-Visual Conf., 1981; project dir. Lambeth Conf. Inter-Anglican Telecommunication Network, 1988; internat. computer network resource leader Religious Communications Congress 90, 1990; bd. dirs. FACTA TV News, Inc.; pres. N.Y. chpt. Religious Pub. Rels. Coun.; telecommunication cons. World Coun. of Chs., Canberra Assembly, 1990-91, Episc. Bd. Theol. Edn., 1993—. Editor: Media Alert newsletter, 1980-86, Luth. Communication newsletter, 1983-87, Episcopal Media Adv. newsletter, 1989—; creator children's TV series Storyline; producer multi-image sequences, Augustana Jubilee, 1980, multi-image program Proclaim, 1984, multi-image effects, Milw. Conv., 1986, (films) Mission on Six Continents, 1975, Room for a Stranger, 1978, Winter Wheat, 1982; exec. producer, One in Mission, 1985, Gathering of the Family, 1988, Doers of the Word, 1988, The Tully-Freeman Report, 1988, Outpourings of Love, 1989, Faith on a Tightrope, 1989, Fresh Winds Blowing, 1989, Prophecy Fulfilled in Me, 1990, President Carter Center Health Video, 1990, To Walk in Beauty, 1990, Pathways for Peace, 1990, Word in the World, 1991, Executive Council Presents, 1991, Cantenbury in North Carolina, 1992. Mem. Metro N.Y. Synod Evangelical Luth. Ch. in Am. Communication Commn., Religious Pub. Rels. Coun.; mem. communication dept. nat. adv. com. Evang. Luth. Ch. in Am.; chair Telecomm. Task Force Lambeth Anglican Bishops Confs., 1988, Bldg. Restoration com. St. John's Episc. Ch., N.Y.C., 1993-95; gov. Inter-Anglican Info. Network Quest Internat. Mgmt. team, 1992—. Recipient award Detroit Press Club Found., 1963, silver medal Internat. Film and TV Festival, 1975, 79, Creative Excellence award U.S. Indsl. Film Festival, 1986, Brit. Telecommunications award, 1988, Polly Bond award, 1989, 90, 91, 92, N.Y. TV Festival finalist, 1990. Mem. Assn. Edn. Communication Tech., Internat. Assn. Bus. Communicators, Internat. TV Assn., World Assn. Christian Communication (chmn. N.Am. broadcast sect. 1975), Nat. Interfaith Cable Coalition VISN (members' com.), Satellite TV Network (bd. dirs.), Episcopal Cathedral Teleconferencing Network (steering com.). Office: Episcopal Ch Nat Office 815 2nd Ave New York NY 10017-4503*

LEE, DAI-KEONG, composer; b. Honolulu, Sept. 2, 1915; s. Lin Fong and Young Kun (Chang) L.; m. Dorothy Isabelle Moncur, May 16, 1974. Student in pre-medicine, U. Hawaii, 1933-36; scholarship student with Roger Sessions, N.Y.C., 1937-38; fellowship student under Frederick Jacobi, Juilliard Grad. Sch., 1938-41; fellowship student under Aaron Copland, Berkshire Music Ctr., summer 1941; M.A. under Otto Luening, Columbia U., 1951. bd. dirs. Am. Music Ctr., N.Y.C., 1960-69. Recorded Prelude, Hula, Symphony No. 1, Polynesian Suite; wrote mus. score for motion picture Letter from Australia, 1945; guest condr., ABC Symphony, Sydney, Australia, 1944-45; composer: orchestral works including Prelude and Hula, 1939, Hawaiian Festival Overture, 1940, Introduction and Allegro for Strings, 1941, Golden Gate Overture for Chamber Orch., 1941, Polynesian Suite, Symphony No. 1, 1941, revised 1947, Symphony No. 2, 1952; chamber works including String Quartet No. 1, 1947, Sonatina for Piano, 1947, Incantation and Dance for Piano and Violin, 1948, Introduction and Allegro for Cello and Piano, 1947; opera Open the Gates, produced by Blackfriars, N.Y.C., 1951; ballet Waltzing Matilda, 1951; mus. score Teahouse of the August Moon, produced by Maurice Evans-George Shaeffer, 1953; Polynesian Suite for Orch., 1958, Violin Concerto, 1947, revised 1955, Mele Olili for Chorus, Solo and Orch., 1960, Canticle of the Pacific, 1968; mus. play Noa-Noa, 1972; Mortal Thoughts of a Buddhist Monk for baritone, chorus and orch., 1976; one-act opera Ballad of Kitty the Barkeep, 1979; mus. plays Jenny Lind, 1981, Gauguin, Maker of Sea and Sky, 1994; Concerto Grosso for string orch., 1952, rev., 1985; contbr. articles to music mags., newspapers. Served with AUS, 1942-45, PTO. Received Albert Metz commn. for violin concerto, 1946; received CBS commn. for Introduction and Allegro for Strings, 1941, Inst. Mus. Art commn. for one-act opera, Poet's Dilemma, 1940; recipient hon. mention Prix de Rome competition Am. Acad. in Rome, 1942; Guggenheim fellow, 1945, 51. Mem. ASCAP, League Composers, Allied MacDowell Club, Dramatists Guild. Composer orchestral, symphonic, chamber music; 1st orchestral work Valse Pensieroso, performed Honolulu Symphony Orch., 1936; works performed by N.Y. Philharm., Eastman Rochester Philharm., Mpls., San Francisco, Cin., CBS, Nat., Montreal, Manila, N.Y.C. Phila., symphony orchs.; under direction of Kurtz, Monteux, Mitropoulos, Goosens, Barlow, Caston, Dixon, Stokowski, Stoessel, Pelletier, Wallenstein, others. Home: 245 W 104th St New York NY 10025-4249

LEE, DAN M., state supreme court justice; b. Petal, Miss., Apr. 19, 1926; s. Buford Aaron and Pherbia Ann (Camp) L.; m. Peggy Jo Daniel, Nov. 27, 1947 (dec. 1952); children, Sheron, Lee Anderson; m. Mary Alice Gray, Sept. 30, 1956; 1 child, Dan Jr. Attended, U. So. Miss., 1946; LLB, Jackson Sch. Law, 1949; JD, Miss. Coll., 1970. Bar: Miss. 1948. Ptnr. Franklin & Lee, Jackson, Miss, 1948-54, Lee, Moore and Countiss, Jackson, Miss., 1954-71; county judge Hinds County, Hinds County, 1971-77; cir. judge Hinds-Yazoo Counties, Hinds-Yazoo Counties, 1977-82; assoc. justice Miss. Supreme Ct., Jackson, 1982-87, presiding justice, 1987-95, chief justice, 1995—. With U.S. Naval Air Corps, 1944-46. Mem. ABA, Hinds County Bar Assn., Miss. State Bar Assn., Aircraft Owners and Pilots Assn., Am. Legion, VFW. Democrat. Baptist. Lodges: Masons, Odd Fellows.

LEE, DANIEL ANDREW, osteopathic physician, ophthalmologist; b. Bklyn., Aug. 20, 1951; s. Jack W. and Lily (Ho) L.; m. Janet Lynne Eng, June 14, 1975 (div. Sept. 1985); children: Jason Matthew, Brian Christopher, Joshua Daniel; m. Kelly Lynne Crego, Sept. 5, 1987; children: Joshua Daniel, Alexandra Nicole Avetkova, Brandon Scott. BS in Psychobiology, SUNY, Stony Brook, 1973; BS in Biology, Westminster Coll., 1973; OD, Pa. Coll. Optometry, 1977; DO, Ohio U., 1984. Cert. in low vision proficiency, ophthalmology; cert. Osteopathic Academy of Opthalmology and Otolaryngology. Instr. Mohawk Valley C.C., Rome, N.Y., 1978-80; pvt. practice optometry, Utica, N.Y., 1978-80, Chauncey, Ohio, 1981-84, Dayton, Ohio, 1984—; intern Grandview Hosp., Dayton, 1984, mem. staff, 1984-85, ophthalmology resident, 1985—; ophthalmolgy chief resident, 1987-88; fellow Ophthalmology Corneal Cons. of Ind., Indpls.; chmn. dept. ophthalmology USNH, Okinawa; assoc. prof. Opthalmology Ohio U. Coll. Osteopathic Medicine; cons. Rome Sch. Dist., Cen. Assn. for Blind, Utica, Kernan Sch. for Multiple Handicapped, Utica, Dept. of Defense Schs.; credentials chmn. Dayton br. Laser Ctrs. Am.; Amelia Earhart student adv. coun., Vestry-All Soul's Episcopal Ch.; speaker various profl. orgns. and confs.; mem. curriculum adv. com. Deer Creek Curriculum Rev. Conf., 1982. Contbr. articles to profl. jours. Mem. adv. bd. ARC, Rome, 1977-80; mem. Mohawk Valley Chinese Cultural Assn., Rome, 1977-80, Dayton Area Chinese Assn., 1985—; nominated People to People Optometry Delegation to People's Republic of China, 1985, India, 1986; co-chmn. Ohio Eye Injury Registry; chmn. pub. health & welfare com. Dayton dist. Acad. Osteo. Medicine. Served with USAF, 1977-80, to lt. comdr. USNR, 1988-91. Fellow Am. Acad. Optometry, Osteopathic Coll. Ophthalmology, Otolaryngology, and Head and Neck Surgery; mem. AMA, Am. Cancer Soc. (mem. bd. dirs. Miami County, Troy chpt.), Am. Osteo. Assn. (student rep. nat. com. on colls. 1984), Ohio Osteo. Assn., Am. Acad. Ophthalmology, Pediatric Keratoplasty Soc., Dayton Area Chinese Assn., Gold Key, Montgomery County Med. Soc., Ohio State Med. Assn., Am. Soc. Cataract and Refractive Surgery, Ohio Opthalmological Soc., Ohio Eyes, Ears, Nose, and Throat Assn. Soc. (pres., program chair 1996), Miami County Medical Soc., Internat. Soc. Refractive Keratoplasty, Assn. Contemporary Optholmology, Internat. Soc. Refractive Surgery, C. of C. Huber Heights and Troy, Order of the Eastern Star, Harmony Lodge, Teikoku Lodge, Aloha and Antioch Shriner's Temples, Scottish Rite, Troy Lions Club, Beta Beta Beta. Episcopalian. Avocations: hunting, fishing, martial arts, photography, playing mandolin. Home: 1495 Fox Run Troy OH 45373-9594 Office: 7371 Brandt Pike Ste B Huber Heights OH 45424-3200

LEE, DANIEL KUHN, economist; b. Kyoto, Japan, Dec. 18, 1946; came to U.S., 1977; s. Chu G. and Myung N. (Lee) L.; m. Kaye K.S. Kwon, Apr. 10, 1976; children: David, Alexander. BS, Kyoto U., Japan, 1970; MA, Seoul Nat. U., Seoul, Republic of Korea, 1973, SUNY, Stony Brook, 1979; PhD, Iowa State U., 1981. Postdoctoral rsch. assoc. Iowa State U., Ames, 1981-82, instr., 1982; sr. economist Miss. Rsch. and Devel. Ctr., Jackson, 1982-88; dir. of econs. Miss. Insts. of Higher Learning, Jackson, 1988-95; sr. fiscal advisor Barents Group, KPMG Peat Marwick, 1995—; adj. prof. Jackson State U., 1986-88; advisor Gov.'s Econ. Task Force, Jackson, 1982-84. Author: A Study of Mississippi Input-Output Model, 1986; contbr. articles to profl. jours. Exec. dir. So. Regional Assn., Washington, 1992—; elder Presbyn. Ch. USA, 1991—. Travel grantee UN Indsl. Devel. Orgn., Vienna, Austria, 1986. Mem. So. Regional Sci. Assn., North Am. Regional Sci. Assn., Am. Econ. Assn., So. Econ. Assn., Gamma Sigma Delta. Avocations: jogging, swimming. Office: Barents Group KPMG Peat Marwick 656 Old Agency Rd Ridgeland MS 39157-9244

LEE, DAVID C., screenwriter. Screenwriter TV series, including The Jeffersons, 1979-85, Cheers, 1984-88, Wings, 1991; exec. prodr. Frasier, 1992— (Emmy award for outstanding comedy series 1995). Office: care The Jim Preminger Agy 1650 Westwood Blvd Ste 201 Los Angeles CA 90024-5613*

LEE, DAVID DEWITT, industrial hygienist; b. Detroit, Feb. 16, 1948; s. Floyd Herbert and Anne Theresa (Damask) L.; m. Lorraine Angeline Wozniak, Sept. 6, 1969; children: Jennifer, Mary, Brian, Jonathan, Sarah. BS Psychology, No. Mich. U., 1975; M Indsl Safety, U. Minn., 1988. Cert. indsl. hygienist, safety profl. Ops. foreman Nat. Steel Pellet Co., Keewatin, Minn., 1976-78, 84-86; safety engr. Hanna Mining Co. Agts., Hibbing, Minn., 1978-81, Butler Tacconite, Nashwauk, Minn., 1981-84; indsl. hygienist Sonora (Calif.) Mining Co., 1988-89, State Indsl. Ins. System, Reno, Nev., 1990-92; indsl. hygienist, safety specialist Univ./C.C. System Nev., Reno, 1992—. Accredited vis., vis. chmn. Mended Hearts, Inc., Reno, 1993-95. With USN, 1967-70, Vietnam. Recipient scholarship Semi-Conductor Safety Assn. Mem. Am. Indsl. Hygiene Assn., Am. Conf. of Govt. Indsl. Hygienist, Am. Acad. Indsl. Hygiene, Am. Bd. Indsl. Hygiene, Am. Soc. Safety Engrs. (chpt. sec. 1994—, chpt. pres.-elect 1995, pres. 1996), Bd. Cert. Indsl. Hygienist and Safety Profls. Republican. Roman Catholic. Avocations: weightlifting, running, bicycling. Office: U Nev Environ Health & Safety MS 328 Reno NV 89557

LEE, DAVID MORRIS, physics educator; b. Rye, N.Y., Jan. 20, 1931; s. Marvin and Annette (Franks) L.; m. Dana Thorangkul, Sept. 7, 1960; children: Eric Bertel, James Marvin. AB, Harvard U., 1952; MS, U. Conn., 1955; PhD, Yale U., 1959. Instr. of physics Cornell U., Ithaca, N.Y., 1959-60, asst. prof. physics, 1960-63, assoc. prof. physics, 1963-68, prof. physics, 1968—; vis. scientist Brookhaven Nat. Lab., Upton, N.Y., 1966-67; vis. prof. U. Fla., Gainesville, 1974-75, 94, U. Calif., San Diego, La Jolla, 1988; vis. lectr. Peking U., Beijing, China, 1981; chair municipal Joseph Fourier U., Grenoble, France, 1994. Contbr. articles to Phys. Rev. Letters, Phys. Rev., Physica and Nature. With U.S. Army, 1952-54. John Simon Guggenheim fellow Guggenheim Found., 1966-67, 74-75, Japan Soc. Promotion of Scis. fellow, 1977; recipient Sir Francis Simon Meml. prize British Inst. of Physics, 1976, shared Nobel prize for physics, 1996. Fellow AAAS, Am. Phys. Soc. (Oliver Buckley prize 1981); mem. Am. Acad. Arts and Scis., Nat. Acad. Scis. Achievements include co-discovery of superfluid 3He, of the tricritical point of 3He-4He mixtures; co-observation of spin waves in spin polarized hydrogen gas. Office: Cornell U Physics Dept Clark Hall Ithaca NY 14853

LEE, DAVID STODDART, investment counselor; b. Boston, Jan. 12, 1934; s. George Cabot and Kathleen Bowring (Stoddart) L.; m. Lucinda Hopkins, Apr. 29, 1972; children: Alexander Putnam, Madeline Jackson, Alice Ingalls. A.B., Harvard U., 1956, M.B.A., 1960. V.p., dir. Lee Higginson Corp., N.Y.C., 1960-65; mng. dir., Scudder, Stevens and Clark, Boston, 1965—; dir., pres., asst. treas. Scudder Investor Svcs., Inc. (formerly Scudder Fund Distbrs.); pres., trustee Scudder Calif. Tax Free Trust, Scudder Cash Investment Trust, Scudder U.S. Treas. Money Fund, Scudder Mcpl. Trust, Scudder State Tax Free Trust, Scudder Tax Free Money Fund, Scudder Tax Free Trust; v.p., trustee Scudder Equity Trust, Scudder GNMA Fund, Scudder Portfolio Trust; v.p. Scudder Securities Trust, Scudder Funds Trust, Scudder Mut. Funds, Inc., Scudder Investment Trust, Scudder Variable Life Investment Fund, The Argentina Fund, Inc., The Brazil Fund, Inc., The Korea Fund, Inc., The L.Am. Dollar Income Fund, Inc., Scudder New Asia Fund, Inc., Scudder New Europe Fund, Inc., Scudder World Income Opportunities Fund, Inc.; v.p., asst. treas. Scudder Global Fund, Inc., Scudder Internat. Fund, Inc.; chmn. dir. Scudder Instnl. Fund, Inc., Scudder Fund, Inc.; v.p., asst. treas. AARP Cash Investment Funds, AARP Growth Trust, AARP Income Trust, AARP Tax Free Income Trust, AARP Managed Investment Portfolios Trust; v.p. Scudder Svc. Corp. Trustee Cotting Sch., Boston, 1974—, New Eng. Med. Ctr., 1974—, The Winsor Sch., 1991—; bd. dirs., treas. Rogerson Cmtys., 1978—; corporator Mass. Gen. Hosp., 1975—. Lt. (j.g.) USN, 1956-58. Mem. Soc. Chartered Fin. Analysts (chartered investment counsellor). Republican. Episcopalian. Clubs: Country, Somerset (Boston).

LEE, DEBORA ANN, elementary school educator, reading specialist; b. Beckley, W. Va., May 2, 1958; d. David Lavon and Edith (Graham) L. AB in Bus. Adminstrn., Beckley Coll., 1978; AB in Arts, Beckley Coll. (Coll. W. Va.), 1982; BS, Concord Coll., 1984; MA, U. W. Va., 1990. Cert. tchr. elem. edn. 1-8, reading specialist k-12, adult. Sec. United Mine Workers Assn., Mullens, W. Va., 1978; receptionist, sec. Ashland Fin., Mullens, 1978-79; tchr. Wyoming County Bd. Edn., Pineville, W. Va., 1984—. Mem. NEA, W. Va. Edn. Assn., Internat. Reading Assn., W. Va. State Reading Coun., Wyoming County Reading Coun. (charter, pres. 1990), Kappa Delta Pi. Democrat. Baptist. Avocations: reading, cooking, needlepoint, music, travel. Office: Mullens Elem Sch 300 Front St Mullens WV 25882-1304

LEE, DEBORAH ROCHE, federal agency administrator. BA, Duke U., 1979; M in Internat. Affairs, Columbia U., 1981. Intern Presdl. Mgmt. Program, Washington, 1981; profl. staff mem. House Armed Svcs. Com., Washington; asst. sec. def. for res. affairs Dept. Def., Washington, 1993—. Office: Reserve Affairs 1500 Defense Pentagon Rm 2E 520 Washington DC 20301-1500*

LEE, DER-TSAI, electrical engineering and computer science educator, researcher, consultant; b. Taipei, Taiwan, Apr. 5, 1949. BSEE, Nat. Taiwan U., Taipei, 1971; MS in Computer Sci., U. Ill., 1976, PhD in Computer Sci., 1978. Asst. prof. elec. engring. and computer sci. Northwestern U., Evanston, Ill., 1978-81, assoc. prof. elec. engring. and computer sci., 1981-86, prof. elec. engring. and computer sci., 1986—; adj. prof. Nat. Taiwan U., 1984-85; program dir. NSF, Washington, 1989-90; vis. rsch. prof. Inst. Info. Sci., Academia Sinica, Taipei, 1984-85; cons., IBM, Yorktown Heights, N.Y., 1982, USDA, New Orleans, 1985-89. Editor: Algorithmic Aspects of VLSI Layout, 1994, Internat. Jour. Computational Geometry and Applications, 1991—. Fellow IEEE, Assn. for Computing Machinery; mem. Soc. Indsl. and Applied Math. Achievements include copyright for Geosheet: A Distributed Visulation Tool for Geometrics Algorithms. Office: Northwestern U EE/CS Dept of ECE 2145 Sheridan Rd Evanston IL 60208-0834 Office: Northwestern U ECE Dept 633 Clark St Evanston IL 60208-0001

LEE, DON YOON, publisher, academic researcher and writer; b. Seoul, Korea, Apr. 7, 1936; came to U.S., 1957; s. Yoo-ehn and Ch'i-ho (Kim) L. BA, U. Wash., 1963; MA, St. John's U., Jamaica, N.Y., 1967; MS, Georgetown U., 1971; MA, Ind. U., 1975, 90. Founder, pub. Eastern Press, Inc., Bloomington, Ind., 1981—. Author: History of Early Relation Between China and Tibet, 1981, An Introduction to East Asian and Tibetan Linguistics and Culture, 1981, Learning Standard Arabic, 1988, An Annotated Bibliography of Selected Works on China, 1981, Light Literature and Philosophy of East Asia, 1982, An Annotated Bibliography on Inner Asia, 1983, An Annotated Archaeological Bibliography of Selected Works on Norther and Central Asia, 1983, Traditional Chinese Thoughts: The Four Schools, 1990, others. Office: Eastern Press Inc PO Box 881 Bloomington IN 47402-0881

LEE, DONALD JOHN, federal judge; b. 1927. AB, U. Pitts., 1950; LLB, Duquesne U., 1954. Bar: Pa. Supreme Ct. 1955; U.S. Supreme Ct. 1984. Assoc. George Y. Meyer and Assocs., 1954-57; law clk. to Hon. Rabe F. Marsh Jr. U.S. Dist. Ct., Pa., 1957-58; assoc. Wilner, Wilner and Kuhn, 1958-61; ptnr. Dougherty, Larrimer & Lee, Pitts., 1961-84, 86-88; judge Ct. Common Pleas of Allegheny County, Pa., 1984-86, 88-90, U.S. Dist. Ct. (we. dist.) Pa., Pitts., 1990—; councilman Borough of Green Tree, 1961-63, solicitor, 1963-84, 86-88; spl. asst. atty. gen. Office of Atty. Gen. Commonwealth of Pa., 1963-74; spl. legal counsel Home Rule Study Commn., Municipality of Bethel Park and Borough of Green Tree, 1973-74, City of Pitts., 1978-80, various municipalities, 1970-86; chmn. Home Rule Charter Transition Com. Bethel Park, 1978. Mem. ad hoc com. Salvation Army. With USN, 1945-47. Mem. ABA, Allegheny County Bar Assn., St. Thomas More Legal Soc., Western Pa. Conservancy, Ancient Order of Hibernians, Knights of Equity, Woodland Hills Swim Club, Gaelic Arts Soc., Tin Can Sailors. Office: US Dist Ct 7th Grant St Rm 916 Pittsburgh PA 15219

LEE, DONALD YOUNG (DON LEE), publishing executive, editor, writer; b. Tokyo, Dec. 11, 1959; s. Victor Young and Jean Ann (Kim) L. BA in English, UCLA, 1982; MFA in Creative Writing, Emerson Coll., 1986. Writing instr. Emerson Coll., Boston, 1985-89; mng. editor Ploughshares, Boston, 1988-92, dir., 1992—; panelist NEA Lit. Program, Washington, 1991-92; cons. AGNI, Boston, 1993, Asian Pacific Am. Jour., 1994. Contbr. short stories, articles to jours. St. Botolph Club Found. fellow, 1990, 91. Mem. PEN Am. New Eng. (bd. dirs.). Democrat. Office: Ploughshares Emerson Coll 100 Beacon St Boston MA 02116-1501

LEE, DONNA JEAN, retired hospice and respite nurse; b. Huntington Park, Nov. 12, 1931; d. Louis Frederick and Lena Adelaide (Hinson) Munyon; m. Frank Bernard Lee, July 16, 1949; children: Frank, Robert, John. AA in Nursing, Fullerton (Calif.) Jr. Coll., 1966; extension student, U. Calif., Irvine, 1966-74; student, U. N.Mex., 1982. RN, Calif.; cert. Intraventous Therapy Assn. U.S.A. Staff nurse Orange (Calif.) County Med. Ctr., 1966-71, staff and charge nurse relief ICU, CCU, Burn Unit, ER, Communicable Disease, Neo-Natal Care Unit, 1969-71, charge nurse communicable disease unit, 1969-70; staff and charge nurse ICU, emergency rm., CCU, med./surg. units Anaheim (Calif.) Meml. Hosp., 1971-74; charge and staff nurse, relief Staff Builders, Orange, 1974-82; agy. nurse Nursing Svcs. Internat., 1978-89; asst. DON Chapman Convalescent SNF, Orange, 1982; geriatric and pedicatrics nurse VNASS, 1985-93; hospice/respite nurse VIA Upjohn Home Healthcare Svcs and VNA Support Svcs. of Orange, 1985-93; ret.; staff relief nurse ICU/CCU various hosps. and labs, including plasmapheresis nurse Med. Lab. of Orange, 1978. Life mem. Republican, pres. task force, 1982—; past mem. Republican adv. com., Rep. Presdl. Trust; active Rep. Nat. Congl. Anti-Smoking Com. Mem. AACN, RNSC, ADA, Aria, Am. Cancer Soc., Am. Lung Assn., Am. Heart Assn., Nat. Multiple Sclerosis Soc., Easter Seal Soc. Baptist. Home: 924 S Hampstead St Anaheim CA 92802-1740

LEE, DOUGLAS A., music educator; b. Carmel, Ind., Nov. 3, 1932; s. Ralph Henley and Flossie Ellen (Chandler) Lee; m. Beverly Ruth Haskell, Sept. 2, 1961. MusB with High Distinction, DePauw U., 1954; MusM, U. Mich., 1958, PhD, 1968; postgrad., U. Md., 1985. Instr. Nat. Mus. Camp, Interlochen, Mich., 1959-62; instr. Mt. Union Coll., Alliance, Ohio, 1959-61, chmn. keyboard instrn., 1959-61; asst. prof. Music Wichita (Kans.) State U., 1964-68, assoc. prof., 1968-74, coord. Music History and Lit., 1968-71, coord. grad. studies in Music, 1969-70, chmn. dept. Musicology, 1971-74, prof. Music, 1974-86, administrv. intern, v.p. bus. affairs, 1983; pvt. practice event coord., 1974-85; prof. Musicology Vanderbilt U., Nashville, 1986—, chmn. Music History and Lit., advisor, 1987—; radio commentator Sta. KMUW-FM, 1969-76; judge various competitions, Mu Phi Epsilon, 1980, Kans. Music Tchrs. Assn., 1975-83, Baldwin Found. awards, 1979, 80; program annotator Nashville Symphony Orch., 1988—; cons. U.S. Dept. Edn. Jacob Javits fellowship program, 1988, 89, United Meth. Publishing Ho., 1988, Mayfield Pub. Co., 1990, Prentice-Hall, Inc., 1993, 97. Author: The Instrumental Works of Christoph Nichelmann: The Thematic Index, 1971, Franz Benda: A Thematic Catalogue of His Works, 1984: editor: Christoph Nichelmann: Clavier Concertos in E Major and A Minor, 1977, Six Sonatas for Violin and Bass by Franz Benda, with Embellishments, 1981; contbr. articles to The New Grove Dictionary of Music and Musicians, 1980, The New Grove Dictionary of Music in the United States, 1986; contbr. articles to profl. jours., chpts. to books. With U.S. Army, 1955-57, Japan. Rector Scholar Found., 1950-54; Rackham fellow U. Mich., 1961-65, fellow NEH, 1980, 85, Am. Philos. Soc., 1980, Kans. Arts Coun., 1985, Tenn. Arts Coun., 1988, 89. Mem. Am. Musicological Soc. (program chmn. Midwest chpt. 1984, South-Ctrl. chpt. 1989, nat. coun. 1986, pres. South-Ctrl. chpt. 1990-91), Music Tchrs. Nat. Assn. (editor 1971-90), Am. Soc. Eighteenth Century Studies, Coll. Music Soc., Sonneck Soc. Am. Music (program coord. 1987-88, editor The Sonneck Soc. Bull. 1988-900. Episcopalian. Avocation: photography. Office: Vanderbilt U 2400 Blakemore Ave Nashville TN 37212-3406

LEE, EDNA PRITCHARD, education educator; b. Windsor, N.C., Oct. 6, 1923; d. Peter Bernard and Edna (Smith) Pritchard; m. Mack Lloyd Lee Sr., May 17, 1945 (dec. Nov. 1970); 1 child, Mack Lloyd Jr.; m. Lee Cross, June 1, 1991. BS, State U. N.C., Elizabeth City; MA, NYU, N.Y.C. Cert. N.Y. Adminstr.-Supr. Tchr. elem. schs. Windsor, N.C., 1944-61; tchr. elem. schs. Mohegan Lake, N.Y., 1961-68, asst. prin. elem. sch., 1968-82; dir. basic edn. Peekskill (N.Y.) High Sch., 1969-80; adj. prof. Mercy Coll., Peekskill, 1985—; vice chmn. bd. dirs. Peekskill Area Health Ctr.; bd. dirs. Family Resource Ctr., Montrose Child Care Ctr. Co-author: Syllabus for 4th Grade Social Studies, 1972. Trustee Mt. Olivet Ch., 1993-96. Named Woman of Yr., NAACP, Peekskill, 1976, Woman Engr. of Yr., Bus. and Profl. Women, Peekskill, 1980; recipient Louis Gregory award Bahai Religion, Peekskill, 1988. Mem. AAUW (v.p. 1970-72), Blacks in Govt., Delta Kappa Gamma, Alpha Kappa Alpha, Tee-Ettes (sec. 1982-88). Avocations: golf, gardening. Home: 101 Dutch St Montrose NY 10548-1517

LEE, EDWARD BROOKE, JR., real estate executive, fund raiser; b. Silver Spring, Md., Oct. 25, 1917; s. E. Brooke Lee and Elizabeth (Wilson) Aspinwall; m. Camilla Edge, Apr. 15, 1944 (dec. Feb. 1983); children: Camilla Lee Alexander, E. Brooke III, Kaiulani Lee Kimbrell, Katherine Blair Lee St. John, Richard Henry, Elizabeth Ashe Somerville; m. Deborah Roche, Apr. 30, 1983; children: Samuel Phillips II, Regina Blair. AB, Princeton U., 1940; student, The Infantry Sch., 1942; postgrad. bus. sch., Harvard U., 1957. Cert. real estate broker Md., D.C., Va. Various indsl. positions to nat. account mgr. Scott Paper Co., Phila., 1940-62; comml. broker Shannon and Luchs, Washington, 1962-83, Merrill Lynch Comml. Realty, Washington, 1983-89, Prudential Preferred Properties, Bethesda, Md., 1989-95; pres. E. Brooke Lee Properties, Inc., Montgomery County, Md., 1979—; fund raiser key gifts Nat. Found. for Cancer Rsch., Bethesda, Md., 1985-95; v.p. Ga. Ave. Properties, Montgomery County, Ga.-Conn., Inc., Montgomery County, Conn. Aspen, Inc., Montgomery County, 1962—; sec.-treas. Brooke Lee Family, Inc., Montgomey County, 1962—. Author numerous sales articles for purchasing mags. Chmn. Drug Action Coalition, Inc., fin. v.p., bd. dirs., 1966-70; rep. candidate for Mayor of Washington, 1982, rep. primary candidate for U.S. Senate, State of Md., 1986. Served to capt. inf. U.S. Army, 1943-45, ETO. Named Realtor Assoc. of Yr., Washington Bd. of Realtors, 1984. Mem. Harvard Bus. Sch. Club (pres. 1962, exec. v.p. 1975), Princeton Club of Washington (sec., bd. dirs. 1970-75), Princeton Club of N.Y., Nat. Account Mktg. Assn. (pres. 1959-62). Republican. Episcopalian. Clubs: Met., Chevy Chase Country (Washington). Lodge: Kiwanis. Avocations: tennis, hunting, swimming, sailing, skating. Home and Office: E Brooke Lee Jr Properties Inc 8806 Connecticut Ave Chevy Chase MD 20815-6737

LEE, EDWARD L., bishop; b. Fort Washington, Pa., 1934; m. Kathryn Fligg, 1961; 1 child, Kathryn E. Grad. cum laude, Brown U., 1956; MDiv, Gen. Theol. Seminary, 1959. Ordained diaconate, priesthood Episc. Ch., 1959. Curate Ch. Holy Trinity, Phila., 1959-64; Episc. advisor Univ. Christian Movement Temple Univ., Phila., 1964-73; rector St. James Ch., Florence, Italy, 1973-82, St. John's Ch., Washington, 1982-89; bishop Diocese We. Mich., Kalamazoo, 1989—; Sunday, pastoral asst. Ch. Annunciation, Phila.; parish cons. St. Peters Ch., Germantown; lectr. homiletics Phila. Divinity Sch.; nat. chair Episc. Peace Fellowship, 1970-73; with Convocation of Am. Chs. Europe, pres. coun. advice; dep. Gen. Conv., 1976, 79; chair Coun. Coll. Preachers; active Washington Diocesan Coun., chmn. exec. com.; com. inquiry on the nuclear issues Diocesan Peace Commn. former chair bd. advisors Am. Internat. Sch. Florence. Office: Episcopal Church Ctn 2600 Vincent Ave Kalamazoo MI 49024-5600*

LEE, E(UGENE) STANLEY, engineer, mathematician, educator; b. Hopeh, China, Sept. 7, 1930; came to U.S., 1955, naturalized, 1961; s. Ing Yah and Lindy (Hsieng) L.; m. Mayanne Lee, Dec. 21, 1957 (dec. June 1980); children: Linda J., Margaret H.; m. Yuan Lee, Mar. 8, 1983; children—Lynn Hua Lee, Jin Hua Lee, Ming Hua Lee. BS, Chung Cheng Inst. Tech., Taiwan, Republic of China, 1953; MS, N.C. State U., 1957; PhDChemE, Princeton U., 1962. Rsch. engr. Phillips Petroleum Co., Bartlesville, Okla., 1960-66; asst. prof. chem. engring. Kans. State U., Manhattan, 1966-67, assoc. prof. indsl. engring., 1967-69; prof. indsl. engring. Kans. State U., 1969—; prof. chem. and elec. engring. U. So. Calif., 1972-76; hon. prof. Chinese Acad. Sci., 1987—; chaired prof. Yuan-ze Inst. Tech., Taiwan, Republic of China, 1993—; cons. govt. and industry. Author: Quasilinearization and Invariant Imbedding, 1968, Coal Conversion Technology, 1979, Operations Research, 1981, Fuzzy and Evidence Reasoning, 1996; editor: Energy Sci. and Tech., 1975—; assoc. editor Jour. Math. Analysis and Applications, 1974—, Computers and Mathematics with Applications, 1974—; editorial bd. Jour. Engring. Chemistry and Metallurgy, 1989—, Jour. of Nonlinear Differential Equations, 1992—, Jour. Chinese Fuzzy Systems Assn., 1995—. Grantee Dept. Def., 1967-72, Office Water Resources, 1968-75, EPA, 1969-71, NSF, 1971—, USDA, 1978-90, Dept. Energy, 1979-84, USAF, 1984-88. Mem. Soc. Indsl. and Applied Math., Ops. Rsch. Soc. Am., N. Am. Fuzzy Info. Processing Soc., Internat. Neural Network Soc., Sigma Xi, Tau Beta Pi, Phi Kappa Phi. Office: Kans State U Dept Indsl Engring Manhattan KS 66506 *Nothing can replace hard work and persistence.*

LEE, FRED C., electrical engineering educator; b. China, 1946; naturalized; BS, Nat. Cheng Kung U., Taiwan, 1968; MSA, Duke U., 1972, PhD, 1974. Tchg. asst. Duke U., Durham, N.C., 1970-72; rsch. asst. Spacecraft Sys. Rsch. Lab., 1972-74; mem. tech. staff TRW Systems, 1974-77; from asst. prof. to prof. Va. Poly. Inst. and State U., Blacksburg, 1977-83, James S. Tucker prof., 1986-94, Lewis A. Hester engring. chair, 1994—, dir. Va. Power Electronics Ctr., 1985—; bd. dirs. Zyetc Corp.; mem. adv. bd. Power Integrations Inc., 1988-94. Fellow IEEE (William E. Newell Power Electronics award 1989, past assoc. editor Trans. on Power Electronics, mem. advt. com.), IEEE Power Electronics Soc. (chmn. meeting com., mem. advt. com., mem. fellow evaluation com., chmn. power electronics specialists conf. 1987, v.p. 1988, pres. 1993-94), IEEE Engrs. Indsl. Applications Soc., Brit. Inst. Engrs. Office: 657 Whitemore Blacksburg VA 24061-0111

LEE, FRED STEVEN, telecommunications engineer; b. Wahiawa Oahu, Hawaii, June 7, 1954; s. Michael T. H. and Annette Kimiko (Ozawa) L.; m. Lynn Marie Gray, Aug. 16, 1985; children: Jennifer L. Pearce, Sandra M. Pearce, Christopher M., Nicole M. BSEE, Cornell U., 1975, MSEE, 1976. Head digital task group Watkins-Johnson, Gaithersburg, Md., 1976-78; prin. engr. Fairchild Space and Electronics, Germantown, Md., 1978-82; dir. engring. DAMA Telecom., Rockville, Md., 1982-86, Data Gen. Telecom., Rockville, 1986-87; pres., owner TransDigital Sys., Inc., Rockville, 1987—; cons. COMSAT Labs., Germantown, 1987—. Tiger Cub leader Cub Scouts Pack 178, Rockville, 1992-93. Achievements include patents for distributed switching architecture and high speed communication processing system. Avocations: scuba, backpacking, spelunking. Office: TransDigital Sys Inc 7753 Barnstable Pl Rockville MD 20855-2537

LEE, GEORGE C., civil engineer, university administrator; b. Peking, China, July 17, 1933; s. Shun C. and J. T. (Chang) L.; m. Grace S. Su, July 29, 1961; children—David S., Kelvin H. B.S., Taiwan U., 1955; M.S. in Civil Engring., Lehigh U., 1958, Ph.D., 1960. Research assoc. Lehigh U., 1960-61; mem. faculty dept. civil engring. SUNY, Buffalo, 1961—; prof. SUNY, 1967—, Samuel P. Capen prof. of engring., 1992—, chmn. dept., 1974-77, dean sch. of engring. and applied scis., 1978-95; sr. univ. advisor for technology SUNY, Buffalo, 1995—; head engring. mechanics sect. NSF, Washington, 1977-78; assoc. dir. Calspan-U. Buffalo Rsch. Ctr., 1985-89; acting dir. Nat. Ctr. for Earthquake Engring. Rsch., 1989-90, dir., 1992—; sci. cons. Nat. Heart Lung and Blood Inst., NSF. Author: Structural Analysis and Design, 1979, Design of Single Story Rigid Frames, 1981, Cold Region Structural Engineering, 1986, Stability and Ductility of Steel Structures Under Cyclic Loading, 1991; contbr. articles to profl. jours. in areas of structural design, nonlinear structural mechanics, biomed. engring. and cold region structural engring. Recipient Adams Meml. award Am. Welding Soc., 1974; Superior Accomplishment award NSF, 1977. Mem. ASCE, Am. Welding Soc., Welding Research Council, Structural Stability Research, Council, Am. Soc. Engring. Edn., AAAS, Sigma Xi, Chi Epsilon, Tau Beta Pi. Office: SUNY Buffalo 429 Bell Hall Buffalo NY 14260-0001

LEE, GILBERT BROOKS, retired ophthalmology engineer; b. Cohasset, Mass., Sept. 10, 1913; s. John Alden and Charlotte Louise (Brooks) L.; m. Marion Corinne Rapp, Mar. 7, 1943 (div. Jan. 1969); children: Thomas Stearns, Jane Stanton, Frederick Cabot, Gilbert Eliot Frazar. BA, Reed Coll., 1937; MA, New Sch. for Social Rsch., 1949. Asst. psychologist U.S. Naval Submarine Base Civil Svc., Psychophysics of Vision, New London, Conn., 1950-53; rsch. assoc. Project Mich., Vision Rsch. Labs., Willow Run, 1954-57; rsch. assoc. dept. ophthalmology U. Mich., Ann Arbor, 1958-72, sr. rsch. assoc., 1972-75, sr. engring. rsch. assoc. ophthalmology, 1975-82, part-time sr. engr. ophthalmology, 1982—; sec. internat. dept., 23d St. YMCA, N.Y.C.; cons. W.K. Kellogg Eye Ctr., Ann Arbor, 1968—. Local organizer, moderator (TV program) Union of Concerned Scientists' Internat. Satellite Symposium on Nuclear Arms Issues, 1986; producer (TV show) Steps for Peace, 1987; designer, builder portable tristimulus Colorimeter; (videotape) Pomerance Awards, UN.; broken lake ice rescue procedure rsch., by one person in a dry suit, all weather conditions, 1966, 89-93 (videotape). Precinct del. Dem. County Conv., Washtenaw County, 1970, 74; treas. Dem. Club, Ann Arbor, Mich., 1971-72, 74-79; vice chmn. nuclear arms control com., 1979; chmn. Precinct Election Inspectors, 1968-75; scoutmaster Portland (Oreg.) area coun. Boy Scouts Am., 1932-39. Capt. AUS, 1942-46, 61-62. Mem. AAAS, Nat. Resources Def. Coun., Fedn. Am. Scientists, N.Y. Acad. Sci., Nation Assocs., ACLU, Sierra Club, Amnesty Internat. Home: 4131 E Pinchot Ave Phoenix AZ 85018-7115

LEE, GLENN RICHARD, medical administrator, educator; b. Ogden, Utah, May 18, 1932; s. Glenn Edwin and Thelma (Jensen) L.; m. Pamela Marjorie Ridd, July 18, 1969; children—Jennifer, Cynthia. B.S., U. Utah, 1953, M.D., 1956. Intern Boston City Hosp.-Harvard U., 1956-57, resident, 1957-58; clin. asso. Nat. Cancer Inst., NIH, 1958-60; postdoctoral fellow U. Utah, 1960-63; instr. U. Utah Coll. Medicine, 1963-64, asst. prof. internal medicine, 1964-68, assoc. prof., 1968-73, prof., 1973-96, assoc. dean for acad. affairs, 1973-76, dean, 1978-83, prof. emeritus, 1996—; chief of staff Salt Lake VA Med. Ctr., 1985-95. Author: (with others) Clinical Hematology, 9th edit, 1993; Contbr. (with others) numerous articles to profl. jours.; editorial bd.: (with others) Am. Jour. Hematology, 1976-79. Served with USPHS, 1958-60. Markle Found. scholar, 1965-70; Nat. Inst. Arthritis, Metabolic and Digestive Disease grantee, 1977-82. Mem. A.C.P., Am. Soc. Hematology, Am. Soc. Clin. Investigation, Western Assn. Physicians, Am. Inst. Nutrition. Mem. LDS Ch. Home and Office: 3781 Ruth Dr Salt Lake City UT 84124-2331

LEE, GRIFF CALICUTT, civil engineer; b. Jackson, Miss., Aug. 17, 1926; s. Griff and Lida (Higgs) L.; m. Eugenia Humphreys, July 29, 1950; children: Griff Calicutt III, Robert H., Carol E. B.E., Tulane U., 1948; M.S., Rice U., 1951. Civil engr. Humble Oil & Refining Co., New Orleans, Houston, 1948-54; design engr. J. Ray McDermott & Co., Inc., New Orleans, 1954-66; chief engr. J. Ray McDermott & Co., Inc., 1966-75, group v.p., 1975-80, v.p., group exec., 1980-83; cons. engr. Griff C. Lee Inc., 1983—; mem. vis. com. dept. civil engring. U. Tex.; mem. adv. bd. Tulane U., Rice U., MIT; mem. marine bd. NRC. Contbr. articles to profl. jours. Served with USN, 1944-46. Named Outstanding Engring. Alumnus Rice U., 1991. Mem. NAE, ASCE (hon.), Am. Bur. Shipping, Am. Concrete Inst., Am. Welding Soc., Soc. Petroleum Engrs., Am. Petroleum Inst., Internat. House Club, City Club, Bienville Club, New Orleans Country Club, Rotary. Presbyterian. Home: 6353 Carlson Dr New Orleans LA 70122-2803 Office: 1010 Common St New Orleans LA 70112-2401

LEE, HENRY C., forensic scientist; b. China, Nov. 22, 1938; came to U.S., 1965; s. An-Fu and Ho-Ming Lee; m. Margaret Song, 1962; children: Sherry, Stanley. Grad., Taiwan Ctrl. Police Coll.; BS in Forensic Sci., SUNY, 1972; MS, NYU, 1974, PhD in Biochemistry, 1975. From police lt. to capt. Taiwan; newspaper reporter, editor; asst. prof. criminal justice U. New Haven, 1975-78, assoc. prof. forensic sci., 1976-78, prof. forensic sci., program chmn., 1978-79; chief criminologist Conn. State Police Forensic Lab., Meriden, 1979—, lab. dir., 1980—; DNA analysis expert in cases including Helle Crafts, William Kennedy Smith, O.J. Simpson, among others; assisted prosecutors across the country and the world with difficult forensic investigations including mass grave identification in Bosnia and Herzegovina, Branch Davidian (Waco, Tex.) cult; guest lectr. several prominent univs. Author and co-author of more than 20 books and monographs on forensic sci.; contbr. more than 200 articles to profl. jours. Docent scholarship fund U. New Haven, Conn. Dept. Pub. Safety. Recipient numerous awards including Criminalistics sect. of Disting. Criminalistics award, 1986, J. Donero award Internat. Assn. Identification, 1989. Fellow Am. Acad. Forensic Sci. Avocations: cooking, gardening, Chinese calligraphy, fossils. Office: Conn State Police Forensic Lab 278 Colony St Meriden CT 06451-2053

LEE, HI YOUNG, physician, acupuncturist; b. Seoul, Korea, Oct. 18, 1941; came to U.S., 1965, naturalized, 1976; s. Jung S. and Hwa J. (Kim) L.; m. Sun M. Lee, June 4, 1965; children: Sandra, Grace, David. M.D., Yon Sei U., Seoul, 1965. Diplomate Am. Bd. Family Practice. Intern Grasslands Hosp., Valhalla, N.Y., 1965-66; resident VA Hosp., Dayton, Ohio, 1966-70; mem. staff Eastern State Hosp., Medical Lake, Wash., 1970-74; practice family medicine, acupuncturist Empire Med. Office, Spokane, Wash., 1974—; active staff St. Lukes Meml. Hosp., Spokane, 1974—, bd. trustees St. Georges Prep Sch., Wash., 1986— ; courtesy staff Deaconess Med. Center, Spokane, 1974—, Sacred Heart Med. Ctr., Spokane, 1974—. Author: Von Recklinghousen's Disease, 1970 (McDermit award); columnist Rainier Forum Korea Post Weekly News, 1996—. Elder First Presbyterian Church, Spokane, 1975. Fellow Am. Acad. Family Practice; mem. ctr. for Chinese Medicine, Spokane County Med. Soc., Nat. Acupuncture Research Soc., Christian Med. Soc. Home: 2006 W Liberty Ave Spokane WA 99205-2570 Office: Empire Med Office 17 E Empire Ave Spokane WA 99207-1707

LEE, HON CHEUNG, physiology educator; b. Hong Kong, May 7, 1950; came to the U.S., 1967; s. Chai Chong and Yee Chin (Ng) L.; m. Miranda Wong, Aug. 1981; 1 child, Cyrus W. BA, U. Calif., Berkeley, 1971, MA, 1973, PhD, 1978. Postdoctoral rschr. U. Calif., Berkeley, 1978-79, Stanford U., Pacific Grove, Calif., 1979-81; asst. prof. U. Minn., Mpls., 1981-86, assoc. prof., 1986-90, full prof., 1990—; mem. Reproductive Biology Study Sect., NIH, Bethesda, Md., 1993—; chmn. Reproductive Biology Spl. Emphasis Panel, NIH, Bethesda, 1994. Contbr. articles to profl. jours. Rsch. grantee NIH, Bethesda, 1983—, 94—, NSF, Washington, 1986-89. Mem. AAAS, Am. Soc. for Cell Biology. Achievements include discovery of Cyclic ADP-ribose and NAADP messenger molecules for regulating cellular calcium; patent for Cyclic ADP-ribose antagonists. Office: Univ Minn Dept Physiology 6-255 Millard Hall Minneapolis MN 55455

LEE, HOWARD DOUGLAS, academic administrator; b. Louisville, Ky., Mar. 15, 1943; s. Howard W. and Margaret (Davidson) L.; m. Margaret Easley, Nov. 20, 1965; children: Gregory Davidson, Elizabeth Anna. BA in English, U. Richmond, 1964; ThM, Southeastern Seminary, Wake Forest, N.C., 1968; PhD in Religion, U. Iowa, Iowa City, 1971. Prof. religion, devel. dir. Va. Intermont Coll., Bristol, 1971-73; dir. univ. relations Wake Forest (N.C.) U., 1973-78; v.p. devel. Stetson U., DeLand, Fla., 1978-80, v.p. planning and devel., 1980-83, exec. v.p., 1984-86, pres.-elect, 1986-87, pres., 1987—. Contbr. articles to profl. jours. Founding dir. Atlantic Ctr. for Arts, New Smyrna Beach, Fla., 1978—; chmn. DeLand C. of C., 1994; chair Volusia Vision Com., 1994-96. Named Cen. Fla. Fundraiser of Yr. Nat. Assn. Fundraising Execs. 1985. Mem. So. Assn. Colls. and Schs. (exec. coun. 1993-94), Rotary, Deland Country Club, Omicron Delta Kappa. Avocations: running, golf, wood carving, woodworking/antiques, reading. Office: Stetson U Campus Box 8258 421 N Boulevard Deland FL 32720

LEE, HUA, electrical engineering educator; b. Taipei, Taiwan, Sept. 30, 1952; came to U.S., 1976; s. Chi-Sun and Min-Eeh (Poon) L.; m. Rayshin Wang, June 5, 1976; children: Michelle, Michael. BS, Nat. Taiwan U., Taipei, 1974; MS, U. Calif., Santa Barbara, 1978, PhD, 1980. Asst. prof. U. Calif., Santa Barbara, 1980-83, prof., 1990—; asst. prof. U. Ill., Urbana, 1983-87, assoc. prof., 1987-90; adv. bd. mem. Acoustical Imaging Conf., 1988—; rev. panel mem. NSF, 1991—, NRC, 1991—. Author: Engineering Analysis, 1988; editor: Imaging Technology, 1986, Modern Acoustical Imaging, 1986, Acoustical Imaging, vol. 18, 1990; editor various jours. Recipient Presdl. Young Investigator award NSF, 1985, award Pattern Recognition Soc., 1993; named Prof. of Yr. Mortar Bd. Honor Soc., U. Calif.-Santa Barbara, 1992. Fellow IEEE, Acoustical Soc. Am.; mem. Am. Soc. Engring. Edn., Eta Kappa Nu. Achievements include development of scanning laser tomographic microscope, of microwave subsurface imaging system for NDE of civil structures, of synthetic-aperture sonar imaging system, and of high-performance imaging techniques. Office: U Calif Santa Barbara Dept Elec Engring Santa Barbara CA 93106

LEE, HWA-WEI, librarian, educator; b. Canton, China, Dec. 7, 1933; came to U.S., 1957, naturalized, 1962; s. Luther Kan-Chun and Mary Hsiao-Wei (Wang) L.; m. Mary F. Kratochvil, Mar. 14, 1959; children: Shirley, James, Pamela, Edward, Charles, Robert. BEd, Nat. Taiwan Normal U., 1954; MEd, U. Pitts., 1959, PhD, 1964; MLS, Carnegie Mellon U., 1961. Asst. libr. U. Pitts. Librs., 1959-62; head tech. svcs. Duquesne U. Libr., Pitts., 1962-65; head libr. U. Pa., Edinboro, 1965-68; dir. libr. and info. ctr. Asian Inst. Tech., Bangkok, Thailand, 1968-75; assoc. dir. librs., prof. libr. adminstrn. Colo. State U., Fort Collins, 1975-78; dean librs., prof. Ohio U., Athens, 1978—; cons. FAO, UNESCO, U.S. AID, World Bank, Internat. Devel. Rsch. Ctr., Asia Found., OCLC; del.-at-large White House Conf. Libr. and Info. Svcs., 1991. Author: Librarianship in World Perspectives, 1991, Fundraising for the 1990s: The Challenge Ahead, 1992, Modern Library Management, 1996; exec. editor Jour. Ednl. Media and Libr. Sci., 1982—; mem. editl. bd. Internat. Comm. in Libr. Automation, 1975-76, Jour. Libr. and Info. Sci., 1975-78, Libr. Acquisition: Practice and Theory, 1976-83; adv. bd. Jour. Info., Comm. and Libr. Sci., 1994—; contbr. articles to profl. jours. Recipient Disting. Svc. award Libr. Assn. of China (Taiwan), 1989. Mem. ALA (councilor 1988-92, 93—, John Ames Humphry/Forest Press award 1991), Acad. Libr. Assn. Ohio, Am. Soc. Info. Sci., Asian-Pacific Am. Librs. Assn. (Disting. Svc. award 1991), Internat. Fedn. Libr. Assns. and Instns. (standing com. univ. librs. and other gen. rsch. librs. 1989-93), Assn. Coll. and Rsch. Librs. Chinese-Am. Librs. Assn. (Disting. Svc. award 1983), Internat. Assn. Orientalist Librs., Ohio Libr. Assn. (bd. dirs. 1991-92, Libr. of the Yr. 1987), Online Computer Libr. Ctr. (users coun. 1987-91), Ohio Chinese Acad. and Profl. Assn. (founding pres. 1988-90). Home: 19 Mulligan Rd Athens OH 45701-3734 Office: Ohio U Alden Libr Athens OH 45701

LEE, IN-YOUNG, lawyer; b. In-Cheon, Kyonggi-do, Korea, Dec. 5, 1952; came to U.S. 1978; s. In-Seok and Hyun-Bo (Rim) L.; m. Young-Lae Hong, July 1, 1978; children: Casey K., Brian K. LLB, Seoul Nat. U., Korea, 1975; LLM, Harvard U., 1980; JD, UCLA, 1983. Bar: Ill. 1983, N.Y. 1987, D.C. 1989, U.S. Ct. Internat. Trade. Assoc. Baker & McKenzie, Chgo.,

1983-86, Marks & Murase, N.Y.C., 1986-87, Baker & McKenzie, N.Y.C., 1987-91; ptnr. Marks & Murase, N.Y.C., 1991-96, McDermott, Will & Emory, N.Y.C., 1996—; gen. counsel Korean C. of C. and Industry in USA, Inc., 1993—, Assn. Korean Fin. Instns. Am., Inc. Articles editor Pacific Basin Law Jour. Presbyterian. Avocations: fishing, golf. Office: McDermott Will & Emery 50 Rockefeller Plaza New York NY 10020-1605

LEE, ISAIAH CHONG-PIE, social worker, educator; b. Ma-kung, Taiwan, Jan. 31, 1934; s. Ju-Nie Chen and Chioh L.; m. Ho-Mei Chen, Feb. 8, 1960; children—Jense, Jenfei. Dr.P.H., UCLA, 1972. Lic. clin. social worker, family, marriage and child counselor. Dist. dir. public health social work Los Angeles County Health Dept., 1970-72; assoc. prof. social work Calif. State U., Long Beach, 1972-78, prof. social work, 1978—, chmn. dept., 1980-86, dir. Internat. Inst. Social Work, 1982—; vis. prof. social work Tunghai U., Tai Chung, 1986-87; vis. prof. family medicine Kaoshiung Med. Coll., 1989, med. sociology, 1993-94. Author: Medical Care in a Mexican American Community, 1972, Health Care Need of the Elderly Chinese in Los Angeles, 1979, Youth Leadership in Immigrant Communities, 1986, Yin-Yang Theory in Chinese Medicine, 1987, Selective Readings in Social Work, 1988, Community Organizing--Chinese-American Perspectives, 1992, The Proceedings of the Conference on Health and Social Policy Research at Kaohsiung Medical College, 1993, The Proceedings of the Conference on Medical Care and Welfare Policy for the Elderly at Kaohsiung Medical College, 1994. Sec. bd. dirs. Oriental Healing Arts Inst., Calif.; founder Formosan Presbyterian Ch. of Orange County, 1978; pres. bd. dirs. Formosan Presbyn. Ch. Orange County, 1978-79; chmn. Asian Presbyn. Council So. Calif., 1980-81; chmn. Internat. Task Force Nat. Comm. on Self-Devel. of People United Presbyn. Ch., 1980-84; advisor social econ. group World Coun. on Chs., Geneva, 1980-84; adv. bd. Asian Am. Community Mental Health Tng. Center, Los Angeles, 1972-77; v.p. Pacific Asian-Am. Center, Santa Ana, Calif., 1981-82, pres., 1982-84; founder Calif. Inst. of Human Care, 1988. 2d lt. Chinese Army, 1954-55. Fellow Soc. Clin. Social Work; mem. Oriental Social Health Soc. (founder, pres. 1970-72), AAUP, Council Social Work Edn., Chinese-Am. Social Workers Assn. USA, (founder, pres. 1985-88), Nat. Assn. Social Workers, Acad. Cert. Social Workers, Taiwanese-Am. Profl. Assn. USA (pres. 1993—). Democrat. Office: Calif State U Dept Social Work Long Beach CA 90840

LEE, J. DANIEL, JR., retired insurance company executive; b. Pitts., Mar. 11, 1938; s. John Daniel and Frances Emma (Schimid) L.; m. Betty Williams, Oct. 22, 1961; children—John, Michael, Julie. A.B., Duke U., 1960; M.B.A., U. N.C., 1963; postgrad., Dartmouth Coll., 1984. Investment analyst, gen. investment mgr. Prudential Ins. Co. Am., Jacksonville, Fla., 1963-70; gen. investment mgr. Prudential Ins. Co Am., Newark, 1974-77; asst. v.p. Tchrs. Ins. and Annuity Assn. of Am., N.Y.C., 1978, 2d v.p., 1978-80, v.p., 1980-83, mgr. securities div., 1983, sr. v.p., 1983, investment area mgr., 1984, exec. v.p., chief investment officer, 1984-96; ret. Avocations: golf; salt-water fishing.

LEE, J. PATRICK, academic administrator; b. Leitchfield, Ky., Nov. 30, 1942; s. Herman G. and Josephine (Pearl) L.; m. Louise Sipple, June 8, 1972. BA, Brescia Coll., 1963; postgrad., U. Paris, 1966-67; PhD, Fordham U., 1971. Asst. prof. French Brescia Coll., Owensboro, Ky., Univ. of Ga., Athens, Ga.; v. p. acad. affairs Belmont N.C. Abbey Coll.; provost Barry Univ., Miami, Fla.; researcher 18th Century French lit., Voltaire works. Woodrow Wilson fellow, 1963, Danforth fellow, 1963-67, Fulbright fellow, 1966-67. Mem. AAUA (exec. bd.), SEASECS (exec. bd., past pres.), Delta Epsilon Sigma (nat. sec./treas.), Phi Beta Kappa. Home: 1341 NE 103rd St Miami FL 33138

LEE, JACK (JIM SANDERS BEASLEY), broadcast executive; b. Buffalo Valley, Tenn., Apr. 14, 1936; s. Jesse McDonald and Nelle Viola (Sanders) Beasley; m. Barbara Sue Looper, Sept. 1, 1961; children: Laura Ann, Elizabeth Jane, Sarah Kathleen. Student, Wayne State U., 1955-57; BA, Albion Coll., 1959. Cert. radio mktg. cons. Announcer Sta. WHUB-AM, Cookeville, Tenn., 1956; news dir., program dir. Sta. WALM-AM, Albion, Mich., 1957-59; radio-TV personality WKZO-Radio-TV, Kalamazoo, 1960-62; prodn. dir. Stas. WKMH-WKNR, Detroit, 1962-63; gen. mgr. Sta. WAUK-AM-FM, Waukesha, Wis., 1963-65; asst. program mgr. Sta. WOKY, Milw., 1965-70; program mgr. Sta. WTMJ-WKTI, Milw., 1970-76; gen. mgr. Sta. WEMP-WMYX, Milw., 1976-88; pres. Jack Lee Enterprises Ltd., Milw., 1977—; pres., CEO, Milw. Area Radio Stas., 1989—; instr. dept. mass comm. U. Wis.-Milw., 1972-81. With U.S. Army, 1959, 61-62; maj. CAP, 1964—. Decorated Army Commendation medal. Mem. AFTRA, Actors Equity, Milw. Advt. Club, Omicron Delta Kappa, Alpha Epsilon Rho. Home and Office: 277 W N Chicory Ln # 2793 Pewaukee WI 53072 *It is a constant struggle to balance my greatest gift—the ability to express myself—with my biggest failing—the inability to keep my mouth shut.*

LEE, JAMES A., health facility finance executive; b. Red Level, Ala., Dec. 19, 1939; s. H. Alton Lee; m. Charlotte Phillips, Dec. 19, 1963 (div. July 1971); children: Phillip, Michele, Jenifer; m. Melanie Cooper, Dec. 14, 1973; children: Christopher, Amanda. BBA in Acctg., Jacksonville State U., 1964; MS in Hosp. and Health Adminstrn., U. Ala., 1980. CPA, Ala. Sr. acct. Macke, Eldredge, McIntosh, Birmingham, Ala., 1964-67, Touche, Ross, Bailey & Smart, Birmingham, 1967-68; bus. functions mgr. Druid City Hosp., Tuscaloosa, Ala., 1968-71; sr. assoc. adminstr., fin. Univ. Ala. Hosp., Birmingham, 1971-94; CFO Montgomery Cardiovasc. Assocs., PC, 1994—; asst. prof. health services adminstrn. Univ. Ala. Birmingham, 1980—; asst. prof. Dept. Pub. Health, Univ. Ala. Birmingham, 1984—. Mem. Health Care Fin. Mgmt. Assn., Ala. Soc. CPA's, Am. Inst. CPA's, Am. Hosp. Assn. Republican. Baptist. Home: 109 Pemberton Pl Pelham AL 35124-2817

LEE, JAMES EDWARD, JR., educational administrator; b. Pitts., Mar. 9, 1939; s. Willard and Gladys Hilda (Jenkins) L.; m. Daisy Mae Tibbs, June 29, 1977; children: Stephen Michael, Monica Michelle, Brian Patrick, Priscilla Demone. BS, Wayne State U., 1962, EdS, 1969; MA, U. Mich., 1964; postgrad., Mich. State U., Wayne State U., U. Minn., U. Colo., 1964-95, Ctrl. Mich. U. Cert. tchr., adminstr., Mich. Tchr. Miller, Durfee and Michael Jr. High Schs., Detroit, 1962-67; team leader Nat. Tchr. Corps, Detroit, 1967-69; dept. head Noble Jr. High Sch., Detroit, 1969-74; asst. prin. MacKenzie High Sch., Detroit, 1974-80; asst. prin. Drew Mid. Sch., Detroit, 1980, prin., 1980-97; prin. Chander Park Acad., 1997—; instr. Wayne State U., Detroit, 1967-69, edn. cons., 1970-71; instr. Wayne C.C., 1967-81; prin. adult evening sch., 1974-80, summer gifted program, Detroit, 1986-92; mem. profl. stds. commn. for sch. adminstrs. Mich. Dept. Edn., 1992-96, mem. adminstrv. waiver com., 1992-94. Contbg. author: The Development of Micro Teaching as an Evaluative Instrument in Teacher Training, 1969, (manual) The Principalship, 1990. Co-chair ednl. audit com. Oak Park (Mich.) Sch., 1988-90; bd. dirs. Scott Community Ctr., Detroit, 1988-97; adv. bd. Adrian/Scott program to inspire readiness for ednl. success, Detroit, 1990-97; adv. coun. Christ Child House, Detroit, 1990-92. With USMC, 1956-58. Recipient Prins. and Educators award Booker T. Washington Bus. Assn., Detroit, 1986, 90, Citation for Outstanding Leadership Detroit Bd. Edn., 1986; named finalist Boss of Yr., Detroit chpt. Am. Bus. Women's Assn., 1987. Mem. Nat. Assn. Secondary Sch. Prins., Nat. Mid. Sch. Assn., Mich. Assn. Supervision and Curriculum Devel., Mich. Assn. Secondary Sch. Prins. (exec. bd. 1986-88, Outstanding Mid. Level Prin. of Yr. 1991), Mich. Assn. Mid. Sch. Educators (bd. dirs. 1988-91). Avocation: tennis. Home: 22580 Saratoga St Apt 2102M Southfield MI 48075-5947 Office: Charles R Drew Mid Sch 9600 Wyoming St Detroit MI 48204-4669

LEE, JAMES JIEH, environmental educator, computer specialist; b. I-Lan, Taiwan, Aug. 27, 1939; came to U.S.A. 1968; s. Yun Ping and Lien Hwa (Kuo) L.; m. Margie J. Feng, March 31, 1965; 1 child: Jean H. BA, Taiwan Normal U., Taipei, 1962; MA, U. Minn., 1970; PhD in Environ. Scis., Greenwich U. Cert. high sch., univ. tchr., Taiwan. Tchr. I-Lan High Sch., 1962-64; instr. Ta-Tung & Taiwan Normal U., 1964-68; rsch. asst. U. Minn., Mlps., 1968-71, rsch. assoc., 1971-77; computer specialist U.S. Dept. Commerce, Silver Spring, Md., 1977-83; sr. computer system analyst U.S. Pub. Health Svc., Rockville, Md., 1983-92; planning dir. Ctr. for Taiwan Internat. Rels., Washington, 1990—; pres. World Fedn. Taiwanese Assns., 1995—; with Internat. Environ. Protection Assn., Washington, 1988-90, also bd. dirs. 1986—; bd. dirs. Asia Resource Ctr., Washington, 1993—; exec. dir. Constitution Movement for Taiwan, Washington, 1993—; chmn. Formosan Human Rights Assn. Washington chpt., 1976—. Co-author: (with others) Introduction to Human Geography, 1966, Yun-Wu Social Sci., 1971; author: Minnesota Taxing Jurisdictions, 1976, Return to Nature, 1991, Taiwan's Ecological Series, Vols. 1-4, 1955. Bd. dirs. Formosan Assn. Pub. Affairs, Washington, 1982-92. Recipient automation data processing/extramural rsch. USPHS, 1991. Mem. World Watch, Nat. Resource Def. Coun., Am. Solar Energy Soc., Union of Concerned Scientists, World Fedn. Taiwanese Assns. (pres. 1995—), Sierra Club. Avocations: traveling, hiking. Home: 14306 Parkvale Rd Rockville MD 20853-2530

LEE, JAMES MATTHEW, Canadian politician; b. Charlottetown, P.E.I., Can., Mar. 26, 1937; s. James Matthew and Catherine (Blanchard) L.; m. Patricia Laurie, July 2, 1960; children: Jason, Laurie Ann, Patti Sue. P.C., St. Dustans U., 1956. Mem. provincial parliament from, 5th Queens Riding, 1975-82; minister Health and Social Service-Province of P.E.I., Charlottetown, from 1979, Tourism, Parks and Conservation, 1980; premier, pres. Exec. Council-Province P.E.I., Charlottetown, 1981-86. Mem. Can. Pension Commn., 1986—, Privy Council Can., 1982. Mem. Can. Jaycees (internat. senate 1983), United Comml. Travellers Am. (past sr. councilor), Coun. for Can. Unity (nat. v.p. 1993). Roman Catholic.

LEE, JAMES MICHAEL, religious education educator, publisher; b. Bklyn., Sept. 29, 1931; s. James and Emma (Brenner) L.; m. Marlene Mayr, Oct. 16, 1976; children: James V, Michael F.X., Patrick John. A.B., St. John's U., 1955; A.M., Columbia U., 1956, Ed.D., 1958. Tchr. gen. sci. N.Y.C. secondary sch., 1955-56, chmn. sci. dept. and coordinator audiovisual aids, 1956-59, substitute tchr. adult edn., 1955-60; lectr. Hunter Coll. Grad. Sch., N.Y.C., 1959-60, Sch. Edn. Seton Hall U., South Orange, N.J., 1959; asst. prof. grad. dept. edn. St. Joseph Coll., West Hartford, Conn., 1959-62, U. Notre Dame, South Bend, Ind., 1962-65; assoc. prof. U. Notre Dame, 1965-68, prof., 1968-77, chmn. dept. grad. studies in edn., 1966-71, dir. religious edn. program, 1967-77; prof. U. Ala. at Birmingham, 1977—, chmn. dept. secondary instrn. and ednl. founds., 1977-79; lectr. Chaplain's Sch., Air U., 1985-88; subject matter expert, lectr. GS-16 Chaplain Corps, USN, 1990-91, hon. chaplain, 1991; mem. Birmingham Diocesan Bd. Edn., 1981-89; founder, pub. Religious Edn. Press, 1974—; cons. in field. Author: Principles and Methods of Secondary Education, 1963, Guidance and Counseling in Schools, Foundations and Processes, 1966, Purpose of Catholic Schooling, 1968, Shape of Religious Instruction, 1971, The Flow of Religious Instruction, 1973, Forward Together, 1973, The Content of Religious Instruction, 1985; sr. author: The Delivery of Religious Education in the Sea Services, 1991; editor, contbr.: Seminary Education in a Time of Change, 1965, Readings in Guidance and Counseling, 1966, Catholic Education in the Western World, 1967, Toward a Future for Religious Education, 1970, The Religious Education We Need, 1977, The Spirituality of the Religious Educator, 1985, Handbook of Faith, 1990; corr. editor Panorama: An Internat. Jour. Religious Edn. and Values. Fulbright sr. research scholar U. Munich, 1974-75; Religious Edn. Assn. Lilly research tng. fellow, 1974-75, 85. Fellow Soc. for Sci. Study Religion; mem. NEA, N.Am. Profs. of Christian Edn., Assn. Profs. and Rschrs. in Religious Edn. (exec. com. 1972-73, 78-80), Am. Ednl. Rsch. Assn., Nat. Soc. Study Edn., Religious Edn. Assn. (rsch. com. 1970-76, bd. dirs. 1979-89), Religious Rsch. Assn., Fulbright Alumni Assn., K.C. (4th degree 1996). Home: 5316 Meadow Brook Rd Birmingham AL 35242-3315

LEE, JANIE C., curator; b. Shreveport, La., Apr. 22, 1937; d. Birch Lee and Joanna (Glassell) Wood; m. David B. Warren, Jan. 2, 1980. Student, Nat. Cathedral Sch., 1951-55; BA, Sarah Lawrence Coll., 1959. Asst. to Cheryl Crawford, Actors Studi o, N.Y.C., 1962-63; co-prodr. Off Broadway Theatre Co., N.Y.C., 1963-65; owner, pres. Janie C. Lee Gallery, Dallas, 1967-74, Houston, 1973-96; owner, pres. Janie C. Lee Master Drawings, N.Y.C., 1983-96; adj. curator of drawings Whitney Mus. Am. Art, 1997—; mem. art appraisal panel IRS, Washington, 1987-94. Prodr. ann. catalogue on 20th Century drawings, 1979-93. Mem. Alumnae Bd. Sarah Lawrence Coll. (1972-74); pres. Nancy Graves Found., 1996—. Mem. Art Dealers Assn. Am. (bd. dirs. 1980-88, 92-94, v.p. 1984-88). Avocation: study of Italian life and culture. Office: 1209 Berthea St Houston TX 77006-6411

LEE, JASON DAVIS, communications executive; b. Portland, Oreg., Oct. 25, 1949; s. Jason Dwight and Dorothy Bernadine (Davis) L.; m. Lauri Scheyer, May 28, 1972; children: Ryan, Rustin, Marit. BA, Reed Coll., 1972; MS in Indsl. Adminstrn., Carnegie-Mellon U., 1974. Sr. assoc. Booz, Allen & Hamilton, Chgo., 1974-79, prin., 1981-88; prin. Braxton Assocs., Boston, 1979-81; asst. v.p. investments and acquisitions Ameritech Devel. Corp., Chgo., 1988-90, v.p. investments and acquisitions, 1990-95; exec. v.p., worldwide mng. dir. Young and Rubicam, N.Y.C., 1995—. Co-chmn. Roycemore Sch. Charity Benefit, Evanston, Ill., 1988. Mem. Info. Industry Assn., Soc. Automotive Engrs. Republican. Home: 1965 Broadway New York NY 10023 Office: Young and Rubicam 285 Madison Ave New York NY 10017-6401

LEE, JEN-SHIH, biomedical engineering educator; b. Kwangtong, China, Aug. 22, 1940; parents Y. and Yao-Ze (Lai) L.; m. Lian-Pin Ma Lee, June 11, 1966; children: Lionel, Grace, Albert. BS, Nat. Taiwan U., 1961; MS, Calif. Inst. Tech., 1963, PhD, 1966. Advance rsch. fellow San Diego Heart Assn., U. Calif., San Diego, 1966-69; asst. prof. dept. Biomedical Engring. U. Va., Charlottesville, 1969-74, assoc. prof., 1974-83, prof., 1983—, chmn. dept. Biomedical Engring., 1988—. Editor: Microvascular Mechanics, 1988; assoc. editor Jour. Biomech. Engring., 1987-93; contbr. articles to Jour. Applied Physiology, Jour. Biomech. Engring., others. Recipient Rsch. Career Devel. award NIH, 1974-80. Fellow ASME, Am. Inst. Med. and Biol. Engring., Am. Physiol. Soc.; mem. IEEE, Microcirculatory Soc., Biomed. Engring. Soc. (bd. dirs. 1991-93, pres. 1994-95), Coun. of Socs. Am. Inst. Med. and Biol. Engring. (bd. dirs. 1995-97, chair 1995-97).

LEE, JEROME G., lawyer; b. Chgo., Feb. 23, 1924; m. Margo B. Lee, Dec. 23, 1947; children—James A., Kenneth M. BSChE, U. Wis., 1947; JD, NYU, 1950. Bar: N.Y. 1950, U.S. Supreme Ct. 1964. Assoc. firm Jeffery, Kimball, Eggleston, N.Y.C., 1950-52; assoc. firm Morgan, Finnegan, Durham & Pine, N.Y.C., 1952-59; ptnr. Morgan, Finnegan, Pine, Foley & Lee, N.Y.C., 1959-86; sr. ptnr. Morgan & Finnegan, N.Y.C., 1986—; lectr. in field. Author: (with J. Gould) Intellectual Property Counseling and Litigation, 1988, USPTO Proposals to Change Rule 56 and the Related Rules Regarding a Patent Applicant's Duty of Candour, Patent World, 1992; contbr. articles to legal jours. in patent and trademark litigation splty. Served to sgt. U.S. Army, 1944-46. Fellow Am. Bar Found.; mem. ATLA, ABA (mem. coun. Intellectual Property Law sect., chmn. com. fed. practice and procedure, chmn. com. Ct. of Appeals Fed. Cir., chmn. com. on ethics and profl. responsibility, stds. com., mem. fed. cir. adv. com. 1992—), Am. Intellectual Property Law Assn. (bd. dirs. 1984-90, pres. 1991), Am. Judicature Soc., Internat. Fedn. Indsl. Property Attys., Found. for Creative Am. (bd. dirs.), N.Y. Bar Assn., Assn. of Bar of City of N.Y., N.Y. County Bar Assn., N.Y. Patent, Trademark and Copyright Law Assn. (bd. dirs. 1975-80, pres. 1981), others. Home: 3328 Sabal Cove Ln Longboat Key FL 34228-4259 Office: Morgan & Finnegan 345 Park Ave New York NY 10154-0004

LEE, JERRY CARLTON, university administrator; b. Roanoke, Va., Nov. 21, 1941; m. Joan Marie Leo; 1 child, Zan. BA, W.Va. Wesleyan Coll., 1963; postgrad., W.Va. U. Grad. Sch. Indsl. Relations, 1963-64, U. Balt. Sch. Law, 1967-69; MA, Va. Poly. Inst., 1975, EdD, 1977; LLD (hon.), Gallaudet U., 1986. Mgmt. trainee Gen. Motors Corp., 1964-65; v.p. adminstrn. Comml. Credit Indsl. Corp., Washington, 1965-71; dir. gen. services Gallaudet Coll., Washington, 1971-77, asst. v.p. bus. affairs, 1978-82, v.p. adminstrn. and bus., 1982-84; pres. Gallaudet U. (formerly Gallaudet Coll.), Washington, 1984-88, Nat. U., San Diego, 1989—. Hon. bd. dirs. D.C. Spl. Olympics; commn. in adminstrn. org. Rehab. Internat.; bd. dirs. People to People, Deafness Research Found., Am. Assn. Univ. Adminstrs., Am. Coun. on Edn. Commn. on Women in Higher Edn.; hon. advocacy bd. Nat. Capital Assn. Coop. Edn.; mem. Personnel Policies Forum Bur. Nat. Affairs. Served with USAR, 1966-72. Recipient Nat. Service award, Hon. Pres. award Council for Better Hearing and Speech, 1986, One-of-a-Kind award People-to-People, 1987, Advancement Human Rights & Fundamental Freedoms award UN, U.S.A., Disting. Alumni award Va. Poly. Inst., 1985, Pres.' award Gallaudet Coll. Alumni Assn., Gallaudet Community Relations award, U.S. Steel Found. Cost Reduction Incentive award Nat. Assn. Coll. and Univ. Bus. Officers, award Am. Athletic Assn. Deaf, 1987. Mem. Am. Assn. Univ. Adminstrs. (Eileen Tosney award 1987), Consortium of Univs. Washington Met. Area (exec. com.), Nat. Collegiate Athletic Assn. (pres.' commn.), Nat. Assn. Coll. Aux. Services (jour. adv. bd., journalism award), Alpha Sigma Pi (Man of Yr. award 1983-84). Lodge: Sertoma (life, found. nat. adv. com.). Avocations: tennis, long distance running, weightlifting. Office: Nat Univ 11255 N Torrey Pines Rd La Jolla CA 92037-1011

LEE, JINHO, research engineer, consultant; b. Seoul, Korea, Sept. 11, 1963; came to U.S., 1976; s. Sangawan and Junghee (Han) L.; m. Joan E. Carletta, Oct. 3, 1994. BS in Engring., SUNY, Buffalo, 1985, PhD in Engring., 1991. Asst. engr. Calspan Co., Buffalo, 1985-91; rsch. engr. Sverdrup Tech. Inc., Brook Park, Ohio, 1991-94; sr. rsch. engr. NYMA, Inc., Brook Park, Ohio, 1994—; cons. engr. Waste Minimization Co., Cleveland, 1991—. Contbr. articles to profl. jours. Mem. AIAA (sr.), ASME. Republican. Methodist. Achievements include co-development of pollution free cleaning system, co-development of NASA combustor analysis tools. Home: 4091 River Ln Rocky River OH 44116-3826 Office: NYMA Inc at Lerc Brookpark OH 44142

LEE, JOE, federal judge. BJ, U. Ky., 1952, JD, 1955. Bar: Ky., U.S. Dist. Ct. (ea. dist.) Ky., U.S. Ct. Mil. Appeals, U.S. Supreme Ct. Law clk. to chief justice Ky. Supreme Ct.; law clk. to dist. judge U.S. Dist. Ct. (ea. dist.) Ky.; counsel to congl. subcom. U.S. Ho. of Reps.; bankruptcy judge U.S. Bankruptcy Ct., Lexington, Ky., 1961—; adj. prof. U. Ky. Coll. Law, 1972-92. Editor-in-chief Am. Bankruptcy Law Jour., 1982-90; author: Bankruptcy Practice Manual, 1981, 84-87; contbr. of more than 40 articles to profl. jours. Treas., bd. dirs. Emerson Ctr., Inc. With USAF, 1943-49. Recipient Henry T. Duncan Meml. award for disting. jud. svc. Fayette County Bar Assn., 1986. Fellow Am. Bar Found.; mem. ABA (chmn. com. on consumer bankruptcy 1977-82), Ky. Bar Assn. (Outstanding Judge award 1991), Fed. Bar Assn. Nat. Bankruptcy Conf. (chmn. com. on individual debtor 1982—), Nat. Conf. Bankruptcy Judges (pres. 1973-74, sec. 1979-90, com. on legis. 1973-77, Herbert M. Bierce Disting. Jud. Svc. award 1983). Office: US Bankruptcy Ct PO Box 1111 Lexington KY 40589-1111

LEE, JOHN EVERETT, physician; b. Charlotte, N.C., May 5, 1932; s. William States Lee and Sarah Everett; m. Ione Coker, July 29, 1961; children: Sarah Lee Elson, Jonathan Coker. AB, Princeton U., 1954; MD, Duke U., 1958. Diplomate Am. Bd. Psychiatry & Neurology, Am. Bd. Sleep Medicine. Chief resident neurology N.Y. Hosp., N.Y.C., 1963-64; mem. neurology faculty Med. Coll. Cornell U., N.Y.C., 1965-72; neurologist Atlanta Neurol. Clinic, 1972-92; sleep disorders practitioner Northside Hosp., Atlanta, 1992—; chief of staff Northside Hosp., 1984-86, bd. dirs. Office: Northside Hosp Sleep Disorders Ctr 5780 Peachtree Dunwoody Rd NE Atlanta GA 30342-1513

LEE, JOHN JIN, lawyer; b. Chgo., Oct. 20, 1948; s. Jim Soon and Fay Yown (Young) L.; m. Jamie Pearl Eng, Apr. 30, 1983. BA magna cum laude, Rice U., 1971; JD, Stanford U., 1975; MBA, 1975. Bar: Calif. 1976. Assoc. atty. Manatt Phelps & Rothenberg, L.A., 1976-77; asst. counsel Wells Fargo Bank N.A., San Francisco, 1977-79, counsel, 1979-80, v.p., sr. counsel, 1980, v.p., mng. sr. counsel, 1981—; mem. governing com. Conf. on Consumer Fin. Law, 1989-93. Bd. dirs. Asian Bus. League of San Francisco, 1981—, gen. counsel, 1981. Fellow Am. Coll. Consumer Fin. Svcs. Attys., Inc., (bd. regents 1995—), mem. ABA (chmn. subcom. on housing fin., com. on consumer fin. svcs., bus. law sect. 1983-90, vice chmn. on subcom. securities products, com. on consumer fin. svcs. bus. law sect. 1993-95, chmn. subcom. on securities products, com. on consumer fin. svcs., bus. law sect. 1995-96, chmn. subcom. on electronic banking, com. on consumer fin. svcs., bus. law sect. 1996—), Consumer Bankers Assn. (lawyers com.), Soc. Physics Students, Stanford Asian-Pacific Am. Alumni/ae Club (bd. dirs. 1989-93, v.p. 1989-91). Democrat. Baptist. Office: Wells Fargo Bank NA Legal Dept 111 Sutter St San Francisco CA 94104-4545

LEE, JOHN MARSHALL, mathematics educator; b. Phila., Sept. 2, 1950; s. Warren W. and Virginia (Hull) L.; m. Pm Weizenbaum, May 26, 1984; children: Nathan Lee Weizenbaum, Jeremy Lee Weizenbaum. AB, Princeton U., 1972; student, Tufts U., 1977-78; PhD, MIT, 1982. Systems programmer Tex. Instruments, Princeton, N.J., 1972-74; Geophys. Fluid Dynamics Lab., NOAA GFDL/NOAA, Princeton, 1974-75; tchr. math. and physics Wooster Sch., Danbury, Conn., 1975-77; programmer and cons. info. processing svcs. MIT, Cambridge, Mass., 1978-82; asst. prof. math. Harvard U., Cambridge, 1982-87; asst. prof. math. U. Wash., Seattle, 1987-89, assoc. prof. math., 1989-96, prof. math., 1996—; sr. tutor Harvard U., Cambridge, 1984-87. Contbr. articles to profl. jours. Rsch. fellow NSF, 1982. Mem. Am. Math. Soc. (Centennial fellow 1989). Avocations: hiking, wine tasting. Home: 5637 12th Ave NE Seattle WA 98105-2603 Office: Univ Wash Math Dept Box 354350 Seattle WA 98195-4350

LEE, JOHN THOMAS, finance educator, financial planner; b. Cleve., May 31, 1942; s. Harry C. and Lucille B. (Varnell) L.; m. Teresa (Susie) Leming, Dec. 18, 1996; children: Andrea, Joanne. BS in Econs., Tenn. Tech U., 1964; MS in Fin., U. Tenn., 1966; PhD in Fin., U. Ga., 1977. CFP. Instr. fin. Tenn. Tech U., Cookeville, 1966-71, asst. prof., 1973-78, assoc. prof., 1978-84; teaching asst. U. Ga., Athens, 1971-73; prof. fin. Mid. Tenn. State U., Murfreesboro, 1984—, Weatherford prof. fin., 1984-91, chmn. dept. econs. and fin., 1991—; mem. faculty 5th Ann. Cash Mgmt. Inst. Nat. Forum, 1984, Grad. Sch. Banking of South, La. State U., 1986, 88, 89, Tenn. Bankers Sch., Vanderbilt U., 1985; spkr., discussant, moderator, presenter numerous profl. orgns. Contbr. numerous articles to profl. jours. Recipient Outstanding Faculty award Tenn. Tech. U. Coll. Bus. Found.; named Prof. of Yr. Coll. of Bus. Mid. Tenn. State U., 1988, 91; Ayers fellow ABA Stonier Grad. Sch. Banking, summer 1987. Mem. Internat. Assn. Fin. Planning (pres. greater Tenn. chpt. 1995-96), Fin. Mgmt. Assn., So. Fin. Assn., Ea. Fin. Assn., Midwest Fin. Assn., Southwestern Fin. Assn., Mid-South Acad. Econs. and Fin. (2d v.p. 1990-91, 1st v.p. 1991-92, pres. 1993-94), Mid. Tenn. Inst. CFP's (bd. dirs. 1996-97), Mid. Tenn. Soc. CFP's (charter), Civitan (pres. Cookeville 1983-84, Stones River 1990-91, lt. gov. Valley dist.), Beta Gamma Sigma (pres. Mid. Tenn. State U. chpt. 1986-87, 92-94), Omicron Delta Epsilon, Sigma Iota Epsilon, Alpha Kappa Psi, Phi Delta Theta. Baptist. Home: 2522 Tomahawk Trce Murfreesboro TN 37129-6502 Office: Mid Tenn State U E Main St Murfreesboro TN 37132

LEE, JOLI FAY EATON, elementary education educator; b. Holdredge, Nebr., Sept. 24, 1951; d. Ray Lee and Lois Illeen (Willoughby) Larkins; m. James Edward Eaton, Aug. 16, 1969 (div. Jan. 1979); children: Threva, James, Beth; m. Chris Lee, Aug. 13, 1991; stepchildren: Michael Lee, Robyn Lee. BS in Elem. Edn., N.Mex. State U., Las Cruces, 1980, MA in Curriculum and Instruction, 1984. Cert. elem. tchr., N.Mex. Tchr. elem. Alamogordo (N.Mex.) Pub. Schs., 1980—; co-chmn. City Elem. Sci. Fair, Alamogordo, 1989-90, chmn., 1990-92; with Summer Sci. Pilot Program, 1992-94. Contbr. articles to profl. jours. Nat. conv. co-chmn. Nat. Speleological Soc., Tularosa, N.Mex., 1986; joint venturer Cave Rsch. Found., 1983—; person. dir., Guadalupe Area Cave Rsch. Found., N.Mex., 1987-90; del. Cave Exploration Del. to People's Republic of China, 1993. Crimson scholar N.Mex. State U., 1980. Mem. NEA, Nat. Speleological Soc. (sec. Southwestern region 1984, 91-92, 93, Southwestern regional chmn. 1985-86). Republican. Episcopalian. Home: 1405 St Francis Dr Tularosa NM 88352-2003 Office: North Elem Sch 1300 Florida Alamogordo NM 88310-6331

LEE, JONATHAN OWEN, financial services company executive, lawyer; b. Boston, Mar. 12, 1951; s. Herbert C. and Mildred (Schiff) L.; m. Barbara Ruth Cole, Mar. 24, 1984; children: Suzanna Cole, Alexander Philip. AB in Architecture, U. Calif., Berkeley, 1973; JD, Boston Coll., 1976. Bar: Mass. 1976. Staff atty. SEC, N.Y.C., 1976-79; pres. Lee Capital Holdings, LLC, Boston, 1979—; chmn. bd. dirs. Globe Metall., Inc., Cleve., 1986—, HSC Hospitality, Inc., Dallas, 1995—, C-Systems, Inc., Boston, 1997—; bd. dirs. So. Energy Homes, Inc., Adison, Ala., 1st Security Svcs., Inc., Boston, Hyde Athletic Industries, Inc., Peabody, Mass., P.A.R. Assocs., Inc., Boston. Bd. dirs. Combined Jewish Philanthropies, Boston, 1987—; mem. bd. overseers Mus. Fine Arts, Boston. Mem. Young Presidents Orgn., Explorers Club. Office: Lee Capital Holdings 1 International Pl Boston MA 02110-2600

LEE, JONG HYUK, accountant; b. Seoul, Korea, May 6, 1941; s. Jung Bo and Wol Sun L. BS Han Yang U., Seoul, Korea, 1964, BA, Sonoma State U. Rohnert Park, Calif., 1971; MBA in Taxation, Golden Gate U., San Francisco, 1976. CPA Calif. m. Easter Kim Jan. 24, 1970. Cost Acct., internal auditor Foremost-McKesson Co., San Francisco, 1971-74, sr. acct. clerk, Wong, Foulkes & Barbieri, CPAs. Oakland , Calif., 1974-77, pres. J.H. Lee Accountancy Corp., Oakland, 1977-89, 95—, Bay Cities Restaurants, Inc., Wendy 's Franchise, 1989-94; Instr., Armstromg Coll., Berkeley, Calif., 1977-78; lectr. acctg., dir. sch. of bus., The U.S. Korea Bus. Inst., San Francisco State U.; adv. bd. mem. Ctr. or Korean Studies, Insts. of East Asian Studies U. Calif.,Berkely; dir. United Labor Bank, Oakland bd. dirs. Korean residents Assn., 1974, Multi-svc. Ctr. for Koreans, 1979, BetterBus. Bur., 1984-87; chmn. cacus Calif.-Nev. ann. conf. United Meth Ch., 1977; commr. Calif. State Office Econ. Opportunity, 1982-86; pres. Korean Am. Dem. Network; mem. Dem. Nat. Fin. Coun.; regional chmn. Adv. Coun. on Peaceful Unification Policy, Republic of Korea; Commr. Asian Art Mus. San Francisco, 1988-91, Commr. Oakland Cmty. and Econ. Devel. 1997; bd., dir., East Bay Asian Local Devel. Corp with Korean Marine Corps, 1961-64; 1st lt. Calif. State Mil. Res. Mem. Am. Inst. CPAs. Nat. Assn. Asian Am. CPAs (bd. dir.), Am. Acctg. Assn., Nat. Assn. Accts., Internat Found. Employee Benifit Plans, Calif. Soc. CPAs, Oakland C. of C., Korean Am. C. of C. (pres. Pacific North Coast Rotary. Democrat. Author tax and bus. column Korea Times, 1980. Home: 180 Firestone Dr Walnut Creek CA 94598-3645 Office: 369 13th St Oakland CA 94612-2636

LEE, JOSEPH EDWARD, history educator; b. Chester, S.C., Sept. 24, 1953; s. Tyre Douglas and Martha Ola (Bankhead) L.; m. Ann-Franklin Hardy, Sept. 24, 1983; 1 child, Elizabeth. BA, Presbyn. Coll., Clinton, S.C., 1975; MA, Winthrop U., 1983; PhD, U. S.C., 1987. Instr. Adult Edn. Program, Chester, 1975-81; ctr. dir. Project Head Start, Chester, 1975-76; edn. coordinator Project Head Start, Rock Hill, S.C., 1978-81, Rock Hill, 1978-81; tchr., coach Chester Sch. Dist., 1976-78; personnel dir. Carolina Community Actions, Rock Hill, 1981-82; grad. asst. Winthrop U., Rock Hill, 1982-83; teaching asst. U. S.C., Columbia, 1983-85; hist. prof. U. N.C., Charlotte, 1985-94; prof. history Winthrop U., Rock Hill, S.C., 1994—; adj. prof. U. S.C., 1985-88, Belmont Abbey Coll., 1987-95; cons. S.C. Com. on the Humanities, Columbia, 1983, N.C. Humanities Coun., 1991; guest lectr. Sacred Heart Coll., Belmont, N.C., 1987. Author: The New Muckrakers, 1996; contbr. articles to profl. jours. Mem. Chester City Council, 1979-83; treas. Chester County Dem. Orgn. 1984-86, vice-chmn. 1976-82; v.p. S.C. Young Democrats, 1982-83; election com. City of Chester, 1976-79; lectr. N.C. Commn. on the Bicentennial of the Const., Charlotte, 1986. Recipient Sen. Olin D. Johnston award, S.C. Dem. Orgn., R. Means Davis Fellow in So. Hist., U. S.C., 1983-85. Mem. So. Hist. Assn., S.C. Hist. Assn. (bd. dirs.), S.C. Hist. Soc., So. Caoliniana Soc., Order of Omega, Friends of Historic Brattonsville, Mus. of York County, Yorkville Hist. Soc., Kiwanis, Sertoma (v.p. Chester club 1981-82), Moose, Phi Alpha Theta, Phi Beta Delta, Kappa Alpha Order, Omicron Delta Kappa. Democrat. Presbyterian. Avocations: tennis, collecting political campaign materials. Home: 202 W Madison St York SC 29745

LEE, JOSEPH WILLIAM, sales executive; b. Florence, S.C., Sept. 19, 1943; s. Warner Lou and Rosalee (Hyman) L.; m. Rita Martin, Sept. 8, 1962; children: Mark Stephen, Allison Lynette. Grad. high sch., Florence. Clk. Atlantic Coast Line R.R., Florence, 1962-69; sales rep. Durham (N.C.) & So. Rwy., 1969-74; dist. sales mgr. Westmoreland Coal Sales Co., Charlotte, N.C., 1974-82; v.p. purchasing Westmoreland Coal Sales Co., Phila., 1982-85, v.p. purchasing distbn., 1985-88, v.p. purchasing and northern sales, 1988-91; sr. v.p. Westmoreland Coal Sales Co., Phila., Pa., 1991, pres., 1991-95; v.p. sales TECO Coal Corp., 1995. Mem. N.C. Coal Inst., So. Coals Conf., Inc. (trustee 1989-92), Norfolk So. Corp. Adv. Bd. Republican.

LEE, JOYCE ANN, administrative assistant; b. Safford, Ariz., Sept. 18, 1942; d. Roy and Minnie R. (Mobley) Brewer; m. Eugene W. Gaddy Jr., Mar. 16, 1970 (div. 1985); children: Carol, Kevin, Aaron; m. Glenn A. Lee, Oct. 16, 1992. AA, Ea. Ariz. Coll., 1980, AAS, 1993; BA in Mgmt., U. Phoenix, 1995. Dispatcher Mohave County Sheriff's Office, Kingman, Ariz., 1969-74; sec. Globe (Ariz.) Mobile Home Sales, 1975-83; data entry supr. SMC & Assocs., Globe, 1985-88; tax preparer H&R Block Co., Globe, 1992; adminstrv. asst. Am. Pub. Co., Globe, 1994—; instr. computer, bus. classes Ea. Ariz. Coll. Gila Pueblo campus, Globe, 1996—. Girls camp dir. LDS Ch., Globe, 1985-90; mem. com. Boy Scouts Am., Globe. Mem. NAFE, Phi Theta Kappa. Democrat. Avocations: hunting, fishing, hiking, archery, camping. Home: Rt 1 CC 179 Globe AZ 85501 Office: Ea Ariz Coll Gila Pueblo Campus Globe AZ 85501-1416

LEE, JUNE WARREN, dentist; b. Boston, Feb. 24, 1952; d. Earl Arnold and Rosemary Regina (Leary) Warren; m. William Lee, July 25, 1976; children: Jaime Michelle, Daniel William. BA, Brandeis U., 1973; DDS, Georgetown U., 1977; student, U.S. Dental Inst., 1985-87. Pvt. practice, Boston, 1977—; chair gen. arrangements YDC 21, Yankee Dental Congress, chair sci. com. YDC 23. Mem. Altrusa Club of Quincy, Mass., 1979-96, Cunningham Sch. PTO, Milton, Mass., 1987—, Parent-Adv. Coun., Collicot Elem. Sch., Milton, 1986-87; dental instr. Cunningham Sch., 1987—; dental screening, Healthworks, Neponset Health Ctr., Boston, 1981-84; bd. dirs. Delta Dental Plan Mass., 1995—. Master Acad. Gen. Dentistry (coun. ann. meetings and internat. confs., past pres. New Eng. Mastertrack program, pres.-elect Mass. chpt., past chmn. editl. rev. bd. Audiodent); fellow Am. Coll. Dentists, Internat. Coll. Dentists, Acad. Dentistry Internat.; mem. ADA, Mass. Dental Soc., South Shore Dist. Dental Soc. (chmn.-elect 1991, chmn. 1992, chmn. program com. 1995-96), Am. Orthodontic Soc., Am. Acad. Gnathologic Orthopedics, Am. Assn. for Functional Orthodontics, Am. Assn. Women Dentists (sec. 1987, v.p. 1988, pres.-elect 1989, pres. 1990, A.T. Cross Co. Women of Achievement award 1985, bd. dirs. Gillette Hayden Meml. Found.), Women's Dental Soc. Mass. (sec. 1978, v.p. 1979-81, pres. 1981-83), Mass. Dentists Interested in Legislation, Chestnut Hill Rsch. Study Club. Roman Catholic. Avocations: travel, geneology, reading, writing, celtic music. Office: 383 Neponset Ave Dorchester MA 02122-3104

LEE, KANG-WON WAYNE, engineer, educator; b. Seoul, Nov. 15, 1947; came to U.S., 1976; s. Chong-Keuk and Jung-Ki (Baik) L.; m. Jee-Bock Hong, Aug. 11, 1979; children: J. Stephen, J. Harold, Grace E. BS, Seoul Nat. U., 1974; MS, Rutgers U., 1978; PhD, U. Tex., Austin, 1982. Civil engr. Lyon Assocs., Inc., Seoul, 1974-76; structural engr. TAMS-Engrs. and Architects, Seoul, 1976; hwy. constrn. inspector N.J. Dept. Transp., East Brunswick, N.J., 1978; rsch. engring. asst. U. Tex., Austin, 1978-82; asst. prof. Kind Saud U., Riyadh, Saudi Arabia, 1982-85; from asst. prof. to prof. dept. civil engring. U. R.I., Kingston, 1985—; vis. rsch. assoc. U. Calif., Berkeley, 1991; vis. prof. Seoul Nat. U., 1991, Korean Advanced Inst. of Sci. and Tech., Daejon, 1992; engring. cons. Lee Engring., Kingston, 1987—; dir. grad. studies, dept. civil engring., U. R.I., Kingston, 1996—. Contbr. articles to profl. jours. including Jour. Transp. Engrs., Jour. of Materials in Civil Engring. Adv. com. mem. New Eng. Transp. Consortium, Rocky Hill, Conn., 1986—; policy com. mem. Region I Univ. Transp. Ctr., Cambridge, Mass., 1988—; mem. R.I. Transp. Joint Rsch. Coun., Providence, 1994—. Recipient Program Devel. award U. R.I., 1987, Murphy Award for faculty excellence, 1990, Meritorious Svc. award RIDOT, 1996. Mem. ASCE (sec. BMC), ASTM, Transp. Rsch. Bd. (chair A2D04 (3)), AAPT, ASEE, ITE, Chi Epsilon. Mem. United Ch. of Christ. Achievements include teaching and research in areas of pavement and transportation engineering. Avocations: gardening, hiking, sports. Office: U RI Dept Civil Engring Kingston RI 02881

LEE, KATE LEARY, financial adviser; b. Hastings, Nebr., Dec. 13, 1946; d. Robert Michael and Alyce Rita (Popp) Leary; widowed; children: Modie Alexander Lee, Marni Sue Lee. AA, Mesa Jr. Coll., 1968; BA in Spl. Edn., U. No. Colo., 1970, MA in Learning Disabilities, 1977, MBA, 1982. Lic. tchr., Colo. Speech pathologist, audiologist Unit 13, Scottsbluff, Nebr., 1971-76; tchr. spl. edn. Sch. Dist. 13, Greeley, Colo., 1977-78; master spl. n. Havern Ctr., Inc., Denver, 1978-80; v.p. R.M. Leary & Co., Inc., Denver, 1980-84, pres., 1984—; sr. arbitrator BBB, 1988—; broker rep. Titan Value Equities Group, Inc., 1983-94. Fin. coun. Notre Dame Cath. Parish, Denver, 1989—; vol. coord. for State of Colo. gubernatorial candidate, 1994. Mem. Western Divsn. Conf. Pensions and Benefits, Colo. Harvard Bus. Sch. Club, Soc. Asset Allocators and Fund Timers, Inc. (dir. 1990-93), Ambassador Club Greater Denver C. of C. Office: RM Leary & Co Inc 1580 Lincoln #800 Denver CO 80203-1510

LEE, KENNETH, physicist; b. San Francisco, July 3, 1937; s. Kai Ming and Ah See Lee; A.B. with honors in Physics, U. Calif., Berkeley, 1959. Ph.D., 1963; m. Cynthia Ann Chu, June 28, 1959; children—Marcus Scott, Stephanie Denise. Research physicist Varian Assocs., Palo Alto, Calif., 1963-68; mem. research staff, mgr. IBM, San Jose, Calif., 1968-83; dir. memory techs. Southwall Techs., Palo Alto, Calif., 1983-84; sr. v.p. product devel. Domain Tech., Milpitas, Calif., 1984-89; chief tech. officer, pres. WSSG Bus. Group, Home: 20587 Debbie Ln Saratoga CA 95070-4827 Office: Quantum Corp 500 Mccarthy Blvd Milpitas CA 95035-7908

LEE, KENNETH STUART, neurosurgeon, educator; b. Raleigh, N.C., July 23, 1955; s. Kenneth Lloyd and Myrtie Lee (Turner) L.; m. Cynthia Jane Anderson, May 23, 1981; children: Robert Alexander, Evan Anderson. BA, Wake Forest U., 1977; MD, East Carolina U., 1981. Diplomate Nat. Bd. Med. Examiners, Am. Bd. Neurol. Surgeons; med. lic. N.C., Ariz. Intern, then resident in neurosurgery Wake Forest U. Med. Ctr., Winston-Salem, N.C., 1981-88; fellow Barrow Neurol. Inst., Phoenix, 1988-89; clin. asst. prof. neurosurgery East Carolina U., Greenville, N.C., 1989-93, clin. assoc. prof. neurosurgery, 1994—, adj. assoc. prof. health edn., 1997—. Assoc. editor Current Surgery, 1990—; contbr. 30 articles to profl. jours. and 5 chpts. to books. Mem. Ethicon Neurosurgical Adv. Panel, 1989—. Bucy fellow, 1988. Fellow ACS, Am. Heart Assn. (stroke coun.); mem. AMA, N.C. Med. Soc., Am. Assn. Neurol. Surgeons, Am. Soc. Stereotactic and Functional Neurosurgery, So. Med. Assn., Congress Neurol Surgeons, N.C. Neurosurg. Soc. (sec.-treas. 1991-93, pres. 1994-95), So. Neurosurg. Soc., Alpha Omega Alpha. Democrat. Baptist. Achievements include research on the efficacy of certain surgical procedures, particularly carotid endarterectomy, in the prevention of strokes. Home: 3600 Baywood Ln Greenville NC 27834-7630 Office: Ea Carolina Neurosurg 2325 Stantonsburg Rd Greenville NC 27834-7534

LEE, KEUN SOK, business educator, consultant; b. Pusan, Korea, May 12, 1954; came to the U.S., 1981; s. Namho and Okki (Ryo) L.; m. Youn Bin Lee, Apr. 15, 1980; children: Grace, Danny. BA, Hankuk U. of Fgn. Studies, Seoul, 1979; MBA, U. No. Iowa, 1983; DBA, U. Ky., 1987; postgrad., Columbia U. Rsch. cons. U. No. Iowa, Cedar Falls, 1982-83; rsch. asst. U. Ky., Lexington, 1983-84, tchg. asst., 1984-85; instr. Hofstra U., Hempstead, N.Y., 1986-87, asst. prof., 1987-93, tenured prof., 1993—. Author numerous publs. in mktg. jours. and confs. Recipient best article award Mu Kappa Tau, 1989, Acad. Mktg. Sci., 1991, best paper award AMS, 1991. Mem. Acad. Mktg. Svc., Am. Mktg. Assn. (assoc.). Avocation: Tae Kwon Do (2d degree Black Belt). Home: 1503 John St Fort Lee NJ 07024-2560 Office: Hofstra U 141 Weller Hall Hempstead NY 11550

LEE, KUO-HSIUNG, medicinal chemistry educator; b. Kaohsiung, Taiwan, Jan. 4, 1940; came to U.S., 1965; s. Ching-Tsung Lee and Chin-Yeh Yang; m. Lan-Huei Chen; children: Thomas Tung-Ying, Catherine Tung-Ling. BS, Kaohsiung Med. Coll., Taiwan, 1961; MS, Kyoto U., Japan, 1965; PhD, U. Minn., 1968. Postdoctoral scholar dept. chemistry UCLA, 1968-70; asst. prof. Sch. Pharmacy, U. N.C., Chapel Hill, 1970-74, assoc. prof., 1974-77, prof. medicinal chemistry, 1977-91, dir. natural products lab., 1983—, Kenan prof. medicinal chemistry, 1992—; adj. prof. Koahsiung Med. Coll., 1977—; mem. devel. therapeutics contract rev. com. Nat. Cancer Inst., NIH, 1984-88, Bio-organic and natural products chemistry study sect., 1990-94, mem. reviewers res., 1994-98; external assessor, res grants coun., Hong Kong, 1994—; cons. natural products program divsn. life scis. NSC, Taiwan, 1986-87, Food and Drug Bur., Dept. Health, Exec. Yuan of Republic of China, Taiwan, 1986-92, Genelabs, Inc., Redwood City, Calif., 1988—, Nat. Rsch. Inst., Chinese Medicine, Taiwan, 1989—, Sphinx Pharms. Corp., Durham, N.C., 1990-94; sci. advisor Nat. Lab. Foods and Drugs, Dept. Health, Exec. Yuan of Republic of China, Taiwan, 1990—; mem. sci. adv. bd. Pharmagenesis, 1992—; mem. acad. adv. com. planning sect. Nat. Health Rsch. Inst., Dept. Health, 1992-95, mem. recruitment and adv. com., 1996—, mem. sci. rev. and sci. coun. com. pharm. and biotech. sect., 1996—; mem. internat. adv. com. Biotechnology Rsch. Inst., Hong Kong U. of Sci. & Tech., 1997—. Mem. editl. adv. bd. Abstracts of Chinese Medicines, 1986—, Oriental Healing Arts Internat. Bull., 1987—, Bot. Bull. Academia Sinica, 1988—, The Chinese Pharm. Jour., 1988—, Jour. Pharm. Scis., 1990-92, Jour. Chinese Medicine, 1990—, Internat. Jour. Oriental Medicine, 1989—, Kaohsiung Jour. Med. Sci., 1992—, Internat. Jour. Pharmacognosy, 1991—, Jour. Nat. Prod., 1994—; contbr. more than 350 articles to profl. jours. Grantee NIH, Am. Cancer Soc., U.S. Army, 1971—; recipient Soine Meml. award U. Minn., 1990, Achievement award Genelabs, 1993, Lifu Acad. award Chinese Medicine, 1994, T.M. Tu Sci. award, 1995, Merit award Nat. Health Rsch. Insts., 1996; named Hon. Prof., Shanghai Inst. Materia Medica, 1996. Mem. Academia Sinica; fellow AAAS, Am. Assn. Pharm. Scientists, Acad. Pharm. Sci.; mem. Am. Chem. Soc., Chem. Soc., Am. Soc. Pharmacognosy, Am. Assn. Pharm. Sci., Am. Assn. Coll. Pharm., Phytochemistry Soc. N.Am., Soc. Syn. Organic Chemistry, Am. Assn. Cancer Rsch. Achievements include patents on synthesis of anti-cancer drugs, anti-fungal agts., anti-AIDS compounds, discovery of more than 1,000 novel plant anti-tumor agts. and synthetic analogs; elucidation of structure-activity relationships, mechanisms of action of bioactive products. Office: U NC Sch Pharmacy Chapel Hill NC 27599-7360

LEE, KYO RAK, radiology educator; b. Seoul, Korea, Aug. 3, 1933; s. Ke Chong and Ok Hi (Um) L.; came to U.S., 1964, naturalized, 1976; MD, Seoul Nat. U., 1959; m. Ke Sook Oh, July 22, 1964; children: Andrew, John. Intern, Franklin Sq. Hosp., Balt., 1964-65; resident U. Mo. Med. Center, Columbia, Mo., 1965-68; instr. dept. radiology U. Mo., Columbia, 1968-69, asst. prof., 1969-71; asst. prof. dept. radiology U. Kans., Kansas City, 1971-76, assoc. prof., 1976-81, prof., 1981—. Served with Republic of Korea Army, 1950-52. Diplomate Am. Bd. Radiology (cert. added qualification in pediat. radiology). Recipient Richard H. Marshak award Am. Coll. Gastroenterology, 1975. Fellow Am. Coll. Radiology; mem. Radiol. Soc. N.Am., Am. Roentgen Ray Soc., Assn. Univ. Radiologists, Kans. Radiol. Soc., Greater Kansas City Radiol. Soc., Wyandotte County Med. Soc., Korean Radiol. Soc. N.Am., Soc., Soc. Pediat. Radiology. Contbr. articles to med. jours. Home: 9800 Glenwood St Shawnee Mission KS 66212-1536 Office: U Kans 39th St and Rainbow Blvd Kansas City KS 66103

LEE, LANSING BURROWS, JR., lawyer, corporate executive; b. Augusta, Ga., Dec. 27, 1919; s. Lansing Burrows and Bertha (Barrett) L.; m. Natalie Krug, July 4, 1943; children: Melinda Lee Clark, Lansing Burrows III, Bothwell Graves, Richard Hancock. BS, U. Va., 1939; postgrad U. Ga. Sch. Law, 1939-40; JD, Harvard U., 1947. Bar: Ga. 1947. Former corp. officer Ga.-Carolina Warehouse & Compress Co., Augusta, 1957-89, pres., chief exec. officer, 1989—, co-owner Ga.-Carolina Warehouse Co. Chmn. bd. trustees James Brice White Found., 1962—; sr. warden Episc. Ch., also chancellor, lay min. Sr. councillor The Altantic Coun. of the U.S.; bd. dirs. Med. Coll. Ga. Found., Kanuga Endowment, Inc. Capt. USAAF, 1942-46. Fellow Am. Coll. Trust & Estate Counsel, Ga. Bar Found.; mem. Harvard U. Law Sch. Assn. Ga. (pres. 1966-67), Augusta Bar Assn. (pres. 1966-67), Soc. Colonial Wars Ga., Ga. Bar Assn. (former chmn. fiduciary law sect.), U.S. Supreme Ct. Hist. Soc., U. Va. Thomas Jefferson Soc. of Alumni, Internat. Order St. Luke the Physician, Augusta Country Club, Harvard Club of Atlanta, The Pres.'s Club of Med. Coll. Ga. Home: 2918 Bransford Rd Augusta GA 30909-3004 Office: Law Offices Lansing B Lee Jr First Union Bank Bldg 699 Broad St Ste 904 Augusta GA 30901-1448

LEE, LESLIE WARREN, marketing executive; b. Mpls., Nov. 21, 1949; s. Adolph Orlando and Eunice Celia (Akerson) L.; m. Kathleen Karen Frie, June 2, 1973; children: Megan Christine, Maren Elisabeth, Matthew Warren. BA in History magna cum laude, Augsburg Coll., Mpls., 1971. CLU, ChFC. Dir. YMCA, Mpls., 1971-73; dist. sales mgr. Chrysler Mtr. Corp., Marshfield, Wis., 1973-75; agt. Northwestern Mut. Life, Marshfield, 1975-81; mgr. advanced underwriting The Rural Cos., Madison, Wis., 1981-83; advanced life mktg. specialist Am. Family Ins., Madison, 1983-95; nat. sales dir. Flexsystem, Madison, 1995—; instr. Dept. Bus., U. Wis., Madison, 1981-82, Dept. Econs., U. Wis., Stevens Point, 1978-91; lectr. in field; cons. in litigation involving life ins. Mem. Nat. Assn. Life Underwriters, Madison Assn. Life Underwriters, Am. Soc. CLU and ChFC. Republican. Lutheran. Avocation: philately. Office: Flexsystem TASC 2302 International Ln Madison WI 53704-3127

LEE, LILLIAN VANESSA, microbiologist; b. N.Y.C., June 1, 1951; d. Wenceslao and Ada (Otero) Cancel; B.S. in Biology, St. Johns U., 1972; M.S. in Microbiology, Wagner Coll., 1974; m. Thomas Christopher Lee, June 11, 1972; children: Tovan, John-Peter, Phillip-Michael. Grad. lab. asst. in microbiology Wagner Coll., S.I., N.Y., 1972-74; clin. microbiology technologist Queens Hosp. Center, Jamaica, N.Y., 1974-81, clin. microbiology supr., 1981-84; sect. head microbiology Nyack (N.Y.) Hosp., 1984-93, acting lab. mgr., 1992-93; microbiology mgr. Beth Israel Med. Ctr., N.Y., 1994-97; microbiology mgr. Cabrini Med. Ctr., N.Y., 1997—. Cert. registered microbiologist and specialist in microbiology, clin. lab. specialist. Mem. Am. Soc. Clin. Pathologists, Am. Soc. Microbiology (N.Y.C. br. coun. mem. 1992—, program com. chair 1993-96, N.Y.C. br. nat. coun. 1996, 97), Am. Acad. Microbiology, Med. Mycology Soc. N.Y., N.Y.C. Soc. Infectious Diseases, Clin. Lab. Mgmt. Assn. (program com. 1996—). Home: 14 Continental Dr West Nyack NY 10994-2803 Office: Beth Israel Med Ctr 1st Ave at 16th St New York NY 10003

LEE, LIN-NAN, communications engineer, engineering executive; b. Kaonsiung, Taiwan, Feb. 24, 1949. BSEE, Nat. Taiwan U., 1970; PhD in Elec. Engring., U. Notre Dame, 1976. Sr. scientist Linkabit Corp., 1975-77; various rsch. and devel. positions COMSAT Labs., 1977-91, chief scientist sys. divsn., 1977-91; asst. v.p., engr. Hughes Network Sys., 1991—. Fellow IEEE (past chmn. Washington/No. Va. sect. info. theory group). Office: Hughes Network Systems B 212/11717 Exploration Ln Germantown MD 20876

LEE, LLOYD ENG-MENG, real estate consultant; b. Tacoma, Wash., Feb. 2, 1971; s. K.J. and Linda (Ho) L. BA, Harvard U., 1992; MS in Hotel Adminstrn., Cornell U., 1995. Assoc. cons. Ernst & Young, N.Y.C., 1995—; asst. cons. to Sultan of Brunei, Juradong, 1994, Longhorn Steaks, N.Y., 1994, Dairy Queen, N.Y.C., 1994. author, dir.: (corp. video) Interstate Hotel TQM, 1993; writer: t.v. commercial, 1992. Vol. tchr. Montessori Sch., Boston, 1992-93; coord. House and Neighborhood Devel., Cambridge, 1990-92. Mem. Assisted Living Fedn. Am., Asian Real Estate Profls. Assn., Nat. Coun. Sr. Housing, Cornell Soc. Hotelmen, Cornell Sch. Hotel Adminstrs. Hospitality Global Task Force, Harvard Club N.Y. Avocation: writing educational books for children. Office: Ernst & Young Kenneth Leventhal Real Estate 1211 6th Ave New York NY 10036

LEE, LOW KEE, electronics engineer, consultant; b. Oakland, Calif., Feb. 12, 1916; s. Hing Wing and Yan Hai (Louie) L.; m. Alice Jing, Nov. 29, 1953; children: Elliott James, Elizabeth Joanne. BS, U. Calif., Berkeley, 1937, MS, 1939; PhD, Calif. Western U., 1977. Group leader Aerophysics Lab., Los Angeles, 1946-50; lab. mgr. Stanford Research Inst., Menlo Park, Calif., 1950-55; asst. to dir. Gen. Mills, Mpls., 1955-57; dept. mgr. product engring. TRW, Redondo Beach, Calif., 1957-62, asst. dir. product assurance, 1962-78, ret., 1978; cons. Omni Corp., Rancho Santa Fe, Calif., 1983—, Control Data Inc., City of Industry, Calif. Co-author: Design and Construction of Electronic Equipment, 1961; contbr. to books, encys. Fellow IEEE, Chinese Am. Inst. Engrs. and Scientists (pres. San Francisco 1945-46, trustee 1979-81, 89-91, Meritorious award 1985), Masons. Home: 4479 Deerberry Ct Concord CA 94521-4513

LEE, MARCIA ELLEN, insurance agent; b. Framingham, Mass., Mar. 27, 1949; d. Robert F. and Lois Ann (Walker) Reeves; m. William G.T. Lee, Nov. 8, 1994. Grad. high sch., Scotia, N.Y. Cert. gen. agt.; acredited customer svc. rep.; errors and omissions cert. trainer. Account exec. Nat. Mortgage and Fin. Co. Ltd., Honolulu, 1980-82; ind. ins. agt. Ins. Specialist of Hawaii, Inc., Honolulu, 1982-89, Beck, Kuklich & Swartman, Inc., Honolulu, 1989-90; pres., mgr. Mutual Gen. Underwriters, Inc., Honolulu, 1990-95; gen. agt., regional mgr. Capitol Am. Life Ins. Co., Honolulu, 1995—; exec. v.p. Internat. Ins. Alliance, Inc. Pres. Kapiolani Jaycees, Honolulu, 1984-86; trustee Honolulu Teater for Youth, 1997—. Recipient Warrior Club Recruitment award Hawaii Jaycees, Honolulu, 1984, 85; named 1st female chpt. pres. Hawaii Jaycees, Honolulu, 1984, pres. of month, 1985, Outstanding Young Woman of Am., 1985, ABI Woman of Yr., 1992. Mem. Hawaii Ind. Ins. Agts. Assn. (conv. chmn. 1987-89, edn. chmn. 1989-91, v.p. 1990, pres.-elect 1991, pres. 1992, Disting. Svc. award 1989), Honolulu Execs. Assn., Amb. Coun. Plz. Club. Avocations: golfing, walking, knitting. Address: 3210 Wauke St Honolulu HI 96815-4449 Office: Pacific Mktg Assocs 1221 Kapiolani Blvd Ste Ph40 Honolulu HI 96814-3503

LEE, MARGARET BURKE, college administrator, English educator; b. San Diego, Dec. 28, 1943; d. Peter John and Margaret Mary (Brown) Burke; m. Donald Harry Lee, June 30, 1973; children: Katherine Louise, Kristopher Donald. BA summa cum laude, Regis Coll., 1966; MA with honors, U. Chgo., 1970, PhD, 1978; IEM Cert. Harvard U., 1992, Seminar for New Pres., 1996. Asst. to humanities MIT, Cambridge, 1969; instr. Dover-Sherborn High Sch., Dover, 1973-75; instr. Alpena Community Coll., Mich., 1975-80, dean liberal arts, 1980-82; dean instrn. Kalamazoo Valley Community Coll., 1982-85; v.p. Oakton Community Coll., Des Plaines, Ill., 1985-95, pres. 1995—; cons. evaluator North Cen. Assn., Chgo., 1982—, commr.-at-large, 1988-92, commn. on inst. of higher edn. bd. dirs., 1992—, vice chair, 1996—; cons., field faculty Vt. Coll., Montpelier, 1982-85; mem. admissions com. Ill. Math and Sci. Acad., 1988—; bd. gov.'s North Cook Ednl. Svc. Ctr., 1988—; bd. dirs. North Cook Ednl. Svc. Ctr., 1989—, vice-chair, 1990-91, chair 1992-94; mem. Bd. Edn. Dist. 39, Wilmette, Ill., 1990-92; Des Plaines Sister Cities, 1995—; mem. bd. dirs. Ill. Cmty. Coll. Atty's. Assn., 1994—. Mem. Career Edn. Planning Dist., Kalamazoo, 1982, Kalamazoo Forum/Kalamazoo Network, 1982, Needs Assessment Task Force, 1984. Ford Found. fellow, 1969-73; Woodrow Wilson Found. fellow, 1975; fed. grantee, 1978-84. Mem. Am. Assn. Community and Jr. Colls., Mich. Assn. Community Coll. Instrnl. Adminstrs. (pres. 1983-85), Mich. Occupational Deans Adminstrs. Coun. (exec. bd. 1983-85), Mich. Women's Studies Assn. (honors selection com. 1984), North Cen. Assn. Acad. Deans (pres. 1988-90), Kalamazoo Consortium Higher Edn. (pres.'s coun. coordinating com. 1982-85), Kalamazoo C. of C. (vocat. edn. subcom. indsl. coun. 1982), North Cen. Assn. Acad. Deans (v.p., pres. 1985-87), Des Plaines C. of C. (mem. bd. dirs. 1995—). Democrat. Lutheran. Avocations: quilt collecting, reading, listening to classical music, sports spectating, theatre-going. Home: 2247 Lake Ave Wilmette IL 60091-1410 Office: Oakton CC 1600 E Golf Rd Des Plaines IL 60016-1234

LEE, MARGARET NORMA, artist; b. Kansas City, Mo., July 7, 1928; d. James W. and Margaret W. (Farin) Lee; PhB, U. Chgo., 1948; MA, Art Inst. Chgo., 1952. Lectr., U. Kansas City, 1957-61; cons. Kansas City Bd. Edn., Kansas City, Mo., 1968-86; guest lectr. U.Mo.-Columbia, 1983, 85, 87, 89, 91, 93-95; one-woman shows Univ. Women's Club, Kansas City, 1966, Friends of Art, Kansas City, 1969, Fine Arts Gallery U. Mo. at Columbia, 1972, All Souls Unitarian Ch. Kansas City, Mo., 1978; two-Woman show Rockhurst Coll., Kansas City, Mo., 1981 exhibited in group shows U. Kans., Lawrence, 1958, Chgo. Art Inst., 1963, Nelson Art Gallery, Kansas City, Mo., 1968, 74, Mo. Art Show, 1976, Fine Arts Gallery, Davenport, Iowa, 1977; represented in permanent collections Amarillo (Tex.) Art Center, Kansas City (Mo.) Pub. Library, Park Coll., Parkville, Mo. Mem. Coll. Art Assn. Roman Catholic. Contbr. art to profl. jours.; author booklet. Home and Studio: 4109 Holmes St Kansas City MO 64110-1127

LEE, MARIANNA, editor; b. N.Y.C., Aug. 23, 1930; d. Isaac and Charlotte (Steiner) Lubow; m. Edward Lee, June 17, 1968 (div. 1978); 1 child, Susanna. BA, Smith Coll., 1952; postgrad, Columbia U., 1952-53; postgrad., Oxford (Eng.) U., 1957-58. Asst. editor Watson-Guptill Publs., N.Y.C., 1958-59; chief copy editor Grolier, Inc., N.Y.C., 1960-61; mng. editor Portfolio & Art News Ann., N.Y.C., 1961-62; assoc. editor Parade Publs., N.Y.C., 1962-66; mng. editor The Johns Hopkins Press, Balt., 1966-68, U. Tex. Press, Austin, 1968-69; sr. publs. mgr. Scripps Inst. of Oceanography, La Jolla, Calif., 1979-82; mng. editor Harcourt Brace & Co., San Diego, 1982—. Contbr. articles to profl. jours. Democrat. Jewish. Avocations: piano, painting, fell walking, speaking. Office: Harcourt Brace and Co 525 B St San Diego CA 92101-4403

LEE, MARILYN (IRMA) MODARELLI, law librarian; b. Jersey City, Dec. 8, 1934; d. Alfred E. and Florence Olga (Koment) Modarelli; m. Alfred

McClung Lee III, June 8, 1957 (div. July 1985); children: Leslie Lee Ekstrand, Alfred McClung IV, Andrew Modarelli. BA, Swarthmore (Pa.) Coll., 1956; JD, Western New Eng. Sch. of Law, 1985. Bar: Mass. 1986. Claims rep., supr. region II Social Security Adminstrn., Jersey City, 1956-59; law libr. County of Franklin, Greenfield, Mass., 1972-78; head law libr. Mass. Trial Ct., Greenfield, 1978—; mem. Franklin County Futures Lab Task Force (Mass. Cts.), 1994—. Chmn. Franklin County (Mass.) Regional Tech., Turners Falls, 1974-76, Sch. Bldg. Com., 1974-76; mem. Franklin County Planning Bd., 1988—, mem. exec. bd., 1992-95; clk. Franklin County Tech. Sch., 1976-81; vice chmn. Greenfield Planning Bd., 1987-95; mem. Greenfield Sch. Bldg. Com., 1995—; mem. Greenfield C.C. Found., 1990—; moderator All Soul's Unitarian Ch., 1996—, treas., 1997—; mem. alumni coun. Swarthmore Coll, 1994-97. Mem. Mass. Bar Assn., Franklin County Bar Assn. (chmn. lawyer referral com. 1992-94, vice chmn. 1994—, chmn. libr. com. 1992—), Law Librs. of New Eng. (treas. 1993-97), Am. Assn. Law Librs., Greenfield Charter (com. clk. 1979-83). Avocations: swimming, gardening. Office: Mass Trial Ct Franklin Law Libr 425 Main St Greenfield MA 01301-3313

LEE, MARTIN YONGHO (KYUNG-JOO LEE), mechanical engineer; b. Apr. 13, 1937; s. Yee Whan and Myo Ryun (Choi) L.; m. Su Ja Bang, Nov. 29, 1969; children: Mu Young, Tae Young. BSME, Han Yang U., Seoul, Republic of Korea, 1964. Lic. stationary engr., N.Y.; lic. energy mgmt. engrs. 1st class, indsl. power boiler-turbine oper. engrs. 1st class, Korea. Start-up engr. Sam-Chuch Power Plant, 1963-66; jr. engr. U.S. Army, Camrhan Bay, Vietnam, 1966-69; startup engr. power plant Korea Electric Power Co., Seoul, 1969-75; stationary engr. CUNY, N.Y.C., 1981-92, Queens, 1981-92; stationary engr. N.Y. Police Dept., N.Y.C., 1992—. Mem. Assn. Energy Engr., Co-Generation Assn. Home: 14628 34th Ave Flushing NY 11354-3134 Office: Police Hdqs NYC 1 Police Plz New York NY 10038-1403

LEE, MATHEW HUNG MUN, physiatrist; b. Hawaii, July 28, 1931; married; 3 children. AB, Johns Hopkins U, 1953; MD, U. Md., 1956; MPH, U. Calif., 1962. Diplomate Am. Bd. Physical Medicine & Rehab. Resident Inst. Physical Medicine & Rehab., NYU, 1962-64, assignee rehab. svc.N.Y. State Health Dept., 1964-65, from asst. prof. to assoc. prof. rehab. medicine, 1965-73, dir. edn. & training dept. rehab. medicine, 1966-68, assoc. dir., 1968, prof. rehab medicine, 1973—; dir. dept. rehab. medicine Goldwater Meml. Hosp., 1968—; assoc. vis. physician Goldwater Meml. Hosp., 1965-68, vis. physician, 1968—, chief electrodiagnosis unit, 1966—, v.p. med. bd., 1969-70, pres., 1971' asst. clin. prof. Coll. Dentistry NYU, 1966-69, clin. asst. prof., 1969-70, clin. assoc. prof., 1970—; cons. Daughters of Israel Hosp., N.Y., 1965-72, Bur. Adult Hygiene, 1965—, Human Resources Ctr., 1966—; asst. attending physician Hosp. NYU, 1968—; med. dir. dept. rehab. medicine N.Y.U., 1989; attending physician Bellevue Hosp. Ctr., 1971—; cons. World Rehab. Fund, Gordon Seagrave & Maryknoll Hosps., Korea, 1969, U.S. Dept. Interior. Fellow Am. Acad. Physical Medicine & Rehab., Am. Coll. Physicians, Am. Pub. Health Assn.; mem. AAAS, Pan-Am. Med. Assn. Office: Jerry Lewis Neuromuscular Dis Ctr Dept Rehab Medicine 400 E 34th St New York NY 10016-4901

LEE, MEREDITH, German literature and language educator; b. St. Louis, July 11, 1945; m. Anthony Battaglia, Nov. 18, 1977. BA summa cum laude, St. Olaf Coll., Northfield, Minn., 1968; MPhil with distinction, Yale U., 1971, PhD, 1976. Asst. prof. U. Calif., Irvine, 1974-81; assoc. prof. U. Calif., 1981-93; prof. U. Calif., Irvine, 1993—, dean undergrad. studies, 1984-88, assoc. dean humanities, 1982-84, chair dept. German, 1991—; sec., treas., dir. Goethe Soc. N.Am., 1979-94, exec. sec., 1994—; chair area adv. com. Coun. for Internat. Exch. Scholars, Washington, 1986-88. Author: Studies in Goethe's Lyric Cycles, 1978; co-editor: Interpreting Goethe's Faust Today, 1994; contbr. articles to profl. jours. Danforth fellow, 1968-74; Fulbright scholar, Göttingen, Fed. Republic Germany, 1972-73. Mem. Am. Assn. Tchrs. German, Am. Soc. for 18th Century Studies, Soc. For Values in High Edn., Modern Lang. Assn., German Studies Assn. (exec. com. 1983-86), Phi Beta Kappa. Lutheran. Office: U Calif Dept German Irvine CA 92697-3150

LEE, MICHELE, actress; b. L.A., June 24, 1942; d. Jack and Sylvia Helen (Silverstein) Dusick; m. James Farentino, Feb. 20, 1966 (div. 1983); 1 son, David Michael; m. Fred Rappoport, Sept. 27, 1987. Actress roles include (Broadway play) How to Succeed in Business Without Trying, 1962-64, Seesaw, 1973, (movies) How to Succeed in Business With Really Trying, 1967, The Love Bug, 1969, Dark Victory, 1975, Bud and Low, 1976, A Letter to Three Wives, 1985, Single Women, Married Men, 1989, The Fatal Image, 1990, My Son Johnny, 1991, (TV movie) Broadway Bound, 1992, When No One Would Listen, 1993, Big Dreams Broken Hearts: The Dottie West Story, 1995, (TV series) Knots Landing, 1979-93 (Outstanding Lead Actress award Soap Opera awards 1992); exec. producer When No One Would Listen, Big Dreams Broken Hearts, The Dottie West Story; exec. producer, co-writer, dir. Color Me Perfect, 1996 (Christopher award, 1997, Gracie Allen award 1997). Recipient Top Star of Tomorrow award Motion Picture Exhibitors of U.S. and Can., 1967, Drama Desk award Broadway Critics, 1973, Outer Critics Circle award, 1973, Christopher award, 1997, Gracie Allen award, 1997; nominated for Antoinette Perry award, 1973-74, Emmy for Knots Landing, 1981-82.

LEE, MORDECAI, political scientist, educator; b. Milw., Aug. 27, 1948; s. Jack Harold and Bernice (Kamesar) L.; 1 child, Ethan. BA, U. Wis., 1970, MPA, Syracuse U., 1972, PhD, 1975. Guest scholar Brookings Instn., Washington, 1972-74; legis. asst. to Congressman Henry Reuss, Washington, 1975; asst. prof. polit. sci. U. Wis.-Whitewater and Parkside, 1976; mem. Wis. Ho. Reps., 1977-82; mem. Wis. Senate, 1982-89; exec. dir. Milw. Jewish Coun. Cmty. Rels., 1990-97; asst. prof. govt. U. Wis.-Milw., 1997—.

LEE, NELDA S., art appraiser and dealer, film producer; b. Gorman, Tex., July 3, 1941; d. Olan C. and Onis L.; A.S. (Franklin Lindsay Found. grantee), Tarleton State U., Tex., 1961; B.A. in Fine Arts, N. Tex. State U., 1963; postgrad. Tex. Tech. U., 1964, San Miguel de Allende Art Inst., Mexico, 1965; 1 dau., Jeanna Lea Pool. Head dept. art Ector High Sch., Odessa, Tex., 1963-68. Bd. dirs. Odessa YMCA, 1970, bd. dirs. Am. Heart Assn., Odessa, 1975; fund raiser Easter Seal Telethon, Odessa, 1978-79; bd. dirs. Ector County (Tex.) Cultural Center, 1979—, Tex. Bus. Hall of Fame, 1980-85; bd. dirs., mem. acquisition com. Permian Basin Presdl. Mus., Odessa, 1978; bd. dirs., chairperson acquisition com. Odessa Art Mus., 1979—; pres. Mega-Tex. Prodns., TV and movie producers; pres. Ector County Democratic Women's Club, 1975, Nelda Lee, Inc., Odessa; appointee Tex. Commn. Arts, 1993—. Group exhbns. include El Paso, Tex., New Orleans. Recipient Designer-Craftsman award El Paso Mus. Fine Arts, 1964. Mem. Am. Soc. Appraisers (sr.), Nat. Tex. Assn. Art Dealers (pres. 1978—), Odessa C. of C. Contbr. articles to profl. jours. Office: Nelda Lee Inc PO Box 4268 Odessa TX 79760-4268

LEE, PAUL CHING-LAI, banker, real estate developer; b. Tainan, Taiwan, Republic of China, Dec. 10, 1943; came to the U.S., 1978; s. Lau Teh and Koy (Lin) L.; m. Mary S. Lin, June 8, 1966; children: Patty S., Kathy S. B in Commerce, Nat. Cheng-Kung U., Tainan, 1966, M in Bibl. Study, 1996. Pres. Oriental Spring Internat. Corp., N.Y.C., 1978-81, Taiwan Christian Svcs., Inc., N.Y.C., 1982—, Teco Industry (USA) Corp., N.Y.C., 1978—; vice chmn. Great Ea. Bank, N.Y.C., 1990—; bd. dirs. Five Giants, Inc., San Francisco, Seven Giants, Inc., N.Y.C., 1984—, 136-09 Realty, Inc., N.Y.C. Lt. U.S. Army, 1966-67, Taiwan. Mem. Am. Reformed Ch. Avocations: golf, travel, tai-chi, swimming, ping-pong. Home: 106 Jarvis Ave Staten Island NY 10312-5772 Office: Great Ea Bank 41-48 Main St Flushing NY 11355-3134

LEE, PAUL LAWRENCE, lawyer; b. N.Y.C., 1946. AB, Georgetown U., 1969; JD, U. Mich., 1972. Bar: N.Y. 1974. Editor-in-chief Mich. Law Rev., 1971-72; law clk. to Hon. Walter R. Mansfield U.S. Ct. Appeals (2d cir.), 1973-74; spl. asst. to gen. counsel U.S. Treasury Dept., 1977-78, exec. asst. to dep. sec., 1978-79; dep. supt. and counsel N.Y. State Banking Dept., 1980-81; ptnr. Shearman & Sterling, N.Y.C., 1982-94; exec. v.p., gen. counsel Republic N.Y. Corp., N.Y.C., 1994—. Office: Republic NY Corp 452 5th Ave New York NY 10018-2706

LEE, PEGGY (NORMA DELORES EGSTROM), singer, actress; b. Jamestown, N.D., May 26, 1920; d. Marvin Engstrom; m. Dave Barbour, 1943 (div. 1951); 1 dau., Nicki; m. Brad Dexter, Jan. 4, 1955 (div. 1955); m. Dewey Martin, Apr. 25, 1956; Jack del Rio, Mar., 1964 (div. 1964). Grad., high sch. Singer Sta. WDAY, Fargo, N.D.; various singing engagements Mpls.; vocalist Will Osborne's band, Doll House, Palm Springs, Ambassador Hotel West, Chgo., Americana Hotel, Basin St. East, Benny Goodman's Band, 1941-43; singer concerts with Benny Goodman at Melodyland Theatre, Anaheim, Calif., Circle-Star Theatre, San Carlos, Calif. Author: (verse) Softly, With Feeling, 1953; screen appearances include Mr. Music, 1950, The Jazz Singer, 1953, Pete Kelly's Blues, 1955; performer Revlon Revues CBS-TV, 1960; actor Gen. Electric Theater, 1960; composer for films including Johnny Guitar, About Mrs. Leslie; composer musical score (cartoon) Tom Thumb; lyricist, voice talent Lady and the Tramp; rschr., program writer, performer The Jazz Tree Philharm. Ctr. for Performing Arts, N.Y.C., 1963; recordings include Golden Earrings, You Was Right Baby, It's A Good Day, Manana, and I Don't Know Enough About You, Is That All There Is (Grammy award 1969), I'm A Woman, Mirrors, There'll Be Another Spring, 1948, 1985, You Can Depend On Me, Seductive, Peggy Lee Sings With Benny Goodman, 1988, Peggy Lee Sings the Blues, 1988, Vol. 1-The Early Years, 1990, Classics, 1993, Love Held Lightly, 1993, Moments Like This, 1993, Peggy Lee with Bing Crosby: It's a Good Day, 1995, Sings For You, 1995, Spotlight on Peggy Lee, 1995. Named Best Female Vocalist by Metronome, Downbeat mags., 1946; recipient Most Popular Vocalist citation Billboard, 1950; Nat. Acad. of Recording Arts & Sciences Lifetime Achievement Award, 1994. Office: care Irvin Arthur & Assoc 9363 Wilshire Blvd Ste 212 Beverly Hills CA 90210-5418 also: Parrot/City Hall 25 Tiburon St San Rafael CA 94901*

LEE, PETER JAMES, bishop; b. Greenville, Miss., May 11, 1938; s. Erling Norman and Marion (O'Brien) L.; m. Kristina Knapp, Aug. 28, 1965; children: Stewart, Peter James Jr. AB, Washington and Lee U., 1960; MDiv, Va. Theol. Sem., 1967; postgrad, Duke U. Law Sch., 1963-64; DD (hon.), Va. Theol. Sem., 1984, St. Paul's Coll., Lawrenceville, Va., 1985, U. of the South, 1993. Ordained priest Episc. Ch., 1968, bishop, 1984. Newspaper reporter, editor Pensacola, Fla., Richmond, Memphis, 1960-63; deacon St. John's Cathedral, Jacksonville, Fla., 1967-68; asst. min. St. John's Ch. LaFayette Sq., Washington, 1968-71; rector Chapel of the Cross, Chapel Hill, N.C., 1971-84; bishop coadjutor Episcopal Diocese of Va., Richmond, 1984-85, bishop, 1985—; pres. trustees of the funds Diocese of Va., 1985—; dir. Presiding Bishop's Fund for World Relief, 1986-93. Rector bd. trustees Episcopal H.S., Alexandria, Va., 1985—; chmn. Meml. Trustees, Richmond, trustee Wash. Nat. Cathedral. Recipient duPont Fund Lifetime Achievement award, 1997. Mem. Phi Beta Kappa, Omicron Delta Kappa. Office: Diocese Va 110 W Franklin St Richmond VA 23220-5010

LEE, PHILIP RANDOLPH, medical educator; b. San Francisco, Apr. 17, 1924; married, 1953; 4 children. AB, Stanford U., 1945, MD, 1948; MS, U. Minn., 1956; DSc (hon.), MacMurray Coll., 1967. Diplomate Am. Bd. Internal Medicine. Asst. prof. clin. phys. medicine & rehab. NYU, 1955-56; clin. instr. medicine Stanford (Calif.) U., 1956-59, asst. clin. prof., 1959-67; asst. sec. health & sci. affairs U. Calif., San Francisco, 1967-69, chancellor, 1969-72, prof. social medicine, 1969-97, dir. inst. health policy studies, 1972-93; asst. sec. U.S. Dept. of Health & Human Services, Washington, D.C., 1993-97; prof. emeritus, sr. advisor Inst. Health Policy, San Francisco, 1997—; mem. dept. internal medicine Palo Alto Med. Clinic, Calif., 1956-65; cons. bur. pub. health svc. USPHS, 1958-63, adv. com., 1978, nat. commn. smoking & pub. policy, 1977-78; dir. health svc. office tech. cooperation & rsch. AID, 1963-65; dep. asst. sec. health & sci. affairs HEW, 1965, asst. sec., 65-69, mem. nat. coun. health planning & devel., 1978-80; co-dir. inst. health & aging, sch. nursing U. Calif., San Francisco, 1980—; pres. bd. dirs. World Inst. Disability, 1984—; mem. population com. Nat. Rsch. Coun.- Nat. Acad. Sci., 1983-86; mem. adv. bd. Scripps Clinic & Rsch. Found., 1980—. Author over 10 books; contbr. articles to profl. jours. Recipient Hugo Schaefer medal Am. Pharm. Assn., 1976. Mem. AAAS, AMA, ACP, Am. Pub. Health Assn., Am. Fedn. Clin. Rsch., Am. Geriatric Soc., Assn. Am. Med. Colls., Inst. Medicine-Nat. Acad. Sci. Achievements include research in arthritis and rheumatism, especially Rubella arthritis, cardiovascular rehabilitation, academic medical administration, health policy. Office: Inst Health Policy 1338 Sutter St 11th Fl San Francisco CA 94109*

LEE, QWIHEE PARK, plant physiologist; b. Republic of Korea, Mar. 1, 1941; came to U.S., 1965; d. Yong-sik and Soon-duk (Paik) Park; m. Ickwhan Lee, May 20, 1965; children: Tina, Amy, Benjamin. MS, Seoul Nat. U., Republic of Korea, 1965; PhD, U. Minn., 1973. Head dept. plant physiology Korea Ginseng and Tobacco Inst., Seoul, 1980-82; instr. Sogang U., Seoul, 1981, Seoul Women's U., 1981; research assoc. U. Wash., Seattle, 1975-79. Exec. dir. Korean Community Counseling Ctr., Seattle, 1983-86. Named one of 20 Prominent Asian Women in Wash. State, Chinese Post Seattle, 1986. Mem. AAAS. Buddhist. Home: 13025 42nd Ave NE Seattle WA 98125-4624 Office: U Wash Dept Pharm SJ-30 1959 NE Pacific St Seattle WA 98195-0004

LEE, RAPHAEL CARL, plastic surgeon, biomedical engineer; b. Sumter, S.C., Oct. 29, 1949; s. Leonard Powell and Jean Maurice (Langston) L.; m. Kathleen Kelley, Feb. 11, 1983; children: Rachel, Catherine. BS, U. S.C., 1971; MS, Drexel U., 1975; MD, Temple U., 1975; ScD, MIT, 1979. Diplomate Am. Bd. Plastic Surgeons, Am. Bd. Surgery. Chief resident gen. surgery U. Chgo. Hosps., 1980-81; assoc. in surgery Brigham and Women's Hosp., 1984-89; assoc. surgeon The Children's Hosp., 1985-89; dir. Electrical Trauma Program, 1991—; med. dir. U. Chgo. Burn Unit, 1991—; asst. prof. of surgery Harvard Med. Sch., 1984-89; Karl R. VanTassel asst. prof. of electrical and bioengring. MIT, 1983-89, asst. prof. of bioengring. and surgery Harvard MIT, Divsn. of Health Scis. and Tech., 1983-89; prof. surgery, anatomy and organismal biology U. Chgo., 1992—; chmn. bd. dirs. Avocet Polymers Techs., Inc., 1996—. Author: Electrical Injury, Multidisciplinary Approach, 1994; editor: Electrical Trauma, Pathophysiology, 1992; editl. bd. Bioelectromagnetics, 1993—; contbr. numerous articles to profl. jours. Recipient Alumni Achievement award Class of 1975 Temple Med. Sch., 1995, Searle Scholar award The Searle Found., 1985-88; named Ams. 100 Brightest Young Scientists Sci. Digest, 1984; MacArthur Prize fellow John D. and Catherine T. MacArthur Found., 1981-86. Fellow ACS (Schering Scholar in Surgery 1978); mem. IEEE, AAAS, Am. Burn Assn. (Linberg award), Am. Phys. Soc., Am. Soc. for Cell Biology, Am. Assn. Plastic Surgeons (James Barrett Brown award 1988), Biophys. Soc., Nat. Med. Assn. (plastic surgery sect chmn. 1989-91), Soc. for Phys. Regulation in Biology and Medicine (scientific program com. 1993, pres. 1995), Soc. of Univ. Surgeons, Tau bet Pi, Alpha Omega Alpha, Sigma Xi. Achievements include 12 patents. Office: U Chgo Hosps Pritzker Sch Medicine-Surgery MC6035 5841 S Maryland Ave Chicago IL 60637-1463

LEE, R(AYMOND) WILLIAM, JR., apparel company executive; b. Richmond, Va., Apr. 24, 1930; s. Raymond William and Sally (Beal) L.; m. Marianne Hollingsworth, June 21, 1952; children: Lelia, Carol, Raymond William, III, Sally. A.B., Duke U., 1951. With Oxford Industries, Inc., Atlanta, 1955—; v.p. men's wear Oxford Industries, Inc., 1970-77, v.p. fin. and adminstrn., 1977-86; adv. bd. Allendale Ins. Co., 1982; mem. adv. com. U.S. Dept. of Commerce, 1982—; exec. v.p. fin. and adminstrn. Oxford Industries, Inc., 1986—; bd. dirs. Major Leasing. Vice-chmn. Ga. Rep. party, 1981-83; bd. dirs. Ga. Coop. Svcs. for Blind, 1974—, pres., 1979-80. With USMCR, 1951-53. Mem. Am. Apparel Mfrs. Assn. (dir. 1964-70), Men's Fashion Assn. (dir. 1974-86), Father's Day Council (dir. 1975-85); dir. Ga. Regents Global Ctr., 1993—. Republican. Episcopalian. Clubs: Cherokee Town and Country (treas. 1977-78, dir. 1979-83, pres. 1982-83); Fripp Island; Dataw; Capitol Hill; Kiwanis; Green Boundary. Home: 6265 Riverside Dr NW Atlanta GA 30328-3623 Office: Oxford Industries Inc 222 Piedmont Ave NE Atlanta GA 30308-3306

LEE, RICHARD DIEBOLD, law educator, legal publisher; b. Fargo, N.D., July 31, 1935; s. Sidney Jay and Charlotte Hannah (Thompson) L.; m. Patricia Ann Taylor, June 17, 1957; children—Elizabeth Carol, Deborah Susan, David Stuart. B.A. with distinction, Stanford U., 1957; J.D., Yale U., 1960. Bar: Calif. 1961. U.S. Dist. Ct. (no. dist.) Calif. 1961, U.S. Ct. Appeals (9th cir.) 1961. Dep. atty. gen. Office of Atty. Gen., Sacramento, 1960-62; assoc. McDonough, Holland, Schwartz, Allen & Wahrhaftig, Sacramento, 1962-66, ptnr., 1966-69; asst. dean U. Calif. Sch. Law, Davis, 1969-73, assoc. dean, 1973-76; assoc. prof. law Temple U. Sch. Law, Phila., 1976-77, vis. prof., 1975-76, prof., 1977-89; dir. profl. devel. Baker & McKenzie, Chgo., N.Y.C., 1981-83; dir. Am. Inst. for Law Tng., Phila., 1985-89; dir. profl. devel. Morrison & Foerster, San Francisco, 1989-93; dir. Continuing Edn. of the Bar, Berkeley, 1993—; mem. Grad. and Profl. Fin. Aid Coun., Princeton, N.J., 1974-80; trustee Law Sch. Admission Council, Washington, 1976-78; mem. internat. adv. com. Internat. Juridical Org., Rome, 1977-88; mem. bd. advisors Lawyer Hiring and Tng. Report, Chgo., 1983-95; vis. prof. law sch. law Golden Gate U., San Francisco, 1988-89. Author: (coursebook) Materials on Internat. Efforts to Control the Environment, 1977, 78, 79, 80, 84, 85, 87. Co-editor: Orientation in the U.S. Legal System annual coursebook, 1982-92. Contbr. articles to profl. jours. Bd. dirs. Lung Assn. of Sacramento-Emigrant Trails, 1962-69, pres., 1966-68; bd. dirs. Sacramento County Legal Aid Soc., 1968-74, pres., 1971-72; chmn. bd. overseers Phila. Theol. Inst., 1984-88, bd. overseers, 1979-80, 84-88; mem. bd. of council Episcopal Community Services, Phila., 1984-88; trustee Grace Cathedral, San Francisco, 1989—, chair bd. trustees, 1992-95; mem. bd. visitors John Marshall Law Sch., Chgo., 1989-93; trustee Grad. Theol. Union, Berkeley, 1991—, vice-chair, 1994—. Mem. ABA (chmn. various coms., spl. coms. on continuing legal edn. MacCrate Task Force on Law Schs. and the Profession: Narrowing the Gap 1991-93), State Bar Calif. (chair standing com. on minimum continuing legal edn. 1990-92, com. mem. 1990-93), Profl. Devel. Consortium (chair 1991-93), Am. Law Inst. Democrat. Episcopalian. Club: Yale (N.Y.C.). Home and Office: 2001 Sacramento St # 4 San Francisco CA 94109-3342 Office: Continuing Edn of the Bar 2300 Shattuck Ave Berkeley CA 94704-1517

LEE, RICHARD KENNETH, building products company executive; b. Birmingham, Eng., Dec. 10, 1942; came to U.S., 1964; s. Kenneth Jesse Lee and Eleanor Margaret (Bellsham) Dean; m. Melinda Elena Noback, Aug. 20, 1966; children: Sonja Eleanor, Alyssa Claire. BSc with upper 2d class honours, No. Poly. U. London, 1964; MS in Inorganic Chemistry, Northwestern U., 1965; PhD in Inorganic Chemistry, U. London, 1968. Various corp. rsch. positions UOP Inc., Des Plaines, Ill., 1965-74, mgr. catalyst R & D automotive products divsn., 1974-77; v.p., gen. mgr. portable battery div. Gould Inc., St. Paul, 1977-82; v.p., gen. mgr. Elgar Corp., an Onan/McGraw Edison Co., San Diego, 1982-85; v.p. R & D, Pharmaseal div. Baxter Healthcare Corp., Valencia, Calif., 1985-88; v.p. strategic bus. ops. Manville Sales Corp., Denver, 1988-92; pres., chief exec. officer Rocklite Inc., Denver, 1992—; adj. prof. masters tech. program U. Coll., U. Denver, 1993-95. Author: (videotape) U.S. Competitiveness—A Crisis?, 1992; patentee for vehicle emission control system. Chmn. Summit 91, Denver, 1991, mem. organizing com. Summit 92, Pacoima, Calif., 1992; bd. dirs. Indsl. Rsch. Inst., Inc., Washington, 1991-92. Recipient IR-100 award Indsl. R & D, 1978; Fulbright travel scholar, 1964-65. Mem. Rocky Mountain World Trade Ctr. (vice chmn. 1992-94, exec. com. 1992-94, bd. dirs. 1990-95), Denver C. of C. Office: Rocklite Inc PO Box 44423 Denver CO 80201-4423 *The quality of life for U.S. citizens in the early 21st Century will be primarily determined by the results of U.S. industry and government efforts to improve our ability to commercialize technology successfully.*

LEE, RICHARD SCOTT, neurologist; b. Bklyn., Sept. 10, 1949. BS in Chemistry, U. Wis., 1970; MD, SUNY, Buffalo, 1974. Diplomate Am. Bd. Neurology, Am. Acad. Pain Mgmt., Am. Bd. Electroencephalography, Am. Bd. Neurophysiology. Intern in str. medicine U. Fla. Hosps., 1974-75; clin. neurologist Martin Meml. Hosp., Stuart, Fla., 1981-90; resident in neurology U. Miami Aff. Hosps., 1975-78; neurologist Physicians Plus HMO, Madison, Wis., 1991; cons. neurologist Reno (Nev.) Neurol. Assocs., 1992-93; dir. neuroscis. Sierra Summit Rehab., Reno, Nev., 1983-94, No. Nev. Med. Ctr., Reno, 1994—; med. dir. No. Nev. Sleep Disorders Ctr., Sparks, 1995—; cons. neurologist Washoe Med. Ctr., Reno, 1992—, St. Mary's Regional Med. Ctr., 1992—. Contbr. articles to profl. jours. Fellow Am. Acad. Neurology, Royal Soc. Medicine; mem. Am. Acad. Pain Mgmt., Am. Assn. for Study of Headache, Internat. Headache Soc., Am. Sleep Disorders Assn. Office: No Nev Med Ctr 2385 E Prater Way Ste 200 Sparks NV 89434-9663

LEE, RICHARD VAILLE, physician, educator; b. Islip, N.Y., May 26, 1937; s. Louis Emerson and Erma Natalie (Little) L.; m. Susan Bradley, June 25, 1961; children: Matthew, Benjamin. BS, Yale U., 1960, MD cum laude, 1964. Diplomate Am. Bd. Internal Medicine, Am. Bd. Family Practice. Intern Grace-New Haven Hosp., 1964-65, asst. resident in internal medicine, 1965-66, 69-70; fellow in inflammatory disease Yale U., New Haven, 1970-71; practice medicine specializing in internal medicine New Haven, 1969-76, Buffalo, 1976—; family practice Poplar, Mont., 1966-68, Chester, Mont., 1968-69; asst. prof. medicine Yale U., 1971-74, assoc. prof. clin. medicine, 1974-76; prof. medicine SUNY, Buffalo, 1976—, prof. pediatrics, 1985—, adj. prof. anthropology, 1989—, prof. obstetrics, 1992—, chief div. gen. internal medicine, 1979-82, chief div. maternal and adolescent medicine, 1982—, chief div. geog. medicine, 1991—; dir. primary care ctr. Yale-New Haven Hosp., 1975-76, dir. med. clinics, 1971-75; chief med. svc. Buffalo VA Hosp., 1976-79; head dept. medicine Children's Hosp. Buffalo, 1979-96; chief med. officer WHO Collaborating Ctr. for Health in Housing, 1995—, fellow, 1985—; cons. internal medicine N.Y. Zool. Soc., 1973—; cons. physician Buffalo Zool. Soc., 1980—; aviation med. examiner, 1980—; med. dir. Ecology and Environment, Inc., Lancaster, N.Y. Sr. editor Current Obstetric Medicine, 1989—; corr. editor Jour. Obstetrics and Gynecology, London, 1989—; mem. editl. bd. Internat. Jour. Environ. Health, 1994—; cons. editor Am. Jour. Medicine, 1976-86; contbr. articles on gen. medicine, infectious diseases, and med. anthropology to med. jours., also articles on med. problems during pregnancy; contbr. chpts. to books on obstetrics. Served with USPHS, 1966-68. Fellow ACP, Explorers Club N.Y.C., Royal Geog. Soc., Royal Soc. Medicine; mem. AMA, Am. Soc. History of Medicine, Yale China Assn. (trustee 1992—, sec. 1995—, sec. 1995—), N.Y. Acad. Sci., Am. Fedn. Clin. Rsch Soc., Gen. Internal Medicine, Am. Soc. Tropical Medicine and Hygiene, Infectious Disease Soc. Am., Soc. Obstetric Medicine (pres. 1991-93), Am. Coll. Occupl. and Environ. Medicine, Great Lakes Interurban Clin. Club, Alpha Omega Alpha. Home: 7664 East Quaker Rd Orchard Park NY 14127-2015

LEE, ROBERT, association executive, former theological educator, consultant, author; b. San Francisco, Apr. 28, 1929; s. Frank and Shee (Fong) L.; m. May Gong, Feb. 4, 1951; children: Mellanie Lynn, Marcus Arthur, Matthew John, Wendy Gale, Michele Miko. A.B., U. Calif.-Berkeley, 1951; M.A., Pacific Sch. Religion, 1953; B.D. magna cum laude, Union Theol. Sem., 1954; Ph.D., Columbia U., 1958. Ordained to ministry United Ch. Christ, 1954; transferred to U.P. Ch., 1961; Western regional exec. sec. Chinese Student Christian Assn., 1949-50; assoc. sec. Stiles Hall, Univ. YMCA, Berkeley, Calif., 1950-52; dir. rsch. Protestant Council N.Y., 1954; from instr. to asst. prof. ch. and community Union Theol. Sem., 1955-61; lectr. philosophy Mills Coll. Edn., 1956-57; Margaret Dollar prof. social ethics, dir. Inst. Ethics and Soc., San Francisco Theol. Sem., 1961-83; v.p. acad. affairs Alaska Pacific U., 1983-85; pres., dir. Enfield Resources, 1985-87; dean Internat. Student Studies Heald Coll. Inst. of Tech., San Francisco, 1987-88; rsch. cons. Ctr. for Pacific Rim, U. San Francisco, 1989—; asst. v.p., dir. Asian Am. Philanthropy, United Way of Bay Area, 1990—; coord. community rels. Peace Corps., 1991-96; prof., area chmn. Grad. Theol. Union, 1962-70; vis. prof. Union Theol. Sem., summer 1964, Internat. Christian U., Tokyo, Japan, 1964-65, Assn. S.E. Asian Sems., Hong Kong, 1966; vis. scholar Stanford Grad. Sch. Bus., 1971-72; co-optd staff World Council Chs. Conf. Ch. and Soc., Geneva, 1966; lectr., TV appearances, 1956—; cons. ISI Corp., 1971-72, World Coll. West, 1977-83, Coun. on Founds., 1989—, Peace Corps, 1991-96; theologian-in-residence Windward Coalition, Kilua, Hawaii, 1980; moderator Inst. Religion and Social Studies, Jewish Theol. Sem., 1960; assoc. Columbia Seminar, 1961; sr. fellow East-West Center, Honolulu, 1972-73; bd. advisors Walden U.; nursing home care specialist Found. Health Corp., 1987; mem. exec. com. Calif. State Bar Ct., 1989—. Author: Social Sources of Church Unity (selected for Kennedy White House Library), 1960, Religion and Leisure in America, 1964, Directory of Centers for the Study of Society, 1965, Stranger in the Land, 1967, The Schizophrenic Church, 1969, The Promise of John C. Bennett, 1969, (with Marjorie Casebier) The Spouse Gap, 1971, Marriage Enrichment Sharing Sessions, 1979, China Journal, 1980, Faith and the Prospects of Economic Collapse, 1981, Guide to Chinese American Philanthropy and Charitable Giving Patterns, 1990; editor: Cities and Churches, 1962, (with Martin E. Marty) Religion and Social Conflict, 1964, The Church and The Exploding Metropolis, 1965, Action/Reaction; Pacific Theol. Rev., (book revs. edit.) East/West; contbr. to profl. jours., books. Mem. adv. com. problems met. soc. U.P. Ch., 1961—, Center Study Democratic Instns., Coll. Marin, 1965—; bd. sponsers Christianity and Crisis; bd. dirs. Chinese for

Affirmative Action, Am. Soc. Christian Ethics, Ctr. for Family in Transition, Family Svc. Agy. of Marin, Festival Theatre Found., Pacific S.W. Student YMCA, ISI Trust Fund, ISI Growth Fund, ISI Income Fund, Found. for Theol. Edn. S.E. Asia; asst. v.p., bd. dirs. Asian Am. and Internat. Philanthropy, United Way Bay Area: bd. dirs. Marin Chinese Culture Ctr.; commn. Marin County Human Rights Comm., 1995—; hon. chairperson U.N 50 Marin Com., 1995—. Recipient Martin Luther King, Jr. Humanitarian award Marin County, 1994. Mem. Religious Rsch. Assn. (book rev. editor jour. 1959-65), Am. Sociol. Assn., Soc. Religion Higher Edn., Soc. for Sci. Study Religion, Center for Ethics and Social Policy, United Presbyn. Found. (trustee), Asians and Pacific Islanders in Philanthropy, Nan Hai Art Ctr. (trustee). Home: 717 Montecillo Rd San Rafael CA 94903-3135

LEE, ROBERT DORWIN, public affairs educator; b. Detroit, Jan. 14, 1939; s. Robert Dorwin Sr. and Virginia (Stanow) L.; m. Barbara Marvin, June 4, 1966; children: Robert, Craig, Cameron. BA, Wayne State U., 1960; MA, Syracuse (N.Y.) U., 1963, PhD, 1967. From asst. to prof. Pa. State U., University Park, 1966—, head pub. adminstrn. dept., 1988-94; prof. hotel, restaurant, and recreation mgmt., 1994—. Author: Public Personnel Systems, 3d edit., 1993; lead author: Public Budgeting Systems, 5th edit., 1994. Avocations: backpacking, swimming, bicycling. Home: 672 Devonshire Dr State College PA 16803-3231 Office: Pa State U Sch Hotel Restaurant & Rec 201 Mateer Bldg University Park PA 16802-1307

LEE, ROBERT EARL, retired physician; b. North Sydney, N.S., Can., Sept. 26, 1928; came to U.S. 1928, naturalized, 1942; s. Matthew and Amy Roberts (Moulton) L.; m. Sally Gosling, June 23, 1953 (annuled 1967); children: Diane, Cynthia, Susan, Robert; m. Elaine Katherine Chapleau, Dec. 15, 1967. AB, Colgate U., 1948; MD, Cornell U., 1952. Diplomate Am. Bd. Internal Medicine. Intern N.Y. Hosp., Cornell Med. Ctr., N.Y.C., 1952-53, resident, 1955-56, asst. clin. prof. internal medicine Med. Coll.; fellow Manhattan VA Hosp., N.Y.C., 1956-57; cons. internal medicine N.Y. Hosp., Cornell Westchester Div., 1958, dir. med. services, 1967-80, attending physician Burke Rehab., White Plains, 1957-71, cons., 1971-93; attending physician White Plains Hosp., N.Y., 1957-93, St. Agnes Hosp., White Plains, 1971-93; ret., 1993; cons. in medicine Dobbs Ferry Hosp., N.Y., 1968-90; pres. White Plains Hosp. Med. Staff, 1975-76; mem. Westchester County Bd. Mgrs., Div. Lab. and Research, 1970, chmn. 1984—. Bd. dirs. Westchester Council Social Agencies, 1972-77; sr. warden Ch. of St. James the Less, Scarsdale, N.Y., 1988; vol. vol. advisor Scarsdale Ambulance Corps., 1977—; v.p. Greenburgh Nature Ctr., Scarsdale, 1982-84. Served to 1st lt. U.S. Army, 1953-55. Named to Am. Soc. Most Venerable Order of St. John of Jerusalem, 1984 (comdr.). Mem. Westchester County Med. Soc., N.Y. State Med. Soc., ACP, Westchester County Med. Soc. (bd. dirs. 1970-72). Republican. Episcopalian. Clubs: Fox Meadow Tennis (Scarsdale) (pres. 1980-81); Union League. Home: 9 Old Windy Bush Rd New Hope PA 18938-1133

LEE, ROBERT LLOYD, pastor, religious association executive; b. Escanaba, Mich., Jan. 3, 1943; s. Lloyd Benjamin and Eleanor Mae (Leece) L.; m. Gloria Jeanne James, June 3, 1967; children: Adam Robert, Amy Vicary Lee Skogerboe. BA, Augsburg Coll., 1965; MDiv, Free Luth. Sem., 1968; ThM, Bethel Theol. Sem., 1988. Ordained min. Luth. Ch., 1968. Pastor Tioga (N.D.) Luth. Parish, 1966-72, Grace & Zion Luth. Chs., Valley City, N.D., 1972-79, Helmar Luth. Ch., Newark, Ill., 1990-92; prof. hist. theology Free Luth. Schs., Mpls., 1979-89; pres. Assn. Free Luth. Congregations, Mpls., 1992—. Author: Fever Saga, 1987; editor: Do the Work of An Evangelist, 1990; editor The Luth. Ambassador, 1990-93. Co-chmn. Luth. Estonian Am. Friends, 1992—. Mem. Valdres Samband, Norwegian-Am. Hist. Assn., N.Am. Manx Assn. Office: Assn Free Luth Congregations 3110 E Medicine Lake Blvd Minneapolis MN 55441-3008

LEE, ROBERT SANFORD, psychologist; b. Bklyn., Nov. 16, 1924; s. Mark and Celia (Edelstein) L.; m. Barbara Kaplan, June 9, 1963 (div. 1980); children: David, Daniel. Student, U. Chgo., 1943-46; B.A., NYU, 1947, Ph.D., 1956. Psychologist, N.Y. Program dir. U.S. Bur. Census, N.Y.C., 1947-50; rsch. assoc. NYU, 1952-58; asst. dir. The Psychol. Corp., N.Y.C., 1959-61; rsch. advisor for comms. IBM, Armonk, N.Y., 1961-81; sr. v.p. McCann-Erickson, Inc., N.Y.C., 1981-84; assoc. prof. mktg. Lubin Grad. Sch. Bus. Pace U., N.Y.C., 1984—. Author: (with Chein, Gerard and Rosenfeld) The Road to H, 1964. Served with U.S. Army, 1943-45. Recipient Kurt Lewin award N.Y. State Psychol. Assn., 1994. Mem. AAAS, APA, Am. Assn. for Pub. Opinion Rsch. (exec. coun. 1967-68, 71-72), N.Y. Assn. for Pub. Opinion Rsch. (pres. 1995-96). Home: 277 W 10th St Ph B New York NY 10014-2562 Office: Pace Univ Lubin Sch Bus 1 Pace Plz New York NY 10038-1502

LEE, ROGER RUOJIA, semiconductor engineer; b. Swatow, Guangdong, China, Sept. 3, 1958; came to U.S., 1981; s. Zen-An and Der-Fan Chow; m. Kathleen Marie Ryan, Jan. 2, 1986 (div. Nov. 1987); 1 child, Adam Ryan; m. Tami Sue Ferdig, May 14, 1989; children: Allan Michael, John Mei-Fong. BS, Iowa State U., 1984, MS, 1985. Device engr. Tex. Instruments, Houston, 1986-87; project leader Micron Tech., Boise, Idaho, 1987—. Mem. IEEE. Mem. Christian Ch. Home: 3936 N Burnstead Pl Boise ID 83704-4482 Office: Micron Tech Inc 2805 E Columbia Rd Boise ID 83716-9624

LEE, RONALD BARRY, marketing company executive, former army officer; b. N.Y.C., May 26, 1932; s. Kermit James and Lillian Bryant (Jackson) L.; m. Nancy Jean Kowalk, Oct. 10, 1985; children: Brett Michael, Brooke Alexandra; 1 child by previous marriage, Dean Eric. .B.S. in Engring, U.S. Mil. Acad., 1954; M.B.A., Syracuse U., 1964; PhD (ABD), Am. Univ., 1975; LL.D., Western New Eng. Coll., 1969; M.A., Am. U., 1977, postgrad., 1977-79. Commd. 2d lt. U.S. Army, 1954, advanced through grades to maj., 1965; communications officer 3d Armored Corps, 1954-56; radio and wire communications constrn. engring. Okinawa, 1956-59; part-time radio announcer Sta. KSBK, Okinawa, 1957-59; instr. orgn. and staff procedures U.S. Army Signal Sch., 1960-61, instr. plans and operations, 1961, chief operations, officer dept., 1961-62; asst. G-3 (operations) adviser Vietnamese 9th Div., 1962-63; chief electronic system sect., evaluation br. systems analysis Army Material Command, 1964-65; White House fellow, 1965-66, resigned commn., 1966; mem. staff Lawrence F. O'Brien, The White House, 1965; asst. to postmaster gen., 1965-66, dir. office planning and systems analysis, 1966-68; asst. provost, dir. Center for Urban Affairs; prof. Mich. State U., 1968-69; asst. postmaster gen. for planning and marketing, 1969-72; with Xerox Corp., Stamford, Conn., 1972-73, White Plains, N.Y., 1973-75; regional mgr. Xerox Corp., Des Plaines, Ill., 1975-78; mgr. govt., edn. and med. mktg. Xerox Corp., Rochester, N.Y., 1978-79; mgr. bus. and community affairs Xerox Corp., Washington, 1979-82; pres. Phoenix Group Internat. Ltd., Washington, 1982-89; exec. v.p. Devl. Mgmt. Group, Inc., Chgo., 1989-90; pres. Vantage Mktg. Internat. Inc., 1991—, Phoenix Group Internat., Ltd., 1991—; exec. v.p. G/DEC Internat., Ltd., 1992—; lectr. in field. Contbr. articles to profl. jours., chpts. to books; poet. Mem. Weston (Conn.) Police Commn., 1973-75; trustee Western New Eng. Coll., 1969-75; bd. advisers, trustee Woodrow Wilson Sch. (Princeton), 1969-75; bd. dirs. Zion Investment Assn., 1970-76, Jr. Achievement Greater Washington, 1979-89, NCCJ, 1980-89, Comty. Found. Greater Washington, 1980-89, Duke Ellington Sch. Arts, 1980-89, Workshops for Careers in the Arts, 1980-89; adv. bd. Nat. Assn. Sickle Cell Diseases, 1972—; chmn. bd. trustees Capital Children's Mus., 1979-89; mem. D.C. Mayor's Pvt. Industry Coun., 1979-89. Decorated Army Commendation medal with oak leaf cluster; named Neighbor of Month Springfield, Mass., June 1950; jr. singles champion New Eng. Tennis Assn., 1950; recipient Arthur S. Flemming award, 1968. Mem. NAACP, Nat. Urban League, Assn. West Point Grads., Assn. Syracuse Army Comptrs., Am. Soc. Pub. Adminstrn., White House Fellows Assn. (1st pres. 1966), Am. Acad. Polit. and Social Sci., Beta Gamma Sigma, Alpha Phi Alpha. Office: Vantage Marketing Internat Inc 4200 Wisconsin Ave NW Washington DC 20016-2143

LEE, RONALD DEMOS, demographer, economist, educator; b. Poughkeepsie N.Y., Sept. 5, 1941; s. Otis Hamilton and Dorothy (Demetracopoulou) L.; m. Melissa Lee Nelken, July 6, 1968; children: Sophia, Isabel, Rebecca. BA, Reed Coll., 1963; MA, U. Calif.-Berkeley, 1967; PhD, Harvard U., 1971. Postdoctoral fellow Nat. Demographic Inst., Paris, 1970-71; asst. prof. to prof. U. Mich., Ann Arbor, 1971-79; prof. demography and econs. U. Calif., Berkeley, 1979—, dir. Berkeley Ctr. on Econs. and Demography of Aging; cons. in field. Peace Corps. vol., Ethiopia, 1963-65. NIH fellow, 1965-67; NSF fellow, 1968-69; Social Sci. Research Council fellow, 1970-71; NIH grantee, 1973—; Guggenheim fellow, 1984-85. Mem. NAS (chair com. on population), Population Assn. Am. (pres. 1987), Am. Econ. Assn., Internat. Union Sci. Study of Population. Democrat. Author: Econometric Studies of Topics in Demographic History, 1978; Population Patterns in the Past, 1977, Population, Food, and Rural Development, 1988, Economics of Changing Age Distributions in Developed Countries, 1988, others; contbr. articles to profl. jours. Home: 2933 Russell St Berkeley CA 94705-2333 Office: U Calif Dept Demography 2232 Piedmont Ave Berkeley CA 94720-2121

LEE, RONALD EUGENE, international air transportation supply executive; b. Seattle, Nov. 29, 1960; s. Clifton Wilmer and Maxine (Meath) L. AA, Everett C.C., 1982; BS in Mfg. Engring. Tech., Ctrl. Wash. U., 1984; MS in Engring. Mgmt., Long Beach State/West Coast U., 1990. Cert. D1-9000 advanced quality sys., just-in-time. world class mfg., total quality mgmt., quality auditing. Assoc. methods engr. indsl. engring. Douglas Aircraft Co., Torrance, Calif., 1984-85, mfg. methods engr., 1985-86, sr. methods engr., 1986-87, mgr., 1987, mgr. JIT mfg., 1987-89, mgr. indsl. engring., 1989; mgr. supplier mgmt. Douglas Aircraft Co., Long Beach, Calif., 1989-91, mgr. bus. planning, 1991-92, mgr. purchasing support, 1992-93; procurement quality assurance rep. Boeing Helicopter Co., Pa., 1992—; lead rep. The Boeing Co., Seattle, 1995-96, mgr., intl. field operations, 1996—. Mem. McDonnell Douglas Mgmt. Club, Soc. Mfg. Engrs. (sr.), Inst. Indsl. Engrs., Am. Soc. Quality Control (cert. quality assurance auditor). Democrat. Roman Catholic. Avocations: golf, weightlifting, skiing, racquetball. Office: The Boeing Co PO Box 3707 M/S 39-CL Seattle WA 98124

LEE, SALLY A., editor-in-chief; m. Rob Niosi. Grad., Durham U., Eng., Clark U., Mass. Reporter Worcester (Mass.) Telegram; mng. editor Worcester (Mass.) Monthly; spl. features editor Woman's World mag., N.Y.C.; articles editor Woman's Day mag., N.Y.C.; sr. editor Redbook mag., N.Y.C.; editor-in-chief YM/Young & Modern mag., N.Y.C., 1994-96, Fitness Mag., N.Y.C., 1996—; corr. E! Entertainment Network. Office: Fitness Mag 110 5th Ave New York NY 10011-5601*

LEE, SARAH TOMERLIN, design executive; b. Union City, Tenn.; d. Charles Granville and Dorothy (Robinson) Tomerlin. B.A., Randolph Macon Women's Coll., 1932. Copyeditor Vogue mag. JBK, N.Y.C., 1939-45; v.p. Lord and Taylor, N.Y.C., 1959-65; pres. Fashion Group, N.Y.C., 1960-63; editor-in-chief House Beautiful mag., N.Y.C., 1965-71; pres. Tom Lee Ltd., N.Y.C., 1971-93, Beyer Blinder, Belle/Tom Lee Interiors, N.Y.C., 1993—; cons. to pres. Fashion Inst. Tech., 1971-74. Editor: American Fashion. Vice pres. N.Y. Landmarks Conservancy. Recipient Penny-Mo. Magazine award, 1967, Fashion Inst. award, 1981, Women Bus. Owners N.Y. Entrepreneurial award, 1981, Am. Inst. Interior Decorators Project award, 1982, Decorators Club medal of honor, 1982, Interior Design Project award Am. Soc. Interior Designers, 1987, award of Spl. Distinction, Restaurant & Instns., 1987, 1st Pl. Resort Splty. award Restaurant Hospitality, 1988, Platinum Circle award, 1988, Interior Design award Restaurant Hospitality, 1989, Interior Design Project award Am. Soc. Interior Designers, 1990; named to Interior Design Mag. Hall of Fame, 1986; named Woman of Yr. by Exec. Women in Hospitality, 1988, Designer of Distinction, Am. Soc. Interior Designers, 1990; recipient Edyth Wharton achievement award, 1996. Mem. Decorators Club (pres. 1995-97), Craft Coun. N.Y. (bd. dirs. 1965-75, emeritus 1983), Cosmopolitan Club, Nat. Arts Club. Office: Beyer Blinder Belle Tom Lee Interiors 41 E 11th St New York NY 10003-4602

LEE, SHERMAN EMERY, art historian, curator; b. Seattle, Apr. 19, 1918; s. Emery H. and Adelia (Baker) L.; m. Ruth A. Ward, Sept. 3, 1938; children: Katharine C. (Mrs. Bryan Reid), Margaret A. (Mrs. Stephen Bachenheimer), Elizabeth K. (Mrs. William Chiego), Thomas W. B.A., M.A., Am. U.; Ph.D., Western Res. U. Curator, Far Eastern art Detroit Inst. Art, 1941-46; with dept. arts and monuments, div. civil info. and edn. sect. Gen. Hdqrs. SCAP, Tokyo, 1946-48; asst. dir., then asso. dir. Seattle Mus. Art, 1948-52; curator Oriental art Cleve. Mus. Art, 1952-83, dir., 1958-83; prof. art Western Res. U., 1983-97; adj. prof. U. N.C., Chapel Hill.. Author: Chinese Landscape Painting, rev. edit., 1962, (with Wen Fong) Streams and Mountains Without End, 1955, Japanese Decorative Style, 1961, History of Far Eastern Art, 5th edit., 1994, (with W.K. Ho) Chinese Art under the Mongols, 1968, Reflections of Reality in Japanese Art, 1983, Past, Present, East and West, 1983; editor: On Understanding Art Museums, 1977. Trustee Amon Carter Mus. Western Art. Served from ensign to lt. (j.g.) USNR, 1944-46. Decorated Legion of Honor; Order North Star; Order of Sacred Treasure 3d class. Mem. Am. Acad. Arts and Scis., Asia Soc. (hon. trustee), Century Assn (N.Y.C.). Home: 102 Dixie Dr Chapel Hill NC 27514-6615 Office: Univ NC Dept Art Chapel Hill NC 27514

LEE, SHEW KUHN, retired optometrist; b. Balt., Apr. 24, 1923; s. Mong Har and Gum Tuey (Wong) L. OD, Ill. Coll. Optometry, 1949; postgrad. Cath. U. Am., 1957, Md. U., 1959; m. Florence Gin Toy, Oct. 29, 1949; children: Wayson Perry, Davin Jeffrey. Pvt. practice optometry, Washington, 1949-88; ret., 1988. Lectr. D.C. Traffic Safety Sch.; v.p. D.C. Bd. Optometry, 1959-65; mem. D.C. Bd. Examiners in Optometry, 1973-84, sec., 1974; mem. Eye Bank Council; vision rsch. cons. HEW, 1973. Bd. dirs. Eye Bank and Rsch. Found., Washington Hosp. Center. With U.S. Army, 1942-45. Decorated Purple Heart, Bronze Star medal with oak leaf cluster; recipient Meritorious Pub. Svc. award Govt. of D.C., 1965. Mem. Am. Optometric Assn. (life, pres. joggers 1968—, Disting. Svc. award 1974), Am. Legion (life, citation of merit 1954, post comdr. D.C. 1960), D.C. Optometric Soc. (sec. 1956-57), Lees Assn. (trustee), Chinese Consol. Benevolent Assn. (founder), Flying Optometrist Assn. Am. (bd. dir. 1974—), Beta Sigma Kappa. Lion (charter pres. Chi-Am. 1960, zone chmn. 1961, dep. dist. gov. 1963, hon. mem. Capitol Hill, Washington Host, Extension award 1960, 75, Presdl. Banner award 1975). Rsch. publs. in field. Home: 2939 McKinley St NW Washington DC 20015-1217

LEE, SHIH-YING, mechanical engineering educator; b. Peking, China, Apr. 30, 1918; came to U.S., 1942, naturalized, 1952; s. Tse-Kung and Pei-Jour (Tao) L.; m. Lena Yin, Aug. 18, 1973; children: Carol Sana, David, Linda Grace, Eileen M. Sc.D., MIT, 1945. Bridge design engr. Chinese Govt., 1940-41, hydraulic power research engr., 1941-42; design engr. Cram & Ferguson Co., Boston, 1945-47; research engr. MIT, Cambridge, 1947-52, mem. faculty, 1952-74, prof. mech. engring., 1966—; chmn., chief exec. officer Setra Systems Inc., Acton, Mass.; Mem. Nat. Acad. Engrs. Inventor field instrumentation, fluid power control. Home: Huckleberry Hl Lincoln MA 01773 Office: Setra Systems 189 Swanson Rd Boxboro MA 01719-1316

LEE, SHUISHIH SAGE, pathologist; b. Soo-chow, Kiang Su, China, Jan. 5, 1948; came to U.S., 1972, naturalized, 1979; d. Wei-ping Wilson and Min-chen (Sun) Chang; m. Chung Seng Lee; children: Yvonne Claire, Michael Chung. MD Nat. Taiwan U., 1972; PhD, U. Rochester, 1976. Resident in pathology Strong Meml. Hosp., Rochester, N.Y., 1976-78, Northwestern Meml. Hosp., Chgo., 1978-79; dir. cytology and electron microscopy Parkview Meml. Hosp., Ft. Wayne, Ind., 1979—; clin. assoc. prof. Ind. U. Med. Sch. Contbr. articles to profl. jours. Fellow Coll. Am. Pathologists, Am. Soc. Clin. Pathologists; mem. AMA, Ind. Med. Assn., N.E. Ind. Pathologists Assn. (sec. 1984), Ind. Assn. Pathologists, N.Y. Acad. Scis., Am. Assn. Pathologists, Am. Soc. Cytology, Internat. Acad. Pathology, Internat. Acad. Cythology, Buckeye Soc. Cytology, Electron Microscopy Soc. Am. Home: 5728 The Prophets Pass Fort Wayne IN 46845-9659 Office: Parkview Meml Hosp 2200 Randallia Dr Fort Wayne IN 46805-4638

LEE, SHUNG-MAN, nephrologist; b. Canton, Peoples Republic of China, Feb. 22, 1949; came to the U.S., 1968; s. Ning-Woo and Shui-Fong Lee; m. Ellen Poon, Aug., 1976; 1 child, Andrew. BS, U. Toronto, 1972, MD, 1976. Diplomate Am. Bd. Nephrology, Am. Bd. Internal Medicine, Nat. Bd. Med. Examiners. Intern Sunnybrook Med. Ctr. U. Toronto, 1976-77, resident, 1977-78; resident Jewish Gen. Hosp. McGill U., Montreal, 1978-79; clin. fellow in nephrology Billings Hosp. U. Chgo., 1979-81, rsch. fellow, 1981-82; pres., med. dir. Biotronics Kidney Ctr., Beaumont, Tex., 1990—; cons. nephrologist, mem. med. staff St. Elizabeth Hosp., Beaumont, Bapt. Hosp. S.E. Tex., Beaumont, Beaumont Med. Surg. Hosp., 1982-90; med. dir. Cmty. Dialysis Svcs., Beaumont, 1986-90; cons. nephrologist, mem. courtesy staff Dr.'s Hosp., Groves, Tex., Bapt. Hosp., Orange, Tex., Park Place Hosp., Port Arthur, Tex.; clin. asst. prof. U. Tex. Med. Br. at Galveston, 1991—; founder, owner Biotronics Kidney Ctr. Beaumont, Inc.; founder, Lake Charles (La.) Dialysis Ctr. Contbr. articles to profl. jours. Organizer, founding mem. Adult Indigent Clinic for S.E. Tex., Beaumont, 1992—. Rsch. fellow Chgo. Heart Assn., 1981; rsch. scholar Ontario Cancer Soc., 1974, Ann Shepard Meml. scholar in biology, 1970. Fellow ACP; mem. AMA, Internat. Soc. Nephrology, Internat. Soc. Peritoneal Dialysis, Am. Soc. Nephrology, Jefferson County Med. Soc., So. Med. Assn., Am. Soc. Internal Medicine, Tex. Med. Assn., Chinese-Am. Soc. Nephrology (pres.), New Century Health Care Internat. (pres.). Office: Biotronics Kidney Ctr 2688 Calder St Beaumont TX 77702-1917

LEE, SIDNEY PHILLIP, chemical engineer, state senator; b. Pa., Apr. 20, 1926; s. Samuel L. and Mollie (Heller) L. B.Sc., U. Pa., 1939; McMullin fellow, Cornell U., 1939-40, then M.Ch.E. Chem. engr. Atlantic Richfield Co., 1938-42; sr. chem. engr., 1942-45; pres. Dallas Labs., 1945—, Asso. Labs., Dallas, 1945—, West Indies Investment Co., 1957—; chmn. exec. com. West Indies Bank & Trust Co.; dir., mem. exec. com. Am. Ship Bldg. Co.; prin. West Indies Investment Co., St. Croix, 1956—. writer of Lee Lets Loose column for local Carribean newspapers. Mem. V.I. Senate, 1976—, now v.p.; chmn. com. govt., chmn. com. on fin. ops. V.I. Govt. Dem. nat. committeeman for V.I., 1969—; mem. V.I. Bd. Edn., 1969-76; mem. Gov.'s Blue Ribbon Commn. for Econ. Devel., 1995—. Fellow Am. Inst. Chemists; mem. AIChE (sr.), AIME (sr.), AARP (chmn. legis. com. 1984—), St. Croix C. of C. (v.p. 1995), Rotary (pres. 1971-73), Lions (pres. 1960), Tau Beta Pi, Sigma Tau. Home and Office: 135 E 54th St Apt 11C New York NY 10022-4511 Office: PO Box 15705 Dallas TX 75215 *In retrospect, elation from supposed triumphs or defeats is blurred in memory; and of greater importance is the quality of one's life or how one played the game.*

LEE, STAN (STANLEY MARTIN LIEBER), cartoon publisher, writer; b. N.Y.C., Dec. 28, 1922; s. Jack and Celia (Solomon) Lieber; m. Joan Clayton Boocock, Dec. 5, 1947; 2 dau., Joan C., Jan (dec.). Student pub. schs., N.Y.C.; hon. degree, Bowling Green State U. Copy writer, then asst. editor, editor Timely Comics (became Atlas Comics), N.Y.C., 1939-42; editor, creative dir. Atlas (became Marvel Comics) Comics, until 1961; creative dir., editor-in-chief Marvel Comics, 1961-70, pub., 1970—; creative dir. Marvel Prodns., 1980-89, chmn. Marvel comics, 1989—; adj. prof. popular culture Bowling Green (Ky.) State U.; coll. lectr., TV script editor. Creator, former writer and editor Fantastic Four, Incredible Hulk, Amazing Spiderman, numerous others; author: Origins of Marvel Comics, 1974, Son of Origins, 1975, Bring On The Bad Guys, 1976, Mighty Marvel Strength & Fitness Book, 1976, Mighty Marvel Superheroes Fun Book, 1976, The Marvel Comics Illustrated Version of Star Wars, 1977, The Amazing Spiderman Vol. No. 3, 1977, The Superhero Women, 1977, The Mighty World of Marvel Pin-up Book, 1978, The Mighty Marvel Superhero Fun Book Vol. No. 3, 1978, The Silver Surfer, How to Draw Comics the Marvel Way, 1978, Marvel's Greatest Superhero Battles, 1978, Incredible Hulk, 1978, Marvelous Mazes to Drive You Mad, 1978, Fantastic Four, 1979, Doctor Strange, 1979, Complete Adventures of Spider-Man, 1979, Captain America, 1979, The Best of the Worst, 1979, Marvel Word Games, 1979, Omnibus Fun Book, 1979, Dunn's Conundrum, 1985, The Best of Spider-Man, 1986, Marvel Team-Up Thrillers, 1987, The Amazing Spiderman, No. 2, 1980, Hulk Cartoons, 1980, Marvel Masterworks Vol. 2: Fantastics Four, 1987, X-Men, 1987, Marvel Masterworks, Vol. 1: Amazing Spider-Man, 1987, Masterworks, Vol. 6: Fantastic Four, 1988, Silver Surfer: Judgement Day, 1988, Silver Surfer: Parable, 1988, Spider-Man, 1988, Avengers, 1988, The God Project, 1990, Silver Surfer: The Enslavers, 1990, Marvel Masterworks, Vol. 13: Fantastic Four, 1990, Best of Marvel Comics, 1991, Night Cat, 1991, Marvel Masterworks, Vol. 17: Daredevil, 1991, Marvel Masterworks, Vol. 18: Thor, 1991, Spider-Man Wedding, 1991, Spider-Man Masterworks, 1992, Uncanny X-Men Masterworks, 1993, Marvels Greatest Super Battles, 1994, The Ultimate Spiderman, 1994, The Very Best of Spiderman, 1994, The Incredible Hulk: A Man-Brute Berserk, 1995, others. Served with AUS, 1942-45. Recipient Alley Award, 1963-68; Comic Art Award, Soc. for Comic Art Rsch. & Preservation, 1968; Eureka Award, Il Targa 1970; Publisher of the Year, Periodical & Book Assn. of America, 1978; ann. award Popular Culture Assn., 1974. Mem. (founder), Acad. Comic Book Arts (award 1973), Nat. Acad. TV Arts and Scis., Nat. Cartoonists Soc., AFTRA. Club: Friars (N.Y.C.). Office: Marvel Comics Group Wilshire Blvd Ste 1400 Los Angeles CA 90024 also: Cowles Syndicate Inc 235 E 45th St New York NY 10017-3305*

LEE, STEPHEN W., lawyer; b. New Castle, Ind., Oct. 25, 1949; s. Delmer W. Lee and Loma F. (Thurston) McCall; m. Pamela A. Summers, Aug. 2, 1969; children: Erin E., Stephanie M. BS, Ball State U., 1971; JD summa cum laude, Ind. U., 1977. Bar: Ind. 1977, U.S. Dist. Ct. (so. dist.) Ind. 1977, U.S. Ct. Appeals (7th cir.) 1977, U.S. Supreme Ct. 1982. Officer, lt.(j.g.) USNR, Phila., 1971-74; law clk. U.S. Dist. Ct. (no. dist.) Ind., Ft. Wayne, 1977-78; assoc. Barnes, Hickam, Pantzer & Boyd, Indpls., 1978-82; assoc. Barnes & Thornburg, Indpls., 1982-83, ptnr., 1984—. Editor-in-chief: Indiana Law Jour., 1976-77. Dir. Ind. Repertory Theatre, Indpls., 1986-91; exec. coun. Ind. U. Alumni Assn., Bloomington, 1989; dir. Ind. U. Sch. of Law Alumni Assn., Bloomington, 1984-90, pres., 1991-92; mem. Ball State U. Coll. Bus. Alumni Bd., 1991—, Ball State U. Entrepreneurship Adv. Bd., 1994—. Mem. Ind. State Bar Assn., Indpls. Bar Assn. (chmn. bus. sect. 1985), Highland Golf & Country Club. Republican. Avocations: golf. Office: Barnes & Thornburg 11 S Meridian St Indianapolis IN 46204-3506

LEE, SUL HI, library administrator; b. Taegu, Korea, July 13, 1936; s. Sang Moo and Won Nim L.; m. Seol Bong Ryu, Sept. 6, 1962; 1 child, Melissa Jemee. B.A., Bowling Green State U., 1961; M.A., U. Toledo, 1964, U. Mich., 1966. Reference libr. Toledo Pub. Libr., 1961-67; supr. info. analysts Owens-Ill., Inc., 1967-68; dir. Ctr. for Libr. and Info. Sys., U. Toledo, 1968-70; assoc. dir. libr. Eastern Mich. U., Ypsilanti, 1970-73; assoc. dir. librs. U. Rochester, N.Y., 1973-75; dean libr. svcs. Ind. State U., Terre Haute, 1975-78; dean univ. librs. U. Okla., Norman, 1978—, prof. Sch. Libr. and Info. Studies, 1988—. Author: Library Orientation, 1972, A Challenge for Academic Libraries, 1973, Planning-Programing-Budgeting System, 1973, Library Budgeting, 1977, Emerging Trends in Library Organization, 1978, Serials Collection Development: Choices and Strategies, 1981, Reference Service: a Perspective, 1983, Library Fundraising, 1984, Issues in Acquisitions, 1984, Access to Scholarly Information, 1985, Pricing and Cost of Monographs and Serials, 1987, Acquisitions, Budgets and Materials Costs, 1988, The Impact of Rising Costs of Serials and Monographs on Library Services and Programs, 1989, Library Material Costs and Access to Information, 1990, Budgets for Acquisitions, 1991, Vendor Evaluation and Acquisitions Budgets, 1992, Collection Assessment and Acquisitions Budgets, 1993, The Role and Future of Special Collections in Research Libraries, 1993, Declining Acquisitions Budgets, 1994, Access, Ownership and Resource Sharing, 1995; editor: Collection Management, 1996—, Jour. Libr. Adminstrn., 1987—. Mem. ALA (com. on accreditation 1981-83, mem. coun. 1986-90, coun. com. on coms. 1988-89), Assn. Rsch. Librs. (chair com. mgmt. rsch. librs. 1987-89, bd. dirs. 1991-94), Greater Midwestern Rsch. Librs. Consortium (chair 1994-95), U. Mich. Sch. Libr. Sci. Alumni Soc. (pres. 1983-84, mem. edtl. com. CAUSE 1995-98). Office: U Okla 401 W Brooks St Norman OK 73069-8824

LEE, T. GIRARD, church growth consultant; b. Washington, Nov. 3, 1938; m. T. Girard and Dorothy (Thomas) L.; m. Paula Stephan, June 17, 1961; children: Kenneth Robert, Jennifer Margaret Dowd, Rebecca Susan Clark, Nancy Elizabeth. BArch, Miami U., 1961. Registered architect M.D., D.C., Va., W.Va. Architect intern various architects offices, Silver Spring, Md., 1965-68; assoc., architect Bagley & Soule Architects, Chevy Chase, Md., 1968-69; sole proprietor Lee & Assoc., Bethesda, Md., 1969-71; ptnr. Bagley, Soule, Lee Architects, Chevy Chase, 1971-84, Lee Warner & Assocs., Annapolis, Md., 1984-90; v.p., treas., prin. Lee-Warner Architects, Inc., Annapolis, Md., 1990-96; pvt. practice architect, cons. Annapolis, 1996—. Chmn. bd. mgmt. Bethesda Chevy Chase YMCA, 1976-77; bd. trustees United Way and Nat. Capitol Area, Washington, 1977-80; bd. dirs. Anne Arundel County YMCA, Annapolis, Md., 1986-91. Mem. AIA (pres. Potomac Valley chpt. 1974-75, treas. Chesapeake Bay chpt. 1985-91), Md. Soc. Architects (pres. 1978-79), Rotary (pres. club 1982-83). Republican. United Methodist. Avocations: golf, tennis, sailing, jogging. Office: 754 Robin Hood Hill Annapolis MD 21405

LEE, TE GYU, neurologist; b. Gyong-sang Province, Tong Young, Korea, Mar. 3, 1962; s. Jong Seok and Young Ae (Kim) L.; m. Hyeon Yi Jung; children: Jun Oh, Jun Seung. MD, Seoul (Korea) Nat. U., 1987, MS, 1995. Diplomate Korean Bd. of Neurology. Intern Seoul Nat. U. Hosp., 1987-88, resident, 1991-95; instr. dept. neurology Gyeong-Sang (Korea) Nat. U., 1995; fellow The Headache Ctr. Cleve. Clinic Found., Cleve., 1995-97; clin. fellow, resch. fellow Mass. Gen. Hosp/Harvard Med. Sch., Boston, 1997—. Lt. Korean Air Force, 1988-91. Am. Acad. Neurology fgn. scholar, 1994; Jr. Headache rsch. awardee Am. Acad. Neurology Edn. and Rsch. Foun., 1997. Mem. N.Y. Acad. Scis., Am. Acad. Neurology (assoc.). Home: 2550 Kemper Rd Apt 109 Shaker Heights OH 44120-1250 Office: The Headache Ctr Desk A50 Cleve Clinic Found Cleveland OH 44195

LEE, THOMAS ALEXANDER, accountant, educator; b. Edinburgh, Scotland, May 18, 1941; s. Thomas Henderson and Dorothy Jane (Norman) L.; m. Ann Margaret Brown, Sept. 14, 1963; children: Sarah Ann, Richard Thomas. Chartered acct., Inst. Chartered Accts.Scotland, Edinburgh, 1964; tax acct., Inst. Tax, Glasgow, Scotland, 1965; MS, U. Strathclyde, Glasgow, Scotland, 1969, DLitt, 1984. Audit asst. Edinburgh, 1959-64, Glasgow, 1964-66; lectr. U. Strathclyde, 1966-69, U. Edinburgh, 1969-73; prof. U. Liverpool, Eng., 1973-76, U. Edinburgh, 1976-90; dir. rsch. Inst. Chartered Accts. Scotland, 1983-84; prof. U. Ala., 1990—, dir. PhD program, 1991—; vis. prof. U. Md., 1986, U. Utah, 1987-88, U. Edinburg, Scotland, 1991-94, Deakin U., 1994—; hon. prof. U. Dundee, Scotland, 1995—. Editor: Internat. Jour. Auditing; assoc. editor Brit. Acctg. Rev.; mem. editl. bd. various jours., 1971—. Trustee Acad. Acctg. Historians, v.p., 1996—. Mem. Fellow Royal Soc. Arts; mem. Inst. Chartered Accts. Scotland (coun. 1989-90), Inst. Taxation. Presbyterian. Avocations: church, road running, cricket history. Office: U Ala PO Box 870220 Tuscaloosa AL 35487-0220

LEE, THOMAS HENRY, electrical engineer, educator; b. Shanghai, China, May 11, 1923; came to U.S., 1948, naturalized, 1953; s. Y. C. and Nan Tien (Ho) L.; m. Kin Ping, June 12, 1948; children—William F., Thomas H. Jr., Richard T. B.S.M.E., Nat. Chiao Tung U., Shanghai, 1946; M.S.E.E., Union Coll., Schenectady, 1950; Ph.D., Rensselaer Poly. Inst., 1954. Registered profl. engr., Pa. Mgr. research and devel. Gen. Electric Co., Phila., 1959-74; mgr. strategic planning Fairfield, Conn., 1974-78, staff exec., 1978-80; prof. elec. engring. MIT, Cambridge, 1980-84, 87—; dir. Internat. Inst. for Applied Systems Analysis, Laxenburg, Austria, 1984-87; pres. Tech. Assessment Group, Schenectady, 1980-84, Ctr. for Quality Mgmt., Cambridge, Mass., 1990—. Author: Physics and Engineering of High Power Switching Devices, 1973, Energy Aftermath, 1989; patentee in field. Recipient Davis medal for outstanding engring. accomplishment Rensselaer Poly. Inst., 1987. Fellow IEEE (Power Life award 1980, Haraden Pratt award 1983), AAAS; mem. NAE, Swiss Acad. Engring. Sci., Power Engring. Soc. (pres. 1974-76).

LEE, TIMOTHY EARL, international agency executive, paralegal; b. Seattle, May 23, 1947; s. Charles Augusta and Esther Letty (Young) L.; m. Marcia Lea Wulff, July 6, 1968 (div. May 1976); children: Vincent Dean, Dante' Claude; 1 stepson, Kevin Paul McCorkle; m. Jayne Elizabeth Ashley, Apr. 28, 1984 (div. Apr. 1995). Cert., Ivy Tech., 1981, Am. Inst. Paralegal Studies, 1988. Mgr. Gen. Fin. Corp., Evanston, Ill., 1970-74, FBT Capital Corp., South Bend, Ind., 1974-76; owner Lee's Internat. Investigative Rsch. Agy., Ft. Wayne, Ind., 1978—. Mem. Heritage Foun., Citizens Against Govt. Waste; spl. adv. Allen Superior Ct. With U.S. Army, 1966-68, Vietnam. Recipient Cert. of Appreciation, DAV, 1968. Mem. VFW, Ind. Assn. Pvt. Detectives (v.p. N.E. region Ind. 1984—), Ind. Sheriff's Assn., Ft. Wayne Allen County Security Assn., Coun. for Inter-Am. Security, Nat. Security Ctr., Nat. Def. Inst., 27th Field Artillery Assn. (v.p., founding father), Am. Legion, Vietnam Vets, Internat. Platform Assn., Concord Coalition. Home: 8516 River Canyon Dr Fort Wayne IN 46835-1015

LEE, TOM STEWART, judge; b. 1941; m. Norma Ruth Robbins; children: Elizabeth Robbins, Tom Stewart Jr. BA, Miss. Coll., 1963, JD cum laude, U. Miss., 1965. Ptnr. Lee & Lee, Forest, Miss., 1965-84; pros. atty. Scott County, Miss., 1968-71; judge Scott County Youth Ct., Forest, 1979-82; mcpl. judge City of Forest, 1982; judge U.S. Dist. Ct. (so. dist.) Miss., Jackson, 1984-96, chief judge, 1996—. Asst. editor: Miss. Law Jour. Deacon, Sunday sch. tchr. Forest Bapt. ch.; pres. Forest Pub. Sch. Bd., Scott County Heart Assn.; bd. visitors Miss. Coll. Law Sch.; lectr. Miss. Coll., 1993. Served to capt. USAR. Named one of Outstanding Young Men Am. Mem. Miss. Bar Assn., Scott County Bar Assn., Hinds County Bar Assn., Fed. Bar Assn., Fed. Judges' Assn., Forest C. of C. (bd. dirs.), Forest Jaycees (past pres., Disting. Service award), Ole Miss. Alumni Assn. (pres.), Miss. Coll. Alumni Assn. (bd. dirs.), Am. Legion. Office: US Dist Ct 245 E Capitol St Ste 110 Jackson MS 39201-2414

LEE, TONG HUN, economics educator; b. Seoul, Nov. 20, 1931; came to U.S., 1955, naturalized, 1968; s. Chong Su and Yun (Lee) L.; m. Yul Jah Ahn, June 11, 1960; children: Bruce Keebeck, James Keewon. B.S., Yon-Sei U., 1955; Ph.D., U. Wis., 1961. Asst. prof. econs. U. Tenn., Knoxville 1962-64; assoc. prof. U. Tenn., 1964-67; prof. econs. U. Wis., Milw., 1967-96, chmn. dept. econs., 1978-82; disting. univ. prof. econs. Ajou U., Suwon, Korea, 1997—. Author: Interregional Intersectoral Flow Analysis, 1973; contbr. articles to profl. jours. NSF grantee, 1965-67, 73-75. Mem. Am. Econ. Assn., Am. Fin. Assn., Am. Statis. Assn., Econometric Soc. Home: Life Apt 703-1602, 242, Kumi-Dong, Boondang-Gu, Sungnam Kyoungki-Do 463-500, Republic of Korea Office: Ajou U Dept Econs, 5 Wonchon-Dong Paldal-Gu, Suwon 442-749, Republic of Korea *Success comes from determination, persistence and hard work, but the ultimate measure of success is derived from the inner life of a person.*

LEE, TSUNG-DAO, physicist, educator; b. Shanghai, China, Nov. 25, 1926; s. Tsing-Kong L. and Ming-Chang (Chang); m. Jeannette Chin, June 3, 1950; children: James, Stephen. Student, Nat. Chekiang U., Kweichow, China, 1943-44, Nat. S.W. Assoc. U., Kunming, China, 1945-46; PhD, U. Chgo., 1950; DSc (hon.), Princeton U., 1958; LLD (hon.), Chinese U., Hong Kong, 1969; DSc (hon.), CCNY, 1978. Research assoc. in astronomy U. Chgo., 1950; research assoc., lectr. physics U. Calif., Berkeley, 1950-51; mem. Inst. for Advanced Study, Princeton (N.J.) U., 1951-53, prof. physics, 1960-63; asst. prof. Columbia U., N.Y.C., 1953-55, assoc. prof., 1955-56, prof., 1956-60, 63—, adj. prof., 1960-62, Enrico Fermi prof. physics, 1963—, Univ. prof., 1984—; Loeb lectr. Harvard U., Cambridge, Mass., 1957, 64. Editor: Weak Interactions and High Energy Nutrino Physics, 1966, Particle Physics and Introduction to Field Theory, 1981. Decorated grande ufficiale Order of Merit (Italy); recipient Albert Einstein Sci. award Yeshiva U., 1957, (with Chen Ning Yang) Nobel prize in physics, 1957, Ettore Majorana-Erice-Sci. for Peace prize, 1990. Mem. NAS, Acad. Sinica, Am. Acad. Arts and Scis., Am. Philos. Soc., Acad. Nazionale dei Lincei, Acad. Sci. China. Office: Columbia U Dept Physics Bldg 538 Morningside Heights W 120th St New York NY 10027*

LEE, VERNON ROY, minister; b. Jackson, Miss., Feb. 1, 1952; s. Samuel Rayford and Evie Mae (Abel) L.; m. Rhonda Sue Parker, Nov. 6, 1970; 1 child, Shannon Grant. Pastor Mt. Moriah Bapt. Ch., Junction City, Ark., 1971-72, Pleasant Grove Bapt. Ch., El Dorado, Ark., 1972-74, Pilgrims Rest Bapt. Ch., Spearsville, La., 1974-76, Bethany Bapt. Ch., Bastrop, La., 1976-78, 1st Bapt. Ch., Taylor, Ark., 1978-83, Farmington Bapt. Ch., Corinth, Miss., 1983-86, Wyatt Bapt. Ch., El Dorado, 1986—. Trustee Southeastern Bapt. Coll., Laurel, Miss., 1983-86, Ctrl. Bapt. Coll., Conway, Ark., 1992-96, asst. chmn. bd. trustees, 1993-95, chmn., 1995-96; vol. Boy's Clubs, El Dorado, 1986-91, YMCA, Corinth, 1983-86. Mem. Bapt. Missionary Assn. Am. (v.p. 1986-88, pres. 1990-92, clk. missionary com. 1989-91, asst. ch. adv. com. 1992-95), Miss. Bapt. Assn. (pres. 1984-86). Avocations: golf, fishing, basketball, softball. Home: 625 Royal Oak El Dorado AR 71730-6768 Office: Wyatt Bapt Ch 4621 W Hillsboro El Dorado AR 71730-6768

LEE, VICTOR HO, lawyer; b. Washington, Dec. 5, 1960; s. Stanley S. and Nancy J. Lee. Student, Oxford (Eng.) U., summer 1981; BS, Georgetown U., 1982, JD, 1985. Bar: N.Y. 1986, D.C. 1988. Intern SEC, N.Y.C., 1983; assoc. Kaye, Scholer, Fierman, Hays & Handler, N.Y.C., summer 1984, 1985-91; ptnr. Bitonti & Wilhelm, Mc Lean, Va., 1991-92; CFO Nap, Inc., N.Y.C., 1992—. Mem. staff The Tax Lawyer, 1983-84, topics editor, mem. editorial bd., 1984-85. Mem. ABA, N.Y. State Bar Assn., D.C. Bar Assn., Nat. Asian Pacific Am. Bar Assn. (co-chmn. judiciary com. 1992-93), Washington D.C. Asian Pacific Am. Bar Assn., Asian-Am. Legal Def. and Edn. Fund, N.Y. Asian-Am. Bar Assn. Home: 188 E 64th St New York NY 10021-7451 Office: NAP Inc 171 Madison Ave New York NY 10016-5110

LEE, WALLACE WILLIAMS, JR., retired hotel executive; b. Nacogdoches, Tex., June 28, 1915; s. Wallace Williams and Caryl (Ames) L.; m. Doris Card, Sept. 19, 1942; children: Doris Lee Bessette, Frederic Williams. B.S. in Hotel Adminstrn, Cornell U., 1936; postgrad. in Advanced Bus. Mgmt, Columbia, 1954. Cert. hotel adminstr. Asst. mgr. Broadmoor Hotel, Colorado Springs, Colo., 1938-42; resident mgr. Hotel Thayer, West Point, N.Y., 1945-47; mgr. Hotel Anderson (Ind.), 1947-48; resident mgr. Hotel Roosevelt, N.Y.C., 1951-53; v.p., gen. mgr. Hotel Roosevelt, 1954; asst. mgr. Waldorf-Astoria, N.Y.C., 1948-51; mgr. Waldorf-Astoria, 1954-59, v.p., resident mgr., 1959-61; v.p., gen. mgr. The Barclay and Park Lane Hotels, N.Y.C., 1961-63; group v.p. accommodations Howard Johnson Co., 1963-80; dir. Smiley Bros., Inc., 1981-96, mem. exec. com., 1982-87. Vice chmn. AH/MA adv. com. to Statler Found., 1966-72; mem. exec. bd. Greater N.Y. coun. Boy Scouts Am., 1960-71, mem. exec. bd. Boston Coun., 1971-79, chmn. camping Northeast region, 1972-73; bd. dirs., 1960-71, v.p. bd. dirs. YMCA of Greater N.Y., 1965-71; bd. dirs. Travelers Aid Soc., N.Y.C., 1959-66; trustee Am. Hotel Found., 1973-78; pres. Hospitality, Lodging and Travel Rsch. Found., 1975-80; trustee Christ Ch. Meth. N.Y.C., 1959-64, chmn. ocfl. bd., 1963-64; trustee Congl. Ch., Sherman, Conn., 1965-68, deacon, 1981-83; assoc. 1st Presbyn. Ch., Orlando, Fla., 1990-97. Served to capt. AUS, 1942-45. Recipient Silver Beaver award Boy Scouts Am., 1964, Disting. Achievement in Edn. and Advancing Profession of Innkeeping award Hotel and Restaurant Mgmt. Soc. NYU, 1964, award of merit Am. Hotel and Motel Assn., Hosp. Travel Rsch. Found., 1980; named Man of Yr. YMCA Neighbor Youth Br. Greater N.Y., 1961; named to Hall of Fame Hospitality Mag., 1965. Mem. Cornell Soc. Hotelmen (pres. 1953-54, trustee Found. 1991—), Am. Security Coun., Conn. Soc. Mayflower Desc., Ednl. Inst., Timber Trails Club (pres. 1966-67). Congregationalist. Home (summer): Tryon Estates Apt B-242 621 Laurel Lake Dr Columbus NC 28722

LEE, WILLIAM CHARLES, judge; b. Fort Wayne, Ind., Feb. 2, 1938; s. Russell and Catherine (Zwick) L.; m. Judith Anne Bash, Sept. 19, 1959; children—Catherine L., Mark R., Richard R. A.B., Yale U., 1959; J.D., U. Chgo., 1962. Bar: Ind. 1962. Ptnr., Parry, Krueckeberg & Lee, Fort Wayne, 1964-70; dep. pros. atty. Allen County, Fort Wayne, 1963-69, chief dep., 1966-69; U.S. atty. No. Dist. Ind., Fort Wayne, 1970-73; ptnr. Hunt, Suedhoff, Borror, Eilbacher & Lee, Fort Wayne, 1973-81; U.S. Dist. judge No. Dist. Ind., Fort Wayne, 1981—; instr. Nat. Inst. Trial Advocacy. Contbd. numerous publications and lectrs. in the field. Co-chmn. Fort Wayne Fine Arts Operating Fund Drive, 1978; past bd. dirs., v.p., pres. Fort Wayne Philharm. Orch.; past bd. dirs., v.p. Hospice of Fort Wayne, Inc.; past bd. dirs. Fort Wayne Fine Arts Found., Fort Wayne Civic Theatre, Neighbors, Inc., Embassy Theatre Found.; past bd. dirs., pres. Legal Aid of Fort Wayne, Inc.; past mem. ch. coun., v.p. Trinity English Lutheran Ch. Council; past trustee, pres. Fort Wayne Community Schs., 1978-81, pres., 1980-81; trustee Fort Wayne Mus. Art, 1984-90; past bd. dirs., pres. Fort Wayne-Allen County Hist. Soc. Griffin scholar, 1955-59; chmn. Fort Wayne Cmty. Schs Scholarship Com.; bd. dirs. Arts United of Greater Fort Wayne, Fort Wayne Ballet. Weymouth Kirkland scholar, 1959-62; named Ind. Trial Judge of the Yr, 1988. Fellow Am. Coll. Trial Lawyers, Ind. Bar Found.; mem. ABA, Allen County Bar Assn., Ind. State Bar Assn., Fed. Bar Assn., Seventh Cir. Bar Assn., Phi Delta Phi (past bd. dirs., 1st pres.), Benjamin Harrison Am. Inn of Ct., North Side High Alumni Assn. (bd. dirs. pres.), Fort Wayne Rotary Club (bd. dir.). Republican. Lutheran. Office: US Dist Ct 2145 Fed Bldg 1300 S Harrison St Fort Wayne IN 46802-3435

LEE, WILLIAM CHIEN-YEH, electrical engineer; b. London, July 20, 1932; married; 2 children. BS, Chinese Naval Acad., Taiwan, 1954; MS, Ohio State U., 1960, PhD, 1963. Mem. tech. staff comms. Bell Labs., 1964-79; sr. scientist, mgr. def. comm. divsn. ITT, 1979-84; v.p. Pactel Cellular, Walnut Creek, Calif., 1985—, Airtouch, Walnut Creek, 1985—; affil. mem. U. Calif., Irvine, 1985—, U. Calif., Davis, 1985—; mem. Nat. Comms. Forum Overseas Coun., 1985—; state apptd. bd. mem. Calif. Sci. and Tech. Coun., 1996—. Author 3 books on mobile comms.; contbr. over 100 articles to profl. publs. Recipient Disting. Alumni award Ohio State U., 1990. Fellow IEEE (Avante Garde award Vehicluar Tech. Soc. 1990, Contbn. award San Francisco sect. 1990); mem. Brit. Inst. Elec. Engrs., Sigma Xi. Office: Airtouch 1340 Treat Blvd Ste 500 Walnut Creek CA 94596-7961 *Use mathematics to solve problems; use physics to interpret results; use counter examples to check outcomes; use pictures to memorize the importance.*

LEE, WILLIAM FRANKLIN, III, association administrator; b. Galveston, Tex., Feb. 20, 1929; s. William Franklin Jr. and Anna Lena (Keis) L.; m. Jacqueline Tyler; children: William Franklin IV, Robert Terry, Patricia Lynn, Peggy Ann. MusB, N. Tex. State U., 1949, MS, 1950; MusM, U. Tex., 1956, PhD, 1956. Prof. music St. Mary's U., San Antonio, 1952-55; asst. to dean fine arts U. Tex., 1955-56; chmn. dept. music Sam Houston State Coll., 1956-64; dean Sch. Music U. Miami (Fla.), 1964-82, provost, exec. v.p., 1982-86, disting. prof., composer in residence, 1986-88; dir. arts Fla. Internat. U., Miami, 1988-90; dean coll. fine arts and humanities U. Tex., San Antonio, 1990-95; exec. dir. Internat. Assn. Jazz Educators, 1995—. Performances with Houston, Dallas symphony orchs., performances with Gene Krupa and Artie Shaw, guest clinician, condr., composer, 1952—; composer, author, arranger more than 100 published works.; author: Music Theory Dictionary, 1962; also articles, music publs.; biographer, discographer of Stan Kenton, 1981; editor, co-founder: Southwestern Brass Jour., 1958, Belwin New Dictionary of Music and Musicians, 1988. Mem. AAUP, ASCAP (recipient 26 awards 1968— including Deems Taylor awards 1981, 85), Nat. Assn. Am. Composers and Condrs., Music Educators Nat. Conf., Am. Fedn. Musicians, Music Tchrs. Nat. Assn., Pi Kappa Lambda, Kappa Kappa Psi, Phi Mu Alpha. Office: Internat Assn Jazz Educator PO Box 724 Manhattan KS 66502-0006

LEE, WILLIAM GENTRY, lawyer; b. St. Louis, Apr. 2, 1944; s. Gentry and Wilma (Elliott) L.; m. Carter Kerr, Aug. 9, 1969; children: William Gentry Jr., Kathryn Carter. BA cum laude, Harvard U., 1966; JD, U. Okla., 1969. Bar: Okla. 1969, Tex. 1972. Assoc. Vinson & Elkins, Houston, 1973-81, ptnr., 1981—; mem. com. on revision of corp. laws bus. law sect. State Bar of Tex., 1975—. Editor: Okla. Law Rev., 1967-69; contbr. articles to profl. jours. Adminstrv. bd. mem. Cho-Yeh Camp and Conf. Ctr., Livingston, Tex., 1990-94; deacon 1st Presbyn. Ch. of Houston, 1979-83, elder, 1984—. Capt. U.S. Army JAGC, 1969-73. Named to Order of Coif U. Okla., 1969. Mem. Allegro, Houston Club, Houston Ctr. Club, River Oaks Country Club, Kiwanis (bd. dirs. 1993-95). Republican. Avocations: tennis, golf. Home: 3665 Overbrook Ln Houston TX 77027-4127 Office: Vinson & Elkins 1001 Fannin St Ste 3635 Houston TX 77002-6706

LEE, WILLIAM JOHN, petroleum engineering educator, consultant; b. Lubbock, Tex., Jan. 16, 1936; s. William Preston and Bonnie Lee (Cook) L.; m. Phyllis Ann Bass, June 10, 1961; children: Anne Preston, Mary Denise. B in Chem. Engring., Ga. Inst. Tech., 1959, MSChemE, 1961, PhD in Chem. Engring., 1963, NAE, 1993, Ga. Tech. Acad. Disting. Engring. Alumni, 1994. Registered profl. engr., Tex., Miss. Sr. rsch. specialist Exxon Prodn. Rsch. Co., Houston, 1962-68; assoc. prof. petroleum engring. Miss. State U., Starkville, 1968-71; tech. advisor Exxon Co., Houston, 1971-77; prof. petroleum engring. Tex. A&M U., College Station, 1977—, holder Noble chair in petroleum engring., 1985-93, Peterson chair in petroleum engring., 1993—; dir. Crisman Inst. for Petroleum Reservoir Mgmt. at Tex. A&M U., 1987-93; exec. v.p. S.A. Holditch & Assocs., Inc., College Station, 1979—. Author: Well Testing, 1982. Recipient award of excellence Halliburton Edn. Found., 1982, Meritorious Engring. Teaching award Tenneco, Inc., 1982, Disting. Teaching award Assn. Former Students, Tex. A&M U., College Station, 1983; Tex. Engring. Experiment Sta. fellow, 1987-88, sr. fellow 1990. Mem. Soc. Petroleum Engrs. (disting., chmn. edn. and accreditation com. 1985-86, disting. lectr. 1980, disting. faculty achievement award 1982, Reservoir Engring. award 1986, Regional service award 1987, disting. svc. award 1992, Carll award 1995, dir. 1996—). Presbyterian. Avocation: travel. Home: 3100 Rolling Gln Bryan TX 77807-3209 Office: Tex A&M U Petroleum Engring Dept College Station TX 77843

LEE, WILLIAM JOHNSON, lawyer; b. Oneida, Tenn., Jan. 13, 1924; s. William J. and Ara (Anderson) L.; student Akron U., 1941-43, Denison U., 1943-44, Harvard U., 1944-45; J.D., Ohio State U., 1948. Bar: Ohio 1948, Fla. 1962. Research asst. Ohio State U. Law Sch., 1948-49; asst. dir. Ohio Dept. Liquor Control, chief purchases, 1956-57, atty. examiner, 1951-53, asst. state permit chief, 1953-55, state permit chief, 1955-56; asst. counsel, staff Hupp Corp., 1957-58; spl. counsel City Attys. Office Ft. Lauderdale (Fla.), 1963-65; asst. atty. gen. Office Atty. Gen., State of Ohio, 1966-70; adminstr. State Med. Bd. Ohio, Columbus, 1970-85, also mem. Federated State Bd.'s Nat. Commn. for Evaluation of Fgn. Med. Schs., 1981-83; Mem. Flex 1/Flex 2 Transitional Task Force, 1983-84; pvt. practice law, Ft. Lauderdale, 1965-66; acting municipal judge, Ravenna, Ohio, 1960; instr. Coll. Bus. Adminstrn., Kent State U., 1961-62. Mem. pastoral relations com. Epworth United Meth. Ch., 1976; chmn. legal aid com. Portage County, Ohio, 1960; troop awards chmn. Boy Scouts Am., 1965; mem. ch. bd. Melrose Park (Fla.) Meth. Ch., 1966. Mem. Exptl. Aviation Assn. S.W. Fla., Franklin County Trial Lawyers Assn., Am. Legion, Fla., Columbus, Akron, Broward County (Fla.) bar assns., Delta Theta Phi, Phi Kappa Tau, Pi Kappa Delta. Served with USAAF, 1943-46. Editorial bd. Ohio State Law Jour., 1947-48; also articles. Home: Apple Valley 704 Country Club Dr Howard OH 43028-9530

LEE, WILLIAM KENDALL, JR., insurance industry executive; b. Washington, May 18, 1949; s. William Kendall and Barbara Marie (Look) L.; m. Marsha Ann Anderson, Jan. 16, 1971 (div. Nov. 1976); children: Eric Dean, Ryan Michael; m. Virginia Ann Fellowes, Oct. 5, 1991. AB in Polit. Sci., Wabash Coll., 1971. Underwriter Meridian Ins., Indpls., 1971-79; cons. Alper Svcs. Inc., Chgo., 1979-80; sr. cons. Peat, Marwick, Mitchell, Chgo., 1980-82, Hales & Assocs., Oak Brook, Ill., 1982-83; v.p. The Middleton Group, Lisle, Ill., 1983-85; sr. mgr. KPMG - Peat Marwick, Chgo., 1985-88; pres. Stetson & Lee, Inc., Wheaton, Ill., 1988-93; v.p. adminstrn. and systems Maginnis & Assocs. KVI, Chgo., 1993—. Contbr. articles to profl. jours. Mem. NRA, Soc. Chartered Property Casualty Underwriters, Aircraft Owners and Pilots Assn., Glen Oak Country Club. Episcopalian. Avocations: flying, gun collecting, golfing. Home: 117 E Farnham Ln Wheaton IL 60187-6401 Office: Maginnis-KVI 332 S Michigan Ave Ste 1400 Chicago IL 60604-4408

LEE, WILLIAM MARSHALL, lawyer; b. N.Y.C., Feb. 23, 1922; s. Marshall McLean and Marguerite (Letts) L.; m. Lois Kathryn Plain, Oct. 10, 1942; children: Marsha (Mrs. Stephen Derynck), William Marshall Jr., Victoria C. (Mrs. Larry Nelson). Student, U. Wis., 1939-40; BS, Aero. U., Chgo., 1942; postgrad., UCLA, 1946-48, Loyola U. Law Sch., L.A., 1948-49; JD, Loyola U., Chgo., 1952. Bar: Ill. 1952. Thermodynamicist Northrop Aircraft Co., Hawthorne, Calif., 1947-49; patent agt. Hill, Sherman, Meroni, Gross & Simpson, Chgo., 1949-51, Borg-Warner Corp., Chgo., 1951-53; ptnr. Hume, Clement, Hume & Lee, Chgo., 1953-72; pvt. practice Chgo., 1973-74; ptnr. Lee and Smith (and predecessors), Chgo., 1974-89, Lee, Mann, Smith, McWilliams, Sweeney & Ohlson, Chgo., 1989—; cons. Power Packaging, Inc. Speaker and contbr. articles on legal topics. Pres. Glenview (Ill.) Citizens Sch. Com., 1953-57; v.p. Glenbrook High Sch. Bd., 1957-63. Lt. USNR, 1942-46, CBI. Recipient Pub. Svc. award Glenbrook High Sch. Bd., 1963. Mem. ABA (chmn. sect. intellectual property law 1986-87, sect. fin. officer 1976-77, sect. sec. 1977-80, sect. governing coun. 1980-84, 87-88), Ill. Bar Assn., Chgo. Bar Assn., 7th Fed. Cir. Bar Assn., Am. Intellectual Property Law Assn., Intellectual Law Assn. Chgo., Licensing Execs. Soc. (pres. 1981-82, treas. 1977-80, trustee 1974-77, 80-81, 82-83, internat. del. 1980—), Phi Delta Theta, Phi Alpha Delta. Republican. Home: 84 Otis Rd Barrington IL 60010-5128 Office: 209 S La Salle St Chicago IL 60604-1202

LEE, WILLIAM SAUL (BILL LEE), artist, writer; b. Bklyn., Nov. 15, 1938; s. Arthur Martin and Clara (Levine) Levy; m. Dona Ruth Johnson-Lee; 1 child, Jennifer Catherine. Grad. high sch., N.Y.C. Humor editor Penthouse Publs., N.Y.C., 1976—; tchr. satiric art Sch. Visual Art; lectr. slide shows of satiric art. Author: 7 books including Insecurity is Better Than No Security at All, (comic strip and lit. format) Investigative Cartooning; featured cartoonist San Francisco Chronicle, Leescapes, The New Yorker, Playboy, Penthouse, Omni, Esquire, Cosmopolitan, Nat. Lampoon, and others; nationally syndicated cartoonist: Lee Scapes, Tribune Media Svcs.; one-man art show at Visual Arts Ctr., N.Y.C., 1974; works exhibited in group shows at Castelli Gallery, N.Y.C., 1972, Motreal Fair, 1974, Hansen Galleries, N.Y.C., 1975, Van Gogh Mus., Holland, 1975, Kew Gardens, London, 1975, Greene St. Gallery, N.Y.C., 1986, Broome St. Gallery, 1987, Atrium Gallery, 1989. Recipient Internat. Humor award Montreal Expo, 1971, 72, Metro Arts Festival, 1986, 87. Mem. Nat. TV Acad., Writers Guild, Motion Picture Acad., Mus. of Broadcasting, Nat. Cartoonist Soc., Soc. Illustrators, Am. Inst. Graphic Arts, Soc. Publ. Designers, Tarreytown Group. Avocations: drawing, writing, painting, sculpting. •

LEE, WON JAY, radiologist; b. Seoul, Korea, Feb. 2, 1938; came to U.S., 1965; s. Kang Sei and Choon Ja (Park) L.; m. Moon Jung, Feb. 24, 1968; children: Julie, Lisa, Jennifer. Dr.med., Yonsei U., Seoul, 1962. Diplomate Am. Bd. Radiology, Am. Bd. Nuclear Medicine. Intern Wyckoff Heights Hosp., Bklyn., 1965-66; resident NYU Med. Ctr., N.Y.C., 1966-69; fellow, asst. radiologist L.I. Jewish Med. Ctr., New Hyde Park, N.Y., 1969-71, staff radiologist, 1975-82, chief uroradiology, 1983—; assoc. radiologist Binghamton (N.Y.) Gen. Hosp., 1971-75; asst. prof. SUNY, Stony Brook, 1975-86, assoc. prof. radiology, 1987-89; prof. radiology Albert Einstein Coll. Medicine, 1989—; cons. in field. Contbr. chpts. to books and articles to profl. jours. First lt. USMC, 1962-65, Korea. Recipient Sci. Paper award Soc. Uroradiology, 1994, Clin. award Can. Assoc. Radiologists, 1979. Fellow Am. Coll. Radiology, Cardiovascular and Interventional Radiology, Soc. Uroradiology; mem. Assn. Univ. Radiologists, Am. Roentgen Ray Soc., Radiol. Soc. N.Am. Democratic. Methodist. Avocations: gardening, golf, traveling. Home: 15 Lucille Ln Huntington Station NY 11746-5848 Office: LI Jewish Med Ctr 270-05 76th Ave New Hyde Park NY 11040-1433

LEE, YEU-TSU MARGARET, surgeon, educator; b. Xian, Shensi, China, Mar. 18, 1936; m. Thomas V. Lee, Dec. 29, 1962 (div. 1987); 1 child, Maxwell M. AB in Microbiology, U. S.D., 1957; MD, Harvard U., 1961. Cert. Am. Bd. Surgery. Assoc. prof. surgery Med. Sch., U. So. Calif., L.A., 1973-83; commd. lt. col. U.S. Army Med. Corps, 1983, advanced through grades to col., 1989; chief surg. oncology Tripler Army Med. Ctr., Honolulu, 1983—; assoc. clin. prof. surgery Med. Sch., U. Hawaii, Honolulu, 1984-92, clin. prof. surgery, 1992—. Author: Malignant Lymphoma, 1974; author chpts to books; contbr. articles to profl. jours. Pres. Orgn. Chinese-Am. Women, L.A., 1981, Hawaii chpt., 1988; active U.S.-China Friendship Assn., 1991—. Recipient Chinese-Am. Engrs. and Scis. Assn., 1987; named Sci. Woman Warrior, Asian-Pacific Womens Network, 1983. Mem. ACS, Soc. Surg. Oncology, Assn. Women Surgeons. Avocations: classical music, movies, hiking, ballroom dancing. Office: Tripler Army Med Ctr Dept Surgery Honolulu HI 96859

LEE, YOUNG BIN, psychiatrist, neurologist; b. Seoul, Korea, Mar. 21, 1937; came to U.S., 1964; s. Suksin and Insik (Kim) L.; m. Moon Chin Cho, Apr. 24, 1965; children: Edward S., Susan E., Ellen M. Pre-med. study coll. sci. and engring., Yonsei U., Seoul, 1955-57, MD, 1961. Diplomate Am. Bd. Neurology and Psychiatry, Am. Bd. Profl. Psychiatry Cons., Am. Bd. Geriatric Psychiatry, Am. Bd. Profl. Disability. Rotating intern Sibley Meml. Hosp., Washington, 1964-65; neurology resident Pa. Hosp., Phila., 1965-68; psychiatry resident Ancora Psychiat. Hosp., Hammonton, N.J., 1968-70, neurologist in charge, 1970—, asst. med. dir., 1972-88; clin. asst. prof. Robert Wood Johnson Med. Sch., Camden, N.J.; cons. in neurology West Jersey Hosp., Berlin, 1971, Vineland (N.J.) Devel. Ctr., 1971-87; cons. in neuropsychiatry Cumberland County Guidance Ctr., Millvile, N.J., 1971-86. With Korean Army, 1962-63. Named Outstanding Asian Am. N.J. Asian Am. Heritage Counsel, Hacketstown, N.J., 1994. Mem. Am. Acad. Neurology, Am. Psychiat. Assn., Am. Electroencephalography Assn., The Capitol Hist. Soc., Korean Am. Assn. So. N.J. (pres. 1988-91), The Fedn. of Korean Am. Assn. N.J. (pres. 1991-93). Achievements include establishment of Korean Language Course at Rutgers U. Avocations: gardening, classical music apreciation, fishing, car repair. Home: 7 Pine Acres Dr Medford NJ 08055-9578 Office: 228 Kings Hwy E Haddonfield NJ 08033-1913

LEE, YOUNG JACK, federal agency administrator; b. Seoul, Republic of Korea, Feb. 25, 1942; came to U.S., 1969; s. Kyung Ho and Taekyo (Chung) L.; m. Kiran Jung, Mar. 31, 1967; children: Hyung Joo, Taejoo J., Minjoo L. BEE, Seoul Nat. U., 1964; MS in Stats., Ohio State U., 1972, PhD in

Stats., 1974. Asst. prof. U. Md., College Park, 1974-79; math. statistician NIH, Bethesda, Md., 1979-89, br. chief, 1989—. Mem. Am. Statis. Soc., Clin. Trial Soc., Biometrics Soc. Office: NIH Bldg 6100 Rm 7B13 Bethesda MD 20892

LEE, YUNG-KEUN, physicist, educator; b. Seoul, Korea, Sept. 26, 1929; came to U.S., 1953, naturalized, 1968; s. Kwang-Soo and Young-Sook (Hur) L.; m. Ock-Kyung Pai, Oct. 25, 1958; children—Ann, Arnold, Sara, Sylvia, Clara. B.A., Johns Hopkins, 1956; M.S., U. Chgo., 1957; Ph.D., Columbia, 1961. Research scientist Columbia U., N.Y.C., 1961-64; prof. physics Johns Hopkins U., Balt., 1964—; vis. mem. staff Los Alamos Sci. Lab., 1971; vis. researcher Institut Scis. Nucléaires, Grenoble, France, 1975; cons. Idaho Nat. Engring. Lab., 1988—. Contbr. articles to profl. jours. Mem. Am. Phys. Soc. Democrat. Methodist. Club: Johns Hopkins. Home: 1318 Denby Rd Baltimore MD 21286-1627 Office: Johns Hopkins U 34th and Charles Sts Baltimore MD 21218

LEEAN, JOSEPH, social services administrator; b. Iola, Wis., Mar. 10, 1942; s. Sidney and Marie (Grosfield) L.; m. Virginia Floor, June 12, 1964; children: Dawn, Miriam, Jana. BA, Augustana Coll., 1964; postgrad., Western Mich. U., 1964-65, U. Wis., 1965-66. High sch. tchr. Waupaca, Wis., 1966-71; owner, pres. Dings Dock, Inc., Waupaca, 1973-83, Clearwater Harbor, Inc., Waupaca, 1974-79; pres. Waupaca Thrills, Inc., Waupaca, 1983-85, Sparkling Springs, Inc., Waupaca, 1985—; mem. Wis. Senate, Madison, 1984-95; sec. Dept. Health and Family Svcs., 1995—. Pres. Chain-o-Lakes Sanitary Dist., Waupaca; mem. Nat. Rep. Party Club, Wis. Rep. Party Club, Waupaca County Rep. Party Club. Mem. Waupaca C. of C. (pres.). Lutheran.

LEEBERN, DONALD M., distilled beverage executive; b. 1938. Pres. Georgia Crown Distributing, Columbus, Ga., 1960—. Office: Georgia Crown Distributing PO Box 7908 Columbus GA 31908-7908*

LEEBRON, DAVID WAYNE, law educator; b. Phila., Feb. 12, 1955. BA, Harvard U., 1976, JD, 1979. Bar: N.Y. 1982, Pa. 1981, Hawaii 1980. Law clk. Judge Shirley Hufstedler, L.A., 1979-80; assoc. Cleary, Gottlieb, Steen & Hamilton, N.Y.C., 1981-83; prof. Sch. Law NYU, 1983-89; prof. Sch. Law Columbia U., N.Y.C., 1989—, dean, 1996—. Office: Columbia U Sch Law 435 W 116th St New York NY 10027-7201

LEECH, CHARLES RUSSELL, JR., lawyer; b. Coshocton, Ohio, July 29, 1930; s. Charles Russell and Edna (Henry) L.; m. Patricia Ann Tubaugh, June 20, 1953; children—Charles Russell III, Timothy David (dec.), Wendy Ann. A.B. cum laude, Kenyon Coll., 1952; J.D., Ohio State U., 1955; M.A., U. Toledo, 1969. Bar: Ohio 1955. Assoc. Fuller & Henry P.L.L. and predecessor firms, Toledo, 1957-64; ptnr. Fuller & Henry and predecessor firms, Toledo, 1964—. Mng. editor: Ohio State Law Jour, 1955. Mem. exec. com. alumni council Kenyon Coll., 1967-72, trustee coll., 1974-80. Served with USNR, 1955-57. Fellow Ohio State Bar Found.; mem. Am., Ohio, Toledo bar assns., Kenyon Coll. Alumni Assn. Maumee Valley (past pres.), Beta Theta Pi, Phi Delta Phi. Republican. Home: 10953 Springbrook Ct Whitehouse OH 43571-9674 Office: 1 Seagate Fl 17 Toledo OH 43604-1558

LEECH, JAMES WILLIAM, technology company executive; b. St. Boniface, Man., Can., June 12, 1947; s. George Clarence and Mary Elizabeth (Gibson) L.; m. Jacqueline Roberts Hilton; children: Jennifer Hilton, Joanna Marjorie, James Andrew Douglas. BS in Math. and Physics with hons., Royal Mil. Coll. Can., 1964; MBA, Queen's U., Can., 1973. Exec. asst. to pres. Commerce Capital Corp., Ltd., Montreal, Que., Can., 1973-74, v.p., 1974-75; exec. v.p. Commerce Capital Trust Co., Calgary, Alta., Can., 1976-78; sr. v.p. Eaton/Bay Fin. Services Ltd., Toronto, Ont., Can., 1979; pres., bd. dirs. Unicorp Canada Corp., Toronto, 1979-88; pres., CEO, bd. dirs. Union Energy, Inc., Toronto, 1985-93, Disys Corp., Toronto, 1993-96; vice chair, bd. dirs. Kasten Chase Applied Rsch. Ltd., Mississauga, Ont., 1996—; bd. dirs. Harris Steel Group, Inc., Winpak Ltd. Vice chmn. adv. coun. sch. bus. Queens U., 1979-83, mem. gen. coun., 1978—, mem. investment com. bd. trustees, 1980—, trustee, 1984-96, mem. fund coun., 1988—; bd. dirs., chmn., pres., mem. exec. com. Can. Stage Co., 1989-94; v.p., bd. dirs. Toronto Arts Coun., 1994—, Toronto Hosp. Found., 1996—. D.I. McLeod scholar, 1971-73; Seagram rsch. fellow, 1983, Samuel Bronfman Found. fellow, 1973, Transp. Devel. Agy. fellow, 1972. Mem. Young Pres. Orgn. (Upper Can. chpt.), The Nat. Club, Granite Club, Muskoka Lakes Golf and Country Club. United Ch. Can. Home: 70 Garfield Ave, Toronto, ON Canada M4T 1E9

LEECH, JOHN DALE, lawyer, health care/corporate consultant; b. Cleve., Apr. 3, 1939; s. George Alfred and Mary Virginia (Merrell) L.; m. Patricia Jeanne Higgins, July 15, 1961; children: Kathryn, Carolyn, Krista, Karlyn. BA with honors, Williams Coll., 1961; LLB, Duke U., 1964. Bar: Ohio 1964, U.S. Dist. Ct. (no. and ea. dists.) Ohio 1965, U.S. Ct. Appeals (6th cir.) 1968, U.S. Ct. Appeals (4th cir.) 1974, U.S. Supreme Ct. 1988. Assoc. Arter & Hadden, Cleve., 1964-72; ptnr. Calfee, Halter & Griswold, Cleve., 1972-95, mem. exec. com., 1989-92, of counsel, 1996—; chmn. health care law sect., antitrust; pres. Riverledge Healthcare Cons. Councilman, pres. coun. Mayfield Village, Ohio, 1970-74, mayor, 1974-75; trustee Regional Income Tax Agy., Cuyahoga County, Ohio, 1974-75; pres. Hillcrest Hosp., Cleve., 1980-84, chmn. bd., 1986-88; bd. dirs. Cleve. Dialysis Ctr., 1984-89; del. Congress Hosp. Trustees, Chgo., 1986-94; trustee Am. Hosp. Assn., 1993-95, mem. exec. com., trustee various coms., Chgo., 1987-95, bd. mentor, 1984—; testimony House Ways and Means Subcom., 1987, 93; trustee Health Hill Hosp., 1988—; bd. commrs. Joint Commn. on Accreditation of Healthcare Orgns., Oakbrook, Ill., 1995—. Mem. ABA (various coms., antitrust and healthcare sects.), Soc. Ohio Hosp. Attys., Ohio Bar Assn., Greater Cleve. Bar Assn., Cleve. Country Club, Union Club. Republican. Avocations: golf, tennis, photography, reading, hiking. Home: Ste 100 10149 Cedar Rd Chesterland OH 44026-3301 Office: Calfee Halter & Griswold 1400 One Donald Investment Cleveland OH 44114-2601

LEECH, NOYES ELWOOD, lawyer, educator; b. Ambler, Pa., Aug. 1, 1921; m. Louise Ann Gallagher, Apr. 19, 1954; children: Katharine, Gwyneth. AB, U. Pa., 1943, JD, 1948. Bar: Pa. 1949. Assoc. Dechert, Price & Rhoads (and predecessors), Phila., 1948-49, 51-53; mem. faculty dept. law U. Pa., Phila., 1949-57; prof. U. Pa., 1957-78, Ferdinand Wakeman Hubbell prof. law, 1978-85, William A. Schnader prof. law, 1985-86, prof. emeritus, 1986—. Co-author: The International Legal System, 3d edit., 1988; gen. editor: Jour. Comparative Bus. and Capital Market Law, 1978-86. Mem. Order of Coif, Phi Beta Kappa. Office: U Pa Law Sch 3400 Chestnut St Philadelphia PA 19104-6204

LEEDER, ELLEN LISMORE, language and literature educator, literary critic; b. Vedado, Havana, Cuba, July 8, 1931; came to U.S., 1959; d. Thomas and Josefina (Jorge) Lismore; m. Robert Henry Leeder, Dec. 20, 1957 (dec. 1994); 1 child, Thomas Henry. D of Pedagogy, U. Havana, Cuba, 1955; MA, U. Miami, 1966, PhD, 1973. Lang. tchr. St. George's Sch., Havana, 1952-59; from part-time instr. to full prof. Spanish Barry U., Miami Shores, Fla., 1960-75, prof. Spanish, 1975—, chmn. dept. for lang., 1975-76, coord. of Fgn. Lang., 1976-89; dir. Spanish immersion program, 1986-88; part-time prof. Miami-Dade C.C., 1974-75; vis. prof. U. Madrid, 1982; prof. Forspro Program Studies Abroad, 1989, 90; cons. HEH, 1981-83; judge Asociación Críticos y Comentaristas del Arte, Miami, 1985—; judge Silver Knight Awards, 1979-83; oral examiner juror Dade County Pub. Schs., Miami, 1986-87. Author: El Desarraigo en Las Novelas de Angel María de Lera, 1978, Justo Sierra y el Mar, 1979, Dimensión Existencial en la Narrativa de Lera, 1992; co-editor: El arte narrativo de Hilda Perera, 1996. Bd. dirs. Vis. Nurse Assn., 1978-80. Mem. MLA, South Atlantic MLA, Am. Coun. Tchg. Fgn. Langs., Am. Assn. Tchrs. Spanish and Portuguese (pres. 1978-84, v.p. 1984-87, pres. Southeastern Fla. chpt.), Fla. Fgn. Assn., Círculo de Cultura Panamericano, Assn. Internat. Hispanistas, Assn. Cubana de Mujeres Universitarias (pres.), Cuban Women Club, Phi Alpha Theta, Kappa Delta Pi, Sigma Delta Xi, Alpha Mu Gamma, Coral Gables Country Club. Avocations: tennis, piano, singing, numismatics. Home: 830 SW 101st Ave Miami FL 33174-2836 Office: Barry Univ 11300 NE 2d Ave Miami FL 33161-6628

LEEDOM, ERIN, dancer. Attended, Am. Ballet Sch., Joffrey Ballet Sch. Dancer Oakland (Calif.) Ballet, until 1988; dancer Ballet West, Salt Lake City, 1988-90, prin. artist, 1990—. Dance performances include Giselle, Coppelia, Death and the Maiden, Green Table Cake Walk, Daphnis and Cloe, Romeo & Juliet, Anna Karenina, The Dream, The Nutcracker, The Gilded Bat, Sleeping Beauty, Rosalinda, Cinderella. Office: Ballet West 50 W 200 S Salt Lake City UT 84101-1642*

LEEDOM, JOHN NESBETT, distribution company executive, state senator; b. Dallas, July 27, 1921; s. Floyd H. and Gladys Lorraine (Nesbett) L.; m. Betty Lee Harvey, Mar. 17, 1956; children: Joann, Judy, Eddie Kennedy, Danny Kennedy, Linda, John Nesbett. B.S.E.E., Rice U., 1943. Engr., Naval Research Lab., Washington, 1943-45; asst. sales mgr. Sprague Products Co., North Adams, Mass., 1945-50; founder, chief exec. officer Wholesale Electronic Supply, Inc., Dallas, 1950—; pres. Levco, Inc., 1973—; mem. Tex. Senate, 1980-96. Chmn. Dallas County Republican Com., 1962-66, mem. state exec. com., 1966-68; mem. Dallas City Council, 1975-80. Author The Group and You. Served to lt. (j.g.), USNR, 1943-45. Mem. Nat. Electronic Distbrs. Assn. (pres. 1971-72), Nat. Assn. Wholesale Distbrs. (pres. 1972-73), IEEE, Mil. Order World Wars, Navy League, Tau Beta Pi. Office: 2809 Ross Ave Dallas TX 75201-2524

LEEDS, CHARLES ALAN, publishing executive; b. Mpls., Aug. 20, 1951; s. Charles Phillips and Irene (Pollard) L.; m. Karen Sue Biggs, Aug. 2, 1986; children: Charles Austin, Tyler Dixon. BA, Drake U., 1973, MPA, 1978. Mktg. coord. Register and Tribune Syndicate Inc., Des Moines, Iowa, 1973-79; sales mgr. Washington Post Writers Group, Washington, 1979-89; pres. and editorial dir. L.A. Times Washington Post News Svc., Washington, 1989—; asst. professorial lectr. George Washington U., Washington, 1986, 88. Mem. nat. adv. bd. Sch. Journalism and Mass Comm. Drake U., 1996—. Recipient Best in Bus. award Am. Journalism Rev., 1995. Mem. Internat. Press Inst. (assoc.), Soc. Profl. Journalists, Sigma Delta Chi, Kappa Tau Alpha. Presbyterian. Avocations: jogging, tennis. Home: 4714 17th St N Arlington VA 22207-2031 Office: LA Times-WA Post News Svc 1150 15th St NW Washington DC 20071-0001

LEEDS, DOUGLAS BRECKER, advertising agency executive, theatre producer; b. N.Y.C., Mar. 15, 1947; s. Richard Henry and Nancy Ann (Brecker) L.; m. Christine Castler, Jan. 14, 1980; 1 child, Victoria Brecker. BS, Babson Coll., 1970. V.p., dir. Auto Data Systems, Inc., Natick, Mass., 1970-72; dir. leasing Beacon Cos., Inc., Boston, 1972-77; account exec. Thomson-Leeds Co., Inc. div. The WPP Group, N.Y.C., 1977-84, exec. v.p., 1985-88, pres., 1988—, chief exec. officer, 1989—; chmn. ednl. rels. com. Point of Purchase Advt. Inst., 1986—, elected bd. dirs., 1989, vice chmn., 1994—; bd. dirs. Checker Board Found. Co-producer: (Broadway musical) Streetheat, 1985; assoc. producer: (Broadway play) Sleight of Hand, 1986; patentee in field. Chmn., founder Lobby Gallery Assocs. Whitney Mus. Am. Art, N.Y.C., 1983-90; trustee Guild Hall of East Hampton (Mus. and Theatre), 1990-92, John Drew Theatre; chmn. men's com. Boys Club N.Y., 1989; bd. dirs. chmn. Friends Henry Street Settlement House, N.Y.C., 1977-80; trustee Whitney Mus. Am. Art, 1992—, co-chmn. membership com., 1993—, Worcester Acad., 1982-85, Babson Coll., 1979-86, also co-chmn. devel. and pub. affairs com.; spl. projects com., The Soc. of Meml. Sloan-Kettering Cancer Ctr.; bd. dirs. Am. Theatre Wing, 1991—, mem. adminstrn. com. Tony Awards. Mem. Babson Coll. Alumni Assn. (bd. dirs., v.p. 1975-79), Union Club, Doubles Club, Royal Tennis Court Club (Middlesex, Eng.). Office: Thomson-Leeds Co Inc 450 Park Ave S New York NY 10016-7320

LEEDS, NORMA S., chemistry educator; b. N.Y.C.; d. Harry Archer and Teenie Sterne; m. Morton W. Leeds, Feb. 4, 1945; 1 child, Valerie Ann. PhD, Rutgers U., 1950. Rsch. assoc. Sloan Kettering Inst. Cancer Rsch., N.Y.C., 1950-55; supr. Gen. Aniline & Film, Linden, N.J., 1955-58; asst. prof. Fairleigh Dickinson U., Florham Park, N.J., 1959-62; assoc. prof. Caldwell (N.J.) Coll. for Women, 1962-64; assoc. prof. chemistry to prof. Kean Coll., Union, N.J., 1964-91, chair dept. chemistry, 1970-72, prof. emeritus, 1991—. Contbr. articles to profl. publs.; editor Opera at Florham Assn., Florham Park, 1992—, OAF, 1992-97.. Cottrell grantee Rutgers U., 1942-50; Univ. Rsch. Coun. fellow Rutgers U., 1946-48. Mem. Fortnightly Club (chair membership 1993-95), Sigma Xi. Unitarian. Home: 6 Sunningdale Ct Maplewood NJ 07040

LEEDS, ROBERT, dentist; b. Newark, Sept. 8, 1930; s. William David and Gertrude (Greene) L.; m. Joyce Sumner, Nov. 28, 1960; children: Deborah Joyce, Robin Elizabeth. AA, U. Fla., 1950; DDS, Emory U., 1954. Gen. practice dentistry, Miami, Fla. Patentee herpes simplex method of therapy. Served to maj. USAF, 1954-56. Mem. ADA, East Coast Dental Assn., Miami Dental Soc., South Dade Dental Soc. Club: Coral Gables Country (Fla.). Lodges: Shriners, Masons. Avocations: sailing; water skiing; snow skiing. Office: 6437 Bird Rd Miami FL 33155-4827

LEEDS, ROBERT LEWIS, JR., marketing and management educator; b. N.Y.C., Feb. 9, 1930; s. Robert Lewis and Elisabeth (Bandler) L.; m. Irene Osterweil, July 9, 1958 (div.); children: Leslie Anne, Robert Lewis III; m. Joan Wrigley, Sept. 27, 1984. B.A., Amherst Coll., 1951; M.B.A., U. Pa., 1953. With Manhattan Industries, Inc. (formerly Manhattan Shirt Co.), N.Y.C., 1955-76; v.p. marketing Manhattan Industries, Inc., 1958-65, exec. v.p., 1965-66, chmn. bd., chief exec. officer, 1966-74; also dir.; v.p. corporate devel. Benrus Corp., 1976-78; adv. bd. Mfrs. Hanover Trust Co., 1973-74; part-time faculty Bklyn. Coll., 1979, Pace U., 1979-81, Marymount Manhattan Coll., 1982—; Disting. lectr. mktg. and mgmt., dir. Exec. MBA Program, U. South Fla., 1982—. Bd. dirs. Hillside Hosp., Glen Oaks, N.Y.; mem. mktg. com. Morton Plant Hosp., 1984—Served with USAF, 1953-55. Recipient award for Civic Endeavour Textile Vets. Assn., 1968; award Young Men's Assn., 1971. Mem. Men's Fashion Assn. (chmn. bd. 1972-74, dir.). Home: 215 Midway Is Clearwater FL 34630-2316

LEEDY, DANIEL LONEY, ecologist; b. Butler, Ohio, Feb. 17, 1912; s. Charles Monroe and Bernice Camilla (Loney) L.; m. Barbara E. Sturges, Nov. 25, 1945 (dec. Mar. 12, 1988); children: Robert Raymond, Kathleen Eleanor; m. Virginia Lee Bittenbender, Sept. 22, 1989. A.B. with honors, Miami U., Oxford, Ohio, 1934, B.Sc., 1935; M.Sc., Ohio State U., 1938, Ph.D., 1940. Asst. geology and zoology depts. Miami U., 1933-35; instr. wildlife mgmt. Ohio State U., 1940-42; leader Ohio Coop. Wildlife Research Unit, 1945-48; biologist charge coop. wildlife research units U.S. Fish and Wildlife Service, Washington, 1949-57; mem. biol. sci. com. Dept. Agr. Grad. Sch., 1950-75; pres. Wildlife Soc., 1952, exec. sec., 1953-57; chief br. wildlife research U.S. Fish and Wildlife Service, 1957-63; chief div. research Bur. Outdoor Recreation, Dept. Interior, 1963-65; water resources research scientist Office Water Resources Research, 1965-74; ret., 1974; sr. scientist Nat. Inst. Urban Wildlife, Columbia, Md., 1975-95. Contbr. over 100 articles to profl. publs. Served to capt. USAAF, 1942-45. Decorated Bronze medal.; Recipient cert. of merit Nash Conservation Awards program, 1953; Am. Motors Conservation award, 1958; U.S. Dept. Interior Disting. Service award, 1972; Disting. Alumni award Ohio State U., 1975; Daniel L. Leedy Urban Wildlife Conservation award established in his honor Nat. Inst. Urban Wildlife, 1985. Fellow AAAS; mem. Wildlife Soc. (hon., Aldo Leopold award for disting. service to wildlife conservation 1983), Am. Ornithologists Union (elective mem.), Wilson Ornithol. Soc., Am. Fisheries Soc., Sigma Xi. Clubs: Field Biologists, Cosmos (Washington). Home: 12401 Ellen Ct Silver Spring MD 20904-2905

LEEDY, ROBERT ALLAN, SR., retired lawyer; b. Portland, Oreg., Aug. 5, 1909; s. Harry E. and Loretta (Viles) L.; m. Annapauline Rea, Sept. 14, 1935; children: Douglas Harry, Robert Allan, Jr. J.D., U. Oreg., 1933. Bar: Oreg. 1933. Practiced in Portland, 1934-86; former mem. firm Bullivant, Houser, Bailey, Pendergrass, and Hoffman, ret.; U.S. commr., 1943-56; Mem. Oreg. Bar Examiners, 1947-48, chmn., 1949. Chancellor Episcopal Diocese Oreg., 1970-83. Mem. ABA, Oreg. Bar Assn. (pres. 1953), Multnomah County Bar Assn., Western Bar Conf. (pres. 1952), Alpha Tau Omega, Phi Delta Phi. Home: 1300 NE 16th Ave #1219 Portland OR 97232 Office: Pioneer Towers Portland OR 97204

LEEF, JAMES LEWIS, biology educator, immunology research executive; b. San Francisco, Mar. 6, 1937; married, 1964; 4 children. BA, U. Calif., San Francisco, 1967; PhD in Biology, U. Tenn., 1974. Sr. investigator cryobiology, head Malaria Rsch. dept. Biomed. Rsch. Inst., Rockville, Md., 1976-82, exec. dir., 1982—; cons. Sci. and Indsl. Rsch. and Devel. Co., 1967-69; guest scientist Navy Med. Rsch. Inst., 1976—. U. Ill. fellow, 1973-76. Mem. AAAS, Soc. Cryobiology, Tissue Culture Assn., Am. Assn. Tissue Banks, N.Y. Acad. Sci. Achievements include research in malariology; mechanisms of freezing injury; study of various developmental stages of malaria and schistosomiasis parasites as antigens in developing a malaria and schistosomiasis vaccine and preservation of these forms at low temperatures. Office: Biomed Rsch Inst 12111 Parklawn Dr Rockville MD 20852-1709*

LEEFE, JAMES MORRISON, architect; b. N.Y.C., Aug. 28, 1921; s. Charles Clement and Suzanne (Bernhardt) L.; m. Miriam Danziger, Oct. 31, 1949; 1 dau., Molly Elizabeth. Cert., U.S. Mcht. Marine Acad., 1943; B.Arch., Columbia U., 1950. Practice architecture San Francisco, 1955-60; chief architect power and indsl. div. Bechtel Inc., San Francisco, 1960-64; prin. urban designer Bechtel Inc., 1974-80; chief architect San Francisco Power div. Bechtel Power Corp., 1980-89; v.p., asst. sec. Bechtel Assos. (P.C.), N.Y., 1978-89; v.p. Bechtel Assos. (P.C.), D.C. and Va., 1978-89; pvt. cons. architect Sausalito, Calif., 1989—; ptnr. Leefe & Ehrankrantz Architects, San Francisco, 1964-68; v.p. Bldg. Systems Devel. Inc., San Francisco and Washington, 1965-70; also dir.; dir. architecture Giffels Assos. Inc., Detroit, 1971-74; lectr. in architecture Columbia U., 1951-52, U. Calif., Berkeley, 1954-60; mem. faculty U. for Pres's., Young Pres's. Orgn., 1967; adj. prof. U. Detroit, 1971-72; mem. adv. bd. Nat. Clearing House for Criminal Justice Planning and Architecture, 1974-76. Works include Mus. West of Am. Craftsmen's Council, San Francisco, 1964 (Archtl. Record award for interior design 1971), Wells Hydrocombine Dam and Power Generating Facility, Columbia River, Wash., 1965, Boundary Dam, Pend Orielle River, Wash., 1965 (Am. Public Power Assn. honor award 1975), Detroit Automobile Inter-Ins. Exchange Corp. Hdqrs, Dearborn, Mich., 1972 (Detroit chpt. AIA honor award 1975), PPG Industries Research Center, Allison Park, Pa., 1973 (Detroit chpt. AIA honor award 1975, Am. Inst. Steel Constrn. Archtl. award of excellence 1975, Mich. Soc. Architects honor award 1976), Gen. Electric Research Center, Twinsburg, Ohio, 1973 (Detroit chpt. AIA honor award 1977), Appliance Buyers Credit Corp. Hdqrs. Office, Benton Harbor, Mich., 1974 (Engring. Soc. Detroit Design award 1976), Standard Tng. Bldg. Commonwealth Edison, 1989-90, Strybing Arboretum, San Francisco, 1990; contbr. articles to profl. jours.; originator various techniques for analysis of human factors in the working environment. Chmn. bd. Mus. West of Am. Crafts Coun., San Francisco, 1966-68; vice chmn. Franklin (Mich.) Hist. Dist. Commn., 1973-74; trustee So. Marin Land Trust. With U.S. Mcht. Marine, 1942-46. Recipient Hirsh Meml. prize Columbia U., 1950, 1st prize (with Miriam Leefe) Dow Chem. Co. Competition for Interior Design, 1960. Fellow AIA; hon. mem. Internat. Union Architects Working Group Habitat, trustee, So. Marin Land Trust. Home and Office: James Leefe FAIA Architect 131 Spencer Ave Sausalito CA 94965-2022 *I think of architecture as a celebration of life, of the buildings we make for ourselves as stepping stones on the path of history. This forces me to be an optimist, always searching to find a manifestation of the joy of being in my work.*

LEEGE, DAVID CALHOUN, political scientist, educator; b. Elkhart, Ind., May 18, 1937; s. Harold Martin and Nellie Josephine (Bliss) L.; m. Patricia Ann Schad, June 8, 1963; children—David McChesney, Lissa Maria, Kurt Johannes. B.A., Valparaiso U., 1959; postgrad., U. Chgo., 1959-60; Ph.D., Ind. U., 1965. Instr. social sci. Concordia Coll., River Forest, Ill., 1962-64; asst. prof. polit. sci., dir. pub. opinion survey unit U. Mo., Columbia, 1964-68; assoc. prof., dir. survey research center SUNY, Buffalo, 1968-70; assoc. prof. U. Ill., Chgo., 1970-72; prof. U. Ill., 1972-76, head dept., 1972-73; prof. govt. and internat. studies U. Notre Dame, Ind., 1976—; dir. center for study of contemporary society U. Notre Dame, 1976-85, dir. London program, 1982, dir. program for research on religion, church and society, 1984—; dir. Hesburgh Program in Pub. Service, 1987-92; program dir. for polit. sci. NSF, 1974-76; vis. prof. York U., Toronto, Ont., Can., 1970, U. Mich., 1971, 73, U. Leuven, Belgium, 1980, Cath. U. Am., 1985-86. Author: (with Wayne Francis) Political Research, 1974, (with Lyman Kellstedt) Rediscovering the Religious Factor in American Politics, 1993; editor: The Missouri Poll, 1965-68, (with Joseph Gremillion) The Notre Dame Study of Catholic Parish Life Report Series, 1984-89; contbr. articles to profl. jours. Mem. bd. overseers Am. Nat. Election Studies, 1990—, chair, 1994-97; del. ICORE, 1993—; mem. coun. ICPSR, 1966-69. Mem. Am. Polit. Sci. Assn. (sect officer, program com., chmn. task force), Midwest Polit. Sci. Assn. (chair nominating com., coun., program co-chair). Lutheran. Home: 51971 S Shoreham Ct South Bend IN 46637-1358 Office: U Notre Dame Dept Govt Notre Dame IN 46556

LEEHEY, PATRICK, mechanical and ocean engineering educator; b. Waterloo, Iowa, Oct. 27, 1921; s. Florance Patrick and Monica (White) L.; m. Dorothy Feltus, Feb. 3, 1944; children—Patrick M., David J., Christopher M., Jonathan R., Susan E., Jennifer A. B.S., U.S. Naval Acad., 1942; postgrad., U.S. Naval Postgrad. Sch., 1946-47; Ph.D., Brown U., 1950. Commd. ensign USN, 1942, advanced through grades to capt., 1962; hydrofoil project officer, 1951-53; design supt. Puget Sound Naval Shipyard, 1956-58; head ship silencing br. USN Bur. Ships, 1958-63; head acoustics lab. David Taylor Model Basin, 1963-64; ret., 1964; assoc. prof. naval architecture MIT, 1964-66, prof., 1966-71, prof. mech. and ocean engring., 1971—; liaison scientist ONR, London, 1984-85; cons. Bath Iron Works, Rand Corp., Litton Industries, Office Naval Research. Mem. Am. Math. Soc., Acoustical Soc. Am., Am. Soc. Naval Engrs. Patentee in field. Home: 48 Bellevue Rd Swampscott MA 01907-1517 Office: MIT Rm 3-262 Cambridge MA 02139

LEEKLEY, JOHN ROBERT, lawyer; b. Phila., Aug. 27, 1943; s. Thomas Briggs and Dorothy (O'Hora) L.; m. Karen Kristin Myers, Aug. 28, 1965 (dec. Mar. 1997); children: John Thomas, Michael Dennis. BA, Boston Coll., 1965; LLB, Columbia U., 1968. Bar: N.Y. 1968, Mich. 1976. Assoc. Curtis, Mallet-Prevost, Colt & Mosle, N.Y.C., 1968-69, Davis Polk & Wardwell, N.Y.C., 1969-76; asst. corp. counsel Masco Corp., Taylor, Mich., 1976-77, corp. counsel, 1977-79, v.p., corp. counsel, 1979-88, v.p., gen. counsel, 1988-96; sr. v.p., gen. counsel Masco Corp., Taylor, 1996—. Bd. visitors Columbia U. Law Sch., N.Y.C., 1994-96; mem. Freedom Twp. Bd. Tax Appeals, 1984-85. Mem. ABA (com. long range issues affecting bus. practice 1976-96), Mich. State Bar Assn. Democrat. Roman Catholic. Avocations: Percheron horse breeding, hunting, fishing, outdoor activities. Office: Masco Corp 21001 Van Born Rd Taylor MI 48180-1340

LEELAND, STEVEN BRIAN, electronics engineer; b. Tampa, Fla., Dec. 27, 1951; s. N. Stanford and Shirley Mae (Bahner) L.; m. Karen Frances Hayes, Dec. 20, 1980; children: Crystal Mary, April Marie. BSEE, MSEE magna cum laude, U. South Fla., 1976. Registered profl. engr., Ariz. Engr. Bendix Avionics, Ft. Lauderdale, Fla., 1976-77; prin. engr., instr. Sperry Avionics, Phoenix, 1977-84; prin. staff engr. Motorola Govt. Electronics Group, Scottsdale, Ariz., 1984-88; engring. fellow, mgr. dept. software engring. Fairchild Data Corp., Scottsdale, 1988—; cons. Motorola Govt. Electronics Group, 1991. Patentee systolic array, 1990; contbr. articles to profl. jours. Mem. IEEE (Phoenix chpt. Computer Soc. treas. 1978-79, sec. 1979-80, chmn. 1980-81, 81-82), Tau Beta Pi, Pi Mu Epsilon, Phi Kappa Phi, Omicron Delta Kappa, Themis. Republican. Adventist. Avocations: chess, computers, biking, exercise, health. Home: 10351 E Sharon Dr Scottsdale AZ 85260-9000 Office: Fairchild Data Corp 350 N Hayden Rd Scottsdale AZ 85257-4601

LEEMAN, CAVIN PHILIP, psychiatrist, educator; b. N.Y.C., Jan. 16, 1932; s. Stephen and May (Cavin) L.; m. Susan Epstein, Aug. 11, 1957 (div. 1983); children: Eve, Jennifer, Raphael; m. Diane Leenheer Zimmerman, Feb. 18, 1984. AB, Harvard U., 1952, MD, 1959. Diplomate Am. Bd. Psychiatry and Neurology. Intern in medicine Mass. Gen. Hosp., Boston, 1959-60; resident in psychiatry Mass. Mental Health Ctr., Boston, 1960-62; resident in psychiatry Beth Israel Hosp., Boston, 1962-64, asst. in psychiatry, 1964-66; instr. in psychiatry Harvard Med. Sch., Boston, 1966-75; chief of psychiatry Framingham (Mass.) Union Hosp., 1973-83; lectr. Harvard Med. Sch., 1975-83; assoc. clin. prof. Boston U. Sch. Medicine, 1974-83; chief of psychiatry VA Med. Ctr., Bklyn., 1983-85; clin. dir. psychiatry Univ. Hosp., Bklyn., 1985-96; clin. prof. psychiatry SUNY Health Sci. Ctr., Bklyn., 1984—; faculty assoc., divsn. humanities in medicine, SUNY Health Sci. Ctr., Bklyn., 1994—; mem. active med. staff Univ. Hosp., Bklyn., 1985—.

Contbr. articles to profl. publs. Fellow Am. Psychiat. Assn. (life), Am. Psychosomatic Medicine; mem. Assn. for Acad. Psychiatry, Am. Assn. Gen. Hosp. Psychiatrists, N.Y. Acad. Medicine, Physicians for Social Responsibility, Physicians for Human Rights, Soc. Bioethics Cons. Office: 344 W 23rd St Apt 1B New York NY 10011-2269

LEEMAN, SUSAN EPSTEIN, neuroscientist, educator; b. Chgo., May 9, 1930; d. Samuel and Dora (Gubernikoff) Epstein; m. Cavin Leeman (div.); children: Eve, Raphael, Jennifer. BA, Goucher Coll., 1951; MA, Radcliffe Coll., 1954, PhD, 1958; DS (hon.), SUNY, Utica, 1992; hon. degree, Goucher Coll., 1993. Instr. Harvard Med. Sch., Boston, 1958-59; postdoctoral fellow Brandeis U., Waltham, Mass., 1959-62, 62-66; rsch. assoc., adj. ast. prof., asst. rsch. prof. Brandeis U., Waltham, Mass., 1966-68, 68-71; asst. prof. Harvard Med. Sch., 1972-73, assoc. prof., 1973-80; prof. U. Mass. Med. Ctr., Worcester, 1980-92, dir. interdept. neurosci. program, 1984-92; prof. Boston U. Sch. Medicine, 1992—; Burroughs Wellcome vis. prof. U.Ky., 1992. Fogarty scholar NAS, 1994; recipient Women in Sci. award N.Y. Acad., 1995. Mem. NAS (197th Lilly lectr. 1994, Fred Conrad Koch award 1994, Women in Sci. award 1995). Office: Boston U Sch Medicine Dept Pharmacology 80 E Concord St Boston MA 02118-2307

LEENEY, ROBERT JOSEPH, newspaper editor; b. New Haven, May 10, 1916; s. Patrick Joseph and Mary Alice (Ross) L.; m. Anne King Coyne, June 28, 1941; children: Robert Joseph, David Coyne, Anne Patricia. Student pub. and pvt. schs.; L.H.D. (hon.), U. New Haven, 1983, Albertus Magnus Coll., 1985. Reporter, book page editor, drama critic New Haven Register, 1940-47, editorial writer, 1947-55; editor editorial page New Haven Jour.-Courier, New Haven Register, 1956-61, exec. editor, 1961-72, editor, 1972-81, editor emeritus, 1981, v.p., dir., 1970—; v.p., sec. Register Pub. Co.; dir. Conn. Savs. Bank.; examiner adminstrv. reports, editor Ofcl. Digest State Reports, Conn., 1951-52. Columnist. Conn. pub. info. chmn. Am. Cancer Soc.; v.p. Arts Council Greater New Haven; mem. Conn. Edn. Council, Edn. Commn. of States, Conn. Commn. on Freedom of Info., 1981-86 ; bd. dirs. St. Raphael's Hosp. Found., Long Wharf Theatre, New Haven, 1990; trustee Albertus Magnus Coll., 1984, Conn. Found. Open Govt. Served with USAAF, World War II. Named to New Eng. Journalism Hall of Fame, 1977; recipient Seal of the City award for disting. cmty. svc., 1994. Mem. Nat. Conf. Editl. Writers, Am. Soc. Newspaper Editors, New Eng. Soc. Newspaper Editors (pres. 1961), New Eng. AP News Execs. Assn. (pres. 1977), Conn. Editl. Assn., Conn. Cir. AP (pres.), New Haven C. of C. (v.p., dir., Disting. Svc. award), Outer Circle, N.H. Colony Hist. Soc., Kiwanis, Woodbridge Club, Mory's Club, Quinnipiak Club, Sigma Delta Chi (pres. Conn. chpt. 1963-69). Home: R 69 424 Carrington Hill Rd Bethany CT 06524 Office: New Haven Register 40 Sargent Dr New Haven CT 06511-6111

LEEPA, ALLEN, artist, educator; b. N.Y.C., Jan. 9, 1919; s. Harvey and Esther (Gentle) L. Student (scholar), The New Bauhaus Sch., 1937-38; scholar, Hans Hofmann Sch., 1938-39; B.S., Columbia U., 1942, M.A. (scholar), 1948, Ed.D., 1960. Art instr. Hull Sch., Chgo., 1937-38, Bklyn. Art Center, 1939-40, Met. Mus., N.Y.C., 1940-41, St. Marks Center, N.Y.C., 1941-42; draftsman Acrotorque Co., Conn., 1942, Glen Martin Aircraft, N.Y.C., 1942-44; prof. art Mich. State U., 1945-84, ret. prof. emeritus; mem. Leepa Gallery of Fine Art, Tarpon Springs, Fla., 1987-90. Author: The Challenge of Modern Art, 1949, 95, Abraham Rattner, 1974; contbr.: (anthologies) The New Art, 1966, 68, The Humanitites in Contemporary Life, 1960, Minimal Art; art editor: The Centennial Rev. Arts and Scis. Jour., 1959-62; one man shows Artists Gallery, N.Y.C., 1953, La Cours D'Ingres, Paris, 1961, Artists Mart, Detroit, 1969, Duke U., 1981; group shows include Mus. Modern Art, N.Y.C., 1953, VII Bienal, São Paulo, Brazil, 1963, Prado Mus., Madrid, Spain, 1956, Detroit Inst. Arts, 1948, 50, 56, 80, Pa. Acad. Fine Arts, 1951, 63; represented in permanent collections Mich. State U., Grand Rapids (Mich.) Mus., South Bend (Ind.) Mus.; lifetime work Tampa Mus. Fine Art, Leepa/Rattner Mus. Fine Arts St. Petersburg (Fla.) Jr. Coll. Fulbright award to Paris, 1950-51; Ford Found. grantee Brazil, 1970; recipient numerous prizes for paintings including: 1st prize statewide mural competition, Mich., 1983; 1st prize abstract painting Guild Hall Mus., East Hampton, N.Y., 1985. Mem. Mich. Acad. Arts, Scis., Letters. Office: Mich State U Art Dept East Lansing MI 48823

LEEPER, DORIS MARIE, sculptor, painter; b. Charlotte, N.C., Apr. 4, 1929; d. Ernest R. Leeper and Pauline A. (Fry) Leeper Harrison. B.A., Duke U., 1951. With graphic arts dept. Charlotte Engraving, 1951-55, PhD (hon.) Duke U., 1997, Stetson U., 1997; artist, salesperson, designer So. Engraving, Atlanta, 1955-61; mem. adv. panels Fla. Arts Council, 1975-93. One-woman shows include Hunter Mus. Art, Chattanooga, 1968, 75, 79, Jacksonville Art Mus., Fla., 1968, 76, Mint Mus. Art, Charlotte, 1968, 76, Duke U. Mus., Durham, N.C., 1969, High Mus. Art, Atlanta, 1975, Greenville County Mus. Art, S.C., 1976, Columbia Mus. Art, S.C., 1976, Ringling Mus. Art, Sarasota, Fla., 1976, Miss. Mus. Art, Jackson, 1979, Mus. Arts and Scis., Daytona Beach, Fla., 1980, LeMoyne Art Found., Tallahassee, 1980, Anniston Mus., Natural History, Ala., 1980, G. McKenna Gallery, Charlotte, 1983, Foster Harmon Galleries, Sarasota, 1984, Atlantic Ctr. for the Arts, New Smyrna Beach, 1984, Albertson Peterson Gallery, Winter Park, 1993, Cornell Fine Arts Mus., Winter Park, 1995, Pensacola (Fla.) Mus. Art, 1996-97; group shows include Jacksonville Art Mus., 1971-72, 72, Albright-Knox Gallery, Buffalo, 1972-73, Miss. Mus. Art, 1978, Am. Acad. and Inst. Arts and Letters, N.Y.C., 1979, N. Miami Mus., Fla., 1984, Ctr. Arts, Vero Beach, Fla., 1986, Sampson Art Gallery, Stetson U., DeLand, 1990, Cornell Fine Arts Mus., Rollins Coll., Winter Park, 1990, Appalachian State U., Boone, N.C., 1990, 91, 2d Internat. Ephemeral Sculptures Exhbn., Fortaleza, Brazil, 1991, Duncan Gallery of Art, DeLand, 1991, Cummer Gallery of Art, Jacksonville, 1992, Cornell Fine Arts Mus., Rollins Coll., Winter Park, 1992, Samuel P. Harn Mus. of Art, Gainesville, 1993, Hodgell Gallery, Sarasota, 1995, Arts on Douglas, New Smyrna Beach, Fla., 1996; commns. include Fla. State Legis. Bldg., IBM, Atlanta, Orlando Internat. Airport, Fla., others; represented in permanent collections Hunter Mus. Art, Chattanooga, Jacksonville Art Mus., Columbus Mus. Art, Ohio, Duke U., Durham, Greenville County Mus. Art, Ill. Wesleyan U., Mint Mus. Art, Miss. Mus. Art, Mus. Arts and Scis., Daytona Beach, Nat. Mus. Am. Art, Washington, Stetson U., Deland, Fla., U. S. Fla., Tampa, Wadsworth Athenaeum, Hartford, Conn., others. Founder Atlantic Ctr. for Arts, New Smyrna Beach, Fla., 1977-78, trustee, 1979-86, adv. coun. 1986-92; trustee Mus. Arts and Scis., Daytona Beach, 1977-78, Fla. Conservation Found., 1981-85; mem. adv. commn. Canaveral Nat. Seashore, 1975-85; bd. dirs. Coastal Ednl. Broadcasters, Inc., New Smyrna Beach, 1983-90; mem. internat. adv. bd. La Napoule Art Found., France, 1987-94. Nat. Endowment Arts fellow, 1972; Fla. Fine Arts Council fellow, 1977; Rockefeller Found. fellow, 1977; recipient Humanist Arts award Am. Humanist Assn., 1990, Fla. Arts Recognition award 1993, Outstanding Alumnae award Zeta Tau Alpha, 1994. Avocations: reading; tennis; environmental affairs. Home: 806 N Peninsula Ave New Smyrna Beach FL 32169-2318

LEEPER, HAROLD HARRIS, arbitrator; b. Kansas City, Mo., July 29, 1916; s. Truman Elmer and Bess Mayburn (Harris) L.; m. Maribelle Potts, Sept. 21, 1941; children: Robert Chester, Marilyn Anne. BSBA, U. Mo., 1937; JD, Oklahoma City U., 1956. Bar: Okla. 1957, U.S. Supreme Ct. 1969. Regional pers. officer VA, Oklahoma City, 1946-52; state adminstrv. officer IRS, Oklahoma City, 1952-56; pers. officer FAA, Oklahoma City, 1956-63; from hearing officer to chief hearing officer FAA, Washington, 1963-71; adminstrv. law judge Social Security Adminstrn., Dallas, 1971-73; freelance labor mgmt. arbitrator Dallas, 1974—. Pres. Way Back House, Inc., Dallas, 1975-77, bd. dirs., 1997—; chmn. pers. com. Wesley Rankin Community Ctr., Dallas, 1989-95. 1st lt. U.S. Army, 1943-46, lt. col. Res. ret. Mem. Fed. Bar Assn. (pres. Dallas chpt. 1982-83), Nat. Acad. Arbitrators (regional chmn. 1990-92), Mil. Order World Wars (comdr. D.C. chpt. 1969-70), Mason, Shriner. Democrat. Methodist. Avocations: golf, sailing, flying, church activities. Home and Office: 6256 Glennox Ln Dallas TX 75214-2144

LEERABHANDH, MARJORIE BRAVO, chemist, educator; b. Negros Occidental, Philippines; came to U.S., 1982.; d. Rustico Ginese and Monica Tolosa (Tolosa) Bravo; m. Sunai Leerabhandh, Oct. 2, 1986. BS in chemistry cum laude, U. Santo Tomas, 1979; PhD in chemistry, U. So. Calif., 1990. Rsch. teaching asst. chem. dept. U. So. Calif., L.A., 1984-89; faculty mem. chem. dept. Moorpark (Calif.) Coll., 1992—; project mgr. Med. Analysis Sys., Inc., Camarillo, Calif., 1989-93, rsch. team leader, 1993-94, mgr. rsch. and devel., 1994—. Author: Nitrogen Tixation Research Progress, 1985, Nitrogen Fixation: 100 Years After, 1988; contbr. articles to profl. jours. Mem. Am. Chem. Soc., Am. Assn. for Clinical Chem., Chem. Soc. U. Santo Tomas Manila (pres., 1979). Achievements include patents for Fructosamine Reagent and Calibrator Systems, Stabilization of Functional Proteins. Office: Med Analysis Sys Inc 542 Flynn Rd Camarillo CA 93012-8027

LEES, BENJAMIN, composer; b. Harbin, China, Jan. 8, 1924; came to U.S., 1925; Studied piano, with K.I. Rodetsky, 1931, Marguerite Bitter, 1945-48; compostion, with Halsey Stevens at U. So. Calif., 1945-48, with George Antheil, 1949-54. Prof. composition Peabody Conservatory, Queen's Coll., Manhattan Sch. Music. Composer: Profile, 1952, Declamations for piano and strings, 1953, Symphony Number 1, 1953, Number 2, 1958, Piano Concerto Number 1, 1955, Divertimento Burlesca, 1957, Songs of the Night for Soprano and Orch, 1952, Violin Concerto, 1958, Prologue, Capriccio and Epilogue, 1958, Concerto for Orch, 1959, Concertante Breve, 1959, Interlude for Strings, 1957, Visions of Poets for Soprano and Tenor Solo; Chorus and Orch., 1961; The Gilded Cage; chamber music String Quartet Number 1, 1952; Evocation for Solo Flute, 1953, Violin Sonata Number 1, 1953, Movement da Camera for Flute, Clarinet, Cello and Piano, 1954, String Quartet Number 2, 1955, Three Variables for Winds and Piano, 1956; piano Sonata for Two Pianos, 1951; Toccata, 1953, Fantasia, 1954, Kaleidoscopes, 1959, Sonata Breve, 1956, Six Ornamental Etudes, 1957; songs Cyprian Songs for baritone, 1961; Concerto for Oboe and Orch, 1964, Piano Sonata 4, 1965, Piano Concerto 2, 1966, Symphony No. 3, 1968; opera Medea in Corinth, 1970; Study for Solo Cello, 1972, Sonata No. 2 for Violin and Piano, 1973, Etudes for Piano and Orch., 1974, Labyrinths for Symphonic Band, 1975, Variations for Piano and Orch., 1975, Passacaglia for Orch., 1976, Concerto for Woodwind Quintet and Orch., 1976, Staves soprano and piano, 1977; Scarlatti Portfolio; transcriptions for orch., 1978; Dialogue for Cello and Piano, 1977, Paumanok for mezzo-soprano with piano, 1980; Omen for soprano with piano, 1981; Sonata for cello and piano, 1981, String Quartet No. 3, 1982, Double Concerto for piano, cello and orch., 1982, Concerto for brass choir and orch., 1983, Portrait of Rodin (orch.), 1984, Symphony No. 4 (Memorial Candles), 1985, Odyssey II for solo piano, 1986, Symphony # 5, 1988, String Quartet No. 4, 1989, Sonata for Violin and Piano # 3, 1989, Concerto for Horn and Orch., 1991, Mirrors for solo piano, 1992, Borealis for orch., 1993, Echoes of Normandy, 1994, Classico (solo guitar, 1995), Celebration (orchestra), 1996, Contellations (orchestra), 1997. Recipient Fromm Found. award, 1953; William and Noma Copley Found. award, 1955; UNESCO award, 1958; Sir Arnold Bax medal, 1958; Composers award Lancaster Symphony Orch., 1985; Guggenheim fellow, 1954, 66; Fulbright fellow, 1956. Address: 2451 A Birdie Way Palm Springs CA 92264

LEES, MARJORIE BERMAN, biochemist, neuroscientist; b. N.Y.C., Mar. 17, 1923; d. Isadore I. and Ruth (Rogalsky) Berman; m. Sidney Lees, Sept. 17, 1946; children: David E., Andrew, Eliot. BA, Hunter Coll., 1943; MS, U. Chgo., 1945; PhD, Harvard U., Radcliffe Coll., 1951. Assoc. biochemist, asst. biochemist McLean Hosp., Belmont, Mass., 1953-62; rsch. assoc. Darmouth Med. Sch., Hanover, N.H., 1962-66; assoc. biochemist McLean Hosp., Belmont, 1966-76; prin. and sr. rsch. assoc. Harvard Med. Sch., Boston, 1966-85; biochemist E.K. Shriver Ctr., Waltham, Mass., 1976—; prof. biochemistry (neurology) Harvard Med. Sch., Boston, 1985—; biochemist Mass. Gen. Hosp., Boston, 1976—; assoc. dir. biochemistry E.K. Shriver Ctr., Waltham, 1982-90, dir. biochemistry, 1990-93, assoc. dir. mental retardation rsch. ctr., 1994—; mem. adv. com. biomed. and behavioral rsch. NASA/NIH, 1993—; mem. sci. adv. com. Nat. Multiple Sclerosis Soc., 1988-93. Chief editor Jour. of Neurochemistry, 1986-90; author (with others) books; contbr. articles to profl. jours. Mem. adv. coun. Nat. Inst. Neurological Disorders, Bethesda, Md., 1979-82; chmn. Radcliffe Grad. Soc., Cambridge, Mass., 1978-80. Predoctoral fellow USPHS, 1947-50, postdoctoral fellow Am. Cancer Soc., 1951-53; Javits Neurosci. grantee NIH, 1983-90, 91-97, prin. grantee NIH, 1962—; named to Hunter Coll. Hall of Fame, 1982. Mem. Am. Soc. Biochemistry and Molecular Biology, Internat. Soc. Neurochemistry, Am. Soc. Neurochemistry (treas. 1975-81, pres. 1983-85), Soc. for Neurosci., Am. Assn. Neuropathology (assoc.), Internat. Soc. Neuroimmunology, N.Y. Acad. Scis., Am. Women in Sci., Phi Beta Kappa. Office: E K Shriver Ctr 200 Trapelo Rd Waltham MA 02154-6332

LEES, MARTIN HENRY, pediatrician, educator; b. London, May 11, 1929; came to U.S., 1958; s. David William and Lilian Thomson (White) L.; m. Elizabeth McMahon, Sept. 5, 1959; children: Deborah Ann, Jacqueline Mary, Christina Beth. MBBS, London U., 1955, MD, 1962. Diplomate: Am. Bd. Pediatrics, Am. Bd. Pediatric Cardiology, Am. Bd. Fetal/Neonatal Medicine. Intern South Devon Hosp., Plymouth, Eng., 1955-57; resident in pediatrics Hosp. Sick Children, 1957; sr. resident, fellow in pediatric cardiology Boston Children's Hosp., 1958-61; asst. prof. McGill U., Montreal, Que., Can., 1961-62; prof. pediatrics U. Oreg. Health Ctr., Portland, 1963-95. Fellow Royal Coll. Physicians (London); mem. Am. Heart Assn., Am. Pediatric Soc., Soc. Pediatric Rsch. Home: 14 Morningview Lane Lake Oswego OR 97035-2340 Office: Pediatric Cardiology 501 N Graham St Ste 330 Portland OR 97227-2001

LEES, SIDNEY, research facility administrator, bioengineering educator; b. Phila., Apr. 17, 1917; s. Charles K. and Bess Rose (Segal) L.; m. Marjorie Berman, Sept. 17, 1947; children—David E.B., P. Andrew, Eliot Jay. A.B., Coll. City N.Y., 1938; S.M., Mass. Inst. Tech., 1948, Sc.D., 1950. Observer U.S. Weather Bur., 1938-40; meteorol. instrument engr. U.S. Signal Corps, 1940-43; research asso. Mass. Inst. Tech., 1947-50, asst. prof. aero. dept., 1950-57; cons. engr., 1957-62; prof. engring. Thayer Sch., Dartmouth, 1962-66; head bioengring. dept., sr. mem. staff Forsyth Inst. Research and Advanced Study, Boston, 1966—; hon. rsch. assoc. dept. med. biophysics U. Manchester, England, 1990—; adj. prof. Northeastern U., 1980; vis. scientist U. Amsterdam, 1975; chmn. Joint Automatic Control Conf., 1965, Rsch. Conf. on Instrumentation Sci., 1971, Conf. on Ultrasonics in Bioengring. and Biophysics, 1978, Internat. Symposium on Acoustical Imaging, 1997. Co-author: Instrument Engineering, 3 vols, 1952-55; Editor: Air, Space and Instruments, Draper Anniversary vol, 1963; Contbr. articles to profl. jours. Served with AUS, 1943-46. Fellow Acoustical Soc. Am. (emeritus); mem. Am. Phys. Soc., ASME, IEEE, Engring. in Medicine and Biology Soc. IEEE (chmn. region I 1980—), Sigma Xi (pres. Dartmouth chpt. 1964-65). Home: 50 Eliot Memorial Rd Newton MA 02158-2704 Office: Forsyth Dental Center 140 Fenway Boston MA 02115-3782

LEESER, DAVID O., materials engineer, metallurgist; b. El Paso, Tex., Aug. 3, 1917; s. Oscar D. and Rose R. (Goodman) L.; m. Marilyn Bachman Kalina, Mar. 18, 1945; children: Barbara H., Joyce N. BSc in Mining, U. Tex., El Paso, 1943; MSc in Materials Sci., Ohio State U., 1950; postgrad., U. Fla., 1962, U. Mich., 1985. Registered profl. engr., Ohio, Calif., Ariz. Mining engr. Bradley Mining Co., Stibnite, Idaho, 1943-44; rsch. engr. Battelle Meml. Inst., Columbus, Ohio, 1944-50; assoc. metallurgist Argonne Nat. Lab., Lemont, Ill., 1950-54; mgr., staff metallurgist Atomic Power Devel. Assn., Detroit, 1954-61; chief scientist, materials Chrysler Corp./Missiles, Cape Canaveral, Fla., 1961-68; chief metallurgist Chrysler Corp., Amplex div., Detroit, 1968-75; sr. staff engr. Burroughs Corp. (Unisys), Plymouth, Mich., 1975-86; prin., materials cons., forensic engr. D.O. Leeser, Profl. Egnr., Scottsdale, Ariz., 1987—; materials cons. fgn. tech. divsn. Wright-Patterson AFB, Dayton, Ohio, 1958-80; charter mem. Missile, Space and Range Pioneers, Cape Canaveral, 1967—; organizer Fla. Indsl. Exhbn., Orlando, 1968; U.S. del. 2d World Metall. Congress, Chgo., 1957, Internat. Conf. on Peaceful Uses of Atom, Geneva, 1958, Internat. Atomic Energy Agy. Conf., Vienna, Austria, 1961. Contbr. articles on nuclear radiation effects on structural materials, flame deflector materials for rockets, forensic investigations to profl. publs. Vice-pres. Manzanita Villas Home Owners Assn., Scottsdale, 1990—. Recipient citation War Manpower Commn., 1945, U.S. Sci. R&D Office, 1946, Appreciation award State of Fla., 1968; Engr. of Yr. Fla. Engring. Soc.-Canaveral Coun. Tech. Socs., 1967, Outstanding Alumnus of Yr., U. Tex. at El Paso, 1969; recipient Apollo Achievement award NASA, 1969, Exemplary Action award Burroughs Corp., 1986. Mem. Am. Soc. materials Internat., Sigma Xi. Achievements include collaboration on development of atomic bomb, Apollo space program, first nuclear-powered naval vessel; pioneering studies on effects of nuclear radiation on materials. Home: 11515 N 91st St Unit 151 Scottsdale AZ 85260-6899

LEE-SMITH, HUGHIE, artist, educator; b. Eustis, Fla., Sept. 20, 1915; s. Luther and Alice (Williams) Smith; m. Mabel Louise Everett, 1940 (div. 1953); 1 child, Christina; m. Helen Nebraska, 1965 (div. 1974); m. Patricia Thomas-Ferry, 1978. Student, Art Sch. of Detroit Soc. Arts and Crafts, 1934-35; grad., Cleve. Inst. Art, 1938; B.S., Wayne State U., 1953; DFA (hon.), Md. Inst. Coll. Art, 1995. Instr. painting Grosse Pointe War Meml., Mich., 1956-66, Studio-on-the-Canal, Princeton, N.J., 1959-64; art tchr. Princeton Country Day Sch., 1964-65; artist-in-residence Howard U., 1969-71; instr. painting Art Students League, N.Y.C., 1972-87, ret., 1987; adj. prof. Trenton State Coll., 1972-73. One-man shows include Detroit Artists Market, Howard U. Gallery, Washington, Grand Central Art Galleries, N.Y.C., Janet Nessler Gallery, N.Y.C., U. Chgo., June Kelly Gallery, N.Y.C., Butler Inst. Am. Art, Youngstown, Ohio, Chgo. Cultural Ctr., Greenville (S.C.) Mus. Art, others; exhibited group shows Cleve. Mus. Art, Detroit Inst. Arts, Butler Inst. Am. Art, Youngstown, Bklyn. Mus., Wadsworth Atheneum, Boston Mus., San Francisco Mus., Mus. Modern Art, Whitney Mus., Am. Acad, and Inst. Arts and Letters, N.Y.; represented in permanent collections Met. Mus., Phila. Mus., Detroit Inst. Arts, Parrish Mus., Southampton, L.I., N.J. State Mus., Standard Oil of Ohio, AT&T, Wadsworth Atheneum, U. Mich., Wayne State U., Schomburg Coll., N.Y.C., Howard U., Nat. Mus. Am Art, U.S. Navy Art Ctr., Chase Manhattan Bank, N.Y.C., Forbes Mag. Collection, N.Y.C., Kidder & Peabody Co., N.Y.C., Mus. Internat. Art, Sofia, Bulgaria, Century Assn., N.Y.C., Lagos (Nigeria) Mus. With USN, 1944-45. Recipient Thomas B. Clark prize NAD, 1959, prize Allied Artists Am., 1958, Emily Lowe award, 1957, Founders prize Detrout Inst. Arts, 1953, cert. of commendation USN, 1974, Art Achievement award Wayne State U., Key to the City of Hartford (Conn.) award, Ranger Fund purchase award NAD, 1977, Audubon Artist prizes, 1982, 83, 85, 86, Medal of Merit Lotos Club, 1996, Benjamin West Clinecdinst Meml. medal Artists Fellowship Inc., 1996; named Mich. Painter of Yr. Detrout News, 1953. Mem. Artists Equity Assn. (bd. dirs.), Allied Artists Am., Princeton Art Assn., Mich. Acad. Sci., Arts and Letters, NAD (mem. coun., awards juries), Audubon Artists (pres. 1980-82, exhbn. coord.), Artists Fellowship (trustee, v.p. 1985-88), Century Assn., Lotos Club (N.Y.C.). Home: 3741 Altez NE Albuquerque NM 87111

LEESON, LEWIS JOSEPH, research pharmacist, scientist; b. Paterson, N.J., Apr. 26, 1927; s. Alfred Elias and Rose (Sandow) L.; m. Barbara Rothstein, Dec. 20, 1953; children: Suzanne, Erica, Alex. BS in Pharmacy, Rutgers U., Newark, 1950, MS in Pharm. Chemistry, 1954; PhD in Pharm. Chemistry, U. Mich., 1957. Registered pharmacist, N.J., N.Y., Mich. Pharmacist Mack Drug Co., Paterson, N.J., 1950-52, Fried's Drugs, Paterson, 1952-54; lab. asst. Rutgers U. Coll. Pharmacy, Newark, 1952-54, U. Mich., Ann Arbor, 1954-57; rsch. pharmacist, project leader Lederle Labs., Pearl River, N.Y., 1955-67; dir. product R & D, Union Carbide Co., Greenburgh, N.Y., 1967-69; asst. dir. product R & D, Geigy Pharm., Suffern, N.Y., 1969-71; dir., sr. dir., sr. rsch. fellow Ciba-Geigy Pharm., Summit, N.J., 1971-84; disting. rsch. fellow Ciba-Geigy Corp., Summit, 1984-93, ret., 1993; pres. LJL Assocs. Inc, Pharm. R&D Cons., Montville, N.J., 1993—; Dean Lou Busse lectr. U. Wis., 1993; mem. USP exec. com., 1990-95; N.J. DURC, 1984-89; prin., chief cons. Cogent Pharm., 1997—. Editor: Dissolution Technology, 1971; contbr. over 40 articles to profl. jours; patentee in field. Recipient Disting. Alumnus award U. Mich., 1990. Fellow Acad. Pharm. Sci., Am. Assn. Pharm. Scientists; mem. Am. Pharm. Assn., Sigma Xi, Rho Chi, Phi Lambda Upsilon. Jewish. Achievements include 14 patents in field. Home and Office: LJL Assocs Inc 134 Ridge Dr Montville NJ 07045-9473

LEET, MILDRED ROBBINS, corporate executive, consultant; b. N.Y.C., Aug. 9, 1922; d. Samuel Milton and Isabella (Zeitz) Elowsky; m. Louis J. Robbins, Feb. 23, 1941 (dec. 1970); children: Jane, Aileen; m. Glen Leet, Aug. 9, 1974. BA, NYU, 1942; LHD (hon.), Coll. Human Svcs., 1988; LLD honoris causa, Marymount Coll., Tarrytown, N.Y., 1991; HHD, Lynn U., 1993; D Humanitarian Svc. (hon.), Norwich U., 1994; DHL, Conn. Coll., 1996. Pres. women's div. United Cerebral Palsy, N.Y.C., 1951-52; bd. dirs. United Cerebral Palsy, 1953-55; rep. Nat. Coun. Women U.S. at UN, 1957-64, 1st v.p., 1959-64, pres., 1964-68, hon. pres., 1968-70; sec., v.p. conf. group U.S. Nat. Orgns. at UN, 1961-64, 76-78, vice chmn., sec., 1962-64, mem. exec. com., 1961-65, 75—, chmn. hospitality info. svc., 1960-66; vice chmn. exec. com. NGO's UN Office Public Info., 1976-78, chmn. ann. conf., 1977; chmn. com. on water, desertification, habitat and environment Conf. NGO's with consultative status with UN/ECOSOC, 1976—; mem. exec. com. Internat. Coun. Women, 1960-73, v.p., 1970-73; chmn. program planning com., women's com. OEO, 1967-72; chmn. com. on natural disasters N.Am. Com. on Environment, 1973-77; N.Y. State chmn. UN Day, 1975; ptnr. Leet & Leet (cons. women in devel.), 1978—; co-founder Trickle Up Program, 1979—, co-pres., 1991—; mem. task force on Africa UN, 1995—. Contbr. articles to profl. jours.; editor UN Calendar & Digest, 1959-64, Measure of Mankind, 1963; editorial bd.: Peace & Change. Co-chmn. Vols. for Stevenson, N.Y.C., 1956; vice chmn. task force Nat. Dem. Com., 1969-72; commr. N.Y. State Commn. on Powers Local Govt., 1970-73; chmn. Coll. for Human Svcs. Audrey Colten Coll., 1985—; former mem. bd. dirs. Am. Arbitration Assn., New Directions, Inst. for Mediation and Conflict Resolution, Spirit of Stockholm; bd. dirs. Hotline Internat.; v.p. Save the Children Fedn., 1986-93; rep. Internat. Peace Acad. at UN, 1974-77, Internat. Soc. Cmty. Devel., 1977—; del. at large 1st Nat. Women's Conf., Houston, 1977; chmn. task force on internat. interdependence N.Y. State Women's Meeting, 1977; mem. Task Force on Poverty, 1977—; chmn. Task Force on Women, Sci. and Tech. for Devel., 1978; U.S. del. UN Status of Women Commn., 1978, UN Conf. Sci. and Tech. for Devel., 1979, Brazzaville Centennial Celebration, 1980; mem. global adv. bd. Internat. Expn. Rural Devel., 1981—; mem. Coun. Internat. Fellows U. Bridgeport, 1982-88; trustee overseas edn. fund LWV, 1983-91; v.p. U.S. Com. UN Devel. Fund for Women, 1983—; mem. Nat. Consultative Com. Planning for Nairobi, 1984-85; co-chmn. women in devel. com. Interaction, 1985-91; mem. com. of cooperation Interam. Commn. of Women, 1986; bd. dirs. Internat. Devel. Conf., 1991—; mem. UN task force informal sector devel Africa,1995—. Recipient Crystal award Coll. Human Svcs., 1983, Ann. award Inst. Mediation and Conflict Resolution, 1985, Woman of Conscience award Nat. Coun. Women, 1986, Temple award Inst. Noetic Scis., 1987, Presdl. Edn Hunger award, 1987, Giraffe award Giraffe Project, 1987, Woman of the World award Eng.'s Women Aid, 1989, Mildred Robbins Leet award Interaction, 1995; co-recipient Rose award World Media Inst., 1987, Human Rights award UN Devel. Fund for Women, 1987, (with Glen Leet) Pres.'s medal Marymount Manhattan Coll., 1988, Leadership award U.S. Peace Corps, Woman of Vision award N.Y.C. NOW, 1990, Matrix award Women in Comm., Inc., Spirit of Enterprise award Rolex Industries, 1990, Ann. award Interaction, 1990, Citation, Pres. Bush's Ann. Points of Light Award, 1992, Internat. Humanity award ARC Overseas Assn., 1992, Excellence award U.S. Com. for UNIFEM, 1992, Champion of Enterprise award Avon, 1994, Achievement award NYU-Washington Square Coll. Alumni Assn., 1995, Lizettte H. Sarnoff Vol. Svc. award Yeshiva U., 1996, Disting. Svc. award N.Y. African Studies Assn., 1996. Mem. AAAS, Women's Nat. Dem. Club, Women's Forum Inc., Cosmopolitan Club, Princeton Club. Home and Office: 54 Riverside Dr New York NY 10024-6509

LEET, RICHARD HALE, oil company executive; b. Maryville, Mo., Oct. 11, 1926; s. Theron Hale and Helen Eloise (Rutledge) L.; m. Phyllis Jean Combs, June 14, 1949; children: Richard Hale II, Alan Combs, Dana Ellen. B.S. in Chemistry, N.W. Mo. State Coll., 1948; Ph.D. in Phys. Chemistry, Ohio State U., 1952. Rsch. chemist Standard Oil Co., Whiting, Ind., 1953-64; dir. long-range and capital planning, mktg. dept. Am. Oil Co., Chgo., 1964-68; mgr. ops. planning, mfg. dept. Am. Oil Co., 1968-70; regional v.p. Am. Oil Co., Atlanta, 1970-71; v.p. supply Am. Oil Co., Chgo., 1971-74; v.p. planning and adminstrn. Amoco Chems. Corp., Chgo., 1974-75; v.p. mktg. Amoco Chems. Corp., 1975-77, exec. v.p., 1977-78, pres., 1978-83; dir. Amoco Corp., Chgo., 1983-91, vice chmn., 1991-92; retired, 1992; bd. dirs. Gt. Lakes Chem., Vulcan Materials Corp., ITW, Landauer, Inc. Former chmn. bd. mgrs. Met. YMCA, Chgo.; former pres. Boy Scouts Am.; former chmn. bd. Am. Indsl. Health Coun.; former bd. visitors Emory U., 1970-71; vice chmn. found. bd. Ohio State U; trustee Brenau U. With USNR, 1944-46. Mem. Am. Chem. Soc., Soc. Chem. Industry (exec. com.), Am. Petroleum Inst. (bd. dirs.), Société Industrielle de Chemie, Chem. Mfrs. Assn. (dir.), Phi Sigma Epsilon, Gamma Alpha. Office: Lighthouse Acres PO Box 1686 Gainesville GA 30503-1686

LEETCH, BRIAN JOSEPH, hockey player; b. Corpus Christi, Tex., Mar. 3, 1968. Student, Boston Coll. With N.Y. Rangers, 1986—; mem. U.S. Olympic hockey team, 1988, Team USA for 1991 Can. Cup Tournament, Stanley Cup championship team, 1994. Named mem. U.S. Coll. first-team All-Am. team, 1987, Sporting News NHL Rookie of Yr., 1989, Player of the Year, Hockey East, 1986-87, Rookie of the Year, 1986-87, Sporting News All-Star team, 1991-92; recipient Calder Meml. trophy for NHL Rookie of Yr.,1988, 1989, James Norris Meml. trophy for best defenseman, 1991, 92, Conn Smythe trophy, 1993-94. Office: NY Rangers Madison Sq Garden 4 Pennsylvania Plz New York NY 10001*

LEETE, WILLIAM WHITE, artist; b. Portsmouth, Ohio, June 12, 1929; s. Bernard Emerson and Lois Trowbridge (Denison) L.; m. Doris Louise Knight, Sept. 19, 1952; children: Amy MacDonald, Robin Schodt. B.A., Yale U., 1951, B.F.A., 1955, M.F.A., 1957. Mem. faculty dept. art U. R.I., Kingston, 1957-95, prof. emeritus, 1995; acting dept. chmn. U. R.I., 1968, 69-70, 76. Represented in permanent collections, De Cordova Mus., Lincoln, Mass., Cleve. Mus., Worcester Mus., R.I. Hosp., Trust Bank, also various pvt. collections. Served with USMC, 1951-53. Mem. AAUP, Coll. Art Assn., Siggraph. Home: 202 Silver Lake Ave Wakefield RI 02879-4231 Office: U RI Dept Art Kingston RI 02881

LEETS, PETER JOHN, outplacement consulting firm executive; b. London, Mar. 12, 1947; came to U.S., 1948; s. Earl Edward and Doris Eileen L.; m. Anne E. Shahinian, May 15, 1982. BS in Mktg., Ind. U., 1969. Salesman Ortho Pharm. Corp., Raritan, N.J., 1969-74; account mgr. Revlon Inc., Indpls., 1974-76; regional dir. Revlon Inc., Cleve., 1976-79; field sales mgr. Revlon Inc., Bay Village, Ohio, 1979-83; nat. field sales mgr. Binney & Smith, Bethlehem, Pa., 1983-85; v.p., dir. sales Dell Pub. Co., Inc., N.Y.C., 1985-87; exec. v.p. Geneva Corp., Irvine, Calif., 1987-88; pres. Geneva Cos., Costa Mesa, Calif., 1988-90; exec. v.p. Exec. Assets Corp., Irvine, Calif., 1990-91; pres. Exec. Assets Corp., 1992-94; mng. prin. Right Assocs., Irvine, Calif., 1994—; bd. dirs. Career Beginnings, Career Transition Ptnrs., Constl. Rights Found. Chairperson Orange County Econ. Outlook Conf.; bd. dirs. Forum for Corp. Dirs., PIHRA Found. Fellow Outplacement Inst.; mem. Internat. Assn. Career Mgmt. Profls. (bd. dirs.), Profls. Human Resources Assn., Ind. U. Alumni (life), U. Calif. Irvine Chancellor's Club (bd. dirs.), Delta Chi. Office: Right Assocs 3333 Michelson Dr Ste 400 Irvine CA 92612-1684

LEEVER, HAROLD, chemical company executive; b. Detroit, May 21, 1914; s. Guy Harold and Mary (MacGregor) L.; m. Ruth Ann Salter, Oct. 5, 1935; children: Suzanne Hart, Thomas, John, Daniel, Andrew. BSChemE, Mich. State U., 1936; PhD (hon.), Post Coll., 1947. From chief chemist to v.p. McDermid Inc., Waterbury, Conn., 1938-54, pres., 1954-77, chmn. bd., 1977—. Patentee in field. Chmn. bd. Post Coll., Waterbury, 1965—; chmn. United Way, Waterbury, 1959, 81. Recipient Hiram Hayden award Boy Scouts Am., Silver Beaver award Boy Scouts Am.; named Industrialist of Yr., Conn. chpt. United Ch. of Christ, Man of the Yr. Waterbury United Way, 1989, Outstanding Fund Raiser of Conn. Nat. Soc. Fund Raising Execs., 1988. Lodge: Rotary. Home: 366 Guilds Hollow Rd Bethlehem CT 06751-1607 Office: MacDermid Inc 245 Freight St Waterbury CT 06702-1802

LEEVY, CARROLL MOTON, medical educator, hepatology researcher; b. Columbia, S.C., Oct. 13, 1920; s. Isaac S. and Mary (Kirkl) L.; m. Ruth S. Barboza, Feb. 4, 1956; children: Carroll Barboza, Maria Secora. AB, Fisk U., 1941; MD, U. Mich., 1944; ScD (hon.), N.J. Inst. Tech., 1973, U. Nebr., 1989; HHD (hon.), Fisk U., 1981; M, Am. Coll. Physicians, 1991. Intern Jersey City Med. Ctr., 1944-45, resident, 1945-48, dir. clin. investigation, 1947-57; fellow Banting-Best Inst., U. Toronto, Ont., Can., 1953; research assoc. Harvard U. Med. Sch., Cambridge, Mass., 1959; assoc. prof. U. Medicine and Dentistry of N.J., 1960-64, prof., 1964, Disting. prof., 1990—; physician in chief Univ. Hosp., 1975-91; dir. Liver Ctr. U. Medicine and Dentistry N.J., 1983-85; dir. div. hepatology and nutrition N.J. Med. Sch., 1959-75, acting chmn. dept. medicine, 1966-68, chief of medicine, 1968-71, chmn. dept. medicine, 1975-91; disting. prof. medicine Univ. Hosp., physician in chief, 1975-91; acting chmn. Sammy Davis Jr. Nat. Liver Inst., 1984-86, pres., sci. dir., 1989—; dir. N.J. Med. Sch. Liver Ctr., 1991—; chief medicine VA Hosp., East Orange, N.J., 1966-71; cons. NIH, 1965—, FDA, 1970-80, VA, 1971—, Alcohol and Nutrition Found., 1970-80, Am. Liver Found., 1979-84; cons. Health Care Fin. Adminstrn., 1990—, mem. adv. com. on liver transplantation, 1991—; mem. Nat. Commn. on Digestive Disease, 1975-78; mem. expert com. on chronic liver disease WHO, 1978; mem. nat. adv. com. digestive disease HHS, 1989-93; chmn. monitoring com. VA Coop. Study on Alcoholic Hepatitis, 1989-94—, VA Rsch. Study on Colchicine Alcoholic Cirrhosis, 1994—; med. dir. Univ. Hosp. Liver Transplant Program, 1989—. Author: Practical Diagnosis and Treatment of Liver Disease, 1957, Evaluation of Liver Function in Clinical Practice, 1965, 2d edit., 1974, Liver Regeneration in Man, 1973, The Liver and Its Diseases, 1973, Diseases of the Liver and Biliary Tract, 1977, Guidelines for Detection of Drug and Chemical-Induced Hepatotoxicity, 1979, Alcohol and the Digestive Tract, 1981, Standardization of Nomenclature, Diagnostic Criteria and Prognosis for Diseases of the Liver and Biliary Tract, 1994; contbr. numerous articles to med., sci. jours.; patentee in field. Bd. dirs. U. Cape Town, South Africa, 1984—; active Cmty. Congl. Ch. Cmdr. USNR, 1954-59. E.V. Gabriel scholar, 1938, Kellog Med. scholar, 1942; recipient Modern Med. award, 1972, Edward Ill award, 1973, United Negro Coll. Fund award, 1980, Key to City of Newark, 1981, Key to City of Columbia, S.C., 1987, Key to City of Secaucus, N.J., 1981, 50th N.J. Achievement award U. Medicine and Dentistry N.J., 1995; 40th Anniversary Faculty Honoree, U. Medicine and Dentistry N.J., 1995. Mem. NAACP, ACP (publs. com. 1969-74, master), AMA (vice-chmn., chmn. program com. sect. on gastroenterology 1971-74), AAAS, Am. Assn. for Study Liver Diseases (pres. 1967-68, chmn. steering com. 1968-74, Disting. Svc. award 1991), Internat. Assn. for Study Liver (pres. 1970-74, chmn. criteria com. 1972—), Am. Gastroenterol. Assn. (edn. and tng. com. 1967-71), Assn. Profs. Medicine (Robert Williams Disting. Chmn. award 1991), Assn. Am. Physicians, Soc. Exptl. Biology and Medicine, Am. Soc. Clin. Nutrition, Am. Inst. Nutrition, Nat. Med. Assn. (award 1987, Centenial award 1995), Am. Fedn. Clin. Rsch., Assn. Acad. Minority Physicians (pres. 1986-88, chmn. bd. trustees 1988—, Disting. Achievement award 1995), Internat. Com. on Informatics in Hepatology (chmn. 1986—), Internal Hepatology Informatics Group (chmn. 1984-93), N.J. Acad. Medicine, N.J. Liver Study Group (chmn. 1996), Phi Beta Kappa, Alpha Omega Alpha, Sigma Pi Phi. Home: 35 Robert Dr Short Hills NJ 07078-1525 Office: UMDNJ Med School 100 Bergen St Newark NJ 07103-2407 *My goal has been to help improve quality of life of all people, the disadvantaged and advantaged. Efforts have been made through medical education and research to decrease the incidence and untoward effects of disease, as well as improve communication and the social environment.*

LEFCO, KATHY NAN, law librarian; b. Bethesda, Md., Feb. 24, 1949; d. Ted Lefco and Dorothy Rose (Fox) Harris; m. Stephen Gary Katz, Sept. 2, 1973 (div. May 1984); m. John Alfred Price, Nov. 24, 1984 (dec. Jan. 1989). BA, U. Wis., 1971; MLS, U. Wis., Milw., 1975. Rsch. asst. Ctr. Auto Safety, Washington, 1971-73; asst. to dir. Ctr. Consumer Affairs, Milw., 1973-74; legis. librarian Morgan, Lewis & Bockius, Washington, 1976-78; dir. library Mulcahy & Wherry, Milw., 1978; paralegal Land of Lincoln Legal Assistance, Springfield, Ill., 1979-80; reference and interlibrary loan librarian Sch. Medicine So. Ill. U., Springfield, 1980; reader svcs. librarian Wis. State Law Library, Madison, 1981-83; ref. librarian Mudge Rose Guthrie Alexander & Ferdon, N.Y.C., 1983-85; sr. legal info. specialist Cravath, Swaine & Moore, N.Y.C., 1985-86; asst. librarian Kaye, Scholer, Fierman, Hays & Handler, N.Y.C., 1986-89; head libr. Parker Chapin Flattau & Klimpl, N.Y.C., 1989-94; dir. library svcs. Winston & Strawn, Chgo., 1994—. Author: (with others) Mobile Homes: The Low-Cost Housing Hoax, 1973. Mem. Law Libr. Assn. Greater N.Y. (sec. 1989-91), Chgo. Assn. Law Librs., Am. Assn. Law Librs. Democrat. Jewish. Avocations: biking, backgammon, politics. Home: 474 N Lake Shore Dr Apt 2504 Chicago IL 60611-3440 Office: Winston & Strawn 35 W Wacker Dr Chicago IL 60601-1614

LEFEBVRE, ALAN J., lawyer; b. Akron, Colo., Mar. 17, 1953; s. Vern L. and Adeline V. (Molacek) L.; m. Eileen Helen Buhmann, Feb. 26, 1987. BA in Polit. Sci. with high honors and departmental distinction, U. Calif., Santa Barbara, 1975; JD, U. San Francisco, 1978. Bar: Calif. 1978, Nev. 1979, U.S. Dist. Ct. Nev. 1979, U.S. Ct. Appeals (9th cir.) 1979, U.S. Supreme Ct. 1992, U.S. Dist. Ct. (cen. dist.) Calif. 1994. Law clk. 8th Jud. Dist. Ct., Las Vegas, Nev., 1978-79; assoc. Jolly, Urga & Wirth, Las Vegas, 1979-80; assoc., ptnr. Beckley, Singleton, DeLanoy Jemison & List, Las Vegas, 1980-89; sr. ptnr. Lefebvre & Barron, Las Vegas, 1989—. Mem. Nev. Commn. on Jud. Discipline, Carson City, 1991—. Mem. Internat. Assn. Def. Counsel. Republican. Roman Catholic. Avocations: boating, fishing, classical music. Office: 301 Clark Ave Ste 600 Las Vegas NV 89101-6537

LEFEBVRE, GABRIEL FELICIEN, retired chemical company executive; b. N.Y.C., Feb. 29, 1932; s. Gabriel F. and Harriett Blanche (Terrill) L.; m. Doris Jeanette Germain, Oct. 26, 1952; children: David Marshall, Richard Terrill, Kathryn Louise. B.S., Webb Inst. Naval Arch., 1952. Registered profl. engr., Ky., Ohio. Ptnr. Leco, Inc., Paducah, Ky., 1962-63; engring. supr. B.F. Goodrich Chem. Group, Calvert City, Ky., 1963-76; plant mgr. B.F. Goodrich Chem. Group, Louisville, 1977-78; gen. mgr. Chlor-Alkali B.F. Goodrich Chem. Group, Cleve., 1978-82, v.p PVC intermediates, 1982-83, gen. mgr. PVC intermediates, 1982-83, v.p. facilities mgmt., 1983-85, pres. Convent Chem Corp., 1978-83, dir., 1978-83; v.p. LaPorte Chem. Corp. B.F. Goodrich Chem. Group, 1982-83; v.p. ops. Geon Vinyl div., 1985-87, v.p. regulatory affairs, 1987-91; tech. mgr. Abadan Petrochem Co., Tehran, Iran, 1976-77. Served to lt. USNR, 1952-56. Mem. ASME, Nat. Soc. Profl. Engrs. Episcopalian. Home: 492-6 Overlook Dr Aurora OH 44202

LEFEBVRE, GREN GORDON, school superintendent; b. Buffalo, May 2, 1943; s. Gordon and Anne B. (Finch-Noyes) L.; m. Mary Margaret Hill, Aug. 20, 1966; children: Lisa Jackman, Christopher. BS, Purdue U., 1966, MS, 1967, EdS, 1982. Lic. sch. supt., Ind. Tchr./coach Darlington (Ind.) High Sch., 1967-70, Coal Creek Cen. High Sch., New Richmond, Ind., 1970-71, North Montgomery High Sch., Crawfordsville, Ind., 1971-76; prin. Waynetown (Ind.) Elem.-Jr. High Sch., 1976-87, Northridge Mid. Sch., Crawfordsville, 1987-91; supt. North Montgomery Community Sch. Corp., Linden, Ind., 1991-96; prin. Lester B. Sommer Elem. Sch., 1996—; cons. on stress mgmt. Mem. Town of Darlington Town Bd., pres., 1977-85; bd. dirs. Montgomery County United Fund, 1984—, Youth Svcs. Bur., Crawfordsville, 1986-92, Montgomery County Boys Club, 1978-84, Montgomery County coun. Boy Scouts Am., 1980-82. Mem. Am. Soc. Notaries, Ind. Assn. Pub. Sch. Supts., Darlington Community Assn., Ind. High Sch. Athletic Assn., Am. Legion, Darlington Conservation Club, Lions, Elks, Phi Beta Kappa. Republican. Episcopalian. Avocations: antiques, travel, raising cats, reading. Home: PO Box 176 Darlington IN 47940-0176 Office: North Montgomery Cmty Sch Corp PO Box 70 Linden IN 47955-0070

LEFEBVRE, PEGGY ANDERSON, advertising executive; b. Springfield, Mo., Dec. 2, 1951; d. Paul William and Norma Jean (Turk) Anderson; m. Donald E. Lefebvre, July 25, 1980. BA in Graphic Arts cum laude, U. Ill., 1974; MBA, Pacific Western U., 1993. Coord. advt. and trade show Bell & Howell, Salt Lake City, 1971-74; designer, prodn. asst. Sta. KUTV, Salt Lake City, 1974; art dir. Associated Advt., Salt Lake City, 1977-80; owner, creative dir. Lefebvre Advt., Anaheim, Calif., 1980—; freelance designer various advt. agys., Chgo.; bd. dirs. Delmark Corp.; past guest lectr. advt. copywriting and bus. devel. Nat. U., Inc. Mag., Orange Coast Coll. One woman shows Ward Gallery, Chgo., 1974, Atrium Gallery, Salt Lake City, 1976. Past bd. dirs. MADD, Orange County Sexual Assault Network; mem. Anaheim Area Visitor and Conv. Bd., Western States Advt. Agy. Assn. Recipient Excellence in Creative Direction award, Bus. and Profl. Advt. Assn., 1989, 94, Outstanding Achievement in Advt. award Western Assn. Conv. & Visitor Burs, Award of Merit Bus. Comms. and Mktg. Assn. L.A., 1991, 95, Award of Excellence, 1995. Mem. DAR. Republican. Office: Lefebvre Advt 1547 E La Palma Ave Anaheim CA 92805-1614

LEFELHOCZ, IRENE HANZAK, nurse, business owner; b. Cleve., Nov. 10, 1926; d. Joseph J. and Gisella Elizabeth (Biro) Hanzak; m. Joseph R. Lefelhocz, Aug. 7, 1948; 1 child, Joseph R. III. RN, St. Luke's Hosp. Sch. Nursing, 1948; BSN, Case Western Res. U., 1963; MEd, John Carroll U., 1971; MSN, Case Western Reserve U., 1973. RN, Ohio, Ala. Pres., mgr. The Joseph House, Gadsen, Ala.; adminstrv. cons. The Episcopal Kyle Home, Gadsen; nurse cons. Ala. Dept. Health, Montgomery, Ala.; supr., evening and night nurse adminstr. Riverview Med. Ctr., Moragne Park, Gadsden; psychology therapist, counselor to inpatient population Mountain View Hosp., Gadsden, mem. spkrs. bur.; counselor Sch. Nursing, Holy Name of Jesus Med. Ctr. Mem. allocations com. United Way, Etowah County; active numerous other community orgns.; bd. dirs., vice chmn. Etowah County chpt. ARC. Mem. NEA, Ohio Edn. Assn., ARC (past pres.). Home: 173 Lakeshore Dr Gadsden AL 35906-8570 Office: Mountain View Hosp 3001 Scenic Hwy Gadsden AL 35904-3047

LEFER, ALLAN MARK, physiologist; b. N.Y.C., Feb. 1, 1936; s. I. Judah and Lillian G. (Gastwirth) L.; m. Mary E. Indoe, Aug. 23, 1959; children—Debra Lynn, David Joseph, Barry Lee and Leslie Ann (twins). BA, Adelphi Coll., 1957, Western Res. U., 1959; PhD (NSF fellow), U. Ill., Urbana, 1962. Instr. physiology, USPHS-NIH fellow Western Res. U., 1962-64; asst. prof. physiology U. Va., 1964-69, assoc. prof., 1969-71, prof., 1972-74; vis. prof. Hadassah Med. Sch., Jerusalem, 1971-72; prof., chmn. dept. physiology Jefferson Med. Coll., Thomas Jefferson U., Phila., 1974—; dir. Ischemia-Shock Research Inst., 1980-95; cons. Merck & Co., Upjohn Co., Genentech Inc., Syntex, Inc., Ciba-Geigy, NIH, Nitromed, Bristol-Myers Squibb, Cytel Corp.; Wellcome Found.; vis. prof. 1985-86, Pfizer vis. prof. cardiovascular medicine, 1995; Nat. Bd. of Med. Examiners, Step 1, 1993-95; vis. prof. U. Calif. San Diego, 1995-96. Author: Pathophysiology and Therapeutics of Myocardial Ischemia, 1977, Prostaglandins in Cardiovascular and Renal Function, 1979, Cellular and Molecular Aspects of Shock and Trauma, 1983; Leukotrienes in Cardiovascular and Pulmonary Function, 1985; mng. editor: Eicosanoids, 1988-93; cons. editor Circulatory Shock, 1973-80; field editor Jour. of Pharmacology and Exptl. Therapeutics Cardiovascular, 1994—; mem. editl. bd. Critical Care Medicine, Shock Am. Jour. Physiology, Endothelium, Cardiovasc. Pathology, Drug News and Perspectives; contbr. to World Book Ency. Sci. Yearbook, 1979; contbr. over 550 sci. articles to profl. jours. Active Acad. Com. on Soviet Jewry, 1970-95; chmn. United Jewish Appeal, 1973-74; coach basketball and baseball Huntingdon Valley Athletic Assn., 1975-78. Recipient Pres. and Visitor's prize in rsch. U. Va., 1970, Disting. Alumnus award U. Ill., 1996. Fellow Am. Coll. Cardiology; mem. AAAS, Am. Physiol. Soc., Am. Soc. Pharmacology and Exptl. Therapeutics, Internat. Heart Rsch. Soc., Am. Heart Assn. (established investigator 1968-73, fellow circulation coun., nat. grant rev. com. 1993-95), Pa. Heart Assn. (rsch. com.), Shock Soc. (chmn. membership com., pres. 1983-84, chmn. devel. com. 1985-89, chmn. internat. rels. com. 1993), Internat. Fed. Shock Socs. (coun. 1994—, pres. 4th internat. shock congress 1996—), Soc. Exptl. Biology and Medicine, Israel Soc. Physiology and Pharmacology, Phila. Physiol. Soc. (pres. 1978-79), Sierra Club, B'nai B'rith (Charlottesville chpt., v.p. 1967-68, chmn. Va. Hillel 1970-71), Sigma Xi. Democrat. Home: 3590 Walsh Ln Huntingdon Valley PA 19006-3226 Office: Thomas Jefferson Univ 1020 Locust St Philadelphia PA 19107-6731

LEFEVER, MICHAEL GRANT, state agency administrator; b. Lancaster, Pa., Sept. 12, 1947; s. Norwood Grant and Frances (Gillespie) LeF.; m. M. Malissa Burnette, 1989; 1 child, Grant Burnette. BA in English, Presbyn. Coll., 1969; MPA, U. S.C., 1976. Claims rep. Underwriters Adjusting Co., Columbia, S.C., 1972-73; project adminstr. CATAYTIC, Inc., Charlotte, N.C., 1973-75; dep. dir. S.C. Dept. Juvenile Placement and Aftercare, Columbia, 1977-81, dir., 1981; asst. commr. for adminstrn. S.C. Dept. Youth Svcs., Columbia, 1981-82, dep. commr., 1982-86; exec. dir. S.C. Worker's Compensation Commn., 1986—; interim commr. S.C. Dept. of Juvenile Justice, 1993; chmn. Serious and Violent Offender Study Com., Columbia, 1981-86; bd. dirs. State Agy. Dirs. Orgn., 1991-96, v.p. 1992, pres. 1993-95; bd. dirs. Ctr. for Cancer Treatment and Rsch. Richland Meml. Hosp., 1992, exec. com. 1994—, vice chmn., 1995-96, chmn., 1997, S.C. State Quality Network, 1992-95; cons. Gov.'s Children Coordinating Cabinet, Columbia, 1981-86. Pres. Palmetto State Alumni chpt. Theta Chi, Columbia, 1973-83, Columbia Area Alumni Assn., Presbyn. Coll., Columbia, 1979, Windcrest Villas Homeowners Assn., North Myrtle Beach, S.C., 1989-90; treas. Planned Parenthood Cen. S.C., 1988-91, Bd. Assocs., 1991—; mem. adv. com. on pub. adminstrn., exec. com. U. S.C., 1988—; mem. bd. trustees Presbyn. Coll., 1996—. Served with U.S. Army, 1970-71. Named Outstanding Pub. Adminstr., 1986. Mem. Nat. Youth Work Alliance (chmn. 1982-83), Am. Soc. for Pub. Adminstrn. (treas. S.C. chpt. 1987—), Mental Health Assn. Midlands, So. Assn. of Worker's Compensation Adminstrs. (exec. com. 1986—), Internat. Assn. Indsl. Accident Bds. and Commns. (chmn. adminstrn. and proc. com. 1989-93, exec. com. 1993—, sec. 1995—, pres. 1996), S.C. Youth Workers Assn. (bd. dirs. 1979-83), Presbyn. Coll. Alumni Assn. (bd. dirs. 1986—, pres. 1988-89, Outstanding Young Alumnus award 1981). Home: 2721 Wheat St Columbia SC 29205-2538

LEFEVRE, DAVID E., lawyer, professional sports team executive; b. Cleve., Oct. 25, 1944; s. Fay A. and Mary (Eaton) LeF. BA, Yale U., 1966; JD, U. Mich., 1971. Bar: N.Y., U.S. Dist. Ct. (so. and ea. dists.) N.Y. Assoc. Reid & Priest, N.Y.C., 1971-78, ptnr., 1979-92; owner Houston Astros Baseball Club, 1979-84, Cleve. Indians Baseball Club, 1984-86; dir. Tampa Bay Lightning, NHL; bd. dirs. TDC (USA), Inc., NHL Pension Soc.; chmn. bd. dirs. Chertsey Corp.; bd. govs. NHL, 1992—; bd. dirs. Fla. Sports Found., 1996—. Bd. dirs. Tampa Downtown Partnership; vol. Peace Corps, Uruguay, 1966-68. Recipient Spl. award Tampa Sports Club.; named Hon. Alumnus, Cleve. State U., 1985. Mem. ABA, Sports Lawyers Assn., Canyon Club (pres. Armonk, N.Y. 1986—), Alexis de Tocqueville Soc., Univ. Club of Tampa. Office: Tampa Bay Lightning 401 Channelside Dr Tampa FL 33602 Also: 303 E 57th St New York NY 10022-4001

LEFEVRE, ELBERT WALTER, JR., civil engineering educator; b. Eden, Tex., July 29, 1932; s. Elbert Walter Sr. and Hazie (Davis) LeF.; m. Joyce Ann Terry, Nov. 28, 1957; children: Terry Ann, Charmaine Rene, George Walter, John Philip. BS in Civil Engring, Tex. A&M U., 1957, MS in Civil Engring, 1961; PhD, Okla. State U., 1966. Registered profl. engr., Ark., Tex. Faculty Tex. A&M U., Bryan, 1958, Tex. Technol. Coll., Lubbock, 1959-63, Okla. State U., Stillwater, 1963-66, U. Ark., Fayetteville, 1966—; head dept. civil engring. U. Ark., 1971-82, dean engring., 1982-83; sr. v.p. Engring. Svcs., Inc., Springdale, Ark., 1973—; dir. Nat. Rural Transp. Study Ctr., 1992-96; mem. Ark. State Bd. Registration for Profl. Engrs. and Land Surveyors, 1984-96, pres., 1989, 94; mem. Nat. Coun. Examiners for Engring. and Surveying, 1984—, v.p. So. zone, 1991-93, mem. accreditation bd. engring. and tech., 1985-91. Served to 1st lt. AUS, 1953-56. Fellow ASCE (pres. Mid-South sect. 1972, chmn. dist. 14 1977-80, dir. dist. 14 1983-86, v.p. zone II 1996—), Inst. Engrs. of Ireland; mem. NSPE (v.p. profl. engrs. in edn. 1982, v.p. S.W. region 1984-86, pres. 1989-90), Transp. Rsch. Bd., Am. Soc. Engring. Edn. (pres. midwest sect. 1976-77), Ark. Soc. Profl. Engrs. (pres. 1979-80, Outstanding Ark. Engr. 1980) Masons, Rotary (pres. 1973), Sigma Xi, Chi Epsilon, Tau Beta Pi, Phi Beta Delta. Home: 300 Paradise Ln Springdale AR 72762-3832 Office: Univ Ark Dept Civil Engring Fayetteville AR 72701 *I owe a great debt to those whose efforts have provided me the opportunity to accomplish these things. Personal relationships dwarf the honors I have received.*

LEFEVRE, GREG, bureau chief; b. Los Angeles, Jan. 28, 1947; s. Robert Bazille and Anna Marie (Violé) L.; m. Mary Deborah Bottoms, July 10, 1971. AA, Valley Coll., 1970; BS, San Diego State U., 1972, postgrad. Asst. news dir. Sta. KDEO, San Diego, 1971-73; reporter Sta. KFMB-TV, San Diego, 1973-75; sr. reporter Sta. KDFW-TV, Dallas, 1976-81; news dir. Sta. KSEE-TV, Fresno, Calif., 1981-83; corr. Cable News Network, San Francisco, 1983-89, bur. chief, 1989—. Mem. AP Broadcasters, Soc. Profl. Journalists, Radio and TV News Dirs. Assn. Club: Dallas Press (v.p. 1978-81). Office: CNN Am Inc 50 California St Ste 950 San Francisco CA 94111-4606

LEFEVRE, PERRY DEYO, minister, theology educator; b. Kingston, N.Y., July 12, 1921; s. Johannes and Faye (McFerran) LeF.; m. Carol Baumann, Sept. 14, 1946; children: Susan Faye, Judith Ann, Peter Gerret. AB, Harvard U., 1943; BD, Chgo. Theol. Sem., 1946, DD, 1992; PhD, U. Chgo., 1951. Ordained to ministry Congl. Ch., 1946. Instr. religion Franklin and Marshall Coll., 1948-49; asst., then assoc. prof. religion Knox Coll., 1949-53, Fed. Theol. Sem., U. Chgo., 1953-61; prof. constructive theology Chgo. Theol. Sem., 1961-92, dean of faculty, 1961-81, acting dean, 1990-91. Author: The Prayers of Kierkegaard, 1956, The Christian Teacher, 1958, Introduction to Religious Existentialism, 1963, Understandings of Man, 1966, Philosophical Resources for Christian Thought, 1968, Conflict in a Voluntary Association, 1975, Understandings of Prayer, 1981, Aging and the Human Spirit, 1981, Radical Prayer, 1982; editor: Paul Tillich: The Meaning of Health, 1984, Spiritual Nurture and Congregational Development, 1984, Daniel Day Williams Essays in Process Theology, 1985, Pastoral Care and Liberation Praxis, 1986, Bernard Meland Essays in Constructive Theology, 1988, Creative Ministries in Contemporary Christianity, 1991, Modern Theologies of Prayer, 1995. Mem. Phi Beta Kappa. Address: 5757 S University Ave Chicago IL 60637-1507

LEFEVRE, THOMAS VERNON, retired utility company executive, lawyer; b. Dallas, Dec. 5, 1918; s. Eugene H. and Callie E. (Powell) L.; m. Lillian Herndon Bourne, Oct. 12, 1946; children: Eugene B., Nicholas R., Sharon A., Margot P. BA, U. Fla., 1939, LLB, 1942; LLM, Harvard U., 1946. Bar: Fla. 1945, N.Y. 1947, D.C. 1951, Pa. 1955, U.S. Supreme Ct. 1953. Atty. IRS and various firms, N.Y.C., Washington, and Phila., 1946-55; ptnr. Morgan, Lewis & Bockius, Phila., 1956-79; pres., chief exec. officer UGI Corp., Valley Forge, Pa., 1979-85, chmn., 1983-89; chmn. G.P. Hospitality, Inc., 1981—; mem. Commr.'s Adv. Group IRS, 1976-77. Bd. dirs. Zool. Soc. Phila., 1982-91, WHYY Inc., 1982-96; chmn. U. Arts, 1986-89; trustee Franklin Inst., 1980-89, Fox Chase Cancer Ctr., 1979-88. With USMC, 1942-46. Fellow ABA (vice chmn. govt. rels. sect. of taxation 1976-79), Am. Bar Found.; mem. Pa. Bar Assn., Merion Cricket Club, Merion Golf Club, Sankaty Head Golf Club, Nantucket Yacht Club. Episcopalian. Office: Fidelity Ct Bldg Ste 105 5 Radnor Corp Ctr Wayne PA 19087-5240

LE FEVRE, WILLIAM MATHIAS, JR., brokerage company executive; b. Muskegon, Mich., Dec. 22, 1927; s. William Mathias and Crystal (Atkinson) LeF.; m. Ada Marie Cannon, 1949 (div. 1973); children—Marie L. Keidel, Jeanne L. Van Vlandren, William Mathias III, Suzanne C. Goldman; m. Mathilda Bock Maguire, 1976. Grad., Phillips Exeter Acad., 1946; student, U. Mich., 1946-48. Floor ptnr. Arthur Wiesenberger & Co., N.Y.C., 1956-60; assoc. oddlot broker DeCoppet & Doremus, N.Y.C., 1961-64; v.p. Carter, Walker & Co. Inc., N.Y.C., 1964-68, Bruns, Nordeman & Co., N.Y.C., 1969-71; dir. research Sade & Co., Washington, 1972-73, Mack Bushnell & Edelman, N.Y.C., 1973-74; v.p. investment strategy Granger & Co., N.Y.C., 1974-80, Purcell, Graham & Co., N.Y.C., 1980-86; sr. v.p. market strategy Advest Inc., N.Y.C., 1986-91, Tucker Anthony Inc., N.Y.C., 1991-93, Sutro & Co., San Francisco, 1991-93; sr. market analyst Ehrenkrantz King Nussbaum Inc., N.Y.C., 1993—; mem. N.Y. Stock Exchange, 1958-64; assoc. mem. Am. Stock Exchange, 1960-62; speaker various colls., univs. and indsl. assns., 1977—. Editor: Monday Morning Market Memo, 1973—; contbr. market commentary radio and TV, 1980—. Mem. Assn. for Investment Mgmt. and Rsch., N.Y. Soc. Security Analysts. Home: 132 E 35th St New York NY 10016-3892 also: 78 Grassy Hill Rd Old Lyme CT 06371-1352 Office: Ehrenkrantz King Nussbaum Inc 598 Madison Ave New York NY 10022-1614

LEFF, ALAN RICHARD, medical educator, researcher; b. Pitts., May 23, 1945; s. Maurice D. and Grace Ruth (Schwartz) L.; m. Donna Rae Rosene, Feb. 14, 1975; children: Marni, Karen, Alison. AB cum laude, Oberlin Coll., 1967; MD, U. Rochester, 1971. Diplomate Am. Bd. Internal Medicine, Am. Bd. Pulmonary Disease. Intern U. Mich. Hosp., Ann Arbor, 1971-72, resident, 1974-76; fellow U. Calif.-San Francisco, 1976-77, postdoctoral fellow, 1977-79; asst. prof. medicine U. Chgo., 1979-85, assoc. prof.medicine and clin. pharm., 1985-89, prof. medicine, anesthesia and critical care and clin. pharm., 1989—, prof. cell physiology, 1992—, prof. pediatrics, 1993—, prof. pharm. and physical scis., 1993—, dir. pulmonary medicine service, 1984-87, dir. Pulmonary Function Lab., 1979-87, chief sect. pulmonary and critical care medicine, 1987—; dir. NIAID Asthma and Allergic Dis. Coop. Rsch. Ctr., Chgo., 1993—; advisor San Francisco Dept. Pub. Health, 1977-79, Chgo. Dept. Health, 1979—; bd. dirs. Chgo. Lung Assn., 1984-93. Cons. editor Jour. Clin. Invest., editorial bd. Am. Jour. Physiology, Jour. Applied Physiology; editor Am. Jour. Respir. Critical Care Medicine, 1994—; assoc. editor Am. Rev. Respiratory Disease, 1989-94, Pulmonary Pharm., 1987; contbr. articles to profl. jours. Served with USPHS, 1972-74. Recipient Citation of merit Chgo. Lung Assn., 1974; Leopold Schepp Found. fellow, 1967-69. Fellow Am. Coll. Chest Physicians; mem. Am. Fedn. Clin. Research (councilor 1983-86), Am. Soc. Clin. Investigation, Am. Physiological Soc., Cent. Soc. for Clin. Investigation, Assn. Am. Physicians, Sigma Xi. Avocation: music. Home: 5730 S Kimbark Ave Chicago IL 60637-1615 Office: U Chgo Pritzker Sch Medicine Div Biological Scis MC 6076 5841 S Maryland Ave Chicago IL 60637-1463

LEFF, DEBORAH, foundation executive; b. Washington, Oct. 25, 1951; d. Sam and Melitta (Jerech) L. AB, Princeton (N.J.) U., 1973; Jd, U. Chgo., 1977. Trial atty. Civil Rights divsn. U.S. Dept. Justice, Washington, 1977-79; dir. office of pub. affairs Fed. Trade Commn., Washington, 1980-81; sr. producer Nightline-ABC News, Washington and London, 1983-89, World News Tonight-ABC News, N.Y.C., 1990-91; pres. The Joyce Found., Chgo., 1992—, also bd. dirs.; bd. dirs. CARE, Inc.; chair Midwest Rhodes Scholars Selection Com., Chgo., 1992. Mem. Coun. on Founds. Office: The Joyce Found 135 S La Salle St Ste 4010 Chicago IL 60603

LEFF, ILENE J(OAN), management consultant, corporate and government executive,; b. N.Y.C., Mar. 29, 1942; d. Abraham and Rose (Levy) L.; BA cum laude, U. Pa., 1964; MA with honors, Columbia U., 1969. Statis./computer analyst McKinsey & Co., N.Y.C., 1969-70, rsch. cons., 1971-74, mgmt. cons., N.Y.C. and Europe, 1974-78; dir. exec. resources Revlon, Inc., N.Y.C., 1978-81, dir. human resources, 1981-83, dir. personnel, 1983-86; cons. APM Inc., 1986-88; mgmt. cons., The Estee Lauder Cos., 1988-92; dep. asst. sec. for mgmt. HUD, Washington, 1993-94; pres. Leff Mgmt. Consulting, 1995—; rsch. asst. U. Pa., Phila., 1964-65; employment counselor State of N.J., Newark, 1965-66; tchr., Newark, 1966-69; lectr. Grad. Program in Pub. Policy, New Sch. for Social Rsch., Wharton Sch., Duke U.; chmn. com. on employment and unemployment, mem. exec. com. Bus. Rsch. Adv. Coun., U.S. Bur. Labor Stats., 1980; sr. del. econ. rels. and trade Sino-U.S. Conf., 1986. Ops. coun. Jr. Achievement Greater N.Y., 1975-78; cons. Com. for Econ. Devel., N.Y. Hosp., Regional Plan Assn., Am. Cancer Soc.; vol. for dep. mayor for ops. N.Y.C., 1977-78. Mem. N.Y. Human Resource Planners (treas. 1984), Fin. Women's Assn. N.Y. (exec. bd., 1977-78, 83-84), The Fashion Group (treas. 1989). Contbr. issue papers and program recommendations to candidates for U.S. Pres., U.S. Senate and Congress, N.Y. State Gov., mayor N.Y.C. Office: 767 5th Ave New York NY 10153-0001

LEFF, JOSEPH NORMAN, yarn manufacturing company executive; b. N.Y.C., Dec. 17, 1923; s. Phillip and Lillian (Wiesen) L.; m. Joyce Hochberg, June 12, 1954 (div. 1958); 1 child, Julie; m. Juanita Hughey, Dec. 17, 1967; 1 child, Valerie. BS, Columbia U., 1944, AB, 1946. Treas. Nat. Spinning Co. Inc., N.Y.C., 1949-63, pres., chief exec. officer, 1963-83, chmn., chief exec. officer, 1983—. Mem. bd. visitors Columbia Coll., N.Y.C., 1987-92; trustee Park Ave. Synagogue, N.Y.C., 1987-95; bd. dirs., pres. 92d St. YM/YWHA, N.Y.C., 1994-97, chmn., 1997—; bd. dirs. Inst. Textile Tech., Va., 1982—. With U.S. Army, 1944-45. Mem. Woolknit Assocs. (bd. dirs.), Acrylic Coun. (pres. 1988-97), Harmonie Club (Pres. 1974-75) (N.Y.C.), Quaker Ridge Golf Club (Scarsdale, N.Y.). Jewish.

LEFF, SANDRA H., gallery director, consultant; b. N.Y.C., Dec. 24, 1939; d. I. Bernard and Rose (Kupfer) L. BA, Cornell U., 1960; MA, Inst. Fine Arts, N.Y.C., 1969. Editorial asst. Indsl. Design Mag., N.Y.C., 1960-61; instr., asst. Mus. of City of N.Y., 1962-65; assoc. print dept. Sotheby Parke Bernet, N.Y.C., 1969-73; rsch. asst. Daniel Chester French Exhibit, Washington, 1975-77; dir. Am. painting Graham Gallery, N.Y.C., 1977-93. Author: (exhbn. catalogs) Thomas Anshutz: Paintings, Watercolors and Pastels, 1979, Guy Pène du Bois: Painter, Draftsman and Critic, 1979, Helen Torr, 1980, John White Alexander: Fin-de-Siècle American, 1980, Jan Matulka & Vaclav Vytlacil, 1992. Ford Found. fellow, 1967. Mem. Phi Beta Kappa. Avocations: reading, traveling, jogging, film, photography.

LEFF, SANFORD ERWIN, cardiologist; b. Buffalo, Apr. 4, 1942; s. Fred and Minnie (Simon) L.; m. Carolyn Rosenfield (div.); children: Jonah, Alex; m. Cathleen Game, June 2, 1990. BA, U. Mich., 1964; MD, SUNY, Buffalo, 1968. Diplomate Am. Bd. Internal Med. Chief of cardiology Interfaith Med. Ctr., Bklyn., 1981—. Office: 47 Plaza St W Brooklyn NY 11217-3905

LEFFEK, KENNETH THOMAS, chemist, educator; b. Nottingham, Eng., Oct. 15, 1934; emigrated to Can., 1959, naturalized, 1966; s. Thomas and Ivy Louise (Pye) L.; m. Janet Marilyn Wallace, Sept. 26, 1958; children: Katharine, Geoffrey. B.S., Univ. Coll., London, 1956, Ph.D., 1959. Asst. prof. chemistry Dalhousie U., Halifax, N.S., 1961-67; assoc. prof. Dalhousie U., 1967-72, prof., 1972-94, dean grad. studies, 1972-90, prof. chemistry, 1990-94, ret., 1994; chmn. Atlantic Provinces Interuniv. Com. on Scis., 1975-77. Author: Sir Christopher Ingold, a Biography; contbr. articles on phys.-organic chemistry to profl. jours. Leverhulme fellow U. Kent (Eng.), 1967-68. Fellow Chem. Inst. Can., Royal Soc. Arts (London; chmn. Atlantic Can. chpt. 1987-91); mem. Chem. Soc. London, Chem. Inst. Can. (nat. dir. tech. and sci. affairs 1980-83, nat. v.p. 1985-86, pres. 1986-87). Home: 980 Kentwood Ter, Victoria, BC Canada V8Y 1A6

LEFFELL, DAVID JOEL, surgeon, medical administrator, dermatologist, educator, researcher; b. Montreal, Feb. 28, 1956; came to U.S., 1973; s. Allen Bernard and Freda (Deckelbaum) L. BS, Yale U., 1977; MD, McGill U., Montreal, 1981. Diplomate Am. Bd. Dermatology, Am. Bd. Internal Medicine. Resident in internal medicine Meml. Sloan-Kettering Cancer Ctr., N.Y.C., 1981-84; instr. medicine Cornell U. Sch. Medicine, N.Y.C., 1983-84; lectr., fellow dermatologic surgery U. Mich., Ann Arbor, 1987-88; resident in dermatology Yale U. Sch. Medicine, New Haven, 1984-86, assoc. prof. dermatology, plastic surgery and otolaryngology, 1988-96, chief Mohs micrographic surgery and laser surgery, 1988—, dir. Yale skin cancer detection program, 1988—, med. dir. faculty practice plan, 1996—; sci. advisor Nat. Hereditary Hemorrhagic Telangiectasia Found., New Haven, 1991—; bd. dirs. Am. Coll. Mohs Micrographic Surgery and Cutaneous Oncology. Contbg. editor: Jour. Dermatologic Surgery and Oncology; assoc. editor Med. and Surg. Dermatology; mem. editl. bd. Archives of Dermatology; assoc. editor: Geriatric Dermatology; inventor laser fluorescence device to measure photoaging; author: Manual of Skin Surgery. Recipient Frederic Mohs award Skin Cancer Found., 1988, 91. Mem. Conn. Dermatology Soc. (pres.). Home: 69 Mumford Rd New Haven CT 06515-2431 Office: Yale Sch Medicine PO Box 208059 New Haven CT 06520

LEFFERTS, GEORGE, writer, producer, director; b. Paterson, N.J.. BA in Engring., Drew U., 1940; BA in English, U. Mich., 1942. Exec. prodr., writer, dir. NBC, 1947-57; pres. George Lefferts Assocs., 1968—; exec. prodr. ABC, 1966-67, Time-Life Films, 1980-81; tchr. John Hopkins U., Balt., 1989-90, Rutgers U., 1992—; prodr., writer, dir. Network for Continuing Med. Edn., 1990—; program cons. ABC, 1981. Exhibited sculpture, Sculpture Gallery, N.Y.C., 1960; producer: series Report from America, U.S. Dept. State, Tactic, Am. Cancer Soc., others; (Recipient Nat. Media award 1961, Fame award 1962, Fgn. Press award 1963, Golden Globe award 1967, Plaudit award Producers Guild 1968, 69, Cine Golden Eagle award 1974, Peabody award 1970, 75, 1st prize San Francisco Film Festival 1970; nominee Humanitas Prize 1988); author: plays Nantucket Legend, 1960, The Boat, 1968, Hey Everybody, 1969; columnist N.Y. Observer, Litchfield County Times, 1984-87 (1st prize New England Journalism award, 1984, 85); also author mag. articles, works on piano method, syndicated columns, others; prodns. include Biographies in Sound (Peabody award 1956), NBC Theatre, (Ohio State award 1955), Kraft Theatre, Armstrong Circle Theatre, Studio One, Lights Out, Frank Sinatra Show; spl. program Pain, 1971, Bravo Picasso!, 1972, What Price Health; program NBC Investigative Reports, 1972 (Albert Lasker award), CBS, Ben Franklin Series (Peabody award 1975, Emmy award 1975), Ryan's Hope, 1977 (Emmy award 1977), Purex Specials, 1966 (Emmy award 1966), The People vs. Jean Harris, 1981; exec. prodr., writer, dir., NBC, Spls. for Women (2 Emmy awards 1965); series (Emmy award 1962), 1961 (Golden Globe award 1961); exec. prodr.: series Breaking Point, 1962-64 (Prodrs. Guild Plaudit award 1963), CBS, Smithsonian Spls., 1974-75, ABC, Wide World of Entertainment, 1973-74, Bing Crosby Prodns., 1962-64; exec. prodr.: Wolper Prodns., 1974-75, Time/Life Films, 1978-79; original films produced include: The Living End, 1959, The Stake, 1960, The Teenager, 1965, The Harness, 1972, The Night They Took Miss Beautiful, 1977, Bud & Lou, 1978, Mean Dog Blues, 1979, The Search for Alexander the Great, 1981, Dressed to Kill, 1980; prodr.: series Hallmark Hall of Fame, 1969-70, Never Say Goodbye, 1987 (Emmy award 1988, Humanitas award nomination 1988), TV play Teacher, Teacher, 1974 (Emmy award 1974). With AUS, 1942-45. William Rose scholar Drew U., 1940. Mem. NATAS, Am. Acad. Motion Picture Arts and Scis., Christopher Morley Knothole Assn. Club: South Bay Cruising (Babylon, (N.Y.).

LEFFERTS, GILLET, JR., architect; b. N.Y.C., May 6, 1923; s. Gillet and Helen Willets (Lambert) L.; m. Lucia Beverly Hollerith, Apr. 21, 1951; children: Helena Gillet (dec.), Robert Beverly, John Willets, Sarah Fox, David Hollerith. AB, Williams Coll., 1947; MFA, Princeton, 1950. Apprentice Moore & Hutchins, N.Y.C., 1947-48, 50-55; assoc. Moore & Hutchins, 1955-66, ptnr., 1967-72; ptnr. Hutchins, Evans & Lefferts, N.Y.C., 1972-89; mem. William A. Hall Partnership, Architecture and Planning, N.Y.C., 1990—; instr. Mechanics Inst., N.Y.C., 1955-58. Architect: master plan and ednl. facilities SUNY-Binghampton, 1956—, Buffalo, 1981-85; master plan Coll. Agr., Malaya, 1970, St. Johnland Nursing Home, L.I., N.Y., 1976, Clark Gymnasium, Cooperstown, N.Y., 1986, Nat. Baseball Hall of Fame and Mus. Expansion, Cooperstown, 1988-89, 93-94, Scholes Libr. Coll. Ceramics, Alfred U., 1992. Mem. zoning bd. appeals Town of Darien, Conn., 1961-69, mem. planning and zoning commn., 1969-77, chmn., 1973-77, mem. bd. selectmen, 1983-89; bd. dirs. Darien Hist. Soc., 1978-83, pres., 1982-83; trustee Darien Pub. Libr., 1991-97; bd. dirs. Darien Nature Ctr., 1997—. With USAAF, 1943-46. Decorated Air medal with oak leaf cluster. Fellow AIA; mem. Fairfield County Alumni Assn. Williams Coll. (v.p. 1965-67), Nat. Inst. Archtl. Edn. (chmn. bd. trustees 1963-65, treas. 1970-73), Delta Psi. Episcopalian. Clubs: Century Assn. (N.Y.C.), Williams (N.Y.C.); Norwalk (Conn.); Yacht. Office: 42 E 21st St New York NY 10010-7216

LEFFERTS, WILLIAM GEOFFREY, physician, educator; b. Towanda, Pa., Mar. 24, 1943; s. William LeRoy and Beatrice (Smith) L.; m. Susan Lynn Hiles, Oct. 31, 1970. B.A., Hamilton Coll., 1965; M.D., Hahnemann Med. Coll., 1969. Intern Hahnemann Hosp., 1969-70; resident in internal medicine Cleve. Clinic Hosp., 1970-73, chief med. resident, 1972-73; asst. prof. internal medicine Hahnemann Med. Coll., 1973-77; assoc. prof. Med. Coll. Pa., 1978-82, dir. primary care unit, 1978-82, dir. div. gen. internal medicine, 1979-82; staff physician Cleve. Clinic Found., 1982—. Fellow ACP. Office: 9500 Euclid Ave Cleveland OH 44195-0001

LEFFLER, CAROLE ELIZABETH, mental health nurse, women's health nurse; b. Sidney, Ohio, Feb. 18, 1942; d. August B. and Delores K. Aselage; children: Veronica, Christopher. ADN, Sinclair Community Coll., Dayton, Ohio, 1975. Cert. psychiat. nurse coord. Nurse Grandview Hosp, Dayton, 1961-76; substitute sch. nurse Fairborn (Ohio) City Schs., 1981-82; dir. nursing Fairborn Nursing Home, 1983; psychiat. nurse coord. Dayton Mental Health Ctr., 1984—; mem. exec. bd. 1199; chmn. disaster mental health com. ARC Ohio. Vol., instr., disaster health nurse ARC, chmn. State of Ohio disaster mental health com.; officer, leader, camp nurse for Girl Scouts, Boy Scouts; Ch. Parish Coun. Recipient Fleur de Lis award Girl and Boy Scouts, Svc. award ARC, Fairborn Mayor's Cert. of Merit for Civic Pride, State of Ohio Govs. award Innovation Ohio. Mem. ANA, Ohio Nurses Assn. Home: 29 W Bonomo Dr Fairborn OH 45324-3407

LEFFLER, MELVYN P., history educator; b. N.Y.C., May 31, 1945; s. Louis and Mollie (Fuchs) L.; m. Phyllis Koran, Sept. 1, 1968; children: Sarah Ann, Elliot. BS, Cornell U., 1966; PhD, Ohio State U., 1972. Asst. prof. Vanderbilt U., Nashville, 1972-77, assoc. prof., 1977-86; internat. affairs fellow Coun. Fgn. Rels. Dept. Def., Washington, 1979-80; prof. U. Va., Charlottesville, 1986-94, Edward R. Stettinius prof. history, 1994—, chmn. hist. dept., 1990—. Author: The Elusive Quest, 1979, A Preponderance of Power, 1992 (Bancroft, Ferrell & Hoover prizes 1993), The Specter of Communism, 1994; contbr. articles to profl. jours. Fellow Woodrow Wilson Internat. Ctr., 1979, Am. Coun. Learned Socs., 1984, Nobel Peace Inst., 1994. Mem. Am. Hist. Assn., Orgn. Am. Hists., Soc. Hists. Am. Fgn. Rels. (v.p. 1993, future pres., Bernath Article prize 1984). Jewish. Home: 1612 Concord Dr Charlottesville VA 22901-3135 Office: U Va History Dept Randall Hall Charlottesville VA 22903

LEFFLER, STACY BRENT, retired government employee; b. Quincy, Ill., May 22, 1944; s. Burl William and Eva Elaine (Wood) L.; m. Shirley Mazer, Oct. 6, 1970; children: Sean Alisha, Bar-El Haim. BS in Math., N.Mex. Inst. Mining & Tech., 1974; MA in Internat. Rels., N.Mex. State U., 1982; postgrad., U. N.Mex. Ops. rsch. analyst Dept. of the Navy, China Lake, Calif., 1974-76; ops. rsch. analyst Dept. of the Army, White Sands Missile Range, N.Mex., 1976-89, Ft. Bliss, Tex., 1989-94; chmn. Joint Svcs. Command and Control Decision Aids Working Group, 1991-92. With U.S. Army, 1963-67. Mem. NRA (life), Jewish War Vets., Mensa, Intertel, Pi Alpha Delta, Pi Sigma Alpha. Jewish. Avocations: shooting sports, scuba diving, computers, reading. Home: PO Box 742 Santa Teresa NM 88008-0742

LEFKO, JEFFREY JAY, hospital administrator; b. St. Paul, July 15, 1945; s Morris and Dorothy (Mindell) L.; m. Philomena M. Corno, Mar. 6, 1970 (div. Dec. 1984); children: Melissa Ann, Benjamin Scott, Ellen Rachael; m. Mary Wilson, Jan. 10, 1986 (div. June 1989); m. Susan H. Shockley, Jan. 5, 1990. BSBA with distinction, U. Nebr., 1967; M in Hosp. Adminstrn., Washington U., St. Louis, 1969. Adminstrv. resident St. John's Mercy Hosp., St. Louis, 1968-69; nat. fellow Health Services Adminstrn. Am. Hosp. Assn.-Blue Cross Assn., Chgo., 1969-70; v.p. planning/ops. Meth. Hosp. of Ind., Indpls., 1970-75; v.p. Jewish Hosp., St. Louis, 1975-78; v.p. planning Greenville (S.C.) Hosp. System, 1979-88; exec. cons. The Lash Group, Greenville, 1988-90; v.p. planning Union Meml. Hosp., Balt., 1990-93; v.p. planning and mktg. St. Joseph Med. Ctr., Balt., 1993—; adj. instr. Washington U., 1976-78; guest lectr. Duke U., Univ. S.C., Clemson U., Ind. U.; instr. Furman U., Greenville, 1982-84, Med. Univ. of S.C. 1989. Contbr. articles to profl. jours.; contbr. to (book) Guide to Strategic Plannin g for Hosps., 1981; mem. edit. bd. Health Care Strategic Mgmt., 1984—. Mem. Am. Hosp. Ass. (pres. Soc. for Hosp. Planning and Mktg. 1984-85), Am. Coll. of Health Care Execs., Carolinas Soc. of Hosp. Planning (founding mem.), Innocents Soc., Beta Gamma Sigma. Lodge: Rotary. Avocations: coaching boys' baseball, basketball clubs, reading, tennis, baseball card collecting. Office: St Joseph Med Ctr 7620 York Rd Baltimore MD 21204-7508

LEFKOVITS, ALBERT MEYER, dermatologist; b. N.Y.C., June 30, 1937; s. Aaron Melchoir and Muriel (Mark) L.; A.B., Cornell U., 1958; M.D. (Lederle research fellow), N.Y. Med. Coll., 1962; m. Cheryl Beth Kornberg, Apr. 25, 1971; children—Ari Nathan, Lauren Blair. Intern, Newark Beth Israel Hosp., 1962-63; resident in dermatology Kings County Hosp. Center, SUNY, Downstate Med. Center, Bklyn., 1963-65; chief resident dermatology Mt. Sinai Hosp., N.Y.C., 1965-66, research fellow in dermatology, 1966-67, asst. attending physician, 1966—; practice medicine specializing in dermatology, N.Y.C., 1966—; asst. attending physician Beekman-Downtown Hosp., N.Y.C., 1968-75; instr. dermatology Mt. Sinai Sch. Medicine, 1966-68, clin. asso. dermatology, 1968-73, asst. prof., 1974, acad. council, 1973-78, 1886—; instr. dermatology N.Y. Med. Coll., 1966-69. Alumni fund-raising chmn. Horace Mann Sch., 1976-78; treas. Mt. Sinai Alumni, 1988-90, sec., 1991-93, v.p., 1993-95, pres. 1995-97. Served to maj. M.C., AUS, 1969-71. Recipient Fredrick Wise Dermatology award N.Y. Acad. Medicine, 1965, Torch of Liberty award Anti-Defamation League, 1987, Maimonides award Keren Or Found. for Handicapped Blind Children, 1994; mem. med. adv. bd. Skin Cancer Found. Mem. Harvey Soc., Soc. Investigative Dermatology, Dermatology Found., Soc. Tropical Dermatology, Am. Acad. Dermatology (task force on therapeutics and FDA liaison com.), AMA, Internat. Soc. Human and Animal Mycology, Mycology Soc. of Ams., N.Y. Acad. Scis., Am. Physicians Fedn. (trustee, exec. com.), Jewish Chautaugua Soc. (life), Dermatology Soc. Greater N.Y. (pres.), N.Y. State Med. Soc., Cornell Alumni Assn. N.Y. (bd. govs. 1974-76) Med. Adv. Bd. Skin Cancer Found., 1986—. Jewish (dir. congregation Emanu-El men's club). Clubs: Harmonie, Town, Cornell (N.Y.C.), Friar's, Lawrence Yacht (fleet surgeon 1982-83, sec. 1984, treas. 1985, commodore 1987). Address: 1040 Park Ave New York NY 10028-1032

LEFKOWITZ, HOWARD N., lawyer; b. Utica, N.Y., Oct. 28, 1936; s. Samuel I. and Sarah Lefkowitz; m. Martha Yelon, June 16, 1958; children: Sarah, David. BA, Cornell U., 1958; LLB, Columbia U., 1963. Bar: N.Y. 1963, Fla. 1979, D.C. 1981. Ptnr. Proskauer Rose Goetz & Mendelsohn LLP, N.Y.C., 1963—; mem. tri-bar opinion com., editl. subcom. Editor Columbia Law Rev., 1963; author New York LLC Forms and Practice Manual, 1994. Served to lt. (j.g.) USN, 1958-61. Kent scholar Columbia U. Law Sch. Fellow Am. Coll. Investment Counsel; mem. ABA (mem. ltd. liability entity subcom. of bus. sect. 1993—), Assn. of Bar of City of N.Y. (chmn. com. on corp. law 1990-93), N.Y. County Lawyers Assn. (chmn. com. on comm. entertainment and arts-related law 1983-86). Office: Proskauer Rose Goetz & Mendelsohn LLP 1585 Broadway New York NY 10036-8200

LEFKOWITZ, IRVING, engineering educator; b. N.Y.C., July 8, 1921; s. Adolph and Celia (Berko) L.; m. Madelyn I. Moinester, July 3, 1955; children: Deborah, Daniel. B.S. in Chem. Engring., Cooper Union, 1943; M.S. in Instrumentation Engring., Case Inst. Tech., 1955, Ph.D., 1958. With J.E. Seagram & Sons, 1943-53, dir. instrumentation research, 1951-53; faculty Case Inst. Tech., 1953-87, prof. engring., 1965-87, prof. emeritus, 1987—, dir. research group in control of complex systems, 1960-85; acting chmn. systems engring. dept. Case Western Res. U., 1972-76, chmn., 1980-83; v.p. techs. devel. Control Soft, Inc., Cleve., 1994—; mem. sci. staff Internat. Inst. Applied Systems Analysis, Austria, 1974-75; Cons. in field, 1959—. Contbr. papers to profl. lit.; Editorial adv. bd.: Jour. Dynamic Systems, Measurement and Control, 1972-77. NATO postdoctoral fellow, 1962-63. Fellow IEEE, AAAS; mem. Systems Sci. and Cybernetics Soc. (adminstr. com. 1969-72), Am. Automatic Control Council (chmn. systems engring. com. 1968-69, Control Heritage award 1982), IFAC (vice-chmn. systems engring. com. 1975-78, chmn. com. 1978-81, vice chmn. tech. bd. 1981-84), IEEE Control Systems Soc. (chmn. control of indsl. systems tech. com. 1983-87 , bd. govs. 1985-86). Home: 3532 Meadowbrook Blvd Cleveland OH 44118-3659 Office: Case Western Res U Systems Engring Dept University Circle Cleveland OH 44106

LEFKOWITZ, JERRY, lawyer, accountant; b. N.Y.C., Jan. 3, 1945; s. Seymour Arthur and Edna (Mann) L.; children: David Scott, Deborah Lynn. BS in Econs., U. Pa., 1966; JD, Boston U., 1969. Bar: N.Y. 1970; CPA, N.Y., 1971. Tax mgr. Arthur Andersen & Co., N.Y.C., 1969-77, KMG Peat, Marwick, N.Y.C., 1977-82; sr. tax ptnr. Rosenblatt, Slavet & Radezky, CPA's, N.Y.C., 1982—; atty. Slavet & Lefkowitz RLLP, N.Y.C., 1982—. Avocations: tennis, golf. Home: 80 Arthur Ct Port Chester NY 10573-3124 Office: 292 Madison Ave New York NY 10017-6307

LEFKOWITZ, MARY ROSENTHAL, Greek literature educator; b. N.Y.C., Apr. 30, 1935; d. Harold L. and Mena (Weil) Rosenthal; m. Alan L. Lefkowitz, July 1, 1956 (div.); children: Rachel, Hannah; m. Hugh Lloyd-Jones, Mar. 26, 1982. BA, Wellesley Coll., 1957; AM, Radcliffe Coll., 1959, PhD, 1961; LHD (honoris causa), Trinity Coll., Hartford, Conn., 1996. Instr. Greek Wellesley (Mass.) Coll., 1960-63, asst. prof. Greek and Latin, 1964-69, assoc. prof. Greek and Latin, 1969-75, prof. Greek and Latin, 1975-79; Andrew W. Mellon prof. in the humanities Wellesley (Mass.) Coll, 1979—; vis. prof. U. Calif., Berkeley, 1978; vis. fellow St. Hilda's Coll., 1979-80, Corpus Christi Coll., 1991. Author: Heroines and Hysterics, 1981, Lives of the Greek Poets, 1981, Women in Greek Myth, 1986, First Person Fictions, 1991, Not Out of Africa, 1996; co-editor: Women's Life in Greece and Rome, 1982, 2d edit., 1992, Black Athena Revisited, 1996. Fellow NEH, 1979-80, 91, ACLS, 1972-73, Hon. fellow St. Hilda's Coll., Oxford, 1994—. Mem. Am. Philol. Assn. (bd. dirs. 1974-77), Class Assn. New Eng. (pres. 1972-73). Home: 15 W Riding St Wellesley MA 02181-6914 Office: Wellesley Coll 106 Central St Wellesley MA 02181-8203

LEFKOWITZ, ROBERT JOSEPH, physician, educator; b. N.Y.C., Apr. 15, 1943; s. Max and Rose (Levine) L.; children: David, Larry, Cheryl, Mara, Joshua; m. Lynn Tilley, May 26, 1991. B.A., Columbia U., 1962, M.D., 1966. Diplomate: Am. Bd. Internal Medicine. Assoc. prof medicine Duke U., Durham, N.C., 1973-77, prof. medicine, 1977—, James B. Duke prof. medicine, 1982—, prof. biochemistry, 1985—; investigator Howard Hughes Med. Inst., Durham, 1976—; vis. prof. NYU, 1996. Author: Receptor Binding Studies in Adrenergic Pharmacology, 1978, Receptor Regulation, 1981, Principles of Biochemistry, 1983. Am. Heart Assn. established investigator, 1973-76, Basic Rsch. prize, 1990; recipient Young Scientist award Passano Found., 1978, George Thorn award Howard Hughes Med. Inst., 1979, Oppenheimer award, 1982, Gordon Wilson medal Am. Clin. and Climatol. Assn., 1982, Lita Annenberg Hazen award, 1983, outstanding rsch. award Internat. Soc. for Heart Rsch., 1985, H.B. van Dyke award Coll. Physicians and Surgeons Columbia U., 1986, Steven C. Beering award Ind. U. Sch. Medicine, 1986, N.C. award in Sci., 1987, Internat. award Gairdner Found., 1988, Novo Nordsk Biotech. award, 1990, Biomed. Rsch.award Assn. Am. Med. Colls., 1990, City of Medecin award, N.C., 1991, Columbia U. Coll. of Physicians and Surgeons Alumnus award for Disting. achievements in medicine, 1992, Bristol-Meyers Squibb award for Disting. achievement in Cardiovascular rsch., 1992, The Giovani Lorenzini Prize for Basic Biomedical Rsch., 1992, Columbia U. coll. of Physicians and Surgeons Joseph Mather Smith Prize, 1993, The Endocrine Soc. Gerald D. Aurbach Lectr. award Inst. of Medicine NAS, 1995, J. David Gladstone Insts. Disting. Lecture award, 1996, Bio/Tech. Winter Symposia Feodor Lynen award, Ciba award Hypertension Rsch. award, 1996. Mem. Am. Soc. Biol. Chemists, Am. Soc. Clin. Investigation (counselor, 1982-85, pres.-elect 1986-87, pres. 1987-88), Assn. Am. Physicians (treas. 1989-94), Am. Soc. Pharmacology and Exptl. Therapeutics (John J. Abel award 1978, Goodman and Gilman award 1986), Endocrine Soc., Am. Fedn. Clin. Research (sec.-treas. 1980-83, mem. nat. council 1978-83), NAS, Am. Acad. Arts and Scis., Japanese Biochem.soc. (hon.), Am. Heart Assn. Basic Rsch. Soc. Office: Duke Univ Med Ctr PO Box 3821 Durham NC 27710-0001

LEFLER, LISA JANE, anthropologist and social sciences educator; b. Gastonia, N.C., Jan. 21, 1959; d. Buddy Allen and Jean (Nations) L. AA in Liberal Arts, Montreat-Anderson Coll., 1979; BA in Psychology, Appalachian State U., 1981; MA in Edn., Western Carolina U., 1988, EDS, 1991; PhD Anthropology, U. Tenn., 1996. Instr. social scis. Southwestern C.C., Sylva, N.C., 1988-93, Haywood C.C., Clyde, N.C., 1990-96; instr. history Western Carolina U., Cullowhee, N.C., 1989, 93, vis. instr. anthropology Dept. Continuing Edn., 1990, instr. dept. anthropology, continuing edn. instr., 1990-96, instr. regional history, 1990-93, lectr. new beginning program, 1989-92, instr. anthropology, 1991—; also counselor asst. upward bound program Western Carolina U., 1989, lectr. new beginning program, 1989-92; chem. dependency curriculum writer, grant writer, lectr. Unity Regional Treatment Ctr./Indian Health Svc., Cherokee, N.C., 1990, 93—; adj. asst. prof. anthropology, U. Okla., 1996, adj. asst. prof. anthropology Appalachian State U., Boone, N.C., 1997; grant writer Indian Health Promotion Dept., U. Okla., 1996; mem. subcom. Project Healthy Cherokee. Chair Mountain Heritage Ctr. Mus. Vols.; former bd. dirs. Catch the Spirit of Appalachia, Inc. Tennis scholar Montreat-Anderson Coll., 1977-79. Mem. Am. Anthrop. Assn., Southeastern Anthrop. Soc., Appalachian Studies Assn. Mem. Worldwide Ch. of God. Avocations: tennis, walking, camping reading. Home: PO Box 662 Dillsboro NC 28725

LEFLER, WADE HAMPTON, JR., ophthalmologist; b. Statesville, N.C., Feb. 27, 1937; s. Wade Hampton and Eunice Trudye (Chilcoat) L.; AB, U. N.C., Chapel Hill, 1959; MD, Bowman Gray Sch. Medicine, 1963; m. Katherine Webb Davis, Apr. 1, 1961; children: Elizabeth Ashley Wilson, Rosemary Kirsten, Ririe. Med. intern N.Y. Hosp., Cornell Med. Center, 1963-64; resident in ophthalmology Duke U. Med. Center, 1966-69; practice medicine specializing in ophthalmology, Hickory, N.C., 1969—; partner Graystone Eye, Ear, Nose, Throat Center, Hickory, 1974—; clin. assoc. prof. ophthalmology Duke Med. Center, 1969—; mem. staff Catawba Meml. Hosp., Hickory, Frye Regional Med. Ctr., Hickory, Western Carolina Center, Morganton, N.C., Duke Eye Center, Durham, N.C., Oteen VA Hosp., Asheville, N.C. Trustee Catawba Meml. Hosp., 1990-94. Served to capt. M.C., U.S. Army, 1964-66. Duke U. Med. Center grantee, 1968-70; diplomate Am. Acad. Ophthalmology. Mem. AMA, N.C. Med. Soc., Catawba County Med. Soc., Med. Alumni Assn. Bowman Gray Sch. Medicine (pres. 1993, Disting. Svc. award 1995), Phi Beta Kappa, Alpha Omega Alpha. Presbyterian. Club: Lake Hickory Country. Home: 1260 6th St NW Hickory NC 28601-2408 Office: PO Box PO Box 2588 Hickory NC 28603-2588

LEFLY, DIANNE LOUISE, research psychologist; b. Denver, July 17, 1946; d. Gordon Eugene Boen and Elizabeth (Welsh) Tuveson. AB, U. No. Colo., 1968; MA, U. Colo., 1980; PhD, U. Denver, 1994. Classroom tchr. Adam County Sch. Dist. #12, Thornton, Colo., 1968-77; rschr. John F. Kennedy Child Devel. Ctr., Denver, 1979-81, U. Colo. Health Scis. Ctr.,

1981-89, U. Denver, 1989—; cons. Colo. Dept. Edn., 1997—, Colo. Dept. Pub. Health and Environ., 1997—. Contbr. articles to profl. jours. Mem. Colo. Rep. Party, Denver, 1968—. Scholarship U. No. Colo., 1964-68; fellowship U. Denver, 1989. Mem. Mensa. Republican. Avocations: computer activities, dancing, hiking, reading. Home: 8650 W 79th Ave Arvada CO 80005-4321 Office: U Denver 2155 S Race St Denver CO 80210-4638

LEFRAK, EDWARD ARTHUR, cardiovascular surgeon; b. Newark, Apr. 21, 1943; s. Bernard David and Lillian (Hollander) L.; m. Trudy Glaser, Aug. 8, 1973; children: Lisa, Allison, Shayna, Ashley, Mikaela. BA cum laude, SUNY, Buffalo, 1965; MD, Ind. U., 1969. Diplomate Am. Bd. Surgery, Am. Bd. Thoracic Surgery. Intern in gen. surgery Baylor Coll. Medicine Affiliated Hosps., Houston, 1969-70, resident in gen. surgery, 1970-75; resident cardiopulmonary surgery U. Oreg. Med. Sch., 1975-77; chief cardiac surgery Va. Heart Ctr. Fairfax Hosp., Falls Church, Va., 1977—, dir. cardiac surgery rsch.; pres. Cardiovascular and Thoracic Surgery Assocs., P.C., Annandale, Va.; clin. assoc. profl. surgery Uniformed Svcs. U. Health Scis., Bethesda, Md.; asst. clin. prof. surgery Georgetown U. Sch. Medicine, Washington; active staff Cardio-Thoracic Surgery Svc. Nat. Naval Med. Ctr., Bethesda; asst. prof. surgery U. Oreg. Med. Sch., 1977; mem. courtesy staff Alexandria (Va.) Hosp.; con. Clin. Ctr. NIH, Bethesda; mem. med. adv. com. Washington Regional Transplant Consortium; dir. heart and lung transplantation Va. Heart Ctr. Fairfax, 1986-86; mem. critical care com. Fairfax Hosp., 1978-93; mem. com. for clin. investigation involving human beings Baylor Coll. Medicine, 1974; jour. cons. Chest, Cancer Chemotherapy Reports. Author: Cardiac Valve Prostheses, 1979; prodr. films in field; contbr. articles to profl. publs. Fellow ACS, Am. Coll. Cardiology, Am. Coll. Chest Physicians, Internat. Coll. Surgeons; mem. AMA, Am. Heart Assn. (bd. dirs. No. Va. chpt. 1978), Albert Starr Surg. Soc., Fairfax County Med. Soc., Med. Soc. Va., Met. Washington Soc. Thoracic and Cardiovascular Surgeons, Michael E. DeBakey Internat. Cardiovascular Soc., Soc. Thoracic Surgeons, Internat. Soc. for Heart and Lung Transplantation, So. thoracic Surg. Assn., Washington Area Transplant Soc., Am. Assn. Thoracic Surgery, Colegio Interamericano de Médicos y Cirujanos. Address: 3301 Woodburn Rd Annandale VA 22003

LEFRAK, SAMUEL J., housing and building corporation executive; b. N.Y.C., Feb. 12, 1918; s. Harry and Sarah (Schwarz) LeF.; m. Ethel Stone, May 14, 1941; children: Denise, Richard, Francine, Jacqueline. Grad., U. Md., 1940; postgrad., Columbia U., Harvard U.; LLD (hon.), U. of Studies, Rome, 1971, N.Y. Law Sch., 1974, Colgate U., 1979; HHD (hon.), Pratt Inst., 1988, U. Md., 1990, Queens Coll., 1994, Mich. State U., 1995. Pres. Lefrak Orgn., 1948—, chmn. bd., 1975—; creator, sponsor, builder Lefrak City, Battery Park City, Gateway Pla., Newport Complex; mem. adv. bd. Sta. WHLI, 1955; commr. Landmarks Preservation Commn., N.Y.C., 1966; commr. pub. works Borough Manhattan, 1956-58; commr. Interstate Sanitation Commn., 1958; Saratoga Springs Commn., 1962—; mem. adv. bd. Chem Bank.; guest lectr. Harvard Grad. Sch. Bus. Adminstrn., 1971, Yale, 1975, NYU, 1977; guest speaker Fin. Women's Assn., N.Y., 1975; guest lectr. Princeton U., U. Haifa, 1983, Oxford U., 1984, Pratt Inst., 1987, Harvard U., 1987, Columbia Sch. Bus., 1988, Wharton Sch. Bus., 1989, Sch. Bus. NYU, 1989; speaker UN, 1988; featured speaker Instl. Investment Real Estate Conf., 1975, Fed. Home Loan Bank Conf., 1990; guest lectr. Japanese Govt., Finnish Govt., Switzerland, 1967; U.S. del. Internat. Conf. Housing and Urban Devel., Switzerland, 1967; dir. N.Y. World's Fair Corp., 1964-65, N.Y. Indsl. Devel. Corp., 1975—, chmn. bd. L.I. Post; pres. N.Y.C. Comml. Devel. Corp., 1967-71, chmn., 1971—; founding mem. World Business Coun., Inc., 1970; mem. Pres.'s Com. Employment Handicapped; spl. cons. urban affairs State Dept., 1969; mem. adv. coun. Real Estate Inst., N.Y. U., 1970—; mem. gov. fin. Pres.'s Club U. Md., 1971, com. N.Y. State Traffic Safety Council, 1966; bd. visitors Sch. Law, Columbia U., 1983; commr. Saratoga-Capital dist. N.Y. State Park and Recreation Commn., 1973; mem. real estate coun. exec. com. Met. Mus. Art, 1982; mem. N.Y.C. Pub. Devel. Corp., Nat. Energy Coun., U.S. Dept. Commerce, Mayor's Com. on Housing Devel., N.Y.C., 1974—; mem. exec. com. Citizen's Budget Com. for N.Y.C., Inc., 1975—; mem. Gov. Cuomo's Adv. Coun., 1983, N.Y. State Gov.'s Task Force on Housing, 1974; establish Lefrak Lecture Series, U. Md., 1982; creator, developer residential and business property. Vice chmn.-at-large ARC, N.Y.; mem. U.S. com. UN Orgn., 1957; chmn. nat. bd. Histadrut, 1967—; mem. Israel Bonds Prime Minister Com., 1980; dir. Ronald McDonald House, 1986; chmn. bldg. com. Saratoga Performing Arts Ctr.; mem. Fifth Ave. Assn.; dir., chmn. real estate div. Greater N.Y. Fund; hon. com. AAU; Queens chmn. United Greek Orthodox Charities, 1973; chmn. Celebrity Sports Night-Human Resources Ctr., 1973-74, Sports Assn. Hebrew U. of Jerusalem, 1979; patron Met. Mus. Art; sponsor Israel Philharm. Orch., Jan Groth Exhibit, Guggenheim Mus.; trustee, dir. Beth-El Hosp.; bd. dirs. USO, Citizens Housing and Planning Council, N.Y., 1957—, Interfaith Movement, Diabetics Found., Queens Cultural Assn., Consumer Credit Counseling Svc. Greater N.Y., Astoria Motion Picture and TV Ctr. Found.; trustee N.Y. Law Sch., Queens Art and Cultural Ctr., Jewish Hosp. at Denver, N.Y Civic Budget Com.; trustee, med. adv. bd. Brookdale Hosp. Med. Ctr., Pace U.; mem. exec. bd. Greater N.Y. couns. Boy Scouts Am.; founder Albert Einstein Sch. Medicine; mem. Bretton Woods Com.; bd. govs. Invest-in-Am. Nat. Coun.; mem. task force on energy conservation Div. Community Housing, 1981—; mem. com. N.Y. State Traffic Safety Coun., 1966; chmn. Scandinavia Today, 1981—; bd. visitors Sch. Law Columbia U., 1983; mem. adv. bd. The Explorer's Club, 1984; mem. Nat. Com. on U.S.-China Rels. Inc.; bd. dirs. Inst. Nautical Archaeology; trustee Queens Coll., 1989; adv. dir. Met. Opera, 1990; conf. bd. Keynote Address-Annual Fin. Seminar, 1987; mem. Lambda Alpha Internat. bd. trustees Guggenheim Mus., 1993; mem. bd. trustees Dana Farber Cancer Inst. Harvard Med. Sch., 1992. Decorated officer Order of Lion of Finland, 1980, Medal of Parliament, 1988; officer Order St. John of Jerusalem Knights of Malta, 1982; Order of the North Star of Sweden, 1982; comdr. Royal Norwegian Order of Merit, 1987; Chevalier des Artes et des Lettres medal, France, 1996; recipient Mayor N.Y.C. award outstanding citizenship, 1960; Nat. Boys Club award, 1960; Citizen of Year award B'nai Brith, 1963; Am. Achievement award, 1984; Disting. Achievement award, 1967; Man of Year award VFW, 1963; Brotherhood award NCCJ, 1964; Chief Rabbi Herzog gold medal; Torah Fellowship citation Religious Zionist Am., 1966; John F. Kennedy Peace award, 1966; Man of Year award Bklyn. Community Hosp., 1967; Builder of Excellence award Brandeis U., 1968; Master Builder award N.Y. Cardiac Ctr., 1968; Disting. Citizen award M Club Found. U. Md., 1970; Disting. Alumnus award U. Md. Alumni Assn., 1970; Disting. Citizen and Outstanding Community Svc. award United Way, 1986; Am. Achievement award Ency. Britannica, 1984; Am. Eagle award nat. coun. Invest-in Am., 1972; Exec. Sportsman award Human Resources Ctr., 1973; Archtl. award Fifth Av. Assn., 1974; Excellence in Design award Queens C. of C., 1974; Flame Truth award Fund Higher Edn., 1986; LeFrak Forum Mich. State U., 1997; elected hon. citizen Md., 1970; Citizen of Yr. award Bklyn. Philharm. Orch., 1983; dedication of Samuel J. LeFrak Hall U. Md., 1982, LeFrak Gymnasium, Amherst Coll., 1986, LeFrak Terrace Explorers Club, 1996, LeFrak Moot Ct., N.Y. Law Sch., 1990, LeFrak Meadow, N.Y.C., 1991, LeFrak Concert Hall, Queens Coll., LeFrak Gallery and Sculpture Terrace, Guggenheim Mus.; LeFrak Lecture Series at U. Md. established, 1982, LeFrak Learning Ctr. Temple Emanuel, 1995; LeFrak Gymnasium and Scholarship Barnard Coll., 1997; Comdr. of the Royal Norwegian Order of Merit, presented by King Olav V, 1987; Rough Riders award Boy Scouts Am., 1987; Torch of Progress Assoc. Builders and Owners Greater N.Y.; award Soc. Fgn. Consuls, 1988, Gold medal and Man of Yr. award Israel Bonds Found., 1990, Developer of the Yr. Associated Builders and Owners of Greater N.Y., 1990; award Assn. Graphics Arts, 1990, Disting. Citizen of World award UN, 1994, Alumni Hall of Fame award U. Md., 1995; named to Nat. Sales Club Hall of Fame, 1990, Songwriter's Hall of Fame, 1997. Mem. Sales Execs. Club N.Y. (dir.), United Hunts Racing Assn., Philharm. Symphony Soc. N.Y., Explorers Club (dir.), Newcomen Soc. U.S., Phi Kappa Phi, Tau Epsilon Phi (established Samuel J. LeFrak scholarship award 1975). Clubs: U. Md. Pres.'s (mem. Gov. N.Y. fin.), Lotos (bd. dirs. 1975—, Merit award 1973), Grand Street Boys, Friars (dir. Found.), Advertising, Economic, Downtown Athletic (N.Y.C.); Town, Turf and Field; Cat Cay (Nassau, Bahamas); Xanadu Yacht (Freeport, Grand Bahamas); Palm Bay (Miami Beach, Fla.); Seawane; Ocean Reef (Key Largo); Sag Harbor Yacht (L.I.). Lodges: Masons (32d degree), Shriners. Office: Lefrak Orgn Inc 97-77 Queens Blvd Rego Park NY 11374-3317

LEFRANC, MARGARET (MARGARET SCHOONOVER), artist, illustrator, editor, writer; b. N.Y.C., Mar. 15, 1907; d. Abraham and Sophie (Teplitz) Frankel; m. Raymond Schoonover, 1942 (div. 1945). Student, Art Students League, N.Y.C., Kunstschule des Westerns, Berlin, NYU Grad. Sch., Andre L'Hote, Paris, Acad. Grande Chaumiere, Paris. Tchr. art Adult Edn., Los Alamos, 1946, Miami (Fla.) Mus. Modern Art, 1975-76. Exhibited in one-person shows at Mus. N.Mex., Santa Fe, 1948, 51, 53, Phlbrook Art Ctr., Tulsa, 1949, 51,, Okla. Art Ctr., 1950, Recorder Workshop, Miami, 1958, St. John's Coll., Santa Fe, 1993, 97, A Lifetime of Imaging (works on paper), 1921-95, Figurative Works, 1920-30, Cline Fine Art Gallery, 1997; group shows include Salon de Tuileries, Paris, 1928, 29, 30, Art Inst. Chgo., 1936, El Paso Mus. Art, 1964, Mus. Modern Art, 1974, North Miami Mus. Contemporary Art, 1984, Miami Collects, 1989, Women's Caucus Invitational, 1990, Gov.'s Gallery, Santa Fe, 1992, Gene Autry Western Heritage Mus, 1995, Gilcrease Mus., Tulsa, 1996, Mus. N.Mex. Santa Fe, 1996, Brigham Young U., Provo, Utah, 1996; in collections at Beiles Artes, Mexico City, Mus. Fine Arts, Santa Fe. Bd. dirs., pres. Artist Equity of Fla., 1964-68; v.p. Miami Art Assn., 1958-60; founder, bd. dirs. Guild Art Gallery, N.Y.C., 1935-37. Recipient Illustration award Fifty Best Books of Yr., Libr. of Congress, Hon. Mention award Rodeo Santa Fe, Mus. N.Mex., others, Gov.'s award for Excellence and Achievement in the Arts, 1996.

LEFSTEIN, NORMAN, lawyer, educator; b. Rock Island, Ill., July 16, 1937; s. George M. and Rose Lefstein; m. Leah M. Lefstein, Apr. 15, 1962 (div.); children: Lisa, Adam, Susan. Student, Augustana Coll., 1955-58; LL.B., U. Ill., 1961; LL.M., Georgetown U., 1964. Bar: Ill. 1961, D.C. 1963. Asst. U.S. atty. Washington, 1964-65; project dir. Nat. Council Juvenile Ct. Judges, Chgo., 1965-68; staff mem. Dept. Justice, Washington, 1968-69; dep. dir. Pub. Defender Service for D.C., 1969-72, dir., 1972-75; assoc. prof. law U. N.C., Chapel Hill, 1975-79, prof., 1979-87; dean, prof. Ind. U. Sch. Law, Indpls., 1988—; vis. prof. Duke U., 1976-77, fall 1978; chmn. Ind. Pub. Defender Commn., 1990—. Bd. editors U. Ill. Law Forum, 1959-61. Mem. ABA (council criminal justice sect. 1979-88 , chmn. 1986-87, reporter Project to Update ABA Criminal Justice Standards 1977-85), Nat. Legal Aid and Defender Assn. (bd. dirs., mem. exec. com. 1975-80), Order of Coif. Home: 3405 Bay Point Dr Indianapolis IN 46240-2442 Office: Ind U Sch Law 735 W New York St Indianapolis IN 46202-5222

LEFTON, DONALD E., hotel executive. Vice chmn. Carnival Hotels & Resorts, Miami, Fla. Office: Carnival Hotels & Resorts 3250 Mary St Miami FL 33133-5232

LEFTON, HARVEY BENNETT, gastroenterologist, educator, author; b. Cleve., May 17, 1944; s. Nat L. and Edith (Waintrup) L.; m. Paulette Lipkowitz, Aug. 24, 1968; children: Allison Rachel, Daniel Adam. BS, U. Pitts., 1966; MD, Jefferson Med. Coll., Phila., 1970. Cert. Nat. Bd. Med. Examiners, Am. Bd. Internal Medicine, Am. Bd. Gastroenterology. Intern medicine Cleve. Clinic, 1970-71, resident internal medicine, 1971-72, fellow gastroenterology, 1972-74; chief gastroenterology Scott AFB, Belleville, Ill., 1974-76; asst. clin. prof. medicine Med. Coll. Pa., Phila., 1976-78, assoc. clin. prof. medicine, 1978-81, clin. prof. medicine, 1981—; cheif gastroenterology Frankford Hosps., Phila., 1997—; cons. gastroenterology Friends Hosp., Belmont Psychiat. Hosp., Pa., 1980—; chief gastroenterology Frankford Hosp., 1997—. Contbr. articles to profl. jours. Maj. USAF, 1974-76. Named Outstanding Vol. Physician, Med. Coll. Pa., 1994. Fellow ACP, Am. Coll. Gastroenterology, Coll. Physicians Phila.; mem. Am. Soc. Gastroenterology Endoscopy, Pa. Soc. Gastroenterology, Omicron Delta Kappa. Home: 559 Long Ln Huntingdon Valley PA 19006-2935 Office: 2 Bala Plz Ste Il 22 Bala Cynwyd PA 19004-1501

LEFTWICH, JAMES STEPHEN, management consultant; b. Stevenage, Eng., Nov. 30, 1956; came to U.S., 1957; s. James Wright and Del Maureen (Thomson) L.; m. Carol Petersen, Nov. 7, 1980 (div. Jan. 1982). AA in Criminal Justice, Butte Coll., Oroville, Calif., 1981; BA, S.W. U., 1993. Lic. internat. accredited safety auditor; cert. hazardous material specialist. Prodn. mgr. Artistic Dyers Inc., El Monte, Calif., 1976-80; mgr. loss control and risk mgmt. Mervyn's Dept. Stores, Hawyard, Calif., 1982-91; dir. risk mgmt. Save Mart Corp., Modesto, Calif., 1991-93; v.p. ops. I.C.S. Corp., San Ramon, Calif., 1993-94; pres. I.C.S. Corp., Irvine, Calif., 1994-95; v.p. Health Systems of Am. Internat., 1995-96; COO CHSI Ins. Svcs., Walnut Creek, Calif., 1996—; cons. R.I.M. Assocs., Walnut Creek, Calif., 1989-96; instr. Claims Mgmt. Inst., 1993; bd. dirs. Am. Real Estate Bur., Walnut Creek. Scriptwriter, tech. advisor 12 safety videos; contbr. articles on safety and risk mgmt. to profl. publs. Res. police officer Cotati (Calif.) Police Dept., 1983-85; fundraiser United Way, Hayward, 1986, Am. Found. for AIDS Rsch., L.A., 1990; bd. dirs. Bay Area Safety Coun., Oakland, Calif., 1987-88; trustee Calif. Safety Ctr., Sacramento, 1990-91, dir., 1991—. Mem. Am. Soc. for Safety Engrs., Nat. Safety Mgmt. Soc., Nat. Fire Protection Assn., Risk and Ins. Mgmt. Soc., Nat. Assn. Chiefs Police, Nat. Environ. Tng. Assn. Avocations: snow skiing, swimming, running, biking. Office: CHSI Insurance Svcs 2121 N California Blvd Ste 290 Walnut Creek CA 94596-7305

LEFTWICH, ROBERT EUGENE, oncological nursing educator; b. Lubbock, Tex., July 2, 1940; s. Eugene L. and Georgia (Kirkpatrick) L. BSN, Baylor U., 1963; MS, Northern Ill. U., 1970; PhD, Clayton U., 1977. Head nurse Baylor U. Med. Ctr., Dallas, 1963-64; supr. U.S. Air Force Nurse Corps, Fla., Tex., 1964-67; instr. nursing Cameron State Coll., Lawton, Okla., 1967-68, Rock Valley Coll., Rockford, Ill., 1968-70; dir. ADN program Kankakee (Ill.) Community Coll., 1970-71, dean health edn., 1971-72; chmn. dept. adult nursing Med. Coll. Ga., Augusta, 1972-75; asst. prof. U. Louisville, 1975-77; prof. nursing Governors State U., University Park, Ill., 1977—; bd. mem. Community Health Planning Bd., Kankakee, 1970-72; curriculum cons. Purdue U., Westville, Ind., 1983; oncology nursing cons. Ingalls Hosp., Harvey, Ill., 1979-85; grievance chairperson Univ. Profls. of Ill., University Park, 1981-83. Author: Nursing, Nutrition and the Adult Client, 1974, Humanistic Teaching Strategies and Nursing Students' Attitudes about Death and Dying, 1977, Self-Care Guide for the Cancer Patient, 1989; primary rschr.: Acuity Levels in an Adult Oncology Unit, 1981, Sexual Harrassment in Nursing Education, 1995; contbr. articles to profl. jours. Organist Trinity United Meth. Ch., Chgo., 1985-87; organist, choirmaster Bethel Covenant Ch., Flossmoor, Ill., 1987-96; organist Immanuel Ch., Evergreen Park, Ill., 1996—. 1st lt. U.S. Air Force, 1963-67. Mem. Univ. Profls. Ill., Am. Guild Organists, Sigma Theta Tau. Avocations: ch. organist, choirmaster, concert organist, pianist, tenor soloist. Office: Governors State U Dept Nursing University Park IL 60466

LEFTWICH, RUSSELL BRYANT, allergist, immunologist, consultant; b. Glasgow, Ky., Nov. 1, 1951; married; 2 children. BSChemE, Arizona State U., 1974; MD, Vanderbilt U., 1978. Diplomate Am. Bd. Allergy and Immunology, Am. Bd. Internal Medicine, Nat. Bd. Med. Examiners. Resident dept. internal medicine Vanderbilt U., Nashville, 1978-81, clin. asst. prof. medicine, 1984—; staff physician Green Hosp., La Jolla, Calif., 1981-83; dir. allergy ctr. Bapt. Hosp.; mem. group practice in allergy and clin. immunology, 1983-84, pvt. practice, 1985—; chief divsn. allergy U. Tenn.-Bapt. Hosp. Internal Medicine Residency, 1989—. Contbr. articles to profl. jours. Chmn. Comm. & Public Svc. Com., 1997—. Summer Rsch. grantee Ariz. Heart Assn., 1974; fellow Scripps Clinic and Rsch. Found., 1981-83, chief clin. fellow, 1982-83. Fellow Am. Acad. Allergy and Immunology (sinusitis com., vice chmn. computers and tech. com.), Am. Coll. Chest Physicians; mem. AMA, Am. Coll. Allergy and Immunology (mem. pub. rels. com., regional coord. pub. rels. network, chmn. computers and tech. com. 1994—), Tenn. Med. Assn. (del. ho. dels. 1990—), Tenn. Soc. Allergy and Immunology (pres. 1989-92), Nashville Acad. Medicine (chmn. young physicians com. 1990-91, mem. comm. and pub. svc. com.), Nashville Soc. Internal Medicine, Nashville Allergy Soc., Southea. Soc. Allergy and Immunology, So. Med. Assn., Alpha Omega Alpha, Tau Beta Pi. Office: Allergy & Asthma Assocs 300 20th Ave N Ste 100 Nashville TN 37203-2132

LEGAN, ROBERT WILLIAM, securities analyst; b. Eugene, Oreg., Mar. 9, 1936; s. John William and Mertha Evelyn (Bagent) L.; m. Janis Carolyn Fosnaugh, Apr. 28, 1957; children: Tracy Legan Kurtz, Lori Legan Mondshine, Dale William. BS, Oreg. State U., 1959, MS in Nuclear Engring., 1965; PhD ChemE, U. Idaho, 1969. Registered profl. engr., Tex. Engr. GE, Richland, Wash., 1959-64, Battelle Northwest, Richland, 1959-71, Phillips Petroleum, Idaho Falls, Iowa, 1964-67; v.p. Houston Rsch., 1973-77, Subsurface Disposal Co., Houston, 1977-79; pres., owner Photox Internat. Inc., Texas City, Tex., 1979-87; commodity and stock market analyst, Texas City, 1987—; pub. The Oracle Stock and Commodity newsletters; presenter investment seminars. Developer computer program forcasting price and time for markets. Republican. Avocations: gardening, bridge. Home and Office: PO Box 2639 Texas City TX 77592-2639

LÉGARÉ, HENRI FRANCIS, archbishop; b. Willow-Bunch, Sask., Can., Feb. 20, 1918; s. Phillippe and Amanda (Douville) L. B.A., U. Ottawa, 1940; theol. student, Lebret, Sask., 1940-44; M.A., Laval U., 1946; Dr. Social Sci., Cath. U. Lille, France, 1950; LL.D. (hon.), Carleton U., Ottawa, 1959, Windsor (Ont.) U., 1960, Queens U., Kingston, Ont., 1961, U. Sask., 1963, Waterloo (Ont.) Luth. U., 1965, U. Ottawa, Can., 1984; Doctor of Univ., U. of Ottawa. Ordained priest Roman Cath. Ch., 1943; prof. sociology Laval U., 1947, U. Ottawa, 1951; exec. dir. Cath. Hosp. Assn. Can., 1952-57; dean faculty social scis. U. Ottawa, 1954-58, pres., 1958-64; provincial Oblate Fathers, Winnipeg, Man., 1966-67; bishop of Labrador, 1967-72; archbishop Grouard-McLennan, Alta., 1972-96. Contbr. articles to profl. jours. Chmn. Canadian Univs. Found., 1960- 62. Decorated grand cross merit Order Malta, 1964; order merit French Lang. Assn. Ont., 1965. Mem. Assn. Canadian Univs. (pres. 1960-62), Can. Conf. Cath. Bishops (pres. 1981-83), Internat. Assn. Polit. Sci. Office: Archbishop's House, CP 388, McLennan, AB Canada T0H 2L0

LEGASPI, JESUSA CRISOSTOMO, agricultural scientist, entomologist; b. Pasay, Manila, Philippines; came to U.S., 1987; m. Benjamin Antonio Legaspi Jr.; 1 child, Michelle Elaine. BS, U. Philippines, Los Banos, 1978; MSc, U. Newcastle-Upon-Tyne, Eng., 1984; PhD, Purdue U., 1991. Rsch. asst. Philippine Coun. for Agr., Los Banos, 1980-82, Internat. Rice Rsch. Inst., Los Banos, 1985-86; grad. rsch. asst. Purdue U., West Lafayette, Ind., 1987-91; rsch. assoc. USDA, Weslaco, Tex., 1992-95; asst. prof. Tex. Agrl. Experiment Sta., Weslaco, 1995—. Contbr. articles to profl. jours. Sci. judge Jackson Elem. Sch., McAllen, Tex., 1992; vol. Ind. State Fair, Indpls., 1990; mem. Fil-Am Assn., Rio Grande Valley, Tex., 1993. David Ross fellow Purdue U., 1987; Colombo Plan scholar Brit. Coun., 1982. Mem. Entomol. Soc. Am., Philippine Assn. of Entomologists, Sigma Xi, Gamma Sigma Delta. Roman Catholic. Avocations: swimming, bowling, reading, travel. Office: Tex Agrl Experiment Sta 2415 E Us Highway 83 Weslaco TX 78596-8344

LEGATE, STEPHEN, ballet dancer; b. Portland, Oreg.. Student, Marylynn's Ballet Arts, Riverside, Calif., Nat. Ballet Sch. With Nat. Ballet Can.; soloist San Francisco Ballet, 1991-92, prin. dancer, 1992—. Appeared in ballets Nanna's Lied, Rubies, The Concert, La Pavane Rouge, Seeing Stars, Handel- a Celebration, Beads of Memory, The Four Seasons, Nutcracker, La Fille mal gardee, Connotations, The End, Don Quixote, Nutcracker, La Ronde, Voluntaries, Daphnis and Chloe, Sphinx, Tagore, Swan Lake, Pastorale, Forgotten Land, Transfigured Night, Blue Snake, The Second Detail, Le Corsaire, Onegin; appeared in TV prodns. The Merry Widow, Alice. Named Best Male Dancer, Internat. Competition for Erik Bruhn Award, 1989. Office: San Francisco Ballet 455 Franklin St San Francisco CA 94102-4438*

LEGATES, GARY A., secondary education educator; b. Wilmington, Del., May 3, 1951; s. James M. and Elmira E. (Dulin) LeG.; m. Ninette O. Mellott, Nov. 20, 1976. BA, Western Md. Coll., 1974, postgrad., 1978-81; MA in Classics, Pa. State U., 1975. Cert. tchr., Md. Fgn. lang. tchr. Westminster (Md.) H.S., 1977—; guest lectr. Western Md. Coll., 1977—. Deacon Westminster Bapt. Ch., 1981-83, 85-87, Sunday sch. supt., 1989-93; bd. dirs. Am. Coun. of Blind of Md., 1988-92. Mem. Am. Classical League, Classical Assn. Atlantic States, Nat. Assn. Blind Tchrs. (sec. 1987-91, 2nd v.p. 1995—), Alumni Assn. Md. Sch. for Blind (pres. 1989-93). Republican. Avocations: swimming, reading, singing, playing instruments, collecting old music. Home: 530 Poplar Ave Westminster MD 21157 Office: Westminster HS 1225 Washington Rd Westminster MD 21157-5803

LEGATES, JOHN CREWS BOULTON, information scientist; b. Boston, Nov. 19, 1940; s. Eber Thomson and Sybil Rowe (Crews) LeG.; m. Nancy Elizabeth Boulton, Apr. 28, 1993. BA in Math., Harvard U., 1962. Edn. svcs. mgr. Telcomp Dept. Bolt Beranek & Newman, Cambridge, Mass., 1966-67; v.p. Washington Engring. Svcs., Cambridge, 1967-69; v.p., co-founder Cambridge Info. Systems, 1968-69; v.p., founder Computer Adv. Svc. to Edn., Wayland, Mass., 1966-72; exec. dir. Educom Interuniversity Communications Coun., Boston, 1969-72; founder, mng. dir. Program on Info. Resources Policy Harvard U., 1973—, founder, pres. Ctr. Info. Policy Rsch., 1978—; mem. Arpanet NWG, core Arpanet/Internet design team, 1970-72; cons. in field. Contbr. articles to profl. jours. Bd. dirs. Nat. Telecommunications Conf., Washington, 1979. Kent fellow, 1964. Mem. NAS/NRC (telecommunications privacy, reliability and integrity panel), IEEE, Nat. Sci. Found., Soc. for Values in Higher Edn. Episcopalian. Club: Nashuba Valley Hunt (Pepperell, Mass.) (pres. 1974-80). Avocations: sailing, fox-hunting, mountaineering, classical music. Home: PO Box 6331 Lincoln MA 01773-6331

LEGENDRE, LOUIS, biological oceanography educator, researcher; b. Montreal, Que., Can., Feb. 16, 1945; s. Vianney and Marguerite (Venne) L. BA, U. Montreal, 1964, BSc, 1967; PhD, Dalhousie U., Halifax, 1971. Postdoctoral fellow U. Paris VI, Villefranche-sur-Mer, 1971-73; rsch. assoc. U. Laval, Quebec City, Que., 1973, asst. prof., 1974-77; assoc. prof. U. Laval, Quebec City, 1977-81, prof., 1981—; v.p. Groupe interuniversitaire de recherches océanographiques du Que., 1989—; group chmn. Natural Scis. and Engring. Rsch. Coun. Can., Ottawa, 1989-92. Co-author: (with P. Legendre) Numerical Ecology, 1983; contbr. articles to profl. jours. Vice-pres. Model Environ., Liege, Belgium, 1993—. Decorated Knight of Malta; recipient Léo-Pariseau award Assn. canadienne-française pour l'avancement des sciences, 1985, Michel-Jurdant award, 1986; Killam Rsch. fellow Can. Coun., 1996—. Fellow Royal Soc. of Can., mem. Am. Soc. Limnology and Oceanography. Office: U Laval, Dept Biology, Sainte Foy, PQ Canada G1K 7P4

LEGERE, DIANE J., art association administrator, alpaca breeder; b. Inglewood, Calif., July 18, 1952; d. Charles E. and June L. Brown; m. Richard M. Legere, July 21, 1984. BA, San Jose State U., 1976. Regional mgr. Am. Internat. Grou Subs., Seattle, 1987-92; exec. dir. Western Art Assn., Ellensburg, Wash., 1992—; dir., curator Clymer Mus. Art, Ellensburg, 1996—; bd. dirs., past 2d v.p., past chair human resources The Clymer Mus. of Art, Ellensburg, Wash., 1992-95, dir., curator, 1996—; bd. dirs., chair promotions com. Laughing Horse Summer Theatre, 1995. Author, editor: (newsletter) Brush Strokes, 1993—. Mem. Tourism Task Force, 1992, Tourism C. of C., Ellensburg, Wash., 1995. Theatre Arts scholar Kiwanas, 1970. Mem. Alpaca Breeders of Am., Wash. Athletic Club. Avocations: painting, sculpture, writing, gardening, antique roses. Office: Western Art Assn PO Box 893 Ellensburg WA 98926-3112 Also: Clymer Mus Art 416 N Pearl St Ellensburg WA 98926

LEGERE, LAURENCE JOSEPH, government official; b. Fitchburg, Mass., Jan. 2, 1919; s. Laurence Joseph and Aurore Hermine (Bean) L.; m. Mary Yesley Keville, Oct. 25, 1973. B.S., U.S. Mil. Acad., 1940; M.P.A., Harvard, 1948, A.M. (Littauer fellow), 1949, Ph.D., 1951. Commd. 2d lt. U.S. Army, 1940, advanced through grades to col., 1959; asst. prof. internat. relations U.S. Mil. Acad., 1945-47; student Nat. War Coll., 1960-61; asst. to mil. rep. of Pres. U.S., Washington, 1961-62; sr. staff mem. NSC, Washington, 1962-63; ret., 1966; sr. staff mem. Center for Internat. Studies, M.I.T., Cambridge, 1966-67; dir. office nat. security studies Bendix Corp., Ann Arbor, 1967-68; dir. internat. and social studies div. Inst. Def. Analyses, Arlington, Va., 1968-74; def. advisor U.S. Mission to NATO, Brussels, 1974-89, ret., 1989; mem. policy panel on Europe UN Assn., 1967-69. Contbg. author, editor: The President and the Management of National Security, 1969; Contbr. numerous articles on foreign and def. policies to profl. jours. Decorated Silver Star, Legion of Merit, Bronze Star, Purple Heart, Disting. Civilian Service medal; recipient Presdl. Service Badge, 1956-57, 61-63, medal Outstanding Pub. Service, 1976, medal Disting. Pub. Service, 1978, 81, 87, Presdl. award for Disting. Fed. Civilian Svc., 1989. Mem. Internat. Inst. Strategic Studies. Clubs: Army-Navy (Washington). Office: 1073 Riverbend Dr Advance NC 27006-8530*

LEGG, BENSON EVERETT, federal judge; b. Balt., June 8, 1947; s. William Mercer Legg and Beverly Bladen (Mann) Mason; m. Kyle Prechtl Legg;

children: Jennifer, Charles, Matthew. AB magna cum laude, Princeton U., 1970; JD, U. Va., 1973. Bar: Md. 1973. Law clk. to Hon. Frank A. Kaufman, Balt., 1973-74; assoc. Venable, Baetjer & Howard, Balt., 1975-81, ptnr., 1982-91; judge U.S. Dist. Ct., Dist. Md., Balt., 1991—; spl. reporter appeals com. and standing com. on rules of practice and procedure Ct. Appeals Md., 1983-85; faculty mem. nine day intensive trial advocacy program Md. Inst. Continuing Profl. Edn. for Lawyers, Inc., 1987—, program on appellate advocacy, 1988; lectr. and panelist in field. Mem. Va. Law Rev.; contbr. articles to profl. jours. Bd. dirs. Ctrl. Md. chpt. ARC, 1979-88, past chpt. gen. counsel; mem. adv. bd. Nat. Aquarium in Balt., 1987—; trustee Balt. Zoo. Mem. ABA (bus. torst litigation com. 1987), Md. State Bar Assn., Inc. (chmn. econs. of litigation com. 1981-82), Bar Assn. Balt. City (vice chmn. CLE com. 1986-87, chmn. 1987-88, exec. coun. 1987-88, judiciary com. 1989-90), The Serjeant's Inn Law Club, Order of Coif. Office: US Dist Ct 101 W Lombard St Ste 340 Baltimore MD 21201-2605

LEGG, REAGAN HOUSTON, lawyer; b. Kaufman, Tex., Nov. 18, 1924; s. Edward and Mary Alta (Coon) L.; m. Norma Jean Eden, July 16, 1949 (div. 1976); children—John, Ellen, Emily, Reagan Houston. BBA, U. Tex.-Austin, 1947, LLB, 1948. Bar: Tex. 1948, U.S. Dist. Ct. (we. dist.) Tex. 1951, U.S. Dist. Ct. (no. dist.) Tex. 1957, U.S. Ct. Appeals (5th cir.) 1960, U.S. Supreme Ct. 1961. County atty. Midland County (Tex.), 1951-55; ptnr. Legg, Saxe & Baskin, Midland, Tex., 1955-79, Legg, Aldridge & Carr, Midland, 1980-84, pvt. practice law, Midland, 1984-89, Kaufman, Tex., 1989—. Trustee Midland Coll., 1971-86 , pres. bd., 1972-75; bd. dirs. Permian Basin Regional Planning Commn., 1977-86 ; pres. Leadership Midland, 1978-80, Tex. Community Coll. Trustees and Adminstrs., 1980-81, Nat. Assn. Community Coll. Trustees, 1982-83. With USN, 1942-46. Named Boss of Yr. Midland Legal Secs. Assn., 1969; recipient M. Dale Ensign Leadership award Assn. Community Coll. Trustees, 1977. Fellow Tex. Bar Found.; mem. ABA, Tex. Bar Assn. (chmn. com. group legal svcs. 1968-74), Midland C. of C. (bd. dir. 1968-73, 78-81), Midland County Bar Assn. (pres. 1967-68), Kaufman C. of C. (bd. dirs. 1993—), Kaufman Cemetery Assn. (bd. dirs. 1992—). Democrat. Methodist. Clubs: Cedar Creek Country, Masons. Office: PO Box 227 Kaufman TX 75142-0227

LEGG, WILLIAM JEFFERSON, lawyer; b. Enid, Okla., Aug. 20, 1925; s. Garl Paul and Mabel (Gensman) L.; m. Eva Imogene Hill, Dec. 16, 1950; children: Melissa Lou, Eva Diane, Janet Sue. Grad., Enid Bus. Coll., 1943; student, Pittsburg State U., 1944; BBA, U. Tex., Austin, 1946; JD, U. Tulsa, 1954. Bar: Okla. 1954, U.S. Supreme Ct., U.S. Ct. Appeals (10th cir.), U.S. Dist. Ct. (we. dist.) Okla. With aviation sales Phillips Petroleum Co., 1946-48; atty. Marathon Oil Co., 1954-61; pvt. practice Oklahoma City, 1962—; ptnr. Andrews Davis Legg Bixler Milsten & Price, Inc. and predecessor firms, Oklahoma City, 1962—, pres., 83-86, also dir., 1973-77, 80-81, 83-86, 90, sec., 1975-80, 82-83, 90, now sr. counsel and adv. dir., 1991—; adj. prof. law Oklahoma City U., 1975-80; lectr. Okla. U. Law Sch., 1986; bd. dirs., v.p. internat. oil cos., Turkey, Australia, Brunei; bd. dirs., gen. counsel N.J. Natural Resources Co., 1986-91; dir. Skillpath Seminars, Kansas City, Mo., 1995—; lectr. energy seminars. Contbr. articles to profl. jours. Ordained Reorganized Ch. of Jesus Christ of Latter Day Saints, 1964, dist. pres., 1975-80, br. pres., 1986-91, evangelist, 1993—; mem. com. Okla. Gov.'s Energy Adv. Council, 1973, Okla. Blue Ribbon Com. on natural gas well allowables, 1983; trustee Am. Inst. Discussion, 1962-88, chmn., 1969-72, now mem. exec. com., counsel; trustee Jenkins Found. Research, sec., 1975-81; trustee Restoration Trails Found., 1975; trustee Graceland Coll., Lamoni, Iowa, 1986—, mem. exec. com., chmn. bus. affairs com., 1988—; trustee Met. Library Endowment Trust, 1986—, treas. 1988—, chmn. investment com.; rsch. fellow Southwestern Legal Found., Dallas, 1989—. With USN, 1943-46, lt. (j.g.) USNR, 1946-66. Mem. ABA, Internat. Bar Assn., Okla. Bar Assn. (past com. chmn.), Oklahoma County Bar Assn. (past com. chmn.), Internat. Assn. Energy Econs., Econ. Club Okla., Men's Dinner Club, Petroleum Club. Home: 3017 Brush Creek Rd Oklahoma City OK 73120-1855 Office: Andrews Davis Legg Bixler Milsten & Price Inc 500 W Main St Oklahoma City OK 73102-2253

LEGGE, CHARLES ALEXANDER, federal judge; b. San Francisco, Aug. 24, 1930; s. Roy Alexander and Wilda (Rampton) L.; m. Janice Meredith Sleeper, June 27, 1952; children: Jeffrey, Nancy, Laura. AB with distinction, Stanford U., 1952, JD, 1954. Bar: Calif. 1955. Assoc. Bronson, Bronson & McKinnin, San Francisco, 1956-64, ptnr., 1964-84, chmn., 1978-84; judge U.S. Dist. Ct. (no. dist.) Calif., San Francisco, 1984—. Served with U.S. Army, 1954-56. Fellow Am. Coll. Trial Lawyers; mem. Calif. Bar Assn. (past chmn. adminstrn. justice com.). Republican. Clubs: Bohemian, World Trade (San Francisco); Orinda (Calif.) Country. Office: US Dist Ct PO Box 36060 Rm 19-5424 450 Golden Gate Ave San Francisco CA 94102*

LEGGETT, DONALD YATES, academic administrator; b. Windsor, N.C., Oct. 31, 1935; s. Turner Carter Leggett and Ruby (Harden) Lanier; m. Nancy Lou Porter, Aug. 17, 1980; 1 stepson, Clayton Porter Johnston. BS in Phys. Edn., Social Studies, East Carolina U., 1958, MA in Edn., 1962; postgrad., N.C. State U., 1966-67. Tchr., coach Benhaven (N.C.) High Sch., 1958-59, Buies Creek (N.C.) High Sch., 1959-64; coach, tchr., Needham B. Broughton High Sch., Raleigh, N.C., 1964-66; asst. prin. Needham B. Broughton High Sch., Raleigh, 1966-70; dir. alumni affairs East Carolina U., Greenville, N.C., 1970-73; dir. alumni affairs and founds. East Carolina U., Greenville, 1973-79, dir. alumni rels., 1979-85, asst. to vice chancellor for instl. advancement, 1985-92, assoc. vice chancellor for alumni rels., 1992—, acting dir. Regional Devel. Inst., 1993; driver tng. coord. Raleigh City Sch. System, 1964-66; mem. numerous coms. at East Carolina U., 1970—. Editor East Carolina U. Alumni pubs. 1979-85; contbr. articles to alumni pubs. Past mem. bd. dirs. Pitt County Boys Club, Pitt-Greenville Arts Coun. (past mem. steering com.); former bd. dirs. Ea. N.C. village of Yesteryear; vice chmn. Pitt-Greenville Conv. and Visitors Authority. Named Boss of Yr. Greenville Jaycees, 1976. Mem. Coun. for Advancement and Support of Edn., East Carolina U. Pirate Club, Pitt-Greenville C. of C., Kiwanis Club (charter mem., past bd. dirs. Univ. City), Greenville Golf and Country Club, Phi Kappa Phi, Phi Delta Kappa. Baptist. Avocations: wood working, gardening. Home: 113 Bells St Greenville NC 27858

LEGGETT, GLENN, former English language educator, academic administrator; b. Ashtabula, Ohio, Mar. 29, 1918; s. Glenn H. and Celinda (Sheldon) L.; m. Doris Ruth James, June 14, 1941 (dec.); children: Leslie Ann Leggett Leonard, Susan Cady Leggett Jones, Celinda Sheldon Leggett Conrad, Joanna Ruth Leggett Sinnwell; m. Russelle Seeberger Jones, Mar. 11, 1973; children: Brian Edward Jones, Sarah Lorene Jones Krumm. A.B., Middlebury (Vt.) Coll., 1940, LL.D., 1971; M.A., Ohio State U., 1941, Ph.D., 1949; L.H.D., Rockford Coll., 1967, Ripon Coll., 1968, Coll. Idaho, 1974, Grinnell Coll., 1975; LL.D., Morningside Coll., 1975; Litt.D., Lawrence U., 1968. Instr. in English Mass. Inst. Tech., 1942-44; instr., then asst. prof. English Ohio State U., 1946-52; asso. prof. English U. Wash., 1952-58, asst. to pres., 1958-61, vice provost, 1961-63, provost, 1963-65; prof. English, pres. Grinnell Coll., 1965-75, pres. emeritus, 1979—; v.p. corporate communications Deere & Co., 1975-79; Mem. commn. English Coll. Entrance Exam. Bd., 1957-65, trustee, 1965-76, vice chmn., 1970-72, chmn., 1972-74; pres. Mayflower Retirement Homes, Inc., 1986-88. Author: (with Mead and Kramer) Handbook for Writers, 12th edit., 1995, A Conservative View, The New Professors, 1960; editor: Twelve Poets, 1959, (with Daniel and Beardsley) Theme and Form: An Introduction to Literature, 4th edit., 1975, (with Daniel) The Written Word, 1960, (with Steiner) Twelve Poets, alt. edit., 1967, Years of Turmoil: Years of Change, 1978, Teacher to Teacher: Selected Papers on Teaching, Writing, and Higher Education, 1979. Chmn. Ill.-Iowa Assn. Children with Learning Disabilities, 1976-79; bd. dirs. Quad-Cities Grad. Study Center, 1975-79, chmn., 1977-79; chmn. Conf. Coll. Composition, 1959, Iowa Coll. Found., pres., 1974-75; trustee Marycrest Coll., 1975-80; curator Stephens Coll., 1976-83; mem. exec. com. Iowa Natural Heritage Found., 1979-93; mem. Iowa Natural Resources Commn., 1982-83; bd. dirs. Stewart Library, pres., 1987-88. Served with USNR, 1944-46. Danforth grantee, 1971; recipient Edward S. Noyes award Coll. Bd., 1979. Mem. MLA, Nat. Council Tchrs. English (chmn. coll. sect. 1963-65, chmn. survey undergrad. curriculum in English 1964-67, task force career edn. 1978-79), Iowa Assn. Pvt. Colls. (pres. 1969-71), Assoc. Colls. Midwest (chmn. 1971-73), Chi Psi. Conglist. Home: 6 College Park Rd Grinnell IA 50112-1207

LEGGETT, GLORIA JEAN, minister; b. Buffalo, June 6, 1941; d. Richard Howard and Mary Alice (Jumper) Pope; m. Arthur William Leggett, June 17, 1961; children: Wendy Irene, Pamela Jean. MusB, Va. Commonwealth U., 1986; MDiv, Wesley Theol. Sem., 1991. Ordained to ministry, Christian Ch., 1991. Choir dir. St. Mark's United Meth. Ch., Richmond, Va., 1974-80; hosp. chaplain Johnston-Willis Hosp., Richmond, Va., 1991—; interim minister Westville Christian Ch., Mathews, Va., 1992-93, Crewe (Va.) Christian Ch.; police chaplain Chesterfield County (Va.) Police Dept., 1995—; pastor Westside Christian Ch., Richmond, Va., 1997—; tchr. music, Richmond, 1972—; supply preacher, keynote speaker Main Line Denomination Chs., Va., 1990—. Rape crisis counselor YWCA, Richmond, 1992; bd. dirs. Va. Wildlife Fedn., 1986-92. Recipient Achievement award Dale Carnegie Course, Richmond, 1979. Mem. NOW, AAUW, Phi Kappa Phi. Avocations: travel, music, crossword puzzles, pets. Home and office: 9216 Groomfield Rd Richmond VA 23236

LEGGETT, JAMES DANIEL, church administrator; b. Williamston, N.C., Oct. 21, 1939; s. James S. and Hazel Louise (Wynn) L.; m. Clara Faye Watts, June 25, 1961; children: James Jr., Joseph Talmadge, Cynthia Faye, John David. BA, Pembroke State U.; ThB, Holmes Coll. of the Bible, hon. doctorate, 1988. Ordained to ministry Pentecostal Holiness Ch., 1960. Pastor Swan Quarter Pentecostal Holiness Ch., 1962-64, Pinetown Pentecostal Holiness Ch., 1962-64, Mt. Olive Pentecostal Holiness Ch., Pembroke, 1964-70, Culbreth Meml. Pentecostal Holiness Ch., Falcon, 1970-86; asst. gen. supt. Internat. Pentecostal Holiness Ch., Bethany, Okla., 1989-93, vice chmn., 1993—; exec. dir. Evangelism USA; pres. Extension Loan Fund; supr. N.C. Conf., 1986-89; mem. Evangelical Curriculum Commn., writer Sunday Sch. lit., instr. extension classes Holmes Coll. of the Bible, Emmanuel Coll. Sec. bd. trustees Holmes Coll. of the Bible, past bd. dirs. Office: Pentecostal Holiness Ch 7300 NW 39th Expy Bethany OK 73008-2340

LEGGETT, JOHN CARL, sociology educator; b. Detroit, Sept. 18, 1930; s. Norval John and Eileen Elizabeth (McVeigh) L.; m. Iris Leja Leggett (div. Feb. 1989); children: Britt Erika, Shannon Kelley. BA, U. Mich., 1954, MA in Polit. Sci., 1956, MA in Sociology, 1958, PhD in Sociology, 1962. Various positions U. Mich., Ann Arbor, 1954-62, lectr. dept. sociology, rsch. assoc. Sch. Social Work, 1961-62; instr. sociology U. Calif., Berkeley, 1962-63, asst. prof., 1963-66, rsch. assoc., 1964-65; asst. prof. Simon Fraser U., Berkeley, 1966-67; assoc. prof. Simon Fraser U., 1967-70; lectr. sociology U. Calif., Davis, 1968, lectr. black studies, 1971; assoc. prof. sociology Rutgers U., New Brunswick, N.J., 1971—; vis. assoc. prof. Sacramento State Coll., 1967-68; prof. U. Conn., 1968-69; vis. lectr. U. B.C. (Can.), Vancouver, 1970; cons. to labor union, including United Farm Union, AFL-CIO. Author: Class, Race and Labor: Working Class Consciousness in Detroit, 1968, paperback edit., 1971, Race, Class and Political Consciousness, 1973, Taking State Power, 1973, (with others) Allende, His Exit and Our Times, 1978, Whither Black Studies, 1971, The American Working Class, 1979, Mining the Field, A Photo History of American Farm Worker Struggles, 1991; co-author (with Suzanne Malm) The Eighteen Stages of Love, 1995; contbr. numerous articles and book revs. prof. publ. Active Free Speech Movement, Berkeley, 1964, Farm Labor Support Com., Berkeley and Delano, Calif., 1965, Vietnam Day Com., Berkeley, 1965-66, Rainbow Coalition Cen. N.J., 1984—; officer, organizer Socialist Youth League, 1951-54; mem. Socialist Party, 1958-64, New Democratic Party, 1967-70, United Farm Workers; candidate for local polit. offices; union ofcl.; chmn. Raritan Inst. With USN, 1949-50. Recipient Disting. Faculty Person award Livingston Coll. Assn. Grads., 1987, Alfred McClung Lee award Sociological Abstracts, Inc./Internat. Sociological Assn., 1994; Ford Found. fellow, 1954-55; grantee Social Sci. Rsch. Coun., 1960-61, 64, Can. Coun., 1968-70, Trans-Action Rsch. grantee, 1984-85. Mem. AAUP (officer, grievance counselor Rutgers U.), Am. Sociol. Soc., So. Sociol. Soc., Midwestern Sociol. Soc., North Cen. Sociol. Soc., Assn. for Humanist Sociology (pres. 1995—), Soc. for Study Social Problems, Students for Dem. Soc. (charter Ann Arbor chpt. 1960). Avocations: white water canoeing, mountain hiking. Home: 320 Lawrence Ave Highland Park NJ 08904-1840 Office: Rutgers U Dept Sociology New Brunswick NJ 08904

LEGGETT, NANCY PORTER, university administrator; b. Greenville, N.C., Aug. 14, 1952; d. Earl Lindeburgh and Louise (Adams) Porter; m. Ted Clayton Johnston, Nov. 19, 1971 (div. Dec. 1979); 1 child, Clayton Porter; m. Donald Yates Leggett, Aug. 17, 1980. Student, East Carolina U., 1971-73, Pitt C.C., Greenville, 1975-76. Sec./coord. grad. ext. and tchr. edn. programs Divsn. Continuing Edn., East Carolina U., Greenville, 1971-80; sect. sec. ambulatory pediatrics Sch. Medicine, East Carolina U., Greenville, 1981-83; adminstrv. sec. to chmn. dept. pediatrics Esat Carolina U., Greenville, 1983-94; resource person dept. pediatrics Sch. Medicine, East Carolina U., Greenville, 1984-94, exec. asst. to chmn. dept. pediatrics, 1994—; mem. traffic appeals com. East Carolina U., Greenville, 1995-96, chair benefits com., 1995—, mem. parking and traffic com., 1996—. Mem. Greenville Cmty. Appearance Commn., 1990-94, Greenville Mus. Art, 1980-82; com. mem. N.C. Symphony, Greenville, 1988-89; mem., mem. steering com. Children's Miracle Network Telethon, Greenville, 1986-90; vol. Friends of Children's Hosp. Greenville, 1986-88; mem. Nat. Scleroderma Found., 1987-88, Hist. Hope Found., Windsor, N.C., 1990—; bd. dirs. Rose H.S. Acad. Boosters, 1994-95. Mem. Greenville Country Club, Kiwanis (charter mem., bd. dirs. 1990-91). Baptist. Avocations: gardening, reading, walking, birdwatching. Home: 113 Bells St Greenville NC 27858 Office: East Carolina Univ Sch of Medicine Dept Pediatrics Greenville NC 27858

LEGGETT, ROBERTA JEAN (BOBBI LEGGETT), social services administrator; b. Kankakee, Ill., Nov. 30, 1926; d. Clyde H. and Sybil D. (Billings) Karns; m. George T. Leggett, Aug. 25, 1956. Sec. Cardov div. Chemetron Corp., Chgo., 1951-60; sec., asst. mgr. Ravisloe Country Club, Homewood, Ill., 1961-65; sec. Nationwide Paper Co., Chgo., 1966-68; exec. dir. Am. Bd. Oral and Maxillofacial Surgery, Chgo., 1969-87. Mem. Chgo. Soc. Assn. Execs., Conf. Med. Soc. Execs. of Greater Chgo., Profl. Secs. Internat. Methodist.

LEGGETT, WILLIAM C., biology educator, academic administrator; b. Orangeville, Ont., Can., June 25, 1939; s. Frank William and Edna Irene (Wheeler) L.; m. Claire Holman, May 9, 1964; children: David, John. BA, Waterloo U. Coll., 1962; MSc, U. Waterloo, 1965; PhD, McGill U., 1969; DSc, U. Waterloo, 1992; LLD, Wilfred Laurier U., 1994. From rsch. scientist to rsch. assoc. Essex (Conn.) Marine Lab., 1965-73; asst. prof. McGill U., Montreal, Que., Can., 1970-72, assoc. prof., 1972-79, prof., 1979—, chmn. dept. biology, 1981-85, dean of sci., 1986-91, acad. v.p., 1991-94; prin., vice chancellor Queen's U., Kingston, Ont., Can., 1994—; chmn. bd. Huntsman Marine Lab., 1980-89; pres. Groupe Interuniversitaire de Recherche Oceanographique du Que., 1986-91; chmn. grant selection com. for population biology Natural Scis. and Engring. Research Council Can., 1980-81, chmn. grant selection com. for oceans, 1986-87; exec. com. Coun. Ontario Univ., 1996—. Mem. editl. bd.: Can. Jour. Fisheries and Aquatic Sciences, 1980-85, Le Naturaliste Canadien, 1980-91, Can. Jour. Zoology, 1982-86; contbr. articles in field. Recipient Dwight D. Webster award Am. Fisheries Soc., 1989, Award for Excellence for Fisheries Edn., 1990, Fry medal Can. Soc. Zoologists, 1990, Outstanding Biologist award Can. Coun. Biol. Chmn., 1993; grantee in field. Fellow Rawson Acad., Royal Soc. Can.; mem. Am. Fisheries Soc. (pres. North-East divsn. 1977-78, EO Sette award 1997), Can. Com. for Fishery Rsch., Can. Soc. Zoologists, Am. Soc. Limnology and Oceanography, Am. Soc. Naturalists. Office: Queen's U, Sci Dept, Kingston, ON Canada K7L 3N6

LEGIDO, AGUSTIN, pediatric neurologist; b. Carinena, Spain, Sept. 9, 1957; came to U.S., 1985; s. Agustin and Maria Luisa (Cameo) L.; m. Elvira Isabel Zuazo, July 31, 1992; 1 child, Agustin Javier. BD, Goya Inst., Zaragoza, Spain, 1974; MD, Zaragoza U., 1980; PhD, Bologna U., 1981, Zaragoza U., 1985. Diplomate Am. Bd. Pediat., Am. Bd. Psychiatry & Neurology. Pediat. fellow Clinica Pediatrica II, Bologna, Italy, 1980-81; pediat. residency Hosp. Clin. Universitario, Zaragoza, 1981-85; pediat. neurology fellow Children's Hosp. Phila., 1985-87; neurology rsch. fellow U. Pa. Sch. Medicine, Phila., 1987-88; pediat. resident St. Christopher's Hosp. for Children, Phila., 1988-89, mem. attending staff, 1990—; neurologist Med. Coll. Pa., Phila., 1989-90, cons. in child neurology, 1992—; asst. prof. pediat. and neurology Temple U. Sch. Medicine, Phila., 1990-95, assoc. prof., 1995—; cons. in child neurology Albert Einstein Med. Ctr., Phila., 1993—. Roman Catholic. Avocations: movies, theatre, reading, restaurants, travel. Office: St Christophers Hosp for Children Dept Neurology Philadelphia PA 19134-1095

LEGINGTON, GLORIA R., middle school educator. BS, Tex. So. U, Houston, 1967; MS, U. So. Calif., L.A., 1973. Cert. adminstr. (life). Tchr., mentor L.A. Unified Sch. Dist., 1991-93; tchr. insvc. classes for area colloquim, parents, tchrs., faculty shared decision making coun., 1993-94, mem. faculty senate, 1992-93, mem. sch. improvement, 1993-94; del. U.S. Spain Joint Conf. on Edn., Barcelona, 1995. Sponsor 8th grade, 1994—. Named semi-finalist Nat. Libr. Poetry, 1997. Mem. NEA, Internat. Reading Assn., Calif. Reading Assn., United Tchrs. L.A., Calif. League of Mid. Schs. Avocations: painting, writing, collecting black memorabilia, reading, traveling.

LEGLER, BOB, publishing company executive. Chmn. bd. First Mktg. Bd., Pompano Beach, Fla. Office: First Mktg Co 3300 Gateway Dr Pompano Beach FL 33069-4841*

LEGLER, MITCHELL WOOTEN, lawyer; b. Alexandria, Va., June 3, 1942; s. John Clarke and Doris (Wooten) L.; m. Harriette Dodson; children: John Clarke, Dorothy Trumbull, Harriette Holland. BA in Polit. Sci. with honors, U. N.C., 1964; JD, U. Va., 1967. Bar: Va. 1967, Fla. 1967. Pres. Commander, Legler, Werber, Dawes, Sadler & Howell, Jacksonville, Fla., 1976-91; mng. ptnr. Foley & Lardner, Jacksonville, 1991-95; chmn. Fla. Bar Consumer Protection Law Com. Editorial bd. Va. Law Rev., 1966-67. Mem. Va. Bar Assn., Fla. Bar Assn. (lectr. continuing legal edn.), Order of Coif, Phi Beta Kappa, Phi Eta Sigma, Delta Upsilon, Delta Theta Phi. Office: Mitchell W Legler PA 1 Independent Dr Ste 3104 Jacksonville FL 32202-5026

LEGO, PAUL EDWARD, retired corporation executive; b. Centre County, Pa., May 16, 1930; s. Paul Irwin and Sarah Elizabeth (Montgomery) L.; m. Ann Sepety, July 7, 1956; children: Paul Gregory, Debra Ann, Douglas Edward, Michael John. B.S. in Elec. Engring, U. Pitts., 1956, M.S., 1958. With Westinghouse Electric Corp., 1956—; gen. mgr. Westinghouse semiconductor div. Westinghouse Electric Corp., Pitts., 1970-74; gen. mgr. electronic tube div. Westinghouse Electric Corp., Elmira, N.Y., 1974-75; bus. unit gen. mgr. electronic components divs. Westinghouse Electric Corp., Pitts., 1975-77; v.p., gen. mgr. lamp divs. Westinghouse Electric Corp., Bloomfield, N.J., 1977-80; exec. v.p. electronics and control group Westinghouse Electric Corp., Pitts., 1980-83, exec. v.p. control equipment, 1983-85, sr. exec. v.p. corp. resources, 1985-87, pres., COO, 1988-90, chmn., CEO, 1990-93, also bd. dirs.; ret., 1993; pres. Intelligent Enterprises, Pitts., 1993—; chmn. bd. Commonwealth Aluminum Corp., Louisville, 1995—; bd. dirs. PNC Bank Realty Holding Co., USX Corp., Consol. Natural Gas Co., Lincoln Electric Co. Trustee U. Pitts.; mem. bd. trustees U. Pitts. Sch. Engring.; bd. overseers N.J . Inst. Tech., Newark, 1979—. With U.S. Army, 1948-52. Recipient Westinghouse Order of Merit 1975, Disting. Alumni award U. Pitts. Sch. Engring., 1986, Bicentennial Medallion of Distinction award U. Pitts., 1987. Mem. Am. Soc. Corp. Execs., Valley Brook Country Club, Duquesne Club, The Club Pelican Bay (Naples, Fla.), Laurel Valley Golf Club, Rolling Rock Club (Ligonier, Pa.). Republican. Roman Catholic. Office: Exec Assocs 1 Ppg Pl Ste 2210 Pittsburgh PA 15222-5401 *I believe that every individual in an organization should take ownership of his or her job and have the authority and responsibility to make continuous improvements in the processes by which the objectives of that job are accomplished. This approach will produce the lowest possible cost for that job and, collectively, for the company, with the highest level of quality and customer service.*

LEGOFFIC, FRANCOIS, biotechnology educator; b. Pluzunet, France, Nov. 10, 1936; s. Jacques and Marie LeGoffic; m. Marie-Thérèse Castel, Nov. 28, 1957; 1 child, Marc. Dr 3e Cycle, U. Paris, 1962, Dr Sci., 1963. Various positions Nat. Ctr. Sci. Rsch., France, 1962-74; prof. Ecole Nationale Supérieure de Chimie de Paris, 1975—; bd. dirs. UA 1389 du Centre Nat. de la Recherche Scientifique; vis. prof. Rolla U., 1975. Contbr. over 350 articles to Organic Chemistry, Biochemistry, Gen. and Environ., Biotechnology and Microbiology; holder 20 patents. Recipient award Chem. Soc. France, 1968, Acad. Pharmacy, 1971, Acad. Scis., 1993; named Officier palmes academiques, 1994. Achievements include rsch. on total synthesis of natural compounds of therapeutic value, mechanism of resistance of bacteria to antibiotics, mechanism of action of antibiotics, enzyme inhibitors as drugs in antibacterial, antifungal and anticancer area, biotechnology, such as new membranes, immobilized enzymes and cells, enzymes in organic synthesis, valorization of molecules from marine origin and the use of antibodies in environmental analytical chemistry and biosensors design as well as the devel. of new bioprocesses for enzymes production and their use in environmental depollution. Home: 42 rue Jean Georget, 92140 Clamart France Office: ENSCP, 11 rue Pierre Marie Curie, 75231 Paris France

LE GRAND, CLAY, lawyer, former state justice; b. St. Louis, Feb. 26, 1911; s. Nicholas and Mary Margaret (Leifeld) Le G.; m. Suzanne Wilcox, Dec. 30, 1935, (wid.); children: Mary Suzanne Le Grand Murray, Julie A. Le Grand Ekstrand, Nicholas W.; m. Margaret Morris Burrows, Dec. 11, 1993. Student, St. Ambrose Coll., Davenport, Iowa, 1928-31; LL.B., Catholic U. Am., 1934. Bar: Iowa 1934. Practice law Davenport, 1934-57; judge Dist. Ct., 1957-67; justice Supreme Ct. Iowa, Davenport, 1967-83; of counsel Stanley, Rehling, Lande & Van Der Kamp, Davenport, 1983-92, Noyes, O'Brien, Gosma and Brooke, Davenport, 1992-95, Noyes & Gosma, Davenport, 1995—; lectr. St. Ambrose Coll., 1957-67. Recipient award for outstanding achievement in field of law and the cts. Cath. U. Am., 1969; award of merit for profl. achievement St. Ambrose Coll., 1976. Mem. Am., Iowa, Scott County bar assns., Am. Judicature Soc., Inst. Jud. Adminstrn. Home: 4130 Northwest Blvd Apt 32 Davenport IA 52806-4234 Office: Noyes & Gosma 4500 N Brady St Ste 200 Davenport IA 52806-4061

LEGRAND, MICHEL JEAN, composer; b. Paris, Feb. 24, 1932; came to U.S., 1955; s. Raymond and Marcelle Legrand; children: Hervé, Benjamin, Eugénie. Diploma, Conservatoire Nationale Superieur de Musique, Paris, 1951. Composer, condr., pianist, 1965—. Composer: (score, song, adaptation) I Will Wait for You, 1965 (3 Acad. award nominations), Windmills of Your Mind, 1968 (Acad. award 1968), film scores include Summer of 42, 1970 (Acad. award 1970), Brian's Song, 1971, Lady Sings the Blues, 1972, The Three Muscateers, 1973, Ode to Billy Joe, 1975, The Other Side of Midnight, 1977, Atlantic City, 1980, The Mountain Men, 1980, Never Say Never Again, 1983, Yentl, 1984 (Acad. award 1984), The Pickle, 1993, Ready to Wear, 1994, also over 100 albums; arranger (album) I Love Paris, 1954; contbr. jazz pianist with numerous orchs. including Pitts. Symphony, Minn. Orch., Buffalo Philharm.; collaborated with various artists including Barbra Streisand, Sarah Vaughan, Jack Jones, Lena Horne, Dame Kiri Te Kanawa, Ray Charles, Miles Davis, Neil Diamond, Johnny Mathis; dir. (film) 5 Days in June, 1989. Mem. Dramatists Guild, Songwriters Guild of Am., Am. Fedn. Musicians, AFTRA, ASCAP, Acad. Motion Picture Arts and Scis. (Oscar award 1967, 70, 83). Avocations: boating, airplane pilot, tennis, horseback riding. Office: c/o Jim DiGiovanni 157 W 57th St Ph B New York NY 10019-2210

LEGRICE, STEPHEN, magazine editor. Exec. editor Star Mag., Tarrytown, N.Y. Office: Star Mag 660 White Plains Rd Tarrytown NY 10591*

LEGUEY-FEILLEUX, JEAN-ROBERT, political scientist, educator; b. Marseilles, France, Mar. 28, 1928; came to U.S., Aug. 1949; s. E. Feilleux and Jeanne (Leguey) Feilleux Levassort; m. Virginia Louise Hartwell, Sept. 19, 1953; children—Michele, Monique, Suzanne, Christiane. M.A., Ecole Superieure de Commerce, France, 1949; Diplome Superieur d'Etudes Coloniales, U. d'Aix-Marseille, France, 1949; M.A., U. Fla., 1951; Ph.D., Georgetown U., 1965. Lectr. Sch. Foreign Service Georgetown U., Washington, 1957-66; dir. research Inst. World Polit. Georgetown U., 1960-66; asst. prof. St. Louis U., 1966-70, assoc. prof., 1970—, chmn. polit. sci. dept., 1983-96; vis. scholar Harvard Law Sch., Cambridge, Mass., 1974-75; chmn. Fulbright Commn. for France Inst. Internat. Edn., N.Y.C., 1974-76; vis. researcher UN, N.Y.C., 1981; mem. academic delegation, Jordan, 1988, Israel, 1990, Syria, Bahrain, Kuwait, 1991, Kuwait, Syria, 1992, Syria, 1993—, Yemen, 1995, Morocco, Tunisia, Spain, 1996. Author (with others): Law of Limited International Conflict, 1965. Contbr. chpt. to books Implications of Disarmament, 1977, Democracy in a High-technology Society, 1988, The

External Environment, 1991, Proceedings of First Gobal Village Conference, 1992, Great Events from History II: Human Rights, 1992, Science and Politics of Food, 1995. Contbr. articles to profl. jours. Author testimony Pres.'s Commn. on 25th Anniversary of UN, 1970. Recipient Medaille d'Or Institut Comml., France, 1949, Fulbright award U.S. State Dept., 1950, Cert. Disting. Service Inst. Internat. Edn., 1976; named Outstanding Educator Nutshell Mag., 1982; Malone fellow in Jordan, 1988. Mem. UN Assn. (mem. nat. coun. chpt. and div. pres. 1972-73, steering com. 1973-75), Am. Biog. Inst. (named to Hall of Fame, 1986), Internat. Human Rights Task Force (chmn. 1975-81), Character Research Assn. (pres. 1980-83, 89-90), Acad. Coun. on UN System, Am. Coun. for UN Univ., Georgetown U. Gold Key Soc., Alpha Sigma Nu, Phi Alpha Theta, Pi Sigma Alpha, Delta Phi Epsilon, Pi Delta Phi. Roman Catholic. Home: 6139 Kingsbury Ave Saint Louis MO 63112-1101 Office: Saint Louis U Dept Polit Sci 221 N Grand Blvd Saint Louis MO 63103-2006

LE GUIN, URSULA KROEBER, author; b. Berkeley, Calif., Oct. 21, 1929; d. Alfred Louis and Theodora (Kracaw) Kroeber; m. Charles A. Le Guin, Dec. 22, 1953; children: Elisabeth, Caroline, Theodore. BA, Radcliffe Coll., 1951; MA, Columbia, 1952. Vis. lectr. or writer in residence numerous workshops and univs., U.S. and abroad. Author: Rocannon's World, 1966, Planet of Exile, 1966, City of Illusion, 1967, The Word For World is Forest, 1976, A Wizard of Earthsea, 1968, The Left Hand of Darkness, 1969, The Tombs of Atuan, 1971, The Lathe of Heaven, 1971, The Farthest Shore, 1972, The Dispossessed, 1974, The Wind's Twelve Quarters, 1975, A Very Long Way from Anywhere Else, 1976, Orsinian Tales, 1976, The Language of the Night, 1979, Leese Webster, 1979, Malafrena, 1979, The Beginning Place, 1980, Hard Words, 1981, The Eye of the Heron, 1983, The Compass Rose, 1982, King Dog, 1985, Always Coming Home, 1985, Buffalo Gals, 1987, Wild Oats and Fireweed, 1988, A Visit from Dr. Katz, 1988, Catwings, 1988, Solomon Leviathan, 1988, Fire and Stone, 1989, Catwings Return, 1989, Dancing at the Edge of the World, 1989, Tehanu, 1990, Searoad, 1991, Blue Moon Over Thurman Street, 1993, Wonderful Alexander and the Catwings, 1994, Going Out With Peacocks, 1994, A Fisherman of the Inland Sea, 1994, Four Ways to Forgiveness, 1995, Unlocking the Air, 1996, (with Diana Bellessi) The Twins, The Dream, 1997, Jane On Her Own, 1997; also numerous short stories, poems, criticism, screenplays. Recipient Howard D. Vursell award Am. Acad. Arts and Letters, 1991, Pushcart prize, 1991, Boston Globe-Hornbook award for excellence in juvenile fiction, 1968, Nebula award (novel) 1969, (novel and story) 1975, (story) 1975, (novel) 1990, Hugo award (novel) 1969, (story) 1973, (novella) 1973, (novelette) 1988, Gandalf award, 1979, Kafka award, 1986, Newbery honor medal, 1972, Nat. Book award, 1972, H.L. Davis award Oreg. Inst. Literary Arts, 1992, Hubbub annual poetry award, 1995, Asimov's Reader's award, 1995, Nebula award, 1996, James Tiptree Jr. Retrospective award, 1996, Locus Readers award, 1996. Mem. Sci. Fiction Research Assn., Sci. Fiction Writers Assn., Authors League, PEN, Writers Guild West, NOW, NARAL, Phi Beta Kappa. Office: care Virginia Kidd Lit Agy PO Box 278 Milford PA 18337-0278 also: care Matthew Bialer William Morris Agy 1350 Avenue Of The Americas New York NY 10019-4702

LEGUM, JEFFREY ALFRED, automobile company executive; b. Balt., Dec. 16, 1941; s. Leslie and Naomi (Hendler) L.; m. Harriet Cohn, Nov. 10, 1968; children: Laurie Hope, Michael Neil. student The Park Sch., 1959; BS in Econs. Wharton Sch., U. Pa., 1963; grad. Chevrolet Sch. Merchandising and Mgmt., 1966. With Park Circle Motor Co., Balt., 1963—, exec. v.p., 1966-77, pres. 1977—; pres. Legum Chevrolet-Nissan, 1977-89, also dir.; ptnr. Pkwy. Indsl. Ctr., Dorsey, Md., 1965-91; ltd. ptnr. Circle Ltd. Partnership, Glen Burnie, Md., 1991; v.p., dir. P.C. Parts Co., 1967—, pres., 1995—; v.p. Westminster Motor Co. (Md.), 1967-72, pres., dir., 1972—; pres. One Forty Corp., Westminster, 1972—; dir., exec. com. United Consol. Industries, 1970-73; dist. chmn. Chevrolet Dealers Council, 1975-77, chmn. Washington zone, 1982-83. Chmn. transp. div. Associated Jewish Charities, Balt., 1966-69; mem. Md. Svc. Acad. Review Bd., 1975-77, Bus. Adv. Bd. to Atty. Gen., 1985-87; trustee The Legum Found., Balt., 1967—; trustee Balt. Mus. Art, 1992—, mem. fine arts accessions com., 1992—, mem. investment com., 1992—, chmn., 1995-96, mem. exec. com., 1993, fin. com., 1995—, contr., 1994-96; sec., treas., 1996—, trustee The Park Sch. Balt., 1979-94, chmn. investment com., 1980-96, mem. investment com., 1980—, mem. exec. com., chmn. fin. com., treas., 1981-91, mem. sr. adv. bd. 1994—; pres.'s com. U. Toronto, 1983—; bd. dirs. Assoc. Placement Bur. (Jewish Vocat. Svc.), Balt., 1964-76, v.p., 1972-76; adv. bd. The Competitive Edge, Albuquerque, 1977-81; mem. investment com. Balt. Hebrew Congregation, 1980—, bd. electors, 1990-93; bd. dirs. Preakness Celebration, Inc., 1988-89, Associated Jewish Community Fedn. Balt., 1992-96; mem. adv. coun., exec. com. Wilmer Eye Inst., The Johns Hopkins Hosp., 1991; mem. instl. rev. bd. for human subjects rsch. Johns Hopkins Bayview Med. Ctr., 1992—; mem. steering com. Govt. House Trust, 1996—. Recipient award of honor Assoc. Jewish Charities of Balt., 1967, 68; Cadillac Master Dealer award, 1980-88, 91; Cadillac Pinnacle of Excellence award, 1986; Young Pres.'s Orgn. Cert. Appreciation, 1984; Nissan Nat. Merit Master award, 1982-88; Chevrolet Nat. Svc. Supremacy award, annually 1979-89, Sales Giant award Automotive News, 1987, Minute of Gratitude The Park Sch. Bd. Trustees, 1994. Mem. Md. New Car and Truck Assn., Young Pres. Orgn. (pres.'s forum 1977-92), World Pres.' Orgn., Benjamin Franklin Assocs., Johns Hopkins Assocs., Carroll County C. of C., Md. Hist. Soc. (exec. com. Library of Md. History 1981-90), Chesapeake Pres.' Orgn., Suburban Club (Baltimore County), U. of Pa., Center Club, U. Toronto Faculty Club (hon.). Home: 10 Stone Hollow Ct Baltimore MD 21208-1860 Office: 1829 Reisterstown Rd Baltimore MD 21208-6320

LEHAN, RICHARD D'AUBIN, English language educator, writer; b. Brockton, Mass., Dec. 23, 1930; s. Ralph A. and Mildred L.; m. Ann Evans, June 11, 1960; 1 son, Edward Scott. B.A., Stonehill Coll., 1952; M.A., Boston Coll., 1953; Ph.D., U. Wis., 1958. Mem. faculty U. Wis.-Madison, 1953-57, U. Tex.-Austin, 1958-62; mem. faculty dept. English UCLA, 1962—, prof. English, 1969—, chmn. dept. English, 1971-73; Fulbright exchange prof. Moscow State U., USSR, 1974-75. Author: F. Scott Fitzgerald, 1966, Theodore Dreiser, 1969, Literary Existentialism, 1973, The Great Gatsby: The Limits of Wonder, 1990. Recipient Disting. Teaching award U. Tex., 1961, UCLA, 1970; Fulbright award, 1975; Guggenheim fellow, 1978-79, Pres.'s Rsch. fellow U. Calif., 1988-89. Home: 333 S Oakhurst Dr Beverly Hills CA 90212-3505 Office: UCLA Dept English Los Angeles CA 90024-1530

LEHISTE, ILSE, language educator; b. Tallinn, Estonia, Jan. 31, 1922; came to U.S., 1949, naturalized, 1956; d. Aleksander and Julie M. (Sikka) L. Dr.Phil., U. Hamburg (Ger.), 1948; Ph.D., U. Mich., 1959; D.Univ. (hon.), U. Essex (Eng.), 1977; Dr. Phil. (hon.), U. Lund (Sweden), 1982, U. Tartu, Estonia, 1989. Lectr. U. Hamburg, 1948-49; assoc. prof. modern langs. Kans. Wesleyan U., 1950-51, Detroit Inst. Tech., 1951-56; rsch. assoc. U. Mich., 1957-63; faculty Ohio State U., Columbus, 1963-87, prof. linguistics, 1965-87, prof. emeritus, 1987—, chmn. dept., 1965-71, 85-87; dir. Linguistic Inst. Ohio State U., 1970; vis. prof. U. Cologne, Germany, 1965, UCLA, 1966, U. Vienna, 1974, U. Tokyo, 1980. Author 11 books; latest being Lectures on Language Contact, 1988; contbr. articles to profl. jours., book revs. Guggenheim fellow, 1969, 75; grantee Am. Council Learned Socs., 1971; fellow Center for Advanced Study in Behavioral Scis., 1975-76. Fellow AAAS, Am. Acad. Arts and Scis., Acoustical Soc. Am.; mem. MLA, Linguistic Soc. Am. (exec. com. 1971-73, pres. 1980), Internat. Soc. Phonetic Scis., Societas Linguistica Europaea. Home: 985 Kennington Ave Columbus OH 43220-4018

LEHMAN, ARNOLD LESTER, museum official, art historian; b. N.Y.C., July 18, 1944; s. Sidney and Henrietta F. L.; m. Pamela Gimbel, June 21, 1969; children— Nicholas Richard, Zachary Gimbel. BA, Johns Hopkins, 1965, MA, 1966; MA, Yale U., 1968, PhD, 1973. Chester Dale fellow Met. Mus. Art, N.Y.C., 1969-70; lectr. art history Cooper Union and Hunter Coll., 1969-72; dir. Urban Improvements Program, N.Y.C., 1970-72, Parks Council of N.Y.C., 1972-74, Met. Mus. and Art Centers, Miami, Fla., 1974-79, Balt. Mus. Art, 1979-97, Bklyn. Mus. Art, 1997—; adj. prof. dept. art history Johns Hopkins U., 1986-93, 1995—; dir. or trustee several corps. and non-profit orgns. Author: The Architecture of Worlds Fairs 1900-1939, 1972, The New York Skyscraper: A History of its Development 1870-1939, 1974; editor: Oskar Schlemmer, 1986; also various mus. catalogs. Trustee several non-profit orgns. Mem. Assn. Art Mus. Dirs. (trustee 1987-93, pres. 1990-91), Harmonie Club (N.Y.C.). Office: Bklyn Mus Art 200 Eastern Pkwy Brooklyn NY 11238-6052

LEHMAN, BRUCE ARTHUR, lawyer; b. Beloit, Wis., Sept. 19, 1945; s. Dean A. Lehman and Wanda R. (Westbrook) Watson. BS, U. Wis., 1967, JD, 1970. Bar: D.C. 1976, U.S. Ct. Appeals (D.C. cir.). Atty. Wis. Legislature, Madison, 1970-71, U.S. Dept. Justice, Washington, 1973-74, Swidler & Berlin, Chtd., Washington, 1983-93; counsel com. judiciary U.S. Ho. Reps., Washington, 1974-83, chief counsel subcom. cts., civil liberties, adminstrn., 1978-83; atty. Swidler & Berlin, Chtd., Washington, 1983-93; asst. sec. commerce, commr. patents and trademarks Dept. Commerce/U.S. Patent Trademark Office, Washington, 1993—. adv. bd. BNA Patent, Trademark and Copyright Law Jour., 1991-93. mem. Clinton/Gore Transition Team, Washington, 1992-93; vice chmn. D.C. Gen. Hosp. Commn., 1987-93, chmn. D.C. Gen. Hosp. Found., 1989-93. 1st lt. U.S. Army, 1971-73. Named Lawyer of Yr. Nat. Law Jour., 1994. Democrat. Office: US Patent & Tademark Office Office of Commr Washington DC 20231

LEHMAN, CHRISTOPHER M., international business consultant; b. Phila., Dec. 15, 1948; s. John F. and Constance (Cruice) L.; m. Maureen Daly, Oct. 1971; children: Brian Thomas, Robert Francis, Christopher M. BA, St. Joseph's Coll., 1971; MA in Law and Diplomacy, Fletcher Sch., 1974, MA in Internat. Rels., 1974, PhD in Internat. Rels., 1993. Research assoc. Fgn. Policy Research Inst., Phila., 1974-76; legis. asst. Senator Harry Byrd, Washington, 1976-78, Senator John Warner, Washington, 1979-81; office dir. Dept. State, Washington, 1981-83; spl. asst. to Pres. The White House, Washington, 1983-85; sr. v.p. Black, Manafort, Stone & Kelly, Alexandria, Va., 1985-87; pres. Commonwealth Cons. Corp., Washington, 1987—. Bd. advisors KIDS Found.; chmn. bd. Northern Va. Scholarship Trust. Served with USNR, 1969-71. H.B. Earhart fellow, 1971, 72, 73.

LEHMAN, DAVID R., children's entertainer. Record prodr., v.p., songwriter Someday Baby Inc., Nashville. Recipient Grammy award for "The Rock-A-Bye Collection, Volume One", 1990, Best Musical Album for Children "Sleepy Time Lullabyes", 1996. Office: Someday Baby Inc 1508 16th Ave S Nashville TN 37212-2906*

LEHMAN, DENNIS DALE, chemistry educator; b. Youngstown, Ohio, July 15, 1945; s. Dale Vern and Coryn Eleanor (Neff) L.; m. Maureen Victoria Tierney, July 19, 1969 (div. Mar. 1981); children—Chris, Hillary; m. Kathleen Kim Kuchta, May 15, 1983. B.S., Ohio State U. 1967; M.S., Northwestern U., 1968, Ph.D., 1972. Prof. chemistry Chgo. City Colls., 1968—, Northwestern U., Evanston, Ill., 1974-94; lectr. biochemistry Northwestern U. Med. Sch., Chgo., 1979-90; cons. Chgo. Bd. Edn. Mem. Am. Chem. Soc., AAAS, Sigma Xi. Author: Chemistry for the Health Sciences, 1981, 7th edit., 1993; Laboratory Chemistry for the Health Sciences, 1981, 7th edit., 1993. Home: 13780 W Elm Ln Wadsworth IL 60083-9410 Office: Chgo City Colls 30 E Lake St Chicago IL 60601-2403

LEHMAN, EDWARD WILLIAM, sociology educator, researcher; b. Regensburg, Germany, Feb. 7, 1936; came to U.S., 1939; s. William and Kate (Hoffman) L.; m. Ethna V. O'Flannery, May 26, 1962; 1 child, Robert. B.S., Fordham U., 1956, M.A., 1959; Ph.D., Columbia U., 1966. Lectr. Fordham U., 1958-59; vis. research sociologist dept. psychiatry Montefiore Hosp., Bronx, N.Y., 1959-61; lectr. Sch. Nursing, Columbia U., N.Y.C., 1964-67; research sociologist Cornell U. Med. Coll., N.Y.C., 1961-67; asst. prof., then assoc. prof. sociology NYU, 1967-78; prof., 1978—, chmn. dept., 1978-84, 93-96; assoc. dir. Ctr. Policy Research, N.Y.C., 1976-85, sr. research assoc., 1969-89; mem. minority adv. com. N.Y. State Dept. Mental Hygiene, 1981-90. Author: Political Society: A Macrosociology of Politics, 1977, Coordinating Health Care: Explorations in Interorganizational Relations, 1975, The Viable Polity, 1992; editor: (with others) A Sociological Reader in Complex Organizations, 1980. Served to capt. U.S. Army, 1957. Mem. Am. Sociol. Assn., Am. Polit. Sci. Assn. Democrat. Roman Catholic. Home: 1 Washington Square Vlg New York NY 10012-1632

LEHMAN, GEORGE MORGAN, food sales executive; b. Chgo., Apr. 28, 1938; s. George Daniel and Margaret Marie (Cunningham) L.; m. Kathleen Marie Loftus, June 30, 1962; children: Robert Patrick, Daniel Joseph, Kathleen Marie, Michael Francis, William Terrance, Marilyn Elizabeth. BS, Marquette U., 1960; postgrad., Marquette Law Sch., 1962. Salesman, area mgr., city mgr. Am. Dist. Telegram Co., Chgo., 1964-79; security cons. A.I.C. Security Systesm, Chgo., 1981-83; exec. acct. mgr. Murphy Butter & Egg Co., Chgo., 1984-90; acct. exec. Badger/Murphy Food Svc., Chgo., 1990—; assoc. mem. Chef's De Cuisine, Chgo., 1985-97. V.p. Sch. Dist. 126, Oak Lawn, Ill.; coach, umpire, v.p. Oak Lawn Little League; coach YMCA Basketball, Oak Lawn Pk. Dist. Basketball. Recipient Those Who Excell in Edn. award Ill. Assn. Sch. Bds., 1991, Cert. of Achievement, 1992. Mem. Beverly Stamp Club, Delta Sigma Pi. Roman Catholic. Avocations: stamps, basketball, darts. Home: 10733 Lawler Ave Oak Lawn IL 60453-5113 Office: Badger/Murphy Food Svc 700 N Western Ave Chicago IL 60612-1218

LEHMAN, HARRY JAC, lawyer; b. Dayton, Ohio, Aug. 29, 1935; s. H. Jacques and Mildred (Benas) L.; m. Linda L. Rocker, June 7, 1964 (div. Mar. 1977); children: Sara Beth, Adam Henry, Matthew Daniel; m. Patricia L. Steele, Aug. 30, 1980; 1 child, Alexandra Steele. BA, Amherst Coll., 1957; JD, Harvard U., 1960. Bar: Ohio 1960. Assoc. Burke, Haber & Berick, Cleve., 1960-61; assoc. Falsgraf, Kundtz, Reidy & Shoup, Cleve., 1961-66, ptnr., 1967-70; of counsel Benesch, Friedlander, Coplan & Aronoff, Cleve., 1971-80; ptnr. Jones, Day, Reavis & Pogue, Columbus, 1980—; adj. prof. law Ohio State U., Columbus, 1980-84, 86-87; mem. Bd. Bar Examiners, State of Ohio, Columbus, 1983-85. Contbr. articles to profl. jours. Mem. Ohio Ho. of Reps., Columbus, 1971-80; chmn. House Judiciary Com., 1975-80; mem. Ohio Elections Com., Columbus, 1983-88, State Underground Parking Com., Columbus, 1983-87, chmn., 1984-86. Served with USAR, 1960-66. Named one of Ten Outstanding Young Men, Cleve. Jaycees, 1968-69; recipient Disting. Service award NAACP, 1968, Outstanding Freshman Legislator award Ohio Legis. Correspondents Assn., 1971-72, Disting. Service award Ohio Edn. Assn., 1972, Most Effective Legislator award Ohio Legis. Correspondents Assn., 1973-74, Pub. Service award Ohio Pub. Defender Assn., 1974, Outstanding Pub. Service award Ohio Pub. Transit Assn., 1978, Disting. Service award ACLU Ohio Found., 1978, Most Effective Legislator 112th Gen. Assembly Ohio award Columbus Monthly Mag., 1980, Most Effective Legislator 113th Gen. Assembly Ohio award Columbus Monthly Mag. Mem. Ohio Bar Assn., Columbus Bar Assn., Cleve. Bar Assn., Columbus Athletic Club, New Albany Country Club. Democrat. Jewish. Avocations: reading, golf, family. Home: 2642 Charing Rd Columbus OH 43221-3628 Office: Jones Day Reavis & Pogue 41 S High St Ste 1900 Columbus OH 43215-6103

LEHMAN, JEFFREY SEAN, law educator; b. Bronxville, N.Y., Aug. 1, 1956; s. Leonard and Imogene (McAuliffe) L.; m. Diane Celeste Becker, May 20, 1979; children: Rebecca Colleen, Jacob Keegan, Benjamin Emil. AB, Cornell U., 1977; M of Pub. Policy, U. Mich., 1981, JD, 1981. Bar: D.C. 1983, U.S. Ct. Appeals (fed. cir.) 1984, U.S. Ct. Appeals (D.C. cir.) 1987, U.S. Supreme Ct. 1987. Law clk. to chief judge U.S. Ct. Appeals (1st cir.), Portland, Maine, 1981-82; law clk. to assoc. justice U.S. Supreme Ct., Washington, 1982-83; assoc. Caplin & Drysdale, Chartered, Washington, 1983-87; asst. prof. U. Mich. Law Sch., Ann Arbor, 1987-92, prof., 1992-93, prof. law and pub. policy, 1993—, dean, 1994—; vis. prof. Yale U., 1993, U. Paris II, 1994. Co-author: Corporate Income Taxation, 1994; editor-in-chief: Mich. Law Rev., 1979-80. Foster parent Arlington County Dept. Human Svcs., 1983-87; trustee Skadden Fellowship Found., 1995—. Henry Bates fellow, 1981. Mem. ABA, Am. Law Inst., Order of Coif. Democrat. Jewish. Office: U Mich Law Sch 324 Hutchins Hall Ann Arbor MI 48109

LEHMAN, JOAN ALICE, real estate executive; b. Jamaica Queens, N.Y., May 8, 1938; d. Hans Newman and Margot (Deutsch) Senen; m. Eugene Lehman, June 17, 1956 (div. Mar. 1990); children: Joel, Peter, Alan, Ira, Helen Ann, Helen Beth, Robert, Jacqueline, John, Steven, Robin, Elizabeth, Jody, Lisa, David, Andy, Jeremy, Jay. AA, Nassau C.C., East Meadow, N.Y., 1971; BS, Nova U., 1982. Lic. real estate broker, Fla. Owner Joan Lehman Real Estate Mgmt. Co., Old Bethpage, N.Y., 1961-82; tchr. Broward County Schs., Ft. Lauderdale, Fla., 1982-86; owner Joan Lehman Real Estate, Plantation, Fla., 1986—; pres. Jo Al 1 Inc., Plantation, —%. Mem. Sunset Sch. Adv. Bd., Ft. Lauderdale, 1994-96; bd. dirs. Property Owners Ctrl. Lauderhill, Fla., 1996; den mother Boy Scouts Am., Old Bethpage, N.Y.; leader Girl Scouts U.S., Old Bethpage. Avocations: bowling, travel, theater. Office: 1841 SW 68th Ave Plantation FL 33317-5020

LEHMAN, JOHN F., JR., industrialist; b. Phila., Sept. 14, 1942; s. John F. and Constance (Cruice) L.; m. Barbara Wieland, 1975; children: John F., Alexandra, Grace. B.S. in Internat. Relations, St. Joseph's Coll., 1964; B.A. in Law with honors, MA in Internat. Law and Diplomacy, Cambridge U., 1967; Ph.D. in Internat. Relations, U. Pa., 1974. Sr. staff mem. Nat. Security Council, 1969-74; dep. dir. U.S. Arms Control and Disarmament Agy., 1975-77; pres. Abingdon Corp., 1977-81; sec. of Navy Washington, 1981-87; mng. dir. Paine Webber, 1988-91; chmn. J.F. Lehman & Co., N.Y.C., 1991—, Sperry Marine Inc., N.Y.C., 1993-96; bd. dirs. Ball Corp., Sedgwick Group, plc, ISO, Inc. Author: Command of the Seas, 1989, Making War, 1992. Capt. USNR, 1968—.

LEHMAN, KARL FRANKLYN, accountant; b. Lowville, N.Y., Aug. 15, 1942; s. Addison E. and Mary L. (Zehr) L.; m. Elaine K. Hartsough, Aug. 2, 1964; children: Karleia Janel, Regan Scott, Anjanette Joy. BA, Goshen Coll., 1963; MBA, Columbia U., 1965. CPA, Ind., N.Y.; cert. real estate broker, Ind. Staff acct., CPA Arthur Andersen & Co., CPA's, N.Y.C., 1965-68; mgr., CPA McGladrey & Co., CPA's, Davenport, Iowa, 1968-71; v.p., sec.-treas. ADM Industries, Inc., Elkhart, Ind., 1971-74; treas., contr. Globestar Industries, Inc., Elkhart, 1974-80; assoc. prof. acctg. Goshen (Ind.) Coll., 1980-83; pres. Karl F. Lehman & Assocs., PC CPA's, Goshen, 1980—, also bd. dirs.; mem. Creation Design and Mfg., Inc., Elkhart, Pioneer Homes, Inc., Goshen, Creation Design, Inc., Goshen, Feed Mill Restaurant, Inc., Shipshewanna, Ind., Family Svcs. of Elkhart (Ind.) County, Inc. Mem. AICPA, N.Y. State Soc. CPA's. Home: 3500 Calumet Ave Elkhart IN 46514-4408 Office: Karl F Lehman & Assocs PC 316 S 3rd St Goshen IN 46526-3710 also: Karl F Lehman & Assocs PC 615 W Bristol St Elkhart IN 46514-2900 also: Karl F Lehman & Assocs PC 445 S Van Buren St Shipshewana IN 46565-9176 also: Karl F Lehman & Assocs PC 1001 N Main St Nappanee IN 46550-1016

LEHMAN, LAWRENCE HERBERT, consulting engineering executive; b. N.Y.C., Apr. 30, 1929; s. Samuel and Shirley (Freiberg) L.; m. Susan E. Green, June 29, 1957; children: Scott Jeffrey, Christopher Adam. BCE, NYU, 1949; MBA, Iona Coll., 1978. Registered profl. engr., N.Y., N.J., Ky., Ill., Mass., Conn., Ind., Pa., Md., Fla., Tenn. Project engr. Andrews & Clark (Cons. Engrs.), N.Y.C., 1951-57; project mgr. Barstow, Mulligan & Vollmer (Cons. Engrs.), N.Y.C., 1957-59; chief engr., ptnr. Vollmer Assos. (Cons. Engrs.), N.Y.C., 1959-67; chief exec. officer, dir. Berger, Lehman Assos. (P.C.), Rye, N.Y., 1967—. Recipient Third award U.S. Steel Corp., 1966, Bridge award Pre-stressed Concrete Inst., 1975, Honor award Nat. ACEC, 1995, others. Fellow ASCE (life); mem. NSPE, N.Y. State Bd. Engrs. and Land Surveyors, Am. Cons. Engrs. Coun., Soc. Am. Mil. Engrs., Transp. Rsch. Bd., Am. Ry. Engring. Assn., Internat. Assn. Bridge and Structural Engrs., Am. Rd. and Transp. Builders Assn., Am. Arbitration Assn. (nat. panel arbitrators), N.Y. Assn. Cons. Engrs. (Engring. Excellence awards 1975, 79, 90, 95), Conn. Engrs. in Pvt. Practice, West County Profl. Engrs. Soc. (Engr. of Yr. award 1991), The Moles, High Speed Rail Assn. Home: 10 Chester Dr Rye NY 10580-2204 Office: 411 Theodore Fremd Ave Rye NY 10580-1410

LEHMAN, ORIN, retired state official; b. N.Y.C., Jan. 14, 1922; s. Allan S. and Evelyn (Schiffer) L.; children: Susan, Brooke, Sage. BA, Princeton U., 1942; MA, NYU, 1956, PhD, 1961; LHD (hon.), Hartwick Coll., 1962, Marist Coll., 1993; LLD (hon.), Manhattan Coll., 1985. Economist Lehman Bros., N.Y.C., 1947-52; pub. and chmn. Colgreene Pub., Inc., Hudson, N.Y., 1951-59; chmn. Colgreene Broadcasting Co., Catskill, N.Y., 1958-75, Picket Prodn., Inc., N.Y.C., 1968-75; commr. N.Y. State Office of Parks, Recreation and Hist. Preservation, Albany, 1975-94; chmn. N.Y. State Commn. for Restoration of the Capitol, 1979; adv. U.S. del. UN Conf. Trade and Devel., 1964-68; chmn. N.Y. State Gov.'s Com. on Employment of Handicapped, 1956-65; mem. public adv. bd. Econ. Cooperation Adminstrn., 1950-52; mem. U.S. Nat. Commn. for UNESCO, 1968-71; chmn. N.Y.C. Bd. Corrections, 1974-75; mem. exec. com. N.Y.C. Criminal Justice Coordinating Com., 1974-75. Trustee, past chmn. New Sch. Social Research, N.Y.C., Parsons Sch. Design; trustee, chmn. Just-One-Break, Inc.; trustee, past exec. dir. Eleanor Roosevelt Meml. Found.; bd. dirs. Ednl. Broadcasting Corp., 1965-74; pres. N.Y. Citizens Com. Public Higher Edn., 1964-68. Served to capt. U.S. Army, 1942-47. Decorated D.F.C., Bronze Star, Purple Heart; recipient Disting. Svc. award Nat. Govs. Assn, 1992, citations Anti-Defamation League, citations N.Y.C. Jaycees, citations N.Y. State Jaycees, citations Pres.'s Com. on Employment of Handicapped, citations CSC U.S., citations CCNY, citations Marist Coll., citations Taft Sch., Pres.'s Pub. Svc. award Nature Conservancy, Pugsley medal Nat. Park Found., 1989. Office: 20 E 69th St Apt 4C New York NY 10021-4960

LEHMAN, RICHARD LEROY, lawyer; b. Johnstown, Pa., Feb. 4, 1930; s. John S. and Deliah E. (Chase) L.; m. Lucia M. Ragnone; children: Ann Laurie, Leslie Ann, Lucia Marie. AB in Social Work, U. Ky., 1957; LLB, U. Detroit, 1960. Bar: Mich. 1961, U.S. Dist. Ct. (ea. dist.) Mich. 1961, U.S. Ct. Appeals (6th cir.) 1961. Pvt. practice Detroit; ptnr. Garan, Lucow, Miller, Lehman, Seward & Cooper, 1961-79; pres. Home Bldg. Plan Svc., Inc., Portland, Oreg., 1979-82; pres., gen. counsel Matvest Inc., Farmington Hills, Mich., 1980-86; pres. Xi Industries, Flint, Mich., 1982-86; ptnr. Lehman & Valentino, P.C., Bloomfield Hills, Mich., 1986-95; pres. Premiere Packaging, Inc., Flint, 1987-91, chmn., CEO, 1990—; vis. lectr. U. Detroit Law Sch., 1970-74, also Inst. Continuing Legal Edn. Mem. exec. com. pres.'s cabinet U. Detroit, 1975-79; mem. Old Newsboys Goodfellow Fund Detroit, 1966—, bd. dirs., 1975-78. 1st lt. AUS, 1947-53. Recipient Algernon Sydney Sullivan Medallion U. Ky., 1957. Mem. ABA, FBA, Mich. Bar Assn., Genesee County Bar Assn. (mem. bench and bar com. 1975-78), Am. Judicature Soc., Am. Arbitration Assn., Assn. Def. Trial Counsel, Def. Rsch. Inst., U. Ky. Alumni Assn., U. Detroit Law Sch. Alumni Assn. (dir. 1970-77, pres. 1974-75), U. Detroit Alumni Assn., 6th Cir. Jud. Conf. (life), Pine Lake Country Club (bd. dirs. 1991—, pres. 1994-95). Roman Catholic. Avocations: golf, downhill skiing, carpentry. Home: 4052 Waterwheel Ln Bloomfield Hills MI 48302-1870 Office: Premiere Packaging 6220 Lehman Dr Flint MI 48507-4678

LEHMAN, (ISRAEL) ROBERT, biochemistry educator, consultant; b. Tauroggen, Lithuania, Oct. 5, 1924; came to U.S., 1927; s. Herman Bernard and Anne (Kahn) L.; m. Sandra Lee Teper, July 5, 1959; children: Ellen, Deborah, Samuel. AB, Johns Hopkins U., 1950, PhD, 1954; MD (hon.), U. Gothenberg, Sweden, 1987; DSc (hon.), U. Pierre et Marie Curie, Paris, 1992. Instr. biochemistry Washington U., St. Louis, 1957-59; asst. prof. Stanford (Calif.) U., 1959-61, assoc. prof., 1961-66, prof., 1966—; sci. adv. bd., dirs. U.S. Biochem. Corp., Cleve., 1984—; sci. adv. RPI, Boulder. Author: Principles of Biochemistry, 6th edit., 1978, 7th edit., 1984. Sgt. U.S. Army, 1943-46, ETO. Recipient ASBMB-Merk award Am. Soc. for Biochemistry, 1995. Mem. NAS, Am. Acad. Arts and Scis., Am. Soc. Biol. Chemistry and Molecular Biology (Merck award 1995). Democrat. Jewish. Home: 895 Cedro Way Palo Alto CA 94305-1002 Office: Stanford U Dept Biochemistry Beckman Ctr Stanford CA 94305

LEHMAN, TOM, professional golfer; b. Austin, Minn.. Profl. golfer, 1982—. Named Ben Hogan Tour Player of Yr., 1991; named to Pres. Cup team, 1994; ; won Reflection Ridge, Gulf Coast Classic, S.C. Classic, Santa Rosa Open, The Meml. Tournament, 1994, Colonial Invitational, 1995, Brit. Open, 1996. Office: c/o PGA Box 109601 100 Ave of Champions Palm Beach Gardens FL 33410

LEHMANN, DORIS ELIZABETH, elementary education educator; b. Ramsey, N.J., Aug. 17, 1933; d. Alfred Harrison and Anna Elizabeth (Gerhold) Rockefeller; m. Victor S. Lehmann, June 25, 1955; children: Joanne E. Cathy Lynn, Victor A., Kristie Sue. BS in Edn. magna cum laude, Wagner Coll., 1955; student in edn., Columbia U., summers 1988-91, Jersey City State, 1990—, William Paterson, 1971. Elem. tchr. Sch. St. Sch., Ramsey, 1955-56; bedside instr. N. Bergen County schs., N.J., 1966-71; elem. tchr. Edith A. Bogert Sch., Upper Saddle River, N.J., 1971—. Author numerous poems; author: (with others) Curriculum for Values Education in

New Jersey, 1991. Indian cons. Bergen County Mus. of Art and Sci., Paramus, N.J., 1983—. Recipient Fellowship of Life award Luth. Layman's Movement, 1955. Fellow Upper Saddle River Edn. Assn. (social sec. 1972-73, v.p. 1974-75, 84-85, liaison to USR hist. soc. 1986—) N.J. Edn. Assn., N.J. North Edn. Assn., Alpha Omicron Pi (life, treas. 1954, v.p. 1955). Republican. Lutheran. Office: Edith A Bogert Sch 395 W Saddle River Rd Saddle River NJ 07458-1622

LEHMANN, ERICH LEO, statistics educator; b. Strasbourg, France, Nov. 20, 1917; came to U.S., 1940, naturalized, 1945; s. Julius and Alma Rosa (Schuster) L.; m. Juliet Popper Shaffer; children: Stephen, Barbara, Fia. M.A., U. Calif. at Berkeley, 1943, Ph.D., 1946; D.Sc. (hon.), U. Leiden, 1985, U. Chgo., 1991. Asst. dept. math. U. Calif. at Berkeley, 1942-43, asso., 1943-46, instr., 1946-47, asst. prof., 1947-51, asso. prof., 1951-54, prof., 1954-55, prof. dept. stats., 1955-88, emeritus, 1988—, chmn. dept. stats., 1973-76; vis. assoc. prof. Columbia, 1950-51, Stanford, 1951-52; vis. lectr. Princeton, 1951. Author: Testing Statistical Hypotheses, 1959, 2d edit., 1986, (with J.L. Hodges, Jr.) Basic Concepts of Probability and Statistics, 1964, 2d edit, 1970, Nonparametrics: Statistical Methods Based on Ranks, 1975, Theory of Point Estimation, 1983. Recipient Fisher award Coms. of Pres. Stats. Socs. in N.Am., 1988; Guggenheim fellow, 1955, 66, 79; Miller research prof., 1962-63, 72-73; recipient Samuel S. Wilks Meml. medal Am. Statis. Assn., 1996. Fellow Inst. Math. Stats., Am. Statis. Assn., Royal Statis. Soc. (hon.); mem. Internat. Statis. Inst., Am. Acad. Arts and Scis., Nat. Acad. Scis. Office: Educational Testing Service Mail Stop 15-T Princeton NJ 08541

LEHMANN, HEINZ EDGAR, psychiatrist, consultant, researcher; b. Berlin, July 17, 1911; came to Can., 1937, naturalized, 1948; s. Richard and Emmy (Grönke) L.; m. Annette Joyal, July 28, 1940; 1 child, François. Abiturium, Mommsen Gymnasium, Berlin, 1929; M.D., U. Berlin, 1935; LL.D. (hon.), U. Calgary, Can., 1980. Clin. dir. Douglas Hosp., Montreal, Que., Can., 1947-66; dir. research Douglas Hosp., 1966-67; prof. psychiatry McGill U., Montreal, 1965—; emeritus prof. McGill U., 1981—, chmn. dept. psychiatry, 1970-74; cons. 4 Montreal hosps., 1976—; dep. commr. research N.Y. State Office Mental Health, Albany, 1980—. Contbr. over 300 articles to profl. jours., chpts. to books. Decorated officer Order of Can.; recipient Albert Lasker award Lasker Found., 1957, Heinz Lehmann Rsch. award N.Y. State Office of Mental Health, 1990, Van Giessom awrd N.Y. Psychiat. Inst., 1991, prix de l'oeuvre scientifique Assn. French-Lang. Physicians in Can., 1992, Thomas William Salmon medal, 1994. Fellow Internat. Coll. Neuropsychopharmacology (pres. 1970-72), Can. Coll. Neuropsychopharmacology (Heinz Lehmann ann. award 1983), Que. Psychiat. Assn. (Heinz Lehmann ann. award 1986); mem. Am. Coll. Neuropsychopharmacology (pres. 1965-66, life), Am. Psychiat. Assn. (life), Royal Soc. Can. Avocations: gemology; astronomy; magic; skiing; scuba diving. Office: 1033 Pine Ave W, Montreal, PQ Canada H3A 1A1

LEHMANN, MICHAEL STEPHEN, film director; b. San Francisco, Mar. 30, 1957; s. Herbert and Minette L.; m. Holland Sutton; children: Alexander, Natalie. BA, Columbia U., 1978; MFA, U. So. Calif., 1985. Mgr. electronic cinema div. Zoetrope, Hollywood, Calif., 1981-83. Dir. (films) Heathers, 1989 (Best First Feature award Ind. Feature Project 1990), Meet the Applegates, 1991, Hudson Hawk, 1991, Airheads, 1994, The Truth About Cats and Dogs, 1996; exec. prodr. (film) Ed Wood, 1994. Office: Creative Artists Agy 9830 Wilshire Blvd Beverly Hills CA 90212-1804

LEHMANN, PHYLLIS WILLIAMS, archaeologist, educator; b. Bklyn., Nov. 30, 1912; d. James Barnes and Florence Lourene (Richmond) Williams; m. Karl Lehmann, Sept. 14, 1944 (dec. Dec. 1960). B.A., Wellesley Coll., 1934, L.H.D., 1976; Ph.D., NYU, 1943; Litt.D., Mt. Holyoke Coll., 1971; D.F.A., Coll. Holy Cross, 1973. Asst. charge classical collection Bklyn. Museum, 1934-36; part-time instr. history art Bennett Jr. Coll., 1936-39; mem. faculty Smith Coll., 1946—, prof. art, 1955-67, Jessie Wells Post prof. art, 1967-72, William R. Kenan, Jr. prof. art, 1972-78, prof. emeritus, 1978—, dean, 1965-70; asst. field dir. excavations conducted by Archaeol. Research Fund of NYU at Samothrace, 1948-60, acting dir., 1960-62, adv. dir., 1962—; research prof. Inst. Fine Arts, NYU, 1961-62; adj. prof. Inst. Fine Arts, N.Y. U., 1965—; Flexner lectr. Bryn Mawr Coll., 1977; Baldwin lectr. Oberlin Coll., 1982. Author: Statues on Coins of Southern Italy and Sicily in the Classical Period, 1946, Roman Wall Paintings from Boscoreale in the Metropolitan Museum of Art, 1953, The Pedimental Sculptures of the Hieron in Samothrace, 1962, Samothrace, vol. 3, 1969, (with Karl Lehmann) Samothracian Reflections. Aspects of the Revival of the Antique, 1973, Skopas in Samothrace, 1973, Cyriacus of Ancona's Egyptian Visit and Its Reflections in Gentile Bellini and Hieronymus Bosch, 1977, Samothrace, Vol. 5, 1982, contbr. Vol. 7, 1992; also articles in profl. jours.; Editor: (with Karl Lehmann) Samothrace, 1961—; asst. editor: Art Bull., 1945-47; book rev. editor, 1949-52. Named hon. citizen of Samothrace, 1968; recipient Wellesley Coll. Alumnae Assn. Achievement award, 1976; Gold medal Pan Samothracian Hearth of Athens, 1981; hon. mem. Pan Samothracian Hearth of Athens, 1979; Fulbright research grantee Italy, 1952-53; Guggenheim fellow, 1952-53; Bollingen fellow, 1960. Fellow Am. Acad. Arts and Scis.; mem. Archaeol. Inst. Am. (trustee 1970-73), Coll. Art Assn. Am., Am. Numis. Soc., Soc. Archtl. Historians (Alice D. Hitchcock award 1969), AAUW, Renaissance Soc. Am., Am. Sch. Classical Studies in Athens (research fellow fall 1970, 76, exec. com. 1970-75, publ. com. 1970-80, chmn. 1977-80), Williamsburg Hist. Soc., Phi Beta Kappa. Club: Cosmopolitan. Home: 127 Main St Haydenville MA 01039-9713 Office: Smith Coll Hillyer Hall Northampton MA 01063

LEHMANN, RUTH PRESTON MILLER, literature educator; b. Ithaca, N.Y., Feb. 18, 1912; d. Ernest Allen and Lillian Allen (Phillips) Miller; m. Winfred P. Lehmann, Oct. 12, 1940; children—Terry Jon, Sandra Lehmann Hargis. B.A., Cornell U., 1932, M.A., 1934; postgrad., Bryn Mawr Coll., 1935-36; Ph.D., U. Wis.-Madison, 1942. Teaching asst. U. Wis., Madison, 1938-42; editor lang. texts U.S. Armed Forces Inst., Washington, 1943-44; instr. George Washington U., Washington, 1944-46; lectr. Washington U., St. Louis, 1946-47; instr. Georgetown U. English Lang. Program, Ankara, Turkey, 1955-56; asso. prof. English Huston Tillotson Coll., Austin, Tex., 1956-58; lectr. English U. Tex., Austin, 1960-67; asso. prof. U. Tex., 1967-72, prof., 1972-80, prof. emeritus, 1980—; delivered Rudolf Thurneysen Meml. lecture, U. Bonn., Fed. Rep. of Germany, 1985. Contbg. author: The Origins of Writing, 1989; editor: Fled Duin na nGed, 1964, (with W.P. Lehmann) Introduction to Old Irish, 1975, Early Irish Verse, 1982, Beowulf: An Imitative Translation, 1988, Blessed Bastard. Mem. MLA, Medieval Acad. Am., Early English Texts. Soc., Phi Beta Kappa (pres. Austin chpt. 1978-79), Phi Kappa Phi, Pi Lambda Theta. Democrat. Home: 3800 Eck Ln Austin TX 78734-1613 Office: U Tex Dept English Austin TX 78712
Happiness is a state of mind and more fun than boredom.

LEHMANN, WILLIAM LEONARDO, electrical engineer, educator; b. Milw., Dec. 17, 1924; s. William Christian and Johanna Alma (Schrumpf) L.; m. Barbara Taylor, June 29, 1948; children: Johanna, William, Katherine, Wendy, Christianne. AB, Haverford (Pa.) Coll., 1944; MS, Syracuse (N.Y.) U., 1948, PhD, 1953. Registered profl. engr., Ohio. Prof. physics acting dean Air Force Inst. Tech., 1951-66; lectr. Ohio State U., 1957-60; dep. for labs. Office Asst. Sec. Air Force Research and Devel., 1966-74; dir. Air Force Office Sci. Research, 1974-78, Air Force Weapons Lab., Kirtland AFB, N.Mex., 1978-81; chief scientist Combat Devel. Experimentation Ctr. U.S. Army Sci. Support Lab, Ft. Ord, Calif., 1982-85; sr. sci. analyst N.Mex. Engring. Research Inst., 1985-93; prof. elec. engring. U. N.Mex., Albuquerque, 1988-93; sr. assoc. Ctr. for Occupational R & D, 1993—; vis. prof. U. N.Mex., 1981-82, also adv. bd. Coll. Engring.; Past mem. Gov. N.Mex. Tech. Excellence Com.; mem. USAF Scientific Adv. Bd., 1985-92. Mem. Beaver Creek (Ohio) Sch. Dist. Bd., 1965-66; trustee Lovelace Med. Found. Served with AUS, 1944-45. Recipient Air Force Exceptional Civilian Service medal with three oak leaf cluster, 1981, Ohio Engr.'s award, 1966, award Ohio Soc. Profl. Engrs., 1965. Fellow AAAS; Mem. Air Force Assn. (citation honor 1978), Am. Soc. Engring. Edn., AIAA, Am. Def. Preparedness Assn., Sigma Xi, Sigma Pi Sigma, Tau Beta Pi. Republican. Episcopalian. Lodge: Rotary. Patentee solar orientation device. Home: PO Box 637 700 Island Retreat Rd Port Aransas TX 78373 Office: Port Aransas High Sch PO Box 1297 Port Aransas TX 78373-1297

LEHMANN, WINFRED PHILIPP, linguistics educator; b. Surprise, Nebr., June 23, 1916; s. Phillip Ludwig and Elenore Friederike (Grosnick) L.; m. Ruth Preston Miller, Oct. 12, 1940; children: Terry Jon, Sandra Jean. BA, Northwestern Coll., Watertown, Wis., 1936; MA, U. Wis., 1938, PhD, 1941; LittD (hon.), SUNY, Binghamton, 1985; DHL (hon.), U. Wis., 1995. From instr. to asst. prof. Wash. U., 1946-49; from assoc. prof. to prof. U. Tex., 1949-63, Ashbel Smith prof. linguistics, 1963-83, Louann and Larry Temple prof. humanities, 1983-86, prof. emeritus, 1986—, chmn. dept. Germanic langs., 1953-65, chmn. dept. linguistics, 1965-72, dir. Linguistics Research Center, 1961—; Jawaharlal Nehru Meml. lectr., New Delhi, 1981; dir. Georgetown English lang. program, Ankara, Turkey, 1955-56; chmn. linguistics del. People's Republic of China, 1974, co-chmn. Social Sci./Humanities Planning Commn., 1981. Author: (with L. Faust) A Grammar of Formal Written Japanese, 1951, Proto-Indo-European Phonology, 1952, The Alliteration of Old Saxon Poetry, 1953, The Development of Germanic Verse Form, 1956, Historical Linguistics: An Introduction, 1962, 3d edit., 1992, Descriptive Linguistics: An Introduction, 1972, 2d edit., 1976, Proto-Indo-European Syntax, 1974, Linguistische Theorien der Moderne, 1981, Language: An Introduction, 1982, Gothic Etymological Dictionary, 1986, Die Gegenwaertige Richtung der Indogermanistischen Forschung, 1992, Theoretical Bases of Indo-European Linguistics, 1993, Residues of Pre-Indo-European Active Structure and Their Implications for the Relationships among the Dialects, 1995; editor: Language and Linguistics in the People's Republic of China, 1974, (with R.P.M. Lehmann) An Introduction to Old Irish, 1975, Syntactic Typology, 1978, (with Yakov Malkiel) Perspectives on Historical Linguistics, 1982, Language Typology, 1985, Language Typology: Systematic Balance in Language, 1987, (with H.J.J. Hewitt) Typological Models in Reconstruction, 1988; contbr. articles to profl. jours. Chmn. bd. dirs. Center for Applied Linguistics, 1973-78. 1st lt. Signal Corps AUS, 1942-46. Decorated Comdr.'s Cross, Order Merit Fed. Republic Germany, 1987; recipient Jakob Grimm prize, 1975, Pro bene Meritis award, U. Tex., 1987; fellow Fulbright Found., Norway, 1950-51, Guggenheim Found., 1972-73. Mem. MLA (exec. coun. 1977-80, pres. 1987), Linguistic Soc. Am. (pres. 1973), Am. Coun. Learned Socs. (sec. bd. 1977-86, Harry H. Ransom award teaching excellence 1989), Danish Acad. Scis. Lutheran. Home: 3800 Eck Ln Austin TX 78734-1613

LEHMANN-HAUPT, CHRISTOPHER CHARLES HERBERT, book reviewer; b. Edinburgh, Scotland, June 14, 1934; came to U.S., 1934; s. Hellmut Otto Emil and Letitia Jane H. (Grierson) Lehmann-H.; m. Natalie S. Robins, Oct. 3, 1965; children: Rachel Louise, Noah Christopher. B.A., Swarthmore Coll., 1956; M.F.A., Yale U., 1959. Editor A.S. Barnes & Co., Inc., N.Y.C., 1961-62, Holt, Rinehart & Winston, 1962-63; sr. editor Dial Press, 1963-65; mem. staff N.Y. Times Book Review, 1965-69; sr. book reviewer N.Y. Times, 1969—; asst. prof. lit. CUNY, 1973-75. Author: Me and Di Maggio, 1986, A Crooked Man, 1995. Club: Century. Office: New York Times 229 W 43rd St New York NY 10036-3913

LEHMBERG, ROBERT HENRY, research physicist; b. Phila., Dec. 4, 1937; s. Henry and Marguerite Elenore (Schock) L.; m. Norma Geder, Dec. 29, 1966; 1 child, Karl Robert. BSc, Pa. State U., 1959; MSc, U. Ariz., 1961; PhD, Brandeis U., 1968. Rsch. physicist Naval Air Devel. Ctr., Warminster, Pa., 1966-72, Naval Rsch. Lab., Washington, 1972—; chmn. program com. Conf. on Lasers and Electro-Optics, Washington, 1991. Contbr. articles to profl. jours.; patentee in field. Fellow Am. Phys. Soc. (Excellence in Plasma Physics Rsch. award 1993); mem. AAAS, IEEE, Sigma Xi. Achievements include development of optical beam smoothing techniques for laser fusion, optical design of the Naval Research Laboratory's Nike laser facility, and research in nonlinear optics and laser-plasma interaction physics. Office: Naval Rsch Lab Plasma Divsn 4555 Overlook Ave SW Washington DC 20375-0001

LEHMBERG, STANFORD EUGENE, historian, educator; b. McPherson, Kans., Sept. 23, 1931; s. Willard Eugene and Helen (Stanford) L.; m. Phyllis Barton, July 23, 1962; 1 son, Derek Grantham. BA, U. Kans., 1953, MA, 1954; PhD, Cambridge (Eng.) U., 1956, DLitt, 1990. Mem. faculty U. Tex., Austin, 1956-69; mem. faculty U. Minn., 1969—, prof. history, 1967—, chmn. dept., 1979-85. Author: Sir Thomas Elyot, Tudor Humanist, 1960, Sir Walter Mildmay and Tudor Government, 1966, The Reformation Parliament, 1970, The Later Parliaments of Henry VIII, 1977, The Reformation of Cathedrals, 1988, The People of the British Isles to 1688, 1991, Cathedrals Under Siege, 1996; also articles, revs. Fulbright scholar, 1954-56; Guggenheim fellow, 1965-66, 85-86. Fellow Royal Hist. Soc.; mem. Am. Hist. Assn., Midwest Conf. Brit. Studies (pres. 1982-84), Renaissance Soc. Am., Am. Soc. Reformation Research. Episcopalian. Home: 2300 Willow Ln S Minneapolis MN 55416-3863 Office: U Minn Dept History Minneapolis MN 55455

LEHNE, PASCAL HORST, chemistry educator, consultant; b. Hamburg, Germany, Apr. 17, 1915; s. Richard Wilhelm and Clarita (Voigt) L.; m. Julita Tapang Dawat, Aug. 4, 1972; 1 child, Rowena. Diploma in chemistry, U. Heidelberg, Germany, 1944. Asst. master Gewerbeschule Hansestadt Hamburg, 1956-65, sr. asst. master, 1966-80, ret., 1980, temporary appointed tutor, 1981-83; hon. co-worker Mus. für Hamburgische Geschichte, Hamburg, 1994—; vice dir. evening sch. English Inst., Heidelberg, 1950-52; subdir., tutor Inst. für Lernsysteme, Hamburg, 1980-86. Author: The Normal Gauge Electric Light Railway Altrahlstedt-Volksdorf-Wohldorf, 4 edits., 1954-86; co-author: Lead and Silver, 1966, 2nd edit., 1975, About the Mariana Islands, 1972; calculator of orbital elements of comet Paraskevopoulos (1941c) from pvt. observations; author numerous edits. Periodic Chart of Elements, 1938-52; contbr. articles to profl. jours. Mem. Gesellschaft Deutscher Chemiker, Bund für Deutsche Schrift, The Planetary Soc. Avocations: preparing Tagalog-German dictionary, compilation of comprehensive collections of elements and inorganic compounds. Home: Hamburger Strasse 110b, 22949 Ammersbek Germany Office: Staatliche Gewerbeschule für Chemie, Billwerder Billdeich 614, 21033 Hamburg Germany

LEHNER, GEORGE ALEXANDER, JR., lawyer; b. Cleve., Aug. 13, 1948; s. George Alexander and Phyllis More (Holbrook) L.; m. Diana Hill Day, May 29, 1971; children: Kristin, Alison. BA, Wesleyan U., Middletown, Conn., 1971; JD, U. Mich., 1976, M in Urban Planning, 1977. Bar: Mich. 1977, D.C. 1979, U.S. Dist. Ct. D.C. 1987, U.S. Ct. Appeals (4th cir.) 1987, U.S. Ct. Appeals (D.C. cir.) 1988, U.S. Ct. Appeals (9th cir.) 1993. Atty., advisor U.S. Dept. State, Washington, 1977-80; assoc. Arent, Fox, Kintner, Plotkin & Kahn, Washington, 1981-87; ptnr. Sloan, Lehner & Ruiz, Washington, 1987-89, Pepper, Hamilton & Scheetz, Washington, 1989—; adj. prof. Georgetown U. Law Ctr., 1990-93; gen. counsel Internat. Women's Media Found., 1990—. Co-author: Europe Without Frontiers: A Lawyer's Guide, 1989. Advisor foreign policy Mondale for Pres., 1984; Watson Fellow. Mem. ABA, Phi Beta Kappa. Avocations: sailing, photography. Home: 508 Woodland Ter Alexandria VA 22302-3317 Office: Pepper Hamilton & Scheetz 1300 19th St NW Washington DC 20036-1609

LEHNER, MARK, archaeologist, educator; b. Fargo, N.D., Apr. 2, 1950; s. Paul William and Ethel Lois (Davy) L.; m. Suzanne Ayad Massoud, July 12, 1975 (div. 1985); children: Ramsi, Luke; m. Julia Cort, July 2, 1995. BA in Anthropology, Am. U., Cairo, 1975; PhD in Egyptology, Yale U., 1990. Field dir. Sphinx and Isis Temple project Am. Rsch. Ctr., Egypt, 1979-83, co-dir. Pyramids radiocarbon dating project, 1984; dir. Giza Plateau mapping project Am. Rsch. Ctr./Oriental Inst. U. Chgo., Egypt, 1984—; dir. Koch-Ludwig Giza Plateau project U. Chgo., 1988—, instr. Egyptian Archaeology Oriental Inst., 1990-91, asst. prof., 1991-95, 1995—; bd. dirs. Ancient Egypt Rsch. Assocs., Inc; archtl. surveyor, draughtsman, area supervisor Nag Hammadi, Faw Qibli Expeditions Claremont Inst. Antiquity and Christianity, 1976-78; surveyor and dir. clearing ops. Sci. and Archaeology project, 1978; supr. mapping, photographer, draughtsman, various excavations in the Sphinx area, 1978; mapper Bayt al-Razzaz project Am. Rsch. Ctr., 1978; surveyor, object restorer, artist, photographer various salvage excavations, 1979; area supr., mapper, photographer, Tell el-Amarna expedition, Egypt Exploration Soc., 1979-80, archtl. surveyor Tomb of Akhenaten epigraphic survey, 1980;surveyor Deir el-Ballas expedition, Mus. Fine arts, Boston, 1983; archtl. surveyor Tombe of Aperia project, Saqqara Ctr. National de Recherches Scientifiques, 1983-85, Abdyos Regional Site Survey, U. Pa., 1983, Nasr. Mohammed Mosque Restoration, The German Archaeological Inst., 1985; cons. Time-Life Books, 1986-87, Field Mus. Nat. History, Chgo., 1987-88, NAS Com. Sphinx conservation study, 1989, Getty Conservation Inst., 1989-90, The Jerde Partnership, 1989-90, Egyptian Antiquities Orgn. Symposium on Sphinx restoration, 1992, materials adv bd. Nat. Rsch. Coun. conservation Egyptian monuments study steering com., 1992; lectr. in field; rsch. assoc. Harvard Semitic Mus. TV appearnaces include PM Mag., 1982, LBS Mysteries of the Pyramids, 1988, National Geographic Explorer, 1992, Nova: This Old Pyramid, 1992, 97, Nova: Obelisk; contbr. articlesto profl. jours. Sterling Prize fellow Yale U., 1986; recipient William J. Horowitz prize Near Eastern Langs. and Civilizations, Yale U. 1991. Office: Harvard Semitic Mus 6 Divinity Ave Cambridge MA 02138-2020

LEHNER, URBAN CHARLES, journalist; b. Grand Rapids, Mich., May 10, 1947; s. Urban Edward and Angeline Grace (Marcy) L.; m. Anne Marie Eding, May 2, 1969 (div. 1976); m. Nancy Ellen Leonard, June 28, 1980; 1 child, Alicia Ann. AB in history, U. Mich., 1969; JD, Georgetown U., 1979. Staff reporter The Wall Street Jour., N.Y.C., Phila., Chgo., Washington, 1969-80; bur. chief. The Wall Street Jour., Tokyo, 1980-83, Detroit, 1983-85; mng. editor The Wall Street Jour. Europe, Brussels, 1985-87; bur. chief The Wall Street Jour., The Asian Wall Street Jour., Tokyo, 1988-92; editor The Asian Wall Street Jour., Hong Kong, 1992—. Editor: Let's Talk Turkey (About Japanese Turkeys) And Other Tales from the Asian Wall Street Journal, 1996. Lt. (j.g.) USNR, 1970-72. Recipient Citation for Excellence with Alan Murray for Strained Alliance Overseas Press Club, 1991. Mem. Fgn. Corrs. Club Japan. Office: The Asian Wall St Jour, 2/F AIA Bldg CPO Box 9825, Hong Kong China

LEHNERT, HERBERT HERMANN, foreign language educator; b. Luebeck, Germany, Jan. 19, 1925; came to U.S., 1958, naturalized, 1971; s. Bernhard Alfred and Elisabeth (Doemel) L.; m. Ingeborg Poth, Aug. 13, 1952; children—Bernard (dec.), Brigitte, Bettina. Ph.D., U. Kiel, Germany, 1952. Lectr. U. Western Ont., Can., 1957; faculty Rice U., 1958-68, prof. German, 1966-68; prof. German U. Kans., 1968-69; prof. German U. Calif., Irvine, 1969—, chmn. dept., 1974-76; vis. prof. Harvard, fall 1970. Author: Thomas Mann: Fiktion, Mythos, Religion, 1965, Struktur und Sprachmagie, 1966, Thomas Mann Forschung, 1969, Geschichte der deutschen Literatur: Vom Jugendstil zum Expressionismus, 1978, Nihilismus der Menschenfreundlichkeit: Thomas Manns Wandlung (with Eva Wessell), 1991; editor: Doctor Faustus: A Novel at the Margin of Modernism (with Peter C. Pfeiffer) 1991; contbr. articles to profl. jours. Nat. Endowment for Humanities fellow, 1973, 78; Guggenheim fellow, 1978-79. Mem. MLA, Am. Assn. Tchrs. German. Home: 8 Harvey Ct Irvine CA 92612-4033 Office: U Calif Dept German Irvine CA 92697-3150

LEHOCZKY, JOHN PAUL, statistics educator; b. Columbus, Ohio, June 29, 1943; s. Paul Nicholas and Thelma Marie (Heisterkamp) L.; m. Mary Louise Zimmerman, Sept. 10, 1966; children: Jennifer Lynne, Jessica Augusta. BA, Oberlin Coll., 1965; MS, Stanford U., 1967, PhD, 1969. Asst. prof. stats. Carnegie Mellon U., Pitts., 1969-73, assoc. prof., 1973-81, prof., 1981-96, head dept., 1984-95; Thomas Lord prof. stats. Carnegie Mellon U., 1997—; assoc. editor IEEE Transactions on Computers, 1995—; cons. in legal stats., statis. anlysis, math. fin. and real-time computing. Dept. editor Mgmt. Sci., 1981-86; assoc. editor Jour. Real-Time Systems, 1989—; contbr. over 90 rsch. papers in various diciplines. Fellow Am. Statis. Assn. (statistician of yr. Pitts. chpt. 1987), Inst. Math. Stats.; mem. IEEE, AAAS, Assn. for Computing Machinery, Internat. Statis. Inst., Informs. Office: Carnegie Mellon Univ Dept Stats Pittsburgh PA 15213

LEHODEY, JOHN FRANCOIS, hotel company executive; b. Paris, July 27, 1933; came to U.S., 1960; s. Jacques and Gabrielle (Godard) L.; 1 child, Jacques. B.S. in Hotel Adminstrn. Hotel Sch., Thonon, France, 1953. Purser S.S. Liberté, S.S. Ile de. France, French Line, Le Havre-N.Y., 1955-60; mgr. rooms div. Waldorf Astoria Hotel, N.Y.C., 1963-71; mgr. Novotel, Paris, 1972-78; gen. mgr., v.p. Sofitel div. Accor N.Am., Mpls., 1979—. Served with French Navy, 1953-55. Mem. French-Am. C. of C., Chaine des Rotisseurs. Home: 5601 W 78th St Minneapolis MN 55439-3105 Office: 2 Overhill Rd Ste 420 Scarsdale NY 10583-5316

LEHOVEC, KURT, electrical engineering educator; b. Ladowitz, Czechoslovakia, June 12, 1918; came to U.S., 1947, naturalized, 1952; married, 1952. BS, Charles U., Prague, Czechoslovakia, 1938, MS, 1940; PhD in Physics, U. Prague, 1951. Head rsch. lab. physics inst. Prague U., 1942-45, rsch. fellow, 1945-46; rsch. fellow U.S. Signal Corps, Ft. Monmouth, N.J., 1947-52; dir. semicondr. R&D Sprague Elec. Co., 1952-66; pres. Inventors & Investors, 1967—; prof. electronics U. So. Calif., L.A., 1971-881971-97, emeritus prof. engring. and material sci., 1988—; adj. prof. Williams Coll., 1967, U. Calif., Irvine, 1980; cons. in field. Fellow IEEE, Am. Phys. Soc. Office: 200 S Westmoreland Ave Los Angeles CA 90004-6110*

LEHR, DENNIS JAMES, lawyer; b. N.Y.C., Feb. 7, 1932; s. Irwin Allen and Teeny (Scofield) L.; m. Enid J. Auerbach, June 10, 1956; children—Austin Windsor, Bryant Paul, Amy Lynn. BA, NYU, 1954, LLM, 1961; LLB, Yale U., 1957. Bar: N.Y. 1959, D.C. 1967. Atty. Allstate Ins. Co., N.Y.C., 1958-59; atty. Regional Office SEC, N.Y.C., 1959-61; assoc. Borden and Ball, N.Y.C., 1961-63; atty. Office Spl Counsel Investment Co. Act Matters SEC, Washington, 1963-64; assoc. chief counsel Office Comptroller Currency U.S. Treasury Dept., Washington, 1964-67; assoc. Hogan & Hartson, Washington, 1967-69, ptnr., 1969-94, of counsel, 1994—; bd. advs. So. Meth. U. Grad. Sch. Banking; adj. prof. Georgetown Law Sch., 1964-68; legal adv. com. Nat. Ctr. on Fin. Svcs., U. Calif.; lectr. Practicing Law Inst.; adv. coun. Banking Law Inst.; pub. mem. Adminstrv. Conf. of the U.S. Bd. contbrs. Fin. Services Law Report. Contbr. articles to profl. jours. Mem. ABA (coun. mem. sect. bus. law, former chmn. com. on Long Range Issues Affecting Bus. Law Practice, former chmn., com. on devels. in investment svcs.). Office: Hogan and Hartson 555 13th St NW Washington DC 20004-1109

LEHR, JANET, art dealer, publisher, author; b. N.Y.C., June 7, 1937; d. Herbert Davis and Florence (Lustig) Cooperman; m. Lewis Lehr, Feb. 22, 1959 (div. 1984); children: Florence Rachel, Michael William, Samuel Joseph. BA, NYU, 1955; JD, Bklyn. Law Sch., 1958. Pvt. practice art dealer 20th century Am. paintings N.Y.C., 1962-72; dir. Janet Lehr Inc., 19th and 20th Century Photographs, N.Y.C., 1972—; ptnr. Vered Gallery, paintings and sculptures by modern Am. masters, emerging artists and Am. rediscovery 1920-70, East Hampton, N.Y., 1988—; co-dir. Gallery 6M, N.Y.C., 1964-72; curator Landscape Photography, State Mus. Munich, 1979. Author: William Henry Jackson, Picture Maker of the American West, William Henry Fox Talbot and the Art of Photo Mechanical Illustration, 1978; exhbns. include Horatio Ross: Scottish Photographs 1850s Yale University, British Ctr. for the Arts, 1993, Masterworks of Photography, Art Gallery of New South Wales, Sydney, Australia, 1994; also 33 quar. issues on history photography, 1976-86. Mem. Assn. Internat. Photography Art Dealers (founding), Antiquarian Book Dealers Am., Internat. Book Dealers Assn. Home and Office: 891 Park Ave New York NY 10021-0326

LEHR, LEWIS WYLIE, diversified manufacturing company executive; b. Elgin, Nebr., Feb. 21, 1921; s. Lewis H. and Nancy (Wylie) L.; m. Doris Stauder, Oct. 13, 1944; children—Mary A. Lehr Makin, William L., Donald D., John M. B.S. in Chem. Engring, U. Nebr., 1947, Sc.D. (hon.), 1977. With 3M Co., St. Paul, 1947—; v.p. med. products div. 3M Co., 1960-72, health care products group, 1972-74, tape and allied products group, 1974-75, pres. U.S. ops., 1975-79, vice chmn., 1979-80, chmn., chief exec. officer, 1980-86; bd. dirs. Jack Eckerd corp., Tampa, Fla., Sci., Inc., Bloomington, Minn., Peregrine, Inc. Trustee U. Nebr. Found. Served with AUS, 1943-46, ETO. Recipient Alumni Achievement award U. Nebr. Alumni Assn., 1976, State of Nebr. Wagon Master award, 1995. Mem. Am. Chem. Soc. Clubs: North Oaks Golf, White Bear Yacht, Minnesota. Address: Minn World Trade Ctr 30 7th St E Ste 3050 Saint Paul MN 55101-4901

LEHRER, JAMES CHARLES, television journalist; b. Wichita, Kans., May 19, 1934; s. Harry Frederick and Lois Catherine (Chapman) L.; m. Kate Staples, June 4, 1960; children: Jamie, Lucy, Amanda. A.A., Victoria Coll., 1954; B.J., U. Mo., 1956. Reporter Dallas Morning News, 1959-61; reporter, columnist, city editor Dallas Times Herald, 1961-70; exec. producer, corr. Sta. KERA-TV, Dallas, 1970-72; pub. affairs coordinator Public Broadcasting Service, Washington, 1972-73; corr. NPACT-WETA-TV, Washington, 1973—; exec. editor, anchor The NewsHour with Jim

Lehrer, 1995—; instr. creative writing Dallas Coll., So. Meth. U., 1967-68. Author: (fiction) Viva Max, 1966, We Were Dreamers, 1975, Kick the Can, 1988, Crown Oklahoma, 1980, The Sooner Spy, 1990, Lost and Found, 1991, Short List, 1992, A Bus of My Own, 1992, Blue Hearts, 1993, Fine Lines, 1994, The Last Debate, 1995, White Widow, 1997, (plays) Chili Queen, 1986, Church Key Charlies Blue, 1987, The Will and Bart Show, 1992. Served with USMC, 1956-59. Recipient Columbia-Dupont award; George Polk award; Peabody award; Emmy award. Mem. Am. Acad. Arts and Scis., Dramatists Guild, Authors Guild, Tex. Inst. Letters, Coun. on Fgn. Rels. Office: Sta WETA-TV PO Box 2626 Washington DC 20013-2626

LEHRER, KENNETH EUGENE, real estate advisor, economic consultant; b. N.Y.C., Apr. 17, 1946; s. Charles Carlton and Evelyn Estelle (Rosenfeld) L.; m. Myrna Sue Newman, Apr. 4, 1981 (div. 1988); m. Geraldine Trudy Fishman, Mar. 18, 1994. BS, NYU, 1967, MBA, 1969, MA, 1972, D in Pub. Adminstrn., 1980. Registered investment advisor; cert. real estate appraiser; lic. real estate broker. Asst. treas. Bankers Trust Co., N.Y.C., 1970-73; dir. devel. Coventry Devel. Corp., N.Y.C., 1974-77; asst. v.p. Affiliated Capital Corp., Houston, 1977-80; dir. fin. Allison/Walker Interests, Houston, 1980-82; mng. dir. Lehrer Fin. and Econ. Adv. Svcs., 1982—; prof. real estate fin. U. Houston Grad. Sch. Bus. Adminstrn., 1985—; chmn. bd. dirs. Acadia Savs. and Loan Assn., Crowley, La., French Market Homestead Savs. Assn., Metairie, La., Twin City Savs. Bank, West Monroe, La., 1st Savs. La., LaPlace, Integrated Resource Techs. Inc., 1992-95. Pres. Cornerstone Mcpl. Utilities Dist., 1978-85; bd. dirs. Ft. Bend County Mcpl. Utility Dist. #106, Houston Caliber Fin. Group, chmn., 1994-96. Mem. Am. Horse Show Assn. (life), Nat. Steeplechase and Hunt Assn. (life), U.S. Tennis Assn. (life), Am. Real Estate and Urban Econs. Assn., Am. Real Estate Soc., Nat. Assn. Bus. Economists, NYU Money Marketeers, Nat. Forensic Ctr., Nat. Assn. Corp. Dirs., Am. Acad. Econ. and Fin. Experts, Internat. Coll. Real Estate Cons. Profls., Internat. Assn. Corp. Real Estate Execs., Nat. Assn. Forensic Economists, Am. Arbitration Assn., Houston Bus. Economists, Western Econ. Assn., Fin. Club. NYC., Real Estate Educators Assn., Am. Econ. Assn., N.Am. Econs. and Fin. Assn., So. Econ. Assn., NYU Alumni Fedn. (bd. dirs. 1974-77), Tex. Rep. Assn., Rep. Senatorial Inner Cir. (life, Medal of Freedom 1994), Houston C. of C. (mem. govtl. relations com.), Princeton Club N.Y., Jockey Club (Miami, Fla.), Capitol Hill Club (Washington). Episcopalian. Home: 5555 Del Monte Dr Apt 802 Houston TX 77056-4117 Office: Lehrer Fin and Econ Adv Svcs 1775 Saint James Pl Ste 110 Houston TX 77056-3403

LEHRER, LEONARD, artist, educator; b. Phila., Mar. 23, 1935; s. Abraham and Bessie Lehrer; m. Marilyn Bigard, May 29, 1977; 1 child, Anna-Katrina Picard; stepchildren: Tracy Peel, Janna Peel, John Peel, Jamye Pawlak. BFA, Phila. Coll. Art, 1956; MFA, U. Pa., 1960. Mem. faculty Phila. Coll. Art, 1956-70, co-dir. found. program, 1965-70; prof. art U. N.Mex., 1970-74, chmn. dept., 1970-73; prof. U. Tex., San Antonio, 1974-77; dir. divsn. art and design U. Tex., 1974-75; prof., dir. Sch. Art, Ariz. State U., Tempe, 1977-90; dir. Visual Art Rsch. Studios, 1984-91; prof. art NYU, 1991-97, chair dept. art and art professions, 1991-96. One-man shows include Utah Mus. Fine Arts, Salt Lake City, 1973, 82, Marian Locks Gallery, Phila., 1974-77, 84, McNay Art Mus., San Antonio, 1975, Galerie Kühl, Hannover, Germany, 1976, 79, 82, 91, Bomann Mus., Celle, Germany, 1980, Marilyn Butler Fine Art, Scottsdale, Ariz., 1980, Assoc. Am. Artists, Phila., 1984, Am. Cultural Affairs Ctr., Madrid, 1984, MyungSook Lee Gallery, N.Y.C., 1997, numerous others; exhibited in group shows including 14th Ljubljana Internat. Print Biennial, 1981, 4th Graphic Arts Biennial of Ams., Cali, Colombia, 1981, 7th Brit. Internat. Print Biennial, Bradford, Eng., 1982, Internat. Printmaking Invitational, San Bernardino, Calif., 1983, XXXV Art Fair, Munich, 1992, XXIV Art Fair, Hannover, 1993; represented in permanent collections Met. Mus. Art, N.Y.C., Mus. Modern Art, N.Y.C., Phila. Mus. Art, Nat. Gallery Art, Fed. Res. Bd., Corcoran Gallery, Libr. of Congress, Washington, Spengel Mus. Art, Hannover; curator Large Scale Am. Prints in Art Multiple Dusseldorf, Germany, 1992; author: (introductory essay) The Art of the Book; works featured in The Art of Leonard Lehrer, 1986; contbr. articles to profl. jours. Mem. bd. trustees, v.p. Internat. Print Ctr. N.Y., Inc.; chair Arts Acad. Adv. Com., The College Bd., 1996—. Recipient 1st prize 4th Miami Internat. Print Biennial, 1980; recipient Western States Art Found. Printmaking Fellowship award, 1979, Heitland Found. prize, Celle, 1980, Gold Medal award Ariz. chpt. Nat. Soc. Arts and Letters, 1981. Office: NYU Dept Art and Art Professions New York NY 10003

LEHRER, STANLEY, magazine publisher, editorial director, corporate executive; b. Bklyn., Mar. 18, 1929; s. Martin and Rose L.; m. Laurel Francine Zang, June 8, 1952; children: Merrill Clark, Randee Hope. BS in Journalism, N.Y. U., 1950; postgrad. in edn, San Antonio Coll., 1952. Editor and pub. Crossroads mag., Valley Stream, N.Y., 1949-50; youth service editor Open Road mag., N.Y.C., 1950-51; mng. editor School & Society, N.Y.C., 1953-68, v.p., 1956-68; pub. School & Society Books, N.Y.C., 1963-86; pres., pub. School & Society mag., N.Y.C., 1968-72; pres., pub. Intellect mag., N.Y.C., 1972-78, editorial dir., 1974-78; founder, pres., pub., editl. dir. USA Today mag., Valley Stream, N.Y., 1978—; pres., pub., editorial dir. Newsview newsletter, 1979—, Your Health newsletter, 1980—, The World of Sci. newsletter, 1980—; cons. Child Care Publs., N.Y.C., 1955. Producer, commentator: (WBAI-FM radio program) Report on Eucation, N.Y.C., 1960-61; author: John Dewey: Master Educator, 1959, Countdown on Segregated Education, 1960, Religion, Government, and Education, 1961, A Century of Higher Education: Classical Citadel to Collegiate Colossus, 1962, Automation, Education, and Human Values, 1966, Conflict and Change on the Campus: The Response to Student Hyperactivism, 1970, Leaders, Teachers, and Learners in Academe: Partners in the Educational Process, 1970, Education and the Many Faces of the Disadvantaged: Cultural and Historical Perspectives, 1972; contbr. articles to nat. mags., newspapers and profl. jours.; exhibited Stanley Lehrer maritime collection on transatlantic ships at N.Y. Yacht Club, 1983, on Cunard Line's 150th anniversary at Forbes Mag. Galleries, N.Y.C., 1989-90, on French Line's Normandie at French Embassy, N.Y.C., 1992, and Bass Mus. Art, Miami, Fla., 1993, on Ships of State: The Great Transatlantic Liners, PaineWebber Art Gallery, N.Y.C., 1994-95, on the Wreck of the Titanic, Nat. Maritime Mus., London, 1994-95, on S.O.S. Safety on Ships: Learning from New York's Maritime Tragedies, Water Street Gallery, Seamen's Church Institute, N.Y.C., 1996; designer of life jackets for Broadway musical Titanic, Lunt-Fontanne Theatre, N.Y.C., 1997. V.p. Garden City Park (N.Y.) Civic Assn., 1961-63; treas. Citizens' Com. Edn., Garden City Park, 1962; mem. nat. jr. book awards com. Boys' Clubs Am., 1954; mem. nat. hon. com. for Richard H. Heindel Meml. Fund, Pa. State U., 1979-80. With Signal Corps, U.S. Army, 1951-53. Recipient non-fiction awards Midwestern Writers Conf., Chgo., 1948. Mem. New Hyde Park (N.Y.) C. of C. (dir. 1961-62), Titanic Hist. Soc., S.S. Hist. Soc. Am., Soc. Advancement of Edn. (treas. 1953—, trustee 1963—, pres. 1968—), Ocean Liner Mus. (N.Y.C.), Psi Chi Omega. Home: 82 Shelbourne Ln New Hyde Park NY 11040-1044 Office: USA Today 99 W Hawthorne Ave Valley Stream NY 11580-6101

LEHRER, WILLIAM PETER, JR., animal scientist; b. Bklyn., Feb. 6, 1916; s. William Peter and Frances Reif (Muser) L.; m. Lois Lee Meister, Sept. 13, 1945; 1 child, Sharon Elizabeth. BS, Pa. State U., 1941; MS in Agr., MS in Range Mgmt., U. Idaho, 1946, 55; PhD in Nutrition and Biochemistry, Wash. State U., 1951; LLB, U. Chgo., 1972, JD, 1974; MBA, Pepperdine U., 1975. Mgmt. trainee Swift & Co., Charleston, W.Va., 1941-42; farm mgr. Maple Springs Farm, Middletown, N.Y., 1944-45; rsch. fellow U. Idaho, Moscow, 1945; asst. prof. to prof. U. Idaho, 1945-60; dir. nutrition Albers Milling Co., L.A., 1960-62; dir. nutrition and rsch. Albers Milling Co., 1962-74, Albers Milling Co. & John W. Eshelman & Sons, L.A., 1974-76, Carnation Co., L.A., 1976-81; ret.; cons. in field; speaker, lectr. more than 40 univs. in U.S. and abroad. Contbr. 115 articles to profl. jours.; co-author: The Livestock Industry, 1950, Dog Nutrition, 1972; author weekly column Desseret News, Salt Lake City. Mem. rsch. adv. co. U.S. Brewers Assn., 1969-81; mem. com. on dog nutrition, com. animal nutrition Nat. Rsch. Coun. NAS, 1970-76. With U.S. Army Air Corps, 1942-43. Named Disting. Alumnus, Pa. State U., 1963, 83, Key Alumnus, 1985; named to U. Idaho Alumni Hall of Fame, 1985; recipient Alumni Achievement award Wash. State U., 1993. Fellow AAAS, Am. Soc. Animal Sci.; mem. Am. Inst. Nutrition, Coun. for Agrl. Sci. & Tech., Am. Registry of Profl. Animal Scientists, Am. Inst. Food Technologists, Animal Nutrition Rsch. Coun., Am. Dairy Sci. Assn., Am. Soc. Agrl. Engrs., Am. Feed Mfrs. Assn. (life, nutrition coun. 1962-81, chmn. 1969-70), Calif. State Poly. U. (adv. coun. 1965-81, Meritorious Svc. award), The Nutrition Today Soc., Am. Soc. Animal Sci., Poultry Sci. Assn., Nat. Block & Bridle Club, Hayden Lake Country Club, Alpha Zeta, Sigma Xi, Gamma Sigma Delta (Alumni Award of Merit), Xi Sigma Pi. Republican. Avocations: river running, hunting, fishing, gardening, restoring furniture. Home: Rocking L Ranch 12180 Rimrock Rd Hayden Lake ID 83835

LEHRMAN, IRVING, rabbi; b. Tiktin, Poland, June 15, 1911; came to U.S. 1916; s. Abraham and Rachel Minnie (Dinowitz) L.; m. Bella Goldfarb, May 21, 1935; children: David Lehrman, Rosalind Lehrman. DHL, Jewish Theol. Sem. of Am., N.Y.C., 1948, DD, 1969; DHL, St. Thomas U., Miami, Fla., 1989; DL, Barry U., Miami, 1992; DHL, Fla. Internat. U., 1992. Ordained rabbi, 1943. Student rabbi Temple Shomrei Emunah, Montclair, N.J., 1939-43; rabbi Temple Emanu-El of Greater Miami, Miami Beach, Fla., 1943-93; founding rabbi, dean Lehrman Day Sch., 1993—; vis. prof. Homiletics Jewish Theol. Sem. Am.; nat. pres. Synagogue Coun. Am.; chmn. United Jewish Appeal Nat. Rabbinic Cabinet; chmn. Greater Miami Combined Jewish Appeal; chmn. bd. govs. Greater Miami State of Israel Bonds; found. chmn. Jewish Nat. Fund; hon. pres. S.E. region Rabbinical Assembly of Am. Author: In the Name of God, collection of sermons, articles, 1979, L'Chaim, thoughts for Jewish living, 1985, Portraits in Charcoal, 1980. Mem. White House Commn. on Obscenity and Pornography, Aging, and Food, Nutrition and Health (co-chmn. religious task force); bd. dirs. Miami Jewish Home and Hosp. for Aged, Internat. Synagogue at JFK Airport, N.Y.C.; nat. v.p. Zionist Orgn. Am.; adv. bd. St. Thomas U., Nat. Conf. Christians and Jews; former mem. exec. com. UNESCO, Greater Miami Community Rels. Bd. Recipient silver medal NCCJ, Prime Min.'s medal State of Israel, Albert Einstein Brotherhood award Technion U., Golda Meir Leadership award State of Israel Bonds, also others; Lehrman Dr. named in his honor, Miami Beach, 1986; Rabbi Irving Lehrman Park established in his honor by Miami Friends of Tel Aviv Found., Tel Aviv, 1988; Rabbi Irving & Belle Lehrman Recreation and Picnic Area established Jabotinsky Park, Shuni, Israel, 1992. Mem. Rabbinical Assn. Greater Miami (past pres.). Office: Temple Emanu-El 1701 Washington Ave Miami FL 33139-7541 *There is one principle that has guided my life and I always share it with others: "No matter how difficult it may seem, you will never be sorry for doing the right thing."*

LEHRMAN, MARGARET MCBRIDE, television news executive, producer; b. Spokane, Wash., Sept. 25, 1944; d. John P. and Ruth A. McBride; m. Michael Lloyd Lehrman, June 27, 1970. BA, U. Oreg., 1966; MS, Columbia U., 1970. Dir. coll. desk Peace Corps, Washington, 1966-69; asst. to exec. editor The Morning News Co., Washington, 1970-72; reporter Albright Communications, Washington, 1973-74; tv assignment editor ABC News, Washington, 1974; press asst. Senator Robert P. Griffin, Washington, 1975-79; researcher Today Show, NBC News, Washington, 1979, assoc. producer, 1979-83, Washington producer, 1983-89, dep. bur. chief, 1989-95, Washington producer, spec. coverage and events, 1995—. Trustee U. Oreg. Found., 1990—. Recipient Edwin M. Hood award for diplomatic reporting (China) adv. bd. Internat. Women's Media Found., Women's Fgn. Policy Group. Office: NBC News 4001 Nebraska Ave NW Washington DC 20016-2733

LEHRMAN, NAT, magazine editor; b. Bklyn., Aug. 5, 1929; s. Louis and Lena (Goldfarb) L.; m. Kazuko Miyajima, Nov. 13, 1956; children: Jerome M., Cynthia H. B.A., Bklyn. Coll., 1953; M.A., NYU, 1961. Travel editor internat. travel dept. Am. Automobile Assn., 1955-57; editor Relax mag., 1958, Dude, also Gent mags., 1959-61; assoc. to sr. editor Playboy mag., Chgo., 1966-71; editor new publs. Playboy Enterprises, 1972; editor, then assoc. pub. Oui mag., 1973-75; sr. v.p., assoc. pub. Playboy mag., 1976-85, dir. mag. divsn., 1980-85, pres. pub. div., 1982-85; pub.'s cons., 1985-87; dir. Essence mag.; tchr. fiction Columbia Coll., Chgo., 1967, chmn. journalism dept., 1987—. Author: Masters and Johnson Explained, 1970. Bd. dirs. Chgo. Chamber Musicians. With U.S. Army, 1953-55. Mem. Chgo. Classical Guitar Soc. (bd. dirs.). Club: Lincoln Park Tennis (pres.). Office: 600 S Michigan Ave Chicago IL 60605-1901

LEHTIHALME, LARRY (LAURI) K., financial planner; b. Montreal, Que., Can., Feb. 26, 1937; came to U.S., 1964; s. Lauri Johann and Selma Maire (Piispanen) L.; m. Elizabeth Speed Smith, Sept. 9, 1961; children: Tina Beth, Shauna Lyn. Student, Sir George Williams U., Montreal, 1960-64, Mission Coll., San Fernando, Calif., 1978-80, Pierce Coll., Woodland Hills, Calif., 1990-92. Lic. in variable annuity, life and disability ins., Calif.; lic. securities series 7 SEC, series 63. Acct., customer svc. cons. No. Electric, Montreal, 1957-64; salesman Remington Rand Systems, Wilmington, Del., 1964-67; account exec., comm. cons. Pacific Tel. & Telegraph Co., L.A., 1968-84; tech. customer support specialist AT&T, L.A., 1984-85; fin. adv., registered rep. Am. Express Fin. Advisors, L.A., 1987—. Mem. ctrl. com. Calif. 39th Assembly Dist. Rep. Com., 1976-81, City of L.A., 12th dist.; pres. North Hills Jaycees, 1969-70; sec.-treas. Com. Ind. Valley City and County Govt., 1978-82; subchmn. allocations United Way, Van Nuys, Calif., 1990; fundraiser North Valley YMCA, 1986—, Kids Safe Edn. Found.; formerly active numerous comty. and polit. orgns. in San Fernando Valley. Named Jaycee of Yr., Newark (Del.) Jaycees, 1966, Granada Hills Jaycees, 1971; recipient cert. of merit U.S. Ho. of Reps., 1973, cert. appreciation City of L.A., 1980, 84, State of Calif., 20th senate dist., 1983, Comty. Spirit award, 1990. Mem. L.A. Olympic Organizing Com. Alumni Assn., Jr. Chamber Internat. (life, senator 1973), U.S. Jaycees (life, Jaycee of Yr. 1965, Outstanding Local Jaycee 1965-66, Presdl. award Honor 1967, Jaycee of Month 1966-67, asst. gen. chmn. 1970-71, state dir. N. Hollywood chpt. 1970-71, Cert. Merit 1971, state gen. chmn., 1971-72, 72-73, Outstanding State Chmn. Calif. dist. 22 1973-74), Granada Hills C. of C. (bd. dirs. 1976-83, Man of Yr. award 1973), Granada Hills Jr. C. of C. Episcopalian. Avocation: community service. Home: 11408 Haskell Ave Granada Hills CA 91344-3959 Office: Am Express Fin Advisors 11145 Tampa Ave Ste 20A Northridge CA 91326-2264

LEHTINEN, MERJA HELEN KOKKONEN, journalist, researcher, publisher; b. N.Y., Feb. 25, 1954; d. Osmo Ilmari and Hilkka Annikki (Kokkonen-Lind) L. AB in Am. Studies, Mt. Holyoke Coll., 1976; student, Dartmouth Coll., 1975; cert. in Finnish and Scandinavian, U. Helsinki, 1978. Assoc. tech. writer The Travelers Ins. Co., Hartford; mng. editor ASHRAE, N.Y.; internat. editor ASCE, N.Y.; dir. publs. Am. Assn. Engring., N.Y.; mng. editor Bill Comms., Inc., N.Y.; news editor McGraw Hill Co., N.Y.; exec. editor Mng. Automation Mag., N.Y.; editor-in-chief, pub. Indsl. Computing Mag. Kruger, McCarthy & Lehtinen, N.Y., 1987-93; founder, pres. Westisle Pub. Co., Westford, Mass., 1993; owner, pub. Discover Conn. Mag. and The Conn. Chronicles, 1993—; USA developer Field Comm. USA, Angel, Angel Bus. Comm., London, 1996; intern for Sen. Strom Thurmond U.S. Senate, Washington, 1973; dir. career guidance Am. Assn. Engring. Scis., N.Y., 1983-84; commr. Econ. Devel. Commn. of Colchester, Conn., 1992-96, hearing officer, 1994—; bd. dirs. Indsl. Computing Soc., Research Triangle Park, N.C., 1993-95. Author: Quality Control, 1977 (award of excellence Soc. Tech. Comms., 1977); ghost writer Exec. Jour., Hewlett-Packard Co., 1996; contbr. articles to profl. jours. and mags. Vice chmn. Rep. Town Com., 1993-96; Rep. candidate for nomination to U.S. Congress 2d dist., 1992; hearing officer Justice of the Peace, Colchester, Conn., 1996—; bd. incorporators Eliza Huntington Meml. Home, Inc., 1993—, bd. dirs., fundraising chmn.; co-chair Internat. Conf. on Indsl. Computing, Toronto, 1992. Recipient rsch. fellow Rep. National Com., Washington, 1975. Mem. Instrument Soc. Am., Indsl. Computing Soc. (founder, mem. bd. dirs. 1993-95). Republican. Avocations: skiing, water & oil painting, gardening.

LEIBACH, DALE W., public relations executive. Reporter Kansas City Star; mgr. pub. affairs Ford Motor Co., Washington; asst. press sec. White House, 1977-81; press sec. to U.S. senator Tom Harkin; sr. v.p., mng. dir. Powell Adams & Rinehart (Ogilvy & Mather), Washington; sr. v.p., chief oper. officer Powell Tate, Washington. Office: Powell Tate 700 13th St NW Ste 1000 Washington DC 20005-3960

LEIBER, GERSON AUGUST, artist; b. Bklyn., Nov. 12, 1921; s. William and Rebecca (Margulis) L.; m. Judith Maria Peto, Feb. 5, 1946. Student Art Students League, N.Y., 1947-52, Bklyn. Mus. Art Sch., 1952-53; DFA (hon.), Bar Ilan U., Israel, 1993. Instr. Newark Sch. Fine and Indsl. Arts; v.p. Judith Leiber, Inc., N.Y.C., 1963—. One-man shows, Oakland (Calif.) Mus., 1960, N.Y.C., 1961, 62, 63, 64, 68, 69, 72, 76, 85, 95, 96, Fine Arts Mus. L.I. (N.Y.), 1991; exhibited in numerous nat. and internat. group shows, prints and paintings represented in pvt. and permanent collections. With AUS, 1942-47. Recipient numerous prizes including Bklyn. Mus. Purchase awards, 1953-66, 2d prize of $1,000, Assoc. Am. Artists Nat. Print Exhbn., 1959, Soc. Washington Printmakers prize, 1962, purchase award Hunterdon County Art Center 6th nat. print exhbn., 1962, Audubon medals of Honor for Graphics, 1963, 65, Sonia Watter award Am. Color Print Soc., 1968, 1000 Purchase award Assn. Am. Artists, 1968, John Taylor Arms Meml. prize NAD, 1971; Tiffany fellow, 1957, 60. Mem. NAD, Soc. Am. Graphic Artists (past pres.), Art Students League N.Y. Home: 7 Park Ave New York NY 10016-4330 Studio: 27 E 31st St New York NY 10016-6810

LEIBER, JERRY, songwriter; b. 1933. Songwriter: (with Mike Stoller) Hound Dog, Loving You, Jailhouse Rock, Searchin', Young Blood, Yakety Yak, Charlie Brown, Along Came Jones, Poison Ivy, Little Egypt, Down in Mexico, D.W. Washburn, Shoppin' for Clothes, That Is Rock & Roll, Smokey Joe's Cafe, Framed, Riot in Cell Block #9, Stand By Me, Spanish Harlem, I (Who Have Nothing), On Broadway, Dance With Me, Drip Drop, Saved, Lucky Lips, Love Potion #9, Only in America, I Keep Forgettin', Kansas City, Ruby Baby, Fools Fall in Love, I'm a Woman, Black Denim Trousers and Motorcycle Boots, Treat Me Nice, (You're So Square) Baby, I Don't Care, Bossa Nova Baby, Santa Claus is Back in Town, She's Not You, Trouble, (single David Bowie's album Tonight album) I Keep Forgetting, 1995, (play) Smokey Joe's Cafe-The Songs of Leiber and Stoller, 1995. Recipient Founders' award ASCAP, 1991, Best Musical Show Album Grammy award, 1996; inducted into Songwriters' Hall of Fame, 1985, Record Producers' Hall of Fame, 1986, Rock & Roll Hall of Fame, 1987; nominated 7 Tony awards. Office: Atlantic Records 75 Rockefeller Plz New York NY 10019-6908*

LEIBER, JUDITH MARIA, designer, manufacturer; b. Budapest, Hungary, Jan. 11, 1921; came to U.S., 1947, naturalized, 1949; d. Emil and Helen (Spitzer) Peto; m. Gerson Leiber, Feb. 6, 1946. Student pvt. schs., Hungary and Eng.; DFA (hon.), Internat. Fine Arts Coll., 1993; PhD (hon.), Bar Ilan U., Israel, 1993, Internat. Fine Arts Coll., Miami, Fla., 1993. Master handbag maker Hungary, 1942; pattern maker, designer Nettie Rosenstein, N.Y.C., 1947-60, Koret, N.Y.C., 1960-61; owner, mgr. Judith Leiber, Inc., N.Y.C., 1963—. Author: Judith Leiber, The Artful Handbag, 1995; designs represented in 30-yr. retrospective F.I.T. Mus., N.Y., 1993-94. Recipient Swarovski award and Am. Handbag Designer award Leather Industries Am., 1970, Coty award Am. Fashion Critics, 1973, Neiman-Marcus award, 1980, Women Who Made a Difference award Fashion Group, 1986, Lifetime Achievement award Dallas Mart, 1991, Am. Acad. Achievement award, 1992, FAAB Lifetime Achievement award, 1992, Ellis Island Medal Honor, 1993, Lifetime Achievement award Coun. Fashion Designers Am., 1993, Fashion Hall of Fame award Shannon Rodgers & Jerry Silverman Sch. Fashion Design and Merchandising, Kent State U., 1995; featured Retrospective of Work New Orleans Mus. Mem. Nat. Handbag Authority (dir. 1972—). Pioneering woman master handbag maker, Hungary; first woman patternmaker Am. handbag industry. Office: 20 W 33rd St New York NY 10001-3305

LEIBERT, RICHARD WILLIAM, special events producer; b. N.Y.C., Nov. 11, 1948; s. Richard William and Rosemarie Martha (Bruns) L. BS, Boston U., 1966-70; student, Northwestern U., 1971. Producer Sta. WBZ AM/FM, Boston, 1968-70; prodn. dir. Sta. WMMR-FM, Phila., 1970; exec. producer Sta. WIND-AM, Chgo., 1970-72; program dir. Sta. KGB AM-FM, San Diego, 1972-80; pres. Events Mktg., Inc., L.A., 1980—; dir. Nat. Fireworks Ensemble, Los Angeles, Calif., 1985—. Creator (mascot, publicity stunts) Sta. KGB Chicken, 1974; creator, producer (radio fireworks show) Sta. KGB Sky Show, 1976; writer, producer (network radio show) New Music News, 1983; creator, dir. (touring co.) Nat. Fireworks Ensemble, 1985. Recipient Emmy award, 1978; named Program Dir. of Yr. Billboard Mag., 1976, Radio Program of Yr. Billboard Mag., 1976. Avocations: sailing, baseball. Office: Events Mktg Inc PO Box 65694 Los Angeles CA 90065-0694

LEIBHOLZ, STEPHEN WOLFGANG, physicist, engineering company executive, entrepreneur; b. Berlin, Jan. 28, 1932; came to U.S., 1936; s. Ernest S. and Louise (Stern) L.; m. Ann Esther Greenberg, May 29, 1958; children: Judith, Robert, Daniel. BA in Physics, NYU, 1952. Prin. engr. Repub. Fairchild Co., Farmingdale, N.Y., 1957-60; mgr. systems design and analysis Auerbach Corp., Phila., 1960-67; founder, chmn. Analytics, Inc., Willow Grove, Pa., 1967-91; advisor, cons. scientist U.S. govt. agys., Washington, 1970—; founder, CEO Chesapeake Tech Labs Inc., 1986—, ACS, Inc., 1987—, Inst. for Global Intelligence, 1995—. Author and editor 7 books; contbr. articles to profl. pubs. Bd. dirs. Jenkintown Music Sch., 1970-74, advisor Kansas City Camerata Chamber Orch. Cons. U. of Arts, Pa. Conv. Ctr.; mem. adv. bd. Inst. for Adv. Psychology. Sr. fellow Fgn. Policy Rsch. Inst. Mem. AAAS, IEEE, Mil. Ops. Rsch. Soc. (past bd. dirs.), Cosmos Club (Washington). Office: 2333 Huntingdon Pike Huntingdon Valley PA 19006-6109

LEIBIN, HARVEY BRUCE, architect; b. Waterbury, Conn., May 7, 1947; s. Samuel and Helen (Blumenfeld) L.; m. Florence Epstein, June 28, 1970; children: Bradford A., Kate E., Kara B. BA, Cornell U., 1969; BS, U. Mich., 1971, MArch, 1973. Registered profl. architect, Conn., Mass., N.Y. Draftsman, designer Daniel Schwartzman & Assocs., N.Y.C., 1973-75; designer, job capt. Van Summern and Weigold, N.Y.C., 1975-77; designer, project architect Russell Gibson von Dohlen, Farmington, Conn., 1977-87; prin., owner Leibin Assocs., Hartford, Conn., 1987-90; prin., ptnr. DuBose Assocs., Inc., Hartford, 1990—. Prin. projects include The North Dormitory Complex Renovation at Conn. Coll., The Univ. Conn. at Stamford, Harman Hall The Loomis Chaffee Sch., The Sci. Ctr. of Conn., Kravis Hall the Loomis Chaffee Sch., Southern Conn. State U., Swing Space Bldg., Security Ins. Corp. Interiors, The Hartfrod Courant Hdgrs., UTC Rsch. Labs. Otis Elevator Rsch. Bldg., single family residences. Mem. East Hartford (Conn.) Design Rev. Bd., 1987-90, Beth El Edn. Com., West Hartford, Conn., 1990-92; chmn. Pond Place Assn. Design Rev., Avon, Conn. Mem. U.S. Army Res., 1969-75. Recipient Downtown Workplace award Hartford Archtl. Conservancy, Aetna Cityplace award, 1986, Landmark Bank/Cityplace award, 1986; named Readers Poll/Best Interior, Interior Design Mag., 1980; Rogow Found. scholar, Hartford. Mem. Conn. Soc. Architects, AIA, NCARB, Bldg. Owners and Mgrs. Assn., Cornell Club of Hartford, Mich. Club of Hartford. Jewish. Home: 65 Buttonwood Hill Rd Avon CT 06001-3241 Office: DuBose Assocs Inc 49 Woodland St Hartford CT 06105-2337

LEIBOLD, ARTHUR WILLIAM, JR., lawyer; b. Ottawa, Ill., June 13, 1931; s. Arthur William and Helen (Cull) L.; m. Nora Collins, Nov. 30, 1957; children: Arthur William III, Alison Aubry, Peter Collins. AB, Haverford Coll., 1953; JD, U. Pa., 1956. Bar: Pa. 1957. With Dechert, Price & Rhoads, Phila., 1956-69, ptnr., 1965-69; ptnr. Dechert, Price & Rhoads, Washington, 1972—; gen. counsel Fed. Home Loan Bank Bd. and Fed. Savs. & Loan Ins. Corp., Washington, 1969-72, Fed. Home Loan Mortgage Corp., 1970-72; lectr. English St. Joseph's Coll., Phila., 1957-59. Contbr. articles to profl. publs. Mem. Pres. Kennedy's Lawyers Com. Civil Rights, 1963, Adminstrv. Conf. U.S., 1969-72; bd. dirs. Marymount Coll. Va., 1974-75; Mem. Phila. Com. 70, 1965-74, Fellowship Commn. Mem. ABA (mem. ho. dels. 1967-69, 79-88, treas. 1979-83, mem. fin. com., mem. bd. govs. 1977-83), Fed. Bar Assn. (mem. nat. coun. 1971-80), D.C. Bar Assn., Phila. Bar Assn., Am. Bar Found. (treas. 1979-83), Am. Bar Retl. Assn. (dir. 1978-83), Am. Bar Endowment (bd. dirs. 1984-97, pres. 1995-97), Internat. Bar Assn., Phila. Country Club (Gladwyne, Pa.), Chester River Yacht & Country Club (Chestertown, Md.), Skating Club Phila., Orpheus Club (Phila.), Order of the Coif, Phi Beta Kappa. Republican. Roman Catholic. Home: 2014 N Kenmore St Arlington VA 22207-3711 Office: Dechert Price & Rhoads 1500 K St NW Ste 500 Washington DC 20005-1209

LEIBOVICH, SIDNEY, engineering educator; b. Memphis, Apr. 2, 1939; s. Harry and Rebecca (Palant) L.; m. Gail Barbara Colin, Nov. 24, 1962; children: Bradley Colin, Adam Keith. BS, Calif. Inst. Tech., Pasadena, 1961; PhD, Cornell U., 1965. NATO postdoctoral fellow U. Coll., London, 1965-66; asst. prof. thermal engring. Cornell U., Ithaca, N.Y., 1966-70, assoc. prof. thermal engring., 1970-78, prof. mech. and aerospace engring., 1978-89, Samuel B. Eckert prof. mech. and aerospace engring., 1989—.

Editor: Nonlinear Waves, 1974; assoc. editor: Jour. Fluid Mechanics, 1982-93; co-editor: Acta Mechanica, 1986-92; mem. editorial bd. Ann. Revs. of Fluid Mechanics, 1989-93; gen. editor Cambridge U. Press Monographs on Mechanics, 1994—. Disting. lectr. Naval Ocean Rsch. Devel. Activity, 1983. Recipient MacPherson prize Calif. Inst. Tech., 1961. Fellow ASME (chmn. applied mechanics div. 1987-88), Am. Phys. Soc. (chmn. div. fluid dynamics 1987-88), Am. Acad. Arts and Scis., U.S. Nat. Com. for Theoretical and Applied Mechanics (chair 1990-92.), Nat. Acad. Engring. Office: Cornell U Upson Hall Ithaca NY 14853

LEIBOW, RONALD LOUIS, lawyer; b. Santa Monica, Calif., Oct. 4, 1939; s. Norman and Jessica (Kellner) L.; m. Linda Bengelsdorf, June 11, 1961 (div. Dec. 1974); children: Jocelyn Elise, Jeffrey David, Joshua Aaron; m. Jacqueline Blatt, Apr. 6, 1986. AB, Calif. State U., Northridge, 1962; JD, UCLA, 1965. Bar: Calif. 1966, U.S. Dist. Ct. (cen. dist.) Calif. 1966, U.S. Dist. Ct. (no., so. and ea. dists.) Calif. 1971. Spl. asst. city atty. City of Burbank, Calif., 1966-67; assoc., then ptnr. Meyers, Stevens & Walters, L.A., 1967-71; ptnr. Karpf, Leibow & Warner, Beverly Hills, Calif., 1971-74, Volk, Newman Gralla & Karp, L.A., L.A., 1979-81, Spector & Leibow, L.A., 1982-84, Stroock & Stroock & Lavan, L.A., 1984-94; ptnr. Kaye, Scholer, Fierman, Hays & Handler, L.A., 1994—, mng. ptnr., 1996—; lectr. law UCLA, 1968-69; asst. prof. Calif. State U., Northridge, 1969-71. Contbr. articles to profl. jours. Pres. Jewish Community Ctr., Greater L.A., 1983-86; v.p. Jewish Community Ctr. Assn. N.Am., N.Y.C., 1988—, Jewish Fedn. Community, Greater L.A., 1988—. Mem. ABA (bus. bankruptcy com.), Phi Alpha Delta. Avocations: writing, tennis, skiing, travel. Office: Kaye Scholer Fierman Hays & Handler 1999 Avenue Of The Stars Fl 16 Los Angeles CA 90067-6022

LEIBOWITZ, ANN GALPERIN, lawyer; b. Balt., Oct. 11, 1940; d. Harold Marcy and Dorothy Rebecca (Trivas) Galperin; m. Howard Marvin Leibowitz, July 3, 1960; children: Ellen Ann, Katherine Leibowitz Kotkin. AB, Goucher Coll., 1960; LLB, U. Md., 1964. Bar: Mass. 1964, U.S. Ct. Appeals (1st cir.) 1984. Patent agt. W.R. Grace & Co., Clarkesville, Md., 1960-63; patent atty. Polaroid Corp., Cambridge, Mass., 1963-72, corporate atty., 1972-77, sr. corporate atty. and labor counsel, 1977-95; prin., founder AGL Assocs., Weston, Mass., 1995—; lectr. Coun. Edn. in Mgmt., Walnut Creek, Calif., 1987—; mem. faculty Mass. Continuing Legal Edn., Boston, 1991—. Bd. trustees Goucher Coll., Towson, Md., 1983-89; chmn. fin. com. Town of Weston, 1989-91, active, 1984-91, chmn. bd. selectmen, 1993—, active, 1991—; mem. exec. adv. bd. Ctr. House, Boston, 1990—; exec. com. bd. trustees Deaconess Waltham Hosp., 1995—. Mem. ABA, Am. Corporate Counsel Assn. (bd. dirs. N.E. chpt. 1988-91), Mass. Bar Assn. (lectr. 1987—), Boston Bar Assn., Indsl. Rels. Rsch. Assn.

LEIBOWITZ, DAVID PERRY, lawyer; b. Bronx, N.Y., Jan. 21, 1950; s. Bernard B. and Annette (Friedman) L.; m. Teri H. Bandala, Aug. 22, 1971; children: Rachel, Saryn. BA in Econs., Northwestern U., 1970; JD cum laude, Loyola U., 1974. Bar: Ill. 1974, U.S. Dist. Ct. (no. dist) Ill. 1974, U.S. Ct. Appeals (7th cir.) 1974, U.S. Supreme Ct. 1982, U.S. Ct. Appeals (11th cir.) 1985. Assoc. Goebel & Kal, Chgo., 1974-75; judicial clerk Ill. Appellate Ct., Chgo., 1975-76; ptnr. Schwartz, Cooper, Kolb & Gaynor, Chgo., 1976-91, Freeborn & Peters, Chgo., 1992—. Contbr. articles to profl. jours., chpts. to books. Mem. bd. edn. Highland Park (Ill.) Sch. Dist., 1987-92; pres. bd. edn. North Shore Sch. Dist. 112, Highland Park, 1992—; pres. bd. trustees Highland Park Pub. Libr., 1991-92. Mem. Am. Bankruptcy Inst., Ill. Bar Assn., Chgo. Bar Assn. Office: Freeborn & Peters 311 S Wacker Dr Ste 3000 Chicago IL 60606-6620

LEIBOWITZ, HERBERT AKIBA, English language educator, author; b. Staten Island, N.Y., Apr. 26, 1935; s. Morris and Rose (Rabinowitz) L.; m. Susan Yankowitz, May 3, 1978; 1 son, Gabriel. B.A., Bklyn. Coll., 1956; M.A., Brown U., 1958; Ph.D., Columbia U., 1966. Asst. prof. English Columbia U., 1967-70; asst. prof. humanities Richmond Coll., Staten Island, N.Y., 1971-73, assoc. prof., 1973-76; assoc. prof. English Coll. S.I., 1976-81; prof. English Coll. Staten Island, CUNY and Grad. Ctr., CUNY, 1981—; prof. English emeritus, 1991—; Fannie Hurst vis. prof. Washington U., St. Louis, 1995. Author: Hart Crane: An Introduction to the Poetry, 1968, Fabricating Lives, 1989; editor: Selected Music Criticism of Paul Rosenfeld, 1970, Parnassus: Poetry in Review, 1972, Parnassus: Twenty Years of Poetry in Review, 1994, Asphodel, That Greeny Flower and Other William Carlos Williams Love Poems, 1994. Recipient Fels award for editorial distinction Coordinating Coun. Lit. Mags., 1975; postdoctoral fellow U. Ill. Ctr. Advanced Study, 1968-69, Chamberlain fellow Columbia U., 1970, fellow N.Y. Inst. Humanities, 1987—, Mellon Seminar fellow NYU, 1988, Guggenheim fellow, 1991-92. Mem. PEN (Nora Magid award for disting. editing of lit. mag. 1995), Nat. Book Critics Circle (bd. dirs. 1988-94, pres. 1992-94). Jewish. Home: 205 W 89th St New York NY 10024-1828 Office: Poetry Rev Found 205 W 89th St Ph 8F New York NY 10024-1841

LEIBOWITZ, JACK RICHARD, physicist, educator; b. Bridgeport, Conn., July 21, 1929; BA, NYU, MS, 1955; PhD in Physics, Brown U., 1962. Rsch. physicist MIT Lincoln Lab., 1956-61, Westinghouse Rsch. Labs., Pitts., 1961-64; asst. prof. U. Md., College Park, 1964-69; assoc. prof. physics Cath. U. Am., Washington, 1969-73, prof. physics, 1974-95, prof. physics emeritus, 1995—, assoc. dean for grad. studies, 1988-93, chmn. art dept., 1882-86, acad. senate; sci. cons. govt. agys., NBC-TV. Fellow Am. Phys. Soc., Washington Acad. Scis.; mem. Sigma Xi. Contbr. numerous rsch. articles to sci. jours. and books. Research in condensed matter physics: superconductivity, electron-phonon interaction, band structure. Home: P O Box 256 Ashton MD 20861 Office: Cath U of Am Dept Physics Washington DC 20064

LEIBOWITZ, MARVIN, lawyer; b. Phila., Jan. 24, 1950; s. Aaron and Ethel (Kashoff) L.; m. Faye Rebecca Liepack, Nov. 12, 1983; children: Cheryl Renée, Ellen Paulette. BA, Temple U., 1971, postgrad., 1971-72; JD, Widener U., 1976. Bar: Pa. 1977, N.J. 1977, U.S. Dist. Ct. N.J. 1977, U.S. Dist. Ct. (we. dist.) Pa. 1980. Atty.-advisor SSA, Pitts., 1977—; pvt. practice law, Pitts., 1979—. Committeeman Phila. Dem. Com., 1973-77. Pa. State Scholar Pa. Higher Edn. Assistance Agy., Harrisburg, 1967-71. Recipient U.S. Dep. Health and Human Svcs. citation, 1994. Mem. Nat. Treasury Employees Union (regional steward 1982—), Pa. Bar Assn., Allegheny County Bar Assn. Democrat. Jewish. Home: 6501 Landview St Pittsburgh PA 15217-3000

LEIBSLA, MELVIN DONALD, data processing executive; b. Cleve., Mar. 27, 1953; s. Melvin Donald and Marguerite (Scribbner) L.; m. Barbara A. Stasko, July 4, 1981; children: Michael, Jason. BS in Applied Sci., Miami U., 1975; grad., Sch. Bank Mgmt., Madison, Wis., 1990. Programmer/analyst Fed. Res. Bank Cleve., 1975-80; system analyst Olympia Brewing, Tumwater, Wash., 1980-82; system analyst/auditor N.W. Pipeline, Salt Lake City, 1982-84; EDP audit mgr. Zions Bancorp, Salt Lake City, 1984—; speaker in field. Contbr. articles to profl. jours. Active in developing digital signatures on internet for the State of Utah. Active local ch. parish coun., Salt Lake City, 1989—. Mem. EDP Auditors Assn. (pres., v.p. 1989-91, bd. dirs. 1989-94), Data Processing Mgmt. Assn. Republican. Roman Catholic. Avocations: marathons, coaching and refereeing soccer, church activities. Office: Zions Bancorp 2200 S 3270 W West Valley City UT 84119-1112

LEIBSON, IRVING, industrial executive; b. Wilkes Barre, Pa., Sept. 28, 1926; s. Henry and Sonia (Rose) L.; m. Lola Pavalow, Feb. 16, 1950; children: Russell, Sandra Eve. B.Chem. Engring. cum laude, U. Fla., 1945, M.S., 1947; M.S. Carnegie Inst. Tech., 1949; D.Sc., Carnegie Inst. Tech., 1952. Registered profl. engr., Calif., Tex. Chem. engr. to supr. Humble Oil and Refining Co., Baytown, Tex., 1952-61, mgr. process engring., 1961-63, tech. mgr., 1963-65, dir. R & D, 1965-67; gen. mgr. ABS div., 1967-68; v.p. Dart Industries Chem. Group, Paramus, N.J., 1969-74; asst. to sr. v.p., investment dept. Bechtel Corp., San Francisco, 1974-75; mgr. process and environment, v.p. C & I/Girdler Inc. (a Bechtel Co.), 1976-78; v.p., mgr. rsch. and engring. Bechtel Nat. Inc., 1978-79; sr. v.p. Bechtel Inc., 1979-81; sr. v.p., mgr. mktg. Bechtel Group Inc., 1981-85, sr. v.p., sr. tech. officer, 1985-87, exec. cons., 1987-94; founder, pres. Bold Techs., 1987—; part-time prof. Rice U., 1957, U. Md., 1954. Contbr. articles to profl. jours. Dist. commr. E. Harris County dist. Boy Scouts Am., 1958-61; vice-chmn. Intersoc. Task Force Energy, 1973; assoc. World Coal Study, 1979-80; assoc. coal industry adv. bd. Internat. Energy Agy., 1980-95; treas., vice chmn., chmn. mem. exec. com. Coun. Alternate Fuels, 1982-87; mem. Nat. Coal Coun., 1985-94, chmn. Coal Policy Commn., 1987-91; mem. exec. com., 1987-95; mem. adv. bd. Ctr. Chem. Process Safety Tech., 1985-88; mem. liquid fuels com. NRC, 1989-90. With AUS, 1953-54. Recipient Disting. Alumnus award U. Fla., 1988. Fellow Am. Inst. Chem. Engrs. (dir. 1967-69, v.p. 1973, pres. 1974, Publ. award S. Tex. chpt. 1957, Founders award 1976, Disting. Svc. award 1996); mem. Am. Chem. Soc., Engrs. Joint Coun. (dir. 1969-78), Engrs. Manpower Commn., Coal and Slurry Tech Assn. (chmn. 1986-89), Round Hill Golf and Country Club (San Francisco), World Trade Club (San Francisco), Sailfish Point Golf Club (Stuart, Fla.), Ary Club (Stuart), Villa Taverna Club (San Francisco). Patentee in field. Home: 2920 SE Dune Dr Stuart FL 34996-1986

LEIBTAG, BERNARD, accountant; b. Balt., Oct. 24, 1950; s. Aaron H. and Rose Sarah (Miller) L.; m. Susan Ann Weintraub, Aug. 4, 1974; children: Gila M., Aaron D., Aliza C. BA in History, Yeshiva U., 1973; MA in History, Columbia U., 1975, M Phil in History, 1976, MBA in Acctg., 1979. CPA, Md. Staff acct. Arthur Young & Co., N.Y.C., 1979; mgr. Grant Thornton, Balt., 1979-86; sr. mgr. KPMG Peat Marwick, Balt., 1987-90; tax dir. Kamanitz, Uhlfelder & Permison, Balt., 1990-95; tax prin. Schiller, Holinsky & Garoyn, P.A., Balt., 1995—; cons. Nat. Bus. Inst., Eau Claire, Wis., 1989—, Balt. Assn. Tax Counsel, 1990—, Comptroller of Treasury, Annapolis, Md., 1985-86; expert witness on tax issues; testified before U.S. Ho. of Reps. Com. on Ways and Means. Contbr. articles to profl. jours.; appeared on TV and radio talk shows about tax matters. Mem. Assn. Jewish Charities Young Leadership Coun., Balt., 1982-84; mem. Associated Way Balt., 1982—, Columbia Bus. Sch. Club Balt. Fellow Nat. Found. Jewish Culture, 1976, Yivo Inst., N.Y.C., 1973-76. Mem. AICPA, Md. Assn. CPAs (mem. state tax com. 1981—, chmn. state tax com. 1989-91, mem. estate and gift tax com. 1992-94, 95-97, cert. appreciation 1989-96), Md. Soc. Accts., Balt. Assn. Tax Counsel, Balt. Estate Planning Coun., Beta Gamma Sigma, Eta Sigma Phi, Pi Gamma Mu. Democrat. Jewish. Office: Schiller Holinsky & Garoyn PA 10451 Mill Run Cir Ste 330 Owings Mills MD 21117-5577

LEIBY, BRUCE RICHARD, secondary education educator, writer; b. Media, Pa., Aug. 30, 1947; s. Edward Charles and Margaret Ellen (Strawbridge) L.; m. Linda Pauline Flounders, June 26, 1971. BSBA, Tusculum Coll., Greeneville, 1969; postgrad. West Chester U., 1970, 72. Tchr. Interboro Sch. Dist., Prospect Park, Pa., 1969-70, Delaware County C.C., Media, 1974; acct., tchr. info. processing Upper Darby (Pa.) Adult Sch., 1970-88, Upper Darby Sch. Dist., 1970—; staff asst. Upper Darby H.S., 1987—, mem. bus. edn. adv. bd., co-sponsor Bus. Club, 1987-88; mem. bus. edn. curriculum com., 1992—. Author for Greenwood Press, Westport, Conn., 1988—; author: Gordon Macrae--A Bio-Bibliography, 1991, Howard Keel--A Bio-Bibliography, 1995. Mem. NEA, Pa. Edn. Assn., Upper Darby Edn. Assn. (past membership chmn.), Am. Film Inst., Suburban Phila. Bus. Edn. Assn., Internat. Friends of Gordon Macrae, Internat. Doris Day Soc., Shirley Jones Fan Club. Republican. Methodist. Avocations: music, reading, collecting performing arts memorabilia, acting. Home: 13 E 6th St Media PA 19063-2501 Office: Upper Darby HS Lansdowne Ave Upper Darby PA 19082-5410

LEICHTLING, MICHAEL ALFRED, lawyer; b. N.Y.C., Mar. 30, 1943; s. Stanley Arthur and Roslyn Priscilla (Fuhr) L.; m. Arlene Dorf, July 30, 1966; children: Julie Karen, Nina Anastasia, Noah James. BA, SUNY, Binghamton, 1963; JD, Northwestern U., 1966; postgrad., Columbia U., 1968. Bar: N.Y. 1969, U.S. Ct. Appeals (2d cir.) 1969. Assoc. Aranow Brodsky Bohlinger Einhorn & Dann, N.Y.C., 1966, Parker Chapin & Flattau, N.Y.C., 1969-77; ptnr. Parker Chapin Flattau & Klimpl, LLP, N.Y.C., 1977—; mem. exec. com. Parker Chapin Flattau & Klimpl, N.Y.C., 1987-92; bd. dirs. H. Warshow & Sons Inc., N.Y.C. Editor Northwestern U. Law Rev., 1965-66, Equipment Leasing Jour., 1986—, Computer Leasing Today, 1989—. Bd. dirs. Friends of Israel Disabled War Vets., N.Y.C., 1986—. With U.S. Army, 1966-68; Vietnam. Decorated Bronze Star; Regents scholar, 1963, Newman scholar, 1963-66. Mem. N.Y. State Bar Assn. (corp. law sect.), N.Y. County Lawyers Assn. (banking law com., secured lending com.), Equipment Leasing (state legis. com.), Ea. Assn. Equipment Lessors (chmn. legal com., gen. counsel 1986—). Avocations: reading, painting, swimming, golf. Home: 148 Quinn Rd Briarcliff Manor NY 10510-2133 Office: Parker Chapin Flattau Klimpl LLP 1211 6th Ave New York NY 10036-8701

LEIDEN, CARL, political scientist, educator; b. Boone, Iowa, Feb. 6, 1922; s. Carl Eric and Christine Olivia (Bergstrom) L.; m. Mary Katherine Rood, Sept. 5, 1945; children: Lisa Ingrid, Derek Stefan. B.S., Iowa State Coll., 1945; M.P.A., Wayne U., 1947; Ph.D., State U. Iowa, 1949. Instr. State U. Iowa, Iowa City, 1946-49; asst. prof. to assoc. prof. Marshall Coll., Huntington, W.Va., 1949-59; assoc. prof. Am. U., Cairo, Egypt, 1959-61; assoc. prof. to prof. polit. sci. U. Tex., Austin, 1961-87, prof. emeritus, 1987—; Fulbright lectr. Peshawar U., Pakistan, 1952-53; vis. assoc. prof. U. Calif.-Berkeley, 1957; prof. Nat. War Coll., Washington, 1972-73. Author or co-author eight books on polit. sci. Volker Found. fellow, 1945-46; Fulbright teaching grantee, 1952-53, 1966; Earhart Found. grantee, 1970. Republican. Home: 3301 Stoneridge Rd Austin TX 78746-7715 Office: Univ Texas Polit Sci Dept Austin TX 78712

LEIDER, GERALD J., motion picture and television company executive; b. Camden, N.J., May 28, 1931; s. Myer and Minnie Leider; m. Susan Trustman, Dec. 21, 1968; children: Matthew Trustman, Kenneth Harold. B.A., Syracuse U., 1953. Theater producer in N.Y.C., London, 1956-59; dir. spl. programs CBS-TV, 1960-61, dir. program sales, 1961-62; v.p. TV ops. Ashley Famous Agy., Inc., N.Y.C., 1962-69; pres. Warner Bros. TV, Burbank, Calif., 1969-74; exec. v.p. fgn. prodn. Warner Bros. Pictures, Rome, 1975-76; ind. producer motion pictures and TV GJL Prodns., Inc., Los Angeles, 1977-82; pres. ITC Prodns., Inc., Los Angeles, 1982-87; pres., chief exec. officer ITC Entertainment Group, Studio City, Calif., 1987-91. Producer: Gielgud's Ages of Man, 1958-59; feature motion pictures include The Jazz Singer (with Neil Diamond), 1980, Trenchcoat, 1983; TV films include And I Alone Survived, 1978, Willa, 1979, The Hostage Tower, 1980. Mem. Bd. Visitors Coll. Visual and Performing Arts, Syracuse U. Recipient Arents Alumni medal Syracuse U., 1977; Fulbright fellow U. Bristol (Eng.), 1954. Mem. Acad. Motion Picture Arts and Scis., Acad. TV Arts and Scis., Am. Film Inst. (second decade council), Hollywood Radio and TV Soc. (pres. 1975-76); mem. steering com. The Caucus for Producers, Writers & Dirs. Office: 11661 San Vicente Blvd Los Angeles CA 90049-5103

LEIDHEISER, HENRY, JR., retired chemistry educator, consultant; b. Union City, N.J., Apr. 18, 1920; s. Henry and Margaret Marie (Steinel) L.; m. Virginia Townsend, Feb. 21, 1944; children: Margaret Frances, Henry III. BS in Chemistry, U. Va., 1941, MS in Phys. Chemistry, 1943, PhD in Phys. Chemistry, 1946. Research associate U. Va., Charlottesville, 1946-49; research chemist, dir. Va. Inst. for Sci. Research, Richmond, 1949-68; prof. chemistry Lehigh U., Bethlehem, Pa., 1968-90, prof. emeritus, 1990—; cons. space science NASA, 1972-84; cons. numerous indsl. orgns. Author or editor of 8 books; 275 publs. in tech. lit.; 7 patents on crystal growth and metal surface treatment. NATO fellow to Cambridge U., England, 1969; recipient J. Shelton Horsley Rsch. award Va. Acad. Sci., 1948, Oak Ridge Inst. Nuclear Studies Rsch. award, 1949, Westinghouse Signal and Brake Award of Inst. Metal Finishing, 1954, Silver medal Am. Electroplaters' Soc., 1978, Arch T. Colwell award Soc. Automotive Engrs., 1979, Humboldt Sr. Scientist award, 1985, Tambour award 11th Congress Metal Finishing, 1984, Silver medal South African Corrosion Inst., 1986, Libsch Rsch. award Lehigh U., 1987, Mattiello Rsch. award Fedn. Soc. Coatings Tech., 1990. Fellow AAAS; mem. Am. Chem. Soc., Electrochem. Soc. (Young Author's award 1948, Rsch. award 1986, 91), Nat. Assn. Corrosion Engrs. (Whitney award 1983), Rotary. Republican. Presbyterian. Avocations: bridge, golf, collecting ceramics. Home: 822 Carnoustie Dr Venice FL 34293-4343

LEIDNER, HAROLD EDWARD, lawyer; b. Cleve., Aug. 23, 1937; s. Nathan Nelson and Therese Loretta (Burdine) L.; children—Kenneth Jason, Andrew Mitchell. A.B., Cornell U., 1959; LL.B., Western Res. U., 1963. Bar: Ohio 1963. Since practiced in Cleve.; prin. Fuerst, Leidner, Dougherty & Kasdan Co., 1968-79; ptnr. firm Benesch, Friedlander, Coplan & Aronoff, 1984—. Law editor: Webster's New World Dictionary of the American Language, 1970. Mem. Am., Ohio, Cleve. bar assns.; Am. Arbitration Assn. Republican. Clubs: Cornell; Commerce (Cleve.); Curzon House (London, Eng.). Home: 2112 Acacia Park Dr Lyndhurst OH 44124-3863 Office: Benesch Friedlander Coplan 2300 BP America Bldg 200 Public Sq Cleveland OH 44114-2301

LEIER, CARL VICTOR, internist, cardiologist; b. Bismarck, N.D., Oct. 20, 1944; married; 3 children. BA, Creighton U., 1965, MD cum laude, 1969. Diplomate Am. Bd. Internal Medicine, Cardiovascular Medicine, Critical Care Medicine, Geriatric Medicine, Nat. Bd. Med. Examiners; lic. med., surgical Nebr., med. Ohio. Intern Ohio State U. Coll. Medicine, Columbus, 1969-70, med. resident (instr.) dept. medicine, 1971-73, chief resident (instr.), 1973-74, fellowship divsn. cardiology, 1974-76; pathology resident dept. pathology St. Vincent Hosp., Worcester, Mass., 1970-71; trainee NIH Tng. Grant, 1974-75; asst. prof. medicine cardiology dept., Ohio State U. Coll. Medicine, Columbus, 1976-80, asst. prof. pharmacology, 1976-80, assoc. prof., 1980-84, faculty mem. grad. sch., 1980—, dir. rsch. divsn. cardiology, 1980-83, James W. Overstreet prof. of medicine, 1983—, prof. of medicine divsn. cardiology, 1984—, prof. pharmacology, dept. pharmacology, 1984—, dir. divsn. cardiology, 1986—; internship selection com. dept. medicine, Ohio State U., 1973-74, hosp. procedures com. Ohio State U. Hosps., 1973-74; mem. pharmacology and therapeutics com. Ohio State U. Hosps., 1976-80; mem. rsch. com. ctrl. Ohio chpt. Am. Heart Assn., 1977-84, bd. trustees, 1979-88, exec. rsch. com., 1979-84, vice chmn. rsch. com., 1980-82, chmn. rsch. peer rev. com., 1982-84, v.p., 1984-86, pres. elect, 1986-88; numerous other coms.; cons. cardiorenal adv. bd. Smith-Kline Labs., 1982-85, com. on cardio-vascular rsch. and devel., 1982-85., AMA on Drugs and Tech., 1985—, Lilly-Elanco devel. ractopamine, 1989; mem. ad hoc adv. com. on carvedilol in congestive heart failure, Smith, Kline and Beacham Pharms., 1991, ad hoc adv. com. on PDEI devel., McNeil Pharms., 1991, ad hoc adv. com. for clin. trials on Ibopamine, Zambon Pharms., 1993, sci. adv. com. Ohio State Univ. Brain Tumor Rsch. Ctr., 1993—, data safety monitoring bd., Otsuka Vesnarinone Trials, 1993— mem. chmn. Annual Sci. Sessions of the Am. Coll. of Cardiolog, 1996-97; vis. prof., lectr. and presenter at numerous sci. confs., insts. in U.S. and internationally. Editor: (book) Cardiotonic Drugs, 1986, 2d rev. edit., 1991; co-author: (with H. Boudoulas) CardioRenal Disorders and Diseases, 1986, 2d edit., 1992 (with J. Vincent) Critical Care Medicine: Recent Advances in Cardiovascular Medicine, 1990; contbr. more than 40 chpts. to other medical books and almost 200 articles to peer reviewed jours. including: Vascular Surgery, Archives of Internal Medicine, Circulation, Brit. Heart Jour., Jour. Electrocardiology, Clinical Pharmacologic Therapy, Chest, Am. Jour. Medicine, Jour. Cardiovascular Pharmacology, Am. Heart Jour., Geriatrics, Annals of Internal Medicine and others; editor in chief Congestive Heart Failure: Index and Revs., 1988—; mem. editorial bds. of ten medical jours. concerned with heart diseases, the review bds. of others including New Eng. Jour. Medicine, Internat. Jour. Cardiology, Jour. of Lab. and Clin. Medicine. Recipient Upjohn award, 1969, Lange Scholar award, 1969, Golden Apple Student Tchg. award, 1973, 75, Young Investigator award Ctrl. Ohio Heart Chpt., Am. Heart Assn., 1976-78, Rsch. Recognition award, 1978; named One of Best Doctors of Columbus, Columbus Monthly, 1992. Fellow Am. Coll. Clin. Pharmacology, Coun. on Clin. Pharmacology, Am. Heart Assn., Am. Coll. Cardiology, Am. Coll. Physicians, Coun. on Geriatric Cardiology; mem. AAAS, Ohio State Med. Assn., Am. Fedn. for Clin. Rsch., Ctrl. Soc. for Clin. Rsch., Am. Soc. Clin. Investigation, Assn. Univ. Cardiologists, Internat. Soc. for Heart Rsch., Internat. Soc. Cardiovascular Pharmacotherapy, Assn. Profs. of Cardiology. Office: Ohio State U Med Ctr Divsn Cardiology 1654 Upham Dr Columbus OH 43210-1250

LEIES, JOHN ALEX, theology educator, clergyman; b. Chgo., Apr. 24, 1926; cre; BS in Edn., U. Dayton, 1948; STB, U. Friborg, Switzerland, 1954, STL, 1956, STD, 1958. Asst. to provincial Soc. of Mary, St. Louis, 1961-64; regional superior Marianist Missions, Peru, 1964-68; prof. theology, dir. campus ministry St. Mary's U., San Antonio, 1974-81, chmn. grad. theology dept., 1980-81, acad. v.p., 1981-85, pres., 1985-88, grad. advisor theology dept., 1977-81, chmn. dept., 1996—, dir. Ctr. for Profl. Ethics, 1991—; dir. Cath. Charismatic Bible Inst., 1977-86, 91—; theologian mem. ethics com. Santa Rosa Hosp., 1978-81, 89-94; mem. gen. chpt. Soc. of Mary, 1966-67, 71, 76, 81, 86, 91; rsch. fellow cons. Pope John Med. Moral Rsch. Ctr., Braintree, Mass., 1988—; trustee Tex. Ctr. for Legal Ethics and Professionalism, 1994-95. Mem. Lambda Chi Alpha, Rotary, Univ. Faculty for Life, Fellowship of Cath. Scholars. Avocation: reading. Address: St Mary's Univ of San Antonio 1 Camino Santa Maria St San Antonio TX 78228-5433

LEIGH, HOYLE, psychiatrist, educator, writer; b. Seoul, Korea, Mar. 25, 1942; came to U.S., 1965; m. Vincenta Masciandaro, Sept. 16, 1967; 1 child, Alexander Hoyle. MA, Yale U., 1982; MD, Yonsei U., Seoul, 1965. Diplomate Am. Bd. Psychiatry and Neurology. Asst. prof. Yale U., New Haven, 1971-75, assoc. prof., 1975-80, prof., 1980-89, lectr. in psychiatry, 1989—; dir. Behavioral Medicine Clinic, Yale U., 1980-89; dir. psychiat. cons. svc. Yale-New Haven Hosp., 1971-89; chief psychiatry VA Med Ctr., Fresno, Calif., 1989—; prof., vice chmn. dept. psychiatry U. Calif., San Francisco, 1989—, head dept. psychiatry, 1989—; cons. Am. Jour. Psychiatry, Archives Internal Medicine, Psychosomatic Medicine. Author: The Patient, 1980, 2d edit., 1985, 3d edit., 1992; editor: Psychiatry in the Practice of Medicine, 1983, Consultation-Liaison Psychiatry: 1990's & Beyond, 1994, Biopsychosocial Approaches in Primary Care: State of the Art and Challenges for the 21st Century, 1997. Fellow ACP, Internat. Coll. Psychosomatic Medicine (v.p.), Am. Acad. Psychosomatic Medicine; mem. AMA, AAUP, World Psychiat. Assn. Avocations: reading, music, skiing. Office: U Calif Dept Psychiat 2615 E Clinton Ave Fresno CA 93703-2223

LEIGH, JANET (JEANETTE HELEN MORRISON), actress; b. Merced, Calif., July 6, 1927; m. Tony Curtis, June 4, 1951 (div. 1962); children: Jamie Lee, Kelly; m. Robert Brandt, 1962. Student, Coll. Pacific. Actress: (films) Romance of Rosy Ridge, 1947, If Winter Comes, 1947, Hills of Home, 1948, Words and Music, 1948, Act of Violence, 1948, Little Women, 1949, That Forsythe Woman, 1949, The Red Danube, 1949, The Doctor and the Girl, 1949, Holiday Affair, 1949, Two Tickets to Broadway, 1951, Strictly Dishonorable, 1951, Angels in the Outfield, 1951, It's a Big Country, 1952, Scaramouche, 1952, Fearless Fagan, 1952, The Naked Spur, 1953, Houdini, 1953, Walking My Baby Back Home, 1953, Confidentially Connie, 1953, Prince Valiant, 1954, The Black Shield of Falworth, 1954, Rogue Cop, 1954, Living It Up!, 1954, My Sister Eileen, 1955, Pete Kelly's Blues, 1955, Just This Once, 1955, Touch of Evil, 1958, The Vikings, 1958, The Perfect Furlough, 1958, Psycho, 1960, Who Was That Lady?, 1960, The Manchurian Candidate, 1962, Bye Bye Birdie, 1963, Wives and Lovers, 1963, Grand Slam, Harper, 1966, Kid Rodello, 1966, Hello Down There, 1968, The Deadly Dream, 1971, One Is a Lonely Number, 1972, Night of the Lepus, 1972, Boardwalk, 1979, Fog, 1980, Other Realms, (TV movies) numerous including The World Series Murders, Death's Head, The Monk, 1969, Honeymoon with a Stranger, 1969, The House on Green Apple Road, 1970, The Chairman, Murdock's Gang, 1973, Telethon, 1977, Mirror, Mirror, 1979, Murder at the World Series, Murder She Wrote, Love Letters, 1991; author: (autobiography) There Really Was a Hollywood, 1984, (novel) House of Destiny, 1995, (stage) Murder Among Friends, 1976, Love Letters, 1991, (non-fiction) Psycho Revisited, Psycho: Behind the Scenes of the Classic Thriller, 1995; rec. (album) Bye Bye, Birdie. Office: Ansel Eisenstadt & Frazier 6310 San Vicente Blvd Ste 401 Los Angeles CA 90048-5426*

LEIGH, JENNIFER JASON (JENNIFER LEIGH MORROW), actress; b. L.A., Feb. 5, 1962; d. Barbara Turner and Vic Morrow. Student, Lee Strasberg Inst. Appearances include (films) Eyes of a Stranger, 1980, Fast Times at Ridgemont High, 1982, Wrong is Right, 1982, Easy Money, 1983, Grandview U.S.A., 1984, Flesh + Blood, 1985, The Hitcher, 1986, The Men's Club, 1986, Sister, Sister, 1987, Under Cover, 1987, Heart of Midnight, 1988, The Big Picture, 1989, Last Exit to Brooklyn, 1989, Miami Blues, 1990, Crooked Hearts, 1991, Backdraft, 1991, Rush, 1992, Single White Female, 1992, Short Cuts, 1993, The Hudsucker Proxy, 1994, Mrs. Parker and the Vicious Circle, 1994, Dolores Claiborne, 1994, Kansas City, 1996, Bastard Out of Carolina, 1996; (TV movies) Angel City, 1980, The Killing of Randy Webster, 1981, The Best Little Girl in the World, 1981, The First Time, 1982, Girls of the White Orchid, 1983, Buried Alive, 1990; prodr., actress Georgia, 1995. Office: ICM c/o Tracey Jacobs 8942 Wilshire Blvd Beverly Hills CA 90211-1934 also: care Elaine Rich 2400 Whitman Pl Los Angeles CA 90068-2464

LEIGH, MARGIE, mortgage company originator; b. Campbellsville, Ky., June 6, 1946; d. Bennie Lawrence and Evelyn Garnetta (Seay) DeWitt; children: Susan Leigh, Tracy Lynne. Grad. in elem. edn., Western Ky. U., 1968; postgrad., U. Ky., Lexington, 1986, U. Ky., Elizabethtown, 1988. Real estate agt. Nat. Realtors Assn., Elizabethtown, Ky., 1986-92; mortgage originator Nat. Bankers Assn., McLean, Va., 1993—, Dynamics Fin., Inc. Mem. adv. bd. Hardin County Sch., Elizabethtown, 1985-87. Recipient Apple award Elizabethtown Sch. Sys., 1985; named to Order of Ky. Cols. Mem. Order Ea. Star, Ky. Cols. Republican. Baptist. Avocations: golf, tennis, writing.

LEIGH, MONROE, lawyer; b. South Boston, Va., July 15, 1919; s. Leander Faulkner and Elizabeth Edmunds (Monroe) L.; m. Mary Gallaher Leigh, Apr. 15, 1951; children: Edward Monroe, Parker McCollester, Elizabeth Faulkner. B.A., Hampden-Sydney Coll., 1940; LL.B., U. Va., 1947. Bar: Va. 1947, D.C. 1948, U.S. Supreme Ct 1950. Assoc. firm Covington, Burling, Rublee, Acheson & Shorb, 1947-51; mem. U.S. del. N. Atlantic Council, London and Paris, 1951-53; dep. asst. gen. counsel Dept. Def., 1953-55, asst. gen. counsel internat. affairs, 1955-59; ptnr. Steptoe and Johnson, Washington, 1961-75, 77—; legal adviser Dept. State, 1975-77; lectr. U. Va. Law Sch., 1964-75, 78-88; mem. Permanent Ctr. of Arbitration, The Hague, 1975-80; mem. adv. Com. Internat. Investment U.S. Trade Rep., 1984-95; mem. Legal Adviser's Adv. Com. on Pub. Internat. Law, 1993—; mem. adv. com. Am. Law Inst. on Fgn. Rels. Law; mem. chmn.'s list of panels of conciliators and arbitrators Internat. Ctr. for Settlement of Investment Disputes. Co-editor: National Treaty Law and Practice, 1995; contbr. articles to profl. jours. Trustee U. Va. Law Sch. Found., 1988-95. Capt. USAAF, 1943-46. Recipient Superior Honor award Sec. of State, 1977. Mem. ABA (Theberge award 1989, chmn. task force on war crimes in Yugoslavia 1993—), Internat. Law Assn., Am. Soc. Internat. Law (pres. 1981-82, hon. pres. 1990-92), Coun. Fgn. Rels., Washington Inst. Fgn. Affairs, Am. Law Inst., Colonnade Club, Cosmos Club, Met. Club, Chevy Chase Club. Episcopalian. Home: 5205 Westwood Dr Bethesda MD 20816-1838 Office: 1330 Connecticut Ave NW Washington DC 20036-1704

LEIGH, SHARI GREER, software consulting firm executive; b. Reading, Pa., Mar. 1, 1959; d. Martin and Francine Rita (Gross) Rothenstein; m. Martin Brad Greer, Dec. 31, 1979; children: Shannon Leigh, Krista Heather. BA in Biochemistry, Wellesley Coll.-MIT, 1980; postgrad. in bus. adminstrn., Colo. State U., 1982-83. Lead thermal engr. Rockwell Internat. Space div., Downey, Calif., 1980-81; systems engr. Martin Marietta Aerospace, Denver, 1981-82, aerospace new bus. analyst, 1982-84; v.p. Miaco Corp. (Micro Automation Cons.), Englewood, Colo., 1984-87, pres., CEO, 1987-97; pres. Miaco Corp., Englewood, 1997—. Co-designer life systems monitor for Sudden Infant Death Syndrome, 1980. Exec. bd. dirs. Mile High chpt. ARC, 1991-96. Recipient Recognition award for 500 fastest growing cos. Inc. Mag., 1990, 91, Blue Chip Enterprise award Am.'s Best Small Bus., U.S. C. of C., 1991; named Bus. Leader to Watch in the 90's Corp. Connection; finalist Colo. Small Bus. of the Yr. award C. of C., 1992-93, Person of Yr., U.S. Small Bus. Bus. Adminstrn., South Metro Small Bus. Person of Yr., 1992-93. Mem. Greater Denver Chamber (coun. mem. small bus. bd. 1991-93), So. Met. C. of C. (bd. dirs. 1994—). Office: Miaco Corp 6300 S Syracuse Way Ste 415 Englewood CO 80111-6724

LEIGH, SHERREN, communications executive, editor, publisher; b. Cleve., Dec. 22, 1942; d. Walter Carl Maurushat and Treva Eldora (Burke) Morris; m. Norman J. Hickey Jr., Aug. 23, 1969 (div. 1985). BS, Ohio U., 1965. Communications dir. Metal Lath Assn., Cleve., 1965-67; creative dir. O'Toole Inc., Chgo., 1967-69; sr. v.p. RLC Inc., Chgo., 1969-77; pres. Leigh Communications Inc., Chgo., 1978—; chmn. Today's Chgo. Woman mag., 1982—; pres. Ill. Ambassadors, Chgo., 1985-86; bd. dirs. Chgo. Fin. Exchange, 1985-87. Author: How to Write a Winning Resume, How to Negotiate for Top Dollar, How to Find, Get and Keep the Job You Want. Bd. dirs. Midwest Women's Ctr., Chgo., 1984-86, Girl Scouts Chgo., 1985-87, Black Women's Hall of Fame Found., Chgo., 1986—, Apparel Industry Bd., Chgo., 1988, Auditorium Theater of Roosevelt U. Recipient Corp. Leadership award YWCA Met. Chgo., 1979, Entrepreneurship award, 1988, Media Advocate of Yr. award U.S. SBA, 1994; named one of 10 Women of Achievement Midwest Women's Ctr., Chgo., 1987, Advt. Woman of Yr. Women's Advt. Club, Chgo., 1988; inducted City of Chgo. Women's Hall of Fame, 1988. Mem. Chgo. Network, Econ. Club Chgo., Execs. Club Chgo., Com. of 200 (founding mem.). Office: Leigh Communications, Inc 150 E Huron St Ste 1225 Chicago IL 60611-2949

LEIGH, STEPHEN, industrial designer; b. N.Y.C., May 21, 1931; s. Herman Lerner and Rhea (Drinkhouse) L.; m. Barbara Lynn Haim, Feb. 14, 1984; children: Harvey Alan, Madeleine Beth. BFA, Cooper Union, 1951. Interior designer Robert Gruen Assocs., N.Y.C., 1951-55; designer, project dir. Michael Saphier Assocs., N.Y.C., 1955-59; pres. Stephen Leigh & Assocs. Inc., N.Y.C., 1959—; interior designers, cons. specializing in comml. usage, United Jewish Appeal, 1963, U.S. Pavilion, Venezuelan Pavilion, N.Y. World's Fair, 1964-65, Random House, 1969, Mitsubishi Internat. Corp., 1980, Rapid Am. Corp., 1982, Bowery Savs. Bank, 1986; lectr. NYU. Columnist Real Estate Weekly, 1963-65, The Office Mag., 1985—; one-man shows of sculpture at Cartier and East River Savings Bank; recent prin. works include Union Chelsea Nat. Bank, Faberge, Fino Restaurant, Il Menestrello Restaurant, Schenley, redesign of landmark facade at 111 8th Ave., 1989; sculpted permanent team trophy for Eisenhower Golf Tournament. Recipient AIA design award for Venezuelan Pavilion N.Y. World's Fair, 1964-65, Excellence award The Archtl. Woodwork Inst., 1988. Mem. Am. Soc. of Interior Designers (N.Y. chpt.), Charge des Missions of the Confrerie de la Chaine des Rotisseurs (Bronze Star of Excellence), Brotherhood of the Knights of the Vine. Avocations: sculpture, painting, cooking, travel, collecting Americana and American flags. Office: 157 E 57th St New York NY 10022-2104

LEIGH-MANUELL, ROBERT ALLEN, training executive, educator; b. Bay Shore, N.Y., Oct. 4, 1942; s. Darrell B. and Rose A. (Sanders) L.-M.; m. Diane W. Frisbee, Mar. 28, 1964 (div. May 1982); children: Nancy D., Timothy J., Charles R.; m. Donna M. McGrath, Oct. 25, 1982; children: Michael N., David A. Student, Kans. State U., 1960-61; BS, SUNY, Oswego, 1964; postgrad., Hofstra U., 1965-66; MA, NYU, 1977. Cert. secondary sch. tchr., N.Y.; cert. sch. adminstr., N.Y. Tchr. Sachem Cen. Sch. Dist., Holtsville, N.Y., 1964-67; tng. mgr. Deutsch Relays, North Port, N.Y., 1967-68; instructional systems engr. Sperry Gyroscope, Great Neck, N.Y., 1968-74; cons. Mind, Inc., N.Y.C., 1974; tchr. Wantagh Sch. Dist., Wantagh, N.Y., 1974-76; adminstrv. intern Mamaroneck (N.Y.) Sch. Dist., 1976; adminstr. Westchester B.O.C.E.S., Port Chester, N.Y., 1976-79; tng. mgr. Data Communication, Farmingdale, N.Y., 1979-84; mgr. program devel. The Southland Corp., Dallas, 1984-92; ind. cons., owner Monarch Assocs., Dallas, Tex., 1992—; com. mem. Commr.'s Task Force for technology in edn. Tex. Edn. Agy., Austin, 1987-88. Mem. Huntington (N.Y.) Sch. Dist. Bd. Edn., 1973-79, pres., 1975-77; vol. fireman West Sayville (N.Y.) Fire Dept., 1960-70. Named an Outstanding Young Man in Am., Jaycees, 1974. Republican. Baptist. Avocations: fishing, hunting. Home: 3439 Meadow Creek Ln Sachse TX 75048-4181 Office: Monarch Assocs Ste 119 9319 Lyndon B Johnson Fwy Dallas TX 75243-3440

LEIGHNINGER, DAVID SCOTT, cardiovascular surgeon; b. Youngstown, Ohio, Jan. 16, 1920; s. Jesse Harrison and Marjorie (Lightner) L.; m. Margaret Jane Malony, May 24, 1942; children: David Allan, Jenny. BA, Oberlin Coll., 1942; MD, Case Western Res. U., 1945. Intern Univ. Hosps. of Cleve., 1945-46, resident, 1949-51, asst. surgeon, 1951-68; rsch. fellow in cardiovascular surgery rsch. lab. Case Western Res. U. Sch. Medicine, Cleve., 1948-49, 51-55, 57-67, instr. surgery, 1951-55, sr. instr., 1957-64, asst. prof., 1964-68, asst. clin. prof., 1968-70; resident Cin. Gen. Hosp., 1955-57; practice medicine specializing in cardiovascular surgery, Cleve., 1957-70; pvt. practice medicine specializing in cardiovascular and gen. surgery Edgewater Hosp., Chgo., 1970-82, staff surgeon, also dir. emergency surg. services, 1970-82; staff surgeon, also dir. emergency surg. svcs. Mazel Med. Ctr., Chgo., 1970-82; emergency physician, Raton, N.Mex. and Trinidad, Colo., 1982-85; assoc., courtesy, or cons. staff Marymount Hosp., Cleve., Mt. Sinai Hosp., Cleve., Geauga Community Hosp., Chardon, Ohio, Bedford Community Hosp (Ohio), 1957-70. Tchr. tng. courses in CPR for med. personnel, police, fire and vol. rescue workers, numerous cities, 1950-70. Served to capt., M.C., AUS, 1946-48. Recipient Chris award Columbus Internat. Film Festival, 1964, numerous other award for sci. exhibits from various nat. and state med. socs., 1953-70; USPHS grantee, 1949-68. Fellow Am. Coll. Cardiology, Am. Coll. Chest Physicians; mem. Mont Reid Surg. Soc. (Cinn.). Contbr. numerous articles to med. jours., chpts. to med. texts; spl. pioneer research (with Claude S. Beck) in physiopathology of coronary artery disease and CPR; developed surg. treatment of coronary artery disease; achieved 1st successful defibrillation of human heart, 1st successful reversal of fatal heart attack; provided 1st intensive care of coronary patients. Home: HC 68 Box 77 Fort Garland CO 81133-9708

LEIGHTEN, EDWARD HENRY, publisher, consultant; b. Montclair, N.J., June 22, 1914; s. Jack and Mariette G. (Ackerman) L.; m. Alice Celia Bowne, Aug. 31, 1940; children: Judith (Mrs. Harvey L. Slade), Jeanne Elizabeth (Mrs. T.E. Card). B.S. in Optics, U. Rochester, 1937. Engr. Universal Camera Corp., N.Y.C., 1938-39; mem. editorial staff Photo Technique and Product Engrng. mags. McGraw-Hill Pub. Co., N.Y.C., 1939-42; tech. editor U.S. Camera mag., N.Y.C., 1946-47; editor, pub. Photo Devels. (now Photo Mktg.) mag. Master Photo Dealers Assn.), Jackson, Mich., 1947-52; editor Flow mag., Flow Quar. mag. and Flow Directory, Indsl. Pub. Co., Cleve., 1952-56; exec. editor Flow mag., Flow Quar. mag. and Flow Directory, Indsl. Pub. Co., 1956-60; with Cahners Pub. Co., Boston, 1960-82; pub. Modern Materials Handling mag., 1960-81, v.p., 1966-80; v.p., group pub. Modern Materials Handling and Traffic Mgmt. mags., 1974-80; staff v.p. Modern Materials Handling and Traffic Mgmt. mags. (Boston div. corp.), 1981-82; pres. Cons. Services Group (communications, mktg., pub. relations); asso. prof. mktg. Cape Cod Community Coll. Mem. Westlake (Ohio) Sch. Bd., 1958-60, Westlake Libr. Bd., 1958-60; vol. J.N. (Ding) Darling Nat. Wildlife Refuge, Sanibel, Fla., 1984—. Lt. USNR, 1942-46. Recipient Honor award for contbns. to materials handling edn. Internat. Material Mgmt. Soc. Mem. Material Handling Inst., Caster and Floor Truck Mfrs. Assn., Nat. Wooden Pallet and Container Assn., Internat. Material Mgmt. Soc. (cert. profl. in material handling and material mgmt.), Material Handling Equipment Dealers Assn., Nat. Council Phys. Distbn. Mgmt., Bus./Profl. Advt. Assn. (cert. bus. communicator), Theta Chi. Home and Office: 531 Riverview Dr Chatham MA 02633-1117 *Full, clear, and honest communication among people—in social, industrial, professional and commercial endeavors—is essential to our social, economic, and political growth, nationally and internationally. To be a good communicator is to be a catalyst for progress in all aspects of life. Opportunities for good communicators abound, but relatively few persons are aware of them early enough in their careers. Too many who have writing abilities or aspirations think only in terms of news or literary careers. Whatever profession, trade or technology a person may choose, training in communications will enhance his development and speed his progress.*

LEIGHTON, ALBERT CHESTER, history educator; b. Chester, N.H., Sept. 6, 1919; s. Arthur Edmund and Sarah Elizabeth (Edwards) L.; m. Estella Ruth Dietel, Jan. 17, 1958; children: Cedric Edmund George. AB, U. Calif., Berkeley, 1960, MA, 1961, PhD, 1964. Enlisted U.S. Army, 1937, commd. 2d lt., 1946, advanced through grades to capt., 1953, ret., 1957; ops. officer, Germany, 1947-50, staff officer Hdqrs., Washington, 1950-53, 55-57, ops. officer, Korea, Japan, Taiwan, 1954-55; assoc. prof. history SUNY-Oswego, 1964-69, prof., 1969-85, prof. emeritus, 1985—; adj. prof., lectr. U. Tex. at San Antonio, 1987—; Fulbright Rsch. prof. U. Munich, 1978-79; faculty exchange scholar SUNY, 1981-85; coordinator internat. rsch. in hist. cryptanalysis, 1969—; speaker Internat. Congress, St. Petersburg formerly Leningrad, 1970, Moscow, 1971, Tokyo, 1974, Edinburgh, 1977. Author: Transport and Communication in Early Medieval Europe, 1972; contbr. Ency. Americana; contbr. articles to profl. jours. Rsch. fellow Ctr. Medieval and Renaissance Studies UCLA, 1984, Medieval Insts. fellow Duke U., 1976, SUNY Binghamton fellow, 1985. Mem. Am. Hist. Assn., Medieval Acad. Am., Am. Cryptogram Assn., Beale Cypher Soc., Ancient and Honorable Arty. Co. Mass., New Eng. Hist. and Genealogical Soc., Ret. Officers Assn. Home: 8406 Burwell San Antonio TX 78250-2538

LEIGHTON, CHARLES MILTON, specialty consumer products executive; b. Portland, Maine, June 4, 1935; s. Wilbur F. and Elizabeth (Loveland) L.; AB, Bowdoin Coll., 1957, LLD (hon.), 1989; M.BA, Harvard U., 1960; children: Julia Loveland, Anne Throop; m. Roxanne Brooks McCormick, May 23, 1992. Product line mgr. Mine Safety Appliances Co., Pitts., 1960-64; instr. Harvard Bus. Sch., 1964-65; group v.p. Bangor Punta Corp., Boston, 1965-69; chmn., CEO CML Group, Inc., Acton, Mass., 1969—; bd. dirs. New England Investment Co., Boston, Met. Life Ins. Co., N.Y. Past pres. Alumni Coun. Harvard Bus. Sch., Cambridge, Mass.; past pres. of trustees Concord (Mass.) Acad. Republican. Episcopalian. Clubs: New York Yacht (commodore 1993-94); Chatham (Mass.) Yacht (vice commodore 1957); Harvard of N.Y.C. and Boston, Harvard Faculty Club, Tarratine, Internat. Golf Club. Home: PO Box 247 Bolton MA 01740-0247 Office: CML Group Inc 524 Main St Acton MA 01720-3593

LEIGHTON, FRANCES SPATZ, writer, journalist; b. Geauga County, Ohio; m. Kendall King Hoyt, Feb. 1, 1984. Student, Ohio State U. Washington corr. Am. Weekly; corr. and Washington editor This Week Mag.; Washington corr. Met. Group Sunday Mags.; contbg. editor Family Weekly; free-lance journalist Metro Sunday Group, Washington; lectr. summer confs. Dellbrook-Shenandoah Coll., Georgetown U., Washington. Author over 30 books on hist. figures, celebrities, Hollywood, psychiatry, the White House and Capitol Hill, 1957—; (with Louise Pfister) I Married a Psychiatrist, 1961, (with Francois Rysovy) A Treasury of White House Cooking, 1968, (with Frank S. Caprio) How to Avoid a Nervous Breakdown, 1969, (with Mary B. Gallagher) My Life with Jacqueline Kennedy, 1969, (with Traphes Bryant) Dog Days at the White House, 1975, (with William Fishbait Miller) Fishbait—the Memoirs of the Congressional Doorkeeper, 1977, (with Lillian Rogers Parks) My 30 Years Backstairs at the White House (made into TV mini-series), 1979, (with Hugh Carter) Cousin Beedie, Cousin Hot--, My Life with the Carter Family of Plains, Georgia, 1978, (with Jerry Cammarata) The Fun Book of Fatherhood-or How the Animal Kingdom is Helping to Raise the Wild Kids at Our House, 1978, (with Natalie Golos) Coping with Your Allergies, 1979, (with Ken Hoyt) Drunk Before Noon—The Behind the Scenes Story of the Washington Press Corps, 1979, (with Louis Hurst) The Sweetest Little Club in the World, The Memoirs of the Senate Restaurateur, 1980, (with John M. Szostak) In the Footsteps of Pope John Paul II, 1980, (with Lillian Rogers Parks) The Roosevelts, a Family in Turmoil, 1981, (with June Allyson) June Allyson, 1982, (with Beverly Slater) Stranger in My Bed, 1985 (made into TV movie), 1987, The Search for the Real Nancy Reagan, 1987, (with Oscar Collier) How To Write and Sell Your First Nonfiction Book, 1990, How to Write and Sell Your First Novel, 1986, 3rd edit., 1997, (with Stephen M. Bauer) At Ease at the White House, 1991; contbr. numerous feature stories on polit., social and govtl. personalities to various publs. Bd. dirs. Nat. Found., from 1963. Recipient Edgar award, 1961. Mem. Senate Periodical Corr. Assn., White House Corr. Assn., Am. News Women's Club, The Writers Club, Nat. Press Club, Writers League of Washington (pres.), Washington League Am. Pen Women (pres.), Washington Ind. Writers, Smithsonian Assocs., Nat. Trust Historic Preservation, Lake Barcroft Women's Club, Delta Phi Delta, Sigma Delta Chi. Unitarian. Office: Lake Barcroft 6336 Lakeview Dr Falls Church VA 22041-1331

LEIGHTON, GEORGE NEVES, retired federal judge; b. New Bedford, Mass., Oct. 22, 1912; s. Antonio N. and Anna Sylvia (Garcia) Leitao; m. Virginia Berry Quivers, June 21, 1942; children: Virginia Anne, Barbara Elaine. AB, Howard U., 1940; LLB, Harvard U., 1946; LLD, Elmhurst Coll., 1964; LL.D., John Marshall Law Sch., 1973, Southeastern Mass. U., 1975, New Eng. U. Sch. Law, 1978; LLD, Loyola U., Chgo., 1989, R.I. Coll., 1992. Bar: Mass. 1946, Ill. 1947, U.S. Supreme Ct. 1958. Ptnr. Moore, Ming & Leighton, Chgo., 1951-59, McCoy, Ming & Leighton, Chgo., 1959-64; judge Circuit Ct. Cook County Ill., 1964-69, Appellate Ct. 1st Dist., 1969-76; U.S. dist. judge No. Dist. Ill., 1976-86; sr. dist. judge U.S. Dist. Ct., No. Dist. Ill., 1986-87; of counsel Earl L. Neal & Assocs., 1987—; adj. prof. John Marshall Law Sch., Chgo., 1965—; commr., mem. character and fitness com. for 1st Appellate Dist., Supreme Ct. Ill., 1955-63, chmn. character and fitness com., 1961-62; joint com. for revision Ill. Criminal Code, 1959-63; chmn. Ill. adv. com. U.S. Commn. on Civil Rights, 1964; mem. pub. rev. bd. UAW, AFL-CIO, 1961-70; Asst. atty. gen. State of Ill., 1950-51; pres. 3d Ward Regular Democratic Orgn., Cook County, Ill., 1951-53; v.p. 21st Ward, 1964. Contbr. articles to legal jours. Bd. dirs. United Ch. Bd. for Homeland Ministries, United Ch. of Christ, Grant Hosp., Chgo.; trustee U. Notre Dame, 1979-83, trustee emeritus, 1983—; bd. overseers Harvard Coll., 1983-89. Capt., inf. AUS, 1942-45. Decorated Bronze Star.; Recipient Civil Liberties award Ill. div. ACLU, 1961; named Chicagoan of Year in Law and Judiciary Jr. Assn. Commerce and Industry, 1964. Fellow ABA (chmn. coun. 1976, mem. coun. sect. legal edn. and admissions to bar); mem. NAACP (chmn. legal redress com. Chgo. br.), Am. Coll. Trial Lawyers, John Howard Assn. (bd. dirs.), Chgo. Bar Assn., Ill. Bar Assn. (joint com. mem. for revision jud. article 1959-62), Nat. Harvard Law Sch. Assn. (mem. coun.), Howard U. Chgo. Alumni Club (chmn. bd. dirs.), Phi Beta Kappa. Office: Earl L Neal & Assocs 111 W Washington St Ste 1700 Chicago IL 60602-2711

LEIGHTON, HENRY ALEXANDER, physician, consultant; b. Manila, Nov. 12, 1929; (parents U.S. citizens).; s. Raymond Harry and Theola Marie (Alexander) L.; m. Helga Maria Hell, Jan. 17, 1970; children: Alan Raymond, Henry Alexander, Michael Ballinger, John, Marni, Tammy Ballinger. BA in History, U. Calif., Berkeley, 1952, MPH, 1971; MD, U. Calif., San Francisco, 1956. Diplomate Am. Bd. Preventive Medicine. Intern So. Pacific Gen. Hosp., San Francisco, 1956-57; resident in surgery Brooke Gen. Hosp., Ft. Sam Houston, Tex., 1960-62; commd. 2d. lt. U.S. Army, 1957, advanced through grades to col., 1971; div. surgeon 8th Inf. div. U.S. Army, Germany, 1964-66; comdr. 15th Med. Bn. U.S. Army, Vietnam, 1966-67, instr. Med. Field Service Sch. U.S. Army, San Antonio, 1968-70; resident preventive medicine U.S. Army, Ft. Ord, Calif., 1971-72, chief preventive medicine, 1973-76; chief preventive medicine U.S. Army-Europe, 1976-79, ret., 1979; chief occupational health MEDDAC U.S. Army, Ft. Ord, 1981-89; pvt. practice Salinas, Calif., 1990—. Neighborhood commr. Boy Scouts Am., 1964-66; bd. dirs. Am. Lung Assn. of Calif., 1982-84, and of affiliate, 1980-86, The Calif. Acad. Preventive Medicine, 1994-96; pres. The Bluffs Homeowners Assn., 1986. Decorated Air medal with oak leaf cluster, Bronze Star, Legion of Merit, Meritorious Service medal. Fellow Am. Coll. Preventive Medicine; mem. Am. Pub. Health Assn., Am. Coll. Occupational Medicine, Assn. Mil. Surgeons, Ret. Officers Assn., Assn. U.S. Army, Theta Xi. Lodges: Masons, Shriners. Office: 14096 Reservation Rd Salinas CA 93908-9208

LEIGHTON, JOSEPH, pathologist; b. N.Y.C., Dec. 13, 1921; m. Rosalind Weinberger, Dec. 15, 1946; children—Daniel A., Edith R. AB, Columbia U., 1942; MD, L.I. Coll. Medicine, Bklyn., 1946. Intern Mt. Sinai Hosp., N.Y.C., 1946-47; resident in pathology Mass. Gen. Hosp., Boston, 1948-49, USPHS Hosp., Balt., 1950; research pathologist Nat. Cancer Inst., Bethesda, Md., 1951-56; mem. faculty dept. pathology U. Pitts. Sch. Medicine, 1956-70; prof. pathology Med. Coll. Pa., Phila., 1971-89, chmn. dept. pathology, 1971-87; pathologist Peralta Cancer Rsch. Inst., 1989-92, Aeron Biotech. Inc., San Leandro, Calif., 1994—. Author: The Spread of Cancer, 1967; inventor radial histophysiologic gradient culture chamber. Served with USPHS, 1948-56. Eleanor Roosevelt Cancer Research fellow, 1970-71. Mem. Am. Assn. Cancer Research, Tissue Culture Assn., Am. Assn. Pathologists, Internat. Acad. Pathology. Home: 2324 Lakeshore Ave Apt 2 Oakland CA 94606-1056 Office: Aeron Biotech Inc 1933 Davis St San Leandro CA 94577-1260

LEIGHTON, LAWRENCE WARD, investment banker; b. N.Y.C., July 1, 1934; s. Sidney and Florence (Ward) L.; m. Mariana Stroock, June 21, 1959; children: Sandra L. Galvin, Michelle Stroock. BSE, Princeton U., 1956; MBA, Harvard U., 1962. V.p. Kuhn Loeb & Co., N.Y.C., 1962-69, Clark, Dodge & Co., Inc., 1970-74; dir. Norton-Simon, Inc., 1974-78; ltd. ptnr. Bear, Stearns & Co., 1978-82; mng. dir. Chase Investment Bank, 1983-88; pres., CEO Union d'Etudes et d'Investissements Mcht. Bank of Credit Agricole, 1989-93; vice chmn. 2I, Inc., 1993-94, mng dir. LM Capital Corp., 1994-96; sr. advisor Bentley Assocs., L.P., 1997—; dir. Corp. Renaissance Group, 1994—; chmn. Princeton Schs. Com. of N.Y., 1965-85. Mem. exec. com. Princeton U. Alumni Coun., 1975-80; vice chmn. nat. schs. com. Princeton U., 1980—; chmn. Harvard Bus. Sch. Fund of N.Y., 1964-65, mem. nat. fin. com. Pete DuPont for Pres., 1986-88; trustee Waterford Inst., 1985—. Served to lt. (j.g.) USN, 1957-60. Clubs: Stanwich (Greenwich, Conn.), Princeton Club of N.Y. (scholarship com. 1970—, bd. govs. 1989-96), Coral Beach and Tennis (Bermuda). Avocations: flying, golf, photography. Home: 1088 Park Ave New York NY 10128-1132 Office: Bentley Assocs 1155 Ave of Americas New York NY 10036-2711

LEIGHTON, RICHARD F., retired dean. BA, Western Md. Coll., 1951; MD, U. Md., 1955. Diplomate Am. Bd. Internal Medicine (Specialty Cardiovascular Disease). Intern U. Hosp., Balt., 1955-56; flight surgeon USN, 1956-58; resident Ohio State U. Hosp., 1959-61, resident, cardiology fellow, 1961-64; from asst. prof. to assoc. prof. medicine Coll. Medicine Ohio State U., 1965-74, dir. coronary care unit, 1968-69, dir. cardiac catheterization labs., 1970-74; prof. medicine, chief cardiology Med. Coll. Ohio, 1974-90, acting chmn. dept. medicine, 1988, vice chmn., 1988-90, v.p. acad. affairs, dean Sch. Medicine, 1990-95, sr. v.p. acad. affairs, dean Sch. Medicine, 1995-97; ret., 1997. Editl. bd. La Lettre du Cardiologue, 1985—; contbr. numerous articles to profl. jours. Fellow ACP, Am. Coll. Cardiology (gov. Ohio chpt. 1985-88), Am. Heart Assn (coun. circulation, epidemiology, clinical cardiology, coun. rep. Ohio 1977-80), Royal Soc. Medicine; mem. Ctrl. Soc. Clin. Rsch., Societe Francaise Cardiologies (corr.), Alpha Omega Alpha. Office: Med Coll Ohio Office of Dean Toledo OH 43699

LEIGHTON, ROBERT, film editor. Editor: (films) Delusion, 1981, (with Peter Thornton) Kill and Kill Again, 1981, Blood Tide, 1982, The House Where Death Lives, 1982, The Being, 1983, (with Mark Goldblatt) Wavelength, 1983, This Is Spinal Tap, 1984, The Sure Thing, 1985, Stand By Me, 1986, The Princess Bride, 1987, (with Adam Weiss) Bull Durham, 1988, When Harry Met Sally..., 1989, Blaze, 1989, Misery, 1990, (with Richard Chew) Late for Dinner, 1991, A Few Good Men, 1992, Life With Mikey, 1993, North, 1994, The American President, 1995, Courage Under Fire, 1996, Ghosts of Mississippi, 1996. Office: care Motion Picture Editors 7715 W Sunset Blvd Ste 200 Los Angeles CA 90046-3912

LEIGHTON, ROBERT JOSEPH, state legislator; b. Austin, Minn., July 7, 1965; s. Robert Joseph Sr. and JoAnn (Mulvihill) L. BA, U. Minn., 1988; JD, U. Calif., Berkeley, 1991. Minn. state rep. Dist. 27B, 1995—. Mem. Big Brothers/Big Sisters, bd. dirs., 1994—; mem. Am. Heart Assn., bd. dirs., 1993—. Presdl. and Waller scholar U. Minn., 1988. Mem. ABA, Minn. Bar Assn., Minn. Trial Lawyers Assn., Phi Beta Kappa. Home: 1007 9th St NW Austin MN 55912 Office: Leighton Meany Cotter & Enger 601 N Main St Austin MN 55912-3319

LEIJONHUFVUD, AXEL STIG BENGT, economics educator; b. Stockholm, Sweden, Sept. 6, 1933; came to U.S., 1960; s. Erik Gabriel and Helene Adelheid (Neovius) L.; m. Marta Elisabeth Ising, June 10, 1955 (div. 1977); m. Earlene Joyce Craver, June 18, 1977; children—Carl Axel, Gabriella Helene, Christina Elisabeth. Fil. kand., U. Lund, Sweden, 1960; M.A., U. Pitts., Pa., 1961; Ph.D., Northwestern U., 1967; Fil. Dr. (hon.), U. Lund, Sweden, 1983; Dr. (hon.), U. Nice, Sophia-Antipolis, France, 1995. Acting asst. prof. econs. UCLA, 1964-67, assoc. prof. econs., 1967-71, prof. econs., 1971—, chair dept. econs., 1980-83, 90-92; dir. Ctr. for Computable Econs., 1992-97; prof. monetary theory and policy U. Trento, Italy, 1995—; co-dir. summer workshops Siena Internat. Sch. Econ. Rsch., 1987-91; participant numerous profl. confs.; cons., lectr., vis. prof. econs. various colls. and univs.; cons. Republic of Tatarstan, 1994. Author: On Keynesian Economics and the Economics of Keynes: A Study in Monetary Theory, 1968, Keynes and the Classics: Two Lectures, 1969, Information and Coordination: Essays in Macroeconomic Theory, 1981, (with D. Heymann) High Inflation, 1995. Mem. econ. expert com. of pres. Kazakhstan, 1991-92. Brookings Instn. fellow, 1963-64; Marshall lectr. Cambridge U., Eng., 1974; Overseas fellow Churchill Coll., Cambridge, 1974; Inst. Advanced Study fellow, 1983-84. Mem. Am. Econ. Assn., Western Econ. Assn., History of Econs. Soc. Office: UCLA Dept Econs Los Angeles CA 90024

LEIKEN, EARL MURRAY, lawyer; b. Cleve., Jan. 19, 1942; s. Manny and Betty G. L.; m. Ellen Kay Miner, Mar. 26, 1970; children: Jonathan, Brian. BA magna cum laude, Harvard U., 1964, JD cum laude, 1967. Asst. dean, assoc. prof. law Case Western Res. U., Cleve., 1967-71; ptnr. Hahn, Loeser, Freedheim, Dean & Wellman, Cleve., 1971-86, Baker & Hostetler, Cleve., 1986—; adj. faculty, lectr. law Case Western Res. U., 1971-86. Pres. Shaker Heights (Ohio) Bd. Edn., 1986-88, Jewish Community Ctr., Cleve., 1988-91, Shaker Heights Family Ctr., 1994—. Named one of Greater

Cleve.'s 10 Outstanding Young Leaders, Cleve. Jaycees, 1972; recipient Kane award Cleve. Jewish Community Fedn., 1982. Mem. ABA, Greater Cleve. Bar Assn. (chmn. labor law sect. 1978). Home: 20815 Colby Rd Cleveland OH 44122-1903 Office: Baker & Hostetler 3200 Nat City Ctr 1900 E 9th St Cleveland OH 44114-3401

LEIMKUHLER, FERDINAND FRANCIS, industrial engineering educator; b. Balt., Dec. 31, 1928; s. Ferdinand Frank and Louise (Kimmel) L.; m. Natalie Therese Morin, July 4, 1956; children: Kristin, Margaret, Jeanne, Benedict, Thomas, Ernest. B.S. cum laude, Loyola Coll., Balt., 1950; B.Engring., Johns Hopkins U., 1952, D.Engring. with distinction, 1962. Mgmt. engr. E.I. DuPont de Nemours & Co., Inc., 1950-57; research engr. Johns Hopkins U., 1957-61; prof. indsl. engring. Purdue U., 1961—, head Sch. Indsl. Engring., 1969-74, 81-93, dir. tech. assistance program, 1993-96; vis. prof. U. Calif., Berkeley, 1968-69, 90; vis. prof. (Fulbright-Hayes sr. lectr.), U. Ljubljana, Slovenia, 1974-75; cons. in field. Served with AUS, 1952-54. Fellow Inst. Indsl. Engrs.; mem. Ops. Rsch. Soc. Am., Inst. Mgmt. Scis., Am. Soc. Engring. Edn., Sigma Xi, Alpha Sigma Nu, Tau Beta Pi. Office: Dept Indsl Engring Purdue U West Lafayette IN 47907-1286

LEIN, MALCOLM EMIL, architect; b. Havre, Mont., July 19, 1913; s. Emil A. and Ruth (Fredeen) L.; m. Miriam Balliet Bend, Apr. 13, 1939; children: Eric Manning, Kristin Anker, R. Kurt Harrison. Student, U. Wis., 1930; BArch, U. Minn., 1936; student, U.S. Army C.I. Sch., 1943, Command & Gen. Staff Sch., U.S. Army, 1943, Nat. War Coll., 1963. Asst. head constrn. dept. F.W. Woolworth Co., Dist. Office, Mpls., 1936-41; pvt. practice architecture and design St. Paul, 1946—; instr. Macalester Coll., St. Paul, 1947-50; dir. Minn. Mus. of Art, St. Paul, 1947-77, pres., 1973-79; pres., founder Design Cons., Inc., St. Paul, 1949—, Mid-West Credit Corp., St. Paul, 1959—, Desconi Corp.; founder, dir. Gallery St. Paul, The Commodore, St. Paul, 1981-85; founder, pres. Madeline Island Art Ctr., La Pointe, Wis., 1991—. Trustee, founder Benlei Found., Scottsdale, Ariz., 1988—; bd. dirs. Phoenix Chamber Music Soc. Col. C.E., AUS, 1935-66, WWII CBI. Mem. Am. Assn. Mus., Am. Fedn. Art, Archives Am. Art, Res. Officers Assn., Air Force Assn., Japan Am. Soc. Minn. (v.p. bd. dirs.), Smithsonian Assocs., Phoenix Art Mus., Asian Art Coun. of Mpls. Art Inst., Planned Parenthood of Cen. & No. Ariz. (chmn. endowment and planned giving com.). Club: University (St. Paul). Home: 6200 E Hummingbird Ln Paradise Vly AZ 85253-3651 Office: 361 Summit Ave Saint Paul MN 55102-2168 *Goals: Find challenging creative work without sacrificing principles. Acknowledge the help and guidance from so many and do as much for others. Appreciate beauty. Live in harmony with nature, God and neighbors. Learn throughout life, Keep an open mind. Acquire wisdom. Remain a free spirit. And "be prepared" to live forever or die tomorrow.*

LEINBACH, PHILIP EATON, librarian; b. Winston-Salem, N.C., Sept. 17, 1935; s. Gray Newton and Martha Elizabeth (Eaton) L.; m. Nancy Lee Yocom, July 27, 1957; children—Jonathan Eaton, David Timothy. A.B., Duke U., 1956; M.A. in History, Ind. U., 1963, M.L.S., 1964. Adminstrv. asst. Harvard U. Library, Cambridge, Mass., 1964-66; asst. librarian for acquisitions Harvard U., Cambridge, 1966-67, specialist in book selection, 1967-71, asst. univ. librarian, 1972-82; univ. librarian Tulane U., New Orleans, 1982—; acting chief libr. Harvard U. Div. Sch., Cambridge, 1978-79; dep. libr. Queen Mary Coll., London, 1970-71. Author: Handbook for Librarians, 1977, Personnel Administration in an Automated Environment, 1990. Served with USNR, 1957-61. Fellow Ind. U., 1963-64; UCLA Grad. Sch. Library and Info. Sci., 1982; NDEA modern lang. fellow, 1962-63. Mem. ALA (council 1984-88), La. Library Assn., Omicron Delta Kappa, Beta Phi Mu, Pi Sigma Alpha. Home: 7530 Saint Charles Ave New Orleans LA 70118-3878 Office: Tulane U Howard-Tilton Memorial Library New Orleans LA 70118-5682

LEINENWEBER, HARRY D., federal judge; b. Joliet, Ill., June 3, 1937; s. Harry Dean and Emily (Lennon) L.; m. Lynn Morley Martin, Jan. 7, 1987; 5 children; 2 stepchildren. AB cum laude, U. Notre Dame, 1959; JD, U. Chgo., 1962. Bar: Ill. 1962, U.S. Dist. Ct. (no. dist.) Ill. 1967. Assoc. Dunn, Stefanich, McGarry & Kennedy, Joliet, Ill., 1962-65, ptnr., 1965-79; city atty. City of Joliet, 1963-67; spl. counsel Village of Park Forest, Ill., 1967-74; spl. prosecutor County of Will, Ill., 1968-70; spl. counsel Village of Bolingbrook, Ill., 1975-77, Will County Forest Preserve, 1977; mem. Ill. Ho. of Reps., Springfield, 1973-83, chmn. judiciary I com., 1981-83; ptnr. Dunn, Leinenweber & Dunn, Joliet, 1979-86; fed. judge U.S. Dist. Ct. (no. dist.) Ill., Chgo., 1986—; bd. dirs. Will County Bar Assn., 1984-86, State Jud. Adv. Coun., 1973-85, sec. 1975-76. Bd. dirs. Will County Legal Assistance Found., 1982-86, Good Shepard Manor, 1981—, Am. Cancer Soc., 1981-85, Joliet (Ill.) Montessori Sch., 1966-74; del. Rep. Nat. Conv., 1980; precinct committeeman, 1966-86. Recipient Environ. Legislator Golden award. Mem. Will County Bar Assn. (mem. jud. adv. coun., 1973-85, sec. 1975-76, bd. dirs. 1984-86), Nat. Conf. Commrs. on Uniform State Laws (exec. com. 1991-93, elected life mem. 1996). Roman Catholic. Office: US Dist Ct 219 S Dearborn St Ste 1946 Chicago IL 60604-1801

LEINIEKS, VALDIS, classicist, educator; b. Liepaja, Latvia, Apr. 15, 1932; came to U.S., 1949, naturalized, 1954; s. Arvid Ansis and Valia Leontine (Brunaus) L. BA, Cornell U., 1955, MA, 1956; PhD, Princeton U., 1962. Instr. classics Cornell Coll., Mount Vernon, Iowa, 1959-62, asst. prof. classics, 1962-64; assoc. prof. classics Ohio State U., 1964-66; assoc. prof. classics U. Nebr., Lincoln, 1966-71, prof. classics, 1971—, chmn. dept. classics, 1967-95, chmn. program comparative lit., 1970-86, interim chmn. dept. modern langs., 1982-83. Author: Morphosyntax of the Homeric Greek Verb, 1964; The Structure of Latin, 1975; Index Nepotianus, 1976; The Plays of Sophokles, 1982, The City of Dionysos, 1996. Contbr. articles to profl. jours. Mem. AAUP, Am. Classical League, Classical Assn. Middle West and South, Am. Philol. Assn. Republican. Home: 2505 A St Lincoln NE 68502-1841 Office: U Nebr Dept Classics Lincoln NE 68588-0337

LEININGER, MADELEINE MONICA, nurse, anthropologist, administrator, consultant, editor, author; b. Sutton, Nebr., July 13, 1925; d. George M. S. and Irene (Sheedy) L. BS in Biology, Scholastic Coll., 1950, LHD, 1976; MS in Nursing, Cath. U. Am., 1953; PhD in Anthropology, U. Wash., 1965; DSc (hon.), U. Indpls., 1990; PhDN (hon.), 1990, U. Kuopio, Finland, 1991. RN; cert. transcultural nurse FAA/Am. Acad. Nursing. Instr., mem. staff, head nurse med.-surg. unit, supr. psychiat. unit St. Joseph's Hosp., Omaha, 1950-54; assoc. prof. nursing, dir. grad. program in psychiat. nursing U. Cin. Coll. Nursing, 1954-60; research fellow Nat. League Nursing, Eastern Highlands of New Guinea, 1960-62, 78, 92; research assoc. U. Wash. Dept. Anthropology, Seattle, 1964-65; prof. nursing and anthropology, dir. nurse-scientist PhD program U. Colo., Boulder and Denver, 1966-69; dean sch. nursing, prof. nursing, lectr. anthropology U. Wash., Seattle, 1969-74; dean coll. nursing, prof. nursing and anthropology U. Utah, Salt Lake City, 1974-80; Anise J. Sorell prof. nursing Troy (Ala.) State U., 1981; prof. nursing, adj. prof. anthropology, dir. Ctr. for Health Research, dir. transcultural nursing offerings Wayne State U., Detroit, 1981-95, prof. emeritus, 1995—; adj. prof. anthropology U. Utah, 1974-81; disting. vis. prof. at 87 univs., U.S. and overseas, 1970—; cons. Saudi Arabia, Brazil, Europe, Japan, Thailand, China, Burnei, Indonesia, Australia, South Africa, Finland, Sweden, The Netherlands, New Guinea, Australia, Jordan, Iran, Africa, 60 health instns. in U.S. Author: 28 books including Nursing and Anthropology: Two Worlds to Blend, 1970, Contemporary Issues in Mental Health Nursing, 1973, Caring: An Essential Human Need, 1981, Reference Sources for Transcultural Health and Nursing, 1984, Basic Psychiatric Concepts in Nursing, 1960, Care: The Essence of Nursing and Health, 1984, Qualitative Research Methods in Nursing, 1985, Care: Discovery and Clinical-Community Uses, 1988, Ethical and Moral Dimensions of Caring, 1990, Culture Care, Diversity and Universality: A Theory of Nursing, 1991, Care: The Compassionate Healer, 1991, Caring Imperative for Nursing Education, 1991, Transcultural Nursing, 1995; editor Jour. of Transcultural Nursing, 1989—; mem. editl. bd. 10 nat. and internat. jours.; editor or contbr. over 200 articles to profl. jours., 47 chpts. to books; lectr. in field. Disting. vis. scholar at 87 univs., U.S. and overseas; recipient Outstanding Alumni award Cath. U. Am., 1969, Recognition award Am. Assn. Colls. of Nursing, 1976, 96, Nurse of Yr. award Dist. 1 Utah Nurses Assn., 1976, Lit. award Utah Nurses Assn., 1978, Trotter Disting. Pub. Lectr. award U. Tex., 1985, Disting. Faculty Tchg. Recognition award Wayne State U., 1985, Outstanding Faculty Rsch. scholar award Wayne State U. and Gerontology Inst., 1985, Gershenson Rsch. award Wayne State U., 1985, Pace Inst. Rsch. award, 1992, Hewlett Packard Rsch. award, 1992, award for Acad. Excellence AAUW-Detroit, 1986, Disting. award Bd. Govs., 1987, Pres. Excellence in Tchg. award, 1988, Women of Sci. award U. Calif. at Fullerton, 1990, Outstanding Univ. Grad. Mentor award Wayne State U., 1995, Nightingale Rsch. award Oakland U., 1995, outstanding nursing leader Russell Sage Coll, Sigma Theta Tau Intl. Disting. scholar award Russell Sage Coll., 1995; libr. and reading sects. at Madenna U. dedicated to Madeleine Leininger, 1996. Fellow ANA, Am. Anthrop. Soc. for Applied Anthropology (exec. com. 1980-84), Am. Acad. Nursing; mem. Am. Assn. Humanities, Am. Applied Anthropol. Soc., Mich. Nurses Assn. (Bertha Culp Human Rights award 1994), Ctrl. States Anthropology, Amnesty Internat., Transcultural Nursing Soc. (founder, bd. dirs., pres. 1974-80), Cultural Cmty. Group Assn. (ethics, humanities heritage study group), Nat. Rsch. Care Confs. (leader human care rsch.), Internat. Assn. Human Caring (founder, pres., bd. dirs.), Nordic Caring Soc. Sweden (hon.), Sigma Xi, Pi Gamma Mu, Sigma Theta Tau (Lectr. of Yr. 1987—), Delta Kappa Gamma, Alpha Tau Delta. Office: 11211 Woolworth Plz Omaha NE 68144-1875

LEIPER, ROBERT DUNCAN, protective services official; b. Houston, July 22, 1953; s. William Harper Leiper and Frances Ann (Wright) Freeman; m. Glynna Dell Wilson, May 18, 1985; children: Kelsey Allison, Chad Wilson. AAS in Fire Protection, San Jacinto Coll., 1983; BA in Pub. Mgmt., U. Houston, 1988. Master fire fighter, Tex. Lt. Spring Br. Fire Dept., Houston, 1973-75; asst. svc. mgr. Archer Motor Sales, Houston, 1975-77; fire fighter Baytown (Tex.) Fire & Rescue, 1977-80, driver, 1980-83, lt., 1983-88, capt., 1988-92, fire chief, 1992—; instr. Tex. A & M U., College Station, 1988-92, Lamar U., Beaumont, Tex., 1990-92. Chmn. bd. Baycoast Med. Ctr., Baytown, Tex., 1994-95. Named Exec. Fire Officer, Nat. Fire Acad.; recipient Fire Fighter of Yr. award VFW, 1987, 90. Mem. Nat. Fire Protection Assn., Baytown Profl. Fire Fighters (v.p. 1982), Hispanic C. of C., Baytown C. of C., Kiwanis Club (pres. 1994, Rookie of Yr. award 1989). Avocations: wood working, camping, photography. Office: Baytown Fire and Rescue Svcs 201 Wye Dr Baytown TX 77521-4121

LEIPOLD, WILLIAM CHARLES, JR., plastics company executive, consultant; b. West Reading, Pa., Mar. 30, 1949; s. William Charles Sr. and Patricia (Feehan) L. BS in Chem. Engring., Ohio State U., 1972; MBA, U. Chgo., 1973. Asst. to mfg. mgr. W.R. Grace & Co., Burlington, Mass., 1973; process engr. polyfibron div. W.R. Grace & Co., Owensboro, Ky., 1974, gen. supr. polyfibron div., 1975; mgr. dept. electronics div. Raychem Corp., Menlo Park, Calif., 1976, engring. mgr., 1977-78; U.S. product mgr. pipe protection div. Raychem Corp., Redwood City, Calif., 1978-79; plant mgr., mgr. rsch. and devel. solar div. Sealed Air Corp., Hayward, Calif., 1981; mgr. ops. Custom Coating & Laminating, Worchester, Mass., 1980; pres., chmn. Columbine Plastics Corp., Boulder, Colo., 1982—; cons. Medac, Inc., Bethesda, Md., 1987-89. Mem. Soc. Plastic Engrs. (sr. mem., sr. pres. 1970-72, Disting. Service award 1972). Libertarian. Club: Boulder Country. Avocations: tennis, skiing, astronomy, photography. Office: Columbine Plastics Corp 3195 Bluff St Boulder CO 80301-2103

LEIPPER, DALE FREDERICK, physical oceanographer, educator; b. Salem, Ohio, Sept. 8, 1914; s. Robert and Myrtle (Cost) L.; m. Virginia Alma Harrison, May 14, 1942; children: Diane Louise, Janet Elizabeth, Bryan Robert, Anita Dale. BS in Edn., Wittenberg Coll., 1937, DSc (hon.), 1968; MA, Ohio State U., 1939; postgrad., UCLA, 1939-40; Ph.D., Scripps Instn. Oceanography, 1950. Tchr. city schs. San Diego, 1940-41; research oceanographer, tchr. Scripps Instn. Oceanography, U. Calif., 1945-49; mem. faculty dept. oceanography and meteorology Tex. A&M U., 1949-68, head dept., 1949-64, prof., 1964-68; prof., chmn. dept. oceanography Naval Postgrad. Sch., 1968-79; rsch. prof. U. Nev., 1996—; supr. rsch. program NSF, Internat. Geophys. Year, Office Naval Rsch.; mem. tech. panel oceanography, exec. vice chmn. meteorology panel U.S. Nat. Com. Internat. Geophys. Year; chmn. com. marine scis. Soc. Regional Edn. Bd., 1952-56; assoc. dir. Tex. A&M Rsch. Found., 1953-54. Contbr. articles on West Coast fog, oceanography, hurricane-ocean interaction, ocean currents to jours. in field. Served as maj. USAAF, 1941-45; weather officer, oceanographer. Mem. Am. Meteorol. Soc., Am. Geophys. Union, Am. Soc. Limnology and Oceanography (pres. 1957-58), Tex. Acad. Sci. (pres. 1955), Nat. Acad. Sci. (panel chmn. 1959-64), Marine Tech. Soc., Am. Soc. Oceanography (pres. 1967-68), U. Corp. for Atmospheric Rsch. (founding mem., bd. dirs.), The Oceanography Soc., Sigma Xi, Phi Kappa Phi. Club: Rotary (pres. Bryan, Tex. 1965-66). Home and Office: 716 Terra Ct Reno NV 89506-9606

LEIPZIG, ARTHUR, photographer, educator emeritus; b. Bklyn., Oct. 25, 1918; s. Julius M. and Esther Pearl (Rubin) L.; m. Mildred Levin, Mar. 21, 1942; children: Joel Myron, Judith Anne. Student, Photo League, 1942-43, Paul Strand Photo Workshop, 1946. Staff photographer PM newspaper, N.Y.C., 1942-46, Internat. News Photos, N.Y.C., 1946; freelance photographer East Meadow, N.Y., 1946—; prof. art, dir. photography C.W. Post Sch. of Arts, L.I. U., Greenvale, N.Y., 1968—. Contbr. photographs to Fortune, Look, Parade, Life, Natural History, Sunday Times, also indsl. mags.; guest editor Infinity Mag., N.Y.C., 1970, mem. editorial bd., 1973-75; interview and photographs included Life Documentary Photo Book, N.Y.C., 1972, 83; exhibited works Mus. Modern Art, 1946-51, 55-58, Met. Mus. Art, 1961, 62, Nassau Mus. Art, 1975, Queens Mus. Art, 1982, Transco Gallery, Houston, 1985, Daniel Wolf Gallery, N.Y.C., Houston Foto Fest, 1986, Photo Find Gallery, Woodstock, Coll. Art Gallery, New Paltz, N.Y., Smithsonian Mus., Washington, 1987, Mus. of the City of N.Y., Children's Games, 1988, Photofind Gallery, N.Y.C., 1990, ICP, Bklyn., 1992; one-man shows include Midtown Y Gallery, 1978, Henry St. Settlement, Arts for Living Ctr., 1986, Frunkin Adams Gallery, N.Y.C., 1990, 92, Photofind Gallery, 1990, Howard Greenberg Gallery, 1991, Salena Gallery, Bklyn., 1992, Port Washington Libr., 1994, Mus. of the City of N.Y., 1995, 96, Albin O. Kuhn Gallery, Balt., Md.; represented in permanent collections Mus. Modern Art, Bklyn. Mus., Eastman House, Nat. Gallery Art, Nassau Mus. Art, Houston Mus. Fine Arts, Midtown Y Gallery, Visual Studies Workshop, Pablo Casals Mus., Internat. Ctr. Photography, Nat. Mus. Am. Art, Washington, Consol. Freightways, San Francisco, Bank of Am. Art Program, San Francisco, Bibliotheque Nationale, Paris, The Jewish Mus., N.Y.C., Mus. Folkwang, Essen, Germany, The Nat. Portrait Gallery, Washington, The Gilman Paper Co., Queens Coll., N.Y., Dreyfus, N.Y.C., Soho Grand Hotel; retrospective exhbn. Hillwood Gallery, Brookville, N.Y., 1989, Musée De La Civilisation, Quebec City, 1990; featured on World of Photography, Sta. WABC-TV; pub. Classic Photographs from the Brooklyn Museum Collection, 1987, Sarah's Daughters, 1988, Master Photographs Photography in Fine Arts Exhbt. Internat. Ctr. Photography, 1988, 92, The Nat. Portrait Gallery, 1992, High Mus., Altlanta, 1992, Growing up in N.Y., 1995. Adv. bd. Midtown Y Gallery, 1983; bd. dirs. Nassau Mus. Fine Art, 1973-75. Recipient Nat. Urban League award, 1962, ORT award, 1976, Nassau County Office Cultural Devel. award, 1982, David Newton Excellence in Teaching award, 1989, Award for Scholarly Achievement, L.I. U. Trustees, 1983, 89. Mem. Am. Soc. Mag. Photographers (bd. govs., trustee 1960-65, treas. 1965). Office: LI Univ CW Post Coll Art Dept Northern Blvd Greenvale NY 11548-1207 *For me, the most important thing is loving what I do. I love photography and I love to teach photography. My success in both areas is due to may passion for my work.*

LEIS, HENRY PATRICK, JR., surgeon, educator; b. Saranac Lake, N.Y., Aug. 12, 1914; s. Henry P. and Mary A. (Disco) L.; m. Winogene Barnette, Jan. 8, 1944; children: Henry Patrick III, Thomas Frederick. BS cum laude, Fordham U., 1936; MD, N.Y. Med. Coll., 1941. Diplomate Am. Bd. Surgery. Intern Flower and Fifth Ave Hosps., N.Y.C., 1941-42, resident, 1943-44, 46-49, attending surgeon, chief breast service, 1960-81; resident in surgery Kanawa Valley Hosp., Charleston, W.Va., 1942-43; attending surgeon, chief breast service Met. Hosp., N.Y.C., 1960-81, emeritus chief breast service, 1982—; attending surgeon Coler Meml. Hosp., N.Y.C., 1960-76; chief breast surgery Cabrini Hosp. Med. Ctr., 1978-85, cons. breast surgery, 1985—; emeritus surgeon Lenox Hill Hosp., N.Y.C., 1980-83, hon. surg. staff, 1984—; hon. surg. staff Drs. Hosp., N.Y.C.; hon. surg. staff, cons. breast surgery Breast Diagnostic Ctr. Columbia Grand Strand Regional Med. Ctr., Myrtle Beach, S.C., 1985—; liason officer Am. Coll. Surgeons Commn. on Cancer; attending surgeon Westchester County Med. Ctr., 1977-81, emeritus surgeon, 1982—; clin. prof. surgery U. S.C. Sch. Medicine, Breast Surg. Oncology, Columbia, 1985—; hon. dir. breast cancer ctr., cons. in breast surgery Winthrop Univ. Hosp., Mineola, 1971—; cons. in breast surgery VA Hosp., Columbia, S.C., 1985—; cons. in breast surgery St. Claires Hosp., N.Y.C., 1979; attending surg. staff Richland Meml. Hosp., Columbia, 1986-90; clin. prof. surgery, 1960-81, prof. emeritus, 1982—, co-dir. Inst. Breast Diseases, 1978-82, emeritus, 1982—, chief breast svc. N.Y. Med. Coll., 1960-81, emeritus, 1982—; cons. in breast surgery SUNY Div. Rehab., 1965—, Med. and Surg. Specialists Plan N.Y.; mem. Am. Joint Com. on Breast Cancer Staging and End Results; v.p. N.Y. Met. Breast Cancer Group, 1975-76, pres., 1977-79; cons. Med. Advs. Selective Svc. System, N.Y.C. Alumni trustee N.Y. Med. Coll., 1971-76; adv. coun. Fordham Coll. Pharmacy, 1968; bd. dirs. Hall Fame and Mus. Surg. History and Related Scis. Author: Diagnosis and Treatment of Breast Lesions: The Breast, 1970, Management of Breast Lesions, 1978, Breast Cancer: Conservative and Reconstructive Surgery, 1989, Breast Lesions: Diagnosis and Treatment, 1988; co-editor: Breast; hon. editor Internat. Surgery Jour.; mem. editorial bd. jour. Senolgia, 1982—, Breast: An Internat. Jour.; contbr. articles to profl. jours. Mem. Women's Cancer Task Force of S.C. Capt. M.C., AUS, 1944-46, PTO. Decorated knight Grand Cross Equestrian Order Holy Sepulchre Jerusalem, knight Mil., Order of Malta, Knight Noble Co. of the Rose; recipient award of Merit Am. Cancer Soc., 1969, 87, cert. and award for outstanding and devoted services to indigent sick City N.Y., 1965, Dr. George Hohman Meml. medal, 1936, N.Y. Apothecaries medal, 1936, Internat. cert. merit for disting. service to surgery, 1970, award of merit N.Y. Met. Breast Cancer Group, 1976, medal of Ambrogino (Italy), 1977, Service award of Honor N.Y. Med. Coll., 1969, medaille d'Honneur (France), medal of City of Paris, 1979, Siver Palm Jerusalem award 1996, citation for svcs. to indigent sick in S.C. Fellow ACS (cancer liaison physician Surgeons commn. on Cancer 1987—, Peruvian Acad. Surgery (hon.), Am. Acad. Compensation Medicine, Am. Soc. Clin. Oncology, Am. Assn. Cancer Rsch., Am. Geriatrics Soc., Indsl. Med. Assn., Internat. Coll. Surgeons (1st v.p. 1973-74, pres. 1977-78, v.p., chmn. coun. examiners U.S. sect. 1962-68, pres. 1971, Svc. award of honor 1971), Internat. Paleopathology Assn. (founder), N.Y. Acad. Medicine, N.Y. Coun. Surgeons, Royal Soc. Health (Eng.); mem. AMA, AAAS, AAUP, Am. Cancer Soc. (com. breast cancer), Am. Med. Writers Assn., Am. Profl. Practice Assn., Assn. Am. Med. Colls., Am. Coll. Radiology (com. mammography and breast cancer), Assn. Mil. Surgeons U.S., Cath. Physicians Guild (pres. N.Y. 1970-78), Gerontol. Soc., Internat. Platform Assn., N.Y. Cancer Soc., N.Y. County Med. Soc., N.Y. Surg. Soc., Pan Am Med. Assn. (v.p. N.Am. sect. on cancer 1967—), Pan Pacific Surg. Assn. (v.p. 1980, Res. Officers Assn. U.S., Soc. Acad. Achievement (editorial bd. 1969—), Nat. Consortium Breast Ctrs. (bd. dirs. 1991—), Soc. Med. Jurisprudence, Soc. Nuclear Medicine Surg. Soc. N.Y. Med. Coll., WHO, World Med. Assn., Alumni Assn. N.Y. Med. Coll. (gov. 1960—, pres. 1971), Assn. Mil. Surgeons U.S., Catholic War Vets Assn., VFW, Hollywood Acad. Medicine (hon.), Alpha Omega Alpha, Phi Chi; hon. mem. Argentine Soc. Mammary Pathology, Argentina Cardiac and Thoracic Surg. Soc., Ecuador Med. Assn., Mo. Surg. Soc., Venezuela Surg. Soc., Italian Surg. Soc., S.C. Oncology Soc., So. Med. Assn. Club: Surf, Rotary. Lodge: K.C. (4th deg.).

LEISER, BURTON MYRON, philosophy and law educator; b. Denver, Dec. 12, 1930; s. Nathan and Eva Mae (Newman) L.; m. Janet A. Johnson, Aug. 12, 1984; children: Shoshana, Illana, Phillip, stepdaughter Sheri Johnson. BA, U. Chgo., 1951; MHL, Yeshiva U., 1956; PhD, Brown U., 1968; JD, Drake U., 1981. Bar: Iowa 1982, N.Y. 1985, U.S. Dist. Ct. (so. dist.) N.Y. 1986, U.S. Supreme Ct. 1986. Instr. Fort Lewis Coll., Durango, Colo., 1963-65; asst. prof. SUNY, Buffalo, 1965-68, assoc. prof., 1968-70; assoc. prof. Sir George Williams U., Montreal, Can., 1969-72; prof., chmn. Drake U., Des Moines, 1972-83; E.J. Mortola prof. philosophy, adj. prof. law Pace U., N.Y.C., 1983-88, disting. prof. philosophy, 1988—; del. UN for Am. Profs. for Peace in the Middle East, 1988-91. Author: Custom, Law and Morality, 1969, Values in Conflict, 1981, Liberty, Justice and Morals, 1986. Chmn. bd. trustees Congregation Bet Am Shalom, White Plains, N.Y., 1990-92; chmn. regional bd. Anti-Defamation League, Westchester-Putnam-Rockland Counties, 1995-97, nat. commr., 1995—. Brown U. fellow 1959-62, NYU fellow 1955-57; grantee NEH, Exxon Ednl. Found. Mem. Am. Profs. for Peace in the Middle East (nat. sec. 1983-89), Am. Soc. Value Inquiry (pres. 1978-80). Republican. Jewish. Avocations: bird watching, music. Office: Pace Univ Philosophy Dept Briarcliff Manor NY 10510 *If God hadn't wanted us to stick our necks out, he wouldn't have given us necks.*

LEISER, ERNEST STERN, journalist; b. Phila., Feb. 26, 1921; s. Monroe Felsenthal and Gertrude (Stern) L.; m. Caroline Thomas Camp, Oct. 26, 1946; children: Nancy, Shelley, Nicholas. AB, U. Chgo., 1941. Reporter City News Bur. Chgo., 1941; asst. picture editor Chgo. Herald-Am., 1941-42, 46; corr. Overseas News Agy., 1947-52; successively corr., producer, dir. TV news, exec. producer CBS News, N.Y.C., 1953-72; sr. producer, producer bicentennial coverage, spl. reports CBS News, 1975-79, v.p. spl. events and polit. coverage, 1979-81, v.p., dep. dir. news, 1981-85; exec. producer ABC News, N.Y.C., 1972-75; sr. fellow Gannett Ctr. for Media Studies, 1987-88. Author: This is Germany, 1950; contbr. articles to mags. Served with AUS, 1942-46. Decorated Bronze Star, Croix de Guerre; recipient Sigma Delta Chi award for TV reporting, 1956, Peabody awards for TV reporting and producing, 1956, 77, Ohio State awards, 1969, 77, Nat. Acad. TV Arts and Scis. award, 1968-71. Home: 15 College Ave South Nyack NY 10960

LEISH, KENNETH WILLIAM, publishing company executive; b. Cambridge, Mass., Dec. 31, 1936; s. Frank and Lillian (Kargir) L.; m. Barbara Lynn Ackerman, Nov. 27, 1966; children: Matthew, Emily, Adam. A.B. magna cum laude, Harvard U., 1958; M.S. in Journalism, Columbia U., 1959. Interviewer Oral History Office, Columbia, 1960; free lance drama reviewer Variety, 1961-66; editor Am. Heritage Pub. Co., Inc., N.Y.C., 1961-69; v.p., gen. mgr. book div. Am. Heritage Pub. Co., Inc., 1971-77; editor-in-chief Am. Heritage Press, 1970-71; mgr. large-format paperbacks Bantam Books Inc., N.Y.C., 1977-81; editor-in-chief Grolier Inc. Project Editorial Group, 1981-87; v.p., dir. product devel. Grolier Internat., Inc., Danbury, Conn., 1988-91; v.p. new product devel. Grolier Inc., Danbury, Conn., 1992-95; v.p., mng. editor Grolier Ednl., Danbury, Conn., 1996—. Author: The White House, 1972, A History of the Cinema, 1974. Served with AUS, 1959-60. Home: 3 Vermont Ave White Plains NY 10606-3507 Office: Grolier Inc Sherman Turnpike PO Box 1788 Danbury CT 06816-1788

LEISING, MARY KATHLEEN, manufacturing executive; b. Corry, Pa., Mar. 15, 1950; d. Francis Morgan and Florence Marie (McEvoy) Coyle; m. David Michael Leising, July 19, 1969; 1 child, Michelle Anne. AS, Regents Coll., 1972, BS, 1975; MBA, St. Bonaventure U., 1990. Tchr.'s aide Lauderdale County Schs., Meridian, Miss., 1972-73; from shipping clk. to coord. synchronous mfg. Valeo Engine Cooling (formerly Blackstone Corp.), Jamestown, N.Y., 1975-90; mgr. inventory control Valeo Engine Cooling, Jamestown, 1991, mgr. logistics, 1991—. Mem. Am. Prodn. and Inventory Control Soc. (cert.). Roman Catholic. Avocations: reading, camping. Office: Valeo Engine Cooling 2258 Allen St Jamestown NY 14701-2326

LEISSA, ARTHUR WILLIAM, mechanical engineering educator; b. Wilmington, Del., Nov. 16, 1931; s. Arthur Max and Marcella E. (Smith) L.; m. Gertrud E. Achenbach, Apr. 11, 1974; children: Celia Lynn, Bradley Glenn. BME, Ohio State U., 1954, MS, 1954, PhD, 1958. Engr., Sperry Gyroscope Co., Great Neck, N.Y., 1954-55; rsch. assoc. Ohio State U., 1955-56, instr. engring. mechanics, 1956-58, asst. prof., 1958-61, assoc. prof., 1961-64, prof., 1964—; vis. prof. Eidgenossische Technische Hochschule, Zurich, Switzerland, 1972-73, USAF Acad., Colorado Springs, Colo., 1985-86, U. Canterbury, Christchurch, N.Z., 1997; Plenary lectr. 2nd Internat. Conf. on Recent Advances in Structural Dynamics, Southampton, Eng., 1984, 4th Internat. Conf. on Composite Structures, Paisley, Scotland, 1987, Dynamics and Design Conf., Japan Soc. Mech. Engrs., Kawasaki, 1990, Energy Sources and Tech. Conf., ASME, Houston, 1992; cons. in field. Author: Vibration of Plates, 1969, Vibration of Shells, 1973, Buckling of Laminated Composite Plates and Shell Panels, 1985; assoc. editor Applied Mechanics Revs., 1985-93, editor-in-chief, 1993—; assoc. editor Jour. Vibration and Acoustics, 1990-93; mem. editl. bd. Jour. Sound and Vibration, 1971—, Internat. Jour. Mech. Sci., 1972—, Composite Structures, 1982—, Applied Mechanics Revs., 1988-93, Jour. Vibration and Control, 1994—; contbr. over 150 articles to profl. jours. Performer Columbus Symphony Orch. Operas, 1971-76; gen. chmn. Pan Am. Congress Applied Mechanics, Rio de Janeiro, 1989; leader Ohio State U. Mt. McKinley Expdn., 1978. Recipient Recognition plaque Inst. de Mecanica Applicada, Argentina, 1977, Centennial cert., Am. Soc. Engring. Edn., 1993. Fellow ASME, Am. Acad. Mechanics (pres. 1987-88), Japan Soc. for Promotion Sci.; mem. Am. Soc. for Engring. Edn., Am. Alpine

Club. Home: 1294 Fountaine Dr Columbus OH 43221-1520 Office: 155 W Woodruff Ave Columbus OH 43210-1117

LEISTEN, ARTHUR GAYNOR, lawyer; b. Chgo., Oct. 17, 1941; s. Arthur Edward Leisten and Mary (Francis) Gaynor; m. Florence T. Kelly, May 11, 1968; children: Thomas, Hillary. AB magna cum laude, Loyola U., Chgo., 1963; JD, Harvard U., 1966; grad. exec. mgmt. program, Northwestern U., Chgo., 1983 and 1986, Pa. State U., 1985. Bar: Ill. 1966, U.S. Dist. Ct. (no. dist.) Ill. 1967, U.S. Ct. Appeals 1967. Assoc. prof. Sch. Law Loyola U., 1966-69; assoc. Chadwell & Kayser, Ltd., Chgo., 1969-74; staff atty. Texaco, Inc., Chgo., 1974-75; atty. USG Corp., Chgo., 1975-78, sr. atty., 1978-82, sr. gen. atty., 1982-85, assoc. gen. counsel, 1985, v.p., assoc. gen. counsel, 1985-86, v.p., gen. counsel, 1986-90, sr. v.p., gen. counsel, 1990-93, sr. v.p., gen. counsel, sec., 1993—. Mem. ABA (corp. counsel com.), Chgo. Bar Assn., Am. Corp. Counsel Assn., Univ. Club, Law Club (Chgo.), Mich. Shores Club (Wilmette, Ill.), Westmoreland Country Club. Office: USG Corp 125 S Franklin St Chicago IL 60606-4605

LEISURE, GEORGE STANLEY, JR., lawyer; b. N.Y.C., Sept. 16, 1924; s. George S. and Lucille E. (Pelouze) L.; m. Joan Casey, June 22, 1949; children: Constance, Timothy, Matthew, George III. B.A., Yale U., 1948; LL.B., Harvard U., 1951. Bar: N.Y. 1953, U.S. Supreme Ct. 1966. Asst. U.S. atty. So. Dist. N.Y., 1954-56; trial atty. antitrust div. Dept. Justice, N.Y.C., 1956-57; partner firm Donovan Leisure Newton & Irvine, N.Y.C., 1957—; spl. counsel to Gen. William Westmoreland in Westmoreland vs. CBS, 1984-85. Served with USN, 1943-46; served to lt. USNR, 1951-53. Fellow Am. Coll. Trial Lawyers (chmn. N.Y. downstate com. 1975-77); mem. Fed. Bar Council (pres. 1976-78), Assn. Bar City N.Y. (exec. com. 1962-66), Fed. Bar Assn., ABA, N.Y. State Bar Assn., N.Y. County Lawyers Assn. Home: Cottage 467 PO Box 30221 Sea Island GA 31561 Office: Donovan Leisure et al 30 Rockefeller Plz New York NY 10112

LEISURE, PETER KEETON, federal judge; b. N.Y.C., Mar. 21, 1929; s. George S. and Lucille E. (Pelouze) L.; m. Kathleen Blair; Feb. 27, 1960; children: Lucille K. (dec.), Mary Blair, Kathleen K. B.A., Yale U., 1952; LL.B., U. Va., 1958. Bar: N.Y. 1959, U.S. Supreme Ct. 1966, D.C. 1979, U.S. Dist. Ct. Conn. 1981. Assoc. Breed, Abbott & Morgan, 1958-61; asst. U.S. atty. So. Dist. N.Y., 1962-66; partner firm Curtis, Mallet-Prevost, Colt & Mosle, 1967-78; ptnr. Whitman & Ransom, N.Y.C., 1978-84; judge U.S. District Court Southern New York, New York, NY, 1984—. Bd. dirs. Retarded Infants Svcs., 1968-78, pres., 1971-75; bd. dirs. Community Coun. of Greater N.Y., 1972-79, Youth Consultation Svcs., 1971-78; trustee Ch. Club of N.Y., 1973-81, 87-90; mem. jud. ethics com. Jud. Conf., 1990-93, fin disclosure com. Fellow Am. Bar Found., Am. Coll. Trial Lawyers; mem. ABA, Am. Law Inst., Am. Judges Assn., D.C. Bar Assn., Fed. Bar Coun. (trustee, v.p. 1973-78), Bar Assn. City of N.Y., Nat. Lawyers Club (hon.). Office: US Dist Ct 1910 US Courthouse 500 Pearl St New York NY 10007-1316

LEITCH, VINCENT BARRY, literary and cultural studies educator; b. Hempstead, N.Y., Sept. 18, 1944; s. Eugene Vincent and Lucile Jean (Amplo) L.; m. Jill Robin Berman, May 20, 1970 (div. May 1987); children: Kristin M., Rory G. BA, Hofstra U., 1966; MA, Villanova U., 1967; PhD, U. Fla., 1972. Postdoctoral fellow Sch. Criticism and Theory, U. Calif., Irvine, 1978; interim asst. prof. U. Fla., Gainesville, 1972-73; from asst. prof. to prof. English Mercer U., Macon, Ga., 1973-86; prof. English Purdue U., West Lafayette, Ind., 1986—, co-dir. English and philosophy doctoral program, 1986-93; sr. Fulbright lectr. U. Tampere, Finland, 1979; reviewer NEH, 1985-88; Moss chair of excellence U. Memphis, 1991; mem. adv. bd. Modern Fiction Studies, 1992-97, Symploke, 1995—. Author: Deconstructive Criticism, 1983, American Literary Criticism from the 1930s to the 1980s, 1988, Cultural Criticism, Literary Theory, Poststructuralism, 1992, Postmodernism: Local Effects, Global Flows, 1996; mem. editl. bd. lit. and film series Fla. State U. Press, 1983—, Purdue Univ. Press, 1988-90; mem. staff Abstracts of English Studies, 1972-75; mem. editl. bd. South Atlantic Rev., 1985-87. Recipient Outstanding Acad. Book award Assn. Coll. and Rsch. Librs., 1988; Am. Philos. Soc. grantee, 1974; fellow NEH, 1980, Mellon Found., 1981, Am. Coun. Learned Socs., 1985-86, Ctr. for Humanistic Studies, Purdue U., 1989, 96. Mem. MLA (publs. com. 1990-93, assembly del. 1990-92, 93-95, chair organizing com. 1995, chair ad hoc com. on governance issues 1995, mem. 1996, exec. com. lit. criticism divsn. 1994—), Soc. for Critical Exch. (bd. dirs. 1978-83), PEN Am. Ctr., Internat. Assn. for Philosophy and Lit., Am. Comparative Lit. Assn. Office: Purdue U Dept English West Lafayette IN 47907

LEITER, EDWARD HENRY, scientist; b. Columbus, Ga., Apr. 17, 1942; m. Susan Shaw, Sept. 5, 1964. BS, Princeton U., 1964; MS, PhD in Cell Biology, Emory U., 1968. Fellow U. Tex., Austin, 1968-71; asst. prof. CUNY, Bkyn., 1971-74; assoc. staff scientist Jackson Lab., Bar Harbor, Maine, 1974-75, staff scientist, 1975-90, sr. staff scientist, 1990—. Recipient rsch. award Am. Diabetes Assn., 1995. Achievements include research in genetics and immunology of diabetes. Office: Jackson Lab Bar Harbor ME 04609

LEITER, ELLIOT, urologist; b. Bklyn., May 24, 1933; s. David and Freda (Pearlman) L.; m. Renee Anita Epstein, June 9, 1963; children: Ariane L., Karen R., Michael E. AB, Columbia U., 1954; MD, NYU, 1957. Diplomate Nat. Bd. Med. Examiners, Am. Bd. Urology. Intern Johns Hopkins Hosp., Balt., 1957-58, resident in surgery, 1958-59; resident in surgery NYU Hosp., 1959-60; resident in urology Bellevue Hosp., N.Y.C., 1960-63; asst. in urology Johns Hopkins Hosp., Balt., 1958-59; asst. in urology NYU, N.Y.C., 1960-63, instr. in urology, 1963; instr. in urology Columbia U., N.Y.C., 1966-67; asst. prof. Mt. Sinai Sch. Medicine, N.Y.C., 1966-69, assoc. prof., 1969-78, prof., 1978-89; clin. prof. urology, 1989—; acting chmn. urology Mt. Sinai Sch. Medicine, N.Y.C., 1982-84; dir. urology Beth Israel Med. Ctr., N.Y.C., 1978-85; attending urologist, dir. pediatric urology Mt. Sinai Hosp., 1976-78; pres. Metro-Litho, Inc., N.Y.C., 1988-91, bd. dirs., 1991—. Contbr. articles to profl. publs., chpts. to books. Pres. Emerald Marine Ltd., Wilmington, Del., 1981; bd. dirs. Brith Milah Bd., 1970. Fellow Am. Urolog. Assn. (com. mem., 1st prize N.Y. sect. 1963, 64, pres. 1985-86), N.Y. Acad. Medicine (chmn. judicial com. urolog. sect. 1976, ACS; mem. Soc. Univ. Urologists, Royal Soc. Health, Soc. Pediatric Urology, Am. Acad. Pediatrics, Internat. Coll. Surgeons, N.Y. Met. Lithotriptor Assn. (pres. 1987), N.Y. Met. Biliary Lithotriptor Assn. (pres. 1989), Saugatuck Harbor Yacht Club, Seven Ses Cruising Assn. Republican. Jewish. Avocations: sailing, skiing, reading, music. Home: 181 Hawks Way Sequim WA 98382-3862 Office: 109 E 38th St New York NY 10016-2601

LEITER, RICHARD ALLEN, law educator, law librarian; b. Sacramento, Mar. 21, 1952; s. Lionel and Lois Rose Leiter; m. Wendy Ellin Werges, Dec. 30, 1978; children: Madeline Rose, Anna Joy, Rebecca Hope. BA in Anthropology and Religious Studies with honors, U. Calif., Santa Cruz, 1976; JD, Southwestern U., 1981; M of Libr. and Info. Sci., U. Tex., 1986. Libr. asst. Irell & Manella, L.A., 1977-78; libr. Hopkins, Mitchell & Carley, San Jose, Calif., 1982-84; head of reference Law Sch., U. Tex., Austin, 1984-86; pub. svcs. libr. Law Sch., U. Nebr., Lincoln, 1986-88; head libr. Littler, Mendelson, Fastiff & Tichy, San Francisco, 1988-91; dir. law libr., assoc. prof. law Regent U. Sch. Law, Virginia Beach, Va., 1991-94, Howard U. Sch. Law, A.M. Daniels Law Libr., Washington, 1994—; mem. Westlaw Acad. Adv. Bd., 1990-93; sec. bd. dirs. StoneBridge Sch., 1993-94; mem. adv. bd. Oceana Publs., Inc., 1994—. Editor: (book sect.) Yellow Pads to Computers, 1986, 91; author: (bibliography) New Frontiers of Forensic & Demonstrative Evidence, 1985; editor: Automatome, 1987-89, The Spirit of Law Librarianship, 1991, National Survey of State Laws, 1993, 2d edit., 1997; editor Southwestern U. Law Review; contbr. articles to profl. jours. Mem. adv. com. StoneBridge Ednl. Found. Mem. ABA, Am. Assn. Law Librs. (so. chpt., automation and sci. devel. spl. interest sect. 1986—, chair 1989-90, indexing of periodical lit. adv. com. 1990-91, chair 1990-91, mem. spl. com. to promote development of resources for legal info. cmty. 1994-96, recruitment com. 1995-97, rsch. com. 1997—), San Francisco Pvt. Law Librs. (steering com. 1989), Consortium Southeast Law Librs. (vice chair), Scribes. Avocations: bicycling, reading, backpacking. Home: 2830 Woodlawn Ave Falls Church VA 22042-2011 Office: Howard U Daniel Law Libr 2900 Van Ness St NW Washington DC 20008-1106

LEITER, ROBERT ALLEN, journalist, magazine editor; b. Phila., Apr. 21, 1949; s. Samuel Simon and Beverly (Agins) L.; m. Barbara Ann Field, May 6, 1973; children: Lauren, James, Rebecca. BA in English and Creative Writing with honors, U. Iowa, 1970. Freelance writer short stories, book revs., feature articles The Nation, The New Republic, Redbook, Am. Scholar, N.Y. Times, Partisan Rev., The Forward, others, 1973—; mng. editor, book columnist Inside mag., Phila., 1983-87; gen. reporter, book editor Jewish Exponent, Phila., 1987—; co-editor Friday, lit. supplement newspaper Jewish Exponent, Phila., 1983-87, mgn. editor Jewish Exponent 100th Anniversary edit., 1987, editor Extra Extra, weekly mag. sect., 1987-94; news editor Jewish Exponent, 1994-95, literary supplement editor, 1995—; contbr. editor Am. Poetry Rev., Phila., 1987—; instr. writing, Am. lit., theater Cheltenham (Pa.) Adult Sch., 1983-87. Author: (with others) Jewish Profiles, 1992. Asst. to vice chmn. U.S. Commn. on Civil Rights, Washington, 1987-88. Recipient Smolar award for excellence in N.Am. Jewish journalism for article series, 1989, Simon Rockower award, 1990, 93, 96, Keystone Press award, 1994. Mem. Phi Beta Kappa. Republican. Jewish. Avocation: collecting books, antique furniture and paintings. Home: 1002 Prospect Ave Elkins Park PA 19027-3058 Office: Phila Jewish Exponent 226 S 16th St Philadelphia PA 19102-3348

LEITER, WILLIAM C., banking executive; b. Akron, Ohio, May 16, 1939; s. Clarence Dailey and Lucille E. (Knecht) L.; m. Sue J. Sullivan, Nov. 5, 1965; children: Brian Robert, Sonja Lou. BS in Bus. Adminstrn., Kent State U., 1961. CPA, Pa. Various positions Coopers & Lybrand, Pitts., 1961-75; fin. v.p. Wendy's Internat. Inc., Dublin, Ohio, 1975-81; sr. v.p., controller Banc One Corp., Columbus, Ohio, 1981—. Mem. Am. Inst. CPAs, Fin. Execs. Inst. (past pres., bd. dirs. 1981—), Assn. Bank Holding Cos. (chmn. acctg. com. 1982—). Republican. Presbyterian. Club: Capital (Columbus). Avocations: fishing, reading, swimming. Office: Bank One Corp 100 E Broad St Columbus OH 43215-3607

LEITH, CECIL ELDON, JR., retired physicist; b. Boston, Jan. 31, 1923; s. Cecil Eldon and Elizabeth (Benedict) L.; m. Mary Louise Henry, July 18, 1942; children: Ann, John, Paul. A.B., U. Calif. at, Berkeley, 1943, Ph.D., 1957. Exptl. physicist Lawrence Radiation Lab., Berkeley, 1946-52; theoretical physicist Lawrence Radiation Lab., Livermore, Calif., 1952-68; sr. scientist Nat. Center for Atmospheric Research, Boulder, Colo., 1968-83; div. dir. Nat. Center for Atmospheric Research, 1977-81; physicist Lawrence Livermore Nat. Lab. (Calif.), 1983-90; Symons Meml. lectr. Royal Meteorol. Soc., London, 1978; chmn. com. on atmospheric scis. NRC, 1978-80, sci. program evaluation com. Univ. Corp. for Atmospheric Rsch., 1991-96; mem. joint sci. com. world climate research program World Meteorol. Organ. and Internat. Council Sci. Unions, 1976-83; mem. program adv. com. Office Advanced Sci. Computing, NSF, 1984-85. Served with AUS, 1944-46. Fellow Am. Phys. Soc., Am. Meteorol. Soc. (Meisinger award 1967, Rossby research medal 1982). Home: 627 Carla St Livermore CA 94550-2316 Office: Lawrence Livermore Nat Lab PO Box 808 Livermore CA 94551-0808

LEITH, EMMETT NORMAN, electrical engineer, educator; b. Detroit, Mar. 12, 1927; s. Albert Donald and Dorothy Marie (Emmett) L.; m. Lois June Neswold, Feb. 17, 1956; children: Kim Ellen, Pam Elizabeth. B.S., Wayne State U., 1950, M.S., 1952, Ph.D., 1978; DSc (hon.), U. Aberdeen, Scotland, 1996. Mem. research staff U. Mich., 1952—, prof. elec. engring., 1968—; cons. several indsl. corps. Contbr. articles to profl. jours. Served with USNR, 1945-46. Recipient Gordon Meml. award S.P.I.E., 1965; citation Am. Soc. Mag. Photographers, 1966; Achievement award U.S. Camera and Travel mag., 1967; Excellence of Paper award Soc. Motion Picture and TV Engrs., 1967; Daedalion award, 1968; Stuart Ballantine medal Franklin Inst., 1969; Distinguished Faculty Achievement award U. Mich., 1973; Alumni award Wayne State U., 1974; cited by Nobel Prize Commn. for contbns. to holography, 1971; Holley medal ASME, 1976; named Man of Year Indsl. Research mag., 1966; Nat. medal of Sci., 1979; Russel lecture award U. Mich., 1981; recipient Dennis Gabor medal Soc. Photo-Instrumentation Engrs., 1983, Gold medal, 1990; Mich. Sci. Trailblazer award, 1986. Fellow Optical Soc. Am. (Wood medal 1975, Herbert Ives medal 1985), IEEE (Liebmann award 1967, Inventor of Year award 1976), Engring. Soc. Detroit (hon.); mem. Nat. Acad. Engring., Sigma Xi, Sigma Pi Sigma. Patentee in field. First demonstrated (with colleague) capability of holography to form high-quality 3-dimensional image. Home: 51325 Murray Hill Dr Canton MI 48187-1030 Office: Univ Mich Inst Sci and Tech PO Box 618 Ann Arbor MI 48106-0618

LEITH, JAMES CLARK, economics educator; b. Brandon, Man., Can., Dec. 9, 1937; s. James Scott and Bertha Miriam (Clark) L.; m. Carole Ann Mason, Aug. 29, 1964; children: James Douglas, Deborah Ann, Jonathan Gregory. B.A., U. Toronto, 1959; M.S., U. Wis., 1960, Ph.D., 1967. Fgn. service officer Trade Commn. Service-Govt. of Can., 1960-67, Santo Domingo, Dominican Republic, 1961-64, Chgo., 1965; asst. prof. econs. U. Western Ont., 1967-71, assoc. prof., 1971-78, prof., 1978—, chmn. dept. econs., 1972-76, v.p. acad. provost, 1980-86; econ. cons. Ministry Fin. and Devel. Planning, Gaborone, Botswana, 1986-88; dir. rsch. Bank of Botswana, 1993-95, sr. policy advisor, 1995-97; vis. lectr. U. Ghana, Legon, 1969-71; sr. research assoc. Nat. Bur. Econ. Research, 1971-75; vis. researcher Inst. Internat. Econ. Studies, Stockholm, 1976-77; vis. prof. Catholic U., Lima, Peru, 1979; vis. scholar Harvard Inst. Internat. Devel., Cambridge, Mass., 1992-93. Author: Foreign Trade Regimes..., Ghana, 1974, Ghana: Structural Adjustment Experience, 1996; co-author: (with P.T. Ellsworth) The International Economy, 1975, 84; co-editor: (with D. Patinkin) Keynes, Cambridge and the General Theory, 1977; contbr. articles to econ. jours. Mem. United Ch. of Can.

LEITH, JOHN HADDON, clergyman, theology educator; b. Due West, S.C., Sept. 10, 1919; s. William H. and Lucy Ann (Haddon) L.; m. Ann Caroline White, Sept. 2, 1943; children—Henry White, Caroline Haddon. A.B., Erskine Coll., 1940, D.D. (hon.), 1972; B.D., Columbia Theol. Sem., 1943; M.A., Vanderbilt U., 1946; Ph.D., Yale U., 1949; D.D. (hon.), Davidson Coll., 1978; D.Litt. (hon.), Presbyn. Coll., 1990. Ordained to ministry Presbyterian Ch. 1943. Pastor chs. in Nashville and Auburn, Ala., 1944-59; Pemberton prof. theology Union Theol. Sem., Richmond, Va., 1959-90; vis. prof. Columbia Theol. Sem., Eckerd Coll., New Coll. at U. Edinburgh; adj. prof. Va. Commonwealth U.; mem. ad interim com. to revise book of ch. order Presbyn. Ch. U.S., 1955-61, mem. com. to write brief statement of faith, 1960-62, mem. com. to prepare brief statement of reformed faith, 1984-91; chmn. com. revision of chpt. 3 of Confession of Faith, 1959-60, mem. permanent nominating com. gen. assembly, 1972-75; chmn. bd. Presbyn. Survey, 1961-70; bd. dirs. Presbyn. Outlook Mag., 1962—; moderator Presbyn. Synod N.C., 1977-78; mem. Gov.'s Commn. on Seasonal and Migrant Farm Workers, 1982-94; mem. adv. coun. Ctr. of Theol. Inquiry, Princeton, N.J., 1989-94. Author: Creeds of the Churches, 1963, 3d. rev. edit., 1982, The Church, A Believing Fellowship, 1965, rev., 1980, Assembly at Westminster, 1973, Greenville Church, The Story of a People, 1973, rev. edit. 1997, The Reformed Tradition, A Way of Being the Christian Community, 2d edit., 1981, John Calvin, the Christian Life, 1984, The Reformed Imperative, 1988, John Calvin's Doctrine of the Christian Life, 1989; editor: Guides to Reformed Theology, The Reformed Imperative, 1988, From Generation to Generation, 1990, Basic Christian Doctrine, 1993; editor (with Stacy Johnson) A Reformed Reader, A Source Book for Christian Theology, 1993, Crisis in the Church, the Plight of Theological Education, 1997. Trustee Erskine Coll.; bd. dirs. Inst. Religion and Democracy, 1985-93; mem. Richmond City com. Dem. Party, 1973-93. Kent fellow, 1946-48; Folger Library fellow, 1964; grantee Advanced Religious Studies Found., 1974. Mem. Calvin Studies Soc. (pres. 1980-83). Home: 3311 Suffolk Rd Richmond VA 23227-4724

LEITMANN, GEORGE, mechanical engineering educator; b. Vienna, Austria, May 24, 1925; s. Josef and Stella (Fischer) L.; m. Nancy Lloyd, Jan. 28, 1955; children: Josef Lloyd, Elaine Michèle. BS, Columbia U., 1949, MA, 1950; PhD, U. Calif., Berkeley, 1956; D Engring. honoris causa, Tech. U. Vienna, 1988; D honoris causa, U. Paris, 1989, Tech. U. Darmstadt, 1990. Physicist, head aeroballistics sect. U.S. Naval Ordnance Sta., China Lake, 1950-57; mem. faculty U. Calif., Berkeley, 1957—, prof. engring. sci., 1963—, prof. grad. sch., 1995—, assoc. dean acad. affairs, 1981-90, assoc. dean rsch., 1990-94, acting dean, 1988, chair of the faculty, 1994—; cons. to aerospace industry and govt. Author: An Introduction to Optimal Control, 1966, Quantitative and Qualitative Games, 1969, The Calculus of Variations and Optimal Control, 1981, others; contbr. articles to profl. jours. Served with AUS, 1944-46, ETO. Decorated Crox de Guerre France, Fourragere Belgium, Comdr.'s Cross of Order of Merit, Germany; recipient Pendray Aerospace Lit. award AIAA, 1979, Von Humboldt U.S. Sr. Scientist award Von Humboldt Found., 1980, Levy medal Franklin Inst., 1981, Mechanics and Control of Flight award AIAA, 1984, Berkeley citation U. Calif.-Berkeley, 1991, von Humboldt medal Von Humboldt Found., 1991, Rufus Oldenburger medal ASME, 1995, Bellman Continuum Soc. award, 1995; named Miller Rsch. prof., 1966. Mem. NAE, Acad. Sci. Bologna, Internat. Acad. Astronautics, Argentine Nat. Acad. Engring., Russian Acad. Natural Sci., Georgian Acad. Engring., Bavarian Acad. Sci., A.V. Humboldt Assn. Am. (pres. 1994-97), Georgian Acad. Sci. Office: U Calif Coll Engring Berkeley CA 94720

LEITNER, ALFRED, mathematical physicist, educator, educational film producer; b. Vienna, Austria, Nov. 3, 1921; came to U.S., 1938, naturalized, 1944; s. Philipp and Lona (Machlup) L.; m. Marzia O'Neil, Nov. 24, 1948; children: Kathleen Adams, Deborah Matulis, David. B.A., U. Buffalo, 1944; M.S., Yale U., 1945, Ph.D., 1948. Research assoc. Courant Inst. Math. Scis., N.Y. U., 1947-51; from asst. prof. to prof. physics Mich. State U., 1951-67; prof. physics Rensselaer Poly. Inst., 1967-88, prof. emeritus, 1988—; research assoc. Harvard U., 1965-66; cons. Harvard project physics, 1966-68; vis. prof. U.S. Mil. Acad., West Point, 1983-85. Author papers on theory spl. functions, boundary value problems, antennas, history of sci., teaching.; Films Liquid Helium, 1963, Superconductivity, 1966, Project Physics, 1965-68; Dispersion, 1973, Fraunhofer (2 films), 1974, A Story of Research, 1981; (videotapes) Our Favorite Physics Demonstrations, 1987. Guggenheim fellow, 1958-59; Deutscher Akademischer Austauschdienst fellow, 1977. Fellow Am. Phys. Soc.; mem. Assn. Physics Tchrs., Am. Assn. Univ. Profs., Phi Beta Kappa, Sigma Xi. Home: 1201 8th Ter N Naples FL 34102-5411

LEITNER, DAVID LARRY, lawyer; b. Bklyn., Feb. 20, 1956; s. Sol and Beatrice (Brodsky) L.; m. Jana L. Grady, Sept. 11, 1983; children: Morgan Blaire, Gabriel Rand. Student, SUNY, Brockport, 1974-75; BA, SUNY, Stony Brook, 1976; JD, U. Iowa, 1979. Bar: Iowa 1979, U.S. Dist. Ct. (no. and so. dists.) Iowa 1979, U.S. Ct. Appeals (2d, 7th and 8th cirs.) 1980, U.S. Tax Ct. 1981, U.S. Supreme Ct. 1994; CPCU. Asst. atty. various counties, Iowa, 1979-81; assoc. Cooper, Sinnard & Cooper, Forest City, Iowa, 1981-83; sole practice Forest City, 1983; atty. Grinnell (Iowa) Mut. Reins. Co., 1983-86, Allied Group Inc. Co., Des Moines, 1986-87; with Davis, Grace, Horvath, Gonnerman and Rowenhorst, Des Moines, 1987-89; pvt. practice Des Moines, 1990—; judicial hospitalization referee Winnebago County, Ia., 1983. Co-author: Automobile Accident Law and Practice, 1988; editor Tort and Ins. Law Jour., 1988-92, Truck Accident Litigation Insurance, Tobacco Litigation Insurace, Managed Care Liability; contbr. articles to profl. jours.; contbg. author: No Fault and Uninsured Motorist, 1992. Mem. ABA (speaker, mem. tort and ins. practice sect., com. chair), Iowa Bar Assn. (bridge gap com., Mason Ladd award com.), Assn. Trial Lawyers, Am. Trial Lawyer Assn., Soc. Chartered Property and Casualty Underwriters, Def. Rsch. Inst. Jewish. Avocations: photography, furniture bldg. Home: 8751 Oakdale Dr Johnston IA 50131-2206 Office: 5850 NW 62nd Ave Johnston IA 50131-1537

LEITNER, PAUL R., lawyer; b. Winnsboro, S.C., Nov. 11, 1928; s. W. Walker and Irene (Lewis) L.; m. Jeannette C. Card, Mar. 16, 1985; children by previous marriage: David, Douglas, Gregory, Reid, Cheryl. AB, Duke U., 1950; LLB, McKenzie Coll., 1954. Bar: Tenn. 1954; cert. civil trial specialist Nat. Bd. Trial Advocacy and Tenn. Commn. on CLE and Specialization. Pvt. practice law Chattanooga, 1954; assoc. firm Leitner, Warner, Moffitt, Williams, Dooley, Carpenter & Napolitan and predecessor firms, 1952-57, ptnr., 1957—; Tenn. chmn. Def. Rsch. Inst., 1978-89. Bd. dirs. Family Service Agy., 1957-63, Chattanooga Symphony and Opera Assn., 1986-89, sec., 1987-89; mem. Chattanooga-Hamilton County Community Action Bd.; mem. Juvenile Ct. Commn., Hamilton County, 1955-61, chmn., 1958-59; chmn. Citizens Com. for Better Schs.; mem. Met. Govt. Charter Commn. Served with U.S. Army, 1946-47. Named Young Man of Yr. Chattanooga Area, 1957. Fellow Am. Coll. Trial Lawyers, Tenn. Bar Found, Chattanooga Bar Found. (founding); mem. ABA, Tenn. Bar Assn., Jaycees (Chattanooga, pres. 1956-57), Fed. Ins. Corp. Counsel, Internat. Assn. Def. Coun., Trial Attys. Am., Tenn. Def. Lawyers Assn. (pres. 1975-76), Am. Bd. Trial Advs. (advocate), U.S. Sixth Cir. Jud. Conf. (life). Methodist. Home: Augusta Dr Lookout Mountain TN 37350

LEITZE, ANNETTE EMILY RICKS, mathematics educator; b. Jacksonville, Ill., May 31, 1951; d. William Brown and Rachel Emily (Husted) Ricks; m. Harold Dean Leitze, Aug. 19, 1972; children: Jason Matthew, Jeremy Michael. BS in Math., Western Ill. U., 1972; MA in Math., Ind. U., 1988, PhD in Math. Edn., 1992. Cert. 6-12 math. tchr., Ill. Tchr. math. Triopia Jr.-Sr. High Sch., Concord, Ill., 1975-80; assoc. instr. dept. math. Ind. U., Bloomington, 1986-88, rsch. asst., assoc. instr. Sch. Edn., 1989-92, instr. math. Sch. Continuing Studies, 1992; prof. Ball State U., Muncie, Ind., 1992—. Author: Mathematical Problem Solving through Children's Literature: The Indian in the Cupboard; contbg. editor: Projects for Real World Problem Solvers, 1991; author software Problem-Solving Data Bank; also articles. Mem. restructuring task force Monroe County Community Sch. Corp., Bloomington, 1989, mem. math. textbook adoption com., 1992. Grad. fellow Ind. U. Sch. Edn., 1989, 90. Mem. Am. Ednl. Rsch. Assn., Spl. Interest Group, Ind. Coun. Tchrs. Math., Math. Assn. Am., Nat. Coun. Tchrs. Math., Psychology of Math. Edn., Sch. Sci. and Math. Assn., Kappa Mu Epsilon, Phi Delta Kappa. Office: Ball State U Dept Math Scis Muncie IN 47306

LEITZEL, JOAN RUTH, university president. BA in Math., Hanover Coll., 1958; MA in Math., Brown U., 1961; PhD in Math., Ind. U., 1965. Instr. math. Oberlin (Ohio) Coll., 1961-62; asst. prof. math. Ohio State U., Columbus, 1965-70, assoc. prof., 1970-84, prof., 1984-92, vice chmn. dept., 1973-79, acting chmn., 1978, assoc. provost, 1985-90; prof. dept. math. and stats. U. Nebr., Lincoln, 1992-96, sr. vice chancellor for acad. affairs, 1992-96, interim chancellor, 1995-96; pres. U. N.H., Durham, 1996—; mem. adv. com. Griffith Ins. Found., 1979-82; cons. Ohio Dept. Edn., 1980-83; participant Am. Coun. on Edn., 1980, 82; cons. Nat. Commn. on Excellence in Edn., U.S. Dept. Edn., 1982; mem. univ. math. edn. del. to China, 1983; dir. divsn. materials devel., rsch. and info. sci. edn. NSF, 1990-92; presenter in field, 1980—; bd. dirs. Am. Assn. Higher Edn., chmn.-elect, 1996-97; mem. interpretive reports adv. bd. Nat. ssessment Ednl. Progress, 1995-98; trustee Consortium on Math. and Its Applications, 1994-95; mem. exec. coun. com. on acad. affairs Nat. Assn. State Univs. and Land-Grant Colls., 1994-96, bd. dir., 1997—, chmn. com. on faculty, 1994-96; mem. coordinating coun. for edn. NRC, 1993-95, mem. bd. on math. scis. edn., 1985-87; numerous others. Bd. dirs. United Way Lincoln, 1995-96, 1st Plymouth Ch., 1996, Lincoln Partnership for Econ. Devel., 1996. Recipient Disting. Alumni award Hanover Coll., 1986, dir.'s award for mgmt. excellence NSF, 1991; grantee NSF, 1976-79, 84-88, Battelle Found., 1981-83, SOHIO, 1983-85. Mem. AAAS (edn. com. 1981-84), Am. Math. Soc. (com. on excellence in scholarship 1993-95), Assn. for Women in Math., Math. Assn. Am. (nominatinig com. 1978-79, com. on tchr. tng. and accreditation Ohio sect. 1976-79, nat. com. on undergrad programs 1982-85, chmn. joint task force on curriculum for grades 11-13 with Nat. Coun. Tchrs. Math. 1986-88), Nat. Coun. Tchrs. Math., Mortar Bd., Sigma Xi, Phi Kappa Phi. Office: U NH Office of Pres Durham NH 03824

LEITZELL, TERRY LEE, lawyer; b. Williamsport, Pa., Apr. 15, 1942; s. Ernest Richard and Inez Mae (Taylor) L.; m. Lucy Acker Emmerich, June 18, 1966; children: Thomas Addison, Charles Taylor, Robert Davies. A.B., Cornell U., 1964; J.D., U. Pa., 1967. Bar: D.C. bar 1967. Consular officer Dept. State, Bombay, India, 1968-70; atty.-adv. for oceans affairs Dept. State, Washington, 1970-77; chief U.S. negotiator UN law of sea negotiations Dept. State, Geneva, also N.Y.C., 1974-77; asst. adminstr. for fisheries and dir. Nat. Marine Fisheries Service, NOAA, Dept. Commerce, Washington, 1978-81; practice law Washington, 1981-92, Seattle, 1992—. Mem ABA, Mem. D.C. Bar Assn., Am. Soc. Internat. Law. Democrat. Home: 3150 W Laurelhurst Dr NE Seattle WA 98105-5346 Office: Bogle & Gates 2 Union Sq Seattle WA 98101-2023

LEITZKE, JACQUE HERBERT, psychologist, corporate executive; b. Watertown, Wis., Dec. 25, 1929; s. Herbert Wilbert and Ruth Valberg

(Stavenow) L.; m. Mary Annis Lacey, June 20, 1950 (div. Nov. 1963); children: Keith Alan, Sari Dawn, Thora Jacquelynne. BS, U. Wis., Madison, 1955; MA, Kent State U., 1958. Lic. psychologist, Wis., Ill., N.Y. Sch. psychologist Bur. Child Guidance, N.Y.C., 1959-61; clin. psychologist Bur. of Child Guidance, Neenah, Wis., 1961-64; clin. psychologist, psychotherapist Winnebago County Guidance Ctr., Neenah, Wis., 1961-64; sch. psychologist Waukegan City (Ill.) Sch. Dist. 61, 1965-66; clin. psychologist Wis., Ill., 1967-78; corp. pres., CEO Psychometrics Internat. Corp., Watertown, 1979—. Author: Definitively Incorporeal Human Intelligence Itself; originator intelligence test Abecedarian Measure of Human Intelligence, 1979. Trustee Human Intelligence Rsch. Found. Served with USAF, 1948-51. Mem. APA, Mensa. Avocation: landscape artist. Home: 1153 Boughton St Apt 807 Watertown WI 53094-3106

LEIWEKE, TIMOTHY, sales executive, marketing professional; b. St. Louis, Apr. 21, 1957; s. John Robert and Helen (Caicuey) L.; m. Pamela Leiweke, Nov. 1, 1984. Grad. high sch., St. Louis. Salesperson New Eng. Mut. Life Ins. Co., St. Louis, 1976-79; asst. gen. mgr. St. Louis Steamers/MISL, 1979-80; gen. mgr. Balt. Blast/MISL, 1980-81; v.p., gen. mgr. Kansas City (Mo.) Comets/MISL, 1981-84; v.p. Leiweke and Co., Kansas City, 1984-85; pres. Kansas City Comets/MISL, 1986-88; v.p. sales and mktg. div. Minn. Timberwolves, Mpls., 1988-91; sr. v.p. of bus. ops. Denver Nuggets, Denver, 1991-92; pres. Denver Nuggets, Denver, CO, 1992-96; pres., CEO LA Kings, Los Angeles, 1996—. Bd. dirs. Kidney Found., Minn., 1989—, Spl. Olympics, Minn., 1989—, Timberwolves Community Found., Minn., 1989—. Named Rookie of the Yr., Mo. Life Underwriters, 1976, Kansas Citian of the Yr., Kansas City Press Club, 1983; recipient William Brownfield award U.S. Jaycees, 1978, William Brownfield award Mo. Jaycees, 1978, Excalibur award Am. Cancer Soc., 1987. Mem. Kansas City Mktg. and Sales Execs., Mpls. Club. Avocations: running, golf, cross-country skiing, soccer, basketball. Home: 1635 Clay St Denver CO 80204-1799 Office: LA Kings NHL 3900 W Manchester Blvd Inglewood CA 90305-2200*

LEIZEAR, CHARLES WILLIAM, retired information services executive; b. Balt., Dec. 15, 1922; s. Charles R. and Nellie Beyer L.; m. Jean Smith, Nov. 26, 1947; children: Robin DeBarry, Kathy King. Charles R. II. B.S. cum laude, Loyola Coll., Balt., 1949. With Burroughs Co., 1949-71; v.p. mktg. data systems Singer Co., N.Y.C., 1972-76; group v.p. cash mgmt. services Nat. Data Corp., Atlanta, 1976-81, exec. v.p. fin. service and systems, 1981-83, exec. v.p. ops., 1983-85, exec. v.p. retail systems, 1984, sr. v.p., 1985-88; mktg. and quality process cons. Charles Assocs., Atlanta, 1989—. Bd. dirs. Lupus Specialists, Inc., Atlanta. With U.S. Army, 1942-45. Recipient Susan Anthony award for highest acad. achievement Loyola U., 1947.

LEJEUNE, DENNIS EDWARD, investment counsel; b. Chgo., Feb. 25, 1942; s. Edward George and Eileen Marie (Donnellan) L.; m. Barbara Katharine Benson, July 24, 1965; children: Angela Marie, Katharine Kelly, Amy Eileen. B.B.A., U. Notre Dame; postgrad., Northwestern U. Internat. banking officer Provident Nat. Bank, Phila., 1971-73; fgn. exch. trader Harris Trust & Savs. Bank, Chgo., 1966-71, asst. v.p., 1973-74, v.p., mgr. IMM div., 1974-80, sr. v.p., mgr. investment dept., 1980-81, exec. v.p., 1981-86; dir. internat. fin. svcs. Stotler & Co., Chgo., 1986-87; pvt. investment counsel Traverse City, Mich., 1987—. Tchr. St. Faith, Hope & Charity Ch., Winnetka, Ill., 1977-81; trustee Glen Arbor Twp., 1992-96; pres. Glen Lake Assn., 1992-93, bd. dirs., 1989-95. Mem. Forex Assn. N.Am. (sec. 1976-80), Pub. Securities Assn. (dir. 1983-85), Bond Club Chgo. (dir., pres. 1988), Rotary. Republican. Roman Catholic. Clubs: Univ. (Chgo.), Glen Lake Yacht, Traverse City Golf and Country. Avocations: sailing, golf, swimming, ancestry. Home: 7366 S Glen Lake Rd Glen Arbor MI 49636 Office: Investment Counsel 12935 S West Bay Shore Dr Traverse City MI 49684-5470

LE JEUNE, FRANCIS ERNEST, JR., otolaryngologist; b. New Orleans, Jan. 3, 1929; s. Francis Ernest and Anna Lynne (Dodds) LeJ.; m. Ena Kay Hudson, Dec. 21, 1963; children: Francis III, Baltzer, Katherine, Ann. B.S., Tulane U., 1950, M.D., 1953. Intern Charity Hosp., La., New Orleans, 1953-54; resident U. Iowa Hosps., Iowa City, 1954-57; mem. staff dept. otolaryngology Ochsner Clinic, New Orleans, 1959-96, chmn. dept. otolaryngology, 1963-89; clin. prof. dept. otolaryngology Tulane U. Sch. Medicine, New Orleans, 1977—. Served with USAF, 1957-59. Mem. ACS, Am. Laryngol. Assn., Am. Laryngol., Rhinol. and Otol. Soc., Am. Broncho-Esophagol. Soc., Am. Soc. Head and Neck Surgery, Am. Acad. Otolaryngology, Head and Neck Surgery, La.-Miss. Ophthalmol. and Otolaryngol. Soc. (pres. 1993-94), So. Yacht Club, Boston Club. Home: 334 Garden Rd New Orleans LA 70123-2004 Office: Tulane U Sch Medicine 1415 Tulane Ave New Orleans LA 70112-2605

LEJINS, PETER PIERRE, criminologist, sociologist, educator; b. Moscow, Jan. 20, 1909; came to U.S., 1940, naturalized, 1944; s. Peter P. and Olga (Makarova) L.; m. Nora Muller, June 6, 1937. M. Philosophy, U. Latvia, 1930, LL.M., 1933; postgrad., U. Paris, 1934; Ph.D. (Rockefeller fellow), U. Chgo., 1938; LLD (hon.), Eastern Ky. U., 1986. Chair criminal law U. Latvia, 1938-40; prof. sociology U. Md., College Park, 1941-79, prof. emeritus, 1979—; acting dept. chmn. U. Md., 1944-46, 61; dir. Inst. Criminal Justice and Criminology, 1969-79; chmn. bd. dirs. Nat. Criminal Justice Ednl. Devel. Consortium, 1975-76; prof. Sch. Criminology, Fla. State U., 1982-84; cons. area human resources USAF, 1951-55; lectr. delinquency and crime Frederick A. Moran Meml. Inst., summers 1956, 57, 63; Mem. exec. com. Correctional Service Assos., 1947-50, Com. for Am. Participation in 2d Internat. Congress Criminology, Paris, 1950; mem. U.S. delegation 12th Internat. Penal and Penitentiary Congress, The Hague, 1950, 1st UN Congress for Prevention Crime and Treatment Delinquents, Geneva, 1955, 2d Congress, London, Eng., 1960; mem. U.S. delegation 3d UN Congress for Prevention Crime and Treatment of Offenders, Stockholm, 1965, 4th Congress, Kyoto, 1970, 5th Congress, Geneva, 1975; ofl. del. various assns. 7th UN Congress on Prevention of Crime and Treatment of Offenders, Milan, 1985; U.S. corr. to UN in social def. matters, 1965-76; vice chmn. bd. Joint Commn. on Manpower and Tng. in Corrections, 1964-70; U.S. rep. Internat. Penal and Penitentiary Found., 1974—, v.p., 1981-90; mem. Task Force Commd. to Study Correctional System, Joint Commn. on Mental Illness and Health, 1956-57; chmn. cons. com. Uniform Crime Reporting, FBI, 1957-58; mem. bd. Criminal Justice Assn., Washington; pres. bd. Md. Prisoners Aid Assn., 1957-60; chmn. Joint Baltic Am. Com., 1961-62, 66; exec. com. corrections sect. United Community Services, Washington; mem. Md. Gov.'s Commn. Prevention and Treatment Juvenile Offenders; mem. exec. bd. profl. coun., counc. rsch., trustee Nat. Coun. Crime and Delinquency, 1968-71; also mem. Md. Coun.; chmn. adv. bd. Md. Children's Ctr., 1959-65; chmn. rsch. com., adv. coun. Inst. Criminological Rsch., Dept. Corrections, D.C.; chmn. adv. bd., mem. governing bd. Patuxent Inst. Defective Delinquents; chmn. subcom. on instns. task force on correction Gov.'s Crime Commn., 1968-70; mem. rsch. and devel. task force Nat. Adv. Commn. Criminal Justice Standards and Goals, Law Enforcement Assistance Adminstrn., 1972-74, Phase II, 1974-76, chmn., 1974-76; vis. prof. Kuwait U., 1973; pres. Am. Assn. Doctoral Programs in Criminal Justice and Criminology, 1976—; mem. Md. Gov.'s Task Force on Alternative Sanctions to Incarceration, 1991. Chief editor: Jour. Rsch. in Crime and Delinquency, 1968-69, bd. editors, 1969-89; contbr. articles to profl. jours. and encys. Chmn. Social Survey Com., Prince Georges County, 1946-47 Community Chest Planning Coun., Prince Georges County, 1949-57; bd. dirs. Health and Welfare Coun. Nat. Capitol Area; 1st v.p. Prince Georges County Regional Com., bd. dirs. Washington Action for Youth, United Planning Orgn., Bok Tower Gardens Found., 1977—; chmn. D.C. Commrs. Com. on Youth Opportunity; pres. bd. dirs. Oscar Freire Inst., Sao Paolo, Brazil, 1974-77. Recipient Alumni Profl. Achievement award U. Chgo., 1973; establishment of annual Peter P. Lejins award for outstanding research in corrections, Am. Correctional Assn., 1987; decorated three stars govt. Republic of Latvia, 1995. Fellow Washington Acad. Sci., Am. Soc. Criminology, Internat. Centre Comparative Criminology; mem. AAUP, Am. Correctional Assn. (dir., mem. exec. com., chmn. com. on research and planning, pres. 1962-63, chmn. research council, E.R. Cass correctional achievement award 1980), Am. Sociol. Soc. (past pres. D.C.), Eastern Sociol. Soc., So. Sociol. Soc., Soc. Advancement Criminology, Nat. Probation Assn., Internat. Soc. Criminology (pres. sci. commn. 1973-80, hon. pres. 1981—, v.p. 1981-90), Latvian Frat. Assn. (past pres.), Am. Latvian Assn. (pres. 1951-70, now hon. pres.), Acad. Sci. Ind. Republic of Latvia (hon. mem. 1990), Free World Latvian Fedn. (pres. 1956-70), Phi Kappa Phi (disting. mem. on nat. level) Omicron Delta Kappa, Alpha Kappa Delta. Clubs: Cosmos (Washington); Faculty (U. Md.) (College Park and Baltimore); Pres. Club (U. Md., U. Chgo.); Colonnade Soc. (U.MD. Coll. Pk.), Lettonia (past pres.). Lodge: Rotary.

LEKAS, MARY DESPINA, retired otolaryngologist; b. Worcester, Mass., May 13, 1930; d. Spyridon Peter and Merciny S. (Manoliou) L.; m. Harold William Picozzi. BA, Clark U., 1949, DS (hon.), 1997; MD, Athens (Greece) U., 1957; MA, Brown U., 1986; student, Boston U. Diplomate Am. Bd. Otolaryngology. Sci. instr. Hahnemann Hosp. Sch. Nursing; rotating intern Meml. Hosp., Worcester, 1957-58; resident in otolaryngology R.I. Hosp., Providence, 1958-62; resident in otolaryngology and otorhinolaryngology U. Pa. Grad. Sch. Medicine, 1960; surgeon in chief, dept. otolaryngology R.I. Hosp., 1984-96; pvt. practice Providence, 1962—; chmn. dept. otolaryngology Brown U., Providnce, 1984, clinical prof. emerita surgery divsn. otolaryngology, head and neck ; cons. Cleft Palate Clin. and Craniofacial of R.I. Hosp., 1964—, VA Hosp., Providence, 1967—, St. Joseph Hosp., Providence, 1983—, Miriam Hosp., Providence, 1984—; lectr. profl. orgns. Mem. editorial bd. Am. Jour. Rhinology, 1987—; contbr. articles to profl. jours. Mem. alumni coun. Clark U. Clark V. Jonas Clark fellow; named R.I. Woman Physician of Yr., 1992; disting. svc. award Providence Med. Assn., 1996. Fellow ACS, Soc. Univ. Otolaryngologists-Head and Neck Surgeons, Triological Soc. (ea. sect. sec., Presdl. Citation 1993), Am. Acad. Otolaryngology-Head and Neck Surgeons, Am. Acad. Facial Plastic and Reconstructive Surgeons, Am. Acad. Broncho-Escophalogy (treas., v.p. 1990); mem. AMA, Assn. Acad. Dept. Otolaryngology-Head and Neck Surgery, Deafness Rsch. Found., Am. Cleft Palate Assn., Am. Med. Women's Assn. (R.I. Woman Physician of Yr. 1992), Am. Broncho-Esophagological Assn. (hon.), Centurian Club, New Eng. Otolaryng. Soc. (pres. 1987-88). Greek Orthodox. Avocations: cycling, swimming, church choir. Home: 129 Terrace Ave Riverside RI 02915-4726 Office: Physicians Office Bldg 110 Lockwood St Providence RI 02903-4801

LELAND, HENRY, psychology educator; b. N.Y.C., Feb. 13, 1923; s. Ida (Miller) L.; m. Helen D. Faitos (div. 1979); children: Colombe, David Jean, Daniel Louis; m. Sherrie Lynn Ireland, Dec. 7, 1980. AB, San Jose State Coll., 1948; PhD, Université de Paris, Paris, 1952. Lic. psychologist, Ohio. Clin. psychologist with Dr. Jean Biro, Paris, 1949-52; sr. clin. psychologist N.Y. State Mental Health Commn., Syracuse, 1952-54; dir. dept. psychol. svc. Muscatatuck State Sch., Butlerville, Ind., 1954-57; chief clin. psychologist Parsons (Kans.) State Hosp. and Tng. Ctr., 1957-63; coord. profl. tng., edn. and demonstration Parsons (Kans.) State Hosp. and Tng. Ctg., 1963-70; assoc. in child rsch. Kansas U. Bur. child Rsch., Lawrence, 1963-70; assoc. prof. psychology Ohio State U., Columbus, 1970-72, prof., 1972-93, prof. emeritus, 1993—, mem. senate, 1985-88; chief psychology Herschel W. Nisonger Ctr., Columbus, 1970-93; tchg. asst. Ind. U. Extension Svc., 1956-57; assoc. prof. Kansas State Coll., 1958-70; dist. vis. lectr. U. So. Calif., L.A., 1969; prin. investigator Adaptive Behavior Project, Ohio Dept. Mental Health and Mental Retardation, 1972-75, cons., 1972-75; bd. examiners State Bd. Psychology Ohio, 1987-88, 93-94, sec., 1988-89, pres., 1989-90, 94-95, active, 1986-95; cons. Cen. Ohio Psychiat. Hosp., 1986-93; com. on acad. misconduct Ohio State U., 1990-93. Author: (wih D. Smith) Play Therapy with Mentally Subnormal Children, 1965, (with others) Brain Damage and Mental Retardation, 1967, (with others) Handbuch der Kinderpsychotherapie, Vol. II, Germany, 1968, (with others) Social Perceptual Training Kit for Community Living, 1968, Impairment in Adaptive Behavior: A Community Dimension, Tracks, Vols. II, 12, 1960-67, (with others) Social Inference Training of Retarded Adolescents at the Pre-Vocational Level, 1968, (with others) Mental Health Services for the Mentally Retarded, 1972, (with others) Sociobehavioral Studies in Mental Retardation, 1973, (with others) Mental Retardation: Current and Future Perspectives, 1974, (with others) Research to Practice in Mental Retardation and Education and Training, II, 1977, (with others) International Encyclopedia of Psychiatry, Psychology, Psychoanalysis and Neurology, II, 1977, (wth others) Psychological Management of Pediatric Problems, 1978, (with Deutsch)Abnormal Behavior, 1980, (with others) Pscychoeducational Assessment of Preschool and Primary Age Children, 1982, (with others) Comprehensive Handbook of Mental Retardation, 1983, (with others) The Foundations of Clinical Neuropsychology, 1983, (with others) Institutions for the Mentally Retarded: A Changing Role in Changing Times, 1986, (with others) AAMR Adaptive Behavior Scale-Residential and Community, 1995, AAMR Adaptive Behavior Scale-School, 1993; cons. editor Am. Jour. Mental Deficiency, 1965-70, Profl. Psychology, 1977-95, Mental Retardation, 1980-84; contbr. articles to profl. jours. Mem. Franklin County bd. Mental Retardation/Development Disabilities, 1980-82; trustee Goodwill Rehab. Ctr., 1975—, mem. exec. com., 1985—. Recipient Disting. Svc. in Mental Deficiency award, Am. Assn. on Mental Deficiency, 1985. Fellow AAAS, APA (councilor 1986-90 , Edgar A. Doll Meml. award div. 33 1990), Am. Assn. on Mental Retardation (councilor 1964-68), Ohio Psychol. Assn., Soc. for Pediatric Psychology, Kans. Psychol. Assn. (pres. 1966), Ctrl. Ohio Psychol. Assn. (pres. 1996). Democrat. Jewish. Avocations: stamp collecting, gourmet cooking. Home: 2120 Iuka Ave Columbus OH 43201-1322

LELAND, JOY HANSON, anthropologist, alcohol research specialist; b. Glendale, Calif., July 29, 1927; d. David Emmett and Florence (Sockerson) Hanson; m. David A. Riegert, Nov. 14, 1993. B.A. in English Lit., Pomona Coll., Claremont, Calif., 1949; M.B.A., Stanford U., 1960; M.A. in Anthropology, U. Nev., 1972; Ph.D. in Anthropology, U. Calif., Irvine, 1975. With Desert Research Inst., U. Nev., 1961—, asst. research prof., 1975-77, assoc. research prof., 1977-79, rsch. prof., 1979-89, rsch. prof. emerita, 1990—. Author: monograph Firewater Myths, Frederick West Lander-A Biographical Sketch; contbg. author: Smithsonian Handbook of North American Indians; also articles, book chpts. NIMH grantee, 1972-73; Nat. Inst. Alcohol Abuse and Alcoholism grantee, 1974-75, 79-81. Mem. Am. Anthrop. Assn., Southwestern Anthrop. Assn., Soc. Applied Anthropology, Soc. Med. Anthropology, Gt. Basin Anthrop. Conf., Phi Kappa Phi. Office: Desert Rsch Inst U Nev System PO Box 60220 7010 Dandini Blvd Reno NV 89512-3901

LELAND, LAWRENCE, insurance executive; b. C., Can., Nov. 13, 1915. AB, Earlham Coll. CLU. Asst. supt. agys. Am. United Life Ins. Co., 1948-58, agy. v.p., 1958-67, dir., 1962-67; from sr. v.p., mem. operating com. to exec. v.p. Nat. Life Ins. Co., Montpelier, Vt., 1967-80; ret. Nat. Life Ins. Co., 1980; dir. Nat. Life Investment Mgmt. Co., Inc.; pres., dir. Equity Service, Inc., Adminstrv. Services, Inc.; exec. com. Audit Nat. Life Ins. Co. Trustee Earlham Coll, 1958-67, acting pres., 1984-85, hon. life trustee, 1985—; mem. Vt. Employment Security Bd.; bd. visitors Guilford Coll., 1980-85. Recipient Outstanding Vol. award Earlham Coll. Mem. Gen. Agts. and Mgrs. Assn., Central Vt. Life Underwriters Assn., Lafayette (Ind.) Life Underwriters Assn. (past pres.), Masons, Ind. Leaders Club, Meridian Hills Country Club. Mem. Soc. of Friends. Home: 12 Westwood Dr Montpelier VT 05602-4211 *Died Aug. 10, 1996.*

LELAND, MARC ERNEST, trust advisor, lawyer; b. San Francisco, Apr. 20, 1938; s. Herbert and Sarah Betty (Robinson) L.; m. Elisabeth Gustava De Rothschild, July 7, 1970 (div. Sept. 1980); children: Natasha Hanna, Olivia Mitzi; m. Jacqueline de Botton, 1989. AB in Govt., Harvard U., 1959; MA in Law, St. John's Coll.-Oxford U., Eng., 1961; JD, U. Calif.-Berkeley, 1963. Ford Found. fellow Inst. Comparative Law-U., Paris, 1963-64; assoc. Cerf Robinson & Leland, San Francisco, 1964-68, ptnr., 1972-76; faculty fellow Harvard U. Law Sch., Boston, 1968-70; gen. counsel Peace Corps, Washington, 1970-71, ACTION, Washington, 1971-72; ACDA rep. Force Reduction Talks, Vienna, Austria, 1976-78; resident ptnr. Proskauer Rose Goetz & Mendelsohn, London, 1978-81; asst. sec. internat. affairs Dept. Treasury, Washington, 1981-84; pres. Marc E. Leland & Assocs., Washington, 1984—. Republican. Jewish. Office: 1001 19th St N Ste 1700 Arlington VA 22209-1722

LELAND, PAULA SUSAN, educational administrator, educator; b. Duluth, Minn., Feb. 10, 1953; d. Clarence Henry and Agnes Gudrun (Feiring) L. BS in Elem. Edn. and Music with honors, U. Minn., Duluth, 1975, BS in English, Lang. Arts and Sec. Edn. with honors, 1979; MS in Edn. Adminstrn. and Edn. summa cum laude, U. Wis., Superior, 1982, MEd in Profl. Devel., English and Language Arts summa cum laude, 1984, Spl. degree in Edn. Adminstrn. summa cum laude, 1988, postgrad., 1988—; postgrad., U. St. Thomas, 1989, U. Minn., Mpls., 1996—. Tchr. elem. gifted children U. Minn., Mpls., 1980; tchr. Hermantown (Minn.) Cmty. Schs. Dist. 700, 1975—, substitute adminstr., 1982-92; mem. staff devel. com. Hermantown (Minn.) Cmty. Schs. Dist. 700, Hermantown, 1987—; dist. coord. and chairperson, planning, evaluating and reporting com., adminstrv. rep. State Dept. of Edn. for Minn. #700, Hermantown, 1984-86; supr. student tchrs. U. Wis., Superior, 1977—, adminstr. practicum, 1981-82; supr. student tchrs. U. Minn., Duluth, 1977—; mem. faculty community adv. com. for student tchrs., 1985—; Coll. St. Scholastica, 1977—; supr. tchr. aides, parent vols., and interpreters, 1980—; fgn. exch. tchr. host, 1982-83; profl. edn. tutor, 1989-90; mem. textbook com. Hermantown Schs., 1977—; writer, reporter Hermantown Star, 1978. Curriculum writer Hermantown Community Schs.; music arranger, composer, lyricist. Mem. Dem. Nat. Conv. supporter, Dem. Party Local Affiliation, Duluth, 1972—, Lake Superior Ctr. Non-Profit Orgn.; choir dir., dir. music Zion Luth. Ch., 1980—, dir./coord. music and handbell, 1983—, asst. dir. 1976-79, co-chair music and co-author music tape for Centennial Celebration, 1988, mem. nominating and worship coms. chairperson, 1992-94, 97, recorder, sec. and choir sec., pastor-selected com. for assoc. in ministry, 1980—, vocalist, 1967—, Sunday Sch. tchr., Bible sch. tchr. 1968-75, substitute asst. dir., 1976-80, coun. mem. 1992—, v.p. 1993-94, 97, pres. 1994-96, chair call com. pastor-elect, 1994-96, found. bd. dirs., 1994-96, v.p. found. bd. dirs., 1997; supporter Reading is Fundamental, 1975—, United Way of Greater Duluth, 1975—; mem. Dairy Coun., Hermantown Arts Coun.; active Goodwill Industries, Salvation Army, Clean Water Action, Minn. Dept. Natural Resource-Wildlife, U. Minn. Legis. Network, 1992—; Archtl. Planner Ednl. Facilities and Creative Activity, 1984; bd. dirs. Duluth Fed. Employees Credit Union, 1994-95. Named to The Nat. Women's Hall of Fame, 1995; Alworth scholar, 1971-75, Denfeld scholar, 1968-71. Mem. AAUW, NAFE, Am. Mus. Nat. Hist., Assn. Lutheran Ch. Musicians (invited), Future Tchrs. Orgn., Red Cross Club (pres, former v.p., svc. award), Sons of Norway (Viking Ship Project), N.Am. Assn. for Environ. Edn., Norwegian Am. Heritage Fund, Minn. Valley Nat. Wildlife Refuge, N.D. Parks and Recreation, Friends of Deep Portage, Arrowhead Reading Coun., Minn. Reading Assn., Hermantown Fedn. Tchrs., Hermantown Sch. Dist. Cont. Edn. (co-chair, former sec., cert. of appreciation 1990), Hermantown Fedn. Tchrs., Minn. Hist. Soc., Midwest Fed. Banking Consortium, U. Minn.-Duluth Alumni Assn., U. Wis.-Superior Alumni Assn., Minn. Naturalists Assn., Tweed Mus. Art, Mpls. Soc. of the Arts, Mpls. Soc. of Fine Arts, Minn. Inst. Art, Internat. Platform Assn., Smithsonian Nat. Assocs., Smithsonian Inst., Charles F. Menninger Soc., Laura Ingalls Wilder Meml. Soc., Midwesterners Club, Alpine Club, Zoofari Club, Queen Mary and Spruce Goose Voyager Club, Kappa Delta Pi, Sigma Alpha Iota, Phi Kappa Phi, Phi Delta Kappa, Delta Kappa Gamma, Beta Sigma Phi, Alpha Delta Kappa. Office: 4289 Ugstad Rd Hermantown MN 55811-3615

LELAND, RICHARD G., lawyer; b. Oceanside, N.Y., Jan. 25, 1949; s. Arnold Joseph and Eunice (Himlyn) L.; children: Jennifer Mara, David Jarett. BS, Cornell U., 1971; JD with distinction, Hofstra U., 1974. Bar: N.Y. 1975, U.S. CT. Appeals (2nd cir.) 1975, U.S. Dist. Ct. (so. and ea. dists.) N.Y. 1976, U.S. Supreme Ct. 1979. Assoc. Winer, Neuburger & Sive, N.Y.C., 1974-76; law sec. to justice Supreme Ct. N.Y. Nassau County, Mineola, 1976-79; assoc. Ruskin, Schlissel, Moscou & Evans, P.C., Mineola, 1979-82, ptnr., 1982-89; ptnr. Rosenman & Colin, N.Y.C., 1989—; faculty dir. Cambridge Inst., Vienna, Va., 1990-91; adj. prof. environ. law Hofstra U., Hempstead, N.Y., 1991—. Contbr. articles to profl. jours. Mem. ABA, N.Y. state Bar Assn., Nassau County Bar Assn. (chmn. com.). Office: Rosenman & Colin LLP 575 Madison Ave New York NY 10022-2511

LELAND, SARA, ballet dancer; b. Melrose, Mass., Sept. 2, 1941; m. Arthur Kevorkian. Student with, E. Virginia Williams, Melrose, Mass. Dancer New England Civic Ballet, Joffrey Ballet, 1959-60; dancer N.Y.C. Ballet, 1960-83, asst. ballet mistress, 1983—. Dancer: (ballets) Les Biches, 1960, Don Quixote, Jewels, 1967, Symphony in Three Movements, 1972, Union Jack, 1976, Vienna Waltzers, Dances at a Gathering, 1969, The Golberg Variations, 1971, Illuminations, The Concert, 1971, Gaspard de la Nuit, 1973, Lost Sonata, 1972, Choral Variations on Bach's Von Himmel Hoch, 1972, Scherzo Fantastique, 1972; ballet master staged works for the Joffrey Ballet, Boston Ballet, the Dance Theater of Harlem. Office: NYC Ballet Inc NY State Theater Lincoln Ctr Plz New York NY 10023*

LELAND, TIMOTHY, newspaper executive; b. Boston, Sept. 24, 1937; s. Oliver Stevens and Frances Chamberlain (Ayres) L.; m. Natasha Bourso, Sept. 26, 1964 (div. 1981); children: Christian Bourso, London Chamberlain; m. Julie S. Hatfield, Nov. 23, 1984. A.B. cum laude, Harvard U., 1960; M.S. with honors, Columbia Sch. Journalism, 1961. Med. editor Boston Herald, 1963-64; sci. editor Boston Globe, 1965-66, State House bur. chief, 1966-67, asst. city editor, 1968-69, investigative reporter, 1970-71, asst. mng. editor, 1972, mng. editor (Sunday), 1976-81, mng. editor (daily), 1981-82, asst. to pub., 1984—, v.p., 1990—. Bd. dirs. Boys and Girls Clubs of Boston, World Affairs Coun. of Boston. Recipient Am. Polit. Sci. award, 1968; Pulitzer Prize for investigative reporting, 1972; Sigma Delta Chi award for civic service (reporting), 1972; award for pub. service A.P. Mng. Editors, 1974; Sevellon Brown award, 1974; U.S.-South African Leader Exchange Program traveling grantee, 1969; Internat. fellow Columbia, 1961. Mem. Harvard Club. Office: Boston Globe 135 Morrissey Blvd Dorchester MA 02107

LELCHUK, ALAN, author, educator; b. Bklyn., Sept. 15, 1938; s. Harry and Belle (Simon) L.; married; 2 children. B.A., Bklyn. Coll., 1960; M.A., Stanford, 1963; Ph.D., Stanford U., 1965; student, U. London, 1963-64. Writer-in-residence Brandeis U., 1966-81; vis. writer Amherst Coll., 1982-84; guest Mishkenot Sha'Ananim, Jerusalem, 1976-77; adj. prof. Dartmouth Coll., 1985—; writer-in-residence Haifa U., Israel, 1986-87; vis. writer CCNY, fall 1991; vis. prof. U. Rome Torvergata, Apr., 1996. Author: American Mischief, 1973, Miriam at Thirty-four, 1974, Shrinking, 1978, Miriam in Her Forties, 1985, (young adult novel) On Home Ground, 1987, Brooklyn Boy, 1990, Playing the Game, 1995; assoc. editor Modern Occasions, 1970-72; editor: Eight Great Hebrew Short Novels, 1983, co-founder Steerforth Press, 1993; manuscript collection Mugar Meml. Libr., Boston U.; contbr. fiction, criticism to lit. mags. Yaddo and MacDowell Colony fellow, 1968-69; Guggenheim fellow, 1976-77; Fulbright grantee, 1986-87. Mem. Authors Guild, P.E.N. Home: RR 2 Canaan NH 03741-9802 Office: care Georges Borchardt 136 E 57th St New York NY 10022-2707

LELCHUK, HOWARD, advertising executive; married; two children. Various positions N.W. Ayer, BBDO, N.Y., Pitts.; v.p. media dir. Kenyon & Eckhardt; exec. media dir., v.p. Ogilvy & Mather Direct, 1983-85, sr. v.p., 1985-94, mem. exec. com., 1992—, worldwide media dir., 1994—; co-chair Resource Bd. Ogilvy & Mather Direct, O&M Direct Hispana, 1990—; bd. dirs. BPA Internat.; spkr. in field. Contbr. articles to profl. jours. Mem. Direct Mktg. Assn. (ethics policy com., privacy task force), AAAA (chmn. direct response media com.). Avocation: tennis. Office: Ogilvy & Mather Direct 309 W 49th St New York NY 10019-7316

LELE, AMOL SHASHIKANT, obstetrician and gynecologist; b. Chhindnara, India, May 23, 1944; came to U.S., 1970; d. Gajanan S. and Sarala S. (Manjrekar) Karande; m. Shashikant Lele, Feb. 28, 1970; children: Kedar, Rajal. MBBS, Bombay U., 1967, MD, 1970; DGO, Coll. Physicians, Bombay, 1969. Diplomate Am. Bd. Ob-Gyn. Clinical ob-gyn. clinic St. Luke's Hosp., Cleve., 1974; instr. SUNY, Buffalo, 1974-76, asst. prof., 1978-84, clin. assoc. prof., 1984—; fellow Children's Hosp., Buffalo, 1976-78, dir. women's svcs., 1976—, dir. outreach program, 1991—; dir. prenatal care Erie County Med. Ctr., Buffalo, 1979—; mem. health com. Planned Parenthood, Buffalo, 1992—; mem. infant mortality task force Health Systems Agy., Buffalo, 1994—. Avocations: reading, theater, light music. Home: 75 Nottingham Ter Buffalo NY 14216 Office: Children's Hosp Buffalo 239 Bryant St Buffalo NY 14222-2006

LELE, PADMAKAR PRATAP, physician, educator; b. Chanda, India, Nov. 9, 1927; came to U.S., 1958; s. Pratap Vasudev and Indira (Prabhudesai) L.; m. Carla Maria Tophoff, Jan. 23, 1959; children: Martin, Malcolm. M.D., Seth G.S. Med. Coll., 1950; D.Phil., Oxford (Eng.) U., 1955. Intern K.E.M. Hosp., Bombay, India, 1950-51; resident K.E.M. Hosp., 1951-52; lectr. Oxford U., 1952-57; vis. scientist NIH, Bethesda, Md., 1958-59; tech. dir. med. acoustics research group and assoc. neurophysiologist Mass. Gen. Hosp., Boston, 1959-69; assoc. in neurosurgery Harvard Med. Sch.; assoc. prof. exptl. medicine MIT, Cambridge, 1969-71; prof. MIT,

1972-94, prof. emeritus, sr. lectr., 1994—; prof. Harvard-MIT Div. Health Scis. and Tech, also prof. exptl. medicine and dir. Hyperthermia Ctr.; cons. NIH. Mem. editl. bd. Ultrasound in Medicine and Biology, 1973-94, In Vivo, 1985—; contbr. articles to med. jours. Recipient History Med. Ultrasound Pioneer award World Fedn. Ultrasound in Medicine and Biology, 1988. Fellow Acoustical Soc. Am., Am. Inst. Ultrasound in Medicine (governing bd. 1973-76, Joseph H. Holmes Pioneer award 1988); mem. IEEE, Am. Soc. Clin. Hyperthermic Oncology, European Soc. for Hyperthermic Oncology, N.Am. Hyperthermia Group, Am. Assn. Physicists in Medicine, Bioelectromagnetics Soc. (charter). Home: 5820 Ravenswood Rd La Jolla CA 92037-7419

LELYVELD, JOSEPH SALEM, newspaper executive editor, correspondent; b. Cin., Apr. 5, 1937; s. Arthur Joseph and Toby (Bookholz) L.; m. Carolyn Fox, June 14, 1959; children: Amy, Nita. BA summa cum laude, Harvard U., 1958, MA, 1959; MS in Journalism, Columbia U., 1960. Reporter, editor N.Y. Times, 1963—, fgn. corr., Johannesburg, New Delhi, Hong Kong, London, 1965-86, columnist mag., staff writer, 1977, 84-85, fgn. editor, 1987-89, mng. editor, 1990-94; exec. editor, 1994—. Author: Move Your Shadow, 1985 (Pulitzer prize, L.A. Times Book prize, Sidney Hillman award, Cornelius P. Ryan award, all 1986). Recipient George Polk Meml. award, 1972, 84; Guggenheim fellow, 1984. Mem. The Century Assn. Office: The NY Times 229 W 43rd St New York NY 10036-3913

LEM, RICHARD DOUGLAS, painter; b. L.A., Nov. 24, 1933; s. Walter Wing and Betty (Wong) L.; B.A., UCLA, 1958; M.A., Calif. State U.-Los Angeles, 1963; m. Patricia Ann Soohoo, May 10, 1958; 1 son, Stephen Vincent. Exhibited in one-man shows at Gallery 818, Los Angeles, 1965; group shows at Lynn Kottler Galleries, N.Y.C., 1973, Palos Verdes Art Gallery, 1968, Galerie Mouffe, Paris, France, 1976, Le Salon des Nations, Paris, 1984, numerous others; represented in permanent collections; writer, illustrator: Mile's Journey, 1983, 2nd edit., 1995; cover illustrator: The Hermit, 1990, The Hermit's Journey, 1993. Served with AUS, 1958-60. Mem. UCLA Alumni Assn. Address: 1861 Webster Ave Los Angeles CA 90026-1229 *Personal philosophy: It requires a great deal of inner strength to pursue your personal vision with single mindedness - it's a challenge that justifies my existence.*

LEMAIRE, JACQUES, professional hockey coach; b. Lasalle, Que., Can., Sept. 7, 1945. Player Montreal Canadiens, 1967-79, head coach, 1983-85; head coach, player Sierre Hockey Club, Switzerland, 1979-81; asst. coach SUNY Coll., Plattsburgh, 1981-82; coach Longueuil Chevaliers, maj. jr. league, Que., 1982-83; dir. of hockey pers. Montreal Canadiens, 1985-87, asst. to mng. dir., 1987-93; head coach N.J. Devils, 1993—; mem. Stanley Cup Championship teams, 1968, 69, 71, 73, 76-79. Named NHL Coach of Yr., Sporting News, 1993, 94. Office: NJ Devils PO Box 504 East Rutherford NJ 07073-0504*

LE MAISTRE, CHARLES AUBREY, internist, epidemiologist, educator; b. Lockhart, Ala., Feb. 10, 1924; s. John Wesley and Edith (McLeod) LeM.; m. Joyce Trapp, June 3, 1952; children: Charles Frederick, William Sidney, Joyce Anne, Helen Jean. BA, U. Ala., 1943, LLD (hon.), 1971; MD, Cornell U., 1947; LLD (hon.), Austin Coll., 1970; DSc (hon.), U. Dallas, 1978, Southwestern U., 1981; D honoris causa, U. Guadalajara (Mex.), 1989. Intern, then resident medicine N.Y. Hosp., 1947-49; research fellow infectious diseases Cornell U. Med. Coll., 1949-51, mem. faculty, 1951-54, asst. prof. medicine, 1953-54; mem. faculty Emory U. Sch. Medicine, 1954-59, prof. preventive medicine, chmn. dept., 1957-59; prof. medicine U. Tex. Southwestern Med. Sch., 1959-78, assoc. dean, 1965-66; vice chancellor health affairs U. Tex. System, Austin, 1966-68; exec. vice chancellor U. Tex. System, 1968-69, dep. chancellor, 1969-70, chancellor, 1971-78, prof. medicine, 1978-96; pres., internist U. Tex. M.D. Anderson Cancer Ctr., 1978-96; cons. epidemiology Communicable Disease Center, USPHS, 1953-69; cons. medicine VA, 1954-59; area med. cons. VA (Atlanta area), 1958-59; vis. staff physician Grady Meml. Hosp., Atlanta, 1954-59, Emory U. Hosp., 1954-59; sr. attending staff mem. Parkland Meml. Hosp., Dallas, 1959-66; med. dir. chest div. Woodlawn Hosp., Dallas, 1959-65; mem. Surgeon Gen.'s Adv. Com. Smoking and Health, 1963-64, AMA-Edn. Research Found. com. research tobacco and health, 1964-66; chmn. Gov. Tex. Com. Tb Eradication, 1963-64; cons. internal medicine Baylor U. Med. Center, Dallas, 1962-66, St. Paul Hosp., Dallas, 1966; cons. div. hosp. and med. facilities USPHS, 1966; mem. N.Y.C. Task Force on Tb, 1967; cons. Bur. Physician, HEW, 1967-70; mem. grad. med. edn. nat. adv. com. Health Resources Adminstrn., 1977-80; mem. Tex. Legislature Dept. Health, Edn. and Welfare, 1967, Tex. Legislature Com. on Organ Transplantation, 1968, Carnegie Commn. on Non-Traditional Study, 1971-73; mem. bd. commrs. Nat. Commn. on Accrediting, 1973-76; mem. joint task force on continuing competence in pharmacy Am. Pharm. Assn.-Am. Assn. Coll. in Pharmacy, 1973-74; mem. exec. com. Legis. Task Force on Cancer in Tex., 1984-86; adv. bd. 6th World Conf. on Smoking and Health. Contbr. med. jours.; contbg. author: A Textbook of Medicine, 10 and 11th edits, 1963, Pharmacology in Medicine, 1958; Translating author: The Tubercle Bacillus, 1955; mem. editorial bd. Am. Rev. Respiratory Diseases, 1955-58. Mem. President's Commn. White House Fellows, 1971; chmn. subcom. on diversity and pluralism Nat. Council on Ednl. Research, 1973-75; bd. dirs. Assn. Tex. Colls. and Univs., 1974-75; mem. devel. council United Negro Coll. Fund, 1974-78; mem. nat. adv. council Inst. for Services to Edn., 1974-78; mem. exec. com. Assn. Am. Univs., 1975-77; mem. Project HOPE com. on Health Policy, 1977; chmn. steering com. Presbyn. Physicians for Fgn. Missions, 1960-62; mem. Ministers Cons. Clinic, Dallas, 1960-62; trustee Austin Coll., 1979-83, Stillman Coll., 1978-84; bd. dirs. Ga. Tb Assn., 1955-59; bd. dirs. Damon Runyon-Walter Winchell Cancer Fund, 1976-85, chmn. exec. com., v.p., 1978, pres., 1979-83; trustee Biol. Humanics Found., Dallas, 1973-82; chmn. health manpower com. Assn. Am. Univs., 1975-78; sec. Council So. Univs., Inc., 1976-78, pres., 1977-78; hon. life trustee Menninger Found.; Host com. Houston Econ. Summit, 1990. Recipient Cornell Univ. Alumni of Distinction award, 1978, Disting. Alumnus award U. Alabama Sch. Medicine, 1982, Pres.' award Am. Lung Assn., 1987, Gibson D. Lewis award for Excellence in Cancer Control Tex. Cancer Coun., 1988, award of Honor Am. Soc. Hosp. Pharmacists, 1988, Svc. to Mankind award Leukemia Soc. Am. Tex. Gulf Coast chpt., 1991, People of Vision award Tex. Soc. to Prevent Blindness, 1991, Outstanding Tex. Leader award 7th Ann. John Ben Sheppard Pub. Leadership Forum, 1991; Inst. Religion's Caring Spirit Tribute, 1993, AMA Disting. Svc. award, 1995; named Houstonian of Yr. Houston Sch. for Deaf Children, 1987. Mem. AMA, (Disting. Svc. award 1995), NASA, NIH (chair joint adv. com. behavioral rsch. 1992), Am. Thoracic Soc. (past v.p.), So. Thoracic Soc. (past pres.), Nat. TB Assn., Tex. Med. Assn., Ga. Med. Assn., Soc. Assn. Oncology (bd. dirs.), Am. Cancer Soc. (tex. bd. dirs. 1977-89, med. and sci. com. 1974, chmn. study com. on tobacco and cancer 1976, pub. edn. com. 1976-87, chmn., mem. various nat. coms., v.p., pres. 1986, med. dir.-at-large 1977-89), Houston C. of C. (dir. 1979-89), Philos. Soc. Tex. (pres. 1980-81), Greater Houston Ptnrship (bd. dirs. 1989-96), Alpha Omega Alpha. Presbyterian. Home: 13104 Travis View Loop Austin TX 78732-1741

LEMAN, LOREN DWIGHT, civil engineer; b. Pomona, Calif., Dec. 2, 1950; s. Nick and Marian (Broady) L.; m. Carolyn Rae Bratvold, June 17, 1978; children: Joseph, Rachel, Nicole. BSCE, Oreg. State U., 1972; MS in Civil, Environ. Enging., Stanford U., 1973. Registered profl. engr., Alaska. Project mgr. CH2M Hill, San Francisco, 1973, Reston, Va., 1973-74, Ketchikan, Alaska, 1974-75, Anchorage, 1975-87; state rep. State of Alaska, 1989-93, state senator, 1993—; owner Loren Leman, P.E., Anchorage, 1987—; mem. Anchorage Hazardous Materials Commn., Local Emergency Planning Com., 1989-93. Contbr. articles to profl. jours. Mem. Breakthrough Com., Anchorage, 1978; del. to conv. Rep. Party of Alaska, 1976-90; basketball coach Grace Christian Sch., Anchorage, 1985-88; commr. Pacific States Marine Fisheries Commn.; past chmn. Pacific Fisheries Legis. Task Force. Mem. ASCE, Alaska Water Mgmt. Assn., Am. Legis. Exch. Coun., Water Environment Fedn., Toastmasters (pres.). Republican. Avocations: reading, fishing, biking, music, basketball. Home: 2699 Nathaniel Ct Anchorage AK 99517-1016 Office: Alaska State Legis 716 W 4th Ave # 520 Anchorage AK 99501-2107

LEMANN, THOMAS BERTHELOT, lawyer; b. New Orleans, Jan. 3, 1926; s. Monte M. and Nettie E. (Hyman) L.; m. Barbara M. London, Apr. 14, 1951; children: Nicholas B., Nancy E. A.B. summa cum laude, Harvard U., 1949, LL.B., 1952; M.C.L., Tulane U., 1953. Bar: La. 1953. Since practiced in New Orleans; assoc. Monroe & Lemann, New Orleans, 1953-58, ptnr., 1958—; bd. dirs. B. Lemann & Bro., Mermentau Mineral and Land Co., So. States Land & Timber Corp., Avrico Inc. Contbr. articles to profl. publs. Mem. council La. State Law Inst., sec. trust adv. com.; chmn. Mayor's Cultural Resources Com., 1970-75; pres. Arts Coun. Greater New Orleans, 1975-80, bd. dirs.; mem. vis. com. art museums Harvard U., 1974-80; trustee Metairie Park Country Day Sch., 1956-71, pres., 1967-70, New Orleans Philharmonic Symphony Soc., 1956-78, Flint-Goodridge Hosp., 1960-70, La. Civil Service League, pres., 1974-76, New Orleans Mus. Art, 1986-92; bd. dirs. Zemurray Found., Hever Found., Parkside Found., Azby Fund, Azby Art Fund, Greater New Orleans Found., Arts Coun. New Orleans, Musica da Camera. Served with AUS, 1944-46, PTO. Mem. ABA, La. Bar Assn. (bd. govs. 1977-78), New Orleans Bar Assn., Assn. Bar City N.Y., Am. Law Inst., Soc. Bartolus, Phi Beta Kappa. Jewish. Clubs: New Orleans Country, Wyvern (New Orleans). Home: 6020 Garfield St New Orleans LA 70118 Office: Monroe & Lemann 201 Saint Charles Ave New Orleans LA 70170-1000

LEMANSKE, ROBERT F., JR., allergist, immunologist; b. Milw., 1948. MD, U. Wis., 1975. Diplomate Am. Bd. Pediats., Am. Bd. Allergy and Immunology. Intern U. Wis. Hosp., Madison, 1975-76, resident in pediats., 1976-78, asst. prof. medicine. Fellow Am. Acad. Pediats., Am. Acad. Allergy and Immunology. Office: Clin Sci Ctr 600 Highland Ave Madison WI 53792-0001*

LEMANSKI, LARRY FREDRICK, medical educator; b. Madison, Wis., June 5, 1943; s. Fredrick Everett and Marjery Ulila (Hill) L.; m. Sharon Lee Wulf, Aug. 6, 1966; children: Scott Fredrick, Jennifer Lee. BS, U. Wis., Platteville, 1966; MS, Ariz. State U., 1968, PhD, 1971. Asst. prof. U. Calif., San Francisco, 1975-77; assoc. prof. U. Wis., Madison, 1977-79, prof., 1979-83; prof., chmn. dept. anatomy and cell biology SUNY, Syracuse, 1983—, dir. cell and molecular biology doctoral tng. program and consortium, 1987—; rsch. prof. biology Syracuse U., 1988—; mem. ad hoc rev. panel NIH. Adult leader for Boy Scouts Am., mem. nat. staff Boy Scout Jamboree 1989, coun. tng. chmn., 1992—. Officer USAR, 1965-69. Recipient Pres'. award Rsch. SUNY HSC, 1987, Disting. Alumnus award U. Wis., 1990, Profl. Excellence award N.Y. State/United Univ. Professions, 1990; NIH fellow, 1968-71, 71-73, Muscular Dystrophy fellow, 1973-75; grantee NIH, 1975—. Mem. AAAS, Am. Heart Assn. (Wis. affiliate rsch. com. 1982-83, Louis N. Katz Rsch. prize 1978, Outstanding Rsch. award 1982, Established Investigator award 1976-81), Electron Microscopy Soc. Am., Am. Assn. Anatomists, Am. Soc. Cell Biology (congrl. liaison com. 1993—), Soc. Devel. Biology, Am. Assn. Anatomy Chmn., N.Y. Acad. Scis., Masons (3d degree master), Sigma Xi, Beta Beta Beta. Methodist. Avocations: gardening, fishing, boating, camping, music. Home: 4163 Coye Rd Jamesville NY 13078-9780 Office: SUNY Coll Medicine Dept Anatomy Cell Biol Syracuse NY 13210

LE MASTER, DENNIS CLYDE, forest economics and policy educator; b. Startup, Wash., Apr. 22, 1939; s. Franklin Clyde and Delores Ilene (Schwartz) Le M.; m. Kathleen Ruth Dennis, Apr. 4, 1961; children: Paul, Matthew. BA, Wash. State U., 1961, MA, 1970, PhD, 1974. Asst. prof. dept. forestry and range mgmt. Wash. State U., Pullman, 1972-74, assoc. prof., 1978-80, prof., chair dept., 1980-88; prof., head dept. forestry and natural resources Purdue U., West Lafayette, Ind., 1988—; dir. resource policy Soc. Am. Foresters, Bethesda, Md., 1974-76; staff counsel subcom. on forests Ho. of Reps., Washington, 1977-78; cons. USDA Forest Svc., Washington, 1978, Com. on Agr., Ho. of Reps., 1979-80, Forest History Soc., Durham, N.C., 1979-83, The Conservation Found., 1989-90, Office Tech. Assessment, Washington, 1989-91, Consultative Group on Biol. Diversity, 1991. Author: Decade of Change, 1984; co-editor 8 books; contbr. articles to profl. jours. Bd. dirs. Pinchot Inst. for Conservation. Mem. AAAS, Soc. Am. Foresters (coun. 1988, chair house of soc. dels. 1982), Inland Empire Soc. of Soc. Am. Foresters (chair 1980-81, Forester of Yr. award 1982), Soc. for Range Mgmt., Forest Products Soc., Omicron Delta Epsilon, Beta Gamma Sigma, Xi Sigma Pi. Democrat. Episcopalian. Avocation: fishing. Home: 824 Lazy Ln Lafayette IN 47904-2722 Office: Purdue U Dept Foresty & Natural Resources West Lafayette IN 47907

LEMAY, JACQUES, lawyer; b. Quebec City, Can., July 10, 1940; s. Gerard and Jacqueline (Lachance) LeM. B.A., Que. Sem., 1959; LL.L., Laval U., 1962; postgrad., U. Toronto, 1964; D.E.S., 1965. Bar: Que. 1963. Practice in Quebec City, 1964—; mem. firm Prevost, Gagne, Flynn, Chouinard & Jacques, 1964-67; ptnr. Flynn, Rivard, Jacques, Cimon, Lessard & LeMay, 1968-86, Flynn, Rivard, 1986—; legal adviser Societe des Ajusteurs d'Assurance, 1969; bd. dirs. Can. 88 Energy Corp. Mem. Societe des Etudes Juridiques (pres. 1969). Club: Cercle de la Garnison (Que.). Home: 2342 Marie-Victorin, Sillery, PQ Canada G1T 2W5 Office: 70 Dalhousie, Bureau 500, Quebec, PQ Canada G1K 7A6

LEMBERG, LOUIS, cardiologist, educator; b. Chgo., Dec. 27, 1916; s. Morris and Frances Lemberg; m. Dorothy Feinstein, 1940 (dec. 1969); children: Gerald, Laura Bott, Paula Saltzman; m. Miriam Mayer, Jan. 29, 1971. B.S., U. Ill.-Chgo., 1938, M.D., 1940. Intern Mt. Sinai Hosp., Chgo., 1940-41, resident, 1945-48; asst. prof. med. 1955-58; assoc. prof. med. 1958-70; prof. clin. cardiology U. Miami Sch. Medicine (Fla.), 1970—, dir. coronary care unit, 1965-75; chief cardiology Mercy Hosp., 1974-79; chief staff Nat. Children's Cardiac Hosp., 1959-66; cons. cardiology VA Hosp., Miami, 1953-64; dir. Cardiology Dade County Hosp., 1953-64, dir. Heart Sta. and Electrocardiography, U. Miami Jackson Meml. Med. Ctr., 1952-75, program dir. Courses in Coronary Care for Practicing Physician, 1970—, Master Approach to Cardiovascular Problems, 1972-82, Cardiology Update for Intensive Care Nurses, 1978-92, Cardiology Update, 1987—. Served to maj. AUS, 1941-55; ETO. Recipient U. St. Torres (Phillippines) Luis Guerrero hon. lectr. award, 1977; Recognition award U. Miami Sch. Medicine; Lifetime Achievement award Jackson Meml. Med. Ctr. U. Miami, 1997; Key to City of Miami Beach, Fla. Fellow ACP, Am. Coll. Cardiology (editorial bd. jour.); mem. Heart Assn. Greater Miami (pres.), Fla. Heart Assn. (pres.), Am. Heart Assn. (fellow Council Clin. Cardiology), AMA (Physician's Recognition award 1970-86, 1986-94, 95—). Democrat. Jewish. Clubs: Palm Bay (Miami), Williams Island. Author: Vectorcardiography, 1969, (1975 2d edit.); Electrophysiology of Pacing and Cardioversion, 1969. Editor-in-chief Current Concepts in Cardiovascular Disorders, 1984-86. Contbr. to med. publs. Pioneer in devel. Demand Pacemaker, 1964, A chair in Cardiology established at the U. Miami Sch. of Medicine entitled The Louis Lemberg Professor of Cardiology, 1990. Home: 720 NE 69th St Apt 18 South Miami FL 33138-5738 Office: Mercy Hosp Professional Office Bldg 3661 S Miami Ave Ste 606 Miami FL 33133-4214

LEMBERGER, AUGUST PAUL, university dean, pharmacy educator; b. Milw., Jan. 25, 1926; s. Max N. and Celia (Gehl) L.; m. Charlyne A. Young, June 30, 1947; children: Michael, Mary, Thomas, Terrence, Ann, Kathryn, Peter. BS, U. Wis., 1948, PhD, 1952. Sr. chemist Merck & Co., Inc., Rahway, N.J., 1952-53; asst. prof. U. Wis. Sch. Pharmacy, 1953-57, asso. prof., 1957-63, prof. pharmacy, 1963-69; prof. pharmacy, dean U. Ill. Coll. Pharmacy, Chgo., 1969-80; prof. pharmacy, dean U. Wis.-Madison Sch. Pharmacy, 1980-91, ret., 1991; sec. Wis. Pharmacy Internship Bd., 1965-69; conf. dir. Nat. Indsl. Pharm. Research Conf., 1966-69; mem. Am. Council on Pharm. Edn., 1978-84, v.p., 1980-84. Served to 1st lt. AUS, 1944-46. Recipient Kiekhofer Meml. Teaching award U. Wis., 1957, citation of merit, 1977, Disting. Pharmacist award Wis. Pharm. Assn., 1969, Higuchi Lecture award Acad. Pharm. Sci. and Tech., Japan, 1989, Pres.' award Wis. Soc. Hosp. Pharmacists, 1991, Alumnus of Yr. award Pharmacy Alumni Assn., 1991. Fellow AAAS, Am. Found. for Pharm. Edn. (Disting. Svc. Profile award 1990), Acad. Pharm. Scis., Am. Assn. Pharm. Scientists; mem. Am. Soc. Hosp. Pharmacists, Am. Assn. Colls. Pharmacy (past com. chmn., exec. com. 1971-74, chmn. coun. deans 1975-77, chmn. sect. tchrs. of pharmacy Conf. Tchrs., hon. pres. 1993-94), Acad. Pharm. Scis. (v.p. 1976-77, pres. 1983-84), Am. Pharm. Assn. (mem. jud. bd. 1976-79, trustee 1985-88, treas. 1989-90, hon. pres. 1996-97), Wis. Pharm. Assn., Sigma Xi, Rho Chi (v.p. 1979-81, pres. 1981-83). Home: 7439 Cedar Creek Trl Madison WI 53717-1538 Office: 425 N Charter St Madison WI 53706-1508

LEMBERGER, LOUIS, pharmacologist, physician; b. Monticello, N.Y., May 8, 1937; s. Max and Ida (Siegal) L.; m. Myrna Sue Diamond, 1959; children: Harriet Felice Schor, Margo Beth. B.S. magna cum laude, Bklyn. Coll. Pharmacy, L.I. U., 1960; Ph.D. in Pharmacology, Albert Einstein Coll. Medicine, 1964, M.D., 1968; Doctorate (hon.), L.I. U., 1994. Pharmacy intern VA Regional Office, Newark, summer 1960; postdoctoral fellow Albert Einstein Coll. Medicine, 1964-68; intern in medicine Met. Hosp. Center, N.Y. Med. Coll., N.Y.C., 1968-69; rsch. assoc. NIH, Bethesda, Md., 1969-71; clin. pharmacologist Lilly Lab. for Clin. Rsch., Eli Lilly & Co., Indpls., 1971-75; chief clin. pharmacology Lilly Lab. for Clin. Rsch., Eli Lilly & Co., 1975-78, dir. clin. pharmacology, 1978-89, clin. rsch. fellow, 1982-93; asst. prof. pharmacology Ind. U., 1972-73, asst. prof. medicine, 1972-73, assoc. prof. pharmacology, 1973-77, assoc. prof. medicine, 1973-77, prof. pharmacology, 1977—, prof. medicine, prof. psychiatry, 1977—, mem. grad. faculty, 1975—; adj. prof. clin. pharmacology Ohio State U., 1975-86; physician Wishard Meml. Hosp., 1976—; cons. U.S. Nat. Commn. on Marijuana and Drug Abuse, 1971-73, Can. Commn. Inquiry into Non-Med. Use of Drugs, 1971-73; mem. Pharm. Mfrs. Assn. Commn. on Medicines for Drug Dependence and Abuse, 1990-93, Ind. Optometric Legend Drug Adv. Com., 1991-96; guest lectr. various univs., 1968—; lectr. U. Minn., 1993—; mem. adv. com. Faseb Life Scis. Rsch. Office, 1993-96. Author: (with A. Rubin) Physiologic Disposition of Drugs of Abuse, 1976; contbr. numerous articles on biochemistry and pharmacology to sci. jours.; editorial bd.; Excerpta Medica, 1972-96, Clin. Pharmacology and Therapeutics, 1976-96, Communications in Psychopharmacology, 1975-91, Pharmacology, Interant. Jour. Exptl. and Clin. Pharmacology, 1978-94, Drug and Alcohol Abuse Rsch., 1979-86, Drug Devel. Rsch., 1980-87, Trends in Pharmcol. Scis., 1980-85. Post adviser Crossroads of Am. council Boy Scouts Am., 1972-77. Served with USPHS, 1969-71. Recipient Disting. Alumnus award Albert Einstein Coll. Medicine, 1989, Disting. Alumnus award L.I. U., 1990. Fellow ACP, AAAS, Am. Coll. Neuropsychopharmacology (chmn. credentials com. 1993) , Am. Coll. Clin. Pharmacology; mem. Am. Soc. Pharmacology and Exptl. Therapeutics (com. div. clin. pharmacology 1972-78, chmn. com. 1978-83, coun. 1980-83, chmn. long-range planning com. 1984-86, pres. 1987-88, ASPET award in Therapeutics, 1985, Harry Gold award for rsch. and teaching excellence in clin. pharmacology 1993), Am. Soc. Clin. Pharmacology and Therapeutics (chmn. sect. neuropsychopharmacology 1973-80, chmn. fin. com. 1976-83, 89-92, v.p. 1981-82, pres. 1983-84, dir. 1975-81, 84-87, Rawls-Palmer award 1986, Henry Elliot Disting. Svc. award 1992), Am. Soc. Clin. Investigation, Collegium Internat. Neuro-Psychopharmacologicum, Am. Fedn. Clin. Rsch. Ctrl. Soc. Clin. Rsch., Soc. Neuroscis., Sigma Xi, Alpha Omega Alpha, Rho Chi. Jewish. Home: 3315 Walnut Creek Dr N Carmel IN 46032-9038 Office: Ind Univ Sch Medicine Dept Pharmacology and Medicine Indianapolis IN 46202

LEMBERIS, THEODORE THOMAS, international law and law educator; b. LaPorte, Ind., Sept. 15, 1948; s. Thomas Theodore and Helen N. (Pappas) L.; m. Renna T. Theodorakas, Nov. 13, 1978; children: Eleni, Stephanie. BA, Purdue U., 1972; MPA, Roosevelt U., 1978; JD, John Marshall Law Sch., Chgo., 1982. Bar: Ill. 1982, U.S. Dist. Ct. (no. dist.) Ill. 1982. Systems analysis Metro. Reclamation, Chgo., 1979-82; pub. defender Cook County, Chgo., 1982-85; assoc. Hinshaw & Culberson, Chgo., 1985-86; ptnr. Keck, Mahin & Cate, Chgo., 1986-94; prof. law Chgo.-Kent Law Sch., 1994-95; ptnr. Arstein & Lehr, Chgo., 1995—; adj. prof. Chgo.-Kent Law Sch., 1995—. Contbr. articles to profl. jours. Mem. Ill. Bar Assn. (sect. counsil mem.). Greek Orthodox. Avocations: tennis, horse-back riding. Office: Arstein & Lehr Ste 1200 120 S Riverside Plz Rm 1200 Chicago IL 60606-3910

LE MEHAUTE, BERNARD JEAN, marine physics educator; b. St. Brieuc, Bretagne, France, Mar. 29, 1927; m. Marie-Josseline Roy; children by previous marriage: Anne, Patrick. Licence es Scis., U. Toulouse, France, 1951, D in Engring., 1951; D in Advanced Study, U. Paris, 1953; PhD, U. Grenoble, France, 1957. Hydraulic engr. Sogreah, Grenoble, 1953-57; asst. prof. Ecole Polytechnique, Montreal, Can., 1957-59; rsch. prof. Queen's U., Kingston, Ont., Can., 1959-61; dir. geomarine div. Nat. Engring. Sch. Cy., Pasadena, Calif., 1963-66; v.p., sr. v.p., corp. chief engr. TeTraTech. Inc., Pasadena, 1966-78, bd. dirs., 1966-81; chmn. ocean engring dept. Rosenstiel Sch. Marine and Atmospheric Scis., Miami, Fla., 1978-85; prof. applied marine physics U. Miami, 1985-92, prof. emeritus, 1992—. Author: Hydrodynamic and Water Waves, 1976, Ocean Engineering Science, 2 vols., 1990, Water Waves Generated by Explosion. Mem. nat. sea grant adv. bd. NOAA, 1971-78; mem. Coastal Engring. Rsch. Bd., C.E., U.S. Army, 1982-88. Mem. NAE, Am. Shore and Beach Preservation Assn. (bd. dirs. 1966-93, dir. emeritus 1993—), Nat. AC Eng. Republican. Roman Catholic.

LEMER, ANDREW CHARLES, engineer, economist; b. Maxwell Field, Ala., Dec. 25, 1944; s. Samuel Theodore and Carol (Oppenheimer) L.; m. Patricia Spear, Aug. 1967 (div. Dec. 1981); m. Jane Felsten, Aug. 1992; children: Elizabeth Catherine, Daniel Evan. SB, MIT, 1967, SM, 1968, PhD, 1971. Assoc. Alan M. Voorhees & Assoc., Inc., McLean, Va., 1971-76; sr. assoc. PRC Planning & Econs., Inc., McLean, 1976-80; chief planner PRC (Nigeria) Ltd., Lagos, 1980-82; div. v.p. PRC Engring., Inc., McLean, 1982-85; pres. Matrix Group, Inc., Washington, 1985—; dir. bldg. rsch. bd. Nat. Acad. Scis., Washington, 1988-94; cons. Fed. Rail Adminstrn., Washington, 1975, FAA, Washington, 1986—, World Bank, Washington, 1980—, Abell Found., Balt., 1993—, Transp. Rsch. Bd., Washington, 1993—; vis. prof. civil engring. Purdue U., West Lafayette, Ind., 1995—. Prin. author: In Our Own Back Yard: Principles for Improving the Nation's Infrastructure, 1993, Toward Infrastructure Improvement: A Research Agenda, 1994, Solving the Innovation Puzzle: Challenges Facing the U.S. Design and Construction Industry, 1996; contbr. articles to profl. jours.; editl. adv. bd. Jour. Infrastructure Sys., Constrn. Bus. Rev., Constrn. Mgmt. and Econs. Mem. ednl. coun. MIT, Washington, 1974—. Loeb fellow Harvard U., 1992-93. Mem. ASCE, Am. Inst. Cert. Planners, Engring. Soc. Balt., Cosmos Club (Washington). Office: 4701 Keswick Rd Baltimore MD 21210-2322

LEMERT, JAMES BOLTON, journalist, educator; b. Sangerfield, N.Y., Nov. 5, 1935; s. Jesse Raymond and Caroline Elizabeth (Brown) L.; m. Rosalie Martha Bassett, Mar. 23, 1972. AB, U. Calif., Berkeley, 1957, M in Journalism, 1959; PhD, Mich. State U., 1964. Newspaper reporter Oakland (Calif.) Tribune, 1955-56, Chico (Calif.) Enterprise-Record, 1957, 58-60; asst. prof. journalism So. Ill. U., Carbondale, 1964-67; asst. prof. U. Oreg., Eugene, 1967-69, assoc. prof., 1969-76, prof. sch. journalism/comm., 1976—, dir. divsn. comm. rsch., 1967-94, dir. grad. program Sch. Journalism, 1983-86, 88-93; chairperson task force to revise faculty governance U. Oreg., 1983-84, mem. senate, 1981-83, 86-88, 93-94, mem. pres.'s adv. coun., 1990-91, chairperson pres.'s adv. coun., 1991-92, mem. grad. coun., 1984-86, 89-90, 94-96, chairperson grad. coun., 1993-94, chairperson task force on rsch. and grad. edn., 1990-91. Prodr., on-air host Old Grooves show Sta. KWAX-FM, 1977-80, 82-84; author: Does Mass Communication Change Public Opinion After All? A New Approach to Effects Analysis, 1981, Criticizing the Media: Empirical Approaches, 1989, News Verdicts, The Debates and Presidential Campaigns, 1991, Politics of Disenchantment: Bush, Clinton, Perot and the Press, 1996; editor Daily Californian, 1957; contbr. articles to profl. jours., newspapers and mags. Mem. Oreg. Alcohol and Drug Edn. Adv. Com., 1968-69; pres. South Hills Neighborhood Assn., 1976-77, bd. dirs., 1982-84, 86-88; bd. dirs. Traditional Jazz Soc. Oreg., 1981-83, 87; v.p. Met. Cable Access Corp., 1983-84; mem. exec. bd. AAUP, 1975-76, 91-94; mem. state exec. com., head chpt. Assn. Oreg. Faculties, 1981-83, 85-87, state v.p., 1987-89, del. to Oreg. Faculties Polit. Action Com., 1986-89. Recipient Outstanding Journalist award Sigma Delta Chi, 1957, Donald M. McGammon Communication Rsch. Ctr. critical rsch. grantee, 1988-89, Allen Family Found. grantee; NSF fellow, 1963, 64; Calif. Newspaper Pubs. fellow, 1957; Butte County Alumni scholar, 1953-54. Mem. Assn. Edn. in Journalism and Mass Comm. (vice chairperson civic journalism interest group 1995-96), Am. Assn. Pub. Opinion Rsch., Am. Polit. Sci. Assn., Phi Beta Kappa (membership chmn. 1985-86, v.p., pres. 1989-91). Home: PO Box 2224 Waldport OR 97394 *Journalism is one of the more tradition-bound crafts. A constant underlying theme in the research and writing I do is that the research might help journalism redefine itself. There certainly is much need for change in long-held journalistic practices. Habit and "we've always done it this way" are no longer good enough reasons— if they ever were.*

LEMESH, NICHOLAS THOMAS, designer, filmmaker; b. McKees Rocks, Pa., May 21, 1946; s. Nicholas and Sophie (Nowak) L. B.F.A. with honors, Carnegie-Mellon U., 1968; M.F.A., NYU, 1971. Asst. program dir. Kingsley Assn., Pitts., 1968-70; art dir. William Sloane House YMCA, N.Y.C., 1969-71; graphic designer Kahn Assos., N.Y.C., 1971; adminstrv. asst. Grad.

Inst. Film and TV, NYU, 1971-72; v.p., film producer Grey Advt., N.Y.C., 1972—. Youth rep. League of Red Cross Socs. to UN; nat. gov. Nat. ARC, 1970-77, chmn. hist. resources com., Washington, bd. dirs. N.Y. chpt.; U.S. rep. Internat. Red Cross Conf., Geneva, 1969. Recipient Internat. Disting. Service award for humanitarian service Macalester Coll., 1970; CLIO award for comml. excellence, 1984, 86; Andy One Show Houston Film Festival award. Mem. Nat. Inst. Social Scis., Broadcast Advt. Producers Soc. Am. Democrat. Mem. Byzantine Cath. Ch. Home: 240 E 35th St New York NY 10016-4282 Office: 777 3rd Ave New York NY 10017

LEMIEUX, CLAUDE, professional hockey player; b. Buckingham, Que., July 16, 1965. Right wing Montreal Canadiens, 1983-90, N.J. Devils, 1990-95, Colo. Avalanche, 1995—; mem. Stanley Cup Championship teams, 1986, 95, 96. Named to Que. Major Jr. Hockey League All-Star second team, 1983-83, first team, 1984-85; recipient Guy Lafleur trophy, 1985, Conn Smythe trophy for most valuable player in playoffs, 1995. Office: Colo Avalanche McNichols Arena 1635 Clay St Denver CO 80204-1743*

LEMIEUX, JEROME ANTHONY, JR., electrical and computer engineer; b. Fond du Lac, Wis., July 9, 1957; s. Jerome Anthony and Janet Ann (Lehman) L.; m. Cynthia Maureen Hahn, Nov. 29, 1980; children: Angela Kay, Jerome Anthony III. BSEE, U. Wis., 1980; MSEE, Miss. State U., 1984, PhD in Elec. Engring., 1987. Commd. 2d lt. USAF, 1980, advanced through grades to maj.; squadron officer sch. residence program USAF, Maxwell AFB, Ala., 1985; T-38 instr. pilot 50th Flying Tng. Squadron USAF, Columbus AFB, Miss., 1982-86; fighter lead in tng. capt. 434th Tactical Fighter Squadron USAF, Hollomon AFB, N.Mex., 1986; fighter pilot capt. 21st and 562nd Tactical Fighter Squadron USAF, George AFB, Calif., 1986-87; F-16C/F-46 combat ready fighter pilot, flight comdr., instr. pilot, capt. USAF, Spangdahlem Air Base, Germany, 1987-90; ret.; tech. staff mem., sys. and signal processing engr. MIT Lincoln Lab., Lexington, Mass., 1990-94, cons. engr., 1994—; airline pilot Delta Air Lines/Atlanta Internat. Airport, N.Y.C., N.Y., 1991—; R&D engr. MITRE Corp., Bedford, Mass., 1994—; adj. prof. elec. engring. Boston U., 1988-91, U. Md., 1987-88; cons. engr. USAF, Electronic Systems Ctr., Hanscom AFB, Mass., 1994—; chmn. 1995 IEEE Internat. Radar Conf., Washington, com. mem., 1993-97; pres. Bus. Ads Online, Internet Consulting and Design Co.; pres. Bus. Ads Online, 1996—, Am. Aviation, An Advanced Electronics R&D Co., 1991—. Editor: Fourier Analysis Textbook, 1994; contbr. numerous articles to profl. jours. Maj. USAFR, 1990—. Decorated Air Force Commendation medal with oak leaf cluster. Mem. IEEE, IEEE Aerospace and Electronics Sys. Soc., IEEE Signal Processing Soc., IEEE Computer Soc., Alpha Delta Phi, Tau Beta Pi, Eta Kappa Nu, Kappa Mu Epsilon. Avocations: running, weightlifting, reading, computer programming, flying. Home: 6 Unicorn Way Nashua NH 03063-3303 Office: USAF Hanscom AFB/FMXS 9 Eglin St Hanscom AFB MA 01731-2143

LEMIEUX, JOSEPH HENRY, manufacturing company executive; b. Providence, Mar. 2, 1931; s. Mildred L. Lemieux; m. Frances Joanne Schmidt, Aug. 11, 1956; children: Gerald Joseph, Craig Joseph, Kimberly Mae Lemieux Wolff, Allison Jo. Student, Stonehill Coll., 1949-50, U. R.I., 1950-51; BBA summa cum laude, Bryant Coll., 1957. With Owens-Ill., Toledo, 1957—, various positions with glass container div. and closure and metal container group; exec. v.p. Owens-Ill. Owens-Ill., Inc., Toledo, 1984, pres. pkg. ops., 1984, pres., chief oper. officer, 1986-90, pres., chief exec. officer, 1990-91, chmn. bd., chief exec. officer, 1991—, also bd. dirs.; bd. dirs. Ohio Citizens Bank, Toledo, Nat. City Corp., Cleve. Vice chmn. bd. govs. Edison Indsl. Systems Ctr. U. Toledo, 1986. Served to staff sgt. USAF, 1951-55. Named one of Outstanding Young Men Am., Jaycees, 1965. Mem. Glass Packaging Inst. (chmn. 1984-86), Inverness Club (Toledo). Roman Catholic. Avocations: golf, tennis. Office: Owens-Illinois Inc 1 Seagate Toledo OH 43604-1558*

LEMIEUX, LINDA DAILEY, museum director; b. Cleve., Sept. 6, 1953; d. Leslie Leo LeMieux Jr. and Mildred Edna (Dailey) Tutt. BA, Beloit Coll., 1975; MA, U. Mich., 1979; assoc. cert., Mus. Mgmt. Program, Boulder, Colo., 1987. Asst. curator Old Salem, Inc., Winston-Salem, N.C., 1979-82; curator Clarke House, Chgo., 1982-84; curator Western Mus. Mining and Industry, Colorado Springs, Colo., 1985-86, dir., 1987—. Author: Prairie Avenue Guidebook, 1985; editor: The Golden Years--Mines in the Cripple Creek District, 1987; contbr. articles to mags. and newspapers. Fellow Hist. Deerfield, Mass., 1974—. Research grantee Early Am. Industries Assn., 1978. Mem. Am. Assn. Mus., Am. Assn. State and Local History, Colo.-Wyo. Mus. Assn., Colo. Mining Assn., Nev. Mining Assn., Mountain Plains Assn. Mus., Women in Mining. Congregationalist. Home: 1337 Hermosa Way Colorado Springs CO 80906-3050 Office: Western Mus of Mining & Industry 1025 N Gate Rd Colorado Springs CO 80921-3018

LEMIEUX, MARIO, former professional hockey player; b. Montreal, P.Q., Can., Oct. 5, 1965; m. Nathalie Asselin, June 26, 1993; 1 child, Lauren. With Pitts. Penguins, 1984-97; mem. NHL All-Star team, 1987-88, 88-89, 92-93, Stanley Cup Championship team, 1991, 92; player NHL All-Star game, 1992-93. Recipient Hart Meml. trophy for most valuable player, 1988, 89, 96, Conn Smythe trophy for most valuable player in playoff, 1991, Art Ross Meml. trophy, 1987-88, 88-89, 91-92, 92-93, 96, Dodge Performance of the Year award, 1987-88, 88-89, Dodge Ram Tough award, 1988-89, Michel Briere trophy, 1983-84, Jean Beliveau trophy, 1983-84, Michael Bossy trophy, 1983-84, Guy LaFleur trophy, 1983-84, Calder Meml. trophy, 1984-85, Lester B. Pearson award, 1985-86, 87-88, 92-93, Pro Set NHL Player of the Year, 1991-92, Bill Masterson Meml. trophy, 1992-93; named Sporting News All-Star team, 1987-88, 88-89, 92-93, Player of the Year Canadian hockey League, 1983-84, All-Star game MVP, 1985, 88, 90, Player of the Year NHL, 1992-93. Office: Pittsburgh Penguins Civic Arena Gate # 9 Pittsburgh PA 15219*

LEMIEUX, RAYMOND URGEL, chemistry educator; b. Lac La Biche, Alta., Can., June 16, 1920; s. Octave L.; m. Virginia Marie McConaghie, 1948; children: 1 son, 5 daus. BS with honors, U. Alta., 1943; PhD in Chemistry, McGill U., 1946; DSc (hon.), U. N.B., 1967, Laval U., Quebec, 1970, U. Ottawa, 1975, U. Waterloo, 1980, Meml. U., Nfld., 1981, Université du Quebec, 1982, Queen's U., Kingston, 1983, McGill U., Montreal, 1984; Dr. honoris causa, Université de Provence, Marseille, France, 1972; LLD (hon.), U. Calgary, 1979, U. Sask., 1993; DSc (hon.), Université de Sherbrooke, 1986, McMaster U., 1986, U. Alta., 1991; PhD (hon.), U. Stockholm, 1988, U. Stockholm, 1988. Postdoctoral fellow Ohio State U., Columbus, 1946-47; asst. prof. U. Sask., Saskatoon, Can., 1947-49; sr. rsch. officer NRC of Can., Saskatoon, 1949-54; prof., chmn. chemistry dept. U. Ottawa, Can., 1954-61; vice dean, faculty of pure and applied sci. U. Ottawa, 1954-61; prof. organic chemistry U. Alta., Edmonton, Can., 1961-81, Univ. prof., 1981-85, prof. emeritus, 1985—. Author 243 published articles in sci. field. Decorated companion Order of Can.; recipient Louis Pariseau medal, Association Canadienne Francaise pour l'Advancement des Sciences, 1961, Centennial of Can. medal, 1968, award of achievement Province of Alta., 1980, diplome d'Honneur Le Groupe Francais des Glucides, Lyon, France, 1981, Izaak Walton Killam award The Can. Coun., 1981, rsch. prize U. Alta., 1982, Sir Frederick Haultain prize, Govt. Alta., 1982, Tishler award lectr. Harvard U., 1983, Gairdner Foun. Internat. award, 1985, Rhone-Poulenc award Royal Soc. Chemistry, Eng., 1989, King Faisal Internat. prize in sci., 1990, Gold medal Nat. Scis. and Engring. Rsch. Coun. Can., 1991, Manning award of distinction, 1992, PMAC Health Rsch. Found. Medal of Honor, 1992, Albert Einstein award World Cultural Coun., 1992, Gt. Can. award, 1993, Alta. Pioneer award Alta. Sci. and Tech. Found., 1993; inauguration of The Lemieux Lectures, U. Ottawa, 1972; inauguration of The Raymond U. Lemieux Lectures on Biotechnology, U. Alta., 1987; inauguration of The R.U. Lemieux Award for Organic Chemistry, Can. Soc. for Chemistry, 1992; inducted into Alta. Order of Excellence, 1990. Fellow Chem. Inst. Can. (hon., 1st div. award div. organic chemistry 1954, Palladium medal, 1964) Royal Soc. Can., Royal Soc. London, Am. Chem. Soc. (C.S. Hudson award 1966), The Chem. Soc. (Haworth medal 1978), medal of hon. Can. Med. Assn., 1985). Home: 7602 119th St, Edmonton, AB Canada T6G 1W3 Office: U Alta, Dept Chem, Edmonton, AB Canada T6G 2G2

LEMKE, ALAN JAMES, environmental specialist; b. Appleton, Wis., May 22, 1945; s. Edwin R. and Ethel Mae (Noe) L.; m. Joyce Eileen Kruse, May 24, 1975; 1 child, David Edwin. BS in chemistry, Coll. Idaho, 1968. Rsch. chemist Am. Med. Ctr., Denver, 1972-74; chemist U.S. Geol. Survey, Denver, 1975-77; chemist II Occupl. Health Lab., Portland, Oreg., 1977-80, State Hygienic Labs., Des Moines, 1980-82; indsl. hygienist Iowa Divsn. Labor, Des Moines, 1982-88; environ. specialist Iowa Dept. Natural Resources, Spencer, 1988—. Author: The Noe Family's Involvement in the Civil War: A History of Wisconsin's 19th Volunteer Infantry Regiment, 1994. Chmn. Elder Bd., Harvest Evang. Free Ch. Republican. Evangelical. Avocations: camping, hiking, fishing, history, reading. Home: 1110 15th Ave W Spencer IA 51301-2943 Office: Iowa Dept Natural Resources 1900 N Grand Ave Spencer IA 51301-2200

LEMKE, JAMES UNDERWOOD, physicist; b. Grand Rapids, Mich., Dec. 26, 1929; s. Andrew Bertram and Frances (Underwood) L.; m. Ann Stickley, Aug. 1, 1953; children: Catherine, Susan, Michael. BS in Physics, Ill. Inst. Tech., 1959; MS in Physics, Northwestern U., 1960; PhD in Physics, U. Calif., Santa Barbara, 1966. From assoc. to tech. v.p. Armour Rsch. Found., Chgo., 1957-60; dir. Bell & Howell Rsch. Labs., Pasadena, Calif., 1960-68; pres. Spin Physics, Inc. subs. Eastman Kodak, San Diego, 1968-82; fellow rsch. labs. Eastman Kodak, Rochester, N.Y., 1982-86; pres. Rec. Physics, Inc., San Diego, 1986—; founder, dir. Visqus Corp., 1989; adj. prof. U. Calif. at San Diego, LaJolla, 1982—. Contbr. numerous sci. and tech. articles to phys. jours.; patentee in field. Bd. dirs. San Diego Aero-Space Mus., 1982—. Recipient Revelle medal U. Calif. San Diego. Mem. NAE, AAAS, Am. Phys. Soc., Magnetic Soc. (IEEE (Reynold Johnson medal 1995). Democrat. Avocation: airplane pilot.

LEMKE, JUDITH A., lawyer; b. New Rochelle, N.Y., Sept. 28, 1952; d. Thomas Francis and Sara Jane (Blish) Fanelli; m. W. Frederick Lemke, Apr. 1, 1980; 1 child, Morgan Frederick. Student, Manhattanville Coll., Purchase, N.Y., 1970-72; BA, Case Western Res. U., Cleve., 1974, MA, 1975, JD, 1978. Sr. cert. pub. acct. Price Waterhouse, Cleve., 1978-81; assoc. Benesch Friedlander Coplan & Aronoff, Cleve., 1981-85; adjunct faculty Cleve. Marshall Coll. Law, 1982-86; ptnr. Benesch Friedlander Coplan & Aronoff, Cleve., 1986-94; prin. Kahn Kleinman Yanowitz & Arnson Co., Cleve., 1994-95; tax mgr. N.Am./L.Am. tax planning and compliance Chiquita Brands Internat., Cin., 1995—; adj. faculty Case Western Res. U. Sch. of Law, 1993-95. Recipient Elijah Watt Sells award for highest distinction AICPA, N.Y.C. 1979. Mem. ABA, Ohio State Bar Assn., Cleve. Bar Assn., Cleve. Tax Club, Internat. Fiscal Assn., Case Western Res. U. Undergrad. Alumni Assn. (exec. com. 1987-95, trustee 1987-95, chmn. spl. events com. 1989-90, pres. 1990-92, v.p. 1993-94). Avocations: kayaking, wilderness canoe camping, guitar. Home: 7119 Saint Edmunds Dr Cincinnati OH 45230-3879 Office: Chiquita Brands Internat 250 E 5th St Cincinnati OH 45202-4119

LEMKE, LAURA ANN, foreign language educator, assistant principal; b. Hollis, L.I., N.Y., May 4, 1964; d. Ronald Louis Zarobinski and Donna Jean (Strayer) Williams; m. David Michael Lemke, Aug. 25, 1984; 1 child, Kelsey Marie. BA in French and Bus. with honors, Mich. State U., 1987, M in Edn. Adminstrn., 1993. Cert. secondary tchr., vocat. and adminstrn. Teaching asst. East Lansing (Mich.) Pub. Schs., 1985-87, French and bus. tchr. comty. edn., 1985-87; tchr. French and bus. Grand Blanc (Mich.) Comty. Schs., 1987&, coord. elem. fgn. lang., 1990-91, coord. K-12 fgn. lang., 1991-94; chair North Cen. accreditation Grand Blanc Mid. Sch., 1990-96. Vol. Flint Internat. Inst., 1987-91, United Way, Flint, 1992. Mem. Nat. Bus. Edn. Assn. (Award of Merit 1987), Am. Assn. of Tchrs. of French, Mich. Fgn. Lang. Assn. (presider's chair 1994-95), Mich. Bus. Edn. Assn. (Outstanding Bus. Educator award 1986-87), Phi Kappa Phi. Avocations: reading mysteries, camping, traveling. Home: 6057 E Maple Ave Grand Blanc MI 48439-9003 Office: Grand Blanc Comty Schs 11920 S Saginaw St Grand Blanc MI 48439-1402

LEMLE, ROBERT SPENCER, lawyer; b. N.Y.C., Mar. 6, 1953; s. Leo Karl and Gertrude (Bander) L.; m. Roni Sue Kohen, Sept. 5, 1976; children: Zachary, Joanna. AB, Oberlin Coll., 1975; JD, NYU, 1978. Bar: N.Y. 1979. Assoc. Cravath, Swaine & Moore, N.Y.C., 1978-82; assoc. gen. counsel Cablevision Systems Corp., Woodbury, N.Y., 1982-84, v.p., gen. counsel, 1984-86, sr. v.p., gen. counsel, sec., 1986-94, exec. v.p., gen. counsel, sec., 1994—; bd. editors Cable TV and New Media Law and Fin., N.Y.C., 1983—, bd. dirs. Cablevision Systems Corp., 1988—. Bd. trustees L.I. Children's Mus., 1990—, pres., 1996—; bd. trustees Oberlin Coll., 1996—. Mem. ABA, N.Y. State Bar Assn. Avocation: real estate. Home: 7 Grace Dr Old Westbury NY 11568-1228 Office: Cablevision Systems Corp 1 Media Crossway Dr Woodbury NY 11797

LEMLY, THOMAS ADGER, lawyer; b. Dayton, Ohio, Jan. 31, 1943; s. Thomas Moore and Elzabeth (Adger) L.; m. Kathleen Brame, Nov. 24, 1984; children: Elizabeth Hayden, Joanna Marsden, Isabelle Stafford, Kate Brame. BA, Duke U., 1970; JD with honors, U. N.C., 1973. Bar: Wash. 1973, U.S. Dist. Ct. (we. dist.) Wash. 1973, U.S. Ct. Appeals (9th cir.) 1975, U.S. Supreme Ct. 1980. Assoc. Davis Wright Tremaine, Seattle, 1973-79, ptnr., 1979—. Contbg. editor Employment Discrimination Law, 1984-87, 94—; editor Wash., Oreg., Alaska and Calif. Employment Law Deskbooks, 1987—. Chmn. Pacific Coast Labor Conf., Seattle, 1983; trustee Plymouth Congregational Ch., 1980-84, Seattle Opera Assn., 1991—. Mem. ABA (labor employment law sect. 1975—, subcom. chmn. 1984-90, liaison com. 1982-89), Seattle-King County Bar Assn. (chmn. labor sect.), Assn. Wash. Bus. (trustee 1992—, chmn. human resources coun. 1993—, chmn. employment law task force 1987-93), U. N.C. Bar Found. (bd. dirs. 1973-76), Seattle Duke Alumni Assn. (pres. 1979-84), Order of Coif, Wash. Athletic Club (Seattle), Rotary. Republican. Congregationalist. Home: 1614 7th Ave W Seattle WA 98119-2919 Office: Davis Wright Tremaine 2600 Century Sq 1501 4th Ave Seattle WA 98101-1662

LEMMON, GEORGE COLBORNE, bishop; b. St. John, N.B., Can., Mar. 20, 1932; m. Lois Jean Foster, June 7, 1957; children: Paul, Marilu, Robert. BA, U. N.B., 1959; Licentiate in Theology, Wycliffe Coll., Toronto, Can., 1962, BD, 1964, DD (hon.), 1991; DD (hon.), King's Coll., Halifax, N.S., Can., 1990. Ordained deacon Anglican Ch. Can., 1962, priest, 1963. Consecrated bishop Diocese of Fredericton (N.B.), Anglican Ch. Can., 1989—; linotype operator, 10 yrs.; mem. nat. exec. com., nat. stewardship com. Anglican Ch. Can. Columnist The Daily Gleaner, 1986—. Active Mayor's Adv. Com. on Econ. Devel., Fredericton, 1991; sec. Crake Found. Inc.; founding mem. Cons for Christ, Fredericton. Mem. Irenaeus Fellowship. Office: Diocese of Fredericton, 115 Church St, Fredericton, NB Canada E3B 4C8 Home: 791 Brunswick St, Fredericton NB Canada E3B 1H8

LEMMON, JEAN MARIE, editor-in-chief; b. Duluth, Minn., Nov. 11, 1932; d. Lawrence Howard and Marie Julien (Gunderson) H.; m. Richard LuVerne LemMon, Apr. 17, 1965 (div. 1976); 1 child, Rebecca Jean. BA, U. Minn., 1954. Editor Better Homes and Gardens Mag., Des Moines, 1961-63, dept. head crafts, 1985-86, editor-in-chief, 1993—; women's editor Successful Farming, Des Moines, 1963-68; pres. Jean LemMon & Assocs., Des Moines, 1968-84; project editor Meredith Pub. Svcs., Des Moines, 1984-85; editor-in-chief Country Home Mag., Des Moines, 1986-93; adv. bd. Drake U. Journalism Sch., 1991—. Mem. ASCAP, Mensa Internat., Am. Soc. Interior Designers. Office: Better Homes and Gardens 1716 Locust St Des Moines IA 50309-3038*

LEMMON, PHILIP DOUGLAS, publishing company executive; b. Pocatello, Idaho, Sept. 4, 1943; s. Eugene and Shirley (Walton) L.; m. M. Kathleen Jensen; Dec. 13, 1943; children: Kari, Steven. Student, Idaho State U., 1961-63, 67. Regular performances Egyptian Theatre; Boise on Robert Morton Theatre Pipe Organ; conductor Church Organist Seminars; recital series for Dunkley Music Boise; Instn. sales dir. Dunkley Music, Boise; tchr., arranger, composer; owner Douglas Pub. Co., Spiral Studios and Prodns., Odyssey Records. Author: By Special Invitation, 1983, Preludes for Workshop I, II, Essentials for Organists, 1986, Beginning Organist Workshop, 1985, Sweet Is the Work, 1991, Biography of J.J. McClellen - Organist of the Mormon Tabernacle. Mem. Egyptian Theatre Organ Found. (chmn.), Am. Guild Organists. Republican. Mem. LDS Ch. Avocations: theatre pipe organ restoration, concerts, workshops for church organists and theatre organists, arranging, oil painting. Home: 8465 Westchester Ave Boise ID 83704-4375

LEMNIOS, ANDREW ZACHERY, aerospace engineer, educator, researcher; b. Newburyport, Mass., Nov. 23, 1931; s. Zaharias Vasilios and Evangelia (Malamoglou) L.; m. Aspasia Soula Hanos, Sept. 26, 1954; children: Karen Eve, Keith Harold. SB, MIT, 1953, SM, 1954; PhD, U. Conn., 1967; grad. advanced mgmt. program, Harvard U., 1983. Rsch. engr. United Techs. Rsch., East Hartford, Conn., 1954-60; sr. analytical engr. Kaman Aerospace Corp., Bloomfield, Conn., 1961-63, chief of fluid mechanics, 1963-68, chief rsch. engr., 1969-76, dir. rsch. and tech., 1976-89, asst. v.p. rsch. and tech. programs, 1989-93; adj. prof. Western New Eng. Coll., Springfield, Mass., 1956-76, U. Mass., Amherst, 1976-78; mem. aeronautics adv. com. NASA, Washington, 1979-84; mem. rotorcraft adv. com. Rensselaer Poly. Inst., Troy, N.Y., 1985-92, rsch. prof., dir., 1993—; mem. rotorcraft adv. com. U. Md., College Park, 1985-92, Ga. Inst. Technology, Atlanta, 1985-92. Patentee controllable twist rotor, rotor trim tab. Fellow AIAA (assoc.); mem. Am. Helicopter Soc. Republican. Greek Orthodox. Avocations: carpentry, gardening, music, reading. Home: 144 Primrose Dr Longmeadow MA 01106-2534 Office: Rensselaer Polytechnic Inst Rotorcraft Tech Ctr Jonsson Engring Ctr Troy NY 12180

LEMOINE, PAMELA ALLYSON, assistant principal; b. Mansura, La., Sept. 6, 1945; d. Levy Paul and Iva Rae (Paul) L. BA in English, Libr. Sci., Nicholls State U., 1967; MEd in Ednl. Tech., McNeese State U., 1976; postgrad., Pepperdine U., 1978-80, Boston U., 1980-82. Libr. Evergreen Jr. High Sch., Houma, La., 1967-69, Zukiran Elem. Sch., Okinawa, Japan, 1969-70, Goose Bay High Sch., Labrador, Can., 1970-72, Matthew Perry Sch., Iwakuni, Japan, 1972-76; head libr., audio-visual specialist Kubasaki High Sch., Okinawa, 1978-80; libr. Bamberg (Germany) Am. High Sch., 1980-82; tchr. Evergreen Jr. High Sch., Houma, 1982-83; libr. Lisa Park Elem. Sch., Houma, 1983-84; audio-visual specialist H.L. Bourgeois High Sch., Houma, 1984-85; asst. prin. Lisa Park Elem. Sch., Houma, 1985—; cons. librarian Dept. Def. Schs., Bamberg, 1980-82. Contbr. articles to mags. Pres. Friends of the Libr., Houma, 1988, Houma-Terrebonne Arts and Humanities Coun., 1992-93, treas., 1989-91; bd. dirs. Terrebonne Libr. Bd. Control., Houma, 1990—. Named Outstanding Tchr. of Yr. Dept. Def. Schs., 1979, 81. Mem. NEA, Terrebonne Prin.'s Assn. (corr. sec. 1991), Phi Delta Kappa, Delta Kappa Gamma. Avocations: gardening, sewing, crafts, writing. Home: 116 Westview Dr Houma LA 70364-2534 Office: Lisa Park Sch 1900 Willie Lou Ave Houma LA 70364-2556

LEMOLE, GERALD MICHAEL, surgeon; b. S.I., N.Y., Dec. 17, 1936; s. Joseph Michael and Mary (Boylan) L.; B.S. in Biology, Villanova U., 1958; M.D., Temple U., 1962; m. Emily Jane Asplundh, Dec. 8, 1962; children—Lisa Jane, Laura Leigh, Emily Anne, Gerald Michael, Samantha Mary, Christopher Robin. Intern, S.I. Hosp., 1962-63; resident in gen. surgery Temple U., Phila., 1963-67; resident in thoracic surgery Baylor Affiliated Hosps., Houston, 1967-69; practice medicine specializing in cardio thoracic surgery, Phila., 1969—, Browns Mills, N.J., 1972-84; chief sect. cardiac and thoracic surgery Temple U. Hosp., Phila., 1970-77; prof. surgery Temple U. Health Scis. Ctr., 1975-77; chmn. dept. surgery Deborah Heart and Lung Ctr., Phila., 1972-84; chief sect. cardiovascular surgery Med. Ctr. Del.; vis. prof. cardiac surgery U. Dublin (Ireland), 1974, U. Istanbul, Turkey, 1982, Mil. Med. Coll., Ankara, Turkey, 1985, Beijing Heart Inst., 1991; clin. prof. surgery U. Pa., 1979, Rutgers Med. Sch. Diplomate Am. Bd. Surgery, Am. Bd. Thoracic Surgery. Recipient Disting. Alumnus award VIllanova U., 1987. Fellow ACS, Am. Coll. Cardiology, Am. Coll. Chest Physicians (cardiovascular com. 1974—); mem. Phila. Coll. Physicians, Am. Assn. Thoracic Surgery, Am. Fedn. Clin. Research, Am., Pan Am. thoracic socs., Internat., Cardiovascular Soc., Denton A. Cooley Cardiovascular Surg. Soc., Am. Coll. Angiology, Pa., Phila. County med. socs., Phila. Acad. Surgery, Phila. Acad. Cardiology (pres. 1976-79, chmn. exec. com. 1976—), Assn. Acad. Surgeons, Soc. Vascular Surgery, Pa. Assn. Thoracic Surgeons, AMA, Am. Heart Assn. (cardiovascular council 1973—, pres. Del. chpt. 1991, chmn. bd. dirs. 1992), Pa. Assn. Thoracic Surgery (program chmn. 1975—). Contbr. numerous articles on cardiovascular surgery and disease to med. jours.; research in cardiovascular physiology. Home: 404 Tomlinson Rd Huntingdon Valley PA 19006-4818 Office: Med Ctr Del 4745 Ogletown Stanton Rd # 20 Newark DE 19713-2067

LEMON, HENRY MARTYN, physician, educator; b. Chgo., Dec. 23, 1915; s. Harvey Brace and Louise (Birkhoff) L.; m. Harriet Tuxbury Qua, May 3, 1941 (dec. Jan. 1976); children—Elizabeth Anne Lemon Snell, Harvey Brace, Stanley Moncrief, David Tuxbury, Jennifer Jane Lemon Dewitt; m. Dorothy Campbell, May 28, 1976. B.S., U. Chgo., 1938; M.D. cum laude, Harvard U., 1940. Diplomate: Am. Bd. Internal Medicine, Am. Bd. Med. Oncology. Intern Billings Hosp., Chgo., 1940-41; asst. resident medicine Billings Hosp., 1941-42; asst. dept. medicine U. Chgo., 1942-43; chief med. resident Univ. Hosp., Boston, 1946-48; instr. medicine Boston U., 1946-48, asst. prof. medicine, 1948-54, assoc. prof., 1954-61; dir. Eugene C. Eppley Cancer Inst. U. Nebr. Coll. Medicine, Omaha, 1961-68, prof. internal Medicine, 1961-86, emeritus prof., 1986—; cons. internal medicine VA, Boston, Omaha, 1950-86; bd. dirs. Mass., Nebr. divs. Am. Cancer Soc. Served to capt. M.C. U.S. Army, 1943-46; col. USAR; ret. Recipient Disting. Service award U. Chgo. Med. Alumni, 1952, awards of merit AMA Sci. Exhibits, 1957, 1962, 1965, Disting. Teaching award U. Nebr. Med. Center, 1976, Meritorious Service award, 1980, Margaret Hay Edwards medal Am. Assn. Cancer Edn., 1989. Fellow ACP; mem. AMA, Am. Assn. Cancer Research, Am. Soc. Clin. Oncology, Endocrine Soc., Soc. Surg. Oncology, Central Soc. Clin. Research, Planned Parenthood Omaha and Council Bluffs (pres. 1990), Res. Officers Assn., Phi Beta Kappa, Phi Beta Kappa Assocs. Omaha (pres. 1985-87), Sigma Xi (Disting. Research award U. Nebr. chpt. 1985), Alpha Omega Alpha. Unitarian. Club: Rotary. Rsch. in air-borne infection, Cytodiagnosis Pancreatic cancer, transplantation human cancer to hamsters, estrogen imbalance in breast cancer, endocrine and chemotherapy cancer, reduction toxicity in cancer chemotherapy, estriol prevention breast cancer, carcinogenesis breast, leukemia and lymphoma. Home: 600 S 42d St Omaha NE 68198-3330 Office: U Nebr Dept Internal Medicine Omaha NE 68198-3330 *My medical life in service, education and research has taken place during the golden age of American medicine, a period of unprecedented growth in our ability to diagnose and treat most diseases. My work has received inestimable benefit from those who were my teachers, and I have found my own greatest reward in attempting to illuminate the paths of my students; this fact and the privilege of serving my patients have been my chief professional guides along the way.*

LEMON, JIM, radio station executive. Gen. mgr. WLUW-FM, Chgo. Office: WLUW-FM 820 N Michigan Ave Chicago IL 60611-2103

LEMON, LESLIE GENE, consumer services company executive; b. Davenport, Iowa, June 14, 1940. BS, U. Ill., 1962, LLB, 1964. Bar: Ill. 1964, Ariz. 1972. Asst. gen. counsel Am. Farm Bur. Fedn., Chgo., 1964-69; sr. atty. Armour and Co., Chgo., 1969-71; with Viad Corp (formerly The Dial Corp and The Greyhound Corp.), Phoenix, 1971—; gen. counsel The Dial Corp (formerly Greyhound Corp.), Phoenix, 1977-96, v.p., 1979—; bd. dirs. FINOVA Group, 1992—. Vestryman All Saints Episcopal Ch., Phoenix, 1975-81; trustee Phoenix Art Mus., 1985—; bd. dirs. Phoenix Children's Hosp., 1985—; bd. visitors U. Calif. Med. Sch., Davis, 1983—. Mem. ABA, Assn. Gen. Counsel, Maricopa County Bar Assn., State Bar Ariz., Phoenix C. of C. (bd. dirs. 1989-95), Am. Arbitration Assn. (bd. dirs. 1996—), Food the Drug Law Inst. (bd. dirs. 1995-97). Home: 1136 W Butler Dr Phoenix AZ 85021-4428 Office: Viad Corp 1850 N Central Ave Phoenix AZ 85004-4527

LEMON, RALPH, choreographer; b. Cin., Aug. 1, 1952; m. Mary Good; 1 child, Chelsea. Student, U. Minn. Worked with Meredith Monk, N.Y.C.; founded troupe Ralph Lemon Co., N.Y.C., 1985-95; founded Mixed Blood Theater Co., Mpls. Worked and performed with Nancy Hauser, Mpls.; selected dances Boundary Water, 1984, Flock, 1986, And the Jungle Will Obliterate the Shrine/Seasons, 1986, Two, 1987, Les Noces, 1987, Wanda in the Awkward Age, 1987, Nightingales and Fishermen, 1987, Happy Trails, 1988, Punchinello, 1988, Joy, 1989, Solo, 1990, Bogus Pomp, 1990, Folkdances, 1991, Persephone, 1991 (Gold medal), Phrases Almost Biblical, 1993, Their Eyes Rolled Back in Ecstacy, 1993, Threestep (Shipwreck), 1995, Killing Tulips, 1995. Recipient Boston Ballet's ann. choreography competition winner, 1988. Office: PO Box 143 New York NY 10011

LEMON, ROBERT GRANVILLE, retired baseball player; b. San Bernadino, Calif., Sept. 22, 1920. Baseball player Cleve. Indians, 1941-58; mgr. Kansas City Royals, 1970-72, Chgo. White Sox, 1977-78, N.Y. Yankees, 1978-82. Named to Baseball Hall of Fame, 1976, Minor League Mgr. of Yr. Sporting News, 1966; mgr. N.Y. Yankees World Series Champions, 1978; selected to Am. League All-Star Team, 1948-54. Office: c/o Nat Baseball Hall Fame PO Box 590 Cooperstown NY 13326-0590

LEMONICK, AARON, physicist, educator; b. Phila., Feb. 2, 1923; s. Samuel and Mary (Ferman) L.; m. Eleanor Leah Drutt, Feb. 12, 1950; children—Michael Drutt, David Morris. B.A., U. Pa., 1950; M.A., Princeton U., 1952, Ph.D., 1954. Asst. prof. physics Haverford Coll., Pa., 1954-57, assoc. prof., 1957-61; assoc. prof. Princeton U., N.J., 1961-64, prof., 1964-94, assoc. chmn. dept. physics, 1967-69, dean grad. sch., 1969-73, dean faculty, 1973-89, dean of faculty emeritus, 1989—; assoc. dir. Princeton-Pa. Accelerator, 1961-67; prof. emeritus Princeton U., N.J., 1994—; v.p. Princeton U. Press, 1973—; dep. dir. Princeton Plasma Physics Lab., 1989-90. Trustee Bryn Mawr Coll., 1988—, Princeton Day Sch. Fellow AAAS, Am. Phys. Soc.; mem. AAUP, Am. Assn. Physics Tchrs., Phi Beta Kappa, Sigma Xi. Office: Princeton U Dept Physics Princeton NJ 08544

LEMONNIER, DANIEL BRIAN, small business owner, entertainer; b. Chgo., Dec. 3, 1955; s. Edwin Peter and Rita Delores (Riordan) LeM; m. Shari L. Smith, May 27, 1995; 1 child, Flynn Jered. BFA, Marquette U., 1978; MFA, DePaul U., 1980. Asst. mgr. DePaul U. Goodman Sch. Children's Theater, Chgo., 1983-86; mascot (Benny the Bull) Chgo. Bulls, 1986—; owner, mgr. Folksongs and Foolery Entertainment, Chgo., 1987—; actor, mem. ensemble Illustrated Theatre Co., Evanston, Ill., 1983-87; mem. ensemble Face to Face Prodns., Chgo., 1988—; promotions mascot Chgo. White Sox, 1984-88; dir. storytelling festival Chgo. Children's Mus., 1992—; creative cons. Kimberly Clark, Appleton, Wis., 1990—; devel. com. Victor C. Neumann Assn., 1993—. Author: (videotape) Grimms in America, 1990; writer plays Prairie Visions, 1991, Mad Anthony and the New Nation, 1992; performed at Pres. Clinton's 1997 Inauguration festivities. Mem. benefit adv. bd. Body Politic Theatre, 1991—; bd. dirs. Diamond Back Theatre, 1993—. Recipient gold medal Operation Snowball, 1988, commendation VA Med. Ctr., North Chicago, Ill., 1990, Soc. Security Admin., 1993, Gale Sayers/Mark Lund Children's Home, 1993; scholar Chgo. Drama League, 1979, Sara Siddons Soc., 1980, Spirit award Marquette U. Club Chgo., 1994. Mem. Nat. Assn. for Preservation and Proliferation Storytelling, Chgo. Assn. Profl. Performing Artists for Children, NOW, Roscoe Village Neighbors Assn., Victor C. Neumann Assn. (bd. dirs.). Avocations: long distance running, travel, reading, playing folk music on guitar, banjo, auto harp, mandolin and dulcimer. Office: Folk Songs and Foolery Entertainment 3443 N Leavitt St Chicago IL 60618-6013

LE MONS, KATHLEEN ANN, portfolio manager, investment broker; b. Trenton, N.J., Apr. 6, 1952; d. Albert Martin and Veronica Grace (Kerr) LeM.; m. Walter Everett Faircloth, Apr. 15, 1978 (div. Dec. 1988); m. Jeffery West Benedict, June 29, 1991. Attended, Rollins Coll., 1970-71, Fla. State U., 1971-76; BSBA magna cum laude, Christopher Newport U., 1995; postgrad., Coll. William and Mary, 1995—. Registered rep. NASD/NYSE, investment advisor; cert. portfolio mgr. Sci. rsch. assoc. NASA, Hampton, Va., 1973-76; fin. cons. Merrill Lynch Pierce Fenner Smith, Hampton, 1985-88; cert. portfolio mgr. Wheat First Butcher Singer, Newport News, Va., 1988—. Pres. James Landing Assn., 1991-95; life mem. Capital Dist. Found., 1992; mem. exec. panel fund distbn. Va. Peninsula United Way, 1996-97; Hampton Rds. chair March of Dimes Walk Am., 1996—; bd. dirs. Greater Hampton Rds. March of Dimes Found., 1997—. George F. Hixson fellow Kiwanis Internat., 1996. Mem. Am. Mktg. Assn., Va. Peninsula C. of C. (transp. task force 1993-97, govtl. affairs task force 1993—), Oyster Point Kiwanis (charter), Coll. of William and Mary Part-Time MBA Assn. (charter, curriculum com. chair 1995—, v.p. 1996—), Christopher Newport U. Pres.' Coun., Christopher Newport Univ. Alumni Soc. (bd. dirs. 1996—), Mensa, James River Country Club (9-hole golf group), Alpha Chi. Republican. Avocations: golf, snowskiing. Home: 61 Queens Ct Newport News VA 23606-2034 Office: Wheat First Butcher Singer 11817 Canon Blvd Newport News VA 23606-2569

LEMONS, L. JAY, academic administrator; b. Chadron, Nebr., Aug. 30, 1959; s. Larry Dean and LaVana Lee (Smith) L.; m. Marsha Louise Shone, May 27, 1984; children: Olivia Jaye, Magdalene Marie. BS, BA, Nebr. Wesleyan U., 1983; MEd, U. Nebr., 1985; PhD, U. Va., 1991. Cert. phys. edn. tchr., health edn. tchr. Hall dir. office residence life Nebr. Wesleyan U., Lincoln, 1982-84; grad. asst. to dir. admissions office admissions and advising U. Nebr., Lincoln, 1984-85; asst. area coord. dept. student affairs Tex. A&M U., College Station, 1985-86, area coord. dept. student affairs, 1986-88; grad. asst. to dean Curry Sch. Edn. U. Va., Charlottesville, 1988-89, intern Curry Sch. Edn. Found., 1989, intern office of pres., 1989-90, asst. to pres., 1990—; chancellor U. Va., Wise, Va., 1992—; summer conf. program chair divsn. student svcs. Tex. A&M, 1987; presenter S.W. Assn. Coll. Univ. Housing Officers Conf., 1987, ann. minority student recruitment and retention conf. Tex. Higher Edn. Coord. Bd., 1988; bd. dirs. S.W. Va. Higher Edn. Ctr., Abingdon, S.W. Va. Pub. Edn. Consortium, Wise, Clinch Valley Coll. Found. Contbr. articles to profl. jours. Recipient Outstanding Young Men of Am. award, 1986, Gov.'s fellowship, 1988-90, Annette Gibbs Rsch. and Publ. award, 1990. Mem. Am. Assn. Counseling and Devel., Am. Coll. Personnel Assn. (presenter nat. conf. 1986), Nat. Assn. Student Personnel Adminstrs. (participant new profl.'s inst. region III 1987, local arrangements com. mem. fall conf. 1988, registration chair Tex. state conf. 1988, program coord. state conf. 1989, 90, presenter region IV west conf. 1986, nat. conf. 1988, region III chief student affairs officers workshop 1988, ann. conf. 1991, Outstanding New Profl. award region III 1987), Assn. Study Higher Edn., So. Assn. Coll. Student Affairs (registration chair devel. theories workshop 1988, presenter ann. conf. 1987), Blue Key Nat. Honor Soc., Kappa Delta Pi (Outstanding Edn. Student award 1983). Office: Univ Va Clinch Valley Coll College Ave Wise VA 24293

LEMOS, RAMON MARCELINO, philosophy educator; b. Mobile, Ala., July 7, 1927; s. Marcelino and Marie Louise (Moore) L.; m. Mamie Lou McCrory, Dec. 26, 1951 (dec. Apr. 1990); children: Noah Marcelino, William Ramon, Christopher Tait, John Paul; m. Anne Craft, Aug. 7, 1994. B.A., U. Ala., 1951; M.A., Duke, 1953, Ph.D., 1955; Fulbright scholar, U. London, Eng., 1955-56. Mem. faculty U. Miami, 1956—, prof. philosophy, 1967—, chmn. dept., 1971-84. Author: Experience, Mind and Value, 1969, Rousseau's Political Philosophy, 1977, Hobbes and Locke: Power and Consent, 1978, Rights, Goods, and Democracy, 1986, Metaphysical Investigations, 1988, The Nature of Value: Axiological Investigations, 1995. Served with USMC, 1945-49. Named Outstanding Tchr. U. Miami, 1968. Mem. Am. Philos. Assn. (program chmn. Eastern div. meeting 1983), Fla. Philos. Assn. (pres. 1963), Phi Beta Kappa, Phi Kappa Phi, Omicron Delta Kappa. Home: 6960 SW 82nd Ct Miami FL 33143-2509 Office: U Miami Dept Philosophy Coral Gables FL 33124

LEMPERT, PHILIP, advertising executive, author, syndicated columnist, TV correspondent; b. East Orange, N.J., Apr. 17, 1953; s. Sol and Lillian E. L.; married Laura Gray; 1 son. BS in Mktg., Drexel U., 1974; degree in Package Design, Pratt Inst., 1978. With Lempert Co., Belleville, N.J., 1974-89; pres. Consumer Insight, Inc., 1990-96; sr. v.p., sr. ptnr. AGE Wave Inc., 1991-93; columnist Chgo. Tribune, 1993—, Knight-Ridder/Tribune Syndicate; correspondent Today Show, WGN-TV, KTLA-TV, WGNX-TV, Tribune TV; Columnist, Supermarket News, founder, CEO Supermarket Alliance, 1993—; adj. prof. Fairleigh Dickinson U., Seton Hall U. Pub., editor newsletter The Lempert Report; also TV corr., lectr. Author: Phil Lempert's Supermarket Shopping and Value Guide, 1996, Top Ten Trends for Baby Boomers for Business, 1997. Chmn. Tribune Food Task Force, 1996—; host Shopping Smart WOR Radio Network. Mem. Am. Assn. Advt. Agencies (bd. govs. 1986-88, legis. liason 1988-90, legis. coord. 1987-90), Nat. Food Brokers Assn. (chmn. food svcs. com.). Office: Tribune Broadcasting 5800 Sunset Blvd Hollywood CA 90028

LEMPERT, RICHARD OWEN, lawyer, educator; b. Hartford, Conn., June 2, 1942; s. Philip Leonard and Mary (Steinberg) L.; m. Cynthia Ruth Willey, Sept. 10, 1967; 1 child, Leah Rose. A.B., Oberlin Coll., 1964; J.D., U. Mich., 1968, Ph.D. in Sociology, 1971. Bar: Mich. 1978. Asst. prof. law U. Mich., Ann Arbor, 1968-72, assoc. prof., 1972-74, prof. law, 1974—, prof. sociology, 1985—, Francis A. Allen collegiate prof. law, 1990—, acting chair dept. sociology, 1993-94, chair dept. sociology, 1995—; Mason Ladd disting. vis. prof. U. Iowa Law Sch., 1981; vis. fellow Centre for Socio-Legal Rsch., Wolfson Coll., Oxford (Eng.) U., 1982; mem. adv. panel for law and social sci. div. NSF, 1976-79, mem. exec. com. adv. com. for social sci., 1979; mem. com. law enforcement and adminstrn. of justice NRC, vice chmn., 1984-87, chmn., 1987-89; mem. adv. panel NSF program on Human Dimensions of Global Change, 1989, 92—; mem. com. on DNA technology in forensic sci. NRC, 1989-92, com. on drug testing in workplace, 1991-93. Author: (with Stepehn Saltzburg) A Modern Approach to Evidence, 1977, 2d edit., 1983; (with Joseph Sanders) An Invitation to Law and Social Science, 1986, Under the Influence, 1993; editor: (with Jacques Normand and Charles O'Brien) Under the Influence? Drugs and the American Work Force, 1994; editorial bd. Law and Soc. Rev., 1972-77, 89-92, editor, 1982-85; editorial bd. Evaluation Rev., 1979-82, Violence and Victims, 1985—, Jour. Law and Human Behavior, 1980-82; contbr. articles to profl. jours. Fellow Ctr. for Advanced Study in Behavioral Scis., 1994-95. Fellow Am. Acad. Arts and Scis.; mem. Am. Sociol. Assn. (chair sect. sociology of law 1995-96), Law and Society Assn. (trustee 1977-80, 90-93, exec. com. 1979-80, 82-87), Soc. Am. Law Tchrs., Order of Coif, Phi Beta Kappa, Phi Kappa Phi. Office: U Mich Law Sch 625 S State St Ann Arbor MI 48109-1215

LEMR, JAMES CHARLES, geriatrics nurse; b. Painesville, Ohio, May 24, 1951; s. James Robert and Helene Gloria (Maycroft) L.; children: Melissa Ann, James Robert. Diploma, Willoughby-Eastlake Sch. Practical Nursing, 1984. Cert. pharmacology, basic life support A.H.A., IV therapy, sports medicine. Charge nurse C.L.P.N. Maple Nursing Home, Chesterland, Ohio, 1991-94, Chardon (Ohio) Quality Care, 1994-96, Mentor (Ohio) Way Care Ctr., 1996—. Mem. Lic. Practical Nurse Assn. Ohio. Home: PO Box 883 Painesville OH 44077-0883

LENAHAN, WALTER CLAIR, retired foreign service officer; b. Everett, Wash., Apr. 20, 1934; s. James Harold and Doris Anne (Larson) L.; m. Patricia Anne Casey, July 6, 1957; children—Karen Diane, Desiree, Lorelei, Casey James. B.A., U. Oreg., 1960. Commd. fgn. service officer Dept. State, 1961; officer Dept. State, Washington, 1961-72, U.S. Embassy, Beijing, People's Republic of China, 1979-81, Dept. Commerce, Washington, 1981-86; dep. asst. sec. for textiles and apparel Dept. Commerce, 1982-86; v.p. Am.-Philippine Fiber Industry, Inc., Manila, 1972-76; pres. Internat. Bus. and Econ. Research Corp., Washington, 1986-95; retired, 1995. Served to sgt. U.S. Army, 1953-56. Recipient Sr. Fgn. Service Presdl. award Dept. State, 1984. Lutheran. Avocations: tennis; contract bridge.

LENARD, GEORGE DEAN, lawyer; b. Joliet, Ill., Aug. 26, 1957; s. Louis George and Jennie (Helopoulos) L.; m. Nancy Ilene Sundquist, Nov. 11, 1989. BS, Ill. State U., 1979; JD, Thomas Cooley Law Sch., 1984. Bar: Ill. 1984, U.S. Dist. Ct. (no. dist.) Ill. 1984, U.S. Supreme Ct. 1990. Asst. states atty. Will County States Attys. Office, Joliet, 1984-88; asst. pub. defender Will County Pub. Defenders Office, Joliet, 1988-95; pvt. practice law Joliet, 1988—. Mem. ABA, ATLA, Nat. Assn. Criminal Def. Lawyers, Ill. State Bar Assn., Chgo. Bar Assn., Phi Alpha Delta (Isaac P. Christiancy chpt.). Avocations: target shooting, golf, baseball. Office: 81 N Chicago St Ste 206 Joliet IL 60432-4383

LENARD, MICHAEL BARRY, merchant banker, lawyer; b. Chgo., May 20, 1955; s. Henry Madart and Jacqueline Jo Anne (Silver) L.; m. Amy Jeanne Rifenbergh, Oct. 10, 1987; children: Madeline M., Nicholas X. BBA, U. Wis., 1977; postgrad., NYU, 1981-82; JD, U. So. Calif., 1982. Assoc. Whitman & Ransom, N.Y.C., 1982-83; assoc. Latham & Watkins, L.A., 1984-91, ptnr., 1992-93; mng. dir., counsellor William E. Simon & Sons, L.A., 1993—; bd. dirs. William E. Simon & Sons (Asia), Hong Kong, Wallem Simon Asian Shipping Investments, Ltd., Hong Kong, Wyle Labs., L.A., Creative Optics, Phoenix, Internat. Logistics, Ltd., Chgo. With So. Calif. Law Rev. mag., 1980-81. V.p. U.S. Olympic Com., 1989-96, mem. exec. com., bd. dirs., 1985-96, mem. athletes' adv. coun., 1981-89, vice chmn. athletes' adv. coun., 1985-89; named to Internat. Coun. for Arbitration of Sport, Internat. Olympic Com., 1994—; bd. dirs. L.A. Sports Coun., 1988—, Atlanta Com. for Olympic Games, 1990—. Named semi-finalist Outstanding Undergrad. Achievement award, 1977, USA Team Handball Athlete of Yr., 1985, USOC Olympian Mag. Team Handball SportsMan of Yr., 1985, Nat. Champion in Team Handball, 1975, 77, 79, 80, 82, 87, 95; recipient Harry A. Bullis scholarship, 1977, Disting. Svc. award U.S. Sports Acad., 1996; mem. 1984 Olympic Team, U.S. Nat. Team, 1977-85 (capt. 1985). Mem. Order of the Coif, Phi Kappa Phi, Beta Gamma Sigma, Beta Alpha Psi, Phi Eta Sigma. Home: 1433 El Bosque Ct Pacific Palisades CA 90272-1915 Office: William E Simon & Sons 10990 Wilshire Blvd Ste 1750 Los Angeles CA 90024-3913

LENARDON, ROBERT JOSEPH, classics educator; b. Fort William, Ont., Can., Sept. 8, 1928; came to U.S., 1949; s. Louis and Nina (Boffa) L. BA with honors in Latin, U. B.C., Can., 1949; MA in Classics, U. Cin., 1950, PhD, 1954. Instr. Greek and Latin Columbia, 1954-57; asst. prof. classics U. Wash., Seattle, 1957-59; mem. faculty dept. classics Ohio State U., Columbus, 1959—; assoc. prof. Ohio State U., 1963-69, prof., dir. grad. studies, 1969-84, prof. emeritus, 1984-92; prof., head dept. classics Siena Coll., 1992-95; vis. prof. U. B.C., summers 1960-61, 66, NYU, 1973, 91-92. Author: (with Mark P.O. Morford) Classical Mythology, 1971, 5th edit., 1995, A Companion to Classical Mythology, 1997; The Saga of Themistocles, 1977; book rev. editor Classical Jour., 1961-68. Taft scholar and fellow, 1950-54; vis. fellow Corpus Christi Coll., Cambridge (Eng.) U., 1971. Mem. Am. Philol. Assn. Home: 62 Willett St Albany NY 12210-1140

LENCEK, RADO L., Slavic languages educator; b. Mirna, Slovenia, Oct. 3, 1921; came to U.S., 1956; s. Ludovik Ivan and Kati (Jaksa) L.; m. Nina A. Lovrencic, May 4, 1946; children: Bibi-Alice, Lena-Maria. Studied Slavic philology, U. Ljubljana, Slovenia, 1940-45, U. Padova, Italy, 1946-47; teaching diploma, Istituto Magistrale, Gorizia, Italy, 1947; MA in Linguistics, U. Chgo., 1959; PhD in Slavic Langs., Harvard U., 1962. Asst. prof. Istituto Magistrale Sloveno, Gorizia-Trieste, Italy, 1944-55; editor USIS-Trieste, Italy, 1951-54; asst. prof. U. Ill., Urbana, 1962-65; asst. prof. Slavic langs. Columbia U., N.Y.C., 1965-69, assoc. prof., 1969-74, prof., 1974-92, prof. emeritus, 1992—; assoc. Averell Harriman Inst. for Advanced Study of the Soviet Union; mem. Inst. on East Cen. Europe; vis. assoc. prof. NYU, 1969-72; vis. prof. Yale U., 1974, U. Ill., Urbana, 1977; coord. Nat. Com. Serbo-Croatian Teaching Materials, 1982—; U.S. coord. for Cooperation Project on Slavistics, 1983—; active U.S.-USSR Commn. on the Humanities and Social Scis., Inst. East Ctrl. Europe; participant Internat. Congs. of Slavists Prague, 1968, Warsaw, 1973, Zagreb-Ljubljana, 1978, Kiev, 1983, Sofia, 1988, Bratislava, 1993; coord. Columbia U. Program in Slavic Cultures, organized symposia Columbia U., 1974, 84, Prato di Resia, Italy, 1979, Northwestern U., 1980, U. Chgo., 1984, Acad. of Scis. USSR, Moscow, 1987, Am. Assn. Tchrs. of Slavic and East European Langs. Annual Convention, San Francisco, 1991, Toronto, Can., 1993; mem. adv. bd. Slovenski jezik-Slovene Linguistic Studies, 1994—. Author: Ob Jadranu, Ethnographic Studies, 1947, The Verb Pattern of Contemporary Slovene, 1966, A Bibliographical Guide to Slavic Civilizations, 1966, An Outline of the Course on Slavic Civilizations, 1970, 2d edit., 1978, The Structure and History of Slovene Language, 1982, Slovenes, The Eastern Alpine Slavs, and Their Cultural Heritage, 1989, The Correspondence Between Jan Baudouin de Courtenay (1845-1929) and Vatroslav Oblak (1864-96), 1992, Izbrane Razprave in Eseji (selected papers and essays), 1996; editor: (with others): Xenia Slavica, Gojko Ruzicic Festschrift, 1975, The Dilemma of the Melting Pot: The Case of the South Slavic Languages, 1976, To Honor Jernej Kopitar, 1780-1980, 1982, A Bibliography of Recent Literature on Macedonian, Serbo-Croatian and Slovene Languages, 1990; co-editor: Who's Who of Slovene Descent in the United States, 1992, 2d edit. 1995; editor U.S. Info. Svcs. Bull., Trieste, Italy, 1951-54, others; editor (series) Papers in Slovene Studies, 1975-76, editl. com., editor book revs. Slovene Studies, 1979—; editl. com. Folia Slavica, 1976-89, Nationalities Papers, 1979—, Geschichte, Kultur und Geisteswelt der Slowenen, Munich, 1982-91, Beiträge zur Kenntnis Südosteuropas, Munich, 1983-91, Münchner Zeitschrift für Balkankunde, 1983-91, Geschichte, Kultur und Geisteswelt der Südslaven, Munich, 1990; mem. coun. jours. Slavisticna revija, 1991—; contbr. numerous articles in field of Slavic linguistics and cultures to scholarly jours. and proceedings of internat. confs., symposiums. (Kopitarjev zbornik) Papers presented in Ljubljana, published in Slovenia: "Kopitar's Uderstanding of Historical Evolutionary Trends of Older Slovens Written Texts", 1996,"An Attempt of Stratification of Early Slovene Christian Terminology of the Oldest EasternAlpine Slavic Text," 1996, (Tretji Trubarjev zbornik) "Sociolinguistic Components of Adam Bhoric's Concept of his Literacy Standard of Written Slovene, 1996. Fulbright fellow, 1986; named Amb. of Rep. of Slovenia for Sci. Ministry for Sci. and Tech. of Rep. of Slovenia, 1995; grantee NSF, 1974, 79, Japan Soc. for Promotion Sci., 1989, Internat. Rsch. Exchs. Bd., 1971, 72, 83, 85, 94; recipient Lit. prize for publ. of Who's Who of Slovene Descent in U.S. 1995 Soc. Slovene Intellectuals of Trieste (Italy), 1996. Fellow Am. Coun. Learned Socs., Bulgarian Acad. Scis.; mem. Slovenska Kulturna Akcija (Buenos Aires), Slavists' Assn. Slovenia (hon. Ljubljana chpt. 1989—), Linguistic Soc. Am., Linguistic Circle N.Y., Am. Assn. Advancement Slavic Studies, Am. Assn. Tchrs. Slavic and East European Langs. (Disting. Scholarly Career award 1994), Soc. Slovene Studies (founder, pres. 1973-83, editor Newsletter 1973-77, editor Letter 1978-83, dir. Ctr. for Rsch. and Documentation 1988—), Inst. on East Ctrl. Europe, N.Y. Acad. Scis., Slovene Acad. Scis. and Arts, Ljubljana, Slovenia, European Acad. Scis. Arts, Salzburg, Austria, Fulbright Assn., Am. Slovene Cong. (orgnl. com. 1993-94, acad. advisor to coun. on acad. activities 1994—). Home: 560 Riverside Dr New York NY 10027-3202 Office: Columbia U 420 W 118th St New York NY 10027-7213

LENDER, ADAM, electrical engineer; b. Gleiwitz, Germany, Sept. 15, 1921; s. Joseph and Regina (Waksberg) L.; m. Lilia Sadowski, Aug. 10, 1945; children: James, Richard. BSEE, Columbia U., 1954, MSEE, 1956; PhDEE, Stanford U., 1972. Mem. tech. staff Bell Telephone Labs., Murray Hill, N.J., 1954-60; project engr. Internat. Tel. & Tel. Labs., Nutley, N.J., 1960-61; head advanced devel. GTE Lenkurt, Inc., San. Carlos, Calif., 1961-84; sr. cons. scientist, sr. mem. Lockheed Rsch. Labs., Palo Alto, Calif., 1984-93; adj. prof. grad. sch. elec. engring. U. Santa Clara (Calif)., 1976-87. Author: (with others) Digital Communications, 1981; contbr. articles to profl. jours.; inventor correlative techniques applied in digital communications and magnetic tape recordings, patentee in field. Recipient Stuart Ballantine medal Franklin Inst., 1984. Fellow IEEE (editor-in-chief Transactions in Comm. 1978-84, sr. tech. editor IEEE Comm. Mag. 1987-94, Donald J. McLellan award 1983, Centennial medal 1984), AIAA (assoc.); mem. Comm. Soc. IEEE (bd. govs. 1977-79, 82-84, Edwin Armstrong Achievement award 1995), Columbia U. Alumni Assn. (N.Y.C.), Stanford U. Aumni Assn., Tau Beta Pi, Eta Kappa Nu. Avocations: music, history. Home: 4124 Briarwood Way Palo Alto CA 94306-4609

LENDERMAN, JOANIE, elementary education educator; b. Medford, Oreg., Jan. 20, 1946; d. Jay Lenderman and Vivian Spencer. BS in Edn., So. Oreg. Coll., Ashland, 1969; MS in Edn., Portland State U., 1972; postgrad., U. Va., 1985. Elem. tchr. Beaverton (Oreg.) Schs., 1972-76, Internat. Sch. Svcs., Isfahan, Iran, 1976-78; ESL instr. Lang. Svcs., Tucker, Ga., 1983-84; tchr. Fairfax (Va.) Schs., 1985-86; elem. tchr. Beaverton (Oreg.) Schs., 1990-96. Mem. Nat. Trust for Hist. Preservation, Hist. Preservation League of Oreg., Portland. Mem. AAAS, AAUW, U.S. Hist. Soc., Platform Soc., Smithsonian Instn., Am. Mus. Natural History, Nat. Mus. Women in Arts, U.S. Hist. Soc., The UN, The Colonial Williamsburg Found., Wilson Ctr., N.Y. Acad. Sci., Nat. Trust for Hist. Preservation, Hist. Preservation League of Oreg. Home: 4920 NW Salishan Dr Portland OR 97229

LENEAU, THOMAS ERVIN, gas company executive; b. Mpls., Aug. 3, 1950; s. Thomas J. and Evelyn F. (Schwantees) LeN. BS in Math., St. Cloud State U., 1972; MEd, U. Minn., 1977; B in Acctg., U. Minn., Duluth, 1979; MBA, Ariz. State U., 1985. CPA, Ariz., Minn. Math. instr. Duluth Pub. Schs., 1972-78; acctg. instr. U. Minn., Duluth, 1978-79; auditor Deloitte, Haskins & Sells, Mpls., 1979-81; v.p. fin. Rio Verde Devel., Scottsdale, Ariz., 1981-86; pres., CEO Black Mountain Gas Co., Cave Creek, Ariz., 1986—, also bd. dirs. Treas. Foothills Community Found., Carefree, Ariz., 1989-94; mem. adv. bd. Desert Foothills Land Trust, Cave Creek, Ariz., 1995—, treas. 1997—; treas. Desert Foothills Land Trust, 1997—. Mem. AICPA. Office: Black Mountain Gas Co PO Box 427 Cave Creek AZ 85331-0427

LENEHAN, ART, newspaper editor. Grad., Columbia U., 1971. Asst. mng. editor electronic news The Star-Ledger, Newark. Office: Newark Morning Ledger Co One Star Ledger Plz Newark NJ 07102-1200*

LENESS, GEORGE CRAWFORD, lawyer; b. N.Y.C., Oct. 10, 1936; s. George John and Christine (Gibbs) L. AB magna cum laude, Harvard U., 1958; LLB, Columbia U., 1961. Bar: N.Y. 1962, D.C. 1972. Assoc. Simpson Thacher & Bartlett, N.Y.C., 1961-66; assoc. Hale Russell & Gray, N.Y.C., 1966-69, ptnr., 1969-85; ptnr. Winthrop, Stimson, Putnam & Roberts, N.Y.C., 1985-92, sr. counsel, 1992—. Sgt. USAR, 1954-60. Mem. N.Y.C. Bar Assn., Harvard Club N.Y.C., Westchester County Club (Harrison, N.Y.). Republican. Office: Winthrop Stimson Putnam et al 1 Battery Park Plz New York NY 10004-1405

LENFANT, CLAUDE JEAN-MARIE, physician; b. Paris, Oct. 12, 1928; came to U.S., 1960, naturalized, 1965; s. Robert and Jeanine (Leclerc) L.; children: Philipe, Bernard, Martine Lenfant Wayman, Brigitte Lenfant Martin, Christine. B.S., U. Rennes, France, 1948; M.D., U. Paris, 1956; D.Sc. (hon.), SUNY, 1988. Asst. prof. physiology U. Lille, France, 1959-60; from clin. instr. to prof. medicine physiology and biophysics U. Wash. Med. Sch., 1961-72; asso. dir. lung programs Nat. Heart, Lung and Blood Inst. NIH, Bethesda, Md., 1970-72; dir. div. lung diseases Nat. Heart, Lung and Blood Inst. NIH, 1972-80; dir. Fogarty Internat. Center NIH, 1980-82, assoc. dir. internat. research, 1980-82; dir. Nat. Heart, Lung and Blood Inst., 1982—. Assoc. editor: Jour. Applied Physiology, 1976-82, Am. Jour. Medicine, 1979-91 ; mem. editorial bd.: Undersea Biomed. Research, 1973-75, Respiration Physiology, 1971-78, Am. Jour. Physiology and Jour. Applied Physiology, 1970-76, Am. Rev. Respiratory Disease, 1973-79; editor-in-chief: Lung Biology in Health and Disease. Fellow Royal Coll. Physicians; mem. Assn. Am. Physicians, Am. Soc. Clin. Investigation, French Physiol. Soc., Am. Physiol. Soc., N.Y. Acad. Scis., Undersea Med. Soc., Inst. of Medicine of Nat. Acad. Sci., USSR Acad. Med. Scis., French Nat. Acad. Medicine. Home: 13201 Glen Rd Gaithersburg MD 20878-8855 Office: Nat Heart Lung & Blood Inst Bldg 31A Rm 5A52 Bethesda MD 20892

LENFEST, HAROLD FITZ GERALD, cable television executive, lawyer; b. Jacksonville, Fla., May 29, 1930; s. Harold Churchill and Rena (FitzGerald) L.; m. Marguerite Brooks, July 9, 1955; children: Diane, H. Chase, Brook. AB, Washington and Lee U., 1953; LLB, Columbia U., 1958. Bar: N.Y. 1959. Assoc. Davis Polk & Wardwell, N.Y.C., 1958-65; assoc. counsel Triangle Publs., Phila., 1965-70; mng. dir. communications div. Triangle Publs., N.Y.C., 1970-74; editorial dir., pub. Seventeen mag., N.Y.C., 1970-74; pres. Suburban Cable TV Co., 1970—, Empire State Cable TV Co., 1970-74, Lenfest Communications, Inc., 1974—; bd. dirs. TCI West, Inc., Seattle, Liberty Media Corp., Cable Advt. Bur., Videopole (France), Australis Media Ltd. (Australia), Voice FX, Inc., C-Span; chmn. Video JukeBox, Inc.; CEO Cable AdNet, Inc., 1981-92, StarNet, Inc., 1989—, TelVue, Inc., 1990—. Bd. dirs., v.p. Columbia U. Sch. Law, N.Y.C., 1960-65, 74-78, mem. bd. visitors, 1992—; trustee Walter Kaitz Found., Oakland, Calif., 1986-88; trustee, nat. campaign chmn. Washington and Lee U., 1990—; mem. bd. regents Mercersburg Acad., 1989—, pres., 1994—; mem. James Madison Coun. Libr. of Congress, 1989—; bd. dirs., mem. exec. com. Phila. Mus. Art, 1993—; bd. dirs. C-SPAN, 1995—; trustee, mem. exec. com. Chesapeake Bay Found., 1995—. Capt. USNR, 1953-76, active duty, 1953-56, 62, ret. Named Man of Yr. Phila. Area Easter Seal Soc., 1992; recipient Disting. Achievement award Columbia U. Sch. Law, 1997. Mem. Pa. Cable TV Assn. (bd. dirs., officer 1976-79), Assn. of Bar of City of N.Y., The Mayflower Soc., Soc. of Colonial Wars. Home: 2445 Oaks Cir Huntingdon Valley PA 19006-5621 Office: The Lenfest Group 200 Cresson Blvd PO Box 989 Oaks PA 19456-0989

LENG, SHAO CHUAN, political science educator; b. Chengtu, China, Feb. 14, 1921; came to U.S., 1945, naturalized, 1953; s. Yin Tung and Nan (Chen) L.; m. Alice Li, Dec. 12, 1944 (dec. 1968); 1 child, David; m. Nora Yen, June 14, 1970. B.A., Nat. Central U. China, 1943; M.A., Yale, 1948; Ph.D., U. Pa., 1950. Lectr. U. Pa., 1949-50; from lectr. to prof. U. Va., Charlottesville, 1950-72; Doherty Found. prof. U. Va., 1972-85, D. Compton prof. gvt. and fgn. affairs, 1985-92, Compton prof. emeritus, chmn. com. Asian studies, 1965-68, 74-92; Fulbright lectr. Doshisha (Japan) U., 1956-57;

adviser Union Research Inst., Hong Kong, 1961; vis. scholar Harvard, 1962; research asso. Duke U. Rule of Law Research Center, 1964-66; Cons. Research Analysis Corp., 1968-71, HEW, 1978; research asso. Harvard Law Sch., 1968-69. Author: Japan and Communist China, 1959, (with Norman D. Palmer) Sun Yat-sen and Communism, 1961, (with others) Sovereignty within the Law, 1965, Justice in Communist China, 1968, Criminal Justice System in Post-Mao China, 1985. Editor: (with Hungdah Chiu) Law in Chinese Foreign Policy, 1972, Post-Mao China and U.S.-China Trade, 1977, (with Hungdah Chiu) China: 70 Years After the 1911 Revolution, 1984, Changes in China: Party, State, and Society, 1989, Coping with Crisis: How Governments Deal with Emergencies, 1990, Chiang Ching-Kuo's Leadership in the Development of the Republic of China on Taiwan, 1992, Reform and Development in Deng's China, 1994; cons. editor: Asian Forum, 1974-81, Asian Affairs, 1983—, Asia Pacific Rev., 1989—, Jour. Chinese Studies, 1984—, World Affairs, 1975-84. Social Sci. Research Council grantee, 1956; research fellow Social Sci. Research Council-Am. Council Learned Socs., 1961-62, 68-69; Fulbright Research scholar Hong Kong and Taiwan, 1977; vis. scholar Wilson Center, 1980; research fellow Inst. for Study of World Politics, 1984; chmn. bd. dirs. U.S.-Asia Research Inst., 1983—. Mem. Am. Polit. Sci. Assn., Am. Soc. Internat. Law, Assn. Asian Studies, Assn. Chinese Social Scientists in N.Am. (pres. 1989-91). Home: 217 Highview Ln Charlottesville VA 22901-1017

LENGA, J. THOMAS, lawyer; b. Toledo, Dec. 16, 1942; s. Casimir M. and Rose C. (Sturniolo) L.; children by previous marriage: Christina M., John Thomas Jr., Peter M. BA, U. Toledo, 1965, JD, 1968. Bar: Mich. 1968, Ohio 1968. Mem. Dykema Gossett PLLC, Detroit, 1972-96; mem Clark Hill L.C., Detroit, 1996—; mem. com. on std. jury instrns. Mich. Supreme Ct.; adv. Am. Bd. of Trial Advs. Capt. JAGC, U.S. Army, 1968-72. Named Disting. Alumnus, Coll. Law, U. Toledo, 1987. Fellow Am. Coll. Trial Lawyers; mem. ABA, Detroit Bar Assn. (pres. 1989-90), State Bar Mich. (bd. commrs. 1992—, treas. 1995-96, v.p. 1996-97), Internat. Assn. Def. Counsel. Office: Clark Hill LC 500 Woodward Ave Ste 3500 Detroit MI 48226-3435

LENGEMANN, FREDERICK WILLIAM, physiology educator, scientist; b. N.Y.C., Apr. 8, 1925; s. Peter and Dorathea Johanna (Wolter) L.; m. J. Joan Doremus, Dec. 23, 1950; children—Frederick William Jr., David Munson. Student, N.Y. State Sch. Agr., Farmingdale, 1942-43; B.S. with distinction, Cornell U., 1950, M.Nutrition Sci., 1951; Ph.D., U. Wis., 1954. Research asso. U. Tenn.-AEC Agrl. Research Program, Oak Ridge, 1954-55; asst. prof. dept. chemistry U. Tenn. Med. Sch., Memphis, 1955-59; prof. dept. physiology N.Y. State Coll. Vet. Medicine, Cornell U., 1959-88, prof. physiology emeritus, 1988—; biochemist div. biology and medicine AEC, 1962-63; cons. FAO-IAEA, Vienna, Austria, 1966-67, 76-77, Fed. Radiation Council, 1964-65, NRC, 1970-73, Nat. Com. on Radiation Protection, 1970-73, 79, 82; IAEA expert U. Nacional Agraria, Peru, 1978; lectr., dir. tng. courses. Contbr. articles to profl. jours. Mem. planning bd. Town of Dryden, N.Y., 1963-68. Served with USNR, 1943-46. Decorated Air medal with 3 stars. Fellow AAAS; mem. Council Agrl. Sci. and Tech., Am. Dairy Sci. Assn., Am. Nutrition Soc., Fed. Am. Socs. for Exptl. Biology, Nat., N.Y. State Christmas tree growers assns., Sigma Xi, Phi Kappa Phi. Home: PO Box 161 Rome PA 18837-0161 Office: Cornell U NY State Coll Vet Medicine Dept Physiology Ithaca NY 14853

L'ENGLE, MADELEINE (MRS. HUGH FRANKLIN), author; b. N.Y.C., Nov. 29, 1918; d. Charles Wadsworth and Madeleine (Barnett) Camp; m. Hugh Franklin, Jan. 26, 1946; children: Josephine Franklin Jones, Maria Franklin Rooney, Bion. A.B., Smith Coll., 1941; postgrad., New Sch., 1941-42, Columbia U., 1960-61; holder 19 hon. degrees. Tchr. St. Hilda's and St. Hugh's Sch., 1960—; mem. faculty U. Ind., 1965-66, 71; writer-in-residence Ohio State U., 1970, U. Rochester, 1972, Wheaton Coll., 1976—, Cathedral St. John the Divine, N.Y.C., 1965—. Author: The Small Rain, 1945, Ilsa, 1946, Camilla Dickinson, 1951, A Winter's Love, 1957, And Both Were Young, 1949, Meet the Austins, 1960, A Wrinkle in Time, 1962, The Moon by Night, 1963, The 24 Days Before Christmas, 1964, The Arm of the Starfish, 1965, The Love Letters, 1966, The Journey with Jonah, 1968, The Young Unicorns, 1968, Dance in the Desert, 1969, Lines Scribbled on an Envelope, 1969, The Other Side of the Sun, 1971, A Circle of Quiet, 1972, A Wind in the Door, 1973, The Summer of the Great-Grandmother, 1974, Dragons in the Waters, 1976, The Irrational Season, 1977, A Swiftly Tilting Planet, 1978, The Weather of the Heart, 1978, Ladder of Angels, 1980, A Ring of Endless Light, 1980, Walking on Water, 1980, A Severed Wasp, 1982, And It Was Good, 1983, A House Like a Lotus, 1984, Trailing Clouds of Glory, 1985, A Stone for a Pillow, 1986, Many Waters, 1986, Two-Part Invention, 1988, A Cry Like a Bell, 1987, Sole Into Egypt, 1989, From This Day Forward, 1988, An Acceptable Time, 1989, The Glorious Impossible, 1990, Certain Women, 1992, The Rock That Is Higher: Story As Truth, 1993, Anytime Prayers, 1994, Troubling a Star, 1994, Penguins and Golden Calves, 1996, A Live Coal in the Sea, 1996, Glimpses of Grace, 1996, Wintersong, 1996, Mothers and Daughters, 1997. Pres. Crosswicks Found. Recipient Newbery medal, 1963, Sequoyah award, 1965, runner-up Hans Christian Andersen Internat. award, 1964, Lewis Carroll Shelf award, 1965, Austrian State Lit. award, 1969, Bishop's Cross, 1970, U. South Miss. medal, 1978, Regina medal, 1985, Alan award Nat. Coun. Tchrs. English, 1986, Kerlan award, 1990; collection of papers at Wheaton Coll. Mem. Authors Guild (mem. council), Authors League (mem. council), Writers Guild Am. Episcopalian. Home: 924 W End Ave Apt 95 New York NY 10025-3534 Office: care Cath St John the Divine 1047 Amsterdam Ave New York NY 10025-1702 *Over the years I've worked out a philosophy of failure which I find extraordinarily liberating. If I'm not free to fail, I'm not free to take risks, and everything in life that's worth doing involves a willingness to take a risk and involves the risk of failure. Each time I start a new book I am risking failure. Although I have had over 40 books published, there are at least 6 full unpublished books which have failed, but which have been necessary for the book which then gets published. The same thing is true in all human relationships. Unless I'm willing to open myself up to risk and to being hurt, then I'm closing myself off to love and friendship.*

LENGYEL, ALFONZ, art history, archeology and museology educator; b. Godollo, Hungary, Oct. 21, 1921; came to U.S., 1957; s. Aurel and Margit (Furedy) L.; m. Hongying Liu. Terminal degree in Law and Polit. Sci., Miskolc Law Acad., Budapest, Hungary, 1944; M.A., San Jose State Coll., 1959; Ph.D., U. Paris, 1964; LL.D., London Inst. Applied Research, 1973. Asst. prof. San Jose State Coll. (Calif.), 1961-63; faculty U. Md. European Div., Paris and Heidelberg, Germany, 1963-68; intern museology Ecole du Louvre, Paris, 1965-66; prof. Wayne State U., Detroit, 1968-72, No. Ky. U., Highland Heights, 1972-77; dean, prof. Inst. Mediterranean Art and Archaeology, Cin., 1977-82; coord. art history Rosemont Coll. (Pa.), 1982-86; research prof. art history, dir. Goebel's Print Collection, 1986-88; pres. Fudan Mus. Found., 1988—; adj. curator Detroit Inst. Arts, 1968-72; cons. Paris Am. Acad., 1963—; dir. UPAO, Washington, 1983—; adv. prof. Fudan U., Shanghai, Peoples Republic of China; cons. prof. Xian Jiaotong U., Xian, Peoples Republic of China, founder Sino-Am. Summer Field Sch. Archaeology. Author: Pub. Rels. for Mus., 1992, Archaeology for Museologists, 1993, Chinese Chronological History, 1993; co-author: The Archaeology of Roman Pannonia, 1983; contbr. numerous articles to profl. jours. Bd. dirs. Hungarian-Am. Fedn., Cleve., 1983-91, exec. v.p., Ft. Laudedale, Fla., 1951—; mem. Republican Presdl. Task Force, Washington, 1982—; mem. adv. bd. U.S. Dept. Interior Nat. Park Service, 1987-91. Rockefeller Found. grantee U. Vienna, 1957; Govt. of France grantee U. Paris, 1962-63; S. H. Kress Found. lectureship Denison U. (Ohio), 1967-68; Smithsonian Instn. grantee, 1968; NEH grantee, 1971, 76. Fellow Internat. Acad. Sci. and Lettres, Arpad Acad. (pres. 1982—), Szechenyi Acad, Am. Assn. Swiss, German, Austrian Profs.; mem. Internat. Coun. Mus., Renaissance Soc Am., Coll. Art Assn. Am., Archaeol. Inst. Am., Nat. Fedn. Hungarian-Ams., Soc. Architectural Historians, N.Y. Acad. Scis., Mich. Acad. Scis. and Letters, Soc. Profl. Archaeologists, Christopher Giest Hist. Soc., Detroit Classical Assn. Republican. Roman Catholic. Home: 135 Pineneedle Dr Bradenton FL 34210 Office: Fudan Mus Found Bradenton FL 34210

LENGYEL, CORNEL ADAM (CORNEL ADAM), author; b. Fairfield, Conn., Jan. 1, 1915; s. Elmer Alexander and Mary Elizabeth (Bismarck) L.; m. Teresa Delaney Murphy, July 10, 1933; children: Jerome Benedict, Paul Joel, Michael Sebastian, Cornelia (Mrs. Charles Burke). LittD (hon.), World Acad. of Arts and Culture, Taiwan, 1991. Editor, supr. Fed. Research Project, San Francisco, 1938-41; music critic The Coast, San Francisco, 1937-41; shipwright, personnel officer Kaiser Shipyard, Richmond, Calif., 1942-44; mgr. Forty-Nine Theatre, Georgetown, Calif., 1946-50; editor W.H. Freeman Co., San Francisco, 1952-54; founder, exec. editor Dragon's Teeth Press, Georgetown, 1969—; vis. prof., lectr. English lit. Calif. State U., 1962-63; writer-in-residence Hamline U., St. Paul, 1968-69; guest lectr. MIT, 1969; transl. from Hungarian; editorial cons. HEW; ednl. dir. ILGWU. Author: (history) American Testament: The Story of the Promised Land, 1956, Four Days in July, 1958, I, Benedict Arnold: The Anatomy of Treason, 1960, Presidents of the U.S.A., 1961, Ethan Allen and the Green Mountain Boys, 1961, Jesus the Galileean, 1966, The Declaration of Independence, 1969; (poetry) Thirty Pieces, 1933, First Psalms, 1950, Fifty Poems, 1965, Four Dozen Songs, 1970, The Lookout's Letter, 1971, Late News from Adam's Acres, 1983, El Dorado Forest: Selected Poems, 1986, Advice to a Future Poet: Poems Early and Late, 1996; (plays) The World's My Village, 1935, Jonah Fugitive, 1936, The Giant's Trap, 1938, The Atom Clock, 1951, Eden, Inc., 1954, rev. edit. The Master Plan, 1963, Will of Stratford, 1964, Three Plays, 1964, The Case of Benedict Arnold, 1975, Doctor Franklin, 1976, The Shadow Trap, 1977, The Second Coming, 1985, Mengele's Passover, 1987, A Clockmaker's Boy: Part One, 1987; (novel) Malunkyaputta: His Quest for Edification, 1996; (essay) The Creative Self, 1971, contbr. to anthologies, The Golden Year, 1960, Interpretation for Our Time, 1966, The Britannica Library of Great American Writing, 1961, The Menorah Treasury, 1964, The Courage to Grow Old, 1988, From These Hills, 1990, Blood to Remember, 1991, Anthology of Contemporary Poets, 1992, World Poetry, 1993, We Speak for Peace, 1993, also Poet Lore, The Coast, The Argonaut, Saturday Rev., Menorah Jour., Kayak, Old Crow, Mandrake Rev. Served with U.S. Merchant Marine, 1944-45. Recipient Albert M. Bender award in lit., 1945; recipient 1st prize Maritime Poetry Awards, 1945, 1st prize Poetry Soc. Va., 1951, Maxwell Anderson award drama, 1950, Di Castagnola award Poetry Soc. Am., 1971, Internat. Who's Who in Poetry award, 1972; Huntington Hartford Found. resident fellow, 1951, 64; MacDowell Colony resident fellow, 1967; Ossabaw Island Found. fellow, 1968; Nat. Endowment for Arts fellow, 1976-77. Mem. MLA, AAUP, PEN, Poetry Soc. Am., Poetry Soc. Eng., Authors Guild. Address: Adam's Acres Georgetown CA 95634 *What would a writer convey through his work? His vision of life, his response to the oddity, terror, humor, beauty, pathos, or grandeur of experience. He would renew our original sense of wonder at the mystery of things and speak in a human voice fittingly of man's mortal adventures amid the immortal dance of the elements . . . To endure, a book must stir a variety of men in any generation. Though all that we do may prove perishable, we must proceed as if . . . Do one thing well enough to endure, we tell ourselves. A thing done well is well done for all time.*

LENGYEL, ISTVÁN, chemist, educator; b. Kaposvar, Hungary, July 12, 1931; came to the U.S., 1958; s. István and Margit (Palásthy) L. Diploma in chemistry, Eotvos Lorand U., 1955; PhD in Organic Chemistry, MIT, 1964. Rsch. chemist G. Richter Pharm. Works, Inc., Budapest, 1953-55; chemist State Geophys. Inst., Budapest, 1955-56; rsch. chemist Biochemie GmbH, Kundl, Austria, 1957-58; rsch. asst. Johns Hopkins Med. Sch., Balt., 1958-59; predoctoral fellow MIT, Cambridge, 1959-63, postdoctoral fellow, 1964; NIH postdoctoral fellow Techn. U., Munich, 1964-65; rsch. assoc. MIT, Cambridge, 1965-67; prof. chemistry St. John's U., Jamaica, N.Y., 1967—, chmn. dept. chemistry, 1985-91; vis. scholar U.S. Nat. Acad. Sci. and Hungarian Acad. Scis., 1973. Recipient award Alexander von Humboldt Found., 1973-74. Avocations: swimming, travel. Home: 84-01 169th St Jamaica NY 11432-2033 Office: Saint Johns U 8000 Utopia Pkwy Jamaica NY 11432-1335

LENHART, CYNTHIA RAE, conservation organization executive; b. Cheverly, Md., Nov. 3, 1957; d. Donald Edward and Vesta Jean (Morris) L.; m. John Charles Doyle Jr., Oct. 24, 1987. BS in Environ. Studies, Coll. William & Mary, 1979; MS in Environ. Sci., SUNY, Syracuse, 1983. Asst. to pres. Environ. Policy Inst., Washington, 1979-81; wildlife policy analyst Nat. Audubon Soc., Washington, 1984-90; exec. dir. Hawk Mountain Sanctuary, Kempton, Pa., 1990—; bd. dirs. Am. Bird Conservancy, Washington. Contbr. chpts. to Audubon Wildlife Report, 1985, 87, 88, 89. Chair Everglades Coalition, Washington, 1986-88; bd. dirs. Pa. Environ. Coun., Phila. Mem. NAFE. Office: Hawk Mountain Sanctuary RR 2 Box 191 Kempton PA 19529

LENHART, JAMES THOMAS, lawyer; b. Cambridge, Mass., Nov. 3, 1946; s. James Wills and Martha Agnes (Everly) L.; m. Lynn Dexter Stevens, June 21, 1969; children—Amanda Brooks, James Edward, Abigail Ames. Cert. in History, U. Edinburgh, Scotland, 1967; A.B., Columbia U., 1968, J.D., 1972. Bar: N.Y. 1973, D.C. 1974. Clk. to judge U.S. Dist. Ct. (so. dist.) N.Y., 1972-73; assoc. Shaw, Pittman, Potts & Trowbridge, Washington, 1973-79, ptnr., 1980—; adj. prof. Cornell Law Sch., 1992-93; instr. Washington Coll. Law of Am. U., Washington, 1976-78. Chair exec. com. Westmoreland Congregational Ch., Washington, 1989, bd. dirs. 1978-79, 83-84. Harlan Fiske Stone scholar Columbia U., 1968-69, 71-72. Mem. Am. Law Inst., D.C. Def. Lawyers Assn., ABA, D.C. Bar Assn., Fed. City Club, The Barristers. Democrat. Mem. United Ch. of Christ. Office: Shaw Pittman Potts & Trowbridge 2300 N St NW Washington DC 20037-1122

LENHERR, FREDERICK KEITH, neurophysiologist, computer scientist; b. N.Y.C., Feb. 4, 1943; s. Frederick Joseph and Thelma Frances (DeFrehn) L. A.B., Harvard U., 1965; M.S., U. Mass., 1973, Ph.D., 1975. Instr. biology and physics Taft Sch., Watertown, Conn., 1965-66; rsch. and devel. engr. No. Rsch. & Engring., Cambridge, Mass., 1966-69; turbine engr. Gen. Electric Co., Lynn, Mass., 1969-70; neurophysiologist, computer scientist Ctr. Systems Neurosci., U. Mass., Amherst, 1974-77; dir. Berkeley Brain Ctr., 1977-80; pres. New Salem (Mass.) Rsch., 1981—; sr. engr. Visual Intelligence, Amherst, Mass., 1982-85; project scientist Harvard U., Cambridge, Mass., 1986-87; microcomputer faculty Holyoke Community Coll., 1991-92; sr. rsch. scientist App. Comp. Sys. Inst. Mass., 1993—. Founding editor: Brain Theory Newsletter, 1975-77. Democrat. Lutheran. Home and Office: W Main St New Salem MA 01355

LENHOFF, HOWARD MAER, biological sciences educator, academic administrator, activist; b. North Adams, Mass., Jan. 27, 1929; s. Charles and Goldie Sarah Lenhoff; m. Sylvia Grossman, June 20, 1954; children: Gloria, Bernard. B.A., Coe Coll., 1950, D.Sc. (hon.), 1976; Ph.D., Johns Hopkins U., 1955. USPHS fellow Loomis Lab., Greenwich, Conn., 1954-56; vis. lectr. Howard U., Washington, 1957-58; rsch. assoc. George Washington U., Washington, 1957-58; postdoctoral fellow Carnegie Instn., Washington, 1958; investigator Howard Hughes Med. Inst., Miami, 1958-63; prof. biology, dir. Lab. for Quantitative Biology U. Miami, Coral Gables, 1963-69; prof. biol. scis. U. Calif., Irvine, 1969-92, prof. polit. sci., 1986-92, assoc. dean biol. scis., 1969-71, dean grad. div., 1971-73, faculty asst. to vice chancellor of student affairs, 1986-88, 90-96, chair faculty senate, 1988-90, prof. emeritus, rsch. prof., 1993—; vis. scientist, Louis Lipsky fellow Weizmann Inst. Sci., Rehovot, Israel, 1968-69; vis. prof. chem. engring., Rothschild fellow Israel Inst. Tech., 1973-74; vis. prof. Hebrew U., Jerusalem, spring 1970, fall 1971, 77-78; Hubert Humphrey Inst. fellow Ben Gurion U., Beersheva, Israel, 1981; sr. rsch. fellow Jesus Coll., U. Oxford, 1988; dir. Nelson Rsch. & Devel. Co., Irvine, 1971-73; bd. dirs. BioProbe Internat., Inc., Tustin, Calif., 1983-89, chmn. bd., 1983-86. Editor/author: Biology of Hydra, 1961, Hydra, 1969, Experimental Coelenterate Biology, 1972, Coelenterate Biology—Review and Perspectives, 1974, Hydra: Research Methods, 1983, Enzyme Immunoassay, 1985, From Trembley's Polyps to New Directions in Research on Hydra, 1985, Hydra and the Birth of Experimental Biology, 1986, Biology of Nematocysts, Conception to Birth, 1988; mem. editorial bd. Jour. Solid Phase Biochemistry, 1976-80. Vice chmn. So. Calif. div. Am. Assn. Profs. for Peace in Middle East, 1972-80; bd. dirs. Am. Assn. for Ethiopian Jews, 1974-93, pres., 1978-82; bd. govs. Israel Bonds Orange County, Calif., 1974-80, Dade County Heart Assn., Miami, 1958-61, So. Calif. Technion Soc., 1976; pres. Hillel Coun. of Orange County, 1976-78; nat. chmn. faculty div. State of Israel Bonds, 1976; mem. sci. adv. bd. Am. Friends of Weizman Inst. Sci., 1980-84; bd. dirs. Hi Hopes Identity Discovery Found., Anaheim, Calif., 1982-87, pres. bd. govs., 1983-85, William Syndrome Found., trustee, 1992, pres., bd. dirs., 1993-95, exec. v.p., 1995—; v.p. edn. Williams Syndrome Assn., 1994, bd. dirs., 1993-94. 1st lt. USAF, 1956-58. Recipient Career Development award USPHS, 1965-69; Disting. fellow Iowa Acad. Sci., 1986. Fellow AAAS; mem. Soc. Physics and Natural History of Swiss Acad. Scis. (hon.), Am. Chem. Soc., Am. Biophys. Soc., Am. Soc. Zoologists, History of Sci. Soc., Am. Soc. Cell Biologists, Am. Soc. Biol. Chemists, Biophysics Soc., Soc. Gen. Physiologists, Soc. Growth and Devel. Home: 304 Robin Hood Ln Costa Mesa CA 92627-2134 Office: U Calif Sch Biol Scis Irvine CA 92697

LENING, JANICE ALLEN, physical education educator; b. Topeka, Mar. 10, 1946; d. John Otis and Bertha May (Simon) Allen; m. Jay Ridley Lening, Dec. 26, 1976; children: Brooke Michelle, Chad Allen. BA in Phys. Edn., U. Denver, 1968; MA in Elem. Edn., U. No. Colo., 1980. Lic. tchr. phys. edn., elem. edn., Colo. Tchr. Denver Pub. Schs., 1968-69; phys. edn. tchr. Jefferson County Schs., Lakewood, Colo., 1969—, gymnastics coach, 1969, 76-79, gymnastics judge, 1970-75; mem. budget com. Shaffer Elem. Sch., Littleton, 1985-86, accountability com., 1985-86; wellnes rep. Shaffer, Colorow, Gov. Racn Elem., Littleton, 1985-97; mem. social com. Lasley, Green Gables, Shaffer, Gov. Ranch Elem. Lakewood and Littleton, 1970-97; student coun. supr. Green Gables Elem., Lakewood, 1978-85, credit union rep., 1980-85. Leader Girl Scouts, Littleton, 1986-87; coach Columbine Soccer Assn., Littleton, 1986-91; judge Odyssey of the Mind, Littleton, 1986-97. Recipient Gold medal Am. Heart Assn., Denver, 1991, Bronze award, 1994-95 State Champion award sch. Pres. Coun. on Phys. Fitness, 1990-96; chairperson Precedures Com., 1994-97. Mem. AAPHERD, NEA, PAC, Colo. Edn. Assn. (mentor tchr. 1997), JCEA. Republican. Avocations: softball, swimming, volleyball, golf, tennis. Home: 6546 W Hoover Pl Littleton CO 80123-3632 Office: Govs Ranch Elem Sch 5354 S Field St Littleton CO 80123-7800

LENKE, JOANNE MARIE, publishing executive; b. Chgo., Aug. 27, 1938; d. August Julian and Dorothy Anna (Gold) L.; B.S., Purdue U., 1960; M.S., Syracuse U., 1964, Ph.D., 1968. Tchr. pub. schs., Evanston, Ill., 1960-63; editor Test Dept., Harcourt, Brace & World, Inc., N.Y.C., 1967-70; research psychologist Harcourt Brace Jovanovich, Inc., N.Y.C., 1970-73, exec. editor, 1973-75; asst. dir. ednl. measurement div. The Psychol. Corp., N.Y.C., 1975-83, dir. ednl. measurement and psychometrics, Cleve., 1983-85, San Antonio, 1986, v.p., dir. Measurement div., 1986-88, sr. v.p., 1988-91, exec. v.p., 1991—; field reader U.S. Office Edn., 1972, NSF grantee, 1963-64. Mem. Nat. Council on Measurement in Edn., Am. Psychol. Assn., Am. Ednl. Research Assn. Adv. editor Jour. of Ednl. Measurement, 1974-78. Home: 1311 Vista Del Monte San Antonio TX 78216-2229 Office: The Psychol Corp 555 Academic Ct San Antonio TX 78204-2455

LENKOSKI, LEO DOUGLAS, psychiatrist, educator; b. Northampton, Mass., May 13, 1925; s. Leo L. and Mary Agnes (Lee) L.; m. Jeannette Teare, July 12, 1952; children—Jan Ellen, Mark Teare, Lisa Marie, Joanne Lee. A.B., Harvard, 1948, spl. student, 1948-49; M.D., Western Res. U., 1953; grad., Cleve. Psychoanalytic Inst., 1964. Intern Univ. Hosps., Cleve., 1953-54, resident in psychiatry, 1956-57, dir. psychiatry, 1970-86, chief of staff, 1982-90; dir. profl. services Horizon Ctr. Hosp., 1980; asst. resident in psychiatry Yale U., New Haven, 1954-56; teaching fellow Case Western Res. U., Cleve., 1957-60, from instr. to prof. psychiatry, 1960-93; prof. emeritus, 1993—; assoc. dean Sch. Medicine Case Western Res. U., Cleve., 1982-93, dir. Substance Abuse Ctr., 1990-93; cons. Cleve. Ctr. on Alcoholism, DePaul Maternity and Infant Home, St. Ann's Hosp., Def. Dept., Cleve. VA Hosp., Psychiat. Edn. br. NIMH; mem. Cuyahoga County Mental Health and Retardation Bd., 1967-73, 94—, Health Planning and Devel. Commn., 1967-73, Ohio Mental Health and Retardation Commn., 1976-78. Contbr. articles to profl. jours. Bd. dirs. Hough-Norwood Health Ctr., Hitchcock Ctr., Hopewell Inn. 1st lt. USAAF, 1943-46. Decorated D.F.C., Air medal with oak leaf cluster.; Career Tchr. grantee NIMH, 1958-60. Fellow Am. Psychiat. Assn. (life), Am. Coll. Psychiatrists, Am. Coll. Psychoanalysts (pres. 1988-89); mem. AMA, AAAS, Ohio Psychiat. Assn. (pres. 1974—), Am. Psychoanalytic Assn., Assn. Am. Med. Colls., Cleve. Acad. Medicine (bd. dirs. 1987-90), Ohio Med. Assn., Pasteur Club, Am. Assn. Chairmen Depts. Psychiatry (pres. 1978-79), Alpha Omega Alpha. Home: 1 Bratenahl Pl Apt 1010 Cleveland OH 44108-1155 Office: 11000 Euclid Ave Cleveland OH 44106-1714

LENMAN, BRUCE PHILIP, historian, educator; b. Aberdeen, Scotland, Apr. 9, 1938; s. Jacob Philip and May (Wishart) L. MA in History with 1st class honors, Aberdeen U., 1960; MLitt, U. Cambridge, 1965, LittD, 1986. Asst. prof. U. Victoria, B.C., Can., 1963; lectr. Queen's Coll., Dundee, Scotland, 1963-67, U. Dundee, 1967-72; lectr. U. St. Andrews, Scotland, 1972-78, sr. lectr., 1978-83, reader, 1983-92, prof. of modern history, 1992—; James Pinckney Harrison prof. history Coll. William and Mary, Williamsburg, Va., 1988-89; mem. econs. and bus. studies panel Scottish Edn. Dept., Ediburgh, 1979-81, humanities sub.-com. Council for Nat. Acad. Awards, London, 1985-87. Author: From Esk to Tweed, 1975, Economic History of Modern Scotland, 1977 (Scottish Arts Coun. award 1977), The Jacobite Risings 1689-1746, 1980 (Scottish Arts Coun. award 1980), Scotland 1746-1832, 1981, The Jacobite Clans of the Great Glen, 1984, The Jacobite Clause, 1986, The Eclipse of Parliament, 1992; co-author: (with John S. Gibson) The Jacobite Threat, 1990; editor: Chambers Dictionary of World History, 1993. Brit. Acad.-Newberry Library fellow, 1982, John Carter Brown Library fellow, 1984, Mellon fellow Va. Hist. Soc., 1990, Mayers fellow Huntington Libr., 1996. Fellow Royal Hist. Soc.; mem. Am. Soc. for 18th Century Scottish Studies, Am. Soc. for 18th Century Studies, Soc. for History of Discoveries, Hakluyt Soc. Clubs: Royal Commonwealth (London); New Golf (St. Andrews). Avocations: golf, hill walking, tennis, swimming. Office: U St Andrews Dept Modern History, St Katharine's Lodge, Saint Andrews KY16 9AL, Scotland

LENN, STEPHEN ANDREW, lawyer; b. Ft. Lauderdale, Fla., Jan. 6, 1946; s. Joseph A. and Ruth (Kreis) L.; 1 child, Daniel Lenn. BA, Tufts U., 1967; JD, Columbia U., 1970. Assoc. Kronish, Lieb, Shainswit, Weiner & Hellman, N.Y.C., 1970-72, Shereff, Friedman, Hoffman & Goodman, N.Y.C., 1972-75; exec. v.p., gen. counsel Union Commerce Bank, Union Commerce Corp., Cleve., 1975-83; ptnr., mng. ptnr. Porter, Wright, Morris & Arthur, Cleve., 1983-88; ptnr Baker & Hostetler, Cleve., 1988—. Trustee Gt. Lakes Sci. Ctr. Mem. ABA (com. on devel. in investment svcs. 1980—), Ohio Bar Assn., Cleve. Bar Assn., N.Y.C. Bar Assn., Calif. Bar Assn., Oakwood Club. Office: Baker & Hostetler 3200 Nat City Ctr 1900 E 9th St Cleveland OH 44114-3401

LENNARZ, WILLIAM JOSEPH, research biologist, educator; b. N.Y.C., Sept. 28, 1934; s. William and Louise (Richter) L.; m. Roberta S. Lozensky, June 16, 1956 (div. June 1973); children: William, Matthew, David; m. Sheila Jackson, July 13, 1973. B.S., Pa. State U., 1956; Ph.D., U. Ill., 1959; research fellow, Harvard, 1959-62. Mem. faculty Johns Hopkins Sch. Medicine, 1962-83, assoc. prof. biochemistry, 1966-70, prof., 1971-83; R.A. Welch prof. and chmn. dept. biochemistry and molecular biology U. Tex. Cancer Ctr., M.D. Anderson Hosp., Houston, 1983-89; leading prof., chmn. dept. biochemistry and cell biology SUNY, Stony Brook, 1989—; cons. NIH. Editorial bd.: Biochem. Biophys. Research Commn., Biosci. Reports. Clayton Found. scholar, 1962-64; Lederle Faculty awardee, 1965-67; recipient Distinguished Young Scientist award Md., 1967. Mem. NAS, Am. Chem. Soc., Am. Soc. Biol. Chemists and Molecular Biologists (pres. 1989-90), Am. Soc. Microbiology, Am. Soc. Cell Biology (pub. affairs com.), Assn. Med. Grad. Sch. Dept. Biochemistry (pres. 1993), Internat. Union Biochemists and Molecular Biologists (exec. com.), Worcester Found. (mem. scientific adv. bd.), Soc. Glycobiology (pres. 1993), Sigma Xi, Phi Kappa Phi, Alpha Chi Sigma. Rsch. biochemistry of cell surface molecules and of fertilization. Home: 43 Erland Rd Stony Brook NY 11790-1124 Office: SUNY at Stony Brook 450 Life Scis Stony Brook NY 11790

LENNES, GREGORY, manufacturing and financing company executive; b. Chgo., Aug. 5, 1947; s. Lawrence Dominic and Genevieve (Karoll) L.; m. Maryann Meskers, July 27, 1968; children: Robert, Sandra, Ryan. BA, U. Ill., 1969, MA, 1971, postgrad., 1971-73. Corp. archivist Navistar Internat. Corp. (formerly Internat. Harvester Co.), Chgo., 1973-80, records mgr., 1980—, asst. sec., 1980—; sec. Navistar Fin. Corp., Schaumburg, Ill., 1980—, Navistar Internat. Transportation Corp., 1987—. Editor: Historical Records in the Farm Equipment Industry, 1977. Mem. Am. Soc. Corp Secs., Assn. Records Mgrs. and Adminstrs., Soc. Am. Archivists, Midwest Archives Conf., Assn. Info. and Image Mgmt. Home: 19641 S Schoolhouse Rd Mokena IL 60448-1700 Office: Navistar Internat Corp 455 N Cityfront Plaza Dr Chicago IL 60611-5503

LENNON, A. MAX, food products company executive; b. Columbus County, N.C., Sept. 27, 1940; m. Ruth Carter; children—Daniel Ray, Robin LuRay. AA, Mars Hill Coll., 1960; BS, N.C. State U., 1962, PhD, 1970. Owner, operator crop and livestock farm, 1962-66; grad. asst. N.C. State U., Raleigh, 1966-70; asst. prof. animal sci. Tex. Tech U., Lubbock, 1970-72, assoc. prof., 1972, prof., chmn. dept. animal sci., 1974-77; asst. dean, dir. rsch. Coll. Agrl. Scis., Tex. Tech U., 1977-79, assoc. dean, dir. rsch., 1979; sr. swine nutritionist Central Soya Co., Decatur, Ind., 1973; dir. swine feeds rsch. Cen. Soya Co., Decatur, Ind., 1974; chairperson dept. animal husbandry U. Mo.-Columbia, 1980, dir. agrl. experiment sta., dean coll. agr., 1980-83; v.p. for agrl. adminstrn., exec. dean for agr., home econs. and natural resources Ohio State U., Columbus, 1983-86; pres. Clemson (S.C.) U., 1986-94; pres., CEO Ea. Foods Inc., Atlanta, 1994—; Seaman A. Knapp lectr. Dallas, 1988; past co-chmn. Ohio Gov.'s Commn. on Agr.; past chmn. N. Cen. region Coun. of Adminstrv. Heads of Agr.; bd. dirs. First Union Corp., Delta Woodside Industries, Inc., Duke Power Co., Escuela Agricola de la Region Tropical Humeda, Baptist Med. Ctr. Found.; past bd. govs. Am. Royal; E.T. York Disting. lectr. Auburn U., 1991. Contbr. articles to profl. jour. Mem. S.E. regional adv. bd. Inst. Internat. Edn.; adv. com. for task force on agriculture devel. and cooperation, Internat. Devel. Agy.; co-chair policy adv. com. Competitive Rsch. Grants; bd. dirs. Farm Found., Nat. Dropout Prevention Fund Devel. Coun., Greenville Tech. Coll. Fed. Devel. Coun., Fellowship Christian Farmers Internat. State Panel, S.C. Women in Higher Edn.; mem. Dept. Def. Clothing & Textile Bd., Adv. Com. for Task Force on Agrl. Devel. and Cooperation; trustee Palmetto Partnership, Found. for Drug Abuse Prevention, adv. bd. McDonald's Initiative, So. Assn. Coll. and Schs. Com. on Intercollegiate Athletics, Internat. Assn. of Agribus; mem. Congl. Office Tech. Assessment Coun., So. Assn. Colls. and Schs., Commn. on Colls. Class of 1994, rep. S.C.'s Exec. Coun.; bd. dirs. Bapt. Med. Ctr. Found. Recipient Disting. Alumnus award Coll. Agr. and Life Scis., N.C. State U., 1989, Nat. 4-H Alumni award, 1989, Thomas Green Clemson medallion Clemson U., 1991. Mem. AAAS, Am. Soc. Animal Sci., Internat. Assn. Agribus., Coun. for Agrl. Sci. and Tech., Farm House Assn., Internat. Devel. Agy., Alpha Zeta, Phi Sigma, Phi Kappa Phi, Gamma Sigma Delta. Address: Press Home M H College Mars Hill NC 28754

LENNON, DONALD RAY, archivist, historian; b. Brunswick County, N.C., Oct. 6, 1938; s. George William and Eula Lee (Rowell) L.; m. Billie Mae Royall, Dec. 20, 1969; children: William Christopher, Mark Whitfield. BS, East Carolina U., 1960, MA, 1962. Cert. archivist Am. Soc. Cert. Archivists. Archivist II N.C. Divsn. Archives and History, Raleigh, 1964-67; dir. manuscript collection East Carolina U., Greenville, N.C., 1967—; coord. spl. collections East Carolina U., Greenville, 1987—; mem. state hist. records adv. bd., Raleigh, 1975-85; mem. Hist. Bath (N.C.) Commn., 1982-88. Co-author: A Quest for Glory, 1991 (Society Cup award 1992); co-editor: The Wilmington Town Book, 1743-1778 (Clarendon Cup award 1974), Harnett, Hooper and Howe, 1979, Politics, Bar and Bench, 1980. Bd. dirs. N.C. Preservation Consortium, Durham, 1989-93. With U.S. Army, 1962-64. Mem. Soc. Am. Archivists, Hist. Soc. N.C. (pres. 1992-93), Soc. N.C. Archivists. Democrat. Baptist. Home: 201 Cherrywood Dr Greenville NC 27858-8611 Office: East Carolina U Joyner Libr Special Collections Department Greenville NC 27858

LENNON, ELIZABETH M., retired educator; b. Chgo., Apr. 29; d. John Joseph and Johanna Amelia (Pfaff) L. AB, Ind. U., 1941; postgrad., Butler U., 1946, N.C. State U., 1956, San Francisco State U., 1960; MA in Edn. of Physically Handicapped, Columbia U., 1947. Elem. tchr., typing tchr. Ind. Sch. for the Blind, 1944-51; lower sch. tchr. Perkins Sch. for the Blind, 1951-53; tchr., insvc. coord. Gov. Morehead Sch., Raleigh, N.C., 1953-54; staff devel. specialist N.C. Commn. for the Blind, 1964-67; asst. prof. blind rehab. Western Mich. State U., Kalamazoo, 1967-78, part-time asst. prof. blind rehab., 1978-81, 88. Author publs. in field. Bd. dirs. Nat. Accreditation Coun. for Agys. Serving the Blind and Visually Impaired, 1976-83; vice chair Mich. Commn. for the Blind, 1978-84; vice chair bd. dirs Shepherd's Ctr. of Greater Kalamazoo, 1989-90, chmn., 1990—; sec. Affiliated Leadership League of and for the Blind of Am., 1978-91; bd. dirs. Southcentral Mich. Commn. on Aging, 1978-91, sec., 1986-88; sec. Am. Coun. of the Blind, 1988-90; bd. dirs. Voluntary Action Ctr. of Greater Kalamazoo, 1986—; bd. dirs., mem. com., founder Kalamazoo Ctr. for Ind. Living, 1980—; pres. Coun. of Citizens with Low Vision, 1985-88. Recipient Robert D. Mahoney award for Outstanding Svc. to Visually Impaired of Mich., Mich. Assn. of Blind and Visually Impaired, 1978, Clare Lynch award Kalamazoo Coun. of the Blind, 1981, George Card award for Outstanding Svc. to Visually Imparied Nationwide, Am. Coun. of the Blind, 1983, Spl. Tribute, State of Mich., 1984, Lifetime Achievement award Kalamazoo Ctr. for Ind. Living, 1987, Outstanding Svc. to the Older Citizens of S.W. Mich., Mich. Legislature, 1990, Jim Neubacher Lifetime Achievement award Kalamazoo Ctr. for Ind. Living, 1991, Golden Bell award J.C. Penney, 1992. Mem. Assn. for Edn. and Rehab. of the Blind and Visually Impaired (mem. various coms. on state and nat. levels), Coun. for Exceptional Children, Mich. Assn. of Transcribers for the Visually Impaired (past pres., editor newletter, bd. dirs., founding mem.). Avocations: reading, music, travel. Home: 1400 N Drake Rd Apt 218 Kalamazoo MI 49006-3911

LENNON, JOSEPH LUKE, college official, priest; b. Providence, Sept. 21, 1919; s. John Joseph and Marjorie (McCabe) L. AB, Providence Coll., 1940; STB, Immaculate Conception Coll., 1946; MA, U. Notre Dame, 1950, PhD, 1953; LLD, Bradford Durfee Coll. Tech., 1963; LittD (hon.), U. Southeastern Mass., 1975; DHL (hon.), Roger Williams Coll., 1980. Ordained priest Roman Cath. Ch., 1947; instr. U. Notre Dame, 1948-50; mem. edn. dept. Providence Coll., 1950-51, 53-56, asst. dean men, 1953, dean of men, 1954-56, dean of coll., 1956-68, v.p. community affairs, 1968-88, ret., 1988; dir. Tchrs. Guild of Thomistic Inst., 1953-56, Pennywise Shop; bd. trustees So. New Eng. Sch. of Law, 1994—. Author: The Role of Experience in the Acquisition of Scientific Knowledge, 1952, The Dean Speaks, 1958, College is for Knowledge, 1959; rev. as 30 Ways to Get Ahead at College, 1964. Mem. adv. council Citizens Edn1. Freedom; adv. bd. Perceptional Edn. and Research Center; co-chmn. Easter Seals, 1968; arbitrator R.I. Bd. Labor; adv. com. Mental Retardation, R.I.; chmn. Nat. Library Week, 1962; mem. R.I. Adv. Com. Vocational Edn.; ann. lectr. Psychology and Everyday Life, WJAR-TV, 1960-75; mem. Gov. R.I. Com. to Study R.I. State Inst. at, Howard; chmn. speaker's bur. United Fund Campaign, 1971; coordinator Civil Rights Affirmative Action Program, 1970-78; mem. Com. Future Jurisprudence in, R.I; com. clergy renewal Diocese Providence; mem. Com. for CROP-Community Hunger Appeal of Ch. World Service, 1974-75; mem. subcom. on family law Gov.'s Commn. on Jurisprudence of Future; mem. membership com. Cancer Control Bd., R.I., 1977; mem. Gov.'s Commn. on Consumer's Council, 1977, Gov.'s Leadership Conf. on Citizen Participation.; bd. dirs. Blue Cross and Blue Shield, Progress for Providence, R.I. Legal Services, Fed. Hill House, Pawtucket YMCA, The Samaritans, Handgun Alert, Vols. in R.I. Schs., Meeting St. Sch., Big Sisters, Big Bros. Assn. R.I., R.I. Easter Seal, Blackstone Valley Surgicare, R.I. Heart Assn.; chmn. 1975 Heart Fund campaign; trustee R.I. chpt. Leukemia Soc. Am.; adv. bd. Parents Without Partners; bd. govs. John E. Fogarty Found., Irish Scholarship Found.; bd. dirs., trustee Big Sisters Assn., R.I.; bd. dirs. Diabetes Assn.; adv. bd. St. Joseph's Merged Hosps.; mem. corp. R.I. Hosp.; trustee Emma Pendleton Bradley Hosp., 1984—, Southern New Eng. Sch. Law, 1994—; chmn. Laborer's Internat. Union North Am. Scholarship Program, 1995—; mem. adv. council Quirk Inst.; mem. Spl. Legis. Commn. Created on Catastrophic Health Ins., 1979-82, Gov.'s Screening Com. for the Judiciary, 1980-89; mem. Save the Bay, 1986-88; bd. dirs. John Burke Scholarship Found., 1973— Scholarship Funds of the Laborers' International Union of North America. Recipient Seal of Approval R.I. Automobile Dealers Assn., 1978. Mem. Nat. Cath. Edn. Assn., Am. Cath. Sociol. Soc., Nat. Soc. Study Edn., Am. Philosophers Edn. Assn., New Eng. Ednl. Assn., New Eng. Guidance and Personnel Assn., Greater Providence Epilepsy Assn., Nat. Soc. Study Edn., Am. Arbitration Assn., Alpha Epsilon Delta, Delta Epsilon Sigma (pres. 1966-69).

LENNON, THOMAS JOHN, retired air force officer, company executive; b. Honolulu, Aug. 16, 1942; s. John Joseph and Alice (Ventura) L.; m. Lynn Elizabeth Schweir, July 2, 1966; children: Thomas John Jr., Timothy James. BS in Biology, Va. Mil. Inst., 1965; MPA, Golden Gate U., 1978; postgrad., Air Command and Staff Coll., 1973, Nat. War Coll., 1983, Harvard U., 1993. Commd. 2d lt. USAF, 1965, advanced through grades to brig. gen.; pilot USAF, Thailand, 1968-69, F-4 aircraft comdr., instr. pilot, 1970-71; F-4 instr., wing ops. officer USAF, George AFB, Calif., 1971-74; F-15 project officer Hdqrs. Tactical Air Command USAF, Langley AFB, Va., 1974-76, chief current ops., asst. ops. officer, 1976-78; asst. dep. comdr. ops. 401st tactical fighter wing USAF, Torrejon Air Base, Spain, 1984-85; dep. comdr. ops. 86th tactical fighter wing USAF, Ramstein Air Base, Germany, 1985-87; dir. joint gen. officer warfighting course USAF, Maxwell AFB, Ala., 1987-88; comdr. 39th tactical group and US forces USAF, Incirlick Air Base, Turkey, 1988-89; comdr. 48th tactical fighter wing USAF, RAF Lakenheath, Eng., 1989-90, Taif, Saudi Arabia, 1990-91; exec. officer dep. comdr. in chief HQ US European command USAF, Stuttgart, Germany, 1991-92; dir. mil. to mil. contact program hdqrs. U European command USAF, Stuttgart, 1992-94, ret., 1994; v.p. Sonalysts, Inc., Alexandria, Va., 1994—; Air Force dep. under sec. NOAA; exec. mem. Next Generation Radar Program Coun.; Dept. Def. agent Space Weather, Weather Modeling and Simulation; mem. Nat. Aviation Weather, Nat. Space Weather Program Coun., Nat. Aviation Icing, Joint Automated Weather Obs. Program Coun.; mem. space coun. on space weather R&D, NAS, mem. rsch. coun. on atmosphere and environ. Decorated Legion of Merit with two oak leaf clusters, DFC with four oak leaf clusters, Air medal with 25 oak leaf clusters, Bronze Star, Republic of Vietnam Gallantry Cross, Palm, Rep. of Vietnam Campaign Medal, Kuwait Liberation medal, Estonian White Star. Mem. Air Weather Assn., Ret. Officers Assn., Air Force Assn. Roman Catholic. Avocations: skiing, golf, running. Home: 4207 Middlebrook St Fairfax VA 22032 Office: Sonalysts Inc 1901 N Beauregard St Ste 350 Alexandria VA 22311-1705

LENNOX, ANNIE, rock musician; b. Aberdeen, Scotland, Dec. 25, 1954; m. Radha Raman, Mar. 1984 (div. 1985). Student, Royal Acad. Music, London. Mem. musical group Catch, Tourists, 1977-80; founding mem. Eurythmics. Albums: (with Eurythmics) In The Garden, 1980, Sweet Dreams, 1983, Touch, 1984, 1984 (For the Love of Big Brother), 1984, Be Yourself Tonight, 1985, Revenge, 1986, Savage, 1988, We Too Are One, 1989, Greatest Hits, 1991, Eurythmics Live, 1993; (solo) Diva, 1992, Medusa, 1994; actress (film) Revolution. Office: care Simon Fuller Mgmt Unit 32, 35-37 Parkgate Rd, London England SW11 4NP

LENNOX, DONALD D(UANE), automotive and housing components company executive; b. Pitts., Dec. 3, 1918; s. Edward George and Sarah B. (Knight) L.; m. Jane Armstrong, June 11, 1949; children: Donald D., J. Gordon. BS with honors, U. Pitts., 1947. CPA, Pa. With Ford Motor Co., 1950-69, Xerox Corp., 1969-80; corp. v.p. and sr. v.p. info. tech. group Xerox Corp., Rochester, N.Y., 1969-73, group v.p. and pres. info. tech. group, 1973-75, group v.p., pres. info. systems group, 1975-80; sr. v.p., sr. staff officer Xerox Corp., Stamford, Conn., 1973-74; sr. v.p. ops. staff Navistar Internat. Corp., Chgo., 1980-81, exec. v.p., 1981-82, pres., chief operating officer, 1982, chmn., chief exec. officer, 1983-87, also bd. dirs.; chmn., chief exec. officer Schlegel Corp., Rochester, N.Y., 1987-89; chmn. Internat. Imaging Materials, Inc., Amherst, N.Y., 1990—; also bd. dirs. Internat. Imaging Materials, Inc., Amherst; bd. dirs. Prudential-Securities Mut. Funds, Gleason Corp. Served with AC USN, 1942-45. Decorated D.F.C. with 2 gold stars, Air medal with 4 gold stars. Mem. Rochester Area C. of C. (pres. 1979), Country Club of Rochester, Genesee Valley Econ. Club, Chgo. Club, Order of Artus, Beta Gamma Sigma. Republican. *What modest success I have enjoyed is the result of hard work and dedication to the success of the organization public or private. Rarely is one's contribution to the success of the organization not recognized or rewarded.*

LENNOX, EDWARD NEWMAN, holding company executive; b. New Orleans, July 27, 1925; s. Joseph Andrew and May Alice (Newman) L.; B.B.A., Tulane U., 1949; m. Joan Marie Landry, Sept. 3, 1949; children: Katherine Sarah, Anne Victoria, Mary Elizabeth, Laura Joan. Mktg. service clk. Shell Oil Co., New Orleans, 1949; with W.M. Chambers Truck Line, Inc., 1950-60 exec. v.p., 1954-60; v.p., gen. mgr. Radcliff Materials, Inc., New Orleans, 1961-71; v.p. Office Pub. Affairs, So. Industries Corp., 1971-88; v.p. Dravo Natural Resources Co., 1982-91, Dravo Corp., 1989-91, ret., 1992; pres. Tidelands Industries, Inc., 1982-85; bd. dir. Home Savings & Loan Assn., 1979-89, pres., 1982-88, chmn., 1984-89; cons. Martin-Marietta Aggregates, 1995—. Pres., La. Tank Truck Carriers, 1954-55; mem. La. Bd. Hwys., 1965-67; chmn. New Orleans Aviation Bd., 1965-66; bd. dirs. Travelers Aid Soc., 1966-68, Met. Area Com., 1967-80, Constrn. Industry Legis. Coun., 1968-85, Miss. Valley Assn., 1969-72; pres. bd. levee commrs. Orleans Levee Dist., 1969-72; pres. Met. New Orleans Safety Coun., 1969-71; bus. and fin. adviser Congregation Sisters of Immaculate Conception; vice chmn. transp. task force Goals for La., 1969-72; mem. New Orleans Bd. Trade, 1971-89; mem. Ala. Gov.'s Adv. Coun. on Econs., 1971-72, Gov.'s Adv. Com. River Area Transp. and Planning Study, 1971-72; area v.p. Pub. Affairs Rsch. Coun. La., 1972-73; mem. exec. com. La. Good Roads Assn., 1972-74; industry del. La. Constl. Conv., 1973; mem. exec. com. Miss. Valley World Trade Coun., 1973-74; bd. dirs., exec. com. Pendleton Meml. Meth. Hosp., 1963-81, dir. emeritus, 1981—; bd. dirs. Boys' Clubs Greater New Orleans, 1973-79; bd. dirs., mem. exec. bd. Goodwill Industries Greater New Orleans, Inc., 1975-79, 81—, treas., 1984-85, first v.p., 1987-88, chmn. 1989-90; bd. dirs. Americanism Forum, 1975—, Tragedy Fund, Inc., 1976—; bd. govs. La. Civil Svc. League, 1974—, pres., 1977-78; dir. chmn. bd. trustees La. Found. Pvt. Colls., 1980-83. Capt. AUS, 1943-46. Recipient Industry Svc. award Assoc. Gen. Contractors Am., 1967, Cert. of Appreciation Constrn. Industry Assn. New Orleans, 1972, New Orleans Jaycees award, 1960, Cert. of Merit Mayoralty of New Orleans, 1964, 67, Monte M. Lemann award La. Civil Svc. League, 1976; named Hon. Life Chmn., 1980, hon. Citizen and Amb. at Large City of Jacksonville, 1966. Mem. NAM (pub. affairs steering com. So. div. 1979—), La. Motor Transport Assn. (pres. 1963-64), Ala. Trucking Assn. (v.p. 1956-60), So. Concrete Masonry Assn. (pres. 1963-68), Greater New Orleans Ready Mixed Concrete Assn. (pres. 1966-68), La. Shell Producers Assn. (pres. 1966-68), C. of C. New Orleans Area (bd. dir. 1968-73, 75-77, pres. elect 1973), Internat. House (bd. dir. 1977-79), Traffic Club New Orleans, Lakeshore Property Owners Assn. (bd. dir. 1974-86, pres. 1976-77, 79-80), Tulane Alumni Assn., Mobile Area C. of C. Club: Metairie Country (bd. govs. 1976-82, 89-92, pres. 1980-81). Home: 862 Topaz St New Orleans LA 70124-3626 Office: 120 Mallard St Ste 150 Saint Rose LA 70087-4016

LENO, JAY (JAMES DOUGLAS MUIR LENO), television personality, comedian, writer; b. New Rochelle, N.Y., Apr. 28, 1950; s. Angelo and Cathryn Leno; m. Mavis Nicholson, 1980. Grad., Emerson Coll., 1973. Worked as Rolls-Royce auto mechanic and deliveryman. Stand-up comedian playing Carneigie Hall, Caesar's Palace, others; numerous appearances on Late Night with David Letterman; exclusive guest host The Tonight Show, NBC-TV, 1987-92, host, 1992— (Emmy award, 1995); host, prodr. Showtime Spl. Jay Leno and the American Dream, 1986, Saturday Night Live, 1986, Jay Leno's Family Comedy Hour (Writers Guild Am. nomination), 1987, Our Planet Tonight; film appearances include: The Silver Bears, Fun with Dick and Jane, 1977, American Hot Wax, 1978, Americathon, 1979, Collision Course, 1988, Dave, 1993, Wayne's World 2, Major League 2, The Flintstones, 1994; (voice) What's up Hideous Sun Demon?, We're Back, 1995. Avocations: antique motorcycles and automobiles. Office: PO Box 7885 Burbank CA 91510-7885 also: ICM 8942 Wilshire Blvd Beverly Hills CA 90211*

LENON, RICHARD ALLEN, chemical corporation executive; b. Lansing, Mich., Aug. 4, 1920; s. Theo and Elizabeth (Amon) L.; m. Helen Johnson, Sept. 13, 1941; children: Richard Allen, Pamela A., Lisa A. BA, Western Mich. Coll., 1941; postgrad., Northwestern U., 1941-42. Mgr. fin. div. Montgomery Ward & Co., Chgo., 1947-56; v.p. fin. Westinghouse Air Brake Co., 1963-67, treas., 1965-67; v.p., treas. Internat. Minerals & Chem. Corp., Skokie, Ill., 1956-63; group v.p. fin. and adminstrn. Internat. Minerals & Chem. Corp., 1967-68, exec. v.p., 1968-70, pres., 1970-78, chmn., 1977-86, chmn. exec. com., 1986-88; chmn. exec. com. IMC Global Inc., 1989-96; bd. dirs. IMC Global Inc. Lt. comdr. USNR, 1942-47. Clubs: University (Chgo.); Glen View (Ill.). Home: 803 Solar Ln Glenview IL 60025-4464 Office: IMC Global Inc 2100 Sanders Rd Northbrook IL 60062-6139

LENOX, ANGELA COUSINEAU, healthcare consultant; b. Vergennes, Vt., Dec. 12, 1946; d. Romeo Joseph and Colombe Mary (Gevry) C.; m. Donald Allen Lenox, Oct. 5, 1969 (div.); 1 child, Tiffanie Jae. RN diploma, Albany Med. Ctr. Sch. Nursing, 1969; BS, Barry U., 1982; M of Health Mgmt., St. Thomas U., 1990. Cert. in profl. healthcare quality. Intravenous therapist Holy Cross Hosp., Ft. Lauderdale, Fla., 1979-91; utilization review coord. North Borward Hosp., Pompano Beach, Fla., 1984-89; med. staff quality mgr. Humana Bennett, Plantation, Fla., 1990-91; med. resource analyst Hermann Hosp., Houston, 1991-93; assoc. mgr. quality improvement The Prudential, Sugar Land, Tex., 1993-95; dir. quality United Healthcare Tex., Houston, 1995—; quantity dir., United Healthcare of Tex., 1997—; cons. ACL Cons., Houston. Contbr. articles to profl. jours. 1st lt. U.S. Army res., 1991—. Mem. Tex. Gold Coast Assn. Healthcare Quality, Tex. Soc. Quality Assurance, Nat. Assn. Healthcare Quality. Avocations: skiing, running, reading, writing. Home: 8523 Dawnridge Dr Houston TX 77071-2441

LENOX, ROGER SHAWN, lawyer; b. Prescott, Ark., June 27, 1961; s. Ollie and Mae Lenox; m. Patricia Mickens; children: Mariah, Maya. BSN cum laude, U. Ala., Huntsville, 1987; JD, U. Mich., 1991. Bar: Tex. 1992, D.C. 1993, U.S. Ct. Appeals (D.C. cir.) 1993, U.S. Dist. Ct. (no., so., ea. and we. dists.) Tex. 1994, U.S. Ct. Appeals (5th cir.) 1995; RN, Ala. Summer assoc. Dykema Gossett, Detroit, 1989-90; assoc. Fulbright & Jaworski, L.L.P., Dallas, 1991-95; pvt. practice Law Office of Roger S. Lenox, Dallas, 1995—. Firm rep. Dallas Black C. of C., 1992-95, The Sci. Place, Dallas, 1993-95; spkr. Greater Tex. chpt. Nat. Assn. Pediatric Nurse Practitioners and Assocs., 1995; atty. mentor for Criminal Cts. Day, Youth Leadership Dallas, 1994; Career Day spkr. Dallas Bus. Magnet H.S., 1993. Lt. (j.g.) USN, 1987-91. Recipient Faculty Award for Clin. Excellence, U. Ala., Huntsville, 1987, Nat. Collegiate Nursing award U.S. Achievement Acad., 1987; U. Mich. Law Sch. Clarence Darrow scholar, 1988-91. Mem. ABA, Tex. Bar, D.C. Bar, Dallas Bar Assn., J.L. Turner Legal Assn., Sigma Theta Tau. Avocations: travel, water skiing, biking, automotive mechanics. Home: 842 Clear Fork Dr Dallas TX 75232 Office: PO Box 222128 Dallas TX 75222-2128

LENT, JOHN ANTHONY, journalist, educator; b. East Millsboro, Pa., Sept. 8, 1936; s. John and Rose (Marano) L.; remarried Rose Kueny, 1988; children: Laura, Andrea, John, Lisa, Shahnon. B.S., Ohio U., 1958, M.S., 1960; Ph.D., U. Iowa, 1972; cert., Press Inst. of India, Sophia U., Tokyo, Japan, U. Oslo, Guadalajara, Mex., Summer Sch. Dir. public relations, instr. English W.Va. Tech., Montgomery, 1960-62; Newhouse research asst. and asst. to dir. communications research Syracuse (N.Y.) U., 1962-64; lectr. De La Salle Coll., Manila, 1964-65; asst. prof. W.Va. Tech., 1965-66; asst. prof. journalism U. Wis., Eau Claire, 1966-67; asst. prof. journalism, head tchrs.' journalism sequence Marshall U., Huntington, W.Va., 1967-69; vis. assoc. prof. U. Wyo., Laramie, 1969-70; asst. editor Internat. Comm. Bull., Iowa City, 1970-72; coord. mass comm. U. Sains Malaysia, Penang, 1972-74; assoc. prof. comm. Temple U., Phila., 1974-76, prof. comm. (journalism), 1976-95, prof. comm. (broadcasting, telecomm., and mass media), 1995—, Benedum vis. disting. prof., 1987. Author: Asian Newspapers Reluctant Revolution, 1971, Asian Mass Communications: A Comprehensive Bibliography, 1975, 78, Third World Mass Media and Their Search for Modernity, 1977, Broadcasting in Asia and Pacific, 1978, Topics in Third World Mass Media, 1979, Caribbean Mass Commmunications: A Comprehensive Bibliography, 1981, Asian Newspapers: Contemporary Trends and Problems, 1982, Videocassettes in the Third World, 1989, Asian Film Industry, 1990, Caribbean Popular Culture, 1990, Caribbean Mass Communications, 1990, Transnational Communications, 1991, Women and Mass Communications: An International Annotated Bibliography, 1991, Bibliographic Guide to Caribbean Mass Communications, 1992, Bibliography of Cuban Mass Communications, 1992, Cartoonmeter, 1994, Animation, Caricature, and Gag and Political Cartoons in the U.S. and Canada: An International Bibliography, 1994, Comic Art of Europe: An International, Comprehensive Bibliography, 1994, Comic Books and Comic Strips in the United States: An International Bibliography, 1994, Asian Popular Culture, 1995, A Different Road Taken, 1995, Comic Art in Africa, Asia, Australia and Latin America: A Comprehensive, International Bibliography, 1996, others; founding editor: Berita, 1975—; founding mng. editor: WittyWorld, 1987—; editor: Westview Press Internat. Comm. series, 1992-95, Asian Cinema, 1994—. Anchor Hocking scholar, 1954-59, U. Oslo scholar, 1962, Fulbright scholar, The Philippines, 1964-65; recipient Benedum award, 1968, Broadcast Preceptor award (2), 1979, Paul Eberman Outstanding Rsch. award, 1988, Ray and Pat Browne Nat. Book award, 1995, Temple U. Exceptional award, 1995; decorated Chapel of Four Chaplains' Legion of Honor. Mem. Malaysia/Singapore/Brunei Studies Group (founding chmn. 1975-82), Caribbean Studies Assn., Assn. Asian Studies, Internat. Assn. Mass Comm. Rsch. (visual and comic art organizer, chair 1984—), Asian Cinema Studies Soc. (chmn. 1994—), Population Culture Assn. (founding chmn. Asian popular culture group 1996—), Sigma Delta Chi, Sigma Tau Delta, Kappa Tau Alpha, Phi Alpha Theta. Home: 669 Ferne Blvd Drexel Hill PA 19026-3110 Office: Temple Univ Journalism Dept Philadelphia PA 19122 *I have cherished the principles of hard work over long hours, accuracy, comprehensiveness, and honesty in my intellectual and scholarly endeavors. I have considered it important to set and meet goals, to share my work with others, to remain untainted by organizations or individuals who, I feel, are not working for the good of mankind. I also cherish, and protect and use, my right to speak out on those issues which I feel are offensive to the public; the result has been that my writings have incurred the wrath of government ministers in at least two countries.*

LENT, NORMAN FREDERICK, JR., former congressman; b. Oceanside, N.Y., Mar. 23, 1931; s. Norman Frederick and Ellen (Bain) L.; m. Barbara Ann Morris, Aug. 4, 1979; children from previous marriage: Norman Frederick 3d, Barbara Anne, Thomas Benjamin. BA, Hofstra U., 1952; LLB, Cornell U., 1957; LLD (hon.), Kyung Hee U., Seoul, Republic of Korea, 1975, Molloy Coll., 1985, Hofstra Coll., 1988. Bar: N.Y. 1957, Fla. 1976. Assoc. police judge East Rockaway, N.Y., 1958-60; confidential law sec. to N.Y. State Supreme Ct., 1960-62; mem. N.Y. State Senate, 1963-70, chmn. joint legislative com. public health, 1966-70; mem. 92nd Congress 5th Dist. N.Y., 1971-73; mem. 93rd-102d Congresses 4th Dist. N.Y., 1973-93; vice chmn. Energy and Commerce com. 100th-102nd Congresses U.S. Ho. Reps., 1986-93, vice chmn. Mcht. Marine subcom., 1987-93; cons. Lent & Scrivner, Washington, 1993—; Rep. exec. leader, East Rockaway, N.Y., 1968-70. Mem. bd. visitors U.S. Mcht. Marine Acad., Kings Point, N.Y. With USNR, 1952-54. Recipient George Estabrook Disting. Service award Hofstra U., 1967, Israeli Prime Minister's medal, 1977, Disting. Achievement medal N.Y.C. Holland Soc., 1987, Tree of Life award Jewish Nat. Fund., 1987, Anatoly Sharansky Freedom award L.I. Com. for Soviet Jewry, 1983. Mem. Fla. Bar Assn. Office: Lent & Scrivner 915 15th St NW Washington DC 20005-2302

LENTHALL, FRANKLYN, theatre historian; b. Nanticoke, Pa., July 14, 1919; s. Samuel Franklyn and Lena (Fraunfelter) L. Student, Cornell U., 1942-44, Am. Acad. Dramatic Arts, 1946. Curator Boothbay Theatre Mus.; Mem. faculty Am. Acad. Dramatic Arts, 1949-54, Am. Theatre Wing, 1958-59; acting curator, cons. theatre Mus. of City of N.Y., 1983-86; regional auditioner Am. Acad. Dramatic Arts, N.Y.C. and Pasadena, Calif., 1995—; Former mem. exec. bd. Theatre Library Assn., Lincoln Center, N.Y.C., 1966-70; mem. Maine Commn. on Arts and Humanities, 1967-73; theatre cons., 1968-69, lectr. on theatre, theatre historian. Appeared in profl. theatre, 1937-51; featured in: movies, including Naked City; producer, dir. with movies, including, Lenthall Players, 1951-58, producer, owner, dir., Boothbay (Maine) Playhouse and Theatre Mus., 1957-74; dir.: off-Broadway prodn. Hello and Goodby (Athol Fugard), N.Y.C., 1977, Oblomov, 1984. Contbr. articles on theatre to various publs; contbg. author: Autographs and Manuscripts: A Collector's Manual, 1978, Theatre and Performing Arts Collection, Playbill Mag., 1981; curator exhbns. The Old Met: A Memory of Opera On Broadway, N.Y.C. Operas First Forty Years. Served with CIC AUS, 1942-44. Recipient Disting. Service award in recognition of dedicated service to theatre Wyo. Sem., 1979. Mem. Drama League N.Y. (adv. bd. 1959—, bd. dirs. 1983-88), Lincoln County Cultural and Hist. Assn. (trustee 1973-77), Polish Theatre Inst. (bd. dirs. 1984-88), Boothbay C. of C. (dir. 1963-70). Methodist (lay Preacher). Home and Office: 3-A Signal Point Village Sea St Boothbay Harbor ME 04538 *Only in recent years have I learned to really appreciate and understand William Blake's lines from his poem ETERNITY: "He who binds to himself a joy Does the winged life destroy; But he who kisses the joy as it flies Lives in eternity's sunrise." Every day of my life I am more fully aware of the importance of the ARTS AND THE HUMANITIES in the lives of all of us. . .in the life of this great country. For too long they have been neglected. I am in complete agreement with Tolstoy who wrote "When someone sees or feels something, and ex-*

presses it in such a form that he who listens, reads, or sees his work feels, sees, and hears the same thing in the same way as the artist, that is art.".

LENTON, ROBERTO LEONARDO, research facility and environmental administrator; b. Buenos Aires, Feb. 28, 1947; s. Leonard Gersham and Katie (McCulloch) L.; m. Julia Anne Frend, June 11, 1971; children: Alexandra, James, Christopher, Jessica. Civil Engr., U. Buenos Aires, 1971; SM in Civil Engring., MIT, 1973, PhD in Water Resources Systems, 1974. Planning asst. Ministry Pub. Works, Buenos Aires, 1970-71; vis. rsch. engr. MIT, Cambridge, 1971-72, rsch. asst., 1972-74, asst. prof., 1974-77; project specialist Ford Found., New Delhi, 1977-80, program officer, 1980-83; program officer Ford Found., N.Y.C., 1983-86; dep. dir. gen. Internat. Irrigation Mgmt. Inst., Kandy, Sri Lanka, 1986-87; dir. gen. Internat. Irrigation Mgmt. Inst., Colombo, Sri Lanka, 1987-94; dir. sustainable energy and environ. divsn. UN Devel. Programme, N.Y.C., 1995—. Co-author: Applied Water Resources Systems Planning, 1979. Bd. dirs., treas. Am. Embassy Sch., New Delhi, 1981-83; bd. dirs. Overseas Children's Sch., Colombo, 1989-93. Mem. ASCE, Am. Geophys. Union, Centro Argentino Ingenieros. Avocations: windsurfing, tennis, running. Home: 48 Rye Rd Rye NY 10580 Office: UN Devel Programme One UN Plz New York NY 10017

LENTS, DON GLAUDE, lawyer; b. Kansas City, Mo., Nov. 4, 1949; s. Donald Victor and Helen Maxine (Draper) L.; m. Peggy Lynn Iglauer, Aug. 27, 1972; children: Stacie Lee, Kelsey Lynn. BA magna cum laude, Harvard U., 1971, JD magna cum laude, 1974. Bar: Mo. 1974, U.S. Dist. Ct. (ea. dist.) Mo. 1975, U.S. Ct. Appeals (8th cir.) 1975. Jr. ptnr. Bryan Cave, St. Louis, 1974-81, ptnr., 1982, 84—; mem. exec. com., 1988—; ptnr. Bryan Cave, London, 1982-84; mgr. internat. dept. Bryan Cave, St. Louis, 1984-88, mgr. corp. and bus. dept., 1988-95, chair corp. and bus. dept., 1995-96, head transactions group, 1996—; instr. law Washington U., 1979-80. Co-author: Missouri Corporate Law and Practice, 1989, 91 and ann. supplements. Bd. dirs. Leadership St. Louis, Inc., 1978-81, 86-91, pres., 1989-91; bd. dirs. Coro Found., St. Louis, Inc., 1986-91, gen. counsel, sec., 1988-90; vol. St. Louis Lawyers and Accts. for Arts, 1988-93, v.p., 1990-92, pres., 1992-93; bd. dirs. Brit. Am. Project, 1989-94, pres., 1993-94; bd. dirs., exec. com. Confluence St. Louis, 1995-96; bd. dirs., exec. com. Focus St. Louis, 1996—. Sheldon fellow Harvard U., 1974-75. Mem. ABA, Mo. Bar Assn. (coun. corp. and bus. law sect. 1987-93, vice chmn. 1988-92), Met. St. Louis Bar Assn. (sec. bus. law sect. 1980-81), Harvard Alumni Assn. (regional dir. 1993-96), Hasty Pudding Club, Harvard Club (exec. com. St. Louis Club 1978-82, v.p. 1987-92, pres. 1992-93). Office: Bryan Cave 1 Metropolitan Sq 211 S Broadway Saint Louis MO 63102-1705

LENTZ, EDWARD ALLEN, consultant, retired health administrator; b. Superior, Wis., May 30, 1926; s. Otto Albert and Martha Mary Ann (Gruhel) L.; m. Margaret Ann Denier, May 30, 1952; 1 child, Elizabeth Ann Clark. BS, U. Cin., 1951; MHA, Wayne State U., Detroit, 1957. Asst. dir. Pub. Health Fedn., Cin., 1954-57; dir. health planning United Cmty. Coun., Columbus, Ohio, 1957-62; asst. dir. Columbus Hosp. Fedn., 1962-65; assoc. exec. dir. Ohio Hosp. Assn., Columbus, 1965-69; exec. dir. Health Planning Assn. of Ohio River Valley, Cin., 1969-70; asst. prof. grad. program in health svcs. adminstrn. Coll. of Medicine, Ohio State U., Columbus, 1970-72, adj. assoc. prof. preventive medicine, 1957—; dep. dir. med. care adminstrn. Ohio Dept. Health, Columbus, 1972-75; pres., CEO Med. Advances Inst., Columbus, 1975-79; v.p. corp. devel. Mt. Carmel Health System, Columbus, 1979-95; cons. Mt. Carmel Health System, 1995-97; cons. cmty. health planning USPHS. Contbr. articles to profl. jours. Mem., chair Ohio Dept. Human Svcs./Ohio Med. Care Adv. Com., Columbus, 1975—; bd. dirs., vice chair Netcare Corp., Columbus, 1989—. Served with USN, 1944-46; 1st lt. U.S. Army, 1951-53, Korea. Recipient Spl. Citation for hosp. planning and mktg. in Ohio and Delbert L. Pugh Conf., Ohio State U. Coll. Medicine and Ohio Hosp. Assn., 1991. Fellow Am. Pub. Health Assn. (bd. dirs., vice chmn. bd. trustees 1979-83); mem. Ohio Pub. Health Assn. (pres. 1969-70), Am. Assn. Areawide Planning Agencies (pres. 1969-70), Ohio Hosp. Assn. Soc. for Hosp. Planning and Mktg. (pres. 1987-88), Columbus Rotary (com. chair). Presbyterian. Avocations: fishing, photography, tennis. Home: 585 Keyes Ln Worthington OH 43085-3503

LENTZ, EDWIN LAMAR, art historian; b. Houston, Mar. 31, 1951; s. Edwin Lonzo and Gerald Dwain (Flack) L. BA, U. Tex., 1973, MA, 1991. Spl. asst. to Harry H. Ransom Harry Ransom Humanities Rsch. Ctr., U. Tex., Austin, 1971-73, curator Coral Maud Oneal Rm., 1975—; mus. registrar Lyndon Baines Johnson Libr. and Mus., Austin, 1974-75; asst. to registrar Mus. Fine Arts, Houston, 1975-76; curator/assoc. mng. dir. Festival-Inst. at Round Top, Tex., 1976—. Author (catalog): Cora Maud Oneal Room, 1979, 85; contbr. articles to profl. jours. Ransom Ctr. rsch. grantee, 1985, 86, 88; Victorian Soc. Am. scholar, 1992. Mem. Coll. Art Assn. (mem. mus. com. 1993—), Am. Friends of Attingham, Victorian Soc. Am., Phi Kappa Phi. Avocations: rare books, theatre. Office: Festival-Inst at Round Top PO Box 89 Round Top TX 78954-0089

LENTZ, THOMAS LAWRENCE, biomedical educator, dean, researcher; b. Toledo, Mar. 25, 1939; s. Lawrence Raymond and Kathryn (Heath) L.; m. Judith Ellen Pernaa, June 17, 1961; children: Stephen, Christopher, Sarah. Student, Cornell U., 1957-60; MD, Yale U., 1964. Instr. in anatomy Yale U. Sch. Medicine, New Haven, 1964-66, asst. prof. of anatomy, 1966-69, assoc. prof. of cytology, 1969-74, assoc. prof. of cell biology, 1974-85, prof. of cell biology, 1985—, asst. dean for admissions, 1976—, vice chmn. cell biology, 1992—; mem. cellular and molecular neurobiology panel NSF, 1987-88, mem. cellular neurosci. panel, 1988-90; mem. neurology B-1 study sect. Nat. Inst. Neurol. Disorders and Stroke, NIH, 1996. Author: The Cell Biology of Hydra, 1966, Primitive Nervous Systems, 1968, Cell Fine Structure, 1971; contbr. over 90 articles to sci. publs. Vice chmn., chmn. Planning and Zoning Commn., Killingworth, Conn., 1979—; active Killingworth Hist. Soc. Recipient Conn. Fedn. Planning and Zoning Agys. award, 1995, Citizen of Yr. award Killingworth Lions Club, 1993; fellow Trumbull Coll., Yale U.; grantee NSF, 1968-92, Dept. Army, 1986, NIH, 1987—. Mem. AAAS, Am. Soc. Cell Biology, Soc. for Neurosci., N.Y. Acad. Scis., Appalachian Mountain Club (trails com., Warren Hart award 1995, White Mountain Four Thousand Footer Club), Appalachian Trail Conf., Mt. Washington Obs., Wonalancet Out Door Club, Alpha Omega Alpha. Republican. Mem. United Ch. of Christ. Achievements include study of primitive nervous systems, identification of neurotoxin binding site on the acetylcholine receptor, identification of cellular receptor for rabies virus. Office: Yale U Sch Medicine Dept Cell Biol 333 Cedar St PO Box 208002 New Haven CT 06520-8002

LENZ, CHARLES ELDON, electrical engineering consultant, author; b. Omaha, Apr. 13, 1926; s. Charles Julius and Hattie Susan (Wageck) L. SB, MIT, 1951; MS, U. Calif., Irvine, 1971; SM, MIT, 1953; PhD, Cornell U., 1957. Registered profl. engr., Mass. Elec. engr. GE, Pittsfield, West Lynn, Mass., Syracuse, Ithaca, N.Y., 1949-56; sr. staff engr. Avco Corp., Wilmington, Mass., 1958-60; mem. tech. staff Armour Rsch. Found., Chgo., 1960-62; sr. staff engr. North Am. Aviation, Inc., Anaheim, Calif., 1962-69; prof. U. Hawaii, Honolulu, 1966-68, U. Nebr., Omaha, 1973-78; sr. engr. Control Data Corp., Omaha, 1978-80; elec. engr. USAF, Offutt AFB, Nebr., 1980-84; sr. rsch. engr. Union Pacific Railroad, Omaha, 1984-87; engring. cons., author, 1987—; guest lectr. Coll. of Aeronautics, Cranfield, Eng., 1969, Cornell U., Ithaca, N.Y., UCLA, U. Minn., Mpls. Contbr. articles to profl. jours. including IEEE Internat. Conv. Record, ISA Conf. Procs., ISA Transactions, Procs. of the IEEE Electronics Conf., Procs. of Internat. Aerospace Instrumentation Symposium, Procs. of Modeling and Simulation Conf., Procs. of IEEE Electronics Conf., Procs. of Nat. Aerospace Electronics Conf., Procs. of Nat. Congress of Applied Mechanics. Program com. mem. N.E. Rsch. and Engring. Meeting, Boston, 1959. With USNR, 1944-46. Recipient 1st prize for tech. papers Am. Inst. Elec. Engrs., 1949; tuition scholar MIT, 1948-51, John McMullen Grad. scholar Cornell U., 1955-56; Charles Bull Earl Meml. fellow Cornell U., 1956-57, postgrad. fellow, U. Calif., Irvine, 1971. Mem. ASCE, IEEE (sr., life, nat. feedback control com., nat. control subcom. on computers), Sci. Rsch. Soc. Am. (life), N.Y. Acad. Scis. (life), Inst. Soc. Am. (sr.), Tau Beta Pi (life), Eta Kappa Nu (life), Sigma Xi (life). Achievements include protoprogramming and patents in the fields of computer safety, storage and testing, phase-angle measurement, radar-signal processing, and ultraprecise control. Home: 5016 Western Ave Omaha NE 68132-1466

LENZ, EDWARD ARNOLD, trade association executive, lawyer; b. White Plains, N.Y., Sept. 28, 1942; s. Frederick and Hildegarde (Bunzel) L.; m. Anna Maria Bartusiak, Mar. 21, 1987; children: Scott, Eric. BA, Bucknell U., 1964; JD, Boston Coll., 1967; LLM, NYU, 1968. Bar: N.Y. 1968, D.C. 1973, Mich. 1982. Trial atty. U.S. Dept. Justice, Washington, 1970-72; assoc. gen. counsel U.S. Cost of Living Coun., Washington, 1973; assoc. Miller & Chevalier, Washington, 1973-80; counsel Health Ins. Assn. Am., Washington, 1980-82; v.p., asst. gen. counsel Kelly Svcs. Inc., Troy, Mich., 1982-89; chmn. legis. com. Nat. Assn. Temp. & Staffing Svcs., Alexandria, Va., 1985-89; sr. v.p., gen. counsel Nat. Assn. Temp. Svcs., Alexandria, Va., 1989-93, sr. v.p. legal and govt. affairs, 1993—. Author: Co-employment--Employer Liability Issues in Staffing Services Arrangements, 1994. Capt. U.S. Army, 1968-70, Vietnam. Decorated Bronze Star. Mem. ABA, N.Y. Bar Assn., D.C. Bar Assn., Am. Corp. Counsel Assn., Pi Sigma Alpha, Sigma Alpha Epsilon. Home: 818 S Lee St Alexandria VA 22314-4334 Office: Nat Assn Temp & Staffing Svcs 119 S St Asaph St Alexandria VA 22314-3119

LENZ, HENRY PAUL, management consultant; b. N.Y.C., Nov. 24, 1925; s. Ernest and Margaret (Schick) L.; m. Norma M. Kull, Jan. 25, 1958; children: Susan, Scott, Theresa. A.B., U. N.C., 1946; M.B.A., Coll. Ins., 1974. Underwriter U.S. Casualty Co., N.Y.C., 1948-55; underwriting mgr. Mass. Bonding & Ins. Co., N.Y.C., 1955-60; with Home Ins. Co., N.Y.C., 1960-85; sr. v.p. Home Ins. Co., 1972-75, exec. v.p., dir., 1975-85; chmn. bd. Lenz Enterprises Ltd., Chatham, NJ, 1985—; former pres., dir. Home Indemnity Co.; pres., dir. Home Ins. Co. Ind., Home Ins. Co. Ill., City Ins. Co., Home Group Risk Mgmt.; chmn. bd. Home Reins. Co., Scott Wetzel Services Inc.; chmn., pres. Cityvest Reins. Ltd., City Ins. Co. (U.K.) Ltd.; trustee Am. Inst. Property and Liability Underwriters, Ins. Inst. Am. Served with USNR, 1944-47, 52-53. Decorated Army Commendation medal. Mem. Soc. CPCU's, Phi Beta Kappa, Sigma Nu. Office: Lenz Enterprises Ltd 42 Edgehill Ave Chatham NJ 07928-1937

LENZ, PHILIP JOSEPH, municipal administrator; b. Monterey Park, Calif., Sept. 15, 1940; s. Philip George and Irene Mary (Bowers) L.; m. Mary Lou Antista, July 16, 1966; children: Brian Joseph, Jonathan Thomas. BA, Calif. State U., L.A., 1966; MS, Pepperdine U., 1974; cert. instr. total quality mgmt., Calif. State U., San Bernardino, 1993. Dir. West Valley div. San Bernardino County (Calif.) Probation Dept., 1977-79, dir. juvenile div., 1979-82, dir. adminstrv. services, 1982-88, dir. dist. services, 1988-90; dep. chief probation officer, 1990—; instr. dept. bus. Calif. State U., San Bernardino; instr. dept. social rels. Loma Linda U., 1988. Sec. bd. trustees Upland (Calif.) Sch. Dist., 1986—, pres. sch. bd., 1989-90, 94-96; mgr., coach Upland Am. Little League, 1981-90, bd. dirs., 1982-90; pres. Fontana (Calif.) Family Svc. Agy., 1972-74; mem. adv. com. corrections Chaffey Coll., Alta Loma, Calif., 1977-97; mem. Upland Parks and Recreation Com., 1986—, chmn., 1989-91; bd. dirs. Highlander Ednl. Found., v.p., 1991-96; mem. Calif. Youth Authority CADRE of Cons. Recipient Tim Fitzharris award Chief Probation Officers of Calif., 1987. Mem. Calif. Probation, Parole and Correctional Assn. (liaison, regional v.p. 1981-83, 2d v.p. 1985-86, 1st v.p. 1986—, pres. 1987—), Probation Bus. Mgr.'s Assn. (regional chmn. 1984-86, v.p. 1987), Western Correctional Assn., Assn. for Criminal Justice Rsch. (bd. dirs.), Probation Adminstrs. Assn. (regional chair 1992-93). Democrat. Roman Catholic. Avocations: baseball, bicycle riding, hiking. Home: 1375 Stanford Ave Upland CA 91786-3147 Office: San Bernardino County Dept Probation 175 W 5th St San Bernardino CA 92401-1401

LENZ, ROBERT WILLIAM, polymer chemistry educator; b. N.Y.C., Apr. 28, 1926; s. Henry B. and Olga A. (Grote) L.; m. Madeleine Leblanc, June 6, 1953; children: Kathleen, Douglas, Cynthia, Suzanne. BSChemE, Lehigh U., 1949; PhD, SUNY, Syracuse, 1956. Rsch. chemist Chicopee Mfg. Co., Chicopee Falls, Mass., 1951-53; rsch. chemist Dow Chem. Co., Midland, Mich., 1955-61, Framingham, Mass., 1961-63; asst. dir. FRL Inc., Dedham, Mass., 1963-66; prof. U. Mass., Amherst, 1996-95, prof. emeritus, 1995—; cons. many cos. in the chem. industry, 1966—; dist. faculty lectr. U. Mass., 1994. Author: Organic Chemistry of Synthetic High Polymers, 1967; assoc. editor Macromolecules, 1982-94, editor-in-chief, 1995—; contbr. over 375 articles to publs. Mem. adv. bd. Petroleum Rsch. Fund, 1989-93, Greve Found., N.Y.C., 1988-94; bd. dirs. Cult Awareness Network, Chgo., 1989-91. Recipient Sr. Humboldt prize, Humboldt Found., Bonn, Fed. Republic of Germany, 1979, Polymer Chemistry award Am. Chem. Soc., 1992, Outstanding Contbns. to Polymer Chemistry award Soc. of Polymer Sci. Japan, 1995; faculty fellow U. Mass., 1984. Achievements include 16 patents in field. Home: 43 Aubinwood Rd Amherst MA 01002-1623 Office: U Mass Polymer Sci Engring Dept Amherst MA 01003

LENZI, MARK, Olympic athlete, springboard diver; b. Huntsville, Ala., July 4, 1968; s. William S. and Mary Ellen L. BS in Gen. Studies, Ind. U., 1990. Mem. U.S. National Diving Team, 1989-93, 95; Olympic springboard diver Barcelona, Spain, 1992, Atlanta, 1996; nat. spokesperson Learn To Fly program Nat. Air Transp. Assn. Recipient Gold medal springboard diving Olympics, Barcelona, 1992, Bronze medal springboard diving Olympics, Atlanta, 1996, 17 internat. titles, 7 nat. titles, 2 World Cups. Achievements include first person to score over 100 points on a single dive; first American to complete a forward 4 1/2 somersault in national competition. Avocations: reading, drawing, hunting and fishing. Office: c/o US Olympic Com 1750 E Boulder St Colorado Springs CO 80909-5724*

LEO, JACQUELINE M., TV executive. Feature writer Singapore Herald, AP; sr. editor Modern Bride; co-founder Child, N.Y.C., 1986, editor-in-chief, 1987-88; editor-in-chief Family Circle, N.Y.C., 1992-94; editl. dir. women's mags. group N.Y. Times Co., N.Y.C., 1994, dir. mag. and media devel., 1994—; editorial dir. Good Morning America ABC-TV News, N.Y.C., 1994—. Author: New Woman's Guide To Getting Married. Bd. dirs. Women's Commn. for Refugee Women and Children, Child Care Action Campaign. Recipient Matrix award Women in Comm., 1993. Mem. Am. Soc. Mag. Editors (bd. dirs.), N.Y. Acad. Scis. (bd. govs.). Office: ABC News/Good Morning Am 147 Columbus Ave New York NY 10023-5900

LEO, JOHN P., columnist; b. Hoboken, N.J., June 16, 1935; s. Maurice M. and Maria M. (Trincellita) L.; m. Stephanie Wolf, Dec. 30, 1967 (div.); children: Kristin, Karen; m. Jacqueline Jasous, Jan. 21, 1978; 1 child, Alexandra. BA, U. Toronto, 1957; LittD (hon.), Marietta Coll., 1996. Reporter Bergen Record, Hackensack, N.J., 1957-60; editor Cath. Messenger, Davenport, Iowa, 1960-63; assoc. editor Commonweal mag., N.Y.C., 1963-67; reporter The New York Times, N.Y.C., 1967-69; dep. adminstr. N.Y.C. Dept. Environ. Protection, 1970-73; press columnist Village Voice, N.Y.C., 1973-74; assoc. editor, sr. writer Time mag., N.Y.C., 1974-88; columnist U.S. News & World Report, N.Y.C., 1988—. Author: How the Russians Invented Baseball, 1989, Two Steps Ahead of the Thought Police, 1994. Mem. ch.-state com. ACLU, 1964-66; bd. advisors Columbia Journalism Rev., 1994—. Office: US News & World Report 1290 6th Ave Ste 600 New York NY 10104

LEO, PETER ANDREW, newspaper columnist, writing educator; b. Teaneck, N.J., Aug. 3, 1943; s. Maurice Matthew and Mary (Trincellita) L.; m. Sylvia Weed, July 26, 1970; children—Steven, Jane. A.B., U. Toronto, 1966; M.A., NYU, 1967. High sch. tchr. Peace Corps, Nairobi, Kenya, 1968-69; reporter AP, N.Y.C., 1970, Greensboro Record (N.C.), 1971-72, Wilmington News-Jour. (Del.), 1973-78; reporter, asst. city editor, columnist Pitts. Post-Gazette, 1978—. Recipient Headliners award Atlantic City Press Club, 1972, Golden Quill award Pitts. Press Club, 1980, Keystone award Pa. Newspaper Pubs. and Editors Assn., 1984. Home: 5266 Beelermont Pl Pittsburgh PA 15217-1010 Office: PG Pub Co 34 Blvd Of The Allies Pittsburgh PA 15222-1204

LEOGRANDE, WILLIAM MARK, political science educator, writer; b. Utica, N.Y., July 1, 1949; s. John James and Patricia Ann (Ryan) LeoG; m. Martha J. Langelan. AB, Syracuse U., 1971, MA, 1973, PhD, 1976. Asst. prof. Hamilton Coll., Clinton, N.Y., 1976-78; dir. polit. sci. Am. U., Washington, 1980-82, asst. prof. polit. sci., 1978-83, assoc. prof., 1984-89, prof., 1989—, chair dept. govt., 1992-96; mem. profl. staff U.S. Senate, 1982-83, cons., 1984-85. Author: Cuba's Policy in Africa, 1980; editor: (with Morris Blachman) Confronting Revolution; Security Through Diplomacy in Central America, 1986, (with Louis Goodman) Political Parties and Democracy in Central America; dir. Latin Am. Rsch. Rev., 1982-86, World Policy Jour., 1983-93. Dir. svc. com. Unitarian-Universalist Ch., Boston, 1983-86; mem. staff Michael Dukakis Presdl. Campaign, 1988. Council Fgn. Relation Internat. Affairs fellow, 1982-83, Pew Faculty fellow, 1994-95. Mem. Coun. Fgn. Rels., Am. Polit. Sci. Assn., Latin Am. Studies Assn. (exec. council 1984-87). Democrat. Home: 7215 Chestnut St Bethesda MD 20815-4051 Office: Am U Sch Pub Affairs Ward Cir Washington DC 20016

LEON, ARTHUR SOL, research cardiologist, exercise physiologist; b. Bklyn., Apr. 26, 1931; s. Alex and Anne (Schrek) L.; m. Gloria Rakita, Dec. 23, 1956; children: Denise, Harmon, Michelle. BS in Chemistry with high honors, U. Fla., 1952; MS in Biochemistry, U. Wis., 1954, MD, 1957. Intern Henry Ford Hosp., Detroit, 1957-58; fellow in internal medicine Lahey Clinic, Boston, 1958-60; fellow in cardiology Jackson Meml. Hosp.-U. Miami (Fla.) Med. Sch., 1960-61; dir. clin. pharmacology research unit Hoffmann-La Roche Inc.-Newark Beth Israel Med. Ctr., 1969-73; from instr. to assoc. prof. medicine Coll. Medicine and Dentistry N.J., Newark, 1967-73; from assoc. prof. to prof. div. epidemiology U. Minn., Mpls., 1973—, H.L. Taylor prof. exercise sci. and health enhancement, dir. lab. physiol. hygiene and exercise sci., div. kinesiology, Coll. Edn., 1991—, dir. applied physiology and nutrition, 1973-91; mem. med. eval. team Gemini and Apollo projects NASA, 1964-67. Editor Procs. of the NIH Consensus Conf. on Phys. Activity and Cardiovasc. Health, 1997; assoc. editor Surgeon Gen.'s Report on Health Benefits of Exercise, 1996; contbr. numerous articles to profl. pubis. Trustee Vinland Nat. Sports Health Ctr. for Disabled, 1978—; mem. gov.'s coun. physical fitness sports, 1979—. Served as officer M.C. U.S. Army, 1961-67, 90-91, col. Res. 1978-92, ret. Recipient Anderson award AAHPER, 1981; Am. Heart Assn. fellow, 1960-61. Fellow Am. Coll. Cardiology, Am. Coll. Chest Physicians, Am. Coll. Clin. Pharmacology, N.Y. Acad. Scis., Am. Coll. Sports Medicine (trustee 1976-78, 82-83, v.p. 1977-79, pres. Northland chpt. 1975-76, Citation award 1995), Am. Assn. Cardiovasc. and Pulmonary Rehab. (trustee 1989-90), Am. Acad. Kinesiology and Phys. Edn.; mem. Am. Physiol. Soc., Am. Soc. Pharmacology and Exptl. Therapeutics, Am. Inst. Nutrition, Am. Heart Assn. (v.p. Hennepin County divsn. 1980-81, pres. 1982-83), Am. Coll. Nutrition, Am. Fedn. Clin. Rsch., Minn. Lung Assn. (trustee 1978-81), Phi Beta Kappa, Phi Kappa Phi. Jewish. Home: 5628 Glen Ave Minnetonka MN 55345-6610 Office: U Minn Sch Kinesiology & Leisure Studies 202 Cooke Hall Minneapolis MN 55455-0136

LEON, BRUNO, architect, educator; b. Van Houten, N.Mex., Feb. 18, 1924; s. Giovanni and Rose (Cunico) L.; m. Louise Dal-Bo, Sept. 4, 1948 (dec. 1974); m. Bonnie Bertram, Sept. 12, 1976; children: Mark Jon, John Anthony, Lisa Rose. Student, Wayne State U., 1942, U. Detroit, 1945-48; LHD (hon.), U. Detroit, 1984; BArch, N.C. State Univ., 1953. Registered architect, Mich., N.C., Mass., N.Y., N.Mex., Fla. Head design staff Fuller Research Found., Raleigh, N.C., 1954-55; archtl. designer I.M. Pei & Assos., N.Y.C., 1955-56; instr. Mass. Inst. Tech., 1956-59; designer Catalano & Belluschi (architects), Cambridge, Mass., 1958-59; asst. prof. U. Ill. at Urbana, 1959-61; dean Sch. Architecture, U. Detroit, 1961-93, dean emeritus, 1993; pvt. practice architecture, 1956—. Served with USAAF, 1942-45. Fellow AIA (dir. Detroit 1963-64); mem. Alpha Sigma Nu (hon.), Phi Kappa Phi. Home: 9 Redonda Ct Santa Fe NM 87505-8308 *I believe the integral quality of the human spirit to be the ability to dream rather than to rationalize.*

LEON, DONALD FRANCIS, university dean, medical educator; b. Washington, Aug. 19, 1932; s. Frank A. and Madeline (Wildman) L.; children: Anne, James, John, Sharon. AB, Georgetown U., 1953, MD, 1957. Diplomate Am. Bd. Internal Medicine, Subspeciality Bds. in Cardiovascular Diseases. Instr. medicine U. Pitts., 1965-67, asst. prof. medicine, 1967-70, assoc. prof., 1971-75, vice chmn. medicine, 1971-75, assoc. prof., 1975-77, exec. assoc. dean, 1975-79, prof. medicine, 1977—, pres. Univ. Health Ctr., 1979-83, dean Sch. Medicine, 1979-84; dean clin. affairs Georgetown U. Hosp., Washington, 1989-94, prof. medicine divsn. cardiology, 1994—; bd. dirs. Blue Cross Western Pa. Co-editor: Pericardial Disease, 1982, Am. Heart Assn. Monograph, 1975. Served to capt. USAF, 1961-63. Am. Heart Assn. scholar, 1968-73. Fellow ACP, Council on Clin. Cardiology, Am. Heart Assn. (fellow Coun. on Circulation), Am. Coll. Cardiology (bd. dirs.); mem. Am. Fedn. for Med. Rsch., Cen. Soc. for Clin. Rsch. Office: Georgetown Univ Hosp 3800 Reservoir Rd NW Washington DC 20007-2113

LEÓN, EDUARDO A., diplomat, business executive; b. Santiago de los Caballeros, Dominican Republic, Oct. 13, 1920; s. Eduardo and Maria León Jimenes; m. Ana Tavares, Feb. 16, 1946. Student, O'Sullivan Bus. Coll., Montreal, Can., 1937; BBA, McGill U., 1939. Under sec. of state industry and Commerce Ministry, Santo Domingo, Dominican Republic, 1953, Fgn. Affairs Ministry, Santo Domingo, Dominican Republic, 1954; ministry of comml. affairs Embassy of Dominican Republic, Washington, 1955; envoy extraordinary and minister Plenipotenciary of Dominican Republic, London, 1956, Otawa, Can., 1957; pres. E. León Jimenes, C. por A., Santiago de los Caballeros, 1939—; ambassador extraordinary Plenipotenciary of Dominican Republic, Washington, 1986-89, Plenipotenciary at Large, Dominican Republic, 1989—. Named to Order of Duarte, Sánchez and Mella in the Grade of Grand Cross, Order of Christopher Columbus in the Grade of Comdr., Order of Cuban Red Cross in Grade of Grand Cross, Decoration of Christopher Columbus in Grade of Grand Cross Silver Plate, 1995; recipient Paul Harris medal Rotary Internat., Gold Ring Philip Morris Inc. Mem. Nat. Coun. Businessmen, Assn Industries of Dominican Republic, Ctrl. Bank Dominican Republic, Bank of Agriculture and Industry, State Coun. of Sugar, Rotary, Met. Club N.Y., Union League Club, Internat. Golf Club, Centro Espanol Club. Roman Catholic. Avocations: tennis, golf, shooting, collector of wines, travel. Office: EPS No B 101 PO Box 02 5360 Miami FL 33102-5360

LEÓN, FELIX IVAN, pulmonologist; b. Santurce, P.R., Mar. 17, 1948; s. Felix Antonio and Irma (Rivero) L.; m. Nicole Lucienne Soto, Mar. 24, 1972; children: Michelle, Annette. Student, U. Colo., 1965-68; MD, U. P.R., 1972. Diplomate Am. Bd. Internal Medicine, Am. Bd. Pulmonary Disease. Instr. in medicine U. P.R. Med. Sch., San Juan, 1975-76; fellow in pulmonary disease Wash. U. Med. Sch., St. Louis, 1976-78; assoc. prof. medicine U. Ctrl. Del Caribe, Cayey, P.R., 1978-84; prof. medicine U. Ctrl. Del Caribe, Bayamon, P.R., 1986-88, head dept. medicine, 1986-88; pvt. practice pulmonology San Juan Office, 1984-86, 93—; chief pulmonary fellowship San Juan City Hosp., 1988-93; sr. respiratory dist. cons. P.R. Indsl. Commn., San Juan, 1978—; treas. 1st Pan Am. Congress Diseases of Chest, San Juan, 1989-96. Capt. U.S. Army, 1977-78. Fellow ACP, Am. Coll. Chest Physicians, Am. Coll. Cardiology. Roman Catholic. Avocations: tennis, model airplanes, swimming. Office: 1329 Jesus J Pinero Caparra Terrace PR 00923

LEON, ROBERT LEONARD, psychiatrist, educator; b. Denver, Jan. 18, 1925; s. Louis and Rae (Brown) L.; m. Willena Lee, Sept. 14, 1947; children: Alexis Kay, Mark Robert, Jeffrey Clayton, Stacy Lee. MD, U. Colo., 1948. Diplomate Am. Bd. Psychiatry and Neurology. Intern U. Mich. Hosp., Ann Arbor, 1948-49; resident in psychiatry U. Colo. Med. Ctr., Denver, 1949-52, child psychiatry fellow, 1951-52; child psychiatry fellow Bur. Mental Hygiene, New Haven, Conn. Dept. Health/Student Health Svc., Yale U., 1952-53; asst. dir., acting dir. child psychiatry Greater Kansas City Mental Health Found., 1953-54; instr. psychiatry U. Kans. Sch. Medicine, Kansas City, 1956-57; asst. prof. psychiatry U. Tex. Health Sci. Ctr. at Dallas, Southwestern Med. Sch., 1957-61, assoc. prof., 1961-65, prof., 1965-67; prof., chmn. dept. psychiatry Sch. Medicine U. Tex. Health Sci. Ctr., San Antonio, 1967-95, interim chmn., 1995-96; Ashbel Smith prof. U. Tex. Health Sci. Ctr., San Antonio, 1990—; chief psychiatry U. Health Sys., Bexar County, San Antonio, 1967-96; cons. psychiatry Audie Murphy Vet.'s Hosp., 1973—; cons. Mental Health Orgn., region IV, HEW, 1957-73; mem. Psychiat. Tng. Rev. NIMH, Rockville, Md., 1970-74; hon. cons. World Health Orgn., Geneva, 1996. Author: Psychiatric Interviewing: A Primer, 1982, 2d edit., 1989; contbr. articles to profl. jours. Sr. surgeon USPHS, 1954-57. Fellow ACP (pres. 1987-88), Am. Psychiat. Assn. (life), Am. Orthopsychiat. Assn. (life), Am. Acad. Child and Adolescent Psychiatry (life), Am. Assn. Social Psychiatry (pres. 1990-92); mem. Am. Assn. Chmn. Depts. Psychiatry (pres. 1982-83), Benjamin Rush Soc., World Assn. for Social Psychiatry. Home: 6866 Stonykirk St San Antonio TX 78240-2743 Office: U Tex Health Sci Ctr 7703 Floyd Curl Dr San Antonio TX 78284-6200

LEÓN, TANIA JUSTINA, composer, music director, pianist; b. Havana, Cuba, May 14, 1943; came to U.S., 1967; d. Oscar and Dora (Ferran) L. BA in Piano and Theory, Peyrellade Conservatory Music, Havana, 1963; MA in Music Edn., Nat. Conservatory Music, Havana, 1965; BA in Acctg., U. Havana, 1965; BS Music Edn., NYU, 1973, BS in Music Edn., 1973, MA in Composition, 1975. Prof. Bklyn. Coll. Conservatory of Music, 1994—; vis. prof. Yale U., New Haven, 1993; vis. lectr. Harvard U., Cambridge, Mass., 1994; resident composer Lincoln Ctr. Inst., 1985, teaching artist, 1982-88; composer in residence Nat. Black Music Festival, 1990, Cabrillo Music Festival, 1990, Yaddo, 1991, Ravinia Festival, 1991, Cleve. Inst., 1992, Bellagio Ctr., Italy, 1992, Cornish Coll., Seattle, 1993, Billings Symphony, 1993, Carnegie Mellon U., Pitts., 1993, Harvard Coll., Cambridge, Mass., 1993, Voices of Change, Dallas, 1993; panelist N.Y. State Council on the Arts, 1980, 81, 86, NEA composing program, 1980-82, recording program, 1985-87; mem. adv. bd. Bklyn. Coll. Conservatory, 1982-84, Meet the Composer, 1983—, Children TV Workshop; artistic dir. Composers Forum Inc., N.Y.C., 1987—; assoc. prof. composition Bklyn. Coll., 1987—; bd. dirs. Am. Music Ctr., N.Y. Found. for Arts; with Cin. Symphony Orch., 1991—, Revson Composer fellow N.Y. Philharmonic, 1993—; U.S. rep. U.S.-Mex. Fund for Culture, 1994. Piano soloist, Cuba, 1964-67; piano soloist, N.Y. Coll. of Music Orch., N.Y.C., 1967, NYU Orch., N.Y.C., 1969, Buffalo Symphony Orch., 1973; staff pianist, condr., Dance Theatre of Harlem, N.Y.C., 1968—, assoc. condr., 1983—, music dir., 1968-79; founder, Dance Theatre of Harlem Orch., 1975; concert series Meet the Performer, 1977; music dir. concert series Dance in Am. Spl., Sta. WNET-TV; guest condr. concert series, Genova (Italy) Symphony Orch., 1972, Juilliard Orch., Festival Two Worlds, Spoleto, Italy, Symphony New World, 1974, Royal Ballet Orch., 1974, 76, BBC Orch., 1974, 76, Halle Orch., 1974, Buffalo Philharm. Orch., 1975, Concert Orch. of L.I., 1979, Sadler's Wells Orch., 1979, London Universal Symphony, 1979, Composer's Forum, 1979, Lincoln Ctr. Outdoor Festival, 1980, Bklyn. Coll. Symphony, 1981, J. F. Kennedy Ctr. Opera House Orch., 1981, 82, Radio City Music Hall, 1982, Spoleto Festival, Charleston, 1983, Orch. of Our Time, N.Y., N.Y. Grand Opera, Colonne Orch., Paris, Mich. Opera, Human Comedy, Royale Theatre, Broadway, Pasadena Orch., P.R. Symphony, Met. Opera Orch., Phoenix Symphony, Columbus Symphony Orch., Fund. Latinoamericana Musica Contemporanea P.R., Am. Women Condr./Composer Symposium, Eugene, Oreg., New Music Am., Houston, New Music in Am., 1989 and Concert in the Pk., 1990 both with Bklyn. Philharm., Cabrillo Festival, 1990, Nat. Black Arts Festival, Atlanta, 1990, La Crosse Symphony, Wis., 1991, Dance Theatre of Harlem, 1991, 92, 93, 25th Anniversary Season-94, Celebrate Bklyn. Festival, 1991, Bklyn. Philharm., 1991, New World Symphony, Miami, Fla., 1991, 94, Cosmopolitan Symphony Orch., N.Y.C., 1991, Beethovenhalle Symphony Orch., Bonn, Germany, 1992, Opera Orch. of Johannesburg, 1992, Nat. Symphony Orch., Johannesburg, 1992, Louisville Symphony, 1992, RIAS Orch., Berlin, 1992, Billings Symphony, 1993, Dance Theater of Harlem, 1993, 94, Carnegie Mellon Orch., 1993, Alvin Ailey 35th Anniversary Season, 1993, Am. Composers Orch. Chamber Ensemble, 1994, Munich Biennale, 1994, others; royal command performer concert series, London Palladium, 1974, 76, Concert Orch. L.I., 1976, concert pianist, Sta. WNYC-FM, 1968-70; conductor coord.: concert series Music by Black Composers Series, Bklyn. Philharmonia, 1978-79; music dir., condr., Bklyn. Philharm. Community Concert Series, 1977—; mus. dir., condr. The Wiz, Broadway Theatre, 1978; music dir. Death, Destruction and Detroit, 1979, Alvin Ailey Am. Dance Theatre, 1983—, Whitney Mus. Contemporary Music Concert Series, 1986, 87; mus. dir., composer: Maggie Magalita, J.F. Kennedy Ctr. Performing Arts, 1980, The Golden Windows, 1982; apptd. music dir. concert series, Intar Theatre, N.Y.C.; condr., mus. dir. concert series Godspell, NYU, 1978, Carmencita, 1978; composer (ballet music) Haiku, 1974, (piano concerto) Tones, 1970, Sailor's Boat, (score for musical) Dougla, 1974, (African ballet) La Ramera de la Cueva, 1974, (score for musical) Namiac Poems, 1974, (for voice, chorus and orch.) Spiritual Suite, 1975, (2 sopranos, chorus and mixed ensemble with narrator), Concerto Criollo, 1976, (concerto for piano, 8 timpanies and orch.) Pet's Suite, 1979, (for flute and piano) I Got Ovah, 1980, (for soprano, piano and percussion, based on poems by Carolyn M. Rodgers) Concerto Criollo, 1980, Four Pieces for Cello, 1981, De-Orishas, 1982, Ascend, Fanfare for Brass and Percussion, 1983, (for solo piano) Momentum, 1984, Bata, 1985, Permutation Seven, 1985, A La Par, 1986, Ritual, 1987, Pueblo Mulato, 1987, Heart of Ours, a piece, 1988, Parajota Delaté, 1988, Kabiosile, 1988, Latin File, 1988, Indigena for instrumental ensemble, 1991, Solisti Chamber Orch N.Y., 1991, Carabali for orch., 1992, Crossings for brass ensemble, 1992, Arenas d'un Tempo for clarinet, cello and piano, 1992, Son Sonora for flute and guitar, 1993, Scourge of Hyacinths: chamber opera, 1994, Para Viola y Orquesta for viola and orch., 1994, Sin Normas Ajenas for chamber orch., 1994; records on CRI, WesternWind, Albany Records, Newport Classics, Leonarda Records. Bd. dirs. Am. Composers Orch. Recipient Young Composers prize Nat. Council Arts, Havana, 1966, Alvin Johnson award Am. Council Emigres in the Profession, 1971, Cintas award in composition, 1974-75, 78-79, Achievement award Nat. Council Women of U.S., 1980, Byrd Hoffman Found. award, 1981, Key to City of Detroit, 1982, Queens Council on Arts award, 1983, Meet The Composer awards, 1978-94, Manhattan Arts award, 1985, Dean Dixon Achievement award, 1985, N.Y. State Coun. on Arts award, 1988, Mayor's citation, City of N.Y., 1989, Celebrate Bklyn. Achievement award, 1990, award in music Am. Acad. and Inst. of Arts and Letters, 1991; Nat. Endowment for Arts fellow, 1975. Mem. ASCAP (Composers award 1978-94), French Soc. Composers, Am. Acad. Poets (bd, dirs.), Am. Composers Orch. (bd. dirs.), Am. Fedn. Musicians, Ctr. New Music, Am. Music Ctr. (bd. dirs. 1985—), Internat. Artists Alliance, Am. Women Composers, AFL-CIO. *

LEONARD, SISTER ANNE C., superintendent, education director; b. N.Y.C., Dec. 22, 1936; d. Patrick A. and Mary T. (McAlpin) L. BS in Edn. and Social Sci., Fordham U., 1962, MA, 1965; CAGS, Boston U., 1972; postgrad., Hunter Coll., U. San Francisco, U. Northern Ill., Notre Dame U. Cert. tchr. K-12, adminstr. N.Y. Tchr., asst. prin., prin. Notre Dame Acad., Staten Island, N.Y., 1957-68; prin. Maternity B.V.M. Sch., Bourbonnais, Ill., 1968-69, St. Jude the Apostle Sch., South Holland, Ill., 1969-78; dir. Cath. Elem. Schs. Archdiocese of Chgo., 1978-83, dir. ednl. svcs., mem. Cardinal Bernadin's cabinet, 1983-90, exec. officer commn. ednl. svcs., 1983-90; supt. schs., dir. edn. Archdiocese of Okla. City, 1990-96; U.S. province leader Congregation of Notre Dame, Ridgefield, Conn., 1996—; chair edn. divisn. Cath. Conf. Ill., 1988-90; del. gen. chpt. Congregation Notre Dame, mem. provincial coun.; mem. edn. com. U.S. Cath. Conf. Bishops, Washington, 1985-88; mem. Nat. Cath. Bishops' Mellennium Com.; speaker in field; lectr., presenter workshops; mem. Fortune 500 panel edn. and bus.; devel. mission statement, just principles compensation, new models compensation for prins., 1987-91; initiated, organized Dirs. Edn. Wis., Ill., Ind., Ohio, Mich.; attended symposia in field; mem. com. prep. Office of Cath. Edn. Conciliation Process; exec. officer local sch. bds.; initiated individually guided edn. program St. Jude Sch. Cons. textbooks William H. Sadlier, Inc.; contbr. articles to profl. jours. Trustee DePaul U., 1986—, bd. dirs., chair acad. affairs com.; bd. dirs. Jr. Achievement, Chgo., 1984-90, Okla. City, 1991-96; mem. NCCJ, 1992—, Gov. Ill. adv. com. on non-pub. schs., Springfield, 1978-82, planning com. Big Shoulders Project. Mem. ASCD, Nat. Cath. Ednl. Assn. (pres. chief adminstrs. Cath. edn. 1991-94, v.p. 1989-91, vice chair bd. 1991—, task force 1990-91, supervision, pers., curriculum, Educator or Yr. award 1990), Archdiocesan Prins. Assn. (pres. 1973-78), Chgo. Coun. Fgn. Rels., Phi Delta Kappa (Educator of Yr. 1984). Avocations: reading, swimming, traveling. Home: 223 W Mountain Rd Ridgefield CT 06877 Office: 222 W Mountain Rd Ridgefield CT 06877-3629

LEONARD, BUCK, retired baseball player; b. Rocky Mount, N.C., Sept. 8, 1907. Baseball player Homestead Grays. Named to Nat. Baseball Hall of Fame, 1972. Office: c/o Nat Baseball Hall Fame PO Box 590 Cooperstown NY 13326-0590

LEONARD, DAVID MORSE, lawyer; b. Akron, Ohio, Dec. 4, 1949; s. Frank O. and Barbara J. (Morse) L.; m. Sharon Elaine Quati, May 7, 1977; children: Michael Morse, Lindsey Marie. BS in Chem. Engring., Purdue U., 1972; JD, Emory U., 1975. Bar: Ga. 1975, U.S. Ct. Appeals (4th, 5th and 11th cirs.), U.S. Dist. Ct. (no., mid. and so. dists.) Ga., U.S. Dist. Ct. (so. dist.) Ala., U.S. Dist. Ct. (we. dist.) La.; cert. mediator, cert. mediation tng. Assoc. Montet & Smith, Atlanta, 1975-79; assoc. Hurt, Richardson, Garner, Todd & Cadenhead, Atlanta, 1979-83, ptnr., 1983-85; of counsel Lord, Bissell & Brook, Atlanta, 1985-87, ptnr., 1987—; mem. panel of arbitrators Am. Arbitration Assn., 1995—. Mem. ABA (litigation sect., tort and ins. practice sect.), Profl. Liability Underwriting Soc., Atlanta Lawyers Club, Atlanta C. of C., Am. Arbitration Assn. (panel of arbitrators). Home: 4152 Club Dr NE Atlanta GA 30319-1116 Office: Lord Bissell & Brook 1201 W Peachtree St NW Ste 3700 Atlanta GA 30309-3400

LEONARD, EDWARD F., chemical engineer, educator; b. Paterson, N.J., July 6, 1932; s. Edward F. and Adelyn (Minder) L.; children—Mary, Edward F., Gerald, Louise, Joseph. S.B. in Chem. Engring., M.I.T., 1953; M.S. in Chem. Engring, U. Pa., 1955, Ph.D., 1960. Mem. faculty Columbia U., 1958—, prof. chem. engring., 1968—, also founder seminar on biomaterials.; dir. Artificial Organs Rsch. Lab., vice chmn. Ctr. for Biomed. Engring., 1995—. Author articles in field. Fellow Am. Inst. Chem. Engrs. (William H. Walker award), Am. Inst. Med. and Biol. Engring. Found.; mem. Am. Soc. Artificial Internal Organs (pres. 1972-73), Biomed. Engring. Soc. (a founder), N.Y. Acad. Medicine. Home: 29 Rossmore Ave Bronxville NY 10708-5615

LEONARD, EDWARD PAUL, naval officer, dentist, educator; b. Greenfield, Mass., Dec. 29, 1935; s. Laurence Francis and Hilda Mae (Coutu) L.; m. Lola Jeanne Ahern, Sept. 6, 1958; children: Lisa Ann, Jeffrey Torbert, Julie Marie, Laurence Edward. Student, St. Joseph's Sem., 1953-56, St. Anselm's Coll., 1956, U. Mass., 1956-58; DDS, Georgetown U., 1962; MS, U. Md., 1968, PhD, 1970; attended, Marymount U., 1990-92. Commd. lt. USN, 1962, advanced through grades to capt., 1979; asst. dental officer Subic Bay Naval Sta. USN, The Philippines, 1970-72; assoc. histopathologist dental rsch. inst. USN, Great Lakes Naval Base, Ill., 1972-76, chief histopathology dental rsch. inst., 1976-80; program mgr. Naval Med. R & D USN, Bethesda, Md., 1980-83; quality assurance officer Office Dir. Naval Med. USN, Washington, 1983-84, dental care analyst Office Dir. Naval Med., 1984-86; exec. officer Naval. Dental Clin. USN, Parris Island, S.C., 1986-88; comdg. officer Naval Dental Clin. USN, Charleston, S.C., 1988—; mem. exec. coun. Mgmt. Devel. Adv. Bd. Navy Surgeon Gen., Washington, 1983-86; grant reviewer div. rsch. grants NIH, Washington, 1981-83; tchr. biology, ecology Hargrave Mil. Acad., asst. basketball coach, sailing club sponsor, astronomy club sponsor; evaluator Va. Ind. Schs. Assn. Contbr. articles to profl. jours. Vol. coach Vienna (Va.) Youth League, 1983-84; coach McLean (Va.) Youth League, 1984. Recipient Carl A. Schlack Rsch. award Assn. Mil. Surgeons of U.S., 1989. Fellow Internat. Coll. Dentists, Am. Coll. Dentists; mem. Internat. Assn. Dental Rsch., Am. Assn. Dental Rsch., Am. Assn. Pub. Health Dentistry, Nat. Assn. Biology Tchrs. Democrat. Roman Catholic. Avocations: sailing, astronomy, historic preservation. Home: 4189 88th Pl S Boynton Beach FL 33436-2320

LEONARD, EDWIN DEANE, lawyer; b. Oakland, Calif., Apr. 22, 1929; s. Edwin Stanley and Gladys Eugenia (Lee) L.; m. Judith Swatland, July 10, 1954; children: Garrick Hillman, Susanna Leonard Hill, Rebecca, Ethan York. BA, The Principia, 1950; LLB, Harvard U., 1953; LLM, George Washington U., 1956. Bar: D.C. 1953, Ill. 1953, N.Y. 1957. Assoc. Davis Polk Wardwell Sunderland & Kiendl, N.Y.C., 1956-61; ptnr. Davis Polk & Wardwell, N.Y.C., 1961—. Trustee the Brearley Sch., N.Y.C., 1980-90. Served to 1st lt. JAGC, 1953-56. Mem. ABA, N.Y. Bar Assn., N.Y. County Bar Assn., Assn. of Bar of City of N.Y. (chmn. various coms.), Millbrook Equestrian Ctr. (pres.). Home: 1148 Fifth Ave New York NY 10128-0807 Office: Davis Polk & Wardwell 450 Lexington Ave New York NY 10017-3911

LEONARD, ELMORE JOHN, novelist, screenwriter; b. New Orleans, Oct. 11, 1925; s. Elmore John and Flora Amelia (Rivé) L.; m. Beverly Claire Cline, Aug. 30, 1949 (div. 1977); children: Jane, Peter, Christopher, William, Katherine; m. Joan Leanne Lancaster, Sept. 15, 1979 (dec. 1993); m. Christine Kent, Aug. 19, 1993. PhB, U. Detroit, 1950. Author over 30 novels including Hombre, 1961, City Primeval, 1980, Split Images, 1982, Cat Chaser, 1982, La Brava, 1983, Stick, 1983, Glitz, 1985, Bandits, 1987, Touch, 1987, Freaky Deaky, 1988, Killshot, 1989, Get Shorty, 1990, Maximum Bob, 1991, Rum Punch, 1992, Pronto, 1993, Riding the Rap, 1995, Out of Sight, 1996; author of screenplays including The Moonshine War, 1970, Joe Kidd, 1972, Mr. Majestyk, 1974, (with Joseph Stinson) Stick, 1985, (with John Steppling) 52 Pick-Up, 1986, (with Fred Walton) The Rosary Murders, 1987, (with Jim Borrelli and Alan Sharp) Cat Chaser, 1990. With USN, 1943-46. Recipient Mystery Writers of Am. Grand Master award, 1992. Mem. Writers Guild of Am., Authors Guild, Mystery Writers of Am., Western Writers of Am. Roman Catholic. Address: Creative Artists Agy 9830 Wilshire Blvd Beverly Hills CA 90212*

LEONARD, EUGENE ALBERT, banker; b. St. Louis, Aug. 27, 1935; s. Albert Hiram and Mary (Crowson) L.; m. Mary Ann Sampson, Aug. 31, 1956 (div. 1994); children: Charles, James, Susan; m. Constance Anne Deschamps, June 3, 1995. BS, U. Mo., 1957, MS, 1958, PhD, 1962; postgrad., Stonier Grad. Sch. Banking, Rutgers U., 1964-66. Instr. agrl. econs. U. Mo. at Columbia, 1959-60; with Fed. Res. Bank St. Louis, 1961-77; v.p., mgr. Fed. Res. Bank St. Louis (Memphis br.), 1967-70, sr. v.p., 1970-71, 1st v.p., 1971-77; on loan to bd. govs. FRS as asst. sec., Washington, 1970-71; sr. v.p. Merc. Bancorp. Inc., St. Louis, 1977-87; pres. Corp. for Fin. Risk Mgmt., St. Louis, 1987—; instr. econs. Central States Sch. Banking, 1962-69, Ill. Bankers Sch., 1962-74, Sch. Banking South, 1970-83, Stonier Grad. Sch. Banking, 1975-80, bd. regents, 1978-81; adj. assoc. prof. econs. Memphis State U., 1969-70. Bd. dirs. Logos Sch., St. Louis, 1977-85, chmn., 1985; bd. dirs. Repertory Theater of St. Louis, 1981-87. Mem. Mo. Bankers Assn. (treas. 1984-85, pres. 1986-87), U. Mo. Columbia Alumni Assn. (nat. pres. 1980-81, bd. dirs. devel. fund 1981-89, Faculty Alumni award 1986), Gamma Sigma Delta, Kappa Sigma. Unitarian. Home: 30 Portland Pl Saint Louis MO 63108-1204 Office: Corp for Fin Risk Mgmt 8675 Olive Blvd Saint Louis MO 63132-2503

LEONARD, GEORGE EDMUND, real estate, bank, and consulting executive; b. Phoenix, Nov. 20, 1940; s. George Edmund and Marion Elizabeth (Fink) L.; m. Gloria Jean Henry, Mar. 26, 1965 (div. Feb. 1981); children: Tracy Lynn, Amy Theresa, Kristin Jean; m. Mary C. Short, Sept. 22, 1990. Student, Ariz. State U., 1958-60; BS, U.S. Naval Acad., 1964; postgrad., Pa. State U., 1969-70; MBA, U. Chgo., 1973. Commd. ensign, USN, 1964, advanced through grades to lt. comdr., 1975; v.p. 1st Nat. Bank Chgo., 1970-75; exec. v.p., chief banking, chief fin. and chief lending officer Mera Bank, Phoenix, 1975-90, also bd. dirs., 1982-90; pres., chief exec. officer Cen. Savs., San Diego, 1985-87; chmn., CEO AmBank Holding Co. of Colo., Scottsdale, Ariz., 1990-91, Consumer Guarantee Corp., Phoenix, 1996; pres., CEO Diversified Mgmt. Svcs., Inc., Phoenix, 1991—, GEL Mgmt. Inc., Phoenix, 1991—; CFO Western Pacific Airlines, Colorado Springs, 1996—, bd. dirs., 1996—; bd. dirs. Beverly Hills (Calif.) Savs., , Am. Nat. Bank of Scottsdale, Bank of Santa Fe, 1990-91, Bank of Colo. Springs. Active Phoenix Thunderbirds, 1979—; bd. dirs. Maricopa C.C.s Found., treas., 2d v.p., 1991-93, 1st v.p., 1993-94, pres., 1994-95, past pres., 1995-96, Camelback Charitable Trust, 1991-92, The Samaritan Found., 1993-96, chmn. fin. com., 1994-96, vice chmn., 1996. Mem. Phoenix Met. C. of C. (bd. dirs. 1975-82), Inst. Fin. Edn. (bd. dirs. 1980-87, nat. chmn. 1985-86), Ariz. State U. Coll. of Bus. Deans Coun. of 100, Paradise Valley Country Club (bd. dirs. 1991—, treas. 1992-95, pres. 1995-97), Univ. Club (San Diego), Kiwanis. Republican. Roman Catholic. Home: 4920 Langdale Way Colorado Springs CO 80906 Office: Western Pacific Airlines Inc 2864 S Circle Dr Ste 1100 Colorado Springs CO 80906-4114

LEONARD, GILBERT STANLEY, oil company executive; b. Kingsport, Tenn., Sept. 3, 1941; s. Robert Spencer and Hope (Palmer) L.; m. Barbara Ann Bell, June 12, 1965 (div. 1982); m. Linda Marie Gremillion, Oct. 27, 1984. BS in Indsl. Mgmt., Purdue U., 1964; MS in Bus., U. Kans., 1970. Summer trainee Tenn. Eastman Co., Kingsport, 1963, prodn. planner, 1966-68; mktg. analyst Exxon Co., USA, Houston, 1970-74, distbn. specialist, 1975-78, staff systems analyst, 1979-81, group supr. applications support, 1982-84, strategic systems planner, 1984-85, supr. applications devel., 1986-89; sys. supr. Exxon Card Ctr., Houston, 1990-95; supr. network & telecommunication divsn. Exxon Computing Svc. Corp., 1994-96; sr. systems supr. Ctr. Expertise client/server systems Exxon Co. USA, 1996—; instr., facilitator team leadership forum Exxon Co., USA, Houston, 1988, instr., faciliator quality forum, 1990-94; advisor, cons. Nat. Jr. Achievement, Houston, 1972-74. Lay reader Episc. Ch. Good Shepherd, Kingwood, Tex., 1975-82; treas. Forrest Lake Townhome Assn., Houston, 1987-88, pres., 1988-89. Lt. USNR, 1964-66. Recognized for excellence in Naval ROTC Chgo. Tribune, 1963. Mem. Quarterdeck Soc. (pres. 1962-63), Beta Gamma Sigma. Avocations: private pilot, golf, running. Office: Exxon Co USA PO Box 2180 Houston TX 77252-2180

LEONARD, GLEN M., museum administrator; b. Salt Lake City, Nov. 12, 1938; s. Burnham J. and Allene (Green) L.; m. Karen Wright, Mar. 15, 1968; children: Cory, Kyle, Keith. BA, U. Utah, 1964, MA, 1966, PhD, 1970. Mng. editor Utah State Hist. Soc., Salt Lake City, 1970-73; sr. rsch. assoc. history divsn. Ch. of Jesus Christ of Latter-day Saints, Salt Lake City, 1973-78; dir. Mus. Ch. History and Art, Salt Lake City, 1979—; mem. adv. bd. editors Utah Hist. Quarterly, Salt Lake City, 1973-88; assoc. editor Jour. Mormon History, Provo, Utah, 1974-80; bd. dirs. Western Studies Ctr., Brigham Young U., Provo. Co-author: The Story of the Latter-day Saints, 1976; contbr. articles to profl. publs. Mem. Hist. Preservation Commn., Farmington, Utah, 1986-92; mem. adv. coun. Mormon Pioneer Nat. Hist. Trail, Nat. Pk. Svc., 1980-86; mem. Utah Pioneer Sesquicentennial Celebration Coordinating Coun., 1995-97. Recipient Dale Morgan Article award Utah State Hist. Soc., 1973, Mormon History Assn. Article awards, 1990, 96. Mem. Orgn. Am. Historians, Western History Assn., Am. Assn. Mus. (mus. assessment program cons.), Western Mus. Assn., Utah Mus. Assn. (bd. dirs. 1980-83), Am. Assn. State and Local History. Avocations: photography, music, gardening. Office: Mus Ch History and Art 45 N West Temple Salt Lake City UT 84150-1003

LEONARD, GUY MEYERS, JR., international holding company executive; b. Bluefield, W.Va., Sept. 22, 1926; s. Guy Meyers and Mabel (Bonham) L.; AB, BS, Morris Harvey Coll., 1949; BDiv, Southwestern Bapt. Sem., 1952; STM, Harvard U., 1957; m. Pat Kirby, June 28, 1949; children: Calvin David, Dinah Lynn. Commd. ensign U.S. Navy, 1952, advanced through grades to capt., 1968, ret., 1972; dir. R & D Ency. Britannica Ednl. Corp., Chgo., 1972-76; pres. Communication Programming Svcs., Inc., Charleston, S.C., 1976—; pres., CEO First Don Trading Co., 1982—; chmn., CEO Transocean Ltd., internat. holding co., 1982-86; pres. GHL, Inc., Pacific rim, Africa, 1991—; cons. drug control programs for schs., cons. Ency. Britannica, Home Mission Bd. and Brotherhood Commn. So. Bapt. Conv. Sec., U.S. Power Squadron, Charleston, 1969; chmn. Spl. Commn. on Drug Abuse for Armed Forces, 1970-72; active Conn. coun. Boy Scouts Am., 1959-62; chmn. stewardship com. Episc. Diocese of S.C., 1994-95. Served with USN, 1943-72. Decorated Legion of Merit, Meritorious Svc. medal, Navy Commendation medal, Disting. Svc. Medal; recipient Disting. Svc. award City of Louisville, 1963. Mem. Harvard Club S.C., C. of C., Trident Chamber (Charleston), Navy League U.S., Ret. Officers Assn. Club: Kiwanis (spl. projects chmn., 1964-65). Designer, produced with Harvard U. and sta. WGBH, Boston, mediated coll. curriculum leading to B.S. degree for use by naval personel.

LEONARD, HERMAN BEUKEMA (DUTCH LEONARD), public finance and management educator; b. Carlisle Barracks, Pa., Dec. 26, 1952; s. Charles Frederick and Margery Alden (Beukema) L.; m. Kathryn Anne Angell, Oct. 9, 1983; children: Whitney Angell, Dana Angell. AB summa cum laude, Harvard U., 1974, AM, 1976, PhD, 1979. Asst. prof. pub. policy John F. Kennedy Sch. Govt., Harvard U., Cambridge, Mass., 1979-83, assoc. prof., 1983-86, George F. Baker prof. pub. mgmt., 1986—, acad. dean for teaching programs, 1992—; mem. Gov.'s Coun. Econ. Policy, Alaska, 1980-82; chmn. Gov.'s Task Force on Coll. Opportunity , Mass., 1987-88; bd. dirs. Mass. Health and Ednl. Facilities Authority, 1988—; mem. adv. bd. N.Y.C. Debt Mgmt., 1990-94. Co-author: Discrimination in Rural Housing, 1976; author: Checks Unbalanced: The Quiet Side of Public Spending, 1986, By Choice or By Chance? Tracking the Values in Massachusetts Public Spending, 1992; contbr. numerous articles on pub. fin. and mgmt. to jours. in field. Recipient grad. fellowship NSF, 1974; jr. fellow Soc. Fellows, Harvard U., 1976-79; Presdl. scholar, 1970. Mem. Phi Beta Kappa. Office: Harvard U John F Kennedy Sch Govt 79 JFK St Cambridge MA 02138-5801

LEONARD, JAMES JOSEPH, physician, educator; b. Schenectady, June 17, 1924; s. James Joseph and Helena (Flood) L.; m. Helen Louise Mitchell, Oct. 24, 1953; children: James Joseph, W. Jeffrey, Paul Mitchell, Kathleen Marie. M.D., Georgetown U., 1950. Intern medicine Georgetown U. Hosp., 1950-51, jr. asst. resident, 1951-52, fellow cardiology, 1953-54; asst. resident medicine Boston City Hosp., 1952-53; resident pulmonary diseases D.C. Gen. Hosp., 1954-55, med. officer, 1955-56; instr. medicine Georgetown U. Med. Sch., 1955-56, Duke Med. Center, 1956-57; asst. prof. medicine, dir. div. cardiology Georgetown U. service D.C. Gen. Hosp., 1957-59; asst. prof. medicine U. Tex. Med. Br., Galveston, 1959-62; asso. prof. medicine Ohio State U. Med. Sch., 1962-63; dir. div. cardiology U. Pitts. Med. Sch., 1963-70, asso. prof. medicine, 1963-67, prof. medicine, 1967-77, acting chmn. dept., 1970, chmn. dept., 1971-77; prof., chmn. dept. medicine Uniformed Services U. of Health Scis., 1977—. Master ACP; mem. So. Soc. Clin. Investigation, Am. Clin. and Climatol. Assn., Central Soc. Clin. Research, Assn. Am. Physicians, Assn. Profs. Medicine, Assn. U. Cardiologists. Home: 3200 Farmington Dr Chevy Chase MD 20815-4827 Office: 4301 Jones Bridge Rd Bethesda MD 20814-4712

LEONARD, JEFFREY S., lawyer; b. Bklyn., Sept. 14, 1945; m. Maxine L. Bortnick, Dec. 28, 1967; children: Deborah, Jennifer. AB in History, U. Rochester, 1967; JD, U. Ariz., 1974. Bar: Ariz. 1974; U.S. Dist. Ct. Ariz. 1974, U.S. Ct. Appeals (9th cir.) 1974, U.S. Supreme Ct. 1985. Law clk. to judge U.S. Dist. Ct. Ariz., 1974-75. Mem. editorial bd. Ariz. Law Rev., 1973-74. Mem. Order of Coif. Office: Leonard Collins & Kelly PC Two Renaissance Sq 40 N Central Ave Ste 2500 Phoenix AZ 85004-4405

LEONARD, JOHN HARRY, advertising executive; b. N.Y.C., June 28, 1922; s. Frederick H. and Florence (Kiechlin) L.; m. Marjorie Jane Haslun, Oct. 19, 1946; children—John Kiechlin, Janet Ann. B.S., N.Y. U., 1942, M.B.A., 1951. Advt. mgr. Autographic Register Co., 1946-47; promotion mgr. Macfadden Pub. Co., 1947-50; successively copywriter, account exec., v.p. and account supr. Batten, Barton, Durstine & Osborn, 1950-64; with DDB Needham Worldwide (formerly Doyle Dane Bernbach, Inc.), N.Y.C., 1964-87, group sr. v.p., 1972-87; lectr. Grad. Sch. Bus., N.Y. U., 1959-61. Bd. dirs., past exec. com. Am. Bible Soc.; past chmn. bd. dirs. Wartburg Home, Mt. Vernon, N.Y.; trustee NYU, 1978-84. With USAAF, 1943-46. Recipient Alumni Meritorious Service award N.Y. U., 1969. Mem. NYU Grad. Sch. Bus. Alumni Assn. (pres.), NYU Commerce Alumni Assn. (pres. 1979-80), Alpha Delta Sigma. Home: 310A Heritage Vlg Southbury CT 06488-1752

LEONARD, JOHN WIRTH, English educator, retailer; b. Balt., July 23, 1946; s. John William and Margaret Mary (Wirth) L.; m. Ellen Louise Brooks, June 21, 1969 (div.); children—Cora Lee, John Joseph. B.S., Loyola Coll., 1968; M. equivalent Towson State U., 1977. Licensed pyrotechnist, Md. Instr. English, Baltimore County Bd. Edn., Towson, Md., 1968—; pres. Pyrotechnics Guild Inc., White Marsh, Md., 1973-76; owner, operator Sparkler City, U.S.A., Perry Hall, Md., 1983—; pyrotechnic operator Zambelli Fireworks, New Castle, Pa., 1979—. Designer fireworks ground display (Plaque for best display), 1975. Mem. Pyrotechnics Guild Internat., Inc. (pres. 1975-77). Republican. Roman Catholic. Clubs: Crackerjacks; Fireworks (Wood Bridge, Va.) (pres. 1982—). Lodge: K.C. (warden 1978-79). Home: 221 Spring Ave Lutherville MD 21093 Office: Baltimore County Bd Edn 1000 S Marlyn Ave Baltimore MD 21221-5939

LEONARD, JUSTIN, professional golfer; b. Dallas, June 15, 1972. Grad., U. Tex. Profl. golfer, 1994—. Won U.S. Amateur Championship, 1992, NCAA Championship, 1994, Buick Open, 1996; only golfer in history to win 4 straight Southwest Conf. titles. Office: c/o PGA Box 109601 100 Ave of Champions Palm Beach Gardens FL 33410

LEONARD, KURT JOHN, plant pathologist, university program director; b. Holstein, Iowa, Dec. 6, 1939; s. Elvin Elsworth and Irene Marie (Helkenn) L.; m. Maren Jane Simonsen, May 28, 1961; children: Maria Catherine, Mary Alice, Benjamin Andrew. BS, Iowa State U., 1962; PhD, Cornell U., 1968. Plant pathologist Agrl. Rsch. Svc. USDA, Raleigh, N.C., 1968-88; dir. Cereal Rust Lab. U. Minn. USDA, St. Paul, 1988—. Author: (with others) Annual Review of Phytopathology, 1980; co-editor: Plant Disease Epidemiology, vol. 1, 1986, vol. 2, 1989; editor-in-chief: Phytopathology,

1981-84, Am. Phytopathol. Soc. Press, 1994-97; contbr. numerous articles to profl. jours. Fellow Am. Phytopathol. Soc. (coun. 1981-84, 94-97); mem. Am. Mycol. Soc., Internat. Soc. Plant Pathology (councilor 1982-93), Brit. Soc. Plant Pathology, Phi Kappa Phi, Sigma Xi, Gamma Sigma Delta. Achievements include description of new species and genera of plant pathogenic fungi; research on spread of disease through crop mixtures, on relationships between virulence and fitness in plant pathogenic fungi. Office: U Minn USDA ARS Cereal Lab Saint Paul MN 55108

LEONARD, MICHAEL A., automotive executive; b. Cadillac, Mich., Aug. 3, 1937; s. Hugel A. and Mildred (Johnson) L.; m. Frances Erickson, June 18, 1960; children: Kristin, Anne. MA, Alma Coll., 1959; MBA, Wayne State U., 1964; MS, MIT, 1971. Exec. Chrysler Corp., Highland Park, Mich., 1959-75; group v.p. Bendix Corp., Southfield, Mich., 1975-83; v.p., group exec. Allied Signal Automotive, Bloomfield Hills, Mich., 1983-91; pres. Harman, Inc., Southfield, Mich., 1991-94; mng. ptnr. Exec. Resources Inc., Bloomfield Hills, Mich., 1994—; bd. dirs. Kalyani Brake Co., Pune, India, Bendix France, Paris, Bendix Italy, and fgn. subs. Trustee Alma (Mich.) Coll.; chmn. Presbyn. Villages of Mich. Sloan fellow, MIT. Mem. Soc. Automotive Engrs., Delta Sigma Phi (pres. 1958-59). Presbyterian. Avocations: swimming, golf, boating. Home: 4375 Barchester Dr Bloomfield Hills MI 48302-2116 Office: Executive Resources Inc PO Box 625 Bloomfield Hills MI 48303-9999

LEONARD, MICHAEL STEVEN, industrial engineering educator; b. Salisbury, N.C., Feb. 2, 1947; s. Charles Thomas and Dorothy Francis (Loflin) L.; m. Mary Elizabeth Stewart, June 21, 1969; children: Dorothy Elizabeth, Amanda Brooke, Gabrielle Francis. B in Engring., U. Fla., 1970, M in Engring., 1972, PhD, 1973. Registered profl. engr., Mo., S.C. Asst. prof. health systems rsch. ctr. Georgia Tech, Atlanta, 1973-75; asst. prof. indsl. engring. U. Mo., Columbia, 1975-79, assoc. prof. indsl. engring., 1979-82, prof. indsl. engring., 1982-90, dept. chmn. indsl. engring., 1985-90; dept. head indsl. engring. Clemson (S.C.) U., 1990-95; engring. accreditation commn. bd. engring. and tech., Balt., 1994—. Editor Jour. Soc. for Health Systems, 1989-91; contbr. articles to profl. jours. evaluation adv. com. Am. Blood Commn., Washington, 1977-80; bd. dirs. Am. Cancer Soc. Boone County Mo. unit, Columbia, 1978-90. Mem. Soc. Health Systems (bd. dirs. 1989-94, pres. elect 1991-92, pres. 1992-93), Inst. Indsl. Engrs. (nat. dir. career guidance 1987—), Mo. Soc. Profl. Engrs. (cen. chpt. treas. 1988-89, v.p. 1989-90). Office: Clemson U Dept Indsl Engring Clemson SC 29634

LEONARD, NELSON JORDAN, chemistry educator; b. Newark, Sept. 1, 1916; s. Harvey Nelson and Olga Pauline (Jordan) L.; m. Louise Cornelie Vermey, May 10, 1947 (dec. 1987); children: Kenneth Jan, Marcia Louise, James Nelson, David Anthony; m. Margaret Taylor Phelps, Nov. 14, 1992. B.S. in Chemistry, Lehigh U., 1937, Sc.D., 1963; B.Sc., Oxford (Eng.) U., 1940, D.Sc., 1983; Ph.D., Columbia U., 1942; D.h.c., Adam Mickiewicz U., Poland, 1980; D.Sc. (hon.), U. Ill., 1988. Fellow and rsch. asst. chemistry U. Ill., Urbana, 1942-43, instr., 1943-44, assoc., 1944-45, 46-47, asst. prof., 1947-49, assoc. prof., 1949-52, prof. organic chemistry, 1952-73, head div. organic chemistry, 1954-63, prof. chemistry and biochemistry, 1973-86, R.C. Fuson prof. chemistry, mem. Ctr. for Advanced Study, 1981-86, R.C. Fuson prof. emeritus, 1986—; investigator antimalarial program Com. Med. Research, OSRD, 1944-46; sci. cons. and spl. investigator Field Intelligence Agy. Tech., U.S. Army and Dept. Commerce, 1945-46; mem. Can. NRC, summer 1950; Swiss-Am. Found. lectr., 1953, 70; vis. lectr. UCLA, summer 1953; Reilly lectr. U. Notre Dame, 1962; Stieglitz lectr. Chgo. sect. Am. Chem. Soc., 1962; Robert A. Welch Found. lectr., 1964, 83; Disting. vis. lectr. U. Calif.-Davis, 1975; vis. lectr. Polish Acad. Scis., 1976; B.R. Baker Meml. lectr. U. Calif., Santa Barbara, 1976; Ritter Meml. lectr. Miami U., Oxford, Ohio; Werner E. Bachman Meml. lectr. U. Mich., Ann Arbor, 1977; vis. prof. Japan Soc. Promotion of Sci., 1978; Arapahoe lectr. U. Colo., 1979; Tanabe rsch. lectr. Scripps Rsch. Inst., La Jolla, Calif., 1993; mem. program com. in basic scis. Arthur P. Sloan, Jr. Found., 1961-66; Philips lectr. Haverford Coll., 1971; Backer lectr., Groningen, Netherlands, 1972; FMC lectr. Princeton U., 1973; plenary lectr. Laaxer Chemistry Conf., Laax, Switzerland, 1980, 82, 84, 88, 90, 92; Calbiochem-Behring Corp. U. Calif.-San Diego Found. lectr., 1981; Watkins vis. prof. Wichita State U. (Kans.), 1982; Ida Beam Disting. vis. prof. U. Iowa, 1983; Fogarty scholar-in-residence NIH, Bethesda, Md., 1989-90; Sherman Fairchild Disting. scholar Calif. Inst. Tech., 1991; Syntex. disting. lectr. U. Colo., 1992; faculty assoc. Calif. Inst. Tech., 1992—; mem. adv. com. Searle Scholars program Chgo. Community Trust, 1982-85; ednl. adv. bd. Guggenheim Found., 1969-88, mem. com. of selection, 1977-88. Editor: Organic Syntheses, 1951-58, mem. adv. bd., 1959—, bd. dirs., 1969—, v.p., 1976-80, pres., 1980-88; editorial bd. Jour. Organic Chemistry, 1957-61, Jour. Am. Chem. Soc., 1960-72; adv. bd. Biochemistry, 1973-78, Chemistry International, 1984-91, Pure and Applied Chemistry, 1984-91; contbr. articles to profl. jours. Recipient medal Synthetic Organic Chem. Mfrs., 1970, Wheland award U. Chgo., 1991, creativity award U. Oreg., 1994, Arthur C. Cope Scholar award Am. Chem Soc., 1995; named to Mt. Vernon (N.Y.) H.S. Hall of Fame, 1985; fellow Rockefeller Found., 1950, Guggenheim fellow, 1959, 67. Fellow Am. Acad. Arts and Scis. (v.p. 1991-93); mem. NAS, AAAS, Polish Acad. Scis. (fgn.), Ill. Acad. Sci. (hon.), Am. Chem. Soc. (award for creative work in synthetic organic chemistry 1963, Edgar Fahs Smith award and lectureship Phila. sect. 1975, Centennial lectr. 1976, Roger Adams award 1981, Paul G. Gassman Disting. Svc. award divsn. organic chemistry 1994, A.C. Cope rsch. scholar award 1995), Am. Soc. for Biochemistry and Molecular Biology, Chem. Soc. London, New Swiss Chem. Soc., Internat. Union Pure and Applied Chemistry (sec. organic chemistry divsn. 1989, v.p. 1989-91, pres. 1991-93), Pharm. Soc. Japan (hon.), Am. Philos. Soc., Phi Beta Kappa, Phi Lambda Upsilon (hon.), Tau Beta Pi, Alpha Chi Sigma. Achievements include patents on synthesis of sparteine; esters of pyridine dicarboxylic acid as insect repellents; fluorescent derivatives of adenine- and cytosine-containing compounds. Home: 389 California Ter Pasadena CA 91105-2463

LEONARD, PATRICIA LOUISE, education educator, consultant; b. Wales Township, Mich., Aug. 26, 1940; d. Leo James and Laurelda Rose (Lashbrook) L. BS, Ea. Mich. U., 1963; MA, Ctrl. Mich. U., 1969; Ednl. Specialist, Mich. State U., 1978; PhD, U. Tenn., 1982. Cert. tchr., Mich.; cert. coop. edn. coord. Tchr. Millington (Mich.) Cmty. H. S., 1963-68, Bullock Creek Schs., Midland, Mich., 1968-69; asst. prof. Ctrl. Mich. U., Mt. Pleasant, 1969-80, 82-83; grad. tchg., rsch. asst. U. Tenn., Knoxville, 1980-82; assoc. prof. Rider U., Lawrenceville, N.J., 1983—; mem. vocat. adv. coun. Mercer County Spl. Svcs. Sch. Dist., Trenton, N.J., 1992—; cons. in edn. and bus., 1982—. Contbr. articles to profl. jours. Mem. Nat. Bus. Edn. Assn., Am. Vocat. Assn., N.J. Bus. Edn. Assn. (bd. dris. 1992—, observer, editor 1994-96), Ea. Bus. Edn. Assn. (gen. co-chair 1988-89), Pi Omega Pi (nat. coun. 1991-95, 97—), Delta Pi Epsilon, Phi Kappa Phi, Phi Delta Kappa, Omicron Tau Theta. Avocations: swimming, reading, needlework, drawing,. Home: RR3 Box 3346 Browns Mills NJ 08015 Office: Rider U 2083 Lawrenceville Rd Lawrenceville NJ 08648-3001

LEONARD, PAUL HARALSON, retired lawyer; b. Houston, Mar. 4, 1925; s. Paul Haralson and Dovie Lore (Shuler) L.; m. Barbara Ann Underwood, Nov. 26, 1948; children: Leslie Ann, Scott Paul. BA, Rice U., 1948; JD, South Tex. Coll. of Law, 1957. Bar: Tex. 1957, U.S. Patent and Trademark Office 1960, U.S. Ct. Appeals (10th cir.) 1963, U.S. Ct. Mil. Appeals 1965, U.S. Supreme Ct. 1965, U.S. Ct. Appeals (5th cir.) 1981, U.S. Ct. Appeals (Fed. cir.) 1982. Acct. Highland Oil Co., Houston, 1948-50; statis. acct. Union Oil and Gas Corp. of La., Houston, 1953-59; assoc. Hayden & Pravel, Houston, 1959-61; patent atty. Halliburton Co., Duncan, Okla., 1961-69; div. patent atty. Ethyl Corp., Baton Rouge, 1969-87; v.p. Cen. Foods, Inc., Baton Rouge, 1979-90, bd. dirs. V.p. Plato Dependent Sch. Dist., Duncan, Okla., 1966-67, pres., 1968. Served to lt. comdr., USNR, 1942-67. Me. Tex. Bar Assn, Masons. Republican. Avocations: U.S. coins, stamp collecting. Home and Office: 10639 Rondo Ave Baton Rouge LA 70815-4847

LEONARD, R. MICHAEL, lawyer; b. Atlanta, Feb. 27, 1953; s. Charles C. and Catherine (Martin) L.; m. Margaret Ellen Mead, June 29, 1985 (div. 1993); 1 child, Sarah Marie. AB, U. N.C., 1975, JD with honors, 1978. Bar: Ala. 1978, N.C. 1987. Assoc. Cabaniss, Johnston, Gardner, Dumas & O'Neal, Birmingham, Ala., 1978-85, ptnr., 1985-86; assoc. Womble Carlyle Sandridge & Rice, Winston-Salem, N.C., 1986-88, ptnr., 1988—. Author: Trail and Naturalist's Guide to Oak Mountain State Park, Alabama, 1982. Bd. dirs. Ala. Conservancy, Birmingham, 1981-85, Piedmont Land Conservancy, Greensboro, n.C., 1989-91; bd. dirs. Ala. Trails Assn., Birmingham, 1985—, founder, pres., 1985-87; trustee N.C. Nat. Heritage Found., Raleigh, 1989-92, Nature Sci. Ctr., Winston-Salem, 1994-95; gov.'s appointee bd. trustees N.C. Natural Heritage Trust Fund, 1994—; nat. adv. coun. Trust for Pub. Land, San Francisco, 1991—; mem. adv. coun. N.C. Yr. of the Mtns., 1995-96; mem. Nat. Coun. Conservation Fund, Arlington, Va., 1997—; pres. Bethania (N.C.) Hist. Property Owners Assn., Inc., 1996—; founding chmn. Ga. Pinhoti Trail Assn., Rome, 1996—; bd. dirs. Bethania Historic Assn., 1996—. Recipient E-Town E-chievement award, Boulder, Colo., 1997, Pres.'s Conservationist of Yr. award Conservation Fund, Arlington, 1996, Oak Leaf award Nature Conservancy, Washington, 1991, Sol Feinstone Environ. award Coll. Environ. Sci. & Forestry, SUNY, Rochester, 1991, Chpt. Svc. award N.C. Chpt. Sierra Club, 1990, Malcolm Stewart Conservationist of Yr. award Ala. Conservancy, Birmingham, 1983. Mem. Ala. Bar Assn., N.C. Bar Assn., Birmingham Bar Assn., Forsyth County Bar Assn., Downtown Rotary Club, Carolina Club, Black Bear Club, Order of Coif, Phi Beta Kappa, Phi Eta Sigma. Democrat. Avocations: writing, hiking, mountain climbing, camping, turkey hunting. Office: Womble Carlyle Sandridge & Rice 200 W 2nd St Winston Salem NC 27101-4019

LEONARD, RICHARD HART, journalist; b. N.Y.C., May 23, 1921; s. Richard Barstow and Stella Burnham (Hart) L.; m. Barbara Klausner, July 11, 1948; children: Laurie, Lisa. BA, U. Wis., 1947. Reporter Milw. Jour., 1947, picture editor, 1948, with Madison (Wis.) bur., 1949-50, state desk, 1951-52, state editor, 1953-62, mng. editor, 1962-66; editor, v.p. Milw. Jour. Co., 1967-85, v.p., 1967-77, sr. v.p., 1977-85, ret., 1986; editor-in-residence East-West Ctr., Honolulu, 1987; sr. fellow East-West Ctr., 1988-89; mem. Pulitzer Prize Bd., 1976-86; prof. journalism Marquette U., 1989—. With AUS, 1942-46. Recipient Carr Van Anda award Ohio U., 1972, East-West Ctr. Disting. Svc. award, Disting. Svc. award U. Wis. Mem. Am. Soc. Newspaper Editors, Internat. Press Inst. (chmn. 1984-86), Milw. Press Club (pres. 1965, elected Hall of Fame), Sigma Delta Chi (nat. pres. 1976), Phi Kappa Phi. Presbyterian. Home: 330 E Beaumont Ave Milwaukee WI 53217-4867

LEONARD, ROY JUNIOR, civil engineering educator; b. Central Square, N.Y., Aug. 17, 1929; s. Roy Jackson and Margaret Elizabeth (Keller) L.; m. Edith Campbell Gilmore; children: Robert J., Constance J. BS, Clarkson Coll. Tech., 1952; MS, U. Conn., 1954; postgrad., Mich. State U., 1954-55; PhD, Iowa State U., 1958. Registered profl. engr., N.Y., Pa., Kans., Mo., Colo.; registered profl. geologist, Mo. Asst. prof. civil engring. U. Del., 1957-59; assoc. prof. Lehigh U., 1959-65; spl. projects engr. Dames and Moore (geotech. cons.), N.Y.C., 1965; prof. civil engring. U. Kans., Lawrence, 1965-95; pres. Alpha-Omega Geotech., Inc., Kansas City, Kans. NSF fellow, 1963-65. Fellow ASCE; mem. NSPE, ASTM (chair com. vitrified clay pipe), Assn. Engring. Geologists, U.S. Com. Large Dams, Soc. Mining Engrs., Nat. Soc. Forensic Engrs., Am. Concrete Inst., Am. Pub. Works Assn., Chi Epsilon. Episcopalian. Home: 25003 Mackey Rd Lawrence KS 66044-7340

LEONARD, SAMUEL WALLACE, oil company and bank executive; b. Cumberland, R.I., Sept. 29, 1922; s. Samuel James and Hazel Della (Flagg) L.; m. Dorothy Wilma Carpenter, Oct. 15, 1949. BS in Acctg. and Fin., Bryant Coll., 1941; BA in Econs., Brown U., 1948; AMP, Harvard Bus. Sch., Soldiers Field, Mass., 1968. Internal auditor Conoco Inc., Ponca City, Okla., 1948-51; asst. dir. employee benefits Conoco Inc., Houston, 1952-54; pres., gen. mgr. Sahara Petroleum Co., Alexandria, Egypt, 1954-60; v.p., treas. Pasa Petroquímica Argentina, Buenos Aires, 1961-66; pres. Conoco Libya, Tripoli, 1966-71, Conoco Española, Madrid, Spain, 1971-72; exec. asst. pres. Conoco Inc., Stamford, Conn., 1972-76; v.p., gen. mgr. Dubai (United Arab Emirates) Petroleum, 1976-82; ret.; chmn. bd. dirs. Security Bank & Trust Co. (merger 4th Fin. Corp. 1993), Ponca city, 1992-93; bd. dirs. Bank IV Okla., Ponca City. Chmn. Little League, Tripoli, Libya, 1966-71; bd. dirs. Ponca City Libr., 1988-94. Staff sgt. U.S. Army, 1942-45, U.S. and Europe. Decorated Purple Heart, Bronze Star Valor. Mem. VFW, Am. Legion, Ponca City Country Club, Elks. Republican. Episcopal. Avocations: hunting, fishing, travel, gardening. Home and Office: PO Box 667 Ponca City OK 74602-0667

LEONARD, SUGAR RAY (RAY CHARLES LEONARD), retired professional boxer; b. Wilmington, N.C., May 17, 1956; s. Cicero and Getha L.; m. Juanita Wilkinson, Jan. 19, 1980 (div. 1990); children: Ray Charles, Jr., Jarrell Giulio. Profl. boxer, 1977-82, 84, 1987-91; pres. SRL Mgmt., Inc.; with Franklin Sports Industries, Inc. Commentator boxing broadcasts; exercise video: Boxout with Sugar Ray Leonard, 1993. Recipient Gold medal Olympic Games, 1976; winner World Boxing Coun. Welterweight Championship, 1979, World Boxing Assn. Championship Jr. Middleweight div., 1981, World Boxing Coun. Championship and World Boxing Assn. Welterweight Championship, 1981, World Boxing Coun. Middleweight Championship, 1987, World Boxing Coun. Light Heavyweight and Super Middleweight Championship, 1988. Address: Ste 303 4401 East West Hwy Bethesda MD 20814-4521*

LEONARD, THOMAS ALOYSIUS, lawyer; b. Phila., Sept. 5, 1946; s. Thomas Aloysius and Mary Teresa (Kelly) L.; m. Kathleen Mary Duffy; children: Sarah, Mary Kate, Tom. BS, Drexel U., 1968; JD, Temple U., 1971. Bar: Pa., U.S. Supreme Ct., U.S. Ct. Appeals (3d cir.), U.S. Dist. Ct. (ea., mid., we. dists.) Pa., U.S. Dist. Ct. (so. dist.) N.J., U.S. Dist. Ct. Utah, U.S. Dist. Ct. (so. dist.) N.Y. Assoc. Dilworth, Paxson, Kalish & Kauffman, Phila., 1972-76, ptnr., 1976-79, 83-87, sr. ptnr., mem. exec. com., 1987—; controller City of Phila., 1987-91; chmn. litigation dept., sr. ptnr., permanent mem. mgmt. com. Obermayer, Rebmann, Maxwell and Hippel, Phila., 1991—; bd. dirs. Fed. Nat. Mortgage Assn., Independence Blue Cross; vice chmn. Phila. Gas Commn., 1979-83; register of wills City of Phila., 1976-79; mem. disciplinary bd. Supreme Ct., Pa., 1991-95, vice chmn., 1995-96, chmn., 1996—. Mem. editorial bd. Amran's Pa. Practice, 1972; contbr. articles to profl. pubs. Mem. Dem. Nat. Com., Washington, 1976-83, mem. fin. com., 1988, vice chair fin., 1993, Pa. fin. chair, 1993—, bd. dirs.; del. Dem. Nat. Conv., 1976, 80, 92, 96; chmn. Pa. fin. com. Clinton for Pres., 1992, 96; co-chair Rendell for Mayor, 1991, 95; mem. coun. Phila. Orch., 1981-86; bd. dirs. Acad. Scis., Phila., 1981-85; pres. Pa. chpt. Irish Am. Partnership. Capt. U.S. Army, 1971-77. Recipient Man of Yr. award Emerald Soc., 1979, Korean-Am. Friendship Soc., 1982, Carmel Humanitarian award Haifa U., 1981, Merit award Chapel of Four Chaplains, 1983. Mem. ABA, Pa. Bar Assn., Phila. Bar Assn. (bd. govs. 1979-82), Union League, Phila. Racquet Club, Serra Club (past pres.). Roman Catholic. Office: Obermayer Rebmann Maxwell and Hippel 1617 John F Kennedy Blvd Fl 19 Philadelphia PA 19103-1821

LEONARD, TIMOTHY DWIGHT, judge; b. Jan. 22, 1940; s. Dwight and Mary Evelyn Leonard; m. Nancy Louise Laughlin, July 15, 1967; children: Kirstin Dione, Ryan Timothy, Tyler Dwight. BA, U. Okla., 1962; JD, 1965; student Mil. Naval Justice Sch., 1966. Bar: Okla. 1965, U.S. Dist. Ct. (no. and we. dists) Okla. 1969, U.S. Ct. Appeals (10th cir.) 1969, U.S. Supreme Ct. 1970. Asst. atty. gen. State of Okla., 1968-70, senator, 1979-88; ptnr. Blankenship, Herrold, Russell et al, Oklahoma City, 1970-71, Trippet, Leonard & Kee, Beaver, 1971-88; of counsel Huckaby, Fleming, et al., Oklahoma City, 1988-89; U.S. atty. Western Dist. Okla., 1989-92; judge U.S. Dist. Ct. (we. dist.) Okla., 1992—; guest lectr., tchr. Oklahoma City U., 1988-89. Mem. U.S. Atty. Gen.'s Adv. Com., 1990-92, chmn. office mgmt. and budget subcom., 1990-92. Co-author: 4 Days, 40 Hours, 1970. Rep. lt. gov. candidate Okla.; minority leader Okla. State Senate, 1985-86; white ho. mil. aide, Washington, 1966-67. Lt. USN, 1965-68, Washington. Named Outstanding Legislator Okla. Sch. Bd. Assn., 1988. Mem. ABA, Okla. Bar Assn., Phi Alpha Delta, Beta Theta Pi. Republican. Methodist. Avocations: basketball, running, reading. Office: US Courthouse 200 NW 4th St Ste 5102 Oklahoma City OK 73102-3031

LEONARD, VENELDA HALL, writer; b. Tifton, Ga., Jan. 7, 1914; d. Alonza Clayton and Bessie Lee (Shiver) Hall; m. James W. Leonard, June 14, 1931; children: James W. Leonard, Jr., Doris Delle Carr, Joan Le Mai Kyser. AA, Gulf Coast C.C., Panama City, Fla., 1964; BS, Fla. State U., 1965, MS, 1966. Instr. English, journalism Mosley H.S., Panama City, Fla., 1969-78; instr. remedial English Gulf Coast C.C., Panama City, 1979. Author: Sourwood, 1995. Mem. Phi Theta Kappa. Home: 2302 Country Club Dr Lynn Haven FL 32444

LEONARD, WALTER RAYMOND, retired biology educator; b. Scott County, Va., July 5, 1923; s. Homer Stanley and Minnie Eunice (Neal) L.; m. Alice Ann McCaskill, Sept. 1, 1951; children—Leslie Ann, Walter Raymond. B.A., Tusculum Coll., Greeneville, Tenn., 1946; M.A., Vanderbilt U., 1947, Ph.D., 1949. Mem. faculty Wofford Coll., Spartanburg, S.C., 1949-93; John M. Reeves prof. biology Wofford Coll., 1954-87, William R. Kenan Jr. prof. biology, 1987-93, William R. Kenan Jr. prof. emeritus, 1993—; instl. rev. bd. mem. Spartanburg Regional Med. Ctr., 1994—; faculty athletic rep. NCAA. Served with USAAF, 1942-43. Named to Sports Hall of Fame, Tusculum Coll., 1983; Walter Raymond Leonard scholarship created Wofford Coll., 1973; W. Ray Leonard award established Beta Beta Beta, 1993; W. Ray Leonard Retirement Fund established Former Students Wofford Coll., 1993. Mem. AAAS, S.C. Acad. Sci., Scabbard and Blade (hon.), Lamda Chi Alpha (named to Hall of Fame 1996), Letterman's Club (hon.). Methodist. Rsch. on cell metabolism. Home: 110 Pinetree Cir Spartanburg SC 29307-2938 Office: Wofford Coll N Church St Spartanburg SC 29301

LEONARD, WILL ERNEST, JR., lawyer; b. Shreveport, La., Jan. 18, 1935; s. Will Ernest and Nellie (Kenner) L.; m. Maureen Laniak; children—Will Ernest III, Sherry Elizabeth, Robert Scott, Stephen Michael, Christopher Anthony, Colleen Mary, Leigh Alison. B.A., Tulane U., 1956, LL.B., 1958; LL.M., Harvard U., 1966. Bar: La. 1958, D.C. 1963, U.S. Supreme Ct. 1963. Announcer sta. WVUE-TV, New Orleans, 1958-60; legislative asst. to U.S. Senator Russell B. Long, 1960-65; profl. staff mem. com. fin. U.S. Senate, 1966-68; mem. Internat. Trade Commn. (formerly U.S. Tariff Commn.), 1968-77, chmn., 1975-76; ptnr. Ablondi, Foster, Sobin & Davidow, Washington, 1996—; Congl. staff fellow Am. Polit. Sci. Assn., 1965-66. Home: 7324 Bradley Blvd Bethesda MD 20817-2130 Office: Ablondi Foster Sobin & 1130 Connecticut Ave NW Washington DC 20036-3904

LEONBERGER, FREDERICK JOHN, electrical engineer, photonics manager; b. Washington, Sept. 25, 1947; s. Melvin Fred and Mary Dorothy (Burchell) L.; m. Janet Marie Bueche, Aug. 8, 1970; children—Gregory, Katharine. B.S.E., U. Mich., 1969; S.M., MIT, 1971, E.E., 1972, Ph.D., 1975. Mem. staff MIT Lincoln Lab., Lexington, 1975-81; group leader MIT Lincoln Lab., 1981-84; mgr. photonics and applied physics United Tech. Rsch. Ctr., East Hartford, Conn., 1984-91; gen. mgr. United Tech. Photonics, Bloomfield, 1991-95; v.p., chief tech. officer UTP, Inc., Bloomfield, 1995—. Contbr. articles to profl. jours.; patentee in field. Fellow IEEE (tech. program com. 1979—, assoc. editor Jour. Quantum Electronics 1983-87), Optical Soc. Am. (tech. program com. 1979—, assoc. editor Optics Letters 1988-91); mem. IEEE Lasers and Electrooptics Soc. (adminstrv. com. 1984-86, pres. 1988, Quantum Electronics award 1993), Sigma Xi, Tau Beta Pi, Eta Kappa Nu. Avocations: tennis; golf; hiking; classical music. Office: UTP 1289 Blue Hills Ave Bloomfield CT 06002-1302

LEONE, GEORGE FRANK, pharmaceutical executive; b. Astoria, N.Y., Aug. 1, 1926; s. George and Fannie K. (Teano) L.; m. Mary Louise Potts, Dec. 14, 1945; children: Pamela Ann, George Frank. BS, Wesleyan U., 1949; postgrad., NYU, 1951; grad. Advanced Mgmt. Program,, Harvard Bus. Sch., 1959; postgrad., U. Tex., 1977; DSc (hon.), Tex. Wesleyan U., 1990. Chemist, Lederle Labs., Pearl River, N.Y., 1949-50; with Alcon Labs., Inc., Ft. Worth, 1950-91; med. sales rep. Alcon Labs., Inc., 1950-54, dist. sales mgr., 1954-58, regional sales mgr., 1958-63, nat. sales mgr., 1963-66, dir. mktg., 1966-69, gen. mgr. domestic, 1969-70, v.p. sci., tech., 1971-81, sr. v.p., 1981-91, also dir.; Pres. Laksmi Corp., Fort Worth, 1989—; pres. Avicon, Inc., 1972-79; exec. com. trustee Alcon Rsch. Inst., 1980—; trustee C.V. Whitney Lab., U. Fla., St. Augustine, 1996—. Pres., commr. Earth County Water Control and Improvement, Dist. 1, 1976-80; trustee Tex. Wesleyan U., fin. com., exec. com., 1985-91, audit and fin. com., 1993; bd. dirs. Tex. Christian U. Rsch. Found., 1976-82; chmn. athletic com. Dan Danciger Jewish Community Ctr.; pres. Peninsula Pecan Growers Assn., 1980-85; mem. fin. com. Fort Worth Acad., 1984-88, bd. dirs., 1986-88. With USN, 1944-46. Named Disting. Alumnus, Tex. Wesleyan U., 1979. Mem. Yoga Soc. N.Y. (pres. 1978-94, bd. dirs. 1978—), Am. Radio Relay League, Alpha Chi. Club: Fort Worth. Home: 4100 Hildring Dr E Fort Worth TX 76109-4714 also: 321 Monika Pl Saint Augustine FL 32084-6441 Office: Laksmi Corp 6201 S Freeway PO Box 1959 Fort Worth TX 76134-2099 also: 4100 Hildring Dr E Fort Worth TX 76109-4714

LEONE, LUCILE P., retired health administrator; b. Ohio, 1902; m. Nicholas C. Leone, 1952. BA, U. Del., 1924; BS, Johns Hopkins U., 1927; MS, Columbia U., 19929. Staff nurse Johns Hopkins Hosp., Balt., 1927-29; instr., prof. U. Minn., Mpls., 1929-41; comdt. Student Nursing Svc. USPHS, 1941-42, dir. Cadet Corps Program, 1942-48, chief nurse officer, asst. surgeon gen., 1948-66; assoc. dean nursing Tex. Woman's Coll., 1967-71; advisor internat. students Sch. Nursing U. Calif., San Francisco, 1978-83. Mem. Inst. Medicine/Nat. Acad. Sci. Address: 1400 Geary Blvd San Francisco CA 94109-6561

LEONE, STEPHEN ROBERT, chemical physicist, educator; b. N.Y.C., May 19, 1948; s. Dominic and Annie Frances (Sappa) L. BA, Northwestern U., 1970; PhD, U. Calif., Berkeley, 1974. Asst. prof. U. So. Calif., L.A., 1974-76; physicist/fellow Nat. Inst. Standards and Tech., Boulder, Colo., 1976-94, acting chief Quantum Physics divsn., 1994-95; adj. prof. U. Colo., Boulder, 1994-96. Contbr. over 200 articles to profl. publs.; mem. editorial bd. Optics Letters, Jour. Chem. Physics, Chem. Revs., Jour. Phys. Chemistry, Molecular Physics, Chem. Physics Letters, Progress in Reaction Kinetics; patentee in field. Recipient silver and gold medals Dept. Commerce, 1980, 85, Coblentz award Coblentz Soc., 1984, Arthur S. Flemming award U.S. Govt., 1986, Samuel Wesley Stratton award Nat. Inst. Standards and Tech., 1992; Alfred P. Sloan fellow Sloan Found., 1977-81, Guggenheim fellow, 1988. Fellow AAAS, Optical Soc. Am., Am. Phys. Soc. (chair div. chem. physics 1987-88, Herbert P. Broida prize 1989); mem. NAS, Am. Chem. Soc. (pure chemistry award 1982, nobel laureate signature award 1983). Office: JILA Univ of Colo Campus Box 440 Boulder CO 80309

LEONE, WILLIAM CHARLES, retired manufacturing executive; b. Pitts., May 3, 1924; s. Joseph and Fortuna (Sammarco) L.; m. Sara Jane Hollenback, Aug. 26, 1950; children: William Charles, David M., Patricia Ann, Mary Jane. BS, Carnegie Inst. Tech., 1944, MS, 1948, DSc, 1952. Asst. prof. engring. Carnegie Inst. Tech., Pitts., 1946-53; mgr. Indsl. Sys. divsn. Hughes Aircraft, L.A., 1953-59; v.p., gen. mgr., dir. Rheem Califone, L.A., 1960, Rheem Electronics, L.A., 1960-68; group v.p. Rheem Mfg. Co., 1968-71; exec. v.p. Rheem Mfg. Co., N.Y.C., 1971-72, pres., 1972-76; also dir. Rheem Mfg. Co.; pres. City Investing Co. Internat., Inc., 1972-76; pres., dir. Farah Mfg. Co., El Paso, Tex., 1976-77; bus. cons., 1977-79; acting vice chmn. McCulloch Oil Corp. (MCO), L.A., 1979-80, also bd. dirs.; pres., dir. MAXXAM Inc. (formerly MCO Holdings, Inc.), 1980-90; vice chmn. MAXXAM Inc., 1990-92; chmn., CEO, dir. Pacific Lumber Co., 1986-90, Horizon Corp., 1984-89. Trustee Carnegie Mellon U., 1986-92. Mem. ASME, IEEE, Am. Inst. Aerospace and Aeronautics, Sigma Xi, Tau Beta Pi, Pi Tau Sigma, Theta Tau, Pi Mu Epsilon. Home: 2209 Chelsea Rd Palos Verdes Peninsula CA 90274-2603

LEONETT, ANTHONY ARTHUR, banker; b. Summit, N.J., Jan. 4, 1929; s. Joseph J. and Margaret (DiGuglielmo) L.; m. Ann Marino, Oct. 6, 1974; 1 son by previous marriage, Anthony Arthur. B.S., Seton Hall U., 1950; certificate, Am. Inst. Banking, 1956; postgrad., U. Wis., 1962. Mgr. First Nat. Bank & Trust Co., Summit, 1950-56; sr. v.p., auditor Nat. State Bank, Elizabeth, N.J., 1956—; instr. principles of auditing and bank operations Am. Inst. Banking; faculty N.J. Data Processing Sch., Princeton, Bank Adminstrn. Sch. of U. Wis. Bd. dirs. N.J. affiliate Am. Heart Assn. Served with U.S. Army, 1951-53. Recipient Irving Grabiel award for outstanding leadership in banking, 1979. Mem. Am. Inst. Banking (dir. chpt.), Bank Adminstrn. Inst. (N.J. state dir. 1977-79, pres. N.J. chpt., dist. dir. 1979-81). Republican. Roman Catholic. Clubs: K.C., Minisink (Chatham). Home: 102 N Hillside Ave Chatham NJ 07928-2825 Office: 68 Broad St Elizabeth NJ 07201-2206

LEONG, G. KEONG, operations management educator; b. Georgetown, Penang, Malaysia, Mar. 10, 1950; s. Eng Loong Leong and Mee Lan Chiew; m. C. Lin Khong; 1 child, Michelle P.Y. BEngring., U. Malaya, Kuala Lumpur, 1973; MBA, U. S.C., 1984, PhD in Bus. Adminstrn., 1987. Trainee exec. Fraser and Neave Co., Kuala Lumpur, 1973-74; project engr. Behn Meyer Engring, Shah Alam, Malaysia, 1974-76, export mgr., 1977; tech. mgr. Behn Meyer Engring., Shah Alam, Malaysia, 1980-82; gen. mgr. Hanseatic Engring. and Trading Co., Bangkok, 1978-80; rsch. asst., teaching asst. U. S.C., Columbia, 1983-87; asst. prof. ops. mgmt. Ohio State U., Columbus, 1987-93; assoc. prof. ops. mgmt. Ohio State U., 1993—; advisor Ohio State U. chpt. Am. Prodn. and Inventory Control Soc., 1989-90, 91—, acad. liaison, 1995—; assoc. dir. Ctr. Excellence in Mfg. Mgmt., 1995—. Coord. United Way Cen. Ohio, Columbus, 1988, 89, 90, 91. Internat. rsch. fellow Internat. Ctr. for Electronic Commerce, Seoul, Korea. Fellow Inst. of Engrs. Malaysia; mem. Decision Scis. Inst. (chair innovative edn. com. 1994-95, track chair in strategic mgmt. 3d internat. mtg., co-track chair Prodn. and Ops. Mgmt. Mfg. 1996, v.p. 1997—, Best Paper award 1990, Stan Hardy Best Paper award 1994, 96), INFORMS, Acad. of Mgmt., Beta Gamma Sigma. Avocation: golf. Home: 246 Caren Ave Worthington OH 43085-2525 Office: Ohio State Univ 1775 S College Rd Columbus OH 43210-1309

LEONG, HELEN VANESSA, systems programmer; b. Chgo., Dec. 14, 1949; d. Linton and Sue Lin (Hong) L.; m. Stephen Occhiuzzo, Aug. 28, 1993. BS in Liberal Arts/Math., Ill. Inst. Tech., 1971. Computer sys. analyst Ill. Bell Tel., Chgo., 1971-76; commd. ensign USN, 1977, advanced through grades to lt. comdr., 1992; pers. officer NAS Glenview, Ill., 1977-78; pub. affairs officer NAS Glenview, 1979-80; computer sys. analyst Space and Naval Warfare Sys. Command, Washington Navy Yard, Washington, 1980-83; program mgr. asst. Dept. of Navy (OP-942) Pentagon, Washington, 1983-86; joint action officer Office Joint Chiefs of Staff (J-6), Pentagon, Washington, 1986-87; exec. officer Naval Regional Data Automation Ctr., Newport, R.I., 1987-89; sys. programmer Stanford (Calif.) Health Svcs., 1989—. mem. Svc. Acad. Adv. Bd. Frank Wolf, Tenth Dist., Va., 1985-87; chairperson energy com. Skyline Condo Assn., Falls Church, Va., 1986. Decorated Navy Achievement medal, 1982, Joint Commendation medal, 1987, Navy Commendation medal, 1989, Nat. Def. medal, 1992. Mem. NAFE, Nat. Sys. Programmers Assn. Avocations: downhill skiing, ice skating, roller blading, knitting, reading. Office: Stanford Health Svcs 300 Pasteur Dr # B Palo Alto CA 94304-2203

LEONG, JO-ANN CHING, microbiologist, educator; b. Honolulu, May 15, 1942; d. Raymond and Josephine Ching; m. Oren T.H. Leong; children: Kara Elise, Jonathan Raymond. BA in Zoology, U. Calif., Berkeley, 1964; PhD in Microbiology, San Francisco Sch. Medicine, 1971. Postdoctoral rsch. assoc. dept. biochemistry U. Calif., San Francisco, 1971-75, asst. rsch. virologist Cancer Rsch. Inst., 1975; asst. prof. Oreg. State U., Corvallis, 1975-80, assoc. prof., 1980-86, prof., 1986-92, disting. prof., 1992—, chairperson, 1996—; grant reviewer Sea Grant, NSF, CRIS, USDA, NIH; cons. Am. Microscan, 1986. Co-author: Retroviruses and Differentiation, 1982, Molecular Approaches to Bacteria and Viral Diseases of Fish, 1983, Fish Vaccination, 1988, Viral Vaccines for Aquaculture, 1993, Human Endogenous Retroviruses, 1994, DNA Vaccines for Fish, 1996; virology editor Diseases of Aquatic Organisms. Coord. Women in Sci. Career Workshop, Portland (Oreg.) State U., 1977. Recipient Dernham Rsch. Fellowship, Am. Cancer Soc., 1973-75, fellowship Giannini Found. for Med. Rsch., 1973, Rsch. award Sigma Xi, 1990; named NORCAS prof. Batelle NW Labs, 1976, Disting Prof. Oreg. State U. Alumni Assn., 1991. Fellow Am. Acad. Microbiology; mem. AAAS, AAUP (exec. bd. 1982), European Assn. of Fish Pathologists, Am. Soc. Microbiology, Am. Soc. Virology, Am. Fisheries Soc. (fish health sect.), Assn. Women in Sci., Am. Assn. Cancer Rsch. Office: Oreg State U Dept Microbiology Corvallis OR 97331-3804

LEONG, LAM-PO (LANBO LIANG), artist, educator; b. Canton, Guangdong, China, July 3, 1961; came to U.S., 1983; BFA in Chinese Brush Painting, Canton Fine Arts Inst., 1983; MFA in Painting with high distinction, Calif. Coll. Arts & Crafts, 1988. Instr. art Calif. Coll. Arts and Crafts, Oakland, 1986-87, U. Calif. Ext. and ASUC, Berkeley, 1989, 90—, San Jose (Calif.) State U. Ext., 1989-91, Chabot Coll., Hayward, Calif., 1989-94; lectr. San Francisco State U., 1988-95, asst. prof., 1996—; instr. Laney Coll., Oakland, Calif., 1997—; artistic dir. Oakland Asian Cultural Ctr., Calif., 1990-92; lectr. and spkr. in field, including TV appearances, Asian Art Mus. San Francisco, Chinese Cultural Ctr., San Francisco, 1985, 90, 92, 93, 95, 96. One-man shows include Markings Gallery, Berkeley, 1984, Sumitomo Bank, Albany, Calif., 1985, Calif. Coll. Arts & Crafts, 1985, Rosicrucian Egyptian Mus., San Jose, 1986, U. Utah, Salt Lake City, 1986, Patrick Gallery, Regina, Sask., Can., 1986, Mus. Macao Luis De Camoes, Macao, 1986, Kai Ping County Mus., Guangdong, 1987, Chinatown Gallery, San Francisco, 1987, Guangzhou Fine Arts Mus., Canton, 1988, The Arlington Gallery, Oakland, 1989, Moy Ying Ming Gallery, Chgo., 1990, Chinese Culture Ctr., San Francisco, 1991, Stanwood Gallery, San Francisco, 1992, Sanuk Fine Asian Collectables, San Francisco, 1992, The Univ. Gallery, San Francisco, 1994, Michael Thompson Gallery, San Francisco, 1995, 97, China Art Expo '95, Guangzhou, China, 1995, Chinese Art Gallery, San Leandro, Calif., 1997, MTC Gallery, Oakland, Calif., 1996, Galerie du Monde, Hong Kong, 1997; exhibited in group shows at Hong Kong Arts Ctr., 1980, Chinese Painting Exhibit Guangdong Province, 1981 (3d Prize award 1981), Macao Artists Assn. Exhbn., 1982, 96, Mus. Canton Fine Arts Inst., 1983, Nat. Mus. Art, Beijing, 1985, Macao Young Artist Exhbn. (Excellence award, 1st prize 1985), Pacific Art Ctr., Seattle, 1985, Chinese Culture Ctr., 1986, Faculty & MFA Show Calif. Coll. Arts & Crafts, San Francisco Campus, 1986, Chinese-Am. Artist Exhbn., Taipei, Taizhong, Taiwan, 1986, Sullivan Galleries, Salt Lake City, 1987, Oriental Gallery, N.Y., 1987, Santa Cruz Art League (Spl. award 1988, 1st prize 1990), Asian Resource Gallery, Oakland, 1988, Nat. Mus. Fine Arts, Beijing, 1988, 90, Chinese Art Gallery, San Leandro, Calif., 1989, Stanwood Gallery, 1989, Gallery Imago, San Francisco, 1990, Sun Gallery, Hayward, 1990, N.Y. Art Expo, N.Y.C., 1991, Gallery 5, Santa Monica, Calif., 1991, Butterfield & Butterfield Auction, San Francisco, 1992, 95-96, Asian Art Mus., San Francisco, 1992, Ke Shan Art Gallery, Taipei, 1993, Wan Fung Art Gallery, Hong Kong, 1993, Gallery On The Rim, San Francisco, 1994, Resource for Art, 1995, Ginsberg Collection, 1995, Macao Art Expo, 1988-96, Acad. Art Coll., San Francisco, 1996, Shanghai Arts Mus., 1997; work represented in various mus., corp. and pvt. collections including Guangzhou Arts Mus., Macao Camoes Mus., Mus. Canton Fine Arts Inst., Asian Art Mus. San Francisco, United Savs. Bank, Calif., Hotel East 21, Tokyo, The Tokyo Westin Hotel, Comml. Bank, San Francisco, Westin Surabaya, Indonesia; author: Brush Paintings of Lam-Po Leong, 1986, Journey of the Heart, 1994; illustrator: Brushstrokes-Styles and Techniques of Chinese Painting, 1993, The Tao of Power, 1986; designer (granite courtyard) New Chinatown Pk., San Francisco, 1993; (multi-image projection) Ctr. Arts Yerba Buena Gardens, San Francisco, 1996. Recipient Outstanding Merit award Young Art Now Competition, 1980, Decade of Achievement award Asian/Pacific Heritage Week, 1988, 2d prize Zunyi Internat. Brush Painting Competition, 1989; inductee Pan-Pacific Asian Hall of Fame at San Francisco Internat. Expo., 1987; grantee City of Oakland Cultural Arts Divsn., 1994-96. Mem. Asian Artists Assn. Am., Oriental Art Assn., U.S.A. (v.p.), Macao Soc. Social Scis., Hai-Ri Artists Assn. (China), Nat. Modern Meticulous Painting Soc. (China), Chinese Am. Culture Exch. Assn. (co-founder, dir. 1992—). Avocations: film, ballroom dance, travel, photography. Office: Brushwork Gallery 166 Palisades Dr Daly City CA 94015-4517

LEONG, SUE, retired community health and pediatrics nurse; b. Alameda, Calif., Feb. 15, 1930; d. Leong Dai Sun and Leong San See. BS, U. Calif., San Francisco, 1953; MPH, U. Mich., 1963; MA, San Francisco Theol. Sem., 1958. Cert. sch. nurse, sch. nurse practitioner, nurse specialist. Head nurse Lafayette Clinic, Detroit; pub. health nurse San Francisco Health Dept.; assoc. dir. Ecumenical Campus Ctr., Ann Arbor, Mich.; sch. nurse practitioner Ann Arbor Pub. Schs.; adj. asst. prof. U. Mich. Contbr. articles to profl. jours. Parish nurse cons., 1996—. Mem. NEA, Mich. Assn. Sch. Nurses (Disting. Svc. award 1990, Dorothy Christy award 1993). Home: 1506 Golden Ave Ann Arbor MI 48104-4327

LEONHARDT, DEBBIE ANN, counselor, writer, minister; b. Valdese, N.C., June 11, 1953; d. Douglas Franklin and Jettie Arcena (Stilwell) L. BA, Lenoir-Rhyne Coll., 1975, MA, 1986; MDiv, Southeastern Bapt. Theol. Sem., 1977. Cert. Nat. Bd. Cert. Conselors, N.C. Bd. Licensed Profl. Counselors; ordained to ministry Bapt. Ch., 1983. Min. edn. Front St. Bapt. Ch., Statesville, N.C., 1978-80; assoc. min. First Bapt. Ch., Taylorsville, N.C., 1980-85; sch. counselor Alexander County Pub. Schs., Taylorsville, N.C., 1985—; pres. Alexander Counseling and Consulting Svcs., Inc., Taylorsville, N.C., 1994—; instr. cont. edn. Catawba Valley C.C., Hickory, N.C., 1993—; cons., seminar leader Catawba County Family Support Network, Hickory, N.C., 1996. Author: Survival Kit: A Guide for Brain Injured Patients, 1995; contbr. article to profl. jour., poems to collection. Vol. chaplain Catawba Meml. Hosp., Hickory, N.C., 1994-95; mem. Smart Start Partnership Task Force, Alexander County, N.C., 1995-96; mem., cons. Catawba County Traumatic Brain Injury Resource Com., Hickory, N.C., 1996. Name Young Career Woman Bus. and Profl. Women's Club, 1984. Mem. Nat. Brain Injury Assn., Nat. Bd. Cert. Counselors (test item writer Master Addictions Counselor, test item review com. 1996), N.C. Bd. Licensed Profl. Counselors, N.C. Sch. Counslors Assn., N.C. Brain Injury Assn. Democrat. Avocations: public speaking, coaching basketball, swimming. Home: Rt 2 Box 443 Curtis Ln Hiddenite NC 28636 Office: Alexander Counseling & Cons Svcs 125 Wilkesboro Rd NW Taylorsville NC 28681-2321

LEONHARDT, FREDERICK WAYNE, lawyer; b. Daytona Beach, Fla., Oct. 26, 1949; s. Frederick Walter and Gaetane Laura L.; m. Victoria Ann Cook, Dec. 27, 1975; children: Ashley Victoria, Frederick Whitaker. BA, U. Fla. 1971, JD, 1974. Bar: Fla. 1974, N.C. 1984, D.C. 1985; cert. real estate lawyer, Fla., 1987. Gen. counsel Fla. House of Reps., 1974-75; ptnr. Cobb, Cole and Bell, Daytona Beach, 1975-79; pres. Leonhardt & Upchurch, 1979-87; ptnr. Holland & Knight, Orlando, Fla., 1987-93; ptnr. Gray, Harris & Robinson, P.A., Orlando and Cocoa Beach, 1993—. Chmn. bd. dirs. Orlando/Orange County Compact, 1989-90; founder Leadership Daytona Beach; grad. Leadership Fla., bd. regents, 1995—; Leadership Orlando, 1992, Leadership Ctrl. Fla., 1995; bd. dirs. Orlando Regional Med. Ctr. Found., 1992—; past chmn. Orlando Area Sports Commn. Mem. ABA (state and local govt. law sect. vice-chmn., past editor sect. newsletter 1991-94), Orange and Volusia Counties Bar Assn., Greater Orlando C. of C. (chmn. 1991-92), Daytona Beach Area C. of C. (pres. 1985), Fla. C. of C. (bd. dirs. 1984-90, 93—), Phi Alpha Delta, Delta Chi. Office: Gray Harris & Robinson PA PO Box 3068 201 E Pine St Ste 1200 Orlando FL 32802

LEONHARDT, THOMAS WILBURN, librarian, technical services director; b. Wilmington, N.C., Feb. 7, 1943; s. Thomas Beauregard and Rachel Virginia (Callicutt) L.; m. Margaret Ann Pullen, Sept. 19, 1966; children: Hilary, Thomas, Rebecca, Benjamin. AA, Pasadena (Calif.) City Coll., 1968; AB, U. Calif., Berkeley, 1970, MLS, 1973. Head gift and exch. div. Stanford (Calif.) U. Librs., 1973-76; head acquisition dept. Boise (Idaho) State U. Libr., 1976-79, Duke U. Librs., Durham, N.C., 1980-82; asst. univ. libr. U. Oreg., Eugene, 1982-87; dean librs. U. of the Pacific, Stockton, Calif., 1987-92; dir. tech. svcs. U. Okla. Librs., Norman, 1992-97; libr. dir. Oreg. Inst. Tech., Klamath Falls, 1997—; editor RTSD Newsletter, Chgo., 1986-89, Info. Tech. & Librs., Chgo., 1990-95. Editor Advances in Collection Development and Resource Management, JAI Press, 1994—; publisher, editor Callicutt Family Chronicle; contbr. articles to profl. jours. Bd. dirs. No. Regional Libr. Facility, Richmond, Calif., 1988-92, Feather River Inst. for Libr. Acquisitions, Blairsden, Calif.; del. Online Computer Libr. Ctr. AMIGOS Bibliog. Coun., Inc., 1996—. Mem. ALA, Assn. Coll. Rsch. Librs. (v.p./pres.-elect 1995—), Libr. and Info. Tech. Assn., Assn. for Libr. Collections and Tech. Svcs., Ctrl. Assn. Librs. (bd. dirs. Stockton chpt. 1987-92). Democrat. Avocations: trumpet, guitar. Home: 204 Terra Ct Norman OK 73069-8641

LEONIS, JOHN MICHAEL, aerospace executive; b. Whittier, Calif., Oct. 21, 1933; s. Michael Arthur and Minnie Augusta (Peterson) L.; m. Edith Ann Pattison, Aug. 30, 1958; children: Susan Elizabeth, Carolyn Ann, Linda Maria. BEE, U. Ariz., 1959. Past pres. Litton Guidance and Control Systems, Woodland Hills, Calif.; chmn., CEO Litton Industries, Inc., Woodland Hills, Calif., 1995—. Mem. AIAA, Inst. Navigation, Air Force Assn., Assn. U.S. Army, Assn. Naval Aviation, Naval Helicopter Assn., Am. Electronics Assn. Office: Litton Industries Inc 21240 Burbank Blvd Woodland Hills CA 91367-6675*

LEONSIS, TED, communications company executive, publishing company executive; b. Vero Beach, Fla., Jan. 8, 1956. BA magna cum laude, Georgetown U., 1976; postgrad. Suffolk U. Law Sch., 1980. Copywriter, advt. mgr. Wang Labs., Inc., 1976-78, corp. publicity/pub. relations dir., 1978-81; dir. mktg. communications Harris Corp., Melbourne, Fla., 1981-83; exec. v.p. Redgate Pub. Co., Vero Beach, Fla., 1983—, also dir.; pres. Redgate Communications Corp., 1986-94; pres. Am. Online Svcs. Co., Vienna, Va., 1994-96, AOL Studios, Vienna, 1996—; founder Collegiate Entrepreneurs Fund; dir. Preview Media Inc., Brevard Venture Fund. Chmn. United Fund campaign, Wang Labs. Inc., 1980; bd. dirs. Big Bros. Brevard County, 1981. Brevard Art Ctr. and Mus., Brevard Council of Arts, 1981, Juvenile Employment Project, Lowell, Mass., Merrimack Regional Theatre. Mem. Pub. Relations Soc. Am. (cert.), Publicity Club Boston, Bus. Profl. Advt. Adminstrs., Am. Mktg. Assn. Author: Software Master for the IBM PC, Mastering The IBM Assistant Series, Software Master for PFS, Blue Magic; pub. The Macintosh Buyer's Guide, Apple II Rev., The Apple IIGS Buyer's Guide, COMPAQ, FYI; The Harris Mag. for Info. Mgmt.; contbr. articles to profl. jours. Office: America Online Svcs Co 8619 Westwood Center Dr Vienna VA 22182-2220

LEONTIEF, WASSILY, economist, educator; b. Leningrad, Russia, Aug. 5, 1906; s. Wassily and Eugenia (Bekker) L.; m. Estelle Helena Marks, Dec. 25, 1932; 1 child, Svetlana Eugenia Alpers. Student, U. Leningrad, 1921-25; grad. Learned Economist; PhD, U. Berlin, 1928; PhD honoris causa, U. Bruxelles, Belgium, 1962, U. York, Eng., 1967, U. Louvain, 1971, U. Paris, 1972, U. Pa., 1976, U. Lancaster, Eng., 1976; D honoris causa, Adelphi Coll., 1988; LHD (hon.), Rensselaer Poly. Inst., 1988; D honoris causa, U. Cordoba, 1990, Humboldt U. of Berlin, 1995. Rsch. economist Inst. Weltwirtschaft U. Kiel, Germany, 1927-28, 30; econ. adviser to Chinese govt. Nanking, 1929; with Nat. Bur. Econ. Rsch., N.Y.C., 1931; instr. econs. Harvard U., Cambridge, Mass., 1932-33; asst. prof. Harvard U., Cambridge, 1933-39, assoc. prof., 1939-46, prof., 1946-75, dir. econ. project, 1948-72, Henry Lee prof. econs., 1953-75; prof. econs. NYU, 1975—, univ. prof., 1983—, founder Inst. Econ. Analysis, 1978-85, mem. rsch. staff, 1986; cons. Dept. Labor, 1941-47, OSS, 1943-45, UN, 1961-62, Dept. Commerce, 1966-82, EPA, 1975-80 , UN, 1980—. Author: The Structure of the American Economy, 1919-29, 2d edit., 1976, Studies in the Structure of the American Economy, 1953, 2d edit., 1977, Input-Output Economics, 1966, 2d edit., 1986, Collected Essays, 1966, Theories, Facts and Policies, 1977, The Future of the World Economy, 1977, (with Faye Duchin) The Future Impact of Automation on Workers, 1986; Contbr. articles to sci. jours. and periodicals U.S. and abroad. Mem. Commn. to Study Orgn. of Peace, 1978; trustee N.C. Sch. Sci. and Math., 1978; mem. issues com. Progressive Alliance, 1979; mem. Com. for Nat. Security, 1980. Decorated officer Order Cherubim U. Pisa; comdr. Order Arts and Letters, Legion of Honor (France); Order of Rising Sun (Japan); recipient Bernhard-Harms prize econs. Fed. Republic of Germany, 1970, Nobel prize in econs., 1973, Takemi Meml. award Inst. Seizon and Life Scis., Japan, 1991, Harry Edmonds award for Life Achievement, 1995; Guggenheim fellow, 1940, 50. Fellow Soc. Fellows Harvard (sr. fellow, chmn. 1964-75), Econometric Soc., Royal Statis. Assn. (hon.), Inst. de France (corr.), N.Y. Acad. Scis.; mem. NAS, AAAS, Am. Philos. Soc., Internat. Statis. Inst., Am. Econ. Assn., Am. Statis. Assn., USSR Acad. Scis. (fgn.), Royal Econ. Soc., Japan Econ. Rsch. Ctr. (hon.), Brit. Acad. (corr.), French Acad. Scis. (corr.), Royal Irish Acad. (hon.), World Acad. for Progress of Planning Sci. (hon. pres. 1993), Academie Universelle des Cultures, Brit. Assn. Advancement of Sci. (pres. Sect. F 1976), USSR Acad. Scis. (fgn.), Soc. of Optimate Italian Culture Inst., Century Club. Mem. Greek Orthodox Church. Office: NYU Dept Econs 269 Mercer St New York NY 10003-6633

LEOPOLD, LUNA BERGERE, geology educator; b. Albuquerque, Oct. 8, 1915; s. Aldo and Estella (Bergere) L.; m. Barbara Beck Nelson, 1973; children: Bruce Carl, Madelyn Dennette. BS, U. Wis., 1936, DSc (hon.), 1980; M.S., UCLA, 1944; Ph.D., Harvard, 1950; D Geography (hon.), U. Ottawa, 1969; DSc (hon.), Iowa Wesleyan Coll., 1971, St. Andrews U., 1981, U. Murcia, Spain. With Soil Conservation Service, 1938-41, U.S. Engrs. Office, 1941-42, U.S. Bur. Reclamation, 1946; head meteorologist Pineapple Research Inst. of Hawaii, 1946-49; hydraulic engr. U.S. Geol. Survey, 1950-71, chief hydrologist, 1957-66, sr. research hydrologist, 1966-71; prof. geology U. Calif. at Berkeley, 1973—. Author: (with Thomas Maddock, Jr.) The Flood Control Controversy, 1954, Fluvial Processes in Geomorphology, 1964, Water, 1974, (with Thomas Dunne) Water in Environmental Planning, 1978; also tech. papers. Served as capt. air weather service USAAF, 1942-46. Recipient Disting. Svc. award Dept. of Interior, 1958, Veth medal Royal Netherlands Geog. Soc., 1963, Cullum Geog. medal Am. Geog. Soc., 1968, Rockefeller Pub. Service award, 1971, Busk medal Royal Geog. Soc., 1983, Berkeley citation U. Calif., David Linton award British Geomorphol. Rsch. Group, 1986, Linsley award Am. Inst. Hydrology, 1989, Caulfield medal Am. Water Resources Assn., 1991, Nat. Medal Sci. NSF, 1991, Palladium medal Nat. Audubon Soc., 1994, Joan Hodges Queneau Palladium medal Am. Assn. Engring. Socs., 1994. Mem. NAS (Warren prize), ASCE (Julian Hinds award), Geol. Soc. Am. (Kirk Bryan award 1958, pres. 1972, Disting. Career award geomorphological group 1991, Penrose medal 1994), Am. Geophys. Union (Robert E. Horton medal 1993), Am. Acad. Arts and Scis., Am. Philos. Soc., Cosmos Club (Washington), Sigma Xi, Tau Beta Pi, Phi Kappa Phi, Chi Epsilon. Home: 400 Vermont Ave Berkeley CA 94707-1722 Office: U Calif Dept Geology Berkeley CA 94720

LEOPOLD, MARK F., lawyer; b. Chgo., Jan. 23, 1950; s. Paul F. and Corinne (Shapira) L.; m. Jacqueline Rood, June 9, 1974; children: Jonathan, David. BA, Am. U., Washington, 1972; JD, Loyola U., Chgo., 1975. Bar: Ill. 1975, U.S. Dist. Ct. (no. dist.) Ill. 1975, Fla. 1976, U.S. Ct. Appeals (7th cir.) 1976, U.S. Ct. Appeals (8th cir.) 1979. Assoc. McConnell & Campbell, Chgo., 1975-79; atty. U.S. Gypsum Co., Chgo., 1979-82, sr. litigation atty., 1982-84; sr. litigation atty. USG Corp., 1985-87, corp. counsel, 1987, sr. corp. counsel, 1987-89; asst. gen. counsel G.D. Searle & Co., 1989-93; asst. gen. counsel Household Internat., Inc., Prospect Heights, Ill., 1993—; adv. bd. Roosevelt U. Legal Asst. Program, 1994—; legal writing instr. Loyola U. Sch. Law, Chgo., 1978-79; pres., bd. dirs. Internat. Policyholders Assn., 1992-93; del. candidate Rep. Nat. Conv., 1996. Mem. Lake County Study Commn. II, Waukegan, Ill, 1989-90; commr. Lake County, Waukegan, Ill., 1982-84, Forest Preserve, Libertyville, Ill., 1982-84, Pub. Bldg. Commn., Waukegan, Ill., 1980-82; chmn. Deerfield Twp. Rep. Cen. Com., Highland Park, Ill., 1984-86, officer, 1981-89; vice chmn. Lake County Rep. Cen. Com., Waukegan, Ill., 1982-84; bd. dirs. Am. Jewish Com., Chgo., 1988-91. Recipient Disting. Svc. award Jaycees, Highland Park, 1983. Mem. ABA (antitrust com. 1976—, litigation com. 1980—, torts and ins. practice com. 1989—), Pi Sigma Alpha, Omicron Delta Kappa. Republican. Office: Household Internat 2700 Sanders Rd Prospect Heights IL 60070-2701

LEPAGE, ROBERT, actor, director, playwright; b. Quebec City, Canada, 1957. Degree in drama, Conservatoire d'Art Dramatique, Quebec, 1978. Actor Ligue Nationale d'Improvisation, 1980-82; actor, dir. Le Théâtre Rep'40re, 1982—; artistic dir. French theatre Nat. Arts Ctr., Ottawa, Can, 1990-92. Prodsn. include (TV) Needles and Opium, 1991, Tectonic Plates, 1990, A Midsummer Night's Dream, 1992, Coriolanus, 1993, Seven Streams of the River Ofa, 1994, (TV series) The Dragon's Trilogy; in theatre: dir., cowriter Circulations, 1984; dir., writer, actor Vinci, 1986; dir. Le Polygraphe, 1988, Echo, 1989, Macbeth, 1993, The Tempest, 1993; actor (film) Jesus of Montreal, 1988, Ding et Dong le Film, 1990, Montreal vu par, 1991. Recipient Gov. Gen.'s Performing Arts award, 1994. *

LEPELSTAT, MARTIN L., lawyer; b. Bklyn., Apr. 10, 1947; s. Larry and Nana (Citrin) L.; m. Audrey A. Fireman, Jan. 18, 1975; children: Rachel M., Michael H. BBA, CCNY, 1968; JD, Cornell U., 1971; MBA, U. Mich., 1970; LLM, NYU, 1976. Bar: N.J. 1978, N.Y. 1972, Fla. 1972. Tax cons. Touche Ross, N.Y.C., 1971-73; assoc. Weil, Gotshal & Manges, N.Y.C., 1973-78, Greenbaum, Rowe, Smith, Woodbridge, N.J., 1978—. Bd. dirs. Winston Towers 300 Assn., Inc., Cliffside Park, N.J., 1978-86. Fellow Am. Coll. of Trust and Estate Counsel, 1991—; mem. ABA (tax and real estate probate com.), N.J. State Bar Assn., Middlesex County Bar Assn. (pres. tax com. 1987-88, pres. probate com. 1986-87, trustee 1988-92), Fla. Bar Assn. Home: 20 Snoden Ln Watchung NJ 07060-6253 Office: Greenbaum Rowe Smith PO Box 5600 Woodbridge NJ 07095-0988

LEPIE, ALBERT HELMUT, chemist, reseacher; b. Malapane, Silesia, Germany, Aug. 6, 1923; came to U.S., 1963; s. Albert and Emilia (Zachlod) L.; m. Claire Kortz, 1956 (div. 1964); 1 child, Karin. Degree in chem. engring., Staatliche Ing. Schule, Essen, Germany, 1953; diploma in chemistry, Tech. Hochschule, Aachen, Germany, 1959; D in Natural Scis., Tech. Hochschule, Munich, Germany, 1961. Chem. engr. Pahl'sche Gummi & Asbest, Düsseldorf, 1953-59; chemist Deutsche Versuchanstalt für Luftfahrt, Munich, 1961-63; rsch. chemist U.S. Naval Propellant Plant, Indian Head, Md., 1963-64; rsch. chemist Naval Weapons Ctr., China Lake, Calif., 1964-95, ret., 1995; chmn. mech. properties panel Joint Army, Navy, NASA, and Air Force Interagy. Rocket Propulsion, 1977-84. Inventor air curtain incinerator for energetic materials and fiber peal force measurement device, flywheel high rate tensile tester for viscoelastic materials. Recipient Joint Army, Navy, NASA, and Air Force award, 1984, William B. McLean award Naval Weapons Ctr. Mem. Am. Chem. Soc. (sec. China Lake chpt. 1968, 69), China Lake Astron. Soc., Sigma Xi. Roman Catholic. Avocations: astronomy, computer programming, motorcycling. Home: 121 S Desert Candles St Ridgecrest CA 93555-4218

LEPINE, JEAN, cinematographer. Dir. photography: (films) Les Amazones, 1990, On a Marche Sur la Lune, 1990, Vincent & Theo, 1990, Montreal Vu Par, 1991, The Player, 1992, Bob Roberts, 1992, A Home of Our Own, 1993, Ready to Wear (Pret-a-Porter), 1994, Habitat, 1995; (TV movies) Tanner 88, 1988, J.F.K. Reckless Youth, 1993, Talking With, 1994, Beyond the Call, 1995. Office: Doug Apatow Agency 11849 W Olympic Blvd Ste 100 Los Angeles CA 90064-1148*

LEPKOWSKI, WIL (WILBERT CHARLES LEPKOWSKI), journalist; b. Salem, Mass., Sept. 3, 1934; s. Charles J. and Alice (Bartnicki) L.; m. Jane Littlefield, Oct. 28, 1961 (div. May 1975); children: David E., Rebecca A., Thomas M.C.; m. Helene Kay Hollander, Feb. 4, 1984; 1 child, Katherine Angela. BS in Chemistry, U. Mass., 1956; MS in Biochemistry, Ohio State U., 1961. Asst. chemist Doeskin Products Inc., Easthampton, Mass., 1956; asst. editor Chem. Abstracts Svcs., Columbus, Ohio, 1956-58; reporter UP Internat., Columbus, 1960, Providence Jour.-Bull., Westerly, R.I., 1961; sci. writer Johns Hopkins Med. Instns., Balt., 1961-63, Newhouse Newspapers, Washington, 1963-65; bur. head, S.E. Chem. & Engring. News, Washington, 1965-69, sr. corr., 1977—; sci. corr. Bus. Week, Washington, 1969-75; freelance writer, cons., 1975-77. Contbr. articles to jours. in field. Sloan/Rockefeller fellow Advanced Sci. Writing Prgram, Columbia U. Grad. Sch. Journalism, 1959-60. Mem. Nat. Press Club, Nat. Assn. Sci. Writers, Am. Sci. Affiliation, Latin Am. Parents Assn., U.S. Assn. for Club of Rome. Roman Catholic. Avocations: natural history, geography, poetry, spiritual reading. Office: Chem & Engring News 1155 16th St NW Washington DC 20036-4800 *Tell the truth.*

L'EPLATTENIER, NORA SWEENY HICKEY, nursing educator; b. N.Y.C., Mar. 16, 1945; 1 child, Brendan Sweeny Hickey. Diploma, Bellevue Mills Sch. Nursing, 1965; BS in Health Sci. summa cum laude, Bklyn. Coll., 1978; MS in Psychiat.-Mental Health Nursing, Adelphi U., 1982, PhD, 1988. RN, N.Y., N.J.; cert. clin. specialist in adult mental health; cert. group therapist; cert. nurse practitioner in psychiatry, N.Y.; Reiki therapist. Dir. psychiat. staff devel. Bellevue Hosp. Ctr., N.Y.C., 1980-82; group psychotherapist Jewish Inst. Geriatric Care, New Hyde Park, N.Y., 1983; staff psychotherapist New Hope Guild, N.Y.C., 1984; assoc. prof. grad. and undergrad. L.I. U. Bklyn., N.Y.C., 1986—; nurse rschr. Englewood (N.J.) Hosp. and Med. Ctr., N.Y., 1994-97; pvt. practice N.Y., 1982—. Maj. USAR, 1977—. Isabel McIsaac scholar, 1983, Am. Legion scholar, 1962. Mem. Ea. Group Psychotherapy Soc., Sigma Theta Tau.

LEPORE, MARIE ANN, home care nurse; b. Bronx, N.Y., Aug. 21, 1946; d. John Paul and Lillian Josephine (Lucenta) LePore; 1 child, Marie Ann Bank. Student, Cambridge Acad., 1982, S.I., N.Y., 1983, Barton Sch., 1986; med. asst. diploma, Laurel Sch., 1986; A of Specialized Bus., I.C.S., Scranton, Pa., 1995, A in Computer Specialist in Sci., 1996; DegreeMed. Dental Asst., Laurel Sch. for Med. Recruit, N.Y. Home care nurse Dept. Social Svcs., N.Y.C., 1975-78; home health care worker Massive Home Health Svcs., Bronx, N.Y., 1978-82; home careworker Puerto Rican Home Care Svcs., Bronx, N.Y., 1982-84; home care nurse Entea Home Care, Bronx,

N.Y., 1986-89, Montefiore Hosp., Bronx, 1989—; dental asst. Recipient numerous professional awards. Home: 3304 White Plains Rd Bronx NY 10467-5703 Office: 925 Oak St Scranton PA 18515-0999

LEPPARD, RAYMOND JOHN, conductor, harpsichordist; b. London, Aug. 11, 1927; came to U.S., 1976; s. Albert Victor and Bertha May (Beck) L. MA, U. Cambridge, Eng., 1955; DLitt (hon.), U. Bath, Eng., 1973; PhD (hon.), U. Indpls., 1991, Purdue U., 1992, Butler U., 1994, Wabash Coll., 1995. Fellow Trinity Coll., Cambridge; lectr. music U. Cambridge, 1958-68. Mus. dir. English Chamber Orch., London, 1959-77; prin. condr. BBC Philharm., Manchester, Eng., 1972-80; condr. symphony orchs. in Am. and Europe, Met. Opera, N.Y.C., Santa Fe Opera, San Francisco Opera, Covent Garden, Blyndebourne, Paris Opera; prin. guest condr. St. Louis Symphony Orch., 1984-90, music dir. Indpls. Symphony Orch., 1987—, European Tour, 1993; rec. artist, composer numerous film scores; author: Authenticity in Music, 1989, Raymond Leppard on Music/An Anthology of Critical and Personal Writings, 1993. Decorated Commendatore Della Repubblica Italiana; comdr. Order Brit. Empire. Office: Colbert Artists Mgmt 111 W 57th St Ste 1416 New York NY 10019-2211 also: Indpls Symphony Orch 45 Monument Cir Indianapolis IN 46204-2907

LEPPER, MARK ROGER, psychology educator; b. Washington, Dec. 5, 1944; s. Mark H. and Joyce M. (Sullivan) L.; m. Jeanne E. Wallace, Dec. 22, 1966; 1 child, Geoffrey William. BA, Stanford U., 1966; PhD, Yale U., 1970. Asst. prof. psychology Stanford (Calif.) U., 1971-76, assoc. prof., 1976-82, prof., 1982—; chmn., 1990-94; fellow Ctr. Advanced Study in Behavioral Scis., 1979-80; chmn. mental health behavioral scis. research rev. com. NIMH, 1982-84, mem. basic sociocultural research rev. com., 1980-82. Co-editor: The Hidden Costs of Reward, 1978; cons. editor Jour. Personality and Social Psychology, 1977-85, Child Devel., 1977-86, Jour. Ednl. Computing Research, 1983—, Social Cognition, 1981-84; contbr. articles to profl. jours. Recipient Hoagland prize Stanford U., 1990; Woodrow Wilson fellow, 1966-67, NSF fellow, 1966-69, Sterling fellow, 1969-70, Mellon fellow, 1975, fellow Stanford U., 1988-90; grantee NSF, 1978-82, 86-88, NIMH, 1978-86, 88—, Nat. Inst. Child Health and Human Devel., 1975-88, 90—, U.S. Office Edn., 1972-73. Fellow APA, Am. Psychol. Soc., Soc. Personality and Social Psychology, Soc. Psychol. Study Social Issues; mem. Am. Ednl. Rsch. Assn., Soc. Exptl. Social Psychology, Soc. Rsch. in Child Devel. Home: 1544 Dana Ave Palo Alto CA 94303-2813 Office: Stanford U Dept Psychology Stanford CA 94305

LEPPERT, RICHARD DAVID, humanities educator; b. Fargo, N.D., Aug. 28, 1943; s. Frederick W. and Eunice I. (Conlon) L. B.A., Moorhead State U., 1966, B.S., B.A., 1966; M.M., Ind. U., 1969, Ph.D., 1973. Asst. prof. humanities U. Minn.-Mpls., 1973-78, assoc. prof., 1978-82, prof., 1982—, chmn. humanities program, 1980-86, chmn. dept. cultural studies & comparative lit., 1993—. Author: Theme of Music in Flemish Paintings of 17th Century, 1977, Arcadia at Versailles, 1978; editor (with others): Music and Society: The Politics of Composition, Performance and Reception, 1987, Music and Image, 1988, The Sight and Sound: Music Representation and the History of the Body, 1993, Art and the Committed Eye: The Cultural Functions of Imagery, 1996. Woodrow Wilson fellow, 1970-71; Fulbright fellow, 1970-72; Guggenheim fellow, 1979-80; Nat. Endowment Humanities sr. fellow, 1986-87. Office: U Minn Dept Cultural Studies & Comp Lit Folwell Hall # 350 Minneapolis MN 55455-0194

LEPPIG, MARY LOUISE, artist; b. McCurtain, Okla., Dec. 14, 1910; d. John Henigman and Louse Rom; m. Gordon Jack Leppig, June 20, 1931 (dec. 1990); children: Ron, Donna. Student, Chgo. Art Inst. Comml. artist Chgo., illustrator, designer. Mem. Nat. Mus. Women in Arts, West Suburbium Art League, West Alexander Art Club, Middle Ga. Art Club.

LEPPIK, MARGARET WHITE, state legislator; b. Newark, N.J., June 5, 1943; d. John Underhill and Laura Schaefer White; m. Ilo Elmar Leppik, June 18, 1967; children: Peter, David, Karina. BA, Smith Coll., 1965. Rsch. asst. Wistar Inst., U. Pa., Phila., 1967-68, U. Wis., Madison, 1968-69; mem. Minn. Ho. Reps., St. Paul, 1990, 92, 94, 96. Commr. Golden Valley (Minn.) Planning Com., 1982-90; mem. Golden Valley Bd. Zoning Appeals, 1985-87. Recipient Citizen of Distinction award Hennepin County Human Svcs. Planning Bd. 1992; named Legislator of Yr., U. Minn. Alumni Assn., 1995. Mem. LWV (v.p., dir. 1984-90), Minn. Opera Assn. (pres. 1986-88), Rotary Internat., Optimists Internat. Republican. Avocations: gardening, hiking. Home: 7500 Western Ave Golden Valley MN 55427-4849 Office: 393 State Office Bldg Saint Paul MN 55155

LEPS, THOMAS MACMASTER, civil engineer, consultant; b. Keyser, W.Va., Dec. 3, 1914; s. Thomas Davis and Grace (King) L.; m. Catherine Mary Sacksteder, June 22, 1940; 1 son, Timothy. B.A., Stanford U., 1936; M.S., MIT, 1939. Jr. and asst. civil engr. Calif. Divsn. Hwys., U.S. C.E., Bur. of Reclamation, 1936-41; Chief civil engr. So. Calif. Edison Co., Los Angeles, 1946-61; chief engr. Shannon & Wilson Co., Seattle, 1961-63; cons. civil engr. U.S. and abroad, Dinuba, Calif., 1963—; mem. over 90 bds. of cons. on hydro, steam and nuclear power projects. Contbr. articles to profl. jours., chpts. to engring books. Served to comdr. USNR, 1943-46, 46-60. Recipient certificate of Appreciation Calif. Dept. Water Resources, 1971. Mem. NAE (life mem., nominations com. for officers 1991), ASCE (life mem., cert. of appreciation 1961), U.S. Com. on Large Dams (life mem. vice-chmn. exec. com. 1980-81), Phi Beta Kappa, Tau Beta Pi. Presbyterian. Address: PO Box 217 Dinuba CA 93618-0217

LE QUESNE, PHILIP WILLIAM, chemistry educator, researcher; b. Auckland, New Zealand, Jan. 6, 1939; came to U.S., 1967; s. Ernest W. B. and Bettie A. (Colwill) Le Q.; m. Mary E. Kinloch, 1965 (dec. 1988); children: Elizabeth Ruth, Martin James. B.S., U. Auckland, 1960, M.S., 1961, Ph.D., 1964, D.Sc. (hon.), 1979. Asst. prof. U. Mich., Ann Arbor, 1967-72; assoc. prof. Northeastern U., Boston, 1973-78, prof., 1978—, chmn. dept. chemistry, 1979-87; assoc. dir. Barnett Inst. for Chem. analysis and Materials Sci., 1993—. Contbr. articles on chemistry to profl. jours. Sr. warden Ch. of the Advent, Boston, 1990-96. Home: 17 Stafford Rd Newton Center MA 02159-1818 Office: Northeastern U Chemistry Dept 360 Huntington Ave Boston MA 02115-5005

LERCH, RICHARD HEAPHY, retired lawyer; b. Balt., Oct. 8, 1924; s. Charles Sebastian and Marguerite Mary (Mullen) L.; m. Marie Therese Logan, Feb. 11, 1950; children—Marie L., Elizabeth L., Ellen C. A.B. magna cum laude, Loyola Coll., Balt., 1947; LL.B., U. Md., 1949. Bar: Md. bar 1948. Since practiced in Balt.; partner Lerch & Huesman, 1959-96; ret., 1996; Pres. Jr. Bar Assn., 1960. Served with AUS, 1944-46, 51-52. Mem. Am., Md., Balt. bar assns., Internat. Assn. Ins. Counsel. Democrat. Roman Catholic. Home: 5906 Meadowood Rd Baltimore MD 21212-2435

LERER, NEAL M., lawyer; b. Chelmsford, Mass., June 20, 1954; m. Rose P. Meegan, July 28, 1991; 1 child, Benjamin Joseph. BA, Brown U., 1976; JD, Duke Law Sch., 1979. Bar: Mass. 1979, U.S. Dist. Ct. Mass. 1980, U.S. Ct. Appeals (1st cir.) 1991. Ptnr. Martin, Magnuson, McCarthy & Kenney, Boston, 1980-96; mng. atty., pvt. practice Chelmsford, Mass., 1996—; corporator Lowell (Mass.) 5 Cents Savings Bank, 1985—. Co-author: Personal Injury and Death, 1980, Damages in Massachusetts, 1990, Personal Injury Litigation in Massachusetts, 1991. Reader Recording for the Blind, Cambridge, Mass., 1987-94. Mem. DRI, Mass. Bar Assn. (ins. com.), Mass. Bar Found., Mass. Def. Lawyers Assn., Brown Club of Boston (bd. dirs.). Office: Law Offices Neal M. Lerer 56 Central Sq Chelmsford MA 01824-3055

LERITZ, LAWRENCE R., choreographer, singer, actor, dancer, producer, director, songwriter; b. Alton, Ill., Sept. 26, 1952; s. Leonard Henry and Marcella Rose (Fravle) L. Student Harkness Ballet Sch., 1973-74; Sch. Am. Ballet, 1975-76. Debut: State Fair, St. Louis Muny Opera, 1969, appeared in Can Can, 1983; TV appearances include: Capitol, 1982, All My Children, 1981-85, Home Sweet, Homeless; Rodney Dangerfield: It's Lonely at the Top, HBO, 1992, various commls.; guest expert on various talk shows including Rolonda, Charles Perez, Maury Povich, Show Biz Today, Am. Muscle Mag.; film debut: Stardust Memories, 1979; appeared in Easy Money, 1982, Stag, 1997; star Leritz and His Girls, 1983-85; Broadway appearances include: Fiddler On the Roof, 1981, Fonteyn and Nureyev on Broadway, 1975; appeared Met. Opera telecast of Manon Lescaut, 1980; choreographer feature film musical The Last Dragon, 1984; choreographer, co-star home video Treehouse Trolls Birthday Day, 1993; dancer with Harkness Ballet, Paris Opera, Hamburg Ballet, Chgo. Ballet, world wide guest star; dir., choreographer own co. Dance Celebration which represented U.S. at Internat. Choreographic Competitions, Paris, 1979; dir. mus. numbers for Shields and Yarnell; creator mus. indsls. for Lily of France, Bausch & Lomb, Christian Dior; pres. Leritz Prodns., Ltd., N.Y.C. and L.A., 1983—; star exercise cruise on Queen Elizabeth II, 1995; rec. artist: It Takes Two to Tango, 1984, Crank It Up, 1989, Bright Light, 1992; song lyricist, composer; east coast prodr. Day of Compassion, 1995-96. Full scholar Sch. Am. Ballet, Harkness Ballet Sch.; Lawrence R. Leritz Day declared, recipient Key to City, Wood River, Ill., 1983, Alton, Ill., 1987; appeared on cover Dance Pages mag., fall 1987, spring 1989 Time Magazine's Local Hero, 1996; writer Muscular Devel. mag., Ironman mag., Men's Fitness mag., Muscle & Fitness mag.; creator, star of video Total Stretch! with Lawrence Leritz, 1992. Mem. AFTRA, ASCAP (Pop Music awards for songwriting 1985—), SAG (mem. film nominating com. 1996), Actors Equity Assn., Am. Guild of Musical Artists (bd. govs. 1979-92, 94—, prodn. supr./choreographer 50th Anniversary Gala 1986, Life Membership award for disting. svc. 1991); choreographer, guest dancer Placido Domingo's L.A. Music Ctr. Opera, 1987. Office: 318 W 45th St Apt 3 New York NY 10036-8343

LERMAN, EILEEN R., lawyer; b. N.Y.C., May 6, 1947; d. Alex and Beatrice (Kline) L. BA, Syracuse U., 1969; JD, Rutgers U., 1972; MBA, U. Denver, 1983. Bar: N.Y. 1973, Colo. 1976. atty. FTC, N.Y.C., 1972-74; corp. atty. RCA, N.Y.C., 1974-76; corp. atty. Samsonite Corp. and consumer products div. Beatrice Foods Co., Denver, 1976-78, assoc. gen. counsel, 1978-85, asst. sec., 1979-85; ptnr. Davis, Lerman, & Weinstein, Denver, 1985-92, Eileen R. Lerman & Assocs., 1993—; bd. dir. Legal Aid Soc. of Met. Denver, 1979-80. Bd. dirs., vice chmn. Colo. Postsecondary Ednl. Facilities Authority, 1981-89; bd. dirs., pres. Am. Jewish Com., 1989-92; mem. Leadership Denver, 1983. Mem. ABA, Colo. Women's Bar Assn. (bd. dir. 1980-81), Colo. Bar Assn. (bd. govs.), Denver Bar Assn. (trustee), N.Y. State Bar Assn., Rhone Brackett Inn (pres.-elect 1996), Denver Law Club, Rutgers U. Alumni Assn., University Club. Home: 1018 Fillmore St Denver CO 80206-3332 Office: Lerman & Assocs LLC 50 S Steele St Ste 420 Denver CO 80209-2809

LERMAN, LEONARD SOLOMON, science educator, scientist; b. Pitts., June 27, 1925; s. Meyer Louis and Freamah (Hoffman) L.; m. Claire Carol Lindegren, July 14, 1952 (div. Sept. 1973); children: Averil, Lisa, Alexander; m. Elizabeth Knox Taylor, May 11, 1974 (div. 1996). BS, Carnegie Inst. Tech., 1945; PhD, Calif. Inst. Tech., 1950. Postdoctoral fellow U. Chgo., 1949-51; from asst. to assoc. prof. U. Colo., Denver, 1951-63, prof. biophysics, 1963-65; prof. molecular biology Vanderbilt U., Nashville, 1965-76; prof., chmn. biology SUNY, Albany, 1976-84; dir. diagnostics Genetics Inst., Cambridge, Mass., 1984-87; sr. lectr. MIT, Cambridge, 1987—; mem. panel Dept. Energy, Washington, 1986-93; mem. Health and Environ. Rsch. Adv. Com. Bd. Bd. Radiation Effects Rsch., NRC, 1988-96. Editor: Molecular and Gen. Genetics jour., 1976-82; mem. editorial bd. Genomics; contbr. articles to profl. jours. Guggenheim Found. fellow, 1971-72. Mem. NAS, AAAS, Am. Acad. Arts & Scis., Am. Soc. Biol. Chemists, Human Genome Orgn., Am. Soc. Human Genetics. Home: 135 Wallis Rd Chesnut Hill MA 02167-3112 Office: MIT Dept Biology Bldg 68 Rm 630 Cambridge MA 02139

LERNER, ABRAM, retired museum director, artist; b. N.Y.C., Apr. 11, 1913; s. Hyman and Sarah (Becker) L.; m. Pauline Hanenberg, Oct. 7, 1940; 1 child, Aline. B.A., NYU, 1935; student, Ednl. Alliance, Art Students League, Bklyn. Mus.; pvt. studies, Florence, Italy. Asso. dir. A.C.A. Gallery and Artist's Gallery, N.Y.C., 1945-57; curator Joseph H. Hirshhorn Collection, N.Y.C., 1957-66; dir. Hirshhorn Mus. and Sculpture Garden, Washington, 1967-85; founding dir. emeritus, ret. Hirshhorn Mus. and Sculpture Garden, Smithsonian Instn., Washington, 1985; Adv. bd. Archives Am. Art, 1970—. Author: Hirshhorn Museum and Sculpture Garden - Inaugural Book, 1974, Gregory Gillespie, 1977; contbr. to mags., mus. catalogues.; one man show, Davis Gallery, N.Y.C., 1958, group shows include, A.C.A. Gallery, Peridot Gallery, Bklyn.-Mus., Pa. Acad., Davis Gallery, represented in pvt. collections. Decorated commandeur in de Orde Van Oranje-Nassau (The Netherlands); chevalier dans L'Ordre des Arts et des Lettres (France). Home: 98 Lewis St Southampton NY 11968-5006

LERNER, ALEXANDER ROBERT, association executive; b. Chicago, Ill., June 26, 1946; s. Peter Lerner and Lillian Orlinsky Joseph; m. Marianne Ryan, Apr. 21, 1979; 1 child, Lindsey Anne. BS, No. Ill. U., 1970. Adminstrv. asst. Gov. of Ill., 1970-72; adminstrv. asst. speaker Ill. Ho. of Reps., Springfield, 1973-74; asst. dir. pub. affairs div. AMA, Chgo., 1974-75; dir. Ill. State Med. Soc., Chgo., 1975-78; pres. Govtl. Affairs, Inc., Chgo., 1978-81; chief exec. officer Ill. State Med. Soc. and Ins. Svcs. Inc., Chgo., 1981—. Chmn. Ill. Sports Facilities Authority, 1992—. Mem. Am. Assn. Med. Soc. Execs., Am. Soc. Assn. Execs., Chgo. Soc. Assn. Execs., Union League Club, Chgo. Yacht Club, Michigan Shores Club, Execs. Club of Chgo. Avocations: nautical antiques, presidential history, travel. Office: Ill State Med Soc 20 N Michigan Ave Chicago IL 60602-4811

LERNER, ALFRED, real estate and financial executive; b. N.Y.C., May 8, 1933; s. Abraham and Clara (Abrahmson) L.; m. Norma Wokloff, Aug. 7, 1955; children: Nancy Faith, Randolph David. BA, Columbia U., 1965. Chmn. bd., chief exec. officer Multi-Amp Corp., Dallas, 1970-80, Realty Refund Trust, Cleve., 1971-90; pres., chief exec. officer Refund Advisers, Inc., 1971—, Town & Country Mgmt. Corp., 1979-93; chmn., dir. Equitable Bancorp., Balt., 1981-90; chmn., bd. dirs. Prog. Corp., Cleve., 1988-93; chmn., CEO MBNA Corp., Newark, 1991—, Town & Country Trust, 1993—; chmn., bd. dirs. MNC Corp., Balt., 1991-93. Trustee Columbia U., Case Western Res. U.; pres. Cleve. Clinic. 1st lt. USMCR, 1955-57. Mem. Young Pres. Orgn., Beechmont Club (Cleve.), Harmonie Club (N.Y.C.). Jewish. Home: 19000 S Park Blvd Cleveland OH 44122-1853 Office: 25875 Science Park Dr Beachwood OH 44122-7304

LERNER, ARNOLD STANLEY, radio station executive; b. Phila., Feb. 17, 1930; s. Joseph C. and Rose L. (Friedmann) L.; m. Maureen Ann Ireland, Aug. 7, 1972; children: Hilary R., Joseph C. BS in Econs., U. Pa., 1951; M in Liberal Studies, Boston U., 1974. Ptnr. Sta. KOMA, Oklahoma City, 1956-58, Sta. KITO, San Bernadino, Calif., 1959, Sta. WORC, Worcester, Mass., 1984-89, Sta. WNVE, Rochester, N.Y., 1986-97, Sta. WJMN, Boston, 1987-94, Sta. WZOU, Gorham, Maine, 1988—, Sta. WQSS, Camden, Maine, 1988—, WTHT, Portland, Maine, 1994—, WLAM-FM, Windham, Maine, 1997—; pres. Sta. WADK, Newport, R.I., 1960-77, Comm. Mgmt., Inc., Hollis, N.H., 1978-87; chmn., gen. mgr. Sta. WSSH, Lowell, Mass., 1963-86, Sta. WLLH, Lowell, 1963—; treas. Stas. WLAM/WKZS, Lewiston, Maine, 1977—; dir. Sta. WKSZ, Media-Phila., 1984—; bd. dirs., exec. com. First Bank, Chelmsford, Mass., 1977-88; vice chmn. Enterprise Bank and Trust, Lowell, 1988—; bd. dirs. Courier Corp.; instr. U. Mass., Lowell, 1996—. Trustee St. Joseph's Hosp., Lowell, 1976-87, Applewild Sch., Fitchburg, Mass., 1979-92, pres., 1985-89; bd. dirs.. Merrimack Valley Goodwill Industries, Lowell, 1972-86, chmn., 1976-78; bd. dirs. Merrimack Repertory Theatre, Lowell, 1988—, v.p., 1989-91, treas. 1992-94. Recipient Meritorious Svc. award Nat. Rehab. Assn., 1975. Mem. Nat. Assn. Broadcasters (bd. dir. 1977-81, chmn. radio bd. 1979-81), Mass. Broadcasters Assn. (bd. dir. 1968-87, pres. 1969-70), Vesper Country Club (Tyngsboro, Mass.), Kiwanis (pres. 1968, Citizen of Yr. award 1979, Lowell). Jewish. Home and Office: 155 Pine Hill Rd Hollis NH 03049-5939

LERNER, DANIEL MERRIL, broadcasting company executive; b. Phila., Nov. 26, 1932; s. Joseph C. and Rose L. (Friedmann) L.; m. Elaine Gomberg, Sept. 11, 1954; children: Ann, Paul, Julie. A.B., U. Pa., 1954, M.A. in Communications, 1961. Personnel officer City of Phila., 1954-60; account exec. Sta. WADK, Newport, R.I., 1961-62, Sta. WFIL-AM/TV, Phila., 1962-63; v.p. Sta. WLLH/WSSH-FM, Boston, 1963-82; chmn. Sta. WPLY-FM, Phila., 1982—; owner, cons. Daniel Lerner Co., Merion, Pa., 1974—; gen. ptnr. Cloverleaf Real Estate Partnership, Media, Pa., 1985—; co-owner Sta. WZOU-FM, Boston, 1987-94, Sta. WQSS-FM, Camden, Maine, 1988—; pres. Greater Media Tower Co., Media, Pa., 1995—. Bd. dirs. Delaware County ARC, Pa., 1985-88, Delaware County YMCA, 1994—. Mem. Broadcast Pioneers, Pa. Assn. Broadcasters, Del. County C. of C. (bd. dirs.). Avocations: boating, tennis. Office: Sta WPLY-FM 1003 Baltimore Pike Media PA 19063

LERNER, HARRY JONAS, publishing company executive; b. Mpls., Mar. 5, 1932; s. Morris and Lena (Liederschneider) L.; m. Sharon Ruth Goldman, June 25, 1961 (dec. 1982); children: Adam Morris, Mia Carol, Daniel Aryeh, Leah Anne; m. Sandra Karon Davis, Aug. 24, 1996. Student, U. Mich., 1952, Hebrew U., Jerusalem, 1953-54; B.A., U. Minn., 1957. Founder Lerner Publs. Co., Mpls., 1959; pres., chief exec. officer, pub. Lerner Publs. Co., 1959—; founder Muscle Bound Bindery, Inc., 1967, chief exec. officer, 1967—; founder Carolrhoda Books, Inc., 1969; pres., gen. mgr. Interface Graphics Inc., 1969—, CEO, 1993—; bd. visitors U. Minn. Press; del. White House Conf. on Libr. and Info. Svcs., 1979; chmn. North Loop Bus. Assn., Mpls., 1972-79, Minn. Book Pubs. Roundtable, 1974; bd. overseers Hill Monastic Manuscript Libr., St. John's U., Collegeville, Minn., 1986-89; bd. dirs., libr. dir. Jewish Community Ctr. Pres. Twin City chpt. Am. Jewish Com., 1980-85; bd. dirs. Fgn. Policy Assn. Minn., 1970-71, bd. dirs. Children's Book Coun., N.Y.C., 1991-94, Minn. Libr. Assn. Found., 1997; bd. advisors Books for Africa, 1996. Recipient Brotherhood award NCCJ, 1961, also numerous graphic arts awards. Mem. ACLU, Mpls. Inst. Art, Walker Art Ctr, St. Paul-Mpls. Com. on Fgn. Affairs, Ampersand Club, Daybreakers Breakfast Club (Mpls.). Home: 2215 Willow Ln N Minneapolis MN 55416-3862 Office: Lerner Pub Co 241 1st Ave N Minneapolis MN 55401-1607

LERNER, JULIUS, mechanical engineer; b. Phila., July 27, 1919; s. Joseph and Gertrude (Leather) L.; children: Nina, Leon. Diploma in mech. engring., Drexel Inst. Tech., 1943, BS, 1953. Registered profl. engr., Calif., Pa.; diplomate, bd. cert. forensic examiner Am. Bd. Forensic Examiners. Machinist apprentice U.S. Navy Yard, Phila., 1940-41; lead machinist Baldwin Locomotive, Eddystone, Pa., 1941-44; sr. staff engr. Sun Oil Co., Newtown Square, Pa., 1946-83; pres. J. Lerner, Inc., Broomall, Pa., 1983—; speaker in field. Contbr. articles to profl. jours. Bd. dirs. Merci Haverford Hosp., Havertown, Pa., 1990—, Congregation Beth El Suburban; leader sr. group Broomall, 1991—; math tutor Chester H.S.; guest spkr. Marple-Newtown H.S.; mem. Marple Planning Commn. Sgt. U.S. Army, 1944-46, ETO. Mem. Am. Soc. Safety Engrs., Instrument Soc. Am., NSPE, Pa. Soc. Profl. Engrs. (bd. dirs. Delaware County br., chmn. selection com. for Delaware County Engr. of Yr.), ASME (life), IEEE, Am. Petroleum Inst. (com. on dynamic measurement), Am. Acad. Forensic Scis. Achievements include 21 U.S. patents, several patents pending. Home and Office: 2516 Parke Ln Broomall PA 19008-2204

LERNER, MARTIN, museum curator; b. N.Y.C., Nov. 14, 1936; s. Joseph and Rose (Kolberg) L.; m. Roberta M. Rubenstein, Feb. 26, 1968; children: Benjamin Louis, Seth Laurence, Jocelyn Ann. BA, Bklyn. Coll., 1959; postgrad., Inst. Fine Arts, NYU, 1961-65. Asst. prof. U. Calif., Santa Barbara, 1965-66; asst. curator Oriental art Cleve. Mus. Art, 1966-72; asst. prof. Case Western Res. U., 1968-72; vice chmn. charge Far Eastern art Met. Mus. Art, N.Y.C., 1972-75; curator Indian and S.E. Asian art Met. Mus. Art, 1978—; cons. in field; internat. lectr. Author: Bronze Sculptures from Asia, 1975, Blue and White: Early Japanese Export Ware, 1978, The Flame and the Lotus, 1984, (with W. Felten) Cambodian and Thai Sculpture: From the 6th to the 14th Century, 1989, Entdeckungen: Skulpturen der Khmer und Thai, 1989, (with S. Kossak), The Lotus Transcendent, 1991, Ancient Khmer Sculpture, 1994; contbr. articles to profl. jours. Served with U.S. Army, 1959-61. Clubs: East India; Devonshire (London). Home: Giglio Ct Croton-on-Hudson NY 10520 Office: Met Mus Art 82nd & Fifth Ave New York NY 10028

LERNER, MICHAEL ALBERS, educator; b. N.Y.C., Oct. 22, 1943; s. Max and Genevieve Edna (Albers) L.; m. Leslie Acoca, 1974 (div. 1981); 1 child, Joshua Hawkes; m. Sharyle Martiel Patton, July 10, 1983. BA, Harvard U., 1965; PhD, Yale U., 1971. Asst. prof. Yale U., New Haven, 1971-72; assoc. Carnegie Coun. on Children, New Haven, 1971-72; exec. dir. Full Circle Sch., Bolinas, Calif., 1973-75; pres. Commonweal, Bolinas, 1975—; dir. Commonweal Cancer Help Program, Bolinas, 1985—; pres. Smith Farm Ctr. for Healing Arts, Washington, 1996—; chief cons. Office of Tech. Assessment, U.S. Congress, Unconventional Cancer Treatments, 1989-91; chmn. bd. Hale Fund, San Francisco, 1991-95; pres. Jenifer Altman Found., 1992—. Author: Choices in Healing, 1992; co-editor: A Reader in Personality and Politics, 1970; contbr. articles to jours. in field. Coord. Californians for Juvenile Justice Reform, 1988-90. Fulbright fellow, Brazil, 1965-66; Woodrow Wilson fellow Yale U., 1971; MacArthur Found. prize fellow, 1983-88. Mem. Ctr. for Advancement Health (trustee inst.), Japan Soc. (U.S.-Japan leadership program 1990). Office: Commonweal PO Box 316 Bolinas CA 94924-0316

LERNER, NATHAN BERNARD, artist; b. Chgo., Mar. 15, 1913; s. Louis Alexander and Ida Lerner; m. Kiyoko Asai, July 1, 1968; children: Michael John, Amy Elizabeth. Student, Nat. Acad. Art, Chgo., 1931, Art Inst. Chgo., 1933-34; B.S., Sch. Design in Chgo., 1941. Head of photo workshop Sch. of Design in Chgo., 1941-43; head of product design workshop, dean of faculty and students Inst. of Design, Chgo., 1945-49; ednl. dir. Inst. of Design, 1946-47; prof. U. Ill., Chgo., 1967-72; pres. Lerner Design Assos., 1949-72. One man shows include Chgo. Mus. Sci. and Industry, 1974, Bauhaus Archives, Berlin, 1975, Pentax Gallery, Osaka, Japan, 1976, Harry Lunn Gallery, Washington, 1977, Frumkin Gallery, Chgo., 1977, G.R. Hawkins Gallery, Los Angeles, 1977, Chgo. Hist. Soc., 1983, Photog. Gallery Internat., Tokyo, 1984, Ill. State Mus., Springfield, Chgo. Cultural Ctr., Ind. State U., Terre Haute, 1974, Bradley U., Peoria, Ill., 1973, Frumkin Gallery, Chgo., 1975, New York, 1976, Inst. of Contemporary Art, Boston, 1978, Augustana Mus., Rockford, Ill., 1987, The Photographers Gallery, London, 1988, Valparaiso U. Mus., 1989, U. Iowa Mus., 1993, Milw. Mus. Fine Art, 1995; represented in permanent collections Art Inst. Chgo., Mus. Modern Art, N.Y.C., Met. Mus. Art, N.Y.C., Mus. Fine Arts, Houston, Mus. Modern Art, Paris, Bibliotheque National, Paris, Eastman House, Rochester, Bauhaus Archive, Berlin, Mpls. Art Inst., Mus. Contemporary Art, Chgo., Nihon U., Tokyo, Seattle Mus. Art, Monterey (Calif.), Inst. Art, Amon Carter Mus., Fort Worth Israel Mus., Jerusalem, Kyoto Mus. Art, Japan, San Francisco Mus. Art, Ill. State Mus. Art, Internat. Ctr. Photography, N.Y.C., Ctr. for Creative Photography, Tucson, Santa Fe Mus. Fine Arts, Milw. Art Mus., Smart Gallery, Chgo., Les Recontres D'Arles, France, Tokyo Met. Mus. Ill. Arts Council grantee 1977-78. Mem. Artists Guild Chgo., Art Inst. Chgo. Alumni Assn. Patentee in field. Address: 849 W Webster Ave Chicago IL 60614-3615*

LERNER, RALPH, architect, university dean; b. N.Y.C., Oct. 17, 1949; s. Irvin Louis and Sonia (Levine) L.; m. Lisa Diana Fischetti, June 20, 1982; children: Sigmund Michael, Esther Diana. BArch, Cooper Union, 1974; MArch, Harvard U., 1975. Registered architect, N.Y., N.J., Mass. Asst. prof. U. Va., Charlottesville, 1975-79; sr. lectr. Poly. Cen. London, 1979-80; assoc. prof. Harvard U., Cambridge, Mass., 1980-83; lectr. Princeton (N.J.) U., 1983-87, assoc. prof., 1987-89, prof., dean Sch. Architecture, 1989—, George Dutton '27 prof. of architecture, 1994—; pvt. practice, Princeton, 1980—. Prin. works include Villa Vasone (Progressive Architecture award 1981), Indira Gandhi Nat. Centre for The Arts, New Delhi, 1986 (1st prize design competition 1986). Recipient 1st prize internat. design competition Epping Town Coun., Essex, Eng., 1984, 1st award Progressive Architecture, 1987, 1st prize Eva's Kitchen and Sheltering Svcs., 1994. Mem. AIA, N.J. Soc. Architects. Office: 306 Alexander St Princeton NJ 08540-7124

LERNER, RICHARD MARTIN, academic administrator, educator; b. Bklyn., Feb. 23, 1946; s. Max and Sara (Goldfarb) L.; m. Jacqueline Rose Verdirame, July 24, 1977; children: Justin, Blair, Jarrett. BA in Psychology with honors, Hunter Coll. of CUNY, 1966, MA, 1967; PhD, CUNY, 1971. Rsch. asst. dept. edn. Bklyn. Coll. of CUNY, 1966-67; sci. rsch. asst. dept. psychology Hunter Coll. of CUNY, 1966-67, lectr. dept. psychology, 1967-69; asst. to assoc. prof. psychology Ea. Mich. U., Ypsilanti, 1969-76; assoc. prof. child devel. Pa. State U., University Park, 1976-80, prof. child and adolescent devel., 1981-91; dir. Inst. Children, Youth and Families Mich. State U., East Lansing, 1991-96, prof. family and child ecology, psychology, pediatrics and human devel., 1991—; Anita L. Brennan prof. edn., dir. Boston Coll. Ctr. for Child, Family and Cmty. Partnerships, Chestnut Hill, Mass., 1996—; vis. scientist Max-Planck-Institut für Bildungsforschung,

Berlin, 1983; co-dir. Ctr. for Advanced Study in the Behavioral Scis., Stanford, Calif., 1984; dir. Ctr. for the Study of Child and Adolescent Devel., Pa. State U., 1984-89, prof.-in-charge Grad. Program in Human Devel. and Family Studies, 1985-87, coord. rsch. Carnegie Corp.-Pa. State U. Policy, Rsch. and Intervention for Devel. in Early Adolescence Program, 1990-91; Lansdowne vis. scholar U. Victoria, B.C., Can., 1989. Author: Concepts and Theories of Human Development, 1976, On the Nature of Human Plasticity, 1984, Final Solutions: Biology, Prejudice and Genocide, 1992; author (with G.B. Spanier) Adolescent Development: A Life-Span Perspective, 1980, (with D.F. Hultsch) Human Development: A Life-Span Perspective, 1983, (with J. Belsky and G.B. Spanier) The Child in the Family, 1984, (with F.W. Vondracek and J.E. Schulenberg) Career Development: A Life-Span Developmental Approach, 1986, (with D.H. Ford) Developmental Systems Theory: An Integrative Approach, 1992; author (with others) Psychology, 1986; editor Mich. Psychologist, 1971-74, Newsletter of the Assn. Aviation Psychologists, 1973-74, Jour. Rsch. on Adolescence, 1991-96, Applied Developmental Sci., 1997—; assoc. editor Internat. Jour. Behavioral Devel., 1984-90; co-editor Life-Span Devel. and Behavior, 1986-93; mem. editorial bd. Child Devel., 1978-88, Devel. Psychology, 1985-90, Devel. Rev., 1986—, Jour. of Applied Devel. Psychology, 1986—, Human Devel., 1988—; contbr. chapters to books; contbr. articles to profl. jours.; pub. monographs. NDEA Title IV Grad. fellow CUNY, 1966-69, fellow Ctr. Advanced Study in the Behavioral Scis., 1980-81; recipient Outstanding Teaching award AMOCO Found., 1982, PhD Alumni Spl. Achievement award CUNY, 1989; named to Hunter Coll. Hall of Fame, 1981. Fellow AAAS, Am. Psychol. Soc. (charter), Am. Psychol. Assn. (divsn. 2, 7, and 9, disting. visitor program), Am. Assn. Applied and Preventive Psychology (charter), Soc. for the Psychol. Study of Social Issues; mem. Internat. Soc. for the Study of Behavioral Devel., Am. Ednl. Rsch. Assn., Am. Home Econs. Assn., Nat. Coun. Family Rels., Ea. Psychol. Assn., N.Y. Acad. Scis., Merrill-Palmer Soc. (charter), Soc. Rsch. on Adolescence, Soc. Rsch. in Child Devel., Soc. for the Study of Social Biology, Kappa Omicron Nu, Sigma Xi, Psi Chi. Office: Boston Coll Ctr for Child Family & Cmty Partnerships Campion Hall III Boston MA 02167

LERNER, STEPHEN ALEXANDER, microbiologist, physician, educator; b. Chgo., Oct. 4, 1938; s. David G. and Florence (Trace) L.; m. June 6, 1963 (div. 1990); children: Deborah, Daniel, Susan; m. Aug. 18, 1991. AB magna cum laude, Harvard U., 1959, MD magna cum laude, 1963. Intern, then resident Peter Bent Brigham Hosp., 1963-65; rsch. assoc. NIH, 1965-68; postdoctoral fellow Stanford (Calif.) U., 1968-71; asst. prof. then assoc. prof. U. Chgo., 1971-86; prof. of medicine Wayne State U., Detroit, 1986—; convenor Soviet-Am. Symposium Antibiotics and Chemotherapy, Moscow, 1988. Editor: Aminoglycoside Ototoxicity, 1981; mem. editl. bd. Antimicrobial Agts. and Chemotherapy, 1981—, European Jour. Clin. Microbiology and Infectious Diseases, 1992—; contbr. articles to profl. jours. With USPHS, 1965-67. Recipient Borden Rsch. award, 1963. Fellow Infectious Disease Soc. Am., Am. Acad. Microbiology (com. on awards 1993-96); mem. Am. Soc. Microbiology (chmn. antimicrobial chemotherapy 1987-88, divsn. group rep. 1990-92, councillor 1990-92, chmn. confs. com. 1993-96, internat. coord. com. 1993—, chmn. 1996—), Inter-Am. Soc. for Chemotherapy (pres. 1986-88, bd. dirs., chmn. 1988-93), Internat. Soc. Chemotherapy (exec. com. 1987-93), Phi Beta Kappa, Sigma Xi, Alpha Omega Alpha. Democrat. Jewish. Avocations: travel photography, Russian language, collecting antique maps. Office: Harper Hosp Div Infectious Diseases 3990 John R St Detroit MI 48201-2018

LERNER, STEVEN PAUL, lawyer; b. Bklyn., Nov. 9, 1958; s. Lloyd J. and Arline May (Solomon) L.; m. Donna Lynn Borges, Sept. 9, 1984; children: Kaitlin Olga, Colin Lane, Cody Layton. BA, L.I. U., 1980; JD, Syracuse U., 1983. Bar: N.Y. 1984, U.S. Dist. Ct. (ea. and so. dists.) N.Y. 1984, U.S. Ct. Appeals (2d cir.) 1984. Assoc. Robert & Schneider, Hempstead, N.Y., 1983-86; ptnr. Robert, Lerner & Robert, Rockville Centre, N.Y., 1986—. Advisor, sponsor Nassau County Rep. Com., Mineola, N.Y., 1990—; sponsor Suffolk County Rep. Com., Riverhead, N.Y., 1992—; vice chmn. budget com. Baldwin (N.Y.) Ednl. Assembly and Baldwin Bd. Edn., 1994; mem., lectr. Nassau/Suffolk Health Sys. Agy., N.Y., 1994. Mem. ABA, Nassau Bar Assn., Suffolk Bar Assn., Kings Bar Assn., Nassau Acad. Law (lectr. 1987—), Nat. Acad. Elder Care Attys. Jewish. Avocations: golf, all sports, my children. Home: 1854 Longfellow St Baldwin NY 11510-2336 Office: Robert Lerner & Robert 100 Merrick Rd Ste 508W Rockville Centre NY 11570-4801

LERNER, THEODORE RAPHAEL, dentist; b. Bklyn., Sept. 28, 1932; s. Meyer and Tillie (Brimberg) L.; student Washington and Jefferson Coll., 1950-53; DDS, U. Pa., 1957; m. Barbara Ellen Bernstein, June 29, 1974; children by previous marriage: Andrea Holly, Evan Andrew. Practice dentistry, specializing in endodontics, Bklyn., 1957-93, Forest Hills, N.Y., 1968-93, Boca Raton, Fla., 1992—. Diplomate Am. Bd. Endodontics. Fellow Internat., Am. colls. dentists, Am. Assn. Endodontists; mem. ADA, 2d Dist. Dental Soc. (pres. 1971), Dental Soc. State of N.Y. (pres. 1983), Fla. Dental Assn. Home: 7040 Lions Head Ln Boca Raton FL 33496-5931 Office: 2499 Glades Rd Ste 204 Boca Raton FL 33431-7201

LERNER, VLADIMIR SEMION, computer scientist, educator; b. Odessa, Ukraine, Sept. 12, 1931; came to U.S., 1990; s. Semion N. and Manya G. (Grosman) L.; m. Sanna K. Gleyzer, Sept. 28, 1954; children: Alex, Tatyana, Olga. BSEE, Odessa Poly. Inst., 1954; MEE, Inst. Problem's Controls, Moscow, 1959; PhD in Elec. Engring., Moscow Power Inst., 1961; D Sci. in Systems Analysis, Leningrad State U., 1974. Prof. elec. engring. Kishinev (Moldova) State U., 1962-64; prof. elec. engring. and control systems Kishinev Poly. Inst., 1964-79; sr. scientist in applied math. Acad. Sci., Kishinev, 1964-79; dir. math. modeling and computer sci. lab. Rsch. Inst., Odessa, 1979-89; sr. lectr. UCLA, 1991-93, rschr., 1993—; chmn. computer sci. dept. West Coast U., L.A., 1993—; mem. adv. bds. Acad. Sci., Kishinev, 1964-79, Poly. Inst., Kishinev, 1964-79; vis. prof. Leningrad State U., 1971-73; cons., mem. adv. bd. Poly. Inst., Odessa, 1979-89; mem. hon. editl. adv. bd. Encyclopedia of Life Support Syss., Informational Macrodynamics. Author: Physical Approach to Control Systems, 1969, Superimposing Processes in Control Problems, 1973, Dynamic Models in Decision Making, 1974, Special Course in Optimal and Self Control Systems, 1977, Lectures in Mathematical Modelling and Optimization, 1995, Mathematical Foundations of Informational Macrodynamics, 1996, Lectures in Informational Macrodynamics, 1996, Informational Macrodynamics: Theory, Numerical Insights and Applications, 1997; contbr. numerous articles to sci. jours.; holder 23 patents; founder new sci. discipline informational Macrodynamics. Recipient Silver medal for rsch. achievements, Moscow, 1961, outstanding achievements in edn., Kishinev, 1975. Avocations: bicycling, travel. Office: West Coast U 440 Shatto Pl Los Angeles CA 90020-1704

LERNER, WARREN, historian; b. Boston, July 16, 1929; s. Max and Rebecca (Rudnick) L.; m. Francine Sandra Pickow, Aug. 16, 1959; children: Suzanne Rachel Knuiman, Amy Florence Coyle, Daniel Joseph. B.S., Boston U., 1952; M.A. and cert. of Russian, Inst. Columbia U., 1954, Ph.D. (Am. Council Learned Socs.-Social Service Research Council fgn. area fellow), 1961. Asst. prof. history Roosevelt U., 1959-61; asst. prof. Duke U., 1961-65, assoc. prof., 1965-72, prof., 1972—, chmn. dept., 1985-90; cons. NEH, 1974-80. Author: Karl Radek: The Last Internationalist, 1970, A History of Socialism and Communism in Modern Times, 1982, rev. edit., 1993; editor: The Development of Soviet Foreign Policy, 1973, (with Clifford M. Foust) The Soviet World in Flux, 1967; contbr. articles to profl. jours.; mem. internat. editorial bd. Studies in Comparative Communism, 1973-91. Served with U.S. Army, 1954-56. Am. Philos. Soc. fellow, 1972, 82; NEH, 1974-75. Mem. Conf. Slavic and East European History (exec. council 1978-80, pres. 1986-87), Am. Assn. Advancement Slavic Studies, Am. Hist. Assn., So. Conf. Slavic Studies. Jewish. Office: Duke U Dept History PO Box 90719 Durham NC 27708-0719

LERNER-LAM, EVA I-HWA, transportation executive; b. N.Y.C., Dec. 27, 1954; d. Sau-Wing and Jean (Lu) Lam; m. Arthur Lawrence Lerner-Lam, Sept. 4, 1977; children: Timothy Chi-Wen, Matthew Ta-Wen, Katherine I-Wen. AB, Princeton U., 1976; MS, MIT, 1978. Asst. planner County of San Diego, San Diego, 1977-78; dir. transp. planning group PRC Toups/Voorhies, La Jolla, Calif., 1978-79; assoc. planner Orange County Transit Dist., Garden Grove, Calif., 1979-80; assoc. planner San Diego Met. Transit Devel. Bd., 1980, sr. planner, 1981, dir. planning and ops., 1982-84; gen. mgr. Regency Motors, Montclair, N.J., 1984-85; asst. v.p., dir. planning and adminstrn. The Dah Chong Hong Trading Corp., N.Y.C., 1985-88; prin., cons. The Palisades Cons. Group Inc., Tenafly, N.J., 1988—; transport sys. advisor Economist Confs. Group, 1994—; mem. coun. on Fgn. Rels., 1996—, bd. adv. ENO Transp. Found., 1997—. Founder, coord. Asian-Am. Admissions Vols. Group, Princeton, N.J., 1985—; chmn. bd. dirs. Si-Yo Music Soc. Found., N.Y.C., 1988—; bd. dirs. Princeton U., 1984-88, founder, bus. mgr. and condr. Princeton U. Jazz Ensemble, 1973-76; mem. Coun. on Fgn. REls., 1996—; bd. advisors Eno Transp. Found., 1997—. Outstanding student fellow State Farm Cos., Princeton, 1974; recipient Outstanding Achievement award Tribute to Women in Industry, San Diego, 1983; named Auto Dealer of Yr., N.J. Living Mag., 1985. Mem. NSF (transp. rsch. bd.), ASCE (vice chmn. planning com. urban transp. divsn. 1987-91, vice chairperson exec. com. 1991-92, chmn. exec. com. 1992-93), Am. Planning Assn., Inst. Transp. Engrs. (best paper award 61st ann. meeting 1991, Innovative Intermodal Solutions for Urban Transp. award 1993, Ivor S. Wisepart Engr. award 1995), IVHS Am. (founding mem.), Asian Alumni of Princeton (Outstanding Achievement award 1988), Campus Club (bd. dirs. 1984-94), San Diego Princeton Club (pres. 1983-84). Avocations: piano, swimming, running, bicycling, hiking.

LEROUX, BETTY VON MOORE, elementary education educator; b. Rockingham County, N.C., Oct. 18, 1938; d. J. Melvin and Callie M. (Edens) Moore; m. Daneel Leon leRoux, July 25, 1959; 1 child, Anna Elizabeth. Student, Appalachian State U., 1957-59, Longwood Coll., 1959-61, U. N.C., Greensboro, 1962; BS, East Carolina U., 1966. English tchr. Appomattox (Va.) County Schs., 1959-61; middle sch. tchr. Madison (N.C.)-Mayodan City, 1961-65; tchr. Pitt County Schs., Greenville, N.C., 1966—; chmn. Middle Sch. Comm., Greenville, 1986—; com. mem. Pitt County Middle Sch. Task Force, Greenville, 1992-93, Pitt County Writing Handbook, Greenville; chmn. Chicod Sch. So. Assn., Greenville. Treas. Rockingham County (N.C.) Dem. Women's Orgn., 1961-65; mem. Jr. Svc. League, Madison, N.C., 1961-65; corr. sec. Bus. and Profl. Women, Greenville, 1972-80. Named Outstanding Young Women of Am., Bus. and Profl. Women's Club, Greenville, 1972. Mem. ASCD, Delta Kappa Gamma Internat. (membership chmn.), Women's Ministries (pres. 1978-81). Avocations: traveling, piano, gardening, antiquing, reading.

LE ROY, BRUCE MURDOCK, historian; b. Hornell, N.Y., June 9, 1920; s. Leland Bruce and Nina Boyce (Murdock) Le R.; m. Esther Buschman, Nov. 7, 1947; children: Philip Alden, Carolyn Sue (dec.). Student, Syracuse U., 1938-40, Transylvania U., 1941-42, Harvard Sch. Overseas Adminstrn., 1943-44; A.B., U. Calif., Berkeley, 1950. Mgr. coll. dept. Found. Press, N.Y.C., 1950; rep. Houghton Mifflin Co., 1950-58; dir. Wash. State Hist. Soc., Tacoma, 1959-84, dir. emeritus, 1985—; vis. lectr. Ft. Steilacoom Coll., 1985-86, U. Puget Sound, 1974-76; cons. U. Wash. Press, 1956-58; chmn. Gov. Wash. Boundary Survey Coun., 1960-61, Wash. Civil War Centennial Commn., 1960-65, Pacific N.W. Hist. Conf., 1960, 63, 78, Wash. Am. Revolution Bicentennial Commn., 1970-76. Author: H.M. Chittenden: A Western Epic, 1961, series Northwest History in Art, 1963-69, Lairds, Bards and Mariners: The Scot in Northwest America, 1978; gen. editor: Pacific Northwest Ethnic History Series, 1975-81; mem. editorial bd. Pacific N.W. Quar., 1958-84, N.W. Today, 1961-70, The American West, 1965-75, Manuscripts, 1978-94. Trustee Tacoma Art Mus., 1960-62, Allied Arts, 1962-65; pres. Tacoma Community Coll. Friends of the Library, 1981-83. Served with USAAF, 1943-46. Recipient award Calif. Writers Club, 1950, Nat. Archives and Record Services, 1958; Wash. Diamond Jubilee award, 1964; Disting. Service award Tacoma Public Library, 1977; John Binns award, 1976. Mem. Manuscript Soc., Am. Assn. State and Local History, Bibliog. Soc. Am., Western History Assn., Am. Studies Assn. (sec.-treas. 1961-64), Coun. Regional Rsch. (sec. 1959-84), Am. Folklore Soc., Am. Antiquarian Soc., SR. Presbyterian. Clubs: Univ. Union (trustee 1966-70), Tacoma, Clan Donald. Home: 10511 Sunnybrook Ln SW Tacoma WA 98498-3743

LEROY, DAVID HENRY, lawyer, state and federal official; b. Seattle, Aug. 16, 1947; s. Harold David and Lela Fay (Palmer) L.; 2 children. B.S., U. Idaho, 1969, J.D., 1971; LL.M., NYU, 1972; JD (hon.), Lincoln Coll., 1993. Bar: Idaho 1971, N.Y. State 1973, U.S. Supreme Ct. 1976. Law clk. Idaho 4th Dist. Ct., Boise, 1969; legal asst. Boise Cascade Corp., 1970; asso. firm Rothblatt, Rothblatt, Seijas & Peskin, N.Y.C., 1971-73; dep. prosecutor Ada County Prosecutor's Office, Boise, 1973-74; pros. atty. Ada County Prosecutor's Office, 1974-78; atty. gen. State of Idaho, Boise, 1978-82, lt. gov., 1983-87; ptnr. Runft, Leroy Coffin & Matthews, 1983-88, Leroy Law Offices, 1988—; candidate for Gov. of Idaho, 1986, U.S. Congress, 1994; U.S. nuclear waste negotiator, 1990-93; U.S. Presdl. elector, 1992; lectr., cons. in field. Mem. State Task Force on Child Abuse, 1975; mem. Ada County Coun. on Alcoholism, 1976; del. Rep. Nat. Conv., 1976, 80, 84; chmn. Nat. Rep. Lt. Gov.'s Caucus, 1983-86; bd. dirs. United Fund, 1975-81; del. Am. Coun. Young Polit. Leaders, USSR, 1979, Am. Coun. for Free Asia, Taiwan, 1980, U.S./Taiwan Investment Forum, 1983; del. leader Friendship Force Tour USSR, 1984; legal counsel Young Reps., 1974-81; candidate for Gov. Idaho, 1986; presdl. elector, 1992; candidate U.S. Ho. Reps. 1st Dist, Idaho, 1994. Mem. Nat. Dist. Attys. Assn., Idaho Prosecutors Assn., Am. Trial Lawyers Assn., Idaho Trial Lawyers Assn., Nat. Assn. Attys. Gen. (chmn. energy subcom., exec. com., del to China 1981), Western Attys. Gen. Assn. (vice chmn. 1980-83, chmn. 1981), Nat. Lt. Govs. Assn. (exec. bd. 1983), Idaho Bar Assn., Sigma Alpha Epsilon. Presbyterian. Office: The Leroy Offices PO Box 193 Boise ID 83701-0193

LEROY, EDWARD CARWILE, rheumatologist; b. Elizabeth City, N.C., Jan. 19, 1933; s. J. Henry and Grace Brown (Carwile) LeR.; m. Garnette DeFord Hughes, June 11, 1960; children: Garnette DeFord, Edward Carwile. BS summa cum laude, Wake Forest Coll., 1955; MS in Pathology, U. N.C., 1958, MD with honors, 1960. Med. intern Presbyn. Hosp., N.Y.C., 1960-61; resident Presbyn. Hosp., 1961-62; clin. asso. Nat. Heart Inst., Bethesda, Md., 1962-65; fellow in rheumatology Columbia U., 1965-67; dir. Edward Daniels Faulkner Arthritis Clinic; asso. attending physician Presbyn. Hosp., N.Y.C., 1970-75; asso. prof. Columbia U. Coll. Phys. and Surg., 1970-75; prof. medicine, dir. div. rheumatology and immunology Med. U. S.C., Charleston, 1975-95, prof., chmn. dept. microbiology and immunology, 1995—; bd. dirs. Arthritis Found. Contbr. articles med. jours. Recipient Alexander von Humboldt prize U. Cologne (Germany), 1995-96. Mem. Am. Coll. Rheumatology (bd. dirs.), AAAS, Am. Fedn. Clin. Research, Harvey Soc., A.C.P., Am. Assn. Immunologists, Soc. Exptl. Biology and Medicine, Am. Soc. Clin. Investigation, Microvascular Soc., N.Y. Acad. Scis., So. Soc. Clin. Investigation, Assn. Am. Physicians, Orthopedic Research Soc. First Scots Presbyterian. Clubs: Yeamans Hall, Carolina Yacht. Office: Med Univ SC Dept Microbiology/Immunol 171 Ashley Ave Charleston SC 29425-0001

LEROY, G. PALMER, art dealer; b. N.Y.C., July 15, 1929; s. John Minturn and Georgiana Kip (Palmer) LeR.; m. Kyra Hawkins, June 18, 1955; children: Kyra, Nina, Pamela. BA, Harvard U., 1951. With N.Y. Times, 1951-52, Frank Best & Co., N.Y.C., 1952-53, Kenyon & Eckhardt, Inc., N.Y.C., 1953-55, Inmont Corp., U.S. and Europe, 1955-83; v.p. sales Inmont Internat., Inc., N.Y.C., 1974-83; ptnr. Clinton R. Howell, Inc. Antiques, Pound Ridge, N.Y., 1984-85; mng. dir. Met. Opera Guild, Inc., N.Y.C., 1985-94; pub. Opera News, N.Y.C., 1985-94; dealer 19th and 20th Century Am. Art Palmer LeRoy Fine Art, Lyme, Conn., 1994—; mem. industry sector adv. com. chem. industry U.S. Commerce Dept., 1976-83. Pres. Friends of John Jay Homestead, Inc., Katonah, N.Y., 1977-95, chmn., 1995—; bd. dirs. The Bedford Assn., 1972-85, pres., 1975-80, bd. dirs. emeritus, 1986—; bd. dirs. Wildlife Preservation Trust Internat., Inc., Phila., 1983-94, pres., 1990-93, emeritus coun., 1994—; bd. dirs. N.Y. br. English Speaking Union, 1993—, chmn., 1997—; sr. warden St. Matthew's Ch., Bedford, 1985-89.

LE ROY, L. DAVID, journalist; b. Tignall, Ga., Jan. 2, 1920; s. Lansing Burrows and Glennie (David) LeR.; m. Mary Margaret Pridgeon, Sept. 2, 1945 (div.); children: David Charles, Gregory Alan; m. Ydoine B. Marholec, Apr. 30, 1988 (div.). A.B., U. Ga., 1941; student, Va. C. C., Shenandoah Coll., 1980. Mng. editor Air Force Times, 1950-53; with U.S. News & World Report, 1953-70, news editor, 1953-64; mem. Capitol Hill staff, 1964-70; publs. dir. Republican Congl. Com., 1970-74, pub. relations dir., 1974-76; exec. dir. Nat. Press Found., 1977-80. Author: Gerald Ford--Untold Story, 1974, The Outdoorsman's Guide to Government Surplus, 1978, World War II As I Knew It, 1994. Active local Boy Scouts Am. Served with AUS, 1941-46. Decorated Purple Heart. Mem. Nat. Press Club (pres. 1967, bd. govs., chmn. bd. govs.), Nat. Rifle Assn., Sigma Delta Chi. Presbyterian. Home: 101 Fox Ln Kearneysville WV 25430

LEROY, MISS JOY, model, designer; b. Riverdale, Ill., Sept. 8, 1927; d. Gerald and Dorothea (Wingebach) Reasor. BS, Purdue U., 1949. Model, sales rep. Jacques, Lafayette, Ind., 1950; book dept. sales rep. Loebs, Lafayette, 1951-52; window trimmer Marshall Field's and Co., Evanston, Ill., 1952-53; sales and display rep. Emerald Ho., Evanston, 1954-55; model, narrator, designer J.L. Hudson Co., GM Corp., Coca Cola Co., Hoover Vacuum Co., Jam Handy Orgn., Am. Motors Corp., Speedway Petroleum Corp., Ford Motors Tractor & Implement Divsn.-The Sykes Co., Detroit, 1958-61; tour guide, model The Christian Sci. Publ. Soc., spl. events coord. Prudential Ins. Co., model Copley 7, Boston, 1962-70. Author: Puzz-its, 1986-96. Founding angel Asolo Theatre, Sarasota, 1960s; mem. Ft. Lauderdale Internat. Film Festival, 1990, Mus. of Art, 1978, Fla. Conservation Assn., Rep. Senatorial Com. Inner Cir., 1990, Congl. Com., 1990, Nat. Trust for Hist. Preservation, 1986, Fla. Trust for Hist. Preservation, 1987, Nat. Wildflower Rsch. Ctr., 1992; one of founding friends 1000 Friends of Fla., 1991; mem. Rep. Presdl. Task Force, 1993; founding mem. Rep. Campaign Coun., 1994, Grand Club Rep. Party Fla., 1996. Mem. Nat. Parks and Conservation Assn., Purdue U. Gold Coast Club, Stratford Shakespearean Festival of Am., USS Constn. Mus. (charter mem. 1993), Purdue U. Alumni Assn., Walt Disney's Magic Kingdom Club, Wilderness Soc., Magic Kingdom Entertainment Club, Maupin Alumni, Heritage Found., Soc. Honorary Mariners, Heralds of Nature Soc., Ducks Unltd., Paddlewheel Steamboatin' Soc. Am., Cunard World Club, Skald Club, Yacht Club, The Crystal Soc., The Cousteau Soc., Covette Club, Coastal Conservation Assn., Captain's Cir., Intravler Club, Internat. Marine Animal Trainers Assn., Am. Queen Inaugural Soc., Zeta Tau Alpha. Avocation: travel. Home: 2100 S Ocean Ln Apt 2104 Fort Lauderdale FL 33316-3827

LERSCH, DELYNDEN RIFE, computer engineering executive; b. Grundy, Va., Mar. 22, 1949; d. Woodrow and Eunice Louise (Atwell) Rife; m. John Robert Lersch, May 9, 1976; children: Desmond, Kristofor. BSEE, Va. Poly. Inst. and State U., 1970; postgrad. Boston U., 1975—. With Stone & Webster Engring. Corp., 1970-91, elec. engr., supr. computer applications, Boston, 1978-80, mgr. computer graphics, 1980-84, mgr. engring. systems and computer graphics, 1984-87, div. chief info. techs., 1987-90, v.p., 1990-91; chief A.D.P. officer Univ. Rsch. Assocs., 1991-94; mgr. Global Electronic Security & Bus. Continuity; CARE Pvt. Mortgage Ins. Sys. Corp. account mgr. Perot Sys. Corp., Dallas, 1994—. Named Stone and Webster's Woman Engr. of Yr., 1976, 79; Mass. Solar Energy Research grantee, 1978; honored by Engring. News Record mag. for contbns. to constrn. industry, 1983. Mem. IEEE (sr.), Assn. Women in Sci., Soc. Women Engrs. (sr.), Women in Sci. and Engring., Energy Communicators, Nat. Computer Graphics Assn., Profl. Council New Eng., Women in Energy (dir. Mass. chpt. 1978, New Eng. region 1979), LWV, Rotary (Rotarian of Yr. 1993-94). Congregationalist. Club: Boston Bus. and Profl. Women's. Author: Cable Schedule Information Systems As Used in Power Plant Construction, 1973, 2d edit., 1975; Information Systems Available for Use by Electrical Engineers, 1976; contbr. articles in field of computer aided design and engring. Home: 1106 Bristol Cir De Soto TX 75115-2818 Office: Perot Sys Corp 12377 Merit Dr Ste 1100 Dallas TX 75251-3233

LERUD, JOANNE VAN ORNUM, library administrator; b. Jamestown, N.D., Nov. 21, 1949; d. Elbert Hiel and Dorothy Arlene (Littrick) Van Ornum; m. Gerald Henry Groenewold, Jan. 15, 1971 (div. Nov. 1978); 1 child, Gerd Heil Groenewold; m. Jeffrey Craig Lerud, Aug. 30, 1980; 1 child, Jesse Currier. BS in Geology, U. N.D., 1971, MS in Geology, 1979; MA in Librarianship and Info. Mgmt., U. Denver, 1979. Assoc. tech. info. specialist Marathon Oil Co., Littleton, Colo., 1980-86; libr. dir. Mont. Coll. Mineral Sci. and Tech., Butte, 1986-89, Colo. Sch. Mines, Golden, 1989—; report investigator in field. NSF grantee, 1970. Mem. Geosci. Info. Soc. (v.p. 1988, pres. 1989). Avocations: reading, needlework, antiques. Office: Colo Sch Mines Arthur Lakes Libr Golden CO 80401

LERUP, LARS G., architecture educator, college dean. Civil engring. diploma, Helsingborg Tech. Coll., Sweden, 1960; BArch, U. Calif., Berkeley, 1968; MArch in Urban Design, Harvard U., 1970. Asst. prof. architecture U. Calif., Berkeley, 1970-77, assoc. prof. architecture, 1977-87, prof. architecture, 1987-93; Harry K. and Albert K. Smith prof. and dean architecture Rice U., Houston, 1993—, dean Sch. of Architecture, 1993—; counselor Assn. Collegiate Schs. Architecture, Western Region, 1972-73, 76-77, 77-78; teaching cons. CCNY Sch. of Architecture, 1974; assoc. dean, chair environ. design program U. Calif., Berkeley, 1978-79; vis. fellow Inst. Architecture and Urban Studies, N.Y.C., 1979-81, dir. ednl. programs, 1981; Andrew Carnegie vis. prof. Cooper Union, N.Y.C., 1980-81; vis. prof. Rice U. Sch. Architecture, Houston, 1983, Caudill vis. prof., 1987; vis. prof. Architecture Assn., London, 1985, So. Calif. Inst. Architecture, L.A. and Vico Morcote, Switzerland, 1985, 91-93, ednl. dir., 1990-93; vis. prof. architecture U. Grenoble, France, 1990; mem. numerous coms. U. Calif., Berkeley, So. Calif. Inst. Architecture, Rice U.; supr. grad. students; lectr., rschr., guest critic in field. Author: Building the Unfinished: Architecture and Human Action, 1977, 3rd edit., 1983, Planned Assaults: Nofamily Hous. Love/House, Texas Zero, 1987, (with others) Fires and Human Behavior, 1980, Designer's Own Homes: Private Residences of Thirty of America's Leading Interior Designers, 1984, Architecture and Body, 1988, Architect's People, 1989, Visionary San Francisco, 1990; contbr. articles to profl. jours. and catalogs; prin. works include Folksam Ins. Co. Hdqrs., Farsta, Sweden, Ecole Maritime, La Rochelle, Bretagne, France, Cmty. Ctr., Eskilstuna, Sweden, Ch., Stora Tuna, Sweden, Bldg. Sci. Rm., U. Calif., also furniture design. Regents Tuition scholar U. Calif., 1966-67, 67-68; Arthur Lehman grantee Harvard U., 1969-70, Gulf Oil grantee, 1969-70; recipient citation for excellence Progressive Architecture Awards Program, 1976, citation Assn. Collegiate Schs. Architecture, 1986. Office: Rice U Sch of Architecture 6100 Main St Houston TX 77005-1827

LESAK, DAVID MICHAEL, safety engineer, educator, consultant; b. Phila., July 5, 1952; s. Joseph Michael and Charlotte (Rockel) L.; m. Lora Jean Schmoyer, June 12, 1976; children: Jana Bryn, Scott David. BS, Kutztown U., 1976. Lab. technician Air Products and Chems. Inc., Trexlertown, Pa., 1976-78; sci. tchr. Parkland Sch. Dist., Orefield, Pa., 1978-79, Quakertown (Pa.) Sch. Dist., 1980; owner, pres. Hazard Mgmt. Assocs., Allentown, Pa., 1981—; adj. prof. Nat. Fire Acad., Emmitsburg, Md., 1981—, devel. team mgr. Hazmat courses; adj. prof. Emergency Mgmt. Inst., Emmitsburg, 1985—; mem. Hazardous Materials Transp. Uniform Safety Act, Nat. Hazardous Materials Curriculum Devel. com. for Nat. Response Team; chief Lehigh County Hazmat Team, 1990—. Author: Chemistry of Hazardous Materials, 1983, (study guide) Fire Chemistry I and II, 1991; author, prodr., narrator: (videotape) Fire Fighter Safety, 1984, (text) Taking Command of Hazardous Materials Strategies and Tactics, 1997; author, presenter: (videotape) Oxidizers, 1991; author GEDAPER emergency ops. decision-making process Nat. Fire Acad.; prodr.: (videos) Container Damage Assessment, 1993, Spill Control, Stop It, Confine It, 1993, Flammable Liquids and Gases, 1993, Flammable Solids and Dusts, 1993, Explosives and Other Unstable Substances, 1993, Alkali and Alkali Earth Metals, 1993. Chmn. Lehigh County Hazardous Materials Adv. Commn., Allentown, 1990-93; fire chief Lower Macangie Twp., Pa., 1984-86. Mem. Am. Soc. Safety Engrs., Pa. Assn. Hazardous Material Techs. (sec. 1994—). Home and Office: Hazard Mgmt Assocs PO Box 3004 Allentown PA 18106-0004

LESAR, HIRAM HENRY, lawyer, educator; b. Thebes, Ill., May 8, 1912; s. Jacob L. and Missouri Mabel (Keith) L.; m. Rosalee Berry, July 11, 1937 (dec. Oct. 1985); children: James Hiram, Albert Keith, Byron Lee; m. Barbara Thomas, Feb. 12, 1987. AB, U. Ill., 1934, JD, 1936; JSD, Yale U., 1938. Bar: Ill. 1936, Mo. 1954, U.S. Supreme Ct. 1960. Asst. prof. law U. Kans., 1937-40, asso. prof., 1940-42; sr., prin. atty. bd. legal examiners U.S. CSC, 1942-44; assoc. prof. law U. Mo., 1946-48, prof., 1948-57; prof. law Washington U., St. Louis, 1957-72, dean Sch. Law, 1960-72; founding dean, prof. law So. Ill. U., Carbondale, 1972-80, interim pres. univ., 1974, acting pres., 1979-80, disting. service prof., 1980-82, prof. emeritus, 1982—, vis. disting. svc. prof., 1983—; disting. vis. prof. McGeorge Sch. Law, 1982-83; vis. prof. law U. Ill., summer 1947, Ind. U., summer 1952, U. So. Calif., summer 1959, U. N.C., summer 1961, NYU, summer 1965. Author: Landlord and Tenant, 1957; Contbr. to: Am. Law of Property, 1952, supplement, 1977, also, Dictionary Am. History, Ency. Brit. Bd. dirs. Legal Aid Soc., St. Louis and St. Louis County, 1960-72, pres. 1966-67; mem. Human Rels. Commn., University City, Mo., 1966-71, chmn., 1966, 67; bd. dirs. Land of Lincoln Legal Assistance Found., 1972-82, pres., 1982, vice chmn., 1988—; mem. Fed. Mediation and Conciliation Svc., other arbitration panels; bd. dirs. Bacone Coll., 1981-87; trustee Lincoln Acad. Ill., 1987—. Lt. comdr. USNR, 1944-46. Recipient Pres.' award Mo. Bar, 1968; named Laureate Lincoln Acad. of Ill., 1985. Fellow Am. Bar Found., Ill. Bar Found.; mem. ABA, AAUP, FBA, Am. Arbitration Assn., Am. Law Inst., Ill. Bar Assn., Mo. Bar Assn., St. Louis Bar Assn., Am. Judicature Soc., Univ. Club St. Louis, Yale Club Chgo., Rotary Internat., Jackson Country Club, Masons, K.T., Shriners, Order of Coif, Phi Beta Kappa, Phi Kappa Phi, Phi Delta Phi (hon.). Baptist. Home: 11 Hillcrest Dr Carbondale IL 62901-2444

LESCH, ANN MOSELY, political scientist, educator; b. Washington, Feb. 1, 1944; d. Philip Edward and Ruth (Bissell) Mosely; BA, Swarthmore Coll., 1966; PhD, Columbia U., 1973. Rsch. assoc. Fgn. Policy Rsch. Inst., Phila., 1972-74; assoc. Middle East rep. Am. Friends Svc. Com, Jerusalem, 1974-77; Middle East program officer Ford Found., N.Y.C., 1977-80, program officer, Cairo, 1980-84; assoc. Univs. Field Staff Internat., 1984-87; prof. Villanova U., 1987—, assoc. dir. ctr. Arab and Islamic studies, 1992-95. Author: The Politics of Palestinian Nationalism, 1973, Arab Politics in Palestine, 1979, Political Perceptions of the Palestinians on the West Bank and Gaza, 1980, (with Mark Tessler) Israel, Egypt and the Palestinians, 1989, Transition to Palestinian Self-Government, 1992; contbr. articles to profl. jours. Bd. dirs. Am. Near East Refugee Aid, 1980-86, Middle East Report, 1989-93, Human Rights Watch/Middle East, 1989—; co-chair middle East Program Com., Am. Friends Svc. Com., 1989-94; mem. Quaker UN Com., 1979-80, U.S. adv. com. Interns for Peace, 1978-82. Fellow Catherwood Found., 1965; NDFL fellow, 1967-71; Am. Rsch. Ctr. grant Egypt, 1988, U.S. Inst. of Peace Rsch. grants, 1990-91, 97, Wilson Ctr. Guest scholar Smithsonian, 1990, Rockefeller Fdn. Bellagio Ctr., 1996. Mem. Middle East Studies Assn. (bd. dirs. 1988-91, pres. 1993-96), Middle East Inst., Am. Polit. Sci. Assn., Sudan Studies Assn. (sec. 1993-96, pres. 1997—), Coun. Fgn. Rels. Unitarian. Office: Villanova U Dept Polit Sci Villanova PA 19085

LESCH, MICHAEL, cardiologist; b. N.Y.C., June 30, 1939; s. Maurice and Rose (Linn) L.; m. H. Bella Samuels, June 25, 1961; children—Leah Deura, Ian Samuel. A.B., Columbia U., 1960; M.D., Johns Hopkins U., 1964. Diplomate: Am. Bd. Internal Medicine, Am. Bd. Cardiology. Intern, then resident in medicine Johns Hopkins Hosp., 1964-66; physician USPHS, 1966-68; chief resident physician, fellow cardiology, asst. prof., then asso. prof. medicine Harvard U. Med. Sch.-Peter Bent Brigham Hosp., 1968-76; Magerstadt prof. medicine Northwestern U. Med. Sch., 1976-89; clin. prof. medicine, chmn. dept. medicine, Henry Ford Hosp. U. Mich., Detroit, 1989—; prof. Medicine Case Western U., Cleve., 1994—; mem. life scis. adv. com. NASA, 1980. Editor: Progress in Cardiovascular Diseases, 1971—; editorial bd. profl. jours. Fellow A.C.P., Am. Coll. Cardiology; mem. Am. Soc. Clin. Investigation, Am. Heart Assn. (gov. 1978-81), Chgo. Heart Assn. (pres. 1982-83). Office: Henry Ford Hosp 2799 W Grand Blvd Detroit MI 48202-2608

LESCH, MICHAEL OSCAR, lawyer; b. Berlin, May 28, 1938; came to U.S., 1940, naturalized, 1946; s. Adolf F. and Maria E. Leschnitzer; m. Judith Willis, Aug. 31, 1965; children—Sara, Benjamin. A.B., Columbia U., 1958; LL.B., Harvard U., 1961. Bar: N.Y. 1961, U.S. Dist. Ct. (so. dist.) N.Y. 1963, U.S. Dist. Ct. (ea. dist.) N.Y. 1965, U.S. Ct. Appeals (2d cir.) 1968, U.S. Supreme Ct. 1975, U.S. Ct. Appeals (3d cir.) 1979, U.S. Ct. Appeals (7th cir.) 1979. Assoc. Shea & Gould and predecessors, N.Y.C., 1961-69; ptnr. Shea & Gould and predecessors, 1970-94, LeBoeuf, Lamb, Greene & MacRae, N.Y.C., 1994—. Contbr. articles to profl. jours. Mem. ABA, N.Y. State Bar Assn., Assn. Bar City N.Y., Fed. Bar Council, Am. Arbitration Assn. (panel of arbitrators). Office: LeBoeuf Lamb Greene & MacRae 125 W 55th St New York NY 10019-5369

LESESNE, JOAB MAULDIN, JR., college president; b. Greenville, S.C., June 21, 1937; s. Joab Mauldin and Henrietta (Fennell) L.; m. Ruth Osborne, Feb. 1, 1958; children: Julia Ruth, Maryrose Lyle, Joab Mauldin III, Henry Herbert. B.A., Erskine Coll., 1959; M.A., U. S.C., 1961, Ph.D., 1967; hon. degree, Lander Coll., 1991. Instr. U. S.C.-Coastal Carolina br., Conway, 1960-62; mem. faculty Wofford Coll., 1964—, dean coll., 1970-72, pres., 1972—; past pres. S.C. Assn. Colls. and Univs.; past chmn. S.C. Tuition Grants Commn., 1972; mem. S.C. Commn. on Archives and History.; pres. So. Univ. Conf.; bd. dirs. Am. Coun. on Edn.; chmn. bd. dirs. NationsBank, N.C. and S.C. Author: History of Erskine College, 1967. Bd. dirs. Spartanburg County Found., United Way, chmn., 1991. Mem. S.C. Hist. Assn. (past pres.), Nat. Assn. Ind. Colls. and Univs. (chmn. 1985-86). Methodist. Office: Wofford Coll Office of Pres 429 N Church St Spartanburg SC 29303-3612

LESH, PHILIP CHAPMAN, musician, composer; b. Berkley, Calif., Mar. 15, 1940; s. Frank Hamilton and Barbara Jewel (Chapman) L.; m. Jill Winifred Johnson, Sept. 12, 1984; children: Graham Hamilton, Brian James. Student, Coll. San Mateo, 1958-61, Mills Coll., 1962. Co-founder, bass and vocals group Grateful Dead, 1965—. Albums include American Beauty, Grateful Dead, 1967, Anthem of the Sun, Aoxomoxoa, 1969, Live Dead, 1970, Workingman's Dead, 1970, The Grateful Dead, 1971, Bear's Choice: History of the Grateful Dead, Vol. 1, 1973, Skeletons From the Closet, 1974, What A Long Strange Trip It's Been: The Best of the Grateful Dead, 1977, Wake Of the Flood, 1973, From Mars Hotel, 1974, Blues for Allah, 1975, Steal Your Face, 1976, Terrapin Station, 1977, Shakedown Street, 1978, Built to Last, 1989, Dead Set, Europe, 1972, Reckoning, 1986, Go To Heaven, In the Dark, 1987, Without a Net, 1990, One From the Vault, Two From the Vault, and others; songwriter (with Robert Hunter) Box of Rain, 1970, (with Robert M. Petersen) New Potato Caboose, 1967, Unbroken Chain, 1974, Pride of Cucamonga, 1974; composer Foci for 4 orchs., 1963. Office: care Grateful Dead Prodns. PO Box 1073 San Rafael CA 94915-1073 also: Arista Records 6 W 57th St New York NY 10019*

LE SHANA, DAVID CHARLES, retired academic administrator; b. Lucknow, India, Nov. 15, 1932; came to U.S., 1949; naturalized, 1958; s. Newman John and Gwendolyn Beatrice (White) Le S.; m. Rebecca Ann Swander, June 8, 1951; children: Deborah Lynn, James David, Catherine Ann, Christine Joy. AB, Taylor U., Upland, Ind., 1953; AM in Edn, Ball State U., 1959; PhD, U. So. Calif., 1967; LHD (hon.), George Fox Coll., 1982; EdD (hon.), Taylor U., 1996; DD (hon.), Western Evang. Sem., 1996. Ordained to ministry Friends Ch., 1953; pastor Ypsilanti (Mich.) Friends Ch., 1953-54; dir. pub. relations, chaplain Taylor U., 1954-61; pastor 1st Friends Ch., Long Beach, Calif., 1961-67; mem. staff George Fox Coll., Newberg, Oreg., from 1967, pres., 1969-82; pres. Seattle Pacific U., 1982-91, pres. emeritus, 1991—; pres. Western Evang. Sem., Portland, Oreg., 1992-96; pres. emeritus Western Evang. Sem., Portland, 1996—; min. Pacific N.W. Conf. of Free Meth. Ch.; bd. dirs. Coun. Ind. Colls., 1971-80, chmn., 1976-78; chmn. commn. higher edn. Nat. Assn. Evangelicals, 1973-75; chmn. Oreg. Ind. Colls. Assn., 1971-72, 81-82; mem. So. Calif. Radio and TV Commn., 1963-67; bd. dirs. Christian Coll. Consortium, chmn., 1984-86; mem. fact-finding group to Bangladesh, 1972; mem. adv. bd. Oriental Missionary Soc.; bd. advs. Latin Am. Mission, Friends Ctr., Azusa Pacific U. Author: Quakers in California, 1969; Rec.: album Songs of Discipleship, 1965. Bd. dirs. Oreg. Ind. Coll. Found., 1969-82, 92—, George Fox Coll. Found., 1971-82, Herbert Hoover Found., Oreg., 1975-82, Ind. Colls. of Wash., 1982-91, Wash. Friends of Higher Edn., 1982-91; bd. assocs. Pacific Sci. Ctr.; mem. Wash. Gives Leadership Coun., 1989-92, mem. edn. commn. States Task Force on State Policy and Ind. Higher Edn., 1986-89; trustee CRISTA Ministries, 1982-88, 90-96, bd. dirs., 1982—; chmn. bd. Christian Coll. Coalition, 1991. Recipient Alumni Service award Taylor U., 1961, Chamber of Achievement award, 1978; Tchr. of Yr. award Ball State U., 1978. Mem. Nat. Assn. Evangs. (bd. dirs. 1980—, chmn. theology com. 1992-94), Portland Rotary Club. Address: 5737 Charles Cir Lake Oswego OR 97035-8714

LESHER, JOHN LEE, JR., consulting services company executive; b. Harrisburg, Pa., Feb. 7, 1934; s. John Lee and Mary Alice (Watkeys) L.; m. Nancy Smith, July 11, 1970; children by previous marriage: John David, James Elam, Andrew Gwynne. BA cum laude, Williams Coll., 1956; MBA, Harvard U., 1958. Budget dir., asst. sec. The Barden Corp., Danbury, Conn., 1958-61; cons. Booz, Allen & Hamilton Inc., N.Y.C., 1961-64, assoc., 1964-66, v.p., 1966-76, pres., 1976-85; pres. Mars & Co. Cons. Inc., Greenwich, Conn., 1985-87, Home Group Fin. Services, N.Y.C., 1987-88; v.p. Cresap, McCormick & Paget, N.Y.C., 1988-89; mng. dir. Korn/Ferry Internat., N.Y.C., 1989-93; pres. Jack Lesher & Assocs., Greenwich, Conn., 1993—. Clubs: Harvard Bus. Sch., Watch Hill Yacht, Misquamicut (Watch Hill, R.I.), Round Hill (Greenwich, Conn.), River (N.Y.C.), Coral Beach (Bermuda).

LESHER, MARGARET, newspaper publisher, songwriter; b. San Antonio, Tex., May 4, 1932; d. Lloyd Elmo Lisco and Dovie Deona (Maynard) Lisco Welch; m. William Jarvis Ryan (dec.); children: Patricia Ryan Simmonds, Wendi Ryan Alves, Jill Ryan Heidt, Roxanne Ryan Gibson; m. Dean Stanley Lesher, Sr., Apr. 2, 1973 (dec.); m. Collin T.C. Thorstenson, Nov. 7, 1996. Dir. cmty. svcs. Contra Costa Times Newspaper, Walnut Creek, Calif., 1973-94; chmn. bd. Lesher Comm., Inc., Walnut Creek, 1974—; pres., ceo, Dean and Margaret Lesher Found. Composer, lyricist gospel song Margaret Lesher Album, 1976 (So. Calif. Motion Picture Coun. Bronze Halo award 1982); author 14 published poems. Regent Holy Names Coll., Oakland, Calif., 1979-86; chief of protocol Contra Costa County, 1980—; dir. Bay Area Sports Hall of Fame, San Francisco, 1982—; bd. overseers U. Calif., San Francisco, 1983-90; bd. dirs. Yosemite Fund; mem. San Francisco Host Com., 1983—, Internat. Host Com. of Calif., 1983-86, Nat. Reading Initiative Coordinating Coun., 1988—; dir. emeritus Alameda-Contra Costa Regional Parks Found.; developed Contra Costa County Citizen Recognition Awards Program with County Police Chiefs Assn.; founded Contra Costa Literacy Alliance; commr. Port of Richmond, Calif., 1983-86; chmn. adv. bd. Crisis Nursery of Bay Area, Concord, 1983-86; adv. bd. Oakland A's Baseball Team, 1984-85, (Battered Women's) Alternatives, 1983—; pres. bd. dirs. Mt. Diablo Hosp. Found., 1980-81; bd. dirs. Contra Costa Council, 1984-90; mem. adv. bd. Las Trampas Sch. Mentally Retarded, chmn., 1984-90; trustee Oakland Symphony Orch., 1985-86; host Informed Viewer pub. svc. program Sta. KFCB-TV. Recipient Spl. Merit award State of Calif., 1982, Charles E. Scripps award Outstanding Contbn. in the Promotion of Literacy, 1988, 2 Internat. Silver Angel awards, 1st pl. for lit. program Calif. Newspaper Pub.'s Assn., 1988; named Calif. Assembly Woman of Yr. Mem. Am. Newspaper Pub. Assn. (ednl. svcs. com. 1988—), Gospel Music Assn., ASCAP, Nat. TV Acad. Arts & Scis., Calif. Cattlemen's Assn., Cancer of the Prostate Cure, Walnut Creek Rotary. Republican. Christian. Avocation: horses. Office: Lesher Comm Inc 244 Glorietta Blvd Orinda CA 94563-3547

LESHER, RICHARD LEE, association executive; b. Doylesburg, Pa., Oct. 28, 1933; s. Richard E. Lesher and Rosalie Orabelle (Meredith) Lesher Ehrhart; m. Agnes Marie Plocki, June 13, 1981; children by previous marriage: Douglas Allen, Laurie Lynn, Betsy Lee, Craig Collin. BBA, U. Pitts., 1958; MS, Pa. State U., 1960; DBA, Ind. U., 1963, LLD (hon.), 1979; D of Pub. Service (hon.), Ferris State Coll., 1981; DBA (hon.), Lawrence Inst. Tech., 1985. Asst. prof. Coll. Commerce and Adminstrn., Ohio State U., Columbus, 1963-64; cons. NASA, Washington, 1964-65; dep. asst. adminstr. NASA, 1965-66, asst. adminstr., 1966-69; bus. and mgmt. cons. Washington, 1969-71; pres. Nat. Ctr. for Resource Recovery, Washington, 1971-75, U.S. C. of C., Washington, 1975—; bd. dirs. G&L Realty Corp., World Heart Corp., Can., AIT, Can., Accugraph Corp., Corel Corp., Can., Iridium; mem. bd. advs. Norfolk So. Corp. Author: Economic Progres...It's Everybody's Business, 1980, Meltdown on Main Street: How Small Business is Leading the Revolution Against Big Government, 1996; syndicated newspaper columnist; participant (syndicated weekly TV show) It's Your Business. Mem. bd. visitors Coll. Bus. Adminstrn. Pa. State U.; mem. Sch. Bus. Dean's Adv. Coun. Ind. U. With U.S. Army, 1954-56. Recipient Superior Achievement award NASA, 1968, Exceptional Svc. award, 1968, Alumni Achievement award Pa. State U., 1976, Acad. of Alumni Fellows award Ind. U., 1977, Religious Heritage award, 1978, Horatio Alger award, 1980, Bicentennial medal of distinction U. Pitts., 1987, Golden Exec. medal Gen. C. of C. of Taiwan, 1988, Disting. Alumni fellow Pa. State U., 1990, Assn. of Yr. award Assn. Trends, 1994. Mem. Am. Soc. Assn. Execs. (Spl. Key award 1992), Washington Soc. Assn. Execs., Am. C. of C. Execs. (bd. dirs.), Congl. Country Club, Met. Club, Phi Alpha Kappa, Beta Gamma Sigma (dir.'s table, nat. award 1977). Avocations: golfing, fishing, horseback riding, tennis. Office: C of C of the USA 1615 H St NW Washington DC 20062-0001

LESHER, ROBERT OVERTON, lawyer; b. Phoenix, Apr. 6, 1921; s. Charles Zaner and Alice Marguerite (Heckman) L.; children: Stephen Harrison, Janet Kay. BA, U. Ariz., 1942, LLB, 1949. Bar: Ariz. 1949, Ill. 1949. Atty. Atcheson, Topeka & Santa Fe Ry., 1949-54; pvt. practice, Tucson, 1954—; ptnr. Lesher & Lesher, PC, Tucson, 1960—; adj. prof. Law Sch., U. Ariz., 1954-84; mem. Supreme Ct. Ariz., 1960. With AUS, 1942-46, 50-52. Fellow Am. Coll. Trial Lawyers; mem. Am. Law Inst., Am. Bd. Trial Advs. (diplomate), Internat. Assn. Ins. Counsel, Tucson Country Club. Home: 659 N Richey Tucson AZ 85716-5102 Office: 3773 E Broadway Blvd Tucson AZ 85716-5409

LESHER, WILLIAM RICHARD, retired academic administrator; b. Carlisle, Pa., Nov. 14, 1924; s. David Luther and Carrie LaVerne (Adams) L.; m. Veda E. Van Etten, June 16, 1946; children—Eileen Fern, Martha Zoe Lesher Keough. Th.B., Atlantic Union Coll., South Lancaster, Mass., 1946; M.A., Andrews U., 1964; Ph.D., NYU, 1970. Ordained to ministry Seventh-day Adventist Ch., 1951. Pastor No. New Eng. Conf. Seventh-day Adventists, 1946-56; pastor, mission dir. Delta sect. Nile Union Seventh-day Adventists, Alexandria, Egypt, 1957-58; prin. Nile Union Acad., Cairo, Egypt, 1959-61; sec. Middle East Div. Seventh-day Adventists Beirut, Lebanon, 1962-64; assoc. prof. religion, dir. summer sch., asst. to pres. Atlantic Union Coll., 1964-71; assoc. dir. Sabbath sch. dept. Gen. Conf. Seventh-day Adventists, Washington, 1971-79; dir. Bibl. Research Inst., Gen. Conf. Seventh-day Adventists, Washington, 1979-84; gen. v.p. Gen. Conf. Seventh-day Adventists, Washington, 1981-84; pres. Andrews U., Berrien Springs, Mich., 1984-94; ret., 1994. Author: Tips for Teachers, 1979; editor adult Sabbath Sch. lessons, 1971-79, studies in sanctuary and atonement, 1980-81; contbr. articles to religious jours. Recipient Founders Day award NYU, 1970. Home: 4703 Greenfield Dr Berrien Springs MI 49103-9566

LESHNER, ALAN IRVIN, scientist administrator; b. Lewisburg, Pa., Feb. 11, 1944; s. Saul S. and Martha (Schmidt) L.; A.B., Franklin and Marshall Coll., 1965; M.S., Rutgers U., 1967, Ph.D., 1969; m. Agnes Farkas, May 18, 1969; children—Sarah, Michael. Asst. prof. psychology Bucknell U., 1969-73, assoc. prof., 1973-78, prof., 1978-82; program assoc. Div. Behavioral and Neural Scis., NSF, Washington, 1979-80, project mgr. Office Dir., 1980-82, dep. exec. dir. Commn. on Precoll. Edn., Nat. Sci. Bd., 1982-83; dep. dir. div. behavioral and neural scis. NSF, 1983-85, dir. div. precoll. materials devel. and research, 1984-85, exec. officer biol., behavioral and social scis., 1985-87; dep. dir. NIMH, 1988—, acting dir., 1990-92; vis. scientist U. Wis., 1976-77, dir. Natl. Inst. on Drug Abuse, HHS, Washington, 1993—; Fulbright lectr. Weizmann Inst. Sci., Rehovoth, Israel, 1977-78; Am.-Hungarian Acads. Sci. exchange scientist Postgrad Med. Sch., Budapest, 1974. Recipient teaching award Bucknell U., 1974, 1978, Nat. Research Service award, 1976. Fellow AAAS, Am. Psychol. Assn., Am. Psychological Soc., N.Y. Acad. Scis., Internat. Soc. Research on Aggression; mem. Phi Beta Kappa. Democrat. Jewish. Author: An Introduction to Behavioral Endocrinology, 1978; contbr. chpts., numerous articles on roles of hormones in behavior, sci. and tech. policy, higher edn. to profl. publs. Office: HHS Natl Inst Drug Abuse 5600 Fishers Ln Rockville MD 20857*

LESHY, JOHN D., lawyer, legal educator, government official; b. Winchester, Ohio, Oct. 7, 1944; s. John and Dolores (King) L.; m. Helen M. Sandalls, Dec. 15, 1973; 1 child, David Alexander. AB cum laude, Harvard U., 1966, JD magna cum laude, 1969. Trial atty. Civil Rights Divsn. Dept. Justice, Washington, 1969-72; atty. Natural Resources Def. Coun., Palo Alto, Calif., 1972-77; assoc. solicitor energy and resources Dept. Interior, Washington, 1977-80; prof. law Ariz. State U., Tempe, 1980—; spl. counsel to chair Natural Resources Com. U.S. Ho. Reps., Washington, 1992-93; solicitor, gen. counsel Dept. Interior, 1993—; cons. Calif. State Land Commn., N.Mex. Atty. Gen., Western Govs. Assn., Congl. Rsch. Svc., Ford Found.; mem. com. Onshore Oil & Gas Leasing, NAS Nat. Rsch. Coun., 1989-90; vis. prof. Sch. Law U. San Diego, 1990. Author: The Mining Law: A Study in Perpetual Motion, 1987, The Arizona State Constitution, 1993; co-author Federal Public Land and Resources Law, 3d edit., 1992; contbr. articles, book chpts. to profl. jours., environ. issues. Bd. dirs. Ariz. Ctr. Law in Pub. Interest, 1981-86, Ariz. Raft Adventures, 1982-92; mem. Gov.'s Task Force Recreation on Fed. Lands, 1985-86, Gov.'s Task Force Environ. Impact Assessment, 1990, City of Phoenix Environ. Quality Commn., 1987-90. Robinson Cox vis. fellow U. Western Australia Law Sch., Perth, 1985, rsch. fellow U. Southampton, Eng., 1986; Ford Found. grantee, Resources for the Future grantee. Democrat. Avocations: piano, hiking, whitewater rafting, photography. Office: Department of the Interior Solicitor 1849 C St NW Washington DC 20240-0001

LESIKAR, RAYMOND VINCENT, business administration educator; b. Rogers, Tex., June 29, 1922; s. Vince E. and Albina J. (Stanislaw) L.; m. Lu Clay Allen, July 7, 1945 (dec July 1993); children: Patricia Lesikar King, Raymond Vincent. B.B.A., U. Tex., 1947, M.B.A., 1948, Ph.D., 1954. With Douglas Aircraft Co., 1941-42, Sears, Roebuck & Co., 1947; instr. Tex. Christian U., 1948-49; asst. prof. U. Tex., 1949-54; faculty La. State U., Baton Rouge, 1954-77; prof. bus. adminstrn. La. State U., 1959—, chmn. dept. mgmt., 1959-77; dean La. State U. (Coll. Bus. Adminstrn.), 1963-64, 72-73, prof. emeritus, 1977—; adj. prof. U. Tex., Austin, 1977-79; prof., chmn. dept. mgmt. U. North Tex., Denton, 1979-88; guest prof. univs., People's Republic China, spring 1982, 83, 84; cons. in field. Author: Business Communication: Theory and Application, 1968, 7th edit. 1993, Report Writing for Business, 10th edit., 1997, Introduction to Business: A Socie Approach, 1972, 3d rev. edit., 1979, Productive Business Writing, 1959, Business Report Writing, 1957, How to Write Reports, 1974, 2d rev. edit., 1984, Basic Business Communication, 1979, 7th rev. edit., 1996; contbr. articles to profl. jours. Served with AUS, 1943-46. Fellow Am. Bus. Communication Assn. (pres. 1961); mem. S.W. Social Sci. Assn. (pres. 1967), Acad. Mgmt., Internat. Communication Assn., Internat. Soc. Gen. Semantics, Horseshoe Bay Country Club, Beta Gamma Sigma, Phi Kappa Phi, Sigma Iota Epsilon. Home and Office: PO Box 7912 Horseshoe Bay TX 78657-9203

LESKO, HARRY JOSEPH, transportation company executive; b. Cleve., Dec. 6, 1920; s. Theodore Prokop and Bertha Barbara (Trojack) L.; m. Evelyn Martha Culley, Feb. 3, 1945; children—Harry Richard, Larry J., Garry E., Mark J., John M., Joseph. B.B.A., Cleve. State U., 1956. Schedule analyst Cleve. Ry. System, 1938-40; pres., dir. Greyhound Lines, Inc., Phoenix, 1940—; pres. Atlantic Greyhound Lines of Va., Inc.; v.p. Gelco Bus Leasing Co., 1979—; pres. Trailways Lines Inc., Dallas, 1979—; pres., dir. The Trailways Corp., Trailways, Inc.; dir. Trailways Lines Inc. (25 subs.), Southeastern Stages, Inc., Atlanta, N.Mex. Transp. Co., Roswell, KG Lines, Tulsa, Okla. Transp. Co., Lubbock, Tex., Jefferson Lines Inc., Mpls., Kerrville Bus. Co., Tex., Continental Lines, Amarillo, Tex., Service Coach Co., Jacksonville, Fla., Gen. Fire and Casualty Co. Served to capt. USMC, 1942-46. Mem. Am. Bus. Assn. (dir.). Republican. Roman Catholic. Club: Brookhaven Country.

LESKO, LEONARD HENRY, Egyptologist, educator; b. Chgo., Aug. 14, 1938; s. Matthew Edward and Josephine Bernice (Jaszczak) L.; m. Barbara Jadwiga Switalski, Dec. 29, 1966. B.A., Loyola U., Chgo., 1961, M.A., 1964; Ph.D., U. Chgo., 1969; M.A. ad eundem, Brown U., 1983. Tchr. Quigley Prep. Sem. South, Chgo., 1961-64; Egyptologist, epigrapher, epigraphic survey Oriental Inst., U. Chgo., Luxor, Egypt, 1964-65; acting instr. U. Calif. at Berkeley, 1966-67, acting asst. prof., 1967-68, asst. prof., 1968-72, asso. prof., 1972-77, prof. Egyptology, 1977-82, dir. Center Nr. Eastern Studies, 1973-75, chmn. dept., 1975-77, 79-81, chmn. grad. program in ancient history and archeology, 1978-79, chmn. humanities council, 1980-81; dir. Seila project, 1981; C.E. Wilbour prof. Egyptology, chmn. dept. Brown U., 1982—; chmn. faculty, faculty exec. com., 1992-93. Author: The Ancient Egyptian Book of Two Ways, 1972, Glossary of the Late Ramesside Letters, 1975, King Tut's Wine Cellar, 1977, Index of the Spells on Egyptian Middle Kingdom Coffins and Related Documents, 1979; co-author: Religion in Ancient Egypt, 1991, Pharoah's Workers: The Villagers of Deir el-Medina, 1994; editor: A Dictionary of Late Egyptian, vol. I, 1982, vol. II, 1984, vol. III, 1987, vol. IV, 1989, vol. V, 1990, Egyptological Studies in Honor of Richard A. Parker, 1986; contbr. articles to profl. pubs. and encys. Recipient award computer oriented rsch. in humanities Am. Coun. Learned Socs., 1973; NEH fellow, 1970-71, grantee, 1975-79, co-dir. Summer Inst., 1995; FIAT faculty fellow U. Torino, 1990. Mem. Am. Rsch. Ctr. in Egypt (gov. 1973-75), Am. Oriental Soc., Archeol. Inst. Am. (pres. San Francisco chpt. 1976-78, pres. Narragansett chpt. 1994-95), Internat. Assn. Egyptologists, Egypt Exploration Soc., Found. Egyptologique Rein Elisabeth, Soc. Francaise d'Egyptologie, U.S. Lighthouse Soc., Lighthouse Preservation Soc., Explorers Club. Office: Brown U Dept Egyptology PO Box 1899 Providence RI 02912-1899

LESKO, RONALD MICHAEL, osteopathic physician; b. Homestead, Pa., Mar. 25, 1948; s. Andrew Paul and Elizabeth Ann (Tarasovic) L.; m. Helena Alexandra Shalayeva, July 29, 1990. BS, U. Pitts., 1970; DO, Coll. Osteo. Medicine & Surgery, Des Moines, 1973; MPH, Loma Linda U., 1985. Diplomate Am. Osteo. Bd. Family Physicians, Am. Osteo. Bd. Preventive Medicine (bd. dirs., chmn. pub. health rep., chmn. bd. exam. com. 1991-97). Family physician pvt. practice Port Richey, Fla., 1974-80; flight surgeon USN, NAS Chase Field Beeville, Tex., 1981-83; resident gen. preventive medicine Loma Linda (Calif.) U. Med. Ctr., 1983-85; pvt. practice family and preventive medicine, pvt. practice, Del Mar, Calif., 1988—; flight surgeon, capt. USNR, NAS Miramar, San Diego, 1988-95; ret. USNR, Loma Linda, Calif., 1996; attending physician ambulatory care svc. J.L. Pettis Meml. VA Hosp., Loma Linda, Calif., 1986-88; staff physician Scripps Meml. Hosp., La Jolla, Calif., 1990—; lectr., 1985—; cons. Jour. Am. Osteo. Assn., Chgo., 1987, phys. rediness div. USN, Washington, 1988; med. advisor blue ribbon adv. com. Nutrition Screening Initiative, Washington, 1991. Contbr. articles to med. jours.; rschr. in nutrition and metabolism in human physiology. Med. adviser March of Dimes Suncoast chpt., New Port Richey, 1977-79; bd. dirs. Fla. Gulf Health Systems Agy., Region IV, 1977-79, Price-Pottenger Nutrition Found., San Diego, 1988—. Fellow Am. Osteo. Coll. Occupational and Preventive Medicine (trustee 1989-91, chmn. pub. health divisional com. 1989-91), Am. Coll. Preventive Medicine; mem. APHA, Am. Osteo. Assn., San Diego Osteo. Med. Assn., Osteo. Physicians and Surgeons Calif., Am. Coll. Family Physicians-Osteo., U.S. Naval Flight Surgeons. Avocations: scuba diving, photography, marksmanship, art, music. Office: 13983 Mango Dr Ste 103 Del Mar CA 92014-3146

LESLIE, DONALD WILMOT, landscape architecture educator; b. Pitts., Dec. 29, 1942; s. Donald and Harriette Rebecca (Wilmot) L.; divorced; children: Robin Elizabeth, Kristen Bogar. BS in Landscape Architecture, Pa. State U., 1965; M Landscape Architecture, U. Mich., 1967. Registered landscape architect, Pa. Landscape architect Simonds & Simonds, Pitts., 1967-71; asst. prof. dept. landscape architecture Pa. State U., University Park, 1971-78, assoc. prof., 1978—, assoc. dean, 1991—; pvt. practice, State College, Pa., 1979—; cons. Comprehensive Design, State Coll., 1986—; master grader Coun. Landscape Archtl. Registration Bds., 1988-90. Contbg. author: Landscape Architectural Construction, 1985. Pres. coun. Trinity Luth. Ch., State College, 1987-88; pres. Forest Edge Townhouse Assn., State College, 1987-92. Recipient Disting. Teaching award Pa. State U., 1975. Fellow Am. Soc. Landscape Architects (pres. Pa. chpt. 1984-85, nat. trustee 1986-89, nat. v.p. 1989-91, nat. pres. 1996-97, Disting. Svc. award Pa. chpt. 1987). Republican. Home: 1210 Westerly Pky State College PA 16801-4158 Office: Pa State U Coll Arts & Architecture 116 Arts Bldg University Park PA 16802-2900

LESLIE, GERRIE ALLEN, immunologist; b. Red Deer, Alta., Can., Nov. 19, 1941; s. John Allen and Lily Elizabeth (von Hollen) L.; m. Anna Magdalene Madsen Ladefoged, July 31, 1965; children: Kirsten, John Gerrie. BS in Pharmacy, U. Alta., 1962, MS in Microbiology, 1965; PhD, U. Hawaii, 1968. Postdoctoral fellow U. Fla., Gainesville, 1968-70; prof. Tulane U. Med. Sch., New Orleans, 1970-74, Oreg. Health Scis. U., Portland, 1974-86; pres., chief exec. officer Immunology Cons. Lab., Lake Oswego, Oreg., 1979—; sci. adviser Epitope Inc., Beaverton, Oreg., 1987-91, Ultra Diagnostics, Seattle, 1987-91; cons. to biotech. cos. S.Am., Thailand, U.S. Author and co-author 110 sci. articles. Grantee NIH,1968-86, NSF, 1970-85, Kroc Found., 1970-86, Cancer Found., Med. Rsch. Found., John Hartford Found., others. Mem. Am. Assn. Immunology, Oreg. Polled Hereford Assn.

(bd. dirs. 1991—, pres. 1996—). Lutheran. Avocations: stamp collection, coin collecting, fishing, farming.

LESLIE, HENRY ARTHUR, lawyer, retired banker; b. Troy, Ala., Oct. 15, 1921; s. James B. and Alice (Minchener) L.; m. Anita Doyle, Apr. 5, 1943; children: Anita Lucinda Leslie Bagby, Henry Arthur Jr. B.S., U. Ala., 1942, J.D., 1948; J.S.D., Yale U., 1959; grad., Sch. Banking, Rutgers U., 1964. Bar: Ala. 1948. Asst. prof. bus. law U. Ala., 1948-50, 52-54; prof. law, asst. dean U. Ala. (Sch. Law), 1954-59; v.p. trust officer Birmingham Trust Nat. Bank, Ala., 1959-64; sr. v.p., trust officer Union Bank & Trust Co., Montgomery, Ala., 1964-73; sr. v.p., sr. loan officer Union Bank & Trust Co., 1973-76, exec. v.p., 1976-78, pres., chief exec. officer, 1978-91, also bd. dirs.; ret., 1991; sole practice Montgomery, Ala., 1991—; mem. Ala. Oil and Gas Bd., 1984-85; dir. First Fin. Mgmt. Corp., 1981—. Pres. Downtown Unltd., 1983-84; mem. Ala. Bd. Bar Examiners, 1973-78, bd. dirs. YMCA, 1992—; chmn. bd. Ala. Bankers Found., 1971-77; trustee Ala. Assn. Ind. Colls. Decorated Bronze Star. Mem. ABA, Ala. Bar Assn., Montgomery Bar Assn. (Liberty Bell award 1989), Ala. Ind. Bankers (chmn. 1983-84), Ala. Bankers Assn. (trust div. pres. 1963-65), Ind. Bankers Assn. Am. (dir. 1983-90), Farrah Order Jurisprudence (pres. 1973), Order of Coif Alumni, Newcomen Soc. N.Am., Montgomery C. of C. (dir. 1983-84, pres. 1987-88), Maxwell Officers Club, Montgomery Country Club, Kiwanis, Delta Sigma Pi, Phi Delta Phi, Omicron Delta Kappa, Pi Kappa Phi. Episcopalian (past sr. warden). Home: 3332 Boxwood Dr Montgomery AL 36111-1702 Office: 3332 Boxwood Dr Montgomery AL 36111-1702

LESLIE, JACQUES ROBERT, JR., journalist; b. L.A., Mar. 12, 1947; s. Jacques Robert and Aleen (Wetstein) L.; m. Leslie Wernick, June 21, 1980; 1 child, Sarah Alexandra. BA, Yale U., 1968. Tchr. New Asia Coll., Chinese U., Hong Kong, 1968-70; free-lance journalist Washington, 1970-71; fgn. corr. L.A. Times, Saigon, 1972-73, Phnom Penh, 1973, Washington, 1974; chief New Delhi (India) bur. L.A. Times, 1974-75, Madrid, 1975-76; chief Hong Kong bur. L.A. Times, 1976-77; freelance journalist, 1977—; contbg. writer Wired Mag., 1993—; contbg. writer Wired mag., 1993—. Author: The Mark: A War Correspondent's Memoir of Vietnam and Cambodia. Recipient Best Fgn. Corr. award Sigma Delta Chi, 1973, citation for reporting Overseas Press Club, 1973. Home: 124 Reed St Mill Valley CA 94941-3448

LESLIE, JOHN WALTER, development consultant; b. Norfolk, Va., Sept. 18, 1929; s. John Walter and Ella Arden (Squires) L.; m. Audrey May Munford, Apr. 9, 1957. B.A., Coll. William and Mary, 1952; student, Mich. State U., 1957-58, U. Oreg., 1962-64; M.A., Am. U., 1968. From copy boy to sports reporter Norfolk Virginian-Pilot, 1944-49; sports reporter Newport News (Va.) Daily Press, 1950-52, asst. sports editor, 1956-57; asst. news editor Mich. State U., 1957-58; asso. dir. Ketchum, Inc., 1958-60; dir. devel. and pub. relations Lewis and Clark Coll., 1960-63; exec. v.p. Am. Coll. Pub. Relations Assn., 1963-74; pres. Instl. Advancement Consultants, Inc., N.Y.C., 1974-80; sr. v.p. Brakeley, John Price Jones, Inc., N.Y.C., 1974-80; v.p. devel. U. Houston System, 1981-85; pres. John W. Leslie Inc., Potomac, Md., 1986—. Author: Focus on Understanding and Support: A Study in College Management, 1969, Seeking the Competitive Dollar, 1971; contbr. articles to profl. jours. Served to 1st lt. USAF, 1952-56. Home: 8004 Grand Teton Dr Rockville MD 20854-4074

LESLIE, JOHN WEBSTER, JR., communications company executive; b. Milw., July 20, 1954; s. John and Joanne Marie (Chamberlain) L.; m. Laura Elizabeth Bafford, June 7, 1986; children: Finn Elizabeth, John Webster III. BS in Fgn. Service, Georgetown U., 1976. Legis. asst. Senator Edward Kennedy, Washington, 1976-80; campaign dir. northeast region Kennedy for Pres., Washington, 1980-81; polit. dir. Senator Edward Kennedy for U.S. Senate, Washington, 1981-82; exec. dir. Fund for Dem. Majority, Washington, 1982-83; pres. Sawyer/Miller Group, N.Y.C., 1983-93; ptnr. Robinson Lerer Sawyer Miller, N.Y.C., 1993-96; Bd. dirs. Internat. Policy Research, Inc., N.Y.C., Creative Media, Inc., N.Y.C.; pres. Bozell Sawyer Miller Group, 1996—. Contbr. articles to profl. jours.; speaker in field. Bd. dirs. Nat. Student Edn. Fund, Washington, 1977-79. Fellow Circumnavigators Found., Am. Assn. Polit. Cons. Roman Catholic. Office: Bozell Sawyer Miller Group 75 Rockefeller Plz Fl 5 New York NY 10019-6908

LESLIE, JOHN WILLIAM, public relations and advertising executive; b. Indpls., Nov. 22, 1923; s. John Edward and Catherine (Harris) L.; m. Joan Williams, Dec. 26, 1970; 1 dau. by previous marriage, Catherine Alexandra. Student, U.S. Naval Acad., 1943-44, George Washington U., 1949, Indsl. Coll. Armed Forces, 1956. Dep. excise adminstr. Ind., 1946-47; pvt. pub. relations bus., 1947-49; dir. pub. relations Ind. Democratic State Central Com., 1948-49, Ind. Dept. Vets. Affairs, 1949; press officer Dept. Labor, 1949-51, acting asst. dir. info., 1951-52, asst. dir., 1952-56, dep. dir., 1956-59, dir., 1959-81; sr. assoc. Kamber Group, Washington, 1981-84, counselor, 1984-88, exec. v.p., COO, 1988-96, vice chmn., sec., 1997—, also bd. dirs.; mem., dir. pub. D.C. Com. Employment Physically Handicapped, 1952-53; charter mem. U.S. Sr. Exec. Svc., 1979—. Author numerous articles in field. Advt. cons. Pres.'s Com. on Youth Employment, 1964-80; U.S. del Internat. Graphic Design Coun., Japan, 1973; trustee Washington chpt. Leukemia Soc. Am., 1976-82; chmn. Pub. Printers Adv. Com. on Printing and Publs, 1977-79. Served with USN and USNR, 1941-46. Recipient commendation President's Com. Employment Physically Handicapped, 1954; Disting. Service award Dept. Labor, 1962; citation outstanding service Navy Dept., 1964; Presdl. citation, 1966; Merit award Internat. Labor Press Assn., 1969; Disting. Career Service award Dept. Labor, 1973; Communications award Ga. chpt. Pub. Relations Soc. Am., 1972; Sec. Labor's Recognition award, 1974; Communicator of Yr. award Nat. Assn. Govt. Communicators, 1981. Mem. Am. Assn. Polit. Cons., Am. League Lobbyists, Nat. Press Club, English Speaking Union. Episcopalian. Home: 4290 Massachusetts Ave NW Washington DC 20016-5558 Office: Kamber Group 1920 L St NW Ste 700 Washington DC 20036-5014

LESLIE, LOTTIE LYLE, retired secondary education educator; b. Huntsville, Ala., Aug. 5, 1930; d. James Peter and Amanda Lacy Burns; children: Thomas E. Lyle Jr., Theodore Christopher Leslie, DeMarcus Miller Leslie. BS, Ala. A and M U., 1953, student, 1960-83; training cert., Learning Ctrs. of Am., 1985. Cert. secondary tchr. Social studies, English, Music. Tchr. Madison County Bd. Edn., Huntsville, Ala. Author: Teaching the Importance of Character Through Poetry, 1968-69, Ways to Teach Language Composition and Literature, Versatility Versus Violence, Families and Foreign Relationships, Musical Instruments of the World From K-12 and Undergraduate to Graduate; contbr. poetry to profl jours. Active St. Joseph's Cmty., 1959—. Recipient Miss Liberty trophy, 1986, Victory pin, 1987, Medal of Honor Commemorating Disting. Lifelong Achievements, 1993, cert. appreciation Indian Creek P.B. Ch., 1994. Mem. NEA, ASCD, NAACP, Ala. Edn. Assn., Madison County Music Edn. Assn., Internat. Black Writers and Artists, Inc., N.Y. Poetry Soc., Am. Poetry Assn. (vol. IV no. 2 summer 1985). Con. sponsor Ednl. Expo 2000. Home: 3207 Farris Dr NW Huntsville AL 35810-3342

LESLIE, LYNN MARIE, secondary education educator; b. Lake City, Fla., Nov. 17, 1948; d. Billy Verlyn Spooner and Dorothy Marie (Odom) Loomis; m. Roy Hamner Leslie, Nov. 25, 1967; children: Kim Ball, Billy Leslie, Dodi Leslie. BS in Edn., Trevecca U., 1970; ME in Spl. Edn., Tenn. State U., 1987, postgrad. in Edn., 1996; postgrad. in Edn., Cumberland U., 1996. Cert. career ladder III, Tenn. Tchr. Leesburg (Fla.) Elem. Sch., 1970-71, Wessington Pl. Elem. Sch., Hendersonville, Tenn., 1974-87, Knox Doss Mid. Sch., Hendersonville, 1987—; mem. Sumner County Ins. Trust, Gallatin, Tenn., 1991-96; tchr, Hall of Fame Jr. Achievement, 1993. Mem. NEA (del.), Tenn. Edn. Assn. (del.), Sumner County Edn. Assn. (pres. 1991-92, 95-96, sec. 1992-95, sec./treas. 1996—, numerous coms. chair, tchr. welfare com. 1990-91). Mem. Ch. of Nazarene. Avocations: reading, travel. Home: 1032 Carriage Hill Pl Hendersonville TN 37075-8728

LESLIE, ROBERT LORNE, lawyer; b. Adak, Alaska, Feb. 24, 1947; s. J. Lornie and L. Jean (Conelly) L.; children—Lorna Jean, Elizabeth Allen. B.S., U.S. Mil. Acad., 1969; J.D., Hastings Coll. Law, U. Calif.-San Francisco, 1974. Bar: Calif. 1974, D.C. 1979, U.S. Dist. Ct. (no. dist.) Calif. 1974, U.S. Ct. Claims 1975, U.S. Tax Ct. 1975, U.S. Ct. Appeals (9th and D.C. cirs.), U.S. Ct. Mil. Appeals 1980, U.S. Supreme Ct. 1980. Commd. 2d lt. U.S. Army, 1969, advanced through grades to maj., 1980; govt. trial atty. West Coast Field Office, Contract Appeals, Litigation Div. and Regulatory Law Div., Office JAG, Dept. Army, San Francisco, 1974-77; sr. trial atty. and team chief Office of Chief Trial Atty., Dept. Army, Washington, 1977-80; ptnr. McInerney & Dillon, Oakland, Calif., 1980—; lectr. on govt. contracts CSC, Continuing Legal Edn. Program; lectr. in govt. procurement U.S. Army Materiel Command. Col. USAR. Decorated Silver Star, Purple Heart. Mem. ABA, Fed. Bar Assn., Associated Gen. Contractors, The Beavers. Office: Ordway Building Fl 18 Oakland CA 94612-3610

LESLIE, SEAVER, artist; b. Boston, Aug. 22, 1946; s. John Frederick and Joan (Warland) L.; m. Anne Cleland Rogers; children: Genevieve, Marion, Frances. BFA, RISD, 1969, MEd, 1970. Exhibited in shows at Hirschl & Adler Gallery, N.Y.C., 1981, Tatistcheff Gallery, N.Y.C., 1982, Decordova Mus., Lincoln, Mass., 1989, Maine Coast Artists, Rockport, 1993, Portland (Maine) Mus. of Art, 1993. Author: 12 Points: Putting the Case for Customary Measure, 1979, Why America Should Not Go Metric, 1993. Founder Ams. for Customary Weight and Measure, N.Y.C., The Morris Farm Trust; co-founder Maine Trans. Coalition, Wicasset. Office: Old Stone Farm Wiscasset ME 04578

LESLIE, SEYMOUR MARVIN, communications executive; b. N.Y.C., Dec. 16, 1922; s. Harry and Fay (Goldstein) L.; m. Barbara Miller, Mar. 30, 1947; children: Ellen, Jane, Carol. EE, Syracuse U., 1945; grad., Advanced Mgmt. Program, Harvard U., 1971; DHL, Hofstra U., 1974. Sales mgr. Voco, Inc., N.Y.C., 1946-52; founder Pickwick Internat., Inc., Woodbury, N.Y., 1953, chmn. bd., pres., 1953-77; chmn. Leslie Group, Inc., 1977—; pres. CBS Video Enterprises div. CBS, Inc., N.Y.C., 1980-82; chmn., pres., chief exec. officer MGM/UA Home Entertainment Group, Inc., 1982-87; co-chmn. Leslie/Linton Entertainment Corp., 1993—; bd. dirs. Shorewood Packaging Corp., Allied Digital Corp., Similar Corp., Songwriters Hall of Fame; vis. disting. prof. Syracuse U. Sch. Music, 1984. Active Boy Scouts Am., 1947-50; mem. corp. adv. coun. Syracuse U.; mem. coun. Hofstra U.; bd. govs. Anti Defamation League, 1960—; v.p., dir. T.J. Martell Found.; v.p. Friars Found.; v.p., bd. dirs. Songwriter's Hall of Fame. Sgt. U.S. Army, 1942-46, PTO. Recipient Presdl. award Nat. Assn. Record Merchandisers, 1976, Disting. Svc. award, 1977, Outstanding Arendts Alumnus award Syracuse U., 1978; named Man of Yr. Time Mag., 1987; named to Video Hall of Fame, 1987. Mem. ASCAP, N.Y. Coun. for Humanities, Record Industry Assn. Am. (profl. group), B'nai B'rith, Friars Club, Harvard Club, Harvard Bus. Club. Office: Leslie Group Inc 1370 Ave Of The Americas New York NY 10019-4602

LESLIE, (ROBERT) TIM, state legislator; b. Ashland, Oreg., Feb. 4, 1942; s. Robert Tabor Leslie and Virginia (Hall) P.; m. Clydene Ann Fisher, June 15, 1962; children: Debbie, Scott. BA in Political Sci., Calif. State U., Long Beach, 1963; MPA, U. Southern Calif., L.A., 1969. Prin. analyst Sacramento County Exec. Office, Calif., 1965-69; cons. Assm. W. & M. Commn., Sacramento, 1965-72; prin. legis. rep. County Sups. Assn., Sacramento, 1972-80; founder bd. dirs. Comm. Act. Against Drg., Sacramento, 1975-83; v.p. Moss & Thompson, Inc., Sacramento, 1980-84; exec. v.p. Kuhl. Corp., Sacramento, 1984-86; assemblyman Calif. State Legislature, Sacramento, 1986-91, senator, 1991—; vice chmn. Appropriations Com., Judiciary Com.; mem. Ins. Com., Natural Resources Com. Recipient Hang Tough award Nat. Tax Limitation Com., Calif., 1987; named Legislator of Yr., Sacramento County Taxpayers League and Osteo. Surgeons of Calif., 1990, Women in Timber, 1994. Republican. Presbyterian. Capital office: 4081 State Capital Sacramento CA 95814 District office: 1200 Melody Ln Ste 110 Roseville CA 95678-5189

LESLIE, WILLIAM BRUCE, history educator; b. Orange, N.Y., July 21, 1944; s. William and Annette (Riedell) L.; children: William Andrew, Sarah Acton; m. Dorothy Kaul. BA, Princeton U., 1966; PhD, Johns Hopkins U., 1971. Asst. prof. history SUNY, Brockport, 1970-79, assoc. prof., 1979-96, prof., 1996—; vis. prof. Jordanhill Coll., Scotland, 1972, dir. grad. studies in history, 1984-90, 97—; co-dir. SUNY Social Sci. Program, London, 1978-79, 82-83, 89; cons. Regents Coll. and ETS, AP Exams. Author: Gentlemen and Scholars, 1993; mem. editl. bd. History of Higher Edn. Ann., 1991—; contbr. articles and revs. to profl jours. Fulbright scholar, Denmark, 1996-97. Mem. Orgn. Am. Historians, Am. Hist. Assn., History of Edn. Soc., Adirondack Mountain Club, Western Monroe Hist. Soc., Amnesty Internat., Princeton Club N.Y., Phi Alpha Theta. Democrat. Avocations: camping, travel, gardening. Office: SUNY History Dept Brockport NY 14420-2956

LESLIE, WILLIAM CAIRNS, metallurgical engineering educator; b. Dundee, Scotland, Jan. 6, 1920; came to U.S., 1925, naturalized, 1940; m. Florence M. Hall, 1948; 1 dau. B.Metall. Engring., Ohio State U., 1947, M.Sc., 1948, Ph.D., 1949. Metallurgist U.S. Steel Research Lab., Kearny, N.J., 1949-53; assoc. dir. staff research and devel. Thompson Products, Inc., Cleve., 1953-54; with U.S. Steel Corp., Monroeville, Pa., 1954-73; mgr. phys. metallurgy E.C. Bain Lab. for Fundamental Research, 1963-73; prof. materials engring. U. Mich., 1973-85, prof. emeritus, 1985—; adj. prof. metallurgy Bklyn. Poly. Inst., 1952-53; Battelle vis. prof. metallurgy Ohio State U., 1964-65; vis. prof. U. Melbourne, Australia, 1979; Am. Soc. Metals and AIME rep. to EJC Metric Council and Am. Nat. Metric Council, 1971-80; mem. ship research com. NRC, 1978-81; Garofalo lectr. Northwestern U., 1977; U.S. rep. Internat. Conf. Strength of Metals and Alloys, 1970-82; mem. Charles Hatchett award panel Metals Soc. Gt. Britain, 1978-81; cons. in field; mem. adv. com. div. metals and ceramics Oak Ridge Nat. Lab., 1974-75; mem. com. on basic research, advisor to Army Research Office, Durham, N.C., 1973-78; mem. ad hoc com. on non-magnetic structural steels Nat. Materials Adv. Bd., 1973-74. Author: The Physical Metallurgy of Steels, 1981; Contbr. articles to profl. jours. Served to 1st lt. C.E. U.S. Army, 1943-46. Named Disting. Alumnus Ohio State U. Coll. Engring., 1967, Disting. Alumnus lectr., 1984. Fellow Am. Soc. Metals Internat. (chmn. publs. com. 1966-68, mem. metals sci. divsn. coun. 1970-75, Pitts. chpt. Andrew Carnegie lectr. 1970, Edward DeMille Campbell lectr. 1971, Phila. chpt. Albert Sauveur lectr. 1975, Cleve. chpt. Zay Jeffries lectr. 1975, hon. mem. 1986, Barrett medal Rocky Mtn. chpt. 1992, Gold medal 1995), Inst. Materials of Gt. Britain (fellow 1984), Metall. Soc. (chmn. Inst. Metals divsn. 1971-72, bd. dirs. 1971-72, sr. fellow), Internat. Metallographic Soc. (Henry Clifton Sorby award 1991); mem. AIME (v.p., dir. 1975), Krumb lectr. 1967), Henry Marion Howe lectr. 1982), AAAS, Sigma Xi, Tau Beta Pi. Patentee in field. Home and Office: RR 7 Box 7416 Palmyra VA 22963-9510

LESLY, PHILIP, public relations counsel; b. Chgo., May 29, 1918; m. Ruth Edwards, Oct. 17, 1940 (div. 1971); 1 son, Craig.; m. Virginia Barnes, May 11, 1984. BS magna cum laude, Northwestern U., 1940. Asst. to news editor Chgo. Herald & Examiner, 1935-37; copywriter advt. dept. Sears, Roebuck & Co., Chgo., 1940-41; asst. dir. publicity Northwestern U., 1941-42; account exec. Theodore R. Sills & Co. (pub. rels.), Chgo., 1942; v.p. Theodore R. Sills & Co. (pub. rels.), 1943, exec. v.p., 1945; dir. pub. rels. Ziff-Davis Pub. Co., 1945-46; exec. v.p. Harry Coleman & Co. (pub. rels.), 1947-49; pres. Philip Lesly Co. (pub. rels.), Chgo., 1949—; lectr. pub. rels., pub. opinion to bus. and sch. groups. Co-author: Public Relations: Principles and Procedures, 1945, Everything and the Kitchen Sink, 1955; author: The People Factor, 1974, Selections from Managing the Human Climate, 1979, How We Discommunicate, 1979, Overcoming Opposition, 1984, Bonanzas and Fool's Gold, 1987; bimonthly Managing the Human Climate; editor: Public Relations in Action, 1974, Public Relations Handbook, 3d rev. edit., 1967, Lesly's Public Relations Handbook, 1971, rev. edit., 1978, 83; Lesly's Handbook of Public Relations and Communications, 1991, 2d edit., 1997; contbr. articles to bus. publs. Recipient Gold Anvil award Pub. Relations Soc. Am., 1979; voted leading active practitioner Pub. Relations Reporter Survey, 1978. Mem. Pub. Rels. Soc. Am., Phi Beta Kappa. Home and Office: 155 N Harbor Dr Apt 5311 Chicago IL 60601-7382 also: 1000 S Collier Blvd #904 Marco Island FL 34145 *One should stand out by focusing on those talents and skills that others cannot demonstrate, rather than by competing with the crowd.*

LESONSKY, RIEVA, editor-in-chief; b. N.Y.C., June 20, 1952; d. Gerald and Muriel (Cash) L. BJ, U. Mo., 1974. Researcher Doubleday & Co., N.Y.C., 1975-78; researcher Entrepreneur Mag., L.A., 1978-80, rsch. dir., 1983-84, mng. editor, 1985-86, exec. editor, 1986-87; editor Entrepreneur Mag., Irvine, Calif., 1987-90, v.p., editor-in-chief, 1990—; rsch. dir. LFP Inc., L.A., 1980-82; speaker, lect. in field. Editor: 184 Businesses Anyone Can Start, 1990, Complete Guide to Owning a Home-based Business, 1990, 168 More Businesses Anyone Can Start, 1991, 111 Businesses You Can Start for Under $10,000, 1991; contbr. articles to mags. Apptd. SBA Nat. Adv. Coun., 1994-96, 96—. Named Dist. Media Advocate of Yr., Small Bus. Adminstrn., 1993, Dist. Women in Bus. Advocate, Small Bus. Adminstrn., 1995. Mem. Women's Network for Entrepreneurial Tng. (bd. dirs., advisor, nat. steering com.), Nat. Assn. Women's Bus. Advocates (bd. dirs.). Avocations: books, magazines, baseball. Office: Entrepreneur Mag Group 2392 Morse Ave Irvine CA 92614-6234

LESS, ANTHONY ALBERT, retired naval officer; b. Salem, Ohio, Aug. 31, 1937; s. Joseph Anthony and Mildred Gertrude (Bair) L.; m. Leanne Carol Kuhl, Mar. 3, 1962; children: Robyn, Pamela, Theresa, Christina. BS in Chemistry, Heidelberg Coll., 1959. Designated naval aviator. Commd. ensign USN, 1960, advanced through grades to vice adm., 1991, ret., 1994; commdg. officer USS Wichita (AOR-1), 1979-81; chief of staff Commdr. 7th Fleet, Yokosuka, Japan, 1983-84; dir. Polit. Mil Br. JCS, Washington, 1985-87; commdr. Carrier Group One, Pacific, 1987-88, Mid. East Force, Manama, Bahrain, 1988-89; dir. Plans and Policy Navy Staff, Washington, 1989-91; comdr. Naval Air Force Atlantic Fleet, Norfolk, Va., 1991-94; pres. Assn. Naval Aviation, Washington, 1995; cons. Kaman Aerospace, Bloomfield, Conn., 1994—; v.p. K-Max mil. ops. Kaman Aerospace Corp., Bloomfield, Conn. Mem. Assn. Naval Aviation (pres. 1994), Soc. Naval Engrs. Roman Catholic. Avocations: racquetball, farming, reading. Office: K-Max Mil Ops Kaman Aerospace Blue Hills Ave Bloomfield CT 06089

LESSARD, MICHEL M., finance company executive; b. Quebec City, Can., Aug. 31, 1939; s. Maurice and Jacqueline (Lacasse) L.; m. Doris Lamoureux; children: Eric, Christine. BA, Laval U., Quebec, 1958, B in Commerce, 1961, M in Commerce, 1962; MBA, Harvard U., 1967. With Can. Ingersoll Rand, Allied Chem. Can., DomGlass Ltd., Montreal, Que., Can.; with Credit Foncier, Montreal, 1970-86, asst. gen. mgr., treas., 1978-79, sr. asst. gen. mgr., 1979-80, exec. v.p., 1980-81, pres., dir., mem. exec. com., 1981-86, pres., chief exec. officer, 1984-86; pres. Sogexfi Inc., 1986—; pres. and CEO Immobiliere Natgen Inc., 1993-95; chmn. Mildev Real Estate Svcs.; bd. dirs. Jonergin Inc., Kree Tech., Inc., Montreal, Overseas Med. Ventures N.V. Mem. Pride Can. Inc. Fellow Trust Cos. Inst., Winchester Club, Club de Golf de la Vallee du Richelieu. Home: 11 O'Reilly Apt 1503, Verdun, PQ Canada H3E 1T6

LESSARD, RAYMOND WILLIAM, bishop; b. Grafton, N.D., Dec. 21, 1930. Student, St. Paul Sem., Am. Coll., Rome. Ordained priest Roman Cath. Ch., 1956. Mem. staff Congregation for Bishops, Roman Curia, 1964-73; consecrated bishop, 1973; bishop Diocese of Savannah Diocese of Savannah, Ga., 1973-95; adj. prof. theology St. Vincent de Paul Sem., Boynton Beach, Fla., 1995—. Office: Catholic Pastoral Ctr 601 E Liberty St Savannah GA 31401-5118

LESSEM, JAN NORBERT, pharmaceuticals executive; b. Malmo, Sweden, Apr. 7, 1948; s. Slom and Frida (Marcus) L.; m. Eva K. Löfquist, July 11, 1976; children: Martin A., Sarah E. MD, U. Lund, 1974, PhD, 1982. Med. diplomate. Intern, then resident in cardiology; assoc. prof. U. Lund, Sweden, 1981-82; med. dir. Merck, Sharp & Dohme, Rahway, N.J., 1982-83, Bristol-Myers, Evansville, Ind., 1983-85; sect. head cardiology div. Syntex Research, Palo Alto, Calif., 1986-87, sr. dept. head cardiology div., 1987-90; dir. clin. investigation SB Pharma., Phila., 1991-95; med. dir. Takeda Am., Princeton, N.J., 1995—. Contbr. over 150 articles to profl. jours. Bd. dirs. Am. Swedish Hist. Mus., Phila., 1992—. Fellow Am. Coll. Cardiology, Coll. of Physicians Phila., Swedish Soc. Cardiology, Royal Swedish Coll. Med. Jewish Youth. Club: Jewish (Malmo) (pres. 1966-73). Avocations: opera, art, books, tennis, travelling. Office: Takeda am 101 Carnegie Ctr Ste 207 Princeton NJ 08540-6231

LESSEN, LARRY LEE, federal judge; b. Lincoln, Ill., Dec. 25, 1939; s. William G. and Grace L. (Plunkett) L.; m. Susan Marian Vaughn, Dec. 5, 1964; children: Laura, Lynn, William. BA, U. Ill., 1960, JD, 1962. Bar: Ill. 1962, U.S. Dist. Ct. (ctrl. dist.) Ill. 1964, U.S. Bankruptcy Ct. 1964, U.S. Tax Ct. 1982, U.S. Ct. Appeals (7th cir.) 1981, U.S. Supreme Ct. 1981. Law clk. to presiding justice U.S. Dist. Ct., 1962-64; asst. state's atty. State of Ill., Danville, 1964-67; mng. ptnr. Sebat, Swanson, Banks and Lessen, Danville, 1967-85; judge U.S. Bankruptcy Ct., Danville, 1973-85, U.S. Magistrate, Danville, 1973-84; chief judge U.S. Bankruptcy Ct., Springfield, Ill., 1985-93; U.S. bankruptcy judge Springfield divsn., 1993—. Mem. ABA, FBA, Sangamon County Bar Assn., Vermilion County Bar Assn, Nat. Conf. Bankruptcy Judges (bd. govs.), Am. Bankruptcy Inst., Lincoln-Douglas Inn of Cts. Office: US Bankruptcy Ct 235 U S Courthouse 600 E Monroe St Springfield IL 62701-1626

LESSEN, MARTIN, engineering educator, consulting engineer; b. N.Y.C., Sept. 6, 1920; s. Philip and Lena (Sukornik) L.; m. Elizabeth Scher, Aug. 27, 1948; children: Margot, Deborah, David. B.S.M.E., CCNY, 1940; M.M.E., NYU, 1942; Sc.D., MIT, 1948. Registered profl. engr. Mech. engr. Bklyn. Navy Yard, 1940-46; aero. research scientist NACA Cleve., 1948-49; prof. aero. engring. Pa. State U., State College, 1949-53; prof. and chmn. applied mechanics U. Pa., Phila., 1953-60; prof., chmn. dept. mech. engring U. Rochester, N.Y., 1960-70; Yates Meml. prof. engring. U. Rochester, 1967-83, Yates Meml. prof. engring. emeritus, 1983—; liaison scientist Office Naval Research, London, 1976-79; cons. Gen. Electric Co., 1954-58, RCA Co., 1957-64, Bausch & Lomb, 1965-75, Eastman Kodak Co., 1964—, Energy div. ORNL, 1984—; advisory com. Oak Ridge Nat. Lab., 1984-87. Author numerous papers in field; patentee in field. Sr. postdoctoral fellow NSF, Cambridge, Eng., 1966; Vollmer Fries hon. fellow Rensselaer Poly. Inst., Troy, N.Y., 1978; exchange lectr. Nat. Acad. Sci., USSR, 1967. Fellow ASME (founding chmn. energetics 1964), Am. Phys. Soc., AAAS. Club: Cosmos (Washington). Home and Office: 12 Country Club Dr Rochester NY 14618-3720

LESSENBERRY, ROBERT ADAMS, retail executive; b. Glasgow, Ky., May 7, 1926; s. Robert Long and Hugh Barret (Adams) L.; m. Mary Lloyd Howard, Dec. 26, 1946; children: Robert Howard, Hugh Barret Adams, Leigh Langford. B.A., Centre Coll. of Ky., 1950. Owner, Lessenberry Realty, Glasgow, 1954—; ptnr. Parkview Devel. Co., Glasgow, 1959-80, owner, 1980—; ptnr. Lessenberry Enterprises, Glasgow, 1968—; pres. Lessenberry Devel. Co., Inc., Glasgow, 1968-92; owner Lessenberry Real Estate, Glasgow, 1972—; pres., chmn. Lessenberry Bldg. Centre, Inc., Glasgow, 1953—, Lessenberry Electric & Plumbing, Inc., 1973—; pres. The Glasgow Ry. Co., 1965—, also dir., treas. Elder, First Presbyn. Ch., Glasgow, 1952—, tchr. sch., 1963-67, choir dir. 1953-68; vice chmn. exec. council Louisville Presbytery, 1962-66; pres., trustee Westminster Terr. Presbyn. Home for Sr. Citizens and Health Care Ctr., Louisville, 1968-79, 83-85; trustee Presbyn. Homes and Services of Ky. Inc., 1985-86; bd. dirs. Barren County (Ky.) Red Cross; pres. Glasgow Community Concert Assn., 1953-58; mem. Glasgow City Council, 1962-66, chmn. fin. 1962-66, mayor, 1966-68, chmn. water commn., 1966-68, dir. mcpl. housing, 1966-68; chmn. Glasgow Electric Plant Bd., 1977—; dir. Barren River Area Devel. Council, 1968-72; chmn. Glasgow Urban Renewal and Community Devel. Agy., 1979-82; trustee Ky. Ind. Coll. Fund, 1967—. Served with AUS, 1944-46, to lt.,1950-53. Decorated Bronze Star with cluster; named hon. citizen Metro Nashville. Mem. Glasgow C. of C. (dir. 1972-74), Glasgow-Barren County Bd. Realtors (dir. 1979—), Ind.-Ky. Hardware Assn. (pres. 1981, dir. 1975-86), Nat. Lumber and Bldg. Material Dealers Assn. (dir. 1977-80), Ky. Retail Lumber Dealers Assn. (pres. 1968-81), Hardware Wholesalers, Inc. (pres. 1973-79), Sigma Chi, Omicron Delta Kappa, Rotary (dir., pres. 1963, Paul Harris Fellow 1987), Masons, Shriners. Office: PO Box 246 Glasgow KY 42142-0246

LESSENCO, GILBERT BARRY, lawyer; b. Balt., June 19, 1929; s. Jacob David and Sarah (Bank) L.; B.S., Johns Hopkins U., 1950; LL.B., Harvard U., 1953; m. Elaine Beitler, Sept. 3, 1952; children: Susan Donna, Amy Gail, Robert Howard. Admitted to D.C. bar, 1953; since practiced in Washington; with Wilner and Bergson, 1955-60; ptnr. Wilner & Scheiner, 1960-90, Semmes, Bowen & Semmes, 1990-95, mng. ptnr., Washington, 1992-95; of counsel Thompson, Hine and Flory, 1995—. Mem., treas. Democratic Central Com., Montgomery County, Md., 1970-74; chmn. Internat. Visitors Service Council, 1962; bd. dirs. Jewish Social Service Agy. of Greater Washington, 1978—, pres., 1984-86; bd. dirs. Mental Health Assn. of Montgomery County, 1980-84, pres., 1981-82; bd. dirs. Friends of Park

Police for Montgomery County, 1996; mem. Johns Hopkins Univ. com. for Washington, 1996; trustee Meridian House Found.; commr. Washington Suburban San. Commn., 1987-93, chmn., 1989-90; co-chmn., fundraiser St. Luke's House, 1989. Served to lt. USAF, 1953-55. Named Outstanding Young Lawyer of Yr., D.C. Jr. Bar, 1965. Mem. Phi Sigma Delta (v.p.). Home: 10731 Gloxinia Dr Rockville MD 20852-3442 Office: 1920 N St NW Washington DC 20036-1601

LESSER, GERSHON MELVIN, physician, lawyer, medical and legal media commentator; b. N.Y.C., Apr. 3, 1933; s. Herman and Dora (Kronfeld) L.; m. Michelle Elyse Lesser; children: Hadrian, Aaron, Jason. BA, UCLA, 1954; MD, U. So. Calif., 1958; JD, UWLA, 1977. Diplomate Am. Bd. Forensic Medicine. Atty. in pvt. practice L.A., 1977-82; med. dir. Westside Hosp., Am. Med. Inc., Beverly Hills, 1964-75; pvt. practice cardiology L.A., 1963-92; mem. pres.'s coun. Salk Inst., La Jolla, Calif.; broadcaster KGIL Radio, San Fernando Valley, 1984-92, KCRW-Nat. Pub. Radio, Santa Monica, Calif., 1980-94; med. broadcaster KTTV, Hollywood, Calif., 1984-86; med. dir. CD, L.A., 1978-89; adj. prof. law U. West L.A. Sch. Law, 1980-87; instr. internal medicine and med. malpractice, U. So. Calif. Sch. Medicine, L.A., 1963-80. Author: Growing Younger, 1987, When You Have Chest Pain, 1989; TV commentator Alive and Well, USA Cable, L.A., 1984-95; host TV program Law, Life and Medicine. Fellow Am. Coll. Legal Medicine, Royal Soc. Health, Am. Coll. Angiology, Am. Coll. Geriatrics; mem. ABA, AMA, Calif. Med. Assn., Am. Acad. Preventive Medicine, Am. Coll. Thoracic Medicine, Am. Coll. Cardiology, Am. Soc. Internal Medicine, Calif. Bar Assn., L.A. Bar Assn., L.A. County Med. Assn.Salerni Collegium, Phi Delta Epsilon. Office: Atkins Agy 8484 Wilshire Blvd Ste 205 Beverly Hills CA 90211-3213

LESSER, JOAN L., lawyer; b. L.A.. BA, Brandeis U., 1969; JD, U. So. Calif., 1973. Bar: Calif. 1973, U.S. Dist. Ct. (cen. dist.) Calif. 1974. Assoc. Irell and Manella, L.A., 1973-80, ptnr., 1980—; mem. planning com. Ann. Real Property Inst., Continuing Edn. of Bar, Berkeley, 1990—; speaker at profl. confs. Trustee Windward Sch.; grad. Leadership L.A., 1992. Mem. Orgn. Women Execs., Order of Coif. Office: Irell and Manella LLP 1800 Avenue Of The Stars Los Angeles CA 90067-4212

LESSER, JOSEPH M., retired business executive, retail store executive; b. N.Y.C., July 27, 1928; s. Jacob and Sonia (Gustow) L.; m. Sonia Rabinowitz, Nov. 26, 1948; children: Brett Paul, Peter John. BS in Social Sci., CCNY, 1949; JD, Bklyn. Law Sch., 1953. With Allied Stores Corp., 1955—, personnel and labor relations advisor, 1955-58, dir. cen. services, 1960-68; asst. to pres., 1958-60; coordinator control and ops. divs. Allied Stores Corp., 1963-65, v.p. control and ops., electronic data processing divs., 1967-80, v.p. food services div., 1967-80, pres. Alcomp Electronic Data Systems div., 1968-75; sr. v.p., exec. group mgr. Allied Stores Corp., N.Y.C., 1980—; dir., sr. v.p. Allied Stores-Penn. Ohio-Inc., N.Y.C., 1981—, Allied Cen. Stores, Inc., N.Y.C., 1984-88; sr. v.p. Allied Stores III, Inc., N.Y.C., 1985-88; dir., exec. v.p. Allied Stores-East, Inc., N.Y.C., 1986-88, ret.; exec. v.p. Internat. Collectibles Inc., 1989-92; ret.; bd. govs. Allied Stores Assocs., 1991—; v.p., sec., treas. The Continental Collection, Inc., 1996—. Pres. Briarcliff Schs., Briarcliff Manor, N.Y., 1973; bd. dirs. North-East Council Schs., N.Y.C., 1967; life trustee Indpls. Mus. Art. Mem. Nat. Retail Mchts. Assn. (bd. dirs. 1977-79), Marco Island Art League, U.S. Power Squadrons (lt.-cruise comdr.) USCG Aux. Flotilla, Marco Island Civic Assn., Princeton Club (N.Y.C.) Calif. Yacht Club, Island Country Club, Hideaway Club (chmn. archtl. rev. com. 1991-93), Marco Bay Yacht Club, Marco Island Cruise Club. Office: 2000 Royal Marco Way #603 Marco Island FL 34145

LESSER, LAURENCE, musician, educator; b. Los Angeles, Oct. 28, 1938; s. Moses Aaron and Rosalyne Anne (Asner) L.; m. Masuko Ushioda, Dec. 23, 1971; children—Erika, Adam. AB, Harvard U., 1961; student of Gaspar Cassadó, Germany, 1961-62; student of Gregor Piatigorsky, 1963-66. Mem. faculty U. So. Calif., Los Angeles, 1963-70, Peabody Inst., Balt., 1970-74; mem. faculty New Eng. Conservatory Music, Boston, 1974—, pres., 1983-96, pres. emeritus, 1997—; former vis. prof. Eastman Sch. Music, Rochester, N.Y.; vis. prof. Toho Gakuen Sch. Music, Tokyo, 1973-95; performed with New Japan Philharm., Boston Symphony, London Philharm., L.A. Philharm. and Marlboro, Spoleto, Casals, Santa Fe and Banff festivals; rec. artist; overseer emeritus Boston Symphony Orch. Trustee emeritus WGBH Ednl. Found.; mem. adv. coun. Chamber Music Am. Recipient prize Tchaikovsky Competition, Moscow, 1966; Fulbright scholar, 1961-62; Ford Found. grantee, 1972. Mem. Am. Acad. Arts and Scis., Harvard Mus. Assn., Tavern Club, Phi Beta Kappa, Pi Kappa Lambda, Sigma Alpha Iota. Jewish. Home: 65 Bellevue St Newton MA 02158-1918 Office: New Eng Conservatory Music 290 Huntington Ave Boston MA 02115-5018

LESSER, LAWRENCE J., advertising agency executive; b. Bklyn., June 1, 1939; m. Joanna Savarese, Aug. 26, 1962; children: Eileen, Kristin. AAS, N.Y.C. Community Coll., 1959. Asst. acct. exec. Friend Reiss Advt., 1959-63; v.p., acct. supr. sr. v.p. L.W. Frohlich, 1963-72; sr. v.p Medicus Comm. Inc., N.Y.C., 1972-76; pres., ceo, chmn. Medicus Group Internat., N.Y.C., 1976-95; exec. v.p. D'Arcy Masius Benton & Bowles, Inc., N.Y.C., 1996—, also bd. dirs., mem. exec. com. Office: D'Arcy Masius Benton & Bowles Inc 1675 Broadway New York NY 10019-5820

LESSER, WENDY, literary magazine editor, writer, consultant; b. Santa Monica, Calif., Mar. 20, 1952; d. Murray Leon Lesser and Millicent (Gerson) Dillon; m. Richard Rizzo, Jan. 18, 1985; 1 stepchild, Dov Antonio; 1 child, Nicholas. BA, Harvard U., 1973; MA, Cambridge (Eng.) U., 1975; PhD, U. Calif., Berkeley, 1982. Founding ptnr. Lesser & Ogden Assocs., Berkeley, 1977-81; founding editor The Threepenny Rev., Berkeley, 1980—; Bellagio resident Rockefeller Found, Italy, 1984. Author: The Life Below the Ground, 1987, His Other Half, 1991, Pictures at an Execution, 1994, A Director Calls, 1997; editor: Hiding in Plain Sight, 1993. Fellow NEH, 1983, 92, Guggenheim fellow, 1988, ACLS, 1996. Democrat. Office: The Threepenny Rev PO Box 9131 Berkeley CA 94709-0131

LESSER, WILLIAM HENRI, marketing educator; b. N.Y.C., Dec. 19, 1946; s. Arthur and Ethel (Boissevain) L.; m. Susan Elizabeth Bailey, Dec. 27, 1975; children: Andrew, Jordan. BA in Geography, U. Wash., 1968; MS in Resource Econs., U. R.I., 1974; PhD in Agrl. Econ., U. Wis., 1978, 1993-94; From asst. to assoc. prof. mktg. Cornell U., Ithaca, N.Y., 1978-91, prof., 1991—; acting exec. dir. Internat. Svc. for Acquisition of Bio-tech Applications, 1994-95; with Internat. Acad. Environ., Geneva, 1993-94; grad. field rep. Dept. Agrl. Econs., Ithaca, 1985-88; dir. Cornell Western Socs. Program, 1991-93; cons. World Bank, Washington, US/AID, Winrock Internat., Morrilton, Ark. Editor: Animal Patents: The Legal Economic and Social Issues, 1990; author: Equitable Patent Protection in the Developing World, 1991, Marketing Livestock and Meat, 1993, Sustainable Use of Genetic Resources under the Correction on Biological Diversity. Zone capt. Dem. com. Town of Ithaca, 1985-90, mem. planning bd., 1987-93. Nat. fellow Kellogg Found., 1988-91. Mem. Am. Agrl. Econ. Assn., Patent & Trademark Office Soc. Avocations: gardening, painting, antique cars. Home: 406 Coddington Rd Ithaca NY 14850-6012 Office: Cornell U Dept Argl Econs 405 Warren Hall Ithaca NY 14853-7801

LESSIN, LAWRENCE STEPHEN, hematologist, oncologist, educator; b. Washington, Oct. 14, 1937; s. Maurice and Anna (Brodsky) L.; m. Judith Ann Lustok, Dec. 23, 1961; children: Jennifer Lynn, Jonathan Lustok, Martine Rose. Student, U. Mich., 1955-58; M.D., U. Chgo., 1962. Diplomate Am. Bd. Internal Medicine (assoc. mem. 1976-82). Intern, resident in internal medicine, chief resident, fellow in hematology Hosp. U. Pa., 1962-67; spl. fellow Nat. Heart Inst., Inst. for Cell Pathology, Paris, 1967-68; asst. prof. medicine Duke U., 1968-70; assoc. prof. medicine and pathology George Washington U., 1970-74, prof. medicine and pathology, dir. div. hematology and oncology, 1974—; dir. George Washington U. Cancer Ctr., Washington, 1991-93; med. dir. Washington Cancer Inst. Washington Hosp. Ctr., 1993—; vis. physician medicine br. Nat. Cancer Inst., 1971-74; cons. hematology Washington VA Hosp., 1971—; cons. ARC Blood Bank, 1972—, Nat. Naval Med. Ctr., Bethesda, Md., 1974—, Nat. Heart, Lung and Blood Inst., 1974; Walter Reed Army Med. Ctr., 1978—; ad hoc cons. Nat. Heart, Lung and Blood Inst., Study Sect. Program-Project Grants, 1977; mem. NASA Biomed. Rev. Panel, 1981-88; chmn. div. blood diseases and resources adv. com. Nat. Heart, Blood and Lung Inst., NIH, 1985-86, mem. inst. scientific rev. com., 1997—; chmn., program dir. Assn. Hematology-Oncology, 1983-87; vol. spl. emphasis panel Comprehensive Sickle Cell SCOR Applications, 1997—. editorial reviewer: Annals of Internal Medicine, 1969—, Nouvelle Revue de Hematologie, 1970—, Blood, Jour. Hematology, 1971—, Archives of Internal Medicine, 1972—, Nature, 1973, Jour. Clin. Investigation, 1973—, New Eng. Jour. Medicine; mem. editorial Blood Cells, 1979—, Hematologic Pathology, 1985—; contbr. articles to profl. jours., chpts. to books. Served to capt. M.C. USAR, 1963-69. Named Intern of Year U. Pa. Hosp., 1963; nominee for Golden Apple award, 1975; Nat. Heart Inst. spl. fellow Paris, 1967-68. Fellow ACP, Internat. Soc. Hematology; mem. Am. Coll. Physicians (chair Hematology Med. Knowledge Self-Assessment program, 1992—), Am. Soc. Hematology, Am. Fedn. Clin. Research, Am. Soc. Clin. Oncology, Am. Blood Commn., Am. Soc. Internal Medicine, D.C. Med. Soc., Internat. Blood Cells Club, Am. Soc. Clin. Oncology, Sigma Xi, Alpha Omega Alpha. Club: Cosmos (Washington). Office: Washington Cancer Inst 110 Irving St NW Washington DC 20010-2931

LESSIN, MICHAEL EDWARD, oral-maxillofacial surgeon; b. Chgo., Jan. 24, 1944; m. Cathy Irene Wilkinson, June 22, 1968; children: Amy Suzanne, Beth Michele. BDS, U. Ill., 1965; DDS, Ill. Coll. Dentistry, 1969. Diplomate Am. Bd. Oral Maxillofacial Surgery. Commd. 1st lt. U.S. Army, 1969, advanced through grades to Col., 1983, retired, 1989; resident in oral and maxillofacial surgery Letterman Army Med. Ctr., San Francisco, 1974-77; clin. assoc. prof. dept. Oral and Maxillofacial Surgery U. Tex., San Antonio, 1985-89; clin. assoc. prof. Surgery W.Va. U., Morgantown, 1990—; assoc. dept. Dental Medicine and Surgery, dept. Pediatrics Geisinger Med. Ctr., Danville, Pa., 1990—; clin. assoc. prof. surgery Med. Coll. Pa., Hahnemann, 1995—; cons. ROK Ctrl. Army Hosp., Seoul, Korea, 1977-79, U.S. Army Dental Activity Gen. Practice Residency Program, Ft. Sill, Okla., 1985-86, 87, to surgeon gen., 1987-89, William Beaumont Army Med. Ctr., El Paso, Tex., 1990-91, Dwight D. Eisenhower Med. Ctr., Augusta, Ga., 1990, residency program, Ft. Campbell, Ky., 1992-93; lectr. in field. contbr. articles to profl. jours. Mem. ADA, Am. Trauma Soc., Pa. Dental Assn., Tri-county Dental Assn., 38th Parallel Dental Soc. Avocations: travel, golf. Office: Geisinger Med Ctr Academy Ave Danville PA 17822

LESSING, BRIAN REID, actuary; b. Miami, Fla., Feb. 2, 1954; s. Kenneth Oliver Ralph and Margaret (Takash) L. AB magna cum laude, Princeton (N.J.) U., 1976; MS, N.Y.U., 1979. Cert. FSA, Soc. Actuaries, 1989, CLU, Am. Coll., 1992. Tech. asst. Mutual of N.Y., 1980-84; actuarial asst. Equitable Life Assurance, N.Y.C., 1984-87; asst. actuary, 1987-89, assoc. actuary, 1989-91, actuary, 1991-93, asst. v.p., 1993—; adj. instr. N.Y. Inst. Tech., 1979, Pace U., N.Y.C., 1979, 80; adj. asst. prof. The Coll. of Ins., N.Y.C., 1989-91. Mem. ch. coun. exec. com. Community Ch. of N.Y., 1984-87, fin. com., 1989—. Recipient Rsch. assistantship N.Y.U., 1976-80. Fellow Soc. of Actuaries; mem. Am. Soc. CLU and ChFC, Am. Acad. Actuaries, Phi Beta Kappa. Unitarian Universalist. Home: 433 W 24th St Apt 5F New York NY 10011-1203 Office: Equitable Life Assurance 14th Flr Location 14.093 1290 Avenue Of The Americas New York NY 10104-0199

LESSING, DORIS (MAY), writer; b. Kermanshah, Persia, Oct. 22, 1919; d. Alfred Cook Tayler and Emily Maude McVeagh; m. Frank Charles Wisdom, 1939 (div. 1943); m. Gottfried Anton Nicholas Lessing, 1945 (div. 1949); children: John W. (dec.), Jean W., Peter L. Educated in, So. Rhodesia; DLitt (hon.), Princeton U., 1989, Durham U., 1990; D Fellow in Lit., Sch., Eng. Am. Studies, U. East Anglia, 1991; DLitt (hon.), Warwick U., 1994; LittD (hon.), Bard Coll., 1994, Harvard U., 1995. Author: (novels) The Grass is Singing, 1950, Five Short Novels, 1953, Retreat to Innocence, 1959, The Golden Notebook, 1962 (Prix Medicis Award for work translated into French, 1976), Children of Violence, 5 vols., 1964-69, Briefing For a Descent Into Hell, 1971, The Summer Before the Dark, 1973, The Memoirs of a Survivor, 1975, Shikasta, 1979, Marriages Between Zones Three, Four and Five, 1980, The Sirian Experiments, 1981 (Booker McConnell Prize nominee, 1981), The Making of the Representative for Planet 8, 1982, Documents Relating to the Sentimental Agents in the Volyen Empire, 1983, The Diaries of Jane Somers (Diary of a Good Neighbour, 1983, and If the Old Could..., 1984, pub. under pseudonym Jane Somers), The Good Terrorist, 1985 (W.H. Smith Lit. Award, 1986; Palermo Prize, 1987; Premio Internazionale Monello, 1987), The Fifth Child, 1988, The Libretto of the Making of the Representative for Planet 8, 1988, The Fifth Child, 1988, Playing the Game, 1995, Love, Again, 1996; (nonfiction) Going Home, 1968, In Pursuit of the English, 1961, Particularly Cats, 1967, Prisons We Choose to Live Inside, 1987, The Wind Blows Away Our Words...and Other Documents Relating to the Afghan Resistance, 1987, Particularly Cats and More Cats...And Rufus, 1991, African Laughter: Four Visits to Zimbabwe, 1992; (autobiography) Under My Skin: Volume One of My Autobiography, to 1949, 1994; (short stories) This Was the Old Chief's Country, 1952, The Habit of Loving, 1957, A Man and Two Women, 1963, African Stories, 1965, The Temptation of Jack Orkney and Other Stories, 1978, The Story of a Non-Marrying Man, 1972, Collected African Stories, 1978, This Was Old Chief Country, 1952, The Sun Between Their Feet, 1981, London Observed: Stories and Sketches (U.K.)/The Real Thing (U.S.), 1992; (collections) To Room 19 (Collected Stories Vols. 1 and 2), 1978, The Doris Lessing Reader, 1990; (plays) Each in His Own Wilderness, 1958, Play with a Tiger, 1973, The Singing Door, 1973; (essays) A Small Personal Voice, 1974; (poetry) Fourteen Poems, 1959; (libretto for opera with music by Philip Glass) The Making of the Representative for Planet 8, 1988; also newspaper reports. Recipient Somerset Maugham award Soc. of Authors, 1954, Austrian State prize for European Lit., 1981, Shakespeare prize, Hamburg, 1982, Grinzane Cavour award, Italy, 1989; named Woman of Yr. Norway, 1995. Fellow MLA (hon.); mem. Nat. Inst. Arts and Letters., Am. Acad. Arts & Letters (assoc. mem. 1974), Inst. Cultural Rsch. Office: care Jonathan Clowes Ltd, 10 Iron Bridge House, Bridge Approach, London NW1 8BD, England

LESSITER, FRANK DONALD, magazine editor; b. Pontiac, Mich., Oct. 5, 1939; s. Milon John and Donalda Belle (Taylor) L.; m. Pamela Ann Fuzak, Nov. 23, 1963; children—Deborah, Susan, Michael, Kelly. B.S. in Dairy Sci, Mich. State U., 1961, postgrad. in Advt., 1962-65. Info. specialist Mich. Coop. Extension Service, East Lansing, 1962-65; exec. editor Agrl. Pubs., Milw., 1965-68; editor Nat. Livestock Producer mag., Chgo., 1969-72, No-Till Farmer, 1972—; v.p., editor Nat. Livestock Producer, 1974-78; editor Rural Builder, 1977-89; exec. v.p. Reiman Assocs., 1977-81; editor Farmer's Digest, 1988—; pres. Am. Farm Bldg. Services, Inc., 1981-89, No-Till Farmer, Inc., 1981—, Lessiter Publs., Brookfield, Wis., 1989—; editor Ridge Till Hotline, 1991-96, Am. Farrier's Jour., 1992—. Author: (with Pamela Ann Fuzak Lessiter) Agricultural Travel Guide, 1971, Horsepower, 1977, 100 Most Common No-Tillage Questions, 1981; editor: Winning Hoops, 1996—; editor, pub. Am. Farriers Jour., 1992—; contbg. author: (with Pamela Ann Fuzak Lessiter) Commodity Yearbook, 1972, 75. Named Farm Mag. Editor of Year Dekalb AgResearch Program, 1972, Newsletter Editor of Year Newsletter Clearing House, 1973, Best Farm Mktg. Writer CIBA-Ceigy Awards Program, 1976, Farm Mag. Writer of Yr., 1977. Mem. Nat. Press Photographers Assn., Nat. Agrl. Mktg. Assn., Am. Agrl. Editors Assn. (Photographer of Year 1975). Home: 16000 Choctaw Trl Brookfield WI 53005-5504 Office: PO Box 624 Brookfield WI 53008-0624

LESTAGE, DANIEL BARFIELD, retired naval officer, physician; b. Jennings, La., July 7, 1939; s. Henry Oscar Jr. and Juliet Xavier (Barfield) L.; m. Helen Newcomer, Mar. 9, 1963; children: Juliet Lestage Hirsch, Diane Lestage Davis, Daniel B. Jr. Grad., La. State U., 1959, MD, 1963; grad., Naval Sch. Aviation, 1964; MPH, Tulane U., 1969; diploma, Indsl. Coll. Armed Forces, 1978. Diplomate Am. Bd. Preventive Medicine (trustee 1988-94), Am. Bd. Family Practice. Commd. ensign USN, 1962, advanced through grades to rear adm., 1986; rotating intern Charity Hosp., New Orleans, 1963-64; resident in family practice Lafayette (La.) Charity Hosp., 1964; student flight surgeon Naval Sch. Aviation Medicine, Pensacola, Fla., 1964; staff flight surgeon/med. officer Carrier Air Wing 16 USS Oriskany, NAS Lemoore, Calif., 1965-67; sr. med. officer Naval Med. Clinic, NAS New Orleans, 1967-68, USS John F. Kennedy, Norfolk, Va., 1971-73; resident in aerospace medicine Naval Aerospace Med. Inst., Pensacola, 1969-71; sr. med. officer Br. Clinic, Jacksonville NAS, 1973-77; chief preventive medicine dept. Naval Regional Med. Ctrs., Jacksonville, 1973-77; spl. asst. to surgeon gen. Navy Bur. Medicine and Surgery Dept. Navy, Washington, 1978-81; head operational medicine br., aeromed. advisor Office of Chief Naval Ops., Washington, 1978-81; dir. clin. svcs., dir. med. edn., exec. officer Naval Regional Med. Ctr., Portsmouth, Va., 1981-83; commanding officer Naval Hosp., Millington, Tenn., 1983-84; comdr. U.S. Naval Med. Command, London, 1984-86; fleet med. officer U.S. Naval Forces Europe, 1984-86; fleet surgeon U.S. Atlantic Fleet, Norfolk, 1986-88; command surgeon U.S. Atlantic Command U.S. Atlantic Command/Supreme Allied Comdr., Norfolk, 1986-89; asst. dir. naval medicine Office of Chief Naval Ops., 1989; insp. gen. Navy Bur. of Medicine and Surgery, 1989-90; comdr. Naval Med. Ctr., Portsmouth, Va., 1990-92; corp. med. dir. Blue Cross/Blue Shield of Fla., Jacksonville, 1992-95, v.p. med. ops., 1995-97, v.p. profl. & orgnl. rels., 1997—; asst. dean Ea. Va. Med. Sch., Norfolk, 1981-83, assoc. dean, 1990-92; del. AMA ho. of dels from Aerospace Med. Assn., 1993—; del. Fla. Med. Assn. ho. of dels. from Fla Soc. Preventative Medicine, 1995—. Dir. Blood Bank, Jacksonville, 1973-77; bd. dirs. Cath. Family Svcs., Portsmouth, 1981-83, Fraser-Millington Mental Health Ctr., Memphis, 1983-84. Decorated Legion of Merit with four oak leaf clusters, Meritorious Svc. medal, Air medal with oak leaf cluster, Navy Commendation medal; recipient Physician's Recognition award AMA, 1972, 75, 78, 81, 85, 88, 91, 94, 97. Fellow Am. Coll. Physicians, Am. Coll. Preventive Medicine, Am. Acad. Family Physicians, Aerospace Med. Assn. (pres. 1988-89); mem. AMA (del. 1993—), Fla. Acad. Family Physicians (bd. dirs. 1995-98), Fla. Soc. for Preventive Medicine (pres. 1995-96), Fla. Med. Assn. (del. 1995—), VFW, Am. Legion, Internat. Acad. Aviation and Space Medicine, Assn. Mil. Surgeons U.S., Soc. Med. Cons. ro Armed Forces, Rotary, Elks. Roman Catholic. Avocations: travel, cooking. Home: 1782 Long Slough Walk Orange Park FL 32073-7033 Office: Blue Cross/Blue Shield Fla 8657 Baypine Rd Jacksonville FL 32256-7513

LESTER, ANDREW WILLIAM, lawyer; b. Mpls., Feb. 17, 1956; s. Richard G. and Marion Louise (Kurtz) L.; m. Barbara Regina Schmitt, Nov. 22, 1978; 1 child, Susan Erika. Student, Ludwig-Maximilians Univ., Munich, 1975-76; BA, Duke U., 1977; MS in Fgn. Service, JD, Georgetown U., 1981. Bar: Okla. 1981, D.C. 1985, Tex. 1990, U.S. Supreme Ct. 1992, Colo. 1995. Cons. Dresser Industries, Inc., Washington, 1979-81; assoc. Conner & Winters, Tulsa, 1981-82; asst. atty. City of Enid, Okla., 1982-84; ptnr. Lester, Loving & Davies, P.L.L.C. and predecessor firms, Edmond, 1984—; adj. prof. Okla. City Univ. Sch. of Law; lectr. in field; U.S. magistrate judge Western Dist. Okla., 1988-96; constl. law specialist Ctrl. and East European Law Initiative, ABA, Ukraine, Belarus and Moldova, 1993. Author: Constitutional Law and Democracy, 1994; contbr. book revs. and articles to profl. jours. Intern Office of Senator Bob Dole, Washington, 1977-78; mem. transition team EEOC Office Pres.-Elect Reagan, Washington, 1980-81; chmn. Enid Police Civil Service Commn., 1985-87; bd. dirs. Enid Habitat for Humanity, 1986-88, Booker T. Washington Community Ctr., Enid, 1987-90; mem. Martin Luther King, Jr. Holiday Commn. of Enid, 1988-91. Fellow Okla. Bar Found.; mem. Okla. Bar Assn., D.C. Bar Assn., Tex. Bar Assn., Colo. Bar Assn., Okla. Assn. Mcpl. Attys. (bd. dirs. 1987-91, 94—, gen. counsel 1987-88, pres. 1988-90, 94—), Oklahoma County Bar Assn., Def. Rsch. Inst. (govt. liability com.), Federalist Soc. (vice chmn. civil rights practice group 1996—, pres. Ctrl. Okla. chpt. 1996—). Republican. Baptist. Avocations: German language, cartography. Office: Lester Loving & Davies PLLC 1505 Renaissance Blvd Edmond OK 73013-3018

LESTER, BARNETT BENJAMIN, editor, foreign affairs officer; b. Toronto, Can., Aug. 7, 1912; came to U.S., 1917; s. Louis and Lena (Rubenstein) L.; m. Rita Constance Hatcher, May 31, 1943 (dec.); m. Claudette Yvonne Gionet, Apr. 19, 1970. Student, Cleve. Coll., Western Res. U., 1933; AB (Miller Scholar), Oberlin Coll., 1934, (grad. scholar), 1934-35; grad. scholar, Nat. Inst. Pub. Affairs, Washington, 1935-36; scholar, Syracuse U., 1935-36, Acad. Internat. Law, The Hague, 1936; student, fellow, Fletcher Sch. Law and Diplomacy, 1935-36; student, Fgn. Service Inst., 1952, 56, Dep. Chiefs Mission Seminar, Dept. State, 1981. Mem. staff, corr. Cleve. Plain Dealer and Cleve. News, 1928-33; feature writer Boston Sunday Post, 1935-38; mng. editor, later editor Exclusive Features Syndicate, Boston, 1936-38; asso. editor The Writer mag., Boston, 1936-38; info. officer Dept. Justice, 1938-41; asst. dir. feature div. Office Inter-Am. Affairs, 1941-45; info. publicist Dept. State, 1945; pub. relations exec. Al Paul Lefton Co., Inc., Phila., 1945-46; info. specialist, chief motion pictures, acting chief audio-visual sect. USPHS, Office Surgeon Gen., 1947-48; info. specialist Fed. Security Agy., 1948-49; chief editorial and prodn. sect. Nat. Heart Inst. (info. specialist, sci. reports br. NIH), 1949-52; pub. info. chief NIH, 1950; review officer Dept. State, 1952-61, supervisory publs. editor, 1961-63, editor-writer, 1963-73, pub. info. officer, 1973-85; assoc. editor Newsletter, 1977-81; assoc. editor State Mag., 1981-86, sr. editor, 1986-89, on contract, 1989; pub. affairs specialist, 1985-89; fgn. svc. res. officer, 1965-73, assigned to policy and pub. info. affairs program, 1962-67; assigned to policy and pub. info affairs program Newsletter and Info. Office, Office Dir. Gen. Fgn. Svc., 1967-81, Office Pub. Affairs and State Mag., Office Dir. Gen. Fgn. Svc., 1981-89, Career counselor Oberlin Coll., 1940—; rep. Office Surg. Gen., USPHS, on Interdepartmental com. med. tng. aids, 1947-48; invited participant U.S. Commr. Edn. Conf. Audio-Visual Aids to Edn., 1948; mem. info. staff Pres.'s Midcentury White House Conf. on Children and Youth, 1950; mem. spl. survey audio-visual tchg. and tng. aids Nat. Heart Inst., USPHS and Assn. Am. Med. Colls., 1951; invited participant symposium The White House: The First 200 Yrs., White House Hist. Assn., 1992. Author: (with others) The Writer's Handbook, 1936. Recipient War Service award Coord. Inter-Am. Affairs, 1945, Meritorious Honor Group award Dept. State, 1967, 40 Year Service award, 1979, Spl. Achievement award, 1979, Superior Honor award, 1983, Superior Honor Group award, 1984; Loy W. Henderson—Joseph C. Satterthwaite award for pub. service, 1987; Bicentennial award Am. Revolution Bicentennial Adminstrn., 1977; award for excellence Soc. Tech. Communications, 1982; award for achievement Soc. Tech. Communication, 1985; 50 Yr. Pin, Fletcher Sch. Law and Diplomacy, 1986; 50 Yr. Svc. award, bronze plaque for 51 yrs. U.S. Govt. Svc., 1989; John Jacob Rogers award for outstanding career achievement, Dept. State, 1989; cert. commendation Dept. State, 1989. Mem. Am. Fgn. Svc. Assn., Am. Polit. Sci. Assn., Am. Acad. Polit. and Social Sci., Acad. Polit. Sci., Diplomatic and Consular Officers Ret., Fed. Editors Assn. (Blue Pencil award 1975), Nat. Assn. Govt. Communicators (Blue Pencil Publs. award 1983), Consular Officers Assn., Marquis Libr. Assn. (adv. mem.), U.S. Diplomatic Courier Assn. (hon., Silver Diplomatic Courier medal and cert. appreciation 1990), Nat. Press Found. (charter), Nat. Trust for Hist. Preservation, U.S. Capitol Hist. Soc., Civil War Trust (charter), Assn. for Diplomatic Studies and Tng., Internat. Club (charter, honored as founding mem.) (Washington), Nat. Press Club, Silver Owl Club (Washington), Am. Fgn. Svc. (Washington). Two suggestions adopted by U.S. Postal Service resulted in issuing Treaty of Paris stamp and Great Seal of U.S. embossed stamped envelope. Home: 2507 N Lincoln St Arlington VA 22207-5223

LESTER, CHARLES TURNER, JR., lawyer; b. Plainfield, N.J., Jan. 31, 1942; s. Charles Turner and Marlyn Elizabeth (Tate) L.; m. Nancy Hudmon Simmons, Aug. 19, 1967; children: Susan Hopson, Mary Elizabeth. B.A., Emory U., 1964, J.D., 1967. Bar: Ga. 1966, U.S. Dist. Ct. (no. dist.) Ga. 1967, D.C. 1970, U.S. Ct. Appeals (5th cir.) 1967, U.S. Ct. Appeals (11th cir.) 1982, U.S. Ct. Appeals (10th cir.) 1984. Assoc. Sutherland, Asbill & Brennan, Atlanta, 1970-77, ptnr., 1977—. Mem. Leadership Atlanta, 1980-81; pres. Atlanta Legal Aid Soc., 1979-80. Lt. JAGC, USNR, 1967-70. Fellow Am. Bar Found; mem. ABA, State Bar of Ga. (pres. young lawyers sect. 1977-78, bd. govs. 1977-78, 80-93, chmn. formal adv. opinion bd. 1987-90, exec. com. 1977-78, 1987-93, pres. 1991-92), Atlanta Bar Assn., Am. Judicature Soc., Lawyers Club Atlanta (treas. 1982-83, exec. com. 1982-90, 2d v.p. 1986-87, 1st v.p. 1987-88, pres. 1988-89), D.C. Bar Assn., Ga. C. of C. (bd. dirs. 1994—). Democrat. Methodist. Home: 1955 Musket Ct Stone Mountain GA 30087-1703 Office: Sutherland Asbill & Brennan 999 Peachtree St NE Atlanta GA 30309-3964

LESTER, JULIUS B., author; b. St. Louis, Jan. 27, 1939; s. W.D. and Julia (Smith) L.; m. Milan Sabatini; children: Jody Simone, Malcolm Coltrane, Elena Milad, David Julius, Lian Brennan. BA, Fisk U., 1960. Prof. Judaic studies U. Mass., Amherst, 1971—. Profl. musician and singer, recording for Vanguard Records, folklorist and writer, dir., Newport Folk Festival, 1966-68; author: (with Pete Seeger) The 12-String Guitar as Played by Leadbelly, 1965, Look Out, Whitey, Black Power's Gon' Get Your Mama, 1968, To Be a Slave, 1968 (Newberry Honor book 1968), Black Folktales, 1969, Revolutionary Notes, 1969, Search for the New Land, 1970, The Knee-High Man and Other Tales, 1972, Long Journey Home: Stories from Black History, 1972, Two Love Stories, 1972, Who I Am, 1974, All Is Well, 1976, This Strange New Feeling, 1982, Do Lord Remember Me, 1985, The Tales of Uncle Remus: The Adventures of Brer Rabbit, 1987, The Tales of Uncle Remus, The Further Adventures of Brer Rabbit, 1988, Lovesong: Becoming a Jew, 1988, How Many Spots Does A Leopard Have?, 1989, Further Tales of Uncle Remus, 1990, Falling Pieces of the Broken Sky, 1990, Last Tales of Uncle Remus, 1994, And All Our Wounds Forgiven, 1994, The Man Who Knew Too Much, 1994, John Henry, 1994 (Boston Globe-Horn Book award 1995), Othello: A Novel, 1995, Sam and the Tigers, 1996; editor: Seventh Son: The Thoughts and Writings of W.E.B. DuBois, vol. 1 and 2, 1971; assoc. editor: Sing Out, 1964-69; contbg. editor: Broadside of New York, 1964-70. Office: U Mass Judaic Studies Herter Hall Amherst MA 01003 *The older I become, the greater the mystery of my life. I think I see my life as journey into mystery, in awe and fear, with joy and apprehension. Whatever my accomplishments, my life is more than and other than, and finally, best expressed by the silence of winter snow, prairie skies, or a feathered serpent. To be as true and eloquent as a drop of water hanging from a twig—that is my ideal.*

LESTER, JUNE, library-information studies educator; b. Sandersville, Ga., Aug. 25, 1942; d. Charles DuBose and Frances Irene (Cheney) L.; 1 child, Anna Elisabeth Engle. B.A., Emory U., 1963, M.Librarianship, 1971; D in Library Sci., Columbia U., 1987; cert. in advanced librarianship Columbia U., 1982. Asst. prof., cataloger U. Tenn. Library, Knoxville, 1971-73; librarian div. library and info. mgmt. Emory U., Atlanta, 1973-81, asst. prof. div. library and info. mgmt., 1976-80, assoc. prof., 1980-87; accreditation officer Am. Library Assn., 1987-91; assoc. dean, assoc. prof. Sch. Libr. and Info. Scis., U. North Tex., Denton, 1991-93; dir., prof. Sch. Libr. and Info. Studies, U. Okla., Norman, 1993—. UCLA sr. fellow, 1987. Mem. ALA (council mem. 1987), Assn. for Libr. and Info. Sci. Edn. (bd. dirs. 1985-87, 94-97, pres. 1995-96), Am. Soc. Info. Sci., Okla. Library Assn., Phi Beta Kappa, Beta Phi Mu. Unitarian. Home: 2006 Trailview Ct Norman OK 73072-6654 Office: U Okla Sch Libr and Info Studies 401 W Brooks St Norman OK 73019-6030

LESTER, LANCE GARY, education educator, researcher; b. Wausau, Wis., Sept. 12, 1943; s. Lawrence Harold and Joanna Susan (Martin) L.; m. Rochelle Damson McDermott, Sept. 25, 1973 (div.); stepchildren: Barbara Ann Brady, John Patrick McDermott. BA in English, St. John's U., 1965, MS in Secondary Edn., 1967; MA in Cinematography, NYU, 1969. Prof. football player N.Y. Jets/Titans, N.Y.C., 1960-61; educator Newtown High Sch., Elmhurst, N.Y., 1965—; mgr. B. S. Klein Real Estate, Bayside, N.Y., 1974—, track coach, 1973—; prof. film St. John's U., Jamaica, N.Y., 1981—; prof. White Magic Moving Pictures & Video, Glendale, N.Y., 1986—; lectr. N.Y. Jet Parking & Chowder Soc., N.Y.C., 1986, Queensborough Coll. Film Forum, Bayside, 1988—. Named N.Y.C. Track Coach of Yr., 1986. Mem. United Fedn. of Tchrs., N.Y.C. Coun. of English, Cinephiles. Roman Catholic. Avocations: Karate, track, travel agent. Office: Newtown High Sch 48-01 90th St Elmhurst NY 11373

LESTER, MALCOLM, historian, educator; b. Georgetown, Ga., Dec. 9, 1924; s. Malcolm Nicholson and Emmie (Bledsoe) L.; m. Pauline Hardeman Domingos, July 7, 1956; 1 dau., Pauline Malcolm (dec.). A.B., Mercer U., 1945; M.A., U. Va., 1946, Ph.D., 1954; Fulbright scholar, U. London (King's Coll.), 1949-50. Instr. history Mercer U., Macon, Ga., 1946-47, asst. prof., 1947-50, assoc. prof., 1950-54, prof., 1954-59, dean Coll. Liberal Arts, 1955-59; prof. history Davidson (N.C.) Coll., 1959-89, Charles A. Dana prof. history, 1977-89, prof. emeritus, 1989—, chmn. history dept., 1962-87; dir. Davidson summer program at Cambridge U., 1981-87. Author: Anthony Merry Redivivus: A Reappraisal of the British Minister to the United States, 1803-6, 1978; contbr. to American National Biography, Dictionary of National Biography; contbr. book revs. to various hist. jours. Elder Presbyn. Ch., 1964—, moderator Mecklenburg Presbytery, 1974; mem. internat. adv. coun. U. Buckingham, England, 1980-89. Recipient Algernon Sydney Sullivan award Mercer U., 1945, Thomas Jefferson award Davidson Coll., 1982. Fellow Royal Hist. Soc. (Eng.); mem. Am. So. Hist. Assns., Orgn. Am. Historians, Nat. Trust (Eng.), Hist. Assn. (Eng.), Conf. Brit. Studies, AAUP, Nat. Assn. Scholars, Soc. Nautical Rsch. (Eng.), English Speaking Union, Raven Soc., Sons Confederate Vets., Colonnade Club (U. Va.), Phi Beta Kappa (sen. United chpts. 1976-82, com. qualifications 1978-82), Omicron Delta Kappa. Republican. Presbyterian. Home: 228 Roundway Down PO Box 548 Davidson NC 28036-0548

LESTER, PAMELA ROBIN, lawyer; b. N.Y.C., Aug. 5, 1958; d. Howard M. and Patricia Barbara (Briger) L. Student, Princeton U., 1978-79; BA cum laude, Amherst Coll., 1980; JD, Fordham U., 1983. Bar: N.Y. 1984, D.C. 1985. With Advantage Internat., Inc., Washington, 1984-89, gen. counsel, 1987-89; assoc. Akin, Gump, Strauss, Hauer & Feld, Washington, 1989-90; sr. v.p. bus. affairs and gen. counsel Time Warner Sports, N.Y.C., 1991—; adj. lectr. sports law Am. U. Law Sch., 1989-91; adj. faculty sports law Fordham U. Law Sch., 1992-96; bd. advisors Ctr. for Protection of Athletes Rights. Contbr. chpt. to: The Law of Professional and Amateur Sports, 1989, 95. Mem. ABA (program and sports divsn. chair forum entertainment and sports industries' governing com. 1992-96, chair elect 1996, governing com. standing com. on forum-coms. 1994—, chair 1997), Assn. Bar City N.Y. (sports law com. 1991-95), Sports Lawyers Assn. (bd. dirs.), N.Y. State Bar Assn., Women's Sports Found. (mem. bd. adv.). Office: Time Warner Sports 1100 Avenue Of The Americas New York NY 10036-6712

LESTER, RICHARD, film director; b. Phila., Jan. 19, 1932; s. Elliott and Ella (Young) L.; m. Deirdre Vivian Smith, 1956; 2 children. B.S., U. Pa. TV dir., CBS, 1951-54, dir., TV Goon Shows, 1956; directed: Running, Jumping and Standing Still Film (Acad. award nomination, 1st prize San Francisco Festival 1960); dir.: feature films It's Trad, Dad, 1962, Mouse on the Moon, 1963, A Hard Day's Night, 1964, The Knack, 1964 (Grand Prix, Cannes Film Festival), Help, 1965 (Best Film award, Best Dir. award Rio de Janeiro Festival), A Funny Thing Happened on the Way to the Forum, 1966, How I Won the War, 1967, Petulia, 1968, The Bed-Sitting Room, 1969 (Ghandi Peace prize, Berlin Festival 1969), The Three Musketeers, 1973, Juggernaut, 1974 (Best Dir., Teheran Festival), The Four Musketeers, 1975, Royal Flash, 1975, Robin and Marian, 1976, The Ritz, 1976, Butch and Sundance—The Early Days, 1978, Cuba, 1979, Superman II, 1980, Superman III, 1982, Finders Keepers, 1984, Return of the Musketeers, 1989, Get Back, 1991. Office: Creative Artists Agy 9830 Wilshire Blvd Beverly Hills CA 90212-1804*

LESTER, RICHARD ALLEN, economist, educator; b. Blasdell, N.Y., Mar. 1, 1908; s. Garra Kimble and Jessie Isabel (Holmes) L.; m. Doris Margaret Newhouse; children: Margaret Wing, Harriet Tarver, Robert A. PhB, Yale U., 1929; AM, Princeton (N.J.) U., 1930, PhD, 1936. With Princeton U., 1931-32, 34-38, prof., 1945-74, prof. emeritus, 1974—; assoc. dean Woodrow Wilson Sch., 1966-68; dean faculty Princeton U., 1968-73, rsch. assoc. Indsl. Rels. sect., 1973—; asst. prof. U. Wash., Seattle, 1938-40; from asst. to assoc. prof. Duke U., Durham, N.C., 1940-45; br. chief War Prodn. Bd. and War Manpower Commn., Washington, 1941-42; manpower cons. Office of Sec. of War, Washington, 1943-44; chmn. N.J. Employment Security Coun., Trenton, 1954-64; N.J. chmn. Pub. Employer-Employee Rels. Study Commn., Trenton, 1974-75; trustee Tchrs. Ins. and Annuity Assn., N.Y.C., 1959-63; v.p. Princeton U. Press, 1969-72. Author: Monetary Experiments, 1939, As Unions Mature, 1958, Economics of Labor, 2d edit., 1964, Labor Arbitration, 1984, Wages, Benefits and Company Employment Systems, 1988. Elected mem. Princeton Borough Coun., 1958-61; trustee Ctr. for Analysis Pub. Issues, Princeton, 1970-83; vice chmn. Pres.'s Commn. on Status of Women, Washington, 1961-63. U.S. Dept. Labor Merit award, 1968. Mem. Indls. Rels. Rsch. Assn. (pres. 1956), Am. Econ. Assn. (exec. com. 1951-53, v.p. 1961), Nat. Acad. Social Ins. Democrat. Avocations: swimming, fishing. Home: Meadow Lakes Apt 46-03U Hightstown NJ 08520-3332 Office: Princeton U Indsl Rels Sect Firestone Libr Princeton NJ 08544

LESTER, RICHARD GARRISON, radiologist, educator; b. N.Y.C., Oct. 24, 1925; s. L. I. and Pauline (Smolan) L.; m. Marion Louise Kurtz, Jan. 17, 1949; children: Elizabeth P., Andrew W. A.B., Princeton U., 1946; M.D., Columbia U., 1948. Intern N.Y.C. Hosp., 1948-49; asst. resident radiology Stanford Hosp., 1950-51, 53-54; from instr. to assoc. prof. radiology U. Minn., 1954-61; prof. radiology, chmn. dept. Med. Coll. Va., 1961-65, Duke Sch. Medicine, 1965-76; prof. radiology U. Tex. Med. Sch., Houston, 1976-84; chmn. dept. U. Tex. Med. Sch., 1977-81; interim pres. Meharry Med. Coll., Nashville, 1981-82; dean Eastern Va. Med. Sch., Norfolk, 1984-89, prof. radiology, 1984-93, chmn. dept., 1989-91; prof. emeritus, 1993—; v.p. acad. affairs Med. Coll. of Hampton Roads, formerly Eastern Va. Med. Authority, Norfolk, 1984-89; trustee Meharry Med. Coll., 1975—. Author: (with others) Congenital Heart Disease, 1965, Exposure of the Pregnant Patient to Diagnostic Radiations, 1985; also numerous articles. Deacon Freemason St. Bapt. Ch. Capt. USAF, 1951-53. Fellow Am. Coll. Radiology, Am. Coll. Chest Physicians; mem. Assn. Univ. Radiologists, Am. Roentgen Ray Soc., Soc. Pediatric Radiology, Radiol. Soc. N.Am. (dir. 1976—, chmn. bd. 1981, pres. 1983). Home: 1362 De Bree Ave Norfolk VA 23517-2131 Office: Ea Va Med Sch PO Box 1980 Norfolk VA 23501-1980

LESTER, RICHARD LEE, elementary education educator, consultant; b. Omaha, June 30, 1946; s. Joseph Clarence Lester and Ruth Alma (Ward) Bax; m. Peggy I. Amole, Jan. 23, 1971; children: Christopher, Michael, Stephen. BEd, Wright State U., 1976; MEd, Miami U., Oxford, Ohio, 1987. Cert. tchr., Ohio. Head electronics technician Litton Industries, Smyrna, Del., 1967-68; head quality control Advance Devel. Corp., Gardena, Calif., 1968-70; asst. mgr. Katz Drug Co., Springfield, Mo., 1970-71; advt. sales Greenfield (Ohio) Daily Times, 1971-72; tchr. Miami Trace Local Schs., Washington Court House, Ohio, 1976—. Author computer programs. Pres. Fayette County Dem. Club, Washington Court House, 1981; chair Fayette County Dem. Party, 1982. Served with USN, 1964-67, Okinawa. Named Outstanding Young Educator, Washington Court House Jaycees, 1979, Outstanding Life Saving Action awardee Lions Club, 1980; Martha Holden Jennings Found. grantee, 1992, 94, Nat. Ctr. for Sci. Teaching and Learning grantee, 1991-93. Mem. Nat. Sci. Tchrs. Assn., Miami Trace Tchrs. Assn. (pres. 1979-80), Elks. Avocation: golf. Home: 39 Allen Ave New Holland OH 43145-9640 Office: Miami Trace Jr High Sch 103 Main St Bloomingburg OH 43106

LESTER, ROBERT CARLTON, religious studies educator; b. Lead, S.D., Feb. 1, 1933; s. Odell and Mary Olivia (Martin) L.; m. Donna Helene Larson, Apr. 15, 1954; children: Paul E., Charles F., R. Timothy. BA, U. Mont., 1955; BD, Yale U., 1958, MA, 1959, PhD, 1963. From asst. prof. to assoc. prof. Am. U., 1962-70; mem. faculty U. Colo., Boulder, 1970—, prof. religious studies, 1972—; vis. prof. Cornell U., 1968-69; vis. lectr. Dept. State., monthly, 1963-70; mem. faculty Humanities Inst, NEH, 1979. Author: Theravada Buddhism in Southeast Asia, 1973, Ramanuja on the Yoga, 1975, Srivacana Bhushana of Pillai Lokacharya, 1979, Buddhism: The Path to Nirvana, 1987. Ford. Found. fellow, 1960-62, Fulbright Hays fellow, 1967, 74-75, faculty fellow U. Colo., 1974-75, Am. Inst. of Indian Studies fellow, 1982-83, 88. Mem. Am. Acad. Religion, Assn. Asian Studies, Soc. Values in Higher Edn., Phi Kappa Phi. Office: U Colo Dept Religious Studies Boulder CO 80309

LESTER, ROBIN DALE, educator, author, former headmaster; b. Holdrege, Nebr., Mar. 1, 1939; s. Earl L. and Evelyn Grace (Robinson) L.; m. Helen Sargent Doughty, Aug. 26, 1967; children: Robin Debevoise, James Robinson. Student, St. Andrews U., Scotland, 1958-61; BA, Pepperdine U., 1962, MA, 1963; MAT, U. Chgo., 1966, PhD, 1971. Resident head, dean students office U. Chgo., 1964-72, Ferdinand Schevill fellow dept. history, 1966-68; asst. prof. history Columbia Coll., Chgo., 1966-70; chmn. social scis. dept. Columbia Coll., 1970-72; chmn. history dept. Collegiate Sch., N.Y.C., 1972-75; headmaster Trinity Sch., N.Y.C., 1975-86, San Francisco U. Sch., 1986-88, Latin Sch. of Chgo., 1989-92; tchr. Francis W. Parker Sch., Chgo., 1994—; adj. prof. Columbia Coll., Chgo., 1992—. Author: Stagg's University, 1995, Wuzzy Takes Off, 1995, Roy Foy, 1996; contbr. to N.Y. Times, 1979, 80, 81, Jour. Am. History, 1980, 95, Chgo. Tribune, 1989, Jour. Sports History, 1991, History of Edn. Quar., 1995, U. Chgo. mag., 1995. Mem. Manhattan Borough Dem. Com., N.Y.C., 1977-86; commr. Commn. on Ednl. Issues, 1980-86; mem. edn. com. Chgo. Hist. Soc., 1991-95; mem. Chgo.-Prague Sister Cities Com., 1991; trustee, treas. St. Andrews U. Am. Found., 1985—; precinct capt. Dem. Party, Chgo., 1964. Lauder fellow Aspen Inst., 1985. Mem. Am. Hist. Assn., Am. Studies Assn., N.Am. Soc. Sport Historians (Book of the Yr. award 1995), Orgn. Am. Historians, Headmaster's Assn., Country Day Sch. Headmaster's Assn., University Club (N.Y.C.), Quadrangle Club. Episcopalian. Home: 2230 N Lincoln Park W Chicago IL 60614-3814 Office: Francis W Parker Sch 330 W Webster Ave Chicago IL 60614-3811

LESTER, VIRGINIA LAUDANO, advocate civil rights consumer protection; b. Phila., Jan. 5, 1931; d. Edmund Francis and Emily Beatrice (Downes) Laudano; children: Pamela Lester Golde, Valerie Lester. BA, Pa. State U., 1952; MEd, Temple U., 1955; PhD, Union Grad. Sch., 1972; JD, Stanford U. Law Sch., 1988. Tchr. pub. schs. Abington, Pa., 1952-55, Greenfield Center, N.Y., 1956; instr. edn. dept. Skidmore Coll., Saratoga Springs, N.Y., 1962-64; dir. endl. research Skidmore Coll., 1967-72, asst. to the pres., 1968-72; asst. dir. Capitol Dist. Regional Supplementary Edn. Center, Albany, N.Y., 1966-67; assoc. dean, asst. prof. state-wide programs Empire State Coll., State U. N.Y., Saratoga Springs, 1973-75; sr. assoc. dean, assoc. prof. Empire State Coll., State U. N.Y., 1975-76, acting dean state-wide programs, 1976; pres., prof. interdisciplinary studies Mary Baldwin Coll., Staunton, Va., 1976-85; cons. to bd. trustees Mary Baldwin Coll., 1985-88; assoc. Hunton & Williams, Richmond, Va., 1988-90; interim pres. Friends World Coll., Huntington, N.Y., 1990-91; dir. presdl. search consultation svc. Assn. of Governing Bds. of Univs. and Colls., 1991-94; counsel spl. projects office of exec. dir. Am. Assn. Retired Persons, 1994—; mem. cons. core faculty Union Grad. Sch., Union for Experimenting Colls. and Univs., Cin., 1975-82; vis. faculty fellow Harvard U. Grad. Sch. Edn., 1976; cons. in field; bd. dirs. So. Bankshares, So. Bank; bd. dirs. Council Advancement of Small Colls., 1977-81, Am. Council Edn., 1983-85. Mem. com. on criminal sexual assault Va. State Crime Commn., 1976; v.p. Costume Collection, Inc., 1971-73; v.p. Warren, Washington, Saratoga Counties Planned Parenthood, 1972-74, bd. dirs., 1970-74; mem. Saratoga Springs Housing Bd. Appeals, 1966-76, Commn. on Future of Va., 1982-84; bd. dirs. Nat. Urban League, 1979-86; pres. commn. NCAA, 1984-85. Mem. Am. Acad. Polit. and Social Scis., Va. Found. Ind. Colls. (trustee, exec. com.), Va. Council Ind. Colls., Am. Council on Edn. (commn. on women in higher edn. 1977-80), Nat. Assn. Ind. Colls. and Univs. (dir.), Assn. Va. Colls. (sec.-treas. 1978-79, pres. 1980-81, dir.), Assn. Ch. Related Colls. and Univs. of South (pres. 1983), Pi Lambda Theta, Pi Gamma Mu, Chimes. Mem. Soc. of Friends.

LESTER, WILLIAM ALEXANDER, JR., chemist, educator; b. Chgo., Apr. 24, 1937; s. William Alexander and Elizabeth Frances (Clark) L.; m. Rochelle Diane Reed, Dec. 27, 1959; children: William Alexander III, Allison Kimberleigh. B.S., U. Chgo., 1958, M.S., 1959; postgrad., Washington U., St. Louis, 1959-60; Ph.D., Cath. U. Am., 1964. Phys. chemist Nat. Bur. Standards, Washington, 1961-64; asst. dir. Theoretical Chemistry Inst. of U. Wis.-Madison, 1965-68; research staff mem. IBM Research Lab., San Jose, Calif., 1968-75; mgr., 1976-78; mem. tech. planning staff IBM T.J. Watson Research Center, Yorktown Heights, N.Y., 1975-76; dir. Nat. Resource for Computation in Chemistry, Lawrence Berkeley (Calif.) Lab., 1978-81, also assoc. dir., staff sr. scientist, 1978-81, faculty sr. scientist, 1981—; prof. chemistry U. Calif., Berkeley, 1981—, assoc. dean Coll. Chemistry, 1991-95; lectr. chemistry U. Wis., 1966-68; cons. NSF, 1976-77, mem. chem. divsn. adv. panel, 1980-83, adv. com. Office Advanced Sci. Computing program, 1985-87, chmn., 1987, sr. fellow for sci. and engring., asst. to dir. for human resource devel., 1995-96; mem. U.S. nat. com. Internat. Union Pure and Applied Chemistry, 1976-79; mem. com. on recommendations for U.S. Army Basic Sci. Rsch. NRC, 1984-87, mem. steering com., 1987-88; chemistry rsch. evaluation panel AF Office Sci. Rsch., 1974-78; chmn. Gordon Conf. Atomic and Molecular Interactions, 1978; mem. NRC panel on chem. physics Nat. Bur. Stds., 1980-83; mem. com. to survey chem. scis. NRC, 1982-84, Fed. Networking Coun. Adv. Com., 1991-95; mem. blue ribbon panel on high performance computing NSF, 1993; mem. com. on high performance computing and comm.: status of a major initiative NRC, 1994-95, mem. com. on math. challenges from computational chemistry, NRC, 1994-95. Editor: Procs. of Conf. on Potential Energy Surfaces in Chemistry, 1971; author: (with Brian L. Hammond and Peter J. Reynolds) Monte Carlo Methods in Ab Initio Quantum Chemistry, 1994; mem. editl. bd. Jour. Phys. Chemistry, 1979-87, Jour. Computational Chemistry, 1980-87, Computer Physics Comm., 1981-86; mem. adv. bd. Sci. Yr., 1989-93, Comms. on Analysis, Geometry and Physics, 1997—. Recipient Alumni award in sci. Cath. U. Am., 1983. Fellow AAAS (com. on nominations 1988-91, nat. bd. dirs. 1993-97), Am. Phys. Soc. (chmn. div. chem. physics 1986); mem. Am. Chem. Soc. (sec.-treas. Wis. sect. 1967-68, chmn. div. phys. chemistry 1979, treas. div. computers in chemistry 1974-77), Nat. Orgn. Black Chemists and Chem. Engrs. (Percy L. Julian award 1979, Outstanding Tchr. award 1986, exec. bd. 1984-87). Home: 4433 Briar Cliff Rd Oakland CA 94605-4624 Office: U Calif Dept Chemistry Berkeley CA 94720 *Perseverance is the watchword-the will to hold on.*

LESTER, W(ILLIAM) BERNARD, agricultural economist, business executive; b. Havana, Fla., Jan. 9, 1939; s. William Duncan and Edith (Blackburn) L.; m. Elaine Purnell, Mar. 30, 1961; 1 child, Mark Alan. BSA, U. Fla., 1961, MSA, 1962; PhD, Tex. A&M U., 1965. Agrl. economist Tex. A&M U., 1965-67; economist rsch. dept. Fla. Citrus Commn. U. Fla., 1967; dir. econ. rsch. Fla. Dept. Citrus, Gainesville, 1968-76, dep. exec. dir., 1976-78, exec. dir., 1979-86; dep. exec. v.p., chief oper. officer Alico Inc., LaBelle, Fla., 1986-87; exec. v.p., chief oper. officer Alico Inc., LaBelle, 1988—. Contbr. numerous rsch. reports to profl. jours. With U.S. Army, 1956. Democrat. Methodist. Office: Alico Inc 640 S Main St PO Box 338 LaBelle FL 33935

LESTINA, GERALD F., wholesale grocery executive. Pres., CEO Roundy's Inc., Pewaukee, Wis. Office: Roundy's Inc 23000 Roundy Dr Pewaukee WI 53072*

LESTINA, ROGER HENRY, English language educator; b. Yosemite Nat. Pk., Calif., Apr. 7, 1940; s. Henry Francis and Mary Roselyn (O'Brien) L.; m. Linda Jeanne Fish, Aug. 24, 1963; children: Deanna, Joseph, Nicholas, Daniel. BA in English, Loyola U., L.A., 1962; MA in English, U. Alaska, 1974. Cert. secondary education tchr., Calif. Commd. 2d lt. USAF, 1962, advanced through grades to maj., 1974, ret., 1984; instr. USAF Acad., Colorado Springs, Colo., 1975-79; parish adminstr. St. John's Cath. Ch., Edmond, Okla., 1984-90; lead instr. freshman composition Okla. State U., Oklahoma City, 1990—. Co-author: (textbook) The Freshman Writer: Finding, Organizing, and Supporting Ideas, 1996; editor: (handbook) The Conservation Officer's Guide to Collection and Preservation of Evidence, 1995. Ch. cantor/choir mem. St. Francis of Assisi Parish, Tinker AFB, Okla., 1991—; sec. faculty coun. Okla. State U.-OKC, 1997—. Recipient Nat. Inst. for Staff and Organizational Devel. Excellence in Tchng. award, 1996. Mem. MLA, AAUP (sec. Okla. State U.-OKC chpt. 1995-97), Nat. Coun. Tchrs. English, S.W. Regional Conf. on English, Ret. Officers Assn. Republican. Roman Catholic. Avocation: singing. Home: 708 Concord Cir Edmond OK 73003 Office: Okla State U 900 N Portland Ave Oklahoma City OK 73107

LESTINGER, ALAN, company executive. Pres., COO, vice chmn. Barnett Banks. Office: 50 N Laura St Jacksonville FL 32202-3664

LESTON, PATRICK JOHN, judge; b. Maywood, Ill., May 2, 1948; s. John R. and Lorraine (McQueen) L.; m. Kristine Brzezinski; children: Alison, Adam. BS in Communications, U. Ill., 1970; JD cum laude, Northwestern U., Chgo., 1973. Bar: Ill. 1973, U.S. Dist. Ct. (no. dist.) Ill. 1973, U.S. Ct. Appeals (7th cir.) 1973. Ptnr. Jacobs & Leston, Villa Park, Ill., 1973-79; pvt. practice Glen Ellyn, Ill., 1979-89; ptnr. Keck, Mahin & Cate, Oakbrook Terrace, Ill., 1989-95; judge 18th Cir. Ct., DuPage County, Ill., 1995—; presenter at profl. confs. Editor Ill. State Bar Assn./Young Lawyers Divsn. Jour., 1983-85. Class rep. Northwestern U. Law Sch. Fund, 1982-88; organizer DuPage County (Ill.) Law Explorers. Fellow ABA (Ill. del. to ABA/Young Lawyers divsn. assembly 1982-85), Ill. Bar Assn. (chmn. fellows 1991-92, mem. bd. govs. 1990—, chmn. young lawyers divsn. 1985, chmn. agenda com. 1986, del. to 18th jud. cir. assembly 1982-88), Ill. Bar Found. (charter), Am. Bar Found.; mem. Chgo. Bar Assn., DuPage County Bar Assn. (pres. 1987, bd. dirs. 1979-84, chmn. judiciary com. 1988, gen. counsel 1989), Lions, Chi Psi. Avocations: volleyball, skiing, scuba diving, travel. Office: 18th Jud Cir Ct 505 N County Farm Rd Wheaton IL 60187-3907

LESZCZYNSKI, JERZY RYSZARD, chemistry educator, researcher; b. Tomaszow, Poland, May 26, 1949; cam to U.S., 1986; s. Leslaw and Hanna (Kaptur) L.; m. Danuta, June 25, 1972; children: Rafal, Magda. MS, Tech. U. Wroclaw (Poland), 1972, PhD, 1975. Lectr. chemistry Tech. U. Wroclaw, 1976-86; vis. sci. U. Fla., Gainesville, 1986-88; rsch. assoc. U. Ala., Birmingham, 1988-90; from asst. to assoc. prof. Jackson (Miss.) State U., 1990-95, prof., 1995—; conf. chmn. organizing com. Current Trends in Computational Chemistry, 1992-96; presenter in field. Author chpts. to books; editor: Computational Chemistry, Reviews of Current Trends, 1995, 96; co-author: Computational Quantum Chemistry, 1988, Combustion Efficiency and Air Quality, 1995, Interaction of DNA Bases and the Structure of DNA, 1996, Molecular Structure and Infrared Spectra of DNA Bases and Their Derivatives: Theory and Experiment, 1997; editor: Electronic Jour. of Theoretical Chemistry; sr. editor Asian Jour. Spectroscopy; guest editor: Structural Chemistry, 1995; referee: Jour. Am. Chem. Soc., Internat. Jour. Quantum Chemistry, Chem. Physics Letters, Structural Chemistry, Jour. Phys. Chemistry, Jour. Molecular Structure, Jour. Computational Chemistry, Jour. Biomolecular Structure and Dynamics; mem. editl. bd. Structural Chemistry; contbr. articles to profl. jours. Recipient Outstanding Faculty award AT&T, 1992. Mem. Am. Chem. Soc., Internat. Soc. Quantum Biology and Pharmacology (exec. com. 1995—), Miss. Acad. Sci. Office: Jackson State U Dept Chemistry 1400 Lynch St Jackson MS 39217-0002

LETAW, HARRY, JR., technology corporation executive; b. Miami, Fla., Aug. 7, 1926; s. Harry and Nina (Cook) L.; m. Joyce Winston Brown, June 4, 1947; children: Anne Winston, Kaye Lynn, John Robert, Mary Jane, Amelia Elizabeth, James Brown. BS in Chemistry with high honors, U. Fla., 1949, MS, 1951, PhD, 1952. Rsch. asst. prof. Elec. Engring. dept., U. Ill., Urbana, 1952-55; mktg. mgr. Raytheon Co., Wayland, Mass., 1955-61; dir. advanced programs Elec. div. Martin Marietta, Middle River, Md., 1961-64; v.p., gen. mgr. Ea. Tech. Ctr., Inc., Bunker-Ramo Corp., 1964-65; pres. Severn Comms. Corp., Millersville, Md., 1965—, Logos Ltd., Arlington, Va., 1968-72; chmn., pres. Radiation Systems, Inc., McLean, Va., 1974-78; pres. Intellinet Corp., Millersville, 1983—; chmn., pres., CEO Essex Corp., Columbia, Md., 1988—, also bd. dirs.; adj. assoc. prof. bus. adminstrn. Drexel Inst., 1963-64; cons. Compagnie Internat. pour L'Informatique, St. Germain-en-Laye, France, 1966-68. Contbr. articles to profl. jours; patentee in field. Bd. dirs. Econ. Opportunity Com., Anne Arundel County, 1969-71; chmn. adv. com. on ednl. aspects of contemporary issues Md. State Dept. Edn., 1969-73; pres. Greater Severna Park Coun., 1972-73; participant DOD Joint Civilian Orientation Conf. 58, 1995. Sgt. U.S. Army, 1944-47; 2d lt. USAR, 1948-50. Emory U. Alumni scholar, 1943-44; U. Fla. rsch. corp. fellow, 1950; U.S. AEC predoctoral fellow Oak Ridge Inst. for Nuclear Studies, 1950-52. Mem. IEEE (sr.), Am. Phys. Soc., Security Affairs Support Assn. (bd. dirs. 1992-95), Phi Beta Kappa, Sigma Xi. Avocations: hiking, reading, public affairs. Office: Essex Corp 9150 Guilford Rd Columbia MD 21046-1803

LETCHER, NAOMI JEWELL, quality engineer, educator, counselor; b. Belle Point, W. Va., Dec. 29, 1924; d. Andrew Glen and Ollie Pearl (Meadows) Presley; m. Frank Philip Johnson, Oct. 5, 1945 (div. Dec. 1953); m. Paul Arthur Letcher, Mar. 6, 1954; children: Frank, Edwin, Richard, David. AA, El Camino Jr. Coll., 1964; BA, Calif. State U., 1971. Inspector N. Am. Aviation, Downey, Calif., 1964-71; substitute tchr. ABC Unified sch. Dist., Artesia, Calif., 1971-72; recurrence control rep. Rockwell Internat., Downey, Calif., 1972-80, quality engr., 1981-86; counselor Forest Lawn Cemeteries, Cerritos, Calif., 1980-81; tech. analyst Northrop, Pico Rivera, Calif., 1986-89; gov. divsn. D-2 area T.M. Internat., Downey, Calif., 1978-79. Author: History of the Letcher Family, 1995. Docent Temecula (Calif.) Valley Mus., 1994—. Mem. AAUW, Nat. Mgmt. Assn., NOW, Srs. Golden Yrs. Club, Alpha Gamma Sigma. Democrat. Baptist. Avocations: genealogy, needlework, stamp collecting, dancing, bowling.

LETEY, JOHN JOSEPH, JR., soil scientist, educator; b. Carbondale, Colo., June 13, 1933; s. John Joseph and Rosine (Tisseur) L.; m. Patricia Kaye Fitzgerald, Sept. 19, 1992; children: Laura, Donald, Lisa. BS in Agronomy, Colo. State U., 1955; PhD in Soil Physics, U. Ill., 1959. Asst. prof. soil physics UCLA, 1959-61; asst. prof., assoc. prof., prof. U. Calif., Riverside, 1961—, chmn. dept. soil and environ. scis., 1975-80; assoc. dir. water and wetlands resources, 1993—; FAO cons. Bulgaria, 1973, Cen. Soil Salinity Rsch. Inst., Karnal, India, 1989; dir. Kearney Found., U. Calif., 1980-85; mem. Soil Sci. Delegation to People's Republic of China, 1983;

keynote speaker Internat. Conf. Soil Salinity Under Irrigation-Processes and Mgmt., Israel, 1984; researcher in field. Author: (with Stahrl Edmunds) Environmental Administration, 1973; contbr. numerous chpts. to books, articles to profl. jours. Fellow AAAS, Soil Sci. Soc. Am. (past chmn. soil physics div., assoc. editor proceedings 1967-73); mem. Am. Soc. Agronomy (soil sci. award 1970). Mormon. Avocation: oil painting. Home: 435 W Campus View Dr Riverside CA 92507-4028 Office: U Calif Dept Soil & Environ Scis Riverside CA 92521

LETHBRIDGE, FRANCIS DONALD, architect; b. Hackensack, N.J., Oct. 5, 1920; s. Berry B. and Florence A. (Lapham) L.; m. Mary Jane Christopher, June 21, 1947; children: Catherine B. (Mrs. Robert A. Grove), Mary P. (Mrs. Christopher G. Cromwell), Christopher B., Margaret F. (Mrs. Arsim Cejku). Student, Stevens Inst. Tech., 1937-40, Yale Sch. Architecture, 1945-46. Ptnr. archtl. firm Keyes, Smith, Satterlee & Lethbridge, Washington, 1951-55, Keyes, Lethbridge & Condon, Washington, 1956-75, Francis D. Lethbridge & Assocs., Washington, 1975-90; mem. fgn. bldgs. archtl. rev. panel U.S. State Dept., 1977-80; mem. archtl. adv. panel Fed. Res. Bd., 1979-83; mem. Potomac Planning Task Force, 1965-67; bd. advisers Nat. Trust for Hist. Preservation, 1969-71; mem. Joint Com. Landmarks Nat. Capital, 1964-79, chmn., 1964-73. Co-author: Guide to the Architecture of Washington, D.C; prin. works include Pine Spring Community, Fairfax County, Va., 1951-54, Potomac Overlook, 1955-58, U.S. Chancery, Lima, Peru, 1957, Forest Industries Bldg., Washington, 1961, Carderock Springs Community, Montgomery County, Md., 1963-65, Unitarian Ch, River Road, Md., 1964, master plan Arlington Nat. Cemetery, 1966-68, Ft. Lincoln New Town, 1968, Visitors Ctr., Arlington Nat. Cemetery, 1988. Trustee Nantucket Atheneum; advisor Nantucket Hist. Assn. Officer, pilot USNR, 1942-45. Decorated D.F.C., Air medal; recipient Design Merit award AIA, 1955, 66, 1st honor award, 1966, Potomac Valley Chpt. archtl. award, 1956, 58, 60, 62, 64, 66, 68, 70, 72, 74, 76, joint award of honor AIA-Nat. Assn. Home Builders, 1960; award in architecture Washington Bd. Trade, 1953, 55, 61, 63, 65, 67, 69, 71, 73; Renchard prize for historic preservation, 1983. Fellow AIA (pres. Washington Met. chpt. 1964, v.p. 1969-70, pres. AIA found. 1971-73); mem. Cosmos Club (Washington). Home and Office: 48 Orange St Nantucket MA 02554-3937

LETICHE, JOHN MARION, economist, educator; b. Uman, Kiev, Russia, Nov. 11, 1918; came to U.S., 1941, naturalized, 1949; s. Leon and Mary (Grossman) L.; m. Emily Kuyper, Nov. 17, 1945; 1 son, Hugo K. BA, McGill U., 1940, MA, 1941; PhD in Econs, U. Chgo., 1951. Rockefeller fellow Council Fgn. Relations, N.Y.C., 1945-46; Smith-Mundt vis. prof. U. Aarhus and U. Copenhagen, Denmark, 1951-52; spl. tech. econ. adv. UN ECA, Africa, 1961-62; prof. U. Calif. at Berkeley, 1960—; cons. AID, U.S. Depts. State, Labor, HUD and Treasury, 1962—; emissary to Japan and Korea, Dept. State, 1971; cons. Econ. Coun. Can., 1972—, World Bank, 1981—, Bank of Eng., London, Bundesbank, Frankfurt, Fed. Republic of Germany; lectr. Stockholm, Paris, Uppsala, Hamburg, Kiel, Oxford (Eng.), 1973—, Vancouver, Toronto, Montreal, Zagreb, 1983, Frankfurt, Bonn, Moscow and Nakhodka Acad. Scis. USSR, 1986, Hong Kong, Shanghai, Wuhan, Beijing, London, Bonn, Frankfurt, De Hague, 1987, Bundesbank, 1992, 93, Peoples Republic China, Beijing, Shanghai, 1988, 90, 94, New Delhi, Addis Ababa, Kuala Lumpur and Seoul, 1996, Acad. Scis., Taipei, 1989, joint session Calif. legis., 1975; ext. examiner adv. degrees U. Hong Kong, U. Calcutta, India. Author: Reciprocal Trade Agreements in the World Economy, 1948, in Japanese, 1951, System or Theory of the Trade of the World, 2d edit., 1957, Balance of Payments and Economic Growth, 2d edit., 1976, A History of Russian Economic Thought, 2d edit., 1977, The Key Problems of Economic Reconstruction and Development in Nigeria, 1970, Dependent Monetary Systems and Economic Development, 1974, Lessons of the Oil Crisis, 1977, Gains from Trade, 1979, Controlling Inflation, Recession, Federal Deficits and the Balance of Payments, 1980, The New Inflation and Its Urban Impact, 1980, Monetary Systems of Africa in the 1980s, 1981, International Economic Policies and Their Theoretical Foundations, 1982, 2d edit., 1992; Russian Statecraft: An Analysis and Translation of Iuril Krizhanich's Politika, 1985, Economics of the Pacific Rim, 1989; editor Royer Lectures, 1980-90, Toward a Market Economy in China, 1992, China's Emerging Monetary and Financial Markets, 1995, India's Economic Reforms, 1996; contbr. articles to encys., congl. coms. and profl. jours. Supervisory bd. Sch. Econs., St. Petersburg, Russia, 1994—. Recipient certificate merit Ency. Brit., certificate merit Inst. World Affairs, certificate merit Internat. Legal Center, U. Mich., U.S. Office Personnel Mgmt. Sr. Fed. Govt. Execs. and Mgrs., U. Calif.-Berkeley; Adam Smith medal U. Verona, 1977; Guggenheim fellow, 1956-57. Mem. Am. Econ. Assn. (nominating com. 1968-69), Econometric Soc., Royal Econ. Soc., U.S.-Asian Econ. Com. (bd. dirs. 1983—), African Studies Assn., Am. Soc. Internat. Law (bd. 1969-72). Home: 968 Grizzly Peak Blvd Berkeley CA 94708-1549

LETKI, ARLEEN, secondary school educator; b. Pitts., Sept. 30, 1949; d. Henry S. and Monica (Kocinski) K. BS, Lambuth Coll., 1971; MA, Glassboro State Coll., 1989; postgrad., Widener U., 1991—. Cert. social studies, English, elem., spl. edn., pupil pers. svcs., supr., prin., N.J., elem. and secondary prin., Pa. 3d, 5th and 6th grade tchr. St. Mary Sch., Camden, N.J., 1971-72; 7th grade tchr. Annunciation Sch., Belmawr, N.J., 1972-74; 7th and 8th grade tchr. St. Rose Sch., Haddon Heights, N.J., 1974-84; spl. edn. tchr. Glassboro (N.J.) Intermediate Sch., 1984-87, lang. arts tchr., 1987-89; social studies tchr. Glassboro (N.J.) H.S., 1989-96; asst. prin. Washington Twp. H.S., 1996—; prin. adult H.S., alternative evening sch., cmty. sch. Mem. ASCD, AAUW, Nat. Coun. for Social Studies. Republican. Roman Catholic. Avocations: calligraphy, gardening, reading, walking. Home: 18 Bells Lake Dr Turnersville NJ 08012-1532 Office: Washington Twp HS Glassboro NJ 08028

LETOURNEAU, DUANE JOHN, biochemist, educator; b. Stillwater, Minn., July 12, 1926; s. John Peter and Olga Margaret (Lange) LeTourneau; m. Phyllis Jean Kaercher, June 22, 1947; children: Bruce Duane, Diane Elaine, Keith George. B.S., U. Minn., 1948, M.S., 1951, Ph.D., 1954. Asst. prof., asst. agrl. chemist U. Idaho, Moscow, 1953-58; assoc. prof., assoc. agrl. chemist U. Idaho, 1958-63, prof., biochemist, 1963-91, asst. dept. head, 1988-89, sec. faculty, 1990-91, sec. faculty, prof. biochemistry emeritus, 1992—; vis. prof. botany U. Sheffield (Eng.), 1973; vis. scientist Nat. Research Council Can., Saskatoon, 1981; Bd. dirs. Idaho Inst. Christian Edn., 1958-62, 73-75, v.p., 1959-62. Author research publs. on plant biochemistry. Bd. dirs. U. Idaho Luth. Campus Coun., 1962-64, 73-75, chmn., 1963-64; trustee FarmHouse Internat. Found., 1974-80, chmn., 1976-80; trustee Gritman Meml. Hosp., 1969-82, v.p., 1977-80; bd. dirs. Gritman Med. Ctr., 1991—, Palouse Regional Health Corp., 1992-96; bd. dirs. Latah County Hist. Soc., 1982-89, 92-96, pres. bd. dirs., 1984-87; trustee Idaho Hist. Soc., 1992—. With USAAF, 1945. Recipient Outstanding Faculty award Asso. Students U. Idaho, 1960-62, 87, Coll. Agr. Outstanding Instr. award, 1962, R.M. Wade Excellence in Teaching award, 1968, 78, Disting. Faculty award, 1982, Prof. of Yr. award, 1983; Citation for Disting. Achievement, U. Idaho, 1984; Nat. Acad. Scis.-NRC sr. postdoctoral fellow, 1964-65. Fellow AAAS, Am. Inst. Chemists; mem. AAUP (v.p. U. Idaho chpt. 1959-60, sec. 1984-87), Am. Chem. Soc., Am. Soc. Plant Physiologists, Am. Inst. Biol. Scis., Am. Phytopath. Soc., Idaho Acad. Sci. (v.p. 1985-86, pres. 1986-87, editor jour. 1983-89), Mycol. Soc. Am., Phytochem. Soc. N.Am., Am. Soc. Plant Physiologists, Iron Wedge, FarmHouse (dir. Idaho chpt. 1957-62, 72-75, 82-90, pres. 1957-62, 74, 82-85, 90; nat. dir. 1960-64, nat. v.p. 1962-64), Lions (bd. dirs. Moscow Central club 1971-74, 90-91, pres. 1973-74), Sigma Xi, Alpha Zeta, Gamma Alpha, Gamma Sigma Delta (pres. U. Idaho chpt. 1979-80), Phi Kappa Phi (v.p. U. Idaho chpt., pres. 1990-91), Phi Sigma (regional v.p. 1993—). Lutheran (chmn. ch. council and congregation, 1966-69). Home: 479 Ridge Rd Moscow ID 83843-2521

LETOURNEAU, GILLES, judge; b. Que., Can., July 14, 1945; s. romeo and Marguerite (Thibault) L.; m. Claudette tremblay, July 1, 1971; children: Simon, christian, Marie-Eve. BA in Arts, Levis (Que.) Coll., 1965; LLL, Laval U., Que., 1968; LLM, London sch. Econs./Polit. Sci., 1972, PhD, 1975. Bar: Que. 1969. Pvt. practice Que., 1969-71, 75-77; faculty law, vice dean Laval U., 1975-77; dir. policy making and legis. drafting Que. Dept. Justice, 1977-84; assoc. gen. sec. Govt. Que., 1984-85; v.p., pres. Law Reform Commn. of Can., Ottawa, Ont., 1985-90, 90-92; judge Fed. Ct. of Can., Ottawa, 1992—. contbr. articles to profl. jours. Recipient Merit award Levis Coll., 1992, Que. Bar, 1992. Avocations: fishing, outdoor activities. Office: Federal Court of Canada, Supreme Ct of Canada Bldg, Wellington St, Ottawa, ON Canada K1A 0H9*

LETOURNEAU, JEAN-PAUL, business association executive and consultant; b. St.-Hyacinthe, Que., Can., May 4, 1930; s. Eugene and Annette (Deslandes) L.; m. Claire Paquin, Sept. 26, 1956. Counsellor in Indsl. Relations, U. Montreal, Que., 1953; cert. c. of c. adminstrn., U. Syracuse, 1962; cert. advanced mgmt. U.S. C. of C, 1965. Mcpl. sec. Mont St.-Hilaire, Que., 1950-53; personnel mgr. Dupuis Freres (mail order house), 1953; editor Jeune Commerce, weekly tabloid Fedn. Que. Jr. C's. of C., 1953; sec. gen. Montreal Jr. C. of C., 1953-56; asst. gen. mgr. Province Que. C. of C., Montreal, 1956-59, gen. mgr., 1959-71, exec. v.p., 1971-90. Author: Quebec, The Price of Independence, 1969, Report on Corporate Social Responsibilities, 1982. Mem. C. of C. Execs. Can. (pres. 1982-83, mem. coun. excellence 1986), Corp. Consellors in Indsl Rels. of Que., Am. C. of C. Execs. (bd. dirs. 1982-83), Can. Exec. Svc. Orgns. (bd. dirs. 1991-95, vice chair 1993-95), Office Persons Handicapped of Que. (bd. dirs. 1992—, exec. com. 1994—), St.-Denis Club. Roman Catholic. Office: 165 Cote Ste-Catherine #202, Outremont, PQ Canada H2V 2A7 *Liberty is priceless; but liberty imposes responsibility, and if one is not responsible he will lose his liberty.*

LETOURNEAU, RICHARD HOWARD, retired college president; b. Stockton, Calif., Jan. 3, 1925; s. Robert G. and Evelyn (Peterson) LeT.; m. Louise Marion Jensen, Feb. 8, 1947; children: Robert Gilmore, Caleb Roy, Linda Louise, Liela Lynn. Student, Wheaton Coll., 1946, LeTourneau Coll., 1956; B.S., Tex. A&M U., 1958, M.S., 1961; Ph.D., Okla. State U., 1970. Gen. mgr. Miss. div. R.G. LeTourneau, Inc., Longview, Tex., 1949-52; v.p. prodn. R.G. LeTourneau, Inc., 1952-57, exec. v.p., 1966, pres., 1966-71; sr. v.p. Marathon Mfg. Co., Houston, 1971-72; dir. Marathon Mfg. Co., 1971-76; pres. Mosley Machinery Co., Waco, Tex., 1972-73; v.p. LeTourneau Found., 1973-75; prof. bus. mgmt. Belhaven Coll., Jackson, Miss., 1993—; mem. Tex. Indsl. Commn., 1959-66; adminstrv. v.p. LeTourneau Coll., 1958-62, pres., 1962-68, 75-85, chancellor, 1985-86, pres. emeritus, 1986—, chmn. bd. trustees, 1968-75; cons. to higher edn., 1986-93. Author: Management Plus, 1973, Keeping Your Cool in a World of Tension, 1975, Success Without Succeeding, 1976, Success Without Compromise, 1977, Democracy in Trouble, 1985, More Than Knowledge, 1985, Laws of Success for Christians, 1985, Finding Your Niche in Life, 1985. Past pres. LeTourneau Found. Served with C.E. AUS, 1944-46, PTO. Mem. Sigma Xi, Phi Kappa Phi, Tau Beta Pi, Alpha Pi Mu. Home and Office: 5225 Wayneland Dr Jackson MS 39211 *As a successful industrialist, educator and author, I have found that life is more than mind and body. Everyone, to have a joyous and truly successful life must also trust Jesus Christ as Lord for a spiritual dimension and overall balance in life. With this element missing, regardless of the profession followed, life will be hollow and meaningless, and an eternity of regret is certain.*

LETSINGER, ROBERT LEWIS, chemistry educator; b. Bloomfield, Ind., July 31, 1921; s. Reed A. and Etna (Phillips) L.; m. Dorothy C. Thompson, Feb. 6, 1943; children: Louise, Reed, Sue. Student, Ind. U., 1939-41; B.S., Mass. Inst. Tech., 1943, Ph.D., 1945; DSc (hon.), Acadia U., Can., 1993. Research assoc. MIT, 1945-46; research chemist Tenn. Eastman Corp., 1946; faculty Northwestern U., 1946—, prof. chemistry, 1959—, chmn. dept., 1972-75, joint prof. biochemistry and molecular biology, 1974—, Clare Hamilton Hall prof. chemistry, 1986-92, Clare Hamilton Hall prof. emeritus chemistry, 1992—; Mem. med. and organic chemistry fellowship panel NIH, 1966-69, medicinal chem. A study sect., 1971-75; bd. on chem. scis. and tech. Nat. Research Council, 1987-90. Mem. bd. editors Nucleic Acids Research, 1974-80; contbr. articles to profl. jours. Guggenheim fellow, 1956; JSPS fellow Japan, 1978; recipient Rosenstiel Medallion, 1985, Humboldt Sr. US Scientist award, 1988, NIH merit award, 1988, Arthur C. Cope scholar award, 1993. Fellow Am. Acad. Arts and Scis., Nat. Acad. Scis., Am. Assn. Arts and Scis.; mem. Am. Chem. Soc. (bd. editors 1969-72, bioconjugate chemistry 1992—, Arthur C. Cope scholar award 1993), Internat. Union Pure and Applied Chemistry, Sigma Xi, Phi Lambda Upsilon (hon. mem.). Home: 316 3rd St Wilmette IL 60091-3461 Office: Northwestern U Chemistry Dept 2145 Sheridan Rd Evanston IL 60208-0834

LETSOU, GEORGE VASILIOS, cardiothoracic surgeon; b. Boston, 1958; s. Vasilios George and Helen (Valacellis) L.; m. Jane Elizabeth Carter, June 1, 1985; children: Christopher George, Philip Taylor, John Carter. AB magna cum laude, Harvard U., 1979; MD, Columbia U., 1983. Diplomate Am. Bd. Surgery, Am. Bd. Thoracic Surgery. Resident in gen. surgery Yale-New Haven Hosp., 1983-88, chief resident and instr. surgery, 1987-88, clin. fellow in cardiothoracic surgery, 1988-89, Cystic Fibrosis Found. fellow cardiopulm. transplantation, 1988-89, Winchester scholar in cardiothoracic surg. rsch., 1989-90, resident in cardiothoracic surgery, 1990-91, chief resident in cardiothoracic surgery, 1991-92; attending surgeon Yale U., New Haven, 1992-95, instr. surgery, 1987-88, 91-92, asst. prof. surgery, 1992-95; attending surgeon Yale-New Haven Med. Ctr., 1992-95, Meth. Hosp., Ben Taub Hosp., Houston, 1995—; assoc. prof. surgery Baylor Coll. Medicine, Houston, 1995—. Mem. AMA, ACS, Am. Coll. Cardiology, Am. Coll. Chest Physicians, Soc. Thoracic Surgeons. Office: Dept Surgery One Baylor Plaza Ste 4040 Houston TX 77030

LETT, CYNTHIA ELLEN WEIN, marketing executive; b. Takoma Park, Md., Dec. 24, 1957; d. Arthur Benjamin and Mary Louise (Barker) Wein; m. Gerald Lee Lett, June 1, 1991. BS, Purdue U., 1979; M, Antioch Sch. Law, 1982-83. Mktg. researcher Sheraton, Washington, 1979-80; sales mgr. Sea Pines Plantation Co., Hilton Head Island, S.C., 1980-81; dir. sales Sheraton Potomac Hotel, Rockville, Md., 1981-82, Ritz Carlton Hotel, Washington, 1982-83; pres. Creative Planning Internat., Washington, 1983—; dir. The Lett Group, 1996—; dir. mem. Great Inns Am., Annapolis, 1987-89; etiquette cons., 1989—; dir. meetings Am. Healthcare Inst., 1991-92; corp. affairs mgr. MCI Telecom Corp., 1992-95; pres. The Lett Group, 1996—. Author: Getaway Innstyle, America's Fifty Best Inns, 1990; editor Travel Inn Style Newsletter, 1990-91, Apropos!, 1996—. Mem. Exec. Women Internat., Profl. Conf. Mgmt. Assn., Washington Conv. and Visitors Assn., Greater Washington Soc. Assn. Execs., Found. for Internat. Meetings (bd. govs. 1985-86), Purdue Club (1982-93). Avocations: classical music, amateur photography, country inns, foreign travel, gardening. Office: Creative Planning Internat 13116 Hutchinson Way Ste 100 Silver Spring MD 20906-5947

LETT, LEON, professional football player; b. Mobile, Ala., Oct. 12, 1968. Student, Hinds Jr. Coll., Emporia (Kans.) State U. Defensive lineman Dallas Cowboys, 1991—. Selected to Pro Bowl, 1994. Mem. Dallas Cowboys Super Bowl Champions, Super Bowl XXVII, 1992, XXVIII, 1993. Office: Dallas Cowboys 1 Cowboys Pkwy Irving TX 75063-4945*

LETT, PHILIP WOOD, JR., defense consultant; b. Newton, Ala., May 4, 1922; s. Philip Wood Sr. and Lily Octavia (Kennedy) L.; m. Katy Lee Howell, June 26, 1948; children: Kathy, Warren, Lisa. B MechE, Ala. Poly. Inst., 1943; MS in Engring., U. Ala., 1947; PhD MechE, U. Mich., 1950; MS in Indsl. Mgmt., MIT, 1960. Registered profl. engr., Mich. Lab. engr., engring. div. Chrysler Corp., 1950-52, project engr., def. engring. div., 1952-54, chief engr., def. engring. div., 1954-61, operating mgr., def. engring. div., 1961-73; head XM1 Tank task force Chrysler Corp., Sterling Heights, Mich., 1973-76; gen. mgr. Sterling Def. div. Chrysler Corp., 1976-79; v.p. engring. Chrysler Def. Inc., Center Line, Mich., 1980-82; v.p. research & engring. Gen. Dynamics Land Systems Div., Center Line, 1982-86, v.p., asst. to gen. mgr., 1986-87; pres. PWL Inc., 1987—; mem. U.S. delegation to NATO Indsl. Adv. Group. Contbr. articles to tech. jours. and to Internat. Def. Rev. Trustee Judson Ctr., 1989—. Capt. U.S. Army, 1943-46. Decorated Cheonsu medal Republic of Korea; awarded membership U.S. NAE, 1984; recipient Outstanding Engr. award Auburn U., 1984, Ben S. Gilmer award, 1991, Silver medal Am. Def. Preparedness Assn., 1989; named Disting. Engring. fellow U. Ala. Coll. Engring., 1992; named to Ala. Engring. Hall of Fame, 1992; Sloan fellow MIT, 1960-61. Mem. Orchard Lake Country Club. Baptist. Home: 1330 Oxford Rd Bloomfield Hills MI 48304-3952 Office: PO Box 2074 Warren MI 48090-2074

LETTERMAN, DAVID, television personality, comedian, writer; b. Indpls., Apr. 12, 1947; s. Joseph and Dorothy L.; m. Michelle Cook, 1969 (div. 1977). Grad., Ball State U., 1969. Radio and TV announcer, Indpls.; performer The Comedy Store, Los Angeles, 1975—; appearances on TV include (variety series) Mary, CBS; frequent guest host The Tonight Show; host (morning comedy/variety program) David Letterman Show, NBC, 1980, Late Night with David Letterman, NBC, 1982-1993, The Late Show with David Letterman, CBS, 1993— (also writer); host, Academy Awards, 1995; writer for TV including Bob Hope Special, Good Times, Paul Lynde Comedy Hour, John Denver Special; author: (with others) The Late Night with David Letterman Book of Top Ten Lists, 1990, An Altogether New Book of Top Ten Lists, 1991; film appearances include: Cabin Boy, 1994. Recipient 6 Emmy awards, 1981-88. Avocations: baseball, basketball, auto racing, running. Office: Late Show with David Letterman Ed Sullivan Theater 1697 Broadway New York NY 10019-5904*

LETTERMAN, ERNEST EUGENE, manufacturers representative company executive; b. Kansas City, Mo., Feb. 24, 1950; s. Emory A. and Zelda L. (Leach) L.; m. Barbara Jean Watkins, June 6, 1970; children: Amy Elizabeth, Rebecca LeAnn. BS in Bus. and Indsl. Mgmt., Ctrl. Mo. State U., 1972. Custodial, maintenance Harmon Industries, Inc., Grain Valley, Mo., 1962-68, prodn. engr., 1969-73, asst. plant mgr., 1974-75; sales mgr. Harmon Industries, Inc., Warrensburg, Mo., 1975-76; sales engr. Pacific Sci., Inc., Anaheim, Calif., 1976-81, regional sales mgr., 1982-86; v.p. TechScience Internat., Inc., Santa Ana, Calif., 1987-91, also bd. dirs; pres., owner Capital Products, Inc., Lee's Summit, Mo., 1991—; dir. Scholer Exec. Bd., Manhattan, Kans., 1991—. Patentee for electrical trailer connector. Cub master Boy Scouts Am., Warrensburg, 1973-75; pres. Lochkirk Home Owners Assn., Lee's Summit, 1986-88; pastor Lee's Summit Reorganized Ch. of Jesus Christ of Latter-day Saints, 1987-91; mem. stake high coun. Santa Fe Stake--Reorganized Ch. Jesus Christ of Latter-day Saints, Independence, Mo., 1991—. Recipient Outstanding Sales award BYK-Gardener, 1988, Ling Electronics, 1988. Mem. Am. Concrete Assn. (pres. 1993, v.p., sec., treas. Kans. chpt.), Air & Waste Mgmt. Assn., Am. Republican. Avocations: swimming, scuba diving. Home: 23900 E 88th St Lees Summit MO 64064-2711 Office: Capital Products Inc 618 SW 3rd St Ste H Lees Summit MO 64063-2277

LETTOW, CHARLES FREDERICK, lawyer; b. Iowa Falls, Iowa, Feb. 10, 1941; s. Carl Frederick and Catherine (Reisinger) L.; m. Sue Lettow, Apr. 20, 1963; children: Renee, Carl II, John, Paul. BS in Chem. Engring., Iowa State U., 1962; LLB, Stanford U., 1968. Bar: Calif. 1969, Iowa 1969, D.C. 1972, Md. 1991. Law clk. to Hon. Ben C. Duniway U.S. Ct. Appeals (9th cir.), San Francisco, 1968-69; law clk. to Hon. Warren E. Burger U.S. Supreme Ct., Washington, 1969-70; counsel Council on Environ. Quality, Washington, 1970-73; assoc. Cleary, Gottlieb, Steen & Hamilton, Washington, 1973-76, ptnr., 1976—; pres. Busy Way Farms, Inc., 1989—. Contbr. articles to profl. jours. Trustee Potomac Sch., McLean, Va., 1983-90, chmn. bd. trustees, 1985-88. 1st lt. U.S. Army, 1963-65. mem. ABA, Am. Law Inst., D.C. Bar Assn., Iowa Bar Assn., Order of Coif. Club: University. Office: 1752 N St NW Washington DC 20036-2907

LETTS, J. SPENCER, federal judge; b. 1934. BA, Yale U., 1956; LLB, Harvard U., 1960. Commd. U.S. Army, 1956, advanced through grades to capt., resigned, 1965; pvt. practice law Fulbright & Jaworski, Houston, 1960-66, Troy, Malin, Loveland & Letts, L.A., 1973-74, Hedlund, Hunter & Lynch, L.A., 1978-82, Latham & Watkins, L.A., 1982-85; gen. counsel Teledyne, Inc., 1966-73, 75-78, legal cons., 1978-82; judge U.S. Dist. Ct. (cen. dist.) Calif., L.A., 1986—. Contbr. articles to profl. jours. Mem. ABA, Calif. State Bar, Tex. State Bar, L.A. Bar Assn., Houston Bar Assn. Office: US Dist Ct 312 N Spring St Ste 243J Los Angeles CA 90012-4704*

LETTVIN, THEODORE, concert pianist; b. Chgo., Oct. 29, 1926; s. Solomon and Fannie (Naktin) L.; m. Joan Rorimer; children: Rory, Ellen, David. Mus. B., Curtis Inst. Music, 1949; postgrad., U. Pa. Head piano dept. Cleve. Music Sch. Settlement, 1957-68; prof. piano New Eng. Conservatory Music, Boston, 1968-77; prof., dir., doctoral program in piano performance U. Mich. Sch. Music, Ann Arbor, 1977-87; disting. prof. dept. music Rutgers U., New Brunswick, N.J., 1987—, dir. doctor of mus. arts and artist's diploma program, 1987-92, studio tchr., coach chamber music, 1992—; vis. lectr. U. Colo., 1956-57; tchr. master classes U. S.E. Mass., summer 1973, U. Calif., San Jose, 1992, 93; mem. faculty Chamber Music Sch., U. Maine, Orono. First appeared as concert pianist, 1931, solo debut with Chgo. Symphony Orch., 1939, solo, orchestral appearances include Boston Symphony Orch., N.Y. Philharm., Phila. Orch., Cleve. Orch., Chgo. Orch., Washington Nat. Symphony, Pitts. Symphony, Seattle Symphony, Mpls. Symphony, Atlanta Symphony, other Am. and European orchs.; radio appearance Bell Telephone Hour, 1948, debut Ravinia Festival, 1951, apprentice condr. William Steinberg, Buffalo Symphony Orch., 1950-51, concertized throughout U.S., Can., Europe, Africa, 1952-85; concert appearances Pitts., Cin., Atlanta, Boston, N.Y.C., Phila., Chgo., Cleve., Mpls. and Chautauqua, Ravinia, Interlochen and New Coll., Town Hall, Alice Tully Hall concerts, in N.Y.C., Boston Symphony Orch.; performances in concert with Bernard Greenhouse, cellist; concert tours, Europe, 1952, 55, 58, 60, 62-85, Israel, 1973, Africa and Japan, 1974; also numerous performances with European orchs., summer festivals, TV; asst. artist: Africa and Japan, Marlboro Music Festival, 1963. Recipient award Soc. Am. Musicians, 1933, Naumberg award, 1948, Michaels Meml. award, 1949, Laureate internat. piano competition Queen Elisabeth of Belgium. Mem. Am. Fedn. Musicians, Am. Guild Mus. Artists, AAUP (exec. com.), Music Tchrs. Nat. Assn., Am. Liszt Soc., Curtis Inst. Music Alumnae Assn. (bd. dirs.). Home: 12 Bernard Rd East Brunswick NJ 08816-1306 Office: Rutgers U Marryott Music Bldg Douglass Campus New Brunswick NJ 08903 also: 463 Rowe Mountain Rd Bradford NH 03221-3408

LETWIN, LEON, legal educator; b. Milw., Dec. 29, 1929; s. Lazar and Bessie (Rosenthal) L.; m. Alita Zurav, July 11, 1952; children—Michael, Daniel, David. Ph.B., U. Chgo., 1950; LL.B., U. Wis., 1952; LL.M., Harvard U., 1964. Bar: Wis. 1952, Calif. 1969. Teaching fellow Harvard Law Sch., Boston, 1963-64; faculty Law Sch. UCLA, 1964—, prof., 1968—. Contbr. articles to profl. jours. Active ACLU. Mem. Lawyers Guild, State Bar Calif. Home: 2226 Manning Ave Los Angeles CA 90064-2002 Office: UCLA Law Sch 405 Hilgard Ave Los Angeles CA 90095-9000

LETZIG, BETTY JEAN, association executive; b. Hardin, Mo., Feb. 18, 1926; d. Robert H. and Alina Violet (Mayes) L. BA, Scarritt Coll., 1950, MA, 1968. Ednl. staff The Methodist Ch., Ark., Okla. Tex., 1953-60; with Internat. Deaconess Exchange Program, London, 1961-62; staff exec. Nat. Div. United Meth. Ch., N.Y.C., 1962-95, ret. 1995; coord. Mission Pers. Support Svcs., 1984-88; exec. sec. Deaconess Program Office, 1989-95. Contbr. articles to profl. jours. Bd. dirs. Global Health Action (INSA), Atlanta, 1974-88, Vellore Christian Med. Coll., N.Y.C., 1984-94; mem. U.S. com. Internat. Coun. Social Welfare, Washington, 1983-89; active Nat. Interfaith Coalition on Aging, Athens, Ga. and Washington, 1972—, pres., 1981-85. Recipient Deaconess Exch. award Commn. Deaconess Work, 1961-62. Mem. Nat. Coun. Aging, Nat. Voluntary Orgns. Ind. Living for Aging (exec. com. 1978-84), Nat. Coun. Social Welfare, Older Women's League. United Methodist. Avocations: travel, beachcombing, photography, needlework. Home: 235 E 22nd St Ofc 1U New York NY 10010-4616 Office: Nat Program Divsn Gen Bd Global Ministries 475 Riverside Dr Ste 300 New York NY 10115-0122

LEU, MING CHUAN, engineering educator; b. Taoyuan, Taiwan, Apr. 27, 1951; came to U.S. 1975; s. Teh-Yung and Tao (Hwang) L.; m. Shu-Hwa Hwang, July 16, 1978; children—Paul W., John W., Karen W. B.S., Taiwan U., 1972; M.S., Pa. State U., 1977; Ph.D., U. Calif.-Berkeley, 1981. Research asst. Pa. State U., 1975-77, U. Calif., Berkeley, 1977-81; asst. prof. engring. Cornell U., Ithaca, N.Y., 1981-87; prof., sponsored chmn. mfg. and productivity N.J. Inst. Tech., 1987—; program dir. NSF, 1996—; program dir. NSF, 1996—; rschr. Moog Inc., East Aurora, N.Y., 1982-89, AT&T, Princeton, N.J., 1988—; faculty advisor Tau Beta Pi, 1983-87. Contbr. 130 articles to profl. jours. and confs. Editor: Computer-Integrated Manufacturing, 1983, Computer Integrated Manufacturing and Robotics, 1984, Robotics and Manufacturing Automation, 1985, Japan-USA Symposium on Flexible Automation, 1992. Earl C. Anthony scholar U. Calif., Berkeley 1977-80; NSF research grantee, 1983—; rsch. grantee Office Naval Rsch., 1992-96; recipient Wood award Forest Product Research Soc. award, 1981; Young Investigator awardee White House and NSF, 1985, Harlan J. Perlis Rsch. award N.J. Inst. Tech., 1993. Mem. Soc. Automotive Engrs. (Ralph R. Teetor ednl. award 1985), ASME (chmn. mfg. engring. divsn. 1989-90, fellow 1993), IEEE, CIRP, SME (Univ. Lead award 1994), Am. Soc. Engring.

Edn., Sigma Xi, Tau Beta Pi, Phi Kappa Phi. Christian and Missionary Alliance. Home: 3 Hamilton Pl Pine Brook NJ 07058-9725 Office: NJ Inst Tech Newark NJ 07102

LEUBERT, ALFRED OTTO PAUL, international business consultant, investor; b. N.Y.C., Dec. 7, 1922; s. Paul T. and Josephine (Haaga) L.; m. Celestine Capka, July 22, 1944 (div. 1977); children: Eloise Ann Cronin, Susan Beth; m. Hope Sherman Drapkin, June 4, 1978 (div. 1982). Student, Dartmouth Coll., 1943; BS, Fordham U., 1946; MBA, NYU, 1950. Account mgr. J.K. Lasser & Co., N.Y.C., 1948-52; controller Vision, Inc., N.Y.C., 1952-53; controller Old Town Corp., 1953-54, sec., controller, 1954-56, sec.-treas., 1956-57, v.p., treas., 1957-58; dir. subsidiaries Old Town Corp. (Old Town Internat. Corp., Old Town Ribbon & Carbon Co., Inc.), Mass. and Calif., 1955-58; v.p., controller Willcox & Gibbs, Inc., N.Y.C., 1958-59; v.p., treas. Willcox & Gibbs, Inc., 1959-65, pres., dir., chief exec. officer, 1966-76; founder, pub., pres. Leubert's Compendium of Bus. (Fin. and Econ. Barometers), 1978-82; pres. Alfred O.P. Leubert Ltd., 1981-82, chmn. CEO, 1993—; chmn., CEO Solidyne, Inc., 1982; chmn. bd., pres., CEO, dir. Chyron Corp., 1983-91; dir. K & E Real Estate Ltd., China, 1994-96; chmn. bd. CEO Leubert & Co. (H.K.) Ltd., 1994—; dir. Laser-Pacific Media Corp., 1995-96; chmn. bd., CEO, bd. dirs. Chyron Group (U.K.) Ltd., 1985-89; dir. Isis Interactive Inc., 1996—; dir., vice chrmn. Advanced Definition Systems, Inc., 1996—; chmn. bd., CEO, bd. dirs. CMX Corp.; bd. dirs. Aurora Systems, 1988-91; vice chmn., dir. Advanced Definition Systems, Inc., 1996; CEO, dir. CGS Units, Inc., 1988-90, chmn. bd., 1989-90; bd. dirs. Digital Svcs. Corp.; vice chmn. bd. dirs. CMX Laser Sys., Inc., 1988-93; instr. accountancy Pace Coll., 1955-57. Bd. dirs. United Fund of Manhasset, 1963-69, pres., 1964-65; bd. dirs. Actor's Studio, 1972-76; adv. bd. St. Anthony's Guidance Clinic, 1967-69. Served to 1st lt., inf. USMCR, 1943-46. Decorated Bronze Star; recipient Humanitarian award Hebrew Acad., N.Y.C., 1971. Mem. AICPA, N.Y. State Soc. CPAs, Fordham U. Alumni Assn. Roman Catholic. Club: N.Y. Athletic (N.Y.C.). Home and Office: 1 Lincoln Plz New York NY 10023-7129

LEUBSDORF, CARL PHILIPP, newspaper executive; b. N.Y.C., Mar. 17, 1938; s. Karl and Bertha (Boschwitz) L.; m. Carolyn Cleveland Stockmeyer, Mar. 26, 1963 (div. 1978); 1 child: Carl Philipp Jr.; stepchildren: Lorna Stockmeyer, E. William Stockmeyer Jr., C. Cleveland Stockmeyer, Claire C. Stockmeyer; m. Susan Page, May 23, 1982; children: Benjamin Page, William Page. BA in Govt., Cornell U., 1959; MS in Jour., Columbia U., 1960. Staff writer AP, New Orleans, 1960-63, Washington, 1963-75; corr. Balt. Sun, Washington, 1976-81; AME Washington bur. chief Dallas Morning News, Washington, 1981—. Mem. White House Corrs. Assn. (pres. 1995-96), Gridiron Club, National Press Club (Washington). Office: Dallas Morning News 1325 G St NW Ste 250 Washington DC 20005-3104

LEUNG, FRANKIE FOOK-LUN, lawyer; b. Guangzhou, China, 1949; married; 1 child. BA in Psychology with honors, Hong Kong U., 1972; MS in Psychology, Birmingham U., Eng., 1974; BA, MA in Jurisprudence, Oxford U., Eng., 1976; JD, Coll. of Law, London, 1977. Bar: Calif. 1987. Barrister Eng. and Hong Kong, 1977—; lectr. Chinese law for businessmen Hong Kong U., 1984-85, 85-86; vis. scholar Harvard U. Law Sch., 1983; barrister, solicitor Supreme Ct. of Victoria, Australia, 1983—, Calif. Bar, 1987—; cons. prof. Chinese Law Diploma Program, U. East Asia, 1986-87; adj. prof. Loyola Law Sch., L.A., 1988—, Pepperdine U. Law Sch., 1989-90; lectr. Stanford U. Law Sch., 1995—. Author 4 books; contbr. numerous articles to profl. jours., chpts. to 4 books. Bd. advisors Hong Kong Archives Hoover Instn.-Stanford U., 1988—. Mem. Calif. State Bar (mem. exec. coun. internat. sect. 1989-92, Wiley W. Manuel award 1993), Hong Kong Bar Assn., European Assn. for Chinese Law (mem. exec. coun. 1986—, country corr. 1985—), Am. C. of C. (chmn. subcom. on Chinese intellectual property law 1985-86), Am. Soc. Internat. Law (judge moot ct. 1984-86). Office: Lewis D'Amato 221 N Figueroa St Ste 1200 Los Angeles CA 90012-2646

LEUNG, KASON KAI CHING, computer specialist; b. Hong Kong, July 2, 1962; came to U.S., 1963; s. Patrick Kin Man and Esther Mo Chee (Shum) L. BA in Computer Sci., U. Calif., 1984. Microcomputer specialist Coopers & Lybrand, San Francisco, 1985-87; freelance computer specialist San Francisco, 1988-90; computer applications specialist T.Y. Lin Internat., San Francisco, 1990-92; tech. specialist Ziff-Davis Labs., Foster City, Calif., 1993-94; tech. analyst PC Mag., Foster City, Calif., 1995; sr. tech. analyst Ziff-Davis Benchmark Operation, Foster City, Calif., 1996, Ziff-Davis Labs., Foster City, Calif., 1997—. Mem. Assn. for Computing Machinery. Avocations: computers, sports, music, reading. Home: 90 Stanford Heights Ave San Francisco CA 94127-2318

LEUPOLD, HERBERT AUGUST, physicist; b. Bklyn., Jan. 6, 1931; s. August John and Josefa (Thalmyer) L. BS in Physics, CUNY-Queens Coll., 1953; AM in Physics, Columbia U., 1958, PhD in Physics, 1964. Instr. physics CUNY-Queens Coll., Flushing, 1957-83; postdoctoral fellow Lawrence Livermore Lab., Livermore, Calif., 1964-67; instr. physics Monmouth Coll., West Long Branch, N.J., 1967-68, 69-70, 84-85; instr. chemistry Trenton (N.J.) State Coll., 1984-85; rsch. physicist U.S. Army Rsch. Lab., Ft. Monmouth, N.J., 1967—. Co-author: Rare Earth Iron Permanent Magnetics, 1996; contbr. over 100 articles to profl. jours. over 80 patents in fields of magnetics and electronics. With U.S. Army, 1953-55. Fellow IEEE (mem. assoc. editors of IEEE transactions), Army Rsch. Lab.; mem. Magnetics Soc. of IEEE (mem. adminstrv. com. 1991-93, mem. various conf. organizing coms.), Am. Phys. Soc., Sigma Xi. Roman Catholic. Office: US Mil Acad Bartlett Hall Rm 300 West Point NY 10996

LEUPP, EDYTHE PETERSON, retired education educator, administrator; b. Mpls., Nov. 27, 1921; d. Reynold H. and Lillian (Aldridge) Peterson; m. Thomas A. Leupp, Jan. 29, 1944 (dec.); children: DeEtte (dec.), Patrice, Stacia, Roderick, Braden. BS, U. Oreg., 1947, MS, 1951, EdD, 1972. Tchr. various pub. schs. Idaho, 1941-45, Portland, Oreg., 1945-55; dir. tchr. edn. Northwest Nazarene Coll., Nampa, Idaho, 1955-61; sch. adminstr. Portland Pub. Schs., 1963-84; dir. tchr. edn. George Fox Coll., Newberg, Oreg., 1984-87; ret., 1987; s; vis. prof. So. Nazarene U., Bethany, Okla., 1988-95; adj. prof. Warner Pacific Coll., Portland, 1996—; pres. Portland Assn. Pub. Sch. Adminstrs., 1973-75; dir.-at-large Nat. Coun. Adminstrv. Women in Edn., Washington, 1973-76; state chmn. Oreg. Sch. Prins. Spl. Project, 1978-79; chair Confdn. Oreg. Sch. Adminstrs. Ann. Conf.; rschr. 40 tchr. edn. programs in colls. and univs.; designer tchr. edn. program George Fox Coll. Author tchr. edn. materials. Pres. Idaho State Aux. Mcpl. League, 1957, Nampa PTA, 1958, Nampa unit AAUW, 1956; bd. dirs. Portland Fedn. Women's Clubs, 1963. Recipient Golden Gift award, 1981; named Honored Tchr. of Okla., 1993, Hazel Fishwood scholar, 1970; Idea fellow Charles Kettering Found., 1978, 80, 87, 91, 92, 93, 94. Mem. ASCD, Am. Assn. Colls. Tchr. Edn., Delta Kappa Gamma (pres. Alpha Rho 1986-88), Phi Delta Kappa, Pi Lambda Theta. Republican. Nazarene. Avocations: travel, crafts, photography. Home: 8100 SW 2nd Ave Portland OR 97219-4602

LEUTHOLD, RAYMOND MARTIN, agricultural economics educator; b. Billings, Mont., Oct. 13, 1940; s. John Henry and Grace Irene L.; m. Jane Hornaday, Aug. 20, 1966; children—Kevin, Gregory. Student, Colo. U., 1958-59; B.S., Mont. State U., 1962; M.S., U. Wis., 1966, Ph.D., 1968. Faculty U. Ill., Urbana-Champaign, 1967—; now prof. dept. agrl. econs. U. Ill., T.A. Hieronymus disting. prof., dir. office futures and options rsch.; vis. scholar Stanford U., 1974, Chgo. Mercantile Exch., 1990, 91. Co-author: The Theory and Practice of Futures Markets, 1989; editor: Commodity Markets and Futures Prices, 1979; co-editor: Livestock Futures Research Symposium, 1980. Served with U.S. Army, 1962-64. Fulbright research scholar Institute de Gestion Internationale Agro-Alimentaire, Cergy, France, 1981. Mem. Am. Econ. Assn., Am. Agrl. Econs. Assn. (Disting. Policy award 1980, Outstanding Instr. award 1986, 88, 90, 92, College Funk award 1993). Office: 305 Mumford Hall 1301 W Gregory Dr Urbana IL 61801-3608

LEUTY, GERALD JOHNSTON, osteopathic physician and surgeon; b. Knoxville, Iowa, July 23, 1919; s. John William and Mable Reichard (Johnston) L.; m. Martha L. Weymouth, Jan. 24, 1940 (div. 1957); children: Maxine Joanne, Robert James, Gerald Johnston Jr., Karl Joseph; m. Norma Jean Hindman, Dec. 30, 1969; children: Barbara Jayne, Patrick Jack. AB, Kemper Mil. Sch., Boonville, Mo., 1939; postgrad., Drake U., Des Moines, 1944-45; DO, Des Moines Coll. Osteopathy, 1949; embalmer, Coll. Mortuary Sci., St. Louis, 1941. Mortician/embalmer Cauldwell-McJihon Funeral Home, Des Moines, 1939-40; aero. engr. Boeing Aircraft Co., Wichita, Kans., 1941-42; osteopathic physician and surgeon Knoxville (Iowa) Osteopathic Clinic, 1949-56; dir. Leuty Osteopathic Clinic, Earlham, Iowa, 1957-77; osteopathic physician and surgeon in pvt. practice Santa Rosa, Calif., 1977—; prof. clin. med. Coll. Osteopathic Medicine of the Pacific, Pomona, Calif., 1985—. With U.S. Army, 1942-46. Named Physician of the Yr., 6th Dist. Iowa Osteopathic Soc., 1975, Disting. Leadership award, Am. Biog. Inst., 1988, others. Fellow Internat. Co. Angiologists; mem. Am. Osteopathic Assn. (ho. of dels., life mem. 1989), Iowa Osteopathic Soc. (pres. 6th dist. 1974), Soc. Osteopathic Physicians, No. Calif. Osteopathic Med. Soc. (pres. 1981), Osteopathic Physicians and Surgeons of Calif. (pres. 1982), Am. Acad. Osteopathy (chmn. component socs. com. 1988, pres. Calif. divsn. 1987, pres. No. Calif. divsn. 1989, 91-93, 95), North Coast Osteopathic Med. Assn. (pres. 1992), Am. Med. Soc. Vienna (life mem.), Am. Legion (6th dist. comdr. 1974-75), Lions (pres. 1946). Republican. Presbyterian. Avocations: photography, travel. Home: 5835 La Cuesta Dr Santa Rosa CA 95409-3914

LEUTZE, JAMES RICHARD, academic administrator, television producer and host; b. Charleston, S.C., Dec. 24, 1935; w. Willard Parker and Magdalene Mae (Seith) L.; m. Kathleen Shirley Erskine, Feb. 13, 1960; children—Magdalene Leigh, Jay Erskine, James Parker. B.A., U. Md., 1957; M.A., U. Miami, 1959; Ph.D., Duke U., 1968. Legis. asst. U.S. Senator Hubert Humphrey, Washington, 1963-64; prof. history U. N.C., Chapel Hill, 1968-87, chmn. curriculum peace, war, and def., 1979-87, Bowman and Gordon Gray prof., 1982, Dowd prof. Peace and War, 1986; TV host-producer N.C. Ctr. for Pub. TV, Chapel Hill, 1984—; pres. Hampden-Sydney (Va.) Coll., 1987-90; chancellor U. N.C. at Wilmington, 1990—. Author: Bargaining for Supremacy: Anglo-American Naval Collaboration, 1937-41, 1977 (Bernath prize 1978), A Different Kind of Victory: The Biography of Admiral Thomas C. Hart, 1981 (John Lyman Book award 1981); editor: London Journal Gen. Raymond E. Lee, 1972, The Role of the Military in a Democracy, 1974; contbr. articles to profl. jours. Served to capt. USAF, 1960-63. Recipient Standard Oil award for teaching U. N.C., 1971, Tanner award for teaching, 1978, Order of Golden Fleece award, 1983, J.W. Pate award for creating environ. awareness, 1995. Mem. Orgn. Am. Historians, Royal U.S. Inst. (London), Am. Hist. Assn., Univ. Club (N.D.), George C. Marshall Found., Phi Beta Kappa. Democrat. Episcopalian. Avocations: sportsman; hunting; fishing. Office: U NC 601 S College Rd Wilmington NC 28403-3201

LEUVER, ROBERT JOSEPH, former government official, association executive; b. Chgo., Feb. 2, 1927; s. Joseph Anthony and Helen Yolanda (Fornaciari) L.; m. Hilda Sanjuana Ortiz, July 29, 1950; 1 dau., Mary Ellen. AB, Loyola U., L.A., 1950; MA, Cath. U. Am., 1954. Exec. v.p., treas. Claretians, Inc., Chgo., 1959-72; chief mgmt. analysis divsn. ACTION, Washington, 1972-74; chief treas. payroll divsn. U.S. Dept. Treasury, Washington, 1974-79; asst. dir. Bur. Engraving and Printing, Washington, 1979-82, dep. dir., 1982, dir., 1983-88; now exec. dir. Am. Numismatic Assn., Colorado Springs, Colo.; mem. Citizens Stamp Adv. Com. to Postmaster Gen., U.S. Postal Service, 1983-88. Bd. dirs. Cath. Journalism Scholarship Fund, N.Y.C., 1967-72; v.p., dir. Southampton Assn., Arlington, Va., 1979-86. Recipient Best Editorial award Cath. Press Assn., 1964, Sr. Exec. award, 1980, 84, 85, Presdl. Meritorious Svc. award U.S. Pres., Washington, 1983, Presdl. Disting. Svc. award, 1986. Mem. Fed. Exec. Inst. (grad.), Sr. Exec. Assn. Roman Catholic. Office: Am Numismatic Assn 818 N Cascade Ave Colorado Springs CO 80903-3208

LEV, ALEXANDER SHULIM, mechanical engineer; b. Tselinograd, USSR, May 4, 1945; came to U.S., 1979; s. Borukh and Golda (Kopitman) L.; m. Polina Zhdanovskaja, Aug. 31, 1968; 1 child, Victoria. MSME, Lvov Polytech Inst., 1968. Project mgr. Glavspetsavtotrans, Lvov, USSR, 1968-78; sr. engr. Machine Plant, Lvov, USSR, 1978-79; metalurgist Ronson Metals Corp., Newark, N.J., 1980-82, foundry quality control mgr., 1982-83, reduction dept. mgr., 1986; project mgr. FMB Systems Inc., Harrison, N.J., 1986-94; v.p. Internat. Fair Share Inc., Rockaway, N.J., 1994—. Patentee in field. Mem. Am. Metals Soc., Metallurgical Soc. Avocations: reading, art, metal work, tennis. Home: 16 Princeton St Maplewood NJ 07040-3517

LEVA, JAMES ROBERT, electric utility company executive; b. Boonton, N.J., May 10, 1932; s. James and Rose (Cocci) L.; m. Marie Marinaro, Dec. 19, 1950; children: James, Daniel, Linda, Michael, Christopher. BSEE, magna cum laude, Fairleigh Dickinson U., 1960; JD, Seton Hall Law Sch., 1980. Lineman Jersey Central Power and Light Co., Morristown, N.J., 1952-60, elec. engring. and operating depts., 1960-62, personnel rep., 1962-68, mgr. employee relations, 1968-69, v.p. personnel and services, 1969-79, v.p. consumer affairs, 1979-82, dir., 1976-82; pres., COO, dir. Pa. Electric Co., Johnstown, 1982-86; pres., COO Jersey Cen. Power & Light Co., Morristown, N.J., 1986-92; chmn., CEO Gen. Pub. Utilities, 1992—, also bd. dirs.; chmn., pres., CEO, bd. dirs. GPU Service Corp., Parsippany, N.J.; chmn. bd. dirs. GPU Nuc. Corp., Parsippany, N.J.; chmn. CEO, bd. dirs. Met. Edison Co., Reading, Pa., Pa. Electric Co., Johnstown, Pa., Utilities Mut. Ins. Co., N.J. Utilities Assn.; chmn. St. Clares Health Care Found.; trustee Tri-County Scholarship Fund, Fairleigh Dickinson U.; chmn. Sch. Planning & Pub. Policy Rutgers U. Served with USMC, 1949-51, Korea. Mem. N.J. Bar, N.J. Bar Assn. Roman Catholic. Club: Mendham (N.J.) Golf & Tennis. Office: Gen Pub Utilities 100 Interpace Pky Parsippany NJ 07054-1149

LEVA, NEIL IRWIN, psychotherapist, hypnotherapist; b. N.Y.C., Sept. 18, 1929; s. Charles and Alice Lee (Peirce) L.; m. Jean Kathryn Walters, Dec. 4, 1952 (div. May, 1988); children: Steven L., Michael N., Scott A.; m. Susan Mary Callagy, Aug. 12, 1988. BA in Govt., U. Tex., 1963; MA in Systems Mgmt., U. So. Calif., 1973; MA in Psychology, Cath. U. Am., 1976; MSW, U. Md., 1990. Diplomate in clin. social work. Commd. 2d. lt. U.S. Army, 1953, advanced through grades to col., 1976, retired, 1976; with psych. factors div. Quadraennial Bd. for Rev. of Mil. Compensation, Washington, 1974-76; psychotherapist Village Counselling Ctr., Potomac, Md., 1978-86, Met. Psychotherapist Group, Bethesda, 1986-90, Village Counseling Ctr., Potomac, Md., 1990—; human factors cons. The Artery Orgn., Washington, 1978-83, Montgomery County Schs., Rockville, Md., 1979-81. Decorated D.F.C., Bronze Star with V device and 4 oak leaf clusters, Air Medal with V device and 10 oak leaf clusters, Purple Heart, Legion of Merit. Mem. NASW, DAV, Am. Assn. Marriage and Family Therapist, Am. Assn. Profl. Hypnotherapist, Internat. Transactional Analysis Assn., Mil. Order of Purple Heart, Am. Legion. Democrat. Avocations: musician, outdoors, fishing. Home: 10011 Counselman Rd Potomac MD 20854-5019 Office: Village Counseling Ctr 10011 Counselman Rd Potomac MD 20854-5019

LEVADA, WILLIAM JOSEPH, archbishop; b. Long Beach, Calif., June 15, 1936; s. Joseph and Lorraine (Nunez) L. B.A., St. John's Coll., Camarillo, Calif., 1958; S.T.L., Gregorian U., Rome, 1962, S.T.D., 1971. Ordained priest Roman Cath. Ch., 1961, consecrated bishop, 1983. Assoc. pastor Archdiocese of L.A., 1962-67; prof. theology St. John's Sem., Camarillo, Calif., 1970-76; ofcl. Doctrinal Congregation, Vatican City, Italy, 1976-82; exec. dir. Calif. Cath. Conf., Sacramento, 1982-84; aux. bishop Archdiocese of L.A., 1983-86; archbishop Archdiocese of Portland, Oreg., 1986-95; Archbishop of San Francisco, 1995—. Trustee Cath. U. Am.; chmn. bd. dirs. Pope John XXIII Med.-Moral Rsch. and Edn. Ctr. Mem. Nat. Conf. Cath. Bishops (com. on doctrine), U.S. Cath. Conf., Cath. Theol. Soc. Am., Canon Law Soc. Am. Office: Archbishop of San Francisco 445 Church St San Francisco CA 94114-1720

LEVAL, PIERRE NELSON, federal judge; b. N.Y.C., Sept. 4, 1936; s. Fernand and Beatrice (Reiter) L. B.A. cum laude, Harvard U., 1959, J.D. magna cum laude, 1963. Bar: N.Y. 1964, U.S. Ct. Appeals 2d Circuit 1964, U.S. Dist. Ct. So. Dist. N.Y 1966. Law clk. to Hon. Henry J. Friendly, U.S. Ct. Appeals, 1963-64; asst. U.S. atty. So. Dist. N.Y., 1964-68, chief appellate atty., 1967-68; assoc. firm Cleary, Gottlieb, Steen & Hamilton, N.Y.C., 1969-74; ptnr. firm, 1973-75; 1st asst. dist. atty. Office of Dist. Atty., N.Y. County, 1975-76; chief asst. dist. atty. Office of Dist. Atty., 1976-77; U.S. dist. judge So. Dist. N.Y., N.Y.C., 1977-93; judge U.S. Ct. of Appeals (2d cir.), N.Y.C., 1993—. Contbr. articles to profl. jours. Served with U.S. Army, 1959. Mem. Am. Law Inst. (council), Assn. Bar City N.Y., N.Y. County Lawyers Assn. Office: US Courthouse Foley Square New York NY 10007-1501

LEVALLEY, GUY GLENN, speech communication educator; b. Phila., Oct. 21, 1942; s. Glenn Henry and Mary Jane (Henderson) LeV.; BA, Glassboro State Coll., 1964; MA, U. Iowa, 1967; m. E. Raye Gerlack, June 17, 1967 (div. 1981); 1 son, Ian G.; m. Page Lacey, Oct. 21, 1995. Designer, tech. dir. Glassboro (N.J.) Summer Theatre, 1963-67, Monticello Coll., Godfrey, Ill., 1967-68; asst. tech. dir. N.Y. Shakespeare Festival Mobile Theatre Unit, N.Y.C., 1967; asst. prof. theatre Prince George's Coll., Largo, Md., 1968-73, assoc. prof. speech communication, designer, tech. dir. theatre, 1974—; lighting designer Murray Spalding Movement Arts Inc., 1975—, City Dance '77; bldg. cons. Church St. Theatre, Capitol Hill Arts Workshop; co-dir. 94th Combat Bomb Wing Research Group. Mem. Am. Theatre Assn., U.S. Inst. Theatre Tech., 8th USAF Hist. Soc., Eastern Communication Assn. Democrat. Quaker. Reviewer, cons. Choice mag., 1974—. Author: Annotated Bibliography of Stage Lighting for the Dance, 1974, 77; Technical Elements of Stage Lighting; Technical Theatre: A Critical Bibliography, 1985; contbg. author: A Handbook of Stage Lighting; contbr. articles to profl. jours. Home: 7305 Hopkins Ave College Park MD 20740-3411 Office: 301 Largo Rd Largo MD 20870

LE VAN, DANIEL HAYDEN, retired gas industry executive; b. Savannah, Ga., Mar. 29, 1924; s. Daniel Hayden and Ruth (Harner) LeV. Grad., Middlesex Sch., 1943; BA, Harvard U., 1950; postgrad., Babson Inst., 1950-51. Underwriter Zurich Ins. Co., N.Y.C., 1951-52; co-owner, dir. Overseas Properties, Ltd., N.Y.C., 1970—; dir. Colonial Gas Co., Lowell, Mass., 1973-97, ret., 1997. With AUS, 1943-46. Mem. Harvard Club (N.Y.C. and Boston).

LEVASSEUR, SUSAN LEE SALISBURY, secondary education educator; b. Wyandotte, Mich., Nov. 20, 1967; d. David Henry and Lynda Lee (Macaulay) Salisbury; m. John Peter LeVasseur, Dec. 19, 1992. BS in Edn., Ctrl. Mich. U., 1990; MEd in Counseling, Wayne State U., 1997. Cert. secondary tchr., Mich. Substitute tchr. Dearborn (Mich.) Schs., 1991, Allen Park (Mich.) Schs., 1991; tchr. sci. Berkley (Mich.) Schs., 1991—. Instr. Mich. Red Cross, Detroit, 1983—; deacon Allen Park Presbyn. Ch., 1991-93; mem. Colitis Found. Am. Mem. ASCD, AAUW, Nat. Counseling Assn., Am. Kennel Club, Nat. Sci. Tchrs. Assn., Mich. Sci. Tchrs. Assn., Mich. Counseling Assn., Mich. Edn. Assn., Kappa Delta Pi, Alpha Phi Omega. Presbyterian. Avocations: figure skating, swimming, dog training. Home: 22436 Cobb St Dearborn MI 48128-1313

LEVASSEUR, WILLIAM RYAN, lawyer; b. Fredericksburg, Va., June 10, 1935; s. George B. and Martha F. (Callegary) L.; m. Joanne Bowers, May 30, 1958; children: William Ryan Jr., John M., Michele Henzi. AA, U. Balt., 1958, JD, 1961. Bar: Md. 1962, U.S. Dist. Ct. Md. 1962, U.S. Supreme Ct. 1972, D.C. 1979, U.S. Ct. Appeals (4th cir.) 1979. Pvt. practice Balt., 1962-69; asst. atty. gen. Md. Atty. Gen.'s Office, Balt., 1969-71; assoc. Semmes, Bowen & Semmes, Balt., 1971-73, ptnr., 1974-94; ptnr. Howell, Gately, Whitney & Carter, Towson, Md., 1994—. Mem. adv. bd. Villa Julie Coll., 1982—, U. Balt. Sch. Law, 1985-91, trustee; trustee Md. Law Rev., 1996-97. With USAFR, 1955-59. Named Alumnus of the Yr. U. Balt. Alumni Assn., 1989. Mem. ABA (tort and ins. practice sect., elected to sect. coun., 1996, minority women and gen. mem. involvement com. 1992-95, women and minority involvement 1995-96, chmn. arrangements com., 1995-96, co-chmn. family life com. 1991-93, mem. pub. rels. com. 1990-93, chmn. liaison jud. adminstrv. divsn. 1986-89, chmn. Profl. Issues, 1987-88, chmn. Scope and Correlation, 1988-89, chmn. workers' compensation and employers' liability commn. and chmn. nat. inst. 1985-86, program chmn. 1983-84, sr. vice chmn. 1987—), Fed. Bar Assn. (mem. nat. coun. 1995—, pres. Md. chpt. 1987-88, chair select com. bench bar 1993-94, cir. officer 4th cir. 1988-92, chair nat. mem., com. 1991-93, mem. 1993-94, nat. mem. svcs. com. 1988-89, nat. nominating com. 1988, ops. rev. com., advisor found. 1991-93, bd. dirs., pres. 1994—), Md. State Bar Assn. (sect. adminstrn., law, litigation, negligence and compensation, mem. fed. dist. ct. com., bd. govs. 1997—), D.C. Bar Assn. (litigation divsn.), Assn. Def. Trial Counsel (workers compensation com.), Assn. Compensation Ins. Attys. (pres. 1982), Bar Assn. Balt. City (sec. 1993-94, v.p. 1990, 94-95, pres. elect 1995-96, pres. 1996-97, treas. 1992, chmn. law sch. activities/funding com. 1983-90, jud. com. 1989-94, chmn. 1991-92, chair legis. com. joint task, force for injured workers rehab. 1987—), Balt. City Bar Found., Md. Inst. for Continuing Profl. Edn. Lawyers (trustee 1995-96), U. Balt. Alumni Assn. (pres. 1983-85, sch. law adv. bd. 1985-91), Md. Assn. Def. Trial Attys., Def. Rsch. Inst., KC. Democrat. Roman Catholic. Home: 1917 Knollton Rd Lutherville Timonium MD 21093-5248 Office: Howell Gately Whitney & Carter 401 Washington Ave Fl 12 Towson MD 21204-4821

LEVAY, SIMON, neurologist, writer, educator; b. Oxford, England, Aug. 28, 1943. BA in Natural Scis., Cambridge U., 1966; PhD in Neuroanatomy, U. Gottingen, 1971. Postdoctoral fellow Harvard U., 1972-74, from instr. to assoc. prof. neurobiology, 1974-84; assoc. prof. Salk Inst. for Biol. Scis., La Jolla, Calif., 1984-92; founder Inst. for Gay and Lesbian Edn., West Hollywood, Calif., 1992—. Author: The Sexual Brain, 1993, Queer Science, 1996, Albrick's Gold, 1997; contbr. articles to profl. jours.; co-author: (with Elisabeth Nonas) City of Friends: A Portrait of the Gay and Lesbian Community in America, 1996. Achievements include research demonstrating that the brains of heterosexual and homosexual men are anatomically different. Avocation: bicycling. Home: 9003 Norma Pl West Hollywood CA 90069 Office: Inst Gay and Lesbian Edn 626 N Robertson Blvd West Hollywood CA 90069-5022

LEVE, ALAN DONALD, electronic materials manufacturing company owner, executive; b. Los Angeles, Dec. 15, 1927; s. Milton Lewis and Etta L.; m. Annette Einhorn, Sept. 3, 1962; children—Laura Michelle, Elise Deanne. BS, UCLA, 1951. CPA, Calif. Staff acct., mgr. Joseph S. Herbert & Co. (C.P.A.s), Los Angeles, 1951-57; ptnr. Joseph S. Herbert & Co. (C.P.A.s), 1957-63; fin. and adminstrv. v.p., sec./treas. Mica Corp., Culver City, Calif., 1963-82, also bd. dirs., 1963-82, chmn. bd., chief exec. officer, 1982-83; v.p., bd. dirs. Micaply Internat. Inc., 1968-1982; v.p. Micaply AG, Switzerland, 1972-83, also bd. dirs., chief exec. officer, also bd. dirs., 1982-83; v.p., bd. dirs. Micaply Internat., Ltd., U.K., 1971-82; chmn. bd., mng. dir., chief exec. officer Micaply Internat. Ltd., U.K., 1982-83; v.p., bd. dirs. Titan Chem. Corp., Edgecraft Corp., Culver Hydro-Press, Inc., L.A., 1963-75; chmn. bd., pres., chief exec. officer Ohmega Techs., Inc., Culver City, Calif., 1983—, Ohmega Electronics, Inc., Culver City, 1986—. Served with USAAF, 1946-47. Home: 16430 Dorado Dr Encino CA 91436-4118 Office: 4031 Elenda St Culver City CA 90232-3723

LEVE, SAMUEL, scenic designer; b. USSR, Dec. 1, 1910; 1 child, Teri. Student, various art schs., N.Y.C, Yale U., Jewish Theol. Sem. Am. instr., lectr. CCNY, Baylor U., Waco, Tex., Yale U., NYU, Fla. State U., Tallahassee, YMHA. Designer over 100 Broadway prodns. for Shurberts, George Abbott, Theatre Guild, Rodgers and Hammerstein, Orson Welles, David Merrick, Saroyan, Met. Opera, Maurice Schwartz (Yiddish Theatre), Habimah, others; design Chanukah Festivals at Madison Square Garden, N.Y.C., McCormick Place, Chgo.; designer two synagogues N.Y.C., St. John the Divine Cathedral, and for five presidents. Address: 277 W End Ave New York NY 10023-2604

LEVEE, JOHN HARRISON, artist, designer; b. Los Angeles, Apr. 10, 1924; s. Michael Charles and Roze L.; m. Claude Marie, Dec. 19, 1964. B.A., UCLA, 1948; postgrad., New Sch. Social Research, N.Y.C., 1949, Acad. Julian, 1950. vis. prof. art U. Ill., 1965, N.Y. U., 1967-68, U. So. Calif., 1971. One-man shows include Konig Galerie, Geneva, 1971, Andre Emmerich Gallery, N.Y.C., 1957-59, 62, 66, Gimpel Fils, London, 1958, 60, 66, Galerie de France, 1961, 62, 64, 69, Nora Gallery, Jerusalem, Haira (Israel) Mus. Art, Moose Gallery, Toronto, 1963, Phoenix Mus. Art, 1964, U. Ill. Krannert Art Mus., 1965, Tel Aviv (Israel) Mus., 1969, Margo Leavin Gallery, L.A., 1970, Galerie la Toabis, Paris, 1975, Palm Springs (Calif.) Mus., 1978, Mus. Nice, France, 1980, Galerie La Closerie des Lilacs, Paris, 1983, 86, Galerie 1900-2000, Paris, Galerie de Poche, Paris, 1990; one-man retrospective Galerie Le Gall, Paris, 1986, retrospective of the 1950's, Gallerie Callu, Paris, 1989, retrospective of the 1960's, 1989, retrospective 1953-93 Toulouse Mus., France, retrospective 1990-1997 Gallerie Roquefeuil-Pallade, Paris; group shows, Salon de Mai, Paris, 1954-79, 96, Salon des Realités Nouvelles, 1954-96, Salon Comparison, 1978-97, Paris, Carnegie Internat., 1955-58, Washington's Corcoran Gallery of Art, 1956, 58, Mus. Modern Art N.Y.C., 1957, Whitney Mus., 1957-59, 65, Arts Club Chgo.,

1958, Guggenheim Mus., 1966, Salon des grands et jeunes d'aujourd'hui 1996, Musee du Grand Palais, L'ecole de Paris, 1945-57, Hqrs. UNESCO, 50th anniversary, Paris, 1996, Salon Grands et Jeunes d'aufourd hurs, Paris, 1978-92, competition Salon Grands et Jeunes Mus. Modern Art, Paris, others, many archtl. projects, France, U.S.A. Served with USAAF, 1944-46. Recipient prizes including Watercolor Assn. Ann. 1955, 56, Commonwealth of Va. Biann. Purchase award 1966, grand prix Woolmark Found. 1974-75, gran prix Biennale de Paris 1969; Ford grantee, 1969; Tamarind fellow Los Angeles, 1969. Jewish. Home: 119 rue Notre Dame des, Champs, 6 Paris France *Most thinkers and artists are not historical geniuses who have broken with previous tradition, perceived relationships hitherto unnoticed, or even invented new relationships or had new visions thus transforming the categories in terms of which human beings think of their place in the universe. But for each historical period there are these men of genius and it is the moral imperative of us all to strive, to reach out in our own way and within our own limits, toward this end.*

LEVEILLE, GILBERT ANTONIO, food products executive; b. Fall River, Mass., June 3, 1934; s. Isidore and Rose (Caron) L.; divorced; children: Michael, Kathleen, Edward; m. Carol A. Phillips, Aug. 7, 1981. B in Vocat. Agr., U. Mass, 1956; MS, Rutgers U., 1958, PhD, 1960. Prof. nutritional biochemistry U. Ill., Urbana, 1965-71; chmn. dept. food sci. and human nutrition Mich. State U., East Lansing, 1971-80; dir. nutrition and health sci. Gen. Foods Corp., Tarrytown, N.Y., 1980-86; v.p. for rsch. and tech. svcs. Nabisco Inc., East Hanover, N.J., 1986-96; pres. Leveille Assocs., Denville, N.J., 1996—. Author: The Set Point Diet, 1985 (N.Y. Times nonfiction bestseller); also over 300 articles. Served to 1st lt. U.S. Army, 1960-62. Recipient rsch. award Poultry Sci. Assn., 1965, Disting. Faculty award Mich. State U., 1980. Mem. AAAS, Am. Chem. Soc., Am. Inst. Nutrition (pres. 1988-89, Mead Johnson rsch. award 1971), Am. Soc. for Clin. Nutrition, Inst. Food Technologists (pres. 1983-84, fellow 1983, Carl Fellers award 1992).

LEVELL, EDWARD, JR., city official; b. Jacksonville, Ala., Apr. 2, 1931; m. Rosa M. (Casellas) L, Aug. 3, 1951; children: Edward III (dec.), Ruben C., Kenneth W., Randy C., Raymond C. (dec.), Cheryl D. Levell Rivera, Michael K. BS, Tuskegee Inst., 1953; MA in Urban Sociology, U. No. Colo., 1972; M in Mgmt., Indsl. Coll./Air War Coll., 1974. Commd. 2d lt. USAF, 1953, advanced through grades to col., 1978, various flight tng., air ops. and command positions, 1953-69; comdr. cadet group, then dep. commandant cadet wing USAF Acad., 1969-73; dep. comdr., wing comdr., vice comdr. 1st spl. ops. wing USAF, 1973-77, wing comdr. 58th tactical air command tng. wing, 1977-78, col., vice comdr., comdr. 20th air divsn., 1978-83, ret., 1983; dep. commr. aviation City of Chgo. Dept. Aviation, 1983-89; dep. dir. aviation, fin. and adminstrn. City of New Orleans Dept. Aviation, 1989-90, dep. dir. aviation, ops. and maintenance, 1990-92, dir. aviation, 1992—. bd. dirs. Tourist & Conv. Commn., New Orleans; trustee Dryades YMCA, New Orleans; mem. transp. com. World Trade Ctr. Decorated Legion of Merit, D.F.C. (2), Meritorious Svc. Medal (2), Air Medal (8), Air Force Commendation Medal; recipient Disting. Svc. award Jacksonville, Ala., 1974, State of Fla. Commn. Human Rels. award for spl. recognition, 1977, Air Force Assn. Spl. Citation of Merit, 1977, Disting. Svc. award City of Chgo. Dept. Aviation, 1986, 87, 88; inducted in Tuskegee Univ. Hall of Fame, 1991. Mem. Airport Ops. Coun. Internat. (task force chmn. ann. conf. New Orleans 1991), Am. Assn. Airport Execs., Gulf Coast Internat. Hispanic C. of C. Home: 1500 W Esplanade Ave Apt 46F Kenner LA 70065-5346 Office: New Orleans Aviation Bd New Orleans Intl Airport Box 20007 New Orleans LA 70141

LEVELT SENGERS, JOHANNA MARIA HENRICA, research physicist; b. Amsterdam, The Netherlands, Mar. 4, 1929; came to U.S., 1963; d. Wilhelmus Henricus and Maria Antonia Josephine (Berger) Levelt; m. Jan V. Sengers, Feb. 21, 1963; children: Rachel Teresa, Adriaan Jan, Maarten Willem, Phoebe Josephine. BS, Municipal U., Amsterdam, 1950, MS, 1954, PhD in Physics, 1958; hon. doctorate, Delft U. Tech., 1992. Rsch. asst. Municipal U., Amsterdam, 1954-63; postdoctoral assoc. U. Wis., Madison, 1958-59; rsch. physicist Nat. Bur. Standards, Gaithersburg, Md., 1963-95, group leader, 1978-88, NIST fellow emeritus, 1995—; vis. prof. U. Louvain, Belgium, 1971; vis. scientist Mcpl. U., Amsterdam, 1974-75; Regents prof. UCLA, 1982. Contbr. 12 chpts. to books and over 100 articles to profl. jours. Recipient DOC silver medal, 1972, DOC gold medal, 1978, WISE award U.S. Interagy. Com., Women in Sci. and Engring., Washington, 1985, A.V. Humboldt Rsch. award Ruhr-U., Bochum, Germany, 1991; Nat. Inst. Standards Tech. fellow, 1983-95. Fellow Am. Phys. Soc.; mem. ASME (nat. del. rsch. com. water and steam 1988—), AIChE, AAAS, NAE, NAS, Royal Netherlands Acad. Scis., Internat. Assn. Properties Water and Steam (v.p. 1988-90, pres. 1990-91, hon. fellow 1994), European Phys. Soc., Am. Chem. Soc. (divsn. phys. chemistry), Sigma Xi. Democrat. Avocations: gardening, hiking, swimming, traveling, reading. Home: 110 N Van Buren St Rockville MD 20850-1861 Office: Nat Inst Standards & Tech Gaithersburg MD 20899

LEVEN, ANN RUTH, arts administrator; b. Canton, Ohio, Nov. 1, 1940; d. Joseph J. and Bessie (Scharff) L. AB, Brown U., 1962; cert. with distinction in program in bus. adminstrn., Harvard-Radcliffe Univs., 1963; MBA, Harvard U., 1964. Product mgr. household products div. Colgate-Palmolive, N.Y.C., 1964-66; account exec. Grey Advt., N.Y.C., 1966-67; fin. asst. Met. Mus. Art, N.Y.C., 1967-69; asst. treas. Met. Mus. Art, 1970-72, treas., 1972-79; v.p., sr. corp. planning officer Chase Manhattan Bank, N.Y.C., 1979-83; pres. ARL Assocs., N.Y.C., 1983—; treas. Smithsonian Instn., 1984-90; dep. treas. Nat. Gallery Art, Washington, 1990-94, treas., 1994—; adj. asst. prof. Grad. Sch. Bus., Columbia U., 1975-77, adj. assoc. prof., 1977-79, adj. prof., 1980-93; exec.-in-residence Amos Tuck Sch., Dartmouth Coll., winter 1976, spring, 1984; dir. Alliance Capital Res., Inc., 1978-79, Short Term Asset Res., 1985-93, Oreg. Tax Free Trust, 1986—, Churchill Tax-Free Fund of Ky., 1987—, Churchill Cash Res. Trust, 1995—, Cascades Cash Fund, 1989-94, Aquila Cascadia Equity Fund, 1996—, Del. Group, 1989—. Artist (awarded prizes for painting and graphic arts); author articles on grad. bus. edn., mgmt. studies on the arts. Mem. exec. bd. new leadership div. Fedn. Jewish Philanthropies, 1968-70; mem. council N.Y. Public Library, mem. exec. com., 1976-79; mem. mus. adv. panel N.Y. State Council on Arts, 1977-79; bd. dirs. Camp Rainbow, 1970-84, v.p., 1976-78, treas., 1982-84; bd. overseers Amos Tuck Sch., 1978-84, chmn. ednl. affairs com., 1979-84; trustee Brown U., 1976—, also mem. fin. and budget com., student life com., devel. com., adv. and exec. coms.; bd. mem. Ctr. for Fgn. Policy Devel., 1989-94; trustee Artists' Choice Mus., 1979-87; bd. dirs. Reading Is Fundamental, 1987-91, adv. coun., 1991-94; mem. vis. com. Harvard U. Bus. Sch., 1979-84; trustee ARC Endowment Fund, 1985-90; bd. dirs. Am. Arts Alliance, 1990-92; bd. dirs. Twyla Tharp Dance Found., 1982-87; bd. overseers Hood Mus.-Hopkins Ctr. Dartmouth Coll., 1984-91, chmn., 1988-91; trustee N.Y. Sch. Interior Design, 1996—; mem. staff Presdl. Task Force on Arts and Humanities, 1981. Recipient Young Leadership award Council Jewish Fedns. and Welfare Funds, 1968; named N.Y. State's Outstanding Young Woman, 1976. Mem. Harvard Bus. Sch. Alumni Assn. (exec. coun. 1976-79, v.p. 1978-79), Women's Fin. Assn., Women's Forum, Econ. Club of Washington, Cosmopolitan Club, Harvard Bus. Sch. Club, Radcliffe Club, Brown Club, Art Table. Home: 785 Park Ave New York NY 10021-3552 Office: Natl Gallery of Art Washington DC 20565

LEVEN, CHARLES LOUIS, economics educator; b. Chgo., May 2, 1928; s. Elie H. and Ruth (Reinach) R.; m. Judith Danoff, 1950 (div. 1970); m. Dorothy Wish, 1970; children: Ronald L., Robert M., Carol E., Philip W., Alice S. Student, Ill. Inst. Tech., 1945-46, U. Ill., 1947; B.S., Northwestern U., 1950, M.A., 1957, Ph.D., 1958. Economist Fed. Res. Bank of Chgo., 1950-56; asst. prof. Iowa State U., 1957-59, U. Pa., 1959-62; asso. prof. U. Pitts., 1962-65; prof. econs. Washington U., St. Louis, 1965-91, chmn. dept. econs., 1975-80, prof. emeritus, 1991—; dir. Inst. Urban and Regional Studies, 1965-85; disting. prof. U. Mo., St. Louis, 1991—; cons. EEC, Ill. Auditor Gen., Polish Ministry of Planning and Constrn., St. Louis Sch. Bd., Ukrainian Ctr. for Markets and Entrepreneurship, European Inst. Comparative Urban Rsch. Author: Theory and Method of Income and Product Accounts for Metropolitan Areas, 1963, Development Benefits of Water Resource Investment, 1969, An Analytical Framework for Regional Development Policy, 1970, Neighborhood Change, 1976, The Mature Metropolis, 1978. Served with USNR, 1945-46. Ford Found. fellow, 1956; grantee Social Sci. Rsch. Coun., 1960; grantee Com. Urban Econ., 1965; grantee NSF, 1968, 73, Merc. Bancorp., 1976, HUD, 1978, NIH, 1985. Mem. Am. Econ. Assn., Regional Sci. Assn. (pres. 1964-65, Walter Isard award for distig. scholarship 1995), Western Regional Sci. Assn. (pres. 1974-75), So. Regional Sci. Assn. (disting. fellow 1991). Home: 7042 Delmar Blvd Saint Louis MO 63130-4301 Office: Washington U Box 1208 1 Brookings Dr Saint Louis MO 63130-4862 also: U Mo 8001 Natural Bridge Rd Saint Louis MO 63121-4401 *Achievement is satisfying, but especially so when one can win without others losing. At the same time, it appears unnecessary to be a failure to prove one's sincerity.*

LEVENDOGLU, HULYA, gastroenterologist; b. Samsun, Turkey, Nov. 20, 1948; came to U.S., 1973; d. Ali Riza and Hidayet (Acar) L.; m. Mustafa Orhan Kaymakcalan, June 21, 1974 (div. 1981). M.D., Hacettepe U., 1972. Diplomate Am. Bd. Internal Medicine; Intern and resident in internal medicine Cook County Hosp., Chgo., 1973-76, fellow, 1976-78, attending physician, 1978-80, chmn. div. gastroenterology, 1983-89; assoc. prof. SUNY Health Sci. Ctr. Bklyn.; chmn. div. gastroenterology Brookdale U. Hosp. Med. Ctr., Bklyn., 1989—; acting chief div. gastroenterology Bklyn. VA Hosp., 1981-83. Contbr. articles to profl. publs. Research grantee SUNY, 1981, Eli Lilly & co., 1984, UpJohn Co., 1985, Ortho Pharmaceutical Co., 1985. Fellow ACP, Am. Coll. Gastroenterology; mem. AAAS, Am. Gastroent. Assn., Am. Soc. for Gastrointestinal Endoscopy, Am. Soc. for Study of Liver Diseases. Moslem. Office: Brookdale U Hosp Med Ctr 1 Brookdale Plz Brooklyn NY 11212-3139

LEVENDUSKY, PHILIP GEORGE, clinical psychologist, administrator; b. Lowell, Mass., Oct. 21, 1946; s. Harry George and Phyllis Mary (Gowgill) L.; m. Cynthia Ann Becton; 1 child, Jason Philip. BA magna cum laude, U. Mass, 1968; MS, Wash. State U., 1971, PhD, 1973. Diplomate Am. Bd. Profl. Psychology. Asst. to dir. Human Rels. Ctr., Wash. State U., Pullman, 1971-73; asst. psychologist McLean Hosp., Belmont, Mass., 1974-82; assoc. psychologist McLean Hosp., Belmont, 1982-92, psychologist, 1992—, dir. cognitive behavior therapy unit, 1974-94, dir. ambulatory care, 1991-95, asst. gen. dir., 1993-95, v.p. network devel., 1995—, chmn. dept. psychology, dir. clin. tng., 1996—; instr. psychiatry Harvard Med. Sch., 1974-88, asst. prof., 1989—; dir. Levendusky and Assocs., Arlington, Mass., 1980—; Bd. dirs. Pullman Mgmt., Manchester, Mass., 1976-80, Feeding Ourselves, 1980, Anorexia Bulemia Care, 1991-93; dir. Bain & Co., Employee Consultation, Boston, 1987—; cons. Va Hosp., Boston, 1977-85, Boston Cardiovascular Health, 1983-85, Mass. Dept. Mental Health, 1987—; mem. Mass. Bd. Psychology, Boston, 1988-93. Contbr. articles to profl. jours., mags., newspapers; author book chpts.; guest numerous TV and Radio programs, Boston. Mem. Am. Psychol. Assn., Assn. Advancement Behavior Therapy, New Eng. Soc. of Behavior Analysis and Therapy (bd. dirs. 1991), Blue Hill Country Club, Phi Beta Kappa. Republican. Roman Catholic. Avocations: skiing, jogging. Office: McLean Hosp 115 Mill St Belmont MA 02178-1041

LEVENFELD, MILTON ARTHUR, lawyer; b. Chgo., Mar. 18, 1927; s. Mitchell A. and Florence B. (Berman) L.; m. Iona R. Wishner, Dec. 18, 1949; children—Barry, David, Judith. Ph.B., U. Chgo., 1947, J.D., 1950. Bar: Ill. 1950. Ptnr. Altman, Levenfeld & Kanter, Chgo., 1961-64, Levenfeld and Kanter, Chgo., 1964-80, Levenfeld, Eisenberg, Janger & Glassberg, Chgo., 1980—; former dir. Bank of Chgo., Garfield Ridge Trust & Savs. Bank; lectr. in fed. taxation. Contbr. articles to profl. jours. Bd. dirs. Spertus Coll. Judaica, Jewish Fedn. Chgo., 1975-84, Am. Israel C. of C., 1st nat. v.p.; chmn. legacies and endowments com., 1982-84; co-gen. chmn. Chgo. Jewish United Fund, 1977, vice chmn. campaign, 1979; gov. mem. Orchestral Assn. Chgo. Symphony Orch.; vis. com. U. Chgo. Law Sch., 1989-91; pres. Am. Israel C. of C. of Met. Chgo., 1993-95, 96—. With USNR, 1944-45. Recipient Keter Shem Tov award Jewish Nat. Fund, 1978. Mem. ABA, Ill. Bar Assn., Chgo. Bar Assn., Am.-Israel C. of C. Home: 866 Stonegate Dr Highland Park IL 60035-5145 Office: 33 W Monroe St Chicago IL 60603-5300

LEVENSON, ALAN BRADLEY, lawyer; b. Long Beach, N.Y., Dec. 13, 1935; s. Cyrus O. and Jean (Kotler) L.; m. Joan Marlene Levenson, Aug. 19, 1956; children: Scott Keith, Julie Jo. AB, Dartmouth Coll., 1956; BA, Oxford U., Eng., 1958, MA, 1962; LLB, Yale U., 1961. Bar: N.Y. 1962, U.S. Dist. Ct. D.C. 1964, U.S. Ct. Appeals (D.C. cir.) 1965, U.S. Supreme Ct. 1965. Law clk., trainee div. corp. fin. SEC, Washington, 1961-62, gen. atty., 1962, trial atty., 1963, br. chief, 1963-65, asst. dir., 1965-68, exec. asst. dir., 1968, dir., 1970-76; v.p. Shareholders Mgmt. Co., L.A., 1969, sr. v.p., 1969-70, exec. v.p., 1970; ptnr. Fulbright & Jaworski, Washington, 1976—; lectr. Cath. U. Am., 1964-68, Columbia U., 1973; adj. prof. Georgetown U., 1964, 77, 79-81, U.S. rep. working party OECD, Paris, 1974-75; adv. com. SEC, 1976-77; mem. adv. bd. Securities Regulation Inst., U. Calif., San Diego, 1973—, vice chmn. exec. com., 1979-83, chmn., 1983-87, emeritus chmn., 1988—; mem. adv. coun. SEC Inst., U. So. Calif., L.A., Sch. Acctg., 1981-85; mem. adv. com. Nat. Ctr. Fin. Svcs,. U. Calif.-Berkeley, 1985-89; mem. planning com. Ray Garrett Ann. Securities Regulation Inst. Northwestern U. Law Sch.; mem. adv. panel to U.S. compt.-gen. on stock market decline, 1987, panel of cons., 1989—; mem. audit adv. com. GAO, 1992—. Mem. bd. editl. advisors U. Iowa Jour. Corp. Law, 1978—; Bur. Nat. Affairs adv. bd. Securities Regulation and Law Report, 1976—; bd. editors N.Y. Law Jour., 1976—; bd. advisors, corp. and securities law advisor Prentice Hall Law & Bus., 1991-95; contbr. articles to profl. jours.; mem. adv. bd. Banking Policy Report. Recipient Disting. Service award SEC, 1972; James B. Richardson fellow Oxford U., 1956. Mem. ABA (adv. com., fed. regulation securities com., task force rev. fed. securities laws, former chair subcom. on securities activities banks), Fed. Bar Assn. (emeritus mem. exec. com. securities law com.), Am. Law Inst., Practicing Law Inst. (nat. adv. com. 1974, adv. com. ann. securities reg. inst.), AICPA (pub. dir., bd. dirs. 1983-90, fin. com. 1984-90, chmn. adv. coun. auditing standards bd. 1979-80, future issues com. 1982-85), Nat. Assn. Securities Dealers (corp. fin. com. 1981-87, nat. arbitration com. 1983-87, gov.-at-large, bd. govs. 1984-87, exec. com. 1986-87, long range planning com. 1987-90, chmn. legal adv. bd. 1988-93, spl. com. governance and structure 1989-90, numerous adv. coms.). Home: 12512 Exchange Ct S Potomac MD 20854-2431 Office: Fulbright & Jaworski LLP 801 Pennsylvania Ave NW Washington DC 20004-2615

LEVENSON, ALAN IRA, psychiatrist, physician, educator; b. Boston, July 25, 1935; s. Jacob Maurice and Frances Ethel (Biller) L.; m. Myra Beatrice Katzen, June 12, 1960 (div. 1993); children: Jonathan, Nancy; m. Linda Ann Nadell, Jan. 30, 1994. AB, Harvard U., 1957, MD, 1961, MPH, 1965. Diplomate: Am. Bd. Psychiatry and Neurology. Intern U. Hosp., Ann Arbor, Mich., 1961-62; resident psychiatry Mass. Mental Health Center, Boston, 1962-65; staff psychiatrist NIMH, Chevy Chase, Md., 1965-66; dir. div. mental health service programs NIMH, 1967-69; prof. psychiatry U. Ariz. Coll. Medicine, Tucson, 1969—, head dept. psychiatry, 1969-89; chief exec. officer Palo Verde Mental Health Svcs., Tucson, 1971-91, chief med. officer, med. dir., 1991-93; chmn. bd. dirs., CEO Psychiatrists' Purchasing Group, 1991—; chmn. bd. dirs. Psychiatrists' Risk Retention Group, 1991—; mem. staff Tucson Med. Ctr., U. Med. Ctr., Tucson. Author: The Community Mental Health Center: Strategies and Programs, 1972; Contbr. papers and articles to psychiat. jours. Bd. dirs. Tucson Urban League, 1971-78, Pima Council on Aging, 1976-83. Served with USPHS, 1965-69. Fellow Am. Psychiat. Assn. (treas. 1986-90), Am. Coll. Psychiatrists (regent 1980-83, v.p. 1983-85, pres.-elect 1985-86, pres. 1982-87), Am. Coll. Mental Health Adminstrn. (v.p. 1980-82, pres. 1982-83); mem. Group for Advancement Psychiatry, Harvard Alumni Assn. (bd. dirs. 1988-91). Office: 75 N Calle Resplendor Tucson AZ 85716-4937

LEVENSON, JACOB CLAVNER, English language educator; b. Boston, Oct. 1, 1922; s. Joseph Mayer and Frances (Hahn) L.; m. Charlotte Elizabeth Getz, June 6, 1946; children: Anne Berthe, Jill Mayer, Paul Getz. AB, Harvard U., 1943, PhD, 1951. Tutor in history and lit. Harvard, 1946-50, vis. lectr. English and gen. edn., 1951-52; instr. English U. Conn., 1950-54; asst. prof. to prof. English U. Minn., 1954-67; Edgar Allan Poe prof. English U. Va., Charlottesville, 1967—; chmn. dept. U. Va., 1971-74; faculty Salzburg (Austria) Seminar in Am. Studies, 1947, 49; Mem. Com. of Cons., Notable Am. Women, 1607-1950, 63-72. Author: The Mind and Art of Henry Adams, 1957, Hist. and Critical Introductions The Works of Stephen Crane, II-V, VII, 1969-76; editor: Stephen Crane: Prose and Poetry, 1984, Mark Twain Life on the Mississippi, 1967, Discussions of Hamlet, 1960, The Letters of Henry Adams I-III, 1982, IV-VI, 1988; mem. editorial bd.; Am. Quar., 1964-70, Va. Quar. Rev., 1968—, New Literary History, 1969—, Am. Lit., 1988-91; contbr. articles to profl. jours. Served with AUS, 1943-45. Decorated Bronze Star medal; Guggenheim fellow, 1958-59; Am. Council Learned Socs. fellow, 1961-62; Am. Philos. Soc. Penrose grantee, 1956; recipient E. Harris Harbison award for disting. teaching Danforth Found., 1966. Mem. MLA, Am. Studies Assn., Signet Soc., Phi Beta Kappa. Home: 1100 Free State Rd Charlottesville VA 22901-1819

LEVENSON, MARC DAVID, optics and lasers specialist, scientist; b. Phila., May 28, 1945; s. Donald William and Ethyl Jean Levenson; m. Naomi Francis Matsuda, Oct. 24, 1971. SB, MIT, 1967; MS, Stanford U., 1968, PhD, 1971. Rsch. fellow Harvard U., Cambridge, Mass., 1971-74; asst. prof. physics U. So. Calif., L.A., 1974-77, assoc. prof., 1977-79; mem. rsch. staff IBM Rsch. div., San Jose, Calif., 1979-93, head mgr. OSC, 1987, mgr. quantum metrology, 1990; v.p. Focused Rsch., Inc., Sunnyvale, Calif., 1993-95; propr., cons. Marc D. Levenson Optics, Saratoga, 1993-95; vis. fellow Joint Inst. for Lab. Astrophysics, U. Colo., Boulder, 1995-96; vis. prof. Rice U., Houston, 1996—. Author: Introduction to Nonlinear Laser Spectroscopy, 1988; editor: Lasers, Spectroscopy, New Ideas, 1987, Resonances, 1991; West Coast editor Solid State Tech. mag., 1993—; editor-in-chief Microlithography World Mag., 1995—; contbr. articles to profl. jours. Alfred Sloan rsch. fellow, 1975. Fellow IEEE, Optical Soc. Am. (Adolph Lomb medal 1976), Am. Phys. Soc., Bay Area Chrome Users Soc./Soc. Photog. and Instrumentation Engrs. (award 1991). Avocations: gardening, reading.

LEVENSON, STANLEY RICHARD, public relations and advertising executive; b. Cin., Dec. 28, 1933; s. Irven Philip and Dorothy (Aftel) L.; m. Barbara Lind, July 23, 1962; children: Laura, Amy. B.A., U. Mich., 1956; postgrad., Am. U. S.W. sales and promotion mgr. DOT Records, Hollywood, Calif., 1959-62; S.W. sales and mktg. rep. Pickwick Internat. Co., 1963-65; pres., chmn. bd. Stan Levenson Assos., Dallas, 1966-76; exec. v.p., gen. mgr. public relations div. S.W., Bozell & Jacobs, Dallas, 1976-81; pres., CEO Levenson & Levenson, Dallas, 1981-83; CEO Levenson Pub. Rels., 1984—; dir. Fidelity Nat. Bank, Dallas; Trustee TACA, 1980, Dallas Alliance, 1988; adj. prof. in pub. relations mgmt. So. Meth. U., 1987-88, mem. adv. bd. Pub. Rels. sequence studies. Group leader comm. task force Dallas Police Dept.; assoc. mem. Dallas Assembly; bd. dirs. Dallas Arboretum, Vis. Nurses Assn., Family Place; mem. adv. bd. Crystal Charity Ball; co-chmn. Dallas Mayor's Task Force on Mktg.; mem. exec. com., bd. dirs. Ctrl. Downtown Assn., Dallas, 1993-94; mem. Dallas Citizens Coun., 1997—. With U.S. Army, 1956-58. Mem. Pub. Rels. Soc. Am. (accredited, North Tex. Teich award), Soc. Profl. Journalists. Home: 4545 Mill Run Rd Dallas TX 75244-6432 Office: Plz Ams S Tower 600 N Pearl St Ste 910 Dallas TX 75201-2872

LEVENSTEIN, ALAN PETER, advertising executive; b. N.Y.C, May 25, 1936; s. Jules David and Mollie Jarvis Levenstein; m. Gail Susan Berman, Sept. 15, 1963; children: Miranda, Jessica, Antony. AB magna cum laude, Amherst Coll., 1956. Copywriter J. Walter Thompson Co., N.Y.C., 1959-60, The Marschalk Co., N.Y.C., 1961-62; with Kenyon & Eckhardt Advt. Inc., N.Y.C., 1964-79, v.p., 1967-79; freelance journalist and advt. cons. N.Y.C, 1979-85; with Bozell, Jacobs, Kenyon & Eckhardt (now Bozell Worldwide), N.Y.C., 1985—; vice chmn. Bozell Worldwide, 1991—. Mem. coun. Nat. Acad. Design, 1993—. Mem. Phi Beta Kappa, Century Assn. Club (N.Y.). Democrat. Jewish. Office: Bozell Worldwide Inc 40 W 23rd St New York NY 10010-5200

LEVENTHAL, BENNETT LEE, psychiatry and pediatrics educator, administrator; b. Chgo., July 6, 1949; s. Howard Leonard and Florence Ruth (Albert) L.; m. Celia G. Goodman, June 11, 1972; children: Matthew G., Andrew G., Julia G. Student, Emory U., 1967-68, La. State U., 1968-70; BS, La. State U., 1972, postgrad., 1970-74, MD, 1974. Diplomate Am. Bd. Psychiatry and Neurology in Psychiatry, Am. Bd. Psychiatry and Neurology, Child Psychiatry; lic. physician N.C., La., Ill., Va. Undergrad. rsch. assoc. Lab. Prof. William A. Pryor dept. chemistry, La. State U., 1968-70; house officer I Charity Hosp. at New Orleans, 1974; resident in psychiatry Duke U. Med. Ctr., Durham, N.C., 1974-78, chief fellow divsn. dept. psychiatry, 1976-77, chief resident dept. psychiatry, 1977-78, clin. assoc. dept. psychiatry, 1978-80; staff psychiatrist, head psychiatry dept. Joel T. Boone Clinic, Virginia Beach, Va., 1978-80; staff psychiatrist, faculty mem. dept. psychiatry Naval Regional Med. Ctr., Portsmouth, Va., 1978-80; asst. prof. psychiatry and pediats. U. Chgo., 1978-85, dir. Child Psychiatry Clinic, 1978-85, dir. Child and Adolescent Psychiatry Fellowship tng. program, 1979-88; psychiat. cons. Caledonia State Prision/Halifax Mental Health Ctr., Tillery, N.C., 1976-77, Fed. Correctional Inst., Butner, N.C., 1977-78; cons. Norfolk Cmty. Mental health Ctr., 1978-80; adj. prof. psychology, biopsychology, and devel. psychology U. Chgo., 1990, adj. assoc. prof. dept. psychology and com. on biopsychology, 1987-90; meed. dir. Child Life and Family Edn. program Wyler Children's Hosp. of U. Chgo., 1983-95; dir. child and adolescent programs Chgo. Lakeshore Hosp., 1986—; Pfizer vis. prof. dept. psychiatry U. P.R., 1992; examiner Am. Bd. Psychiatry and Neurology in Gen. Psychiatry and Child Psychiatry, 1982—; mem. steering com. Harris Ctr. for Devel. Studies, U. Chgo., 1983—; mem. com. on evaluation of GAPS project AMA, 1993—; treas. Chgo. Consortium for Psychiat. Rsch., 1994; pres. Ill. Coun. Child and Adolescent Psychiatry, 1992-94; vis. scholar Hunter Inst. Mental Health and U. New Castle, NSW, Australia, 1995; mem. Gov.'s Panel on Health Svcs., 1993-94; prof. psychiatry & pediats. U. Chgo., 1990—, chmn. dept. psychiatry, 1991—; presenter in field. Mem. editl. bd. Univ. Chgo. Better Health Letter, 1994—; cons. editor: Jour. Emotional and Behavioral Disorders, 1992-96; reviewer: Archives of Gen. Psychiatry, 1983—, Biol. Psychiatry, 1983—, Am. Jour. Psychiatry, 1983—, Jour. AMA, 1983—, Jour. Am. Acad. Child and Adolescent Psychiatry, 1983—, Sci., 1983—; book rev. editor Jour. Neuropsychiatry and Clin. Neuroscis., 1989-92, mem. editl. bd., 1989-92; contbr. articles to profl. jours. Lt. comdr. M.C., USNR, 1978-80. Recipient Crystal Plate award Little Friends, 1994, Individual Achievement award Autism Soc. Am., 1991, Merit award Duke U. Psychiat. Resident's Assn., 1976, Bick award La. Psychiat. Assn., 1974; Andrew W. Mellon Found. faculty fellow U. Chgo., 1983-84; John Dewey lectr. U. Chgo., 1982. Fellow Am. Acad. Child and Adolescent Psychiatry (Outstanding Mentor 1988, dep. chmn. program com. 1979—, chmn. arrangements com. 1979—, new rsch. subcom. for ann. meeting 1986—, mem. work group on rsch. 1989—), Am. Psychiat. Assn. (Falk fellow, mem. Ittleson Award Bd. 1994-97, mem. Am. Psychiat. Assn./Wisniewski Young Psychiatrists Rsch. Award Panel 1994—), Am. Acad. Pediats., Am. Orthopsychiat. Assn.; mem. AAAS, Am. Coll. Psychiatrists, Brain Rsch. Inst., Ill. Coun. Child and Adolescent Psychiatry, Ill. Psychiat. Soc., Soc. for Rsch. in Child Devel., Soc. of Profs. of Child and Adolescent Psychiatry, Soc. Biol. Psychiatry, Nat. Bd. Med. Examiners, Mental Health Assn. Ill. (profl. adv. bd. 1991—), Sigma Xi. Office: U of Chgo Pritzker Sch of Medicine 5841 S Maryland Ave Chicago IL 60637-1463

LEVENTHAL, CARL M., neurologist, consultant, retired government official; b. N.Y.C., July 28, 1933; s. Isidor and Anna (Semmel) L.; m. Brigid Penelope Gray, Feb. 4, 1962 (wid. Feb. 1994); children: George Leon, Sarah Elizabeth Roark, Dinah Susan, James Gray. A.B. cum laude, Harvard U., 1954; M.D., U. Rochester (N.Y.), 1959. Diplomate: Am. Bd. Psychiatry and Neurology. Fellow in anatomy U. Rochester, 1956-57; intern, then asst. resident in medicine Johns Hopkins Hosp., 1959-61; asst. resident, then resident in neurology Mass. Gen. Hosp., Boston, 1961-64; commd. officer USPHS, 1963-96, asst. surgeon gen., 1979-83; asso. neuropathologist Nat. Inst. Neurol. Diseases and Blindness, 1964-66; neurologist Nat. Cancer Inst., 1966-68; asst. to dep. dir. sci., 1968-73; acting dep. dir. sci. NIH, 1973-74; dep. dir. bur. drugs FDA, Rockville, Md., 1974-77; dep. dir. Nat. Inst. Arthritis, Diabetes and Digestive and Kidney Diseases, 1977-81; div. dir. Nat. Inst. Neurol. Disorders and Stroke, 1981-96; sr. policy analyst for life scis. Office of Sci. and Tech. Policy, Exec. Office of Pres., 1983; asst. clin. prof. neurology Georgetown U. Med. Sch., 1966-76. Recipient Commendation medal USPHS, 1970, Meritorious Svc. medal, 1974, 77, 91, Outstanding Svc. medal, 1988, dir.'s award NIH, 1992, Disting. Svc. medal, 1997. Fellow Am. Acad. Neurology; mem. Am. Assn. Neuropathologists, Am. Neurol. Assn., Soc. for Exptl. Neuropathology, Alpha Omega Alpha. Home: 10924 Brewer House Rd Rockville MD 20852-3422

LEVENTHAL, ELLEN IRIS, portfolio manager, financial services executive; b. N.Y.C., Feb. 17, 1949; d. Harry and Laura (Schapira) L. BA, Barnard Coll., N.Y.C., 1971; MA, Columbia U., 1973; MBA, NYU, 1978; student, Harvard U., 1968. Registered rep. NASD. Sr. investment analyst Comptrollers Office City of N.Y., 1978-79; asst. investment officer Chem.

Bank, N.Y.C., 1980-81; v.p., portfolio mgr. E.F. Hutton, N.Y.C., 1981-87, Shearson Lehman Bros., N.Y.C., 1987-89, Ellaure Corp., N.Y.C., 1989—; portfolio mgr. Delta Capital Mgmt., 1993—. Mem. Investment Tech. Assn., N.Y. Soc. Security Analysts, NYU Bus. Forum, NYU Fin. Club, Money Marketeers of NYU, Princeton Club of N.Y., Barnard Coll. Club of N.Y., City Club of N.Y., Women's City Club of N.Y., Kappa Delta Pi. Avocations: golf, piano, ballet, tennis.

LEVENTHAL, LAWRENCE JAY, rheumatologist, educator; b. N.Y.C., June 5, 1958; s. Samuel and Anne Leventhal; m. Linda Currao, May 15, 1988; 2 children. BA in Biology magna cum laude, Brandeis U., 1980; MD, Hahnemann U., 1984. Resident in internal medicine Albert Einstein Med. Ctr., Phila., 1984-87; fellow in rheumatology U. Pa., Phila., 1987-90; clin. assoc. in medicine U. Pa., 1989-91, clin. asst. prof. medicine, 1989-91, 91—; clin. asst. prof. Med. Coll. Pa., Phila., 1990—; dir. arthritis rsch. edn. Presbyn. Hosp., Phila., 1990-93; assoc. chief rheumatology Grad. Hosp., Phila., 1993—. Author: Primer of Rheumatic Disease, 1994; editor: Jour. Clin. Rheumatology; contbr. articles to profl. jours. Named one of Best Drs. in Am., 1996-97. Fellow ACP, Am. Coll. Rheumatology, Phila. Coll. Physicians; mem. AMA (physicians recognition award 1987—), Am. Soc. Internal Medicine, Phila. Rheumatism Soc. (pres. 1996), Arthritis Found. (exec. bd.). Office: Grad Hosp 1800 Lombard St Philadelphia PA 19146-1414

LEVENTHAL, NATHAN, performing arts executive, lawyer; b. N.Y.C., Feb. 19, 1943; s. Harry and Fay (Bronstein) L.; m. Gretchen Dykstra, Feb. 12, 1993. B.A. in Pub. Affairs, Queens Coll., 1963; J.D. cum laude, Columbia U., 1966. Bar: N.Y. 1967. Commr. Rent and Housing Maintenance, N.Y.C., 1972-73; chief counsel U.S. Senate Subcom. Adminstrv. Practice and Procedure, Washington, 1973-74; assoc. and ptnr. Poletti, Freidin, Prashker, Feldman & Gartner, N.Y.C., 1974-78; commr. Housing Preservation and Devel., N.Y.C., 1978-79; dep. mayor ops. City of N.Y., 1979-84; pres. Lincoln Ctr. for Performing Arts, N.Y.C., 1984—; lectr. govt. housing policy New Sch. Social Research, N.Y.C., 1979; lectr. health care and pub. policy Columbia Law Sch., N.Y.C., 1971. Editor-in-chief: Columbia Law Rev., 1965-66. Bd. visitors City Univ. Law Sch., N.Y.C., 1983—, Columbia Law Sch., 1989—, The New Sch., N.Y.C., 1992—; chmn. Citizens Union, 1994—; active Council on Jud. Adminstrn., Bar Assn. N.Y. City, 1983-90; dir. Nat. Youth Service Corp. for N.Y.C., 1983-85; commr. N.Y.C. Charter Revision Commn., 1986-89, N.Y. State Commn. on Constl. Revision, 1993—; dir. Queen's Coll. Found., 1988—; chair David M. Dinkins Mayoral Transition Com., 1989-90. Harlan Fiske Stone scholar Columbia Law Sch., 1963-65, Jerome Michael scholar, 1965-66; Disting. Service award Citizens Housing and Planning Council, N.Y.C., 1984, Am. Soc. Pub. Adminstrn. outstanding pub. adminstr. award 1982, Columbia Univ. Medal for Excellence, 1985.

LEVENTHAL, RUTH, academic administrator, dean emeritus, educator; b. Phila., May 23, 1940; d. Harry Louis Mongin and Bertha (Rosenberg) Mongin Blai; children: Sheryl Anne, David Alan. BS, U. Pa., 1961, PhD, 1973, MBA, 1981; HHD (hon.), Thomas Jefferson U., 1995. Cert. med. technologist, clin. lab. scientist. Trainee NSF, 1971, USPHS, 1969-70, 73; asst. prof. med. tech. U. Pa., Phila., 1974-77; acting dean U. Pa., 1977-81; dean Hunter Coll., N.Y.C., 1981-84; provost, dean, prof. biology Capital Coll. Pa. State U., Middletown, 1984-95; prof. biology Pa. State Hershey Med. Ctr., 1996—; site visitor Middle State Assn. Colls. and Secondary Schs., Phila., 1983—. Author: (with Cheadle) Medical Parasitology: A Self Instructional Text, 1979, 2d edit., 1985, 3rd edit., 1991, 4th edit., 1995; contbr. chpt. to book and articles to profl. jours. Chmn. founds. Tri-County United Way, South Central Pa., 1996, 97; mem. health found. bd. Harrisburg Hosp., Pa., 1984-92; bd. dirs. Tri-County Planned Parenthood, 1984-87, Harrisburg Acad., Wormleysburg, Pa., 1984-88, Metro Arts of Harrisburg, 1984-87, Pa. Power and Light, Inc., 1988—, Mellon Bank Commonwealth Region, 1990—; founding chair Coun. Pub. Edn., 1984—. Recipient Alice Paul award Women's Faculty Club, U. Pa., 1981; Recognition award NE Deans of Schs. of Allied Health, 1984, Athena award Capital Region C. of C., 1992, John Baum Humanitarian award Am. Cancer Soc., 1992, Lifetime Achievement award Family and Children's Svcs., 1996; named Disting. Dau. Pa. by Gov. Thomas Ridge, 1995. Mem. Am. Soc. Parasitologists, AAUW (bd. dirs. Pa. br. 1985—), Sigma Xi. Avocations: skiing, painting, sculpture. Office: Pa State U Milton S Hershey Med Ctr 500 University Dr PO Box 850 Hershey PA 17033

LEVENTIS, NICHOLAS, chemistry educator, consultant; b. Athens, Greece, Nov. 12, 1957; came to U.S., 1980; s. Spyro and Efrosine (Nenou) L.; m. Chariklia Sotiriou, Nov. 12, 1988; 1 child, Theodora. BS in Chemistry, U. Athens, Greece, 1980; PhD in Chemistry, Mich. State U., 1985; grad. cert. in adminstrn. and mgmt., Harvard U., 1992. Grad. asst. Mich. State Univ., East Lansing, 1980-85; rsch. assoc. MIT, Cambridge, Mass., 1985-88; project dir. Molecular Displays, Inc., Cambridge, 1988-90, v.p. R & D, 1990-93; prof. chemistry U. Mo., Rolla, 1994—; cons. Igen, Inc., Rockville, Md., 1987-94; Hyperion Catalysis Internat., Cambridge, 1988-94, Delta F Corp., Woburn, Mass., 1992-94, Moonwatch Inc., 1995—. Contbr. articles on electrochromic phenomena and devices to Yearbook of Ency. of Sci. & Tech., Jour. Mat. Chem., Chem. of Materials, Jour. Electrochem. Soc., Polymer News. Recipient Greek Inst. State Scholarships awards Greek Govt. Dept. Edn., 1976-79, Katie Y. F. Yang prize Harvard U., Cambridge, 1992; named Ethyl Corp. fellow Mich. State U., East Lansing, 1983, Yates Meml. fellow Mich. State U., East Lansing, 1984. Mem. Am. Chem. Soc. (Arthur K. Doolittle award 1993), Electrochemical Soc., Internat. Union Pure & Applied Chemistry (affiliate mem.), Soc. for Info. Display. Greek Orthodox. Achievements include patents for electrochromic, electroluminescent and electrochemiluminescent displays; electrically conductive polymer composition, method of making same and device incorporating same; apparatus for conducting a plurality of simultaneous measurements of electrochemiluminescent phenomena. Home: 1604 McCutchen Dr Rolla MO 65401-2651 Office: U Mo Dept Chemistry Rolla MO 65401

LEVER, ALVIN, health science association administrator; b. St. Louis, Jan. 27, 1939; s. Jack I. and Sabina (Vogel) L.; m. Norine Sue Schwedt, Jan. 27, 1963; children: Daniel Jay, Michael Leonard. BS in Archtl. Scis., Washington U., St. Louis, 1961, BArch, 1963; MA in Applied Psychology, U. Santa Monica, 1992. Registered architect, Mo., Ill. Project designer Sir Basil Spence, Architects, Edinburgh, Scotland, 1963-65; sr. project designer Hellmuth, Obata & Kassabaum, St. Louis, 1965-68, v.p., project mgr., 1968-72; v.p. facility devel. Michael Reese Med. Ctr., Chgo., 1972-74; v.p., gen. mgr. Apelco Internat., Ltd., Northbrook, Ill., 1974-90; dir. membership and fin. Am. Coll. Chest Physicians, Northbrook, 1990-92, exec. dir., 1992-95, exec. v.p., CEO, 1995—; pub. jour. Chest. Pub. Chest. Bd. dirs. Chest Found., 1997; v.p. Congregation B'nai Tikvah, 1987-91, pres., 1993-95. Mem. Profl. Conv. Mgmt. Assn., Am. Soc. Med. Soc. Execs., Am. Soc. Assn. Execs., Chgo. Soc. Assn. Execs., Chgo. Assn. Healthcare Execs., Alliance for Continuing Med. Edn. Avocations: scuba diving, bicycling, travel., golf. Office: Am Coll Chest Physicians 3300 Dundee Rd Northbrook IL 60062-2303

LEVERE, RICHARD DAVID, physician, academic administrator, educator; b. Bklyn., Dec. 13, 1931; s. Samuel and Mae (Fain) L.; m. Diane L. Gonchar, Jan. 15, 1978; children: Elyssa C., Corinne G., Scott M. Student, NYU, 1949-52; MD, SUNY, N.Y.C., 1956. Intern Bellevue Hosp., N.Y.C., 1956-57, resident, 1957-58; resident Kings County Hosp., 1960-61; asst. prof. medicine SUNY Downstate Med. Center, 1965-69, assoc. prof., 1969-73, prof., 1973-77, vice-chmn. dept. medicine, 1975-77, chief hematology/oncology div., 1970-77; asst. prof. Rockefeller U., 1964-65; prof., chmn. dept. medicine N.Y. Med. Coll., 1977-93, vice dean, 1991-93; med. dir. Westchester County Med. Ctr., 1991-92; v.p. med. affairs St. Agnes Hosp., 1991-93; sr. v.p. The Bklyn. Hosp. Ctr., 1994—; assoc. dean, prof. medicine NYU Sch. Medicine, 1994—; adj. prof. Rockefeller U., 1973—. Contbr. articles to profl. jours. Bd. dirs. Leukemia Soc. Am., 1970-85, Am. Heart Assn., 1978-94; trustee Our Lady of Mercy Med. Ctr., 1993-96. NIH grantee, 1971-76, 65-86. Fellow ACP (gov. N.Y. State 1990-94, pres. N.Y. State chpt. 1992-93, Physician Recognition award 1986), N.Y. Acad. Medicine; mem. Harvey Soc., Am. Soc. Clin. Investigation, Soc. Study of Blood (pres. 1973-74), Soc. Devel. Biology, Am. Soc. Pharm. Exptl. Therapeutics (William Dock Teaching award, Tinsley Harrison Rsch. award), Den Tiroler Adler-Ordern of Austria, Alpha Omega Alpha. Home: 5 Seymour Pl W Armonk NY 10504-2516 Office: Bklyn Hosp Ctr 121 Dekalb Ave Brooklyn NY 11201-5425

LEVERENZ, HUMBOLDT WALTER, retired chemical research engineer; b. Chgo., July 11, 1909; s. Paul Frederick and Lydia (Humboldt) L.; m. Edith Ruggles Langmuir, Nov. 30, 1940; children: David, Edith, Julia, Ellen. BA in Chemistry, Stanford U., 1930; postgrad., U. Muenster, 1930-31. Rsch. engr. RCA Mfg. Co., Camden, Harrison, N.J., 1931-42; rsch. engr. RCA Labs., Princeton, N.J., 1942-54, dir. physics and chem. rsch. lab., 1954-57, asst. dir. rsch., 1957-59, dir. rsch., 1959-61, assoc. dir., 1961-68; staff v.p. RCA Corp., Princeton, 1968-74; mem. Materials Adv. Bd., Washington, 1964-68. Author: Luminescence of Solids, 1950, 70; contbr. articles to profl. publs. Named Modern Pioneer Nat. Assn. Manufacturers, 1940; recipient Frank P. Brown medal Franklin Inst., 1954. Fellow Am. Phys. Soc., Optical Soc. Am., IEEE; mem. Nat. Acad. Engring., Am. Chem. Soc., Sigma Xi. Achievements include 67 patents; devel. of phosphors and luminescent screens used in fluorescent lamps and picture tubes, ferrites for TV receivers. Home: 2240 Gulf Shore Blvd N Apt K4 Naples FL 34102-1613

LEVERING, EMMA GERTRUDE, special education educator; b. Bryn Mawr, Pa., Feb. 17, 1946; d. William Joseph and Mary Kathryn (Smith) L. BA, Ursinus Coll., 1968; MEd, Millersville State Coll., 1973. Tchr. of socially/emotionally disturbed students Montomery County Intermediate Unit, Norristown, Pa., 1969-94; tchr. learning/emotional support students Jarrettown Elem. Sch., 1993—. Recipient Annie Sullivan award Montgomery County Intermediate Unit, 1990. Mem. Coun. Exceptional Children (mem. chmn. chpt. 388 1988-93, Honor award 1988), Assn. Learning Disabilities, ASCD, Children with Attention Deficit Disorders. Avocations: gardening, embroidery, reading.

LEVERT, FRANCIS EDWARD, nuclear engineer; b. Tuscaloosa, Ala., Mar. 28, 1940; s. John Clemins and Bessie Leona (Williams) LeV.; m. Faye Burnett, June 5, 1965; children: Francis Edward, Gerald Clemins, Lisa Ann. BSME, Tuskegee Inst., 1964; MS in Nuclear Engring., U. Mich., 1966; PhD in Nuclear Engring., Pa. State U., 1971. Registered profl. engr, Tenn. Assoc. prof., head mech. engring. dept. Tuskegee (Ala.) Inst., 1972-73; nuclear engr. Commonwealth Edison, Chgo., 1973-74, Argonne (Ill.) Nat. Lab., 1974-79; sr. scientist Tech. for Energy Corp., Knoxville, Tenn., 1979-85; v.p. K.E.M.P. Corp., Knoxville, 1985—. Author: (book) Literature Review and Commercial Source Evaluation of AM.-261 (AEC-ORO-4333), 1973, (book) A Guide to Patent Applications, (Van Nostrand Reinhold 1993); contbr. over 60 articles to tech. publs. AEC fellow, 1964-66, Def. Nat. Edn. Act fellow, 1968-70, Am. Soc. Engring. Edn. Ford Found. fellow, 1973-74. Mem. Am. Soc. Mech. Engrs. (exec. com. Plant Main div. 1989—). Achievements include 14 patents for Heat Flux Monitor, Slag Depositor Monitor, Level Gages, Solid State Neutron Sensor, Directional Sensitive Self-power Gamma Detectors, self-power hair curlers, upwardly deployed venetian blinds. Home: 1909 Matthew Ln Knoxville TN 37923-1340 Office: KEMP Corp Knoxville TN 37917

LEVERT, JOHN BERTELS, JR., investment executive; b. Birmingham, Ala., Apr. 16, 1931; s. John Bertels Sr. and Jacqueline (Tutwiler) L.; m. Anne Barrington King, Dec. 27, 1954; children: John Bertels III, Anne Lee. BA, Tulane U., 1954. Salesperson Carl E. Woodward Constrn. Co., New Orleans, 1956-58; from salesperson to exec. v.p. Metal Bldg. Product Co., Inc., New Orleans, 1958-70; stockbroker Howard Weil LaBouisse Friedrichs, New Orleans, 1970-75, pres., chief exec. officer, 1975-86, chmn., chief exec. officer, 1986—. Pres. United Way of Greater New Orleans, 1979-80; chmn. Archbishops Community Appeal, New Orleans, 1984; chmn. bd. trustees Loyola U., New Orleans, 1986—; chmn. fin. svc. survey com. New Orleans New Bus. Initiative, 1989—. 1st lt. U.S. Army, 1954-56. Recipient Humanitarian award Arthritis Found., 1989. Mem. N.Y. Stock Exch. (allied, regional firms adv. com. 1983-86), So. Yacht (commodore 1987-89). Republican. Roman Catholic. Avocations: sailing, flying. Office: Howard Weil LaBouisse Friedrichs 1100 Poydras St Ste 900 New Orleans LA 70163-1100

LEVESON, IRVING FREDERICK, economist; b. N.Y.C., June 28, 1939; s. Hyman Wolf and Minnie L.; m. Barbara Diane Wurtzelman, Jan. 28, 1961; children: Stephen Martin, Scott Owen. BA (N.Y. State Regents scholar), CCNY, 1960, MBA, 1963; PhD, Columbia U., 1968. Rsch. analyst, rsch. asst. Nat. Bur. Econ. Rsch., 1963-67; rsch. economist N.Y.C. Health Svcs. Adminstrn., 1967-68; economist RAND Corp., 1968-69; dir. rsch. Office Comprehensive Planning, N.Y.C., Planning Commn., 1969-71; asst. adminstr. health systems planning N.Y.C. Health Services Adminstrn., 1971-74; sr. profl. staff, dir. econ. studies Hudson Inst., Croton-on-Hudson, N.Y., 1974-84; sr. v.p., dir. rsch. Hudson Strategy Group, N.Y.C., 1984-90; pres. Leveson Cons., Marlboro, N.J., 1990—; mem. Gov. N.Y. health adv. coun., 1975-78, mem. adv. commn. on budget realities for the 80s, 1983-84; lectr., cons. in field. Author: The Future of the Financial Services Industry, 1982, American Challenges: Business and Government in the World of the 1990s, 1991; editor: Quantitative Explorations in Drug Abuse Policy, 1980; co-editor: Analysis of Urban Health Problems, 1976, Western Economies in Transition, 1980. Trustee Monmouth Heights Civic Assn., 1971-77. Mem. Am. Econ. Assn., Nat. Assn. Bus. Economists, Assn. Social Scis. in Health (exec. council 1973-82). Jewish. Home and Office: 23 Prescott Dr Marlboro NJ 07746-1351

LEVESQUE, LOUIS, bishop; b. Amqui, Que., Can., May 27, 1908; s. Philippe and Catherine (Beaulieu) L. B.A., Laval U., 1928, Ph.L., 1930, Th.D., 1932; S.S.L., Bib. Inst., Rome and Jerusalem, 1935. Ordained priest Roman Cath. Ch., 1932; tchr. holy scripture Rimouski, Que., 1936-51; bishop of Hearst, Ont., 1952-64; archbishop of Rimouski, 1964-73, retired archbishop, 1973—; Chmn. Canadian Cath. Conf., 1965-67; mem. Congregation Bishops, Rome, 1968-73. Mem. Cath. Bibl. Assn. Am. Home: 83 Saint John Baptist W, Rimouski, PQ Canada G5L 4G2*

LEVESQUE, RENE JULES ALBERT, retired physicist; b. St. Alexis, Que., Can., Oct. 30, 1926; s. Albert and Elmina Louisa (Veuilleux) L.; m. Alice Farnsworth, Apr. 6, 1956 (div.); children: Marc, Michel, Andre; m. Michèle Robert, Feb., 1992. B.Sc., Sir George Williams U., 1952; Ph.D., Northwestern U., 1957. Research assoc. U. Md., 1957-59; asst. prof. U. Montreal, 1959-64, assoc. prof., 1964-67, prof., 1967-87, dir. nuclear physics lab., 1965-69, chmn. dept. physics, 1968-73, vice dean arts and scis., 1973-75, dean, 1975-78, v.p. research, 1978-85, v.p. research and planning, 1985-87, prof. emeritus, 1987; mem. Atomic Energy Control Bd., Ottawa, Can., 1985-87, pres., 1987-93; ret., 1993; mem. adv. com. ING project Atomic Energy of Can. Ltd., 1966-69; mem. adv. bd. physics NRC Can., 1972-74, pres. nuclear physics grant selection, 1973; mem. adv. bd. on TRIUMF, 1979-87; v.p. Commn. Higher Studies Que. Ministry Edn., 1976-77, Natural Scis. and Engring. Research Council Can., 1981-87; v.p. bd. dirs. Can.-France-Hawaii Telescope Corp., 1979-80, pres., 1980-81; pres. permanent research com. Conf. Rectors and Prins. Que. Univs., 1979-80; pres. Mouvement Laïc de Langue française, 1961. Mem. Can. Assn. Physicists (pres. 1976-77), U. Montreal Faculty Assn. (pres. 1971), Fedn. Que. Faculty Assn. (pres. 1971-72), Interciencia Assn. (v.p. bd. dirs. 1979-80), Assn. Scis., Engring. and Tech. Comty. Can. (v.p. 1979-80, pres. 1980-81). Home: 190 Willowdale PH 1, Outremont, PQ Canada H3T 1G2

LEVETOWN, ROBERT ALEXANDER, lawyer; b. Bklyn., July 20, 1935; s. Alfred A. and Corinne L. (Cohen) L.; m. Roberta S. Slobodkin, Oct. 18, 1959. Student, U. Munich, Fed. Republic Germany, 1954-55; AB, Princeton U., 1956; LLB, Harvard U., 1959. Bar: D.C. 1960, N.Y. 1982, Va. 1984, Pa. 1985. Assoc. Pierson, Ball & Dowd, Washington, 1960-62; asst. U.S. atty. Washington, 1962-63; atty. Chesapeake & Potomac Telephone Cos., Washington, 1963-66, gen. atty., 1966-68, gen. solicitor, 1968-73, v.p., gen. counsel, 1975-83; exec. v.p., gen. counsel Bell Atlantic, 1983-91, vice chmn., 1991-92, also bd. dirs., 1989-92; bd. dirs. Telecom NZ, 1992—; chmn. of H.R. com., 1995—. Mem. ABA (vice chmn. comm. com., pub. utility law sect. 1986-93), Washington Met. Corp. Counsels' Assn. (bd. dirs. 1981-83), Nat. Legal Ctr. (legal adv. coun. 1986-92). Republican. Jewish.

LEVEY, GERALD SAUL, physician, educator; b. Jersey City, N.J., Jan. 9, 1937; s. Jacob and Gertrude (Kantoff) L.; m. Barbara Ann Cohen, June 4, 1961; children: John, Robin. AB, Cornell U., 1957; MD, N.J. Coll. Medicine, 1961. Diplomate: Am. Bd. Internal Medicine. Med. intern Jersey City Med. Ctr., 1961-62, asst. med. resident, 1962-63; postdoctoral fellow dept. biol. chemistry Harvard U. Med. Sch., 1963-65; med. resident Mass. Gen. Hosp., Boston, 1965-66; clin. assoc. clin. endocrinology br. Nat. Inst. Arthritis and Metabolic Diseases NIH, Bethesda, Md., 1966-68, clin. assoc. Nat. Heart and lung Inst., 1968-69, sr. investigator Nat. heart and Lung Inst., 1969-70; assoc. prof. medicine U. Miami Sch. Medicine, Fla., 1970-73, prof. medicine, 1973-79; prof., chmn. dept. medicine U. Pitts. Sch. Medicine, 1979-91; physician-in-chief Presbyn.-Univ. Hosp., Pitts., 1979-91; sr. v.p. for med. and sci. affairs Merck and Co., Inc., Whitehouse Sta., N.J., 1991-94; provost med. scis., dean Sch. of Medicine UCLA, 1994—; Harold Jeghers lectr. N.J. Coll. Medicine, 1977; Marian Blankenhorn lectr. Cin. Soc. Internal Medicine, 1982; co-prin. investigator Nat. Study of Internal Medicine Manpower, 1984—. Mem. editorial bd.: Endocrinology, 1972-76, Am. Jour. Physiology, 1972-76, Jour. Applied Physiology, 1972-76, Annals of Internal Medicine, 1981-84; cons. editor: Hosp. Medicine, 1981-91; contbr. articles to profl. jours. Bd. dirs. Am. Jewish Com., Miami, 1975-79; mem. United Jewish Fedn. Pitts. Leadership Devel., 1981-82; bd. dirs. Jewish Family and Children's Services, 1982-83. NIH grantee, 1971-91; Fla. Heart Assn. grantee, 1971-74. Fellow ACP; mem. AMA, Am. Thyroid Assn. (mem. membership com. 1977-80), Am. Fedn. Clin. Rsch. (councillor so. sect. 1973-76, pres. so. sect. 1977-78), Am. Soc. Clin. Investigation, Endocrine Soc., Assn. Profs. Medicine (chmn. ad hoc com. for use of animals in rsch., 1982-85, chmn. task force on internalmedicine manpower 1983-90, nat. pres. 1990-91), So. Soc. Clin. Investigation, Soc. Gen. Internal Medicine, Assn. Am. Physicians, Alpha Omega Alpha. Home: 1132 Laurel Way Beverly Hills CA 90210-2221 Office: UCLA 10833 Le Conte Ave Los Angeles CA 90095-3075*

LEVEY, ROBERT FRANK, newspaper columnist; b. N.Y.C., June 2, 1945; s. Stanley Victor and Sylvia Rose (Frank) L.; m. Jane Ellen Freundel, May 17, 1980; children: Emily Susanna, Alexander Freundel. B.A., U. Chgo., 1966. Reporter Albuquerque Tribune, 1966-67; reporter, editor Washington Post, 1967-81, columnist, 1981—; vis lectr. Duke U., Durham, N.C., 1979—; adviser journalism Cath. U. Am., Washington, 1979-81. Talk show host Sta. WRC-AM, 1981-83, Sta. WTTG-TV, Washington, 1982-87, Sta. WBAL, 1988-92, Sta. WMAL, 1993-96; commentator Sta. WASH-FM, 1983-84, Sta. WJLA-TV, 1984-86, Sta. WETA-FM, 1985-90, Sta. WTOP, 1997—. Woodrow Wilson fellow. Mem. Reporters Com. for Freedom of the Press, Newspaper Guild (chmn. Washington Post unit 1972-75), AFTRA, U. Chgo. Alumni Assn. (bd. govs. 1992—), Sigma Delta Chi. Jewish. Office: Washington Post 1150 15th St NW Washington DC 20071-0001

LEVEY, SAMUEL, health care administration educator; b. Cape Town, South Africa, July 11, 1932; came to U.S., 1949, naturalized, 1954; s. Harry and Esther (Turecka) L.; m. Linda Anne Madison, Dec. 26, 1965; children: Eric B., Andrea E., Sara B. A.B., Bowdoin Coll., 1955; A.M., Columbia U., 1956; M.A., U. Iowa, 1959, Ph.D., 1961; M.S., Harvard U., 1963. Adminstrv. assoc. U. Iowa hosps. and Clinics, Iowa City, 1958-60; instr. U. Iowa, 1960-61, asst. prof., 1961-62; dir. div. Mass. Dept. Public Health, Boston, 1963-67; asst. dir. med. care planning Harvard Med. Sch., Boston, 1967-68; lectr. health service adminstrn. Harvard Sch. Public Health, 1967-69; asst. commr. Mass. Dept. Public Welfare, Boston, 1968-69; prof., chmn. grad. program in health care adminstrn. CUNY, 1969-77; prof., adminstr. medicine Mt. Sinai Sch. Medicine, N.Y.C., 1973-77; G. Hartman prof. and head of grad. program in hosp. and health adminstrn. Ctr. for Health Services Research Coll. Medicine and Grad. Coll., U. Iowa, Iowa City, 1977-91; G. Hartman prof. Coll. Medicine and Grad. Coll., U. Iowa, 1991—; hosp. and health cons. Author: (with N.P. Loomba) Health Care Administration: A Managerial Perspective, 1973, 2d edit., 1984, Health Care Administration: A Selected Bibliography, 1973, (with H. Rosen and J. Metsch) The Consumer and the Health Care System, 1977, (with N.P. Loomba) Long Term Care Administration, vols. 1, 11, 1977, (with T. McCarthy) Health Management for Tomorrow, 1980, Hospital Leadership and Accountability, 1992, The Rise of University Teaching Hospital: A Leadership Perspective, 1997; sr. editor: Spectrum series on Heath Systems Management, 1974-86; editor: Hosp. and Health Services Adminstrn., 1987-92. Named Otho Ball fellow Am. Coll. Hosp. Adminstrs., 1958-59; Faculty fellow Found. Econ. Edn., 1962; HHS trainee, 1962-63. Mem. Assn. Univ. Programs in Health Adminstrn. (dir. 1979-80, chmn. bd. 1980-81), Am. Pub. Health Assn., Internat. Hosp. Fedn., Am. Coll. Healthcare Execs., Am. Hosp. Assn. Home: 336 Macbride Dr Iowa City IA 52246-1716 Office: U Iowa Steindler Bldg Iowa City IA 52242

LEVI, BARBARA GOSS, physicist, editor; b. Washington, May 5, 1943; d. Wilbur H. and Mildred C. (Wallin) Goss; m. Ilan M. Levi, Sept. 10, 1966; children: Daniel S., Sharon R. BA, Carleton Coll., 1965; MS, Stanford U., 1967, PhD, 1971. Assoc. editor Physics Today Am. Inst. Physics, N.Y.C., 1969-70, cons. editor Physics Today, 1970-89, assoc. editor Physics Today, 1987-88; sr. assoc. editor Physics Today, N.Y.C., 1989-93, sr. editor, 1993—; mem. tech. staff Bell Labs, Holmdel, N.J., 1982-83; mem. rsch. staff Ctr. for Energy and Environ. Studies Princeton U., 1981-82, 83-87; lectr. Ga. Tech., Atlanta, 1976-80, Fairleigh Dickinson U., Madison, N.J., 1970-75; vis. prof. Rutgers U., Piscataway, N.J., 1988-89; cons. U.S. Office Tech. Assessment, Washington, 1976-93. Editor: (with others) Energy Sources: Conservation and Renewables, 1985, The Future of Land-Based Strategic Missiles, 1989, Global Warming: Physics and Facts, 1992. Treas. LWV, Holmdel and Colts Neck, N.J., 1983-94. Fellow AAAS (mem. steering com. physics group 1997—), Am. Phys.Soc. (edn. com. 1989-91, chmn. forum on physics and soc. 1988-89, forum councilor, 1992-95, mem. exec. bd. 1994-95, Lilienfeld prize com. 1993-95, chair 1995, com. on coms. 1994-96, chair 1996, mem. exec. com. forum edn. 1997—); mem. AAUW (nuclear energy task force 1975-77), Fedn. Am. Scientists (gov. bd. 1985-89), Am. Assn. Physics Tchrs. Avocations: tennis, traveling, hiking, skiing.

LEVI, DAVID F., federal judge; b. 1951. BA, Harvard U., MA, 1973; JD, Stanford U. Bar: Calif. 1983. U.S. atty. ea. dist. State of Calif., Sacramento, 1986-90; judge U.S. Dist. Ct. (ea. dist.) Calif., 1990—; chmn. task force on race, religious and ethnic fairness U.S. Ct. Appeals (9th cir.), 1994—, mem. jury com., 1993-95. Adv. com. on Civil Rules, 1994—; vis. com. U. Chgo. Law Sch., 1995—. Mem. Am. Law Inst., Milton L. Schwartz Inn of Ct. (pres. 1992-95). Office: 2504 Fed Bldg 650 Capitol Mall Sacramento CA 95814

LEVI, HERBERT WALTER, biologist, educator; b. Frankfurt, Germany, Jan. 3, 1921; came to U.S., 1938, naturalized, 1945; s. Ludwig and Irma (Hochschild) L.; m. Lorna Rose, June 13, 1949; 1 child, Frances. Student, Art Students League, N.Y.C., 1938-39; B.S., U. Conn., 1946; M.S., U. Wis., 1947, Ph.D., 1949; MA (hon.), Harvard U., 1970. Instr., then asst. prof. to asso. prof. zoology, extension div. U. Wis., 1949-56; asst. curator arachnology Mus. Comparative Zoology Harvard U., 1956-57, assoc. curator, 1957-66, curator, 1966-91, prof. biology, 1970-91, Agassiz prof. zoology, 1972-91, prof. emeritus, 1991—; sec. Rocky Mountain Biol. Lab., 1959-65; vis. prof. Hebrew U., Jerusalem, 1975; bd. govs. Nature Conservancy, 1956-62; taxonomic cons. Smithsonian projects, 1979; cons. Syntax, Cambridge, Mass., 1986. Author: (with L.R. Levi) Spiders and Their Kin, 1968, 69, Aranas y especies afines, 1971; also numerous articles; translator, editor: Invertebrate Zoology (Kaestner), 3 vols.; bd. reviewers Pacific Insects, 1980-85; bd. editors Psyche, 1957-92, Zoomorphology, 1980-85, Sci. Bull. de Mus., Paris, 1980—, (internat.) Annales Zoologici Warszawa Poland, 1993—, Memorias do Instituto Butantan, São Paulo, Brazil, 1994—. Fellow AAAS; mem. Am. Soc. Zoologists, Soc. Study Evolution, Soc. Systematic Zoology (councillor 1967-69), Am. Micros. Soc. (bd. reviewers 1973-94), Am. Arachnol. Soc. (hon. mem., bd. editors 1974—, dir. 1975-83, pres. 1979-81), Am. Ecol. Soc., Am. Inst. Biological Scis., Wildlife Soc., Am. Ornithol. Union, Assn. Systematics Collections (council nat. systematic collections and resources 1975), British Arachnological Soc., Cambridge Entomology Club, Centre International de Documentation Arachnologique (v.p. 1965-68, pres. 1980-83, hon. mem. 1995—), Japanese Arachnological Soc. (hon.), Soc. Systematic Biologists, Spider Club So. Africa (hon.), Wilson Ornithological Soc., Wilderness Soc. Home: 45 Wheeler Rd Pepperell MA 01463-1025 Office: Harvard U Mus Comparative Zoolog Cambridge MA 02138

LEVI, ILAN MOSCHE, computer and communications company consultant; b. Haifa, Israel, July 17, 1943; came to U.S., 1956; s. Seligman P. and Ruth (Bril) L.; m. Barbara Goss, Sept. 10, 1966; children: Daniel Steven,

Sharon Ruth. BSME, The Cooper Union, 1965; MS in Aeros. and Astronautics, Stanford U., 1966, PhD in Structural Mechanics, 1968. Rsch. assoc. dept. aeros. and astronautics Stanford U., Calif., 1968-69; mem. tech. staff engring. mechanics and physics dept. Bell Labs., Whippany, N.J., 1969-71, supr., 1971-80, dept. head, 1980-85; dir. Bell Labs., Holmdel, N.J., 1985—; dir. bus. terminals devel. lab AT&T Labs., Holmdel, 1985-88; dir. customer systems devel. lab. AT&T Bell Labs., Middletown, N.J., 1988-94; cons. dir., product devel. AT&T Global Bus. Comm. Systems, 1994-95; retired Lucent Techs./Bell Labs., 1996, product devel. cons., 1996—; cons. Lawrence Radiation Lab., Livermore, Calif., 1968-69, N.J. Com. on Sci. and Industry, Trenton, 1985-86. Contbr. articles to profl. jours., chpts. to books. NSF fellow, 1965. Jewish. Avocations: tennis, backpacking, bicycling, photography. Home and Office: 1616 La Vista Del Oceano Santa Barbara CA 93109-1790

LEVI, ISAAC, philosophy educator; b. N.Y.C., June 30, 1930; s. Eliezer Asher and Eva (Lunenfeld) L.; m. Judith S. Rubins, Dec. 25, 1951; children: Jonathan Abram, David Isser. B.A., NYU, 1951; student, Jewish Theol. Sem., 1947-52; M.A., Columbia, 1953, Ph.D., 1957; PhD honoris causa, Lund U., 1988. Part-time instr. Rutgers U., 1954-56; lectr. CCNY, 1956-57, asst. prof. philosophy, 1962-64; asst. prof. philosophy Western Res. U., 1957-62, assoc. prof., 1964-67, prof., 1967-70, chmn. dept., 1968-70; prof. philosophy Columbia U., 1970—, chmn. dept., 1973-76, 89-91; vis. scholar Corpus Christi Coll., Cambridge (Eng.) U. 1973, vis. fellow Darwin Coll., 1980, 93; vis. rsch. fellow Australian Nat. U., 1987; vis. fellow All Souls Coll., Oxford (Eng.) U., 1988; vis. fellow Inst. Advanced Study, Hebrew U. Jerusalem, 1994, Wolfson Coll., Cambridge, 1997. Author: Gambling With Truth, 1967, The Enterprise of Knowledge, 1980 Decisions and Revisions, 1984, Hard Choices, 1986, The Fixation of Belief and Its Undoing, 1991, For the Sake of the Argument, 1996; contbr. articles to profl. jours. Fulbright scholar, 1966-67; Guggenheim fellow, 1966-67; NEH fellow, 1979-80. Fellow Am. Acad. Arts and Scis.; mem. AAUP, Am. Philos.Assn., Philosophy of Sci. Assn., Brit. Soc. Philosophy of Sci., Phi Beta Kappa, Pi Mu Epsilon. Democrat. Home: 25 Claremont Ave New York NY 10027-6827

LEVI, JAMES HARRY, real estate executive, investment banker; b. Boston, Oct. 28, 1939; s. Robert Emmett and Doris (Cohen) L.; m. Constance Jo Adler, Dec. 30, 1967; children: James H. II, Andrew R., Deanne D., Constance Jo. AB, Harvard U., 1961, MBA, 1964. Past pres. Value Properties Inc., N.Y.C.; now pres. Levi Co., Larchmont, N.Y.; chmn. bd. dirs. New Millenium Energies, Inc., St. Louis; pres. Gt. Train Store co., Dallas, others; prof. Bus. Sch. Columbia U., N.Y.C.; past pres. Oppenheimer Properties, Inc., N.Y.C.; exec. v.p., mem. exec. com. Oppenheimer & Co., Inc.; pres., chmn. bd. dirs. numerous affiliated cos. Mem. Bus. Sch. coun. Tulane U., N.Y.; mem. bd. govs. Hebrew Union Coll./Jewish Inst. Religion; mem. bd. overseers Sch. Architecture, Ill. Inst. Tech.; mem. exec. bd. Westchester Putnam coun. Boy Scouts Am.; mem. traffic commn. Village of Larchmont, N.Y.; mem. joint planning commn. Villages of Larchmont and Mamaroneck; trustee Larchmont Hist. Soc. Ensign USN, 1961-62. Named Man of Yr., St. Louis Rabbinical Coll., 1986. Mem. Real Estate Securities and Syndication Inst. (former gov.), Nat. Assn. Realtors, Nat. Assn. Rev. Appraisers (cert.), Soc. for Indsl. Archeology, Soc. Archtl. Historians, Nat. Assn. Security Dealers (registered prin.), Sheldrake Yacht Club (past treas.). Avocations: boating and sailing, collecting antiques, travelling, opera, kinetic sculpture. Home: 85 Larchmont Ave Larchmont NY 10538-3748 Office: Levi Co 85 Larchmont Ave Larchmont NY 10538-3748

LEVI, JOHN G., lawyer; b. Chgo., Oct. 9, 1948; s. Edward H. and Kate (Sulzberger) L.; m. Jill Felsenthal, Oct. 7, 1979; children: Benjamin E., Daniel F., Sarah K.H. AB, U. Rochester, 1969; JD, Harvard U., 1972, LLM, 1973. Bar: Ill. 1973. Ptnr. Sidley & Austin, Chgo. Vice chmn. bd. Weiss Mem. Hosp., Chgo.; v.p. trustee Francis W. Parker Sch., Chgo.; bd. dirs. Chgo. Child Care Sco.; vis. com. U. Chgo. Coll.; mem. Citizens Com. Juvenile Ct., Chgo. Mem. ABA, Ill. Bar Assn., Chgo. Bar Assn., Law Club Chgo. Office: Sidley & Austin 1 First Natl Plz Chicago IL 60603-2003

LEVI, JOSEF ALAN, artist; b. New York, Feb. 17, 1938; s. Jacob and Evelyn D. (Speizer) L. B.A., U. Conn., 1959; postgrad., Columbia U., 1960. Artist in residence Appalachian State U., N.C., 1969, vis. prof. art, Pa. State U., 1976. One-man shows of paintings include Stable include N.Y.C., 1966, 67, 68, 69, 70, Arts Club of Chgo., 1967, J.B. Speed Art Mus., Louisville, Ky., 1968, Appalachian State U., Boone, N.C., 1969, Lambert Gallery, Los Angeles, 1971, Gertrude Kasle Gallery, Detroit, 1971, Jacobs Ladder Gallery, Washington, 1972, Images Gallery, Toledo, Ohio, 1972, A.M. Sachs Gallery, N.Y.C., 1975, 76, 78, O.K. Harris Gallery, N.Y.C., 1983, 85, 87, 90, 92, 94, 96, Adams-Middleton Gallery, Dallas, 1986, Harmon Meek Gallery, Naples, Fla., 1996; numerous group shows, 1965—, latest being, Balt. Mus. Art, 1975, Mus. Art, R.I. Sch. Design, 1976, Art Mus., U. N.C., Greensboro, 1977, Russell Sage Coll., Troy, N.Y., 1977, Washington U., St. Louis, 1977, Whitney Mus., N.Y.C., 1978-79, Meml. Art Gallery, U. Rochester, N.Y., 1979, Aldrich Mus. Contemporary Art, Ridgefield, Conn., 1980, Western Assn. Art Museums, 1981, Worcester (Mass.) Art Mus., 1981, Palace Theatre of Arts Gallery, Stamford, Conn., 1984, Randolph Macon Coll., Ashland, Va., 1985, Robert I. Kidd Galleries, Birmingham, Mich., 1985, Elaine Benson Gallery, Bridgehampton, N.Y., 1985; others; represented in numerous permanent collections including, Aldrich Mus. Contemporary Art, Albright-Knox Gallery, Buffalo, N.Y., Mus. Modern Art, N.Y.C., Krannert Art Mus., U. Ill., Urbana, Va. Mus. Fine Arts, Richmond, AT&T, N.Y.C., Corcoran Gallery, Washington, U. Md., College City, Chrysler Corp., Detroit., Spellman Coll., Atlanta, Exxon Corp., N.Y.C., Minolta Corp., N.Y.C., Des Moines Art Ctr., Newark Mus., Dartmouth Coll., Hanover, N.H., Storm King Art Ctr., Mountainville, N.Y., U. Notre Dame Art Gallery, South Bend, Ind., J. B. Speed Art Mus., Louisville, Bank of N.Y., N.Y.C., Lewis and Clark Coll., Portland, Oreg., Technimetrics Inc., N.Y.C., Best Products Corp., Ashland, Va., Southland Corp., Dallas, TRW Corp., Cleve., Bklyn. Mus. Art, Worcester (Mass.) Art. Mus., Albion (Mich.) Coll., Prudential Ins. Co. Am., Newark. Served to 1st. lt. Adj. Gen. Corps U.S. Army, 1959-60. Mem. N.Y. Artist Equity Assn.

LEVI, KURT, retired banker; b. Wiesbaden, Germany, May 20, 1910; came to U.S., 1937, naturalized, 1942; s. Josef and Martha (Kahn) L.; m. Ruth Neumann, Feb. 17, 1938; 1 son, Peter. LL.B., U. Frankfurt, Germany, 1931. Mdse. mgr. Consol. Retail Stores, Kansas City, Mo., 1937-55; with United Mo. Bank, Kansas City, 1956-80; sr. v.p. United Mo. Bank, 1971-80, Traders Bank, Kansas City, 1980-85; adj. prof. Park Coll., Parkville, Mo., 1984-85. Gen. and area chmn. Kansas City (Mo.) United campaign, 1962; chmn. finance com. Camp Fire Girls Am., 1964; chmn. Kansas City Mayor's Prayer Breakfast Club, 1968; gen. chmn. Greater Kansas City Bonds for Israel, 1959; chmn. Greater Kansas City Conf. Soviet Jewry, 1966; vice chmn., mem. exec. bd. Community Relations Bur., 1972; pres. Heart Am. chpt., Religious Zionists Am., 1971; bd. govs. Jewish Fedn. and Council Kansas City, 1972-88, div. chmn. Fedn. campaign, 1986; bd. govs. Kansas City chpt. Am. Jewish Com., nat. bd. dirs.; pres., chmn. bd. Kehilath Israel Synagogue, lifetime hon. Gabbi; bd. govs., ombudsman Temple Sholom, Pompano Beach, Fla., 1988-94. Mem. Kansas City C. of C., B'nai B'rith (pres. Kansas City lodge 1984 1965, Greater Kansas City Coun. 1966, pres. Dist. II 1975-76, exec. v.p., bd. dirs., pres. Ft. Lauderdale 1990-92, pres. Kol Haverim lodge 1990-97), Kiwanis (v.p. Kansas City 1955), Legion of Honor, Playa del Sol Social Club (pres. 1989-90). Home: Playa del Sol 3500 Galt Ocean Dr Apt 2405 Fort Lauderdale FL 33308-6809 also: 121 W 48th St Kansas City MO 64112

LEVI, MAURICE DAVID, economics educator; b. London, Sept. 28, 1945; came to U.S., 1967; s. Karl and Louisa Hannah (Magson) L.; m. Kathleen Birkinshaw, Jan. 14, 1979; children—Adam Julian, Naomi Anne, Jonathan Karl. B.A. in Econs. with 1st class honors, U. Manchester, Eng., 1967; M.A., U. Chgo., 1968, Ph.D., 1972. Vis. prof. Hebrew U., Jerusalem, 1978; vis. assoc. prof. U. Calif.-Berkeley, 1979; vis. scholar MIT, Cambridge, 1980; prof. business U. B.C., Vancouver, Can., 1972—; vis. prof. London Bus. Sch., 1985. Author: Economics Deciphered, 1981, Thinking Economically, 1985, International Finance, 3rd edit., 1996, Economics and the Modern World, 1994; contbr. articles to profl. jours. Mem. Vancouver Mayor's Econ. Adv. Commn., 1983-84, Fed. Provincial Initiative, 1987-90. Recipient Seagram award, 1978; grantee Ford Found., 1969-70, Can. Coun., 1978, 80, 85; Nomura fellow U. Exeter, 1990. Jewish. Avocations: astronomy; salmon fishing.

LEVI, PETER STEVEN, chamber of commerce executive, lawyer; b. Washington, June 3, 1944; s. Kurt and Ruth (Neumann) L.; m. Enid Goldberg, Jan. 26, 1969; children: Joshua, Jeff. BA, Northwestern U., 1966; JD, U. Mo., Kansas City, 1969, LLM in Urban Legal Affairs, 1971. Bar: Mo. 1969. Gen. counsel Mid Am. Regional Coun., Kansas City, 1971-77, exec. dir., 1977-90; pres. Greater Kansas City C. of C., 1990—; participant internat. local govt. mgmt. exch. program with Israel, Internat. City Mgmt. Assn., 1985-86. Author: Model Subdivision Regulations, 1975; contbr. numerous articles to legal and pub. adminstrn. jours. Bd. dirs. Starlight Theatre, Kansas City Area Devel. Coun., Downtown Coun., Kansas City region NCCJ, Full Employment Coun., City of Fountains, Project NEIGHBORH.O.O.D., Am. Royal Assn.; mem. policy adv. group Bus.-Edn. Expectations; past pres. Kehilath Israel Synagogue; trustee Avila Coll. Recipient Pub. Adminstr. of Yr. award Am. Soc. Pub. Adminstrn., 1985, L.P. Cookingham Pub. Adminstrn. award, 1989; Walter Scheiber Regional Leadership award Nat. Assn. Regional Couns., 1990; fellow U.S. Dept. Transp., 1975. Mem. Assn. C.C. Execs., Rotary. Home: 3720 W 119th Ter Leawood KS 66209-1046 Office: Greater Kans City C of C 911 Main St Ste 2600 Kansas City MO 64105-2009

LEVI, VICKI GOLD, picture editor, historical consultant, actress; b. Atlantic City, Sept. 16, 1941; d. Albert and Beverly Valentine Gold; m. Alexander Hecht Levi, May 31, 1970; 1 child, Adam Hecht Levi. Student, Montclair State Coll., 1959-60, New Sch. Social Rsch., N.Y.C., 1970-73, Sch. Visual Arts, N.Y.C., 1972, Lee Strass Berg Sch. Acting, N.Y.C., 1961. Actress Atlantic City, N.Y.C and L.A., 1945—; asst. to pres. Family Fare, Inc., N.Y.C., 1966; advt. rep. Cosmopolitan Mag., N.Y.C., 1967; publicity dir. Misty Harbor, Ltd., N.Y.C., 1968; freelance picture researcher, 1972—; contbg. picture editor Esquire Mag., N.Y.C., 1980—, Mirabella Mag., N.Y.C., 1991—, Atlantic City Mag., 1988—, New Woman Mag., 1995—; story cons. Alvin Cooperman Prodns., N.Y.C., 1985—; hist. cons. various Atlantic City, N.Y.C., 1994—; lectr. on Atlantic City, 1979—; guest exhibitor Internat. Ctr. Photography, N.Y.C., 1979; guest exhibitor and lectr. Cooper Hewitt, N.Y.C., 1980; guest curator Songwriters Hall of Fame, N.Y.C., 1979; guest lectr. Mcpl. Art Soc., N.Y.C., 1979; co-founder Atlantic City Hist. Mus., 1985—, bd. dirs., exhibit dir., 1995—; hist. cons. Toast to Times Square Com., N.Y.C., 1988—; curator Atlantic City Playground of the Nation, Atlantic City Hist. Mus., 1994; co-curator Charles K. Doble's Atlantic City, 1994, Images of African Americans in Atlantic City, 1995, Severty-Five Years of Miss America in Pictures, 1995, The Al Gold Years, 1996, Bettmann on the Boardwalk, 1997, Atlantic City Hist. Mus., 1996; bd. dirs. Hecht-Levi Found. Co-author: Atlantic City: 125 Years of Ocean Madness, 1979, rev. edit., 1994, Live and Be Well: A Celebration of Yiddish Culture in America, 1982, You Must Have Been a Beautiful Baby, 1992; columnist Phila. Bull., The Way It Was, 1980; prodr., dir. (hist. video) Boardwalk Ballyhoo, 1992 (Am. Assn. State and Local History award 1995, Atlantic City Tourism Coun. Resolution award 1995, Tourism Advocacy award Greater Atlantic City Region Tourism Coun. 1996); rschr.: Miss America, The Dream Lives On, 1995; hist. cons. (prodn.) Atlantic City Experience, 1995, (Broadway prodn.) Having Our Say, 1995, Time and Again; hist. image cons. (PBS prodn.) I Hear America Singing, 1996; hist. rschr. (Disney World prodn.) BoardWalk Resort, 1996, (Broadway prodn.) Steel Pier. Reviewer of grants, Nat. Endowment for Humanities, Washington. Recipient Author's Citation, N.J. Inst. Tech., Divsn. Continuing Edn., 1980, Senate Resolution, N.J. State Senate, 1979, Outstanding Achievement award, Atlantic City Women's C. of C., 1981, Proclamation from mayor of Atlantic City, 1981; named An Atlantic City Treasure, Atlantic City Women's C. of C., 1989; named to Atlantic County Woman's Hall of Fame, 1997. Mem. NATAS (Emmy judge 1987—, spl. events com. 1989-90), SAG, Am. Fedn. TV and Radio Artists, Am. Soc. Picture Profls. (bd. dirs. 1984), Ziegfeld Club. Democrat. Jewish. Avocations: world travel, memorabilia collecting. Home and Office: 211 Central Park W New York NY 10024-6020

LEVI, YOEL, orchestra conductor; b. Sotmar, Rumania, Israeli, Aug. 16, 1950; naturalized U.S. citizen, 1987; m. Jacqueline; 3 children. MA in Violin and Percussion, U. Tel Aviv, 1975; grad. degree, Jerusalem Acad. Music, 1976; studied with, Mendi Rodan; Diploma, Guildhall Sch. Music and Drama, London, 1978; studied with Franco Ferrara, Siena, Acad. Santa Cecilia, Rome and Kiril Kondrashin, Hilversum. Percussionist Israel Philharmonic Orch., 1975, conducting asst., 1978-80; resident condr. Cleve. Orch., 1980-84; music dir. Atlanta Symphony Orch., 1988—; guest condr. N.Am. and European orchs. Albums include The Artistry of Yoel Levi: The Telarc Collection, Vol. 8; recs. with Angel-EMI, Schwann, Telarc. Recipient 1st prize Condrs. Internat. Competition, Besancon, 1978. Office: care Harold Hope Ltd, 31 Sinclair Rd, London England W14 ONS also: Columbia Artists Mgmt Foster Divsn 165 W 57th St New York NY 10019-2201*

LEVICH, ROBERT ALAN, geologist; b. Bklyn., Apr. 16, 1941; s. Leonard Walter and Dinah (Cohen) L.; m. Stella Araba Nkrumah, June 10, 1964; children: Alexander Kwamina, Walter Abraham, Leo Augustine. BS in Geology, CUNY, Bklyn., 1963; MA in Geol. Scis., U. Tex., 1973. Cert. profl. geologist. Vol. Peace Corps Ghana 3 Geologists, Kade, Ghana, 1963-65; tchg. asst. in geology U. Tex., Austin, 1965-67, rsch. asst. in chem. engring., 1967-68; geologist Ghana Geol. Survey, Sunyani, 1969-72, U.S. Atomic Energy Commn., Austin,, Tex., Spokane, Wash., 1973-81; regional mgr. Apache Energy & Minerals Co., Spokane, 1981-82; cons. expert East Africa Internat. Atomic Energy Agy., Vienna, Austria, 1982-83; geologist, phys. scientist U.S. Dept. Energy, Argonne, Ill., Las Vegas, Nev., 1984-88; chief tech. analysis br. U.S. Dept. Energy/YMP, Las Vegas, Nev., 1988-89; internat. programs mgr. U.S. Dept. Energy/YMP, Las Vegas, 1989-96; mgr. Yucca Mountain Site Description Document, 1996—; U.S. rep., joint tech. com. Internat. Stripa Project, Stockholm, 1989-92; lead U.S. del. OECD/Nuclear Energy Agy. Site Evaluation and Design Experiments, Paris, 1990—; U.S. Dept. Energy rep., joint tech. com. OECD/NEA Alligator Rivers Analogue Project, Sydney, NSW, Australia, 1990-92; project dir. USDOE/Atomic Energy, Can. Ltd. Subsidiary Agreement, 1991-95; tech. coord. USDOE/Switzerland Nat. Co-op. for Disposal Radioactive Waste Project Agreement, 1991-96; project dir. USDOE/Swedish Nuclear Fuel & Waste Mgmt. Co. Hard Rock Lab. Project Agreement, 1993-96. Author, co-author, editor reports. Fellow Geol. Soc. Am., Soc. Econ. Geologists; mem. Am. Nuclear Soc. (Internat. High Level Radioactive Waste Mgmt. Conf. program com., steering com.), Assn. Geoscientists for Internat. Devel., Am. Inst. Profl. Geologists (v.p. Nev. sect. 1993, 94, mem. nat. screening bd. 1994-96, chmn. nat. screening bd. 1996—), Nat. Peace Corps. Assn. Achievements include development of international radioactive waste natural analogue study; developed and negotiated international bilateral technical cooperative projects in geologic disposal of radioactive waste with Canada, Switzerland, Sweden, Japan, Spain and France; managed development of Yucca Mountain Site Description Document. Office: US Dept Energy YMP 1551 Hillshire Dr Las Vegas NV 89134-6321

LEVIE, HOWARD S(IDNEY), lawyer, educator, author; b. Wolverine, Mich., Dec. 19, 1907; s. J. Walter and Mina (Goldfarb) L.; m. S. Blanche Krim, July 24, 1934. A.B., Cornell U., 1928, J.D., 1930; LL.M., George Washington U., 1957. Bar: N.Y. 1931, Mo. 1965, U.S. Dist. Ct. (ea. dist.) N.Y. 1934, U.S. Dist. Ct. (so. dist.) N.Y. 1935, U.S. Supreme Ct. 1947, U.S. Ct. Appeals (D.C. cir.) 1949, U.S. Ct. Mil. Appeals 1953. Assoc. Weit & Goldman, N.Y.C., 1931-42; with JAGC, U.S. Army, 1942, advanced through grades to col., 1954; staff officer UN Command Armistice Del., Korea, 1951-52; chief internat. affairs div. Office of JAG, 1954-58; legal adviser U.S. European Command, Paris, 1959-61; ret. 1963; prof. law St. Louis U., 1963-77, prof. emeritus, 1977—; prof. U.S. Naval War Coll., Newport, R.I., 1971-72, Charles H. Stockton prof. internat. law, 1971-72; instr. internat. law Salve Regina Coll., Newport, R.I., 1984-88; adj. prof. Naval War Coll., 1991—. Author: Prisoners of War in International Armed Conflict (Internat. Soc. for Mil. Law and the Law of War Ciardi prize 1982), 1979, Documents on Prisoners of War, 1980, Protection of War Victims, 4 vols., 1979-81, The Status of Gibraltar, 1983, The Code of International Armed Conflict, 1986, The Law of Non-International Armed Conflict, 1987, The Law of War and Neutrality: A Selected English-Language Bibliography, 1988, Mine Warfare at Sea, 1992, Terrorism in War: The Law of War Crimes, 1993; editor vols. 7-12: Terroism: Documents of International and Local Control, 1997. Decorated Legion of Merit, Bronze Star; grantee Ctr. for Advanced Rsch., Naval War Coll., 1980-82, U.S. Inst. Peace, 1991; Howard S. Levie Mil. Chair of Operational Law established by U.S. Naval War Coll., 1994; recipient Outstanding Civilian Svc. medal Dept. of the Army, 1995; named Disting. Mem. of Judge Advocate Gen.'s Corps Regiment, 1995. Mem. ABA, Am. Soc. Internat. Law (exec. coun. 1969-70), Internat. Law Assn., Ret. Army Judge Advs. Assn., Internat. Soc. for Mil. Law and Law of War, Phi Beta Kappa. Home and Office: 41 Sherman St Newport RI 02840-2959

LEVIE, JOSEPH HENRY, lawyer; b. N.Y.C.; s. Mortimer Joseph and Pearl (Seelig) L.; m. Hallie Ratzkin, Jan. 26, 1963; children: Matthew Benjamin, Jessica Ruth. AB, Columbia U., 1949, LLB, 1951. Bar: N.Y. 1952, U.S. Supreme Ct. 1954. Assoc. Laporte & Meyers, N.Y.C., 1955-59; asst. gen. counsel Loew Theatres Inc., N.Y.C., 1959-63; from assoc. to ptnr. Rathheim, Hoffman, Kassel & Levie, N.Y.C., 1964-81; ptnr. Rogers & Wells, N.Y.C., 1982-94, ret., 1994, sr. counsel, 1995—; lectr. banking and related subjects to various profl. groups. Contbr. articles to profl. jours. With JAGC, U.S. Army, 1952-55. Fellow Am. Coll. Comml. Fin. Attys.; mem. Columbia Coll. Alumni (pres. class of 1949). Home: 131 Riverside Dr New York NY 10024-3713 Office: Rogers & Wells 200 Park Ave New York NY 10166-0005

LEVIEN, DAVID HAROLD, surgeon; b. N.Y.C., Aug. 4, 1948; s. Maurice Berryl and Gloria Anita (Siff) L.; m. Merril Ann Lirette, Aug. 6, 1977; children—Michael, William, Rachel. B.A., Johns Hopkins U., 1970; M.D., Georgetown U., 1974. Diplomate Am. Bd. Surgery, Am. Bd. Med. Examiners. Resident Mt. Sinai Hosp., N.Y.C., 1974-76; coordinated surg. resident U. Mass., 1976-79; surg. edn. coordinator New Rochelle Hosp., N.Y., 1980-88 ; instr. surgery N.Y. Med. Coll., Valhalla, 1980-83, asst. prof. surgery, 1983-90, clin. assoc. prof., 1990-91; cons. in surgery Castle Point VA Hosp., 1980-90. clin. assoc. prof. surgery Med. Coll. Pa./Hahnemann U., 1991—, Jefferson Med. Coll., 1996—; dir. surgery Episcopal Hosp. Author textbook on surgery; contbr. articles to profl. jours. Mem. alumni admissions com. Johns Hopkins U., Balt., 1984-90. Fellow ACS; mem. AMA, Soc. Critical Care Medicine, Assn. Acad. Surgery, Westchester Acad. Medicine.

LE VIEN, JOHN DOUGLAS (JACK LE VIEN), motion picture and television producer, director; b. N.Y.C., July 18, 1918; s. Christopher Luke and Rose Jeanette Le V. Chmn. bd. TCA Travel Corp. Am., 1979—; chmn. bd. Electronic Pub. Co., London. Div. News editor: Pathé News, 1946-57; ind. motion picture and TV dir. and producer, 1958—; producer: (TV series) Valiant Years, 1959-60; exec. producer: (film) Black Fox, 1962 (Acad. award); producer and dir.: (films) Finest Hours, 1963-64, A King's Story, 1965, Churchill Centenary, 1974; (TV shows) Other World of Winston Churchill, 1964, The Gathering Storm, 1973, The Amazing Voyage of Daffodil and Daisy, 1974, Cicero, 1975, Where the Lotus Fell, 1976, Flames Over the Sahara, 1977, Children of the Lotus, 1978, Churchill and The Generals, 1980; pres., exec. producer TV movies, Le Vien Internat. Prodns. Ltd., N.Y.C., 1958—; chmn. bd., exec. producer TV shows, Le Vien Films Ltd., London, Eng., 1963—; author: The Valiant Years, 1961, The Finest Hours, 1964, (with Lady Mosley) The Duchess of Windsor, 1979, (with Barrie Pitt) Churchill and The Generals. Served to col. AUS, World War II, ETO; col. Res. Decorated Legion of Merit, Bronze Star; Legion of Honor; Croix de Guerre France). Mem. Brit. Acad. Film & Television Arts. Club: Overseas Press (N.Y.C.). Home: 15 Chesterfield Hill, London W1, England

LE VIEUX, JANE STUART, pediatrics nurse; b. Washington, May 1, 1956; d. Richard Stuart and Jane Marie (O'Connell) Le V.; m. Gary B. Elliott, Sept. 4, 1982; children: Julianne, Aimée. BSN, U. South Ala., 1979; MS in Child Devel., U. North Tex., 1989, MEd in Counseling and Play Therapy, 1991. Lic. profl. counselor; registered play therapist, Tex. Staff nurse ICU Children's Med. Ctr., Dallas, 1979-81, RN cardiac cath lab., 1981-84, bone marrow transplant child life specialist, 1991—; supr. cardiac cath lab. Humana Hosp.-Medical City, Dallas, 1984-86, pediatric clin. nurse educator, 1986-87; child and family therapist The Caring Ctr., Dallas, 1992—; children's grief therapist and cons. Family Hospice, 1993—; clin. instr. Tex. Woman's U. Coll. Nursing, 1995—; therapist Grief Camp El Tesoro De La Vida, First Tex. coun. Camp Fire Girls, 1995. Active Weekend to Wipe Out Cancer, Dallas, Children's Cancer Fund, Jr. League of Dallas; bd. dirs. Trinity Ministry to the Poor. Author: (with others) A Handbook for Practitioners, 1993. Mem. Assn. for Play Therapy, ANA, Tex. Nurses Assn., Child Life Coun., Assn. for Care of Children's Health, Phi Delta Kappa. Roman Catholic. Avocations: windsurfing, running, tennis, needlepoint. Home: 10019 Rockhill Ln Dallas TX 75229-4208 Office: The Caring Ctr 8222 Douglas Ave Ste 777 Dallas TX 75225-5938

LEVIN, A. LEO, law educator, retired government official; b. N.Y.C., Jan. 9, 1919; s. Isaachar and Minerva Hilda (Shapiro) L.; m. Doris Feder, Dec. 28, 1947; children—Allan, Jay Michael. BA, Yeshiva Coll., 1939; JD, U. Pa., 1942; LLD (hon.), Yeshiva U., 1960, NY Law Sch., 1980, Quinnipiac Coll., 1995; PhD (hon.), Bar-Ilan U., Israel, 1990. Bar: N.Y. 1947, U.S. Supreme Ct. 1982. Instr., then asst. prof. law U. Iowa, 1947-49; law faculty U. Pa., Phila., 1949-69, 70-89, Meltzer prof. law, 1987-89, Meltzer prof. emeritus, 1989—, vice provost, 1965-68; v.p. for acad. affairs Yeshiva U., N.Y.C., 1969-70; dir. Fed. Jud. Ctr., Washington, 1977-87; chmn. Pa. State Legis. Reapportionment Commn., 1971-73; founding dir. Nat. Inst. Trial Advocacy, 1971-73; conf. coord. Nat. Conf. on Causes of Popular Dissatisfaction with Adminstrn. of Justice (Pound Conf.); chmn. bd. cert. Circuit Execs., 1977-87; mem. adv. bd. Nat. Inst. Corrections, 1977-87. Author: (with Woolley) Dispatch and Delay: A Field Study of Judicial Administration in Pennsylvania, 1961; (with Cramer) Problems on Trial Advocacy, 1968; editor: (with Schuchman and Yablon) Cases on Civil Procedure, 1992, Supplement, 1994. Hon. trustee Bar Ilan U., Ramat Gan, Israel, 1967—; hon. pres. (former pres.) Jewish Publ. Soc. Am. Served to 1st lt. USAF, 1942-46, ETO. Recipient Mordecai Ben David award Yeshiva U., 1967, Disting. Svc. award U. Pa. Law Sch. Alumni, 1974, Bernard Revel award Yeshiva Coll., 1963, Justice award Am. Judicature Soc., 1995; White lectr. La. U., 1970, Jeffords lectr., N.Y. Law Sch., 1980, Murrah Lectr. U. Pa. Law Sch., 1989. Fellow Am. Acad. Arts and Scis.; mem. Am. Law Inst., Am. Judicature Soc. (pres. 1987-89), Order of Coif (nat. pres. 1967-70). Jewish. Office: U Pa Law Sch 3400 Chestnut St Philadelphia PA 19104-6204

LEVIN, AARON REUBEN, pediatrician, educator; b. Johannesburg, Transvaal, Republic of South Africa, Mar. 19, 1929; came to U.S., 1964; s. Louis and Fanny (Galgut) L.; m. Lenore Zhita Gladstone, Dec. 6, 1955; children: Sheryl Rina, Terry Larice, Serle Kevin. BS, Witwatersrand U., 1948, MB, BCh, 1953, MD, 1969. Diplomate Am. Bd. Pediatrics, Pediatric Cardiology. Intern Edenvale Hosp., Johannesburg, 1954-55; sr. med. officer Fever Hosp., Johannesburg, 1955-56; registrar in pediatrics Coronation Hosp., Johannesburg, 1956-61, Charing Cross Hosp., London, 1961-62; attending pediatrician Edenvale Hosp., Johannesburg, 1962-64; instr. in pediatrics Duke Univ. Med. Sch., Durham, N.C., 1964-66; asst.-assoc. prof. pediatrics Cornell Univ. Med. Coll., N.Y.C., 1966-73, prof. pediatrics, 1973-94; prof. pediatrics N.Y. Med. Coll., 1994—; attending pediatrician N.Y. Hosp. Cornell Med. Ctr., 1966-94, also dir. pediatric catheterization labs. 1966-94; cons. cardiologist Englewood (N.J.) Hosp., 1980-90; cons. pediatric cardiologist St. Lukes Hosp., Newburgh, N.Y., 1982—, New Rochelle (N.Y.) Hosp., 1994—, Pascack (N.J.) Hosp., 1994—; assoc. attending pediatric cardiologist Westchester County Med. Ctr., 1994—. Contbr. articles and papers to profl. jours. Pres. Beth Emeth Synagogue, Larchmont, N.Y., 1973, Pediatric Cardiology Soc. Greater N.Y., 1978. Fellow Am. Heart Assn., Am. Coll. Cardiology, N.Y. Heart Assn., Am. Angiology Soc., Royal Coll. Physicians (Edinburgh, Scotland). Avocations: stamp collecting, reading, gardening.. Home: 701 Fairway Green Old Post Rd Mamaroneck NY 10543 Office: NY Med Coll 601 Munger Pavilion Valhalla NY 10595

LEVIN, ALAN M., television journalist; b. Bklyn., Feb. 28, 1926; s. Herman and Shirley (Levinstein) L.; m. Hannah Alexander, Oct. 30, 1948; children: Marc, Nicole, Danielle, Juliet. BA, Wesleyan U., Middletown, Conn., 1946. Reporter, columnist Plainfield (N.J.) Courier News, 1957-60; statehouse corr. AP, Trenton, N.J., 1960-61; writer N.Y. Post, 1961-63; press sec. Sen. Harrison Williams, Washington, 1963-64; news producer, writer WABC-TV, N.Y.C., 1965-67; owner Levin Mediaworks Inc., producers documentaries for comml. and pub. TV, N.Y.C. Documentary film maker, NET, N.Y.C., 1968-69, documentary film maker, pub. affairs, news writer, dir., producer,

WNET-TV, N.Y.C., 1969-82. Served with AUS, 1944-46. Recipient numerous awards including George Polk Meml. award, Dupont Columbia award, Emmy awards. Home: 88 Claremont Ave Maplewood NJ 07040-2024 Office: Blowback Prodns Inc 601 W 26th St 17th Fl New York NY 10001

LEVIN, ALAN SCOTT, pathologist, allergist, immunologist, lawyer; b. Chgo., Jan. 12, 1938; s. John Bernhard and Betty Ruth (Margulis) L.; m. Vera S. Byers, June 15, 1971. BS in Chemistry, U. Ill., Champaign-Urbana, 1960; MS in Biochemistry, U. Ill., Chgo., 1963, MD, 1964; JD, Golden Gate U., 1995. Diplomate Am. Bd. Allergy and Immunology, Am. Bd. Pathology; bar: Calif. 1995. Intern Children's Hosp. Med. Ctr., Boston, 1964-65; adj. instr. pediatrics U. Calif., San Francisco, 1971-72, asst. prof. immunology dept. dermatology, 1972-78, adj. assoc. prof., 1978-88; dir. lab. immunology U. Calif. & Kaiser Found. Rsch. Inst. Joint Program Project, San Francisco, 1971-74; attending physician dept. medicine Mt. Zion/U. Calif. San Francisco Hosps., 1971—; dir. div. immunology Western Labs., Oakland, Calif., 1974-77; med. dir. MML/Solano Labs. Div. Chemed-W.R. Grace, Inc., Berkeley, Calif., 1977-79; med. dir. Levin Clin. Labs., Inc., San Francisco, 1979-81; pvt. practice San Francisco, 1981—. Contbr. articles to profl. jours., chpts. to books. Lt. USN, 1966-69, Vietnam. Decorated Bronze Star, Silver Star, 4 Air medals; Harvard Med. Sch. traineeship grantee, 1964, USPHS hematology tng. grantee U. Calif., San Francisco Med. Ctr., 1969-71; recipient Faculty Rsch. award Am. Cancer Soc., 1970-74. Fellow Coll. Am. Pathologists, Am. Coll. Emergency Physicians, Am. Soc. Clin. Pathologists; mem. AMA, Am. Acad. Allergy and Immunology, Am. Coll. Allergy and Immunology, Am. Assn. Clin. Chemists, Am. Acad. Environ. Medicine, Calif. Med. Assn., San Francisco Med. Soc. Jewish. Office: Immunology Inc 500 Sutter St Ste 512 San Francisco CA 94102-1114

LEVIN, ALVIN IRVING, composer, educator; b. N.Y.C., Dec. 22, 1921; s. David and Frances (Schloss) L.; m. Beatrice Van Loon, June 5, 1976 (div. 1981). BMus in Edn., U. Miami (Fla.), 1941; MA, Calif. State U., L.A., 1955; EdD with honors, UCLA, 1968. Composer, arranger for movies, TV, theater Allied Artists, Eagle-Lion Studios, Los Angeles, 1945-65; tng. and supervising tchr. Los Angeles City Schs., 1957-65, adult edn. instr., 1962-63; research specialist Los Angeles Office Supt. edn., 1965-67; asst. prof. ednl. research Calif. State U., Los Angeles, 1968; asst. prof. elem. edn. Calif. State U., Northridge, 1969-73; self-employed, Northridge, 1973—; founder, pres. Alvin Irving Levin Philanthropic Found., 1973—, ordained to ministry Ch. of Mind Sci., 1975; founder, pres. Divine Love Ch. An Internat. Metaphys. Ch., 1977—, Meet Your New Personality, A Mind Expansion Program, 1975-77. Bd. overseers Calif. Sch. Profl. Psychology, 1974—; gen. chmn., producer Fiftieth Anniversary Pageant of North Hollywood Park, 1977. Author: My Ivory Tower, 1950, Symposium: Values in Kaleidoscope, 1973, (TV series) America, America!, 1978-79, (docudrama) One World, 1980; composer: Symphony for Strings, 1984, Tone Poem for MaleChorus and Brass, 1984, Hymn to the United Nations for chorus and Male Chorus and Brass, 1984, Hymn to the United Nations for chorus and symphonyorch., 1991, Hiawatha Suite for Chorus and Symphony Orch., 1994, We Are Not Alone, Chorus and Symphony Orchestra, 1996, North Hollywood: Metamorphosis, A Symphonic Suite, 1996-97, Introspection for Symphony Orchestra, 1997 (music-drama) Happy Land, 1971, (musical plays) A Tale of Two Planets, 1988, Blueprint for a New World Model, 1991; prodr. UN Festival Calif. State U., Northridge, 1991; compiler, contbr. U.S. Dept. Edn. reports Adult Counseling and Guidance, 1967, Parent Child Preschool Program, 1967, English Classes for Foreign Speaking Adult Professionals, 1967, Blueprint for New World Order, 1991. Recipient plaque State of Calif., 1977, Golden Merit medal. Rep. Presdl. Task Force, 1985.Named to Rep Task Force Presdl. Commn., 1986. Mem. Nat. Soc. for Study Edn., AAUP, Am. Statis Assn., Internat. Coun. Edn. for Tchg., L.A. World Affairs Coun., Internat. Platform Assn., World Federalist Assn. (pres. San Fernando Valley chpt. 1991—), North Hollywood C. of C. (dir. 1976—), Phi Delta Kappa. Home and Office: 5407 Colfax Ave Apt 223 North Hollywood CA 91601-5209 *Personal philosophy: Always dream the impossible dream; then make it come true, with every possible action!.*

LEVIN, ARNOLD MURRAY, social worker, psychotherapist; b. Bklyn., Dec. 26, 1924; s. William and Pauline Levin; m. Elaine M. Zimmerman, Dec. 19, 1946 (dec. Aug. 1971); children: Michael, Nancy Jo Noteman, Amy Louise. BA, U. Mass., 1948; MA, U. Chgo., 1950, PhD, 1975; Cert., Chgo. Inst. Psychoanalysis, 1955. ACSW, LCSW, BCD. Case worker Jewish Family Svcs., Chgo., 1950-53; group therapist Portal House Clinic Alcoholism, Chgo., 1952-55; exec. dir. Family Svc., Mental Health Ctr. So. Cook County, Park Forest, Ill., 1953-60; pvt. practice in social work Chgo., 1960—; founder, pres. Inst. Clin. Social Work, Chgo., 1979—; bd. dirs. Jewish Childrens Bur., Chgo., 1987—; founder, pres., Ill. Soc. Clin. Social Workers, Chgo., 1971-76; mem. 90 for the 90's, Ill. Author: Private Practice of Psychotherapy, 1983. Sgt. U.S. Army, 1943-46. NIMH grantee, 1971; recipient Gov.'s award, Chgo., 1975, Alumnus of Yr. award U. Chgo., 1976. Mem. Nat. Registry of Health Care Providers in Clin. Social Wk. (bd. dirs. 1985-88), Nat. Fedn. Socs. for Clin. Social Work (founder 1971-75). Avocations: acting, theatre. Home: 3180 N Lake Shore Dr #11G Chicago IL 60657 Office: 151 N Michigan Ave Apt 809 Chicago IL 60601-7543

LEVIN, BERNARD, physician; b. Johannesburg, Republic of South Africa, Apr. 1, 1942; came to U.S. 1966, naturalized 1972; m. Ronelle DuBrow; children: Adam, Katherine. MD, U. Witwatersrand, 1964. Resident Presbyn. St. Lukes Hosp., Chgo., 1966-68; rsch. fellow U. Chgo., 1968-71; NIH fellow U. Chgo., 1971-72; instr. medicine U. Chgo., 1971-73, asst. prof. medicine, 1973-78, assoc. prof., 1979-84; prof. med., chmn. dept gastrointestinal oncology and digestive diseases, U. Tex. Med. Ctr. M.D. Anderson Hosp., Houston, 1984-94, Robert R. Herring prof., 1986-91, Ellen F. Knisely chair, 1991-94, v.p. for Cancer Prevention (ad interim), 1992-94, v.p. for Cancer Prevention, 1994—, Betty Marcus chair 1994—; mem. large bowel cancer working group Nat. Cancer Inst., 1984-85; cons. spl. study sect. Nat. Cancer Inst., 1976-84, chair nat. adv. com. on colorectal cancer, 1990—. Contbr. articles to profl. jours.; mem. editorial bd. Pancreas, Jour. Nat. Cancer Inst. J. Clin. Oncology USPHS grantee, 1976-80; Melamid Found. Gift, U. Chgo., 1978-83; NCI grantee, 1980-84, others. Fellow ACP, Am. Coll. Gastroenterology; mem. AAAS, Am. Assn. Cancer Rsch., Am. Gastroenterol. Assn., Am. Soc. Gastrointestinal Endoscopy, Am. Pancreatic Assn, Am. Soc. Preventive Oncology, Am. Soc. Clin. Oncology, Am. Cancer Soc. (chair nat. adv. com. on colorectal cancer), Sigma Xi. Jewish. Office: UT M D Anderson Cancer Ctr 1515 Holcombe Blvd # 203 Houston TX 77030-4009

LEVIN, BETSY, lawyer, educator, university dean; b. Balt., Dec. 25, 1935; d. M. Jastrow and Alexandra (Lee) L. AB, Bryn Mawr (Pa.) Coll., 1956; LLB, Yale U., 1966. Bar: D.C. 1967, Colo. 1982. Research geologist U.S. Geol. Survey, Washington, 1956-63; law clk. to judge U.S. Ct. Appeals (4th cir.), Balt., 1966-67; spl. asst. to U.S. Amb. to UN, Arthur J. Goldberg N.Y.C., 1967-68; dir. edn. studies Urban Inst., Washington, 1968-73; prof. law Duke U., Durham, N.C., 1973-80; gen. counsel U.S. Dept. Edn., Washington, 1980-81; dean, prof. law U. Colo., Boulder, 1981-87; exec. v.p. Assn. Am. Law Schs., Washington, 1987-92; Arch T. Allen vis. disting. prof. law U. N.C. Sch. Law, Chapel Hill, 1993; vis. prof. law Am. U. Washington Coll. Law, 1994, Georgetown U. Law Ctr., Washington, 1994; disting. vis. prof. sch. law U. Balt., 1995-96; vis. prof. law Howard U. Sch. Law, Washington, 1996—; mem. Nat. Coun. Ednl. Rsch., 1978-79; mem. civil rights reviewing authority HEW, 1979-80. Co-author: Educational Policy and the Law, 2d edit., 1982, 3d edit., 1991; editor: Future Directions for School Finance Reform, 1975; co-editor: The Courts, Social Science and School Desegregation, 1977, School Desegregation: Lessons of the First 25 Years, 1979. Bd. dirs. Nat. Inst. for Dispute Resolution. White House fellow, 1967-68. Fellow Am. Bar Found.; mem. ABA, Nat. Assn. Women Judges (program com. 1985-92), Am. Law Inst. (coun.), Order of Coif. Office: Howard U Sch Law 2900 Van Ness St NW Washington DC 20008-1106

LEVIN, BURTON, diplomat; b. N.Y.C., Sept. 28, 1930; s. Benjamin and Ida (Geller) L.; m. Lily Lee, Jan. 4, 1960; children: Clifton, Alicia. BA, CUNY, 1952; M Internat. Affairs, Columbia U., 1954; postgrad., Harvard U., 1964; LLD (hon.), Carleton Coll., 1993. Commd. fgn. service officer Dept. State, 1954; counselor/econ. officer Am. Embassy, Taipei, Taiwan, 1954-56, polit. officer, 1969-74; intelligence research specialist Dept. State, Washington, 1956-58, dir. Republic China affairs, 1974-77; polit. officer Am. Embassy, Jakarta, Indonesia, 1959-63; polit. officer Am. Consulate Gen. Hong Kong, 1965-69, dep. chief mission, 1977-78, consul gen., 1981-86; dep. chief mission Am. Embassy, Bangkok, Thailand, 1978-81; amb. to Burma, 1987-90; dir. Asia Soc. Hong Kong Ctr., 1990-95; vis. prof. Carleton Coll., 1995; vis. fellow Stanford U., 1974; vis. lectr. Harvard U., 1986, Carleton Coll., 1994; bd. dirs. Mansfield Found., China Fund, Yaohan Food Processing and Trading Co. Ltd.; mem. coun. Nanjing U. Ctr. for Chinese and Am. Studies Johns Hopkins U. Mem. Am. Fgn. Service Assn. Clubs: Am., Hong Kong Country. Home: 314 2nd St E Northfield MN 55057-2204

LEVIN, CARL, senator; b. Detroit, June 28, 1934; m. Barbara Halpern, 1961; children: Kate, Laura, Erica. BA, Swarthmore Coll., 1956; JD, Harvard U., 1959. Ptnr. Grossman, Hyman & Grossman, Detroit, 1959-64; asst. atty. gen., gen. counsel Mich. CRC, 1964-67; chief appellate defender City of Detroit, 1968-69, mem. coun., 1970-73, pres. coun., 1974-77; ptnr. Schlussel, Lifton, Simon, Rands & Kaufman, 1971-73, Jaffe, Snider, Raitt, Garratt & Heuer, 1978-79; U.S. senator from Mich., 1979—; past instr. Wayne State U., U. Detroit; ranking mem. Armed Svcs. Com., Govtl. Affairs Com., Com. on Small Bus., Senate Dem. Steering & Coordination Com., Senate Select Com. on Intelligence. Mem. Mich. Bar Assn., D.C. Bar. Democrat. Office: US Senate 459 Russell Senate Off Washington DC 20510

LEVIN, CARL, public and government relations consultant; b. Ringgold, La.; m. Doris Wechsler; m. Sonia Atlas, Oct. 13, 1958; children: Judith Friedman, Richard (dec.), Virginia, Alan Schwartzbach. Student, CCNY, 1930-33. Corr. CCNY N.Y. Herald Tribune, 1930-34, staff reporter, 1934-43, Washington corr., 1943-45, 46-50; war and fgn. corr. N.Y. Herald Tribune, Europe, 1945-46; free lance mag. writer, 1942-50; Washington mgr. William H. Weintraub & Co. (advt. and pub. relations), 1950-52; charge Washington activities Schenley Industries, Inc., 1952-62, v.p., 1955-62; dir. pub. support Trade Expansion Act, White House, 1962; pres. Carl Levin Assos., Inc., 1962-68; v.p., gen. mgr. Burson-Marsteller, Washington, 1968-72; v.p., sr. cons. Burson-Marsteller, 1972-83, sr. v.p., 1983-87; mem. Nat. Small Bus. Adv. Coun., 1964-68; cons. in field. Collaborator books on journalism, postwar security investigations; contbr. to nat. mags. Active in founding Am.-Israel Pub. Affairs Soc.; bd. dirs. Interracial Coun. Bus. Opportunity, 1972-75; mem. bd. Com. Accuracy on Middle East Reporting in Am., 1985-91, Am. Gas Index Fund, 1990—; trustee Opera Soc. Washington, 1963-70, Ford's Theater, Washington, 1975-81; co-chmn. Citizens Com. Opera, 1963. Mem. Soc. Profl. Journalists, Lotos Club (N.Y.C.). Home: Apt 809 5450 Whitley Park Ter Bethesda MD 20814-2057

LEVIN, CHARLES EDWARD, lawyer; b. Chgo., Oct. 6, 1946; m. Barbara Serwer, Dec. 28, 1975. BA with high honor, DePaul U., 1968; JD cum laude, Northwestern U., Chgo., 1971. Bar: Ill. 1971. Asst. instr. legal writing and rsch. Northwestern U. Law Sch., 1970-71; assoc. D'Ancona & Pflaum, Chgo., 1971-76, ptnr., 1977-90; ptnr. Jenner & Block, Chgo., 1990—; mem. governing bd. Comml. Fin. Assn. Edn. Found., 1990—; asst. instr. legal writing, rsch. Northwestern U., 1970-71. Mem. bd. editors Northwestern U. Law Rev., 1970-71. Mem. aux. bd. Chgo. Architecture Found., 1989—; mem. governing bd. Comml. Fin. Assn. Edn. Found., N.Y. Mem. ABA (bus. sect. 1992—), Chgo. Bar Assn. (vice chmn. architecture and law com. 1974-75, vice chmn. divsn. D, mem. exec. com. fed. tax com. 1983-84, comml. fin. and trans. com. 1990—, Article 9 drafting subcom.), Assn. for Corp. Growth, East Bank Club Chgo., 410 Club. Avocations: acquisition fine arts, support arts organizations, jogging. Office: Jenner & Block 1 E IBM Plz Fl 4400 Chicago IL 60611-3586

LEVIN, CHARLES LEONARD, state supreme court justice; b. Detroit, Apr. 28, 1926; s. Theodore and Rhoda (Katzin) L.; children: Arthur, Amy, Fredrick. B.A., U. Mich., 1946, LL.B., 1947; LL.D. (hon.), Detroit Coll. of Law, 1980. Bar: Mich. 1947, N.Y. 1949, U.S. Supreme Ct. 1953, D.C. 1954. Pvt. practice law N.Y.C., 1948-50, Detroit, 1950-66; ptnr. Levin, Levin, Garvett & Dill, Detroit, 1951-66; judge Mich. Ct. Appeals, Detroit, 1966-73; assoc. justice Mich. Supreme Ct., 1973—; mem. Mich. Law Revision Commn., 1966. Trustee Marygrove Coll., 1971-77, chmn., 1971-74; mem. vis. coms. to Law Schs., U. Mich., U. Chgo., 1977-80, Wayne State U. Mem. Am. Law Inst. Office: Mich Supreme Ct 500 Woodward Ave Fl 20 Detroit MI 48226-3423*

LEVIN, DAVID ALAN, lawyer; b. Cheverly, Md., Nov. 16, 1947; s. Jacob Solomon and Elaine (Astrin) L.; m. Pamela Evelyn Ruff, Sept. 18, 1976; 1 child, Michael Brian. BS, U. Md., 1968, JD, 1972. Bar: Md. 1972, U.S. Ct. Appeals (4th cir.) 1975. Ptnr. Levin & Levin, Langley Park, Md., 1972-75, O'Malley, Miles, Largo, Md., 1975-84, Wharton, Levin, Ehrmantraut, Klein & Nash, Annapolis, Md., 1984—. Fellow Am. Coll. Trial Lawyers. Office: Wharton Levin et al PO Box 551 104 West St Annapolis MD 21404-0551

LEVIN, EDWARD JESSE, lawyer; b. Balt., Oct. 31, 1951; s. Cyril and Virginia Lee (Kremer) L.; m. Cheri Wyron, Feb. 18, 1973; children: Paul Clifford, Benjamin Lawrence. BA, Johns Hopkins U., 1973; JD, U. Va., 1976. Bar: Md. 1976, U.S. Supreme Ct. 1980. Assoc. Piper & Marbury LLP, Balt., 1976-84; ptnr. Piper & Marbury, Balt., 1984—. Co-author: Maryland Real Estate Leasing Forms and Practice, 1988. 1st v.p. Balt. Bd. of Jewish Edn., 1987-89, pres., 1989-91. Fellow Am. Coll. Real Estate Lawyers (chmn. attys.' opinions com. 1992—); mem. Md. State Bar Assn. (chmn. sect. real property, planning and zoning 1988-90. co-chmn. spl. joint com. lawyers' opinions comml. transactions 1989—), Balt. City Bar Assn. (co-chmn. spl. joint com. lawyers' opinions comml. transactions 1989—). Democrat. Jewish. Office: Piper & Marbury LLP 36 S Charles St Baltimore MD 21201-3020

LEVIN, EDWARD M., lawyer, government administrator; b. Chgo., Oct. 16, 1934; s. Edward M. and Anne Meriam (Fantl) L.; children from previous marriage: Daniel Andrew, John Davis; m. Margot Aronson, Apr. 4, 1993. BS, U. Ill., 1955; LLB, Harvard U., 1958. Bar: Ill. 1958, U.S. Supreme Ct. 1968. Mem. firm Ancel, Stonesifer, Glink & Levin and predecessors, Chgo., 1958, 61-68; draftsman Ill. Legis. Reference Bur., Springfield, 1961; spl. asst. to regional adminstr. HUD, Chgo., 1968-71, asst. regional adminstr. community planning and mgmt., 1971-73; asst. dir. Ill. Dept. Local Govt. Affairs, Chgo., 1973-77; of counsel Holleb, Gerstein & Glass, Ltd., Chgo., 1977-79; chief counsel Econ. Devel. Adminstrn., U.S. Dept. Commerce, Washington, 1979-85, 97—; sr. fellow Nat. Gov's. Assn., 1985-86; sr. counsel U.S. Dept. Commerce, Washington, 1987-96; lectr. U. Ill., 1972-73, adj. assoc. prof. urban scis., 1973-79; lectr. Loyola U., 1976-79, No. Va. law Sch., 1988. Assoc. editor Assistance Mgmt. Jour., 1990-95; contbr. articles to profl. jours. Mem. Ill. Nature Preserves Com., 1963-68, Northea. Ill. Planning Commn., 1974-77, Ill.-Ind. Bi-State Commn., 1974-77; bd. dirs. Cook County Legal Assistance Found., 1978-79, D.C. Appleseed Ctr., 1994—; mem. Ill. divsn. ACLU, 1965-68, 77-79, v.p., 1977-78. With AUS, 1958-60. Mem. ABA (chmn. fed. assistance com. 1995-96), FBA (chmn. fed. grants com. 1991-95), Ill. Bar Assn. (Lincoln award 1977), Nat. Grants Mgmt. Assn. (bd. dirs. 1988-92, Pres.'s award 1994), Appleseed Found. (bd. dirs., mem. exec. com. 1994—). Home: 3201 Porter St NW Washington DC 20008-3212 Office: 14th & Constitution Ave NW Washington DC 20230-0002

LEVIN, FRANK S., physicist, educator; b. N.Y.C., Apr. 14, 1933; s. James J. and Celia (Aronovitch) L.; m. Madeline Carol McMurrough, Apr. 1973; 4 children. B.A., Johns Hopkins U., 1955; Ph.D., U. Md., 1961. Research assoc. Rice U., Houston, 1961-63, Brookhaven Nat. Lab., Upton, N.Y., 1963-66, U.K. Atomic Energy Authority, Harwell, Eng., 1965-67; mem. faculty Brown U., Providence, 1967—; prof. physics Brown U., 1977—; co-organizer 9th Internat. Conf. on Few-Body Problems, 1980. Co-editor (series): Finite Systems and Multiparticle Dynamics. Recipent Sr. U.S. Scientist award Alexander von Humboldt Stiftung, 1979. Fellow Am. Phys. Soc. (founder, 1st chmn. topical group on few body systems and multiparticle dynamics). Office: Brown U Physics Dept PO Box 1843 Providence RI 02912-1843

LEVIN, GEOFFREY ARTHUR, botanist; b. Los Alamos, N.Mex., Dec. 7, 1955; s. Jules Samuel and Jane Walden (Settle) L.; m. Renée Patricia Papini, May 24, 1981; children: Tobias, Madeline. BA, Pomona Coll., 1977; MS, U. Calif., Davis, 1980, PhD, 1984. Asst. prof. Ripon (Wis.) Coll., 1982-84; curator, chmn. botany dept. San Diego Natural History Mus., 1984-93; lectr. U. San Diego, 1984-90; asst. profl. scientist Ill. Natural History Survey, Champaign, 1994-96, assoc. profl. scientist, dir. Ctr. for Biodiversity, 1996—; adj. asst. prof. dept. plant biology U. Ill., 1995—, adj. asst. prof. dept. natural resources and environ. studies, 1995—; rsch. assoc. Mo. Bot. Garden, 1994—. Contbr. articles to jours. in field. Bd. dirs. Fond du Lac Audubon Soc., 1983-84, San Diego Audubon Soc., 1986-87; pres. Summit Unitarian Universalist Fellowship, El Cajon, Calif., 1989-91; treas. Unitarian Universalist Ch., Urbana, Ill., 1996—. Recipient Jesse M. Greenman award. Mo. Bot. Garden, 1987; NSF grad. fellow, 1977-81. Mem. Am. Inst. Biol. Scis., Am. Soc. Plant Taxonomists, Bot. Soc. Am., Soc. Systematic Biologists, Calif. Bot. Soc. (bd. editors 1992-95), Phi Beta Kappa, Sigma Xi. Democrat. Office: Ill Natural History Survey Ctr for Biodiversity 607 E Peabody Dr Champaign IL 61820-6917

LEVIN, GERALD MANUEL, media and entertainment company executive; b. Phila., May 6, 1939; s. David and Pauline (Schantzer) L.; m. Carol S. Needleman, Aug. 30, 1959 (div. Aug. 1970); children: Laura, Leon, Jonathan; m. Barbara J. Riley, Oct. 11, 1970; children: Michael, Anna. BA, Haverford Coll., 1960; LLB, U. Pa., 1963; LLD (hon.), Tex. Coll., 1985; LLD (hon.), Middlebury Coll., 1994; LHD (hon.), U. Denver, 1995. Assoc. Simpson, Thacher & Bartlett, N.Y.C., 1963-67; gen. mgr., chief operating officer Devel. and Resources Corp., N.Y.C., 1967-71; rep. Internat. Basic Economy Corp., Tehran, Iran, 1971-72; v.p. programming Home Box Office, N.Y.C., 1972-73, pres., chief exec. officer, 1973-76, chmn., chief exec. officer, 1976-79; group v.p. video Time, Inc., N.Y.C., 1979-84, exec. v.p., 1984-88, vice chmn., dir., 1988-90; vice chmn., dir. Time Warner Inc., N.Y.C., 1990—, chief oper. officer, 1991-92, pres., co-chief exec. officer to chmn. and CEO, 1992—; trustee emeritus Hampshire Coll. Trustee Haverford Coll., 1983-95, chmn. bd. dirs., 1990-95; bd. dirs., treas. N.Y. Philharm., Ronald H. Brown Found., A Living Meml. to the Holocaust—Mus. of Jewish Heritage. Mem. The Aspen Inst., N.Y. City Partnership, Nat. Cable TV Ctr. and Mus. and A Living Memorial to the Holocause-Mus. of Jewish Heritage (coun. on fgn. rels.), The Trilateral Commn., Corp. Governance Task Force of the Bus. Roundtable, Phi Beta Kappa. Avocations: reading, jogging. Office: Time Warner Inc 75 Rockefeller Plz New York NY 10019-6908

LEVIN, GILBERT VICTOR, health information, services and products; b. Balt., Apr. 23, 1924; s. Henry I. and Lillian R. (Richman) L.; m. Karen Bloomquist, Oct. 25, 1953; children: Ron L., Henry L., Carol Y. BE, Johns Hopkins U., 1947, MS, 1948, PhD, 1963. Registered profl. engr., D.C., Md. With Md. State Dept. Health, 1948-50, Calif. Dept. Health, 1950-51, D.C. Dept. Pub. Health, 1951-55; v.p. Resources Research, Inc., Washington, 1955-63; dir. life systems div. Hazleton Labs., Inc., Reston, Va., 1963-67; chief exec. officer, chmn. bd. Biospherics Inc., Beltsville, Md., 1967—. Contbr. 100 articles to profl. jours.; mem. editorial bd. BioScience, 1960-63. Trustee John Hopkins U., 1982-85. Merchant Marine USCG, 1944-46. Recipient Pub. Svc. medal NASA, 1977; Whiting medal Johns Hopkins U., 1987, Disting. Alumnus award, 1995. Fellow Am. Pub. Health Assn.; mem. ASCE, AAAS (Newcomb Cleveland prize 1977), Am. Water Works Assn., Water Pollution Control Fedn., Am. Soc. Microbiology, N.Y. Acad. Scis. Club: Cosmos. NASA experimenter Mariner 9 mission, 1971, Viking Mission Labeled Release Life Detection expt., 1976; mem. team Mars oxident expt. for Russian Mars lander, 1996; patentee in field; inventor PhoStrip process for wastewater nutrient removal, microbial radiorespirometry, nonfattening sweeteners use of D-Tagatose as antihyperglycemic agent and in diabetes treatment; application of firefly bioluminescent assay for adenosine triphosphate bioassays to biomass determination and to microbial enumeration. Home: 3180 Harness Creek Rd Annapolis MD 21403-1614 Office: Biospherics Inc 12051 Indian Creek Ct Beltsville MD 20705-1261 *Man's ability to accumulate information through learning and to pass it on to his descendents frees his generations from endless repetition. He may hope to understand the universe and his place in it.*

LEVIN, HAL ALAN, psychiatrist; b. Bklyn., Feb. 13, 1935; s. David and Rose M. (Rosen) L.; children of former marriage: Julie Levin Keith, Susan Levin Davis, Mark D. Levin; m. Sharon Greenleaf, Feb. 9, 1973; children: Anne Levin Warrick, Julie Elizabeth, Alisa M., Kimberly L. Grimes, Christopher Lenk. BS, Roosevelt U., 1958; MD, Tulane Med. Sch., New Orleans, 1967. Diplomate Am. Bd. Psychiatry and Neurology, Am. Bd. Forensic Examiners, Am. Bd. Forensic Medicine. Intern Norfolk (Va.) Gen. Hosp., 1967-68; resident in psychiatry Sheppard & Enoch Pratt Hosp., Towson, Md., 1968-70, Crownsville (Md.) Hosp., 1970-71; fellow in forensic psychiatry U. So. Calif., L.A., 1983-84; staff psychiatrist Atascadero (Calif.) State Hosp., 1971-72; pvt. practice psychiatry San Bernardino, Calif., 1972-85; asst. prof. clin. psychiatry Mich. State U., East Lansing, 1985-86; asst. dir. mental health State of Mich., Lansing, 1985-86; dir. mental health State of Ariz., Phoenix, 1986-87; pvt. practice psychiatry Tempe, Ariz., 1987—; cons. psychiatrist San Bernardino County Hosp., 1972-85, San Bernardino Superior Ct., 1972-85; dir. Desert Valley Clinic, Apple Valley, Calif., 1973-80; med. dir. Big Bear (Calif.) Psychiat. Clinic, 1980-84; med. dir. Ctr. for Behavioral Health, Tempe, 1989—. cons. Jewish Family Svcs., Tempe, 1990—, Interfaith Counseling, Mesa, Ariz., 1991—. Mem. AMA, Am. Psychiat. Assn., Ariz. Med. Assn., Am. Acad. Psychiatry & the Law, Am. Bd. Forensic Examiners, Friends of Phoenix Symphony. Democrat. Avocations: computers, film, reading, swimming, music. Office: 5410 S Lakeshore Dr # 103 Tempe AZ 85283-2171

LEVIN, HARVEY JAY, financial institutions design and construction specialist, developer, auctioneer; b. Fitchburg, Mass., Apr. 27, 1936; s. Abe and Ila L.; children: Kimberly, Tara, Robin, Vanessa. Student Brandeis U., Boston U., U. Md., Ind. U.; BBA in Fin., U. Mass., 1960; MA in Econs., U. N.H., 1970; PhD LaSalle U., PhD in Bus. Mgmt., 1996. Lic. real estate broker, Mass., N.H.; lic. comml. pilot; lic. auctioneer, Maine, Mass., N.H., Vt., Accredited Auctioneer Real Estate, CAI. Pres. Central Tool Warehouse, Leominster, Mass., 1959-66; dir. mktg. and sales Spacemakers, Canton, Mass., 1970-72, New Eng. Homes, Biddeford, Maine, 1973-74; gen. mgr. Great No. Homes, Boston, 1966-70; cons. service mgr. Bank Bldg. Corp., St. Louis, 1974-80; v.p. Shelter Resources, Birmingham, Ala., 1972-73; v.p. Fin. Concepts, Natick, Mass., 1980-85; pres. Am. Bank Design, Inc., and Credit Union Bldg. Corp., Portsmouth, N.H., Harv Levin, Inc., Auctioneers, 1986—; cons. Republic Homes, Truro, Can., 1974. Author, lectr. personal and profl. seminars. Chmn. sch. bldg. com. Kensington, N.H., 1985; pres. Pheasant Run Condominium Assn., 1993—; chairperson Parents Fund, U. N.H., 1993-95, pres.- elect Parents Coun., 1995—. Served with U.S. Army, 1955-57. Recipient Award of Honor, Bank Bldg. Corp. of Am., 1976, 1st Place Design award Bank Bldg. Corp. of Am., 1977, Best Mktg. and Sales Plan award Automation in Housing Assn., 1972, FMHA award for Best Elderly Housing Project (Hazel Dell Apts., Alfred, Maine); named Hon. Lt. Col. Aide-de-Camp by Gov. of Ala., 1978. Mem. Aircraft Owners and Pilots Assn., Phi Sigma Kappa. Clubs: The River (Kennebunkport, Maine); Hampton River Boat, Portsmouth Power Squadron. Lodge: Masons. Office: Am Bank Design Inc and 6 Greenleaf Woods Dr Portsmouth NH 03801-5443

LEVIN, HENRY MORDECAI, economist, educator; b. N.Y.C., Dec. 7, 1938. B.S. cum laude, NYU, 1960; M.A., Rutgers U., 1962, Ph.D., 1967. assoc. research scientist, Grad. Sch. Pub. Adminstrn., NYU, 1965-66; research assoc. social econs. Econ. Studies div. Brookings Inst., Washington, 1966-68; asst. prof. edn. and econs. Stanford U., Calif., 1968-69, assoc. prof. econs., 1969-75, prof. econs. and edn., 1975—, David Jacks Prof. of Higher Edn. and Econs., 1992—, fellow Ctr. for Advanced Studies in Behavioral Scis., 1976-77, dir. Inst. Research on Ednl. Fin. and Governance, 1978-84; Fulbright prof. U. Barcelona, 1989; vis. scholar Russell Sage Found., 1996-97. Office: Stanford U Ctr Edn Rsch CERAS Bldg 109 Stanford CA 94305

LEVIN, HERBERT, diplomat, foundation executive; b. N.Y.C., Jan. 14, 1931; m. Cornelia Rose, Feb. 21, 1954; children: Martha Levin Flynn, Jonathan C. BA, Harvard U., 1952; MA, Fletcher Sch. Law Diplomacy, 1956. Internat. economist Dept. of State, 1956-58; Chinese lang. and area tng. Taichung, Taiwan, 1959-61; econ. officer Am. Consulate Gen., Hong Kong, 1961-64; polit. officer Am. Embassy, Taipei, 1964-67, Tokyo, 1967-70; staff mem. East Asia Nat. Security Coun., 1970-71; deputy dir. Japanese affairs Dept. of State, 1971-74; deputy chief mission Am. Embassy, Dar-es-Salaam, 1975-77, Colombo, 1977-79, New Delhi, 1979-81; asst. nat. intelligence officer East Asia East and South Asia Nat. Intelligence Coun., 1981-83; staff mem. policy planning coun. Dept. State, 1983-85; staff dir. subcom. Asian and Pacific Affairs Ho. Reps., 1985; diplomat-in-residence, dir. studies Asia Found., San Francisco, 1986-88; spl. asst. Office of Sr. Rep. for

Strategic Tech. Policy Dept. State, 1988-90, exec. asst. to amb.-at-large and spl. asst. to sec. of state for non-proliferation and nuclear energy affairs, 1990-91; spl. advisor to UN under-sec. gen. Ji Chaozhu N.Y.C., 1991-94; exec. dir. Am.- China Soc., N.Y.C., 1994—; adviser U.S. Del. to 14th Gen. Assembly of UN, 1985; presenter in field. With U.S. Army, 1953-55. Fellow Ctr. Internat. Affairs, Harvard U., 1974-75. Mem. Am. Fgn. Svc. Assn. (life), Asia Soc., Assn. Asian Studies (life), UN Assn. N.Y. (bd. dirs.), Harvard Club N.Y., Cosmos Club, Dar-es-Salaam Yacht Club (life), Sri Lanka, Hill Club (life), Hong Kong Cricket Club (life), Lake Mansfield Trout Club (life). Office: Am-China Soc 350 Park Ave Fl 4 New York NY 10022-6022 Home (summer): Long Meadow Hill Calais VT 05648

LEVIN, IRA, author, playwright; b. N.Y.C., Aug. 27, 1929; s. Charles and Beatrice (Schlansky) L.; m. Gabrielle Aronsohn, Aug. 20, 1960 (div. 1968); children: Adam, Jared, Nicholas; m. Phyllis Finkel, Aug. 26, 1979 (div. 1982). Student, Drake U., Des Moines, 1946-48; A.B., N.Y. U., 1950. Freelance writer, 1950—; author: A Kiss Before Dying, 1953, Rosemary's Baby, 1967, This Perfect Day, 1970, The Stepford Wives, 1972, The Boys from Brazil, 1976, Sliver, 1991, Son of Rosemary, 1997; playwright: No Time for Sergeants, 1955, Interlock, 1958, Critic's Choice, 1960, General Seeger, 1962, Drat! the Cat, 1965, Dr. Cook's Garden, 1967, Veronica's Room, 1973, Deathtrap, 1978, Break a Leg, 1979, Cantorial, 1989. Served with U.S. Army, 1953-55. Recipient Edgar Allan Poe award, 1953, 80, Bram Stoker award, 1997. Mem. Dramatists Guild (council mem. 1980—). Office: care Harold Ober Assocs 425 Madison Ave New York NY 10017-1110

LEVIN, JACK, physician, educator, biomedical investigator; b. Newark, Oct. 11, 1932; s. Joseph and Anna (Greengold) L.; m. Francine Corthesy, Apr. 13, 1975. B.A. magna cum laude, Yale U., 1953, M.D. cum laude, 1957. Diplomate: Am. Bd. Internal Medicine. Intern in medicine Grace-New Haven Hosp., 1957-58, asst. resident in medicine, 1960-62; chief resident in medicine Yale-New Haven Med. Ctr., 1964-65; clin. assoc. Nat. Cancer Inst., Bethesda, Md., 1958-60; fellow in hematology Johns Hopkins U. Sch. Medicine and Hosp., Balt., 1962-64, mem. faculty, 1965-82, prof. medicine, 1978-82; prof. lab. medicine, prof. medicine U. Calif. Sch. Medicine, San Francisco, 1982—; dir. hematology lab. and blood bank San Francisco VA Med. Ctr., 1982-93, dir. flow cytometry facility, 1987-90; cons. in field. Author: (with P.D. Zieve) Disorders of Hemostasis, 1976; editor: (with E. Cohen and F.B. Bang) Biomedical Applications of the Horseshoe Crab (Limulidae), 1979, (with S.W. Watson and T.J. Novitsky) Endotoxins and Their Detection with the Limulus Amebocyte Lysate Test, 1982, Detection of Bacterial Endotoxins with The Limulus Amebocyte Lysate Test, 1987, (with others) Bacterial Endotoxins. Structure, Biomedical Significance, and Detection with the Limulus Amebocyte Lysate Test, 1985, Megakaryocyte Development and Function, 1986, Bacterial Endotoxins. Pathophysiological Effects, Clinical Significance, and Pharmacological Control, 1988, Molecular Biology and Differentiation of Megakaryocytes, 1990, Bacterial Endotoxins: Cytokine Mediators and New Therapies for Sepsis, 1991, Bacterial Endotoxin: Recognition and Effector Mechanisms, 1993, Bacterial Endotoxins: Basic Science to Anti-Sepsis Strategies, 1994, Bacterial Endotoxins: Lipopolysaccharides from Genes to Therapy, 1995; mem. editorial bd. Blood, Jour. Endotoxin Rsch.; contbr. numerous articles to profl. jours; developer (with F.B. Bang) Limulus test for bacterial endotoxins. Mem. Yale Alumni Schs. Com. for Md., 1967-82, for San Francisco, 1986—; mem. sci. adv. bd. Nat. Aquarium, Balt., 1978-82; mem. corp. Marine Biol. Lab., 1965—; trustee Marine Biol. Lab., 1988-93; mem. panel ind. assessors for rsch. project grants awards Nat. Health and Med. Rsch. Coun. Australia, 1982—. Served with USPHS, 1958-60. Markle scholar, 1968-73; recipient USPHS Rsch. Career Devel. award, 1970-75; Royal Soc. Medicine fellow Oxford (Eng.) U., 1972; Josiah Macy Jr. Found. faculty scholar, 1978-79; Frederik B. Bang award for rsch. in bacterial endotoxins, 1986. Fellow ACP; mem. Am. Soc. Hematology, Am. Soc. Clin. Investigation, Internat. Soc. Hematology, Internat. Soc. Explt. Hematology, Am. Soc. Investigative Pathology, Am. Fedn. Clin. Rsch., Soc. Exptl. Biology and Medicine, Internat. Endotoxin Soc., So. Soc. Clin. Investigation, Western Assn. Physicians, Soc. Invertebrate Pathology, Soc. Analytical Cytology, Cell Kinetics Soc., Internat. Soc. Artificial Cells, Blood Substitutes and Immobilization Biotech., Calif. Acad. Medicine, Phi Beta Kappa, Sigma Xi. Clubs: 14 W Hamilton St, Tudor and Stuart; Yale (San Francisco).

LEVIN, JACK S., lawyer; b. Chgo., May 1, 1936; s. Frank J. and Judy G. (Skerball) L.; m. Sandra Sternberg, Aug. 24, 1958; children: Lisa, Laura, Leslie, Linda. B.S. summa cum laude, Northwestern U., 1958; LL.B. summa cum laude, Harvard U., 1961. Bar: Ill. 1961; C.P.A. (gold medalist), Ill., 1958. Law clk. to chief judge U.S. Ct. of Appeals 2d Circuit, N.Y.C., 1961-62; asst. for tax matters to Solicitor Gen. of U.S., Washington, 1965-67; assoc. law firm Kirkland & Ellis, Chgo., 1962-65, ptnr., 1967—; Frequent lectr. on legal aspects of venture capital transactions, mergers, acquisitions, buyouts, workouts, fed. income tax matters; vis. com. Harvard Law Sch., 1987-93, lectr., 1997—; lectr. Law Sch. U. Chgo., 1988—. Author book on structuring venture capital, pvt. equity and entrepreneurial transactions; co-author multi-volume treatise on mergers, acquisitions and buyouts; case editor Harvard Law Rev., 1959-61; contbr. numerous articles to legal jours. and chpts. to law books. Parliamentarian Winnetka (Ill.) Town Meetings, 1974-83, 89, 93-96; chmn. nat. fundraising drives Harvard Law Sch., 1985-86, 90-91, 95-96, chmn. lawyer's divsn. Jewish United Fund Chgo., 1993-95. Mem. ABA (chmn. subcom. 1968-79), Fed. Bar Assn., Chgo. Bar Assn. (exec. com. 1985—), Am. Coll. Tax Counsel. Clubs: Mid-Am. (bd. dirs. 1985-88), Birchwood (Highland Park, Ill.) (pres. 1980-82). Home: 1220 Sunset Rd Winnetka IL 60093-3628 Office: Kirkland & Ellis 200 E Randolph St Chicago IL 60601-6436

LEVIN, JACOB JOSEPH, mathematician, educator; b. N.Y.C., Dec. 21, 1926; s. David and Rose (Kaplan) L.; m. Avis Harriet Ofstrock, Sept. 7, 1952; children—Debra F., Kenneth E., Claire B. B.E.E., Coll. City N.Y., 1949; Ph.D., Mass. Inst. Tech., 1953. Instr. math. Purdue U., 1953-55; lectr. Mass. Inst. Tech., 1955-56; staff mem. Lincoln Lab. of Mass. Inst. Tech., 1956-63; prof. math. U. Wis., 1963—; vis. prof. U. B.C., Vancouver, Can., 1977-78. Contbr. articles to profl. jours. Served with AUS, 1945-46. NSF sr. postdoctoral fellow, 1970-71. Mem. Am. Math. Soc., Soc. Indsl. and Applied Math., Sigma Xi. Home: 1110 Frisch Rd Madison WI 53711-3120

LEVIN, LINDA ROSE, mental health counselor; b. Des Moines, June 29, 1951; d. Morris Sam and Betty Francis (Burns) Nemirovski; m. Michael Arthur Levin, Feb. 25, 1971; children: David Bradley, Shane Michael. Student, Grandview Jr. Coll., 1969-70; BS in Psychology, Ottawa Univ., 1992, MA in Counseling, 1994. Cert. hypnotherapist, advanced hypnotherapist. Asst. dir. trade practice Better Bus. Bur., Phoenix, 1980-83; program coord. Carnation Health and Nutrition Ctr., Phoenix, 1983-85; v.p. AAA Telephone Answering Svc., Phoenix, 1985-90; past state of Ariz. rep. Toughlove, Phoenix, 1988-90; counselor level II, resident advisor Wayland Family Ctrs., Phoenix, 1990-91; case mgr. for the serious mentally ill Community Care Network, Phoenix, 1991-92; pvt. practice in hypnotherapy Counseling Ctr. for Personal Growth, Phoenix, 1992—. Vol. arbitrator Better Bus. Bur., 1983—. Mem. Am. Arbitration Assn. Democrat. Jewish. Avocations: swimming, reading, karate (brown belt), aerobics. Office: Counseling Ctr for Personal Growth 13231 N 35th Ave # A-2 Phoenix AZ 85029-1233

LEVIN, MARK JAY, director of photography, lighting designer, cinematographer, writer; b. Mpls., July 30, 1957; s. Myron Yale and Phyllis (Goodman) L. BA, U. Wis., 1979. Lighting dir., cameraman Sta. WHA-TV, Madison, Wis., 1978-79, NBC, 1980, ABC, Hollywood, 1982-89; dir. photography Columbia Pictures TV, 1989-93; dir. photography comedy, dramatic, music, variety, news and talk format prodns. Numen Lumen Prodns., Burbank, 1991—, IFA West, 1994—, Disney TV, 1994—; lighting dir. Bob Booker/Universal TV, 1984, Platypus Prodn., 1983-85, Dick Clark Prodn., 1982-83, Sta. KABC-TV, 1984-86; dir. photography Amos Prodn., 1982; pres. Numen Lumen Prodns., Burbank, Calif.; agt. IFA West, Glendale, Calif., 1994—. Lighting designer, dir. photography numerous TV series spls. and CD Rom games including The New Love American Style, 1985, Charmed Lives, 1986, Sweet Surrender, 1986, The Charmings, 1986-87, Facts of Life, 1987, Women in Prison, 1987-88, Who's the Boss ?, 1985-92 (6 Emmy award nominations 1986-91, Emmy award 1989), The Martin Short Show, 1994, Treasure Quest CD Rom 1995, Who Makes You Laugh ?, 1995, Kelsey Grammer's Look at Parenthood, 1995, Unhappy Ever After 1994-97, Cleghorne, 1994-95, High School USA, 1996, General Hospital, 1984-89, 91, 92, Living Dolls, 1989, Faerie Tale Theater, 1983-85 (Ace award 1983), American Bandstand, 1983-86, The Love Boat Spl., 1984, Home Movies, 1982, The Love Connection, 1984-85, ABC's World News Tonight, 1984-86, Married With Children, Nat. Cerebral Palsey Telethon, 1985, 87, 89, One of the Boys, 1989, numerous local prodns.; dir. of photography Married People, 1990, Guys Next Door, 1990; lighting designer Up With People, 1990, Countdown, 1990; dir. of photography Rap Tap, 1991, Vinnie and Bobby, 1992, Hangin' with Mr. Cooper, 1992, The Hannigans, 1992; (pilot) Country Comfort, (pilot) Beakmans World, 1992, Letting Go, 1992, Hangin' With Mr. Cooper, 1992-93, George, 1993, (pilot) Family, 1993, Who Makes You Laugh?, 1994, The Martin Short Show, 1994, The Jerry Springer Show, 1994, The Dirs. Round Table, 1994, Romance Theatre, 1994, Bill Cosby-In Concert, 1994, Christmas from the Los Angeles Music Ctr., 1995-96, The Iceman Cocketh (pilot), 1996, It Ain't Easy (pilot), 1996, Starz, 1996; contbg. editor Lighting Dimensions mag., 1980-85; author: Cosmos the Space Ship, News Lighting; contbr. articles to profl. jours. Active Big Bros. of Greater L.A., 1984-91. Recipient ACE award for Lighting Design in a Dramatic Presentation, 1983, Patriotic Svc. award U.S. Dept. of the Treasury, 1984, Outstanding Excellence award Am. Soc. Lighting Designers, 1988-91, Outstanding Artistic Achievement (4), 1989, Emmy award Outstanding Lighting Dir., 1989. Mem. Am. Soc. of Lighting Designers, Internat. Assn. Theatrical Stage Employees, World Underwater Fedn., Nat. Assn. Broadcast Employees and Technicians, Soc. Operating Cameramen, Profl. Assn. Diving Instrs. (divemaster), Underwater Photographic Soc., Internat. Photographers Guild (I.A.T.S.E. local 600), Soc. TV Lighting Dirs. (Can.), Nat. Assn. Underwater Instrs. (divemaster), Soc. Motion Picture and TV Engrs. Home: 9318 Via Ferrara Burbank CA 91504-1509 also: Numen Lumen Prodns 859 N Hollywood Way Ste 172 Burbank CA 91505-2814 also: IFA West 229 N Central Ave Ste 333 Glendale CA 91203-2537

LEVIN, MARSHALL ABBOTT, judge, educator; b. Balt., Nov. 22, 1920; s. Harry Oscar and Rose (DeLaviez) L.; m. Beverly Edelman, Aug. 6, 1948; children: Robert B., Susan R. Lieman, Burton H. BA, U. Va., 1941; JD, Harvard Law Sch., 1947. Bar: Md. 1947, U.S. Dist. Ct. Md. 1947, U.S. Ct. Appeals (4th cir.) 1950, U.S. Supreme Ct. 1953. Bill drafter, legis. asst. Dept. Legis. Reference, Annapolis, Md., 1948-49; rsch. asst. Workers Compensation Commn., 1951, police magistrate, 1951-55, magistrate housing ct., 1955-58; ptnr. Levin & Levin, Balt., 1947-66; pvt. practice Balt., 1966-68; ptnr. Edelman, Levin, Levy & Rubenstein, Balt., 1968-71; judge cir. ct. City of Balt., 1971-87, judge for asbestos litigation, 1987—; lectr. nationally on toxic torts, complex litigation, asbestos; lectr. Nat. Conf. on Child Abuse, 1976; dir. Legal Aid Soc., Balt., 1979-81; chmn. jud. bd. sentencing State of Md., 1979-83, chmn. sentencing guidelines bd., 1983-87; instituted One Trial/One Day jury system, Balt., 1983; adj. prof. mass torts, legal & ethical studies grad. sch. U. Balt., 1979—; charter mem. faculty coun., coord. and faculty general jurisdiction, current issues in civil litigation Nat. Jud. Coll., 1980—; mem. vis. faculty trial advocacy workshop Harvard Law Sch. Contbr. articles to law revs. Mem. Jud. Disability Commn., 1980-87; chmn. Mass Tort Litigation Com., 1991-95. NEH fellow, 1976. Mem. ABA (vice chmn. mass tort and litigation com.), Md. State Bar Assn. (Leadership award 1984), Balt. City Bar Assn. (commendation 1982). Home: 6106 Ivydene Ter Baltimore MD 21209-3522 Office: 245 Courthouse Ct Baltimore MD 21204-4702

LEVIN, MARTIN P., publishing executive, lawyer; b. Phila., Dec. 20, 1918; s. Harry and Sarah (Haimovitz) L.; m. Marcia Obrasky, Apr. 2, 1939; children: Jeremy, Wendy, Hugh Lauter. B.S., Temple U., 1950, postgrad. (personnel Council fellow), 1950; J.D., N.Y. Law Sch., 1983. Adminstrv. officer U.S. War Dept., 1940-44, VA, 1945-50; sr. v.p. Grosset & Dunlap, Inc., N.Y.C., 1950-66; pres. book pub. div. Times Mirror Co., N.Y.C., 1966-83; cons. Times Mirror; counsel Cowan, Leibowitz and Latman, P.C.; adj. prof. N.Y. Law Sch.; resident fellow pub. course Stanford U.; cons. Ford Found., India, 1957-58; mem. Pres.'s Working Com. on Books and Publs. Abroad; mem. exec. com. Ctr. for the Book, Libr. of Congress; trustee Harvard U. Press; mem. Assn. Am. Pubs. delegation to USSR, 1976, to People Republic of China, 1979; former chmn. Franklin Book Programs. Author: Be Your Own Literary Agent, 1995; contbr. articles to profl. jours. Trustee William Alanson White Inst.; chmn. Assn. Am. Book Pubs., 1982. With AUS, 1944-45. Recipient Pub. of Yr. award ADL, 1980, Friend of Jerusalem award, 1985. Mem. Assn. Am. Pubs. (chmn., dir. exec. com.), Pubs. Lunch Club (past pres.), Friars Club. Home: 221 Kirby Ln Rye NY 10580-4321 also: 9150 Blind Pass Rd Sarasota FL 34242-2978 Office: Cowan Leibowitz & Latman 1133 Avenue Of The Americas New York NY 10036-6710

LEVIN, MARVIN EDGAR, physician; b. Terre Haute, Ind., Aug. 11, 1924; s. Benjamin A. and Bertha Levin; m. Barbara Yvonne Symes; 3 children. BA, Washington U., St. Louis, 1947, MD, 1951. Diplomate Am. Bd. Internal Medicine. Intern Barnes Hosp., St. Louis, 1951-52, asst. resident in internal medicine, 1952-53; Nat. Polio Found. fellow in metabolism and endocrinology Sch. Medicine, Washington U., St. Louis, 1953-55; prof. clin. medicine emeritus, assoc. dir. Endocrine, Diabetes and Metabolism Clinic, Washington U., St. Louis; attending physician emeritus Barnes-Jewish Hosp., St. Louis; vis. prof. endocrinology and diabetes People's Republic China, 1982, Jakarta, Indonesia, Taipei, 1994, Cairo, 1992, Malvern, Eng., 1996; cons. endocrine panel U.S. Pharmacopeia: med. dir. Harry and Flora D. Freund Meml. Found. Co-editor: (with L.W. O'Neal and J. Bowker) The Diabetic Foot, 1973, 5th edit., 1993; contbr. numerous articles to profl. jours., book chpts. Fellow ACP, Soc. Vascular Medicine and Biology; mem. AMA, Am. Diabetes Assn. (nat. bd. dirs. 1984-86, chmn. publ. com. 1986-87, bd. dirs. Mo. chpt. 1987-93, editor in chief Clin. Diabetes 1988-93, co-editor Diabetes Spectrum 1988-93), St. Louis Clin. Diabetes Assn. (pres. 1965-66), Am. Thyroid Assn., Endocrine Soc., Am. Fedn. for Clin. Rsch. (emeritus), St. Louis Soc. Internal Medicine, St. Louis Internist Club (pres. 1972), Sigma Xi, Alpha Omega Alpha. Avocations: golf, collecting Belle Epoque French prints. Office: 732 Fairfield Lake Dr Chesterfield MO 63017-5928

LEVIN, MICHAEL STUART, steel company executive; b. N.Y.C., Aug. 2, 1950; s. Morton Sheldon and Ruth Jean (Leff) L.; m. Laurence Diane deBardon deSegonzac, Dec. 13, 1984; children: Alex Rene-Philippe, Max-André Simon, Sebastien Pierre. B.A. with honors, U. Wis., 1972; M.B.A., Harvard U., 1974. Asst. trader Titan Indsl. Corp., N.Y.C., 1974-75, trader, 1975-76, export mgr., 1976-78, v.p., 1978-80, sr. v.p., 1980-82, pres., 1982—, mem. coun. on fgn. rels.; dir. Aiesec USA, Inc. Chmn. Erick Hawkins Dance Found. Clubs: Gulfstream Polo, N.Y. Yacht, Mashomack Fish and Game Preserve, Millbrook G & T. Avocations: polo, sailing, skiing, shooting. Office: Titan Industrial 555 Madison Ave 10th Fl New York NY 10022-3301*

LEVIN, MORTON D(AVID), artist, printmaker, educator; b. N.Y.C., Oct. 7, 1923; s. Louis and Martha (Berusch) L. B.S. in Art Edn, CCNY, 1948; student in painting, Andre LHote, Paris, 1950; in sculpture, Ossip Zadkine, 1950; etching and engraving, Federico Castellon, N.Y.C., 1948, Stanley W. Hayter, Paris, 1951; student in lithography, Pratt Graphic Art Center, N.Y.C., 1966. Founder, dir., instr. printmaking, painting Morton Levin Graphics Workshop, San Francisco, 1972-91. One-man shows include Galerie Breteau, Paris, 1952, Winston Gallery, San Francisco, 1972, 80, 83, 85-97; exhibited in group shows at Seattle Art Mus., 1946-49, Libr. of Congress, Washington, 1946, 49, Pa. Acad. Fine Arts, 1948, Mus. Modern Art, Paris, 1951, Pallazzo del Academia, Genoa, Italy, 1951; represented in permanent collections at N.Y. Pub. Libr., Libr. of Congress, History of Medicine Divsn. Nat. Libr. Medicine; work featured in Jour. Erotic Arts, Yellow Silk #34, 1990. Served with inf. U.S. Army, 1943-45. Recipient Bryan Meml. prize Villager Travel Exhbn., N.Y.C., 1964, 3d prize Washington Sq. Art Exhbn., 1964. *My goal has been to define our world and the primal forces of desire, love, procreation, death, and rebirth. To this end, I have created a universe in my art inhabited by the natural and fantastic. Humans, birds, and beasts, male and female, interact and strive on an elemental level. In a romantic expressionistic style, I have attempted to illuminate the human condition.*

LEVIN, MURRAY SIMON, lawyer; b. Phila., Feb. 8, 1943; s. Sidney Michael and Eva (Goldstein) L.; m. Jalond Marie Robinson, June 9, 1968; children—Adrianne Lesley, Alexandra Amber-Rose. BA, Haverford Coll., 1964; MA, Harvard U., 1968, LLB, 1968; cert., Hague Internat. Acad. Law, 1967. Bar: Pa. 1968, U.S. Dist. Ct. (ea. dist.) Pa. 1970, U.S. Ct. Appeals (3d cir.) 1970, U.S. Supreme Ct. 1979. Instr. English Harvard U., 1965-68; law clk. to U.S. Dist. Ct. Judge, 1968-70; instr. govt. Haverford Coll., 1970-71; litigation ptnr. Pepper, Hamilton & Scheetz, Phila., 1970—, mem. firm exec. com., 1993-95; overseas lectr., U.K., Sweden, Germany, Senegal, Kenya, Cameroon, Morocco, Israel, Vietnam, 1988—; law seminar speaker. Weekly commentator radio Sta. WCAU Dick Clayton Show, TV program Morningside, 1973-76; weekly host, interviewer Sta. WHYY, 1974-79; TV commentator O.J. Simpson trial, 1995; contbr. articles to profl. jours. Chmn. Phila. Coun. Expt. in Internat. Living, 1967-70; mem. Phila. Urban Coalition Housing Task Force, 1968-80; chmn. coll. divsn. Allied Jewish Appeal, 1968-70; pres. Ctrl. Phila. Reform Dems., 1973-74; bd. dirs. Grad. Hosp. Phila., 1975-97, Friends Ctrl. Sch., 1988-96, divsn. Fgn. Policy Rsch. Com. Mid. East Coun., 1992-94, Mid. East Forum, 1994—. Root-Tilden fellow, 1964. Mem. ABA, Pa. Bar Assn. (ho. of dels.), Phila. Bar Assn. (young lawyers exec. bd. 1973, bd. govs. 1985-88, zone del. 1988—, chmn. profl. guidance com. 1989-92, co-chmn. internat. human rights com. 1990-91), Phila. Trial Lawyers Assn., Assn. Internat. des Jeunes Avocats Brussels (bd. dirs. 1981-85, 1st Am. pres. 1985-88), Union Internationale des Avocats Paris (advisor to pres., mem. exec. com. 1993—, pres. Am. chpt. 1995—, congress pres. 1997), Am. Law Inst., Am. Judicature Soc., Phi Beta Kappa. Office: Pepper Hamilton & Scheetz 3000 2 Logan Sq 18th & Arch Sts Philadelphia PA 19103-2799

LEVIN, PETER J., hospital administrator, public health professor; b. N.Y.C., Apr. 25, 1939; s. Sol and Kate (Gottlieb) L.; m. Judith S. Bolton, June 3, 1967; children: Edward, Gael, Karen. B.A., Harvard U., 1961; M.P.H., Yale U., 1965; Sc.D., Johns Hopkins U., 1969. Asso. exec. dir. Bronx (N.Y.) Municipal Hosp. Center, 1970-72; exec. dir. New Haven Health Care, Inc., 1972-74; assoc. commr. Dept. Health, N.Y.C., 1974-77; assoc. v.p. med. affairs, exec. dir. Stanford U. Hosp., 1977-81; asst. clin. prof. dept. epidemiology and pub. health Yale Med. Sch., 1973-75; assoc. clin. prof. dept. community health Albert Einstein Coll. Medicine, 1976-77; clin. assoc. prof. dept. family, community and preventive medicine Stanford U., 1978-81; dean Coll. Pub. Health, prof. health adminstrn. U. Okla., Oklahoma City, 1982-84; dean Coll. Pub. Health U. South Fla., Tampa, 1984-94, prof. pub. health, 1984-97; vis. scholar Hoover Inst., Stanford U., 1994-95; mem. health policy counsel to Senator Connie Mack U.S. Senate, 1997—. Chmn. Hosp. Cost Containment Bd., State of Fla., 1985-88, Fla. HMO Quality Care Interagy. Task Force, 1987, Hillsborough County Health Care Adv. Bd., 1990-92; Served with U.S. Army, 1961-65, USPHS, 1965-67. Office: US Senate 517 Hart Washington DC 20510

LEVIN, RICHARD C., lawyer; b. Dallas, June 15, 1945; s. Paul Michael and Yetta Gail (Caplan) L.; m. Kay Robins, June 18, 1982; children: Edward C., Henry A. BA, Tulane U., 1967; JD, Georgetown U., 1970. Bar: Tex. 1975. Law clerk 5th cir. U.S. Ct. Appeals, 1970-71; assoc. Sulivan & Cromwell, N.Y.C., 1971-74; assoc. Akin, Gump, Strauss, Hauer & Feld L.L.P., Dallas, 1974-77, ptnr., 1978—; with Dallas Mgmt. com., 1989—; co-head litigation sect. Akin, Gump, Strauss, Hauer & Feld, head antitrust sect., internat. litigation sect.; spkr. in field. Contbr. articles to profl. jours. Former mem. exec. bd. Dallas Opera; former mem. bd. govs. Dallas Symphony; corp. com. Dallas Mus. Fine Arts; former mem., v.p. bd. trustees Hist. Preservation League; former mem. Landmark Com. City Dallas, bd. trustees Arts Magnet Sch.; former mem., dep. vice chmn., mgmt. com. Arts Dist. in Dallas; former chmn. Task Force Multi-Purpose Performing Arts Hall Dallas Opera, Dallas Ballet; bd. dirs. Dallas Opera, Salzburg Music Festival. Mem. Dallas Bar Assn. (coun. mem. Antitrust, Trade Regulation sect. 1987—, internat. law sect. 1990—). Jewish. Avocations: classical music, art, sports. Home: 4408 Saint Johns Dr Dallas TX 75205-3825 Office: Akin Gump Strauss Hauer & Feld 1700 Pacific Ave Ste 4100 Dallas TX 75201-4624

LEVIN, RICHARD CHARLES, academic administrator, economist; b. San Francisco, Apr. 7, 1947; s. D. Derek and Phylys M. (Goldstein) L.; m. Jane Ellen Aries, June 24, 1968; children: Jon, Daniel, Sarah, Rebecca. BA, Stanford (Calif.) U., 1968; LittB, Oxford (Eng.) U., 1971; PhD, Yale U., 1974; LLD (hon.), Princeton U., 1993, Harvard U., 1994. With Yale U., New Haven, 1974—, pres., 1993—, chmn. econs. dept., 1987-92, Frederick William Beinecke prof. econs., 1992—, dean Grad. Sch., 1992-93; rsch. assoc. Nat. Bur. Econ. Rsch., Cambridge, Mass., 1985-90; program dir. Internat. Inst. Applied Sys. Analysis, Vienna, 1990-92; mem. exec. com. Consortium on Financing Higher Edn.; dir. Yale-New Haven Health Svcs. Corp., Inc., 1993—; trustee Tanner Lectures on Human Values; cons. numerous law and bus. firms. Trustee Hopkins Sch., New Haven, 1988-95. Yale-New Haven Hosp., 1993—, Univs. Rsch. Assn., 1994—; bd. dirs. Yale-New Haven Health Svcs. Corp., Inc., 1993—. Fellow Merton Coll. Oxford U., 1996. Mem. Am. Econ. Assn., Econometric Soc. Democrat. Jewish. Office: Yale U 105 Wall St New Haven CT 06511-6608

LEVIN, RICHARD LOUIS, English language educator; b. Buffalo, Aug. 31, 1922; s. Bernard and Meta (Block) L.; m. Muriel Abrams, June 22, 1952; children: David, Daniel. B.A., U. Chgo., 1943, M.A., 1947, Ph.D., 1957. Mem. faculty U. Chgo., 1949-57, asst. prof. English,, 1953-57; prof. English, SUNY at Stony Brook, 1957—, acting chmn. English dept., 1960-63, 65-66; mem. adv. bd. World Center for Shakespeare Studies.; mem. acad. adv. council Shakespeare Globe Ctr.; Fulbright lectr., 1984-85. Author, cons. in field.; Editor: Tragedy: Plays, Theory and Criticism, 1960, The Question of Socrates, 1961, Tragedy Alternate, 1965, (by Thomas Middleton) Michaelmas Term, 1966, The Multiple Plot in English Renaissance Drama, 1971, New Readings vs. Old Plays: Recent Trends in the Reinterpretation of English Renaissance Drama, 1979. Served to lt. (j.g.) USNR, 1943-46, ETO. Recipient Explicator award, 1971; Am. Council Learned Socs. fellow, 1963-64; research fellow State U. N.Y., 1961, 65-68, 71, 73; NEH sr. fellow, 1974; Guggenheim fellow, 1978-79, Nat. Humanities Ctr. fellow, 1987-88; SUNY faculty exchange scholar. Mem. MLA (mem. adv. com. publs., mem. del. assembly), Internat. Shakespeare Assn., Shakespeare Assn. Am. (trustee), N.Y. Shakespeare Soc., Malone Soc., Joseph Crabtree Found., Marlowe Soc. Am., Medieval and Renaissance Drama Soc. (mem. council), AAUP, Inst. for Renaissance Interdisciplinary Studies. Democrat. Jewish. Home: 26 Sparks St Melville NY 11747-1727 Office: SUNY Humanities Bldg Stony Brook NY 11794

LEVIN, ROBERT E., financial management company executive. Student, U. Bordeaux, France, 1975-76; BA in French Civilization, U. Calif., Berkeley, 1978; MBA in Fin. and Internat. Bus., NYU, 1985. Sr. analyst, commodities trader Chilewich Corp., N.Y.C., 1979-87; mem. trading and sales tng. program Salomon Bros, Inc., N.Y.C., 1987-88; sr. analyst, spl. advisor Tudor Investment Corp., N.Y.C., 1988-89; trading strategist Moore Capital Mgmt., Inc., N.Y.C., 1989-93; pres. EuroCapital Mgmt., Inc., 1990—, Sierra Capital Mgmt., Inc., N.Y.C., 1990—; adj. asst. prof. internat. affairs Columbia U., 1990—; lectr. in field; founder, chmn. Internat. Forum, N.Y.C., 1980; mem. U.S. Congl. delegation anti-Defamation League, Israel and Ireland, 1986; founder Environ. Fin. Group, 1989. Author: Bill Clinton, 1992; editor: Democratic Blueprints; contbr. articles to Futures Mag. Founder, chmn. Wall St. Dems., 1983-86; mem. N.Y. County Dem. Com.; trustee Am. Place Theatre, 1986; co-chair fundraiser Dukakis Campaign, 1988; issues rschr., speech writer Congl. candidate George Hirsch, 1984; mem. N.Y. regional bd. Anti-Defamation League B'nai B'rith, 1986-88; membership chmn. New Leadership, Ben-Gurion U. of the Negev, Israel, 1989-90. Avocations: tennis, cross country skiing, hiking, horseback riding, writing. Office: Columbia U SIPA Internat Affairs Blvd 420 W 118th St Fl 13 New York NY 10027-7213

LEVIN, ROBERT JOSEPH, retail grocery chain store executive; b. Everett, Mass., Mar. 19, 1928; s. Edward A. and Rose E. L.; m. Carrol Silverman, June 21, 1948; children: Richard J., Cathy Levin Shuman. B.A. cum laude, U. Wis., 1948. From dir. store ops. and purchasing to pres., treas. C.B. Perkins Tobacco Co., Boston, 1948-73; from dir. store ops. and purchasing to pres., treas. C.B. Perkins Tobacco Co. (co. merged with Stop & Shop), Boston, 1970; v.p., then pres. Medi Mart div. Stop & Shop, 1971-75; group v.p. Stop & Shop Cos., Inc., Boston, 1975-79; sr. v.p. Stop & Shop Cos., Inc., 1979-82, vice. chmn., 1982—, also dir.; bd. dirs. S.A.Y. Industries, Sterling Inc.; chmn. bd. S.A.Y. Packaging, 1988—. Bd. dirs. U. Wis. Found. Mem. Nat. Mass Retailing Inst. (dir.). Jewish. Home: 4762 Exeter Estate

Ln Lake Worth FL 33467-8105 Office: 1776 Heritage Dr Quincy MA 02171-2119 also: PO Box 369 Boston MA 02101-0369

LEVIN, RONALD MARK, law educator; b. St. Louis, May 11, 1950; s. Marvin S. and Lois (Cohn) L.; m. Anne Carol Goldberg, July 29, 1989. BA magna cum laude, Yale U., 1972; JD, U. Chgo., 1975. Bar: Mo. 1975, D.C. 1977. Law clk. to Hon. John C. Godbold U.S. Ct. Appeals, 5th cir., 1975-76; assoc. Sutherland, Asbill & Brennan, Washington, 1976-79; asst. prof. law Washington U., St. Louis, 1979-80, assoc. prof. law, 1980-85, prof. law, 1985—, assoc. dean, 1990-93; cons. Adminstrv. Conf. U.S., 1979-81, 93-95. Co-author: Administrative Law and Process, 4th edit., 1997. Chair senate coun. Washington U., 1988-90. Mem. ABA (coun. sect. adminstrv. law and regulatory practice 1986-89), Assn. Am. Law Sch. (chair sect. adminstrv. law 1993, chair sect. legis. 1995). Home: 7352 Kingsbury Blvd Saint Louis MO 63130-4142 Office: Wash Univ Sch Law Campus Box 1120 Saint Louis MO 63130

LEVIN, SANDER M., congressman; b. Detroit, Sept. 6, 1931; s. Saul R. and Bess (Levinson) L.; m. Victoria Schlafer, 1957. B.A., U. Chgo., 1952; M.A., Columbia U., 1954; LL.B., Harvard U., 1957. Supr. Oakland County Bd. Suprs., Mich., 1961-64; mem. Mich. Senate, 1965-70; fellow Kennedy Sch. Govt., Inst. Politics, Harvard U., Cambridge, Mass., 1975; asst. adminstr. AID, Washington, 1977-81; mem. 98th-105th Congresses from 17th (now 12th) Mich dist., 1983—; mem. ways and means com., subcoms. oversight and human resources; adj. prof. law Wayne State U., Detroit, 1971-74. Chmn. Mich. Dem. Com., 1968-69; Dem. Candidate for Gov., 1970, 74. Office: US Ho of Reps 2209 Rayburn HOB Washington DC 20515-2212*

LEVIN, SIMON, lawyer; b. Newark, Aug. 4, 1942; m. Barbara Leslie Lasky, Dec. 21, 1989; children: David, Jennifer Menken, Yale, Michael, Jacob. BS cum laude, Lehigh U., 1964; JD, NYU, 1967, LLM in Taxation, 1974. Bar: N.J. 1967, U.S. Tax Ct. 1971, U.S. Ct. Claims 1972, N.Y. 1980. Assoc. Shanley & Fisher, Newark, 1970, Hannoch Weisman, Newark, 1970-73; ptnr. Robinson, Wayne, Levin, Riccio & La Sala, Newark, 1973-88; mem., co-chmn. tax dept. Sills Cummis Zuckerman Radin Tischman Epstein & Gross, Newark, 1988—; civilian aide to Sec. Army for N.J., 1992-95; mem. N.J. Dept. Treasury Transition Team for Gov. Christine Todd Whitman, 1993-94; mem. treas. adv. group N.J. Dept. of Treasury, 1995—; lectr., panelist numerous orgns. Co-author: Taxation Investors in Securities and Commodities, 1983, 2d edit., 1984, supplement, 1986, Estate Planning and Administration in New Jersey, 1987; contbr. articles to profl. jours. Trustee, mem. exec. com. Jewish Comty. Found., MetroWest, Whippany, N.J., pres., 1979-83; trustee, mem. exec. com. Israel Bond Campaign MetroWest, Livingston, N.J., 1988—, chmn., 1988-89; commr. N.J. Vietnam Vets. Meml. Commn., Princeton, 1994—. Capt. U.S. Army, 1968-69, Vietnam. Recipient Cohn Leadership award Jewish Fedn. MetroWest, 1982, Endowment Achievement award Coun. Jewish Fedns., 1986, N.J. Meritorious Svc. medal, 1995. Fellow Am. Coll. Tax Counsel; mem. ABA, N.J. Bar Assn. (chmn. commodities sect. 1982-86), Essex County Bar Assn. (chmn. sect. taxation 1974-76), Monmouth County Bar Assn., Phi Delta Phi. Avocations: tennis, skiing, politics, opera, community service. Office: Sills Cummis Zuckerman Radin Tischman Epstein Gross 1 Riverfront Plz Newark NJ 07102-5401

LEVIN, SIMON ASHER, mathematician, ecologist, educator; b. Balt., Apr. 22, 1941; s. Theodore S. and Clara G. L.; m. Carole Lotte Leiffer, Aug. 4, 1964; children: Jacob, Rachel. BA in Math., Johns Hopkins U., 1961; PhD in Math. (NSF fellow), U. Md., 1964; DSc (hon.), Ea. Mich. U., 1990. Teaching asst. U. Md., 1961-62, research assoc., 1964, visitor, 1968; NSF fellow U. Calif., Berkeley, 1964-65; asst. prof. math. Cornell U., 1965-70, assoc. prof. applied math., ecology, theoretical and applied math., 1971-77, prof. applied math. and ecology, 1977-92, Charles A. Alexander prof. biology, 1985-92, adj. prof., 1992—, chmn. sect. ecology and systematics div. biol. scis., 1974-79, dir. Ecosystems Rsch. Ctr., 1980-87, dir. Ctr. for Environ. Rsch., 1987-90; George Moffett prof. biology Princeton U., 1992—, associated faculty applied math., 1992—; dir. Princeton Environ. Inst., 1993—; vis. scholar U. Wash., 1973-74; vis. scientist Weizmann Inst., Rehovot, Israel, 1977, 80; hon. prof. U. B.C., 1979-80; Lansdowne lectr. U. Victoria, 1981; disting. vis. scientist SUNY, Stony Brook, 1984; vis. fellow All Souls Coll., U. Oxford, 1988; Ostrom lectr. Washington State U., Pullman, 1994; lectr. Third Annual Stanislaw Ulam Meml., Santa Fe Inst., 1996; co-chmn. Gordon Conf. on Theoretical Biology, 1970, chmn. Gordon Conf. on Theoretical Biology and Biomath., 1971; c hmn. Am. Math. Soc./Soc. Indsl. and Applied Maths. Com. on Maths. in Life Scis., 1973-79; mem. core panel on math. in biol. scis., program com. Internat. Congress Mathematicians, 1977-78; co-convenor Biomath. Conf., Oberwolfach, W. Ger., 1978; co-dir. Internat. Ctr. for Theoretical Physics Autumn Course on Math. Ecology, Trieste, Italy, 1988, 92, 96; mem. adv. com. divsn. environ. scis. Oak Ridge Nat. Lab., 1978-81; vice chmn. math. Com. Concerned Scientists, N.Y.C., 1979—; mem. sci. panel Hudson River Found., 1982-86, chmn., 1985-86, bd. dirs., 1986—; mem. Commn. on Life Scis., NRC, 1983-89, mem. com. ecosys. mgmt. of sustainable marine fisheries ocean studies bd., 1995—; mem. Health and Environ. Rsch. Adv. Com. Dept. of Energy, 1986-90; prin. lectr. Conf. Bd. on Math. Scis. course on math. ecology, 1985; mem. oversight rev. bd. U.S. Nat. Acid Precipitation Assessment Program; spkr. commencement address Ea. Mich. U., 1990; sci. bd. Santa Fe Inst., 1991—; bd. dirs. Beijer Inst., 1994—; bd. dirs. The H. John Heinz III Ctr. for Sci., Econs. and the Environment, 1994—. Editor: Lectures on Mathematics in Life Sciences, vols. 7-12, 1974-79, Ecosystem Analysis and Prediction, 1974, (with R.H. Whittaker) Niche: Theory and Application, 1975, Studies in Mathematical Biology, 2, vols., 1978, New Perspectives in Ecotoxicology, 1983, Mathematical Population Biology, 1984, Mathematical Ecology, 1984, Math Ecology: An Introduction, 1986, (with others) Mathematical Ecology, 1988, Ecotoxicology: Problems and Approaches, 1989, Perspectives in Theoretical Ecology, 1989, (with T. Hallam and L. Gross) Applied Mathematical Ecology, 1989, (with T. Powell and J.H. Steele) Patch Dynamics, 1993, Frontiers in Mathematical Biology, 1994; editor-in-chief Ecological Applications, 1988-95; editor: Ecology and Ecol. Monographs, 1975-77; editor Jour. Math. Biology, 1976-79, mng. editor, 1979-95; mng. editor Biomath., 1976-95, Lecture Notes in Biomath., 1973-95; mng. editor Princeton U. Press, Monographs in Population Biology, 1992—; assoc. editor Theoretical Population Biology, 1976-84; mem. editl. bd. Evolution Theory, 1976—, Ecol. Issues, 1995—, Conservation Ecology, 1995—, Discrete Applied Math., 1978-87, Internat. Jour. Math. and computer Modelling, 1979—; mem. editl. bd. Princeton U. Press, Complexity series, 1992—; mem. adv. bd. Jour. Theoretical Biology, 1977—, Ecological Rsch., 1996—, Ecosystems, 1996—; also various other editl. positions. Bd. dirs. N.J. chpt. Nature Conservancy, 1995—. Guggenheim fellow, 1979-80, Japanese Soc. for Promotion of Sci. fellow, 1983-84; recipient Disting. Statis. Ecologist award Internat. Assn. Ecology, 1994. Fellow AAAS (bd. dirs. 1994—), Am. Acad. Arts and Scis.; mem. Ecol. Soc. Am. (chmn. Mercer awards subcom. 1976, mem. coun. 1975-77, ad hoc com. to evaluate ecol. consequences of nuclear war 1982-83, pres.-elect 1989-90, pres. 1990-91, MacArthur award 1988), Soc. and Indsl. and Applied Math. (mem. coun. 1977-79, coun. exec. com. 1978-79, coun. rep. to bd. trustees 1978-79, chmn. human rights com. 1980-83, mng. editor Jour. Applied Math. 1975-79), Am. Inst. Biol. Scis., Am. Math. Soc. (dir. short course on math. population biology 1983), Am. Soc. Naturalists, Soc. Math. Biology (pres. 1987-89), Brit. Ecol. Soc., Soc. Study Evolution, U.S. Com. for Israel Environ., Sigma Xi. Jewish. Home: 11 Beechtree Ln Princeton NJ 08540-7428 Office: Princeton U Dept Ecology & Evolutionary Biology Eno Hall Princeton NJ 08544-1003

LEVIN, SUSAN BASS, lawyer; b. Wilmington, Del., July 18, 1952; d. Max S. and Harriet C. (Rubin) Bass; children: Lisa, Amy. BA, U. of Rochester, 1972; JD, George Washington U., 1975. Bar: D.C. 1975, U.S. Ct. Claims 1975, N.J. 1976, Pa. 1981, U.S. Ct. Appeals (3d cir.) 1983, U.S. Supreme Ct. 1984. Law clk. to assoc. justice U.S. Ct. Claims, Washington, 1975-76; assoc. Covington & Burling, Washington, 1976-79; pvt. practice Cherry Hill, N.J., 1979-87; counsel Ballard, Spahr, Andrews & Ingersoll, Phila., Camden (N.J.), 1993-96, Pepper Hamilton & Sheetz, Phila. and Cherry Hill, Pa., 1996—. Pres. Cherry Hill (N.J.) Twp. Council, 1986-88; mayor City of Cherry Hill, 1988—; trustee N.J. Coalition of Small Bus. Orgns., 1985-87; del. Dem. Presdl. Conv., 1992, 96; Bd. trustees 21 Fund 1996—, Delegate to President's Summit on America's Future, chair Pam's List; trustee N.J. Alliance for Action, South Jersey Devel. Coun. Recipient Woman of Achievement award Camden County Girl Scouts, 1986, Barbara Boggs Sigmuno award N.J. Women Polit. Caucus, 1996. Mem. Tri County Women Lawyers (pres. 1984-85), N.J. Assn. Women Bus. Owners (state pres. 1984-85 named Woman of Yr. 1985), Phi Beta Kappa, Order of Coif. Office: 820 Mercer St Cherry Hill NJ 08002-2638

LEVIN, WARREN MAYER, family practice physician; b. Phila., Aug. 20, 1932; s. Israel and Clara Deborah (Cherim) L.; m. Marsha Ann Beinstein, Dec. 24, 1955 (div. 1975); children: Beth Ann, Julie Ruth; m. Frances Susan Teitler, Mar. 20, 1982; 1 child, Erika Alexandra. BS, Ursinus Coll., 1952; MD, Jefferson Med. Coll., 1956. Diplomate Am. Bd. Family Pracitce, Am. Bd. Bariatric Medicine, Am. Bd. Environ. Medicine, Am. Bd. Chelation Therapy. Intern U.S. Naval Hosp., Newport, R.I., 1956-57; pvt. practice S.I., N.Y., 1959-74; founder, med. dir. Heights Holistic Health Ctr., Bklyn., 1974-79, World Health Med. Group, N.Y.C., 1979-94; physician Physicians for Complementary Medicine, N.Y.C., 1994—. Contbr. to books: Nutrition in Pregnancy, 1981, Challenging Orthodoxy, 1991, Alternative Medicine, 1994. Bd. govs. Internat. Coll. Applied Nutrition, 1974-76; chmn. med. adv. bd. Survive with a Cure. Lt. Med. Corps USNR, 1956-59. Recipient Disting. Pioneer in Alternative Medicine award Found. for Advancement of Innovative Medicine Fund, 1995, Presdl. Commendation, Am. Coll. for Advancement in Medicine, 1995. Fellow Am. Assn. Environ. Medicine, Am. Coll. Nutrition, Am. Acad. Family Practice; mem. am. coll. Advancement Medicine (treas.), Am. Soc. Bariatric Medicine (v.p. 1980-82). Avocations: ice skating, sailing, swimming. Office: Physicians ComplementaryMedicine 24 W 57th St Ste 701 New York NY 10019-3918

LEVIN, WILLIAM COHN, hematologist, former university president; b. Waco, Tex., Mar. 2, 1917; s. Samuel P. and Jeanette (Cohn) L.; m. Edna Seinsheimer, June 23, 1941; children: Gerry Lee Levin Hornstein, Carol Lynn Levin Cantini. B.A., U. Tex., 1938, M.D., 1941; M.D. (hon.), U. Montpellier, 1980. Diplomate: Am. Bd. Internal Medicine. Intern Michael Reese Hosp., Chgo., 1941-42; resident John Sealy Hosp., Galveston, Tex., 1942-44; mem. staff U. Tex. Med. Br. Hosps., Galveston, 1944—, assoc. prof. internal medicine, 1948-65, prof., 1965—; Warmoth prof. hematology U. Tex. Med. Br., 1968-86, Ashbel Smith prof., 1986—, pres., 1974-87; past chmn., past mem. cancer clin. investigation rev. com. Nat. Cancer Inst., past. mem. Bd. Sci. Counselors. Exec. com., mem. nat. bd. Union Am. Hebrew Congregations; trustee Houston-Galveston Psychoanalytic Found., 1975-78, Menil Found., 1976-83. Recipient Nicholas and Katherine Leone award for adminstrv. excellence, 1977; decorated Palmes Académiques France. Fellow ACP, Internat. Soc. Hematology; mem. Am. Fedn. Clin. Research, Central Soc. Clin. Research, Am. Soc. Hematology, Phi Beta Kappa, Sigma Xi, Alpha Omega Alpha. Office: Am Indemnity Co PO Box 1259 Galveston TX 77553-1259

LEVINE, ALAN, lawyer; b. Middletown, N.Y., Jan. 17, 1948; s. Jacques and Florence (Tananbaum) L.; m. Nancy Shapiro, June 7, 1971; children: Emily Jane, Malcolm Andrew. BS in Econs., U. Pa., 1970; JD, NYU, 1973. Bar: N.Y. 1974, U.S. Dist. Ct. (so. dist.) N.Y. 1974, U.S. Dist. Ct. (ea. dist.) N.Y. 1980, U.S. Tax Ct. 1980, U.S. Ct. Appeals (2d cir.) 1975. Law clk. U.S. Dist. Ct. (so. dist.) N.Y., N.Y.C., 1973-75; asst. U.S. atty, U.S. Attys. Office, so. dist. N.Y., Dept. Justice, N.Y.C., 1975-80; assoc. Kronish, Lieb, Weiner & Hellman, N.Y.C., 1980-82, mem., 1982—. Chmn. bd. Park Ave. Synagogue, N.Y.C., 1993—; bd. dirs. Jewish Theol. Sem. Rabbinical Sch.; bd. dirs. MYF Legal Svcs., Inc., 1990-93. Law chmn. N.Y. County Rep. Com., 1991-93. Recipient Atty. Gen. Dirs. award U.S. Dept. Justice, 1980, Torch of Learning award Am. Friends Hebrew U., 1995. Fellow Am. Bar Found., Am. Coll. Trial Laywers; mem. ABA (ho. of dels. 1983-84, chmn. spl. com. youth edn. for citizenship, 1988-91, vice chmn. white collar crime com. 1996—), N.Y. State Bar Assn. (chmn. com. on citizenship edn. 1979-84, ho. of dels. 1982-84, award of achievement 1984). Republican. Jewish. Club: Sunningdale Country (bd. trustees 1988-90 Scarsdale, N.Y.); Mask and Wig (Phila.). Home: 1185 Park Ave New York NY 10128-1308 Office: Kronish Lieb Weiner & Hellman 1114 Avenue Of The Americas New York NY 10036-7703

LEVINE, ALAN J., entertainment company executive; b. L.A., Mar. 8, 1947; s. Phil and Shirley Ann (Lauber) L.; m. Judy B. Birnbaum, July 18, 1973; children: Andrea, Jay. BS in Bus., U. So. Calif., L.A., 1968, JD, 1971. Bar: Calif. 1972, U.S. Dist. Ct. (so. dist.) Calif. 1972. Ptnr. Pacht, Ross, Warne, Bernhard & Sears, L.A., 1971-78, Schiff, Hirsch & Schreiber, Beverly Hills, Calif., 1978-80, Armstrong, Hirsch & Levine, L.A., 1980-89; pres., COO, SONY Pictures Entertainment, Inc., Culver, Calif., 1989—; v.p. cinema circulus dept. cinema and TV, U. So. Calif., L.A., 1988-90, bd. councilors of dept., 1991—; bd. dirs. UCLA Entertainment Symposium, 1986-89. Chmn. cabinet entertainment div. United Jewish Fedn., L.A., 1990-93; bd. govs. Cedars-Sinai Med. Ctr., L.A., 1989—. Mem. Calif. State Bar Assn., L.A. County Bar Assn., Beverly Hills Bar Assn., Acad. Motion Picture Arts and Scis., Acad. TV Arts and Scis. Democrat. Office: SONY Pictures Entertainment Inc 9601 Wilshire Blvd Ste 630 Beverly Hills CA 90210-5208*

LEVINE, ARNOLD MILTON, retired electrical engineer, documentary filmmaker; b. Preston, Conn., Aug. 15, 1916; s. Samuel and Florence May (Clark) L.; m. Bernice Eleanor Levich, Aug. 31, 1941; children: Mark Jeffrey, Michael Norman, Kevin Lawrence. BS in Radio Engring., Tri-State U., Angola, Ind., 1939, DSc, 1960; MS, U. Iowa, 1940. Head sound lab. CBS, N.Y.C., 1940-42; asst. engr., div. head ITT, N.Y.C. and Nutley, N.J., 1942-65; lab. head, lab. dir. ITT, San Fernando, Calif., 1965-71; v.p. aerospace, gen. mgr., sr. scientist ITT, Van Nuys, Calif., 1971-86; ret., 1986. Patentee fiber optics, radar, motion picture digital sound, communications and TV fields. Past mem. bd. dirs., v.p., pres. Am. Jewish Congress, L.A. Recipient San Fernando Valley Engr. of Yr. award, 1968; Profl. designation Motion Picture Art & Scis., UCLA, 1983. Fellow IEEE (life), Soc. Motion Picture and TV Engrs., USCG Aux. (vice comdr. 1990-91, flotilla cmdr. 1992-94). Avocations: sailing, amateur radio, filmmaking, swimming. Home: 10828 Fullbright Ave Chatsworth CA 91311-1737

LEVINE, ARTHUR ELLIOTT, academic administrator, educator; b. N.Y.C., June 16, 1948; s. Meyer and Katherine (Kalman) L.; m. Linda Christine Fentiman, Aug. 18, 1974; children: Jamie Sloan Fentiman, Rachel Elizabeth Fentiman. B.A. in Biology, Brandeis U., 1970; Ph.D., SUNY-Buffalo, 1976; LHD (hon.), U. Puget Sound, 1981, U. New Eng, Biddeford, Maine, 1983, Unity Coll., Maine, 1984, Greensboro Coll., N.C., 1988, Bradford Coll., 1989, Capital U., 1991, Taitung Tchrs. Coll., Taiwan, 1991, Albright Coll., 1993, William Jewell Coll., 1995, U. N.H., 1995. Sr. fellow Carnegie Council on Policy Studies in Higher Edn., Berkeley, Calif., 1975-80, Carnegie Found., Washington, 1980-82; pres. Bradford Coll., Mass., 1982-89; chmn. Inst. for Edn. Mgmt. Harvard U., Cambridge, Mass., 1989-94; pres. Tchrs. Coll., Columbia U., N.Y.C., 1994—; cons. to numerous colls., univs., U.S. Co-author: Reform of Undergraduate Education, 1973 (Am. Coun. on Edn. Book of Yr. award 1974), Quest for Common Learning, 1982, Opportunity in Adversity, 1985, Shaping Higher Education's Future, 1989, Higher Learning in America, 1993, Beating the Odds, 1996; author: Handbook on Undergraduate Curriculum, 1978, Why Innovation Fails, 1980, When Dreams and Heroes Died, 1980. Recipient Edn. Press Assn. Am. award, 1981, 89, 90, 94; book named Book of Yr., Am. Coun. on Edn., 1974; Spencer fellow, 1979. Office: Tchrs Coll Columbia U 525 W 120th St New York NY 10027-6625

LEVINE, ARTHUR SAMUEL, physician, scientist; b. Cleve., Nov. 1, 1936; s. David Alvin and Sarah Ethel (Rubinstein) L.; m. Ruth Eleanor Rubin, Oct. 14, 1959; children: Amy Elizabeth, Raleigh Hannah, Jennifer Leah. AB, Columbia U., 1958; MD, Chgo. Med. Sch., 1964. Diplomate Am. Bd. Pediatrics, Am. Bd. Pediatric Hematology-Oncology. Intern in pediatrics U. Minn., Mpls., 1964-65, resident in pediatrics, 1965-66, USPHS fellow in hematology and genetics, 1966-67; capt. USPHS, 1967-92, rear adm., asst. surgeon gen., 1992—; clin. assoc. div. cancer treatment Nat. Cancer Inst., Bethesda, Md., 1967-69, sr. staff fellow, 1969-70, sr. investigator, 1970-73, head sect. infectious disease, pediatric oncology br., 1973-75, chief pediatric oncology br., 1975-82; sci. dir. Nat. Inst. Child Health and Human Devel., Bethesda, 1982—; clin. prof. medicine and pediatrics Georgetown U., Washington, 1975—; clin. prof. pediatrics Uniformed Svcs. U. Health Scis., Bethesda, 1983—; vis. prof. Cold Harbor Spring Lab., N.Y., 1973, Benares Hindu U., India, 1975, U. Minn., 1974, Hebrew U., Israel, 1981, U. Bologna, 1989, Northwestern U., 1992, Moscow State U., 1996; Karon meml. lectr. U. So. Calif., 1983; Seham lectr. U. Minn., 1983; Harris lectr. Va. Commonwealth U., 1995; Markey lectr. Wash. U., 1996. Author: Cancer in the Young, 1982; editor-in-chief The New Biologist, 1989-92; contbr. articles to profl. jours. Recipient Disting. Alumnus award Chgo. Med. Sch., 1972, NIH Dir.'s award, 1984, Meritorious Svc. award USPHS, 1987, Disting. Svc. award, 1991, Surgeon Gen.'s Exemplary Svc. award, 1993. Mem. Am. Soc. Clin. Investigation, Soc. Pediatric Research, Am. Assn. Cancer Research, Am. Soc. Hematology, Am. Soc. Clin. Oncology, Am. Fedn. Clin. Research, AAAS, Am. Soc. Microbiology, Am. Soc. Pediatric Hematology/Oncology. Office: Nat Inst Child Health and Human Devel 9000 Rockville Pike Bethesda MD 20814-1436

LEVINE, BARBARA GERSHKOFF, early childhood education educator, consultant; b. Providence, June 2, 1950; d. Aaron and Miriam Charlotte (Blackman) Gershkoff; m. Alan Marshal Levine, Aug. 22, 1971 (div. Sept. 1986); children: Adam Jonathan, Matthew Corey Gershkoff; m. H. Michael Mogil, Feb. 6, 1988. BS in Early Childhood Edn., Wheelock Coll., 1972; MA in Elem. Sci. and Math. Edn., Hood Coll., 1995. Head tchr. Town & Country Schs., College Park, Md., 1973-74, head tchr., supr., 1974-75; head tchr. Early Childhood Ctr., Rockville, Md., 1987-95; tchr. 2d grade, elem. sch. sci./math coord. Sandy Spring Friends Sch., 1995—; cons. How the Weatherworks, Rockville, 1987—; co-chair Project Sky Awareness Week, Think Weather, Inc., Rockville, 1991—. Co-author: (videotape, tchr.'s guide) Our Sea of Clouds, 1992, (videotape, tchr.'s manual) A Hurricane: Through the Eyes of Children, 1993, Weather Study Under a Newspaper Umbrella, 1989, (books) The Amateur Meteorologist, 1993, Anytime Weather Everywhere, 1996; contbr. articles to profl. jours. Mem. Nat. Assn. for Educating Young Children, Nat. Sci. Tchrs. Assn., Nat. Coun. Tchrs. Maths. Avocations: bridge, bicycling, travel, reading. Home and Office: How the Weatherworks 1522 Baylor Ave Rockville MD 20850-1025

LEVINE, BARRY WILLIAM, internist; b. Everett, Mass., Mar. 21, 1940; s. Irvine and Betty (Nemon) L.; m. Ellen S. Haas, June 30, 1963; children: Susan, Rachel. BA, Dartmouth Coll., 1962, BS in Medicine, 1963; MD, Harvard U., Boston, 1965. Diplomate Am. Bd. Internal Medicine, Am. Bd. Pulmonary Disease. Intern Presbyn. St. Lukes Hosp., Chgo., 1965-66; resident Harvard Svc./Boston City Hosp., 1966-68; fellow in pulmonary disease Mass. Gen. Hosp., Boston, 196870; intern Presbyn.-St. Lukes Hosp., Chgo., 1965-66, resident in medicine, 1966-67; resident in medicine Boston City Hosp.-Harvard U., 1967-68; fellow Mass. Gen. Hosp., Boston, 1968-70; asst. in medicine Mass. Gen Hosp., Boston, 1970-80, assoc. physician, 1980—. Bd. dirs. North Haven Devel. Corp., 1984—. Fellow ACP; mem. Masons, Shriners. Avocations: sailing, jogging, collectingh art, gardening, model building. Home: 14 Manor House Rd Newton MA 02159-1520

LEVINE, BERYL JOYCE, state supreme court justice; b. Winnipeg, Man., Can., Nov. 9, 1935; came to U.S., 1955; d. Maurice Jacob and Bella (Gutnik) Choslovsky; m. Leonard Levine, June 7, 1955; children: Susan Brauna, Marc Joseph, Sari Ruth, William Noah, David Karl. BA, U. Man., Winnipeg, 1965; JD with distinction, U. N.D., 1974. Bar: N.D. 1974. Assoc. Vogel, Branther, Kelly, Knutson, Weir & Bye, Ltd., Fargo, N.D., 1974-85; justice N.D. Supreme Ct., Bismarck, 1985-1996; chmn. jud. planning com. Joint Procedure Com., Bismarck. Bd. dirs. Fargo Youth Commn., 1974-77, Hospice of Red River Valley, Fargo; chmn. Gov.'s Commn. of Children at Risk, 1985, co-chair N.D. Gender Fairness Com. Named Outstanding Woman in N.D. Law, U. N.D. Law Women's Caucus, 1985, ABA Comm. on Margaret Brent award, 1996. Mem. Cass County Bar Assn. (pres. 1984-85), N.D. State Bar Assn., Burleigh County Bar Assn., Order of Coif.

LEVINE, C. BRUCE, lawyer; b. Liberty, N.Y., Aug. 20, 1945. Student, Stanford U.; BA magna cum laude, UCLA, 1967; JD cum laude, Harvard U., 1971. Bar: Calif. 1971. Mem. Greenberg, Glusker, Fields, Claman & Machtinger, L.A. Editor Harvard Law Rev., 1970-71. Mem. State Bar Calif., L.A. County Bar Assn. (chmn. income tax com. tax sect. 1979-80), Beverly Hills Bar Assn. (chmn. taxation com. 1977-78), Phi Beta Kappa, Pi Gamma Mu. Office: Greenberg Glusker Fields Claman & Machtinger 1900 Avenue Of The Stars Fl 20 Los Angeles CA 90067-4301

LEVINE, CARL MORTON, motion picture exhibition, real estate executive; b. Bklyn., Sept. 24, 1931; s. Joseph M. and Frances Pearl (Smith) L.; m. Judith Ann Pollack, June 12, 1955 (div.); m. Miriam Scott Zeldman Duberstein, June 24, 1973; children: Jonathan Mark, Suzanne Beth; stepchildren: Debra Wiley-Hart, Douglas Reed Duberstein. BA, Bklyn. Coll., 1953; M in Dramatic Arts, Columbia U., 1955. Unit mgr., fl. and stage mgr., asst. dir., assoc. producer Sta. WRCA-TV NBC, N.Y.C., 1952-57; theatre mgr., asst. mgr. Forty Second St. Co. Lawbin Theatre Corp., Inc., N.Y.C., 1958-62, supr., 1963-65, gen. mgr., 1965-74; owner, mgr. Double L Ranch, Adirondack Mountains, 1958-62; v.p., gen. mgr. Midtown Theatre Corp. Brandt Theatres, N.Y.C., 1974-86; gen. mgr., dir. theatre ops. Sameric Mgmt. Corp., Phila., 1986; comml. ops. mgr. Newmark & Co. Real Estate, Inc., N.Y.C., 1987-88; mng. dir. Loews 84th St. Sixplex Theater, N.Y.C., 1988-89; dir. ops. Eugene M. Grant & Co., N.Y.C., 1989-96; ret., 1996; founder, producer, v.p., treas. Mirca Prodns. Ltd., N.Y.C., 1981-88; bd. dirs. Variety Club, N.Y.C., 1981-86, entertainment div. UJA-Fedn., N.Y.C., 1985; mem. Nat. Commn. Anti-Defamation League, 1965-86; v.p. Queens Coun. on Arts, 1977-80, pres., 1980-81. Chmn. producer Vets. Com. Variety Shows, VA Hosp., 1968-71; mem. adv. bd. Nassau County Fine Arts Mus., 1981-83. Mem. Acad. TV Arts and Scis., Variety Internat., Motion Picture Pioneer (life), Ind. Theatre Owner's Assn. (v.p. 1967-85), League N.Y. Theatres and Producers (labor negotiation com. 1980-83), Cinema B'nai B'rith (pres. 1970-72). Republican. Jewish.

LEVINE, CHARLES MICHAEL, publishing company executive, consultant; b. Buffalo, Dec. 19, 1942; s. Abraham and Rose (Ackman) L.; 1 child, Gabriel Lee. B.A., Columbia U., 1963; M.A., Ind. U., 1966. With Peace Corps, 1967-69; editor McGraw Hill F.E.P., Singapore, 1972-75; mng. dir. APA Publs., Singapore, 1976-78; former dir. gen. ref. and sci. Macmillan Pub. Co. Inc., N.Y.C., from 1978; formerly with Simon & Schuster; v.p., exec. pub. John Wiley & Sons, to 1994; with Random House Inc., N.Y.C., 1994—. Mem. Phi Beta Kappa. Office: Random House Reference Mail Drop 3-2 201 E 50th St New York NY 10022-7703

LEVINE, DANIEL BLANK, classical studies educator; b. Cin., July 22, 1953; s. Joseph and Elizabeth (Blank) L.; m. Judith Robinson, Aug. 14, 1984; children: Sarah Ruth, Amy Elizabeth. Student, Am. Sch. Classical Studies, Athens, 1974, 78-89; BA in Greek and Latin magna cum laude, U. Minn., 1975; PhD in Classics, U. Cin., 1980. Seymour fellow Am. Sch. Classical Studies, 1978-79; asst. prof. U. Ark., 1980-84, assoc. prof., 1984—; dir. Summer Session Am. Sch. Classical Studies, Athens, 1987, 95; dir. study tour in Greece Vergilian Soc., 1990; referee Classical Jour., 1984-88, Helios, 1984-88, Cornell U. Press, 1988-89, 91—, Classical Outlook, 1988-89; panelist NEH, Washington, 1986; co-dir., instr. gifted and talented H.S. students summer program State of Ark. Dept. Edn. Grant, 1988; mem. mng. com. Am. Sch. Classical Studies Athens, 1991—. Contbr. articles to profl. jours. Grantee NEH 1981, 82, 83, 84, 92; recipient Outstanding Tchr. award Mortar Bd. Sr. Honor Soc., U. Ark., 1991, Master Tchr. award Fulbright Coll., 1995. Mem. Am. Philological Assn. (Excellence in Teaching Classics award 1992), Am. Classical League, Classical Assn. Mid. West and South (Ovatio 1996, v.p. com. promotion Latin in Ark. 1980-86, 91—, chmn. regional rep. com. for promotion Latin, Outstanding State V.P. for 1982-83), U. Ark. Teaching Acad., Phi Beta Kappa. Home: 904 Park Ave Fayetteville AR 72701-2027 Office: U Ark Dept Fgn Langs 425 Kimpel Hall Fayetteville AR 72701

LEVINE, DAVID M., newspaper editor; b. Newark, Oct. 2, 1949; s. Seymour I. and Fay D. Levine; m. Arleen Weintraub, Apr. 5, 1987. BA, Montclair State Coll., 1971; MS, Columbia U., 1973. Reporter, state house corr. Herald-News, Passaic, N.J., 1971-74; editorial writer Phila. Bull., 1974-79; night mng. editor Trenton (N.J.) Times, 1979-83; exec. fin. editor Washington Times, 1983-85; exec. editor Lebhar-Friedman Co., N.Y.C., 1985-86; editor Daily Jour., Elizabeth, N.J., 1986-87, Hudson Dispatch, Union City, N.J., 1987-91, The Daily Jour., Elizabeth, N.J., 1990-92; editor, v.p. The Herald-News, Passaic, N.J., 1992-94; editor-in-chief Mariner Cmty. Newspapers, 1995-96; editor-in-chief, v.p. Tribune-Democrat Pub. Co., Johnstown, Pa., 1997—; adj. instr. English dept. Rutgers U., Newark, 1987—;

prin. Jour. Publs., Trenton, 1971—, Levine Publs., Trenton, 1974—. Author: Editorial Style, 1974.

LEVINE, DONALD NATHAN, sociologist, educator; b. New Castle, Pa., June 16, 1931; s. Abe and Rose (Gusky) L.; m. Joanna Bull, Nov. 6, 1955 (div. 1967); children: Theodore, William; m. Ruth Weinstein, Aug. 26, 1967; 1 child, Rachel. AB, U. Chgo., 1950, MA, 1954, PhD, 1957; postgrad., U. Frankfurt, Germany, 1952-53. Asst. prof. sociology U. Chgo., 1962-65, assoc. prof., 1965-73, prof., 1973-86, dean of Coll., 1982-87, Peter B. Ritzma prof., 1986—. Author: Wax and Gold: Tradition and Innovation in Ethiopian Culture, 1965, Georg Simmel on Individuality and Social Forms, 1971, Greater Ethiopia: The Evolution of a Multiethnic Society, 1974, Simmel and Parsons: Two Approaches to the Study of Society, 1980, The Flight from Ambiguity: Essays in Social and Cultural Theory, 1985, Visions of the Sociological Tradition, 1995; editor: The Heritage of Sociology series, 1988—. Recipient Quantrell award U. Chgo., 1971, Cert. of award Ethiopian Rsch. Coun., 1993, Amoco Found. award for disting. contbn. to undergrad. tchg., 1996; Guggenheim fellow, 1980; fellow Ctr. for Advanced Study in Behavioral Scis., 1980-81. Mem. Internat. Soc. Comparative Study Civilization, Am. Sociol. Assn. (chair theory sect. 1996-97). Jewish. Office: U Chgo 1126 E 59th St Chicago IL 60637-1539

LE VINE, DUANE GILBERT, petroleum company executive; b. Balt., July 5, 1933; s. Harry B. and Frances Annette (Culleton) LeV.; m. Patricia J. Allman, Aug. 10, 1957; children: Duane Gilbert, Michele P., William A., James D., Erin A., Megan K. B.S. in Chem. Engring., Johns Hopkins U., 1956, M.S., 1958. With Exxon Research & Engring. Co., 1959—; dir. fuels products research lab. Exxon Research & Engring. Co., Linden, N.J., 1971-74; mgr. gasoline and lube processes div. Exxon Research & Engring. Co., Florham Park, N.J., 1974-76; gen. mgr. Baytown (Tex.) research and devel. site, 1976-78, exec. dir. corp. research sci. labs., 1979-84; mgr. worldwide environ. affairs Exxon Corp., N.Y.C., 1984-90; mgr. sci. and strategy devel. Exxon Corp., Dallas, 1990—; mem. Nat. Air Pollution Rsch. Adv. Com., 1971-74, Tex. Energy and Natural Resources Adv. Coun., 1976-78; mem. com. energy tech. assessment NASA, 1974; participant UN/industry-sponsored conf. on environ. mgmt., Versailles, France, 1984; chmn. Rene Dubos Internat. Forum on Mng. Hazardous Materials, N.Y.C., 1988, Rene Dubos Internat. Forum on Global Urbanization, N.Y.C., 1989; mem. adv. com. Calif. Inst. Tech., Johns Hopkins U., Rene Dubos Ctr.; chmn. Internat. Petroleum Industry Global Climate Change Symposium, Rome, 1992; chmn. Symposium on Critical Issues in the Econs. of Climate Change, Paris, 1996. Author: (with Upton) Management of Hazardous Agents, 1992, The City as a Human Environment, 1994; patentee, author combustion, electrochemistry, environ. petroleum/synthetic fuels. Fellow Am. Inst. Chemists; mem. AIChE, AAAS, Internat. Combustion Inst., Am. Chem. Soc., Am. Petroleum Inst., N.Y. Acad. Scis., Internat. Petroleum Industry Environ. Conservation Assn. (exec. com. 1984—, vice chmn. 1994-95, chmn. and chief officer 1996—), Sigma Xi, Tau Beta Pi, Phi Lambda Upsilon. Achievements include research on automotive emission control catalyst systems, on evaporative loss control devices, on exhaust recycle systems for NOx control, on catalytic coal gasification, on donor solvent coal liquifaction, and on direct synthesis of hydrocarbon liquids from CO/H2. Office: Exxon Corp 5959 Las Colinas Blvd Rm 3314 Irving TX 75039-4202

LEVINE, EDWIN BURTON, retired classics educator; b. Chgo., Nov. 11, 1920; s. Benjamin and Bertha (Kauffman) L.; m. Myra Estrin, Apr. 22, 1944; children—William Alan, Patricia Ann. A.B., U. Chgo., 1949, A.M., 1950, Ph.D., 1953. Instr. classics U. Nebr., 1951-52; instr., then asst. prof. Wayne State U., Detroit, 1955-60; instr. Detroit Bd. Edn., 1960-61, New Trier High Sch., Winnetka, Ill., 1962-64; vis. lectr. U. Ill. at Chgo. Circle, 1964-65, mem. faculty, 1965—, prof. classics, 1968-87, prof. emeritus, 1987—, founder and 1st head dept., 1969-74. Author: Introduction to Classical Greek, 1968; prin. compiler: Follett World-Wide Latin-English Dictionary, 1968, Hippocrates, 1971, Landor's Latin Poetry, 1968. Served with AUS, 1943-46. Fellow AAAS; mem. Am. Philol. Assn., Soc. for History of Medicine, Archaeol. Inst. Am., Chgo. Classical Club (pres. 1967-69). Home: 701 Forum Sq Apt 509 Glenview IL 60025-3866

LEVINE, ELLEN R., magazine editor; b. N.Y.C., Feb. 19, 1943; d. Eugene Jack and Jean (Zuckman) Jacobson; m. Richard U. Levine, Dec. 21, 1964; children: Daniel, Peter. Student, Wellesley Coll. Reporter The Record, Hackensack, N.J., 1964-70; editor Cosmopolitan mag., N.Y.C., 1976-82; editor in chief Cosmopolitan Living mag., N.Y.C., 1980-81, Woman's Day mag., N.Y.C., 1982-91, Redbook mag., N.Y.C., 1991-94, Good Housekeeping, N.Y.C., 1994—; dir. N.J. Bell, Newark; commr. U.S. Atty. Gen.'s Commn. on Pornography, 1985-86. Author: Planning Your Wedding, Waiting for Baby, Rooms That Grow With Your Child. Mem. exec. com. Senator Bill Bradley, 1984—. Named to Writers Hall of Fame, 1981, Acad. Women Achievers, YWCA, 1982; recipient Outstanding Profl. Achievement award N.J. coun. Girl Scouts U.S., 1984, Woman of Achievement award N.J. Fedn. Women's Clubs, 1984, Matrix award N.Y. Women in Communications, Inc., 1989, honor award Birmigham So. Coll., 1991. Office: Good Housekeeping 959 8th Ave New York NY 10019-3737*

LEVINE, GEORGE LEWIS, English language educator, literature critic; b. N.Y.C., Aug. 27, 1931; s. Harris Julius and Dorothy Sara (Podolsky) L.; m. Margaret Bloom, Aug. 19, 1956; children: David Michael, Rachel Susan. B.A., NYU, 1952; M.A., U. Minn., 1953, Ph.D., 1958. Instr. Ind. U., Bloomington, 1959-62, asst. prof., 1962-65, assoc. prof., 1965-68; prof. English Rutgers U., New Brunswick, N.J., 1968—, chmn. dept., 1979-83; Kenneth Burke prof. Rutgers U., New Brunswick, 1985—; vis. prof. U. Calif.-Berkeley, 1968, Stanford U., Calif., 1974-75; vis. research fellow Girton Coll., Cambridge U., Eng., 1983; dir. Ctr. for Critical Analysis of Contemp. Culture. Author: Boundaries of Fiction, 1968, The Endurance of Frankenstein, 1975, The Realistic Imagination, 1981, One Culture, 1987, Darwin and the Novelists, 1988, Lifebirds, 1995; author, editor: The Art of Victorian Prose, 1968, Mindful Pleasures, 1975, Constructions of the Self, 1992, Realism and Representation, 1993, Aesthetics and Ideology, The Politics of Research, 1994; editor: Victorian Studies, 1959-68. Served with U.S. Army, 1953-55. Guggenheim Found. fellow, 1971-72; NEH fellow, 1978-79; Rockefeller Found. fellow, 1983; Rockefeller Found. Bellagio fellow, 1997. Mem. MLA, AAUP. Democrat. Jewish. Home: 419 Lincoln Ave Highland Park NJ 08904-2728 Office: Rutgers U Ctr Critical Analysis Cont New Brunswick NJ 08903

LEVINE, GEORGE RICHARD, English language educator; b. Boston, Aug. 5, 1929; s. Jacob U. and Rose Lillian (Margolis) L.; m. Joan Adler, June 8, 1958 (div. 1977); children—David, Michael; m. Linda Rashman, Apr. 17, 1977. B.A., Tufts Coll., Medford, Mass., 1951; M.A., Columbia, 1952, Ph.D., 1961. Lectr. English Columbia, 1956-58; instr. Northwestern U., 1959-63; mem. faculty State U. N.Y., Buffalo, 1963—; prof. English State U. N.Y., 1970—, dean faculty arts and letters, 1975-81. Author: Henry Fielding and The Dry Mock, 1967; editor: Harp on the Shore: Thoreau and the Sea, 1985, Jonathan Swift: A Modest Proposal and Other Satires, 1995; contbr. articles to profl. jours. Chmn. bd. dirs. Youth Orch. Found., Buffalo, 1974-75; trustee Buffalo Chamber Music Soc., Arts Devel. Svcs.; bd. dirs. Buffalo Philharm. Orch. With AUS, 1952-54. Univ. fellow Columbia U., 1958-59; Faculty Research fellow SUNY, 1966, 67; Fulbright lectr. W. Ger., 1969-70; recipient Chancellor's award excellence in teaching SUNY, Buffalo, 1973-74. Mem. MLA, Am. Soc. 18th Century Studies, Internat. Assn. Univ. Profs. English. Jewish. Clubs: Adirondack Mountain. Home: 18 St Andrew's Walk Buffalo NY 14222-2010 Office: SUNY Dept English 306 Clemens Hall Buffalo NY 14260

LEVINE, GERALD RICHARD, mortgage investment and merchant banker, financial advisor; b. N.Y.C., Nov. 7, 1936; s. Irving Arthur and Lillian (Kronstadt) L.; m. Linda L. Paige, May 17, 1991.; children from previous marriage: Jodi Levine Avergun, Debby Levine Rifkin, James H. AB, Brown U., 1958; MBA, GM Inst. Tech., Flint, Mich., 1960; postgrad., Pohs Inst. Ins., N.Y.C., 1978, Securities Tng. Inst., N.Y.C., 1981; postgrad. real estate, NYU, 1993. Pres. Town and Country Motors (Div. KLZ Corp.), Woodmere, N.Y., 1959-78, TAR Brokerage Corp., 1977—; nat. mktg. dir. Performance Dynamics Inc., N.Y.C., 1978-81; v.p. Oppenheimer & Co., N.Y.C., 1981-84; sr. v.p. Twenty-First Securities Corp., N.Y.C., 1984-89; assoc. nat. dir. corp. and instl. investment programs Devel. Corp. for Israel, N.Y.C., 1989-91; assoc. dir. estate planning div. Prudential Securities/Ins., N.Y.C., 1991-92; dir. corp. philanthropy Anti-Defamation League, N.Y.C., 1992-93; dir. Sealy Hoffman & Sheehan Inc., 1993-94; sr. mng. dir. Investment Adv. Group, N.Y.C., 1994-97; field acctg. mgr. N.Y. office wholesale divsn. Long Beach Mortgage Co., Long Beach Fin. Svcs., Orange, Calif., 1997—. Pres. 5 Towns div. Salvation Army, Woodmere, 1968-85; mem. exec. com., adv. bd. commerce and industry div. State of Israel Bonds, N.Y.C., 1988-89; mem. exec. com. Brown Ann. Fund, Providence, 1987-89, 92-94, Brown Corp. Com. on Devel., 1987-89, 92-94, major gifts chmn. 30th Reunion, 1988, 35th Reunion, 1993, N.Y.C. Brown Reg. Devel. Com., 1988-93; advisor Brown U. Sports Found., 1987—; bd. dirs. Brown U. Football Assn., Providence, 1988-92; bd. dir. Head Marshall Alumni Divsn. 1983-84, 88-89, head class agt. 1978-88, treas. class of 1958, 1988-93, pres. class of '58, 1993—, Alumni Marshall, 1993. Recipient Disting. Alumni Svc. award Brown U., 1988. Mem. Brown U. Alumni Assn. (exec. bd. assn. class officers 1994—), Brown U. Club N.Y. (pres. 1990-92, v.p., exec. dir. 1989-90), K.P. (mem. at large), Princeton Club, Nat. Arts Club. Republican. Jewish. Avocations: golf, fishing, antique car restorations, woodworking, chess. Office: Long Beach Mortgage Co 80-02 Kew Gardens Rd Ste 1050 Kew Gardens NY 11415

LEVINE, GUILLERMO, computer scientist, educator; b. Guadalajara, Mex., Apr. 27, 1953; s. Leo and Aurora (Gutierrez) L. Electronic Engr., U. Guadalajara, 1975; MSc in Computer Sci., Nat. U. Mex., 1979. Prof. U. Guadalajara, 1973-75, Met. U., Mexico City, 1976-86, Nat. U., Mexico City, 1980-89; rsch. dir. Micrologica, Mexico City, 1982-90, gen. dir., 1990-91; founder, 1st dir. computer sci. faculty U. Guadalajara, 1991-95; cons. Internat. Ctr. of Social Security Studies, OAS, UN, Mexico City, 1983-85; acad. cons. Red Uno, Mex., 1994—. Author: Introduction to Computer Science, 1984, Introduction to Programming, 1989, Elements of Computing, 1993, Fundamental Structures of Computing, 1996; coord. nat. report Computer Sci. Edn., 1988, 97. Mem. IEEE, Assn. Computing Machinery. Jewish. Avocations: reading, classical music. Home and Office: PO Box 1-953 Centro, 44100 Guadalajara Mexico

LEVINE, HAROLD, lawyer; b. Newark, Apr. 30, 1931; s. Rubin and Gussie (Lifshitz) L.; children: Brenda Sue, Linda Ellen Levine Gersen, Louise Abby, Jill Anne Levine Zuvanich, Charles A., Cristina Gussie, Harold Rubin II; m. Cristina Cervera, Aug. 29, 1980. B.S. in Engring., Purdue U., 1954; J.D. with distinction, George Washington U., 1958. Bar: D.C. 1958, Va., 1958, Mass. 1960, Tex. 1972, U.S. Patent Office, 1958. Naval architect, marine engr. U.S. Navy Dept., 1954-55; patent examiner U.S. Patent Office, 1955-58; with Tex. Instruments Inc., Attleboro, Mass., 1959-77, asst. sec., Dallas, 1969-72, asst. v.p. and gen. patent counsel, 1972-77; ptnr. Sigalos & Levine, Dallas, 1977-93; prin. Levine & Majorie LLP, 1994—; chmn. bd. Vanguard Security, Inc., Houston, 1977—; chmn. Tex. Am. Realty, Dallas, 1977—; lectr. assns., socs.; del. Geneva and Lausanne (Switzerland) Intergovtl. Conf. on Revision, Paris Pat. Conv., 1975-76. Mem. U.S. State Dept. Adv. Panel on Internat. Tech. Transfer, 1977. Mem. ABA (chmn. com. 407 taxation pats. and trdmks. 1971-72), Am. Patent Law Assn., Dallas Bar Assn., Assn. Corp. Pat. Csl. (sec.-treas. 1971-73), Dallas-Fort Worth Patent Law Assn., Pacific Indsl. Property Assn. (pres. 1975-77), Electronic Industries Assn. (pres. pat. com. 1972), NAM, Southwestern Legal Inst. on Patent Law (planning com. 1971-74), U.S. C. of C., Dallas C. of C., Alpha Epsilon Pi, Phi Alpha Delta. Republican. Jewish. Club: Kiwanis. Contbr. chpt. to book, articles to profl. jours. Editor: George Washington U. Law Rev., 1956-57; mem. adv. bd. editors Bur. Nat. Affairs, Pat., Trdmk. and Copyright Jour., 1979-87. Office: Levine and Majorie LLP 12750 Merit Dr Ste 1000 Dallas TX 75251-1243

LEVINE, HENRY DAVID, lawyer; b. N.Y.C., June 7, 1951; s. Harold Abraham and Joan Sarah (Price) L.; m. Barbara Wolgel, Aug. 28, 1976; children: David, Rachel, Daniel. AB, Yale U., 1972; JD, M in Pub. Policy, Harvard U., 1976. Bar: N.Y. 1977, D.C. 1978, U.S. Supreme Ct. 1980. Assoc. Wilmer, Cutler & Pickering, Washington, 1976-80; assoc. Morrison & Foerster, Washington, 1981-83, ptnr., 1983-92; ptnr. Levine, Blaszak, Block & Boothby, Washington, 1993—; cons. to GSA on FTS2000 Successor System, 1994—. Editor Telematics, 1984-89. Mem. Nat. Rsch. Coun. Com on High Tech. Bldgs., 1985-88. Named one of the twenty-five most powerful people in networking Network World, 1996. Mem. ABA, Fed. Communication Bar Assn., Forum Com. on Comm. Law. Home: 5208 Edgemoor Ln Bethesda MD 20814-2342 Office: Levine Blaszak Block & Boothby 1300 Connecticut Ave NW Ste 500 Washington DC 20036-1708

LEVINE, HOWARD ARNOLD, state supreme court justice; b. Mar. 4, 1932; m. Barbara Joan Segall, July 25, 1954; children: Neil Louis, Ruth Ellen, James Robert. B.A., Yale U., 1953, LL.B., 1956. Bar: N.Y. 1956. Asst. in instrn., research asso. in criminal law Yale Law Sch., 1956-57; asso. firm Hughes, Hubbard, Blair, Reed, N.Y.C., 1957-59; practiced in Schenectady, 1959-70; asst. dist. atty. Schenectady County, N.Y., 1961-66, dist. atty., 1967-70; judge Schenectady County Family Ct., 1971-80; acting judge Schenectady County Ct., 1971-80; adminstrv. judge family cts. N.Y. State 4th Jud. Dist., 1974-80; asso. justice appellate div. 3d dept. N.Y. State Supreme Ct., 1982-93; asso. judge N.Y. Ct. of Appeals, 1993—; vis. lectr. Albany Law Sch., 1972-81; mem. N.Y. Gov.'s Panel on Juvenile Violence, N.Y. State Temp. Commn. on Child Welfare, N.Y. State Temp. Commn. on Recodification of Family Ct. Act, N.Y. State Juvenile Justice Adv. Bd., 1974-80; mem. ind. rev. bd. N.Y. State Div. for Youth, 1974-80; mem. rules and adv. com. on family ct. N.Y. State Jud. Conf., 1974-80. Contbr. articles to law revs. Bd. dirs. Schnecatady County Child Guildance Ctr., Carver Community Ctr., Freedom Forum of Schnectady. Mem. Am. Law Inst., N.Y. State Bar Assn. (chmn. spl. com. juvenile justice), Assn. Family Ct. Judges State N.Y. (pres. 1979-80). Home: 2701 Rosendale Rd Niskayuna NY 12309-1300 Office: County Bldg 620 State St Schenectady NY 12305-2112

LEVINE, HOWARD HARRIS, health facility executive; b. Bklyn., Sept. 30, 1949; s. Roy and Lucille Levine. MPH in Hosp. Administrn., UCLA, 1974; BBA in Mktg., Baruch Coll., 1972. Adminstrv. resident Inter-Community Hosp., Covina, Calif., 1973-74; adminstrv. asst. to exec. dir. John F. Kennedy Med. Ctr., Edison, N.J., 1974-75; assoc. exec. dir. John F. Kennedy Med. Ctr., Edison, 1975-78; adminstr. Robert Wood Johnson Jr. Rehab. Inst., Edison, 1975-78; asst. dir. Beth Israel Med. Ctr., N.Y.C., 1978-81, assoc. dir., 1981-84, sr. assoc. dir. for ops., 1984-87; v.p. Staten Island Univ. Hosp., 1988, sr. v.p., chief oper. officer, 1988-91; CEO Chapman Med. Ctr., Orange, Calif., 1992-96; v.p. OrNda Health Corp., 1994-95; pres., CEO Columbia West Hills (Calif.) Med. Ctr., 1996—; adj. lectr. dept. health care adminstrn. Bernard M. Baruch Coll./Mt. Sinai Sch. Medicine, N.Y.C., 1982-93; Health Profl. adv. com. March of Dimes, 1992—; joint com. patient svcs. Calif. Hosp. Assn., 1992—; guest lectr. svcs. Calif. Hosp. Assn., 1992—; guest lectr. NYU Grad. Sch. Pub. Adminstrn., 1984-86; mem. mental health and substance abuse com. Greater N.Y. Health Adminstrn., 1988-91, profl. affairs and hosp. ops. com., 1989-91, chmn. com. on utilization rev., 1988-91; exec. and planning com. Hosp. Coun. So. Calif., 1992—, coun. on profl. practices N.J. Hosp. Assn., Princeton, 1977-78, dist. bd. Health Svcs. Adminstrn., N.Y.C., 1979-80. Mem. editorial adv. bd. The Malpractice Reporter, N.Y.C., 1980-88. Mem. ins. profl. adv. com. Fedn. Jewish Philanthropies Ins., 1981-87; mem. tech. adv. panel N.J. State Health Coordinating Coun., Princeton, 1976-78; bd. dirs. Meals-on-Wheels Program, Metuchen, Edison and Woodbridge, N.J., 1974-76; mem. budget com. United Crusade L.A., 1973-74. Fellow Am. Coll. Healthcare Execs.; mem. Coun. Hosp. Adminstrs. (pres. 1986-87), Met. Health Adminstrs. Assn. (pres. 1980-82), Am. Coll. Healthcare Mktg., Hosp. Adminstrs. Discussion Group. Home: 865 Comstock Ave # 14 B Los Angeles CA 90024 Office: Columbia West Hills Med Ctr 7300 Med Ctr Dr West Hills CA 91307

LEVINE, IRVING RASKIN, news commentator, university dean, author, lecturer; b. Pawtucket, R.I.; s. Joseph and Emma (Raskin) L.; m. Nancy Cartmell Jones, July 12, 1957; children—Jeffrey Claybourne Bond, Daniel Rome, Jennifer Jones. BS, Brown U., 1944, LHD (hon.), 1969; MS, Columbia, 1947; LHd (hon.), Bryant Coll., 1974; D.Journalism (hon.), Roger Williams Coll., 1985; LLD (hon.), U. R.I., 1988; LHD (hon.), Lynn U., 1992; LLD (hon.), Northeastern U., 1993; D in Journalism (hon.), R.I. Coll., 1996. Writer obits. Providence Jour., 1940-43; fgn. news editor Internat. News Service, 1947-48; chief Vienna (Austria) bur., 1948-50; with NBC, 1950-95; war corr. NBC, Korea, 1950-52; radio anchor World News Roundup, Moscow, 1953-54; chief corr. NBC, Moscow, 1955-69, Rome, 1968-71, London, 1967-68; chief econs. corr. NBC, Washington, 1971-95; dean Sch. Internat. Studies, Lynn U., Boca Raton, Fla., 1995—; commentator Consumer News and Bus. Channel Cable TV affiliate svc. NBC TV News, 1990-96; commentator Pub. Broadcasting Sys., WPBT, Miami, 1997—; spl. writer London Times, 1955-59; covered assignments in Can., China, Czechoslovakia, Bulgaria, Poland, Japan, Vietnam, Formosa, Thailand, Eng., France, Germany, Switzerland, Algeria, Congo, Israel, Turkey, Tunisia, Greece, Yugoslavia, Union of South Africa, Denmark, Sweden, Ireland; press group with pres. Ford, Carter, Reagan, Bush, Clinton; attended G-7 Econ. Summits, 1975-95; lectr. univs., bus. groups, cruise ships. Author: Main Street, USSR, 1959, Travel Guide to Russia, 1960, Main Street, Italy, 1963, The New Worker in Soviet Russia, 1973; contbr. articles to nat. mags.; guest on numerous TV shows including Murphy Brown, 1989, David Letterman Show, 1990, Jay Leno Show, 1990. With Signal Corps, U.S. Army, 1944-47, Philippines, Japan. Recipient award for best radio-TV reporting from abroad Overseas Press Club, 1956, award for outstanding radio network broadcasting Nat. Headliners Club, 1957, 50th Anniversary award Columbia Sch. Journalism, 1963, Emmy citation 1966, Martin R. Gainsbrugh award for best eco. reporting, 1978, William Rogers award Brown U., 1988, Silver Circle award Nat. Acad. TV Arts and Scis., 1990, 93; named one of 10 Outstanding Young Men, U.S. Jaycees, 1956; named to R.I. Hall of Fame, 1972, Pawtucket Hall of Fame, 1986, Nat. Broadcasters Hall of Fame Lifetime Achievement award, 1995; honoree Loyola Coll.'s Beta Gamma Sigma, 1994,. Mem. Coun. on Fgn. Rels. (fellowship 1952-53), Cosmos, Phi Beta Kappa, Beta Gamma Sigma. Office: Lynn U 3601 N Military Trl Boca Raton FL 33431-5507

LEVINE, ISRAEL E., writer; b. N.Y.C., Aug. 30, 1923; s. Albert Ely and Sonia (Silver) L.; m. Joy Elaine Michael, June 23, 1946; children: David, Carol. BS, CCNY, 1946. Asst. dir. pub. rels. CCNY, 1946-54, dir., 1954-77, editor Alumnus Mag., 1952-74, 87-89; editor Health Care Week, 1977-79, William H. White Publs., 1979-81; dir. communications Am. Jewish Congress, 1981-87; COO Richard Cohen Assocs., N.Y.C., 1987—. Author: (with A. Lateiner) The Techniques of Supervision, 1954; The Discoverer of Insulin: Dr. Frederick G. Banting, 1959, Conqueror of Smallpox: Dr. Edward Jenner, 1960, Behind the Silken Curtain: The Story of Townsend Harris, 1961, Inventive Wizard: George Westinghouse, 1962, Champion of World Peace: Dag Hammarskjold, 1962, Miracle Man of Printing: Ottmar Mergenthaler, 1963, Electronics Pioneer: Lee DeForest, 1964, Young Man in the White House: John Fitzgerald Kennedy, 1964, 91, Oliver Cromwell, 1966, Spokesman for the Free World: Adlai Stevenson, 1967, Lenin: The Man Who Made a Revolution, 1969, The Many Faces of Slavery, 1975; contbr. over 200 articles to mags. Mem. exec. com. Com. for Pub. Higher Edn., N.Y.C., 1987—. 2d lt., navigator USAAF, 1943-45, ETO. Decorated Air medal with 3 oak leaf clusters, 3 battle stars USAAF; recipient 125th Anniversary medal; CCNY, 1972, Svc. medal CCNY Alumni Assn., 1974. Mem. The Authors Guild, Authors' League Am., Soc. of Silurians, 2d Air Divsn. Assn. Jewish. Avocation: gardening. Address: Richard Cohen Assocs 40 W 55th St Ste 503 New York NY 10019-5316

LEVINE, JACK, artist; b. Boston, Jan. 3, 1915; s. Samuel Mayer and Mary (Grinker) L.; widowed; 1 child, Susanna Levine Fisher. AFD, Colby Coll., Waterville, Maine, 1956. One-man shows include Downtown Gallery, N.Y.C., 1938, Artists, 1942, Mus. Modern Art, N.Y.C., 1943; exhibited in group shows at Jeu de Paume, Paris, 1938, Carnegie Internat. exhbns., 1938-40, Artists for Victory, Met. Mus., N.Y.C., 1942, retrospective at Jewish Mus., N.Y.C., 1978-79; represented in permanent collections Mus. Modern Art, Met. Mus. Art, N.Y.C., William Hayes Foggs Mus., Harvard U., Addison Gallery, Andover, Mass., Mus. Vatican, D.C. Moore Gallery, N.Y. With AUS, 1942-45. Mem. Am. Acad. Arts and Letters (pres., chancellor), Inst. Arts and Letters (pres. 1993), Nat. Acad. Design, Century Club.

LEVINE, JACK ANTON, lawyer; b. Monticello, N.Y., Dec. 23, 1946; s. Milton and Sara (Sacks) L.; m. Eileen A. Garsh, Sept. 7, 1974; children: Matthew Aaron, Dara Esther. BS with honors, SUNY, Binghamton, 1968; JD with honors, U. Fla., 1975, LLM in Taxation, 1976. Bar: Fla. 1975, U.S. Ct. Appeals (11th cir.) 1981, U.S. Tax Ct., 1982. Tax atty. legis. and regulations divsn. Office chief counsel IRS, Washington, 1977-81; assoc. Holland & Knight, Tampa, Fla., 1981-83, ptnr., 1984—; lectr. in field. Contbr. articles to profl. jours. Mem. ABA, Fla. Bar Assn. (sect. taxation exec. coun. 1984—, chmn. ptnrship. com. 1985-88, chmn. taxation regulated public utilities com. 1988-92, co-chmn. corps. and tax-exempt orgns. com. 1992—, bd. cert. in tax law 1984—). Democrat. Jewish. Avocations: golf, reading, traveling. Home: 10905 Carrollwood Dr Tampa FL 33618-3903 Office: Holland & Knight 400 N Ashley Dr Ste 2300 Tampa FL 33602-4327

LEVINE, JAMES, conductor, pianist, artistic director; b. Cin., June 23, 1943; s. Lawrence M. and Helen (Goldstein) L. Studied piano with Rosina Lhevinne and Rudolf Serkin, studied conducting with Jean Morel, Fausto Cleva and Max Rudolf, studied theory and interpretation with Walter Levin; student, Juilliard Sch. Music; hon. degree, U. Cin., New Eng. Cons., Northwestern U., SUNY, Potsdam. Music dir. Ravinia Festival, 1973-93; artistic dir. Met. Opera, 1986—; guest lectr. Sarah Lawrence Coll., Harvard U., Yale U. Piano debut with Cin. Symphony, 1953; conducting debut at Aspen Music Festival, 1961; Met. Opera debut, 1971; Chgo. Symphony debut at Ravinia Festival, 1971; regularly appears throughout U.S. and Europe as condr. and pianist, including Vienna Philharm., Berlin Philharm., Chgo. Symphony, Phila. Orch., Boston Symphony, N.Y. Philharm., Dresden Staatskapelle, Philharmonia Orch., Israel Philharm., Wagner Festival at Bayreuth; made Bayreuth debut in new prodn. Parsifal, 1982; condr. Salzburg Festival, 1975-93; Salzburg premieres include Schönberg's Moses und Aron, 1987, Offenbach's Tales of Hoffmann, 1980, Mahler's Seventh Symphony, Mendelssohn's Elijah; condr. Met. premiere prodns. of Verdi's I Vespri Siciliani, Stiffelio, I Lombardi, Weill's The Rise and Fall of the City of Mahagonny, Stravinsky's Oedipus Rex, Berg's Lulu, Mozart's Idomeneo and La Clemenza di Tito, Gershwin's Porgy and Bess, Schönberg's Erwartung, world premiere Corigliano/Hoffman The Ghosts of Versailles, 1991; subject of documentary for PBS; artistic dir. Met. Opera. Recipient Smetana medal, 1987, 8 Grammy awards. Office: Met Opera Assn Inc Met Opera House Lincoln Ctr New York NY 10023

LEVINE, JEROME, psychiatrist, educator; b. N.Y.C., July 10, 1934; s. Abraham and Sadie (Glowatz) L.; children: Ross W., Lynn R., Andrew R. BA, U. Buffalo, 1954, MD, 1958. Intern, then psychiat. resident E.J. Meyer Meml. Hosp., Buffalo, 1958-61; sr. psychiat. resident St. Elizabeth's Hosp., Washington, 1961-62; staff psychiatrist USPHS Hosp., Lexington, Ky., 1962-64; research psychiatrist, asst. chief psychopharmacology research br. NIMH, 1964-67, chief of br., 1967-81, chief pharmacologic and somatic treatments research br., 1981-84; research prof. psychiatry U. Md. Sch. Medicine, Balt., 1985-94; dep. dir. Nathan Kline Inst. for Psychiat. Rsch., Orangeburg, N.Y., 1994—; rsch. prof. psychiatry NYU, 1994—; instr. psychiatry Johns Hopkins Med. Sch., 1964-72; vis. prof. U. Pisa, Italy, 1977. Author books and papers on psychopharmacology, clin. trial methodology, somatic treatment assessment for psychiat. disorders. Mem. Soc. Clin. Trials, Am. Psychiat. Assn. (Hofheimer Research prize 1970), Am. Coll. Neuropsychopharmacology, Collegium Internationale Neuropsychopharmacologicum, Am. Soc. Clin. Pharmacology and Therapeutics. Home: 15 Stony Hollow Chappaqua NY 10514-2014 Office: Nathan Kline Inst Bldg 37 140 Old Orangeburg Rd Ste 37 Orangeburg NY 10962-1157

LE VINE, JEROME EDWARD, retired ophthalmologist, educator; b. Pitts., Mar. 23, 1923; s. Harry Robert and Marian Dorothy (Finesilver) L.; m. Marilyn Tobey Hiedovitz, Apr. 14, 1957; children: Loren Robert, Beau Jay, Janice Lynn. B.S., U. Pitts., 1944; M.D., Hahnemann Med. Sch., Phila., 1949; postgrad. in ophthalmology U. Pa., 1951-52. Diplomate Am. Bd. Disability Cons., Am. Bd. Quality Assurance & Utilization Rev. Intern, St. Francis Hosp., Pitts., 1949-50; resident in ophthalmology Jefferson U. Med. Sch. Hosp., Phila., 1952-54; ophthalmologist Leech Farm VA Hosp., Pitts., 1955-59; chief eye dept. Stanocola Clinic, Baton Rouge, 1959-64; sole practice medicine specializing in ophthalmology, Baton Rouge, 1959-86; cons. La. State U., East La. State Hosp. Infirmary, Villa Feliciana Geriatric Hosp., disability dept. Social Security Adminstrn., div. blind La. State Pub. Welfare dept.; mem. staff Our Lady of the Lake Hosp., Baton Rouge Gen. Hosp., Women's Hosp.; instr. spl. edn. U. Southeastern La., 1971. Mem. Am. Bd. Quality Assurance and Utilization Rev., 1990. Served with MC, AUS, 1942-44. Fellow Am. Geriatric Soc., Royal Soc. Health; mem. AMA, La. State

Med. Soc., East Baton Rouge Parish Med. Soc., 6th Dist. Med. Soc., New Orleans Acad. Ophthalmology, So. Med. Assn., La. Med. Soc., Baton Rouge Parish Med. Soc., Pi Lambda Phi, Phi Delta Epsilon. Democrat. Jewish. Office: PO Box 66787 Baton Rouge LA 70896-6787

LEVINE, LAINIE See **KAZAN, LAINIE**

LEVINE, LAURENCE BRANDT, investment banker; b. N.Y.C., Dec. 17, 1941; s. Martin and Beulah (Brandt) L.; m. Laura Lynn Vitale; 1 child, Blair Brandt. BA (Francis Biddle prize 1961), Princeton U., 1964; LLB, Stanford U., 1967. V.p., voting shareholder Drexel Burnham Lambert, N.Y.C., 1968-71; corp. planning officer Office of Chmn., Ogden Corp., N.Y.C., 1971-73; pres. Investment Research Assos., West Chester, Pa., 1973-80; sr. v.p., dir. investment banking Kramer Capital Cons., Inc., N.Y.C., 1981; exec. v.p. Henry Ansbacher Inc., N.Y. and London, 1982-84; sr. v.p. Rothschild Inc., N.Y., 1984-86; exec. v.p. and dir. corp. fin. Smith New Ct. Inc., N.Y. and London, 1986-90; chmn. Blair Corp., N.Y. and London, 1990—, dir. First Internat. Fin. Group, Hamburg, London and Bermuda, Landmark Funds Svcs., Inc., N.Y.C.; dir., vice chmn. Signature Fin. Group, Boston; Bd. visitors Stanford U. Law Sch., 1968-71, exec. com., 1970; dir. Musica Sacra, N.Y., 1981-86, Concert Artists Guild, N.Y., 1989-92, Ballet Fla., 1992—; pres. Palm Beach Sch. Arts Found., 1993—; adv. bd. Kravis Ctr., 1991—. Office: 250 Royal Palm Way Ste 205 Palm Beach FL 33480-4315

LEVINE, LAURENCE HARVEY, lawyer; b. Cleve., Aug. 23, 1946; s. Theodore and Celia (Chaikin) Levine; m. Mary M. Conway, May 13, 1978; children: Abigail, Adam, Sarah. BA cum laude, Case Western Res. U., 1968; JD, Northwestern U., 1971. Bar: Ill. 1971, U.S. Dist. Ct. (no. dist.) Ill. 1972, U.S. Ct. Appeals (6th, 7th, 10th and D.C. cirs.). Law clk. to presiding judge U.S. Ct. Appeals (6th cir.), Detroit, 1971-72; assoc. Kirkland & Ellis, Chgo., 1972-76; ptnr. Latham & Watkins, Chgo., 1976—. Bd. editors Northwestern Law Rev., 1968-71. Mem. ABA, Chgo. Bar Assn., Mid-Am. Club. Office: Latham & Watkins Sears Tower Ste 5800 Chicago IL 60606

LEVINE, LAURENCE WILLIAM, lawyer; b. N.Y.C., Apr. 9, 1931; s. Robert L. and Molly (Brunner) L. B.A., Union Coll., 1952; LL.B., Harvard U., 1955. Bar: N.Y. 1958. Teaching fellow Def. Studies Program, Harvard U., 1955-56; aide to Adlai Stevenson N.Y.C., 1956-57; office mgr. N.Y. com. Stevenson, Kefauver, Wagner, 1956; sec. N.Y. com. for Dem. Voters, 1962-66; ptnr. Walsh & Levine (merged with Bigham Englar Jones & Houston 1990), N.Y.C., 1958—; sec.-treas. Kabuki Japanese Restaurant, N.Y.C., 1958-80; counsel Northeast Airlines, N.Y.C., 1958-67, Brit. Eagle Airlines, 1963-69, Aerolineas Argentinas, 1960—, Banco de la Nacion Argentina, N.Y.C., 1972-79, Banco de Intercambio Regional Argentina, 1977-80; ptnr. San Francisco Mdse. Mart, 1964-84, Holiday Inn-Union Sq., 1969-89, Kaanapoli Hotel, Hawaii, Hilton Hotel, Pasadena, Calif., 1969-88, Gray Lines, Inc., San Francisco, 1980—, Investco Mortgage Co. of Boston, 1975—, Southern Cone Pub. Co., 1980-86, Arion Press, San Francisco, 1979—, Calix and Corolla; dir. Alaska Airline, 1966-68, Stanley Aviation Corp., 1966-73, Foothill Group, 1972-80, Security Nat. Bank, 1983-84, Pan Australian Fund, 1972-74, N.Y. Venture Fund., Venture Income Plus, R.P. F. Funds of Am., 1984—; liquidator Transcontinental Airlines, 1960-63; chmn. creditors com. Am. Hydrofoil Co., 1965-68, Imperial 400 Motels, 1967-74, Harvard Industries; treas., co-owner Games Mag., 1980-81; sec., dir. Games Mag., 1978-80; pub. mem. Blue Cross/Blue Shield, Downtown Eye and Ear Hosp. N.Y.C., 1978-93; sec. Sale Tilney (N.A.), Inc., 1987-90. Author: Gullibles Travels Thru Harvard, 1955, U.S.-China Relations, 1972; contbr. to: East-Europe mag., 1969, Cambio Mag., Argentina, Harvard Law Sch. Bull, N.Y. Times; Argentine newspapers Rev. of River Plate. Treas. Citizens for McCarthy, 1968; mem. Coun. on State Priorities State N.Y., 1982; trustee Bklyn. Poly. Prep. Country Day Sch., 1992. Mem. Assn. of Bar of City of N.Y., N.Y. County Lawyers Assn., Argentine-Am. C. of C. (pres. 1985-87, bd. dirs. 1972-94), Downtown Assn., Georgetown Club, Harvard Club. Home: 245 Everglades Ave Palm Beach FL 33480-3719 Office: Bigham Englar Jones et al 14 Wall St 22nd Fl New York NY 10005-2101

LEVINE, LAWRENCE STEVEN, lawyer; b. Bklyn., Mar. 30, 1934; s. Harry and Bess (Feiner) L.; m. Linda Robbins, June 16, 1957; children: Lauren Victoria, Audrey Elizabeth, Hilary Anne. AB, Colgate U., 1955; LLB, Yale U., 1958. Bar: N.Y. 1958, U.S. Supreme Ct. 1973. Asst. U.S. Atty. Ea. Dist. N.Y. U.S. Dept. Justice, N.Y.C., 1958-62; assoc. firm Kronish & Lieb, N.Y.C., 1962-63, ptnr. Beldock Levine & Hoffman, N.Y.C., 1964—; vis. instr. Harvard Law Sch., 1991. Bd. dirs. Jewish Fund for Justice, 1984—, chair, 1989—; mem. nat. bd. New Jewish Agenda, 1980-89, New Outlook Mag., 1982-90; trustee YM-YWHA's Greater N.Y., Harry Levine Meml. Found., 1965—, Riverdale Coutnry Sch., 1979-89. Mem. Fed. Bar Assn., N.Y. County Lawyers Assn., N.Y. Civil Liberties Union (cooperating counsel), Yale Club. Democrat. Home: 122 E 76th St New York NY 10021-2833 Office: Beldock Levine & Hoffman 99 Park Ave New York NY 10016-1601

LEVINE, LOUIS DAVID, museum director, archaeologist; b. N.Y.C., June 4, 1940; s. Moe Wolf and Jeanne (Greenwald) L.; m. Dorothy Abrams, Dec. 30, 1962 (div. 1991); children: Sarra L., Samuel E. Student, Brandeis U., 1960; BA with honours, U. Pa., 1962, PhD with distinction, 1969. Instr. of Hebrew U. Pa., Phila., 1966-69; asst. curator Royal Ont. Mus., Toronto, Can., 1969-75, assoc. curator, 1975-80, curator, 1981, assoc. dir., 1987-90; asst. commr., dir. N.Y. State Mus., Albany, 1990—; vis. sr. lectr. Hebrew U., Jerusalem, 1975-76; vis. prof. U. Copenhagen, 1985; asst. prof. U. Toronto, 1969-74, assoc. prof. U. Toronto, 1974-81, prof., 1981-90; dir. Seh Gabi Expdn., western Iran, 1971-73, dir. Mahidasht Project, western Iran, 1975-79. Author: Two Stelae from Iran, 1972, The Neo-Assyrian Zagros, 1974; editor: Mountains and Lowlands, 1977; contbr. articles to profl. jours. NDEA fellow U. Pa., 1962-65, Fulbright fellow, 1965, W.F. Albright fellow, Am. Schs. of Oriental Rsch., 1966, fellow Inst. for Advanced Studies, Hebrew U. Mem. Brit. Inst. of Persian Studies, Brit. Sch. of Archaeology in Iraq, Am. Assn. Mus., Am. Oriental Soc. Jewish. Avocations: woodworking, music. Office: NY State Mus Cultural Edn Ctr Rm 3099 Albany NY 12230

LEVINE, MACY IRVING, physician; b. Johnstown, Pa., May 19, 1920; s. Elliott B. and Ida (Leuin) L.; m. Evelyn B. Levine, June 28, 1948; children: Alan, Amy, Paul, Robert. BS, U. Pitts., 1940, MD, 1943. Diplomate Am. Bd. Internal Medicine, Am. Bd. Internal Medicine in Allergy. Intern U. Pitts. Med. Ctr., 1944; resident in allergy VA Hosp., Aspinwall, Pa., 1947-48, resident in medicine, 1948-49; fellow in medicine Lahey Clinic, Boston, 1950-51; USPHS postdoctoral fellow in medicine Peter Bent Brigham Hosp.-Harvard Med. Sch., Boston, 1951-52; pvt. practice Pitts., 1952—; clin. prof. medicine U. Pitts. Sch. Medicine. Editor: Monograph on Insect Allergy, 1995; editor Bull. of the Allegheny County MEd. Soc., 1975-86, Pitt Medicine Med. Alumni Assn., U. Pitts., 1987—; contbr. more than 70 articles to profl. jours. Bd. dirs. Self Help Group Network, 1989-95, B'nai Israel Congregation, Pitts., 1965-71, Hebrew Free Loan Assn. Pitts., 1980—. Capt. U.S. Army, 1944-46, PTO. Recipient Disting. Svc. award Am. Acad. Allergy and Immunology, 1987, Frederick M. Jacob, M.D. Physician Merit award for Outstanding Svc. Allegheny County Med. Soc., 1988. Fellow Am. Acad. Allergy, Asthma and Immunology (v.p. 1982-83, Outstanding Vol. Clin. Faculty award 1996), Pa. Allergy Assn. (pres. 1970-71, Spl. Recognition award 1989), fellow, ACP; mem. Pitts. Allergy Soc. (pres. 1959-61), U. Pitts. Med. Alumni Assn. (pres. 1976-77), U. Pitts. Alumni Assn. (pres. 1984-85). Avocations: stamp collecting, tennis, bridge. Home: 220 N Dithridge St Apt 400 Pittsburgh PA 15213

LEVINE, MADELINE GELTMAN, Slavic literatures educator, translator; b. N.Y.C., Feb. 23, 1942; d. Herman and Nettie (Kritman) Geltman; m. Steven I. Levine; children: Elaine, Daniel. B.A., Brandeis U., 1962; M.A., Harvard U., 1964, Ph.D., 1971. Asst. prof. Grad Sch. CUNY, N.Y.C., 1971-74; assoc. prof. U. N.C., Chapel Hill, 1974-80, prof., 1980-94, Kenan prof. Slavic lits., 1994—, chmn. dept. Slavic langs., 1979-87, 94—; chmn. joint com. on Ea. Europe, Am. Coun. Learned Socs.-Social Sci. Rsch. Coun., 1989-92. Translator: A Memoir of the Warsaw Uprising (Miron Bialoszewski), 1977, 2d edit. 1991, The Poetry of Osip Mandelstam: God's Grateful Guest (Ryszard Przybylski), 1987, Beginning With My Streets: Essays and Recollections (Czeslaw Milosz), 1992, A Year of the Hunter (Czeslaw Milosz), 1994; translator with Francine Prose: A Scrap of Time and Other Stories (Ida Fink), 1986, 2d edit., 1995; author: Contemporary Polish Poetry, 1925-75, 1981. NEH fellow, 1984; recipient (with Francine Prose) award for lit. translation PEN-America, 1988. Mem. Am. Assn. for Advancement of Slavic Studies, Polish Inst. of Arts and Scis. Am., Am. Assn. Tchrs. of Slavic and East European Langs., Am. Literary Translators Assn., Pen-Am. Home: 5001 Whitehorse Rd Hillsborough NC 27278-9399 Office: U NC 421 Dey Hall CB # 3165 Chapel Hill NC 27599

LEVINE, MARK LEONARD, lawyer; b. Bath, Maine, Mar. 6, 1945; s. Saul and Sophie Gertrude (Greenblatt) L.; m. Stephanie M. von Hirschberg, Nov. 9, 1989. AB, Columbia U., 1966, MS in Journalism, 1979; JD, NYU, 1969. Bar: N.Y. 1969, U.S. Dist. Ct. (so. and ea. dists.) N.Y. 1971. Assoc. White & Case, N.Y.C., 1969-78; pub. Scarf Press, N.Y.C., 1979-85; pvt. practice law N.Y.C., 1981-85; of counsel Sullivan & Worcester, N.Y.C., 1985-88; ptnr. Sullivan & Worcester, LLP, N.Y.C., 1988—. Author: Negotiating a Book Contract: A Guide for Authors, Agents and Lawyers, 1988; co-editor: The Tales of Hoffman, 1970, The Complete Book of Bible Quotations, 1986; contbg. editor Small Press Mag., 1986; contbr. articles to profl. jours. Campaign coord. McCarthy for Pres., Marshfield, Wis., 1968; dep. campaign mgr. Perrotta for Comptr./Com. to Re-elect John Lindsay Mayor, N.Y.C., 1969; cons. McGovern for Pres. Com., Albany, N.Y., 1972. Recipient Citation of Appreciation Laymen's Nat. Bible Com., 1979. Mem. Assn. of Bar of City N.Y., Authors Guild, Am. Book Producers Assn. (bd. dirs. 1984-87, v.p. 1986-87), B'nai B'rith Youth Orgn. (internat. v.p. 1963-64). Democrat. Jewish. Avocations: reading, chess, movies. Office: Sullivan & Worcester LLP 767 3rd Ave New York NY 10017-2023

LEVINE, MELDON EDISES, lawyer, former congressman; b. Los Angeles, June 7, 1943; s. Sid B. and Shirley B. (Blum) L.; children: Adam Paul, Jacob Caplan, Cara Emily. AB, U. Calif., Berkeley, 1964; MPA, Princeton U., 1966; JD, Harvard U., 1969. Bar: Calif. 1970, D.C. 1972. Assoc. Wyman, Bautzer, Rothman & Kuchel, 1969-71; legis. asst. U.S. Senate, Washington, 1971-73; ptnr. Levine Krom & Unger, Beverly Hills, Calif., 1973-77; mem. Calif. Assembly, Sacramento, 1977-82, 98th-102d Congresses from 27th Calif. dist., Washington, 1983-93; ptnr. Gibson, Dunn & Crutcher, L.A., 1993—. Author: The Private Sector and the Common Market, 1968; contbr. articles to various publs. Co-pres. Builders for Peace; mem. governing bd. U.S.-Israel Sci. and Tech. Commn., So. Calif. chpt. Anti-Defamation League, So. Calif. chpt. Am. Jewish Com., So. Calif. chpt. Am. Jewish Congress, So. Calif. chpt. NAACP Legal Def. Fund, U. Judaism, City of Hope, U. Calif. Alumni Coun.; mem. amateur baseball team Hollywood Stars, 1971—. Mem. Calif. Bar Assn., Los Angeles Bar Assn.

LEVINE, MELVIN CHARLES, lawyer; b. Bklyn., Nov. 12, 1930; s. Barnet and Jennie (Iser) L. BCS, NYU, 1952; LLB, Harvard U., 1955. Bar: N.Y. 1956, U.S. Supreme Ct. 1964. Assoc., Kriger & Haber, Bklyn., 1956-58, Black, Varian & Simons, N.Y.C., 1959; sole practice, N.Y.C., 1959—; devel. multiple dwelling housing. Mem. N.Y. County Lawyers Assn. (civil ct. com., housing ct. com., uniform housing ct. rules com., liaison to Assn. Bar City of N.Y. on selection of housing and civil ct. judges, com. on judiciary, task force on tort reform). Democrat. Jewish. Home: 146 Waverly Pl New York NY 10014-3848 Office: 271 Madison Ave Ste 1404 New York NY 10016-1001

LEVINE, MICHAEL, public relations executive, author; b. N.Y.C., Apr. 17, 1954; s. Arthur and Virginia (Gaylor) L. Student, Rutgers U., 1978. Owner, operator TV News Mag., Los Angeles, 1977-83; owner Levine/Schneider Pub. Rels., now Levine Comms. Office, Inc., Los Angeles, 1982—; mem. Gov.'s adv. bd. State Calif., Sacramento, 1980-82; pres., owner Aurora Pub., L.A., 1986—; moderator Thought Forum; lectr. in field; founder, moderator L.A. Media Roundtable. Author: The Address Book: How to Reach Anyone Who's Anyone, 1984, The New Address Book, 1986, The Corporate Address Book, 1987, The Music Address Book, 1989, Environmental Address Book, 1991, Kid's Address Book, 1991, Guerrilla P.R., Lessons at Halfway Point, Take It From Me; pub., writer For Consideration newsletter. Mem. Ronald Reagan Pres.'s Libr.; founder The Actor's Conf., Aurora Charity, 1987; bd. dirs. Felice Found., Micah Ctr.; adv. bd. Dare America. Mem. TV Acad. Arts and Scis., Entertainment Industries Coun., Musician's Assistance Program, West Hollywood C. of C. (bd. dirs. 1980-82). Jewish. Office: 433 N Camden Dr Fl 4 Beverly Hills CA 90210-4426

LEVINE, MURRAY, psychology educator; b. Bklyn., Feb. 24, 1928; s. Israel and Birdie (Cutler) L.; m. Adeline Gordon, June 15, 1952; children: David Israel, Zachary Howard. BS, CCNY, 1949; MA in Psychology, U. Pa., 1951, PhD in Psychology, 1954; JD, SUNY, Buffalo, 1983. Bar: N.Y. 1984; lic. psychologist, N.Y.; diplomate in clin. psychology Am. Bd. Profl. Psychology. Psychologist VA, Phila., 1949-57, Devereux Schs., Devon, Pa., 1957-63; from asst. to assoc. prof. psychology Yale U., New Haven, 1963-68; prof. SUNY, Buffalo, 1968—, Disting. Svc. prof., 1995—. Author: Community Psychology, 1987, 2d edit., 1997, Helping Children, 1992; contbr. articles to profl. jours. Chmn. bd. dirs. Citizens Cleaning House Hazardous Wastes, Falls Church, Va., 1983—; U.S. adv. bd. Child Abuse and Neglect. Recipient Seymour Sarason award SCRA, 1997, Kurt Lewin award NYSPA, 1997. Mem. APA (fellow sects. 12, 27, 41, disting. contbns. award 1987, teaching and mentoring award 1992), APLS. Home: 74 Colonial Cir Buffalo NY 14213-1467

LEVINE, NAOMI BRONHEIM, university administrator; b. N.Y.C., Apr. 15, 1923; d. Nathan and Malvina (Mermelstein) Bronheim; m. Leonard Levine, Apr. 11, 1948; 1 dau., Joan. B.A., Hunter Coll., 1944; LL.B., Columbia, 1946, J.D., 1970. Bar: N.Y. bar 1946. With firm Scaadrett, Tuttle & Chalaire, N.Y.C., 1946-48, Charles Gottlieb, N.Y.C., 1948-50; with Am. Jewish Congress, 1950-78, exec. dir., 1972-78; v.p. to sr. v.p. external affairs NYU, 1978—; asst. prof. law and police sci. John Jay Coll., N.Y.C., 1969-73, L.I. U., 1965-69. Author: Schools in Crisis, 1969, The Jewish Poor-an American Awakening, 1974, Politics, Religion and Love, 1990; mem. editorial staff Columbia Law Rev., 1945-46. Bd. dirs. Jewish Cmty. Rels. Coun., Am. Women's Econ. Devel. Council; trustee N.Y. UJA-Fedn. Recipient Constl. Law prize Hunter Coll., 1944; named to Hall of Fame, 1972. Office: 70 Washington Sq S New York NY 10012-1019

LEVINE, NORMAN GENE, insurance company executive; b. N.Y.C., Sept. 14, 1926; s. Harris J. and Dorothy S. (Podolsky) L.; m. Sandra Leibow, Dec. 11, 1969; children—Linda, Daniel, Donald. Student, U. Wis.-Madison, 1943-48. Agt. Aetna Life Ins. Co., N.Y.C., 1948-56; supr. Aetna Life Ins. Co., 1956-59, gen. agt., 1959-75; mng. gen. agt. Mut. Benefit Life Ins. Co. in N.Y.C., San Francisco, 1975-91; br. mgr. Sun Life of Can., 1991-97; pres. Levine Fin. Group, 1975—, Levine Enterprises, San Francisco, 1994—; internat. speaker in field; past div. v.p. Million Dollar Round Table; nat. chmn. Life Underwriters Tng. Council, 1983-84; nat. pres. Gen. Agts. and Mgrs. Conf., 1986-87. Author: How to Build a $100,000,000 Agency in Five Years or Less, Yes You can, Life Insurance to Diversification, Selling with Silk Gloves Not Brass Knuckles; editor: b i-weekly news report Probe; contbr. numerous articles to profl. jours.; author tapes on ins., mgmt., photography, Americanism. Past mem. bd. dirs. Calif. Law Enforcement Needs Com.; chmn. Gama Found.; chmn. Million Dollar Round Table Mentoring Coun. Served with AUS, 1944-46, ETO. Recipient Julian Myrick award, 1969, John Newton Russell Meml. award, 1986; named to Hall of Fame Gen. Agts. and Mgrs. Conf., 1982. Mem. N.Y.C. Assn. Life Underwriters (pres. 1967-68), N.Y. State Assn. Life Underwriters (pres. 1968-69), Nat. Assn. Life Underwriters (pres. 1974-75, dir. polit. action com. 1967-69), N.Y.C. Life Mgrs. Assn. (pres. 1974-75), Assn. Advanced Life Underwriters, Am. Soc. C.L.U.s, San Francisco Gen. Agts. and Mgrs. Assn. (pres. 1983), Golden Key Soc., Linnaean Soc., San Francisco C. of C., Audubon Soc., Am. Israel Friendship League (trustee). Mem. Order B'nai Zion (pres. 1964-67). Home: 251 Crest Rd Woodside CA 94062-2310 Office: 1 California St San Francisco CA 94111-5401 *Profit and concern for people are not mutually exclusive and, in fact, people working in a synergistic relationship produce greater profit and general well-being. Democracy with all its problems is still clearly the best of all available methods of government; capitalism and free enterprise create the competition and reward that best challenge the human mind and body; and freedom to "stand tall" with faith, integrity and dignity are the basis for one's conscience and a guide for society's morality.*

LEVINE, PAMELA GAIL, business owner; b. Alameda, Calif., Nov. 20, 1942; d. Carl B. and Lucille N. (Lua) Leverenz; m. George David Barth (div. 1974); children, Claudia Anne, Shanette Michelle; m. Leonard Stuart Levine; children: Leslie, Julie, Susan, Stuart Carl. BA in Archtl. Design/Fine Arts, U. Calif., Berkeley, 1965. Designer Trude of Calif., San Francisco, 1965-66; tchr. TWA, Kansas City, Mo., 1966-69; ptnr., owner, archtl. designer Leverenz of N.Y., 1970—; owner, designer Ressco, Katonah, N.Y., 1974—; cons. archtl. design and real estate devel.; founder, owner Sintec-Internat. Bus. Opportunities, 1989—. Designer of Sets/Costumes, Chappaqua Drama Group, 1973—. Devel. com. Mount Holyoke Coll., S. Hadley, Mass., 1987—; co-founder Looking Glass Players, Mt. Kisco, N.Y., 1985—; active Jr. League, Caramoor, Katonah Mus. Mem. No. Westchester Ctr. for the Arts (exec. com., v.p. bd. dirs., bd. dirs. devel. com., co-chmn. bldg. com.), Chappaqua Drama Group (bd. dirs.). Republican. Avocations: painter, costume design, set design, doll design, artist. Home: RR 6 Katonah NY 10536-9806 Office: Real Estate Support Svcs PO Box 574 Katonah NY 10536-0574

LEVINE, PAUL MICHAEL, paper industry executive, consultant; b. Bklyn., Apr. 15, 1934; s. Isaac Bert and Jessie Sue (Palevsky) L.; m. Lois Jaffin, June 11, 1954 (div.); children: Daniella Sarah, Julie Ann, Carl Joseph; m. 2d Noelle Tenedou, July 14, 1974; children: Simone Allana, Alexander Owen. A.B. in Econs., Harvard Coll., 1954; A.M. in Internat. Econs., Fletcher Sch. Internat. Law and Diplomacy, 1955. Sales mgr. U.S. Industries, Stamford, Conn., 1956-61; chief exec. officer subs. cos. Parsons and Whittemore-Black Clawson, N.Y.C., 1962-69; dep. adminstr. City of N.Y., 1970-72; v.p. S&S Corrugated Paper Machinery Co., Bklyn., 1973-76, Continental Group, Stamford, Conn., 1977-83; chmn. New Lehigh Corrugated Products, Farmingdale, N.Y., United Container Corp., Phila.; lectr., fellow Yale U., U. Conn., Fordham U., 1979-90; Neeltran Inc., New Milford, Conn., Shulz Electric Corp., New Haven, Conn., Gulf Copper Mfg. Co., Port Arthur, Tex. Author: Proceedings 6th World Forestry Congress, 1966; editor: Study of Peoria County Model Program, 1970, Practical Exporting, 1962, The Role of Venture Capital in Europe and the World. Trustee Hartman Regional Theatre, Stamford, 1981-82; bd. dirs. Ridgefield Orch., 1978-83, Bklyn. Arts and Culture Assn., 1973-92. Mem. Turnaround Mgmt. Assn., Explorers Club. Democrat. Jewish. Office: Paul M Levine & Assocs 466 Ridgebury Rd Ridgefield CT 06877-1228 *Creativity, innovation and laughter are the glories of the world.*

LEVINE, PEGGY AYLSWORTH, psychotherapist, writer, poet; b. Newark, May 2, 1921; d. Roscoe Nichols and Helen (Dorsen) Aylsworth; m. Samuel Schultz, Mar. 29, 1950 (div. 1979); children: Christie Romero, Ronald M. Schultz; m. Norman Philip Levine, Sept. 20, 1986. BA in Psychology, Lindenwood Coll., 1977; MA in Psychology, Antioch West Coll., L.A., 1978. Rschr. Carl Byoir & Assocs., N.Y.C., 1941-43; rsch. editor True Mag., Fawcett Publs., N.Y.C., 1944-45; adminstr. Valley Ctr. of Arts, Encino, Calif., 1966-69; pub. rels. dir. Comsky Gallery, L.A., 1970; pvt. practice psychotherapy Santa Monica, Calif., 1980—. Author: (children's album) The Glooby Game, 1949, (poetry) Letters to the Same Address, 1989, Along These Lines, 1995, (novels) Morning in the Long Night City, 1992, Among These Several, 1996; contbr. poems to various mags., revs. V.p. Valley Ctr. of Arts, 1956-57, publicity dir., 1955-65; publicity dir. Alliance for Survival, Santa Monica, 1979-81. Avocations: art collecting, reading, ephemera and stamp collecting, reading plays, photography. Home and Office: 606 Raymond Ave Apt 1 Santa Monica CA 90405-4530

LEVINE, PETER HUGHES, physician, health facility administrator; b. Everett, Mass., Nov. 13, 1938; s. Louis and Helen (Hughes) L.; m. Catherine Brooks Holst, Aug. 26, 1962; children: Thomas H., William H., James L. BS, Tufts U., 1960; MD, Tufts U., Boston, 1964. Diplomate Am. Bd. Internal Medicine, Am. Bd. Hematology. Hematology fellow Tufts - N.E. Med. Ctr., Boston, 1967-69; hematologist Andrews AFB Referral Hosp., Washington, 1969-71; dir. blood coagulation lab. and hemophilia ctr. Tufts - N.E. Med. Ctr., Boston, 1971-75; chmn. dept. medicine Worcester (Mass.) Meml. Hosp., 1975-90, dir. Blood Rsch. Lab., 1975—; pres., chief exec. officer Med. Ctr. of Cen. Mass., Worcester, 1990—; asst. prof. medicine Tufts U. Sch. Medicine, Boston, 1971-75; prof. medicine U. Mass. Med. Sch., Worcester, 1975—. Contbr. 164 articles to med. jours., 131 published abstracts in area of hematology. Med. dir. Nat. Hemophilia Found., N.Y.C., 1983-87; pres. Worcester County Music Assn., 1989-92; trustee Worcester Poly. Inst., 1990—, Mass. Biotech. Rsch. Inst., 1990—, Worcester Bus. Devel. Com., 1992—, United Way Ctrl. Mass., 1993—; trustee and exec. com. mem. Mass. Hosp. Assn., 1992—. Maj. USAF, 1969-71. Recipient Disting. Tchr. award Tufts U. Sch. Medicine, Boston, 1973, 75, Outstanding Med. Educator, U. Mass. Med. Sch., Worcester, 1981, 85, 86, 88, 89, 91, House Staff Disting. Tchr., Worcester Meml. Hosp., 1980, 87, 88, Murray Thelin Award for Rsch. Nat. Hemophilia Found., 1987. Fellow ACP; mem. Am. Soc. Hematology, Am. Fedn. Clin. Rsch. Achievements include patent pending on cure of hemophilia by gene therapy; development of model program for home therapy of hemophilia; research on production and effects of leukocyte-generated oxidants, on omega-3 fatty acids, prostanoids, and platelet and leukocyte function. Office: Med Ctr Ctrl Mass 119 Belmont St Worcester MA 01605-2903

LEVINE, PHILIP, poet, educator; b. Detroit, Jan. 10, 1928; s. A. Harry and Esther Gertrude (Priscol) L.; m. Frances Artley, July 12, 1954; children: Mark, John, Teddy. B.A., Wayne State U., 1950, A.M., 1955; M.F.A., U. Iowa, 1957, studied with John Berryman, 1954. Instr. U. Iowa, 1955-57; instr. Calif. State U., Fresno, 1958—; prof. English Calif. State U., 1969-92, Tufts U.; tchr. Princeton U., Columbia U., U. Calif., Berkeley.; Elliston lectr. poetry U. Cin.; poet-in-residence Vassar Coll., Nat. U. Australia; chmn. lit. panel Nat. Endowment Arts, 1985; adj. prof. NYU, Spring, 1984; Univ. prof. Brown U., spring 1985; tchr. NYU, U. Iowa, Vanderbilt U. Author: On the Edge, 1961, Silent in America: Vivas for Those Who Failed, 1965, Not This Pig, 1968, 5 Detroits, 1970, Thistles, 1970, Pili's Wall, 1971, Red Dust, 1971, They Feed They Lion, 1972, 1933, 1974, On The Edge & Over, 1976, The Names of the Lost, 1976 (Lenore Marshall award Best Am. Book Poems 1976), 7 Years from Somewhere, 1979 (Nat. Book Critics Circle prize 1979, Notable Book award Am. Libr. Assn. 1979), Ashes, 1979 (Nat. Book Critics Circle prize 1979, Nat. Book award 1979), Don't Ask, 1979, One for the Rose, 1981, Selected Poems, 1984, Sweet Will, 1985, A Walk with Tom Jefferson, 1988 (Bay Area Book Reviewers award), What Work Is, 1991 (L.A. Times Book Prize 1991, Nat. Book award for poetry, 1991), New Selected Poems, 1991, Earth, Stars, and Writers, 1992, The Bread of Time: Toward an Autobiography, 1994, Simple Truth, 1994 (Pulitzer Prize for poetry 1995); editor: (with Henri Coulette) Character and Crisis, 1966, (with E. Trejo) The Selected Poems of Jaime Sabines, (with Ada Long) Off the Map, The Selected Poems of Gloria Fuertes, 1984, (with D. Wojahn and B. Henderson) The Pushcart Prize XI, 1986, The Essential Keats, 1987. Active anti-Vietnam war movement. Recipient Joseph Henry Jackson award San Francisco Found., 1961, The Chaplebrook Found. award, 1968, Frank O'Hara Meml. prize, 1973; Amer. Academy of Arts and Letters Award of Merit, 1974; Levinson Prize, 1974; Harriet Monroe Meml. prize for poetry, 1976; Golden Rose award New Eng. Poetry Soc., 1985, Ruth Lilly Poetry Prize, Modern Poetry Assn. and Am. Council Arts, 1987, Elmer Bobst award NYU, 1990, Lit. Lion New York Public Library 1993; named outstanding lectr. Calif. State U., Fresno, 1971, outstanding prof. Calif. State U. System, 1972; Stanford U. poetry fellow, 1957, Nat. Inst. Arts and Letters grantee, 1973, Guggenheim fellow, 1973-74, 80; Nat. Endowment for Arts grantee, 1969, 70 (refused), 76, 81, 87. *My hope is to write poetry for people for whom there are no poems.**

LEVINE, PHILIP, classics educator; b. Lawrence, Mass., Sept. 8, 1922; s. Samuel and Jennie (Derdak) L.; m. Dinnie Moseson, June 19, 1955; children—Jared Elliott, Harlan Alcon. A.B., Harvard, 1946, A.M., 1948, Ph.D., 1952; DHL (hon.), U. Judaism, 1986. Instr., asst. prof. classics Harvard, 1952-59; assoc. prof. classical langs. U. Tex. at Austin, 1959-61; assoc prof., prof. classics UCLA, 1961-91, prof. emeritus, 1991—; dean div. humanities U. Calif. at Los Angeles, 1965-83; Biggs resident lectr. Washington U., 1993; info. officer Coun. U. Calif. Emeriti Assn. Author: Lo Scriptorium Vercellese da S. Eusueblo ad Attone, 1958, St. Augustine, City of God, Books 12-15, 1966; editor: Latin lt. sect. Twayne World Author Series, 1964—; adv. editor, U. Calif. Publs. in Classical Studies, 1963-72; assoc. editor, contbr. to U. Calif. Studies in Classical Antiquity, 1967-75, sr. co-editor, 1975-78; mem. editorial bd. Classical Antiquity, 1986-93. Mem. rev. com., sr. fellowship program Nat. Endowment for Humanities, 1966-70;

bd. govs. U. Judaism, 1968-90, coun. visitors, 1990-94, acad. adv. coun., 1994—. With AUS, 1943-46. Sheldon fellow Italy; Guggenheim fellow; Fulbright Research grantee; recipient Bromberg Humanities award; decorated Cavaliere dell' Ordine al Merito della Repubblica Italiana. Mem. Am. Philol. Assn. (dir. 1968-70), Mediaeval Acad. Am. (exec. council 1969-72), Renaissance Soc., Am. Philol. Assn., Pacific Coast (chmn. gen. lit. 1964-65), Phi Beta Kappa. Home: 224 S Almont Dr Beverly Hills CA 90211-2507 Office: U Calif Dept Classics Los Angeles CA 90095

LEVINE, RACHMIEL, physician; b. Poland, Aug. 26, 1910; came to U.S., 1936, naturalized, 1944; s. Solomon and Bessie (Benzion) L.; m. Anne Gussack, Mar. 4, 1943; children—Judith Ann, Daniel Saul. B.A., McGill U., 1932, M.D., 1936. Intern, then resident Michael Reese Hosp., Chgo., 1936-38; research fellow Michael Reese Hosp., 1939, dir. dept. metabolism, 1942-60, chmn. dept. madicine, 1952-60, dir. med. edn., 1952-60; professorial lectr. physiology U. Chgo., 1945-60; prof., chmn. dept. medicine N.Y. Med. Coll., 1960-71; exec. med. dir. City of Hope Med. Center, Duarte, Calif., 1971-78; dir. research City of Hope Med. Center, 1978—; Active United Jewish Appeal, Chgo., 1959-60; Cons. NSF, 1956-59, mem. bd. found. fund psychiat. research, 1958-61; Jakobaeus lectr. Karolinska Inst., Stockholm, 1963. Contbr. numerous articles to profl. jours. Fellow Am. Acad. Arts and Scis.; mem. Am. Physiol. Soc., Nat. Acad. Scis., Endocrine Soc. (Upjohn award 1957), A.C.P., Assn. Am. Physicians, N.Y. Acad. Medicine, Chgo. Inst. Medicine, Am. Diabetes Assn. (Banting medal 1961, council 1958, pres. 1964-65), Internat. Diabetes Assn. (pres. 1967-70, hon. pres. 1970—), Harvey Soc. (pres. 1967-68, Gairdner award 1971, Joslin medal 1972). Home: 2024 Canyon Rd Arcadia CA 91006-1503 Office: City of Hope Med Ctr Duarte CA 91010

LEVINE, RAPHAEL DAVID, chemistry educator; b. Alexandria, Egypt, Mar. 29, 1938; brought to U.S., 1939; s. Chaim S. and Sofia (Greenberg) L.; m. Gillah T. Ephraty, June 13, 1962; 1 child, Ornah T. MSc, Hebrew U., Jerusalem, 1959; PhD, Nottingham (Eng.) U., 1964; DPhil, Oxford (Eng.) U., 1966; PhD honoris causa, U. Liege, Belgium, 1991, Tech. U., Munich, Germany, 1996. Vis. asst. prof. U. Wis., 1966-68; prof. theoretical chemistry Hebrew U., Jerusalem, 1969—, chmn. research ctr. molecular dynamics, 1981—, Max Born prof. natural philosophy, 1985—; Battelle prof. chemistry and math. Ohio State U., Columbus, 1970-74; Brittingham vis. prof. U. Wis., 1973; adj. prof. U. Tex., Austin, 1974-80, MIT, 1980-88, UCLA, 1989—; Arthur D. Little lectr. MIT, 1978; Miller rsch. prof. U. Calif., Berkeley, 1989, A.D. White prof. at large Cornell U., 1989—. Author: Quantum Mechanics of Molecular Rate Processes, 1969, Molecular Reaction Dynamics, 1974, Lasers and Chemical Change, 1981, Molecular Reaction Dynamics and Chemical Reactivity, 1986, Algebraic Theory of Molecules, 1995; mem. editorial bds. several well known scientific jours.; contbr. articles to profl. jours. Served with AUS, 1960-62. Recipient Ann. award Internat. Acad. Quantum Molecular Sci., 1968, Landau prize, 1972, Israel prize in Exact Scis., 1974, Weizman prize, 1979, Rothschild prize, 1992, Max Planck prize for Internat. Cooperation, 1996; co-recipient Chemistry prize Wolf Found., 1988; Ramsay Meml. fellow, 1964-66, Alfred P. Sloan fellow, 1970-72. Fellow Am. Phys. Soc.; mem. Israel Chem. Soc., Israel Acad. Scis., Max Planck Soc. (fgn. mem.), Academia Europaea (fgn.), Am. Acad. Arts and Scis. (fgn. hon. mem.), Am. Philos. Soc. (fgn.), Royal Danish Acad. Scis. and Letters (fgn.). Office: UCLA Dept Of Chemistry Los Angeles CA 90095-1569 also: Hebrew U Jerusalem, 91904 Jerusalem Israel

LEVINE, RHEA JOY COTTLER, anatomy educator; b. N.Y.C., Nov. 26, 1939; d. Zachary Robert Cottler and Hildreth (Abramson) Cottler Rosenfeld; m. Stephen Maxwell Levine, June 16, 1960; children: Elizabeth, Michael Gordon, Zachary Thomas. AB summa cum laude, Smith Coll., 1960; MS, NYU, 1963, PhD, 1966. Lab. instr. NYU Sch. Commerce, N.Y.C., 1963-64; postdoctoral fellow, instr. histology Yale U. Sch. Medicine, New Haven, 1966-68; rsch. assoc. U. Pa. Sch. Medicine, Phila., 1968-69; asst. prof. anatomy Med. Coll. Pa., Phila., 1969-74, assoc. prof. anatomy, 1974-80, prof. anatomy, 1980—, vice chmn., 1988-89; manuscript reviewer numerous sci. journals, Washington and N.Y.C., 1975—; reviewer grant proposals NSF, Washington, 1975—, mem. NIH Study Sect., 1980-84. Contbr. sci. articles to profl. jours. Trustee Richard Stockton Coll. N.J., Pomona, 1983—, chmn. bd. trustees, 1991-94; trustee Smith Coll., 1996—; bd. dirs. Hollybush Festival, Glassboro, N.J., 1987-91, Smith Coll. Friends of Libr., Northampton, Mass., 1968-72. NYU Sch. Medicine summer rsch. fellow, 1960, NSF grad. fellow, 1960-65, A.H. Robins rsch. fellow, 1966, USPHS fellow, 1966-68; grantee Women's and Program project NIH, NSF, 1973—; recipient Founder's Day award NYU, 1966, Smith Coll. medal, 1994. Mem. AAAS, Coalition Jewish Profl. Women South N.J. (steering com.), Am. Assn. Anatomists, Am Soc. Cell Biology, Biophys. Soc. (coun. 1991-94, chair pub. sci. policy com. 1992-94), Histochem. Soc., Soc. Gen. Physiology, Wilderness Med. Soc., N.Y. Acad. Scis., Smith Coll. Club, Woodcrest Country Club (house chair 1983-84), Phi Beta Kappa, Sigma Xi. Jewish. Office: MCP Hahnemann Sch of Medicine Allegheny U of Health Scis 3200 Henry Ave Philadelphia PA 19129-1137

LEVINE, RICHARD E., lawyer; b. Flushing, N.Y., Aug. 6, 1950; s. Sol and Betty (Broad) L.; m. Lori A. Balter, Oct. 28, 1979; 1 child, Jamie Balter. BS in Mech. Engring., Bucknell U., 1972; JD, U. Md., 1975; LL.M. in Taxation, Georgetown U., 1978. Bar: Md. 1975, U.S. Tax Ct. 1979, D.C. 1980, U.S. Supreme Ct. 1983, U.S. Ct. Appeals (4th cir.) 1984. Assoc. Miles & Stockbridge, Balt., 1978-83, prin., 1983—; adj. prof. U. Md. Law Sch., Balt., 1988. Contbr. articles to profl. jours. Bd. dirs. Har Sinai West Sr. Citizens Housing, Balt., 1983-92. Fellow Am. Coll. Tax Counsel; mem. ABA (tax sect., chair partnerships 1990-92), Md. State Bar Assn. (tax sect. coun. 1983-86), The Center Club (house com. 1990—, bd. govs. 1996—). Avocations: golf, music. Office: Miles & Stockbridge 10 Light St Baltimore MD 21202-1435

LEVINE, RICHARD JAMES, publishing executive; b. N.Y.C., Jan. 24, 1942; s. Irving Joseph and Dorothy Joyce (Thome) L.; m. Neil Ann Stuckey, June 1, 1963; children: Jonathan Donald, Russell Neilan. BS, Cornell U., 1962; MS with high honors, Columbia U., 1963. Gen. assignment reporter Wall St. Jour., Washington, 1966-67, labor corr., 1967-70, mil. writer, 1970-75, chief econ. writer, outlook columnist, 1975-80; editl. dir./data base pub. Dow Jones & Co., Princeton, N.J., 1980-87, v.p. info. svcs. group, 1987-89, v.p. and editl. dir. info. svcs. group, mem. mgmt. com., 1989-92, v.p., mng. editor info. svcs. segment, mem. mgmt. com., Dow Jones & Co., N.Y.C., 1992-95; v.p. fin. info. svcs. group, mng. editor Dow Jones News Svcs., Dow Jones & Co., N.Y.C., 1995—; pres. Dow Jones AER Co., Inc., 1994—; pres. Econ. Rsch. Co. Inc., 1994-97; v.p., mng. editor Dow Jones Newswires, Dow Jones & Co., Jersey City, 1997—; dep. chmn. VWD GmbH. Author: (with others) The Wall Street Journal Views America Tomorrow, 1977. 1st lt. U.S. Army, 1964-66. Columbia U. Pulitzer fellow, 1963-64. Mem. Cornell U. Tower Club, Soc. Profl. Journalists, Cornell Club (N.Y.C.), Princeton Indoor Tennis Ctr. Home: 108 Parkside Dr Princeton NJ 08540-4815 Office: Harborside Fin Ctr 600 Plaza Two Jersey City NJ 07311-1103

LEVINE, ROBERT A., cardiologist; b. N.Y.C., Jan. 29, 1953; s. Jules and Shirley (Krupnick) L. AB summa cum laude, Harvard Coll., 1974; MD, Harvard Med. Sch., 1978. Diplomate Am. Bd. Internal Medicine. Intern, resident in medicine Beth Israel Hosp., Boston, 1978-81; fellow in cardiology Mt. Sinai Hosp., N.Y.C., 1981-83; clinical & rsch. fellow Mass. Gen. Hosp., Boston, 1983-85; instr. in medicine Harvard Med. Sch., Boston, 1985-87; asst. prof. medicine Harvard Med. Sch., 1987-94, assoc. prof. medicine, 1994—; staff physician cardiac unit Mass. Gen. Hosp., Boston, 1985—, dir. cardiac ultrasound labs., 1995—; sci. session abstract chmn. Am. Soc. Echocardiography, 1993-95, program chmn., 1996—, bd. dirs. 1995—; adj. prof. bioengring. Ga. Inst. Tech., Atlanta, 1995—. Editl. bd. Jour. Am. Coll. Cardiology, 1991-95, Circulation, 1996—. Recipient awards NIH, 1985, 87, 95; clinician-scientist, est. investigator Am. Heart Assn., 1986, 91. Office: Mass Gen Hosp Cardiac Ultrasound VBK523 Boston MA 02114

LEVINE, ROBERT ARTHUR, economist, policy analyst; b. Bklyn., July 7, 1930; s. Isaac Bert and Jessie Sue (Palevsky) L.; m. Esther Carol Knudsen, Mar. 2, 1953; children: David Knudsen, Peter Kemmerer, Joseph Karl. BA, Harvard U., 1950, MA, 1951; PhD, Yale U., 1957. Economist Rand Corp., 1957-61, sr. economist, 1962-65, 69-73, 87—, sr. economist emeritus, 1994—; research assoc. Harvard U. Center Internat. Affairs, 1961-62; asst. dir. for research, plans, programs and evaluation OEO, Washington, 1966-69; pres. N.Y.C.-Rand Inst., 1973-75; dep. dir. Congl. Budget Office, Washington, 1975-79; v.p. System Devel. Corp., Santa Monica, Calif., 1979-85; pres. Canyon Analysts, 1985—; sr. fellow Nat. Security Studies Program, UCLA, 1964-65; vis. prof. public policy Stanford U. Grad. Sch. Bus., 1972; adj. prof. econs. Pepperdine U. Sch. Bus. and Mgmt., 1984. Author: The Arms Debate, 1963, The Poor Ye Need Not Have With You, 1971, Public Planning: Failure and Redirection, 1972, Evaluation Research and Practice, 1981, Still the Arms Debate, 1990, Turmoil and Transition in the Atlantic Alliance, 1991. With USN, 1951-54. Ford Found. grantee, 1969, 85; German Marshall Fund grantee, 1979; Carnegie Corp. grantee, 1986. Mem. Inst. Strategic Studies. Club: Beverly Glen Democratic. Home and Office: 10321 Chrysanthemum Ln Los Angeles CA 90077-2812

LEVINE, ROBERT JAY, lawyer; b. Hackensack, N.J., Aug. 7, 1950; s. Nathan R. and Naomi (Bendel) L.; m. Joan Beth Mirviss, Aug. 10, 1975. AB, Brown U., 1972; JD, U. Pa., 1975. Bar: N.Y. 1976, U.S. Dist. Ct. (so. and ea. dist.) N.Y. 1976. Assoc. Davis Polk & Wardwell, N.Y.C., 1975-82, ptnr., 1983—; pres. and dir. Sylvan Winds, Inc. Mem. ABA, N.Y. State Bar Assn., Assn. of Bar of City of N.Y., Phi Beta Kappa. Democrat. Jewish. Club: Brown of N.Y.C. Avocations: golf, travel, cooking, film. Home: 115 Central Park W New York NY 10023-4153 Office: Davis Polk & Wardwell 450 Lexington Ave New York NY 10017-3911

LEVINE, ROBERT JOHN, physician, educator; b. N.Y.C., Dec. 29, 1934; s. Benjamin Bernard and Ruth Florence (Schwartz) L.; m. Jeralea Fooshee Hesse, Nov. 28, 1987; children from previous marriage: John Graham, Elizabeth Hurt Braun. Student, Duke U., 1951-54; MD with distinction, George Washington U., 1958. Diplomate Am. Bd. Internal Medicine. Med. house officer Peter Bent Brigham Hosp., Boston, 1958-59, asst. resident in medicine, 1959-60; clin. assoc. Nat. Heart Inst., Bethesda, Md., 1960-62, investigator, 1963-64; chief med. resident VA Hosp., West Haven, Conn., 1962-63; mem. faculty depts. medicine and pharmacology Yale U., New Haven, 1964-73, chief sect. clin. pharmacology, 1966-74, prof. medicine, lectr. pharmacology, 1973—; mem. med. staff Yale-New Haven Med. Ctr., 1964-68, attending physician, 1968—; mem. Conn. Adv. Com. on Foods and Drugs, 1967-82, sec. 1969-71, chmn., 1971-73; mem. adv. com. AIDS program U.S. HHS, 1989-95; cons. Nat. Commn. Protection of Human Subjects of Biomed. and Behavioral Rsch., 1974-78; bd. dirs. Medicine in the Pub. Interest, Inc., 1976—, sec., 1983—. Author: Ethics and Regulation of Clinical Research, 1981, 2d edit., 1986; co-editor: Ethics and Research on Human Subjects: International Guidelines, 1993; editor Clin. Rsch., 1971-76, IRB: Rev. Human Subjects Rsch., 1978—; contbr. numerous articles to profl. jours. Mem. Conn. Humanities Coun., 1983-89, chmn. 1988-89, Coun. Internat. Orgn. Med. Scis., co-chmn. steering com. revision internat. ethical guidelines for biomed.rsch. involving human subjects, 1991-93. Multiple rsch. grantee. Fellow ACP, The Hastings Ctr., AAAS (coun. del. 1987-91); mem. Am. Soc. Clin. Investigation, Am. Soc. Clin. Pharmacology and Therapeutics (bd. dirs. 1981-85), Am. Fedn. Clin. Rsch. (nat. coun. 1967-76, exec. com. 1971-76), Am. Soc. Pharmacology and Exptl. Therapeutics (exec. com. 1974-77), Am. Soc. Law, Medicine and Ethics (bd. dirs., pres. 1989-90, 94-95), Pub. Responsibility in Medicine and Rsch. (bd. dirs.), Soc. for Bioethics Consultation (bd. dirs. 1988-94), Sigma Xi, Alpha Omega Alpha. Office: Yale U Sch Medicine 333 Cedar St New Haven CT 06510-3206

LEVINE, ROBERT JOSEPH, secondary school administrator; b. Bklyn., Jan. 7, 1945; s. Robert J. Sr. and Thelma Lillian (Myatt-Coates) L.; m. Marilyn Barbara Sokol, Dec. 24, 1965 (div. Apr. 1970); m. Martha Klein Levine, May 24, 1981; children: Justin David, Ryan Michael. BA in Anthropology, U. Ariz., 1967; MS in Edn., CUNY, 1974, advanced cert. edn. adminstrn./super., 1976. Cert. adv. prof., Md.; supr. and prin., guidance, social studies, N.Y.; supr., prin. Tchr. social studies Intermediate Sch. 128M, N.Y.C., 1968-70, Prospect Heights H.S., Bklyn., 1970-71; tchr. social studies, English, Spanish, TESOL John Jay H.S., Bklyn., 1971-76; guidance counselor Lake Clifton H.S., Balt., 1976-79, Ea. H.S., Balt., 1980-83, Francis M. Wood Alternative H.S., Balt., 1983-85; guidance counselor Balt. Poly. Inst., 1988-92, asst. prin., 1992—; dir. summer opportunity program Friends Sch. of Balt., 1978-86; chmn. guidance adv. panel Balt. City Pub. Schs., 1981-85; chmn. Balt. Nat. Coll. Fair, 1989-96. Author: (curriculum document) The History of Brooklyn, 1975. Mem. exec. bd. Hist. Balt. Soc., 1989-92; parent com. Cub Scout Pack 18, Balt., 1990-92; referee U.S. Soccer Fedn. Mem. Nat. Assn. Secondary Sch. Prins., Nat. Assn. Coll. Admission Counselors, Soc. for Applied Anthropology, Pipe Club of Gt. Britain (life). Avocations: bicycling, music, chess. Home: 14 Strongwood Rd Owings Mills MD 21117-2442 Office: Balt Poly Inst 1400 W Cold Spring Ln Baltimore MD 21209-4904

LEVINE, ROBERT SIDNEY, chemical engineer; b. Des Moines, June 4, 1921; s. George Julius and Betty (Dennen) L.; m. Sharon Lorraine White; children: George, Gail, Tamara, Michelle, James. B.S. in Chem. Engring, Iowa State U., 1943; S.M. (Standard Oil Co. Ohio fellow 1947-48), M.I.T., 1946, Sc.D., 1949. With Rocketdyne div. Rockwell Internat. Co., 1948-66; assoc. research dir. NASA, 1966-74; chief liquid rocket tech. Nat. Bur. Standards, Washington, 1974—; chief fire dynamics Nat. Bur. Standards (now Nat. Inst. Standards and Tech.), Washington, 1975—; mem. faculty UCLA, 1962-64, George Washington U., 1977; pres. Combustion Inst., 1974-78; chmn. Am. and Soviet Com. on Fire Rsch. in Housing, 1977-82. Author papers in field; mem. Washington editl. rev. bd. NIST, 1976—. Named Engr. of Year Los Angeles sect. Am. Inst. Chem. Engrs., 1961. Mem. Am. Chem. Soc., AIAA, Nat. Fire Prevention Assn. Home: 19017 Threshing Pl Gaithersburg MD 20879-2150 Office: Nat Inst Standards & Tech Gaithersburg MD 20899

LEVINE, RONALD H., physician, state official; b. N.Y.C., Mar. 30, 1935; m. Elizabeth P. Kanof; children—Mitchell, Rebecca Ann. BS, Union Coll., Schenectady, N.Y., 1955, DSc (hon.), 1990; MD, SUNY-Bklyn., 1959; MPH, U. N.C., 1967. Officer USPHS, Raleigh, N.C., 1963-65; chief communicable disease br. N.C. State Bd. Health, Raleigh, 1965-67, chief community health sect., 1968-73; asst. dir., dep. dir. N.C. Div. Health Services, Raleigh, 1974-81, state health dir., 1981—. Recipient Stevens award N.C. Assn. Local Health Dirs., 1982. Fellow Am. Acad. Pediatrics, Am. Pub. Health Assn., Am. Coll. Preventive Medicine, mem. N.C. Pub. Health Assn. (pres. 1974-75, Reynolds award 1973), Wake County Med. Soc. (pres. 1978), N.C. Med. Soc. Office: Dept Environ Health & Natural Resources PO Box 27687 512 N Salisbury St Raleigh NC 27604-1118

LEVINE, RONALD JAY, lawyer; b. Bklyn., June 23, 1953; s. Louis Leon and Marilyn Priscilla (Markovich) L.; m. Cindy Beth Israel, Nov. 18, 1979; children: Merisa, Alisha. BA summa cum laude, Princeton U., 1974; JD cum laude, Harvard U., 1977. Bar: N.Y. 1978, U.S. Dist. Ct. (so. and ea. dists.) N.Y. 1978, D.C. 1980, N.J. 1987, U.S. Supreme Ct. 1982, U.S. Ct. Apeals (2d cir.) 1983, N.J. 1987, U.S. Dist. Ct. N.J. 1987, U.S. Dist. Ct. (we. dist.) N.Y. 1991, U.S. Ct. Appeals (3d cir.) 1991, Pa. 1995. Assoc. Phillips, Nizer, Benjamin, Krim & Ballon, N.Y.C., 1977-80, Debevoise & Plimpton, N.Y.C., 1980-84; assoc. Herrick, Feinstein, N.Y.C., 1984-85, ptnr., 1985—; gen. counsel Greater N.Y. Safety Council, N.Y.C., 1979-81; arbitrator Small Claims Ct. of Civil Ct. of City of N.Y., 1983-85. Mem. Site Plan Rev. Adv. Bd., West Windsor, N.J., 1986, planning bd., 1987. Mem. ABA (litigation sect.), N.Y. State Bar Assn. (chmn. com. on legal edn. and bar admission 1982-92, com. on profl. discipline 1989-90), N.J. State Bar Assn. (product liability com. 1991—, profl. responsibility com. 1992-96), Assn. of Bar of City of N.Y. (coun. jud. adminstrn. 1994-95, com. on profl. responsibility 1980-83, com. on legal assistance 1983-86, product liability com. 1987-91, trustee career devel. awards 1989-90), Phi Beta Kappa. Home: 6 Arnold Dr Princeton Junction NJ 08550-1521 Office: Herrick Feinstein 2 Park Ave New York NY 10016-5675

LEVINE, RUTH ROTHENBERG, biomedical science educator; b. N.Y.C.; d. Jacob and Jeannette (Bandel) Rothenberg; m. Martin J. Levine, June 21, 1953. BA magna cum laude, Hunter Coll., 1938; MA, Columbia U., 1939; PhD, Tufts U., 1955. Asst. prof. sch. medicine Tufts U., 1955-58; asst. prof. pharmacology sch. medicine Boston U., 1958-61, assoc. prof. sch. medicine, 1961-65, prof. sch. medicine, 1965—, univ. prof., 1972—; chmn. grad. div. med. and dental scis. Boston U. Sch. Medicine, 1964-89, assoc. dean grad. biomed. scis., 1981-89, assoc. dean emeritus, 1989—; mem. sci. adv. bd. U.S. EPA, 1976-82, Internat. Joint Commn., State Dept., 1983-89. Author: Pharmacology, Drug Actions and Reactions, 1973, 5th edit., 1990; coord. internat. symposia of subtypes of muscarinic receptors. Named to Hall of Fame, Hunter Coll. of City of N.Y. Fellow AAAS; mem. Am. Soc. Pharmacology and Exptl. Therapeutics (sec.-treas. 1975-76), Biophys. Soc., Am. Chem. Soc., Am. Pharm. Assn., Acad. Scis., Phi Beta Kappa, Sigma Xi. Home: 212 Crafts Rd Chestnut Hill MA 02167-1452 Office: Boston U Sch Medicine Div Med and Dental Scis Boston MA 02118

LEVINE, SANFORD HAROLD, lawyer; b. Troy, N.Y., Mar. 13, 1938; s. Louis and Reba (Semegren) L.; m. Margaret R. Appelbaum, Oct. 29, 1967; children—Jessica Sara, Abby Miriam. A.B., Syracuse U., 1959, J.D., 1961. Bar: N.Y. 1961, U.S. Dist. Ct. (no. dist.) N.Y. 1961, U.S. Dist. Ct. (we. dist.) N.Y. 1979, U.S. Dist. Ct. (ea. and so. dists.) N.Y. 1980, U.S. Ct. Appeals (2d cir.) 1962, U.S. Supreme Ct. 1967. Law asst. to assoc. judge N.Y. Ct. Appeals, Albany and to justice N.Y. Supreme Ct., 1962-66; law asst. to assoc. judge N.Y. Ct. Appeals, Albany, 1964; asst. counsel N.Y. State Temporary Commn. on Constl. Conv., N.Y.C., 1966-67; assoc. counsel SUNY System, Albany, 1967-70, dep. univ. counsel, 1970-78, acting counsel, 1970-71, acting univ. counsel, 1978-79, univ. counsel and vice chancellor legal affairs, 1979-97, svc. prof. Sch. of Edn., dir. program in edn. and law, 1997—; adj. prof. Sch. of Edn. State U. N.Y., Albany, 1992-97; mem. paralegal curriculum adv. com. Schenectady County Community Coll., 1975—. Fellow Am. Bar Found., N.Y. Bar Found.; mem. ABA (ho. dels. 1987-89), N.Y. State Bar Assn., Albany County Bar Assn., Nat. Assn. Coll. and Univ. Attys. (exec. bd. 1979-82, bd. dirs. 1982-89, pres. 1986-87), Am. Soc. Pub. Adminstrn., Am. Acad. Healthcare Attys., Nat. Health Lawyers Assn. Editorial bd. Syracuse U. Law Rev., 1960-61; editorial adv. bd. Jour. Coll. and Univ. Law, 1977-81. Home: 1106 Godfrey Ln Schenectady NY 12309-2712

LEVINE, SEYMOUR, lawyer; b. Bklyn., Jan. 29, 1924; s. Abraham and Lena (Gitlin) L.; m. Anna Baron, Sept. 6, 1952; children: Ronnie Livia, Alison M. BBA, CCNY, 1949; JD, Harvard U., 1952. Bar: N.Y. 1952, Fla. 1974. Tax lawyer S.D. Leidesdorf and Co., N.Y.C., 1952-58; assoc. Parker, Chapin, Flattau and Klimpl, N.Y.C., 1958-1967, ptnr., 1967-92, of counsel, 1993—; adj. assoc. prof. Inst. of Paralegal Studies, NYU, 1978-86, mem. adv. com.; chmn. of faculty, lectr. Practicing Law Inst., N.Y., Chgo., San Francisco, 1981-85; lectr. on estate planning, N.Y.C., San Francisco, Chgo. Contbr. articles to profl. jours. Pres., bd. dirs. Met. Jewish Geriatric Ctr., Bkyn., 1969—; active Vols. of Legal Svcs., Inc., N.Y.C., 1988—. Sgt. USMC, 1943-46. Fellow Am. Coll. Trust and Estates Counsel; mem. ABA, Fla. Bar Assn., N.Y. State Bar Assn., Assn. of Bar of City of N.Y., Harvard Club of N.Y. Avocation: tennis. Office: Parker Chapin Flattau & Klimpl 1211 Avenue Of The Americas New York NY 10036-8701

LEVINE, SOLOMON BERNARD, business and economics educator; b. Boston, Aug. 10, 1920; s. Isaac William and Sybil (Mannis) L; m. Elizabeth Jane Billett, Dec. 24, 1943; children: Janet Ruth Levine Thal, Michael Alan, Samuel Billett, Elliott Mannis. AB magna cum laude, Harvard Coll., 1942; cert. Japanese Lang., U. Colo., 1944; MBA with honors, Sch. Bus. Adminstrn., Harvard U., 1947; postgrad., MIT, 1947-49, Ph.D. in Indsl. Econs., 1951. Teaching asst. dept. econs. and social sci. MIT, 1947-49; faculty U. Ill., 1949-69, prof. labor and indsl. relations and Asian studies, 1964-69; prof. bus. and econs. U. Wis.-Madison, 1969-89, prof. emeritus, 1989—, mem. East Asian Studies Program, chmn., 1968-77, co-chmn., 1982-88, dir. Nat. Resource Ctr. for East Asian Studies, 1985-87, participating faculty mem. Indsl. Relations Research Inst.; Fulbright prof. Keio U., Tokyo, 1959; vis. prof. dept. econs. Pa. State U., 1960; vis. prof. labor relations dept. econs. MIT, 1962-63; vis. prof. econs. U. Singapore, 1968; vis. lectr. and research scholar various univs., Indonesia, 1973, Australia, 1973, N.Z., 1973, vis. scholar univs., Japan, 1978, Australia, 1978, N.Z., 1978, Singapore, 1978, South Korea, 1978; vis. prof., sr. scholar Monash U., Australia and Japan, 1981-82, vis. research scholar Macquarie U., Australia, 1985; vis. prof. Internat. U. Japan, 1984; vis. prof. Nanzan U., Nagoya, Japan, 1989-91, U. Hawaii, Manoa, 1991; vis. fellow Swinburne Inst. Tech., Australia, 1992; vis. scholar Japan Ctr. for Mich. Univ., Japan, 1994. labor arbitrator. Author: Industrial Relations in Postwar Japan, 1958, Japanese transl., 1959, (with Hishashi Kawada) Human Resources in Japanese Industrial Development, 1980; co-editor, co-author: chpts. and preface Workers and Employers in Japan: The Japanese Employment Relations System, 1973, (with Koji Taira) Japan's External Economic Relations: Japanese Perspectives, 1991; contbr. to sect. Ency. Americana; chpts. to books, articles to publs. Treas. Stevenson for Pres. Campaign, Champaign-Urbana, Ill., 1952; mem. Community Integration Council, 1965-69. Sheldon traveling fellow Harvard U., Mex., 1942; Social Sci. Rsch. Coun. tng. fellow, 1948-49; Fulbright rsch. scholar and Ford Found. rsch. fellow Hitotsubashi U., Tokyo, 1953-54; Social Sci. rsch. Coun. fellow Carnegie Inst. Tech., 1957; life fellow Found. Keio U., 1961; Fulbright-Hays faculty rsch. scholar Japan, 1968, 73, 78, Singapore, 1968, 78, Australia, 1978; Fulbright-Hays faculty scholar N.Z., 1978; Japan Found. scholar, 1978; hon. Fulbright sr. scholar Australia, 1981. Mem. Indsl. Rels. Rsch. Assn., Am. Econ. Assn., Assn. for Asian Studies, Midwest Conf. of Asian Affairs (pres. 1961), Japan Soc., Internat. House of Japan, Internat. Indls. Rels. Assn., Japan Illini Club (hon. life), Wis. Alumni Assn. Japan (pres. 1990), Phi Beta Kappa, Beta Gamma Sigma. Home: 916 Van Buren St Madison WI 53711-2167

LEVINE, STUART GEORGE, editor, English literature educator, author; b. N.Y.C., May 25, 1932; s. Max and Jean (Berens) L.; m. Susan F. Matthews, June 6, 1962; children: Rebecca, Aaron, Allen. A.B., Harvard U., 1954; M.A., Brown U., 1956, Ph.D., 1958. Teaching fellow Brown U., 1956-57; instr. in English U. Kans., Lawrence, 1958-61; asst. prof. U. Kans., 1961-64, assoc. prof. Am. studies, 1964-66, prof., 1966—, founder, chmn. dept. Am. Studies, 1963-70, prof. English, 1976-92, Exxon intra-univ. vis. prof. dept. music history, 1981-82, prof. emeritus, 1992—; Fulbright disting. lectr., Naples chair U. Naples, Italy, 1994-95; Fulbright prof. U. La Plata (Argentina), 1962, U. Costa Rica, 1965, 67, Nat. Autonomous U. Mexico, 1973, several univs. in Chile, 1985; exch. professorship U. West Indies, 1988; scholar-in-residence U. Ariz., 1972-73; profl. concert musician, 1955-58, 73—, also artist; dir. NEH Summer Seminar for Coll. Tchrs., 1978; also cons. panels; vis. prof. various univs. Author: (with N.O. Lurie) The American Indian Today, 1968, Caffin's The Story of American Painting, 1970, Edgar Poe: Seer and Craftsman, 1972, (fiction) The Monday-Wednesday-Friday Girl and Other Stories (Gross-Woodley competition winner 1994); also author short stories pub. in various mags.; editor in chief Am. Studies, 1960-89, founding editor, 1989—; editor (with Susan F. Levine) The Short Fiction of Edgar Allan Poe: An Annotated Edition, 1976, 90; one-man shows include Regents Ctr. Gallery, Kansas City, 1983, Lawrence Arts Ctr., 1984; French horn player Lawrence Woodwind Quintet, Lawrence Symphony Orch., Lawrence Mcpl. Band, CottonWood Winds. Recipient Anisfield Wolf award (with others) Saturday Rev., 1968, citation NCCJ, 1969; grantee Kans. Com. for Humanities, 1982-83, 83-84. Mem. Am. Studies Assn. (exec. com. nat. meeting 1965-66, publs. com. nat. meeting 1965-66, Gabriel and Bode prize coms. 1983, chmn. both coms. 1984-85), Mid-Am. Am. Studies Assn. (exec. and editorial bds. 1960—), MLA, Am. Fedn. Musicians. Home: 1644 University Dr Lawrence KS 66044-3150 *Open exchange of great ideas and of decent people were as important as economic failure in toppling the Iron Curtain. We cannot yet know whether humane ideals and rational discourse can trump ancient fears and old hatreds. Looked to for leadership, our nation is uncertain of its course. I worry that at this critical time we allow deterioration in the quality of our ideas, perhaps even in our ability to reason. The dangerous irrationality of our contemporary political life may reflect failure to insist on highest standards early in our citizens' education-our poorest citizens' especially. Schoolteachers themselves clumsy of thought, ignorant of history and culture, frightened of science and mathematics, cannot train the bright creators of ideas which our country and the interlocked world need. Our best people, our best effort, should be engaged in doing better.*

LEVINE, SUMNER NORTON, industrial engineer, educator, editor, author, financial consultant; b. Boston, Sept. 5, 1923; s. Frank and Lillian (Gold) L.; m. Caroline Gassner, Nov. 27, 1952; 1 dau., Joanne. B.S., Brown U., 1946; Ph.D., U. Wis., 1949; postgrad., M.I.T., 1956. Instr. U. Chgo., 1949-50; sr. research fellow Columbia, 1950-54; dir. research labs. VA, East Orange, N.J., 1954-56; adv. scientist comml. atom power div. Westinghouse Electric Co., Pitts., 1956; dir. chemistry Metallurgy and Materials Labs.; also staff adv. engr. Gen. Engring. Labs., Am. Machine & Foundry Co., Greenwich, Conn., 1956-58; sect. head, materials and advanced electronic devices RCA, 1958-61; chmn. materials scis. dept., prof. engring., also prof., dir.

grad. program in indsl. adminstrn. SUNY, Stony Brook, 1961-91; dir. urban research, vis. prof. CUNY Grad. Center, 1967-68; Danforth vis. lectr., 1968-69; vis. prof. Yale Sch. Orgn. and Mgmt., 1976; prof. fin. Coll. Urban and Policy Scis., SUNY, Stony Brook, 1978—; cons. to industry; bd. dirs. Norteck Assocs.; editorial adviser Ocean Engring. Author textbooks, profl. articles; editor: Financial Analysts Handbook, 1975, 2d edit., 1987, Investment Manager's Handbook, Dow Jones-Irwin Bus.and Investment Almanac, 1976—, Acquisition Manual, 1990, Turnaround and Bankruptcy Investing, 1991, Handbook of Global Investing, 1992, Internat. Bus. and Investment Almanac, 1992—; editor-in-chief Jour. Biomed. Materials Rsch., 1966-78, Jour. Socio-Econ. Planning Scis., 1966, Advances in Biomed. Engring. and Med. Physics, 1966. Recipient award for distinguished contbn. to biomed. materials research, 1973. Mem. IEEE, World Conf. Planning Scis., Am. Chem. Soc., Am. Soc. Metals, Electrochem. Soc., Ops. Research Soc. Am., Inst. Mgmt. Scis., Fgn. Policy Assn., N.Y. Acad. Scis. (chmn. conf. materials in biomed. engring. 1966, chmn. colloquia socioecon. planning 1966-68), Soc. for Biomaterials (dir. 1974-76), N.Y. Soc. Security Analysts (chmn. edn. and seminar com., Vols. award 1984), Mus. Modern Art, Met. Mus. of Art, Princeton Club N.Y., Brown U. Club, Sigma Xi. Office: PO Box 2118 Setauket NY 11733-0883

LEVINE, SUSAN MICHELLE, social worker; b. Bklyn., July 29, 1963; d. Norman and Barbara Ellen (Fishman) L.; life ptnr. Karen J. Docherty, Dec. 14, 1993. BA in Psychology, SUNY, Stony Brook, 1986, MSW, 1990; MPA, Ga. State U., 1993. Lic. clin. social worker, Ga. Foster care worker Angel Guardian Home, Bklyn., 1986-87; child protective svcs. worker N.Y.C. Dept. Human Resources, 1987-88; cmty. asst. Chapin Apt. Complex, Stony Brook, 1989-90; sr. caseworker Fulton County Family and Children's Svcs., Atlanta, 1991-92; clin. social worker Ga. Mental Health Inst., Atlanta, 1992—; guest lectr. Ga. State U. Dept. Mental Health, 1994; clinician mobile crisis psychiat. assessment team Brawner Hosp., 1995, Charter Peachford, 1996. Disaster mental health counselor ARC, Atlanta, 1996. Mem. NASW (continued edn. com. 1991—, legis. com. 1992, panel mem. com. on inquiry Ga. chpt. 1995—, counselor for depression hotline 1992), Am. Soc. Pub. Adminstrs., Pi Alpha Alpha. Avocations: travel, hiking, bicycling, attending concerts and plays. Office: Ga Mental Health Inst 1256 Briarcliff Rd NE Atlanta GA 30306-2636

LEVINE, SUZANNE BRAUN, magazine editor; b. N.Y.C., June 21, 1941; d. Imre and Esther (Bernson) Braun; m. Robert F. Levine, Apr. 2, 1967; children: Joshua, Joanna. BA with honors, Radcliffe Coll., 1963. Reporter Seattle mag., 1963-65; reporter, researcher Time/Life Books, N.Y.C., 1965-67; features editor Mademoiselle, N.Y.C., 1967-68, McCalls mag., N.Y.C., 1968-69; free-lance writer, 1970; mng. editor Sexual Behavior mag., 1971-72, MS. mag., N.Y.C., 1972-88; editor Columbia Journalism Rev., N.Y.C., 1989-97; adj. prof. Columbia Grad. Sch. Journalism. Co-editor: The Decade of Women, A Ms History of the Seventies, 1980; exec. producer: Ms. HBO TV spl., 1981, She's Nobody's Baby, TV documentary, 1981 (Peabody award). Woodrow Wilson guest lectr. coord. Chautauqua Conf. on Families. Mem. Am. Soc. Mag. Editors (v.p.), Women's Media Group. Office: Columbia U Columbia Journalism Rev 700 Journalism Bldg New York NY 10027

LE VINE, VICTOR THEODORE, political science educator; b. Berlin, Dec. 6, 1928; came to U.S., 1938; s. Maurice and Hildegard (Hirschberg) LeV.; m. Nathalie Jeanne Christian, July 19, 1958; children: Theodore, Nicole. BA, UCLA, 1950, MA, 1958, PhD, 1961. Research assoc. UCLA, 1958-60; prof., head dept. polit. sci. U. Ghana, Legon, 1969-71; vis. prof. Hebrew U., Jerusalem, 1978, U. Tex., Austin, 1980; Fulbright prof. U. Yaounde, Cameroon, 1981-82; prof. polit. sci. Washington U., St. Louis, 1961—; cons. U.S. Dept. State, Dept. Def., 1971—; lectr. USIA, 1981—; mem. U.S. Nat. Cmemn. UNESCO, 1964; dir. Office Internat. Studies, Washington U., 1975-76; vis. lectr. Fudan U., U. Nanjing (China), 1987, Ibn Saud and King Abdulazziz Univs., Saudi Arabia, 1990; mem. Carter Ctr. Internat. monitoring team to Ghana nat. elections, 1992. Author: Cameroons: Mandate to Independence, 1964, 70, Cameroon Federal Republic, 1971, Political Corruption: Ghana, 1975, (with Timothy Luke) Arab-African Connection, 1979; (with Heidenheimer and Johnston) Political Corruption: A Handbook, 1990. Mem., dir. UN Assn., St. Louis, 1964-74; mem. Coun. on World Affairs, 1969—; pres. Ctr. for Internat. Understanding, 1988—. With U.S. Army, 1951-54. Ford. Found. fellow Cameroon, 1960-61; Hoover Instn. fellow, 1974; Lester Martin fellow Truman Instn., Jerusalem, 1978; Fulbright lectr. U.S. Fulbright Commn., Yaounde, Cameroon, 1981-82. Mem. Am. Polit. Sci. Assn., African Studies Assn., Mideast Studies Assn., Midwest Polit. Sci. Assn., Mo. Polit. Sci. Assn. Office: Washington U Dept Polit Sci Saint Louis MO 63130

LEVINE, WILLIAM SILVER, electrical engineering educator; b. Bklyn., Nov. 19, 1941; s. Louis Nathan and Gertrude (Silver) L.; m. Shirley Johannesen, Feb. 14, 1963; children: Bruce Jonathan, Eleanor Joan. BEE, MIT, 1962, MEE, 1965, PhD in Elec. Engring., 1969. Project engr. Data Tech. Inc., Cambridge, Mass., 1962-64; grad. asst. MIT, Cambridge, 1964-69; asst. prof. U. Md., College Park, 1969-73, assoc. prof., 1973-81, prof., 1981—; cons. IBM Fed. System Div., Gaithersburg, Md., 1972-75, Computational Engring. Inc., Laurel, Md., 1980-90. Co-author: Using MATLAB to Analyze and Design Control Systems, 1992, 2d edit., 1995; editor: The Control Handbook, 1996; contbr. articles to profl. jours. Recipiet numerous rsch. grants, 1969—. Fellow IEEE, IEEE Control Systems Soc. (pres. 1990, disting. mem. 1990); mem. IEEE Medicine and Biology Soc. (disting. lectr. 1991), Soc. for Indsl. and Applied Math. Office: U Md Dept Elect Engring College Park MD 20742

LEVINGER, JOSEPH SOLOMON, physicist, educator; b. N.Y.C., Nov. 14, 1921; s. Lee J. and Elma (Ehrlich) L.; m. Gloria Edwards, Aug. 14, 1943; children—Sam, Laurie, Louis, Joe. B.S., U. Chgo., 1941, M.S., 1944; Ph.D., Cornell U., 1948. Physicist Metall. Lab., U. Chgo., 1942-44, Franklin Inst., Phila., 1945; instr. Cornell U., 1948-51, vis. prof., 1961-64; from asst. prof. to prof. La. State U., 1951-61; prof. physics Rensselaer Poly. Inst., 1964-92, prof. emeritus, 1992—; Fulbright fellow, asso. prof. U. Paris—Sud, 1972-73. Author: Nuclear Photo-disintegration, 1961, Secrets of the Nucleus, 1967, The Two and Three Body Problem, 1974. Guggenheim fellow, 1957-58. Fellow Am. Phys. Soc. Home: Red Mill Rd Rensselaer NY 12144-3010 Office: Rensselaer Poly Inst Dept Physics Troy NY 12180

LEVINGS, THERESA LAWRENCE, lawyer; b. Kansas City, Mo., Oct. 24, 1952; d. William Youngs and Dorothy (Neer) Frick; m. Darryl Wayne Levings, May 25, 1974; children: Leslie Page, Kerry Dillon. BJ, U. Mo., 1973; JD, U. Mo., Kansas City, 1979. Bar: Mo. 1979, U.S. Dist. Ct. (we. dist.) Mo. 1979, U.S. Ct. Appeals (8th cir.) 1982, U.S. Ct. Appeals (10th cir.) 1986, U.S. Dist. Ct. (ea. dist.) Mo. 1989. Copy editor Kansas City Star, 1975-78; law clk. to judge Mo. Supreme Ct., Jefferson City, 1979-80; from assoc. to ptnr. Morrison & Hecker, Kansas City, 1980-94; founding ptnr. Badger & Levings, L.C., Kansas City, 1994—; mem. fed. practice com. U.S. Dist. Ct. (we. dist.), 1990-95; mem. fed. adv. com. U.S. Ct. Appeals (8th cir.), 1994—. Leadership grad. Kansas City Tomorrow; account exec. United Way; bd. dirs. Jr. League, Housing Info. Ctr. Recipient Outstanding Svc. award young lawyers coun. Mo. Bar, 1985, 86, Pres.' award, 1989. Mem. Mo. Bar (bd. govs. 1990—, young lawyers coun. 1982-89, chair 1988-89), Assn. Women Lawyers Greater Kansas City (pres. 1986-87, Woman of Yr. 1993), Lawyers Assn. Greater Kansas City (bd. dirs. young lawyers sect. 1982-83), Kansas City Met. Bar Assn. (chair civil practice and procedure com. 1988-89, chair fed. practice com. 1990-91). Avocations: antiques, history, cooking. Office: Badger & Levings LC 1101 Walnut St Kansas City MO 64106-2134

LEVINS, ILYSSA, public relations executive; b. New Hyde Park, N.Y., Dec. 3, 1958; d. Jack and Marlene (Newman) L. BA, NYU, 1980. Asst. account exec. Gross, Townsend, Frank, Hoffman, Inc., N.Y.C., 1982, account exec., 1983, sr. account exec., 1984, account supr., 1985, group account supr., 1986, v.p., dir. pub. rels., 1987-88, sr. v.p., dir. pub. rels., 1988-90, pres. pub. rels. divsn., 1990-94; mng. dir., 1994—. Mem. Pub. Rels. Soc. Am., Am. Soc. for Hosp. Mktg. and Pub. Rels., Women in Communications, Pharm. Advt. Coun., Food and Drug Law Inst., Am. Med. Writer's Assn., Am. Soc. for Health Care Mktg. and Pub. Rels. Jewish. Avocations: poetry, biking, swimming. Office: Gross Townsend Frank Hoffman Inc 114 5th Ave New York NY 10011-5604

LEVINS, JOHN RAYMOND, investment advisor, management consultant, educator; b. Jersey City, Aug. 4, 1944; s. Raymond Thomas and Catherine (Kelly) L. BS in Acctg., U. N.H., 1973; MBA, U. N.H., Plymouth, 1976. Registered investment advisor; cert. mgmt. cons., enrolled to practice IRS; cert. licensing instr., real estate and multiple lines ins. broker, comml. arbitration panelist; accredited tax advisor. Mgmt. risk analyst Express Treaty Mgmt. Corp., N.Y.C., 1962-67; asst. risk mgr. Bigelow-Sanford, Inc., N.Y.C., 1967-71; cons., broker BYSE, Inc., Laconia, N.Y., 1971-74; asst. prof. Nathaniel Hawthorne Coll., Antrim, N.H., 1975-82, Keene (N.H.) State Coll., 1982—; prin. Levins & Assocs., Concord, N.H., 1986—; investment advisor Reality Techs., Internat. Fin., Concord, 1991—; dir. Small Bus. Inst. Keene State Coll., 1982-86; exec. seminar leader Strategic Mgmt. Group, Inc., 1986—, Boston U., 1986—; gen. securities rep. H.D. Vest Fin. Svcs., 1990; mem. bd. advisors Am. Biog. Inst.; pvt. practice real estate, ins. cons., Concord, 1981; panelist securities arbitration Nat. Assn. Security Dealers, Am. Stock Exch.; consumer affair mediator Dept. Justice, Office of Atty. Gen., N.H.; mortgage banker; comml. financing broker; mem. SEC, spkr., seminar leader in field. Author: Finance and Accounting, 1979 (Excellence award 1980), Financial Analysis, 1981 (Excellence award 1980), Managing Cash Flow, 1988 (Excellence award 1988), Finance and Management, 1989. Incorporator Spaulding Youth Ctr., Tilton, N.H., 1990; colleague Found. for Acctg. Edn., assoc., profl. standing, 1988; mem. Nat. Consortium Edn. and Tng., Madison, Wis., 1989. With USN, 1969-71, S.E. Asia. Named Outstanding Support Leader U.S. Small Bus. Adminstrn., Concord, 1985, Outstanding Svc. Leader Community Leaders Am., N.H., 1990, One of Outstanding Young Men Am. U.S. Jaycees Bd. Adv.'s, 1983. Mem. AICPA (mem. Profl. Devel. Inst., sponsor trainer 1988-89), Investment Co. Inst. (assoc., nat. standing 1987), Inst. Mgmt. Cons. (assoc., nat. standing 1985), Nat. Soc. Pub. Accts. (del., profl. standing 1985), Nat. Soc. Non-Profit Orgns. (svc. provider 1989, colleague), Accreditation Coun. for Accountancy (fed. taxation accreditation 1987, colleague). Avocations: boating, teaching, community service, athletics. Home and Office: Levins & Associates PO Box 442 624 Alton Woods Dr Concord NH 03302-0442

LEVINS, RICHARD, science educator; b. N.Y.C., June 1, 1930; s. Ruben and Ruth (Sackman) L.; m. Rosario Morales, June 10, 1950; children: Aurora, Ricardo, Alejandro. A.B., Cornell U., 1951; Ph.D., Columbia U., 1965. Farmer, P.R., 1951-56; research assoc. U. Rochester, N.Y., 1960-61; assoc. prof. biology U. P.R., 1961-66; assoc. prof. biology and math. biology U. Chgo., 1967-68, prof., 1969-75; John Rock prof. population sci. Harvard Sch. Pub. Health, 1975—; mem. sci. adv. council natural resources P.R. Dept. Pub. Works, 1970-72; mem. adv. bd. N.Y. Marxist Sch. Author: Evolution in Changing Environments, 1968; co-author: (with R.C. Lewontin) The Dialectical Biologist, (with C. Puccia) Qualitative Modeling of Complex Systems, (with Yrjo Haila) Humanity and Nature, 1992; editorial bd.: La Escalera, 1965-72, Am. Naturalist, 1968-71, Theoretical Population Biology, 1970—. Coffee region organizer P.R. Communist Party, 1952-54; mem. Partido Socialista Puertorriqueño; bd. dirs. Concilio Hispano, 1986-94, Oxfam Am., 1988-95, Grassroots Internat., 1996—. Recipient Arthur Felberbaum award Brecht Forum, 1995; Edinburgh medal The Wider Soc., 1996, Award Inst. of Fundamental Rsch. in Tropical Agrl., 1996. Mem. Am. Acad. Arts and Sci., New World Agr. and Ecol. Group, Sci. for Vietnam, N.E. Organic Farmers Assn., Cuban Botanical Assn. (corr. mem.). Home: 107 Amory St Cambridge MA 02139-1229 *Understand the world in order to change it, and in changing it get to understand it better.*

LEVINSKY, NORMAN GEORGE, physician, educator; b. Boston, Apr. 27, 1929; s. Harry and Gertrude (Kipperman) L.; m. Elena Sartori, June 17, 1956; children—Harold, Andrew, Nancy. A.B. summa cum laude, Harvard U., 1950, M.D. cum laude, 1954. Diplomate Am. Bd. Internal Medicine. Intern Beth Israel Hosp., Boston, 1954-55; resident Beth Israel Hosp., 1955-56; commd. med. officer USPHS., 1956; clin. assoc. Nat. Heart Inst., Bethesda, Md., 1956-58; NIH fellow Boston U. Med. Center, 1958-60; practice medicine, specializing in internal medicine and nephrology Boston, 1960—; chief of medicine Boston City Hosp., 1968-72, 93-97; physician-in-chief, dir. Boston U. Med. Ctr. Hosp., Boston, 1972-97; asst. prof., then assoc. prof. medicine Boston U., 1960-68, Wesselhoeft prof., 1968-72, Wade prof. medicine, 1972-97, chmn. dept. medicine, 1972-97, prof. medicine, assoc. provost, 1997—; mem. drug efficacy panel NRC; mem. nephrology test com.-Am. Bd. Internal Medicine, 1971-76: mem. gen. medicine B rev. group NIH; mem. comprehensive test com. Nat. Bd. Med. Examiners, 1986-89; chmn. com. to study end-stage renal disease program Nat. Acad. Scis./Inst. Medicine, 1988-90, chmn. com. on Xenografts, 1995. Editor (with R.W. Wilkins) Medicine: Essentials of Clinical Practice, 3d edit., 1983, (with R. Rettig) Kidney Disease and the Federal Government, 1991; contbr. chpts. to books, sci. articles to med. jours. Recipient Distinguished Teacher awd., Am. Coll. of Physicians, 1992. Master ACP; mem. AAAS, Am. Fedn. Clin. Rsch., Am. Soc. Clin. Investigation, Am. Heart Assn., Assn. Am. Physicians, Am. Physiol. Soc., Assn. Profs. Medicine (sec., treas. 1984-87, pres.-elect 1987-88, pres. 1988-89), Am. Soc. Nephrology, Inst. Medicine NAS, Interurban Clin. Club (pres. 1985-86), Phi Beta Kappa, Alpha Omega Alpha. Home: 20 Kenwood Ave Newton MA 02159-1439 Office: Boston U Med Ctr 75 E Newton St Boston MA 02118-2340

LEVINSON, ARNOLD IRVING, allergist, immunologist; b. Balt., 1944. MD, U. Md. Sch. Medicine, 1969. Diplomate Am. Bd. Internal Medicine, Am. Bd. Allergy and Immunology. Intern Balt. City Hosps., 1969-70, resident internal medicine, 1970-71; fellow U. Pa., Phila., 1971-73, 73-75, prof. medicine and neurology, 1987—; fellow U. Calif., San Francisco, 1972-73. Mem. AAAAI, AAI, AFCR, AFEB, ASCI, CIS, Brit. Soc. Immunology. Office: U Pa Hospital 3400 Spruce St Philadelphia PA 19104

LEVINSON, ARTHUR DAVID, molecular biologist; b. Seattle, Mar. 31, 1950; s. Sol and Malvina (Lindsay) L.; m. Rita May Liff, Dec. 17, 1978; children: Jesse, Anya. BS, U. Wash., 1972; PhD, Princeton U., 1977. Postdoctoral fellow U. Calif., San Francisco, 1977-80; sr. scientist Genentech, South San Francisco, 1980-84, staff scientist, 1984—, dir. cell genetics dept., 1988-89, v.p. rsch., 1990-93, sr. v.p. rcsh. and devel., 1993-95; pres., CEO Genentech, Co., 1995—. Mem. editorial bd. Virology, 1984-87, Molecular Biology and Medicine, 1986-90, Molecular and Cellular Biology, 1987—, Jour. of Virology, 1988-91. Mem. Am. Soc. Microbiology, Am. Soc. Biochemistry and Molecular Biology. Office: Genentech Inc 460 Point San Bruno Blvd South San Francisco CA 94080-4918

LEVINSON, BARRY L., film director; b. Balt., Apr. 6, 1942. Ed., Am. U., Washington. film writer, actor: Silent Movie, 1976, High Anxiety, 1978; writer: ...And Justice for All, 1979, Inside Moves, 1980, Best Friends, 1982, Unfaithfully Yours, 1984; dir.: The Natural, 1984, Young Sherlock Holmes, 1985, Good Morning Vietnam, 1987, Rain Man, 1988 (Academy award 1989, Dirs. Guild Am. award 1989); screenwriter, dir.: Diner, 1982, Tin Men, 1987, Avalon, 1990 (Writers Guild Am. award 1990); co-prodr., dir. Bugsy, 1991, Disclosure, 1994; co-writer, dir., prodr. Toys, 1992; writer, dir., prodr. Jimmy Hollywood, 1994 (also actor), Sleepers, 1996; actor: Quiz Show, 1994; dir., exec. prodr. (TV) Homicide: Life on the Street, 1993 (Emmy award, Outstanding Individual Achievement in Directing in a Drama Series, 1993, Peabody award 1993); prodr. Donnie Brasco. Mem. Dirs. Guild Am., Writers Guild Am. Address: c/o Baltimore Pictures Bldg 81-200 4000 Warner Blvd Burbank CA 91522

LEVINSON, DANIEL RONALD, lawyer; b. Bklyn., Mar. 24, 1949; s. Gerald Sam and Risha Rose (Waxer) L.; m. Luna Frances Lambert, Sept. 13, 1980; children: Luna Claire, Hannah Louise. AB, U. So. Calif., 1971; JD, Georgetown U., 1974; LLM, George Washington U., 1977. Bar: N.Y. 1975, Calif. 1976, D.C. 1976, U.S. Supreme Ct. 1978. Law clk. appellate divsn. N.Y. Supreme Ct., Bklyn., 1974-76; assoc. McGuiness & Williams, Washington, 1977-81, ptnr., 1982-83; dep. gen. counsel U.S. Office Personnel Mgmt., Washington, 1983-85; gen. counsel U.S. Consumer Product Safety Commn., Washington, 1985-86; chmn. U.S. Merit Sys. Protection Bd., Washington, 1986-93; of counsel Shaw Bransford & O'Rourke, Washington, 1993-94; chief of staff U.S. Rep. from Ga. Bob Barr, Washington, 1995—; adj. lectr. Am. U., Washington, 1981-82, Cath. U. Am., Washington, 1982. Notes and comments editor Am. Criminal Law Rev., 1973-74; contbr. articles to profl. jours. Bd. dirs. Washington Hebrew Congregation, 1993-96; prin. Coun. for Excellence in Govt., 1993-94. Mem. ABA, Adminstrv. Conf. U.S. (govt. mem. 1984-93), Phi Beta Kappa. Republican. Home: 3529 Woodbine St Chevy Chase MD 20815-4047 Office: 1130 Longworth Ho Offc Bldg Washington DC 20515

LEVINSON, HARRY, psychologist, educator; b. Port Jervis, N.Y., Jan. 16, 1922; s. David and Gussie (Nudell) L.; m. Roberta Freiman, Jan. 11, 1946 (div. June 1972); children—Marc Richard, Kathy, Anne, Brian Thomas; m. Miriam Lewis, Nov. 23, 1990. BS, Emporia (Kans.) State U., 1943, MS, 1946; PhD, U. Kans., 1952. Coordinator profl. edn. Topeka State Hosp., 1950-53, psychologist, 1954-55; dir. div. indsl. mental health Menninger Found., Topeka, 1955-68; visiting prof. MIT, 1961-62, U. Kans. Bus. Sch., 1967, Texas A&M U., 1976; Thomas Henry Carroll-Ford Found. distinguished vis. prof. Harvard Grad. Sch. Bus., Boston, 1968-72; adj. prof. Coll. Bus. Adminstrn., Boston U., 1972-74; lectr. Harvard Med. Sch., 1972-85; adj. prof. Pace U., 1972-83; clin. prof. psychology Harvard Med. Sch., 1985-92, emeritus prof., 1992—; head sect. orgnl. mental health Mass. Mental Health Ctr., 1983-92; pres. The Levinson Inst., 1968-91, chmn. bd., 1991—; mem. Am. Bd. Profl. Psychology, 1972-80, chmn., 1978-80; Ford Found. prof. Mathur Inst., Jaipur India, 1974; conducted internat. course on social psychiatry Finnish Govt. Inst., 1979. Author: Emotional Health In the World of Work, 1964, Executive Stress, 1970, The Exceptional Executive (McKinsey Found. and Acad. Mgmt. awards), 1968 (James A. Hamilton Hosp. Adminstrs. Book award), Organizational Diagnosis, 1971, The Great Jackass Fallacy, 1973, Psychological Man, 1976, Casebook for Psychological Man; (with S. Rosenthal) CEO: Corporate Leadership in Action (Am. Coll. Health Care Adminstrs. Book award 1986), 1984, Ready, Fire, Aim, 1986, Designing and Managing Your Career, 1989, Career Mastery, 1992. Chmn. Kans. adv. com. U.S. Civil Rights Commn., 1962-68; chmn. Topeka Human Relations Commn., 1967-68. Served with F.A. AUS, 1944-46. Recipient Perry Rohrer Cons. Psychology Practice award, 1984, Career award Mass. Psychol. Assn., 1985, First award Soc. Psychologists in Mgmt.; Eminent scholar in bus. Fla. Atlantic U., 1995. Fellow APA (award for disting. profl. contbn. to knowledge 1992); mem. AAAS, Acad. Mgmt., Authors Guild. Home: 225 Brattle St Cambridge MA 02138-4623

LEVINSON, HERBERT SHERMAN, civil and transportation engineer; b. Chgo., Sept. 25, 1924; s. Israel and Tillie (Gash) L.; m. Sally Farver, July 3, 1977. BSCE, Ill. Inst. Tech., 1949; cert. in hwy. traffic, Yale U., 1952. Jr. traffic engr. Chgo. Park Dist., 1949-51; from assoc. to sr. v.p. Wilbur Smith & Assocs., New Haven, 1952-80; prin. Herbert S. Levinson Transp. Cons., New Haven, 1980—; prof. civil engring. U. Conn., Storrs, 1980-86; prof. transp. Poly. Inst. of N.Y., N.Y.C., 1986-88, rsch. prof., 1988—; vis. lectr. Yale U., New Haven, 1961-80; transp. cons. Author: Transportation and Parking for Tomorrow's Cities, 1966, (with D. Votaw) Elementary Sampling for Traffic Engrs., 1961, (with R. Weant) Urban Transportation Perspectives and Prospects, 1983, Parking, 1990; contbr. numerous articles to profl. jours. Served as cpl. USAF, 1943-46. Recipient Presdl. Design award Nat. Endowment for the Arts, 1988. Fellow ASCE (Benjamin Wright award 1993), Inst. Transp. Engrs. (Transp. Engr. of Yr. 1976, Tech. Coun. award 1982, Theodore M. Matson award 1997); mem. NAE, Transp. Rsch. Bd., Am. Planning Assn., Conn. Acad. Sci. and Engring.

LEVINSON, JOHN MILTON, obstetrician, gynecologist; b. Atlantic City, Aug. 17, 1927; m. Elizabeth Carl Bell; children: Patricia Anne, John Carl, Mark Jay. BA, Lafayette Coll., Easton, Pa., 1949; MD, Thomas Jefferson U., 1953. Diplomate Am. Bd. Ob-Gyn. Intern Atlantic City Hosp., 1953-54; Am. Cancer Soc. clin. fellow Jefferson Med. Coll. Hosp., Phila., 1954-55; resident in ob-gyn. Del. Hosp., Wilmington, 1955-57; pvt. practice ob-gyn. Wilmington, 1957-85; prof. dept. ob-gyn. Jefferson Med. Coll., Thomas Jefferson U., Phila., hon. clin. prof., 1990—; sr. attending physician emeritus Med. Ctr. Del., Wilmington, 1986—; attending chief dept. ob-gyn. St. Francis Hosp., Wilmington, chief emeritus, 1986-92; founder, pres. Aid for Internat. Medicine, Inc., 1966—; med. dir., chief surgeon Quark Expeditions, 1991-95; cons. Riverside Hosp., 1972-86, Wilmington Pa. Blue Shield, 1982—: cons. gynecology U.S. VA, 1974-85; founding mem., treas., bd. dirs. Physicians Health Svcs., Del., Ltd., 1985-87; vis. prof., cons., ship's surgeons, practicing physician various orgns. in Africa, Antarctica, Arctic regions, Ctrl. Am., Europe, S.E. Asia,, S.W. Asia, 1963—; lectr. in field; internat. med. cons. to Sen. Edward M. Kennedy, 1967—; chmn. Antarctic expdns. study group to advise NSF, 1992-93; co-chmn. Com. for Safety in Arctic and Antarctic Frontier Expeditions, 1992-93. Author: Shorebirds: The Birds, the Hunters, the Decoys, 1991; contbr. articles to profl. jours., book chpts. Bd. dirs. Del. com. Project H.O.P.E., 1965-75, ARC, 1968-70, Charles A. Lindbergh Fund, Inc., 1985-90; trustee Blue Cross/ Blue Shield Del., Inc., 1968-86, Brandywine Coll., 1972-77; bd. dirs. Nat. Assn. Blue Shield Plans, 1971-77; mem adv. com. Trinity Alcohol and Drug Program, 1978-85; mem. Del. Gov.'s Commn. on Health Care Cost Mgmt., 1985-87; bd. dirs. founding mem. World Affairs Coun. Wilmington Inc, v.p., 1981-86; pres. Rockland Mills Cmty. Assn., 1992-94. With USN, 1945-47; col. M.C., USAFR, 1984-87. Recipient Brandywine award Brandywine Coll., 1968, cert. of appreciation for med. svcs. Ministry of Health, Republic of Vietnam, 1963-66, commendation Pres. of U.S., 1971, The Eisenhower award People to People Internat., 1986, Commemorative medal Charles A. Lindbergh Fund, 1987, Phila. Explorers award 1987, Citation for Outstanding Contbn. to People of Del., Med. Soc. Del., 1992. Fellow Am. Assn. Ob.-Gyns., Royal Geog. Soc. London; mem. AMA, Am. Assn. Gyn. Laporoscopists (founding, bd. dirs.), Del. Obstetric Soc. (pres. 1980-82), Phila. Obstetric Soc., Med. Soc. Del. (Citation of Merit award 1992), New Castle County Med. Soc., Soc. Ob-Gyn. Vietnam (hon.), Ducks Unltd. (sponsor, mem. Del. com. 1980-92), Explorers Club (fellow 1966—, chmn. Phila. chpt. 1983-85, bd. dirs. 1981-88, pres. N.Y.C. 1985-87), Univ. and Whist Club Wilmington (life, bd. govs. 1961-64), Rotary (bd. dirs. local club 1991-93), Theta Chi (pres. 1945) Phi Beta Pi (pres. 1952), Kappa Beta Phi (pres. 1952). Avocations: hunting, polar history, sailing, collecting, bird decoys. Home: 55 Millstone Ln Rockland DE 19732

LEVINSON, LAWRENCE EDWARD, lawyer, corporation executive; b. N.Y.C., Aug. 25, 1930; s. Samuel Keever and Sara Lee (Tarvin) L.; m. Margaret Anne Bishop, Aug. 20, 1989; children: Elizabeth, Suzanne, Lucia. BA magna cum laude, Syracuse U., 1952; LLB, Harvard U., 1955. Bar: N.Y. 1957, U.S. Supreme Ct. 1958. Atty. Office Sec. Air Force, Washington, 1957-63; spl. assignments Office Sec. Def., Washington, 1963-65; dep. counsel to Pres. U.S., Washington, 1965-69; sr. v.p. Paramount Communications, Inc., N.Y.C., 1969-94; sr. Washington counsel VIACOM Internat., 1994-95; ptnr. Verner, Liipfert, Bernhard, McPherson and Hand, Washington, 1995—; mem. Nat. Council on Health Planning and Devel., Washington, 1978-84; host pub. affairs TV program Capital Notebook, 1991—. Mem. bd. visitors Syracuse U. Coll. Arts and Scis., 1981—. Served with Judge Adv. div. U.S. Army, 1955-57. Mem. Assn. Am. Pubs. (bd. dirs. 1989-95), Army-Navy Country Club (Washington). Home: 5715 Little Falls Rd Arlington VA 22207-1554

LEVINSON, L(ESLIE) HAROLD, lawyer, educator; b. Bournemouth, Eng., Oct. 17, 1929; s. Abraham and Ada (Bloomberg) L.; m. Joan Gluck, Mar. 28, 1965; children: Andrea, Lara. BBA, 1957; LLB, U. Miami, 1962; LLM, NYU, 1964; JSD, Columbia U., 1974. Bar: Fla. 1962, N.Y. 1964; CPA. Ptnr. acctg. firm Miami, Fla., 1958-62; instr. acctg. NYU, 1962-64; lectr. on devel. financing UN, N.Y.C. and Geneva, summers 1963-65; asst. to legal dir. ACLU, N.Y.C., summers 1964-65; asst. prof. U. Fla., 1966-67, assoc. prof., 1967-70, prof., 1970-73; vis. prof. Vanderbilt U. Sch. Law, Nashville, 1973-74, prof., 1974—; mem. Fla. Law Rev. Coun., 1972-74; cons. Adminstrv. Conf. U.S. 1976-86; reporter 1981 Revision Model State Adminstrv. Proc. Act., Nat. Conf. Commrs. Uniform State Laws, 1978-81; vis. prof. NYU Sch. Law, 1994. Mem. ABA, Am. Law Inst., Am. Inst. CPA's. Office: Vanderbilt U Sch Law 21st Ave S Nashville TN 37240

LEVINSON, PETER JOSEPH, lawyer; b. Washington, June 11, 1943; s. Bernard Hirsh and Carlyn Virginia (Krupp) L.; m. Nanette Susan Segal, Mar. 30, 1968; children: Sharman Risa, Justin David. AB in History cum laude, Brandeis U., Waltham, Mass., 1965; JD, Harvard U., 1968. Bar: Hawaii 1971, U.S. Supreme Ct. 1975. Summer supr. Harvard Legal Aid Bur., Cambridge, Mass., 1968; research asst. Harvard Law Sch., 1968-69; teaching fellow Osgoode Hall Law Sch., York U. (Can.), 1969-70, research assoc., 1969-70, asst. prof., 1970-71; dep. atty. gen. State of Hawaii, 1971-75; vis. fellow Harvard U., 1976-77; ptnr. Levinson and Levinson, Honolulu, 1977-79; spl. asst. to dir. Office Program Support, Legal Services Corp., Washington, 1979; cons. Select Commn. on Immigration and Refugee Policy,

Washington, 1980-81; minority counsel subcom. on immigration, refugees and internat. law com. on judiciary, U.S. Ho. of Reps., Washington, 1981-85, minority counsel subcom. monopolies and comml. law, 1985-89, minority counsel subcom. econ. and comml. law, 1989-95, counsel com. on judiciary, 1995—. Trustee, Hawaii Jewish Welfare Fund, 1972-75, chmn. fund drive, 1972; trustee Temple Emanu-El, Honolulu, 1973-75; mem. alumni admissions council Brandeis U., 1978-82. Recipient award of merit United Jewish Appeal, 1974. Mem. Hawaii State Bar Assn. (chmn. standing com. on continuing legal edn. 1972, chmn. standing com. on jud. adminstrn. 1979), ABA, Am. Judicature Soc. Contbr. articles to profl. jours. Office: B353 Rayburn House Office Bldg Washington DC 20515

LEVINSON, ROBERT ALAN, textile company executive; b. Balt., July 26, 1925; s. Louis and Frieda (Kellert) L.; m. Patricia S. Schulte, Apr. 23, 1954; children: Margot, Andrew, John. AB, Dartmouth Coll., 1946, MBA, 1946; postgrad., London Sch. Econs., 1946-47. With Burlington Industries, N.Y.C., 1949-51; v.p., dir. Bangor Punta, Inc., N.Y.C., 1964-68; chmn. bd. Duplan Corp., N.Y.C., 1968-79; chmn. Andrex Industries Corp., N.Y.C.; cons. Dillon Yarn Corp.; chmn., pres. Levcor Internat.; dir., chmn., mem. exec. com. Belding Heminway Corp. Trustee Bklyn. Mus., chmn., 1972-84; chmn. Harlem Sch. of Arts, Nat. Dance Inst.; bd. dirs., exec. com., vice chmn. Nat. Commn. on U.S.-China Relations. With USNR, 1943-45, 52-54. Home: 1035 5th Ave New York NY 10028-0135 Office: 1071 6th Ave New York NY 10018-3704

LEVINSON, SHAUNA T., financial services executive; b. Denver, Aug. 1, 1954; d. Charles and Geraldine D. Titus; m. Kenneth L. Levinson, Dec. 21, 1986. BA cum laude, U. Puget Sound, 1976; M Bank Mktg. with honors, U. Colo., 1986. Cert. fin. planner. Fin. planning analyst Swift and Co., Chgo., 1977-79; from credit analyst to asst. v.p. Ctrl. Bank of Denver, 1979-84; v.p. fin. svcs. First Nat. Bank S.E. Denver, 1984-94; dir. mktg. First Nat. Banks, 1991-94; pres., CEO Fin. Directions, Inc., Denver, 1994—; mem. bankers edn. com. Colo. Bankers Assn., Denver, 1992-94. Contbr. articles to profl. jours. Chmn. human resources com., mem. adminstrv. coun. Jr. League of Denver, 1983—; mem. cmty. assistance fund, placement adv. com.; fundraiser Women's Libr. Assn. U. Denver, 1990-94, 96—, Good Shepherd Cath. Sch., 1986-95, Jewish Cmty. Ctr., Denver, 1990-95, St. Mary's Acad., 1995—, Theodore Herzl Day Sch., 1996—. Recipient Gold Peak award Am. Bankers Assn.-Bank Mktg. Assn., 1987; named Businessperson of Week Denver Bus. Jour., 1995. Mem. AAUW, Am. Inst. Banking, Jr. League Denver, U. Denver Pioneer Hockey Club, Kappa Alpha Theta (Chgo. NW alumnae 1977-79, program chair 1979), Phi Kappa Phi. Office: 1624 Market St Ste 475 Denver CO 80202-1518

LEVINSON, STEPHEN ELIOT, electrical engineer; b. N.Y.C., Sept. 27, 1944; s. Benjamin Adler and Doris Ruth (Goldstein) L.; m. Diana Elaine Sheets, June 6, 1976. AB, Harvard U., 1966; MS, U. R.I., 1972, PhD, 1974. J.W. Gibbs instr. Yale U., New Haven, 1974-76; Disting. mem. tech. staff Bell Labs., Murray Hill, N.J., 1976—, head linguistics rsch. dept., 1990—; vis. researcher NTT Labs., Tokyo, 1979; vis. fellow Cambridge U., U.K., 1984. Editor Computer Speech and Language jour., 1986—; patentee in speech recognition field. Fellow IEEE, Acoustical Soc. Am.; mem. AAAS, Assn. for Computing Machinery, N.Y. Acad. Sci., Sigma Xi (rsch. award U. R.I. chpt. 1973). Avocations: violin, sailing, skiing.

LEVINSON, STEVEN HENRY, judge; b. Cin., June 8, 1946. BA with distinction, Stanford U., 1968; JD, U. Mich., 1971. Bar: Hawaii 1972, U.S. Dist. Ct. Hawaii 1972, U.S. Ct. Appeals (9th cir.) 1972. Law clk. to Hon. Bernard H. Levinson Hawaii Supreme Ct., 1971-72; pvt. practice Honolulu, 1972-89; judge Hawaii Cir. Ct. (1st cir.), 1989-92; assoc. justice Hawaii Supreme Ct., Honolulu, 1992—. Staff mem. U. Mich. Jour. Law Reform, 1970-71. Active Temple Emanu-El. Mem. ABA (jud. adminstrn. divsn. 1989—), Hawaii State Bar Assn. (dir. young lawyers divsn. 1975-76, dir. 1982-84), Nat. Jud. Coll. (state jud. leader 1991—). Jewish. Address: Ali'iolani Hale 417 S King St Honolulu HI 96813

LEVINSON, WARREN MITCHELL, broadcast journalist; b. Bklyn., Feb. 23, 1953; s. Abraham and Roslyn Anne (Bell) L.; m. Debra Lynn Galant, Sept. 1, 1985; children: Margot, Noah. BA, Duke U., 1975. Reporter Sta. WCHL Radio, Chapel Hill, N.C., 1974-77; news dir. Sta. WBLG/WKQQ Radio, Lexington, Ky., 1977-78; newswriter AP, N.Y.C., 1979-82; corr. AP Radio, N.Y.C., 1982—. Co-host (radio talk program) Newsweek on Air, 1985—. Recipient Silver medal for News Mag. Internat. Radio T.V. Soc., 1989. Avocations: bicycling, poetry. Office: Associated Press 50 Rockefeller Plz New York NY 10020-1605

LEVINTHAL, ELLIOTT CHARLES, physicist, educator; b. Bklyn., Apr. 13, 1922; s. Fred and Rose (Raiben) L.; m. Rhoda Arons, June 4, 1944; children—David, Judith, Michael, Daniel. B.A., Columbia Coll., 1942; M.S., Mass. Inst. Tech., 1943; Ph.D., Stanford U., 1949. Project engr. Sperry Gyroscope Co., N.Y.C., 1943-46; research assoc. nuclear physics Stanford (Calif.) U., 1946-48, sr. scientist dept. genetics Sch. Medicine, 1961-74, dir. Instrumentation Research Lab., 1961-80, assoc. dean for research affairs, 1970-73, adj. prof. genetics Sch. Medicine, 1974-80, research prof. mech. engring., dir. Inst. Mfg. and Automation Sch. Engring., 1983-90, assoc. dean for research Sch. Engring., 1986-90, assoc. dean spl. programs, 1990-91, prof. emeritus, 1991—; research physicist Varian Assocs., Palo Alto, Calif., 1949-50, dir. research, 1950-52; chief engr. Century Electronics, Palo Alto, 1952-53; pres. Levinthal Electronics, Palo Alto, 1953-61; dir. def. scis. office Def. Advanced Projects Agy., Dept. Def., Arlington, Va., 1980-83; mem. NASA Adv. Coun., 1980-84, space studies bd., NRC, 1989-91, mem. human exploration, 1991-92, army sci. bd., 1989-91; cons. HEW. Recipient NASA Public Service medal, 1977. Mem. AAAS, IEEE, Am. Phys. Soc., Optical Soc. Am., Biomed. Engring. Soc., Sigma Xi. Democrat. Jewish. Home: 59 Sutherland Dr Atherton CA 94027-6430 Office: Stanford U Sch of Engring 530 Duena St Rm 104 Stanford CA 94305-3030

LEVINTON, JEFFREY S., biology educator, oceanographer; b. N.Y.C., Mar. 20, 1946; s. Nathan and Lillian (Moshman) L.; m. Joan Miyeko Miyazaki, Mar. 30, 1979; children: Nathan Toshi, Andrew Koji. BS, CCNY, 1966; M in Philosophy, Yale U., 1969, PhD, 1971. Asst. prof. biology SUNY, Stony Brook, 1970-75, assoc. prof., 1975-83, prof., 1983—, head dept., 1984-90, 91-93; vis. prof. U. Arhus, Denmark, 1966-67, Uppsala (Sweden) U., 1981, U. Cambridge, England, 1983; chmn. panel Hudson River Found, 1986-90. Author: Marine Ecology, 1982, Genetics, Paleontology, and Macroevolution, 1988, Marine Biology, 1995; reviewer, contbr. over 100 articles to profl. jours. Mem. Environ. Policy Com. Conn., 1969. NSF fellow, 1969, Sterling hon. fellow, 1969, John Simon Guggenheim fellow, 1983. Mem. Ecol. Soc. Am. (editor 1986-93), Am. Soc. Naturalists (editor 1974-79). Democrat. Office: SUNY Dept Ecology & Evolution Stony Brook NY 11794-5245

LEVIS, ALEXANDER HENRY, systems engineer, educator, consultant; b. Yannina, Greece, Oct. 3, 1940; came to U.S., 1959; s. Henry N. and Jeannette (Matathia) L.; m. Ilze E. Sedriks, Mar. 26, 1970 (dec. 1994); children: Livia, Philip. AB, Ripon Coll., 1963; BS, MIT, 1965, MS, 1965, ME, 1967, ScD, 1968. Asst. prof. Poly. Inst. Bklyn., 1968-73, assoc. prof., 1973-74; mgr. systems rsch. dept. Systems Control, Inc., Palo Alto, Calif., 1973-79; sr. rsch. scientist MIT, Cambridge, 1979-90, prof., 1996—; prof. George Mason U., 1990-96, chair, systems engring. dept., 1992-94, 96—. Assoc. editor IEEE Transactions on Automatic Control, 1975-77, Automatica Jour., 1980-85. Editor five books; contbr. articles to sci. jours. Recipient Exceptional Civilian Svc. Medal Air Force, 1994, Disting. Svc. Edn. award AFCEA, 1996. Fellow IEEE Control Systems Soc. (v.p. 1984-85, pres.-elect 1986, pres. 1987, Disting. Mem. award 1987), AAAS; mem. AIAA (sr.), Air Force Sci. Adv. Bd., 1990-94. Home: 10607 Springvale Ct Great Falls VA 22066-1740 Office: George Mason U C3I Ctr Fairfax VA 22030

LEVIS, DONALD JAMES, psychologist, educator; b. Cleve., Sept. 19, 1936; s. William and Antoinette (Stejskal) L.; children: Brian, Katie. Ph.D., Emory U., 1964. Postdoctoral fellow clin. psychology Lafayette Clinic, Detroit, 1964-65; asst. prof. psychology U. Iowa, Iowa City, 1966-70, assoc. prof., dir. research and tng. clinic, 1970-72; prof. SUNY-Binghamton, 1972—. Author: Learning Approaches to Therapeutic Behavior Modification, 1970, Implosive Therapy, 1973; cons. editor: Jour. Abnormal Psychology, 1974-80, Jour. Exptl. Psychology, 1976-77, Behavior Moedifications, 1977-81, Behavior Therapy, 1974-76, Clin. Behavior Therapy Rev., 1978—; contbr. articles to profl. jours. Served to capt. AUSR, 1958-66. Fellow Behavior and Therapy Research Soc. (charter, clin.), Am. Psychol. Assn.; mem. Assn. Advancement Behavior Therapy (publ. bd. 1979-82), AAAS, Psychonomic Soc., N.Y. State Psychol. Assn., Sigma Xi. Home: 48 Riverside Dr Binghamton NY 13905-4402 Office: SUNY at Binghamton Dept Psychology Binghamton NY 13901

LEVIS, RICHARD GEORGE, middle school educator; b. Kenosha, Wis., Nov. 20, 1946; s. Elso R. and Valentina (Maraccini) L.; m. Diane Rose Christie, June 12, 1971; 1 child, Maureen R. BS, U. Wis., 1968, MS, 1973. Tchr. social studies Parker Jr. High Sch., Janesville, Wis., 1969, Washington Jr. High Sch., Kenosha, 1969—; mem. com. on vandalism and mid. schs. Kenosha Unified Schs.; jr. h.s. rep. Kenosha Ednl. Found., 1994. Co-author: (with James Hansen) United Nations Resource Materials and Bibliographies, 1974. V.p. Kenosha Tchrs. Union, 1971-73; exec. bd. Kenosha Dem. Party, 1969-86; mem. canvass bd., Kenosha; rep. United Fund, 1985—. Mem. NEA, Nat. Coun. Social Studies, Wis. Social Studies Coun., Wis. Edn. Assn., Kenosha Edn. Assn. (bd. dirs. 1975-77), Phi Delta Kappa. Democrat. Catholic. Avocations: golf, reading, watching sports, politics, travel. Home: 3520 14th Pl Kenosha WI 53144-2939 Office: Washington Jr H S 811 Washington Rd Kenosha WI 53140-2846

LEVI-SETTI, RICCARDO, physicist, director; b. Milan, July 11, 1927; married, 1959; 2 children. Doctor Degree in Physics, U. Pavia, Italy, 1949; Libera Docenza in Physics, U. Rome, 1955. Asst. prof. U. Pavia, Italy, 1949-51; rsch. mem. Nat. Inst. for Nuclear Rsch. U. Milan, 1951-56; rsch. assoc. Enrico Fermi Inst. U. Chgo., 1956-57, asst. prof., 1957-62, assoc. prof., 1962-65, prof. physics, 1965—, dir. Enrico Fermi Inst., 1992—; Guggenheim fellow CERN, Geneva, 1963; hon. rsch. assoc. Field Mus. Natural History, Chgo., 1976—. Decorated Commendatore dell'Ordine al Merito (Italy); John Simon Guggenheim fellow, 1963, Angelo della Riccia fellow Italian Phys. Soc., 1954. Fellow Am. Phys. Soc.; mem. Phi Beta Kappa. Office: U Chgo Enrico Fermi Inst 5640 S Ellis Ave Chicago IL 60637-1433

LEVIT, EDITHE JUDITH, physician, medical association administrator; b. Wilkes-Barre, Pa., Nov. 29, 1926; m. Samuel M. Levit, Mar. 2, 1952; children: Harry M., David B. BS in Biology, Bucknell U., 1946; MD, Woman's Med. Coll. of Pa., 1951; DMS (hon.), Med. Coll. Pa., 1978; DSc (hon.), Wilkes U., 1990. Grad. asst. in psychology Bucknell U., 1946-47; intern Phila. Gen. Hosp., 1951-52, fellow in endocrinology, 1952-53, clin. instr., assoc. in endocrinology, 1953-57, dir. med. edn., 1957-61, cons. med. edn., 1961-65; asst. dir. Nat. Bd. Med. Examiners, Phila., 1961-67; assoc. dir., sec. bd. Nat. Bd. Med. Examiners, 1967-75, v.p., sec. bd., 1975-77, pres., chief exec. officer, 1977-86, pres. emeritus, life mem. bd., 1987—; cons. in field, 1964—; mem. adv. coun. Inst. for Nuclear Power Ops., Atlanta, 1988-93; bd. dir. Phila. Electric Co. Contbr. articles to profl. jours. Bd. dirs. Phila. Gen. Hosp. Found., 1964-70; bd. dirs. Phila. Council for Internat. Visitors, 1966-72; bd. sci. counselors Nat. Library Medicine, 1981-85. Recipient award for outstanding contbns. in field of med. edn. Commonwealth Com. of Woman's Med. Coll., 1970; Alumni award Bucknell U., 1978; Disting. Dau. of Pa. award, 1981; Spl. Recognition award Assn. Am. Med. Colls., 1986; Disting. Service award Fedn. State Med. Bds., 1987; Master A.C.P. Fellow Coll. Physicians of Phila.; mem. Inst. Medicine of Nat. Acad. Scis., AMA, Pa., Phila. County med. socs., Assn. Am. Med. Colls.; Phi Beta Kappa, Alpha Omega Alpha, Phi Sigma. Home: The Rittenhouse 210 W Rittenhouse Sq Philadelphia PA 19103-5726

LEVIT, HELOISE B. (GINGER LEVIT), art dealer, fine arts and media consultant; b. Phila., Apr. 2, 1937; d. Elmer and Claire Frances (Schwartz) Bertman; m. Jay Joseph Levit, July 14, 1962; children: Richard Bertman, Robert Edward, Darcy Francine. BA in French Literature, U. Pa., 1959; MA in French Literature, U. Richmond, 1975; Cert., Alliance Française, Paris, 1991, Chambre de Commerce et d'Industrie de Paris, 1991, La Sorbonne, Paris, 1994, Instituto Lorenzo di Medici Firenze, Italy, 1996; post grad., art history, Va. Commonwealth U., Richmond, 1994—. Arts broadcaster Richmond, Va., 1976-82; dir. Fine Arts Am., Inc., Richmond, 1982-84; tchr. Henrico County Pub. Schs., Richmond, 1984-88; dir. devel. Sta. WVST-FM Va. State U., Petersburg, 1987-88; mgr., dir. devel. Richmond Philharm. Orch., 1988-94; fine arts and media cons. Art-I-Facts, Richmond, 1988—. Author: Moments, Monuments & Monarchs, 1986 (Star award 1986); arts writer Richmond Rev., 1989-90; anchor, producer (syndicated radio series) Va. Arts Report, 1978-83, Va. Women, 1984 (Va. Press Women award 1986). V.p. Va. Mus. Collector's Cir., Richmond, 1986-91, mem. steering com.; pres. Richmond Area Dem. Women's Club, 1992-93; mem. Va. Mus. Coun., Richmond; mem. Richmond Symphony Orch. League. Mem. Am. Assn. Tchrs. of French, Va. Capitol Corrs. Assn., Va. Press Women, U. Pa. Alumni Club (v.p. 1980-90, Ben Franklin award 1990), Am. Symphony Orch. League, Amicale Francaise, Alliance Francaise (cert. 1989, 91), La Table Francaise (chmn. 1996), Va. Writers Club. Avocations include tennis, art collecting, classical music, foreign travel. Home and Office: Art-I-Facts 1608 Harborough Rd Richmond VA 23233-4720

LEVIT, JAY J(OSEPH), lawyer; b. Phila., Feb. 20, 1934; s. Albert and Mary Levit; m. Heloise Bertman, July 14, 1962; children: Richard Bertman, Robert Edward, Darcy Francine. AB, Case Western Res. U., 1955; JD, U. Richmond, 1958; LLM, Harvard U., 1959. Bar: Va. 1958, D.C. 1961, U.S. Supreme Ct. 1961. Trial atty. U.S. Dept. Justice, Washington, 1960-64; sr. atty. Gen. Dynamics Corp., Rochester, N.Y., 1965-67; ptnr. Stallard & Levit, Richmond, Va., 1968-77, Levit & Mann, Richmond, 1978—; instr. U. Mich. Law Sch., Ann Arbor, 1964-65; adj. assoc. prof. U. Richmond Law Sch., 1974-77; adj. lectr. Va. Commonwealth U., Richmond, 1970-85; lectr. in field. Contbg. editor The Developing Labor Law-Bur. Nat. Affairs, 1974—. Mem. ABA (labor com.), Va. Bar Assn. (labor com.), Fed. Bar Assn. (labor com.). Avocations: art collecting, jogging, swimming, travel. Home: 1608 Harborough Rd Richmond VA 23233-4720 Office: Levit & Mann 1301 N Hamilton St Richmond VA 23230-3945

LEVIT, MAX, food service executive. V.p., 1958-1993; pres. Grocers Supply Co., Houston, 1993—. Office: Grocers Supply Co 3131 Holcombe Blvd Houston TX 77021-2116*

LEVIT, MILTON, grocery supply company executive; b. 1924; married. Grad., U. Tex., 1946. With Grocers Supply Co. Inc., Houston, 1946—, v.p., 1947-75, pres., 1975—, CEO, 1993—, also chmn. bd., dir. Served with USN. Office: Grocers Supply Co Inc 3131 E Holcombe Blvd Houston TX 77021-2116*

LEVIT, VICTOR BERT, lawyer, foreign representative, civic worker; b. Singapore, Apr. 21, 1930; s. Bert W. and Thelma (Clumeck) L.; m. Margery K. Blum, Oct. 26, 1986; children: Carson, Victoria; m. Margery K. Blum, Oct. 26, 1996. A.B. in Polit. Sci. with great distinction, Stanford, 1950; LL.B., Stanford U., 1952. Bar: Calif. 1953. Assoc. Long & Levit, San Francisco and Los Angeles, 1953-55, ptnr., 1955-83; mng. ptnr. Long & Levit, San Francisco and L.A., 1971-83; ptnr. Barger & Wolen, San Francisco, L.A. and Newport Beach, 1983—; assoc. and gen. legal counsel U.S. Jaycees, 1959-61; legal counsel for consul gen. Ethiopia for San Francisco, 1964-71; hon. consul for Ethiopia for San Francisco, Ethiopia, 1971-76; guest lectr. Stanford U. Law Sch., 1958—, Haile Selassie I Univ. Law Sch., 1972-76; mem. com. group ins. programs State Bar Calif., 1980—; Mem. Los Angeles Consular Corps, 1971-77; mem. San Francisco Consular Corps, 1971-77, vice dean, 1975-76; Grader Calif. Bar Exam., 1956-61; del. San Francisco Mcpl. Conf., 1955-63, vice chmn., 1960, chmn., 1961-63. Author: Legal Malpractice in California, 1974, Legal Malpractice, 1977, 2d edit., 1983; Note editor: Stanford Law Rev, 1952-53; legal editor: Underwriters' Report, 1963—; Contbr. articles to legal jours. Campaign chmn. San Francisco Aid Retarded Children, 1960; mem. nat. com. Stanford Law Sch. Fund, 1959—; mem. Mayor's Osaka-San Francisco Affiliation Com., 1959-65, Mayor's Com. for Mcpl. Mgmt., 1961-64; mem. San Francisco Rep. Country Cen. Com., 1956-63; assoc. mem. Calif. Rep. Cen. Com., 1956-63, 70-72; campaign chmn. San Francisco Assemblyman John Busterud, 1960; bd. dirs. San Francisco Comml. Club, 1967-70, San Francisco Planning and Urban Renewal Assn., 1959-60, San Francisco Planning and Urban Renewal Assn. Nat. Found. Infantile Paralysis, 1958, Red Shield Youth Assn., Salvation Army, San Francisco, 1960-70, bd. dirs. NCCJ, San Francisco, 1959—, chmn., No. Calif., 1962-64, 68-70; mem. nat. bd. dirs., 1964-75; bd. dirs. San Francisco Tb and Health Assn., 1962-70, treas., 1964, pres., 1965-67; bd. dirs. San Francisco Assn. Mental Health, 1964-73, pres., 1968-71; mem. com. Nat. Assn. Mental Health, 1969-71; trustee United Bay Area Crusade, 1966-74, Ins. Forum San Francisco; bd. visitors Stanford Law Sch., 1969-75; mem. adv. bd. Jr. League San Francisco, 1971-75. Named Outstanding Young Man San Francisco mng. editors San Francisco newspapers, 1960, One of Five Outstanding Young Men Calif., 1961. Fellow ABA (chmn. profl. liability com. for gen. practice sect. 1979-81, council gen. practice sect. 1982-86, sec.-treas. gen. practice sect. 1986-87); mem. San Francisco Bar Assn. (chmn. ins. com. 1962, 73, chmn. charter flight com. 1962-66), State Bar Calif. (com. on group ins. programs 1980—, chmn. gen. practice sect. 1988—), Consular Law Soc., Am. Arbitration Assn. (arbitrator), World Assn. Lawyers (chmn. parliamentary law com. 1976—), Am. Law Inst. (adviser restatement of law governing lawyers 1985—), Internat. Bar Assn., San Francisco Jr. C. of C. (dir. 1959, pres. 1958), U.S. Jaycees (exec. com. 1959-61), Jaycees Internat. (life, senator), Calif. Scholarship Fedn., U.S. C. of C. (labor com. 1974-76), San Francisco C. of C. (dir.), Phi Beta Kappa, Order of Coif, Pi Sigma Alpha. Clubs: Commercial (San Francisco) (dir.); Commonwealth (quar. chmn.), California Tennis; World Trade; Bankers. Home: 2063 Broadway San Francisco CA 94115 Office: Barger & Wolen 101 California St Ste 4725 San Francisco CA 94111-5875

LEVIT, WILLIAM HAROLD, JR., lawyer; b. San Francisco, Feb. 8, 1938; s. William Harold and Barbara Janis (Kaiser) L.; m. Mary Elizabeth Webster, Feb. 13, 1971; children: Alison Jones, Alexandra Bradley, Laura Elizabeth Fletcher, Amalia Elizabeth Webster, William Harold, III. BA magna cum laude, Yale U., 1960; MA Internat. Rels., U. Calif., Berkeley, 1962; LLB, Harvard U., 1967. Bar: N.Y. 1968, Calif. 1974, Wis. 1979. Fgn. service officer Dept. State, 1962-64; assoc. firm Davis Polk & Wardwell, N.Y.C., 1967-73; assoc., then ptnr. firm Hughes Hubbard & Reed, N.Y.C. and Los Angeles, 1973-79; sec. and gen. counsel Rexnord Inc., Milw., 1979-83; ptnr., dir., chair internat. practice group Godfrey & Kahn, Milw., 1983—; substitute arbitrator Iran-U.S. Claims Tribunal, The Hague, 1984-88; lectr. Practicing Law Inst., ABA, Calif. Continuing Edn. of Bar, State Bar of Wis. Contbr. to: Mergers and the Private Antitrust Suit: The Private Enforcement of Section 7 of the Clayton Act, 1977. Bd. dirs. Wis. Humane Soc., 1980-90, pres., 1986-88; bd. dirs. Vis. Nurse Corp., Milw., 1980-90, chmn., 1985-87; bd. dirs. Vis. Nurse Found., 1986-95, chmn., 1989-91; bd. dirs. Aurora Health Care Inc., 1988-93, Wis. Soc. to Prevent Blindness, 1981-91, Columbia Coll. Nursing, 1992—, Aurora Health Care Ventures, 1993—; rep. Assn. Yale Alumni, 1976-79, 81-84, 90-93; pres. Yale Club So. Calif., 1977-79; mem. neutral advisor panel CPR Inst. for Dispute Resolution. Ford Found. fellow U. Pa., 1961-62, NDEA fellow U. Calif., Berkeley, 1962. Mem. ABA (com. on corp. counsel litigation sect.), Am. Soc. Corp. Secs. (pres. Wis. chpt. 1982-83, dir. 1981-92), Am. Arbitration Assn. (panel arbitrators 1977—), Assn. of Bar of City of N.Y., State Bar Calif. (com. on continuing edn. of bar 1977-79), L.A. County Bar Assn. (ethics com. 1976-79), State Bar Wis. (dir. internat. bus. transactions sect. 1985-92, dist. 2 bd. attys. profl. responsibility com. 1985-94, chmn. 1993-94), Bar Assn. 7th Cir. (gen. chair com. on rules and practice 1995—), Am. Br. Internat. Law Assn., Nat. Assn. Security Dealers (bd. arbitrators 1988—), Chartered Inst. Arbitrators (assoc., London), N.Y. Stock Exch. (panel arbitrators 1988—), N.Am. Coun. London Ct. of Internat. Arbitration, Am. Soc. Internat. Law, Inst. Jud. Adminstrn., Milw. Club, Milw. Athletic Club, Town Club, Phi Beta Kappa. Office: 780 N Water St Ste 1500 Milwaukee WI 53202-3512

LEVITAN, DAVID M(AURICE), lawyer, educator; b. Tver, Lithuania, Dec. 25, 1915; (parents Am. citizens); m. Judith Morley; children: Barbara Lane Levitan, Stuart Dean Levitan. B.S., Northwestern U., 1936, M.A., 1937; Ph.D., U. Chgo., 1940; J.D., Columbia U., 1948. Bar: N.Y. 1948, U.S. Supreme Ct. 1953. Various U.S. Govt. adminstrv. and advisory positions with Nat. Youth Adminstrn., Office Price Adminstrn., War Prodn. Bd., Fgn. Econ. Adminstrn. Supreme Hdqrs. Allied Expeditionary Force, and Cen. European div. Dept. State, 1940-46; cons., sec. joint-com. of 5th and 6th coms., 2d Gen. Assembly, dir. com. of experts for establishing adminstrv. tribunal UN, 1946-47; cons. pub. affairs dept., producer series of pub. affairs programs on TV and radio ABC, 1946-53; pvt. practice N.Y.C., 1948-66; counsel Hahn & Hessen, N.Y.C., 1966-68, ptnr., 1968-86; instr. U. Chgo., 1938-41; adj. prof. public law Columbia U., 1946-65; adj. prof. John Jay Coll. Criminal Justice, CUNY, 1966-75; adj. prof. polit. sci. Post Coll., 1964-66; adj. prof. law Cardozo Sch. Law, 1978-82; pvt. practice, 1995—; asst. to Ill. state adminstr. Nat. Youth Adminstrn., chief budget sect., Washington, 1940-41; mgmt. analyst Office of Price Adminstrn., 1941; spl. asst. to chmn. War Prodn. Bd., 1942-43; chief property control divsn. Fgn. Econ. Adminstrn., Washington, 1944-45; with U.S. Group of Control Coun. for Germany at SHAEF, London, 1944; advisor Ctrl. European divsn. U.S. Dept. State, 1945; cons. UN, 1946-47, Sect. Joint Com. 5th and 6th Coms., 1946-47, 2d session of 1st Gen. Assembly, 1946-47; dir. Com. of Experts on Establishment of Adminstrn. Tribunal, 1946-47; cons. pub. affairs dept. ABC, 1946-53. Contbr. articles to legal jours. Mem. Nassau County (N.Y.) Welfare Bd., 1965-69; chmn. Planning Bd., Village of Roslyn Harbor, N.Y., 1965-66; chmn. Bd. of Zoning Appeals, Village Roslyn Harbor, 1967-86. Recipient Demobilization award Social Sci. Rsch. Coun., 1946-48. Fellow Am. Coll. Trust and Estate Counsel; mem. ABA, Am. Polit. Sci. Assn., Am. Soc. Internat. Law, Am. Law Inst., Assn. Bar City N.Y. Home: 103 N E 19th Ave Deerfield Beach FL 33441 Office and Home: 250 Scudeters Ln Roslyn NY 11576

LEVITAN, IRWIN BARRY, neuroscience educator, academic administrator; b. Jan. 13, 1947; came to U.S., permanent resident; married; two children. BSc in Biochemistry with first class honors, McGill U., Montreal, 1967, MSc in Biochemistry, 1968, PhD in Biochemistry, 1970. Rschr. in lab. of Dr. T. E. Webb, cancer rsch. unit McGill U., 1967-70; rschr. in lab of prof. H. Hyden, Inst. Neurobiology U. Goteborg, Sweden, 1970-72; rschr. in lab. of Dr. S. H. Barondes, dept. psychiatry U. Calif. San Diego, 1972-74; permanent staff and group leader Friedrich Miescher Institut, Basel, Switzerland, 1974-82; assoc. prof. biochemistry Brandeis U., Waltham, Mass., 1982-85, prof. biochemistry, 1985—, Nancy Lurie Marks Prof. neuroscience, 1992—, pres., dir. Volen Ctr. for Complex Sys., 1989—; dir. biochem. seminar McGill U., 1969-70; instr. neurochemistry U. Calif. San Diego, 1972-73; coord. and instr. introductory neurobiology Friedrich Miescher Institut, 1975-77, mem. exec. com., 1975-78; instr. introductory neurobiology Biozentrum, U. Basel, 1975-82; instr. introductory and advanced neurobiology Brandeis U., 1983—, coord. and dir. neurosci. program, 1983—, dir. ctr. complex sys., 199—; vis. prof. cellular neurology MIT, 1987-93; co-dir. summer course in neurobiology Marine Biolog. Lab., Woods Hole, Mass., 1990-94; chmn. Gordon Conf. on Ion Channels, 1986; mem. adv. bd. Whitney Lab. Marine Biology-U. Fla., nominating com. Bristol Myers Squibb award for disting. achievement in neurosci.; disting. vis. prof. Duke U., Durham, N.C., 1993, Dana Alliance for Brain Initiatives Charles A. Dana Found., 1994. Author: (with L. K. Kaczmarek) Neuromodulation: the Biochemical Control of Neuronal Excitability, 1987, (with L. K. Kaczmarek) The Neuron: Cell and Molecular Biology, 1991; editor (with P. D. Evans) Ion Channels and Receptors, 1986; mem. editorial bd. Jour. Neuroscience, Jour. Molecular Biology, Jour. Exptl. Biology, Neuron; contbr. numerous articles to profl. jours. and chapters to books. Mem. adv. bd. Cystic Fibrosis Rsch. Ctr.-U. Ala. Woodrow Wilson fellow 1967; Centennial fellow Med. Rsch. Coun. Can., 1970-73; Quebec scholar, 1968, 69; scholar McGill U., 1963, 66, 67; bursar Nat. Rsch. Coun. Can., 1967, studentship, 1968, 69; named Helen Wendler Deane Disting. lectr. Wellesley Coll., 1988, J. H. Quastel Disting. Vis. prof. McGill U., 1989, Rushton lectr. Fla. State U., 1991, Cooper lectr. Yale U., 1992, Disting. Vis. prof. in Pharmacology and Neurobiology, Duke U., 1993; recipient Jacob Javits Neuroscience Investigator award NIH, 1985, 1992. Office: Brandeis Univ Volen Cte Complex Sys 415 South St Waltham MA 02154-2728

LEVITAN, JAMES A., lawyer; b. N.Y.C., Mar. 24, 1925; s. Leo and Della (Brody) L.; m. Ruth Terry White, Jan. 30, 1951; children—Deborah A., Judith T., Susan J. B.S. in Chem. Engring, M.I.T., 1948; LL.B. (mem. bd. Law Rev. 1950-51), Columbia U., 1951. Bar: N.Y. bar 1951. Since practiced in N.Y.C.; ptnr. Skadden, Arps, Slate, Meagher & Flom, 1965-95, of counsel, 1995—; life mem. MIT Corp., Cambridge, Mass., 1995—, chmn. audit com., 1994—; regional chmn. N.Y.C. MIT Ednl. Coun., 1974-90; lectr. in field of tax. Served with USNR, 1944-46. Stone scholar, 1948-51; Kent scholar, 1950. Mem. N.Y. State Bar Assn., Assn. Bar City N.Y., Tau Beta Pi. Home: 26 Wake Robin Ln Stamford CT 06903-4611 Office: Skadden Arps Slate Meagher & Flom 919 3rd Ave New York NY 10022

LEVITAN, LAURENCE, lawyer, former state senator; b. Washington, Oct. 22, 1933; s. Maurice Land Nathlie (Rosenthal) L.; BS, Washington and Lee U., 1955; JD, George Washington U., 1958; m. Barbara E. Levin, 1957; children: Jennifer, Michelle, Lisa. Admitted to Md. bar, 1964; with Levitan, Cramer & Weinstein, 1959-72, Levitan Ezrin, West & Kenxton, 1973-85, Beckett Cromwell & Myers, 1985-90, Frank Bernstein Conaway & Goldman, 1990-92; of counsel Baker & Hostetler, 1992-95; ptnr. Rifkin, Livingston, Levitan and Silver, LLC, Annapolis, Md., 1995—; mem. Md. Ho. of Dels., 1971-74; mem. Md. Senate, 1975-94, chmn. budget and taxation com., policy com., spending affordability com., mem. joint com. on mgmt. pub. funds., legis. com. on budget and audit, gov.'s commn. to rev. state taxes & taxes structure, joint legis. com. on tax reform, govtl. commn. to revise annotated code of Md., joint subcom. on program open space, chmn. drunk and drugged driving task force, chmn. joint com. on ins. tax reform; mem. Montgomery County Exec.'s Commn. for Higher Edn. in High Tech.; past mem. Gov.'s Commn. To Study Unification of Circuit Ct., Gov.'s Commn. to Study Condominium Laws, Gov.'s Commn. Law Enforcement and Adminstrn. Justice, Gov.'s Subcom. on Revenue Structure of Task Force to Study State-Local Relationships; mem. Gov.'s Commn. To Study Feasibility of Biennial Budget, Gov.'s Task Force on Real Property Closing Costs, Task Force To Study Md. Tax Ct., Gov.'s Commn. Sch. Funding, Joint Task Force on Md.'s Procurement Law; apptd. co-chmn. transition team on budget review Gov. Glendening. Mem. ABA, D.C. Bar Assn., Md. Bar Assn., Nat. Conf. State Legislatures (mem. subcom. on fed. budget and taxation com., fiscal affairs govt. oversight com.), So. Legis. Conf. (chmn. fiscal affairs and govt. ops. steering com. 1992-93), Am. Legis. Exch. Coun. (tax task force). Democrat. Jewish. Office: 163 Conduit St Annapolis MD 21401-2512 also: 11426 Georgetowne Dr Potomac MD 20854-3722

LEVITAN, MAX FISHEL, geneticist, anatomy educator; b. Tverai, Telsiu Aps, Lithuania, Mar. 1, 1921; came to U.S., 1928; s. Solomon Leib Hannah (Siev) L.; m. Beth Sheva German, Oct. 25, 1947; children: Eve Leah Gerber, Sara Ann, Marjorie Ruth Gross. AB, U. Chgo., 1943; MA, U. Mich., 1946; PhD, Colmubia U., 1951. Asst. in zoology Columbia U., N.Y.C., 1946-49; assoc. prof. biology Va. Poly. Inst., Blacksburg, 1949-55; asst. prof. anatomy Woman's Med. Coll. Pa., Phila., 1955-58, assoc. prof., 1958-60, prof. anatomy and med. genetics, 1960-66, acting chmn. anatomy dept., 1964-66; prof. biology, chmn. dept. George Mason U., Fairfax, Va., 1966-68; assoc. prof. anatomy Mt. Sinai Sch. Medicine, CUNY, N.Y.C., 1968-70, prof. anatomy, 1970—, prof. human genetics, 1995—. Author: Textbook of Human Genetics, 1971, 3rd edit. 1988; contbng. author: Clinical Genetics, 1973, Genetics and Biology of Drosophila, 1982, Drosophila Inversion Polymorphism, 1992, Encyclopedia of Human Biology, 1992, 1997, Encyclopedia of Science and Technology, 1992, 1997, Genetics of Natural Populations, 1995; assoc. editor Evolution, 1977-79; contbr. numerous articles to sci. jours. Named Edward Everett Just Meml. lectr. Howard U., Washington, 1968; recipient Rsch. Career Devel. award NIH, 1963. Fellow AAAS; mem. Genetics Soc. Am., Soc. for Study of Evolution, Am. Soc. Naturalists, Sigma Xi (sec. VPI chpt. 1954-55, sec.-treas. Mt. Sinai chpt. 1975—). Jewish. Achievements include rsch. in linkage disquilibria in inversion systems, unique chromosomal breakage factor. Home: 1212 5th Ave New York NY 10029-5210 Office: Mt Sinai Sch Medicine CUNY 1 Gustave L Levy Pl New York NY 10029-6504

LEVITAS, MITCHEL RAMSEY, editor; b. N.Y.C., Dec. 1, 1929; s. Samuel M. and Fira (Zilboorg) L.; m. Gloria Barach, Dec. 24, 1950; children: Anthony, Daniel. AB, Bklyn. Coll., 1951. With Dept. State, 1951-53; reporter N.Y. Post, 1953-60; asst. editor Time mag., 1960-64; editor, writer N.Y. Times Mag., 1965-70; editor Metropolitan, 1976; editor Week in Rev. N.Y. Times, from 1977; editor Sunday Book Rev., 1983-89; sr. editor weekends N.Y. Times, 1989—; editor Op-Ed page N. Y. Times, 1990-95; editl. dir. N.Y. Times Book Devel., 1995—; vis. scholar Woodrow Wilson Found., 1979—. Author: America in Crisis. Recipient George Polk award investigative reporting, 1957; Woodrow Wilson fellow, 1951, Nieman fellow, 1958. Mem. Century Assn., Coun. Fgn. Rels., Phi Beta Kappa. Office: NY Times Co 229 W 43rd St New York NY 10036-3913*

LEVITCH, JOSEPH See **LEWIS, JERRY**

LEVITETZ, JEFF, food wholesaler. CEO Purity Wholesale Grocers, Boca Raton, Fla. Office: Purity Wholesale Grocers 6413 Congress Ave Ste 250 Boca Raton FL 33487-2840*

LEVITHAN, ALLEN B., lawyer; b. 1946. AB, Lafayette Coll., 1968; JD cum laude, Harvard U., 1971. Bar: N.J. 1972. Legal sec. to Hon. Joseph Weintraub N.J. Supreme Ct., 1971-72; with Lowenstein, Sandler, Kohl, Fisher & Boylan A Profl. Corp., Roseland, N.J. Pres. Jewish Family Svc. of MetroWest, 1981-84. Mem. ABA, N.J. State Bar Assn. Office: Lowenstein Sandler Kohl Fisher & Boylan 65 Livingston Ave Roseland NJ 07068-1725

LEVITIN, LEV BEROVICH, scientist, educator; b. Moscow, Sept. 25, 1935; U.S., 1981; s. Ber L. and Tzetzilia (Gushansky) L.; m. Yulia Shmukler, 1959 (div. 1970); 1 son, Boris. M.Sc., Moscow U., 1960; Ph.D., Acad. Scis. of USSR, 1969. Sr. research scientist Inst. Info. Transmission Problems, USSR Acad. Scis., 1961-73; sr. lectr. Tel-Aviv U., 1974-80; vis. prof. Bielefeld U., W. Ger., 1980-81, Syracuse (N.Y.) U., 1981-82; prof. engring. Boston U., 1982-86; disting. prof. engring. sci., 1986—; vis. scientist Heinrich-Hertz Inst., Berlin, 1980, Institut fü r Optoelektronik, Oberpfaffenhofen, W.Ger., 1981; cons. Vishay Israel, Ltd., Tel-Aviv, 1979, SEL Forschungszentrum, Stuttgart, Germany, 1987. Editor: Principles of Cybernetics (in Russian), 1967; contbr. articles sci. jours. Fellow IEEE; mem. AAUP, Am. Math. Soc., Assn. Computing Machinery, Soc. Indsl. and Applied Math., N.Y. Acad. Scis., Am. Soc. for Engring. Edn., Math. Assn. Am., AAAS, Memento, Resistance Internat., Amnesty Internat. Office: Boston U Coll Engring 44 Cummington St Boston MA 02215-2407

LEVITON, ALAN EDWARD, museum curator; b. N.Y.C., Jan. 11, 1930; s. David and Charlotte (Weber) L.; m. Gladys Ann Robertson, June 30, 1952; children: David A., Charlotte A. AB, Stanford U., 1949, MA, 1953, PhD, 1960; student, Columbia U., summers 1947, 48, 53, NYU, 1948, U. Nebr., 1954. Asst. curator herpetology Calif. Acad. Scis., San Francisco, 1957-60, assoc. curator, 1960-61, chmn., curator, 1962-82, 89-92, curator, 1983-88, 93—, chmn. computer svcs., 1983-92, editor sci. publs., 1994-97; assoc. curator zool. collections Stanford U., 1962-63, lectr. biol. sci., 1963-70; professorial lectr. Golden Gate U., 1953-63; adj. prof. biol. sci. San Francisco State U., 1967-97. Author: North American Amphibians, 1970, Reptiles of the Middle East, 1992, T.H. Hittel's California Academy of Sciences, 1997; contbr. numerous articles to sci. and profl. jours. Am. Philos. Soc. grantee, 1960, NSF grantee, 1960-61, 77-79, 80, 83-86, 86-89, 91-93, Belvedere Sci. Fund grantee, 1958-59, 62. Fellow AAAS (coun. 1976-97, com. coun. affairs 1983-85, sec.-treas. Pacific divsn. 1975-79, exec. dir. 1980-98), Calif. Acad. Scis., Geol. Soc. Am. (vice chmn. history geology divsn. 1989-90, chmn. 1990-91); mem. Am. Soc. Ichthyologists and Herpetologists (mem. bd. govs. 1960-84), Soc. Systematic Zoology (sec.-treas. Pacific sect. 1970-72), Forum Historians of Sci. Am. (coord. com. 1986-88, sec.-treas. 1988-90), Herpetologists League (pres. 1961-62), History of Sci. Soc. Home: 571 Kingsley Ave Palo Alto CA 94301-3225 Office: Calif Acad Scis Golden Gate Park San Francisco CA 94118

LEVITSKY, MELVYN, ambassador; b. Sioux City, Iowa, Mar. 19, 1938; s. David and Mollie (Schwartz) L.; m. Joan Daskovsky, Aug. 12, 1962; children: Adam, Ross Josh. BA, U. Mich., 1960; MA, U. Iowa, 1963. Polit. officer U.S. Embassy, Moscow, 1972-75; officer-in-charge Soviet-U.S. bilateral relations Dept. State, Washington, 1975-78, dep. dir. UN polit. affairs, 1978-80, dir. UN polit. affairs, 1980-82, dep. asst. sec. for human rights and humanitarian affairs, 1982-83; dep. dir. Voice of Am., Washington, 1983-84; dep. assoc. dir. broadcasting USIA, Washington, 1983-84; U.S. amb. to Bulgaria, 1984-87; exec. sec., spl. asst. to sec. Dept. State, Washington, 1987-89, asst. sec. state internat. narcotics matters, 1989-94; U.S. amb. to Brazil, 1994—. Recipient Meritorious Honor award Dept. State, 1968, Superior Honor award Dept. State, 1975, 82, Presdl. Meritorious Svc. awards, 1986-91. Mem. Am. Fgn. Service Assn.

LEVITT, ARTHUR, JR., federal agency administrator, securities and publishing executive; b. Bklyn., Feb. 3, 1931; s. Arthur and Dorothy (Wolff) L.; m. Marylin Blauner, June 12, 1955; children: Arthur III, Lauri. BA, Williams Coll., 1952, LLD (hon.), 1980; LLD (hon.), Pace U., 1980, Hamilton Coll., 1981, L.I. U., 1984, Hofstra U., 1985. Asst. promotion dir. Time, Inc., N.Y.C., 1954-59; exec. v.p., dir. Oppenheimer Industries, Inc., Kansas City, Mo., 1959-62; with Shearson Hayden Stone Inc. (now Shearson Lehman Bros., Inc.), N.Y.C., 1962-78, pres., 1969-78; chmn., chief exec. officer, dir. Am. Stock Exchange, N.Y.C., 1978-89; chmn. Levitt Media Co., N.Y.C., 1989-93, N.Y.C. Econ. Devel. Corp., 1990-93, SEC, Washington, 1993—. Chmn. President's Pvt. Sector Survey on Cost Control, 1982-84, President's Task Force on Pvt. Sector Initiatives, 1981-82, White House Small Bus. Conf. Commn., 1978-80; mem. N.Y. State Coun. on Arts, 1969—; chmn. bd. dirs. Spl. Adv. Task Force on Future Devel. West Side Manhattan, President's Base Closure and Realignment Commn.; trustee Williams Coll.; bd. dirs. Revson Found. With USAF, 1952-54, maj. Res. Recipient Medal of Excellence Bd. Regents State of N.Y. Mem. Am. Bus. Conf. (chmn. 1980-89), Phi Beta Kappa. Office: SEC 450 5th St NW Washington DC 20001-2739

LEVITT, B. BLAKE, medical and science writer; b. Bridgeport, Conn., Mar. 25, 1948; d. John Joseph and Beatrice Dolores (Rozanski) Blake; m. Andrew Levitt, Dec. 20, 1968 (div. May 1977); m. Jon P. Garvey, Nov. 19, 1983. BA in English magna cum laude, BA in History summa cum laude, Quinnipiac Coll., 1972; postgrad., Yale U., 1988. Instr. English as fgn. lang. U. Khon Kaen, Thailand, 1968-69; market researcher Lyons Bakeries Ltd., London, summer 1971; traffic mgr., copywriter Provocatives Advt. Agy., Danbury, Conn., 1976-78; tech. writer tng. divsn. Jack Morton Prodns., N.Y.C., 1978-82; freelance feature and med. writer Litchfield County Times, New Milford, Conn., 1982-85, N.Y. Times, N.Y.C., 1985-89; freelance writer med. and sci. books, 1989—. Author: Electromagnetic Fields: A Consumer's Guide to the Issues and How to Protect Ourselves, 1995 (Will Solimene Book award for excellence 1996), 50 Essential Things to Do When the Doctor Says It's Infertiltiy, 1995; co-author: (with John R. Sussman M.D.) Before You Conceive, The Complete Pre-Pregnancy Guide, 1989 (Will Solimeme Book Award of Excellence 1991); contbr. articles to N.W. Hills Mag., New Eng. Monthly, Con. Mag. Founding mem., bd. dirs. Warren (Conn.) Land Trust, 1989-91; mem. Dem. Town Com., Warren, 1993—; vice-chmn. zoning bd. appeals Town of Warren, 1993-95. Mem. Nat. Assn. Sci. Writers, Bioelectromagnetics Soc., Am. Med. Writers Assn., Author's Guild, Author's League. Avocations: architectural design and renovation, reading, hiking, gardening.

LEVITT, GEORGE, retired chemist; b. Newburg, N.Y., Feb. 19, 1925; m. Julie Zeto; children: Barbara Klein, Jeffrey, David, Gregory. BS, Duquesne U., 1950, MS, 1952; PhD, Mich. State U., 1957. Rsch. chemist Exptl. Sta. E.I. du Pont de Nemours & Co., Inc., 1956-63, rsch. chemist Stine Lab., 1963-66, rsch. chemist Exptl. Sta., 1966-68, sr. rsch. chemist, 1968-80, rsch. assoc., 1981-86; instr. Del. Tech. and C.C., 1975-80. Pres. We Care in Del., 1986-87, bd. dirs., 1986-94. Recipient Internat. pesticide rsch. award Swiss Soc. Chem. Industries, 1982, Chesapeake chpt. Nat. Agrl. Mktg. Assn., 1987, Disting. Alumnus of Yr. award Duquesne U. Coll. Arts and Sci., 1988, Nat. Medal of Tech., 1993, Disting. Inventor award Intellectualproperty Owners Am., 1983. Mem. AAAS, Am. Chem. Soc. (Creative Invention award 1989, Kenneth Spencer award 1991), Internat. Union Pure & Applied Chemistry, Sigma Xi. Achievements include research in organic syntheses, herbicides, fungicides, medicinals, pesticides; synthesis of heterocyclic compounds; characterization and identification of novel organic compounds for biological evaluation; defined and optimized chemical structure-biological activity relationships and sulfonylurea herbicides. Home: 110 Downs Dr Greenville DE 19807-2556

LEVITT, GERALD STEVEN, natural gas company executive; b. Bronx, N.Y., Mar. 21, 1944; s. Charles and Beatrice (Janet) L.; m. Natalie Lillian Hoppen; children: Mark, Roy. B in Mgmt. Engring., Rensselaer Poly. Inst., 1965; MBA, DePaul U., 1972. Registered profl. engr., Ill. Tech. rep. Worthington Air Conditioning Co., Ampere, N.J., 1965-67; indsl. sales engr. Peoples Gas Light & Coke Co., Chgo., 1967-71; planning specialist Peoples Gas Co., Chgo., 1971-72; v.p. Stone & Webster Mgmt. Cons., Inc., N.Y.C., 1972-82; exec. v.p., chief staff officer South Jersey Gas Co., Folsom, N.J., 1982—; v.p., CFO South Jersey Industries, Inc., Folsom, N.J., 1987—. Bd. dirs. Camden County coun. Boy Scouts Am., West Collingswood, N.J., Rowan Coll. Found. Mem. Am. Gas Assn., Greater Atlantic City C. of C. (past bd. dirs.), N.J. State C. of C. (bd. dirs.). Office: S Jersey Gas Co 1 S Jersey Plz Hammonton NJ 08037-9109

LEVITT, GREGORY ALAN, education educator; b. Memphis, Jan. 12, 1952; s. Robert Riley and Martha Lorraine (Swincher) L.; m. Billie Diane Tomblin (div. June 1985); 1 child, Joshua Paul; m. Yueping Guo, June 3, 1994; 1 child, Maya Guo. BA, Capital U., Columbus, Ohio, 1975; MA, Ohio State U., 1988, PhD, 1990. Cert. secondary sch. tchr., adminstr., Ohio; cert. tchr. Chinese lang. Beijing Lang. Inst. Tchr. Wehrle H.S., Columbus, 1975-85; grad. teaching assoc. Ohio State U., Columbus, 1985-90; cons./rschr. CBS News, Beijing, China, 1989; dir. fgn. tchrs. Beijing U. of Aero. and Astron. Engring., 1988-90; assoc. prof. U. New Orleans, 1990—; assoc. dir. Ctr. for the Pacific Rim, New Orleans, 1990—; dir. A World of Difference Inst., New Orleans, 1994—. Mem. editl. rev. bd. Teaching About Asia Jour., 1993—; contbr. articles to profl. jours., chpts. to books and computer software. Bd. dirs. Tyomey Ctr. for Peace Through Justice, New Orleans, 1994—; mem. cmty. bd. Success Dropout Prevention, New Orleans, 1990—; coll. organizer AIDS Walk, U. New Orleans, 1993-94. Grantee U.S. Dept. Edn., 1994, East-West Ctr., Honolulu, 1994, La. Endowment for Humanities, 1993. Mem. ASCD, Nat. Coun. for the Social Studies, Assn. for Asian Studies, Nat. Assn. for Multicultural Edn., La. Coun. for the Social Studies, La. Ednl. Rsch. Assn., Phi Beta Delta, Phi Delta Kappa (advisor 1994—). Avocations: golf, racquetball, tennis, snorkeling, swimming. Home: 5421 Hewes St New Orleans LA 70125 Office: Univ of New Orleans Coll of Edn Dept of C&I New Orleans LA 70148

LEVITT, IRVING FRANCIS, investment company executive; b. Braddock, Pa., July 3, 1915; s. Charles and Frances (Goretsky) L.; m. Florence Chaikin, Oct. 10, 1937; children: Robert Bruce, Linda Ann (Mrs. Stanley L. Ehrenpreis). B.S. (hon.) in journalism, U. Mich., 1936. Advt. mgr. feature writer Braddock (Pa.) Free Press, 1936-37; advt. mgr. Levitt Bros. Furniture Stores, 1936-38; partner, exec. adminstr. stores in Levitt Bros. Furniture Stores, Braddock, Vandergrift and New Kensington, Pa., 1938-55; exec. asst., v.p. Levinson Steel Co., Pitts., 1942-44; real estate, indsl. devel., 1938-82; pres. Lepar, Inc., 1950-80; pres., chmn. bd. Union Screw & Mfg. Co., Pitts.; chmn. bd. Investment Capital Corp., Pitts., 1955—, Radix Orgn., Inc., N.Y., Radix Real Estate, Inc., RRE Enterprises, Inc.; pres. Kirwan Heights Land Co., King Land Co., Ind., Blawnox Realty Co.; chmn. bd. Apollo Industries, Inc., 1959-68; chmn. bd., dir. Apollo Internat. Corp.; pres., dir. Apollo-Peru S.A., Oakland Investment Corp., Pitts.; v.p., dir. Apollo Indsl., Inc., Apollo Investment Co., Pitts.; sr. v.p. Parker-Levitt Corp., Sarasota, Fla., Marble Island, Inc., Vt.; ptnr. Oliver-Smithfield Venture, Pitts., Nineteen Hundred Group Ltd., Sarasota, Fla.; bd. dirs. Comml. Bank & Trust Co., Pitts., Nuclear Materials & Equipment Corp., Ednl. Audio Visual, Inc., N.Y., London, Radix Ventures, N.C., N.Y.; chmn. bd., dir. Lido Beach Devel. Co., Inc., Sarasota, Fla.; partner One Hundred Kennedy Ltd., Tampa, Fla., SMP, Ltd., Pine Run Devel., Inc., Sarasota; mem. Pitts. Bd. Realtors, New Kensington Indsl. Devel. Corp., Smaller Mfrs. Coun. Bd. dirs. Massanutten Mil. Acad., Woodstock, Va., United Jewish Fedn. Finance, Pitts., Irene Kaufman Settlement Bd.; trustee Levitt Found. Pitts., Rodef Shalom Temple, Pitts. Mem. Nat. Sales Execs. Club (dir. 1952-82), Am. Jewish Com., Chautauqua Soc., Am. Arbitration Assn. (panel of arbitrators), Nat. Assn. Securities Dealers (bd. arbitration). Clubs: Westmoreland Country (Export, Pa.) (v.p. 1948-83); Metropolis Country (White Plains, N.Y.); Longboat Key Country; Marco Polo (N.Y.C.); Standard (Pitts.) (dir.), Pitts. Athletic Assn. (Pitts.); Belfry New Century (London); Univ. (Sarasota). Office: Investment Capital Corp 595 Bay Isles Rd Ste 120-G Longboat Key FL 34228-3102 also: 230 Park Ave Rm 630 New York NY 10169-0699

LEVITT, ISRAEL MONROE, astronomer; b. Phila., Dec. 19, 1908; s. Joseph and Jennie (Marriner) L.; m. Alice Gross, July 3, 1937; children: Peter Leighton, Nancy Bambino. BSME, Drexel U., 1932, DSc, 1958; MA, U. Pa., 1937, PhD, 1948; DSc, Temple U., 1958, Phila. Coll. Pharmacy and Sci., 1963. Astronomer, Fels Planetarium of The Franklin Inst., Phila., 1934-39; asst. asso. dir. Fels Planetarium of The Franklin Inst., 1939-49, dir., 1949-72, v.p. inst., 1970-72; exec. dir. Phila. Mayor's Sci. and Tech. Adv. Council, 1972-93; sr. lectr. astronomy U. Pa., 1977; astronomer The Flower Obs., 1946-48; dir. (Sci. Council), 1953—; sci. cons. to City of Phila., 1956-63; chmn. Air Pollution Control Bd. Phila., 1965—. Author: Precision Laboratory Manual, 1932, (with Roy K. Marshall) Star Maps for Beginners, 1942, Space Traveler's Guide to Mars, 1956, Target for Tomorrow, 1959, Exploring The Secrets of Space, 1963, (with Dandridge M. Cole) Beyond the Known Universe, 1974; developer NASA Spacemobile; inventor oxygen mask, pulse counting photoelectric photometer (with William Blitzstein); contbr. articles in jours., mags. on sci. subjects; author: internationally syndicated space & sci. column for Gen. Features. Recipient USN Ordnance Devel. award, 1945; Henry Grier Bryant gold medal Geog. Soc. Phila., 1962; Joseph Priestley award Spring Garden Inst., Phila., 1963; Writing award Aviation/Space Writers Assn., 1965; Samuel S. Fels Medal award, 1970; cert. of recognition NASA, 1977. Fellow AAAS, Am. Astronautical Soc., Brit. Interplanetary Soc.; mem. AIAA, Am. Astron. Soc., Rittenhouse Astron. Soc. (past pres.), Acad. Scis. Phila. (v.p. 1993), Nat. Assn. Sci. Writers, Aviation Writers Assn., Explorers Club, Pi Tau Sigma. Home: 3900 Ford Rd Apt 19D Philadelphia PA 19131 Office: 1515 Market St Fl 17 Philadelphia PA 19102-1921

LEVITT, JERRY DAVID, medical educator; b. Phila., Apr. 11, 1941; s. Abraham and Nettie (Dash) L.; m. Julie Meranze, June 2, 1967; children: Rachel, Daniel, Gabriel. BA, U. Pa., 1962, MD, 1966. Diplomate Am. Bd. Anesthesiology; lic. physician, Pa., Maine. Intern Mt. Sinai Hosp., N.Y.C., 1966-67; resident in anesthesia U. Pa. Hosp., Phila., 1967-69, rsch. fellow, 1971-72; instr. anesthesia U. Pa., phila., 1972-73, asst. prof. anesthesia, 1973-82; assoc. prof. anesthesiology Allegheny U. Health Scis., Hahnemann Sch. Medicine, Phila., 1982—. Author: (with others) Basic Pharmacology in Medicine, 1990; contbr. articles to profl. jours. With USPHS, 1969-71. Avocations: photography, hiking, music. Office: Allegheny U Hosps Hahnemann Broad & Vine Sts Philadelphia PA 19102

LEVITT, LEROY PAUL, psychiatrist, psychoanalyst; b. Wilkes-Barre, Pa., Jan. 8, 1918; s. Samuel and Paula (Goldstein) L.; divorced; children: Steven C., Susan M., Jeremy W., Sara H.; m. Jane A. Glaim, Apr. 7, 1971. B.S., Pa. State U., 1939; M.D., Chgo. Med. Sch., 1943; postgrad., Inst. Psychoanalysis, Chgo., 1950-59. Diplomate: Am. Bd. Psychiatry and Neurology. Intern Beth David Hosp., N.Y.C., 1943; resident Elgin (Ill.) State Hosp., 1947-49; pvt. practice, specializing in psychiatry and psychoanalysis Chgo., 1949—; prof. psychiatry Chgo. Med. Sch., 1949-76, dean, 1966-73; dir. Ill. Dept. Mental Health, 1973-76; v.p. Mt. Sinai Hosp. Med. Ctr., Chgo., 1976-82, chmn. dept. psychiatry, 1982-87, dir. med. edn., 1987-88; prof. psychiatry Rush Med. Coll., 1977-89, prof. emeritus, 1989—; mem. staff Naples Community Hosp., 1989-95; cons. Blue Cross-Blue Shield, 1977-80, Nat. Council Aging, Ill. Psychiat. Inst.; mem. Mayor's Commn. on Aging, 1955-60. Pres. Chgo. Bd. Health, 1979-83; bd. dirs. Med. Ctr. YMCA, Med. Careers Council; bd. govs. Inst. of Medicine of Chgo. Med. Soc. Served to capt. M.C. AUS, 1944-46. Named Prof. of Year Chgo. Med. Sch., 1964, Tchr. of Year Ill. Psychiat. Inst., 1966, Chicagoan of Yr. in Medicine, 1970; WHO fellow Europe, 1970; recipient Sinai Health Service award, 1986. Fellow Am. Psychiat. Assn. (life), Am. Acad. Psychoanalysis, Am., Internat. psychoanalytic assns., Ill. Psychiat. Soc. (pres.), Chgo. Inst. Medicine, Am. Coll. Psychiatrists, Am. Coll. Psychoanalysts (pres. 1983, Laughlin award 1985), Sigma Xi, Alpha Omega Alpha, Phi Lambda Kappa (Gold medal sci. award). Home: 222 Harbour Dr Naples FL 34103-4022

LEVITT, MIRIAM, pediatrician; b. Lampertheim, Germany, June 10, 1946; came to U.S., 1948; d. Eli and Esther (Kingston) L.; m. Harvey Flisser, June 25, 1967; children: Adam, Elizabeth, Eric. AB, NYU, 1967; MD, Albert Einstein Coll. Medicine, Yeshiva U., 1971. Diplomate Am. Bd. Pediatrics. Intern Montefiore Med. Ctr., Bronx, N.Y., 1970-71, resident in pediatrics, 1971-73, attending pediatrician, 1975—; dir. outpatient svcs. pediatrics Bronx-Lebanon Hosp., N.Y.C., 1973-77; instr. pediatrics Albert Einstein Coll. Medicine, N.Y.C., 1973-76, asst. prof. clin., 1976—; med. staff Lawrence Hosp., Bronxville, N.Y., 1978—, dir. pediatrics, 1988—; sch. physician Bronxville Bd. Edn., 1983—. Fellow Am. Acad. Pediatrics; mem. Westchester County Med. Soc. Office: 1 Pondfield Rd Bronxville NY 10708-3706

LEVITT, MITCHELL ALAN, management consultant; b. N.Y.C., June 20, 1944; s. Ben and Rhea (Brody) L. BA, CUNY, 1967; MA, Temple U., 1969. Sr. ptnr., pres. Klein Consultants, N.Y.C., 1979—; bd. dirs. Hyde Products, Cleve. Mem. Am. Psychol. Assn., Inst. Mgmt. Cons. Home: 1675 York Ave New York NY 10128-6752 Office: Klein Cons 305 Madson New York NY 10165

LEVITT, RAYMOND ELLIOT, civil engineering educator; b. Johannesburg, Republic of South Africa, Aug. 7, 1949; came to U.S., 1972; s. Barnard and Riva Eleanor (Lazarus) L.; m. Kathleen Adele Sullivan, Nov. 26, 1976; children: Benjamin John, Joanna Maurine, Zoë Ellen. BSCE, U. Witwatersrand, Johannesburg, 1971; MSCE, Stanford U., 1973, PhDCE, 1975. Project engr. Christiani & Neilsen, Cape Town, Republic of South Africa, 1971-72; asst. prof. civil engring. MIT, Cambridge, 1975-79, assoc. prof., 1979-80; assoc. prof. Stanford (Calif.) U., 1980-88, prof., 1988—; assoc. dir. Ctr. for Integrated Facility Engring.; chmn. bd. Design Power, Inc., Cupertino, Calif., Vite, Stanford, Calif.; advisor U.S. Dept. Labor, Washington, 1976-77, Calif. Pub. Utilities Commn., San Francisco, 1982-84. Co-author: Union and Open-Shop Construction, 1978, Construction Safety Management, 1987, 2d edit., 1993, Knowledge-Based Systems in Engineering, 1990. Pres. Stanford Homeowners Assn., 1981-83. Recipient Marksman award Engring. News Record, N.Y.C., 1985, Commitment to Life award Nat. Safe Workplace Inst., 1987. Mem. ASCE (Huber Prize award 1982), Am. Assn. Artificial Intelligence, Project Mgmt. Inst. Unitarian. Avocations: swimming, trout fishing, tennis, music. Office: Stanford U Dept Civil Engring # 4020 Stanford CA 94305

LEVITT, ROBERT E., gastroenterologist; b. Phila., Oct. 22, 1948; s. Martin E. and Miriam G. (Elson) L.; m. Linda Levitt, Mar. 13, 1976; children: Adam, Ashley. BA summa cum laude, Temple U., 1970, MD, 1974. Diplomate Am. Bd. Internal Medicine, Am. Bd. Gastroenterology. Chief hepatology and gastrointestinal rsch. Presbyn. U. of Pa. Med. Ctr., Phila., 1979-88, staff gastroenterologist, 1979—, assoc. dir. Inst. Gastroenterology, 1981-89; chief svc. gastroenterology Bryn Mawr (Pa.) Hosp., 1985—, chief gastrointestinal sect. dept. medicine, 1988—, dir. endoscopy ste., 1988—; asst. prof. medicine U. Pa. Sch. Medicine, 1979—; dir. endoscopy suite Bryn Mawr Hosp., 1988—. Contbr. articles to med. jours., chpts. to med. books; mem. editorial adv. bd. Post-Grad. Medicine. Fellow ACP; mem. AMA (Physicians Recognition award 1978, others), Am. Gastroenterol. Assn., Am. Coll. Gastroenterology, Am. Soc. for Gastrointestinal Endoscopy, Pa. Soc. Gastroenterology, Med. Club Phila., Phi Eta Sigma, Alpha Omega Alpha. Office: 933 E Haverford Rd Bryn Mawr PA 19010-3819

LEVITT, SERENA FARR, nursing administrator; b. Washington, June 10, 1938; d. James Franklin and Evelyn Estelle (Richards) Farr; m. Edward Isaac Levitt, Jan. 2, 1966; children: Daniel Clifford, Richard Curtis, Lynette Cecelia, David Samuel Charles. AAS in Nursing, N. Va. C.C., Annandale, Va., 1977. Registered nurse. Clk. typist U.S. Dept. of Agr., Washington, 1956-58; pubs. asst. Jansky & Bailey Atlantic Rsch., Springfield, Va., 1960-61; spl. asst. avionics pubs., prodn. supr. Howard Rsch., Arlington, Va., 1962-64; tech. writer Computer Usage, Washington, Va., 1964-65; pubs. supr. Tracor, Rockville, Md., 1965; pubs. engr. Fairchild-Hiller, Bladensburg, Md., 1965-66; dir. documentation, program mgr. Krohn-Rhodes Rsch. Inst., Washington, 1966-67, Documentation Logistics Corp., Fairfax, Va., 1967-74; supr. Leewood Nursing Home, Annandale, Va., 1977-78; med. liaison Dept. Navy, Yokosuka, Japan, 1986-88; nursing supr., office mgr. Dr. Bruce E. Lessin, MD, McLean, Va., 1990-94. Recipient scholarship Zonta Club of Arlington, 1956. Mem. ANA, AAAS, IEEE, Am. Assn. Office Nurses, Nat. League Nursing, Soc. Tech. Writers and Pubs. Jewish. Avocations: jewelry design, painting, crafts, crochet, sewing. Home: 9920 Farr Dr Fairfax VA 22030-2020

LEVITT, SEYMOUR HERBERT, physician, radiology educator; b. Chgo., July 18, 1928; s. Nathan E. Levitt and Margaret (Chizever) D.; m. Phillis Jeanne Martin, Oct. 31, 1952 (div. Oct. 1981); children: Mary Jeanne, Jennifer Gaye, Scott Hayden; m. Solveig I. Ostberg, Feb. 6, 1983. B.A., U. Colo., 1950, M.D., 1954. Diplomate: Am. Bd. Radiology (trustee). Intern

Phila. Gen. Hosp., 1954-55; resident in radiology U. Calif. at San Francisco Med. Center, 1957-61; instr. radiation therapy U. Mich., Ann Arbor, 1961-62, U. Rochester, N.Y., 1962-63; asso. prof. radiology U. Okla., Oklahoma City, 1963-66; prof. radiology, chmn. div. radiotherapy Med. Coll. Va., Richmond, 1966-70; prof., head dept. therapeutic radiology U. Minn., Mpls., 1970—; cons. in field. Exec. bd. Am. Joint Com. for End Result Reporting and Cancer Staging; com. radiation oncology studies Nat. Cancer Inst. Bd. dirs., mem. exec. com. Am. Cancer Soc., 1990-95. With M.C., AUS, 1955-57. Recipient Disting. Svc. award U. Colo., 1988. Fellow Am. Coll. Radiology (bd. chancellors, Gold medal 1995), Royal Coll. Radiology (hon.); mem. Am. Radium Soc. (sec. 1981-83, pres. 1983-84, Janeway medal 1989), Radiol. Soc. N.Am. (bd. dirs. 1991—, chmn. bd. dirs. 1997—), Am. Assn. Cancer Rsch., Am. Cancer Soc. (pres. Minn. divsn. 1979-80, nat. bd., exec. com.), Am. Roentgen Ray Soc., Soc. Chairmen of Acad. Radiation Oncology Programs (pres. 1974-76), Internat. Soc. Radiation Oncology (pres. 1981-85), Soc. Nuclear Medicine, Am. Soc. Clin. Oncology, Am. Soc. Therapeutic Radiologists (exec. bd. 1974-78, pres. 1978-79, chmn. bd. 1979-80, Gold medal 1991), Deutsche Rontgengesellschaft Gesellschaft fur Medizinische Radiologie E.V. (hon.), Phi Beta Kappa, Sigma Xi., Alpha Omega Alpha. Home: 7233 Lewis Ridge Pkwy Minneapolis MN 55439-1933 Office: U Minn PO Box 436 Minneapolis MN 55455

LEVITZ, PAUL ELLIOT, publishing executive; b. Bklyn., Oct. 21, 1956; s. Alfred Lazarus and Hannah (Brenner) L.; m. Jeanette Francine Cusimano, Nov. 2, 1980; children: Nicole, Philip, Garret. Student, N.Y. U., 1973-76. Editor, pub. The Comic Reader, Bklyn., 1971-73; writer, asst. editor Nat. Periodical Publs., Inc., N.Y.C., 1973-76; editor, editorial coordinator, writer DC Comics, N.Y.C., 1976-80, mgr. bus. affairs, 1980-82, v.p. ops., 1982-84, exec. v.p., 1984-89, exec. v.p., pub., 1989—; exec. v.p., pub. MAD mag., 1993—. Jewish. Home: 23 Stony Hollow Chappaqua NY 10514 Office: DC Comics 1700 Broadway New York NY 10019-5905

LEVOVITZ, PESACH ZECHARIAH, rabbi; b. Poland, Sept. 15, 1922; came to U.S., 1923; s. Reuben and Leah Zlate (Kustanowitz) L.; m. Bluma D. Feder, Feb. 5, 1945 (dec. 1970); children: Sivya, Yaakov; m. Eleanore Herman Klugmann, 1972 (dec. Nov. 1980); children: Maurice, Danny, Renee, Jackie; m. Frayde Twersky Perlow, Dec. 18, 1989; stepchildren: Yitzchok, Faige, Joseph. B.A., Yeshivah U., 1942. Rabbi Mesivtha Tifereth Jerusalem Rabbinical Sem., 1943, Congregation Sons of Israel, Lakewood, N.J., 1944—; founder, 1945; since dean Bezalel Day Sch.; Pres. Rabbinical Council Am., 1966-68, chmn. commn. on internat. affairs, 1972; asso. chmn. Soviet Jewry commn., 1980; mem. exec. com. Synagogue Council Am., 1953—; standing com. Conf. European Rabbis and Asso. Rabbis, 1964—; steering com. World Conf. Ashkenazi and Sephardi Synagogues; Co chmn. rabbinic cabinet Bonds for Israel, 1972; chaplain Lakewood Police Dept., 1950—; vis. chaplain Naval Air Sta., Lakehurst, N.J., 1945—; nat. chmn. ann. conv. Rabbinical Council of Am., 1971; v.p. Religious Zionists Am., 1974; nat. chmn. Vaad Haroshi Religious Zionists Am., 1975; pres. Beth Din of Am., 1986. Mem. adv. bd. Lakewood Housing Council, Nat. Community Relations Adv. Council, United Jewish Appeal; chmn. bd. Sons of Israel Sr. Citizens Housing Inc., 1980; mem. N.J. Drug Utilization Council.; chmn. adv. council on protection kosher legislation to Atty. Gen., State of N.J.; mem. exec. Ocean County Jewish Fedn., 1988; co-chmn. BLue Ribbon Panel Lakewood Twp., 1992—. Recipient Revel Meml. award in religion and religious edn. Yeshivah Coll. Alumni Assn., 1967; award for outstanding rabbinic leadership Union of Orthodox Jewish Congregations Am., 1969; Nat. Assn. Hebrew Day Schs., 1980; chief Rabbi Issas Halevi Herzog Torah Fellowship award Religious Zionists Am., 1972; chmn. nat. conv., 1974; named Rabbi of Yr., Israel Bond Orgn., 1991. Mem. Conf. Presidents Nat. Jewish Orgns., Am. Conf. Soviet Jewry. Home: 403 6th St Lakewood NJ 08701-2705 Office: Congregation Sons of Israel Madison Ave Lakewood NJ 08701

LEVOWITZ, BERNARD SAMUEL, surgeon, administrator; b. Bklyn., July 17, 1926; s. Daniel Joseph and Gertrude Ruth (Fried) L.; m. Eunice Henri Tevlov, June 29, 1957; children: Lisa Eve, Joyce Eden. BS, CCNY, 1944; MD, N.Y. Med. Coll., 1949. Chief thoracic surgery Maimonides Med. Ctr., Bklyn., 1962-66; dir. surg. svcs. and dept. surgery Jewish Hosp. and Med. Ctr., Bklyn., 1966-76; dir. dept. surgery Brookdale Hosp., Bklyn., 1976-84, Caledonian Hosp., Bklyn., 1984-89; chmn. dept. surgery Woodhull Med. and Mental Health Ctr., Bklyn., 1989—. Lt. med. corps USN, 1950-53. Recipient Am. Cancer Soc. fellowship SUNY, Bklyn., 1957. Mem. ACS, Bklyn. Surg. Soc. (pres. 1974-75), N.Y. Cardiovascular Soc., N.Y. Surg. Soc., Thoracic Surgeons Soc., Am. Assn. Thoracic Surgeons. Avocations: fitness, computers, photography. Office: Woodhull Hosp 760 Broadway Brooklyn NY 11206-5317

LEVOY, MYRON, author; b. N.Y.C., Jan. 30, 1930; s. Bernard and Elsie (Schwartz) L.; m. Beatrice Fleischer, Jan. 27, 1952; children: David, Deborah. BS in Chem. Engring., CCNY, 1952; MS in Chem. Engring., Purdue U., 1953. Engr. Pratt & Whitney Aircraft Co., East Hartford, Conn., 1953-56; project engr. Reaction Motors Inc., Rockaway, N.J., 1956-67; engr. specialist Polytech. Design, Livingston, N.J., 1973-81; writer, 1955—. Author: (novel) A Necktie in Greenwich Village, 1968; Penny Tunes and Princesses, 1972, The Witch of Fourth Street and Other Stories, 1972 (Book World Honor Book 1972), Children's Book Showcase award 1973), Alan and Naomi, 1977 (Boston Globe-Horn Book award, Honor Book 1978, Jane Addams Honor Book award 1978, Am. Book award finalist 1980, Silver Pencil award The Netherlands 1981, Austrian State prize for children's lit 1981, German State prize for young adult lit. 1982, Buxtenhuder Bulle award Fed. Republic Germany 1982), A Shadow Like a Leopard, 1981 (ALA Best Book for Young Adults 1981), Three Friends, 1984, The Hanukkah of Great-Uncle Otto, 1984, Pictures of Adam, 1986 (ALA Best Book for young adults 1986, Internat. Reading Assn. young adult choice 1986), The Magic Hat of Mortimer Wintergreen, 1988 (Jr. Lit. Guild selection 1988), Kelly 'N' Me, 1992, also poetry and plays; contbr. articles to profl. jours. Mem. PEN, The Authors Guild, The Dramatists Guild. Jewish. Avocations: tennis, cross-country skiing, swimming, museums, films. Office: Writers House Inc 21 W 26th St New York NY 10010-1003

LEVY, ALAIN M., record company executive; b. France, Dec. 19, 1946. Grad., Ecole des Mines, France; MBA, U. Pa. Asst. to the pres. CBS Internat., N.Y.C., 1972-73; v.p. mktg. for Europe CBS Internat., Paris, 1973, v.p. of creative ops. for Europe; also mgr. CBS/Italy, 1978; mng. dir. CBS Disques, France, 1979; chief exec. officer PolyGram France, 1984; exec. v.p. PolyGram group, France and Fed. Republic of Germany, 1988; mgr. U.S. ops. PolyGram group, 1990—; pres., chief exec. officer, mem. bd. mgrs. PolyGram USA, 1991—; apptd. to group mgmt. com. Phillips Electronics, majority shareholder of PolyGram USA, 1991—. Office: PolyGram Records Inc 825 8th Ave New York NY 10019-7416 also: 30 Berkeley Sq, London W1X 5HA, England*

LEVY, ALAN DAVID, real estate executive; b. St. Louis, July 19, 1938; s. I. Jack and Natalie (Yawitz) L.; grad. Sch. Real Estate, Washington U., 1960; m. Abby Jane Markowitz, May 12, 1968; children: Jennifer Lynn, Jacqueline Claire. Property mgr. Solon Gershman Inc., Realtors, Clayton, Mo., 1958-61; gen. mgr. Kodner Constrn. Co., St. Louis, 1961-63; regional mgr. Tishman Realty & Constrn. Co., Inc., N.Y.C., 1963-69, v.p., Los Angeles, 1969-77; exec. v.p., dir. Tishman West Mgmt. Corp., 1977-88; pres. Tishman West Cos., 1988-92, chmn. Tishman Internat. Cos., 1993—; guest lectr. on real estate mgmt. to various forums. Mem. L.A. County Mus. Art; former chmn. Am. Art Coun.; trustee Archives Am. Art, Harvard-Westlake Sch.; bd. govs. W.L.A. coun. Boy Scouts Am. Mem. Bldg. Owners and Mgrs. Assn. L.A. (dir.), N.J. (co-founder, hon. dir.), Inst. Real Estate Mgmt. (cert. property mgr.), Urban Land Inst., Internat. Council Shopping Centers. Contbr. articles on property mgmt. to trade jours. Office: 10900 Wilshire Blvd Ste 510 Los Angeles CA 90024-6528

LEVY, ALAN JOSEPH, editor, journalist, writer; b. N.Y.C., Feb. 10, 1932; s. Meyer and Frances (Shield) L.; m. Valerie Wladaver, Aug. 7, 1956; children: Monica, Erika. A.B., Brown U., 1952; M.S. in Journalism, Columbia U., 1953. Reporter Louisville Courier-Jour., 1953-60; free-lance contbr. Life, Sat. Eve. Post, N.Y. Times, others, 1960-91; investigator Carnegie Commn. Ednl. TV, Boston, 1966-67; fgn. corr. Life, N.Y. Times mags., Prague, Czechoslovakia, 1967-71; freelance author, dramatist, corr. Vienna, 1971-90; dramaturg Vienna's English Theatre, 1977-82; founding editor in chief The Prague Post (Eng. language weekly newspaper), 1991—; lectr. on theatre Salzburg Seminar in Am. Studies, Austria, 1981; adj. prof. lit. and journalism Webster U., Vienna, 1983—; lectr.-in-residence Gritti Palace, Venice, Italy, 1987; prof. non-fiction Ctrl. European U. Summer Writers' Workshop, Prague, 1994, Charles U. Summer Writers' Workshop, Prague, 1996—. Author: Draftee's Confidential Guide, 1957, 2d edit., 1966, Operation Elvis, 1960, The Elizabeth Taylor Story, 1961, Wanted: Nazi Criminals at Large, 1962, Interpret Your Dreams, 1962, 2d edit., 1975, Kind-Hearted Tiger, 1964, The Culture Vultures, 1968, God Bless You Real Good, 1969, Rowboat to Prague, 1972, 2d edit. titled So Many Heroes, 1980, Good Men Still Live, 1974, The Bluebird of Happiness, 1976, Forever, Sophia, 1979, 2d edit., 1986, Treasures of the Vatican Collections, 1983, Ezra Pound: the Voice of Silence, 1983, W.H. Auden: In the Autumn of the Age of Anxiety, 1983, Vladimir Nabokov: The Velvet Butterfly, 1984, Ezra Pound: A Jewish View, 1988, The Wiesenthal File, U.K. edit. 1993, U.S. edit. 1994 (U.S. Author of the Year Am. Soc. of Journ. and Authors, 1995); dramatist The World of Ruth Draper, 1982; librettist Just an Accident?, 1983 (Ernst Krenek prize City of Vienna, 1986). Trustee Thomas Nast Found., Landau, Germany, 1978—, Saving Our Heritage Assn., Oberdorf, Switzerland, 1994—. Served with U.S. Army, 1953-55. Recipient New Republic Younger Writer award, 1958, Best Enterprise Reporting award Sigma Delta Chi, 1959, golden Johann Strauss medal City of Vienna, 1981, travel writing awards Pacific Area Travel Assn., 1978, Govt. of Malta, 1985, Franz Kafka medal European Franz Kafka Circle, Prague, 1996, T.G. Masaryk medal Masaryk Acad. of the Arts, Prague, 1996; Bernard De Voto fellow Middlebury Coll., 1963. mem. Am. Soc. Journalists and Authors, Authors Guild and Dramatists Guild of Authors League of Am., Overseas Press Club Am., PEN, Fgn. Press assns. Vienna, Prague, Austrian Soc. Authors, Composers and Music Pubs., Czech Union Journalists. Democrat. Jewish. Office: Wallace Literary Agency 177 E 70th St New York NY 10021-5109 Address: The Prague Post, Na Porici 12, CZ-11530 Prague 1, Czech Republic

LEVY, ALBERT, family physician; b. Stanleyville, Congo, Zaire, Nov. 8, 1948; came to U.S., 1977; s. Moise and Eugenie J. (Menache) L.; children: Antonia G., Eric M. MD, Fed. U. Brazil, Rio de Janeiro, 1973, MS in Field Medicine, 1976. Diplomate Am. Bd. Family Physicians, Am. Bd. Family Practice, Am. Bd. Geriatric Medicine. Chief family medicine sect. Our Lady of Mercy Hosp., Bronx, N.Y., 1989-96; pvt. practice family medicine Manhattan Family Practice, N.Y.C., 1990—; physician Montefiore Med. Ctr., Bronx, 1994—; asst. clin. prof. dept. family medicine Albert Einstein Coll. Medicine, Bronx, N.Y., 1994—; asst. prof. N.Y. Med. Coll., Valhalla, N.Y., 1994—; with Beth Israel Med. Ctr., 1986, St. Luke's/Roosevelt Med. Ctr., 1986, Lenox Hill Hosp., 1995. Fellow Am. Acad. Family Physicians, Royal Soc. Medicine, (Eng.), N.Y. Acad. Medicine; mem. AMA, Am. Geriatric Soc., World Orgn. Nat. Colls./Acads. Family Physicians, N.Y. Acad. Scis., Med. Soc. State of N.Y., N.Y. County Acad. Family Physicians (v.p. 1992), Soc. Tchrs. Family Medicine. Jewish. Avocations: tennis, opera, travel, wind surfing. Home: 311 Wilton Rd Westport CT 06880-1426 also: 25 Sutton Pl S New York NY 10022 Office: Manhattan Family Practice 911 Park Ave New York NY 10021-0337

LEVY, ARNOLD S(TUART), real estate company executive; b. Chgo., Mar. 15, 1941; s. Roy and Esther (Scheff) L.; m. Eva Cichosz, Aug. 8, 1976; children: Adam, Rachel, Deborah. BS, U. Wis., 1963; MPA, Roosevelt U., 1970. Dir. Neighborhood Youth Corps, Chgo., 1966-68; v.p. Social Planning Assn., Chgo., 1968-70; planning dir. Office of Mayor Chgo., 1970-74; dep. dir. Mayor's Office Manpower, Chgo., 1974-75; sr. v.p. Urban Investment & Devel. Co., Chgo., 1975-93; pres., CEO Stone-Levy, LLC, Chgo., 1994—; mem. S-L Hospitality Group, LLC, 1995—; pres. JMB/Urban Hotels, Hotel and Resort Devel. Group, JMB/Urban Devel. Co., 1985-93; ptnr. Pierce and Co., 1994—; bd. dirs. Hostmark Mgmt. Group, Inc.; mem. Urban Land Inst. Pres. Ark, Chgo., 1970-72, Parental Stress Svcs., Chgo., 1978-79; past lectr. DePaul U., Roosevelt U., Loyola U.; v.p. Inst. Urban Life, Chgo., 1983—. Co-editor: The Professionals' Guide to Commercial Property Development, 1988. Bd. dirs. Mus. Broadcast Communications, Chgo. Coun. of Urban Affairs, Am Shalom, pres. Ill. Humane Soc. ; steering com. Radio Hall of Fame; chmn. Spertus Inst. Jewish Studies, Glencoe Plan Commn., Carlton Club (Chgo.), Twin Orchard Club. Home: 535 Park Ave Glencoe IL 60022-1501 Office: Stone-Levy & Co LLC 630 Dundee Rd Ste 220 Northbrook IL 60062-2750

LEVY, ARTHUR JAMES, public relations executive, writer; b. Bklyn., Dec. 23, 1947; s. Bernard and Bernice (Lipner) L.; m. Andrea Susan Hall, May 11, 1980; children: Zoe Jess, Jake Benjamin. BA, Brandeis U., 1969. Account exec., disc jockey Sta. WBUS-FM, Miami Beach, Fla., 1971; pop music critic Magic Bus Newspaper, Miami Beach, 1971; sr. editor, writer Zoo World mag., Ft. Lauderdale, Fla., 1971-74; chief writer Atlantic Records, N.Y.C., 1975-78; assoc. dir. Press and Pub. Info. dept. Columbia Records, N.Y.C., 1978-88, nat. dir. media services, publicity dept., 1988-93; v.p. Sony Music Entertainment Comms. Dept., N.Y.C., 1993-95; so. regional v.p. Rock Writers of the World, 1973-74; seminar panelist United Jazz Coalition, N.Y.C., 1983—, CMJ Folk, 1987—, New Music Seminar Folk, 1989—; ind. music publicity cons., writer, 1995—. Writer, researcher album and video liner notes for Rolling Stones, Blue Öyster Cult, Eric Andersen, Johnny Cash, Herbie Mann, Taj Mahal, Al Kooper, Robert Johnson, Jan Hammer, Julio Iglesias, Manfred Mann, Jimmy Webb, Pete Seeger, Montreux Festival '77, Elvis Presley: Golden Celebration, 1985 (Grammy nomination), Songs of the Civil War, Iggy Pop; appeared on album session (Finnadar Records) Idil Biret's New Line Piano, 1978, (Columbia) Jaroslav Jakubovic's Checkin' In, 1978. Named Publicist of Yr. Columbia Records, 1982, 87, Media Man of Yr. Record World mag., N.Y.C., 1981. Mem. NARAS (gov. N.Y. chpt., Grammy voting com., crafts com.), Rock and Roll Hall of Fame (nominating com., mus. experts com.), Nat. Acad. Popular Music. Avocation: record collecting.

LEVY, BERNARD C., electrical engineer, educator; b. Princeton, N.J., July 31, 1951. Ingenieur civil des mines, Paris, 1974; PhD in Elec. Engring., Stanford U., 1979. Prof. dept. elec. and computer engr. U. Calif. Fellow IEEE (image and multidimensional signal processing tech. com. 1992—). Office: Univ of California Davis Dept Electrical & Computer Eng Davis CA 95616*

LEVY, BURTON See LANE, BURTON

LEVY, DALE PENNEYS, lawyer; b. Phila., Sept. 10, 1940; d. Harry M. and Rosalind (Fried) Penneys; m. Richard D. Levy, Dec. 20, 1970; children: Jonathan D., Michael Z. BA, Wellesley Coll., 1962; JD, U. Pa., 1967. Bar: Pa. 1967, U.S. Ct. Appeals (3rd cir.) 1971. Assoc. Blank, Rome, Comisky & McCauley, Phila., 1967-76, ptnr., 1976—; bd. dirs. Phila. Sch., Phila. Indsl. Devel. Corp. Contbr. articles to profl. jours. Bd. dirs., chair Women in Transition, 1983-85, active adv. bd., 1985—; chair Women's Rights Com., 1978; bd. dirs. Phila. Sr. Ctr., 1994—, Phila. Theatre. Co., 1995—. Mem. ABA, Pa. Bar Assn., Phila. Bar Assn. (past chair women's rights com.). Mem. ABA (real property, probate and trust law sect., chairperson com. on pub.-pvt. ventures/privatization), Phila. Bar Assn. (real estate, corp., banking and bus. law sect., mem. women's rights com.). Office: Blank Rome Comisky & McCauley 4 Penn Center Plz Philadelphia PA 19103-2521

LEVY, DANIEL, economics educator; b. Tschakaia, Georgian Republic, Georgia, Nov. 13, 1957; came to U.S., 1983; s. Shabtai and Simha (Leviashvili) L.; m. M. Sarit Adler, Sept. 10, 1981; children: Avihai, Eliav. BA, Ben-Gurion U., Beer-Sheva, Israel, 1982; MA, U. Calif., Irvine, 1989, PhD, 1990. Lectr. U. Minn., Mpls., 1983-88, St. Olaf Coll., Northfield, Minn., 1986-88, The Coll. St. Catherine, St. Paul, 1987-88; prof. Pepperdine U., Irvine, 1989-90, U. Calif., Irvine, 1990-91, Union Coll., Schenectady, N.Y., 1991-92, Emory U., Atlanta, 1992—; computer software programmer Mac Cartuli, 1989. Contbr. articles to profl. jours. Treas. Minn. Student Orgn., 1984-85. Mem. Internat. Inst. Forecasters, Am. Econ. Assn., Soc. Econ. Dynamics and Control, Econometric Soc., Western Econ. Assn., Mensa. Avocations: basketball, tennis, chess, computers, piano. Office: Emory U Dept Economics Atlanta GA 30322

LEVY, DAVID, lawyer, insurance company executive; b. Bridgeport, Conn., Aug. 3, 1932; s. Aaron and Rachel (Goldman) L. BS in Econs., U. Pa., 1954; JD, Yale U., 1957. Bar: Conn. 1958, U.S. Supreme Ct. 1963, D.C. 1964, Mass. 1965, N.Y. 1971, Pa. 1972; CPA, Conn. Acct. Arthur Andersen & Co., N.Y.C., 1957-59; sole practice Bridgeport, 1959-60; specialist tax law IRS, Washington, 1960-64; counsel State Mut. Life Ins. Co., Worcester, Mass., 1964-70; assoc. gen. counsel taxation Penn Mut. Life Ins. Co., Phila., 1971-81; sole practice Washington, 1982-87; v.p., tax counsel Pacific Mut. Life Ins. Co., Newport Beach, Calif., 1987—. Author: (with others) Life Insurance Company Tax Series, Bureau National Affairs Tax Management Income Tax, 1970-71. Mem. adv. bd. Tax Mgmt., Washington, 1975-90, Hartford Inst. on Ins. Taxation, 1990—; bd. dirs. Citizens Plan E Orgn., Worcester, 1966-70. With AUS, 1957. Mem. ABA (vice-chmn. employee benefits com. 1980-86, ins. cos. com. 1984-86, torts and ins. practice sect., subcom. chair ins. cos. com. tax sect. 1994—), Assn. Life Ins. Counsel, AICPA, Beta Alpha Psi. Jewish.

LEVY, DAVID, broadcasting executive; b. Phila.; s. Benjamin and Lillian (Potash) L.; m. Lucile Alva Wilds, July 25, 1941 (div. 1970); children: Lance, Linda; m. Victoria Robertson, Apr. 23, 1987; 1 stepchild, Kate Jolson. BS in Econs., U. Pa., 1934, MBA, 1935. With Young & Rubicam, Inc., N.Y.C., 1938-59, v.p., assoc. dir. radio-TV dept., mem. agy. plans bd.; v.p. charge network programs and talent NBC, N.Y.C., 1959-61; exec. producer Filmways, L.A., 1964-68, Goodson-Todman Prodns., West Coast, 1968-69; exec. v.p., dir. Golden Orange Broadcasting Co., Anaheim, Calif., 1969-88, bd. dirs.; exec. v.p. charge TV activities Four Star Internat., Inc., Beverly Hills, Calif., 1970-72; pres. Wilshire Prodns. Inc., Beverly Hills, 1972—; mem. faculty Calif. State U., Northridge, 1973-77; TV advisor Citizens for Eisenhower, 1952, 56, Haig for Pres., 1988; dir. radio and TV for Citizens for Eisenhower-Nixon, 1956; prodr., writer 3-network program for closing Rep. campaign broadcast Four More Years, 1956; writer, co-prodr. closing program election eve behalf of Wendell Willkie, 1940; cons. Sec. Treasury, 1944-46; chief radio sect. war fin. divsn. Treasury Dept. Exec. prodr. Double Life of Henry Phyffe, 1965; exec. prodr., creator TV series Addams Family, 1964-66, The Pruitts of Southampton ABC-TV, 1966-67; prodr. world premier Sarge, also exec. prodr., creator TV series Universal Studios NBC, 1971-72; creator Hollywood Screen Test, Bat Masterson, Appointment with Adventure, Outlaws, The Americans, Real West, The Kate Smith Daytime Hour, others; launched Maverick, Shirley Temple, National Velvet, Father Knows Best, Godfrey's Talent Scouts, People's Choice, I Married Joan, Life of Riley, Dr. Kildare, Bonanza, Hitchcock Presents, Thriller, Saturday Night at the Movies, Walt Disney's Wonderful World of Color, Robert Taylor and the Detectives, The Deputy, Car 54, 1st Bob Newhart Show, 1st Phil Silvers Show, Goodyear TV Playhouse, Peter Pan (starring Mary Martin), What's My Line, Make the Connection, Say When, others; prodr. Paramount TV, 1972-73, Hanna Barbera Prodns. NBC, 1973-74; creative cons. Name That Tune, Ralph Edwards Prodns. and Sandy Frank Prodns., 1974-81; creative cons. You Asked For It, Battle of the Planets; TV cons. Mark Goodson Prodns., 1989—; co-creator, exec. prodr. Face the Music TV series, 1980-81; author: (novels) The Chameleons, 1964, The Network Jungle, 1976, The Gods of Foxcroft, 1970, Potomac Jungle, 1990; contbr. short stories to popular mags. Lt. USNR, 1944-46. Recipient Treasury medal and disting. svc. citation U.S. Treasury Dept., 1946. Mem. ASCAP, TV Acad., Writers Guild Am., Prodrs. Guild Am. (past sec., bd. dirs.), Hollywood Radio-TV Soc. (pres. 1969-70, award 1970), Caucus for Prodrs., Writers and Dirs. (sec., steering com., exec. dir. 1974—, Disting. Svc. award 1985, Spl. award of merit for 20 yrs. svc. 1994). Republican. Jewish. Avocation: writing. Office: 210 S Spalding Dr Beverly Hills CA 90212-3608

LEVY, DAVID, lawyer; b. Atlanta, July 7, 1937; s. Meyer and Elsie (Reisman) L.; m. Diane L. Lerner; children: Jeffrey Marc, Robert William, Danielle Beth, Margo Shaw; stepchildren: Mitchell S. Haber, Cort A. Haber. B.A., Emory U., 1959, LL.B., 1961; LL.M., Georgetown U., 1964. Bar: Ga. 1961. Atty. SEC, Washington, 1961-65; assoc., partner Arnstein, Gluck, Weitzenfeld & Minow, Chgo., 1965-71; partner Kaler, Karesh & Frankel, Atlanta, 1971-73; exec. v.p. adminstrn., counsel, dir. Nat. Svc. Industries, Inc., Atlanta, 1973—; also bd. dirs. Nat. Service Industries, Inc., Atlanta. Mem. Am., Ga. bar assns. Office: Nat Svc Industries Inc 1420 Peachtree St NE Atlanta GA 30309-3002

LEVY, DAVID ALFRED, immunology educator, physician, scientist; b. Washington, Aug. 27, 1930; s. Stanley A. and Blanche B. (Berman) L.; m. Annette Levy-Badoux; children: Jill, William, Stanley. BS, U. Md., 1952, MD, 1954. Diplomate Am. Bd. Internal Medicine, Am. Bd. Allergy and Immunology. Intern, resident in medicine U. Hosp., Balt., 1954-59; physician VA Hosp., Balt., 1961-62; fellow dept. microbiology Sch. Medicine Johns Hopkins U., 1962-66, asst. prof. radiol. sci. Sch. Hygiene and Pub. Health, Sch. Medicine, 1966-68, assoc. prof. Sch. Hgiene and Pub. Health, Sch. Medicine, 1968-71, prof. radiol. sci. and epidemiology Sch. Hygiene and Pub. Health, Sch. Medicine, 1972-73, prof. biochemistry Sch. Hygiene and Pub. Health, Sch. Medicine, 1973-82, with joint appointments in epidemiology and medicine Sch. Medicine, 1973-82, in pathobiology Sch. Medicine, 1980-82, prof. immunology and infectious diseases Sch. Medicine, 1982-86; mem. FDA Panel on Rev. of Allergenic Extracts, 1975-83; mem. allergy and immunology rev. com. Nat. Inst. Allergy and Infectious Diseases, 1975-77; adj. dir. Centre d'Immunologie et de Biologie, Pierre Fabre, S.A., 1985-90; cons. to pharm. industry, 1990—. Editorial bd. Clin. Immunology and Immunopathology, 1971-76, Revue d'Allergologie Française; contbr. articles to med. jours. and books. Sci. dir. Centre d'Allergie, Hopital Rothschild, Paris, 1991—. With U.S. Army, 1959-61. Fellow Am. Acad. Allergy and Immunology; mem. Internat. Union Immunol. Socs. (vice chmn. allergen standardization subcom. 1980-83), Am. Assn. Immunologists, French Soc. Allergology, Sigma Xi. Home and Office: 11 Quai St Michel, 75005 Paris France

LEVY, DAVID MATTHEW, lawyer; b. Boston, Feb. 13, 1954; s. Harold and Lillian (Kruger) L.; m. Keily Downey, June 14, 1986. BA, Cornell U., 1975; JD, U. Mich., 1979. Bar: D.C. 1979, U.S. Ct. Appeals (D.C. and 10th cirs.) 1980, U.S. Ct. Appeals (3rd cir.) 1982, U.S. Ct. Appeals (9th cir.) 1986, U.S. Supreme Ct. 1989. Assoc. Sidley & Austin, Washington, 1979-86, ptnr., 1986—. Contbr. articles to profl. jours. Mem. ABA (vice-chair postal matters com. adminstrv. law sect. 1991-92, chair 1992-95). Office: Sidley & Austin 1722 I St NW Washington DC 20006-3705

LEVY, DAVID STEVEN, college administrator; b. L.A., Mar. 9, 1955; s. Henry and Gloria Grace (Barouh) L. BA, Occidental Coll., 1977; MA, 1979. Asst. dir. fin. aid Calif. State Coll., San Bernardino, 1978-79; fin. aid counselor Calif. State U.-Northridge, 1979-80; assoc. dir. student fin. aid Calif. State U.-Dominguez Hills, 1980-82; dir. fin. aid Occidental Coll., L.A., 1982-88; dir. fin. aid Calif. Inst. Tech., Pasadena, Calif., 1988—, assoc. dean of students, 1991—; mem. Title IA Adv. Com. Calif., 1977-80; negotiator U.S. Dept Edn. Mem. life-long learning com. Calif. Postsecondary Edn. Commn., 1980—, mem. student fin. aid issues com., 1984—; mem. Sallie Mae Fin. Aid Adv. Bd., 1994—. Richter fellow Princeton U., 1976; Calif. State U. adminstrv. fellow, 1981—. Mem. Nat. Assn. Student Fin. Aid. Adminstrs. (Meritorious Achievement award 1988, bd. dirs. 1991—, commn. dir. 1994-95), Mortar Board Alumni Assn. (pres. 1977—), Calif. Assn. Student Fin. Aid Adminstrs. (ind. segmental rep. 1984, sec. 1985, treas. 1986-88, lifetime mem. 1996, Pres.'s award 1986, 93, Meritorious Svc. award 1994, Segmental Leadership award 1992, Creative Leadership award 1990), Western Assn. Student Fin. Aid Adminstrs. (Disting. Svc. award 1990, Pres. Disting. Svc. award 1992), Nat. Assn. Student Fin. Aid Adminstrs., Phi Beta Kappa, Delta Phi Epsilon, Psi Chi, Phi Alpha Theta, Sigma Alpha Epsilon. Jewish. Co-editor Calif. Student Aid Commn. Student Aid Workbook, 1977—; co-author, contbr. Playing the Selective College Admissions Game, 1994; contbr. Paying Less for College, Top Colleges for Science. Home: 2704 Franklin St La Crescenta CA 91214 Office: CalTech 515 S Wilson Ave Pasadena CA 91106-3212

LEVY, DONALD HARRIS, chemistry educator; b. Youngstown, Ohio, June 30, 1939; s. Gabriel and Minnie (Lerner) L.; m. Susan Louise Miller, June 14, 1964; children—Jonathan G., Michael A., Alexander B. B.A., Harvard U., 1961; Ph.D., U. Calif.-Berkeley, 1965. Asst. prof. chemistry U. Chgo., 1967-74, assoc. prof., 1974-78, prof., 1978—, chmn. dept. chemistry, 1983-85, Ralph and Mary Otis Isham prof., 1994-97, Albert A. Michelson Dist. Svc. prof., 1997—; mem. chemistry adv. com. NSF. Assoc. editor Jour. Chem. Physics, 1983—. Fellow Am. Phys. Soc., AAAS; mem. Am. Chem. Soc., Optical Soc. Am., Am. Acad. Arts and Scis., Nat. Acad. Scis. Office: U Chgo Dept Chemistry 5640 S Ellis Ave Chicago IL 60637-1433

LEVY, EDWARD CHARLES, JR., manufacturing company executive; b. Detroit, Nov. 14, 1931; s. Edward Charles and Pauline (Birndorf) L.; m. Julie Ruth Honigman, July 11, 1955; 2 children. SB, MIT, 1952. From staff to exec. v.p. Edward C. Levy Co., Detroit, 1952-70; pres. Edward C. Levy Co., 1970—. Bd. dirs. Edward C. Levy Found., Karmanos Cancer Inst., Detroit, Round Table of Christians and Jews, Mackinac Ctr. for Pub. Policy; trustee Children's Hosp. of Mich., Citizens Rsch. Coun. Mich., Washington Inst. for Near East Policy; officer Am. Israel Pub. Affairs Com. Mem. ASTM, Am. Concrete Inst., Engring. Soc. Detroit, Detroit Club, Renaissance Club, Franklin Hills Country Club. Jewish. Office: Edward C Levy Co Inc 8800 Dix St Detroit MI 48209-1093

LEVY, EDWARD KENNETH, mechanical engineering educator. BS, U. Md., 1963; MS, MIT, 1964, ScD, 1967. Prof. mech. engring. Lehigh U., 1967—; assoc. prof. NAE. Mem. AIChE, ASME, Am. Nuclear Soc. Achievements include research in fluid mechanics, heat transfer and applied thermodynamic aspects of energy with emphasis on power generation systems. Office: Lehigh U Energy Rsch Ctr 117 Atlss St Bethlehem PA 18015-4728

LEVY, EUGENE, actor, director, screenwriter; b. Hamilton, Ont., Can.. Appearences include (films) Cannibal Girls, 1972, Running, 1979, Nothing Personal, 1980, Heavy Metal, 1981, Strange Brew, 1983, Going Berserk, 1983, National Lampoon's Vacation, 1983, Splash, 1984, Armed and Dangerous, 1986, The Canadian Conspiracy, 1986, Club Paradise, 1986, Speed Zone, 1989, Father of the Bride, 1991, Once Upon A Crime, 1992, Stay Tuned, 1992, I Love Trouble, 1994, Father of the Bride, Part II, 1995, Waiting for Guffman, 1996, Multiplicity, 1996; (TV) The Lovebirds, 1979, From Cleveland, 1980, George Burn's Comedy Week, 1985, Dave Thomas: The Incredible Time Travels of Henry Osgood, 1986, Billy Crystal-Don't Get Me Started, 1986, Bride of Boogedy, 1987, Ray Bradbury Theatre, 1988; actor, dir.: (TV) Second City TV, 1977-81, SCTV Network, 1981-83, The Last Polka, 1985, Autobiographies: The Enigma of Bobby Bittman, 1988; dir.: (TV) Second City's 50th Anniversary Special, 1988, Partners in Love, 1992, Sodbusters, 1994, Harrison Bergeron, 1995. Office: William Morris Agy 151 S El Camino Dr Beverly Hills CA 90212-2704*

LEVY, EUGENE PFEIFER, architect; b. Little Rock, Dec. 14, 1936; s. Emmanuel Gabe and Elizabeth (Pfeifer) L.; m. Gertrude Watkins Cromwell, June 24, 1959; children: Edwin Cromwell, Andrew Stewart, Charles Pfeifer. B.Arch., U. Va., 1959. Registered architect, Ark., Calif., Ga., Tex. Apprentice Erhart, Eichenbaum, Rauch & Blass, Little Rock, 1959-60; architect, pres. Cromwell, Truemper, Levy, Thompson & Woodsmall, Inc., Little Rock, 1962—. Bd. dirs. Little Rock Boys' Club, 1973—, bd. dirs. Temple B'nai Israel, Little Rock, 1975-78, Little Rock chpt. NCCJ, 1984; chmn. Ctrl. Ark. chpt. ARC, 1989. Capt. U.S. Army, 1960-62. Recipient numerous awards including: U.S. Corps. of Engrs. 1985 Design award for Resident Office and Visitors Ctr., Greers Ferry Lake, Ark., USAG 1985 First Honor award for commissary, Camp Foster, Okinawa, Japan, AIA 1980 Design award for Master Plan and First Phase Design for Multi Agy. Office Bldg., State of Ark. Capitol Ground, Little Rock, AIA Honorable Mention award for Systematics, Inc., Corp. Hdqrs., 1982, AIA Design award for Winthrop Rockefeller Meml. Gallery Ark. Arts Ctr., Little Rock, 1982, AIA Design for Commissary, USAF Acad., Colo., 1983, Little Rock Riverfront Belvedere, AIA Design award, 1987, AIA Design award for Itzkowitz residence, Little Rock, 1991. Fellow AIA (Design award Commissary USAF; mem. Greater Little Rock C. of C. (com. 1983-84). Clubs: Little Rock Country, Little Rock Athletic. Home: 5415 Sherwood Rd Little Rock AR 72207-5333 Office: Cromwell Truemper Levy Thompson Woodsall Inc 101 S Spring St Little Rock AR 72201-2413

LEVY, EZRA CESAR, aerospace scientist, real estate broker; b. Habana, Cuba, Sept. 22, 1924; s. Mayer D. and Rachel Levy; m. Gaynor D. Popejoy, 1980; children from previous marriage: Daniel M., Diana M. Levy Friedman, Linda R. Levy Brenden. MS, UCLA, 1951. Sect. head Douglas Aircraft Co., Santa Monica, Calif., 1951-54; dept. head Lockheed Aircraft Co., Van Nuys, Calif., 1954-56, Librascope, Glendale, Calif., 1956-57, Radioplane, Van Nuys, 1957-58; asst. dept. mgr. Space Tech. Labs., Redondo Beach, Calif., 1958-60; asst. divsn. dir. TRW, Redondo Beach, Calif., 1960-74; now real estate broker Regency Realty Corp., Temple City, Calif. Author: Laplace Transform Tables, 1958; contbr. articles to profl. jours. Cpl. U.S. Army, 1944-46. Mem. Temple City C. of C. (bd. dirs. 1992-97), Masons (past master and sec.). Democrat. Jewish. Avocations: art, music, philately.

LEVY, GERHARD, pharmacologist; b. Wollin, Germany, Feb. 12, 1928; came to U.S., 1948, naturalized, 1953; s. Gotthold and Eliesabeth (Luebeck) L.; m. Rosalyn Mincer, June 8, 1958; children: David, Marc, Sharon. B.S., U. Calif. at San Francisco, 1955, Pharm.D., 1958; Dr. honoris causa, Uppsala (Sweden) U., 1975, Phila. Coll. Pharmacy and Sci., 1979, L.I. U., 1981, U. Ill., 1986, Hoshi U., Japan, 1996. Asst. prof. pharmacy U. Buffalo, 1958-60; asso. prof. pharmacy State U. N.Y. at Buffalo, 1960-64, prof. biopharmaceutics, 1964-72, distinguished prof. pharmaceutics, 1972-75, chmn. dept. pharmaceutics, 1966-70, univ. disting. prof. emeritus, 1995; vis. prof. Hebrew U., Jerusalem; cons. WHO, 1966, Bur. Drugs Adv. Panel System, FDA, 1971-74; mem. com. on problems of drug safety NRC, 1971-75; mem. pharmacol.-toxicol. com. NIH, 1971-75. Mem. editorial bd. Jour. Pharm. Sci, 1970-75, Clin. Pharmacology and Therapeutics, 1969—, Internat. Jour. Clin. Pharmacology, 1968-78, Drug Metabolism and Disposition, 1973-78, Jour. Pharmacokin Biopharm, 1972—, Internat. Jour. Pharm., 1977-95, Jour. Pharmacobi-Dynamics, 1979-93, Pharm. Res., 1983-95; contbr. articles to profl. jours. Served with AUS, 1950-51. Recipient Ebert prize, 1969, Am. Pharm. Assn. Research Achievement award, 1969, McKeen Cattell award Am. Coll. Clin. Pharmacology, 1978, Host-Madsen medal Internat. Pharm. Fedn., 1978, Oscar B. Hunter award in exptl. therapeutics Am. Soc. Clin. Pharmacology and Therapeutics, 1982, Volwiler Research Achievement award Am. Assn. Colls. Pharmacy, 1982, Scheele award Swedish Acad. Pharmaceutical Scis., 1992, 1st Lifetime Achievement in the Pharm. Scis. award Internat. Pharm. Assn., 1994; named Alumnus of Year U. Calif. Sch. Pharmacy Alumni Assn., 1970. Fellow Am. Pharm. Assn., Acad. Pharm. Scis. (Takeru Higuchi Research prize 1983), AAAS; mem. Inst. Medicine of Nat. Acad. Scis., Am. Assn. Pharm. Scientists (Dale E. Wurster Rsch. award 1992), Am. Soc. Exptl. Pharmacology and Therapeutics. Home: 169 Surrey Run Buffalo NY 14221-3321 Office: SUNY Sch Pharmacy Amherst NY 14260

LEVY, H. RICHARD, biochemistry educator; b. Leipzig, Germany, Oct. 22, 1929; came to U.S., 1946; s. Berthold and Charlotte Agnes Hedwig (Frank) L.; m. Betty Louise Samuels, June 12, 1960; 1 child, Karen. BSc in Chemistry, Rutgers U., 1950; PhD in Biochemistry, U. Chgo., 1956. Instr. Ben May Lab. for Cancer Rsch., U. Chgo., 1959-61, asst. prof., 1961-63; asst. prof. dept. bacteriology and botany Syracuse (N.Y.) U., 1963-66, assoc. prof. dept. bacteriology and botany, 1966-70, assoc. prof. dept. biology, 1970-71, prof. of biochemistry, 1971—; chmn. dept. biology, 1993—. Contbr. articles and revs. to profl. publs. Grantee NIH, NSF, 1963—. Mem. AAAS, AAUP, Am. Chem. Soc., Am. Soc. for Biochemistry and Molecular Biology, Protein Soc. Home: 144 Lewis Ave Syracuse NY 13224-2232 Office: Syracuse U Biology Dept 130 College Pl Syracuse NY 13210-2819

LEVY, HAROLD BERNARD, pediatrician; b. Shreveport, La., Apr. 27, 1918; s. Phillip and Ida (Sperling) L.; m. Betty Ann Friedenthal, Nov. 29, 1942; children—James, Charles, Roger, Judy Levy Harrison. B.S., La. State U., 1937; M.D., 1940. Diplomate Am. Bd. Pediatrics. Intern, Tri-State Hosp., Shreveport, 1940-41; resident in pediatrics Shreveport Charity Hosp., 1946-48; practice medicine specializing in pediatrics, Shreveport, La., 1948—; co-med. dir. Caddo Found. for Exceptional Children, 1953—; founder, dir. spl. clinic for learning disabilities La. Handicapped Children's Services, 1955—; clin. assoc. prof. pediatrics La. State U. Med. Sch., Shreveport, 1973—; faculty mem. Nat. Coll. Juvenile Justice, Reno, 1975—; mem. staff Schumpert, Willis-Knighton, Doctors, La. State U. hosps.; Pres., Shreveport Summer Theater, 1953; pres. Caddo-Bossier Safety Council, 1959-60. Served to maj. M.C., USAAF, 1942-46. Recipient Brotherhood citation NCCJ, 1976; Spl. recognition award La. Assn. Children with Learning Disabilities, 1976; Axson-Choppin award La. Pub. Health Assn., 1983. Mem. Am. Acad. Cerebral Palsy and Devel. Medicine (pres. 1983), Am. Acad. Pediatrics, La. Med. Soc., So. Med. Assn., AMA, Orton Dyslexia Soc., Sigma Xi. Republican. Jewish. Club: East Ridge Country. Author: Square Pegs, Round Holes, The Learning Disabled Child in the Classroom and at Home, 1973; contbr. articles to profl. jours. Home: 6026 Dillingham Ave Shreveport LA 71106-2131 Office: 865 Margaret Pl Ste 316 Shreveport LA 71101-4542

LEVY, HAROLD JAMES, physician, psychiatrist; b. Buffalo, Feb. 15, 1925; s. Sidney Harold and Evelyn (Sperling) L.; m. Arlyne Adelstein, July 3, 1958; children: Sanford Harvey, Richard Alan, Kenneth Lee. MD, U. Buffalo, 1946. Diplomate in psychiatry Am. Bd. Neurology and Psychiatry. Intern Erie County Med. Ctr., Buffalo, 1946-47, asst. resident in psychiatry, 1947-48, asst. chief psychiatry, 1953-58, attending psychiatrist, 1957-90; cons. psychiatrist Erie County Med. Ctr., 1990—; fellow in psychosomatic medicine Med. Sch. U. Buffalo, Erie County Med. Ctr., 1950-53; psychiatrist Buffalo, 1950—; mem. courtesy staff Millard Fillmore Hosp., 1957, clin. asst., 1958, asst. attending physician, 1959-63, assoc. attending physician, 1963-64, attending physician, 1964-90, chmn. dept. psychiatry, 1968-90, cons., 1990—; attending psychiatrist BryLin Psychiat. Hosp. (formerly Linwood Bryant Hosp.), Buffalo, 1955—, clin. dir. psychiatry, 1966-91; staff psychiatrist Psychiat. Clinic, Family Ct. Erie County, N.Y., 1959-63, psychiat. dir. clinic, 1963-80; mem. courtesy staff in psychiatry St. Joseph's Intercommunity Hosp., Buffalo, 1969-71, cons. in psychiatry, 1971—; cons. in psychiatry St. Francis Hosp., 1972-91, Sisters of Charity Hosp., 1985—; asst. in psychiatry Med. Sch. SUNY, Buffalo, 1950-52, instr. 1952-55, assoc. 1955-70, clin. asst. prof. 1970-86, clin. assoc. prof., 1986—; mem. psychiat. staff Rosa Coplon Jewish Home and Infirmary, 1957-72, chmn. dept. psychiatry, 1969-72; staff psychiatrist Chronic Disease Rsch. Inst., sect. on alcoholism Med. Sch. SUNY, Buffalo, 1950-53; psychiat. cons. Dent Clinic Found. Millard Fillmore Hosp., 1967—, Lafayette Gen. Hosp., Buffalo, 1973-85. Pres. Lemezo Enterprises Inc., Buffalo, 1970, Sanricken Enterprises Inc., Buffalo, 1970—; mem. exec. com. Blue Shield Western N.Y. Served to capt. M.C., AUS, 1948-50. Fellow Am. Psychiat. Assn. (life, pres. Western N.Y. dist. br. 1969-70), Am. Soc. Psychoanalytic Physicians, Am. Soc. Advancement Electrotherapy; mem. AMA, Israel Med. Assn., N.Y. State Med. Soc., Erie County Med. Soc. (chmn. com. on mental health, econs. com., publ. com. for bull. 1959-78), Buffalo Acad. Medicine, Maimonides Med. Soc. (pres. 1968-69), N.Y. State Soc. Med. Rsch., Western N.Y. Neuropsychiat. Soc. (pres.-elect 1965-66), Western N.Y. Psychiat. Assn. (pres. 1974-75), Gen. Alumni Assn. SUNY, Buffalo (treas. exec. bd. 1967-69, numerous offices), SUNY-Buffalo Sch. Medicine Alumni Assn. (past pres., numerous offices), Med. Students' Aid Soc. (past nat. pres., chmn. bd. dirs. 1990-92), B'nai B'rith (exec. com. Anti Defamation League), Cherry Hill Colf and Country Club, Alpha Omega Alpha, Phi Lambda Kappa (nat. dir., past nat. v.p., past nat. pres., chmn. bd. dirs. 1990-92), Beta Sigma Rho. Home: 47 Longleat Dr Buffalo NY 14226-4114 Office: Psychiat Assocs of Western NY 2740 Main St Buffalo NY 14214-1702

LEVY, HERBERT MONTE, lawyer; b. N.Y.C., Jan. 14, 1923; s. Samuel M. and Hetty D. L.; m. Marilyn Wohl, Aug. 30, 1953; children: Harlan A., Matthew D., Alison Jill. A.B., Columbia U., 1943, LL.B., 1946. Bar: N.Y. 1946, U.S. Dist. Ct. (so. dist.) N.Y. 1946, U.S. Ct. Appeals (2d cir.) 1949, U.S. Dist. Ct. (ea. dist.) N.Y. 1949, U.S. Supreme Ct. 1951, U.S. Ct. Appeals (10th cir.) 1956, U.S. Tax Ct. 1973, U.S. Ct. Appeals (4th cir.) 1988. Assoc. Rosenman, Goldmark, Colin & Kaye, 1946-47, Javits & Javits, 1947-48; staff counsel ACLU, 1949-56; sole practice, 1956-64; ptnr. Hoffman, Gartlir, Hoffheimer, Gottleib & Gross, 1965-69; sole practice, N.Y.C., 1969—; bd. dirs. Music Outreach; faculty N.Y. County Lawyers Assn.; former lectr. Practising Law Inst. Exec. com. on law and social action Am. Jewish Congress, 1961-66; trustee Congregation B'nai Jeshurun, 1987—, chmn. bd. trustees 1988-91, gen. counsel bd. trustees, 1991-92. Mem. Fed. Bar Coun. (past trustee), Bar Assn. City N.Y., N.Y. County Lawyers Assn., 1st Amendment Lawyers Assn., Assn. Trial Lawyers Am., Democrat. Author: How to Handle an Appeal (Practising Law Inst.), 1968, rev. edit. 1982, 2d rev. edit., 1990; also legal articles. Home: 285 Central Park W Apt 12W New York NY 10024-3006 Office: 60 E 42nd St Rm 4210 New York NY 10165-4299

LEVY, JACQUES, educator, theater director, lyricist, writer; b. N.Y.C., July 29, 1935; s. Milton and Jean (Brandler) L.; m. Claudia Carr, Apr. 27, 1980; children: Maya, Julien. BA, CCNY, 1956; MA, Mich. State U., 1958, PhD, 1961. Moderator dirs./playwrights unit The Actors Studio; co-dir. Open Theater Workshop, N.Y.C.; tchr. play analysis, lyric writing New Sch. Social Rsch.; tchr. acting, directing, playwriting Hunter Coll., N.Y.C.; tchr. directing Tisch Sch Arts NYU, Grad. Dept. Theater Columbia U., Sch. Drama Yale U.; head univ. theater program Colgate U., Hamilton, N.Y., prof. Eng. Dir.: (Broadway plays) Oh! Calcutta!, Almost an Eagle, Doonesbury; dir., writer: (off-Broadway, regional, European plays) Turtlenecks, Back Country, Miami Lights; dir.: (off-Broadway, regional, European plays) America Hurrah, Scuba Duba, Red Cross (Obie award for disting. direction), La Turista, Geography of a Horse Dreamer, Rock Garden, Where Has Tommy Flowers Gone?, American Days, Sleep, Mensch Meyer, The Golden Land, The Potsdam Quartet, The Bed Was Full, Green Pants, K2, The Glass Menagerie, Exact Change, Blood Wedding, A Chekhov Concert, The Beggar's Opera, The Rolling Thunder Review; playwright, lyricist: Miami Lights, Berchtesgaden, Back Country, Just a Season, (adaptation) Alcestis, Eyes in the Heat, Tell the Rain; lyricist: (Byrds'album) Byrdmaniax, Untitled, (Roger McGuinn's solo album) Thunderbyrd, (Bob Dylan's album) Desire, Fame...the Musical, The Golden Land. Recipient Obie award disting. direction, Obie award group achievement as co-dir. Open Theater, Drama Desk directing award nominations, Outer Critics Circle directing award nominations, Grammy award lyricist nominations; BMI grantee (5). Office: Colgate U Univ Theater 13 Oak Dr Hamilton NY 13346-1338

LEVY, JEROME, dermatologist; retired naval officer; b. Bklyn., Aug. 17, 1926; s. Alexander and Pauline (Wollkof) L.; m. Leona Elsie Eligator, June 6, 1948; children—Andrew B., Eric J., Peter C., David J. Student, Wesleyan U., 1944-45; postgrad., 1952-54; A.B., Yale U., 1947; M.D., Albany Med. Coll., 1958. Diplomate Am. Bd. Dermatology. Commd. ensign M.C., U.S. Navy, 1957, advanced through grades to capt., 1972; intern U.S. Naval Hosp., Newport, R.I., 1958-59; resident U.S. Naval Hosp., Phila., 1960-62, U. Pa. Grad. Sch. Medicine, Phila., 1962-63; chief dept. dermatology U.S. Naval Hosp., Memphis, 1963-67, Yokosuka, Japan, 1967-70, Long Beach, Calif., 1974-75; head outpatient dermatology clinic San Diego Naval Hosp., 1970-72; sr. med. officer Keflavik, Iceland, 1972-74; ret., 1975; med. dir. dermatology Westwood Pharm Co., Buffalo, 1975-82; acting chief dermatology dept. Buffalo Gen. Hosp., 1981-82; cons. Erie County Health Dept., 1979-82; clin. assoc. prof. SUNY, Buffalo Med. Sch., 1980-82; practice medicine specializing in dermatology, Coronado, Calif., 1982-90. Contbr. articles to med. jours. Decorated Navy Commendation medal, Joint Service Commendation medal; Knight's Cross of the Order of Falcon (Iceland). Fellow Am. Acad. Dermatology, ACP; mem. AMA, So. Med. Assn., Assn. Mil. Surgeons, U.S., Navy League, Alpha Omega Alpha. Republican. Jewish. Home: 3352 Lucinda St San Diego CA 92106-2932

LEVY, JOSEPH, lawyer; b. N.Y.C., June 9, 1928; s. Morris Joseph and Dora (Cohen) L.; m. Gertrud C. Roeder, Jan. 20, 1967; children—Diana N., Susan R. BBA cum laude, Coll. City N.Y., 1950; JD cum laude, N.Y. U., 1954. Bar: N.Y. 1955, D.C. 1968. Asso. Parker, Chapin and Flattau, N.Y.C., 1954-62; ptnr. firm Rivkin, Sherman & Levy (and predecessors), N.Y.C., 1962-84, Schnader, Harrison, Segal & Lewis, 1984-93; v.p., sec., dir. Trecom Bus. Sys., Inc., Edison, N.J., 1993—; sec., dir. Horizons Comms. Corp., 1970-78, Quad Typographers, Inc., 1965-79; sec. Savin Bus. Machines Corp., 1959-84, On-Line Systems, Inc., 1968-78, Lambda Tech., Inc., 1970-78, Programming Methods, Inc., 1969-72, Kreisler Mfg. Cor., 1969-72, Peck & Peck, 1970-73, v.p., sec., dir. Trecom Bus. Systems, Inc., 1985—. Served to capt. AUS, 1951-53. Home: 254 University Way Paramus NJ 07652-5516 Office: Trecom Bus Sys Inc 333 Thornall St Edison NJ 08837-2220

LEVY, JOSEPH LOUIS, publishing company executive; b. Bklyn., June 21, 1947; s. Myron M. and Miriam M. (Glick) L.; m. Carol A. Arschin, July 3, 1973; children: Darren Ross, Marissa Darcel. BBA, Pace U., 1970. Dir. mktg. Frost & Sullivan Inc., N.Y.C., 1966-71; v.p. Internat. Data Corp., Waltham, Mass., 1972-80, v.p. mktg., Framingham, Mass, 1980-86; pres. Pub. and Communications Group, 1986-87, group pres. Internat. Data Corp., 1987; pres., group pub. CIO Comms., 1988—. Contbr. spl. reports on computer industry and tech. to Fortune mag., 1975-86, Industry Week mag., 1984-85, US News and World Report, 1986, Forbes mag, 1987—. Named Young Exec. of Yr., Internat. Data Corp., 1972-76. Mem. Am. Mktg. Assn. (Mktg. Man of Yr. 1970), Am. Mgmt. Assn., Soc. Info. Mgmt., Sales Execs. Club. Republican. Office: 492 Old Connecticut Path Framingham MA 01701-4584

LEVY, JOSEPH WILLIAM, department stores executive; b. Fresno, Calif., 1932; m. Sharon Sorokin; children: Felicia, Jody, Bret. BS, U. So. Calif., 1954. Asst. merchandising mgr., then mgr. Gottschalks, Inc., Fresno, 1956-72, exec. v.p., 1972-82, chmn., chief exec. officer, 1982—; chmn. exec. com. Frederick Atkins Inc., N.Y.C., 1992—, also bd. dirs. Chmn. Fresno Econ. Devel. Corp., 1982-83; mem. Calif. Transp. Commn., 1983-91, chmn., 1986-87; sec. City of Fresno Equipment Corp.; mem. bus. adv. coun. Sch. Bus. and Adminstrv. Scis., Calif. State U., Fresno; trustee Community Hosps. Cen. Calif. With USNR, 1950-58. Mem. Calif. C. of C. (bd. dirs.), Fresno County and City C. of C. (transp. com.), U. So. Calif. Sch. Bus. Alumni Assn., San Joaquin Country Club, U. Sequoia-Sunnyside Country Club, Downtown Club (Fresno). Home: 6475 N Sequoia Dr Fresno CA 93711-1232 Office: Gottschalks Inc PO Box 28920 Fresno CA 93729-8920

LEVY, KENNETH, music educator; b. N.Y.C., Feb. 26, 1927; s. Meyer and Sylvia Levy; m. Clara Brooks Emmons, Jan. 25, 1956; children: Robert Brooks, Helen Gardner. A.B., Queens Coll., 1947; M.F.A., Princeton U., 1949, Ph.D., 1956. Instr. music Princeton (N.J.) U., 1952-54; from asst. prof. to Fredrick R. Mann. prof. Brandeis U., Waltham, Mass., 1954-66; prof. music Princeton U., 1966—, chmn. dept. music., 1967-70, 88, Scheide prof. music history, 1988-95. Author: Music: A Listener's Introduction, 1983, Gregorian Chant and the Carolingians, 1997; assoc. editor: Anthologie de la Chanson Parisienne au Seizieme Siecle, 1953; mem. editorial bd. Monumenta Musicae Byzantinae, 1968—, Grove's Dictionary, 6th edit, Early Music History, 1980—; contbr. articles to profl. jours. With USNR, 1945-46. Recipient Fulbright award Italy, 1962-63, Howard T. Behrman award for disting. achievements in humanities, 1983, Deems Taylor award ASCAP, 1989, Pres.'s Disting. Teaching award Princeton U., 1995; Guggenheim fellow, 1955-56, Am. Coun. Learned Socs. fellow, 1970-71, sr. fellow Dumbarton Oaks, Harvard U., 1992-96; vis. fellow Cambridge U., 1995. Fellow Medieval Acad. Am.; mem. Am. Philos. Soc. Office: Princeton U Dept Music Woolworth Ctr Mus Studies Princeton NJ 08544

LEVY, KENNETH JAMES, advertising executive; b. Cleve., June 15, 1949; s. Morton Leonard and Joan (Beitman) L.; m. Carol Wallisa, Sept. 7, 1974; children: Michael, Allison. BSBA, Ohio State U., 1971, MBA, 1973. Asst. account exec. Ketchum Advt., Pitts., 1973-75, account exec., 1975-77, account supr., 1977-78; account exec. Grey Advt., N.Y.C., 1978-79, account supr., 1979-80, v.p., mgmt. supr., 1980-84, v.p., group mgmt. supr., 1984-87, sr. v.p., 1987-94; exec. v.p., 1994—. Advisor Jr. Achievement Pitts., 1979; vol. Give Kids the World Village. Mem. Ohio State U. Alumni Assn., Whippoorwill Country Club (Armonk, N.Y.). Avocations: golf, physical fitness, biographical reading. Home: 3 Carolyn Pl Armonk NY 10504-1101

LEVY, KENNETH JAY, psychology educator, academic administrator; b. Dallas, Sept. 18, 1946; s. Reuben and Ruth (Okon) L.; children: Ryan S., Scott D. BA, U. Tex., 1968, MA, 1969; PhD, Purdue, 1972. Asst. prof. psychology SUNY, Buffalo, 1972-75, assoc. prof., 1976-78, prof., 1979—, chmn. dept. psychology, 1976-78, dean social scis., 1978-82, various adminstrv. positions, 1985—, assoc. provost, 1987—. Contbr. numerous articles to profl. jours.; editorial cons. Psychometrika. Home: 39 Shire Dr S East Amherst NY 14051-1816 Office: SUNY at Buffalo Capen Hall Buffalo NY 14260

LEVY, LEAH GARRIGAN, federal official; b. Miami, Fla., Apr. 29, 1947; d. Thomas Leo and Mary (Flaherty) Garrigan; m. Roger N. Levy, May 2, 1977; children: Philip, Aaron. Student, George Mason U. Mem. legis. staff U.S. Ho. Reps., 1973-75; mem. scheduling staff U.S. Senate, 1975-77, mem. adminstrv. scheduling staff, 1977-81; staff asst. pub. liaison The White House, 1982-84; spl. asst. U.S Dept. Transport, Washington, 1984-89, U.S. Dept. Housing, Washington, 1989—; scheduling asst. Empower Am., Washington, 1993-94; scheduler majority leader Dick Armey U.S. Ho. of Reps., Washington, 1995—. Contbr. to Rep. Nat. Com., Washington. Contbr. Rep. Nat. Conv. Va. Rep. Party, Washington; del. Va. State GOP Conv., Richmond, 1994. Roman Catholic. Avocations: tennis, golf, reading (nonfiction).

LEVY, LEON, investment company executive; b. N.Y.C., Sept. 13, 1925; s. Jerome and Sadie (Samuelson) L.; m. Roxanne Wruble, Dec. 13, 1959 (div.); m. Shelby White, Aug. 12, 1983. BSS, City Coll., 1948. Security analyst Hirsch & Co., N.Y.C., 1948-51; gen. ptnr. Odyssey Ptnrs. (formerly Oppenheimer & Co.), N.Y.C., 1951—; chmn. bd. dirs. Oppenheimer Mutual Funds; chmn. bd. dirs. Avatar Holdings, Inc.; bd. dirs. United Kingdom Fund; lectr. CCNY, 1952-59. Trustee Bard Coll., Inst. Fine Arts, NYU; pres. Inst. Advanced Studies, Rockefeller U., Jerome Levy Inst. for Econ. Rsch., N.Y.C.; bd. dirs. Internat. Found. Art Rsch., John Simon Guggenheim Found. Office: Odyssey Ptnrs LP 31 W 52nd St New York NY 10019-6118

LEVY, LEONARD WILLIAMS, history educator, author; b. Toronto, Ont., Can., Apr. 9, 1923; s. Albert and Rae (Williams) L.; m. Elyse Gitlow, Oct. 21, 1944; children: Wendy Ellen, Leslie Anne. BS, Columbia U., 1947, MA, 1948, PhD (Univ. fellow), 1951; LHD, Brandeis U., 1987; DHL (hon.), Claremont Grad. Sch., 1991. Research asst. Columbia U., 1950-51; instr., asst. prof., asso. prof., prof. Brandeis U., Waltham, Mass., 1951-70, first incumbent Earl Warren chair constl. history, 1957-70, dean Grad. Sch. Arts and Scis., 1958-63, dean faculty arts and scis., 1963-66; Andrew W. Mellon prof. humanities, history, chmn. grad. faculty history Claremont (Calif.) Grad. Sch., 1970-90, prof. emeritus, 1990—; Disting. scholar in residence So. Oreg. State Coll., 1990—; Reiser lectr. U. Chgo. Law Sch., 1964; Gaspar Bacon lectr. Boston U., 1972; Elliott lectr. U. So. Calif. Law Sch., 1972; Hugo Black lectr. U. Ala., 1976; Bicentennial lectr., City of St. Louis, 1976; disting. lectr. U. Cin., 1978. Author: The Law of the Commonwealth and Chief Justice Shaw, 1957, Legacy of Suppression; Freedom of Speech and Press in Early American History, 1960, Jefferson and Civil Liberties; The Darker Side, 1963, Origins of the Fifth Amendment, 1968 (Pulitzer Prize in history 1969), Judgments: Essays on American Constitutional History, 1972, Against The Law: The Nixon Court and Criminal Justice, 1974, Treason Against God: History of the Offense of Blasphemy, 1981, Emergence of a Free Press, 1985, Constitutional Opinions, 1986, The Establishment Clause, 1986, Original Intent and the Framers' Constitution, 1988, Blasphemy: Verbal Offense Against the Sacred, 1993, Seasoned Judgments, 1994, A License to Steal: The Forfeiture of Property, 1995; editor: Major Crises in American History, 1962, The American Political Process, 1963, The Presidency, 1964, The Congress, 1964, The Judiciary, 1964, Parties and Pressure Groups, 1964, Freedom of the Press from Zenger to Jefferson, 1966, American Constitutional Law, 1966, Judicial Review and the Supreme Court, 1967, Freedom and Reform, 1967, Essays on The Making of the Constitution, 1969, rev. edit. 1987, The Fourteenth Amendment and the Bill of Rights, 1970, The Supreme Court Under Earl Warren, 1972, Jim Crow in Boston, 1974, Essays on the Early Republic, 1974, Blasphemy in Massachusetts, 1974, The Framing and Ratification of the Constitution, 1987, The American Founding, 1988, American Constitutional History, 1989; co-editor: Ency. Am. Presidency, 4 vols., 1993; gen. editor: Am. Heritage Series, 60 vols., Harper Documentary History of Western Civilization, 40 vols.; editor-in-chief Ency. Am. Constn., 4 vols., 1986, supplement, 1991; gen. editor: Bicentennial History of the American Revolution; adv. bd.: Revs. in Am. History, John Marshall Papers, Salmon P. Chase Papers; contbr. articles to profl. jours. Mem. nat. bd. Commn. on Law and Social Action, Am. Jewish Congress; mem. U.S. Bicentennial Commn. Am. Revolution, 1966-68; mem. exec. council Inst. for Early Am. History and Culture; mem. nat. adv. council ACLU, Pulitzer prize juror, chmn. biog. jury, 1974, history jury, 1976. With AUS, 1943-46. Recipient Sigma Delta Chi prize for journalism history, 1961, 86; Frank Luther Mott prize Kappa Tau Alpha, 1961; Pulitzer prize for history, 1969; Commonwealth Club prize for nonfiction, 1975; Oboler Meml. Prize of Am. Library Assn. for Intellectual Freedom, 1986; Cert. Merit ABA, 1986; Henry L. Mencken award Free Press Assn., 1986; Dartmouth Medal Am. Library Assn., 1987, 95; Guggenheim fellow, 1957-58; Center For Study Liberty in Am. fellow Harvard, 1961-62; Am. Bar Found. sr. merit fellow, 1973-74; Am. Coun. Learned

Socs. fellow, 1973; NEH sr. fellow, 1974. Mem. Am. Hist. Assn. (Littleton-Griswold com. legal history), Orgn. Am. Historians, Am. Soc. Legal History (dir.), Am. Antiquarian Soc., Soc. Am. Historians, Inst. Early Am. History and Culture (exec. coun.), Mass. Hist. Soc., Kappa Delta Pi. Democrat. Home: 1025 Timberline Ter Ashland OR 97520-3436

LEVY, LOUIS EDWARD, retired accounting firm executive; b. Cleve., Nov. 16, 1932; s. Jerome and Bessie (Goldberg) L.; m. Sandra Harris, Mar. 4, 1956; children: Jerold, Richard, Lawrence. BBA, Case Western Res. U., 1956. CPA, N.Y. Agt. IRS, Cleve., 1956; ptnr., vice chmn. KPMG Peat Marwick, N.Y.C., 1958-90; bd. dirs. Household Internat. Inc., Kimberly-Clark Corp., Alex Brown./Flag Investors Group; former mem. emerging issues task force Fin. Acctg. Standards Bd.; former adj. prof. Columbia U. Grad. Sch. Bus. Chmn. emeritus Nat. Multiple Sclerosis Soc., N.Y.C., 1978—; fellow Brandeis U., Boston, 1981—. Recipient Braden award Weatherhead Sch. Mgmt. Case Western Res. U., 1984, Community Svc. award Brandeis U., 1980. Mem. AICPA (chmn. quality control inquiry com.), Ohio Soc. CPA's, Maplewood Country Club (N.J.), Sky Club. Republican. Jewish. Avocations: tennis, boating.

LEVY, MARK IRVING, lawyer; b. Chgo., June 28, 1949; s. Kenneth Warren and Arleen (Langhaus) L.; m. Judith Jarrell Levy, Sept. 8, 1979; children: Elizabeth Sara, Mitchell Bennett. BA summa cum laude/hons. ex. distinction, Yale U., 1971, JD, 1975. Bar: D.C. 1976, U.S. Dist. Ct. D.C. 1977, U.S. Supreme Ct. 1980, Ill. 1986, U.S. Ct. Appeals (D.C. cir.) 1990, U.S. Ct. Appeals (6th, 7th and 8th cirs.) 1990, U.S. Tax Ct. 1990, U.S. Ct. Appeals (9th cir.) 1993, U.S. Ct. Appeals (2d, 4th and 10th cirs.) 1994, U.S. Ct. Appeals (3d, 5th, 11th and Fed. cirs.) 1996. Law clk. Judge Gerhard A. Gesell, Washington, 1975-76; assoc. Covington & Burling, Washington, 1976-79, 81-83; asst. to solicitor gen. U.S. Dept. Justice, Washington, 1979-81, 83-86; ptnr. Mayer, Brown & Platt, Chgo., 1987-93; dep. asst. atty. gen. Civil Div. U.S. Dept. Justice, Washington, 1993-95; ptnr. Howrey & Simon, Washington, 1995—. Exec. editor Yale Law Jour., 1974-75. Recipient Israel H. Peres prize Yale Law Sch., 1975. Mem. Am. Acad. Appellate Lawyers, Law Club of Chgo., Yale Law Sch. Alumni Assn. (former treas., exec. com. mem. 1987-90), Phi Beta Kappa. Home: 7609 Winterberry Pl Bethesda MD 20817-4847 Office: Howrey & Simon 1299 Pennsylvania Ave NW Washington DC 20004

LEVY, MARK RAY, lawyer; b. Denver, Mar. 2, 1946; s. Richard C. and Hilde (Lindauer) L.; m. Patricia Loeb, June 13, 1971; children: Betsy, Robert. BA, U. Colo., 1968, JD, 1972. Bar: Colo. 1972, U.S. Dist. Ct. Colo. 1972. Assoc. Holland & Hart LLP, Denver, 1972-78, ptnr., 1978—; adj. prof. the lawyering process U. Denver Law Sch., 1990-93; mem. spl. adv. com. Colo. Securities Bd., 1996—. Author: (with others) Colorado Corporations Manual, 1987, Colorado Corporation Law and Practice, 1990. Trustee Congregation Emanuel, Denver, 1984-90, mem. legal com., 1989—; chmn. Denver Alumni Phonathon U. Colo. Law Sch., 1989-90, mem. alumni bd., 1992-96, chmn. alumni bd., 1994-95; trustee Nat. Repertory Orch., 1995-96. Mem. ABA, Colo. Bar Assn. (Blue Sky Law task force 1980-81, co-chmn. Colo. securities law rev. com. 1988-91, Article 8 of UCC com. 1995-96), Denver Bar Assn., Rockies Venture Club. Office: Holland and Hart LLP 555 17th St Ste 3200 Denver CO 80202-5555

LEVY, MARVIN DANIEL, professional football coach, sports team executive; b. Chgo., Aug. 3, 1929. BA, Coe Coll., 1950; MA, Harvard U., 1951. High sch. coach St. Louis, 1951-52; asst. football coach Coe Coll., Cedar Rapids, Iowa, 1953-55; asst. coach, then head coach U. N.Mex., 1956-59; head coach U. Calif., Berkeley, 1960-63, Coll. William & Mary, Williamsburg, Va., 1964-68; asst. coach Phila. Eagles, NFL, 1969, Los Angeles Rams, NFL, 1970, Washington Redskins, NFL, 1971-72; head coach Montreal (Que., Can.) Alouetts, Can. Football League, 1973-77, Kansas City (Mo.) Chiefs, NFL, 1978-82, Chgo. Blitz, U.S. Football League, 1984; head coach Buffalo Bills, NFL, 1986—, v.p., 1995—. Office: Buffalo Bills 1 Bills Dr Orchard Park NY 14127-2237*

LEVY, MARVIN DAVID, composer; b. Passaic, N.J., Aug. 2, 1932; s. Benjamin and Bertha (Tramberg) L. B.A., N.Y. U., 1954; M.A., Columbia U., 1956; pupil, Philip James, Otto Luening. Asst. dir. Am. Opera Soc., 1952-61; music critic Mus. Am. Herald Tribune, 1952-58; assoc. prof. of music Bklyn. Coll., 1974-76. Composer: orchestral Caramoor Festival Overture, 1958, Symphony, 1960, Kyros, 1961, One Person, 1962, Piano Concerto, 1970, Trialogus, 1972, In Memoriam: W.H. Auden, 1974, Canto de los Maranos, 1978, Pascua Florida, 1987, Arrows of Time, 1988; oratorios For The Time Being, 1959, Sacred Service, 1964, Masada (Nat. Symphony commn.); operas Mourning Becomes Electra (Met. Opera commn.), 1967, Escorial, 1958, Sotoba Komachi, 1957, The Tower, 1956; musical The Grand Balcony, 1990, 95; film theater scores; chamber music; artistic dir. Ft. Lauderdale Opera, 1989-94. Recipient Prix de Rome, 1962, 65, N.Y.C. Scroll award for Disting. and Exceptional Svc., 1967; Guggenheim grantee, 1960, 64, Ford Found. grantee, 1965, Damrosch grantee, 1961, NEA grantee, 1974, 78. Mem. ASCAP. Office: care Sheldon Soffer Mgmt 1507 Argyle Dr Apt 107 Fort Lauderdale FL 33312-1575*

LEVY, MATTHEW DEGEN, consumer products executive, management consultant; b. N.Y.C., Dec. 5, 1958; s. Herbert Monte and Marilyn (Wohl) L.; m. Laura Ann Goldin, Aug. 20, 1989; 1 child, Ely Samuel. BA magna cum laude and spl. honors, Tufts U., 1980; M in Pub. and Pvt. Mgmt., Yale U., 1983. Rsch. assoc. State St. Cons., Boston, 1980-81; cons. to vice chmn. Yankelovich, Skelly & White, Inc., Stamford, Conn., 1982; staff fin. analyst IBM Corp., White Plains, N.Y., 1983-86; co-founder, prin. WSY Cons. Group, Inc., Greenwich, Conn., 1986-93; area dir. and mng. cons. Renaissance Strategy Group, N.Y.C., 1993-95; dir. bus. planning and devel. Sara Lee Corp., N.Y.C., 1995—; cons. Yale Sch. Mgmt. Alumni Assn., 1989; bus. mgr., anchorman WMFO Radio, Medford, Mass., 1977-80; co-instr. course on decision-making Tufts U., 1977. Contbr. articles to mags. Bd. dirs. DOROT, N.Y.C., 1986—, pres. bd., 1991-94; mem. allocations com. United Way of Greenwich, 1984-86. Mem. Yale Club of N.Y. Avocations: running, political button collecting. Home: 415 E 85th St New York NY 10028-6355 Office: Sara Lee Corp 516 W 34th St New York NY 10001-1311

LEVY, MICHAEL B., business educator; b. Balt., July 12, 1947; m. Bonny B. Wolf; 1 child. BA, Brown U., 1969; PhD, Rutgers U., 1979. Tchr. social studies, coach Loyola High Sch., Balt., Md., 1973-76; teaching asst. Rutgers U., New Brunswick, N.J., 1977-78, instr., 1978-84; asst. prof. Tex. A&M Univ., College Sta., 1978-84, assoc. prof. polit. sci., 1984-85; economist joint econ. com. U.S. Congress, Washington, 1985-87; adminstrv. asst. to Sen. Lloyd Bentsen U.S. Senate, Washington, 1987-93; asst. sec. legis. affairs U.S. Dept. Treasury, Washington, 1993-95; adj. instr. Georgetown U., Washington, 1986-93, disting. vis. prof., 1995—; legis. cons. Brownstein, Hyatt, Farber and Strickland, Denver and Washington, 1995—. Editor: Political Thought in America, 1981, 87, (with Philip Abbot) The Liberal Future in America: Essays in Renewal, 1985, (with Edward Portis) Handbook of Political Theory and Policy Sciences, 1989; contbr. articles to profl. jours. Bevier fellow Rutgers U., 1979; R.J. Reynolds fellow for So. High Sch. Tchrs. Office: Georgetown U Sch Bus 37th & O NW Washington DC 20057

LEVY, MICHAEL RICHARD, publishing executive; b. Dallas, May 17, 1946; s. Harry Aaron and Florence (Friedman) L.; m. Rebecca Gloria Schulman, Jan. 19, 1969 (div. 1993); children: Anne Rachel, Tobin Janel and Mara Elizabeth (twins). BS, U. Pa., 1968; JD, U. Tex., 1972. Bar: Tex. 1972. Pres. Mediatex Communications Corp., Austin, Tex., 1972—; founder, pub. Tex. Monthly mag., 1973—. Mem. bd. visitors M.D. Anderson Cancer Ctr.; trustee Capital of Tex. Pub. Telecomms. Coun., Austin; mem. Austin EMS Quality Assurance Com.; bd. dirs. St. Marks Sch. Tex. Named One of Outstanding Amss. under 40, Esquire mag., 1984; recipient Excellence in Media award Susan G. Komen Found., 1989, Disting. Alumnus award St. Mark's Sch. Tex., 1994, Katherine Ripley award for print media Planned Parenthood Dallas, 1996. Mem. State Bar Tex., Mag. Pubs. Am. (bd. dirs.), World Pres.' Orgn., Ex-Students' Assn. U. Tex. (life), Met. Club, Rockefeller Ctr. Club, Crescent Club, Westwood Country Club, Headliners Club. Home: PO Box 146 Austin TX 78767-0146 Office: Texas Monthly PO Box 1569 Austin TX 78767-1569

LEVY, NELSON LOUIS, physician, scientist, corporate executive; b. Somerville, N.J., June 19, 1941; s. Myron L. and Sylvia (Cohen) L.; m. Joanne Barnett, Dec. 21, 1963 (div. 1972); children: Scott, Erik, Jonathan; m. Louisa Douglas Stiles, Dec. 21, 1974; children: Michael, Andrew, David. BA/BS summa cum laude, Yale U., 1963; MD, Columbia U., 1967; PhD, Duke U., 1972. Diplomate Am. Bd. Allergy and Immunology. Intern, U. Colo. Med. Ctr., Denver, 1967-68; resident Duke U. Med Ctr., Durham, N.C., 1970-73; rsch. assoc. NIH, Bethesda, Md., 1968-70; asst. prof. immunology Duke U. Med. Ctr., 1972-75, assoc. prof. immunology and neurology, 1975-80, prof., 1980-81; dir. biol. rsch. Abbott Labs., Abbott Park, Ill., 1981, v.p. rsch., 1981-84; pres. Nelson L. Levy Assocs., Inc., 1984-87; chief exec. officer The CoreTechs Corp., Lake Forest, Ill., 1987-92; pres., Fujisawa Pharm., Deerfield, Ill., 1992-93; CEO Ill. Tech. Devel. Corp., 1993-95; chmn. bd. dirs., CEO The Core Techs Corp., Lake Forest, 1995—; chmn. bd. dirs. Horizon Quest, Inc., Laguna Hills, Calif., 1996—; cons. Upjohn Co., Inc., Kalamazoo, 1976-77, G.D. Searle Inc., Skokie, Ill., 1984-87, Erbamont Inc., Stamford, Conn., 1984-90, Eastman Kodak, Rochester, N.Y., LyphoMed, Inc., Rosemont, Ill., 1985-89, The Nutrasweet Co., Skokie, Ill., 1985-88, Bayer AG, 1987-89, Fujisawa Pharm. Co., 1988-92, Alcide Corp., 1991—, Ameritech, 1993—, several venture cos.; bd. dirs. Intek Diagnostics, Inc., Helis, Inc., Bionica Pty, Ltd., Software Care Mgmt. Systems, Inc., Heybach Enterprises, Inc., Saniguard Products Corp., MedVac, Inc., Anthra Pharms., Inc., Myotech Corp., ChemBridge Corp., Mei-Rui Pharma, Ltd. Editor several books; contbr. articles to profl. publs., chpts. to books. Coach Little League, Am. Youth Soccer Orgn.; corp. adv. bd. Family Svc. of South Lake County, 1991—. Surgeon USPHS, 1968-70. Grantee Am. Cancer Soc., 1970-75, NIH, 1971-81, Nat. Multiple Sclerosis Soc., 1974-81, Ill. Dept. Commerce and Cmty. Affairs, 1993—. Mem. Am. Assn. Immunologists, Am. Assn. Cancer Rsch., Licensing Execs. Soc., Rotary, Phi Beta Kappa, Sigma Xi, Alpha Omega Alpha, Phi Gamma Delta. Avocations: triathlons, tennis, biking, sailing. Office: 1391 Concord Rd Lake Forest IL 60045-1506

LEVY, NORMAN, motion picture company executive; b. Bronx, N.Y., Jan. 3, 1935; s. Irving and Helen (Saunders) L.; m. Hirsch, Nov. 11, 1962; children—Jordan, Brian, Matthew. BA, CCNY. Salesman Universal Pictures, 1957-67, Nat. Gen. Pictures, 1967-74; gen. sales mgr. Columbia Pictures, Burbank, Calif., 1974-75; exec. v.p. in charge domestic sales Columbia Pictures, 1975-77, exec. v.p. mktg., 1977-78, pres. domestic distbn., 1978-80, pres. Twentieth Century Fox Entertainment Group, 1980-81, vice chmn., 1981-85; mktg., distbn. cons., 1985—; chmn. New Century/Vista Film Co. L.A., 1985-91; chmn., chief exec. officer Domino Entertainment, L.A., 1991-92; pres., CEO Creative Film Enterprises, L.A., 1992—. Served with U.S. Army, 1955-57. Office: Creative Film Enterprises Ste 1201 1801 Avenue Of The Stars Los Angeles CA 90067-5806

LEVY, NORMAN B., psychiatrist, educator; b. N.Y.C., 1931; s. Barnett Theodore and Lena (Gulnick) L.; m. Lya Weiss (dec.); children: Karen, Susan, Joanne; m. Carol Lois Spiegel, 1 son, Robert Barnett. B.A. cum laude, NYU, 1952; M.D., SUNY. Diplomate: Am. Bd. Psychiatry and Neurology (examiner). Intern Maimonides Med. Center, Bklyn.; resident physician in medicine U. Pitts.-Presbyn. Hosp.; resident in psychiatry Kings County Hosp. Center, Bklyn.; instr. psychiatry SUNY Downstate Med. Ctr. Coll. Medicine, Bklyn.; asst. prof. SUNY Downstate Med. Ctr. Coll. Medicine, assoc. prof.; prof. State U. N.Y. Downstate Med. Center Coll. Medicine, 1980-95; presiding officer faculty SUNY Downstate Med. Ctr. Coll. Medicine, assoc. dir. med-psychiat. liaison service, 1965-80; prof. psychiatry, medicine, surgery and coordinator psychiat. liaison services N.Y. Med. Coll.; clin. prof. psychiatry, adj. prof. of medicine Health Science Ctr. SUNY, Bklyn., 1992—; dir. liaison psychiatry divsn. Westchester County Med. Ctr., 1980-95, mem. exec. com. med. staff, 1981-85, 89-92; dir., consultation-liaison and emergency psychiatry Coney Island Hosp., Bklyn., 1996—; vis. prof. psychiatry and medicine So. Ill. U. Sch. Medicine; vis. prof. psychiatry John A. Burns Sch. Medicine, U. Hawaii, 1981; coord. 1st Internat. Conf. Psychol. Factors in Hemodialysis and Transplantation, 1978, 2d-9th Internat. Confs. on Psychonephrology; cons. NIMH; chief med. svcs. USAF Hosp., Ashiya, Japan; clin. prof. psychiatry, adj. prof. medicine SUNY Health Sci. Ctr., Bklyn., 1996—. Author: (with others), editor: Living or Dying: Adaptation to Hemodialysis, 1974, Psychonephrology I: Psychological Factors in Hemodialysis and Transplantation, 1981, Men in Transition: Theory and Therapy, 1982, Psychonephrology II: Psychological Problems in Kidney Failure and their Treatment, 1983; contbr. articles to jours., chpts. to textbooks in field.; assoc. editor: Gen. Hosp. Psychiatry, 1978-82, sect. editor, 1982—; sect. editor: Internat. Jour. Psychiatry in Medicine, 1977-78; mem. editorial bd., book rev. editor Jour. Dialysis and Transplantation, 1979—; mem. editorial bd. Resident and Staff Physician, 1981-91, Internat. Jour. Artificial Internal. Organs, 1983-93, Geriatric Nephrology and Urology, 1990—, Kidney: A Current Survey of World Literature, 1990—. Served to capt. M.C., USAF. Served to capt. M.C., USAF. Recipient Willaim A. Console Master Tchr. award, SUNY, Brooklyn, 1991; Thomas P. Hackett award Acad. Psychosomatic med., 1993. Fellow ACP, Am. Coll. Psychiatrists, Am. Psychiat. Assn. (pres. Kings County dist. br. 1981-82), Internat. Coll. Psychosomatic Medicine, Acad. Psychosomatic Medicine; mem. AAAS, Am. Psychosomatic Soc. (coun. 1994—), N.Y. Acad. Scis., Psychonephrology Found. (pres. 1978—), Assn. Acad. Psychiatry, Internat. Soc. Nephrology, Am. Soc. Nephrology, Am. Assn. Artificial Internal Organs, Soc. Liaison Psychiatry (bd. dirs. 1979-80, sec. 1980-81, pres.-elect 1991-92, pres. 1992-94, bd. dirs. 1995—), Phi Beta Kappa, Sigma Xi. Home: 169 Westminster Rd Brooklyn NY 11218-3445 Office: Coney Island Hosp Dept Psychiatry Brooklyn NY 11235

LEVY, NORMAN JAY, investment banker, financial consultant; b. N.Y.C., Aug. 14, 1942; s. Benjamin and Sophie (London) L.; m. Rene S. Cohen; children—Ellen, David. B.B.A., U. Cin., 1964; M.B.A., Columbia U., 1966. Assoc., v.p. Salomon Bros., N.Y.C., 1966-77, spl. ptnr., 1977-79, gen. ptnr., 1979-81; sr. v.p. Wertheim & Co., N.Y.C., 1982; mng. dir. L.F. Rothschild, Unterberg, Towbin, N.Y.C., 1983-84; private practice investment cons. Tenafly, N.J., 1985—. Mem. Securities Industry Assn. (com. on acctg. 1977-79). Home: 40 Mayflower Dr Tenafly NJ 07670-3130

LEVY, PETER, cinematographer. Cinematographer: (films) A Nightmare on Elm Street Part 5: The Dream Child, 1989, Dangerous Game, 1989, Predator 2, 1990, Ricochet, 1992, Judgment Night, 1993, Blown Away, 1994. Office: Int'l Creative Mgmt 8942 Wilshire Blvd Beverly Hills CA 90211-1934*

LEVY, RALPH, engineering executive, consultant; b. London, Apr. 12, 1932; came to U.S., 1967, naturalized, 1978; s. Alfred and Esther L.; m. Barbara Dent, Dec. 12, 1959; children: Sharon E., Mark S. B.A., Cambridge U., 1953, M.A., 1957; Ph.D., Queen Mary Coll. U. London, 1966. Mem. sci. staff GEC, Stanmore, Middlesex, Eng., 1953-59; mem. sci. staff Mullard Research Labs., Redhill, Eng., 1959-64; lectr. dept. elec. and electronic engring. U. Leeds, 1964-67; v.p. research Microwave Devel. Labs., Inc., Natick, Mass., 1967-84; v.p. engring. KW Engring., San Diego, 1984-88; v.p. research Remec Inc., San Diego, 1988-89; R. Levy Assocs., 1989—. Author: (with J.O. Scanlan) Circuit Theory, 1970, 2d vol., 1973; contbr. articles in field. Fellow IEEE (editor Transactions on Microwave Theory and Techniques 1986-88, Career award IEEE Microwave Theory and Techniques Soc. 1997); mem. Instn. Elec. Engrs. (London). Patentee in field. Office: 1897 Caminito Velasco La Jolla CA 92037-5725

LEVY, RICHARD HERBERT, lawyer; b. Chgo., Sept. 15, 1943; s. Milton David and Sophie (Lippert) L.; m. Ilyse Powell; children: Joshua, Rachel, Stacey. BS, So. Ill. U., 1966; JD magna cum laude, DePaul U., 1976. Bar: Ill. 1976, Colo. 1994. Ptnr. Felwell, Galper & Lasky, Chgo., 1976, Rudnick & Wolfe, Chgo., 1983-88, Vedder, Price, Kaufman & Kammholz, Chgo., 1992—; counsel to exec. bd. Home Builders Chgo., Oak Brook, Ill., 1986—. Mem. ABA, Chgo. Vol. Lawyers Soc., Practising Law Inst. (real estate law adv. com.). Home: 1205 Wincanton Dr Deerfield IL 60015-3140 Office: Vedder Price Kaufman & Kammholz 222 N La Salle St Chicago IL 60601-1002

LEVY, RICHARD PHILIP, physician, educator; b. Hempstead, N.Y., Nov. 3, 1923; s. Edward I. and Elma (Nathan) L.; m. Barbara Quint, Sept. 15, 1945; children: Donald Martin, Ellen Susan, Charles Edward. B.S., Yale U., 1944, M.D., 1947. Intern, resident Univ. Hosps. of Cleve., 1947-53; faculty Case Western Res. Med. Sch., Cleve., 1953—, prof. medicine, 1977-78, clin. prof. medicine, 1978—, prof. internal medicine, 1978—, chmn. dept. internal medicine, 1983-89; prof. internal medicine endocrinology Coll. Medicine Northeastern Ohio U., Akron, Ohio, 1978—; svc. chief endocrinology St. Thomas Med. Ctr., Akron, 1985-92; med. editor Webster's New World Dictionary, 1970. Contbr. articles to profl. jours. Served with USNR, 1949-51. Fellow ACP; mem. Thyroid Assn., Endocrine Soc., Am. Diabetes Assn., Am. Coll. Clin. Endocrinology, Ohio Med. Assn., Sigma Xi. Office: 444 N Main St Akron OH 44310-3110

LEVY, ROBERT EDWARD, engineering consultant; b. Cin., May 23, 1939; s. Aaron F. and Elizabeth W. (Hirsch) L.; m. Candace Ann Wolfe, June 20, 1970; children: Brian D., Jessica A. BChemE, Cornell U., 1962; PhDChemE, U. Calif. at Berkeley, 1967. Various positions, including mgr. synthetic fuels devel., rsch. and engrng. Exxon Co., Florham Park, N.J., 1967-80, 84-86; mgr. tech. dept. Lago Oil & Transport Co., Esso Interam. div. Exxon Co., Aruba, Netherlands Antilles, 1980-84; v.p., dir. tech. devel. M.W. Kellogg Co., Houston, 1987-93; v.p. govt. and regulatory affairs Energy Biosystems Corp., The Woodlands, Tex., 1993-97; engrng. cons. Houston, 1997—; cons. in field. Patentee in field. Indsl. mem. Comm. for Prevention of Shoreline Pollution by Oil, Aruba, 1982-84. Mem. AIChE, Indsl. Rsch. Inst. (bd. editors 1992-95, pre-coll. edn. com. 1995-97, chmn., 1996-97), Sigma Xi (pres. Kellogg chpt. 1991-92). Avocations: tennis, jogging, sailing.

LEVY, ROBERT ISAAC, physician, educator, research director; b. Bronx, N.Y., May 3, 1937; s. George Gerson and Sarah (Levinson) L.; m. Ellen Marie Feis, 1958; children: Andrew, Joanne, Karen, Patricia. B.A. with high honors and distinction, Cornell U., 1957; M.D. cum laude, Yale U., 1961. Intern, then asst. resident in medicine Yale-New Haven Med. Ctr., 1961-63; clin. assoc. molecular diseases Nat. Heart, Lung and Blood Inst., Bethesda, Md., 1963-66, chief resident, 1965-66, attending physician molecular disease br., 1965-80, head sect. lipoproteins, 1966-80, dep. clin. dir. inst., 1968-69, chief clin. services molecular diseases br., 1969-73, chief lipid metabolism br., 1970-74, dir. div. heart and vascular diseases, 1973-75, dir. inst., 1975-81; v.p. health scis., dean Sch. Medicine Tufts U., Boston, 1981-83, prof. medicine, 1981-83; v.p. health scis. Columbia U., N.Y.C., 1983-84, prof., 1983-88, sr. asst. v.p. health scis., 1985-87; pres. Sandoz Research Inst., East Hanover, N.J., 1988-92; pres. Wyeth-Ayerst Rsch. Wyeth-Ayerst Labs div. Am. Home Products, Phila., 1992—; attending physician Georgetown U. med. div. D.C. Gen. Hosp., 1966-68; spl. cons. anti-lipid drugs FDA. Editor: Jour. Lipid Rsch., 1972-80, Circulation, 1974-76, Am. Heart Jour., 1980-90; contbr. articles to profl. jours. Served as surgeon USPHS, 1963-66. Recipient Kees Thesis prize Yale U., 1961; Arthur S. Flemming award, 1975; Superior Service award HEW, 1975; Rsch. award and Van Slyke award Am. Soc. Clin. Chemists, 1980; Roger J. Williams award, 1985; award Humana Heart Found., 1988. Mem. Am. Heart Assn. (mem. coun. on atherosclerosis), Am. Inst. Nutrition, Am. Fedn. Clin. Rsch., N.Y. Acad. Scis., Am. Soc. Clin. Nutrition, Am. Soc. Clin. Investigation, Am. Coll. Cardiology, Inst. Medicine of Nat. Acad. Scis., Am. Soc. Clin. Pharmacology and Therapeutics, Assn. Am. Physicians, Phi Beta Kappa, Sigma Xi, Alpha Omega Alpha, Alpha Epsilon Delta, Phi Kappa Phi. Office: Wyeth-Ayerst Rsch PO Box 8299 Philadelphia PA 19101-0082

LEVY, ROBERT MICHAEL, neurosurgeon, researcher; b. Tyndall AFB, Fla., Oct. 22, 1954; s. Ira Mortimer and Rheda Bertha (Fisch) L. BA summa cum laude, Northwestern U., 1976, MS, 1976; PhD, Stanford U., 1980; MD, Stanford Medical Sch., 1981. Diplomate Am. Bd. Neurological Surgery, Nat. Bd. Medical Examiners. Intern general surgery Stanford U Medical Ctr., Stanford, Calif., 1981-82; postgrad. rsch. surgeon dept. neurological surgery U. Calif., San Francisco, 1982-87, resident dept. neurosurgery, 1982-87; chief resident San Francisco Gen. Hosp., 1984; chief resident neurological surgery VA Medical Ctr., San Francisco, 1986, U. Calif., San Francisco, 1987; acting chief div. neurological surgery Northwestern U. Medical Sch., Chgo.; cons. Medtronics, Mpls.; asst. prof. dept. surgery, Northwestern U. Medical Sch., 1987-90, asst. prof. dept. physiology, 1987-90, charter mem. Inst. Neuroscience, 1988—, dir. Northwestern Comprehensive Pain Clinic Northwestern Medical Faculty Found., 1987—; head sect. of stereotactic/functional neurosurgery, 1987—; assoc. prof. dept. surgery, 1990—, assoc. prof. dept. physiology, 1990—; deputy chief div. neurosurgery, 1991-93, rsch. dir. dept. surgery, 1992-94, dir. residency training program div. neurosurgery, 1993-95. Co-author: AIDS and Nervous System, 1988, The Neurosurgery of Chronic Pain, 1996, AIDS and the Nervous System 2d edit., 1996; contbr. numerous articles to profl. jours. Recipient Rsch. award Nat Inst. Health, 1974, Henry B. Newman award San Francisco Neurological Soc., 1983, First Annual Clinical Neuroscience Trainee award L.A. Soc. Neurology & Psychiatry, 1987, William H. Sweet Young Investigators award, Am. Assn. Neurological Surgeons, 1993; recipient numerous rsch. grants. Mem. Am. Assn. Neurological Surgeons, Am. Coll. Surgeons, Am. Epilepsy Soc., AMA, Am. Pain Soc., Am. Soc. Stereotactic and Functional Neurosurgery, Calif. Medical Assn., Chgo. Neurological Soc., Congress Neurological Surgeons, Internat AIDS Soc., Internat. Narcotics Rsch. Congress, Internat. Assn. Study of Pain, Am. Assn. of Neurological Surgeons and Congress of Neurological Surgeons, Soc. Magnetic Resonance in Medicine, World Soc. Stereotactic and Functional Neurosurgery, Internat. Coll. Surgeons. Office: Northwestern U Medical Sch 233 E Erie St Ste 614 Chicago IL 60611-5934

LEVY, ROBIN CAROLE, elementary guidance counselor; b. Berlin, Apr. 13, 1964; parents Am. citizens; d. Kenneth and Henrietta Nan (Weithorn) Kaplan; m. Guy Glickson Levy, July 27, 1986; 1 chld, Clare Sydney. BS, Fla. State U., 1986; MEd, Coll. William and Mary, 1991. Cert. tchr., Va. Presch. tchr. Talent House Pvt. Sch., Fairfax, Va., 1986-87; 4th grade tchr. Mt. Vernon Elem. Sch., Tabb, Va., 1987-92; elem. counselor Bethel Manor Elem. Sch., LAFB, Va., 1992-95; family mediator Dispute Settlement Ctr., Norfolk, Va., 1993—, Dispute Resolution Ctr., Richmond, Va., 1994—. Past pres., v.p. Denbigh Jaycees, Va., 1987-94 (Project Mgr. of Yr. 1991, 93, Outstanding Local Pres. 1994), sec., treas. Mem. ASCD, ACA, Va. Counselors Assn., Va. Sch. Counselors Assn., Peninsula Counselors Assn. Democrat. Jewish. Avocations: jogging, swimming, reading. Home: 463 Cheshire Ct Newport News VA 23602-6404

LEVY, ROCHELLE FELDMAN, artist; b. N.Y.C., Aug. 4, 1937; d. S. Harry and Eva (Krause) Feldman; m. Robert Paley Levy, June 4, 1955; children: Kathryn Tracey, Wendy Paige, Robert Paley, Angela Brooke, Michael Tyler. Student Barnard Coll., 1954-55, U. Pa., 1955-56; BFA, Moore Coll. Art, 1979. Mgmt. cons. Woodlyne Sch., Rosemont, Pa., 1983-84; sr. ptnr. DRT Interiors, Phila., 1983—; ptnr. Phila. Phillies, 1981-94. One-woman shows: Watson Gallery, Wheaton Coll., Norton, Mass., 1977, U. Pa., 1977, Med. Coll. Pa., Phila., 1982, Aqueduct Race Track, Long Island, N.Y., 1982, 68, Phila. Art Alliance, 1983, Moore Coll. Art, Phila., 1984, Phila. Art Alliance, 1994. Pres., League of Children's Hosp., Phila., 1969-70; bd. overseers Ctr. for Judaic Studies U. Pa., 1993-96. Recipient G. Allen Smith Prize, Woodmere Art Gallery, Chestnut Hill, Pa., 1979; Woman honoree Samuel Paley Day Care Ctr., Phila., 1990, Jefferson Bank Declaration award, 1991, Nat. Philanthropy honoree The Nat. Soc. of Fund Raising Execs. Greater Phila. chpt., 1994. Trustee Moore Coll. Art, 1979—, chmn. bd. trustees, 1988—; mem. selections and acquisitions com. Pa. Acad. Fine Arts, 1979—; bd. mgrs., 1975—, chmn. exec. com., 1982—, bd. trustees, 1990—. Mem. Allied Artists Am., Artist's Equity, Phila. Art Alliance, Phila. Mus. Art (assoc.), Phila. Print Club. Office: 2 Logan Sq Ste 2525 Philadelphia PA 19103-2707

LEVY, S. WILLIAM, dermatologist; b. San Francisco, Sept. 28, 1920; s. Joseph and Dora (Taylor) L.; m. Elisabeth Rellstab, Mar. 17, 1974; children: David Lewis, Ann Louise. BS, U. Calif., San Francisco, 1943, MD, 1949. Practice medicine specializing in dermatology San Francisco; research dermatologist Biomechanics Lab., U. Calif., San Francisco; mem. staff Children's Hosp., Mt. Zion Hosp. and Med. Center; cons. to Letterman Army Hosp.; central med. adv. Calif. Blue Shield, San Francisco; clin. prof. dermatology U. Calif.; cons. in field. Author: Skin Problems of the Amputee, 1983; co-author: The Skin in Diabetes, 1986, Dermatology, 3rd edit., 1992, Dermatology in General Medicine, 4th edit., 1993, Atlas of Limb Prosthetics, 2d edit., 1992, Cutis, 1995. Served with USN, 1943-46. Recipient Lehn and Fink Gold Medal award. Fellow Am. Acad. Dermatology (Gold medal); mem. San Francisco Dermatol. Soc. (pres.), Pacific Dermatologic Assn. (v.p.), AMA, Calif. Med. Assn. (sci. council 1977-84), San Francisco Med. Soc. Office: Ste 305 599 Sir Francis Drake Blvd Greenbrae CA 94904-1732

LEVY, SAM MALCOLM, advertising executive; b. Henderson, Ky., Nov. 26, 1901; s. Mike Meyer and Hattie Belle (Wile) L.; m. Isabel Helen Cone, Apr. 22, 1929; 1 child, Sue Levy Klau. Student, U. Mo., 1919-21; PhB, U. Chgo., 1921-23; postgrad., Harvard Coll., 1926. Exec. McCann Erickson, N.Y.C., 1923-30; adv. dir. News & Record, Greensborough, N.C., 1930-31; v.p. dir. Keelor & Stites, Cin., 1931-46; lectr. speech U. Cin., 1940-44; pres. Assoc. Adv. Agy., Cin., 1946-71; sr. v.p. Sive Inc. - A Div. Young & Rubicam, 1971-89; ret. Sive Inc.-A Div. Young & Rubicam, 1989; life trustee Clean Cin. Inc., bd. govs. Big Bros. Assn., Glen Manor Home for Aged, 1963—; instr. advt. evening coll. U. Cin., 1945-48. Editor: Socony Monthly Mag., 1925-27. Active Friend of Serengeti Aftrica; mem. Cin. Art Mus. Named to Hon. Order of Ky. Cols., 1984; donated Glass Gallery to Cin. Art Mus., 1980, Floral Clock to Cin. Park Bd., 1988; recipient Key to the City of Cin., 1988, Emerald award, 1993. Mem. Advts. Club Cin., Black Friars Club Chgo., Bankers Club, Losanti Ville Country Club Cin., Founders Soc., Cin. Symphony Orch., Thomas Schippers Soc., Zeta Beta Tau (pres., grad club). Republican. Home: 2444 Madison Rd Cincinnati OH 45208-1256

LEVY, STANLEY HERBERT, lawyer; b. Phila., Apr. 11, 1922; s. Max and Rose (Cohen) L.; m. Gloria Kamber, Dec. 20, 1953; children: Steven M., Peter B. B.A., Cornell U., 1943; LL.B., Harvard U., 1949, J.D., 1968. Bar: N.Y. 1949, U.S. Dist. Ct. (ea. and so. dists.) N.Y., U.S. Treasury 1949, U.S. Supreme Ct. 1949. Practiced in N.Y.C., 1949—. Mem. Republican Town Com., Scarsdale, 1963-65, Temple Emanu-el, Westchester, N.Y. Served to 1st lt. F.A., AUS, 1943-47. Mem. Assn. Bar City N.Y., Confrérie des Chevaliers du Tastevin (officier commandeur), Commanderie de Bordeaux (comdr.), Harvard Club, Yale Club, Century Country Club (Purchase, N.Y.), Westchester Flying Club (White Plains, N.Y.), Mashomack Fish and Game Preserve (Pine Plains, N.Y.). Home: 3 Richbell Rd Scarsdale NY 10583-4421 Office: 521 5th Ave New York NY 10175

LEVY, STEPHEN RAYMOND, high technology company executive; b. Everett, Mass., May 4, 1940; s. Robert George and Lillian (Berfield) L.; m. Sandra Helen Rosen, Aug. 26, 1961; children: Phillip, Susan. B.B.A., U. Mass., 1962. Chmn. emeritus, dir. Bolt Beranek and Newman Inc., Cambridge, Mass.; bd. dirs. Thermo Optek Corp., One Wave, Inc., Boston Renaissance Charter Pub. Sch., Epicon, Inc.; chmn. bd. dirs. Koon Interactive Corp. Mem. Gov.'s Coun. Econ. Growth and Tech. (chmn. com. telecomms. devel.); chmn. Mass. Telecomms. Coun.; bd. dirs. Mass. High Tech. Coun.; bd. overseer Boston Symphony Orch. With AUS, 1963-66. Decorated Army Commendation medal. Mem. Am. Electronics Assn. (chmn. 1986), Mass. High Tech. Coun. (chmn. 1987-89). Home: 300 Boylston St Apt 1204 Boston MA 02116-3923 Office: The Apogee Group Inc 150 Cambridgepark Dr Cambridge MA 02140-2322

LEVY, STEVE, sports anchor, studio host; b. Mar. 12, 1965. BS in Comms., Oswego State U., 1987. Reporter Sta. WTOP-TV, Oswego, N.Y., 1983-87; sports dir. Sta. WTOP-TV, Oswego, 1986-87; play-by-play commentator Oswego State's hockey team Sta. WOCR-Radio, Oswego; part-time reporter various sports events Sta. WABC-Radio, 1987; prodr., host pregame show NHL Radio Network, 1988-89; host intermission updates for N.Y. Rangers and Knicks' games Sta. WNBC-Radio, N.Y.C., 1987-88; weekend sports reporter, host The NFL in Action Sta. WFAN-Radio, N.Y.C., 1986-93; sports anchor/reporter Sta. WCBS-TV, N.Y.C., 1992-93; host Sports Desk Madison Sq. Garden Network, N.Y.C., 1989; SportsCenter anchor, NHL studio host ESPN, 1993—, Sports Radio GameDay anchor, 1993—, host NHL show Nat. Hockey Night, 1993—, NFL co-host Sports Radio's Game Day, 1993—. Office: c/o ESPN ESPN Pla Bristol CT 06010

LEVY, (ALEXANDRA) SUSAN, construction company executive; b. Rockville Centre, N.Y., Apr. 26, 1949; d. Alexander Stanley and Anna Charlotte (Galasieski) Jankoski; m. William Mack Levy, Aug. 12, 1977. Student, Suffolk Community Coll., Brentwood, N.Y., 1976. Cert. constrn. assoc. Supr. N.Y. Telephone Co., Babylon, 1970-74; v.p. Aabbacco Equipment Leasing Corp., Lindenhurst, N.Y., 1974-81; pres., owner Femi-9 Contracting Corp., Lindenhurst, 1981—. Mem. affirmative action adv. coun. N.Y. State Dept. Transp., Albany, 1984-88, human resources adv. panel Long Island Project 2000; mem. Presdl. Task Force, Washington, 1982—; mem. Leadership Am., 1994-95. With U.S. Army, 1967-69. Recipient Henri Dunant Corp. award ARC Suffolk County, 1986, Race to the Top award Bridgestone Tire Corp., 1992, Nawbo award Nat. Assn. Women Bus. Owners, 1993; named honoree Women on the Job, 1989. Mem. Nat. Assn. Women in Constrn. (founder L.I. chpt., pres. 1983-85, regional chmn. woman-owned bus. enterprise com., nat. chmn. pub. rels. and mktg. com., nat. dir. Region 1 1988-89, Mem. of Yr. L.I. chpt. 1987, Exec. of Yr. L.I. chpt., nat. dir., 1988-89, nat. treas. 1991-93, nat. v.p. 1993-94, nat. pres.-elect 1994-95, pres. 1995-96), Nassau Suffolk Contractors Assn. (sec. 1984-87, sec.-treas. 1987-96, bd. dirs.), Nat. Assn. Women Bus. Owners (charter, Top Woman Bus. Owner award 1993), Am. Plat form Assn. Republican. Roman Catholic. Avocations: reading, writing, golf. Home: 133 Hollins Ln East Islip NY 11730-3006 Office: Femi-9 Contracting Corp 305 E Sunrise Hwy Lindenhurst NY 11757-2521

LEVY, WALTER JAMES, oil consultant; b. Hamburg, Germany, Mar. 21, 1911; s. Moses and Bertha (Lindenberger) L.; m. Augusta Sondheimer, Apr. 11, 1942 (dec.); children: Robert Alan (dec.), Susan Clementine. Student, U. Heidelberg, 1929-30, U. Berlin, 1930-31, U. Kiel, 1931-32. Asst. to editor Petroleum Press Bur., London, Eng., 1936-41; free lance economist N.Y.C., 1941-42; chief petroleum sect. OSS, Washington, 1942-45; asst. office intelligence research Dept. State, 1945-48, cons., also Pres. com. fgn. aid, 1948; chief oil br. ECA, 1948-49, cons., 1949-51; econ. cons., 1949—, NSRB, 1950; pres. Materials Policy Commn., 1951; cons. policy planning staff Dept. State, 1952-53, ICA, 1956-57; cons. office Under Sec. and Asst. Secs., 1960-80, Office Civil and Def. Moblzn., 1960, European Econ. Community, 1970; fgn. econ. adviser Socony-Vacuum Oil Co., 1948; adviser to Mr. Harriman on mission to Iran, 1951; Petroleum adviser U.S. del. Council Fgn. Ministers meeting, 1947; mem. U.S. del. of Austrian Treaty Commn., 1947, State Dept. del. for oil discussions with U.K., 1946, U.S. del. trade discussion with Sweden, 1945, U.S. world programming group on petroleum, 1945; mem. enemy oil com. Joint Chiefs Staff, 1943-45; oil adviser to spl. emissary of Pres. Kennedy to Pres. of Indonesia, 1963; Mem. adv. council to Sch. Advanced Internat. Studies Johns Hopkins U. Author (Oil Strategy and Politics, 1941-81 1982); Contbr. articles to profl. publs. Recipient spl. plaque in grateful appreciation for invaluable contbr. to welfare U.S., Sec. State, 1968; decorated Dato Setia haila Jasa Sultan Brunei, 1968; Order of Taj Iran, 1969; hon. companion Order St. Michael and St. George, Eng.; insignia of comdr.'s cross Order of Merit Fed. Republic of Ger., 1979; President's certificate of merit. Mem. Council on Fgn. Relations. Home: 300 Central Park W New York NY 10024-1513

LEVY, WALTER KAHN, management consultant executive; s. Benn Barnet and Beatrice (Kahn) L.; m. Anita von Bachelle, July 23, 1955; children: Gregg W., Evonne A. BA, Washington & Jefferson Coll., 1952; MS in Retail, NYU, 1966. Cert. mgmt. cons. Mgmt. trainee Burlington Mills, N.Y.C., 1952; buyer, merchandiser Bloomindale Bros., N.Y.C., 1953-65; cons. Cresap, McCormack & Padget, N.Y.C., 1965-68; v.p. ops. Bonwit Teller, N.Y.C., 1968-71; cons., chmn. Walter K. Levy & Robert E. Kerson Assocs., Inc., N.Y.C., 1971-95; cons. Goldman Sachs, N.Y.C. Trustee Washington & Jefferson Coll., Washington, Pa., 1980—; bd. dirs. Sch. Bd. Selection Com., Larchmont, N.Y., 1973-76. Sgt. USAR, 1954-62. Mem. Japan Soc., Larchmont Yacht Club. Avocations: history, reading, travel, tennis. Home: 35 Ellsworth Rd Larchmont NY 10538-1414

LEW, JOYCELYNE MAE, actress; b. Santa Monica, Calif., Feb. 25, 1962; d. George and Mabel Florence (Lum) L. BA in Theatre Arts, UCLA, 1981, teaching credential, 1982; MA in Urban Edn., Pepperdine U., 1984; bilingual cert., U. So. Calif., 1983; postgrad., Stella Adler Acad., 1988; studied with, The Groundlings Improv Group, 1987. Appeared in films Tai-Pan, 1987, Fatal Beauty, 1989, The Royal Affair, 1993, Shattered Image, 1993, Dr. Boris and Mrs. Duluth, 1994, Hindsight, 1996, Fire in My Heart, 1996; TV programs The Young and the Restless, 1990, Phil Donahue Show, 1993, Hard Copy, 1994, Current Affair, 1995, Gordon Elliott, 1995, Married With Children, 1997, True Hollywood Stories, 1997, E Entertainment; voice over artist, mag. model, body double, dancer; appeared in comml. Good Seasons, 1996, Pillsbury Doughboy, 1996, Pacific Bell, 1996; co-writer film script They Still Call Me Bruce, 1986 (award); song lyricist Nighttime Blues. Mem. judging com. for film grants Nat. Endowment for Arts, 1986; mem. L.A. Beautiful, 1993. Mem. AFTRA, SAG, AEA, ATAS (blue ribbon com. for Emmy awards 1986-96), Assn. Asian Pacific Am. Artists (treas. 1983-89), Nat. Asian Am. Telecomms. Assn., Am. Film Inst. Conservatory Workshop, Calif. PTA (life). Avocations: calligraphy, makeup art and hair, charcoals, fashion and interior design. Home and Office: 1958 N Van Ness Ave Los Angeles CA 90068-3625

LEW, ROGER ALAN, manufacturing company executive; b. N.Y.C., Mar. 16, 1941; s. Louis Arthur and Estelle Bebe (Marcus) L.; m. Marilyn Drourr, May 29, 1962; children—William, Jeffrey, Richard. B.S. in Fin, NYU, 1963. With Franklin Nat. Bank, N.Y.C., 1963-66; sr. v.p. Security Nat. Bank, N.Y.C., 1966-75; v.p. NVF Co., N.Y.C., 1975-78; sr. v.p. NVF Co., 1978-81, treas., 1979-81; pres., dir. Wormuth Bros. Foundry, Inc., Athens, N.Y., 1981—; pres., bd. dirs. Mirage Fin., Inc., 1985—, transmission Gear Sales, Inc., 1985—, Hudson Valley Buyers, Inc., 1985—; former sr. v.p., treas. Sharon Steel Corp., Pa. Engrng. Corp., DWG Co., Southeastern Pub. Svc. Co.; former sr. v.p., treas., bd. dirs. Wilson Bros.; former mem. small bus. and agr. adv. coun. to N.Y. Fed. Res. Bank. Trustee, former exec. v.p. Universal Housing & Devel. Co.; former v.p. Security Mgmt. Corp. Served with U.S. Army, 1959-60. Mem. Am. Iron and Steel Inst. Clubs: Colonie Country (Voorhees, N.Y.); Sag Harbor (N.Y.) Yacht. Office: Howard Hall Rd PO Box 171 Athens NY 12015

LEW, RONALD S. W., federal judge; b. L.A., 1941; m. Mamie Wong; 4 children. BA in Polit. Sci., Loyola U., L.A., 1964; JD, Southwestern U., 1971. Bar: Calif. 1972. Dep. city atty. L.A. City Atty's. Office, 1972-74; ptnr. Avans & Lew, L.A., 1974-82; commr. fire and police pension City of L.A., 1976-82; mcpl. ct. judge County of L.A., 1982-84, superior ct. judge, 1984-87; judge U.S. Dist. Ct. (cen. dist.) Calif., L.A., 1987—; Bar: Calif. 1971. Mem. World Affairs Council of L.A., 1976—, Christian Businessmen's Com. of L.A., 1982—. 1st lt. U.S. Army, 1967-69. Recipient Vol. award United Way of L.A., 1979, cert. of merit L.A. Human Relations Commn., 1977, 82. Mem. Am. Judicature Soc., Calif. Assn. of Judges, So. Calif. Chinese Lawyer's Assn. (charter mem. 1976, pres. 1979), Chinese Am. Citizens Alliance, San Fernando Valley Chinese Cultural Assn., Delta Theta Phi. Office: US Dist Ct 312 N Spring St Los Angeles CA 90012-4701

LEW, SALVADOR, radio station executive; b. Camajuani, Las Villas, Cuba, Mar. 6, 1929; came to U.S., 1961; s. Berko and Clara (Lewinowicz) L.; m. Laura F. Lew; 1 child, Esther Maria. JD magna cum laude, U. Havana, 1952. Editor Sch. Mural Newspaper, Camajuani, Cuba, 1941-43; pres. youth sect. and nat. sec. Cuban People's Party, Cuba, 1948-53; Latin Am. cons. Walters, Moore & Costanzo, Miami, Fla., 1961-72; news dir. Sta. WMIE and Sta. WQBA, Miami, 1961-70; gen. mgr., news dir. Sta. WRHC, Miami, 1973-89; host talk show, 1989—; pres. adv. bd. Cuba Broadcasting, 1992.Trustee, dir. United Way, 1985—. Recipient Lincoln Marti award Sec. HEW, 1964; FBI Award for Community Svcs., 1983; community svc. awards various orgns., 1973-84. Mem. Cuban Lawyers Assn. Exile. Jewish. Home: 2863 SW 23rd St Miami FL 33145-3309

LEWALLEN, WILLIAM M., JR., ophthalmologist; b. McGregor, Tex., Aug. 31, 1927; s. William M. and Lois Pauline (Sherrill) L.; m. Katherine Louise Mosley, June 12, 1947 (div. Nov. 1985); children: Margaret Anne, William Michael, Susan, Cynthia. BS, Southern Meth. Univ., 1944; MD, Southwestern Med. Coll. Tex., 1947. Diplomate Am. Bd. Otolaryngology, Am. Bd. Ophthalmology. Internship Baylor Univ., Dallas, 1947-48; residency otolarygology Southwestern Medical Coll., Dallas, 1948-50; residency ophthalmology Jefferson Davis Hosp., Houston, 1953-54; pvt. practice Pueblo, Colo., 1955—; asst. clin. prof. Univ. Colo. Medical Sch., Denver, 1956—; cons. Colo. State Hosp., Pueblo, 1956—, U.S. VA Hosp., Ft. Lyon, Colo., 1956—; chief ophthalmology St. Mary-Corwin Hosp., 1970-72, exec. com., 1970-74; bd. dirs. Republic Nat. Bank, Centenial Bank Pueblo & Blende. Contbr. articles to profl. jours. Bd. dirs. YMCA, Pueblo, 1958-60; pres. bd. dirs. Rocky Mountain Coun. Boy Scout Am., 1960-72; mem. sch. bd. Pueblo Sch. Bd. Dist. 60, 1959-71, pres. sch. bd., 1967-69; pres., chmn. bd. dirs. Pueblo Blvd. Bank, 1979-93; pres. Rotary Club, 1975-76, dir., 1974-77. Lt. comdr. U.S. Navy, 1950-52. Fellow Am. Acad. Ophthalmology. Republican. Protestant. Avocations: bicycling, fishing, hiking, skiing. Home and Office: 205 Dunsmere Ave Pueblo CO 81004

LEWAND, F. THOMAS, lawyer; b. San Diego, July 24, 1946; s. Barbara (Boening) L.; m. Kathleen Sullivan, Aug. 3, 1968; children: Thomas, Kevin, Kristen, Carrie. BA, U. Detroit, 1968; JD, Wayne State U., 1970. Bar: Mich. 1970, U.S. Dist. Ct. (ea. dist.) 1970. Law clk. to presiding justice U.S. Ct. Appeals (6th cir.), Detroit, 1970; commr. Oakland County, Pontiac, Mich., 1978-80; chief of staff to Gov. J. Blanchard Lansing, Mich., 1982-83; ptnr. Jaffe, Raitt & Heuer, Detroit, 1970-92, Bodman, Longley & Dahling, Detroit, 1992—; trustee Gov. Blanchard Found., Lansing, 1982—, U. Detroit Mercy, 1996—; bd. dir. Met. Realty Corp., Detroit, 1988—. Campaign mgr. Gov. James J. Blanchard, MIch., 1978; chmn. Mich. Dems., 1989-91. Mem. State Bar Mich., Nat. Assn. Bond Lawyers. Office: Bodman Longley & Dahling 100 Renaissance Ctr Fl 34 Detroit MI 48243-1003

LEWANDOWSKI, ANDREW ANTHONY, utilities executive, consultant; b. Kiel, Germany, Nov. 29, 1946; came to U.S., 1949; s. Kazimierz and Emily (Lewandowski) L.; m. Mary Ann Zuza; 1 child, Adam Christopher. Student, Rutgers U., 1964-66; BS in Mech. Engring., N.J. Inst. Tech., 1969; postgrad., Pa. State U., 1969-70; MS in Mech. Engring., N.J. Inst. Tech., 1973. Registered profl. engr., N.J.; cert. profl. planner, N.J. NSF trainee N.J. Inst. Tech., 1970-72; Engr. I DeLeuw, Cather & Co., Newark, 1970; gas utilities engr. DeLeuw, Cather & Co. of N.Y., Inc., N.Y.C., 1972, specifications writer, 1972-74, chief specifications, 1974-75; supv. engr. Elizabethtown Gas Co., Iselin, N.J., 1976-79; mgr. planning, system improvement Elizabethtown Gas Co., Iselin, 1979-81, mgr. planning, budgets, 1981-86; internal cons., computer mgmt. Elizabethtown Gas Co., Elizabeth, N.J., 1986-87; internal cons. ops., engring. Elizabethtown Gas Co., Iselin, N.J., 1987-89; internal cons. engring., budgets Elizabethtown Gas Co., Union, N.J., 1989-95, sr. planning engr., 1995—. Editor Jaycee newsletter, 1979-80, local Rep. newsletter, 1986; monthly contbr. Film Score Monthly, 1993—. Den leader, asst. cubmaster Cub Scouts Boy Scouts Am., sec. troop com., merit badge counselor; active various local govt. religious, polit. and charitable orgns. Recipient Dir. of Yr. award South Plainfield Jaycees, 1972, Disting. Svc. award, 1975, Outstanding Young Man of Yr. award N.J. Jaycees. 1975, South Plainfield Jaycees, 1976, den leader award Boy Scouts Am. 1994; inducted into South Plainfield H.S. Hall of Fame, 1997. Mem. NSPE, ASME, KC, Internat. Platform Assn., South Plainfield Polish Nat. Home, Soc. Preservation of Film Music. Republican. Roman Catholic. Home: 1910 Murray Ave South Plainfield NJ 07080-4713 Office: Elizabethtown Gas Co 1 Elizabethtown Plz Union NJ 07083-7136

LEWANDOWSKI, THEODORE CHARLES, psychology educator; b. Phila., Apr. 26, 1945; s. Theodore A. and Teresa M. Lewandowski; m. Regina F. Blake, Sept. 21, 1968; children: Michael T., Joan T. BA, Villanova U., 1967, MS, 1969; CAGS, Temple U., 1979. Lic. psychologist, Pa. Lectr. Villanova (Pa.) U., 1974-79; prof. Delaware County Coll., Media, Pa., 1969—; lectr. Thomas Jefferson U., Phila., 1981—; credential evaluator Pa. State Bd. Psychology, Harrisburg, 1987—, vice-chairperson, 1980-86; mem. Pa. Drug, Device and Cosmetic Bd., Harrisburg, 1987-92. Author: Abnormal Psychology Case Interviews, 1971; co-author: Instructor's Manual to accompany Understanding Abnormal Behavior, 1971. Emergency coord. for Ea. Pa. Am. Radio Relay League, Newington, Conn., 1989-92. Mem. APA (state liaison 1970-72), Am. Ednl. Rsch. Assn., Am. Psychol. Soc., Ea. Psychol. Assn., Pa. Psychol. Assn. (stds. com. 1973-74), Pa. Ednl. Rsch. Assn. Office: Delaware County Coll 901 Media Line Rd Media PA 19063-1027

LEWARK, CAROL ANN, special education educator; b. Fort Wayne, Ind., Mar. 8, 1935; d. Lloyd L. and Elizabeth J. (Arthur) Meads; m. Paul N. Lewark, Aug. 20, 1955; children: David P., Laura, Beth, Daniel A. BA, St. mary of Woods, 1978; MS, Ind. U., 1981. Cert. elem. educator, spl. educator mentally retarded K-12, learning disabilities K-12, Ind.; cert. home tng. specialist, Wis. Home tng. specialist Madison Wis. ARC, Madison, 1968-70; nursery sch. cons. Allen County ARC, Ft. Wayne, Ind., 1971-73; early childhood spl. edn. dir. Allen County ARC, Ft. Wayne, 1973—; cons. in field; presenter in field; apptd. by Ind. Gov. to State Interagy. Coordinating Coun. for Infants and Toddlers, 1992-95; apptd. to Higher Ed Coun. for Early Childhood and Spl. Edn. Contbr. articles to profl. jours. Apptd. to Leadership Ft. Wayne, 1994; v.p. ARC Allen County, 1995; apptd. Ft. Wayne to Citizens adv. bd. Cmty. Devel. Block Grant. Named Model Project Site 99-457 Early Intervention Ind. State Dept. Mental Health, 1987; Tech. Assistance grantee Georgetown U., 1991-93. Mem. Ind. Coun. for Exceptional Children (sec. 1990-94), First Steps of Allen County (facilitator 1989—), Leadership Fort Wayne. Avocations: painting, needle work, travel. Home: 910 Kensington Blvd Fort Wayne IN 46805-5312 Office: ARC of Allen County 2542 Thompson Ave Fort Wayne IN 46807-1051

LEWCOCK, RONALD BENTLEY, architect, educator; b. Brisbane, Australia, Sept. 27, 1929; s. Harry Kingsley and Ena (Orrock) L.; m. Barbara Sansoni, Aug. 8, 1981. Student, U. Queensland, 1947-49; BArch, Capetown U., South Africa, 1951; PhD, U. Cape Town, South Africa, 1961; MA, Cambridge U., Eng., 1970; Eliza Howard vis. fellowship, Columbia U., 1963. Pvt. practice architecture, 1951—; Whitehead research fellow Clare Hall, Cambridge U., Eng., 1970-72, ofcl. fellow, 1976-84; research officer Middle East Centre, Cambridge, 1973-80; Aga Khan prof. architecture for Islamic culture, dir. program in architecture for Islamic socs. MIT, Cambridge, 1984-91; chmn. Aga Khan program for Islamic architecture MIT and Harvard U., 1985-87; prof. architecture Ga. Inst. Tech., Atlanta, 1991—; cons. UNESCO, Habitat, World Bank, British Coun., Am. Rsch. Cen., Egypt, 1976—; lectr. U. Natal, 1952-57, sr. lectr., 1958-69; lectr., examiner Cambridge U., 1973-85; unit leader design in developing world Archtl. Assn., London, 1977-81; lectr. Archtl. Assocs. Sch., London, 1971-82; vis. prof. grad. sch. architecture Ga. Inst. Tech., 1979-84, Harvard, 1984, Louvain U., 1984; vis. Aga Khan prof., MIT, 1991-93, UQT, Australia, 1996. Author: Early 19th Century Architecture in South Africa, 1963, Traditional Architecture in Kuwait and the Northern Gulf, 1978, 2d edit. 81, Wadi Hadramawt and the Walled City of Shibam, 1986, The Old World City of San'a', 1986, The Architecture of an Island—Sri Lanka, 1996; editor: (with R.B. Serjeant) San'a' an Arabian Islamic City, 1983; contbr. articles to profl. jours., Architecture in the Islamic World, 1976, New Grove Dictionary of Music and Musicians, 1980, 97. Mem. coun. Inst. History and Archaeology East Africa, London, 1976-86, Middle East Centre, Cambridge, Eng., 1981-88, British Sch. Archaeology in Jerusalem, London, 1981—; tech. coord. Internat. Campaign for the Conservation of Sana'a in Yemen Arab Rep. and Shibam and Wadi Hadramaut in Peoples Dem. Rep. of Yemen, 1978-93, UNESCO/UNDP Campaign for Conservation of Monuments and Cities in Uzbekistan, 1994—; steering com. mem. Aga Khan award, 1990-93, Aga Khan Trust for Culture, Geneva, 1993—. Mem. Royal Inst. British Architects (assoc.).

LEWELL, PETER A., international technology executive, researcher; b. St. John, N.B., Can.. Exec. dir. N.B. Rsch. and Productivity Coun., Fredericton, N.B., Can.; bd. dirs. Incutech, Ctr. Nuclear Energy Rsch. Office: NB Rsch & Productivity Coun, 921 ch College Hill Rd, Fredericton, NB Canada E3B 6Z9

LEWELLEN, WILBUR GARRETT, management educator, consultant; b. Charleroi, Pa., Jan. 21, 1938; s. Anthony Garrett and Cozie Harriett (Watson) L.; m. Jean Carolyn Vanderlip, Dec. 8, 1962 (div. 1982); children—Stephen G., Jocelyn A., Jonathan W., Robyn E.; m. Eloise Evelyn Vincent, Mar. 5, 1983. B.S., Pa. State U., University Park, 1959; M.S., MIT, Cambridge, 1961, Ph.D., 1967; LhD (hon.), Budapest U. of Econ. Scis., 1996. Asst. prof. mgmt. Purdue U., West Lafayette, Ind., 1964-68, assoc. prof. mgmt., 1968-72, prof., 1972-83, Loeb prof. mgmt., 1983-88; Krannert disting. prof. mgmt. Purdue U., 1988—; dir. exec. edn. programs Purdue U., West Lafayette, Ind., 1985—; cons. Bank Am., San Francisco, 1975—, Ind. Bell tel. Co., Indpls., 1976—, Am. Water Works Co., Wilmington, Del., 1978—, Indpls. Power and Light Co., 1993—; bd. dirs. USF & G Corp. Author: Executive Compensation in Large Industrial Corporations, 1968, Ownership Income of Management, 1971, The Cost of Capital, 1981. Recipient Salgo-Noren award as Outstanding Tchr. in Grad. Profl. Programs, Salgo-Noren Found., 1973, 77, 79, 84. Mem. Fin. Mgmt. Assn. (v.p. 1973-74), Am. Fin. Assn., Strategic Mgmt. Soc., AAUP, Western Fin. Assn., Lafayette Country Club, Ford's Colony Country Club. Methodist. Home: 3809 W Capilano Dr West Lafayette IN 47906-8881 Office: Purdue Univ Grad Sch Mgmt West Lafayette IN 47907

LEWENT, JUDY CAROL, pharmaceutical executive; b. Jan. 13, 1949. BA, Goucher Coll., 1970; MS in Mgmt., MIT, 1972. With corp. fin. dept. E.F. Hutton & Co., Inc., 1972-74; asst. v.p. for strategic planning Bankers Trust Co., 1974-75; sr. fin. analyst corp. planning Norton Simon, 1975-76; div. contr. Pfizer, Inc., 1976-80; dir. acquisitions and capital analysis Merck & Co., Inc., Whitehouse Station, N.J., 1980-83, asst. contr., 1983-85, exec. dir. fin. evaluation and analysis, 1985-87, v.p., treas., 1987-90, v.p. fin., CFO, 1990-92, sr. v.p., CFO, 1993—. Office: Merck & Co Inc PO Box 100 One Merck Dr Whitehouse Station NJ 08889-0100

LEWERT, ROBERT MURDOCH, microbiologist, educator; b. Scranton, Pa., Sept. 30, 1919; s. Philip John and Nell (Bertholf) L.; m. Evelyn P. Allen, Feb. 19, 1948; children—Philip Allen, Barbara Joan. B.S., U. Mich., 1941; M.S., Lehigh U., 1943; Sc.D., Johns Hopkins, 1948. Diplomate: in parasitology Am. Bd. Microbiologists. Instr. biology Lehigh U., 1941-43, Hobart and William Smith Colls., Geneva, N.Y., 1943-44; instr. dept. bacteriology and parasitology U. Chgo., 1948-52; asst. prof. U. Chgo., 1952-56, assoc. prof. microbiology, 1957-61, prof., 1961-85, prof. emeritus dept. molecular genetics and cell biology, 1985—; Vis. prof. parasitology U. Philippines Inst. Hygiene, 1961, 63-66; mem. com. on parasitic diseases Armed Forces Epidemiological Bd., 1955-73; cons. to surgeon gen. Dept. Army, 1956-75; cons. on parasitic diseases Hines (Ill.) VA Hosp., 1975-82; mem. tropical medicine and parasitology study sect. USPHS, 1965-69, allergy and infectious diseases tng. grant com., 1969-73. Mem. editorial bd.: Jour. Parasitology, 1958-64, Abstracts of Bioanalytic Tech, 1959-63, Jour. Infectious Disease, Am. Jour. Epidemiology, Am. Jour. Tropical Medicine and Hygiene. Served with USNR, 1944-46. Fulbright fellow, 1961; Guggenheim fellow, 1961; recipient U. Chgo. Med. Alumni Gold Key award, 1997. Mem. Am. Acad. Microbiology, Am. Soc. Parasitologists, Am. Soc. Tropical Medicine and Hygiene, AAAS, Royal Soc. Tropical Medicine and Hygiene, N.Y. Acad. Scis., Nippon Bijitsu Token Hozon Kyokai (life), Japanese Sword Soc. of U.S. (chmn. 1977-83), Nihontoken Hozon Kai, Kunzan-Sensei Ni Manabu-Kai, Token Soc. Gt. Britian, Sigma Xi. Research on immunity to schistosomiasis, histochem. and cytochem. studies on invasiveness of parasites, biochemistry of host-parasite relationships. Home: 37 Henry Mountain Rd Brevard NC 28712-9705 Office: 920 E 58th St Chicago IL 60637-1432

LEWEY, SCOT MICHAEL, gastroenterologist, army officer; b. Kansas City, Mo., Sept. 10, 1958; s. Hugh Gene and Janice Vivian (Arnold) L.; divorced; children: Joshua Michael, Aaron Scot, Rachel Anne; m. Jennifer L. Hill. BA in Chemistry, William Jewell Coll., 1980; DO, U. Health Scis., 1984. Diplomate Am. Bd. Internal Medicine, Am. Bd. Gastroenterology, Am. Bd. Hepatology, Am. Bd. Pediat. Commd. 2d lt. U.S. Army, 1980, advanced through grades to lt. col., 1994; resident internal medicine and pediatrics William Beaumont Army Med. Ctr., El Paso, Tex., 1985-89; asst. chief pediatric svc. Irwin Army Hosp., Ft. Riley, Kans., 1989-90; asst. chief dept. medicine Irwin Army Hosp., Ft. Riley, 1990, chief emergency med. svcs., 1990; comdr. F co. 701st support bn. 1st inf. Operation Desert Shield Operation Desert Storm U.S. Army, Saudi Arabia, 1990-91; chief dept. pediatrics Munson Army Hosp., Ft. Leavenworth, Kans., 1991-92, chief dept. medicine, 1992-93; fellow in gastroenterology Fitzsimons Army Med. Ctr., Aurora, Colo., 1993-95, staff gastroenterology svc., 1995-96; chief gastroenterology svc. Evans Army Hosp., Ft. Crason, Colo., 1996—; clin. instr. medicine U. Colo. Health Scis. Ctr. Sch. Medicine. Decorated Bronze STar; named Outstanding Young Man of Am.; recipient Jr. Scientist Rsch. award William Baumont Soc. of Army Gastroenterologists, 1994. Fellow ACP, Am. Acad. Pediatrics; mem. AMA (physician recognition award), Am. Coll. Gastroenterology, Am. Osteo. Assn., Am. Gastroenterol. Assn., Am. Soc. Gastrointestinal Endoscopy, Assn. Mil. Osteo. Physicians and Surgeons. Republican. Mem. Christian Ch. Avocations: racquetball, golf, running, genealogy, reading. Office: Evans Army Hosp Gastroenterology Svc Fort Carson CO 80913

LEWIN, ANN WHITE, museum director, educator; b. Boston, Dec. 19, 1939; d. Albert and Florence (Levy) White; m. Robert S. Benham; 1 child,

Daniel Lewin. AB, Bryn Mawr Coll., 1960. Tchr., adminstr. Montessori Sch., Annandale, Va., 1965-69; dir. staff devel. Nat. Child Research Ctr., Washington, 1969-70; founder, adminstr. Parkmont Sch., Washington, 1970-75; exec. dir., founder Capital Children's Mus., Washington, 1975-95; founder, pres. The Nat. Learning Ctr., Washington, 1983-95; cons. Arlington County Pub. Schs., Va., 1970-75, George Washington U., Washington, 1970-71; exec. dir. The Leadership Inst. Memphis, 1995—. Contbr. articles to profl. jours. Named Washingtonian of Yr., Washingtonian Mag., 1979, Women of Dist. award Nat. Conf. for Coll. Women Student Leaders, 1990, Creative Person of the Year award Odyssey of the Mind, 1991. Mem. Am. Assn. Mus., Cultural Alliance, Assn. Sci. and Tech. Ctrs. (bd. dirs. 1982), Nat. Assn. Edn. Young Children, Assn. Childhood Edn. Internat. Home: 1577 Cherry Park Dr Memphis TN 38120-4322

LEWIN, GEORGE FOREST, former insurance company executive; b. Plainfield, N.H., Oct. 25, 1916; s. George Forest and Maude (Welch) L.; m. Barbara DeFord, May 26, 1943. A.B., Middlebury Coll., 1940; LL.B., J.D., Georgetown U., 1951. Claims adjuster Liberty Mut. Ins. Co., 1940-41; exec. trainee Provident Mut. Life Ins. Co., 1941-43; asst. Washington rep. Anthracite Coal Industry, 1943-45; asst. traffic mgr. Aircraft Industries Assn., 1945-47; with Govt. Employees Ins. Co., Washington, 1947-73; v.p., sec. Govt. Employees Ins. Co., 1963-70, sr. v.p., 1970-73; v.p. Govt. Employees Life Ins. Co., Govt. Employees Ins. Co., Govt. Employees Financial Corp., 1974-76; sec. Criterion Ins. Co., 1964-70, exec. v.p., 1973-74, pres., 1974-81, also former dir.; ret., 1981. Trustee Kimball Union Acad., Meriden, N.H., 1977-82. Mem. Am., Va. bar assns., Newcomen Soc., Phi Alpha Delta, Kappa Delta Rho. Republican. Methodist. Home: 5225 Connecticut Ave NW Washington DC 20015-1845

LEWIN, K(ATHERINE) TAMAR, reporter; b. Cleve., Dec. 6, 1949; d. David Victor and Doris (Shapiro) L.; m. Robert L. Krulwich, June 29, 1980; children: Nora, Jesse. BA, Barnard Coll., 1971; JD, Columbia U., 1974. Bar: N.Y. 1975, D.C. 1978. Reporter, Bergen Record, Hackensack, N.J., 1975-77; investigative researcher Common Cause, Washington, 1977-78; Washington Bur. chief Nat. Law Jour., 1978-80, mng. editor, N.Y.C., 1980-82; legal affairs reporter, nat. corr. N.Y. Times, N.Y.C., 1982—.

LEWIN, KLAUS J., pathologist, educator; b. Jerusalem, Israel, Aug. 10, 1936; came to U.S., 1968; s. Bruno and Charlotte (Nawratzki L.; m. Patricia Coutts Milne, Sept. 25, 1964; children: David, Nicola, Bruno. Attended, King's Coll. U. London, 1954-55; MB, BS, Westminster Med. Sch. London, Eng., 1959; MD, U. London, 1966. Diplomate Am. Bd. Pathology, Royal Coll. Pathologists (London), lic. Calif. Casualty officer Westminster Med. Hosp., 1960; resident Westminster Hosp. Med. Sch., London, 1960-68; pediatric house physician Westminster Hosp. Med. Sch., Westminster Children's Hosp., 1961; house physician St. James Hosp., Balham, London, 1961; asst. prof. pathology Stanford (Calif.) U., 1970-76; assoc. prof. pathology UCLA, L.A., 1977-80; attending physician Dept. Medicine Gastroenterology divsn. UCLA, Wadsworth, Va., 1978—; prof. pathology UCLA Med. Sch., L.A., 1980—, prof. dept. medicine divsn. gastroenterology, 1986—; divsn. surg. pathology UCLA Ctr. Health Scis.; resident pathologist clinical chemistry, bacteriology, hematology, blood transfusion, serology, Westminster Hosp. Med. Sch., 1961-62, registrar dept. morbid anatomy, 1962-64, rotating sr. registrar morbid anatomy, Royal Devon, Exeter Hosp., 1964-68; vis. asst. prof. pathology, Stanford U. Med. Sch., 1968-70; vice chmn. pathology UCLA, L.A., 1979-86; pres. L.A. Soc. Pathologists Inc., 1985-86; mem. curriculum com. U. Calif. Riverside, 1977-84; cons. Wadsworth VA Hosp., L.A., carcinoma of esophagus intervention study, Polyp Prevention study, Nat. Cancer Inst., Cancer Preservation Studies br., Bethesda, Md., Sepulveda VA Hosp.; mem. various coms. UCLA in field; rschr. structure, function, pathologic disorders of gastrointestinal tract and liver. Author: (with Riddel R., Weinstein W.) Gastrointestinal Pathology and Its Clinical Implications, 1992, (with Henry Appelman) Atlas of Tumor Pathology: Tumors of the Esophagus and Stomach, 1996; editl. bd. Human Pathology, 1986—, Am. Jour. Surg. Pathology, 1990—; reviewer Gastroenterology and Archives of Pathology; contbr. papers, abstracts, revs. to profl. jours., chpts. in books; lectr., presenter in field. Dir. diagnostic Immonuhistochemistry Lab.; mem. diagnostic surg. Pathology svc. Recipient Chesterfield medal Inst. Dermatology, London, 1966; named Arris and Gale lectr. Royal Coll. Surgeons, London, 1968; Welcome Trust Rsch. grantee, 1968; fellow Found. Promotion Cancer Rsch., Tokyo, 1992. Fellow Royal Coll. Pathologists (Eng.); mem. Pathological Soc. Great Britain, Am. Gastroenterology Soc., Gastrointestinal Pathology Soc. (founder, pres. 1985-86, exec. com., edn. com. 1990—), U.S. Acad. Pathology, Can. Acad. Pathology, Assn. Clin. Pathologists, Pathological and Bacteriological Soc. Great Britain, Internat. Acad. Pathology, L.A. Pathology Soc. (bd. dirs.), Calif. Soc. Pathology (edn. com. 1983—), So. Calif. Soc. Gastrointestinal Endoscopy, Arthur Purdy Stout Soc., Gastrointestinal Pathology Soc. (pres., by-laws com., chmn. edn. com., exec. com.). Avocations: internat. travel, geographic pathology, hiking, swimming. Home: 333 N Las Casas Ave Pacific Palisades CA 90272-3307 Office: UCLA Sch Medicine Dept Pathology 10833 Le Conte Ave Los Angeles CA 90095-3075

LEWIN, LEONARD, electrical engineering educator; b. Southend-On-Sea, Eng., July 22, 1919; came to U.S., 1968; s. Abraham and Leza (Roth) L.; m. Daphne Smith, June 26, 1943; children: David Ian, Wendy Patricia. Student, pub. schs., Southend; D.Sc., U. Colo., 1967. Chartered elec. engr., U.K. Sci. officer Brit. Admiralty, Witley, Surrey, Eng., 1941-45; sr. engr. Standard Telecommunication Labs., Harlow, Essex, Eng., 1946-50, head microwave dept., 1950-60, asst. mgr. transmission research, 1960-66, sr. prin. research engr., 1967-68; prof. elec. engring. U. Colo., Boulder, 1968-86, prof. emeritus, 1987—; cons. Standard Telecommunication Labs., 1968-90, Medion Ltd., London, 1970-90, Nat. Bur. Standards, Boulder, 1978-90, Nuclear Protection Adv. Group, London, 1980-90, MIT Lincoln Labs., 1984-90, NOAA, 1984-93; Nat. Prestige lectr. Inst. Elec. Engring, New Zealand, 1987. Author: Theory of Waveguides, 1975, Polylogarithms and Associated Functions, 1981; editor: Telecommunications in the U.S.: Trends, 1981, Telecommunications: Interdisciplinary, 1985, Structural Properties of Polylogarithms, 1991. Mem. Accountability Com. Boulder Valley Schs., 1979-81; active Colo. Assn. for Gifted and Talented, Boulder, 1976-90. Grantee U.K. Sci. Research Council, 1973, 75; grantee Fulbright Commn., 1981. Fellow IEEE (Microwave award, W.G. Baker 1963, Microwave Career award 1993), Brit. Interplanetary Soc.; mem. Instn. Elec. Engrs. U.K. (Premium award 1952, 60), Internat. Sci. Radio Union (U.S. nat. com.). Home: 980 Mcintire St Boulder CO 80303-2725 Office: U Colo Campus Box 425 Boulder CO 80309 *Essential ingredients in developing a constructive and fruitful life are generosity, unselfishness, and thoughtful consideration for others. Avoid being hypnotized by the logic of words. Understanding supersedes imagination!.*

LEWIN, MOSHE, historian, educator; b. Wilno, Poland, Nov. 6, 1921; came to U.S., 1978; s. Leo J. and Fima L. (Koltunova) L. B.A., Tel Aviv U., 1961; Ph.D., Sorbonne, Paris, 1964. Dir. study Ecole des Hautes Etudes, Paris, 1965-66; sr. fellow Columbia U., N.Y.C., 1967-68; research prof. Birmingham U., Eng., 1968-78; prof. history U. Pa., Phila., 1978—; mem. acad. council Kennan Inst. for Russian Studies, Washington, 1981-84. Author: Russian Peasant and Soviet Power, 1968, Lenin's Last Struggle, 1968, Political Undercurrents in Soviet Economic Debates, 1974, 2d edit., The Making of the Soviet System, 1985, The Gorbachev Phenomenon, 1988, expanded edit., 1991, Stalinism and the Roots of Reform, 1991, Russia-USSR-Russia, 1995, (with Ian Kershaw) Stalinism and Nazism: Dictatorships in Comparison, 1997. Fellow Inst. for Advanced Studies, Princeton, N.J., 1972-73, Wilson Kennan Ctr., Washington, 1976-77, John Simon Guggenheim Found., 1995. Mem. AAUP, AAAS, Am. Hist. Assn., Inst. d'Etudes Slaves (Paris), The Authors' Guild, Inc. Home: 309 S 25th St Philadelphia PA 19103-6403

LEWIN, PETER ANDREW, electrical engineer, educator; b. Oct. 27, 1945. BSc and MSc, U. Denmark, 1969, PhD, 1979. Project leader Bruel & Kjaer Naerum, Copenhagen, Denmark, 1969-78; project mgr. Danish Inst. Biomed. Engring., Copenhagen, 1978-80; rsch. fellow U. Denmark, 1980-83; prof. dept. elec. and computer engr. Drexel U., 1983—. Fellow IEEE (mem. tech. com. IEEE Ultrasonics Symposium 1985, mem. stds. subcom. on ultrasonics, sensors, session chmn. IEEE Ultrasonics Symposia, session chmn./organizer, Lithotripsy, Engring. in Medicine and Biology conf. 1990, co-chmn. med. ultrasound track EMBS conf. 1990, co-chmn. indsl. exhibits com. EMBS conf. 1990, co-editor IEEE Med. Ultrasound Parameter Measurement Guide 1984-88, reviewer IEEE Transactions, co-editor spl. issue IEEE Transactions on Ultrasonics, Frequency and Frequency Control 1988). Office: Drexel University Dept Electrical & Computer Eng Philadelphia PA 19104

LEWIN, RALPH ARNOLD, biologist; b. London, Apr. 30, 1921; came to U.S., 1947; s. Maurice and Ethel Lewin; m. Joyce Mary Chismore, June, 1950 (div. 1965); m. Cheng Lanna, June 3, 1969. BA, Cambridge U., Eng., 1942, MA, 1946; PhD, Yale U., 1950; ScD, Cambridge U., Eng., 1973. Instr. Yale U., New Haven, Conn., 1951-52; sci. officer Nat. Research Council, Halifax, N.S., Can., 1952-55; ind. investigator NIH, Woods Hole, Mass., 1956-59; assoc. prof., now prof. U. Calif., La Jolla, 1960—. Editor: Physiology and Biochemistry of Algae, 1962, Genetics of Algae, 1976, Biology of Algae, 1979, Biology of Women, 1981, Origins of Plastids, 1993, Internacia Vortaro de Mikroba Genetiko, 1994; co-editor: Prochloron, a microbial enigma, 1989; transl. Winnie-La-Pu (Esperanto), 1972, La Dektri Horlogoj, 1993. Served with British Army, 1943-46. Mem. Phycological Soc. Am. (pres. 1970-71, Darbaker prize 1963). Avocations: Esperanto, recorders, badminton. Home: 8481 Paseo Del Ocaso La Jolla CA 92037-3024 Office: U Calif San Diego Scripps Inst Oceanogra # 0202 La Jolla CA 92093

LEWIN, SEYMOUR ZALMAN, chemistry educator, consultant; b. N.Y.C., Aug. 16, 1921; s. Charles and Ida (Lazaroff) L.; m. Pearl Goldman, Oct. 17, 1943; children: David, Jonathan. BS, CCNY, 1941; MS, U. Mich., 1942, PhD, 1950; Prof. (hon.), Instituto Químico de Sarria, Spain, 1961. Lectr. U. Mich., Ann Arbor, 1947-48, rsch. fellow, 1948-50; instr. NYU, N.Y.C., 1950-51, asst. prof., 1951-54, assoc. prof., 1954-59, prof. chemistry, 1959-91, emeritus, 1991—; cons. in field; vis. prof. Internat. Ctr. Conservation, Venice, Italy, 1974—. Author: Earth, Air, Fire, Water and DNA, 1970; Editor: Chemists' Dictionary, 1963; Funk & Wagnall Ency., 1972-77. Patentee in field. With U.S. Army, 1943-45. Recipient K. Fajans prize U. Mich., 1954, Golden Dozen Teaching Excellence awards NYU, 1960, 89, Oscar Foster prize N.Y. Chemistry Tchrs. Soc., 1973; Belgian-Am. Found. fellow, 1962. Fellow N.Y. Acad. Scis. (Cressy Morisson prize 1958), Am. Inst. Chemists; mem. Am. Chem. Soc. (chmn. analytical group N.Y. sect. 1973-74, tour speaker of yr. 1970-71), Am. Assn. Cereal Chemists, Sigma Xi (pres. NYU chpt. 1965-66), Inst. Food Technologists. Home: 4231 N Walnut Ave Arlington Heights IL 60004-1302

LEWIN, TED BERT, writer, illustrator; b. Buffalo, N.Y., May 6, 1935; s. Sidney Walter and Berenece (Klehn) L.; m. Betsy Reilly, 1963. BFA, Pratt Inst., 1956. Author: I Was a Teenage Professional Wrestler, 1993 (ALA Notable award 1993); illustrator: Island of the Blue Dolphins, 1990, Bird Watch, 1990 (ALA Notable award), Herds of Thunder Manes of Gold, 1989, National Velvet, 1985, The Day of Ahmed's Secret, 1990 (ALA Notable award), I Wonder if I'll See a Whale?, 1991, The Potato Man, 1991, Faithful Elephants, 1988, Brother Francis and the Friendly Beasts, 1991, Sami and the Time of the Troubles, 1992, Matthew's Meadow, 1992, Matthew Wheelock's Wall, 1992, The Great Pumpkin Switch, 1992, Cowboy Country, 1993, The Always Prayer Shawl, 1993, Pepe the Lamplighter, 1993 (Caldecott Honor award 1994), Just in Time for Christmas, 1994, Lost Moose, 1994, Seawatch, 1996, Ali, Child of the Desert, 1997; author, illustrator: Tiger Trek, 1990, When the Rivers Go Home, 1992, Amazon Boy, 1993, The Reindeer People, 1994, Sacred River, 1995, Market!, 1996, American Too, 1996. Home and Office: 152 Willoughby Ave Brooklyn NY 11205-3729

LEWINS, STEVEN, security analyst, investment advisor, corporate officer; b. N.Y.C., Jan. 22, 1943; s. Bruno and Kaethe (Czhoeck) L.; m. Rayna Lee Kornreich, July 4, 1968 (div. 1991); children: Shani Nicole, Scott Asher. BA, Queens Coll., CUNY 1964, MA in Diplomatic-Econ. History, 1966, postgrad. in bus. adminstrn., 1969-72; postgrad. cert. in public adminstrn. NYCSC, SUNY, 1967. Park ranger-historian Nat. Park Svc., Statue of Liberty, N.Y.C., 1964-66; traffic asst. AT&T, White Plains, N.Y., 1966; adminstrv. intern N.Y. State, Albany, 1966-67; asst. to commr. N.Y. State Narcotics Addiction Control Commn., N.Y.C., 1967-69; security analyst Value Line Investment Survey, N.Y.C., 1969-71, assoc. rsch. dir., 1971-74, rsch. dir., directing editor Value Line Investment Survey, 1974-80, v.p. Value Line Data Svcs., 1975-80 (created Value Line Financial Data Base, 1974); v.p. Arnold Bernhard & Co., 1975-80, dir., 1976-80, mem. exec. com., 1977-80; ptnr. Ray-Lux Products, 1978-80; pres. RayLux Assocs., 1980-81, dir., 1980-86; founder RayLux Fin. Svc., 1980 (1st SEC-registered electonic investment adv. svc.); v.p., unit head investment div. Citibank N.A., 1981-86, v.p. Citicorp Investment Mgmt., Inc., 1986-88; v.p. transp. and aerospace investment mgmt. Chancellor Capital Mgmt., 1988-92; mng. dir., rsch. dir., head of equity First Capital Advisers/F.C. Fin. Svcs., N.Y.C., 1992-93; v.p. Investment Rsch. Gruntal & Co., Inc., 1994—; adv. corp. disclosure com. SEC, 1977-78, ICC, 1982-92, Dept. Transp., 1982-92, 95—, internal funds investment consultant, 1997—, Dept. Justice, 1982-92, 95-96, Dept. State, 1986-92, Surface Transp. Bd. Legal Panel, 1996—; advisor Air Transport Assn., 1965—, Fed. Res. Bd., 1996—, infrastructure com. U.S. Ho. of Reps., 1997—. Participant U.S.-USSR Emigration/Jackson Vanek, 1984-91, U.S.-USSR Pan Am-Aeroflot Aviation Agreement, 1985, USSR Student Exchg., 1985-86, U.S.-USSR Anti-Internat. Terrorism, 1985-91, U.S.-USSR Rights of Terrorists, 1985, U.S.-USSR Trans-Siberian-CSX Corp. Initiative, 1989, TRW, Inc-Energia N.P.O. Look Down Satellite Agreement, 1989-90, U.S.-USSR Orbital Space Coop., 1989-90, U.S.- USSR Def. Conv. Projects, 1990-93, Reagan-Gorbachev Summit Preparations, 1986, 87, 88, Bush-Gorbachev Summit Preparation, 1990, U.S.-USSR AMR Corp.-Aeroflot Bilateral Discussion, 1989, U.S.-USSR Spl. Mission/Secure Info. Negotiation, 1983-92, U.S.-Japan airline bilateral negotiation, 1996, CSX Corp./CIS indsl. negotiation, 1996—; sponsor U.S.-USSR Pace U., rsch. exch., 1990; Citicorp liaison USSR mission to UN, 1982-88, Inst. U.S. and Can., Acad. Scis. USSR, 1985-88, econs. dept. Acad. Scis. USSR, 1988; liaison Chancellor Capital Mgmt., USSR, 1988-92; overseas fact-finding visits include Saudi Arabia, Egypt, Jordan, Israel, 1979, Peoples Republic of China, Japan, Hong Kong, 1981, USSR, 1985, 86, 89, 90, Georgia SSR, 1985, 90, Uzbekistan SSR, 1986, Baykhal, Irkutsk, Olha, Siberia, 1989, Kazakhstan SSR, Republic of Georgia, Baykonour-Soyuz Launch Ctr., 1990. Acting col. S.I.N., USAF, M.A.C., 1990. Recipient Commendation award U.S. Dept. of Justice for spl. assistance in pursuit of U.S.-USSR rels., 1990, U.S. Presdl. Commendation citation for Gulf War, 1992, USSR Supreme Soviet election for 50th birthday award in svc. to USSR for peace, 1990. Mem. Croton-on-Hudson Narcotics Guidance Coun., 1972-75, Cortland Indsl. Com., 1975-77; dist. leader Dem. Party, 1979-83; founding mem. Challenger Found., 1987. Fellow Fin. Analyst Fedn. Mem. N.Y. Soc. Security Analysts (sr. security analyst, membership com., computer applications symposium, airline splinter group, motor carrier splinter group, aerospace splinter group), Bus. Economists Coun., Washington Transp. Roundtable, Assn. Computer Users, Internat. Platform Assn., N.Y. Assn. Bus. Economists, Nat. Assn Bus. Economists, Nat. Planetary Soc., Nat. Space Soc., Nat. Air and Space Mus., Tau Delta Phi (pres. 1963, 64, undergrad. of yr. 1963, spl. student senate recognition 1964, Coll. Distinction medal French 1964). Democrat. Author: Fashoda Crisis of 1898, 1966, Knowing Your Common Stocks, 1979, The Social Overhaul of the USSR, 1986, Economics Can Bind U.S.-USSR, 1986, Economic Reform in the U.S.S.R., 1990, USA: 21st Century World Transportation Crossroads, 1994, U.S. Needs World-Class Transportation System, 1994, Transports as Economic Indicators, 1995, The New Union Pacific, 1996, Transportation Trends into 21st Century, 1996, The Global Terrorist Threat, 1996, The Boeing Company: Firing on All Cylinders, 1997, U.S. Transportation "Consolidations" and "Surprise", 1997, Secular Trends in Global Transportation, 1997; co-author: (with Parkanskii) US-USSR Summit Agenda, 1995, (with Bogdanov and Bobrakov) US-USSR Anti-International Terrorist Protocol, 1989, (with Bogdanov and Bobrakov) Rights of Terrorist, 1990, (with Bogdanov, Bobrakov) U.S.-USSR Space Cooperation, 1990; editor: Megatrends, 1980, Witch Doctor of Wall Street, 1990. Speaker security analysis, econs., transp., aerospace, def., corp. disclosure, deregulation, air traffic control and safety, fin. data svcs., U.S. megatrends, USSR Glastnost and Perestroika, C.I.S., resurgent economy. Home: 66 Grand St Croton On Hudson NY 10520-2519 Office: Gruntal & Co Inc 14 Wall St Fl 15 New York NY 10005-2101

LEWINTER, MARTIN M., cardiologist; b. Bklyn., May 9, 1944; s. Aaron E. and Miriam (Kaplan) LeW.; m. Barbara J. Weinstein, June 25, 1967; children: Andrea, Rubin, Michelle. BA, Columbia U., 1965; MD, NYU, 1969. Resident NYU-Bellevue Med. Ctr., 1969-72; fellow in cardiology U. Calif., San Diego, 1972-75, from asst. prof. to assoc. prof. medicine, 1975-85; prof. medicine, dir. cardiology unit U. Vt., Burlington, 1985—; trustee Flexher Allen Health Care, Burlington, 1995—. Author, editor: Left Ventricular Diastolic Distinction and Heart Failure, 1993, Cardiac Energetics, 1995; contbr. articles to profl. jours. Trustee Vt. affiliate Am. Heart Assn., 1987-90. Maj. USAR, 1970-77. Fulbright Found. fellow, 1983-84. Fellow Am. Coll. Cardiology, Am. Heart Assn. (coun. on circulation, coun. on clin. cardiology); mem. Assn. Univ. Cardiologists (councillor 1995-97), Assn. Profs. Cardiology (data base chair 1996—). Avocations: music, sports. Office: Fletcher Allen Health Care Cardiology Unit 111 Colchester Ave Burlington VT 05401-1473

LEWIS, A. DUFF, JR., investment executive; b. Pitts., May 3, 1939; s. A. Duff and Helen Radey (Woolford) L.; m. Nancy Bastian, May 3, 1969; children: Amie D., Jennifer E., Katherine E., Jonathan K. BSME, Grove City Coll., 1962; MS, Purdue U., 1965. Chartered fin. analyst. Project engr. Bailey Meter Co., Wickliffe, Ohio, 1962-64; from fin. analyst mfg. to fin. analyst corp. Eastman Kodak Co., Rochester, N.Y., 1965-82, pension investment coord., 1982-91; mng. dir. Rogers, Casey & Assocs., Darien, Conn., 1992-96; investment officer U. Rochester, N.Y., 1996—. Mem. Inst. Chartered Fin. Analysts, Fin. Analysts Fed., Rochester Soc. Security Analysts, Mill Creek Community Club, Inc. (co-founder, treas.). Republican. Lutheran. Home: 1231 Stockbridge Rd Webster NY 14580-9145 Office: U Rochester Treasurer's Office Adminstrn Bldg Rm 263 Rochester NY 14627

LEWIS, ALAN JAMES, pharmaceutical executive, pharmacologist; b. Newport Gwent, UK. BSc, Southampton U., Hampshire, 1967; PhD in Pharmacology, U. Wales, Cardiff, 1970. Postdoctoral fellow biomedical sci. U. Guelph, Ont., Can., 1970-72; rsch. assoc. lung rsch. ctr. Yale U., 1972-73; sr. pharmacologist Organon Labs., Ltd., Lanarkshire, Scotland, 1973-79; rsch. mgr. immunoinflammation Am. home products Wyeth-Ayerst Rsch., Princeton, N.J., 1979-82, assoc. dir. exptl. therapeutics, 1982-85, dir., 1985-87, asst. v.p., 1987-89, v.p. rsch., 1989-93; pres. Signal Pharms. Inc., San Diego, 1994-96, pres., CEO, 1996—. Editor allergy sect. Agents & Actions & Internat. Archives Pharmacodynamics Therapy; reviewer Jour. Pharmacology Exptl. Therapy, Biochemical Pharmacology, Can. Jour. Physiol. Pharmacology, European Jour. Pharmacology, Jour. Pharm. Sci. Mem. Am. Soc. Pharmacological and Exptl. Therapeutics, Am. Pheumatism Assn., Mid-Atlantic Pharmacology Soc. (v.p. 1991-93, pres. 1993-94), Pulmonary Rsch. Assn., Inflammation Rsch. Assn. (pres. 1986-88), Pharm. Mfrs. Assn., Internat. Assn. Inflammation Socs. (pres. 1990-95). Achievements include research in mechanisms and treatment of inflammatory diseases including arthritis and asthma cardiovascular diseases, metabolic disorders, central nervous system diseases, osteoporosis and viral diseases. Office: Signal Pharms Inc 5555 Oberlin Dr Ste 100 San Diego CA 92121-3746

LEWIS, ALEXANDER, JR., oil company executive; b. Danville, Pa., July 21, 1916; s. Alexander and Elizabeth (Mason) L.; m. Alice Kabakjian, May 1, 1942; children—Alexander III, Dennis James, Brady Mason. B.S., Ursinus Coll., 1938; M.S., U. Pa., 1940; Ph.D., U. Pitts., 1951. Chemist refinery tech. div. Gulf Oil Corp., Phila., 1938-42; chief product devel. engr. Gulf Oil Corp., Pitts., 1951-54; mgr. chem. mktg. Gulf Oil Corp., 1954-58, mgr. petrochems. dept., 1958—, v.p., 1960-64, sr. v.p., 1964-78; pres. Internat. Trade and Tech., 1978—; dir. Tri Century Ins. Corp., 1985—; mem. Pa. Gov.'s Sci. Adv. Com., 1965-75, Pa. State Com. for Nuclear Energy Devel. and Radiation Control, 1969-79, Pa. State Bd. Edn., 1969-77; pres. Gulf Oil Found., 1973-78; v.p. World Petroleum Congresses, London, 1975-79. Trustee Ursinus Coll., 1972, Point Park Coll., 1973; bd. regents Georgetown U.; bd. dirs. St. Clair Meml. Hosp., Pitts., Internat. Mgmt. and Devel. Inst., Washington. Served to lt. USNR, 1942-46. Fellow Mellon Inst. Indsl. Research, 1946-51. Mem. Am. Chem. Soc., Am. Petroleum Inst., Soc. Automotive Engrs., AAAS, Pitts. Chemists Club, Explorers Club, Duquesne Club, Univ. Club (Pitts.), Downtown Club (Pitts.), Longue Vue Club, Frosty Valley Country Club (Danville, Pa.), Sigma Psi, Phi Lambda Upsilon.

LEWIS, ALEXANDER INGERSOLL, III, lawyer; b. Detroit, Apr. 10, 1946; s. Alexander Ingersoll Jr. and Marie T. (Fuger) L.; m. Gretchen Elsa Lundgren, Aug. 8, 1970; children: Jennifer L., Katherine F., Elisabeth M., Alexander Ingersoll IV. BA with honors, Johns Hopkins U., 1968; JD cum laude, U. Pa., 1971. Bar: Md. 1972, U.S. Dist. Ct. Md. 1972, U.S. Ct. Appeals (4th cir.) 1975, U.S. Supreme Ct. 1976, D.C. 1982. Assoc. Venable, Baetjer & Howard, LLP, Balt., 1972-75, 78-80, ptnr., 1981—; head estate and trust practice group Venable, Baetjer & Howard LLP, Balt., 1993—; asst. atty. gen. State of Md., Balt., 1975-77; cons. subcom. on probate rules, standing com. on rules and procedures Md. Ct. Appeals, 1976—; mem. Md. Gov.'s Task Force to Study Revision of Inheritance and Estate Tax Laws, 1987-88; lectr. Md. Inst. Continuing Profl. Edn. Lawyers, 1978—, Nat. Bus. Inst., 1986-87, 92—, Cambridge Inst., 1986-90, Nat. Law Found., 1988—. Contbr. articles to legal jours. Vice chmn. Md. Gov.'s Task Force on Long-Term Fin. Planning for Disabled Individuals, 1990-94. 1st lt. U.S. Army, 1972. Fellow Am. Coll. Trust and Estate Counsel; mem. ABA, Md. Bar Assn. (chmn. probate reform and simplification com. estates and trusts coun. 1984-86, sec. 1987-88, chmn. 1989-90, com. on laws 1994—), D.C. Bar Assn., Bar Assn. City Balt., Immigration Lawyers Assn., Balt. Estate Planning Coun., Johns Hopkins Club. Republican. Roman Catholic. Avocations: canoeing, camping, tennis. Home: 922 Army Rd Ruxton MD 21204-6703 Office: Venable Baetjer & Howard LLP 1800 Two Hopkins Plz Baltimore MD 21201

LEWIS, ANDRE LEON, artistic director; b. Hull, Que., Can., Jan. 16, 1955; s. Raymond Lincoln and Theresa L. Student, Classical Ballet Studio, Ottawa, Royal Winnipeg (Man.) Ballet Sch., 1975; studies with David Moroni, Arnold Spohr, Rudi van Dantzig, Jiri Kylian, Peter Wright, Hans van Manen, and Alicia Markova, among others. Mem. corps de ballet Royal Winnipeg (Man.) Ballet, 1979-82, soloist, artistic coord., 1984-89, interim artistic dir., 1989-90, assoc. artistic dir., 1990-95, artistic dir., 1995—; staged Danzig's Romeo and Juliet, Teatro Comunale, Florence, Italy, Greek Nat. Opera, Athens. Dancer, soloist (ballets) Song of a Wayfarer, Fall River Legend, Nuages Pas de deux, Lento A Tempo E Appassionatto, Nutcracker, Four Last Songs, Romeo and Juliet, Belong Pas de deux, Ectasy of Rita Joe, (TV and films) Fall River Legend, Giselle, Heartland, Romeo and Juliet, The Big Top, Firebird, Belong Pas De Deux; performed at many events including the opening Gala performance of the Internat. Ballet competition in Jackson, Miss., Le Don Des Etoiles, Montreal, a spl. gala honoring Queen Beatrix of Holland and at a Gala performance in Tchaikovsky Hall, Moscow; appeared as a guest artist throughout N.Am., the Orient and USSR. Avocation: listening to opera. Office: Royal Winnipeg Ballet, 380 Graham Ave, Winnipeg, MB Canada R3C 4K2

LEWIS, ANDREW LINDSAY, JR. (DREW LEWIS), transportation and natural resources executive; b. Phila., Nov. 3, 1931; s. Andrew Lindsay and Lucille (Bricker) L.; m. Marilyn S. Stoughton, June 1, 1950; children: Karen Lewis Sacks, Russell Shepherd, Andrew Lindsay IV. BS, Haverford (Pa.) Coll., 1953; MBA, Harvard U., 1955; postgrad., MIT, 1968. With Henkels & McCoy, Inc., Blue Bell, Pa., 1955-60, Am. Olean Tile Co., Inc., Lansdale, Pa., 1960-68, Nat. Gypsum Co., Buffalo, 1960-70; chmn. Simplex Wire & Cable Co., Boston, 1970-74, chief exec. officer, 1972-74; pres., chief exec. officer Snelling & Snelling, Inc., Boston, 1972-74; fin. and mgmt. cons. Lewis & Assocs., Plymouth Meeting, Pa., 1974-81; sec. U.S. Dept. Transp., Washington, 1981-83; chmn. Warner Amex Cable Communications Inc., N.Y.C., 1983-86; chmn., chief exec. officer Union Pacific R.R., Omaha, 1986; pres. Union Pacific Corp., N.Y.C., 1986-87; chmn., CEO Union Pacific Corp., Bethlehem, Pa., 1987—; bd. dirs. Am. Express, Ford Motor Co., Lucent Technologies FPL Group Inc., Gannett Co., Inc., Gulfstream Aerospace Corp.; trustee Com. for Econ. Devel. Rep. candidate for gov., Pa., 1974; mem. Rep. Nat. Com., 1976-90, dep. chmn., 1980; dep. polit. dir. Reagan-Bush Campaign Com., 1980; co-chmn. Nat. Econ. Commn., 1988-89; chmn. The Bus. Roundtable, 1990-92; mem. nat. exec. bd. Boy Scouts of Am. Mem. Phila. Club, Sunnybrook Golf Club (Plymouth Meeting, Pa.), Saucon Valley Country Club (Bethlehem, Pa.), Bohemian Club (San Francisco). Office: Union Pacific Corp Martin Tower 8th & Eaton Ave Bethlehem PA 18018

LEWIS, ANDREW MORRIS, JR., virologist; b. Cheriton, Va., Nov. 28, 1934; s. Andrew Morris and Wilsye (Hamilton) L.; m. Gladys Ruth Shorrock, June 8, 1960; children: T. Reid Lewis, Andrew M. III. BA, Duke U., 1956, MD, 1961. Intern Pediatrics Duke Host., 1961-62, resident, 1962-63; scientist Nat. Inst. Allergy and Infectious Diseases/Lab. Immunopathology/NIH, Bethesda, Md., 1963-86; head viral pathogenesis sect. NIAID/LIP/NIH, Bethesda, Md., 1986-95; chief DNA virus lab. office vaccines, rsch. & rev. Ctr. Biol. Evaluation and Rev., FDA, Rockville, Md., 1997—; Capt. USPHS, 1963. Decorated Commendation medal. Mem. Am. Soc. Microbiology, Am. Soc. Virology, Am. Assn. Immunologists, AAAS, Am. Assn. Cancer Rsch. Achievements include development of nondefective adeno-SV40 hybrids and biometric models to associate viral oncogene functions with tumorigenicity. Office: DVRR/CBER/FDA HFM 400 1401 Rockville Pike Rockville MD 20852-1428

LEWIS, ANNE MCCUTCHEON, architect; b. New Orleans, Oct. 15, 1943; d. John Tinney and Susan (Dart) McCutcheon; m. Ronald Burton Lewis, Oct. 2, 1971; children: Matthew, Oliver. BA magna cum laude, Radcliffe Coll., 1965; MArch, Harvard U., 1970. Registered architect, D.C. Designer and planner Skidmore, Owings & Merrill, Washington, 1969-72, Keyes, Lethbridge & Condon, Washington, 1972-75; prin. Anne McCutcheon Lewis AIA, Washington, 1976-81; ptnr. McCartney Lewis Architects, Washington, 1981—. Mem. Harvard U. Grad. Sch. Design Alumni Coun., Cambridge, Mass., 1979-82; bd. dirs. Friends Non-Profit Housing, Washington, 1981—, Washington Humane Soc., 1990—. Fellow AIA (Design awards 1979, 83, 89, 90, 91, 92, 93, 96, dir.-at-large Washington chpt. 1982-84). Mem. Soc. of Friends. Office: McCartney Lewis Architects 1503 Connecticut Ave NW Washington DC 20036-1103

LEWIS, ANNICE MOORE, middle school language arts educator; b. Dallas, Sept. 18, 1947; d. Eugene T. and Darlene (Sanford) Moore; m. Olan H. (Bud) Lewis, Aug. 23, 1969; children: Dane, Lora. BA, East Tex. Bapt. U., 1969. Cert. secondry sch. Tchr. English, Music, Tex. Tchr. English, reading (high sch.) White Oak (Tex.) Ind. Sch. Dist., 1969-71, tchr. English, reading, speech (middle sch.), 1975-77; tchr. English Marshall (Tex.) Ind. Sch. Dist., 1972-73; tchr. English, reading, speech Sequoyah Middle Sch., Broken Arrow, Okla., 1979-81; music sec., coord. children.s choir 1st Bapt. Ch., Texarkana, Tex., 1981-83; tchr. lang. arts, reading, Tex. studies Hawkins (Tex.) Ind. Sch. Dist., 1986—; coord. UIL, coach Middle Sch., Hawkins, 1987—, lang. arts coord., mentor, 1989—; mem. Dist. Wide Improvement Coun., Hawkins, Tex., 1991—, Outcome Based Edn. Curriculum Devel. Com., 1992—; presenter Middle Sch. Kaleidescope Conf., Henderson, Tex., 1990—. Author: lang. arts planning guides (middle schs.), 1969—; asst. producer (religious drama) The Promise, 1984. Soloist adult choir 1st Bapt. Ch., Tex., Okla., Ark., 1969—; mem. handbell choirs, 1969-94; dir. 1st-3rd grade choir 1st Bapt. Ch., Gladewater, Tex., 1984-86. Mem. Tex. Assn. Supervision and Curriculum Devel., Assn. Tex. Profl. Educators (pres. 1992-94, region 7 v.p.), Nat. Coun. Tchrs. English (N.E. Tex. chpt.), Internat. Reading Assn. (local pres. region 7 1992-94, v.p., bd. dirs. 1995—),. Home: PO Box 1592 Gladewater TX 75647-1592 Office: Hawkins Mid Sch Drawer L Hawkins TX 75765

LEWIS, ANTHONY, newspaper columnist; b. N.Y.C., Mar. 27, 1927; s. Kassel and Sylvia (Surut) L.; m. Linda Rannells, July 8, 1951 (div.); children: Eliza, David, Mia; m. Margaret H. Marshall, Sept. 23, 1984. A.B., Harvard U., 1948. Deskman Sunday dept. N.Y. Times, 1948-52; staff Democratic Nat. Com., 1952; reporter Washington Daily News, 1952-55, Washington bur. N.Y. Times, 1955-64; chief London bur. N.Y. Times, 1965-72; editorial columnist, 1969—; lectr. on law Harvard U., 1974-89; James Madison vis. prof. Columbia U., 1983—. Author: Gideon's Trumpet, 1964 (award as best fact-crime book Mystery Writers Am.), Portrait of a Decade: The Second American Revolution, 1964, Make No Law: The Sullivan Case and the First Amendment, 1991; contbr. articles to profl. jours. Recipient Heywood Broun award, 1955, Pulitzer prize for nat. reporting, 1955, 63; Nieman fellow, 1956-57. Mem. Am. Acad. Arts and Scis., Tavern Club. Office: NY Times 2 Faneuil Hall Marketplace Boston MA 02109-1648

LEWIS, ARTHUR DEE, corporation executive; b. Greenville, Tex., Sept. 13, 1918; s. Carl Hamilton and Maxie (Curtis) L.; m. Hildegard Bair, Dec. 7, 1946; children: Gregory Scott, Kimberly Kealani. Student, U. Tex., 1935-41, Advanced Mgmt. Program, Harvard, 1952; Sc.D., Clarkson Coll. Tech. With Am. Airlines, 1941-55, beginning as cargo research analyst, successively supr. spl. projects, mgr. econ. analysis br., dir. econ. planning div., 1941-54, asst. v.p. planning, 1954-55; exec. v.p. Hawaiian Airlines, 1955, pres., dir., chief exec. officer, 1955-64; sr. v.p., gen. mgr., dir. Eastern Air Lines, 1964-67, pres., chief operating officer, dir., 1967-69; gen. partner F. S. Smithers & Co., 1969—; chmn., pres., chief exec. officer F. Smithers & Co., 1969-73; chmn., chief exec. officer U.S. Ry. Assn., 1974-77; pres., dir., chief exec. officer Am. Bus Assn., 1977-82; chmn., chief exec. officer U.S. Africa Airways, 1990-94, bd. dirs., chmn. emeritus, cons.; chmn. bd. Airline Media Assocs., Inc.; organizer Consol. Ry. Corp.; organizer Nat. Ry. Passenger Corp.; dir. Riegel Paper Corp., Rexham Corp., Bankers Security Life Ins. Soc., Bank of Commerce, Iroquois Brands Ltd., C. Brewer & Co., Bishop Trust Co., Internat. Bank; chmn. Mid Pacific Airlines, Honolulu; cons. airline mobizn., transp. div. Nat. Security Resources Bd., Korean War; cons. Def. Air Transp. Adminstrn., 1951-55, Dept. Transp., 1969. Bd. regents U. Hawaii; bd. govs. Pacific and Asian Affairs Council, Iolani Sch. Boys; bd. dirs. Hawaii Visitors Bur.; trustee, chmn. emeritus Clarkson Coll. Tech. Mem. Am. Mgmt. Assn. (dir., mem. exec. com.), Honolulu C. of C. (dir. 1958-59), Young Pres. Orgn., World Bus. Coun. (pres., dir. 1973-74), Conquistadores del Cielo (dir.), Burning Tree Club (Bethesda, Md.), Soc. of Sr. Aerospace Execs., Inc. (pres., dir. 1995-97).

LEWIS, AUDREY GERSH, financial marketing/public relations consultant; b. Phila., Dec. 1, 1933; d. Benjamin and Augusta (Fine) Gersh; divorced; children: Jamie Lewis Keith, Ruth-Ellen. Student, Temple U., 1951-53. Asst. mgr. accounts payable/receivable Turner Constrn. Co., Louisville, 1953-55; rep. sales, mktg., fin. depts. Benjamin Gersh Wholesaler Jeweler, Wyncote, Pa., 1955-69; registered rep. Seaboard Planning Corp. (formerly B.C. Morton Broker Del.), Greenwich, Conn. and Wyncote, 1969-72; placement counselor sales and mktg. dept. Greyhound Permanent Pers. subs. Greyhound Corp., Stamford, Conn., 1974-77; asst. v.p. Am. Investors Corp., Greenwich, 1977-85; founder, pres. Audrey Gersh Lewis Cons. Ltd., Greenwich, 1985—. Chair Cancer Fund, Wyncote, United Fund Leadership Award, Wyncote; asst. treas. Republican Town Com., Greenwich, 1981-82; mem. Greenwich Town Alarm Appeals Bd., 1985—. Mem. Assn. Corp. Growth (bd. dirs., v.p. mktg. and pub. rels. N.Y. chpt. 1989-92, mem. nat. ann. meeting planning com. 1992, 93, 94), Fin. Women's Assn., Women's Econ. Round Table, Greenwich C. of C. (mem. pub. rels. com. 1990—, corp. devel. com. 1991—), Centre for the Study of the Presidency (nat. adv. coun.), N.Y. Hong Kong Assn., Am. C. of C. in Hong Kong, World Trade Centres in Can. Avocations: antiquing, walking, reading. Office: Audrey Gersh Lewis Cons Ltd PO Box 4644 Greenwich CT 06831-8644

LEWIS, BERNARD, Near Eastern studies educator; b. London, May 31, 1916; s. H. Lewis; m. Ruth Helene Oppenhejm, 1947 (div. 1974); 2 children. BA, U. London, PhD; postgrad., univs. of London and Paris; hon. doctorate, Hebrew U., Jerusalem, 1974, Tel Aviv U., 1979, SUNY, Binghamton, 1987, U. Pa., 1987, Hebrew Union Coll., 1987, Yeshiva U., 1991, Haifa U., 1991, Bar-Ilan U., 1992, Brandeis U., 1993, Ben-Gurion U., 1996, Ankara U., 1996. Asst. lectr. in Islamic history Sch. Oriental Studies U. London, 1938, prof. history Near and Middle East, Sch. Oriental and African Studies, 1949-74, hon. fellow, 1986; Cleveland E. Dodge prof. nr. ea. studies Princeton U., 1974-86, prof. emeritus, 1986—; A.D. White prof. at large Cornell U., 1984-90; dir. Annenberg Rsch. Inst., Phila., 1986-90; Ataturk prof. (hon.) Princeton (N.J.) U., 1992-93; vis. prof. history UCLA, 1955-56, Columbia U., 1960, Ind. U., 1963; vis. prof. College de France, 1980, Ecole des Hautes Etudes, Paris, 1983-86; Class of 1932 lectr. Princeton U., 1964; vis. mem. Inst. for Advanced Study, Princeton, N.J., 1969, long-term mem., 1974-86; Gottesman lectr. Yeshiva U., 1974; Jefferson lectr. NEH, 1990; Tanner lectr. Oxford U., 1990; Weizmann lectr. in Humanities, 1991; Henry M. Jackson meml. lectr., 1992; Siemens Stiftung lectr., Munich, 1993; Merle-Curti lectr., Madison, Wis., 1993; lectr. N.Y. Pub. Libr., 1993. Author: The Origins of Ismailism, 1940, Turkey Today, 1940, British Contributions to Arabic Studies, 1941, Handbook of Diplomatic and Political Arabic, 1947, The Arabs in History, 1950, new edit., 1993, Notes and Documents from the Turkish Archives, 1952, The Emergence of Modern Turkey, 1961, rev. edit., 1968, (transl. from Ibn Gabirol) The Kingly Crown, 1961, Istanbul and the Civilization of the Ottoman Empire, 1963, The Middle East and the West, 1964, The Assassins, 1967, Race and Color in Islam, 1971, Islam in History, 1973, new edit., 1993, Islam from the Prophet Muhammad to the Capture of Constantinople, 2 vols., 1974, History Remembered, Recovered, Invented, 1975, Studies in Classical and Ottoman Islam, 7th-16th centuries, 1976, The Muslim Discovery of Europe, 1982, The Jews of Islam, 1984, Semites and Anti-Semites, 1986, The Political Language of Islam, 1988, Race and Slavery in Islam, 1990, Islam and the West, 1993, The Shaping of the Modern Middle East, 1994, Cultures in Conflict: Christians, Muslims and Jews in the Age of Discovery, 1995, The Middle East: A Brief History of the Last 2000 Years, 1996; (with Amnon Cohen) Population and Revenue in the Towns of Palestine in the Sixteenth Century, 1978; author, editor: Land of Enchanters, 1948, The World of Islam: Faith, People, Culture, 1976; author, co-editor: Historians of the Middle East, 1962, Ency. of Islam, 1956-87; editor: (with others) The Cambridge History of Islam, vols. 1-11, 1971; co-editor: Muslims in Europe, 1992, Religionsgespräche im Mittelalter, 1992; also articles. Served with Royal Armoured Corps and Intelligence Corps, Brit. Army, 1940-41; with dept. Fgn. Office, 1941-45. Recipient Cert. of Merit for svcs. to Turkish culture, Turkish Govt., 1973, Harvey prize, 1978; Univ. Coll. of London fellow, 1976. Fellow Brit. Acad., Royal Hist. Soc., Turkish Hist. Soc. (hon.), Sch. of Oriental and African Studies (hon.); mem. Am. Acad. Arts and Scis., Am. Philos. Soc., Am. Hist. Assn., Soc. Asiatique (hon.), Inst. d'Egypte (Cairo, assoc.), Inst. de France (corr.), Turkish Acad. Scis. Office: Near East Studies Dept Princeton Univ Princeton NJ 08544

LEWIS, BERNARD LEROY, electronic scientist, consultant; b. Storm Lake, Iowa, Dec. 19, 1923; s. Leo Leroy and Francis Mae (Cutchael) L.; m. Dorothy Louise Simonezux, Feb. 16, 1946 (dec. Feb. 1985); children: David Leroy, Michael Peter, Patrick Daniel, Timothy Mark; m. Marilyn W. McCullum, Oct. 10, 1990. BS in Physics, Tulane U., 1947, MS in Physics, 1948; postgrad., U. Md., 1953-56. Sect. head Naval Rsch. Lab., Washington, 1948-57; cons. Systems Inc., Orlando, Fla., 1957-60; prin. engr. Radiation Inc., Orlando, 1960-61; design engr. Martin Marietta Co., Orlando, 1961; chief engr. Airtronics, Washington, 1961-63; prin. engr. Harris Intertype, Melbourne, Fla., 1963-69; bus. ptnr. McDowell Assocs., Melbourne, 1969-72; sr. scientist Naval Rsch. Lab., Washington, 1972-84; radar cons. Bernard L. Lewis Assocs., Melbourne, Fla., 1984—; cons. Sperry Rand, Great Neck, N.Y., 1984-87, Naval Rsch. Lab., Washington, 1987-88; adj. prof. Fla. Inst. Tech., Melbourne, Fla., 1984-89. Author: Aspects of Radar Signal Processing; contbr. over 72 tech. papers to profl. jours.; patentee in field. Lt. USN, 1957. Recipient Disting. Civilian Svc. award USN Rsch. Lab., 1981, 5 times Best Paper of the Yr. award Naval Rsch. Lab., 1972-82, Outstanding Alumnus award Tulane U., 1984. Fellow IEEE. Democrat. Roman Catholic. Avocations: physics theory, bridge, golf. Home and Office: 817 Villa Dr Melbourne FL 32940-7037

LEWIS, BOYD DE WOLF, publisher,editor, writer; b. Boston, Aug. 18, 1905; s. Harry Braddock and Margaret De Wolf (Wade) L.; m. Hazel Reviere Bestick, Sept. 1, 1929; children: David De Wolf, Patricia Ann. Student, Boston U., 1923-27. Reporter, editor and bur. mgr. UP Assns., 1927-45; war corr. with Canadian, Brit. and Am. forces, 1944-45; 1 of 3 Am. press assn. reps. at German surrender Rheims, France, 1945; European news mgr. UP, 1945; exec. editor Newspaper Enterprise Assn., N.Y.C., 1945—; v.p. Newspaper Enterprise Assn., 1949-63, pres., 1963-72; v.p. pub. info. Nat. Safety Council, 1949-57; pub. The World Almanac, 1966-72; Sec. bd. Wolf Trap Found., 1975-76; trustee Cooper Inst., Naples, Fla.; cons. editor and columnist Maturity News Service, 1987—. Author: autobiography Not Always a Spectator, 1981. Mem. Mayflower Descs. Am. Address: 9319 Old Courthouse Rd Vienna VA 22182-2015

LEWIS, BRIAN KREGLOW, computer consultant; b. Durban, Republic of South Africa, Sept. 2, 1932; s. Arthur Armington and Isabel (Kreglow) L.; m. Mary Helen Kidwell, July 14, 1953; children: Brian E., James A., Charles A., Carol J., Robert E., Sharon H. BS, Ohio State U., 1954; PhD, Tufts U., 1971. Biology tchr. Lincoln-Sudbury (Mass.) Regional High Sch., 1965-66; rsch. assoc. May Inst. for Med. Rsch., Cin., 1971-75; from asst. to assoc. prof. health sci. Grand Valley State U., Allendale, Mich., 1975-81; prin. Lewis Assocs., Sarasota, Fla., 1984—; adj. asst. prof. physiology Cin. Coll. Medicine, 1972-75; assoc. prof. Ponce (P.R.) Sch. Medicine, 1981-84, prof., chmn. physiology, 1987-91; instr. Macintosh computer for beginners Sarasota County Tech. Inst., 1995—. Contbr. revs. and articles to Computer Shopper, Proceedings Soc. Exptl. Biology Medicine, Am. Heart Jour., Atherosclerosis; developer business and ednl. software. Cubmaster, scoutmaster Boy Scouts Am., 1963-78; mem. fin. com., ch. choir St. Andrew Ch., Sarasota, 1984—; bd. dirs. Sarasota chpt. Soc. Preservation and Encouragement Barbershop Quartet Singing in Am., 1994, sec., 1995—; active Village Voices, Greenhills, Ohio, 1972-75. Lt. Supply Corps USN, 1954-62. NIH fellow, 1965-71. Mem. Endocrine Soc., Soc. for Study Reproduction, Soc. for Study Fertility, Sarasota IBM PC Users Group (spreadsheet SIG leader 1993-94, software reviewer 1992—, moderator TechForum 1996—), Sigma Xi. Office: 6423 Caracara St Sarasota FL 34241-9104

LEWIS, BROCK, investment company executive; b. New Bedford, Mass., July 16, 1930; s. Frank Edward and Mary (Brock) L.; m. Susan Wahl, Sept. 4, 1954; children: Juliana D., Christopher B., Josiah E., Victoria D. BA, Dartmouth Coll., 1952; LLB, Boston U., 1955; postgrad., NYU, 1959-61. Asst. v.p. Fidelity Union Trust Co., Newark, 1955-64; v.p., trust officer County Nat. Bank, Poughkeepsie, N.Y., 1964-67, Capital Nat. Bank, Houston, 1967-69; v.p. Lionel D. Edie & Co., Houston, 1969-72, Dominick Mgmt. Co., N.Y.C., 1972-75, Marine Midland Bank, N.Y.C., 1975-80; 1st v.p. Lehman Mgmt. Co., N.Y.C., 1980-82; owner, pres. Brock Lewis Assocs. Ltd., Lawrenceville, N.J., 1982—; chmn., CEO Skandii Group, Inc., Princeton, N.J., 1991—; pres. SGI Internat., Inc., Lawrenceville, 1991—; cons. State of N.J. Adminstrn. Office of Cts., Trenton, 1993—; bd. dirs. Pacific Nat. Bank, Nantucket, Mass., Pacific Nat. Bank, Nantucket, Mass.; dir. Inst. Social and Econ. Policy Middle East, Cambridge, Mass., 1993—. Pres. Greater Trenton Symphony, 1993—; dir. Steinway Soc., Princeton, 1990; trustee Tabor Acad., Marion, Mass. Mem. Nat. Assn. Bus. Economists (chmn. internat. Bus. Rish Mgmt., Danish Am. C. of C., Swedish Am. C. of C., Finnish Am.C. of C., European Am. C. of C., Princeton C. of C., Mercer County C. of C., Nat. U.S.-Arab C. of C., Global Bus. Assn., Tabor Acad. Alumni Assn. (chmn. 1995—, trustee 1995—), Nassau Club, Pacific Club, Dartmouth Clubs of N.Y. and Princeton, Dartmouth Rowing Club, Union Boat Club Boston.

LEWIS, C. A., church administrator. Exec. sec. Ch. of the Living God Exec. Bd. *

LEWIS, CALVIN FRED, architect, educator; b. Chgo., Mar. 27, 1946; s. Howard George and Fern Teresa (Voelsch) L.; m. L. Diane Johnson, Aug. 24, 1968; children: Nathan, Miller, Cooper, Wilson. B of Architecture, Iowa State U., 1969. Architect Charles Herbert and Assocs., Des Moines, 1970-86; prin. Herbert Lewis Kruse Blunck Architecture, Des Moines, 1987—; arch., lectr. Inter Market Sq., Mpls., 1985, Nat. Tile Conf., L.A., 1987, Am. Soc. Landscape Archs., 1988, Iowa State U., 1985, 89; awards juror Dallas AIA, Kans. AIA, Nebr. AIA. Projects published in profl. jours. Chmn. profl. adv. bd. Iowa State U. Recipient Best in Design award Time Mag., 1982; named one of Top Young Architects in Country, Met. Home mag., 1983. Fellow AIA (more than 50 design awards 1972—). Avocations: sports, photography. Office: Herbert Lewis Kruse Blunk Architecture 202 Fleming Bldg Des Moines IA 50309-4081

LEWIS, CARL (FREDERICK CARLTON LEWIS), Olympic track and field athlete; b. Birmingham, Ala., July 1, 1961; s. Bill and Evelyn (Lawler) L. Student, U. Houston. Competed in Europe and U.S.; track meets include: Nat. Collegiate Athletic Assn. indoor championships, Baton Rouge, La., 1981, Nat. Outdoor Championships, Knoxville, Tenn., 1982, Nat. Sports Festival, 1982, Athletic Congress Outdoor Championships, Indpls., World Championships, Helsinki, 1983, Millrose Games, N.Y., 1984, Summer Olympics, 1980, 1984, 88, 92, 96; recorded album Break it Up, 1986. Recipient James E. Sullivan award best amateur athlete, 1981, Jesse Ownes award, 1982, Athlete of Yr. award Assoc. Press Sports, 1983; named World Athlete of the Decade Track & Field News, 1980-89, U.S. Athlete of the Yr., 1981, 82, 83, 84, 87, 88, 91, World Athlete of the Yr., 1982, 83, 84; winner 1 Bronze medal Pan Am. Games, 1979, 2 Gold medals, 1981, 1 Gold medal World Cup, 1981, 3 Gold medals World Championships, 1983, 9 Gold medals Olympics, 1984, 88, 92, 96, 1 Silver medal, 1988; named to U.S. Olympic Hall of Fame, 1985; world record holder in 4x100 relay, 1981, 83, 84, 91, 92, in 4x200 relay, 1989, 100 meter dash, 1991; Am. record holder in 4x100 relay, 1981, 83, 84, 90, 91, in 200 meter dash, 1983, 100 meter dash, 1987, 88, 91, 4x200 relay, 1989; world and Am. indoor record holder in long jump, 1981, 82, 84, in 60 yd. dash, 1983. Office: Carl Lewis Internat Fan Club PO Box 57-1990 Houston TX 77257-1990

LEWIS, CEYLON SMITH, JR., physician, educator; b. Muskogee, Okla., July 19, 1920; s. Ceylon Smith and Glenn (Ellis) L.; m. Marguerite Dearmont, Dec. 20, 1943; children: Sarah Lee Lewis Lorenz, Ceylon Smith III, Carol D. Lewis Kast. BA, Washington U., 1942, MD, 1945. Diplomate: Am. Bd. Internal Medicine, bd. govs., 1976-82. Intern Salt Lake Gen. Hosp., Salt Lake City, 1945-46, fellow in cardiovascular disease, 1950-51; resident in internal medicine VA Hosp., Salt Lake City, 1948-50; pvt. practice specializing in internal medicine and cardiology Tulsa, 1951—; mem. staff St. John's Hosp., Tulsa, 1952—, chief of staff, 1963, chmn. dept. medicine, 1970-71, mem. teaching staff, 1952—; cons. in internal medicine and cardiology Indian Health Svc., Claremore (Okla.) Indian Hosp., 1956—, USAID for Czech Republic, Slovak Republic, 1993—; vis. staff Hillcrest Medical Ctr., Tulsa, 1953—, St. Francis Hosp., Tulsa, 1963—, Univ. Hosp., Oklahoma City, 1973—; med. dir. St. John's Med. Ctr., Tulsa, 1976-78; asst. clin. prof. medicine Okla. U., 1970-74, assoc. clin. prof., 1975-76; clin. prof. U. Okla. Coll. Medicine, Tulsa, 1976—, dir. Internat. Studies in Medicine, 1990—; adj. clin. prof. med. scis. U. Tulsa Coll. Nursing, 1978—; mem. Okla. Physician Manpower Tng. Commn. Contbr. articles to profl. jours. Trustee Coll. Ozarks, 1962-72, chmn., 1964-66; bd. dirs. United Way, Tulsa, 1973-81, St. John Medical Ctr., 1974-84, Okla. Found. Peer Review., 1973-79, treas., 1973—; bd. dirs. Med. Benevolence Found., 1993—;pres. Tulsa Med. Edn. Found., Inc., 1973-77, 82-84, Presbyn Med. Mission Fund, Inc., Woodville, Tex., 1973-77, 82-84, bd. dirs. 1972-89; elder 1st Presbyn. Ch., Tulsa, 1959—;. Fellow Royal Australian Coll. Physicians, 1986; recipient Heart of Yr. award Okla. Heart Assn., 1974, Disting. Svc. award Am. Heart Assn., 1976. Fellow ACP (chmn. bd. govs. 1978-79, bd. regents 1980—, treas. 1983-85, pres.-elect 1985-86, pres. 1986-87, immediate past pres. 1987-88, pres. emeritus 1988—), Am. Coll. Cardiology, Am. Coll. Chest Physicians, Royal Australasian Coll. Physicians (hon.); mem. Tulsa County Med. Soc. (pres. 1971), Am. Clin. and Climatological Assn., Okla. Med. Assn. (pres. 1977-78), Inst. Medicine Nat. Acad. Scis. (1984—), AMA, Am. Fedn. Clin. Rsch., Okla. Soc. Internal Medicine (pres. 1971-72), Am. Soc. Internal Medicine, Tulsa County Heart Assn (dir. 1952-74, pres. 1956-57, Okla. Heart Assn. (dir. 1952—, pres. 1959-60), Am. Heart Assn. (fellow council clin. cardiology, v.p. 1974-75), Royal Soc. Medicine (London), Action in Internat. Medicine (v.p. 1991—); So. Hills Country Club. Office: 2300 Riverside Dr Tulsa OK 74114

LEWIS, CHARLES A., investment company executive; b. Orange, N.J., Oct. 23, 1942; s. F. Donald and Edna H. L.; m. Gretchen Smith, July 1967 (div.); m. Penny Bender Sebring, June 9, 1984. BA, Amherst Coll., 1964; MBA, U. Pa., 1966. Asst. to pres. Computer Tech., Inc., Skokie, Ill., 1969-70; 1st v.p. White, Weld, & Co., 1970-78; vice chmn. investment banking Merrill Lynch & Co., Chgo., 1978—. Trustee Amherst Coll., 1989—, Chgo. Symphony Orch., 1989—, Ravinia Festival, 1995—; assoc. Northwestern U., 1989—; life dir. Juvenile Diabetes Found., Met. Chgo. Mem. Chgo.Club, Glen View Club, Econ. Club Chgo. Office: Merrill Lynch & Co 5500 Sears Tower Chicago IL 60606-6325

LEWIS, CHARLES ARLEN, financial services company executive; b. Columbus, Ga., Nov. 7, 1943; s. Harlin B. and Dorothy A. (Elliott) L.; m. Linda L. McDowell, Dec. 5,1964; 1 child, Bryan C. Security trader White & Co. Investments, St. Louis, 1964-67; dist. sales mgr. Horizon Corp., Overland Park, Kans., 1967-73; mgr. U.S. Realty & Investment Co., St. Louis, 1973-75; fin. cons. Profesco, Inc., St. Louis, 1975-77; pres., CEO Am. Econ. Svcs., Ltd., St. Louis, 1977-82, Nat. Investment Corp., St. Louis, 1982-88; pres., CEO Le Bryan Corp., Washington, 1988-93, bd. dirs.; pres., CEO Integrated Mgmt. Sys., Inc., Lancaster, Calif., 1994—, also chmn. bd., 1994—; bd. dirs. Grimm Fin. Resources Inc., McLean, Va., Elliott, McDowell & Davis, Ltd., St. Louis, IMS Techs. & Svcs., Inc., Lancaster. Adv. bd. mem. Child Find Internat., St. Louis, 1987-88; chmn. bd. World Practical Taekwondo Fedn., Hong Kong, 1986—. 2d lt. U.S. Army, 1961-64. Recipient Disting. Svc. award Hong Kong Taekwondo Assn., 1982, Outstanding Svc. award World Practical Taekwondo Fedn., 1984, 87. Avocations: flying, golf.

LEWIS, CHARLES D., insurance executive, rancher, consultant; b. Denver, June 22, 1936; s. Harry Thompson and Margretta (Borrmann) L.; m. Penelope Hall, June 18, 1956; children: C. Randel, Christina, Vanda H. Student, Dartmouth Coll., 1954-55; BSBA, U. Denver, 1959, MBA, 1961. Tax mgr. Arthur Andersen & Co., Denver, 1959-64; exec. v.p., treas. Vail (Colo.) Assocs., Inc., 1964-67, Writer Constrn. Corp., Denver, 1967-69; pres., chief exec. officer, founder Copper Mountain (Colo.), Inc., 1969-82; gen. ptnr. W.F.R. Ltd., Kremmling, Colo., 1979—; gen. ptnr., dir. Boettcher & Co., Denver, 1982-85; pres. L.W.P. Svcs., Inc., Golden, Colo., 1985-95; pres., dir. Arlberg Holding Co., 1990—; pres. Arlberg Ins. Co., 1990—; mng. mem. Eldora Enterprises L.L.C., 1990—, C.D. Lewis LLC, 1997—; bd. dirs. Eire County Investment Co. Chmn. Copper Mountain Water & Sanitation Dist., 1972-82, Copper Mountain Met. Dist., 1972-82; mem. Colo. Passenger Tramway Bd., 1974-82, chmn., 1976-82. Recipient Industry and Environ. award Rocky Mountain Ctr. on Environment, 1974; named Outstanding Design, Ski Mag., 1975, Colo. Ski Hall of Fame, 1989. Mem. Am. Arbitration Assn., Colo. Soc. CPAs, Nat. Ski Areas Assn. (chmn. 1981-83), Colo. Ski Country USA (chmn. 1978-79), Am. Ski Fedn. (vice chmn. 1980-82), Colo. Wildlife Commn. Republican. Episcopalian. Avocations: climbing, fishing. Home: 19752 US Hwy 40 Kremmling CO 80459-9603 Office: LWP Svcs Inc 575 Union Blvd Ste 310 Lakewood CO 80228-1242

LEWIS, CHARLES EDWIN, physician, educator; b. Kansas City, Dec. 28, 1928; s. Claude Herbert and Maudie Friels (Holaday) L.; m. Mary Ann Gurera, Dec. 27, 1963; children—Kevin Neil, David Bradford, Matthew Clinton, Karen Carleen. Student, U. Kans., 1948-49; M.D., Harvard, 1953; M.S., U. Cin., 1957, Sc.D., 1959. Diplomate Am. Bd. Preventive Medicine (Occupl. Medicine). Intern, resident U. Kans. Hosp., 1953-54; trainee USPHS, 1956-58; fellow occupational health Eastman Kodak Co., 1958-59; asst. clin. prof. epidemiology Baylor U. Sch. Medicine, 1960-61; asso. prof. medicine U. Kans. Med. Sch., 1961-62, prof., chmn. dept. preventive medicine, 1962-69; coordinator Kan. Regional Med. Program, 1967-69; prof. social medicine Harvard Med. Sch., 1969-70; prof. pub. health, head div. health adminstrn. UCLA Med. Sch., 1970-72, prof. medicine, div. head, 1972-90; prof., 1972-89; prof. nursing Sch. Nursing UCLA Med. Sch., 1973—, head div. preventive and occupational medicine, 1991-93; dir. Health Svcs. Rsch. Ctr., 1991-93, UCLA Ctr. Health Promotion and Disease Prevention, 1991—; chair acad. senate UCLA, 1995-96; chmn. acad. senate UCLA, 1995-96; cons. Getty Trust, Walt Disney Prodns.; mem. Nat. Bd. Med. Examiners, 1964-68, 8-83, Jt. Commn. on Accreditaiton Health Care Orgns., 1989-95; mem. health svcs. rsch. study sect. USPHS, 1968-76; vis. scholar Annenberg Sch. Comm., U. So. Calif., 1980-81; mem. adv. bd. Hosp. Rsch. and Edn. Trust, 1972-75. Contbr. articles to profl. Jours. Served to capt. USAF, 1954-56. Recipient Ginsberg prize medicine U. Kans., 1954, Glasier award Soc. Gen. Internal Medicine, 1988. Fellow APHA, Acad. Occupl. Medicine; mem. ACP (regent 1988-94, Rosenthal award 1980, Laureate award So. Calif. III 1994, mastership, 1996), Internat. Epidemiology Soc., Assn. Tchrs. Preventive Medicine (pres. coun. 1977-80), Am. Assn. Physicians. Home: 221 S Burlingame Ave Los Angeles CA 90049-3702

LEWIS, CHARLES JOSEPH, journalist; b. Bozeman, Mont., July 10, 1940; s. Vern Edward James and Mary (Brooke) L.; m. Sarah Withers; children: Peter, Patrick, Barbara. BS in Humanities with Honors, Loyola U., Chgo., 1962; JD, Columbia U., 1965. Bar: Ill. 1965. Atty. McDermott, Will & Emery, Chgo., 1965-67; reporter City News Bur., Chgo., 1967-68; reporter, editor Chgo. Sun-Times, 1968-73; with AP, 1974-89, reporter, editor, Washington, 1974-78, reporter, editor, L.A., 1978-80, personnel mgr.,

N.Y.C., 1981-83, bur. chief, Hartford, Conn., 1980-81, bur. chief, Washington, 1984-89; bur. chief Hearst Newspapers, Washington, 1989—. Bd. dirs. Nat. Press Found., Washington, 1985—, treas., 1987-88, vice chmn., 1988-90, chmn., 1990-92; dir. Reporters Com. for Freedom of the Press, 1993—, SDX Found. Washington, 1996—. Lance cpl. USMCR, 1963-67. Mem. Am. Soc. Newspaper Editors, Gridiron Club, Sigma Delta Chi (v.p. Washington chpt. 1988-89). Office: Hearst Newspapers 1701 Pennsylvania Ave NW Washington DC 20006-5805

LEWIS, CHARLES LEONARD, psychologist; b. Wellsville, Ohio, Jan. 6, 1926; s. Cleo L. and Charlotte (Hahn) L.; m. Charlotte J. Wynn, Sept. 8, 1948 (dec. Mar. 1987); children: Stephen C., Janet J., Judith A.; m. Jane E. McCormick, Oct. 1, 1988. B.S. in Edn. with honors, Ohio U., 1949; M.A., U. Minn., 1953, Ph.D., 1955. Assoc. dir. activities U. Minn., 1950-55; dean student affairs, assoc. prof. psychology U. N.D., 1955-62; exec. dean, assoc. prof. ednl. psychology U. Tenn., 1962-67; v.p. student affairs Pa. State U., 1967-72; exec. dir. Am. Personnel and Guidance Assn., Washington, 1972-74, exec. v.p., 1974-83, exec. v.p. emeritus, 1984—; pres. Charles L. Lewis & Assocs., Annandale, Va., 1983-85, Chuck Lewis et al, Lancaster, Pa., 1985—; guest prof. U. Md., 1973; mem. Nat. Adv. Com. for Devel. Guidance Components-Career Edn., 1972-76. Founding editor Jour. Coll. Students Pers., 1958-64; mem. editl. bd. Pers. and Guidance Jour., 1954-57. Mem. Pres.'s Com. for Handicapped, 1972-80; bd. dirs. Ctr. Cmty. Hosps., Bellefonte, Pa. With U.S. Army, 1944-47. Recipient George Hill Disting. Alumni award Ohio U., 1981, Outstanding Alumnus Coll. Edn. Ohio U., 1988. Mem. APA, AAUP, Am. Assn. Higher Edn., Am. Coll. Pers. Assn. (pres. 1968-69), Nat. Assn. Student Pers. Adminstrs., Nat. Assn. Woman Deans and Counselors, Am. Pers. and Guidance Assn. (dir. 1967-70), Am. Assn. Univ. Adminstrs. (dir. 1973), Coun. Advancement of Stds. (bd. dirs.), Ohio U. Alumni Soc. and Friends Coll. Edn. (coun. 1985-92, bd. dirs. 1986-92), Psi Chi, Kappa Delta Pi, Beta Theta Pi, Chi Sigma Iota (founding dir. 1984-90). Episcopalian.

LEWIS, CHRISTINA LYNN, human services administrator; b. Brook Park, Ohio, June 19, 1963; d. Albert Joseph and Gail Ann (Kohler) Urbas; m. Timothy Allen Lewis, Aug. 3, 1989; 1 child, Cherie Ann. AA, Pasco Hernando C.C., Brooksville, Fla., 1996; student, Thomas Edison State Coll., 1996—. Owner, operator Spl. Touch Day Care, Olmsted Twp., Ohio, 1986-89, Spring Hill, Fla., 1989-94; dir., tng. coord. United Cerebral Palsy, Brooksville, 1994-96; mentor, tng. advisor child care outreach program United Cerebral Palsy, Brooksville, Fla., 1993—; advisor, instr. Child Devel. Assn. Credential Program, Brooksville, 1991—; coun. mem. Pre-K Interagy. Coun., Brooksville, 1994—; CPR, First Aid instr. ARC, 1994—; area supr. Head Start, Inverness, Fla., 1996—. Author (tng. packet) CDA: Everything You Need to Know to Get Started, 1992. Dep. registrar Supr. Elections, Hernando County, 1994; vol. instr. ARC. Recipient Resolution 91-70 award Hernando County Commr., Brooksville, 1991. Mem. Nat. Assn. for the Edn. Young Children, Assn. for Better Child Care (founding mem., newsletter editor 1990, sec., resource and referral 1989-93, Tchr. of Yr. 1990), Phi Theta Kappa. Republican. Avocations: snorkeling, pottery, camping. Home: 9063 Spring Hill Dr Spring Hill FL 34608-6241 Office: Childhood Devel Svcs 613 Us Highway 41 S Inverness FL 34450-6074

LEWIS, CLAUDE AUBREY, columnist; b. N.Y.C., Dec. 14, 1936; s. Robert George Lewis and Hazel (Perkinson) Gray; m. Beverly McKelvey, Oct. 18, 1953; children: Pamela, Bryan, Craig, Beverley. AB in English, CCNY, 1958; LHD (hon.), Thomas Jefferson U., 1986. From editorial asst. to asst. editor Newsweek, N.Y.C., 1953-64; reporter N.Y. Herald Tribune, N.Y.C., 1964-65, NBC, Phila., 1965-67; assoc. editor, columnist Phila. Bull., 1967-82; editor, pub. Nat. Leader, Phila., 1982-84; columnist, mem. editorial bd. Phila. Inquirer, 1984—. Author: Muhammad Ali, 1962, Adam Clayton Powell, 1965, Benjamin Banneker, 1968; co-author: New York City in Crisis, 1966. Bd. dirs. Valley Forge Med. Ctr., Phila., Met. Hosp., Phila., Djonge McNair Health Fund, Phila. Recipient Gold Typewriter award Schaefer, 1964, 67; 1st pl. award Phila. Med. Soc., 1967, Martin Luther King Jr. award Nat. Orgn. of Unions, 1967. Mem. Nat. Assn. Black Journalists (founder). Avocations: photography, reading. Office: Phila Inquirer 400 N Broad St Philadelphia PA 19130-4015*

LEWIS, CLINTON, federal agency administrator; b. Eastman, Ga., Sept. 24, 1931; s. Theo and Lucy Victoria (Smith) L.; m. Jane Ivelyn Cadwell Evans, Aug. 18, 1950 (div. Aug. 1967); children: Jerry Thomas, David Theo; m. Ruth Grace Waller, June 19, 1969; children: Gwendolyn Elaine Gay, Clinton Jr. BBA, Ga. Coll., 1973; diploma, Air War Coll., 1979. Chief mgmt. evaluation office USAF, Robins AFB, Ga., 1971-73, supt. aircraft components repair, 1973, chief aircraft scheduling, inventory br., 1973-74, chief aircraft planning, engring. br., 1974-75, chief indsl. products and life support sys. divsn., 1975-76, dep. chief aircraft divsn., 1976-81, dep. dir. directorate of distbn., 1981-84, dep. dir. directorate of maintenance, 1984-90, dir. tech. and indsl. support directorate, 1990—. Chmn. Civilian Non-Appropriated Funds Coun., Robins AFB, 1988—; treas. Parkerson Bapt. Ch., Eastman, Ga, 1978—. Recipient Presdl. Rank of Meritious Exec., Pres. of U.S., 1988, Disting. Civilian Svc. award Dept. of Def., 1995, Vocat. award for Civil Svc., Warner Robins, Ga. Rotary Club, 1996. Mem. Air Force Assn., Fed. Mgrs.' Assn. (Outstanding Fed. Mgr. of Yr. 1995), Sr. Exec. Svc. Avocations: baseball, softball, golf, swimming. Home: Rt 4 Eastman GA 31023 Office: WR-ALC/TI 420 2nd St Ste 100 Robins AFB GA 31098-1640

LEWIS, CLYDE A., lawyer; b. Hoquiam, Wash., June 20, 1913; s. J.D. Clyde and Loretta C. (Adelsperger) L.; A.B., U. Notre Dame, 1934; J.D., Harvard U., 1939; m. Helen M. Judge, Sept. 22, 1936 (dec. Sept. 1985); m. Patricia Davis Judge, Oct. 1, 1988; children: Clyde A., John E. Admitted to N.Y. bar, 1940, U.S. Supreme Ct. bar, 1959; mem. Lewis & Rogers, and predecessor firms, Plattsburgh, N.Y. Comdr. in chief VFW, 1949-50, also served as sr. and jr. vice comdr. in chief, mem. nat. legis. com. Served to maj. USAAF, 1942-45. Decorated D.F.C. with 2 oak leaf clusters, Air medal with 4 oak leaf clusters; USAF Exceptional Svc. award; Croix de Guerre (France); invested Knight of Malta. Mem. Am. Legion, Am., N.Y. State bar assns., Notre Dame, Harvard alumni assns., U.S. Strategic Inst., Def. Orientation Conf. Assn. Republican. Roman Catholic. Clubs: Capitol Hill, K.C., Elks. Home: 93 Lighthouse Rd Plattsburgh NY 12901-7018 Office: 53 Court St Plattsburgh NY 12901-2834

LEWIS, DALE KENTON, retired lawyer, mediator; b. Goodland, Kans., June 20, 1937; s. W. Homer and L. (Fern) L.; m. Constance L. Coover, Dec. 27, 1958; children—James W., Bari Lynn, Brad Kenton. B.A., State U. Iowa, 1959; J.D., Colo. U., 1962. Bar: Colo. 1962, Ind. 1968. Mem. firm Lewis & Ausenhus, Loveland, Colo., 1962-67; with Eli Lilly and Co., 1967-90; counsel Elanco Products Co., 1969-77; gen. counsel, sec. Elizabeth Arden, Inc., 1977-81, corp. asst. sec. and asso. gen. counsel, 1981-83, corp. asst. sec., dep. gen. counsel, 1983-86, sec., dep. gen. counsel, 1986-89; v.p., sec., gen. counsel DowElanco, Indpls., 1989-95; ret., 1995. Mem. Am. Corp. Counsel Assn., Order of Coif. Episcopalian.

LEWIS, DAN ALBERT, education educator; b. Chgo., Feb. 14, 1946; s. Milton and Diane (Sabath) L.; m. Stephanie Riger, Jan. 3, 1982; children: Matthew, Jake. BA cum laude, Stanford U., 1968; PhD, U. Calif., Santa Cruz, 1980. Rsch. assoc. Arthur Bolton Assocs., Sacramento, 1969-70; survey contr. Sci. Analysis Corp., San Francisco, 1971; dir. Stanford Workshops on Polit. and Social Issues Stanford (Calif.) U., 1971-74; projects adminstr. Ctr. Urban Affairs and Policy Rsch., Northwestern U., Evanston, Ill., 1975-80, asst. prof. edn., 1980-86, assoc. prof. edn., 1986-90, assoc. dir., chair grad. program human devel./social policy, 1987-90, prof. edn., 1990—; vis. scholar Sch. Edn., Stanford U., 1990-91; mem. task force on restructuring mental health svcs. Chgo. Dept. Health, 1982; mem. human rights authority Ill. Guardianship and Advocacy Commn., 1980-82; adv. mem. com. on planning and inter-agy. coordination Commn. Mental Health and Devel. Disabilities, 1979; interim adv. com. on mental health City of Chgo., 1978; adv. mem. Gov.'s Commn. to Revise Mental Health Code Ill., 1975-77; presenter at profl. confs.; presenter workshops. Editor: Reactions to Crime, 1981; co-author: Fear of Crime: Incivility and the Production of a Social Problem, 1986, The Social Construction of Reform: Crime Prevention and Community Organizations, 1988, The Worlds of the Mentally Ill, 1991, The State Mental Patient in Urban Life, 1994, Race and Educational Reform, 1995; contbr. articles, book revs. to profl. publs. Bd. dirs. Designs for Change, Ill. Mental Health Assn.; rsch. adv. com. Chgo. Urban League, Chgo. Panel Pub. Sch. Finances, 1989-91; needs assessment tech. com. United Way Chgo., 1989-90; ednl. coun. Francis W. Parker Sch., Chgo., 1988-90; task force on restructuring mental health svcs. Chgo. Dept. Health, 1982; com. on mentally disabled Ill. State Bar Assn., 1983-89; rsch. policy com. Ill. Dept. Mental Health, 1978; bd. dirs. Mental Health Assn. Greater Chgo., 1977-84, v.p. pub. policy, 1979-83. Office: Northwestern Univ 2040 Sheridan Rd Evanston IL 60208-0855

LEWIS, DANA KENNETH, trading company executive, consultant, author; b. L.A., Aug. 24, 1945; s. Kenneth Robert and Ouida Jo (Norris) L.; m. Yoko Koshio, Sept. 12, 1969; 1 child, Michelle Cynthia. BA, Friends World Coll., Huntington, N.Y., 1976; MA, Goddard Coll., Plainfield, Vt., 1980. Cons. to pres. Emile, Inc., Osaka, Japan, 1976-77; residential houseparent Bethany Children's Home, Womelsdorf, Pa., 1977-78, cottage life supr., 1978-86, dir. home life, adminstr., 1986-94; co-founder, pres. Lewis Mktg., Inc. (formerly Pacific Rim Enterprises, Inc.), Fleetwood, Pa., 1989—; founder The Metalog Group, Fleetwood, Pa., 1993—; instr. Pa. State U., 1981-83, Family Life Devel., Cornell U., 1982-85; presenter Treischman Conf., Boston, 1989. Author: Working with Children, 1981; author, speaker, audio cassettes Child Care and Communications, 1979—; mem. editorial bd. Jour. 1984; book reviewer, 1988; contbr. articles to profl. jours. Lectr. various local facilities, 1978—. Served as staff sgt., USAF. Mem. Child Care Assn. of Pa. (trainer, presenter 1979-87, keynote speaker Regional Confs. 1986, Dedicated Service award 1986). Avocations: computers, reading, poetry, writing, travelling. Home and Office: Lewis Mktg Inc 22 Bick Rd Fleetwood PA 19522-9611

LEWIS, DANIEL EDWARD, systems engineer, computer company executive; b. Cleve., May 24, 1955; s. Arthur Edward and Vivian Jeanette (Davis) L.; m. Kimber Lea Thacher, Dec. 30, 1993. BSEE, Ohio State U., 1981; MBA, U. Akron, 1988. Registered profl. engr., Ohio. Sys. engr. Firestone Tire & Rubber, Akron, Ohio, 1981-83; software devel. mgr. Diebold Corp., Canton, Ohio, 1983-85; computer product sales Arrow Electronics, Solon, Ohio, 1985-86; sr. sys. analyst Bristol Petroleum, Cleve., 1986-89; product mgr. Telxon Corp., Fair Lawn, Ohio, 1989-93; sr. mktg. mgr. Norand Corp., Cedar Rapids, Iowa, 1993-95, dir. mktg., 1995—. Contbr. articles to profl. jours. Mem. IEEE, Am. Mgmt. Assn., Assn. for Computing Machinery. Avocations: travel, skiing, sailing. Home: 3602 Caribou Ct NE Cedar Rapids IA 52402-2525 Office: Norand Corp 550 2nd St SE Cedar Rapids IA 52401-2023

LEWIS, DARRELL L., retail executive; b. Mason City, Iowa, Nov. 20, 1931; s. Milton Loren and Blanche Ione (Wilson) L.; m. Mary Jo Bahnsen, Oct. 22, 1950; children—John L., Lonnette Ann, Sherri Jo. MBA, Stanford U., 1970. With Osco Drug, Inc. subsidiary Jewel Cos., Inc., 1949-62; with Jewel Turn-Style, 1962; pres. Turn-Style Family Centers, Franklin Park, Ill., 1967-74; head Jewel Hypermarket Turn-Style Family Centers, 1974; pres. Osco Drug, Inc., 1974-75, v.p. store and sales devel., 1976-77; pres. D.L. Lewis Drug Co. Inc., Bensenville, Ill., 1978—, chmn. bd., 1987—. Home: 12338 Sunset Dr Three Rivers MI 49093-9580 Office: DL Lewis Drug Co 1325 W Irving Park Rd Bensenville IL 60106-1764

LEWIS, DAVID CARLETON, medical educator, university center director; b. Hartford, Conn., May 19, 1935; s. Theodore and Lillian (Levin) L.; m. Eleanor Grace Levinson, Aug. 23, 1959; children: Deborah, Steven. AB magna cum laude, Brown U., 1957; MD, Harvard U., 1961. Intern Beth Israel Hosp., Boston, 1961-62, jr. resident, 1962-63, chief med. resident, 1966-67, dir. emergency unit and med. outpatient dept., 1969-71; sr. resident U. Hosps. Cleve., 1963-64, Parkland Meml. Hosp., Dallas, 1964-66; fellow U. Tex. Southwestern Med. Hosp., Dallas, 1964-66; Sloan Found. fellow Harvard Med. Sch., Boston, 1971-72; med. dir. Washingtonian Ctr. for Addictions, Boston, 1972-77; dir. div. alcohol and substance abuse Roger Williams Gen. Hosp., Providence, 1976—; dir. program in alcoholism and drug abuse Brown U., Providence, 1976-82, prof. medicine and community health, 1982—, Donald G. Millar prof. alcohol and addiction studies, 1987—, chmn. dept. community health, 1981-86, dir. Ctr. Alcohol and Addiction Studies, 1982—; mem. nat. adv. coun. Nat. Alcohol Inst., Rockville, Md., 1981-85, cons. to dir., 1985—; mem. sci. adv. bd. Children of dir., 1985—; cons. WHO,, 1986—, mem. WHO cocaine global adv. com., 1992-95; chair Physician Consortium on Substance Abuse Edn., 1989—; mem. Carnegie Substance Abuse Adv. com., 1989-92; scholar-in-residence Nat. Inst. Med., 1991-92; mem. adv. panel to U.S. Pharmacopoeia, 1995—; mem. Drug Strategies Nat. Adv. Panel, 1994—; mem. nat. adv. com. Robert Wood Johnson Found. Fighting Back program, 1996—. Author: The Drug Experience: Data for Decision Making, 1970; editor: Providing Care for Children of Alcoholics, 1986; editor Brown U. Digest of Addiction Theory and Application, 1986—; exec. editor Substance Abuse jour., 1984—; contbr. numerous articles to profl. jours. Med. dir. Beacon Hill Free Clinic, Boston, 1968-71; chmn. Mayor's Coun. on Drug Abuse, Boston, 1972-80; mem. nat. adv. com. for fighting back program Robert Wood Johnson Found., 1996—. Grantee Nat. Alcohol and Drug Insts., 1986—, Edward John Noble fellow Harvard U. Med. Sch., 1957-91. Fellow ACP; mem. NAS, Inst. Medicine Study on Treatment Alcohol Problems, Assn. Med. Edn. and Rsch. in Substance Abuse (pres. 1983-88, Excellence in Medicine award 1986), Am. Soc. Addiction Medicine (chair core curriculum com. 1989-96, chair sect. on internal medicine 1990—, bd. dirs.), U.S. Pharmacopea (mem. adv. panel), Brown Med. Alumni Assn. (pres. 1974-76), Phi Beta Kappa, Sigma Xi. Avocations: choral singing, sailing, photography. Office: Brown Univ Ctr Alcohol & Addiction Studies Box G Providence RI 02912

LEWIS, DAVID JOHN, lawyer; b. Zanesville, Ohio, Feb. 4, 1948; s. David Griff and Barbara Ann (Hoy) L.; m. Susan G. Smith; 1 child, Ann Elizabeth. BS in Fin., U. Ill., 1970, JD, 1973. Bar: Ill. 1973, D.C. 1974. Law clk. to Judge Philip W. Tone U.S. Dist. Ct. For North Dist. Ill., Chgo., 1973-74; assoc. Sidley & Austin, Washington, 1974-80, ptnr., 1980—. Mem. ABA. Office: Sidley & Austin 1722 I St NW Washington DC 20006-3705

LEWIS, DAVID KELLOGG, philosopher, educator; b. Oberlin, Ohio, Sept. 28, 1941; s. John Donald and Ewart (Kellogg) L.; m. Stephanie Robinson, Sept. 5, 1965. BA, Swarthmore Coll., 1962; MA, Harvard U., 1964, PhD, 1967; DLitt (hon.), U. Melbourne, 1995. Asst. prof. philosophy UCLA, 1966-70; mem. faculty Princeton U., 1970—, prof. philosophy, 1973—; cons. Hudson Inst., 1962-75; Fulbright lectr., Australia, 1971; Locke lectr. Oxford U., 1984.; Kant lectr. Stanford U., 1988. Author: Convention: A Philosophical Study, 1969, Counterfactuals, 1973; On the Plurality of Worlds, 1986, Philosophical Papers, vol. I, 1983, vol. II, 1986, Parts of Classes, 1991. Fulbright rsch. fellow N.Z., 1976, Santayana fellow Harvard U., 1988; Recipient Matchette prize for philos. writing, 1972. Mem. AAAS, AAUP, NAS, Brit. Acad., Australian Acad. Humanities. Office: Princeton U Dept Philosophy Princeton NJ 08544

LEWIS, DAVID LANIER, business history educator; b. Bethalto, Ill., Apr. 5, 1927; s. Donald F. and Edith (Jinkinson) L.; m. Florence Yuri Tanaka, Apr. 5, 1953; children: Kim, Leilani, Sumi, Lance. B.S., U. Ill., 1948; M.S., Boston U., 1955; M.A., U. Mich., 1956, Ph.D., 1959; postgrad. (Fulbright scholar), London Sch. Econs., 1956-57. Reporter Edwardsville (Ill.) Intelligencer, 1948; bur. chief, state editor Alton (Ill.) Telegraph, 1948-50; editor employee publs. St. Louis Lincoln-Mercury Plant, 1950-51; press relations rep. Borden Co., N.Y.C., 1952, Ford Motor Co., Dearborn, Mich., 1952-55; pub. relations exec. Gen. Motors Corp., Detroit, 1959-65; asso. prof. bus. history U. Mich., Ann Arbor, 1965-68; prof. U. Mich., 1968—. Author: The Public Image of Henry Ford: An American Folk Hero and His Company, 1976, The Automobile and American Culture, 1983, Ford, 1903 to 1984, 1984, Ford Country, 1987, Ford Chronicle: A Pictorial History From 1893, 1992, The Car and The Camera, 1996; assoc. editor, columnist: Cars & Parts; guest editor: Mich. Quar. Rev, 1980-81. Trustee Nat. Automotive History Collection, Detroit. Served with USNR, 1945-46. Mem. Mich. Hist. Soc., Soc. Automotive Historians (past pres.), Am. Hist. Assn., Bus. Hist. Conf. Home: 2588 Hawthorn Rd Ann Arbor MI 48104-4032 Office: U Mich Bus School Ann Arbor MI 48109-1234

LEWIS, DAVID LEVERING, history educator; b. Little Rock, May 25, 1936; s. John Henry and Alice Urnestine (Bell) L.; m. Sharon Lynn Siskind, 1965 (div. Oct. 1988); children: Eric, Allison, Jason; m. Ruth Ann Stewart, Apr. 15, 1994; 1 child, Allegra. BA in History/Philosophy, Fisk U., 1956; MA in U.S. History, Columbia U., 1959; PhD in Modern Europe/France, London Sch. Econs. & Polit. Sci., 1962. Lectr. European history U. Ghana, Legon, 1963-64; from assoc. prof. to prof. U. D.C., 1970-80; prof. U. Calif. San Diego, La Jolla, 1981-85; M.L. King, Jr. Univ. prof. Rutgers U., New Brunswick, N.J., 1985—; commr. Nat. Portrait Gallery, Smithsonian Instn., Washington, 1989-94; bd. dirs. Nat. Humanities Ctr. 1993-97. Author: King: A Biography, 1970, Prisoners of Honor: The Dreyfus Affair, 1974, District of Columbia: A Bicentennial History, 1976, When Harlem Was in Vogue, 1981, The Race to Fashoda: European Colonialism and African Resistance in the Scramble for Africa, 1988, W.E. DuBois: Biography of a Race, 1868-1919, Vol. I, 1993 (Pulitzer prize 1994), The Civil Rights Movement in America, 1986, Harlem Renaissance: Black Art of America, 1987, Bridges and Boundaries: African Americans and American Jews, 1992. With U.S. Army, 1962-63. Recipient Bancroft prize Columbia U., 1994, Francis Parkman prize Soc. Am. Historians, 1994; fellow Woodrow Wilson Internat. Ctr. Scholars, Smithsonian Instn., 1977-78, 90-91, Ctr. Advanced Study Behavioral Scis., 1980-81, Nat. Humanities Ctr., 1983-84, Guggenheim Meml. Found., 1986-87; Ralph Waldo Emerson prize Phi Beta Kappa, 1994. Mem. AAUP, Am. Hist. Assn., African Studies Assn., Orgn. Am. Historians, Soc. French Hist. Studies, So. Hist. Assn., Century Club, Phi Beta Kappa (chmn. Am. scholar com., 1991-93, senator united chpts. 1991—). Avocations: traveling, cycling. Office: Rutgers U Dept History Van Dyck Hall New Brunswick NJ 08903*

LEWIS, DELANO EUGENE, broadcast executive; b. Arkansas City, Kans., Nov. 12, 1938; s. Raymond Ernest and Enna (Wordlow) L.; m. Gayle Carolyn Jones; children: Delano Jr., Brian, Geoffrey, Phillip. BA, U. Kansas, 1960; JD, Washburn U., 1963; LHD (hon.), Marymount U., 1988; D of Humane Letters, Bowie State U., 1992; D of Pub. Svc., George Washington U., 1991; DHL (hon.), Barry U., 1994, Kent State U., 1995, Lafayette Coll., 1996. Staff atty. U.S. Dept. of Justice, Washington, 1963-65, EEOC, Washington, 1965-66; assoc. dir., country dir. U.S. Peace Corps., Nigeria, Uganda, 1966-69; legis. asst. Sen. Edward Brooke Mass., Washington, 1969-71; adminstrv. asst. Congressman Walter Fauntroy, Washington, 1971-73; mgr. pub. affairs Chesapeake & Potomac Telephone Co., Washington, 1973-76, asst. v.p., 1976-83, v.p., 1983-88, pres., 1988-93; pres., CEO Nat. Public Radio, Washington, 1994—; bd. dirs. Apple Computer, Guest Svcs., Inc., Black Entertainment TV, Colgate-Palmolive, Halliburton Co. Pres. Greater Washington Bd. Trade, 1988; chmn. Mayor's Transition Com., 1978, D.C. Youth Employment Adv. Coun., 1992; co-chair D.C. Vocational Edn. and Career Opportunities Com., 1991, NPR Found.; mem. emeritus bd. Washington Performing Arts Soc., 1990—, Nat. Bd. AFRICARE, 1990—; bd. dirs. Lincoln Theatre. Named Washingtonian of Yr. Washingtonian mag., 1978, Man of Yr., Greater Washington bd. trustees, 1992; recipient Pres. medal Cath. U., Washington, 1978, Tree of Life award NCCJ, 1989, Social Responsibility award George Washington U. Sch. Bus., 1990, Spl. award Women of Washington, Disting. Alumni Citation U. Kans. Mem. Kans. Bar Assn., D.C. Bar Assn., Georgetown Club. Democrat. Roman Catholic. Avocations: jogging, tennis, racquetball. Office: Nat Public Radio 635 Massachusetts Ave NW Washington DC 20001-3752

LEWIS, DELBERT O'NEAL, disability consultant, former state official; b. Searcy, Ark., Oct. 15, 1947; s. Scott and Viola Marie (Hodges) L. BA in Psychology and Sociology, Harding U., 1969; 2M Rehab. Counseling, Ark. State U., 1972. Cert. rehab. counselor. With divsn. rehab. svcs. Ark. Dept. Human Svcs., Little Rock, 1972-90, planning specialist, 1978-90; ret., 1990, cons. on disability issues to govt., legal, ednl., and pvt. orgns., 1990—; former staff and advisor Ark. Com. on Equal Access for Handicapped, Interdeptl. Task Force on Rights of Handicapped, D.C. Govt., Washington, others; former rehab. specialist Disability Determination Svcs. Social Security Adminstrn., Little Rock; former mem. planning coun. CETA and Job Tng. Partnership Act, Little Rock and Pulaski County; guest lectr. on disability issues U. Ark., Little Rock; founding mem., past pres. Ark. Environ. Barriers Coun.; mem. Ark. Adv. Com. to U.S. Commn. on Civil Rights; cons. Emerging Issues Project Inst. for Info. Studies, Washington. Contbr. articles to profl. publs. First pub. mem. Ark. Bd. Architects; former bd. dirs. OurWay, Inc., Little Rock; active Ark. Child Find to Implement Edn. for Handicapped Children Act., others. Recipient plaque of appreciation for svcs. as pres. Ark. br. Nat. Rehab. Counseling Assn., 1976, certs. City of Little Rock, 1975-85, First Mover and Shaker award Ark. Gov.'s Commn. on People with Disabilities, 1978, recognition of svc. plaque Ark. Rehab. Assn., 1990, dedicated svc. plaque Ark. Divsn. Rehab. Svcs. Consumer Adv. Coun., 1990, pub. svc. plaque ARKLA Gas Co., 1991, Cert. of svc. award U.S. Commn. on Civil Rights, Washington, 1995. Mem. Found. for Sci. and Disability, Gazette Internat. Networking Inst.-Internat. Polio Network, Drug Policy Found. Avocations: disability rights and access advocate, writing, anti war on drugs, supporter of Alliance for Cannabis Therapeutics. Home and Office: 2400 Riverfront Dr Apt 12-F Little Rock AR 72202

LEWIS, DENNIS CARROLL, public relations executive; b. Milw., Jan. 7, 1940; s. Carroll and Alyce Mae (Bryce) Lewis Paxton; m. Marie Benedicte Denizet, Nov. 1, 1973 (div. Dec. 1982); 1 son, Benoit. Student U. Wis. 1957-61; BS, San Francisco State Coll., 1967. Computer programmer, analyst Levi Strauss, San Francisco, 1969-72; freelance book editor, San Francisco, 1972-73; book editor Miller Freeman Publishing Co., San Francisco, 1973-76; pub. rels. account exec. Paul Purdom & Co., San Francisco, 1977-81; ptnr. Hi-Tech. Publicity, San Francisco, 1981-84; pres. Hi-Tech Pub. Relations, Inc., San Francisco, 1984-90 (acquired by Shandwick Plc, 1988); healing Tao instr. and Chi Nei Tsang practitioner, 1993—. Author: The Tao of Natural Breathing, 1997; co-editor: Sacred Tradition and Present Need, 1975; On the Way to Self-Knowledge, 1976; also articles in newspapers and profl. jours. Co.-pub., editor Computer Publicity News, San Francisco, 1981-90. Club: San Francisco Tennis.

LEWIS, DONALD EMERSON, banker; b. Orange, N.J., Apr. 3, 1950; s. Donald Emerson Lewis and Marie (Gannon) Slaght; m. Suzanne Kimm, Oct. 12, 1974; children: Andrew Gannon, Meredith Marie, Carolyn Ann. AB, Villanova U., 1972; MBA, Boston Coll., 1974. V.p. Citibank N.A., N.Y.C., 1974-85, Boston Safe Deposit & Trust Co., N.Y.C., 1985-87; sr. v.p. United Jersey Banks, Princeton, N.J., 1987-91; v.p. Fleet Bank, N.A., Glen Rock, N.J., 1991—. Republican. Roman Catholic. Club: Canoe Brook Country. Avocations: golf, platform tennis. Office: Fleet Bank NA 208 Harristown Rd Glen Rock NJ 07452-3306

LEWIS, DONALD JOHN, mathematics educator; b. Adrian, Minn., Jan. 25, 1926; s. William J. and Ellanora (Masgai) L.; m. Carolyn Dana Hauf, Dec. 28, 1953. BS, Coll. St. Thomas, 1946; PhD, U. Mich., 1950. Instr. Ohio State U., Columbus, 1950-52; asst. prof. U. Notre Dame (Ind.), 1953-57, assoc. prof., 1957-61; assoc. prof. U. Mich., Ann Arbor, 1961-63, prof. maths., 1963—, dept. chair, 1983-94; dir. Divsn. Math. Scis. Nat. Sci. Found., 1995—; mem. Inst. for Adv. Study, 1952-53, 90-91; vis. scientist U. Manchester (Eng.), 1959-61, Cambridge (Eng.), 1960-61; vis. fellow Trinity Coll., Cambridge, 1965-69, Japanese Soc. for Promotion of Sci., Tokyo, 1974; visitor U. Heidelberg, Germany, 1980-81, 83; adv. bd. math. sci. NSF, 1983-86, math panel sci., 1993. Author: Introduction to Algebra, 1965, Calculus and Linear Algebra, 1970; editor: Proceedings of Symposia in Pure Math., 1971; contbr. 55 articles on number theory to profl. jours. Recipient Humboldt Preis award Alexander von Humboldt Soc., Germany, 1980, Disting. Svc. award Am. Math. Soc., 1995; fellow NSF, 1952-53, 59-61. Roman Catholic. Avocations: gardening. Home: 2250 Glendaloch Rd Ann Arbor MI 48104-2832 Office: U Mich Math Dept Ann Arbor MI 48109-1003

LEWIS, DOUGLAS, art historian; b. Centreville, Miss., Apr. 30, 1938; s. Charles Douglas and Beatrice Fenwick (Stewart) L. B.A. in History; B.A. in History of Art, Yale U., 1960, M.A., 1963, Ph.D., 1967; B.A. in Fine Arts, Clare Coll., Cambridge (Eng.) U., 1962, M.A., 1966. Asst. in instrn. Yale U., 1962-64; asst. prof. art Bryn Mawr Coll., 1967-68; vis. lectr. U. Calif., Berkeley, spring 1970, fall 1979; adj. prof. Johns Hopkins U., 1973-77; curator sculpture and decorative arts Nat. Gallery Art, Washington, 1968—; professorial lectr. Georgetown U., 1980-93; adj. prof. U. Md., 1989-91, 93—; mem. art adv. coms. Bayly Art Mus. U. Va., Mt. Holyoke Coll. Art Mus., Lawrenceville Sch.; vice-chmn. nat. citizens stamp adv. com. U.S. Postal Svc.; adv. bd. Centro Palladiano, Vicenza, Italy. Author: The Late Baroque Churches of Venice, 1979, The Drawings of Andrea Palladio, 1981, intro. to Renaissance Master Bronzes, 1986. Mem. Am. fellowship com. Belgian-Am. Ednl. Found. Recipient Copley medal Nat. Portrait Gallery, 1981; Chester

Dale fellow; David E. Finley fellow Nat. Gallery Art, 1964-67; Rome Prize fellow Am. Acad. Rome, 1964-66, Bruce Curatorial fellow Nat. Gallery Art, 1997-98. Mem. Coll. Art Assn. Am., Soc. Archtl. Historians, Nat. Trust Historic Preservation, Washington Collegium for the Humanities (adv. bd.), Manuscript Soc., Assn. Art History. Episcopalian. Clubs: Yale (N.Y.C.); Falcons (Cambridge U.). Office: Nat Gallery Art Washington DC 20565-0001

LEWIS, EDWARD ALAN, religious organization adminstrator; b. Brazil, Ind., July 22, 1946; s. Edward and Ruth Margaret (Eberwein) L. B in Music Edn., Grace Coll., 1969; M in Divinity, Grace Sem., 1973. Asst. to pastor, youth dir. Grace Brethren Ch., Winona Lake, Ind., 1969-73; nat. dir. youth ministries Grace Brethren Ch. Christian Edn., Winona Lake, 1973-85; dir. candidate personnel Grace Brethren Fgn. Missions, Winona Lake, 1982-88; exec. dir. Grace Brethren Ch. Christian Edn., Winona Lake, 1985—. Mem. Grace Brethren Ch., Winona Lake, 1969—, exec. mem. denominational youth com., 1984—; moderator Nat. Fellowship of Grace Brethren Chs., 1994-95. Mem. Grace Sem. Alumni Assn. (pres. 1984-85), Ind. Dist. Ministerium, Nat. Ministerium Assn. Avocations: music, piano, singing, jogging, travel. Home and Office: PO Box 365 Winona Lake IN 46590-0365

LEWIS, EDWARD B., biology educator; b. Wilkes-Barre, Pa., May 20, 1918; s. Edward B. and Laura (Histed) L.; m. Pamela Harrah, Sept. 26, 1946; children: Hugh, Glenn (dec.), Keith. B.A., U. Minn., 1939; Ph.D., Calif. Inst. Tech., 1942; Phil.D., U. Umea, Sweden, 1982; DSc, U. Minn., 1993. Instr. biology Calif. Inst. Tech., Pasadena, 1946-48, asst. prof., 1949-56, prof., 1956-66, Thomas Hunt Morgan prof., 1966-88, prof. emeritus, 1988—; Rockefeller Found. fellow Sch. Botany, Cambridge U., Eng., 1948-49; mem. Nat. Adv. Com. Radiation, 1958-61; vis. prof. U. Copenhagen, 1975-76, 82; researcher in developmental genetics, somatic effects of radiation. Editor: Genetics and Evolution, 1961. Served to capt. USAAF, 1942-46. Recipient Gairdner Found. Internat. award, 1987, Wolf Found. prize in medicine, 1989, Rosenstiel award, 1990, Nat. Medal of Sci. NSF, 1990, Albert Lasker Basic Med. Rsch. award, 1991, Louisa Gross Horowitz prize Columbia U., 1992, Nobel Prize in Medicine, 1995. Fellow AAAS; mem. NAS, Genetics Soc. Am. (sec. 1962-64, pres. 1967-69, Thomas Hunt Morgan medal), Am. Acad. Arts and Scis., Royal Soc. (London) (fgn. mem.), Am. Philos. Soc., Genetical Soc. Great Britain (hon.). Home: 805 Winthrop Rd San Marino CA 91108-1709 Office: Calif Inst Tech Div Biology 1201 E California Blvd Pasadena CA 91125-0001

LEWIS, EDWARD SHELDON, chemistry educator; b. Berkeley, Calif., May 7, 1920; s. Gilbert Newton and Mary (Sheldon) L.; m. Fofo Catsinas, Dec. 21, 1955; children—Richard Peter, Gregory Gilbert. B.S., U. Calif., Berkeley, 1940; M.A., Harvard U., 1947, Ph.D., 1947. NRC postdoctoral fellow UCLA, 1947-48; from asst. prof. to prof. chemistry Rice U., Houston, 1948-90, prof. emeritus, 1990—, chmn. dept. chemistry, 1963-67, 80-85; Vis. prof. U. Southampton, Eng., 1957, Phys. Chem. Lab., Oxford (Eng.) U., 1967-68, U. Kent, Canterbury, Eng., 1977, H.C. Ørsted Inst., U. Copenhagen, 1980. Contbr. articles to profl. jours.; Editor: Investigation of Rates and Mechanisms of Reactions, 1974. Served with USNR, 1944-46. Guggenheim fellow, 1968. Fellow AAAS, Royal Irish Acad.; mem. Am. Chem. Soc. (S.W. regional award 1987), Royal Soc. of Chemistry, Phi Beta Kappa, Sigma Xi, Phi Lambda Upsilon. Home: 5651 Chevy Chase Dr Houston TX 77056-4004

LEWIS, EDWIN REYNOLDS, biomedical engineering educator; b. Los Angeles, July 14, 1934; s. Edwin McMurtry and Sally Newman (Reynolds) L.; m. Elizabeth Louise McLean, June 11, 1960; children: Edwin McLean, Sarah Elizabeth. AB in Biol. Sci., Stanford U., 1956, MSEE, 1957, Engr., 1959, PhD in Elec. Engring., 1962. With research staff Librascope div. Gen. Precision Inc., Glendale, Calif., 1961-67; mem. faculty dept. elec. engring. and computer sci. U. Calif., Berkeley, 1967—, dir. bioengring. tng. program, 1969-77, prof. elec. engring. and computer sci., 1971-94, prof. grad. sch., 1994—, assoc. dean grad. div., 1977-82, assoc. dean interdisciplinary studies coll. engring., 1988-96, prof. Grad. Sch., 1996—; chair joint program bioengring. U. Calif., Berkeley and San Francisco, 1988-91. Author: Network Models in Population Biology, 1977, (with others) Neural Modeling, 1977, The Vertebrate Inner Ear, 1985, Introduction to Bioengineering, 1996; contbr. articles to profl. jours. Grantee NSF, NASA, 1984, 87, Office Naval Rsch., 1990-93, NIH, 1975—; Neurosci. Rsch. Program fellow, 1966, 69; recipient Disting. Teaching Citation U. Calif., 1972; Jacob Javits neurosci. investigator NIH, 1984-91. Fellow IEEE, Acoustical Soc. Am.; mem. AAAS, Assn. Rsch. in Otolaryngology, Soc. Neurosci., Toastmasters (area lt. gov. 1966-67), Sigma Xi. Office: Dept Elec Engring & Computer Scis U Calif Berkeley CA 94720

LEWIS, ELEANOR ROBERTS, lawyer; b. Detroit, Jan. 5, 1944; d. David Edward and Patricia Mary (Easterbrook) Roberts; m. Roger Kutnow Lewis, June 24, 1967; 1 child, Kevin Michael. B.A., Wellesley Coll., 1965; MA, Harvard U., 1966; JD, Georgetown U., 1974. Bar: D.C. 1975, U.S. Dist. Ct. D.C. 1975, U.S. Ct. Appeals (D.C. cir.) 1975, U.S. Ct. Appeals (10th cir.) 1976, U.S. Supreme Ct. 1980. Secondary sch. tchr., Mass., Md., 1966-71; atty. HUD, Washington, 1974-76, asst. gen. counsel, 1979-82; atty. Brownstein Zeidman & Schomer, Washington, 1976-79; chief counsel internat. commerce U.S. Dept. Commerce, Washington, 1982—. Author, editor (with others) Street Law, 1975. Contbr. chpts. to books, articles to legal and fin. jours. Commr. D.C. Adv. Neighborhhod Comm. Bd. dirs. Dana Place Condominium, Washington. Mem. ABA (U.S. govt. liaison to internat. sect.), D.C. Bar Assn., Sr. Execs. Assn. (nat. bd. dirs.). Home: 5034 1/2 Dana Pl NW Washington DC 20016-3441 Office: US Dept Commerce 14th & Constitution Ave NW Washington DC 20230-0002

LEWIS, EMANUEL RAYMOND, historian, psychologist, retired librarian; b. Oakland, Calif., Nov. 30, 1928; s. Jacob A. and Rose (Grossman) L.; m. Joan R. Wilson, Feb. 7, 1954; 1 son, Joseph J.; m. Eleanor M. Gamarsh, Aug. 24, 1967. B.A., U. Calif., Berkeley, 1951, M.A., 1953; Ph.D., U. Oreg., 1962. Asst. prof. psychology Oreg. Coll. Edn., 1961-62, Oreg. State U., 1962-67; project mgr. System Devel. Corp., Falls Church, Va., 1968-69; vis. postdoctoral research asso. in Am. history Smithsonian Instn., Washington, 1969-70; chief historian, dir. research Contract Archeology, Alexandria, Va., 1971-73; librarian U.S. Ho. of Reps., Washington, 1973-95, libr. emeritus, 1995—. Author: Seacoast Fortifications of the United States, 1970, 2d edit. 1979, 3d edit. 1993; editor: The Educational Information Center, 1969. Served with M.I. U.S. Army, 1954-56. NIMH research fellow, 1960.

LEWIS, ENID SELENA, educator; b. Jamaica, W.I., Aug. 6, 1928; arrived in U.S., 1989; d. Thomas Vivian and Carlena Agatha (Hemmings) Davis; m. George Nathaniel Lewis, Aug. 12, 1953; children: Patrick, Heather, Peter, Charmaine, George Jr., Suzanne. BA in Early Childhood Edn., Univ. Coll. W.I., 1983. Primary sch. tchr. Ministry of Edn., Jamaica, 1949-70, trainer tchr. early childhood and spl. edn., 1970-80, edn. officer early childhood and spl. edn., 1980-83, edn. officer spl. edn., 1983-88; tchr. Archdiocese of N.Y., 1989—; field work in edn. Swasiland, Africa, 1976; adv. bd. Edn., Jamaica, 1986-88. Recipient Nat. award scholarships Jamaica Gov., 1982, Israel Assn. Internat Coop. to Israel, 1974-75, U. Kans., 1983, U. West Indies, 1979, 80. Baptist. Avocations: cooking, music, church activities, reading. Home: 391A Decator St Brooklyn NY 11233 Office: Sacred Heart of Jesus Sch 456 W 52nd St New York NY 10019-6302

LEWIS, FELICE FLANERY, lawyer, educator; b. Plaquemine, La., Oct. 5, 1920; d. Lowell Baird and E. Elizabeth (Lee) Flanery; m. Francis Russell Lewis, Dec. 22, 1944. BA, U. Wash., 1947; PhD, NYU, 1974; JD, Georgetown U., 1981. Bar: N.Y. 1982. Dean L.I. Univ., Liberal Arts & Scis., Bklyn., 1974-78; assoc. Harry G. English, Bklyn., 1983-85, 91—; adj. prof., polit. sci. L.I. Univ., Bklyn., 1983—. Author: Literature, Obscenity and Law, 1976; co-editor: Henry Miller, Years of Trial & Triumph, 1962-64, 1978. Home: 28 Whitney Cir Glen Cove NY 11542-1316 Office: Harry G English 7219 3rd Ave Brooklyn NY 11209-2131

LEWIS, FLORA, journalist; b. Los Angeles; d. Benjamin and Pauline (Kallin) L.; m. Sydney Gruson, Aug. 17, 1945 (div.); children—Kerry, Sheila, Lindsey. B.A., UCLA, 1941; M.S., Columbia U., 1942, LHD (hon.), 1984; LL.D., Princeton U., 1981; hon. doctorate, Mt. Holyoke Coll., Bucknell U., Muhlenberg Coll., Manhattan Marymount. Reporter Los Angeles Times, 1941, A.P., N.Y., Washington, London, 1942-46; free lance or contract for Observer, Economist, Financial Times, France-soir, Time Mag.; free lance or contract for N.Y. Times Mag., London, Warsaw, Berlin, Hague, Mexico City, Tel Aviv, 1946-54, Prague, Warsaw, 1956-58; editor McGraw-Hill, N.Y.C., 1955; bur. chief Washington Post, Bonn, London, N.Y.C., 1958-66; syndicated columnist Newsday, Paris, N.Y.C., 1967-72; bur. chief N.Y. Times, Paris, 1972-80; European diplomatic corr. N.Y. Times, 1976-80, fgn. affairs columnist, 1980-90, sr. columnist, 1990—. Author: Case History of Hope, 1958, Red Pawn, 1964, One of Our H-Bombs is Missing, 1967, Europe: A Tapestry of Nations, 1987, Europe: A Road to Unity, 1992; contbr. to anthologies, books, mags. Arthur D. Morse fellow in communications and society Aspen Inst. for Humanistic Studies, 1977; decorated chevalier Legion d'Honneur; recipient awards for best interpretation fgn. affairs, 1956, best reporting fgn. affairs, 1960; Overseas Press Club award; Columbia Journalism Sch. 50th Anniversary Honor award, 1963; award for disting. diplomatic reporting George Washington U. Sch. Fgn. Service, 1978, Carr Van Anda award Ohio State U. Sch. Communications, 1982, Fourth Estate award Nat. Press Club, 1985, Matrix award for Newspapers N.Y. Women in Communications Inc., 1985, Elmer Holmes Bobst award in Arts and Letters NYU, 1987, Internat. House award, 1990; named hon. fellow UCLA Coll. Arts and Scis. Mem. Coun. on Fgn. Rels., Internat. Inst. for Strategic Studies (coun.), Inst. for East-West Security Studies, Phi Beta Kappa. Office: Am University in Paris, 34 Ave de New York, 75014 Paris 75116, France

LEWIS, FLOYD WALLACE, former electric utility executive; b. Lincoln County, Miss., Sept. 23, 1925; s. Thomas Cassidy and Lizzie (Lofton) L.; m. Jimmie Etoile Slawson, Dec. 27, 1949; children: Floyd Wallace, Gail, Julie, Ann, Carol, Michael Paul. B.B.A., Tulane U., 1945, LL.B., 1949. Bar: La. 1949. With New Orleans Pub. Service Inc., 1949-62, v.p., chief fin. officer, 1960-62; v.p. Ark. Power & Light Co., Little Rock, 1962-63; sr. v.p. Ark. Power & Light Co., 1963-67; exec. v.p., dir. La. Power & Light Co., New Orleans, 1967-68; pres. La. Power & Light Co., 1968-70, chief exec. officer, 1968-71, chmn. bd., 1970-72; pres. Middle South Utilities, Inc., 1970-79, 80-85, chmn. bd., 1979-85, also dir., chief exec. officer, 1972-85; pres., dir. Middle South Services, Inc., New Orleans, 1970-75, chmn., 1975-85, chief exec. officer, 1972-79; pres., dir. Middle South Energy, Inc., 1974-85; chmn. bd. System Fuels, Inc., 1972-85; dir. New Orleans br. Fed. Res. Bank, 1974-75, chmn., 1975; past dir. Fed. Res. Bank of Atlanta, Breeder Reactor Corp., New Orleans Pub. Service Inc., Ark. Power and Light Co., La. Power & Light Co., Miss. Power and Light Co., U.S. Chamber Commerce; mem. adv. com. Elec. Cos. Advt. Program, 1969-72, chmn., 1970-71; mem. electric utility adv. com. to Fed. Energy Adminstrn., 1975-76; chmn. Edison Electric Inst., 1976-77, mem. exec. com., 1974-78; mem. exec. com. Assn. Edison Illuminating Cos., 1973-80; dir. Electric Power Research Inst., 1977-82, chmn., 1979-81; dir. Am. Nuclear Energy Council, 1982-86. Mem. exec. bd. New Orleans area council Boy Scouts Am., 1967-80, v.p., 1970-74, pres., 1975-76, mem. regional exec. com., 1968-80; v.p. Com. for a Better La., 1975-76, sr. v.p., 1976-77, pres., 1977-78; bd. dirs. La. World Expn. Inc., 1976-89, chmn., 1980-81, 83-89, pres., 1981-83; chmn. Utility Nuclear Power Oversight Com., 1979-81; vice chmn. campaign United Fund, New Orleans, 1970, chmn., 1971; bd. dirs. New Orleans Symphony Soc., 1974-75, Atomic Indsl. Forum, 1982-86, vice chmn., 1985-86; bd. dirs. Pub. Affairs Research Council of La.; pres. New Orleans Bapt. Sem. Found., 1973-76, 91-92; trustee La. Coll., 1984-90; New Orleans Baptist Theol. Sem., 1954-62, 1968-78, v.p., 1970-78; bd. adminstrs. Tulane U., 1973-88, bd. visitors, 1968-71; bd. govs. Med. Center, 1969-73, vice chmn., 1969-71; chmn. alumni adv. council Grad. Sch. Bus., 1970-73; bd. dirs. U.S. Com. Energy Awareness, 1982-85, vice-chmn., 1983-84, chmn., 1985; v.p. Internat. House, 1970; trustee Com. Econ. Devel., 1972-87; mem. bd. Ochsner Med. Found., 1976-96, mem. exec. com., 1977-96; 1st chmn. Parents Council, Furman U.; mem. Parents Council, Wake Forest U., 1980-81; trustee La. Bapt. Foudn., 1995-97, chmn. 1996. Served to ensign USNR, 1945-46. Recipient Silver Beaver, Silver Antelope Boy Scouts Am.; Oliver Townsend medal Atomic Indsl. Forum; Outstanding Alumni award Grad. Sch. Bus., 1970; Disting. Alumnus award Tulane U., 1983. Mem. Tulane Alumni Assn. (exec. com., treas. 1970), Order of Coif, Beta Gamma Sigma, Omicron Delta Kappa, Beta Theta Pi, Phi Delta Phi. Baptist (deacon).

LEWIS, FRANK HARLAN, botanist, educator; b. Redlands, Calif., Jan. 8, 1919; s. Frank Hooker and Mary Elizabeth (Smith) L.; m. Margaret Ruth Ensign, Aug. 2, 1945 and Aug. 2, 1984; children: Donald Austin, Frank Murray; m. Ann Gibbons, Dec. 23, 1968 (dec. 1983). AA, San Bernardino Valley Coll., 1939; BA, UCLA, 1941, MA, 1942, PhD, 1946; postgrad., Calif. Inst. Tech., 1942-44. Mem. faculty UCLA, 1946-82, prof. botany, 1956-82, prof. emeritus, 1982—, systematist expt. sta., 1956-62, chmn. dept., 1959-62, dean of life scis., 1962-82, dean emeritus, 1982—; Cons. genetics NSF, 1958-61, specialized biol. facilities, 1963-68. Bd. editors: Evolution, 1951-53; editor, 1972-74; bd. editors: Am. Jour. Botany, 1964-66, Am. Naturalist, 1965-67, 77-79; chmn. bd. editors U. Calif. publs. in botany, 1958-62. Trustee Graeme Joseph Revolving Scholarship Fund, 1968-86. NRC fellow John Innes Hort. Instn., London, 1947-48; Guggenheim fellow, 1954-55. Fellow AAAS (council mem. 1974-76), Calif. Acad. Sci.; mem. Bot. Soc. Am. (pres. Pacific div. 1959, Merit award 1972), Soc. Study Evolution (pres. 1961), Internat. Orgn. Plant Biosystematists (exec. com. 1961-81, v.p. 1964-69, pres. 1969-75), Am. Soc. Naturalists (pres. 1971), Am. Soc. Plant Taxonomists (pres. 1969), Internat. Soc. Plant Taxonomists, Phi Beta Kappa, Sigma Xi. Home: 14280 W Sunset Blvd Pacific Palisades CA 90272-3933

LEWIS, FRANK LEROY, electrical engineering educator, researcher; b. Wurzburg, Germany, May 11, 1949; s. Frank Leroy and Ruth Evangeline (Shirley) L.; MBA in Elec. Engring. and Physics, Rice U., 1971, MEE, 1971; MS in Aero. Systems, U. West Fla., 1977; PhD in Elec. Engring., Ga. Tech., 1981. asst. prof. elec. engring. Ga. Inst. Tech., Atlanta, 1981-86, assoc. prof. 1986-90, prof., 1990; Moncrief-O'Donnell prof. electrical engring. U. Tex. Arlington, 1990—; cons. Lockheed-Ga., Marietta, 1983-87; cons./lectr. UN Umbrella Project, Warsaw, Poland, 1991. Author: Optimal Control, 1986, 2d edit. 1995; Optimal Estimation, 1986, Aircraft Simulation and Control, 1992, Applied Optimal Control and Estimation, 1992, Robot Control, 1992, Control of Robot Manipulators, 1993; assoc. editor: J. Circuits, Systems Signal Proc., 1986; editl. bd. Internat. Jour. Intelligent Control and Systems, 1995—, Internat. Jour. of Control, 1995—, others; contbr. 104 articles to tech. jours. Served to lt. USN, 1971-77. NSF grantee, 1982, 86, 88, 90, 92; Fulbright Internat. Exchange scholar, 1988; recipient Terman award Am. Soc. Engring. Edn., 1989, Moncrief-O'Donnell endowed chair in robotics U. Tex., Arlington, 1990, Halliburton Outstanding Rsch. award UTA, 1992, Best Paper award ARRI, 1992, 93, Excellence in Teaching award Eta Kappa Nu, 1981. Fellow IEEE (awards); mem. AAAS, Control Systems Soc. of IEEE, Soc. Indsl. and Applied Math., Sigma Xi (M. Ferst awards 1981, 84, Monie A. Ferst Best Paper award 1990). Current work: intelligent control, robotics, manufacturing, Subspecialty: Systems engineering, robotics, automation. Home: 2482 Meadow Park Cir # 212 Bedford TX 76021

LEWIS, FRANK R., JR., surgeon, hospital administrator; b. Willards, Md., Feb. 23, 1941; m. Janet Christiansen, 1996. AB in Physics, Princeton U., 1961; MD, U. Md., 1965; PhD in Med. Physics, U. Calif., Berkeley, 1970. Surg. dir. M/SICU San Francisco Gen. Hosp., 1973-80, dir. emergency dept., 1980-83, chief of staff, 1983-85, asst. chief of surgery, 1981-86, chief of surgery, 1986-92; prof. surgery Case Western Res. U., Cleve., 1994—; chmn. dept. surgery Henry Ford Hosp., Detroit, 1992—. Fellow ACS (1st v.p. 1995-96, gov. 1988-93); mem. Cen. Surg. Soc., Western Surg. Soc., Am. Surg. Assn., Shock Soc. (pres., coun. mem. 1978—). Office: Henry Ford Hosp 2799 W Grand Blvd Detroit MI 48202-2608

LEWIS, GENE DALE, historian, educator; b. Globe, Ariz., Feb. 20, 1931; s. Abner E. and May J. (Hyatt) L.; m. Dottie Ladd Bidlingmeyer, Aug. 3, 1963. BA, Ariz. State U., 1951, MA, 1952; PhD, U. Ill., 1957. Lectr. Ariz. State U., 1953, So. Ill. U., 1957-58; vis. assoc. prof. history U. Ill., Urbana, 1965, Case Western Res. U., Cleve., 1966; prof. history U. Cin., 1958—, acting head dept., 1981-82, dir. grad. studies, 1989, head dept., 1989—; sr. v.p., provost, 1973-76. Author: Charles Ellet Jr., Engineer as Individualist, 1968; editor: New Historical Perspectives: Essays on the Black Experience in Antebellum America, 1984; co-editor Greater Cincinnati Bicentennial History Series, 1988—. Recipient Barbour award for excellence U. Cin., 1969, Nat. award Omicron Delta Kappa, 1968. Mem. AAUP, So. Hist. Assn., Am. Hist. Assn., Orgn. Am. Historians. Home: 444 Rawson Woods Ln Cincinnati OH 45220-1142 Office: U Cin Dept History Cincinnati OH 45221

LEWIS, GENE EVANS, retired medical equipment company executive; b. Terrell, Tex., May 17, 1928; s. John Evans and Helen Elizabeth (Paterson) L.; m. Sonya Dolishny, Jan. 21, 1950; children: Robert, Melissa. BSEE, Tex. A&M U., 1949. Sales, mktg. and engring. mgr. GE, Schenectady, Dallas, Pittsfield, Holyoke, Lynn, 1950-68; gen. mgr. various bus. GE, Milw., 1970-77; group product mgr. Picker X-Ray, Cleve., 1968-70; pres. sci. instruments div. Am. Optical Corp., Southbridge, Mass., 1977-78; pres. internat. div. Am. Optical Corp., 1978-79, pres., 1979-84; pres. Baker Instruments Corp., Allentown, Pa., 1985-88; chmn., CEO Novecon Technologies, 1994—; bd. dirs. Alpine Group, Inc.; exec. mem. The Holly Inn. With Signal Corps U.S. Army, 1949. Mem. Calibogue Club, Sea Pines Country Club. Home: 25 Spartina Cres Hilton Head Island SC 29928-2925 Office: Novecon Technologies 12030 Sunrise Valley Dr Ste 300 Reston VA 20191-3409

LEWIS, GEORGE RAYMOND, state agency administrator, clinical social worker; b. Bridgeton, N.J., July 7, 1944; s. Raymond and Evelyn Rhoda (Mitchell) L.; m. Tenelia Kay Boykin, Sept. 3, 1966. BA, U. N.Mex., 1966; MSW, Our Lady of the Lake Coll., 1971. Cert. social worker; lic. ind. social worker. With N.Mex. Health and Social Services Dept., 1971-92; dist. tng. officer N.Mex. Health and Social Services Dept., Roswell, 1972-73, field office mgr., 1973-75, social worker cons., 1975-84, dist. ops. mgr., 1984-92; clin. dir. Assurance Home Inc., 1992—; behavioral sci. specialist Cmty. Guidance Ctr., San Antonio, 1971; ajd. instr. N.Mex. State U., Las Cruces, 1971, 83, 85, 94, 95, Ea. N.Mex. U., Roswell, 1973-76, 92; clin. dir. Chaves County 1st Offender Program, Roswell, 1974-77; field instr. Tex. Tech. U., Lubbock, 1981; bd. dirs. Assurance Home Inc., Roswell; mem. N.Mex. Bd. Social Work Examiners, 1989-91; N.Mex. del. to Am. Assn. State Social Work Bd., 1990-93. Bd. dirs. Chaves County Home Health Agy. Inc., Roswell, 1973-76, Parents Anonymous of N.Mex. Inc., 1978-79; mem. State N.Mex. Acupuncture Bd., 1994-95. Named an Outstanding Young Man of Am., U.S. Jaycees, 1978, 81. Mem. Nat. Assn. Social Workers (New Mexico Rose Praisner award, 1992), Acad. Cert. Social Workers, Order of the Arrow, Blue Key. Democrat. Baptist. Avocations: greenhouse gardening, camping, fishing, hunting. Home: 1018 N Plains Park Dr Roswell NM 88201-2516 Office: Assurance Home Inc 100 E 18th St Roswell NM 88201

LEWIS, GEORGE WITHROW, business executive; b. Berwyn, Ill., May 13, 1929; s. George Edward and Katherine (Withrow) L.; m. Ellen Freer Baker, Sept. 14, 1963 (div. Apr. 1987); children: George Baker, Martha Freer; m. Elizabeth Morgan Williams, Dec. 26, 1992. A.B., Princeton, 1951; M.B.A., Harvard, 1955. With Ford Motor Co., 1955-62; cons. McKinsey & Co., N.Y.C., 1962-64; mng. dir. Rolls-Royce Motors Internat. Div., 1964-83. Vice-pres. fin. Eisenhower Exchange Fellowships, 1985-92; dir. Rolls-Royce Found. 1st lt., arty. AUS, 1952-53, Korea. Mem. Harvard Bus. Sch. Club of Phila. (past pres.). Episcopalian (vestryman). Home: 1325 Lombard St Philadelphia PA 19147-1003

LEWIS, GERALD JORGENSEN, judge; b. Perth Amboy, N.J., Sept. 9, 1933; s. Norman Francis and Blanche M. (Jorgensen) L.; m. Laura Susan McDonald, Dec. 15, 1973; children by previous marriage: Michael, Marc. AB magna cum laude, Tufts Coll., 1954; JD, Harvard U., 1957. Bar: D.C. 1957, N.J. 1961, Calif. 1962, U.S. Supreme Ct. 1968. Atty. Gen. Atomic, LaJolla, Calif., 1961-63; ptnr. Haskins, Lewis, Nugent & Newnham, San Diego, 1963-77; judge Mcpl. Ct., El Cajon, Calif., 1977-79; judge Superior Ct., San Diego, 1979-84; assoc. justice, Calif. Ct. of Appeal, San Diego, 1984-87; dir. Fisher Scientific Group, Inc., 1987—, Bolsa Chica Corp., 1991-93, Gen. Chemical Group, Inc., 1996—; of counsel Latham & Watkins, 1987-97; dir. Wheelabrator Techs., Inc., 1987-93, Henley Mfg., Inc., 1987-89; adj. prof. evidence Western State U. Sch. Law, San Diego, 1977-85, exec. bd., 1977-89; faculty San Diego Inn of Ct., 1979—, Am. Inn of Ct., 1984—. Cons. editor: California Civil Jury Instructions, 1984. City atty. Del Mar, Calif., 1963-74, Coronado, Calif., 1972-77; counsel Comprehensive Planning Orgn., San Diego, 1972-73; trustee San Diego Mus. Art., 1986-89; bd. dirs. Air Pollution Control Dist., San Diego County, 1972-76. Served to lt. comdr. USNR, 1957-61. Named Trial Judge of Yr., San Diego Trial Lawyers Assn., 1984. Mem. Am. Judicature Soc., Soc. Inns of Ct. in Calif., La Jolla Wine and Food Soc., Confrerie des Chevaliers du Tastevin, Order of St. Hubert (Knight Commdr.), Friendly Sons of St. Patrick. Republican. Episcopalian. Clubs: Bohemian; LaJolla Country (dir. 1980-83); Venice Island Hunt Club; Prophets. Home: 6505 Caminito Blythefield La Jolla CA 92037-5806 Office: Latham & Watkins 701 B St Ste 2100 San Diego CA 92101-8116

LEWIS, GERRI, newspaper columnist; b. Stamford, Conn., Apr. 2, 1948; d. John Nance and Eileen Francis Karwoski; m. Robert L. Lewis, Aug. 30, 1970; children: Tyson, Christian, Gillian. B Gen. Studies, U. Conn. Publicist Ridgefield (Conn.) Coalition Community Action, 1984-87, election campaign, 1993; newspaper columnist, feature writer, food and drink editor The Acorn Press, Ridgefield, 1987—; also freelance writer. Mem. Soc. Profl. Journalists (feature story award Conn. chpt. 1996, First Place award 1996, 97). Home: 400 W Mountain Rd Ridgefield CT 06877

LEWIS, GLADYS SHERMAN, nurse, educator; b. Wynnewood, Okla., Mar. 20, 1933; d. Andrew and Minnie Elva (Halsey) Sherman; R.N., St. Anthony's Sch. Nursing, 1953; student Okla. Bapt. U., 1953-55; AB, Tex. Christian U., 1956; postgrad. Southwestern Bapt. Theol. Sem., 1959-60, Escuela de Idiomas, San Jose, Costa Rica, 1960-61; MA in Creative Writing, Central (Okla.) State U., 1985; PhD in English Okla. State U. 1992; m. Wilbur Curtis Lewis, Jan. 28, 1955; children: Karen, David, Leanne, Cristen. Mem. nursing staff various facilities, Okla., 1953-57; instr. nursing, med. missionary Bapt. mission and hosp., Paraguay, 1961-70; vice-chmn. edn. commn. Paraguay Bapt. Conv., 1962-65; sec. bd. trustees Bapt. Hosp., Paraguay, 1962-65; chmn. personnel com., handbook and policy book officer Bapt. Mission in Paraguay, 1967-70; trustee Southwestern Bapt. Theol. Sem., 1974-84, chmn. student affairs com., 1976-78, vice-chmn. bd. 1978-80; ptnr. Las Amigas Tours, 1978-80; writer, conference leader, campus lectr., 1959—; adj. prof. English Cen. State U., Okla. (name changed to U. Cen. Okla.), 1990-91; faculty mem., asst. prof. English U. Cen. Okla., 1991-95, assoc. prof., 1996—. Active Dem. com., Evang. Women's Caucus, 1979-80; leader Girl Scouts U.S.A., 1965-75; Okla. co-chmn. Nat. Religious Com. for Equal Rights Amendment, 1977-79; tour host Meier Internat. Study League, 1978-81. Mem. AAUW, Internat. and Am. colls. surgeons women's auxiliaries, Okla. State, Okla. County med. auxiliaries, Am. Nurse Assn., Nat. Women's Polit. Caucus, 1979-80. Author: On Earth As It Is, 1983; Two Dreams and a Promise, 1984, Message, Messenger and Response, 1994; also religious instructional texts in English and Spanish; editor Sooner Physician's Heartbeat, 1979-82; contbr. articles to So. Bapt. and secular periodicals. Home: 14501 N Western Ave Edmond OK 73013-1828

LEWIS, GOLDY SARAH, real estate developer, corporation executive; b. West Selkirk, Man., Can., June 15, 1921; d. David and Rose (Dwor) Kimmel; m. Ralph Milton Lewis, June 12, 1941; children: Richard Alan, Robert Edward, Roger Gordon, Randall Wayne. B.S., UCLA, 1943; postgrad., U. So. Calif., 1944-45. Pvt. practice acctg. L.A., 1945-57, law office mgr., 1953-55; dir., exec. v.p. Lewis Homes, Upland, Calif., 1955—, Lewis Construction Co. Inc., Upland, 1959—, Lewis Bldg. Co., Inc., Las Vegas, 1960—, Republic Sales Co., Inc., 1956—, Kimmel Enterprises, Inc., 1959—; mng. partner Lewis Homes of Calif., 1973—; mng. ptnr. Lewis Homes of Nev., 1972—, Western Properties, 1972—, Foothill Investment Co., 1971—, Republic Mgmt. Co., 1978—. Contbr. articles to mags., jours. Mem. Dean's Coun. UCLA Grad. Sch. Architecture and Urban Planning; mem. UCLA Found., Chancellor's Assocs.; endowed Ralph and Goldy Lewis Ctr. for Regional Policy at UCLA, 1989, Ralph and Goldy Lewis Hall of Planning and Devel. at U.S.C., 1989, others. Recipient 1st award of distinction Am. Builder mag., 1963, Homer Briggs Svc. to Youth award West End YMCA, 1990, Spirit of Life award City of Hope, 1993; co-recipient Builder of Yr. award Profl. Builder Mag., 1988, Housing Person of Yr. award Nat. Housing Conf., 1990, Entrepreneur of Yr. award Inland Empire, 1990; Ralph and Goldy Lewis Sports Ctr. named in their honor City of Rancho Cucamonga, 1988, also several other parks and sports fields including Lewis Park in Claremont.; named one of Woman of Yr. Calif. 25th Senate Dist., 1989, (with husband Ralph M. Lewis) Disting. Chief Exec. Officer, Calif. State U., San Bernardino, 1991, Mgmt. Leaders of the Yr. Univ. Calif., Riverside, 1993. Mem. Nat. Assn. Home Builders, Bldg. Industry Assn. So. Calif. (Builder of Yr. award Baldy View chpt. 1988), Internat. Coun. Shopping Ctrs., Urban Land Inst. Office: Lewis Homes PO Box 670 Upland CA 91785-0670

LEWIS, GORDON CARTER, auditor; b. Billings, Mont., June 14, 1960; s. Gene Eskil and Vanda (Carter) L. Student, U. Utah, 1978-79, 81-82; AA, LDS Bus. Coll., 1984; BBA, Nat. Coll., Denver, 1986. Market rsch. interviewer Colo. Market Rsch. Svcs. Inc., Denver, 1984-87, 93-94; mgmt. trainee Yellow Front Stores, Aurora, Colo., 1987; auditor, 1987-93; computer office coord. US EPA, Denver, 1989-91; store mgr. Trans Pacific Stores, Denver, 1994-97. Ch. leadership, 1979—, bowling league officer. Mem. Assn. Govt. Accts., Am. Bowling Congress, Am. Philatelic Soc. Republican. Mem. LDS Ch.

LEWIS, GORDON GILMER, golf course architect; b. Shawnee, Okla., Sept. 7, 1950; s. Ted Eugene and Janet Garvin (Panner) L.; m. Karen Louise McKenzie, June 2, 1973 (div. Dec. 1981); children: Melanie Marie Lewis-Lehr, Katie McKenzie Lewis-Lehr; m. Susette Mamie London, June 11, 1988; children: London Marshall, Sarah June Victoria. B of Landscape Architecture, Kans. State U., 1974. Registered landscape architect, Ala., Kans., Fla. Golf course architect David Gill, St. Charles, Ill., 1974-75, Charles M. Graves Orgn., Atlanta, 1975-78, Gordon G. Lewis, Naples, Fla., 1978—. Prin. works include Meadowbrook Links, Rapid City, S.D. (Top 50 Pub. Courses in U.S.), The Hulman Links at Los Creek, Terre Haute, Ind. (Top 50 Pub. Courses in U.S.), Lagoon Park, Montgomery, Ala. (Top 75 Pub. Courses in U.S.), The Forest, Ft. Myers, Fla. (Top 50 Courses in Fla.), The Vines, Estero, Fla. (Golf Digest One of Top New Courses 1986), Worthington, Bonita Springs, Fla., Tsai-Hsing, Taipei, Taiwan, others. Republican. Presbyterian. Avocation: golf. Home: 598 Henley Dr Naples FL 34104

LEWIS, GREGORY WILLIAMS, scientist; b. Seattle, Mar. 3, 1940; s. Delbert Srofe and Eileen Julianne (Williams) L.; m. Stephanie Marie Schwab, Sept. 18, 1966; children: Jeffrey Williams, Garrick Peterson. BS, Wash. State U., 1962, MA, 1965, PhD, 1970. Tchr., rsch. asst. Wash. State U., Pullman, 1965-69; prin. investigator U.S. Army Med. Rsch. Lab., Ft. Knox, Ky., 1970-74; prin. investigator USN Pers. R & D Ctr., San Diego, 1974—, head neurosci. lab., 1980-95, leader security sys., 1981-83, head neurosci. projects office, 1987-89, divsn. head neurosci., 1989-95, sr. prin. scientist, 1995—; cons. in field. Contbr. articles to profl. jours. Bd. dirs., pres. Mesa View Homeowners Assn., Calif., 1980-82; bd. dirs. Santa Fe Homeowners Assn., Calif., 1994-96. Capt. U.S. Army, 1967-74. Fellow Internat. Orgn. Psychophysiology; mem. AAAS, Soc. Neurosci., Internat. Brain Rsch. Orgn., N.Y. Acad. Scis., Soc. Psychophysiol. Rsch., Sigma Xi, Alpha Kappa Delta, Delta Chi, Psi Chi. Achievements include research in ophthalmic ultrasonography, neuroelectric research and development of brain activity and variability for improving the evaluation of education and training materials, personnel assessment, and prediction of job performance; physiological correlates of performance; psychophysiology of individual differences; neuromagnetic research directed toward individual differences and personnel performance; neuroelectric and neuromagnetic data acquisition and analysis; patent for development of neuroelectric and neuromagnetic method and system for individual identification and impairment of function using artificial neural network analyses; patent pending for development of neuroelectric and neuromagnetic method and system to objectively evaluate an individual's interest level in education, training, and other materials; developing personnel performance models for use in preliminary design and rapid prototyping of ship systems. Avocations: music, electronics, working on timber land and vacation log home. Home: 410 Santa Cecelia Solana Beach CA 92075-1505 Office: US Navy Pers R&D Ctr 53335 Ryne Rd San Diego CA 92152-7207

LEWIS, HAROLD ALEXANDER, insurance company executive; b. Kingston, Jamaica, Feb. 25, 1953; came to U.S., 1980; s. Frankie Lewis and Kathlene (Smith) Benjamin. Student, Mt. St. Benedict, Trinidad, W.I., 1978-80, Don Bosco Coll., Newton, N.J., 1980-82. With Brit. Caribbean Inc., Kingston, 1972-74, 76-78; substitute tchr. St. Philip Neri Elem. Sch., Houston, 1982-83; licensing examiner Nat. Benefit Life Ins. Co., N.Y.C., 1983-89, mgr. microsystems and records retention, 1989-92; licensing adminstr., 1992-95; pres. Consulting Mgmt., Bronx, N.Y., 1995—. Vice chmn. Health Ins. Plan-HMO Consumer Coun., Bronx, 1984—; sec. Bronx Regional Coun., 1986-89; mem. Scout Assn. of Jamaica (W.I.), 1976-78; bd. dirs. Health Ins. Plan of Greater N.Y., mem. coun., 1990—. Named Consumer of Yr., HIP, 1987. Mem. NAFE, Assn. of Records Mgrs. and Adminstrs. Avocations: playing guitar and organ, reading, tennis, charitable work. Home: 1210 Sherman Ave Apt 6C Bronx NY 10456-3044 Office: Consulting Mgmt P O Box 31 Bronx NY 10456

LEWIS, HENRY RAFALSKY, manufacturing company executive; b. Yonkers, N.Y., Nov. 19, 1925; s. Jasper R. and Freda (Rafalsky) L.; m. Barbara Connolly, June 15, 1957; children—Peter, Susan, Abigail. AB, Harvard U., 1949, MA, 1951, PhD, 1957. Group head Ops. Evaluation Group, Washington, 1955-57; mem. staff Electronic Rsch. Lab. RCA, Princeton, N.J., 1957-66, dir., 1966-70; v.p. rsch./devel. Itek Corp., Lexington, Mass., 1970-74; pres. Optel Corp., Princeton, N.J., 1974; sr. v.p. Dennison Mfg. Co., Waltham, Mass., 1974-85, vice chmn., 1986-91, also bd. dirs.; CEO Celadon Scis. Inc., Boston, 1996—; bd. dirs. Delphax Sys., Randolph, Mass., Cenzyme Corp., Cambridge, Mass., Dyax Corp., Cambridge, Celadon Sci., Boston. Contbr. articles to profl. jours. Chmn. investment com. Powers (Mass.) Music Sch., 1978-90; mem. Harvard Grad. Soc. Coun., 1992-95. With U.S. Army, 1944-46. Mem. IEEE, Am. Phys. Soc., Phi Beta Kappa, Sigma Xi. Club: Harvard. Home: 35 Clover St Belmont MA 02178-2410

LEWIS, HENRY WILKINS, university administrator, lawyer, educator; b. Jackson, N.C., Nov. 7, 1916; s. Edmund Wilkins and Jane Crichton (Williams) L. A.B., U. N.C., 1937; J.D., Harvard, 1940. Bar: N.C. bar 1940. Practice in Jackson, 1940-41; mem. staff Inst. of Govt., U. N.C., 1946-51, research prof. pub. law and govt., 1951-57, prof., 1957-73; acting v.p. U. N.C., 1968-69; dir. Inst. Govt., 1973-78, Kenan prof. pub. law and govt., 1975-78, emeritus, 1978—; v.p., bd. dirs. Wilkins Texas Corp., 1967-92. Author: Property Tax Collection in North Carolina, 1951, rev. edit., 1957, The General Assembly of North Carolina: Organization and Procedure, 1952, Legislative Committees in North Carolina, 1952, Basic Legal Problems in the Taxation of Property, 1958, (with Robert G. Byrd) In Rem Property Tax Foreclosure, 1959, An Introduction to County Government, 1963, rev. edit., 1968, Primary and General Election Law and Procedure, 11 edits., latest, 1968, Property Tax Exemptions and Classifications, 1970, The Property Tax: An Introduction, 1972, rev. edits., 1975, 78, Northampton Parishes, 1951, The Doctor and Mrs. Lewis, 1980, More Taste Than Prudence: A Study of John Evans Johnson (1815-1870), 1983, Compelled to Wander, 1987, That Sally Brodnax, 1990, A Candid Confederate, 1997; contbr. articles to profl. jours. Counsel N.C. Elections Laws Commn., 1967; counsel N.C. Commn. for Study Local and Ad Valorem Tax Structure, 1970, N.C. Commn. for Study Property Tax Exemptions and Classifications, 1973; mem. N.C. Criminal Justice Tng. and Standards Council, 1973-78, N.C. Criminal Justice Edn. and Tng. System Council, 1973-78, N.C. Commn. on Productivity in State Govt., 1976-77; Mem. adv. bd. N.C. State Art Soc., 1962-63; mem. Com. for Restoration St. John's Ch., Williamsboro, N.C., 1950-79; mem. adv. bd. Ackland Art Center, U. N.C., 1957-78, mem. vis. com. 1987—; trustee Va. Episcopal Sch., 1974-80, U. N.C. Center for Public TV, 1980-88; bd. dirs. N.C. Pub. TV Found., 1987-88. Served to capt. AUS, 1941-46. Mem. Lincoln's Inn Soc., N.C. Bar Assn., N.C. Lit. and Hist. Assn. (v.p. 1972-75), N.C. Collectors (pres. 1965-66), N.C. Soc. (dir.), Roanoke-Chowan Group (convenor 1962-65), Nat. Sporting Libr. (hon. life), Va. Hist. Soc., Jamestowne Soc., Order of Gimghouls, Phi Beta Kappa, Alpha Tau Omega. Episcopalian (parish conv. del. intermittently 1948-95, mem. diocesan standing com. intermittently 1957-91, com. on constitution and canons 1973—, dep. Gen. Conv. 1967, 69, 70, 76, 79, 82, 85). Home: 386 Fearrington Post Pittsboro NC 27312-8518

LEWIS, HERBERT SAMUEL, anthropologist, educator; b. Jersey City, May 8, 1934; s. Frederic and Estelle (Sachs) L.; m. Marcia Barbash, June 23, 1957; children—Tamar Anne, Paula Miriam, Joshua Daniel. A.B., Brandeis U., 1955; Ph.D., Columbia U., 1963. Instr. Northwestern U., Evanston, Ill., 1961-63; lectr. anthropology Columbia U., N.Y.C., 1961; from asst. to full prof. anthropology U. Wis., Madison, 1963-73, prof., 1973-96, dir. African studies program, 1993-95, prof. emeritus, 1996—; vis. prof. Hebrew U., Jerusalem, 1969-70; cons. AID, Africare, 1981-84. Author: A Galla Monarchy, 1965, After the Eagles Landed: The Yemenite Jews of Israel, 1989, (monograph) Leaders and Followers: Anthropological Perspectives, 1974, The Origins of the Galla and Somali; contbr. articles to profl. jours. Research grantee Ford Found., Ethiopia, 1958-60, NSF, Ethiopia, 1965-66, Israel, 1975-77; Fulbright research grantee, 1987. Fellow Am. Anthropol. Assn., Royal Anthropol. Inst. of Gt. Britain and Ireland, African Studies Assn. Home: 1009 Tumalo Trl Madison WI 53711-3024 Office: U Wis Dept Anthropology Social Sci Bldg Madison WI 53706

LEWIS, HOWARD FRANKLIN, chiropractor; b. Havre de Grace, Md., July 27, 1944; s. Walter Lee and Ruby Jane (Moretz) L.; m. Margaret Colleen Bush, Apr. 8, 1963 (div. 1969); 1 child, Vaughn; m. Cynthia Marie Hoover, Apr. 4, 1970; children: Amy, David. D of Chiropractic, L.A. Coll. Chiropractic, 1971. Diplomate Am. Bd. Chiropractic Radiology; lic. chiropractor Calif., Md. Pvt. practice Lewis Chiropractic Ctr., Bel Air, Md., 1974-85, Fallston, Md., 1985—. Fellow Internat. Coll. Chiropractors; mem. Am. Chiropractic Assn. (mem. coun. on diagnostic imaging, coun. on nutrition), Am. Chiropractic Coll. Radiology, Md. Chiropractic Assn. (chmn. bd. dirs. 1985-86, v.p. 1986, pres. 1987-89, Leadership award 1989, Chiropractor of Yr. award 1990), Md. State Bd. Chiropractic Examiners (v.p. 1994-96, pres. 1996—), Sacro Occipital Rsch. Soc. (bd. dirs. 1992-95, cert.), Christian Chiropractors Assn., Found. Chiropractic Edn. and Rsch. Republican. Office: Lewis Chiropractic Ctr 1621 Bel Air Rd Fallston MD 21047-2727

LEWIS, HUEY (HUGH ANTHONY CREGG, III), singer, composer, bandleader; b. N.Y.C., July 5, 1951; s. Hugh Anthony II and Magda Cregg; m. Sidney Conroy, 1983; children: Kelly, Austin. Student, Cornell U. Mem. Clover, 1972-77; singer, composer leader Huey Lewis and the News, 1978—. Rec. artist: (with Clover) Clover, 1977, Unavailable, 1977, Love on the Wire, 1977, (with Huey Lewis and the News) Huey Lewis and the News, 1980, Picture This, 1982, Sports, 1983, Fore, 1986, Small World, 1988, Hard at Play, 1991, Best of Huey Lewis and the News, 1992, Four Chords and Several Years Ago, 1994; hit singles include Do You Believe in Love?, Workin' for a Living, I Want a New Drug, The Heart of Rock 'n' Roll, Heart and Soul, Walking on a Thin Line, Hip To Be Square, I Know What I Like, (single from Back to the Future soundtrack) The Power of Love; contbr. (single and video) We Are the World, 1984; appeared in films: Back to the Future, 1985, Short Cuts, 1993. Office: care Capito-EMI Records 1750 Vine St Hollywood CA 90028-5209*

LEWIS, HUNTER, financial advisor, publisher; b. Dayton, Ohio, Oct. 13, 1947; s. Welbourne Walker and Emily (Spivey) L.; m. Elizabeth Sidamon-Eristoff, July 3, 1993. AB magna cum laude, Harvard U., 1969. Asst. to office of pres. Boston Co., 1970, v.p., 1972-73; pres. Boston Co. Fin. Strategies, Inc., 1971-72; co-founder Cambridge Assocs. Inc. and Cambridge Capital Advisors, Inc., Washington, 1973—; former dir., chmn. bd. Shelburne Farms Inc. Former trustee, chmn. fin. com. Groton Sch.; former chmn. adv. bd. Dumbarton Oaks, affiliate of Harvard U.; pres. emeritus, trustee Am. Sch. Classical Studies at Athens; former mem. pension fin. com. World Bank; bd. dirs., treas. World Wildlife Fund; former dir. Worldwide Fund for Nature; chmn. bd. dirs. Worldwatch Inst.; chmn. fin. com., trustee Pierpont Morgan Libr., N.Y.C.; former trustee Thomas Jefferson Found., Monticello; chmn., bd. dirs. Trearne Found.; trustee Culpeper Found. With USMC, 1969-70. Author: The Real World War, 1982, A Question of Values, 1990; contbr. articles to N.Y. Times, Atlantic Monthly, Washington Post, other mags. and newspapers; author monographs on specialized fin. subjects. Mem. Univ. Club (N.Y.C.), Knickerbocker Club (N.Y.C.), Union Boat Club (Boston), Met. Club (Washington). Office: 1110 N Glebe Rd Ste 1100 Arlington VA 22201-4795

LEWIS, HYLAN GARNET, sociologist, educator; b. Washington, Apr. 4, 1911; s. Harry Wythe and Ella (Wells) L.; A.B., Va. Union U., 1932; A.M. (Social Sci. Research Council fellow 1932, Rosenwald Found. fellow 1939-41), U. Chgo., 1936, Ph.D., 1951; m. Leighla Whipper, Oct. 4, 1935 (div. May 1945); 1 dau., Carole Ione Lewis Bovoso; m. Audrey Carter, Nov. 2, 1946; 1 son, Guy Edward. Instr. sociology Howard U., Washington, 1934-41, prof. sociology, 1964-67; prof. social sci. Talladega (Ala.) Coll., 1941-42; info. specialist OWI, 1942-45; asso. prof. Hampton Inst., 1945-48; asso. prof. sociology Atlanta U., 1948-55, prof., 1955-57; asso. dir. community services Unitarian Service Com., Inc., Boston, 1957-59; dir. child rearing study Health and Welfare Council, Washington, 1959-64; mem. delinquency grants rev. com. NIMH, 1963-67, mem. social problems research rev. com., 1969-73; mem. devel. behavioral scis. study sect. NIH, 1974-76; prof. sociology Bklyn. Coll. 1967-77, prof. emeritus, 1977—; vis. prof. Grad. Center, CUNY, 1977—; Michael Harrington prof. Queens Coll. CUNY, 1990-91, vis. prof. sociology, 1991-92; sr. cons. Clark, Phipps, Clark & Harris, Inc., 1975-85; sr. assoc. Kenneth B. Clark & Assocs., 1985—; sr. v.p. Met. Applied Research Center, Inc., 1967-75; vis. scholar Russell Sage Found., 1974-75. Research asso. Inst. for Research in Social Sci., U. N.C., 1947-48; cons. Volta River Project Preparatory Commn., Gold Coast, 1954; Ashmore project Fund for Advancement Edn., 1953, So. Regional Council, 1954-58, Commn. on Race and Housing, 1956-57; cons. disaster study com. NRC, 1955-56; mem. adv. com. grants program U.S. Children's Bur., 1962-66; mem. adv. panel small grants program U.S. Dept. Labor, 1963-83; chief cons. family panel White House Conf. Civil Rights Planning, 1965; mem. rev. panel U.S. Office Edn., 1965-67; mem. Head Start research adv. com. Office Econ. Opportunity, 1965-67; mem. grants adv. com. Nat. Endowment for the Humanities, Nat. Found. Arts and Humanities, 1967-68, others. Fund for Advancement Edn. fellow, 1955-56. Fellow AAAS; mem. Am. Sociol. Assn. (DuBois-Johnson-Frazier award 1976), Soc. Rsch. Assn., Eastern Sociol. Soc. (merit award 1979), Alpha Phi Alpha. Author: Blackways of Kent, 1955. Home: 372 Central Park W New York NY 10025-8240

LEWIS, JACK (CECIL PAUL LEWIS), publishing executive, editor; b. North English, Iowa, Nov. 13, 1924; s. Cecil Howell and Winifred (Warner) L.; m. Roselle Gilbout; children: Dana Claudia, Brandon Paul, Scott Jay, Suzanne Marie. B.A., State U. Iowa, 1949. Publicist savs. bonds U.S. Treasury Dept., Des Moines, 1948-49; reporter Santa Ana (Calif.) Register, 1949-50; motion picture writer Monogram Pictures, 1950; reporter Daily Pilot, Costa Mesa, Calif., 1956-57; editor Challenge Pub., North Hollywood, Calif., 1957-60; pres. Gallant/Charger Publs. Inc, Capistrano Beach, Calif., 1960—; editor, pub. Gun World, 1960-97. Author 8 novels, 25 other books, 11 TV shows, 8 motion pictures; editor 26 books; contbr. articles to mags. Served to lt. col. USMCR, 1942-46, 50-56, 58, 70. Decorated Bronze Star, Air medal (3), Meritorious Service medal, Navy Commendation medal. Mem. Writers Guild Am., U.S. Marine Corps Combat Corrs. Assn. (pres. 1970-71, 73-74, 80-81, chmn. bd. 1972-78), Sigma Nu, Sigma Delta Chi. Republican. Home: 405 Avenida Teresa San Clemente CA 92672-2234

LEWIS, JACQUELYN ROCHELLE, quality administrator; b. Portsmouth, Va., Feb. 24, 1956; d. Everet Darl and Frances Emaline (Pettit) Johnson; m. Philip Alden Lewis Jr., May 20, 1978. Nursing diploma, Iowa Meth. Hosp. Sch. Nursing, 1985; BS, Purdue U., 1979; MBA, Thomas Coll., 1997. RN; cert. prof. in healthcare quality. Staff nurse Iowa Lutheran Hosp., Des Moines, 1985-87, U.S. Naval Hosp., Groton, Conn., 1987, Ctrl. Maine Med. Ctr., Lewiston, 1988; quality coord. Kennebec Valley Med. Ctr., Augusta, Maine, 1988—. V.p. Ctrl. Maine Dressage Assn., Auburn, 1996—, sec. 1993-95; usher Prince of Peace Luth. Ch., 1991—. Mem. Maine Assn. Healthcare Quality (skpr.). Avocations: horseback riding, hiking, cross country skiing, travel. Office: Kennebec Valley Med Ctr 6 E Chestnut St Augusta ME 04330-5717

LEWIS, JAMES EARL, investment banker; b. Chgo., Aug. 1, 1939; s. J. Earl and Elsie L. (Danneberg) L.; m. Patricia Ann Martin, Jan. 19, 1980. BA, DePauw U., 1961; MBA, U. Chgo., 1966. Analyst Harris Trust & Savs. Bank, Chgo., 1966-68; v.p. Paine, Webber, Jackson & Curtis, Boston, 1968-70; mgr. corp. loan component Gen. Electric Credit Corp., Stamford, Conn., 1971-77; v.p. Rauscher Pierce Refsnes Inc., Dallas, 1978-82; sr. v.p., mgr. corp. fin. dept. First Oklahoma Bancorp. Inc., Dallas and Oklahoma City, 1982-84; v.p., mgr. corp. fin. group PNC Mcht. Banking Co., Phila., 1984-87; v.p., dir. corp. fin. Ferris & Co., Inc., Washington, 1987-88; v.p. Washington Sq. Capital Markets Inc., Bala Cynwyd, Pa., 1988-90; pres., founder Mid. Atlantic Capital, Wayne, Pa., 1990-94; founder, mng. dir. Phila. Factors, Inc., 1993—; bd. dirs. Phila. Factors. With U.S. Army, 1962-64. Mem. Phila. Fin. Assn., Delaware Valley Venture Group, Orpheus Club. Home: 852 Briarwood Rd Newtown Square PA 19073-2620 Office: 6 S Bryn Mawr Ave Bryn Mawr PA 19010-3215

LEWIS, JAMES HISTED, retired foreign service officer; b. Carbondale, Pa., Dec. 18, 1912; s. Edward Butts and Laura (Histed) L.; m. Betty Prater, Dec. 12, 1943; children—Jane, Marie, David, Jon. AB., George Washington U., 1935, A.M., 1939. Asst. in polit. sci. George Washington U., Washington, 1934-36; mem. staff div. trade agreements U.S. Dept. State, Washington, 1936-42; fgn. service aux. officer, spl. asst. amb. Am. Embassy, London, 1942-44; economist div. comml. policy U.S. Dept. State, Washington, 1944-45, sec. Sec. State's Staff Com., 1945-46, advisor econs. U.S. Del. of Paris Peace Conf. and Council Fgn. Ministers, 1946, chief Brit. Commonwealth br. div. comml. policy, 1947-49, with Office Brit. Commonwealth and No. European Affairs, 1949-54; mem. U.S. del. GATT trade negotiations, Annecy, France, 1949; head negotiator GATT trade negotiations, Torquay, England, 1950-51, Geneva, 1956, 61; commd. fgn. service officer U.S. Dept. State, Washington, 1954, 1st sec. Am. embassy and consul in London, 1954-57, counselor econ. affairs Am. embassy in Copenhagen, 1957-61, chief div. trade agreements, 1961-62, chief div. comml. policy and treaties, 1962-63, dep. dir. Office Internat. Trade, 1963-65, minister-counselor for econ. affairs U.S. mission to Geneva, also dep. head U.S. del. Kennedy round trade negotiations, 1965-67, dep. dir. gen. with personal rank of ambassador GATT Secretariat in Geneva, 1967-69, counselor Am. embassy in Bonn, Fed. Republic Germany, 1969-70, dep. amb. Am. embassy in Helsinki, 1970-73, ret., 1973; cons. multilateral trade matters, 1975—. Mem. Am. Fgn. Service Assn., Pi Gamma Mu, Delta Phi Epsilon. Presbyterian. Home: 8800 Clifford Ave Bethesda MD 20815-4745

LEWIS, JAMES LEE, JR., actuary; b. Toungoo, Burma, June 11, 1930; s. James Lee and Lilly (Ryden) L.; m. Tamra Dell Johns, June 30, 1954; children: James Lee III, David Alexander, Stephen John, Susan Kim, Michael Ryden. BA, U. Mich., 1952, MA, 1956. Actuary Lincoln Nat. Life Ins. Co., Ft. Wayne, Ind., 1956-74; sr. v.p. Mutual Security Life Ins. Co., Ft. Wayne, 1974-83; v.p., actuary Montlife Corp., Itaska, Ill., 1983-84; v.p., sr. actuary Covenant Life Ins. Co., Phila., 1984-94; actuary provident Mut. Life Ins. Co., Phila., 1994-96; ret., 1996. Pres. Associated Chs., Ft. Wayne., 1982; chmn. Project Commitment, Ft. Wayne, 1969. With U.S. Army, 1952-54. Fellow Soc. of Actuaries (com. chair 1988-91); mem. Am. Acad. of Actuaries (charter), Phila. Actuaries Club. Baptist. Avocations: racquetball, barbershop singing.

LEWIS, JEROME A., petroleum company executive, investment banker; b. Wichita, Kans., 1927; married. BA in Engring., U. Okla. Geologist Shell Oil Co., 1950-51; pres. Lewmont Drilling, Inc., 1951-65, Border Exploration Co., 1965-68; pres., chmn. bd., chief exec. officer Petro-Lewis Corp., 1968-87; pres. Princeps Ptnrs., Inc., 1987—; also dir. DenverAmerican Petrol. 1991—. Bd. dirs. Denver Leadership Found., Trinity Forum, Downing St. Found. Mem. Ind. Petroleum Assn. Am., Oil Investment Inst. (founding gov.), World Pres.' Orgn., Am. Assn. Petroleum Geologists, Am. Petroleum Inst., Chief Execs. Orgn. Office: Princeps Ptnrs Inc 1775 Sherman St Ste 1450 Denver CO 80203-4316

LEWIS, JERROLD See BOCK, JERRY

LEWIS, JERRY, congressman; b. Oct. 21, 1934. BA, UCLA, 1956. Former underwriter life ins. underwriter; field rep. for former U.S. Rep. Jerry Pettis; mem. Calif. State Assembly, 1968-78; vice chmn. rules com., chmn. subcom. on air quality; mem. 96th-103rd Congresses from 35th (now 40th) Calif. dist., 1979—; chmn. appropriation com. Va.-HUD subscom., mem. defense subcom., select com. on intelligence, chmn. subcom. on human intelligence; co-chair Calif. Congl. Delegation. Presbyterian. Office: 2112 Rayburn Bldg Washington DC 20515-0540

LEWIS, JERRY (JOSEPH LEVITCH), comedian; b. Newark, Mar. 16, 1926; s. Danny and Mona Levitch; m. Patti Palmer, 1944 (div.); children: Gary, Ron, Scott, Chris, Anthony, Joseph; m. Sandra Pitnick, 1983; 1 child, Danielle Sara. Edn., Irvington (N.J.) High Sch.; DHL (hon.), Mercy Coll., 1987. Prof. cinema U. So. Calif.; pres. JAS Prodns., Inc., P.J. Prodns., Inc. Began as entertainer with record routine at Catskill (N.Y.) hotel; formed comedy team with Dean Martin, 1946-56; performed as a single, 1956—; formed Jerry Lewis Prodns. Inc., prod., dir., writer, star, 1956; films include: My Friend Irma, 1949, My Friend Irma Goes West, 1950, At War with the Army, 1950, That's My Boy, 1950, Sailor Beware, 1951, The Stooge, 1952, Jumping Jacks, 1952, Scared Stiff, 1953, The Caddy, 1953, Money From Home, 1953, Three Ring Circus, 1954, Living it Up, 1954, You're Never Too Young, 1955, Artists and Models, 1955, Partners, 1956, Hollywood or Bust, 1956, The Delicate Delinquent, 1957, The Sad Sack, 1957, The Geisha Boy, 1958, Rockabye Baby, 1958, Don't Give Up the Ship, 1959, Li'l Abner, 1959, Visit to a Small Planet, 1960, The Bellboy, 1960, Cinderfella, 1960, The Ladies Man, 1961, It's Only Money, 1962, The Errand Boy, 1962, It's a Mad, Mad, Mad, Mad World, 1963, The Nutty Professor, 1963, Who's Minding The Store, 1963, The Patsy, 1964, The Disorderly Orderly, 1964, The Family Jewels, 1965, Boeing-Boeing, 1965, Three On A Couch, 1965, Way ... Way ... Out, 1966, The Big Mouth, 1967, Don't Raise the Bridge, Lower the Water, 1968, Hook, Line and Sinker, 1969, One More Time, 1969, Which Way To the Front?, 1970, Hardly Working, 1981, King of Comedy, 1983, Smorgasbord, 1983, Slapstick, 1984, To Catch A Cop, 1984, How Did You Get In?, 1985, Cookie, 1989, Arrowtooth Waltz, 1991, Mr. Saturday Night, 1992; appeared on Broadway in Damn Yankees, 1995, on tour, 1995—; author: The Total Film-Maker, 1971, Jerry Lewis in Person, 1982; principal TV appearances include master of ceremonies ann. Labor Day Muscular Dystrophy Telethon, 1966—. Comdr. Order of Arts & Letters, France, 1984; nat. chmn. Muscular Dystrophy Assn. Recipient most promising male star in TV award Motion Picture Daily's 2nd Ann. TV poll, 1950, (as team), one of TV's 10 money making stars award Motion Picture Herald - Fame poll, 1951, 53-54, 57, best comedy team award Motion Picture Daily's 16th annual radio poll, 1951-53, Nobel Peace Prize nomination, 1978. Mem. Screen Producers Guild, Screen Dirs. Guild, Screen Writers Guild. Office: Jerry Lewis Films Inc 3160 W Sahara Ave # 16C Las Vegas NV 89102-6003 also: William Morris Agy Inc 151 S El Camino Dr Beverly Hills CA 90212-2704

LEWIS, JERRY LEE, country-rock singer, musician; b. Ferriday, La., Sept. 29, 1935; s. Elmo and Mary Ethel L.; m. Kerrie Lee; children: Phoebe, Jerry Lee Jr. Student, Waxahachie (Tex.) Bible Inst. Rock and roll performer, recs. on Sun Records label, Whole Lotta Shakin' Goin' On, 1957, Great Balls of Fire, Mercury/Phonogram, 1963-78, Elektra Records, 1978-81; shifted to country and rock repertoire: recs. include Golden Hits, Odd Man In, Country Class, Roll Over Beethoven, High Heel Sneakers, Jerry Lee Lewis, Southern Roots, Good Rockin' Tonight, Taste of Country, Sunday After Church, Rural Route #1, Drinkin Wine Spo Dee O Dee, Golden Cream of Country, Monsters, Old Tyme Country Music, Rockin with From the Vaults of Sun; appeared in films American Hot Wax, Disc Jockey Jamboree, High School Confidential; albums include Sold Gold, 1986, The Killer Rocks On, 1987, Rocket, 1988, 1992, Killer: The Mercury Years Vol. One, Vol. Two, Vol. Three, 1989, Great Balls of Fire, 1989, Whole Lotta Shakin' Goin' On, 1992, Rockin' My Life Away, 1992, Heartbreak, 1992, All Killer, No Filler: The Anthology, 1993, Young Blood, 1995, Back to Back, 1996. Named to Rock and Roll Hall of Fame, 1986. Office: Warner Bros Records 75 Rockefeller Plz New York NY 10019*

LEWIS, JERRY M., psychiatrist, educator; b. Utica, N.Y., Aug. 18, 1924; s. Jerry M. and Margaret (Miller) L.; m. Patsy Ruth Price, Sept. 24, 1949; children: Jerry M., Cynthia Lewis-Reynolds, Nancy Minns, Tom. MD, Southwestern Med. Sch., Dallas, 1951. Diplomate Am. Bd. Psychiatry and Neurology. Staff psychiatrist Timberlawn Psychiat. Hosp., Dallas, 1957-63, chief women's svc., 1963-66, chief adolescent svcs., 1966-70, dir. profl. edn., 1970-79, psychiatrist-in-chief, 1979-88, dir. rsch., 1988-93; dir. rsch. and tng. Timberlawn Psychiat. Rsch. Found., Dallas, 1967-88, sr. rsch. psychiatrist, 1988—; clin. prof. psychiatry, family practice and cmty. medicine Southwestern Med. Sch.; cons. in psychiatry Baylor U. Med. Ctr., Dallas. Author: No Single Thread, 1976, How's Your Family, 1978, To Be a Therapist, 1979, The Long Struggle, 1983, Swimming Upstream: Teaching Psychotherapy in a Biological Era, 1991, The Monkey-Rope, 1995, Marriage as a Search for Healing: Theory, Assessment & Therapy, 1997. Served with USN, 1943-45.

Fellow Am. Coll. Psychiatrists (pres. 1985), Am. Psychiat. Assn., So. Psychiat. Assn. (pres. 1979); mem. Group for Advancement of Psychiatry (pres. 1987), Benjamin Rush Soc. (pres. 1994-95), AMA, Tex. Med. Assn. Office: PO Box 270789 Dallas TX 75227-0789

LEWIS, JESSICA HELEN (MRS. JACK D. MYERS), physician, educator; b. Harpswell, Maine, Oct. 26, 1917; d. Warren Harmon and Margaret (Reed) L.; m. Jack D. Myers, Aug. 31, 1946; children: Judith Duane (dec.), John Lewis, Jessica Read, Elizabeth Reed, Margaret Anne. A.B., Goucher Coll., 1938; M.D., Johns Hopkins U., 1942. USPHS Research fellow U. N.C., 1947-48, research assoc. dept. physiology, 1948-55; assoc. dept. medicine Duke Med. Sch., 1951-55; research assoc. dept. medicine U. Pitts., 1955-58, faculty, 1958-92, research assoc. prof., 1965-70, prof. medicine, 1970-92, prof. medicine emeritus, 1992—; dir. research Central Blood Bank Pitts., 1969-74, v.p., 1974-85, med. dir. and sr. v.p., 1985-89, sci. dir., sr. v.p., 1985-92, sr. v.p., med. and sci. dir. emeritus, 1992—; dir. Hemophilia Center Western Pa., 1973-81. Author: Comparative Hemostasis in Vertebrates, also more than 250 sci. papers. Mem. Am. Physiol. Soc., Am. Soc. Clin. Investigation, Am. Fedn. Clin. Research, Soc. for Exptl. Biol. Medicine, Internat. Soc. Hematology, Am. Soc. Hematology, Sigma Xi. Rsch. on mechanism blood coagulation, fibrinolysis, hemorrhagic and thrombotic diseases and comparative vertebrate coagulation. Home: Dithridge House 220 N Dithridge St Apt 900 Pittsburgh PA 15213-1424 Office: Central Blood Bank Pitts 812 5th Ave Pittsburgh PA 15219-4701

LEWIS, JOHN BRUCE, lawyer; b. Poplar Bluff, Mo., Aug. 12, 1947; s. Evan Bruce and Hilda Kathryn (Kassebaum) L.; m. Diane F. Grossman, July 23, 1977; children: Samantha Brooking, Ashley Denning. BA, U. Mo., 1969, JD, 1972; LLM in Labor and Employment Law, Columbia U., 1978; diploma, Nat. Inst. Trial Advocacy, 1982. Bar: Mo. 1972, U.S. Ct. Appeals (8th cir.) 1973, U.S. Dist. Ct. (ea. dist.) Mo. 1974, U.S. Dist. Ct. (no. dist.) Ohio 1979, Ohio 1980, U.S. Ct. Appeals (6th cir.) 1982, U.S. Dist. Ct. (ea. dist.) Mich. 1983, U.S. Ct. Appeals (3d cir.) 1987, U.S. Supreme Ct. 1987, U.S. Dist. Ct. (no. dist.) Calif. 1987, U.S. Ct. Appeals (7th cir.) 1990. Assoc. Millar, Schaefer & Ebling, St. Louis, 1972-77, Squire, Sanders & Dempsey, Cleve., 1979-85; ptnr. Arter & Hadden, Cleve., 1985—; chair Labor and Employment Law Practice Group, 1987—; lectr. in field. Contbr. articles to legal jours. Mem. Cleve. Council on World Affairs. Mem. ABA (sec. labor and employment law, com. EEO law, comm. law forum), Ohio State Bar Assn. (sec. labor and employment law), Greater Cleve. Bar Assn. (sec. labor law), St. Louis Met. Bar Assn., Am. Law Inst., Def. Rsch. Inst., Selden Soc., Ohio C. of C. (labor adv. com.). Office: Arter & Hadden 925 Euclid Ave Cleveland OH 44115

LEWIS, JOHN CLARK, JR., manufacturing company executive; b. Livingston, Mont., Oct. 15, 1935; s. John Clark and Louise A. (Anderson) L.; m. Carolyn Jean Keesling, Sept. 4, 1960; children: Robert, Anne, James. BS, Fresno (Calif.) State U., 1957. With Service Bur. Corp., El Segundo, Calif., 1960-70, Computer Scis. Corp., 1970; with Xerox Corp., El Segundo, 1970-77, pres. bus. systems div., 1977; pres. Amdahl Corp., Sunnyvale, Calif., 1983-87, chief exec. officer, 1983—, chmn., 1987—. Served with USNR, 1957-60. Roman Catholic. Office: Amdahl Corp 1250 E Arques Ave Sunnyvale CA 94086-5401*

LEWIS, JOHN FRANCIS, lawyer; b. Oberlin, Ohio, Oct. 25, 1932; s. Ben W. and Gertrude D. Lewis; m. Catharine Monroe, June 15, 1957; children: Ben M., Ian A., Catharine G., William H. B.A., Amherst Coll., 1955; J.D., U. Mich., 1958. Bar: Ohio 1958, U.S. Dist. Ct. (no dist.) Ohio 1959, U.S. Supreme Ct. 1973. Assoc. firm Squire, Sanders & Dempsey, Cleve., 1958-67; ptnr. Squire, Sanders & Dempsey LLP, 1967—, mng. ptnr. Cleve. office, 1985—. Co-author: Baldwin's Ohio School Law, 1980-91, Ohio Collective Bargaining Law, 1983. Trustee, chmn. Ohio Found. Ind. Colls., Case Western Res. U.; trustee Playhouse Sq. Found., chmn., 1980-85; mem. exec. com. Greater Cleve. Growth Assn.; trustee Musical Arts Assn.; hon. chmn. Found. for Sch. Bus. Mgmt., Leadership Cleve., 1977-78. Recipient Malcolm Daisley Labor-Mgmt. Rels. award, 1991, Tree of Life award Jewish Nat. Fund, 1993, Nat. Conf. award, 1995. Mem. Cleve. Bar Assn., Ohio Bar Assn., ABA (com. pub. edn.), Nat. Sch. Bd. Assn., Nat. Orgn. Legal Problems (past pres.), Ohio Assn. Sch. Bus. Ofcls. (hon. life), Fifty Club of Cleve., Ohio Council Sch. Bd. Attys. Episcopalian. Home: 2001 Chestnut Hills Dr Cleveland OH 44106-4601 Office: Squire Sanders & Dempsey 4900 Key Tower 127 Public Sq Cleveland OH 44114-1216

LEWIS, JOHN FURMAN, retired lawyer, oil company executive; b. Fort Worth, Apr. 24, 1934; s. Ben B. and Minnie W. (Field) L.; children: Joyce Ann, George Field, William Patrick. Student, Tex. Christian U., summer 1955; B.A. in Econs., Rice U., 1956; J.D. with honors, U. Tex., 1962; postgrad., Princeton U., 1965-66; M.B.A., Bowling Green State U., 1971. Bar: Tex. 1962, U.S. Dist. Ct. 1965, U.S. Supreme Ct. 1967, Ohio 1968, U.S. Ct. Mil. Appeals 1971, Okla. 1987. Atty. Atlantic Richfield Co., 1962-67; with Marathon Oil Co., Findlay, Ohio, 1967-86, gen. atty., 1978, sr. atty., 1978-81, assoc. gen. counsel, 1981-83, v.p., gen. counsel, 1983-84, v.p., gen. counsel, sec., 1985-86; sr. v.p., gen. counsel The Williams Cos., Tulsa, 1986-96; retired, 1996; mem. adv. bd. Internat. Oil and Gas Ednl. Ctr. of Southwestern Legal Found. Contbr. articles to profl. jours. Mem. exec. com., trustee United Way of Hancock County, Findlay, Ohio, 1984-86; bd. dirs. No-We-Oh coun. Camp Fire, Inc., Findlay, 1974-86, Okla. Green Country coun., Tulsa, 1987-89; mem. Arts and Humanities Coun., Tulsa, 1991-95. Lt. (j.g.) USN, 1956-59. Mem. ABA (subcom. chmn. 1984-85), Tex. Bar Assn., Am. Petroleum Inst. (lawyer-adviser mktg. com. 1982-84, gen. law com. 1983—), Ohio Bar Assn., U. Tex. Law Sc. Alumni Assn. (bd. dirs. 1994-96), Am. Club Lisbon. Republican. Avocations: jogging, tennis, golf.

LEWIS, JOHN HARDY, JR., lawyer; b. East Orange, N.J., Oct. 31, 1936; s. John Hardy and Sarah (Ripley) L.; m. Mary Ann Spurgeon, June 25, 1960; children: Peter, David, Mark. AB magna cum laude, Princeton U., 1958; JD cum laude, Harvard U., 1961. Bar: Pa. 1962. Assoc. Morgan, Lewis & Bockius, Phila., 1965-69, ptnr., 1969—. trustee Blair Acad., Blairstown, N.J.; rector's warden All Saints' Ch., Wynnewood, Pa. Served to major USAF, 1962-65. Fellow Am. Coll. Trial Lawyers. Home: 1000 Green Valley Rd Bryn Mawr PA 19010-1912 Office: Morgan Lewis & Bockius 2000 One Logan Sq Philadelphia PA 19103

LEWIS, JOHN MILTON, cable television company executive; b. nr. Slocomb, Ala., Mar. 29, 1931; s. Phil Truman and Vermell Beatrice (Avery) L.; grad. high sch.; m. Mary Lee Robledo, June 9, 1951; children: Janet Lee, Lee Michael. With Gulf Power Co., Panama City, Fla., 1949-56; self employed vehicle svc. co., Panama City, 1956-58; v.p., bd. dir., Burnup & Sims of Fla., Inc., West Palm Beach, 1958-70; pres., bd. dir. Wometco Cable Corp., Miami, Fla., 1970-94; pres., CEO SPI Holding, Inc., Richardson, Tex., 1988-89, also bd. dirs.; CEO Spectradyne, Inc., Richardson, 1988-89; pres. Key Capital Group, Inc., Miami, 1995—, St. Joe Comms., Inc., Port St. Joe, Fla., 1996—. bd. dirs. Allied Waste Mgmt., Phoenix; pres. St. Joe Telephone Co., Inc., Port St. Joe, Fla.; cons. in field. Recipient Tower Club award So. TV Assn. Mem. Cable TV Pioneers, Masons. Republican. Office: Key Capital Group Inc PO Box 561009 9500 S Dadeland Blvd Ste 603 Miami FL 33156

LEWIS, JOHN PRIOR, economist, educator; b. Albany, N.Y., Mar. 18, 1921; s. Leon Ray and Grace (Prior) L.; m. June Estelle Ryan, July 12, 1946; children—Betsy Prior, Sally Eastman, Amanda Barnum. Student, St. Andrews U., Scotland, 1939-40; A.B., Union Coll., Schenectady, 1941; M.Pub. Adminstrn., Harvard, 1943, Ph.D. in Polit. Economy and Govt, 1950; D.C.L., Union Coll., 1970. Instr., asst. prof. econs. and govt. Union Coll., Schenectady, 1946-50; mem. staff, asst. to chmn. Council Econ. Advisers, Exec. Office of Pres., Washington, 1950-53; cons. UN Korean Reconstrn. Agy., Pusan, Korea, 1953; assoc. prof. Ind. U., 1953-56, prof. bus. econs. and pub. policy, 1956-64, disting. service prof. bus. econs. and pub. policy, 1964, chmn. dept., 1961-63; mem. Council Econ. Advisers, Exec. Office of Pres., Washington, 1963-64; minister-dir. USAID mission to India, 1964-69; dean Woodrow Wilson Sch. Pub. Affairs, 1969-74; prof. econs. and internat. affairs Princeton (N.J.) U., 1969-91, prof. emeritus, 1991—; on leave as chmn. devel. assistance com. OECD, Paris, 1979-81; as DAC chmn. ann. OECD vols. on devel. cooperation OECD, 1979-81; sr. advisor Overseas Devel. Coun., 1981—; sr. staff mem. in India Brookings Instn., Washington, 1959-60; mem. UN Com. on Devel. Planning, 1970-83, rapporteur, 1972-78. Author: Business Conditions Analysis, 1959, 2d edit., (with R.C. Turner), 1967, Quiet Crisis in India: Economic Development and American Policy, 1962, (with Ishan Kapur) Multilateral Aid, and the 1970's, 1973, (with V. Kallab) U.S. Foreign Policy and the Third World, 1983, Development Strategies Reconsidered, 1986, Strengthening the Poor, 1988, India's Political Economy, 1995, (with Devesh Kapur and Richard Webb) The World Bank: Its First Half Century, 1997. Served to lt. USNR, 1943-46, PTO. Home: 61 County Rd 518 Princeton NJ 08540 Office: Princeton U Woodrow Wilson Sch Princeton NJ 08544

LEWIS, JOHN R., congressman; b. Pike County, Ala., Feb. 21, 1940; m. Lillian Miles, 1968; 1 child, John-Miles. BA, Am. Bapt. Theol. Sem., Nashville, 1961, Fisk U., 1963. Mem. City Coun., Atlanta, 1982-86, 100th-105th Congresses from 5th Ga. dist., Washington, 1986—; former chief dep. majority whip. Civil rights leader; mem. Martin Luther King Ctr. for Social Change, African Am. Inst., Robert F. Kennedy Meml. Office: US Ho of Reps 229 Cannon Bldg Washington DC 20515-1005*

LEWIS, JOHN WILSON, political science educator; b. King County, Wash., Nov. 16, 1930; s. Albert Lloyd and Clara (Lewis) Seeman; m. Jacquelyn Clark, June 19, 1954; children: Cynthia, Stephen, Amy. Student, Deep Springs Coll., 1947-49; AB with highest honors, UCLA, 1953, MA, 1958, PhD, 1962; hon. degree, Morningside Coll., 1969, Lawrence U., 1986, Russian Acad. Sci., 1996. Asst. prof. govt. Cornell U., 1961-64, assoc. prof., 1964-68; prof. polit. sci. Stanford U., 1968—, William Haas prof. Chinese politics, 1972—, co-dir. arms control and disarmament program, 1971-83, co-dir. NE Asia U.S. Forum on Internat. Policy, 1980-90, co-dir. Ctr. for Internat. Security and Arms Control, 1983-91, sr. fellow, 1991—, dir. Project on Peace and Cooperation in the Asian-Pacific Region; chmn. Internat. Strategic Inst., 1983-89; chmn. joint com. on contemporary China Social Sci. Rsch. Coun.-Am. Coun. Learned Socs., 1976-79; mng. dir. Generation Ventures, 1994—; former vice chmn., bd. dirs. Nat. Com. on U.S.-China Rels.; cons. Senate Select Com. on Intelligence, 1977-81, Los Alamos Nat. Lab., Lawrence Livermore Nat. Lab., Dept. of Def., 1994-96; mem. Def. Policy Bd., 1994-96; chmn. com. advanced study in China Com. Scholarly Comm. with People's Republic of China, 1979-82; mem. com. on internat. security and arms control Nat. acad. Scis., 1980-83; organizer first univ. discussion arms control and internat. security matters Chinese People's Inst. Fgn. Affairs, 1978, first academic exch. agreement Dem. People's Repb. of Korea, 1988; negotiator first univ. tng. and exch. agreement People's Rep. of China, 1978. Author: Leadership in Communist China, 1963, Major Doctrines of Communist China, 1964, Policy Networks and the Chinese Policy Process, 1986; co-author: The United States in Vietnam, 1967, Modernization by Design, 1969, China Builds the Bomb, 1988, Uncertain Partners: Stalin, Mao, and the Korean War, 1993, China's Strategic Seapower: The Politics of Force Modernization in the Nuclear Era, 1994; editor: The City in Communist China, 1971, Party Leadership and Revolutionary Power in China, 1970, Peasant Rebellion and Communist Revolution in Asia, 1974; contbr.: Congress and Arms Control, 1978, China's Quest for Independence, 1979, others; mem. editl. bd. Chinese Law and Govt., China Quar., The Pacific Rev. Served with USN, 1954-57. Mem. Assn. Asian Studies, Am. Polit. Sci. Assn., Coun. Fgn. Rels. Home: 541 San Juan St Stanford CA 94305-8432 Office: Stanford U 320 Galvez St Stanford CA 94305-6105

LEWIS, JONATHAN, health care association administrator. BS Applied Behavioral Scis., U. Calif., Davis. Founder, mng. ptnr., pres. JLA Advocates, Inc.; exec. dir. Calif. Commn. on Tchg. Profession; chief cons. State of Calif. State Senate Commn. on Property Tax Equity, 1990-91; exec. dir. Calif. Assn. Health Maintenance Orgns., Sacramento, 1990-93; founder, pres. Acad. for Internat. Health Studies, Inc., Davis, Calif., 1993—; vis. faculty U. Calif., Berkeley; budget cons. State of Calif. Senate Pres. Office: Acad Internat Health Study 621 Georgetown Pl Davis CA 95616-1821

LEWIS, JONATHAN JOSEPH, surgical oncologist, molecular biologist; b. Johannesburg, South Africa, May 23, 1958; s. Myer Philip and Maisie (Bagg) L.; m. Nanci Lynn Vicedomini, May 20, 1990. MB BCH, Witwatersrand U., Johannesburg, 1982; PhD, Med. Sch., South Africa, 1990. Registrar in surgery Witwatersrand U. Sch. Medicine, 1982-87; postdoctoral assoc. Yale U. Sch. Medicine, New Haven, Conn., 1987-90; chief resident, surgery Yale U. Sch. Medicine, New Haven, 1990-92; fellow dept. surgery Meml. Sloan-Kettering Cancer Ctr., N.Y.C., 1992-94, attending surgeon, asst. mem., 1994—; asst. prof. surgery Cornell Univ. Med. Coll., 1994—. Contbr. articles to profl. jours. Recipient Abelheim medal Med. Coun., 1982, Trubshaw medal Coll. of Surgeons, Johannesburg, 1984; Winston fellow Sloan-Kettering Inst., 1994-95. Fellow ACS, Royal Coll. Surgeons; mem. Am. Soc. Cell Biology, Am. Assn. Cancer Rsch., Am. Soc. Clin. Oncology (Young Investigator award 1994), Assn. Acad. Surgeons, Soc. Surg. Oncology, N.Y. Acad. Scis. Jewish. Achievements include research in oncogenes, growth factors, signal transduction , immunotherapy, gene therapy. Home: 504 E 63rd St Apt 37S New York NY 10021-7929 Office: Meml Sloan-Kettering Cancer Dept Surgery 1275 York Ave New York NY 10021-6007

LEWIS, JULIETTE, actress; b. Fernando Valley, Calif., June 21, 1973; d. Geoffrey and Glenis Batley L. TV appearances include Homefires (Showtime miniseries), I Married Dora, 1988, A Family For Joe, 1990; TV Movies include Too Young To Die, 1989; films include My Stepmother is an Alien, 1988, Meet the Hollowheads, 1989, National Lampoons Christmas Vacation, 1989, Cape Fear, 1991 (Academy Award nomination best supporting actress 1991), Crooked Hearts, 1991, Husbands and Wives, 1992, Kalifornia, 1993, That Night, 1993, What's Eating Gilbert Grape, 1993, Romeo is Bleeding, 1994, Natural Born Killers, 1994, Mixed Nuts, 1994, Strange Days, 1995, The Basketball Diaries, 1995, From Dusk Till Dawn, 1996, The Evening Star, 1996, The Audition, 1996. Office: William Morris Agy 151 S El Camino Dr Beverly Hills CA 90212-2704

LEWIS, KAREN MARIE, writer, editor; b. Syracuse, N.Y., Oct. 29, 1965; d. Stephan Joseph and Mary Josephine (Scully) L. Student, Simon's Rock of Bard Coll., 1982-83; BA cum laude, Barnard Coll., 1986; MA, Brandeis U., 1989. Prodn. asst. Claremont Rsch. and Pub., N.Y.C., 1984-86; tchg. asst. Barnard Coll., N.Y.C., 1984-86; teaching asst. Brandeis U., Waltham, Mass., 1988; freelance writer Great Barrington, Mass., 1989-95; editl. asst. o.blek, Great Barrington, 1992-93; ESL algebra tutor Lenox (Mass.) Meml. High, 1995; editor Construct, Inc., Great Barrington, 1994—, tutor adult edn., 1996; prodn. asst. The Artful Mind, Great Barrington, 1997—. Contbr. articles to anthologies, newspapers and poetry jours. Mem. Poets and Writers. Roman Catholic. Home: PO Box 1094 Great Barrington MA 01230-6094

LEWIS, KATHRYN HUXTABLE, pediatrician; b. Lakewood, Ohio, July 23, 1934; d. Harold Stafford and Otillie Louise (May) H.; m. Samuel T. Lewis III, Apr. 8, 1967 (dec. Sept. 1994); children: Samuel T. IV, Stephen A., Anne E. Student, Cornell U., 1952-55; MD, Yale U., 1959; MPH, Johns Hopkins U., 1964. Diplomate Nat. Bd. Med. Examiners, Am. Bd. Pediatrics. Intern Univ. Hosps., Cleve., 1959-60, resident in pediatrics, 1961-62, chief resident in pediatrice, 1962-63; resident in pediatrict Children's Hosp. of Phila., 1960-61, Cleve. Met. Gen. Hosp., 1961-62; tchg. fellow in pediatrics Western Res. U., Cleve., 1962-63, sr. instr. dept. pediatrics, 1965-67, sr. clin. instr. dept. preventive medicine, 1965-66, sr. instr. dept. preventive medicine, 1966-67; tchg. fellow in pediatrics Johns Hopkins U., Balt., 1963-64; rsch. assoc. Sch. Hygiene and Pub. Health Johns Hopkins U., Lahore, Pakistan, 1964-65; tchg. assoc. Ford Found., Lahore, 1964-65; clin. asst. prof. dept. pediatrics/dept. preventive medicine U. Pitts. Sch. Medicine, 1967-75; asst. dir. out-patient dept. Children's Hosp. of Pitts., 1967-75; dir. pediatric clinics ambulatory svcs. Cleve. Met. Gen. Hosp., 1966-67; cons. in field.; sch. physician Tyrone Area Bd. Edn., 1976—; dir. Pediatric Outpatient Ctr. Tyrone Hosp., 1975-92, Pediatric Outpatient Ctr. Geisinger Tyrone divsn., 1992—. Contbr. articles to profl. jours. Recipient Disting. Alumni award in sci. Lakewood H.S., 1993. Fellow Am. Acad. Pediatrics, APHA ; mem. Pa. Med. Soc., Phi Beta Kappa. Office: Geisinger Med Group 1 Hospital Dr Tyrone PA 16686-1810

LEWIS, KIRK MCARTHUR, lawyer; b. Schenectady, N.Y., Jan. 3, 1957; s. David MacArthur and Eleanor Burrows (Smith) L.; m. Barbara Jean Lewis, June 12, 1982; children: John Christopher, Kerry Elizabeth. BS, Cornell U., 1979; JD, Syracuse U., 1985. Bar: N.Y. 1986, U.S. Dist. Ct. (no. dist.) N.Y. 1988, U.S. Dist. Ct. (ea. dist.) N.Y. 1991, U.S. Ct. Appeals (2d cir.) 1989. Jud. clk to Hon. Conrad K. Cyr U.S. Dist. Ct. Maine, Bangor, 1985-87; assoc. DeGraff, Foy, Holt, Harris, Mealey & Kunz, Albany, N.Y., 1987-93, ptnr., 1993—. Bd. dirs., v.p., pres. Schenectady (N.Y.) Assn. for Retarded Citizens, 1990—. Mem. ABA, N.Y. State Bar Assn. Home: 30 Washington Rd Scotia NY 12302 Office: DeGraff Foy Holt Harris Mealey & Kunz 90 State St Albany NY 12207

LEWIS, LARRY LISLE, human resources specialist company executive; b. 1945. With Homefinders Inc., Jackson, Miss., 1970-90; pres. People Lease Inc., Jackson, Miss., 1984—. With U.S. Army, 1968-70. Office: People Lease Inc 4735 Old Canton Rd Jackson MS 39211-5520

LEWIS, LOIDA NICOLAS, food products holding company executive; b. The Philippines, Dec. 23, 1942; m. Reginald Lewis, 1969. BA, St. Theresa's Coll., 1963; LLB, U. Philippines, 1967. Immigration atty. N.Y.C.; with Immigration and Naturalization Svc.; chmn., CEO TLC Beatrice Internat., N.Y.C., 1994—. Author: How the Filipino Veteran of World War II Can Become a U.S. Citizen (According to the Immigration Act of 1990), 1991, One Hundred One Legal Ways to Stay in the U.S.A.: or, How to Get a Green Card According to the Immigration Act of 1990, 1992, How to Get a Green Card: Legal Ways to Stay in the U.S.A., 1993. Office: TLC Beatrice Internat 9 W 57th St Fl 39 New York NY 10019-2701*

LEWIS, LOIS A., health services administrator; b. Tuskegee, Ala.; d. Arthur J. and Katie (Cephus) Long; m. Charles Lewis; children: Robin Jordan, Michelle Allen. BSN, U. Conn., 1959, MS, 1974; PhD, Columbia Pacific, 1989. CNAA. Community health nurse Hartford VNA, Conn., 1967-68, 70-71; sch. nurse Clark County Schs., Las Vegas, 1968-70; dir. job corps. Community Renewal Team, Hartford, 1971-72; sr. nurse Cap. Reg. Mental Health, Hartford, 1974-75; exec. dir. Manchester (Conn.) VNA, 1975-87; br. dir. Vis. Nurse and Home Care, Inc., Hartford, 1987-88; dir. community nursing and home health State Dept. Health, Hartford, 1988-96; ret., 1996; chairperson Cedarcrest Hosp., Newington, Conn., 1980-95; mem. adv. bd. dirs. U. Ct. Health Ctr., Farmington, 1982—, Hartford Hosp., 1992-96. Contbr. articles to profl. jours. Bd. dirs. ARC, Farmington, Conn., 1989—; mentor Career Beginnings, Hartford, 1989, 90. With USN, 1959-61. Mem. Nat. Assn. for Home Care (bd. dirs. 1980-83, 85-88), Conn. League for Nursing, Conn. Pub. Health Assn., Am. Pub. Health Assn., Sigma Theta Tau, Chi Eta Phi. Democrat. Methodist. Avocations: swimming, reading, knitting.

LEWIS, LUCINDA, musician; b. Kansas City, Mo., May 8, 1953; d. William Merle and Beverly (Hampton) L. MusB, Manhattan Sch. Music, N.Y.C., 1970, MusM, 1974. Prin. horn N.J. Symphony, Newark, 1977—. *

LEWIS, MARGARET M., marketing professional; b. Bridgeport, Conn., Sept. 27, 1959; d. Raymond Phillip and Catherine Helen (Gayda) Palovchak; m. William A. Lewis Jr., Oct. 4, 1980. BS summa cum laude, Sacred Heart U., 1986; postgrad., U. Bridgeport; AS, Katherine Gibbs Sch., 1980. Program mgr. sales svc. group Newspaper Coop. Couponing, Inc., Westport, Conn., 1985-87; sales adminstr. Supermarket Communication Systems, Inc., Norwalk, Conn., 1987-88, mgr. mktg. support, 1988-89; asst. project mgr. sales promotion Mktg. Corp. Am., Westport, 1989-91, account exec., 1991-92; mgr. program svcs. Ryan Partnership, Westport, 1992-93, sr. program mgr., 1993-95, mng. dir., 1995-96; account dir. Creative Alliance, Westport, Conn., 1996-97; promotion mktg. cons. CSC Weston Group, Wilton, Conn., 1997—. Mem. NAFE, Direct Mktg. Assn., Am. Mgmt. Assn. Democrat. Roman Catholic. Home: 16 Nickel Pl Monroe CT 06468-3005 Office: CSC Weston Group Ten Westport Rd Wilton CT 06897

LEWIS, MARIANNE H., psychiatric nurse practitioner; b. Frankfurt, Germany, Feb. 8, 1921; d. Emil B. and Jessie (Falk) Horkheimer; m. Harold S. Lewis, July 10, 1943; children: Harold S., Jr., Dale G. AAS in Nursing, Pace U., White Plains, N.Y., 1970; BS, 1976; MSN in Adult Psychiatric Nursing, Yale U., 1980. Registered profl. nurse, Conn., advance nurse practitioner, Fla., cert. ANA specialist in psychiatric-mental health nursing, 1983. Sr. staff nurse Psychiatry N.Y.U. Med. Ctr., 1971-73; dir. White Plains (N.Y.) Med. Ctr. Day Hosp., 1973-78; asst. clin. prof. Yale U. Sch. Nursing, 1981-91; clin. specialist Dept. Psychiatry VA Med. Ctr., West Haven, Conn., 1980-83; nurse counseling group Northwalk, Conn., 1983-88; clin. specialist Grand View Psychiatric Resource Ctr. Waterbury (Conn.) Hosp., 1988-90; psychiatric review specialist Aetna Life and Casualty Ins. Co., Middletown, Conn., 1991-92; advanced registered nurse practitioner Vis. Nurse Asn. of Southwest Fla., 1995-96. Spkr. Pace U. Dedication of Lienhard Sch. Nursing Bldg., Pleasantville, N.Y., 1974; mem. recorder consort Ft. Myers, Fla., Sarasota Recorder chpt. Mem. ANA, Coun. Clin. Specialists, Fla. Nurses Assn. Avocation: early music. Home: 3030 Binnacle Dr Apt 309 Naples FL 34103-4157

LEWIS, MARILYN WARE, water company executive; b. 1943. Former pres. Solanco Pub. Co.; vice chmn. Am. Water Works Co., Inc., Voorhees, N.J., now chmn., also bd. dirs.; bd. dirs. Penn Fuel Gas Co., Cigna Corp. Office: Am Water Works Co Inc 2 E Main St Strasburg PA 17579-1410

LEWIS, MARK EARLDON, city manager; b. Boston, June 27, 1951; s Frederick Cole Lewis and Barbara (Forsyth) Corrigan; m. Kristine Mietzner, May 1, 1983; children: Anna Kristine, Benjamin Mark. BA, Washington State U., 1975; BS, We. State U., 1993, JD, 1995. Bar: Calif. 1996. Adminstrv. asst. City and Borough of Juneau, Alaska, 1975-77; city mgr. City of Valdez, Alaska, 1978-82; commr. State of Alaska Dept. of Community and REgional Affairs, Juneau, 1982-83; dep. city mgr. City of South San Francisco, Calif., 1984-87, city mgr., 1987-88; city mgr. City of Monterey Park, Calif., 1988-91, City of Colton, Calif., 1991-93, Union City, 1995—. Dir. Monterey Park Boys' and Girls' Club, 1990; vice chmn. allocation team United Way, 1990, area group chmn. 1989-90; exec. com. mem. Calif., colo., Ariz. and Nev. Innovation Group, 1987. Mem. State Bar Calif., Calif. City. Mgrs. Assn. (exec. com. 1996). Avocation: sailing. Home: 4350 Coventry Ct Union City CA 94587 Office: 34009 Alvarado Niles Rd Union City CA 94587-4452

LEWIS, MARTIN EDWARD, shipping company executive, foreign government concessionary; b. Chgo., Dec. 27, 1958; s. Martin Luther and Anna Adlene (Gaines) L. BA, Johns Hopkins U., 1981; postgrad., Rush Med. Coll., 1983-85. Chmn. bd., chief exec. officer Internat. Financier Inc., Chgo., 1987—; co. rep. Assn. S.E. Asia Nations Secretariat Gen., Jakarta, Indonesia, 1995—; co. rep. OPEC, Vienna, 1988—, Supreme Coun. States of Cooperation Coun., Summit Confs. Countries of Cooperation Coun. for Arab States of Gulf, Secretariat Gen., Riyadh, Saudi Arabia, 1989—; corp. amb. plenipotentiary GM Overseas Ops., N.Y.C., 1977, Adam Opel, Russelsheim, Fed. Republic Germany, 1977. Mem. Asia Soc., Japan Soc. Republican. Avocations: golf, tennis, yachting, scuba diving.

LEWIS, MARTIN R., paper company executive, consultant; b. N.Y.C., Feb. 14, 1929; s. William and Ida (Goldman) L.; m. Renee Raines, Aug. 13, 1950 (div.); children: Jeffrey, Wendy, Lisa; m. Diane Carol Brandt, July 4, 1975. BA, NYU, 1949, LLB, 1951; LLM, U. Mich., 1952. CEO Williamhouse-Regency, Inc., N.Y.C., 1955-95; cons., N.Y.C., 1995—. Bd. dirs. McBurney br. YMCA, N.Y.C. Mem. Envelope Mfg. Assn., Paper Club N.Y.C. Jewish.

LEWIS, MARY JANE, communication educator, writer; b. Kansas City, Mo., July 22, 1950; d. J.W. Jr. and Hilda (Miller) L. BA, Stephens Coll., Columbia, Mo., 1971; MA, NYU, 1984, PhD, 1996. Cert. video prodr. The Corp. for Cmty. TV, Honolulu. Office mgr. Crazy Shirts, Inc., Honolulu, 1974-79; creator Exotic Exports, Honolulu, 1979-80; asst. buyer Bloomingdale's, N.Y.C., 1980-82; office mgr., media dir. Andiamo, Inc., N.Y.C., 1982-85; freelance stylist Condé Nast, Inc., N.Y.C., 1985-86; lectr. U. Hawaii, Honolulu, 1988; tchg. fellow NYU, 1989-90, asst. prof., 1990-92; prof. U. Hawaii, Kapiolani C.C., Honolulu, 1992—, U. Hawaii, Honolulu C.C., 1994—; mem. adj. faculty Fashion Inst. Tech., N.Y.C., 1983; lectr. U. Hawaii, adult edn. programs, 1986—; lectr. NYU Sch. Continuing Edn., 1991-94; video stylist, asst. prodr. State of Hawaii Dept. Edn., Honolulu, 1994—, Kapiolani C.C.; developer numerous adult edn. comm. courses.

Author: (book) Careers in Fashion Manual, 1994, (TV/movie script) The Last Rose of Summer, 1992; creator, prodr., dir., host U. Hawaii, Svc. Learning Comm. TV Program, 1997; creator, prodr., host (cmty. TV program) Comm. Solutions, 1997. Mem. AAUW, NEA, Writers Guild Am., Women in Comm., The Fashion Group Internat., Inc., U. Hawaii Profl. Assn., Film and Video Assn. Hawaii, Cmty. TV Prodrs. Assn. State of Hawaii, U. Hawaii Women's Campus Club, Honolulu Acad. Arts, NYU Alumni Assn., Kappa Alpha Theta (pres. pledge class 1968—). Avocations: psychic tarot readings, gourmet vegetarian cooking, sailing, gardening, cats. Home: 91-513 B Hapalua St Ewa Beach HI 96706 Office: U Hawaii Kapiolani C C 4303 Diamond Head Rd Honolulu HI 96816

LEWIS, MELVIN, psychiatrist, pediatrician, psychoanalyst; b. London, May 18, 1926; came to U.S., 1956; s. Abraham George and Kitty (Merrick) L.; m. Dorothy S. Otnow, May 30, 1963; children: Gillian Io, Eric Anthony. M.B., B.S., Guy's Hosp. Med. Sch., London, 1950; D.C.H., 1954; M.A. (hon.), Yale U., 1972. Diplomate Am. Bd. Psychiatry and Neurology, Am. Bd. Child Psychiatry; cert. in psychoanalysis, child and adolescent psychoanalysis. Intern Lambeth Hosp., 1950, Fulham Hosp., 1951 (both Eng); resident in pediatrics Yale U. Sch. Medicine, 1956-57, resident in psychiatry and child psychiatry, 1957-61; instr. psychiatry Yale U. Child Study Center, New Haven, 1961-63; asst. prof. pediatrics and psychiatry Yale U. Child Study Center, 1963-67, assoc. prof., 1967-70, prof. child psychiatry and pediats., 1971—, dir. med. studies, 1970—. Author: Clinical Aspects of Child and Adolescent Development, 1971, 3d edit. (with Fred Volkmar), 1991; editor: Jour. Am. Acad. Child & Adolescent Psychiatry, 1975-87, Child and Adolescent Psychiatry, A Comprehensive Textbook, 1991, 2d edit., 1996; cons. editor: Child and Adolescent Psychiatric Clinics of North America, 1991—. Served with M.C. Royal Army, 1951-53. Fellow Am. Acad. Child and Adolescent Psychiatry, Am. Psychiat. Assn., Royal Coll. Psychiatrists; mem. Royal Soc. Medicine, Am. Pediatric Soc., Am. Psychoanalytic Assn. Home: 10 St Ronan Ter New Haven CT 06511-2315 Office: Yale U Child Study Ctr 333 Cedar St New Haven CT 06510-3206

LEWIS, MO, professional football player; b. Atlanta, Ga., Oct. 21, 1969. Student, U. Georgia. With N.Y. Jets, 1991—. Office: New York Jets 1000 Fulton Ave Hempstead NY 11550-1030*

LEWIS, NANCY LOUINE LAMBERT, school counselor; b. Austin, Tex., Jan. 28, 1938; d. Claud Standard and Audrey Louine (Jackson) Lambert; m. Raymond Clyde Lewis, Dec. 27, 1958; children: Laura Lewis Maloy, John Lambert. BA in English with highest honors, U. Tex., 1958, MEd in Guidance and Counseling, 1964. Lic. tchr. secondary English, counselor; lic. profl. counselor. Tchr. English Allan Jr. High Sch. Austin Ind. Sch. Dist., 1958-62, counselor Univ. Jr. High Sch., 1963-65; counselor Gary Job Corps Ctr., San Marcos, Tex., 1965-67; supr. student tchrs. English dept. curriculum and instrn. U. Tex., Austin, 1968-69, editor, writer, group leader Ctr. Pub. Sch. Ethnic Studies, 1969-76; counselor Allan Jr. High Sch. Austin Ind. Sch. Dist., 1976-80, counselor Martin Jr. High Sch., 1980-86, counselor Fulmore Mid. Sch., 1986-87, counselor Mendez Mid. Sch., 1987—; instr. corr. studies U. Tex., Austin, 1968—. Contbr. articles to profl. jours. Vol. Dem. party, Austin, 1973—, First United Meth. Ch., Austin, 1955—; mem. Mayor's Task Force on Gangs, Crime and Drugs, City of Austin, 1990-91. Mem. ACA, NEA, Am. Sch. Counselors Assn. (editl. bd. Sch. Counselor 1989-96), Tex. State Tchrs. Assn., Tex. Sch. Counselors Assn. (senator 1981-84, pres. 1985-86, chair counseling advocacy com. 1991-93, Mid. Sch. Counselor of Yr. 1993), Tex. Counseling Assn. (senator 1981-84, publs. com. chair 1981-84, membership com. chair 1994-96), Ctrl. Tex. Counseling Assn. (pres. 1982-83), Austin Assn. Tchrs. (cons. com. 1990-93, Human Rels. award 1989-90), Pathways (bd. dirs.), Delta Kappa Gamma (pres. Lambda Iota chpt. 1990-92), Phi Beta Kappa, Phi Delta Kappa. Avocations: travel, reading, playing bridge. Home: 1427 Salem Meadow Cir Austin TX 78745-2911 Office: Mendez Mid Sch 5106 Village Square Dr Austin TX 78744-4462

LEWIS, NATHAN SAUL, chemistry educator; b. L.A., Oct. 20, 1955. BS in Chemistry with highest honors, MS in Chemistry, Calif. Inst. Tech., 1977; PhD in Chemistry, MIT, 1981. Asst. prof. chemistry Stanford (Calif.) U., 1981-86, assoc. prof., 1986-88; assoc. prof. Calif. Inst. Tech., 1988-90, prof., 1990—; cons. Lawrence Livermore (Calif.) Nat. Lab., 1977-81, 84-88, Solar Energy Rsch. Assocs., Santa Clara, Calif., 1981-85, Am. Hosp. Supply, Irvine, Calif., 1983-85, Molecular Devices, Palo Alto, Calif., 1983-88; mem. U.S. Japan Joint Conf. Photochemistry and Photoconversion, 1983, Chem. Revs. Adv. Bd., 1989-92, long range planning com. Electrochem. Soc., 1991-94, Adv. Bd. Progress Inorganic Chemistry, 1992-94, vis. com. dept. applied sci. Brookhaven Nat. Lab., 1993—. Divisional editor Jour. Electrochemical Soc., 1984-90; mem. editorial adv. bd. Accounts Chem. Rsch., 1993—. Recipient Presdl. Young Investigator award, 1984-88, Fresenius award Phi Lambda Upsilon, 1990, Pure Chemistry award Am. Chem. Soc., 1991; Achievement Rewards Coll. Scientists Found. scholar Calif. Inst. Tech., 1975-77, Calif. State scholar, 1976-77, Carnation Co. Acad. Merit scholar, 1976-77, Camille and Henry Dreyfus Tchr. scholar, 1985-90; Fannie and John Hertz Found. fellow MIT, 1977-81, Alfred P. Sloan Rsch. fellow, 1985-87. Office: Calif Inst Tech Dept Chem 127-72 Pasadena CA 91125

LEWIS, NORMAN, English language educator, writer; b. N.Y.C., Dec. 30, 1912; s. Herman and Deborah (Nevins) L.; m. Mary Goldstein, July 28, 1934; children—Margery, Debra. B.A., CUNY, 1939; M.A., Columbia U., 1941. Instr., lectr CUNY, N.Y.C., 1943-52; assoc. prof. English NYU, N.Y.C., 1955-64; instr. Compton Coll., Calif., summers 1962-64, UCLA, 1962-69; prof. English Rio Hondo Coll., Whittier, Calif., 1964-91, chmn. communications dept., 1964-75. Author: (with others) Journeys Through Wordland, 1941, Lessons in Vocabulary and Spelling, 1941, (with Wilfred Funk) Thirty Days to a More Powerful Vocabulary, 1942, rev. edit., 1970, Power with Words, 1943, How to Read Better and Faster, 1944, rev. edit., 1978, The Lewis English Refresher and Vocabulary Builder, 1945, How to Speak Better English, 1948, Word Power Made Easy, 1949, rev. edit., 1978, The Rapid Vocabulary Builder, 1951, rev. edit., 1980, 3d edit., 1988, How to Get More Out of Your Reading, 1951, Twenty Days to Better Spelling, 1953, The Comprehensive Word Guide, 1958, Dictionary of Correct Spelling, 1962, Correct Spelling Made Easy, 1963, rev. edit. 1987, Dictionary of Modern Pronunciation, 1963, New Guide to Word Power, 1963, The New Power with Words, 1964, Thirty Days to Better English, 1964, The Modern Thesaurus of Synonyms, 1965, RSVP-Reading, Spelling, Vocabulary, Pronunciation (books I-III), 1966, 77, See, Say, and Write! (books I and II), 1973, Instant Spelling Power, 1976, R.S.V.P. for College English Power (books I-III), 1977-79, R.S.V.P. with Etymology (books I and II), 1980-81, Instant Word Power, 1980, New American Dictionary of Good English, 1987; editor: New Roget's Thesaurus of the English Language in Dictionary Form, 1961; also numerous articles in nat. mags.

LEWIS, NORMAN G., academic administrator, researcher, consultant; b. Irvine, Ayrshire, Scotland, Sept. 16, 1949; Came to U.S., 1985; s. William F. and Agnes H. O. L.; m. Christine I. (div. Oct. 1994); children: Fiona, Kathryn. BSc in Chemistry with honors, U. Strathclyde, Scotland, 1973; PhD in Chemistry 1st class, U. B.C., 1977. NRC postdoctoral fellow U. Cambridge, Eng., 1978-80; rsch. assoc. chemistry dept. Nat. Rsch. Coun., Can., 1980; asst. scientist fundamental rsch. divsn. Pulp and Paper Rsch. Inst. Can., Montreal, 1980-82, group leader chemistry and biochemistry of woody plants, grad. rsch. chemistry divsn., 1982-85; assoc. prof. wood sci. and biochemistry Va. Poly. Inst. and State U., Blacksburg, 1985-90; dir. Inst. Biol. Chemistry, Wash. State U., Pullman, 1990—; Eisig-Tode disting. prof.; cons. NASA, DOE, USDA, NIH, NSF, Am. Inst. Biol. Scis., other industries, 1985—. Mem. editl. bd. Holzforschung, 1986, TAPPI, 1986, 89, Jour. Wood Chemistry and Tech., 1987—, Polyphenols Actualities, 1992—; mem. editl. bd., N.Am. assoc. editor Phytochemistry, 1992—; author or co-author more than 100 publs., books, articles to profl. jours. Hon. mem. Russian Assn. Space and Mankind. Recipient ICI Merit awards Imperial Chem. Industries, 1968-69, 69-70, 70-71, 71-72, ICI scholar, 1971-73, Chemistry awards Kilmarnock Coll., 1969-70, 70-71; NATO/SRC scholar U. B.C., 1974-77; named Arthur M. and Kate E. Tode Disting. Prof. Mem. Am. Chem. Soc. (at-large cellulose divsn., organizer symposia, programme sub-com. cellulose, paper and textile divsn. 1987-90, editorial bd.), Am. Soc. Plant Physiologists, Am. Soc. Gravitational and Space Biology, Phytochemical Soc. N.A. (phytochemical bank com. 1989—), Chem. Inst. Can. (treas. Montreal divsn. 1982-84, Am. Inst. Chemists and Chem. Inst. Can. Montreal conf. 1982-84), Can. Pulp and Paper Assn., Tech. Assn. of Pulp and Paper Industry, Societe de Groupe Polyphenole, Gordon Rsch. Conf. (vice-chmn. raenewable resources com. 1993—). Presbyterian. Achievements include 2 patents in field. Home: 1710 NE Upper Dr Pullman WA 99163-4624 Office: Washington State U Inst Biol Chemistry Clark Hall Pullman WA 99164

LEWIS, ORME, JR., investment company executive, land use advisor; b. Phoenix, Apr. 26, 1935; s. Orme and Barbara (Smith) L.; m. Elizabeth Bruening, Oct. 17, 1964; children: Joseph Orme, Elizabeth Blaise. BS, U. Ariz., 1958. Assoc. Coldwell Banker, Phoenix, 1959-64; v.p. Braggiotti Constrn., Phoenix, 1964-65; pvt. practice investment brokerage Phoenix, 1966-69; dep. asst. sec. Dept. Interior, Washington, 1969-73; dir. devel. Ariz. Biltmore Estates, 1973-76; exec. World Resources Co., Phoenix and McLean, Va., 1978-91; mng. mem. Applewhite Laflin & Lewis, Phoenix, 1979-96; gen. ptnr. Equity Interests, Phoenix, 1982—; mng. dir. Select Investments, Phoenix, 1996—; bd. dirs. Biofoam Corp., Phoenix; co-chmn. U.S. Adv. Com. on Mining and Mineral Rsch., Washington, 1982-94; mem. U.S. Emergency Minerals Adminstrn., 1987—, Disease Control Rsch. Commn., 1995—, Gov.'s Regulatory Rev. Coun., 1992-95, State Plant Site Transmission Line Com., Phoenix, 1974-85. Mem. Ariz. Senate, 1955-59; chmn. Phoenix Children's Hosp., 1981—; mem. governing bd. Polycystic Kidney Rsch. Found., Kansas City, Mo., 1983—, Ariz. Cmty. Found., 1986-91, Ariz. Parks and Conservation Coun., 1985—, Ariz. State U. Found., Tempe, 1981—, Ariz. Hist. Found., 1984—, Desert Bot. Garden, 1987-89, Men's Art Coun., 1983-85. Recipient Dept. Interior Conservation Svc. award, 1996. Mem. Ariz. C. of C. (dir. 1990-96), Met. Club (Washington), Ariz. Valley Field Riding and Polo Club, Paradise Valley Country Club, Rotary. Republican. Home: 4325 E Palo Verde Dr Phoenix AZ 85018-1127 Office: Select Investments 4350 E Camelback Rd Ste 260-e Phoenix AZ 85018

LEWIS, PAUL LE ROY, pathology educator; b. Tamaqua, Pa., Aug. 30, 1925; s. Harry Earl and Rose Estella (Brobst) L.; m. Betty Jane Bixby, June 2, 1953; 1 child, Robert Harry. AB magna cum laude, Syracuse U., 1950; MD, SUNY, Syracuse, 1953. Diplomate Am. Bd. Pathology. Intern Temple U. Hosp., Phila., 1953-54; resident in pathology Hosp. of U. Pa., Phila., 1954-58, asst. instr., 1957-58; instr. pathology Thomas Jefferson U. Coll. Medicine, Phila., 1958-62, asst. prof., 1962-65, assoc. prof., 1965-75, prof., 1975-93, prof. emeritus, 1993—; pathologist Thomas Jefferson U. Hosp., 1958-91; attending pathologist Meth. Hosp., Phila., 1975-93, dir. clin. labs., chmn. dept. pathology, 1975-92, consulting pathologist, 1993—; pathologist pvt. practice Phila., 1993—; pres. Penndel Labs. Inc., Ardmore, Pa., 1974-85; cons. VA Hosp., Coatesvillle, Pa., 1976-85; mem. med. adv. com. ARC Blood Bank, Phila., 1978—. Contbg. author: Atlas of Gastrointestinal Cytology, 1983; contbr. articles to med. jours. 2d lt. USAAF, 1943-46. Fellow Am. Soc. Clin. Pathologists, Coll. Am. Pathologists; mem. AMA, Pa. Med. Soc., Philadelphia County Med. Soc., Internat. Acad. Pathology, Am. Soc. Cytology, Masons, Phi Beta Kappa, Alpha Omega Alpha, Nu Sigma Nu. Republican. Methodist. Avocations: photography, hiking. Home and Office: 521 Baird Rd Merion Station PA 19066-1301

LEWIS, PEIRCE FEE, geographer, educator; b. Detroit, Oct. 26, 1927; s. Peirce and Amy Lois (Fee) L.; m. Felicia Louise Stegeman, Feb. 2, 1952; 1 child, Hugh Gilchrist. BA summa cum laude, Albion Coll., 1950; MA, U. Mich., 1953, PhD, 1957. Geographer, U.S. Army Forces, Tokyo, 1953-55; lectr. U. Mich., Ann Arbor, 1958; NSF fellow, U. Wash., Seattle, 1957-58; vis. prof. U. Calif., Berkeley, 1976-77; asst. prof. Pa. State U., University Park, 1958-62, prof. geography, 1962—, prof. emeritus, 1995—; John Hannah prof. Integrative Studies, Mich. State U., E. Lansing, 1992; cons., author Smithsonian Instn., Washington, 1974-77, Smithsonian Instn. Books, 1989-90, Ency. Britannica, Chgo., 1973-74, 81-83, 89-90, Pa. Pub. TV, 1982-83; cons. Nat. Geog. Soc., 1981—, Nat. Mus. Am. History, Washington, 1990—, Nat. Rural Studies Com., 1991, So. Living Mag.; cons. Strong Mus., Rochester, N.Y., Newberry Libr., Chgo.; mem. steering com. Pioneer Am. Soc. vols. on Nat. Rd. Author: New Orleans: Making An Urban Landscape, 1976; editor: Visual Blight in America, 1973; contbr. articles to profl. jours. Mem. Borough Planning Commn., State College, Pa., 1967-76, mem. traffic commn., 1968-70; bd. dirs. Pa. Roadside Council, 1969-74. Served with U.S. Army, 1945-47. Recipient First Prize essay Internat. Geog. Congress, Stockholm, 1960; Lindback Teaching award Pa. State U., 1981; Disting. Teaching award Nat. Council for Geog. Edn., 1982; Nat. Honors award Assn. Am. Geographers, 1977, Trustee of Am. award Ctr. for Hist. Preservation, Mary Washington Coll., 1987, Disting. Geographer award Pa. Geog. Soc., 1991; rsch. assoc. U. Calif., Berkeley, 1986; John Simon Guggenheim Fellow, 1986-87, Woodrow Wilson fellow Woodrow Wilson Internat. Ctr. for Scholars, Smithsonian Inst., 1988, John Bracken fellow Pa. State U., 1993—. Mem. Assn. Am. Geographers (pres. 1983-84, nat. councillor 1981-82, 84-85, vis. geog. scientist, chmn. J.B. Jackson prize com.), Am. Geog. Soc., Nat. Council for Geog. Edn., Phi Beta Kappa. Democrat. Club: State College Literary. Avocation: travel. Home: 1377 Penfield Rd State College PA 16801-6420 Office: Pa State Univ Dept Geography 302 Walker Bldg University Park PA 16802-5011

LEWIS, PERRY JOSHUA, investment banker; b. San Antonio, Feb. 11, 1938; s. Perry Joshua and Zelime L. L.; m. Memrie Taylor Mosier, May 12, 1962 (div. 1994); children—Perry Joshua, IV, Memrie Fraser. B.A., Princeton U., 1959. Registered rep. Lee Higginson Corp., N.Y.C., 1960-63; comml. project mgr. Parsons & Whittemore, Inc., N.Y.C., 1964-67; sr. v.p., mgr. corp. fin. div. Smith Barney, Harris Upham & Co. Inc., N.Y.C., 1967-79; pres. MacKay-Lewis Inc., N.Y.C., 1980-81; ptnr. Morgan Lewis Githens & Ahn, Conn., N.Y.C., 1982—; bd. dirs. Aon Corp., Chgo., Evergreen Media Corp., ITI Techs., Inc., North St. Paul, Stuart Entertainment, Inc., Gradall Industries, Inc., New Philadelphia, Ohio. With U.S. Army, 1959-60, 61-62. Clubs: Knickerbocker of N.Y., Doubles N.Y., Field (Greenwich, Conn.). Office: Morgan Lewis Githens & Ahn 2 Greenwich Plz Greenwich CT 06830-6353

LEWIS, PETER A., energy consultant; b. Somerville, N.J., Feb. 18, 1938; s. Albert Lincoln and Frances Lavinia (Westervelt) L.; m. Gretchen Louise Gunkel, May 31, 1958; children: Sharon Lynn Lewis Ranson, Jeffrey Scott, Timothy Brian. BSEE, Lehigh U., 1959; MS in Mgmt. Engring., Newark Coll. Engring. (now N.J. Inst. Tech.), 1969. Registered profl. engr., N.J. Engr. Pub. Svc. Electric and Gas Co., Newark, 1963-71, sr. engr., 1971, asst. mgr. R & D, 1971-78, mgr. energy utilization R & D, 1978-88, mgr. R & D planning, 1988-92; mgr. dir. ednl. activities IEEE, Piscataway, N.J., 1992—; cons. Electric Power Rsch. Inst., Palo Alto, Calif. 1973-86, Gas Rsch. Inst., Chgo., 1988-91; chmn. tech. com. Fuel Cell Users Group, Washington, 1979-87; vice chmn. Commn. on Tech. Edn. for N.J., 1987-97. Author: Financing Nuclear Fuel Requirements of Utilities, 1969. Bd. govs. Greater Trenton Symphony Orch., N.J. 1986-89. Capt. USAF, 1959-63. Fellow IEEE (mem. various coms.); mem. Electrochem. Soc., NSPE (rep. to N.J. Inventors Congress and Hall of Fame, chmn. selection com.), Engrs. Club. Avocations: hiking, classical music, tennis, photography. Office: IEEE PO Box 1331 Piscataway NJ 08855-1331

LEWIS, PETER BENJAMIN, insurance company executive; b. Cleve., Nov. 11, 1933; s. Joseph M. and Helen (Rosenfeld) L.; married, June 19, 1955 (div. 1980); children: Ivy, Jonathan, Adam. A.B., Princeton U., 1955. With Progressive Ins. Cos., 1955—; pres., CEO Progressive Casualty Ins. Co., The Progressive Corp., Ohio, 1965—, Mayfield Village, 1965-94; chmn. bd., pres., CEO Progressive Corp., 1993—. Mem. Soc. C.P.C.U. Clubs: Ceve. Racquet, Oakwood, Union. Office: Progressive Corp 6300 Wilson Mills Rd Cleveland OH 44143-2109*

LEWIS, PHILIP, educational and technical consultant; b. Chgo., Oct. 23, 1913; s. Solomon and Fannie (Margolis) L.; m. Geraldine Gisela Lawenda, Sept. 1, 1947; 1 child, Linda Susan. BS, DePaul U., Chgo., 1937, MA, 1939; EdD, Columbia Tchrs. Coll., 1951. Chmn. dept. edn. Chgo. Tchrs. Coll.; also asst. prin., tchr. South Shore High Sch., Chgo., 1940-51; prin. Herman Felsenthal Elementary Sch., Chgo., 1955-57; dir. Bur. Instructional Materials, Chgo. Pub. Schs., 1957-63, Bur. Research Devel. and Spl. Projects, 1963-67; pres. Instructional Dynamics Inc., Chgo., 1967-89, ret., 1989; ednl. and tech. cons., 1991—; nat. cons. TV and instructional techniques, 1955—; ednl. cons. to accrediting bur. Health Edn. Schs., 1971-89; chmn. adv. com. U.S. Office Edn., Title VII, 1964-67. Author: Educational Television Guidebook for Electronics Industries Association, 1961, also numerous articles.; mem. editorial bd. Nation's Schs. and Colls; multimedia tech. editor: Tech. Horizons in Edn; cons.: Jour. Ednl. Tech. and Communications; producer ednl., multimedia, tng. and mental health and human devel. materials. Served to lt. comdr. USNR, 1942-45. Mem. Soc. Programmed and Automated Learning (pres. 1960-65), NEA (v.p. dept. audiovisual instrn., chmn. commn. on tech. standards dept. audiovisual instrn. 1965-85), Nat. Assn. Ednl. Broadcasters, Am. Legion, Council for Ednl. Facilities Planners (editorial adv. bd. 1972-80) Ill. C. of C. (edn. com. 1970-77), Chgo. Assn. Commerce and Industry (chmn. edn. com. 1970-80), Nat. Audio-Visual Assn. (profl. devel. bd. 1969-76, chmn), Chgo. Press Club, Masons, Shriners, Rotary, Phi Delta Kappa. Home: 2 E Oak St Apt 3201 Chicago IL 60611-1216

LEWIS, PHILLIP HAROLD, museum curator; b. Chgo., July 31, 1922; s. Bernard and Sonia (Pimstein) L.; m. Sally Leah Rappaport, Aug. 25, 1949; children—David Bernard, Betty Alice and Emily Ruth (twins). B.F.A., Art Inst. Chgo., 1947; M.A., U. Chgo., 1953, Ph.D., 1966; postgrad. (Fulbright ednl. grant), Australian Nat. U., Canberra, 1953-54. Conducted field research projects on art and soc. of New Ireland, 1953-54, 70, 81; asst. curator primitive art Field Mus. Natural History, Chgo., 1957-59; asso. curator Field Mus. Natural History, 1960, curator, 1961-67, curator primitive art and Melanesian ethnology, 1968-92, ret., 1992, chmn. dept. anthropology, 1975-79, co-chmn. dept., 1980-81, acting chmn. dept., 1987; curator emeritus, 1994—. Served with USAAF, 1942-45. Fellow Royal Anthrop. Inst. Gt. Britain and Ireland, Am. Anthrop. Assn. Home: 1118 Main St Evanston IL 60202-1649 Office: Field Mus Natural History Roosevelt Dr Chicago IL 60605

LEWIS, RALPH JAY, III, management and human resources educator; b. Balt., Sept. 25, 1942; s. Ralph Jay and Ruth Elizabeth (Schmeltz) L. BS in Engring., Northwestern U., 1966; MS in Adminstrn., U. Calif., Irvine, 1968; PhD in Mgmt., UCLA, 1974. Rsch. analyst Chgo. Area Expressway Surveillance Project, 1963-64, Gen. Am. Transp. Co., Chgo., 1965-66; assoc. prof. mgmt. and human resources mgmt. Calif. State U., Long Beach, 1972—; cons. Rand Corp., Santa Monica, Calif., 1966-74, Air Can., Montreal, Que., 1972-73, Los Angeles Times, 1973;. Co-author: Studies in the Quality of LIfe, 1972; author instructional programs, monographs; co-designer freeway traffic control system. Bd. dirs. Project Quest, Los Angeles, 1969-71. Mem. AAAS, APA, The World Future Soc., Soc. of Mayflower Descendants, SAR (Ill. Soc.), Beta Gamma Sigma. Democrat. Office: Calif State U Dept Human Resources Mgmt Long Beach CA 90840

LEWIS, RALPH MILTON, real estate developer; b. Johnstown, Pa., Nov. 9, 1919; s. Morris and Sarah (Galfond) L.; m. Goldy Sarah Kimmel, June 12, 1941; children: Richard Alan, Robert Edward, Roger Gordon, Randall Wayne. AA, Los Angeles City Coll., 1939; BS, UCLA, 1941; postgrad., U. So. Calif., 1945-48. Bar: Calif. 1952. Pvt. practice acctg. Los Angeles, 1945-55, pvt. practice law, 1953-55; founder Lewis Homes, 1957; chmn. bd. Lewis Construction Co., Inc., Upland, Calif., 1959—, Lewis Bldg. Co., Inc., Las Vegas, 1960—, Republic Sales Co. Inc.; dir., v.p. Kimmel Enterprises, Inc., 1959—; mng. partner Lewis Homes of Calif., 1973—, Lewis Homes of Nev., 1972—, Western Properties, Upland, 1972—, Foothill Investment Co., Las Vegas, 1971—, Republic Mgmt. Co., Upland, 1978-86; dir. Gen. Telephone Co. Calif., 1981-86; mem. adv. bd. Inland divsn. Bank of Am.; instr. U. So. Calif., UCLA, L.A. City Coll., 1948-54, Dooley Law Rev. Course, 1953-54; guest lectr. numerous colls., univs. Author: Land Buying Checklist, 1981, 85, 88, 90; contbr. articles to mags., jours. Mem., com. chmn. Calif. Commn. of Housing and Community Devel., 1965-67; mem. Calif. Gov.'s Task Force on the Home Bldg. and Construction Industry, 1967; pres. Bd. of Edn. Citrus Community Coll. Dist., Azusa, Calif., 1969, 73, mem., 1967-73; mem. Citizens Planning Council, Los Angeles County Regional Planning Commn., 1972-73, UCLA Found., Chancellor's Assoc.; mem. dean's council UCLA Grad. Sch. Architecture and Urban Planning; trustee U. Calif. Riverside Found.; bd. dirs. Regional Research Inst. So. Calif., 1983-84; chmn. land use and planning com. Citizens' Adv. Council, Calif. Senate Housing Com., 1983-84; founding mem. Rancho Cucamonga Community Found., 1987-88; donated $5 million to Lewis Ctr. for Regional Policy Studies Grad. Sch. UCLA, 1989, $5 million to the Ralph and Goldy Lewis Hall of Planning and Devel. Sch. Urban and Regional Planning U. So. Calif., 1989; funded Goldy & Ralph Lewis Edn. Ctr. Temple Beth Israel, Pomona, Calif.; land donor to City of Claremont, Calif., City of Rancho Cucamonga, Calif., City of Ontario, Calif.; bd. dirs. Calif. Community Colls., 1992—. Recipient Profl. Achievement commendation Calif. State Assembly, 1977, Humanitarian award NCCJ, 1979, Builder of Year award Bldg. Industry Assn. So. Calif., 1970; named as U. So. Calif.'s 1st Developer in Residence, 1988 at Lusk Ctr. for Real Estate Devel., (with wife Goldy) Entrepreneur of Yr., Inland Empire, 1990, 92, Housing Person of Yr. Nat. Housing Conf., 1990; recipient Good Scout award Old Baldy council Boy Scouts Am., 1984, (with wife) Builder of Yr. award Profl. Builder mag., 1987, Disting. chief exec. officer award Calif. State U., San Bernardino, 1991, Calif. State Legis. recognition Outstanding Leadership in the Bus. World, 1991, Spirit of Life award City of Hope, 1993, Mgmt. Leaders of Yr. award U. Calif., Riverside, 1993; inducted Nat. Housing Ctr.'s Hall of Fame, Washington, 1988; named Builder of Century, U. Calif., Irvine and Sumigarden Group, 1991. Mem. Am. Bar Assn., Calif. Soc. C.P.A.'s, Nat. Assn. Home Builders (dir.), Calif. Bldg. Industry Assn. (dir., chmn. affordable housing task force 1978-80, named to Hall of Fame 1987), Bldg. Industry Assn. So. Calif. (past treas., pres., dir., Bldg. Industry Assn. Medal of Honor, 1986, Builder of Yr. 1988).). Office: Lewis Homes 1156 N Mountain Ave Upland CA 91786-3633

LEWIS, RAMSEY EMANUEL, JR., pianist, composer; b. Chgo., May 27, 1935; s. Ramsey Emanuel and Pauline (Richards) L.; m. Geraldine Taylor, Apr. 7, 1954 (div. Mar. 1989); children—Vita Denise, Ramsey Emanuel III, Marcus Kevin, Dawn, Kendall, Frayne, Robert; m. Janet Tamillow, June 10, 1990. Student, Chgo. Music Coll., 1947-54, U. Ill., 1953-54, De Paul U., 1954-55; DHL (hon.), De Paul U., 1993, U. Ill., Chgo., 1995, DePaul U., Chgo., 1993; ArtsD (hon.), U. Ill., 1995. Mgr. record dept. Hudson-Ross, Inc., Chgo., 1954-56. Organizer Ramsey Lewis Trio, 1956; now solo artist; 1st profl. appearance, Chgo. 1957, appeared N.Y.C., 1958—, San Francisco, 1962, played Randall's Island Jazz Festival, N.Y.C., 1959, Saugatuck (Mich.) Jazz Festival, 1960, Newport (R.I.) Jazz Festival, 1961, 63, numerous jazz concerts at various festivals and univs. since 1961; toured with New Sounds of 1963; appeared in film Save the Children, 1973; recipient Grammy awards for The In Crowd 1965, Hold It Right There 1966, Hang on Sloopy 1973); albums include Another Voyage, 1970, The Piano Player, 1970, Them Changes, 1970, Back To The Roots, 1971, Upendo Ni Pamoja, 1972, Funky Serenity, 1973, Legacy, 1978, Best of Ramsey Lewis, 1981, Salongo, 1976, Sun Goddess, 1974, Tequila Mockingbird, 1977, Ramsey, 1979, Routes, 1980, (with Nancy Wilson) The Two of Us, 1984, Fantasy, 1985, Keys to the City, 1987, A Classic Encounter (with London Philharm. Orch.), 1988, Urban Renewal, 1989, We Meet Again (with Billy Taylor), 1989, The Electric Collection, 1991, Ivory Pyramid, 1992, Sky Island, 1993, Maiden Voyage, 1994, Urban Knights, 1995, Between The Keys, 1996, Urban Knights II, 1997; composer: Sound of Spring, Fantasia for Drums, Look-a-Here, Sound of Christmas; organizer, Rams' L Prodns., Inc., Chgo., 1966, Ramsel Pub. Co., Chgo., 1966, Ivory Pyramid Prodns., Inc., 1995; host weekly jazz TV show, Sta. B.E.T. (cable TV) Ramsey Lewis on Jazz Ctrl., 1990—; host weekly jazz radio show The Ramsey Lewis Show, 1990-97, Sta. WNUA, Chgo., syndicated in various cities throughout the U.S., Legends of Jazz with Ramsey Lewis, 1997—; artistic dir. Jazz series at Ravinia Festival Chgo., 1993—; numerous TV appearances; lectr. various univs.; performance at White House, 1995. Named Person of Week ABC Nightly News, 1995; elected laureate Lincoln Acad., Springfield, Ill., 1997. Address: 180 N La Salle St Ste 2200 Chicago IL 60601-2702

LEWIS, RANDOLPH VANCE, molecular biologist, researcher; b. Powell, Wyo., Apr. 8, 1950; s. William (Jack) Fredrick and Evelyn Jean (Vonburg) L.; m. Lorrie Dale Emery, May 27, 1972; children: Brian, Daryl (dec.), Karren. BS in Chemistry, Calif. Inst. Tech., 1972; MS in Chemistry, U. Calif., San Diego, 1974; PhD in Chemistry, U. Calif., 1978. Postdoctoral fellow Roche Inst. Molecular Biology, Nutley, N.J., 1978-80; asst. prof. molecular biology U. Wyo., Laramie, 1980-84, assoc. prof., 1984-89, head dept., 1986-91, prof., 1989—; dir. NSF EPSCOR Program, 1990—; cons. NIH, Bethesda, Md., 1985-91, Hoffmann-LaRoche, Nutley, N.J., 1990-93, DuPont, Wilmington,Del., 1990-94, Protein Polymer Techs., San Diego, 1988-94; pres. Wyobigen, Laramie, Wyo., 1994—. Author chpts. to books; contbr. articles to profl. jours. Mem. Jr. Livestock Sale Com., Laramie,

1991—; pres. Albany County 4-H Coun., Laramie, 1994—. Sloan Found. fellow, 1985; recipient Research Career Devel. award NIH, 1985, Jr. Faculty award Am. Cancer Soc., 1985, Burlington-North Faculty award U. Wyo., 1986. Mem. Am. Chem. Soc., Am. Soc. Biochemists and Molecular Biologists, N.Y. Acad. Scis., Protein Soc. Republican. Methodist. Achievements include discovery of opioid peptide precursor; sequencing of first spider silk protein genes; five products licenses; patents pending. Avocations: fly fishing, bird hunting. Home: 1948 Howe Rd Laramie WY 82070-6885 Office: U Wyo PO Box 3944 Laramie WY 82071-3944

LEWIS, RICHARD, actor, comedian; b. Bklyn., June 29, 1948; s. Bill and Blanche L. Student, Ohio State U., 1970. Head copywriter N.J. advt. agency, 1970-71; appearances include Greenwich Village club, The Improv, The Tonight Show. Co-writer: (TV special) Diary of a Young Comic; actor (TV series) Harry, 1987, King of the Building, 1987, Anything But Love, 1990-92, Daddy Dearest, 1993, over 40 appearances on Late Night With David Letterman, 1982; appeared in (cable special) I'm In Pain, 1985, I'm Exhausted, 1988 (ACE award nomination 1988), All-Star Toast to the Improv, 1988, I'm Doomed, 1990; films include The Wrong Guys, 1988, That's Adequate, 1989, Once Upon a Crime, 1992, Robin Hood: Men in Tights, 1993, Wagons East, 1994, Leaving Las Vegas, 1995, Drunks, 1995, Hugo Pool, 1997; A Weekend in the Country, 1996 (TV Movie). Office: 1999 Ave Of Stars Ste 2850 Los Angeles CA 90067-6082*

LEWIS, RICHARD, SR., securities broker, consultant; b. Macon, Ga., Jan. 18, 1930; s. William Chapman and Florida (Zelius) L.; m. Iris Joy Clements, Sept. 10, 1949; children: Richard Jr., Linda Lee. Cert. investments securities broker, pistol and rifle instr. State trooper Fla. Hwy. Patrol, various cities, 1951-72; pres. Gateway Shooters Supply, Inc., Jacksonville, Fla., 1972-82; broker Global Investments Securities Inc., Miami, 1985-86, Investacorp, Inc., Miami Lakes, Fla., 1986-89. Lobbyist Fla. Assn. of State Troopers, Tallahassee, 1988-89. With U.S. Army, 1952-54. Recipient cert. of appreciation, State of Fla., Tallahassee, 1972; Demolay Cross of Honor, Internat. Coun., Kansas City, Mo., 1973; cert. of commendation, State of Fla., 1972. Mem. NRA (life), Fla. Assn. State Troopers (legis. chmn. retirees 1987), V.F.W., Jacksonville Pistol Club (pres. 1968-72), Marion Dunn Masonic Lodge, Elks, Sons Am. Revolution, Sons Confederate Vets., Mil. Order Stars and Bars, Fraternal Order Police, Scottish Rite, Nobles Mystic Shrine (Ambassador-at-large). Republican. Methodist. Avocations: fishing, photography, competitive pistol shooting. Home: 461 High Meadow Tr Cleveland GA 30528

LEWIS, RICHARD ALLAN, financial planner, business consultant; b. Pitts., Feb. 25, 1952; s. Harry C. and Vera E. (Williams) L. BS in Econs., Allegheny Coll., 1974; MBA in Fin., U. Pitts., 1978. CFP. Trainee Mellon Bank, Pitts., 1974-75, various positions with, 1975-84, v.p. N.Am. ops., 1984-86; pres., COO WorkWell, Pitts., 1987-89; sr. fin. planner The Acacia Group, Pitts., 1989—. Mem. exec. com., bd. dirs. Arthritis Found., 1989—. Mem. Nat. Automated Clearing House Assn. (bd. dirs. 1981-86), Tri-State Automated Clearing House Assn. (pres. 1984-86, treas. 1980-83, v.p. 1984-85), Masons, Blue Lodge, Phi Beta Kappa, Delta Tau Delta (pres. house corp. 1976—). Republican. Methodist. Avocations: skiing, jogging, travel, gourmet cooking. Home: 106 Fairway Landings Dr Canonsburg PA 15317-9567 Office: Acacia Group Acacia Bldg Pittsburgh PA 15220

LEWIS, RICHARD HARLOW, urologist; b. San Diego, May 14, 1951; s. Charles William Jr. and Gene (Harlow) L.; m. Deanna Elma Boggs, March 14, 1950; children: Richard Harlow Jr., Sara-Grace Dean. BS, Guilford Coll., 1973; MD, Duke U., 1977. Intern Bethesda (Md.) Naval Hosp., 1977-78, residence, 1978-82, chief urology, 1982-85; pvt. practice McIver Clinic, Jacksonville, Fla., 1985—; mng. ptnr. McIver Clinic divsn. Urology Clinic of Fla., Jacksonville, 1994—. Mem. Christian Coalition, Duval County, Fla., 1987—; Rep. precinct rep., Duval County, 1987-90. Lt. comdr. USNR, 1973-85. Winner, Karl Storz Endoscope Photography Contest Karl Storz Corp., 1983. Fellow ACS, Am. Soc. Laser Medicine Surgery, Am. Bd. Laser Surgery, S.E. Surg. Soc.; mem. Am. Urol. Assn. Avocations: tennis, computers, wine, travel. Home: 4900 Arapahoe Ave Jacksonville FL 32210-8336 Office: McIver Clinic 710 Lomax St Jacksonville FL 32204-4004

LEWIS, RICHARD KNOX, city official; b. Auburn, N.Y., June 25, 1946; s. Harry C. and Jean E. (Knox) L.; m. Barbara, Dec. 28, 1968; children: Wendy, Adam. AA, Auburn Community Coll., 1968; BA, U. Miss., 1970, MA, 1972. Project planner Mo. Dept. Community Affairs, Jefferson City, Mo., 1971-73; planning dir. City of Ocala, Fla., 1973-79; asst. city mgr., airport mgr. City of Ocala, 1979-96; dep. city mgr., airport mgr. City of Ocala, Fla., 1996—. Past pres. Vol. Svc. Bur. Bd., Ocala, 1991, United Way of Marion County, Ocala, 1984-85, past campaign chmn., 1981-82; chmn. United Way Fla., 1995-96; bd. dirs. Ocala Civic Theatre. Recipient Community Svc. award Marion County Jaycees, 1986. Mem. Am. Planning Assn., Am. Inst. Cert. Planners, Assn. Urban Planners, Fla. Airport Mgrs. Assn. (bd. dirs.), Am. Assn. Airport Execs., Statewide Continuing Fla. Divsn. Sys. Plan Com. Episcopalian. Office: City of Ocala 151 SE Osceola Ave Ocala FL 34471-2148

LEWIS, RICHARD M., lawyer; b. Gallipolis, Ohio, Dec. 11, 1957; s. Denver E. and Mary Esther (Mobley) L.; m. Cheryl F. Hickman (div.); m. Diane K. Williams, Apr. 26, 1986. BA in Polit. Sci., Ohio State U., 1979; JD, Capital U., 1982. Bar: Ohio 1982, U.S. Dist. Ct. (so. dist.) Ohio 1984, U.S. Supreme Ct. 1986; cert. civil trial advocacy Nat. Bd. Trial Advocacy. Pvt. practice law, 1982-83; assoc. Mary Bone Kunze, Jackson, Ohio, 1983-85; pvt. practice law Jackson, 1985-86; ptnr. Ochsenbein, Cole & Lewis, Jackson, 1986-96, Cole & Lewis, Jackson, 1996—; lectr. in field; expert witness. Mem. ABA, ATLA, Ohio State Bar Assn., Jackson County Bar Assn. (past pres.), Ohio Acad. Trial Lawyers (bd. trustees 1993-94, 94-95, 95-96, 96-97, 97—, budget com. 1993-94, supreme ct. screening com. 1994, vice-chairperson family law com. 1994-95, chairperson-elect family law com. 1995—, chairperson family law com. 1995-96, exec. com., chair mem. com. 1996-97, co-chair regional CLE seminars 1997). Home: 603 Reservoir Rd Jackson OH 45640-8714 Office: Cole and Lewis 295 Pearl St Jackson OH 45640-1748

LEWIS, RICHARD PHELPS, physician, educator; b. Portland, Oreg., Oct. 26, 1936; s. Howard Phelps and Wava Irene (Brown) L.; m. Penny A. Brown, Oct. 12, 1982; children: richard Phelps, Heather Brown. BA, Yale U., 1957; MD, U. Oreg., 1961. Intern Peter Bent Brigham Hosp., Boston, 1961-62, resident, 1962-63; Howard Irwin fellow in cardiology U. Oreg., Portland, 1963-65; sr. resident Stanford U., 1965-66, instr. dept. medicine, 1968-69; asst. chief cardiology Madigan Gen. Hosp., Tacoma, 1966-68; asst. prof. medicine div. cardiology Ohio State U., 1969-71, assoc. prof., 1971-75, prof., 1975—, dir. Divsn. Cardiology, 1972-86, dir., 1972-86, assoc. chmn. for hosp. and clin. affairs, 1980-86; mem. cardiovascular sect. Am. Bd. Internal Medicine, 1981-87, critical care medicine, 1988-92. Contbr. articles to profl. jours. Served with M.C. U.S. Army, 1966-68, col. res. Decorated Army Commendation medal. Fellow ACP (gov. Ohio chpt. 1976-80, chmn. MKSAP cardiovascular sect. 1989-82), Am. Heart Assn. (coun. on clin. cardiology), Am. Coll. Cardiology (Ohio gov. 1988-91, chmn. bd. govs. 1990-91, trustee 1991—, chmn. self assessment program, v.p. 1994-95, pres.-elect 1995-96, pres. 1996-97), Am. Clin. and Climatological Assn.; mem. Am. Fedn. Clin. Rsch., Ctrl. Soc. Clin. Rsch., Laennec Soc., Am. Heart Assn., Assn. U. Cardiologists, Alpha Omega Alpha. Republican. Episcopalian. Home: 5088 Stratford Ave Powell OH 43065-8771 Office: 466 W 10th Ave Columbus OH 43210-1240

LEWIS, RICHARD STANLEY, author, former editor; b. Pitts., Jan. 8, 1916; s. S. Morton and Mary L. (Lefstein) L.; m. Louise G. Silberstein, June 8, 1938; children: Jonathan, David. B.A., Pa. State U., 1937. Reporter Cleve. Press, 1937-38; rewrite man, drama critic Indpls. Times, 1938-43, reporter, city editor, 1946-49; reporter St. Louis Star-Times, 1949-51; mem. staff Chgo. Sun-Times, 1951-68, sci. editor, 1967-68; mng. editor Bull. Atomic Scientists, Chgo., 1968-70; editor Bull. Atomic Scientists, 1971-74; writing cons. earth sci. curriculum project NSF, summers 1964-65. Author: The Other Child, 1951, (rev. edit, 1960), A Continent for Science, 1965, Appointment on The Moon, 1968, rev. edit., 1969, The Nuclear Power Rebellion, 1972, The Voyages of Apollo, 1974, From Vinland to Mars: 1000 Years of Exploration, 1976, The Other Child Grows Up, 1977, The Voyages of Columbia, 1984, Challenger: The Final Voyage, 1987, Space in the 21st Century, 1990; prin. author: The New Illustrated Encyclopedia of Space Exploration; editor: Man on the Moon, 1969, Alamogordo Plus 25 Years, 1970, Frozen Future, 1972, The Energy Crisis, 1972, The Environmental Revolution, 1973. Mem. Indialantic Town Council, 1980-82, apptd. dep. mayor, 1980. Served with AUS, 1943-46, ETO. Fellow Brit. Interplanetary Soc. (London); Mem. Authors Guild, Authors League Am. Club: Nat. Press (Washington); Canaveral Press (Cocoa Beach, Fla.) (pres. 1985). Home: 1401 S Magnolia Ave Indialantic FL 32903-3510

LEWIS, RICHARD WARREN, advertising executive; b. N.Y.C., June 8, 1951; s. Stanley and Janet (Sweet) L.; m. Isabel Ellen Abrams, Mar. 19, 1977; children: Ariane, Amanda, Sam. BA, Hofstra U., 1973; MBA, NYU, 1978. Advt. exec., pres. GGK New York, 1978-84; mgmt. supr. Lois/GGK, N.Y.C., 1985-86; exec. v.p., mgmt. supr. TBWA Chiat/Day, N.Y.C., 1987—. Author: Absolutbook: The Absolut Vodka Advertising Story, 1996. Coach Dobbs Ferry (N.Y.) Baseball League, 1990-91. Recipient Clio award, 1989, Andy award Advt. Club N.Y., 1989, Kelly award Mag. Pubs. Am., 1989. Mem. Am. Advt. Fedn. (speaker). Home: 256 Clinton Ave Dobbs Ferry NY 10522-3007 Office: TBWA Advt Inc 180 Maiden Ln New York NY 10038-4925

LEWIS, RITA HOFFMAN, plastic products manufacturing company executive; b. Phila., Aug. 6, 1947; d. Robert John and Helen Anna (Dugan) Hoffman; 1 child, Stephanie Blake. Student Jefferson Med. Coll. Sch. Nursing, 1965-67, Gloucester County Coll., 1993—; Gen. mgr. Sheets & Co., Inc. (now Flower World, Inc.), Woodbury, N.J., 1968-72; dir., exec. v.p., treas. Hoffman Precision Plastics, Inc., Blackwood, N.J., 1973—; ptnr. Timber Assocs.; commr. N.J. Expressway Authority, 1990—, sec., 1990-91, treas., 1991—, chmn. pers., 1991—; apptd. mem. N.J. Senate Forum on Budget and Revenue Alternatives, 1991; guest speaker various civic groups, 1974; poetry editor SPOTLIGHTER Innovative Singles Mag. Author: That Part of Me I Never Really Meant to Share, 1979; In Retrospect: Caught Between Running and Loving; columnist Innovative Singles mag., 1989—. Mem. Com. for Citizens of Glen Oaks (N.J.), 1979—, Gloucester Twp. Econ. Devel. Com., 1981—, Gloucester Twp. Day Scholarship Com., 1984—; mem. adv. coun. Gloucester Twp. Econ. Adv. Coun., 1995—; chairperson Gloucester Twp. Day Scholarship Found., 1985-96; bd. dirs. Diane Hull Dance Co. Recipient Winning Edge award, 1982, Mayor's award for Womens' Achievement, 1987, Outstanding Cmty. Svc. award Mayor, Coun. and Com., 1987, Don L. Stackhouse Achievement award, 1996. Mem. NAFE, Sales Assn. Chem. Industry, Blackwood Businessmen's Assn., Soc. Plastic Engrs. Roman Catholic.

LEWIS, ROBERT, periodical editor, journalist; b. Montreal, Que., Can., Aug. 19, 1943; s. Leon R. and Margaret (Horan) L.; m. Sara Lewis, May 27, 1967; children: Christopher Robert, Timothy O'Neill. BA, Loyola Coll., 1964. Gen. reporter Montreal Star, 1964-65, Ottawa corr., 1965-66; chief Montreal bur. Time mag., 1967-68, Ottawa corr., 1968-70, Boston corr., 1970-72, chief Toronto bur., 1972-74; chief Ottawa bur. Maclean's Mag., 1975-82, mng. editor, 1982-93, editor, 1993—. Home: 31 Brooke Ave, Toronto, ON Canada M5M 2J5 Office: Maclean's Mag, 777 Bay St, Toronto, ON Canada M5W 1A7

LEWIS, ROBERT DAVID, ophthalmologist, educator; b. Thomasville, Ga., Aug. 27, 1948; s. Ralph N. and E. Margaret (Klaus) L. BS, St. Louis Coll. Pharmacy, 1971; MD, St. Louis U., 1975. Diplomate Am. Bd. Ophthalmology; registered pharmacist. Intern, Cardinal Glennon Hosp. Children, St. Louis, 1975-76; resident St. Louis U., 1976-79; practice medicine specializing in ophthalmology, St. Louis, 1979—; dir. pediatric ophthalmology St. Louis U., 1980-82, 85, asst. prof., 1980-88, assoc. prof., 1988—; pres. St. Louis Ophthalmological Soc., 1991-92; dir. pediatric ophthalmology Cardinal Glennon Hosp. for Children, St. Louis, 1980-82, 85; mem. adv. bd. Delta Gamma Found. for Visually Handicapped Children. Recipient St. Louis U. Award for Teaching, 1982. Fellow ACS; mem. AMA, Mo. Med. Assn., St. Louis Med. Soc., Am. Acad. Ophthalmology, Contact Lens Assn. Ophthalmology, Internat. Assn. Ocular Surgeons, Am. Intraocular Implant Soc., Am. Bd. Club. (pres. 1991-92). Office: 12700 Southfork Rd Ste 205 Saint Louis MO 63128-3201 also: 3915 Watson Rd Saint Louis MO 63109-1251

LEWIS, ROBERT DAVID GILMORE, editor; b. Chgo., Jan. 16, 1932; s. James Lee and Betty (Ryden) L.; m. Georgia Demopoulos, Aug. 4, 1956 (div. July 1988); children: Peter, Sarah, Mary, John, Elizabeth, Daniel, Susan; m. Jacqueline Mc Gregor, July 15, 1988. BA, Mich. State U., 1955. Reporter, city editor Galesburg (Ill.) Register-Mail, 1955-59; reporter, bus. editor Kalamazoo Gazette, 1960-64; state capitol corres. Booth Newspapers, Lansing, Mich., 1964-66; Washington corres. Booth Newspapers, Washington, 1966-87, Newhouse Newspapers, Washington, 1987-91; sr. editor Am. Assn. Retired Persons Bull., Washington, 1991—; bd. vis. Les Aspin Ctr. for Govt., Washington, Marquette U., 1996—. Mem. Soc. Profl. Journalists (chmn. freedom info. com. 1978-83, sec.-treas., pres.-elect then pres., 1983-86, Wells Meml. Key award 1980), White House Corres. Assn., Nat. Press Club (chmn. bd. govs. 1975-77), Sigma Delta Chi Found. (bd. dirs. 1986-88). Avocations: antique furniture collecting, fishing. Home: 301 Maryland Ave NE Washington DC 20002-5711 Office: AARP Bulletin 601 E St NW Washington DC 20049-0001

LEWIS, ROBERT EDWIN, JR., pathology immunology educator, researcher; b. Meridian, Miss., Mar. 11, 1947. BA in Biology and Chemistry, U. Miss., 1969, MS in Microbiology, 1973, PhD in Pathology, 1976; specialty tng., Barnes Hosp., U. Miami Med. Ctr., U. Tenn. Ctr. for Health Scis., City of Memphis Hosps., St. Jude Children's Research Hosp. Instr. pathology, anesthesiology U. Miss. Med. Ctr., Jackson, 1976-77, asst. prof. pathology, 1977-84, asst. prof. anesthesiology, 1977-85, asst. dir. clin. immnuopathology lab., 1978-81, assoc. dir. tissue typing lab., 1980-84, dir. paternity testing lab., 1981—, assoc. dir. clin. immunopathology lab., 1981-84, asst. prof. nurse anesthesiology, 1981-85, assoc. prof. pathology, 1984-91, prof., 1991—, co-dir. clin. immunology, tissue typing lab., 1984—, mem. grad. council, 1981—, prof., 1991—. Co-author: Illustrated Dictionary of Immunology, 1995; editor: (with J.M. Cruse) Concepts in Immunopathology, Vols. 1-8, 1985-91, The Year in Immunology-1984-85, 1985, The Year in Immunology-1986-87, 1987, The Year in Immunology-1988, 1989, The Year in Immunology-1989-90, 1990, Progress in Experimental Tumor Research, Vol. 32, 1987, Contributions to Microbiology and Immunology, Vol. 8, 1986, Vol. 9, 1987, Vol. 10, 1989, Vol. 11, 1989, The Year in Immunopathology, 1987, Complement Profiles, Vol. 1, 1992; sr. editor Pathology and Immunopathology Research, 1982-90, Immunologic Research, 1981—, Transgenics, 1993; series editor Concepts in Immunopathology, The Year in Immunology, Contributions to Microbiology and Immunology; vol. editor Progress in Experimental Tumor Research; immunology editor Dorland's Illustrated Medical Dictionary, 26th and 27th edits.; dep. editor-in-chief Pathobiology, 1990—; contbr. chpts. to books. Am. Cancer Soc. grantee, NIH grantee, Wilson Found. grantee, 1990-95. Fellow Royal Soc. Health; mem. AAAS, Am. Assn. Pathologists, Am. Assn. Immunologists, Clin. Immunology Soc., Can. Soc. Immunology, Reticuloendothelial Soc., Am. Soc. Microbiology, Am. Soc. Histocompatibility and Immunogenetics (co-chmn. publs. com., co-chmn. 1987-95), Exptl. Biology and Medicine, N.Y. Acad. Scis., Miss. Acad. Scis., Sigma Xi. Office: U Miss Med Ctr Pathology Dept 2500 N State St Jackson MS 39216-4500

LEWIS, ROBERT ENZER, lexicographer, educator; b. Windber, Pa., Aug. 12, 1934; s. Robert Enzer and Katharine Torrence (Blair) L.; m. Julie Fatt Cureton, May 14, 1977; children: Perrin Lewis Rubin, Torrence Evans Lewis; stepchildren: Sarah Cureton Kaufman, James S. Cureton. BA, Princeton U., 1959; MA, U. Pa., 1962, PhD, 1964. Tchr. English Mercersburg (Pa.) Acad., 1959-60; teaching fellow U. Pa., Phila., 1961-63; lectr. Ind. U., Bloomington, 1963-64, asst. prof., 1964-68, assoc. prof., 1968-75, prof. English, 1975-82; prof. English U. Mich., Ann Arbor, 1982—. Author: (with A. McIntosh) Descriptive Guide to the Manuscripts of the Prick of Conscience, 1982, (with others) Index of Printed Middle English Prose, 1985; editor: De Miseria Condicionis Humane (Lotario dei Segni), 1978; co-editor: Middle English Dictionary, 1982-83, editor-in-chief: vols. 8, 9, 10, 11, 1983—; gen. editor: Chaucer Libr., 1970—, chmn. editl. com., 1978-89; mem. editl. bd. New Oxford English Dictionary, 1984—. Bd. regents Mercersburg Acad., 1975-87. U.S. Army, 1954-56. Vis. rsch. fellow Inst. Advanced Studies in the Humanities, U. Edinburgh, 1973-74; Am. Coun. Learned Socs. fellow, 1979-80. Mem. Medieval Acad. Am. (mem. publs. com. 1987-92), Dictionary Soc. N.Am., New Chaucer Soc. Episcopalian. Office: Middle English Dictionary 555 S Forest Ave Ann Arbor MI 48104-2531

LEWIS, ROBERT KAY, JR., fundraising executive; b. Danville, Ky., Aug. 10, 1935; s. Robert K. and Mona (Hyden) L.; m. Wendy Gardiner, June 18, 1960; children: Mary Elizabeth, Mona Hyden, Robert K. III. BA, Ctr. Coll., Danville, 1957; MS, George Washington U., 1972. Advanced through ranks to lt. U.S. Navy, 1958-63; alumni/annual giving dir. Ctr. Coll., 1963-67; served to capt. U.S. Navy, 1967-81; alumni/pub. affairs dir. Ctr. Coll., 1981-83; pub. affairs dir. Va. Tech., Blacksburg, 1983-87; sr. v.p. Host Comm., Lexington, 1987-89; pres. Ky. C. of C., Frankfort, 1990, Global Advancement, Lexington, Ky., 1991—. Trustee Severn Sch., Severna Park, Md., 1979-83; bd. visitors McCallie Sch., Chattanooga, 1983-86; bd. dirs. Ky. Advocates for Higher Edn., Lexington, 1990—. Mem. Nat. Soc. Fund Raising Execs. (bd. dirs. Lexington chpt. 1991—), Henry Clay Found. (bd. dirs. Lexington, 1994—), Nat. Press Club, Coun. Advancement and Support of Edn. (Ky. bd. dirs. 1991—), Lexington Rotary Endowment (bd. dirs. 1996—). Presbyterian. Home: Forest Hill Farm 2667 Lexington Rd Danville KY 40422 Office: Global Advancement 333 W Vine St Ste 300 Lexington KY 40507-1626

LEWIS, ROBERT LAWRENCE, lawyer, educator; b. N.Y.C., Sept. 25, 1919; s. Isador and Sadie (Holzinger) L.; m. Frieda Friedman, Nov. 24, 1940 (dec. 1961); children—Brian S., Paul E., David N.; m. Joanne Marcia Waxman, June 16, 1963; children—Pavia S., Eraclea S. A.B., Hamilton Coll., 1940; LL.B., Case Western Res. U., 1948. With firm Ulmer & Berne, Cleve., 1948-64, ptnr., 1956-64; ret., 1964; prof. law, dir. grad. div. Cleve.-Marshall Law Sch. (now Cleve. State U.), 1948-53; bd. dirs. Banner Industries, Inc., Cleve.; scholar-in-residence, prof. classics Cuyahoga C.C.; adj. prof. nonprofit governance Case Western Res. U., Cleve. Author: Five Angry Women, 1990, Agatharcus, 1993. Cons., evaluator North Central Assn. Colls. and Schs., Middle States Assn. Mem. Cleve. Area Arts Council, 1971-73; pres. Fairmount Center for Creative and Performing Arts, 1973-75; trustee, chmn. bd. Cuyahoga Community Coll.; trustee Cuyahoga Community Coll. Found., Playhouse Sq. Found., Cleve., Cleve. Commn. Higher Edn., Lake Erie Coll., Council for Interinstnl. Leadership, Pace Assn., New Orgn. for Visual Arts; bd. dirs. Assn. Governing Bds. Univs. and Colls.; bd. advisers Cleve. Ballet; trustee, v.p. New Cleve. Opera Co. Served to 1st lt., arty. and ordnance corps AUS, 1942-46, NATOUSA. Decorated Legion of Merit, Purple Heart. Mem. Exec. Order Ohio Commodore, Phi Beta Kappa. Home: 2425 N Park Blvd Apt 4 Cleveland OH 44106-3154 Office: 900 Bond Ct Bldg Cleveland OH 44114 *There is neither a standard nor a uniform set of qualities which best fits one to be a member of society, and anyone who contends to the contrary, may be equated with the infamous and mythical Procrustes. I for one prefer the preservation of individuality. No one of us should be fitted to the bed of Procrustes. I prefer that we shall all survive; and each of us shall then be the richer for the survival of the other.*

LEWIS, ROBERT LEE, lawyer; b. Oxford, Miss., Feb. 26, 1944; s. Ernest Elmo and Johnice Georgia (Thirkield) L.; children: Yolanda Sherice, Robert Lee Jr., Dion Terrell, Viron Lamar, William Lovell. BA, Ind. U., 1970, JD, 1973; M in Pub. Service, West Ky. U., 1980. Bar: Ind. 1973, Ky. 1979, U.S. Ct. Claims, U.S. Ct. Internat. Trade, U.S. Tax Ct., U.S. Ct. Mil. Appeals, U.S. Ct. Appeals (fed. cir.), U.S. Supreme Ct. Sole practice Evansville, Ind., 1973-75, Gary, Ind., 1980—; atty., army officer U.S. Army, Ft. Knox, Ky., 1975-78; appellate referee Ind. Employment Security Div., Indpls., 1978-80. Mem. adv. com. Vincennes (Ind.) U., 1983—; bd. dirs. Opportunities Industrialization Ctr., Evansville, 1973-75. Served to sgt. JAGC, USMC, 1962-66, Vietnam, sgt. U.S. Army, 1975-78, lt. col. USAR. Named Ky. Col. Mem. ABA, Ind. Bar Assn., Ky. Bar Assn., Nat. Bar Assn., Ind. Bd. Realtors, Ind. U. Alumni Assn., Phi Alpha Delta. Methodist. Home and Office: 2148 W 11th Ave Gary IN 46404-2306

LEWIS, ROGER KUTNOW, architect, educator, author; b. Houston, Jan. 9, 1941; s. Nathan D. and Betty (Kutnow) L.; m. Eleanor Draper Roberts, June 24, 1967; 1 child, Kevin Michael. BArch, MIT, 1964, MArch, 1967. Registered architect, D.C., Va., Md. Vol. architect Peace Corps, Nabeul, Tunisia, 1964-66; designer Wilkes & Faulkner, Washington, 1967-68; ptnr. Chavarria/Lewis Assocs., Washington, 1968-71; prin. Roger K. Lewis AIA & Assocs., Washington, 1971-80; pres. Pecla Corp., Washington, 1971-81; ptnr. Chesapeake Design Group, Balt., 1980-81; prin. Roger K. Lewis FAIA, Architect & Planner, Washington, 1981—; prof. U. Md. Sch. Arch., 1968—; mem. D.C. Com. on Design Arts, Washington, 1988-92. Author: Architect? A Candid Guide to the Profession, 1985, Shaping the City, 1987; co-author Growth Management Handbook, 1989; author articles in jours.and periodicals, chpts. in books, encys.; columnist The Washington Post, 1984—. Recipient Fed. Design Achievement award Nat. Endowment for the Arts, Washington, 1988, numerous awards Am. Planning Assn., AAUW, 1985—. Fellow AIA (numerous design awards 1973—); mem. Washington Area Architecture Group (co-founder), Faberge Arts Found. (bd. advs.), Cosmos Club, Lambda Alpha. Home: 5034 1/2 Dana Pl NW Washington DC 20016-3441 Office: Univ Md Sch of Architecture College Park MD 20742

LEWIS, RON, congressman; b. Greenup County, Ky., Sept. 14, 1946; m. Kayi Gambill, 1966; children: Ronald Brent, Allison Faye. Student, Morehead State U.; BA in History and Polit. Sci., U. Ky., 1969; MA in Higher Edn., Morehead State U., 1981; student, USN Officer Candidate Sch. Ordained to ministry Bapt. Ch. With Ky. Hwy. Dept., Ea. State Hosp.; with sales various cos.; tchr. Watterson Coll., 1980-85; pastor White Mills Bapt. Ch.; owner small bus. Elizabethtown, Ky.; mem. 103d-104th Congresses from 2d Ky. Dist., 1994—; mem. mil. procurement and mil. pers. subcoms., nat. security com., mem. risk mgmt. and splty. crops and resource conservation, rsch. and forestry subcoms., agr. com. Past pres. Hardin and Larue County Jail Ministry. Named Guardian of Srs.' Rights, Tax Fairness Srs.; honoree U.S. Term Limits, League Pvt. Property Rights, Coun. Citizens Against Govt. Waste, Nat. Fed. Ind. Bus. Mem. Severus Valley Ministerial Assn., Elizabethtown C. of C. Office: US Ho of Reps 223 Cannon Bldg Ofc Bld Washington DC 20515-1702

LEWIS, RONALD CHAPMAN, record company executive; b. Louisville, Aug. 20, 1950; s. William June and Mildres A. (Lewis) Miller; m. Laquetta W. Lewis; 1 child, Keith. A. in Music, Jeff Community Coll., Louisville, 1975. Pres. Mr. Wonderful Prodns., Inc., Louisville, 1984—, Louisville Assn. Music Performers, 1987—. Served with USN, 1969-71. Home and Office: Mr Wonderful Prodns Inc 1730 Kennedy Rd Louisville KY 40216-5110

LEWIS, ROY ROOSEVELT, physicist; b. Richmond, Va., Mar. 4, 1935; s. Jesse NMN and Elizabeth (Lewis) L.; m. Debra Blondell, Sept. 21, 1968 (div. Aug. 1974); 1 child, Roy Jr.; m. Linda Eleanor, Dec. 19, 1985. BS, Va. Union U., Richmond, 1958; MS, Howard U., 1962, UCLA, 1969; PhD, UCLA, 1972. Mem. tech. staff Hughes Rsch. Lab., Malibu, Calif., 1972-75, Aerospace Corp., El Segundo, Calif., 1977-81, TRW, Redondo Beach, Calif., 1981-82; dir. minority engring. Calif. State U., Long Beach, 1982-83; assoc. prof. Calif. State U., 1982-86, Calif. State Polytech. U., Pomona, Calif., 1986-89; faculty fellow Jet Propulsion Lab. Cal. Inst. Tech., Pasadena, Calif., 1987-89; mem. tech. staff Jet Propulsion Lab. Cal. Inst. Tech., 1989-93; pres. Roy Lewis & Assocs., a sci. cons. firm, Inglewood, Calif., 1993—. Author: LewLearns, Science Lessons For Children, 1977; contbr. articles to profl. jours. Mem. Am. Soc. Engring. Edn., Nat. Soc. Black Physicists, L.A. Coun. Black Engrs., IEEE, Inglewood Dem. Club, Sigma Xi, Alpha Phi Alpha, Sigma Phi Sigma. Episcopalian. Home: 1401 Overhill Dr Inglewood CA 90302-1346

LEWIS, RUSSELL CARL, JR., family nurse practitioner; b. Charlotte, N.C., Nov. 8, 1946. AS, Cen. Piedmont Community Coll., Charlotte, 1972; cert. family nurse practitioner, U. N.C., 1976. Cert. BCLS, ACLS. Adminstr., healthcare provider, owner Downtown Med. Ctr., Charlotte; staff nurse, mem. emergency room computer com. Carolinas Med. Ctr., Charlotte; prin. in design of downtown med. ctr. With USNR, 1964-70.

LEWIS, RUSSELL T., newspaper publishing executive. Pres., gen. mgr. The N.Y. Times, N.Y.C., 1993—, pres., COO. Office: NY Times 229 W 43rd St New York NY 10036-3913*

LEWIS, SAMUEL WINFIELD, retired government official, former ambassador; b. Houston, Oct. 1, 1930; s. Samuel Winfield and Sue Roselle (Hurley) L.; m. Sallie Kate Smoot, June 20, 1953; children: Pamela Gracelle, Richard Winfield. BA magna cum laude, Yale U., 1952; MA, Johns Hopkins U., 1954; PhD (hon.), Tel Aviv U., 1985, Hebrew U. Jerusalem, 1985, Weizman Inst. Sci., 1985; DHL (hon.), Hebrew Union Coll., 1986, Balt. Hebrew U., 1988; LLD (hon.), Salem-Teikyo U., 1991. Exec. asst. Am. Trucking Assn., Washington., 1953-54; fgn. svc. officer Dept. State, Washington, 1954-85; consular officer Naples, Italy, 1954-55; consul Florence, Italy, 1955-59; officer-in-charge Italian affairs Washington, 1959-61, spl. asst. to undersec. state, 1961, spl. asst. to spl. rep. of pres., 1961-63; dep. asst. dir. US AID Mission to Brazil, Rio de Janeiro, 1964-65; exec. officer embassy, Rio de Janeiro, 1965-67; dep. dir. Office Brazil Affairs, Washington, 1967-68; sr. staff mem. for Latin Am. Affairs Nat. Security Council, White House, Washington, 1968-69; spl. asst. for policy planning Bur. Inter-Am. Affairs, Washington, 1969; spl. asst. to dir. gen. Fgn. Svc., 1970-71; dep. chief mission and counselor embassy Kabul, Afghanistan, 1971-74; dep. dir. policy planning staff Dept. State, 1974-75, asst. sec. state for internat. orgn., 1975-77; U.S. ambassador to Israel, 1977-85; lectr., diplomat-in-residence Johns Hopkins Fgn. Policy Inst., Washington, 1985-86; pres. U.S. Inst. of Peace, Washington, 1987-93; dir. policy planning staff U.S. Dept. State, Washington, 1993-94; cons. U.S. Dept. State, 1994-95; sr. internat. fellow The Dayan Ctr., Tel Aviv U., 1986-87; chmn. bd. overseers Harry S. Truman Rsch. Inst. for Advancement of Peace, Hebrew U., 1986-91; guest scholar The Brookings Inst., Washington, 1987; mem. bd. advisors Washington Inst. Near East Policy, 1986-93, counselor, 1995—; adv. com. Initiative for Peace and Cooperation on the Mid. East, Washington, 1994—; vis. prof. Hamilton Coll., spring 1995, fall 1997, adj. prof. Sch. Fgn. Svc., Georgetown U., 1996. Author: Making Peace Among Arabs and Israelis, 1991; contbg. author: The Middle East: Ten Years After Camp David, 1988, Soviet-American Competition in the Middle East, 1988, Israel: The Peres Era, 1987; contbr. articles to profl. jours., also N.Y. Times, Washington Post. Bd. dirs. Inst. for Study Diplomacy, Georgetown U., 1994—; vice chmn. Ctr. Preventive Action, Coun. Fgn. Rels., 1994—. Recipient William A. Jump award for outstanding service in pub. adminstrn., 1967, Meritorious Honor award Dept. State, 1967, Meritorious Honor award AID, 1967, Pres.' Mgmt. Improvement cert., 1971, Distinguished Honor award Dept. State, 1977, 85, Disting. Alumnus award Johns Hopkins U., 1980, Wilbur J. Carr award Dept. State, 1985; vis. fellow Princeton U., 1963-64. Mem. Am. Acad. Diplomacy (vice chmn. bd. dirs. 1995—), Am. Fgn. Svc. Assn., UN Assn., Coun. Fgn. Rels., Middle East Inst., Assn. Diplomatic Studies and Tng. (bd. dirs. 1995—), Cousteau Soc., Sierra Club, Phi Beta Kappa. Episcopalian.

LEWIS, SCOTT P., lawyer; b. Chgo., 1950. BA magna cum laude, Yale U., 1971; JD cum laude, Harvard U., 1974. Bar: Mass. 1974. Mem. Palmer & Dodge LLP, Boston. Office: Palmer & Dodge 1 Beacon St Boston MA 02108-3107

LEWIS, SHARI, puppeteer, entertainer; b. N.Y.C., Jan. 17, 1934; d. Abraham B. and Ann (Ritz) Hurwitz; m. Jeremy Tarcher, Mar. 15, 1958; 1 child, Mallory. Star weekly NBC-TV show The Shari Lewis Show, 1960-63, weekly TV show BBC, London, 1969-75, weekly show for ind. network, Gt. Britain, 1970, weekly syndicated series The Shari Show, daily PBS series Lamb Chop's Play-Along, 1991-96 (named TV Guide's Best of Best for Children, TV Guide's Top 10 Children's Shows 1993); writer, prodr., star NBC spl. A Picture of Us, 1971, spls. on PBS, including Lamb Chop in the Haunted Studio 1994, Lamb Chop's Special Chanukah 1995, Shari's Special Passover 1997; CD-Rom Lamb Chop Loves Music, 1995; performer or condr. with over 100 symphonies in U.S., Can., Japan, 1977—; command performances, London, 1970, 73, 78; author 60 pub. books, including 15 One Minute Bedtime Stories (best-selling series); 24 home video cassettes, including 101 Things for Kids to Do, Shari's Christmas Concert, Don't Wake Your Mom, 1992, Let's Make Music, 1994; appeared in mus. prodns., including Bye Bye Birdie, Funny Girl. Past nat. bd. dirs. Girl Scouts U.S.; past internat. bd. dirs. Boy Scouts Am.; past pres. Am. Ctr. Films for Children; past hon. chmn. bd. trustees Internat. Reading Found.; past trustee Greater L.A. Zoo Assn. Recipient 12 Emmy awards, including awards for best program and outstanding female personality, 1989, for outstanding performer in a children's program, 1992, outstanding writing in children's series, 1993, outstanding performer in a children's series, 1993, 94, 95, daytime Emmy for performer in a children's series; Peabody award, 1960, 50th Anniversary Dir.'s award Ohio State Award Com., 1988, Monte Carlo Internat. TV award, 1963, Radio-TV Mirror award, 1960, Kennedy Ctr. award for excellence in arts for young people, 1996, Video Choice award, 1988, 12 Parents Choice awards, 1992. Office: care Jim Golden 3128 Cavendish Dr Los Angeles CA 90064-4743

LEWIS, SHEILA MURIEL O'NEIL, retired communications management specialist; b. Glendive, Mont., Sept. 23, 1937; d. John Edward and Muriel Christine (Johnson) O'Neil; m. Lyndell W. Lewis, Dec. 14, 1957 (div. 1973); children: Sheri Lynne, Debra Lynne, Linda Marie, Valerie Jean. AA, Colo. Women's Coll., 1957; BS, U. No. Colo., 1976; postgrad., Stanford U. Adminstrv. asst. DAFC/Dept. Defense DOT/FAA, Denver, 1956-64; substitute tchr. Portland (Oreg.) Public Schs., 1964-72; communications operator Denver Air Rt. Traffic Control Ctr., 1972-78, communications specialist, 1978-80, computer programmer, 1980-82, air traffic controller, 1982-86; communications specialist Air Force Space Command, Falcon AFB, Colo., 1986-95, retired, 1995. Troop leader Campfire Girls, Las Vagas, 1964-72, pres. PTA, Las Vegas, 1964-72. Mem. AAUW, Armed Forces Communications and Electronics Assn., Aviation Space Edn. Assn., Civil Air Patrol, Univ. Aviation Assn., Order of Eastern Star, Order of White Shrine Jerusalem, Chi Omega. Democrat. Lutheran. Avocations: pilot, travel, history, archeology, anthropology. Home: 4934 Daybreak Cir Colorado Springs CO 80917-2657

LEWIS, SHELDON NOAH, technology consultant; b. Chgo., July 1, 1934; s. Jacob Joseph and Evelyn (Mendelsohn) Iglowitz; m. Suzanne Joyce Goldberg, June 17, 1957; children: Sara Lynn, Matthew David, Rachel Ann. BA with honors, Northwestern U., 1956, MS (Univ. fellow), 1956; PhD (Eastman Kodak fellow), UCLA, 1959; postgrad. (NSF fellow), U. Basel, Switzerland, 1959-60; postgrad. cert. in research mgmt, Indsl. Research Inst., Harvard U., 1973. With Rohm & Haas Co., 1960-78, head lab., 1963-68, research supr., 1968-73, dir. splty. chem. research, 1973-74; gen. mgr. DCL Lab. AG subs., Zurich, Switzerland, 1974-75; dir. European Labs. Valbonne, France, 1975-76; corp. dir. research and devel. worldwide for polymers, resins and monomers Spring House, Pa., 1976-78; with The Clorox Co., Oakland, Calif., 1978-91, v.p. R&D, 1978, group v.p., 1978-84, exec. v.p., 1984-91, also bd. dirs.; pres. SNL Inc., Lafayette, Calif., 1991—; mem. indsl. panel on sci. and tech. NSF. Referee: Jour. Organic Chemistry; patentee in field; contbr. articles to profl. publs. Mem. Calif. Inst. Adv. Bd., World Affairs Council, UCLA Chemistry Adv. Council, Bay Area Sci. Fair Adv. Bd., Mills Coll. Adv. Council for Sci. and Math. Recipient cert. in patent law Phila. Patent Law Assn., 1962, Roon award for coatings research Fedn. Socs. Coatings Tech., 1966, cert. of service Wayne State U. Polymer Conf. Series, 1967, cert. in mgmt. by objectives Am. Mgmt. Research, Inc., 1972. Mem. Soap and Detergent Assn. (bd. dirs.), Chem. Ind. Inst. of Toxicology (bd. dirs.), Indsl. Rsch. Inst., Am. Chem. Soc. (chmn. Phila. polymer sect. 1970-71), Soc. Chem. Industry London, Sigma Xi. Jewish. Office: SNL Inc 3711 Rose Ct Lafayette CA 94549-3030

LEWIS, SHERMAN RICHARD, JR., investment banker; b. Ottawa, Ill., Dec. 11, 1936; s. Sherman Richard and Julia Audrey (Rusteen) L.; m. Dorothy Marie Downie, Sept. 9, 1967; children: Thomas, Catherine, Elizabeth, Michael. AB, Northwestern U., 1958; MBA, U. Chgo., 1964. With investment dept. Am. Nat. Bank & Trust Co., Chgo., 1961-64; v.p. Halsey, Stuart & Co., N.Y.C., 1964-70, v.p. in charge corp. fin. dept., 1970-73; v.p. C.J. Lawrence & Sons, N.Y.C., 1970; ptnr. Loeb, Rhoades & Co., N.Y.C., 1973-76, ptnr. in charge corp. fin. dept., 1975-76, exec. v.p., bd. dirs., 1976-77, pres., co-chief exec. officer, 1977-78; vice chmn., co-chief exec. officer Loeb Rhoades, Hornblower & Co., N.Y.C., 1978-79; pres. Shearson/Am. Express Inc., N.Y.C., 1979-82, vice chmn., 1983-84; vice chmn. Shearson Lehman/Am. Express Inc., 1984-85, Shearson Lehman Bros. Inc., 1985-87, Shearson Lehman Hutton Inc., 1988-89; co-chief exec. officer, vice chmn., chmn. exec. com. Lehman Bros., 1990; vice chmn. Shearson Lehman Bros. Holdings, Inc., N.Y.C., 1990-93, Lehman Bros. Holdings, Inc., Lehman Bros., Inc., 1993—. Mem. Pres.'s Commn. on Housing, 1981-82, Pres.'s Coun. on Internat. Youth Exch., 1982-88; trustee Northwestern U., 1992—, regent, 1990—; mem. vis. com. Coll. Arts and Scis., Northwestern U., 1981—, chmn., 1990-96; mem. coun. Grad. Sch. Bus., U. Chgo., 1991—; bd. dirs. The Korea Soc., U.S.-Greek Bus. Coun. Commd. officer USMC, 1958-61, U.S.-Portugal Investment Adv. Coun. Mem. N.Y. Soc. Security Analysts, The Pilgrims, Bond Club, Ridgewood Country Club, Univ. Club, Quogue Field Club. Office: Lehman Bros Inc 3 World Financial Ctr New York NY 10285-0001

LEWIS, STEPHEN RICHMOND, JR., economist, academic administrator; b. Englewood, N.J., Feb. 11, 1939; s. Stephen Richmond and Esther (Magan) L.; children: Virginia, Deborah, Mark. BA, Williams Coll., 1960, LLD, 1987; MA, Stanford U., 1962, PhD, 1963; LHD, Doshisha U., 1993. Instr. Stanford U., 1962-63; research advisor Pakistan Inst. Devel. Econs., Karachi, 1963-65; asst. prof. econs. Harvard U., 1965-66; asst. prof. econs. Williams Coll., 1966-68, assoc. prof., 1968-73, prof., 1973-76, Herbert H. Lehman prof., 1976-87, provost of coll., 1968-71, 73-77, spl. asst. to pres., 1979-80, dir. Williams-Botswana Project, 1982-88, chmn. dept. econs., 1984-86; vis. sr. research fellow Inst. Devel. Studies, Nairobi, Kenya, 1971-73; econ. cons. to Ministry of Finance and Devel. Planning, Govt. of Botswana, 1, 1975—; vis. fellow Inst. Devel. Studies, Sussex, Eng., 1986-87; pres., prof. econs. Carleton Coll., Northfield, Minn., 1987—; cons. econs. Ford Found., Edna McConnell Clark Found., World Bank, Orgn. Econ. Coop. and Devel., Govts. of Kenya, Philippines, Botswana; trustee Carnegie Endowment for Internat. Peace, 1988—. Author: (with others) Relative Price Changes and Industrialization in Pakistan, 1969, Economic Policy and Industrial Growth in Pakistan, 1969, Pakistan: Industrialization and Trade Policy, 1970, Williams in the Eighties, 1980, Taxation for Development, 1983, South Africa: Has Time Run Out?, 1986, Policy Choice and Development Performance in Botswana, 1989, The Economics of Apartheid, 1989; editorial bd. Jour. Econ. Lit., 1985-87. Contbr. chpts. to books, articles to profl. jours. Exec. com. Indianhead coun. Boy Scouts Am., 1989—. Decorated Presdl. Order of Meritorious Svc. (Botswana), 1983; Danforth Found. fellow, 1960-63; Ford Found. dissertation fellow, 1962-63; recipient Disting. Eagle Scout award, 1993. Mem. Council on Fgn. Relations, Nat. Tax Assn., Am. Econ. Assn., Phi Beta Kappa. Office: Carleton Coll Office Pres 1 N College St Northfield MN 55057-4001*

LEWIS, STEVE, Olympic athlete, track and field. Olympic track and field participant Seoul, Korea, 1988, Barcelona, Spain, 1992. Recipient 400m Track and Field Gold medal Olympics, Seoul, 1988, 400m Track and Field Silver medal Olympics, Barcelona, 1992, 4x400m relay Gold medal Olympics, Seoul, 1988, Barcelona, 1992. Office: US Olympic Com 1750 E Boulder St Colorado Springs CO 80909-5724*

LEWIS, SYLVIA DAVIDSON, association executive; b. Akron, Ohio, Apr. 28; d. Harry I. and Helen E. (Stein) Davidson; m. Allen D. Lewis, Oct. 12, 1947; children: Pamela Lewis Kanfer, Randy, Daniel, Cynthia. Student, U. Mich., 1945-47, U. Akron, 1961-62. Editor Akron Jewish News, 1948-50; tchr. Revere Rd. Congregation, Akron, 1964-70; office mgr. Acme Lumber & Fence Co., Akron, 1970-85; nat. pres. NA'AMAT (Movement of Working Women & Vols.), N.Y.C., 1993—. V.p. Planned Parenthood Summit County, 1997—; founding mem. Govt. Affairs Com., Columbus, Ohio, 1981—, mem. exec. com., 1988-89; v.p. Akron Jewish Cmty. Fedn., 1988-95, pres. women's divsn., 1987-90. Inducted into Ohio Women's Hall of Fame, 1995; recipient Golden Rule award J.C. Penney, 1994, Vol. of Yr. award Lippman Cmty. Day Sch., 1992, Commendation of Honor award Ohio Gen. Assembly, 1993. Democrat. Jewish. Avocations: reading, writing, travel, grandchildren. Home: 277 Keith Ave Akron OH 44313-5301 Office: NA'AMAT USA 200 Madison Ave New York NY 10016-3903

LEWIS, SYLVIA GAIL, journalist; b. N.Y.C., Apr. 8, 1945; d. Ben and Clara Lewis. BA, Cornell U., 1967; MA, U. Wash., Seattle, 1968; MS in Journalism, Northwestern U., 1974. Reporter Seattle-Post Intelligencer, 1968-69; asst. editor Cowles Book Co., N.Y.C., 1969-70; with Am. Planning Assn., Chgo., 1974—, mng. editor Planning mag., 1975-77, dir. pubs. Planning mag., 1977—, editor, pub. Planning mag., 1997—. Contbr. articles to profl. jours. Bd. dirs. Bright New City, 1995—. Mem. Soc. Profl. Journalists, Chgo. Headline Club (pres. 1992-93), Soc. Nat. Assn. Publs. (pres. Chgo. chpt. 1986-87, nat. bd. dirs. 1989-91), Northwestern U. Alumni Assn., Cornell Club of Chgo., Phi Beta Kappa. Office: Am Planning Assn 122 S Michigan Ave Chicago IL 60603-6107

LEWIS, THOMAS B., specialty chemical company executive; b. Cleve.; s. Bryn H. and Margaret (Connaughton) L.; m. Mary C. Lewis. B.S., John Carroll U., M.S.; Ph.D., MIT; postdoctoral fellow, Cornell U.; postgrad. Exec. Program, Stanford U., 1983. With Monsanto Co., St. Louis, 1966-88, sr. rsch. chemist, rsch. group leader, project mgr., mgr. comml. devel., dir. corp. rsch. labs. & R&D, gen. mgr. Rubber Chem. divsn.; corp. v.p. Celgene Corp., Warren, N.J., 1988-92; pres., CEO Chiral Techs. Inc., Exton, Pa., 1992—; pres. Akron Polymer Lecture Group, 1977-78. Mem. AAAS, Am. Chem. Soc., Am. Phys. Soc., Soc. Chem. Industries, N.Y. Acad. Sci., Sigma Xi. Roman Catholic. Office: Chiral Techs Inc PO Box 564 Exton PA 19341-0564

LEWIS, THOMAS PROCTOR, law educator; b. Ashland, Ky., Mar. 26, 1930; s. Blaine and Hallie Maud (Heal) L.; m. Nancy Ann Magruder, Sept. 27, 1949; children: Jean, Catherine, Jennifer, Blaine. A.B., U. Ky., 1959, LL.B., 1954; S.J.D., Harvard U., 1964. Asst. prof. law U. Ky., 1957-59, assoc. prof., 1959-60, prof., 1961-65, acad. asst. to pres., 1964-65, dean Coll. of Law, 1976-82, prof., 1982—; prof. law U. Minn., 1965-72, Boston U., 1972-76; of counsel Wyatt, Tarrant & Combs, 1982-86 ; vis. prof. U. Chgo., 1962, U. Wash., 1963-64; labor arbitrator, 1965—; spl. justice Ky. Supreme Ct., 1995. Author: (with R. Levy, P. Martin) Social Welfare and the Individual, 1971; contbr. articles to law jours. Served with USNR, 1954-57. Mem. Ky., Mass. bar assns., Nat. Acad. Arbitrators, Am. Law Inst. Office: U Ky Law Coll Lexington KY 40506

LEWIS, TIMOTHY K., federal judge; b. 1954. BA, Tufts U., 1976; JD, Duquesne U., 1980. Asst. dist. atty. Allegheny County Dist. Attys. Office, Pa., 1980-83; asst. U.S. atty. U.S. Attys. Office (we. dist.) Pa., 1983-91; fed. judge U.S. Dist. Ct. (we. dist.) Pa., 1991-92, U.S. Ct. Appeals (3d cir.), Pitts., 1992—; vis. com. mem. U. Chgo. Law Sch., 1993-96. Former bd. dirs. Ctr. Victims Violent Crime; former mem. Aid Citizen Enterprise. Mem. Pa. Bar Assn. (del. to PBA ho. of dels. 1989-91), Allegheny County Bar Assn. (mem. jud. com. 1988-90, mem. profl. ethics com., mem. planning com., chmn. subcom. minorities in law of planning com., mem. nominating com., mem. fin. com., mem. minorities mentor program, mem. women in law com., fed. ct. sect.), Homer S. Brown Bar Assn., The Boule, Alpha House (former bd. dirs.). Office: US Ct of Appeals 3rd Cir 1014 US Courthouse 7th Ave and Grant St Pittsburgh PA 15219*

LEWIS, WALTER DAVID, historian; b. Towanda, Pa., June 24, 1931; s. Gordon Cleon and Eleanor Esther (Tobias) L.; m. Carolyn Wyatt Brown, June 12, 1954 (div. 1980); children: Daniel Kent, Virginia Lorraine, Nancy Ellyn; m. Patricia L. Freeman, Apr. 26, 1986. BA cum laude, Pa. State U., 1952, MA, 1954; PhD, Cornell U., 1961. Instr. pub. speaking Hamilton Coll., Clinton, N.Y., 1954-57; fellowship coordinator Eleutherian Mills-Hagley Found., Wilmington, Del.; also lectr. history U. Del., 1959-65; assoc. prof. history SUNY, Buffalo, 1965-71, prof., 1971; Hudson prof. history and engring. Auburn (Ala.) U., 1971-95, disting. Univ. prof., 1994—; dir. univ. project tech., human values and so. future, 1974-79; sr. fellow in Am. civilization Cornell U., 1958-59; vis. prof. history U. Tex.-Dallas, summer 1982, 83, 84; pres., dir. conf. on history of civil and comml. aviation (ICCA 92), Swiss Transport Mus., Lucerne, Switzerland, 1992; Charles A. Lindbergh prof. of aerospace history Nat. Air and Space Mus., 1993-94. Exec. co-prodr. (documentary film): About Us: A Deep South Portrait, 1977; author: From Newgate to Dannemora: The Rise of the Penitentiary in New York, 1965, Iron and Steel in America, 1976, Sloss Furnaces and The Rise of the Birmingham District: An Industrial Epic, 1994; co-author: Delta: The History of an Airline, 1979, Hopewell Furnace, 1983, The Airway to Everywhere: A History of All American Aviation, 1937-53, 1988; contbg. author: The Professions in America, 1965, Technology in Western Civilization, 1967, The Development of an American Culture, 1969, Notable American Women, 1971, Great Engineers and Pioneers in Technology, 1981, Technology in America, 2d edit., 1990, Science-Technology Relationships, 1993, Eli Whitney's Cotton Gin, 1793-1993, 1994, Bring History Alive, 1996; co-editor: Economic Change in the Civil War Era, 1965, The Southern Mystique: Technology and Human Values in Changing Region, 1977; gen. editor Procs. of the Internat. Conf. on the History of Civil and Commercial Aviation, 1995; contbr. articles to profl. jours. Grantee NEH, 1973-79, 80—, Delta Airlines Found. 1973-79, Eleutherian Mills Hist. Libr., 1970-73, 80; postdoctoral fellow Nat. Humanities Inst., U. Chgo., 1978-79, Mellon fellow Va. Hist. Soc., 1988, 89, 92; recipient Leonardo da Vinci medal, (Soc. for the Hist. of Tech., 1993). Mem. Soc. History Tech., Ala. Hist. Assn., Lexington Group Transp. Historians, Phi Beta Kappa. Episcopalian. Home: 210 Lee Dr Auburn AL 36832-6722 Office: Auburn U Dept History 310 E Thach Ave Auburn AL 36830-5415

LEWIS, WILBUR CURTIS, surgeon; b. Okmulgee, Okla., Sept. 10, 1930; s. Charles D. and Eula Alice (Cole) L.; m. Gladys Sherman, Jan. 28, 1955; children: Karen Kay, Mark David, Leanne Gwynneth, Cristen Sue. BS, Okla. Bapt. U., 1952; MD, Okla. U., 1955. Diplomate Am. Bd. Family Practice (charter); ordained to ministry Bapt. Ch. as pastor, 1953. Intern Harris Hosp., Ft. Worth, 1955-56; resident in surgery VA Hosp., Dallas, 1956-57, Univ. Hosp., Oklahoma City, 1965-67; med. missionary So. Bapt. Conv., Costa Rica and Paraguay, 1959-70; pvt. practice medicine specializing in surgery, Oklahoma City, 1970—; leader med. disaster relief team, Honduras, 1975, Guatemala, 1976, Dominican Republic, 1977; surgeon, lectr. Maraciabo, Venezuela, 1989, Taxila, Pakistan, 1990, Bangalore, India, 1990, Guito, Ecuador, 1991, Signatepeque and Teguigalpa, Honduras, 1993; mem. staff Bapt. Hosp., Deaconess Hosp., Mercy Hosp., St. Anthony Hosp., Oklahoma City Hosp.; deacon, mem. meml. trust com. 1st Bapt. Ch., Oklahoma City; former chmn. deacons and social ministries com.; former pastor various chs., Okla. and Paraguay; co-founder, former pres. Baptist Med. Dental Fellowship; lectr. on surgery and burn care topics in Venezuela, Pakistan, India and Equador and Honduras. Past pres. Midwest City C. of C. Capt. USAF, 1957-59. Decorated knight Knights of Malta. Fellow ACS, Internat. Coll. Surgeons; mem. AMA, Internat. Fedn. Surgical Colls., Okla. State Med. Assn. (former del. and alt. del.), Christian Med. and Dental Soc. (former del.), Oklahoma City Surg. Soc., Am. Burn Assn., Internat. Soc. Burn Injuries (burn care com.), Oklahoma City Clin. Soc. Democrat. Home: 14501 N Western Ave Edmond OK 73013-1828 Office: 3141 NW Expressway St Oklahoma City OK 73112-4143

LEWIS, WILBUR H., educational management consultant; b. Belmont, Ohio, Sept. 16, 1930; s. Charles W. and Lily B. (Dunfee) L.; m. Jean E. Lewis, Aug. 23, 1958; children—David, Deretta, Denise, Dawn, Darrin. Student, Miami U., Oxford, Ohio, 1948-51; B.S.B.A., Ohio State U., 1953; M.Ed., Ohio U., 1961, Ph.D., 1964. Tchr. pub. schs. Scioto County, Ohio, 1957; tchr., adminstr. public schs. Belmont County, Ohio, 1958-60; grad. asst. Ohio U., 1960-61; prin. high sch., adminstrv. asst. to supt. public schs. Athens, Ohio, 1961-64; asst. prof., adviser to Govt. of Nigeria, 1964-66; asst. supt. pub. schs. Athens, Ohio, 1966-67; prin. high sch. public schs. Wilmington, Ohio, 1967-68; with Parma (Ohio) City Schs., 1968-77, asst. to supt., 1968-70, asst. supt., 1970-72, assoc. supt., 1972-75, supt., 1975-77; supt. Tucson Unified Sch. Dist., 1977-79; cons. ednl. mgmt. Tucson, 1979—; vice chmn. nat. adv. coun. Edn. Disadvantaged Children, 1972-80; supt. Ariz. State Schs. for Deaf and Blind, 1974-94. Planning divsn. United Way, Tucson, 1978-80; bd. dirs. Jr. Achievement, 1978-80. With U.S. Army, 1954-56. Recipient numerous civic awards for community service; Kettering Found. fellow, 1970. Mem. Am. Assn. Sch. Adminstrs., Buckeye Assn. Sch. Adminstrs., Masons, Shriners, Rotary Internat. (v.p. Tucson 1987—, past pres., dist. gov.'s rep. group study exch. dist. 9120 Nigeria, dist. 550 1990, chmn. group study exch. dist. 5490 1991-93), Phi Delta Kappa, Lambda Chi Alpha, Sigma Phi Epsilon. Rsch. in orgnl. devel., adminstrv. behavior patterns, tchr. job satisfaction, student achievement. Home: PO Box 31690 Tucson AZ 85751-1690 *To achieve one must aspire. To aspire one must dream. But if dreams and aspirations are to become achievements one must persevere. The perseverance necessary to turn dreams and aspirations into achievements has always been made easier for me knowing that children and youth were the benefactors of my efforts.*

LEWIS, WILLIAM HEADLEY, JR., manufacturing company executive; b. Washington, Sept. 29, 1934; s. William Headley and Lois Maude (Bradshaw) L.; BS in Metall. Engring., Va. Poly. Inst., 1956; postgrad. Grad. Sch. Bus. Adminstrn., Emory U., 1978; m. Carol Elizabeth Cheek, Apr. 22, 1967; children: Teresa Lynne, Bret Cameron, Charles William, Kevin Marcus. Various positions Lockheed Corp., Marietta, Ga. 1956-1987; mgr. engring. tech. services, 1979-83, dir. engring. Getex div., 1983-86; gen. mgr. Inspection Systems div. Lockheed Air Terminal, Inc., 1986-87; pres., CEO Measurement Systems Inc., Atlanta, 1987—; chmn. Lockheed Corp. Task Force on NDE, 1980-86; mem. Com. to Study Role of Advanced Tech. in Improving Reliability and Maintainability of Future Weapon Systems, Office of Sec. of Def., 1984-85; co-founder, dir., exec. v.p. Applied Tech. Svcs., Inc., 1967—; pres. CEO Applied Tech. Fin. Corp., Atlanta, 1993-96; mng. ptnr. Tech. Fin. Co., LLC; lectr. grad. studies and continuing edn. Union Coll., Schenectady, 1977-82. Served to 1st lt. USAF, 1957-60. Registered profl. engr., Calif. Fellow Am. Soc. for Non-destructive Testing (nat. dir. 1976-78, chmn. nat. tech. council 1977-78, chmn. aerospace com. 1972-74, nat. nominating com. 1982-83, 1984-85); mem. Am. Inst. Aeronautics and Astronics, Am. Soc. for Metals, Nat. Mgmt. Assn., NAS (mem. com. on compressive fracture 1981-83), Brotherhood of the Knights of the Vine, St. Ives Country Club, Country Club Sapphire Valley. Editor: Prevention of Structural Failures: The Role of Fracture Mechanics, Failure Analysis, and NDT, 1978; patentee detection apparatus for structural failure in aircraft. Home: 3127 St Ives Country Club Pky Duluth GA 30097 Office: 2262 Northwest Pky Ste B Marietta GA 30067-9306

LEWIS, WILLIAM HENRY, JR., lawyer; b. Durham, N.C., Nov. 12, 1942; s. William Henry Sr. and Phyllis Lucille (Phillips) L.; m. Jo Ann Whitsett, Apr. 17, 1965 (dis. Sept. 1982); 1 child, Kimberly N.; m. Peyton Cockrill Davis, Nov. 28, 1987. Student, N.C. State U., 1960-63; AB in Polit. Sci., U. N.C., 1965, JD with honors, 1969. Bar: Calif., D.C., U.S. Dist. Ct. (cen. dist.) Calif., U.S. Ct. Appeals (D.C. cir., 2nd and 5th cirs.), U.S. Supreme Ct. Assoc. Latham & Watkins, Los Angeles, 1969-74; exec. officer Calif. Air Resources Bd., Los Angeles and Sacramento, Calif., 1975-78; dir. Nat. Com. on Air Quality, Washington, 1978-81; counsel Wilmer, Cutler & Pickering, Washington, 1981-84; ptnr. Morgan, Lewis & Bockius LLP, Washington, 1984—; spl. advisor on environ. policy State of Calif., L.A. and Sacramento, 1975; lectr. Law Sch. U. Va., 1993—. Bd. dirs. For Love of Children, Inc., Washington, 1985-95, pres., 1987-91; bd. dirs. Advs. for Families, Washington, 1985-87, Hillandale Homeowners Assn., Washington, 1986-87, Thurgood Marshall Ctr. Trust, Washington, 1989-95; mem. EPA Clean Air Act Adv. Com., 1994—. Mem. ABA. Home: 3900 Georgetown Ct NW Washington DC 20007-2127 Office: Morgan Lewis & Bockius LLP 1800 M St NW Washington DC 20036-5802

LEWIS, WILLIAM LEONARD, food products executive; b. Providence, Apr. 8, 1946; s. George Dawson and Margaret Eleanor (Cuddigan) L.; m. Barbara Jane Fournier, July 20, 1968; children: Hillary, Megan. BBA, Gonzaga U., 1973; MBA, Dartmouth Coll., 1975. With product mgmt. dept. Frito-Lay div. Pepsico, Dallas, 1975-80; product mgr. grocery products div. Ralston-Purina Co., St. Louis, 1981-83, brand dir., 1983-84, group dir., 1985-86, dir. mktg., 1986-87; exec. v.p. grocery products div. Ralston-Purina Can., Inc., Mississauga, Ont., 1987-89, pres. grocery products div., 1989-90, pres. parent co., 1990—. With U.S. Army, 1968-71. Office: Ralston Purina Can Inc, 2500 Royal Windsor Ave, Mississauga, ON Canada L5J 1K8

LEWIS, WILLIAM WALKER, management consultant; b. Roanoke, Va., Mar. 29, 1942; s. William Walker and Nancy Katherine (Phipps) L.; m. Jutta Maria Schwarzkopf, Dec. 27, 1966; children: Christopher William, Monica Gisela. BS in Physics with honors, Va. Poly. Inst. and State U., 1963; PhD in Theoretical Physics, Oxford U., 1966. Mem. staff Office of Asst. Sec. for Systems Analysis, Dept. Def., Washington, 1966-69; asso. provost for resource planning, lectr. public and internat. affairs Princeton U., 1969-71; dir. office of analytical studies U. Calif., Berkeley, 1971-73; sr. ops. officer World Bank, 1973-77; prin. dep. asst. sec. for program analysis and evaluation Dept. Def., Washington, 1977-79; asst. sec. policy and evaluation Dept. Energy, Washington, 1979-81; pres. Dist. Heat and Power, Inc., Washington, 1981-82; ptnr. McKinsey & Co., Inc., Washington, 1982—; dir. McKinsey Global Inst., Washington, 1990—. Trustee George C. Marshall Found.

Rhodes scholar, 1963-66. Office: 1101 Pennsylvania Ave NW Washington DC 20004-2514

LEWIS, WILMA ANTOINETTE, federal agency administrator; b. Santurce, P.R.. BA with distinction, Swarthmore Coll., 1978; JD, Harvard U., 1981. Assoc. Steptoe & Johnson, Washington, 1981-1986; asst. U.S. atty. civil divsn. U.S. Atty.'s Office, Washington, 1986-1993; assoc. solicitor divsn. gen. law U.S. Dept. Interior, 1993-95, inspector gen., 1995—; mem. civil justice reform act adv. group U.S. Dist. Ct. D.C., mem. adv. com. on local rules; lectr., instr. George Washington U. Nat. Law Ctr.; mem. faculty Coll. Trial Advocacy. Mem. Phi Beta Kappa. Office: US Dept Interior Office Inspector Gen 1849 C St NW # 5341 Washington DC 20240-0001

LEWISON, EDWARD FREDERICK, surgeon; b. Chgo., Feb. 11, 1913; s. Maurice and Julia (Trockey) L.; m. Elizabeth Oppenheim, July 24, 1938 (wid. 1947); 1 child, John Edward; m. Betty Fleischmann, Mar. 21, 1948; children: Edward M., Robert S., Richard J. BS, U. Chgo., 1932; MD, Johns Hopkins U., 1936. Lic. MD Ill., Md., Fla.; diplomate Am. Bd. Surgery. Chief, Breast Clin. Johns Hopkins Hosp., Balt., 1948-72; asst. prof. surgery Johns Hopkins U. Sch. Med., Balt., 1954-69, assoc. prof. surgery, 1969-80, assoc. prof. surgery, emeritus, 1980—; vice-chmn. breast cancer comm., WHO, Geneva, 1968-70; chmn. nat. conf. breast cancer, Am. Cancer Soc., Washington, 1969, Swiss Cancer League, Lucerne, 1976; mem. H.S. Nat. Comm. of the Nat. Rsch. Coun., Washington, 1983-87; mem. adv. bd. Annie Casey Found., 1996—. Author: Breast Cancer and Its Diagnosis and Treatment, 1955; editor: Breast Cancer, 1977, Conference on Spontaneous Regression of Cancer, 1974; co-author: Diagnosis and Treatment of Breast Cancer, 1981. Bd. dirs. United Way of Md., Balt., 1986-94. Named Humanitarian of Yr., Wyman Guild, Balt., 1990, Disting. Citizen, Gov. State Md., 1980; recipient Cert. of Merit award European Theater Ops., 1945; Johns Hopkins hosp. oncology libr. named in honor of Edward F. Lewison. Fellow AMA, Royal Soc. Medicine, Am. Coll. Surgeons; mem. Am. Cancer Soc. (hon. life, Vol. Leadership award 1984, Premier award 1995), N.Y. Acad. Scis. Achievements include invention of rayable gauze for surgery. Home: 4100 N Charles St Baltimore MD 21218

LEWIS-WHITE, LINDA BETH, elementary school educator; b. Fresno, Calif., June 30, 1950; d. Lloyd Ernest and Anne Grace (Barkman) Lewis; m. Francis Everett White, Feb. 15, 1975; children: Anna Justine, Christopher Andrew Arthur. BA in Home Econs., Calif. State U., Sacramento, 1972, MA in Social Scis., 1973; postgrad., Tex. Women's U., 1976-79; PhD in Reading, East Tex. State U., 1994. Cert. bilingual and elem. edn. tchr., Tex. Tchr. bilingual Arlington Sch. Dist., 1977-96; asst. prof. reading Eastern Mich. U., 1996—; adj. prof. reading Tex. Women's U., Denton, 1989, adj. prof. ESL East Tex. State U., 1993; mem. tchr. trainer cadre, Dallas Ind. Sch. Dist., 1985-92; freelance cons., 1987—; presenter TESOL Internat. Conf., San Antonio, 1989. Cons., writer (book) Ciencias-Silver Burdett, 1988. Troop leader Girl Scouts U.S., Dallas, 1980-82. Mem. Nat. Reading Conf., Nat. Writing Project, Internat. Reading Assn., Tchrs. of English to Spkrs. of Other Langs. (nominating com. 1990-91), TEXTESOL V (chair elem. edn. com. 1989-91), Tex. Assn. Bilingual Edn., Phi Delta Kappa, Pi Mu. Mem. Christian Ch. Avocations: sewing, knitting, quilting, reading, gourmet cooking. Office: Eastern Mich U 714 Pray Harrold Hall Ypsilanti MI 48197-2210

LEWITT, MICHAEL HERMAN, physician, educator; b. Hartford, Conn., Nov. 27, 1948; s. Bernard and Celeste (Garfunkel) LeW.; m. Lynne Rubin, Apr. 1, 1979; children: Mattea, Jeremy, Rachel. BA, Lafayette Coll., 1970; MD, Jefferson Med. Coll., 1974; MPH, Med. Coll. Wis., 1997. Diplomate Am. Bd. Preventive Medicine, Am. Bd. Emergency Medicine, Am. Bd. Family Practice. Med. dr. FMC Group, 1975-78; physician U.S. Steel Corp., 1978-81; staff physician Jeanes Hosp., 1981-84; emergency medicine physician Chester County Hosp., 1984-90; instr. dept. medicine, dept. surgery Jefferson Med. Coll., Phila., 1983—; pvt. practice, 1990—; cons., 1990—. Fellow Phila. Coll. Physicians, Am. Coll. Emergency Physicians, Am. Coll. Occupational and Environ. Medicine, Am. Acad. Family Practice; mem. Am. Coll. Physicians. Office: Paoli Hosp Occupl Med 255 W Lancaster Ave Paoli PA 19301-1763

LEWITT, SOL, artist; b. Hartford, Conn., 1928. B.F.A., Syracuse U., 1949. Instr. Mus. Modern Art Sch., 1964-67, Cooper Union, 1967, Sch. Visual Arts, N.Y.C., 1969-70, NYU, 1970. Contbr. articles on sculpture, drawing, conceptual art to jours., mags.; one-man shows include, Visual Arts Mus., N.Y.C., 1976, San Francisco Mus. Art, 1975, Wadsworth Atheneum, Hartford, Conn., 1981, Musee d'Art Contemporain, Bordeaux, France, 1983, retrospective travelling exhbn., Mus. Modern Art, N.Y.C., 1990-95, Mus. Contemporary Art, Montreal, Krannert Mus., Champaign, Ill., Mus. Contemporary Art, Chgo., La Jolla (Calif.) Mus., 1978-79, Stedelijk Mus., Amsterdam, 1984, Stedelijk Van Abbe Mus., Eindhoven, 1984, Musee d'Art Moderne de la ville de Paris, 1987, Tate Gallery, 1986, Walker Art Ctr., Mpls., 1988, Kunstalle Bern, Switzerland, 1989, Touko Mus., 1990, Porticus, Frankfort, Fed. Republic Germany, 1990, Drawings 1958-92 Haags Gemeentemus., The Hague and tour, Structures 1962-93 Mus. Modern Art, Oxford and tour, 25 Years of Wall Drawings 1968-93 Addison Gallery, Phillips Acad., Andover, Mass., Paints 1970-95 Mus. Modern Art, N.Y.C.; group exhbns. include Sculpture Ann, Whitney Mus. Am. Art, N.Y.C., 1967, Minimal Art, The Hague, 1968, Documenta, Kassel, W. Ger., 1968, 72, 77, 82, Prospect, 1968, Dusseldorf, 1968, Stadtische Kuntshalle, Dusseldorf, 1969, La Jolla Mus. Contemp. Art, 1970, Tokyo Biennale, 1970, Guggenheim Internat., N.Y.C., 1971, Whitney Biennial, Whitney Mus. Am. Art, N.Y.C., 1979, Hayward Gallery, London, 1980, Internat. Sculpture exhbn., Basel, Switzerland, 1980, Westkunst, Cologne, Fed. Republic Germany, 1981, Musee Nat. d'Art Moderne, Paris, 1981, Art Inst. Chgo., 1982, Mus. Modern Art, N.Y.C., 1983, Mus. Contemporary Art, Los Angeles, 1986, Whitney Biennial, 1987, Skulptur Projekt, Münster, Fed. Republic Germany, 1987, Venice (Italy) Biennale, 1988, Zeitlos, Hamburg, Fed. Republic Germany; represented in permanent collections, Stedelijk Mus., Albright-Knox Art Gallery, Buffalo, Art Gallery Ont., Toronto, Los Angeles County Mus. Art, Los Angeles, Mus. Modern Art, N.Y.C., Tate Gallery, London, Centre Georges Pompidou, Paris, Whitney Mus. Am. Art, N.Y.C., Met. Mus. Art, N.Y.C., Art Inst. Chgo.; work also in German, Swiss, Australian, Dutch, Belgian and Am. mus. Office: care Susanna Singer 50 Riverside Dr New York NY 10024-6555

LEWITZKY, BELLA, choreographer; b. Los Angeles, Jan. 13, 1916; d. Joseph and Nina (Ossman) L.; m. Newell Taylor Reynolds, June 22, 1940; 1 child, Nora Elizabeth. Student, San Bernardino Valley (Calif.) Jr. Coll., 1933-34; hon. doctorate, Calif. Inst. Arts, 1981; PhD (hon.), Occidental Coll., 1984, Otis Parsons Coll., 1989, Juilliard Sch., 1993; DFA, Santa Clara U., 1995; DFA (hon.), Calif. State U., Long Beach, 1997. Chmn. dance dept., chmn. adv. panel U. So. Calif., Idyllwild, 1956-74; founder Sch. Dance, Calif. Inst. Arts, 1969, dean, 1969-74; vice chmn. dance adv. panel Nat. Endowment Arts, 1974-77, mem. artists-in-schs. adv. panel, 1974-75; mem. Nat. Adv. Bd. Young Audiences, 1974—, Joint Commn. Dance and Theater Accreditation, 1979; com. mem. Am. chpt. Internat. Dance Coun. of UNESCO, 1974—; trustee Calif. Assn. Dance Cos., 1976—, Idyllwild Sch. Music and Arts, 1986-95, Dance/USA, 1988-95, Calif. State Summer Sch. of Arts, 1988—; cons. the dance project WNET, 1987—. Co-founder, co-dir. Dance Dance Assocs., L.A., 1951-55; founder, 1966; artistic dir. Lewitzky Dance Co., L.A.; choreographer, 1948—; founder, former artistic dir. The Dance Gallery, L.A.; contbr. articles in field; choreographed works include Trio for Saki, 1967, Orrenda, 1969, Kinaesonata, 1971, Pietas, 1971, Ceremony for Three, 1972, Game Plan, 1973, Five, 1974, Spaces Between, 1975, Jigsaw, 1975, Inscape, 1976, Pas de Bach, 1977, Suite Satie, 1980, Changes and Choices, 1981, Confines, 1982, Continuum, 1982, The Song of the Woman, 1983, Nos Duraturi, 1984, 8 Dancers/8 Lights, 1985, Facets, 1986, Impressions #1, 1987, Impressions #3, 1988, Agitime, 1989, Impressions #3, 1989, Episode #1, 1990, Glass Canyons, 1991, Episode #2, 1992, Episode #3, 1992, Episode #4, 1993, Meta 4, 1994, Four Women in Time, 1996. Mem. adv. com. Actors' Fund of Am., 1986—, Women's Bldg. Adv. Council, 1985-91, Calif. Arts Council, 1983-86, City of Los Angeles Task Force on the Arts, 1986—; mem. artistic adv. bd. Interlochen Ctr. for Arts, 1988—. Recipient Mayoral Proclamation, City of L.A., 1976, 1982, ann. award Dance mag., 1978, Dir.'s award Calif. Dance Educators Assn., 1978, Plaudit Award, Nat. Dance Assn., 1979, Labor's Award of Honor for Community Svc., L.A. County AFL-CIO, 1979, L.A. Area Dance Alliance and L.A. Junior C. of C. Honoree, 1980, City of L.A. Resolution, 1980, Distguished Artist Award, City of L.A. and Music Ctr., 1982, Silver Achievement award YWCA, 1982, California State Senate Resolution, 1982, 1984, Award of Recognition, Olympic Black Dance Festival, 1984, Distinguished Women's Award, Northwood Inst., 1984, California State U. Distinguished Artist, 1984, Vesta Award, Woman's Bldg, L.A., 1985, L.A. City Council Honors for Outstanding Contributions, 1985, Woman of the Year, Palm Springs Desert Museum, Women's Committee, 1986, Disting. Svc. award Western Alliance Arts Adminstrs., 1987, Woman of Achievement award, 1988, Am. Dance Guild Ann. award, 1989, So. Calif. Libr. for Social Studies & Rsch. award, 1990, Am. Soc. Journalists & Authors Open Book award, 1990, Internat. Soc. Performing Arts Adminstrs. Tiffany award, 1990, Burning Bush award U. of Judaism, 1991, 1st recipient Calif. Gov.'s award in arts for individual lifetime achievement, 1989; honoree L.A. Arts Coun., 1989, Heritage honoree, Nat. Dance Assn., 1991, Vaslav Nijinsky award, 1991, Hugh M. Hefner First Amendment award, 1991, Artistic Excellence award Ctr. Performing Arts U. Calif., 1992, Lester Horton Lifetime Achievement award Dance Resource Ctr. of L.A., 1992, Occidental Coll. Founders' award, 1992, Dance/USA honor, 1992, Visual Arts Freedom of Expression award Andy Warhol Found., 1993, Artist of Yr. award L.A. County High Sch. Arts, 1993, Freedom of Expression honor Andy Warhol Found. Visual Arts, 1993, Calif. Alliance Edn. award, 1994, Lester Horton Sustained Achievement award, 1995 Danie Resource Ctr. of L.A., Lester Horton award for Restaging and Revival, Dance Resource Ctr. of L.A., 1996, Disting. Artists of 1996, High Sch. of Performing Arts, Houston Tex., Bill of Rights award, Am. Civil Liberties Union of So. Calif., Nat. Medal of Arts, 1996, Gypsy award Profl. Dancers Soc., 1997, Nat. Medal Arts, 1997; grantee Mellon Found., 1975, 81, 86, Guggenheim Found., 1977-78, NEA, 1969-94; honoree Women's Internat. League Peace and Freedom, 1995; presented with Key to the City, Cin., 1997. Mem. Am. Arts Alliance (bd. dirs. 1977), Internat. Dance Alliance (adv. council 1984—), Dance/USA (bd. dirs. 1988), Phi Beta (hon.). Office: Lewitzky Dance Co 1055 Wilshire Blvd Ste 1140 Los Angeles CA 90017-2498 *Dance is communicative of personal, emotive knowledge-- of sensory information common to all. The feel of the wind, the exhilaration of clear space, the headiness of an enormous height, the marvel of human power, one's personal worth-- can take shape and be illuminated in dance. How wonderful to work at something you love! How remarkable to be given the opportunity to utilize one's whole being, one's physical knowledge, intellectual capacity, imagination and creativity in a single persuit. How good to practice dance and know that it will not engage you in mass murders of warfare; it will not destroy our environment. It is capable of healing, celebrating, and sharing human resources. My philosophy is predicated on the belief that choreography is the taskmaster of us all. In each work, I attempt to discover again the truth of that statement.*

LEWKOWITZ, KAREN HELENE, orthodontist; b. Bklyn., Dec. 26, 1956; d. William A. and Janet B. (Kagan) L.; m. Robert Louis Shpuntoff, Dec. 18, 1983; children: Hilana Megan, Ariana Elizabeth. BA magna cum laude, CUNY, 1978; DDS, Columbia U., 1982; cert. in orthodontics, NYU, 1984. Researcher W. M. Krogman Ctr., Children's Hosp. Phila., Pa., 1976; ptnr. Bayside (N.Y.) Orthodontic Assocs., 1984—; pres. med. awareness com. Queens Coll.-CUNY, 1977-78; attending orthodontist, lectr. Jamaica (N.Y.) Hosp., 1984—. Mem. Temple Torah, Little Neck, N.Y., 1988-94, Temple Israel, Great Neck, N.Y., 1994—, Hadassah, Great Neck, 1990—; v.p. of programming Orgn. Rehab. Thru Tng., Lake Success, N.Y., 1991. Mem. ADA, Acad. Gen. Dentistry, Am. Assn. Women Dentists, Am. Assn. Orthodontists, Queens County Dental Soc. (trustee 1985—, historian 1990, treas. 1991, sec. 1992, v.p. 1993, pres.-elect 1994, pres. 1995), Alpha Omega (pres. Columbia U. chpt. 1980-82, pres. Queens-Nassau chpt. 1984-87, Presdl. citation 1986, regent N.Y. met. area 1990, 91). Avocations: piano, tennis. Office: Bayside Orthodontic Assocs 59-01 Springfield Blvd Bayside NY 11364

LEWTER, ALICE JENKINS, history and political science educator; b. Roanoke Rapids, N.C., Aug. 16, 1946; d. Thomas George and Parthenia (Jones) Jenkins; m. Dennis Lacon Lewter, Oct. 3, 1980; 1 child, Sonya Desett Jenkins. BA, N.C. Ctrl. U., 1969, MA, 1975; EdD, N.C. State U., 1995. Cert. tchr. adult and c.c. adminstrn. Instr. Halifax County (N.C.) Schs., 1969-70, Durham (N.C.) City Schs., 1970-72; adminstrv. asst. Found. for Rsch. and Edn. in Sickle Cell Disease, N.Y.C., 1972-73; instr. history/polit. sci. Halifax C.C., Weldon, N.C., 1973—, divsn. chair, 1986-90; program dir. MSIP U.S. Dept. Edn., Washington, 1986-89; adj. prof. Chowan Coll., Murfreesboro, N.C., 1994—; advisor African-Am. Soc., Weldon, 1990-93. Co-author: American History: An Introduction, 1996. Judge Precinct #11, Bd. of Elections, Halifax County, 1978-87; coord. 5-A-Day program Black Chs. United for Better Health, Raleigh, 1992—. Named Educator of the Yr., Halifax-Northampton Opportunities Indsl. Corp., 1994; U.S. Dept. Edn. Minority Sci. Improvement grantee, 1986-89. Mem. Am. Coll. and Univ. Women, Am. Assn. Polit. Scientists, Am. Assn. Women in C.C.'s, The Smithsonian Club, Alpha Kappa Alpha. Democrat. Baptist. Avocations: dancing, bowling, reading, travel, walking. Home: 120 Carmichael Cir Roanoke Rapids NC 27870 Office: Halifax Community College PO Drawer 809 Weldon NC 27890

LEWTER, BILLY RAY, psychology educator; b. Louisville, Aug. 17, 1936; s. Robert Lee and Lena Pearl (Hannah) L.; m. Mary Josephine Knecht, Aug. 17, 1963; children: Jonathan, Amy, Elizabeth, Rachel, David. BA, U. Louisville, 1966; MA, Eastern Ky. U., 1973; PhD, U. Ky., 1979; DLitt, Oxford Grad. Sch., 1985. Assoc. dir. acads. Hong-Kong Christian Coll., 1965-68; instr. psychology Cen. Inst., Manila, 1968-70; asst. prof. psychology Southeastern Coll., Winchester, Ky., 1972-79; assoc. prof. psychology Bryan Coll., Dayton, Tenn., 1980-85; prof. psychology Palm Beach Atlantic Coll., West Palm Beach, Fla., 1985—. Fulbright scholar U.S. Dept. Edn., 1983, 87, 89. Mem. Am. Psychol. Assn. Republican. Home: 2370 Bimini Dr West Palm Beach FL 33406-7760 Office: Palm Beach Atlantic Coll PO Box 24708 West Palm Beach FL 33416-4708

LEWTER, HELEN CLARK, elementary education educator; b. Millis, Mass., Jan. 14, 1936; d. Waldimar Kenville and Ida Mills (Currier) Clark; m. Alvin Council Lewter, June 18, 1966; children: Lois Ida, David Paul, Jonathan Clark. BA, U. Mass., 1958; MS, Old Dominion U., 1978. Postgrad. profl. cert. reading specialist, sociology, elem. grades 1-7. Tchr. Juniper Hill Sch., Framingham, Mass., 1960-63, Aragona Elem. Sch., Virginia Beach, Va., 1963-65, Park Elem., Chesapeake, Va., 1965-67; edn. specialist Riverview Sch., Portsmouth, Va., 1977-78; reading tchr. Truitt Jr. H.S., Chesapeake, 1979-83; reading resource tchr. Southeastern Elem., Chesapeake, 1983-86; tchr. Deep Creek Elem. Sch., Chesapeake, 1986—; pers. task force Chesapeake (Va.) Pub. Schs., 1984-85, textbook adoption com., 1984-85, employee handbook com., 1986-87, K-6 writing curriculum com., 1988-89. Tchr., workshop leader, dir., mem. various coms. Fairview Heights Bapt. Ch., Deep Creek Bapt. Ch., Va. So. Bapt. Retreats, 1968—; mem. mayor's adv. coun. City of Chesapeake, Va., 1988-89; mem. summer missionary Va. So. Bapts., 1993; active PTA. Mem. NEA, Va. Edn. Assn., Chesapeake Edn. Assn., Chesapeake Reading Assn. (v.p., pres., honor and merit coun., chmn. various coms.), Internat. Reading Assn., Va. Reading Assn., Delta Kappa Gamma (legis. chmn.), Kappa Delta Pi, Phi Kappa Phi. Republican. Avocations: church related activities, reading. Home: 428 Plummer Dr Chesapeake VA 23323-3116 Office: Deep Creek Elem Sch 2809 Forehand Dr Chesapeake VA 23323-2005

LEWY, JOHN EDWIN, pediatric nephrologist; b. Chgo., Apr. 22, 1935; s. Stanley B. and Lucile (Mayer) L.; m. Rosalind Portnoy, June 9, 1963; children—Karen, Steven. B.A., U. Mich., 1956; M.D., Tulane U., 1960. Diplomate Am. Bd. Pediatrics (oral examiner 1985-89, oral examination com. 1987-91, certifing examination com. on clin. problems 1989—), Am. Bd. Pediatric Nephrology (credentials com. 1981-83). Intern Michael Reese Hosp. Med. Center, Northwestern U., 1960-61, resident in pediatrics, 1961-62; resident in pediatrics Michael Reese Hosp. Med. Center, 1963-64, chief resident, 1964, pediatric nephrology fellow, 1965, dir. sect. pediatric nephrology, 1967-70; fellow dept. pediatrics Cornell U. Med. Coll., 1966, research fellow physiology, 1966-67, asst. prof. pediatrics, 1970-71, asso. prof., 1971-75, prof., 1975-78, dir. div. pediatric nephrology, 1970-78; prof., chmn. dept. pediatrics Tulane U. Hosp., New Orleans, 1978—; physician-in-chief Tulane Hosp. for Children, New Orleans, 1993—; mem. staff Children's Hosp., Med. Ctr. La.; pediatrician La. Handicapped Children's Program; bd. dirs., sci. adv. com. La. End Stage Renal Disease Council. Assoc. editor Jour. Dialysis, 1978—, Jour. Pediatric Nephrology, 1979—; contbr. over 200 articles and abstracts to profl. jours. Mem. profl. adv. com. Nat. Found. March of Dimes; sci. adv. com. U.S. Renal Data System, HHS, 1990—. Served with M.C., USAF, 1962-63. Named Intern of Year Michael Reese Hosp. Med. Center, 1961; recipient award La. Pediatric Soc., 1960. Mem. Inst. Medicine (end stage renal disease com. 1989-91), Am. Acad. Pediatrics, Soc. Pediatric Research, Am. Pediatric Soc., Am. Soc. Pediatric Nephrology (sec.-treas. 1974-80, pres. 1980-81, pub. policy com. 1991—), Am. Soc. Nephrology, Internat. Soc. Nephrology, Midwest Soc. Pediatric Research, AAAS, Salt and Water Club, N.Y. Acad. Scis., Internat. Pediatric Nephrology Assn. (asst. sec. gen. 1977-78), La. State Med. Soc., Assn. Med. Sch. Pediatric Dept. Chairmen, Am. Soc. Artificial Internal Organs, Orleans Parish Med. Soc., Greater New Orleans Pediatric Soc., Nat. Kidney Found. (health and sci. affairs com. 1989—), So. Soc. Pediatric Research, Kidney Found. La. (bd. dirs., med. adv. bd. 1981—, sci. adv. bd. 1982—), Tulane Clin. Sci. Council (chmn. 1980-90, Tulane senate com. on honors 1982-83, senator 1987-90), Alpha Omega Alpha. Home: 700 S Peters St New Orleans LA 70130-1663 Office: 1430 Tulane Ave New Orleans LA 70112-2699

LEWY, RALPH I., hotel executive; b. Leiwen, Trier, Germany, May 28, 1931; s. Rudolf Reuben and Isabella (Haas) L.; m. Doris J. Laser, Apr. 12, 1964; children: Reuben Mark, Gary Daniel. B.S. in Commerce, Roosevelt U., 1953. C.P.A., Ill. Partner, Katz, Wagner & Co. (C.P.A.s), Chgo.; Partner Grant Thornton (C.P.A.s), Chgo., 1970-76; sr. v.p. Americana Hotels Corp., Chgo., 1976-87; pres. Ralph Lewy Ltd., Chgo., 1987—. Sec., treas., bd. dirs. Albert Pick Jr. Fund; trustee Emanuel Congregation, Chgo.; v.p., bd. dirs. Lois and Leonard Laser Charitable Found. Mem. AICPA. Jewish. Office: 180 N La Salle St Ste 2401 Chicago IL 60601-2704

LEWY, ROBERT MAX, physician; b. N.Y.C., Oct. 18, 1945; s. Martin and Ellen (Newmark) L.; m. Barbara, Oct. 4, 1987; children: Jennifer, Sarah. AB, U. Rochester, 1967; MD, U. Medicine and Dentistry N.J., Newark, 1971; MPH, Columbia U., 1977. Diplomate Nat. Bd. Med. Examiners, Am. Bd. Family Practice. Intern Dartmouth Affiliated Hosps., Hanover, N.H., 1971-72; resident Maine-Dartmouth Family Practice Program, Augusta, 1974-75; clin. scholar Columbia U., N.Y.C., 1975-77; dir. employee health svcs. Presbyn. Hosp., Columbia-Presbyn. Med. Ctr., N.Y.C., 1977-88, dir. office physician affairs, 1988-91, sr. v.p. med. affairs, 1991—; assoc. prof. medicine Columbia U., N.Y.C., 1991—. Author: Preventive Primary Medicine, 1981, Employees at Risk, 1991; contbr. articles to profl. jours. With USPHS, 1972-74. Fellow Am. Occupational Med. Assn. (sec. chmn. 1984-88), Am. Coll. Preventive Medicine; mem. Am. Pub. Health Assn., N.Y. Occupational Med. Assn. (bd. dirs. 1985—). Home: 864 Bradley Pky Blauvelt NY 10913-1127 Office: Presbyn Hosp 622 W 168th St New York NY 10032-3702

LEWYN, THOMAS MARK, lawyer; b. N.Y.C., July 2, 1930; s. Oswald and Agnes (Maas) L.; m. Ann Salfeld, July 15, 1955; children—Alfred Thomas, Mark Henry. B.A., Stanford, 1952, postgrad., 1952-54; LL.B., Columbia, 1955. Bar: N.Y. 1957. Since practiced in N.Y.C.; assoc. Simpson, Thacher & Bartlett, N.Y.C., 1957-64, ptnr., 1965-75, sr. ptnr., 1976-90, of counsel, 1991—; bd. dirs. Metro-Goldwyn-Mayer, Inc. Contbr. articles to profl. jours. Served to 1st lt., F.A. AUS, 1955-57. Mem. ABA, Assn. of Bar of City of N.Y., N.Y. State Bar Assn. Home: 911 Park Ave New York NY 10021-0337 Office: Simpson Thacher & Bartlett 425 Lexington Ave New York NY 10017-3903

LEY, BOB, sports network anchor, reporter. BA in Comms. magna cum laude, Seton Hall U., 1976. Dir. sports/pub. affairs Suburban Cablevision (TV-3), East Orange, N.J., 1976-79; prodn. mgr. Sta. WOR-AM, N.Y.C., 1975-77; ET Sports Ctr. ESPN, 1988-92, NCAA basketball studio host, 1980-89, corr. NCAA basketball Final Four games, 1980—, corr. World Series, 1989, host NFL Draft coverage, 1980-89, host World Cup Soccer, Australian Rules Football Grand Final, play-by-play commentator coll. basketball, boxing, soccer, host Outside the Lines series, 1990—, regular co-anchor SportsCenter, 1979—; pub. address announcer for Cosmos of the N.Am. Soccer League; sportswriter Passaic (N.J.) Herald-News. Recipient four Cable ACE awards, two Sports Emmy awards for Sports Journalism, 1990, 91. Office: c/o ESPN ESPN Pla Bristol CT 06010

LEY, HERBERT LEONARD, JR., retired epidemiologist; b. Columbus, Ohio, Sept. 7, 1923; s. Herbert Leonard and Laura (Spencer) L. M.D., Harvard U., 1946, M.P.H., 1951. Commd. 1st lt. M.C., U.S. Army, 1947, advanced through grades to lt. col., 1955; resigned, 1958; ret. col. USAR, 1983; prof. microbiology George Washington U. Sch. Medicine, 1958-61; civil service with U.S. Army Research Office, 1961-63; asso. prof. epidemiology and microbiology Harvard Sch. Pub. Health, 1963-66; dir. Bur. Medicine, FDA, 1966-68, commr. food and drugs, 1968-69; cons. to food and drug industry, 1969-93. Contbr. sci. articles to profl. jours., chpts to med. texts. Decorated Bronze Star. Fellow Am. Coll. Preventive Medicine; mem. Am. Acad. Microbiology. Office: 4816 Camelot St Rockville MD 20853-3018

LEY, RONALD, psychologist, educator; b. Buffalo, N.Y., Oct. 19, 1929; s. August Andreas and Marie (Jerge) L.; m. Carmen De Brito, Jan. 16, 1965; 1 child, Jessica Elizabeth. BA, U. Buffalo, 1951; PhD, Syracuse U., 1963. Rsch. dir. Madison Area Project, Syracuse, 1962-63; asst. prof. psychology No. Ill. U., DeKalb, 1963-64, Grad. Faculty, New Sch. for Social Rsch., N.Y.C., 1964-66; prof. psychology and stats. SUNY, Albany, 1966—; cons. Nat. Inst. for Occupational Safety and Health; vis. prof. psychology U. P.R., 1969, cardiac dept., Charing Cross Hosp., London, 1988. Author: A Whisper of Espionage, 1990, Rumores de Espionaje: Wolfgang Köhler y los Monos en Tenerife, 1995; editor: Behavioral and Psychological Approaches to Breathing Disorders, 1994; mem. editl. bd. Jour. Behavior Therapy and Exptl. Psychiatry, 1993—, Applied Psycholphysiology and Biofeedback, 1997—; guest editor: Biofeedback and Self-Regulation, 1994; contbr. articles to profl. jours. Bd. dirs. Father's Assn. of the Albany Acad. for Girls, 1981-84. Rsch. fellow SUNY, 1967-68, 70, 74, 76, 78, 91, Rsch. grantee, 1967-72, 74-76, 78, 87-88, 91-92, 96-97, Nat. Inst. Occupl. Safety and Health grantee, 1982-83, 87-88, others. Fellow Behavior Therapy and Rsch. Soc.; mem. APA, Am. Psychol. Soc., Am. Statis. Assn., Assn. Advancement Behavior Therapy, Assn. Applied Psychophysiology and Biofeedback, Author's Guild, Author's League Am., Ea. Psychol. Assn., Internat. Soc. Advancement Respiratory Psychophysiology (pres. 1993-96), New Eng. Soc. Behavior Analysis and Therapy, Psychol. Assn. Northeastern N.Y. (sec. 1967-68, pres. 1983-84, Disting. Psychologist award 1996), N.Y. Acad. Scis., Soc. Psychophysiol. Rsch., Psychonomic Soc., Sigma Xi. Home: 22 Marion Ave Albany NY 12203-1823 Office: SUNY 1400 Washington Ave Albany NY 12222-0100

LEYDA, JAMES PERKINS, pharmaceutical company executive; b. Youngstown, Ohio, Oct. 2, 1935; s. Walter Cletus and Dorothy Eleanor (Perkins) L.; m. Barbara Marie Dykstra, Sept. 9, 1967; children: Jason Walter, Jeffrey Albert, Justin Michael. B.S. in Pharmacy, Ohio No. U., 1957; M.Sc. in Pharmacy, Ohio State U., 1959, Ph.D., 1962. Registered pharmacist, Ohio. Devel. chemist Lederle Labs., Pearl River, N.Y., 1962-66; mgr. new product devel. Cyanamid Internat., Pearl River, 1966-69; dir. new product devel. Merrell Internat., N.Y.C. also Westport, Conn., 1969-81, dir. pharmacy research Merrell Dow Pharm., Cin., 1981-84, dir. comml. devel., 1984-89; assoc. dir. product approval Marion Merrell Dow Inc. (name changed to Hoechst Marion Roussel, Inc.), Cin., 1989-92; mgr. strategic rsch. alliances Hoescht Marion Roussel, Inc., 1992—. Author: Pharmaceutical Chemistry, 1964; contbr. articles to profl. jours. Recipient Ohio No. U./Bristol Labs. Bristol award, 1957; Richardson Merrell Inc. Lunsford Richardson award, 1960; NIH Predoctoral Fellowship award, 1960. Mem. Am. Pharm. Assn., Acad. Pharm. Scis., N.Y. Acad. Scis., AAAS, Sigma Xi. Avocations: Tennis, golf. Home: 10597 Tanagerhills Dr Cincinnati OH 45249-3634 Office: Hoechst Marion Roussel Inc 2110 E Galbraith Rd Cincinnati OH 45237-1625

LEYDEN, NORMAN, conductor; m. Alice Leyden; children: Robert, Constance. Grad., Yale U., 1938; MA, Columbia U., EdD, 1968. Bass clarinetist New Haven Symphony; arranger Glenn Miller Air Force Band, Eng., France; chief arranger Glenn Miller Orch., 1946-49; freelance arranger N.Y.C.; mus. dir. RCA Victor Records, Arthur Godfrey, 1956-59; with Oreg. Symphony, 1970—, assoc. conductor, 1974—; music dir. Seattle Symphony Pops, 1975-93; tchr. Columbia U.; guest condr. over 40 Am.

symphony orchs. including Boston Pops, Minn. Orch., Pitts. Symphony, St. Louis Symphony, San Diego Symphony, San Francisco Symphony, Nat. Symphony, Utah Symphony; condr. Army Air Force. Office: Oreg Symphony Orch 711 SW Alder St Ste 200 Portland OR 97205

LEYDET, FRANÇOIS GUILLAUME, writer; b. Neuilly-sur-Seine, France, Aug. 26, 1927; came to U.S., 1940, naturalized, 1956; s. Bruno and Dorothy (Lindsey) L. AB, Harvard, 1947, postgrad. Bus. Sch., 1952; postgrad. Johns Hopkins Sch. Advanced Internat. Studies, 1952-53; Bachelier-es-lettres-philosophie, U. Paris (France), 1945; m. Patience Abbe, June 17, 1955 (div.); step-children: Catherine Abbe Geissler, Lisa Amanda O'Mahony; m. Roslyn Carney, June 14, 1970; step-children: Walter E. Robb IV, Rachel R. Avery, Holly H. Prunty, Mary-Peck Peters. Past dir. Marin County Planned Parenthood Assn., Planned Parenthood Center Tucson; docent Ariz.-Sonora Desert Mus. 1st lt. French Army, 1947-48. Mem. Nat. Parks Assn., Wilderness Soc., Sierra Club, Nat. Audubon Soc., World Wildlife Fund, Am. Mus. Natural History, Environ. Def. Fund, Ariz.-Sonora Desert Mus., Ariz. Hist. Soc., LWV, Ariz. Opera League, Commonwealth Club. Author: The Last Redwoods, 1963, Time and the River Flowing: Grand Canyon, 1964, The Coyote: Defiant Songdog of the West, 1977; editor: Tomorrow's Wilderness, 1963; editor Noticias; contbr. to Nat. Geog. mag. Died Mar. 4, 1997. Home: 5165 N Camino Real Tucson AZ 85718-5026

LEYDORF, FREDERICK LEROY, lawyer; b. Toledo, June 13, 1930; s. Loftin Herman and Dorothy DeRoyal (Cramer) L.; m. Mary MacKenzie Malcolm, Mar. 28, 1953; children: Robert Malcolm, William Frederick, Katherine Ann, Thomas Richard, Deborah Mary. Student, U. Toledo, 1948-49; B.B.A., U. Mich., 1953; J.D., UCLA, 1958. Bar: Calif. 1959, U.S. Supreme Ct. 1970. Assoc. Hammack & Pugh, L.A., 1959-61; ptnr. Willis, Butler, Scheifly, Leydorf & Grant, L.A., 1961-81, Pepper, Hamilton & Scheetz, L.A., 1981-83, Hufstedler & Kaus, L.A., 1983-95; lectr., cons. Calif. Continuing Edn. of Bar, 1965-92; mem. planning com. Probate and Trust Conf., U. So. Calif., 1984-92. Contbg. author: California Non-Profit Corporations, 1969; contbr. articles to profl. jours. Chmn. pub. adminstr.-pub. guardian adv. commn. Los Angeles County Bd. Suprs., 1972-73; bd. dirs. J.W. and Ida M. Jameson Found., 1967—, Western Ctr. on Law and Poverty, Inc., 1980-82, L.A. Heart Inst., 1988-90; mem. legal com. Music Ctr. Found., 1980-95; mem. lawyers adv. coun. Constl. Rights Found., 1982-85; mem. devel. adv. bd. U. Mich. Sch. Bus. Adminstrn., 1984-90; mem. adv. bd. UCLA-CEB Estate Planning Inst., 1979-92; Lt. USNR, 1953-55. Mem. ABA, L.A. County Bar Assn. (bd. trustees 1973-75), State Bar Calif. (chmn. conf. dels. 1977, Alumnus of Yr. award, conf. of dels. 1983, mem. exec. com. estate planning, trust and probate law sect. 1979-80), L.A. County Bar Found. (pres. 1977-79, bd. dirs. 1975-87), Am. Coll. Trust and Estate Counsel, Internat. Acad. Estate and Trust Law (v.p. N.Am. 1978-82), Life Ins. and Trust Coun. L.A. (pres. 1983-84), UCLA Law Alumni Assn. (pres. 1982), L.A. World Affairs Coun., Chancery Club (pres. 1991-92), Jonathan Club, Laguna Hills Golf Club, Phi Delta Phi, Phi Delta Theta. Republican. Lutheran. Home: 3078-D Via Serena S Laguna Hills CA 92653-2771

LEYH, GEORGE FRANCIS, association executive; b. Utica, N.Y., Oct. 1, 1931; s. George Robert and Mary Kathleen (Haley) L.; m. Mary Alice Mosher, Sept. 17, 1955; children—Timothy George, Kristin Ann. B.C.E., Cornell U., 1954; M.S. (Univ. fellow), 1956. Structural engr. Eckerlin and Klepper, Syracuse, N.Y., 1956-59; asso. dir. engring. Martin Marietta Corp., Chgo., 1959-63; structural engr. Portland Cement Assn., Chgo., 1963-67; dir. mktg. Concrete Reinforcing Steel Inst., Chgo., 1967-75; exec. v.p. Am. Concrete Inst., Detroit, 1975—; editor jour. Am. Concrete Inst., 1975—. Mem. Planning Commn., Streamwood, Ill., 1960-68; chmn. Lake Bluff (Ill.) Citizens Com. for Conservation, 1972. Recipient Bloem Disting. Service award Am. Concrete Inst., 1972. Mem. ASCE, Am. Soc. Assn. Execs. (chmn. key profl. assns. com. 1989-90), Nat. Inst. Bldg. Scis., Am. Ry. Engring. Assn., Am. Nat. Standards Inst. (bd. dirs. 1986—), Am. Soc. for Concrete Constrn. (bd. dirs. 1984—), Phi Kappa Phi. Clubs: North Cape Yacht, Lake Bluff Yacht (dir. 1969-74, commodore 1973). Home: 1327 Lone Pine Rd Bloomfield Hills MI 48302-2756 Office: Am Concrete Inst PO Box 9094 Farmington Hills MI 48333

LEYH, RICHARD EDMUND, SR., retired investment executive; b. Union City, N.J., Mar. 25, 1930; s. Louis Anthony and Grace Agnes (Barringer) L.; m. Patricia Ann Ryan, Apr. 18, 1949; children: Gail, Gloria, Anne, Teresa, Richard, Elizabeth, David. Student, Rutgers U., 1948-49. Sr. clk. Jersey Cen. Power and Light Co., Asbury Park, N.J., 1949-52; dist. mgr. N.J. Natural Gas Co., Asbury Park, 1952-56; methods analyst Univac, Newark, 1957-60; adv. systems engr. IBM, N.Y.C., 1960-65; mgr. real time systems N.Y. Stock Exchange, N.Y.C., 1965-66; dir. ops. Carlisle DeCoppet and Co., N.Y.C., 1967-76; exec. v.p., chief ops. officer Securities Industry Automation Corp., N.Y.C., 1976-91. Mem. Am. Mgmt. Assn., Inst. for Certification Computer Profls. Democrat. Roman Catholic. Avocations: bridge, golf, swimming. Home: 149 Ocean Hollow Ln Saint Augustine FL 32095 Office: Securities Industry Automation Corp Two MetroTech Ctr Brooklyn NY 11201

LEYHANE, FRANCIS JOHN, III, lawyer; b. Chgo., Mar. 29, 1957; s. Francis J. and Mary Elizabeth (Crowley) L.; m. Diana M. Urizarri, May 8, 1982; children: Katherine, Francis J. IV, Joseph, Brigid Rose, James Matthew. BA, Loyola U., Chgo., 1977, JD, 1980. Bar: Ill. 1980, U.S. Dist. Ct. (no. dist.) Ill. 1980, U.S. Ct. Appeals (7th cir.) 1986. Assoc. Condon, Cook & Roche, Chgo., 1980-87; ptnr. Condon & Cook, Chgo., 1988—. Contbr. articles to profl. jours. Mem. Sch. bd. Immaculate Conception Parish, Chgo., 1993-96. Fellow Ill. Bar Found.; mem. Appellate Lawyers Assn. Ill., Ill. State Bar Assn. (mem. assembly 1987-90), Chgo. Bar Assn., Blue Key. Office: Condon & Cook 745 N Dearborn St Chicago IL 60610-3826

LEYLAND, JAMES RICHARD, professional baseball team manager; b. Toledo, Dec. 15, 1944; m. Katie Leyland. Player various minor league teams Detroit Tigers, 1964-69, coach minor league system, 1970-71, mgr. minor league system, 1971-81; coach Chgo. White Sox, 1981-85; mgr. Pitts. Pirates, 1985-96, Fla. Marlins, 1997—. Christmas chmn. Salvation Army, 1990-91. Named Nat. League Mgr. of Yr. Baseball Writers' Assn. Am., 1988, 90, Sporting News, 1990, Man of Yr. Arthritis Found., 1989, Epilepsy Found., 1991. Office: Fla Marlins 2267 NW 199th St Miami FL 33056*

LEYLEGIAN, JACK H., II, investment management company executive; b. Providence, Oct. 26, 1935; m. Dorothy Patricia Aprahamian, July 21, 1957; children: George A., Debra A. BSBA, Boston U., 1957; MBA, U. So. Calif., 1960. Vice pres. No. Trust Co., Chgo., 1966-71; pres. Dreyfus Mgmt. Inc., N.Y.C., 1971-77, Bank Am. Investment Mgmt. Co., San Francisco, 1977-81, Leylegian Investment Mgmt. Inc., Menlo Park, Calif., 1981—; bd. dirs. Imperial Bank, Los Angeles. Mem. Chartered Fin. Analysts Soc., San Francisco Security Analysts Soc. Office: Leylegian Investment Mgmt 601 Gateway Blvd Ste 700 South San Francisco CA 94080-7007

LEYMASTER, GLEN R., former medical association executive; b. Aurora, Nebr., Aug. 17, 1915; s. Leslie and Frances (Wertman) L.; m. Margaret Hendricks, June 20, 1942; children: Mark H., Mary Beth, Lynn F. A.B., U. Nebr., 1938; M.D., Harvard, 1942; M.P.H., Johns Hopkins U., 1950. Intern, asst. resident, resident Harvard Med. Service, Boston City Hosp., 1942-44; mem. faculty Johns Hopkins Med. Sch., 1944-48; instr., asst. prof. bacteriology Sch. Pub. Health and Hygiene, 1946-48; asso. prof. pub. health, instr. medicine U. Utah Sch. Medicine, 1948-50, prof., head dept., preventive medicine, asst. prof. medicine, also dir. univ. health service, 1950-60; adviser med. edn.- preventive medicine ICA, Bangkok, Thailand, 1956-58; asso. sec. council med. edn. and hosps. AMA, Chgo., 1960-63; pres., dean Women's Med. Coll. Pa., 1964-70; dir. dept. undergrad. med. edn. AMA, 1970-75; exec. dir. Am. Bd. Med. Spltys., Evanston, Ill., 1975-81; ret. exec. dir., 1981. Contbr. articles to profl. jours. Mem. AMA, Ill. Med. Assn., Inst. Medicine Chgo., Phi Beta Kappa, Sigma Xi, Alpha Omega Alpha. Home: 93 Kendal Dr Kennett Square PA 19348-2327

L'HEUREUX, JOHN CLARKE, English language educator; b. South Hadley, Mass., Oct. 26, 1934; s. Wilfred Joseph and Mildred (Clarke) L'H.; m. Joan Ann Polston, June 26, 1971. AB, Weston Coll., 1959, Licentiate in Philosophy, 1960; MA, Boston Coll., 1963; Licentiate in Sacred Theology, Woodstock Coll., 1967; postgrad., Harvard U., 1967-68. Ordained priest Roman Catholic Ch., 1966, laicized, 1971; writer in residence Georgetown U., 1964-65, Regis Coll., 1968-69; staff editor The Atlantic, 1968-69, contbg. editor, 1969-83; vis. prof. Am. lit. Hamline U., 1971, Tufts Coll., 1971-72; vis. asst. prof. Harvard U., 1973; asst. prof. Stanford U., 1973-79, assoc. prof., 1979-81, prof., 1981—, Lane prof. humanities, 1985-90, dir. creative writing program, 1976-89. Author: Quick as Dandelions, 1964, Rubrics for a Revolution, 1967, Picnic in Babylon, 1967, One Eye and a Measuring Rod, 1968, No Place for Hiding, 1971, Tight White Collar, 1972, The Clang Birds, 1972, Family Affairs, 1974, Jessica Fayer, 1976, Desires, 1981, A Woman Run Mad, 1988, Comedians, 1990, An Honorable Profession, 1991, The Shrine at Altamira, 1992, The Handmaid of Desire, 1996. Office: Stanford U Dept English Stanford CA 94305

L'HEUREUX-DUBÉ, CLAIRE, judge; b. Quebec City, Que., Can., Sept. 7, 1927; d. Paul H. and Marguerite (Dion) L'H.; m. Arthur Dubé (dec. 197u); children: Louise, Pierre (dec. 1994). BA magna cum laude, Coll. Notre-Dame de Bellevue, Que., 1946; LLL cum laude, Laval U., Que., 1951, LLD (hon.), 1984; LLD (hon.), Dalhousie U., 1981, Montreal U., 1983, Ottawa U., 1988, U. Que., 1989, U. Toronto, 1994. Bar: Que. 1952. Ptnr. Bard, L'Heureux & Philippon, 1952-73; sr. ptnr. L'Heureux, Philippon, Garneau, Tourigny, St.Arnaud & Assocs., from 1969; Puisne judge Superior Ct. Que., 1973-79, Ct. Appeal of Que., 1979-87, Supreme Ct. Can., Ottawa, 1987—; commr. Part II Inquiries Act Dept. Manpower and Immigration, Montreal, 1973-76; del. Gen. Coun. Bar of Que., 1968-70, com. on adminstrn. justice, 1968-73, others; pres. family law com. Family Ct. com. Que Civil Code Rev. Office, 1972-76; pres. Can. sect. Internat. Commn. Jurists, 1981-83, v.p., 1992—. Editor: (with Rosalie S. Abella) Family Law - Dimensions of Justice, 1983; chmn. editorial bd. Can. Bar Rev., 1985-88; author articles, conf. proc., book chpt. Bd. dirs. YWCA, Que., 1969-73, Ctr. des Loisirs St. Sacrement, 1969-73, Ctr. Jeunesse de Tilly-Ctr. des Jeunes, 1971-77; v.p. Can. Consumers Coun., 1970-73; v.p. Vanier Inst. of the Family, 1972-73; lifetime gov. Found. Univ. Laval, 1980, bd. dirs., 1984-85; mem. Comité des grandes orientations de l'Univ. Laval, 1971-72; mem. nat. coun. Can. Human Rights Found., 1980-82, 82-84; mem. Can. del. to Peoples Republic China on Status of Women, 1981; pres. Can. sect. Internat. Commn. Jurists, 1981-83, v.p. internat. bd., 1992—. Apptd. Queen's Counsel, 1969; recipient Medal of the Alumni, U. Laval, 1986, Médaille du Barreau de Que., 1987. Mem. Can. Bar Assn. Can. Inst. Adminstrn. Justice, Internat. Soc. Family Law (bd. dirs. 1977-88, v.p. 1981-88), Internat. Fedn. Women Lawyers, Fedn. Internat. des Femmes Juristes, L'Assn. des Femmes Diplômées d'Univ., Assn. Québécoise pour l'Étude Comparative du Droit (pres. 1984-90), Am. Coll. Trial Lawyers (hon.), Am. Law Inst., Phi Delta Phi. Roman Catholic. Office: Supreme Ct Can, Wellington St, Ottawa, ON Canada K1A 0J1*

LHEVINE, DAVE BERNARD, radiologist, educator; b. Tulsa, May 20, 1922; s. Morris Boise and Sarah Fannie (Piatt) L.; m. Mary Helen Orr, Dec. 19, 1963 (div. July 1986); children: Rhonda Dean, Paul Morris; m. Catherine Marie Garvey, Mar. 28, 1992. BA, Okla. U., 1943, MD, 1945. Diplomate Am. Bd. Radiology. Intern U.S. Naval Hosp., Bklyn., 1945-46; resident in radiology St. Louis City Hosp., Bklyn., 1948-51, 1948-51; dir. dept. radiology Hillcrest Med. Ctr., Tulsa, 1951-83, dir. dept. radiation therapy, 1983-86; clin. prof. dept. radiation oncology Okla. U., Oklahoma City, 1987-95; vice chmn. dept. radiology Okla. U. Sch. Medicine Tulsa Med. Coll., 1978—; corp. sec. Sterling Oil Co. of Okla., Tulsa, 1987-94. Active Tulsa County Dem. politics. Elected chmn. Tulsa County Dem. Com., 1995. Lt. (j.g.) USN, 1942-47. Fellow Am. Coll. Radiology (hon., emeritus); mem. AMA, Radiol. Soc. of N.Am., Okla. State Radiol. Soc. (pres. 1958). Democrat. Avocations: sailing, painting, photography, computers. Home: 2716 E 26th Pl Tulsa OK 74114-4308

LHOTKA, SIDNEY BRUNO, tax accountant; b. Sevetin, Bohemia, Czechsolvakia, Apr. 4, 1926; came to U.S., 1956; s. Vaclav Vojtech and Helena (Valkova) L.; m. Jana M. Lhotka, Mar. 29, 1958. A in Acctg., U. Queensland, Australia, 1958, B in Comm., 1959. Acct., acctg. mgr. Bechtel Corp., San Francisco, 1956-61, product svcs. mgr., 1964-66, 68-83; asst. svcs. mgr. Transport Co. of Tex., Kwajalein, Mich., 1962-64; office mgr. systems and procedures RMK-BRJ Vietnam, Saigon, 1966-68; prin. Fin. and Tax Svcs., Concord, Calif., 1983—. Fellow Australian Soc. of Cert. Practicing Accts.; mem. Nat. Soc. of Pub. Accts., Nat. Assn. of Enrolled Agts., Internat. Assn. of Fin. Planning. Avocations: bicycle riding, swimming, walking. Home: 1314 Corte De Los Vecinos Walnut Creek CA 94598-2902 Office: Fin and Tax Svcs Concord CA 94520

L'HUILLIER, PETER (PETER), archbishop; b. Paris, Dec. 3, 1926; came to U.S., 1980; s. Eugene Henry and Emilienne (Haslin) L'H. Diploma, Inst. St. Denys, Paris, 1949; License of Theology, Moscow Theol. Acad., 1962, D of Canon Law, 1985. Ordained priest Russian Orthodox Ch. in Western Europe, 1954. Lectr. St. Denys Inst., Paris, 1949-50, Three Hierarchs Sem., Villemoisson, France, 1952-62; priest Russian Ch., Paris, 1954-68; prof. Cath. U., Paris, 1966-78; bishop of Chersonese, Diocese of France Russian Ch., Paris, 1968-79, archbishop of Chersonese, 1979; aux. bishop of Bklyn. Orthodox Ch. in Am., N.Y.C., 1979-81; bishop N.Y. and N.J. Orthodox Ch. in Am., 1981-89; archbishop of N.Y. and N.J. Orthodox Ch. in Am., N.Y.C., 1990—; chmn. dept. external affairs Orthodox Ch. in Am., Syosset, N.Y., 1990—; adj. prof. St. Vladimir's Orthodox Sem., Crestwood, N.Y., 1980—; canonical advisor, chmn. theol. edn. commn. Standing Conf. Canonical Orthodox Bishops in Am., N.Y.C. Author: The Church of the Ancient Councils, 1996. Office: Orthodox Ch in Am 33 Hewitt Ave Bronxville NY 10708-2333

LI, CHAOYING, biomedical researcher; b. Jingshan, Hubei, China, July 20, 1958; came to U.S., 1990; s. Yi Li and Yulan Liu; m. Chuli Yi, June 10, 1985; 1 child, Shu. MD, Tongji Med. U., Wuhan, Hubei, China, 1983, MS in Neurobiology, 1989. Asst. Tongji Med. U., Wuhan, 1983-89, lectr., 1989-90; vis. fellow NIH, Rockville, Md., 1990-94, intramural rsch. training award fellow, 1994-95, sr. staff fellow, 1995—. Author: Alcohol, Cell Membranes and Signal Transolution, 1993; contbr. articles to profl. jours. Mem. Soc. Neurosci. Achievements include demonstration for the first time that alcohols affect the function of a neuronal membrane receptor by a direct interaction with the receptor protein, zinc potentiates excitatory action of ATP, copper enhances the function of P2X purinoceptors, protons potentiate ATP-gated ion channel responses to ATP and zinc, and magnesium inhibits the function of P2X purinoceptors by decreasing the affinity of the receptor for ATP. Home: 110 Apple Blossom Way Gaithersburg MD 20878 Office: NIH/NIAAA/LMCN 12501 Washington Ave Rockville MD 20852-1823

LI, CHING-CHUNG, electrical engineering, computer science educator; b. Changshu, Kiangsu, China, Mar. 30, 1932; came to U.S., 1954, naturalized, 1972; s. Lung-Han and Lien-Tseng (Hwa) L.; m. Hanna Wu, June 10, 1961; children: William Wei-Lin, Vincent Wei-Tsin. B.S.E.E., Nat. Taiwan U., 1954; M.S.E.E., Northwestern U., 1956, Ph.D., 1961. Jr. engr. analytical dept. Westinghouse Electric Corp., East Pittsburgh, Pa., 1957; inst. fellow Northwestern U., Evanston, Ill., 1957-59; asst. prof. elec. engring. U. Pitts., 1959-62, assoc. prof., 1962-67; vis. assoc. prof. elec. engring. U. Calif.-Berkeley, 1964; vis. prin. scientist Alza Corp., Palo Alto, Calif., 1970; faculty rsch. participant Pitts. Energy Tech. Ctr., Dept. Energy, Pitts., 1982, 83, 85, 88, 89; prof. elec. engring. U. Pitts., 1967—, prof. computer sci., 1977—; mem. Ctr. Multivariate Analysis, 1982-87, Ctr. for Parallel and Distributed Intelligent Systems, 1986—; sabbatical leave Lab. for Info. and Decision Systems, MIT, 1988; mem. sci. adv. com. Horus Therapeutics, Inc., 1995—. Guest editor Jour. Cybernetics and Info. Sci., 1979, Computerized Med. Imaging and Graphics, 1991; assoc. editor Pattern Recognition, 1985—; contbr. articles to profl. jours. Co-recipient cert. of merit Radiol. Soc. N.Am., 1979; rsch. grantee NSF, 1975-81, 85-87, Pa. Dept. Health, 1977-79, We. Pa. Advanced Tech. Ctr., 1983-84, 86-88, Health Rsch. and Svc. Found., 1985-86, Air Force Office Sci. Rsch., 1990-93. Fellow IEEE (tech. com., com. chmn. 1967—); mem. Biomed. Engring. Soc., AAAS, N.Y. Acad. Sci., Pattern Recognition Soc., Sigma Xi, Eta Kappa Nu. Home: 2130 Garrick Dr Pittsburgh PA 15235-5033 Office: U Pitts Dept Elec Engring Pittsburgh PA 15261

LI, CHU-TSING, art history educator; b. Canton, China, 1920; came to U.S., 1947; m. Yao-wen; children: Ulysses, Amy. B.A., U. Nanking, 1943; M.A. in English Lit., U. Iowa, 1949, Ph.D. in Art History, 1955. Instr. U. Iowa, 1954-55, 56-58, asst. prof., 1958-62, assoc. prof., 1962-65, prof., 1965-66; prof. art history U. Kans., Lawrence, 1966-78, dept. chmn., 1972-78, Judith Harris Murphy Disting. prof., 1978-90, prof. emeritus, 1990—, dir. NEH summer seminar on Chinese art history, 1975, 78, coordinator Mellon faculty seminar, 1979; acting asst. prof. Oberlin Coll., 1955-56; asst. prof. Ind. U., summer 1956; coordinator N.Y. state faculty seminar on Chineses Art History, SUNY, 1965; research curator Nelson Gallery of Art, Kansas City, 1966—; vis. prof. fine arts Chinese U., Hong Kong, 1972-73, summer 1971, leader China visit group, 1973; vis. prof. Grad. Inst. Art History, Nat Taiwan U., 1990; vis. Andrew W. Mellon prof. U. Pitts., 1995; dir. NEH Summer Inst. Modern Chinese Art and Culture, 1991; participant Internat. Symposiums on Chinese Painting, Nat. Palace Mus., Taipei, 1970, Cleve. Mus. Art, 1981, Huangshan Sch. Painters, Hefei, Ahnui, Rep. China, 1984, on Words and Images in Chinese Painting, Met. Mus. Art, N.Y.C., 1985, on the Elegant Brush: Chinese Painting under the Qianlong Emperor, Phoenix Art Mus., 1985, to celebrate 60th anniversary Nat. Palace Mus., Taipei, Taiwan, 1985, on History of Yuan Dynasty, Nanjing U., China, 1986, on art of Badashanren (Chu Tua), Nanchang, China, 1986; on Dunhuang Grottoes, China, 1987; on the Four Monk Painters, Shanghai Mus., 1987; on art of Chang Dai-chien, Nat. Mus. History, Taipei, 1988; Symposium on Contemporary Artistic Development, Nanjing, 1988; Symposium on Chinese Painting of Ming Dynasty Chinese U. Hong Kong, 1988; Symposium on Chinese Painting of the Ming and Qing Dynasties from the Forbidden City, Cleve. Mus. Art, 1989, Symposium on Hist. Studies, since 1911, Nat. Taiwan U., 1989, Symposium on 40th Anniversary of Founding of Liaoning Provincial Mus., Shenyang, China, 1989, Symposium on Painting of Wu Sch., Palace Mus., Beijing, 1990; Internat. Colloquium on Chinese Art History, Nat. Palace Mus. Taipei, 1991, Internat. Symposium on Art of Four Wangs, Shanghai, 1992, VIIeme Colloque Internat. de Sinologie, Chantilly, France, 1992, Symposium Painting at Close Qing Empire, Phoenix, 1992, Symposium on Ming & Qing Painting, Beijing, Symposium on Art of Zhao Meng-fu, Shanghai, 1995, Symposium on 20th Century Chinese Painting, Hong Kong Mus. Art, 1995; spl. cons. Chinese U., Hong Kong, 1971, Symposium on Painting and Calligraphy by Ming Loyalists, Early Ch'ing Period, 1975. Author: books and exhbn. catalogues including The Autumn Colors on the Ch'iao and Hua Mountains, A Painting by Chao Meng-fu, 1254-1322, 1965, Liu Kuo-sung: The Development of a Modern Chinese Artist, 1970, A Thousand Peaks and Myriad Ravines: Chinese Paintings in the Charles A. Drenowatz Collection, 2 vols., 1974, Trends in Modern Chinese Painting, 1979; co-editor, contbr. Chinese Scholar's Studio: Artistic Life in Late Ming, Asia Soc., N.Y.C., 1987; editor, contbr.: Artists and Patrons: Some Social and Economic Aspects of Chinese Painting, 1990; contbr. articles to books and catalogues. Ford Found. Fgn. Area Tng. fellow, 1959-60; grantee Am. Council Learned Socs. and Social Sci. Research Council, 1963-64, NEH, 1975, 78, 91, Com. for Scholarly Communication with People's Republic of China Nat. Acad. Scis., 1979, Am. Council Learned Socs., 1980, Asian Cultural Council, N.Y., 1981, Kans. U., summers 1966-80; U. Iowa research prof., 1963-64; Fulbright-Hayes faculty fellow, 1968-69. Mem. Coll. Art Assn. Am., Assn. for Asian Studies, Midwest Art History Soc., Internat. House of Japan, Min-chiu Soc. Hong Kong, Phi Tau Phi, Phi Beta Kappa (hon.), Phi Beta Delta. Home: 1108 Avalon Rd Lawrence KS 66044-2506 Office: Univ Kans Kress Found Dept Art History Lawrence KS 66045

LI, DAVID WAN-CHENG, cell biologist; b. Heng Shan, Peoples Republic of China, Sept. 2, 1960; came to the U.S., 1986; s. Xi-Lin and Xin-Tao (Guo) L.; m. Lilly Liu, June 17, 1986; children: Flora, Jesse. BS, Hunan Normal U., 1982, MS, 1985; PhD, U. Wash., 1992. Lectr. in biology Hunan Normal U., Chang Sha, Peoples Republic of China, 1987-94, adj. prof. biology, 1995—; teaching asst. U. Alta., Edmonton, Can., 1986; teaching and rsch. asst. U. Wash., Seattle, 1986-92; rsch. scientist Columbia U., N.Y.C., 1992-95, asst. prof. ophthalmology, 1996—. Contbr. articles to profl. jours. Exec. pres. June 4th Found., Seattle, 1990-92, bd. dirs., 1989—. Mem. AAAS, Am. Soc. Cell Biology, Am. Soc. Biochemistry and Molecular Biology, Soc. Devel. Biology, Internat. Soc. Eye Rsch., N.Y. Acad. Sci., Assn. for Rsch. in Vision and Ophthalmology. Achievements include devel. of a set of biol. stds. for the hybrid yue carp and its parents; identification of pair of duplicated genes coding for two different isoelectric forms of insect pigment protein and cloning of these genes; discovery of a common cellular mechanism for non-congenital cataract formation in humans and animals. Mailing Address: PO Box 263 Audubon Sta New York NY 10032 Office: Columbia U Dept Ophthalmology 630 W 168th St New York NY 10032-3702

LI, FU, electrical engineering educator, editor; b. Chengdu, Sichuan, China, Sept. 12, 1958; came to U.S., 1985; s. Zhi and Xiu-Juan (Ding) L.; m. Grace Hui Fang, Mar. 18, 1984; children: Susan J., Karen M. BS in Physics, Sichuan U., 1982, MS in Physics, 1985; PhD in Elec. Engring., U. R.I., 1990. Profl. engr., Oreg. Rsch./teaching asst. U. R.I., Kingston, 1986-89; rsch. staff Philips Labs., Briarcliff Manor, N.Y., summer 1987; tech. staff Prime Computer, Inc., Bedford, Mass., 1989-90; asst. prof. elec. engring. Portland (Oreg.) State U., 1990-94, assoc. prof. elec. engring., 1994—. Author chpts. to 4 books, 1991-94; contbr. articles to profl. jours. Recipient Faculty Devel. award Portland State U., 1991, Pew Teaching Leadership award 2d Nat. Conf. on Teaching Assts., 1989, Excellent Paper award Chinese Assn. Sci. and Tech., 1986. Mem. NSPE, IEEE (sr., assoc. editor Transactions on Signal Processing 1993—, organizer Oreg. chpt. 1993, chair 1993-95, exec. com. 1993—, session chair internat. conf. on acoustice, speech and signal processing 1993-96, session chair statis. signals and array processing workshop 1992, 94, tech. com. on statis. signals and array processing 1992—, chair tech. subcom. power spectrum estimation 1992—, chair 1994—, recognition award 1993, chpt. chmn. award 1994, outstanding counselor award 1995), Eta Kappa Nu. Avocations: thinking, reading, playing computer, swimming, investing. Office: Portland State Univ Dept Elec Engring 1800 SW 6th Ave Portland OR 97201-5204

LI, GERALD, architect, film producer and director; b. Washington, Mar. 4, 1942; s. Chen Sheng and Gloria (Mark) L.; m. Annemarie van Kersen, Oct. 31, 1972 (div. 1990); children: Alexis, Madison. BS, Rensselaer Poly. Inst., 1963, BArch, 1965. Architect Edward Larabee Barnes, N.Y.C., 1965-67; with Romaldo Guirgola, N.Y.C., 1967-68, Brown-Daltas, Rome, 1969-70, Conklin-Rossant, N.Y.C., 1970-72; chief designer Odell Assocs., Charlotte, N.C., 1972-73; prin. Clark Tribble Harris and Li, Charlotte, N.C., 1973-86; chmn., CEO Tribble Harris Li, Inc., Charlotte, N.C., 1986-90, Washington, N.Y.C., and London; dir. Young Pres'. Orgn., N.Y.C., L.A., 1988-90, Covell Matthews Wheatley, PLC, London, 1987-90, THL, Inc., Delaware, 1986-90. Prin. works include Saatchi-Saatchi World Hdgrs., Georgetown Park Shopping Mall, N.W. Mut. Office Bldg., Milw., Ritz Carlton Hotel, Aspen, Bank of Spain, N.Y.C.; dir. short film Cafe Argentina, 1995; prodr. (feature films) Nightwitches, 1997, Peking Story, 1995; screenwriter Wolf Whistle, 1994. Recipient Young Profls. Design award Building Design Construction Mag., 1980. Fellow AIA (Honor award for Discovery Place Mus. 1984); mem. Nat. Coun. Archtl. Registration Bds. Home: 929 E 2nd St Ste 202 Los Angeles CA 90012-4337

LI, GONG-SONG, cardiac surgeon, educator; b. Shanghai, People's Republic China, Feb. 18, 1827; s. Zi-shi and Ji-yao (Wang) L.; m. Lan-fang Tang; children: Ning, Dong. MD, Medical Sch. St. John's Univ., Shanghai, 1950. Cons. P.U.M.C. Hosp., 1954, Inst. Chest Diseases, Beijing, 1956-59; chief dept. thoracic surgery Gen. Hosp., 1972; chief dept. cardvas surgery Great Wall Hosp., 1978; prof. Graduate Medical Coll., 1978—; bd. dirs. Chin. Soc. Thoracic Cardvs Surgery, 1987—. Editor: Extracorporeal Circulation; contbr. articles to profl. jours. Mem. World Soc. Surgeons. Avocations: tennis, swimming, riding, bicycling, music. Office: Great Wall Hosp, 28 Fu Xing Rd, 100853 Beijing China

LI, GUOSONG, mechanical engineering educator; b. Gaoyou, Jiangsu, China, May 9, 1965; s. Jiqing and Guixiang (Xu) L.; m. Aibin Liu, Mar. 24, 1993. BSc, Jiangsu Inst. Tech., Zhenjiang, China, 1985; MSc, Jiao Tong U., Shanghai, 1988, D Engring., 1991. Asst. prof. Jiao Tong U., Shanghai, 1991-92, assoc. prof. mech. engring., 1993—, dep. dir. mfg. engring. divsn. dept. mech. engring., 1994—; mem. youth commn. Prodn. Engring. Instn., 1992—. Contbr. articles to profl. jours. Recipient Grade 2-prize for sci. and tech. progress The State Commn. of Edn. of People's Republic of China, Shanghai, 1993. Mem. AIAA, ASME, SME, Chinese Mech. Engring. Soc. Avocations: classical music, Chinese chess, philosophy, fishing. Home: Apt 218 251 W Dayton Yellow Springs Fairborn OH 45324 Office: Jiao Tong U, 1954 Hua Shan Rd, Shanghai 200030, China Office: Dept Mech and Material Engring Wright State Univ Dayton OH 45435

LI, HUA HARRY, computer scientist; b. Tianjin, People's Republic of China, Nov. 22, 1956; came to U.S., 1982; s. Hua Sheng and Bao Ai Li; m. Maiying Lu, Nov. 4, 1982; children: Alen Lee, Kevin Lee. BS in Elec. and Computer Engring., Tianjin U., 1982; MSECE, U. Iowa, 1984, PhD in ECE, 1989. Lectr. Tianjin U., 1982; asst. prof. computer science Tex. Tech U., Lubbock, 1989-95, assoc. prof. computer sci., 1995—; computer cons., 1990—. Author, editor: Vision Computing with VLSI Circuits, 1994, Fuzzy Logic and Intelligent Systems, 1995, Video Compression, 1996, (prototype system) Realtime Fuzzy Controller, 1994 (Neural Network award). Mem. IEEE. Avocations: camping, piano, fishing. Home: 5102 78th St Lubbock TX 79424 Office: Tex Tech U Computer Sci Dept University Ave Lubbock TX 79409

LI, JAMES CHEN MIN, materials science educator; b. Nanking, China, Apr. 12, 1925; came to U.S., 1949; s. Vei Shao and In Shey (Mai) Li; m. Lily Y.C. Wang, Aug. 5, 1950; children—Conan, May, Edward. B.S., Nat. Central U., China, 1947; M.S., U. Wash., 1951, Ph.D., 1953. Research assoc. U. Calif.-Berkeley, 1953-55; supr. Mfg. Chemists Assn. project Carnegie Inst. Tech., Pitts., 1955-56; phys. chemist Westinghouse Electric Co., Pitts., 1956-57; sr. scientist U.S. Steel Corp., Monroeville, Pa., 1957-69; mgr. strength physics Allied Chem. Co., Morristown, N.J., 1969-71; A.A. Hopeman prof. engring. U. Rochester, N.Y., 1971—; vis. prof. Columbia U., N.Y.C., 1964-65, adj. prof., 1965-71; adj. prof. Stevens Inst. Tech., Newark, 1971-72; vis. prof. Ruhr U., Bochum, Fed. Republic Germany, 1978-79. Holder 5 patents:hemisphere Laue camera and pulsed annealing of amorphous metals with applied magnetic fields; author 2 books; editor 1 book; contbr. 300 articles to profl. jours. Recipient Alexander von Humboldt award, 1978, Acta Metallurgica Gold medal, 1990, Grad. Teaching award U. Rochester, 1993. Fellow TMS/AIME (Robert F. Mehl medal and lectr. 1978, Champion H. Mathewson Gold medal 1972, Structural Materials Divsn. luncheon speaker, 1993, chmn. phys. mutall. com. 1992-95), ASM Internat. (chmn. materials sci. div. 1982-84), Am. Phys. Soc.; mem. Chinese Soc. for Materials Sci. (Lu Tse-Hon medal, 1988). Office: U Rochester Dept Mech Engring Rochester NY 14627-0133

LI, JIANMING, molecular and cellular biologist; b. Xinxiang, Henan, China, Oct. 23, 1956; came to U.S., 1983; s. Zhonghe and Zhimei (Liang) L.; m. Wei Xiao, Sept. 27, 1982; children: Christina Bo, Tracy. BS, Wuhan U., 1982; PhD, CUNY, 1989. Assoc. rsch. scientist Yale U., New Haven, 1989—. Contbr. articles to Jour. Cell Biology, Gene, Jour. Bacteriology, others. Recipient Swebilius cancer rsch. award Yale U., 1991. Mem. AAAS, Am. Assn. Cancer Rsch., Am. Soc. Microbiology, N.Y. Acad. Scis. Achievements include cloning genes in heme biosynthetic pathway, demonstration of role of granulocyte colony-stimulating factor receptor in leukemia cell differentiation; characterization of induction effect of LiCl on leukemia differentiation, synergistic effects of G-CSF and retinoic acid. Office: Yale U Sch Medicine 333 Cedar St New Haven CT 06510-3206

LI, NAI-YI, mechanical engineer, researcher; b. Shinchu, Taiwan, Oct. 1, 1958; children: Catherine, Christopher. BS, Nat. Cheng-Kung U., Taiwan, 1981; MS, U. Mich., 1985, PhD, 1990. Rsch. asst. U. Mich., Ann Arbor, 1985-90, lectr., 1986-90; mech. engr. Aluminum Co. of Am., Alcoa Ctr., Pa., 1990-91, sr. mech. engr., 1991-96, staff engr., 1996—; co-prin. investigator NSF, Washington, 1993—. Asst. editor Orgn. Chinese Ams., 1993; assoc. editor Audio Arts; contbr. articles to profl. jours. Sci. grantee Alcoa Found., 1993-95. Mem. ASME, Soc. Engring. Sci., Sigma Xi. Achievements include continuous slab casting process and equipment design; thermomechanical interface modelling; alumina smelting pot design; aluminum intensive vehicle parts heat treatment process; fatique of metal-matrix composites; gear drive system rating and design. Office: Alcoa Tech Ctr 100 Technical Dr New Kensington PA 15069

LI, NORMAN N., chemicals executive; b. Shanghai, China, Jan. 14, 1933; came to U.S.; naturalized, 1969.; s. Lieh-wen and Amy H. Li; m. Jane C. Li, Aug. 17, 1963; children: Rebecca H., David H. BSin Chem. Engring., Nat. Taiwan U., Taipei, 1955; MS, Wayne State U., 1957; PhD, Stevens Inst. Tech., 1963. Sr. scientist Exxon Rsch. and Engring. Co., Linden, N.J., 1963-81; dir. separation sci. and tech. UOP, Des Plaines, Ill., 1981-88; dir. engineered products and process tech. Allied-Signal Inc., Des Plaines, Ill., 1988-92, dir. rsch. and tech., 1993-95; pres., CEO NL Chem. Technology, Inc., 1995—; mem. NRC, 1985-89; lectr. Am. Inst. Chem. Engrs., 1975-86. Editor 13 books on separation sci. and tech.; contbr. articles to jours. in field; patentee in field. Fellow AICE (dir. divsn. food, pharms. and bioengring. 1988-91, Alpha Chi Sigma rsch. award 1988, bd dirs 1992-94, Ernest Thiele award 1995); mem. NAE, Am. Chem. soc. (Seperation Sci. and Tech. award 1988), N.Am. Membrane Soc. (pres. 1991-93), Academia Sinica. Home: 620 Rolling Ln Arlington Heights IL 60004-5820

LI, PEARL NEI-CHIEN CHU, information specialist, executive; b. Jiangsu, China, June 17, 1946; came to U.S., 1968; d. Ping-Yung and Yao-Hwa (Li) Chu; m. Terry Teng-Fang Li, Sept. 20, 1969; children: Ina Ying, Ping Li. BA, Nat. Taiwan U., Taipei, 1968; MA, W.Va. U., 1971; cert. advanced study in info. studies, Drexel U., 1983. Cert. sr. libr., N.J. Instr. Nat. Tchr.'s Coll., Chang-Hua, Taiwan, 1977-78; reference libr. Camden County Libr., Voorhees, N.J., 1981-82; libr. Kulzer and Dipadova, P.A., Haddonfield, N.J., 1982-87; libr. dir. Am. Law Inst., Phila., 1987-92; gen. mgr., info. specialist Unitek Internat. Corp. (Am.), Mt. Laurel, N.J., 1992—; tchr. South Jersey Chinese Sch., Cherry Hill, N.J., 1978-82. Editor: CLE Around the Cuontry (annually), 1988-92; contbr. articles to profl. jours. Bus. mgr. Chinese Community Ctr., Voorhees, 1981. Mem. NAFE, N.J. Entrepreneurial Network, Inc., Spl. Librs. Assn., Soc. Competitive Intelligence Profls. Home: 1132 Sea Gull Ln Cherry Hill NJ 08003-3113 Office: Unitek Internat Corp 131A Gaither Dr Mount Laurel NJ 08054

LI, SHU, business executive. Chief rsch. officer Polytronics Inc., Richardson, Tex. Office: Polytronics Inc 805 Alpha Dr Richardson TX 75081-2850

LI, TINGYE, electrical engineer; b. Nanjing, China, July 7, 1931; came to U.S., 1953, naturalized, 1963; s. Chao and Lily Wei-peng (Sie) L.; m. Edith Hsiu-hwei Wu, June 9, 1956; children: Deborah Chunroh, Kathryn Dairoh. BSEE, U. Witwatersrand, South Africa, 1953; MS, Northwestern U., Evanston, Ill., 1955, PhD, 1958; DEng (hon.), Nat. Chiao Tung U., Hsinchu, Taiwan, 1991. Mem. tech. staff AT&T Bell Labs., Holmdel, N.J., 1957-67; dept. head repeater techniques research dept. Bell Labs., 1967-76, lightwave media research dept., 1976-84, lightwave systems research dept., 1984-96; dept. head lightwave networks rsch. dept. AT&T Labs.-Rsch., Holmdel, N.J., 1996—; divsn. mgr. AT&T Labs.-Rsch., Middletown, N.J., 1997—; hon. prof. Tsinghua U., Shanghai Jiao Tong U., Beijing U. Posts and Telecomms., U. Electronic Sci. and Tech. of China, Qufu Normal U., No. Jiao Tong U., Tianjin U., Nankai U., Fudan U. Assoc. editor Optics Letters, 1977-78, topical editor, 1989-91; assoc. editor Jour. of Lightwave Tech., 1983-86; editor book series: Optical Fiber Communications; mem. editorial bd. Procs. IEEE, 1974-83, Microwave and Optical Tech. Letters, 1987—, Internat. Jour. High Speed Electronics, 1990—; contbr. articles on microwave antennas and propagation, lasers, coherent optics, optical communications, optical-fiber transmission to sci. jours., chpts. in books. Recipient Alumni Merit award Northwestern U., 1981. Fellow IEEE (W.R.G. Baker prize 1975, David Sarnoff award 1979), AAAS, Photonics Soc. Chinese-Ams., Optical Soc. Am. (chmn. optical comms. tech. group 1979-80, bd. dirs. 1985-87, chmn. internat. activities com. 1988-90, chmn. photonics divsn. 1991-92, pres. 1995, John Tyndall award 1995, Frederic Ives medal 1997); mem. NAE, Chinese Inst. Engrs. U.S.A. (bd. dirs. 1974-78, Achievement award 1978), Academia Sinica (Taiwan), Chinese Acad. Engring., Chinese Am. Acad. and Profl. Assn. (bd. dirs. 1985-89, Achievement award 1983), Electromagnetics Acad., Sigma Xi, Eta Kappa Nu, Phi Tau Phi (pres. East Am. chpt. 1991-93). Club: F.F. Fraternity. Patentee in field. Office: AT&T Labs-Rsch Newman Springs Lab 100 Schultz Dr Red Bank NJ 07701-6750

LI, TZE-CHUNG, lawyer, educator; b. Shanghai, China, Feb. 17, 1927; came to U.S., 1956; s. Ken-hsiang Li and Yun-hsien (Chang) Li; m. Dorothy In-lan Wang, Oct. 21, 1961; children—Lily, Rose. LL.B., Soochow U., Shanghai, 1948; Diploma, Nat. Chengchi U., Nanking, 1949, China Research Inst. of Land Econs., Taipei, 1952; M.C.L., So. Meth. U., Dallas, 1956; LL.M., Harvard U., Cambridge, 1958; M.S., Columbia U., N.Y.C., 1965; Ph.D., New Sch. for Social Research, N.Y.C., 1963. Judge Hwa-lien Dist. Ct., Hwa-lien, Taiwan, Republic of China, 1949-51; dist. atty. Ministry of Justice, Tapei, 1951-52; chief law sect. Ministry of Nat. Def., Tapei, 1952-56; asst. prof. library sci. Ill. State U., Normal, 1965-66; asst. prof. polit. sci., library sci. Rosary Coll., River Forest, Ill., 1966-69, assoc. prof. library sci., 1969-70, 72-74, prof. library sci., 1974-82, dean, prof. Grad. Sch. Library and Info. Sci., 1982-88, prof., 1988—; vis. assoc. prof. law Nat. Taiwan U., 1969; vis. assoc. prof. polit. sci. Soochow U., Taipei, 1969; dir. Nat. Central Library, Taipei, 1970-72; chmn. Grad. Inst. Library Sci., Nat. Central Library, Taipei, 1971-72; commr. Ministry of Examination, Examination Yuan, Taipei, 1971; chmn. com. on library standards, Ministry of Edn., Taipei, 1972; library cons. Soochow U., Nat. Chengchi U., Dr. Sun Yat-sen Meml. Library; mem. library adv. com. Ency. Britannica, 1982-95; hon. prof. library and info. sci. Jiangxi U., People's Republic of China, 1985—; vis. prof. law Suzhou U., Peking U., 1991, Nat. Taiwan U., 1991; hon. cons. univ. library, 1985—; hon. cons. Jiangxi Med. Coll., 1985—; adv. prof. East China Normal U., 1987—; cons. Nova U., 1987-88; mem. ad hoc adv. com. Chgo. Pub. Library Bldg. Planning, 1987-88. Author books including: Social Science Reference Sources, 1980, 2d edit., 1990, Mah Jong, 1982, 2d edit., 1991, An Introduction to Online Searching, 1985; also numerous articles in profl., scholarly jours.; editor Third World Librs., 1996—; founding editor Jour. Library and Info. Sci., 1975-80, mem. editl. bd. 1986-90; founding chmn., mem. editl. bd. Internat. Jour. of Revs., 1984-89; editor: World Libraries, 1996—. Pres. Chinese Am. Ednl. Found., Chgo., 1968-70; chmn. Com. for Chinatown Library, Chgo., 1966-67; advisor Friends of Soochow, Los Angeles, 1974-87; bd. dirs. Asian Human Services, Inc., Chgo., 1978; co-chmn. Com. for Expansion of Chinatown Library, Chgo., 1984-86; pres. China Council on Cultural Renaissance, Midwest chpt., 1974-85. Recipient Govt. Citation Republic of China, 1956, 1972, Philip D. Sang Excellence in Teaching award Rosary Coll., 1971, Disting. Service award Phi Tau Phi, Chgo., 1982, Service award HUD, Chgo. region, 1985, Disting. Service award Chinese Am. Librarians Assn., 1988. Mem. ALA1 Am. Soc. Info. Sci., Assn. Coll. and Research Libraries, Assn. Library ad Info. Sci. Edn., Chinese Am. Librarians Assn. (founding pres. 1976-80), Library Assn. China (Taipei), Phi Tau Phi (pres. 1985-87). Republican. Roman Catholic. Home: PO Box 444 Oak Park IL 60303-0444 Office: Dominican U 7900 Division St River Forest IL 60305-1066

LI, VICTOR ON-KWOK, electrical engineering educator; b. Hong Kong, Oct. 11, 1954; came to the U.S., 1973; s. Chia-Nan and Wai-Ying (Chan) L.; m. Regina Yui-Kwan Wai, Aug. 14, 1977; children: Ronald, Nathan. SB in Elec. Engring. and Computer Sci., MIT, 1977, SM in Elec. Engring. and Computer Sci., 1979, ScD in Elec. Engring. and Computer Sci., 1981. Asst. prof. dept. elec. engring. U. So. Calif., L.A., 1981-87, assoc. prof. dept. elec. engring., 1987-92, prof. dept. elec. engring., 1992—, comm. group leader dept. elec. engring., 1988-91, co-dir. dept. elec. engring. Comm. Scis. Inst., 1991-93, dir., 1993-94, 95—; Disting. lectr. Nat. Sci. coun., Taiwan, 1993; hon. speaker IEE, 1995; keynote spkr. Internat. Conf. Personal, Mobile, and Spread Spectrum Comm., 1996, Multimedia Tech. and Applications Conf., 1996; lectr. and cons. in field. Editor: IEEE Networks, 1986-92, ACM/Baltzer Wireless Networks, 1993—, Telecom.Sys., 1991-95; guest editor spl. issue IEEE Jour. on Selected Areas in Comm., 1987, 97; contbr. articles to profl. jours. Named Disting. lectr. Calif. Poly. Inst., Pomona, 1990. Fellow IEEE (Svc. award 1984, 85, gen. chmn., tech. program chmn. 4th Annual Computer Comm. Workshop, Dana Point, Calif., Oct. 1989, Comm. Soc. tech. com. on computer comm. 1987-89, chmn. L.A. chpt. IEEE Info. Theory Soc. 1983-85, steering com. chair Internat. Conf. on Computer Comm. and Networking, 1992—, tech. program chair symposium on personal comm. svcs., 1995, keynote spkr. internat. conf. 1996), Inst. for Advancement Engring. Office: Univ So Calif Dept Elec Engring Los Angeles CA 90089-2565

LI, YI, staff investigator; b. Beijing, China, May 28, 1947; came to U.S., 1989; d. Zhiyuan and Yunpeng (Zhao) L.; m. Songshun Zhu, Aug. 13, 1970; children: Harry, Jing. MD, Tainjin Med. Coll., 1970, MS, 1981. Physician Tianjin (China) Binjiang Hosp., 1970-72; psychiatrist Tianjin Psychiat. Hosp., 1972-78; neurologist Tianjin Med. Coll. Hosp., 1978-89; asst. rsch. scientist Tianjin Neurol. Inst., 1981-89; rsch. scientist U. Hong Kong, 1986-87; asst. staff investigator Henry Ford Hosp., Detroit, 1991-92, assoc. staff investigator, 1992—. Author: Apoptosis in Cerebral Ischemia, 1995; contbr. articles to profl. jours. Geneva Cantonal U. Ctr. Lab. fellow, 1988-89, Henry Ford Hosp. fellow, 1990-91. Office: Henry Ford Hosp Dept Neurol E & R 3019 2799 W Grand Blvd Detroit MI 48202-2608

LIACOS, PAUL JULIAN, retired state supreme judicial court chief justice; b. Peabody, Mass., Nov. 20, 1929; s. James A. and Pitsa K. (Karis) L.; m. Maureen G. McKean, Oct. 6, 1954; children: James P., Diana M., Mark C., Gregory A. AB magna cum laude, Boston U. Coll. Liberal Arts, 1950; LLB magna cum laude, Boston U., 1952; LLM, Harvard U., 1953; diploma, Air Command and Staff Sch., 1954; LLD (hon.), Suffolk U., 1984, New Eng. Sch. Law, 1985; LHD (hon.), Salem State Coll., 1988; LLD (hon.), Northeastern U., 1991, Boston U., 1996. Bar: Mass. 1952, U.S. Dist. Ct. Mass. 1954, U.S. Ct. Mil. Appeals 1955, U.S. Ct. Appeals (1st cir.) 1971, U.S. Supreme Ct. 1980. Ptnr. firm Liacos and Liacos, Peabody, Mass., 1952-76; prof. law Boston U., 1952-76, adj. prof. law, 1976-89; assoc. justice Mass. Supreme Jud. Ct., 1976-89, chief justice, 1989-96; Distinguished lectr. on law U.S. Mil. Acad., West Point, N.Y., 1972; lectr. Suffolk U. Sch. Law, 1978-79; U.S. Constn. Bicentennial lectr. Boston Pub. Library, 1987; cons. to atty. gen. Mass. on staffing and personnel, 1974-75; lectr. on criminal evidence Boston Police Acad., 1963-64; reporter New Eng. Conf. on Def. of the Indigent, Harvard Law Sch., 1963; reader and cons. on legal manuscripts Little, Brown & Co., Boston, 1968-76; editorial cons. Warren, Gorham & Lamont, 1968-69; mem. steering com. Lawyers Com. for Civil Rights under Law, Boston, 1969-72; chmn. com. on discrimination in the cts. Conf. of Chief Justices, 1993-96. Author: Handbook of Massachusetts Evidence, 6th edit., 1994, supplement, 1996; contbr. articles in field to legal jours.; book rev. editor Boston U. law Rev., 1952. Trustee Suffolk U., Boston, 1993—; trustee, mem. exec. com. Chamberlayne Sch. and Jr. Coll., Boston, 1982-84; trustee Anatolia Coll., Salonika, Greece, 1980—, exec. com., 1986-89; hon. trustee Deree-Pierce Colls., Athens, 1976—; corp. mem. MIT, 1989-96. Named Man of Yr. Boston Law Sch., 1952, Man of Yr. Alpha Omega, 1977, Mem. Colleguum Disting. Alumni Boston U. Coll. Liberal Arts, 1974; recipient Disting. Pub. Svc. award Boston U. Alumni, 1980, Allied Profl. award Mass. Psychol. Assn., 1987, Man of Vision award Nat. Soc. to Prevent Blindness, 1988, State Bill of Rights award Nat. Assn. Criminal Def. Lawyers, 1988, Good Neighbor award Mishkan Tefila Brotherhood, 1990, Founders' award Lawyers Com. for Civil Rights Under the Law, Boston Bar Assn., 1993, citation of jud. excellence Boston Bar Assn., 1995, Ehrman award Mass. Crime and Justice Found., 1996, award Fed. Bar Assn., 1996, Mass. Jud. Conf. award, 1996, Social Law Libr. award, 1996. Mem. ABA (jud. cert. of appreciation 1994), ATLA (editor 1968-73, Outstanding State Appellate Judge 1982), Mass. Bar Assn. (criminal law com. 1964-66), Essex County Bar Assn., Peabody Bar Assn., Greater Lowell Bar Assn. (hon.), Harvard Law Sch. Assn., Mass. Supreme Jud. Ct. Hist. Soc. (chmn. 1996—), Boston U. Law Sch. Alumni Assn. (Silver Shingle award 1977), Phi Beta Kappa. Democrat. Mem. Greek Orthodox Ch.

LIAKOS, JAMES CHRIST, business manager; b. Washington, Feb. 10, 1933; s. Christ and Xantippe (Franks) L.; m. Alexandra Avayanos, Jan. 1, 1956 (div. Jan. 1960); 1 child, Stephanie; m. Roberta Sue Katzman, May 31, 1963. B Comml. Scis., Benjamin Franklin U., 1956. Supr. acctg. dept. Bakery & Confectionery Union Industry Internat. Welfare and Pension Funds, Washington, 1955-66; adminstrv. asst. Am. Physiol. Soc., Bethesda, Md., 1966-76, asst. bus. mgr., bus. mgr., 1985—. With U.S. Army, 1953-54, ETO. Mem. Nat. Soc. Pub. Acctg., Am. Soc. Assn. Execs. Greek Orthodox. Home: 11001 Lopa Ln North Potomac MD 20878-2542 Office: Am Physiol Soc 9650 Rockville Pike Bethesda MD 20814-3998

LIANG, EDISON PARKTAK, astrophysicist, educator, researcher; b. Canton, Republic of China, July 22, 1947; came to U.S., 1964; s. Chi-Sen and Siu-Fong (Law) L.; m. Lily K. Yuen, Aug. 7, 1971; children: Olivia, James, Justin. BA, U. Calif., Berkeley, 1967, PhD, 1971. Rsch. scientist U. Tex., Austin, 1971-73; assoc. instr. U. Utah, Salt Lake City, 1973-75; asst. prof. Mich. State U., East Lansing, Mich., 1975-76, Stanford (Calif.) U., 1976-79; physicist, group leader Lawrence Livermore Nat. Lab., Livermore, Calif., 1980-88; assoc. div. leader Lawrence Livermore Nat. Lab., Livermore, 1988-91; prof. Rice U., Houston, Tex., 1991—; mem. NASA Rev. Panels, Washington, 1988—. Editor: (book) Gamma Ray Bursts, 1986. Named Sci. fellow and Anthony scholar U. Calif., Berkeley, 1967-69. Fellow Am. Physical Soc.; mem. Am. Astron. Soc., Internat. Astron. Union, Phi Beta Kappa, Sigma Xi. Office: Rice U MS 108 Houston TX 77005-1892

LIANG, JASON CHIA, research chemist; b. Beijing, Peoples Republic China, Feb. 24, 1935; came to U.S., 1978, naturalized 1984; s. Tsang Truan and Shulin (Tang) L.; m. Joan Chorng Chen, June 11, 1960; children: Cheryl, Chuck. BS in Pharm. Chemistry, U. Beijing, 1957; postgrad., Pharm. Research Instn., Beijing, 1961; MS in Organic Chemistry, U. Oreg., 1980. Chemist Beijing Chem. Factory, 1961-71; rsch. chemist Beijing Pharm. Factory, 1971-78; rsch. chemist Tektronix Inc., Beaverton, Oreg., 1980-85, sr. rsch. chemist, 1985-88; sr. rsch. chemist Kalama (Wash.) Chem. Inc., 1988—; rschr. in flavor and fragrance chemistry. Contbr. articles to profl. jours.; patentee in field. Fellow Am. Inst. Chemists; mem. Am. Chem. Soc. (organic chemistry divsn., paper presenter 1984-95), Internat. Union Pure and Applied Chemistry (affiliate), Inst. Food Technologists (food chemistry divsn.). Office: Kalama Chem Inc 1296 NW 3rd St Kalama WA 98625-9701

LIANG, JEFFREY DER-SHING, retired electrical engineer, civil worker, diplomat; b. Chungking, China, Oct. 25, 1915; came to U.S., 1944, naturalized, 1971; s. Tze-hsiang and Sou-yi (Wang) L.; m. Eva Yin Hwa Tang, Jan. 2, 1940; 1 child, Shouyu. BA, Nat. Chengchih U., Chungking, 1940; BAS, U. B.C., Vancouver, 1960. Office asst. Ministry of Fgn. Affairs, Chungking, 1940-43; vice consul, Chinese consulate Ministry of Fgn. Affairs, Seattle, 1944-50; consulate-gen. Ministry of Fgn. Affairs, San Francisco, 1950-53; consul, Chinese consulate-gen. Ministry of Fgn. Affairs, Vancouver, 1953-56; engr.-in-tng. Can. Broadcasting Corp., Vancouver, 1960-65; assoc. engr. Boeing Co., Seattle, 1965-67, rsch. engr., 1967-70, engr., 1970-73, sr. engr., 1973-75, specialist engr., 1975-78; cons. Seattle, 1979-81. Mem. chancelor's cir. Wesbrook Soc. U. B.C., Vancouver, 1986—, Seattle-King County Adv. Coun. on Aging, 1984-88, Gov.'s State Coun. on Aging, Olympia, 1986-88, Pres. Coun., Rep. Nat. Com.; permanent mem. Rep. Nat. Senatorial Com., Washington State Rep. Party, Seattle Art Mus.; life mem. Am. Assn. Individual Investors, Rep. Presdl. Task Force; sustaining mem. Rep. Nat. Congl. Com., Rep. Presdl. Adv. Com.,. Mem. IEEE (life), Heritage Found., Nat. Trust Hist. Preservation, Hwa Sheng Chinese Music Club (v.p. 1978-79, chmn. nomination com. 1981-88, 90-94). Republican. Mem. Christian Ch. Avocations: Chinese calligraphy, opera, poetry, physical fitness. Home: 1750 152d Ave NE Apt 302 Bellevue WA 98007-4270 *Always try to do one's best since that is a sure way to go through life without regrets.*

LIANG, JEROME ZHENGRONG, radiology educator; b. Chongging, Sichuan, China, June 23, 1958; came to U.S., 1981; BS, Lanzhou U., China, 1982; PhD, CUNY, 1987. Rsch. instr. Albert Einstein Coll. Medicine, Bronx, N.Y., 1986-87; rsch. assoc. Duke U. Med. Ctr., Durham, N.C., 1987-89; asst. med. rsch. prof. Duke U. Med. Ctr., 1990-92; asst. prof. SUNY, Stony Brook, 1992-97, assoc. prof., 1997—. Contbr. articles to profl. jours. Grantee Soc. Thoracic Radiology, 1994-95, ADAC Rsch. Lab., 1995-96, N.Y. State BioCenter, 1996—; recipient NIH awards, 1990-94, 95—, AHA award, 1996—, N.Y. State Biotech award 1996—. Mem. Assn. Chinese-Am. Sr. Profls., Inc. (trustee 1994—). Achievements include devel. of Bayesian image processing, quantitative emission computed tomography, tissue segmentation from magnetic resonance images. Avocations: swimming, fitness, tennis. Office: Dept Radiology SUNY Stony Brook 4th Fl Rm 092 Stony Brook NY 11794

LIANG, JUNXIANG, aeronautics and astronautics engineer, educator; b. Hangzhou, Zhejiang, China, Aug. 17, 1932; s. Yigao and Yunruo (Yu) L.; m. Junxian Sun, Jan. 27, 1960; 1 child, Song Liang. Grad., Harbin Inst. Tech., 1960. Head control dept. Shenyang (Liaoning, China) Jet Engine R&D Inst., 1960-70, China Gas Turbine Establishment, Jiangyou, Sichuan, China, 1970-78; assoc. chief engr. China Gas Turbine Establishment, Jiangyou, 1978-83; vis. scientist MIT, Cambridge, Mass., 1984-86; prof. China Aerospace Inst. Systems Engring., Beijing, China, 1986—; grads. supr. Beijing U. Aero-Astronautics, Beijing, 1986—; chief engr. Full Authority Digital Elec. Engine Control China Aerospace Industry Ministry, Beijing, 1986-93; mem. China Aerospace Sci. and Tech. Com., Beijing, 1983-94, Aero-engine R&D Adv. Bd., Beijing, 1991-95; bd. dirs. China Aviation Ency. Editl. Bd., Beijing, 1991-95; tech. support supr., mgmt. info. svc. mgr. Am. PC, Inc., Union City, Calif., 1993—. Author: Nonlinear Control System Oscillation, 1964; contbr. articles to Jour. Aeronautics and Astronautics, Jour. Propulsion Tech., Internat. Aviation, Acta Aeronautica et Astronautica Sinica. Recipient Nat. Sci. and Tech. 2d award, China Nat. Sci. and Tech. Com., Beijing, 1965, Sic. and Tech. Progress award, China Aerospace Industry Ministry, 1991, Nat. Outstanding Sci. and Tech. Contbn. award, 1992. Mem. AIAA, Chinese Soc. of Aeronautical, Astronautical Engine Control (mem. commn. 1987—). Achievements include solution of oscillation problem on nonlinear control system; formulation of aircraft overall strategy, study and control of High Thrust/Weight Engine Rsch. Program. Home: 2973 Carmel St Oakland CA 94602-3410

LIANG, MATTHEW H., medical director; b. Santa Monica, Calif., May 24, 1944. AB in Philosophy and Chemistry, Johns Hopkins U., 1965; BMS, Dartmouth U., 1967; MD, Harvard U., 1969, MPH, 1972. Diplomate Am. Bd. Internal Medicine. Intern in medicine U. Minn. Hosps., Mpls., 1969-70, resident in medicine, 1970-71; resident in medicine Harvard Med. Svc., Boston City Hosp., 1972-73; physician People's Riverside Free Clinic, Mpls., 1969-71, Cambridgeport Free Clinic, Cambridge, Mass., 1971-73; interist Family Health Ctr. Boston City Hosp., 1972-73, assoc. med. dir. Nursing Home Telemedicine, 1972-73; with med. corps Office Gen. Surgeon, U.S. Army, Ft. Belvoir, Va., 1973-74; asst. chief med. clinic Walter Reed Army Med. Ctr., Washington, 1974-75, mem. attending staff, 1974-75; clin. instr. Sch. Medicine, Georgetown U., Washington, 1974-75; mem. attending staff Georgetown Med. Svc., D.C. Gen. Hosp., Washington, 1974-75; asst. prof. medicine dept. rheumatology and immunology Harvard Med. Sch., Brigham Womens's Hosp., Boston, 1977-86, assoc. prof. medicine, 1986; lectr. dept. health svcs. Sch. Pub. Health, Harvard U., 1977-79, lectr. dept. health policy and mgmt., 1979; mem. staff Peter Bent Brigham Hosp., Boston, 1977-79, Robert B. Brigham Hosp., Boston, 1977-79, The Hosp. at Parker Hill, Boston, 1979-82, Brigham and Women's Hosp., Boston, 1979—, Brockton (Mass.) VA Hosp., 1980-82, Dana-Farber Cancer Inst., Boston, 1984-86; assoc. dir. Robert B. Brigham Multipurpose Arthritis Ctr., Boston, 1979-80, dir., 1980—; med. dir. rehab. svcs. Brigham and Women's Hosp., Boston, 1982—, med. dir. acute rehab. program, 1984-86; prof. health policy and mgmt. Harvard, Boston, 1995, prof. medicine, 1996—; mem. exec. com. Mass. chpt. Arthritis Found., 1979-81, mem. govtl. affairs com., 1981-82, co-chmn., 1984, bd. trustees 1982—, mem. med. and sci. com. 1982—, chmn. grants subcom. 1990—, mem. rsch. com. 1991—, chmn. Mass. chpt. 1993; mem. arthritis interagency coordinating com., data systems subcom. NIH, 1979, mem. spl. rev. com., 1980-81, mem. nat. arthritis adv. bd. 1985-88, co-chmn. adv. com. on rehab., 1990; mem. adv. panel on allergy, immunology and connective tissue disease U.S. Pharmacopoa Conv., Inc., 1980-82; mem. musculoskeletal panel Social Security Adminstrn., 1985; mem. med. adv. com. Blue Shield Bd. Dirs., Boston, 1986-89; mem. adv. com. Maternal and Child Health Improvement Project, Boston, 1986; chmn. statewide adv. com. on vocat. rehab., 1986; mem. musculoskeletal and skin disease task force on lupus in high risk populations Nat. Inst. Arthritis, 1988—, chmn. health svcs., behavioural and ednl. rsch. steering com. 1990; mem. rsch. grants rev. com. Scleroderma Found., 1989-90; mem. practice guidline panel on low back dysfunction Agy. Health Care Policy and Rsch., 1991—, mem. health svcs. rsch. tng adv. com. 1992; mem. hip fracture and replacement patient outcomes Assessment Rsch. Team Nat. Adv. Bd., 1991—; mem. steering com. assessment program on low back pain L'Institute de recherche en Sante et en Securite du travail du Quebec, 1989-92; chmn. external monitoring com. Multicenter Clin. Trial Hydroxychloroquine in Early Rheumatoid Arthritis, 1989—; mem. grants rev. com. Med. Found., 1990—, mem. clin. rsch. com., 1993, mem. community health and edn. com., 1993; Kellogg Fellowship lectr., 1986—; Kare Bergling lectr. in Rheumatology U. Lund, Sweden, 1990; A.S.B. Bank vis. prof. in Rheumatology/Rehab., Auckland, New Zealand, 1990; Highton Oration lectr., Queenstown, New Zealand, 1990; Matilda G. Irving Meml. lectr., Providence, 1991; Kovacs vis. prof. Royal Soc. Medicine, London, 1994; active Quebec Taskforce on Whiplash Injuries; med. cons. Internat. Grenfell Mission, Newfoundland, 1971. Editor Rheumatology Rev., 1990—, Jour. Orthopaedic Rheumatology, 1990-92; assoc. editor Arthritis and Rheumatism, also mem. editorial bd., 1983-88; mem. editorial bd. Annals of the Rheumatic Diseases, 1989—, Brit. Jour. Rheumatology, 1989—, Lupus, 1990—; mem. adv. bd. Current Med. Lit., 1982-87, Arthritis Info. Mag., 1986, Spine, 1993—. Rsch. fellow in clin. cardiology Royal Postgrad. Sch., Hammersmith Hosp., London, 1969, Clin. fellow in rheumatology Stanford (Calif.) U. Sch. Medicine, 1975-77, Travelling fellow WHO, 1977, 83, Med. Found. fellow, 1979-81; Robert Wood Johnson Clin. scholar, Stanford (Calif.) U. Med. Ctr., 1975-77. Mem. APHA, ACP, Royal Coll. Medicine, Am. Fedn. Clin. Rsch., Am. Coll. Rheumatology (mem. glossary com. 1979-89, mem. com. on health svcs. and health tech. 1980—, mem. orthopaedic coun. 1982-83, chmn. adv. com. med. info. system 1981-83, mem. program com. 1983-84, mem. coun. rehab. rheumatology 1984—, mem. subcom. revision of criteria for classification rheumatoid arthritis 1984-85, councilor northeast region 1984, chmn. subsect. health svcs. rsch. program com. 1985, mem. sr. rheumatology scholar award com. 1985, mem. ad hoc com. for rheumatologic tng. 1986, mem. subcom. on synovial fluid analyses cert. 1989, mem. subcom. on disease activity in systemic lupus eythematosus 1989, mem. allied health profl. assn. rsch. com. 1989-91, mem. com. health care rsch. 1990, mem. coun. rsch. 1992), Mass. Pub. Health Assn., New Eng. Rheumatism Soc., Can. Arthritis Soc. (mem. epidemiology health scis. panel 1990-92, chmn. 1992—), Arthritis Health Professions Assn., Soc. Rsch. and Edn. in Primary Care Internal Medicine, Heberden Soc., Ankylosing Spondylitis Assn. (mem. med. adv. bd. 1986—), Newton Choral Soc. (mem. adv. bd. 1983—), N.Am. Spine Soc. (mem. outcome com. 1991—). Office: Brigham Multipurpose Arthritis Ctr 75 Francis St Boston MA 02115-6110

LIANG, QINGJIAN JIM, petroleum engineer; b. Dalian, China, Apr. 18, 1957; came to U.S., 1988; s. Jishun Liang and Shuzhen Sui; m. Huang Xiaozhong, Apr. 14, 1983; 1 child, Zheng Liang. BS, Daqing (China) Petroleum Inst., 1982; MS, Mont. Coll. Mineral Sci./Tech., 1989; DEng, La. Tech. U., 1993. Drilling engr. Daqing No. 3 Drilling Co., Daqing, 1982-87; rsch. asst. La. Tech. U., Ruston, 1989-93; divsn. engr. Sonat Offshore Drilling Inc., Morgan City, La., 1993—. Assoc. mem. SPE. Achievements include development of new experimental methodology of transport coefficients measurement for two-phase flow in porous media; derived analytical model of two-phase immiscible fluids flow in capillary tube model porous media, discovered evidence of coupling effect. Avocations: fishing, painting, playing volleyball. Office: Offshore Turnkey Ventures Inc Corporate Plaza 110 Capitol Dr Ste 100 Lafayette LA 70508-3826

LIAO, MEI-JUNE, biopharmaceutical company executive; came to U.S., 1974; BS, Nat. Tsing-Hua U. Taiwan, 1973; MPh, Yale U., 1977, PhD, 1980. Tchg. asst. Nat. Taiwan U., 1973-74, Temple U., Phila., 1974-75; tchg. asst. Yale U., New Haven, 1975-76, rsch. asst., 1976-79; postdoctoral assoc. MIT, Cambridge, 1980-83; sr. scientist Interferon Scis., Inc., New Brunswick, N.J., 1983-84; group leader Interferon Scis. Inc., New Brunswick, N.J., 1984-85, dir. cell biology, 1985-87; dir. R&D Interferon Scis., Inc., New Brunswick, N.J., 1987-94, v.p. rsch. & deve., 1995—. Contbr. articles to profl. jours.; inventor in field. Mem. Am. Soc. Biochemistry and Molecular Biology, Internat. Soc. Interferon and Cytokine Rsch., Soc. Chinese Bioscientists in Am., N.Y. Acad. Sci. Office: Interferon Sci Inc 783 Jersey Ave New Brunswick NJ 08901-3605

LIAO, PAUL FOO-HUNG, electronics executive; b. Phila., Nov. 10, 1944; s. Tseng Wu and Tung Mei (Lin) L.; m. Karen Ann Pravetz, Aug. 31, 1968; children: Teresa S., Joanna S. BS, MIT, 1966; PhD, Columbia U., 1973. Rsch. assoc. Columbia U., N.Y.C., 1972-73; mem. tech. staff Bell Labs., Holmdel, N.J., 1973-80, dept. head., 1980-83; div. mgr. Bell Communications Rsch., Red Bank, N.J., 1984-89, asst. v.p., 1989-93, gen. mgr., 1993-95, v.p., 1995-96; chief tech. officer Matsushita Elec. Corp. Am., 1996—; pres. Panasonic Techs., Inc., 1996—. Co-editor: Academic Press Quantum Electronics Book Series; contbr. over 75 articles to profl. jours.; holder over 12 patents in field. Bd. trustees Brookdale C.C. Fellow IEEE, Optical Soc. Am. (editor jour.), Am. Phys. Soc.; mem. Lasers and Electro Optic Soc. of IEEE (pres. 1987). Office: Panasonic Techs Inc 2 Research Way Princeton NJ 08540-6628

LIAO, SHUTSUNG, biochemist, oncologist; b. Tainan, Taiwan, Jan. 1, 1931; s. Chi-Chun Liao and Chin-Shen Lin; m. Shuching Liao, Mar. 19, 1960; children: Jane, Tzufen, Tzuming, May. BS in Agrl. Chemistry, Nat. Taiwan U., 1953, MS in Biochemistry, 1956; PhD in Biochemistry, U. Chgo., 1961. Rsch. assoc., 1960-63; asst. prof. U. Chgo., 1964-69; assoc. prof. dept. biochemistry Ben May Lab. Cancer Rsch., U. Chgo., 1969-71; prof. depts. biochemistry, molecular and cancer biology Ben May Inst. for Cancer Rsch., 1972—; cons. in field. Mem. editorial bd. Jour. Steroid Biochemistry and Molecular Biology, The Prostate, and Receptors; assoc. editor Cancer Research, 1982-89; contbr. over 200 articles to profl jours. V.p. Chgo. Formosan Fed. Credit Union, 1977-79; trustee Taiwanese United Fund in U.S., 1981—; mem. adv. com. Taiwan-U.S. Cultural Exch. Ctr., 1984—. Recipient Sci-Tech. Achievement prize Taiwanese-Am. Found., 1983, Pfizer Lecture fellow award Clin. Rsch. Inst. Montreal, 1972, Gregory Pincus medal and award Worcester Found. for Exptl. Biology, 1992, Tzongming Tu award Formosan Med. Assn., 1993, C.H. Li Meml. Lecture award, 1994; NIH grantee, 1962—; Am. Cancer Soc. grantee, 1971-81. Fellow Am. Acad. Art and Scis.; mem. Am. Soc. Biochemistry and Molecular Biology, Am. Assn. Cancer Rsch., Endocrine Soc., N.Am.-Taiwanese Profs. Assn. (pres. 1980-81, exec. dir. 1981—), Academia Sinica. Achievements include discovery of androgen activation mechanism and androgen receptors; cloning and structural determination of androgen receptors and other novel nuclear receptors, and their genes, and receptor gene mutation in hereditary abnormalities and cancers; rsch. on regulation of hormone-dependent gene expression and cell growth, molecular bases of cancer cell growth and progression, chemoprevention, and therapeutic treatment of hormone-sensitive and insensitive cancers and diseases. Home: 5632 S Woodlawn Ave Chicago IL 60637-1623 Office: U Chgo Ben May Inst Cancer Rsch 5841 S Maryland Ave Chicago IL 60637-1463

LIARD, JEAN-FRANCOIS, cardiovascular physiologist, researcher, educator; b. Pompaples, Vaud, Switzerland, Dec. 20, 1943; came to U.S., 1983; s. Heli Albert and Jeanne (Meystre) L.; m. Fanny Suzanne Klaiber, July 9, 1966; children: Monique Florence, Gisele Catherine. MD, U. Lausanne, Switzerland, 1968. Rsch. asst. Dept. Pharmacology, Lausanne, 1968-71; rsch. fellow dept. physiology Sch. Medicine, Jackson, Miss., 1971-73; rsch. fellow Cleve. Clinic, 1973-74; assoc. prof. INSERM U. Paris, 1974-77; prof. Inst. Rsch. Cardio-Angiology, Fribourg, Switzerland, 1977-83; prof. dept. physiology Med. Coll. Wis., Milw., 1983-93; dir. office scientific affairs Otsuka Am. Pharm., Rockville, Md., 1993-97. Contbr. articles to Circulation Rsch., Am. Jour. Physiology. Recipient Marc Dufour award U. Lausanne, 1973, ann. award Swiss Soc. Cardiology, 1975, rsch. grant Swiss Nat. Sci. Found., 1977-83, NIH, 1983-93. Fellow High Blood Pressure Coun.; mem. Internat. Soc. Hypertension, Am. Physiol. Soc. Achievements include research on role of sodium excretion in reversal of renal hypertension, on models of cardiogenic hypertension in dogs, on role of renal innervation in spontaneously hypertensive rats, on role of vasopressin in cardiovascular control and cardiac output regulation, on extrarenal vasopressin V2 receptors, on the use of allosteric effectors of hemoglobin, on the clinical use of vasopressin antagonists.

LIAU, GENE, medical educator; b. Hsing-Chu, Taiwan, Nov. 28, 1954; came to U.S., 1965; BS in Biology, U. N.C., 1977; DPhil, Vanderbilt U., 1982. Postdoctoral fellow Lab. Molecular Biology Nat. Cancer Inst. NIH, Bethesda, Md., 1982-85; assoc. mem. Dept. Cell Biology Revlon Biotech. Rsch. Ctr., Rockville, Md., 1985-87; scientist I Dept. Molecular Biology Am. Red Cross Jerome H. Holland Lab., Rockville, 1987-90, scientist II, 1990-96, sr. scientist, 1996—; assoc. prof. dept. anatomy George Washington U. Med. Ctr., Washington, 1995—; mem. AHA Vascular Wall Biology Rsch. Study Com., 1992-96, Pathology A Study Sect. NIH, 1994—; invited spkr. in field. Contbr. articles to profl. jours. Arthritis Fund. fellow, 1982-85; pub. health svc. grantee, 1988—; recipient Nat. Rsch. Svc. award NIH, 1977-81, Rsch. Career Devel. award, 1990-95. Mem. AAAS, Am. Soc. Cell Biology, Am. Heart Assn. Coun. Basic Sci. (Established Investigator 1990, Grant-in-Aid 1992-95, 95—), Soc. Chinese Bioscientists, Sigma Xi. Home: 14900 Kelley Farm Dr Darnestown MD 20874 Office: Dept Molecular Biology Holland Lab 15601 Crabbs Branch Way Rockville MD 20855-2736

LIBA, PETER MICHAEL, communications executive; b. Winnipeg, Man., Can., May 10, 1940; s. Theodore and Rose Liba; m. Shirley Ann Collett, May 4, 1963; children: Jennifer, Jeffrey, Christopher. Reporter, news editor The Daily Graphic, Portage la Prairie, Man., 1957-59; reporter The Winnipeg Tribune, 1959-67, city editor, 1967-68; ind. communications cons. Winnipeg, 1968-73; v.p. pub. affairs CanWest Broadcasting Ltd., Winnipeg, 1974-75, exec. v.p., 1979—; asst. gen. mgr. Sta. CKND-TV, Winnipeg, 1975-79, mgr., 1980-87, gen. mgr., 1987-92; pres., CEO CKND TV Inc./SaskWest TV Inc., Winnipeg, 1988-94; exec. v.p. CanWest Global Comm. Corp., Winnipeg, 1993—; bd. dirs. Global Comm. Ltd., Toronto, CanWest Broadcasting Ltd., Winnipeg, CanWest TV, Inc., Winnipeg, CanWest Prodns., Ltd., Winnipeg, CanWest Properties Ltd., Winnipeg, CanWest Maritime TV, Inc., Halifax, TV 3 Network, New Zealand, Network Ten (alternate), Australia; pres. Peli Ventures, Inc., 1975—, Peli Mgmt. Inc., 1982—. Trustee Transcona-Springfield Sch. div., Winnipeg, 1964-67; bd. dirs. Conv. Ctr. Corp., Winnipeg, 1976-86, Atomic Energy of Can., Ltd., Ottawa, Ont., Can., 1981-86, St. Boniface Gen. Hosp., Winnipeg, 1987—, chmn. bd., 1992—. Decorated Order of Can., 1984; recipient Presdl. citation Variety Clubs Internat., 1983, Internat. Media award Variety Clubs Internat., 1986, commemorative medal 125th Anniversary Can., 1992; named Manitoban of Month, Mid-Can. Commerce mag., 1982. Mem. Broadcasters Assn. Man. (pres. 1981-82), Western Assn. Broadcasters (pres. 1984-85, Broadcaster of Yr. award 1991, Broadcaster of Decade award 1994), Can. Assn. Broadcasters (chmn. bd. 1990-92), St. Charles Cluntry Club, Man. Club, Variety Club Man. (chief barker 1984-85). Office: CanWest Global Comm Corp, 201 Portage Ave 31st Fl TD Ctr, Winnipeg, MB Canada R3B 3L7

LIBASSI, FRANK PETER, lawyer; b. N.Y.C., Apr. 20, 1930; s. Frank G. and Mary (Marino) L.; m. Mary Frances Steen, July 10, 1954; children: Thomas, Timothy, Jennifer. B.A. cum laude with honors in Polit. Sci, Colgate U., 1951; LL.B., Yale U., 1954. Bar: N.Y. 1955, Conn. 1980. Enforcement atty. N.Y. State Housing and Rent Commn., 1954-56; regional dir. N.Y. State Commn. on Human Rights, Albany, 1956-62; dep. staff dir. U.S. Commn. on Civil Rights, 1962-66; spl. asst. to sec., dir. office for civil rights HEW, Washington, 1966-68; exec. v.p. The Urban Coalition, Washington, 1968-71; v.p. Am. City Corp., Columbia, Md., 1971-72; pres., chief exec. officer Greater Hartford Process Inc. (Greater Hartford Community Devel. Corp.), 1971-77; gen. counsel HEW, Washington, 1977-79; partner firm Verner, Liipfert, Bernhard and McPherson, Washington, 1979-82; sr. v.p. Travelers Corp., Hartford, Conn., 1982-93; of counsel Verner, Liipfert, Bernhard & McPherson, Washington, 1993—; dean Barney Sch. of Bus. and Pub. Adminstrn., U. Hartford, West Hartford, Conn., 1993-96; pres. Children's Fund of Conn., Hartford, 1996—; v.p. Ctr. for Global Bus. Studies, Paris, 1996—; mem. Urban Land Inst., 1971-77; adv. bd. Bur. Nat. Affairs Housing and Cmty. Devel. Reporter, 1972-77; vis. lectr. Anderson Coll., Chatham Coll., Goddard Coll., Ohio Wesleyan U., 1974-76; adj. faculty Grad. Sch. Bus. and Pub. Adminstrn. U. Hartford, 1976-77; chmn. bd. dirs. Forstmann Corp., 1994—. Author: The Negro in the Armed Forces, 1963, Family Housing and the Negro Serviceman, 1963, Equal Opportunity in Farm Programs, 1965, Revitalizing Central City Investment, 1977. Bd. dirs. legis. com. Am. Coun. Life Ins., 1987-90; bd. dirs., exec. com. Ins. Inst. Hwy. Safety, 1984-88; mem. pub. rels. policy com. Health Ins. Assn. Am., 1988-93; incorporator Inst. Living, 1973—, Hartford Hosp., 1973—, St. Francis Hosp., 1990—, Wheeler Clinic, 1996—, Hartford Seminary, 1993-95; mem. adv. com. Dem. Nat. Com., 1974-77; chmn. Ct. Cmty. Care, Inc., 1980-86; mem. Mt. Sinai Hosp., 1982-90; mem. com. on an aging soc. NAS, 1982-86; mem. exec. com. Downtown Coun. Hartford, 1983-86, Greater Hartford Arts Coun., 1983-86; chmn. Gov.'s Commn. on Financing Long Term Care, 1986-87; mem. nat. consumer adv. com. Am. Health Care Assn., 1985-86; mem. com. on elderly people living alone The Commonwealth Fund, 1985-91; mem. Sec. Bowen's Task Force on Long-term Health Care Policies of Health Care Financing Adminstrn., 1986-87; bd. dirs. Alliance for Aging Rsch., 1986-91; mem. Nat. Retirees Vol. Ctr., 1988-90; mem. Pew Commn. on future of health profls., 1990-93; mem. pub. affairs rsch. coun. conf. bd., 1990-93; mem. United Srs. Health Cooperative, 1990-91; mem. health adv. coun. Johns Hopkins U., 1990-96, mem. com. predicting future diseases Inst. Medicine, 1991-93, bd. advisors Nat. Acad. on Aging, 1992-95; trustee Conn. Pub. Expenditure Coun., 1991-95; mem. adv. com. on health care reform The Commonwealth Fund, 1993—; mem. Duncaster Cmty., 1993—. Recipient Superior Performance award U.S. Commn. on Civil Rights, 1963, Meritorious Svc. award, 1965; Sec.'s spl. citation, 1967; Disting. Svc. award HEW, 1968, Friend of La Casa de Puerto Rico, Hartford, award, 1992; Woodrow Wilson sr. fellow, 1973-77. Mem. ABA, Fed. Bar Assn., N.Y. State Bar Assn., Conn. Bar Assn., Am. Assn. Retired Persons (nat. steering com. for new roles in soc. 1987-90), Greater Hartford C. of C. (bd. dirs. 1985-93, exec. com.). Club: Hartford. Home: 580 Mountain Rd Apt J West Hartford CT 06117-1827

LIBBEY, DARLENE HENSLEY, artist, educator; b. La Follette, Tenn., Jan. 9, 1952; d. Charles Franklin and Geneva (Chitwood) Hensley; children: Michael Damon McLaughlin, Marina Auston. BFA in Painting, San Francisco Art Inst., 1989; MFA in Painting/Drawing, U. Tenn., 1994. Grad. asst. Alliance of Ind. Colls., N.Y.C., 1989; gallery asst. Holley Solomon Gallery, N.Y.C., 1989; teaching assoc., instr. U. Tenn., Knoxville, 1991-94; lectr., instr. U. Tex.-Pan Am., 1994—, South Tex. Cmty. Coll., 1995—; curator Belleza Salon, Knoxville, 1993-94; invitational rep. San Francisco Art Inst., N.Y. Studio Program, Alliance Ind. Colls., 1989; organizer Multi-Media Group Exhbn., San Francisco; lectr., instr. South Tex. C.C., McAllen. One-woman shows include U. Tex.-Pan Am., 1995, 96; exhibited in group shows at San Francisco Art Inst., 1985, 86, 87, 88, 89, Pacific Ctr., San Francisco, 1988, alliance of Ind. Colls., N.Y.C., 1989, San Francisco Mus. Modern Art, 1990, Bluxom Studios, San Francisco, 1991, Gallery 1010, Knoxville, 1991, 92, Ewing Gallery, U. Tenn., Knoxville, 1991, 92, 93, 94, SUNY, Syracuse, 1992, Printers Mark, Knoxville, 1993, Unitarian Ch., Knoxville, 1993, Tomato Head, Knoxville, 1994, Belleza Salon, Knoxville, 1994, U. Pan Am., 1995, 96; group show Museo Historico de Reynosa, Tamalipus, Mex., 1996. Vol. San Francisco Mus. Modern Art, 1990-91; founding mem. Grad. Student Union, U. Tenn., Knoxville, 1993; vol. instr. Knox County Schs., Knoxville, 1992-93; vis. artist Marin County Schs., San Anselmo, Calif., 1989. Tuition scholar San Francisco Art Inst., 1987; materials grantee U. Tenn., 1993, grantee Buck Found., 1987-89. Mem. Coll. Art Assn. Democrat. Unitarian. Avocations: cooking, reading. Home: 1118 W Upas Ave Mcallen TX 78501 Office: U Tex-Pan Am Art Dept 1201 W University Dr Edinburg TX 78539-2909

LIBBEY, ROBERT DAVID, television producer; b. Bangor, Maine, Feb. 28, 1962; s. Fred Harold and Alice Virginia (Keirstead) L.; m. Denise Marie O'Connel, Oct. 8, 1988. BA in Theatre and Broadcasting, U. Maine, 1984. Videographer Community Broadcasting Svc., Bangor, 1985-87; TV producer Maine Pub. Broadcasting Network, Bangor, 1987—; bd. dirs. Bangor Community Theatre, 1988—. Producer TV shows Painting in Maine, 1989-90, The Air We Breathe, 1990. Democrat. Avocations: tennis, dance, acting. Office: Maine Pub Broadcasting 65 Texas Ave Bangor ME 04401-4324*

LIBBIN, ANNE EDNA, lawyer; b. Phila., Aug. 25, 1950; d. Edwin M. and Marianne (Herz) L.; m. Christopher J. Cannon, July 20, 1985; children: Abigail Libbin Cannon, Rebecca Libbin Cannon. AB, Radcliffe Coll., 1971; JD, Harvard U., 1975. Bar: Calif. 1975, U.S. Dist. Ct. (cen. dist.) Calif. 1977, U.S. Dist. Ct. (no. dist.) Calif. 1979, U.S. Dist. Ct. (ea. dist.) Calif. 1985, U.S. Ct. Appeals (2d cir.) 1977, U.S. Ct. Appeals (5th cir.) 1982, U.S. Ct. Appeals (7th cir.) 1976, U.S. Ct. Appeals (9th cir.) 1976, U.S. Ct. Appeals (D.C. cir.) 1978. Appellate atty. NLRB, Washington, 1975-78; assoc. Pillsbury Madison & Sutro LLP, San Francisco, 1978-83, ptnr., 1984—; dir. Alumnae Resources, San Francisco. Mem. ABA (labor and employment sect.), State Bar Calif. (labor law sect.), Bar Assn. San Francisco (labor law sect.), Anti-Defamation League (ctrl. Pacific regional adv. bd.), Radcliffe Club (San Francisco). Office: Pillsbury Madison & Sutro 235 Montgomery St San Francisco CA 94104-2902

LIBBY, GARY RUSSELL, museum director; b. Boston, June 7, 1944; s. Charles W. and Sylvia P. L. BA, U. Fla., 1967, MA (NDEA fellow), 1968; MA, Tulane U., 1972. Instr. English Tulane U., 1968-71; asst. prof. Stetson U., Deland, Fla., 1972-77, vis. prof., 1977-86; dir. Mus. Arts and Scis., Daytona Beach, Fla., 1977—; reviewer Inst. Mus. Svcs., mem. panel Mus. Assessment Program; reviewer Accreditation Commn. of Am. Assn. of Mus. Author: Two Centuries of Cuban Art, 1985; editor: Archipenko: Themes and Variations, 1989, Chihuly: Form From Fire, 1994 (Southeastern Mus. Conf. award 1994), A Century of Jewelry and Gems, 1995, Celebrating Florida, 1995, Cuba: A History in Art, 1997. Trustee Cuban Found.; mem. visual arts panel, youth and children's mus. panel, sci. mus. panel A.D.A. statewide panel Fla. Arts Coun.; panelist Challenge Grant Program; panelist Cultural Instns. Program; mem. hist. mus. grants panel Fla. Divsn. History. Mem. Fla. Art Mus. Dirs. Assn. (govt. liaison 1990, pres. 1995-96, 96-97), Fla. Assn. Mus. (bd. dirs. 1992—, sec. 1995-96, 96-97), Fla. Cultural and Ednl. Alliance (bd. dirs. 1995), Am. Assn. Mus. (accreditation commn. 1994—). Home: 419 Jessamine Blvd Daytona Beach FL 32118-3740 Office: Mus of Arts & Scis 1040 Museum Blvd Daytona Beach FL 32114-4510

LIBBY, JOHN KELWAY, financial services company executive; b. Washington, June 13, 1926; s. John H.and Violet K. (Bamber) L.; m. Mary Seymour Kindel, Dec. 30, 1960; children: Carolyn K., Anne K., Virginia K. BA, Haverford Coll., 1945; postgrad., Harvard U., 1946. With U.S. Dept. State, Washington, 1947-48, Capital Airlines Inc., 1949-51, S.G. Warburg & Co., London, 1954; assoc. and v.p. Kuhn Loeb & Co., N.Y.C., 1955-66, gen. ptnr., 1967-77; mng. dir. Lehman Bros. Kuhn Loeb, Inc., N.Y.C., 1977-80, adv. dir., 1981-84; gen. ptnr. K.L. Assocs., N.Y.C., 1985—; adviser Cen. Bank Venezuela, 1974-75; bd. dirs. various corps. Trustee Brearley Sch., N.Y.C., 1977-85. Lt. USN, 1944-46, PTO, 1951-53. Office: K L Assocs 450 Park Ave New York NY 10022-2605

LIBBY, LAUREN DEAN, foundation executive; b. Smith Center, Kans., Jan. 9, 1951; s. Dean L. and Elizabeth V. (Hansen) L.; m. June Ellen Hofer, Apr. 29, 1979; 1 child, Grant Lauren. BS in Agrl. Econs., Kans. State U., 1973; MBA, Regis U., 1988. Radio sta. employee, 1968-72; asst. program dir. info. br. Kans. State Extension Svc., Manhattan, 1969-73; economist Howard Houk Assocs., Chgo., 1973-75; asst. to pres. The Navigators, Colorado Springs, Colo., 1975-78, ministry devel. coord., 1979-86, dir. min. advancement, 1986-90, v.p., 1990—; pres. New Horizons Found., Colorado Springs, 1990—; bd. dirs. Navigators, Colorado Springs, 1993—; founding bd. dirs. Sta. KTLF-FM/Ednl. Comms. of Colorado Springs, 1987—; cons. 22 listener-supported radio stas., 1989—. Contbr. articles to mags. Bd. dirs. Christian Stewardship Assn., 1995—. Mem. Nat. Soc. Fundraising Execs., Ctrl. States VHF Soc. (pres. 1995). Avocation: amateur radio. Home: 6166 Del Paz Dr Colorado Springs CO 80918-3004 Office: The Navigators 3820 N 30th St Colorado Springs CO 80904-5001

LIBBY, PETER, cardiologist, medical researcher; b. Berkeley, Calif., Feb. 13, 1947; s. Henry and Vivian (Green) L; m. Beryl Rica Benacerraf, Nov. 22, 1975; children: Oliver, Brigitte. BA, U. Calif., Berkeley, 1969; MD, U. Calif., San Diego, 1973; MA (hon.), Harvard U., 1996. Diplomate Am. Bd. Internal Medicine and Cardiovascular Disease. Intern Peter Bent Brigham Hosp., Boston, 1973-74, resident, 1974-76; fellow Harvard Med. Sch., Boston, 1976-79, Brigham & Women's Hosp., Boston, 1979-80; asst. Prof. Tufts U. Sch. Sch. Medicine, Boston, 1980-86, assoc., 1986-90; asst. physician New Eng. Med. Ctr., Boston, 1980-87, physician, 1987-90; dir. vascular medicine and atherosclerosis unit Brigham and Women's Hosp., Boston, 1990—, physician, 1992—; assoc. prof. medicine Harvard Med. Sch., Boston, 1990-96, prof. medicine, 1996—; mem. ad hoc peer rev. com. NIH, Bethesda, Md., mem. pathology A study sect., 1988-92; mem. advisor W.W. Smith Charitable Trust, Phila., 1985-88; mem. peer rev. com. Am. Heart Assn., Mass., 1982-88, chmn. 1992-94, chmn. rsch. com. 1994-96; mem. Nat. Insts. of Health, Bethesda; mem. bd. sci. counselors Nat. Heart, Lung and Blood Inst., 1996—; inaugural basic sci. lectr. European Soc. Cardiology, Birmingham, Eng., 1996, E.B. Raftery Meml. lectr. Royal Coll. Physicians, London, 1996, Durrer Meml. lectr. Acad. Med. Ctr., Amsterdam, 1997, Teichman Meml. lectr. Tel Aviv U., 1997. Recipient Established Investigator award Am. Heart Assn., 1986-91; MERIT award Nat. Heart, Lung, Blood Inst., 1993—; S.A. Levine fellow Am. Heart Assn., Mass., 1976-77, Med. Found., Inc. fellow, Boston, 1980-82, fellow Council Arteriosclerosis, Am. Heart Assn. and Coun. on Circulation. Fellow Am. Coll. Cardiology; mem. Am. Soc. Clin. Investigation, Am. Physiol. Soc., Assn. Am. Physicians, Am. Soc. Cell Biology, Am. Assn. Immunologists, N. Am. Vascular Biology Orgn., Internat. Soc. and Fedn. Cardiology, Assn. Am. Physicians. Home: 111 Perkins St Jamaica Plain MA 02130-4313 Office: Brigham & Women's Hosp 221 Longwood Ave Boston MA 02115-5822

LIBBY, RONALD THEODORE, political science educator, consultant, researcher; b. L.A., Nov. 20, 1941; s. Theodore Harold and Patricia Mildred (Griswold) L.; m. Kathleen Christina Jacobson, June 3, 1982; children: Kathleen Elizabeth Libby, Erin Kristin Jenne. BA, Wash. State U., 1965; MA, U. Wash., 1966, PhD, 1975. Lectr. U. Bostwana, Lesotho and Swaziland, 1973-75, U. Malawi, Zomba, 1975-76, U. Zambia, Lusaka, 1976-79; asst. prof. U. Notre Dame, South Bend, Ind., 1981-83; sr. lectr. U. West Indies, Kingston, Jamaica, 1983-85; assoc. prof. Northwestern U., Evanston, Ill., 1985-86; sr. rsch. fellow Australian Nat. U., Darwin, 1986-87; sr. lectr. Victoria U., Wellington, New Zealand, 1987-89; prof. S.W. State U., Marshall, Minn., 1989-96; prof., chair St. Joseph's U., Phila., 1996—; treas. New Zealand Polit. Sci. Assn., Wellington, 1988-89. Author: Towards an Africanized U.S. Policy for Southern Africa, 1980, The Politics of Economic Power in Southern Africa, 1987, Hawke's Law, 1989 (Choice award 1991), Protecting Markets: U.S. Policy and the World Grain Trade, 1992, ECO-WARS: Counteracting the Power of Business, 1997; contbr. articles to profl. jours. With U.S. Army, 1962-64. Rsch. grantee Carnegie Endowment, 1971. Mem. Am. Polit. Sci. Assn., Internat. Studies Assn., Australian Polit. Sci. Assn. Roman Catholic. Avocations: tennis, handball, piano, singing. Office: St Joseph's U Dept Polit Sci Philadelphia PA 19131-1395 *Through the many travails of life the one abiding principle that has guided me is intellectual honesty and integrity.*

LIBBY, SANDRA CHIAVARAS, special education educator; b. Clinton, Mass., Apr. 8, 1949; B.S. in Spl. Edn., Fitchburg (Mass.) State Coll., 1970, M.Ed. in Reading, 1976; postgrad. (fellow) Clark U., 1981-83; 2 children. Tchr. spl. class Webster (Mass.) Schs., 1970-73, asst. coord. program materials, resource room, 1974, tchr./coord. primary spl. needs program, 1975-78, tchr. jr. high English, 1978-79, reading tchr. jr. high, 1979-80 adminstrv. asst. intern Shepherd Hill Regional Sch., Dudley, Mass., 1980-81; dir., owner Teddy Bear Day Care Ctr., Dudley, Mass., 1983-85; devel. specialist Ft. Devens Post Learning Ctr., Shirley, Mass., 1985-86; resource room tchr. Murdock High Sch., Winchendon, Mass., 1986; tchr. behavioral modification Middle Sch., Winchendon, 1986-87; coord., tchr. gifted and talented Lancaster Pub. Schs., 1987-90; tchr. learning disabilities Leominster Pub. Sch., 1990-91, tchr. primary level behavior modification, 1991—. Sec. Samoset Sch. PTO, Leominister, Mass., 1995—; mem. Edn. Reform Change Team, 1996—. Mem. Nat. Edn. Assn., Mass. Tchrs. Assn., Leominster Tchrs. Assn. (bldg. rep. 1992-95, negotiating com. 1993—, sec. 1995—), Internat. Reading Assn. (v.p. 1994-95, chairperson celebrate literacy award 1994-95), Mass. Reading Assn. (mem. North Worcester County coun. 1994-95), Webster Emblem Club (pres. 1984-85), Phi Delta Kappa (Horace Mann grant 1989-90). Cert. in elem. and spl. edn., reading, reading supervision, learning disabilities, English (secondary), Mass. Home: 29 Chapman Pl Leominster MA 01453-6149

LIBERATI, MARIA THERESA, fashion production company executive; b. Phila., July 16, 1965; d. Edward Michael and Anna Maria Liberati. Student, Laval U., Que., Can., 1984; BS in Fgn. Lang. Edn., Temple U., 1986. Pres., bd. dirs. Sierra Ctr., Feasterville, Pa., 1988—; pres. M.T.L. Prodns., Phila., 1989—; spokesperson Compassion for Animals, Phila., 1988—. Author: Fashion, Fun and Fitness, 1989; editor mab. Better Nutrition for Today's Living, 1990—. Named Miss Pa., 1985, Miss World, 1986; recipient Merit award Actors and Artists Assn., Rome. Mem. AFTRA, NAFE (adv. bd. 1988—). Avocations: reading, cooking. Office: Sierra Ctr divsn MTL Prodns PO Box 52193 Philadelphia PA 19115

LIBERATORE, NICHOLAS ALFRED, business consultant; b. N.Y.C., June 19, 1916; s. Alexander and Angelina (Laspagnoletta) L.; m. Jean Talbot MacAdam, June 6, 1943 (dec.); children: Virginia, George, Nicholas, Elliott, Mark; m. Marianne Westpalm van Hoorn Jewett, Feb. 10, 1973. Student, NYU; MA, Fairfield U., 1975. CFO Cia Chilena de Elec., Santiago, Chile, 1949-54, Cia Aux. de Elec., Rio de Janeiro, 1954-56; Vice pres. Ebasco Internat. Co., N.Y.C., 1956-58; pres. Raymond Concrete Pile Co. Am., N.Y.C., 1958-59; chmn. operating com. Brown-Raymond-Walsh, Madrid, Spain, 1959-62; v.p. Raymond Internat. Inc., N.Y.C., 1962-65; sr. v.p., pres. internat. Group Lone Star Industries, Inc., Greenwich, Conn., 1965-74; sr. v.p. Ebasco Services Inc., N.Y.C., 1974-77; exec. v.p. Genstar Ltd., San Francisco, 1977-83; cons. Royal Bank of Can., Toronto, 1983-90; bd. dirs.

Internat. Mining Corp. Bd. dirs. Fgn. Trade Coun. Served to capt. C.E., AUS, 1943-46. Decorated Bronze Star medal, Army Commendation medal; Cross of Isabel the Catholic, (Spain). Mem. Internat. Coun. (conf. bd.), Brazilian-Am. C. of C. (founder), Pan. Am. Soc. (pres.), Argentine-Am. C. of C. (pres.), Chile-U.S. C. of C. (pres.), St. Francis Yacht Club, Econ. Club N.Y., Bankers' Club San Francisco, Recess Club. Home: 4 Mayflower Ln Weston CT 06883-2632

LIBERMAN, ALVIN MEYER, psychology educator; b. St. Joseph, Mo., May 10, 1917; s. Max and Lotte (Korbholz) L.; m. Isabelle Yoffe, June 1, 1941; children—Mark Yoffe, Michael Charles, Sarah Ivy. A.B., U. Mo., 1938, M.A., 1939; Ph.D., Yale U., 1942. Prof. emeritus Psychology U. Conn., Storrs, 1949—; prof. emeritus Linguistics Yale U., Storrs, 1950-87; Alumni Assn. Disting. prof. U. Conn., Storrs, 1979—; pres., dir. rsch. Haskins Labs., New Haven, 1975-86, sr. v.p., 1986—. Contbr. articles to profl. jours. Guggenheim fellow, 1964-65. Fellow Am. Acad. Arts and Scis.; mem. Nat. Acad. Scis., Soc. Exptl. Psychologists (Warren medal 1975), Acoustical Soc. Am., Am. Psychol. Assn. (Disting. Sci. Contbn. award 1980, F.O. Schmitt medal and prize in neuroscience 1988). Address: 614 Storrs Rd Mansfield Center CT 06250-1225

LIBERMAN, GAIL JEANNE, editor; b. Neptune, N.J., Feb. 26, 1951; d. Si and Dorothy (Gold) L.; m. Alan Lavine, Dec. 20, 1991. BA, Rutgers U., 1972. Youth editor AP, N.Y.C., 1972-73; writer United Feature Syndicate, N.Y.C., 1973; reporter, broadcast editor UPI, Phila. and Hartford, Conn., 1973-75; reporter Courier-Post, Camden, N.J., 1976-80, Bank Advt. News, North Palm Beach, Fla., 1981-82; editor Bank Rate Monitor, North Palm Beach, 1982—. Author: Improving Your Credit and Reducing Your Debt, 1994 (endorsed Inst. CFPs), The Complete Idiot's Guide to Making Money With Mutual Funds, 1996; columnist: Boston Herald, 1994—, America Online, 1996—.

LIBERMAN, ROBERT PAUL, psychiatry educator, researcher, writer; b. Newark, Aug. 16, 1937; s. Harry and Gertrude (Galowitz) L.; m. Janet Marilyn Brown, Feb. 16, 1973; children: Peter, Sarah, Danica, Nathaniel, Annalisa. AB summa cum laude, Dartmouth Coll., 1959, diploma in medicine with honors, 1960; MS in Pharmacology, U. Calif.-San Francisco, 1961; MD, Johns Hopkins U., 1963. Diplomate Nat. Bd. Med. Examiners, Am. Bd. Psychiatry and Neurology. Intern Bronx (N.Y.) Mcpl. Hosp.-Einstein Coll. Medicine, 1963-64; resident in psychiatry Mass. Mental Health Ctr., Boston, 1964-68; postdoctoral fellow in social psychiatry Harvard U., 1966-68, teaching fellow in psychiatry, 1964-68; mem. faculty group psychotherapy tng. program Washington Sch. Psychiatry, 1968-70; with Nat. Ctr. Mental Health Svc., Tng. and Rsch., St. Elizabeths Hosp., also mem. NIMH Clin. and Rsch. Assocs. Tng. Program, Washington, 1968-70; asst. clin. prof. psychiatry UCLA, 1970-72, assoc. clin. prof., 1972-73, assoc. rsch. psychiatrist, 1973-76, rsch. prof. psychiatry, 1976-77, prof. psychiatry, 1977—; dir. Camarillo-UCLA Clin. Rsch. Unit, 1970-97, dir. Clin. Rsch. Ctr. Schizophrenia and Psychiat. Rehab., 1977—; chief Rehab. Medicine Svc., West L.A. VA Med. Ctr., Brentwood divsn., 1980-92; cons. div. mental health and behavioral scis. edn. Sepulveda (Calif.) VA Hosp., 1975-80; practice medicine specializing in psychiatry, Reston, Va., 1968-70, Thousand Oaks, Calif., 1977—; staff psychiatrist Ventura County Mental Health Dept., 1970-75; staff psychiatrist Ventura County Gen. Hosp.; mem. med. staff UCLA Neuropsychiatric Inst. and Hosp., Ventura Gen. Hosp., Camarillo State Hosp., 1970-97, West Los Angeles VA Med. Ctr.; dir. Rehab. Rsch. and Tng. Ctr. Mental Illness, 1980-85. Bd. dirs. Lake Sherwood Community Assn., 1978—, pres., 1979-81, 90-92, v.p., 1992-95; mem. Conejo Valley Citizens Adv. Bd., 1979-81, sec., 1995—. Served as surgeon USPHS, 1964-68. Recipient Noyes award for Rsch. in Schizophrenia, 1992, Kolb award in Schizophrenia, 1994. Research grantee NIMH, SSA, NIDA, VA, 1972—. Mem. Assn. Advancement Behavior Therapy (exec. com. 1970-72, dir. 1972-79), Am. Psychiat. Assn. (Hibbs and Van Ameringen awards, Inst. Psychiat. Svcs. Significant Achievement award), Assn. Clin. Psychosocial Research (mem. coun. 1985—, pres. 1975-77), Phi Beta Kappa. Author: (with King, DeRisi and McCann) Personal Effectiveness: Guiding People to Assert Their Feelings and Improve Their Social Skills, 1975; A Guide to Behavioral Analysis and Therapy, 1972; (with Wheeler, DeVisser, Kuehnel and Kuehnel) Handbook of Marital Therapy: An Educational Approach to Treating Troubled Relationships, 1980, Psychiatric Rehabilitation of Chronic Mental Patients, 1987, (with De Risi and Mueser) Social Skills Training for Psychiatric Patients, 1989, (with Kuehnel, Rose and Storzbach) Resource Book for Psychiatric Rehabilitation, 1990, Handbook of Psychiatric Rehabilitation, 1992, (with Yager) Stress in Psychiatric Disorders, 1993, (with Corrigan) Behavior Therapy in Psychiatric Hospitals, 1994; mem. editorial bd. Jour. Applied Behavior Analysis, 1972-78, Jour. Marriage and Family Counseling, 1974-78, Jour. Behavior Therapy and Exptl. Psychiatry, 1975—, Behavior Therapy, 1979-84, Assessment and Invervention in Devel. Disabilities, 1980-85; assoc. editor Jour. Applied Behavior Analysis, 1976-78, Schizophrenia Bull., 1981-87; Internat. Rev. Psychiatry, 1988—, Psychiatry, 1993—; contbr. over 300 articles to profl. jours., chpts. to books. Home: 528 Lake Sherwood Dr Thousand Oaks CA 91361-5120 Office: Cmty & Rehab W LA Psychiatry VA Med Ctr (116 AR) 11301 Wilshire Blvd Los Angeles CA 90073-1003

LIBERT, DONALD JOSEPH, lawyer; b. Sioux Falls, S.D., Mar. 23, 1928; s. Bernard Joseph and Eleanor Monica (Sutton) L.; m. Jo Anne Murray, May 16, 1953; children: Cathleen, Thomas, Kevin, Richard, Stephanie. B.S. magna cum laude in Social Scis., Georgetown U., 1950, LL.B., 1956. Bar: Ohio. From assoc. to ptnr. Manchester, Bennett, Powers & Ullman, Youngstown, Ohio, 1956-65; various positions to v.p., gen. counsel and sec. Youngstown Sheet & Tube Co., 1965-78; assoc. group counsel LTV Corp., Youngstown and Pitts., 1979; v.p. and gen. counsel Anchor Hocking Corp., Lancaster, Ohio, 1979-87. Served to lt. (j.g.) USN, 1951-54. Mem. Ohio Bar Assn. (former chmn. sr. lawyers com.), Fairfield County Bar Assn. (chmn. bus. law com.), Lancaster Country Club, Rotary. Republican. Roman Catholic. Office: 127 W Wheeling St Lancaster OH 43130-3737

LIBERTH, RICHARD FRANCIS, lawyer; b. Bklyn., Mar. 1, 1950; s. S. Richard and Frances J. (Falconer) L.; m. Lisa M. Feenick, June 8, 1974; children: Andrew R., Erica M. BS in Bus. Adminstrn., U. Denver, 1972; JD, Bklyn. Law Sch., 1976. Bar: N.Y. 1977, U.S. Dist. Ct. (so. and ea. dists.) N.Y. 1981, U.S. Dist. Ct. (no. dist.) N.Y. 1991. Staff atty. Mental Health Legal Svcs., Poughkeepsie, N.Y., 1976-78; sr. asst. dist. atty. Rockland County Dist. Attys. Office, N.Y.C., 1978-81; prin. Drake, Sommers, Loeb, Tarshis & Catania, Newburgh, N.Y., 1981—. Dir. Legal Aid Soc. Orange County, Goshen, N.Y., 1982-84, Orange County Cerebral Palsy Assn., Goshen, 1986-89; mem. Rep. Nat. Com., Washington, 1990—. Mem. N.Y. Bar Assn., Newburgh Bar Assn. (pres. 1991), Orange County Bar Assn. (v.p. 1995, pres. 1997), Woodbury Lions Club (Central Valley, N.Y.) (past pres.). Avocations: golf, tennis, reading, collecting. Home: 50 Buena Vista Terr Central Valley NY 10917 Office: Drake Sommers Loeb Tarshis & Catania One Corwin Ct Newburgh NY 12550

LIBERTINY, THOMAS GABOR, mechanical engineer, administrator; b. Miami, Mar. 26, 1966; s. Geroge Z. and Anna (Vizvardi) L.; m. Susan Fryc. BSME, Lawrence Tech. U., 1990. Applications engr. Octal, Inc., Southfield, Mich., 1987-88; mgr. Tensor Systems, Inc., Dearborn, 1988-92; engr. GSE Inc., Farmington, Mich., 1992-94; project mgr. Lucas Assembly and Test Sys., Livonia, Mich., 1994—; lectr. in field. Mem. ASME (full mem., chmn. elect design edn. com.), NSPE, Mich. Soc. Profl. Engrs., Soc. Automotive Engrs. (full mem.), Soc. Mfg. Engrs., Soc. Exptl. Mechanics. Avocation: pvt. pilot.

LIBERTO, JOSEPH SALVATORE, banker; b. Balt., Apr. 26, 1929; s. Cosimo and Anna (Serio) L.; m. Mary Jane Colandro, May 20, 1962; children—Joseph C., Grace Ann. Student, Balt. City Coll., 1945-47; certificate accounting, Balt. Coll. Commerce, 1949; grad., Nat. Assn. Bank Auditors, and Comptrollers Sch. Banking, U. Wis., 1968. With Signet Bank, Md., Balt., 1954—; auditor Union Trust Co. Md., 1963—, asst. v.p., security officer, 1979—. Served with AUS, 1951-53, Japan. Mem. Bank Adminstrn. Inst. (pres. Balt. 1968—), Inst. Internal Auditors. Home: 5609 Biddison Ave Baltimore MD 21206-3442 Office: Signet Bank Baltimore St Baltimore MD 21202-1603

LIBIN, ALVIN G., business executive. LLD, U. Calgary. Co-owner Calgary Flames; chmn. Crownx Properties, Inc.; dir. Extendicare, Inc. (N.Am.), Crown Life Ins. Co. Chmn. Alberta Heritage Found. for Med. Rsch., Can.; chair ACTC Technologies, Inc. Office: Calgary Flames, 255-5 Ave SW # 3200, Calgary, AB Canada T2P 3G6

LIBIN, PAUL, theatre executive, producer; b. Chgo., Dec. 12, 1930; m. Florence Rowe, Sept. 25, 1956; children: Charles, Claire, Andrea. Student, U. Ill.; B.F.A., Columbia U., 1956. Producing dir., v.p. Jujamcyn Theaters, N.Y.C., 1990—. Producer (plays) including The Crucible, 1958, Six Characters in Search of an Author, 1963, Royal Hunt of the Sun, 1965, Circle in the Sq. Theatre, N.Y.C., 1965-90; co-producer (plays) Uncle Vanya, 1973, The Iceman Cometh, 1973, Death of a Salesman, 1975, The Lady from the Sea, 1976, The Night of the Iguana, 1976, The Club, 1976, Tartuffe, 1977, The Inspector General, Man and Superman, Spokesong, Loose Ends, 1978, Major Barbara, Past Tense, The Man Who Came to Dinner, 1979, The Bacchae, John Gabriel Borkman, The Father, Scenes and Revelations, 1980, Candida, MacBeth, Eminent Domain, 1981, Present Laughter, The Queen and the Rebels, The Misanthrope, 1982, The Caine Mutiny Court-Martial, Heartbreak House, Awake and Sing, 1983, Design for Living, 1984, Arms and the Man, Marriage of Figaro, 1985, You Never Can Tell, 1986, Coastal Disturbances, 1987, A Streetcar Named Desire, Juno and the Paycock, 1988, The Night of the Iguana, 1988, The Devil's Disciple, 1988, Ghetto, 1989, Sweeney Todd, 1989, Zoya's Apartment, 1990, The Miser, 1990; producing dir. plays I Hate Hamlet, 1991, Secret Garden, 1991, La Bete, 1991, Two Trains Running, 1992, Jelly's Last Jam, 1992, Tommy, 1993, Angels in America, 1993, My Fair Lady, 1993, Grease, 1994, Love! Valour! Compassion!, 1995, Smokey Joe's Cafe, 1995, My Thing of Love, 1995, Moon Over Buffalo, 1995, Patti LuPone on Broadway, 1995, Seven Guitars, 1996, A Funny Thing Happened on the Way to the Forum, 1996, Present Laughter, 1996, David Copperfield, Dreams and Nightmares, 1996, Annie, 1997, Young Man from Atlanta, 1997. Served with U.S. Army, 1953-55. Recipient Obie award The Club, Village Voice, 1977, Tony award, 1976, 92, 93, 94, 95. Mem. 2d League Off Broadway Theatres and Producers (pres. emeritus), 1st League Am. Theatres and Producers (officer, exec. com., bd. govs.). Office: Jujamcyn Theatres St James Theatre 246 W 44th St New York NY 10036-3910

LIBKA, ROBERT JOHN, educational director, consultant; b. Pigeon, Mich., Sept. 19, 1951; s. Neil August and Joan Lois (Frank) L.; m. Bonnie Rae Borcher, June 16, 1973; children: Michelle, Kimberly, Jennifer. Cadet, U.S. Coast Guard Acad., 1969-71; BA in Edn., Concordia U., River Forest, Ill., 1975, MA in Edn., 1978. Cert. tchr. elem. & secondary schs., Ill., spl. guidance cert. Dir. residence hall Concordia U., River Forest, Ill., 1975-79; dir. student activities Concordia U., River Forest, 1975-87; dir. student ctr. dir. Koehneke Community Ctr., River Forest, 1975-88; project coord. Khusrau translation Harvard U. and Smithsonian Instn., Boston, Washington, 1988-89; pres. Attitudinal Dynamics Internat., Inc., Maywood, Ill., 1970—; dir. guidance Walther Lutheran High Sch., Maywood, Ill., 1989—; exec. dir. Luth. H.S. Assn. Kane and DuPage Counties, St. Charles, Ill., 1993—; cons. Harvard U., Smithsonian Instn., Century Insur., Cook Cty. Sheriff's Officeand others, 1970—. Author: (Book) India: Price of Adventure, 1990; producer: Many videos of Internat. Religions and Cultures, 1988—; contbr. numerous articles to profl. and religious jours. Leader ARC, Chgo., 1975-85; mem. N. Maywood (Ill.) Community Orgn., 1975-85; pres. St. Paul Luth. Ch., 1987-88. Recipient Rsch. grant Smithsonian Instn., New Delhi, India, 1988. Mem. Am. Mgmt. Assn., Am. Personnel & Guidance Assn., Ill. Assn. Coll. Admissions Counselors, Luth. Edn. Assn. (life mem.), Gospel Music Assn., Nat. Assn. Campus Activities (bd. dirs. 1985-87). Avocations: travel, video production, distance running, photography. Home: 805 N 6th Ave Maywood IL 60153-1046 Office: Fox Valley Luth Acad 2400 E Main St Saint Charles IL 60174-2415

LIBMAN, STEVEN BRADLEY, performing arts administrator; b. Providence, Oct. 5, 1959; s. Herman and Marilyn Kayla (Zettel) L.; m. Keitha Ann Grace, Aug. 17, 1980; 1 child, Tracy. BA magna cum laude, R.I. Coll., 1980; Asst. mng. dir. R.I. Coll., Providence, 1978-80; box office mgr. Trinity Sq. Repertory Co., Providence, 1980-81; mng. dir. Auburn Civic Theatre, N.Y., 1981-83, Fulton Opera House, Lancaster, Pa., 1983-86; devel. dir. Pitts. Ballet Theatre, 1987-91, exec. dir., 1991—; adj. faculty arts mgmt. Carnegie Mellon U.; guest lectr. Non-Profit Mgmt. U., Pitts. Trustee Citizens for Arts in Pa., Harrisburg, 1984—, Regent Theatre, 1993-97, Dance/USA, (co-chmn. mgr's. coun. 1994-97); mem. theatre panel Pa. Council on the Arts, 1986-88 mem. Dance Discipline Rev. Panel, Nat. Endowment for the Arts, 1996; mem. adv. com. arts mgmt. program Carnegie Mellon U., Pitts., 1993— . Recipient Theatre Mgmt. award R.I. Coll., 1979. Jewish. Home: 716 Kewanna Ave Pittsburgh PA 15234-1205 Office: Pitts Ballet Theatre 2900 Liberty Ave Pittsburgh PA 15201-1511

LIBOFF, RICHARD LAWRENCE, physicist, educator; b. N.Y.C., Dec. 30, 1931; s. William and Sarah (Mell) L.; m. Myra Blatt, July 4, 1954; children: David, Lisa. A.B., Bklyn. Coll., 1953; Ph.D., NYU, 1961. Asst. prof. physics NYU, 1961-63; prof. applied physics, applied math. and elec. engring. Cornell U., 1964—; prin. investigator Air Force Office Sci. Research, 1978-83, Army Research Office, 1984—; cons. Batelle Columbus Lab. Author: Introduction to the Theory of Kinetic Equations, 1969, 79, Russian edit., 1974, Introductory Quantum Mechanics, 1980, 2d edit., 1991, Korean edit., 1992, Waveguides, Transmission Lines and Smith Charts, 1984, Kinetic Theory: Classical, Quantum and Relativistic Descriptions, 1990. Served with Chem. Corps U.S. Army, 1953-55. Recipient Founders Day cert. N.Y. U., 1961; Solvay fellow, 1972; Fulbright scholar, 1984. Fellow Am. Phys. Soc.; mem. IEEE (sr.), Sigma Xi. Office: Cornell U Phillips Hall Ithaca NY 14853

LIBONATI, MICHAEL ERNEST, lawyer, educator, writer; b. Chgo., May 25, 1944; s. Roland V. and Jeannette K. Libonati; m. Yvonne M. Barber, Sept. 30, 1967; children: Michael, Emma. LLB, Yale U., 1967, LLM, 1969. Bar: D.C. 1968, Ill. 1975, Pa. 1976. Prof. law Temple U., Phila., 1972-90, Carnell prof. law, 1990—; cons. U.S. Adv. Commn. Intergovernmental Rels.; vis. prof. law U. Ala., Tuscaloosa, summer 1976, Cornell U., Ithaca, N.Y., spring 1977, Coll. William and Mary, Williamsburg, Va., fall 1987. Author: (with Sands and Martinez) Local Government Law, 4 vols., 1981-82, (with Hetzel and Williams) Legislative Law and Process, 2d edit., 1993, Local Government Autonomy, 1993, Japanese edit. 1997; asst. editor articles Am. Jour. Legal History, 1971-82. Recipient Williams prize for Excellence in Teaching, 1985, 90; named Hon. Editor Temple U. Law Quarterly, vol. 59, 1986. Mem. NAS (nat. rsch. bd., highway law project adv. commn.), ABA (coun. urban state and local govt. law sect. 1979-83), Am. Law Inst., Nat. Assn. Atty.'s Gen. (state constitution law project adv. bd.). Office: Temple U Sch Law 1719 N Broad St Philadelphia PA 19122-6002

LIBOUS, THOMAS WILLIAM, state senator; b. Binghamton, N.Y., Apr. 16, 1953; s. William Abraham and Kathrine (Haddad) L.; m. Frances Pianella, Sept. 27, 1975; children: Matthew, Nicholas. AAS in Mktg., Broome Community Coll., 1973; BS in Mktg. and Fin., SUNY, Utica, 1975. Dir. mktg. Chase Lincoln First Bank, Binghamton, 1975-83; v.p. mktg. Johnson City Pub. Co., Binghamton, 1983-88; senator N.Y. State Legislature, Albany, 1989—. Minority leader Binghamton City Coun., 1985-88; del. Rep. Nat. Conv., 1992, 96. Mem. Rotary, KC. Republican. Roman Catholic. Office: 1607 State Office Bldg 44 Hawley St Binghamton NY 13901-4400

LICATA, ARTHUR FRANK, lawyer; b. N.Y.C., June 16, 1947. BA in English, Le Moyne Coll., 1969; postgrad., SUNY, Binghampton, 1969-71; JD cum laude, Suffolk U., 1976. Bar: Mass. 1977, N.Y. 1985, U.S. Ct. Appeals (1st cir.) 1977, U.S. Dist. Ct. Mass. 1977, admitted Frank B. Murray, Jr. Inns of Ct. 1990-92. Assoc. Parker, Coulter, Daley & White, Boston, 1977-82; pvt. practice Arthur F. Licata P.C., Boston, 1982—; prin. Ardlee Internat. Trading Co., Ea. and Ctrl. Europe and Russia, 1989—; del. White House Conf. on Trade and Investment on Cen. Europe, Cleve., 1995; lectr. Mass. Continuing Legal Edn., Boston, 1982-90, mem. trial adv. com., 1984-88; mem. working group on drinking and drunk driving Harvard Sch. Pub. Health Ctr. for Health Comms., 1986; spkr. Conv. Nat. Fedn. Paralegal Assns., Boston, 1987; del. U.S.-People's Republic of China Joint Session on Trade, Investment and Econ. Law, Beijing, 1987; co-sponsor Estonian legal del. visit to Mass. and N.H. correctional instns., 1990; Boston host former Soviet legal del. visit, 1989; legal advisor Czech Anglo-Am. Bus. Inst., Prague, Czech Republic, 1989—, Russian Children's Fund, 1992-94, Estonia Acad. for Pub. Safety, 1992-94; adv. bd. Ford Found.'s Legal Resource Ctr adv. com. Czech Republic, 1994-96; participant U.S.-Russian Investment Symposium, Harvard U., 1997. Panel mem. sta. WBZ TV, Boston; contbr. articles to profl. jours. U.S. Del. 6th People to People Juvenile Justice Program to USSR, Moscow, 1989; legal advisor Mass. chpt. MADD, Plymouth County, 1984-87; mem. State Adv. Com. Med. Malpractice, Boston, 1985; bd. dirs. Boston Ctr. for the Arts, 1990-94; mem. profl. adv. bd. Mass. Epilepsy Assn., 1986-93; counsel state coord. commn. MADD, Mass., 1984-86. Recipient Outstanding Citizen award Mothers Against Drunk Driving, 1986. Fellow Mass. Bar Found.; mem. ABA, ATLA, Mass. Bar Assn. (bd. dirs., young lawyers sect. 1979-80, 21st Century Club 1984), Nat. Bd. Trial Advocacy (bd. cert. civil trial advocate 1992—), Mass. Acad. Trial Attys. (bd. dirs. 1991—), U.S.-Russia C. of C. of Boston. Avocation: travel. Office: Fed Res Plz 600 Atlantic Ave Boston MA 02210-2211

LICATA, PAUL JAMES, health products executive; b. Chgo., July 4, 1957; s. Alfonso and Carmela (Castrogiovanni) L.; m. Sandra Lynn Phinney, June 18, 1988; children: Julie Lynn, Andrea Carmela. BA in Econs., Bus. Adminstrn., Calif. State U., Fullerton, 1979, MBA, 1982. Gen. mgr. Calif. Nutritional Products, Huntington Beach, Calif., 1979—; project mgr. Schaads Hydro Ptnrs., Huntington Beach, 1985—, Fullerton Hydro Ptnrs., Ltd., Huntington Beach, 1986—; pres. World Organics Corp., Fountain Valley, Calif., 1989—, Nutrition Masters Inc., Huntington Beach, 1991—; CFO Nat. Inst. Nutrition Edn., Denver, 1986-88. Mem. Calvary Ch., Santa Ana, Calif., 1982—, class pres., 1982-84, 89-90, 95-96. Mem. Nat. Nutritional Foods Assn. (chmn. 1982-84, bd. dirs. 1986-91, pres. 1989-90), Golden West Nutritional Foods Assn. (pres. 1986-87), Soc. for Advancement Mgmt. (pres. Orange County 1984-86, v.p. west region 1987-91, Mgmt. Honor Soc. award 1986). Republican. Avocations: travel, ch. related activities. Office: World Organics Corp 5242 Bolsa Ave Ste 3 Huntington Beach CA 92649-1054

LICENS, LILA LOUISE, administrative assistant; b. Puyallup, Wash., Feb. 18, 1949; d. C.L. and Joan L. (Rubert) Vormestrand. Cert., Knapp Bus. Coll., 1968. Cert. profl. sec. Adminstrv. asst. Weyerhaeuser Co., Tacoma, 1968-93, adminstrv. asst. bleached paperboard, 1993—. Mem. adv. bd. Bates Tech. Coll., 1994—. Mem. Profl. Sec. Internat. (pres. Mt. Rainier chpt. 1994—, pres. Wash.-Alaska divsn. 1990-91, pres.-elect 1989-90, sec. 1987-89, pres. Sea-Tac chpt. 1985-87), Fed. Way Women's Network (treas. 1988, sec. 1989, pes. 1995, 96). Avocations: travel, photography, reading. Home: 771 108th St S Tacoma WA 98444-5666

LICETTI, MARY ELIZABETH, business analysis director; b. N.Y.C., Nov. 2, 1954; d. Philip Carmelo and JoAnn (Milner) Licetti; m. George Guy Colagreco, Apr. 22, 1995. BS in Acctg., Rutgers U., 1985; postgrad., Duke U., 1991, 92, Kenan Flagler Bus. Sch., Chapel Hill, N.C., 1995. Sr. acct. Johns-Manville, Manville, N.J., 1972-80; acctg. supr. Ortho Diagnostic Syss. (Johnson & Johnson), Raritan, N.J., 1981-87, bus. unit fin. mgr., 1988-90, project mgr., 1991-92, USA contr., 1992-95, dir. bus. analysis and fin. sys., 1995—; chmn. supervisory com. Johns-Manville Employees Credit Union, Manville, 1977-80. Treas. Johns-Manville Employee Club; vol. audit com. United Way, Somerset, N.J., 1991-92; dir. Am. Liver Found., Commack, N.Y., 1995—. Mem. NAFE, Inst. Mgmt. Accts., Am. Mgmt. Assn., Soc. Competitive Intelligence Profls. Avocations: bicycling, photography, art, musical composition. Home: 30 Madison Ave Flemington NJ 08822-3306 Office: Ortho Diagnostic Sys US Hwy 202 Raritan NJ 08869

LICH, GLEN ERNST, writer, business executive, public education consultant; b. Fredericksburg, Tex., Nov. 5, 1948; s. Ernst Perry and Thelma Olive (Woolfley) L.; m. Lera Patrick Tyler, Sept. 5, 1970; children: James Ernst Lich-Tyler (dec.), Stephen Woolfley Lich-Tyler, Elizabeth Erin Lich-Tyler. Student, U. Vienna, Austria, 1969-70; BA, Southwestern U., 1971; MA, U. Tex., 1976; MA, S.W. Tex. State U., 1978; PhD, Tex. Christian U., 1984; grad., U.S. Army Command and Gen. Staff Coll., 1984. Instr. U. New Orleans, 1979-80; asst. prof. Schreiner Coll., 1980-87; assoc. prof. and dir. regional studies Baylor U., 1987-90; prof. and chair U. of Winnipeg, 1990-93; exec. dir. Hill Country Inst., 1992—; dir. World Heritage Tours, 1978—; pres., CEO The Sagres Group Inc., Kerrville, Tex., 1996—; adj. faculty U.S. Army Command and Gen. Staff Coll., 1987-97; vis. fellow Yale U., 1987, German Fgn. Ministry, 1983; rsch. fellow Mosher Inst. Internat. Policy Studies, Tex. A & M U., 1988-93; sr. rsch. fellow Ctr. Socioeconomic Rsch. U. Coahuila, Mexico, 1990-95; coord. Standing Conf. Ethnic Chairs and Professorships in Can., 1991-92; cons. in field. Author: The German Texans, 1981, The Humanities and Public Issues, 1990, Fred Gipson at Work, 1990, The Women of Viscri, 1997; editor: (with Dona Reeves-Marquardt) Retrospect and Retrieval: The German Element in Review: Essays on Cultural Preservation, 1978, German Culture in Texas: A Free Earth, 1980, The Cabin Book, 1985, (with Dona Reeves-Marquardt) Texas Country: The Changing Rural Scene, 1986, (with Joseph A. McKinney) Region North America: Canada, United States, Mexico, 1990, Regional Studies: The Interplay of Land and People, 1992; assoc. editor Jour. German-Am. Studies, 1977-80, Yearbook of German-Am. Studies, 1981-93; editor: Jour. Am. Studies Assn. Tex., 1988-90; contbr. articles to profl. publs. Served with U.S. Army, 1972-75, lt. col. USAR, asst. attache to Portugal, 1987-92, asst. attache to Germany, 1992-94; project officer U.S. Embassy, Bucharest, Romania, 1993, Ljubljana, Slovenia, 1993-94; dir. internat. programs Adj. Gen.'s Dept. of State of Tex., 1994-95. Recipient Gold Def. Medal Republic of Slovenia, 1994; NEH rsch. grantee, 1978, 86-87; Fed. Republic Germany, 1983, 87; Swiss Humanities Acad., 1988; Tex. Com. Humanities, 1988, 89; Am. Coun. of Learned Socs., 1988; Embassy of Can., 1988; Max Kade Found., 1989-92; Joint Econ. Com. of U.S. Congress, 1989-91; Ministry of Multiculturalism and Citizenship of Can., 1991-92; Soc. Scis. and Humanities Rsch. Coun. Can., 1991-92, Interactivity Found., 1996—. Mem. MLA, Am. Studies Assn., Assn. Am. Geographers, Am. Folklore Assn., Am. Assn. Tchrs. German, Nat. Coun. Tchrs. English, Soc. for Romanian Studies, Assn. for Can. Studies in U. S., Can. Ethnic Studies Assn., Oral History Assn., Tex. Folklore Soc., Tex. State Hist. Assn., German Studies Assn., Pi Kappa Alpha. Office: Hill Country Inst PO Box 1850 Kerrville TX 78029-1850

LICHACZ, SHEILA ENIT, diplomat, artist; b. Monagrillo, Panama, Oct. 9, 1942. BS, Our Lady of the Lake U., San Antonio, 1965; MA in Edn., Inter-Am. U., San German, P.R., 1968. Amb. at large (extraordinary and plenipotiary) Republic of Panama, 1995—. One-person shows include Mus. of Man, Panama City, Panama, 1979, Nat. Inst. Culture, Panama City, 1980, 81, Mus. Modern Art Latin Am., Washington, 1981, Habitante Gallery, Panama City, 1982, Santa Fe (N.Mex.) East Gallery, 1984, Reina Torres de Araux Mus. Anthropology, Panama City, 1986, Fine Arts Gallery, U. Calif., Irvine, 1989, Feingarten Galleries, L.A., 1989, Robert Mondavi Ctr., Costa Mesa, Calif., 1990, Ventana Fine Art, Santa Fe, 1990, North-South Ctr. Art Gallery, U. Miami, 1992, Vanidades Gallery, Miami, 1992, Art Gallery, Dudley House, Harvard U., Cambridge, Mass., 1993, Ctr. Fine Arts, Miami, 1994, Art Mus. Americas, Washington, 1996, others; exhibited in group shows at Mus. Contemporary Art, Panama City, 1985, Habitante Gallery, Panama City, 1985, 86, 90, Galeria Espacio, San Salvador, 1985, Newport Harbor Art Mus., 1988, Valerie Miller Fine Arts Gallery, Palm Desert, Calif., 1989, Palm Springs (Calif.) Desert Mus., 1989, Bacardi Art Gallery, Miami, 1991, Am. Cath. Mus., N.Y.C., 1992, Instituto Mexicano de Artes, Washington, 1993, Jerusalem Mcpl. Art Gallery, 1996, others; represented in permanent collections at Vanidades Gallery, Miami, Fine Arts Gallery, U. Calif. Irvine, Palm Springs Desert Mus., Nat. Gallery Contemporary Art, Mus. Art, San Jose, Costa Rica, Archer M. Huntington Art Gallery, U. Tex. Austin, Vatican Mus., Mus. of Man., Panama City, Nat. Inst. Culture, Panama City, El Escorial, Madrid, St. Michael's Ch., Monagrillo, Presdl. Palace, Panama City, others; commd. Govt. of Panama for King Juan Carlos, 1977 Pope John Paul II, 1983, Pres. Peru, 1986. Named Pride of Panama and the Americas Pres. of Panama, 1980, Hon. Mayor of San Antonio, 1982, Cultural Amb. at Large Republic of Panama, 1983, Meritorious Citizen of Chitre, Panama, 1983, Outstanding Alumna of Yr. Our Lady of the Lake U., San Antonio, 1985; recipient Key to City of Surf Side, Fla., 1992, Hispanic Achievement award Hispanic Mag., 1996. Home: Hamilton on the Bay #2405 555 NE 34th St Miami FL 33137 Office: 1200 Brickell Ave Miami FL 33131-3214

LICHLITER, WARREN EUGENE, surgeon, educator; b. Murphysboro, Ill., Jan. 24, 1952; s. Gene Estel and Dorothy Colleen (Williams) L.; m.

Carol Jane Loftin, Nov. 3, 1979; children: Gary Edward, Christopher Warren, Adrienne Leigh, Abigail Meredith. BA, U. Tenn., 1974; MD, U. Tex., Galveston, 1978. Intern and resident in gen. surgery Baylor U. Med. Ctr., Dallas, 1979-83, resident in colon rectal surgery, 1983-84, mem. attending staff dept. colon rectal surgery, 1984—, assoc. dir. surg. edn., 1984—, assoc. dir. dept. colon rectal surgery, 1991—; clin. asst. prof. surgery health sci. ctr. U. Tex., Dallas, 1990—. Mem. adv. bd. Am. Cancer Soc., Dallas. Fellow ACS, Am. Soc. Colon Rectal Surgeons; mem. Tex. Surg. Soc., Dallas Soc. Surgeons, Alpha Omega Alpha. Avocations: running, cycling, sailing, kayaking, swimming. Office: 3409 Worth St Ste 500 Dallas TX 75246-2041

LICHT, PAUL, zoologist, educator; b. St. Louis, Mar. 12, 1938; s. Harry and Betty L.; m. Barbara Margaret Morrison, June 30, 1963; children: Andrew Stephen, Rachael Margaret, Carolyn Ann. BA, Washington U., St. Louis, 1959; PhD, U. Mich., 1964. Asst. prof. zoology U. Calif., Berkeley, 1964-68; asso. prof. U. Calif., 1968-72, prof., 1972—, chmn. dept. zoology, 1977-82; dean divsn. biol. scis. U. Calif., Berkeley, 1994—. Numerous publs. in field, 1961—; editor McGraw Hill Book Series, 1976-78; mem. editorial bds. Gen. Comparative Endocrinology, 1978—, Jour. Exptl. Zoology, 1990—; author/owner microcomputer bibliographic program REFMENU. Recipient Grace Pickford medal Soc. Comparative Endocrinology, 1980. Fellow AAAS, Calif. Acad. Sci.; mem. Am. Soc. Zoology (chmn. divsn. comparative endocrinology 1992-93). Office: U Calif Dept Zoology Berkeley CA 94720

LICHT, RICHARD A., lawyer; b. Providence, Mar. 25, 1948; s. Julius M. Licht and Irene (Lash) Olson; m. Roanne Sragow; children: Jordan David, Jeremy Michael, Jaclyn Rose. AB cum laude, Harvard U., 1968, JD cum laude, 1972; LLM in Taxation, Boston U., 1975. Law clk. to chief justice R.I. Supreme Ct., Providence, 1973-74; ptnr. Letts, Quinn & Licht, Providence, 1974-84; mem. R.I. Senate, Providence, 1975-84, chmn. judiciary com. and rules com., 1984; lt. gov. State of R.I., Providence, 1985-89; ptnr. Licht & Semonoff, Providence, 1989—; former chmn. R.I. Commn. on Racial, Religious and Ethnic Harrassment, Dr. Martin Luther King Jr. Holiday Commn., State Energy and Tech. Study Commn. rules com.; chmn. Coun. of State Govt., Intergovtl. Affairs Com., Nat. Focus Team, Bd. Gov. Higher Edn.; bd. regents Elem. and Secondary Edn.; mem. Pub. Telecom. Authority R.I., Univ. R.I. Found., Community Coll. R.I. Found. Bd. dirs. Roger Williams Hosp.; advisor Community Prep. Sch.; corporator Roger Williams Hosp.; trustee Save the Bay, Inc., Emma Pendleton Bradley Hosp.; bd. dirs. Temple Emanuel, Providence, Jewish Fedn. R.I., Samaritans; chmn. Small Bus. Adv. Council, Task Force on Teenage Suicide Prevention, CD Civil Preparedness Adv. Council, Urban League R.I., 1980-82, John Hope Settlement House, 1976-81; chair Am. Cancer Soc. Ball, 1989, Jewish Fedn. R.I. Passage to Freedom, 1989; chair R.I. chpt. Anti-Defamation League; mem. Meeting St. Sch. steering com. for capital fund drive, 1989-92; mem. Women and Infants Corp., Dorcas Place, PARI, UNITAM, NCLG task force of Youth Suicide Prevention, Jewish Home for the Aged of R.I., bd. govs. for the handicapped; active YWCA of Greater R.I., Vols. in Action, Inc., Big Sister Assn. of R.I., Big Bros. R.I.; coordinator vols. gubernatorial campaigns Frank Licht, 1968, 70; active Jewish Community Ctr., Providence, 1975-83, E. Side Sr. Citizens Ctr., 1975-76, R.I. Youth Guidance Ctr., Inc., 1987, Block Island Conservancy, Inc., Notre Dame Health Care Corp., 1987; Dem. candidate for U.S. Senate, 1988; ann. campaign chair Meeting St. Sch., 1990-91. Named an Outstanding Young Man of R.I., R.I. Jaycees, 1979; recipient David Ben Gurion award State of Israel Bonds, 1977, Outstanding Pub. Service award Temple Torat Yisrael, 1985, Disting. Services to the Hispanic Community award Casa Puerto Rico, 1985, Hon. Pub. Service award Meeting St. Sch., 1986, Recognition award R.I. Day Care Dirs. Assn., 1986, award of Appreciation Child Care/Human Services, 1986, Govtl. Services award Ocean State Residences for the Retarded, 1987. Mem. R.I. Bar Assn., Corp. Womens' and Infants' Hosp., Corp. Roger Williams Hosp., Vols. in Action, Inc. Democrat. Office: Licht & Semonoff One Park Row Providence RI 02903

LICHTBLAU, JOHN H., economist; b. Vienna, Austria, June 26, 1921; came to U.S., 1939; s. Ernst and Alice (Fischer) Lichtblau-Lind; m. Charlotte M. Adelberg, Apr. 12, 1944; 1 child, Claudia L. Payne. B in Social Sci., CCNY, 1949; postgrad., NYU, 1950-53. Economist U.S. Dept. Labor, Washington, 1951-53, Conf. Bd., N.Y.C., 1953-54, Walter J. Levy Assocs., N.Y.C., 1955-56; research dir. Petroleum Ind. Research Found. Inc., N.Y.C., 1956-61, exec. dir., 1961-72, chmn., 1972—; chmn. Petroleum Ind. Research Assocs. Inc., N.Y.C., 1977—; co-chmn. energy forum grad. ctr. CUNY, 1996—. Mem. editorial bd. Energy Policy (London), 1987—; contbr. articles to profl. jours., book chpts. Served with U.S. Army, 1944-47, ETO. Mem. Am. Petroleum Inst., Nat. Petroleum Council, Am. Econ. Assn., Internat. Assn. for Energy Economics (5th Ann. award for outstanding contbns. 1986), Council on Fgn. Relations. Office: Petroleum Industry Rsch Found 122 E 42nd St New York NY 10168-0002

LICHTBLAU, MYRON IVOR, language educator; b. N.Y.C., Oct. 10, 1925; s. Samuel and Sadonia (Weinberg) L.; m. Bernice Glanz, June 23, 1956; children: Mark (dec.), Anita, Eric. BA, CCNY, 1947; MA, U. Nacional Mex., 1948; PhD, Columbia U., 1957; diploma (hon.), U. de Nuevo Leon, Mex., 1964. Tchr. spanish secondary schs., N.Y.C., 1948-57; instr. Ind. U., Bloomington, 1957-59; prof. Syracuse U., N.Y., 1959—, chmn. dept. fgn. langs., 1967-74, 86-88; vis. prof. Colgate U., Hamilton, N.Y., 1970, SUNY-Binghamton, 1975; coordinator language program Peace Corps, 1966. Author: The Argentine Novel in the Nineteenth Century, 1959, El Arte estilistico de Eduardo Mallea, 1967, Manuel Galvez, 1972, A Practical Reference Guide to Reading Spanish, 1977, Rayuela y a la creatividad artistica, 1989, An Annotated Bibliography of the Argentine Novel, 1997; editor: Manuel Galvez: Las dos vidas del Pobre Napoleon, 1963, E. Caballero Calderon: Manuel Pacho, 1980, Eduardo Mallea Ante La Critica, 1985, Emigration and Exile in Twentieth-Century Hispanic Literature, 1988, Mario Vargas Llosa: A Writer's Reality, 1990, Manuel Galvez: La maestra normal, 1991; editor Symposium, 1995—, book rev. editor, 1966-94; translator: Eduardo Mallea: History of an Argentine Passion, 1983; book rev. editor: Hispania, 1974-83; mem. editl. bd.: Critica Hispánica, 1985—. Bd. dirs. Syracuse Jewish Community Ctr., 1973; pres. Rabbi Jacob Epstein Sch. Jewish Studies, 1981-83; trustee Temple Beth Sholom, 1987-88. With U.S. Army, 1944-46. Mem. AAUP, MLA, Am. Assn. Tchrs. of Spanish and Portuguese (assoc. editor 1974-83), Inst. Internat. de Lit. Iberoamericana (exec. sec. 1959-63). Jewish. Avocation: tennis. Office: Syracuse U Dept Lang and Lit Syracuse NY 13244

LICHTENBERG, BYRON K., futurist, manufacturing executive, space flight consultant, pilot; b. Stroudsburg, Pa., Feb. 19, 1948; s. Glenn John and Georgianna (Bierei) L.; m. Lee Lombard, July 25, 1970 (divorced); children—Kristin, Kimberly. Sc.B., Brown U., 1969; M.S., MIT, 1975, Sc.D., 1979. Rsch. scientist MIT, Cambridge, 1978-84; pres. Payload Systems, Inc., Cambridge, 1984-89, chief scientist, 1989-91; pres., chief exec. officer Omega Aerospace Inc., Virginia Beach, Va., 1991-96; pilot S.W. Airlines, 1994—. Contbg. author NASA Payload Specialist, 1979-92, Flew on Space Shuttle Mission #9, #45; contbr. articles to profl. jours. Served to lt. col. USAF, Mass. Air N.G., 1969-93. Recipient NASA Space Flight award, 1983, 92, Spaceflight award VFW, 1983, Haley Spaceflight award AIAA, 1983. Mem. Tau Beta Pi, Sigma Xi. Avocations: golf; racquetball; windsurfing; skiing.

LICHTENBERG, MARGARET KLEE, publishing company executive; b. N.Y.C., Nov. 19, 1941; d. Lawrence and Shirley Jane (Wicksman) Klee; m. James Lester Lichtenberg, Mar. 31, 1963 (div. 1982); children: Gregory Lawrence, Amanda Zoe. BA, U. Mich., 1963; postgrad., Harvard U., 1963. Book rev. editor New Woman mag., 1972-73; assoc. editor children's books Parents Mag. Press, 1974; editor, rights dir. Books for Young People, Frederick Warne & Co., N.Y.C., 1975-78; sr. editor Simon & Schuster, N.Y.C., 1979-80; dir. sales promotion Grosset & Dunlap, N.Y.C., 1980-81; ednl. sales mgr. Bantam Books, N.Y.C., 1982-84; dir. mktg. and sales Grove Press, N.Y.C., 1984-86; dir. of sales Grove Press, 1986-87; dir. sales Weidenfeld & Nicolson, N.Y.C., 1986-87; mktg. dir. Beacon Press, Boston, 1988-95; book mktg. coach, pers. bus. coach, 1995—; writer, freelance critic, 1961—. Contbr. articles, essays, stories, poetry, revs. to mags., newspapers and anthologies. Bd. dirs. Children's Book Council, 1978. Recipient 2 Avery Hopwood awards in drama and fiction, 1962, 2 in drama and poetry, 1963; coll. fiction contest award Mademoiselle mag., 1963; Woodrow Wilson fellow, 1963. Mem. Women's Nat. Book Assn. (past pres. N.Y. chpt.). Home and Office: PO Box 268 Santa Fe NM 87504

LICHTENBERGER, H(ORST) WILLIAM, chemical company executive; b. Yugoslavia, Nov. 5, 1935; came to U.S., 1950, naturalized, 1955; s. Andrew W. and Hella L.; m. Patricia Ann Thomas, June 15, 1957; children: Erich, Lisa. B.A., U. Iowa, 1957, B.S. in Chem. Engring., 1959; M.B.A., SUNY, Buffalo, 1962. With Union Carbide Corp., 1959-1992; bus. mgr. Union Carbide Corp., N.Y.C., 1972-75; v.p., gen. mgr. Linde div. Union Carbide Corp., Geneva, 1975-80; v.p. mktg. Union Carbide Corp., N.Y.C., 1980-82; v.p., gen. mgr. gas products Union Carbide Corp., 1982-85, pres. Solvents and Coatings div., 1985-1992, pres. Chemicals and Plastics group, 1986-92; pres., CEO Praxair Inc., 1992—; also chmn. Praxair Inc., Danbury, C.T. Mem. Iowa N.G., 1954-62. Mem. Am. Iron and Steel Inst., Chem. Mfg. Assn. Republican. Achievements include patentee storage cryogenic fluids. Office: Praxair Inc 39 Old Ridgebury Rd Danbury CT 06810-5108 *Progress is best achieved by encouraging people to innovate and to take prudent risks.*

LICHTENSTEIN, ELISSA CHARLENE, legal association executive; b. Trenton, N.J., Oct. 23, 1954; d. Mark and Rita (Field) L. AB cum laude, Smith Coll., Northampton, Mass., 1976; JD, George Washington U., 1979. Bar: D.C. 1980, U.S. Dist. Ct. (D.C. dist.) 1980, U.S. Ct. Appeals (D.C. cir.) 1980. Law clk. U.S. EPA, Washington, 1978-79; staff dir. ABA, Washington, 1979—, assoc. dir. pub. svcs. div., 1981-85, dir., 1985—. Editor, contbr.: Common Boundary/Common Problems: The Environmental Consequences of Energy Production, 1982, Exit Polls and Early Election Projections, 1984, The Global Environment: Challenges, Choices and Will, 1986, (newsletter) Environ. Law; co-editor, contbr. The Environ. Network; co-editor: Determining Competency in Guardianship Proceedings, 1990, Due Process Protections for Juveniles in Civil Commitment Proceedings, 1991, Environmental Regulation in Pacific Rim Nations, 1993, The Role of Law in the 1992 UN Conference on Environment and Development, 1992, Trade and the Environment in Pacific Rim Nations, 1994, Public Participation in Environmental Decisionmaking, 1995, Endangered Species Act Reauthorization: A Biocentric Approach, 1996, Sustainable Development in the Americas: The Emerging Role of the Private Sector, 1996, Environmental Priorities in Southeast Asian Nations, 1997, numerous others. Mem. Nat. Trust for Hist. Preservation. Named Outstanding Young Woman of Am., 1982. Mem. ABA, NAFE, Am. Soc. Assn. Execs., Washington Coun. Lawyers, Assn. Women in Communications, Inc., Environ. Law Inst. (assoc.), Met. Washington Environ. Profls. (pres. 1986-96), D.C. Bar Assn. Democrat. Jewish. Office: ABA Div Pub Svcs 740 15th St NW Washington DC 20005-1019

LICHTENSTEIN, HARVEY, performing arts executive; b. Bklyn., Apr. 9, 1929; s. Samuel and Jennie (Meiner) L.; m. Phyllis Holbrook, Nov. 14, 1971; children: Saul, John. BA, Bklyn. Coll., 1951, LHD (hon.), 1986; postgrad., Bennington (Vt.) Coll., 1953; ArtsD (hon.), L.I. U., 1989; MusD (hon.), Mannes Coll. Music, 1989; LHD (hon.), Pratt Inst., 1993. Subscription and group sales mgr. N.Y.C. Ballet, also N.Y.C. Opera, 1965-67; pres., exec. producer Bklyn. Acad. Music, 1967—; Am. dir. Spoleto (Italy) Festival, 1971-73. Mem. Century Assn. (N.Y.C.). Office: Bklyn Acad Music 30 Lafayette Ave Brooklyn NY 11217-1430

LICHTENSTEIN, LAWRENCE MARK, allergy, immunology educator, physician; b. Washington, May 31, 1934; s. Samuel and Lillian (Colodny) L.; m. Carolyn Eggert, June 15, 1956; children: Elizabeth, Joshua, Rebekah. MD, U. Chgo., 1960; PhD, Johns Hopkins U., 1965. Diplomate: Am. Bd. Allergy and Immunology. Intern, Johns Hopkins Hosp., 1960-61, resident in medicine, 1965-66; asst. prof. medicine Johns Hopkins U. Sch. Medicine, 1966-70, assoc. prof., 1970-75, prof., 1975—, dir. Johns Hopkins Asthma and Allergy Ctr.; mem. Nat. Adv. Allergy and Infectious Diseases Coun. Mem. editorial bd.: Clin. Immunology and Pathology, Immunology, Pulmonary, Allergy; editor 11 books; contbr. articles to profl. jours. Fellow ACP; mem. Am. Soc. Pharmacology and Exptl. Therapeutics, Am. Assn. Immunology (sec., treas.), Am. Fedn. Clin. Rsch., Am. Soc. Clin. Investigation, Am. Acad. Allergy and Immunology (past pres.), Am. Soc. Exptl. Pathology, Collegium Internat. Allergologicum (pres.), Assn. Am. Physicians. Democrat. Jewish. Home: 1600 The Terraces Baltimore MD 21209-3637 Office: John Hopkins Asthma & Allergy Ctr 5501 Hopkins Bayview Cir Baltimore MD 21224-6821

LICHTENSTEIN, ROBERT JAY, lawyer; b. Phila., Jan. 23, 1948; s. Irving M. and Marjorie J. (Weiss) L.; m. Sandra Paley, Aug. 14, 1971; children: David P., Kate. BS in Econs., U. Pa., 1969; JD, U. Pitts., 1973; LLM in Taxation, NYU, 1974. Bar: Pa. 1974, U.S. Tax Ct. 1978, U.S. Dist. Ct. (ea. dist.) Pa. 1979, U.S. Ct. Appeals (3rd cir.) 1982, U.S. Ct. Appeals (4th cir.) 1987. Ptnr. Saul, Ewing, Remick & Saul, 1978-88; assoc. Morgan, Lewis & Bockius, Phila., 1974-78, ptnr., 1988—; dir. Maritrans Inc.; instr. Main Line Paralegal Inst., Wayne, Pa., 1984-87, Paralegal Inst., Phila., 1987-90; adj. prof. law Villanova U. Sch. Law, 1991—. Trustee Temple Brith Achim, King of Prussia, Pa., 1986-91. Mem. ABA, Pa. Bar Assn., Phila. Assn., Locust Club. Democrat. Avocations: skiing, tennis, reading. Office: Morgan Lewis Bockius LLP 2000 One Logan Sq Philadelphia PA 19103

LICHTENSTEIN, ROY, artist; b. N.Y.C., Oct. 27, 1923; s. Milton and Beatrice (Werner) L.; m. Isabel Wilson, June 12, 1949 (div.); children: David, Mitchell; m. Dorothy Herzka, Nov. 1, 1968. BFA, Ohio State U., 1946, MFA, 1949; DFA (hon.), Calif. Inst. Arts., 1977, Ohio State U., 1988, Bard Coll., 1989. Instr. Ohio State U., 1946-51; asst. prof. SUNY-Oswego, 1957-60, Douglass Coll., Rutgers U., 1960-63. Pop art and other themes derived from comic strip techniques; one-man shows include Leo Castelli Gallery, N.Y.C., 1962, 63, 65, 67, 71, 72, 73, 74, 75, 77, 79, 81, 83, 85, 86, 87, 89, 92, Galerie Ileana Sonnabend, Paris, 1963, 65, 70, 75, Pasadena (Calif.) Art Mus., 1967, Walker Art Ctr., Mpls., 1967, Stedelijk Mus., Amsterdam, 1967, Tate Gallery, London, 1968, Guggenheim Mus., N.Y.C., 1969, Nelson Gallery, Kansas City, Mo., 1969, Mus. Contemporary Art, Chgo., 1970, Centre National D'Arte Contemporain, Paris, 1975, and traveling to: Nationalgalerie Staatliche Museum Kulterbesitz, Berlin, Seattle Art Mus., 1976, Inst. Contemporary Art, Boston, 1979, Portland Ctr. for Visual Arts, 1980, St. Louis Art Mus., 1981, Fundacion Juan March, Madrid, 1982, Walker Art Ctr., Mpls., 1986, 'The Drawings of Roy Lichtenstein', Mus. Modern Art, N.Y.C., 1987, and traveling to: Mus. Overholland, Amsterdam, 1987, Tel Aviv Mus., Israel, 1987, Schirn Kunsthalle, Frankfurt, 1988, Mus. Modern Art, Oxford, Eng., 1988, Corcoran Gallery of Art, Washington, 1988; group shows include Whitney Mus. Am. Art, N.Y.C., 1966, 67, 68, 70, 72, 73, 74, 75 (Downtown), 77, 78, 80, 82, 83, 84, 85, 87, Mus. Modern Art, N.Y.C., 1966, 67, 68, 74, 76, 80, 85, 88, Solomon R. Guggenheim Mus., N.Y.C., 1965,76, Venice Biennale, 1966, Corcoran Gallery Art 36th Biennale, Washington, D.C., 1978, Solomon R. Guggenheim MUs., N.Y.C., 1965, 76, Hirschorn Mus., Washington, 1980, Bklyn. Mus. Art, N.Y.C., 1981, Nat. Mus. Am. Art, Smithsonian Inst., Washington, 1984, Palacio Velazquez, Madrid, Spain, 1991, Galerie Martine Queval, Paris, 1992, Galerie Joachim Becker, Paris, 1992; represented in permanent collections: Mus. Modern Art, N.Y.C., Whitney Mus. Am. Art, N.Y.C., Corcoran Gallery Art, Washington, Hirschorn Mus. and Sculpture Garden, Washington, Libr. Congress, Washington, Nat. Gallery Art, Washington, Chgo. Art Inst., Smithsonian Inst., Washington, Victoria and Albert Mus., London, Seibu Art Mus., Tokyo, Ludwig Mus., Cologne, Stedelijk Mus., Amsterdam, Norton Simon Mus., Pasadena, Yale U., New Haven, Walker Art Ctr., Mpls., San Francisco Mus. Modern Art, Albright Knox Gallery, Buffalo; created outside wall for Circarama, N.Y. State Pavillion, N.Y. State World's Fair, 1963, large Painting for Expo '67, Montreal, 1967, Brushstroke Murals for Dusseldorf U. Med. Ctr., 1970, 'Mermaid' (NEA grantee), pub. sculpture for Theatre Performing Arts in Miami Beach, Fla., 1979, 'Brushstrokes in Flight', Port Columbus Airport, Columbus, Ohio, 1984, 'Mural with Blue Brushstroke', Equitable Life Assurance Bldg. with Whitney Mus. Art, 1985, 'Coups de Pinceau', Caisse des Depots and Consignations, Paris, 1988, Tel Aviv Mus. Art, Tel Aviv, 1989. With AUS, 1943-46. Recipient Skowhegan medal for painting, 1977. Mem. Am. Acad. and Inst. Arts and Letters. Office: care Leo Castelli Gallery 420 W Broadway New York NY 10012-3764*

LICHTENSTEIN, SARAH CAROL, lawyer; b. East Orange, N.J., May 25, 1953; d. Carl and Hilda Ruth (Warshaw) L. BA, Wellesley Coll., 1975; JD, Columbia U., 1978. Bar: N.Y. 1979, U.S. Dist. Ct. (ea. and so. dists.) N.Y. 1979, U.S. Ct. Appeals (2d cir.) 1981. Assoc. Milbank, Tweed, Hadley & McCloy, N.Y.C., 1978-84; assoc. Dreyer and Traub, N.Y.C., 1984-87, ptnr., 1987-93; ptnr. Shea & Gould, N.Y.C., 1993-94; arbitrator small claims ct. Civ. Ct. of the City of New York, 1988—; ptnr. Morrison Cohen Singer & Weinstein LLP, N.Y.C., 1994—; dir. Eleven Riverside Dr. Corp., 1986-89, pres., 1988-89; mem. panel of chpt. 7 trustees So. Dist. of N.Y. Contbr. articles to profl. jours. Trustee Stephen Wise Free Synagogue, 1987—, officer, 1990—. Wellesley scholar, 1975, Stone scholar Columbia U., 1977-78. Mem. ABA, Assn. of Bar of City of N.Y. (com. on sex and law, sec. 1981-85, com. on state legis. 1986-89, com. on state cts. of superior jurisdiction 1989-92, coun. on jud. adminstrn. 1992-95, com. on state legislation chair 1994-97).

LICHTER, EDWARD ARTHUR, physician, educator; b. Chgo., June 5, 1928; s. Joseph and Eva (Wise) L.; m. Charlotte Sells, Sept. 7, 1952; children: Michael, Jay. PhB, U. Chgo., 1947; BS, Roosevelt U., 1949; MS, U. Ill., 1951, MD, 1955. Intern Fitzsimons Army Hosp., Denver, 1955-56; resident internal medicine U. Ill., Chgo., 1958-61, assoc. prof. preventive medicine and community health Med. Ctr., 1966-69, prof., dept. head preventive medicine and community health, 1969-86, prof., dept. head health care svcs., 1972-79, prof. community health scis., 1979—, prof. internal medicine, assoc. chief Sect. of Gen. Internal Medicine, 1986—, mem. exec. com., 1990—; mem. exec. com. Univ. Senates Conf., 1992-95; practice medicine specializing in internal medicine and preventive medicine Chgo., 1966—; fellow in immunology NIH, 1961-63, USPHS officer, mem. staff immunology, 1963-66. Served with AUS, 1955-58. Fellow ACP, APHA, Am. Coll. Preventive Medicine; mem. Am. Coll. Epidemiology, Cen. Soc. for Clin. Rsch., Assn. Tchrs, Preventive Medicine, Chgo. Heart Assn., Alpha Omega Alpha. Home: 1310 Maple Ave Evanston IL 60201-4325 Office: Dept Med MC 787 840 S Wood St Chicago IL 60612-7317

LICHTER, PAUL RICHARD, ophthalmology educator; b. Detroit, Mar. 7, 1939; s. Max D. and Buena (Epstein) L.; m. Carolyn Goode, 1960; children: Laurie, Susan. BA, U. Mich., 1960, MD, 1964, MS, 1968. Diplomate Am. Bd. Ophthalmology. Asst. to assoc. prof. ophthalmology U. Mich., Ann Arbor, 1971-78, prof., chmn. dept. ophthalmology, 1978—; chmn. Am. Bd. Ophthalmology, 1987. Editor-in-chief Ophthalmology jour., 1986-94. Served to lt. comdr. USN, 1969-71. Fellow Am. Acad. Opthalmology (bd. dirs. 1981—, pres. 1996, sr. honor award 1986); mem. AMA, Pan Am. assn. Opthalmology (bd. dirs. 1988—, sec.-treas. English speaking countries 1991-95), Mich. State Med. Soc., Washtenaw County Med. Soc., Mich. Opthalmol. Soc. (pres. 1993-95), Assn. Univ. Profs. Opthalmology (trustee 1986-93, pres. 1991-92), Alpha Omega Alpha. Office: U Mich Med Sch Kellogg Eye Ctr 1000 Wall St Ann Arbor MI 48105-1912

LICHTERMAN, MARTIN, history educator; b. N.Y.C., July 18, 1918; s. Joseph Aaron and Esther S. (Schacknowitz) L.; m. Charlotte Rottenberg, Oct. 7, 1945; children: Joshua David, Andrew Marc. B.S., Harvard U., 1939, A.M., 1947; Ph.D., Columbia U., 1952. Instr. Rutgers U., Newark, 1948-51; instr., lectr. Princeton U., 1953-55; mem. research staff Princeton U. (Center for Research on World Polit. Instns.), 1951-53; asst. prof. M.I.T., 1955-60; dir. research to gov. Mass., 1959-60; exec. sec., dir. New Eng. Bd. Higher Edn., Winchester, Mass., 1961-66; dean Center Humanities and Social Scis. Union Coll., Schenectady, 1966-71; acting dean faculty Union Coll., 1971-72, dean faculty, 1972-76; prof. history Center Humanities and Social Scis. Union Coll., 1966-76, distinguished prof. history and higher edn., 1976-78; dean Empire State Coll., 1978-82, prof. history, 1982-83, prof. emeritus, 1983—; pres. Alternative Lifelong Learning, Berkeley, Calif., 1989-91; cons. 20th Century Fund, N.Y.C., 1955-57, Friends World Coll., 1984-86; mem. Mass. Bd. Collegiate Authority, 1961-66. Author: To the Yalu and Back, 1963; co-author: Political Community in the North Atlantic Area, 1957; contbr. articles to profl. jours. Vice chmn. bd. Mass. Com. Children and Youth, 1963-66, mem. exec. bd., 1961-66; adv. bd. Civil Liberties Mass., 1963-66; chmn. bd. New Eng. Council Advancement Sch. Adminstrn., 1961-63; vice chmn. Capital Dist. Civil Liberties Union, 1966-67; chmn. Freedom Forum, Inc., 1970-71, Schnectady Renewals, Inc., 1972-76; bd. dirs. Suffolk County chpt. N.Y. Civil Liberties Union, 1981-87; bd. dirs. Della Corte Internat., Inc., 1983-88. Mem. Orgn. Am. Historians. Home: 2587 Hilgard Ave Berkeley CA 94709-1104

LICHTIG, LEO KENNETH, health economist; b. Bklyn., Oct. 20, 1953; s. Samuel and Alyne Norma (Strauss) L.; m. Susan Mary Walsh, May 15, 1977; children: Brielle Joy, Danica Jill. BS, MS, Rennselaer Poly. Inst., 1974, PhD, 1976. Asst. prof. SUNY, Albany, 1976-77; project specialist, econometrician N.J. State Dept. Health, Trenton, 1977-82; dir. utilization econs. and rsch. Empire Blue Cross/Blue Shield, Albany, 1982-90; v.p. rsch. and demonstration Health Care Rsch. Found., Albany, 1982-90; v.p. Network, Inc., Randolph, N.J., Latham, N.Y., 1990-94; sr. v.p., chief info. officer Network, Inc., Randolph, N.J., 1994-97, Latham, N.Y., 1997—; pvt. practice cons., Latham, 1982-90; mem. nat. diagnosis related group, steering com. health care fin. adminstrn. Yale U., Washington, 1979-81; mem. adj. faculty Russell Sage Grad. Sch. Health Adminstrn., Albany, 1986—, Union Coll. Grad. Mgmt. Inst., Schenectady, N.Y., 1991-92; expert reviewer Health Care Financing Adminstrn., Washington, 1987, 89. Author: Hospital Information Systems for Case Mix Management, 1986; contbg. editor (newsletter) Nat. Report on Computers & Health, 1982-85; contbr. articles to profl. jours. Mem. tech. adv. com. Statewide Planning and Rsch. Coop. System, N.Y. State Dept. Health. Mem. Assn. for Health Svcs. Rsch., Am. Statis. Assn. (com. on privacy and confidentiality 1981-84, subcom. on quality and productivity measures 1988-90), Healthcare Fin. Mgmt. Assn. Avocation: Arthurian legends. Office: Network Inc 8 South Morris St Ste 202 Dover NJ 07801

LICHTIN, (JUDAH) LEON, pharmacist; b. Phila., Mar. 5, 1924; s. Aaron and Rosa (Rosenberg) L.; m. Beverly I. Cohen, Aug. 6, 1950; children—Benjamin Lloyd, Alan Eli. B.S. in Pharmacy, Phila. Coll. Pharmacy and Sci., 1944, M.S. in Pharmacy, 1947; Ph.D. in Pharmacy, Ohio State U., 1950. Asst. prof. pharmacy U. Cin., 1950-51, assoc. prof., 1951-64, prof., 1964—, Andrew Jergens prof. pharmacy, 1971-91, Andrew Jergens prof. pharmacy emeritus, 1991—; cons. in cosmetic sci. Contbr. articles to pharm. jours.; composer string music, vocal music. Past pres. No. Hills Synagogue, Cin. Fellow AAAS, Soc. Cosmetic Chemists; mem. Sigma Xi, Rho Chi. Achievements include patents in field. Home: 801 Cloverview Ave Cincinnati OH 45231-6017

LICHTIN, NORMAN NAHUM, chemistry educator; b. Newark, Aug. 10, 1922; s. James Jechiel and Clara (Greenspan) L.; m. Phyllis Selma Wasserman, May 30, 1947; children—Harold Hirsh, Sara Marjorie Boyd, Daniel Albert. B.S., Antioch Coll., 1944; M.S., Purdue U., 1945; Ph.D., Harvard U., 1948. Faculty Boston U., 1947-93, prof. chemistry, 1961-93, prof. emeritus, 1993—, Univ. prof., 1973-93, chmn. dept. chemistry, 1973-84, dir. Div. Engring. and Applied Sci., 1983-87; chief scientist Synlize, Inc., 1987-90, Project Sunrise Inc., 1990-92, Photox Corp., Boston, 1993-96, Zentox Corp., Boston, 1997—; vis. chemist Brookhaven Nat. Lab., Upton, N.Y., 1957-58, research collaborator, 1958-70; guest scientist Weizmann Inst. Sci., Rehovoth, Israel, 1962-63; vis. prof. Inst. Phys. and Chem. Research, Wako, Japan, 1980, Hebrew U., Jerusalem, 1962-63, 70-71, 75, 76, 80; Coochbehar lectr. Indian Assn. Cultivation of Sci., Calcutta, 1980. Assoc. editor Solar Energy, 1976-93; rsch. and publs. on mechanisms of chem. reactions including reaction of atomic nitrogen with organic compounds, influence of high energy radiation on organic compounds and photoredox reactions of dyes; photochem. conversion solar energy, ionization processes and ionic reactions in solutions in liquid sulfur dioxide, photo assisted solid-catalysis; catalytic and photocatalytic decomposition of organic and inorganic pollutants of air and water. Alumni bd. Antioch Coll., 1996—. NSF fellow, 1962-63. Fellow AAAS; mem. Am. Chem. Soc., Inter-Am. Photochem. Soc., Internat. Solar Energy Soc., Sigma Xi, Phi Beta Kappa (hon.). Home: 195 Morton St Newton MA 02159-1522 Office: 590 Commonwealth Ave Boston MA 02215-2521

LICHTMAN, ALLAN JAY, historian, educator, consultant; b. Bklyn., Apr. 4, 1947; s. Emanuel and Gertrude Louise (Cohen) L.; m. Katherine Martin Crane, June 6, 1970 (div.); 1 child, Kara Martin; m. Shelia Bradford, 1980 (div.); m. Karyn Lynn Strickler, June 8, 1991; 1 child, Samuel Allan. BA magna cum laude, Brandeis U., 1967; PhD, Harvard U., 1973. Dir. forensics Brandeis U., Waltham, Mass., 1968-71, Harvard U., Cambridge, Mass., 1971-72; asst. prof. history The Am. U., Washington, 1973-77; assoc. prof.

history The Am. U., Washington, 1977-78, prof. of history, 1978—, assoc. dean faculty and curricular devel. coll. arts & scis., 1985-87, chair dept. history, 1997—; instr. Brandeis U., 1970; cons. Smithsonian Instn., 1974-79, John Anderson campaign for Pres., 1980, George Washington U., 1983, U.S. Dept. Justice, Washington, 1983—, V.P. Albert Gore, Jr., Washington, 1994-95; advisor Ted Kennedy for Pres. campaign, 1980; cons., commentator NBC spl. project on the history of the Am. Presidency; polit. commentator NBC News Nightside, Voice of Am., USIA, Am.'s Talking Cable Network; expert witness Com. for Civil Rights Under Law, 1983—, U.S. Dept. Justice, 1983—, pvt. attys., 1986—, various state, mcpl. and county jurisdictions, 1986—, ACLU, 1987—, So. Poverty Law Ctr., 1990, Legal Def. Fund, 1991, Puerto Rican Legal Def. and Edn. Fund, 1991—, NAACP, 1993-94, Reform Party, 1996; chmn. Dept. History, 1997; columnist Montgomery Jour., Rockville, Md., 1990—, Reuters News Svc., 1996; appeared on various radio and TV programs; spkr. at more than 50 confs. Author: Your Family History: How to Use Oral History, Personal Family Archives, and Public Documents to Discover Your Heritage, 1978, Prejudice and the Old Politics: The Presidential Election of 1928, 1979, The Keys to the White House, 1996; co-author (with Valerie French) Historians and the Living Past: The Theory and Practice of Historical Study, 1978, (with Laura Irwin Langbein) Ecological Inference, 1978; co-editor (with Joan Challinor) Kin and Communities: Families in America, 1979, (with Ken DeCell) The 13 Keys to the Presidency, 1990; contbr. articles to profl. jours. and popular mags. Tchg. fellow Harvard U., 1969-73; rsch. grantee Am. U., 1978, 82; recipient Outstanding Young Men of Am. award U.S. C. of C. 1979-80, Top Spkr. award Nat. Conv. Internat. Platform Assn., 1983, 84, 87; Sherman Fairchild Distinguished Visiting scholar Calif. Inst. Tech., 1980-81; defeated twenty opponents on TIC TAC DOUGH, 1981. Mem. Am. Historian Assn., Orgn. Am. Historians, Social Sci. History Assn., Fed. City Club, Phi Alpha Phi, Phi Beta Kappa. Democrat. Jewish. Home: 9219 Villa Dr Bethesda MD 20817 Office: The Am Univ Washington DC 20016

LICHTMAN, DAVID MICHAEL, military officer, health care administrator, orthopedist, educator; b. Bkyln., Jan. 14, 1942; s. Harry S. and Frances (Rubin) L.; m. Frances Lubin; children: James Matthew, Elisabeth Jill. Student, Tufts Coll., 1962; MD, SUNY, Bklyn., 1966. Diplomate: Am. Bd. Orthopaedic Surgery. Intern U. Minn. Hosp., 1966-67, Naval Aerospace Med. Inst., Pensacola, Fla., 1967; commd. lt. USN, 1967, advanced through grades to rear adm., 1988, flight surgeon Air Wing 3, 1968-69; mem. staff orthopaedic svc. Nat. Naval. Med. Ctr., Bethesda, Md., 1974-77, chmn. dept. orthopaedic surgery, head, hand surgery svc., 1984-87; dir. orthopaedic residency program Nat. Naval Med. Ctr., Bethesda, Md., 1984-87; asst. chmn. dept. orthopaedic surgery Nat. Naval. Med. Ctr., Bethesda, Md., 1975-77, chmn. dept. orthopaedic surgery, head hand surgery svc., dir. orthopaedic residency program, 1984-87; chmn. dept. orthopaedic surgery and rehab. Naval Hosp., Oakland, Calif., 1977-83, dir. orthopaedic residency program/dir. navy hand fellowship, 1977-83, head hand and microsurgery svc., 1977-83; mem. staff orthopaedic surgery, sr. hand/microsurgery cons., 1988-91, commanding officer, 1989-91; comdr. San Francisco Med. Command, Oakland, 1988-91; promoted to Rear Adm. (lower half), 1989, Rear Adm. (upper half), 1991; retired USN, 1994; John Dunn prof. orthopedic hand surgery Baylor Coll. Medicine, Houston, 1994—; cons. orthopaedic surgery asst. sec. def. for health affairs Dept. Def., Washington, 1988-94; specialty advisor naval surgeon gen. for orthopaedic surgery and hand surgery Bur. Medicine and Surgery Dept. Navy, Washington, 1983-86; prof. surgery and head divsn. orthopaedic surgery Uniformed Svcs. U. of Health Scis., Bethesda, 1984-94, ex-officio mem. bd. regents, 1991-94. Editor: The Wrist and Its Disorders, 1988, Hand and Wrist Sect. Current Opinion in Orthopaedics.; contbr. articles to profl. jours. Mem. ACS (bd. govs.), Am. Acad. Orthopaedic Surgeons, Am. Soc. for Surgery of the Hand Assn., Am. Orthopaedic Assn. (hon.), Mil. Surgeons U.S. (Philip Hench award 1982), Soc. Naval Flight Surgeons, Soc. Mil. Orthopaedic Surgeons (bd. dirs.). Home: 45 Briar Hollow #11 Houston TX 77027 Office: Dept Orthopedic Surgery Baylor Coll Medicine 6550 Fannin St Ste 2525 Houston TX 77030-2709*

LICHTMAN, MARSHALL ALBERT, medical educator, physician, scientist; b. N.Y.C., June 23, 1934; s. Samuel and Vera L.; m. Alice Jo Maisel, June 23, 1957; children—Susan, Joanne, Pamela. AB, Cornell U., 1955; MD, U. Buffalo, 1960. Diplomate Am. Bd. Internal Medicine. Resident in medicine Strong Meml. Hosp., 1960-63; surgeon USPHS and postdoctoral research assoc. Sch. Pub. Health, U. N.C., 1963-65; chief resident and instr. medicine Strong Meml. Hosp., 1965-66; sr. instr. medicine, research trainee in hematology U. Rochester Sch. Medicine, N.Y., 1966-67, asst. prof. medicine, spl. postdoctoral research fellow in hematology, 1968-70, assoc. prof. medicine and radiation biology and biophysics, 1971-74, prof. medicine and radiation biology and biophysics, 1974—, chief hematology unit dept. medicine, 1975-77, co. chief, 1977-89; sr. assoc. dean for acad. affairs and research, 1979-89, dean Sch. of Medicine and Dentistry, 1990-95; exec. v.p. rsch. and med. affairs Leukemia Soc. Am., Inc., 1996—; vis. prof. univs.; lectr. in field. Leukemia Soc. Am. scholar, 1969-74; recipient contracts U.S. Army Research, 1972-78, U.S. Dept. Energy, 1972-80; USPHS grantee, 1971-95. Editor: Abnormalities of Granulocytes and Monocytes, 1975, Hematology for Practitioners, 1978, Hematology and Oncology, 1980, (with W.J. William, E. Beutler, A.J. Erslev) Hematology, 3d edit., 1983, 4th edit., 1990, (with E. Beutler, B. Coller, T.J. Kipps) 5th edit., 1995; (with H.J. Meiselman and P.L. LaCelle) White Cell Mechanics: Basic Science and Clinical Aspects, 1984. Contbr. articles to profl. jours. Master ACP; mem. NIH (hematology study sect., 1982-86), Am. Fedn. Clin. Research, AAAS, Am. Soc. Hematology (pres. 1989), Internat. Soc. Hematology, N.Y. Acad. Scis., Am. Soc. Clin. Investigation, Assn. Am. Physicians, Am. Assn. for Cancer Research, Am. Physiol. Soc., Reticuloendothelial Soc., Soc. Exptl. Biology and Medicine, Am. Soc. Cell Biology. Home: 64 Woodbury Pl Rochester NY 14618-3445 Office: U Rochester Sch Medicine & Dentistry Box 610 601 Elmwood Ave Rochester NY 14642-9999

LICHTWARDT, ROBERT WILLIAM, mycologist; b. Rio de Janeiro, Nov. 27, 1924; s. Henry Herman and Ruth Moyer Lichtwardt; m. Elizabeth Thomas, Jan. 27, 1951; children: Ruth Elizabeth, Robert Thomas. AB, Oberlin Coll., 1949; MS, U. Ill., 1951, PhD, 1954. Postdoctoral fellow NSF, Panama, Brazil, 1954-55; postdoctoral rsch. assoc. Iowa State U., Ames, 1955-57; asst. prof. U. Kans., Lawrence, 1957-60, assoc. prof., 1960-65; sr. postdoctoral fellow NSF, Hawaii, Japan, 1963-64; prof. U. Kans., Lawrence, 1965-94, prof. emeritus, 1994—. Author: The Trichomycetes, Fungal Associates of Arthropods, 1986; contbr. 95 articles to profl. jours. Mem. Mycological Soc. Am. (life, pres. 1971-72, editor-in-chief 1965-70, William H. Weston award for tchg. excellence in mycology 1982, Disting. Mycologist award 1991), Brit. Mycological Soc. (hon.), Japan Mycological Soc. (hon.). Office: U Kans Dept Of Botany Lawrence KS 66045

LICK, DALE WESLEY, educator; b. Marlette, Mich., Jan. 7, 1938; s. John R. and Florence M. (Baxter) L. (dec.); m. Marilyn Kay Foster, Sept. 15, 1956; children: Lynette (dec.), Kitty, Diana, Ronald. BS with honors, Mich. State U., 1958, MS in Math, 1959; PhD in Math, U. Calif., Riverside, 1965. Research asst. physics Mich. State U., East Lansing, 1958; teaching asst. math. Mich. State U., 1959; instr., chmn. dept. math. Port Huron (Mich.) Jr. Coll., 1959-60; asst. to comptroller Mich. Bell Telephone Co., Detroit, 1961; instr. U. Redlands, 1961-63; teaching asst. math. U. Calif., Riverside, 1964-65; asst. prof. math. U. Tenn., Knoxville, 1965-67; postdoctoral fellow Brookhaven Nat. Lab., Upton, N.Y., 1967-68; assoc. prof. U. Tenn., 1968-69; assoc. prof., head dept. math. Drexel U., Phila., 1969-72; adj. assoc. prof. dept. pharmacology Med. Sch., Temple U., Phila., 1969-72; v.p. acad. affairs Russell Sage Coll., Troy, N.Y., 1972-74; prof. math. and computing scis. Old Dominion U., Norfolk, Va., 1974-78; also dean Old Dominion U. (Sch. Scis. and Health Professions); pres., prof. math. and computer sci. Ga. So. Coll., Statesboro, 1978-86; pres., prof. math. U. Maine, Orono, 1986-91; pres., prof. math. Fla. State U., Tallahassee, 1991-93, univ. prof., 1993—; cert. in tng. and cons., mng. orgnl. change. Author: Fundamentals of Algebra, 1970; contbr. articles to profl. jours. Bd. dirs. Statesboro/Coll. Symphony, 1978-86, Statewide Health Coordinating Coun. Va., 1976-78; chmn. higher edn. adv. bd. Reorganized Ch. of Jesus Christ of Latter Day Sts., 1986—; mem. planning com. Bulloch Meml. Hosp., 1979-86; active Coastal Empire coun. Boy Scouts Am., 1982-86, Kataldin coun., 1986-91; bd. dirs. Health Care Ctrs. Am., Virginia Beach, Va., 1978, Ea. Va. Health Systems Agy., 1976-78; chmn., bd. dirs. Assembly Against Hunger and Malnutrition, 1977-78, pres., 1977-78. Mem. AAUP, AAAS, Am. Math. Soc., Math. Assn. Am., Am. Assn. Univ. Adminstrs., Am. Soc. Allied Health Professions, Am. Assn. State Colls. and Univs. (chmn. com. agr. resources and rural devel. 1981-86), Am. Assn. Higher Edn., Sigma Xi, Phi Kappa Phi, Pi Mu Epsilon (governing coun. 1972-77), Beta Gamma Sigma, Pi Sigma Epsilon. Mem., high priest Reorganized LDS Ch. Office: Learning Systems Inst Fla State U 2318 University Ctr Tallahassee FL 32306-4041

LICKHALTER, MERLIN EUGENE, architect; b. St. Louis, May 4, 1934; s. Frank E. and Sophia (Geller) L.; m. Harriet Braen, June 9, 1957; children: Debra, Barbara. BArch, MIT, 1957. Registered arch., Mo., Ill., Calif., Fla., Mich., Wis., Nev., Tex., Ala., Okla., Va. Ptnr. Drake Partnership, Architects, St. Louis, 1961-77; pres. JRB Architects, Inc., St. Louis, 1977-81; sr. v.p., mng. dir. Stone, Marraccini & Patterson, St. Louis, 1981-93; sr. v.p., dir. Cannon, 1993—; owner, pres. mgmt. program Harvard U. Bus. Sch., 1992; cons. Dept. Def., Washington, 1977-78; lectr. Washington U. Sch. Medicine, 1989—. Trustee United Hebrew Cong., St. Louis, 1980-88, 93—; exec. com. bd. dirs. Arts & Edn. Coun. St. Louis, 1991—. Capt. U.S. Army, 1957-59. Recipient Renovation Design award St. Louis Producers Coun., 1976, USAF Europe Design Award, 1990. Mem. AIA (nat. acad. architect for health, chmn. 1993), Am. Hosp. Assn., Am. Assn. for Health Planning, St. Louis Regional Growth Assn., Hawthorn Found., St. Louis Club, St. Louis Ambs., Frontenac Racquet Club, Masons. Jewish. Home: 2 Warson Ln Ladue MO 63124-1251 Office: Cannon One City Ctr Saint Louis MO 63101

LICKLE, WILLIAM CAUFFIEL, banker; b. Wilmington, Del., Aug. 2, 1929; m. Renee Carpenter Kitchell, Nov. 24, 1950; children: Sydney L. Garrison duPont, Ashley L. O'Neil, Kemble L. O'Donnell. BA, U. Va., 1951, LLB, 1953. Bar: Va. 1953. Chmn., CEO Laird, Bissell & Meeds, Inc., 1952-73; sr. v.p., dir. Dean Witter & Co. Inc., 1973-77; chmn., CEO Del. Trust Co., Wilmington, 1977-88; chmn. J.P. Morgan Fla., 1989-93, J.P. Morgan Internat. Holdings, 1989-92; pres. Thomasson Grant & Lickle Pub., 1996—; vice chmn. M.P. Morgan Del., 1989-92; chmn. Register Transfer Co., 1963-65; bd. dirs. Marvin Palmer Assoc. Bd. dirs., treas. Blue Cross-Blue Shield Del., 1963-68; commr. New Castle County (Del.) Airport, 1964-67, New Castle County Transp. Commn., 1967-69; bd. vice chmn., founder Better Bus. Bur. Del., 1966-72; hon. dir. Boys' Club Wilmington, 1963—; trustee Thomas Jefferson U., Phila., 1971-78, Med. Ctr. Del., 1965—, Breeder's Cup Ltd., Lexington, Ky., 1984-95, Winterhur Mus., 1989-94; mem. Pres. Reagan's Export Coun., 1988-89; pres. U. Va. Alumni Assn., 1987-94; spl. asst. Gov.'s Econ. Devel. for State of Del., 1987-91; bd. dirs. Raymond F. Kravis Ctr., Palm Beach, Fla., 1990-95. Clubs: Vicmead Hunt (Del.); Everglades, Bath and Tennis (Palm Beach, Fla.); Saratoga Golf and Polo, Reading Room (Saratoga, N.Y.); Springdale Hall (Camden, S.C.). Home: 568 Island Dr Palm Beach FL 33480-4747 Address: 23 Brandywine Falls Rd Wilmington DE 19806-1001

LIDDELL, DONALD MACY, JR., retired investment counsellor; b. Elizabeth, N.J., Mar. 11, 1907; s. Donald M. and Edith (Stabler) L.; m. Jane Hawley Hawkes, Mar. 30, 1940; children: Jane Liddell Bass, Donald Roger Brooke. B.S., Princeton U., 1928; grad. student, Am. Inst. Banking, N.Y. U. Statistician Banker's Trust Co., N.Y.C., 1928-29, White, Weld & Co., 1929-33; security analyst Fidelity Union Trust Co., Newark, 1935-40; v.p., dir. Templeton, Dobbrow & Vance, Inc., 1946-51, exec. v.p., 1951-60, chmn. bd., 1960-74; dir. 930 Park Ave. Corp., Nat. State Bank of Elizabeth, 1950-88; dir. N.Y. Sch. Interior; dir., fin. adviser Smoke, Fire and Burn Inst., 1950—, cons., 1983—. Contbr. articles to profl. publs. Bd. dirs., fin. adviser Youth Found., 1985—. Res. officer U.S. Army, 1933-35; lt. col. AUS, 1940-45; fin. officer Ea. Def. Command, 1944-45. Mem. Soc. Colonial Wars (treas.-gen. 1969-78, gov. N.J. Soc. 1986-88), Mil. Order Loyal Legion (comdr.-in-chief 1961-62), Sons of Revolution, Mil. Order Fgn. Wars, Order Colonial Lords of Manors in Am. (treas. 1969-88, pres. 1972-75), Lords of Md. Manors, Conf. Patriotic and Hist. Socs. (treas. 1974-84), Pilgrims of U.S., Colonial Order of the Acorn, Down Town Assn., Union Club, Badminton Club, Univ. Club, Ch. Club (all N.Y.C), Nassau Club (Princeton, N.J.). Republican. Episcopalian. Home: 930 Park Ave New York NY 10028-0209

LIDDELL, JANE HAWLEY HAWKES, civic worker; b. Newark, Dec. 8, 1907; d. Edward Zeh and Mary Everett (Hawley) Hawkes; AB, Smith Coll., 1931; postgrad. in art history, Harvard U., 1933-35; MA, Columbia U., 1940; Carnegie fellow Sorbonne, Paris, 1937; m. Donald M. Liddell, Jr., Mar. 30, 1940; children: Jane Boyer, D. Roger Brooke. Pres., Planned Parenthood Essex County (N.J.), 1947-50; trustee Prospect Hill Sch. Girls, Newark, 1946-50; mem. adv. bd., publicity and public relations chmn. N.J. State Mus., Trenton, 1952-60; sec., then v.p. women's br. N.J. Hist. Soc.; women's aux. prodn. chmn. Englewood (N.J.) Hosp., 1959-61; pres. Dwight Sch. Girls Parents Assn., 1955-57; v.p. Englewood Sch. Boys Parents Assn., 1958-60; mem. Altar Guild, women's aux. bd., rector's adv. council St. Paul's Episcopal Ch., Englewood, 1954-59; bd. dir. N.Y. State Soc. of Nat. Soc. Colonial Dames, 1961-67, rep. conf. Patriotic and Hist. Socs., 1964—; bd. dirs. Huguenot Soc. Am., 1979-86, regional v.p., 1979-82, historian, 1983-84, co-chmn. Tercentennial Book, 1983-85; bd. dirs. Soc. Daus. Holland Dames, 1965-82; nat. jr. v.p. Dames of Loyal Legion, USA; bd. dirs., mem. publs. com. Daus. Cin., 1966-72; bd. dirs. Ch. Women's League Patriotic Service, 1962—, pres., 1968-70, 72-74; bd. dirs., chmn. grants com. Youth Found., N.Y.C., 1974—; chmn. for Newark, Smith Coll. 75th Ann. Fund, 1948-50; pres. North N.J. Smith Club, 1956-58; pres. Smith Coll. Class 1931, 1946-51, 76-81, editor 50th anniversary book, 1980-81. Author: (with others) Huguenot Refugees in the Settling of Colonial America, 1982-85; contbr. The Dutch Contribution to the Development of Early Manhattan, 1969. Recipient various commendation awards. Republican. Mem. Colonial Dames Am. (N.Y.C. chpt.). Clubs: Colony, City Gardens, Church (N.Y.C.); Jr. League N.Y.; N.Y. Jr. League; Needle and Bobbin, Nat. Farm and Garden . Editor: Maine Echoes, 1961; research and editor asst., Wartime Writings of American Revolution Officers, 1972-75.

LIDDELL, LEON MORRIS, librarian, educator; b. Gainesville, Tex., July 21, 1914; s. Thomas Leon and Minnie Mae (Morris) L. B.A., U. Tex., 1937, J.D., 1937; B.L.S., U. Chgo., 1946; postgrad., Columbia U., 1948. Bar: Tex. bar 1937. Practiced in Gainesville, 1938-39; with claims dept. Hartford Accident & Indemnity Co., 1937-38, Pacific Mut. Life Ins. Co., 1939-41; asst. prof. law, law librarian U. Conn., 1946-47; asst. prof. law U. Minn., 1949-50, assoc. prof., 1950-54, prof. law, 1954-60, law librarian, 1949-60; prof. law, law librarian U. Chgo., 1960-74, prof. law, law librarian emeritus, 1974—; prof. law, law librarian Northwestern U. Law Sch., 1974-80. Maj. AUS, 1941-46; lt. col. USAR, 1946-62. Mem. Am. Bar Assn., Am. Assn. Law Libraries, Chgo Assn. Law Libraries (past pres.), Spl. Libraries Assn. Club: Mason. Home: 4718 Hallmark Dr Apt 504 Houston TX 77056-3911

LIDDELL, W. KIRK, specialty contracting and distribution company executive, lawyer; b. Lancaster, Pa., July 24, 1949; m. Pamela E. Trow; four children. AB in Econs. magna cum laude, Princeton U., 1971; MBA, U. Chgo., 1976, JD, 1976. Assoc. Covington & Burling, Washington, 1976-80; gen. counsel, v.p. AC and S Inc/Irex Corp., Lancaster, 1980-83; pres., chief exec. officer Irex Corp., 1984—; bd. dirs. High Industries Inc., Penn Fuel Gas, Inc.; Chmn. Lancaster City Ptnrship., 1986; chmn. Lancaster County C. of C. & Industry, 1991; bd. dirs., fin. com. Pa. C. of C. & Industry; bd. dirs. The Lancaster Alliance; bd. dirs., pres. Econ. Devel. Co. Lancaster County; campaign chmn. United Way of Lancaster County, 1995. Lt. USAR, 1971-73. Leon Carol Marshall scholar U. Chgo. Grad. Sch. Bus., 1974-76; named Scholar-Athlete Nat. Football Found. Office: Irex Corp 120 N Lime St Lancaster PA 17602-2951

LIDDICOAT, RICHARD THOMAS, JR., professional society administrator; b. Kearsarge, Mich., Mar. 2, 1918; s. Richard Thomas and Carmen (Williams) L.; m. Mary Imogene Hibbard, Sept. 21, 1939. BS in Geology, U. Mich., 1939, MS in Mineralogy, 1940; grad. gemologist, Gemological Inst. Am., 1941; MS in Meteorology, Calif. Inst. Tech., 1944. Cert. gemologist (hon.) Am. Gem Soc. With Gemological Inst. Am., L.A., 1940-42, 46-76, Santa Monica, Calif., 1976—; dir. edn. Gemological Inst. Am., 1942, 46-49, asst. dir., 1950-52, exec. dir., 1952-83, pres., 1970-83, chmn. bd., 1983—, also author courses; editor Gem and Gemology, 1952—; hon. mem. rsch. staff L.A. Mus. Natural History, 1968—; U.S. dep. to Internat. Gem Conf., 1960, 64, 66, 68, 70, 72, 75, 77, 79, 81, 83, 85, 89; del. Pres.'d Conf. on Small Bus., 1957. Author: Handbook of Gem Identification, 12th edit, 1987, (with others) The Diamond Dictionary, 1960, 2d edit., 1977, (with Copeland) Jewelers Manual, 2d edit. 1967; numerous articles.; contbr. to Ency. Britannica Jr., Ency. Americana, McGraw-Hill Ency. of Sci. and Tech. Trustee Nat. Home Study Coun., 1983-88. Recipient Lifetime Achievement award Modern Jeweler's mag., 1985, award Internat. Soc. Appraisers, 1985, Spl. award Internat. Colored Stone Assn., 1984, Lifetime Achievement award Morris B. Zale, 1987; named Man of Yr., Consol. Jewelers Assn. Greater N.Y., 1984; named to Nat. Home Study Coun. Hall of Fame, 1991; Liddicoatite species of tourmaline group named for him. Fellow Mineral. Soc. Am., Geol. Soc. Am., Gem Assn. Gt. Britain (hon.); mem. AAAS, Am. Gem Soc. (supr. ednl. sessions ann. conclaves 1948-83, Shipley award 1976), Am. Gem Trade Assn. (hon.), Gem Assn. Australia (hon. v.p.), Gem Testing Lab. Gt. Britain (1st hon. life mem.), Bel Air Country Club (bd. dirs. 1980-83, Twenty-Four Karat Club (N.Y.C. and So. Calif.), Sigma Xi, Sigma Gamma Epsilon. Developer system of diamond grading. Home: 1484 Allenford Ave Los Angeles CA 90049-3614 Office: Gemological Inst Am 5345 Armada Dr Carlsbad CA 92008-4602

LIDDLE, ALAN CURTIS, architect; b. Tacoma, Mar. 10, 1922; s. Abram Dix and Myrtle (Maytum) L. B.Arch., U. Wash., 1948; postgrad., Eidgenoissche Technische Hochschule, Zurich, Switzerland, 1950-51. Asst. prof. architecture U. Wash., 1954-55; prin. Liddle & Jones, Tacoma, 1957-67, Alan Liddle (architects), Tacoma, 1967-90, Liddle & Jacklin, Tacoma, 1990—. Architect oceanography bldgs, U. Wash., 1967, Tacoma Art Mus., 1971, Charles Wright Acad., Tacoma, 1962, Pacific Nat. Bank Wash., Auburn, 1965. Pres. bd. Allied Arts Tacoma, 1963-64, Civic Arts Commn. Tacoma-Pierce County, 1969; commr. Wash. Arts Commn., 1971; Bd. dirs. Tacoma Art Mus., 1969-73, Tacoma Zool. Soc., Tacoma Philharmonic, Inc. Served with AUS, 1943-46. Fellow A.I.A. (pres. S.W. Wash. chpt. 1967-68); mem. Wash. Hist. Soc., U. Wash. Alumni Assn. (all life). Home: 12735 Gravelly Lake Dr SW Tacoma WA 98499-1459 Office: 703 Pacific Ave Tacoma WA 98402-5207

LIDE, DAVID REYNOLDS, handbook and database editor; b. Gainesville, Ga., May 25, 1928; s. David Reynolds and Laura Kate (Simmons) L.; m. Mary Ruth Lomer, Nov. 5, 1955 (div. Dec. 1988); children: David Alston, Vanessa Grace, James Hugh, Quentin Robert; m. Bettijoyce Breen, 1988. BS, Carnegie Inst. Tech., 1949; PhD, Harvard U., 1952, AM, 1951. Physicist Nat. Bur. Standards, Washington, 1954-63, chief molecular spectroscopy sect., 1963-69; dir. standard reference data Nat. Bur. Standards, Gaithersburg, Md., 1969-88; editor-in-chief Handbook of Chemistry and Physics, CRC Press, 1988—; pres. Com. on Data for Sci. and Tech., Paris, 1986-90. Author: Basic Laboratory and Industrial Chemicals, 1993, Handbook of Organic Solvents, 1995, (with G.W.A. Milne) Handbook of Data on Organic Compounds, 3rd edit., 1993, (with H.V. Kehiaian) Handbook of Thermophysical and Thermochemical Data, 1994, (with G.W.A. Milne) Names, Synonyms, and Structures of Organic Compounds, 1995, (with Milne) Handbook of Data on Common Organic Compounds, 1995, Properties of Organic Compounds and Properties of Organic Solvents Databases, 1996; editor Jour. Phys. and Chem. Reference Data, 1972-92. Recipient Skolnik award for Chem. Info., Am. Chem. Soc., 1988, Patterson-Crane award, 1991, Presdl. Rank award in sr. exec. svc., 1986. Mem. Internat. Union Pure and Applied Chemistry (pres. phys. chemistry div. 1983-87). Achievements include use of microwave spectroscopy for studying hindered internal rotation, explanation of HCN laser, development of electronic databases of physical and chemical properties. Home and Office: 13901 Riding Loop Dr North Potomac MD 20878-3879

LIDICKER, WILLIAM ZANDER, JR., zoologist, educator; b. Evanston, Ill., Aug. 19, 1932; s. William Zander and Frida (Schroeter) L.; m. Naomi Ishino, Aug. 18, 1956 (div. Oct., 1982); children: Jeffrey Roger, Kenneth Paul; m. Louise N. DeLonzor, June 5, 1989. B.S., Cornell U., 1953; M.S., U. Ill., 1954, Ph.D., 1957. Instr. zoology, asst. curator mammals U. Calif., Berkeley, 1957-59; asst. prof., asst. curator U. Calif., 1959-65, assoc. prof., assoc. curator, 1965-69; assoc. dir. Mus. Vertebrate Zoology, 1968-81, acting dir., 1974-75, prof. zoology, curator mammals, 1969-89, prof. integrative biology, curator of mammals, 1989-94, prof., curator emeritus, 1994—. Contbr. articles to profl. jours. Bd. dirs. No. Calif. Com. for Environ. Info., 1971-77; bd. trustees BIOSIS, 1987-92, chmn., 1992; N.Am. rep. steering com., sect. Mammalogy IUBS, UNESCO, 1978-89; chmn. rodent specialist group Species Survival Commn., IUCN, 1980-89; mem. sci. adv. bd. Marine World Found. at Marine World Africa USA, 1987—; pres. Dehnel-Petrusewicz Meml. Fund, 1985—. Fellow AAAS, Calif. Acad. Scis.; mem. Am. Soc. Mammalogists (dir., 2d v.p. 1974-76, pres. 1976-78, C.H. Merriam award 1986, elected hon. mem. 1995), Am. Soc. Naturalists, Berkeley Folk Dancers Club (pres. 1969, tchr. 1984—), Westwind Internat. Folk Ensemble (dancer 1994—), others. Office: U Calif Mus Vertebrate Zoology Berkeley CA 94720

LIDOFSKY, STEVEN DAVID, medical educator; b. Bklyn., Jan. 19, 1954; s. Leon Julian and Eleanor Helen (Liebman) L.; m. Elisabeth Tang Barfod, May 3, 1982; children: Benjamin Barfod, Anna Barfod. BA, Columbia U., 1975, PhD, 1980, MD, 1982. Bd. cert. in gastroenterology and internal medicine Am. Bd. Internal Medicine. Intern U. Colo., Denver, 1982-83, resident, 1983-85, chief med. resident, 1985-86; fellow in gastroenterology U. Calif., San Francisco, 1986-90, asst. prof. medicine, 1990—. Contbr. articles to profl. jours. Recipient Liver Scholar award Am. Liver Found., 1990-93, Rsch. award Am. Diabetes Assn., 1996. Mem. Am. Assn. for Study of Liver Diseases, Am. Fedn. for Clin. Rsch., Am. Gastroenterol. Assn. (Fiterman Found. Rsch. award 1994), Calif. Acad. Medicine, Western Soc. Clin. Investigation. Avocations: cartooning, cooking, running. Office: Univ Calif San Francisco GI Unit S357 San Francisco CA 94143-0538

LIDSTONE, HERRICK KENLEY, JR., lawyer; b. New Rochelle, N.Y., Sept. 10, 1949; s. Herrick Kenley and Marcia Edith (Drake) L.; m. Mary Lynne O'Toole, Aug. 5, 1978; children: Herrick Kevin, James Patrick, John Francis. AB, Cornell U., 1971; JD, U. Colo., 1978. Bar: Colo. 1978, U.S. Dist. Ct. Colo. 1978. Assoc. Roath & Brega, P.C., Denver, 1978-85, Brenman, Epstein, Raskin & Friedlob, P.C., Denver, 1985-86; shareholder Brenman, Raskin & Friedlob, P.C., Denver, 1986-94; mem. Friedlob Sanderson Raskin Paulson & Tourtillott, LLC, Denver, 1995—; adj. prof. U. Denver Coll. Law, 1985—; speaker in field various orgns.; fluent in Spanish. Editor U. Colo. Law Rev., 1977-78; co-author: Federal Income Taxation of Corporations, 6th edit.; contbg. author: Legal Opinion Letters Formbook, 1996; contbr. articles to profl. jours. Served with USN, 1971-75, with USNR, 1975-81. Mem. ABA (Am. Law Inst.), Colo. Bar Assn., Denver Bar Assn., Denver Assn. Oil and Gas Title Lawyers. Office: Friedlob Sanderson Raskin Paulson & Tourtillott LLC 1400 Glenarm Pl Denver CO 80202-5050

LIDTKE, DORIS KEEFE, computer science educator; b. Bottineau County, N.D., Dec. 6, 1929; d. Michael J. and Josephine (McDaniels) Keefe; m. Vernon L. Lidtke, Apr. 21, 1951. BS, U. Oreg., 1952; MEd cum laude, Johns Hopkins U., 1974; PhD, U. Oreg., 1979. Programmer analyst Shell Devel. Co., Emeryville, Calif., 1955-59, U. Calif., Berkeley, 1960-62; asst. prof. Lansing (Mich.) Community Coll., 1963-68; ednl. specialist Johns Hopkins U., Balt., 1968; assoc. program mgr. NSF, Washington, 1984-85; program dir., 1992-93; sr. mem. tech. staff Software Productivity Consortium, Reston, Va., 1987-88; asst. prof. Towson State U., Balt., 1968-80, assoc. prof., 1980-90, prof. computer sci., 1990—. Named Outstanding Educator, Assn. for Ednl. Data Systems, 1986. Mem. Assn. for Computing Machinery (edn. bd. 1980—, coun. 1984-86, 94—, spl. interest group bd. 1985—, chair 1994—, Recognition Svc. award 1978, 83, 85, 86, 90, 91, Outstanding Contbn. award 1995), Computer Soc. of IEEE (Outstanding Contbn. award 1986, 92, Golden Core), Nat. Ednl. Computer Conf. (steering com., vice chmn. 1983-85, chmn. 1985-89, Recognition award 1988, 92, 95), Computing Scis. Accreditation Bd. (v.p. 1993-95, pres. 1995—). Home: 4806 Wilmslow Rd Baltimore MD 21210-2328 Office: Towson State U Computer & Info Scis Baltimore MD 21204

LIDTKE, VERNON LEROY, history educator; b. Avon, S.D., May 4, 1930; s. Albert William and Aganeta (Boese) L.; m. Doris Eileen Keefe, Apr. 21, 1951. B.A., U. Oreg., 1952, M.A., 1955; Ph.D., U. Calif., Berkeley, 1962. Tchr. high sch. Riddle, Oreg., 1953-55; instr. social sci. U. Calif., Berkeley, 1960-62; asst. prof. history Mich. State U., 1962-66, assoc. prof., 1966-68; vis. asst. prof. U. Calif., Berkeley, 1963; asso. prof. Johns Hopkins U., 1968-73, prof., 1973—, chmn. dept. history, 1975-79; chair Friends of the German Historical Inst., Washington, 1991-94; chair Modern European Sect., Am. Hist. Assn., 1992. Author: The Outlawed Party: Social

Democracy in Germany, 1878-1890, 1966, The Alternative Culture: Socialist Labor in Imperial Germany, 1985; editorial bd.: Jour. Modern History, 1973-76, Central European History, 1982-89, Internat. Labor and Working Class History, 1984-89; contbr. articles to profl. jours. Fulbright research fellow, 1959-60, 66-67; Nat. Endowment Humanities fellow, 1969-70; fellow Wissenschaftekolleg zu Berlin, 1987-88, Max-Planck-Institut fü Geschichte, Göttingen, 1996. Mem. AAUP, Am. Hist. Assn., Coll. Art Assn., Conf. Group for Cen. European History (v.p. 1985, pres. 1986), Conf. Group German Politics (officer 1975-83), Johns Hopkins Club. Home: 4806 Wilmslow Rd Baltimore MD 21210-2328 Office: Johns Hopkins U Dept History Baltimore MD 21218

LIDZ, CHARLES WILMANNS, sociologist; b. Balt., Feb. 1, 1946; s. Theodore and Ruth (Wilmanns) L.; m. Christine MacDougall, June 18, 1967 (div. 1978); m. Lynn C. Brown, May 26, 1979; children: James H. Carwile, Heather M. Carwile, Molly E.M. Lidz. BA, Yale U., 1967; MA, Harvard U., 1968, PhD, 1974. Asst. prof. psychiatry and sociology U. Pitts., 1974-80, assoc. prof., 1980-86, prof., 1986-96, assoc. dir. rsch. Ctr. for Med. Ethics, 1987-96; rsch. prof. psychiatry U. Mass., Worcester, 1996—. Editor, Qualitative Sociology, 1987-91; co-author: Connections: Notes from the Heroin World, 1974, Heroin, Deviance and Morality, 1980, Informed Consent: A Study..., 1984, Informed Consent: Legal Theory and Clinical Practice, 1987, The Erosion of Autonomy in Long-Term Care, 1992. Co-founder New Haven Half-Way House, 1967; bd. dirs. Am. Chronic Pain Assn., Rocklin, Calif., 1982—, pres., 1987, 89; bd. dirs. Transitional Svcs., Inc., Pitts., 1986-93, 95-96, v.p., 1991-92. Grantee NIMH, 1976-79, 85-94, 97—, Pres. Commn. on Bioethics, 1981-82, Retirement Rsch. Found., 1987-89, MacArthur Found., 1990-96. Mem. Soc. for Study of Social Problems, Am. Sociol. Assn. Office: U Mass Med Sch Dept Psychiatry 55 Lake Ave N Worcester MA 01655-0002

LIEB, ELLIOTT HERSHEL, physicist, mathematician, educator; b. Boston, July 31, 1932; s. Sinclair M. and Clara (Rosenstein) L.; m. Christiane Fellbaum; children: Alexander, Gregory. BSc, MIT, 1953; PhD, U. Birmingham, Eng., 1956; DSc (hon.), U. Copenhagen, 1979; Dr. (hon.), Ecole Poly. Fed. Lausanne, Switzerland, 1995. With IBM Corp., 1960-63; sr. lectr. Fourah Bay Coll., Sierra Leone, 1961; mem. faculty Yeshiva U., 1963-66, Northeastern U., 1966-68; mem. faculty MIT, Cambridge, 1968-75, prof. physics, 1963-68, prof. math., 1968-73, prof. math. and physics, 1973—; prof. math. and physics Princeton (N.J.) U., 1975—. Author: (with D.C. Mattis) Mathematical Physics in One Dimension, 1966, (with B. Simon and A. Wightman) Studies in Mathematical Physics, (with M. Loss) Analysis; also articles. Recipient Boris Pregel award chem. physics N.Y. Acad. Scis., 1970; Dannie Heineman prize for mathematical physics Am. Inst. Physics and Am. Phys. Soc., 1978; Prix Scientifique, Union des Assurances de Paris, 1985; Birkhoff prize Am. Math. Soc. and Soc. Indsl. Applied Math., 1988; Max-Planck medal German Phys. Soc., 1992; Guggenheim Found. fellow, 1972, 78. Fellow Am. Phys. Soc.; mem. NAS, Austrian Acad. Scis., Danish Royal Acad., Am. Acad. Arts and Scis., Internat. Assn. Math. Physics (pres. 1982-84, 97-99). Office: Princeton U Jadwin Hall-Physics Dept PO Box 708 Princeton NJ 08544-0708

LIEB, MICHAEL, English educator, humanities educator. AB in Eng. Lit., Rutgers U., 1962, AM in Eng. Lit., 1964, PhD in Eng. Lit., 1967; student, U. Iowa, 1962-63, U. Chgo. Divinity Sch., 1974-75, Spertus Coll. of Judaica, 1987-92. Asst. prof. Eng. Coll. of William and Mary, Williamsburg, Va., 1967-70; assoc. prof. Eng. U. Ill., Chgo., 1970-75, prof. Eng., 1975-88, rsch. prof. humanities, prof. Eng., 1988—; vis. professorial lectr. U. Chgo. Divinity Sch., 1979; bd. dirs. Friends of Milton's Cottage; mem. exec. com. U. Chgo. Renaissance Seminar, 1977—; mem. exec. com. Divsn. 17th Century Eng. Lit. MLA, 1982-86, Divsn. Religious Approaches to Lit., 1987-91; mem. exec. com. Ctr. Renaissance Studies Newberry Libr., 1979—, mem. com. Brit. Acad. Fellowships, 1982-83, mem. search com. for dir., 1984; mem. adv. com. 2d Internat. Milton Symposium, 1983, 4th, 1990; campus rep. Woodrow Wilson Found., 1982-83; mem. numerous coms. U. Ill. Author: The Dialectics of Creation: Patterns of Birth and Regeneration in Paradise Lost, 1970, Poetics of the Holy: A Reading of Paradise Lost, 1981 (James Holly Hanford award Milton Soc. Am.), The Sinews of Ulysses: Form and Convention in Milton's Works, 1989, The Visionary Mode: Biblical Prophecy, Hermeneutics and Cultural Change, 1991, Milton and the Culture of Violence, 1994; co-editor, contbg. author: Achievements of the Left hand: Essays on the Prose of John Milton, 1974, Eyes Fast Fixt: Current Perspectives in Milton Methodology, 1975, Literary Milton: Text, Pretext, Context, 1994, The Miltonic Samson, 1996; contbr. articles to profl. jours.; symposia speaker in field; panelist; invited speaker; cons. edit. bds., univ. presses, profl. jours., librs., depts. Eng., Comparative Lit., Divinity. Pres., co-founder Oak Park Housing Ctr., 1971-73, Advocate award 1992; mem. hon. com. Ill. Humanities Coun., 1986; mem. Am. Jewish Com. Academicians Seminar, Israel, 1986. NEH U. Tchrs. fellow, 1991-92, John Simon Guggenheim Meml. Found. fellow 1987-88, U. Ill. Chgo. Inst. for Humanities sr. fellow 1983, Newberry Libr. Nat. Endowment for Humanities sr. fellow 1981-82, NEH Younger Humanist Study fellow 1974-75; recipient Am. Coun. Learned Societies Grant-in-Aid, 1985, Am. Philosophical Soc. Grant-in-Aid, 1983, Folger Shakespeare Libr. fellow, 1970, 74; Honors Coll. U. Ill. Chgo. fellow 1986—; others. Mem. Milton Soc. Am. (chair James Holly Hanford awards com. 1991-93, treas. 1973-77, v.p. 1980, pres. 1981, honored scholar 1992), Modern Lang. Assn., Milton Soc. of Japan, Southeastern Renaissance Conf., Renaissance Soc. of Am., Calif. Renaissance Conf., Northeastern Modern Lang. Assn., Newberry Libr. Milton Seminar (co-founder, co-chair 1986—), Newberry Libr. Dante Lectures. Home: 212 S Ridgeland Ave Oak Park IL 60302-3226 Office: U Ill Chgo Dept Eng M/C 162 Chicago IL 60607

LIEBELER, SUSAN WITTENBERG, lawyer; b. New Castle, Pa., July 3, 1942; d. Sherman K. and Eleanor (Klivans) Levine; BA, U. Mich., 1963, postgrad. U. Mich., 1963-64; LLB (Stein scholar), UCLA, 1966; m. Wesley J. Liebeler, Oct. 21, 1971; 1 child, Jennifer. Bar: Calif. 1967, Vt. 1972, D.C. 1988. Law clk. Calif. Ct. of Appeals, 1966-67; assoc. Gang, Tyre & Brown, 1967-68, Greenberg, Bernhard, Weiss & Karma, L.A., 1968-70; assoc. gen. counsel Rep. Corp., L.A., 1970-72; gen. counsel Verit Industries, L.A., 1972-73; prof. of law law sch. Loyola U., L.A., 1973-84; spl. counsel, chmn. John S. R. Shad, SEC, Washington, 1981-82; commr. U.S. Internat. Trade Commn. Washington, 1984-88, vice chmn., 1984-86, chmn., 1986-88; ptnr. Irell & Manella, L.A., 1988-94; sr. v.p. Legal Rsch. Network, Inc., L.A., 1994-95; pres. Lexpert Rsch. Svcs., L.A., 1995—; vis. prof. U. Tex., summer 1982; cons. Office of Policy Coordination, office of Pres.-elect, 1981-82; cons. U.S. Ry. Assn., 1975, U.S. EPA, 1974, U.S. Price Commn., 1972; mem. Adminstrv. Conf. U.S., 1986-88. Mem. editorial adv. bd. Regulation mag. CATO Inst. Mem. ABA, State Bar Calif. (treas., vice chair, chair exec. com. internat. law sect.), L.A. County Bar Assn., Practicing Law Inst. (internat. law adv. com.), Washington Legal Found. (acad. adv. bd.), bd. dirs. Century City Hosp., adv. bd. U. Calif. Orientation in U.S.A. Law, Order of Coif. Jewish. Sr. editor UCLA Law Review, 1965-66; contbr. articles to legal publ.

LIEBELER, WESLEY J., law educator, lawyer; b. 1931. B.A., Macalester Coll., 1953; J.D., U. Chgo., 1957. Bar: N.Y. 1958. Assoc. Carter, Ledyard & Milburn, N.Y.C., 1958-64; prof. UCLA Sch. Law, 1965—; dir. Office Policy Planning FTC, Washington, 1974-75; cons. in field; asst. counsel Pres.'s Commn. on Assassination Pres. Kennedy, 1964. Served with U.S. Army. Mem. Western Econ. Assn., Order of Coif. Past articles editor U. Chgo. Law Rev. Office: UCLA Law Sch 405 Hilgard Ave Los Angeles CA 90095-9000

LIEBENSON, HERBERT, economist, trade association executive; b. Chgo., July 26, 1920; s. Michael and Evelyn (Zimmerman) L.; m. Gloria Rachel Krasnow, Mar. 11, 1944; children: Lauren Ward, Lynn Green. B.A., Roosevelt U., 1948; postgrad., U. Chgo., 1948, Am. U., 1949-52. Research assoc. United Mineworkers Pension and Welfare Fund, Washington, 1948-52; employee benefit/labor relations analyst C. of C. U.S., Washington, 1952-58; with Nat. Small Bus. Assn., Washington, 1958—; v.p. Nat. Small Bus. Assn., 1958-80, pres., 1980-86, sr. cons., 1986—; exec. dir. Small Bus. Legis. Council, 1980-86, chmn. tech. for new products and jobs, 1986—; mem. exec. com., chmn. com. on taxation SBA Nat. Adv. Council, 1982-86; pres. del. White House Conf. on Small Bus., 1986; mem. Sec. Labor's mgmt. adv. com. on Landrum-Griffin Act, U.S. Employment Service Adv. Com.; mem. adv. com. on jobs Dept. Commerce Com. on Product Standards; alt. mem. Presdl. Pay Bd., 1973-74; mem. steering com. Nat. Com. to Preserve Family Bus., 1981; mem. nat. com. Am. Energy Week, 1981. Served with USAAF, 1942-46. Mem. Indsl. Relations Research Assn. (pres. chpt. 1961-62), Bus. Adv. Council Fed. Reports (bd. govs. 1970-85), Am. Soc. Assn. Execs. Jewish. Club: Internat. Home: 2703 Unicorn Ln NW Washington DC 20015-2233

LIEBER, CHARLES DONALD, publisher; b. Scheveningen, The Netherlands, Jan. 30, 1921; came to U.S., 1941, naturalized, 1944; s. Edmund Z. and Gabrielle (Lifczis) L.; m. Miriam Levin, July 17, 1960; children: John Nathan, James Edmund, George Theodore, Anne Gabrielle. Student, U. Brussels, 1938-40; B.A., New Sch. for Social Research, 1948. With H. Bittner & Co. (Pubs.), N.Y.C., 1947-49; with Alfred A. Knopf, Inc., N.Y.C., 1949-52, dir. coll. dept., 1960-64; dir. coll. dept. Random House, N.Y.C., 1952-64; pub. Atherton Press, N.Y.C., 1964-67; pres. Atherton Press, Inc., N.Y.C., 1967-70; v.p. Aldine-Atherton, Inc., N.Y.C., Chgo., 1971-72; pres. Lieber-Atherton, Inc., N.Y.C., 1972—; gen. mgr. Hebrew Pub. Co., 1980-85, pres., 1985—; pres. Lieber Publs., Inc., N.Y.C., 1981—. Author: (with A.D. Murphy) Great Events of World History, 1964; chmn. publ. com., mem. editl. bd. Reconstructionist mag., 1983-93. Chmn. West Side Jewish Cmty. Coun., Manhattan, 1978-82, mem.-at-large, 1974—; exec. bd. Jewish Reconstrn. Found., 1978-83, vice chmn., 1979-80, chmn., 1980-83, nat. bd. dirs., 1983-92; trustee St. Ann's Sch., 1983-89, Soc. for Advancement Judaism, 1974-90, treas., 1976-79, co-chmn., 1979-81; bd. dirs. Hebrew Arts Sch., 1974-82, Fedn. Reconstructionist Congregations, 1983-91; founding mem. Lenox Hill Club, 1957. Lt. AUS, 1942-46, CBI. Recipient Mordecai M. Kaplan award Jewish Reconstructionist Found., 1988. Mem. Coll. Pubs. Group (chmn. 1965-66), Assn. Jewish Book Pubs. (pres. 1988-90). Office: Hebrew Publishing Co PO Box 222 Spencertown NY 12165-0222

LIEBER, CHARLES SAUL, physician, educator; b. Antwerp, Belgium, Feb. 13, 1931; came to U.S., 1958, naturalized, 1966; s. Isaac and Lea (Maj) L.; m. M. A. Leo; children: Colette, Daniel, Leah, Samuel, Sarah. Candidate in natural and med. sci., U. Brussels, 1951; M.D., 1955. Intern, resident U. Hosp., Brugmann, Brussels, Belgium, 1954-56; research fellow med. found. Queen Elizabeth, 1956-58; research fellow Thorndike Meml. Lab., Harvard Med. Sch., 1958-60, instr., 1961; assoc. Harvard U., 1962; assoc. prof. medicine Cornell U., 1963-68; dir. liver disease and nutrition unit Bellevue Hosp., N.Y.C., 1963-68; chief sect. liver disease, nutrition and GI-Liver Tng. Program VA Hosp., Bronx, N.Y., 1968—; prof. medicine Mt. Sinai Sch. Medicine, 1969—, prof. pathology, 1976—, dir. Alcohol Research and Treatment Ctr., 1977—; assoc. vis. physician Cornell Med. div. Bellevue, Meml., James Ewing hosps., 1964-69; Am. Coll. Gastroenterology disting. lectr., 1978, Henry Baker lectr., 1979. Recipient award of Belgian Govt. for rsch. on gastric secretion, 1956, Rsch. Career Devel. award NIH, USPHS, 1964-68, E.M. Jellinek Meml. award, 1976, A. Boudreau award Laval U., 1977, W.S. Middleton award, 1977, Leahy Rsch. award, highest honor for med. rsch. Dept. Vets. Affairs, 1994, first Mark Keller award, NIAAA-NIH, 1996. Fellow AAAS, Am. Soc. Nutritional Sci.; mem. ACP, Assn. Am. Physicians, N.Y. Gastroent. Assn. (pres. 1974-75), Am. Soc. Biochemistry and Molecular Biology, Am. Soc. Addictive Medicine (pres. 1974-77, Sci. Achievement award 1989, Disting. Scientist award 1996), Assn. Clin. Biochemists (Kone award 1994), Am. Soc. Clin. Nutrition (McCollum award 1973, pres. 1975-76, Robert H. Herman Meml. award 1993), Am. Soc. Clin. Investigation, Am. Soc. Pharmacol. Exptl. Therapy, Am. Gastroent. Assn. (Disting. Achievement award 1973, Hugh R. Butt award for liver/nutrition 1992), Rsch. Soc. on Alcoholism (pres. 1977-79, Sci. Excellence award 1980, Disting. Svc. award 1992), Am. Coll. Nutrition (Outstanding Achievement award 1990, Am. Assn. Study Liver Diseases. Home: 6 Johnson Ave Englewd Clfs NJ 07632-2107 Office: 130 W Kingsbridge Rd Bronx NY 10468-3992

LIEBER, DAVID LEO, university president; b. Stryj, Poland, Feb. 20, 1925; came to U.S., 1927, naturalized, 1936; s. Max and Gussie (Jarmush) L.; m. Esther Kobre, June 10, 1945; children—Michael, Daniel, Deborah, Susan. B.A., CCNY, 1944; B.Hebrew Lit., Jewish Theol. Sem. Am., 1944, M.Hebrew Lit., 1948, D. Hebrew Lit., 1951; M.A., Columbia, 1947; postgrad., U. Wash., 1954-55, UCLA, 1961-63; L.D.H. hon., Hebrew Union Coll., 1982—. Ordained rabbi, 1948. Rabbi, 1948, Sinai Temple, Los Angeles, 1950-54; dir. (B'nai B'rith Hillel), Seattle, Cambridge, 1954-56; dean students U. Judaism, Los Angeles, 1956-63; Samuel A. Fryer prof. Bible, pres. U. Judaism, 1963-92, Skovron Disting. Svc. prof. Bibl. lit., 1990—, pres. emeritus, 1992—; pres. emeritus U. Judaism, L.A., 1992—; lectr. Hebrew UCLA, 1957-90; vice chancellor Jewish Theol. Sem., 1972-92; mem. exec. coun. Rabbinical Assembly, 1966-69, v.p., 1994-96, pres., 1996—; vice chmn. Am. Jewish Com., L.A., 1972-75; bd. dirs. Jewish Fedn. Coun., L.A., 1980-86, bd. govs., 1986—. Mem. editorial bd.: Conservative Judaism, 1968-70. Served as chaplain USAF, 1951-53. Recipient Torch of Learning award Hebrew U., 1984. Mem. Assn. Profs. Jewish Studies (dir. 1970-71), Phi Beta Kappa. Office: U Judaism 15600 Mulholland Dr Los Angeles CA 90077-1519

LIEBER, DAVID LESLIE, journalist; b. Gastonia, N.C., June 26, 1957; s. Stanley J. and Denise (Berwald) L.; m. Karen Pasciutti, Feb. 18, 1995; stepchildren: Desiree Lauren, Jonathan Lawrence; 1 child, Austin James. BA in Am. Civilization, U. Pa., 1979. Feature writer, media columnist Ft. Myers (Fla.) News-Press, 1980-81; statehouse reporter Charleston (W.Va.) Gazette, 1981-83; staff writer Phila. Inquirer, 1983-93; metro columnist, mem. editl. bd. Ft. Worth (Tex.) Star-Telegram, 1993—. Co-founder Summer Santa Charity. Named Outstanding Journalist W.Va. Trial Lawyers Assn., 1982-83; recipient Smolar award Coun. Jewish Fedns., 1989, Best Commentary award Assn. Black Communicators, 1995. Mem. Investigative Reporters and Editors, Soc. Profl. Journalists, Pen and Pencil, Nat. Soc. Newspaper Columnists (1st prize writing contest 1995; sec./newsletter editor), Lonesome Dove Cemetery Assn. Avocation: political memorabilia collector. Office: Ft Worth Star-Telegram 3201 Airport Fwy Bedford TX 76021-6036

LIEBER, ROBERT JAMES, political science educator, writer; b. Chgo., Sept. 29, 1941; m. Nancy Isaksen; 2 children. BA in Polit. Sci. with high honors, U. Wis., 1963; postgrad. in Polit. Sci., U. Chgo., 1963-64; PhD in Govt., Harvard U., 1968; postgrad. St. Antony's Coll., Oxford (Eng.) U., 1969-70. Asst. prof. Polit. Sci. U. Calif., Davis, 1968-72, assoc. prof., 1972-77, chmn. dept. Polit. Sci., 1975-76, 77-80, prof., 1977-81; prof. Georgetown U., Washington, 1982—, chmn. dept. govt., 1990-96; vis. prof. Oxford U., 1969, Fudan U., Shanghai, 1988; rsch. assoc. Ctr. Internat. Affairs, Harvard U., 1974-75; cons. U.S. Dept. State and Dept. Def., 1975—. Author: British Politics and European Unity, 1970, Theory and World Politics, 1972, Oil and the Middle East War: Europe in the Energy Crisis, 1976, The Oil Decade: Conflict and Cooperation in the West, 1983, No Common Power: Understanding International Relations, 1988, 3d edit., 1995; co-author: Contemporary Politics: Europe, 1976; editor, contbg. author: Eagle Adrift: American Foreign Policy at the End of the Century, 1997; co-editor, contbg. author: Eagle Entangle d: U.S. Foreign Policy in a Complex World, 1979, Eagle Defiant: U.S. Foreign Policy in the 1980s, 1983, Eagle Resurgent? The Reagan Era in American Foreign Policy, 1987, Eagle in a New World: American Grand Strategy in the Post-Cold War Era, 1992; editor: Will Europe Fight for Oil?, 1983; contbr. articles to Harper's, Politique, étrangère, N.Y. Times, Washington Post, Christian Sci. Monitor, others, and profl. jours. Advanceman nat. campaign staff McCarthy for Pres., 1968; fgn. policy advising presdl. campaigns of Sen. Edward Kennedy, 1979-80, Walter Mondale. 1984, Bill Clinton, 1991-92; coord. Mid. East Issues presdl. campaign Michael Dukakis, 1988. Woodrow Wilson fellow, 1963, fellow NDEA, 1963-64, Harvard U., 1964-68, Social Sci. Rsch. Coun., 1969-70, Coun. Fgn. Rels., 1972-73, Guggenheim fellow, 1973-74, Rockefeller Found., 1978-79, Wilson Ctr. Smithsonian Inst., 1980-81, Ford Found., 1981; vis. fellow Atlantic Inst. Internat. Affairs, Paris, 1978-79; guest scholar Brookings Inst., 1981. Mem. Coun. on Fgn. Rels., Internat. Inst. for Strategic Studies, Phi Beta Kappa. Office: Georgetown U Dept of Government Washington DC 20057-1034

LIEBER, STANLEY MARTIN See LEE, STAN

LIEBERMAN, ARCHIE, photographer, writer; b. Chgo., July 17, 1926; s. Sol and Rose (Schiff) L.; m. Esther Kraus, Jan. 11, 1948; children: Eric Joseph, Robert Charles Vories, Kurt Murrow. Student, Inst. Design, Chgo., 1946-48. Contract photographer Time Mag., Chgo., 1950-51; staff photographer Black Star Pub. Co., N.Y.C., 1951-61; adj. prof. Chgo. Theol. Sem., 1976-74; instr. Columbia Coll., Chgo., 1968-74. One man shows include Presbyn.-St. Luke's Hosp., Chgo., Chapel Hill Shopping Ctr., Akron, Ohio Mchts. Assn., Flint, Mich., Arie Crown Theater, Chgo., Carson Pirie Scott & Co., Chgo., Prudential Bldg., Chgo., Agr. U.S.A., Soviet Union, U. Ill., Lake Forest Coll., Kodak Gallery, Grand Central Sta., N.Y.C., Rizzoli Gallery, Chgo., U. Dubuque (retrospective), 1987, Dubuque Mus. Art, Lands End Gallery, Dodgeville, Wis., 1991, Ford Ctr. Fine Art-Knox Coll., 1993, Elveahjem Mus., Madison, Wis., 1994, Freeport Art Mus., 1994, Lake Forest Coll., 1995; group shows include Jewish Mus., N.Y.C., Tower Gallery, Chgo., Garrett Bible Inst., Evanston, Met. Mus. Art, N.Y.C., Expo '67, Montreal, Art Inst. Chgo., 1986, Photography in Fine Arts, N.Y.C., San Diego Mus. Photographic Arts, 1986, Mitchell Mus., Mt. Vernon, Ill., 1987, 88, The Art Inst. of Chgo., 1986, 92, numerous others; author, photographer: The Israelis, 1965 (One of Best 50 Books award), Farm Boy (Friends of Lit. award), Neighbors, 1993; photographer books: Shalom, A Solitary Life, The Future of Religions, The Eternal Life, Holy Holy Land, The Story of Israel, Chicago In Color, Chicago, God Make Me Brave For Life, (with Ray Bradbury) The Mummies of Guanajuato, Chicago: A Celebration, 1990; photojournalist for mags. including: Look, Life, Saturday Evening Post, Collier's, Ladies Home Jour., Fortune, London Illustrated, Redbook, Farm Jour., Pageant, Parade, Bus. Week, Am. Weekly, Venture, U.S. News & World Report, Newsweek, Paris Match, Chgo. Mag.; indsl. photographer for corps. including Inland Steel, Acme Steel, Lands' End, Harvester, Gould Inc., McDonald's, Motorola, Grumman Corp., Internat. Minerals & Chem. Corp.; advt. photographs for: Allstate Ins., Phillip Morris, Schlitz, United Airlines, Jack Daniel, others. Recipient Peter Lisagor award Headline Club of Sigma Delta Chi, 1980; Sinai Health Service award Mt. Sinai Hosp. Med. ctr., Chgo., 1985; various award U. Mo. Sch. Journalism. Clubs: Arts of Chgo., Chgo. Press, Tavern Club, Galena Artists Guild. Office: PO Box 61 Scales Mound IL 61075-0061 *People are not creative. There was only one creative act-The making of somethingout of a void-The creation itself. What people do is to discover that which hasalways been and position it in a new way. Therefore we must be discoverers to invent new things.*

LIEBERMAN, CAROL, healthcare marketing communications consultant; b. St. Louis, June 14, 1938; d. Norman Leonard and Ethel (Silver) Mistachkin; m. Malcolm P. Cooper, Aug. 25, 1962 (div. June 1977); children: Lawrence, Edward, Marcus; m. Edward Lieberman, Apr. 1992. BS, U. Wis., 1959; MA, N.Y. Inst. Tech., 1992. Media buyer Lennen and Newell, Los Angeles, 1959-61; advt. mgr. Hartfield-Zodys, Los Angeles, 1961-62, Haggarty's, L.A., 1962-63; sales rep. Abbott Labs., Bklyn., 1974-75; edn. dir. N.Y. and N.J. Regional Transp. Program, N.Y.C., 1975-78; account exec. Med. Edn. Dynamics, Woodbridge, N.J., 1978-79; dir. program devel. Kallir, Phillips & Ross Info. Media, N.Y.C., 1979-81; exec. v.p. sales and mktg. Audio Visual Med. Mktg., N.Y.C., 1981-85; exec. v.p. Park Row Pubs./John Wiley & Sons Med. Div., N.Y.C., 1985-88; pres., prin. Park Row Pubs., N.Y.C., 1988-91; healthcare mktg. communications cons., Southampton, N.Y., 1991—; cons., prof. comms. and speech N.Y. Inst. Tech., 1991-95; exec. sec. Cardiopulmonary Bypass Consensus Panel, 1993—; cons. Am. Acad. Physician Assts., Washington, 1986-87, Am. Soc. Anesthesiologists, Chgo., 1986-88, Am. Acad. Family Physicians, 1987-91, Am. Psychiat. Assn., 1988, Am. Coll. Gen. Practitioners, 1988, N.Am. Soc. pacing and Electrophysiology, 1988-91, Internat. Immunocompromised Host Soc., 1996—. Editor pub. med. papers, med. films, med. jours. for pharmaceutical cos.; pub. CME Press. Mem. Am. Women in Radio and TV, Soc. Tchrs. Family Medicine (cons.), Pharm. Advt. Council, Nat. Council Jewish Women, Hadassah. Avocations: tennis, writing fiction, classical piano. Home and Office: 41 Barkers Island Rd Southampton NY 11968-2702

LIEBERMAN, CHARLES, economist; b. Landsburg, Bavaria, Germany, July 25, 1948; s. Leo and Tola (Melcer) L.; m. Anne Rosenberg, Aug. 26, 1972; children: David, Michael, Jeremy. BS, MIT, 1970; AM in Econs., U. Pa., 1972, PhD in Econs., 1974. Asst. prof. U. Md., College Park, 1974-79; vis. assoc. prof. Northwestern U., Evanston, Ill., 1978-79; economist Fed. Res. Bank N.Y., N.Y.C., 1979-81; sr. economist Morgan Stanley, N.Y.C., 1981-83; v.p., sr. economist Shearson Lehman Bros., N.Y.C., 1983-86; mng. dir., dir. fin. market rsch. Chem. Securities Inc./Mfrs. Hanover Securities Corp., N.Y.C., 1986-96; chief economist The Global Bank, Chase Manhattan Bank, 1996—; econs. commentator CNBC. Author: (newsletter) Market Commentary; contbr. articles to profl. jours. Sgt. U.S. Army Res., 1970-76. Stonier fellow, 1973, Fellow NSF, 1971. Mem. Forecasters Club N.Y. (treas. 1987-89, v.p. 1990-91, pres. 1991-92), Money Marketeers NYU (bd. govs., v.p., pres. 1992-93). Jewish. Avocations: tennis, skiing, classical music. Office: Chase Securities 270 Park Ave New York NY 10017-2014 *Work hard, play hard, and enjoy life.*

LIEBERMAN, EDWARD JAY, lawyer; b. Evansville, Ind., Apr. 8, 1946; s. Heiman George and Anna Sharp (Blacker) L.; m. Ellen Ackerman Wequsen, June 1, 1969; 1 child: Laura Amy. BSBA, Washington U., St. Louis, 1968, JD, 1971. Bar: Mo. 1971. Jr. ptnr. Bryan Cave, St. Louis, 1972-76; assoc. counsel 1st Nat. Bank in St. Louis, 1976-80; ptnr. Lowenhaupt, Chasnoff, Armstrong & Mellitz, St. Louis, 1980-84, Husch & Eppenberger, St. Louis, 1984—. Mem. ABA, Mo. Bar, Bar Assn. Met. St. Louis, Am. Coll. Mortgage Attys., Nat. Health Care Lawyers Assn. Office: Husch & Eppenberger 100 N Broadway Ste 1300 Saint Louis MO 63102-2706

LIEBERMAN, ELLIOTT, urologist; b. Paterson, N.J., May 14, 1951; s. Benjamin and Henrietta (Reback) L.; children: Brian Howard, Dana Elyse. BA in Biochemistry cum laude with distinction, Cornell U., 1972; MD, SUNY, Bklyn., 1976. Diplomate Am. Bd. Urology. Intern, gen. resident in surgery Mt. Sinai Hosp., N.Y.C., 1976-78; resident in urology SUNY-Downstate Med. Ctr., Bklyn., 1978-81; active attending staff North Shore U. Hosp., various cities, N.Y.; co-chief divsn. urology North Shore U. Hosp., Plainview, N.Y., 1992—; mem. adv. bd. Vis. Nurse Svc. N.Y.; mem. quality assurance com. White Oaks Nursing Home, Woodbury, N.Y. Mem. AMA, Med. Soc. State N.Y., Nassau County Med. Soc., N.Y. State Urol. Soc., Alpha Omega Alpha. Avocations: jogging, wine, music. Office: 875 Old Country Rd Ste 301 Plainview NY 11803-4934

LIEBERMAN, FREDRIC, ethnomusicologist, educator; b. N.Y.C., Mar. 1, 1940; s. Stanley and Bryna (Mason L.). MusB, U. Rochester, 1962; MA in Ethnomusicology, U. Hawaii, 1965; PhD in Music, UCLA, 1977; diploma in Electronics, Cleve. Inst. Electronics, 1973; cert. Inst. for Ednl. Mgmt., Harvard U., 1984. Asst. prof. music Brown U., Providence, 1968-75; assoc. prof. U. Wash., Seattle, 1975-83, chmn. dir. ethnomusicology, 1977-80, dir. sch. music, 1981-83; prof. U. Calif., Santa Cruz, 1983—, dir. divsn. arts, 1983-85, provost Porter Coll., 1983-85, chmn. dept. music, 1988-92; expert witness and forensic musicology cons. Virgin Records and others, 1991—; fieldworker, Taiwan and Japan, 1963-64, Sikkim, winter 1970, Madras, India, winters 1977, 78, 82, 83; mem. folk arts panel Nat. Endowment for Arts, 1977-80, internat. panel, 1979-80; panelist basic rsch. divsn. NEH, 1982-84, Calif. Arts Coun., 1993, Mass. Cultural Coun., 1995; fieldworker, presenter Smithsonian Instn. Festival Am. Folklife, 1978-82; reviewer Ctr. for Scholarly Comm. with China, 1979-91; exch. lectr. U. Warsaw, Poland, spring 1980; co-dir. summer seminar for coll. tchrs. NEH, 1977; dir. Am. Mus. Heritage Found., 1991-96. Author: Chinese Music: An Annotated Bibliography, 1970, 2d edit, 1979, A Chinese Zither Tutor: The Mei-An Ch-in-P'u, 1983, (with Mickey Hart) Drumming at the Edge of Magic, 1990, Planet Drum: A Celebration of Percussion and Rhythm, 1991, Lou Harrison: Composing a World, 1997; editor: (with Fritz A. Kuttner) Perspectives on Asian Music: Essays in Honor of Lawrence Picken, 1975; gen. editor Garland Bibliographies in Ethnomusicology, 1980-86; mem. editl. bd. Musica Asiatica, 1984—; contbr. numerous articles and revs. to profl. publs.; composer: Suite for Piano, 1964, Sonatina for Piano, 1964, Two Short String Quartets, 1966, Leaves of Brass (for brass quartet), 1967, Psalm 136: By the Rivers of Babylon (for chorus), 1971; records include China I: String Instruments, 1969, China II: Amoy Music, 1971, Music of Sikkim, 1975; ethnomusicology cons. 360 Degrees Prodns., 1988—; filmer, editor (with Michael Moore) Traditional Music and Dance of Sikkim, Parts I and II, 1976; prodr., dir., editor videotape Documenting Traditional Performance, 1978, South Indian Classical Music House Concert, 1994. Mem. exec. bd. Pub. Radio Sta. KRAB-FM, Seattle, 1977-78; mem. King County Arts Commn., Seattle, 1977-80. Grantee Nat. Endowment for the Arts, 1978, NEH, 1978, 80, 95-97, N.Y. State Regents fellow, 1958-62, East-West Ctr. fellow and travel grantee, 1962-65, UCLA Chancellor's tchg. fellow, 1965-69,

John D. Rockefeller 3d Fund rsch. fellow, 1970-71. Mem. NARAS, Soc. for Ethnomusicology (editor Ethnomusicology 1977-81, nat. coun. 1970-72, 74-76, 78-81, 83-86), Soc. for Asian Music (editorial bd. Asian Music 1968-77, editor publs. series 1968-83), Assn. Rsch. Chinese Music (mem. adv. bd. 1987—), Coll. Music Soc. (nat. coun. 1973-75, exec. bd. 1974-75, 76-77), Conf. on Chinese Oral and Performing Lit. (exec. bd. 1971-74, 78-80), ASCAP, Internat. Coun. Traditional Music, Am. Musical Heritage Found. (treas. 1991-96), Phi Mu Alpha Sinfonia. Avocations: amateur radio N7AX, photography. Office: U Calif Porter Coll Santa Cruz CA 95064

LIEBERMAN, GAIL FORMAN, investment company executive; b. Phila., May 26, 1943; d. Joseph and Rita (Groder) Forman. BA in Physics and Math., Temple U., 1964, MBA in Fin., 1977. Dir. internat. fin. Standard Brands Inc., N.Y.C., 1977-79; staff v.p. fin. and capital planning RCA Corp., 1979-82; CFO, exec. v.p. Scali McCabe Sloves, Inc., 1982-93; v.p. finance, CFO, mng. dir. Moody's Investors Svc., N.Y.C., 1994-96; CFO TFPPG Thomson Corp., Boston, 1996—; bd. dirs. Allied Devices, Inc. Bd. dirs. Vineyard Theater Group, N.Y.C. Mem. Fin. Execs. Inst. Office: Thomson TFPPG 22 Pittsburgh St Boston MA 02210

LIEBERMAN, GERALD J., statistics educator; b. N.Y.C., Dec. 31, 1925; s. Joseph and Ida (Margolis) L.; m. Helen Herbert, Oct. 27, 1950; children—Janet, Joanne, Michael, Diana. B.S. in Mech. Engring., Cooper Union, 1948; A.M. in Math. Stats., Columbia U., 1949; Ph.D., Stanford U., 1953. Math. statistician Nat. Bur. Standards, 1949-50; mem. faculty Stanford U., 1953—, prof. statistics and indsl. engring., 1959-67, prof. statistics and operations research, 1967—, chmn. dept. operations research, 1967-75, assoc. dean Sch. Humanities and Scis., 1975-77, acting v.p. and provost, 1979, vice provost, 1977-85, dean research, 1977-80, dean grad. studies and research, 1980-85, provost, 1992-93; cons. to govt. and industry, 1953—. Author: (with A.H. Bowker) Engineering Statistics, 1959, 2d edit., 1972, (with F.S. Hillier) Introduction to Operations Research, 1967, 6th edit., 1995. Ctr. Advanced Studies in Behavioral Scis. fellow, 1985-86. Fellow Am. Statis. Assn., Inst. Math. Statistics, Am. Soc. Quality Control (Shewhart medal 1972), AAAS; mem. Nat. Acad. Engring., Inst. Mgmt. Sci. (pres. 1980-81), Ops. Research Soc. Am., Sigma Xi, Pi Tau Sigma. Home: 811 San Francisco Ter Stanford CA 94305-1021

LIEBERMAN, HARVEY MICHAEL, hepatologist, gastroenterologist, educator; b. N.Y.C., Feb. 24, 1949; s. Louis and Ellie (Miller) L.; m. Lewette Alexandra Fielding, Nov. 24, 1985. BA magna cum laude, NYU, 1972, MD, 1976. Intern Bronx (N.Y.) Mcpl. Hosp./Albert Einstein Coll. Medicine, N.Y.C., 1976-77, jr. and sr. resident, 1977-79; fellow in gastroenterology and liver disease Albert Einstein Coll. Medicine, 1979-81, rsch. assoc. Liver Rsch. Ctr., 1983; asst. prof. Albert Einstein Coll. Medicine, Bronx, N.Y., 1984-86; dir. gastroenterology Gouverneur Hosp., N.Y.C., 1986-90; asst. chief gastroenterology Lenox Hill Hosp., N.Y.C., 1992—, founding dir. liver clinic, 1992—; dir. hepatology program, 1994—; ednl. coord. Lenox Hill Hosp., N.Y.C., 1995—; clin. asst. prof. NYU Sch. Medicine, 1986-93, clin. assoc. prof., 1993—; prin. investigator Liver Rsch. Ctr. Albert Einstein Coll. Medicine, 1984-87, vis. scientist, 1992—; med. adv. bd. Crohn's and Colitis Found. of Am., Am. Liver Found., N.Y. chpts., 1987—; researcher in molecular biology of hepatitis B virus and relationship to viral infection and liver cancer. Author: Relationship of Hepatitis B Viral Infection in Serum to Viral Replication, 1983. Recipient Clin. Investigator award NIH, 1984-87. Fellow ACP, Am. Coll. Gastroenterology, N.Y. Acad. Gastroenterology (pres. 1990-91). Achievements include development of assay to measure DNA of hepatitis B virus directly in serum; first to note its greater sensitivity in measuring active viral replication liver disease compared to conventional serological tests. Office: 345 E 37th St New York NY 10016-3217

LIEBERMAN, JAMES, federal agency administrator; b. Providence, Nov. 24, 1945. BSME, U. R.I., 1967; MS in Thermal Engring., Cornell U., 1969; JD with honors, George Washington U., 1974. Bar: Va. 1974, D.C. 1976. Engr. Combustion Engring. Co., Windsor, Conn., 1967; devel. engr. Eastman Kodak Co., Rochester, N.Y., 1968-71; legal asst. Berlin, Roisman & Kessler, Washington, 1973; law clk. McKean, Whitehead & Wilson, Washington, 1973-74; atty. Office of Exec. Legal Dir. NRC, Washington, 1974-81, dir. enforcement staff Office Inspection and Enforcement, 1982, chief counsel for regional ops. and enforcement, 1982-86, asst. gen. for enforcement, chief counsel regional ops., 1986-87, dir. Office of Enforcement, 1987—. Contbr. articles to profl. publs. John McMullen fellow, 1967-69. Office: NRC Office of Enforcement Washington DC 20555

LIEBERMAN, JOSEPH I., senator; b. Stamford, Conn., Feb. 24, 1942; s. Henry and Marcia (Manger) L.; m. Hadassah Freilich, Mar. 20, 1983; children: Matthew, Rebecca, Ethan, Hana. B.A., Yale U., 1964, J.D., 1967. Bar: Conn. 1967. Mem. Conn. Senate, 1971-81, senate majority leader, 1975-81; ptnr. Lieberman, Segaloff & Wolfson, New Haven, 1972-83; atty. gen. State of Conn., Hartford, 1983-89; U.S. senator from Conn., 1989—; mem. armed svcs. com., environment and pub. works com., govtl. affairs com., small bus. com., senate Dem. policy com. Author: The Power Broker, 1966, The Scorpion and the Tarantula, 1970, The Legacy, 1981, Child Support in America, 1986. Democrat. Jewish. Office: 706 Hart Senate Office Bldg Washington DC 20510

LIEBERMAN, LAURENCE, poet, educator; b. Detroit, Feb. 16, 1935; s. Nathan and Anita (Cohen) L.; m. Bernice Clair Braun, June 17, 1956; children—Carla, Deborah, Isaac. BA, U. Mich., 1956, MA in English, 1958; postgrad., U. Calif.-Berkeley. Prof. English Coll. V.I., 1964-68; prof. English and creative writing U. Ill., Urbana, 1968—; U. Ill. Ctr. for Advanced Study Creative Writing fellow, Japan, 1971-72. Author: The Unblinding, 1968, The Achievement of James Dickey, 1969, The Osprey Suicides, 1973, Unassigned Frequencies: American Poetry in Review (1964-77), 1977, God's Measurements, 1980, Eros At the World Kite Pageant, The Mural of Wakeful Sleep, 1985, (poems) The Creole Mephistopheles, 1989, The Best American Poetry, 1991 (award), New and Selected Poems, 1962-92), 1993, The St. Kitts. Monkey Feuds, 1995, Beyond the Muse of Memory: Essays on Contemporary Poets, 1995, Dark Songs: Slave House and Synagogue, 1996; poetry editor poetry books program U. Ill. Press, 1970—; contbr. poetry to lit. jours., popular mags. Recipient award for Best Poems of 1968, Nat. Endowment for Arts, 1969, Jerome P. Shestack award Am. Poetry Rev., 1986; creative writing fellow U. Ill. Ctr. for Advanced Study, Nat. Endowment Arts, 1986-87. Office: U Ill English Dept 608 S Wright St Urbana IL 61801-3613

LIEBERMAN, LEONARD, retired supermarket executive; b. Elizabeth, N.J., Jan. 23, 1929; s. Joseph Harry and Bessie (Bernstein) L.; m. Arlene Ginsberg; children: Elizabeth Susan, Nancy Ellen, Anne Judith. B.A., Yale U., 1950; J.D., Columbia U., 1953; grad., Advanced Mgmt. Program, Harvard U., 1970. Bar: N.J. bar 1954. Assoc., then partner firms in Newark and Orange, 1954-65; v.p., gen. counsel, dir. Supermarkets Operating Co., Union, N.J., 1963-66; v.p., gen. counsel Supermarkets Gen. Corp., Woodbridge, N.J., 1966-69, sr. v.p., 1969-81, chmn. Pathmark div., 1977-79, exec. asst. to pres., 1979-80, chief adminstrv. and fin. officer, 1980-82, exec. v.p., 1981-82, pres., 1982-87, chief exec. officer, 1983-87, chmn., 1986-87; bd. dirs. Outlet Comm., Inc., chmn., CEO, 1991; bd. dirs. Celestial Seasonings, Inc., Republic N.Y. Corp., La Petite Acad., Inc., Sonic Industries; instr. Am. Inst. Banking, 1954-55; co-chmn. joint industry com. on uniform comm. sys. for the grocery industry, 1978-81, com. to improve shipping container design, 1984-86; co-chmn. Gov. Florio's task force on local partnerships, 1991-92. Trustee Jewish Counseling and Svc. Agy. Essex County, 1968-73; trustee Fund for N.J., 1987—, chmn., 1997—; trustee Ctr. for Analysis of Pub. Issues, 1987-97, chmn. 1990-92; trustee Newark Beth Israel Med. Ctr., Newark, 1971-82, treas., 1972-73, pres., 1973-78, hon. pres., 1982—; bd. dirs. Newark Performing Arts Corp., 1987-91; commr. N.J. Pub. Broadcasting Authority, 1982-86, 1st v.p., 1983-86; chmn. N.J. Acad. for Aquatic Scis., Inc., 1989-92; mem. coun. for N.J. affairs, Princeton U., 1988—; bd. regents Seton Hall U., 1989-90; trustee, mem. exec. com., treas. N.J. Ctr. for Performing Arts, 1989—; mem. N.J. com. Regional Plan Assn., 1982-96; task force chmn. Gov.'s Mgmt. Improvement Program, 1982-83; mem. Partnership for N.J., 1983-95; assoc. gov. Hebrew U., 1983-84, bd. govs., 1984-90; bd. dirs. Ctr. Excellence in Govt., 1981-83; trustee Victim Svc. Agy., 1986-96; mem. N.J. State Planning Commn., 1986-90; bd. dirs. Ctr. for Hosp. Care Strategies, Wash., 1996—. Recipient Justice Louis D. Brandeis Humanitarian award N.J. region Zionist Orgn. Am., 1977. Mem. Food Mktg. Inst. (dir. exec. com. 1983-87), Regional Plan Assn. (dir. 1985-95). Office: 1 Gateway Ctr Ste 106 Newark NJ 07102-5311

LIEBERMAN, LESTER ZANE, engineering company executive; b. Newark, July 4, 1930; s. Herman P. and Cecile A. (Ashenfeld) L.; m. Judith Mazor, Aug. 11, 1957; children—Susan, Jane. BS in Mech. Engring., Newark Coll. Engring., 1951, postgrad., 1953-58; DHL (hon.), Clarkson U., 1991. Registered profl. engr., N.J., Pa. Pres. Crest Engring. Inc., Newark, 1955-60; chmn., pres. Atmos Engring. Co. Inc., Kenilworth, N.J., 1960-78; pres., chief exec. officer Clarkson Industries, Inc., N.Y.C., 1978-90; bd. dirs. Lazard Fund, Cives Steel Corp. Trustee Clarkson U., Potsdam, N.Y.; chmn. Beth Israel Med. Ctr., Newark, 1970-96, MBI Healthcare Found., Inc., 1996—. Named Alumnus of Yr., Newark Coll. Engring., 1980. Mem. ASHRAE (pres. 1964-65), Nat. Soc. Profl. Engrs., N.J. Soc. Profl. Engrs., Assn. Energy Engrs., Am. Acad. Environ. Engrs. (diplomate), Mason., Mountain Ridge Country Club (N.J.), Stockbridge Country Club (Mass.), Cornell Club (N.Y.), Morristown Club, Tau Beta Pi (Key award 1982). Jewish. Lodge: Masons. Avocations: skiing, sailing, tennis, golf. Home: Spring Valley Rd Morristown NJ 07960-7011 Office: 70 S Orange Ave Ste 110 Livingston NJ 07039-4903

LIEBERMAN, LOUIS (KARL LIEBERMAN), artist; b. Bklyn., May 7, 1944; s. Abraham and Jeannette (Feinberg) L. BFA, R.I. Sch. Design, 1969; cert., Bklyn. Mus. Art Sch., 1964; BA, Bklyn. Coll., 1966. Adj. lectr. Bklyn. Coll., 1971-78, Lehman Coll., Bronx, N.Y., 1972-75; vis. artist Ill. State U., Normal, 1978, Hamilton Coll., Clinton, N.Y., 1982. One-man shows include Vancouver Art Gallery, B.C., Can., 1969, James Yu Gallery, N.Y.C., 1973, 74, Nina Freudenheim Gallery, Buffalo, 1976, Root Art Ctr., Hamilton Coll., Clinton, N.Y., 1980, Harm Bouckaert Gallery, N.Y.C., 1981, John Davis Gallery, Akron, Ohio, 1983, 85, Columbus Mus. Art, Ohio, 1983, John Davis Gallery, N.Y.C., 1986; group shows include Aldrich Mus. Contemporary Art, Ridgefield, Conn., 1973, 74, Johnson Mus. Art, Ithaca, N.Y., 1981, Fine Arts Mus. L.I., Hempstead, N.Y., 1982, Cleve. Inst. Art, 1982, Met. Mus. Art, N.Y.C., 1983, Byer Mus. Art, Evanston, Ill., 1982, Visual Arts Ctr., Beer-Sheva, Israel, 1985, Kunsthauses, Zurich, Switzerland, McNay Art Mus., San Antonio, Phila. Mus. of Art, 1988, Erie (Pa.) Art Mus., 1988, Art Mus. of Santa Cruz, Calif., 1988, Hunter Mus., Chattanooga, 1989, others; represented in permanent collections including Kenan Ctr., Lockport, N.Y., Aldridge Mus. Contemporary Art, Ridgefield, Conn., Met. Mus. Art, N.Y.C., Phila. Mus. Art, Stamford (Conn.) Mus., Bklyn. Mus., Mus. Fine Arts, Budapest, Hungary, Istvan Kiraly Mus., Budapest, Ackland Art Mus., Chapel Hill, N.C.; art critic N.Y. Arts Jour., 1978-79. Recipient Sculpture award Creative Artist Pub. Service Found., 1971-72, Graphics award Creative Artist Pub. Svc. Found., 1980-81, Graphics award N.Y. Found. Arts, 1984-85; visual arts fellow Nat. Endowment for Arts, 1979-80; Pollack-Krasner Found. fellow, 1987; Adolf and Esther Gottlieb Found. grantee, 1989.

LIEBERMAN, MARK JOEL, lawyer; b. Chgo., Apr. 12, 1949; s. Eugene and Pearl Naomi (Feldman) L.; children: Amy, Kevin. BA, DePaul U., 1971, JD, 1974. Bar: Ill. 1974, Calif. 1980, Tex. 1989. House counsel Mercantile Fin. Corp., Chgo., 1974-80; sr. atty. Assocs. Comml. Corp., Chgo., 1981-84; v.p., asst. gen. counsel Assocs. Comml. Corp., Dallas, 1984—. Mem. ABA, Calif. State Bar Assn. Republican. Jewish. Avocation: woodcarving. Office: Assocs Comml Corp 300 E Carpenter Fwy Irving TX 75062

LIEBERMAN, MICHAEL A., electrical engineer, educator; b. N.Y.C., Oct. 3, 1940; married; two children. BS, MS, MIT, Cambridge, 1962; PhD, MIT, 1966. Prof. Electronic Rsch. Labs. U. Calif., Berkeley, 1977-80; asst. prof. biochem. dept. nutrition Harvard Sch. Pub. Health, Boston, 1981-83; assoc. prof. molecular genetics, biochemistry & microbiology Coll. Medicine U. Cin., 1983—; mem. study sect. cellular biology & physiology NIH, 1986-89. Fellow IEEE (award for contbns. to rsch. in plasma-assisted materials processing, nonlinear dynamics and controlled fusion). Office: Univ California Berkeley Electronics Rsch Lab 253 Cory Hall Berkeley CA 94720-1771*

LIEBERMAN, PAUL, aeronautical engineer, engineering research company executive; b. Bklyn., Dec. 25, 1932; s. Benjamin and Frances (Firestone) L.; m. Ilse-M.; children by previous marriage—Naomi Ruth, Leah, Micah Benjamin. B.S. in Aero. Engring., NYU, 1954; M.S. in Aero. Engring., Princeton U., 1956; Ph.D. in Applied Mechanics, Ill. Inst. Tech., 1964. Engr. Bell Aircraft Corp., Buffalo, 1954; sr. scientist Ill. Inst. Tech. Research Inst., Chgo., 1957-69, project engr. devel. of instrumentation; sr. project mgr. TRW, Redondo Beach, Calif., 1969-81; chief scientist Nat. Tech. Systems, Saugus, Calif., 1981—. Contbr. numerous articles on thermodynamics, applied mechanics, optics and air force systems to profl. jours. Author reports in field. Served to 1st lt. USAF, 1955-57. Guggenheim fellow, 1954-55. Mem. Sigma Xi. Jewish. Home: 19815 Mildred Ave Torrance CA 90503-1121 Office: Nat Tech Systems 1536 E Valencia Dr Fullerton CA 92831-4734

LIEBERMAN, SEYMOUR, biochemistry educator emeritus; b. N.Y.C., Dec. 1, 1916; s. Samuel D. and Sadie (Levin) L.; m. Sandra Spar, June 5, 1944; 1 child, Paul B. B.S., Bklyn. Coll., 1936; M.S., U. Ill., 1937; Ph.D. (Rockefeller scholar 1939-41), Stanford U., 1941; Traveling fellow, U. Basle, Switzerland, Eidgenoess. Tech. Hochschule, Zurich, Switzerland, 1946-47. Chemist Schering Corp., 1938-39; spl. research asso. Harvard U., 1941-45; assoc. mem. Sloan-Kettering Inst., 1945-50; mem. faculty Columbia Coll. Physicians and Surgeons, N.Y.C., 1950—; prof. biochemistry Columbia Coll. Physicians and Surgeons, 1950-87, prof. emeritus, 1987—, vice provost, 1988, assoc. dir. office sci. and tech., 1991—; assoc. dean Inst. Health Scis. St. Luke's Roosevelt Hosp. Ctr., 1984-90; pres. Inst. Health Scis., St. Luke's Roosevelt Hosp. Center, 1981-97; Pfizer traveling fellow McGill U., 1968; Syntex lectr. Mexican Endocrine Soc., 1970; mem. Am. Cancer Soc. panel steroids, 1945-49, hormones, 1949-50, mem. com. pathogenesis of cancer, 1957-60; mem. endocrine study sect. NIH, 1959-63, chmn., 1963-65, mem. gen. clin. research centers, 1967-71; mem. med. adv. com. Population Council, 1961-73; mem. endocrinology panel Cancer Chemotherapy Nat. Service Center, 1958-62; cons. WHO human reprodn. unit, 1972-74, Ford Found., 1974-77; hon. pres. 6th Internat. Congress on Hormonal Steroids, 1982. Editor Jour. Clin. Endocrinology and Metabolism, 1963-67, editorial bd., 1958-63, 68-70, Jour. Biol. Chemistry, 1975-80; contbr. articles to profl. jours. Recipient Disting. Alumnus award Bklyn. Coll., 1971, Disting. Svc. award Columbia U., 1991. Fellow N.Y. Acad. Scis., NAS; mem. Am. Soc. Biol. Chemists, Am. Chem. Soc., Internat. Soc. Endocrinology (U.S. del. central com.), Endocrine Soc. (Ciba award 1952, Koch award 1970, council 1970-73, pres. 1974-75, Roussel prize 1984, Dale medal 1986, Boehringer-Mannheim award lectr. 1992), Harvey Soc. Home: 515 E 72nd St New York NY 10021-4032 Office: 432 W 58th St New York NY 10019-1102

LIEBERMAN-CLINE, NANCY, retired basketball player; b. Bklyn., July 1, 1958. Grad., Old Dominion U. Basketball player Lady Monarchs, Dallas Diamonds, Springfield Fame, 1986-87, Washington Gens., 1987-88. Named to Basketball Hall of Fame, 1996, 3 time All-Am.; recipient Wade Trophy Winner, Boderick Cup Winner Top Female Athlete, Silver Medal U.S. Olympics, 1976; mem. Women's Am. Basketball Championship team, 1985; first female to play men's profl. league, first female inducted to N.Y. C. Basketball Hall Fame; youngest basketball player to medal in Olympics. Office: c/o Basketball Hall Fame PO Box 179 Springfield MA 01101-0179

LIEBERMANN, LOWELL, composer, pianist, conductor; b. N.Y.C., Feb. 22, 1961. D in Musical Arts, Juilliard Sch.; studied with David Diamond, Vincent Persichetti, Jacob Lateiner, Laszlo Halasz. Composer (orchestra) War Songs for Bass Voice and Orch. Op. 7, 1981, Concertino for Cello and Chamber Orch. Op. 8, 1982, Symphony No. 1 Op. 9 (BMI award, 1st prize Juilliard Orch. Competition 1987), 1982, Three Poems of Stephen Crane Op. 11 for baritone, string orch., two horns, harp (Devora Nadworney award Nat. Fed. Music Clubs 1986) 1983, Concerto No. 1 for Piano and Orch. Op. 12, 1983, Sechs Gesaenge Nach Gedichten Von Nelly Sachs Op. 18 for soprano and orch., 1986, The Domain of Arnheim Op. 33, 1990, Concerto No. 2 for Piano and Orch. Op. 36, 1992, Flute Concerto Op. 39, 1992, Revelry for Orch. Op. 47, 1995, Concerto for Flute, Harp, and Orch. Op. 48, 1995; (opera) The Picture of Dorian Gray Op. 45, 1995, (chorus) Two Choral Elegies Op. 2 for SATB a capella (Fred Waring Choral award Nat. Fed. Music 1978), 1977, Missa Brevis Op. 15 for SATB chorus, tenor and baritone solos, organ (3d prize Ch. and Artist Composers Competition 1987), 1985; (piano solo) Piano Sonata Op. 1 (Outstanding Composition award Yamaha Music Found. 1982, 1st prize Nat. Composition Contest Music Tchrs. Nat. Assn. 1978), 1977, Piano Sonata No. 2 Sonata Notturna Op. 10, 1983, Variations on a Theme by Anton Bruckner Op. 19, 1987, Nocturne No. 1 Op. 20, 1987, Four Apparitions Op. 17, 1987, others; (chamber music) Sonata for Violoncello and Piano Op. 3, 1978, Two Pieces for Violin and Viola Op. 4, 1978, Sonata for Viola and Piano Op. 13 (1st Place Victor Herbert/ASCAP awards Nat. Fed. Music Clubs 1986, Brian Israel prize Soc. for New Music 1986), 1984, Sonata for Contrabass and Piano Op. 24, 1987, Fantasy on a Fugue by J.S. Bach Op. 27 for flute, oboe, clarinet, horn, bassoon, piano, 1989, Quintet for Piano and Strings Op. 34 for piano and string quartet, 1989, others; also organ music, voice and piano. Mem. ASCAP, Corp. Yaddo (dir.). Democrat. Office: 820 W End Ave Apt 10B New York NY 10025-5384

LIEBERSON, STANLEY, sociologist, educator; b. Montreal, Que., Can., Apr. 20, 1933; s. Jack and Ida (Cohen) L.; m. Patricia Ellen Beard, 1960; children—Rebecca, David, Miriam, Rachel. Student, Bklyn. Coll., 1950-52; MA, U. Chgo., 1958, PhD, 1960; MA (hon.), Harvard U., 1988; LHD (hon.), U. Ariz., 1993. Asso. dir. Iowa Urban Community Research Center, U. Iowa, 1959-61, instr., asst. prof. sociology, 1959-61; asst. prof. sociology U. Wis., 1961-63, asso. prof., 1963-66, prof., 1966-67; prof. sociology U. Wash., 1967-71, dir. Center Studies Demography and Ecology, 1968-71; prof. sociology U. Chgo., 1971-74, assoc. dir. Population Research Center, 1971-74; prof. sociology U. Ariz., Tucson, 1974-83, head dept., 1976-79; prof. sociology U. Calif., Berkeley, 1983-88; prof. sociology Harvard U., 1988-91, Abbott Lawrence Lowell prof. sociology, 1991—; vis. prof. Stanford U., summer 1970; Claude Bissell disting. vis. prof. U. Toronto, 1979-80; mem. com. on sociolinguistics Social Sci. Research Council, 1964-70; mem. sociology panel NSF, 1978-81. Author: (with others) Metropolis and Region, 1960, Ethnic Patterns in American Cities, 1963; editor: Explorations in Sociolinguistics, 1967, (with Beverly Duncan) Metropolis and Region in Transition, 1970, Language and Ethnic Relations in Canada, 1970, A Piece of the Pie, 1980, Language Diversity and Language Contact, 1981, Making It Count, 1985, (with Mary C. Waters) From Many Strands, 1988; assoc. editor: Social Problems, 1965-67, Sociol. Methods and Research, 1971—; editorial cons. Sociol. Inquiry, 1965-67; adv. editor: Am. Jour. Sociology, 1969-74; editorial bd. Lang. in Society, 1972-74, Internat. Jour. Sociology of Lang, 1974—, Canadian Jour. Sociology, 1975—, Social Forces, 1980-83; adv. council Sociol. Abstracts, 1972-73, Language Problems and Language Planning, 1984-87; mem. editorial com. Ann. Rev. Sociology, 1992-96. Recipient Colver Rosenberger Ednl. prize, 1960; Guggenheim fellow, 1972-73, fellow Ctr. for Advanced Study in Behavioral Scis., 1995-96. Fellow NAS, Am. Acad. Arts and Scis.; mem. Am. Sociol. Assn. (coun. mem. 1985-87, pres. 1990-91, Disting. Contbn. to Scholarship award 1982), Am. Sociol. Found. (trustee 1992-96), Population Assn. Am. (dir. 1969-72), Internat. Population Union, Pacific Sociol. Assn. (v.p. 1984-85, pres. 1986-87), Sociol. Rsch. Assn. (exec. com. 1976-81, pres. 1981), Am. Name Soc., Oakland Sch. Sociology. Home: 5 Mystic Lake Dr Arlington MA 02174-2305 Office: Harvard U Dept Sociology William James Hall Cambridge MA 02138

LIEBERT, ARTHUR EDGAR, retired hospital administrator; b. Milw., Nov. 18, 1930; married. B, Lake Forest Coll; MHA, Northwestern U. Adminstrv. resident Rochester (N.Y.) Gen. Hosp., 1953-54, adminstrv. asst., 1954, asst. adminstr., 1957-65, assoc. dir., 1965-70, exec. dir., 1970-73, pres., 1973-93; pres. Greater Rochester Health Care, 1993-95; co-pres. Greater Rochester Health Sys. Inc., Rochester, 1995-96; bd. dirs. Rochester Gen. Hosp. Mem. Am. Hosp. Assn. (del.), Hosp. Assn. N.Y. (del.). Home: 611 Dewitt Rd Webster NY 14580-1333

LIEBERT, LARRY STEVEN, journalist; b. St. Louis, Apr. 30, 1950; s. Charles Bernard and Tobie Lee (Londe) L.; m. Evelyn Ann Hsu, Mar. 26, 1983; children: Rachel Hsu, Emily Hsu. BA in Polit. Sci., Stanford U., 1972. Reporter San Francisco Chronicle, 1972-73, urban affairs reporter, 1973-75, Sacramento bur. chief, 1975-78, polit. writer, 1978-79, chief polit. writer, 1979-87, Washington bur. chief, 1987-90; news editor, weekly reporter Congl. Quar., Washington, 1990-94, editor CQ Monitor, 1994—; Washington columnist Calif. Jour., Sacramento, 1987-94. Office: Congl Quar 1414 22nd St NW Washington DC 20037-1003

LIEBERT, PETER S., pediatric surgeon, consultant; b. N.Y.C., Feb. 27, 1936; s. Louis M. and Sonia F. (Wolfe) L.; m. Phyllis J. Farkas, Sept. 6, 1960 (div. 1982); 1 child, Peter S., Jr.; m. Mary Ann Rosenfeld, Jan. 22, 1984; 1 stepchild, Lewis Charles. AB, Princeton U., 1957; MD, Harvard Med. Sch., Boston, 1961. Diplomate Am. Bd. Surgery; cert. of spl. competence pediat. surgery. Practice medicine specializing in pediatric surgery Eastchester, N.Y., 1961—; clin. assoc. prof. surgery Columbia U. Coll. Physicians and Surgeons. Author: Color Atlas of Pediatric Surgery; editor: Emergency and Office Pediatrics., Edtl Bd. Jour. Peddiatric Surgery. Dir. Med. Network for Missing Children. Home: 67 Pleasant Ridge Rd Harrison NY 10528-1232 Office: 270 White Plains Rd Eastchester NY 10707-4412

LIEBES, RAQUEL, import/export company executive, educator; b. San Salvador, El Salvador, Aug. 28, 1938; came to the U.S., 1952, naturalized, 1964; d. Ernesto Martin and Alice (Philip) L.; m. Richard Paisley Kinkade, June 2, 1962 (div. 1977); children: Kathleen Paisley, Richard Paisley Jr., Scott Philip. Exch. student, Radcliffe Coll., 1957; BA, Sarah Lawrence Coll., 1960; MEd, Harvard U., 1961; MA, Yale U., 1963, postgrad., 1963-65; PhD, Oxford (Eng.) U., 1994. Tchg. fellow in Spanish Sarah Lawrence Coll., Bronxville, N.Y., 1958-60; exchange student Radcliffe Coll., Cambridge, Mass., 1961; econ. tchg. fellow Yale U., New Haven, 1964-65, instr. Spanish dept., 1964-66; exec. stockholder Import Export Co., San Salvador, 1968-89, also bd. dirs.; adj. prof. Am. U., Washington, 1989-91, dept. fgn. lang. and linguistics dept. fgn. studies Georgetown U., Washington, 1989-93. Contbr. glossary of Spanish med. terms. Hon. consul Govt. of El Salvador, 1977-80; docent High Mus. of Art, Atlanta, 1972-77; vol. Grady Hosp., Atlanta, 1966-71; instr. Spanish for med. drs. Tucson Med. Ctr., 1966-71; chmn. Atlanta Coun. for Internat. Visitors, 1966-71; mem. Outreach Group on Latin Am., Washington, 1982-86; founding mem. John Kennedy Ctr. for Performing Arts, 1980—; mem. Folger/Shakespeare Libr., Smithsonian Inst., Agape, El Salvador. Econ. fellow Yale U., 1964-65; Corcoran Mus. Art fellow, 1984-85; Smithsonian Mus. awardee, 1981-96. Mem. MLA, Am. Biog. Inst. Rsch. Assn. (hon. consul of El Salvador, dep. gov. 1978-80, bd. advisors 1994), Jr. League of Washington, Harvard Club, Yale Club. Republican. Avocations: comparative literature, languages, international business, English literature, Shakespeare. Office: V I P Sal # 148 P O Box 52-5364 Miami FL 33152-5364 *Throughout my life, I have applied the tradition of ethics in each and every one of my activities and have expected. The self-same principle in each and everyone of those with whom I have surrounded myself. The persons I know, as well as writers I admire and love.*

LIEBIG, RICHARD ARTHUR, retired manufacturing company executive; b. Quincy, Ill., Sept. 2, 1923; s. Arthur William and Florence Ann (Parrott) L.; m. Peggy O. Shiley, Aug. 4, 1946; children: Lynn Margaret, Ann Kay. BS, U. Ill., 1949; LLD (hon.), Culver-Stockton Coll., 1989. With Moorman Mfg. Co., Quincy, 1949-88, credit mgr., 1958-60, mgr. fin. adminstrn., 1960-64, treas., 1960-76, bd. dirs., 1960-93, v.p. fin. adminstrn., 1964-75, sec., mem. exec. com., 1971-75, exec. v.p. fin., 1975-76, pres., COO, 1976-77, pres., CEO, 1977-84, chmn. bd., CEO, 1984-87, chmn. bd., 1987-88; bd. dirs. Quincy Soybean Co., 1961-93, sec., 1961-76, v.p., 1968-76, mem. exec. com., 1963-93; v.p. Moorman Co. Fund, 1960-75; mem. exec. com. Moorman Found., 1969-90, 1st v.p., 1972-80, pres., 1980-90, also bd. dirs. 1969-90; pres., mem. exec. com. CFM Found., 1990—, also bd. dirs.; mem. St. Louis adv. bd. Liberty Mut. Ins. Co., 1980, 93; mem. adv. coun. Coll. Commerce and Bus. Adminstrn. U. Ill., Urbana, 1974—; mem. exec. com. Convocom, 1983—, sec., 1990—, also bd. dirs. Mem. adv. coun. Culver-Stockton Coll., Canton, Mo., 1971-82, trustee, 1983—, mem. exec. com., chmn. bd. trustees, 1989—; vice chmn. Profit Sharing Coun. Am., 1979, bd. dirs., 1972-82; mem. Sch. Dist. 172 Bd. Edn., 1963-69, pres., 1969; trustee Quincy Found. for Quality Edn., 1989—; bd. dirs., treas. ednl. revolving fund Blessing Hosp., Quincy, 1963-85; mem. adv. bd. YWCA, 1984—; bd. dirs. Inst. Humane Studies, 1985—. With AUS, 1943-47. Paul Harris fellow, 1987, 97. Mem. Fin. Execs. Inst., Ill. MFrs. Assn. (bd. dirs. 1982-88), Ill. State C. of C. (bd. dirs. 1980-86), Indsl. Assn. Quincy (2nd v.p., mem. exec. com. 1969-71, 75-88, trustee Profit Sharing Rsch. Found. 1986-92), Rotary (bd. dirs. Quincy chpt.). Methodist. Home: 2311 Vermont St Quincy IL 62301-3163

LIEBLER, ARTHUR C., automotive executive; b. Pitts., June 19, 1942; s. Arthur Cyril and Frances (Coyle) L.; m. Nancy Elizabeth Cullen, Sept. 19, 1964; children: Molly, Katie, Patrick. AB in Journalism, Marquette U., 1964; postgrad., Wayne State U. Reporter WRJN Radio Racine Journal Times, Wis., 1964; jr. acct. exec. The Selz Orgn., Chgo., 1965-66; staff reporter, employer Ford Motor Co., Dearborn, Mich., 1966-67, corporate pub. rels. staff, 1967-76; sr. v.p. acct. mgmt. and supv. Ross Roy Inc., Detroit, Mich., 1976-80; dir. corp. mdse. Chrysler Corp., Detroit, 1980-82, dir. communications programs, 1982, gen. mktg. mgr., 1983-87, dir. mktg. svcs., 1987—. Bd. dirs. Common Ground (Drug Prevention) Birmingham Mich., 1966-70; committeeman Dem. Party Chectenham Township Pa., 1971-72; miscellaneous Sch. Bd. Activities, Birmingham Mich., 1974-77. Mem. Detroit Adcraft Club (accredited, bd. dirs.), Pub. Rels. Soc. Am. (bd. dirs.), Am Advt. Fedn. (bd. dirs.), Detroit Golf Club.

LIEBLER, EDWARD CHARLES, veterinarian, construction company executive; b. Brown City, Mich., Apr. 6, 1939; s. Harris D. and Golda Elfleda (Hollenbeck) L.; m. Carol Sue Kerrins, Sept. 10, 1960 (div. 1972); children: Juli Kristina, Edward Jae; m. Sharon D. Willis, Nov. 2, 1973 (div. 1985); m. Karla Christianson (div. 1990); m. Constance M. Montgomery, Aug. 24, 1995. BS, Mich. State U., 1962, DVM, 1964; JD, Thomas A. Cooley Law Sch., 1984. Bar: Mich. lic. pilot. Pvt. practice vet. medicine Caro and Lansing, Mich., 1964-72; founder, pres. Liebler Constrn. Co., 1966—; pvt. practice vet. medicine Caro Land Devel. Corp., 1971-73; veterinarian Vaccination Ctr., 1993—; pvt. practice in law Lansing; v.p. Caro Computer Corp., 1983-84, 87-90; bd. dirs. Caro Devel. Corp., Data Mgmt. Solutions Corp.; founder AAA Four Paws Boarding Kennel, 1997; owner A-1 Economy Storage, Mine Storage, 1996. Chmn. Citizens Com. to Become City, 1969-70; bd. dirs. Mich. Eye Collection Ctr., Inc.; mem. exec. com. Tuscola County Rep. Party, 1976-79; apptd. by Gov. Engler Mich. Higher Edn. Facilities Authority, 1990; vice chair Ingham County Rep. Party, 1997, vice chair 8th Dist., 1997. Mem. Mich. Vet. Med. Assn. (ethics com. 1969-70, dir. 1986-71), Am. Vet. Med. Law Assn. (founding mem., exec. sec. 1994), Thumb Vet. Med. Assn. (pres. 1967-68), Home Builders Assn. Thumb (pres. 1971), Nat. Home Builders Assn. (dir. 1974-75, 77-79), Masons, Lions (pres. local club 1968-69, zone chmn. 1972-73, dept. dist. gov. 1973-75), Amateur Radio Club, Pinehurst Golf and Country Club, N.C. Birchwood Farm Estates Golf and Country Club, Olds Forge Flyers Flying Club. Avocation: travel. Home: 320 N Sycamore St Lansing MI 48933-1063 Office: Capitol City Airport 3317 W Hangar Dr Lansing MI 48906-2135

LIEBLING, JEROME, photographer, educator; b. N.Y.C., Apr. 16, 1924; s. Maurice and Sarah (Goodman) L.; married, Nov. 11, 1949 (div. 1969); children: Madeline, Tina, Adam, Daniella, Rachel Jane. Student, Bklyn. Coll., 1942, 46, 48, New Sch. for Social Research, N.Y.C., 1948-49; LLD (hon.), Portland (Maine) Sch. Art, 1989. Prof. photography U. Minn., Mpls., 1949-69; prof. SUNY-New Paltz, 1957-58, Yale U., New Haven, 1976-77, Hampshire Coll., Amherst, Mass., 1970—. Author, photographer: Jerome Liebling Photographs (Best of Yr. 1982), Aperture, N.Y.C., 1988, The People Yes, The Photographs of Jerome Liebling, Aperture, 1995; editor: Photography-Current Perspective, 1977, Jerome Liebling: The Minnesota Photographs, 1997. Served with U.S. Army, 1942-45, ETO, Africa. Fellow Mass. Arts Found., 1975; fellow Nat. Endowman Arts, 1979, Guggenheim, 1977, 81. Mem. Soc. Photog. Edn. Home: 39 Dana St Amherst MA 01002-2208 Office: Hampshire Coll West St Amherst MA 01002-2954

LIEBMAN, HOWARD MARK, lawyer; b. L.A., Dec. 20, 1952; s. Martin Irving and Frances (Weiner) L.; m. Alena Bekova, Aug. 16, 1975 (div. Dec. 17, 1990); 1 child, Peter. AB, Colgate U., 1974, AM, 1975; JD, Harvard Law Sch., 1977. Cons. Office of Tax Analysis, U.S. Treasury Dept., Washington, 1975; assoc. Paul, Weiss, Rifkind, Wharton & Garrison, N.Y.C., 1976, Covington & Burling, Washington, 1977-79; ptnr. Oppenheimer, Wolff & Donnelly, Brussels, 1979-94; mng. ptnr. Morgan, Lewis & Bockius, Brussels, 1994—; mem. div. coun. on fin. and banking Mgmt. Ctr. Europe, Brussels, 1984—; adv. mem. N.Am. Free Trade & Investment Rep., 1988—. Co-author: Business Operations in the European Union; contbg. editor Tax Planning Internat. Rev., 1982—, Jour. Strategy in Internat. Taxation, 1984-86. Bd. dirs. Harvard Club of Belgium, Brussels, 1989-95, pres., 1993-95; co-chmn. Dukakis for Pres. Belgian Campaign. Fulbright Commn. fellow, 1979. Mem. ABA, Am. C. of C. in Belgium asbl. Democrat. Home: 30 Ave de Boetendael, 1180 Brussels Belgium Office: Morgan Lewis & Bockius, rue Guimard 7, 1040 Brussels Belgium

LIEBMAN, LANCE MALCOLM, law educator, lawyer; b. Newark, Sept. 11, 1941; s. Roy and Barbara (Trilinsky) L.; m. Carol Bensinger, June 28, 1964; children: Jeffrey, Benjamin. BA, Yale U., 1962; MA, Cambridge U., 1964; LLB, Harvard U., 1967. Bar: D.C. 1968, Mass. 1976, N.Y., 1995. Asst. to Mayor Lindsay, N.Y.C., 1968-70; asst. prof. law Harvard U., 1970-76, prof., 1976-91, assoc. dean, 1981-84; dean, Lucy G. Moses prof. law Columbia U. Sch. Law, N.Y.C., 1991-96, prof., dir. Parker Sch. Fgn. Law,, 1996—. Successor trustee Yale Corp., 1971-83. Office: Columbia U Sch Law 435 W 116th St New York NY 10027-7201

LIEBMAN, NINA R., economic developer; b. Toledo, Ohio, May 27, 1941; d. Jules Jay and Phyllis Gertrude (Kasle) Roskin; m. Theodore Liebman, Oct. 27, 1968; children: Sophie, Hanna, Tessa. Student, U. Marseilles, Aix-en-Provence, France, 1959-60, Skidmore Coll., 1960-61, NYU, 1961-63; cert. labor negotiator, Cornell U., 1993. Pub. info. officer Young Adult Inst., N.Y.C., 1978-81; U.S.A. dir. Rhone-Alps Econ. Devel. Assn., N.Y.C. and Lyon, France, 1981-85; internat. mktg. specialist N.Y. State Dept. Econ. Devel., N.Y.C., 1985-89, chief internat. programs, 1989-95; cons. Russian Fedn. Housing Project-The World Bank, Moscow, 1995—; prin. Trade Svcs. & Investment Attraction Inc., Bklyn., 1997—. Co-author: Biz Speak: A Dictionary of Business Terms, Slang and Jargon, 1986. Vol., trained mediator Bklyn. Mediation Ctr.; mem. internat. adv. coun. Eisenhower Found.; mem. internat. adv. bd. Nat. Minority Bus. Coun. Fellow Eisenhower Exch. Fellowship Program, 1993. Mem. Nat. Assn. Export Cos. (exec. dir. 1997—), Alliance Am. and Russian Women, U.S. Com. for UN Devel. Fund for Women, Minority Internat. Network for Trade, Bklyn. C. of C. (bd. dirs., internat. advisor), Bklyn. Heights Assn., Mcpl. Arts Soc., Grace Choral Soc. (bd. dirs. 1993—). Democrat. Jewish. Avocation: choral singing.

LIEBMAN, RONALD STANLEY, lawyer; b. Balt., Oct. 11, 1943; s. Harry Martin and Martha (Altgenug) L.; m. Simma Liebman, Jan. 8, 1972; children: Shana, Margot. BA, Western Md. Coll., Westminster, 1966; JD, U. Md., 1969. Bar: Md. 1969, D.C. 1977, U.S. Dist. Ct. (ea. dist.) Va. 1970, U.S. Dist. Ct. Md. 1970, U.S. Dist. Ct. D.C. 1982, U.S. Dist. Ct. (no. dist.) Calif. 1994, U.S. Ct. Appeals (4th cir.) 1972, U.S. Ct. Appeals (D.C. cir.) 1982, U.S. Ct. Appeals (2d cir.) 1988, U.S. Ct. Appeals (9th cir.) 1992, U.S. Ct. Appeals (5th cir.) 1985, U.S. Ct. Appeals (2d cir.) 1988, U.S. Supreme Ct. 1995. Law clk. to chief judge U.S. Dist. Ct. Md., 1969-70; assoc. Melnicove, Kaufman & Weiner, Balt., 1970-72; asst. U.S. atty. Office of U.S. Atty., Dept. Justice, Balt., 1972-78; ptnr. Sachs, Greenebaum & Tayler, Washington, 1978-82, Patton Boggs, L.L.P., Washington, 1982—. Author: Grand Jury, 1983; co-editor: Testimonial Privileges, 1983. Recipient spl. commendation award U.S. Dept. Justice, 1978. Mem. ABA, D.C. Bar Assn., Md. Bar Assn. Club: Sergeants Inn (Balt.). Office: Patton Boggs LLP 2550 M St NW Washington DC 20037-1301

LIEBMAN, THEODORE, architect; b. Newark, May 7, 1939; s. Edward and Miriam (Applebaum) L.; m. Nina Roskin, Oct. 27, 1968; children—Sophie, Hanna, Tessa. B.Arch., Pratt Inst., 1962; M.Arch., Harvard U., 1963. Registered architect, Mass., N.Y., Colo., Ind. Fla. Project design officer Boston Redevel. Authority, Mass., 1963-64; project dir. David A. Crane, Architect, Phila., 1966-69; chief architect N.Y. State Urban Devel. Corp., N.Y.C., 1969-75; prin. urban design and archtl. adviser Harvard Inst. Internat. Devel., Tehran, Iran, 1975-77; pres. HAUS Internat., Inc., N.Y.C., 1977-79, The Liebman Melting Partnership, Architects and Planners, N.Y.C., 1979—, land devel. mgr. Russian Fed. Housing Project, Moscow, 1995-96; bd. advisers Inst. Urban Design, N.Y.C., 1980-84; assoc. prof. urban design Pratt Inst., Bklyn., 1983-88. Mem. editorial bd. Metropolis, N.Y.C., 1981-88. Contbr. articles to mags. Fellow Am. Acad. in Rome, 1966; Wheelwright travelling fellow Harvard U., 1971. Fellow AIA (pres. N.Y. chpt. 1983-84); mem. Urban Land Inst., Urban Land Inst. Internat. Coun. Home: 105 Montague St Brooklyn NY 11201-3459 Office: The Liebman Melting Partnership 330 W 42nd St New York NY 10036-6902

LIEBMANN, GEORGE W(ILLIAM), lawyer; b. N.Y.C., June 20, 1939; s. William Liebmann and Margaret (Hirschman) Cook; m. Anne-Lise Grimstad, Apr. 29, 1967; children: Pamela Dione, George William, Franklin Alexander. AB, Dartmouth Coll., 1960; JD, U. Chgo., 1963. Bar: Md. 1964, Ill. 1964. With Chaucer Head Book Shop, Inc., N.Y.C., 1958-59; law clk. to chief judge Ct. Appeals Md., 1963-64; with Frank, Bernstein, Conaway and Goldman, Balt., 1964-79; asst. atty. gen. State of Md., Balt., 1967-69; exec. asst. to Gov. Md., Annapolis, 1979-80; sole practice Balt., 1980—; lectr. U. Md. Law Sch., 1977-78, Johns Hopkins U., 1991-92; faculty assoc. Lincoln Inst. for Land Policy, 1996—; asst. reporter Md. Commn. on Criminal Law and Procedure, 1965-70; mem. Gov.'s Commn. to Revise Annotated Code Md., 1974-83; alt. mem. State Planning Coun. on Radioactive Waste Mgmt., 1980-82; chmn. Gov.'s Task Force on Local Govt. Antitrust Liability, 1982-83, Gov.'s Commn. Health Care Providers' Profl. Liability Ins., 1983-84; gen. coun. Md. Econs. Devel. Corp., 1985—; vis. fellow U. Salford, Eng., 1996, Wolfson Coll., Cambridge, 1996. Author: Maryland District Court Law and Practice, 2 vols., 1976, Maryland Civil Practice Forms, 2 vols., 1984, The Little Platoons: Sub-Local Governments in Modern History, 1995, The Gallows in the Grove: Civil Society in American Law, 1997; mng. editor U. Chgo. Law Rev., 1962-63; mem. adv. bd. Accessory Housing, 1990—; contbr. articles to law jours. Sec. Coalition Against the SST, Washington, 1969; trustee Hist. Annapolis Found., 1991—. Simon indsl. and profl. fellow U. Manchester, Eng., 1993-94. Mem. Am. Law Inst., Fed. Jud. Conf. 4th Cir., Libr. Co. Balt. Bar (bd. dirs. 1967—, pres. 1975-77), Engring. Soc. Md. (assoc.). Office: 8 W Hamilton St Baltimore MD 21201-5008

LIEBMANN, MARTHA, psychotherapist; b. Bklyn., Apr. 13, 1938; d. Edward M. and Elsa (Henner) Heyman; m. Jordan C. Schreiber, Dec. 25, 1958 (div. Dec. 1971); children: Eric, Nancy; m. Richard O. Liebmann, Aug. 25, 1990. BA, Queens Coll., 1957; MSW, Columbia U., 1959; PhD, Union Inst., Cin., 1989. Cert. social worker, N.Y.; lic. marriage and family counselor, N.J. Staff therapist group and indivdual therapy Washington Square Inst., N.Y.C., 1968-96, dir. psychiat. social svcs., sr. supr., mem. faculty, 1980—; pvt. practice, 1974-96; mem. faculty Inst. for Psychoanalysis and Psychotherapy of N.J., Bergenfield, 1996—. Mem. Am. Group Psychotherapy Assn., Nat. Assn. for Advancement Psychoanalysis, Coun. Psychoanalytic Psychotherapists. Jewish. Home: 229 Franklin St Haworth NJ 07641-1411 Office: 80 E 11th St Ste 304 New York NY 10003-6000 Office: Psychotherapy Assocs 253 S Washington Ave Bergenfield NJ 07621-3739

LIEBMANN, SEYMOUR W., construction consultant; b. N.Y.C., Nov. 1, 1928; s. Isidor W. and Etta (Waltzer) L.; m. Hinda Adam, Sept. 20, 1959; children: Peter Adam, David W. BSME, Clarkson U. (formerly Clarkson Coll. Tech.), 1948; grad. Indsl. Coll. Armed Forces, 1963, U.S. Army Command and Gen. Staff Coll., 1966, U.S. Army War Coll., 1971. Registered profl. engr., N.Y., Mass., Ga. Area engr. constrn. div. E.I. DuPont de Nemours & Co., Inc., 1952-54; constrn. planner Lummus Co., 1954-56; prin. mech. engr. Perini Corp., 1956-62; v.p. Boston Based Contractors, 1962-66; v.p. A.R. Abrams, Inc., Atlanta, 1967-74, pres., 1974-78, also bd. dirs.; founder Liebmann Assocs., Inc., Atlanta, 1979—; mem. nat. adv. bd. Am. Security Council. Author: Military Engineer Field Notes, 1953, Prestressing Miter Gate Diagonals, 1960; contbr. articles to publs. Mem. USO Council, Atlanta, 1968—, v.p., 1978, mem. exec. com., 1975-79; mem. Nat. UN Day Com., 1975; sr. army coord., judge Sci. Fair, Atlanta Pub. Schs., annually 1979-88, 92—; asst. scoutmaster troop 298 Atlanta area council Boy Scouts Am., 1980-87, Explorer advisor, 1982-86, unit commr., 1985, dist. commr. North Atlanta Dist., Atlanta Area Council, 1988-90, asst. coun. commr., 1990-95, mem. faculty Commrs. Coll., 1985-88, 92, mem. North Atlanta Dist. com. BSA, 1996—; mem. alumni adv. com. Clarkson Coll. Tech., 1981—, alumni bd. govs., 1983-94, Disting. Alumni Golden Knight award, 1983; mem. exec. com., zoning chmn. neighbor planning unit City of Atlanta, 1982—, chmn., 1988, 95, 96, 97, vice-chmn., 1989; pres. West Paces/Northside Neighborhood Assn., 1991—; apptd. civil engr. mem. to City of Atlanta Water and Sewer Appeals Bd., 1992—; apptd. mem. to Mayor's Bond Oversight Com. City of Atlanta, 1995-96. Col. AUS Ret. Corps Engrs., 1948-52, Korea, Germany. Decorated Legion of Merit, Meritorious Service medal, U.S. Army Res. medal, 1975; elected to Old Guard of Gate City Guard, 1979; recipient cert. of Achievement Dept. Army, 1978, USO Recognition award, 1979, Order of Arrow award Boy Scouts Am., 1983, 87, Scouters Key Boy Scouts Am., 1988, North Atlanta Dist. Merit award Boy Scouts Am., 1989, Silver Beaver award, 1991, Disting. Commn. award, 1991, Engring. Profl. award Am. Inst. Plant Engrs., 1987; named Met. Atlanta Engr. of Yr. in Pvt. Practice Ga., 1991, Engr. of Yr. in Pvt. Practice, 1991. Fellow Soc. Am. Mil. Engrs. (bd. dirs. 1986—, chmn. readiness com. 1986-88, program chmn. Atlanta post 1980-81, v.p. 1982, pres. 1983, program chmn. 1988 nat. meeting, asst. regional v.p. for readiness So. region 1991—, Nat. award of Merit 1982-83, Atlanta post Leadership award 1988, life dir. Atlanta Post, 1994, elected nat. dir. 1994-97, James Lucas Chair Atlanta Post, 1994, life mem.); mem. ASTM, NSPE, Am. Cons. Engrs. Coun. (state and nat. pub. rels. coms., nat. ethics com., state legis. liaison com.), Am. Concrete Inst., Soc. 1st U.S. Inf., Res. Officers Assn. (life mem.), U.S. Army War Coll. Found. (life mem.), Nat. Def. Univ. Found., U.S. Army War Coll. Alumni Assn. (life), Ga. Soc. Profl. Engrs. (bd. dirs. Buckhead chpt., state ethics com.), Engrs. Club Boston, Assn. U.S. Army, Def. Preparedness Assn., Am. Arbitration Assn. (panel arbitrators 1979—, constrn. adv. com. 1984—), Cobb C. of C., Downtown Atlanta Kiwanis, Mil. Order World Wars, Order of Engr., Army Engr. Assn. (life), Appalachian Trail Conf., Benyton Mackaye Trail Assn., Ga. Conservancy, Atlanta Hist. Soc., NRA. Republican. Jewish. Clubs: Ft. McPherson Officers; Ga. Appalachian Trail. Lodges: Masons (32 deg.), Shriners, Nat. Sojourners, Heros of '76, Elks, Civitan. Home: 3260 Rilman Dr NW Atlanta GA 30327-2224 Office: Ste 700 210 Interstate North Pkwy SE Atlanta GA 30339-2111

LIEBOVICH, SAMUEL DAVID, warehouse executive; b. Rockford, Ill., Sept. 19, 1946; s. Albert A. and Dorothy (Pollard) L.; m. Erna Susan Horewitch, Oct. 1, 1966; children: Elaine Beth, Mitchell Phillip. BS magna cum laude, Bradley U., 1969; postgrad., U. Ill., 1969-70. Asst. dir. purchasing Liebovich Bros. Inc., Rockford, 1970-80, v.p. purchasing and inventory, 1980-82, pres. nat. sales, 1982—. Bd. dirs. Rockford Symphony Orch., 1994-97; mem. allocations com. United Way, Rockford, 1987-88; bus. chmn. Statue of Liberty Com., Rockford, 1986-87; fin. sec., bd. dirs. Temple Beth El, Rockford, 1975-79, treas., 1993-94; v.p. Temple Bethel, 1995-96; chair United Jewish Appeal Greater Rockford Area, 1988-89; pres. Ohave Shalom Synagogue, Rockford, 1977-79, pres. Greater Rockford Jewish Fedn., 1989-92, Wallenberg Com., Rockford, 1988-89; adv. dir. Mother House. Mem. ASTM, Nat. Assn. Aluminum Distbrs. (nat. com. 1979-85), Nat. Assn. Steel Distbrs. (bd. dirs. 1990-92, v.p. 1992-93, exec. v.p. 1994-95, pres. 1995-96, Pres. award 1993, 94, Steel Man of Yr. award 1996-97), Am. Soc. for Metal, Internat. Kiwanis (fellow award), Alpine Kiwanis (bd. dirs., sec., v.p., pres.-elect 1988-95, pres.), Ill.-Iowa Dist. 6 Kiwanis (lt. gov.-elect divsn. 12 1995-96, lt. gov. dist. 12 1996-97, George Hickson award, Hickson Diamond award), Rockford B'nai B'rith (pres. 1973-76), Masons, Shriners, Mau-Nah-Tee-See Country Club. Republican. Jewish. Avocations: golf, racquetball, fishing, boating. Home: 5540 Roanoke Rd Rockford IL 61107-1748 Office: Liebovich Bros Inc 2116 Preston St Rockford IL 61102-1975

LIEBOW, JOANNE ELISABETH, marketing communication coordinator; b. Cleve., May 15, 1926; d. Arnold S. and Rhea Eunice (Levy) King; m. Irving M. Liebow, June 30, 1947 (div. Jan. 1972); children: Katherine Ann Liebow Frank, Peter. Student, Smith Coll., 1944-47; BA, Case Western Res. U., 1948. Cleve. reporter Fairchild Publs., N.Y.C., 1950-51; freelance pub. rels., Cleve., 1972-78; pub. info. specialist Cuyahoga Community Coll., Cleve., 1979—. Founder, pres. Mt. Sinai Hosp. Jr. Women's Aux., Cleve., 1948-50; pres. PTA, Bryden Elem. Sch., Beachwood, Ohio, 1964; mem. bd., pres. Beachwood Bd. Edn., 1968-76. Recipient Exceptional Achievement award Coun. for Advance Edn., 1982, Citation award, 1982, Grand Prize, 1983; Sophia Smith scholar Smith Coll., 1946, Cleve. Communicator's award Women in Communications, Inc., 1982. Home: 23511 Chagrin Blvd Apt 211 Cleveland OH 44122-5538 Office: Cuyahoga Community Coll Ea Campus 4250 Richmond Rd Cleveland OH 44122-6104

LIEBOW, PHOEBE AUGUSTA RECHT, nursing educator, school nurse; b. Pitts., Aug. 1, 1925; d. Nathan and Frieda (Laufe) Recht; m. Ely Milton Liebow, June 27, 1948; children: Wendy Faith Liebow Burson, Cynthia Hope Liebow, Franette Liebow. RN, Garfield Meml. Hosp., Washington, 1946; BA, Northeastern Ill. U., Chgo., 1972; MA, 1981. Asst. night supr. Garfield Meml. Hosp., Washington, 1946-47; head nurse, med./surg., 1947-48; vis. nurse Chgo., 1948-49, VNA of Ea. Union County, Elizabeth, N.J., 1948-51; clinic nurse North End Clinic, Detroit, 1951-52; substitute sch. nurse Dist. # 113, Highland Park, Deerfield, Ill., 1968-73; cert. sch. nurse Dist. # 39, Wilmette, Ill., 1973-91; mem. adj. faculty as field supr. Nat. Louis U., Wheeling, Ill., 1992—; coord. and facilitator for anorexia nervosa peer support group northeastern Ill. U., Project Hope, Chgo., 1977-84; mem. health and safety curriculum com. Sch. Dist. 39, Wilmette, Ill., 1988-91. Co-author: (1 chpt.) Nursing Care Plan Workbook, 1985; contbr. articles to profl. jours. Vol. crisis line North Shore Help Line, Deerfield, Ill., 1970-71. Recipient Nursing on the Move plaque, ANA, 1990; grantee Creative Nutrition Edn. Tng., Ill., 1988. Fellow Am. Orthopsychiatric Assn.; mem. Ill. Assn. Sch. Nurses, Cert. Health Edn. Specialist, Garfield Meml. Hosp. Alumnae Assn., Nat. Found. for Osteoprosis, Congregation Solel. Avocations: reading, travel, swimming, attending conferences on Sherlock Holmes and Conan Doyle and popular culture. Home: 1694 Elmwood Dr Highland Park IL 60035-2320

LIEBOWITZ, NEIL ROBERT, psychiatrist; b. Bklyn., Feb. 5, 1956; s. Harold and Gertrude Liebowitz; m. Judith Linda Ross, Oct. 21, 1952; children: Sarah Michelle, Daniel Geoffery. BA, U. Va., 1978; MD, SUNY, Stony Brook, 1982. Cert. Am. Bd. Psychiatry and Neurology. Intern Greenwich Hosp. Assn., Greenwich, Conn., 1982-83; psychiatry fellow Yale Dept. Psychiatry, New Haven, 1982-86; chief resident psychiatry Yale New Haven Hosp., 1985-86; dir. consultation liaison psychiatry Newington VA Med. Ctr., Newington, Conn., 1986-87; chief mental hygiene clinic Newington VA Med. Ctr., 1986-88; asst. prof. psychiatry U. Conn., Farmington, 1986-92, asst. clin. prof. psychiatry, 1993—; dir. inpatient psychiatry Newington VA Med. Ctr., 1988-89; dir. ambulatory psychiatry John Dempsey Hosp., Farmington, 1989-91; cons. psychiatrist Rocky Hill (Conn.) Vets. Home and Hosp., 1987-88; attending New Britain Gen. Hosp., 1992—; dir. Conn. Anxiety & Depression Treatment Ctr., Farmington, 1994—; founding mem., bd. dirs. PsychCare, Inc., 1996—. Contbr. articles to profl. jours.; co-investigator clin. research Clin. Psychopharmocology, 1988—. Mem. Am. Psychiat. Assn., Conn. Psychiat. Soc., Hartford Psychiat. Soc. (pres. 1997), Phi Beta Kappa. Office: Conn Anxiety & Depression Treatment Ctr Farmington CT 06032

LIEBTAG, BENFORD GUSTAV, III (BEN LIEBTAG), engineer, consultant; b. Pitts., Sept. 20, 1941; s. Benford Gustav and Alice Mildred (Hunt) L.; children: Cindy, Ben. BSEE, U. Pitts., 1964. Sr. heating and air-conditioning engr. Duquesne Light Co., Pitts., 1964-79; dir. energy mgmt. Van Wagenen and Searcy, Inc., Jacksonville, Fla., 1979-80, v.p., 1980-81; pres. Liebtag, Robinson, and Wingfield, Inc., Jacksonville and Gainesville, Fla., 1981. Mem. ASHRAE (Merit award, Disting. Service award), Assn. Energy Engrs., Soc. Am. Mil. Engrs. Methodist. Lodges: Masons, Kiwanis. Home: 4084 Big Hollow Ln Jacksonville FL 32277

LIECHTY, ERIC, church administrator. Youth dir. The Missionary Church, Fort Wayne, Ind. Office: The Missionary Ch 526 N Main St Elburn IL 60119-8985

LIEDERMAN, DAVID SAMUEL, child welfare administrator; b. Malden, Mass., Apr. 26, 1935; s. Harry A. Liederman; married; children: Wendy, Keith, Larry. BA, U. Mass., 1957; MEd, Springfield Coll., 1958; MSW, U. Pitts., 1962. Teenage supr. Youngstown (Ohio) Jewish Community Ctr., 1958-62; dir. extension services Roxbury (Mass.) Neighborhood House, 1962-64; asst. dir. Roxbury Fedn. Neighborhood Ctrs., 1964-66; dir. family relocation United South End Settlements, Boston, 1966-69; state rep. Mass. Ho. Reps., Boston, 1969-73; dir. Mass. State Office for Children, Boston, 1973-75; chief of staff Mass. Gov. Michael S. Dukakis, Boston, 1975-79; exec. dir. pub. affairs Fedn. Jewish Philanthropies, N.Y.C., 1979-84; exec. dir. Child Welfare League Am., Washington, Boston, Chgo., and L.A., 1984—. Contbr. numerous articles to profl. jours. Bd. dirs. Nat. Assembly, Washington, 1984—; mem. United Way Am. Leadership 18, Alexandria, Va., 1984—; chair Nat. Collaboration for Youth, 1990-94; co-chair Generations United, 1987—. Recipient Disting. Alumni award U. Pitts., 1975, Nat. Mgmt. Excellence award for Social Work Execs. and Mgrs., Nat. Assn. Social Workers, 1987, Nat. Assembly's award for Excellence in Nat. Exec. Leadership, 1996, numerous others. Office: Child Welfare League Am 440 1st St NW Washington DC 20001-2028

LIEF, HAROLD ISAIAH, psychiatrist; b. N.Y.C., Dec. 29, 1917; s. Jacob F. and Mollie (Filler) L.; m. Myrtis A. Brumfield, Mar. 3, 1961; Caleb B., Frederick V., Oliver F.; children from previous marriage: Polly Lief Goldberg, Jonathan F. BA, U. Mich., 1938; MD, NYU, 1942; cert. in psychoanalysis, Columbia Coll. Physicians and Surgeons, 1950; MA (hon.), U. Pa., 1971. Intern Queens Gen. Hosp., Jamaica, N.Y., 1942-43; resident psychiatry L.I. Coll. Medicine, 1946-48; pvt. practice psychiatry N.Y.C., 1948-51; asst. physician Presbyn. Hosp., N.Y.C., 1949-51; asst. prof. Tulane U., New Orleans, 1951-54, asso. prof., 1954-60, prof. psychiatry, 1960-67; prof. psychiatry U. Pa., Phila., 1967-82, prof. emeritus, 1982—; dir. div. family study U. Pa., 1967-81; dir. Marriage Council of Phila., 1969-81, Ctr. for Study of Sex. Edn. in Medicine, 1968-82; mem. staff U. Pa. Hosp., 1967-81, Pa. Hosp., 1981—; clin. prof. psychiatry Jefferson Med. U., 1994—. Author: (with Daniel and William Thompson) The Eighth Generation, 1960; Editor: (with Victor and Nina Lief) Psychological Basis of Medical Practice, 1963, Medical Aspects of Human Sexuality, 1976, (with Arno Karlen) Sex Education in Medicine, 1976, Sexual Problems in Medical Practice, 1981, (with Zwi Hoch) Sexology: Sexual Biology, Behavior and Therapy, 1982, (with Zwi Hoch) International Research in Sexology, 1983, Human Sexuality With Respect to AIDS and HIV Infection, 1989; contbr. numerous articles to publs. Bd. dirs. Ctr. for Sexuality and Religion; mem. La. State Commn. Civil Rights, 1958-67. Maj. M.C. U.S. Army, 1943-46. Commonwealth Fund fellow, 1963-64; recipient Gold Medal award Mt. Airy Hosp., 1977, Lifetime Achievement award Phila. Psychiat. Soc., 1992. Fellow Phila. Coll. Physicians, Am. Psychiat. Assn. (50 yr. life), N.Y. Acad. Scis., AAAS, Am. Acad. Psychoanalysis (charter, past pres.), Am. Coll. Psychiatrists (founding), Am. Coll. Psychoanalysts (charter); mem. Am. Assn. Marriage and Family Therapists, Sex Info. and Edn. Council U.S. (past pres.), Group Advancement Psychiatry (life), Am. Soc. Adolescent Psychiatry, Am. Psychosomatic Soc., Assn. Psychoanalytic Medicine (life), Internat. Acad. Sex Rsch., Soc. Sci. Study of Sex, Am. Soc. Sex Educators, Counselors and Therapists, Soc. Sex Therapists and Researchers, World Assn. Sexology (past v.p.), Soc. Exploration of Psychotherapy Integration (adv. bd.), Columbia Club, Mich. Club of Greater Phila., Penn Club of N.Y., Sigma Xi, Alpha Omega Alpha, Phi Eta Sigma, Phi Kappa Phi. Home: 101 S Buck Ln Haverford PA 19041-1104 Office: 987 Old Eagle School Rd Ste 719 Wayne PA 19087-1708 *The conflict between individual gratification and the needs of society, between competition and cooperation, appears to me to be the most fundamental issue confronting mankind. My goal in life has been to steer a course that fosters service to others and to society without undue sacrifice of individual aspirations.*

LIEF, THOMAS PARRISH, sociologist, educator; b. N.Y.C., Oct. 4, 1931; s. Alfred and Zola Nina (Vogel) L. BA, U. N.Mex., 1955, MA, 1961; PhD, Tulane U., 1970. Bd. cert. substance abuse counselor, La.; case presentation evaluator. Counselor, archaeology asst. U. N.Mex., Albuquerque, 1959-60, 60-61; tchg. asst. dept. sociology Tulane U., New Orleans, 1961-64; instr. to asst. prof. dept. sociology Loyola U., New Orleans, 1964-69; assoc. prof. to prof. dept. sociology So. U., New Orleans, 1968—; cons. on curriculum devel. Tuskegee Inst. Drug Abuse Human Svcs. Manpower Devel. Tng., 1973-78; adj. prof. sociology, assoc. grad. faculty mem. U. New Orleans, 1975-76; cons. various orgns., 1981-82; vis. prof. dept. sociology Tulane U., New Orleans, 1986; rev. com. mem. Alcohol, Drug Abuse & Mental Health Adminstrn. Office, 1987—; bd. dirs. Nat. Assn. Alcoholism and Drug Abuse Counselors, 1990-91; pres. La. Assn. Substance Abuse Counselor and Trainers, 1990-91; adv. bd. Michael Halbrook Recovery Ctr. East Lake

Hosp., 1990-92; mem. La. State Bd. Certification for Substance Abuse Counselors, 1988-92, Adv. Com. for Historically Black Colls. and Univs. Program for Substance Abuse Tng., 1987-89; tng. cons. Am. Indian Tng. Inst., Sacramento, Calif., 1985—; mem. La. Commn. on Alcohol and Drug Abuse, 1984-91, 97—; mem. L.A. Drug Control and Violent Crime Policy Bd., 1993—; contract cons. Ctr. for Substance Abuse Treatment, 1994—; founder, bd. dirs. Accreditation Coun.: Alcohol and Drug Counselor Program in Higher Edn.; cons. in field. Contbr. numerous articles to profl. jours.; mem. editl. rev. com. Counselor, 1986-92; co-author: Academic Linkages Resource Manual. Co-chair La. State-Wide Taskforce Counselor Manpower, 1984-90; pres., founder Nat. Assn. Substance Abuse Trainers and Educators, 1983—; bd. dirs. Nat. Commn. on Accreditation of Alcoholism and Drug Abuse Counselors, 1982-90, Certification Reciprocity Consortium/Alcohol and Other Drug Abuse, Inc., 1981-82; pres., founder La. Cert. Examining Bd. of La. Assn. Substance Abuse Counselor & Trainers, 1978-82; mem. Child Abuse Com. Dist. Atty.'s Office, 1976-80; co-dir. Insight House Adv. Bd., 1976-80. Mem. Am. Sociol. Assn., Am. Acad. Polit. and Social Scis., La. Assn. Substance Abuse Counselors and Trianers, La. Alcohol and Drug Abuse Assn., Nat. Assn. Alcoholism and Substance Abuse Counselors, Nat. Assn. Substance Abuse Trainers and Educators, Soc. for Applied Anthropology, Soc. for Study of Social Problems, So. Sociol. Soc., Substance Abuse Counselor Orgn., Nat. Commn. on Accreditation of Alcoholism and Drug Abuse Counselors Credentialing Bodies. Office: 6400 Press Dr New Orleans LA 70126-1009

LIEGL, JOSEPH LESLIE, lawyer; b. Fond du Lac, Wis., Jan. 20, 1948; s. Melvin Theodore and Verna Lavinia (Jagdfeld) L.; m. Janet L. Meyer, Feb. 1, 1969; children: Matthew, Jeremy. BA with distinction, U. Wis., 1970, JD cum laude, 1973. Bar: Wis. 1973, U.S. Supreme Ct. 1976, Ohio 1978, U.S. Dist. Ct. (no. dist.) Ohio 1978, U.S. Ct. Claims 1978, U.S. Tax Ct. 1978. Assoc. Muchin & Muchin S.C., Manitowoc, Wis., 1973-74; trial atty. U.S. Dept. Justice, Washington, 1974-78; assoc. Jones, Day, Reavis & Pogue, Cleve., 1978-83, ptnr., 1984-96; ptnr. Coopers & Lybrand, LLP, Detroit, 1996—. Mem. ABA (taxation sect.), Cleve. Bar Assn. (chmn. tax sect. 1987-88), Cleve. Tax Inst. (chmn. 1994), Cleve. Tax Club (v.p. 1993-95, pres. 1995-96, past bd. dirs.), Order of Coif, Phi Eta Sigma, Phi Kappa Phi. Avocation: music. Home: 983 Coldspring Dr Northville MI 48167

LIEM, DARLENE MARIE, secondary education educator; b. Lorain, Ohio, June 25, 1941; d. Frederick August and Mary Jane (Derby) Kubishke; m. Frans Robert Liem; children: Dorothea Saliba, Frans Liem, Raymond Liem, Bryan Liem, Shannon Daniel. BS in Edn., Ohio State U., 1963; ME, Wright State U., 1980. Cert. secondary tchr., Ohio. Sci. tchr. Southwestern City Schs., Grove City, Ohio, 1963-66, Greeneview High Sch., Jamestown, Ohio, 1973—; advisor Quick Recall Team, Jamestown, 1984—, NASA Student Shuttle Projects, Regional winners, 1981, 82; dir. Ramblers Drill Team, Jamestown, 1973-77; adv. TEAMS, 1991—. Contbr. articles to profl. jours. Mem. Huber Heights (Ohio) Community Chorus, 1989-90; girl scout leader Huber Heights Girl Scout Troop, 1976-78; children's choir dir., Huber Heights, 1980-84, Sunday sch. tchr., Huber Heights, 1978-83; summer camp dir. Kirkmont Presbyn. Camp, Bellefontaine, Ohio, 1978-83; ordained elder Presbyn. Ch. Named Outstanding Educator Green County Bd. Edn., 1988-89, 92, Woman of Yr. Am. Bus. Women's Assn., 1988, West Region Project Discovery Tchr.-Leader, 1992—, Tandy Tech. Hon. Mention Tchr., 1994; named to Hall of Fame, Miami Valley Sci. and Engring., 1994. Mem. Nat. Sci. Tchrs. Assn., Sci. Edn. Coun. Ohio (bd. dirs. 1981-83), Am. Assn. Physics Tchrs. (South Ohio sect.), Western Ohio Sci. Tchrs. Assn. (pres. 1981-83), Delta Kappa Gamma, Phi Delta Kappa, Kappa Delta Pi. Avocations: chorus, crafts, camping, gardening, reading. Home: 7056 Montague Rd Dayton OH 45424-3044 Office: Greeneview High Sch 53 N Limestone St Jamestown OH 45335-1550

LIEM, KHIAN KIOE, medical entomologist; b. Semarang, Java, Indonesia, Jan. 11, 1942; came to U.S., 1969; s. Coen Ing T and Marie Soei-Nio (Goei) L.; m. Anita Tumewu, Apr. 3, 1980; children: Brian Dexter, Tiffany Marie, Jennifer Amanda, Ashley Elizabeth. BS, Bandung Inst. Tech., Bandung, Indonesia, 1964; MS, Bandung Inst. Tech., 1966, Eastern Ill. U., 1970; PhD, U. Ill., 1975. Registered profl. entomologist, vector ecologist. Grad. teaching asst. Bandung Inst. Tech., 1964-66, grad. instr., 1966-68; grad. rsch./teaching asst. Eastern Ill. U., 1969-70; grad. teaching asst. U. Ill., 1970-74; med. entomologist South Cook County Mosquito Abatement Dist., Harvey, Ill., 1974-76; mgr./dir. med. entomologist South Cook County Mosquito Abatement Dist., Harvey, 1977—; cons. U.S. AID, Washington, 1979—. Recipient Community Svc. award Asian Am. Coalition, 1993. Mem. Am. Mosquito Control Assn. (chmn. resolution com. 1977-78, mem. editorial bd. 1980-83, mem. worldwide com. 1987—), Ill. Mosquito Control Assn. (pres. 1979-81), Entomol. Soc. Am. (com. on book revs.), Am. Tropical Medicine and Hygiene Assn., Am. Registry of Profl. Entomologists, Scientists Inst. Pub. Info., Soc. Vector Ecology, Sigma Xi, Phi Sigma. Roman Catholic. Avocations: soccer, tennis, martial arts, camping, classical music. Home: 8012 Binford Dr Orland Park IL 60462-2300 Office: Mosquito Abatement Dist 15440 Dixie Hwy Harvey IL 60426-2801

LIEN, BRUCE HAWKINS, minerals and oil company executive; b. Waubay, S.D., Apr. 7, 1927; s. Peter Calmer and LaRece Catherine (Holm) L.; m. Deanna Jean Browning, May 4, 1978. BS in Bus., Wyo. U., 1953; D of Bus. (hon.), S.D. Sch. Mines & Tech., 1996. Chmn. bd. Pete Lien & Sons, Inc., Rapid City, S.D., 1944-84, bd. chmn., 1984—; chmn. Concorde Gaming Corp., 1990—, Browning Resources U.S., 1989—. Chmn. Community Chest, Rapid City, S.D., 1956; pres., nat. council Boys Club Am., Rapid City, S.D., N.Y.C., 1968; commr. Presdl. Scholars Commn., Washington, 1982; pres. U. Wyo, Found., 1989-90; life bd. dirs. Salvation Army. Served to 1st lt. U.S. Army, 1945-47, 50-52. Recipient Disting. Service award S.D. Sch. Mines, Rapid City, 1972, Disting. Service award Cosmopolitan Internat., Rapid City, 1983; named Disting. Alumnus, Wyo. U., Laramie, 1982, 96. Mem. Internat. Lime Assn. (pres. 1973-75), Nat. Lime Assn. (pres. 1973-75, Merit award 1973, bd. dirs.), VFW, Am. Legion. Republican. Lutheran. Club: Cosmopolitan (Rapid City, S.D.). Lodges: Masons, Elks. Home: PO Box 440 Rapid City SD 57709-0440 Office: Pete Lien & Sons Inc I 90 & Deadwood Ave PO Box 440 Rapid City SD 57709-0440

LIEN, ERIC JUNG-CHI, pharmacist, educator; b. Kaohsiung, Taiwan, Nov. 30, 1937; came to U.S., 1963, naturalized, 1973; m. Linda L. Chen, Oct. 2, 1965; children: Raymond, Andrew. B.S. in Pharmacy (Frank Shu China Sci. scholar), Nat. Taiwan U., 1960; PhD in Pharm. Chemistry, U. Calif., San Francisco, 1966; postdoctoral fellow in bio-organic chemistry, Pomona Coll., Claremont, Calif., 1967-68. Hosp. pharmacist 862 Hosp. of Republic of China, 1960-61; asst. prof. pharmaceutics and biomedicinal chemistry U. So. Calif., L.A., 1968-72; assoc. prof. U. So. Calif., 1972-76, prof., 1976—, coord. sects. biomedicinal chemistry and pharms., 1975-78, coord. sect. biomedicinal chemistry, 1975-84; cons. Internat. Medication Sys., Ltd., 1978, NIH, 1971, 82-87, 92, 94, Inst. Drug Design, Inc., Calif., 1971-73, Allergan Pharms., Inc., 1971-72, EPA, 1985, 89, Ariz. Disease Control Rsch. Commn., 1986—; sci. adv. nat. labs. Dept. Health, Foods and Drugs, Exec., Yuan, China, Dept. Health Taipei, Taiwan, 1992-94; referee Jour. Pharmacokinetics and Biopharmaceutics, Jour. Medicinal Chemistry, Jour. Food Agr. Chemistry, Jour. Pharm. Sci., Pesticide Biochemistry and Physiology, Chem. Resv., Jour. Organic Chemistry, Pharm. Rsch., Jour. Drug Target, Internat. Jour. Oriental Medicine, Am. Jour. Pharm. Edn. Author 3 books; mem. editorial bd. Jour. Clin. Pharmacy and Therapeutics, 1979—, Internat. Jour. Oriental Medicine, Med. Chem. Rsch., 1991—, Chinese Pharm. Jour., 1991-93, Acta Pharmaceutica, 1992—; contbr. numerous articles to profl. jours. Grantee Merck, 1970, Abbott, 1971-72, NSF, 1972-74, 76-77, IMS, 1979, H & L Found., 1989-96. Fellow AAPS, AAAS, Louis Pasteur Found.; mem. Am. Assn. Cancer Rsch., Acad. Pharm. Scis., Am. Chem. Soc., Am. Assn. Pharm. Scientists, Internat. Union Pure and Applied Chemistry, Sigma Xi, Rho Chi, Phi Kappa Phi. Office: U So Calif Sch Pharmacy 1985 Zonal Ave Los Angeles CA 90033-1058

LIEN, ERIC L., pharmaceutical executive; b. Hammond, Ind., Apr. 9, 1946; s. Arthur P. and Rowena (Woltz) L.; m. Winifred A. Latham, July 23, 1987; children: Caroline, Steven, Janet, Elizabeth, Jeffrey, Alison. BA, Coll. of Wooster, 1968; MSc, U. Ill., 1971, PhD, 1972. Postdoctoral fellow Sch. Medicine U. Pa., Phila., 1972-75; rsch. biochemist Wyeth Labs., Phila., 1975-82, mgr. metabolic disorders, 1982-87, assoc. dir. nutritional rsch., 1987-90; dir. nutritional rsch. Wyeth-Ayerst Labs., Phila., 1990-93, sr. dir. nutritional rsch., 1993—; mem. U.S. delegation CODEX Alimentarius, Washington and Rome, 1988—; mem. tech. adv. group com. on nutrition Am. Acad. Pediatrics, Oak Park, Ill., 1988-94; mem. Com. on Nutritional Scis. Infant Formula Coun., Atlanta, 1988—. Contbr. articles to profl. publs., chpts. to books. Recipient award Am. Heart Assn., 1974. Mem. AAAS, Am. Soc. Parenternal and Enteral Nutrition, Am. Inst. Nutrition, Phi Beta Kappa. Episcopalian. Avocations: hiking, canoeing, French horn, flower gardening. Home: 1 Anthony Dr Malvern PA 19355-1973 Office: Wyeth-Ayerst Labs PO Box 8299 Philadelphia PA 19101-8299

LIENEMANN, DELMAR ARTHUR, SR., accountant, real estate developer; b. Papillion, Nebr., May 17, 1920; s. Arthur Herman and Dorothea M. (Marth) L.; m. Charlotte Peck, Jun 17, 1944; children: Delmar Arthur Jr., David (dec.), Diane, Douglas, Dorothy, Daniel, Denise. BS, U. Nebr., 1941. CPA, Nebr. Acct. Wickstrom Supply, Lincoln, Nebr., 1941, L.L. Coryell & Sons, Lincoln, 1942, Lester Buckley, CPA, Lincoln, 1943-45; pvt. practice Lincoln, 1945—. Pres., v.p., sec., treas., bldg. chmn., charter mem. Christ Luth. Ch., Lincoln, 1949-70; co-commr. Lancaster County, Lincoln, 1954-58; pres. Lincoln Symphony Orch. Found., 1984—, Ethel S. Abbott Charitable Found. Mem. AICPAs, N.E. Soc. CPAs, Colo. Soc. CPAs, Tex. Soc. CPAs, Sertoma (sec.-treas. Lincoln chpt. 1952-68, Internat. Sertoman of Yr. 1962), Hillcrest Country Club, Nebr. Club, Nebr. Chancelors Club, Nebr. Touchdown Club, Nebr. Power Club, Nebr. Rebounders Club. Republican. Avocation: travel. Office: PO Box 81407 Lincoln NE 68501-1407

LIENHARD, JOHN HENRY, IV, mechanical engineering educator; b. St. Paul, Aug. 17, 1930; s. John Henry and Catherine Edith Lienhard; m. Carol Ann Bratton, June 20, 1959; children: John Henry V, Andrew Joseph. A.S., Multnomah Jr. Coll., 1949; BS, Oreg. State Coll., 1951; MS in M.E., U. Wash.-Seattle, 1953; PhD in Mech. Engring., U. Calif.-Berkeley, 1961. Assoc. prof. mech. engring. Wash. State U., Pullman, 1961-67; prof. mech. engring. dept. U. Ky., Lexington, 1967-80; Clyde chair prof. U. Utah, Salt Lake City, summer 1981; prof. mech. engring. U. Houston, 1980-89; M.D. Anderson prof. mech. engring. and history, 1989—. Recipient Portrait award Am. Women in Radio and TV, 1990. Mem. ASME (hon., heat transfer meml. award, Charles Russ Richards award, Ralph Coats Roe medal), Am. Soc. Engring. Edn. (Ralph Coates Roe Teaching medal). Episcopalian. Author 4 books; author/host of program on Pub. Radio, The Engines of Our Ingenuity, also numerous articles in profl. jours. Home: 3719 Durhill St Houston TX 77025 Office: U Houston Dept Mech Engring Houston TX 77204-4792

LIENHART, DAVID ARTHUR, geologist, consultant, laboratory director; b. Cin., Sept. 28, 1939; s. Arthur C. and Grace H.J. (Burger) L.; m. Donna Paula Klosterman, June 12, 1964; children—Devin Scott, Dana Ann. B.A., U. Cin., 1961, M.S., 1964. Cert. profl. geologist, Ind.; registered geologist, Del.; lic. profl. geologist, N.C. Petrographer Ohio River Div. Lab., Cin., 1964-70, geologist, 1970-76; geologist, lab. dir. Ohio River Div. Lab., 1976-90; hydrologist geotech. HTRW div. U.S. Army Corps Engrs., 1990-95; cons. constrn. rock properties and evaluation of rock for erosion control, 1995—; ptnr. Rock Products Cons.; agy. chmn. Combined Fed. Campaign, 1982-84, 89; guest spkr. internat. tech. seminars. Contbr. articles to profl. jours.; author and editor tech. publs. U. Cin. Dept. Army fellow, 1986-87; recipient Outstanding Pub. Svc. award, City of Cin., 1994. Fellow Geol. Soc. Am., Geol. Soc. London; mem. ASCE, ASTM (Excellence in Symposium and Publ. Mgmt. 1995), Assn. Engring. Geologists, Nat. Ground Water Assn., Geol. Soc. Ky., Internat. Soc. Engring. Geologists, Sigma Xi. Methodist. Avocations: fishing, music. Office: 7229 Longfield Dr Cincinnati OH 45243-2209

LIEPMANN, HANS WOLFGANG, physicist, educator; b. Berlin, Germany, July 3, 1914; came to U.S. 1939, naturalized, 1945.; s. Wilhelm and Emma (Leser) L.; m. Kate Kaschinsky, June 19, 1939 (div.); m. Dietlind Wegener Goldschmidt, 1954; 2 children. Student, U. Istanbul, 1933-35, U. Prague, 1935; Ph.D., U. Zurich, 1938; Dr. Engring. (hon.), Tech. U. Aachen, 1985. Research fellow U. Zurich, 1938-39; mem. faculty Calif. Inst. Tech., Pasadena, 1939, prof. aeronautics, 1949—, dir. Grad. Aeronautical Labs., 1972-85, Charles Lee Powell prof. fluid mechanics and thermodynamics, 1976-83, Theodore von Kármán prof. aeronautics, 1983-85, Theodore von Kármán prof. aeronautics emeritus, 1985—; mem. research and tech. adv. com. on basic research NASA. Co-author: (with A.E. Puckett) Aerodynamics of a Compressible Fluid, 1947; (with A. Roshko) Elements of Gas-dynamics, 1957. Contbr. articles to profl. jours. Recipient Physics prize U. Zurich, 1939, Pradtl Ring, German Soc. Aeros. and Astronautics, 1968, Worcester Reed Warner medal ASME, 1969, Michelson-Morley award Case Inst. Tech., 1979, Nat. Medal of Sci., U.S. Dept. Commerce, 1986, Guggenheim medal, Daniel Guggenheim Med. Bd. of Award, 1986, Nat. Medal of Tech., U.S. Dept. Commerce, 1993. Address: Calif Inst Tech Dept Aeronautics Pasadena CA 91125

LIETZ, JEREMY JON, educational administrator, writer; b. Milw., Oct. 4, 1933; s. John Norman and Dorothy B. (Drew) L.; m. Cora Fernandez, Feb. 24, 1983; children: Cheryl, Brian, Angela, Andrew, Christopher. BS, U. Wis., Milw., 1961; MS, U. Wis., Madison, 1971; EdD, Marquette U., 1980. Tchr. Milw. Pub. Schs., 1961-63, diagnostic counselor, 1968-71; sch. adminstr., 1971-95; Tchr. Madison (Wis.) Pub. Schs., 1964-65; rsch. assoc. U. Wis., Madison, 1965-67; instr. Marquette U., Milw., 1980-82; lectr. HEW Conf. on Reading, Greeley, Colo., 1973, NAESP Conf. on Reading, St. Louis, 1974, various state and nat. orgns.; co-founder, bd. dirs., cons. Ednl. Leadership Inst., Shorewood, Wis., 1980—; dir. Religious Edn. Program, Cath. Elem. East, Milw., 1985-86. Author: The Elementary School Principal's Role in Special Education, 1982; contbr. numerous articles, chpts., tests, revs. to profl. jours. V.p. PTA, 1961-62. With U.S. Army, 1954-56, ETO. Recipient Cert. of Achievement award NAESP, 1974. Mem. AAAS, Assn. Wis. Sch. Adminstrs. (mem. state planning com. 1977-79, lectr. 1982), Adminstrs. and Suprs. Coun. (mem. exec. bd. dist. 1977-79, mem. contract negotiations com. 1991-95), Filipino Am. Assn. Wis., U. Wis. Alumni Assn. (Madison), Milw. Mcpl. Chess Assn., U.S. Chess Fedn., Phi Delta Kappa. Home: 2205 N Summit Ave Milwaukee WI 53202-1213 Office: Ednl Leadership Inst PO Box 11411 Milwaukee WI 53211-0411

LIETZEN, JOHN HERVY, human resources executive, health agency volunteer; b. Kansas City, Kans., July 17, 1947; s. Walter Edwin and Kathleen Mae (Griffith) L.; children: Gwendolyn Therese, Anne Gabrielle, Sarah Kathleen. BS, Mo. Valley Coll., 1974; MS, U. Mo., 1976; postgrad, U. Nebr., 1982-88. With Union Pacific R.R., 1971—; yard condr. Union Pacific R.R., Kansas City, Kans., 1971-77; pers. officer Union Pacific R.R., Omaha, 1977-78; pers. dir. Union Pacific R.R., Cheyenne, Wyo., 1978-79, sr. tng. officer dept. claims, 1979-83, mgr. staffing, 1983-84, mgr. affirmative action, 1984-86; human resources tng. and devel. cons. Union Pacific R.R., Omaha, 1986-89, 94—, Salt Lake City, 1989-94. Bd. dirs. Berkshire Village, Kansas City, 1976-77; mem. bd. ministries Valley View Meth. Ch., Overland Park, Kans., 1976-77; pastor and staff rels. com. Hanscom Pk. United Meth. Ch., 1980-81, lay leader, 1983; asst. leader Wyo. coun. Girl Scouts U.S.A., Cheyenne, 1978-79, asst. leader, Omaha, 1980-89, Salt Lake, 1989—, bd. dirs. Great Plains Girl Scout Coun., 1987-89; exec. bd. Nebr. affiliate Am. Diabetes Assn., 1981-89, pres. Midlands chpt., 1982-84, mem. planning and orgn. com., 1986-87, bd. dirs. Utah affiliate, 1990-94, co-founder Omaha Insulin Pump Club, 1986; loaned exec. United Way of Midlands, 1984. Sgt. U.S. Army, 1968-71, Germany. Mem. ASTD, Am. Soc. Pers. and Guidance Assn., Adult and Continuing Edn. Assn. Nebr. (mem. planning com. 1982-84), Nat. Soc. for Performance and Instrn. Republican. Office: 1416 Dodge-OTC Omaha NE 68179

LIETZKE, MILTON HENRY, chemistry educator; b. Syracuse, N.Y., Nov. 23, 1920; s. Henry Robert and Emma (Gutknecht) L.; m. Marjorie Helen Padrutt, May 31, 1943; children: Kathryn Ann, Milton Henry, Carol Lynn; m. Eleanor Jean Hawkins, May 29, 1965; adopted children: Susan Lucinda, Mary Lindl. B.A., Colgate U., 1942; M.S., U. Wis., 1944, Ph.D., 1949. Lab. supr. Tenn. Eastman Corp., Oak Ridge, 1944-47; group leader chemistry div. Oak Ridge Nat. Lab., 1949-74, sr. scientist, 1978-83; prof. chemistry U. Tenn., Knoxville, 1964-90, prof. emeritus, 1990—. Contbr. numerous articles and reports to profl. jours. Bd. dirs. Oak Rige Festival, 1962-64. Fellow Am. Inst. Chemists, N.Y. Acad. Scis.; mem. Am. Chem. Soc. (D.A. Shirley award East Tenn. sect. 1991), Sci. Research Soc. Am., Tenn. Acad. Sci., Alpha Chi Sigma. Home: 7600 Twining Dr Knoxville TN 37919-7127 Office: U Tenn Dept Chemistry Knoxville TN 37916

LIFFERS, WILLIAM ALBERT, retired chemical company executive; b. Union City, N.J., Jan. 12, 1929; s. William F. and Gertrude (Wildemann) L.; m. Mary Rafferty, Sept. 5, 1953; children—Steven, Linda, Wendy. BS in Bus. Adminstrn, Seton Hall U., 1953. With Am. Cyanamid Co., Wayne, N.J., 1953—; v.p. Cyanamid Internat., 1972-74; pres. Cyanamid Internat. (Cyanamid Americas/Far East), 1974-76, corp. v.p., 1976-77, sr. v.p., dir., 1977-78, vice chmn., 1978-93; ret., 1993; sr. advisor UN Devel. Programme, 1994; bd. dirs. Great Atlantic & Pacific Tea Co. Bd. dirs. Nat. Policy Assn., N.J. Inst. Tech. With Fin. Corps U.S. Army, 1951-53.

LIFKA, MARY LAURANNE, history educator; b. Oak Park, Ill., Oct. 31, 1937; d. Aloysius William and Loretta Catherine (Juric) L. B.A., Mundelein Coll., 1960; M.A., Loyola U., Los Angeles, 1965; Ph.D., U. Mich., 1974; postdoctoral student London U., 1975. Life teaching cert. Prof. history Mundelein Coll., Chgo., 1976-84, coordinator acad. computer, 1983-84, prof. history Coll. St. Teresa, Winona, Minn., 1984-89, Lewis U., Romeoville, Ill., 1989—; chief reader in history Ednl. Testing Service, Princeton, N.J., 1980-84; cons. world history project Longman, Inc., 1983—; cons. in European history Coll. Bd., Evanston, Ill., 1983—; mem. Com. on History in the Classroom. Author: Instructor's Guide to European History, 1983; contbr. articles to publs. Mem. Am. Hist. Assn., Ednl. Testing Service Devel. Com. of History. Democrat. Roman Catholic. Office: Lewis U RR 53 Romeoville IL 60446

LIFLAND, BURTON R., federal judge. BA, Syracuse U.; LLB, Fordham U. Bar: N.Y. Pvt. practice N.Y.C.; former chief judge U.S. Bankruptcy Ct. (so. dist.) N.Y., N.Y.C.; chief judge bankruptcy appellate U.S. Ct. Appeals (2d cir.), N.Y.C.; adj. faculty Nat. Jud. Coll.; lectr. Practicing Law Inst., others; condr. seminars, retreats; mem. faculty N.Y. Inst. Credit; mem. jud. conf. subcom. Bankruptcy Case Mgmt. on Bankruptcy; U.S. del. to UN Commn. on Internat. Trade Law. Contbg. author: Chapter 11 Theory and Practice: A Guide to Reorganization; contg. editor: Norton Bankruptcy Law and Practice. Fellow Am. Coll. Bankruptcy. Office: US Bankruptcy Ct US Customs House One Bowling Green 6th Fl New York NY 10004-1408

LIFLAND, JOHN C., federal judge; b. 1933. BA, Yale U., 1954; LLB, Harvard U., 1957. Pvt. practice law, 1957-59; law sec. to Hon. Thomas F. Meaney U.S. Dist. Ct. N.J., 1959-61; mem. firm Stryker, Tams & Dill, 1961-88; dist. judge U.S. Dist. Ct., Newark, 1988—; mem. N.J. State Bd. Bar Examiners, 1968-77. 1st lt. U.S. Army, 1958. Fellow Am. Bar Found., Assn. Fed. Bar (v.p. 1986—), N.J. State Bar Assn., Essex County Bar Assn.; mem. ABA (antitrust sect. publs. com., books editor/co-editor Antitrust Law Jour. 1981-87), Clearwater Seim Club, Essex Club, Harvard Law Sch. Assn. Office: US Dist Ct M L King Fed Bldg & Cthouse PO Box 999 Newark NJ 07101-0999*

LIFLAND, WILLIAM THOMAS, lawyer; b. Jersey City, Nov. 15, 1928; s. Charles and Carolyn (Francks) L.; m. Nancy Moffat, May 29, 1954; children—Carol M., Charles C., J. Kerin, David T. B.S., Yale U., 1949; J.D., Harvard U., 1952. Bar: D.C. 1954, N.Y. 1955, N.J. 1965. Law clk. to Justice John M. Harlan U.S. Supreme Ct., 1954-55; assoc. Cahill Gordon & Reindel, N.Y.C., 1955-58, Paris, 1958-60; ptnr. Cahill Gordon & Reindel, N.Y.C., 1965—; adj. prof. Fordham Law Sch., N.Y.C. Served as lt. USAF, 1952-54. Mem. ABA, N.Y. State Bar Assn., N.J. Bar Assn., D.C. Bar Assn., N.Y. County Lawyers Assn., Assn. Bar City N.Y. Clubs: India House (N.Y.C.), Nassau Club (Princeton, N.J.). Office: Cahill Gordon & Reindel 80 Pine St New York NY 10005-1702

LIFSCHULTZ, PHILLIP, financial and tax consultant, accountant, lawyer; b. Oak Park, Ill., Mar. 5, 1927; s. Abraham Albert and Frances Rhoda (Siegel) L.; m. Edith Louise Leavitt, June 27, 1948; children: Gregory, Bonnie, Jodie. BS in Acctg., U. Ill., 1949; JD, John Marshall Law Sch., 1956. Bar: Ill. 1956; CPA, Ill. Tax mgr. Arthur Andersen & Co., Chgo., 1957-63; v.p. taxes Montgomery Ward & Co., Chgo., 1963-78; fin. v.p., contr. Henry Crown & Co., Chgo., 1978-81; prin. Phillip Lifschultz & Assocs., Chgo., 1981—; exec. dir. Dodi Orgn., 1987-90; v.p. Altra Travel, Northbrook, Ill., 1995—; pres. Great Lakes Shoe Co., Bannockburn, Ill., 1996—. Mem. adv. coun. Coll. Commerce and Bus. Adminstrn. U. Ill., Urbana-Champaign, 1977-78; chmn., Civic Fedn. Chgo., 1980-82; chmn. adv. bd. to Auditor Gen. of Ill., 1965-73; project dir. Exec. Service Corps of Chgo., Chgo. Bd. Edn. and State of Ill. projects, 1980-87. With U.S. Army, 1945-46. Mem. Ill. Bar Assn., Chgo. Bar Assn., Am. Inst. CPA's, Ill. CPA Soc., Am. Arbitration Assn. (comml. panel 1983-94), Nat. Retail Merchants Assn. (chmn. tax com. 1975-78), Am. Retail Fedn. (chmn. taxation com. 1971), Standard Club. Home and Office: 976 Oak Dr Glencoe IL 60022-1427

LIFSON, KALMAN ALAN, management consultant, retail executive; b. Mpls., Oct. 15, 1926; s. Maurice Kalman and Gertrude (Shulkin) L.; m. Irene Londer, June 17, 1950 (dec. July 1968); m. Judith Abrams, Sept. 3, 1969; children: Valerie Leftwich, Kipp, Ione Spear, Stacey Dorfman, Grant Dorfman. BS in Naval Tech., U. Minn., 1946, MABA, 1949; PhD in Psychology, Purdue U., 1951. Commd. ensign USN, 1945, lt. (j.g), 1952; engring. officer Panama Canal Zone, 1945-46; supr. indsl. engring. Temco Aircraft, Dallas, 1951-52; mgmt. engring. officer USN, Washington, 1953-54, resigned; prin. Lifson, Wilson, Ferguson & Winick, Dallas, 1954-94, Pers. Decisions, Inc., Dallas, 1995—; chmn. Harris'Dept. Stores, San Bernadino, Calif., 1980-94, Tex. Rsch. and Electronic Corp. and successors, Dallas, 1962-94, Electronic Mgmt. Info. Sys., 1970-94; chmn. emeritus B.R. Blackmarr & Assocs., Dallas, 1986—; chmn. Fed. Home Loan Bank of 9th Dist., Little Rock, 1979-80; bd. dirs. Bioseparations Inc., Tucson, Ariz., Century Univ., Albuquerque; speaker in fields of psychology, retailing, banking, ops. rsch. Contbr. articles to profl. jours. Chmn. Congl. Commn. on Guaranteed Student Loans, Washington, 1975, Commn. on Orgn. of U.S. Dept. Labor, Washington, 1976; mem. Tex. Commn. on State Employee Productivity, Austin, Tex., 1985. Mem. Am. Psychol. Assn., World Pres. Orgn., Columbian Club (treas. 1950—), Crescent Club, Sigma Xi. Jewish. Office: Pers Decisions Inc 600 Las Colinas Blvd E Ste 1700 Irving TX 75039-5624 *"Winners" are those who can make the big play, who can turn the game around, who can conceive and institute dramatic changes. Those few of us who have been so endowed and developed must use our winnership to effect significant improvements to the well-being of those within our spheres of influence.*

LIFTIN, JOHN MATTHEW, lawyer; b. Washington, June 25, 1943; children: Eric, Hilary. AB, U. Pa., 1964; LLB, Columbia U., 1967. Bar: N.Y. 1967, D.C. 1974, U.S. Dist. Ct. D.C. 1975, U.S. Ct. Appeals (D.C. cir.) 1975, U.S. Supreme Ct. 1980. Assoc. Sullivan & Cromwell, N.Y.C., 1967-71; spl. counsel to chmn. SEC, Washington, 1971-72, assoc. dir. market reg. div., 1972-74; ptnr. Rogers & Wells, Washington, 1974-85; pres. Quadrex Securities Corp., N.Y.C., 1985-87; sr. v.p., gen. counsel Kidder, Peabody Group Inc., N.Y.C., 1987-96; mem. adv. bd. securities regulation and law reports Bur. Nat. Affairs, Inc., Washington, 1979—. Contbr. articles on securities law to profl. jours. Mem. ABA (chmn. com. on fed. regulation securities), Univ. Club.

LIFTON, ROBERT JAY, psychiatrist, author; b. N.Y.C., May 16, 1926; s. Harold A. and Ciel (Roth) L.; m. Betty Jean Kirschner, Mar. 1, 1952; children: Kenneth Jay, Natasha Karen. Student, Cornell U., 1942-44; MD, N.Y. Med. Coll., 1948, DHL, 1977; DSc (hon.), Lawrence U., 1971, Merrimack Coll., 1973; DHL (hon.), Wilmington Coll., 1975, N.Y. Med. Coll., 1977, Marlboro Coll., 1983, Maryville Coll., 1983, Iona Coll., 1984; DSc (hon.), U. Vt., 1984, Amerika Institut Der Universitat, Munich, 1989; DHL (hon.), U. New Haven, 1986. Intern Jewish Hosp., Bklyn., 1948-49; resident psychiatry State U. N.Y. Downstate Med. Center, 1949-51; mem. faculty Washington Sch. Psychiatry, 1954-55; research assoc. psychiatry, also assoc. East Asian studies Harvard U., 1956-61; Found.'s Fund for research psychiatry assoc. prof. Yale Med. Sch., 1961-67, research prof., 1967—; disting. prof. psychiatry and psychology, dir. Ctr. on Violence and Human Survival John Jay Coll. Criminal Justice, the Grad Sch. and Univ. Ctr. and Mt. Sinai Sch. Medicine, CUNY, 1985—; cons. behavioral scis. study sect. NIMH, 1962-64; com. invasion of privacy N.Y. State Bar Assn., 1963-64, various law firms, Columbia seminars modern Japan and Oriental thought and religion,

1965-70; Peter B. Lewis lectr., Princeton U., 1988; Gay lectr. Harvard Med. Sch., 1976, Messenger lectr. Cornell U., 1980. Author: Thought Reform and the Psychology of Totalism: A Study of Brainwashing in China, 1961, 1989, Revolutionary Immorality: Mao Tse-Tung and the Chinese Cultural Revolution, 1968, Death in Life: Survivors of Hiroshima (Nat. Book award), 1969, 1991, (Van Wyck Brooks award), History and Human Survival, 1970, Boundaries: Psychological Man in Revolution, 1970, Home from the War: Vietnam Veterans—Neither Victims Nor Executioners, 1973 (Nat. Book award nominee), (with Eric Olson) Living and Dying, 1974, The Life of the Self, 1976, (with Shuichi Kato and Michael Reich) Six Lives/Six Deaths: Portraits from Modern Japan, 1979, The Broken Connection: On Death and the Continuity of Life, 1979, (with Richard A. Falk) Indefensible Weapons: The Political and Psychological Case Against Nuclearism, 1982, 1991; humorous cartoons Birds, 1969, PsychoBirds, 1979, (with Nicholas Humphrey) In a Dark Time, 1984 (Brit. edit. selected Top Twenty Nat. Peace Book Week, Martin Luther King award, Eng.), The Nazi Doctors: Medical Killing and Psychology of Genocide, 1986 (Nat. Jewish Book award, Los Angeles Times Book prize for history 1987, Lisl and Leo Eitinger award, Oslo, Norway, 1988), German edit. 1988, The Future of Immortality and Other Essays for a Nuclear Age, 1987; (with Eric Markusen) The Genocidal Mentality: Nazi Holocaust and Nuclear Threat, 1990, The Protean Self: Human Resilience in an Age of Fragmentation, 1993, (with G. Mitchell) Hiroshima in America: Fifty Years of Denial, 1995; editor: Woman in America, 1965, America and the Asian Revolutions, 1970, (with R.A. Falk and G. Kolko) Crimes of War, 1971, (with Eric Olson) Explorations in Psychohistory: The Wellfleet Papers, 1975, (with Eric Chivian, Suzanna Chivian, John E. Mack) Last Aid: Medical Dimensions of Nuclear War, 1982, The Genocidal Mentality: Nazi Doctor and Nuclear Threat, 1990. Organizer redress group opposing Vietnam War IAEA, Vienna, 1975. Served to capt. USAF, 1951-53. Recipient Pub. Svc. award N.Y. Soc. Clin. Psychologists, Alumni medal N.Y. Med. Coll., 1970, Karen Horney lectr. award, 1972, Disting. Svc. award Soc. Adolescent Psychiatry, 1972, Mt. Airy Found. Gold medal, 1973, Hiroshima Gold medal, 1975, Gandhi Peace award, 1984, Bertrand Russell Soc. award, 1985, Holocaust Meml. award, 1986, 1st Ann. Nuc. Psychology Rsch. award Harvard U., 1986, Brit Hadorot Convenant of Generations award, 1987, Max A. Hayman award Am. Orthopsychiat. Assn., 1992, Nat. Living Treasure award Psychiat. Inst., 1994, Outstanding Achievement award Armenian Am. Soc. for Studies on Stress and Genocide, 1996. Fellow Am. Acad. Arts and Scis., Am. Psychiat. Assn. (Oskar Pfister award 1987); mem. Assn. Asian Studies, AAAS, Group Study Psychohist. Process (coordinator), Fedn. Am. Scientists, Soc. Psychol. Study of Social Issues. Office: John Jay Coll Criminal Justice 899 10th Ave New York NY 10019-1029

LIFTON, ROBERT KENNETH, diversified companies executive; b. N.Y.C., Jan. 9, 1928; s. Benjamin and Anna (Pike) L.; m. Loretta J. Silver, Sept. 5, 1954; children: Elizabeth Gail Lifton Hooper, Karen Grace Lifton Healy. BBA magna cum laude, CCNY, 1948; LLB, Yale U., 1951; doctorate (hon.), Bar Ilan U., Israel, 1993. Bar: N.Y. 1952. Assoc. Kaye, Scholer, Fierman, Hays & Handler, N.Y.C., 1955-56; asst. to pres. Glickman Corp., N.Y.C., 1956-57; pres. Robert K. Lifton, Inc., N.Y.C., 1957-61; chmn. bd. Terminal Tower Co., Inc., Cleve., 1959-63; pres. Transcontinental Investing Corp., N.Y.C., 1961-72, chmn. bd., 1969-72; ptnr. Venture Assocs., 1972-89; pres. Preferred Health Care Ltd., 1983-88; chmn. bd. dirs. Marcade Group, Inc., 1986-91, Medis El, 1993—, Cell Diagnostics, Inc., 1992—, Medis Inc., 1992—; pres., chmn. bd. dirs. Team Am., Inc., 1983-85; treas. Consol. Accessories Corp., 1980-88, Caron's Connection, Inc., 1985-89; bd. dirs. Bank Leumi Trust co., N.Y.C.; mem. faculty Columbia U. Law Sch., 1973-78, Yale U. Law Sch., 1972-75; guest lectr. Practicing Law Inst., Yale Law Sch., Pace Inst., NYU; founder Nat. Exec. Conf., Washington, Inc.; chmn. oversight com. for Masters Degree, NYU Real Estate Inst., 1987-88. Author: Practical Real Estate: Legal Tax and Business Strategies, 1978; contbr. articles to profl. jours. and handbooks. Mem. McGovern econ. adv. com., 1972-73; chmn. parents com. Barnard Coll., 1976-78; mem. com. of the collection Whitney Mus., 1976-79; trustee Yale U. Sch. Fund, 1974-77, NYU Real Estate Inst., 1983-89; chmn., bd. dirs. Fund for Religious Liberty, 1987-88; pres. Am. Jewish Congress, 1988-94; chmn. Internat. Bd. U.S. Mid. East Project coun. fgn. rels., 1994—; pres. Israel Policy Forum, 1994—, chmn. bd., 1996—; bd. dirs. Builders for Peace, 1993—, Abraham Fund, 1993—, Tel Aviv Mus., 1996—, Besa Inst., 1994—, HIAS, 1990-96; mem. exec. com. AIPAC, 1990—; vice-chmn. NJCRAC, 1994—; exec. com. AIPAC, 1993-96; trustee Am. Friends of Bar Ilam U., 1996—; bd. dirs. Pub. Health Rsch. Inst., 1996—. Lt. (j.g.) USN, 1952-55. Recipient Achievement award Sch. Bus. Alumni Soc. CCNY, James Madison award Fund for Religious Liberty, 1987, Stephen S. Wise award Am. Jewish Congress, 1993. Mem. Order of Coif, Beta Gamma Sigma. Home: 983 Park Ave New York NY 10028-0808 Office: 805 3rd Ave New York NY 10022-7513

LIFTON, WALTER M., psychology and education consultant; b. Bklyn., Nov. 2, 1918; s. Samuel S. and Sarah G. (Berman) L.; m. Ruth S. Knoppow, Oct. 1, 1940; children: Hazel Miriam Kroesser Palmer, Robert William. B.A., Bklyn. Coll., 1942; M.A., NYU, 1947, Ph.D., 1950. Sr. vocat. appraiser Vets. Guidance Center, Hunter Coll., 1946-48; psychologist, research div. NYU, 1948-50; assoc. prof. edn., guidance and counseling U. Ill., 1950-59; dir. guidance publs. and services Sci. Research Assocs., Chgo., 1959-63; coordinator pupil personnel services Rochester City Sch. Dist., N.Y., 1964-70; prof. edn. dept. counseling psychology and student devel. SUNY-Albany, 1970-82, prof. emeritus, 1982—; edn. and psychology cons., 1982—; disting. vis. prof. Coll. Grad. Studies, W.Va., 1985-86; vis. prof., lectr. guidance and counseling 34 colls. and univs.; cons. in field. Author: Keys to Vocational Decisions, 1964, Working With Groups, 2d edit, 1966, Educating for Tomorrow—The Role of Media, Career Devel. and Society, 1970, Groups—Facilitating Individual Growth and Societal Change, 1972; film Just Like a Family, 1979; contbr. articles to profl. jours. Mem. White House Conf. on Children and Youth, 1969-70; cons. Title III ESEA project, Knox County, Tenn., 1967; interim dir. Action for a Better Community, Rochester, 1964-65, Center for Coop. Action in Urban Edn., 1966; apptd. to Durham County Youth Svcs. Bd., 1994. Served with AUS, 1942-46. Fellow Assn. for Specialists in Group Work (sec. 1976—, pres. 1980-81, Eminent Career award 1986); mem. Nat. Assn. Pupil Personnel Adminstrs. (pres. 1970), Nat. Vocat. Guidance Assn. Home and Office: 2701 Pickett Rd Apt 3036 Durham NC 27705-5651 *As a person in the mental health field my focus has been increasingly concerned with prevention rather than remediation, and with helping people shape their environments not just adjust to the status quo.*

LIGARE, KATHLEEN MEREDITH, strategy and marketing executive; b. Providence, Aug. 29, 1950; d. Kenneth MacAllister and Carol (Smith) Ligare. BA, Carleton Coll., 1972; MS, Yale U., 1976; MBA, Northwestern U., 1982. Sr. assoc. Booz, Allen & Hamilton, Chgo., 1978-82; mgr. mktg. and product devel. GE Capital Corp., Barrington, Ill., 1982-83, planning mgr., 1983-84, region mgr., 1984-85; sr. v.p. sales and mktg. Gen. Electric Capital Corp., Barrington, Ill., 1992-93, sr. v.p. internat., 1993-96; prin. KML Enterprises, Inc., Chgo., 1985-92; dir. sales and mktg. GE Capital Europe, Brussels, Belgium, 1995-97; sr. v.p., mng. dir. GE Capital Asia Pacific, Hong Kong, Hong Kong, 1997—. Author: Illinois Women's Directory, 1977. Bd. dirs. Midwest Women's Ctr., Chgo., 1978-89; chair, bd. dirs. alumni ann. fund Carleton Coll., 1990-93, bd. dirs., 1987-94, mem. alumni bd., 1989, trustee, 1993—. Mem. Chgo. Fin. Exch. Office: GE Capital Asia Pacific Ltd Corp, 161F Three Exchange Sq, Hong Kong China

LIGETT, WALDO BUFORD, chemist; b. Middletown, Ohio, Nov. 2, 1916; s. Waldo Buford and Mabel Louise (Berkley) L.; m. Ann Elizabeth Hartwell, Aug. 29, 1940; children: Robert A., John D., Michael T., Steven D., Daniel L. B.S., Antioch Coll., 1939; M.S., Purdue U., 1941, Ph.D., 1944, D.Sc. (hon.), 1965; grad., Advanced Mgmt. Program, Harvard U., 1967. Chemist Eastman Kodak Co., Rochester, N.Y., 1935-38; research supr. Ethyl Corp., Detroit, 1944-51; asst. dir. chem. Ethyl Corp., 1951-52, asso. dir. chem., 1952-62, dir. research and devel., 1962-63; v.p. Celanese Chem. Co., Corpus Christi, Tex., 1963-64; v.p. tech. and mfg. Celanese Chem. Co., 1964-66; tech. dir. Celanese Corp., N.Y.C., 1966-67; v.p. Celanese Corp., 1967-72, Franklin Inst., Phila., 1973-81; pres. Franklin Inst. Research Labs., 1975-81; dir. Franklin-Hahnemann Inst., 1974-81. Fellow Am. Inst. Chemists; mem. Am. Chem. Soc., AAAS, Indsl. Research Inst., Research Soc. Am., N.Y. Assn. Research Dirs., Am. Nuclear Soc., Atomic Indsl. Forum. Patentee in field. Home: 377 Carolina Meadows Villa Chapel Hill NC 27514-7521

LIGGETT, HIRAM SHAW, JR., retired diversified industry financial executive; b. St. Louis, Jan. 12, 1932; s. Hiram Shaw and Lucille (Gardner) L.; m. Margaret McGinness, Jan. 21, 1961; children: Lucille Gardner, Frances Shelby. BA, Colo. Coll., 1953; LLD (hon.), Maryville U., 1991. Cashier Brown Group, Inc., St. Louis, 1957-64, asst. treas., 1964-68, treas., 1968—, v.p., 1983—; bd. dirs. Roosevelt Fed. Savs. and Loan, St. Louis. Past trustee, vice chmn. bd. dirs. McKendree Coll., Lebanon, Ill., 1980-88; trustee, past chmn. bd. trustees Maryville U., St. Louis, 1982-91; past chmn. Provident Counseling, 1983; past v.p., bd. dirs. Jr. Achievement Miss. Valley, 1983; past dir. bi-state chpt. ARC, 1983; bd. dirs., pres. Cardinal Ritter Inst.; bd. dirs., chmn. devel. bd. Paraquad. Capt. USNR, 1953-79. Mem. Fin. Execs. Inst. (pres., dir. 1983—), St. Louis Coun. Navy League (bd. councilors 1982), Univ. Club (St. Louis, chmn. house com. 1975-78), Strathalbyn Farms Club (chmn. house com., pres. bd. dirs.), Alpha Kappa Psi, Tau Kappa Alpha. Republican. Presbyterian. Home: 64 Chesterfield Lakes Rd Chesterfield MO 63005-5400

LIGGETT, LAWRENCE MELVIN, vacuum equipment manufacturing company executive; b. Denver, June 22, 1917; s. Thomas Harrison and Mary Deacon (Taylor) L.; m. Edith Irene Harris, June 20, 1943; children: Pamela Jane Liggett Schwartz, Betty Sue Liggett Brooks El Gammal. A.B., Central Coll., Pella, Iowa, 1938; Ph.D. in Chemistry, Iowa State Coll., 1943. Research chemist NDRC, Iowa State Coll., 1941-43; plant mgr. Cardox Corp., Claremore, Okla., 1943-48; dir. inorganic research Wyandotte Chems. Corp., 1948-55; dir. research, v.p. tech. dir. Airco Speer div. Airco, Inc., 1955-70, pres. Airco Electronics div., 1970-75; pres. Airco Temescal div. BOC Group, Berkeley, Calif., 1975-82; cons. bus. and tech., 1982—. Author. Mem. Am. Chem. Soc., Electronic Industries Assn. Republican. Patentee in field. Home: 1856 Piedras Cir Danville CA 94526-1329

LIGGETT, THOMAS JACKSON, retired seminary president; b. Nashville, May 27, 1919; s. Thomas Jackson and Lola Cleveland (Ballentine) L.; m. Virginia Corrine Moore, Aug. 12, 1941; children: Thomas Milton, Margaret Ann Liggett Herod. A.B., Transylvania U., 1940; M.Div., Lexington Theol. Sem., 1944; postgrad., Union Theol. Sem. and Columbia U., 1950-52; LL.D., Interam. U., 1965, Culver-Stockton Coll., 1959, Butler U., 1975; D.H.L., Transylvania U., 1969; D.D., Eureka Coll., 1971, Phillips U., 1989. Ordained to ministry Christian Ch., 1940; pastor in Danville, Ky., 1943-45; missionary Argentina, 1946-57; prof. Union Theol. Sem., Buenos Aires, 1948-57; pres. Evang. Sem. of P.R., 1957-65; exec. sec. for Latin Am. Christian Ch., 1965-67, chmn. div. world mission, 1967-68; pres. United Christian Missionary Soc., 1968-74; pres. Christian Theol. Sem., Indpls., 1974-86, ret., 1986; del. World Council Chs. assembly in Uppsala, 1968, adviser assembly, Nairobi, Kenya, 1975; mem. governing bd. Nat. Council Chs., 1969-75, 85-87; moderator Disciples of Christ, 1985-87. Author: Where Tomorrow Struggles to be Born, 1970; Editor: Cuadernos Teologicos, 1954-55. Co-chmn. McGovern Task Force on Fgn. Policy in Latin Am., 1972, Democratic precinct committeeman, 1970-72. Mem. Disciples of Christ Hist. Soc. (life), Theta Phi. Home: 647 W Harrison Ave Claremont CA 91711-4537

LIGGETT, TWILA MARIE CHRISTENSEN, academic administrator, public television company executive; b. Pipestone, Minn., Mar. 25, 1944; d. Donald L. Christensen and Irene E. (Zweigle) Christensen Flesher. BS, Union Coll., Lincoln, Nebr., 1966; MA, U. Nebr., 1971, PhD, 1977. Dir. vocal and instrumental music Sprague (Nebr.)-Martell Pub. Sch., 1966-67; tchr. vocal music, pub. schs., Syracuse, Nebr., 1967-69; tchr. Norris Pub. Sch., Firth, Nebr., 1969-71; cons. fed. reading project, pub. schs., Lincoln, 1971-72; curriculum coord. Westside Community Schs., Omaha, 1972-74; dir. State program Right-to-Read, Nebr. Dept. Edn., 1974-76; asst. dir. Nebr. Commn. on Status of Women, 1976-80; asst. dir. project adminstrn./devel. Great Plains Nat. Instructional TV Libr., U. Nebr., Lincoln, 1980—; exec. prodr. Reading Rainbow, PBS nat. children's series, 1980— (9 Nat. Daytime Emmy awards 1990-96, Nat. Primetime Emmy nomination 1996); cons. U.S. Dept. Edn., 1981; Far West Regional Lab., San Francisco, 1978-79; panelist, presenter AAAS, NEA, NEH, NSF, Corp. Pub. Broadcasting, Internat. Reading Assn., Blue Ribbon panelist, Acad. TV Arts & Scis., 1991-96, final judge Nat. Cable Programming Awards, 1991-92. Author: Reading Rainbow's Guide to Children's Books: The 101 Best Titles, 1994, rev. edit., 1996. Bd. dirs. Planned Parenthood, Lincoln, 1979-81. Recipient Grand award N.Y., 1993, Gold medal award Internat. Film and TV Festival, 1996, World Gold medal N.Y. Internat. Film & TV, 1995, Coun. on Internat. Nontheatrical Events Golden Eagle award, 1995, Image award NAACP, 1994, 96. Mem. NATAS, Internat. Reading Assn. (Spl. award Contbns. Worldwide Literacy 1992), Am. Women in Film and TV,Phi Delta Kappa. Presbyterian. Home: 301 E 79th St 23P New York NY 10021-0944 also: 282 W Lakeshore Dr Lincoln NE 68528 Office: PO Box 80669 Lincoln NE 68501-0669

LIGGINS, GEORGE LAWSON, microbiologist, diagnostic company executive; b. Roanoke, Va., June 19, 1937; m. Joyce Preston Liggins, Sept. 3, 1966; 1 child, George Lawson Jr. BA, Hampton U., 1962; cert. med. technician, Meharry Med. Sch., 1963; MPH, U. N.C., 1969; PhD, U. Va., Charlottesville, 1975. Med. technician Vets. Hosp., Hampton, Va., 1963-66; rsch. technician U. N.C. Med. Sch., Chapel Hill, 1966-69; postdoctoral fellow Scripps Clinic, La Jolla, Calif., 1975-76, Salk Inst., La Jolla, 1976-77; rsch. mgr. Hyland div. Baxter, Costa Mesa, Calif., 1977-78; R & D dir. diagnostics div. Baxter, Roundlake, Ill., 1978-83; pres., COO Internat. Immunology, Murrieta, Calif., 1983-86; chmn., CEO Bacton Assay Systems, Inc., San Marcos, Calif., 1986—; cons. Beckman Instruments, Inc., Brea, Calif., 1987-90, Paramax divsn. Baxter, Irvine, Calif., 1988-90, Scantibodies Lab., Santee, Calif., 1990-92; presenter in field; mem. virology study Cold Spring Harbor Lab., L.I., N.Y., 1974. Contbr. articles to profl. jours. Fellow NIH, 1975, Am. Cancer Soc., 1976. Mem. Am. Soc. Microbiology, Am. Assn. Clin. Chemistry, Van Slyke Soc. of Am. Assn. Clin. Chemistry (chmn. elect 1997. program chmn. San Diego Conf. Nucleic Acids 1996), Am. Heart Assn., Nat. Hampton Alumni Assn. (v.p. 1996—), Omega Psi Phi. Republican. Methodist. Avocations: music, golf, tennis, literature. Office: Bacton Assay Systems Inc 772 N Twin Oaks Valley Rd San Marcos CA 92069-1714

LIGGIO, CARL DONALD, lawyer; b. N.Y.C., Sept. 5, 1943. AB, Georgetown U., 1963; JD, NYU, 1967. Bar: N.Y. 1967, D.C. 1967, Wis. 1983. Cons. Arent, Fox, Kintner, Plotkin & Kahn, Washington, 1968-69; assoc. White & Case, N.Y.C., 1969-72; gen. counsel Arthur Young & Co., N.Y.C., 1972-89, Ernst & Young, N.Y.C., 1989-94; ptnr. Dickinson, Wright, Moon, Van Dusen & Freeman, Chgo., 1995—; mem. Brookings Civil Justice Reform Task Force, 1988—. Mem. editl. bd. Rsch. in Acctg. Jour.; contbr. articles to profl. jours. Trustee Fordham Prep. Sch. Mem. ABA, N.Y. State Bar Assn., D.C. Bar Assn., Am. Corp. Counsel Assn. (chmn. bd. dirs. 1984, mem. exec. com. 1982-95), Am. Judicature Soc. (bd. dirs. 1988-92), Coll. Law Mgmt. Home: 233 E Walton St Chicago IL 60611-1526 Office: 225 W Washington St Chicago IL 60606-3418

LIGGIO, JEAN VINCENZA, adult education educator, artist; b. N.Y.C., Nov. 5, 1927; d. Vincenzo and Bernada (Terrusa) Verro; m. John Liggio, June 6, 1948; children: Jean Constance, Joan Bernadette. Student, N.Y. Inst. Photography, 1965, Elizabeth Seton Coll., 1984, Parsons Sch. of Design, 1985. Hairdresser Beauty Shoppe, N.Y.C., 1947-65; freelance oil colors and portraits N.Y.C., 1958-75; instr. watercolor N.Y. Dept. Pks., Recreation and Conservation, Yonkers, 1985-89, Bronxville (N.Y.) Adult Sch., 1989—; substitute tchr. cosmetology Yonkers Bd. Edn., 1988-89. Paintings pub. by Donald Art Co., C.R. Gibson Greeting Card Co.; 12 watercolor paintings for Avon Calendar, Avon Cosmetics Co., 1994, 96; 12 florals for Avon-Can. Publ., 1996, 97; 12 floral paintings published by Enesco Corp., 1996; 2 floral greeting cards published by C.R. Gibson Co. Publ., 1996; floral and still life images on mesh interlock canvas and sold in needlework kits published by Candamar Designs Inc., 1997; floral greeting card printed by C.R. Gibson Co., 1997; pub. is Friends Jour. Mag., Phila. Recipient numerous awards. Mem. Mt. Vernon Art Assn. (pres. membership com. 1983—), Mamaroneck Artist's Guild, Hudson River Contemporary Artist's, Scarsdale Art Assn. (publicity chmn. 1984-89), New Rochelle (N.Y.) Art Assn. Avocation: collect antiques. Home and Office: 166 Helena Ave Yonkers NY 10710-2524

LIGHT, ALFRED ROBERT, lawyer, political scientist, educator; b. Atlanta, Dec. 14, 1949; s. Alfred M. Jr. and Margaret Francis (Asbury) L.; m. Mollie Sue Hall, May 25, 1977; children: Joseph Robert, Gregory Andrew. Student Ga. Inst. Tech., 1967-69; BA with highest honors, Johns Hopkins U., 1971; PhD, U. N.C., 1976; JD cum laude, Harvard U., 1981. Bar: D.C. 1981, Va. 1982. Tax clk. IRS, 1967; lab. technician Custom Farm Services Soils Testing Lab., 1968; warehouse asst. State of Ga. Mines, Mining and Geology, 1970; clk.-typist systems mgmt. div., def. contract adminstrv. services region Def. Supply Agy., Atlanta, 1971, research and teaching asst. dept. polit. sci. U. N.C., Chapel Hill, 1971-74; research asst. Inst. Research in Social Sci., 1975-77; program analyst Office of Sec. Def., 1974; asst. prof. polit. sci., research scientist Ctr. Energy Research, Tex. Tech U., Lubbock, 1977-78; research asst. grad. sch. edn., Harvard U., 1978-79; assoc. Butler, Binion, Rice, Cook & Knapp, Houston, summer 1980, Bracewell & Patterson, Washington, summer 1980, Hunton & Williams, Richmond, Va., 1981-89, of counsel, 1989-93, 95-96; assoc. prof. St. Thomas U. Sch. Law, Miami, Fla., 1989-93, prof., 1993—, interim dean, 1993-94. Bd. advisors Toxics Law Reporter, Bur. Nat. Affairs, Washington, 1987—; contbr. articles to profl. jours. Charter mem. West Broward Community Ch. Capt. USAR, 1971-85. Grantee NSF, Inst. Evaluation Research, U. Mass., Ctr. Energy Research, Tex. Tech U., 1977-78; recipient Julius Turner award Johns Hopkins U., 1971, William Anderson award Am. Polit. Sci. Assn., 1977. Mem. ABA (vice-chmn. tort and ins. practice sect. 1988—, nat. res. and environ. sect. 1993—), Fed. Bar Assn., Va. Bar Assn., Richmond Bar Assn., Phi Beta Kappa, Phi Eta Sigma. Democrat. Home: 1042 Woodfall Ct Fort Lauderdale FL 33326-2832 Office: St Thomas U Sch Law 16400 NW 32nd Ave Opa Locka FL 33054-6459

LIGHT, ARTHUR HEATH, bishop; s. Alexander Heath and Mary Watkins (Nelson) L.; m. Sarah Ann Jones, June 12, 1954; children: William Alexander, Philip Nelson, John Page, Sarah Heath. BA, Hampden-Sydney Coll., 1951, DD, 1987; MDiv, Va. Theol. Sem., 1954, DD, 1970; DD, St. Paul's Coll., 1979. Ordained priest Episcopal Ch., 1955. Rector West Mecklenburg Cure, Boydton, Va., 1954-58, Christ Ch., Elizabeth City, N.C., 1958-63, St. Marys Ch., Kinston, N.C., 1963-67, Christ and St. Luke's Ch., Norfolk, Va., 1967-79; bishop Diocese of Southwestern Va., Roanoke, 1979-96; pres. Province III Episcopal Ch., 1984-93; mem. adv. coun. to presiding bishop, 1985-93; nominating com. 25th presiding bishop of the Episcopal Ch., 1994-97. Author: God, The Gift, The Giver, 1984. Bd. dirs. United Cmty. Fund, 1969-79, Norfolk Seamen's Friends Soc., 1969-79, Tidewater Assembly on Family Life, 1970-79, Friends of Juvenile Ct., 1975-79, Va. Inst. Pastoral Care, 1971-72; bd. dirs., exec. com. Va. Coun. Chs., 1979—; bd. dirs. Roanoke Valley Coun. Cmty. Svcs., 1980-83, Virginians Organized for Informed Cmty. Effort, 1981—; bd. dirs. Appalachian People's Svc. Orgn., 1981-91, pres., 1981-85, v.p., 1989-91; bio-med. ethics com. Ea. Va. Med. Sch., 1973-79, Lewis Gale Hosp., Salem, 1988—, Cmty. Hosp. Roanoke Valley, 1990-94; trustee Va. Episc. Sch., Lynchburg, 1979-96, Episc. H.S., Alexandria, 1979-96, Boys' Home, Covington, 1979-96, Stuart Hall Sch., Staunton, 1979-96, St. Paul's Coll., Lawrenceville, 1979-88; chmn. com. on continuing edn. Va. Theol. Sem., Alexandria, 1985-96, v.p. bd. trustees, 1987-96; bd. dirs., co-chmn. rural residency program Appalachian Ministries Ednl. Resource Ctr., Berea, Ky., 1985-87; mem. coord. cabinet Va. Coun. Churches, 1988-96, chmn. com. on church and soc., 1989-92; mem. Am. com. Kiyosato Ednl. Experiment Project, 1990—, v.p., 1991—; mem. Gen. Conv. Standing Com. on World Mission, 1988-94, chmn., 1991-94; trustee Kanuga Conf. Ctr., 1991—; bd. dirs. Conflict Resolution Ctr., 1996—; cmty. rels. task force City of Roanoke, 1995—. Named Young Man of Yr., Jaycees, 1961, 63; fellow St. George's Coll., Jerusalem, 1978, 89, fellow in biomed. ethics U. Va., 1989. Democrat.

LIGHT, BETTY JENSEN PRITCHETT, former college dean; b. Omaha, Sept. 14, 1924; d. Lars Peter and Ruth (Norby) Jensen; m. Morgan S. Pritchett, June 27, 1944 (dec. 1982); children: Randall Wayne, Robin Kay Pritchett Church, Royce Marie Pritchett Creech; m. Kenneth F. Light, Nov. 23, 1985. B.S., Portland State U., 1965; M.B.A., U. Oreg., 1966; Ed.D., Oreg. State U., 1973. Buyer Rodgers Stores, Inc., Portland, Oreg., 1947-62; chmn. bus. div. Mt. Hood Community Coll., Gresham, Oreg., 1966-70, dir. evening coll., 1970-71, assoc. dean instn., 1972-77, dean humanities and behavioral scis., 1977-79, dean devel. and spl. programs, 1979-83; dean communication arts, humanities and social scis. Mt. Hood Community Coll., 1983-86; mem. state com. for articulation between cmty. colls. and higher edn., 1976-78; mem. Gov.'s Coun. on Career and Vocat. Edn., 1977-86; owner Effective Real Estate Mgmt., 1982—. Author: Values and Perceptions of Community College Professional Staff in Oregon, 1973; contbg. author: (case study) The Pritchett Study in Retailing, An Economic View, 1969. Mem. Gresham City Council, 1983-86. Mem. Oreg. Bus. Edn. Assn., Am. Assn. Higher Edn., Nat. Assn. Staff and Oreg. Devel., Oreg. Women's Polit. Caucus, Am. Vocat. Assn., Oreg. Vocat Assn., Danish Heritage Soc. Club: Soroptimist (pres. 1974-75, 81-82). Home: 1635 NE Country Club Ave Gresham OR 97030-4432

LIGHT, CHRISTOPHER UPJOHN, writer, computer musician, photographer; b. Kalamazoo, Jan. 4, 1937; s. Richard and Rachel Mary (Upjohn) L.; m. Lilykate Victoria Wenner, June 22, 1963 (div. 1986); children: Victoria Mary, Christopher Upjohn Jr.; m. Margo Ruth Bosker, Jan. 2, 1994. AB, Carleton Coll., 1958; MS, Columbia U., 1962; MBA, We. Mich. U., 1967; PhD, Washington U., 1971. Editor, pub. The Kalamazoo mag., 1963-66; pres. Mich. Outdoor Pub. Co., Kalamazoo, 1965-68; product planner The Upjohn Co., Kalamazoo, 1967-68; asst. prof. U. Utah, Salt Lake City, 1971-72; assoc. prof., chmn. fin. dept. Roosevelt U., Chgo., 1975-78; vis. prof. fin. No. Ill. U., 1978-79; freelance writer, computer musician, 1979—; editor Charles Dickens' Village Coquettes, 1992; mgr. spl. projects Sarasota Music Archive, 1992-96. Trustee Harold and Grace Upjohn Found., 1965-85, 94—, pres. 6 yrs.; trustee Kalamazoo Symphony Orch. Assn., 1990—, Sarasota Music Archive, 1990-95, Kalamazoo Coll., 1991-93, Am. Symphony Orch. League, 1992—, sec. 1996—. Recipient ann. press award Mich. Welfare League, 1967. Mem. ASCAP, NARAS (voting com.), Fin. Mgmt. Assn., Soc. Profl. Journalists. Contbr. articles to profl. and microcomputer jours.; music compositions include Ten Polyrhythmic Etudes 1991, Piano Sonata # 1, 1992, record albums include Apple Compote, 1983, One-Man Band, 1985, Ultimate Music Box, Vol. I, 1988, Vol. II, 1993; photographic exhibits include Aspects of Flowers, Ann Arbor, Mich., 1996, E. Lansing, Mich., 1997, Kalamazoo, Mich., 1997. Mem. U. Club Chicago, Gull Lake Country Club. Office: 136 E Michigan Ave Kalamazoo MI 49007

LIGHT, DOROTHY KAPLAN, lawyer, insurance executive; b. Alden, Iowa, May 20, 1937; d. Edward T. and Bessie (Nachazel) Kaplan; m. Ernest Isaac Light, Dec. 28, 1959; children: Christina, William, Samuel, David (twins). B.A., U. Iowa, 1959, J.D., 1961, hon. degree Georgian Ct. Coll., 1991. Bar: Iowa 1961, N.J. 1973; C.P.C.U., CLU. Pvt. practice, Marshalltown, Iowa, 1962-63, Iowa City, 1963-71; with U.S. Army, N.J., 1972-74; asst. gen. counsel Prudential Property & Casualty Ins. Co., Holmdel, N.J., 1974-77, assoc. gen. counsel, dir. corp. services, 1977-82, dir. pub. affairs mktg. dept., 1979-82, dir. pub. affairs, 1982-83, v.p. govt. affairs, 1982-87; v.p. The Prudential Ins. Co. Am., Newark, 1987-90, v.p. and corp. sec., 1990—; chmn. Prudential Found.; bd dirs. Ctr. for N.J. Resources, trustee N.J. Ctr. Analysis of Public Issues, N.J. Supreme Ct. adv. comm. Profl. ethics; Mem. N.J. govs'. transition team, N.J. econ. master plan commn.., N.J. econ. devel. task force, Am. Soc. Corp. Secs. Republican. Roman Catholic. Office: Prudential Ins Co Am 751 Broad St Newark NJ 07102-3777

LIGHT, JAMES FOREST, English educator; b. Memphis, Nov. 5, 1921; s. Luther and Lois Ginevra (Billings) L.; m. Norma Rowena Neal, Mar. 8, 1948 (dec. 1959); children—Sheldon Neal, Matthew Forest, Jama Rowena; m. Amy Marcella Wolf, Dec. 20, 1959. B.A., U. Chgo., 1945, M.A., 1947; Ph.D., Syracuse U., 1953. Instr. U. Ky., 1947-48, Syracuse U., 1948-53; assoc. Radford Coll., 1953-56; asst. prof. Ind. State U., 1956-59, assoc., 1959-61, prof., 1961-65; Bernhard prof., chmn. dept. English U. Bridgeport, 1965-71; dean Sch. of Humanities of Calif. State U.-Fresno, 1971-72; dean of faculties Lehman Coll., CUNY, 1972-73, provost, 1973-79; dean Coll. Liberal Arts So. Ill. U., Carbondale, 1979-85, prof. English, 1979-88, prof. emeritus, 1988—; Fulbright prof. Keele U., Eng., 1963-64; vis. prof. CUNY, summers 1966-69; Fulbright prof. Canterbury U., N.Z., 1986. Author: Nathanael West: an Interpretive Study, rev. edit, 1971, John William DeForest, 1965, J.D. Salinger, 1967; editor The Modern Age, 4th rev. edit, 1981, Studies in All the Kings Men, 1971; contbr. articles to profl. jours. Fellow Found. Econ. Edn., Yaddo Writers and Artists Colony.; mem. MLA, AAUP, Nat. Council Tchrs. English, Ind. Coll. English Assn. (pres. 1962-

63), New Eng. Coll. English Assn. (dir. 1969-71). Democrat. Office: 47 Dogwood Dr Apt 301 Nashua NH 03062-4413

LIGHT, JO KNIGHT, stockbroker; b. DeQueen, Ark., Mar. 15, 1936; d. Donald R. and Auda (Waltrip) Knight; m. Jerry T. Light, June 21, 1958 (dec. 1979); m. Victor E. Menefee Jr., Nov. 18, 1981; 1 child, Jerry T. BA cum laude, U. Ark., 1958. Cert. fin. planner. Travel cons. Comml. Nat. Bank, Little Rock, 1971-76; dist. mgr. Am. Express Co., N.Y.C., 1976-82; account exec. Dean Witter Reynolds, N.Y.C., 1982—, v.p. investments, 1987—, registered investment advisor, 1996—. Mem. Jr. League of Little Rock; vol. Happiness Singers. Mem. Inst. Cert. Fin. Planners, Internat. Assn. Fin. Planners (bd. dirs. 1992-98, pres. bd. 1995-96), U. Ark. Alumni Assn. (bd. dirs. 1974-77), Little Rock Country Club, Razorback Club, Phi Beta Kappa, Kappa Kappa Gamma. Avocations: music, tennis, sailing, snow skiing. Office: Dean Witter Reynolds 401 W Capitol Ave Ste 101 Little Rock AR 72201-3437

LIGHT, JOHN CALDWELL, chemistry educator; b. Mt. Vernon, N.Y., Nov. 24, 1934; s. Robert Fredrich and Alice (Caldwell) L.; m. Phyllis M. Kittel, Dec. 17, 1978; children: David C., Robert S., Erik G. B.A., Oberlin Coll., 1956; Ph.D., Harvard U., 1960. Postdoctoral rsch. assoc. U. Libre de Bruxelles, 1959-61; instr. U. Chgo., 1962-63, asst. prof., 1963-66, assoc. prof., 1966-70, prof. chemistry, 1970—, chmn. dept. chemistry, 1980-82; mem. adv. bd. Petroleum Rsch. Fund, 1981-86; cons. Inst. Def. Analyses, 1962-65, IBM Rsch Labs., San Jose, 1975, Lawrence Livermore Lab., 1979—; adv. com. Army Rsch. Office, Durham, N.C., 1966-72; vis. prof. Yale U., New Haven, 1968; vice chmn. Theoretical Chemistry Conf., Boulder, 1978, chmn., 1981; vis. scientist JILA, U. Colo., Boulder, 1976-77, others. Editor: Jour. Chem. Physics, 1983—. NSF predoctoral/postdoctoral fellow, 1956-61; Alfred P. Sloan Found. fellow. Fellow AAAS, Am. Phys. Soc., Am. Chem. Soc.; mem. Internat. Acad. Quantum Molecular Sci. Home: 1034 E 49th St Chicago IL 60615-1814 Office: 5640 S Ellis Ave Chicago IL 60637-1433

LIGHT, KEN, photojournalist, educator; b. N.Y.C., Mar. 16, 1951; s. Stanley and Dorothea (Gottfried) L.; m. Carmen Lising, June 1976 (div. Aug. 1985); children: Stephen, Allison Rose; m. Melanie Hastings, Aug. 1, 1992. BGS, Ohio U., 1973. Instr. Contra. Costa Coll., San Pablo, Calif., 1974-84; photographer Labor Occ. Health Program, Berkeley, Calif., 1975-81; mem. staff Alameda Neighborhood Arts Program, Oakland, Calif., 1975-81; dir. ctr. for photography Grad. Sch. Journalism U. Calif., Berkeley, 1986—; cons. photographer Libr. Congress Folklife Ctr., 1989-90; faculty San Francisco Acad. Art Coll, 1977-96; lectr., dir. Ctr. for Photography, Berkeley Grad. Sch. Journalism, 1983—; founder fund Documentary Photography, 1988—. Author: To the Promised Land, 1988, With These Hands, 1986, In the Fields, 1984, Delta Time, 1995, Texas Death Row, 1997. Recipient Meritorious Achievement award Media Alliance, 1990, Thomas More Storke Internat. Journalism award World Affairs Coun., 1989; nominnee Pulitzer Prize Feature Photography, 1993; grantee Am. Film Inst., 1979; NEA fellow, 1982, 86, Dorothea Lange fellow. Mem. Soc. Photog. Edn., ASMP, fellow Erna and Victor Hasselblad Found. Home: 3107 Deakin St Berkeley CA 94705-1950

LIGHT, KENNETH B., manufacturing company executive; b. N.Y.C., June 2, 1932; s. Max and Mollie (Schein) Lichtenholtz; m. Judith Klein, May 28, 1961; children: Corey, Randi Beth, Allison. B.S., NYU, 1954, LL.B. cum laude, 1957; M.B.A., U. Chgo., 1976. Bar: N.Y. 1957. Partner firm Light & Light, Bklyn., 1958-61; asst. sec. Gen. Bronze Corp., Garden City, N.Y., 1961-69; sec., gen. counsel Allied Products Corp., Chgo., 1969-76; v.p., gen. counsel Allied Products Corp., 1976-79, sr. v.p., 1979-83, exec. v.p., 1983-93; dir. Allied Products Corp., Chgo., 1993—; exec. v.p., CFO Allied Products Corp., 1995—; pres. Midwest Steel Processing, Inc., 1982-84; dir. Aurora Corp. Ill., Chgo.; vice chmn. Family Res. Ctr., Chgo., 1989-94, chmn., 1994-96; v.p., dir. Verson Corp., Bush Hog Corp. Mem. N.Y.C. Subcontractors Assn. (v.p. 1967-69), Am. Subcontractors Assn. (dir. 1967-68), Chgo. Assn. Commerce and Industry. Home: 1825 Cavell Ave Highland Park IL 60035-2202 Office: Allied Products Corp 10 S Riverside Plz Chicago IL 60606-3708

LIGHT, KENNETH FREEMAN, college administrator; b. Detroit, Jan. 22, 1922; s. Delbert Bertram and Hilma (Stolt) L.; m. Shirley Claire Bower, Jan. 7, 1944 (dec. 1984); children—Karen Christine, Kevin Harold, Brian Curtis; m. Betty Jensen Pritchett, Nov. 23, 1985. B.S., U. Ill., 1949; M.A., Mich. State U., 1952, Ph.D., 1967. Instr. mech. engring. dept. Mich. Tech. U., 1956-60, assoc. prof., coord. for tech. edn., 1960-65; vice chancellor for acad. affairs, v.p. for acad. affairs Lake Superior State Coll., Sault Ste. Marie, Mich., 1965-76; pres. Lake Superior State Coll., 1982-86, Oreg. Inst. Tech., Klamath Falls, 1976-82. Pres. Upper Peninsula Health Edn. Corp., 1975-76; mem. Mich. Manpower Commn., 1973-74, Vocat. Edn. Adv. Council, 1973-76, Oreg. Career and Vocat. Adv. Council, 1977-82, Oreg. Manpower Commn., 1978-80; mem. Econ. Devel. Corp. Chippewa County, 1982-86. Served with USAF, 1942-45, to maj., USAFR. Mem. AAUP, Am. Soc. Engring. Edn., Am. Soc. Mil. Engrs., Air Force Assn., Phi Delta Kappa. Home (summer): 6 Partridge Dr Kincheloe MI 49788-1303

LIGHT, MURRAY BENJAMIN, newspaper editor; b. Bklyn., Oct. 14, 1926; s. Paul and Rose (Liatsk) L.; m. Joan M. Cottrell; children: Lee Light Monier, Laura Light Arbogast, Jeffrey Eugene. B.S., Bklyn. Coll., 1948; M.S. in Journalism, Northwestern U., 1949. Copy editor New York Wold-Telegram, 1949; with Buffalo Evening News, 1949—, news editor, 1962-69, mng. editor for news, 1969-79, editor, v.p., 1979—, sr. v.p., 1983—; mem. Temporary State Commn. on Constl. Revision, 1993-95; mem. arts adv. coun. SUNY, Buffalo, 1987-94, N.Y. State Jud. Screening Com. for 4th Dept., 1983-93; mem. nominating jury for journalism Pulitzer Prize, 1990, 01. Mem. adv. coun. to pres. on journalism St. Bonaventure U., 1980—; mem. cmty. adv. coun. SUNY, Buffalo, 1979—; steering com. State Citizen Bee, 1990—. With AUS, WWII. Mem. N.Y. State Soc. Newspaper Editors (pres. 1977), Am. Soc. Newspaper Editors, A.P. Mng. Editors Assn., N.Y. Fair Trial Free Press Conf. (past chmn.). Office: Buffalo News PO Box 100 1 News Plz Buffalo NY 14203-2994

LIGHT, RICHARD JAY, statistician, education educator; b. N.Y.C., Sept. 10, 1942; s. Solomon Julius and Muriel (Szwarcman) L.; m. Patricia Kahn, June 27, 1965; children: Jennifer Susan, Sarah Elizabeth. BS, U. Pa., 1962, AM, 1964; PhD, Harvard U., 1969; LLD (hon.), U. Winnipeg, Can., 1991. Mem. faculty Harvard U., Cambridge, Mass., 1969—, prof. stats., 1975—; dir. faculty studies John F. Kennedy Inst. Politics, 1971-76; mem. panel children's and family policy Nat. Acad. Scis., 1977—, chmn. panel on evaluation, 1982; panel program evaluation Social Sci. Research Council, 1977—; bd. dirs Huron Inst., Cambridge, Mass., 1971—; cons. World Bank, 1975—; dir. Harvard Assessment Seminar, Cambridge, 1986—. Co-author: Data for Decisions, 1982, Summing Up, 1984, By Design, 1990, Meta-analysis for Explanation, 1992; editor: Learning from Experience, 1982, Evaluation Studies Rev., 1983. Trustee Buckingham, Browne and Nichols Sch., Cambridge, 1977—; mem. policy adv. group Mass. Office of Children, 1977—; bd. dirs. Fund for Improvement Post-Secondary Edn., 1992-95. N.Y. State Advanced Coll. Teaching fellow, 1965; vis. fellow Ctr. Analysis Health Practices, Harvard U. Sch. Pub. Health, 1977-78; Sr. Research award Spencer Found., Chgo., 1978-84; research fellow Ford Found., N.Y.C., 1981; recipient Paul Lazarsfeld award for contbns. to sci., 1992. Mem. Am. Assn. Higher Edn. Assn., Am. Ednl. Rsch. Assn., Am. Sociol. Assn., Am. Evaluation Assn. (pres. 1986), Coun. Applied Social Rsch., Evaluation Rsch. Soc. (Paul Lazarsfeld award 1991), Am. Assn. for Higher Edn. (nat. bd.), Fund for Improvement Postsecondary Edn. (nat. bd.). Home: 31 Dunbarton Rd Belmont MA 02178-2458 Office: John F Kennedy Sch Govt Harvard U Cambridge MA 02138

LIGHT, TERRY RICHARD, orthopedic hand surgeon; b. Chgo., June 22, 1947. BA, Yale U.; MD, Chgo. Med. Sch. Asst. prof. Yale U., New Haven, 1977-80; asst. prof. Loyola U., Maywood, Ill., 1980-82, assoc. prof., 1982-88, prof., 1988-90, Dr. William M. Scholl prof., chmn. dept. orthop. surgery, 1991—; attending surgeon Hines (Ill.) VA Hosp., 1980—, Shriner's Hosp., Chgo. and Tampa, Fla., 1981—, Foster McGaw Hosp., Maywood, 1981—; hand cons., mem. med. adv. bd. DuPage Easter Seals, Villa Park, Ill., 1980—; hand cons. Chgo. White Sox, 1986—; bus. mgr. Jour. Hand Surgery, 1995—. V.p. Frank Lloyd Wright Home and Studio Found., Oak Park, Ill., 1985-88, pres., 1988-90. Fellow ACS, Am. Acad. Orthop. Surgeons; mem. Am. Soc. for Surgery of the Hand, Am. Assn. Hand Surgery (bd. dirs. 1989-91), Chgo. Soc. for Surgery of the Hand (sec. 1985-87, pres.-elect 1987-88, pres. 1988-89), Twenty-First Century Orthop. Assn. (pres. 1979—). Avocations: collecting American arts and crafts. Office: Loyola U Med Ctr 2160 S 1st Ave Maywood IL 60153-3304

LIGHTBURN, ANITA LOUISE, dean, social work educator; b. San Diego, Jan. 2, 1946; d. Kenneth E. and Ann Lorraine (Rosepiler) Schimp; m. Kenneth Dale Lightburn, Aug. 25, 1973; children: Tiffany, Kara. BA, Wheaton Coll., 1968; MS, Columbia U., 1972, MEd, 1988, EdD, 1989. Social worker Mass. Divsn. Child Guardianship, Boston, 1968-70; supr. psychiat. social work McMahon Meml. Shelter, N.Y.C., 1972-73; lectr. Flinders U., Adelaide, Australia, 1973-85; asst., then assoc. prof. Columbia U., N.Y.C., 1989-94; dean, prof. Sch. Social Work Smith Coll., Northampton, Mass., 1994—; vis. prof. U. Conn., West Hartford, 1985, Columbia U., N.Y.C., 1986-88; cons., clinician, therapist in field. Author chpts. to books; contbr. articles to profl. jours. Mem. NASW. Home: 22 Main St Hatfield MA 01038-9784 Office: Smith Coll Sch Social Work Rilly Hall Northampton MA 01063*

LIGHTBURN, FAYE MARIE, genealogist; b. Oakland, Calif., Aug. 9, 1928; d. Lloyd Michael and Alma Leone (Dennis) Brown; m. Jesse Leon Lightburn, Apr. 2, 1946; children: Sandra Jean Lightburn Stein (dec.), Steven Douglas, Marcia Faye Lightburn Scarborough, Janet Lightburn Powers. Student, Sacramento Jr. Coll., Mercy Hosp. Nursing, Sacramento. Food svc. mgr. Duval County Sch. Bd., Jacksonville Beach, Fla., 1964-86. Compiler and editor: Revolutionary Soldier Samuel Brown and some of His Family, 1993, supplement, 1994; compiler: The Palms Presbyterian Church History 1956-1996. Mem. DAR, Nat. Geneal. Soc., Mo. Geneal. Assn., Howard County Geneal Soc., St. Augustine Geneal. Soc., Federated Geneal. Soc., Va. Geneal. Soc., Assn. Profl. Genealogists, Boonslick Hist. Soc. Democrat. Presbyterian. Avocations: reading, traveling, gardening, researching.

LIGHTELL, KENNETH RAY, education educator; b. Oak Park, Ill., Nov. 13, 1944; s. Ray and Mildred (Miller) L.; m. Charlotte Hawkins, Aug. 3, 1989. BA, North Ctrl. Coll., Naperville, Ill., 1966; grad. studies in edn., U. Mo., 1969; grad. studies in computers, Depaul U., 1983; MLA, Houston Bapt. U., 1995. Tchr., coach Roycemore Sch., Evanston, Ill., 1966-68; dir. middle sch. Bklyn. Friends Sch., 1969-81; dir. Olympia (Wash.) Ind. Sch., 1982-83; tchr., coach The Lexington (Ky.) Sch., 1984-88; prin. Charles Wright Acad., Tacoma, 1988-89; dir. of mid. sch. John Cooper Sch., Woodlands, Tex., 1989-92; headmaster St. James Episcopal Sch., Houston, 1993-94, The McClelland Sch., Pueblo, Colo., 1995—; owner, dir. Washinee Woods Camp, Taconic, Conn., 1975-81, Wilderness Adventures, Bklyn., 1970-75; pres., CEO S.L.K. Inc., N.Y.C., 1975-83. Editor: N.C.C. Spectrum, 1966; dir. Festival of the Arts, 1986. Pres. NCC Young Rep., Naperville, Ill., 1964-65; trustee Assn. Colo. Ind. Schs., Pueblo Day Nursery Found. Mem. B.P.O.E. Elks, Nat. Mid. Sch. Assn., Alpha Sigma Lambda. Avocations: sailing, wooden boat building, photography, travel. Home: 415 S Pin High Dr Pueblo West CO 81007

LIGHTFOOT, DAVID WILLIAM, linguistics educator; b. Looe, Eng., Feb. 10, 1945; s. William Richard and Peggy May (Stevens) L.; m. Sarah Elizabeth Hairs, Feb. 7, 1946 (div. 1980); children: Kirsten, Heidi; m. Sari Ruth Hornstein, Nov. 24, 1955; children: Eric, Alexander. BA with honors, U. London, 1966; MA, U. Mich., 1968, PhD, 1971. Asst. prof. McGill U., Montreal, Que., Can., 1970-75; assoc. prof. McGill U., Montreal, Que., 1975-78; prof. U. Utrecht, The Netherlands, 1978-83, U. Md., College Park, 1983—. Author: Natural Logic and Greek Moods, 1975, Principles of Diachronic Syntax, 1979, Explanation in Linguistics, 1981, The Language Lottery, 1982, How to Set Parameters, 1991, Verb Movement, 1994. Mem. Linguistic Soc. Am., Linguistic Assn. Gt. Britain. Home: 7208 Heatherhill Rd Bethesda MD 20817-4657 Office: Univ Md Dept Linguistics College Park MD 20472

LIGHTFOOT, JAMES ROSS, former congressman; b. Sioux City, Iowa, Sept. 27, 1938; s. Elmer and Altha Lightfoot; m. Nancy Lightfoot; children: Terri,Jamie, Allison, James. Customer engr. IBM, 1957-59; police officer City of Tulsa, 1959-61; broadcaster, 1961-70; Mgr. farm equipment plant Corsicana, Tex., 1970-76; small bus. owner Shenandoah, Iowa, 1976-96; mem. 99th-104th Congress from 5th (now 3rd) Iowa dist., 1985-96, appropriations com., chmn. treas., postal svc. and gen. govt. subcom., fgn. ops. appropriations subcom., sub. appropriations, trans.; participant numerous world confs. to promote agriculture. Farm editor Sta. KMA-Radio, Shenandoah, Iowa, 1976-84. Served with U.S. Army, then USAR, 1956-64. Mem FAA (Outstanding Svc. award, vol. safety counselor), Farm Bur., U.S. Feed Grains Coun., Soybean Assn., Nat. Agr. Mktg. Assn. (agr. spokesman of the yr. award), Iowa Pork Prodrs. Assn., Iowa Cattleman's Assn. (broadcasting award). *

LIGHTFOOTE, MARILYN MADRY, molecular immunologist; b. Jacksonville, Fla.; d. Arthur Chester and Janie (Cowart) Madry; m. William Edward Lightfoote II, Oct. 23, 1971; 1 child, Lynne Jan-Maria. BA in Chemistry magna cum laude, Fisk U.; MS in Biochemistry, Georgetown U.; PhD in Microbiology and Immunology, U. Va., 1983. Staff fellow Lab. Immunogenetics Nat, Inst. Allergy Infectious Diseases, NIH, Bethesda, Md., 1983-85, staff fellow Lab. Immunoregulation, 1985-87; rsch. faculty dept. biochemistry George Washington U., 1987-90; molecular immunologist FDA, Rockville, Md., 1990—; Graves meml. lectr. biology dept. N.C. A&T Coll., Greensboro; NSF tng. fellow U. Va., 1979-83; presenter various orgns., workshops and symposiums. Author: Biology of Light, 1992; issue editor Immunomethods, 1992-93. Dir. fund raising Jack and Jill of Am., Reston, Va., 1986-90; dir. Project Lead, Links Inc., Reston, 1990; mem. vestry St. Paul's Episcopal Ch., Alexandria, Va., 1987-90. Mem. AAAS, Am. Assn. Immunology, Mortarboard, Sigma Xi. Achievements include development and characterization of cell lines for study of HIV virus; first isolation and publication of amino acid analysis of HIV Reverse Transcriptase. Home: 827 Swinks Mill Rd Mc Lean VA 22102-2124 Office: FDA 12709 Twinbrook Pky Rockville MD 20852-1719

LIGHTMAN, ALAN PAIGE, physicist, writer, educator; b. Memphis, Nov. 28, 1948; s. Richard Lovis and Jeanne (Garretson) L.; m. Jean Greenblatt, Nov. 28, 1976; children: Elyse, Kara. AB, Princeton U., 1970; PhD in Physics, Calif. Inst. Tech., 1974. Postdoctoral fellow Cornell U., Ithaca, N.Y., 1974-76; asst. prof. Harvard U., Cambridge, Mass., 1976-79; staff scientist Smithsonian Astrophys. Obs., Cambridge, 1979-88; prof. sci. and writing MIT, Cambridge, 1988-95; John E. Burchard prof., 1995—; chair sci. panel NRC Astron. and Astrophys. Survey for 1990's. Author: Problem Book in Relativity and Gravitation, 1974, Radiative Processes in Astrophysics, 1976, Time Travel and Papa Joe's Pipe, 1984, A Modern Day Yankee in Connecticut Court, 1986, Origins: The Lives and Worlds of Modern Cosmologists, 1990 (Most Outstanding Sci. Book in Phys. Sci. award Assn. Am. Pubs.), Ancient Light, 1991, Great Ideas in Physics, 1992, Time for the Stars, 1992, Einstein's Dreams, 1993, Good Benito, 1995, Dance for Two, 1996. Recipient Gemant award Am. Inst. of Physics, 1996; Lit. Light of Boston Pub. Libr., 1995. Fellow AAAS, Am. Acad. Arts and Scis., Am. Phys. Soc.; mem. Am. Astron. Soc. (chmn. high energy astrophysics divsn. 1991). Office: MIT 77 Massachusetts Ave Cambridge MA 02139-4301

LIGHTMAN, HAROLD ALLEN, marketing executive; b. Gloucester, Mass., Oct. 23, 1925; s. Abraham and Gertrude (Chait) L.; m. Irma Shorell, Feb. 19, 1954; children: Timothy, Harold, Jr., Stacey. Student, Norwich U., 1943; student, Cambridge U., Eng., 1946; BBA, U. Miami, 1949; postgrad., Oxford (Eng.) U., 1996. Acct. exec. Grant Advt., Miami, Fla., 1948-50; advt. dir. Sears Roebuck & Co., Tampa, Fla., 1950-51; account exec. Robert Otto Internat., N.Y.C., 1952-53; account exec., field supr. Amos Parish & Co., N.Y.C., 1954-56; acct. exec. Dowd, Redfield & Johnstone, N.Y.C., 1957-59; chmn. bd. dirs. H. Allen Lightman Inc., N.Y.C., 1959—; bd. dirs. Irma Shorell Inc., N.Y.C.; pres., bd. dirs. Ind. Cosmetic Mfg. and Distbrs. U.S.A., v.p. nat. legis. affairs, 1974—; exec. v.p. Alfin Fragrances, Inc., 1985-87; pres. I.S. Labs. Inc., 1987—. Author newspaper column: Seen & Heard, 1965-83; producer: Cable TV program Seen & Heard, 1978—. Publicity, pub. rels. dir. Miami Jr. C. of C., 1948-50. Sgt. U.S. Army, 1943-46, ETO. Decorated Purple Heart, Bronze Star (2), Combat Infantry Badge; recipient Pub. Rels. Gold Key award, 1987. Fellow Winston Churchill Meml. Libr., Harry S. Truman Meml. Libr.; mem. Nat. Fedn. Ind. Bus. (del. 1979), Internat. Platform Assn., Alpha Delta Sigma (founder, 1st pres. 1947-48), Miami Jr. C. of C. (publicity, pub. rels. dir. 1948-50), DAV, Am. Legion (vice comdr. 1948-49), Vets. of the Battle of the Bulge, The Jockey Club. Office: 75 E End Ave New York NY 10028-7909

LIGHTSTONE, RONALD, lawyer; b. N.Y.C., Oct. 4, 1938; s. Charles and Pearl (Weisberg) L.; m. Nancy Lehrer, May 17, 1973; 1 child, Dana. AB, Columbia U., 1959; JD, NYU, 1962. Atty. CBS, N.Y.C., 1967-69; assoc. dir. bus. affairs CBS News, N.Y.C., 1969-70; atty. NBC, N.Y.C., 1970; assoc. gen. counsel Viacom Internat. Inc., N.Y.C., 1970-75; v.p., gen. counsel, sec. Viacom Internat. Inc., 1976-80; v.p. bus. affairs Viacom Entertainment Group, Viacom Internat., Inc., 1980-82, v.p. corp. affairs, 1982-84, sr. v.p., 1984-87; exec. v.p. Spelling Entertainment Inc., L.A., 1988-91, CEO,, 1991-93; chmn. Multimedia Labs. Inc., 1994—; CEO, Dove Entertainment, Inc., 1997—; bd. dirs. Dave Entertainment, Inc. Served to lt. USN, 1962-66. Mem. ABA (chmn. TV, cable and radio com.), Assn. Bar City N.Y., Fed. Communications Bar Assn.

LIGOMENIDES, PANOS ARISTIDES, electrical and computer engineering educator, consultant; b. Pireaus, Greece, Apr. 3, 1928; came to U.S., 1955; s. Aristides P. and Sonia (Akritides) L.; m. Danae J. Tsarmaklis, Dec. 29, 1973;children: Katerina, Christina. BSc in Physics with high honors, U. Athens, 1951, MSc in Radio Engring., 1952; MSc in Elec. Engring., Stanford U., 1956, PhD in Elec. Engring. and Physics, 1958. Registered profl. engr. Research engr. IBM, Poughkeepsie, N.Y., 1958-59, San Jose, Calif., 1959-64; asst. prof. elec. engring. UCLA, 1964-69; adj. prof. elec. engring. Stanford U., Calif., 1969-71, Fulbright prof., 1970-71; disting. vis. prof. U. Md., College Park, 1971-72, prof. elec. engring., 1971-93, prof. emeritus, 1993—, chmn. computer engring., elec. engring. dept., 1972-76; prof. U. Patras, Greece, 1993—; pres., Computer Engring. Cons., Lanham, Md., 1976-80; dir. Cybernetics Rsch. Lab., 1982—; v.p. Caelum Rsch. Corp., 1988-93; cons. to various industries and govt. orgns.; elected chair of informatics, Acad. of Athens, Greece, 1993; pres. Acad.'s Applied Sci. Divsn., Greece, 1995. Author: Information Processing Machines, 1969, Notions, Measures of Probability, 1978, Axiomatic Probability Theory, 1979, Computer Application in Industry and Management, 1981, Management and Office Information Systems, 1984, Visual Languages, 1986, Uncertainty in Knowledge-Based Systems, 1987; assoc. editor sci. jours.; contbr. over 200 articles to sci. and engring. books, jours., conf. proceedings; patentee pathfinder algorithm. Lt. Greek Navy, 1952-54. OECD fellow, 1965, 74; Ford Found. fellow, 1966-68; Salzburg Seminar fellow, 1971; recipient grants and contracts for rsch. in computers and artificial intelligence. Mem. IEEE (life, sr.), N.Y. Acad. Sci. Home: 39 Bakoyianni St, 15235 Vrilissia Greece Office: Acad Athens, 28 Panepistimiou Ave, 10679 Athens Greece

LIGUORI, FRANK NICKOLAS, temporary personnel company executive; b. Bklyn., July 2, 1946; s. August and Mary (Perotto) L.; m. JoAnn Scioscia, July 7, 1968; children: Frank Jr., Mark. BS in Acctg., St. Francis Coll., Bklyn., 1964. CPA, N.Y. Sr. auditor Coopers & Lybrand, N.Y.C., 1964-71; successively controller, treas., sr. v.p., exec. v.p., pres., CEO, chmn. Olsten Corp., Westbury, N.Y., 1971—, also bd. dirs., CEO, chmn. bd. dirs.; bd. dirs. WLIW 21, Plainview, N.Y. Mem. Am. Inst. CPAs, N.Y. State Soc. CPAs, Nat. Assn. Temporary Services (bd. dirs.). Home: 2 Talisman Ct Huntington Station NY 11746-5320*

LIJINSKY, WILLIAM, biochemist; b. Dublin, Ireland, Oct. 19, 1928; came to U.S., 1951; s. Morris and Rebecca (Hershman) L.; m. Rosalie K. Elespuru, June 10, 1973; 1 dau., Catherine Elizabeth; 1 dau. by previous marriage, Sharon Anne. B.Sc. with honours, U. Liverpool, Eng., 1949, Ph.D., 1951. Asst. prof., then assoc. prof. Chgo. Med. Sch., 1955-68; prof. biochemistry U. Nebr. Med. Sch., Omaha, 1968-71; group leader carcinogenesis program Oak Ridge Nat. Lab., 1971-76; dir. chem. carcinogenesis program Frederick (Md.) Cancer Research Facility, 1976-91; expert Nat. Inst. Environ. Health Scis., N.C., 1991-92. Author research papers, revs. Mem. Biochem. Soc., Am. Chem. Soc., Am. Assn. Cancer Research, Am. Soc. Biol. Chemists, Environmental Mutagen Soc., Soc. Occupational and Environ. Health, Sigma Xi. Home: 11398 High Hay Dr Columbia MD 21044-1029

LIJOI, PETER BRUNO, lawyer; b. Suffern, N.Y., Sept. 2, 1953; s. Salvatore and Josephine (Gentile) L.; m. Christine Louise Confroy, Aug. 19, 1978; children: Jonathan Peter, Christopher Andrew. BA in History and Econs., Montclair State Coll., 1975; postgrad. in urban planning, Rutgers U., 1975-76; JD, Pace U., 1979; postgrad., Harvard U., 1992. Bar: N.J. 1981, N.Y. 1988. Rsch. intern N.J. Dept. Edn., Trenton, 1976; intern Office U.S. Atty., N.Y.C., 1977-78; energy coord. Rockland County, 1979-80; dep. dir., of counsel Pvt. Industry Coun., Pearl River, N.Y., 1980-91; pvt. practice law Summit, N.J., 1981—; dir., counsel County of Rockland Indsl. Devel. Agy., 1981-95; v.p., gen. counsel Rockland Econ. Devel. Corp., Pearl River, 1990-91; cons. U.S. Dept. Energy, Washington, 1980; mem. program of instrn. for lawyers Law Sch., Harvard U., 1992; legal counsel K. Hovnanian Cos. North Jersey, Inc., 1993-95, K. Hovnanian Cos. Northeast, Inc., 1995—. Guest writer The Bond Buyer. Bd. dirs. Rockland County coun. Girl Scouts U.S., 1982-92; pres. Washington Elem. Sch. PTA, Summit, 1986—; mem. Summit Planning Bd., desegregation grant adv. com. Summit Bd. Edn., 1992—. Mem. ABA, N.J. Bar Assn., N.Y. Bar Assn., Union County Bar Assn., Assn. Trial Lawyers Am., Nat. Assn. Bond Lawyers. Roman Catholic. Avocations: running, coaching youth soccer. Home: 124 Canoe Brook Pky Summit NJ 07901-1436 Office: 110 Fieldcrest Ave Edison NJ 08837-3620

LIKENS, GENE ELDEN, biology and ecology educator, administrator; b. Pierceton, Ind., Jan. 6, 1935; s. Colonel Benjamin and Josephine (Garner) L.; m. Phyllis Craig; children: Kathy, Gregory, Leslie. BS, Manchester (Ind.) Coll., 1957, DSc (hon.), 1979; MS, U. Wis., 1959, PhD, 1962; DSc (hon.), Rutgers U., 1985, Plymouth State Coll., U. N.H., 1989, Miami U., 1990; LHD (hon.), Union Coll., 1991; DSc (hon.), U. Bodenkultur, Vienna, Austria, 1993, Marist Coll., 1993. Asst. zoology Manchester Coll., 1955-57; grad. teaching asst. U. Wis., 1957-59, vis. lectr., 1963; instr. zoology Dartmouth Coll., 1961, instr. biol. scis., 1963, asst. prof., then assoc. prof., 1963-69; mem. faculty Cornell U., 1969-83, prof. ecology, 1972-83, Charles A. Alexander prof. biol. scis., 1983, adj. prof., 1983—; v.p. N.Y. Botanical Garden, 1983-93; dir. Inst. Ecosystem Studies, Millbrook, N.Y., 1983—, pres., 1993—; dir. Mary Flagler Cary Arboretum, 1983—; prof. biology Yale U., 1984—; prof. grad. field of ecology Rutgers U., 1985—; vis. prof. Ctr. Advanced Rsch., also dept. environ scis. U. Va., Charlottesville, 1978-79; lectr. Williams Summer Inst. Coll. Tchrs., 1966, 67, Drew Summer Inst. Coll. Tchrs., 1968, Cornell U. Alumni Assn., 1978; Paul C. Lemon ecology lectr. SUNY, Albany, 1978; chmn. New Eng. div. task force conservation aquatic ecosystems U.S. Internat. Biol. Program, 1966-67; vis. assoc. ecologist Brookhaven Nat. Lab., 1968; C.P. Snow lectr. Ithaca Coll., 1979, 89; Robert S. Campbell lectr. U. Mo., 1980; A.E. Waller lectr. Ohio State U., 1990; Disting. Ecologist lectr. N.C. State U., 1980; Henry J. Oosting lectr. Duke U., 1985; Rilett vis. scholar Ill. State U., 1985; vis. scholar James Madison U., 1988; Class of 1960 vis. scholar, Williams Coll., Williamstown, Mass., 1988; Jack R. Hargis lectr. U. Minn., Duluth, 1988; Robert H. Woodworth lectr. in sci. Bennington (Vt.) Coll., 1988; mem. Nat. Commn. on Environment, 1991; Olin lectr. Environ. Fairfield U., 1990; lectr. Golden Series, Universität für Bodenkultur, 1991; William V. Kaesar Meml. scholar U. Wis., Madison, 1991; disting. scientist lecture series Bard Coll., 1991; Donnell Foster Hewett Lecture series Lehigh U., 1992; Miles C. Horton spl. lect. Va. Polytech. Inst., State U., 1993, Marine Biological Lab. Fri. evening lecture series Woods Hole, 1993; Granville Sewell disting. lectr. Columbia U., 1994; vis. disting. ecologist, Colo. State U., 1994; Raymond Lindeman Meml. lectr. U. Minn., 1996, Hans Jenny Meml. lectr. U. Calif., Berkeley; lectr. in field; cons. in field; mem. numerous govt. and sci. panels, participant numerous confs. Author 13 books and more than 335 sci. jour. publs. Recipient Conservation award Am. Motors Corp., 1969, 75th Anniversary award U.S. Forest Svc., 1980, Disting. Achievement award Lab. Biomed. and Environ. Studies, UCLA, 1982, Regents medal of excellence SUNY, 1984, award N.Y. Acad. Scis., 1986, Internat. ECI prize for Limnetic Ecology, 1989, Disting. Svc. award N.Y. Bot. Garden, 1989, Disting. Svc. award Am. Inst. Biol. Scis., 1990, The Garden Club Am. Spl. Citation, 1992, The Tyler World Environment prize U. So. Calif., 1993, Australia Prize, 1994; NATO sr. fellow, 1969, Guggenheim fellow, 1972-73; grantee NSF, EPA, Dept.

Energy, USDA Forest Svc., NOAA. Fellow AAAS; mem. NAS (chmn. sect. 27 1986-89), Ecol. Soc. Am. (chmn. study com. 1971-74, v.p. 1978-79, pres. 1981-82, eminent ecologist award 1995), AAAS, Am. Soc. Limnology and Oceanography (pres. 1976-77, 1st G.E. Hutchinson award for excellence in rsch. 1982), Internat. Assn. Theoretical and Applied Limnology (nat. rep., Naumann-Thienemann medal 1995), Royal Swedish Acad. Scis., Am. Polar Soc., Explorers Club, Freshwater Biol. Assn., Internat. Assn. Gt. Lakes Rsch., Internat. Water Resources Assn. (charter), Australian Soc. Limnology, Am. Water Resources Assn. (hon.), Br. Ecol. Soc. (hon.), Am. Inst. Biol. Scis., Royal Danish Acad. Sci., Sigma Xi, Gamma Alpha, Phi Sigma. Methodist. Office: Inst Ecosys Studies Box AB Millbrook NY 12545

LIKENS, JAMES DEAN, economics educator; b. Bakersfield, Calif., Sept. 12, 1937; s. Ernest LeRoy and Monnie Jewel (Thomas) L.; m. Janet Sue Pelton, Dec. 18, 1965 (div.); m. Karel Carnohan, June 4, 1988 (div.); children: John David, Janet Elizabeth. BA in Econs., U. Calif., Berkeley, 1960, MBA, 1961; PhD in Econs., U. Minn., 1970. Analyst Del Monte Corp., San Francisco, 1963; economist 3M Co., Mpls., 1968-71; asst. prof. econs. Pomona Coll., 1969-75, assoc. prof. econs., 1975-83, prof. econs., 1983-85, Morris B. Pendleton prof. econs., 1989—; vis. asst. prof. econs. U. Minn., 1970, 71, vis. assoc. prof., 1976-77; pres., dean Western CUNA Mgmt. Sch., Pomona Coll., 1975—; chmn. bd. 1st City Savs. Fed. Credit Union, 1978—; coord. So. Calif. Rsch. Coun., L.A., 1980-81, 84-85; mem. adv. coun. Western Corp. Fed. Credit Union, 1993—; cons. in field. Author: (with Joseph LaDou) Medicine and Money, 1976, Mexico and Southern California: Toward A New Partnership, 1981, Financing Quality Education in Southern California, 1985; contbr. articles to profl. jours. Served with USCG, 1961-67. Rsch. grantee HUD-DOT, Haynes Found. Mem. ABA, Am. Econ. Assn., Western Econ. Assn. Home: 725 W 10th St Claremont CA 91711-3719 Office: Pomona Coll Dept Econs Claremont CA 91711

LIKINS, PETER WILLIAM, academic administrator; b. Tracy, Calif., July 4, 1936; s. Ennis Blaine and Dorothy Louise (Medlin) L.; m. Patricia Ruth Kitsmiller, Dec. 18, 1955; children: Teresa, Lora, Paul, Linda, Krista, John. BCE, Stanford U., 1957, PhD in Engring. Mechanics, 1965; MCE, MIT, 1958; hon. doctorates, Lafayette Coll., 1983, Moravian Coll., 1984, Med. Coll. Pa., 1990, Lehigh U., 1991, Allentown St. Francis de Sales, 1993; hon. doctorate, Czech Tech U., 1993. Devel. engr. Jet Propulsion Lab., Pasadena, Calif., 1958-60; asst. prof. engring. UCLA, 1964-69, assoc. prof., 1969-72, prof., 1972-76, asst. dean, 1974-75, asso. dean, 1975-76; dean engring. and applied sci. Columbia U., N.Y.C., 1976-80, provost, 1980-82; pres. Lehigh U., Bethlehem, Pa., 1982—; engring. cons. U.S. and fgn. corps. and govt. agys., 1965—. Author: Elements of Engineering Mechanics, 1973, Spacecraft Dynamics, 1982; Contbr. articles to profl. jours. Mem. U.S. Pres.'s Coun. Advisers Sci. and Tech., 1990-93. Ford Found. fellow, 1970-72; named to Nat. Wrestling Hall of Fame. Fellow AIAA; mem. Nat. Acad. Engring., Phi Beta Kappa, Sigma Xi, Tau Beta Pi. Office: Lehigh U 27 Memorial Dr W Bethlehem PA 18015-3005

LILES, FRANK, professional boxer; b. North Hollywood, Calif., Feb. 14, 1965. Named WBA Super Middleweight Champion, 1994. Achievements include record of 29 wins and 1 loss, with 18 knock-outs. Office: c/o Consejo Mundial de Boxeo, Genova 33 Despacho # 503, 06600 Mexico City Mexico

LILEY, PETER EDWARD, mechanical engineering educator; b. Barnstaple, North Devon, Eng., Apr. 22, 1927; came to U.S., 1957; s. Stanley E. and Rosa (Ellery) L.; m. Elaine Elizabeth Kull, Aug. 16, 1963; children: Elizabeth Ellen, Rebecca Ann. B.Sc., Imperial Coll., U. London, 1951, Ph.D. in Physics, 1957, D.I.C., 1957. With Brit. Oxygen Engring., London, 1955-57; asst. prof. mech. engring. Purdue U., West Lafayette, Ind., 1957-61, assoc. prof., 1961-72; assoc. sr. researcher Thermophys. Properties Research Ctr., Purdue U., West Lafayette, Ind., 1961-72, prof. mech. engring., 1972—; sr. rschr. Ctr. for Info. and Numerical Data Analysis and Synthesis, Purdue U., West Lafayette, Ind., 1972-92; cons. in field. Author: Sect. 3 Perry's Chemical Engineers Handbook, 7th edit., 1997, (with Hartnett et al.) Handbook of Heat Transfer Fundamentals, 2d edit., 1985, (with others) Marks Mechanical Engineers Handbook, 10th edit., 1996, Schaums 2000 Solved Problems in Mechanical Engineering Thermodynamics, 1988, Tables and Charts for Thermodynamics, 1995, Kutz Mechanical Engineers Handbook, 1986; co-author: Steam and Gas Tables with Computer Equations, 1985, Thermal Conductivity of Nonmetallic Liquids and Gases, 1970, Properties of Nonmetallic Fluid Elements, 1981, Properties of Inorganic and Organic Fluids, 1988; editor, mem. editl. bd. Internat. Jour. Thermophysics, 1980-86; contbr. chpts. to handbooks in field; contbr. articles to profl. jours.; reviewer profl. jours. Served with Royal Corps Signals, Brit. Army, 1945-48. Lutheran. Home: 3608 Mulberry Dr Lafayette IN 47905-3937 Office: Purdue U Dept Mech Engring Purdue University IN 47907

LILIEN, ELLIOT STEPHEN, secondary education educator; b. Maplewood, N.J.; s. Bernard Banner and Judith Batson (Mulally) L.; m. Louise Anne Hoehl, Jan. 29, 1965 (div. July 1968); m. Nancy Goddard Pierce, July 21, 1985. BA, U. Chgo., 1961; JD, Columbia U., 1964; MAT, Harvard U., 1965. Tchr. Concord (Mass.)-Carlisle H.S., 1965—, head coach fencing, 1965-85, head coach tennis, 1989—; head coach fencing Brown U., Providence, 1987-93; dir. Concord-Acad. Fencing Camp, 1975—. Author: German History 1815-1945, 1972, History of Greece and Rome, 1979, Competition Experiment, 1986. Commr. Northeast Fencing Conf., Boxboro, Mass., 1993—. Grantee Coun. for Basic Edn., 1983. Mem. Four Sch. Consortium (founder, pres. 1987), Concord-Carlisle Tchrs. (pres. 1972-94). Avocations: tennis, WWI poster collecting, swords, beer steins, autographs. Home: 62 Chester Rd Boxboro MA 01719-1808 Office: Concord-Carlisle H S 500 Walden St Concord MA 01742-3617

LILIEN, MARK IRA, publishing, retailing and systems executive; b. Kew Gardens, N.Y., Sept. 7, 1953; s. Robert Samuel and Annette Audrey (London) L. BS in Labor Relations, Cornell U., 1974; MBA in Entrepreneurial Mktg., U. Pa., 1976. Buyer, mdse. controller Korvettes Dept. Stores, N.Y.C., 1976-79; dir. mdse. adminstrn. Walden Books, Stamford, Conn., 1979-84; sr. assoc. Booz Allen & Hamilton, N.Y.C., 1985-86; v.p. Penguin USA, N.Y.C., 1986-89, Barnes & Noble Bookstores, N.Y.C., 1989-92, Lechters, 1992-94, McGraw-Hill, N.Y.C., 1994-96; cons., 1997—. Mem. editorial bd. Retail Systems Alert Newsletter, 1991-94. Schirer fellow Wharton Sch. Bus. U. Pa., 1975-76. Mem. Book Industry Systems Adv. Com. (vice chmn. 1983-84, chmn. 1988-89), Book Industry Study Group, Assn. Am. Pubs. (bus. mgrs. com., Pubnet com. 1986-89), Nat. Retail Fedn. (chmn. SpecNet com. 1990-92). Avocations: theatre, films. Home: 350 Bleecker St Apt 3E New York NY 10014-2631

LILIENFIELD, LAWRENCE SPENCER, physiology and biophysics educator; b. Bklyn., May 5, 1927; s. Henry Jacob and Lee (Markman) L.; m. Eleanor Marion Russ, Oct. 22, 1950; children: Jan, Adele, Lisa. BS, Villanova (Pa.) U., 1945; MD, Georgetown U., 1949, MS, 1954, PhD, 1956. Diplomate Nat. Bd. Med. Examiners, Am. Bd. Internal Medicine. Intern Georgetown U. Hosp., Washington, 1949-59, 1949-50, resident in internal medicine, 1950, 52-54, rsch. fellow, 1954-55; instr. medicine Sch. Medicine Georgetown U., Washington, 1955-56, asst. chief cardiovascular rsch. lab., dept. medicine, 1956-63, asst. chief cardiovascular rsch. lab. dept. medicine, 1956-63, assoc. prof. physiology, biophysics and medicine Sch. Medicine, 1961-64, prof. physiology and biophysics Sch. Medicine, 1964-95, prof., chmn. dept. physiology and biophysics Sch. Medicine, 1963-93, prof. emeritus, 1996—; attending physician VA Hosp., Washington, 1956-70; cons. USPHS, 1964-69, NASA, 1964-70, U.S. Dept. State, 1967-74; established investigator Am. Heart Assn., 1958; vis. prof. faculty of medicine U. Saigon, Republic of Korea, 1965-74. Contbr. numerous articles to profl. jours. Bd. dirs. Washington Heart Assn., 1962-67, chmn., 1966. With USN, 1945; capt. USAF, 1950-52. Recipient Established Investigator award Am. Heart Assn., 1958; Rsch. Career Devel. award USPHS, 1963, Rsch. Career award, 1963, Kaiser-Permanente Teaching award, 1987; USPHS rsch. and rsch. tng. grantee, 1987. Fellow ACP; mem. Am. Soc. for Clin. Investigation, Am. Physiol. Soc., Am. Fedn. for Clin. Rsch. (chair ea. sect. 1965-66). Avocations: computers in education. Office: Georgetown U Sch Medicine 3900 Reservoir Rd NW Washington DC 20007-2195

LILIENTHAL, ALFRED M(ORTON), author, historian, editor; b. N.Y.C., Dec. 25, 1913; s. Herbert and Lottye (Kohn) L. BA, Cornell U., Ithaca, N.Y., 1934; LLB, Columbia U., 1938, JD, 1969. Bar: N.Y. 1938. With Bennett, House & Couts, N.Y.C., 1939-41, State Dept., 1942-43, 45-48; cons. U.S. del. UN San Francisco Conf., 1945; adminstrv. practice, 1947-50; counsel Am.-Arab Assn. Commerce & Industry, 1960-65; editor, pub. Middle East Perspective (monthly newsletter), 1967-85; lectr. on Middle East at numerous colls. and clubs throughout U.S. and fgn. countries, 1951-94, frequent guest TV and radio news commentator on Middle East devels., 1951-91; lectr. cultural symposium United Arab Emirates, Libya, Lebanon, Vienna, Baghdad, Prague; polit. columnist daily Al Qabas, Kuwait, 1976-77; accredited corr. to UN; chmn. Am. Coun. on the Middle East; cons. UN Internat. Conf. on Question Palestine, Geneva, 1983; participant Model Internat. Conf. on Middle East, Prague, 1988, 27 Middle East trips including West Bank and Gaza, 1953-94; guest of UN Sec.-Gen. at 50th Commemorative meeting, San Francisco, 1995. Author: Which Way to World Government, 1949, What Price Israel?, 1954, There Goes the Middle East, 1957, Studies in Twentieth Century Diplomacy, 1959, The Other Side of the Coin, 1965, The Zionist Connection, 1978, The Zionist Connection II, 1982, rev. Czechoslovakian edit., 1989, Japanese edit., 1991, This I Do Believe, 1994; contbr. to: book Zionism-The Dream and the Reality, 1974; monthly commentaries Washington Report on Middle East Affairs, 1988—; also numerous mag. articles and syndicated newspieces. Pres. Rep. First Voters League, 1940; Fusion Party candidate for N.Y.C. Coun., 1941; leader fight against Communist controlled Am. Youth Congress, 1941. With AUS, 1943-45. Papers housed in archives of Hoover Instn., Stanford, Calif. Mem. Nat. Rep. Club, Univ. Club, Capitol Hill Club, Nat. Press Club, Cornell Club Washington. Home and Office: 800-25th St NW Washington DC 20037

LILJEBECK, ROY C., transportation company executive; b. 1937; married. BA, U. Puget Sound, 1961. Acct. Touche Ross Bailey and Smart, 1961-67; with Pacific Air Freight Inc., 1967-68; treas. Airborne Freight Corp., Seattle, 1968-88, v.p., 1968-73, sr. v.p., 1973-79, exec. v.p., 1979—, chief fin. officer, 1984—. Office: Airborne Freight Corp PO Box 662 Seattle WA 98111-0662

LILJEGREN, FRANK SIGFRID, artist, art association official; b. N.Y.C., Feb. 23, 1930; s. Josef Sigfrid and Ester (Davidsson) L.; m. Donna Kathryn Hallam, Oct. 12, 1957. Student, Art Students League, N.Y.C., 1950-55. Instr. painting, drawing, composition Westchester County Center, White Plains, N.Y., 1967-77, Art Students League, 1974-75, Wassenberg Art Center, Van Wert, Ohio, 1978-80, Wright State U. Br. Western Ohio Campus, Celina, Ohio, 1981—; corr. sec. Allied Artists Am., N.Y.C., 1967, exhbn. chmn., 1968—, pres., 1970-72, also dir. Exhibited at Suffolk Mus., Stonybrook, N.Y., Springfield (Mass.) Mus., Marion Kugler McNay Art Inst., San Antonio, Philbrook Mus., Tulsa, N.A.D., N.Y.C., New Britain (Conn.) Mus. Art, Ft. Wayne (Ind.) Mus. Art; represented in permanent collections Art Students League, Univ. Mus., S.E. Mo. State U., Manhattan Savs. Bank, N.Y.C., Am. Ednl. Pubs. Inst., N.Y.C., New Britain Mus. Am. Art, Conn., Cape Girardeau, Mo. Served with AUS, 1951. Recipient numerous awards for still life oil paintings. Mem. Fine Arts fedn. N.Y, Art Students League (life), Acad. Artists Assn., Coun. Am. Artists Socs., Artists Fellowship, Salmagundi. Office: Liljegren Galleries 203 S Cherry St Van Wert OH 45891-2006 *The best advice I could give young artists is to first learn their craft to the fullest so that they can then be free to express themselves in what ever style and medium they then choose to work. Last but not least, they should have self-respect and great love for what they are doing.*

LILLARD, JOHN FRANKLIN, III, lawyer; b. Cheverly, Md., Aug. 2, 1947; s. John Franklin, Jr. and Madeline Virginia (Berg) L.; m. Shannon Leslie Oliver, June 1, 1991; 1 child, John F. Lillard IV. B.A., Washington and Lee U., 1969, J.D., 1971. Bar: N.Y. 1972, D.C. 1974, Md. 1975. Assoc. Donovan, Leisure, Newton & Irvine, N.Y.C., 1971-74, Pierson, Ball & Dowd (merged into Reed, Smith, Shaw & McClay), Washington, 1974-76; trial atty. civil div. Dept. Justice, Washington, 1976-77; ptnr. Lillard & Lillard, Washington, 1977—. instr. Dale Carnegie Course, 1988—. Vice chair Village Council of Friendship Heights, Chevy Chase, Md., 1975-77; candidate U.S. Congress from 5th dist. Md., 1981; chair Am. Solar Energy Assn.; founding mem. Nat. Adv. Coun. Ctr. for the Study of The Presidency, 1970—, Md. State Adv. Bd. on Spl. Tax Dists., 1976-77, alcoholic beverage adv. bd. Montgomery County, 1977-79; chair Eisenhower Centennial Meml. Com., 1990—. Served to 1st lt. USAF Aux., 1973-77. Recipient Eastman award Am. Arbitration Assn., 1971. Mem. Md. Bar Assn., Prince George's County Bar Assn., Anne Arundel County Bar Assn. Republican. Episcopalian. Clubs: Metropolitan (Washington); Tred Avon Yacht (Oxford, Md.); Marlborough Hunt (Upper Marlboro, Md.). Office: Lillard & Lillard 124 South St Annapolis MD 21401-2624

LILLARD, MARK HILL, III, computer consulting executive, former air force officer; b. Jacksonville, Fla., Sept. 1, 1943; s. Mark Hill Jr. and Cornelia Kingman (Callaway) L.; m. Marie-Jacques Le Guyader, June 3, 1972; children: Mark Hill IV, Michael Robert. BA, Bowling Green U., 1965; MS, St. Mary's U., San Antonio, 1976; MBA, Auburn U., 1977. Commd. 2d lt. USAF, 1965, advanced through grades to brig. gen., 1991; dir. spl. actions Combined Forces Command, Republic of Korea, 1980-83; comdr. 596 BMS, Barksdale AFB, La., 1983-85; dep. comdr. OPS, 2 BMS, Barksdale AFB, La., 1985; chief force mgmt. Strategic Air Command Hdqrs, Offutt, Nebr., 1985-87; comdr. 64 ABG, Reese AFB, Tex., 1987, 64 FTW, Reese AFB, Tex., 1987-88; exec. to chief of staff SHAPE (NATO), Mons Belgium, 1988-91; comdr. 57th Air Div., Minot AFB, N.D., 1991; ret., 1991; exec. v.p. Pilot Rsch. Assocs., Inc., Vienna, Va., 1991—, also bd. dirs. Author: Simulation, 1976. Decorated Legion of Merit, Def. Superior Svc. medal, Def. Meritorious Svc. medal; Samil medal (Republic of Korea). Mem. Air Force Assn., Lions, Kiwanis, Phi Delta Theta. Republican. Avocations: tennis, golf. Home: 9516 Locust Hill Dr Great Falls VA 22066-2021 Office: Pilot Rsch Assocs Inc 1953 Gallows Rd Ste 350 Vienna VA 22182-3934

LILLEHEI, C. WALTON, surgeon; b. Mpls., Oct. 23, 1918; s. Clarence Ingewald and Elizabeth Lillian (Walton) L.; m. Katherine Ruth Lindberg, Dec. 31, 1946; children—Kimberle Rae (Mrs. Allen Loken), Craig Walton, Kevin Owen, Clark William. B.S., U. Minn., 1939, M.D., 1942, M.S. in Physiology, 1951, Ph.D. in Surgery, 1951; Dr. Medicinae h.c., U. Oslo, 1976; hon. degree, Faculte De Medecinae De Montpellier, France, 1977; Dr. honoris causa, Sorbonne U., Paris, 1986, U. Rome, 1991; LHD (hon.), Oklahoma City U., 1987; DSc, W.Va. U., 1993. Diplomate: Am. Bd. Surgery, 1951, Am. Bd. Thoracic Surgery, 1954. Pvt. practice medicine, 1942—, specializing gen., thoracic and cardiovascular surgery, 1945—; instr. dept. surgery U. Minn. Med. Sch., 1949-51, asso. prof. surgery, 1951-56, prof. surgery, 1956-67, clin. prof. surgery, 1967—; dir. med. affairs St. Jude Med. Sch., St. Paul, 1979—; chmn. dept. surgery Cornell U. Med. Center, N.Y.C., 1967-74, Lewis Atterbury Stimson prof. surgery Med. Coll., 1967-74; surgeon-in chief N.Y. Hosp., N.Y.C., 1967-70; bd. dirs. Getz Bros. Med., Tokyo. Served lt. col. M.C., AUS, 1942-46. Decorated Bronze Star; officer Order of Leopold (Belgium); recipient Theobald-Smith award AAAS, 1951, Ida B. Gould award, 1957, 1st prize Am. Coll. Coll. Chest Physicians, 1952, Lasker award, 1955, Hektoen Gold medal AMA, 1957, Oscar B. Hunter award Am. Therapeutic Soc., 1958, Purdue Frederick Med. Achievement Travel award Internat. Consul for Health, 1958, Malcom F. Rogers Meml. award Wis. Heart Assn., 1962, Cummings Humanitarian award Am. Coll. Cardiology, 1963, Gairdner Found. Internat. award, 1963, Honor award Stevens Inst. Tech., 1967, Gold Plate award Am. Acad. Achievement, 1968, Bio-Med. Tech. Innovative Contbn. award Congl. Inst. for Space, Sci., and Tech., 1985, Outstanding Achievement award Bd. of Regents, U. Minn., 1991, Markowitz award Acad. Surg. Rsch., 1994, Harvey prize in sci. and tech. Technion, Israel, 1996; Lillehei Endowed Chair in thoracic and cardiovascular surgery named in his honor U. Minn. Med. Sch., 1988, Lillehei Libr. named in his honor, 1991; named to Minn. Inventors Hall of Fame, 1993. Fellow A.C.S., Am. Coll. Chest Physicians, Am. Coll. Cardiology (pres. 1966-67), Am. Coll. Angiology, Am. Heart Assn., Halsted Soc., Internat. Soc. Surgery, Allen O. Whipple Surg. Soc., Pan Am. Med. Soc., Royal Soc. Medicine (Gt. Britain), Soc. Thoracic Surgery; mem. AMA (Billings silver medal 1972), Am. Surg. Assn., Acad. Surg. Rsch., Am. Assn. Thoracic Surgery, Soc. U. Surgeons, Soc. Exptl. Biology and Medicine, AAAS, Internat. Cardiovascular Soc., Soc. Vascular Surgery, Sigma Xi. Home: 73 Otis Ln Saint Paul MN 55104-5645

LILLESAND, THOMAS MARTIN, remote sensing educator; b. Laurium, Mich., Oct. 1, 1946; m. Theresa Hofmeister, 1968; children: Mark, Kari, Michael. BS, U. Wis., 1969, MS, 1970, PhD in Civil Engring., 1973. Prof. remote sensing SUNY, Syracuse, 1973-78, U. Minn., 1978-82, U. Wis., Madison, 1982—; cons., 1973—. Mem. ASCE (pres.-elect), Am. Soc. Photogrametry and Remote Sensing (Alan Gordon award 1979, 93, Talbert Abrams award 1984, Fennell award 1988), Soc. Am. Foresters, Am. Congress on Surveying and Mapping. Office: U Wis Environ Remote Sensing Ctr 1225 W Dayton St Rm 1239B Madison WI 53706-1612

LILLESTOL, JANE BRUSH, career development company executive; b. Jamestown, N.D., July 20, 1936; d. Harper J. and Doris (Mikkelson) Brush; m. Harvey Lillestol, Sept. 29, 1956; children: Kim, Kevin, Erik. BS, U. Minn., 1969, MS, 1973, PhD, 1977; grad. Inst. Ednl. Mgmt., Harvard U., 1984. Dir. placement, asst. to dean U. Minn., St. Paul, 1975-77; assoc. dean, dir. student acad. affairs N.D. State U., Fargo, 1977-80; dean Coll. Human Devel. Syracuse (N.Y.) U., 1980-89, v.p. for alumni rels., 1989-95, project dir. IBM Computer Aided Design Lab., 1989-92; prin. Lillestol Assocs.; charter mem. Mayor's Commn. on Women, 1986-90; NAFTA White House Conf. for Women Leaders, 1993. Bd. dirs. Univ. Hill Corp. Syracuse, 1983-93; mem. steering com. Consortium for Cultural Founds. of Medicine, 1980-89; trustee Pebble Hill Sch., 1990-94, Archbold Theatre, 1990-95, N.D. State U., 1992—. Recipient award U.S. Consumer Product Safety Commn., 1983, Woman of Yr. award AAUW, 1984, svc. award Syracuse U., 1992. Roman Catholic. Office: 8046 E Via De Los Libros Scottsdale AZ 85058

LILLEVANG, OMAR JOHANSEN, civil engineer; b. Los Angeles, Sept. 8, 1914; s. Gunnar Johansen and Nina (Christiansen) L.; m. D. Miriam Guest, Sept. 10, 1939 (dec. Sept. 1990); children—Ralph Glen, Carol Ellen. A.A., Los Angeles Jr. Coll., 1935; B.S., U. Calif., Berkeley, 1937, postgrad., 1950-51. Registered profl. engr., Alaska, Calif., Hawaii, N.J., Oreg., Utah, Wash., Wis. Topographic surveyor Calif. Hwy. Commn., 1937; asst. engr. Coachella Valley County (Calif.) Water and Stormwater Dist., 1938; harbor constrn. engr., 1939-40, cantonment design and constrn. engr., 1941, constrn. engr. dams, aqueduct, tunnel, pump plants, 1942, water resources analyst, 1943; with Leeds, Hill, Barnard and Jewett (Cons. Engrs., and successors), Los Angeles, 1938-43, 46-61; supervising engr. Leeds, Hill, Barnard and Jewett (Cons. Engrs., and successors), 1950-61; v.p., dir. Leeds, Hill & Jewett Inc. (Cons. Engrs.), Los Angeles, 1961-64; cons. civil engring., especially for harbors, rivers, lakes, seas, coastal processes L.A., Whittier, 1964—; mem. advisory panel for shore erosion protection U.S. Army Chief Engrs. Contbr.: articles to profl. jours. including Shore & Beach mag. Trustee, chmn. bldg. com. Plymouth Congregational Ch. of Whittier, Calif. Served with USN, 1943-46. Fellow ASCE (mem. task groups, John G. Moffatt-Frank E. Nichol Meml. award 1981); mem. Am. Shore Beach Preservation Assn., Permanent Internat. Assn. Navigation Congresses, U.S. Power Squadrons. Club: Rotary Internat. Home: 14318 Eastridge Dr Whittier CA 90602-2721 Office: PO Box 4382 Whittier CA 90607-4382

LILLEY, ALBERT FREDERICK, retired lawyer; b. Harrisburg, Pa., Dec. 21, 1932; s. Frederick Anthony and Jane Sander (Ingham) L.; m. Judith Carter Pennock, Sept. 1, 1956; children: Kirk Anthony, Kristin Sander, James Alexander. A.B., Bowdoin Coll., 1954; LL.B., U. Va., 1959. Assoc. Milbank, Tweed, Hadley & McCloy, N.Y.C., 1959-67, ptnr., 1967-96; ret., 1997. Trustee No. Highlands Regional H.S., Allendale, N.J., 1964-65; mem. Allendale Bd. Zoning Adjustment, 1965-66; bd. overseers Bowdoin Coll., 1976-88, overseer emeritus, 1988—; trustee Valley Hosp., Ridgewood, N.J., 1978-92, vice chmn. bd., 1985-89, chmn. bd., 1989-92; bd. dirs. Valley Care Corp., 1992—, Valley Home and Cmty. Health Care, Inc., 1992—; mem. alumni coun. U. Va. Law Sch., 1991-94, U.S. Can. Law Project Adv. Bd. 1st lt. U.S. Army, 1954-56. Mem. ABA, Am. Law Inst., U. Va. Law Sch. Alumni Assn. (fund class mgr.). Home: 204 Laurel Hill Rd Chapel Hill NC 27514-4325

LILLEY, JOHN MARK, academic administrator, dean; b. Converse, La., Mar. 24, 1939; s. Ernest Franklin and Sibyl Arrena (Geoghagan) L.; children: Sibyl Elizabeth, Myles Durham; m. Geraldine Murphy; stepchildren: Benjamin Murphy, Jason Murphy. B in Music Edn., Baylor U., 1961, MusB, 1962, MusM, 1964; D of Musical Arts, U. So. Calif., 1971. Mem. faculty Claremont McKenna, Harvey Mudd, Pitzer and Scripps Colls., Claremont, Calif., 1966-76; asst. dean faculty Scripps Coll., 1973-76; asst. dean arts and scis. Kans. State U., Manhattan, 1976-80; provost, dean Pa. State U., Erie, 1980—; bd. dirs. Erie Conf., 1980—, Erie Plastics Corp., 1994—; mem. N.W. Pa. Indsl. Resource Ctr., 1987—. Condr. 1st performances Kubik, 1972, 76, Ives, 1974, (recording) Kubik, 1974. Bd. dirs., v.p. So. Calif. Choral Music Assn., L.A., 1971-76; mem. Archtl. Commn., Claremont, 1974-76; bd. dirs. Erie Philharm., 1980-86, United Way, Erie County, 1981—, Sta. WQLN Pub. Broadcasting of N.W. Pa., 1992—; mem. Regents Commn. on Nursing Edn., Kansas City, Kans., 1978-79; pres. Pacific S.W. Intercollegiate Choral Assn., L.A., 1969-70. NEH grantee, 1978. Mem. Am. Assn. Higher Edn., Coll. Music Soc., Am. Choral Dirs. Assn., Am. Assn. State Colls. and Univs. (vice chair confs. and profl. devel. com. 1989, chair 1990, bd. dirs. 1995—, govs. tuition account program adv. bd. 1996—), Erie Club, Kahkwa Club, Rotary (bd. dirs. Manhattan club 1979-80, Erie club 1981-88), Phi Mu Alpha Sinfonia, Omicron Delta Kappa. Presbyterian. Avocation: golf. Home: 601 Pasadena Dr Erie PA 16505-1038 Office: Pa State U Behrend Coll Station Rd Erie PA 16563

LILLEY, THEODORE ROBERT, financial executive; b. Paterson, N.J., Jan. 11, 1923; s. Ernest Raymond and Antoinette Eleanor (Hartmann) L.; m. Marguerite Anne Gallman, Jan. 27, 1951; children—Cheryl Anne, Wayne Robert, Ross Warren. B.A. cum laude, N.Y. U., 1946; M.B.A., Columbia U., 1948. Chartered financial analyst. With Standard Oil Co., N.J., 1948-64; investment mgr. Standard Oil Co., 1956-62, fin. mgr., 1962-64; asst. treas. Esso Internat. Inc., 1964-69; v.p. Tchr. Ins. and Annuity Assn. and Coll. Retirement Equities Fund, 1969-72; exec. dir. Fin. Analysts Fedn., N.Y.C., 1972-73; pres. Fin. Analysts Fedn., 1973-81, T.R. Lilley Assocs., 1981—; mem. advisory council Fin. Acctg. Standards Bd., 1976-80. Mem. bd. nat. missions United Presbyn. Ch. U.S.A., 1966-72; mem. United Presbyn. Found., 1972-81; trustee Englewood Hosp., 1979-85; bd. dirs. Near East Found., 1970—; trustee Ramapo Coll., 1977-95, chmn. bd., 1980-82. 1st lt. inf. AUS, 1943-46, ETO. Decorated Bronze Star, Purple Heart. Mem. Phi Beta Kappa, Phi Lambda Upsilon, Beta Gamma Sigma. Office: TR Lilley Assos PO Box 426 Tenafly NJ 07670-0426

LILLEY, WILLIAM, III, communications business consultant; b. Phila., Jan. 14, 1938; s. William, Jr. and Ida Weaver (Macklin) L.; m. Eve Auchincloss, Mar. 12, 1977; children—Buchanan Morgan, Brooke Carole, Whitman Elisa, Justin Weaver. B.A. magna cum laude, U. Pa., 1959; M.A., Yale U., 1961, Ph.D., 1965. Asst. prof. history Yale U., New Haven, 1962-69; prof. govt. U. Va., Charlottesville, 1977; co-founder, editor Nat. Jour., Washington, 1969-73; dep. asst. sec. HUD, Washington, 1973-75; dep., then dir. Council Wage and Price Stability, Washington, 1975-77; staff dir. Com. on Budget, Ho. of Reps., Washington, 1977-78; v.p. CBS, Inc., Washington, 1980-81; v.p. corporate affairs CBS, Inc., N.Y.C., 1981-84, sr. v.p. corporate affairs, 1985-86; pres. Am. Bus. Conf., 1986-88, Policy Communications Inc., Washington, 1988—; chmn., chief exec. officer InContext, Inc., Washington, 1992—; bd. dirs. Ply Gem Industries, Inc., Econ. and Social Rsch. Inst., Madison Ctr. for Ednl. Affairs. Co-author: New Technologies Affecting Broadcasting, 1981, Economic and Social Impacts of Media Advertising, 1989, Impact of Advertising on the Competetive Structure of the Media, 1990, Impact of Media Advertising on International Competetiveness, 1991, Geographic Distribution of U.S. Businesses Which Advertise Heavily, 1991, Almanac of State Legislatures, 1994, State Atlas of Political and Cultural Diversity, 1996, State Legislative Elections: Voting Patterns and Demographics, 1996; contbr. articles to profl. jours. Recipient U.S. Govt. Disting. Svc. award 1975, 76; Samuel F.B. Morse Rsch. fellowship, 1967-68; George Washington Eggleston prize; Most Disting. PhD Dissertation humanities divsn., Yale U., 1965; Woodrow Wilson Fellowship, 1959-61. Mem. Yale Club, Merion Cricket, Cosmos, River Club, Chevy Chase, Met. Club. Clubs: Yale, Merion Cricket, Cosmos, River, Chevy Chase. Office: Policy Communications Inc 1615 L St NW Washington DC 20036-5610

LILLIBRIDGE, JOHN LEE, retired airline executive; b. Dover, Okla., Nov. 3, 1924; s. John Lee and Myra Ina (Munger) L.; m. Audrey Rae Hart,

Aug. 22, 1948; 1 son, John Lee III. B.S. in Mech. Engring., Okla. A&M Coll., 1950; B.S. in Civil Engring., Tex. A&M Coll., 1956. Enlisted in U.S. Army, 1943, advanced through grades to col., 1970, ret., 1973—; officer Corps of Engrs., 1950-73; v.p. Eastern Airlines, Miami, Fla., 1973-86. Democrat.

LILLIE, CHARISSE RANIELLE, lawyer, educator; b. Houston, Apr. 7, 1952; d. Richard Lysander and Vernell Audrey (Watson) L.; m. Thomas L. McGill, Jr., Dec. 4, 1982. B.A. cum laude, Conn. Wesleyan U., 1973; J.D., Temple U., 1976; LL.M., Yale U., 1982. Bar: Pa. 1976, U.S. Dist. Ct. (ea. dist.) Pa. 1977, U.S. Ct. Appeals (3d cir.) 1980. Law clk. U.S. Dist. Ct. (ea. dist.) Pa., Phila., 1976-78; trial atty., honors program, civil rights div. Dept. Justice, Washington, 1978-80; dep. dir. Community Legal Services, Phila., 1980-81; asst. prof. law Villanova U. Law Sch., Pa., 1982-83, assoc. prof., 1983-84, prof., 1984-85; asst. U.S. atty. U.S. Dist. Ct. (ea. dist.) Pa., 1985-88; gen. counsel Redevel. Authority City of Phila., 1988-90; city solicitor Law Dept. City of Phila., 1990-92; ptnr. litigation dept. Ballard, Spahr, Andrew and Ingersoll, 1992—, exec. com. bd. dirs., 1994—; mem. 3d Cir. Lawyers Adv. Com., 1982-85, legal counsel Pa. Coalition of 100 Black Women, Phila., 1983-88; bd. dirs. Juvenile Law Center, Phila., 1982—, Pa. Intergovernmental Coop. Authority, 1992—, Fed. Res. Bank Phila., 1996—; commr. Phila. Ind. City Charter Commn., 1991-94; trustee Women's Law Project, Phila., 1984-90; mem. Mayor's Commn. on May 13 MOVE Incident, 1985-87. Bd. dirs. Women's Way, Phila. Davenport fellow, 1973; Yale Law Sch. fellow, 1981; recipient Equal Justice award Community Legal Svcs., Inc, 1991, J. Austin Norris award Barristers Assn., 1991, Outstanding Alumna award Wesleyan U., 1993, Elizabeth Dole Glass Ceiling award ARC, Phila. chpt., 1994; named One of the Top Three Phila. Labor Mgmt. Attys. Phila. Mag., 1994. Mem. ABA, Nat. Bar Assn., Fed. Bar Assn. (1st v.p. Phila. chpt. 1982-84, pres. Phila. chpt.1984-86, 3rd cir. rep. 1991—), Nat. Conf. Black Lawyers (pres. 1976-78, Outstanding Service award 1978, vice chmn. ABA commn. on minorities 1997—), Am. Law Inst., Phila. Bar Assn. (vice chair bd. govs. 1994, chair, bd. of govs., 1995—), Hist. Soc. U.S. Dist. Ct. (ea. dist.) Pa. (dir. 1983, 1993-96), Barristers Assn. (J. Austin Norris award 1991). Home: 7000 Emlen St Philadelphia PA 19119-2556 Office: Ballard Spahr Andrews Ingersoll 1735 Market St Ste 51 Philadelphia PA 19103-7501

LILLIE, HELEN, journalist, novelist; b. Glasgow, Scotland, Sept. 13, 1915; came to U.S., 1938; d. Thomas and Helen Barbara (Lillie) L.; m. Charles S. Marwick, Sept. 20, 1956. MA, U. Glasgow, 1938; postgrad., Yale U., 1938-40. Rsch. asst. info. divsn. Brit. Info. Svcs., N.Y.C., 1942-45, Brit. Security Coord., N.Y.C., 1945-46; asst. U.S. mgr., writer Media Reps., Inc., N.Y.C., 1947-54; with advt. dept. Family Cir. Mag., N.Y.C., 1955-56; Am. corr. The Glasgow Herald (name now The Herald), 1956-94; freelance feature writer, book reviewer Detroit Free Press, 1965-66. Author: The Listening Silence, 1970, Call Down the Sky, 1973, Home to Strathblane, 1993, Strathblane and Away, 1996, (columns) Inside USA, Helen Lillie's Washington Letter. V.p., acting pres. Cosmopolitan B PM Club of DC, 1972-73. Mem. Am. News Women's Club D.C., Soc. Women Geographers, Advt. Women of N.Y. (various coms.). Presbyterian. Avocations: music, politic watching, travel, theater, reading. Home and Office: 3219 Volta Pl NW Washington DC 20007-2732

LILLIE, MARSHALL SHERWOOD, college safety and security director, educator; b. Corry, Pa., May 23, 1953; s. Lloyd G. and Jalean R. (Sherwood) L.; m. Anita M., Aug 16, 1975; children: Amanda M., Sarah N., Rebekah L., Reuben L. ASB, Erie Bus. Ctr., Pa., 1974; BA, Olivet Nazarene U., Kankakee, Ill., 1980; MS, Mercyhurst Coll., Erie, Pa., 1984. Cert. mcpl. police officer trainer. Dir., security Olivet Nazarene U., Kankakee, Ill., 1977-81; administr. asst. Mercyhurst Coll., Erie, Pa., 1981-86; dir., security Thiel Coll., Greenville, Pa., 1986—; chmn. Western Pa. Security Dirs., 1989-90; instr. Thiel Coll., Greenville, Pa., 1990—, Mercyhurst Coll., Erie, 1992—; defensive tactics instr. Pressure Point Control Sys., 1995—; defensive driving instr. Nat. Safety Coun. Master Sunday Sch. Supr. Ch. of Nazarene, 1991; Mayor's Adv. com., Greenville, Pa., 1990. Mem. NRA, N.E. Coll. and Univ. Security Assn. (editor The Clipboard 1993-94, bd. dirs. 1992-96), Western Pa. Coll., Security Dirs. Assn., Am. Soc. Law Enforcement Trainers, Am. Soc. Indsl. Security (chmn. Lake Erie chpt. 1990-91). Republican. Mem. Ch. of Nazarene. Office: Thiel Coll 75 College Ave Greenville PA 16125-2186

LILLO, JOSEPH LEONARD, osteopath, family practice physician; b. Mt. Gilead, Ohio, Aug. 12, 1954; s. Joseph and Betty Jean (Rogers) L.; m. Barbara Anne Burn, June 25, 1976; children: Marie, Michael, Laura. BS in Zoology, Ariz. State U., 1976; DO, Kirksville Coll. Osteo. Med., 1979. Diplomate Am. Bd. Family Practice, Nat. Bd. Examiners in Osteo. Medicine and surgery. Intern Phoenix Gen. Hosp., 1979-80; physician/surgeon Med. Arts P.A., Scottsdale, Ariz., 1980—; mng. ptnr. Granite Reef Devel. Corp., Scottsdale, 1986-88; adminstr. Scottsdale Cmty. Hosp., 1988-89; chmn. dept. family practice Tempe St. Luke's Hosp., 1992-93, chmn. credentials com., 1994-95; med. dir. Scottsdale Convalescent Plaza, 1988-89. Chmn. bd. Am. Cancer Soc., Scottsdale, 1990, bd. dirs., 1987-93; guest faculty Christ the King Cath. Sch., 1987—. Named Physician of the Yr. Scottsdale Cmty. Hosp., 1986. Mem. Am. Coll. Osteo. Family Physicians, Am. Osteo. Assn., Ariz. Osteo. Med. Assn. Republican. Roman Catholic. Avocations: running, basketball, computers, gardening, reading. Home: 3433 E Contessa Cir Mesa AZ 85213 Office: Medical Arts PA 1525 N Granite Reef Rd Ste 16 Scottsdale AZ 85257-3998

LILLY, EDWARD GUERRANT, JR., retired utility company executive; b. Lexington, Ky., Oct. 29, 1925; s. Edward Guerrant and Elisabeth Read (Frazer) L.; m. Nancy Estes Cobb, Nov. 25, 1961; children: Penelope Read, Edward Guerrant III, Collier Cobb (dec.), Steven Clay. B.S., Davidson Coll., 1948; M.B.A., U. Pa., 1949. Credit analyst Citizens and So. Nat. Bank, Charleston, S.C., 1949-50; asst. v.p. Wachovia Bank and Trust Co., Charlotte, 1952-55, v.p., 1956; v.p., loan adminstrv. officer Wachovia Bank and Trust Co., Wilmington, N.C., 1956-60; sr. v.p., area exec. Wachovia Bank and Trust Co., Kinston, N.C., 1961-62, Durham, N.C., 1963-70; sr. v.p., mgr. trust investment svcs. dept. Wachovia Bank and Trust Co., Winston-Salem, N.C., 1970-71, also bd. dirs., 1971-88; sr. v.p., group exec. Carolina Power and Light Co., Raleigh, N.C., 1971-76, sr. v.p., chief fin. officer, 1976-81; exec. v.p., chief fin. officer Carolina Power and Light Co., Raleigh, 1981-90; also bd. dirs. Carolina Power and Light Co., Raleigh, N.C.; bd. dirs. N.C. Enterprise Corp. Mem. U. N.C. bd. visitors, 1974-87; bd. dirs. Rsch. Triangle Found., Research Triangle Park; trustee Davidson Coll., 1976-88, Union Theol. Seminary. Served to Lt. USNR, 1950-52,. Mem. Edison Electric Inst. (chmn. fin. group 1979). Presbyterian. Lodge: Rotary (Raleigh).

LILLY, ELIZABETH GILES, mobile park executive; b. Bozeman, Mont., Aug. 5, 1916; d. Samuel John and Luella Elizabeth (Reed) Abegg; m. William Lilly, July 1, 1976; children: Samuel Colborn Giles, Elizabeth Giles. *Samuel Colburne Giles owned five filling stations-as a Seventh Day Adventist closed the stations on Saturday, the busiest day. Never would sell cigarettes. The year he passed away at 34 years old he did 4 million dollars business. Dr. Elizabeth Giles, a dental surgeon, of Riverside, California, also raises Arabian horses. Her horse, "Bo Gaz" was the 1996 national champion at the U.S. National Arabian Show .* RN, Good Samaritan Hosp., Portland, Oreg., 1941; student, Walla Walla Coll., Lewis and Clark Coll. Bus., Portland. ARC nurse, tchr. area high schs., Portland; owner Welton Studio Interior Design, Portland; in pub. rels. Chas. Eckelman, Portland, Fairview Farms-Dairy Industry; owner, builder Mobile Park Plaza, Inc., Portland. Del. platform planning com. Rep. Party; mem. Sunnyside Seventh Day Adventist Ch. Recipient Svc. award Multnomah County Commrs., 1984. Mem. Soroptimist Internat. (local bd. dirs., bd. dirs. Women in Transition), Rep. Women's Club (pres.), C. of C., World Affairs Coun., Toastmistress (pres.), Oreg. Lodging Assn. (pres. bd. dirs.), Rep. Inner Circle (life). Address: 19825 SE Stark St Portland OR 97233-6039

LILLY, JOHN RICHARD, II, lawyer; b. Phila., July 20, 1962; s. John Richard Sr. and Elizabeth Anne (Brown) L.; children: John Richard III, Cameron Ludwig. BA, Geoge Washington U., 1987; JD, U. Balt., 1991. Bar: Md. 1992, U.S. Dist. Ct. Md. 1995, U.S. Ct. Mil. Appeals 1994. Law clk. 7th Jud. Cir. Md., Upper Marlboro, 1991-92; asst. state's atty. State's Atty.'s Office Prince George's County Md., Upper Marlboro, 1992—; chmn., co-founder Prince George's County Task Force on Environ. Crimes, Upper Marlboro, 1994—. Comments editor U. Balt. Jour. Environ. Law. Chmn. Oakland Mills Village Bd., Columbia, Md., 1990-92; pres. St. Stephen's Area Civic Assn., Crownsville, Md., 1994-95. Lt. USNR, 1988—. Mem. ABA, Md. Bar Assn., Prince George's County Bar Assn., Anne Arundel Bar Assn. Avocations: tennis, sailing, woodworking, biking, racquetball. Home: 1306 Eva Gude Dr Crownsville MD 21032 Office: State's Atty's Office Ct House Upper Marlboro MD 20772

LILLY, KRISTINE MARIE, soccer player; b. Wilton, Conn., July 27, 1971. Grad., U. N.C., 1993. Midfielder Washington Warthog, Landover, Md., 1995—, U.S. Women's Nat. Soccer Team, Chgo., 1987. Recipient Hemann Trophy, 1991; named Most Valuable Offensive Player NCAA Championship, 1989, 91, U.S. Soccer's Female Athlete of the Yr., 1993, U.S. Nat. Team All-Time Appearance Leader (more than 90 games); mem. FIFA Women's World Championship Team, 1991. Office: US Soccer Fedn US Soccer House 1801 S Prairie Ave Chicago IL 60616-1319*

LILLY, MARTIN STEPHEN, university dean; b. New Albany, Ind., Aug. 31, 1944; s. Raymond John and Amy Elizabeth (Peake) L.; m. Marilyn Ann MacDougall, Jan. 8, 1966; children—Matthew William, Mark Christopher, Rachel Marie, Martin Stephen, Jason Wood. B.A., Bellarmine Coll., Louisville, 1966; M.A., Peabody Coll., Nashville, 1967, Ed.D., 1969. Instr. dept. spl. edn. Peabody Coll., 1967-69; asst. prof. edn. U. Oreg., 1969-71; research coordinator N.W. Regional Spl. Edn. Instructional Materials Center, 1969-71; research coordinator div. research Bur. Edn. for Handicapped U.S. Office Edn., 1971-72; assoc. prof. dept. spl. edn. U. Minn., Duluth, 1972-75; assoc. prof., chmn. dept. spl. edn. U. Ill., Urbana-Champaign, 1975-79, prof., chmn., 1979-81, assoc. dean grad. studies Coll. Edn., 1981-84; dean Coll. Edn. Wash. State U., Pullman, 1984-90, Calif. State U., San Marcos, 1990—; cons. in field; U.S. Office Edn. fellow, 1966-69; pres. Tchr. Edn. Coun. State Colls. and Univs.; co-chair strategic action com. San Diego County Childrens Initiative. Author: Children with Exceptional Needs: A Survey of Special Education, 1979, (with C.S. Blankenship) Mainstreaming Students With Learning and Behavior Problems, 1981; assoc. editor: Exceptional Children, 1969-79; cons. editor: Edn. Unltd, 1979-81; reviewer: Jour. Tchr. Edn, 1980—; mem. editorial bd. Tchr. Edn. and Spl. Edn, 1980-83, co-editor, 1983-84; contbr. chpts. to books, articles to profl. jours. Mem. Coun. for Exceptional Children, Assn. Tchr. Educators, Am. Assn. Colls. Tchr. Edn., Phi Delta Kappa. Democrat. Roman Catholic. Office: Calif State U San Marcos CA 92096-0001

LILLY, MICHAEL ALEXANDER, lawyer, author; b. Honolulu, May 21, 1946; s. Percy Anthony Jr. and Virginia (Craig) L.; m. Kathryn I. Collins, Aug. 10, 1991; children: Michael Jr., Cary J., Laura B., Claire F., Winston W. AA, Menlo Coll., Menlo Park, Calif., 1966; BA, U. Calif., Santa Cruz, 1968; JD with honors, U. of Pacific, 1974. Bar: Calif. 1974, U.S. Dist. Ct. (no., so. and ea. dists.) Calif. 1974, U.S. Ct. Appeals (9th cir.) 1974, Hawaii 1975, U.S. Dist. Ct. Hawaii 1975, U.S. Ct. Appeals (D.C. cir.) 1975, U.S. Supreme Ct. 1978, U.S. Ct. Appeals (7th cir.) 1979. Atty. Pacific Legal Found., Sacramento, 1974-75; dep. atty. gen. State of Hawaii, Honolulu, 1975-79, 1st dep. atty. gen., 1981-84, atty. gen., 1984-85; ptnr. Feeley & Lilly, San Jose, Calif., 1979-81, Ning, Lilly & Jones, Honolulu, 1985—. Author: If You Die Tomorrow-A Layman's Guide to Estate Planning. Pres., dir. Diamond Head Theatre; Lt. USN, 1968-71, Vietnam; capt. USNR. Named hon. Ky. col. Mem. Nat. Assn. Attys. Gen., Hawaii Law Enforcement Ofcls. Assn., Navy Res. Assn. (pres. 14th dist. 1986-89), Navy League (nat. dir., contbg. editor Fore 'N Aft mag., dept. judge adv. to bd. Honolulu coun.), Outrigger Canoe Club. Home: 2769 Laniloa Rd Honolulu HI 96813-1041 Office: Ning Lilly & Jones 707 Richards St Ste 700 Honolulu HI 96813-4623 *Personal philosophy: Always do what you are afraid to do. Never give up. Forgive your enemies.*

LILLY, PETER BYRON, coal company executive; b. Beckley, W.Va., Sept. 26, 1948; s. Wallace Byron and Mabel Elizabeth (Dodson) L.; m. Brenda Jean Ernst, June 20, 1970; children: Lauren E., Peter E. BS in Engring., U.S. Mil. Acad., 1970; MBA, Harvard U., 1977. Commd. 2d lt. U.S. Army, 1970, advanced through grades to capt., served in Vietnam, resigned, 1975; mgmt. cons. Emory Ayers Assocs., N.Y.C., 1977-80; mgr. maintenance Kerr-McGee Coal Corp., Okla. City, 1980-81, dir. adminstrn., 1981-83; gen. mgr. Galatia Mine Kerr-McGee Coal Corp., Galatia, Ill., 1983-88; v.p. mktg. and planning Kerr-McGee Coal Corp., Oklahoma City, 1988-89, pres., 1989-91; sr. v.p. Kerr-McGee Coal Corp., Oklahoma City, 1989-91; pres. Ea. Associated Coal Corp., Charleston, W.Va., 1991-94; exec. v.p Peabody Holding Co., St. Louis, 1994-95, pres., COO, 1995—. Decorated Bronze Star, Purple Heart; Cross of Gallantry (South Vietnam). Mem. Nat. Coal Assn. (bd. dirs. 1989—), Am. Mining Congress (bd. dirs. 1989-91), Nat. Coal Coun. Office: Peabody Holding Co 701 Market St Ste 700 Saint Louis MO 63101-1826

LILLY, THOMAS GERALD, lawyer; b. Belzoni, Miss., Sept. 17, 1933; s. Sale Trice and Margaret Evelyn (Butt) L.; m. Constance Ray Holland, Dec. 29, 1962; children: Thomas Gerald Jr., William Holland, Carolyn Ray. BBA, Tulane U., 1955; LLB, U. Miss., 1960, JD, 1968. Bar: Miss. 1960. Assoc. firm Stovall & Price, Corinth, Miss., 1960-62; asst. U.S. atty. No. Dist. Miss., Oxford, 1962-66; assoc. firm Wise Carter Child & Caraway (and predecessor), Jackson, Miss., 1966-67; ptnr. Wise Carter Child & Caraway (and predecessor), 1967-94, Lilly & Wise, Jackson, 1994—. Served with USNR, 1955-58; rear adm. Res. ret. Decorated Legion of Merit, Navy Commendation medal. Mem. ABA, Fed. Bar Assn. (nat. coun. 1972—, rec. sec. 1975-76, gen. sec. 1976-77, 2d v.p. 1977-78, pres.-elect 1978-79, pres. 1979-80), Hinds County Bar Assn., Miss. State Bar, Miss. Bar Found., Internat. Bar Assn., Am. counsel Assn., Democracy Devel. Initiative (bd. dirs. 1995—), Internat. Trade Club Miss. (bd. dirs. 1995-96), Res. Officers Assn. (pres. Miss. dept. 1982-83), Naval Res. Assn., Naval Order of U.S., Navy Supply Corps Assn., Navy League (pres. Ctrl. Miss. Coun. 1993), Mil. Order World Wars, Southeastern Legal Found. (legal adv. bd. 1988-95), Lamar Order, Newcomen Soc., English-Speaking Union, Omicron Delta Kappa, Phi Delta Phi, Sigma Nu. Office: Lilly & Wise 2180 Deposit Guaranty Plz 210 E Capitol St Jackson MS 39201-2306

LILLY, WESLEY COOPER, marine engineer, ship surveyor; b. Phila., May 23, 1933; s. Richard Gladstone and Margaret Jane L.; m. Barbara Joan Newton, Mar. 15, 1953 (div. Nov. 24, 1978); children: Pamela Lynn, Barbara Joan. BS in Engring., Pa. Mil. Coll., 1956-61. Apprentice machinist Phila. Naval Shipyard, 1951-53, prodn. shipbuilding, 1955-66, planning, design divsn., 1966-68; mem. shipbldg. and testing specifications staff Naval Weapons Svc. Office, 1968-70; procurement prodn. Navy Dept. Navsea, Washington, 1970-86; pres., owner Marine Assocs., St. Augustine, Fla., 1972—; pres., founder Saturn Marine Engring., St. Augustine, Fla., 1986—; programmer Fortran and Cobol rev. bus. computech programs. Inventor, patentee in field. Served with U.S. Army, 1953-55. Mem. Soc. Naval Archs. and Marine Engrs. (chmn. com. for small and medium shipyards/shipbuilding), Tech. Exch. Marine Profls., Putnam Co. Computer Group, Palatka Yacht Club, Navy Dept. Computer Club. Republican. Episcopalian. Avocations: accounting, computers, cruising, sailing. Home: 2757 First Ave Fernandina Beach FL 32034 Office: Marine Assocs Fernandina Beach FL 32034

LILLY, WILLIAM ELDRIDGE, government official; b. Liberty, Tex., Aug. 25, 1921; s. Lawrence C. and Maude (McKinney) L.; m. Blanche Elizabeth Bromert, Jan. 18, 1944; children—Lizbeth Kristine, William Michael. A.B., U. Calif. at Berkeley, 1950, grad. student, 1950-51. Program analyst Naval Ordnance Test Sta., China Lake, Calif., 1950-52; head estimates and analysis Naval Bur. Ordnance, Washington, 1952-54; dep. budget officer Nat. Bur. Standards, 1954-56; asst. dir. plans and programs Navy Polaris program, 1956-60; with NASA, 1960—, asst. administr. for adminstrn., 1967-72, comptroller, 1972-82, cons., 1982—. Pres. Arlington County (Va.) Youth Orgn., 1966-69. Served with USN, 1940-46. Recipient Exceptional Service medal NASA, 1966, 69, Distinguished Service medal, 1973, 81; Career Service award Nat. Civil Service League, 1978; presdl. rank of Disting. Exec., 1980. Mem. Phi Beta Kappa, Pi Sigma Alpha. Home: PO Box 2028 Arlington VA 22202-0028 Office: P100 L'Enfant Plz N SW Washington DC 20024

LILLY-HERSLEY, JANE ANNE FEELEY, nursing researcher; b. Palo Alto, Calif., May 31, 1947; d. Daniel Morris Sr. and Suzanne (Agnew) Feeley; children: Cary Jane, Laura Blachree, Claire Foale; m. Dennis C. Hersley, Jan. 16, 1993. BS, U. Oreg., 1968; student, U. Hawaii, 1970; BSN, RN, Sacramento City Coll., 1975. Cert. ACLS, BCLS. Staff and charge nurse, acute rehab. Santa Clara Valley Med. Ctr., San Jose, Calif., staff nurse, surg. ICU and trauma unit; clin. project leader mycophenolate mofetil program team Syntex Rsch., Palo Alto; pres. Clin. Rsch. Consultation, Santa Cruz, Calif. Co-founder, CFO and dir. scientific rsch. Citizens United Responsible Environmentalism, Inc., CURE (internat. non-profit edn./rsch. orgn.). Mem. AACN.

LILLYMAN, WILLIAM JOHN, German language educator; b. Sydney, Australia, Apr. 17, 1937; came to U.S., 1963, naturalized, 1974; s. John and Christina Mary (Munro) L.; m. Ingeborg Wolz, Sept. 14, 1962; children: Gregory, Christina. AB, U. Sydney, 1959; PhD, Stanford U., 1964. Asst. prof. Stanford (Calif.) U., 1964-67; assoc. prof. U. Calif., Santa Cruz, 1967-72; prof. German U. Calif., Irvine, 1972—, dean humanities, 1973-81, vice chancellor acad. affairs, 1981-82, exec. vice chancellor, 1982-88. Author: Otto Ludwig's Zwischen Himmel und Erde, 1967, Otto Ludwig: Romane und Romanstudien, 1977, Reality's Dark Dream The Narrative Fiction of Ludwig Tieck, 1979, Goethe's Narrative Fiction, 1983; co-editor; Probleme der Moderne, 1983, Horizonte Festschrift für H. Lehnert, 1990, Critical Architecture and Contemporary Culture, 1994. Mem. MLA, Am. Assn. Tchrs. German. Office: U Calif Dept German Irvine CA 92697-3150

LILMAN, ALAN B., restaurant company executive; b. South Bend, Ind., Sept. 24, 1930; s. Sol M. and Lee R. (Rintzler) G.; m. Phyllis Schrager, Feb. 16, 1951; children: Bruce, Jeffrey, Lynn. A.B. with highest honors (Raymond Charles Stoltz scholar), Ind. U., 1952, M.B.A. (John H. Edwards fellow), 1954. With Lazarus Co. div. Federated Dept. Stores, Inc., Columbus, Ohio, 1954-64; div. mdse. mgr. Lazarus Co. div. Federated Dept. Stores, Inc., 1961-64; with Sanger Harris div., 1965-74, chmn. bd., chief exec. officer, 1970-74, corp. v.p., 1974-80; with Abraham & Straus div., 1975-80, chmn. bd., chief exec. officer, 1978-80; pres. Murjani Internat. Ltd., N.Y.C., 1980-85; pvt. investor, 1985-87; chmn. At Ease of Newport Beach (Calif.) Inc., 1988-91; pres., chief exec. officer Consol. Products Inc., 1992—, Steak 'n Shake Inc. Vice chmn. bd. dirs. Ind. U. Found., nat. chmn. ann. giving, 1983, mem. presdl. search com., 1987-88; chmn. dean's adv. coun. Ind. U. Grad. Sch. Bus., 1976-86; mem. dean's adv. coun. Coll. Arts and Scis., Ind. U., 1989—, pres.'s cabinet, 1995; bd. dirs., pres., mem. exec. com. Greater N.Y. Fund-United Way, 1984-87; bd. dirs., mem. exec. com., chmn. strategic planning com. United Way of N.Y.C., 1982-88. Recipient Humanitarian of Yr. award Juvenile Diabetes Found., 1979, Disting. Alumni Svc. award Ind. U., 1996. Mem. Young Pres. Orgn. 49'er, Ind. U. Acad. Alumni Fellows, World Bus. Council, Phi Beta Kappa Assocs., Phi Alpha Theta, Beta Gamma Sigma (charter mem. dirs. table). Home: 2730 Brigs Bnd Bloomington IN 47401-4402 Office: 500 Century Bldg 36 S Pennsylvania St Indianapolis IN 46204-3634 *Value intellectual curiosity, an open mind, the greater import of tomorrow over yesterday, and recognize rapid change as the definition of opportunity while maintaining a sense of humor and honest humility.*

LIM, ALEXANDER RUFASTA, neurologist, clinical investigator, educator, writer; b. Manila, Philippines, Feb. 20, 1942; s. Benito P. and Maria Lourdes (Cuyegkeng) L.; m. Norma Sue Hanks, June 1, 1968; children: Jeffrey Allen, Gregory Brian, Kevin Alexander, Melissa Gail. AA, U. Santo Tomas, Manila, Philippines, 1959, MD, 1964. Intern Bon Secours Hosp., Balt., 1964-65; resident in internal medicine Scott and White Clinic, Temple, Tex., 1965-67; resident in neurology Cleve. Clinic, 1967-69, chief resident in neurology, 1969-70, fellow clin. neurophysiology, 1970-71, clin. assoc. neurologist, 1971-72; neurologist, co-founder, co-mng. ptnr. Neurol. Clinic, Corpus Christi, Tex., 1972—; pres., CEO Neurology, P.A., Corpus Christi, 1972-92; chief neurology Meml. Med. Ctr., Corpus Christi, 1975-90, Spohn Hosp., Corpus Christi, 1974-90, Reynolds Army Hosp., Ft. Sill, Okla., 1990-91; clin. assoc. prof. Sch. Medicine U. Tex. Health Sci. Ctr., San Antonio. Mem. editl. bd. Coastal Bend Medicine, 1988-95; cons., reviewer Tex. Medicine, 1995—. Lt. col. Med. Corps, 1990-91. Recipient Army Commendation medal, 1991, Nat. Def. medal U.S. Army, 1991. Mem. AMA, Tex. Med. Assn. (chmn. neurology 1985-86), Tex. Neurol. Soc. (sec. 1986-88, pres. 1989-90), Am. Acad. Neurology, Am. Epilepsy Soc., Am. Acad. Clin. Neurophysiology, Am. Electroencephalographic Soc., So. Electroencephalographic Soc., Am. Acad. Pain Mgmt., Physician Com. Responsible Medicine, Doctors of the World, Am. Legion, Internat. Platform Assn., KC. Republican. Roman Catholic. Avocations: tennis, philately, travel, snow skiing, bonsai. Home: 4821 Augusta Cir Corpus Christi TX 78413-2711 Office: The Neurological Clinic 3006 S Alameda St Corpus Christi TX 78404-2601

LIM, DANIEL VAN, microbiology educator; b. Houston, Apr. 15, 1948; s. Don H. and Lucy (Toy) L.; m. Carol Lee, Sept. 2, 1973. BA in Biology, Rice U., 1970; PhD in Microbiology, Tex. A&M U., 1973. Postdoctoral fellow Baylor Coll. Medicine, 1973-76; asst. prof. U South Fla., Tampa, 1976-81, assoc. prof. microbiology, 1981-87, chmn. dept. biology, 1983-85, prof. 1987—; pres. Micro Concepts Rsch. Corp; dir. Inst. Biomolecular Sci., 1988-93; cons. in field. Author: Microbiology, 1989, Introduction to Microbiology, 1995; inventor bacteriological broth. Recipient Outstanding Ph.D. Dissertation in U.S. award Phi Sigma, 1974, Outstanding Contbn. in Sci. and Tech. award Fla. Gov. Fellow Am. Acad. Microbiology; mem. Inter-Am. Soc. Chemotherapy (v.p. 1983-88), Am. Soc. Microbiology (pres. southeastern br. 1990-91, Carski award com. 1983-86, Margaret Green Outstanding Tchr. award). Office: U South Fla 4202 E Fowler Ave # 136 Tampa FL 33620-9900

LIM, DAVID JONG-JAI, otolaryngology educator, researcher; b. Seoul, Republic of Korea, Nov. 27, 1935; came to U.S., 1964; s. Yang Sup Lim and Cha Nang Yoo; m. Young Sook Hahn, May 14, 1966; children: Michael, Robert. AB, Yonsei U., Seoul, 1955, MD, 1960. Research fellow in otolaryngology Mass. Eye & Ear Infirmary, Boston, 1965-66; research assoc. dept. otolaryngology Ohio State U. Coll. Medicine, Columbus, 1966-67, asst. prof., 1967-71, assoc. prof., 1971-76, prof. dept. otolaryngology, 1976-91, dir. otological research labs., 1967-91, prof. cell biology, neurobiology and anatomy, 1977-91, prof. emeritus otolaryngology, 1992—; rsch. prof. cell and neurobiology U. So. Calif., 1996—; dir. intramural rsch. program Nat. Inst. on Deaf and Other Communication Disorders, NIH, Bethesda, Md., 1992-94, chief lab cellular biology, 1993-95; exec. v.p. House Ear Inst., L.A., 1995—; mem. nat. adv. neurol. and communicative disorders and stroke coun. NIH, Bethesda, Md., 1979-83; mem. adv. bd. Nat. Inst. Deafness and Other Communication Disorders, 1989-91; cons., bd. dirs. Rsch. Fund Am. Otol. Soc., 1982-87; mem. adv. bd. Cen. Inst. for Deaf, 1989-91. Contbr. articles to profl. jours., chpts. to textbooks. Pres. Korean Assn. in Columbus, 1970; chmn. bd. dirs. Cen. Ohio Korean Lang. Sch., Columbus, 1986; bd. dirs. Deafness Rsch. Found., N.Y.C., 1980—. Fogarty Internat. fellow Karolinska Inst., Stockholm, 1982; recipient Disting. Scholar award Ohio State U., 1985, Javits award NIH, 1985, Guyot prize U. Groningen, 1994; grantee various orgns., 1969-91. Fellow Am. Acad. Otolaryngology (Gold award 1972); mem. Assn. for Research in Otolaryngology (sec./treas. 1973-75, pres. 1976-77, editor-historian 1980-93, historian, 1993—, Merit award 1993), Am. Laryngol. Rhinol. and Otol. Soc., Collegium Oto-rhino-laryngologicum Amicitiae Sacrum (Shambaugh prize 1993), Am. Otol. Soc., Soc. Neurosci., Am. Soc. Cell Biology, Histochem. Soc., Soc. for Mucosal Immunology, Flint Canyon Tennis Club (La Canada). Methodist. Avocations: tennis, skiing. Home: 775 Panorama Pl Pasadena CA 91105-1020 Office: House Ear Inst 2100 W 3rd St Los Angeles CA 90057-1922

LIM, HENRY WAN-PENG, physician; b. Bandung, Indonesia, July 19, 1949; s. Budiman Ruslim and Nietje Tedjasuryani; m. Mamie Wong-Lim, July 20, 1975; children: Christopher T., Kevin T. BS in Biochemistry with honors, McGill U., 1971; MD cum laude, SUNY, Bklyn., 1975. Diplomate in dermatology, dermatol. immunology/diagnostic and lab. immunology Am. Bd. Dermatology; diplomate Nat. Bd. Med. Examiners. Intern Albert Einstein Coll. Medicine, Bronx, N.Y., 1975-76; resident dept. dermatology NYU Sch. Medicine, 1976-79, NIH fellow in dermatology, 1979, Dermatology Found. fellow, 1979-80, from instr. to assoc. prof. dermatology, 1979-93, prof. dermatology, 1993-97, asst. dean for vet. affairs, 1993-97; chmn. and Clarense S. Livingood chair dermatology Henry Ford Med. Ctr., Detroit, 1997—; chief dermatology svc. N.Y. VA Med. Ctr., N.Y.C., 1985-94, chief staff, 1993-97, staff physician dermatology svc., 1994-97; chmn. dermatology Henry Ford Med. Ctr., 1997—. Mem. editl. bd. Photodermatology, Photoimmunology and Photomedicine, 1990—, Jour.

Am. Acad. Dermatology, 1993—; cons. editor Sun and Skin News, 1994; contbr. numerous articles to profl. jours. Recipient numerous awards; McGill U. scholar, 1968-70. Mem. AAAS, AMA, Am. Acad. Dermatology (mem. environ. coun. 1995—), Soc. for Investigative Dermatology, Nat. Assn. VA Dermatologists, Dermatology Found., Am. Dermatology Assn., Am. Fedn. for Clin. Rsch., Am. Soc. for Photobiology, Am. Assn.Immunologists, Am. Coll. Physician Execs., Photomedicine Soc. (pres. 1996—), Alpha Omega Alpha, others. Avocations: travel. Office: Henry Ford Hosp Dept Dermatology 2799 W Grand Blvd Detroit MI 48202-2608

LIM, JAE SOO, engineering educator, information systems; b. Taegu, Korea, Dec. 2, 1950. SB, 1974, SM, 1975, ScD, 1978. Prof. elec. engring. and computer sci. MIT. Recipient Sr. award ASSP Soc., 1984. Fellow IEEE (sec. 1979-83, chmn. 1983-85, tech. com. on digital signal processing, session chmn. 1980-83, registration chmn. 1981-83, internat. conf. on acoustics, speech and signal processing, tech. program co-chmn. workshop on M-D signal processing 1982-83, registration chmn. 1983, session chmn. 1984, tech. program co-chmn. 1985 Internat. Conf. on Acoustics, Speech and Signal Processing, chmn. workshop on digital signal processing 1983-85, tech. com. on multidimensional signal processing 1983-86, sec./treas. 1986-87). Office: MIT 77 Massachusetts Ave Rm 653 Cambridge MA 02139-4301*

LIM, ROBERT CHEONG, JR., surgeon, educator; b. San Francisco, Aug. 27, 1933; s. Robert Cheong and Helen (Ho) L.; m. Carolee Yee, Aug. 23, 1959; children: Gregory Matthew, Jonathan Robert. A.B., U. Calif., Berkeley, 1956; M.D., U. Calif., San Francisco, 1960. Diplomate: Am. Bd. Surgery. Intern U. Calif., San Francisco, 1960-61; asst. resident in surgery U. Calif., 1963-64, VA Hosp., San Francisco, 1961-63; chief resident VA Hosp., 1964-65, NIH fellow in vascular surgery, 1965-66; practice medicine specializing in gen. trauma and vascular surgery San Francisco; asst. prof. U. Calif., San Francisco, 1968-74; asso. prof. U. Calif., 1974-78, prof., 1978—; mem. staffs U. Calif. Hosps., San Francisco Gen. Hosp. Contbr. articles on surgery to profl. jours. Mem. ACS (gov.), Am. Burn Assn., Am. Assn. Surgery of Trauma (v.p. 1996), Am. Surg. Assn., Am. Trauma Soc., Internat. Cardiovascular Soc., Calif. Med. Assn., Assn. Acad. Surgery, Howard C. Naffziger Surg. Soc. (pres. 1995), Pacific Coast Surg. Assn., Pan Pacific Surg. Assn., San Francisco Surg. Soc. (past pres.), Soc. Univ. Surgeons, Soc. Vascular Surgery, Western Surg. Assn., Western Vascular Soc., Alpha Omega Alpha. Presbyterian. Office: U Calif PO Box 780 # U San Francisco CA 94143

LIM, SHUN PING, cardiologist; b. Singapore, Jan. 12, 1947; came to U.S., 1980; s. Tay Boh and Si Moi (Foo) L.; m. Christine Sock Kian Ng; children: Corinne Xian-li, Damien John Xian-ming, Justin David Xian-an. MBBS with honors, Monash U., Clayton, Australia, 1970, PhD, 1981; M in Medicine, Nat. U. Singapore, 1975; M, Royal Australasian Coll. Physicians, 1975. Rsch. scholar Australian Nat. Health and Med. Rsch. Coun., Canberra, 1978-79; fellow in cardiology Michael Reese Hosp., Chgo., 1980-82; chief noninvasive cardiovascular imaging Cin. V.A.M.C., 1982-86; asst. prof. U. Cin., 1982-86; cardiologist Quain and Ramstad Clinic, Bismarck, N.D., 1986-88; clin. asst. prof. U. N.D., Bismarck, 1986-90; pvt. practice cardiovascular diseases, 1988-91; assoc. prof. medicine U. N.D., 1991-93; clin. assoc. prof. Ohio State U., Columbus, 1993—; dir. catheterization lab. Marion (Ohio) Gen. Hosp., 1991-93; med. dir. Cardiovasc. Cons., Columbus, 1993—; pres. Inst. for Advanced Med. Tech., 1990—, Am. Med. Investments, Inc., 1994—; chmn. ICU com. VA Med. and Regional Office Ctr., Fargo, N.D., 1991-93, chief cardiology sect., 1991-93; founder, med. dir. Cardiovascular Cons., Singapore, 1993—; v.p. Acad. Medicine, Marion, 1996-97, pres., 1997—. Contbr. articles to profl. jours.; catheter tip polarographic lactic acid and lactate sensor. Fellow ACP, Am. Coll. Cardiology, Internat. Coll. Angiology, Am. Coll. Angiology, Royal Australian Coll. Physicians, Am. Coll. Chest Physicians, Coun. on Clin. Cardiology of Am. Heart Assn., Soc. Critical Care Medicine, Acad. Medicine Singapore; mem. Am. Fedn. Clin. Rsch., Am. Soc. Echocardiography, Am. Heart Assn. (grantee 1984-85), Ohio State Med. Assn., N.Y. Acad. Scis. (life). Methodist. Office: Cardiovascular Cons Ohio Ste 220 3545 Olentangy River Rd Columbus OH 43214-3907

LIM, SONIA YII, minister; b. China, Jan. 1, 1924; arrived in The Philippines; d. Edward C. C. and King Hua (Co) Yii; m. Teddy T. Lim, Jan. 3, 1943; children: Dorothy, DoraMay Cantada, Sally Jane, Teddy Jr., Nellie Ann L. Tan, Raymond, Roger. AB, Am. Bordner Sch., Manila, 1944; postgrad., St. Thomas U., Manila, 1948, Cornell U., 1972; DD (hon.), Am. Fellowship Ch., Monterey, Calif., 1982; D of Prayer Tech., World Inst., Manila, 1989. Ordained to ministry Full Gospel Ch., 1981. Min. Internat. Fellowship of Clergy, Alta Vista, Calif., 1980-84; founder, pres. Dove Found. Internat. Inc., 1982—; min. Gospel Crusade Ministerial Fellowship Inc., Bradenton, Fla., 1983—; underwriter Insular Life Ins., Pasay, The Philippines, 1991—; Bishop, first lady in Asia, Christian Ch. Fellowship Internat., amb. of goodwill to all nations; conductor ann. Nat. Week of Prayer, Philippines, 25th Ann. World Prayer Congress for Peace, Unity and Progress; chmn. Golden Mother's Day and Golden Father's Day celebrations; group dir. Giorelli Internat., 1992; condr. tng. seminars. V.p., award chmn. Consumers Union of The Philippines, 1944—, bd. dirs. 1971—; chaplain, chmn. internat. rels. Mother's Day and Father's Day Coun., Manila, 1988—; ann. awards chmn. Ann. Grand Tribute to Achievers Parangal ng Bayan, 1995, 96; chmn. Young Achievers Awards, Golden Scroll Awards, Top Entertainers Awards, Golden Heart Awards, Internat. Citation Awards, Grand Achievement Awards, Golden Parents Awards, Celebrity Parents Awards, Family and Parents Week Celebration. Recipient Angel award Religion in Media, 1984, Golden Leadership award Humanitarian Ctr. The Philippines, 1988, award Internat. Cops for Christ Inc., 1990, Grand Achievement award Young Achiever's Found., 1994, 95, Top Prodr.'s award CAP, 1994, Trophy of Distinction award and Century Club Qualifier award IL Assurance Co. Ltd., 1995, Grand Achievement award Parangal ng Bayan, 1995, Asian Mother award Gintong Ina Found., 1996, Key to City of Detroit, Flint, Mich., Jacksonville, Fla., Covina, Calif., Wilson, N.C., Las Vegas, Ft. Worth, Corsicana, Tex., Manila, Mandaluyong, Baguio, Davao, Quezon City, Olongapo, Subic Bay, Cavite, others; named Mother of Yr., Gintong Ina Found., 1988, hon. mayor Oklahoma City. Mem. Philippine Bible Soc. (life), mem. Union Ch. of Manila (Life), Info. and Referral Svcs. The Philippines (life), Makati C. of C. and Industry (bd. dirs. 1968-72), Manila Bay Breakfast Club (bd. dirs. 1976—), Makati Breakfast Club (chaplain 1988—), Manila Overseas Press Club (assoc.), Nat. Prestige Club. Mem. Movers Party. Office: Dove Found Internat Sunset View Towers, 2230 Roxas Blvd Ste 402, Pasay Metro Manila, The Philippines

LIMA, LUIS EDUARDO, tenor; b. Cordoba, Argentina, Sept. 12, 1950; s. Horacio and Yayi (Junyent) L.; m. Caterin de Virgilio, Feb. 18, 1979; children: Rodrigo, Camila, Martin-Geronimo Leandro. B.A. in Music, Teatro Colon, Argentina, 1971; student voice, Carlo Guichandut, Buenos Aires, Gina Cigna, Italy. Am. debut Carnegie Hall, 1976; appeared in maj. opera houses throughout the world, including La Scala, Milan, Italy, 1978, N.Y.C. Opera, 1978-79, Met. Opera, N.Y.C., 1978, 84-85, San Francisco Opera, 1980, 83-91, Covent Garden, London, 1984-91, Vienna State Opera, 1988-93; performances at maj. festivals; author: Poems, 1982; recs.: Donizetti: Gemma di Vergy, Le Roi de Laohr, La Traviata, Requiem; appeared in films: Cossi fan Tutte, Carmen, Don Carlo. Mem. Am. Guild Musicians. Roman Catholic. Avocations: painting; horseback riding. Office: 1950 Redondela Dr Palos Verdes Peninsula CA 90275-1028 also: ICM Artists Inc 40 W 57th St New York NY 10019-4001*

LIMA, ROBERT, Hispanic studies and comparative literature educator; b. Havana, Cuba, Nov. 7, 1935; came to U.S., 1945; BA in English and Philosophy, Villanova U., 1957, MA in Theatre Arts and Drama, 1961; PhD in Romance Lits., NYU, 1968. Prof. Spanish and comparative lits. Pa. State U., University Park, 1965—; fellow Inst. for Arts and Humanistic Studies Pa. State U., 1986—; vis. prof. comparative lit. Pontificia Universidad Católica del Peru; poet-in-residence Universidad Nacional Mayor de San Marcos, Peru, 1976-77; lectr. Romance langs. and lits. Hunter Coll. CUNY, 1962-65, USIA lectr., Peru, Cameroon, Equatorial Guinea. Author: The Theatre of Garcia Lorca, 1963, An Annotated Bibliography of Ramon del Valle-Inclan, 1972, (poetry) Fathoms, 1981, The Olde Ground, 1985, Mayaland, 1992, Dark Prisms Occultism in Hispanic Drama, 1995, The International Annotated Bibliography of Ramon del Valle-Inclan, 1997, Valle-Inclan. El Teatro de su Vida, 1995, (biography) Valle-Inclan. The Theatre of His Life, 1988; co-author: Dos Ensayos Sobre Teatro Español de los Veinte, 1984; editor, translator: Borges the Labyrinth Maker (A.M. Barrenechea), 1965, Valle-Inclan: Autobiography, Aesthetics, Aphorism, 1966; editor, contbr. Borges and the Esoteric, 1993; translator: The Lamp of Marvels, Aesthetic Meditations (Ramon del Valle-Inclan), 1986, Savage Acts: Four Plays (Valle-Inclan), 1993; co-editor Readers Ency. Am. Lit., 1962, Homenaje/Tribute to Martha T. Halsey, 1995; contbr. numerous articles, essays, book revs., poetry, plays, and poetry translations to profl. jours.; prodr., cons., TV and radio programs Centro de Estudios de Television de la Univ. Catolica, Lima, Peru, 1976-77, Voice of Am., N.Y.C., 1961-62, Pendulum Prodns., 1960-61. Bd. dirs. Pa. Ctr. for Book. Recipient Founders Day award NYU, 1968, Play Translation prize Modern Internat. Drama, cert. of merit Writer's Digest Mag., 1982; Rsch. grantee Fund for Rsch. Pa. State U., Inst. for Arts and Humanistic Studies; Cintas Found. fellow in poetry Inst. Internat. Edn., 1971-72, fellow Commonwealth Speakers Program Pa. Humanities Coun., Sr. Fulbright fellow Coun. Internat. Exch. Scholars, 1976-77; others. Fellow Inst. for Arts and Humanistic Studies, Phi Kappa Phi (hon.), Phi Sigma Iota (hon.); mem. Internat. PEN, Poetry Soc. Am., Am. Assn. Tchrs. Spanish and Portuguese, Archaeol. Inst. Am., Am. Comparative Lit. Assn., Internat. Comparative Lit. Assn., Galician Studies Assn., Internat. Assn. Valleinclanistas, Am. Name Soc., Am. Soc. Sephardic Studies, Poets and Writers, Hermetic Text Soc., Beast Fable Soc., Pa. Humanities Coun., N.Am. Acad. Spanish Lang., Fulbright Alumni Assn., Alpha Psi Omega. Home: 485 Orlando Ave State College PA 16803-3477 Office: Pa State U N-346 Burrowes Bldg University Park PA 16802

LIMACHER, MARIAN CECILE, cardiologist; b. Joliet, Ill., May 4, 1952; d. Joseph John and Shirley A. (Smith) L.; m. Timothy C. Flynn, May 17, 1980; children: Mary Katherine Flynn, Brian Patrick Flynn. AB in Chemistry, St. Louis U., 1973, MD, 1977. Diplomate Am. Bd. Internal Medicine, Am. Bd. Cardiovascular Diseases. Resident in internal medicine Baylor Coll. Medicine, Houston, 1977-80, cardiology fellow, 1980-83, instr. medicine, 1983-84; dir. cardiology non-invasive labs. Ben Taub Hosp., Houston, 1983-84; asst. prof. medicine U. Fla., Gainesville, 1984-91, assoc. prof., 1991-97, prof., 1997—; dir. non-invasive labs. Gainesville VA Med. Ctr., 1984—, chief cardiology, 1995—; dir. preventive cardiology program U. Fla., 1987—. Author: (with others) Cardiac Transplantation: A Manual for Health Care Professionals, 1990, Geriatric Cardiology, 1992, The Role of Food in Sickness and in Health, 1993, Clinical Anesthesia Practice, 1994, Primary Care, 1994; mem. editorial bd. Clin. Cardiology, 1990—; contbr. articles to profl. jours. Mem. bioethics commn. Diocese of St. Augustine, Jacksonville, Fla., 1990-94. Recipient Preventive Cardiology Acad. award NIH, 1987-92; grantee for Women's Health Initiative, NIH, 1994—. Fellow ACP, Am. Coll. Cardiology (chair ad hoc com. women cardiology 1994—), Coun. Geriatric Cardiology; mem. Am. Soc. Preventive Cardiology (pres.-elect 1996—), Am. Heart Assn. (fellow coun. clin. cardiology, bd. dirs., pres. Alachua County divsn. 1986-89). Roman Catholic. Avocations: tennis, jogging, snow skiing, playing piano. Office: U Fla Coll Medicine PO Box 100277 Gainesville FL 32610-0277

LIMAN, ARTHUR LAWRENCE, lawyer; b. N.Y.C., Nov. 5, 1932; s. Harry K. and Celia L.; m. Ellen Fogelson, Sept. 20, 1959; children: Lewis, Emily, Douglas. A.B., Harvard U., 1954; LL.B., Yale U., 1957. Bar: N.Y. bar 1958. Asst. U.S. atty. So. Dist. N.Y., 1961-63, spl. asst. U.S. atty., 1965; with firm Paul, Weiss, Rifkind, Wharton & Garrison, N.Y.C., 1957-61, 63—; ptnr. Paul, Weiss, Rifkind, Wharton & Garrison, 1966—; chief counsel N.Y. State Spl. Commn. on Attica, 1972; chmn. Legal Action Center, N.Y.C., 1975; v.p. Legal Aid Soc., N.Y.C., 1973; pres. Legal Aid Soc., 1983-85; chmn. Gov. N.Y. Adv. Commn. Adminstrn. Justice in N.Y. State, 1981-83; mem. N.Y. State Exec. Adv. Com. Sentencing, 1977; mem. adv. com. civil rules U.S. Jud. Conf., 1980-85; mem. commn. on reduction costs and delay U.S. 2d Cir., 1976-80; bd. dirs. Continental Grain Co., Equitable Life Assurance Soc. U.S.; chmn. bd. dirs. Capital Defenders Office, 1995—; chmn. mayor's com. on appointments, 1990-93; chief counsel U.S. Senate select com. on secret mil. assistance to Iran and tne Nicaraguan Opposition, Washington, 1987. Contbr. articles to legal jours.; bd. editors: Nat. Law Jour, 1979—. Bd. overseers Harvard U., 1988-94. Fellow Am. Coll. Trial Lawyers, Am. Bar Found.; mem. ABA, N.Y. State Bar Assn., Bar Assn. City N.Y. (exec. com., Lawyers Com. Civil Rights Under Bd. Overseers, Harvard U., 1988-94). Home: 1060 Fifth Ave New York NY 10128-0104 Office: Paul Weiss Rifkind Wharton & Garrison 1285 Avenue Of The Americas New York NY 10019-6028

LIMAN, ELLEN, painter, writer, arts advocate; b. N.Y.C., Jan. 4, 1936; d. David and Gertrude (Edelman) Fogelson; m. Arthur Liman, Sept. 20, 1959; children: Lewis, Emily, Doug. BA, Barnard Coll., 1957; student, N.Y. Sch. Interior Design, 1959. In pub. rels. Tex McCrary, Inc., 1957; interior designer Malanie Kahane Assocs., 1958-60; cons. on grants to the arts The Joe and Emily Lowe Found., 1975-92, pres./trustee, 1993—; exec. asst. Adv. Commn. for Cultural Affairs, N.Y.C., 1981-82; dir. spl. projects, dir. City Gallery for N.Y.C. Dept. Cultural Affairs, 1980-84; chair N.Y.C. Adv. Commn. for Cultural Affairs, 1991-93. Author: The Money Savers Guide to Decorating, 1972, Decorating Your Country Place, 1973, Decorating Your Room, 1974, The Spacemaker Book, 1977, The Collecting Book, 1980, Babyspace, 1984, others; contbr. editor: Kid Smart Mag., 1995-96; contbr. articles to nat. mags. Founding trustee Internat. Ctr. of Photography, 1973—; trustee The Jewish Mus., 1974—, hon. trustee, 1993—; trustee The Ctr. for Arts Info., 1985-86; mem. N.Y.C. Commn. for Cultural Affairs, 1986-89; bd. dirs. Art Table, Inc., 1987-90, Trust for Cultural Resources, 1993-96, Am. Fedn. of Arts, 1994—.

LIMARZI, JOSEPH, artist; b. Chgo., Sept. 15, 1907; s. Joseph and Mary Della (Guardia) LiM. With Mus. Fine Arts, Springfield, Mass.; instr. painting High Sch. Art & Design, N.Y., 1952-73. Commn. works include HIst. Fed. Govt., Fed. Bldg., Wapokeneta, Ohio, 1937, Fed. Govt., Staten Island, N.Y., 1942; Royal Scarlet Foods, N.Y., 1951; Gen. Cables, Inc., N.Y., 1952; exhibits include Art Inst. Chgo., Bklyn. Mus. Nat., Pa. Acad. Fine Arts; one man shows include Comtemporary Arts, N.Y., Simon's Rock, Mass. & Lehman Gallery, Red Rock, N.Y., 1975; Cleve. Art Inst., Mus. Modern Art, N.Y.; liberal Arts Ctr., Newport, N.H., Berkshire Mus., Pittsfield, Mass., Spencertown Acad., N.Y. Recipient Hon. award Fed. Govt., 1937. Mem. Painters and Sculptors Soc. N.J., Audubon Artists of N.Y., Am. Soc. Contemporary Artists. Avocations: classical, jazz and folk music, history Jefferson and Lincoln. Home: PO Box 144 East Chatham NY 12060-0144 Office: Ella Lerner Gallery 17 Franklin St Lenox MA 01240-2303

LIMATO, EDWARD FRANK, talent agent; b. Mt. Vernon, N.Y., July 10, 1936; s. Frank and Angelina (Lacerra) L. Grad. high sch., Mt. Vernon. With Ashley Famous, 1966, I.F.A., N.Y.C., William Morris Agy., L.A.; talent agt. Internat. Creative Mgmt., N.Y.C., L.A. Mem. Acad. Motion Picture Arts & Scis. (assoc.). Republican. Roman Catholic. Office: Internat Creative Mgmt 8942 Wilshire Blvd Beverly Hills CA 90211-1934*

LIMBACH, WALTER F., construction company executive; b. Pitts., June 17, 1924; s. Emil and Sarah Limbach; m. Sarah Z. Minard, June 16, 1976; children by previous marriage: Elsa, Kurt. B.S., Lehigh U., 1947. With Limbach Co., Pitts., 1947-80; v.p. Limbach Co., 1955-57, pres., 1957-81, dir., 1955-84; chmn., chief exec. officer, dir. Limbach Inc., Pitts., 1980-86; chmn., chief-exec.-officer, dir. Limbach Holdings, Inc., Pitts., 1986-88; dir. Contractors Mut. Assn., Washington, 1971-84; vice chmn. Contractors Mut. Assn., 1973-78, chmn., 1978-84. Bd. dirs. Hill House Assn., Pitts., v.p., 1968-73, 75-80; bd. dirs. Vocat. Rehab. Ctr., Pitts., 1975—, chmn. 1991-93; bd. dirs. Nat. Constrn. Employers Coun., Washington, 1979-84; bd. dirs. Neighborhood Ctrs. Assn., Pitts., 1989—, treas., 1990—. Served with USNR, 1943-46. Mem. Sheet Metal and Air Conditioning Contractors Nat. Assn. (pres. 1958-59), ASME. Home: 123 Beechmont Rd Pittsburgh PA 15206-4513

LIMBACK, E(DNA) REBECCA, vocational education educator; b. Higginsville, Mo., Mar. 23, 1945; d. Henry Shobe and Martha Pauline Rebecca (Willard) Ernstmeyer; m. Duane Paul Limback, Nov. 9, 1963; children: Lisa Christine, Derek Duane. BE, Cen. Mo. State U., 1968, MEd, 1969, EdS, 1976; EdD, U. Mo., 1981. Cert. bus., English and vocat. tchr. Supervising tchr. Lab. Sch. Cen. Mo. State U., Warrensburg, 1969-76, asst. to grad. dean, 1977-79, asst. prof., asst. to bus. dean, 1981-83, assoc. prof. computer and office info. systems, 1984-95, 1986-95, prof. computer and office info. sys., 1996—; mem. manual editing/revision staff State of Mo., Jefferson City, 1989-90; textbook reviewer Prentice-Hall, Englewood Cliffs, N.J., 1990-91. Author various curriculum guides; mem. editl. bd. Cen. Mo. State U. Rsch., 1982-92. Active Warrensburg Band Aides, 1989-93. Grantee RightSoft Corp., 1988. Mem. DAR, Nat. Bus. Edn. Assn. (mem. conf. profl. opportunities com. 1989, info. processing editor Bus. Edn. Forum 1991), Am. Vocat. Assn., North Cen. Bus. Edn. Assn. (Mo. rep., Collegiate Disting. Svc. award 1993), Mo. Bus. Edn. Assn. (all-chpt. pres. 1988-89, Postsecondary Tchr. of Yr. 1992), Assn. Bus. Comms., Warrensburg Athletic Booster Club, Phi Delta Kappa (all-chpt. pres. 1985), Delta Pi Epsilon (rsch. rep. 1989-92, nat. publs. com. 1993—). Lutheran. Avocations: archaeology, oil painting. Home: 1102 Tyler Ave Warrensburg MO 64093-2049 Office: Dockery 200-1/COIS Dept Cen Mo State U Warrensburg MO 64093

LIMBAUGH, RONALD HADLEY, history educator, history center director; b. Emmett, Idaho, Jan. 22, 1938; s. John Hadley and Evelyn E. (Mortimore) L.; m. Marilyn Kay Rice, June 16, 1963; 1 child, Sally Ann. BA, Coll. Idaho, 1960; MA, U. Idaho, 1962, PhD, 1967. Hist. libr. Idaho State Hist. Soc., Boise, 1963-66; instr. Boise Coll., 1964-66; asst. prof. history U. of the Pacific, Stockton, Calif., 1966-71; archivist, curator U. of the Pacific, Stockton, 1968-87, prof. history, 1977—, Rockwell Hunt chair of Calif. history, 1989—; dir. Holt-Atherton Ctr., U. of the Pacific, Stockton, 1984-87; exec. dir. Conf. of Calif. Hist. Socs., Stockton, 1973-76, 77-78, 82-86, 90-97; dir. John Muir Ctr. for Regional Studies, U. of Pacific, Stockton, 1989—; cons., evaluator NEH, 1983-86. Author: Rocky Mountain Carpetbaggers, 1982, John Muir's Stickeen and the Lessons of Nature, 1996; co-editor: (microform) John Muir Papers, 1986, (book) Guide to Muir Papers, 1986; contbr. articles to profl. jours. With U.S. Army, 1955-56. NDEA fellow, 1960; grantee Calif. Coun. Humanities, 1976, Nat. Hist. Publs. and Records Commn., 1980-82, NEH, 1983, Inst. European Studies, 1989, Hoover Libr. Assn., 1997. Mem. AAUP, Western History Assn., Orgn. Am. Historians, Phi Kappa Phi (pres. UOP chpt. 1988), Mining History Assn. Christian Humanist. Avocations: hiking, golf. Office: Univ Pacific 3601 Pacific Cir Stockton CA 95211-0110

LIMBAUGH, RUSH HUDSON, radio and talk show host; b. Cape Girardeau, Mo., 1951; s. Rush Hudson Jr. and Millie Limbaugh; m. Marta Fitzgerald, May 27, 1994. Various disc jockey positions, 1960-88; host The Rush Limbaugh Show on 480 radio stations nationwide, 1988—. Author: The Way Things Ought To Be, 1992, See, I Told You So, 1993; TV syndicated show The Rush Limbaugh Show, 1992—; publisher, monthly newsletter, The Limbaugh Letter, 1995—. Office: Sta WABC 210 Penn Plaza 17th Flr New York NY 10121*

LIMBAUGH, STEPHEN NATHANIEL, federal judge; b. Cape Girardeau, Mo., Nov. 17, 1927; s. Rush Hudson and Bea (Seabaugh) L.; m. DeVaughn Anne Mesplay, Dec. 27, 1950; children—Stephen Nathaniel Jr., James Pennington, Andrew Thomas. B.A., S.E. Mo. State U., Cape Girardeau, 1950; J.D., U. Mo., Columbia, 1951. Bar: Mo. 1951. Prosecuting atty. Cape Girardeau County, Mo., 1954-58; judge U.S. Dist. Ct. (ea. and we. dists.) Mo., St. Louis, 1983—. Served with USN, 1945-46. Recipient Citation of Merit for Outstanding Achievement and Meritorious Service in Law, U. Mo., 1982. Fellow Am. Coll. Probate Counsel, Am. Bar Found.; mem. ABA (ho. of dels. 1987-90), Mo. Bar Assn. (pres. 1982-83). Republican. Methodist. Office: US Dist Ct 1114 Market St Rm 315 Saint Louis MO 63101-2038

LIMBAUGH, STEPHEN NATHANIEL, JR., judge; b. Cape Girardeau, Mo., Jan. 25, 1952; s. Stephen N. and Anne (Mesplay) L.; m. Marsha Dee Moore, July 21, 1973; children: Stephen III, Christopher K. BA, So. Meth. U., 1973, JD, 1976. Bar: Tex. 1977, Mo. 1977. Assoc. Limbaugh, Limbaugh & Russell, Cape Girardeau, 1977-78; pros. atty. Cape Girardeau County, Cape Girardeau, 1979-82; shareholder, ptnr. Limbaugh, Limbaugh, Russell & Syler, Cape Girardeau, 1983-87; cir. judge 32d Jud. Cir., Cape Girardeau, 1987-92; judge Supreme Ct. Mo., Jefferson City, 1992—. Mem. ABA, State Bar Tex., Mo. Bar. Office: Supreme Ct Mo 207 W High St Jefferson City MO 65101-1516

LIMERICK, PATRICIA NELSON, history educator; b. Banning, Calif., May 17, 1951. BA, U. Calif., Santa Cruz, 1972; PhD, Yale, 1980. Prof. history dept. U. Colo., Boulder; chmn. bd. dirs. Ctr. Am. West. Author: (books) Desert Passages: Encounters With the American Deserts, 1985, The Legacy of Conquest: The Unbroken Past of the American West, 1987. MacArthur fellow, 1995. Office: Univ CO Boulder Dept History Box 234 Boulder CO 80309*

LIMON, LAVINIA, social services administrator; b. Compton, Calif., Mar. 5, 1950; d. Peter T. and Marie W. Limon; m. Mohamad Hanon. BA in Sociology, U. Calif., Berkeley, 1972. Asst. dir., office mgr. Ch. World Svc., Camp Pendleton, Calif., 1975-77; chief Vietnamese refugee sect. Internat. Rescue Com., Bangkok, 1977-79; dir. Internat. Rescue Com., L.A., 1983-86, 1983-86; asst. dir. ops. Am. Coun. for Nationalities Svcs., L.A., 1979-83; exec. dir. Internat. Inst., L.A., 1986-93; dir. office refugee resettlement and office family assistance Adminstrn. for Children and Families Dept. HHS, Washington, 1993—; bd. dirs. Am. Coun. for Nationalities Svc., 1992, chair standing com. of profl. coun., 1992; organizer U.S. refugee conf. Am. Coun. Vol. Agys., Manila, 1982; cons. Dept. of State, 1979, 80. Mem. bd. human rels. hate violence response alliance City of L.A., 1992; chair corp. coun. execs. United Way of L.A., 1992, mem. task force fund on devel., 1990; mem. citizen's adv. com. Eastside Neighborhoods Revitilazation Study, 1992; mem. steering com. Coalition for Humane Immigration Rights of L.A., 1992; mem. steering com. Jerusalem Coop. Cities Project, 1991; chair Refugee Forum L.A. County, 1984-85, chair vol. agy. com., 1983-84; treas. Calif. Refugee Forum, 1985-86. Democrat. Home: 4508 Flintstone Rd Alexandria VA 22306-1204 Office: Refugee Resettlement Office 370 Lenfant Plz SW Washington DC 20447-0001

LIMÓN ROJAS, MIGUEL, Mexican government official; b. Veracruz, Mex., Dec. 17, 1943. BA in Law, Nat. Autonomous U., 1967. Lawyer, 1968—; dep. dir. demographics, population Ministry of Govt. of Mex., 1971, dir. demographics, population, 1973; pvt. sec. to undersec. to pres., prof. constl. law Govt. Mex., 1970, advisor to sec. edn., negotiator nat. ednl. plan, 1982-88, undersec. population and migration, 1988-93, sec. agrarian reform, 1993-94, sec. pub. edn., 1995—; dir. Inst. Indigenous Peoples, 1983-88; dir. dept. humanities, Autonomous U.; acad. sec. U. Pedagógica Nat. Mem. Instl. Revolutionary Party. Office: Office of the Secretariat 2nd Fl, Del Cautemoc Argentina # 28, Mexico City 06029, Mexico*

LIMPERT, JOHN H., JR., fund raising executive; b. Bklyn., May 14, 1933; s. John H. and Sophia (Douropoulos) L.; A.B., Harvard U., 1955, postgrad., 1955-56; children: Alexandra Michelle, John Harold III. Public relations mgr. Frankfort Distillers Co. div. Seagram, N.Y.C., 1959-63; account exec. McCann-Erickson, Inc., N.Y.C., 1963-65, account dir., 1965-68; v.p. Ted Bates & Co., Inc., N.Y.C., 1968-71; mgr. lectrs. and speakers Keedick Lecture Bur., Inc., N.Y.C., 1971-73; dir. membership and devel. Mus. Modern Art, N.Y.C., 1973-83, dir. devel., 1983-86; v.p. for devel. and mktg. The N.Y. Bot. Garden, 1986-88; v.p. devel. Lincoln Ctr. for the Performing Arts Inc., 1988-89; assoc. fund counsel Charles H. Bentz Assocs., Inc., N.Y.C., 1990—; —; trustee Children's Aid Soc., 1966-74, Festival Orch. and Chorus, 1967-69, Schola Cantorum, 1963-65; bd. dirs. Assoc. Harvard Alumni, 1967-69, 73-74; bd. dirs. Bronx C. of C., 1988-91; vestryman Grace Episcopal Ch., Plainfield, 1992-95; bd. dirs. NY chpt., Nat. Soc. Fund Raising Execs., 1989-93. With U.S. Army, 1956-58. Cert. fund raising exec. Office: 1111 Park Ave Plainfield NJ 07060-3006

LIMPITLAW, JOHN DONALD, retired publishing executive, clergyman; b. N.Y.C., Jan. 4, 1935; s. Robert and Olga (Lang) L.; m. Susan Elizabeth Glover, May 21, 1960; children: Alison, Amy Elizabeth. BA, Trinity Coll., Hartford, Conn., 1956; MA in Religion, Yale U., 1992. With Marine Midland Bank Trust Co. N.Y., N.Y.C., 1956-61, Celanese Corp., N.Y.C., 1961-63; mgr. personnel Westvaco Corp., N.Y.C., 1963-69; v.p. Warnaco Inc., Bridgeport, Conn., 1969-77, Macmillan Inc., N.Y.C., 1977-89; vicar Parish of Christ's Ch., Easton, Conn., 1992—; dir. St. Mark's Day Care Ctr., Bridgeport, 1995—; seminarian Yale Divinity Sch., New Haven, Conn.,

1989-92; trustee Episcopal Investment Funds; bd. dirs. Inter-Ch. Residences, Inc., 3030 Park, Inc. Democrat. Episcopalian. Avocations: sailing; skiing. Home: 120 Chelsea St Fairfield CT 06430-4941

LIN, ALICE LEE LAN, physicist, researcher, educator; b. Shanghai, China, Oct. 28, 1937; came to U.S., 1960, naturalized, 1974; m. A. Marcus, Dec. 19, 1962 (div. Feb. 1972); 1 child, Peter A. AB in Physics, U. Calif., Berkeley, 1963; MA in Physics, George Washington U., 1974. Statis. asst. dept. math. U. Calif., Berkeley, 1962-63; rsch. asst. in radiation damage Cavendish Lab. Cambridge (Eng.) U., 1965-66; info. analysis specialist Nat. Acad. Scis., Washington, 1970-71; teaching fellow, rsch. asst. George Washington U., Catholic U. Am., Washington, 1971-75; physicist NASA/Goddard Space Flight Ctr., Greenbelt, Md., 1975-80, Army Materials Tech. Lab., Watertown, Mass., 1980—. Contbr. articles to profl. jours. Mencius Ednl. Found. grantee, 1959-60. Mem. AAAS, N.Y. Acad. Scis., Am. Phys. Soc., Am. Ceramics Soc., Am. Acoustical Soc., Am. Men and Women of Sci., Optical Soc. Am. Democrat. Avocations: rare stamp and coin collecting, art collectibles, home computers, opera, ballet. Home: 28 Hallett Hill Rd Weston MA 02193-1753 Office: Army Materials Tech Lab Bldg 39 Watertown MA 02172

LIN, CHIN-CHU, physician, educator, researcher; b. Taichung, Taiwan, Oct. 24, 1935; came to U.S., 1969; naturalized, 1977; s. Kung Yen and Nung (Chiang) L.; m. Sue S. Hsu; children: Jim, John, Juliet. BS, Nat. Taiwan U., 1956, MD, 1961. Diplomate Am. Bd. Ob-Gyn., Am. Bd. Maternal-Fetal Medicine (bd. examiners 1986-89). Rsch. fellow SUNY Downstate Med. Ctr., N.Y.C., 1969-71; resident in ob-gyn Columbia U., N.Y.C., 1972-74; fellow in maternal-fetal medicine Albert Einstein Med. Coll., 1974-76; lectr., staff Nat. Taiwan U. Hosp., Taipei, 1966-69, 1971-72; staff, asst. prof. U. Chgo., 1976-80, assoc. prof., 1980-87, prof., 1987—; maternal-child health adv. com. Dept. of Health, Chgo., 1985-88; frequent keynote spkr. numerous internat. confs. including 12th Asian and Oceanic Congress on Ob-Gyn., 1989, 8th Congress of Fedn. Asian Oceanic Perinatal Soc., Taiwan, 1994, 5th World Congress Ultrasound in Ob-Gyn., Japan, 1995, 29th Internat. Congress Pathophysiology of Pregnancy, Japan, 1997; vis. prof. univs. in U.S., Japan, China, Taiwan 1981—; keynote spkr., prof. S.J. Chiu Meml. lectures, Taiwan, 1989. Author: Interauterine Growth Retardation, 1984, The High Risk Fetus, 1993; editor in chief Taiwan Tribune Med. Issues, 1986-89; contbr. over 80 articles to profl. jours., 17 chpts. to books; reviewer for Am. Jour. Ob-Gyn., Jour. Perinatal Medicine, Obstetrics and Gynecology, Jour. Maternal-Fetal Medicine, Jour. Formosan Med. Assn.; pres. 10th ann. meeting N.Am. Taiwanese Profs. Assn., Taiwan, 1990. People to People Ob-Gyn del. to USSR, 1987; bd. dirs. Taiwanese United Fund, 1980—, pres. 1984-85. Recipient disting. scholar lectr. award Formosa Med. Assn., 1981, Kenote Speaker award Asia-Oceanic Congress Perinatology, 1986, 94, 2d Internat. Symposium on Obstetrics and Perinatal Medicine, Beijing, 1988, 28th Sci. Meeting Assn. Ob-gyn., Taiwan, 1988, 12th Asian Oceanic Congress on Ob-GYn., 1989, 33d Ann. Meeting Assn. Ob-gyn., Taiwan, 1993, 5th World Congress Ultrasound in Ob-Gyn., Japan, 1995, Excellence in Tchg. award Assn. Profs. Ob-Gyn., 1996. Mem. Am. Coll. Ob.-Gyn. (jour. reviewer 1982—, Purdue Frederick award 1978), N.Am. Taiwanese Profs. Assn. (bd. dirs. 1988-91, bull. editor 1980—, v.p. 1988-89, pres. 1989-90, pres. 10th ann. meeting Taiwan 1990), N.Am. Taiwanese Med. Assn. (chmn. ednl. com. 1984-88, bd. dirs. 1991-93, chmn. scientific program 1994), Taiwanese United Fund (bd. dirs. 1980—, pres. 1984-85), Cen. Assn. Ob.-Gyn., Soc. Perinatal Obstetricians, Internat. Soc. Study Hypertension in Pregnancy, Am. Inst. Ultrasound in Medicine, Chgo. Gynecol. Soc. Avocations: tennis, golfing, walking, non-professional writing. Office: U Chgo Dept Ob-Gyn 5841 S Maryland Ave Chicago IL 60637-1463

LIN, EDWARD DANIEL, anesthesiologist, inventor; b. Apr. 19, 1953; s. Henry and Ruth Lin. BS magna cum laude, SUNY, Fredonia, 1973; Woodburn fellow, Roswell Park Cancer Inst., Buffalo, 1974-76; DO, U. Osteopathic Medicine and Health Scis., Des Moines, 1980. Intern. in gen. medicine Millard Fillmore Hosp., Buffalo, 1980-81, emergency physician, 1981-82; resident in anesthesiology Yale-New Haven Med. Ctr., Yale U. Sch. Medicine, 1982-84; attending anesthesiologist Doctors Hosp., Massillon, Ohio, 1984-89; chmn. dept. anesthesiology Massillon Cmty. Hosp., 1991; dep. coroner Stark County, Ohio, 1984-90; assoc. prof. anesthesiology Ohio U. Coll. Osteopathic Medicine, Athens, 1984—; guest lectr. on spinal opiates and pain therapy nat. profl. meetings; founder, pres. Ingenious Techs. Corp, 1991—. Achievements include numerous inventions and patents in medical, telecommunications and consumer fields. Office: Ingenious Techs Corp 556 Roxbury Ave NW Massillon OH 44646-3281

LIN, FRANK CHIWEN, computer science educator; b. Shanghai, China, Aug. 28, 1936; came to U.S., 1953; s. Elmer C. and Virginia (Chang) Ling; m. Margareta Lundgren, Mar. 8, 1968 (div. Aug. 1979); children: Ulrika Lin, Sigrid Lin; m. Helen M. Baldado, Mar. 17, 1987. BECE, Yale U., 1957; postgrad., U. Goettingen (Germany), 1958; PhD in Theoretical Physics, Yale U., 1965; grad. studies in computer sci., Polytech. U. N.Y., 1980, 81, 82. Rsch. assoc. dept. theoretical physics Chalmers Tech. U., Goeteborg, Sweden, 1965-70; vis. prof. physics Nat. Taiwan U., Taipei, 1970; asst. to pres. Biomed. Scis. Inc., Fairfield, N.J., 1971-75; instr. physics, engring., and computer sci. L.B. Wallace State Jr. Coll., Andalusia, Ala., 1976-84; assoc. prof. computer sci. Western Conn. State U., Danbury, 1984-85; from asst. to assoc. prof. computer sci. U. Md., Princess Anne, Md., 1986—. Author: Elementary FORTRAN with Scientific and Business Applications, 1983, Structured BASIC for Mini- and Micro-Computers, 1985; contbr. numerous articles to profl. jours. Prin. investigator numerous grants, 1981-93. Mem. IEEE (treas./sec. local chpt. 1989-90, vice-chmn. local chpt. 1990-91), Assn. Computing Machinery, Yale Sci. and Engring. Assn., N.Y. Acad. Scis., Am. Assn. for Artificial Intelligence, Internat. Neural Network Soc., Am. Med. Informatics Assn., Tau Beta Pi. Avocation: classical music. Home: 711 Riverside Pines Ct Salisbury MD 21801-6727

LIN, HUNG C., electrical engineer educator; b. Shanghai, China, Aug. 8, 1919. BSEE, Chiao Tung U., 1941; MSE, U. Mich., 1948; D in Engring., Poly. Inst. Bklyn., 1956. Engr. Ctrl. Radio Works of China, 1941-44, Ctrl. Broadcasting Adminstrn. China, 1944-47; rsch. engr. RCA, 1948-56; mgr. appliance CBS Semiconductor Ops., 1956-59; lectr. U. Md., College Park, 1966-69, vis. prof. elec. engring., 1969-71, prof. elec. engring., 1971—; adv. engr. Rsch. Lab., Westinghouse Corp., Balt., 1959-63; adj. prof. U. Pitts., 1959-63; vis. lectr. U. Calif., Berkeley, 1965-66. Achievements include research in semiconductor and integrated circuits. Fellow IEEE (Ebers award Electron Device Soc. 1978), Sigma Xi. Office: Univ Maryland Electrical Eng Dept College Park MD 20742

LIN, JAMES CHIH-I, biomedical and electrical engineer, educator; b. Dec. 29, 1942; m. Mei Fei, Mar. 21, 1970; children: Janet, Theodore, Erik. BS, U. Wash., 1966, MS, 1968, PhD, 1971. Engr. Crown Zellerbach Corp., Seattle, 1966-67; asst. prof. U. Wash., Seattle, 1971-74; prof. Wayne State U., Detroit, 1974-80; prof. U. Ill.-Chgo., 1980—, head dept. bioengring., 1980-92, dir. robotics and automation lab., 1982-89, dir. spl. projects Coll. Engring., 1992-94, NSC rsch. chair, 1993-96; vis. prof. in Beijing, Rome, Shan Dong, Taiwan Univs.; lectr. of short courses, 1974—; cons. Battelle Meml. Inst., Columbus, Ohio, 1973-75, SRI Internat., Palo Alto, Calif., 1978-79, Arthur D. Little, Inc., Cambridge, Mass., 1980-83, Ga. Tech. Rsch. Inst., Atlanta, 1984-86, Walter Reed Army Inst. Rsch., 1973, 87, 88, Naval Aerospace Med. Rsch. Labs., Pensacola, 1982-83, U.R.S. Corp., San Francisco, 1985-87, CBS, Inc., N.Y., 1988, U. Va., 1991-92, ACS, Inc., Santa Clara, Calif., 1989-90, Luxtron Corp, Mountainview, Calif., 1991-92, Commonwealth Edison, Chgo., 1991-95; program chmn. Frontiers of Engring. and Computing Conf., Chgo., 1985; chmn., convener URSI Joint Symposium Electromagnetic Waves in Biol. Systems, Tel-Aviv, 1987, Internat. Conf. on Sci. and Tech., 1989-91; chmn. Chinese-Am. Acad. and Profl. Conv., 1993; mem Congrl. Health Care Adv. Coun., 13th dist. Ill., 1987—; mem. citizen's adv. coun. Hinsdale Cen. High Sch., 1988-93. Author: Microwave Auditory Effects and Applications, 1978, Biological Effects and Health Implications of Radiofrequency Radiation, 1987, Electromagnetic Interaction with Biological Systems, 1989, Mobile Comm. Safety, 1996; assoc. editor Jour. Microwave Power and Electromagnetic Energy, 1988-90; editor Advances in Electromagnetic Fields in Living Systems; guest editor EMB Mag., 1997—, Wireless Networks, 1996-97; also numerous papers. Panelist NSF Presdl. Young Investigator award com., Washington, 1984, 89, mem. NIH diagnostic radiology, 1981-85, chmn. SBIR study sect., 1986-94; mem. U.S. Nat. Commn. for URSI, NAS, 1980-82, 90—, chair Commn. K, 1990—; mem. Pres. Com. Nat. Medal of Sci., 1992-93; mem. Nat. Coun. Radiation Protection and Measurement, 1992—, chmn. radio frequency scientific com., 1995—; mem. NAS Extremely Low Frequency Field Monitoring com., 1995—, chmn. Internat. Union of Radio Scis Commn., Electromagnetics in Biology and Med., 1996—; chmn. Internat. Sci. Meeting on Electromagnetics in Medicine, 1997. Recipient IEEE Transaction Best Paper award, 1975; Nat. Rsch. Svcs. award, 1982, Disting. Svc. award, Outstanding Leadership award Chinese Am. Acad. and Profl. Assn. MidAm., 1989 (pres. 1991-92, UIC Best Advisor award, 1993). Fellow AAAS, AIMBE, IEEE (tech. policy coun. 1990-91, chmn. com. on man and radiation 1990-91, assoc. and guest editor transactions on biomed. engring., guest editor transactions on microwave theory and techniques, disting. lectr. engring. in medicine and biology 1991-93); mem. NSPE, Biomed. Engring. Soc. (sr. mem.), Robotics Internat. (sr. mem.), Am. Soc. Engring. Edn., Bioelectromagnetics Soc. (charter, pres.-elect 1993-94, pres. 1994-95, chmn. ann. meeting 1994), Electromagnetics Acad., Golden Key, Sigma Xi, Phi Tau Phi (v.p.), Tau Beta Pi. Office: U Ill Coll Engring 1030 SEO MC/154 851 S Morgan St Chicago IL 60607-7042

LIN, JONATHAN CHUNG-SHIH, computer scientist; b. Taipei, Taiwan, Jan. 20, 1952; came to U.S., 1977; s. Chia-Hsung and Ho (Yang) L.; m. Ling-Li, May 10, 1980; children: Jennifer, Edward. BS, Fu-Jen Catholic U., Taipei, Taiwan, 1975; MS in Computer Sci., Am. U., 1985. Programmer/analyst DLM & Assoc., Annandale, Va., 1977-79; rsch. analyst DSAI, Rockville, Md., 1979-85, project mgr., 1985-92, sr. staff/project mgr., 1992-96, v.p., 1996—; instr. No. Va. C.C., Alexandria, 1986; lectr. Montgomery Coll., Rockville, Md., 1987; adj. prof. Johns Hopkins U., Balt., 1987-92. Contbr. articles to internat. jours. Mem. (voting) Assn. Computing Machinery, Inst. Elec. and Electronic Engrs. (computer soc.), North Am. Taiwanese Prof. Assn. Avocations: soccer, tennis. Home: 14731 Soft Wind Dr North Potomac MD 20878 Office: DSAI 350 Fortune Ter Rockville MD 20854-2981

LIN, JOSEPH PEN-TZE, neuroradiologist, clinical administrator, educator; b. Foochow, China, Nov. 25, 1932; came to U.S., 1959, naturalized, 1974; s. Tai Shui and Chin Sien Lin; m. Lillian Y. Hsu, Dec. 23, 1959; children: James S., Carol W., Julia W. MD, Nat. Taiwan U., 1957. Diplomate Am. Bd. Radiology. Rotating intern Robert B. Green Meml. Hosp., San Antonio, 1959-60; resident in radiology Santa Rosa Med. Center, San Antonio, 1960-61, Bellevue Hosp. Center, N.Y.C., 1961-63; fellow in neuroradiology NYU Med. Ctr., N.Y.C., 1963-65; instr. radiology NYU Med. Ctr., 1965-67, asst. prof., 1967-70, assoc. prof., 1970-74, prof., 1974—; dir. neuroradiology sect. Univ. Hosp., N.Y.C., 1974—; cons. Manhattan VA Hosp., N.Y.C., 1974—, Booth Meml. Hosp., N.Y.C., 1978-84, St. Vincent's Hosp., S.I., N.Y., 1978-85, New Rochelle (N.Y.) Hosp., 1978-85. Contbr. articles on neuroradiology to med. jours. Fellow Am. Coll. Radiology, Am. Heart Assn. (stroke coun.); mem. Am. Chinese Med. Soc. (pres. 1978), Am. Soc. Neuroradiology, Radiol. Soc. N.Am., Assn. Univ. Radiologists. Home: 15 Oxford Rd New Rochelle NY 10804-3712 Office: NYU Med Ctr 550 1st Ave New York NY 10016-6481

LIN, MARIA C. H., lawyer; b. Yunnan, Kunming, China, Jan. 27, 1942. BSc, Coll. Mount St. Vincent, 1966; MSc, U. Kans., 1970; JD, Fordham U., 1978. Bar: N.Y. 1979, U.S. Dist. Ct. (so. and ea. dists.) N.Y. 1979, U.S. Ct. Appeals (Fed. cir.) 1982, U.S. Patent and Trademark Office, U.S Supreme Ct. 1985. Atty. Morgan & Finnegan, N.Y.C. Mem. ABA, N.Y. State Bar Assn., N.Y. Patent, Trademark and Copyright Law Assn. (bd. dirs. 1979-88, internat. law and practice China com. 1979-85, fgn. patent law and practice 1986—, chmn. 1990-91), Am. Intellectual Property Law Assn. (Chinese rels. com. 1983-87, internat. patent law and practice 1988—, chmn. 1995-96, co-chmn., China study group, 1997—). Office: Morgan & Finnegan 345 Park Ave New York NY 10154-0004

LIN, MIN-CHUNG, obstetrician-gynecologist; b. Nan-Tou, Republic of China, Aug. 24, 1944; s. Chi-Hsien and Yue (Chen) L.; m. Miaw-Chyung, June 26, 1971; children: Susie, Judy, Nancy, Frances. MD, Tapei Med. Coll., Republic of China, 1970. Diplomate Am. Bd. Ob-Gyn. Chmn. ob-gyn dept. Cuba (N.Y.) Meml. Hosp., 1976-80, Ira Davenport Meml. Hosp., Bath, N.Y., 1980-95; med. staff ob-gyn. dept. Corning (N.Y.) Hosp., 1995—. Fellow Am. Coll. Ob-Gyn; mem. AMA. Republican. Presbyterian. Office: 163 E 2nd St Corning NY 14830-2801

LIN, MING SHEK, allergist, immunologist; b. Taipei, Taiwan, Oct. 11, 1937; came to U.S., 1965; s. Joseph and Tong-Kai (Chan) Lynn; m. Mary Liao, Nov. 22, 1969; children: Jerry, Michael. MD, Nat. Taiwan U., 1964; PhD, U. Pitts., 1974. Diplomate Am. Acad. Allergy and Immunology, Am. Bd. Pediatrics. Asst. prof. U. Pitts. Grad. Sch. Pub. Health, 1976-80; asst. and assoc. prof. dept. pediatrics U. Pitts. Sch. Medicine, 1981—; chief sect. of allergy and immunology Forbes Health System, Pitts., 1987—; pres. Pitts. Allergy Soc., 1994—. Contbr. articles to Jour. Allery and Immunology, Internat. Congress of Immunology, Jour. Allergy, Jour. Pediatrics, Jour. Cellular Immunology, Immunology. Named Winklestan lectr., 1976. Fellow Am. Soc. for Microbiology; mem. AMA, Am. Acad. Allergy and Immunology. Home: 81 Locksley Dr Pittsburgh PA 15235-5117 Office: 4099 William Penn Hwy Ste 805 Monroeville PA 15146-2518

LIN, MING-CHANG, physical chemistry educator, researcher; b. Hsinpu, Hsinchu, Taiwan, Oct. 24, 1936; came to U.S., 1967, naturalized, 1975; s. Fushin and Tao May (Hsu) L.; m. Juh-Huey Chern, June 26, 1965; children: Karen, Linus H., Ellena J. BSc, Taiwan Normal U., Taipei, 1959; PhD, U. Ottawa, Ont., Can., 1966. Postdoctoral rsch. felloww U. Ottawa, 1965-67; postdoctoral rsch. assoc. Cornell U., Ithaca, N.Y., 1967-69; rsch. chemist Naval Rsch. Lab., Washington, 1970-74, supervisory rsch. chemist, head chem. kinetics sect., 1974-82, sr. scientist for chem. kinetics, 1982-88; Robert W. Woodruff prof. phys. chemistry Emory U., Atlanta, 1988—; mem. adv. bd. Internat. Jour. Chem. Kinetics, 1990-93, Chemistry, World Sci. Pub. Co., Singapore, 1991—, Inst. Atomic and Molecular Sci., Taipei, 1991—; mem. young presdl. award com. NSF, Washington, 1990. Contbr. over 300 articles to profl. jours. 2d lt. Taiwan ROTC, 1960-62. Recipient Civilian Meritorious award USN, 1979, Humboldt award Humboldt Found., 1982, prize in sci. tech. Taiwanese-Am. Found., 1989; Guggenheim fellow, 1982. Mem. Am. Chem. Soc. (Hillebrand prize 1975), Combustion Inst., Am. Vacuum Soc., Materials Rsch. Soc., N.Am. Taiwanese Profs. Assn., Sigma Xi (Pure Sci. award 1976 Naval Rsch. Lab. chpt.). Achievements include discovery of numerous chemical lasers, use of lasers to elucidate mechanisms of combustion, propulsion and gas-surface reactions; first use of lasers to ionize non-fluorescing radicals and to probe for radicals formed in heterogeneous catalytic reactions. Office: Emory Univ Dept Of Chemistry Atlanta GA 30322

LIN, PEN-MIN, electrical engineer, educator; b. Liaoning, China, Oct. 17, 1928; came to U.S., 1954; s. Tai-sui and Tse-san (Tang) L.; m. Louise Shou Yuen Lee, Dec. 29, 1962; children: Marian, Margaret, Janice. B.S.E.E., Taiwan U., 1950; M.S.E.E., N.C. State U., 1956; Ph.D. in Elec. Engring., Purdue U., 1960. Asst. prof. Purdue U., West Lafayette, Ind., 1961-66, assoc. prof., 1966-74, prof. elec. engring., 1974-94, prof. emeritus, 1994—. Author: (with L.O. Chua) Computer Aided Analysis of Electronic Circuits, 1975, Symbolic Network Analysis, 1991, (with R.A. DeCarlo) Linear Circuit Analysis, 1995. Fellow IEEE (life). Home: 3029 Covington St West Lafayette IN 47906-1107 Office: Purdue Univ Sch Of Elec Engring West Lafayette IN 47907

LIN, PING-WHA, engineering educator, consultant; b. Canton, China, July 11, 1925; m. Sylvia Lin; children: Karl, Karen. BS, Jiao-Tong U., Shanghai, China, 1947; PhD, Purdue U., 1951. Engr. various, 1951-61; cons., engr. WHO, Geneva, 1962-66, 84, project mgr., 1980-82; Laurence L. Dresser chair, prof. Tri-State U., Angola, Ind., 1966-95, prof. emeritus, 1995—; pres. Lin Techs Inc., Angola, 1989—. Contbr. articles to profl. jours., including articles on or related to Lin's Theory of Flux. Grantee Dept. of Energy, 1983-84. Fellow ASCE (past pres. Ind. chpt.); mem. Am. Chem. Soc., Am. Water Works Assn. (life), N.Y. Acad. Scis., Sigma Xi. Achievements include patents in the fields. Home: 506 S Darling St Angola IN 46703-1707

LIN, SHU, electrical engineering educator; b. May 20, 1936; came to U.S., 1961; s. Hsiang-Ju Li; m. Aug. 17, 1963; children: Julian J., Patrick S., Michelle S. BSEE, Nat. Taiwan U., Taipei, 1959; MSEE, Rice U., 1964, PhDEE, 1965. Prof. Tex. A&M U., College Station, 1981-82, Irma Runyon prof., 1986-87; asst. prof. elec. engring. U. Hawaii, Honolulu, 1965-69, assoc. prof., 1969-73, prof., 1973-81, 82-86, 87—, chmn. dept., 1989—; vis. scientist IBM Watson Rsch. Lab., Yorktown, N.Y., 1978-79; vis. chair telecom. Tech. U. Munich. Author: Introduction to Error Correcting Codes, 1971; co-author: Error Conto Coding: Fundamentals and Applications, 1983; also over 200 articles; patentee in field. Recipient Disting. Merit award State of Hawaii, 1983, Alesander von Humboldt Rsch. prize for U.S. sr. scientist, 1996; grantee NSF, 1966—, NASA, 1981-93. Fellow IEEE; mem. IEEE Info. Theory Soc. (pres. 1991). Home: 1076 Kamaole St Honolulu HI 96825-2816 Office: U Hawaii 2540 Dole St Honolulu HI 96822-2303

LIN, SHU-FANG HSIA, librarian; b. Kweiling, China, Jan. 7, 1939; came to U.S., 1962; d. Chien-chen and Yu-chia (Sun) Hsia; m. George Chwen-Chen Lin, Nov. 12, 1966; children: Michael, Lawrence. BA, Tunghai U., 1961; MA, Vanderbilt U., 1963, St. John's U., 1981. Internat. law diplomate. Contbr. articles to profl. jours. Mem. AAUP, ALA, Cath. Libr. Assn., Chinese Am. Librs. Assn., Metro Govt. Docs. Interest Group. Avocations: travel, movies, opera, reading. Office: St John's U Libr 8000 Utopia Pky Jamaica NY 11432-1335

LIN, TUNG HUA, civil engineering educator; b. Chungkin, China, May 26, 1911; s. Yao-Ching and Yue (Kuo) L.; m. Susan Z. Chiang, Mar. 15, 1939; childern: Rita P., Lin Chiou, Robert P., James P. B.S., Tangshan Coll., Chiaotung U., 1933; S.M., MIT, 1936; D.Sc., U. Mich., 1953. Prof. Tsing Hua U., China, 1937-39; chief engr. Chinese 2d Aircraft Co., Nancheun, Szechuan, 1939-44; prodn. mgr. Mfg. Factory, China, 1940-44; mem. tech. mission in charge of jet aircraft design, 1945-49; prof. aero. engring. U. Detroit, 1949-55; prof. engring. and applied scis. UCLA, 1955-78, prof. emeritus, 1978—; cons.N.Am. Aviation, N.Am. Rockwell, L.A., 1964-74, Atomic Internat., Canoga Park, Calif., 1965-68, ARA Inc., Industry City, Calif., 1964-94. Author: Theory of Inelastic Structure, 1968; contbr. articles to profl. jours.; mem. editorial bd.: Jour. Composite Materials, 1966-75; patentee in field. Chinese Nat. fellow Tsing-Hua U., 1933; recipient medal for Design of 1st Chinese twin-engine airplane, 1944, Disting. Svc. award Applied Mechanics Rev. ASME, 1966, NSF grantee, 1954-78; named prin. investigator Office Naval Rsch., 1985-93, Air Force Office of Sci. Rsch., 1988—. Fellow ASME, Am. Acad. Mechanics; mem. ASCE (life, gen. chmn. engring. mechanics conf. 1965, Theodore von Karman award 1988); mem. NAE, Academia Sinica. Home: 906 Las Pulgas Rd Pacific Palisades CA 90272-2441 Office: UCLA Dept Civil Engring 405 Hilgard Ave Los Angeles CA 90095-9000

LIN, TUNG YEN, civil engineer, educator; b. Foochow, China, Nov. 14, 1911; came to U.S., 1946, naturalized, 1951; s. Ting Chang and Feng Yi (Kuo) L.; m. Margaret Kao, July 20, 1941; children: Paul, Verna. BS in Civil Engring., Chiaotung U., Tangshan, Republic of China, 1931; MS, U. Calif., Berkeley, 1933; LLD, Chinese U. Hong Kong, 1972, Golden Gate U., San Francisco, 1982, Tongji U., Shanghai, 1987, Chiaotung U., Taiwan, 1987. Chief bridge engr., chief design engr. Chinese Govt. Rys., 1933-46; asst., then assoc. prof. U. Calif., 1946-55, prof., 1955-76, chmn. div. structural engring., 1960-63, dir. structural lab., 1960-63; chmn. bd. T.Y. Lin Internat., 1953-87, hon. chmn. bd., 1987-92; pres. Inter-Continental Peace Bridge, Inc., 1968—; cons. to State of Calif., Def. Dept., also to industry; chmn. World Conf. Prestressed Concrete, 1957, Western Conf. Prestressed Concrete Bldgs., 1960; chmn. bd. Lin Tung Yen, China, 1993—. Author: Design of Prestressed Concrete Structures, 1955, rev. edit., 1963, 3d edit. (with N.H. Burns), 1981, (with B. Bresler, Jack Scalzi) Design of Steel Structures, rev. edit., 1968, (with S.D. Statesbury) Structural Concepts and Systems, 1981, 2d edit., 1988; contbr. articles to profl. jours. Recipient Berkeley citation award, 1976, NRC Quarter Century award, 1977, AIA Honor award, 1984, Pres.'s Nat. Med. of Sci., 1986, Merit award Am. Cons. Engrs., Coun., 1987, John A. Roebling medal Bridge Engring., 1990, Am. Segmental Bridge Inst. Leadership award, 1992, Outstanding Paper of Yr. award Internat. Assn. Bridge and Structural Engring., 1993, Lifetime Achievement award Asian Am. Archs. and Engring. Assn., 1993, Outstanding Achievement award AAAE Assn. of So. Calif., Prix Albert Caquot award Assn. Française pour Construction, 1995; fellow U. Calif. at Berkeley; named Alumnus of Yr. U. Calif. Alumni Assn., 1994. Mem. ASCE (hon., life, Wellington award, Howard medal), NAt. Acad. Engring., Chinese Acad. Sci., Academia Sinica, Internat. Fedn. Prestressing (Freyssinet medal), Am. Concrete Inst. (hon.), Prestressed Concrete Inst. (medal of honor), Chinese Acad. Sci. Home: 8701 Don Carol Dr El Cerrito CA 94530-2734 Office: 315 Bay St San Francisco CA 94133-1923 *Fear incites fear; complex breeds complex. If one learns to control one's own fear and complex, and at the same time understands those of others, one will have gone a long way toward success and happiness.*

LIN, WILLIAM WEN-RONG, economist; b. Pintung, Taiwan, Sept. 5, 1942; came to U.S., 1967; naturalized, 1976; s. Ming-Lay and Shyr-Mey (Chow) L.; m. Kimy Kuei-mei Juan, Oct. 5, 1964; children: Susan, George, Roger. BS, Chung-Hsing U., Taichung, Taiwan, 1964; MS, U. Calif.-Davis, 1969, PhD, 1973. Economist Oak Ridge Nat. Labs., Tenn., 1974-76; agrl. economist U.S. Dept. Agriculture, Washington, 1976-80, sect. head Econ. Rsch. Svc., 1982-92; sr. agrl. economist, 1992—; economist U.S. Dept. Energy, Washington, 1980-81, U.S. Dept. Interior, 1981-82; leader livestock feed del. to China, 1991, OECD, 1991; cons. in field. Contbr. articles to profl. jours. Mem. Taiwanese Am. Assn., 1976-86; legis. affairs com. Saratoga Cmty. Assn., Springfield, Va., 1983; pres. Chinese-Am. Profl. Assn. Met. Washington, 1995. U. Calif. fellow, 1967-68, Disting. scholar, 1969-71; Merit award U.S. Dept. Agr., 1979, 85, 90, 92. Mem. Am. Agrl. Econ. Assn. (productivity com. 1978-80, lectr. 1977), Am. Econs. Assn., Chinese-Am. Profls. Assn. (bd. dirs. 1994), Western Agrl. Econ. Assn. (lectr. 1979), Southern Agrl. Econ. Assn. Home: 9404 Crosstimber Ct Fairfax Station VA 22039-3175 Office: USDA Econ Rsch Svc 1301 New York Ave NW Rm 832 Washington DC 20005-4708

LIN, Y. K., engineer, educator; b. Foochow, Fukien, China, Oct. 30, 1923; came to U.S., 1954, naturalized, 1964; s. Fa Been and Chi Ying (Cheng) L.; m. Ying-yuh June Wang, Mar. 29, 1952; children: Jane, Della, Lucia, Winifred. BS, Amoy U., 1946; MS, Stanford U., 1955, PhD, 1957; Dr. Engring. honoris causa, U. Waterloo, Can., 1994. Tchr. Amoy U., China, 1946-48, Imperial Coll. Engring., Ethiopia, 1957-58; engr. Vertol Aircraft Corp., Morton, Pa., 1956-57; research engr. Boeing Co., Renton, Wash., 1958-60; asst. prof. U. Ill., Urbana, 1960-62, assoc. prof., 1962-65, prof. aero. and astron. engring., 1965-83; Charles E. Schmidt Eminent scholar chair Coll. Engring., dir. Ctr. for Applied Stochastics Rsch. Fla. Atlantic U., Boca Raton, 1984—; vis. prof. mech. engring. M.I.T., 1967-68; sr. vis. fellow Inst. Sound and Vibration Research, U. Southampton, Eng., 1976; cons. Gen. Motors Corp., Boeing Co., Gen. Dynamics Corp., TRW Corp., Brookhaven Nat. Lab. Author: Probabilistic Theory of Structural Dynamics, 1967, Stochastic Structural Mechanics, 1987, Stochastic Approaches in Earthquake Engineering, 1987, Stochastic Structural Dynamics, 1990, Probabilistic Structural Dynamics: Advanced Theory and Applications, 1995; contbr. articles to profl. jours. Sr. postdoctoral fellow NSF, 1967-68. Fellow ASCE (Alfred M. Freudenthal medal 1984), Am. Acad. Mechs., Acoustical Soc. Am., AIAA (assoc.); mem. Sigma Xi, Internat. Assn. for Structural Safety and Reliability (stochastic dynamics rsch. award 1993). Home: 2684 NW 27th Ter Boca Raton FL 33434-6001 Office: Fla Atlantic U Coll Engring Boca Raton FL 33431

LIN, YEOU-LIN, engineer, consultant; b. Taipei, Taiwan, July 2, 1957; came to U.S., 1981; s. Chuan and Chiao-Chen (Chang) L.; m. Ting-Ting Yao, June 25, 1983; children: Cheryl Chang, Calvin Yao. BSEE, Nat. Chiao-Tung U., Hsinchu, Taiwan, 1979; MSEE, U. Pitts., 1982; PhD in Elec. and Computer Engring., Carnegie Mellon U., 1987. Image processing analyst Internat. Robomation Intelligence, Carlsbad, Calif., 1987; computer scientist Four PI Systems Corp., San Diego, 1987-89, sr. vision scientist, 1991-92; sr. systems engr., program mgr. Taiwan Aerospace Corp., Taipei, Taiwan, 1992-94; with Pacific Iradium, Taipei, 1994—; owner Global Linking Tech. Svcs., San Diego, 1991—. Home: 13584 Jadestone Way San Diego CA 92130-2815

LINABERGER, ANNE, television producer; b. Pitts., Sept. 18, 1962; d. James Thomas and Elsa Ann (Held) L.; m. Thomas Joseph Mazula, Nov. 28, 1987. BA in Comm., Allegheny Coll., Meadville, Pa., 1984. Local news anchor WAMO AM & FM, Pitts., 1984-88; network news anchor Sheridan Broadcasting, Pitts., 1987-90; anchor, reporter WDTV-TV, Clarksburg, W.Va., 1988-89, WTAE-AM, Pitts., 1990-93; reporter, prodr. WTAE-TV, Pitts., 1991-93, exec. prodr. news, 1993—; cons. Presbyn. Media Mission, Pitts., 1992—, Emerging Internat. Cities Conf., Pitts., 1993; cons., mem. Presbytery Com. on Comm., Pitts., 1995—. Newsletter editor Mendelssohn Choir Pitts., 1990-93. Mem. Mendelssohn Choir Pitts., 1985—; class leader ann. fund campaign Allegheny Coll., Meadville, Pa., 1984—; elder Northmont United Presbyn. Ch., Pitts., 1990—; bd. dirs. Crisis Ctr. North, Pitts., 1991-94. Recipient awards Prodr. Best Regularly Scheduled Newscast, W.Va. AP, 1989, Reporter Best Spot News Coverage Radio, Pa. AP, 1991, Exec. Prodr. Best Investigation, Soc. Profl. Journalists, Pitts., 1993, Exec. Prodr. Best Spot News Coverage, Pa. AP, 1993. Republican. Avocations: skiing, golf, gardening, antique repair and refinishing. Home: 828 Harden Dr Pittsburgh PA 15229 Office: WTAE-TV 400 Ardmore Blvd Pittsburgh PA 15221-3019

LINAHON, JAMES JOSEPH, music educator, musician; b. Mason City, Iowa, Sept. 6, 1951; s. Robert Eugene and Teresa Darlene (Mulaney) L.; m. Kathryn Anne Tull, Apr. 12, 1987; children: Michael, Katie, Joseph. BA in Music, U. No. Iowa, 1973; M in Music Edn., North Tex. State U., 1975. Assoc. dir. jazz studies Chaffey Coll., Rancho Cucamonga, Calif., 1975-80; prof. music, dir. jazz studies Fullerton (Calif.) Coll., 1980—; cons. U. No. Colo., U. Alaska, U. Calif., U. Ariz., U. Hawaii, DePaul U., Chgo., U. So. Calif., Wash. State U., S.D. State U., 1978—; cons., artist Playboy Jazz Festival, Reno Internat. Jazz Festival, Queen Mary Jazz Festival, Disneyland, All That Jazz; record producer MCA, Warner Bros, ABC, Columbia; performer for Frank Sinatra, Henry Mancini, Beverly Sills, Ella Fitzgerald, Sarah Vaughan, Tony Bennett, Merv Griffin; U.S. Jazz amb., worldwide, 1996. Artist, producer: (jazz compact disc) Time Tripping, 1984 (Album of Yr. Downbeat Mag., 1987), (classical compact disc) Gradus Ad Parnassum, 1990, (compact disk) Season of Our Lives, 1994; composer: (musical composition) Snow Wisp, 1986 (finalist Columbia Artists search). Performer, producer Theatre Palisades, Pacific Palisades, Calif., 1986, Claremont (Calif.) Community Found., 1992; guest soloist Claremont (Calif.) Symphony Orch., 1991. Recipient Major Landers scholarship Iowa Band Master's Assn., Iowa, 1969; named Dee Bee Album of Yr. (5 awards) Downbeat Mag., 1978-87. Mem. NARAS (Oustanding Recordings 1989), Internat. Assn. Jazz Educators (higher edn. rep. 1992-93), Internat. Trumpet Guild, Internat. Assn. Jazz Edn., Am. Soc. Composers, Authors and Publishers, Nat. Assn. Coll. Wind and Percussion Instrs., Am. Fedn. Musicians. Roman Catholic. Avocations: gourmet cooking, home improvement, travel. Home: 560 W 10th St Claremont CA 91711-3714 Office: Fullerton College 321 E Chapman Ave Fullerton CA 92832-2011

LINAWEAVER, WALTER ELLSWORTH, JR., physician; b. San Pedro, Calif., Oct. 16, 1928; s. Walter Ellsworth and Catherine Breathed (Bridges) L.; m. Lydia Anne Whitlock, Oct. 6, 1957; children: Catherine Ann, Nancy Alyn, Walter E. III. BA cum laude, Pomona Coll., 1952; MD, U. Rochester, 1956. Diplomate Am. Bd. Allergy and Immunology, Am. Bd. Pediatrics, Am. Bd. Pediatric Allergy. Intern pediatrics Med. Ctr. U. Rochester, N.Y., 1956-57, resident pediatrics Med. Ctr., 1958-59; asst. resident pediatrics Med. Ctr. UCLA, 1957-58; fellow allergy and immunology Med. Ctr. U. Colo., Denver, 1959-61, instr. pediatrics Sch. Medicine, 1961; pvt. practice Riverside (Calif.) Med. Clinic, 1962—; asst. clin. prof. pediatrics Loma Lida U. Med. Sch., 1965—. Elder Presbyn. Ch. Staff sgt. U.S. Army, 1946-48. Inducted into Athletic Hall of Fame Pomona Coll., Claremont, Calif., 1979. Fellow Am. Acad. Allergy, Asthma & Immunology, Am. Acad. Pediat., Southwestern Pediat. Soc. (emeritus, v.p. 1978), L.A. Acad. Medicine; mem. Riverside County Med. Soc. (councillor), Riverside County Heart Assn. Republican. Avocations: gardening, American and British military history. Home: 1296 Tiger Tail Dr Riverside CA 92506-5475 Office: Riverside Med Clinic 3660 Arlington Ave Riverside CA 92506-3912

LINCE, JOHN ALAN, pharmacist; b. Cleve., Sept. 15, 1940; s. John Alexander and Isabelle Stella (Wirbalas) Lincewicz; m. Katherine Ann Hudson, Sept. 9, 1961 (div. Aug., 1984); children: John Jr., Karen, Mark; m. Shirley Ann Baker, Jan. 18, 1985. BS in Pharmacy, Ohio State U., 1964. Registered pharmacist, Ohio. Pharmacist, owner Hill & Dale Pharmacy, Columbus, Ohio, 1964-75, Franklin Park Med. Pharmacy, Columbus, 1975—. Pharmacy Mktg. award Johnson & Johnson, N.J., 1964. Mem. Coop. of Ohio Pharmacies (charter mem., pres. 1991—), Am. Pharm. Assn., Nat. Assn. Retail Druggists, Ohio Pharmacists Assn., Acad. Pharmacy Ctrl. Ohio (trustee 1994-95, pres. 1995-97), Ohio State Alumni Assn., Ohio State U. Coll. Pharmacy Alumni Assn. (charter), Mid-Ohio Combat Shooters Assn. (pres. 1985-88), Rho Chi. Avocations: photography, woodworking, target shooting. Home: 4645 Meekison Dr Columbus OH 43220-3038 Office: Franklin Park Med Pharmacy 1829 E Long St Columbus OH 43203-2066

LINCHITZ, RICHARD MICHAEL, psychiatrist, pain medicine specialist, physician; b. Bklyn., Mar. 29, 1947; m. Rita A. Colao, Sept. 22, 1973; children: Elise Ann, Michael Benjamin, Jonathan Adam. BA cum laude in Psychology, Cornell U., 1967, MD, 1973; student L.I. Univ., 1967-68, U. Lausanne Med. Sch., 1968-71. Diplomate Am. Bd. Psychiatry and Neurology, Am. Acad. Pain Mgmt., AM. Bd. Pain Medicine. Intern, Moffit Hosp., San Francisco, 1973-74; resident in psychiatry Langley Porter Neurospychiat. Inst., San Francisco, 1974-77; practice medicine specializing in treatment of chronic pain conditions and psychiatry, Carle Place, N.Y., 1978—; med. dir. Roslyn Mental Health Ctr. (N.Y.), 1978—, Pain Alleviation Center, Carle Place, 1978—. Recipient letter of commendation White House, 1977; Nathan Seligman award Cornell U. Med. Coll., 1973; Nat. Psychiat. Endowment Fund award Langley Porter Neuropsychiat. Inst., 1977; Langley Porter Youth Service award, 1977. Fellow Am. Coll. Pain Medicine; mem. Am. Psychiat. Assn., Acad. Pain Research, Am. Pain Soc., Nassau Psychiat. Soc., Am. Acad. of Pain Medicine (bd. dirs.), Am. Acad. Pain Mgmt. (cert.), Alpha Omega Alpha. Author: Life Without Pain, 1987. Office: 179 Westbury Ave Carle Place NY 11514-1227

LINCICOME, BERNARD WESLEY, journalist; b. Zanesville, Ohio, Sept. 13, 1941; s. Robert Parr and Mary Edith Lincicome; m. Jaye Slaughter, Sept. 21, 1963; children: Romey, David. B.S. in Edn., Ohio State U., 1963. Staff writer Sun-Sentinel, Ft. Lauderdale, Fla., 1968-70, sports editor, 1970-73; sports editor Ft. Lauderdale News, 1973-83; columnist Chgo. Tribune, 1983—. Served with USAF, 1958-61. Recipient Best Sports Column award Fla. Press Club, 1981; Column writing award AP Sports Editors, 1982, 85, 88; Best Sports Column award AP, 1984; Peter Lisagor award, 1985, 87. Mem. Fla. Sportswriters Assn. (pres. 1977, Sportswriter of Yr. award 1973, 75, 79, 81). Office: Chgo Tribune Co 435 N Michigan Ave Chicago IL 60611*

LINCICOME, DAVID RICHARD, biomedical and animal scientist; b. Champaign, Ill., Jan. 17, 1914; s. David Rosebery and Olive Iola (Casper) L.; m. Dorothy Lucile Van Cleave, Sept. 1, 1941 (dec. Nov. 1952); children: David Van Cleave, Judith Ann; m. Margaret Stirewalt, Dec. 29, 1953. BS, MS with high honors, U. Ill., 1937; PhD in Tropical Medicine, Tulane U., 1941. Diplomate (emeritus) Am. Bd. Microbiology; diplomate Am. Coll. Animal Physiology; cert. animal scientist Am. Registry Profl. Animal Scientists. Asst. instr. U. Ill., 1937; asst. instr. tropical medicine Tulane U. Med. Sch., 1937-41; asst. prof. parasitology U. Ky., 1941-47, U. Wis. Med. Sch., 1947-49; sr. rsch. parasitologist Du Pont Co., 1949-53; from asst. prof. to full prof. biol. Scis. Howard U., 1953-70; vis. sci. NIH, 1965-66; registrar, Jacob Sheep Conservancy, 1989-96, bd. dirs., 1990—, pres., 1996; vis. scholar Nat. Agrl. Libr. USDA, 1990-92; guest scientist USDA Exp. Sta., Beltsville, Md., 1978—, Naval Med. Rsch. Inst., 1954-62. Founder, editor Exptl. Parasitology, 1949-76; editor Transactions of the Ky. Acad. Sci., 1946-49, Transactions of the Am. Microscopical Soc., 1970-71, Internat. Rev. Tropical Medicine, 1953-63; founder Virology, 1950, Advances in Vet. Sci., 1952. Lt. col. Med. Svc. Corps, U.S. Army, World War II, PTO. Recipient Anniversary award Helminthological Soc., 1975; rsch. grantee NIH, 1958-68. Fellow AAAS, Explorers Club (nat., N.Y.); mem. Helminthological Soc. (pres. 1958, emeritus), Am. Physiol. Soc. (emeritus), Soc. Invertebrate Zoology (emeritus), Am. Soc. Zoologists (emeritus), Am. Soc. Parasitologists, Am. Soc. Cell Biology, Am. Microscopical Soc. (emeritus), Royal Soc. Tropical Medicine (emeritus), Am. Soc. Tropical Medicine (emeritus), Am. Goat Soc. (bd. dirs. 1990-96), Am. Dairy Goat Assn. (founder., 1st sec. rsch. found. 1979, bd. dirs. 1972-87), Nat. Pygmy Goat Assn. (bd. dirs. 1976-92, pres. 1979), Natural Colored Wool Growers Assn. (bd. dirs. 1988-94), Jacob Sheep Breeders Assn., Jacob Sheep Soc. (Eng.), Nat. Tunis Sheep Registry (bd. dirs. 1991-93, sec. 1991-92), Soft-coated Wheaten Terrier Club of Am. (mem rescue com. 1993—), Greater Washington D.C. Area Soft-Coated Wheaten Terrier Club (founder, pres. 1991-92), Am. Livestock Breeds Conservancy (bd. dirs. 1994—), Va. State Dairy Goat Assn. (founder, pres. 1976), Midwestern Conf. Parasitologists (founder, 1st sec. 1949), Soc. Exptl. Biology & Medicine (sec. D.C. chpt. 1996, emeritus), Phi Beta Kappa, Sigma Xi (assoc. mem. 1936, mem. 1941, pres. Howard U. chpt. 1962). Achievements include breeding of two rare and endangered breeds of sheep, Jacob and Tunis and a rare dog the soft coated Wheaten Terrier; founder and first sec. The Rsch. Found. of the Am. Dairy Goat Assn.; founder Midwestern Conf. of Parasitologists. Home: Frogmoor Farm 3032 Courtney Sch Rd Midland VA 22728-9748 also: PO Box 13 4419 Cambria Ave Garrett Park MD 20896 Office: 3032 Courtney School Rd Midland VA 22728-2413

LINCK, CHARLES EDWARD, JR., English language educator; b. Lowemont, Kans., June 6, 1923; s. Charles Edward and Grace Elizabeth (Miller) L.; m. Alice Eugenie Meyer (div. Feb. 1964); 1 child, Charles Edward Lincoln; m. Ernestine Marie Porcher Sewell, Aug. 23, 1970. AB magna cum laude, St. Benedict's Coll., Atchison, Kans., 1951; MS, Kans. State Coll., 1953; PhD in English, U. Kans., 1962. Prof. English East Tex. State U., Commerce, 1958-91, prof. emeritus, 1991—; owner, pub. Cow Hill Press. Author, editor: Edgar Rye: North Central Texas Cartoonist and Journalist, 1972; co-editor: Bibliography of Evelyn Waugh, 1984; editor, pub. Evelyn Waugh in Letters by Terence Greenridge, 1994, Edgar Rye; Colleen, The Mountain Maid - A Story of War and Feud in Kentucky, 1994. With USN, 1943-46, PTO. Mem. MLA, Tex. Coll. English Assn. (pres. 1972), Am. Studies Assn., Tex. Folklore Soc. (pres. 1984). Democrat. Roman Catholic. Avocations: antique printing, native American Indian arts and crafts, photography. Home: Tex A&M U PO Box 3002 Tex A&M U Commerce TX 75429-3002

LINCOLN, ANNA, company executive, foreign languages educator; b. Warsaw, Poland, Dec. 13, 1932; came to U.S., 1948; d. Wigdor Aron and Genia (Zalkind) Szpiro; m. Adrian Courtney Lincoln Jr., Sept. 22, 1951; children: Irene Anne, Sally Linda, Allen, Kirk. Student, U. Calif., Berkeley, 1949-50; BA in French and Russian with honors, NYU, 1965; student, Columbia Tchrs. Coll., 1966-67. Tchr. Waldwick (N.J.) H.S., 1966-69; chmn. Tuxedo Park (N.Y.) Red Cross, 1969-71; pres. Red Cross divsn. Vets. Hosp.; pres. China Pictures U.S.A. Inc., Princeton, N.J., 1994—; prof. fgn. rels. Fudan U., Shanghai, 1994—, prof. English and humanitarian studies, 1996—; adv. bd. guidance dept. Waldwick (N.J.) H.S., 1966-69; hon. bd. dirs. Shanghai Fgn. Lang. Assn., 1994; hon. prof. Fudan U., Shanghai, 1994; leader seminars pm Chinat at top univs., 1996—. Author: Escape to China, 1940-48, 1985, Chinese transl., 1985, The Art of Peace, 1995; dir. devel. of film The Bridge, 1996—. Hon. U.S. Goodwill amb. for peace and friendship, China, 1984, 85, 86, 88. Named Woman of Yr. Am. Biog. Soc., 1993; recipient Peace Through the Arts prize Assn. Internat. Mujeres en las Artes, Madrid, 1993. Mem. AAUW, Women's Coll. Club (publicity chmn. 1991-96), Lit. Club Princeton (chmn.), Present Day Club. Avocations: reading, swimming, bridge, seminars, ballroom dancing. Home and Office: China Pictures USA Inc 550 Rosedale Rd Princeton NJ 08540-2315

LINCOLN, BLANCHE LAMBERT, congresswoman. Mem. from Ark. U.S. Ho. of Reps., Washington. Office: US Ho of Reps 1204 Longworth Ho Off Bldg Washington DC 20515

LINCOLN, EDMOND LYNCH, investment banker; b. Wilmington, Del., Aug. 3, 1949; s. Edmond Earl and Mary Margaret (Lynch) L.; B.A. magna cum laude, Harvard U., 1971, M.B.A., with distinction, 1974; m. Pamela Wick, Sept. 3, 1977; children: Lucy Arms, Emily Lord. Acting rare book librarian Henry Francis duPont Winterthur Mus. (Del.), 1971-72; with Kidder Peabody & Co., Inc., N.Y.C., 1974-94, asst. v.p., 1977-79, v.p. 1979-91, sr. v.p., 1991-94, mgr. govt. agy. fin., 1984-86, transp. group, 1986-94; mng. dir. PaineWebber Inc., N.Y.C., 1994—; pub. interest dir. Fed. Home Loan Bank of N.Y., 1987-89. Recipient Washburn History prize, Harvard U., 1971. Treas., Fed. Hall Meml. Assocs., 1981-87; mem. vis. com. Harvard Coll. Library, 1981-86, 88-94; exec. com. Friends of Harvard U. Track, 1972—, sec., 1976-87. Mem. Investment Assn. N.Y., Friends of Winterthur (trustee 1976-81, 87-93, sec. 1978-81, Winterthur Mus. acad. affairs com. 1992—), Assn. Internationale de Bibliophilie, Assn. of Fellows, The Pierpont Morgan Library, Club of Odd Volumes, Bond Club of N.Y., Grolier Club, Harvard Club (N.Y.C.), India House, Wilmington Club, Wilmington Country Club, Soc. of Naval Architects and Marine Engrs. (assoc.), Phi Beta Kappa. Republican. Roman Catholic. Home: 161 E 79th St New York NY 10021-0421 Office: PaineWebber Inc 1285 Avenue Of The Americas New York NY 10019-6028

LINCOLN, LARRY W., automotive executive; b. 1944. BS in psychology, Mich. Univ., 1965, MA in psychology, bus., 1980. Gen. superintendent Truck and Bus/Chevrolet, Chevrolet Bay City, 1965-86; gen. superintendent Pontiac West Assembly Truck and Bus General Motors Corp., Pontiac, Mich., 1986-93; CEO Mark III Industries, Ocala, Fla., 1993—. Office: Mark 111 Ind PO Box 2525 Ocala FL 34478-1868*

LINCOLN, SANDRA ELEANOR, chemistry educator; b. Holyoke, Mass., Mar. 11, 1939; d. Edwin Stanley and Evelyn Ida (Mackie) L. BA magna cum laude, Smith Coll., 1960; MSChem, Marquette U., 1970; PhD in Inorganic Chemistry, SUNY, Stony Brook, 1982. Tchr., prin. Oak Knoll Sch., Summit, N.J., 1964-74; tchr. Holy Child High Sch., Waukegan, Ill., 1974-76; lectr. chemistry, dir. fin. aid Rosemont (Pa.) Coll., 1976-78; teaching asst. SUNY, Stony Brook, 1978-82; assoc. prof. chemistry U. Portland, Oreg., 1982-96, prof. chemistry, 1997—. Contbr. articles to profl. jours. Cath. sister Soc. Holy Child Jesus, 1963—. Recipient Pres.'s award for Teaching, SUNY, Stony Brook, 1981; Burlington No. Outstanding scholar, 1987. Mem. Am. Chem. Soc., Phi Beta Kappa, Sigma Xi. Democrat. Home: 5431 N Strong St Portland OR 97203-5711 Office: U Portland 5000 N Willamette Blvd Portland OR 97203-5743

LINCOLN, WALTER BUTLER, JR., marine engineer, educator; b. Phila., July 15, 1941; s. Walter Butler and Virginia Ruth (Callahan) L.; m. Sharon Platner, Oct. 13, 1979; children: Amelia Adams, Caleb Platner. BS in Math., U. N.C., 1963; Ocean Engr., MIT, 1975; MBA, Rensselaer Poly. Inst., 1982; MA, Naval War Coll., 1994. Registered profl. engr., N.H., Conn.; chartered engr., U.K. Ops. rsch. analyst Applied Physics Lab. Johns Hopkins U., Silver Spring, Md., 1968-70; grad. asst. MIT, Cambridge, 1971-75; ocean engr. USCG R&D Ctr., Groton, Conn., 1976-78, chief marine syss. & environ. tech. divsn., 1983—; prin. engr. Sanders Assocs., Nashua, N.H., 1978-83; lectr. U. Conn., Avery Point, 1986—; master, U.S. Mcht. Marine. Contbr. articles to profl. jours. Comdr. USNR, 1963—. Fellow MIT, 1971. Mem. SAR, Am. Soc. Naval Engrs., Am. Geophys. Union, N.Y. Acad. Scis., Nat. Assn. Underwater Instrs. (instr. 1971—), Royal Inst. Naval Architects, Soc. Naval Architects & Marine Engrs. (chmn. New Eng. sect. 1996—), Marine Tech. Soc. (exec. bd. New Eng. sect. 1980), Navy League, Naval War Coll. Found., Navy Sailing Assn. (ocean master), Pi Mu Epsilon. Achievements include rsch. in integrated systems modeling and engring. of deep ocean systems; devel. of algorithms for simulation of hydromechs. of ocean systems and ships; engring. mgmt. of ship and marine environmental response systems, rsch., devel., test and evaluation. Office: USCG R&D Ctr 1082 Shennecossett Rd Groton CT 06340-6048

LIND, CARL BRADLEY, retired museum director; b. Bethel, Vt., Apr. 22, 1929; s. Carl Olaf and Signe Alfield (Anderson) L.; m. Barbara Ann Eskridge, Oct. 22, 1951; children: Carl Garrett, Susan Ann, Craig Ira. BA, Norwich U., 1951; cert., Command and Gen. Staff Coll., Fort Leavenworth, Kans., 1960; MA, Columbia U., 1963; cert., NATO Def. Coll., Rome, 1976. Commd. 2nd lt. U.S. Army, advanced through grades to col., 1968; asst. prof. U.S. Mil. Acad., West Point, N.Y., 1961-64; comdr. 1st Squadron 3rd Armored Cavalry Rgt. U.S. Army, Fed. Republic Germany, 1965-67; sr. advisor Vietnamese Nat. Mil. Acad. U.S. Army, Dalat, Vietnam, 1967-68; chief Congl. Inquiry divsn. Office Sec. of the Army U.S. Army, Washington, 1968-71; area comdr. 2nd ROTC Region U.S. Army, Fort Knox, Ky., 1973-75; exec. for interoperability to SACEUR, SHAPE NATO, Mons, Belgium, 1977-79; exec. v.p. Evans Llewellyn Securities, Bellevue, Wash., 1979-81; dep. dir. Mus. of History and Industry, Seattle, 1984-87, exec. dir., 1988-91, also bd. dirs. Contbr. articles to jours. in field. Neighborhood commr. Boys Scouts Am., Baumholder, Fed. Rep. Germany, 1965-66; pres. PTA, Baumholder, 1965-66; commr. King County (Wash.) Landmarks & Heritage Commn., 1992-96, Wash. State Heritage Caucus, 1990—; bd. dirs. Coast Guard Mus. Northwest, Seattle, 1991—, Hydroplane and Antique Race Boat Mus., Seattle, 1993—; mem. exec. bd. Bigelow House Preservation Assn., Olympia, Wash., 1993-95; mem. adv. coun. Puget Sound Blood Ctr., 1997—. Decorated Bronze star, Dept. Def. Superior Svc. medal. Legion of Merit, Meritorious Svc. medal. Mem. VFW (comdr. Mercer Island, Wash. post 5760 1984-85), Assn. of U.S. Army, U.S. Armor Assn., Ret. Officer Assn., Am. Assn. State and Local History, Lions, Rotary. Home: 3023 Country Club Rd NW Olympia WA 98502-3738

LIND, JAMES FOREST, surgeon, educator; b. Fillmore, Sask., Can., Nov. 22, 1925; s. James Forest and Isabella (Pringle) L.; m. Dorothy Anne Berlette, Aug. 23, 1950; children: Heather, James, Scott, Robert, Gregory. M.D., C.M., Queen's U., 1951. Intern Hamilton (Ont.) Gen. Hosp., 1951-52, resident in pathology, 1952-53; fellow in anatomy Queen's U., 1953-54, fellow in medicine, 1954-55; fellow in surgery, 1955-56; registrar in surgery Liverpool, 1956-58; fellow in physiology Mayo Found., 1958-60; lectr. in surgery U. Man., 1960-62, asst. prof. surgery, 1962-64, assoc. prof., 1964-66, prof., 1966-72, head dept. surgery, 1969-72; prof., chmn. dept. surgery McMaster U., 1972-79; prof., chmn. dept. surgery Eastern Va. Med. Sch., 1979-94, prof. emeritus, 1994—; dir. surgery Med. Center Hosps., Norfolk, Va., 1979-94; chief surgery Sentara Hosps., 1991—; hon. cons. attending staff Norfolk Gen. Hosp., Leigh Meml. Hosp., Norfolk, De Paul Hosp., Norfolk; practice medicine specializing in surgery Norfolk, 1979-95; vis. prof. U. B.C., 1966, U. Alta., 1967, U. Sask., 1968, Royal Victoria Hosp., 1969, McGill U., 1969, U. Calgary, 1969, Meml. U., Newfoundland, 1973, Harvard U., 1972, numerous others. Contbr. numerous articles to med. jours. Served with RCAF, 1943-45; lt. comdr. RCN(R), 1948-65. John S. McEashern fellow Can. Cancer Soc., 1956-57; recipient George Christian Hoffman award Queen's U., 1957-58; John and Mary Markle scholar, 1960; other honors. Mem. Royal Coll. Phys. and Surg. Can., Can. Assn. Clin. Surgeons, Can. Assn Gastroenterology (pres. 1972), Can. Soc. Clin. Investigation, Am. Surg. Assn., Central Surg. Assn., Mayo Alumni Assn., Soc. Surg. Chmn., Soc. Univ. Surgeons, Soc. Surgery Alimentary Tract, A.C.S., AMA, Va. Med. Soc., Va. Surg. Soc., Southeastern Surg. Congress, Soc. Am. Gastrointestinal Endoscopic Surgeons (pres. 1986), Am. Motility Soc., Assn. Acad. Surgery, Norfolk Medicine Acad., Esophageal Club. Home: 4044 Sherwood Ln Virginia Beach VA 23455-5613 Office: 825 Fairfax Ave Norfolk VA 23507-1914

LIND, JON ROBERT, lawyer; b. Evanston, Ill., July 4, 1935; s. Robert A. and Ruth (Anderson) L.; m. Jane Langfitt, Aug. 29, 1959; children: Jon Robert Jr., Elizabeth Neal, Susan Porter. AB, Harvard U., 1957, LLB, 1960; diploma in comparative law, Cambridge (Eng.) U., 1961. Bar: Ill. 1961. Assoc. Isham, Lincoln & Beale, Chgo., 1961-68, ptnr., 1968-88; ptnr. McDermott, Will & Emery, Chgo., 1988-96, of counsel, 1997—. Atty. Winnetka (Ill.) Park Dist., 1973-78; bd. dirs. Swedish-Am. Mus. Ctr., 1988-96. Mem. ABA, Chgo. Bar Assn., Harvard U. Alumni Assn. (sec. 1970-73), Econ. Club Chgo., Legal Club Chgo., Law Club Chgo. Home: 644 Walden Rd Winnetka IL 60093-2035 Office: McDermott Will & Emery 227 W Monroe St Chicago IL 60606-5016

LIND, LEVI ROBERT, classics educator, author; b. Trenton, N.J., July 29, 1906; s. John Edward and Lydia (Nieminen) L.; m. Elena Marchant y Riquelme, Aug. 25, 1929; 1 dau., Rosa Elena (Mrs. D.C. Fuchs). B.A., U. Ill., 1929, M.A., 1932, Ph.D., 1936. Asst. prof., assoc. prof. classics Wabash Coll., Crawfordsville, Ind., 1929-40; successively asst. prof., assoc. prof., prof., Univ. Disting. prof. classics U. Kans., Lawrence, 1940—; chmn. dept. U. Kans., 1940-64; vis. research prof. history medicine UCLA, summer 1959, U. Ill., summer 1937, 45; sec. Am. Com. on Medieval Latin Dictionary, UAI, 1937-41; U. Kans. rep. to advis. council Am. Acad. in Rome; pres. Central Labor Union, AFL, Lawrence, 1948-49. Author: Medieval Latin Studies: Their Nature and Possibilities, 1941, The Vita Sancti Malchi of Reginald of Canterbury: a critical edition, 1942, The Epitome of Andreas Vesalius, 1949, Lyric Poetry of the Italian Renaissance: an Anthology With Verse Translations, 1954, Ten Greek Plays in Contemporary Translations, 1957, Latin Poetry in Verse Translation, 1957, Ecclesiale by Alexander of Villa Dei, 1958, Berengario da Carpi, A Short Introduction to Anatomy, 1959, Vergil's Aeneid, 1963, Aldrovandi on Chickens: The Ornithology of Ulisse Aldrovandi (1600), 1963, Epitaph for Poets and Other Poems, 1966, Twentieth Century Italian Poetry: a Bilingual Anthology, 1974, Johann Wolfgang von Goethe, Roman Elegies and Venetian Epigrams, 1974, Studies in Pre-Vesalian Anatomy, 1975, Ovid, Tristia, 1975, André Chénier, Elegies and Camille, 1978, Gabriele Zerbi, Gerontocomia: On the Care of the Aged and Maximianus, Elegies on Old Age and Love, 1988, The Letters of Giovanni Garzoni: Bolognese Humanist and Physician (1419-1505), 1992, Berengario da Carpi, On Fracture of the Skull or Cranium, 1990, An Epitaph Years After, 1990; editor: Problemata Varia Anatomica, 1968. Fulbright research grantee Rome, Italy, 1954-55; NIH grantee in history of medicine, 1960-63; Am. Council Learned Socs. fellow, 1940. Mem. Am. Philol. Assn., Classical Assn. Middle West and South, Medieval Acad. Am., Soc. Ancient Medicine, Phi Beta Kappa (com. qualifications united chpts. 1955-61). Club: Discussion. Home: 4817 Baja Court NE Albuquerque NM 87111

LIND, MARSHALL L., academic administrator. Dean Sch. Extended and Grad. Studies U. Alaska, Juneau, until 1987, chancellor, 1987—. Office: U of Alaska Southeast Office of Chancellor 11120 Glacier Hwy Juneau AK 99801-8625*

LIND, NIELS CHRISTIAN, civil engineering educator; b. Copenhagen, Mar. 10, 1930; s. Axel Holger and Karen (Larsen) L.; m. Veronica Claire Hummel, Nov. 29, 1957 (div. 1979); children: Julie Wilhelmina, Peter Christian, Adam Conrad; m. Virginia Patricia Cano Reynoso, Jan. 26, 1985 (div. 1996); 1 child, Andreas. MSc, Tech. U. Denmark, 1953; PhD, U. Ill., 1959. Design engr. Dominia Ltd., Copenhagen, 1953-54; engr. I Bell Telephone Co., Montreal, 1954-55; field engr. Drake-Merritt, Labrador, Nfld., 1955; asst. prof. U. Ill., Urbana, 1959-60; assoc. prof. civil engring. U. Waterloo, Ont., 1960-62, prof., 1962-91, disting. prof. emeritus, 1992, dir. Inst. Risk Research, 1982-88; adj. prof. U. Victoria, B.C., 1993-95. Recipient Ostenfeld gold medal, 1978; recipient Cancam award Can. Congress Applied Mechanics, 1981. Fellow Royal Soc. Can., Am. Acad. Mechanics (pres. 1972-73). Home: 504-640 Montreal St, Victoria, BC Canada V8V 1Z8

LIND, THOMAS OTTO, barge transportation company executive; b. New Orleans, Apr. 24, 1937; s. Henry Carl Lind and Elinor (Rooney) Messersmith; m. Eugenia Niehaus, June 8, 1963; children: Elinor Ashley, Elizabeth Kelly. BSME, Tulane U., 1959, LLB, 1965. Cert. mech. engr., 1959. Assoc. Jones, Walker, Waechter, Poitevent, Carrere and Denegre, New Orleans, 1965-66; v.p., sec., counsel Ingram Corp., New Orleans, 1966-84; v.p. Gulf Fleet Marine Corp., New Orleans, 1984-85; v.p., regulatory counsel, sec. and asst. treas. New Orleans Pub. Svc., Inc. and La. Power and Light Co., 1985-92; regional counsel for La. Entergy Svcs., Inc., 1993-94; risk mgr., sec. Canal Barge Co., Inc., New Orleans, 1994—. Trustee Metairie Park Country Day Sch., 1991-95; mem. bd. govs. Trinity Sch., New Orleans, 1982-85; vestryman Trinity Ch., New Orleans, 1987-91; active Family of Cmty. and Utility Supporters, New Orleans, 1987-94. Lt. (j.g.) USN, 1959-62; comdr. USNR, 1962-79. Mem. ABA (mem. ho. dels. 1996—), La. State Bar Assn. (bd. dirs. corp. law sect. 1973-75), New Orleans Bar Assn. (bd. dir. 1989—, 2d v.p. 1989-90, sec. 1992-93, 1st v.p. 1993-94, pres.-elect 1994-95, pres. 1995-96, bd. dirs. New Orleans B-Pro Bono project 1994-96), La. Orgn. for Jud. Excellence (bd. dirs.), New Orleans Lawn Tennis Club (pres. 1986-88). Republican. Episcopalian. Avocations: tennis, jogging, numismatics. Home: 1126 Octavia St New Orleans LA 70115-3129 Office: Canal Barge Co Inc 835 Union St New Orleans LA 70112-1401

LINDA, GERALD, advertising and marketing executive; b. Boston, Nov. 25, 1946; s. Edward Linda and Anne Beatrice (Lipofsky) Coburn; m. Claudia Wollack, Sept. 24, 1978; children—Jonathan Daniel Rezny, Jessica Simone. BS in Bus. Adminstrn., Northeastern U., 1969, MBA, 1971; postgrad., U. Mich., 1971-75. Faculty U. Ky., Lexington, 1975-77; ptnr. Tatham-Laird & Kudner, Chgo., 1977-80; v.p. Marsteller, Chgo., 1980-84; sr. v.p. HCM, Chgo., 1984-86; pres. Gerald Linda & Assocs., Chgo., 1986-89; prin. Kurtzman/Slavin/Linda, Inc., Chgo., 1990-93, Kapuler Mkgt.

Rsch., Chgo., 1993-94; pres. Gerald Linda & Assocs., Glenview, Ill., 1994—. Mem. editorial review bd. Jour. Current Issues and Rsch. in Advt., 1984—. Mem. Am. Mktg. Assn. (exec.), Assn. for Consumer Rsch.

LINDAHL, THOMAS JEFFERSON, university dean; b. Norwalk, Wis., July 4, 1937; s. Gust Adolf and Mabel Louise (Zietlow) L.; m. Lee Ann Snowberry, Dec. 22, 1962; children: Gary, Mark. BS, U. Wis., 1960; MEd, U. Ill., 1970; PhD, Iowa State U., 1977. Instr. Stockton (Ill.) Community High Sch., 1968-74, Highland Community Coll., Freeport, Ill., 1968-74; instr. Iowa State U., Ames, 1974-75; chmn. dept. Area I Vocat.-Tech. Sch., Calmar, Iowa, 1975-77; assoc. prof., chmn. agrl. bus. dept. U. Minn., Waseca, 1977-83, vice chancellor, 1983-90, acting chancellor, 1990-91; dean Coll. Agriculture U. Wis., Platteville, 1991-94, dean Coll. Bus. Industry, Life Sci. and Agr., 1994—; cons., evaluator North Ctrl. Assn. Commn. on Instns. Higher Edn., Chgo., 1985—; numerous presentations in field. Author: (with Bennie L. Byler) Professional Education In-Service Needs of Agriculture Instructors in Iowa Post Secondry Area Vocational Schools, 1977, (with Wayne Robinson and N.J. Guderon) Cooperative College of Kenya Feasibility Study for Expansion, 1980, (with Myron A. Eighmy) An Individualized Course in Getting Started, 1980, (with James L. Gibson) Associate Instructor Handbook, 1980; also articles and corr. courses. Lay speaker United Meth. Ch., 1980—; v.p. Am. Assn. Colls. & Schs. Agr., 1995-96pres. 1996-97; pres. Wis. Rural Leadership Program Bd., 1995-97. Recipient hon. state degree Wis. Future Farmers Am., 1993. Fellow Nat. Assn. Coll. Tchrs. Agr. (exec. com., v.p. 1991-92, pres. 1992-93); mem. NEA, Nat. Vocat. Agrl. Tchrs. Assn., Am. Vocat. Assn., Wis. Vocat. Assn., Minn. Vocat. Agrl. Tchrs. Assn. (25-yr. Tchg. award 1985), Iowa Vocat. Agrl. Tchrs. Assn. (15-yr. Membership award), Wis. Assn. Inst. Agr., Am. Assn. Colls. and Schs. Agr. and Renewable Resources (pres. 1996-97), Phi Delta Kappa, Kappa Delta Pi, Phi Kappa Phi. Home: 295 Flower Ct Platteville WI 53818-1915 Office: U Wis Coll Agr University Plz Platteville WI 53818

LINDAMOOD, JOHN BEYER, lawyer; b. Columbus, Ohio, Jan. 18, 1941; s. H. Ray and Betty B. (Beyer) L.; children: Jennifer, J. Brad. AB, DePauw U., 1963; JD, Western Res. U., 1966. Bar: Ohio 1966, U.S. Dist. Ct. (no. dist.) Ohio 1968, U.S. Ct. Appeals (6th cir.) 1984, U.S. Supreme Ct. 1986. Assoc. Carson, Vogelgesang & Sheehan, Canton, Ohio, 1966-71; ptnr. Vogelgesang, Howes & Lindamood, Canton, 1971-79, Vogelgesang, Howes, Lindamood & Brunn, Canton, 1979—. Editor Western Res. Law Rev., 1965-66. Pres. Canton Exch. Club, 1970; v.p. Canton Jaycees, 1970-71; pres. Stark County Bar Assn., Canton, 1989-90. Fellow Ohio State Bar Found.; mem. ABA, Def. Rsch. Inst., Ohio State Bar Assn. (exec. com. 1982-85), Ohio Assn. Civil Trial Attys. Office: Vogelgesang Howes Lindamood & Brunn 400 Tuscarawas St W Canton OH 44702-2018

LINDARS, LAURENCE EDWARD, retired health care products executive; b. N.Y.C., Oct. 14, 1922; s. Arthur John and Florence Vera (Cunard) L.; m. Mary Gibson Grandy, Jan. 22, 1972; children—John L., William A., Nancy E. Student, Dartmouth Coll., 1943-44; B.S., Columbia U., 1947. Sr. auditor Arthur Young & Co., N.Y.C., 1947-51; chief acct. Deering, Milliken & Co., 1951-53; treas., dir. Poloron Products, Inc., New Rochelle, N.Y., 1953-58; controller Atlas Gen., Inc., N.Y.C., 1958-59; controller, treas., dir. fin. planning Pepperidge Farm, Inc., Norwalk, Conn., 1959-67; with C.R. Bard, Inc., Murray Hill, N.J., 1967-88; dir. C.R. Bard, Inc., 1972-92, vice chmn., 1983-88; mem. adv. bd. of Summit Trust Co., 1970-84. Trustee Overlook Hosp., 1973-79, Found., 1988-91, treas., 1989-90; trustee Epilepsy Found. N.J., 1985-90, pres., 1986-87, chmn., 1988-90. Lt. (j.g.) USNR, 1943-46. Mem. Fin. Execs. Inst., Canoe Brook Country Club, Harbour Ridge Yacht and Country Club, Delta Upsilon. Presbyterian.

LINDAU, JAMES H., grain exchange executive; b. Red Wing, Minn., May 21, 1933; s. Gottfrid and Stasia J. (Holmstrom) L.; m. Barbara Ann Marie Braaten, June 12, 1955; 1 child, James H. Jr. BA, Grinnell Coll., 1955. Mgmt. trainee The Glidden Co., Indpls., 1955-56; adminstrv. asst. Honeywell, Mpls., 1959-60; commodity merchandising v.p. The Pillsbury Co., Fresno, Mpls., 1960-83; mayor City of Bloomington, Minn., 1977-88; pres. Mpls. Grain Exch., 1988—; bd. dirs. Nat. Futures Assn., Chgo., mem. exec. com., 1996—; bd. dirs. Nat. Grain Trade Coun., Washington, vice chmn., 1996; owner franchise Burger King Restaurant, Burnsville, 1983—; mem. agrl. tech. adv. com. Depts. of Agriculture and Trade, 1990-94; bd. dirs. Can./Minn. Bus. Coun. Mem. Bloomington Bd. Edn., 1972-75, chmn., 1973-75; mem. Hennepin County Vo-Tech. Sch. Bd., Mpls., 1972-75, Hennepin Parks Found., 1990-92; candidate for lt. gov. Minn. (Rep., primary), 1982; candidate for gov. Minn. (Rep., primary), 1986; pres. Bloomington Minn. Port Authority, 1982-87. Capt. USAF, 1956-59. George F. Baker scholar Grinnell Coll., 1951-55; recipient Outstanding Leader award City of Bloomington, 1986, Good Neighbor award WCCO Radio, Mpls., 1987. Mem. Am. Swedish Inst., Svenska Sallskapet, Swedish Am. C. of C. (pres. Minn. chpg. 1990-94), Grand Nat. Quail Club (treas. 1986). Lutheran. Avocations: hunting, fishing, golfing, cooking, politics. Office: Mpls Grain Exch 400 Grain Exchange Minneapolis MN 55415-1411

LINDAUER, JOHN HOWARD, II, newspaper publisher; b. Montclair, N.J., Nov. 20, 1937; s. John Howard and Louise (Platts) L.; m. Jacqueline Shelly, Sept. 2, 1960 (dec. 1992); children: Susan, John Howard; m. Dorothy Oremus, Sept. 1995. BS, Ariz. State U., 1960; PhD in Econs., Okla. State U., 1964. Asst. prof. econs. Occidental Coll., L.A., 1964-66; assoc. prof. Claremont (Calif.) Men's Coll. and Grad Sch., 1966-70, prof., chmn. econs., 1970-74; dean Coll. Bus. Murray (Ky.) State U., 1974-76; chancellor U. Alaska, Anchorage, 1976-78; commr. Alaska Pipeline, Anchorage, 1978; pres., chief exec. officer Alaska Industry and Energy Corp., Anchorage, 1978—; mem. Alaska Ho. of Reps., 1983-84; Rep. candidate for gov., 1990; bd. dirs. various cos.; owner various newspapers and radio sta.; cons. econ. policy and devel. U.S. Congress; cons. econs. U.S. corps; mem. AF Adv. Bd. Author: Macroeconomics, 1968, 71, 76, Economics: The Modern View, 1977, Land Taxation and the Indian Economic Development, 1979; editor Macroeconomic Readings; contbr. articles to profl. jours. Co-founder, vice chmn. Group against Smog Pollution, 1968; pres. So. Calif. Econ. Assn., 1974. With Army U.S., 1955-57. Fulbright prof., India, 1972; vis. prof. U. Sussex, Eng., 1972-73. Home: 3933 Geneva Pl Anchorage AK 99508-5055

LINDBERG, CHARLES DAVID, lawyer; b. Moline, Ill., Sept. 11, 1928; s. Victor Samuel and Alice Christine (Johnson) L.; m. Marian J. Wagner, June 14, 1953; children: Christine, Breta, John, Eric. AB, Augustana Coll., Rock Island, Ill., 1950; LLB, Yale U., 1953. Bar: Ohio 1954. Assoc. Taft, Stettinius & Hollister, Cin., 1953-61, ptnr., 1961-85; mng. ptnr. Taft, Stettinius & Hollister, 1985—; dir. Cin. Bengals Profl. Football Team, Gibson Greetings, Inc., Knowlton Constrn. Co.; chmn. bd. dirs. Schonstedt Instrument Co., 1994-97. Editor Nat. Law Jour., 1979-90. Sec. Good Samaritan Hosp., Cin.; bd. dirs. Taft Broadcasting Co., Cin., 1973-87, Dayton Walther Corp., 1986-87; bd. dirs. Augustana Coll., 1978-87, 91—, sec., 1981-82, vice-chmn., 1982-83, chmn., 1983-86; pres. Cin. Bd. Edn., 1971, 74, Zion Luth. Ch., Cin., 1966-69; chmn. policy com. Hamilton County Rep. Com., 1981-90; mem. exec. com. Ohio Rep. Fin. Com., 1989-90; trustee Greater Cin. Ctr. Econ. Edn., 1976-91, pres., 1987-89, chmn., 1989-91; chmn. law firm divsn. Fine Arts Fund, 1985; trustee Pub. Libr. Cin. and Hamilton County, 1982—, pres., 1989, 96. Mem. Ohio Bar Assn., Cin. Bar Assn., Greater Cin. C. of C. (trustee 1985, exec. com., vice chmn. govt. and cmty. affairs com. 1989-91), Ohio Libr. Trustees Assn. (bd. dirs. 1986-87), Ohio C. of C. (bd. dirs. 1988-89), Queen City Club (sec. 1989-91), Commonwealth Club, Comml. Club (sec. 1994-96), Cin. Country Club, Optimists. Office: 1800 Star Bank Ctr 425 Walnut St Cincinnati OH 45202

LINDBERG, DONALD ALLAN BROR, library administrator, pathologist, educator; b. N.Y.C., Sept. 21, 1933; s. Harry B. and Frances Seeley (Little) L.; m. Mary Musick, June 8, 1957; children: Donald Allan Bror, Christopher Charles Seeley, Jonathan Edward Moyer. AB, Amherst Coll., 1954, ScD (hon.), 1979; MD, Columbia U., 1958; ScD (hon.), SUNY, 1987; LLD (hon.), U. Mo., Columbia, 1990. Diplomate Am. Bd. Pathology, Am. Bd. Med. Examiners (exec. bd. 1987-91). Rsch. asst. Amherst Coll., 1954-55; intern in pathology Columbia-Presbyn. Med. Ctr., 1958-59, asst. resident in pathology, 1959-60; asst. in pathology Coll. Physician and Surgeons Columbia U., N.Y.C., 1958-60; instr. pathology Sch. of Medicine U. Mo., 1962-63, asst. prof. Sch. of Medicine, 1963-66, assoc. prof. Sch. of Medicine, 1966-69, prof. Sch. of Medicine, 1969-84, dir. Diagnostic Microbiology Lab. Sch. of Medicine, 1960-63, dir. Med. Ctr. Computer Program Sch. of Medicine, 1962-70, staff, exec. dir. for health affairs Sch. of Medicine, 1968-70, prof., chmn. dept. info. sci. Sch. of Medicine, 1969-71; dir. Nat. Libr. of Medicine, Bethesda, Md., 1984—; adj. prof. pathology U. Md. Sch. Medicine, 1988—, clin. prof. pathology U. Va., 1992—; dir. Nat. Coord. Office for High Performance Computing and Comms., exec. office of Pres., Office Sci. & Tech. Policy, 1992-95; mem. computer sci./engring. bd. Nat. Acad. Sci., 1971-74, chmn. Nat. Adv. Com. Artificial Intelligence in Medicine, Stanford U., 1975-84; U.S. rep. to Internat. Med. Info. Assn./Internat. Fedn. Info. Processing, 1975-84; bd. dirs. Am. Med. Info. Assn., 1992—; adv. coun. Inst. Medicine, 1992—. Author: The Computer and Medical Care, 1968; The Growth of Medical Information Systems in the United States, 1979; editor: (with W. Siler) Computers in Life Science Research, 1975; (with others) Computer Applications in Medical Care, 1982; editor Methods of Info. in Medicine, 1970-83, assoc. editor, 1983—; editor Jour. Med. Systems, 1976—, Med. Informatics Jour., 1976—; chief editor procs. 3d World Conf. on Med. Informatics, 1980; editorial bd. Jour. of AMA, 1991—; contbr. articles to jours. Recipient Silver Cord award Internat. Fedn. for Info. Processing, 1980, Walter C. Alvarez award Am. Med. Writers Assn. 1989, PHS Surgeon Gen.'s medallion, 1989, Nathan Davis award AMA, 1989, Presdl. Disting. Exec. Rank award, Sr. Exec. Svc., Outstanding Svc. medal Uniformed Svcs. U. Health Scis., 1992, Computers in Healthcare Pioneer award, 1993, recognition award High Performance Computing Industry, 1995, silver award U.S. Nat. Commn. on Librs. and Info. Scis., 1996, meritorious award Coun. Biol. Editors, 1996; Simpson fellow Amherst Coll., 1954-55; Markle scholar in acad. medicine, 1964-69. Fellow AAAS; mem. Inst. Medicine of NAS, Coll. Am. Pathologists (commn. on computer policy and coordination 1981-84), Mo. Med. Assn., Assn. for Computing Machines, Salutis Unitas (Am. v.p. 1981-91), Am. Assn. for Med. Systems and Informatics (internat. com. 1982-89, bd. dirs. 1982, editor conf. procs. 1983, 84), Gorgas Meml. Inst. Tropical and Preventive Medicine (bd. dirs. 1987—), Am. Med. Informatics Assn. (pres. 1988-91), Sigma Xi. Democrat. Club: Cosmos (Washington). Avocations: photography; riding. Home: 13601 Esworthy Rd Germantown MD 20874-3319 Office: Nat Libr of Medicine 8600 Rockville Pike Bethesda MD 20894-0001

LINDBERG, DUANE R., minister, historian, church body administrator; b. Thief River Falls, Minn., Apr. 16, 1933; s. Edgar and Alice (Amundson) L.; m. E. Mardell Kvitne, June 6, 1954; children: Erik Duane, Karen Kristin Kelle, Karl Stephen, Martha Alice Stone, Kristian John. BS in Chemistry, U. N.D., 1954; MDiv in Theology, Luther Sem., St. Paul, 1961; MA in Am. Studies, U. Minn., 1969, PhD in Am. Studies, 1975. Rsch. chemist DuPont Co., 1954; tchg. asst. chemistry dept. U. Wis., Madison, 1956-57; chemist Minn. Farm Bur. Lab., St. Paul, 1957-59; pastor Epping and Wheelock (N.D.) Luth. Chs., 1961-68; rsch. historian Minn. State Hist. Soc., St. Paul, 1969-71; pastor Zion Luth. Ch., West Union, Iowa, 1971-78; sr. pastor Trinity Luth. Ch., Waterloo, Iowa, 1978-87, Acension Luth. Ch., Waterloo, 1987—; presiding pastor Am. Assn. Luth. Chs., Mpls., 1987—; vis. prof. Upper Iowa U., Fayette, 1976-77; adj. prof. Am. Luth. Theol. Sem., St. Paul, 1996-97. Author: Uniting Word, 1969, Men of the Cloth, 1980; contbr. articles to profl. jours. Bd. dirs. Palmer Meml. Hosp., West Union, Iowa, Allen Meml. Hosp., Waterloo, 1979—; founder, bd. mem. Buffalo Trails Mus., Epping, N.D., 1964-68; founder, bd. mem. Fayette County Hist. Soc., West Union, 1975-78; dean Decorah Conf. Am. Luth. Ch., 1976-78, exec. com. Iowa Dist., 1976-78; bd. dirs. Great Plains Inst. Theology, 1965-68. With U.S. Army, 1955-56. Recipient award of commendation Concordia Hist. Inst., St. Louis, Nehemiah award Abiding World Ministries, Mpls., 1990, award of excellence Allen Meml. Hosp., Waterloo, 1995. Mem. numerous profl. ministerial groups and ch. bds., Rotary, Sons of Norway. Office: Amer Assn of Lutheran Churches 10800 Lyndale Ave S Ste 120 Minneapolis MN 55420 also: Am Assn Luth Chs 2211 Maynard Ave Waterloo IA 50701

LINDBERG, GEORGE W., federal judge; b. Crystal Lake, Ill., June 21, 1932; s. Alger Victor and Rilla (Wakem) L. BS, Northwestern U., 1954, JD, 1957. V.p., legal counsel John E. Reid & Assocs., Chgo., 1955-68; ptnr. Franz, Franz, Wardell & Lindberg, Crystal Lake, 1968-73; comptr. State of Ill., Springfield, 1973-77; dep. atty. gen. State of Ill., Chgo., 1977-78; justice Ill. Appellate Ct., Elgin, 1978-89; dist. judge U.S. Dist. Ct. (no. dist.) Ill., Chgo., 1989—; chmn. Ill. House Com. on Judiciary, Com. on Ethics, Springfield, 1970-73. Holder numerous govt. offices, 1966—. Office: US Dist Ct 219 S Dearborn St Ste 1460 Chicago IL 60604-1705*

LINDBERG, RICHARD CARL, editor, author, historian; b. Chgo., June 14, 1953; s. Oscar Waldemar and Helen Marie (Stone) L.; m. Denise Kay, July 1, 1978. BA, Northeastern Ill. U., Chgo., 1974, MA, 1987. Mgr. Sears Roebuck, Chgo., 1971-84; scriptwriter Signature Group, Schaumburg, Ill., 1984-88; sr. editor Crime Books, Inc., Wilmette, Ill., 1989-92; editor-in-chief Ill. Police and Sheriffs News, Palatine, Ill., 1992—; team historian Chgo. White Sox Baseball Team, 1985—; speaker and lectr. on Chgo. history and baseball, Chgo. Author: Stuck on the Sox, 1978, Who's on Third?, The Chicago White Sox Encyclopedia, 1984, Chicago Ragtime: Another Look at Chicago 1880-1920, 1985, re-pub. as: Chicago by Gaslight: A History of Chicago's Netherworld 1880-1920, 1996, To Serve and to Collect: Chicago Politics and Police Corruption 1855-1960, 1991, Passport's Guide to Ethnic Chicago, 1992, Stealing First in a Two Team Town: The White Sox from Comisky to Reinsdorf, 1994, Quotable Chicago, 1996, The White Sox Encyclopedia, 1997; contbg. writer Encyclopedia of Major League Team Histories, 1991, The Ballplayers, 1990, A Kid's Guide to Chicago, 1980, Encyclopedia of World Crime, 1990; contbr. articles to Chigo. History, USA Today mag., others. Mem. Soc. Midland Authors (v.p.), Chgo. Crime Commn. Chgo. Press Vet. Assn., Phi Alpha Theta (pres. chpt. 1988-91, Robert Zegger Meml. award 1987). Republican. Methodist. Home: 5915 N Navarre Ave Chicago IL 60631-2628 Office: Combined Cos Police Assn 55 S Northwest Hwy Palatine IL 60067-6230

LINDBERG, TOD MARSHALL, editor, writer; b. Syracuse, N.Y., Feb. 25, 1960; s. Robert Sheridan and Dorothy Louise (Farris) L.; m. Christine Ann Tedeschi, Apr. 29, 1989; children: Abby Marshall, Molly Robins. B.A., U. Chgo., 1982. Asst. editor Pub. Interest, N.Y.C., 1982-83, mng. editor, 1983-85; exec. editor Nat. Interest, Washington, 1985-86; sr. editor Insight, Washington, 1986, exec. editor news, 1987-90, dep. mng. editor, 1990-91; edtl. page editor The Washington Times, 1991—; contbg. editor The Weekly Standard, 1995-96; media fellow The Hoover Instn., 1996; editorial cons. Manhattan Inst., N.Y.C., 1983, Inst. for Ednl. Affairs, N.Y.C., 1983-85, Simon & Schuster, Pubs., N.Y.C., 1985. Contbr. articles to profl. jours. Office: The Washington Times 3600 New York Ave NE Washington DC 20002-1947

LINDBLAD, RICHARD ARTHUR, retired health services administrator, drug abuse epidemiologist; b. Atlantic, Iowa, July 15, 1937; s. Clifford Robert and Emma Ruth (Dunham) L.; children: Julie, Richard, Mark. B.S., San Jose State Coll., 1961; M.S., U. Colo., 1965; M.P.H., Johns Hopkins U., 1971, Dr.P.H., 1974. Capt. USPHS, 1961, col., 1975, ret. capt., 1961-94; various assignments including adminstrn., epidemiology, research and prevention of substance abuse disorders Fed. Drug Abuse Treatment Hosp., Ft. Worth, Denver; now dir. internat. programs Nat. Inst. on Drug Abuse, Rockville, Md.; cons. in drug abuse epidemiology WHO, UN; designed and supervised devel. of UN Internat. Drug Abuse Assessment System; cons. on drug abuse rsch. and program devel. Designed and supervised devel. of the International Visiting Scientist and Technical Exchange program of the dept. of Health and Human Svcs.; Contbr. articles to profl. jours. Mem. Am. Public Health Assn., Md. Public Health Assn., Commd. Officers Assn. USPHS, Nat. Assn. Uniformed Services. Home: PO Box 179 Libertytown MD 21762-0179

LINDBURG, DAYTHA EILEEN, physician assistant; b. Emporia, Kans., June 24, 1952; d. Kenneth Eugene and Elsie Eileen (Smith) L. BS cum laude, Kans. State U., 1974; BS magna cum laude, Wichita State U., 1976. Registered cert. physician asst. Physician asst. in family practice Fredrickson Clinic, Lindsborg, Kans., 1976-93; physician asst. in ob/gyn. Mowery Clinic, Salina, Kans., 1993—; cons. McPherson County (Kans.) Health Dept., 1983—. Mem. adv. bd. Riverview Estates Nursing Home, 1980-86; bd. dirs. McPherson County Humane Soc., 1989-93; choir mem. Messiah Luth. Ch., Lindsborg, 1981—, liturgist, 1991—, mem. Altar Guild, 1976—, mem. music and worship com., 1981-88. Kans. Bd. Regents scholar, 1970-71, Kans. State U. scholar, 1972, 73, Smurthwaite scholar, 1970-74. Mem. Assn. of Physician Assts. in Obstetrics and Gynecology, Kans. Acad. Physician Assts., Am. Acad. Physician Asst., McPherson County-Kans. State U. Alumni Assn. (bd. dirs. 1996—). Avocations: crafts, floral arranging, piano, reading, drawing.

LINDE, HANS ARTHUR, state supreme court justice; b. Berlin, Germany, Apr. 15, 1924; came to U.S., 1939, naturalized, 1943; s. Bruno C. and Luise (Rosenhain) L.; m. Helen Tucker, Aug. 13, 1945; children: Lisa, David Tucker. BA, Reed Coll., 1947; JD, U. Calif., Berkeley, 1950. Bar: Oreg. 1951. Law clk. U.S. Supreme Ct. Justice William O. Douglas, 1950-51; atty. Office of Legal Adviser, Dept. State, 1951-53; pvt. practice Portland, Oreg., 1953-54; legis. asst. U.S. Sen. Richard L. Neuberger, 1955-58; from assoc. prof. to prof. U. Oreg. Law Sch., 1959-76; justice Oreg. Supreme Ct., Salem, 1977-90, sr. judge, 1990—; Fulbright lectr. Freiburg U., 1967-68, Hamburg U., 1975-76; cons. U.S. ACDA, Dept. Def., 1962-76; mem. Adminstrv. Conf. U.S., 1978-82. Author: (with George Bunn) Legislative and Administrative Processes, 1976. Mem. Oreg. Constl. Revision Commn., 1961-62, Oreg. Commn. on Pub. Broadcasting, 1990-93; bd. dirs. Oreg. Pub. Broadcasting, 1993—. With U.S. Army, 1943-46. Fellow Am. Acad. Arts and Scis.; mem. Am. Law Inst. (council), Order of Coif, Phi Beta Kappa.

LINDE, LUCILLE MAE (JACOBSON), motor-perceptual specialist; b. Greeley, Colo., May 5, 1919; d. John Alfred and Anna Julia (Anderson) Jacobson; m. Ernest Emil Linde, July 5, 1946 (dec. Jan. 27, 1959). BA, U. No. Colo., 1941, MA, 1947, EdD, 1974. Cert. tchr. Calif., Colo., Iowa, N.Y.; cert. ednl. psychologist; guidance counselor. Dean of women, dir. residence C.W. Post Coll. of L.I. Univ., 1965-66; asst. dean of students SUNY, Farmingdale, 1966-67; counselor, tchr. West High Sch., Davenport, Iowa, 1967-68; instr. grad. tchrs. and counselors, univ. counselor, researcher No. Ariz. U., Flagstaff, 1968-69; vocat. edn. and counseling coord. Fed. Exemplary Project, Council Bluffs, Iowa, 1970-71; sch. psychologist, counselor Oakdale Sch. Dist., Calif., 1971-73; sch. psychologist, intern Learning and Counseling Ctr., Stockton, Calif., 1972-74; pvt. practice rsch. in motor-perceptual tng. Greeley, 1975—; rschr. ocumeter survey Lincoln Unified Sch. Dist., Stockton, 1980, 81, 82, Manteca (Calif.) H.S., 1981; spkr. Social Sci. Edn. Consortium, U. Colo., Boulder, 1993; presenter seminars in field. Author: Psychological Services and Motor Perceptual Training, 1974, Guidebook for Psychological Services and Motor Perceptual Training (How One May Improve in Ten Easy Lessons!), 1992, Manual for the Lucille Linde Ocumeter: Ocular Pursuit Measuring Instrument, 1992, Motor-Perceptual Training and Visual Perceptual Research (How Students Improved in Seven Lessons!), 1992, Effects of Motor Perceptual Training on Academic Achievement and Ocular Pursuit Ability, 1992; inventor ocumeter, instrument for measuring ocular tracking ability, 1989, target for use, 1991; patentee in field. Mem. Rep. Presdl. Task Force, 1989-96, trustee, 1991-92, charter mem., 1994—, life mem., 1994-95; mem. Rep. Nat. Com., 1990, 93-96, 97, Rep. Nat. Com. on Am. Agenda, 1993, Nat. Rep. Congl. Com., 1990, 92, 93, 95, 96, Nat. Fedn. Rep. Women, Greeley Rep. Women, 1996; advisor Senator Bob Dole for Pres.; charter mem. Rep. Newt Gingrich's Speaker's Task Force, Senator Phil Gramm's Presdl. Steering Com.; at-large-del. Rep. Platform Planning Com.; team leader Nat. Rep. Rapid Response Network, Campaign America, 1996; active Heritage Found., Attention Deficit Disorder Adv. Group, Christian Bus. Men's Assn., Friends U. N.C. Librs., Citizens Against Govt. Waste, 1996, Concerns of Police Survivors, 1996, Nat. Assn. of Police Org. Recipient Presdl. medal of merit and lapel insignia, 1990, Nat. Rep. Senatorial Com., 1991-96, cert. of appreciation Nat. Rep. Congl. Com., 1992, 95, lapel pin Rep. Senatorial Inner Circle, 1990-96, Rep. Presdl. commemorative honor roll, 1993, Rep. Senatorial Freedom medal, 1994, Rep. Legion of Merit award, 1994, 96, Rep. Congl. Order of Freedom award, 1995, Convention medallion Rep. Senatiroial Inner Cir., 1996, Lapel Pin award RNC, 1996, Leadership citation Rep. Senatorial Inner Cir./ Rep. Nat. Conv., 1996, Legion of Merit Rep. Presdl. exec. com., 1996, Honor cert. House Spkr. Newt Gingrich, 1996; named to Rep. Nat. Hall of Honor, 1992. Mem. AAUP, NAFE, Nat. Assn. Sch. Psychologists and Psychometrists (spkr. at conf. 1976), Rep. Senatorial Inner Cir. (name engraved on Ronald Wilson Reagan Eternal Flame of Freedom, 1995, on the Nat. Rep. Victory Monument, Washington, 1996, Rep. Sen. Inner Cir. Conv. Medallion 1996, RNG Mems. Only pin 1996), The Smithsonian Assocs., Nat. Trust for Hist. Preservation, Am. Pers. and Guidance Assn., Nat. Assn. Student Pers. Adminstrs., Nat. Assn. Women Deans and Counselors, Calif. Tchrs. Assn., Internat. Platform Assn., Independence Inst., Assn. Children Learning Disabilities (conf. spkr. 1976), Learning Disabilities Assn. (spkr. internat. conv. 1976), Greeley Rep. Women's Club, Pi Omega Pi, Pi Lambda Theta. Avocations: music, archtl. design. Home: 1954 18th Ave Greeley CO 80631-5208

LINDE, MAXINE HELEN, lawyer, business executive, private investor; b. Chgo., Sept. 2, 1939; d. Jack and Lottie (Kroll) Stern; B.A. summa cum laude, UCLA, 1961; J.D., Stanford U., 1967; m. Ronald K. Linde, June 12, 1960. Bar: Calif. 1968. Applied mathematician, reseach engr. Jet Propulsion Lab., Pasadena, Calif., 1961-64; law clk. U.S. Dist. Ct. No. Calif., 1967-68; mem. firm Long & Levit, San Francisco, 1968-69, Swerdlow, Glikbarg & Shimer, Beverly Hills, Calif., 1969-72; sec., gen. counsel Envirodyne Industries, Inc., Chgo., 1972-89; pres. The Ronald and Maxine Linde Found., 1989—; vice chmn. bd., gen. counsel Titan Fin. Group, LLC, Chgo., 1994—. Mem. bd. visitors Stanford Law Sch., 1989-92, law and bus. adv. coun., 1991-94, dean's adv. coun. 1992-94. Mem. Order of Coif, Phi Beta Kappa, Pi Mu Epsilon, Alpha Lambda Delta.

LINDE, ROBERT HERMANN, economics educator; b. Schlewecke, Germany, July 22, 1944; s. Robert and Emma (Lohmann) L.; m. Sabine Rinck, Mar. 12, 1976 (div. 1985); children: Niels Christian, Johanne Cornelia; m. Ingrid Windus, June 30, 1987. Diploma in Econs., U. Gottingen, Fed. Republic Germany, 1969, D in Polit. Sci., 1977, D in Habilitation, 1981. Asst. U. Gottingen, 1976-81, lectr., 1981-86, prof. econs., 1986-87; prof. econs. U. Luneburg, Fed. Republic Germany, 1987—. Author: Theory of Product Quality, 1977, Pay and Performance, 1984, Introduction to Microeconomics, 3rd edit., 1996; co-author: Production Theory, 1976. Mem. Am. Econ. Assn., Verein für Socialpolitik, European Econ. Assn. Office: U Luneburg, Scharnhorststrasse 1 Haus 4, 21332 Luneburg Germany

LINDE, RONALD KEITH, corporate executive, private investor; b. L.A., Jan. 31, 1940; s. Morris and Sonia Doreen (Hayman) L.; m. Maxine Helen Stern, June 12, 1960. BS with honors, UCLA, 1961; MS (Inst. scholar), Calif. Inst. Tech., 1962, PhD (ARCS scholar, Rutherford scholar), 1964. Cons. Litton Industries, L.A., 1961-63, engr., 1961; materials scientist Poulter Labs., Stanford Rsch. Inst., Menlo Park, Calif., 1964; head solid state rsch. Stanford Rsch. Inst., Menlo Park, Calif., 1965-67; chmn. shock wave physics dept., mgr. tech. svcs. Poulter Labs., 1967, dir. shock and high pressure physics div., 1967-68, chief exec. labs., 1968-69; dir. phys. scis. Stanford Rsch. Inst., 1968-69; chmn. bd., CEO Envirodyne Industries, Inc., Chgo., 1969-89; chmn. bd. The Ronald and Maxine Linde Found., Chgo., 1989—; co-chmn. bd. Titan Fin. Group, LLC, Chgo., 1994—; law and bus. adv. coun. Stanford Law Sch., 1991-94, dean's adv. coun. 1992-94. Contbr. articles to various publs.; patentee in field. Mem. adv. bd. ARCS Found., Chgo., 1993—; mem. Northwestern U. Assocs., 1978—; trustee Calif. Inst. Tech., 1989—, Harvey Mudd Coll., 1989—, vice chmn., bd. trustees, 1993—. Mem. Sigma Xi, Tau Beta Pi, Phi Eta Sigma. Office: Linde Found Unit 5801 180 E Pearson St Chicago IL 60611-2130

LINDEGREN, JACK KENNETH, elementary and secondary education educator; b. Fresno, Calif., Feb. 9, 1931; s. Henry Jack and Katherine (Metzler) L.; m. Betty Jo Rowland, Dec. 1960 (div. Apr. 1963); m. Elaine Finnegan, Apr. 27, 1963; children: Susan Carol, Karen Ann. BA, Fresno State Coll., 1954; MA, Calif. State U., Fresno, 1976. Educator, adminstr. Fresno County, Firebaugh, Calif., 1954-5; educator Calaveras County Schs., San Andreas, Calif., 1964-66, Kings County Schs., Corcoran, Calif., 1966-80, Kern County Schs., Bakersfield, Calif., 1985-87, L.A. Unified Schs., 1985—; educator L.A. Unified Schs., 1977-92; instr. ARC, Hanford, Calif., 1974-79.; instr. County Sci. Insvc., 1985. Inventor electroanalysis device Chrysler award., 1965. Participant Desert Opera, Palmdale, Calif., 1986-88; bd. mem., chmn. ARC, Hanford, 1973-78. Sgt. U.S. Army, 1955-57. Mem. NAS, AAAS, NEA, Nat. Assn. Legions of Honor, Nat. Space Soc., Tehran Shrine, Fresno East/West Game Corcoran Band Club, Santa Clara U.

Alumni Assn., Internat. DeMolay Alumni Assn. (life), Assn. Calif. Sch. Adminstrs., Calif. State U. of Fresno Alumni Assn. (life), Scottish Rite (life), Corcoran/Tulare Masons (life, Bethel guardian 1978-80, Pin 1980), Odd Fellows (30 Yr. Mem. award 1991), Mensa (elder, deacon bushop, 10 v.p. Membership award). Presbyterian. Avocations: reading, science and religious literature (Mensa spl. interest groups in religion).

LINDELL, EDWARD ALBERT, former college president, religious organization administrator; b. Denver, Nov. 30, 1928; s. Edward Gustaf and Estelle (Lundin) L.; m. Patricia Clare Eckert, Sept. 2, 1965; children—Edward Paul, Erik Adam. B.A., U. Denver, 1950, M.A., 1956, Ed.D., 1960, L.H.D. (hon.), 1975; Litt.D. (hon.), Tusculum Coll., 1979; D.H.L. (hon.), Roanoke Coll., 1981; Litt.D (hon.), Christ Coll., Irvine, 1992. Tchr. N. Denver High Sch., 1952-61; asst. dean Coll. Arts and Scis., U. Denver, 1961-65, dean, 1965-75; pres. Gustavus Adolphus Coll., St. Peter, Minn., 1975-80, Luth. Brotherhood Mut. Funds, Mpls., Minn., 1980—; v.p. Lutheran Brotherhood Found., 1980—, exec. dir. Mem. exec. bd. Rocky Mountain Synod Lutheran Ch. Am., 1968—, also pres. bd. coll. edn. and ch. vocations.; Trustee Midland Luth. Coll., Fremont, Nebr., Kans. Wesleyan U., Colo. Assn. Ind. Colls. and Univs., Luth. Med. Center, Wheatridge, Colo., Luth. Sch. Theology, Chgo., 1975—, St. John's U., Minn., 1978—; bd. dirs. Pacific Luth. Theol. Sem., 1978-80, Loretto Heights Coll., Colo., 1978-86, Swedish Council Am., 1978—, Gettysburg Theol. Sem., 1981-83; exec. bd. Luth. Council U.S.A., v.p., 1975—; mem. adv. bd. Royal Swedish Acad. Scis., 1980; v.p. Am.-Swedish Inst., 1980; exec. v.p. for external affairs Luth. Brotherhood, 1981—; pres. Nat. Fraternal Congress Am., 1988—; bd. dirs. Wittenberg U., 1988, Bethany Coll., 1991—, Minn. Orch., 1983—, Am. Scandinavian Found., 1982—, Fairview Hosp., 1982—, U.S. Swedish Found. Internat. Sci. Rsch., 1981— (v.p. 1986—), Habitat for Humanity Internat., 1992—. Named Outstanding Faculty Mem. Coll. Arts and Scis., U. Denver, 1964; decorated knight King of Sweden, 1976; recipient Suomi Disting. Svc. award, 1989. Mem. Swedish Pioneer Hist. Soc. (dir. 1979—), U. Denver Alumni Assn. (Career Alumni Achievement award 1994), Phi Beta Kappa. Office: Luth Brotherhood Mut Funds 625 4th Ave S Minneapolis MN 55415-1624

LINDEMANN, EDNA MEIBOHM, museum director, art consultant; b. Buffalo, N.Y., Feb. 25, 1915; d. Carl H. and Pearl (Nason) Meibohm; m. Fred H. Lindemann (dec.). BS in Art with distinction, U. Buffalo, 1936; MA in Art magna cum laude, Northwestern U., 1939; studies with Eliel Saarinen, Cranbrook Acad., 1940-42; EdD in Art, Columbia U., 1956. Instr. U. Buffalo, N.Y., 1936-47, U. Vt., Burlington, 1945-46, NYU, 1949-56; prof. design SUNY, Buffalo, 1956-66, dir. cultural affairs, 1960-66; founding dir. Burchfield Art Ctr., Buffalo, 1967-85; pvt. practice art appraiser, 1986—; dir. emeritus Burchfield Art Ctr., 1985—; rschr. artist's museums. Organizer exhbns., including Burchfield Internat. Exhbn., 1968, Edwin Dickinson Tribute Exhbn., 1977, 150 Yrs. of Portraiture in Western N.Y., 1981, Design in Buffalo, 1982, Nevelsons of Western N.Y., 1984, Niagara Falls, New Impressions, 1985, Robert N. Blair, A Soldier's Portfolio, 1985; curator exhbn., author catalog The Art Triangle-Burchfield, His Dealer and His Colleagues, 1989. Mem. Creative Leadership Council, Buffalo, 1969—; founding mem., bd. dirs. Maude Gordon Homes Arboretum, Buffalo, 1966-78; trustee Buffalo State Coll. Found., 1969-85. Recipient Focus award Buffalo Courier-Express, 1976, Outstanding Patron award Buffalo Soc. Artists, 1981, Achievement award AAUW, 1983; named Citizen of Yr. Buffalo News, 1985. Mem. Appraisers Assn. Am. Inc., Gallery Assn. N.Y. State (founding, chair 1969-79), Assoc. Coll. and U. Mus. (recording sec. 1980-83). Avocations: landscape and architectural design. Home and Office: 52 Behm Rd West Falls NY 14170-9741

LINDEMER, LAWRENCE BOYD, lawyer, former utility executive, former state justice; b. Syracuse, N.Y., Aug. 21, 1921; s. George F. and Altamae (Reimers) L.; children—Lawrence Boyd, David G. Student, Taft Sch., 1939, Hamilton Coll., 1939-41; A.B., U. Mich., 1943, LL.B., 1948. Bar: Mich. 1948. Asst. pros. atty. Ingham County, 1949-51; asst., commn. on orgn. Exec. Br. Govt., Hoover Comm., 1953-55; partner Foster, Lindemer, Swift & Collins (and predecessor firm), 1955-75; justice Mich. Supreme Ct., Lansing, 1975-76; sr. v.p., gen. counsel Consumers Power Co., 1977-86. Mem. Mich. Ho. of Reps., 1951-52; Republican state chmn., 1957-61; mem. Rep. Nat. Com., 1957-61; Rep. candidate atty. gen. Mich., 1966; bd. regents U. Mich., 1968-75; trustee Gerald R. Ford Found., 1985—. Served with USAAF, 1943-45. Mem. ABA, State. Bar Mich. (commr. 1963-70), Mich. State Bd. Ethics, U. Mich. Alumni Assn. (pres. 1983-85), Am. Automobile Assn. (bd. dirs. 1987-96, chmn. 1993-95), Auto Club Mich. (b.d dirs. 1977-96, chmn. bd. 1985-87). Presbyterian (elder). Home: PO Box 667 Stockbridge MI 49285-0667 Office: Foster Swift Collins & Smith PC 313 Washington Sq S Lansing MI 48933-2122

LINDEN, HENRY ROBERT, chemical engineering research executive; b. Vienna, Austria, Feb. 21, 1922; came to U.S., 1939, naturalized, 1945; s. Fred and Edith (Lermer) L.; m. Natalie Govedarica, 1967; children by previous marriage: Robert, Debra. BS, Ga. Inst. Tech., 1944; MChemE, Poly. U., 1947; PhD, Ill. Inst. Tech., 1952. Chem. engr. Socony Vacuum Labs., 1944-47; with Inst. of Gas Tech., 1947-78, various rsch. mgmt. positions, 1947-61, dir., 1961-69, exec. v.p., dir., 1969-74, pres., trustee, 1974-78; various acad. appointments Ill. Inst. Tech., Chgo, 1954-86, Frank W. Gunsaulus Disting. Prof. chem. engring., 1987-90, McGraw prof. energy and power engring. and mgmt., 1990—, interim pres., CEO, 1989-90, interim chmn., CEO Ill. Inst. Tech. Rsch. Inst., 1989-90; COO, GDC, Inc., Chgo., 1965-73; CEO Gas Devel. Corp. subs. Inst. Gas Tech., Chgo., 1973-78, also bd. dirs.; pres., dir. Gas Rsch. Inst., Chgo., 1976-87, exec. advisor, 1987—; bd. dirs. Centennial Holdings, Inc., AES Corp., Proton Energy Systems, Inc. Author tech. articles; holder U.S. and fgn. patents in fuel tech. Recipient award of merit oper. sect. Am. Gas Assn., 1956, Disting. Svc. award, 1974, Gas Industry Rsch. award, 1982, R&D award Nat. Energy Resources Orgn., 1986, Homer H. Lowry award for excellence in fossil energy rsch. U.S. Dept. Energy, 1991, award U.S. Energy Assn., 1993, Walton Clark medal Franklin Inst., 1972, Bunsen-Pettenkofer-Ehrentafel medal Deutscher Verein des Gas und Wasserfaches, 1978, Alumni medal Ill. Inst. Tech., 1995, Lifetime Achievement award The Energy Daily jour., 1996; named to Hall of Fame, Ill. Inst. Tech., 1982, Engring. Hall of Fame Ga. Tech., 1996. Fellow AIChE, Inst. Energy; mem. NAE, Am. Chem. Soc. (recipient H.H. Storch award, chmn. divsn. fuel chemistry 1967, councilor 1969-77), So. Gas Assn. (hon. life). Office: Ill Inst Tech PH 135 10 W 33rd St Ph 135 Chicago IL 60616-3730 also: Gas Rsch Inst 8600 W Bryn Mawr Ave Chicago IL 60631-3505

LINDENBAUM, SANDFORD RICHARD, lawyer; b. N.Y.C., July 6, 1948; s. Sidney Lewis and Ruth Jane (Krauskopf) L.; m. Leslie Sircus, Jan. 17, 1982; children: Dara, David. BA, Franklin & Marshall Coll., 1970; JD with honors, George Washington U., 1973. Bar: N.Y. 1974, U.S. Dist. Ct. (so. dist.) N.Y. 1975, U.S. Dist. Ct. (no. dist.) N.Y. 1985. Asst. dist. atty. County of Westchester, White Plains, N.Y., 1973-78; from assoc. to ptnr. Bower & Gardner, N.Y.C., 1978-94; assoc. Garbarini & Scher, N.Y.C., 1994—. Mem. ABA, N.Y. State Bar Assn. Office: Garbarini and Scher 1114 Avenue Of The Americas New York NY 10036-7703

LINDENBAUM, S(EYMOUR) J(OSEPH), physicist; b. N.Y.C., Feb. 3, 1925; s. Morris and Anne Lindenbaum; m. Leda Isaacs, June 29, 1958. AB, Princeton U., 1945; MA, Columbia U., 1949, PhD, 1951. With Brookhaven Nat. Lab., Upton, N.Y., 1951—, sr. physicist, 1963-96, sr. physicist emeritus, 1996—, group leader high energy physics research group, 1954-89; vis. prof. U. Rochester, 1958-59; Mark W. Zemansky chair in physics CCNY, 1970-75, Zemansky prof. emeritus, 1985—; cons. Centre de Etudes Nucleaire de Saclay, France, 1957, CERN, Geneva, 1962; head CCNY Experimental High Energy Physics Rsch. Group, 1970—; dep. for sci. affairs ERDA, 1976-77. Author: Particle Interaction Physics at High Energies, 1973. Contbr. articles to profl. jours. Fellow Am. Phys. Soc.; mem. N.Y. Acad. Scis., AAAS. Achievements include discovering nucleon isobars dominated high energy particles interactions, isobar model; inventor on line computer technique in scientific experiments; proved experimentally that Einstein's special theory of relativity was correct down to subnuclear distances one hundredth the radius of a proton; discovered the glueball states predicted by quantum chromodynamics. Office: Brookhaven Nat Lab Dept Physics Upton NY 11973 *I was always fascinated by the orderly and powerful laws of nature. Thus I decided to concentrate on one of mankind's greatest intellectual endeavours—scientific inquiry into the physical laws which govern our universe.*

LINDENBERG, STEVEN PHILLIP, counselor, consultant; b. Lancaster, Pa., Dec. 6, 1945; s. Sidney David and Ruth Lillian (Levine) L.; m. Linda Kathleen Young, Aug. 26, 1967; children: Sara Michelle, Karen Rebecca, Elisabeth Claudine. BS, Millersville U., 1968; MEd, Shippensburg State U., 1974; PhD, U. Ga., 1977. Cert. clin. mental health counselor, Nat. Acad. Cert. Clin. Health Counseling, cert. counselor Nat. Bd. Cert. Counselors, cert. sch. psychologist, Pa. Jr. high sci. tchr. Chambersburg (Pa.) Area Sch. Dist., 1972-74; grad. asst. dept. counseling edn. Univ. Ga., Athens, 1974-77; ptnr., cert. clin. mental health counselor Hershey (Pa.) Psychiat. Assocs., 1977-93; founder Lindenberg Inst. for Therapy, 1993—; co-founder, 1st vice-chair Nat. Acad. Cert. Clin. Mental Health Counselors, Falls Church, Va., 1978-80; founder Lindenberg & David, Assocs., Hershey, 1990—; bd. dirs. Ctrl. Pa. Behavioral Health Network; mem. focus group task force Alternate Paths to Justice for 21st Century Pa. State Supreme Ct., 1996. Mem. editorial bd.: Jour. Mental Health Counseling, 1991-94, author: Group Psychotherapy with People Who Are Dying, 1983; contbr. articles to profl. jours. Founding bd. mem. Hospice of En. Pa., Enola, 1978-87, past pres., mem. bereavement com. 1978-93; mem. profl. devel. com. Am. Cancer Soc., Harrisburg, Pa., 1986-87; past pres., mem. bd. sch. dirs. No. Lebanon Sch. Dist., Fredericksburg, Pa., 1988-93. Decorated Am. Spirit of Honor medal Citizens Com. for Army, Navy and Air Force, Inc., Lackland AFB, Tex., 1968; recipient Jesse Heiges Disting. Alumnus award Shippensburg U., 1996. Mem. AACD (bd. dirs. 1979-80), Am. Mental Health Counselors Assn. (pres. 1979-80, profl. recognition awards 1981, 89, charter mem.), Pa. Mental Health Counselors Assn. (treas. 1993-95, pres. 1995—, eminent practitioner 1988), Pa. Alliance Counseling Profls. (pres.-elect 1995-96, pres. 1996-98), Dauphin County Bar Assn. (task force mem. 1994—), Phi Kappa Phi, Kappa Delta Pi. Avocations: writing, music composition and performance, gardening. Office: Lindenberg Inst Therapy 218 W Governor Rd Hershey PA 17033-1726

LINDENBERGER, HERBERT SAMUEL, writer, literature educator; b. L.A., Apr. 4, 1929; s. Hermann and Celia (Weinkrantz) L.; m. Claire Flaherty, June 14, 1961; children: Michael James, Elizabeth Celia. BA, Antioch Coll., Yellow Springs, Ohio, 1951; PhD, U. Wash., Seattle, 1955. From instr. to prof. English and comparative lit. U. Calif., Riverside, 1954-66; prof. German and English, chmn. program comparative lit. Washington U., St. Louis, 1966-69; Avalon prof. humanities Stanford (Calif.) U., 1969—, chmn. program comparative lit., 1969-82; dir. Stanford Humanities Ctr., 1991-92. Author: On Wordsworth's Prelude, 1963, Georg Büchner, 1964, (play) Lear and Cordelia at Home, 1968, Georg Trakl, 1971, Historical Drama: The Relation of Literature and Reality, 1975, Saul's Fall: A Critical Fiction, 1979, Opera: The Extravagant Art, 1984, The History in Literature: On Value, Genre, Institutions, 1990; contbr. articles to profl. jours. Fulbright scholar Austria, 1952-53; Guggenheim fellow, 1968-69; Nat. Endowment Humanities fellow, 1975-76, 82-83; Stanford U. Humanities Ctr. Fellow, 1982-83. Mem. MLA (pres. 1997—), Am. Comparative Lit. Assn. Office: Stanford U Dept Comparative Lit Stanford CA 94305

LINDENFELD, PETER, physics educator; b. Vienna, Austria, Mar. 10, 1925; came to U.S., 1948, naturalized, 1957; s. Bela and Elda (Lachs) L.; m. Lore Kadden, May 31,1953; children: Thomas, Naomi. Student, U. Man., Can., 1942-43; B.A.Sc., U.B.C., Can., 1946, M.A. Sc., 1948; Ph.D., Columbia U., 1954. Vis. lectr. Drew U., Madison, N.J., 1952-53; instr. Rutgers U., 1953-55, asst. prof. physics, 1955-61, asso. prof., 1961-66, prof., 1966—; cons. summer inst. AID, Tirupati, India, 1965; regional counselor N.J. Am.. Inst. Physics, 1963-71; dir. NSF In-svc. Insts. High Sch. Tchrs., 1964-66; Rutgers Rsch. Coun. fellow and guest scientist Faculte de Scis., U. Paris-Sud, Orsay, France, 1970-71; vis. scholar Kyoto U., Japan, 1982. Contbr. articles to profl. jours. Recipient Warren I. Susman award for excellence in teaching, 1988, Robert A. Millikan Lecture award and medal Am. Assn. Physics Tchrs., 1989. Fellow Am. Phys. Soc.; mem. AAUP, Am. Assn. Physics Tchrs. (hon. mem. N.J. sect.). Home: 121 Harris Rd Princeton NJ 08540-3375 Office: Rutgers U Dept Physics and Astronomy Piscataway NJ 08855-0849

LINDENLAUB, J.C., electrical engineer, educator; b. Milw., Sept. 10, 1933; m. Deborah Hart, 1957; children: Brian, Mark, Anne, David. BS, MIT, 1955, MS, 1957; PhD in Elec. Engring., Purdue U., 1961. From asst. prof. to prof. Purdue U., West Lafayette, Ind., 1961-72, prof. elec. engring., 1972—, dir. Ctr. Instrnl. Devel. Engring., 1977-81; mem. tech. staff Bell Telephone Labs., 1968-69; cons. Western Elec., N.Y. State Bd. Regents, Control Data Corp., J. Warren Rsch. in Higher Edn., Nat. Technol. U. Contbr. articles to profl. jours. Recipient Helen Plants award Frontiers in Edn. Conf., 1980, 87, 93; Danforth Found. assoc., 1966. Fellow IEEE (Edn. Soc. Achievement award 1984, Schmitz award FIE Conf.), Am. Soc. Engring. Edn. (Chester F. Carlson award 1988, Disting. Svc. citation 1993). Office: Purdue Univ Electrical Eng School Lafayette IN 47907

LINDENMEYER, MARY KATHRYN, secondary education educator; b. Denver, Dec. 9, 1952; d. Edward L. and Margaret Mary (Hogan) L. BA in English and History, St. Mary Coll., Leavenworth, Kans., 1975; MA in History, U. No. Colo., 1990; grad. reading specialist, U. Phoenix, 1997. Cert. tchr., Mo., Colo., N.Mex. Tchr. Bishop Hogan H.S., Kansas City, Mo., 1976-82, St. Pius X H.S., Kansas City, Mo., 1982-84, Machebeuf Cath. H.S., Denver, 1984-89; prin. Trinidad (Colo.) Cath. H.S., 1989-90; tchr. Navajo Pine H.S., Navajo, N.Mex., 1990—, chair dept. lang. arts, 1992-96; mem. adj. faculty Navajo C.C., Window Rock, Ariz., 1991—. Recipient Dickerson award U. No. Colo. History Fellowship, 1989; named Disting. Tchr., Gallup-McKinley County, 1993; NEH scholar, 1985, 89. Mem. ASCD, Nat. Coun. Tchrs. English. Roman Catholic. Avocations: writing, reading, yard work, photography. Office: Navajo Pine High Sch PO Box 1286 Gallup NM 87305-1286

LINDER, BERTRAM NORMAN, foundation administrator, horse-breeder, actor; b. N.Y.C., Nov. 24, 1915; s. Albert Aaron and Bess (Newman) L.; m. Eleanor Jones (dec.); children: Robert Allan (dec.), Denise J.; m. Mary Ellen Smith. BA cum laude, Williams Coll., 1936; postgrad., Yale U., 1937-38, Columbia U., 1938-39. V.p. Linder Bros., Inc., Scranton, Pa., 1940-65, pres., treas., 1965-80; pres., treas. Albert A. & Bertram N. Linder Found., Inc., N.Y.C., 1965—; owner Hickory Hill Farm, Dalton, Pa., 1947—. Author: Songs to the Night, 1941. Pres. Jewish Fedn., Scranton, 1949-52; pres., co-founder Child Guidance & Psychiatry Ctr., Lackawanna County, Pa.; chmn. adv. bd. Salvation Army, Scranton, 1947-50; pres. United Way, Lackawanna County, 1960-63. 1st lt. inf. U.S. Army, 1943-46, ETO. Decorated Bronze Star, Combat Inf. badge, Purple Heart, Belgian Fourragere; recipient Community Svc. award Scranton C. of C., 1949, Salvation Army, 1950, Citizenship award AFL-CIO, 1962, 65, Americanism award B'nai B'rith, 1965. Mem. AFTRA, SAG, Thoroughbred Owners and Breeders Assn., Thoroughbred of Am. Club (Lexington, Ky.), N.Y. Thoroughbred Breeders, Ky. Thoroughbred Assn., Penn Horse Breeders Assn., 4th U.S. Inf. Divsn. Assn., B'nai B'rith, Phi Beta Kappa. Republican. Jewish. Avocations: fishing, travel. Home: Hickory Hill Farm W Main St Dalton PA 18414-9522 Office: Linder Found Inc 305 E 40th St New York NY 10016-2189

LINDER, JOHN E., congressman, dentist; b. Deer River, Minn., Sept. 2, 1942; s. Henry and Vera Elizabeth Davis L.; m. Lynne Leslee Peterson, 1963; children: Kristine Kerry, Matthew John. BS, U. Minn., 1963, DDS, 1967. Pvt. practice Atlanta, Ga., 1967-82; mem. Ga. Ho. of Reps., 1975-80, 82-90; pres. Linder Fin. Corp., 1977-92; mem. 103d-104th Congress from 4th Ga. Dist., 1993—, 105th Congress from 11th Ga. Dist., 1996—; house rules com., subcom. on legis. process, Rep. steering com., NRCC exec. com. U.S. Ho. of Reps. Founder I Care, 1970. Capt. USAF, 1967-69. Mem. ADA, Ga. Dental Assn., No. Dist. Dental Soc., Rotary. Republican. Presbyterian. Office: US Ho of Reps 1005 Longworth Bldg Washington DC 20515-1004

LINDER, STU, film editor. Editor: (films) The Fortune, 1975, (with Susan Martin) First Family, 1980, My Bodyguard, 1980, Six Weeks, 1982, Diner, 1982, The Natural, 1984, Young Sherlock Holmes, 1985, Code Name: Emerald, 1985, Good Morning, Vietnam, 1987, Tin Men, 1987, Rain Man, 1988 (Academy award nomination best film editing 1988), Avalon, 1990, Bugsy, 1991, Toys, 1992, Quiz Show, 1994. Office: care Motion Picture Editors 7715 W Sunset Blvd Ste 200 Los Angeles CA 90046-3912*

LINDERMAN, JEANNE HERRON, priest; b. Erie, Pa., Nov. 14, 1931; d. Robert Leslie and Ella Marie (Stearns) Herron; m. James Stephens Linderman; children: Mary Susan, John Randolph, Richard Webster, Craig Stephens, Mark Herron, Elizabeth Stewart. BS in Indsl. and Labor Rels., Cornell U., 1953; MDiv magna cum laude, Lancaster Theol. Sem., 1981; postgrad., clin. pastoral edn., Del. State Hosp., New Castle, 1981. Ordained priest, Episcopal Ch. Mem. pers. staff Hengerer Co., Buffalo, 1953-55; chaplain Cathedral Ch. St. John, Wilmington, Del., 1981-82; priest-in-charge Christ Episcopal Ch., Delaware City, Del., 1982-87; vicar Christ Episcopal Ch., 1987-91; assoc. rector St. Andrew's Episcopal Ch., Wilmington, Del., 1991-95, priest in charge, 1995-96; chair human sexuality task force, Diocese of Del., 1981-82, mem. clergy compensation com. and diocesan coun., 1982-86, pres. standing com., 1991—, com. on constitution and canons, 1989. Author, editor hist. study papers. Bd. dirs. St. Michael's Day Nursery, Wilmington, 1985-88; mem. secondary schs. com. Cornell U., bd. dirs., chmn. pers. com. Geriatric Svcs. of Del., 1989—, sec. bd., 1993-96. Mem. Episcopal Women's Caucus, Del. Episcopal Clergy Assn., Nat. Assn. Episcopal Clergy, DAR (v.-regent Caesar Rodney chpt. 1996—), Mayflower (elder, surgeon 1983-95), Dutch Colonial Soc. Del., Stoney Run Questers (pres.), Cornell Women's Club Del. (pres. 1966), Women of St. James the Less (pres. 1972-73), Women's Witnessing Cmty. at Lambeth, Patriotic Soc. in Del. (sec.-treas. conv. 1965-68), Chi Omega. Republican. Avocations: history, genealogy, travel. Home: 307 Springhouse Ln Hockessin DE 19707-9691 Office: St Andrews's Episcopal Ch Eighth And Shipley St Wilmington DE 19801

LINDESMITH, LARRY ALAN, physician, administrator; b. Amarillo, Tex., July 27, 1938; s. Lyle J. and Imogene Agnes (Young) L.; m. Patricia Ann Brady, June 6, 1959 (div. Mar. 1973); children: Robert James, Lisa Ann; m. Diane Joyce Bakken, Nov. 22, 1973; children: Abigail Arleen, Nathan Lyle, David Alan. BA, U. Colo., 1959; MD, Bowman-Gray Sch. Medicine, Winston-Salem, N.C., 1963. Diplomate Am. Bd. Internal Medicine, Am. Bd. I.M.-Pulmonary Disease; Nat. Inst. Occupational Safety and Health B Reader; provider ACLS, advanced trauma life support. Medical intern U. Chgo. Hosps., Clinics, 1963-64; I.M. resident U. Colo. Med. Ctr., Denver, 1964-66; pulmonary disease fellowship U. Colo. Med. Ctr., Webb-Waring Lung Inst., Denver, 1966-67; asst. dir. infectious and pulmonary disease svc. Madigan Gen. Hosp., Tacoma, Wash., 1967-69; chief pulmonary disease Gundersen Clinic, Ltd., La Crosse, Wis., 1969-87, chief pulmonary and occupational medicine, 1979-89, chmn. dept. medicine, 1987-93; chief occupational health, preventive medicine, 1988—; med. dir. of employee health and safety Gundersen Luth. Med. Ctr., 1997—; bd. govs. Gundersen Clinic, Ltd., 1987-93; adj. prof. phys. therapy U. Wis., La Crosse, 1977-92; cons. VA Hosp., Tomah, Wis., 1977-93, Comty. Meml. Hosp., Winona, Minn., 1996—, Tomah Meml. Hosp., 1995—; clin. asst. prof. internal medicine U. Wis., Madison, 1982-92, clin. assoc. prof., 1992—; med. dir. RESTOR U. Wis., La Crosse, 1986-95, Svcs. to Bus. and Industry Gundersen/Luth. Med. Ctr., La Crosse, 1987-94; mem. occupational medicine boardwriting com. Am. Bd. Preventive Medicine, 1992-96. Contbr. book chpts. and articles to profl. publs. Mem. Air Pollution Control Coun. State of Wis. Dept. Natural Resources, 1978-81; vice-chmn. Bd. Control Luther High Sch., Onalaska, Wis., 1990-93. Maj. USAR, 1968-69; chmn. bd. dirs. Greater La Crosse Area C. of C., 1991. Boettcher Found. scholar, 1955-59; named Pagliara Tchr. of Yr. Gundersen Med. Found., 1984; recipient Dist. Svc. award Am. Lung Assn. Wis., 1988. Fellow Am. Coll. Chest Physicians, Am. Coll. Occupational and Environ. Medicine (assoc., chmn. pvt. practice coun., chmn. occupational lung disorders com., treas. med. ctr. occupl. health com. 1996—); mem. AMA, Am. Bd. Preventive Medicine (occupational medicine com. 1991-95), Am. Assn. Respiratory Therapy, Clin. Sleep Soc., Am. Thoracic Soc. (Wis. counselor 1978-81), Ctrl. States Occupational Medicine Assn. (bd. govs. 1984-95, pres. 1991), Am. Lung Assn. Wis. (pres. 1975-77), Wis. Thoracic Soc. (gen. conf. chmn. 1987), State Med. Soc. Wis. (chmn. environ. and occupational health com. 1989-91). Republican. Lutheran. Avocation: photography. Home: W 4965 Woodhaven Dr La Crosse WI 54601 Office: Gundersen Luth Med Ctr 1836 South Ave La Crosse WI 54601-5429

LINDGREN, A(LAN) BRUCE, church administrator; b. Grand Rapids, Mich., July 1, 1948; m. Carole Coonce; children: Stacey, Michael, David (dec.). BS in Sociology, Mich. State U., 1970; MDiv, St. Paul Sch. Theology, 1975. Ordained high priest. Campus minister Park Coll., 1975-77; dir. ministerial edn. Temple Sch., 1986-92; exec. min., World Ch. sec., exec. asst. to 1st presidency Reorganized Ch. of Jesus Christ of Latter Day Saints, 1992—; dir. devel. basic leadership curriculum Temple Sch., 1977-86. Editor: Leaders Handbook, 1985-92. Office: Reorganized Ch of Jesus Christ PO Box 1059 Independence MO 64051-0559

LINDGREN, D(ERBIN) KENNETH, JR., retired lawyer; b. Mpls., Aug. 25, 1932; s. Derbin Kenneth and Margaret (Anderson) L.; m. Patricia Ann Ransier, Dec. 17, 1955; children—Christian Kenneth, Carol Ann, Charles Derbin. BS, U. Minn., 1954, JD, 1958. Bar: Minn. 1958, U.S. Supreme Ct. 1968, U.S. Tax Ct. 1959, U.S. Ct. Appeals (D.C. cir.) 1981. Gen. practice law Mpls., 1958—; mem. Larkin, Hoffman, Daly & Lindgren, Ltd., Mpls., 1960-95, of counsel, 1995; ret., 1995. Contbr. articles to profl. jours. Active Ind. Sch. Dist. 287 Bd. Edn. (Area Vocat. Tech. Coll.), 1979-83, Ind. Sch. Dist. 274 Bd. Edn., Hopkins, Minn., 1970-76, chmn., 1972-76; trustee Mpls. Soc. Fine Arts, 1982-88, Minn. Landscape Arboretum Found., 1989—, pres., 1992-95; bd. overseers Mpls. Inst. Art, 1986-88, Mpls. Coll. Art and Design, 1980-86, vice-chmn., 1982-83, chmn., 1983-86, trustee, 1988-96; active Govs. Commn. on Reform Govt., 1983. Lt. USAF, 1955-57. Fellow Am. Coll. Trust and Estate Counsel; mem. ABA, Minn. Bar Assn., Hennepin County Bar Assn., Mpls. Ahtletic Club, Interlachen Country Club, Troon Golf and Country Club, Alpha Delta Phi, Phi Delta Phi. Congregationalist. Home: 4804 France Ave S #2 Edina MN 55410 also: 11003 E Desert Vista Dr Scottsdale AZ 85255 Office: 1500 Norwest Financial Ctr 7900 Xerxes Ave S Minneapolis MN 55431-1106

LINDGREN, JOHN RALPH, philosophy educator; b. Oak Park, Ill., Oct. 8, 1933; s. Francis L. and Leona (Toussaint) Nichols; m. Shirley Ann Tryon, Dec. 27, 1958; children: J. Thomas, Michael B., David J., Timothy P., Kathryn A. B.S. in Bus. Adminstrn., Northwestern U., 1959; M.A. in Philosophy, Marquette U., 1961, Ph.D. in Philosophy, 1963. Instr. dept. philosophy Holy Cross Coll., Worcester, Mass., 1962-64, asst. prof., 1964-65; asst. prof. Lehigh U., Bethlehem, Pa., 1965-69, assoc. prof., 1969-79, chmn. dept. philosophy, 1973-85, dir. law and legal instns. program, 1978-94, prof., 1979-95, William Wilson Selfridge prof., 1985-88, Clara H. Stewardson prof., 1989-95; vis. scholar Oxford U., 1986, U. Pa. Law Sch., Phila., 1977-78. Author: Social Philosophy of Adam Smith, 1973, Sex Discrimination in Higher Education, 1984, The Law of Sex Discrimination, 1988, 2d edit., 1993; editor: Early Writing of Adam Smith, 1967, Horizons of Justice, 1996, Ritual and Semiotics, 1997. Mem. adv. bd. Alternatives to Violence Project University City Sci. Ctr., Phila., 1980-83. Served with U.S. Army, 1953-55. Mem. Am. Philos. Assn., Internat. Soc. for Philosophy of Law (exec. bd. dirs. 1981-83), Soc. for Philosophy and Pub. Affairs (exec. bd. 1987-95). Democrat. Office: Lehigh U Dept Philosophy 15 University Dr Bethlehem PA 18015-3057

LINDGREN, KERMIT LYLE, nurse; b. Stromsburg, Nebr., Sept. 20, 1953; s. Kermit Lloyd and Agnes Lucille (Black) L. AA, Meth. Coll., 1979; AS, U. Nebr. Med. Ctr., 1982; BS, Nebr. Wesleyan U., 1982; cert. family nurse practitioner, U. N.D., 1985. ACLS, ATLS; cert. physician asst. Teaching assoc. U. Nebr. Coll. Nursing, Lincoln, 1980-82; staff burn/trauma nurse St. Elizabeth Community Health Ctr., Lincoln, 1982-89; RN III Topeka State Hosp., 1989-92, family nurse practitioner, 1992—; instr. prep for parenthood ARC, Lincoln, 1980-89, disaster nurse, 1982-89; nurse practitioner Planned Parenthood, Lincoln, 1985-86; sr. staff nurse II Security Hosp., Lincoln, 1986-88; rural health cons. Johnson County Health Dept., Tecumseh, Nebr., 1984-85; disaster coord. Johnson County Emergency Med. Svc., Tecumseh, 1984-85; BLS instr. Am. Heart Assn., Topeka, 1990—. Capt. U.S. Army Res., 1974—. Decorated Expert Field Med. Badge, Purple Heart. Mem. Am. Burn Assn. Methodist. Avocation: private pilot, parachutist.

LINDGREN, TIMOTHY JOSEPH, supply company executive; b. N.Y.C., Dec. 7, 1937; s. Carl Herbert and Ruth Elizabeth (Pickering) L.; m. Barbara Fiorini, Feb. 7, 1957; children: Sharon, Mark, Susan. AA, Pierce Coll., Woodland Hills, Calif., 1959; BS in Prodn. Mgmt., Calif. State U., Northridge, 1961; MBA in Indsl. Relations, UCLA, 1962. Registered profl. engr., Calif. cert. tchr., Calif. Systems analyst, methods acct. Pacific Tel. & Tel., Van Nuys, Calif., 1964-65; dir. mfg. Olga Co., Van Nuys, 1965-69; dir. prodn. Calif. Almond Orchards, Bakersfield, 1970-72, gen. mgr., 1972-73; pres. United Wholesale Lumber Co., Montebello, Calif., 1973-77; pres., chief exec. officer Fruit Growers Supply Co., Sherman Oaks, Calif., 1978—. Mem. Calif. C. of C. (chair com. on natural resources). Office: Fruit Growers Supply Co 14130 Riverside Dr Sherman Oaks CA 91423-2313

LINDGREN, WILLIAM DALE, librarian; b. Peoria, Ill., Mar. 8, 1936; s. Hugh Gottfried and Olive Kathryn (Myer) L. BA, Bradley U., 1958, MA, 1959; MSLS, U. Ill., 1967. Tchr. Limestone High Sch., Bartonville, Ill., 1960-68; asst. dir. Learning Resources Ctr. Ill. Cen. Coll., East Peoria, 1968-73, dir., 1973—; mem. transition bd. merger of four systems, 1993-94; bd. dirs. Alliance Libr. Sys.; mem. Ill. State Libr. Com. on Resolving the Unserved Problem, 1996—. Singer Ephphetha Schola Cantorum Gregoriana, 1996—. Chmn. East Peoria Oral History Com., 1983-84, Resource Sharing Alliance West Ctrl. Ill. Adv. Coun., 1985—; v.p. Ill. Valley Libr. System, pres. bd., 1988, 90—, treas., 1989, bd. dirs., 1990—; regional chair recruitment com. Am. Heart Assn., 1996—. Mem. ALA, Ill. Libr. Assn. (co-chair cracker barrels program ann. conf. 1989, 90, 91), Assn. Ednl. Media Tech., Assn. Ednl. Media and Tech. Ill., Coun. Libr. Tech., Creve Coeur Club (Peoria).

LINDH, PATRICIA SULLIVAN, banker, former government official; b. Toledo, Oct. 2, 1928; d. Lawrence Walsh and Lillian Winifred (Devlin) Sullivan; m. H. Robert Lindh, Jr., Nov. 12, 1955; children: Sheila, Deborah, Robert. B.A., Trinity Coll., Washington, 1950, LL.D., 1975; LL.D., Walsh Coll., Canton, Ohio, 1975, U. Jacksonville, 1975. Editor Singapore Am. Newspaper, 1957-62; spl. asst. to counsellor to Pres., 1974, spl. asst. to Pres., 1975-76; dep. asst. sec. state for ednl. and cultural affairs Dept. State, 1976-77; v.p., dir. corp. comms. Bank Am., L.A., 1978-84; corp. pub. rels. Bank Am., San Francisco, 1985-93. Trustee La. Arts and Sci. Center, 1970-73, Calif. Hosp. Med. Ctr., 1979-84; bd. dirs. Jr. League of Baton Rouge, 1969, Children's Bur. Los Angeles, 1979, 84, USO Northern Calif.; Rep. state vice chairwoman La., 1970-74; Rep. nat. committeewoman, La., 1974; mem. pub. affairs com. San Francisco World Affairs Coun., 1985; adv. bd. Jr. League Los Angeles, 1980-84; bd. visitors Southwestern U. Sch. Law. Roman Catholic. Home: 12380 Grandee Ct San Diego CA 92128

LINDHEIM, JAMES BRUCE, public relations executive; b. Cleve., Nov. 26, 1945; s. John Arthur and Lois (Reinitz) L.; m. Barbara Levitz, June 6, 1970 (div. May 1978). BA, Williams Coll., 1967; MS in Pub. Affairs, Princeton U., 1970. Asst. dean Woodrow Wilson Sch. Pub. and Internat. Affairs Princeton (N.J.) U., 1971-73; rsch. assoc. Mathematica, Inc., Princeton, 1973-75; dir. corp. priorities svc. Yankolovich, Skelly and White, N.Y.C., 1975-80; exec. v.p., dir. pub. affairs Burson-Marsteller, N.Y.C., 1981-88; dir. corp. svcs. Europe Burson-Marsteller, London, 1989; dir. corp. svcs Europe Burson-Marsteller, Paris, 1990-92, vice-chmn., 1990-92; chmn. Burson-Marsteller, Europe, Paris, 1992-94; chmn. bd. Burson-Marsteller, 1994-95; pres. JLindheim & Co., N.Y.C., 1995—. Home and Office: 832 Broadway New York NY 10003-4813

LINDHEIM, RICHARD DAVID, television company executive; b. N.Y.C., May 28, 1939; s. Gilbert R. and Pearl (Gruskin) L.; m. Elaine Lavis, Dec. 22, 1963; children: Susan Patricia, David Howard. B.S., U. Redlands, 1961; postgrad, U. So. Calif., 1963. Adminstrv. asst. story dept. CBS, L.A., 1962-64; project dir. entertainment testing ASI Market Rsch., L.A., 1964-69; v.p. program research NBC, L.A., 1969-78, v.p. dramatic programs, 1978-79; producer Universal TV, L.A., 1979-81, v.p. current programs, 1981-85, sr. v.p. series programming, 1986-87, exec. v.p. creative affairs, 1987-91; exec. v.p. program strategy MCA TV Group, 1991-92; exec. v.p. Paramount TV Group, 1992—; asst. prof. Calif. State U.; sr. lectr. U. So. Calif.; lectr. UCLA; reviewer NEH; bd. dirs. Am. Fgn. Svc. Intercultural Program-USA. Author: (with Richard Blum) Primetime: Network Television Programming, 1987, Inside Television Producing, 1991; contbr. articles to profl. jours. Mem. Acad. TV Arts and Scis., Producers Guild Am., Writers Guild Am. Democrat. Jewish. Avocations: model railroading, photography, music, traveling. Office: Universal Studios 100 Universal City Plz Universal Cty CA 91608-1002 *In this sophisticated society there are fewer and fewer opportunities for the individual. Technology has made most tasks too complex for one man. As a result the ability to work with other people and to provide leadership and management to groups of people has become vital. The key ingredients are communication, respect for others, and a feeling of belonging, while working in a relaxed, casual environment, where the leader is responsible and receptive.*

LINDHOLM, CLIFFORD FALSTROM, II, engineering executive, mayor; b. Passaic, N.J., Dec. 8, 1930; s. Albert William and Edith (Neandross) L.; m. Margery Nye (div.); children: Clifford, Elizabeth, John; m. Karen Cooper, Oct. 7, 1989. BS in Engring., Princeton U., 1953; M in Engring., Stevens Inst. Tech., 1957. Supr. prodn. GM, Linden, N.J., 1953-56; chmn. bd. Falstrom Co., Passaic, N.J., 1956—; Bd. dirs. N.J. Mfg. Ins. Co., Trenton. Mayor Twp. Montclair, N.J., 1988-92; pres. Montclair Bd. Edn., 1968-72; bd. dirs. Albert Payson Terhune Found., N.J., 1976—. Mem. N.J. Bus. and Industry Assn. (bd. dirs. 1977—), Upper Montclair Golf Club, Mantoloking Yacht Club. Republican. Mem. Ch. of Christ. Home: 10 Mountainside Park Ter Montclair NJ 07043-1209 Office: Falstrom Co 3 Falstrom Ct Passaic NJ 07055

LINDHOLM, DWIGHT HENRY, lawyer; b. Blackduck, Minn., May 27, 1930; s. Henry Nathanial and Viola Eudora (Gummert) L.; m. Loretta Catherine Brown, Aug. 29, 1958; children: Douglas Dwight, Dionne Louise, Jeanne Marie, Philip Clayton, Kathleen Anne. Student, Macalester Coll., 1948-49; BBA, U. Minn., 1951, LLB, 1954; postgrad., Mexico City Coll. (now U. of Ams.), 1956-57. Bar: Minn. 1954, Calif. 1958. Sole practice Los Angeles, 1958-65, 72-81, 84—; ptnr. Lindholm & Johnson, Los Angeles, 1965-69, Cotter, Lindholm & Johnson, Los Angeles, 1969-72; sole practice Los Angeles, 1972-81; of counsel Bolton, Dunn & Moore, Los Angeles, 1981-84. Mem. Calif. Republican Central Com., 1962-63, Los Angeles Republican County Central Com., 1962-66; bd. dirs. Family Service Los Angeles, 1964-70, v.p., 1968-70; bd. dirs. Wilshire YMCA, 1976-77; trustee Westlake Girls Sch., 1978-81; hon. presenter Nat. Charity League Coronet Debutante Ball, 1984; bd. dirs. Calif. State U.-Northridge Trust Fund, 1989-93; bd. dirs. Queen of Angeles/Hollywood Presbyn. Med. Ctr., 1990—; chmn., CEO Queen of Angels, Hollywood Presbyn. Found., 1997—. Served as capt. JAG Corps USAF, 1954-56. Recipient Presdl. award Los Angeles Jr. C. of C., 1959. Mem. ABA, Calif. Bar Assn., L.A. County Bar Assn., Wilshire Bar Assn. (bd. govs. 1989-91), Internat. Genealogy Fellowship of Rotarians (founding pres. 1979-86), Calif. Club, Ocean Cruising Club Eng. (Newport Harbor port officer), Rotary (dir. 1975-78), Delta Sigma Pi, Delta Sigma Rho, Delta Theta Phi (state chancellor 1972-73). Presbyterian. Avocations: sailing, offshore cruising. Office: 3580 Wilshire Blvd Fl 17 Los Angeles CA 90010-2501

LINDHOLM, FREDRIK ARTHUR, electrical engineering educator; b. Tacoma, Wash., Feb. 26, 1936; s. George Fred and Evelyn Blanche (Faul) L.; m. Susanne Shroad Howry, Aug. 22, 1959 (div. July 1966); m. Merle Elizabeth Flannery, Dec. 20, 1969. BS, Stanford U., 1958, MS, 1960; PhD, U. Ariz., 1963. Sr. engr. Motorola Corp., Phoenix, 1963-66; asst. prof. U. Ariz., Tucson, 1963-64, assoc. prof., 1964-66; prof. U. Fla., Gainesville, 1966—; vis. prof. U. Leuven, Belgium, 1973-74; gen. chmn. Internat. Electron Devices Meeting Conf., Washington, 1974; program chmn. Internat. Photovoltaics Specialists Conf., Washington, 1978; cons. Jet Propulsion Lab., Pasadena, Calif., 1978-87, Los Alamos (N.Mex.) Nat. Lab., 1981-86. Author: Principles and Applications of Semiconductor Device Modeling, 1971; contbr. numerous articles to profl. jours.; patentee high-low emitter solar cell. Recipient Best Paper award Internat. Solid-State Cirs. Conf., 1963, 65, Outstanding Engring. Faculty award U. Fla., 1975, univ. tchr.-scholar, 1988. Fellow IEEE; mem. Am. Phys. Soc. Home: 4406 SW 17th Ter Gainesville FL 32608-3910 Office: Dept Elec & Computer Engr Univ Fla Gainesville FL 32611

LINDHOLM, JOHN VICTOR, business executive; b. Kane, Pa., Dec. 29, 1934; s. John Edwin and Mary (Nord) L.; m. Ann Christine Lundquist, Apr. 27, 1957; children: Scott Benjamin, Kristine Ann, John Edwin. BBA, Upsala Coll., 1956; postgrad., NYU, 1960-66. Loan officer Irving Trust Co., N.Y.C., 1960-61, coord. spl. svcs., 1969-72, exec. dir., 1972-74; pres., exec. dir. EOPI, 1974—; dir. fin. Guideposts Assocs., Inc., 1975-91, chief fin. officer, exec. dir., 1991, dir. fin. and support svcs., 1992-95; pres. Econ. Svcs., Inc., 1995; dir. fin. and support svcs. Christian Children's Fund, Richmond, Va.; bd. dirs. Naromi Land Trust, Sherman, Conn., Country Bank, Carmel, N.Y.; chmn. bd. dirs. Country Bank, Carmel, 1988-93; pres., dir. Country Bank, 1993; pres. Putnam Alliance, 1980-82. Treas. Putnam Alliance, 1978-80; trustee Bethel Meth. Home, 1978-85, 87—; dir. fin. Christian Children's Fund, Inc., 1992—. Lt. USNR, 1956-59. Mem. W.O. Assn. (pres. 1994—). Home: 6400 Buckhill Rd Richmond VA 23225-1320 Office: Christian Children's Fund 2821 Emerywood Pky Richmond VA 23294-3726

LINDHOLM, RICHARD THEODORE, economics and finance educator; b. Eugene, Oreg., Oct. 5, 1960; s. Richard Wadsworth and Mary Marjorie (Trunko) L. m. Valaya Nivasananda, May 8, 1987. BA, U. Chgo., 1982, MA, 1983, PhD, 1993. Ptnr. Lindholm and Osanka, Eugene, 1986-89, Lindholm Rsch., Eugene, 1989—; guest lectr. Nat. Inst. Devel. Adminstrn., Bangkok, Thailand, 1989; pres. Rubicon Inst., Eugene, 1988—; adj. asst. prof. U. Oreg., Eugene, 1988—. Campaign co-chmn. Lane C.C. Advocates, Eugene, 1988; coord., planner numerous state Rep. Campaigns, Oreg., 1988—; campaign mgr. Jack Roberts for Oreg. State Labor Commn., 1994; mem. staff Oreg. Senate Rep. Office, 1989-90; precinct committeeperson Oreg. Rep. Party, 1987-92, 94—; bd. dirs. Rubicon Soc., Eugene, 1987—, pres., 1993—. Republican. Lutheran. Home: 3335 Bardell Ave Eugene OR 97401-8021

LINDHOLM, ULRIC SVANTE, engineering research institute executive, retired; b. Washington, Sept. 11, 1931; s. Svante Godfred and Hedwig (Krueger) L.; m. Laura Ann Carranza, July 6, 1962; children: Karl, Kirsten, Jon, Siri. BS, Mich. State U., 1953, MS, 1955, PhD, 1960. Rsch. instr. Mich. State U., East Lansing, 1959-60; sr. engr., mgr., dir., v.p. Southwest Rsch. Inst., San Antonio, 1960-94, ret., 1994; lectr. St. Mary's U., San Antonio, 1961-62. Assoc. editor Soc. Exptl. Stress Analysis Exptl. Mechanics, 1979-82; contbr. numerous articles to profl. jours.; patentee in field. Chmn. bd. dirs. Healy-Murphy Ctr., San Antonio, 1970-81. With USN, 1955-57. Fellow ASME (assoc. editor Jour. Applied Mechanics 1981-83), AAAS; mem. Am. Soc. Metals. Democrat. Avocations: woodworking, antiques. Home: 110 Honey Bee Ln San Antonio TX 78231-1205

LINDIG, BILL M., food distribution company executive; b. 1936; married. Attended, U. Tex. With Sysco Corp., Houston, 1969—, exec. v.p., from 1984, COO, 1984—, now pres., CEO.; chmn. Sysco Avard Food Svcs., Inc., Union City, Calif., Santa Fe Pacific Corp., Schaumburg, Ill. Office: Sysco Corp 1390 Enclave Pkwy Houston TX 77077-2025*

LINDLEY, F(RANCIS) HAYNES, JR., foundation president, lawyer; b. L.A., Oct. 15, 1945; s. Francis Haynes and Grace Nelson (McCanne) L.; m. Hollinger McCloud Lindley, Apr. 1, 1977; 1 child, Anne Hollinger Lindley. BA, Claremont (Calif.) Men's Coll., 1967; MFA, Claremont (Calif.) Grad. Sch., 1972; JD, Southwestern U., L.A., 1976. Bar: Calif. 1976, U.S. Supreme Ct. 1980. Deputy pub. defender Office of Pub. Defender, L.A., 1977-79; staff atty., Dept. Trial Counsel The State Bar of Calif., L.A., 1979-81; pvt. practice, 1981-90; pres. John Randolph Haynes and Dora Haynes Found., L.A., 1987-97; trustee John Randolph Haynes and Dora Haynes Found., L.A., 1978—. Mem. bd. dirs. TreePeople, L.A., 1985-87, So. Calif. Assn. Philanthropy, L.A., 1985-89; mem. bd. fellows Claremont (Calif.) U. Ctr. and Grad. Sch., 1987—; mem. bd. dirs. Marin Agrl. Land Trust, 1995—. Recipient Disting. Svc. award The Claremont (Calif.) Grad. Sch., 1994. Mem. The Calif. Club. Avocation: sailing, art history, banjo. Home: PO Box 1404 Ross CA 94957-1404 Office: John Randolph Haynes and Dora Haynes Found 888 W 6th St Ste 1150 Los Angeles CA 90017-2737

LINDLEY, NORMAN DALE, physician; b. Henrietta, Tex., July 18, 1937; s. Hardie Lindley and Hope (Clement) Mourant; m. Luise Ann Moser, May 29, 1964; children: Norman Dale Jr., Roger Paul. BS, N.Mex. Highlands U., 1960; MD, U. Colo., 1964. Diplomate Am. Bd. Ob-Gyn. Rotating intern Kans. City (Mo.) Gen. Hosp., 1964-65; resident in ob-gyn. St. Joseph Hosp., Denver, 1965-68; med. officer USAF, Cheyenne, Wyo., 1968-70; pvt. practice physician Alamogordo, N.M., 1970—; dir. N.Mex. Found. for Med. Care, Albuquerque, 1985-88, N.Mex. Med. Rev. Assn., Albuquerque, 1985-88; physician liaison Am. Assn. Med. Assts., Chgo., 1987-93; physician advisor N.Mex. Soc. Med. Assts., 1984—. Bd. dirs. Otero County Boys and Girls Club, Alamogordo, 1977—, pres., 1979-81; bd. dirs. Otero County Assn. for Retarded Citizens, 1985-91, pres., 1989-90; bd. dirs. Otero County chpt. Am. Cancer Soc., 1970-72. Capt. USAF, 1968-70. Rsch. grantee NSF, 1959, 60. Fellow Am. Coll. Ob-Gyn.; mem. AMA, Am. Fertility Soc., Am. Inst. Ultrasound in Medicine, Am. Soc. Colposcopists and Cervical Pathologists, N.Mex. Med. Soc. (councilor 1985-88), Otero County Med. Soc. (pres. 1972-73, 83-84), Rotary (pres. White Sands chpt. 1981-82, bd. dirs. 1988-89, Svc. Above Self award 1979, Paul Harris fellow 1987). Avocations: watercolor painting, leatherworking, foreign languages. Home: 2323 Union Ave Alamogordo NM 88310-3849 Office: Thunderbird Ob-Gyn 1212 9th St Alamogordo NM 88310-5842

LINDLEY, THOMAS ERNEST, environmental lawyer, law educator; b. Danville, Ill., July 15, 1948; s. Oscar Ernest and Helen (Milewski) L. BA, U. Ill., 1970; postgrad., U. Tex., 1970-71; JD, Vanderbilt U., 1977. Bar: Ill. 1977, U.S. Dist. Ct. (no. dist.) Ill. 1978, U.S. Dist. Ct. (cen. dist.) Ill. 1983, U.S. Ct. Appeals (7th cir.) 1978, U.S. Supreme Ct. 1982, Oreg. 1985, U.S. Dist. Ct. Oreg. 1985, Trial Bar No. Dist. Ill. 1985, U.S. Ct. Appeals (9th cir.) 1985, Wash. 1987, U.S. Dist. Ct. (we. dist.) Wash. 1987, U.S. Dist. Ct. (ea. dist.) Wash. 1988. Asst. dir. div. EMS Tenn. Dept. Health, Nashville, 1972-74; lawyer Jenner & Block, Chgo., 1977-83, Balbach, Fehr & Lindley, Urbana, Ill., 1983-84, Miller, Nash, Wiener, Hager & Carlsen, Seattle, Portland, Oreg., 1985—; adj. prof. Lewis & Clark Northwestern Sch. Law, Portland, 1991—; lectr. ITT-Kent Coll. Law, Chgo., 1981-83; extern Supreme Ct. Tenn., Nashville, 1976-77; co-chair and author 7th Ann. EPA/Lewis & Clark Hazardous Waste Law & Mgmt. Conf., 1990, 8th Ann. Conf., 1991; chair Assoc. Oreg. Industries' Environ. Crimes Task Forces, 1993, 97; com. chair on internat. environ. crimes Internat. Ctr. for Criminal Reform and Justice, 1994; mem. U.S. Del. 9th Conf. of Parties of Cites, 1994; chair Assn. Oreg. Industries, Water Quality and Water Quantity Subcom., 1995—. Author: Contracting for Environmental Services, 1991, Reducing Lender Liability, 1994; co-author: Oregon's Environmental Audit Privilege: Traveling the Path to Consensus: Preventive Law Reporter, 1994, Oregon Environmental Law--Crimes and Contracting, 1994, Environmental Audit Privilege: BNA, 1993; editor: Oregon Environmental Law--Insurance Coverage, 1991. Bd. dirs. Oreg. Environ. Tech. Assn., 1993-96, sec., 1994-96, United Way Columbia-Willamette, Oreg., 1990-91, United Cerebral Palsy, Oreg., 1987-90, 95—, mem., 1987—, Mental Health Svcs. West, Oreg., 1985, Ill. Pub. Action Coun., 1980-83; chmn. Adv. Bd. CANPAC, 1981; coord. counsel Kennedy for Pres., Ill., 1979-80; vol. Cook County Spl. Bail Project, Ill., 1978-79; candidate U.S. Congress, Ill., 1983-84. Mem. ABA (natural resource sect., litig. sect.), Wash. State Bar Assn. (land use and environ. law sect.), Oreg. State Bar (environ. law sect.). Avocations: backpacking, cross country skiing, theater, politics. Office: Miller Nash Wiener et al 3500 US Bancorp Tower 111 SW 5th Ave Portland OR 97204-3604

LINDLY, DOUGLAS DEAN, elementary school educator, administrator; b. San Diego, Aug. 22, 1941; s. George A. and Jessie V. L.; m. Brenda J., Oct. 22, 1971; children: Elizabeth, David. MA in Curriculum, Pepperdine U., 1967, student, 1975; credential edn., USC, 1971; student, U. Oreg., 1981-85, Oreg. State U., 1981-85; credential adminstrn., Calif. State U., Fullerton, 1991; cert. in spl. edn., Calif. State U., L.A., 1994. Cert. in profl. adminstrv. svcs., Calif., gen. teaching, Calif., standard designated adult edn., Calif., standard elem. teaching, Oreg., standard adminstrv., Oreg.; cert. lang. devel. specialist, Calif., Learning Handicapped and Resource Specialist credential. Supervising tchr. Imperial Schs., Pasadena, Calif., 1965-70; tchr. Charter Oak Unified Sch. Dist., Covina, Calif., 1970-78, Sweet Home (Oreg.) Unified Sch. Dist., 1978-81, Rialto (Calif.) Unified Sch. Dist., 1989-90; prin. Lewis and Clark Sch. Dist., Astoria, Oreg., 1981-86, Barstow (Calif.) Unified Sch. Dist., 1986-89; spl. edn. dir. River Delta Unified Sch. Dist., Walnut Grove, Calif., 1988-89; resource specialist Los Angeles Unified Sch. Dist., 1990—; tchr. motivational program Great Kids Club, 1982—. Author: A Handbook for Parents, 1967, Summer Education Handbook, 1970; contbr. numerous articles on ednl. programs to newspapers and mags., 1970-89. Vol. ARC, Pasadena/Covina, 1970-78; cubmaster Boy Scouts Am., Astoria and Barstow, 1982-88 (Outstanding Svc. award 1988); coach Little League, Astoria, 1985; leader youth group Ch. of God, 1975-81. Grantee Adventures in Success, 1976-78; scholar Future Tchrs. Am. and Eugene Tchrs. Assn., 1959; named San Gabriel Valley Outstanding Educator, San Gabriel Valley Endl. Consortium, 1977; recipient Outstanding Speaker award Toastmasters Internat., 1986, Outstanding Svc. award PTA, 1988. Mem. NEA, ASCD, Assn. Am. Educators, Calif. Assn. Gifted, Calif. Tchrs. Assn., Assn. Calif. Sch. Adminstrs. (assoc.), Kappa Delta Pi. Avocations: family physical fitness, grandparenting, reading, travel. Home: PO Box 1058 962 E Mountain View Ave Glendora CA 91741-2871

LINDMARK, RONALD DORANCE, retired federal agency administrator; b. Clearwater County, Minn., May 3, 1933; s. John G. and Aaste L. (Torgerson) L.; m. Lynette C. Larson, Dec. 16, 1961; children: Eric Karl, Kirstin Sigrid. BS in Forestry, U. Minn., 1961, MS, 1963; PhD in Agrl. Econs., Ohio State U., 1971. Forestry aide No. Pacific Rwy., Seattle, 1959-60; rsch. asst. U. Minn., St. Paul, 1961-63; scientist Ctrl. State Forest Experiment Sta., Columbus, Ohio, 1963-66, No. Ctrl. Forest Experiment Sta., Duluth, Minn., 1966-69; scientist, project leader No. Ctrl. Forest Experiment Sta., Carbondale, Ill., 1969-74; asst. dir. Intermountain Forest Experiment Sta., Ogden, Utah, 1974-77; staff asst., dep. chief Forest Svc. Rsch., Washington, 1977-81; dir. Forest Environ. Rsch., Washington, 1982-87, No. Ctrl. Forest Experiment Sta., St. Paul, 1987-93; ret., 1993; legis. fellow to Congressman from Ohio, 1981. Contbr. articles to profl. jours. With USN, 1952-56. Avocations: travel, photography, outdoor recreation, woodcraft. Home: 1140 Amble Dr Arden Hills MN 55112-5713

LINDMO, TORE, biophysicist; b. Steinkjer, Norway, Apr. 30, 1947; s. Hans and Svanhild (Hustad) L.; m. Siri Haagensen, Feb. 14, 1970; children: Hans Christian, Karine. MS, Norwegian Inst. Tech., Trondheim, 1972; PhD, U. Oslo, 1982. Rschr. OECD Halden reactor Project, Halden, Norway, 1972-73, The Norwegian Radium Hosp., Oslo, 1973-85, 87-88; cons. Skatron, Lier, Norway, 1986-87; prof. Norwegian Inst. Technology, Trondheim, 1989-95, 1996—; Fogarty fellow NIH, NCI, Bethesda, Md., 1983-84; dean Faculty of Physics and Math., Norwegian Inst. Technology, Trondheim, 1993-96; rsch. scholar U. Calif., Irvine, 1996-97. Editor: Flow Cytometry and Sorting, 1990; patentee in field; contbr. articles to profl. jours.; editl. bd.: Cytometry Jour., 1980—. Mem. Internat. Soc. Analytical Cytology, Instn. of Physics and Engring. in Medicine and Biology, Royal Norwegian Soc. Scis. and Letters, Norwegian Acad. Technol. Scis. Office: Dept Physics, Norwegian U Sci and Tech, 7034 Trondheim Norway

LINDNER, CARL HENRY, JR., financial holding company executive; b. Dayton, Ohio, Apr. 22, 1919; s. Carl Henry and Clara (Serrer) L.; m. Edith Bailey, Dec. 31, 1953; children: Carl Henry III, Stephen Craig, Keith Edward. Co-founder United Dairy Farmers, 1940; pres. Am. Fin. Corp., Cin., 1959-84, chmn., 1959—, chief exec. officer, 1984—; now chmn. bd., CEO Am. Fin. Group, Cin.; chmn., chief exec. officer, chmn. exec. com. United Brands Co. (now Chiquita Brands Internat. Inc.), N.Y.C., 1984—; chmn. Penn Cen. Corp. (now American Premier Underwriters), Cin., 1983—, chief exec. officer, 1987-1994, also bd. dirs.; chmn., chief exec. officer Gt. Am. Communications Co., Cin., 1987—; bd. dirs. Mission Ins. bd. advs. Bus. Adminstrn. Coll., U. Cin. Republican. Baptist. Office: Charter Co 1 W Charter Plz Jacksonville FL 32202-3106*

LINDNER, JOSEPH, JR., physician, medical administrator; b. Cin., Apr. 5, 1929; s. Joseph and Mary (Apger) L.; m. Doris G. Beatty, July 29, 1961; children: Laura Lynn, Karen Leslie. AB, Dartmouth Coll., 1951; MD, U. Cin., 1955; MPH, Harvard U., 1977. Intern Cin. Gen. Hosp., 1955-56, resident in medicine, 1958-60, fellow in cardiology, 1960-61; mem. faculty dept. medicine U. Cin. Coll. Medicine, 1961-79, prof., 1975-79; sr. assoc. v.p. U. Cin., 1975-79, sr. assoc. dir., 1977-79; pres., chief exec. officer St. Barnabas Med. Ctr., Livingston, N.J., 1979-85, Trimark Corp., West Orange, N.J.; ptnr. Cons. Assocs., Inc., 1991-92; pres. J. Lindner, Inc., Hilton Head, S.C., 1992—. Trustee Mt. St. Joseph Coll., 1972-76, The Asheville Sch., 1995—; bd. visitors, chmn. The Ashville Sch., 1995—. With USN, 1956-58. Fellow Am. Coll. Physician Execs.; mem. N.J. Med. Soc., Commonwealth Club, Cin. Country Club, Baltusrol Golf Club, Country Club Hilton Head, Bear Creek Golf Club, Short Hills Club. Home and Office: 31 Old Fort Dr Hilton Head Island SC 29926

LINDNER, KENNETH EDWARD, academic administrator and chemistry educator emeritus; b. LaCrosse, Wis., Nov. 29, 1922; s. Henry B. and Cora (Ward) L.; m. Ila M. Jacobson, Feb. 28, 1947 (div.); children: Diane, Charles, Barbara, Nancy, John, Sara; m. Marcia A Lee, March 17, 1990. B.S., Wis. State U., 1949; M.A., U. Iowa, 1953, Ph.D., 1966; HHD (hon.), Tex. Chirpractic Coll., 1994. High sch. chemistry tchr. Black River Falls, Wis., 1949-55; prof. chemistry Wis. State U., LaCrosse, 1956-67; head acad. affairs Wis. State U. System, Madison, 1967-70; chancellor U. Wis.-LaCrosse, 1971-79, chancellor emeritus, Disting. prof., 1983—; chmn. Council Chancellors U. Wis. System, 1978-79; sec. Wis. State Dept. Adminstrn., 1979-82; chmn. bd. Digicators Systems, Inc., 1985-90; adv. bd. Deli Corp., 1980-90; v.p. adminstrn.-provost Tex. Chiropractic Coll., Pasadena, Tex., 1993-94, advisor to pres., 1994—; cons. N.Y. Chiropractic Coll., 1994-95; cons. for closure Coll. St. Teresa, Winona, Minn., 1988-90; cons.-examiner North Ctrl. Assn. Colls. and Secondary Schs., 1972-79, commr., 1976-79; cons. data processing Sentry Ins. Co., 1983, govt. relations Gateway Foods, Inc., LaCrosse, Wis.; cons. radiation chemistry Dairyland Power Coop., LaCrosse Boiling Water Reactor, 1966-67; cons. radiation safety Gunderson Clinic, Luth. Hosp., LaCrosse, 1966-67; exec. v.p. Fastlink Internat., Denver, 1996—. Chmn. bd. trustees Coll. St. Teresa, Winona, Minn., 1986-88. Served with AUS, 1942-45. Mem. Internat. Radiation Protection Soc., Am. Chem. Soc., Health Physics Soc. Home: 3407 Shadow Meadows Dr Houston TX 77082

LINDNER, ROBERT DAVID, finance company executive; b. Dayton, Ohio, Aug. 5, 1920; s. Carl Henry and Clara (Serrer) L.; m. Betty Ruth Johnston, Mar. 29, 1947; children—Robert David, Jeffrey Scott, Alan Bradford, David Clark. Grad. high sch. Chmn. bd. United Dairy Farmers, Cin., 1940—; With Am. Financial Corp., Cin., 1950-95, former v.p., vice chmn. bd., now vice chmn. bd. dirs. Trustee No. Bapt. Theol. Sem. Served with U.S. Army, 1942-45. Mem. Masons (33 degree). Home: 6950 Given Rd Cincinnati OH 45243-2840 Office: United Dairy Farmers 3955 Montgomery Rd Cincinnati OH 45212-3733

LINDNER, WILLIAM H., state official. Sec. Fla. Dept. Mgmt. Svcs., Tallahassee. Office: State of Fla Dept Mgmt Svcs Ste 250 Bldg 4050 4050 Esplanade Way Tallahassee FL 32399-0999

LINDO, DELROY, actor. Appeared in films Malcolm X, 1992, Mr. Jones, 1993, Crooklyn, 1994, Clockers, 1995, Get Shorty, 1995, Broken Arrow, 1996, Feeling Minnesota, 1996. Office: Internat Creative Mgmt 8942 Wilshire Blvd Beverly Hills CA 90211*

LINDO, J. TREVOR, psychiatrist, consultant; b. Boston, Feb. 12, 1925; s. Edwin and Ruby Ianty (Peterson) L.; m. Thelma Elaine Thompson, Sept. 22, 1962. BA, NYU, 1946; cert. in pre-clin. studies, U. Freibourg, Switzerland, 1953; MD, U. Lausanne, Switzerland, 1957. Lic. psychiatrist, N.Y., Conn. Clin. instr. Columbia U., N.Y.C., 1965-75, asst. clin. prof., 1975-82, assoc. clin. prof., 1982-85; attending psychiatrist Bedford-Stuyvesant Cmty. Mental Health Clinic, Bklyn., 1976-86, med. dir., 1986—; attending psychiatrist Harlem Hosp. Ctr., N.Y.C., 1964-75; vis. psychiatrist Interfaith Hosp., Bklyn., 1976-85; psychiat. cons. Bklyn. Bur. Cmty. Svc., 1980, Marcus Garvey Manor, Bklyn., 1982-86; candidate Nat. Bd. Forensic Examiners, 1995. Co-chairperson com. Dr. Thomas Matthew, N.Y.C., 1974. With U.S. Mcht. Marine, 1947-51. Fellow Am. Coll. Internal Physicians; mem. Nat. Med. Assn., Am. Psychiat. Assn., Provident Clin. Soc. (v.p. 1980-82, parliamentarian 1982—), Bklyn. Psychiat. Soc., Black Psychiatrists of Am. Avocations: travel, African art, sailing, swimming. Office: 1265 President St Brooklyn NY 11213-4237 also: Bedford Stuyvesant Cmty Mental Health Ctr 1406 Fulton St Brooklyn NY 11216-2606

LINDQUIST, CLAUDE S., electrical and computer engineering educator; b. Des Moines, Mar. 13, 1940; s. Claude R. and Eva E. (Cox) L.; children: Todd, Tad. BA, U. Redlands, 1963; BSEE, Stanford U., 1963; MSEE, Oreg. State U., 1964, PhD, 1968. Design engr. Collins Radio, Newport Beach, Calif., 1968-71; prof. Calif. State U., Long Beach, 1971-84; prof. elec. and computer engring. U. Miami, Fla., 1984—; cons. Phoenix Data, Computer Automation, Edwards Pacemaker Systems, Bournes, KVB Equipment Systems, Vega Electronics, Datanetics, 1973-81, SHAPE Tech. Ctr., 1993; pres. E&H Electronics, Long Beach, 1979-84; vis. prof. U. Calif., Irvine, 1983-84. Author: Active Network Design, 1977, Adaptive and Digital Signal Processing, 1989; contbr. over 100 tech. papers. Mem. IEEE (sr.), CAS Soc., AASP Soc., Omicron Delta Kappa, Phi Beta Delta, Alpha Epsilon Lambda. Republican. Mem. Assemblies of God Ch. Avocations: church out-reach programs, boating. Office: U Miami Elec and Computer Engring Dept PO Box 24-8294 Miami FL 33124

LINDQUIST, EVAN, artist, educator; b. Salina, Kans., May 23, 1936; s. E.L. and Linnette Rosalie (Shogren) L. B.S.E., Emporia State U., 1958; M.F.A., U. Iowa, 1963; m. Sharon Frances Huenergardt, June 8, 1958; children: Eric, Carl. One man shows include Mo. Arts Council, 1973-75, Albrecht Art Mus., St. Joseph, Mo., 1975, 89, S.E. Mo. State U., 1977, Sandzen Gallery, Lindsborg, Kans., 1978, Galerie V. Kunstverlag Wolfbrum, Vienna, 1979, Poplar Bluff, Mo., 1987, Gallery V, Kans. City, Mo., 1988, Northwest Mo. State U., 1991, U. Iowa, Iowa City, 1995, WR Harper Coll., Palatine, Ill., 1996; group shows include Benjamin Galleries, Chgo., 1976, City of Venice, 1977, Boston Printmakers, 1971-87, Visual Arts Ctr. of Alaska, Anchorage, 1979, Western Carolina U., 1980, Pa. State U., 1980, Kans. State U., 1980, U. N.D., 1981 & 92, Ariz. State U., 1981, 93, Barcelona, Cadaques, Girona, 1990, 93, 94, Tulsa, 1982, Jay Gallery, N.Y.C., 1983, Artists Books, German Dem. Republic, 1984, U. Tenn.-Knoxville, 1985, Memphis State U., 1985, Ark. Arts Ctr., 1983-83, Miss. State U., 1986, Hunterdon Art Ctr., Clinton, N.J., 1986-87, 94, 95, Washington, 1988, Soc. of Am. Graphic Artists/Printmakers, 1988-94, Boston, 1989-94, John Szoke Gallery, 1989, Woodstock, N.Y., 1990, 92, Silvermine Guild Galleries, New Canaan, Conn., 1992, 93, Woodstock Artists Assn., Littman Gallery, Portland State U., Galeria Brita Prinz, Madrid, Spain, 1992, U. Nebraska, 1992, Parkside National, Kenosha, Wis., 1993, 95, Minot, N.D., 1994, Fla. Community Coll., Jacksonville, Fla., 1995, Stonemetal Press, San Antonio, Tex., 1995, San Diego Art Inst., 1995, Schenectady (N.Y.) Mus., 1995, Fla. Printmakers, Jacksonville, 1996, Clemson U., S.C., 1996, U. Tex., Tyler, 1996; represented in permanent collections Albertina, Vienna, Art Inst. Chgo., Nelson-Atkins, Kansas City, Phoenix Art Mus., Uffizi Gallery, Florence, Municipal Gallery, Dublin, San Francisco Art Mus., Whitney Mus. Am. Art, N.Y.C., St. Louis Art Mus., Museo Reina Sofia, Madrid, others; staff artist Emporia State U., 1958-60; prof. Ark. State U., 1963—, pres.'s fellow, 1981-82, 84-85; exhibition dir. Delta Nat. Small Prints Exhibition Ark. State U., 1996. Mem. Soc. Am. Gr. Artists, Coll. Art Assn. Am., MidAm. Coll. Art Assn., Visual Artists and Galleries Assn. Office: PO Box 2782 State University AR 72467-2782

LINDQUIST, MICHAEL ADRIAN, career military officer; b. Cheyenne, Wyo., Nov. 12, 1946; s. Swen George and Beryl Esme (Edwards) L.; m. Frances Eleanor Arnold, Apr. 14, 1968; children: Michella, Michael, Patricia. BS in Econs., U. Tampa, 1975; MS in Logistics Mgmt., Fla. Inst. Technology, Melbourne, 1985. Enlisted U.S. Army, 1966, advanced through ranks to col.; staff officer 3d Support Command U.S. Army, Frankfurt, West Germany, 1980-83; exec. officer 8th Maintenance Group U.S. Army, Hanru, West Germany, 1983-85; cmdr. 601st Ord BN U.S. Army, Aberdeen Proving Ground, Md., 1986-88, dep. dir. tests Test & Evaluation Command, 1988-89; action officer The Joint Staff U.S. Army, Pentagon, 1990-93; comdr. Tobyhanna (Pa.) Army Depot U.S. Army, 1993-95; comdr. Combat Equipment Group Asia U.S. Army, Charleston, S.C., 1995—. Mem. Assn.U.S. Army, VFW, Ret. Officers Assn., Ordnance Assn., Am. Def. Preparedness. Avocations: golf, coin collecting, stamp collecting. Office: Strategic Mobility & Logistics Base 103 Guidance Rd Goose Creek SC 29445-6060

LINDQUIST, RAYMOND IRVING, clergyman; b. Sumner, Nebr., Apr. 14, 1907; s. Rev. Elmer H. and Esther (Nyberg) L.; m. Ella Sofield, Sept. 16, 1930; children: Ray Irving, Ruth Elizabeth Lindquist McCalmont. Student, Kearney State Coll., 1925; A.B., Wheaton Coll., Ill., 1929; student, Columbia U. Law Sch., 1929-30; A.M., Princeton U., 1933; Th.B. (Hugh Davies prize homiletics; Erdman prize Bible; Zwemer fellow Comparative Religions), Princeton Sem., 1933; D.D., Cumberland U., 1939, Ursinus Coll., 1980; LL.D., Bloomfield Coll., N.J., 1957, Eastern Coll., 1977; L.H.D., Calif. Coll. Medicine, 1963. Ordained to ministry Presbyn. Ch., 1934; dir. religious edn. Third Presbyn. Ch., Newark, 1931-34; minister Old First Presbyn. Ch., Orange, N.J., 1934-53, Hollywood First Presbyn. Ch., 1953-71; vis. prof. homiletics Bloomfield Sem., N.J., 1945-53; lectr. Princeton Sem., Pittcairn-Crabbe, Pitts., U. Iowa, USAF, Israel, Germany, Johnston Island, UCLA, U. Soc. Calif., Pentagon, Northwestern U., Chgo. Sunday Evening Club, Westminster Coll., Mo., Tel Aviv, Zurich, Switzerland; pres. bd. nat. missions United Presbyn. Ch., 1955-62, gen. coun., 1955-62; v.p. Templeton Found. Author: Notes for Living. Bd. dirs. Covenant Life (formerly Presbyn. Ministers Fund), Phila., chmn. bd., 1980—; bd. dirs. Presbyn. Med. Center, Hollywood, Calif., 1954—, Met. YMCA, Los Angeles; trustee Princeton Theol. Sem., So. Calif. Presbyn. Homes., Olmstead Trust, Hollywood, Calif., 1954—. Recipient Gold medal Religious Heritage Am., 1984. Mem. Phi Kappa Delta. Clubs: Rotary (Los Angeles) (bd. dirs.), Los Angeles Country (Los Angeles); Symposium (Princeton); Glen Lake (Sparta, N.J.), Sunset Rock (Sparta, N.J.); Shadow Mountain (Palm Desert, Calif.). Home: 19191 Harvard Ave Regents Point Windcrest Irvine CA 92612 *Faith is not jumping to conclusions: it is concluding to jump...The thought of God swings the world like a rock on a rope.*

LINDQUIST, RICHARD JAMES, portfolio manager; b. East Orange, N.J., June 22, 1960; s. Chester Edward and Rose Theresa (Grosso) L.; m. Clare Jacangelo, June 21, 1987; children: Matthew Cole, Kimberly Rose. BS, Boston Coll., 1982; MBA, U. Chgo., 1986. CFA; chartered investment counselor. Investment rsch. analyst N.Y. Life Ins. Co., N.Y.C., 1982-84; bond trader, v.p. T. Rowe Price Assocs., Inc., Balt., 1986-88; portfolio mgr., v.p. Prudential Ins. Co. Am., Newark, 1989; mng. dir. portfolio mgr. CS 1st Boston Investment Mgmt., N.Y.C., 1989-95; exec. dir., portfolio mgr. BEA Assocs., N.Y.C., 1995—. Mem. Assn. Investment Mgmt. & Rsch., Fin. Analysts Fedn., Inst. CFAs, Investment Coun. Assn. Am., Balt. Soc. Security Analysts, N.Y. Athletic Club, Spray Beach Yacht Club. Avocations: golf, cycling, chess. Office: BEA Assocs One Citicorp Ctr 153 E 53rd St New York NY 10022-4611

LINDROS, ERIC BRYAN, professional hockey player; b. London, Ont., Can., Feb. 28, 1973; s. Carl and Bonnie L. Student, York U., Toronto. With Detroit Compuware, 1989—, Phila. Flyers, 1992—; mem. Canadian Olympic Team, 1992, Cup All-Star team, 1989-90, OHL All-Star team 1990-91, NHL All-Star team, 1992-93; player NHL All-Star game, 1992-93. Recipient Plus/Minus award Canadian Hockey League, 1990-91, Red Tilson trophym 1990-91, Eddie Powers Meml. trophy, 1990-91; named Most Valuable Player World Jr. Hockey Championships, 1990, Most Valuable Player Ont. Jr. Hockey Assn., 1991, Player of the Year Canadian Hockey League, 1990-91, Hart Trophy, 1995, Lester B. Pearson Award, 1995, Nat. Hockey League. Office: Core States Ctr 3601 N Broad St Philadelphia PA 19140-4107*

LINDROTH, LINDA (LINDA HAMMER), artist, curator, writer; b. Miami, Sept. 4, 1946; d. Mark Roger and Mae Lang Hammer; m. David George Lindroth, May 26, 1968 (div. Mar. 1985); m. Craig David Newick, June 6, 1987; 1 child, Zachary Eran Newick. BA in Art, Douglass Coll., 1968; MFA in Art, Rutgers U., 1979. Exhibits include Aetna Gallery, 1987, 89, 91, Franklin Furnace, N.Y.C., 1977, Conn. Commn. Arts, Hartford, 1985, 96, Aldrich Mus. Contemporary Art, Ridgefield, Conn., 1987, 95, Downey (Calif.) Mus. Art, 1989, Zimmerli Art Mus. Rutgers U., 1989, Wesleyan U. Ctr. for the Arts, 1990, Boston Pub. Libr., 1991, John Michael Kohler Art Ctr., Sheboygan, Wis., 1992, Joseloff Gallery U. Hartford, 1994, Artspace, New Haven, 1991, 92, 93, 94, 95, DeCordova Mus., Lincoln, Mass., 1995, Urban Glass, Bklyn., 1996, others; represented in permanent collections The Mus. Modern Art, N.Y.C., The Met. Mus. of Art, N.Y.C., The Mus. City of N.Y., Polaroid Collection/Artist Program, N.J. State Mus., Trenton, The Bibliotheque Nationale, Paris, Ctr. for Creative Photography, Tucson, The Newark Mus., The Jane Voorhees Zimmerli Art Mus., New Brunswick, N.J., High Mus. Art, Atlanta, Yale U. Dir. Artspace, Inc., New Haven; mem. Mayor's Task Force on Pub. Art, New Haven. Recipient Ann. Design Rev. award ID Mag., 1990, 91, 93, Honorable Mention, Nat. Peace Garden Design Competition, 1989, Pitts. Corning Archtl. Design Competition, 1988, Individual Artist fellow N.J. State Coun. on Arts, 1974-75, 83-84; grantee Found. for Contemporary Performance Arts, Inc., 1989, 90, Fission Fusion NEA InterARts, 1989, grantee New Eng. Found. for Arts, 1992, Fairfield U., 1995; Conn. Commn. Arts fellow, 1995, New Eng. Found. Arts/NEA Regional Photography fellow, 1995-96, Arch. League of N.Y., 1996. Studio: Lindroth & Newick 219 Livingston St New Haven CT 06511-2209

LINDSAY, BRUCE GEORGE, statistics educator; b. The Dalles, Oreg., Mar. 7, 1947; s. George Speers and Geneva Elizabeth (Davis) L.; m. Teresa Ann Goff, Aug. 23, 1969 (div. 1995); children: Dylan Brantley, Camden James. BA, U. Oreg., 1969; PhD, U. Wash., 1978. Postdoctoral fellow Imperial Coll., London, 1978-79; asst. prof. Pa. State U., University Park, 1979-85, assoc. prof., 1985-87, prof. stats., 1987-91, disting. prof. stats., 1992—. Assoc. editor Annals Stats., 1985-91, 93—, Annals Stat. Math., 1987—, Math. Methods Stats., 1992—; contbr. articles to profl. jours. Scoutmaster Boy Scouts Am., State College, Pa., 1988-89. With USCG, 1970-74. Recipient Humboldt Sr. scientist award, 1990; Guggenheim Found. fellow, 1996. Fellow Inst. Math. Stats.; mem. Am. Statis. Assn., Math. Assn. Am., Internat. Statis. Inst. Democrat. Avocations: running, hiking, reading. Office: Pa State U Dept Stats 326 Classroom Bldg University Park PA 16802-2111

LINDSAY, CAROL FRANCES STOCKTON, art specialist; b. Haileyville, Okla., Dec. 25, 1940; d. Buel Benjamin and Natalie Frances (Bailey) Stockton; m. Robert Carr Lindsay, Oct. 15, 1961; children: Matthew Robert, Mark Stockton, Michael George. AA, Stockton Coll., 1960; BA, Calif. State U., Sacramento, 1970; MEd, U. Nev., 1982, EdS, 1990. Cert. tchr., adminstr., Calif. Tchr. 2d grade Taft Elem. Sch., Stockton, Calif., 1966-67; tchr. 2d and 3rd grades Dry Creek Joint Elem. Sch., Roseville, Calif., 1967-69; tchr. 1st-5th grades Chartville Elem. Sch., Linden, Calif., 1970-77; tchr. 1st grade Northside Elem. sch., Fallon, Nev., 1977-80; tchr. 3rd grade West End Elem. Sch., Fallon, 1980-83; tchr. 5th-8th grades Roosevelt Roads Midd./High Sch., Ceiba, P.R., 1983-85, fine arts dept. coord., 1984-85; student svcs. coord., tchr. Stead Elem. Sch., Reno, 1986-89; student svcs. coord. Silver Lake Elem. Sch., Reno, 1989-93, dean students, 1993-94; art specialist Clark County Sch. Dist., 1994-95; sch. rep. Antilles Consolidated Sch. System Curriculum Coun., Ceiba, P.R., 1983-85. Co-author: Art Goals and Objectives, 1989; author: Site Based Management, 1990. Co-chairperson Muscular Dystrophy Telethon, Fallon, 1980-82; neighborhood supr. Am. Heart Assn., Reno, 1985-86; mem. PTA. Named one of Outstanding Tchr. of Am., 1972. Mem. AAUW, ASCD, Linden Edn. Assn. (bldg. rep., exec. bd. dirs. 1970-77), Churchill County Edn. Assn. (bldg. rep., exec. bd. dirs. 1980-83), Nev. Assn. Sch. Adminstrs., Internat. Reading Assn., Washoe County Tchrs. Assn. (Disting. Svc. award 1988, Dedicated Svc. award 1992, bldg. rep. 1989-92), Clark County Classroom Tchrs. Assn., Nat. Art Edn. Assn. Avocations: art, music, golfing.

LINDSAY, CHARLES JOSEPH, banker; b. Bklyn., Mar. 21, 1922; s. George Patrick and Evelyn (Roth) L.; m. Marie A. Faraone, Jan. 19, 1947; children—George, Charles, Mary Ann. Student, U. Mo., 1943; grad., Am. Savs. and Loan Inst., 1947, Savs. and Loan Grad. Sch., Ind. U.; Profl. Studies in Bus. Adminstrn; Degree with high distinction, Pace U., 1973. With Nassau Fed. Savs. formerly Serial Fed. Savs. & Loan Assn., N.Y.C., 1947—, successively teller, supr., asst. v.p., asst. sec., sec., v.p. and sec., sr. v.p. and dir., pres., 1965—; ret. as pres. Nassau Fed. Savs., 1986, bd. dirs.; former mem. faculty, bd. govs. Savs. and Loan Inst. Mem. pres.'s adv. coun. Pace U. Served with USAAF, World War II. Decorated Air medal with cluster; recipient Alumnus of Year award Pace U., 1975. Mem. State League Savs. Assn. (former dir.), Nat. League Savs. Assns. (exec. com., former dir.), Alumni Assn. Pace U. (pres. 1977—, dir.). Club: Aspetuck Country (Weston, Conn.). Home: Winter Leaves 4 Lilac Ln Weston CT 06883-3008 also: 100 Worth Ave Palm Beach FL 33480-4447

LINDSAY, DALE RICHARD, research administrator; b. Bunker Hill, Kans., Aug. 9, 1913; s. Charles Edwin and Iva (Missimer) L.; m. Sybil Anne McCoy, June 6, 1937; children—Martha Lou Lindsay Cover, Judith Anne Lindsay Clapp, Patricia Dale. A.B., U. Kans., 1937, M.A., 1938; Ph.D., Iowa State Coll., 1943. Entomologist Dept. Agr., summers 1937-39; teaching fellow, instr., research asso. Iowa State Coll., 1938-43; commd. officer USPHS, 1943—, scientist dir., 1955; assigned malaria control in war areas, 1943-45; entomologist charge operations Communicable Disease Center Activies, Pharr, Tex., 1945-48; chief Thomasville (Ga.) field sta., 1948-53; chief program evaluation sect., div. research grants NIH, 1953-55, asst. chief div., 1955-60, chief div., 1960-63; dep. to gen. dir. Mass. Gen. Hosp., Boston, 1963-65; spl. asst. to chancellor health scis. U. Calif. at Davis, 1965-67, asst. chancellor research and health scis., 1968-69; asso. commr. sci. FDA, 1969-71; asso. dir. med. and allied health edn. Duke U., 1971-75; asst. dir. for sci. coordination Nat. Center for Toxicol. Research, Jefferson, Ark., 1975-76; adj. prof. medicine U. Ark. Med. Sch., 1975-76; asso. dept. family and community medicine U. Ariz., 1977-82; Agrl. bd. Nat. Acad. Sci.-NRC, 1970-73; mem. exec. com., public trustee Nutrition Found., 1972-76, Environ. and Agrl. Found., 1974-79; chmn. sci. adv. bd. Nat. Center for Toxicol. Research, 1972-74. Fellow AAAS, Am. Public Health Assn.; mem. Entomol. Soc. Am. (gov. bd. 1958-62), Commd. Officer Assn. USPHS (treas. nat. exec. com. 1959-61) , Sigma Xi, Phi Kappa Phi, Gamma Sigma Delta.

LINDSAY, DAVID BREED, JR., aircraft company executive, former editor and publisher; b. Fayetteville, N.C., Dec. 25, 1922; s. David Breed and Helen Carter (Dodson) L.; m. Elizabeth Hotchkiss Girvin, June 19, 1944; children: David G.B., Robert A., Ann C., Edward H. B.S., Purdue U., 1947. Reporter/photographer Marion (Ind.) Chronicle, 1947-48; editor, gen. mgr. Sarasota (Fla.) Herald Tribune, 1948-55, editor, pres., 1955-82; pres. Cavalier Aircraft Corp., 1955-70, Lindair, Inc., 1971—; designer, test pilot Enforcer Aircraft; cons. Piper Aircraft Corp. Founder, trustee New Coll., Sarasota, 1950-75. Served with U.S. Army, 1943-46. Decorated Army Commendation medal. Mem. Am. Newspaper Pubs. Assn. (dir.), Am. Newspaper Pubs. Assn. Found. (pres.), Inter Am. Press Assn. (dir.), Soc. Exptl. Test Pilots., Sigma Delta Chi. Episcopalian. Clubs: Met. (Washington); Old Capital (Monterey, Calif.). Inventor various aircraft systems, including Enforcer Aircraft. Office: 4930 Bay Shore Rd Sarasota FL 34234-3719

LINDSAY, DIANNA MARIE, educational administrator; b. Boston, Dec. 7, 1948; d. Albert Joseph and June Hazelton (Mitchell) Raggi; m. James William Lindsay III, Feb. 14, 1981. BA in Anthropology, Ea. Nazarene Coll., 1971; MEd in Curriculum and Instrn., Wright State U., 1973, MEd in Social Studies Edn., 1974, MEd in Edn. Adminstrn., 1977; EdD in Urban History, Ball State U., 1976. Supr. social edn. Ohio Dept. Edn., Columbus, 1976-77; asst. prin. Orange City Schs., Pepper Pike, Ohio, 1977-79; prin. North Olmsted (Ohio) Jr. High Sch., 1979-81; dir. secondary edn. North Olmsted City SChs., 1981-82; supt. Copley (Ohio)-Fairlawn City Schs., 1982-85; prin. North Olmsted High Sch., 1985-89, New Trier High Sch., Winnetka, Ill., 1989-96, Worthington Kilbourne H.S., Columbus, Ohio, 1996—; bd. dirs. Harvard Prins. Ctr., Cambridge, Mass. Contbr. articles to profl. jours. Bd. dirs. Nat. PTA, Chgo., 1987-89 (Educator of Yr. 1989), Found. Human Potential, Chgo.,; bd. trustee Columbus Jewish Country Day Sch. Named Prin. of Yr. Ohio Art Tchrs., 1989, one of 100 Up and Coming Educators, Exec. Educator Mag., 1988; recipient John Vaughn Achievements in Edn. North Cen. Assn., 1988. Mem. AAUW, Ill. Tchrs. Fgn. Lang., Rotary Internat., Phi Delta Kappa. Methodist. Avocations: stained glass, reading, travel, biking, harpist. Office: Worthington Kilbourne High Sch 1499 Hard Rd Columbus OH 43235-1991

LINDSAY, DONALD PARKER, former savings bank executive; b. Spokane, Aug. 31, 1915; s. Alexander John and Alice Maude (Kelly) L.; m. Patricia Lally, Oct. 2, 1940; children: Karen, Bridget, Monica. Student, U. Wash., 1934-35. With Lincoln Mut. Savs. Bank, Spokane, 1935-85; pres. Lincoln Mut. Savs. Bank, 1962-80, chief exec. officer, 1969-80, chmn., 1978-85; past dir. First Nat. Bank, Spokane; cons. AID Mission to Iran, 1964. Chmn. United Red Feather drive, Spokane, 1952; past pres. Spokane Philharmonic; trustee Spokane Unltd.; past trustee Mcpl. League Spokane; past chmn. Champagne Ball Charities; chmn. adv. com. on bond issues Spokane Sch. Bd., 1978; mem. bus. adv. com. Wash. State U. Coll. Bus. and Econs., 1979—; mem. Spokane Arts Com., 1976-85, chmn., 1984-85. Served from pvt. to 1st lt. USAAF, 1942-46. Mem. Wash. Savs. League (pres. 1961-62), Nat. Assn. Mut. Savs. Banks (past dir.), Savs. and Loan Found. (past mem. nat. bd.), Mut. Savs. Bank Assn. Wash. (pres. 1979), U.S. League Savs. Assns. (mut. instns. com.), Nat. League Insured Savs. Assn. (mem. bd. govs. 1966-76, mem. exec. com. 1974-76), Soc. Residential Appraisers (pres. Spokane chpt. 1952), Spokane C. of C. (trustee, exec. com. 1970-72, 78-82, sec.-treas. 1979, vice chmn. 1980-81, chmn. 1981-82). Clubs: University (past pres.), Spokane Country (past pres.), Spokane, Manito Golf and Country, Empire, Prosperity, Spokane. Office: 905 W Riverside Ave Spokane WA 99201-1006

LINDSAY, FRANKLIN ANTHONY, business executive, author; b. Kenton, Ohio, Mar. 12, 1916; s. Harry Wyatt and Ruth (Andrews) L.; m. Margot Coffin, Dec. 17, 1948; children: Catherine, Alison (dec.), John Franklin. A.B., Stanford U., 1938; postgrad., Harvard U., 1946. With Columbia div. U.S. Steel Corp., 1938-39; exec. asst. to Bernard Baruch, U.S. del. UN Atomic Energy Commn., 1946; cons. Ho. of Reps. Select (Herter) Com. on Fgn. Aid, 1947-48, ECA, Paris; rep. to exec. com. OEEC, 1948-49; with CIA, 1949-53; with pub. affairs program Ford Found., 1953-56; prin. McKinsey & Co., Inc., N.Y.C., 1956-61; exec. v.p., dir. Itek Corp., Lexington, Mass., 1961-62, pres., dir., 1962-75, chmn. bd., 1975-81, chmn. exec. com., 1981-83; chmn. Engenics, Inc., Menlo Park, Calif., 1983-85; rsch. Assoc. Inst. Politics, Harvard U., 1967-71; cons. 2d Hoover Commn., 1954, The White House, 1955; mem. Rockefeller Spl. Studies Panel Econ. Policy, 1956, Gaither Com. Nat. Security Policy, 1957; asst. staff dir. President's Com. World Econ. Policy, 1958; mem. President Elect's Task Force on Disarmament, 1960; dir. Com. for Nat. Trade Policy, 1956-71; adv. coun. dept. econs. Princeton U., 1961-64; mem. Wilson Ctr. Adv. coun. Smithsonian Instn., 1980-94; trustee Bennington Coll., 1963-73; chmn. bd. trustees Edn. Devel. Ctr., 1967-73; mem. vis. com. dept. econs. Harvard U., 1976-80; mem. President's Adv. Com. on Trade Negotiations, 1976-79; bd. dirs. Nat. Bur. Econ. Rsch., 1976-93, mem. exec. com., 1980—, chmn. 1983-86; mem. adv. coun. Gas Rsch. Inst., 1977-83; vice chmn. energy and raw materials, bus. and industry adv. com. OECD, 1977-82, chmn. 1980, mem. adv. bd. Pub. Agenda Found., 1978-84; mem. NRC Commn. Engring. Systems, 1978-84, panel on balancing nat. interest NAS, 1985-87; bd. dirs. Resources for the Future, 1978-86; assoc. Ctr. for Internat. Affairs, Harvard U., 1988-96; vis. scholar Woodrow Wilson Ctr. for Scholars, Washington, 1987-88, 90; adj. prof. Internat. Mgmt. Inst., Kiev, Ukraine, 1993—; mem. standing policy group on Russia and Eurasia, The Atlantic Coun. of the U.S., 1996—. Author: New Techniques of Management Decision Making, 1958, Beacons in the Night: War and Revolution in Yugoslavia 1941-45, 1993; contbg. author: Preparing Tomorrow's Business Leaders Today, The Conscience of the City, Removing Obstacles to Economic Growth; contbr. articles on nat. and fgn. policy to profl. jours. Vis. scholar Woodrow Wilson Ctr. for Scholars, Washington, 1987-88, 90. Lt. col. AUS, 1940-45; with guerrilla forces 1944-45, Europe (OSS); chief U.S. Mil. Mission to Yugoslavia, 1945. Decorated Legion of Merit; recipient Gold Freedom medal Republic of Slovenia. Mem. Nat. Planning Assn. (vice chmn. com. arms control 1959-62), Coun. Fgn. Rels., Inst. Strategic Studies (London), Com. for Econ. Devel. (trustee 1967—, vice chmn. 1974-88, mem. rsch. and policy com. 1968—), Can.-Am. Com., Hudson Inst. (pub. mem.), Saturday Club (Boston), Century Club (N.Y.), Phi Beta Kappa, Tau Beta Pi.

LINDSAY, GEORGE CARROLL, former museum director; b. Cochranville, Pa., Sept. 28, 1928; s. J. George and M. Elizabeth (Copeland) L.; m. Mary-Edythe Shelley, June 27, 1953. BA, Franklin and Marshall Coll., 1950; student, Dickinson Sch. Law, 1950-53; M.A. (Wintherthur fellow early Am. culture 1953-55), U. Del., 1955. Asst. to dir. Henry Francis du Pont Wintherthur Mus., Del., 1955-56; asst. curator ethnology Smithsonian Instn., 1956-57, asso. curator cultural history, 1957-58, curator mus. service, 1958-66; dir. mus. services N.Y. State Mus., 1966-81, dir., 1981-83, dir. planning and program devel., 1983-86; exec. dir. Vanderbilt Mus., 1986-89; lectr. early Am. decorative arts and architecture; cons. in field; v.p. Alexandria Assn., Va., 1961-62, pres., 1962-63, bd. dirs., 1963-66; bd. dirs. Greater Washington Ednl. TV Assn., 1964-66, mem. programming com., 1965-66; bd. dirs. No. Va. Fine Arts Assn., 1964-66, Mus. Audio-Visual Applications Group, 1962-70; mem. com. furnishing ofcl. reception room State Dept., 1960-75. Bd. dirs. Menands (N.Y.) Pub. Libr., 1970-86, Albany Symphony Orch., 1969-72, ARC, Albany, 1977-86; active Strasburg (Pa.) Borough Coun., 1992-96, pres., 1994-95; trustee Octoraro United Presbyn. Ch., 1993—, Strasbourg Heritage Soc., 1997—. Mem. Am. Assn. Mus. (coun. 1969-72, v.p. 1970-71, chmn. profl. rels. com. 1974-80), N.Y. State Assn. Mus. (sec. 1968-77, pres. 1977-79, coun. 1985-89), N.E. Mus. Conf. (bd. govs. 1982-85, chmn. long range planning com. 1983-85), St. Andrew's Soc. (pres. Albany 1983-85), St. Andrew's Soc. Phila. Mem. Soc. of Friends. Address: 255 Wallingford Rd Strasburg PA 17579-1448

LINDSAY, GEORGE EDMUND, museum director; b. Pomona, Calif., Aug. 17, 1916; s. Charles Wesley and Alice (Foster) L.; m. Geraldine Kendrick Morris, 1972. Student, San Diego State Coll., 1936-39; B.A., Stanford U., 1951, Ph.D., 1956. Dir. Desert Bot. Gardes, Phoenix, 1939-40, San Diego Natural History Mus., 1956-63; Dir. Calif. Acad. Scis., San Francisco, 1963-82, dir. emeritus, 1982—. Served to capt. USAAF, 1943-46. Decorated Air medal with 3 clusters, Bronze Star. Fellow San Diego Soc. Natural History, Zool. Soc. San Diego, Calif. Acad. Scis., A.A.A.S., Cactus and Succulent Soc. Spl. rsch. taxonomy desert plants, Cactaceae of Baja Calif., Mex. Home: 87 Barbaree Way Tiburon CA 94920-2223 Office: Calif Acad Scis San Francisco CA 94118

LINDSAY, GEORGE PETER, lawyer; b. Bklyn., Feb. 22, 1948; s. Charles Joseph and Marie Antionette (Faraone) L.; m. Sharon Winnett, Sept. 8, 1973; children: William Charles, Kimberly Michelle. BA, Columbia U., 1969; JD, Harvard U., 1973. Bar: N.Y. 1974, Mass. 1985, U.S. Dist. Ct. (so. dist.) N.Y. 1974, U.S. Ct. Appeals (2d cir.) 1975. Assoc. White & Case, N.Y.C., 1973-82; ptnr. Miller, Wrubel & Dubroff, N.Y.C., 1982-83, Sullivan & Worcester LLP, N.Y.C., 1983—. Mem. ABA, Assn. Bar City of N.Y., N.Y. State Bar Assn. Office: Sullivan & Worcester LLP 767 3rd Ave New York NY 10017-2023

LINDSAY, HELEN MILLS, psychotherapist; b. Cleve., June 2; d. Don Parmenter Mills and Grace Elidia Stroup; m. Harry Anderson Lindsay, July 21, 1991. BA, Case Western Ress. U., 1932; MS of Social Sci., Boston U., 1947. Lic. clin. social worker. Sr. sen. Calif. Sr. Legislature, 1985—; pres. Aux. Laguna Hills Adult Day Health Care, 1993—. Mem. Leisure World Dem. Club (pres. 1984-85, Leisure Worlder of Month 1996). Avocations: playing piano, gardening. Address: 801 Ronda Mendoza Unit A Laguna Hills CA 92653-5902

LINDSAY, JAMES WILEY, agricultural company executive; b. Des Moines, Sept. 13, 1934; s. Worthington U. Lindsay and Marsha E. (Wiley) Asher; m. Shirley L. Shutt, July 2, 1953 (div. May 1985, dec. 1990); children: Elizabeth Lindsay Foster, James W. II, Jennifer, Lindsay; m. Jean M. Baumann, Aug. 2, 1986; 1 child, Amanda Marie. Mgr. ops. Archer, Daniels, Midland, Fredonia, Kans., 1968-70, Lincoln, Nebr., 1970-72; mgr. export Archer, Daniels, Midland, Decatur, Ill., 1972-74; v.p. western region Archer, Daniels, Midland, Lincoln, 1974-76; v.p. ops. Archer, Daniels, Midland, Cedar Rapids, Iowa, 1979-80; ops. mgr. Archer, Daniels, Midland, Decatur, 1980-83; pres. Brazil ops. T.V.P., Inc., Campinas, Brazil, 1976-79; chief exec. officer AG Processing Inc., Omaha, 1983—; bd. dirs. ABC Ins., Des Moines; mem. adv. bd. FirstBank; v.p. bd. dirs. Proagro and Protinal, Caracas, Venezuela. Mem. Nat. Soybean Processors Assn. (chmn. 1987-91), Jaycees (pres. Fredonia chpt. 1963-64, bd. dirs. Des Moines chpt. 1960). Republican. Roman Catholic. Lodge: Masons. Office: AG Processing Inc PO Box 2047 Omaha NE 68103-2047

LINDSAY, JOHN, IV, principal; b. Trenton, N.J., Oct. 31, 1960; s. John III and Dolores (Hambright) L.; m. Mandy Jane Ablitt, Aug. 23, 1982; children: John V, James Stirling, Cameron Sinclair. BS, Trenton State Coll., 1982; MS, U. North Tex., 1993. Cert. tchr., adminstr., Tex., N.J. Tchr. Dallas Ind. Sch. Dist., 1984-91, asst. prin. Pearl C. Anderson Mid. Sch., 1991-95; prin.Aledo (Tex.) Elem. Sch. Aledo Ind. Sch. Dist., 1995—;

demonstration tchr. Project CARE, Dallas, 1985-88; team leader Leadership Devel. Acad. Dallas Ind. Sch. Dist., 1989. Mem. ASCD, Tex. State Tchrs. Assn., Phi Delta Kappa. Avocations: reading, golf. Home: 213 Scenic Trail Willow Park TX 76087 Office: Aledo Elem Sch 12 Vernon Rd Aledo TX 76008-3103

LINDSAY, JOHN VLIET, former mayor, former congressman, author, lawyer; b. N.Y.C., Nov. 24, 1921; s. George Nelson and Eleanor (Vliet) L.; m. Mary Harrison, June 18, 1949; children—Katharine, Margaret, Anne, John Vliet. Grad., St. Paul's Sch., Concord, N.H., 1940; B.A., Yale U., 1944, LL.B., 1948; LL.D. (hon.), Harvard U., 1969, Williams Coll., 1968. Bar: N.Y. State 1949, N.Y. Dist. Ct. (so. dist.) N.Y 1950, U.S. Supreme Ct. 1955, D.C. 1958. Mem. firm Webster & Sheffield, N.Y.C., 1953-60, 74-91, presiding ptnr., 1989-91; of counsel Mudge Rose Guthrie Alexander & Ferdon, N.Y.C., 1991-94, ret., 1994; exec. asst. to U.S. atty. gen., 1955-56; mem. 86th-89th Congresses from 17th Dist. N.Y.; mayor N.Y.C., 1965-73; Commentator on TV. Author: Journey Into Politics, 1966, The City, 1970, The Edge, 1976. Bd. mem. emeritus Lincoln Ctr. for Performing Arts; chmn. emeritus bd. dirs. Lincoln Ctr. Theatre Co. Lt. USNR, 1943-46. Mem. Assn. of Bar of City of N.Y. (exec. com. 1956-60), ABA, N.Y. State Bar Assn., Assn. Former Mems. Congress (pres. 1987-88). Episcopalian. Democrat.

LINDSAY, JUNE CAMPBELL MCKEE, communications executive; b. Detroit, Nov. 14, 1920; d. Maitland Everett and Josephine Belle (Campbell) McKee; BA with honors in Speech (McGregor Fund Mich. grantee), U. Mich., 1943; Electronics Engring. certificate Signal Corps Ground Signal Svc., 1943; postgrad. (Inst. Gen. Semantics grantee), U. Chgo., 1944-45, N.Y. U. (Armour grantee), 1945-46, Columbia U., 1946-47, Wayne State U., 1960-64, U. Mich., 1964-70, 78—; MA, Specialist-in-Aging Cert., Inst. of Gerontology, 1982; m. Powell Lindsay, Nov. 25, 1967; 1 child, Kristi Costa-McKee. Coord., activator McKee Prodns., Detroit, 1943-56, Being Unltd., 1957—, InterBeing, Inc., 1979—, M.U.T.U.A.L. A.I.D., 1981—; info. dir. Suitcase Theatre, Inc., Lansing and Ann Arbor, Mich. Cons. Cornelian Corner Detroit, Inc., 1957-63, Islamic Ctr. Found. Soc., Detroit, 1959-62, City Ann Arbor Human Rels. Commn., 1966-68, Urban Adult Edn. Inst., Detroit, 1968-69, Mich. Bell Tel. Co., Detroit, 1969, African Art Gallery Founders, Detroit Inst. Arts, 1964, WKAR-TV, Mich. State U., 1971—. Mem. Nat. Caucus, Ctr. for Black Aged; bd. dirs. Mus. Youth Internat., Saline, Mich., Ann Arbor Community Devel. Corp. Chaplain's asst. Univ. Hosp., Ann Arbor, 1971-72; program dir. People-to-People, Ann Arbor, 1971-72; Suitcase Theatre tour coord. Brit. Empire's Leprosy Relief Assn., 1972—; assembly cons. Baha'i Faith, 1960—; mem. Comprehensive Health Planning Coun. S.E. Mich., Baha'i Internat. Health Agy., Inst. for Advancement of Health, Mission Health, Catherine McAuley Health Ctr. Share and Care Support Group. Recipient Award for Excellence Mich. Ednl. Assn., 1971, Mich. Assn. Classroom Tchrs., 1972; exec. dir. Powell Lindsay Meml. Program in Theatre and Communications, Louhelen Baha'i Sch. and Residential Coll., U. Mich., Flint, Mott Community Coll., 1988—. Mem. ACLU, Soc. for Individual Responsibility, Am. Women in Radio and TV, Broadcast Pioneers, Am. Fedn. Advt., Internat. Platform Assn., Gray Panthers, Planetary Citizens, Am. Assn. Adult and Continuing Edn., Am. Pub. Health Assn., Wellness Assocs., Mich. Assn. Holistic Health, Internat. Health Found., Inst. Study Conscious Evolution, Am. Soc. on Aging, Mich. Health Coun., Nat. Coun. on Aging, U.S., Assn. Humanistic Psychology, Assn. Holistic Health, Internat. Soc. for the Study of Subtle Energies and Energy Medicine, Nat. Inst. for the Clin. Application of Behavioral Medicine, Assn. Baha'i Studies, Interfaith Coun. Peace and Justice, Mental Health Assn. in Mich., Mich. League Human Svcs., Mich. Soc. Gerontology, Comprehensive Health Planning Coun. Southeastern Mich., Subarea Adv. Coun., Washtenaw County Council on Aging, Nat. Coun. Sr. Citizens, Am. Assn. Ret. Persons, Nat. Assn. Pub. Health Policy, People's Med. Soc., Alliance for Democracy and Diversity, Giraffe Soc., Living Tao Found., World Future Soc., Nat. Trust for Hist. Preservation, Orgn. Devel. Inst. (registered orgn. devel. profl. 1988), UN Assn. of the U.S.A. Home: 2339 S Circle Dr Ann Arbor MI 48103-3442

LINDSAY, LESLIE, packaging engineer; b. Amsterdam, N.Y., Oct. 30, 1960; d. R. Gardner and Dorothy (Loucks) L. BA in Advt., Mich. State U., 1981, BS in Package Engring., 1982. Cert. profl. engr. in packaging. Constrn. inspector N.Y. State Dept. Transp., Albany, 1983; sr. package design engr. Wang Labs., Inc., Lowell, Mass., 1983-90; sr. packaging engr. Apple Computer, Inc., Santa Clara, Calif., 1990—; conf. speaker Internat. Safe Transit Assn., 1994. N.Y. State Regents scholar, 1977; recipient Silver Ameristar award for electronics packaging, 1993, ID mag. packaging award, 1993, Ameristar judges award for merit, 1995. Mem. Soc. Packaging Profls., Inst. Packaging Profls. (mem. reduction, reuse, and recycling of protective packaging task group), Boston Women's Rugby Club (tour chmn. 1985), Wang Ultimate Frisbee (social chmn. 1986-89). Home: 210 Sondra Way Campbell CA 95008 Office: Apple Computer Inc 20650 Valley Green Dr Cupertino CA 95014-1763

LINDSAY, NATHAN JAMES, aerospace company executive, retired career officer; b. Monroe, Wis., May 24, 1936; s. Ralph Allen and Gertrude (Wartenweiler) L.; m. Shirley Rae Montgomery, Feb. 2, 1958; children: Lori E. Lindsay Smith, Anne, Nathan J. Jr., Susan E. BS in Mech. Engring., U.Wis., 1958, MS in Mech. Engring., 1965; MS in Systems Mgmt., U. So. Calif., L.A., 1976. Commd. 2d lt. USAF, 1958, advanced through grades to maj. gen., 1988; munitions officer USAF Weapons Ctr., Tripoli, Libya, 1959-61; weapons logistics officer USAF Europe, Wiesbaden, Germany, 1961-63; Titan III propulsion officer USAF Space Systems Divsn., L.A., 1965-69; aircraft guns devel. officer Air Force Armament Lab., Fla., 1969-70; grad. Armed Forces Staff Coll., Norfolk, Va., 1970; mgmt. auditor Air Force Systems Command, Andrews AFB, Md., 1971-73; grad. Def. Systems Mgmt. Coll., Ft. Belvoir, Va., 1973; space systems policy officer Air Force Office Special Projects, L.A., 1973-74, launch systems integration mgr., 1974-78; dir. policy and adminstrn. Air Force Office Space Systems, Pentagon, Washington, 1978-80; dir. space ops. support Air Force Space Divsn., L.A., 1980-82, program mgr. launch and control systems, 1982-84; comdr. Ea. Space and Missile Ctr., Patrick AFB, Fla., 1985-86; dep. comdr. for space launch and control systems Air Force Space Divsn., L.A., 1986-87; dir. office spl. projects Office Sec. of Air Force, L.A., 1987-92; v.p. comml. programs Lockheed Martin Astrospace; mem. investigation task force NASA Challenger Accident, Kennedy Space Ctr., 1986. Co-chmn. Brevard County, Fla. Civilian-Mil. Affairs Coun., Cocoa Beach, 1984-86; elder Presbyn. Ch. Decorated D.S.M., Def. Superior Svc. medal, Legion of Merit with one oak leaf cluster, Meritorious Svc. medal with one oak leaf cluster, Joint Svc. Commendation medal, Air Force Commendation medal with one oak leaf cluster, Def. Disting. Svc. medal, NASA Disting. Svc. medal, Gen. Thomas White USAF Space trophy, 1992, AAS Mil. Astronautics award, 1993. Mem. AIAA, Am. Astronautical Soc., Air Force Assn. (Bernard A. Shriever Space award 1989), Nat. Space Club (bd. dirs. 1992-94), U. Wis. Alumni Assn., Am. Legion. Avocations: hiking, travelling, fishing, reading. Home: 48 Madison Dr Plainsboro NJ 08536-2318

LINDSAY, PATRICIA MAE, physician, medical administrator; b. Kilbourne, Ill., Aug. 26, 1942; d. William Louden and Virginia Mae (Sutton) L. BA, Drake U., 1964; MD, U. Ill., 1971. Assoc. med. dir. Ill. State U. Med. Ctr., Normal, 1978-81; chief of hypertension City of Faith, Tulsa, 1981-86; ptnr. Glass-Nelson Med. Clinic, Tulsa, 1986-88; med. dir. Med. Missions, Tulsa, 1983—; asst. prof. U. Okla. Med. Sch.; assoc. with med. dir. various med. hosps. and clinics, St. Petersburg, Russia, 1991-96, also internat. clinics. Vol. physician homeless children, St. Petersburg, Russia, 1997. NIH fellow, 1967-68; recipient Chem. Rubber Co. Physics Achievement award Drake U., 1961-62; Vsevolesk Hosp. wing named in her honor, St. Petersburg, Russia, 1994. Mem. AMA, ACP, Geriat. Med. Soc., Okla.Med. Soc., Tulsa Med. Soc., Beta Beta Beta. Office: Med Missions 2918 E 78th St Tulsa OK 74136-8732

LINDSAY, ROGER ALEXANDER, investment executive; b. Dundee, Scotland, Feb. 18, 1941; s. Archibald Carswell Lindsay and Edith Paterson Bissett. Student, The Morgan Acad., Dundee, Queen's Coll. U. St. Andrews, Scotland. Asst. acct., office mgr. Andrew G. Kidd Ltd., Dundee, 1964; head office acct. Associated British Foods Ltd., London, 1966; sec., treas. Wittington Investments, Ltd., Toronto, 1971-95; exec. v.p. Wittington Investments Ltd., Toronto, 1991-95; pres. Fort House Investments, Toronto, 1989; bd. dirs. Loblaw Cos. Ltd., Intercon Security Ltd., United World Coll. Internat. Can., Inc., The W. Garfield Weston Found., Benedictine Heritage Ltd., Veritel Can., Inc. Trustee Presbyn. Ch. of Can. Knight, Comdr. The Sov. Order of St. John, Serving Bro. Ven. Order Hosp. St. John. Fellow Inst. Mgmt., Inst. Dirs., Soc. Antiquaries Scotland; mem. Inst. Chartered Accts. Scotland, Royal Overseas League, The Nat. Club (pres. Toronto), Coral Beach Club (Bermuda), Montes Club (London). Avocations: heraldry, antique silver, genealogy. Office: Fort House Investments, 150 Heath St W Ste 1302, Toronto, ON Canada M4V 2Y4

LINDSAY, WILLIAM KERR, surgeon; b. Vancouver, B.C., Can., Sept. 3, 1920; s. James Arthur and Lottie Mary (Early) L.; m. Frances Beatrice Ferris, Feb. 15, 1945; children—William Arthur, Barbara Susanne, Katherine Mary, Anne Louise. M.D., U. Toronto, 1945, BS in Medicine, 1949, M.S., 1959. Intern Toronto Gen. Hosp., 1945-46; resident Toronto Gen. Hosp. and Hosp. Sick Children, 1948-51, Montreal Gen. Hosp., 1951-52, Baylor U. Hosp., 1952-53; practice medicine, specializing in plastic surgery Toronto, 1953—; staff surgeon to head divsn. plastic surgery Hosp. for Sick Children, 1953-86, cons., 1986—; project dir. Research Inst., 1954-85; faculty dept. surgery U. Toronto Faculty of Medicine, 1953-86, prof., 1968-86, chmn. interhospital com. for plastic surgery, 1965-86, prof. emeritus, 1986—; Chmn. med. dental staff com. Ont. Hugh MacMillan Treatment Ctr. (formerly Crippled Childrens Ctr.), 1958-63. Trustee McLaughlin Found., 1986—. With M.C., Royal Can. Army, 1943-46; surg. lt. Royal Can. Navy, 1946-47. Recipient Arbor award, 1994; Hon. head burn and plastic surgery dept. Gansu Provincial People's Hosp., Lanzhou City, China, 1994—. Fellow ACS, Royal Coll. Surgeons Can.; mem. Am. Assn. Plastic Surgeons (pres. 1970-71, Hon. award 1995), Can. Soc. Plastic Surgeons (pres. 1963), Easter Seal Soc. Ont. (chmn. med. adv. com. 1957-65, cons. 1952-95, mem. rsch. inst. 1979-95, Gold award 1995), Am. Soc. Plastic and Reconstructive Surgeons (Spl. Achievement award 1979), Am. Soc. Surgery of Hand, Am. Cleft Palate Assn., Brit. Soc. Surgery of Hand. Home: 77 Clarendon Ave, Toronto, ON Canada M4V 1J2 Office: 555 University Ave, Toronto, ON Canada M5G 1X8

LINDSETH, PAUL DOUGLAS, aerospace educator, flight instructor, farmer; b. Rugby, N.D., Dec. 3, 1952; s. Olaf and Ingred Marie (Midtmoen) L.; m. Glenda Norine Sletto, July 27, 1974; 1 child, Brad. BS, N.D. State U., 1974; MA, Cen. Mich. U., 1984; PhD, U. Mich., 1996. Cert. flight instr. Tchr. Hillsboro (N.D.) High Sch., 1974-75; commd. 2d lt. USAF, 1974, advanced through grades to maj.; jet instr. pilot, check pilot USAF, Reese AFB, Tex., 1976-79; dir. ops. USAF, Minot AFB, N.D., 1980-83; dir. standardization and evaluation light lift helicopters USAF, Scott AFB, Ill., 1983-85; flight instr., assoc. prof. Ctr. for Aerospace Scis. U. N.D., Grand Forks, 1985—; farmer, Grand Forks. Contbr. articles to profl. jours. Youth basketball coach YMCA, Grand Forks, 1984-88; mem. Sharon Luth. Ch., Grand Forks, 1984—. Liaison officer CAP USAFR, 1990—. Fellow U. Mich., 1992; leadership finalist Bush Found., 1991. Mem. Am. Assn. Higher Edn., Univ. Aviation Assn., Aerospace Med. Assn., Res. Officers Assn. Avocations: cross-country skiing, water skiing. Home: 2018 Belmont Rd Grand Forks ND 58201-7314 Office: U ND Ctr Aerospace Scis Univ and Tulane Grand Forks ND 58202-8216

LINDSEY, ALFRED WALTER, federal agency official, environmental engineer; b. Camden, N.J., Jan. 10, 1942; s. Alfred Hazel Lindsey and May Marquerite (Ergood) Warrington; m. Kathleen Francis Leighton, Aug. 15, 1964; 1 child, Amy Elizabeth. BS in Pulp and Paper Tech., N.C. State U., 1964. Dep. dir. tech. div. Office of Solid Waste EPA, Washington, 1979-85, dep. dir. Office Environ. Engring., 1985-88, dir. Office Environ. Engring., 1988-95, environ. tech. exec., 1995, dep. dir. Office Wastewater Mgmt., 1996—. Contbr. articles to profl. jours. Bagpiper Prince Georges Police Pipes and Drums. Mem. Sr. Execs. Assn., Nature Conservancy. Republican. Methodist. Office: EPA 4201 401 M St SW Washington DC 20460-0001

LINDSEY, CASIMIR CHARLES, zoologist; b. Toronto, Ont., Can., Mar. 22, 1923; s. Charles Bethune and Wanda Casimira (Gzowski) L.; m. Shelagh Pauline Lindsey, May 29, 1948. B.A., U. Toronto, 1948; M.A., U. B.C., Vancouver, 1950; Ph.D., Cambridge (Eng.) U., 1952. Div. biologist B.C. Game Dept., 1952-57; with Inst. Fisheries, also dept. zoology U. B.C., 1953-66; prof. zoology U. Man., Winnipeg, 1966-79; dir. Inst. Animal Resource Ecology, U. B.C., 1980-85; mem. Fisheries and Oceans Adv. Council, 1981-86; prof. emeritus U. B.C., 1988—; bd. govs. Vancouver Public Aquarium, 1956-66, 80-95; external assessor univs. S ingapore and Nanyang, 1979-81; cons. in field. Author papers in field. Served with Can. Army, 1943-45. Recipient Publ. award Wildlife Soc., 1972; Saunderson award for excellence in teaching U. Man., 1977; Rh Inst. award, 1979; Nuffield Found. grantee, 1973; Killam sr. fellow, 1985-86. Fellow Royal Soc. Can.; mem. Can. Soc. Zoologists (pres. 1977-78), Can. Soc. Environ. Biologists (v.p. 1974-75), Am. Soc. Ichthyologists and Herpetologists (gov.). Office: U BC Dept of Zoology, 6270 University Blvd, Vancouver, BC Canada V6T 1Z4

LINDSEY, D. RUTH, physical education educator; b. Kingfisher, Okla., Oct. 26, 1926; d. Lewis Howard and Kenyon (King) L. BS, Okla. State U., 1948; MS, U. Wis., 1954; PEd, Ind. U., 1965. Registered kinesiotherapist, 1970. Instr. Okla. State U., Stillwater, 1948-50, Monticello Coll., Alton, Ill., 1951-54, DePauw U., Greencastle, Ind., 1954-56; prof. Okla. State U., Stillwater, 1956-75; vis. prof. U. Utah, Salt Lake City, 1975-76; prof. phys. edn. Calif. State U., Long Beach, 1976-88; prof. emeritus phys. edn. Calif. State U., 1988—; freelance author, cons. Westminster, Calif. Co-author: Fitness for the Health of It, 6th edit., 1989, Concepts of Physical Fitness, 9th edit., 1997, Fitness for Life, 4th edit., 1997, Concepts of Physical Fitness and Wellness, 2d edit., 1997, The Ultimate Fitness Book, 1984, Survival Kit for Those Who Sit, 1989, A Menu of Concepts: Physical Fitness Concepts, Toward Active Lifestyles and Fitness and Wellness Concepts, Toward Health Lifestyles, 1996; editor, pub.: Why Don't You Salt the Beans, 1997; editor: Perspectives: Jour. of Western Soc. for Phys. Edn. Coll. Women, 1988-95. Amy Morris Homans scholar, 1964; recipient Disting. and Meritorious Svc. Honor award Okla. Assn. Health, Phys. Edn. and Recreation, 1970, Meritorious Performance award Calif. State U., 1987, Julian Vogel Meml. award Am. Kinesiotherapy Assn., 1988. Fellow AAHPERD, Am. Kinesiotherapy Assn., Calif. Assn. Health, Phys. Edn., Recreation and Dance, Nat. Coun. Against Health Fraud, Orange County Nutrition Coun., Tex. and Acad. Authors Assn., Western Soc. for Phys. Edn. of Coll. Women (Hon. Mem. award 1995), Phi Kappa Phi. Republican. Baptist. Avocations: golf, travel, writing.

LINDSEY, DAVID HOSFORD, lawyer; b. Kingsville, Tex., July 25, 1950; s. Ernest Truman and Helen Elizabeth (Hosford) L.; m. Marilyn Kay Williams, June 8, 1974; children: Seth Williams, Brooks Daniel. BS in Bus. Adminstrn., U. Mo., 1972; JD, Washburn U., 1975. Bar: Mo. 1975. With trust dept. Commerce Bank, Kansas City, Mo., 1974-75, asst. v.p., 1979-83, v.p., 1983-85, sr. v.p., 1985-94, chief credit officer, 1989—; mgr., sales dept. Pioneer Pallet, Inc., North Kansas City, Mo., 1976; asst. cashier Nat. Bank, North Kansas City, 1977, asst. v.p., 1977-78, v.p., 1978-79. Vice chmn. planning and zoning com. City of Liberty, Mo., 1981-93; bd. dirs. Kansas City Met. YMCA (treas., mem. exec. com.). Mem. Mo. Bar Assn., Lawyers Assn. Kansas City, Kansas City Met. Bar Assn., Robert Morris Assn. (bd. dirs. Kansas City chpt.), Kansas City C. of C., Kansas City Alumni Assn. (bd. dirs.), Clayview Country Club, Phi Gamma Delta, Omicron Delta Kappa. Baptist. Home: 602 Camelot Dr Liberty MO 64068-1176 Office: Commerce Bank 1000 Walnut St Kansas City MO 64106-2107

LINDSEY, DOTTYE JEAN, marketing executive; b. Temple Hill, Ky., Nov. 4, 1929; d. Jesse D. and Ethel Ellen (Bailey) Nuckols; m. Willard W. Lindsey, June 14, 1952 (div.). BS, Western Ky. U., 1953, MA, 1959. Owner, Bonanza Restaurant, Charleston, W.Va., 1965; tchr. remedial reading Alice Waller Elem. Sch., Louisville, 1967-75, tchr., 1953-67, 1975-84, contact person for remedial reading, 1968—; regional mgr. A.L. Williams Fin. Mktg. Co., 1988—; profl. model Cosmo/Casablancas Modeling Agy., Louisville, 1984-89; with Primerica Fin. Svcs. (formerly A.L. Willams Fin. Svcs.), Louisville, 1988—; model, 1984-89; regional mgr. Primerica Fin. Svcs., 1988—. Treas. Met. Louisville Women's Polit. Caucus, 1980-88, Ky. Women's Polit. Caucus, 1988-91; bd. sponsor ROTC Western Ky. U., 1950; local precinct capt., 1987—; election officer, 1984—; treas. Ky. Women's Polit. Caucus, 1988-91; elected at-large mem. exec. com. Louisville/Jefferson County Dem., 1996. Named Miss Ky., 1951. Mem. NEA, Ky. Edn. Assn., Jefferson County Tchrs. Assn., various polit. action coms., Internat. Reading Assn., Am. Childhood Edn. Assn. Baptist.

LINDSEY, JACK LEE, III, curator; b. June 7, 1958; s. Charles Edward and Ruth Jacquelyn (Hensley) L. BA in Am. Social and Cultural History with honors, BA in Studio Art with honors, Guilford Coll., 1980; MA in Am. Civilization and Curatorial Studies, U. Pa., 1986, postgrad., 1986—. Asst. curator exhibitions Guilford Coll., Greensboro, N.C., 1978-80; chmn. dept. art and history Atlantic Friends Sch., Northfield, N.J., 1981-85; field rschr., archivist U. Pa., Phila., 1986-87, instr. depts. Am. civilization and folklore and folklife, 1986-89; asst. curator Am. decorative arts Phila. Mus. Art, 1986-88, assoc. curator Am. decorative arts, 1988-89, curator Am. decorative arts, 1990—; chmn. adv. bd. Phila. Folklore Project, 1989-91; lectr. in field. Contbr. articles to profl. jours. Recipient Outstanding Educators award Friends Coun. in Edn., 1984, 85; Newlin Grad. History scholar Guilford Coll., 1980; Rotary Internat. Edn. scholar, 1980-81; rsch. grantee NEA, 1980; Edward Maverick fellow Attingham Trust, 1987. Mem. Am. Folklore Soc. (vice chmn. adv. bd. 1989-90). Office: Phila Mus Art 26th And The Pky Philadelphia PA 19130

LINDSEY, JOHN HORACE, insurance executive, museum official; b. Waxahachie, Tex., July 28, 1922; s. Harry E. and Marie (Smith) L.; m. Sara Houstoun, Aug. 30, 1946; children: Edwin (dec.), David C. BA, Tex. A&M U., 1944. Propr. Lindsey Ins. Agy., Houston, 1953—; bd. of regents Texas A&M U System. Former v.p. Houston Mus. Fine Arts; former pres. Alley Theatre; bd. dirs. South Tex. Coll. Law, Tex. A&M Rsch. Found., College Station; pres. Tex. A&M U. Alumni, 1964; vice chmn. bd. visitors U.S. Mil. Acad.; bd. dirs. George Bush Presdl. Libr. Found. Recipient Disting. Alumni award Tex. A&M U. Home: 3640 Willowick Rd Houston TX 77019-1114 Office: 1st City Bldg Tex Am Bldg 1021 Main St Ste 1740 Houston TX 77002

LINDSEY, JONATHAN ASMEL, development executive, educator; b. Bulloch County, Ga., June 9, 1937; s. Joel Wesley and Ethel Iora (Stickland) L.; m. Edythe Annette Loewer, Apr. 3, 1965; children—Julianna Elizabeth, Jonathan Edward. A.B., George Washington U., 1961; B.D., So. Bapt. Sem., Louisville, 1964; Ph.D., So. Bapt. Sem., 1968; M.S.L.S., U. Ala., 1975. Assoc. prof., librarian Judson Coll., Marion, Ala., 1967-77; assoc. dean, librarian Meredith Coll., Raleigh, N.C., 1977-83; librarian Baylor U., Waco, Tex., 1983-89, dir. found. devel., 1989-95; dir. donor info./recognition, 1995—. Author: (monographs) Free To Be, 1975, Change and Challenge, 1978, (with others) Professional Ethics and Librarians, 1985, Performance Evaluation: A Management Basic, 1986; editor: N.C. Libraries (H.W. Wilson award 1981), 1979-83, Publications in Librarianship, 1988-93; contbr. articles and book revs. to profl. publs. Mem. Waco Peace Alliance, PTA. Mem. ALA, Nat. Soc. Fund Raising Execs., Coun. for Advancement and Support of Edn., Tex. Libr. Assn. Home: 8265 Mosswood Dr Waco TX 76712-2407 Office: Baylor U PO Box 97026 Waco TX 76798-7026

LINDSEY, LAWRENCE BENJAMIN, economist; b. Peekskill, N.Y., July 18, 1954; s. Merritt Hunt and Helen Ruth (Hissam) L.; m. Susan Ann McGrath, Aug. 28, 1982; 2 children. AB magna cum laude, Bowdoin Coll., Brunswick, Maine, 1976; MA, Harvard U., 1981, PhD, 1985; JD (hon.), Bowdoin Coll., 1993. Economist Coun. Econ. Advisers, Washington, 1981-84; from asst. prof. to assoc. prof. Harvard U., Cambridge, Mass., 1984-90; faculty rsch. fellow Nat. Bur. Econ. Rsch., Cambridge, 1984-89; from assoc. dir. to spl. asst. to Pres., Office of Policy Devel., The White House, Washington, 1989-91; gov. Fed. Res. Bd., Washington, 1991-97; resident scholar Am. Enterprise Inst., 1997—; mng. dir. Econ. Strategies, Inc., 1997—. Author: The Growth Experiment, 1990; contbr. articles to profl. jours. Recipient Walter Wriston award Manhattan Inst., 1988, Disting. Pub. Svc. award Boston Bar Assn., 1994. Office: Am Enterprise Inst 1150 17th St NW Washington DC 20036

LINDSEY, ROBERTA LEWISE, music researcher, historian; b. Munich, Apr. 23, 1958; d. Fred S. and Elsie E. (White) L. BMus, Butler U., 1980, MMus, 1987; PhD, Ohio State U., 1996. Pres., owner Profl. Typing Svcs./Indpls., 1980-84; mktg. specialist Merchants Mortgage Corp., Indpls., 1985-87; exec. asst. Ind. Arts Commn., Indpls., 1988-90; GTA Ohio State U., Columbus, 1990-94, music libr. asst., 1991-93, student coord. music in Ohio festival, 1993, vol. tutor coord., 1994-95; lectr. Ohio State U., Marion, 1995; rep. Susan Prter Meml. symposium Ohio State U., Columbus, 1995; vis. rsch. fellow Am. Musci Rsch. Ctr., 1997. Contbr. articles to profl. jours. Reader Ctrl. Ind. Radio Reading, Inc., Indpls., 1985-90; co-founder, mem. Grad. Music Students Assn., Ohio State U., Columbus; mem. multicultural diversity com. Coun. of Grad. Students, Columbus, 1992, mem. orgns. and elections com., 1992, co-chair orientation com., 1993. Sinfonia Rsch. grantee Sinfonia Found., 1993; recipient Grad. Student Alumni Rsch. award Ohio State U., 1993. Mem. Sonneck Soc., Am. Musicological Soc., Coll. Music Soc., Soc. of Ethnomusicology. Presbyterian.

LINDSEY, STEVEN FRANK, banker; b. Herrin, Ill., Jan. 7, 1955; s. Frank Jr. and Dorene (Pattarozzi) L.; m. Nancy Beth Lawrence, Nov. 11, 1977; children: Jill Ellen, Andrea Maria. BA in Econs. and Bus. Adminstrn., Coe Coll., 1977; student, Ill. Bankers Sch., 1984-85, Herbert V. Prochnow Sch. Bank., 1985-87. Teller Bank of West Frankfort, Ill., 1977-79; loan officer Bank of Zeigler, Ill., 1979; v.p. lending Banterra Bank of West Frankfort, 1979—. Mem., advisor task force Treas. of State of Ill., Springfield, 1992. Mem. Ill. Small Bus. Growth Corp. (chmn. bd. dirs. 1991—, Lender of Yr. for State of Ill. 1993, 94), U.S. Small Bus. Adminstrn. (cert. lending status, preferred lending status, SBA Fin. Svcs. Advocate of Yr. for Ill. 1995), Moose (lodge # 795), Franklin County Country Club. Southern Baptist. Avocations: golf, gardening. Office: Banterra Bank West Frankfort 110 E Oak St West Frankfort IL 62896-2741

LINDSEY, SUSAN LYNDAKER, zoologist; b. Valley Forge, Pa., Aug. 23, 1956; d. Howard Paul and Lillian Irene (Whitman) Lyndaker; m. Kevin Arthur Lindsey, July 17, 1982; 1 child, Ryan Howard. BS in Biology, St. Lawrence U., 1978; MA in Zoology, So. Ill. U., Carbondale, 1980; PhD in Zoology, Colo. State U., 1987. Rschr. St. Lawrence U., Kenya, East Africa, 1978; tchr. Beth Jacob H.S., Denver, 1986-87; rschr. mammal dept. Dallas Zoo, 1988-93; exec. dir. Wild Canid Survival and Rsch. Ctr., Eureka, Mo., 1993—; adj. prof. Cedar Valley Coll., 1992-93, So. Ill. U., Carbondale, 1996—; propagation group mem. Red Wolf Species Survival Plan, Tacoma, Wash., 1994—, Mexican Gray Wolf Species Survival Plan, Albuquerque, 1993—; rsch. coord. Okapi Species Survival Plan, 1997—. Contbr. articles to profl. jours. Docent Denver Zool. Found., Denver Zoo, 1985-88. Mem. Am. Zoo and Aquarium Assn., Am. Behavior Soc., Am. Soc. of Mammalogists, Beta Beta Beta, Phi Beta Kappa, Psi Chi. Avocations: horseback riding, canoeing, gardening, photography, travel. Office: Wild Canid Survival Rsch Ctr Wash U PO Box 760 Eureka MO 63025

LINDSEY, TANYA JAMIL, secondary education administrator; b. New Orleans, Tex., Sept. 10, 1961; d. Fredrick Jr. and Ruthie Lee (Leach) Lindsey. BS, Xavier U., New Orleans, 1985; MEd in Ednl. Adminstrn., U. North Tex., 1992. Cert. in sci., middle mgmt., Tex. Tchr. sci. Dallas Ind. Sch. Dist., 1988—; with Leadership Devel. Acad. Dallas Ind. Sch. Dist., 1993—. Youth vol. Voters League, New Orleans. Mem. ASCD, NAACP, Tex. Middle Sch. Assn., Profl. Adminstrs. and Suprs. Coun., Nat. Alliance of Black Sch. Educators, Alpha Kappa Alpha. Avocations: theatre, reading. Home: 2626 Duncanville Rd Dallas TX 75211

LINDSKOG, DAVID RICHARD, lawyer; b. New Haven, Aug. 4, 1936; s. Gustaf Elmer and Charlotte (Birely) L.; m. Elisabeth Lagg, Jan. 28, 1978; 1 child, Stefanie. B.A., Yale U., 1958; LL.B., U. Va., 1965. Bar: N.Y. 1966, conseil juridique France 1978, avocat 1992. Assoc., Curtis, Mallet-Prevost, Colt & Mosle, N.Y.C., 1965-72, ptnr., 1973—. Served to lt. USNR, 1958-62. Mem. Internat. Bar Assn. Episcopalian. Club: Yale (N.Y.C.). Home: 22 Shore Acre Dr Old Greenwich CT 06870-2130 Office: Curtis Mallet-Prevost Colt & Mosle 101 Park Ave New York NY 10178

LINDSKOG, NORBERT F., business and health administration educator, consultant; b. St. Cloud, Minn., Aug. 2, 1932; s. Magnus Alf and Dorthey Ann (Donken) L. BS, St. Cloud State U., 1954, MS, 1957; MHA,

Northwestern U., 1960; DEd, Ariz. State U., 1977. Bus. tchr. Minn. High Schs. and Santa Barbara (Calif.) City Coll., 1954-58; adminstrv. extern Louis A. Weiss Meml. Hosp., Chgo., 1958-59, exec. v.p., 1960-66; adminstrv. resident St. Luke's Hosp., St. Paul, 1959-60; mgmt. cons. in Health & Med. Adminstrn. Booz Allen & Hamilton, Inc., Chgo., 1966-68; cons. in Hosp. adminstr., assoc. for Edn. Ill. Hosp. Assoc., Chgo., 1968-71; faculty assoc. Ctr. for Health Svcs. Adminstr. Grad. Sch. Bus., Ariz. State U., Tempe, 1974-75; asst. prof. bus. Harold Washington Coll. City Colls. of Chgo., 1968-71, assoc. prof. bus., 1971-76, prof. bus., health adminstrn., 1976—, chmn. dept. bus., 1970-82; bd. dirs. Shoreline Corp., 1988—; lectr. Harold Washington Coll., 1962-68; Cen. YMCA Coll., Chgo, 1973-78, cons. 1978; adj. prof. Internat. Acad. Merchandising & Design, 1978—. Prepub. editor and reviewer for many recent bus. related texts; contbr. to profl. jours. Fellow Royal Soc. Health, Am. Assn. Health Care Execs.; mem. Nat. Assn. Mgmt. Educators, Ill. CPA Found., Am. Soc. for Health Manpower Edn. and Tng., Nat. Bus. Edn. Assn., Ill. Bus. Edn. Assn., Chgo. Bus. Edn. Assn., Am. Hosp. Assn., Northwestern U. Health Adminstrn. Alumni Assn., Ariz. State U. Alumni Assn., St. Cloud State U. Alumni Assn., Masons, Phi Delta Kappa, Delta Pi Epsilon, Alpha Delta Mu, Kappa Delta Pi, Pi Omega Pi, Pi Delta Epsilon, Apha Pi Omega. Home: 6301 N Sheridan Rd Chicago IL 60660-1728 Office: Harold Washington Coll 30 E Lake St Chicago IL 60601-2403

LINDSLEY, DONALD BENJAMIN, physiological psychologist, educator; b. Brownhelm, Ohio, Dec. 23, 1907; s. Benjamin Kent and Mattie Elizabeth (Jenne) L.; m. Ellen Ford, Aug. 16, 1933; children: David Ford, Margaret, Robert Kent, Sara Ellen. A.B., Wittenberg Coll. (now Univ.), 1929, D.Sc. (hon.), 1959; A.M., U. Iowa, 1930, Ph.D., 1932; Sc.D. (hon.), Brown U., 1958, Trinity Coll., Hartford, Conn., 1965; D.Sc. (hon.), Loyola U. Chgo., 1969; Ph.D. (hon.), Johannes Gutenberg U., Mainz, W.Ger., 1977. Instr. psychology U. Ill., 1932-33; NRC fellow Harvard U. Med. Sch., 1933-35; research assoc. Western Res. U. Med. Sch., 1935-38; asst. prof. psychology Brown U.; also dir. psychol. and neurophysiol. lab. Bradley Hosp., 1938-46; dir. war research project on radar operation Yale, OSRD, Nat. Def. Research Com., Camp Murphy and Boca Raton AFB, Fla., 1943-45; prof. psychology Northwestern U., 1946-51; prof. psychology, physiology, psychiatry and pediatrics UCLA, 1951-77, prof. emeritus, 1977—, mem. Brain Research Inst., 1961—, chmn. dept. psychology, 1959-62; William James lectr. Harvard, 1958; Univ. Research lectr. U. Calif. at Los Angeles, 1960; Phillips lectr. Haverford Coll., 1961; Walter B. Pillsbury lectr. psychology Cornell U., 1963; vis. lectr. Kansas State U., 1966, Tex. A & M U., 1980; Mem. sci. adv. bd. USAF, 1947-49; undersea warfare com. NRC, 1951-64; cons. NSF, 1952-54; mem. mental health study sect. NIMH, 1953-57; neurol. study sect. Nat. Inst. Neurol. Diseases and Blindness, 1958-62; cons. Guggenheim Found., 1963-70, mem. ednl. adv. bd., 1970-78; chmn. behavioral scis. tng. com. Nat. Inst. Gen. Med. Scis., 1966-69; mem. behavioral biology adv. panel AIBS-NASA, 1966-71; mem. space sci. bd. NAS, 1967-70; mem. com. space medicine, 1969-71; mem. Calif. Legis. Assembly Sci. and Tech. Coun., 1970-71. Cons. editor Jour. Exptl. Psychology, 1947-68, Jour. Comparative and Physiol. Psychology, 1952-62, Jour. Personality, 1958-62; mem. editorial bd. Internat. Jour. Physiology and Behavior, 1965-77, Exptl. Brain Rsch., 1965-76, Developmental Psychobiology, 1968-82, Neurosci. and Behavioral Physiology, 1976—; contbr. numerous articles on physiol. psychology, neurosci., brain and behavior to sci. jours., also numerous chpts. in books. Trustee Grass Found., 1958-95, emeritus trustee, 1996—. Awarded Presdl. Cert. of Merit (for war work), 1948; recipient Disting. Sci. Achievement award Calif. Psychol. Assn., 1977, Disting. Sci. Contbn. award Soc. Psychophysiol. Rsch., 1984, Disting. Grad. award Dept Psychology U. Iowa, 1987, Disting. Alumnus award for Achievement U. Iowa, 1988, Gerard prize (with H.W. Magoun) Soc. Neurosci., 1988, Gold Medal award Am. Psychol. Found., 1989, Hon. Life Mem. award Dept. Psychobiology, U. Calif., Irvine, 1989; Guggenheim fellow Europe, 1959, hon. fellow UCLA Sch. Medicine, 1986. Mem. Nat. Acad. Scis. (chmn. com. long duration missions in space 1967-72, mem. space sci. bd.), Am. Psychol. Assn. (Disting. Sic. Contbn. award 1959), Am. Physiol. Soc., Soc. Exptl. Psychologists, Am. Electroencephalographic Soc. (pres. 1964-65, hon. mem. 1980—, Herbert Jasper award 1994), AAAS (v.p. 1954, chmn. sect. J. 1977), Midwest Psychol. Assn. (pres. 1952), Am. Acad. Cerebral Palsy, We. Soc. Electroencephalography (hon. mem. with great distinction, pres. 1957, Wilder Penfield award and lectr. 1996), We. Psychol. Assn. (pres. 1959-60), Am. Acad. Arts and Scis., Internat. Brain Rsch. Orgn. (reas. 1967-71), Soc. Neuroscis. (Donald B. Lindsley prize in behavioral neurosci. established in his name), Finnish Acad. of Sci. and Letters (fgn. mem.), Sigma Xi, Alpha Omega Alpha, Gamma Alpha, Phi Gamma Delta. Conglist. Home: 471 23rd St Santa Monica CA 90402-3125

LINDSLEY, JOHN MARTIN, chemical engineer; b. Syracuse, N.Y., Sept. 4, 1914; s. Floyd Adelbert and Katherine Agusta (Birch) L.; m. Lois Dorothy Eshleman, May 6, 1939; children: Katherine Virginia Lindsley Scherer, Nancy Sarah Morris, Karen Jean Knowles. Diploma, Mechanics Inst. (now R.I.T.), 1940; certificate, John Huntington Polytech. Inst, 1940-41; student, U. Pitts., 1944-46. Registered profl. engr., N.Y. Pipe fitter, design draftsman Eastman Kodak Kodak Park, Rochester, N.Y., 1935-40; design engr. chem. plant Carbide and Carbon Chems., South Charleston, W.Va., 1940-42; engr. design Koppers Co., Pitts., 1942-46; new plant ops. Buffalo, Houston, Granite City, Ill., 1943-45; project engr. Eastman Kodak, Kodak Park, Rochester, 1947-55, dept. head construction & maintaince div., 1955-67, dept. head utilities, engring., process design, ops., waste disposal solid and liquid, 1967-75; design ops. assignment Kodak Carbide Carbon, Oak Ridge, Tenn., 1951-54; chair subcom. incineration, Kodak rep. Mfg. Chemist Assn., Washington, 1968-75; vice chmn. Monroe County Sewer Agy./Pure Waters Agy, 1964-73. Mem., chair Gates, Chili Ogden Sch. Bd., Monroe County, Rochester, 1959-68; rep. dist. 21 Republican Party, St. Lucie County, Fla., 1980-85, chair exec. com., 1983-85; mem. Gates Town Planning Bd., Monroe County, 1956-62, 67-75, Monroe County Pure Waters Bd., 1973-75, St. Lucie County Water/Sewer Authority, 1986-92. Mem. AIChE (cert., emeritus). Achievements include designing, built and conceived thin film climbing film evaporator single-pass for heat sensitive and hazardous materials-high vacuum. 90 million Btu/hr. chemical waste incinerator for hazardous/toxic waste, liquid and solid upgraded to 120 million Btu/hr in 1986. EPA approved -no violations in 22 years of operation; conceived, designed, built and put into operation in cooperation with Dow Chem. and 3M.

LINDSTEDT-SIVA, (KAREN) JUNE, marine biologist, environmental consultant; b. Mpls., Sept. 24, 1941; d. Stanley L. and Lila (Mills) Lindstedt; m. Ernest Howard Siva, Dec. 20, 1969. Student, U. Calif.-Santa Barbara, 1959-60, U. Calif.-Davis, 1960-62; B.A., U. So. Calif., 1963, M.S., 1967, Ph.D., 1971. Asst. coordinator Office Sea Grant Programs U. So. Calif., 1971; environ. specialist So. Calif. Edison Co., Rosemead, 1971-72; asst. prof. biology Calif. Luth. U., 1972-73; sci. advisor Atlantic Richfield Co., L.A., 1973-77, sr. sci. advisor, 1977-81, mgr. environ. scis., 1981-86, mgr. environ. protection, 1986-96; sr. environ. cons. ENSR, Camarillo, Calif., 1996—; mem. Nat. Sci. Bd., 1984-90; mem. panels on environ. issues Nat. Rsch. Coun.; mem. Polar Rsch. Bd., 1994—; mem. EPA Panel on Environ. Risk Reduction, 1992-94; mem. NAS Alaska Panel; mem. biology adv. coun. Calif. State U.-Long Beach, 1980-92; bd. dirs. So. Calif. Acad. Scis., 1983-93, pres., 1990-92; mem. Marine Scis.; adv. coun. U. So. Calif. Inst. Coastal and Marine Scis.; trustee Bermuda Biol. Sta. for Rsch.; chmn. Oil Spill Conf., San Antonio, 1989, API Oil Spills Com. Contbr. articles to profl. jours. Recipient Calif. Mus. Sci. and Industry Achievement award, 1976, Trident award for Marine Scis., 11th Ann. Rev. Underwater Activites, Italy, 1970, Achievement award for Advancing Career Opportunities for Women, Career Planning Council, 1978; research grantee; distg. scholar biology Calif. Lut. U. Colloquim Scholars, 1988. Fellow AAAS, ASTM (award of merit 1990), So. Calif. Acad. Scis., Soc. Petroleum Industry Biologists (pres. 1976-80); mem. Marine Tech. Soc., Calif. Native Plant Soc., Am. Inst. Biol. Sci., Phi Beta Kappa, Sigma Xi, Phi Kappa Phi.

LINDSTROM, DONALD FREDRICK, JR., priest; b. Atlanta, July 18, 1943; s. Donald Fredrick Sr. and Elizabeth (Haynes) L.; m. Marcia Pace, Dec. 30, 1983; children: Christopher, Eric, Ashley, Ellison. ABJ, U. Ga., 1966; MDiv, Va. Theol. Sem., 1969; JD, Woodrow Wilson Coll. Law, 1977; postgrad., U. West Fla., 1984. Lic. marriage and family therapist. Broadcast journalist radio and TV Atlanta and N.Y.C., 1961-68; priest Episcopal ch., 1969—; rector Episcopal Ch. Mediator, Meridian, Miss., 1991—; pvt. practice as marriage and family therapist, Pensacola, Fla., 1983-91; ecumenical officer Diocese of Ctrl. Gulf Coast, 1989-91, Miss., 1992—; bd. visitors Kanuga Conf. Ctr., 1993—; guest chaplain U.S. Ho. of Reps., 1994; mem. ecumenical staff gen. conv. Episcopal Ch., 1994. Writer, producer The Cry for Help, The Autumn Years. Chaplain Atlanta Police Dept., 1975-78, Meridian Police Dept., 1995—; pres. N.W. Fla. chpt. Nat. Kidney Found., 1987-88; mem. Leadership Atlanta, 1975; bd. dirs. Leadership Pensacola; trustee Fla. Trust for Hist. Preservation. Mem. Am. Assn. for Marriage and Family Therapy (clin.), Mental Health Assn. (life, bd. dirs. Pensacola 1986-88), Navy League, Order of Holy Cross (assoc.), Regional Chambellan, Confrerie de la Chaine des Rotisseurs, Bailli, Bailliage de Meridian, Alpha Tau Omega, Sigma Delta Chi, Delta Gamma Kappa. Avocations: music, photography, traveling, fly fishing. Office: Episcopal Ch Mediator 3825 35th Ave Meridian MS 39305-3617

LINDSTROM, GREGORY P., lawyer; b. Hollywood, Calif., Aug. 4, 1953. AB summa cum laude, UCLA, 1975; JD, U. Chgo., 1978. Bar: Calif. 1978. Ptnr. Latham & Watkins, Costa Mesa, Calif. Mem. Phi Beta Kappa. Office: Latham & Watkins 650 Town Center Dr Ste 2000 Costa Mesa CA 92626-1905

LINDTEIGEN, SUSANNA, rancher, state official; b. Bismarck, N.D., Oct. 3, 1947; d. Casper J. and Lillian Rose (Gross) Kraft; m. Richard Lindteigen; children: Robin Lee, Rhonda Wendy. BS, Mary Coll., 1979; MPA, U. N.D., 1981. Bookkeeper Cen. Bottling Co., Bismarck, 1966-71; office mgr. Jobbers Warehouse/Allied Van Lines, Bismarck, 1971-72; account clk. Hwy. Patrol, Bismarck, 1972-75, per. sec., 1976-78; legal sec. Pub. Svc. Commn. State of N.D., Bismarck, 1979-80, grants and contracts officer Pub. Svc. Commn., 1980-91. Sec. Dist. 8 Rep. Exec. Com., 1995-97, chmn., 1997—; senate edn. com. clk. N.D. Legislature, 1997. Recipient Excellence in Pub. Svc. award Gov. of N.D., 1987, South McLean County Soil Conservation award, 1994. Mem. Pheasants Forever, Westerners Club. Republican. Avocations: hunting, skiing, reading, gardening. Home and Office: RR 1 Box 115 Turtle Lake ND 58575-9774

LINDZEN, RICHARD SIEGMUND, meteorologist, educator; b. Webster, Mass., Feb. 8, 1940; s. Abe and Sara (Blachman) L.; m. Nadine Lucie Kalougine, Apr. 7, 1965; children: Eric, Nathaniel. A.B., Harvard U., 1960, S.M., 1961, Ph.D., 1964. Research assoc. U. Wash., Seattle, 1964-65; Research asso. U. Oslo, 1965-66; with Nat. Center Atmospheric Research, Boulder, Colo., 1966-68; mem. faculty U. Chgo., 1968-72; prof. meteorology Harvard U., 1972-83, dir. Center for Earth and Planetary Physics, 1980-83; Alfred P. Sloan prof. meteorology MIT, 1983—; Lady Davis vis. prof. Hebrew U., 1979; Sackler prof. Tel Aviv U., 1992; Vikram Sarabhai prof. Phys. Rsch. Lab., Ahmendabad, India, 1985; Lansdowne lectr. U. Victoria, 1993; cons. NASA, Jet Propulsion Lab., others; mem. bd. on atmospheric scis. and climate NRC, corr. mem. com. on human rights NAS. Author: Dynamics in Atmospheric Physics; co-author: Atmospheric Tides; contbr. to profl. jours. Recipient Macelwane award Am. Geophys. Union, 1968. Fellow NAS, AAAS, Am. Geophys. Union, Am. Meteorol. Soc. (Meisinger award 1969, councillor 1972-75, Charney award 1985, Haurwitz lectr. 1997), Am. Acad. Arts and Scis., Norwegian Acad. Scis. and Letters; mem. Internat. Commn. Dynamic Meteorology, Woods Hole Oceanographic Instn. (corp.), Institut Mondial des Scis. (founding mem.). Jewish. Office: MIT 54 1720 Cambridge MA 02139

LINDZEY, GARDNER, psychologist, educator; b. Wilmington, Del., Nov. 27, 1920; s. James and Marguerite (Shotwell) L.; m. Andrea Lewis, Nov. 28, 1944; children: Jeffrey, Leslie, Gardner, David, Jonathan. AB, Pa. State U., 1943, MS, 1945; PhD, Harvard U., 1949; LHD (hon.), U. Colo., 1990; DSc (hon.), Rutgers U., 1992. Research analyst OSRD, 1944-45; instr. psychology Pa. State U., 1945-46; teaching fellow Harvard U., Cambridge, Mass., 1946-47, research fellow, 1947-49, research assoc., asst. prof., 1949-53, lectr., chmn. psychol. clinic staff, 1953-56, prof., chmn. dept., 1972-73; prof. psychology Syracuse (N.Y.) U., 1956-57, U. Minn., 1957-64; prof. psychology U. Tex., 1964-72, chmn., 1964-68, v.p. acad. affairs, 1968-70, v.p. ad interim, 1971, v.p., dean Grad. Studies, prof. psychology, 1973-75; dir. Ctr. for Advanced Study in Behavioral Scis., Stanford (Calif.) U., 1975-89, dir. emeritus, 1989—; mem. psychopharmacology study sect. NIMH, 1958-62, mem. program-project com., 1963-67, mem. adv. com. on extramural research, 1968-71; mem. com. faculty research fellowships Social Sci. Research Council, 1960-63, bd. dirs., 1962-76, mem. com. problems and policy, 1963-70, 72-76, chmn., 1965-70, mem. exec. com., 1970-75, chmn., 1971-75, mem. com. genetics and behavior, 1961-67, chmn., 1961-65; mem. com. biol. bases social behavior, 1967—; mem. com. work and personality in middle years, 1972-77; mem. sociology and social psychology panel NSF, 1965-68, mem. spl. commn. social scis., 1968-69, mem. adv. com. research, 1974—, mem. Waterman award com., 1976-79; mem. exec. com., assembly behavioral and social sci. NAS-NRC, 1970—, mem. com. life sci. and pub. policy, 1968-74, mem. panel nat. needs for biomed. and behavioral research personnel, 1974—, mem. com. social sci. in NSF, 1975—, mem. Inst. Medicine, 1975—; mem. com. on drug abuse Office Sci. and Tech., 1962-63; mem. Presdl. Com. Nat. Medal Sci., 1966-69; bd. dirs. Found.'s Fund Research in Psychiatry, 1967-70; bd. dirs. Am. Psychol. Found., 1968-76, v.p., 1971-73, pres., 1974-76. Author: (with Hall) Theories of Personality, 1957, 70, 78; (with Allport and Vernon) Study of Values, 1951, 60; Projective Techniques and Cross-Cultural Research, 1961; (with J.C. Loehlin and J.N. Spuhler) Race Differences in Intelligence, 1975; (with C.S. Hall and R.F. Thompson) Psychology, 1975; also articles; editor: Handbook of Social Psychology, Vols. 1 and 2, 1954, Vols. 1-5, 1969, Assessment of Human Motives, 1958, Contemporary Psychology, 1967-73, History of Psychology in Autobiography, Vol. 6, 1974, vol. 7, 1980, vol. 8, 1989; assoc. editor Psychol. Abstracts, 1960-62, Ency. Social Scis., 1962-67; co-editor Century Psychology Series, 1960-74, Theories of Personality: Primary Sources and Research, 1965, History of Psychology in Autobiography, Vol. V, 1968, Behavioral Genetics: Methods and Research, 1969, Contributions to Behavior-Genetic Analysis, 1970. Fellow Ctr. Advanced Study Behavioral Scis., Stanford, 1955-56, 63-64, 71-72, Inst. Medicine, 1975—. Fellow Am. Psychol. Assn. (bd. dirs. 1962-68, 70-74, mem. publs. bd., 1956-59, 70-73, chmn. 1958-59, mem. council of reps. 1959-67, 68-74, pres. divsn. social and personality psychology 1963-64, mem. policy and planning 1975, 78, pres. assn. 1966-67, mem. council of editors 1968-73, chmn. com. sci. award 1968-69, pres. divsn. gen. psychology 1970-71), Am. Acad. Arts and Scis., Am. Philos. Soc., Inst. Medicine, NAS, AAAS; mem. Am. Eugenics Soc. (bd. dirs. 1962-70), Soc. Social Biology (bd. dirs. 1972—, pres. 1978—), Am. Psychol. Assn. (dir. ins. trust 1973—), Univs. Research Assn. (bd. dirs. 1973-75). Home: 109 Peter Coutts Cir Palo Alto CA 94305-2517

LINEBERGER, WILLIAM CARL, chemistry educator; b. Hamlet, N.C., Dec. 5, 1939; s. Caleb Henry and Evelyn (Cooper) L.; m. Katharine Wyman Edwards, July 31, 1979. BS, Ga. Inst. Tech., 1961, MSEE, 1963, PhD, 1965. Rsch. physicist U.S. Army Ballistic Rsch. Labs., Aberdeen, Md., 1967-68; postdoctoral assoc. Joint Inst. for Lab. Astrophysics U. Colo., Boulder, 1968-70, from asst. prof. to prof. chemistry, 1970-83, E.U. Condon prof. chemistry, 1983—; Phi Beta Kappa nat. lectr., 1989. Capt. U.S. Army, 1965-67. Fellow AAAS, Joint Inst. for Lab. Physics, Am. Phys. Soc. (H.P. Broida prize 1981, Bomen Michelson prize 1987, Optical Sci. Am. Meggers prize 1988, Plyler prize 1992, Irvin Langmuir prize 1996); mem. NAS, ACS (Irving Langmuir prize 1996), Am. Chem. Soc., Am. Acad. Arts and Scis., Sigma Xi. Office: U Colo Joint Inst Lab Astrophysics CB 440 Boulder CO 80309-0440

LINEBERRY, PAUL F., JR., secondary education music educator; b. Waynesville, N.C., Aug. 6, 1944; s. Paul F. and Elmorene L. Lineberry; m. Jane Bulla, Aug. 27, 1966; children: Scott Eric, Brittnay Anne. MusB Edn., East Carolina U., 1966, MusM Edn., 1967. Cert. music tchr. K-12, Pa., supvr. pub. sch. music, Pa. Adj. graduate faculty Music Dept., Trenton State Coll., N.J.; dist. coord. music edn. Coun. Rock Sch. Dist., Richboro, Pa.; instrumental music instr. Coun. Rock H.S., Newtown, Pa., 1991—, chairperson music dept., 1993—; dir. sch. bands in performance in U.S. and Western Europe; cons. pub. sch. music programs, Bucks County, Pa.; lectr. in field. Curriculum devel. com. Coun. Rock Sch. Dist., Richboro, Bucks County Int. Unit Task Force on Music Edn., 1991—; mem. Pa. State Profl. Stds. Com. in Music Edn., 1990—. Recipient graduate study grant Fed. HEW Dept. Mem. NEA, ASCD, Music Educators Nat. Conf., Pa. Music Educators Assn. (com. chmn., Citation of Excellence in Teaching award 1991), Bucks County Music Edn. Assn. (past pres. and com. chmn.), Coun. Rock Edn. Asns., Pa. Edn. Assn., Phi Mu Alpha, Phi Beta Mu. Home: 197 Fletcher Dr Morrisville PA 19067-5968

LINEBERRY, SANDRA BEECH, accountant; b. Battle Creek, Mich., Nov. 22, 1946; d. Raymond August and Betty Jean (Bailey) Wank; m. James E. Beech, June 19, 1964 (div. June 1977); children: James Michael, Daniel Lee, Christina Rena; m. Terry Lineberry, Sept. 10, 1977 (div. June 1983). AA, Kellogg C.C., 1976; BA, Fla. Atlantic U., 1981. Bookkeeper Henry D. Bogaton, Lantana, Fla., 1978-81; acct. Darling & Rosasco CPA's, Palm Beach Garden, Fla., 1981-84, Rosasco & Lineberry CPA's, Royal Palm Beach, Fla., 1984-86, Peterson, Peterson & Rioux, Lake Worth, Fla., 1987—. Mem. AICPA, Fla. Inst. of CPA's. Republican. Methodist. Avocations: bowling, bike riding, jogging, softball, crocheting. Home: 200 NE 5th Ct Delray Beach FL 33444 Office: Peterson Peterson & Rioux CPAs 3003 S Congress Ave Ste 2C Lake Worth FL 33461-2169

LINEHAN, ALLAN DOUGLAS, prosthodontist; b. L.A., Dec. 30, 1954; s. Charles K. and P. Alene (Rohrbaugh) L.; m. Anita J. Peterson, Aug. 1, 1981; children: Chelsea L., Keegan H. BA, Lewis and Clark Coll., 1978; D in Dental Medicine, Oreg. Health Scis. U., 1983; MS in Prosthodontics, U. Tex., 1993. Diplomate Am. Bd. Prosthodontics. Gen. dental officer USAF Clinic Kadena, Okinawa, Japan, 1983-86, USAF Clinic Bitburg, Bitburg, Germany, 1986-90; prosthodontic resident Wilford Hall USAF Medical Ctr. Lackland Air Force Base, San Antonio, 1990-93; chief of prosthodontics 10th Dental Squadron USAF Acad., Colorado Springs, Colo., 1993—. Contbr. articles to profl. jours. Dir. for fundraising Explorer Elem. Sch., Colo. Springs, 1995—. Recipient John J. Sharry Prosthodontic Rsch. competition award Am. Coll. Prosthodontics, 1993, Tylman Rsch. grant Am. Acad. Fixed Prosthodontics, 1992. Fellow Am. Coll. Prosthodontics; mem. Acad. Gen. Dentistry, Psi Omega (v.p. 1979-83). Avocations: automotive restoration, antique restoration, woodworking, metalworking, long distance running. Home: 3337 Birnamwood Dr Colorado Springs CO 80920 Office: 10th Medical Group SGD 2348 Sijan Dr Ste 2a41 USAF Academy CO 80840-8200

LINEHAN, PATRICK FRANCIS, JR., financial planner; b. Jefferson Heights, N.Y., July 31, 1945; s. Patrick Francis and Dorothy Frances (Rowland) L.; m. Jane Elizabeth Uftring, Nov. 18, 1967; children: Patrick Francis III, Colleen Elizabeth, Erin Kathleen. BS in Edn., St. John's U., Jamaica, N.Y., 1966, MS in Edn., 1970. CFP; registered fin. cons.; cert. investment specialist. Math tchr. Bellmore (N.Y.)-Merrick Sch. Dist., 1967-85; fin. planner Amityville, N.Y., 1984—; ocean lifeguard Jones Beach-State Park, Babylon, N.Y., 1965-86; speaker Estate Planning and Seminars, Coll. Fin. Plan Seminars, Tchr. Retirement Seminars. Editor (quar. newsletter) Think About It, 1967—. Mem. Inst. of CFP, Internat. Assn. of Fin. Planners, Internat. Assn. Profl. Fin. Cons., Elks, K.C. Roman Catholic. Avocations: reading, music, golf, swimming. Home: 142 Richmond Ave Amityville NY 11701-4209 Office: Planning for Life 142 Richmond Ave Amityville NY 11701-4209

LINEMEYER, DAVID LEE, molecular biologist; b. Denver, Apr. 19, 1949; s. Clarence Brockman and Frances Pauline (Whitlock) L. BS with highest distinction, Colo. State U., 1971; MS, U. Wash., 1973, PhD, 1977. Staff fellow Nat. Cancer Inst., Bethesda, Md., 1977-80, sr. staff fellow, 1980-81; rsch. fellow Merck Rsch. Labs., Rahway, N.J., 1981-89, assoc. dir., 1989-95; dir. Synaptic Pharm. Corp., Paramus, N.J., 1995-96, Bayer Corp., West Haven, Conn., 1996—. Contbr. articles to sci. jours.; patentee mutant acidic fibroblast growth factor and G-protein coupled receptor field. Scholar Colo. State U., 1967-71. Mem. AAAS, Am. Soc. for Biochemistry and Molecular Biology, Soc. for Neurosci., Phi Kappa Phi. Office: Bayer Corp-B24 400 Morgan Ln West Haven CT 06516-4140

LINER, RONALD SIMS, middle school administrator; b. Concord, N.C., Sept. 20, 1946; s. James Harold and Agnes Matilda (Sims) L.; m. Judy Ann Greene, June 7, 1969; 1 child, Matthew Scott. BS, Appalachian State U., 1968, MA, 1972, EdS, 1989. Cert. tchr., mentor, adminstr., N.C. Elem. tchr. Winston Salem (N.C.), Forsyth County Schs., 1968-72, 75-90, jr. high sch. tchr., coord., 1972-74; adminstr., 1990—; tchr., adminstr. Trinity High Sch., Winston Salem, 1974-75; counselor N.C. Dept. Corrections, Winston Salem, N.C., 1969-74; mentor tchr. Winston Salem Forsyth County Schs., 1966—, A.M.A. Task Force, 1981-82, supts. adv. com. mem., 1988-90, evaluation instr., 1989-90. Scoutmaster, Boy Scouts Am., Winston Salem, N.C., 1973-76. Named Tchr. of Yr. Oak Summit Elem. Sch., 1981, '82, Jefferson Elem. Sch. 1986, finalist for Tchr. of Yr. Winston Salem/ Forsyth County Schs., 1981, '86. Mem. ASCD, NEA, Internat. Reading Assn., N.C. Edn. Assn., Forsyth Assn. Classroom Tchrs. (bldg. rep.), Masons, Phi Delta Kappa (historian 1988-90, treas. 1992-95). Democrat. Presbyterian. Avocations: golf, fishing, bridge, dancing, carpentry. Home: 5555 Alma Dr Winston Salem NC 27105-9601 Office: Hanes Middle Sch 2900 Indiana Ave Winston Salem NC 27105-4426

LINFORD, RULON KESLER, physicist, engineer; b. Cambridge, Mass., Jan. 31, 1943; s. Leon Blood and Imogene (Kesler) L.; m. Cecile Tadje, Apr. 2, 1965; children: Rulon Scott, Laura, Hilary, Philip Leon. BSEE, U. Utah, 1966; MS in ElecE, Mass. Inst. Tech., 1969, PhD in ElecE, 1973. Staff CTR-7 Los Alamos (N.Mex) Nat. Lab., 1973-75, asst. group leader CTR-7, 1975-77, group leader CTR-11, 1977-79, program mgr., group leader compact toroid CTR-11, 1979-80, program mgr., asst. div. leader compact toroid CTR divsn., 1980-81, assoc. CTR divsn. leader, 1981-86, program dir. magnetic fusion energy, 1986-89, program dir., div. leader CTR div. office, 1989-91, program dir. nuclear sys., 1991-93; staff LER, 1993-94, U. Calif. coord. sci. and tech., 1994—. Contbr. articles to profl. jours. Recipient E. O. Lawrence award Dept. of Energy, Washington, 1991. Fellow Am. Physical Soc. (exec. com. 1982, 90-91, program com. 1982, 85, award selection com. 1983, 84, fellowship com. 1986); mem. Sigma Xi. Office: Los Alamos Nat Lab PO Box 1663 MS F673 Los Alamos NM 87545

LING, DAVID CHANG, international book dealer; b. Shanghai, Feb. 17, 1939; s. H.C. and Katherine (Chang) L.; m. Janine Peters, June 20, 1970 (div. Feb. 1975). BA, U. Ore., 1962; MA, U. Wis., 1964, PhD, 1971. Vis. instr. U. of the South, Sewanee, Tenn., 1964-65; asst. prof. U. Wis., Kenosha, 1969-73; owner Ling's Internat. Books, San Diego, 1974—. Mem. Phi Beta Kappa. Democrat. Home: 5012 Westminster Ter San Diego CA 92116-2103 Office: Ling's Internat Books 7531 Convoy Ct San Diego CA 92111-1113

LING, ROBERT MALCOLM, banker, publishing executive; b. Akron, Ohio, July 6, 1931; s. Howard George and Catherine Zola (Smith) L.; m. Lois Claire Fisher Ling, Nov. 1, 1992; children: Shelly, Robert Jr., Amy, Beth, Patricia. BA in Journalism, Mich. State U., 1952. Asst. pres. Dike-O-Seal, Inc., Chgo., 1955-56; gen. mgr. Vollwerth Marquette (Mich.) Co., 1956-58, pres., 1958-75; pres. Vandco Incorp., Marquette, 1975-85, Cable American Corp., Rancho Cordova, Calif., 1985-89, Romali Holdings, Inc., Rancho Cordova, Calif., 1989—; chmn. Gold River Bank, Fair Oaks, Calif., 1990-92, Sacramento Safety Ctr., Inc., 1996—; publisher Grapevine-Independent newspaper, Rancho Cordova, Calif. Mayor City of Marquette, 1980-83, City of Rancho Cordova, Calif., 1986-87. Capt. U.S. Army, 1952-55. Republican. Home: 6032 Puerto Dr Rncho Murieta CA 95683-9313 Office: Romali Holdings Inc 3338 Mather Field Rd Rancho Cordova CA 95670-5966

LING, ROBERT WILLIAM, JR., academic director; b. Oakland, Calif., Jan. 31, 1954; s. Robert William Ling and Jacqueline Laura (Roberts) Ling Mullen; m. Beverly Jean Cass, May 5, 1972 (div. Aug., 1994); children: Tami, Sheri, Robin, Cassandra, Amanda. AAS in Med. Tech., C.C. of Air Force, Maxwell AFB, Ala., 1981; BS in Biology, No. Mich. U., 1983, MA in Biology, 1985. Mem. adv. bd. Clear Lake Edn. Ctr., Escanaba, Mich., 1992—, dir., 1993—; mem. adv. bd. Northwoods Math.-Sci. Ctr., Escanaba, 1992—, Delta Menominee Ground Water Edn. Ctr. Escanaba, 1994—. Author: USAFE History of Desert Shield/Storm, 1991; (with others) Clec Master Plan Permit, 1993; contbr. articles to profl. jours. Capt. USAF, 1985-92. Mem. VFW, Soc. for the Study of Amphibians and Reptiles, Kiwanis, Sigma Xi. Democrat. Roman Catholic. Avocations: herpetoculture, hunting. Office: Clear Lake Edn Ctr 2525 3rd Ave S Escanaba MI 49829-1258

LING, TA-YUNG, physics educator; b. Shanghai, Feb. 2, 1943; married, 1969; 3 children. BS, Tunghai U., Taiwan, 1964; MS, U. Waterloo, Ont., Can., 1966; PhD in Physics, U. Wis., 1971. Teaching asst. physics U. Waterloo, 1965-66, U. Wis., Madison, 1966-67; rsch. asst. U. Wis., 1967-71; rsch. assoc. physics U. Pa., Phila., 1972-75, asst. prof., 1975-77; from asst. prof. to assoc. prof. Ohio State U., Columbus, 1977-83, prof. physics, 1983—. Recipient Outstanding Jr. Investigator award Dept. of Energy, 1977. Mem. Am. Phys. Soc. Achievements include research in experimental high energy physics; deep inelastic neutrino-nucleon scattering, neutrino masses and mixing, neutrino oscillations, deep inelastic electron-proton scattering, high energy proton-proton collisions. Office: Ohio State U High Energy Physics Lab Physics Dept/Smith Lab 174 W 18th Ave Columbus OH 43210-1106*

LINGAFELTER, EDWARD CLAY, JR., chemistry educator; b. Toledo, Mar. 28, 1914; s. Edward Clay and Winifred (Jordan) L.; m. Roberta Crowe Kneedler, Apr. 30, 1938; children—Robert Edward (dec. 1996), Thomas Edward, James Edward, Richard Edward, Daniel Edward. B.S., U. Calif.-Berkeley, 1935, Ph.D., 1939. Mem. faculty U. Wash., Seattle, 1939—; prof. chemistry U. Wash., 1952-84, prof. emeritus, 1984—, assoc. dean Grad. Sch., 1960-68. Contbr. articles to profl. jours. Mem. Am. Chem. Soc., Am. Crystallographic Assn. (pres. 1974), Assn. Italian Cristallografia. Rsch. on solutions, molecular structures of paraffin-chain and coordination compounds. Home: 5323 27th Ave NE Seattle WA 98105-3105 Office: U Wash Dept Chemistry Box 351700 Seattle WA 98195-1700

LINGEMAN, RICHARD ROBERTS, editor, writer; b. Crawfordsville, Ind., Jan. 2, 1931; s. Byron Newton and Vera Frances (Spencer) L.; m. Anthea Judy Nicholson, Apr. 3, 1965; 1 child, Jenifer Kate. BA, Haverford Coll., 1953; postgrad., Yale U. Law Sch., 1956-58, Columbia U. Grad. Sch. Comparative Lit., 1958-60. Exec. editor Monocle mag., N.Y.C., 1960-69; assoc. editor, columnist N.Y. Times Book Review, 1969-78; exec. editor The Nation, N.Y.C., 1978-95, sr. editor, 1995—; bd. dirs. Small Town Inst., Ctr. Middletown Studies. Author: Drugs from A to Z, 1969, Don't You Know There's A War On?, 1971, Small Town America, 1980, Theodore Dreiser: At the Gates of the City 1871-1907, 1986, Theodore Dreiser: An American Journey, 1908-1945, 1990 (Chgo. Sun-Times Book of Yr.). With U.S. Army, 1953-56. Mem. PEN, Authors Guild, Soc. Am. Historians, Nat. Book Critics Cir., N.Y. Hist. Soc., Phi Beta Kappa. Office: Nation 72 5th Ave New York NY 10011-8004

LINGENFELTER, SHERWOOD GALEN, university provost, anthropology educator; b. Hollidaysburg, Pa., Nov. 18, 1941; s. Galen Miller and Kathern Margaretta (Rogers) L.; m. Judith Elaine Beaumont, Aug. 10, 1962; children: Jennifer Elaine, Joel Sherwood. BA, Wheaton Coll., 1963; PhD, U. Pitts., 1971. Dir. acad. advising U. Pitts., 1964-66; instr. SUNY, Brockport, N.Y., 1966-67; asst. prof SUNY, Brockport, 1969-74, assoc. prof., 1974-82, prof. anthropology, 1982-83; NIH predoctoral fellow U. Pitts., 1967-69; prof. Biola U., La Mirada, Calif., 1983-88, provost, sr. v.p., 1988—; cons. in anthropology Summer Inst. Linguistics, Dallas, 1977-96; tng. cons. Liebenzell Mission of Am., Schooleys Mountain, N.J., 1981-89; evaluating cons. Trust Terr. of the Pacific Islands, Saipan, Mariana Islands, 1969-74. Author: Yap: Political Leadership, 1975, The Deni of Western Brazil, 1980, Ministering Cross-Culturally, 1986, Transforming Culture, 1992, Agents of Transformation, 1996; editor: Political Development in Micronesia, 1974, Social Organization of Sabah Societies, 1990. Bd. dirs. Christian Scholars Rev., 1989-95, Grace Brethren Internat. Missions, 1994—. Recipient Disting. Teaching award Biola U., 1987-88; grantee NSF, 1967-69, 79-81, SUNY Rsch. Found., 1970. Fellow Am. Anthrop. Assn., Soc. for Applied Anthropology, Am. Ethnol. Soc.; mem. Assn. Social Anthropology Oceania, Am. Conf. Acad. Deans. Democrat. Mem. Grace Brethern Ch. Office: Biola U Office of Provost 13800 Biola Ave La Mirada CA 90639-0002

LINGERFELT, B. EUGENE, JR., minister; b. Highland Park, Mich., Dec. 18, 1955; s. Beecher Eugene and Nellie Beatrice (Sampson) L.; m. Suzanne Marie Martin, Aug. 7, 1976; children: Austin Stuart, Krystina Marie. BA, Cen. Bible Coll., Springfield, Mo., 1976; MDiv, Tex. Christian Univ., 1980; D of Ministry, Southwestern Bapt. Theol., Seminary, Ft. Worth, 1984. Ordained min. Cathedral of Praise Ch., 1984. Assoc. pastor Bethel Temple, Ft. Worth, 1978-82; missionary, guest lectr. East Africa Sch. of Theology, Nairobi, Kenya, 1982-83; marriage enrichment seminar speaker, 1983; founder and sr. pastor Cathedral of Praise, Arlington, Tex., 1984—; founder Cathedral Christian Acad., 1988—; founder Overcoming Faith TV, 1994—. Co-author: Money: A Spiritual Force, 1985, The Spirit of Excellence, 1994, Compromise in the Church, 1995; contbr. articles to religious jours. Named to Outstanding Young Men of Am., 1980. Republican. Office: Cathedral of Praise PO Box 121234 Arlington TX 76012-1234

LINGL, FRIEDRICH ALBERT, psychiatrist; b. Munich, Germany, Apr. 4, 1927; came to U.S., 1957, naturalized, 1962; s. Friedrich Hugo and Marie Luise (Lindner) L.; m. Leonore E. Trautner, Nov. 15, 1955; children—Herbert F., Angelika M. M.D., Ludwig-Maxim U., Munich, 1952. Diplomate Am. Bd. Psychiatry and Neurology, Am. Bd. Med. Psychotherapists (fellow); cert. mental health adminstr. Intern Edward W. Sparrow Hosp., 1957-58; resident internal medicine City Hosp., Augsburg, Germany, 1953-54; resident psychiatry Columbus (Ohio) State Hosp., 1958-61; supt. Hawthornden State Hosp., Northfield, Ohio, 1963-66; dir. Cleve. Psychiat. Inst., 1966-72; pvt. practice, 1972-92; med. dir. Windsor Hosp., 1976-92, med. dir. emeritus, 1992—; asst. clin. prof. Case Western Res. U., Cleve., 1970—. Contbr. articles to med. jours. Fellow Am. Psychiat. Assn. (life); mem. AMA, Ohio Med. Assn., Ohio Psychiat. Assn., Am. Assn. Psychiat. Adminstrs., N.Y. Acad. Scis., Cleve. Psychiat. Soc. Address: 40 Farwood Dr Chagrin Falls OH 44022-6848

LINGLE, CRAIG STANLEY, glaciologist, educator; b. Carlsbad, N.Mex., Sept. 11, 1945; s. Stanley Orland and Margaret Pearl (Ewart) L.; m. Diana Lynn Duncan, Aug. 21, 1972; 1 child, Eric Glenn. BS, U. Wash., 1967; MS, U. Maine, 1978; PhD, U. Wis., 1983. Nat. rsch. coun. resident rsch. assoc. Coop. Inst. for Rsch. in Environ. Scis., U. Colo., Boulder, 1983-84, rsch. assoc., 1984-86; program mgr. polar glaciology divsn. polar programs NSF, Washington, 1986-87; cons. Jet Propulsion Lab., Pasadena, Calif., 1987-88; nat. rsch. coun. resident rsch. assoc. NASA Goddard Space Flight Ctr., Oceans and Ice Branch, Greenbelt, Md., 1988-90; rsch. assoc. prof. Geophys. Inst., U. Alaska, Fairbanks, 1990—. Contbr. articles to profl. jours. Recipient Antarctic Svc. medal of U.S., NSF, 1987, Rsch. Project of Month award Office of Health and Environ. Rsch., U.S. Dept. Energy, 1990, Group Achievement award NASA, 1992. Mem. AAAS, Internat. Glaciological Soc., Am. Geophys. Union, Sigma Xi. Avocations: downhill and cross-country skiing, canoeing, hiking. Office: Geophys Inst Univ Alaska PO Box 757320 Fairbanks AK 99775-7320

LINGLE, MURIEL ELLEN, elementary education educator; b. Sundown Twp., Minn.; d. Harold O. and Carrie H. (Ewald) Anderson; m. Dale A. Lingle, Aug. 21, 1946; children: Barbara Jean, Tamara Jane. BS with distinction, Union Coll., Lincoln, Nebr., 1968; MA, U. Nebr., Lincoln, 1976. Cert. tchr., Nebr. Elem. tchr. Hallam, Nebr., 1959-62; tchr. Cen. Elem. and High Sch., Sprague-Martell, Nebr., 1963-67, Helen Hyatt Elem. Sch., Lincoln, 1968-70; elem. tchr. Crete (Nebr.) Sch. System, 1970-91; ret., 1991. Recipient award for excellence in teaching Cooper Found., 1990-91, Internat. Woman of Yr. award, 1993-94. Avocations: reading, sewing, music, antique cars, collecting plates and die-cast precision automobile and truck models. Home: 4730 Hillside St Lincoln NE 68506-6431

LINGLE, SARAH ELIZABETH, research scientist; b. Woodland, Calif., July 22, 1955; d. John Clayton and Dorothy Adelaide (Dubois) L.; m. Thomas Pratt Washington IV, May 20, 1989. BS, U. Calif., Davis, 1977; MS, U. Nebr., 1978; PhD, Washington State U., 1982. Lab. asst. U. Calif., Davis, 1975-77; rsch. asst. U. Nebr., Lincoln, 1977-78; rsch., teaching asst. Wash. State U., Pullman, 1979-82; rsch. assoc. Agrl. Rsch. Svc., USDA, Fargo, N.D., 1982-84; supr. plant physiologist USDA, Weslaco, Tex., 1984—, acting rsch. leader, 1991-92. Assoc. editor Crop Sci.; contbr. articles to profl. jours. Mem. AAAS, Am. Soc. of Plant Physiologists, Am. Soc. Agronomy, Crop Sci. Soc. of Am., Sigma Xi. Episcopalian. Achievements include research in biochemistry and physiology of sugar deposition in sucrose-storing plant tissues. Office: USDA Agrl Rsch Svc 2413 E US Hwy 83 Weslaco TX 78596-8344

LINHARDT, ROBERT JOHN, medicinal chemistry educator; b. Passaic, N.J., Oct. 18, 1953; s. Robert J. and Barbara A. (Kelley) L.; m. Kathryn F. Burns, May 31, 1975; children: Kelley, Barbara. BS in Chemistry, Marquette U., 1975; MA in Chemistry, Johns Hopkins U., 1977, PhD in Organic Chemistry, 1979; postgrad., Mass. Inst. Tech., 1979-82. Rsch. assoc. Mass. Inst. Tech., Cambridge, 1979-82; asst. prof. U. Iowa, Iowa City, 1982-86, assoc. prof., 1986-90, prof. medicinal and natural products chemistry, 1990—, prof. chem. and biochem. engring., 1996—, F. Wendell Miller Disting. prof., 1996; cons. in field.; interacad. exchange scientist to USSR NAS, 1988. Mem. editl. bd. Applied Biochemistry and Biotech., 1985—, Carbohydrate Rsch., 1990—, Analytical Biochemistry, 1991—, Jour. Biol. Chem., 1995—; contbr. numerous articles to profl. jours. Johnson and Johnson fellow MIT, 1981; NIH grantee, 1982-95. Mem. AAAS, Am. Chem. Soc. (Horace S. Isbell award Carbohydrate Chemistry 1994), Soc. Glycobiology. Office: U Iowa Coll Pharmacy Phar # 303A Iowa City IA 52240

LINHARES, JUDITH YVONNE, artist, educator; b. Pasadena, Calif., Nov. 2, 1940; d. Helen Evangeline (Frew) Coe.; m. Philip E. Linhares June 15, 1961 (div. July, 1971); 1 child, Amanda Linhares Mason. Student, LA Otis Art Inst., 1960, San Francisco Art Inst., 1963; BFA, Calif. Coll. Arts & Crafts, 1964, MFA, 1970. Art tchr. San Francisco State Coll., 1969-71, San Jose City Coll., 1971-72, U. Calif., Davis, Berkeley, 1979, U. San Francisco, San Francisco Art Inst. other univs., Calif., N.Y., La., 1978—, Sch. of Visual Arts, N.Y.C., 1981—, NYU, 1990—; lectr. at univs. and art insts. nationwide, 1974—. Artist: one-person exhibitions include, Berkeley Gallery, San Francisco, 1972, San Francisco Art Inst., 1976, Paule Anglim Gallery, San Francisco, 1978, 80, 82, 84, 88, 89, 94, Nancy Lurie Gallery, Chgo., 1981, 89, 90, Concord Gallery, N.Y.C., 1982, 83, Ruth Siegel Gallery, N.Y., 1985, Mo David Gallery, N.Y., 1985, L.A. Louver Gallery, Venice, Calif., 1988, Julie Sylvester Edition, N.Y., 1989, The Gaibreath Gallery, Lexington, Ky., 1993, Greenville (S.C.) County Mus. of Art, 1994, (survey exhibition 1971-93), Sonoma (Calif.) State U., 1994, Edwart Thorp Gallery, N.Y.C., 1997; selected group exhibitions San Francisco Art Inst., 1973, Indpls. Mus. of Art, 1984, Peninsula Mus., Monterey, Calif., 1987, Michael Walls Gallery, N.Y., 1987, Rosenberg Gallery, N.Y.C., 1992; represented in pub. collections including Greenville (S.C.) County Mus. of Art, Oakland (Calif.) Mus., Butler Inst. of Am. Art, Youngstown, Ohio, Crocker Art Mus., Sacramento, Calif., San Francisco Mus. of Modern Art, City of San Francisco Airport Commn.,. Recipient Adeline Kent award San Francisco Art Inst., 1976; grantee: Nat Endowment for Arts, 1979, 87, 93-94, Gottleib 1993.

LINHART, JOSEPH WAYLAND, cardiologist, educational administrator; b. N.Y.C., Feb. 7, 1933; s. Joseph and Myrla Watson (Wayland) L.; m. Marilyn Adele Voight, Sept. 1, 1956; children: Joseph, Mary-Ellen, Richard, Jennifer, Donna-Lisa, Daria. BS, George Washington U., 1954, MD, 1958. Diplomate Am. Bd. Internal Medicine with subspecialty in cardiovascular diseases. Intern Washington Hosp. Ctr., 1958-59; resident George Washington U. Hosp., Washington, 1959-60, Duke U. Hosp., Durham, N.C., 1961; fellow Duke U. Hosp., Durham, 1960, 62-63, Nat. Heart Inst./Johns Hopkins Hosp., Bethesda/Balt., Md., 1963-64; asst. prof. medicine U. Fla., Gainesville, 1964-67; clin. assoc. prof. U. Miami, Fla., 1967-68; assoc. prof. medicine U. Tex., San Antonio, 1968-71; prof., dir. cardiology Hahnemann Med. Coll., Phila., 1971-75; prof., chmn. dept. medicine Chgo. Med. Sch., 1975-79, Oral Roberts U., Tulsa, 1979-83; prof. medicine U. South Fla., Tampa, 1983-92; prof., regional chmn. medicine Tex. Tech. U., Odessa, 1992-93; prof. medicine La. State U., Shreveport, 1993—; chief med. svc. VA Med. Ctr., Shreveport, 1993—, acting chief of staff, 1996—; cons. in cardiology and med./legal questions. Contbr. articles to profl. jours.; author 4 books. Mem. med. adv. com. YMCA, Niles, Ill., 1976-79; bd. govs. Phila. Heart Assn., 1972-75; mem. rsch. coun. Okla. Heart Assn., Tulsa, 1980-83. Fellow ACP, Am. Coll. Cardiology; mem. AAAS, Planetary Soc., Nat. Space Soc., Astron. Soc. of Pacific, Alpha Omega Alpha. Republican. Avocations: astronomy, history, model building, organ playing, music. Home: 625 Red Cedar Ct NE Saint Petersburg FL 33703 Office: Overton Brooks VA Med Ctr 510 E Stoner Ave Shreveport LA 71101-4243

LINHART, LETTY LEMON, editor; b. Pittsburg, Kans., Sept. 22, 1933; d. Robert Sheldon and Lois (Wise) Lemon; m. Robert Spayde Kennedy, June 8, 1955 (div. 1978); children: Carole Shea, Nancy Schrimpf, Nina Kennedy; m. Daniel Julian Linhart, June 9, 1986. BS, BA in English and Journalism, U.Kans., 1955; MS in Journalism, Boston U., 1975. Reporter Leavenworth (Kans.) Times, 1954; editor Human Resources Rsch. Office George Washington U., Washington, 1955-56; editor Behavior Rsch. Lab. Harvard Med. Sch., Boston, 1956-58; instr. Boston YMCA, 1960-64; freelance writer and columnist, 1975—; editor Somerville (Mass.) Times, 1975-77; pub. rels. dir. Lettermen of Lexington, Mass., 1978; instr. English Rollins Coll., Winter Park, Fla., 1978-79, Valencia Community Coll., Orlando, Fla., 1978-82, U. Cen. Fla., Orlando, 1979-82; tech. writer Kirschman Software, Altamonto Springs, Mass., 1980-81, Dynamic Control Software, Winter Park, Fla., 1981-82; editor Fla. Specifier, Winter Park, 1982-85, Mobile Home News, Maitland, Fla., 1985-86; instr. English Seminole C.C., Sanford, Fla., 1986-94; Elderhostel instr. Canterbury Rsch. Ctr., 1994—; editor Oviedo (Fla.) Voice, 1994-95, 96; radio talk show host Sta. WALE, Providence, 1997; resource person Am. on Line, 1996—. Author: Are These Extravagant Promises, 1989, Clues for the Clueless, 1996; contbr. articles to profl. jours.; radio host WALE, Providence, 1997—. Pres. MIT Dames Boston, 1958-59, Boston Alumnae of Delta Delta Delta, 1959-62; dist. pres Delta Delta Delta, Tex., 1962-65; mem. Friends of Cornell Mus., Winter Park, Fla.; svc. provider Am. On Line Addiction and Recovery Network, 1996—. Named Outstanding Collegiate Delta Delta Delta, 1955. Mem. NAFE, Ctrl. Fla. Jazz Soc. (bd. dirs. 1983-93), Internat. Platform Soc., Soc. Women Execs., Altrusa Club (publicity com. 1980-83), Orlando Press Club (bd. dirs.), Univ. Club Winter Park, Mortar Bd., Phi Beta Kappa (Belmont, Mass. pres. 1965-78), Theta Sigma Phi, Sigma Delta Chi, Delta Sigma Rho. Avocations: swimming, singing, jazz. Home: PO Box 621131 Oviedo FL 32762-1131

LINICK, ANDREW S., direct marketing executive; b. 1945. PhD in Indsl. Psychology, NYU, 1972. Chmn. bd. dirs. Linick Group Inc., Middle Island, N.Y. Office: Linick Group Inc Linick Bldg PO Box 102 Middle Island NY 11953-0102

LINK, ARTHUR STANLEY, history educator, editor; b. New Market, Va., Aug. 8, 1920; s. John William and Helen Elizabeth (Link) L.; m. Margaret McDowell Douglas, June 2, 1945; children: Arthur Stanley, James Douglas, Margaret McDowell, William Allen. A.B. with highest honors, U. N.C., 1941, Ph.D., 1945; postgrad., Columbia U., 1944-45; M.A., Oxford (Eng.) U., 1958; Litt.D., Bucknell U., 1961, Bethany Coll., 1994; U. N.C., Washington and Lee U., 1965; L.H.D., Washington Coll., 1962, Eastern Ill. U., 1983, Northwestern U., 1984, Monmouth Coll., N.J., 1993; H.H.D. (hon.), Davidson Coll., 1965; Westminster Coll. (Pa.), 1984. Instr. N.C. State Coll., 1943-44; instr. Princeton U., 1945-48, asst. prof., 1948-49; mem. (Inst. Advanced Study), Princeton, 1949, 54-55; assoc. prof. Northwestern U., 1949-54, prof., 1954-60; prof. Princeton U., 1960-65, Edwards prof. Am. history, 1965-76, George H. Davis '86 prof. Am. history, 1976-91, prof. emeritus, 1991—; disting. adj. prof. Am. history U. N.C., Greensboro, 1992—; historian Bowman Gray Sch. Medicine, 1993—; Albert Shaw lectr. Johns Hopkins, 1956; Harmsworth prof. Am. history Oxford U., 1958-59; Commonwealth Fund lectr. U. London, 1977; mem. Nat. Hist. Publs. Commn., 1968-72; pres. Nat. Commn. on Social Studies in Schs., 1987-90. Author: Wilson: The Road to the White House, 1947, (with R. W. Leopold and Stanley Coben) Problems in American History, 1972, Woodrow Wilson and the Progressive Era, 1954, 63, 88, (with William B. Catton and William A. Link) American Epoch, 2 vols., 1986, Wilson: The New Freedom, 1956, Wilson the Diplomatist, 1957, Wilson: The Struggle for Neutrality, 1914-15, 1960, La Política de los Estados Unidas en América Latina, 1960, (with D.S. Muzzey) Our American Republic, 1963, Our Country's History, 1964, Woodrow Wilson, A Brief Biography, 1963, Wilson: Confusions and Crises, 1915-1916, 1964, Wilson: Campaigns for Progressivism and Peace, 1916-17, 1965; editor: (with R.W. Patrick) Writing Southern History, 1967, The Growth of American Democracy, 1968, Woodrow Wilson, A Profile, 1968, The Impact of World War I, 1969, (with W.M. Leary, Jr.) The Diplomacy of World Power: The United States, 1889-1920, 1970, (with Stanley Coben) The Democratic Heritage: A History of the United States, 1971, The Higher Realism of Woodrow Wilson and Other Essays, 1970, (with William M. Leary, Jr.) The Progressive Era and the Great War, 1978, Woodrow Wilson: Revolution, War, and Peace, 1979, Woodrow Wilson and a Revolutionary World, 1913-1921, 1982, (with Richard L. McCormick) Progressivism, 1983, (with W.A. Link) The Twentieth Century: An American History, 1991, Brother Woodrow: A Memoir of Woodrow Wilson (Stockton Axson), 1993; editor: Papers of Woodrow Wilson, 69 vols., 1966-94; editor, sr. writer: A Concise History of the American People, 1984, The American People: A History, 1987; translator, editor: Paul Mantoux, The Deliberations of the Council of Four, 2 vols., 1992; mem. bd. editors Jour. So. History, 1955-58, 63-66, Jour. Am. History, 1967-70; contbr. articles to popular and profl. jours. Trustee Westminster (Pa.) Coll., 1971-82, Warren Wilson Coll., 1993—. Recipient Bancroft prize for biography, 1957, 61; Guggenheim fellow, 1950-51; hon. fellow Jagiellonian U., Cracow, Poland. Fellow Am. Acad. Arts and Scis., Soc. Am. Historians; mem. Am. Philos Soc. (Thomas Jefferson medal 1994), Am. Hist. Assn. (pres.-elect 1983-84, pres. 1984), So. Hist. Assn. (v.p. 1967-68, pres. 1968-69), Orgn. Am. Historians (pres.-elect 1983-84, pres. 1984-85), Nat. Coun. Chs. (v.p. 1963-66), Mass. Hist. Soc. (corr.), Assn. Documentary Editors (pres. 1978-79), Soc. Colonial Wars, Nassau Club, Cosmos Club, Phi Beta Kappa. *I have no thoughts on life that do not stem from my Christian faith. I believe that God created me to be a loving, caring person to do His work in the world. I also believe that He called me to my vocation of teacher and scholar.*

LINK, GEORGE HAMILTON, lawyer; b. Sacramento, Calif., Mar. 26, 1939; s. Hoyle and Corrie Elizabeth (Evans) L.; m. Betsy Leland; children—Thomas Hamilton, Christopher Leland. AB, U. Calif., Berkeley, 1961; LLB, Harvard U., 1964. Bar: Calif. 1965, U.S. Dist. Ct. (no., ea., ctrl. and so dists.) Calif. 1965, U.S. Ct. Appeals (9th cir.) 1965. Assoc. Brobeck, Phleger & Harrison, San Francisco, 1964-69, ptnr., 1970—; mng. ptnr. Brobeck, Phleger & Harrison, L.A., 1973-93; mng. ptnr. firmwide Brobeck Phleger & Harrison, 1993-96; chmn. Pacific Rim Adv. Coun., 1992-95. Bd. regents U. Calif., 1971-74; trustee Berkeley Found., Jr. Statesmen Am.; bd. govs. United Way, 1979-81; trustee, v.p. Calif. Hist. Soc., 1987—. Fellow Am. Bar Found.; mem. ABA, Calif. Bar Assn., L.A. Bar Assn., U. Calif. Alumni Assn. (pres. 1972-75), Calif. Club, Bohemian Club, Jonathan Club. Republican. Methodist. Home: 315 N Carmelina Ave Los Angeles CA 90049-2701 Office: Brobeck Phleger & Harrison 550 S Hope St Los Angeles CA 90071-2627

LINK, O(GLE) WINSTON, photographer; b. Bklyn., Dec. 16, 1914; s. Ernest Albert L. and Ann Winston (Jones) L.; m. Marteal Oglesby 1942 (div. 1946); 1 child, Winston Conway L.; m. Conchita Mendoza, 1983 (div. 1993). BSCE, Poly. Inst. of Bklyn., 1937. Photographer Carl Boyir and Assocs., 1937-42; engr., photographer Airborne Instruments Lab., Columbia U., 1942-45; free-lance indsl. photographer, 1945-83, railroad photographer, 1955-60. Collection of railroad photography include: Steam, Steel and Stars: America's Last Steam Railroad, 1987, The Last Steam Railroad in America, 1995. Office: c/o Thomas H Garver PO Box 3493 Madison WI 53704-0493

LINK, ROBERT JAMES, lawyer, educator; b. Washington, May 25, 1950; s. Robert Wendell and Barbara Ann (Bullock) L.; m. Cheryl Ann Brillante, Apr. 22, 1978; children: Robert Edward, Holden James. BA, U. Miami, 1972, JD, 1975. Bar: Fla. 1975, U.S. Dist. Ct. (mid. dist.) Fla. 1980, U.S. Ct. Appeals (5th cir.) 1980, U.S. Ct. Appeals (11th cir.) 1981, U.S. Supreme Ct. 1984, U.S. Dist. Ct. (no. dist.) Fla. 1989. Asst. pub. defender City of Miami, Fla., 1975-78, City of Jacksonville, Fla., 1978-82; ptnr. Greenspan, Goodstein & Link, Jacksonville, 1982-84, Goodstein & Link, Jacksonville, 1984-85; sole practice Jacksonville, 1985-88; assoc. Howell, Liles & Milton, Jacksonville, 1988-89; ptnr. Pajcic & Pajcic P.A., 1990—; guest instr. U. Miami, 1976, U. Fla., 1979-88, Stetson Law Sch., 1984, Jacksonville U., 1987-88, U. North Fla., 1991. Atty. legal panel ACLU, Jacksonville, 1982-88; bd. dirs. Jacksonville Legal Aid, 1990-92. Mem. Fla. Bar Assn. (chmn. com. for representation of indigents criminal law sect. 1980, cert. criminal trial lawyer 1989), Jacksonville Bar Assn. (criminal law sect.), Nat. Assn. Criminal Def. Lawyers (vice-chmn. post conviction com. 1990), Fla. Pub. Defender Assn. (death penalty steering com. 1980-82, instr. 1979-89). Democrat. Methodist. Avocations: sailing, fishing, diving, softball. Home: 3535 Carlyon St Jacksonville FL 32207-5836 Office: 1900 Independent Sq Jacksonville FL 32202-5013

LINK, WILLIAM THEODORE, television writer, producer; b. Phila., Dec. 15, 1933; s. William Theodore and Elsie (Roerecke) L.; m. Margery Nelson, Sept. 5, 1980. B.S., U. Pa., 1956. bd. govs. The TV Acad., 1976. Writer, creator, producer (with ptnr. Richard Levinson) TV series Columbo, Mannix, McCloud, Murder, She Wrote, also others; writer, producer: made-for-TV movies The Storyteller; My Sweet Charlie, That Certain Summer, The Execution of Private Slovik, The Gun, Crisis at Central High, The U.S. vs. Salim Ajami, The Boys, The Bill Cosby Mysteries; Author: Fineman, 1973, Stay Tuned, 1981, The Playhouse, 1985, Off-Camera, 1986. Served with SIgnal Corps U.S. Army, 1956-58. Recipient Emmy awards Acad. TV Arts and Scis., 1970, 72, Golden Globe awards Hollywood Fgn. Press Assn., 1972 (2), Peabody award, Edgar Allan Poe award Mystery Writers Am., 1980, 81, 83, 84; Paddy Chayefsky Laurel award, 1986, Ellery Queen Lifetime Achievement award, 1989, Bouchercon Performance in the Arts award, 1989; inductee TV Hall of Fame, 1995. Mem. SAG, Writers Guild Am., Dramatists Guild, Mystery Writers Am.

LINKE, RICHARD A., systems engineer, researcher; b. Plainfield, N.J., Feb. 15, 1946; married; 2 children. BA, Columbia U., 1968, MS, 1970, PhD in Physics, 1972. Mem. tech. staff radio physics rsch. Bell Telephone Labs., 1972-86, head lightware comm. rsch. dept., 1986-89; sr. rsch. scientist NEC Rsch. Inst., 1989—. Fellow IEEE , Optical Soc. Am. Office: Nec Rsch Inst 4 Independence Way Princeton NJ 08540-6634

LINKEN, DENNIS C., lawyer; b. Newark, Oct. 15, 1947. Student, Seton Hall U.; BBA, Temple U., 1970; JD, Rutgers U., 1973. Bar: N.J. 1973. Ptnr. Stryker, Tams & Dill, Newark. Address: Stryker Tams & Dill LLP 2 Penn Plz E Newark NJ 07105-2246

LINKER, KERRIE LYNN, systems engineer; b. Poughkeepsie, N.Y., Dec. 12, 1966; d. William Landes and Charlotte Louise (Scofield) Linker. BS in Physics and Math., Susquehanna U., Selinsgrove, Pa., 1989; MEng in Ops. Rsch. and Indsl. Engring., Cornell U., 1992. Prin. tech. staff mem. AT&T, Holmdel, NJ., 1989—. Mem. Inst. for Ops. Rsch. and Mgmt. Scis. Office: AT&T Rm 2f-512 101 Crawfords Corner Rd Holmdel NJ 07733-1900

LINKLATER, ISABELLE STANISLAWA YAROSH-GALAZKA (LEE LINKLATER), foundation administrator; b. Chgo., Sept. 15, 1939; d. Baron Stanislaw and Isabelle Lydia (Yarosh) Galazka. BE, Chgo. State U., 1959. Cert. tchr., Ill. Pub. rels. coord. Kelling Co., Chgo., 1955-57; tchr. Chg. Bd. Edn., 1957-89, coord. computer lab., 1989—; founder, pres., exec. dir. Assisi Animal Found. Edn. writer, coord. Elsa Internat. Wild Animal Appeal, Ill., 1985—; writer Lakeland Press, 1992. Bd. dirs. Townsquare Players, Woodstock (Ill.) Opera House, 1989-91. Recipient Outstanding Citizen award CBS Broadcasting, 1992. Mem. McHenry County Defenders (bd. dirs. 1989-91), East African Wildlife Soc. (U.S. rep.). Avocations: travel, music, theater. Office: Assisi Animal Found PO Box 143 Crystal Lake IL 60039-0143

LINKLATER, WILLIAM JOSEPH, lawyer; b. Chgo., June 3, 1942; s. William John and Jean (Connell) L.; m. Dorothea D. Ash, Apr. 4, 1986; children: Erin, Emily. BA, U. Notre Dame, 1964; JD, Loyola U., 1968. Bar: Ill. 1968, Calif. 1981, U.S. Dist. Ct. (no. dist.) Ill. 1968, U.S. Ct. Appeals (7th cir.) 1971, U.S. Supreme Ct. 1971, U.S. Ct. Appeals (6th cir.) 1990, U.S. Ct. Appeals Washington 1978, Calif. 1981, U.S. Dist. Ct. (cen. dist.) Calif. 1981, U.S. Tax Ct. 1982, U.S. Dist. Ct. (no. dist.) Calif. 1983, U.S. Dist. Ct. (ea. dist.) Mich. 1989, U.S. Dist. Ct., Colo. 1990, U.S. dist. Ct. Hawaii, 1992. Atty. Fed. Defender Project, Chgo.; assoc. Baker & McKenzie, Chgo., 1968-75, ptnr., 1975—. Contbr. articles to profl. jours. Mem. ABA (past co-chmn. com. on internat. criminal law criminal justice sect., mem. criminal practice and procedure com. antitrust sect.), FBA, Ill. Bar Assn., 7th Cir. Bar Assn., Chgo. Bar Assn. (bd. mgrs., past v.p. jud. candidates evaluation com., chmn. large law firm com., Internat. Inst.), Calif. Bar Assn., Colo. Bar Assn., Am. Coll. Trial Lawyers, Am. Bd. Criminal Lawyers, Chgo. Inn of Ct., Wong Sun Soc. San Francisco (internat. proctor), Alpha Simga Nu. Office: Baker & McKenzie 1 Prudential Plz Ste 3000 Chicago IL 60601

LINKLETTER, ARTHUR GORDON, radio and television broadcaster; b. Moose Jaw, Sask., Can., July 17, 1912; s. Fulton John and Mary (Metzler) L.; m. Lois Foerster, Nov. 25, 1935; children: Jack, Dawn, Robert (dec.), Sharon, Diane (dec.). A.B., San Diego State Coll., 1934. Program dir. Sta. KGB, San Diego, 1934; program dir. Calif. Internat. Expn., San Diego, 1935; radio dir. Tex. Centennial Expn., Dallas, 1936; San Francisco World's Fair, 1937-39; pres. Linkletter Prodns.; ptnr., co-owner John Guedel Radio Prodns.; chmn. bd. Linkletter Enterprises; owner Art Linkletter Oil Enterprises. Author: theme spectacle Cavalcade of Golden West, 1940; author and co-producer: theme spectacle Cavalcade of Am, 1941; writer, producer, star in West Coast radio shows, 1940-55; former star, writer: People Are Funny, NBC-TV and radio, Art Linkletter's House Party, CBS-TV and radio; Author: People Are Funny, 1953, Kids Say The Darndest Things, 1957, The Secret World of Kids, 1959, Confessions of a Happy Man, 1961, Kids Still Say The Darndest Things, 1961, A Child's Garden of Misinformation, 1965, I Wish I'd Said That, 1968, Linkletter Down Under, 1969, Oops, 1969, Drugs at My Door Step, 1973, Women Are My Favorite People, 1974, How to be a Super Salesman, 1974, Yes, You Can!, 1979, I Didn't Do It Alone, 1979, Public Speaking for Private People, 1980, Linkletter on Dynamic Selling, 1982, Old Age is not for Sissies, 1988; lectr. convs. and univs. Nat. bd. dirs. Goodwill Industries; commr. gen. to U.S. Exhibit at Brisbane Expo 88, Australia, 1987; amb. to The 200th Anniversary Celebration, Australia, 1987—; bd. regents Pepperdine U.; pres. bd. advisors Ctr. on Aging, UCLA; chmn. bd. French Found. for Alzheimers Rsch. Recipient numerous awards. Address: 8484 Wilshire Blvd Ste 205 Beverly Hills CA 90211-3220

LINKNER, MONICA FARRIS, lawyer; b. Detroit, Dec. 2, 1947; d. Bernard and Madelyn (Lederer) Farris; m. Robert V. Linkner, Dec. 27, 1967 (div. May 1973); 1 child, Joshua Morgan Linkner; m. Dennis J. Dlugokinski, June 4, 1984; 1 child, Matthew Scott Dlugokinski. Student, U. Mich., 1965-67; BA magna cum laude, Wayne State U., 1972, JD, 1977. Bar: Mich. 1977, U.S. Dist. Ct. (ea. dist.) Mich. 1977, U.S. Ct. Appeals (6th cir.) 1985. Asst. to reporter State of Mich. Standard Criminal Jury Instrns. Com., Detroit, 1973-74; clin. student atty. Wayne State Univ. Employment Discrimination, Detroit, 1977; clk. Mich. Ct. Appeals, Detroit, 1977-78; assoc. Lampert, Fried & Levitt, PC, Birmingham, Mich., 1978-80, Lopatin, Miller, Freedman, et. al., Detroit, 1980-88; pvt. practice Berkley, Mich., 1988—; prin. atty. Adoption Law Ctr., P.C., 1993—. Editor: Winning Final Arguments, 1985. Advocate Parents for Pvt. Adoption, Lathrup Village, Mich., 1990—; vol. tchr. Peoples Law Sch., Detroit, 1985, Women's Prison Legal Edn. Project, Ypsilanti, Mich., 1975-77. Mem. ATLA, ACLU, Am. Acad. Adoption Attys. (trustee 1995—), Mich. Trial Lawyers Assn. (sustaining; handicappers law reform advocate 1988-90, chair amicus curiae com. 1988-94), State Bar (family law sect. adoltion com.), 1995—, Disability Rights Bar Assn., Women Lawyers Assn. Mich., Family Tree (pres.), Amnesty Internat., Phi Beta Kappa, Alpha Lambda Delta. Avocations: hiking, sailing, cooking, reading. Office: 3250 Coolidge Hwy Berkley MI 48072-1634

LINKONIS, SUZANNE NEWBOLD, pretrial case manager, counselor; b. Phila., Aug. 24, 1945; d. William Bartram and Kathryn (Taylor) Newbold; m. Bertram Lawrence Linkonis, May 29, 1966; children: Robert William, Deborah Anne, Richard Anthony. AA in Psychology, Albany (Ga.) Jr. Coll., 1979; BA in Psychology, Albany (Ga.) State Coll., 1981; MS in Indsl. Psychology, Va. Commonwealth U., 1986. Office mgr., media buyer Long Advt. Agy., Richmond, Va., 1981-84; media mgr. Clarke & Assocs., Richmond, 1984-85; human resources asst. Continental Ins., Richmond, 1985; rsch. assoc. Signet Bank, N.A., Richmond, 1986-87; program coord. Med. Coll. Va., Richmond, 1988; personnel mgr. Bur. Microbiology, Richmond, 1988-89; pers. specialist Va. State Dept. Corrections, Richmond, 1989-90; human rights adv. Va. State Dept. Youth and Family Svcs., Richmond, 1990-92, rehab. counselor, 1992-94, sr. rehab. counselor, 1994; pre-trial case mgr./counselor Henrico County Govt., Richmond, 1994—; future dir., cons. Mary Kay Cosmetics, Springfield, Va., 1975-77. Mem. NAFE, APA. Republican. Roman Catholic. Avocations: professional jours. in applied psychology, networking groups, walking, tennis. Home: 401 Saybrook Dr Richmond VA 23236-3621 Office: 8600 Dixon Powers Dr Richmond VA 23228-2735

LINKOUS, WILLIAM JOSEPH, JR., lawyer; b. Roanoke, Va., July 17, 1929; s. William Joseph and Mary Virginia (Lester) L.; m. Anita Marie Stedronsky, Oct. 15, 1960; children—William Joseph III, Brian Keith. BA, Roanoke Coll., Salem, Va., 1951; MA in Econs., U. Va., 1954, JD, 1956. Bar: Va. 1956, Ga. 1957. Assoc. Powell, Goldstein, Frazer & Murphy, Atlanta, 1956-62, ptnr., 1962-79, 85—, mng. ptnr., 1979-85. Trustee Holy Innocents Episcopal Sch., Atlanta, 1974-80, Roanoke Coll., 1980-95, emeritus 1995—. Fellow Am. Coll. Trust and Estate Counsel, Am. Bar Found.; mem. State Bar Ga. (past chmn. fiduciary sect., co-chmn. Ga. trust law revision com. 1988-91, chmn. Ga. probate code revision com. 1991-97, chmn. Ga. guardianship code revision com.1997—), Va. State Bar, Am. Law Inst., Internat. Acad. Estate and Trust Law, Atlanta Estate Planning Coun. (pres. 1983-84). Avocation: tennis. Home: 730 Langford Ln NW Atlanta GA 30327-4732 Office: Powell Goldstein Frazer & Murphy 191 Peachtree St NE Ste 16 Atlanta GA 30303-1740

LINMAN, JAMES WILLIAM, retired physician, educator; b. Monmouth, Ill., July 20, 1924; s. Chester E. and Ruth L. (Pearson) L.; m. Frances Firth, Aug. 31, 1946; children—John, Jean, James, Jeffrey. B.S., U. Ill., 1945, M.D., 1947. Intern, resident internal medicine Med. Sch., U. Mich., Ann Arbor, 1947-51, fellow in hematology, 1951-52, 54-56, asst. prof. internal medicine, 1955-56; chief hematology sect. VA Research Hosp. Chgo.; assoc. prof. medicine Med. Sch., Northwestern U., Evanston, Ill., 1956-65; prof. internal medicine Mayo Grad. Sch. Medicine, U. Minn., Mpls.; cons. hematology and head spl. hematology sect. Mayo Clinic-Found., Rochester, Minn., 1965-72; prof. medicine, dir. Osgood Leukemia Ctr., Health Sci. Ctr., U. Oreg., Portland, 1972-79, head hematology div., 1974-78; prof. medicine John A. Burns Sch. Medicine, U. Hawaii, Honolulu, 1979-92; emeritus prof., 1992—; chmn. admissions com. John A. Burns Sch. Medicine, U. Hawaii, Honolulu, 1983-92, asst. dean for admissions, 1988-92; chmn. State of Hawaii Adv. Commn. on Drug Abuse and Controlled Substances, 1986-88; dir. med. edn. The Queen's Med. Ctr., Honolulu, 1987-88. Author: Principles of Hematology, 1966, Factors Controlling Erythropoiesis, 1960, The Leukemias, 1971, Hematology, 1975; Contbr. articles to profl. jours. Served with USAF, 1952-54. Recipient Tchr. of Year award Mayo Fellows Assn., 1970, Tchr. of Year award U. Hawaii, 1980, 81. Mem. Am. Soc. Clin. Investigation, Central Soc. Clin. Research, Am., Internat. socs. hematology, A.C.P., Western Assn. Physicians, Western Soc. Clin. Research, Pacific Interurban Clin. Club, Alpha Omega Alpha, Phi Kappa Phi. Club: Oahu Country. Home: 2130 Pililani Pl Honolulu HI 96822-2513

LINN, DIANA PATRICIA, elementary education educator; b. Perth, Australia, Dec. 31, 1943; came to U.S., 1948; d. Evan Andrew and Grace Henrietta (Springhall) Jarboe; m. Jim F. Erlandsen, July 9, 1966 (div. Mar. 1989); children: Rebecca, Tim, Jenny; m. Richard George Linn, Mar. 31, 1990; 1 stepchild, Cristal. AA, Olympic Coll., 1963; BA in Elem. Edn., Western Wash. U., 1965; MEd, U. Ariz., 1969. Cert. tchr., Wash. Tchr. 3d grade Neomi B. Willmore Elem., Westminster, Calif., 1965-66; tchr. English and sci. 7-8th grade Sunnyside Jr. H.S., Tucson, 1966-70; tchr. kindergarten All Seasons, Tucson, 1972-74; tchr. K-1st grade St. Cyril's, Tucson, 1974-77; tchr. 1st grade Grace Christian Sch., Tucson, 1977-80; tchr. K-1st grade, reading K-6th grade Ridgeview Christian Ctr., Spokane, Wash., 1983-85, Spokane Christian Schs., 1985-87; dir. Ridgeview Christian Learning Ctr., Spokane, 1987-88; tchr. kindergarten Arlington Elem., Spokane, 1988—; mem. curriculum study com. Sunnyside Sch. Dist., Tucson, 1967-68; chmn. accreditation and sch. bd. St. Cyril's Sch., Tucson, 1976-77; chair faculty involvement group, chair staff devel., chair wellness com. Arlington Elem., Spokane, 1992-93, sch. reporter, 1994-95; instr. reading readiness Family Learning Fair, Home Schooling Seminar, Spokane Falls C.C., Spokane, 1988; chair, coord. pre-sch. coop. Arlington Elem. with Spokane Falls C. C. of Spokane C.C., 1992-93; chair faculty involvement group, Arlington Elem., Spokane, 1995—, Grant Elem. Sch., 1996-97; chmn. Imagination Celebration, 1994, 95; mem. early childhood com. equity com. Grant Elem., Spokane, 1996-97. Coord. Christian edn. Valley Foursquare Ch., Spokane, 1982-87; coord. children's ch. Victory Faith Fellowship, Spokane, 1993—; Brownie troop leader Willmore Elem., Westminster, 1965-66; edn1. restructuring rep. for Arlington Elem., Spokane Sch. Dist. # 81, 1992-93; mem. equity com. Early Childhood Com.,1996-97. Scholar Naval Officer's Wives Club, 1961-62; recipient Eisenhower grant, 1990, 94, 96-97. Mem. ASCD, NEA, Wash. Edn. Assn., Spokane Edn. Assn. (Arlington Elem. rep. 1991-93), CPA Wives Club (sec., ball chair 1983-84), Alpha Delta Kappa (membership chair 1994-95, program planning chmn., corr. sec. 1996—). Republican. Avocations: collecting dolls, plates, swimming, quilt-making. Home: 2403 E Illinois Ave Spokane WA 99207-5655 Office: Grant Elem Sch 1300 E 9th Ave Spokane WA 99202-2409

LINN, EDWARD ALLEN, writer; b. Boston, Nov. 14, 1922; s. Hyman and Gertrude (Ober) L.; m. Ruth Goldberg, June 12, 1949; children: Michael, David, Hildy. B.S. in Journalism, Boston U., 1950. With USIS, Washington, 1951-52; asst. editor Macfadden Publs., 1952-53; contbg. writer Sat. Eve. Post, 1964-68. Free-lance writer, 1953-63; author: The Eternal Kid, 1961, Veeck-as in Wreck, 1962, The Last Loud Roar, 1964, The Hustler's Handbook, 1965, Koufax, 1966, Masque of Honor, 1969, Thirty Tons a Day, 1972, The Adversaries, 1973, Big Julie of Vegas, 1974, Out of the Fire, 1975, Nice Guys Finish Last, 1975, Where The Money Was, 1976, Inside the Yankees, The Championship Season, 1978, Steinbrenner's Yankees, 1982, A Great Connection, 1988, The Great Rivalry, 1991, Hitter, 1993, The Life and Turmoils of Ted Williams, A Great Connection-Globalization, 1997. Named Mag. Sportswriter of Year, Nat. Sportscasters and Sportswriters Assn., 1963; recipient Oppie award, 1975. Address: 1150 Anchorage Ln San Diego CA 92106

LINN, GARY DEAN, golf course architect; b. Wichita, Kans., May 11, 1955; s. Richard W. and Marilyn (Hanson) L.; m. Vicki Duncan, Aug. 6, 1977; children: Rachel, Jason, Nathan. B of Landscape Architecture, Kans. State U., 1978. Registered landscape architect Kans., 1979. Mem. Am. Soc. Landscape Architects, Am. Soc. Golf Course Architects. Avocations: family, golf, sports cards, coaching youth sports. Office: 705 Forest Ave Palo Alto CA 94301-2102

LINN, JAMES HERBERT, retired banker; b. Jacksonville, Fla., Nov. 22, 1925; s. Herbert P. and Evelyn Lucile (Gore) L.; m. Betty J. Thatcher, Oct. 22, 1949; children: David, Donald, Charles, Craig, Jill. BA in Liberal Arts, U. Mo., Kansas City, 1948. With various coms. Commerce Bancshares, Inc., Kansas City, 1948, vice-chmn., 1970-90; ret., 1990; bd. dirs. Commerce Bank NA, Hays, Manhattan and Leavenworth, Kans. Dir. Eye Found. of Kansas City. Mem. Robert Morris Assos. Home: 10261 Rosewood Dr Overland Park KS 66207-3456

LINN, JUDY NMN, photographer; b. Detroit, 1947. BFA, Pratt Inst., 1969. Exhibitor in the collections of Getty Collection, L.A., Detroit Art Inst., Dallas Mus. Fine Art, Whitney Mus. Am. Art; adj. asst. prof. photography Pratt Inst., Bklyn., 1974-85. Exhibited in one-person shows and group shows at Dallas Mus. Fine Arts, 1976; Padigione d'Arte Contemporanea, Milan, Italy, 1980, New Wave,N.Y.C., 1981, Susane Hilberry Gallery, Birmingham, 1982, Detroit Art Inst., 1985, Gallery 55, N.Y.C., 1985, Sandra Berler Gallery, Chevy Chase, Md., 1986, Feature Gallery, N.Y.C., 1995. Grantee Bob and Stephanie Scull, 1985, Line 11, 1986. Mailing Address: Feature Inc 76 Greenest New York NY 10012

LINN, MARCIA CYROG, education educator; b. Milw., May 27, 1943; d. George W. and Frances (Vanderhoof) Cyrog; m. Stuart Michael Linn, 1967 (div. 1979); children: Matthew, Allison; m. Curtis Bruce Tarter, 1987. BA in Psychology and Stats., Stanford U., 1965, MA in Ednl. Psychology, 1967, PhD in Ednl. Psychology, 1970. Prin. investigator Lawrence Hall Sci. U. Calif., 1970-87, prin. investigator Sch. Edn., 1985—, asst. dean Sch. Edn., 1983-85, prof., 1989—; Fulbright prof. Weizmann Inst., Israel, 1983; exec. dir. seminars U. Calif., 1985-86, dir. instnl. tech. program, 1988-96, chair cognition and devel., 1996—; cons. Apple Computer, 1983—; mem. adv. com. on sci. edn. NSF, 1978—, Ednl. Testing Svc., 1986—, Smithsonian Instn., 1986—, Fulbright Program, 1983-86, Grad. Record Exam. Bd., 1990-94; chair Cognitive Studes Bd. McDonell Found., 1994-97; mem. computing svcs. adv. bd. Carnegie Mellon U., 1991—; mem. steering com. 3d Internat. Math. and Sci. Study, U.S., 1991—. Author: Education and the Challenge of Technology, 1987; co-author: The Psychology of Gender--Advances Through Meta Analysis, 1986—, Designing Pascal Solutions, 1992—, Designing Pascal Solutions with Data Structures, 1996; contbr. articles to profl. jours. Sci. advisor Parents Club, Lafayette, Calif., 1984-87; mem. Internat. Women's Forum, Women's Forum West, 1992—, membership com., 1995—. Recipient fellow Ctr. for Adv. Study in Behavior. Scis. 1995-96. Fellow AAAS (bd. dirs. 1996—), APA, Am. Psychol. Soc.; mem. Nat. Assn. Rsch. in Sci. and Teaching (bd. dirs. 1983-86, assoc. editor jour., Outstanding Paper award 1978, Outstanding Jour. Article award 1975, 83, Disting. Contbns. to Sci. Edn. Through Rsch. award 1994), Am. Ednl. Rsch. Assn. (chmn. rsch. on women and edn. 1983-85, Women Educators Rsch. award 1982, 88, edn. in sci. and tech. 1989-90, ann. mtg. program com. 1996, Willystine Goodsell award 1991), Nat. Sci. Tchrs. Assn. (mem. rsch. agenda com. 1987-90, task force 1993-94), Soc. for Rsch. in Child Devel. (editl. bd. 1984-89), Soc. Rsch. Adolescence, Sierra Club. Avocations: skiing, hiking. Office: U Calif Sch Edn 4611 Tolman Hall Berkeley CA 94720

LINN, RICHARD, lawyer; b. Bklyn., Apr. 13, 1944; s. Marvin and Enid (Rowe) L.; m. Patricia Madden, Aug. 8, 1966; children: Sandra Joan, Deborah Anne. BEE, Rensselaer Poly. Inst., 1965; JD, Georgetown U., 1969. Bar: Va. 1969, D.C. 1970, N.Y. 1994, U.S. Dist. Ct. (ea. dist.) Va. 1969, U.S. Dist. Ct. D.C. 1970, U.S. Ct. Appeals (4th cir.) 1970, U.S. Ct. Appeals (D.C. cir.) 1970, U.S. Ct. Appeals (fed. cir.) 1982, U.S. Supreme Ct. 1994. Patent examiner U.S. Patent and Trademark Office, Washington, 1965-68; patent agent Office Naval Rsch., Washington, 1968-69; assoc. Brenner, O'Brian, Guay & Connors, Arlington, Va., 1969-71, Stepno & Neilan, Arlington, 1971-72; ptnr. Stepno, Schwab & Linn, Arlington, 1972-74; pvt. practice Washington, 1974-77; ptnr. Wender, Murase & White (name changed to Marks & Murase), Washington, 1977, mng. ptnr. Washington office, 1982-97; ptnr. Foley & Lardner, Washington, 1997—. Mem. ABA, Am. Intellectual Property Law Assn., Internat. Trademark Assn., Va. Bar Assn. (founding bd. govs. Intellectual Property sect. 1971), Rensselaer Washington Alumni Assn. (chmn. 1972). Avocations: swimming, woodworking. Office: Foley & Lardner 3000 K St NW Ste 500 Washington DC 20007-5109

LINN, STUART MICHAEL, biochemist, educator; b. Chgo., Dec. 16, 1940; s. Maurice S. and Pauline L.; m. Priscilla K. Cooper; children: Matthew S., Allison D., Meagan S. B.S. with honors in Chemistry, Calif. Inst. Tech., 1962; Ph.D. in Biochemistry, Stanford U., 1967. Asst. prof. biochemistry U. Calif., Berkeley, 1968-72, assoc. prof., 1972-75, prof., 1975-87, head div. biochemistry and molecular biology, 1987-90, 95—. Mem. editorial bd. Nucleic Acids Rsch., 1974—, Jour. Biol. Chemistry, 1975-80, Molecular and Cellular Biology, 1987-91; contbr. articles to profl. jours., chpts. to books. Helen Hay Whitney fellow, 1966-68; John Simon Guggenheim fellow, 1974-75; recipient USPHS Merit Grant award, 1988—. Mem. AAAS, Am. Soc. Biol. Chemists (coun.), Am. Soc. Microbiologists. Office: U Calif Divsn Biochem & Molec Bio Barker Hall Berkeley CA 94720

LINNA, TIMO JUHANI, immunologist, researcher, educator; b. Tavastkyro, Finland, Mar. 16, 1937; came to U.S., 1968, naturalized, 1981; foster s. Gustaf Lennart and Anne-Marie (Forsstrom) Ackell; m. Rhoda Margareta Popova, May 20, 1961; children: Alexander, Fredrik, Maria. MB, U. Uppsala, Sweden, 1959, MD, 1965, PhD, 1967. Intern, resident hosps. Sweden, pvt. practice medicine hosps. and clinic; asst. prof. histology U. Uppsala, 1967-71; asst. prof. microbiology and immunology Temple U., Phila., 1970-71; dir. lab. clin. immunology hosps. Temple U., 1970-72, adviser clin. immunology, 1972-80; assoc. prof. microbiology, immunology Temple U., Phila., 1971-78; prof. Temple U., 1978-80, research prof., 1980-90; group leader immunology central research and devel. dept. E.I. duPont de Nemours & Co., Wilmington, Del., 1980-84, research supr., 1984-85, mgr. med. research products dept., 1986-87, assoc. med. dir., 1987-90; sr. dir. cellular immunology Applied Immune Scis., Inc., Menlo Park, Calif., 1990-91; sr. assoc. med. dir. inst. clin. immunology and infectious diseases, devel. rsch., Syntex (USA) Inc., Palo Alto, Calif., 1992-94, dir. med. rsch., 1994-95; dir. med. rsch. Roche Global Devel., Palo Alto, Calif., 1995-96; transplant med. liaison Roche Labs., Palo Alto, 1996—; immunology cons. UNDP/World Bank/WHO Spl. Program for Research and Tng. in Tropical Diseases, WHO, Geneva, 1978-79; mem. sci. adv. coun. Internat. Inst. Immunology Tng. and Research, Amsterdam, Netherlands, 1975-81. Author books; contbr. articles to profl. publs. USPHS Internat. postdoctoral research fellow, 1968-70; spl. research fellow U. Minn., 1970; Eleanor Roosevelt Am. Cancer Soc. fellow, 1976; grantee Swedish Med. Research Council, 1969-71; grantee NIH, 1972-80. Mem. Am. Assn. Cancer Research, Am. Assn. Immunologists (chmn. edn. com. 1975-80), Am. Assn. Pathologists, Am. Soc. Microbiology, Internat. Soc. Exptl. Hematology, Internat. Soc. Lymphology, N.Y. Acad. Scis., Reticuloendothelial Soc., Royal Lymphatic Soc. Uppsala, Scandinavian Soc. Immunology, Soc. Swedish Physicians, Swedish Med. Assn. Lutheran. Home: 260 Highland Ave San Carlos CA 94070-1911 Office: PO Box 10850 3401 Hillview Ave Palo Alto CA 94303

LINNAN, JUDITH ANN, psychologist; b. Pasadena, Calif., July 11, 1940; d. Robert Emmet Linnan and Jane Thomas (Shutz) H.; m. Ralph Theodore Comito, Feb. 1, 1964 (div. Mar. 1975); children: Matthew, Andrew, Kristine. BA, U. Portland, 1962; MS, Calif. State U., Long Beach, 1974; PhD, CCI Internat. U., 1982; postgrad., Newport Psychoanalytical Inst., 1984-87, 95—. Lic. marriage family child couns., pupil pers. lifetime, lic. rsch. psychoanalyst. Probation officer L.A. County Probation Dept., 1962-63; social worker L.A. County Dept. Probation and Social Svcs., 1963-69; counselor Huntington Beach (Calif.) Free Clinic, 1970-73, counseling ctr., Calif. State U., Long Beach, 1973-74; psychologist Fullerton (Calif.) Union High Sch. Dist., 1975-80, Psychiat. Med. Group, Orange County, Calif., 1981-82; psychologist, dir. Berkeley Psychol. Svcs., Placentia, Calif., 1982—; pvt. practice psychotherapist Huntington Beach, 1975—; founder, dir. Pacific Acad., Fullerton, 1981-82; dir. human resources So. Calif. Coll. Optometry, Fullerton, 1986—; cons., expert witness Orange County Social Svcs., 1992—; dir. student parent program Placentia Sch. Dist., 1993—. Democrat. Roman Catholic. Avocation: horses. Office: Berkeley Psychol Svcs 101 N Kraemer Blvd Ste 125 Placentia CA 92870-5000

LINNELL, ROBERT HARTLEY, environment, safety consultant; b. Kalkaska, Mich., Aug. 15, 1922; s. Earl Dean and Constance (Hartley) L.; m. Myrle Elizabeth Talbot, June 17, 1950; children: Charlene LeGro, Lloyd Robert, Randa Ruth, Dean Maxfield. BS, U. N.H., 1944, MS, 1948; PhD, U. Rochester, 1950. Asst. instr. U. N.H., 1942-44, instr., 1947; asst. prof. chemistry Am. U., Beirut, 1950-52; assoc. prof., chmn. chemistry dept. Am. U., 1952-55; v.p. Tizon Chem. Corp., Flemington, N.J., 1955-58; assoc. prof. chemistry U. Vt., 1958-61; dir. Scott Research Labs., Plumsteadville, Pa., 1961-62; program dir. phys. chemistry NSF, 1962-65, planning assoc., 1965-67, program mgr. departmental sci. devel., 1967-69; dean Coll. Letters, Arts and Scis., U. So. Calif., Los Angeles, 1969-70; dir. Office Instl. Studies U. So. Calif., 1970-82, chmn. safety sci. dept., 1982-85, prof. emeritus, 1985—; pres. Harmony Inst., 1985-92; cons. Reheis Corp., 1958-61, Coll. Chemistry Cons. Service, 1970-76, EPA, 1971-73, Lake Erie Environment Program, 1971-73. Author: Graduate Student Support and Manpower Resources in Graduate Science Education, 1968, Air Pollution, 1973, Hydrogen Bonding, 1971, Dollars and Scholars, 1982, Meeting The Needs of The Non-Smoking Traveler, 1986, Ignition Interlock Devices: An Assessment of Their Application to Reducing DUI, 1991; contbr. articles to profl. jours. Mem. traffic adv. com. Auto Club So. Calif., 1985-93; treas. Norwich Congl. Ch., 1995-96, chair bus. com. 1996—; coord. Concord Coalition, Upper Valley, N.H. and Vt., 1995—; mem. devel. bd. Upper Valley Tchr. Tng. Program, 1995—; mem. scholarship com. Upper Valley Cmty. Found., 1996—. Recipient Outstanding Achievement award Coll. Tech., U. N.H., 1969. Fellow AAAS; mem. AAUP, Am. Chem. Soc. (program chmn. Washington 1968, divsn. chem. edn. 1971), Am. Assn. Higher Edn., Assn. Instl. Rsch., Am. Soc. Safety Engrs., Nat. Safety Mgmt. Soc., Am. Assn. Univ. Adminstrs., Am. Lung Assn. (bd. dirs. 1986-92, pres. 1991-92), Upper Valley Habitat for Humanity (bd. dirs. 1993-95), Rotary. Patentee in chemistry field. Home: 255 Kings Hwy W White River Junction VT 05001-3200

LINNEN, THOMAS FRANCIS, international strategic management consulting firm executive; b. Carbondale, Pa., Sept. 29, 1925; s. John Joseph and Marie Dolores (Fitzpatrick) L.; m. Mary Joanne, Dec. 28, 1951 ; children: Nancy, Paula, Michele, Thomas F. Jr., Mary J. Jr. BS, Georgetown U., 1949; postgrad., Am. U., Washington, 1951, U. Rochester, 1988. Writer Congl. News Reports, Washington, late 40's; congl. press asst. Washington, 1949; asst. for pub. relations office of pres. Georgetown U., 1950; officer psychol. and spl. ops. Aide Office Sec. Army USAF and U.S. Army, Ft. Bragg, N.C., 1951-55; mgr. Retail Credit Company, Atlanta, 1953-56, 59-72; various managerial assignments GM Equifax Inc., Chgo., 1972-80; regional mgr. ops. and sales Equifax Inc., Upstate, N.Y., 1980-89; pres. The NORAM Group Ltd., Buffalo, 1990-94, vice chmn., 1992, chmn., 1993, 94; pres. Am. Auto. Exports Inc., Russia, 1993, chmn., CEO, 1994; chmn. AIG, Moscow, ABC, Moscow; bd. dirs. Gaflin Communication Group, Inc., Chgo.; on spl. assignment CIA, 1956-59; cons. to Russian govtl. units on market economy transition, 1952—; various positions with world affairs couns. and internat. insts. Pub. Russian internat. bus. newsletter "The Ural Region Focus"; contbr. articles to jours. and mags. Mem. adv. bd. Barat Coll., Buffalo Coun. on World Affairs, Internat. Inst. Buffalo, Chgo. Coun. Fgn. Rels., United Way Crusade of Mercy, Heart Fund Campaigns and other civic orgns.; chairmanship role in John F. Kennedy, Jimmy Carter and Jack Kemp campaigns for the Presidency. Maj. USAR ret. Mem. Res. Officers Assn. U.S. (former nat. officer), Mortgage Bankers Assn. Republican. Roman Catholic. Avocations: tennis, golf. Home and Office: 191 Wellington Dr Palm Coast FL 32164 Office: The NORAM Group Ltd 1333 Statler Towers Buffalo NY 14202-2913 *Democracy, with all its warts and imperfections, remains the best form of government known to man. Yet, democracy, eroded by unbridled freedom in its name and by corrupt self-interests, lethally turns in upon itself. And freedom, devoid of individual responsibility and in mindless confrontation with man's God, will, over time, kill the democratic body politic itself.*

LINNEY, BEVERLY See HALLAM, BEVERLY

LINNEY, ROMULUS, author, educator; b. Phila., Sept. 21, 1930; s. Romulus Zachariah Linney and Maitland (Thompson) Clabaugh; m. Laura Callanan; children: Laura, Susan. BA, Oberlin Coll., 1953, LittD (hon.), 1994; MFA, Yale U., 1958; DLitt. (hon.), Applachian State U., 1995. Prof. Actors Studio MFA New Sch., N.Y.C.; lectr. U. N.C., Chapel Hill, Raleigh, U. Pa., Bklyn. Coll., Conn. Coll., Princeton U., Hunter Coll. Author: (novels) Heathen Valley, 1962, Slowly, By Thy Hand Unfurled, 1965, Jesus Tales 1980, (plays) The Sorrows of Frederick, 1968, Democracy and Esther, and the Love Suicide at Schofield Barracks, 1973, Holy Ghosts, and The Sorrows of Frederick, 1977, Old Man Joseph and His Family, 1978, The Captivity of Pixie Shedman, 1981, Tennessee, 1981 (Obie award), Childe Byron, 1981, The Death of King Philip, 1983, Laughing Stock, 1984, Sand Mountain, 1985, A Woman Without a Name, 1986, Pops, 1987, Juliet, Yance and April Snow, 1989, Three Poets, 1989, Unchanging Love, 1990, '2', 1990, Ambrosio, 1991 (Obie award Sustained Excellence in Playwriting), Spain, 1993, True Crimes, 1995, Oscar Over Here, 1995, Mock Trial, 1996, Mountain Memory, 1996, A Christmas Carol (from Dickens), 1996. With U.S. Army, 1954-56. Grantee NEA, Guggenheim Found., Rockefeller Found., others; recipient Lit. award AAAL. Mem. Dramatists Guild (coun.), Ensemble Studio Theatre, Fellowship of So. Writers, Corp of Yaddo (bd. dirs.). Address: 67 E 11th St #212 New York NY 10003

LINOWES, DAVID FRANCIS, political economist, educator, corporate executive; b. N.J., Mar. 16, 1917; m. Dorothy Lee Wolf, Mar. 25, 1946; children: Joanne Linowes Alinsky, Richard Gary, Susan Linowes Allen (dec.), Jonathan Scott. BS with honors, U. Ill., 1941. Founder, ptnr. Leopold & Linowes (name now BDO Siedman), Washington, 1946-62; cons. sr. ptnr. Leopold & Linowes, 1962-82; nat. founding ptnr. Laventhol & Horwath, 1965-76; chmn. bd, chief exec. officer Mickleberry Comm. Corp., 1970-73; chmn., CEO Perpetual Investment Co., Inc., 1950-88; dir. Horn & Hardart Co., 1971-77, Piper Aircraft, 1972-77, Saturday Rev./World Mag., Inc., 1972-77, Chris Craft Industries, Inc., 1958—, Work in Am. Inst., Inc.; prof. polit. economy, pub. policy, bus. adminstrn. U. Ill., Urbana, 1976—, Boeschenstein prof. emeritus, 1987—; cons. DATA Internat. Assistance Corps., 1962-68, U.S. Dept. State, UN, Sec. HEW, Dept. Interior; chmn. Fed. Privacy Protection Commn., Washington, 1975-77, U.S. Commn. Fair Market Value Policy for Fed. Coal Leasing, 1983-84, Pres.'s Commn. on Fiscal Accountability of Nation's Energy Resources, 1981-82; chmn. Pres.' Commn. on Privatization, 1987-88; mem. Council on Fgn. Relations; cons. panel GAO; adj. prof. mgmt. NYU, 1965-73; Disting. Arthur Young Prof.

U. Ill., 1973-74; emeritus chmn. internat. adv. com. Tel Aviv U.; headed U.S. State Dept. Mission to Turkey, 1967, to India, 1970, to Pakistan, 1968, to Greece, 1971 ; U.S. rep. on privacy to Orgn. Econ. Devel. Intergovtl. Bur. for Informati cs, 1977-81, cons., N.Y.C., 1977-81; U.S. State Dept. mission to Chile, Argentina and Uruguay, July, 1988, Yugoslavia, May, 1991. Author: Managing Growth Through Acquistion, Strategies for Survival, Corporate Conscience; commn. report Personal Privacy in Information Society, Fiscal Accountablility of Nation's Energy Resources; editor: The Impact of the Communication and Computer Revolution on Society, Privacy in America, 1989; contbr. articles to profl. jours. Trustee Boy's Club Greater Washington, 1955-62, Am. Inst. Found., 1962-68; assoc. YM-YWHA's Greater N.Y., 1970-76; chmn. Charities Adv. Com. of D.C., 1958-62; emeritus bd. dirs. Religion in Am. Life, Inc.; former chmn. U.S. People for UN; chmn. citizens com. Combat Charity Rackets, 1953-58. Served to 1st lt. Signal Corps, AUS, 1942-46. Recipient 1970 Human Relations award Am. Jewish Com., U.S. Pub. Service award, 1982, Alumni Achievement award U. Ill., 1989, CPA Distinguished Pub. Svc. award, Washington, 1989. Mem. AICPA (v.p. 1962-63), U. Ill. Found. (emeritus bd. dirs. 1), Coun. Fgn. Rels., Cosmos Club (Washington), Phi Kappa Phi (nat. bd. dirs.), Beta Gamma Sigma. Home: 803 Fairway Dr Champaign IL 61820-6325 Office: U Ill 308 Lincoln Hall Urbana IL 61801 also: 9 Wayside Ln Scarsdale NY 10583-2907

LINOWITZ, SOL MYRON, lawyer; b. Trenton, N.J., Dec. 7, 1913; s. Joseph and Rose (Oglenskye) L.; m. Evelyn Zimmerman, Sept. 3, 1939; children: Anne, June, Jan, Ronni. AB, Hamilton Coll., 1935; JD, Cornell U., 1938; LLD (hon.), Allegheny Coll., Amherst Coll., Bucknell U., Babson Inst., Brandeis U., Colgate U., Curry Coll., Dartmouth Coll., Elmira Coll., Georgetown U., Hamilton Coll., Hebrew Union Coll., Ithaca Coll., Marietta Coll., Johns Hopkins U., Oberlin Coll., St. John Fisher Coll., St. Lawrence U., Jewish Theol. Sem., Washington U., St. Louis, U. Miami, Muskingum Coll., Notre Dame U., U. Pacific, U. Pa., Rutgers U., Pratt Inst., Rider Coll., Roosevelt U., Chapman Coll., U. Mich., Govs. State U., U. Mo., Syracuse U.; LHD (hon.), Am. U., Loyola U., U. Rochester, Yeshiva U., U. Judaism, Wooster Coll.; PhD (hon.), U. Haifa. Bar: N.Y. 1938. Asst. gen. counsel OPA, Washington, 1942-44; ptnr. Sutherland, Linowitz & Williams, 1946-58, Harris, Beach, Keating, Wilcox & Linowitz, Rochester, N.Y., 1958-66; chmn. Nat. Urban Coalition, 1970-76; chmn. bd. dirs., chmn. exec. com., gen. counsel Xerox Corp., 1958-66; chmn. bd. dirs. Xerox Internat., 1966; sr. ptnr. Coudert Bros., 1969-84, sr. counsel, 1984-94; ambassador to OAS, 1966-69; hon. chmn. Acad. Ednl. Devel., Washington, 1992—; co-negotiation Panama Canal treaties, 1977-78; spl. Middle East negotiator for Pres. Carter, 1979-81; chmn. Am. Acad. of Diplomacy, 1984-89; co-chmn. Inter-Am. Dialogue, 1981-92; hon. chmn. Acad. for Ednl. Devel., 1986—; pres. Fed. City Coun., 1974-78; chmn. Pres. Commn. World Hunger, 1978-79; bd. dirs., co-founder Internat. Exec. Svc. Corps; chmn. State Dept. Adv. Com. on Internat. Orgns., 1963-66. Author: The Betrayed Profession, 1994, (memoir) The Making of a Public Man, 1985, This Troubled Urban World, 1974; contbr. articles to profl. jours. Trustee Hamilton Coll., Cornell U., Johns Hopkins U., Am. Assembly; chmn. bd. overseers, bd. dirs. Jewish Theol. Sem., 1971-79. Lt. USNR, 1944-46. Fellow Am. Acad. Arts and Scis.; mem. Am. Assn. for UN (pres. N.Y. State), Rochester Assn. for UN (pres. 1952), Rochester C. of C. (pres. 1958), ABA, N.Y. Bar Assn., Rochester Bar Assn. (v.p. 1949-50), Am. Assn. UN (bd. dirs.), Council on Fgn. Relations, Order of Coif, Phi Beta Kappa, Phi Kappa Phi. Office: Acad for Ednl Devel 1875 Connecticut Ave NW Washington DC 20009-5728

LINSCOTT, JACQUELINE C., education consultant, retired educator; b. Franklin, N.C., Feb. 26, 1941; d. Clyde W. and Katherine (Ray) Clark; m. Leonard Lee Linscott, Aug. 16, 1964; 1 child, Laura Leigh Linscott Bledsoe. BS in Edn., U. N.C., 1964; M in Elem. Edn., Adminstrn. Supr., Stetson U., 1980. Edn. Cert., Fla. Tchr. Riverview Elem. Sch., Titusville, Fla., 1964-66, Jackson Middle Sch., Titusville, Fla., 1966-67, Coquina Elem. Sch., Titusville, Fla., 1967-86; tchr. Challenger 7 Elem. Sch., Cocoa, Fla., 1986-89, PRIME specialist, 1989-91, YRE coord., 1991-96; cons. on yr.-round edn. Dept. Edn., Tallahassee, 1990—. Author: Blue Bell Paper Weights and Other Bells, 1990, rev. edit., 1992, addendum, 1995. Grantee PAC-MAN Reading Program Brevard Pub. Schs., Melbourne, Fla., 1982, Caring Adults Reading with Elem. Students, Brevard Pub. Schs., 1990. Mem. ASCD, Nat. Assn. Yr.-Round Edn. (presenter confs. 1993—), Fla. Assn. Yr.-Round Edn. (presenter conf. 1991—, pres.), Alpha Delta Kappa. Avocations: antique collecting, reading, crafts, Longaberger basket consultant. Home: 3557 Nicklaus Dr Titusville FL 32780-5356

LINSENMEYER, JOHN MICHAEL, lawyer; b. Columbus, Ohio, June 20, 1940; s. John Cyril and Ruth Theresa (Motz) L.; m. Barbara Panish, Aug. 12, 1961; children: Ann Elizabeth Linsenmeyer Nelson, Thomas More, Barbara Mary Linsenmeyer Malone. AB, Georgetown U., 1961, JD, 1964. Bar: Va. 1964, N.Y. 1965, U.S. Supreme Ct.1967, D.C. 1975. Assoc. Cravath, Swaine & Moore, N.Y.C., 1966-75; ptnr. Forsyth, Decker, Murray & Broderick, N.Y.C., 1975-80, Morgan, Lewis & Bockius, N.Y.C., 1980—. Columnist Southern Conn. Newspapers, Greenwich, 1984—; contbr. articles to profl. jours. Police officer, sgt. Greenwich Police Dept. Special Div., 1966-87; cons. firearms Presdl. Commn. on the Causes and Prevention of Violence, 1968-69; bd. dirs. Fairfield County Fish and Game Agy., Newtown, Conn., 1973-77. Mem. N.Y. State Bar Assn., N.Y.C. Fed. Cts. Com., N.Y.C. Fed. Bar Coun., Univ. Club (N.Y.C.), Can. Club (N.Y.C.), Squadron A (N.Y.C.), Rocky Point (Old Greenwich, Conn.), Royal Can. Milit. (Toronto). Republican. Roman Catholic. Clubs: University (N.Y.C.), Squadron A (N.Y.C.), Rocky Point (Old Greenwich, Conn.), Royal Can. Mil. (Toronto), Can. Club of N.Y. Avocations: hunting, shooting, horses, military history. Home: 9 Hendrie Ave Riverside CT 06878-1808 Office: Morgan Lewis & Bockius 101 Park Ave New York NY 10178

LINSEY, NATHANIEL L., bishop; b. Atlanta, July 24, 1926; s. Samuel and L. E. (Forney) L.; m. Mae Cannon Mills, June 8, 1951; children: Nathaniel Jr., Ricarldo Mills, Julius Wayne, Angela Elise. BS, Paine Coll., 1948, LLD (hon.), 1990; BD, Howard U., 1951; MA in Evangelism, Scarritt Coll., 1974; DD (hon.), Miles Coll., 1975, Tex. Coll., 1985. Ordained to ministry Christian M.E.Ch., 1948. Nat. dir. youth Christian M.E.Ch., 1951-52; pastor Rock of Ages Christian M.E.Ch., 1952-53; presiding elder Columbia (S.C.) dist. Christian M.E.Ch., 1953-55; pastor Vanderhorst Christian M.E.Ch., 1955-56, Mattie E. Coleman Christian M.E.Ch., 1956-62, Thirgood Christian M.E.Ch., 1962-66; gen. sec. evangelism Christian M.E.Ch., 1966-78, chmn. bd. lay activities, 1978-82, chmn. fin. com., 1982-86, elected 39th bishop, 1978—, sr. bishop, CEO, presiding bishop 2d dist., 1994, founder Congress on Evangelism, chmn. dept. fin., 1982-86, chmn. bd. evangelism, missions and human concerns, chmn. Coll. of Bishops, 1980, 92; v.p. Interfaith Christian Coun., Washington, 1979-82; mem. presidium World Meth. Coun.; regional sec. N.Am. sect. world evangelism com. World Methodist Coun. Pres. local chpt. NAACP, Knoxville, Tenn., 1957; trustee Miles Coll., Birmingham, Ala.; mem. Wared Coun. of Chs., Nat. Coun. of Chs., Ky. Coun. of Chs. Recipient Disting. Alumni award Paine Coll., 1978, Presdl. citation Nat. Assn. for Equal Opportunities in Higher Edn., 1979, Disting. Svc. award Govt. D.C., 1984, Pub. Svc. award Tex. Coll., 1984, Disting. Missionary award Calif. conf. M.E.Ch., 1985; chieftancy of Obong Uwanna Ibibio Tribe, Nigeria, 1992—. Mem. World Meth. Coun., So. Calif. Ecumenical Coun. Chs. (pres. L.A. chpt. 1984). Democrat. Home: 5115 Rollman Estate Dr Cincinnati OH 45236-1457

LINSK, MICHAEL STEPHEN, real estate executive; b. L.A., Apr. 20, 1940; s. Abe P. and Helen Linsk; BS in Bus. Adminstrn., U. So. Calif., 1965, MBA, 1969; m. Wilma M. Stahl, Aug. 11, 1979; children by previous marriage: Cari E., Steven D. CFO Larwin Group, Inc., Encino, Calif., 1970-75; v.p. fin., dir. Donald L. Bren Co., Los Angeles, 1976-78; v.p., CFO, treas., dir. Wilshire Mortgage/Wilshire Diversified, Burbank, Calif., 1980-81, pres., dir. subs. Wilshire Mortgage Corp., Burbank, 1981-84; pres., dir. Wilshire Realty Investments, Burbank, 1981-84, Glenfed Investments Inc., subs. Glendale Fed. Savs., 1982-84; pres. Eastern Pacific Fin. Group, Los Angeles, 1984-85; sr. v.p. Leisure Tech., Inc., Los Angeles, 1985-87, CEO, Investec Realty Group, Inc., Encino, Calif., 1987-88; sr. v.p. L.A. Land Co., 1988-91, dir. real estate consulting Price Waterhouse, 1992—; dir. Presdl. Savs. Bank, dir. Jewel City Ins., Glendale, Verdugo Services, Inc., Glendale. Treas. Temple Judea, Tarzana, Calif., 1982-83, trustee, 1981-83; treas., bd. dirs. Am. Theater Arts; bd. dirs. North Hollywood Cultural Ctr., Inc. Mem. Bldg. Industry Assn. (dir. Los Angeles chpt. 1981-88), AICPA, Calif. Soc. CPAs, Urban Land Inst., Appraisal Inst., Beta Gamma Sigma. Office: Price Waterhouse 400 S Hope St Los Angeles CA 90071-2801

LINSKY, MARTIN ALAN, state official; b. Brookline, Mass., Aug. 28, 1940; s. Harold Max and Ruth Doran L.; m. Helen Roberts Strieder, Dec. 10, 1964 (div. Jan. 1979); children: Alison, Sam; m. Lynn H. Staley, July 7, 1979; 1 child, Max. BA, Williams Coll., Williamstown, Mass., 1961; JD, Harvard U., 1964. Asst. atty. gen. Commonwealth of Mass., Boston, 1967, chief sec. to the gov., 1992—; mem. and asst. minority leader Mass. Ho. of Reps., Boston, 1967-72; editorial writer and reporter The Boston Globe, 1973-75; editor-in-chief The Real Paper, Cambridge, Mass., 1975-79; asst. dir. Inst. of Politics, John F. Kennedy Sch., Cambridge, 1981-85; instr. in law Boston Coll., Newton, Mass., 1973-85; lectr. in pub. policy John F. Kennedy Sch. of Govt. at Harvard, Cambridge, 1985-92; coord. seminars Ethics Ctr., Poynter Inst. for Media Studies, St. Petersburg, Fla., 1987-88; project dir. Revson Found., N.Y.C., 1982-85; cons. Brookline, 1979-92. Author: Impact: How the Press Affects Federal Policy Making, 1986, How the Press Affects Federal Policy Making: 6 Case Studies, 1986; consulting editor: (books) Getting to Yes, 1981, Beyond the Hotline, 1985; editorial bd.: (pub. broadcasting system program) Frontline, 1985—. Bd. dirs., selection com. Cavallo Found., Cambridge, 1988—; bd. dirs. Ford Hall Forum, Boston, 1989-92; regular polit. commentator Monitor Network, Boston, 1992, WHDH-TV, CBS affiliate, Boston, 1990. Recipient cash prize, second place essay competition, Woodrow Wilson Ctr. for Media Studies, Washington, 1990; selected to teach leadership workshops to acads., John F. Kennedy Sch. of Govt., Cape Town, S. Africa, 1992. Mem. Inst. for Alternative Journalism (bd. dirs. 1983—), Poynter Inst. for Media Studies (bd. advisors 1981—). Avocations: running marathons, Mexican food, collecting baseball cards. Home: 333 Central Park W Apt 26 New York NY 10025-7104 Office: Office of Chief Secretary State House Rm 259 Boston MA 02133

LINSTONE, HAROLD ADRIAN, management and systems science educator; b. Hamburg, Fed. Republic Germany, June 15, 1924; came to U.S., 1936; s. Frederic and Ellen (Seligmann) L.; m. Hedy Schubach, June 16, 1946; children: Fred A., Clark R. BS, CCNY, 1944; MA, Columbia U., 1947; PhD, U. So. Calif., 1954. Sr. scientist Hughes Aircraft Co., Culver City, Calif., 1949-61, The Rand Corp., Santa Monica, Calif., 1961-63; assoc. dir. planning Lockheed Corp., Burbank, Calif., 1963-71; prof. Portland (Oreg.) State U., 1970—; pres. Systems Forecasting, Inc., Santa Monica, 1971—; cons. 1973—. Author: Multiple Perspectives for Decision Making, 1984; co-author: The Unbounded Mind, 1993, The Challenge of the 21st Century, 1994; co-editor The Delphi Method, 1975, Technological Substitution, 1976, Futures Research, 1977; editor-in-chief Technol. Forecasting Social Change, 1969—. NSF grantee, Washington, 1976, 79, 85. Mem. Inst. Mgmt. Scis., Ops. Rsch. Soc., Internat. Soc. Systems Scis. (pres. 1993-94). Avocation: photography. Office: Portland State U PO Box 751 Portland OR 97207-0751

LINSTROTH, TOD B., lawyer; b. Racine, Wis., Feb. 19, 1947; s. Eugene and Gloria L.; m. Jane Kathryn Zedler, June 23, 1972; children: Kathryn, Krista, Kassandre, Kyle. BBA in Acctg., U. Wis., 1970, JD, 1973. Bar: Wis. Assoc. Michael, Best & Friedrich, Madison, Wis., 1973-79, ptnr., 1980—. Mem. Madison Plan Commn., 1978-82, Wis. Gov.'s Task Force Am. Motors Corp., Madison, 1986; bd. visitors Univ. Wis. Sch. Bus., 1991-94; mem. Wis. Gov.'s Sci. and Tech. Coun., Madison, 1993-95; pres. Madison Repertory Theatre. 1st lt. USAR,. Mem. Madison Club (bd. dirs.). Republican. Avocation: sailing. Office: Michael Best & Friedrich 1 S Pinckney St # 700 Madison WI 53703-2808

LINTON, FREDERICK M., strategic planning consultant; b. Stanton, Mich., 1932; m. Peggy Jensen, May 27, 1954; children: Michael, Melinda, Margaret. B.A., Mich. State U., 1959, M.A., 1960. Tchr. San Diego, 1960-66; with AMCORD, Inc., 1966-69, Peat, Marwick & Mitchell, Los Angeles, 1969-70; sr. v.p. Shareholders Capital Corp., Los Angeles, 1970-72; pres., chief exec. officer Boyden Assos. Inc., N.Y.C. and Los Angeles, 1972-74; pres., chmn. Delta Group Inc., Mission Viejo, Calif., 1974—; dir Irvine Indsl. League. Ret. USAF. Mem. F86 Sabre Pilots Assn. Home: 26851 Salazar Dr Mission Viejo CA 92691-5011

LINTON, GORDON J., federal agency administrator. BS in Econs., Lincoln U.; MS in Counseling, Antioch U. Mem. Pa. Ho. Reps., Harrisburg, 1980-93; administrator Fed. Transit Administration, Washington, 1993—; past vice chmn. Ho. Appropriations Com., Pa. Ho. of Reps., chmn. transp. com. on pub. trnsp., chmn. Pa. legis. black caucus; bd. dirs. Southeastern Pa. Transp. Authority. Mem. Conf. Minority Transp. Officials (nat. legis. dir.). Democrat. Office: Fed Transit Auth 400 7th St SW Washington DC 20590-0001*

LINTON, JACK ARTHUR, lawyer; b. N.Y.C., May 29, 1936; s. Paul Phillip and Helen (Feller) L.; m. Nancy A., Sept. 1, 1957; children: Ann Deborah Linton Wilmot, James Paul, John Michael. BA, Albright Coll., 1958; JD, NYU, 1961, LLM in Taxation, 1966. Bar: Pa. 1962, N.Y. 1963, U.S. Tax Ct. 1966, U.S. Dist. Ct. (ea. dist.) Pa. 1978, U.S. Ct. Appeals, 1984. Assoc. DeLong, Dry & Binder, Reading, Pa., 1961-63; asst. ho. counsel Bob Banner Assocs., Inc., N.Y.C., 1963-66; ptnr. DeLong, Dry, Cianci & Linton, Reading, 1967-70, Williamson, Miller, Murray & Linton, Reading, 1970-72, Gerber & Linton, P.C., Reading, 1972-88, Linton, Giannascoli, Barrett & Distasio, P.C., Reading, 1989—; solicitor Reading Parking Authority, 1967-76, City of Reading, 1980-96; bd. dirs. The Group, Inc., Small Bus. Coun. Am., Inc., chmn. polit. action com., 1988—, numerous med. profl. corps., Reading area; lectr. nat. seminars on tax problems for small bus.; co-founder, mem. Estate Planning Coun. Berks County, 1978—. Editor Tax Law Rev., 1965-67; contbr. articles to profl. jours. Pres. Berks County Mental Health Assn., 1968-69, Reading Jewish Community Ctr., 1980-82; mem. Mental Health/Mental Retardation Bd. Berks County, 1974-80; treas., bd. dirs. Reading-Berks Youth Soccer League, 1982-85; bd. dirs. Gov. Mifflin Sch. Dist., Shillington, 1985-93. Kenneson fellow NYU Sch. Law, 1965-67. Mem. ABA (mem. personal svc. orgn. com., tax sect. 1981—, chairperson task force for repeal top-heavy rules 1987-89, vice chmn. personal svc. orgn. com. 1990-92, chmn. personal svc. orgn. com. 1992-94), Pa. Bar Assn., Berks County Bar Assn. (treas. 1969-72), Berks County C. of C. (mem. nat. affairs com.). Democrat. Jewish. Avocations: sports, photography, horticulture. Office: Linton Giannascoli Barrett & Distasio PC PO Box 461 1720 Mineral Spring Rd Reading PA 19603-0461

LINTON, ROY NATHAN, graphic arts company executive; b. Jamestown, Ohio, Jan. 22, 1918; s. Lindley Vanniman and Pearl Candice (Jackson) L.; m. Joyce Sandra Phillips, Dec. 11, 1945; children—Michael, Philip. A.B., Cedarville Coll., 1938; postgrad., Ohio State U., 1938-40. Tchr. math. Blanchester (Ohio) High Sch., 1938-41; with Standard Register Co., Dayton, 1947-83; v.p. ops. Standard Register Co., 1971-72, exec. v.p., 1972-77, pres., 1977-83, chief exec. officer, 1981-83, also dir. Past trustee Miami Valley Hosp., Dayton. Maj. field arty. AUS, 1941-46. Republican. Clubs: Masons (Jamestown), Rotary (San Diego). Office: 5969 Madra Ave San Diego CA 92120-3954

LINTZ, PAUL RODGERS, physicist, engineer, patent examiner; b. Dallas, Feb. 8, 1941; s. Norman Edmund and Sarah Kathleen (Powers) L.; m. Mary Grace Caggiano, Nov. 27, 1965; children: Matthew Thomas, Eileen Sarita, Jerome Peter, Elizabeth Irene. BA cum laude, U. Dallas, 1963; MS, Cath. U. Am., 1965, PhD, 1977. Mem. tech. staff Tex. Instruments, Dallas, 1965-67; rsch. physicist Teledyne Geotech. Co., Alexandria, Va., 1967-74; scientist Planning Systems Inc., McLean, Va., 1974-76; prin. investigator Sci. Applications Internat. Corp., McLean, 1976-84; systems engr. Mitre Corp., McLean, 1984-87; ind. cons. Vienna, Va., 1987-92; patent examiner U.S. Patent and Trademark Office, Washington, 1992—. Mem. Providence Dist. Dem. Com., Vienna, 1985; com. mem. Vienna area Boy Scouts Am., 1986-90; pres. Tysons Woods Civic Assn., Vienna, 1991. Mem. IEEE, D.C. Bar Assn. (social mem.), Internat. Platform Assn., Sigma Xi. Roman Catholic. Achievements include development of digital signal processing techniques for defense purposes in seismic detection of underground nuclear blasts, submarine sonar signal processing, passive bistatic radar signal processing, detection, tracking. Home: 2222 Craigo Ct Vienna VA 22182-5038 Office: US Dept Commerce Patent and Trademark Office ART Unit 2307 Box 13 Washington DC 20231 *The optimist argues the glass is half full of water. The pessimist argues it is half empty. The pragmatic, being thirsty drinks the water.*

LINTZ, ROBERT CARROLL, financial holding company executive; b. Cin., Oct. 2, 1933; s. Frank George and Carolyn Martha (Dickhaus) L.; m. Mary Agnes Mott, Feb. 1, 1964; children—Lesa, Robert, Laura, Michael. B.B.A., U. Cin., 1956. Staff accountant Alexander Grant, Cin., 1958-60; dist. mgr. Uniroyal, Memphis, 1960-65; v.p. Am. Fin. Corp., Cin., 1965—; dir. Rapid-American Corp., McGregor Corp., Faberge Inc., all N.Y.C., H.R.T. Industries Inc., Los Angeles. Fisher Foods Inc., Cleve., Am. Agronomics, Tampa, Fla. Trustee, St. Francis-St. George Hosp., Cin., 1974-81. Served to capt. U.S. Army, 1956-58, 61-62. Republican. Roman Catholic. Home: 5524 Palisades Dr Cincinnati OH 45238-5620 Office: Am Fin Corp 1 E 4th St Cincinnati OH 45202-3717

LINVILL, JOHN GRIMES, engineering educator; b. Kansas City, Mo., Aug. 8, 1919; s. Thomas G. and Emma (Crayne) L.; m. Marjorie Webber, Dec. 28, 1943; children: Gregory Thomas, Candace Sue. A.B., William Jewell Coll., 1941; S.B., Mass. Inst. Tech., 1943, S.M., 1945, Sc.D., 1949; Dr. Applied Sci., U. Louvain, Belgium, 1966; DSc, William Jewell Coll., 1992. Asst. prof. elec. engring. Mass. Inst. Tech., 1949-51; mem. tech. staff Bell Telephone Labs., 1951-55; assoc. prof. elec. engring. Stanford U., 1955-57, prof., dir. solid-state electronics lab., 1957-64, prof., chmn. dept. elec. engring., 1964-80, prof., dir. Center for Integrated Systems, 1980-90—, Canon USA prof. engring., 1988-89, prof. emeritus, 1989—; co-founder, dir. Tele Sensory Corp.; dir. Read-Rite Corp. Author: Transistors and Active Circuits, 1961, Models of Transistors and Diodes, 1963; inventor Optacon reading aid for the blind. Recipient citation for achievement William Jewell Coll., 1963, John Scott award for devel. of Optacon, City of Phila., 1980, Medal of Achievement Am. Electronics Assn., 1983, Louis Braille Prize Deutscher Blindenverband, 1984. Fellow IEEE (Edn. medal 1976), AAAS; mem. Nat. Acad. of Engring., Am. Acad. of Arts and Scis. Home: 30 Holden Ct Portola Valley CA 94028-7913 Office: Stanford U Dept Elec Engring Stanford CA 94305

LINVILLE, RAY PATE, logistics analyst, editor; b. Winston-Salem, N.C., Feb. 27, 1946; s. Clyde Burton and Nellie Pearl (Helm) L.; m. Mary Ann Slordal, July 30, 1970; children: Russell Pate, Rachel Ann. BA in Journalism, U. N.C., 1967; MS in Logistics Mgmt. with distinction, Air Force Inst. Tech., 1973. Commd. 2d lt. USAF, 1967, advanced through grades to col., 1989; materials mgr. USAF, Madrid, 1973-76; mem. staff Tactical Air Command, Hampton, Va., 1976-79; plans officer UN Command, Seoul, Korea, 1980-81; staff analyst USAF, Washington, 1981-85; rsch. fellow Harvard U., Cambridge, Mass., 1985-86; chief combat support analysis Joint Chiefs of Staff, Washington, 1986-89; dir. logistics plans Strat. Air Command, Omaha, 1989-92; chief logistics plans and programs Air Combat Command, Hampton, 1992-93; ret. USAF, 1994; analyst Logistics Mgmt. Inst., McLean, Va., 1993—; adj. prof. U. Va., Falls Church, 1986-88; grad. prof. Webster U., Washington, 1988—; adj. grad. prof. U. So. Calif., L.A., 1981. Author: (monograph) Command and Control of Forces..., 1987; editor, asst. editor, lit. editor, mem. rev. bd. Logistics Spectrum, 1990—; contbr. articles to profl. jours. Dir., v.p., treas. Danbury Forest Com. Assn., Springfield, Va., 1982-84; youth group advisor, deacon Presbyn. Ch., Omaha and Fairfax, Va., 1986—. Decorated Legion of Merit; recipient Outstanding Young Man of Am. award U.S. Jaycees, 1978. Mem. Soc. Logistics Engrs. (sr., life, cert. profl. logistician, chpt. chmn. 1990-91, Bronze award 1991, Pres.'s award for Merit 1996), Air Force Assn. (life), Mil. Ops. Rsch. Soc., Retired Officers Assn., U. N.C. Gen. Alumni Assn. (life), U.S. Chess Fedn. (life), Sigma Iota Epsilon. Avocations: writing, golf, piano, chess. Home: 5231 Capon Hill Pl Burke VA 22015-1615 Office: Logistics Mgmt Inst 2000 Corporate Rdg Ste 5012 Mc Lean VA 22102

LINXWILER, LOUIS MAJOR, JR., retired finance company executive; b. Blackwell, Okla., Mar. 7, 1931; s. Louis Major and Flora Mae (Horton) L.; m. Susan Buchanan, July 27, 1963; children: Louis Major III, Robert William. BS, Okla. State U., 1953. Mgr. credit dept. Valley Nat. Bank, Tucson, 1957-60; sales rep. Vega Industries, Syracuse, N.Y., 1960-62; program dir. Am. Cancer Soc., Phoenix, 1962-67; v.p., mgr. credit dept. United Bank Ariz., Phoenix, 1967-76; dean edn. Am. Inst. Banking, Phoenix, 1976-80; cons. Phoenix, 1980-81, United Student Aid Funds Inc., Phoenix, 1981-82; founder, pres., chief exec. officer Ariz. Student Loan Fin. Corp., Phoenix, 1982-88, also bd. dirs.; founder, chmn., chief exec. officer Western Loan Mktg. Assn., Phoenix, 1984-90, also bd. dirs.; pres. Precision Design and Engring., Inc., Escondido, Calif., 1993—, Circulator Motor Co., Phoenix, 1996—. Editor: Money and Banking, 1978. Pres. City Commn. Sister Cities, Phoenix, 1986-87, Am. Inst. Banking, Phoenix, 1973-74, Phoenix YMCA Bd. Dirs., 1974-75; v.p. North Mountain Behavioral Inst., Phoenix, 1975-77. Served to 1st lt. U.S. Army, 1954-56. Mem. Shriners, Hiram Club, Rotary (bd. dirs. 1982-83, 93-94, 96-97), Beta Theta Pi. Republican. Presbyterian. Avocations: restoring automobiles, World War II history, travel. Home: 3311 E Georgia Ave Phoenix AZ 85018-1424

LINZ, ANTHONY JAMES, osteopathic physician, consultant, educator; b. Sandusky, Ohio, June 16, 1948; s. Anthony Joseph and Margaret Jane (Ballah) Linz; m. Kathleen Ann Kovach, Aug. 18, 1973; children: Anthony Scott, Sara Elizabeth. BS, Bowling Green State U., 1971; D.O., U. Osteo. Med. and Health Scis., 1974. Diplomate Nat. Bd. Osteo. Examiners; bd. cert., diplomate Am. Osteo. Bd. Internal Medicine, Internal Medicine, Med. Diseases of Chest and Critical Care Medicine. Intern Brentwood Hosp., Cleve., 1974-75, resident in internal medicine, 1975-78; subsplty. fellow in pulmonary diseases Riverside Meth. Hosp., Columbus, Ohio, 1978-80; med. dir. pulmonary svcs. Sandusky (Ohio) Meml. Hosp., 1980-85; med. dir. cardio-pulmonary svcs. Firelands Community Hosp., Sandusky, 1985—; cons. pulmonary, critical care and internal medicine, active staff sect. internal medicine, chmn. dept. medicine, head div. pulmonary medicine Firelands Community Hosp., 1985—; cons. staff dept. medicine Good Samaritan Hosp., 1982-85, sect. internal medicine specializing pulmonary diseases; cons. pulmonary, critical care, and internal medicine Providence Hosp., Sandusky, Mercy Hosp., Willard, Ohio; clin. prof. internal medicine Ohio U. Coll. Osteo. Medicine; clin. prof. medicine Univ. Health Scis. Coll. Osteo. Medicine, Kansas City, Mo.; clin. asst. prof. med. Med. Coll. of Ohio at Toledo; adj. prof. applied scis. Bowling Green State U.; mem. respiratory tech. adv. bd. Firelands Campus, Bowling Green State U., 1983—; med. dir. Respiratory Therapy program., Bowling Green State U., 1984—; prof. osteopathic medicine U. Osteopathic Medicine and Health Scis., Des Moines. Author, contbr. articles and abstracts to profl. jours. Water safety instr. ARC, 1965—; med. dir., clin. rsch. investigator Camp Superkid Asthma Camp, 1984—; bd. trustees Stein Hospice, 1986-90. Recipient Edward Ruff Comty. Svc. award Am. Lung. Assn., 1985, Master Clinician award Ohio U. Coll. Osteopathic Medicine, 1987, Golden Rule award J.C. Penney, 1990, Disting. Alumna/Alumnus award Firelands Coll., Bowling Green State U., 1995. Fellow Am. Coll. Chest Physicians, Am. Coll. Critical Care Medicine, Am. Coll. Osteo. Internists; mem. AAAS, European Thoracic Soc., Am. Osteo. Assn., Ohio Osteo. Assn. (past pres., past v.p., past sec.-treas., acad. trustees 5th dist. acad.), Am. Heart Assn., Am. Thoracic Soc., Ohio Thoracic Soc., Am. Lung Assn. (pres., 1st v.p., med. adv. bd. chmn., exec. bd. dirs., bd. dirs. Ohio's So. Shore sect. 1984—), Nat. Assn. Med. Dirs. Respiratory Care, Ohio Soc. Respiratory Care (med. adviser/dir. 1982—), So. Critical Care Medicine, Am. Coll. Physicians (Ohio chpt.), Found. Critical Care (mem. Founder's Cir.), Sandusky Yacht Club, Sandusky chpt.), Alpha Epsilon Delta, Beta Beta Beta, Pi Kappa Alpha, Atlas Med. Fraternity. Roman Catholic.

LIONAKIS, GEORGE, architect; b. West Hiawatha, Utah, Sept. 5, 1924; s. Pete and Andriani (Protopapadakis) L.; student Carbon Jr. Coll., 1942-43, 46-47; BArch., U. Oreg., 1951; m. Iva Oree Braddock, Dec. 30, 1951; 1 dau., Deborah Jo. With Corps Engrs., Walla Walla, Wash., 1951-54; architect Liske, Lionakis, Beaumont & Engberg, Sacramento, 1954-86, Lionakis-Beaumont Design Group, 1986—. Mem. Sacramento County Bd. Appeals, 1967—, chmn., 1969, 75, 76; pres. Sacramento Builders Exchange, 1976. Served with USAAF, 1943-46. Mem. AIA (pres. Central Valley chpt., 1972—), Constrn. Specifications Inst. (pres. Sacramento chpt., 1962; nat. awards, 1962, 63, 65), Sacramento C. of C. (code com., 1970—). Club: North Ridge Country (pres. 1987). Lodge: Rotarian (pres. East Sacramento 1978-79). Prin. works include Stockton (Calif.) Telephone Bldg., 1968, Chico (Calif.) Main Telephone Bldg., 1970, Mather AFB Exchange Complex

Sacramento, 1970, Base Chapel Mather AFB, Sacramento, 1970, Woodridge Elementary Sch., Sacramento, 1970, Pacific Telephone Co. Operating Center Modesto, Calif., 1968, Sacramento, 1969, Marysville, Calif., 1970, Red Bluff, Calif., 1971, Wells Fargo Banks, Sacramento, 1968, Corning, Calif., 1969, Anderson, 1970, Beale AFB Exchange Complex, Marysville, 1971, Cosumnes River Coll., Sacramento, 1971, base exchanges at Bergstrom AFB, Austin, Tex., Sheppard AFB, Wichita Falls, Tex., Chanute AFB, Rantoul, Ill., McChord AFB, Tacoma, Wash., health center Chico State U., Sacramento County Adminstrn. Center, Sacramento Bee Newspaper Plant. Home: 160 Breckenwood Way Sacramento CA 95864-6968 Office: Lionakis Beaumont Design Group 1919 19th St Sacramento CA 95814-6714

LIONETTI, DONALD MICHAEL, career military officer; b. Jersey City, Mar. 6, 1940; s. Norman and Alice Rose (Spano) L.; m. Roberta Ann Tibbett, June 11, 1961; children: Donald M., Laura, Christopher. BS, U.S. Mil. Acad., West Point, N.Y., 1961; MS, Ariz. State U., 1971. Commd. 2nd lt. U.S. Army, 1961, advanced through grades to lt. gen.; brigade cmdr. 9th Divsn. Air Def. Artillery U.S. Army, Ft. Lewis, 1983-85; dep. to cmdr. gen. U.S. Army, Ft. Bliss, 1986-88; dir. plans U.S. Space Command U.S. Army, 1988-89; commanding gen. Air Def. Artillery Ctr. U.S. Army, Ft. Bliss, 1989-91; chief of staff U.S. Army Tng. & Doctrine Command U.S. Army, 1991-92, commanding gen. U.S. Army Space & Strategic Def. Command, 1992-94. Home: 8955 Magnolia Chase Tampa FL 33647

LIOTTA, LANCE ALLEN, pathologist; b. Cleve., July 12, 1947; married; 2 children. BA in Gen. Sci. and Biology, Hiram Coll., 1969; PhD in Biomed. Engring. and Biomath., Case Western U., 1974, MD, 1976. Cert. basic life support Am. Heart Assn., advanced life support Am. Heart Assn. Instr. pathology for inhalation therapists dept. pathology St. Luke's Hosp., Cleve., 1972-74; sr. instr. pulmonary pathology Phase I and Phase II, Sch. Medicine Case Western Reserve U., 1973-74; USPHS resident physician Lab. Pathology, Nat. Cancer Inst. NIH, Bethesda, Md., 1976-78, pathologist, expert/cons. Lab. Pathophysiology, Nat. Cancer Inst., 1978-80, sr. investigator, pub. health svc. officer Lab. Pathophysiology and Pathology, Nat. Cancer Inst., 1980-82, chief tumor invasion and metastases sect. Lab. Pathology and Lab. Pathology, Nat. Cancer Inst., 1982—, dir. anatomic pathology residency program Lab. Pathology, Nat. Cancer Inst., 1982—, dep. dir. intramural rsch., 1992-93; adj. clin. prof. pathology Sch. Medicine George Wash. U.; mem. adj. faculty Sch. Medicine Georgetown U.; invited faculty mem. Rockefeller U., 1979; speaker in field. Author: (with others) Cancer Invasion and Metastasis, 1977, Pulmonary Metastasis, 1978, Metastatic Tumor Growth, 1980, Bone Metastasis, 1981, Cell Biology of Breast Cancer, 1980, New Trends in Basement Membrane Research, 1982, Tumor Invasion and Metastasis, 1982, Progress in Clinical and Biological Research, 1982, Growth of Cells in Hormonally Defined Media, 1982, Understanding Breast Cancer: Clinical and Laboratory Concepts, 1983, The Role of Extracellular Matrix in Development, 1984, Basic Mechanisms and Clinical Treatment of Tumor Metastasis, 1985, Hemostatic Mechanisms and Metastasis, 1984, Biological Responses in Cancer, vol. 4, 1985, The Cell in Contact: Adhesions and Junctions as Morphogenetic Determinants, 1985, Rheumatology, vol. 10, 1986, Progress in Neuropathology, vol. 6, 1986, Cancer Metastasis: Experimental and Clinical Strategies, 1986, Biochemistry and Molecular Genetics of Cancer Metastasis, 1986, Basement Membranes, 1985, 1986 Year Book of Cancer, New Concepts in Neoplasia as Applied to Diagnostic Pathology, 1986, Head and Neck Management of the Cancer Patient, 1986, Cancer Metastasis: Biological and Biochemical Mechanisms and Clinical Aspects, 1988, Important Advances in Oncology, 1988, Breast Cancer: Cellular and Molecular Biology, 1988, Cancer: Principles and Practice of Oncology, vol. 1, 3d edit., 1989, Molecular Mechanisms in Cellular Growth and Differentiation, 1991, Peptide Growth Factors and Their Receptors, 1990, Molecuar Genetics in Cancer Diagnosis, 1990, Cancer Surveys-Advances & Prospects in Clinical, Epidemiological and Laboratory Oncology, vol. 7, no. 4, 1988, Genetic Mechanisms in Carcinogenesis and Tumor Progression, 1990, Molecular and Cellular Biology, Host Immune Responses and Perspectives for Treatment, 1989, Origins of Human Cancer: A Comprehensive Review, 1991, Cancer and Metastasis Reviews, vol. 9, 1990, Comprehensive Textbook of Oncology, 1991, Textbook of Internal Medicine, 2d edit., vol. 2, 1992, Molecular Foundations in Oncology, 1991, Genes, Oncogenes, and Hormones: Advances in Cellular and Molecular Biology of Breast Cancer, 1991, Cell Motility Factors, 1991, Oncogenes and Tumor Suppressor Genes in Human Malignancies, 1993, Principles and Practice of Gnecologic Oncology, 1992, Cancer Medicine, 3d edit., 1993; contbr. articles to profl. jours. NIH Pre-doctoral fellow; recipient Arthur S. Flemming award, 1983, Flow award lectureship Soc. Cell Biology, 1983, Nat. award and lectureship Am. Assn. Clin. Chemistry, 1987, Rsch. award Susan G. Komen Found., 1987, Disting. Lectr. award Rush Cancer Ctr., 1987, George Hoyt Whipple award and lectureship Sch. Medicine U. Rochester, 1988, Karen Grunebaum Symposium award lectureship Hubert H. Humphrey Cancer Rsch. Ctr., 1988, Cancer Rsch. award Milken Family Med. Found., 1988, William M. Shelly Meml. award and lectureship Centennial Johns Hopkins Med. Inst., 1989, Josef Steiner Cancer Found. prize, 1989, Basic Rsch. award Am. Soc. Cytology, 1989, Officer's Recognition award Equal Employment Opportunity, 1990, John W. Cline Cancer Rsch. award and lectureship U. Calif., 1990, Herman Pinkus award lectureship Am. Soc. Dermatology, 1990, Simon M. Shubitz award U. Chgo. Cancer Ctr., 1991, Stanley Gore Rsch. award, 1991, Lila Gruber Cancer Rsch. award Am. Acad. Dermatology, 1991, Am.-Italian Found. Cancer Rsch. award, 1992, Scie. Achievement medal U.S. Surgeon Gen., 1994. Mem. Am. Assn. Cancer Rsch. (bd. dirs., 6th Ann. Rhoads Meml. award 1985), Am. Assn. Pathologists (Warner-Lambert/Parke-Davis award 1984), Am. Soc. Cell Biology, Am. Soc. Clin. Investigation, Internat. Acad. Pathology, Internat. Assn. Metastasis Rsch. (pres. 1990-93), Sigma Xi, Phi Beta Kappa. Achievements include patents for method and device for determining the concentration of a material in a liquid, method for isolating bacterial colonies, test method for separating and/or isolating bacteria and tissue cells, device and method for detecting phenothiazine-type drugs in uring, in vitro assay for cell invasiveness, enzyme immunoassay with two-zoned device having bound antigens, metalloproteinase peptides, matrix receptors role in diagnosis and therapy of cancer, genetic method for predicting tumor aggressiveness, therapeutic application of an anti-invasive compound; patents for role of tumor motility factors in cancer diagnosis, role of tumor metalloproteinases in cancer diagnosis, peptide inhibitor of metalloproteinases, protein inhibitors of metalloproteinases, autotaxin motility stimulating proteins diagnosis and therapy, motility receptor protein and gene diagnosis and therapy. Office: Lab of Pathology Nat Cancer Inst 9000 Rockville Pike Bethesda MD 20814-1436

LIOTTA, RAY, actor; b. Newark, NJ, Dec. 18, 1955; s. Alfred and Mary L. Grad., U. Miami. TV appearances: Another World, NBC, 1978-80, Hardhat & Legs, CBS movie, 1980, Crazy Times, ABC pilot, 1981, Casablanca, NBC, 1983, Our Family Honor, NBC, 1985-86, Women Men = In Love There Are no Rules, 1991.; films: The Lonely Lady, 1983, Something Wild, 1986, Arena Brains, 1987, Dominick and Eugene, 1988, Field of Dreams, 1989, Goodfellas, 1990, Article 99, 1992, Unlawful Entry, 1992, No Escape, 1994, Corrina, Corrina, 1994, Operation Dumbo Drop, 1995, Unforgettable, 1996, Turbulence, 1997, Phoenix, 1997, Copland, 1997. mem. SAG, AFTRA. Office: ICM care Toni Howard 8942 Wilshire Blvd Beverly Hills CA 90211*

LIOU, KUO-NAN, atmospheric science educator, researcher; b. Taipei, Taiwan, Republic of China, Nov. 16, 1944; m. Agnes L.Y. Hung, Aug. 3, 1968; children: Julia C.C., Clifford T.C. BS, Taiwan U., 1965; MS, NYU, 1968, PhD, 1970. Rsch. assoc. Goddard Inst. for Space Studies, N.Y.C., 1970-72; asst. prof. atmospheric sci. U. Wash., Seattle, 1972-74; assoc. prof. U. Utah, Salt Lake City, 1975-80, prof., 1980—, dir. grad. studies in meteorology, 1981-84, dir. Ctr. for Atmospheric and Remote Sounding Studies, 1987—, rsch. prof. physics, 1992—; adj. prof. geophysics, 1992—; vis. prof. UCLA, 1981, U. Ariz., Tucson, 1995; affiliated prof. Peking U., Beijing, China, 1991—; vis. scholar Harvard U., 1985; cons. NASA Ames Rsch. Ctr., Moffett Field, Calif., 1984-94, Los Alamos (N.Mex.) Nat. Lab., 1984-88. Author: An Introduction to Atmospheric Radiation, 1980, Radiation and Cloud Processes in the Atmosphere, 1992; editor: Atmospheric Radiation Progress and Prospects, 1987; contbr. articles to profl. jours. Fellow NRC, Washington, 1970, David Gardner fellow U. Utah, Salt Lake City, 1978; recipient Founders Day award NYU, 1971, NSF grant, 1974—. Fellow Optical Soc. Am., Am. Meterol. Soc. (chmn. atmospheric radiation com. 1982-84), Am. Geophys. Union; mem. AAAS. Home: 4480 Adonis Dr Salt Lake City UT 84124-3923 Office: U Utah Dept Meteorology Salt Lake City UT 84112

LIOU, MING-LEI, electrical engineer; b. Tinghai, Chekiang, China, Jan. 6, 1935; came to U.S., 1958, naturalized, 1971; s. Ih-Min and Hsiao-Pao (Cheng) L.; m. Pearl B. Shen; children: Michael, Christopher, Derek. B.S.E.E., Nat. Taiwan U., 1956; M.S.E.E., Drexel U., 1961; Ph.D. E.E., Stanford U., 1964. Communications engr. Chinese Govt. Radio Adminstrn., Taiwan, 1957-58; instr. dept. elec. engring. Drexel U., Phila., 1958-61; research asst. Stanford Electronics Labs., Stanford U., 1961-63; mem. tech. staff Bell Labs., North Andover, Mass., 1963-66; supr. AT&T Bell Labs., 1966-84; dir. Bell Communications Research, Red Bank, N.J., 1984-92; prof. Hong Kong U. Sci. and Tech., 1992—; dir. Hong Kong Telecom. Inst. Info. Tech., 1993—. Contbr. chpts. to engring. books. Served to 2d lt. ROTC Chinese Air Force, 1956-57, Taiwan. Fellow IEEE, Hong Kong Inst. Engrs.; mem. IEEE Cirs. and Sys. Soc. (chmn. publs. bd. 1981-85, co-chmn. awards com. 1981-83, exec. v.p. 1986, pres. 1988, founding editor Trans. on Cirs. and Sys. for video tech. 1991-95, spl. prize paper award 1973, Darlington prize paper award 1977, Disting. Svc. award 1991, editor Trans. on Cirs. and Sys. 1979-81), Hong Kong Inst. Sci., Sigma Xi, Eta Kappa Nu. Office: The Hong Kong U Sci and Tech, Dept EEE, Clear Water Bay, Kowloon Hong Kong

LIOY, PAUL JAMES, environmental health scientist; b. Passaic, N.J., May 27, 1947; s. Nicholas Paul and Jean Elizabeth (Licurse) L.; m. Mary Jean Yonone, June 13, 1971; 1 child, Jason. BA in Physics and Edn., Montclair State Coll., 1969; MS in Physics and Applied Math., Auburn U., 1971; MS in Environ. Sci., Rutgers U., 1973, PhD in Environ. Sci., 1975. Sr. engr. air pollution Interstate Sanitation Commn., N.Y.C., 1975-78; asst. to assoc. prof. Inst. Environ. Medicine/NYU Med. Ctr., N.Y.C., 1978-85; dep. dir. lab. of aerosol rsch. Inst. Environ. Medicine/NYU Med. Ctr., 1982-85; assoc. prof. to prof. Robert Wood Johnson Med. Sch. U. Medicine and dentistry of N.J., Piscataway, N.J., 1985—; dir. exposure measurement and assessment divsn. Environ. and Occupational Health Scis. Inst. (EOHSI), Piscataway, 1986-94; dep. dir. Environ. and Occupational Health Scis. Inst. (EOHSI), 1995—; mem. grad. faculty Rutgers U., 1986—, admissions chair in environ. scis., 1993—; cons. bd. environ. studies and toxicology NRC, NAS, Washington, 1989-92, mem. numerous coms., 1984—; chmn. Clean Air Coun., N.J. Dept. Environ. Protection, Trenton, 1981-94; mem. Internat. Air Quality Bd., Internat. Joint Commn. U.S.-Can., 1992—; mem. sci. adv. bd. U.S. EPA, 1991—; mem. European Cmty. Air Pollution Exposure Adv. Com., 1996—; mem. dean's adv. bd. Coll. Sci. and Math. Auburn U., Ala., 1996—; adj. asst. prof. Bklyn. Coll., 1977-78; adj. prof. Med. U. S.C., 1996—; sci. cons. on environ. health, indoor air pollution and hazardous waste investigations and remediations. Author 150 scientific publs., 1975—, chpts. in 6 books; author: (book) Toxic Air Pollution, 1987, co-editor: (with M.J. Yonone-Lioy) Air Sampling Instruments, 1985; exec. editor: Atmospheric Environment jour., 1989-94; assoc. editor: Environ. Rsch., 1995—; patentee, 1994. Chair Cranford (N.J.) Environ. Commn., 1978; treas. Cranford Little League, 1984-85. Rsch. grantee EPA, NIH, CDC, ATSDR, N.J. Dept. Environ. Protection, API, DOE, 1978—. Mem. Air Waste Mgmt. Assn. (chmn. editorial bd. 1978-80), Am. Conf. Gov. Indsl. Hygiene (chmn. air sample inst. com. 1984-87), Am. Assn. Aerosol. Rsch. (editorial bd. 1990-93), Internat. Soc. Environ. Epidemiology (bd. councilors 1988-89), Internat. Soc. Exposure Analysis (pres. 1993-94, treas. 1990-91, exec. com. 198995); Soc. of Risk Analysis. Avocations: restoration of houses, tennis, automobiles. Office: Environ/Occup Hlth Scis Inst 681 Frelinghuysen Rd 3rd Fl Piscataway NJ 08855

LIOZ, LAWRENCE STEPHEN, lawyer, accountant; b. N.Y.C., Sept. 24, 1945; s. William and Irma (Berksohn) L.; m. Carol Renee Skolnik, Nov. 20, 1971; children: Adam Russell, Randall Eric. BS, SUNY, Albany, 1967; JD, SUNY, Buffalo, 1970; LLM in Taxation, NYU, 1975. Bar: N.Y.; CPA, N.Y. Mgr. Ernst & Whinney, N.Y.C., 1970-79; dir. tax affairs Azcon Corp., N.Y.C., 1979-82; mgr. Deloitte Haskins & Sells, N.Y.C., 1982-83, ptnr., 1983-84; ptnr. Deloitte Haskins & Sells, Woodbury, N.Y., 1984-87, Margolin, Winer & Evens L.L.P., Garden City, N.Y., 1987—; speaker various tax seminars, 1986—. Contbr. articles on tax to profl. jours. Pres. Rolling Wood Civic Assn., Roslyn, N.Y., 1983—; trustee Flower Hill (N.Y.) Assn., 1985-87, Village of Flower Hill, 1987-92; treas. Roslyn Sch. Dist., 1986—. Mem. ABA, AICPAs, N.Y. State Bar Assn., N.Y. State Soc. CPAs (chmn. fed. tax com. Nassau chpt. 1989-92, exec. bd. 1992—), L.I. Assn. Advancement for Commerce and Industry (dir.), L.I. Housing Partnership (dir.). Jewish. Avocations: skiing, golf. Home: 84 Knollwood W Roslyn NY 11576-1319 Office: Margolin Winer & Evens LLP 400 Garden City Plz Garden City NY 11530-3336

LIPCON, CHARLES ROY, lawyer; b. N.Y.C., Mar. 20, 1946; s. Harry H. and Rose Lipcon; m. Irmgard Adels, Dec. 1, 1974; children: Lauren, Claudia. B.A., U. Miami, 1968, J.D., 1971. Bar: Fla. 1971, U.S. Dist. Ct. (so. dist.) Fla. 1971, U.S. Ct. Appeals (5th cir.) 1972, U.S. Supreme Ct. 1976, U.S. Ct. Appeals (D.C. cir.) 1980, U.S. Dist. Ct. (so. dist.) Tex. 1982, U.S. Ct. Appeals (11th cir.) 1994. Pvt. practice, Miami, Fla., 1971—; lectr. U. Miami Sch. Law; moderator Am. On Line section on Admiralty Law. Author: Help for the Auto Accident Victim, 1984, Seaman's Rights in the United States When Involved in An Accident, 1989. Named Commodore of High Seas, Internat. Seaman's Union. Mem. Fla. Bar Assn., Am. Trial Lawyers Assn., ABA, Fla. Trial Lawyers, Dade County Bar Assn., Dade County Trial Lawyers. Club: Rotary (Key Biscayne). Contbr. articles to profl. jours. Office: 2 S Biscayne Blvd Ste 2480 Miami FL 33131-1803

LIPELES, MAXINE INA, lawyer; b. N.Y.C., Sept. 26, 1953; d. David Arthur and Pauline (Cooper) L.; m. Joel Kramer Goldstein, Aug. 31, 1980; children: Rachel, Joshua. AB, Princeton U., 1975; JD, Harvard U., 1979. Bar: Mass. 1980, Mo. 1982, U.S. Dist. Ct. (ea. dist.) Mo. 1982, U.S. Dist. Ct. Mass., U.S. Ct. Appeals (1st cir.) 1980, U.S. Ct. Appeals (8th cir.) 1982. Law clk. U.S. Dist. Ct. (no. dist.) Calif., San Francisco, 1979-80; asst. atty. gen. State of Mass., Boston, 1980-82; assoc. Husch & Eppenberger, St. Louis, 1982-86, ptnr., 1986-94, of counsel, 1995—; part-time prof. environ. regulation and policy sch. engring. Washington U., St. Louis, 1990—; dir. environ. engring. program Wash. U., St. Louis, 1994—. Co-author: Hazardous Waste, 1992, Water Pollution, 1993, Environmental Law Anthology, 1996. Mem. ABA, Mo. Bar Assn., Bar Assn. Met. St. Louis (chmn. environ. law com. 1986-88). Office: Husch & Eppenberger 100 N Broadway Ste 1300 Saint Louis MO 63102-2706

LIPFORD, ROCQUE EDWARD, lawyer, corporate executive; b. Monroe, Mich., Aug. 16, 1938; s. Frank G. and Mary A. (Mastromarco) L.; m. Marcia A. Griffin, Aug. 5, 1966; children: Lisa, Rocque Edward, Jennifer, Katherine. BS, U. Mich., 1960, MS, 1961, JD with distinction, 1964. Bar: Mich. 1964, Ohio 1964. Instr. mech. engring. U. Mich., 1961-63; atty. Miller, Canfield, Paddock & Stone, Detroit, 1965-66; asst. gen. counsel Monroe Auto Equipment Co., 1966-70, gen. counsel, 1970-72, v.p., gen. counsel, 1973-77; v.p., gen. counsel Tenneco Automotive, 1977-78; ptnr. firm Miller, Canfield, Paddock & Stone, Detroit, 1978—, mng. ptnr., 1988-91; bd. dirs. La-Z-Boy Chair Co., Monroe Bank & Trust, Kincaid Furniture Co., Q.E.D. Environ. Systems, Ferrous Environ. Recycling Corp. Mem. Mich. Bar Assn., Legatus, Knights of Malta, North Cape Yacht Club, Monroe Golf and Country Club, Otsego Ski Club, Ocean Reef Club, Tau Beta Pi, Pi Tau Sigma. Home: 1065 Hollywood Dr Monroe MI 48162-3045 Office: Miller Canfield Paddock & Stone 214 E Elm Ave Monroe MI 48162-2653

LIPINSKI, ANN MARIE, newspaper editor. Assoc. mng. editor for met. news. Chgo. Tribune, now dep. mng. editor, now mng. editor, 1995—. Recipient Pulitzer prize for series on politics and conflicts of interest Chgo. City Coun., 1988. Office: Chgo Tribune 435 N Michigan Ave Chicago IL 60611

LIPINSKI, BARBARA JANINA, psychotherapist, psychology educator; b. Chgo., Feb. 29, 1956; d. Janek and Alicja (Brzozkiewicz) L.; m. Bernard Joseph Burns, Feb. 14, 1976 (div. 1985). B of Social Work, U. Ill., Chgo., 1978; MFCC, MA, U. Calif., Santa Barbara, 1982; PhD, U. So. Calif., 1992. Diplomate Am. Bd. Forensic Medicine; cert. tchr., Calif., psychology tchr., Calif.; cert. adminstr., non-pub. agent; lic. marriage, family and child therapist; bd. cert. forensic examiner. Police svc. officer Santa Barbara (Calif.) Police Dept., 1978-79; peace officer Airport Police, Santa Barbara, 1979-80; emergency comms. Univ. Police, Santa Barbara, 1980-82; facilitator, instr. Nat. Traffic Safety Inst., San Jose, Calif., 1981-87; assoc. dir. Community Health Task Force on Alcohol and Drug Abuse, Santa Barbara, 1982-86; instr. Santa Barbara C.C., 1987-88; patients' rights adv. Santa Barbara County Calif. Mental Health Adminstrn., 1986-89; pvt. practice psychotherapist Santa Barbara, 1985—; faculty mem., clin. coord. Pacifica Grad. Inst., Carpinteria, Calif., 1989—; intern clin. psychology L.A. County Sheriff's Dept., 1991-92, cons. Devereaux Found., Santa Barbara, 1993-95, Ctr. for Law Related Edn., Santa Barbara, 1986; cons., trainer Univ. Police Dept., Santa Barbara, 1987, 89. Vol. crisis work Nat. Assn. Children of Alcoholics, L.A., 1987; crisis intervention worker Women in Crisis Can Act, Chgo., 1975-76; vol. counselor Santa Barbara Child Sexual Assault Treatment Ctr.-PACT, Santa Barbara, 1981-82. Recipient Grad. Teaching assistanship U. So. Calif., 1990-92. Mem. APA, Am. Profl. Soc. on Abuse of Children, Am. Coll. Forensic Examiners, Internat. Critical Incident Stress Found., Calif. Assn. Marriage and Family Therapists, Internat. Soc. for Traumatic Stress Studies. Avocations: writing, dancing, hiking, ecology, pottery. Home: 301 Los Cabos Ln Ventura CA 93001-1183 Office: Pacifica Grad Inst 249 Lambert Rd Carpinteria CA 93013-3019

LIPINSKI, WILLIAM OLIVER, congressman; b. Chgo., Dec. 22, 1937; s. Oliver and Madeline (Collins) L.; m. Rose Marie Lapinski, Aug. 29, 1962; children: Laura, Daniel. Student, Loras Coll., Dubuque, Iowa, 1957-58. Various positions to area supr. Chgo. Parks, 1958-75; alderman Chgo. City Coun., 1975-83; mem. 98th-104th Congresses from 5th (now 3rd) Dist. Ill., 1983—; ranking minority mem., mem. transp. and infrastructure subcom. on railroads. Dem. ward committeeman, Chgo., 1975—; del. Dem. Nat. Midterm Conv., 1974, Dem. Nat. Conv., 1976, 84, 88; pres. Greater Midway Econ. and Community Devel. Com.; mem. Chgo. Hist. Soc., Art Inst., Chgo., pres.'s coun. St. Xavier Coll.; mem. Congl. Competitive Caucus, Congl. Caucus for Women's Issues, Congl. Hispanic Caucus, Congl. Human Rights Caucus, Congl. Populist Caucus, Dem. Study Group, Export Task Force, Inst. for Ill., Maritime Caucus, N.E.-Midwest Congl. Coalition, Urban Caucus. Named Man of Yr. Chgo. Park Dist. 4, 1983; recipient Archer Heights Civic Assn. award 1979, 23d Ward Businessmen and Mchts. award Chgo., 1977, Garfield Ridge Hebrew Congregation award Chgo., 1975-77, Installing Officer award Vittum Park Civic Assn., 23d Ward Minuteman award, Friends of Vittum Park Polish award, Nathan Hale Grand award from S.W. Liberty Soc., S.W. Am. Edn. and Recreation program award, Sentry of Yr. award Stars & Stripes Soc., Ill. State Minuteman award 1991. Mem. Polish Nat. Alliance, Kiwanis (Disting. Svc. award, pres., Peace Through Strength Leadership award 1991). Democrat. Roman Catholic. Office: US Ho of Reps 1501 Longworth House Bldg Washington DC 20515-1303 also: 5832 S Archer Ave Chicago IL 60638-1637

LIPKIN, BERNICE SACKS, computer science educator; b. Boston, Dec. 21, 1927; d. Milton and Esther Miriam (Berchuck) Sacks; m. Lewis Edward Lipkin; children: Joel Arthur, Libbe Lipkin Englander. BS in Biology, Chemistry, Northeastern U., 1949; MA in Psychology, Boston U., 1950; PhD in Experimental Psychology, Columbia U., 1961. Rsch. and devel. scientist Directorate Sci. and Tech., CIA, Washington, 1964-70; scientist dept. computer sci. U. Md., Greenbelt, 1971-72; health sci. adminstr. NIH, Bethesda, Md., 1972-88; cons. computerized text analysis, data exploration L+B and Co., Bethesda, 1989—. Author: String Processing and Text Manipulation in C, 1994; editor: Picture Processing and Psychopictorics, 1970; contbr. articles on computer-based text searches and data analysis to profl. publs. Cerebral Palsy Soc. fellow in neurophysiology, 1961-62; NIH trainee, 1955-58. Mem. AAAS, IEEE, APA, Soc. Neurosci., Optical Soc. Am., Assn. Computing Machinery, Sigma Xi. Jewish. Achievements include design of system for manipulation and analysis of text data files, documentation and instruction manuals; teaching children computer concepts and programming. Office: 9913 Belhaven Rd Bethesda MD 20817-1733

LIPKIN, DAVID, chemist; b. Phila., Jan. 30, 1913; s. William and Ida (Zipin) L.; m. Silvia Stantic Alvarez, Nov. 10, 1973; children—Jeffrey Alan, Edward Walter. B.S., U. Pa., 1934; Ph.D., U. Calif., Berkeley, 1939. Research chemist Atlantic Refining Co., Phila., 1934-36; research fellow U. Calif., Berkeley, 1939-42; research chemist Manhattan Project, Berkeley, 1942-43; research chemist, group leader Los Alamos Sci. Lab., 1943-46; mem. faculty Washington U., St. Louis, 1946—; prof. chemistry Washington U., 1948-66, chmn. dept., 1964-70, William Greenleaf Eliot prof., 1966-81, emeritus, 1981—; sr. vis. fellow Agrl. Research Council, Cambridge, Eng., 1960; vis. research scientist John Innes Inst., Norwich, Eng., 1971, 78; trustee Argonne Univs. Assn., 1969-71; cons. in field. Author. Guggenheim fellow, 1955-56. Mem. Am. Chem. Soc. (St. Louis award 1970), AAUP, Sigma Xi, Tau Beta Pi, Pi Mu Epsilon. Patentee in field. Office: Washington Univ Chemistry Dept Saint Louis MO 63130

LIPKIN, DAVID LAWRENCE, physician; b. Bklyn., Mar. 9, 1938; s. Herman and Celia (Granate) L.; m. Nicole Van Laere, Sept. 23, 1962; children—Lawrence, Elline, Diane. A.B. in Biology, Clark U., Worcester, Mass., 1957; M.D., Catholic U. Louvain (Belgium), 1964. Diplomate Am. Bd. Phys. Medicine and Rehab. Intern, Lutheran Med. Ctr., Bklyn., 1963-64; resident in pediatrics N.J. Coll. Medicine, Jersey City, 1964-66; resident rehab. medicine Albert Einstein Coll. Medicine, Bronx, N.Y., 1966-68, chief resident, 1968-69; clin. instr. U. Miami, 1974-80, clin. asst. prof., 1980—; med. dir. rehab. Parkway Regional Med. Center Humana Hosp., Biscayne, Fla., 1974-88; med. dir. Bon Secours Hosp., North Miami, Fla., 1984-88; chief dept. rehab. medicine Sinai Med. Ctr.; cons. in field. Chmn. stroke com. Am. Heart Assn., Monroe and Dade Counties, Fla., 1980-82; bd. dirs. Multiple Sclerosis Soc, Dade, 1987, Villa Maria Nursing Ctr, 1986. NIH fellow, 1966-69. Mem. Dade County Med. Assn., Fla. Med. Assn., Fla. Soc. Phys. Medicine and Rehab. (pres. 1976-78, 1989—), Am. Rheumatism Assn., Am. Acad. Phys. Medicine and Rehab. Fla. Rheumatology Soc., So. Soc. Phys. Medicine and Rehab. Home: 2714 Oakmont Fort Lauderdale FL 33332-1805

LIPKIN, MARTIN, physician, scientist; b. N.Y.C., Apr. 30, 1926; s. Samuel S. and Celia (Greenfield) L.; m. Joan Schulein, Feb. 16, 1958; children—Richard Martin, Steven Monroe. A.B., NYU, 1946, M.D., 1950. Diplomate: Nat. Bd. Med. Examiners. Practice medicine specializing in internal medicine, gastroenterology and neoplastic diseases N.Y.C.; mem. staff N.Y. Hosp., Meml. Hosp. for Cancer and Allied Diseases, 1972-96; prof. medicine Cornell U. Med. Coll., 1978—, prof. Grad. Sch. Med. Scis., 1978—; mem. and attending physician Meml. Sloan-Kettering Cancer Ctr., 1985-96; dir. clin. rsch. Strang Cancer Prevention Ctr., N.Y.C., 1996—; vis. physician Rockefeller U. Hosp., 1981—; hon. lectr. Israel Med. Assn. and Gastroenterology Soc., 1982; nominator Nobel Prize for Physiology and Medicine, 1982; bd. dirs., officer The Med. Ednl. and Sci. Found. of N.Y.; chmn. bd. Irving Weinstein Found. Mem. editorial bd. Cancer Epidemiology, Biomarkers and Prevention, Cancer Rsch., Internat. Jour. Oncology; editor: Gastrointestinal Tract Cancer, 1978, Inhibition of Tumor Induction and Development, 1981, Gastrointestinal Cancer: Endogenous Factors, 1981, Calcium, Vitamin D and Prevention of Colon Cancer, 1991, Cancer Chemoprevention, 1992; contbr. articles to profl. jours. Served as officer USN, 1953-55. Recipient NIH career devel. award, 1962-71; Albert F.R. Andresen ann. award and lectureship N.Y. State Med. Soc., 1971. Fellow ACP, Am. Coll. Gastroenterology; mem. Med. Soc. State of N.Y. (chmn. sci. program com. 1990-91, chmn. edn. com. 1991—), Digestive Diseases Soc. (founder), Internat. Soc. for Cancer Prevention (founder), Am. Soc. Clin. Investigation, Am. Physiol. Soc., Am. Assn. Cancer Rsch., Am. Gastroenterol. Assn., Soc. for Exptl. Biology and Medicine, Harvey Soc. Office: 1230 York Ave New York NY 10021-6307

LIPKIN, MARY CASTLEMAN DAVIS (MRS. ARTHUR BENNETT LIPKIN), retired psychiatric social worker; b. Germantown, Pa., Mar. 4, 1907; d. Henry L. and Willie (Webb) Davis; m. William F. Cavenaugh, Nov. 8, 1930 (div.); children: Molly C. (Mrs. Gary Oberbillig), William A.; m. Arthur Bennett Lipkin, Sept. 15, 1961 (dec. June 1974). Student, Pa. Acad. Fine Arts, 1924-28; postgrad., U. Wash., 1946-48, Seattle Psychonalytic Assn., 1959-61. Nursery sch. tchr. Miquon (Pa.) Sch., 1940-45; caseworker Family Soc. Seattle, 1948-49, Jewish Family and Child Service, Seattle, 1951-56; psychiat. social worker Stockton (Calif.) State Hosp., 1957-58; supr. social service Mental Health Research Inst., Fort Steilacoom, Wash., 1958-59; engaged in pvt. practice, Bellevue, Wash., 1959-61. Former mem. Phila.

Com. on City Policy. Former diplomate and bd. mem. Conf. Advancement of Pvt. Practice in Social Work; former mem. Chestnut Hill women's com. Phila. Orch; mem. Bellevue Art Mus., Assoc. Am. Assn. of U. Women, Wing Luke Mus. Mem. ACLU, LWV, Linus Pauling Inst. Sci. and Medicine, Inst. Noetic Scis., Menninger Found., Smithsonian Instn., Union Concerned Scientists, Physicians for Social Responsibility, Center for Sci. in Pub. Interest, Asian Art Council, Seattle Art Mus., Nature Conservancy, Wilderness Soc., Sierra Club. Home: 10022 Meydenbauer Way SE Bellevue WA 98004

LIPKIN, SEYMOUR, pianist, conductor, educator; b. Detroit, May 14, 1927; s. Ezra and Leah (Vidaver) L.; m. Catherine Lee Bing, Dec. 27, 1961 (div. 1983); 1 son, Jonathan Michael. Mus. B., Curtis Inst. Music, 1947; studied piano with, David Saperton, 1938-41, Rudolf Serkin, Mieczyslaw Horszowski, 1941-47; conducting with, Serge Koussevitzky, Berkshire Music Center, 1946, 48, 49. Piano tchr. Juilliard Sch. Music, N.Y.C., 1986—; mem. faculty Manhattan Sch. Music, 1965-70, 72-86, NYU, 1980-86; mem. piano faculty Curtis Inst. Music, 1969—, New Eng. Conservatory, 1984-86, faculty music dept. Marymount Coll., Tarrytown, N.Y., 1963-72, chmn. music dept., 1968-71. Condr. Bklyn. Coll. Orch., 1973-74; Ford Found. commn. to perform concerto by Harold Shapero, 1959; debut with Detroit Civic Orch., 1937; apprentice condr. to George Szell, Cleve. Orch., 1947-48; appearances as pianist other U.S. orchs. including Boston Symphony in Tanglewood; ann. tours including soloist, Buffalo and Nat. Symphony, soloist, asst. condr. N.Y. Philharm. tour, Europe and Russia, 1959; conducting debut Detroit Symphony, 1944; recitalist, 92d St YMHA, N.Y.C., 1981, 83, soloist N.Y. Philharm., N.Y.C., 1983, participant in chamber music, Spoleto Festivals, 1982, 83, co-condr. Curtis Inst. Orch., 1952-53, asst. condr. Goldovsky Opera Co. on tour, 1953, condr. N.Y.C. Opera Co., 1958, 1 of 3 asst. condrs. New York Philharm., 1959-60; mus. dir. Teaneck Symphony, N.J., 1961-70, L.I. Symphony, 1963-79, Scarboro Chamber Orch., N.Y., 1964-65, Joffrey Ballet, N.Y. City Center, 1966-68, 1972-79, prin. guest condr., 1968-72; artistic dir. Kneisel Hall Summer Chamber Music Sch. and Festival, 1987— (performed cycle of 32 Beethoven Sonatas 1988-90, Gardner Mus., Boston, 1996—, Beethoven Soc., N.Y., 1997—, 10 Beethoven Violin Sonatas with Andrew Dawes 1995, Uto Ughi, Santa Cecilia, Rome, 1995, 5 cello sonatas with David Soyer 1989, Laurence Lesser, 1996, 5 piano concertos with Santa Fe Symphony 1993); appearances as opera condr. Curtis Inst., Teatro Petruzzelli, Bari, Italy, 1986-87; participant in chamber music Norfolk Fest., 1984-85, Marlboro Fest., 1986; recorded Stravinsky Piano Concerto with N.Y. Philharm., Grieg, Saint-Saens, Strauss sonatas with Aaron Rosand (violin), Grieg, Dohnanyi, Weiner sonatas with Oscar Shumsky (violin), Franck Sonata, Chausson Concerto with Rosand, Hindemith Sonata with Rafael Hillyer (Viola), Beethoven Sonatas op106 and 109 (solo), Schubert Works and Weber Sonatas with Arnold Steinhardt (violin); artistic dir. internat. piano festival and William Kapell competition U. Md., 1988-92. Recipient 1st prize Rachmaninoff Piano Competition, 1948. Mem. Am. Guild Mus. Artists, Am. Fedn. Musicians. Home: 420 W End Ave New York NY 10024-5708 Office: Perform Artist Internat 500 Main St Ste 700 Fort Worth TX 76102-3944

LIPKIN, WILLIAM JOEL, controller, history educator; b. Newark, June 27, 1939; s. Jack N. and Martha (Schartoff) L.; m. Barbara B. Brooks, July 11, 1965; children: Jeffrey, Glen. BA, Rutgers U., Newark, 1960; MA, Rutgers U., 1962, PhD (equivalency), 1963; postgrad in Edn., Kean Coll., 1963-65. Controller Hagin & Koplin, Inc., Newark, 1961-72; pres., CFO Allcar Leasing Corp., Springfield, N.J., 1972-87; controller, CFO Thomas Lincoln Mercury, Westfield, N.J., 1987—; cons. Am. Internat. Rent-A-Car, Springfield, N.J., 1980-86; instr. history Kean Coll., Union, N.J., 1962-73, Union County Coll., 1989—. Recipient Teaching fellowship Rutgers U., 1961, 62. Mem. Am. Hist. Assn., Nat. Notary Assn., N.J. Auto Accts. Assn., B'nai Brith. Avocations: computers, music, sports. Home: 921 Sheridan St Union NJ 07083-6537 Office: Thomas Lincoln Mercury Inc 369 South Ave E Westfield NJ 07090-1465

LIPMAN, BERNARD, internist, cardiologist; b. St. Joseph, Mo., June 14, 1920; s. Harry and Sarah K. (Kross) L.; m. Leslie Joy Garber, Apr. 23, 1949; children: Lawrence Alan, Robert Bruce, Bradford Craig, William Lloyd. A.B., Washington U., 1941, M.D., 1944. Diplomate: Am. Bd. Internal Medicine, Am. Bd. Cardiology. Intern Barnes Hosp., St. Louis, Newington Hosp.-Yale Med. Sch.; resident in medicine Barnes Hosp., 1947-49; teaching fellow U. Wash. Med. Sch., 1949-50; mem. faculty Emory U. Sch. Medicine, Atlanta, 1950—; clin. prof. medicine Emory U. Sch. Medicine, 1978-83, clin. prof. emeritus, 1983—; mem. staff St. Joseph Hosp., Grady Hosp., Piedmont Hosp., Emory U. Hosp., West Paces Ferry Hosp.; dir. heart sta. St. Joseph Hosp.; co-dir. Giddings Heart Clinic. Co-author Lipman-Massie Clinical Electrocardiography, 8th edit., 1989, ECG Pocket Guide, 1987; contbr. articles to med. jours. Co-trustee Albert Steiner Found. Served to capt. M.C. AUS, 1945-47. Fellow A.C.P., Am. Coll. Cardiology (emeritus); mem. Am. Heart Assn. (mem. council clin. cardiology), Am. Fedn. Clin. Research, Am. Soc. Internal Medicine, Phi Beta Kappa, Sigma Xi, Alpha Omega Alpha. Home: 2652 Brookdale Dr NW Atlanta GA 30305

LIPMAN, DAVID, multimedia consultant for publishing company; b. Springfield, Mo., Feb. 13, 1931; s. Benjamin and Rose (Mack) L.; m. Marilyn Lee Vittert, Dec. 10, 1961; children: Gay Ilene, Benjamin Alan. BJ, U. Mo., 1953, LHD (hon.), 1997. Sports editor Jefferson City (Mo.) Post-Tribune, 1953, Springfield Daily News, 1953-54; gen. assignment reporter Springfield Leader and Press, 1956-57; reporter, copy editor Kansas City (Mo.) Star, 1957-60; sports reporter St. Louis Post-Dispatch, 1960-66, asst. sports editor, 1966-68, news editor, 1968-71, asst. mng. editor, 1971-78, mng. editor, 1979-92; chmn. Pulitzer 2000 Pulitzer Pub. Co., St. Louis, 1992-96, multimedia cons., 1997—; bd. dirs. RXL Pulitzer; guest lectr. Am. Press Inst., Columbia U. Journalism Sch., 1967-70; chmn. bd. advisors U. Mo. Sch. Journalism, chmn. bd. dirs. multi-cultural mgmt. program, 1995—; bd. dirs. Columbia Missourian. Author: Maybe I'll Pitch Forever, The Autobiography of LeRoy (Satchel) Paige, 1962, reissued, 1993, Mr. Baseball, The Story of Branch Rickey, 1966, Ken Boyer, 1967, Joe Namath, 1968; co-author: The Speed King, The Story of Bob Hayes, 1971, Bob Gibson Pitching Ace, 1975, Jim Hart Underrated Quarterback, 1977. Bd. dirs. Mid-Am. Press Inst., 1973-97, chmn., 1975-77; trustee United Hebrew Congregation, 1975-77; chmn. com. 21st Century, U. Mo., 1993-94; vice chair Mo. Gov.'s Commn. on Info. Tech., 1994-95; mem. ethics commn. City of Creve Coeur; cons. Mo. Press-Bar Commn., 1995—. 1st lt. USAF, 1954-56. Recipient Univ. Mo. Faculty and Alumni award, 1988, Univ. Mo. Disting. Svc. in Journalism medal, 1989, St. Louis Jermiah award, 1991. Mem. Am. Soc. Newspaper Editors, Newspaper Assn. Am. (mem. industry devel. com. 1993-96), Interactive Svcs. Assn. (bd. dirs. 1994-96), Mo. Editors and Pubs. Assn. (pres. 1990-91), Mo. Soc. Newspaper Editors (bd. dirs. 1990-97, vice chmn. 1992-93, chmn. 1993), Mo. Press Assn. (1st v.p. 1994-95, pres. 1997), Mo. AP Mng. Editors Assn. (pres. 1990), U. Mo. Sch. Journalism Nat. Alumni Assn. (chmn. 1980-83), Press Club of St. Louis (chmn. 1987-94), Soc. Profl. Journalists (pres. St. Louis chpt. 1976-77), Kappa Tau Alpha, Omicron Delta Kappa. Jewish. Office: Pulitzer Pub Co 900 N Tucker Blvd Saint Louis MO 63101-1069

LIPMAN, FREDERICK D., lawyer, writer, educator; b. Phila., Nov. 16, 1935; s. Charles S. and Beatrice (Sanderow) L.; m. Gail Heller, July 25, 1965; children—L. Keith, Darren A. AB, Temple U.; LLB, Harvard Law Sch. Bar: Pa. 1960. Sole practice Phila., 1960-62; corp. counsel AEL Industries, Inc., Colmar, Pa., 1962-69; ptnr. Blank, Rome, Comisky & McCauley, Phila., 1972—; lectr. U. Pa. Law Sch., 1989—, Temple U. Law Sch., 1989-94; bd. dirs. Penjedel. Author: Going Public, 1994, Audit Committees, 1995, How Much Is Your Business Worth, 1996, Venture Capital and Junk Bond Financing, 1996. Bd. dirs. Phila. Ch. of Bezalel, 1989-91. Harvard Law Sch. scholar, 1957; Temple U. scholar, 1953. Mem. Phila. Bar Assn. (bd. govs. 1984-85), Greater Phila. C. of C. (bd. dirs., mem. exec. com. 1980-90, chmn. tech. council 1983-85), Harvard Law Sch. Assn. Greater Phila. (pres. 1988-89). Democrat. Jewish. Lodge: Masons. Avocation: tennis. Office: Blank Rome Comisky & McCauley 4 Penn Center Plz Philadelphia PA 19103-2521

LIPMAN, IRA ACKERMAN, security service company executive; b. Little Rock, Nov. 15, 1940; s. Mark and Belle (Ackerman) L.; m. Barbara Ellen Kelly Couch, July 5, 1970; children: Gustave K., Joshua S, M Benjamin. Student, Ohio Wesleyan U., 1958-60; LLD (hon.), John Marshall U., Atlanta, 1970; LLD (Hon.), Northeastern U., Boston, 1996. Salesman, exec. Mark Lipman Svcs. Inc., Memphis, 1960-63; v.p. Guardsmark, Inc., Memphis, 1963-66; pres. Guardsmark, Inc., 1966—, CEO, 1968—, chmn. bd., 1968—; bd. dirs. Nat. Coun. on Crime and Delinquency, 1975—, chmn. fin. com., treas., 1978-79, vice chmn. bd. dirs., 1982-86, chmn. exec. com., 1986-93, chmn. bd. dirs., 1993-94, chmn. emeritus, 1995—, hon. chmn. 1997—; bd. dirs. Greater Memphis Coun. Crime and Delinquency, 1976-78, entrepreneurial fellow Memphis State U., 1976; mem. environ. security com., pvt. security adv. coun. Law Enforcement Assistance adminstrn., 1975-76; mem. conf. planning com. 2d Nat. Law Enforcement Explorer Conf., 1980. Author: How to Protect Yourself From Crime, 1975, 3d edit., 1989, 4th edit., 1997; contbr. numerous articles to profl. jours., mags. and newspapers. Bd. dirs. Memphis Jewish Cmty. Center, 1974, Memphis Shelby County unit Am. Cancer Soc., 1980-81, Memphis Orchestral Soc., 1980-81, Memphis Jewish Fedn., 1974-83; chmn. Shelby County com. U.S. Savs. Bonds, 1976; mem. president's coun. Memphis State U., 1975-79;, mem. visual arts coun., 1980-82; Memphis mct. chmn. Nat. Alliance Businessmen, 1970-71; mem. task force Reform Jewish Outreach, Union Am. Hebrew Congregations, 1979-83; mem. young leadership cabinet United Jewish Appeal, 1973-78, mem. S.E. regional campaign cabinet, 1980; exec. bd. Chickasaw council Boy Scouts Am., 1978-81; bd. dirs., exec. com. Tenn. Ind. Coll. Fund, 1979; trustee Memphis Acad. Arts, 1977-81; mem. president's club Christian Bros. Coll., 1979; bd. dirs. Future Memphis, 1980-83, 83-86; nat. trustee NCCJ, 1980-92, exec. com., 1981-92, nat. Jewish co-chmn., 1985-88, nat. chmn., 1988-92, hon. chmn., past nat. chmn. nat. conf. Christians and Jews, 1992—; bd. dirs. Memphis chpt., 1980-85, life bd. dirs. Memphis chpt. 1985—; group II chmn. for 1982 campaign United Way Greater Memphis, 1981; v.p. exec. com. Internat. Coun. Christians and Jews, 1992-94; bd. govs. United Way of Am., 1992—, bd. gov.'s liaison, 1991-92, chmn. ethics com., 1992-97, mem. exec. com., 1992-97, co-chmn. vol. involvement com., 1992—, mem. strategic planning com., 1994-96; chmn. UWLC steering com. 1995-96; mem. Alexis de Tocqueville Soc. Nat. Leadership Coun., 1992—, mem. Second Century Initiative Vol. Involvement com., 1987-91; chair Task Force on Critical Markets, 1987-91, mem. exec. cabinet, 1990-91; trustee Memphis Brooks Mus. Art, 1980-83, Yeshiva U.; trustee Simon Wiesenthal Ctr., 1982—, chmn. campaign com., 1983—, mem. fin. and audit com., 1993—; bd. dirs. Nat. Alliance against Violence, 1983-85, Nat. Ctr. Learning Disabilities, 1989-94, United Way of Greater Memphis, 1984-85, gen. campaign chmn., 1985-86; founder, bd. overseers B'nai Brith, 1980; bd. dirs. Tenn. Gov.'s Jobs for High Sch. Grads. Program, 1980-83; trustee Ohio Wesleyan U., 1988—; vice chmn. spl. task force on endowment growth Ohio Wesleyan U., 1990—; mem. bd. overseers Wharton Sch., U. Pa., 1991—, devel. com., 1995—; assoc. trustee U. Pa., 1991—; mem. exec. com. Am. Israel Pub. Affairs Com., 1991—. Recipient Humanitarian of Yr. award NCCJ, 1985, Outstanding Cmty. Sales award Sales and Mktg. Execs. Memphis, 1987, Jr. Achievement Master Free Enterprise award, 1987, Alexis de Tocqueville Soc. award, 1995; one of 10 cited as Best Corp. Chief Exec. of Achievement, Gallagher Pres.'s Report, 1974. Mem. Internat. Assn. Chiefs Police, Am. Soc. Criminology, Internat. Soc. Criminology, Am. Soc. Indsl. Security (cert. protection profl.), 100 Club, B'nai B'rith, Ridgeway Country Club, Racquet Club, Summit Club, Econ. Club (bd. dirs. 1980-85, v.p. 1983-84, pres. 1984-85, chmn. exec. com. 1984-85), Internat. Club (Washington). Republican.

LIPNER, HARRY, retired physiologist, educator; b. N.Y.C., Aug. 26, 1922; s. Samuel and Sarah L.; m. Ethel Lapis, Nov. 11, 1949 (dec. Nov. 1979); children—Laura Jean, Sandra Lea, William F., Michael A.; m. Janet C.A. Mauney, July 10, 1981. BS, L.I. U., 1942; MS, U. Chgo., 1947; PhD, U. Iowa, 1952. Instr. Chgo. Med. Sch., 1954-55; asst. prof. physiology and endocrinology Fla. State U., Tallahassee, 1955-60; asso. prof. Fla. State U., 1960-67, prof., 1967-89, prof. emeritus, 1990—; potter/glazemaker Art ctr., Fla. State U., 1992—; vis. prof. Harvard U. Med. Sch., 1969-70 mem. rev. panel regulatory biology program NSF, 1984-87. Mem. editorial bd.: Endocrinology, 1968-74; contbr. chpts. to textbooks, articles to profl. jours. NIH fellow, 1952-55; Spl. postdoctoral fellow, 1969-70; Fulbright lectr. India, 1974-75. Mem. AAAS, Am. Physiol. Soc., Endocrine Soc., Sigma Xi. Office: Fla State U Dept Biol Sci Tallahassee FL 32306

LIPO, THOMAS A., electrical engineer, educator; b. Milw., Feb. 1, 1938; married; 4 children. BEE, Marquette U., 1962, MSEE, 1964; PhD, U. Wis., 1968. Grad. trainee Allis-Chalmers Mfg. Co., Milw., 1962-64, engring. analyst, 1964; instr. U. Wis., Milw., 1964-66; NRC rsch. fellow U. Manchester (Eng.) Inst. Sci. and Tech., 1968-69; elec. engr. Gen. Electric Co., Schenectady, 1969-79; prof. Purdue U., West Lafayette, Ind., 1979-80; prof. U. Wis., Madison, 1981-90, W.W. Grainger prof. pwoer electronics and elec. machines, 1990—; co-dir. Wis. Elec. Machines and Power Electronics Consortium, 1981—. Fellow IEEE, IEEE Power Engring. Soc., IEEE Indsl. Applications Soc., IEEE Power Electronics Soc. Office: U Wis Dept Elec & Comp Eng 1415 Engineer Dr Madison WI 53706-1607*

LIPOWSKI, ZBIGNIEW JERZY, retired psychiatrist, educator; b. Warsaw, Poland, Oct. 26, 1924; emigrated to Can., 1955, naturalized, 1960; s. Jerzy Ignacy and Zofia (Szeliski) L.; m. Ingrid Thiessen, Nov. 27, 1978; children: Christopher John, Anna Christina. M.B., B.Ch., U. Coll., Dublin, 1954; Diploma in Psychiatry, McGill U., 1959; M.D. (hon.), U. Helsinki, 1981; M.A. (hon.), Dartmouth Coll., 1981. Resident in psychiatry Allan Meml. Inst., Montreal, Que., Can., 1955-58, Mass. Gen. Hosp., Boston, 1958-59; teaching fellow in psychiatry Harvard U., Boston, 1958-59; demonstrator in psychiatry McGill U., Montreal, 1959-62; lectr. McGill U., 1962-65, asst. prof., 1965-67, assoc. prof., 1967-71; dir. psychiat. cons. service Royal Victoria Hosp., Montreal, 1959-71; prof. psychiatry Dartmouth Med. Sch., Hanover, N.H., 1971-83; prof. psychiatry U. Toronto, Ont., Can., 1983-90, prof. emeritus psychiatry, 1990—; cons. psychiatrist Montreal Neurol. Inst., 1968-71; vis. prof. psychiatry Med. U. S.C., Charleston, 1977-78. Author: Delirium: Acute Brain Failure in Man, 1980, Psychosomatic Medicine and Liaison Psychiatry. Selected Papers, 1985, Delirium: Acute Confusional States, 1990; mem. editorial bd.: Gen. Hosp. Psychiatry, 1978—, Jour. Psychosomatic Research, 1981—, Advances in Psychosomatic Medicine, 1968— ; editor: Psychosocial Aspects of Physical Illness, 1973, (with D.R. Lipsitt and P.C. Whybrow) Psychosomatic Medicine: Current Trends and Clinical Applications, 1977, (with E. Kurstak and P.V. Morozov) Viruses, Immunity and Mental Disorders, 1987; contbr. numerous articles to profl. jours. Recipient Lapinlahti medal Finland, 1980; Mona Shenkman Bronfman fellow, 1958-59. Fellow Royal Coll. Physicians Can., Am. Psychiatric Assn. (life, task force on nomenclature 1975-79, Spl. Presdl. Commendation 1987), Acad. Psychosomatic Medicine; mem. Am. Psychosomatic Soc., Polish Inst. Arts and Scis. in Am.

LIPPARD, LUCY ROWLAND, writer, lecturer; b. N.Y.C., Apr. 14, 1937; d. Vernon William and Margaret Isham (Cross) L.; m. Robert Tracy Ryman, Aug. 19, 1961 (div. 1968); 1 child, Ethan Isham Ryman. BA, Smith Coll., 1958; MA in Art History, NYU, 1962; DFA, Moore Coll. Art, 1972, San Francisco Art Inst., 1984, Maine Coll. Art, 1994. Freelance writer, lectr., curator, 1964—; prof. Sch. Visual Arts, N.Y.C., Williams Coll., Queensland U., Brisbane, Australia, U. Colo., Boulder; mem. adv. bd. Franklin Furnace, N.Y.C., 1979—; bd. dirs. Printed Matter, N.Y.C., Ctr. for Study of Polit. Graphics, L.A., Time & Space Ltd., Hudson, N.Y.; co-founder W.E.B., Ad Hoc Women Artist's Com., Artists Meeting for Cultural Change, Heresies Collective and Jour., Artists Call Against U.S. Intervention in Ctrl. Am., Polit. Art Documentation/Distbn. Author: Overlay: Contemporary Art and the Art of Prehistory, 1983, Mixed Blessings: New Art in a Multicultural America, 1990, Pop Art, 1966, The Graphic work of Philip Evergood, 1966, Changing: Essays in Art Criticism, 1971, Tony Smith, 1972, Six Years: The Dematerialization of the Art Object, 1973, From the Center: Feminist Essays on Women's Art, 1976, Eva Hesse, 1976, (with Charles Simonds) Cracking (Brüchig Werden), 1979, Ad Reinhardt, 1981, Get the Message? A Decade of Art for Social Change, 1984, A Different War: Vietnam in Art, 1990, The Pink Glass Swan: Selected Feminist Essays on Art, The Lure of the Local: Senses of Place in a Multicultural Society, 1997, (with Alfred Barr and James Thrall Soby) The School of Paris, 1965, (novel) I See/You Mean, 1979; author, editor: Partial Recall: Photographs of Native North Americans, 1992; editor: Surrealists on Art, 1970, Dadas on Art, 1971; contbg. editor: Art in Am.; contbr. monthly columns Village Voice, 1981-85, In These Times, Z Mag., also numerous articles to mags., anthologies, and mus. catalogs, 1964—. Mem. Dem. Socialists Am., Atlatl, Nat. Writers Union. Recipient Frederick Douglass award North Star Fund, 1994, Frank Jewett Mather award for criticism Coll. Art Assn., 1974, Claude Fuess award for pub. svc. Phillips Andover Acad., 1975, curating award Penny McCall Found., 1989, citation N.Y.C. mayor David Dinkins, 1990, Smith Coll. medal, 1992; Guggenheim fellow, 1968. Avocations: hiking, amateur archaeology, sailing. Home and Office: HC 75 Box 77 Galisteo NM 87540

LIPPARD, STEPHEN JAMES, chemist, educator; b. Pittsburgh, Pa., Oct. 12, 1940; s. Alvin I. and Ruth (Green) L.; m. Judith Ann Drezner, Aug. 16, 1964; children: Andrew (dec.), Joshua, Alexander. BA, Haverford Coll., 1962; PhD, MIT, 1965; DSc (hon.), Tex. A&M U., 1995. Postdoctoral research fellow chemistry MIT, Cambridge, 1965-66, prof. chemistry, 1983-89, Arthur Amos Noyes prof. chemistry, 1989—, head chemistry dept., 1995—; asst. prof. chemistry Columbia U., N.Y.C., 1966-69; asso. prof. Columbia U., 1969-72, prof., 1972-82; dept. head MIT, Cambridge, 1995—; mem. study sect. metallobiochemistry NIH, 1973-77. Editor: Progress in Inorganic Chemistry, 1967-92; mem. editorial bd. Inorganic Chemistry, 1981-83, 89-91, assoc. editor, 1983-88; mem. editorial bd. Account Chem. Res., 1986-88; contbr. articles to profl. jours. Coach Demarest Borough Soccer Team, 1975-82, league adminstr., 1979-82. NSF fellow, 1962-66; Alfred P. Sloan fellow, 1968-70; Guggenheim fellow, 1972; recipient Tchr.-Scholar award Camille and Henry Dreyfus Found., 1971-76, Henry J. Albert award Internat. Precious Metals Inst., 1985, Alexander von Humboldt U.S. Sr. Scientist award, 1988, Am. Chem. Soc. award for Disting. Svc. in the Advancement of Inorganic Chemistry, 1994; sr. internat. fellow John E. Fogarty Internat. Center, 1979. Fellow AAAS; mem. NAS, Am. Acad. Arts and Sci., Nat. Inst. Medicine, Am. Chem. Soc. (chmn. bioinorganic subdiv. 1987-88, Inorganic Chemistry award 1987, Remson award 1987, Mallinckrodt Disting. Svc. award 1994, William H. Nichols medal 1995, assoc. editor jour. 1989—, chmn. inorganic div., chmn. 1992), Am. Crystallographic Assn., Am. Soc. Biol. Chemists, Nat. Inst. Medicine, Chem. Soc. (London), Biophys. Soc., Italian Chem. Soc., Phi Beta Kappa. Home: 15 Humboldt St Cambridge MA 02140-2804 Office: MIT 77 Massachusetts Ave Cambridge MA 02139-4301

LIPPARD, THOMAS EUGENE, lawyer; b. Pitts., 1943. Student Haverford Coll., 1960-64; B.A., U. Pitts., 1965; J.D., U. Chgo., 1968. Bar: Pa. 1968, U.S. Dist. Ct. (we. dist.) Pa. 1968, U.S. Ct. Appeals (3d cir.) 1968, U.S. Tax Ct. 1984. Assoc. Houston, Cooper, Speer & German, 1968-73, ptnr., 1973-74; ptnr. Cohen, Cohen & Lippard, 1974-76; ptnr. Houston, Cohen, Harbaugh & Lippard, P.C., Pitts., 1976-85; ptnr. Thorp Reed & Armstrong, 1986—; sr. v.p. fin. and adminstrn., gen. counsel Tube City, Inc., Glassport, Pa, 1997—. Mem. Allegheny County Bar Assn., Pa. Bar Assn., ABA (chmn. com. on devel. law of union adminstrn. and procedure Sect. Labor Relations Law 1975, mgmt. co-chmn. for formulation and editing of com. report of com. on law of union and adminstrn. and procedure sect. labor and employment law 1980-85). Office: Thorp Reed & Armstrong One Riverfront Ctr Pittsburgh PA 15222

LIPPE, MELVIN KARL, lawyer; b. Chgo., Oct. 21, 1933; s. Melvin M. and Myrtle (Karlsberg) L.; children: Suzanne, Michael S., Deanna; m. Sandra M. Bauer, Jan. 5, 1974. B.S., Northwestern U., 1955, J.D., 1958; grad. cert., Grad. Sch. Banking, U. Wis., 1965; cert., Sr. Bank Officers Seminar, Harvard U., 1966. Bar: Ill. 1958; C.P.A. Assoc. D'Ancona, Pflaum, Wyatt & Riskind, Chgo., 1958-61; asst. to chmn. bd. Exchange Nat. Bank of Chgo., 1961-62, asst. v.p., 1962-64, v.p., 1964-66, sr. v.p., sec. to bd. dirs., 1966-69, exec. v.p., dir., 1969-74, vice chmn. bd., 1974-76, also dir.; dir. Am.-Israel Bank, Ltd., 1974-76; ptnr. Antonow & Fink, Chgo., 1977-88, Altheimer and Gray, Chgo., 1988—; instr. Ill. Inst. Tech., 1960-63. Bd. dirs. Jewish Cmty. Ctrs. Chgo., 1972—, pres., 1980-82; bd. dirs. Chgo. chpt. Am. Jewish Com., 1974-78; life bd. dirs. Jewish Coun. for Youth Svcs., Chgo., pres., 1971; bd. dirs. Family Focus, 1992—. With Ill. N.G., 1959. Mem. ABA, Chgo. Bar Assn., Phi Epsilon Pi, Beta Gamma Sigma. Jewish. Office: Altheimer & Gray 10 S Wacker Dr Chicago IL 60606-7407

LIPPE, PHILIPP MARIA, physician, surgeon, neurosurgeon, educator, administrator; b. Vienna, Austria, May 17, 1929; s. Philipp and Maria (Goth) L.; came to U.S., 1938, naturalized, 1945; m. Virginia M. Wiltgen, 1953 (div. 1977); children: Patricia Ann Marie, Philip Eric Andrew, Laura Lynne Elizabeth, Kenneth Anthony Ernst; m. Gail B. Busch, Nov. 26, 1977. Student Loyola U., Chgo., 1947-50; BS in Medicine, U. Ill. Coll. Medicine, 1952, MD with high honors, 1954. Rotating intern St. Francis Hosp., Evanston, Ill., 1954-55; asst. resident gen. surgery VA Hosp., Hines, Ill., 1955, 58-59; asst. resident neurology and neurol. surgery Neuropsychiat. Inst., U. Ill. Rsch. and Ednl. Hosps., Chgo., 1959-60, chief resident, 1962-63, resident neuropathology, 1962, postgrad. trainee in electroencephalography, 1963; resident neurology and neurol. surgery Presbyn.-St. Luke's Hosp., Chgo., 1960-61; practice medicine, specializing in neurol. surgery, San Jose, Calif., 1963—; instr. neurology and neurol. surgery U. Ill., 1962-63; clin. instr. surgery and neurosurgery Stanford U., 1965-69, clin. asst. prof., 1969-74, clin. assoc. prof., 1974-96, clin. prof. 1996—; staff cons. in neurosurgery O'Connor Hosp., Santa Clara Valley Med. Ctr., San Jose Hosp., Los Gatos Cmty. Hosp., El Camino Hosp. (all San Jose area); chmn. divsn. neurosugery Good Samaritan Hosp, 1989—; founder, exec. dir. Bay Area Pain Rehab. Center, San Jose, 1979—; clin. adviser to Joint Commn. on Accreditation of Hosps.; mem. dist. med. quality rev. com. Calif. Bd. Med. Quality Assurance, 1976-87, chmn., 1976-77. Served to capt. USAF, 1956-58. Diplomate Am. Bd. Neurol. Surgery, Nat. Bd. Med. Examiners, Am. Bd. Pain Medicine. Fellow ACS, Am. Coll. Pain Medicine (bd. dirs. 1991-94, v.p. 1991-92, pres. 1992-93); mem. AMA (Ho. of Dels. 1981—), Am. Coll. Physician Execs., Calif. Med. Assn. (Ho. of Dels. 1976-80, sci. bd., council 1979-87, sec. 1981-87, Outstanding Svc. award 1987), Santa Clara County Med. Soc. (coun. 1974-81, pres. 1978-79, Outstanding Contbn. award 1984, Benjamin J. Cory award 1987), Chgo. Med. Soc., Congress Neurol. Surgeons, Calif. Assn. Neurol. Surgeons (dir. 1974-82, v.p. 1975-76, pres. 1977-79, Pevehouse disting. svc. award 1997), San Jose Surg. Soc., Am. Assn. Neurol. Surgeons (chm. sect. on pain 1987-90, dir. 1983-86, 87-90, Disting. Svc. award 1986, 90), Western Neurol. Soc., San Francisco Neurol. Soc., Santa Clara Valley Profl. Standards Rev. Orgn. (dir., v.p., dir. quality assurance 1975-83), Fedn. Western Socs. Neurol. Sci., Internat. Assn. for Study Pain, Am. Pain Soc. (founding mem.), Am. Acad. Pain Medicine (sec. 1983-86, pres. 1987-88, Philipp M. Lippe Disting. Svc. award 1995, exec. med. dir. 1996—), Am. Bd. Pain Medicine (pres. 1992-93, exec. v.p., 1994—), Alpha Omega Alpha, Phi Kappa Phi. Assoc. editor Clin. Jour. of Pain; contbr. articles to profl. jours. Pioneered med. application centrifugal force using flight simulator. Office: 2100 Forest Ave Ste 106 San Jose CA 95128-1422

LIPPER, KENNETH, investment banker, author, producer; b. N.Y.C., June 19, 1941; s. George and Sally (Hollander) L.; m. Evelyn Rebecca Gruss, June 12, 1966; children: Joanna Helene, Daniella, Tamara, Julie. BA, Columbia U., 1962; JD, Harvard U., 1965; LLM, NYU, 1966; postgrad., Faculté de Droit et Economique, Paris, 1967. Bar: N.Y. 1965. Assoc. Fried, Frank, Harris, Shriver & Jacobson, N.Y.C., 1967-68; dir. industry policy Office Fgn. Direct Investment, Washington, 1968-69; assoc., ptnr. Lehman Bros., N.Y.C., 1969-75; mng. dir., ptnr. Salomon Bros., N.Y.C., 1976-82; dep. mayor City of N.Y., 1983-85; chmn. Lipper & Co., 1986—; adj. prof. internat. affairs Sch. Internat. and Pub. Affairs, Columbia U., N.Y.C., 1976-83, 87—; mem. adv. bd. Fed. Res. Bank N.Y., 1994—, Chase Manhattan Bank, 1994—. Author: (novel) Wall Street, 1987 and chief tech. advisor movie, 1987; author, screenwriter, producer City Hall, 1996; produer film and play The Winter Guest, 1997. Trustee Sch. Orgn. and Mgmt., Yale U., 1983—, Rockefeller Bros. Fund, 1991—; mem. adv. bd. John F. Kennedy Sch. Govt., Harvard U., 1994—; bd. dirs. New Holland N.V., Lincoln Ctr. Performing Arts, Sundance Inst. Recipient medal of distinction City of N.Y., 1985. Mem. Internat. Inst. Strategic Studies, Coun. Fgn. Rels., Econ. Club N.Y., Century Assn., Phi Beta Kappa. Office: Lipper & Co 101 Park Ave New York NY 10178

LIPPERT, CHRISTOPHER NELSON, dentist, consultant; b. N.Y.C., Apr. 17, 1952; s. Raymond Joseph and Shirley Ann (Nelson) L.; m. Valerie Jo Schlager, Nov. 4 1989. BS, U. Cin., 1975; DDS, Emory U., 1979. Dentist John W. Regenos DDS, Inc., Cin., 1979-87; pres., dentist Lippert & Wilkes DDS, Inc., Cin., 1987—; cons. Teret's Syndrome Found., Cin., 1983—, Health Am., Cleve., 1985-90; lectr. Ohio State U., 1981-89. Bd. dirs. Creekwood Condominiums, Cin., 1985-86. Mem. ADA, Am. Acad. Fixed Prosthodontists, Ohio Dental Assn., Ohio Acad. Practice Adminstrn., Cin. Dental Soc. (peer rev. com. 1985—), Midwest Med. Found. (bd. dirs. 1984-88), Phi Eta Sigma, Sigma Alpha Epsilon, Psi Omega. Avocations: sailing, fishing, restoration of classic cars.

LIPPERT, JOHN RICHARD, magazine editor; b. Pitts., Mar. 28, 1952; s. John Jacob and Thelma Rose (Watzlaf) L.; m. Abla Mawoussi Gbedegbebou, June 29, 1977 (div. June 1987); 1 child, Brigitte Akossi; m. Jane Marie Young, Jan. 1, 1990. BA, U. Pitts., 1974, M Pub. and Internat. Affairs, 1979. Secondary sch. tchr. U.S. Peace Corps, Togo, West Africa, 1974-76; rschr. Grad. Sch. Pub. and Internat. Affairs U. Pitts., 1978; intern analyst City of Pitts., 1979; info. mgr., advisor, solar energy inquiry coord., cons. Vols. in Tech. Assistance, Arlington, Va., 1980-87; project mgr., supr., sr. writer Advanced Scis. Inc., Arlington, 1987-94; mng. editor Consumers' Checkbook mag. Ctr. for the Study of Svcs., Washington, 1994—; reviewer, advisor walls subcom. Bldg. Environ. and Thermal Envelope Coun., Washington, 1993. Contbr. articles to profl. publs. and mags. Tchr. religion class St. Bernard's Cath. Ch., Riverdale, Md., 1995—. Mem. Am. Solar Energy Soc., Md., D.C., Va. Solar Energy Industries Assn. (assoc.), Electric Vehicle Assn. of Greater Washington, N.E. Sustainable Energy Assn., Ctr. for Analysis and Dissemination of Demonstrated Energy Techs. Avocations: socially responsible investing, residential energy efficiency and renewable energy, swimming, gardening.

LIPPERT, ROBERT J., administrator and culinary arts educator, consultant; b. Alma, Mich., May 17, 1932; s. Ackley William Matthew and Myrtle (Boddy) L.; m. Marie Alphonsine Mantei, Apr. 2, 1956; children: Robert Jr., Jeffrey Paul, Mark Edward. BS, Ctrl. Mich. U., 1959, MA, 1965, EdS, 1977. Exec. chef Mt. Pleasant (Mich.) Country Club, 1983-86, Riverwood Golf Course, Mt. Pleasant, 1986-90, The Embers, Inc., Mt. Pleasant, 1957-67; instr. Mt. Pleasant Pub. Schs., 1959-67; dir./ culinary arts instr. Mt. Pleasant Tech. Ctr., 1968-95; inst. Ferris State U., Mt. Pleasant, Mich., 1996; exec. banquet chef The Embers, Inc., 1967—; pres. Lippert Consulting and Svc., Mt. Pleasant, 1983—. Writer, editor, dir. TV program Ask The Chef, 1989-90; contbr. articles to profl. jours. Active ch. fund raisers, Mt. Pleasant, 1973—, State Spl. Olympics, 1982-87; chef banquets for sr. citizens. With USN, 1951-54, Korea. Inducted into Mt. Pleasant Pub. Schs. Hall of Fame, 1994. Mem. Internat. Food Svc. Execs. Assn., Am. Acad. Chefs (Svc. award 1990), Am. Culinary Fedn. (Ctrl. Regional Profl. Chef award 1990), Capitol Profl. Chefs (pres. 1985-89, chmn. of bd. 1990-91, Chef of Yr. award 1987), Food Svc. Tchrs. (pres. 1980, 81, 84, bd. dirs. 1979-89), Golden Toque, Mich. Restaurant Assn. (bd. dirs. 1980-82, 84-85, 93—, Food Tchr. of Yr. award 1981, Disting. Svc. award 1996), Mich. Occupational Edn. Assn. (bd. dirs. 1980-87, Vocat. Tchr. of Yr. award 1986), Mich. Chefs (Jefferson medal 1986). Roman Catholic. Home: 1214 Glenwood Dr Mount Pleasant MI 48858-4328 Office: Ferris State U 1214 Glenwood Pl Mount Pleasant MI 48858-4328

LIPPES, GERALD SANFORD, lawyer, business executive; b. Buffalo, Mar. 23, 1940; s. Thomas and Ruth (Landsman) L.; m. Sandra Franger; children: Tracy E., David S., Adam F. Student, U. Mich., 1958-61; JD, U. Buffalo, 1964. Bar: N.Y. 1964. Sr. ptnr. Lippes, Silverstein, Mathias & Wexler, Buffalo, 1964—; sec., dir., gen. counsel Mark IV, Industries, Inc., Amherst, N.Y., 1969—; chmn. Del. Photographic Products, Buffalo, 1970-88, Ingram Software, Buffalo, 1982-86, Abels Bagels, Inc., Buffalo, 1972-75; bd. dirs. Mark IV Industries, Inc., Amherst, N.Y., Gilbraltar Steel Corp., Buffalo Nat. Health Care Affiliates, Inc. Bd. dirs. Buffalo Fine Arts Acad., Children's Hosp. Buffalo; chmn. bd. dirs. Roswell Park Meml. Inst., Buffalo; chmn. U. Buffalo Law Sch., Found. Jewish Philanthropies, Inc., U. Buffalo Found. Recipient Disting. Alumni award U. Buffalo Law Sch., Jaeckle award SUNY, 1995, Katherine Gioia award Roswell Park Alliance Found. 1997, Nat. Conf. of Christians and Jews Citation award 1997; named Entrepreneur of Yr., 1993. Mem. N.Y. State Bar Assn., Erie County Bar Assn., Am. Soc. Corp. Secs. Office: Lippes Silverstein Mathias & Wexler 28 Church St Buffalo NY 14202-3908

LIPPINCOTT, JAMES ANDREW, biochemistry and biological sciences educator; b. Cumberland County, Ill., Sept. 13, 1930; s. Marion Andrew and Esther Oral (Meeker) L.; m. Barbara Sue Barnes, June 2, 1956; children—Jeanne Marie, Thomas Russell, John James. A.B., Earlham Coll., 1954; A.M., Washington U., St. Louis, 1956, Ph.D., 1958. Lectr. botany Washington U., 1958-59; Jane Coffin Childs Meml. fellow Centre Nat. de la Recherche Scientifique, France, 1959-60; asst. prof. biol. scis. Northwestern U., Evanston, Ill., 1960-66; assoc. prof. Northwestern U., 1966-73, prof., 1973-81, prof. biochemistry, molecular biology and cell biology, 1981-94; prof. emeritus Northwestern U., Evanston, Ill., 1994—; assoc. dean biol. scis. Northwestern U., 1980-83; vis. assoc. prof. U. Calif., Berkeley, 1970-71; vis. prof. Inst. Botany U. Heidelberg (Germany), 1974. Contbr. articles to profl. jours. Grantee NIH, NSF, Am. Cancer Soc., USDA. Mem. Am. Soc. Biol. Chemists, Am. Soc. Plant Physiologists, Bot. Soc. Am., Am. Soc. Microbiology. Office: Dept Biochem Molecular Biol & Cell Biol Northwestern University Evanston IL 60208

LIPPINCOTT, JONATHAN RAMSAY, healthcare executive; b. Cin., Dec. 26, 1946; s. Morss d'Isay and Virginia Yvonne (Peugnet) L.; m. Nancy Todd Smith, Feb. 22, 1975; children: Jonathan J.E., Michael R.T. BA, Yale U., 1968; MLitt, Oxford U., 1972. Program research analyst human resources adminstrn. City of New York, 1973-76; exec. asst. to dir. med. ctr. U. Cin. Med. Ctr., 1977, asst. sr. v.p., 1977-84; fellow in HMO planning policy & mgmt. Harvard Community Health Plan, Brookline, Mass., 1985-86; assoc. sr. v.p. U. Cin. Med. Ctr., 1984-94; assoc. dir. U. Cin. Hosp., 1993-94; sr. v.p., chief strategic officer Health Alliance Greater Cin., 1994-97, exec. v.p. for bus. devel., 1997—, exec. v.p. bus. devel., 1997—; exec. dir. bus. devel. Alliance Ptnrs., 1996—; chmn., bd. Southwestern Ohio Sr. Svcs. Inc., Maple Knoll Village, 1993-96, trustee, 1988-97; bd. dirs., sec., treas. Univ. Health Maintenance Orgn., Inc., 1989-93; exec. bd. dirs. The Health Initiative, Cin.; co-dir. U. Cin. Inst. Health Policy and Health Svcs. Rsch., 1993-96. Contbr. articles to cons. and acad. mags. Pres., bd. trustees Little Miami, Inc., Cin., 1984-85; steering com., chmn. health & human svcs. session Leadership Cin., 1983-84; vice chmn. Cin. Transp. Study Com., 1984-85. Mem. Am. Assn. Med. Colls. (midwest regional chmn. group on inst. planning 1991-93), Am. Coll. Health Care Execs., Cin. C. of C. (health care com.). Office: Health Alliance Greater Cin 2060 Reading Rd Ste 400 Cincinnati OH 45202-1456

LIPPINCOTT, JOSEPH P., photojournalist, educator; b. Somerset, Pa., Mar. 12, 1940; s. Joseph Britton and Louise Frances (Picking) L.; widowed; children: Douglas B., David S. BA in Journalism, U. Iowa, 1968. Staff photographer The Miami (Fla.) Herald, 1964-67; pub. rels. dir. Lock Haven (Pa.) State Coll., 1967-68; mag. editor Caterpillar Tractor Co., Peoria, Ill., 1968-69; photo editor, photographer The Detroit Free Press, 1969-75; photo advisor The State News Mich. State U., East Lansing, 1975-84; instr. Lansing C.C., 1977-84; photo editor The Detroit News, 1984-87, The Patriot Ledger, Quincy, Mass., 1988-95; lectr. Boston U., 1990—. Author: An Introduction to Camera Maintenance, 1980. Mem. Nat. Press Photographers Assn. (chmn. nat. portfolio critique 1994-96, Pictures of the Yr. awards), Boston Press Photographers Assn. Avocation: unique photographic equipment. Home: 95 Old Colony Ave # 291 Quincy MA 02170-3831

LIPPINCOTT, PHILIP EDWARD, retired paper products company executive; b. Camden, N.J., Nov. 28, 1935; s. J. Edward and Marjorie Nix (Spooner) L.; m. Naomi Catherine Prindle, Aug. 22, 1959; children: Grant, Kevin, Kerry. BA, Dartmouth Coll., 1957; MBA with distinction, Mich. State U., 1964. With Scott Paper Co., Phila., 1959-94, staff v.p. corp. planning, 1971, div. v.p., consumer products mktg., 1971-72, corp. v.p., mktg., 1972-75, sr. v.p., mktg., 1975-77, v.p., group exec. packaged products div., 1977, dir., 1978-94, pres., COO, 1980-94, chief exec. officer, 1982-94, chmn., 1983-94; ret., 1994; bd. dirs. Campbell Soup Co., Exxon Corp.; trustee Penn Mut. Life Ins. Co. Bd. overseers Dartmouth Inst.; chmn. bd. trustees Fox Chase Cancer Ctr., Phila.; mem. The Bus. Coun. Capt. U.S. Army, 1957-59. Mem. Pine Valley Country Club, Stone Harbor Country Club, Kappa Kappa Kappa, Pi Sigma Epsilon, Beta Gamma Sigma. Mem. Society of Friends.

LIPPINCOTT, SARAH LEE, astronomer, graphologist; b. Phila., Oct. 26, 1920; d. George E. and Sarah (Evans) L.; m. Dave Garroway (dec.); m. Christian Zimmerman. Student, Swarthmore Coll., 1938-39, M.A., 1950; B.A., U. Pa., 1942; D.Sc. (hon.), Villanova U., 1973. Research asst. Sproul Obs., Swarthmore (Pa.) Coll., 1941-50, research asso., 1951-72, dir., 1972-81, prof., 1977-81, prof. and dir. emeritus, 1981—, research astronomer, 1981—; vis. assoc. in astronomy Calif. Inst. Tech., 1977. Author: (with Joseph M. Joseph) Point to the Stars, 1963, 3d edit., 1977, (with Laurence Lafore) Philadelphia, the Unexpected City, 1965; contbr. articles to profl. jours. Mem. Savoy Opera Co., Phila., 1947—; bd. mgrs. Societe de Bienfaisance de Philadelphie, 1966-69. Recipient achievement award Kappa Kappa Gamma, 1966; Disting. Daus. of Pa. award, 1976; Fulbright fellow Paris, 1953-54; Jessie Kovalenko scholar, 1953-54. Mem. Am. Soc. Profl. Graphologists (treas. 1988-93), Rittenhouse Astron. Soc. (sec. 1946-48), Am. Astron. Soc. (lectr. 1961-84), Internat. Astron. Union (v.p. commn. 26, 1970-73, pres. 1971-730, Disting. Daus. Pa. (sec. 1988—), Sigma Xi (pres. chpt. 1959-60). Home: 29 Kendal Dr Kennett Square PA 19348-2323

LIPPINCOTT, WALTER HEULINGS, JR., publishing executive; b. Phila., Jan. 16, 1939; s. Walter Heulings and Helen B. (Howe) L.; m. Caroline Seebohm, June 8, 1974 (div. June 1993); children: Sophie, Hugh. A.B., Princeton U., 1960. With Morgan Guaranty Trust Co., N.Y.C., 1960-63; coll. traveler Harper & Row Pubs., 1963-65, editor, 1965-70, editor-in-chief, coll. dept., 1970-74; editorial dir. Cambridge Univ. Press, N.Y.C., 1974-81; assoc. dir. Cornell Univ. Press, 1982, dir., 1983-86; dir. Princeton U. Press, N.J., 1986—. Club: Knickerbocker (N.Y.C.). Home: 1 River Knoll Dr Titusville NJ 08560-1308 Office: Princeton U Press 41 William St Princeton NJ 08540-5237

LIPPITT, ELIZABETH CHARLOTTE, writer; b. San Francisco; d. Sidney Grant and Stella L. Student Mills Coll., U. Calif.-Berkeley. Writer, performer own satirical monologues, nat. and polit. affairs for 85 newspapers including Muncie Star, St. Louis Globe-Dem., Washington Times, Utah Ind., Jackson News, State Dept. Watch. Singer debut album Songs From the Heart; contbr. articles to 85 newspapers including N.Y. Post, L.A. Examiner, Orlando Sentinel, Phoenix Rep., The Blue Book; author: 40 Years of American History in Published Letters 1952-1992. Mem. Commn. for Free China, Conservative Caucus, Jefferson Ednl. Assn., Presdl. Adv. Commn. Recipient Congress of Freedom award, 1959, 71-73. Mem. Amvets, Nat. Trust for Hist. Preservation, Am. Security Coun., Internat. Platform Assn., Am. Conservative Union, Nat. Antivivisection Soc., High Frontier, For Our Children, Childhelp U.S.A., Free Afghanistan Com., Humane Soc. U.S., Young Ams. for Freedom, Coun. for Inter.-Am. Security, Internat. Med. Corps, Assn. Vets for Animal Rights, Met. Club, Olympic Club. Home: 2414 Pacific Ave San Francisco CA 94115-1238 *Personal philosophy: I believe in freedom of the individual.*

LIPPMAN, SHARON ROCHELLE, art historian, curator, art therapist, writer; b. N.Y.C., Apr. 9, 1950; d. Emanuel and Sara (Goldberg) L. Student, Mills Coll., 1968; BFA, New Sch. Social Rsch., 1970, CCNY, 1972; MA in Cinema Studies, NYU, 1976, postgrad., 1987. Cert. secondary tchr., N.Y. Instr., dir., founder Sara Sch. of Creative Art, Sayville, N.Y., 1976-85; founder, exec. dir., tchr. Art Without Walls, Inc., Sayville and N.Y.C., 1985—; exec. dir., curator Profl. Artist Network for Artists Internationally; organizer Profl. Artist Network for Nat./Internat. Artists, 1994; curator Pub. Art in Pub. Spaces. Author: Patterns, 1968, College Poetry Press Anthology, 1970; contbr. articles to profl. jours.; recipient Nat. Poetry Press award, 1996. Vol. Good Samaritan Hosp., 1984, Southside Hosp., 1983, U. Stony Brook Hosp., 1985, Schneider Children's Hosp., New Hyde Park, N.Y., 1992, New Light-AIDS Patients, Smithtown, N.Y., 1993, Helen Keller Svcs. for the Blind, Hempstead, N.Y., 1993-94, St. Charles Hosp. and Rehab. Ctr., 1996; mem. Whitney Mus., Guggenheim Mus., among others. Recipient Suffolk County New Inspiration award, 1990, Am. Artist Art Svc. award Am. Artists mag., 1993, Suffolk County Legis. proclamation, 1993, Newsday Leadership Vol. award Newsday newspaper, 1994, Nat. Women's Month award Town of Islip, 1996, Disting. Women's award Town of Islip, 1996, Nat. Poetry Press award, 1996. Mem. Orgn. Through Rehab. and Tng., Coll. Art Assn., Met. Mus. Art, Mus. Modern Art Univ. Film Assn. Avocations: fine art, books, cinema, political science, inventions. Office: Art Without Walls Inc PO Box 341 Sayville NY 11782-0341 also: PO Box 6344 FDR Sta New York NY 10150-1902

LIPPMAN, WILLIAM JENNINGS, investment company executive; b. N.Y.C., Feb. 13, 1925; s. Henry J. and Fanny (Schapira) L.; m. Doris Kaplan, July 11, 1948; children—Howard Mark, Deborah Ellen. B.B.A. cum laude, Coll. City N.Y., 1947; M.B.A., N.Y.U., 1957. Marketing mgr. Pavelle Color, Inc., N.Y.C., 1947-50; sales mgr. Terminal Home Sales Corp., N.Y.C., 1950-55; div. mgr. King Merritt & Co., Inc., Englewood, N.J., 1955-60; pres., dir. Pilgrim Distbrs. Inc., Ft. Lee, N.J., 1960-86; pres. L.F. Rothschild Managed Trust L.F. Rothschild Fund Mgmt. Inc., N.Y.C., 1986-88, also dir.; pres. Franklin Managed Trust, New York, 1988—; mem. faculty Fairleigh Dickinson U. Sch. Bus. Adminstrn., 1957-69; bd. govs. Investment Co. Inst. Contbg. author: Investment Dealer Digest. Mem. Nat. Assn. Securities Dealers (investment cos. com.). Home: 18 Daniel Dr Englewood NJ 07631-3736 Office: Franklin Managed Trust 1 Parker Plz Fort Lee NJ 07024-2937

LIPPMANN, BRUCE ALLAN, rehabilitative services professional; b. Balt., Aug. 29, 1950; s. Allan L. and Phyllis Marie (Bunyea) L.; m. Barbara Jean Wood, May 26, 1973 (div. Aug. 1979); m. Susan K. Shampanier, Feb. 1, 1981 (div. Nov. 1990); m. Frances G. Scruggs, Dec. 31, 1991; children: Joshua Rae Holt, Stuart Holt, Joshua Lippmann, Grant Lippmann. BA, U. Md., Catonsville, 1972; MS, Loyola U., 1979; cert., San Diego Inst., 1989; postgrad., Calif. Sch. Profl. Pyschology, 1992-93, Nat. U., 1996—. Cert. rehab. counselor, ins. rehab. specialist. Social worker Md. Children's Ctr., Catonsville, 1970-72; vocat. cons. St. Md. Workers Compensation Commn., Balt., 1975-79; sr. counselor McGuinness Assocs., Fresno, Calif., 1980-84; pres., CEO Sierra Rehab. Svcs. Inc., Fresno, 1984-91; vocat. counselor Fresno, 1991-94; health care mgr. GAB Robins N.Am. Inc., Fresno, 1994-96; cons. Healthcare and Workplace Mgmt., Woodlake, 1996—; resource specialist Rowell Elem. Sch., Fresno, 1996-97; spl. edn. resource specialist tchr., varsity wrestling coach Woodlake H.S., 1997—; cons. Doctors Med. Ctr., Modesto, Calif., 1989-92, Calif. Ctr. Rehab. Svcs., Fresno, 1986-89, U.S Dept. Labor, San Francisco, 1984—; curriculum cons. Microcomputer Tng. Inst., Fresno, 1986-91. Mem. Metro Circle-Fresno Metro Mus., 1986—, Fresno Zool. Soc., 1985—, Fresno Arts Mus., 1984—, Bulldog Found., Fresno State U., 1985-91. With U.S. Army, 1972-75. Mem. APA, Central Calif. Rehab. Assn. (pres. 1984-85), Nat. Assn. Rehab. Profls. (Counselor of Yr. 1987, Pvt. Sector Rehab. Counselor or Yr. 1988), Calif. Nat. Assn.Rehab. Profls. Pvt. Sector (membership com. 1984-85, Meritorious Svc. 1985, Cert. of Recognition 1986), Calif. Assn. Rehab. Profls., Nat. Rehab. Assn., Nat. Rehab Counseling Assn. Democrat. Jewish. Avocations: musician, snow skiing, mountain biking, camping. Office: Woodlake H S 400 W Whitney Ave Woodlake CA 93286 also: Rowell Elem Sch 3460 E McKenzie Fresno CA 93702

LIPPOLD, RICHARD, sculptor; b. Milw., May 3, 1915; s. Adolph and Elsa (Schmidt) L.; m. Louise Greuel, Aug. 24, 1940; children—Lisa, Tiana, Ero. Student, U. Chgo., 1934-37; B.F.A., Art Inst. Chgo., 1937; D.F.A. (hon.), Ripon Coll., 1968. Tchr. Layton Sch. Art, Milw., 1940-41, U. Mich., 1941-44, Goddard Coll., 1945-47; head art sect. Trenton (N.J.) Jr. Coll., 1948-52; prof. Hunter Coll., N.Y.C., 1952-67. Works exhibited Inst. Arts, Detroit, 1946-47, St. Louis City Mus., 1946, Toronto (Ont.) Mus., 1947, Whitney Mus., N.Y.C., 1947, 49, 51-53, 76, Calif. Palace Legion of Honor, San Francisco, 1948, Fundacao de Arte Moderne, Sao Paulo, Brazil, 1948, Mus. Modern Art, N.Y.C., 1951-53, 63, Tate Gallery, London, 1953, Musée d'Art Moderne, Paris, 1955, Nat. Collection Fine Arts, Washington, 1976, Nat. Air and Space Mus., Washington, 1976, Biennale, Venice, 1988; one-man show Willard Gallery, N.Y.C., 1947-48, 50, 53, 62, 68, 73, Arts Club, Chgo., Layton Art Gallery, Milw., 1953, Haggerty Mus., Milw., 1990; represented in collections Addison Gallery Am. Art, Andover, Mass., Fogg Mus., Harvard U., Wadsworth Atheneum, Hartford, Mus. Modern Art, Whitney Mus., N.Y.C., Newark Mus., Met. Mus. Art, N.Y.C., Detroit Art Inst., Des Moines Art Inst., Brooks Gallery, Memphis, Mobile (Ala.) Art Mus., Musée de Vin, Pavillac, France, Munson-Williams-Proctor Inst., Utica, N.Y., Va. Mus. Fine Arts, Milw. Art Center, Yale U. Art Gallery, others, also pvt. collections, U.S. and Europe; commns. include Harvard U., 1950, Inland Steel Bldg, Chgo., 1958, Four Seasons Restaurant, Seagram Bldg., N.Y.C., 1959, Stage Set, Spoleto, Italy, 1959; Portsmouth (R.I.) Priory Ch, 1960, Pan Am Bldg., N.Y.C., 1961, Avery Fisher Hall, Lincoln Center, N.Y.C., 1961, Jesse Jones Hall, Houston, 1965, St. Mary's Cathedral, San Francisco, 1967, Christian Sci. Center, Boston, 1974, Hyatt Regency Atlanta, 1975, Fairlane Plaza, Dearborn, Mich., 1975; 115 foot stainless steel sculpture on mall in front, Air and Space Mus., Washington, 1976; King's Retiring Room, Riyadh, Saudi Arabia, 1977, Columbia (S.C.) Mall, 1977, Kish Island, Iran, 1978, Hyatt Regency, Milw., 1980, Shiga Sacred Garden, Kyoto, Japan, 1981; 250 foot sculpture Park Ave Atrium Bldg., N.Y.C., 1981, One Fin. Ctr., Boston, 1984, Deutsche Bank, Frankfurt, W. Ger., 1985, First Interstate Bank, Seattle, 1985, Sohio Hdqrs., Cleve., 1986, 200 foot high outdoor sculpture, Seoul, South Korea, 1986, Atrium Sculpture for Crystal City, Va., 1986, Marina Square, Singapore, 1986, Orange County Ctr. for Performing Arts, Costa Mesa, Calif., 1987, Atrium Sculpture and Tapestry, Alexandria, Va., 1988, Atrium Sculpture, San Diego, 1990, 95, Haggerty Mus. Retrospective, Marquette U., Milw., 1991, Montrone Residence, La Jolla, 1992, Conv. Ctr., Charlotte, N.C., 1995. Recipient 3d prize Internat. Sculpture Competition, Inst. Contemporary Arts, London, 1953, Creative Arts award Brandeis U., 1958, Silver medal Archtl. League N.Y., 1960, Honor award Mcpl. Art Soc. N.Y., 1963, Fine Arts medal AIA, 1970. Mem. Nat. Inst. Arts and Letters (v.p. 1966). Address: PO Box 248 Locust Valley NY 11560-0248

LIPPS, JERE HENRY, paleontology educator; b. L.A., Aug. 28, 1939; s. Henry John and Margaret (Rosaltha) L.; m. Karen Elizabeth Loeblich, June 25, 1964 (div. 1971); m. Susannah McClintock, Sept. 28, 1973; children: Jeremy Christian, Jamison William. BA, UCLA, 1962, PhD, 1966. Asst. prof. U. Calif., Davis, 1967-70, assoc. prof., 1970-75, prof., 1975-88; prof. U. Calif., Berkeley, 1988—, prof. paleontology, 1988-89, prof. integrative biology, 1989—; dir. Mus. Paleontology, Berkeley, 1989—; dir. Inst. Ecology U. Calif., Davis, 1972-73, chmn. dept. geology, 1971-72, 79-84, chmn. dept. integrative biology, Berkeley, 1991-94. Contbr. articles to sci. publs. Fellow, dir. Cushman Found. Recipient U.S. Antarctic medal NSF, 1975; Lipps Island, Antarctica named in his honor, 1979. Fellow AAAS, Calif. Acad. Scis., Geol. Soc. Am., Cushman Found.; mem. Paleontol. Soc. (pres. 1996-97), Coun. for Media Integrity. Avocation: scuba diving. Office: Mus Paleontology U Calif 1101 Valley Life Scis Bldg Berkeley CA 94720

LIPS, H. PETER, systems engineer director; b. Nov. 6, 1939. BEE, Technische Hochschule Darmstadt, Germany, MEE. Dep. dir. Siemens Ag. Mem. IEEE (mem. DC and flexible AC transmission subcom., working group on performance and testing of HVDC transmission sys., working group on econs. and operating strategies, Uno Lamm award com., substas. com., DC converter stas. subcom., working group on clearance and creepages in HVDC stas., past chmn. working group on power losses in HVDC converter stas., working group on static var compensators), Power Engrng. Soc. (sec.). Office: Siemens Ag/ASI I G TH, Frauenaurachestr 80, 91056 Erlangen Germany

LIPSCHUTZ, ILSE HEMPEL, language educator; b. Bönnigheim, Wurttemberg, Germany, Aug. 19, 1923; came to U.S., 1946; d. Joseph Martin Paul and Fanny (Würzburger) Hempel; m. Lewis D. Lipschutz, Feb. 6, 1952; children: Elizabeth, Marion, Marc Hempel, Margaret Hempel. Diplôme Institut des Professeurs de Français à l'Etranger, Sorbonne U., Paris, 1942, Licence ès Lettres, 1943, Diplôme d'Etudes Supérieures Lettr, 1944; Diploma de Estudios Hispánicos, U. Complutense, Madrid, 1945; MA, Harvard U., 1949, PhD, 1958. Teaching fellow Radcliffe Coll. Harvard U., 1947-50; instr. Vassar Coll., Poughkeepsie, N.Y., 1951-58, asst. prof., 1958-63, assoc. prof., 1963-72, prof., 1972-92, Andrew W. Mellon prof. Humanities, 1981-92; prof. emerita Vassar Coll., 1992—, chair dept., 1975-82; cons., collaborator Spanish Ministry of Culture, Madrid, 1979; lectr. Frick Collection, N.Y.C., 1976, Prado Mus., Madrid, 1983, Met. Mus., N.Y.C., 1989, Universidad Internacional Menéndez Pelayo, Santander, Spain, 1990, Fundación Ramón Areces, Madrid, 1991; vis. prof. U. Complutense, Madrid, 1990; invited mem. Ctr. Rsch. Origines de l'Espagne Contemporaine, Sorbonne, U. Paris, 1992. Author: Spanish Painting and the French Romantics, 1972, rev. Spanish edit., 1988, (with others) La Imagen romántica de España, 1981, Goya, nuevas visiones, 1987, Viajeros románticos a Andalucía, 1987; contbr. articles to profl. jours. Spanish Govt. fellow U. Madrid, 1945; N.Y. State fellow AAUW, 1950-51; Ann. Radcliffe fellow Radcliffe Coll.-Harvard U., 1950-51; faculty fellow Vassar Coll., 1960-61, 67-68; rsch. scholar U.S.-Spain Common. on Edn., 1979-80; sr. rsch. fellow Fulbright-Hays Commn., 1983-84 (nat. fellowship com. 1972-75, 84-87); chevalier Palmes Académiques, 1984. Mem. AAUP, AAUW (nat. fellowship com. 1961-67), Soc. Théophile Gautier (bd. dirs. 1986—), Soc. Etudes Romantiques, Am. Soc. for Hispanic Art Hist. Studies, Soc. for Spanish and Portuguese Hist. Studies. Home: 11 Park Ave Poughkeepsie NY 12603-3101 Office: Vassar Coll Box # 394 124 Raymond Ave Poughkeepsie NY 12604

LIPSCHUTZ, MICHAEL ELAZAR, chemistry educator, consultant, researcher; b. Phila., May 24, 1937; s. Maurice and Anna (Kaplan) L.; m. Linda Jane Lowenthal, June 21, 1959; children: Joshua Henry, Mark David, Jonathan Mayer. B.S., Pa. State U., 1958; S.M., U. Chgo., 1960, Ph.D., 1962. Gastdocent U. Bern, Switzerland, 1964-65; asst. prof. chemistry Purdue U., West Lafayette, Ind., 1965-68, assoc. prof., 1968-73, prof., 1973—, chmn. inorganic chemistry, 1978-82, assoc. head dept. of chemistry, 1993—; dir. chemistry ops. Purdue Rare Isotope Measurement Lab. (PRIME), 1990—; vis. assoc. prof. Tel Aviv U., 1971-72; vis. prof. Max-Planck Inst. fuer Chemie, Mainz, Fed. Republic Germany, 1987; mem. panel space sci. experts Com. on Space Rsch., Space Agy. Forum of the Internat. Space Yr., Internat. Coun. Sci. Unions, 1990-92; cons. in field. Assoc. editor 11th Lunar and Planetary Sci. Conf., 3 vols., 1980; fin. editor: Meteoritics and Planetary Sci., 1992—; contbr. numerous articles to profl. jours. Served to 1st lt. USAR, 1958-64. Recipient Cert. of Recognition, NASA, 1979, Cert. of Spl. Recognition, 1979, Group Achievement award, 1983, Cert. Appreciation, Nat. Commn. on Space, 1986; postdoctoral fellow NSF, 1964-65, NATO, 1964-65; Fulbright fellow, 1971-72. Fellow Meteoritical Soc. (treas. 1978-84, mem. joint com. on pubs. of Geochem. and Meteoritical Socs. 1985-93, fin. officer 1985-93, chmn. 1988-90); mem. AAAS, Am. Chem. Soc., Am. Geophys. Union, Planetary Soc., Internat. Astron. Union (U.S. rep. 1988—), Sigma Xi. Minor planet named in honor of Lipschutz by Internat. Astronomical Union, 1987. Office: Purdue U Dept Chemistry West Lafayette IN 47907

LIPSCOMB, ANNA ROSE FEENY, entrepreneur, arts organizer, fundraiser b. Greensboro, N.C., Oct. 29, 1945; d. Nathan and Matilda (Carotenuto) L. Student langs., Alliance Francaise, Paris, 1967-68; BA in English and French summa cum laude, Queens Coll., 1977; diploma advanced Spanish, Forester Instituto Internacional, San Jose, Costa Rica, 1990; postgrad. Inst. Allende San Miguel de Allende, Mex., 1991. Reservations agt. Am. Airlines, St. Louis, 1968-69, ticket agt., 1969-71; coll. rep. CBS, Holt Rinehart Winston, Providence, 1977-79, sr. acquisitions editor Dryden Press, Chgo., 1979-81; owner, mgr. Historic Taos (N.Mex.) Inn, 1981-89, Southwest Moccasin and Drum, Taos; pres., co-owner Southwest Products, Ltd., 1991—; owner, pres. All One Tribe, Inc., 1996—; fundraiser Taos Arts Celebrations, 1989—; bd. dirs. N.Mex. Hotel and Motel Assn., 1986—; sem. leader Taos Women Together, 1989; founder All One Tribe Foundation, 1994, All One Tribe Drumming Festival, 1991—; mem. adv. bd. Drum Bus. Mag., 1996—. Editor: Intermediate Accounting, 1980; Business Law, 1981. Contbr. articles to profl. jours.; patentee in field. Bd. dirs., 1st v.p. Taos Arts Assn., 1982-85; founder, bd. dirs. Taos Spring Arts Celebration, 1983—; founder, dir. Meet-the-Artist Series, 1983—; bd. dirs. and co-founder Spring Arts N.Mex., 1986; founder Yuletide in Taos, 1988, A Taste of Taos, 1988; bd. dirs. Music from Angel Fire, 1988—; founding mem. Assn. Hist. Hotels, Boulder, 1983—; organizer Internat. Symposium on Arts, 1985; bd. dirs. Arts in Taos, 1983, Taoschool, Inc., 1985—; mem. adv. bd. Chamisa Mesa Ednl. Ctr., Taos, 1990—; founder All One Tribe Found., 1994; bd. dirs. Roadrunner Recyclers, 1995—. Recipient Outstanding English Student of Yr. award Queens Coll., 1977; named Single Outstanding Contbr. to the Arts in Taos, 1986. Mem. Millicent Rogers Mus. Assn., Taos Lodgers Assn. (mktg. task force 1989), Taos County C. of C. (1st v.p. 1988-89, bd. dirs. 1987-89, advt. com. 1986-89, chmn. nominating com. 1989), Internat. Platform Assn., Taos Women Bus. Owners, Phi Beta Kappa. Home: Talpa Rte Taos NM 87571 Office: PO Drawer N Taos NM 87571

LIPSCOMB, JEFFREY JON, fund specialist, insurance agent; b. San Diego, May 8, 1946; s. Willis L. and Marjorie (Jones) L.; m. Jo Ann Elaine Nielsen, Oct. 1, 1983; 1 child, Amanda Nielsen. Student, Occidental Coll., 1964-68, Harvard U., 1971, New England Conservatory Music, 1972. Chief cash flow analyst St. Johnsbury Co., Cambridge, Mass., 1970-81; pvt. investor San Diego, 1981-88; registered rep. New England Securities, Sacramento, 1988—; registered investment specialist Bankamerican Investment Svcs., West Sacramento, Calif., 1997—; registered investment specialist Bankam. Investment Svcs., 1997—. Columnist (fin. commentary) The Bus. Jour. Sacramento, 1990-91. Mem. East Sacramento (Calif.) Improvement Assn., 1988-97; pianist celebrity benefit concerts Stanford Children's Home, Sacramento, 1989. Mem. Inst. Cert. Fund Specialists, Internat. Assn. Fin.

Planning (practitioner divsn. 1993—), Nat. Assn. Life Underwriters, Sacramento Assn. Life Underwriters, New Eng. Leaders Assn., Sutter Lawn Tennis Club (pres. 1992-93), The Sutter Club, Investment Trust Boston Cornerstone Club. Republican. Presbyterian. Avocations: chamber music, genealogy, tennis, chess. Office: 1551 W Capitol Ave West Sacramento CA 95691-3217

LIPSCOMB, OSCAR HUGH, archbishop; b. Mobile, AL, Sept. 21, 1931; s. Oscar Hugh and Margaret (Saunders) L. STL, Gregorian U., Rome, 1957; PhD, Cath. U. Am., 1963. Ordained priest Roman Cath. Ch., 1956; consecrated bishop Roman Cath. Ch., 1980. Asst. pastor Mobile, 1959-65; tchr. McGill Inst., Mobile, 1959-60, 61-62; vice chancellor Diocese of Mobile-Birmingham, 1963-66, chancellor, 1966-80; pastor St. Patrick Parish, Mobile, 1966-71; lectr. history Spring Hill Coll., Mobile, 1971-72; asst. pastor St. Matthew Parish, Mobile, 1971-79, Cathedral Immaculate Conception, Mobile, 1979-80; adminstr. sede vacante Diocese of Mobile, 1980, now archbishop; pres. Cath. Housing Mobile, Mobile Senate Priests, 1978-80; chmn. com. on doctrine Nat. Conf. Cath. Bishops, 1988-91. Author articles, papers in field. Pres. bd. dirs. Mobile Mus., 1966-76; trustee Ala. Dept. Archives and History, Cath. U. Am., Washington, 1983—, Spring Hill Coll., Mobile; chmn. NCCB Com. on Ecumenical and Interreligious Affairs, 1993-96, Cath. Common Groung Com., 1996—; chmn. bd. govs. N.Am. Coll., Rome, 1982-85. Mem. Am. Cath. Hist. Assn., So. Hist. Assn., Ala. Hist. Assn. (pres. 1971-72, exec. com. 1981-88), Hist. Mobile Preservation Soc., Lions. Address: PO Box 1966 36633 400 Government St Mobile AL 36602-2332

LIPSCOMB, PAUL ROGERS, orthopedic surgeon, educator; b. Clio, S.C., Mar. 23, 1914; s. Paul Holmes and Mary Emma (Rogers) L.; m. Phyllis M. Oesterreich, July 20, 1940; children—Susan L. Nachbaur, Paul Rogers. B.S., U. S.C., 1935; M.D., Med. U. S.C., 1938; M.S. in Orthopaedic Surgery, Mayo Found., U. Minn., 1942. Diplomate Am. Bd. Orthopaedic Surgery (sec. 1968-71, pres. 1971-73). Intern Cooper Hosp., Camden, N.J., 1938-39; resident in orthopaedic surgery Mayo Clinic, Rochester, Minn., 1939-43, asst. to staff orthopaedic surgery, 1941-43, staff assoc., 1943-69, v.p. staff, 1963; cons. Methodist, St. Mary's hosps., 1943-69; mem. faculty Mayo Grad. Sch. U. Minn., 1944-69, prof. orthopaedic surgery, 1961-69; mem. univ. senate from U. Minn. (Mayo Grad. Sch.), 1963-67; past mem. grad. and admissions com. and joint com. Grad. Sch. U. Minn. and Mayo Grad. Sch.; prof., chmn. dept. orthopedic surgery (Sch. of Medicine, U. Calif.), Davis, 1969-81, prof. emeritus, 1981—; pres. staff Sacramento Med. Center, 1980-81; mem. staff Woodland Clinic, 1981-86; ret., 1992; v.p. Woodland Clinic Research and Edn. Found., 1982-84, pres., 1984-85; hon. vis. prof. orthopaedics U. Auckland, New Zealand, 1978; cons. Disability Evaluation Group, Sacramento, 1988-92. Contbr. numerous articles to profl. jours. Mem. Am. Acad. Orthopedic Surgery (chmn. com. sci. investigation 1955-56, chmn. instrl. course com., editor instrl. course lectures 1961-63, chmn. com. on arthritis 1970), Orthopaedic Rsch. Soc. (chmn. membership com., mem. exec. com. 1956), AMA (chmn. orthopaedic sect. 1965), ACS, Am. Orthopaedic Assn. (pres. 1974-75), Western Orthopaedic Soc., Internat. Soc. Orthopaedic Surgery and Traumatology, Ctrl., Internat. orthopaedic clubs, New Zealand Orthopaedic Assn. (corr.), Sacramento County, Yolo County med. socs., Sterling Bunnell Found. (trustee 1984-86), Calif. Med. Assn., Sigma Xi, Alpha Omega Alpha. Presbyterian. Home: 749 Sycamore Ln Davis CA 95616-3432

LIPSCOMB, ROSALIND TARVER, artist; b. Spartanburg, S.C., Apr. 12, 1920; d. Virgil Wood and Rosalind (Tarver) L.; m. Richard Bethune Zimmerman, Sr., June 24, 1941 (div. Jan. 1969); children: Richard Bethune Jr., Rosalind; m. Alfred Alonzo Forrest, Jan. 25, 1971 (div. June 1972). BFA, U. Ga., 1940; MA, Auburn U., 1968. Tchr. English Ga. Southwestern Coll., Americus, 1965-75, Sumter County H.S., Americus, 1975-80; profl. artist Americus, 1980—. Portrait artist of Drs. of Sumter Regional Hosp., 1994—. Mem. Nat. Mus. Women in Arts (charter), Portrait Soc. Atlanta (charter), Jr. Svc. League. Republican. Episcopalian. Avocations: travel, reading, art workshops.

LIPSCOMB, THOMAS HEBER, III, information technology executive; b. Washington, Sept. 12, 1938; s. Thomas Heber and Louise Buchanan (Heiss) L.; m. Christine Young Jones, Aug. 22, 1981; children: Peter Scott, Adrienne Clare. B.A., Coll. William and Mary, 1961; M.A., Ind. U., 1965. Editor Bobbs-Merrill Co., 1965-67, Stein & Day Pubs., 1967-69; sr. editor Prentice-Hall, Inc., 1969-70; exec. editor, editor-in-chief Dodd, Mead & Co., 1970-73; pres. Mason & Lipscomb Pubs., 1973-74; ptnr. Hamilton Assocs., 1974-76; pres., CEO N.Y. Times Book Co., 1976-81; chmn. bd. New Capital Pubs., Inc., 1981-85; pres. Delphi Assocs., N.Y.C., 1985-87; pres., CEO Cryptologics Internat., 1988-91; pres., CEO Infosafe Sys., Inc., N.Y.C., 1992-96, chmn., 1996—; chmn. bd. Atlantech Aquaculture Ltd. Contbr. articles to N.Y. Times, Wall St. Journal, Washington Post, and others. Mem. N.Y. Rep. County Com., 1971-80; mem. exec. bd. Am. Ctr. PEN, 1973-79; trustee Robert Coll., Istanbul, Turkey, 1973-81; mem. panel of advisors George Polk Award, 1977—; chmn. N.Y. Vet.'s Leadership Program, 1985-88; dir. Giraffe Project, 1989—, NYU Ctr. Copyright in New Media, Columbia U. New Media Tech. Ctr. Served to lt. U.S. Army, 1961-64. Mem. Council on Fgn. Relations, Internat. Broadcast Inst., East-West Inst. Security Studies, Gibraltar-Am. Coun., St. Nicholas Soc., N.Y. Acad. Scis., Holland Lodge, Mid-Atlantic Club, Nat. Press Club, Met. Club. Episcopalian. Office: Infosafe Sys 342 Madison Ave New York NY 10173

LIPSCOMB, WILLIAM NUNN, JR., retired physical chemistry educator; b. Cleveland, Ohio, Dec. 9, 1919; s. William Nunn and Edna Patterson (Porter) L.; m. Mary Adele Sargent, May 20, 1944; children: Dorothy Jean, James Sargent; m. Jean Craig Evans, 1983; 1 child, Jenna. BS, U. Ky., 1941, DSc (hon.), 1963; PhD, Calif. Inst. Tech., 1946; DSc (hon.), U. Munich, 1976, L.I. U., 1977, Rutgers U., 1979, Gustavus Adolphus Coll., 1980, Marietta Coll., 1981, Miami U., 1983, U. Denver, 1985, Ohio State U., 1991; Transylvania U., 1992. Phys. chemist Office of Sci. R&D, 1942-46; faculty U. Minn., Mpls., 1946-59, asst. prof., 1946-50, assoc. prof., 1950-54, acting chief phys. chemistry div., 1952-54, prof. and chief phys. chemistry div., 1954-59; prof. chemistry Harvard U., Cambridge, Mass., 1959-71, Abbott and James Lawrence prof., 1971-90, prof. emeritus, 1990—; mem. U.S. Nat. Commn. for Crystallography, 1954-59, 60-63, 65-67; chmn. program com. 4th Internat. Congress of crystallography, Montreal, 1957; mem. sci. adv. bd. Robert A. Welch Found.; mem. rsch. adv. bd. Mich. Molecular Biology Inst.; mem. adv. com. Inst. Amorphus Studies; mem. sci. adv. com. Nova Pharms., Daltex Med. Svc., Gensia Pharms., Binary Therapeutics. Author: The Boron Hydrides, 1963, (with G.R. Eaton) NMR Studies of Boron Hydrides and Related Compounds, 1969; assoc. editor: (with G.R. Eaton) Jour. Chemical Physics, 1955-57; contbr. articles to profl. jours.; clarinetist, mem.: Amateur Chamber Music Players. Guggenheim fellow Oxford U., Eng., 1954-55; Guggenheim fellow Cambridge U., Eng., 1972-73; NSF sr. postdoctoral fellow, 1965-66; Overseas fellow Churchill Coll., Cambridge, Eng., 1966, 73; Robert Welch Found. lectr., 1966, 71; Howard U. distinguished lecture series, 1966; George Fisher Baker lectr. Cornell U., 1969; centenary lectr. Chem. Soc., London, 1972; lectr. Weizmann Inst., Rehovoth, Israel, 1974; Evans award lectr. Ohio State U., 1974; Gilbert Newton Lewis Meml. lectr. U. Calif., Berkeley, 1974; also lectureships Mich. State U., 1975, U. Iowa, 1975, Ill. Inst. Tech., 1976, numerous others; also speaker confs.; Recipient Harrison Howe award in Chemistry, 1958; Distinguished Alumni Centennial award U. Ky., 1965; Distinguished Service in advancement inorganic chemistry Am. Chem. Soc., 1968; George Ledlie prize Harvard, 1971; Nobel prize in chemistry, 1976; Disting. Alumni award Calif. Inst. Tech., 1977; sr. U.S. scientist award Alexander von Humboldt-Stiftung, 1979; award lecture Internat. Acad. Quantum Molecular Sci., 1980. Fellow Am. Acad. Arts and Scis., Am. Phys. Soc.; mem. NAS, Am. Chem. Soc. (Peter Debye award phys. chemistry 1973, chmn. Minn. sect. 1949-50), Am. Crystallographic Assn. (pres. 1955), The Netherlands Acad. Arts and Scis. (fgn.), Math. Assn. Bioinorganic Scientists (hon.), Academie Europeenne des Sciences, des Arts et des Lettres, Royal Soc. Chemistry (hon.), Phi Beta Kappa, Sigma Xi, Alpha Chi Sigma, Phi Lambda Upsilon, Sigma Pi Sigma, Phi Mu Epsilon. Office: Harvard U Dept Chemistry 12 Oxford St Cambridge MA 02138-2902

LIPSCOMB-BROWN, EDRA EVADEAN, retired childhood educator; b. Marion, Ill., Aug. 3, 1919; d. Edgar and Anna Josephine (Wiesbrodt) Turnage; m. July 5, 1939 (div. Sept. 1950); 1 son, H. Alan; m. Mark S. Brown, 1981. B.S., So. Ill. U., 1955; M.A., U. Mich., 1955; Ed.D., Ind. U., 1962; postgrad., U. Minn. Tchr. Benton (Ill.) Elem. Schs., 1939-54, DeKalb (Ill.) Consol. Schs., 1955-56; mem. faculty No. Ill. U., DeKalb, 1956-81; prof. elem. edn. No. Ill. U., 1967-81, chmn. elem. and childhood edn., 1978-81, ret., 1981; ednl. cons. to various schs., No. Ill.; mem. vis. accreditation com. Nat. Council Accreditation Tchr. Edn., Kent State U., 1974, U. Wis.-Stout, 1975; co-author, director numerous projects sponsored by U.S. Office Spl. Edn., 1979-81. Author: Lipscomb Teacher Attitude Scale; Contbr. articles to profl. jours. Research grantee No. Ill. U., 1965, 73; Research grantee State of Ill., 1972-73. Mem. Internat. Reading Assn., Internat. Assn. Supervision and Curriculum Devel., NEA, Ill. Edn. Assn., Assn. Higher Edn., Am. Ednl. Research Assn., Pi Lambda Theta. Democrat. *Throughout my life, I have striven toward professional achievement and personal happiness. I tried never to let disappointments become bitterness, life's traumas to become defeat or sadness to become self-pity.*

LIPSET, SEYMOUR MARTIN, sociologist, political scientist, educator; b. N.Y.C., Mar. 18, 1922; s. Max and Lena (Lippman) L.; m. Elsie Braun, Dec. 26, 1944 (dec. Feb. 1987); children: David, Daniel, Carola; m. Sydnee Guyer, July 29, 1990. BS, CCNY, 1943; PhD, Columbia U., 1949; MA (hon.), Harvard U., 1966; LLD (hon.), Villanova U., 1973, Hebrew U., 1981, U. Buenos Aires, 1987, Free U., Brussels, 1990, U. Judaism, 1991, Hebrew Union Coll., 1993, Boston Hebrew Coll., 1993, U. Guelph, 1996. Lectr. U. Toronto, 1946-48; asst. prof. U. Calif., Berkeley, 1948-50; asst., then assoc. prof. grad. faculty Columbia U., 1950-56, asst. dir. Bur. Applied Social Research, 1954-56; prof. sociology U. Calif., Berkeley, 1956-66, dir. Inst. Internat. Studies, 1962-66; vis. prof. social rels. and govt. Harvard U., 1965-66, prof. govt. and sociology, exec. com. Ctr. Internat. Affairs, 1966-75, George Markham prof. Ctr. Internat. Affairs, 1974-75; sr. fellow Hoover Inst. Stanford U., 1975—, prof. polit. sci. and sociology, 1975-92, Caroline S.G. Munro prof., 1981-92; Hazel prof. pub. policy George Mason U., Fairfax, Va., 1990—; Henry Ford vis. research prof. Yale U., 1960-61; Paley lectr. Hebrew U., 1973; Fulbright program 40th Anniversary Disting. lectr., 1987; vis. scholar Russell Sage Found., New York, 1988-89. Author: Agrarian Socialism, 1950, (with others) Union Democracy, 1956, (with R. Bendix) Social Mobility in Industrial Society, 1959, expanded edit., 1991, Political Man, 1960, expanded edit., 1981, The First New Nation, 1963, expanded edit., 1979, Revolution and Counter Revolution, 1968, expanded edit., 1988, (with Earl Raab) The Politics of Unreason, 1970, expanded edit., 1978, Rebellion in the University, 1972, (with Everett Ladd) Academics and the 1972 Election, 1973, Professors, Unions and American Higher Education, 1973, The Divided Academy, 1975, (with David Riesman) Education and Politics at Harvard, 1975, (with I.L. Horowitz) Dialogues on American Politics, 1978, (with William Schneider) The Confidence Gap, 1983, expanded edit., 1987, Consensus and Conflict, 1987, Continental Divide: The Institutions and Values of the United States and Canada, 1990, The Educational Background of American Jews, 1994; (with Earl Raab) Jews and the New American Scene, 1995, American Exceptionalism: A Double-Edged Sword, 1996; co-editor: Class, Status and Power, 1953, Labor and Trade Unionism, 1960, Sociology: The Progress of a Decade, 1961, Culture and Social Character, 1961, The Berkeley Student Revolt, 1965, Class, Status and Power in Comparative Perspective, 1966, Social Structure, Mobility and Economic Development, 1966, Elites in Latin America, 1967, Party Systems and Voter Alignments, 1967, Students in Revolt, 1969, Issues in Politics and Government, 1970, Failure of a Dream? Essays in the History of American Socialism, 1974, rev. edit., 1984; co-editor: Democracy in Developing Countries, 3 vols., Africa, Asia and Latin America, 1988, 89, Politics in Developing Countries, 1990, 95, The Encyclopedia of Democracy, 4 vols., 1995; co-editor Public Opinion mag., 1977-89, Internat. Jour. Pub. Opinion Rsch., 1989—; editor: Students and Politics, 1967, Politics and Social Science, 1969, Emerging Coalitions in American Politics, 1978, The Third Century, 1979, Party Coalitions in the Eighties, 1981, Unions in Transition, 1986, American Pluralism and the Jewish Community, 1990; adv. editor: various jours. including Sci., Comparative Politics. Mem. Bd. Fgn. Scholarships, 1968-71; bd. dirs. Aurora Found., 1985—, U.S. Inst. Peace, 1996—; nat. chmn. B'nai B'rith Hillel Found., 1975-79, chmn. nat. exec. com., 1979-84; assoc. pres. Am. Profs. for Peace in the Middle East, 1976-77, nat. pres., 1977-81; co-chmn. exec. com. Internat. Ctr. Peace in Middle East, 1982-92; co-chmn. Com. for Effective UNESCO, 1976-81; chmn. Com. for UN Integrity, 1981-83; chmn. nat. faculty cabinet United Jewish Appeal, 1981-84; pres. Progressive Found., 1991-95. Recipient Gunyar Myrdal prize, 1970, Townsend Harris medal, 1971, 125th Anniversary alumni medal CCNY, 1963, M.B. Rawson award, 1986, No. Telecom. Gold Medal for Can. Studies, 1987, Marshall Sklare award Assn. Social Sci. Study of Jewry, 1993; fellow Social Sci. Rsch. Coun., 1945-46, Ctr. Advanced Study Behavioral Sci. fellow, 1971-72, Woodrow Wilson Ctr. for Internat. Scholars fellow, 1995-96. Fellow NAS, AAAS (v.p. 1974-78, chmn. sect. on econ. and social sci. 1975-76, 95-96), Nat. Acad. Edn., Am. Sociol. Assn. (coun. 1959-62, MacIver award 1962, pres. 1992-93), Japan Soc.; mem. Sociol. Rsch. Assn. (exec. com. 1981-84, pres. 1985), Am. Polit. Sci. Assn. (coun. 1975-77, pres. 1981-82, Leon Epstein prize 1989), Internat. Polit. Sci. Assn. (coun. 1981-88, v.p. 1982-88), Internat. Soc. Polit. Psychology (pres. 1979-80), Internat. Sociol. Assn. (chmn. com. polit. sociology 1959-71), World Assn. Pub. Opinion Rsch. (v.p. and pres.-elect 1982-84, pres. 1984-86), Am. Philos. Soc., Finnish Acad. Sci. (hon.), Paul Lazarsfeld Gesellschaft (social rsch. 1994—), Soc. for Comparative Rsch. Office: George Mason U Inst of Policy Studies Pohick Module Fairfax VA 22030 also: Stanford U 213 Herbert Hoover Meml Bu Stanford CA 94305

LIPSEY, HOWARD IRWIN, law educator, justice, lawyer; b. Providence, Jan. 24, 1936; s. Harry David and Anna (Gershman) L.; children: Lewis Robert, Bruce Stephen. AB, Providence Coll., 1957; JD, Georgetown U., 1960. Bar: R.I. 1960, U.S. Dist. Ct. R.I. 1961, U.S. Supreme Ct. 1972. Assoc. Edward I. Friedman, 1963-67, Kirshenbaum & Kirshenbaum, 1967-82; ptnr. Abedon, Michaelson, Stanzler, Biener, Skolnik & Lipsey, 1972-83; ptnr. Lipsey & Skolnik, Esquires, Ltd., Providence, 1983-93; assoc. justice R.I. Family Ct., 1993—; lectr. trial tactics Nat. Coll. Adv., 1986, U. Bridgeport Law Sch., Yale U., U. Denver Law Sch., Suffolk U. Law Sch., 1987—; adj. prof. U. Houston Law Sch., 1994—; adj. prof. family law Roger Williams U. Law Sch., 1996—. Served to capt. JAGC, USAR, 1960-71. Fellow Am. Coll. Trial Lawyers, Am. Acad. Matrimonial Lawyers; mem. ABA (chair trial advocacy inst., 1994-97, coun. mem. 1995—), R.I. Bar Assn., Assn. Trial Lawyers Am. Clubs: B'nai B'rith (Anti-Defamation League). Contbg. author: Valuation and Distribution of Marital Property, 1984. Office: RI Family Ct 1 Dorrance Plz Providence RI 02903-3922

LIPSEY, JOHN C. (JACK LIPSEY), insurance company executive; b. Chgo., Oct. 1, 1930; s. Albert Ellis and Mae (Smikler) L.; m. Elise Sandra Gross, Apr. 15, 1956; children—William, Laura, Abby. Ph.B., U. Chgo., 1948; postgrad., NYU, 1949-50. C.L.U.; chartered fin. cons. Spl. agt., mgr., v.p. Prudential Co., Chgo. and N.Y.C., 1956-80; sr. v.p. Home Life Ins. Co., N.Y.C., 1980-82, exec. v.p., 1982-84; pres. HL Fin. Services of N.Y., N.Y.C., 1984-88; v.p. Personal Lines Ins. Co., 1988—; pres. PLI Ins. Agy. of Fla., Inc., 1996—. Bd. govs. Am. Jewish Com., Boca Raton, Fla., 1991—, v.p. 1992-95, pres. 1995—. With Army N.G., 1950-52. Mem. Am. Soc. C.L.U.s, Internat. Assn. Fin. Planners, Nat. Assn. Life Underwriters, Round Table of N.Y., Mountain Ridge Country Club, Delaire Country Club. Republican. Jewish. Avocations: golf; travel. Office: Personal Lines Ins 7777 Glades Rd Ste 112 Boca Raton FL 33434-4150

LIPSEY, JOSEPH, JR., water bottling executive, retail and wholesale corporation executive; b. Selma, Ala., Sept. 12, 1934; s. Joseph and Anna (Bendersky) L.; m. Betty Fay Wellan, June 5, 1960; children: Debora, Joseph III, Elizabeth, Tami. BA, La. State U., 1955, LLB, 1957. Bar: La. 1957, U.S. Dist. Ct. La. 1957, Korea 1959, Ryukyu Island 1958. Ptnr., Howell & Lipsey, Baton Rouge, 1960-65; ptnr. IsraAm Venture Group, Tel Aviv; v.p. Lipsey's Wholesale, Baton Rouge, 1977—; pres. So. Media Rsch. Co., Monroe, La., 1984-92; chmn. Composite Analysis Group, Inc., Alexandria, 1989—; CEO Lipsey Mountain Spring Water, Atlanta, 1990—, Nantahala Spring Water Bottling Co., Highlands, N.C., 1994—; chmn. EAS Pub. Co., Inc.; speaker OPM 10 Harvard U., 1985; lectr. La. State U. Law Sch., Baton Rouge, 1961-63; chmn. Fashion Mchts. Conf., N.Y.C., 1977-81; chmn., sec.-treas. EAS Pub. Co., Inc., 1994—. Mem. exec. com. Com. for a Better La., Baton Rouge, 1971-86; pres. La. State U. Found., 1980-81. Inducted into La. State U. Law Sch. Hall of Fame, 1987. Capt. USAF, 1957-60. Mem. La. State C. of C. (pres. 1973-75), Alexandria C. of C. (pres. 1971-72), Rotary. Democrat. Jewish.

LIPSEY, RICHARD GEORGE, economist, educator; b. Victoria, B.C., Can., Aug. 28, 1928; s. Richard Andrew and Faith Thirell (Ledingham) L.; m. Diana Louise Smart, Mar. 17, 1960; children: Mark Alexander (stepson), Mathew Richard, Joanna Louise, Claudia Amanda. B.A. with honours, U. B.C., 1950; M.A., U. Toronto, 1953; Ph.D., London Sch. Econs., 1958; LL.D. (hon.), McMaster U., 1984, Victoria U., 1985, Carleton U., 1986, Qeens U., 1990; D.Sc. (hon), Toronto U., 1992; D.Litt., Guelph U., 1993; LL.D (hon.), U. Western Ont., 1994, U. Essex, 1996. Research asst. B.C. Dept. Trade and Industry, 1950-53; from asst. lectr. to prof. econs. London Sch. Econs., 1955-63; prof. econs., chmn. dept., dean Sch. Social Studies, U. Essex, Eng., 1965-69; vis. prof. U. B.C., 1969-70, U. Colo., 1973-74; Irving Fisher vis. prof. Yale U., 1979-80; Sir Edward Peacock prof. econs. Queens U., Kingston, Ont., 1970-87; prof. Simon Fraser U., Vancouver, B.C., 1989—; sr. rsch. advisor C.D. Howe Inst., 1983-89; dir. rsch. into growth in U.K. Nat. Econ. Devel. Coun. U.K., 1961-63; mem. coun. and planning com. Nat. Inst. Econ. and Social Rsch. U.K., 1962-69; mem. bd. Social Sci. Rsch. Coun. U.K., 1966-69. Author: An Introduction to Positive Economics, 8th edit, 1995, The Theory of Customs Unions: A General Equilibrium Analysis, 1971; co-author: An Introduction to a Mathematical Treatment of Economics, 3d edit, 1977, Economics, 11th edit., 1995, Mathematical Economics, 1976, An Introduction to the U.K. Economy, 1983, 4th edit., 1993, Common Ground for the Canadian Common Market, 1984, Canada's Trade Options in a Turbulent World, 1985, Global Imbalances, 1987, First Principles of Economics, 1988, 2d edit., 1992, Evaluating the Free Trade Deal, 1988, The NAFTA, What's In, What's Out, What Next, Business Economics, 1997; editor: Rev. Econ. Studies, 1962-64. Decorated officer Order of Can.; Can. Inst. for Advanced Rsch. fellow, 1989—. Fellow Econometric Soc., Royal Soc. Can., Can. Inst. for Advanced Rsch.; mem. Royal Econ. Soc. (council 1967-71), Econ. Study Soc. (chmn. 1965-69), Am. Econ. Assn., Can. Econ. Assn. (pres. 1980-81), Atlantic Econ. Soc. (chmn. 1986-87). Office: Simon Fraser U Harbour Centre, 515 W Hastings St, Vancouver, BC Canada V6B 5K3

LIPSEY, ROBERT EDWARD, economist, educator; b. N.Y.C., Aug. 14, 1926; s. Meyer Aaron and Anna (Weinstein) L.; m. Sally Irene Rothstein, Nov. 24, 1948; children: Marion (Mrs. William Greenlee), Carol (Mrs. William Hersh), Eleanor (Mrs. William Ho). B.A., Columbia, 1944, M.A., 1946, Ph.D., 1961. Research asst. Nat. Bur. Econ. Research, N.Y.C., 1945-53; research assoc. Nat. Bur. Econ. Research, 1953-60, sr. research staff, 1960—, v.p. research, 1970-75, dir. internat. studies, 1975-78, dir. N.Y. Office,, 1978—; lectr. econs. Columbia U., 1961-64; prof. econs. Queens Coll. and Grad. Ctr., CUNY, 1967-95, prof. emeritus, 1995—; cons. Dept. Commerce, Fed. Res. Bd., UN, World Bank; mem. Pres. Adv. Bd. on Internat. Investment, 1977-78; bd. dirs. Rsch. Found. CUNY, 1994-95; exec. com. European Union Studies Ctr., CUNY, 1994—. Author: Price and Quantity Trends in the Foreign Trade of the U.S, 1963, (with Raymond W. Goldsmith) Studies in the National Balance Sheet of the U.S, 1963, (with Doris Preston) Source Book of Statistics Relating to Construction, 1966, (with Irving B. Kravis) Price Competitiveness in World Trade, 1971, (with Phillip Cagan) Financial Effects of Inflation, 1978, (with Irving B. Kravis) Saving and Economic Growth: Is the U.S. Really Falling Behind, 1987; editor: (with Helen Stone Tice) The Measurement of Saving, Investment and Wealth, 1989, (with Magnus Blomström and Lennart Ohlsson) Economic Relations Between the U.S. and Sweden, 1989; assoc. editor Rev. of Econs. and Stats., 1989-92; mem. editorial bd. Rev. of Income and Wealth, 1992—; contbr. articles to profl. jours. Fellow Am. Statis. Assn., Internat. Trade and Fin. Assn. (pres. 1997), N.Y. Acad. Scis.; mem. Acad. Internat. Bus., Nat. Assn. Bus. Economists, Am. Econ. Assn., Internat. Assn. for Rsch. in Income and Wealth, Conf. on Rsch. in Income and Wealth, Econometric Soc., Western Econ. Assn. (bd. dirs. 1996—), European Econ. Assn. Home: 70 E 10th St New York NY 10003-5102 Office: 50 E 42 St New York NY 10017-5405

LIPSHUTZ, ROBERT JEROME, lawyer, former government official; b. Atlanta, Dec. 27, 1921; s. Allen A. and Edith (Gavronski) L.; m. Barbara Sorelle Levin, Feb. 16, 1950 (dec.); children: Randall M., Judith Ann, Wendy Jean, Debbie Sue; m. Betty Beck Rosenberg, Feb. 10, 1973; stepchildren: Robert, Nancy Fay. J.D., U. Ga., 1943. Bar: Ga. 1943, D.C. 1980. Practice in Atlanta, 1947-77, 79—; ptnr. firm Lipshutz, Greenblatt & King, 1979—; counsel to Pres. U.S., Washington, 1977-79. Past vice chmn. Ga. Bd. Human Resources; treas., legal counsel Jimmy Carter Presdl. campaign com., 1976; trustee The Carter Ctr.; adv. com. Jimmy Carter Libr. Capt. AUS, 1944-46. Mem. Am., Ga., Atlanta, D.C. bar assns., Atlanta Lawyers Club, Atlanta., B'nai B'rith (past pres., Disting. Svc. award). Jewish (past pres. The Temple). Office: Lipshutz Greenblatt & King Harris Tower Peachtree Ctr Ste 2300 Atlanta GA 30303

LIPSIG, ETHAN, lawyer; b. N.Y.C., Dec. 11, 1948; s. Daniel Allen and Haddassah (Adler) L. BA, Pomona Coll., 1969; postgrad., Oxford U., 1969-70; JD, UCLA, 1974. Bar: U.S. Dist. Ct. (cen. dist.) Calif. 1974, U.S. Ct. Appeals (9th cir.) 1974, U.S Tax Ct. 1978. Author: Individual Retirement Arrangements, 1980, Downsizing, 1996. Mem. ABA (tax and labor rels. sect.), Western Pension and Benefits Conf., Calif. C. of C., Order of Coif, Ctrl. City Assn., Soc. Fellows of Huntington Libr., Calif. Club, L.A. Men's Garden Club. Avocations: travel, horticulture, wine, music, art. Home: 280 California Ter Pasadena CA 91105-1515 Office: Paul Hastings Janofsky & Walker LLP 555 S Flower St Fl 23 Los Angeles CA 90071-2300

LIPSITT, LEWIS PAEFF, psychology educator; b. New Bedford, Mass., June 28, 1929; s. Joseph and Anna Naomi (Paeff) L.; m. Edna Brill Duchin, June 8, 1952; children: Mark, Ann. BA, U. Chgo., 1950; MS, U. Mass., 1952; PhD, U. Iowa, 1957. Instr. dept. psychology Brown U., Providence, 1957, asst. prof., 1958-61, assoc. prof., 1961-66, prof., 1966-96, dir. Child Study Ctr., 1967-92, Wriston lectr., 1993—, prof. emeritus psychology, med. sci. and human devel., 1996—, rsch. prof. psychology, 1996—; mem. Gov.'s Adv. Commn. on Mental Retardation, 1963-66; cons. NIH; mem. edn. task force Model Cities Program, Providence, 1969-71; fellow Stanford Ctr. for Advanced Study in Behavioral Scis., 1979-80; vis. scientist NIMH, 1986-87; chair steering com. nat. child care project NICHHD, 1994—. Co-author: Child Development, 1979; founder, editor: Infant Behavior and Devel., 1978-82; founding co-editor: Advances in Child Development and Behavior, 1963-70, 78-82; co-editor: Research Readings in Child Psychology, 1963, Experimental Child Psychology, 1971, Advances in Infancy Research, Self-regulatory Behavior and Risk Taking, 1991; contbr. articles to profl. jours. Bd. dirs. Providence Child Guidance Clinic, 1960-63; trustee Butler Hosp., Providence, 1965-84; mem. bd. sci. counselor Nat. Ins. Child Health and Human Devel., 1984-88; nat. co-dir. Lee Salk Family Ctr., Kidspeace, Allentown, Pa., 1993—. Recipient Mentor award for lifetime achievement AAAS, 1995, Profl. Achievement citation U. Chgo., 1995; USPHS Spl. Rsch. fellow, 1966, Guggenheim fellow, 1972-73, USPHS fellow, 1973. Fellow AAAS (Lifetime Mentor award 1994), APA (exec. com. divsn. devel. psychology 1967-70, pres.-elect divsn. devel. psychology 1979-80, pres. divsn. devel. psychology 1980-81, bd. sci. affirs 1985-88, exec. dir. for sci. 1990-91, sci. officer 1991-92, Nicholas Hobbs award 1990); mem. AAUP, Soc. Rsch. in Child Devel., Internat. Soc. Study of Behavioral Devel. (membership sec. 1981-83, exec. com. 1984-89), Am. Psychol. Soc. (founding mem., charter fellow, bd. dirs. 1989-90), Can. Inst. for Advanced Rsch. (chair adv. com. human devel. group 1995—).

LIPSKY, STEPHEN EDWARD, engineering executive, electronic warfare engineer; b. N.Y.C., Jan. 18, 1932; s. Arthur Arnold and Sophie (Malsbrook) L.; m. Laura Roher, May 11, 1958 (div. 1978); children—Janice, Sharon, David; m. Hyla Schaffer, Apr. 7, 1979. B.E.E., NYU, 1953, M.E.E., 1962; PhD in Elec. Engring., Drexel U., 1993. Project engr. Fisher Radio Corp; div. mgr., staff scientist Loral Electronics, Yonkers, N.Y., 1958-63; corp. v.p. Polarad-Radiometrics, Lake Success, N.Y., 1963-70; dir. advanced systems Gen. Inst. Corp., Hicksville, N.Y., 1970-79; chief tech. officer, sr. v.p. Am. Electronic Labs., Lansdale, Pa., 1979-93; founder, chief tech. officer Bynetics Corp., Jenkintown, Pa., 1993—; adj. univ. prof. elec. engring. Drexel U., Phila.; expert witness RF Comms. Author: Microwave Passive Direction Finding, 1987; patentee; contbr. articles to profl. jours. Served to lt. U.S. Army, 1953-55. Decorated Bronze AFCEA medal. Fellow IEEE (life), IEE (London/assoc.); mem. Assn. Old Crows (charter mem., bd. dirs. 1972-74, sr. Gold cert. merit 1990), Am. Radio Relay League, Masons, Navy League, Army Assn. Republican. Avocations: radio amateur, color photography, stamp collecting, antique radios.

LIPSON, LESLIE MICHAEL, political science educator; b. London, Nov. 14, 1912; came to U.S., 1947, naturalized, 1953; s. Alexander and Caroline Rachel (Goodman) L.; m. Helen M. Fruchtman, Oct. 2, 1980; 1 son by previous marriage, David Roger. B.A., Oxford U., 1935, M.A., 1945; Ph.D., U. Chgo., 1938. Prof. polit. sci. and dir. Sch. Public Adminstrn., Victoria U., Wellington, N.Z., 1939-46; prof. polit. sci. Swarthmore (Pa.) Coll., 1947-49, U. Calif., Berkeley, 1950-83; chmn. undergrad. program dept. polit. sci. U. Calif., 1977-80, prof. emeritus, 1980—; mem. faculty Fromm Inst. for Lifelong Learning, San Francisco, 1983—, acad. advisor, 1989—; civilian guest lectr. Nat. War Coll., Washington, 1948-75, Air War Coll., Montgomery, Ala., 1954-86; prof. polit. sci. UN program tech. assistance in L.Am., Fundacao Getulio Vargas, Rio de Janeiro, 1953; vis. prof. Columbia U., 1961, Stanford U., 1963, U. Copenhagen, 1970-71, also others; vis. lectr. Oxford U., Inst. Commonwealth Studies, London, U. Inst. Internat. Higher Studies, Geneva, U. Pavia, U. Zagreb, also others; panelist, reporter Brit. Press on PBS program World Press, Sta. KQED-TV, San Francisco, 1963-75; seminar leader Danforth Assocs. Conf., Estes Park, Colo., 1970; panelist weekly radio program World Affairs Coun., 1986-87; cons. in field. Author: The American Governor, 1939, reprinted, 1968, The Politics of Equality, 1948, The Great Issues of Politics, 1954, 10th edit., 1997, The Democratic Civilization, 1964, The Ethical Crises of Civilization, 1993, (with Elizabeth M. Drews) Values and Humanity, 1971, I Do Not Itch to Etch, Views in Verse, 1987, Not Yet the Yeti: Rhymes for the Times, 1997; contbr. articles to profl. jours. and Ency. Brit. Trustee World Affairs Council No. Calif., 1979-87. Served with Home Guard, 1941-44, N.Z. Commonwealth Fund fellow Harkness Found., 1935-38; Rockefeller fellow, 1955-56, 59-60, grantee, 1967. Mem. NOW, UN Assn. (bd. dirs. San Francisco chpt. 1988-92). Democrat. Jewish. Home: 25 Stoddard Way Berkeley CA 94708-1719 Office: U Calif Dept Polit Sci Berkeley CA 94720

LIPSON, MELVIN ALAN, technology and business management consultant; b. Providence, R.I., June 1, 1936; s. Nathan and Esta (Blumenthal) L.; m. Jacqueline Ann Barclay, July 2, 1961; children: Donna, Robert, Michelle, Judith. BS, U. R.I., 1957; PhD, Syracuse U., 1963. Chemist ICI Organics, Providence, 1963, Philip A. Hunt Chem. Co., Lincoln, R.I., 1964-67; rsch. mgr. Philip A. Hunt Chem. Co., Lincoln, 1967-69; tech. dir. Dynachem div. Morton Thiokol Inc., Tustin, Calif., 1969-72; v.p. Morton Thiokol Inc., Tustin, 1979-82, sr. v.p., 1972-82, 1982-85, exec. v.p., 1985-86, pres., 1986-89; v.p. tech. devel. Morton Internat. Inc., Chgo., 1989-92; pres. Lipson Assocs., Newport Beach, Calif., 1993-96; chmn. bd., CEO Aurelon, Inc., Huntington Beach, Calif., 1993-96, Pivotech., Inc., Newport Beach, Calif., 1996—. Home and Office: 1715 Plaza Del Sur Newport Beach CA 92661-1417

LIPSON, STEVEN MARK, cliniical virologist, educator; b. Bklyn., May 25, 1945; s. Jonas and Ana (Soltz) L.; m. Heleen P. Bleiweiss, Apr. 21, 1971; children: Tracy J., Jennifer B. BS in Biology, Long Island U., 1967; MS in Microbiology, Marine Sci., C.W. Post Coll., 1972; PhD in Cell Biology, Microbiology, N.Y.U., 1981. Radioactive materials cert., N.Y. State Dept. Health. Rsch. assoc. immunology lab. Dept. Neoplastic Diseases Mt. Sinai Sch. Medicine, N.Y.C., 1980-84; chief virology lab., assoc. dir. divsn. microbiology Nassau County Med. Ctr. Dept. of Pathology, East Meadow, N.Y., 1984-90; dir. virology lab., asst. prof. microbiology in medicine North Shore U. Hosp. N.Y.U. Sch. of Medicine, Manhasset, N.Y., 1990—; acting dir. Flow Cytometry/Cellular Immunology Lab. North Shore U. Hosp. N.Y.U. Sch. of Medicine, Manhasset, 1995—; cons. Enzo Biochem, N.Y.C., Becton, Dickenson and Co., Research Triangle Park, N.C., Roche Diagnostic Systems, Nutley, N.J., BioMerieux Vitek, Inc., Rockland, Mass; mem. profl. adv. panel Med. Lab. Advisor, 1994—, adjunct edtl. bd. Clin. Reviews in Microbiology, 1995, Manual of Clin. Microbiology, 1995. Author: Clinical Microbiology Procedures Manual (Virology), 1993; contbr. articles to 42 profl. peer reviewed publs.; presenter over 60 abstracts at sci. meetings. Vol. lectr. Kiwanis Club, Long Island, 1985-90; vol. N.Y. Hall of Sci., Queens, 1996. Mem. Am. Soc. for Microbiology (N.Y. City Br.), Nat. Soc. for Microbiology, Long Island Infectious Dis. Soc. Avocations: stamp collecting, swimming, riflery, travel, restaurants. Office: North Shore U Hosp NYU Sch Medicine Labs Dept 300 Community Dr Manhasset NY 11030-3801

LIPSTEIN, ROBERT A., lawyer; b. Wilmington, Del., Dec. 6, 1954; s. Eugene Joseph and Leona (Feld) L.; m. Cheryl A. Artibee-Wedlake, July 30, 1978; children: Rebecca Lynn, Matthew Wedlake. BA in Econs., Stanford U., 1975, JD, 1978. Bar: D.C. 1978, U.S. Dist. Ct. D.C., 1979, U.S. Ct. Appeals (D.C. cir.) 1980, U.S. Ct. Internat. Trade, 1984, U.S. Ct. Appeals (fed. cir.), U.S. Supreme Ct. 1990. Assoc. Morgan, Lewis & Bockius, Washington, 1978-84, Coudert Bros., Washington, 1984-86; ptnr. Coudert Bros., 1987-94; mng. ptnr. Lipstein, Jaffe & Lawson, L.L.P., 1994—. Mem. ABA (antitrust sect.), D.C. Bar Assn., Phi Beta Kappa. Avocations: golf, wood working, Tae Kwon Do (black belt). Home: 511 Stonington Rd Silver Spring MD 20902-1545 Office: Lipstein Jaffe & Lawson LLP 1615 M St NW Ste 710 Washington DC 20036-3220

LIPSTONE, HOWARD HAROLD, television production executive; b. Chgo., Apr. 28, 1928; s. Lewis R. and Ruth B. (Fischer) L.; m. Jane A. Nudelman, Apr. 7, 1957; children—Lewis, Gregory. BA in Cinema, U. So. Calif., 1950. Asst. to gen. mgr. Sta. KTLA, Los Angeles, 1950-54; program dir. Sta. KABC-TV, Los Angeles, 1955-61, film and program dir., 1961-63; exec. asst. to pres., exec. producer Selmur Prodns., Inc. subs. ABC-TV, Los Angeles, 1963-69; exec. v.p. Ivan Tors Films and Studios, Inc., 1969-70; pres. Alan Landsburg Prodns., Inc., Los Angeles, 1970-85; pres., chief oper. officer The Landsburg Co., Los Angeles, 1985—. Mem. NATAS, Soc. Motion Picture and TV Engrs., Motion Picture Acad. Arts and Scis., Radio Club Am. Office: The Landsburg Co 11811 W Olympic Blvd Los Angeles CA 90064-1113

LIPTON, ALLEN DAVID, retail executive; b. Bklyn., Aug. 10, 1940; s. Moses Meyer and Pearl (Schiff) L.; m. Nanci Mayer, Feb. 24, 1963 (div. 1991); 1 child, Dawn Natalie; m. Vicky Jordan, Sept. 9, 1995. AAS, N.Y.C. Community Coll., 1961. Salesman Bakers Shoe Store, N.Y.C., 1961, Fabrex, N.Y.C., 1962-63, Sporteens, N.Y.C., 1963; asst. buyer Hammacher & Schlemmer, N.Y.C., 1961-62, Gimbels Dept. Store, N.Y.C., 1963-65; area mgr. Gimbels Dept. Store, Paramus, N.J., 1965-69; corp. buyer Stone & Thomas Dept. Store, Charleston, W.Va., 1969—; seminar spokesperson Draperies & Window Coverings Mag., N. Palm Beach, Fla., 1984; chmn. steering com. Fredrick Atkins Wholesale Buying Office. Author: Drapery and Curtain Department Store Training Manual, 1972, Buying Curtains and Draperies, 1987, Buying Carpet, Broadloom and Orentical Rugs, 1991. Firefighter, Parsippany-Troy Hills (N.J.) Vol. Fire Assn., 1966-69. With N.Y. Nat. Guard, 1962-68. Recipient Leadership award Kirsch Co., 1983. Mem. Kanawha Valley Aquarium Soc. (pres. 1972, v.p. 1973, treas. 1975), Lions Club (v.p. Charleston 1996-97), Phi Kappa Rho (sec. 1960). Democrat. Jewish. Avocations: fishing, collecting and breeding tropical fish, collecting stamps and fish, coins. Home: 1619 Quarrier St Apt A Charleston WV 25311-2136 Office: Stone & Thomas Dept Store Lee at Dickinson Charleston WV 25326

LIPTON, BRONNA JANE, marketing communications executive; b. Newark, May 10, 1951; d. Julius and Arlene (Davis) L.; m. Sheldon Robert Lipton, Sept. 23, 1984. BA in Spanish, Northwestern U., 1973. Tchr. Spanish Livingston (N.J.) H.S., 1973-78; profl. dancer Broadway theater, film, TV, N.Y.C., 1978-82; v.p., mgr. Hispanic mktg. svcs. Burson-Marsteller Pub. Rels., N.Y.C., 1982-89; exec. v.p. Lipton Comm. Group, Inc., N.Y.C., 1989—, Latin Reports, 1996—, LCG Latino, 1997—; mem. minority initiatives task force Am. Diabetes Assn., Alexandria, Va., 1987-90, mem. pub. rels. com., 1990-91, mem. visibility and image task force, 1991-92, bd. dirs. N.Y. Downstate affiliate, chmn. visibility and image com., 1992-93. Mem. rev. panel Hispanic Designers, Inc. Recipient Pinnacle award Am. Women in Radio and TV (N.Y. Chpt.), 1984, Value Added awards Burson-Marsteller, N.Y.C., 1982, 83, 84. Mem. Hispanic Pub. Rels. Assn. Avocations: ballet, jazz dance, tennis, fgn. travel, birding. Home: 1402 Chapel Hill Rd Mountainside NJ 07092-1405

LIPTON, CHARLES, public relations executive; b. N.Y.C., May 11, 1928; s. Jack B. and Bertha (Lesser) L.; m. Audrey Williams, Nov. 11, 1951; children—Susan, Jack. AB, Harvard U., 1948. Market researcher Cecil & Presbury, Inc., N.Y.C., 1948-49; spl. events dir. 20th Century Fox Film Corp., N.Y.C., 1949-52; account exec. Ruder & Finn, Inc., N.Y.C., 1953-58; v.p. Ruder & Finn, Inc., 1958-63, sr. v.p., 1963-69, vice-chmn., 1969-95; sr. counsel, 1995—, also bd. dirs.; guest lectr. Boston U., 1967-68. Mem. coun. Ctr. for Vocat. Arts, Norwalk, Conn., 1966-74; trustee Norwalk Jewish Ctr., 1966-70; treas., mem. exec. com. Norwalk Symphony Soc., 1972-85; chmn. parent's counsel Washington U., St. Louis, 1976-77, trustee, 1977—. Mem. Am. Soc. Colon and Rectal Surgeons (trustee), Internat. Pub. Rels. Assn., USIA (pub. rels., pvt. sector com. 1988-93), Nat. Emphysema Soc. (trustee), Nat. Investor Rels. Inst., Harvard Club, Harvard Varsity Club. Home: 4502 Hazleton Ln Lake Worth FL 33467-8633 Office: Ruder Finn Inc 301 E 57th St Fl 3 New York NY 10022-2900

LIPTON, CHARLES JULES, lawyer; b. N.Y.C., Oct. 26, 1931; m. Alice Garretson; children: Leah Jane, Emma Ely. AB, Syracuse (N.Y.) U., 1951; LLB, Yale U., 1954; LLM in Internat. Law, NYU, 1966. Bar: N.Y. 1954, U.S. Supreme Ct. 1958. Assoc. Hughes, Hubbard and Reed, N.Y.C., 1954-55; judge advocate, trial atty. U.S. Dept. of Air Force, Washington, 1955-57; assoc. Breed, Abbott and Morgan, N.Y.C., 1957-62; counsel Freeport Minerals Co., N.Y.C., 1962-69; interregional legal advisor UN, N.Y.C., 1969-74; sr. cons. UN Center on Transnational Corps., N.Y.C., 1976-90, chief legal adviser, 1991-92; spl. counsel Am. Indian Coun. Energy Resource Tribes, Denver, 1978-84; bd. dirs. Havelock Asbestos Mines (Swaziland) Ltd., Sun Internat. of Lesotho Pty., Ltd., Dokolowayo Diamond Mines Ltd., Emaswati Coal Pty., Ltd.; cons. U.S. Commr. of Edn., 1965; legal advisor, cons. numerous govts. and internat. orgns.; comml. legal advisor to the Govt. of Lesotho, 1967—; legal advisor to Kings of Swaziland, 1969—; adj. prof. law NYU, 1975-88; vis. prof. law U. Swaziland, 1977-88, Nat. U. Lesotho, 1984-88; vis. lectr. in law U. Calif., Berkeley, 1974-82; vis. fellow U. NSW, Sydney, Australia, 1987; lectr. in field, participant in numerous workshops; Fulbright prof. law U. Tartu (Estonia), 1996. Contbr. articles to profl. jours. Capt. USAF, 1955-57. Mem. Am. Soc. Internat. Law, Am. Fgn. Law Assn., ABA (chmn. African law com. sect. on internat. and comparative law 1964-67), Assn. of Bar of City of N.Y., African Law Assn. in Am. (bd. dirs. 1969-72. Home: 1136 Fifth Ave New York NY 10128-0122

LIPTON, CLIFFORD CARWOOD, retired glass company executive; b. Huntington, W.Va., Jan. 30, 1920; s. Clifford Carwood and Zerelda (Adkins) L.; m. Alyce Jo Anne Eckley, Jan. 3, 1943 (dec. July 1975); children: Clifford Carwood III, Thomas Denton, Michael Forrester; m. Marie Hope Mahoney, May 26, 1976. B in Engring. Sci., Marshall U., 1948; postgrad. exec. mgmt. program, Pa. State U., 1959. Staff engr. Owens-Ill. Inc., Huntington, 1948-52; supr. engring. Owens-Ill. Inc., Streator, Ill., 1952-55; chief engr. divsn. Owens-Ill. Inc., Toledo, 1955-66; gen. mgr. Giralt Laporta SA, Madrid, 1966-71; dir. mfg. United Glass Ltd., London, 1971-74; mfg. and tech. dir. Owens-Ill. Internat., Geneva, 1974-82; dir. internat. devel. Owens-Ill. Inc., Toledo, 1982-83; ret., 1983; cons. Owens-Ill., Inc., China, Greece and U.S., 1983-85, Internat. Exec. Svc. Corps., 1986—. Mem. sch. bd. Am. Sch., Barcelona, Spain, 1966-67, Madrid, 1967-70; pres. Highland Trails Home-owners Assn., Southern Pines, N.C., 1987-93. 1st lt. Parachute Inf., U.S. Army, 1942-45. Mem. Benevolent and Protective Order Elks, 101st Airborne Divsn. Assn. Republican. Presbyterian. Avocations: travel, golf, reading, music, model engineering. Home: 104 Selkirk Trl Southern Pines NC 28387-7230

LIPTON, DANIEL BERNARD, conductor; b. Paris; s. Gerald David and Germaine (Chaison) L.; m. Olga Lucia Gaviria, Mar. 7, 1983 (div. Oct. 1985). BS in Music, Juilliard Sch., 1963, Mannes Coll., 1965; postgrad., Accademia Chigiana, Siena, Italy, 1965, 67, Ecole Normale Superieure, Paris, 1967. Artistic dir. Opera Hamilton, Ont., Can., 1986; prof. McMaster U., Hamilton, 1988. Condr. Am. Ballet Theater, 1968, Denver Symphony Orch., 1969-70, Teatro Comunale, Firenze, Italy, 1970-71, Teatro Comunale, Bologna, Italy, 1972, Opernhaus Zürich, 1973-75, Teatro del Liceo, Barcelona, Spain, 1979-82, Grand Theatre, Dijon, France, 1980-81, 83, Theatre de l'Opera, Nice, 1982-83, 87, Châtelet, Paris, Teatro de la Zarzuela, Madrid, Teatro La Fenice, Venezia, 1982, Utah Opera, 1983-85, Orch. de l'Opera de Paris, 1986, Bayerische Staatsoper, München, Germany, 1986-87, National theater Mannheim, 1988, 90, Teatro Regio di Parma, Teatro San Carlo, Napoli, Opera in Seoul, Republic of Korea, 1988, world premiere G.C. Menotti's Il Giorno di Nozze, Oper Dortmund, Festival in Jesi, Italy, Opera Buffalo, Oper Köln; artistic dir. Orquesta Sinfonica de Colombia, Opera de Colombia, 1975-83, Opera Hamilton, 1986—, San Antonio Internat. Festival of Arts, 1986-89, dir. music Houston Grand Opera, 1984-85, Spoleto Festival, 1991, Deutsche Oper, Berlin, 1992—; gen. music dir. Dessau, Germany, 1992; music dir., prin. condr. Anhaltische Philharmonie, Germany, 1992-96, Hannover Opera, 1995, Wiesbaden Opera, 1996, Vlaamse Opera, 1996, Nürnberg Opera, 1997, others. Decorated Cruz de Boyaca (Colombia); recipient award Italian Govt.; named Best Condr. of Yr., Opernwelt, 1993, 94; Besançon conducting grantee, Fulbright grantee. Office: Opera Hamilton, 110 King St W, Hamilton, ON Canada L8P 4S6

LIPTON, ERIC, reporter. With Hartford Courant; now county govt. reporter The Washington Post, Fairfax, Va. Recipient Pulitzer Prize for explanatory journalism, 1992. Office: The Washington Post Fairfax County Bureau 4020 University Dr Ste 220 Fairfax VA 22030-6802

LIPTON, JOAN ELAINE, advertising executive; b. N.Y.C., July 12; 1 child, David Dean. B.A., Barnard Coll. With Young & Rubicam, Inc., N.Y.C., 1949-52, Robert W. Orr & Assocs., N.Y.C., 1952-57, Benton & Bowles, Inc., N.Y.C., 1957-64; assoc. dir. Benton & Bowles, Ltd., London, Eng., 1964-68; with McCann-Erickson, Inc. (advt. agy.), N.Y.C., 1968-85; v.p. McCann-Erickson, Inc (advt. agy.), 1970-79, sr. v.p., creative dir., 1979-85; pres. Martin & Lipton Advt. Inc., 1985—. Mem. Bus. Coun. for the UN Decade for Women, 1977-78; bd. vis. PhD program in bus. CUNY, 1986—. Named Woman of Yr. Am. Advt. Fedn., 1974; recipient Honors award Ohio U. Sch. Journalism, 1976; Matrix award, 1979; YWCA award for women achievers, 1979; named Advt. Woman of Yr., 1984. Mem. Advt. Women N.Y. (1st v.p. 1975-76, v.p. Found. 1977-78), Women's Forum (bd. dirs. 1988-90), Women in Communications (pres. N.Y. chpt. 1974-76, named Nat. Headliner 1976). Office: 163 E 62nd St New York NY 10021-7613

LIPTON, LEAH, art historian, educator, museum curator; b. Kearny, N.J., Mar. 22, 1928; d. Abraham and Rose (Berman) Shneyer; m. Herbert Lipton, Sep. 19, 1951 (dec. 1979); children: David, Ivan, Rachel. BA, Douglass Coll. Rutgers U., New Brunswick, N.J., 1949; MA, Harvard U., Cambridge, Mass., 1950; postgrad., Harvard U., 1970-73, Wellesley Coll., 1970-73. Photo, library researcher Mus. Fine Arts, Boston, 1950-53, lectr., division edn., 1965-70; instr. Boston Coll., 1968-69; faculty, full prof. Framingham State Coll., Mass., 1969-94; ret., 1994; interim dir. Danforth Mus. Art, 1994-95; mem. bd. trustees Danforth Mus. Art, Framingham Mass., 1975—; curator Am. art Danforth Mus. Art, Framingham Mass., 1994—; chair exhibitions Com.; Collections Com. Danforth Mus., Framingham Mass., 1988, guest curator Nat. Portrait, Wash., 1985. Author: Book, 1985, Exhibition Catalogues, 1988-94; contbr. articles to profl. jours., 1981—. Co-Founder Danforth Mus. Art., Mass. 1973-75. Recipient Distinguished Service award Framingham State Coll., Mass. 1978, 87. Mem. Coll. Art Assn., Am. Studies Assn. Office: Danforth Mus of Art 123 Union Ave Framingham MA 01702-8223

LIPTON, LESTER, ophthalmologist, entrepreneur; b. N.Y.C., Mar. 14, 1936; s. George and Rita (Steinberg) L.; m. Harriet Arfa, June 25, 1960; children: Sherri, Brandi, Shawn. BA, NYU, 1959; MD, Chgo. Med. Sch. 1964. Rsch. fellow Chgo. Med. Sch., 1959-60; intern Brookdale Hosp. Ctr., Bklyn., 1964-65; resident Harlem Eye and Ear Hosp., N.Y.C., 1965-68; assoc. attending Polyclinic French hosps., N.Y.C., 1968-75; asst. attending physician, ophthalmologist, surg. instr. St. Clare's Hosp., N.Y.C., 1975—; attending ophthalmologist Cabrini Med. Ctr., N.Y.C., 1982—, St. Vincent's Hosp., N.Y.C., 1995—; founder Lipton Eye Clinic, N.Y.C., 1981—; v.p. Van Arfa Realty, N.Y.C., 1984-88; pres. H&L Realty, Suffern, N.Y., 1981—; mem. bd. dirs. Salisbury (Conn.) Pub. Health Nursing Assn. Mem. U.S. Congl. Adv. Bd.; mem. bd. deacons Congregationalist Ch. With AUS, 1956-58. Named Internat. Amigo, OAS; recipient Presdl. Citation for outstanding community svc., 1991. Mem. N.Y. Med. Soc., Am. Assn. Individual Investors, Bronx High Sch. Sci. Alumni Assn., Sharon Country Club, United Shareholders Assn., Internat. Platform Assn., Wider Quaker Fellowship, Vanderbilt U. Cabinet Club. Republican. Home: Interlaken Estates Lakeville CT 06039 also: 1199 Park Ave New York NY 10128-1711 Office: Lipton Eye Clinic 51 E 90th St New York NY 10128-1205

LIPTON, LOIS JEAN, lawyer; b. Chgo., Jan. 14, 1946; d. Harold Lypski and Bernice (Reiter) Farber L.; m. Bertram Kraft, June 13, 1968 (div. 1977); 1 child, Rachel; m. R. Peter Carey, May 30, 1978; 1 child, Sara. B.A., U. Mich., 1966; J.D. summa cum laude, DePaul Coll. Law, Chgo., 1974; post-grad. Sheffield U., Eng., 1966. Bar: Ky. 1974, U.S. Dist. Ct. (we. dist.) Ky. 1974, U.S. Ct. Appeals (6th cir.) 1974, Ill. 1975, U.S. Dist. Ct. (no. dist.) Ill., 1975, U.S. Ct. Appeals (7th cir.) 1976. Staff counsel Roger Baldwin Found. of ACLU, Inc., Chgo., 1975-79, dir. reproductive rights project, 1979-83; atty. McDermott, Will & Emery, Chgo., 1984-86, G.D. Searle, Skokie, Ill., 1988-90; sr. atty. AT&T, Chgo., 1990—. Del White House Conf. on Families, Mpls., 1980. Recipient Durfee award, 1984. Mem. Am. Judicature Soc., ACLU (bd. dirs. Ill.), Chgo. Bar Assn., Chgo. Council Lawyers. Office: AT&T 227 W Monroe St Chicago IL 60606-5016

LIPTON, MARTIN, lawyer; b. N.J., June 22, 1931; s. Samuel D. and Fannie L.; m. Susan Lytle, Feb. 17, 1982; children: James, Margaret, Katherine, Samantha. BS in Econs., U. Pa., 1952; LLB, NYU, 1955. Bar: N.Y. 1956. Ptnr. Wachtell Lipton Rosen & Katz, N.Y.C., 1965—; mem. coun. Am. Law Inst. Trustee NYU; pres. bd. trustees NYU Law Sch.; hon. chmn. Jerusalem Found.; chmn. bd. dirs. Prep for Prep; dir. Inst. Jud. Adminstrn. Office: Wachtell Lipton Rosen & Katz 51 W 52nd St New York NY 10019-6119

LIPTON, RICHARD M., lawyer; b. Youngstown, Ohio, Feb. 25, 1952; s. Sanford Y. Lipton and Sarah (Kentor) Goldman; m. Jane Brennan, May 24, 1981; children—Thomas, Anne, Martin, Patricia. B.A., Amherst Coll., 1974; J.D., U. Chgo., 1977. Bar: Ill. 1977, D.C. 1978, U.S. Dist. Ct. (no. dist.) Ill. 1979, U.S. Ct. Appeals (D.C. and 7th cirs.) 1979, U.S. Tax Ct. 1977, U.S. Ct. Claims 1979. Law clk. to judge Hall, U.S. Tax Ct., Washington, 1977-79; assoc. Isham, Lincoln & Beale, Chgo., 1979-83; ptnr. Ross & Hardies, Chgo., 1983-86; v.p. Pegasus Broadcasting, Chgo., 1986-88; ptnr. Sonnenschein Nath & Rosenthal, Chgo., 1988—. Contbr. articles to profl. jours. Recipient Order of Coif award U. Chgo. Law Sch., 1977. Fellow Am. Coll. Tax Counsel; mem. ABA (coun. dir. 1990-93, vice chair taxation sect. 1993-96), Chgo. Bar Assn. (subcom. chair, chair fed. taxation com. 1991-92). Republican. Clubs: Union League, Mich. Shores, Conway Farms. Office: Sonnenschein Nath Rosenthal 233 S Wacker Dr Ste 8000 Chicago IL 60606-6342

LIPTON, ROBERT STEVEN, lawyer; b. N.Y.C., May 12, 1946; s. Max and Mildred (Goodman) L.; m. Stephanie F. Kass, Aug. 8, 1971. BA, NYU, 1967, JD, 1971. Bar: N.Y. 1972, U.S. Ct. Appeals (2d cir.) 1972, U.S. Dist. Ct. (so. dist.) N.Y. 1973, U.S. Supreme Ct. 1975. Assoc. Curtis, Mallet-Prevost, Colt & Mosle, N.Y.C., 1971-80, ptnr., 1980—. Editor NYU Law Rev., 1969-71. Mem. ABA, Fed. Bar Council, N.Y. State Bar Assn., Assn. of Bar of City of N.Y., Phi Beta Kappa. Club: India House (N.Y.C.). Office: Curtis Mallet-Prevost Colt & Mosle 101 Park Ave New York NY 10178

LIPTON, STUART ARTHUR, neuroscientist; b. Danbury, Conn., Jan. 11, 1950; s. Harold and Evelyn Ruth (Stein) L.; m. Elisabeth Kay Ament, Aug. 10, 1980; children: Jennifer Ann, Jeffrey Harris. BA, Cornell U., 1971; MD, U. Pa., 1977, PhD, 1977; postgrad., Cornell U., 1971, U. Oxford (Eng.), 1972, Harvard U., 1974-76. Diplomate Am. Bd. Psychiatry and Neurology. Intern Beth Israel Hosp. and Harvard Med. Sch., Boston, 1977-78; resident in neurology Beth Israel, Brigham and Women's, Children's Hosp., Boston, 1978-80, chief neurology resident, 1980-81; research fellow in neurobiology Harvard Med. Sch., Boston, 1980-83, instr. in neurology, 1981-83, asst. prof. neurology and neurosci., 1983-87, assoc. prof. neurology and neurosci., 1987-97; chief Cerebravascular and Neurosci. Inst. Brigham and Women's Hosp., Harvard Med. Sch., Boston, 1997—; dir. cellular and molecular neurosci. Children's Hosp., Harvard Med. Sch.; neurologist Mass. Gen. Hosp., Brigham and Women's Hosp., Beth Israel Hosp., Children's Hosp., Boston. Contbr. articles to profl. jours.; patentee in field; composer of popular songs including one that sold 1.5 million copies, 1968. Established investigator Am. Heart Assn., 1988-93. Hartford Found. fellow, 1981, 82, 83, 84, NIH fellow, 1984, 85, 86, 87, 88, 89; NIH grantee, 1984—; Rhodes scholar Oxford (Eng.) U., 1971-72; recipient Pattison award, 1989; Nobel lectr. Karolinska Inst., 1994. Mem. AAAS, Am. Acad. Neurology, Am. Neurol. Assn., Soc. for Neurosci., Assn. for Rsch. in Vision and Opthalmology, Biophys. Soc., Phi Beta Kappa, Alpha Omega Alpha. Avocations: musical composition, soccer. Office: Childrens Hosp & Harvard Med Sch 300 Longwood Ave Boston MA 02115-5724

LIPTON, SUSAN LYTLE, investment banker, lawyer; b. Ft. Warren, Wyo., Oct. 23, 1945; d. James and Bette Lytle; m. Martin Lipton, Feb. 17, 1982. AB, U. Miami, 1967, JD, 1970; LLM, Harvard U., 1971. Bar: Fla. 1970, N.Y. 1984. From assoc. to ptnr. Greenberg Traurig Askew, Miami, Fla., 1970-77; from assoc. to v.p. Goldman Sachs & Co., N.Y.C., 1977-81; from v.p. to mng. dir. L.F. Rothschild, Unterberg, Towbin, N.Y.C., 1981-86; trustee Jewish Mus., 1986—, Brearley Sch., 1991—, Wildlife Conservation Soc., 1991—; trustee, pres. Jewish Communal Fund, 1992—.

LIPTZIN, BENJAMIN, psychiatrist; b. N.Y.C., Sept. 17, 1945; s. David Murray and Mollie (Brody) L.; m. Sharon Leslie Rothstein, June 10, 1968; children: Shoshanna, Daniel, Deborah. BA, Yale U., 1966; MD, U. Rochester, N.Y., 1971. Diplomate Am. Bd. Psychiatry and Neurology. Resident in psychiatry U. Va. Hosp., Charlottesville, 1971-74; med. officer NIMH, Rockville, Md., 1974-78; dir. geriatric psychiatry McLean Hosp., Belmont, Mass., 1978-89, asst. gen. dir., 1989-90; chief dept. psychiatry Baystate Med. Ctr., Springfield, Mass., 1990—; prof., dep. chmn. dept. psychiatry Tufts U. Sch. Medicine, 1990—. Contbr. articles to profl. jours. With USPHS, 1972-78. Recipient Acad. award NIMH, 1983. Fellow Am. Psychiat. Assn. (trustee-at-large 1992-95), Gerontol. Soc. Am.; mem. AMA, Am. Coll. Psychiatrists. Democrat. Jewish. Office: Baystate Med Ctr Dept Psychiatry 140 High St Springfield MA 01199-1000

LIS, ANTHONY STANLEY, business administration educator; b. Easthampton, Mass., Aug. 11, 1918; s. Anthony Stanley and Anna Barbara (Kaczmarczyk) L.; m. Jane Ann Mikus, June 25, 1951 (dec.); children: Anthony, Judith A., Patricia Ann, Sandra J.; m. Sophie A. Pobieglo, June 24, 1983. B.S., Mass. State Coll., Salem, 1950; M.S., Okla. State U., 1951; Ph.D., U. Minn., 1961. Asst. prof. Okla. State U., Stillwater, 1951-55; assoc. prof. U. Tulsa, 1956-62; mem. faculty U. Okla., Norman, 1962-86, prof. bus. adminstrn., 1967-86, prof. emeritus, 1986—; vis. prof. Central Sch. Planning/Stats., Warsaw, Poland, 1984; del. II Congress Scholars of Polish Descent, Warsaw, 1979, III Congress, 1989 ; cons. to numerous bus. and govtl. agencies. Served with U.S. Army, 1937-40, 1942-46. Decorated Bronze Star; recipient Superior Profl. and Univ. Service award U. Okla., 1981; Summer fellow Found. Econ. Edn., 1954. Mem. Am. Bus. Comm. Assn., Polish Am. Hist. Assn., Adminstrv. Mgmt. Soc., Southwestern Social Sci. Assn., Delta Pi Epsilon, Beta Gamma Sigma, Delta Sigma Pi. Roman Catholic. Lodge: Lions. Home: 1827 Peter Pan St Norman OK 73072-5837 Office: U Okla Coll Bus Adminstrn Norman OK 73019

LIS, EDWARD FRANCIS, pediatrician, consultant; b. Chgo., Apr. 1, 1918; s. Stephen and Stephanie L.; m. Sonne Nadine Kowalsen, Apr. 3, 1944; children—Jeffrey Warren, James Bryan. Student, DePaul U., 1936-37; B.S., M.D., U. Ill. Pvt. practice Park Forest, Ill., 1949-51; faculty U. Ill. Coll. Medicine, 1951-90, prof. pediatrics, also dir. div. services crippled children, 1959-90, prof. emeritus, 1990—; dir. center handicapped children Univ. Hosp., U. Ill., 1955-90; cons. in field. Contbr. to profl. jours. Chmn. research adv. com. Children's Bur., HEW, 1964-67; mem. Ill. Commn. Children. Served to capt. AUS, 1944-46. Fellow Am. Acad. Pediatrics, Am. Pub. Health Assn.; mem. Sigma Xi. Home: 3003 Balmoral Cres Flossmoor IL 60422-1404

LISA, ISABELLE O'NEILL, law firm administrator, mergers and acquisitions executive; b. Phila., Mar. 12, 1934; d. Thomas Daniel and Margaret Marie (Hayes) O'Neill; m. Donald Julius Lisa, June 15, 1957; children: Richard Allan, Steven Gregory. Student, Harper Community Coll., Rolling Meadows, Ill., 1976, Scottsdale Community Coll., 1980, Ariz. State U., 1981-82. Cost control clk. Curtis Pub. Co., Phila., 1952-56; sec. United Ins. Co.,

Annapolis, Md., 1956-57; firm adminstr., legal sec. Law Offices Donald J. Lisa, Bloomingdale, Ill., 1987; legal sec. Lisa & Kubida, P.C., Phoenix, 1987-88, firm adminstr., 1987-89; firm adminstr. Lisa & Assocs., Phoenix, 1989-90, Lisa & Lisa, Phoenix, 1990-91, Lisa & Assocs., Scottsdale, Ariz., 1991-95, Law Offices of Donald J. Lisa, Scottsdale, 1995-96; v.p. adminstrn. Lisa & Co., Scottsdale, 1987-97; pres. IAWYA, Ltd., Scottsdale, 1996—; pres. IAWYA, Ltd., Scottsdale, 1996. Den mother Cub Scouts Am., Millburn, N.J., 1965; founder, pres. Pro-Tem Rutgers U. Law Wives Assn., 1962-63; bd. advisors Am. Inst., Phoenix, 1991—. Mem. NAFE, Maricopa County Bar Assn. (legal adminstrs. sect. 1992-95), Internat. Platform Assn., Rotary. Republican. Roman Catholic. Avocations: painting, drawing, graphic design, photography. Home and Office: 8661 E Carol Way Scottsdale AZ 85260

LISANBY, JAMES WALKER, retired naval officer; b. Princeton, Ky., Jan. 31, 1928; s. Alvin and Rebecca L.; m. Gladys Elnora Kemp, Nov. 18, 1951; children: Elizabeth Ann, Sarah Hollingsworth. B.S. in Elec. Engring, U.S. Naval Acad., 1950; Engrs. Degree in Naval Architecture, MIT, 1953-56; student, Program for Mgmt. Devel., Harvard U., 1967. Commd. ensign U.S. Navy, 1950, advanced through grades to rear adm., 1977; ship supt. Charleston Naval Shipyard, 1956-59; main propulsion asst. U.S.S. Antietam (CVS 36), 1959-61; asst. for ship materials, staff, comdr.-in-chief Atlantic Fleet, 1961-63; asst. for new constrn. cruisers and destroyers Naval Ship Systems Command, Dept. Navy, Washington, 1963-65; head procurement and prodn. br., fast deployment logistic ship project office Naval Ship Systems Command, Dept. Navy, 1965-68, exec. asst. to comdr., 1969-70; dir. indsl. engring. office of asst. sec. of navy, installations and logistics, 1968-69; supr. shipbldg. Pascagoula, Miss., 1970-73; asst. for ship design, office chief naval ops., 1973-74, project mgr. LHA class amphibious assault ships, 1974-77; comdr. Naval Ship Engring. Center Navy Dept., Washington, 1977-79; dep. comdr. ship design and integration Naval Sea Systems Command, Dept. Navy, Washington, 1979-81; prin. dep. acquisition Naval Sea Systems Command, Dept. Navy, 1981-83, ret., 1983; founder, pres. Naval Services Internat. Inc., Washington, 1983—, pres., chief exec. officer; chmn. Tech. Financing Inc. Recipient Engr. of Yr. award Soc. Mfg. Engrs., 1979; decorated Legion of Merit. Mem. Am. Soc. Naval Engrs. (nat. v.p. 1979-81), Soc. Naval Architects and Marine Engrs., Sigma Xi, Tau Beta Pi. Office: PO Box 15515 Arlington VA 22215-0515

LISBOA-FARROW, ELIZABETH OLIVER, public and government relations consultant; b. N.Y.C., Nov. 25, 1947; d. Eleuterio and Esperanza Oliver; student pvt. schs., N.Y.C.; m. Jeffrey Lloyd Farrow, Dec. 31, 1980; 1 child, Hamilton Oliver Farrow; 1 stepchild, Maximillian Robbins Farrow. With Harold Rand & Co. and various other public rels. firms, N.Y.C., 1966-75; dir. pub. rels. N.Y. Playboy Club and Playboy Clubs Internat., 1975-79; pres., CEO Lisboa Assocs., Inc., N.Y.C., 1979—; founder, pres. Lisboa Prodns., Inc., Washington, 1994—; counselor Am. Woman's Devel. Corp. Sec. Nat. Acad. Concert and Cabaret Arts; mem. nat. adv. coun. SBA, 1980-81, apptd., 1994—; exec. dir. Variety Club of Greater Washington, Inc., 1985-90, Children's Charity; bd. dirs. Variety Myoelectric Limb Bank Found., 1990-91; trustee Hispanic Coll. Fund, 1995—, vice chair, 1996—; vice chairperson bd. trustees Southea. U., 1996—; bd. dirs. Montgomery County Police Found., 1996—; mem. adv. bd. Indsl. Bank, N.A., 1996; bd. dirs. Montgomery County Police Found., 1996—; active Women and Heart Disease Task Force. Recipient Disting. award of Excellence SBA, 1992, Women Bus. Enterprise award U.S. Dept. Transp. Nat. Hwy. Transp. Safety Adminstrn., 1994, Excellence in Entrepreneurship award Dialogue on Diversity, Inc., 1995; named Pub. Rels. Woman of Yr., Women in Pub. Rels., Hispanic Bus. Woman of Yr., Nat. Hispanic Bus. Coun., 1996. Mem. SAG, NATAS, U.S. Hispanic C. of C. (Hispanic Businesswoman of Yr. 1996), Small Bus. Advisory Coun., U.S. C. of C. (Blue Chip Enterprise award 1993), Advt. Coun., Am. Heart Assn., Hispanic Bus. and Profl. Women's Assn., Ibero-Am. C. of C. (bd. dirs. 1993—, v.p. 1995—, pres. 1997—, Small Bus. award 1993, chair, pres. Greater Washington chpt. 1997—), City Club Washington. Office: 1317 F St NW Washington DC 20004-1105

LISCHER, LUDWIG FREDERICK, retired consultant, former utility company executive; b. Darmstadt, Germany, Mar. 1, 1915; came to U.S., 1923, naturalized, 1933; s. Ludwig J. and Paula (Stahlecker) L.; m. Helen Lucille Rentz, Oct. 1, 1938; 1 dau., Linda Sue. B.S. in Elec. Engring., Purdue U., 1937, D.Eng. (hon.), 1976. With Commonwealth Edison Co., Chgo., 1937-80; v.p. charge engring., research and tech. activities Commonwealth Edison Co., 1964-80; ret., 1980; cons. and mem. adv. com. to engring. tech. div. Oak Ridge Nat. Lab., 1980-84; cons. energy and electric utility fields; past mem. various tech. adv. coms. to fed. agys. and Edison Electric Inst.; past chmn. rsch. adv. com. Electric Power Rsch. Inst. Contbr. articles to profl. jours. Past bd. dirs. Chgo. Engring. and Sci. Center; former trustee Ill. Inst. Tech. Served to lt. col. AUS and USAAF, 1941-45. Fellow IEEE; mem. ASME, Nat. Acad. Engring., Am. Nuclear Soc., Tau Beta Pi, Eta Kappa Nu. Home: 441 N Park Blvd Apt 5A Glen Ellyn IL 60137-4646

LISÉE, JEAN-FRANÇOIS, political scientist, writer; b. Sherbrooke, Que., Can., Feb. 13, 1958; s. Jean-Claude and Andrée (Goulet) L.; m. Catherine Leconte, July 24, 1982. Degree in Law, U. Que., Montreal, 1979, M.Comm., 1990; postgrad., Ctr. De Formation Journalistes, Paris, 1982. Reporter Can. Press/Radio, Montreal, 1979-81; fgn. corr. Radio Canada/Radio Paris, 1982-85, La Presse (Montreal daily), L'Evénement (Paris weekly), Washington, 1985-89; sr. reporter L'Actualité Mag., Montreal, 1990-93; author/commentator Montreal, 1993-94; sr. advisor Prime Minister of Que., Montreal, Quebec City, 1994—. Author: In the Eye of the Eagle, 1990 (Gov. Gen.'s award for non-fiction 1991), Carrefour Amerique, 1990, Les Prétendants, 1993, Le Tricheur, 1994, Le Naufrageur, 1994, The Trickster, 1994. Recipient Prix Jules Fournier, Office de la Langue française, 1990. Office: Conseil Executif, 885 grande-Allée Est, Quebec City, PQ Canada G1A 1A2

LISENBY, DORRECE EDENFIELD, realtor; b. Sneads, Fla., Dec. 2, 1942; d. Neal McLendon and Linnie (McCroan) Edenfield; m. Wallace Lamar Lisenby, Nov. 18, 1961; children: Pamela Ann, Wallace Neal. BS in Tech. Bus. magna cum laude, Athens (Ala.) State Coll., 1991. Stenographer State of Fla., Tallahassee and Miami, Fla., 1960-62, Gulf Oil Corp., Coral Gables, Fla., 1962-64, Gulf Power Co., Pensacola, Fla., 1965-68; loan svc. asst. First Fed. Savs. and Loan Assn., Greenville, S.C., 1969-70; various real estate positions Greenville, 1978-85; adminstrv. asst. Charter Retreat Hosp., Decatur, Ala., 1986-91; realtor assoc. Ferrell Realty Plus, Inc., Tallahassee, Fla., 1995—. Mem. Am. Legion (Citizenship award 1957), Tallahassee Symphony Soc., Avondale Forest Cmty. Club (pres. Taylors, S.C. chpt. 1969), Taylor's Garden Club (pres. Taylor's chpt. 1975-76), P.E.O. Sisterhood, Killearn Ladies Club. Republican. Baptist. Avocations: reading, music, bridge, gardening. Home: 2925 Shamrock St S Tallahassee FL 32308-3226

LISH, GORDON, author, educator, editor; b. Hewlett, N.Y., Feb. 11, 1934; s. Philip and Regina (Deutsch) L.; m. Loretta Frances Fokes, Nov. 7, 1956 (div. May 1967); children: Jennifer, Rebecca, Ethan; m. Barbara Works, May 30, 1969 (dec. Sept. 8, 1994); 1 son, Atticus. LittD (hon.), SUNY, 1993. Editorial dir. Genesis West, 1961-65; editor in chief, dir. linguistic studies Behavioral Research Labs., Menlo Park, Calif., 1963-66; with Ednl. Devel. Corp., Palo Alto, 1966-69; fiction editor Esquire mag., N.Y.C., 1969-77; with Alfred A. Knopf, Inc., 1977-95; lectr. Yale U., 1970-74, guest fellow, 1974-80; tchr. fiction writing Columbia U., 1980—; prof. NYU Coll. Arts and Scis. Author fiction and non-fiction under several pen-names: English Grammar, 1964, The Gabbernot, 1965, Why Work, 1966, A Man's Work, 1967, New Sounds in American Fiction, 1969, Self-Imitation of Myself, 1997, Peru, 1997, Mourner at the Door, 1997; author: (short stories) What I Know So Far, 1981, 84, Mourner at the Door, 1988, The Selected Stories of Gordon Lish, 1996; author (novels): Dear Mr. Capote, 1983, Peru, 1986, Extravaganza, 1989, My Romance, 1991, Zimzum, 1993, Epigraph, 1996, Dear Mr. Capote, (revised), 1996, What I Know So Far, (revised), 1996, Peru (revised), 1997, Mourner at the Door (revised), 1997, Extravaganza (revised), 1997; editor: The Secret of Life of Our Times, 1973, All Our Secrets Are the Same, 1976; editor-in-chief The Quarterly, 1987-97; editor-in-chief Chrysalis Rev., 1959-61.

LISHER, JAMES RICHARD, lawyer; b. Aug. 28, 1947; s. Leonard B. and Mary Jane (Rafferty) L.; m. Martha Gettelfinger, June 16, 1973; children: Jennifer, James Richard II. AB, Ind. U., 1969, JD, 1975. Bar: Ind. 1975, U.S. Dist. Ct. (so. dist.) Ind. 1975. Assoc. Rafferty & Wood, Shelbyville, Ind., 1976, Rafferty & Lisher, Shelbyville, 1976-77; dep. prosecutor Shelby County Prosecutor's Office, Shelbyville, 1976-78; ptnr. Yeager, Lisher & Baldwin, Shelbyville, 1977-96; pvt. practice, Shelbyville, 1996—; pros. atty. Shelby County, Shelbyville, 1983-95. Speaker, faculty advisor Ind. Pros. Sch., 1986. Editor: (seminar manual) Traffic Case Defenses, 1982. Bd. dirs. Girls Club of Shelbyville, 1979-84, Bears of Blue River Festival, Shelbyville, 1982—. Recipient Citation of Merit, Young Lawyers Assn. Mem. Nat. Assn. of Criminals, State Bar Assn. (bd. dirs.), Ind. Pub. Defender Assn., Ind. State Bar Assn. (bd. dirs. young lawyer sect 1979-83, bd. dirs. gen. practice sect. 1996-97), Shelby County Bar Assn. (sec./treas. 1986, v.p. 1987, pres. 1988), Ind. Pros. Attys. Assn. (bd. dirs. 1985-95, sec./treas. 1987, v.p. 1988, pres.-elect 1989, pres. 1990), Masons, Elks, Lions. Democrat. Home: 106 Western Trce Shelbyville IN 46176-9765 Office: Courthouse Rm 303 Shelbyville IN 46176

LISHER, JOHN LEONARD, lawyer; b. Indpls., Sept. 19, 1950; s. Leonard Boyd and Mary Jane (Rafferty) L.; m. Mary Katherine Sturmon, Aug. 17, 1974. B.A. with honors in History, Ind. U., 1975, J.D., 1975. Bar: Ind. 1975. Dep. atty. gen. State of Ind., Indpls., 1975-78; asst. corp. counsel City of Indpls., 1978-81; assoc. Osborn & Hiner, Indpls., 1981-86; ptnr. Osborn, Hiner & Lisher, 1986—. Vol. Mayflower Classic, Indpls., 1981—; pres. Brendonwood Common Inc.; asst. vol. coord. Marion County Rep. Com., Indpls., 1979-80; vol. Don Bogard for Atty. Gen., Indpls., 1980, Steve Goldsmith for Prosecutor, Indpls., 1979, 83, Sheila Suess for Congress, Indpls., 1980. Recipient Outstanding Young Man of Am. award Jaycees, 1979, 85, Indpls. Jaycees, 1980. Mem. ABA, Ind. Bar Assn., Indpls. Bar Assn. (membership com.), Assn. Trial Lawyers Am., Ind. U. Alumni Assn., Hoosier Alumni Assn. (charter, founder, pres.), Ind. Trial Lawyers Assn., Ind. Def. Lawyers Assn., Ind. U. Coll. Arts and Scis. (bd. dirs. 1983-92, pres. 1986-87), Wabash Valley Alumni Assn. (charter), Founders Club, Presidents Club, Phi Beta Kappa, Eta Sigma Phi, Phi Eta Sigma, Delta Xi Alumni Assn. (charter, v.p., sec., Delta Xi chpt. Outstanding Alumnus award 1975, 76, 79, 83), Delta Xi Housing Corp. (pres.), Pi Kappa Alpha (midwest regional pres. 1977-86, parliamentarian nat. conv. 1982, del. convs. 1978-80, 82, 84, 86, trustee Meml. Found. 1986-91. Presbyterian. Avocations: reading; golf; jogging; Roman coin collecting. Home: 5725 Hunterglen Rd Indianapolis IN 46226-1019 Office: Osborn Hiner Lisher PC Ste 380 8330 Woodfield Crossing Indianapolis IN 46240-2494

LISI, MARY M., federal judge. BA, U. R.I., 1972; JD, Temple U., 1977. Tchr. history Prout Meml. High Sch., Wakefield, R.I., 1972-73; hall dir. U. R.I., 1973-74; law clerk to Prof. Jerome Sloan Temple U., Phila., 1975-76; law clerk U.S. Atty., Providence, R.I., 1976, Phila., 1976-77; asst. pub. defender R.I. Office Pub. Defender, 1977-81; asst. child advocate Office Child Advocate, 1981-82; also. pvt. practice atty. Providence, 1981-82; dir. office ct. appointed spl. advocate R.I. Family Ct., 1982-87; dep. disciplinary counsel office disciplinary counsel R.I. Supreme Ct., 1988-90, chief disciplinary counsel, 1990-94; mem. Select Com. to Investigate Failure of R.I. Share and Deposit Indemnity Corp., 1991-92. Recipient Providence 350 award, 1986, Meritorious Svc. to Children of Am. award, 1987. Office: Fed Bldg and US Courthouse 1 Exchange Ter Rm 113 Providence RI 02903-1720

LISIO, DONALD JOHN, historian, educator; b. Oak Park, Ill., May 27, 1934; s. Anthony and Dorothy (LoCelso) L.; m. Susanne Marie Swanson, Apr. 22, 1958; children: Denise Anne, Stephen Anthony. B.A., Knox Coll., 1956; M.A., Ohio U., 1958; Ph.D., U. Wis., 1965. Mem. faculty overseas div. U. Md., 1958-60; asst. prof. history Coe Coll., Cedar Rapids, Iowa, 1964-69, assoc. prof., 1969-74, prof., 1974—, chmn. dept., 1973-81, Henrietta Arnold prof. history, 1980—. Author: The President and Protest: Hoover, Conspiracy, and the Bonus Riot, 1974, Hoover, Blacks, and Lily-Whites: A Study of Southern Strategies, 1985; contbg. author: The War Generation, 1975; contbr. articles to hist. jours. Mem. exec. com. Cedar Rapids Com. Hist. Preservation, 1975-77. Served with U.S. Army, 1958-60. Recipient Outstanding Tchr. award Coe Coll., 1969, Charles J. Lynch Outstanding Teaching award Coe Coll., 1991, Favorite Prof. award, 1996; William F. Vilas rsch. fellow U. Wis., 1963-64; NEH fellow, 1969-70, rsch. fellow, 1984-85; Am. Coun. Learned Socs. grantee, 1971-72, fellow, 1977-78; U.S. Inst. of Peace rsch. grantee, 1990. Mem. Orgn. Am. Historians, Am. Hist. Assn., AAUP, ACLU. Roman Catholic. Home: 4203 Twin Ridge Ct SE Cedar Rapids IA 52403-3950 Office: Coe Coll Cedar Rapids IA 52402

LISKA, GEORGE, political science educator, author; b. Pardubice, Czechoslovakia, June 30, 1922; came to U.S., 1949, naturalized, 1957; s. Bedrich and Karla (Slezakova) L.; m. Suzy Colombier, June 30, 1962; children: Ian Pierre, Anne Fernande. Dr.Jr., Charles U., Prague, Czechoslovakia, 1948; Ph.D. in Polit. Sci, Harvard U., 1955. Sec. to sec. gen. Czechoslovak Ministry Fgn. Affairs, 1946-48; exec. asst. Council Free Czechoslovakia, Washington, 1949-52; asst. prof. polit. sci. U. Chgo., 1958-61; prof. polit. sci. Johns Hopkins U. and Sch. Advanced Internat. Studies, Washington; also research assoc. Johns Hopkins' Washington Ctr. Fgn. Policy Research (succeeded by Fgn. Policy Inst.), 1964—. Author: International Equilibrium, 1957, The New Statecraft, 1960, Nations in Alliance, 1972, Europe Ascendant, 1964, Imperial America, 1967, War and Order, 1968, States in Evolution, 1973, Beyond Kinninger, 1975, Quest for Equilibrium, 1977, Career of Empire, 1978, Russia and World Order, 1980, Russia and the Road to Appeasement, 1982, Rethinking U.S.-Soviet Relations, 1987, Ways of Power, 1990, Fallen Dominions, 1990, The State and Foreign Policy, 1992, Return to the Heartland and Rebirth of the Old Order, 1994,. The Restoration of Politics, 1996. Recipient Sumner prize Harvard U., 1955. Office: 1740 Massachusetts Ave NW Washington DC 20036-1903 also: Johns Hopkins U Dept Polit Sci Baltimore MD 21218 *The impetus behind my efforts as a writer on and academic teacher of international relations has been the effort to convert the impossibility of actual participation—due to the loss of an official role in my native Czechoslovakia—into a deepened insight into the processes ultimately responsible for my expatriation.*

LISKAMM, WILLIAM HUGO, architect, urban planner, educator; b. N.Y.C., Sept. 10, 1931; s. William J. and Johanne (Herz) L.; m. Karen Elizabeth Nunn, May 1979; children: Amanda Nunn, Mason Nunn; children by previous marriage—Erika, Thea, Fiona. B.Arch., Pratt Inst., 1954; Fulbright scholar, Technische Hochschule, Stuttgart, Germany, 1954-55; M.Arch., Harvard, 1956. Project architect maj. archtl. and urban planning programs Calif. and N.Y., 1958-63; exec. v.p. Okamoto & Liskamm, Inc. (planners and architects), San Francisco, 1963-71; ind. archtl. and urban planning cons., 1971-74; pres. William H. Liskamm, AIA, AIP, Inc., 1974—; dir. planning Woodward-Clyde Consultants, San Francisco, 1978-79; dir. campus planning office U. Calif., Berkeley, 1984-90; asst. prof. dept. architecture Coll. Environ. Design, U. Calif. at Berkeley, 1963-69, vice chmn., 1965-67, vis. sr. lectr. U. Coll., London, 1967-68; chmn. bd. Archtl. Found. No. Calif.; chmn. design rev. bd. San Francisco Bay Conservation and Devel. Commn., State of Calif., 1970-80; chmn. archtl. adv. com. Golden Gate Bridge Hwy. and Transp. Dist., 1980-81; prof., advisor major planning and design competitions Nat. Endowment for the Arts. Author: Appearance and Design Element, California Coastal Plan, 1974. Served to 1st lt. C.E. AUS, 1956-58. Recipient awards for profl. projects HUD; Am. Inst. Planners award for San Francisco Urban Design Plan, 1972; Wheelwright fellow Harvard, 1967-68; Nat. Endowment for Arts grantee. Mem. AIA (coll. of fellows).

LISMAN, ERIC, publishing executive, lawyer. V.p. and gen. counsel Cahners Pub. Co., now sr. v.p., gen. counsel. Office: Cahners Pub Co 275 Washington St Newton MA 02158-1646*

LISNEK, MARGARET DEBBELER, artist, educator; b. Covington, Ky., Sept. 26, 1940; d. Aloysius Frank and Mary Elizabeth (Haubold) Debbeler; m. Schiller William Lisnek, June 26, 1966 (dec. May 1995); 1 child, Kimberly Anne. AA with honors, Mt. San Antonio Coll., 1985; BA in Art with honors, Calif. State U., Fullerton, 1991. Cert. substitute tchr. Freelance artist, 1985—; tchr. art Rorimer Elem. Sch., La Puente, Calif., 1992-93, City of Walnut (Calif.) Recreation Svcs., 1992—, Christ Luth. Sch., West Covina, Calif., 1993—, Los Molinos Elem. Sch., Hacienda Heights, Calif., 1993—, Los Altos Elem. Sch., Hacienda Heights, 1993—; mem. Getty Inst. Insvc. Resource Team. One-woman shows include Calif. State U., Fullerton, 1990; exhibited in group shows. Sec., treas., social chair PTA, Los Altos Elem. Sch., Hacienda Heights, 1972-73; membership and social chair Friends of Libr., Hacienda Heights, 1974-75; active Nat. Mus. Women in the Arts, L.A. County Art Mus., Norton Simon Mus., Pasadena, Calif. Mem. Calif. Art Edn. Assn. Avocations: world travel, art history, collecting stamps, foreign languages, dancing.

LISOWITZ, GERALD MYRON, neuropsychiatrist; b. Johnstown, Pa., May 28, 1930; s. Charles Gerson and Tillie (Cohen) L.; m. Amelia Josephine Rozzando, Mar. 1, 1976 (div. June 1967); children: Mara, Scott, Laurie, Carlyn, Linda. BS magna cum laude, U. Pitts., 1953, MD, 1955. Diplomate Am. Bd. Neurology in Psychiatry. Intern Montefiore Hosp., Pitts., 1955-56; psychiat. resident, teaching fellow Western Psychiatric Inst. & Clinic, 1956-59; psychoanalytic trainee Phila. Psychoanalytic Inst., 1958, Pitts. Psychoanalytic Inst., 1962-72; clin. instr. dept. psychiatry Sch. Medicine U. Pitts., 1961-80; pvt. practice gen. psychiatry, 1969—; ptnr. Psychiat. Assocs., Pitts., 1969-83; cons. in field; mem. staff Montefiore U. Hosp., U. Pitts. Med. Sch., St. Francis Gen. Hosp., Pitts., Westmoreland Hosp., Greensburg, Pa.; chief neuropsychiatry U.S. Army Hosp., Ft. Lee, Va.; founder Mental Health Clinic; sr. staff Western Psychiat. Inst., U. Pitts. Med. Sch.; clin. dir. drug and alcohol rehab. St. Francis Gen. Hops., Pitts.-Monroeville, 1990; staff Montefiore U. Hosp., Pitts. Contbr. articles to profl. jours. Bd. dirs., advisor Westmoreland County Mental Health Dept., Greensburg, 1970-85. Capt. U.S. Army, 1959-61. Recipient rsch. award Ciba-Geigy, 1980. Mem. AMA, Am. Psychiat. Assn., Am. Assn. Clin. Psychiatrists, Pa. Med. Soc., Pa. Psychiat. Assn., Westmoreland County Med. Soc., Western Pa. Psychiat. Soc. (pres. 1985-89), Phila. Psychiat. Assn., Pitts. Psychiat. Soc., Pitts. Med. Forum, Phi Delta Epsilon, Phi Beta Kappa. Avocations: music, golf, chess. Home: 3 Foxwood Ln Greensburg PA 15601

LISS, HERBERT MYRON, newspaper publisher, communications company executive; b. Mpls., Mar. 23, 1931; s. Joseph Milton and Libby Diane (Kramer) L.; m. Barbara Lipson, Sept. 19, 1954; children: Lori-Ellen, Kenneth Allen, Michael David. BS in Econs., U. Pa., 1952. With mktg. mgmt. Procter & Gamble Co., Cin., 1954-63, Procter & Gamble Internat., various countries, 1963-74; gen. mgr. Procter & Gamble Comml. Co., San Juan, P.R., 1974-78; v.p., mgr. internat. ops. InterAm. Orange Crush Co. subs. Procter & Gamble Co., Cin., 1981-84; pres. River Cities (Ohio) Communications Inc, 1985—; pub. The Downtowner newspaper and others, Cin., 1985-96. Bd. dirs. Charter Com., Cin., 1958-63, Promotion and Mktg. Assn. U.S., 1978-81, Jr. Achievement, Cin., 1980-87; bd. dirs. Downtown Coun., Cin., 1985-94, treas., 1991-92; bd. dirs. Downtown Cin. Inc., 1995—, mem. DCI retail mktg. com., 1995—. Mem. Manila Yacht Club, Manila Polo, Club Escuela de Equitación De Somos Aquas (Madrid), Rotary Club. (Cin.), Cin. Racquet Club. Home: 8564 Wyoming Club Dr Cincinnati OH 45215-4243

LISS, WALTER C., JR., television station executive. Pres., gen. mgr. WABC-TV, N.Y.C. Office: WABC-TV 7 Lincoln Sq New York NY 10023

LISSAKERS, KARIN MARGARETA, federal agency administrator; b. Aug. 16, 1944; married; 2 children. BA in Internat. Affairs, Ohio State U., 1967; MA in Internat. Affairs, Johns Hopkins U., 1969. Mem. staff com. fgn. rels. U.S. Senate, Washington, 1972-78, mem. staff subcom. multinat. corps., 1972, staff dir. subcom. fgn. econ. policy, 1977; dep. dir. econ. policy planning staff U.S. Dept. State, Washington, 1978-80; sr. assoc. Carnegie Endowment for Internat. Peace, N.Y.C., 1981-83; lectr. internat. banking, dir. internat. bus. and banking program Sch. Internat. Pub. Affairs Columbia U, N.Y.C., 1985-93; U.S. exec. dir. Internat. Monetary Fund, Washington, 1993—. Author: Banks, Borrowers and the Establishment, 1991; contbr. articles to profl. jours. Office: Internat Monetary Fund 700 19th St NW Rm 13-320 Washington DC 20431-0001

LISSAUER, JACK JONATHAN, astronomy educator; b. San Francisco, Mar. 25, 1957; s. Alexander Lissauer and Ruth Spector. SB in Math., MIT, 1978; Phd in Applied Math., U. Calif., Berkeley, 1982. NAS-NRC resident rsch. assoc. NASA-Ames Rsch. Ctr., Moffett Field, Calif., 1983-85; asst. rsch. astronomer U. Calif., Berkeley, 1985; vis. postdoctoral researcher dept. physics Inst. for Theoretical Physics U. Calif., Santa Barbara, 1985-87; asst. prof. astronomy program, dept. earth and space scis. SUNY, Stony Brook, 1987-93, assoc. prof., 1993-96; space scientist NASA Ames Rsch. Ctr., 1996—; rep. Univs. Space Rsch. Assn., SUNY, Stony Brook, 1987-96; vis. scholar dept. planetary scis. and lunar and planetary lab. U. Ariz., Tucson, 1990; professeur invité dept. de physique Univ. de Paris VII et Observatoire de Paris, Meudon, France, 1990; mem. Lunar and Planetary Geoscis. Rev. Panel, 1989, 91; vis. asst. rsch. physicist Inst. for Theoretical Physics, U. Calif., Santa Barbara, 1992, organizer Program on Plant Formation, 1992; rsch. assoc. Inst. d'Astrophysique, Paris, 1993; vis. scholar dept. astronomy U. Calif., Berkeley, 1994-95; adj. assoc. prof. SUNY, Stony Brook, 1996—. Contbr. numerous articles on planet and star formation, spiral density wave theory, rotation of planets and comets to jours. including Nature, Astron. Jour., Icarus, Science, Astrophys. Jour. Letters, Astrophys. Jour., Jour. Geophys. Rsch., Astron. Astrophysics, Ann. Rev. Astron. Astrophysics, others. NASA Grad. student fellow, 1981-82, Alfred P. Sloan Found. fellow, 1987-91. Mem. Am. Astronomical Assn. (divsn. planetary scis., divsn. dynamical astronomy, Harold C. Urey prize divsn. planetary scis. 1992), Internat. Astronomical Union, Am. Geophys. Union. Achievements include research in planetary accretion, dynamics of planetary rings, cratering, binary and multiple star systems, circumstellar disks, resonances and chaos. Office: NASA Ames Rsch Ctr Space Sci Divsn 245-3 Moffett Field CA 94035

LISSENDEN, CAROLKAY, pediatrician; b. Newark, Aug. 22, 1937; d. George Cyrus Sr. and Irene Elizabeth (Hempel) L.; m. Bart Albert Barré, June 13, 1964; children: Lisa Kim Barré-Quick, Bart Christopher Barré. BA, U. Pa., 1959; MD, Med. Coll. Pa., 1964. Pediat. intern St. Luke's Hosp., N.Y.C., 1964-65; pediat. resident Columbia-Presbyn. Hosp., N.Y.C., 1965-67; pvt. practice Mountainside, N.J., 1967—. Fellow Am. Acad. Pediats.; mem. AMA, N.J. Med. Assn., Union County Med. Assn. Republican. Presbyterian. Avocations: gardening, roller skating, sewing. Home and Office: 135 Wild Hedge Ln Mountainside NJ 07092-2520

LISSIMORE, TROY, historic site director. BA in Polit. History, MA in Polit. History, MS in Environ. Sci. and Edn.; JD, John Marshall Law Sch. Historian Gettysburg Nat. Mil. Pk., 1966; pk. mgr. William Howard Taft Nat. Hist. Site; chief interpretation Jamaica Bay; mgr. Jamaica Wildlife Refugee Gateway Nat. Recreational Area; supt. Tuskegee Inst. Nat. Hist. Site; chief of interpretation, asst. supt. Martin Luther King Jr. Nat. Hist. Site; supt., staff pk. ranger S.E. regional office Martin Luther King Jr. Nat. Hist. and Preservation Dist., 1992—. Office: Martin Luther King Nat Hist 526 Auburn Ave NE Atlanta GA 30312-1900*

LISSMAN, BARRY ALAN, veterinarian; b. N.Y.C., June 13, 1952; s. George Joseph and Helene Anna (Freilich) L.; m. Wendy Louise Cooper, June 8, 1975; children: Erica Beth, Rachel Danielle. BS, Cornell U., 1974, DVM, 1977. Lic. veterinarian N.Y., Mass., N.J., Fla. Pvt. practice L.I., N.Y., 1977—; owner, dir. Sachem Animal Hosp. and L.I. Mobile Vet. Clinics, Holbrook, N.Y., 1981—, Animal Med. Clinic, Centereach, N.Y. Contbr. to vet. text books, profl. jours. Mem. AVMA (Practitioner Rsch. award 1989), N.Y. State Vet. Med. Assn. (outstanding svc. to vet. medicine award 1992), L.I. Vet. Med. Assn. (Merit award 1994), Assn. Avian Veterinarians, Am. Assn. House Call Veterinarians (v.p.). Discoverer 1st clin. cases Rocky Mountain spotted fever in dogs, 1979, Lyme disease in dogs, 1983. Home: 15 Quaker Hill Rd Stony Brook NY 11790-1546 Office: Sachem Animal Hosp 227 Union Ave Holbrook NY 11741-1806

LIST, ERICSON JOHN, environmental engineering science educator, engineering consultant; b. Whakatane, New Zealand, Mar. 27, 1939; came to U.S., 1962; s. Ericson Bayliss and Freda Helen (Sunkel) L.; m. Olive Amoore, Feb. 3, 1962; children: Brooke Meredith, Antonia Michael. B.E. with honors, U. Auckland, N.Z., 1961, B.Sc., 1962, M.E., 1962; Ph.D., Calif. Inst. Tech., 1965. Registered profl. engr., Calif. Sr. lectr. U. Auckland, 1966-69; asst. prof. Calif. Inst. Tech., Pasadena, 1969-72, assoc. prof., 1972-78, prof. environ. engring. sci., 1978—, exec. officer, 1980-85; dir. Fluid Kinetics Corp., Ventura, Calif., 1972-82; bd. chmn. Flow Sci. Inc., Pasadena, 1983—; cons. So. Calif. Edison, Rosemead, Calif., 1973—, City and County of San Francisco, 1974—. Author: (with Hugo B. Fischer et al), Mixing in Inland and Coastal Waters, 1979, (with W. Rodi) Turbulent Jets and Plumes, 1982, (with Roscoe Moss Co.) Handbook of Ground Water Development, 1990. Mem. Blue Ribbon Commn. City of Pasadena, 1976-78. Recipient Spl. Creativity award NSF, 1982. Fellow ASCE (editor Jour. Hydraulic Engring. 1984-89). Republican. Club: Athenaeum (Pasadena) (chmn. wine com. 1981-83). Office: Calif Inst Tech 1201 E California Blvd Pasadena CA 91125-0001

LIST, NOEL DAVID, medical educator; b. Apr. 25, 1940; m. Lesley Ellen Strauss; children: David, Jessica, Nancy, Melanie. BS, NYU, 1960; MD, SUNY, N.Y.C., 1965; MPH, Harvard U., 1967. Asst. prof. medicine and preventive medicine U. Md. Sch. Medicine, Balt., 1972-84; assoc. prof. medicine, sr. fellow Ctr. on Aging Duke U. Med. Sch., Durham, N.C., 1984-89; assoc. prof. medicine, chief geriatric medicine Chgo. Med. Sch., 1989-94, head geriatric ctr., 1989-94; prof. medicine divsn. of geriatric medicine U. S.C. Sch. Medicine, Columbia, 1994—, prof. family and preventive medicine, 1994—, assoc. fellow Ctr. on Bioethics, 1994—; chair ethics and guardmanship consul State of Md., Balt., 1980-83. Fellow Am. Geriatric Soc.; mem. AMA, Assn. of Tchrs. of Preventive Medicine, Am. Gerontol. Soc., Gerontol. Soc. S.C., Columbia Med. Soc. Home: 3740 North Shore Rd Columbia SC 21206 Office: JF Byrnes Ctr Geri Med Ed Box 119 2100 Bull St Columbia SC 29202

LIST, ROLAND, physicist, educator, former UN official; b. Frauenfeld, Thurgau, Switzerland, Feb. 21, 1929; s. August Joseph and Anna (Kaufmann) L; m. Gertrud K. Egli, Apr. 14, 1956 (dec. Mar. 1996); children: Beat R., Claudia G. List Woolner. Diploma physics ETH, Swiss Fed. Inst. Tech., 1952, Dr. Sci. Nat., 1960. Head hail sect. Swiss Fed. Inst. for Snow and Avalance Rsch., Davos, Switzerland, 1952-63; prof. dept. physics U. Toronto, 1963-82, 84-94, prof. emeritus, 1994—; assoc. chmn. dept. physics U. Toronto, Can., 1968-73; dep. sec.-gen. World Meteorol. Orgn., Geneva, 1982-84; sec.-gen. Internat. Assn. Meteorology and Atmospheric Scis., 1995—; chmn. World Meteorol. Orgn.-EC Panels on Cloud Physics/Weather Modification, 1969-82, Italian Sci. Com. for Rain Enhancement, 1990—; vis. prof. Swiss Fed. Inst. for Tech., Zurich, Switzerland, 1974; bd. dirs. Univ. Corp.for Atmospheric Rsch., Boulder, Colo., 1974-77; mem. Sci. Coun. Space Shuttle Program, 1979-82. Author more than 220 papers in atmospheric and classical physics. Recipient Sesquicentennial medal St. Petersburg U., Russia, 1970, Patterson medal Can. Meterol. Soc., 1979, Recognition plaque Govt. of Thailand, 1986. Fellow Can. Acad. Sci./Royal Soc. Can., Royal Meteorol. Soc. (U.K.), Am. Meteorol. Soc.; mem. Can. Meteorol. Oceanic Soc., Am. Geophysics Soc., Am. Physics Soc., Swiss Phys. Soc., Swiss Acad. Natural Scis., Rotary. Home: 58 Olsen Dr, Toronto, ON Canada M3A 3J3 Office: U Toronto, Dept Physics, Toronto, ON Canada M5S 1A7

LISTACH, PATRICK ALAN, professional baseball player; b. Natchitoches, La., Sept. 12, 1967. Student, Ariz. State U. Baseball players Milwaukee Brewers, 1988—. Named Am. League Rookie of the Year, 1992. Office: Milw Brewers County Stadium PO Box 3099 Milwaukee WI 53201-3099*

LISTER, EARLE EDWARD, animal science consultant; b. Harvey, N.B., Can., Apr. 14, 1934; s. Earle Edward and Elizabeth Hazel (Coburn) L.; m. Teresa Ann Moore, June 4, 1983. BSc in Agriculture, McGill U., Montreal, Can., 1955, MSc in Animal Nutrition, 1957; PhD in Animal Nutrition, Cornell U., 1960. Feed nutritionist Ogilvie Flour Mills, Montreal, 1960-65; rsch. scientist rsch. br. Animal Rsch. Ctr. Agriculture Can., Ottawa, 1965-74, dep. dir. rsch. br. Animal Rsch. Ctr., 1974-78, program specialist ctrl. region rsch. br., 1978-80; dir. gen. Atlantic region rsch. br. Agriculture Can., Halifax, N.S., 1980-85; dir. gen. plant health and plant products and pesticides, food prodn. and inspection br. Agriculture Can., Ottawa, 1985-87, dir. rsch. br. Animal Rsch. Ctr., 1987-91; dir. Ctr. Food and Animal Rsch., 1991-92; cons., 1992—; former mem. Ont. Agrl. Rsch. and Svc. Coms.; former chmn. Beef Rsch. Com.; invited presenter Atlantic Livestock Conf., 1968, Ea. CSAS meeting, 1969, Can. Com. Animal Nutrition, 1976, CSAS Symposium Laval U., 1974, Guelph Nutrition Conf., 1973, 74, Asst. Dep. Minister Dairy Rev. meeting, Toronto, 1985, U. Guelph ethics conf., 1991, Can. Consumers Assn., Saskatchewan, 1991. Contbr. 54 articles to profl. jours. co-chmn. United Way/Health Ptnrs. for Agriculture Can., Ottawa, 1991; former dir. N.S. Inst. Agrologists. McGill U. scholar, 1953-55; recipient Nat. Rsch. Coun. Post Grad. Spl. scholarship Cornell U., 1957-59. Mem. Am. Soc. Animal Sci., Am. Dairy Sci. Assn., Assn. Advancement Sci. in Can., Agrl. Inst. Can., Can. Soc. Animal Sci. (former dir.), Ont. Inst. Agrologists. Achievements include research in the determination of nutrient requirements of beef cows during winter pregnancy, determination of protein and energy levels and appropriate sources of nutrients fot young dairy calves for optimal growth; development of intensive feeding system for raising high quality beef from Holstein male calves. Home: 390 Hinton Ave, Ottawa, ON Canada K1Y 1B1 Office: Ctr for Food and Animal Rsch, NCC Driveway Bldg #55, Ottawa, ON Canada K1A 0C6

LISTER, HARRY JOSEPH, financial company executive, consultant; b. Teaneck, N.J., Jan. 27, 1936; s. Harry and Arline Audrey (Pinera) L.; m. Erika Anna Maria Englisch, Sept. 3, 1960; children: Harry Joseph Jr., Karen P. Lister Lawson, Leslie M. Lister Fidler, Andrea A. Lister Lytle, Michael P. BS in Fin. and Econs., Lehigh U., 1958. Security analyst Calvin Bullock, Ltd., N.Y.C., 1959-61, assoc. dir. estate planning, 1961-65, dir. estate planning, 1965-72, asst. v.p., 1969-72; v.p. N.Y. Venture Fund, Inc., N.Y.C., 1970-72; registered rep. Johnston, Lemon & Co., Inc., Washington, 1972—, dir., 1978-90, v.p., 1978-83, corp. sec., 1978-85, sr. v.p., 1984-90; v.p. Wash. Mgmt. Corp., 1972-81, corp. sec., 1978-81, exec. v.p., 1981-85, pres., 1985—, dir., 1978—; pres. JL Fin. Svcs., Inc., Washington, 1975-90; v.p. Washington Mut. Investors Fund, Inc., Washington, 1972-81, corp. sec., 1978-81, exec. v.p., 1981-85, pres., dir., 1985—; pres. The Growth Fund of Washington, Inc., 1985—, also bd. dirs.; registered prin., bd. dirs. Washington Funds Distbrs., Inc., 1985-93, pres., 1992-93; pres., trustee The Tax Exempt Fund of Md., 1986—, The Tax Exempt Fund of Va., 1986—; chmn., bd. dirs. Washington Investment Advisors, Inc., 1991—; cons. Capital Group, Inc., L.A., 1972—; regent Coll. for Fin. Planning, Denver, 1979-84, mem. exec. com., 1980-84, chmn. bd. regents, 1981-83; bd. dirs. Internat. Bd. Standards and Practices for Cert. Fin. Planners, 1985-86. Author: Your Guide to IRAs and 14 Other Retirement Plans, 1985. Bd. dirs. cen. Bergen chpt. ARC, Hackensack, N.J., 1968-72, chmn. exec. com., 1970-72; bd. dirs. Westwood, N.J. Planning Bd., 1969-72, vice-chmn., 1970-72; bd. dirs. Westwood N.J. Zoning Bd. Adjustment, 1970-72, ICI Edn. Found., 1996—. Mem. Investment Co. Inst. (pension com., chmn. 1976-81, tax com., rsch. com.), Nat. Assn. Securities Dealers, Inc. (investment cos. com. 1984-87, bd. arbitrators 1987—), Met. Club, Univ. Club. Home: Spinnaker Ct Reston VA 22191 Office: 1101 Vermont Ave NW Washington DC 20005-3521

LISTER, KEITH FENIMORE, publishing executive; b. Clio, Iowa, Aug. 29, 1917; s. W. Frank and Maude (Fenimore) L.; m. Margaret Boman, Sept. 1, 1941 (dec. 1995); children: Janet, Priscilla. Student, Drake U., 1936-41. Pres. Lister Investment Co., San Diego, 1955-61, Southcoast Capital Co., San Diego, 1961-65, City Bank San Diego, 1965-69; pub. San Diego Daily Transcript, 1972-94. Mem. San Diego Yacht Club, Univ. Club. Presbyterian. Avocation: sailing.

LISTER, MARK WAYNE, clinical laboratory scientist; b. Panama City, Fla., June 30, 1954; s. Heamon Lee and Virginia (Hughes) L.; m. Elizabeth Ann Steger, Oct. 4, 1984; 1 child, Andrew Mark. Student med. tech. program, Monaco Med. Labs., Panama City, Fla., 1973-75; grad. with honors, Gulf Coast Coll., Panama City, Fla., 1976-79. Cert. med. technologist, Fla.; clin. lab. scientist, Nat. Cert. Agy. Lab. dir. Calhoun Gen. Hosp., Blountstown, Fla., 1979-82; evening shift supr. Hosp. Lab. Devel. Corp., Plantation, Fla., 1982-83; med. technologist Manatee (Fla.) Gen. Hosp., 1983-84, Las Olas Hosp., Ft. Lauderdale, Fla., 1984; blood bank supr., coord. continuing edn. Fla. Med. Ctr., Lauderdale, Fla., 1984-89; evening shift supr. hosp. and reference lab. Westside Regional Med. Ctr., Plantation, 1989—, coord. continuing edn., 1989—, coord. ancillary blood glucose testing program, 1989—; mem. Broward County Tech. Adv. Com.; coord. continuing edn.; inspector Coll. Am. Pathologists; presenter 10th Internat. Conf. on AIDS, Yokohama, Japan, 1994. Rschr. in human immunodeficiency virus; rsch. in immunology. Active Christ Ch. United Meth., Ft. Lauderdale, 1990—, Imperial Point Homeowners Assn., Ft. Lauderdale, 1991—; host parent Westminster Acad., Ft. Lauderdale, 1993. Mem. Am. Assn. Blood Banks, Fla. Assn. Blood Banks, Am. Med. Technologist, Fla. Soc. Med. Technologist. Avocations: woodworking, swimming, fishing, bicycling. Home: 2125 NE 56th Pl Fort Lauderdale FL 33308-2504

LISTER, SARA ELISABETH, lawyer; b. St. Paul, May 10, 1940; d. Joseph H. and Elisabeth R. Ball; m. Charles E. Lister, June 23, 1961; children—Penny Margaret, Jennifer Mary. A.B., Radcliffe Coll., 1961; M.A. in Polit. Sci., George Washington U., 1966, J.D., 1974. Bar: D.C. Ct. Appeals 1974, U.S. Dist. Ct. 1975, U.S. Cir. Ct. Appeals 1979, U.S. Supreme Ct. 1980. Assoc. Leva, Hawes, Symington, Martin & Oppenheimer, Washington, 1974-77; dep. gen. counsel U.S. Navy, Washington, 1977-79; dep. spl. asst. to sec. def. U.S. Dept. Def., Washington, 1979; gen. counsel U.S. Army, Washington, 1979-81; ptnr. Patterson Belknap Webb & Tyler, 1982-85; gen. counsel Washington Met. Area Transit Authority, 1985—; now asst. sec. Dept. Army divsn. Manpower & Reserve Affairs, Washington. Editor George Washington Law Rev., 1974; contbr. articles to profl. jours. Mem. ABA, D.C. Bar Assn. Office: Pentagon 111 Army Pentagon Washington DC 20310-0111*

LISTER, THOMAS MOSIE, composer, lyricist, publishing company executive, minister; b. Empire, Ga., Sept. 8, 1921; s. Willis Waller and Orena Pearl (Holl) L.; m. Jewel Wylene Whitten, June 2, 1946; children—Brenda (Mrs. James Milton Vann), Barbara (Mrs. David Miller Williams). Attended, Rennsalaer Poly. Inst., 1944-45, Middle Ga. Coll., 1945-46, U. South Fla., 1968; studied privately at, Tampa U., 1958-63. Ordained to ministry Bapt. Ch., 1975. Founder, pres. Mosie Lister Publs., Atlanta, 1952-56, Tampa, 1956—; choral dir. Composer, lyricist numerous gospel songs, 1940—; singer, Tampa, Fla., and Atlanta, 1941, 46-47; Compiler song. collections, hymnbooks, and others; arranger religious music for choral groups and ensembles; songs include I'm Feeling Fine, Where No One Stands Alone, His Hand in Mine; contbg. arranger profl. singing groups. Served with USNR, 1942-45. Named Bapt. Layman of Year for Tampa, 1971; inducted into Gospel Hall of Fame, 1976; recipient Humanist award Sesac, Inc., 1976; Mosie Lister Day named in his honor Tampa, 1974. Mem. Gospel Music Assn. (dir. 1970-71), Fla. Bapt. Ministers of Music Assn. (hon. life). Democrat. Address: 17008 Winners Cir Odessa FL 33556-1828

LISTERUD, (LOWELL) BRIAN, choir director, music educator; b. Duluth, Minn., Mar. 20, 1951; s. Lowell Fred Listerud and Carol May (Tuttle) Alseth; m. Christine Joyce Gunvaldson, Aug. 24, 1973; children: L. Jason, Bjorn C., Solveig C. BS, Mankato State U., 1973; MMus, Ariz. State U., 1979, postgrad., 1984—; postgrad., U. Mont., 1985-89. Cert. tchr., Mont.; nat. registered music educator. Dir. Presbyn. Ch. Choir, Wolf Point, Mont., 1974-79; tchr. music Wolf Point High Sch., 1974-79; dir. handbell choir Trinity Luth., Phoenix, 1989-90; dir. choral activities Great Falls (Mont.) High Sch., 1979-80; dir. Random Ringers Handbells, Missoula, Mont., 1986—; dir. choirs Big Sky High Sch., Missoula, 1980—; dir. Aesirian Alumni Choir, Missoula, 1991—; adjudicator Mont. H.S. Assn., 1979—; clinician dist. music festivals and honor choirs; clinician N.W. Music Educators Regional Conf., Billings, Mont., 1979, N.W. Music Educators Nat. Conf., Portland, Oreg., 1987, 93, Am. Choral Dirs. Assn., Spokane, 1982, Portland, 1984, Louisville, 1989, Internat. Choral Dir. Exch., Germany, 1988, Sweden, 1992, Argentina, 1994. Dir. several concerts; contbr. articles to profl. jours. Mem. Mont. Arts Coun., Helena, 1985-89. Recipient scholarships, letters of commendation, awards. Mem. Am. Choral Dirs. Assn. (Mont. pres. 1987-89), Mont. Music Edn. Assn. (bus. mgr. 1980-85), Mont. Edn. Assn. (faculty rep. 1985-87), Internat. Fedn. Choral Music, Am. Guild of English Handbell Ringers (state chmn. 1992-94, clinician, historian N.W. region 1997), Nat. Assn. Tchrs. Singing, Mankato State U. Alumni Assn., Ariz. State U. Alumni Assn., Sons of Norway (pres. Normendon lodge), Good Samaritans, Carpenters for Christ, Phi Mu Alpha (pres. Lambda Tau chpt. 1972-73). Presbyterian. Avocations: music, travel, building, running, tennis. Office: Big Sky Sch 3100 South Ave W Missoula MT 59804-5106

LISTERUD, MARK BOYD, retired surgeon; b. Wolf Point, Mont., Nov. 19, 1924; s. Morris B. and Grace (Montgomery) L.; m. Sarah C. Mooney, May 26, 1954; children: John, Mathew, Ann, Mark, Sarah, Richard. BA magna cum laude, U. Minn., 1949, BS, 1950, MB, 1952, MD, 1953. Diplomate Am. Bd. Surgery. Intern King County Hosp., Seattle, 1952-53; resident in surgery U. Wash., Seattle, 1953-57; practice medicine specializing in surgery Wolf Point, 1958-93; mem. admission com. U. Wash. Med. Sch., Seattle, 1983-88; instr. Dept. Rural and Community Health, U. N.D. Med. Sch., 1991. Contbr. articles to med. jours. Mem. Mont. State Health Coordinating Council, 1983, chmn. 1986—; bd. dirs. Blue Shield, Mont., 1985-87. Served with USN, 1943-46. Fellow Am. Coll. Surgeons, Royal Soc. Medicine; mem. N.E. Mont. Med. Soc. (pres.), Mont. Med. Assn. (pres. 1968-69), AMA (alt. del., del. 1970-84). Clubs: Montana, Elks. Avocations: fishing, hunting. Home: Rodeo Rd Wolf Point MT 59201 Office: 100 Main St Wolf Point MT 59201-1530

LISTGARTEN, MAX ALBERT, periodontics educator; b. Paris, May 14, 1935; came to U.S., 1968; s. Samuel and Etla (Weber) L.; m. Eileen Anne Gregory, July 3, 1963; children: Karen, Sheralyn, Michael. DDS, U. Toronto, 1959; cert. in periodontics, Harvard U., 1963; MA (hon.), U. Pa., 1971; PhD (hon.), U. Athens, 1993. Research assoc. Harvard U., Boston, 1963-64; asst. prof. periodontics U. Toronto, Can., 1964-67, assoc. prof., 1967-68; assoc. prof. U. Pa., Phila., 1968-71, prof., 1971—; vis. prof. U. Gothenburg, Sweden, 1976-77, U. Berne, 1988-89; cons. Nat. Inst. Dental Research, Bethesda, Md., 1979-88, FDA, Rockville, Md., 1992—; cons. in field. Author textbooks and numerous articles on various aspects of periodontal anatomy, microbiology, histopathology, and diagnosis. Recipient Periodontology award William J. Gies Found., 1981; named Disting. Alumnus, Harvard U., 1986, U. Pa., 1994. Fellow AAAS, Am. Acad. Periodontology (Clin. Rsch. award 1987); mem. ADA, Am. Assn. for Dental Rsch. (pres. 1991-92), Internat. Assn. Dental Rsch. (award for basic rsch. in periodontology 1973). Jewish. Avocations: swimming, skiing, hiking, photography. Office: U Penn-School of Dental Medicine Dept of Periodontics 4001 Spruce St Philadelphia PA 19104-4118

LISTON, MARY FRANCES, retired nursing educator; b. N.Y.C., Dec. 17, 1920; d. Michael Joseph and Ellen Theresa (Shaughnessy) L. BS, Coll. Mt. St. Vincent, 1944; MS, Catholic U. Am., 1945; EdD, Columbia, 1962; HHD (hon.), Allentown Coll., 1987. Dir. psychiat. nursing and edn. Nat. League for Nursing, N.Y.C., 1958-66; prof. Sch. Nursing, Cath. U. Am., Washington, 1966-78; dean Sch. Nursing, Cath. U. Am., 1966-73; prof. Marywood Coll., 1984-87; spl. assignment Imperial Med. Center, Tehran, Iran, 1975-78; dep. dir. for program affairs Nat. League for Nursing, N.Y.C., 1978-84. Mem. Sigma Theta Tau. Home: 182 Garth Rd Scarsdale NY 10583-3863

LIT, ALFRED, experimental psychologist, vision science educator, engineering psychology consultant; b. N.Y.C., Nov. 24, 1914; s. Oscar Zachery and Elsie (Jaro) L.; m. Imogene Speegle, Jan. 27, 1947. B.S., Columbia U., 1938, A.M., 1943, Ph.D., 1948. Lic. psychologist, N.Y., optometrist, N.Y. Prof. optometry Columbia U., N.Y.C., 1946-56; rsch. psychologist U. Mich., Ann Arbor, 1956-59; head human factors Bendix Systems Div., Ann Arbor, 1959-61; prof. psychology Southern Ill. U., Carbondale, 1961-83; prof. emeritus, 1983—; research prof. optometry Schnurmacher Inst. for Vision Research, State Coll. Optometry, SUNY, 1984-86; mem. adv. bd. Emeritus Coll., So. Ill. U., Carbondale, 1986—. Contbr. chpts in books and articles on vision sci. and psychology to sci. jours. Adv. NRC Com. on vision Nat. Acad. Sci., Washington, 1960—. Served to 1st lt. U.S. Army, 1943-46, PTO. Recipient Research award Sigma Xi, So. Ill. U., 1972; Outstanding Educator of Am. award So. Ill. U., 1975. USPHS, NSF grantee, 1962-85. Fellow Am. Optometric Assn., Am. Psychol. Assn., AAAS, Optical Soc. Am., N.Y. Acad. Scis., N.Y. Acad. Optometry (hon.), Soc. Engring. Psychology. Achievements include developing a portable-computer-operated visual display system useful in the early detection of pathology in the visual centers or pathways. Avocation: music. Home: 451 E Lake Dr Murphysboro IL 62966-5956 Office: So Ill Univ Dept Psychology Carbondale IL 62901

LITAN, ROBERT ELI, lawyer, economist; b. Wichita, Kans., May 16, 1950; s. David and Shirley Hermine (Krischer) L.; BS in Econs. (Class of 1946 award, W. Gordon award 1972, Albert A. Berg award 1971, 72), Wharton Sch., U. Pa., 1972; MPhil in Econs., Yale U., 1976, JD (Felix S. Cohen award 1976), 1977, PhD in Econs., Yale U., 1987. Bar: D.C. 1980. m. Avivah D. Swirsky, Aug. 12, 1980. Res. asst. Brookings Instn., 1972-73; instr., then lectr. econs. Yale U., 1975-75; energy cons. Nat. Acad. Scis., 1975-77; regulation and energy specialist President's Council Econ. Advs., 1977-79; assoc. Arnold & Porter, Washington, 1979-82, assoc., then ptnr. and counsel, Powell, Goldstein, Frazer & Murphy, Washington, 1982-90; sr. fellow Brookings Instn., Washington, 1984-92; dir. Ctr. for Econ. Progress, Brookings Inst., 1987-93; dep. asst. atty. gen. U.S. Dept. Justice, 1993-95, assoc. dir. Office of Mgmt. and Budget, 1995-96; dir. econ. studies Brookings Inst., 1996—; cons. Inst. Liberty and Democracy, Lima, Peru, 1985-88; visiting lectr., Yale U. Law Sch., 1985-86; mem. Presdl. Congl. Commn. on Causes of the Savs. and Loan Crisis, 1991-92. Recipient Silver medal Royal Soc. Arts, 1972; Thouron fellow, Eng., 1972. Mem. ABA, Am. Econs. Assn. Democrat. Author or co-author: Energy Modeling for an Uncertain Future, 1978; Reforming Federal Regulation, 1983; Saving Free Trade: A Pragmatic Approach, 1986, What Should Banks Do?, 1987, Liability: Perspectives and Policy, 1988, American Living Standards: Threats and Challenges, 1988, Blueprint for Restructuring America's Financial Institutions, 1989, Banking Industry in Turmoil, 1990, The Revolution in U.S. Finance, 1991, The Liability Maze, 1991, The Revolution in U.S. Finance, 1991, Down in the Dumps: Administration of the Unfair Trade Laws, 1991, The Future of American Banking, 1992, Growth with Equity, 1993, Assessing Bank Reform, 1993, Verdict, 1993, Financial Regulation in a Global Economy, 1994, Footing the Bill for Superfund Cleanups, 1995; contbr. articles to profl. publs. Home: 3 Golden Crest Ct Rockville MD 20854-2982 Office: Brookings Instn 1775 Massachusetts Ave NW Washington DC 20036-2188

LITCHFORD, GEORGE B., aeronautical engineer; b. Long Beach, Calif., Aug. 12, 1918. BA, Reed Coll., 1941. Fellow IEEE (past chmn. awards com. K.I. sect., Pioneer award AES-S 1974, Lamme medal 1981, AIAA (Wright Bros. medal/lectureship 1978); mem. Aerospace and Electronic Sys. Soc. Office: Litchstreet Co 32 Cherrylawn Ln Northport NY 11768-1138

LITES, JAMES, professional hockey team executive; b. Pentwater, Mich.; m. Denise Lites; children: Brooke, Samuel. BA, U. Mich., 1975; JD, Wayne State U., 1978. Exec. v.p. Detroit Red Wings, 1982-93; v.p. Little Caesar's Internat., Inc.; president Dallas Stars, 1993—; team rep. bd. govs. NHL. Office: Dallas Stars 211 Cowboys Pkwy Irving TX 75063-5931*

LITHERLAND, ALBERT EDWARD, physics educator; b. Wallasey, Eng., Mar. 12, 1928; emigrated to Can., 1953, naturalized, 1964; s. Albert and Ethel (Clement) L.; m. Anne Allen, May 12, 1956; children: Jane Elizabeth, Rosamund Mary. B.Sc., U. Liverpool, Eng., 1949, Ph.D., 1955. Rutherford scholar Atomic Energy of Can., Chalk River, Ont., 1953-55; sci. officer Atomic Energy of Can., 1955-66; prof. physics U. Toronto, 1966-79, Univ. prof., 1979-93, Univ. prof. emeritus, 1993—. Contbr. articles to profl. jours. Recipient Rutherford medal Inst. Physics, London, 1974, Silver medal for accelerator-based dating techniques Jour. Applied Radiation and Isotopes, 1980; Guggenheim fellow, 1986-87. Fellow Royal Soc. Can. (Henry Marshall Tory medal 1993), Royal Soc. London, AAAS, Am. Phys. Soc.; mem. Can. Assn. Physicists (Gold medal for achievement in physics 1971). Home: 3 Hawthorn Gardens, Toronto, ON Canada M4W 1P4 Office: 60 Saint George St, Toronto, ON Canada M5S 1A7

LITKE, ARTHUR LUDWIG, business executive; b. Torrington, Conn., Apr. 4, 1922; s. Gustav and Julia (Weiman) L.; m. Stephanie Eleanore Lojewski, June 9, 1951; children: Arthur Lawrence, Suzanne Elizabeth. B.S. in Econs, Trinity Coll., 1944; M.B.A., U. Pa., 1947; grad., Advanced Mgmt. Program, Harvard U., 1961. CPA, N.C.; cert. govt. fin. mgr. With GAO, 1946-64, asso. dir. civil accounting and auditing div., 1963-64; chief accountant, chief Office Accounting and Fin., FPC (FERC), 1964-73; mem. Fin. Acctg. Standards Bd., 1973-78; asso. adminstr. econ. and regulatory adminstrn. Dept. Energy, Washington, 1978; cons. to comptroller gen. of U.S. GAO, 1978-81, 92-96; sr. v.p. Zinder Assocs., 1981-93; v.p. and sec. Zinder Cos., 1985-89, sec., treas., 1990-92, vice chmn., 1993-96; mem. teaching staff econs. dept. Cath. U. Am., 1966-67; professorial lectr. acctg. George Washington U., 1967-73; adj. prof. acctg. Georgetown U., 1981-83; pres. Internat. Consortium on Govtl. Fin. Mgmt., 1981-84. Contbr. articles to profl. jours. Bd. dirs. Potomac Swimming and Recreation Assn., 1958-72, McLean Citizens Assn., 1990—; adv. bd. Conn. State Opera Assn., 1973-78. Recipient Meritorious Service award GAO, 1959; Meritorious Service award FPC, 1969; Disting. Service award, 1973; Disting. Leadership award Assn. Govt. Accts., 1969; Robert W. King Meml. gold medal, 1975. Mem. AICPA (com. on auditing procedure 1967-70, ethics com. 1971-73), D.C. Inst. CPAs, Assn. Govt. Accts. (nat. pres. 1972-73, bd. dirs. Washington chpt. 1969-72), Am. Arbitration Assn., Am. Accts. Assn., World Affairs Coun., Rotary, Pi Kappa Alpha. Lutheran (council). Home: 1422 Lady Bird Dr Mc Lean VA 22101-3227 Office: 1828 L St NW Washington DC 20036-5104

LITKE, DONALD PAUL, business executive, retired military officer; b. Denver, Nov. 7, 1934; s. Walter Monroe and Alice Vivian (Fowler) L.; m. Myrna Kay McDonald, July 1, 1956; children—Bradley, Susan, Lisa. B.S. in Econs., Colo. A&M U., 1956; MS in Internat. Affairs, George Washington U., 1966. Ops. and staff positions U.S. Air Force, 1956-79; vice comdr. Oklahoma City Air Logistics Ctr., 1979-81; dep. dir. logistics and security assistance U.S. European Command, Stuttgart, Germany, 1981-83; comdr. U.S. Logistics Group, Ankara, Turkey, 1983-85; dep. dir. Def. Logistics Agy., Alexandria, VA., 1985-86; pres. Bus. Devel. Internat., Alexandria and Niceville, Fla., 1986—. Contbr. articles to profl. jours. Mem. Air Force Assn. (Middle Mgr. of Yr. 1970, award of excellence 1977), Alpha Tau Omega. Methodist. Avocations: automobile restoration; racquet sports. Home and Office: 2422 Edgewater Dr Niceville FL 32578-2305

LITMAN, BERNARD, electrical engineer, consultant; b. N.Y.C., Oct. 26, 1920; s. Nathan and Gussie (Friedman) L.; m. Ellen Ann Kaufman, Feb. 27, 1949; children—Barbara, Richard. B.S. in Elec. Engring, Columbia U., 1941, Ph.D., 1949; M.S., U. Pitts., 1943. Design engr. energy equipment Westinghouse Electric Co., Pitts., 1941-47; with AMBAC Industries div. United Tech. Corp., Garden City, N.Y., 1949-83; tech. dir. guidance equipment Atlas inter-continental missile AMBAC Industries div. United Tech. Corp., 1962-63, chief engr. systems devel. and research, 1964-83; dir. advanced tech. Gull Electronics Systems Div., Parker Hannifin Corp., 1983-93; tech. cons., 1994-96, ret., 1996; Westinghouse lectr. U. Pitts., 1944; lectr. Adelphi U., Garden City. Co-author: Gyroscopics, 1961. William Petit Trobridge fellow, 1948. Asso. fellow Am. Inst. Aeros. and Astronautics (Achievement award L.I. sect. 1966); mem. IEEE (sr.), Am. Automatic Control Council, N.Y.-N.J. Trail Conf., Sigma Xi. Jewish. Patentee rotary amplifiers, axial motors, gravity pendulums, inductors, 2 axis accellerometers, ballistic missile safety devices, gyro attenuators, thrust retainers. Home: 228 Wagon Wheel Ln Columbus NJ 08022-1119

LITMAN, BRIAN DAVID, communications executive; b. Kansas City, Mo., May 9, 1954; s. Marvin Wilbur and Louise Diane (Raskin) L. BJ, U. Mo., 1977. Promotion mgr. Atlanta br. CBS Records, Atlanta, 1977-78; promotion mgr. CBS Records, Cleve., 1978-79; dir. mktg. Am. TV and Communications (subs. Time, inc. Cable), Pitts., 1980-81; account mgr. Group W Satellite Communications, Stamford, Conn., 1981-82; regional mgr. Hearst/ABC, N.Y.C., 1982-84; dir. nat. accounts Hearst/ABC/NBC, N.Y.C., 1985-86; dir. nat. accounts, western divsn. Hearst/ABC/NBC, L.A., 1986-90; pres. Entertainment and Comm. Holdings Orgn., West Hollywood, Calif., 1990-94; v.p. U.S. West/Interactive Video Enterprises, San Ramon, Calif., 1994-95; pres. Entertainment & Comms. Holdings Orgn.; prin. Internat. Media Group, Beverly Hills, 1996—, Network Devel. Group, Beverly Hills, 1996—. Dir. editorial bd. Emmy mag. Mem. L.A. World Affairs Coun., 1991—. Mem. Acad. TV Arts and Scis. (chmn. cable com. 1989—), Hollywood Radio and TV Soc., L.A. Advt. Club, U.S.-Russia Trade and Econ. Coun. Office: Entertainment & Comm Holdings PO Box 16298 Beverly Hills CA 90209

LITMAN, HARRY PETER, lawyer, educator; b. Pitts., May 4, 1958; s. S. David and Roslyn M. (Margolis) L. BA, Harvard U., 1981; JD, U. Calif., Berkeley, 1986. Bar: Calif. 1987, U.S. Ct. Appeals (D.C. cir.) 1987, Pa. 1988, D.C. 1989, U.S. Ct. Appeals (9th cir.) 1990, U.S. Dist. Ct. (so. dist.) Tex. 1992, U.S. Supreme Ct. 1992, U.S. Dist. Ct. (ea. and we. dists.) Pa.

1993, U.S. Ct. Appeals (7th cir.) 1994. Prodn. asst. feature films N.Y.C., 1980-82; newsman, clk. baseball desk AP, N.Y.C., 1982-83; sports reporter AP, 1983-86; law clk. to Hon. Abner J. Mikva U.S. Ct. Appeals (D.C. cir.), 1986-87; law clk. to Hon. Thurgood Marshall U.S. Supreme Ct., Washington, 1987-88, law clk. to Hon. Anthony M. Kennedy, 1989; asst. U.S. atty., dep. chief appellate sect. Dept. Justice, San Francisco, 1990-92; dep. assoc. atty. gen. Dept. Justice, Washington, 1992-93, dep. asst. atty. gen., 1993—; adj. prof. Boalt Hall Sch. Law U. Calif., Berkeley, 1990-92, Georgetown U. Law Ctr., 1996—. Editor-in-chief Calif. Law Rev., Vol. 73; author various articles. Presdl. scholar, 1976. Mem. Pa. Bar Assn., State Bar Calif., D.C. Bar, Order of Coif. Office: Dept of Justice 10th & Constitution Ave NW Washington DC 20530-0001

LITMAN, RAYMOND STEPHEN, financial services consultant; b. Kingston, Pa., Nov. 2, 1936; s. Stephen Vincent and Mary Helen (Wisnewski) L.; m. Ann Mae Kosik, Nov. 24, 1960; children: Raymond Stephen II, A. Christine. BS in Commerce, Wilkes Coll., 1961. Credit mgr. Sears Roebuck & Co., eastern div., 1961-66; banking officer Phila. Nat. Bank, 1966-69; dir. Decision Dynamics Corp., Marlton, N.J., 1969-71; asst. v.p. Bankers Trust Co., N.Y.C., 1971-75; sr. banking officer Girard Bank, Phila., 1975-77; pres. World Wide Cons. Svcs., Plymouth Meeting, Pa., 1977-78; asso. dir. bank card divsn. Am. Bankers Assn., 1978-80; mng. dir. Chemical Bank, N.Y.C., 1981-92, pres., chief oper. officer, ECC Mgmt. Svcs. Inc., King of Prussia, Pa., 1992-93; pres., CEO Litman Assocs., Inc. Fin. Svcs. Cons.; mem. adv. coun. Credit Rsch Ctr. Purdue U. Served with USN, 1954-57; ETO. Mem. Am. Bankers Assn. (mem. bank card div. exec. com.), Govt. Rels. Coun. and Banking Leadership, Internat. Assn. Credit Card Investigators (pres. Del. Valley chpt. 1976-77, dir. nat. chpt. 1976-77, life mem.), Montgomery County Police Chiefs Assn., Police Chiefs Assn. Southeast Pa., Plymouth Meeting Hist. Soc., VFW, Am. Legion, Frat. Order of Police. Republican. Roman Catholic. Home: 2057 Sierra Rd Plymouth Meeting PA 19462-1826

LITMAN, ROBERT BARRY, physician, author, television and radio commentator; b. Phila., Nov. 17, 1947; s. Benjamin Norman and Bette Etta (Saunders) L.; m. Niki Thomas, Apr. 21, 1985; children: Riva Belle, Nadya Beth, Caila Tess, Benjamin David. BS, Yale U., 1967, MD, 1970, MS in Chemistry, 1972, MPhil in Anatomy, 1972, postgrad. (Life Ins. Med. Rsch. Fund fellow) Yale U., Univ. Coll. Hosp., U. London, 1969-70; Am. Cancer Soc. postdoctoral rsch. fellow Yale U., 1970-73. Diplomate Am. Bd. Family Practice. Resident in gen. surgery Bryn Mawr (Pa.) Hosp., 1973-74; USPHS fellow Yale U. Sch. Medicine, 1974-75; pvt. practice medicine and surgery, Ogdensburg, N.Y., 1977-93, San Ramon, Calif., 1993—; mem. med. staff A. Barton Hepburn Hosp., 1977-93, John Muir Med. Ctr., 1993—, San Ramon (Calif.) Regional Med. Ctr., 1993—, also chmn. med. edn.; commentator Family Medicine Stas. WWNY-TV and WTNY-Radio, TCI Cablevision, Contra Costa T.V.; clin. preceptor dept. family medicine State Univ. Health Sci. Ctr., Syracuse, 1978—. Author: Wynnefield and Limer, 1983, The Treblinka Virus, 1991, Allergy Shots, 1993; contbr. articles to numerous sci. publs. Pres. Am. Heart Assn. No. N.Y. chpt., 1980-84. Fellow Am. Coll. Allergy, Asthma, and Immunology, Am. Acad. Family Physicians; mem. AMA (Physicians Recognition award 1970—), Calif. State Med. Assn., Alameda-Contra Costa County Med. Assn., Joint Coun. Allergy and Immunology, Nat. Assn. Physician Broadcasters (charter), Acad. Radio and TV Health Communicators, Book and Snake Soc., Gibbs Soc. of Yale U. (founder), Sigma Xi, Nu Sigma Nu, Alpha Chi Sigma. Home and Office: PO Box 1857 San Ramon CA 94583-6857

LITMAN, ROSLYN MARGOLIS, lawyer, educator; b. N.Y.C., Sept. 30, 1928; d. Harry and Dorothy (Perlow) Margolis; m. S. David Litman, Nov. 22, 1950; children: Jessica, Hannah, Harry. BA, U. Pitts., 1949, JD, 1952. Bar: Pa. 1952. Practiced in Pitts., 1952—; ptnr. firm Litman, Litman, Harris & Brown, P.C., 1952—; adj. prof. U. Pitts. Law Sch., 1958—; permanent del. Conf. U.S. Circuit Ct. Appeals for 3d Circuit; past chair dist. adv. group U.S. Dist. Ct. (we. dist.) Pa., 1991-94, mem. steering com. for dist. adv. group, 1991—; chmn. Pitts. Pub. Parking Authority, 1970-74; mem. curriculum com. Pa. Bar Inst., 1986—, bd. dirs., 1972-82. Recipient Roscoe Pound Found. award for Excellence in Tchg. Trial Advocacy, 1996. Mem. ABA (del., litigation sect., anti-trust health care com.), ACLU (nat. bd. dirs..), Pa. Bar Assn. (bd. govs. 1976-79), Allegheny County Bar Assn. (bd. govs. 1972-74, pres. 1975), Allegheny County Acad. Trial Lawyers (charter), United Jewish Fedn. (cmty. rels. com., co-chair ch./state com.), Order of Coif. Home: 5023 Frew Ave Pittsburgh PA 15213 Office: 3600 One Oxford Centre Pittsburgh PA 15219

LITOW, JOEL DAVID, strategic planning and financial analyst; b. N.Y.C., Feb. 10, 1947; s. Herbert and Jean (Zaller) L.; m. Lorraine Aziz; children: Jason, Jennifer. BChemE, CCNY, 1968; MBA, Rutgers U., 1973. Chem. engr. Airco, N.Y.C., 1968-69, fin. analyst, 1969-73; mgr. fin. analysis Bali Co., N.J., 1973-75; mgr. cost acctg. M&T Chems. Inc., Rahway, N.J., 1976-77, dir. control devel., 1978-79, controller, 1979-86, v.p. fin., controller, 1986-90; v.p. fin. EIF Atochem N.A., 1990-93, v.p. strategic planning, 1994—. Avocations: tennis, basketball, softball.

LITRENTA, FRANCES MARIE, psychiatrist; b. Balt., June 25, 1928; d. Frank P. and Josephine (DeLuca) L. AB, Coll. Notre Dame Md., 1950; MD, Georgetown U., 1954. Diplomate Am. Bd. Psychiatry and Neurology. Rotating intern St. Agnes Hosp., Balt., 1954-55, asst. resident in psychiatry, 1955-56; fellow in psychiatry Univ. Hosp., Balt., 1956-57; fellow in child psychiatry Georgetown U. Hosp., Washington, 1957-59; clin. instr. psychiatry Med. Ctr. Georgetown U., Washington, 1959-63; clin. asst. prof. Med. Ctr. Georgetown U., 1963-72, clin. assoc. prof. psychiatry Med. Ctr., 1972-87; pvt. practice Balt., 1959—; cons. St. Vincent's Infant Home, Balt., 1965-75; mem. coun. to dean Georgetown U. Sch. Medicine, 1977-93. Fellow Am. Acad. Child and Adolescent Psychiatry, Am. Orthopsychiat. Assn. (life); mem. Am. Psychiat. Assn. (life), Md. Psychiat. Soc. (life), Georgetown Med. Alumni Assn. (nat. comm. chmn. 1987-90, class co-chmn. 1974-87, class comm. chmn. 1987—, bd. dirs. 1989—, gov. 1989-95, senator 1995—, Founder's award 1994). Office: 6110 York Rd Baltimore MD 21212-2600

LITROWNIK, ALAN JAY, psychologist, educator; b. Los Angeles, June 25, 1945; s. Irving and Mildred Mae (Rosin) L.; m. Hollis Merle, Aug. 20, 1967; children: Allison Brook, Jordan Michael. BA, UCLA, 1967; MA, U. Ill., Champaign-Urbana, 1969, PhD, 1971. Psychologist Ill. Dept. Mental Health, Decatur, 1970-71; asst. prof. psychology San Diego State U., 1971-75, assoc. prof., 1975-78, prof., 1978—, chmn. dept. psychology, 1981-87, assoc. dean for curriculum and acad. planning, North County Campus, 1987-88; co-dir. Ctr. for Behavioral and Community Health Studies, San Diego, 1989—; cons. San Diego County Dept. Edn. Program Evaluation, 1975-81; project dir. Self-Concept and Self-Regulatory Processes in Developmentally Disabled Children and Adolescents, 1975-78; co-dir. Child Abuse Interdisciplinary Tng. Program, 1987—; project dir. tobacco use prevention in youth orgns., 1989-92. Research, publs. in field. Contbr. chpts. to books. Mem. San Diego County Juvenile Justice Comm., 1989-92; mem. juvenile systems adv. group San Diego County Bd. Suprs., 1989-91. Grantee U.S. Office Edn., 1975-78, 80-81, Nat. Ctr. Child Abuse, 1987—, Calif. Dept. Health, 1989-92, U. Calif. Tobacco-Related Disease Rsch. Program, 1992-94. Office: Ctr Behavioral/Comm Health Studies 9245 Sky Park Ct San Diego CA 92123-4311

LITSCHGI, A. BYRNE, lawyer; b. Charleston, S.C., Dec. 31, 1920; s. Albert William and Mary Catherine (Byrne) L.; m. Mary Elaine Herring, Sept. 13, 1952. B.B.A., U. Fla., 1941; J.D., Harvard U., 1948. Bar: Fla. 1948, D.C. 1950. Atty. Office Gen. Counsel, Treasury Dept., Washington, 1949-52; legis. asst. to U.S. senator, 1952; mem. firm Hedrick & Lane, Washington, 1953-60, Coles, Himes & Litschgi, Tampa, Fla., 1960-62, Shackleford, Farrior, Stallings & Evans, 1962-87, Dykema Gossett, Tampa, Fla., 1988-92; chmn. SL Industries, Inc., 1976-92; mem. firm Holland & Knight, Tampa, 1992—; incorporator, dir. Communications Satellite Corp., 1962-64; mem. Fla. Jud. Council, 1965-68, U.S. Internal Revenue Commn. Adv. Group, 1967-68. Mem. Harvard Law Sch. Assn. (nat. council 1956-61), ABA (chmn. excise and miscellaneous tax com. tax sect. 1956-59), Fla. Bar, Bar Assn. D.C. Home: PO Box 1288 Tampa FL 33601-1288 Office: Holland & Knight PO Box 1288 Tampa FL 33601-1288

LITSCHGI, RICHARD JOHN, computer manufacturing company executive; b. St. Louis, July 1, 1937; s. William J. and Mary F. (Eynatten) L.; m. Christine Ewert, Aug. 21, 1968. BS, St. Louis U., 1959; MS, U. Okla., 1964. Cert. meteorology St. Louis U./USAF. Supr., Bellcomm, Inc., Washington, 1964-67; mgr. Computer Scis., Brussels, 1967-68, Intranet Computing Co., L.A., 1968-71, Xerox Corp., El Segundo, Calif., 1971-76; dir. Honeywell, Inc., L.A., 1976-80, v.p., Phoenix, 1980-85, v.p. Mpls., 1985-87, v.p. Honeywell Bull Inc., 1987-88, v.p. Bull HN Inc., Boston, 1988-89; v.p. Groupe Bull, Boston and Paris, 1990-93; v.p. Vanguard Automation Inc., Tucson, 1993-94; ret., 1994. Bd. dirs. Arizonians for Cultural Devel., 1981-85; trustee Phoenix Art Mus., 1982-85 . Served to capt. USAF, 1959-62. Democrat. Home: 24 Tupelo Rd Falmouth MA 02540-1945

LITSKY, BERTHA YANIS, microbiologist, artist; b. Chester, Pa., Jan. 2, 1920; d. Edward Bernard and Hattie (Howell) Meade; m. Martin Yanis, June 27, 1942 (dec.); children: Libby Nesvold, Rosalind Yanishevsky; m. Warren Litsky, July 27, 1965 (dec. July 1994). BSc, Phila. Coll. Pharmacy, 1942; MPA, NYU, 1964; PhD, Walden U., 1974. Lic. med. technologist. Head dept. bacteriology Assoc. Labs., Phila., 1942-44; asst. supr. prodn. Nat. Drug Co., Swiftwater, Pa., 1944-45; rsch. bacteriologist U. Pa., Phila., 1945-50; cons. microbiologist Phila., 1950-56; head dept. bacteriology S.I. Hosp., N.Y.C., 1956-65; rsch. assoc. U. Mass., Amherst, 1965—; nurse cons. Bingham Assocs. Fund New Eng. Med. Ctr. Hosp., Boston, 1965-85. Author: An Administrative Program for Hospital Sanitation, 1966, Food Service Sanitation, 1973; contbr. chpts. to books; contbr. more than 115 articles to profl. jours. Troop mother Girl Scouts USA, S.I., 1953-60; judge Acad. Sci., N.Y.C., 1953-60; aided students in project for Sci. Fair, N.Y.c., 1953-62; mem. animal control com. Town of Amherst, 1978-80; sanitation cons. Town Hall, Amherst, 1994—; v.p. Friends of Amherst Stray Animals, 1980—; mem. fundraising com. MSPCA, Boston, 1995. Recipient scholarship NYU, 1964, Editl. award, Hosp. Mgmt., 1964, 65, 68, Annual Alumni award Phila. Coll. Pharmacy and Sci., 1979, Leonard A. Leipus award Am. Soc. for Hosp. Ctrl. Svc. Pers., 1982, 9th Annual Dr. John J. Perkins Meml. award Surgicot, Inc., 1983, Pub. Svc. award Assn. Surg. Technologists, 1983, 85, Appreciation award N.C. Assn. for Hosp. Ctrl. Svc. Pers., 1987, Pioneer in Infection Control award Smith Bros. Whitehaven, Ltd., 1992, among others. Mem. APHA, Am. Hosp. Assn., Am. Soc. Microbiology, Internat. Assn. for Hosp. Ctrl. Svc. Material Mgmt. (Pres.'s award 1992), Amherst Club. Avocations: painting, working with homeless animals, playing the violin, teaching art history, international hospital work. Home: 9 Kettle Pond Rd Amherst MA 01002-1642 Office: U Mass Amherst MA 01003

LITSTER, JAMES DAVID, physics educator, dean; b. Toronto, Ont., Can., June 19, 1938; s. James Creighton and Gladys May (Byers) L.; m. Cheryl Ella Schmidt, June 26, 1965; children: Robin Joyce, Heather Claire. B Engring., McMaster U., Hamilton, Ont., 1961; PhD, MIT, 1965. Instr. physics MIT, Cambridge, Mass., 1965-66, asst. prof. physics, 1966-71, assoc. prof. physics, 1971-75, prof. physics, 1975—, head div. atomic, condensed matter and plasma physics, dept. physics, 1979-83, dir. Ctr. for Materials Sci. and Engring., 1983-88, dir. Francis Bitter Nat. Magnet Lab., 1988-92, interim assoc. provost, v.p. for rsch., 1991, v.p., dean for rsch., 1991-95; v.p. rsch., dean grad. edn. MIT, Cambrdige, Mass., 1996—; mem. rsch. staff Thomas J. Watson Rsch. Ctr. IBM, 1969, cons. to liquid crystal group Thomas J. Watson Rsch. Ctr., 1969-70; vis. prof. U. Paris, 1971-72; lectr. in physics Harvard Med. Sch., 1974-75; mem. ad hoc oversight com. Solid State Chemistry, NSF, 1977-78; cons. N.Y. State Edn. Dept., 1978; vis. scientist Risø Nat. Lab., Denmark, 1978; mem. condensed matter scis. subcom. NSF, 1978-81, materials rsch. adv. com., 1978-81, chmn., 1980-81; mem. solid state scis. panel NRC, 1986-95, chmn., 1991-92. Regional editor Molecular Crystals and Liquid Crystals, 1986-93. Recipient Gold medal Assn. Profl. Engrs. Ont., 1961, Chancellor's Gold medal McMaster U., 1961, Irving Langmuir Chem. Physics prize Am. Chemical Soc., 1993; Kennecott Copper Co. fellow, 1964-65, John Simon Guggenheim Meml. fellow, 1971-72. Fellow AAAS, Am. Phys. Soc., Am. Acad. Arts and Scis. Office: MIT 77 Massachusetts Ave Rm 3-240 Cambridge MA 02139-4301

LITT, IRIS FIGARSKY, pediatrics educator; b. N.Y.C., Dec. 25, 1940; d. Jacob and Bertha (Berson) Figarsky; m. Victor C. Vaughan, June 14, 1987; children from previous marriage: William M., Robert B. AB, Cornell U., 1961; MD, SUNY, Bklyn., 1965. Diplomate Am. Bd. Pediatrics (bd. dirs. 1989-94), sub-specialty bd. cert. in adolescent medicine. Intern, then resident in pediat. N.Y. Hosp., N.Y.C., 1965-68; assoc. prof. pediat. Stanford U. Sch. Medicine, Palo Alto, Calif., 1982-87, prof., 1987—, dir. divsn. adolescent medicine, 1976—, dir. Inst. for Rsch. on Women and Gender, 1990-97. Editor Jour. Adolescent Health. Mem. Soc. for Adolescent Medicine (charter), Am. Acad. Pediatrics (award sect. on adolescent health), Western Soc. Pediatric Rsch., Soc. Pediatric Rsch., Am. Pediatric Soc., Inst. of Medicine/NAS. Office: 750 Welch Rd Ste 325 Palo Alto CA 94304-1510

LITT, MITCHELL, chemical engineer, educator, bioengineer; b. Bklyn., Oct. 11, 1932; s. Saul and Mollie (Steinbaum) L.; m. Zelda Sheila Levine, Sept. 6, 1955; children: Ellen Beth, Steven Eric. A.B., Columbia U., 1953, B.S. in Engring, 1954, M.S., 1956; D.Engring. Sci., Columbia, 1961. Research engr. Esso Research and Engring. Co., 1958-61; faculty U. Pa., 1961—, asso. prof. chem. engring., 1965-72, prof., 1972—, prof. bioengring., 1977—, chmn. dept. bioengring., 1981-90; vis. prof. environ. medicine Duke, 1971-72; vis. prof. Weizmann Inst., Israel, 1979; v.p. research and devel. KDL Med. Techs. Inc., 1984—. Co-editor: Rheology of Biological Systems, 1973; asso. editor: Biorheology; contbr. articles to profl. engrs. Mem. IEEE (engring. in medicine and biology soc.), Am. Inst. Chem. Engrs., Am. Soc. Engring. Edn., Am. Chem. Soc., Biomed. Engring. Soc., Internat. Soc. Biorheology, N.Am. Soc. Biorheology, Am. Inst. Med. Biol. Engring., Phi Beta Kappa, Sigma Xi, Tau Beta Pi, Phi Lambda Upsilon, Theta Tau. Spl. research biorheology transp. processes, chemically reacting systems, med. aspects engring. Home: 2420 Spruce St Philadelphia PA 19103-6423 Office: Univ Pa Dept Bio Engring Philadelphia PA 19104

LITT, MORTON HERBERT, macromolecular science educator, researcher; b. N.Y.C., Apr. 10, 1926; s. Samuel Bernard and Minnie (Hertz) L.; m. Lola Natalie Abrahamson, July 7, 1957; children: Jonathan S., Jennifer A. B.S., CCNY, 1947; M.S., Bklyn. Poly. Inst., 1953, Ph.D., 1956. Turner and Newall fellow U. Manchester, Eng., 1956-57; sr. research fellow N.Y. State Coll. Forestry, Syracuse, N.Y., 1958-59; sr. scientist Allied Chem. Corp., Morristown, N.J., 1960-64, assoc. dir. research, 1965-67; assoc. prof. Case Western Res. U., Cleve., 1967-76, prof. macromolecular sci., 1976—; cons. Allied-Signal Corp., Morristown, N.J., 1967-93, 96—, GAF Corp., 1969-71, Internat. Playtex, Inc., 1972-78, Air Products and Chems. Corp., 1973-83, Dow Chem., 1975-77, 79-83, Church & Dwight Corp., 1980-92, Vistakon, Jacksonville, Fla., 1980—, Polaroid Corp., Cambridge, Mass., 1987-90, Lawrence Livermore Lab., DOE, 1987-89, Argonne Nat. Lab., 1997—. Patentee in field. Fellow AAAS, Am. Inst. Physics; mem. Am. Chem. Soc., Chem. Soc. London, J. Polymer Sci. Polymer Chem. (adv. bd.). Home: 2575 Charney Rd Cleveland OH 44118-4402 Office: Case Western Res U Kent H Smith Bldg Cleveland OH 44106-7202

LITTEER, HAROLD HUNTER, JR., lawyer; b. Rochester, N.Y., Nov. 13, 1943; s. Harold Hunter and Winifred Gladys (Gemming) L.; m. Kathleen May Dool, July 14, 1964; children: Harold H. III, Raymond J. BS, Empire State Coll., 1988; JD, Syracuse U., 1990. Bar: N.Y. 1991. Ptnr. Murray & Litteer, Batavia, N.Y., 1991—. Mem. Wheatland Zoning Bd., Scottsville, N.Y.; town justice Town of Wheatland, Scottsville, N.Y. Mem. ABA, N.Y. State Bar Assn., N.Y. State Defenders Assn., Lions (bd. dirs. Caledonia-Mumford club). Democrat. Baptist. Avocations: golf, fishing, sports, music. Home: 460 Armstrong Rd Mumford NY 14511 Office: Murray & Litteer 23 Jackson St Batavia NY 14020-3201

LITTELL, FRANKLIN HAMLIN, theologian, educator; b. Syracuse, N.Y., June 20, 1917; s. Clair F. and Lena Augusta (Hamlin) L.; m. Harriet Davidson Lewis, June 15, 1939 (dec. 1978); children: Jennith, Karen, Miriam, Stephen; m. 2d Marcia S. Sachs, 1980. BA, Cornell Coll., 1937, DD, 1953; BD, Union Theol. Sem., 1940; PhD, Yale U., 1946; Dr. Theology (hon.), U. Marburg, 1957; ThD (hon.), Thiel Coll., 1968; other hon. degrees, Widener Coll., 1969, Hebrew Union Coll., 1975, Reconstructionist Rabbinical Coll., 1976, Gratz Coll., 1977, St. Joseph's U., 1988, Stockton State Coll., 1991, U. Bridgeport, 1996. Dir. Lane Hall, U. Mich., 1944-49; chief protestant adviser to U.S. High Commr., other service in Germany, 1949-51, 53-58; prof. Chgo. Theol. Sem., 1962-69; pres. Iowa Wesleyan Coll., 1966-69; prof. religion Temple U., 1969-86; adj. prof. Inst. Comtemporary Jewry, Hebrew U., Israel, 1973-94; Ida E. King disting. vis. prof. Holocaust Studies Richard Stockton Coll., 1990, 91, 96-97, Robert Foster Cherry disting. vis. prof. Baylor U., 1993-94, guest prof. numerous univs. Author numerous books including The Anabaptist View of the Church: an Introduction to Sectarian Protestantism (Brewer award Am. Soc. Ch. History), 1952, rev. edit., 1958, 64, From State Church to Pluralism, 1962, rev., 1970; (with Hubert Locke) The German Church Struggle and the Holocaust, 1974, 90; The Crucifixion of the Jews, 1975, 86, The Macmillan Atlas History of Christianity, 1976, German edit., 1976, 89 , (with Marcia Sachs Littell) A Pilgrim's Interfaith Guide to the Holy Land, 1981; A Half-Century of Religious Dialogue: Amsterdam 1939-1989; editor or assoc. editor numerous jours. including Jour. Ecumenical Studies, A Jour. of Ch. and State and Holocaust Genocide Studies; author weekly syndicated columns, also over 300 major articles or chpts. of books in field of modern religious history. cons. NCCJ, 1958-83; mem. exec. com. Notre Dame Colloqium, 1961-68; vice chmn. Ctr. for Reformation Research, 1964-77; nat. chmn. Inst. for Am. Democracy, 1966-69, sr. scholar, 1969-76; co-founder, officer Ann. Scholars' Conf. on Ch. Struggle and Holocaust, 1970—; pres. Christians Concerned for Israel, 1971-78, Nat. Christian Leadership Conf. for Israel, 1978-84, pres. emeritus 1985—; founder, chmn. ecumenical com. Deutscher Evangelischer Kirchentag, 1953-58; co-founder, cons. Assn. Coordination Univ. Religious Affairs, 1959—; mem. U.S. Holocaust Meml. Council, 1979-93; founder, pres. Nat. Inst. on Holocaust, Temple U., 1975-83, Anne Frank Inst., Phila., 1983-89; co-founder, pres. Phila. Ctr. on Holocaust, Genocide and Human Rights, 1989—; mem. exec. com. Remembering For The Future, Oxford and London, 1988, Berlin, 1994; named observer to Vatican II; mem. Internat. Bd. of Yad Vashem, Jerusalem, 1981—. Decorated Grosse Verdienstkreuz (Fed. Republic Germany); recipient Jabotinsky medal, Israel, Ladislaus Laszt Internat. Ecumenical award Ben Gurion U. of Negev, 1991, Buber Rosenzweig medal, Germany, 1996. Mem. PEN, European Assn. Evang. Acads. (co-founder), Locust Club, Pen and Pencil Club, Phi Beta Kappa, Phi Beta Kappa Assocs. Home: PO Box 10 Merion Station PA 19066

LITTELL, MARCIA SACHS, educator, educational administrator; b. Phila., July 12, 1937; d. Leon Harry Sobel and Selma Fisher Goldstein Lipson; m. Robert L. Sachs, Apr. 3, 1955 (div. June 1978); children: Jonathan R., Robert L. Jr., Jennifer Sachs-Dahnert; m. Franklin H. Littell, Mar. 23, 1980; children: Jennith Lawrence, Karen, Miriam, Stephen. BS in Edn., Temple U., 1971, MS in Edn., 1975, EdD, 1990. Cert. tchr. secondary and social studies, Pa. Tchr. Lower Merion Sch. Dist., Ardmore, Pa., 1972-74; regional exec. dir. Brit. European Ctr., Paris, 1974-78; dir. confs. Bryn Mawr (Pa.) Coll., 1976-80; internat. exec. dir. Anne Frank Inst., Phla., 1981-89; adj. prof. Temple U., Phla., 1990—; exec. dir. Ann. Scholars' Conf. on the Holocaust & the Chs., Merion, Pa., 1990—; vis. prof. Phila. C.C., 1974-76; dir. Phila. Ctr. on the Holocaust, Genocide and Human Rights, 1989—; exec. com. Remembering for the Future, Oxford, Eng. and Berlin, 1986—; mem. edn. com. U.S. Holocaust Meml. Mus., Washington, 1987—, chmn.'s adv. com., 1985. Editl. adv. bd. Holocause & Genocide Studies, Oxford U. Press, volume I, 1987—, Bridges: An Interdisciplinary Journal of Theology, Philosophy, History and Science, 1995—; editor: Holocaust Education: A Resource for Teachers and Professional Leaders, 1985, Liturgies on the Holocaust: An Interfaith Anthology, 1986, rev. edit., 1996 (Merit of Distinction award), The Holocaust: Forty Years After, 1989, The Netherlands and Nazi Genocide, 1992, From Prejudice to Destruction: Western Civilization in the Shadow of Auschwitz, 1995, Remembrance and Recollection: Essays on the Centennial Year of Martin Neimoller and Reinhold Niebuhr, 1995, The Uses and Abuses of Knowledge: The Holocaust and the German Church Struggle, 1997, The Holocaust: Lessons For the Third Generation, 1997, Holocaust and Church Struggle: Religion, Power and the Politics of Resistance, 1996. Exec. com. YM/YWHA Arts Coun., Phila., 1980—; adv. bd. Child Welfare, Montgomery County, 1975-80; bd. govs. Lower Merion Scholarship Fund, 1972-80. Named Woman of the Yr., Brith Sholom Women, Phila., 1993, Eternal Flame award Anne Frank Inst., 1988, Hall of Fame award Sch. Dist. of Phila., 1988. Fellow Nat. Assn. Holocaust Educators, Assn. of Holocaust Orgns. (founding sec. 1985-88), Nat. Coun. for the Social Studies. Democrat. Jewish. Avocations: walking, travel, reading. Office: PO Box 10 Merion Station PA 19066-0010

LITTERER, WILLIAM EDWARD, III, physician; b. Davenport, Iowa, Apr. 28, 1953; s. William Edward and Shirley Marie (Schneider) L.; m. Stephanie Anita Magliacano. AB in Biochemistry, Rutgers U., 1975; DO, Kirksville Coll. Osteo. Med., 1979. Diplomate Am. Bd. Internal Medicine, Am. Bd. Osteopathic Internal Medicine, Am. Bd. Geriatrics. Rotating intern Meml. Gen. Hosp., Union, N.J., 1979-80; resident in internal medicine St. Michael's Med. Ctr., Newark, 1980-83; pvt. practice Colonia, N.J., 1983-90, Falmouth, Mass., 1990—; med. dir. Freedom Crest Nursing Home. Fellow ACP. Office: 332 Gifford St Falmouth MA 02540-2948

LITTIG, LAWRENCE WILLIAM, psychologist, educator; b. Madison, Wis., June 30, 1927; s. Lawrence Victor and Elsie Louise (Rosanske) L.; m. Iris Mark, June 15, 1957; children—Eve Alexandra, Amy Victoria, Sharon Elizabeth. B.S., U. Wis., 1950, M.S., 1955; Ph.D., U. Mich., 1959. Instr. dpet. psychology U. Mich., Ann Arbor, 1958-59; Asst. prof. psychology U. Buffalo, 1959-62; asst. program dir. instl. programs NSF, Washington, 1962-63; social psychologist W.E. Upjohn Inst. Employment Research, Washington, 1963-65; prof. social psychology Howard U., Washington, 1965-92, prof. emeritus social psychology, 1992—; prof. psychology Md. Inst. Coll. of Art, Balt., 1993—; Fulbright prof. U. Nottingham, 1961-62; vis. scholar U. London, 1971-72; cons. Brookings Instn., 1968-70, Dept. Labor, 1968-70; vis. prof. U. Wis., 1970. Cons. editor: Jour. Cross Cultural Psychology, 1969-74; contbr. articles to profl. jours. Port warden City of Annapolis, 1994—. U.S. Office Edn. grantee, 1965-70; NIMH research grantee, 1968-69; NSF research grantee, 1961-62; Nat. Inst. Child Health and Human Devel. grantee, 1971-73. Fellow AAAS, Am. Psychol. Assn., Am. Psychol. Soc., Soc. for Personality and Social Psychology; mem. Psychonomic Soc., Brit. Psychol. Soc., Sigma Xi. Clubs: Cosmos (Washington); Md. Capital Yacht, Eastport Yacht (Annapolis, Md.); Amateur Fencing (London). Home: 2 Wells Lndg Annapolis MD 21403-2316 Office: Howard U Dept Psychology Washington DC 20059

LITTLE, ALAN BRIAN, obstetrician, gynecologist, educator; b. Montreal, Que., Can., Mar. 11, 1925; emigrated to U.S., 1951, naturalized, 1959; s. Herbert Melville and Mary Lizette (Campbell) L.; m. Nancy Alison Campbell, Aug. 20, 1949 (div.); children: Michael C. (dec.), Susan MacF. and Deborah MacF. (twins), Catherine E., Jane A., Mary L.; m. Bitten Stripp, Mar. 31, 1983. BA, McGill U., 1948, MD, CM, 1950. Intern Montreal Gen. Hosp., 1950-51; resident Boston Lying-in and Free Hosp. for Women, 1951-55, asst. obstetrician, asso. obstetrician and gynecologist, 1955-65; teaching fellow, asst. prof. Harvard Med. Sch., 1952-65; prof. ob-gyn, then Arthur H. Bill prof. ob-gyn Case Western Res. U. Sch. Medicine, Cleve., 1965-82; chmn. dept. reproductive biology Case Western Res. U. Sch. Medicine, 1972-82; prof. gynecology McGill U., Montreal, 1983—, chmn. dept. ob-gyn., 1983-94; clin. prof. ob-gyn. U. Medicine and Dentistry N.J., Newark, 1994—; dir. dept. ob-gyn. Univ. Hosps., Cleve., to 1982, Royal Victoria Hosp., Montreal, 1983-94; mem. nat. adv. com. Nat. Inst. Child Health and Human Devel. Author: (with B. Tenney) Clinical Obstetrics, 1962; editor: (with others) Gynecology and Obstetrics-Health Care for Women, 1975, 2d edit., 1982; (with D. Tulchinsky) Maternal Fetal Endocrinology, 2d edit., 1994; contbr. articles to profl. jours. Served with RCAF, 1943-45. Fellow ACS, Royal Coll. Surgeons, Am. Coll. Obstetricians and Gynecologists; mem. AMA, Endocrine Soc., Am. Gynecol. and Obstet. Soc., Am., Central assns. ob-gyn., Assn. Profs. Ob-Gyn., Soc. Gynecol. Investigation, Soc. Ob-Gyn. Can. Office: 687 Pine Ave W, Montreal, PQ Canada H3A 1A1

LITTLE, ARTHUR DEHON, investment banker; b. Providence, Feb. 13, 1944; s. Royal and Augusta Willoughby (Ellis) L.; m. E. Jann Leeming, Sept. 6, 1974; children: Cameron Royal, Kimberley Murray. B.A. in History, Stanford U., 1966. With Narragansett Capital Corp., Providence, 1967—, asst. to pres., 1968-69, v.p., 1969-73, exec. v.p., treas., 1975-76, pres., treas., chief operating officer, dir., 1976-77, pres., treas., chief exec. officer, dir., 1977-80, pres., chief exec. officer, dir., 1980, chmn. bd., chief exec. officer, 1980-86; mng. dir. Narragansett Capital, Inc., Providence, 1986—; prin. The Little Investment Co., Boston, 1992—; bd. dirs. A.T. Wall Co., JDR Holdings, Inc., R.I. Zool. Soc., Lyford Cay Found., New Eng. chpt. Am. Liver Found., Jr. Achievement No. New Eng., Jr. Achievement Nat. Bd.; chmn. bd. dirs. Digital Vision, Inc., L & K Acquisitions, Quantum Internat., JDR

Holdings, Inc. Chmn. JDR Holdings, Inc. Mem. Lyford Cay Club, Somerset Club, Kittansett Club, Bald Peak Colony Club. Office: 33 Broad St Ste 10 Boston MA 02109-4216

LITTLE, BRIAN F., oil company executive; b. Moncton, N.B., Can., Oct. 28, 1943; s. George E. and Marion M. (McCartney) L.; m. Dianne E. Rogers, Oct. 11, 1969; children: Michael William, Sara Elizabeth. BA, Am. Internat. Coll., 1966; LLB, Osgoode Hall Law Sch., 1974; LLM, London Sch. Econs., Eng., 1975. Indsl. devel. asst. Can. Nat., Moncton and Montreal, Can., 1967-71; articling student McMillan Binch, Toronto, Ont., Can., 1975-76, assoc., 1977-82, ptnr., 1982-83; v.p., gen. counsel Dome Petroleum, Calgary, Alta., Can., 1983-88; v.p. law and external affairs Amoco Can. Petroleum Co. Ltd., Calgary, 1988-89, sr. v.p. law, 1989-92, sr. v.p. law, gen. counsel, 1992—. Trustee Can. Athletic Found. Mem. Can. Bar Assn., Law Soc. Upper Can., Osgoode Hall Law Sch. Alumni Assn. (bd. dirs.). Office: Amoco Can Petroleum Co Ltd, 240 Fourth Ave SW, Calgary, AB Canada T2P 4H4

LITTLE, BRIAN W., pathology educator, administrator; b. Boston, Dec. 15, 1945; m. Pamela Little; children: Kristin B., Eric W. BA in Physics, Cornell U., 1967; MD, U. Vt., 1973, PhD in Biochemistry, 1977. Diplomate in neuropathology and anatomic and clin. pathology Am. Bd. Pathology; lic., Pa. Attending pathologist neuropathology SUNY, Stony Brook, 1984-87, Lehigh Valley Hosp., Allentown, Pa., 1987—; assoc. prof. pathology Hahnemann U. Sch. Medicine, Phila., 1989-94; dir. of edn. Lehigh Valley Hosp., Allentown, 1991-94; assoc. prof. pathology-neuropathology Med. Coll. of Pa./Hahnemann U., Phila., 1994—, assoc. dean for affiliate affairs, 1994-95, sr. assoc. dean for affiliate affairs and grad. med. edn., 1995—. Office: Med Coll Pa/Hahnemann U Broad and Vine Philadelphia PA 19102-1192

LITTLE, CARL MAURICE, performing arts administrator; b. Campbellton, N.B., Can., Mar. 17, 1924; s. George Everett and Ada (Boucher) L.; m. Frances R. Corner, Aug. 27, 1949; children: Christine, Jennifer, Geoffrey, Stephen; m. Barbara Wolfond, Dec. 8, 1978. B.Sc., Dalhousie U., Halifax, N.S., Can., 1945, Licentiate of Music, 1945, Diploma Engring., 1944; Asso., Royal Coll. Music, London, 1952; Licentiate, Royal Acad. Music, London, 1952. Tchr. music public schs. Outremont, Que., Can., 1949-50; pvt. tchr. music Montreal, Que., 1946-59, Toronto, Ont., 1959-70; producer music CBC Radio, Montreal, 1952-59; producer music CBC Radio, Toronto, 1959-65, nat. network supr. serious music, 1965-75; mgr. Nat. Arts Centre Orch., Ottawa, 1975-78; co-founder, pres. Little Gallery of the Arts, Ottawa, 1979-80; pres. Arts Connection, Victoria, B.C., 1980—; exec. dir., festival adminstr. Courtenay Youth Music Centre (B.C.), 1983; organist Holy Trinity Anglican Ch., Saanichton, B.C., 1984-93. Pianist, 1945-52; juror for internat. music competitions including Scriabin Piano Competition, Oslo, Norway, Internat. String Quartet, Stockholm, Sweden, Let The Peoples Sing, Choir, London; jury chmn. Kathaumixw Internat. Choral Festival Powell River, B.C., Can. Mem. Royal Can. Coll. Organists (program chmn. 1985), Can. Conf. of Arts, Can. Music Council, Can. Amateur Musicians Assn. (dir.; co-founder), Ont. Choral Fedn., Nat. Arts Centre Orch. Assn. Instrumental in founding and adminstrn. of CBC competitions, CBC music projects and programs. Address: 109-134 5th Ave E, Qualicum Beach, BC Canada V9K 1Y7

LITTLE, DANIEL EASTMAN, philosophy educator, university program director; b. Rock Island, Ill., Apr. 7, 1949; s. William Charles and Emma Lou (Eastman) L.; m. Ronnie Alice Friedland, Sept. 12, 1976 (div. May 1995); children: Joshua Friedland-Little, Rebecca Friedland-Little. BS in Math. with highest honors, AB in Philosophy with high honors, U. Ill., 1971; PhD in Philosophy, Harvard U., 1977. Asst. prof. U. Wis.-Parkside, Kenosha, 1976-79; vis. assoc. prof. Wellesley (Mass.) Coll., 1985-87; vis. scholar Ctr. Internat. Affairs Harvard U., 1989-91, assoc. Ctr. Internat. Affairs, 1991-95; asst. prof. Colgate U., Hamilton, N.Y., 1979-85, assoc. prof., 1985-92, prof., 1992-96, chmn. dept. philosophy and religion, 1992-93, assoc. dean faculty, 1993-96; assoc. Ctr. for Population and Devel. Studies, Harvard U., 1996—; v.p. academic affairs Bucknell U., Lewisberg, Pa., 1996—, prof. philosophy, 1996—; teaching fellow Harvard U., 1973-76; participant internat. confs. Ctr. Asian and Pacific Studies, U. Oreg., 1992, Social Sci. Rsch. Coun./McArthur Found., U. Calif., San Diego, 1991, Budapest, Hungary, 1990, Morelos, Mex., 1989, Rockefeller Found., Bellagio, Italy, 1990, U. Manchester, Eng., 1986; mem. screening com. on internat. peace and security Social Sci. Rsch. Coun./MacArthur Found., 1991-94; manuscript reviewer Yale U. Press, Cambridge U. Press, Princeton U. Press, Oxford U. Press, Westview Press, Harvard U. Press, Can. Jour. Philosophy, Philosophy Social Scis., Synthese, Am. Polit. Sci. Rev.; grant proposal reviewer NSF, Social Sci. Rsch. Coun., Nat. Endowment for Humanities; tenure and promotion reviewer U. Tenn., Bowdoin Coll., Duke U. Author: The Scientific Marx, 1986, Understanding Peasant China: Case Studies in the Philosophy of Social Science, 1989, Varieties of Social Explanation: An Introduction to the Philosophy of Social Science, 1991 (Outstanding Book award Choice 1992), On the Reliability of Economic Models, 1995; contbr. articles to profl. jours., books. Social Sci. Rsch. Postdoctoral fellow MacArthur Found., 1989-91, Rsch. grantee NSF, 1987, Woodrow Wilson Grad. fellow, 1971-72. Mem. Am. Philos. Assn., Am. Soc. for Polit. & Legal Philosophy, Assn. Asian Studies, Internat. Assn. Philosophy of Law & Social Philosophy, Internat. Devel. Ethics Assn., Phi Beta Kappa. Office: VPAA Marts Hall Bucknell U Lewisburg PA 17837

LITTLE, DON BARRON, clergyman; b. Rosebud, Tex., Sept. 5, 1936; s. Leonard Barron and Idamartha (Busse) L.; 1 child, Beth Ann; m. Eleanor Ann Wisler, Aug.24, 1958; 1 child, Donna Ruth Bennett. BA, Southwestern U., 1958; ThM, So. Meth. U., 1961; D Ministry, McCormick Sem., Chgo., 1987. Ordained elder United Meth. Ch., 1961. Sr. minister Van (Tex.) United Meth. Ch., 1970-74, 1st United Meth. Ch., Texas City, Tex., 1974-78, Pollard United Meth. Ch., Tyler, Tex., 1978-84, Lakewood United Meth. Ch., Houston, 1984-91, Pasadena (Tex.) 1st United Meth. Ch., 1991-94, 1st United Meth. Ch., Conroe, Tex., 1994—. Chaplain U.S. Army, 1967-70, Vietnam. Decorated Bronze Star, Air medal; recipient Copeland Evangelism award Tex. Ann. Conf., United Meth. Ch., 1986, 92. Office: 1st United Meth Ch 207 W Phillips St Conroe TX 77301-2815

LITTLE, EMILY BROWNING, architect; b. Austin, Tex., June 4, 1951; d. Betty (Browning) L. BA in Cultural Anthropology, U. Tex., 1973, MArch, 1979. Registered architect, Tex. Archtl. apprentice Austin Design Assocs., 1980-81; project mgr. Nutt, Wolters & Assocs., Austin, 1981-84; prin. Emily Little Architects, Inc., Austin, 1984—. Prin. works include numerous residences, hist. restorations and comml. bldgs. Mem. citizens adv. com. Travis County Juvenile Ct., Austin, 1984-86; mem. adv. bd. Deborah Hay Dance Co., Austin, 1984—; chmn. Austin Design Commn., 1987-89. Recipient Archtl. Merit award Austin Bd. Realtors, 1989. Mem. AIA (commr. Austin chpt. 1987-88, Outstanding Young Arch. of Tex. 1993), Tex. Soc. Archs. (honors com. 1992, Design award 1996), Austin Women in Arch. (pres. 1985-86), Nat. Trust for Hist. Preservation, Tex. Fine Arts Assn. (pres. 1990-92), Heritage Soc. Austin (bd. dirs. 1989—, pres. 1995, Bldg. award 1988, 90, 92, 93). Democrat. Avocations: travel, swimming. Office: 1001 E 8th St Austin TX 78702-3248

LITTLE, GEORGE DANIEL, clergyman; b. St. Louis, Dec. 18, 1929; s. Henry and Agathe Cox (Daniel) L.; m. Joan Phillips McCafferty, Aug. 22, 1953; children: Deborah Philips, Cynthia McCafferty (dec.), Alice Annette, Daniel Ross, Benjamin Henry. AB, Princeton U., 1951; MDiv, McCormick Theol. Sem., Chgo., 1954; LLD (hon.), Huron Coll., 1977. Ordained to ministry Presbyn. Ch., 1954; pastor East London Group Ministry, Presbyn. Ch. Eng., 1954-56, Friendship Presbyn. Ch., Pitts., 1956-62; assoc. dir. dept. urban ch., planning assoc. Bd. Nat. Missions, United Presbyterian Ch. U.S.A., N.Y.C., 1962-72; assoc. for budgeting Gen. Assembly Mission Council, 1973-76, exec. dir. council, 1976-84; pastor First Presbyn. Ch., Ithaca, N.Y., 1984-93; interim pres. McCormick Theol. Sem., Chgo., 1993-94; pastor-in-residence Village Presbyn. Ch., Prairie Village, Kans., 1995-96; ret., 1996. Home: PO Box 4302 Ithaca NY 14852-4302

LITTLE, JOHN BERTRAM, physician, radiobiology educator, researcher; b. Boston, Oct. 5, 1929; s. Bertram Kimball and Nina (Fletcher) L.; m. Francoise Cottereau, Aug. 4, 1960; children—John Bertram, Frederic Fletcher. A.B. in Physics, Harvard U., 1951; M.D., Boston U., 1955. Diplomate Am. Bd. Radiology. Intern in medicine Johns Hopkins Hosp., Balt., 1955-56; resident in radiology Mass. Gen. Hosp., Boston, 1958-61; fellow Harvard U., Cambridge, Mass., 1961-63; from instr. to assoc. prof. radiobiology Harvard Sch. Pub. Health, Boston, 1963-75; prof. Harvard Sch. Pub. Health, 1975—, chmn. dept. physiology, 1980-83, James Stevens Simmons prof. radiobiology, 1987—; dir. Kresge Ctr. Environ. Health, Boston, 1982—; cons. radiology Mass. Gen. Hosp., Boston, 1965—, Brigham and Women's Hosp., Boston, 1968—; chmn. bd. sci. counsellors Nat. Inst. Environ. Health Sci., 1982-84; bd. sci. counsellors Nat. Toxicology Program, 1988-92; mem. sci. coun. Radiation Effects Rsch. Found., Hiroshima, Japan, 1993—; chmn. bd. dirs. on radiation effects rsch. Nat. Acad. of Scis. Mem. editorial bd. numerous nat. and internat. jours.; contbr. chpts. to books and articles to profl. jours. Mem. coun. Nat. Coun. on Radiation Protection and Measurements, 1993—; trustee various hist. and cultural orgns. Capt. U.S. Army, 1956-58. Am. Cancer Soc. grantee, 1965-68; recipient numerous rsch. and grants NIH, 1968—; named one of Outstanding Investigator grantee Nat. Cancer Inst., 1988—. Mem. AAAS (coun. in med. scis. 1988-91), Radiation Rsch. Soc. N.Am. (pres.-elect 1985, pres. 1986-87), Am. Assn. Cancer Rsch., Am. Physiol. Soc., Health Physics Soc., Am. Soc. Photobiology, Internat. Assn. Radiation Rsch. (coun.). Avocations: music, architectural history. Office: Harvard U Dept Radiobiology 665 Huntington Ave Boston MA 02115-6021

LITTLE, JOHN DUTTON CONANT, management scientist, educator; b. Boston, Feb. 1, 1928; s. John Dutton and Margaret (Jones) L.; m. Elizabeth Davenport Alden, Sept. 12, 1953; children: John Norris, Sarah Alden, Thomas Dunham Conant, Ruel Davenport. SB in Physics, MIT, 1948, PhD, 1955; PhD (hon.), U. Liege, Belgium, 1992. Engr. Gen. Electric Co., Schenectady, 1949-50; asst. prof. ops. research Case-Western Res. U., 1957-60, assoc. prof., 1960-62; research asst. MIT, 1951-54, assoc. prof. mgmt., 1962-67, prof., 1967-78, George M. Bunker prof. mgmt., 1978-89, Inst. prof., 1989—, dir. Ops. Research Ctr., 1969-76, head mgmt. sci. group Sloan Sch. Mgmt., 1972-82, head behavioral and policy scis. area, 1982-88; pres. Mgmt. Decision Systems, Inc., 1967-80, chmn. bd. dirs., 1967-85; dir., advisor to bd. dirs. Info. Resources, Inc., 1985—; cons. ops. rsch. indsl. govtl. orgns., 1958—; vis. prof. mktg. European Inst. Bus. Adminstrn., Fontainebleau, France, fall 1988; researcher math. programming, queuing theory, mktg., traffic control, decision support systems. Assoc. editor: Mgmt. Sci, 1967-71; contbr. articles to profl. jours. Trustee Mktg. Sci. Inst., 1983-89. Served with AUS, 1955-56. Fellow AAAS; mem. NAE, Ops. Rsch. Soc. Am. (coun. 1970-73, pres. 1979-80), Inst. Mgmt. Scis. (v.p. 1976-79, pres. 1984-85), Inst. for Ops. Rsch. and the Mgmt. Scis. (pres. 1995), Am. Mktg. Assn., Sigma Xi. Home: 37 Conant Rd RR 3 Lincoln MA 01773 Office: MIT Sloan Sch Mgmt Cambridge MA 02142-1347

LITTLE, JOHN WILLIAM, plastic surgeon, educator; b. Indpls., Mar. 12, 1944; s. John William Jr. and Naida (Jones) L.; m. Patricia Padgett Lea, May 26, 1969 (div. 1974); m. Teri Ann Tyson, Feb. 28, 1981 (div. 1982). AB, Dartmouth Coll., 1966, B. in Med. Scis., 1967; MD, Harvard U., 1969. Diplomate Am. Bd. Med. Examiners, Am. Bd. Surgery, Am. Bd. Plastic Surgery. Intern affiliated hosps. Case Western Res. U., Cleve., 1969-70, resident in surgery, 1970-74, resident in plastic surgery, 1973-75; fellow in plastic surgery affiliated hosp. U. Miami, 1975-77; asst. prof. Georgetown U., Washington, 1977-82, assoc. prof., 1982-87, prof., 1987-92, clin. prof., 1992—, dir. div. plastic surgery, residency tng. program, plastic surgeon-in-chief univ. hosp., 1979-92; dir. Nat. Capital Tng. Program in Plastic Surgery affilitated hosps. Georgetown U. and Howard U., 1988-92; dir. Georgetown Plastic Surgery Fellowship in Breast and Aesthestic Surgery, 1990-92; chief plastic surgery Medlantic Ctr. for Ambulatory Surgery, Inc., 1993—; cons. Nat. Cancer Inst., NIH, Bethesda, Md., 1977-92, Washington VA Med. Ctr., 1981-92, Reach to Recovery program Nat. Capital chpt. Am. Cancer Soc., 1981—, RENU program in breast reconstrn., 1982; specialist site visitor plastic surgery residency rev. com. Accreditation Coun. for Grad. Med. Edn., 1982—; vis. lect. various insts. Contbr. numerous articles to profl. jours.; manuscript reviewer Plastic and Reconstructive Surgery, Annals of Plastic Surgery. Bd. dirs. Triann reconstructive surgery teams to Caribbean and S.Am., 1981—, Georgetown Tissue Bank, 1986-88, Operation Luz del Sol, 1992—, Reconstructive Surgeons Vol. Program, 1993—; trustee Washington Opera, 1993—, mem. artistic com., 1994—. Mem. AMA, ACS (coord. plastic surgery audiovisual program Ann. Clin. Congress 1988-90, 92-93, Met. Washington chpt. councillor 1985-94, chmn. sci. program com. 1990-91, v.p. 1991-92, pres. 1992-93), Nat. Capital Soc. Plastic Surgeons (sec. treas. 1982-83, pres. 1984-85), Am. Soc. Plastic and Reconstructive Surgeons (audiovisual program dir. ann. meeting 1984-86, strategic planning com. 1987-96, fin. com. 1989-94, conv. policy com. 1993-96, ops. com. 1993-96, chmn. 1994-95, spokesperson network steering com. 1994-96, bd. dirs. 1994-96, exec. com. 1995-96), Am. Assn. Plastic Surgeons (co-chmn. various coms.), Plastic Surgery Ednl. Found. (bd. dirs. 1985—, devel. com. 1991—, chmn. 1997—, chmn. various coms., rep. to Coun. Plastic Surg. Orgns. 1989-95, parlimentarian 1992-93, v.p. 1993-94, presdl. adv. coun. 1993-96, commr. various commns., pres.-elect, 1995, pres. 1995-96), Med. Soc. D.C. (chmn. plastic surgery sect. 1985), D.R. Millard Surg. Soc. and Ednl. Found. (pres. 1985-87), Am. Cleft Palate Assn., Am. Soc. Maxillofacial Surgeons, Washington Acad. Surgeons (coun. 1988-90), Am. Soc. Aesthetic Plastic Surgery, NE Soc. Plastic Surgeons (chmn. various coms., v.p. 1991-92, pres. 1992-93, historian 1995—), Internat. Soc. Aesthetic Plastic Surgery (chmn. bylaws com. 1990-93, 95—, parliamentarian 1990-93, mem. membership com. 1993—, chmn. 1993-95), Am. Alpine Workshop in Plastic Surgery (founder, pres. 1991-92, historian 1995—), Internat. Fedn. Plastic Reconstructive and Aesthetic Surgery, Internat. Plastic, Reconstructive and Aesthetic Found., Aesthetic Surgery Edn. and Rsch. Found., Nat. Endowment Plast Surgery (bd. govs. 1995—). Republican. Presbyterian. Home: 4200 Massachusetts Ave NW Washington DC 20016-4744 Office: 1145 19th St NW Ste 802 Washington DC 20036-3700

LITTLE, LARRY CHATMON, head football coach; b. Groveland, Ga., Nov. 2, 1945; s. George Chatmon and Ida Mae (Haynes) L.; m. Rose DeJesus, Apr. 15, 1978; children: Damita, Learon. BS, Bethune-Cookman Coll., 1967; DSc, Biscayne Coll., 1972. Pro-football player San Diego Chargers, 1967-69, Miami Dolphins, 1969-80; athletic dir. Miami (Fla.) Edison High Sch., 1981-83; head football coach Bethune-Cookman Coll., Daytona Bch., Fla., 1983-92, Ohio Glory World League, Columbus, 1992, N.C. Ctrl. U., Durham, 1993—. Amb. City of Medicine, Durham, N.C., 1997. Named All Pro, 1971, 72, 73, 74, 75, 76, Off Lineman of Yr. by NFL, 1971, 72, 73, Fla. Hall of Fame by Fla. Sports Writers, 1978, NFL Hall of Fame, 1993. Democrat. Baptist. Home: 5310 Lacy Rd Durham NC 27713-1626 Office: NC Ctrl U PO Box 19705 Durham NC 27707-0099

LITTLE, LESTER KNOX, historian, educator; b. Providence, Oct. 21, 1935; s. Arthur Foster and Edith Caroline (Hyde) L.; m. Lella Gandini, Apr. 7, 1972; stepchildren: Andrea Dell'Antonio, Ian Dell'Antonio. AB, Dartmouth Coll., 1957; MA, Princeton U., 1960, PhD, 1962. History instr. Princeton U., 1961-63; asst. prof. history U. Chgo., 1963-69, assoc. prof., 1969-71; assoc. prof. history Smith Coll., Northampton, Mass., 1971-76, prof., 1976-82, Dwight W. Morrow prof. history, 1982—, chmn. dept. history, 1986-89; dir. Smith Coll. in Italy, 1989-91; vis. prof. history U. Calif., Berkeley, 1988, Yale U., 1995, Ecole des Hautes Etudes en Scis. sociales, Paris, 1996. Author: Religious Poverty and the Profit Economy in Medieval Europe, 1978, Liberty, Charity, Fraternity: Lay Religious Confraternites at Bergamo in the Age of the Commune, 1988, Benedictine Maledictions: Liturgical Cursing in Romanesque France, 1993; co-editor, translator: Nature, Man and Society in the Twelfth Century, 1968. Fellow Inst. Advanced Study, 1969-70, Am. Coun. Learned Socs., 1970-71, Guggenheim Found., 1983, NEH, 1992, resident Am. Acad. in Rome, 1995; grantee Am. Philos. Soc., 1974-75, NEH, 1982. Mem. Am. Hist. Assn., Medieval Acad. Am. Home: 33 Washington Ave Northampton MA 01060-2822 Office: Smith College Dept History Northampton MA 01063

LITTLE, LOREN EVERTON, musician, ophthalmologist; b. Sioux Falls, S.D., Oct. 28, 1941; s. Everton A. and Maxine V. (Alcorn) L.; m. Christy Gyles; 1 child, Nicole Moses; children from previous marriage: Laurie, Richard. BA, Macalester Coll., 1963; BS, U. S.D., 1965; MD, U. Wash., 1967. Prin. trumpeter Sioux Falls Mcpl. Band, 1956-65; trumpeter St. Paul Civic Orch., 1960-62; leader, owner Swinging Scots Band, St. Paul, 1960-63; trumpeter Edgewater Inn Show Room, Seattle, 1966-67, Jazztet-Arts Council, Sioux Falls, 1970-71, Lee Maxwell Shows, Washington, 1971-74; residency in ophthalmology Walter Reed Med. Ctr., Washington, 1974; co-leader, trumpeter El Paso (Tex.) All Stars, 1975; freelance trumpeter, soloist various casinos and hotels, Las Vegas, Nev., 1977—. Trumpeter (album) Journey by R. Romero Band, 1983, Sizenter, 1997; soloist for numerous entertainers including Tony Bennett, Burt Bacharach, Jack Jones, Sammy Davis Jr., Henry Mancini, Jerry Lewis Telethon, for video Star Salute to Live Music, 1989; with Stan Mark Band Nat. Pub. Radio Broadcast, 1994, 95; soloist on video Stan Mark Live at the 4 Queens Hotel, Las Vegas; prodr. Carl Saunders Solo Album Out Of the Blue, 1996. Trustee Nev. Sch. of the Arts, Las Vegas, 1983—; pres. S&L Music SNL Rec. Served to lt. col. U.S. Army, 1968-76, Vietnam. Decorated Silver Star, Purple Heart, Bronze Star, Air medal; fellow Internat. Eye Found., 1974; Dewitt Wallace scholar Readers Digest, 1963-65. Fellow ACS, Am. Acad. Ophthalmology; mem. Am. Fedn. Musicians, Nat. Bd. Med. Examiners. Presbyterian. Avocations: history, music, medicine, sports, skiing.

LITTLE, LOYD HARRY, JR., author; b. Hickory, N.C., Sept. 12, 1940; s. Loyd Harry and Rebecca Lillian (Bailey) L.; m. Kris Petesch, 1993. BA in Journalism, U. N.C., 1962, postgrad., 1967-68. Editor Lumbee weekly newspaper, Pembroke, N.C., 1966; med. reporter Winston-Salem (N.C.) Jour., 1967-69; bus. editor Raleigh (N.C.) News and Observer, 1969; editor Carolina Fin. Times, Raleigh, 1970-75; spl. projects editor Durham (N.C.) Morning Herald, 1976-79; tchr. creative writing courses U. N.C., 1979-82; asst. city editor Greenville (S.C.) News, 1990-93; mng. editor Carteret County News-Times, Morehead City, N.C., 1993—. Author: Parthian Shot, 1975 (Ernest Hemingway award), In the Village of the Man, 1978, Smokehouse Jam, 1988. Chmn. Orange Grove Precinct Republican Com., 1972-73. With Green Berets U.S. Army, 1962-65. Decorated Commendation medal; Vietnamese Bronze Star medal; Hickory Daily Record scholar U. N.C., 1962. Mem. Chez Hickory Club. Home: 1403 Dairyland Rd Chapel Hill NC 27516

LITTLE, MARK MCKENNA, financial management executive; b. Hoisington, Kans., Mar. 30, 1957; s. Freed Sebastian Little and Jana Vaye (Jones) Hansen; m. Peggy Louise Kelly, June 24, 1988; 1 child, McKenna Louise. B of Gen. Studies, Tex. Christian U., 1980. Account exec. Liberty Mut. Ins. Co., San Antonio, 1981-83; cons. M. Little Fin. Enterprises, San Antonio, 1983-89; chmn., chief exec. officer Wall St. Svcs., Inc., San Antonio, 1989—; pres./CEO Waterhouse Fin. Mgmt. Group, Inc., 1995—; mem. bd. advs. Clear Lake Nat. Bank. Bd. dirs. Mental Health Assn. in Greater San Antonio, United Way, 1988-92, pres., chmn., 1990, KLRN TV Cmty. Adv. Bd., San Antonio, 1990-94, pres., 1992-93; bd. dirs. N.E. Ind. Sch. Dist., Kids Involvement Network, San Antonio, 1990—, chmn., 1990-93; bd. dirs. N.E. Ind. Sch. Dist.-Wide adv. bd., 1991—, pres., 1991-92; del., bd. dirs. Jaycees Internat., Taipei, Taiwan, 1983; elected del. Tex. State Rep. Conv., 1992, White House Conf. Small Bus., mem. exec. coun. Tex. del.; mem. bd. trustees N.E. Ednl. Found.; vice chair allocattions panel United Way, San Antonio, 1994; apptd. del. U.S. Securities and Exch. Commn.-Govt. Forum on Small Bus. Capital Formation, Providence, 1995, Washington, 1996; del., program co-chair Tex. Gov.'s Conf. on Small Bus., 1996; appointed delegate U.S. Securities & Exch. Comm., govt. forum on small bus. capital formation, 1995-96. Mem. San Antonio Area Coun. Pres., North San Antonio C. of C. (bd. dirs. 1991—, vice chmn. bd. 1991-92, 95, chmn. bd. elect 1996, 97, Edith Caldwell award 1995), San Antonio Jaycees (bd. dirs. 1982-83), North San Antonio Toastmasters (pres. 1990-91, world affairs coun. 1992-93), Delta Tau Delta (Larry Abrahms award), Clear Lake Natl. Bank Board of Adv. Office: Wall St Svcs Inc 12042 Blanco Rd Ste 330 San Antonio TX 78216-5438

LITTLE, RHODA SMELTZER, nursing administrator; b. Harrisburg, Pa., Jan. 31, 1938; d. Charles Anderson and Rhoda May (Lepperd) Smeltzer; m. Lawrence Jess Little, May 26, 1962; children: Robin Kimberly, Jonathan Sanders. Diploma in nursing, Thomas Jefferson U. Hosp., Phila., 1960; BSN, Grace Coll., 1960; MSN in Nursing Adminstrn., U. Ill., 1979. RN, Pa., Ill., N.J., Fla. Divsnl. dir. nursing and staff devel. Silver Cross Hosp., Joliet, Ill., 1978-82; dir. nursing svcs. Forkosh Meml. Hosp., Chgo., 1982-83; dir. edn. and nursing quality assurance Loyola U. Med. Ctr.-Mulcahy Outpatient Ctr., Maywood, Ill., 1985-88; asst. adminstr. patient care, dir. nursing, maternal/child, emergency and edn. Polyclinic Med. Ctr., Harrisburg, Pa., 1989-96; quality improvement health svcs. divsn. Health Am., Harrisburg, 1996—; cons. St. Francis Hosp., Blue Island, Ill., 1983-84. Contbr. articles to profl. jours. Recipient Edn. award Pa. Hosp. Assn., 1992. Mem. Am. Orgn. Nurse Execs., Pa. Orgn. Nurse Execs., Pa. South Ctrl. Orgn. Nurse Execs. (program and mktg. coms., mem.-at-large exec. com.), Sigma Theta Tau. Presbyterian. Avocations: decorating, music. Home: 833 Tallyho Dr Hershey PA 17033-1828

LITTLE, ROBERT ANDREWS, architect, designer, painter; b. Brookline, Mass., Sept. 9, 1915; s. Clarence Cook and Katherine Day (Andrews) L.; m. Ann Murphy Halle, Dec., 27, 1940; children: Sam Robertson, Revere (dec.). A.B. cum laude, Harvard U., 1937, M.Arch., 1939. Designer G.H. Perkins, Cambridge, Mass., 1939-41; architect U.S. Navy, Washington, 1941-43; ops. analyst Air Staff Intelligence, Washington, 1943-45; prin. Robert A. Little & Assos., Cleve., 1946-58, 67-69; partner Little & Dalton, Cleve., 1958-67; dir. design Dalton-Dalton-Little-Newport, Cleve., 1969-78; owner Robert A. Little, Design and Architecture, 1978—; tchr., lectr. Harvard, U. Pa., Carnegie Inst. Tech., U. Mich., Smith Coll., U. Notre Dame, Kent State U. Exhibited art and graphics in Cleve., Phila., Boston., since 1970; works include Air Force Mus., Dayton, Ohio, Supreme Ct. and Tower, Columbus, Ohio.; one-person shows in Ohio, Maine, Mass. Trustee Cleve. Mus. Sci., 1952-56, Cleve. Inst. Music, 1956-58; mem. Cleve. Fine Arts Com. Served with U.S. Army, 1940. Fellow AIA (pres. Cleve. chpt. 1966-68, nat. and state design awards), Harvard Sch. of Design Alumni Assn. (past pres., internat. dir. of devel.). Home: 5 Pepper Ridge Rd Cleveland OH 44124-4904 Office: Robert A Little FAIA Design 5 Pepper Ridge Rd Cleveland OH 44124-4904 *As a child, I drew pictures all the time—and they were my current ideal—a face I thought pretty, a massive locomotive, a pine tree against the sea, or a castle in the sky. As an adult Designer and Artist, too, I have spent my whole life dreaming of beauty, and trying to create it—and, of course, never fully succeeding. But the great satisfaction has not been the results, but rather the breathless moments of the search itself, and the boundless horizons of the dream.*

LITTLE, ROBERT COLBY, physiologist, educator; b. Norwalk, Ohio, June 2, 1920; s. Edwin Robert and Eleanor Thresher (Colby) L.; m. Claire Campbell Means, Jan. 20, 1945; children—William C., Edwin C. A.B., Denison U., 1942; M.D., Western Res. U., 1944, M.S., 1948. Intern Grace Hosp., Detroit, 1944-45; USPHS postdoctoral research fellow Western Res. U., 1948-49; resident internal medicine Crile VA Hosp., Cleve., 1949-50; asst. prof. physiology, then assoc. prof. physiology and medicine U. Tenn. Sch. Medicine, 1950-54; rsch. participant Oak Ridge Inst. Nuclear Studies, 1952; dir. clin. research Mead Johnson & Co., 1954-57; lectr. medicine U. Louisville, 1955-57; dir. cardio pulmonary labs. Scott and White Clinic, Scott Sherwood and Brindley Found., Temple, Tex., 1957-59; prof. physiology, asst. prof. medicine Seton Hall Coll. Medicine and Dentistry, 1957-64, acting chmn. dept. physiology, 1961-63; prof. physiology, chmn. dept., also asst. prof. medicine Ohio State U. Sch. Medicine, 1964-73; prof. physiology, prof. medicine Med. Coll. Ga. Sch. Medicine, Augusta, 1973-89, chmn. dept. physiology, 1973-86, prof., chmn. emeritus, 1989—; cons. in field. Author: Physiology of the Heart and Circulation, 1977, 2d edit., 1981, 3d edit., 1985, 4th edit., 1989; editor: Physiology of Atrial Pacemakers and Conductive Tissues, 1980; contbr. chpts. to books and articles to profl. jours. Served to capt. M.C. AUS, 1945-47. Mem. AMA, Am. Physiol. Soc., So. Soc. Clin. Investigation, Am. Heart Assn., Soc. Exptl. Biology and Medicine, Am. Fedn. Clin. Research, Sigma Xi, Sigma Chi, Alpha Kappa Kappa, Alpha Omega Alpha. Home: 523 Brandon Village 4275 Owens Rd Evans GA 30809

LITTLE, ROBERT DAVID, library science educator; b. Milw., July 11, 1937; s. Kenneth Edwin and Grace Elizabeth (Terwilliger) L. BA, U. Wis., Milw., 1959; MA, U. Wis., 1964, PhD, 1972. Tchr., sch. librarian Sevastapol Pub. Schs., Sturgeon Bay, Wis., 1959-62; sch. librarian Highland Park (Ill.) High Sch., 1962-63; supr. sch. libraries Sevastapol/Gilbraltor Pub. Sch., Sturgeon Bay, 1963-65; state sch. library supr. Wis. Dept. Pub. Instrn., Madison, 1965-69, program adminstr., 1969-70; asst. prof. libr. sci. U. Wis., Milw., 1970-71, acting dir. Sch. Libr. Sci., 1971; assoc. prof. libr. sci. Ind. State U., Terre Haute, 1971-77, prof., 1977-97, chmn. dept., 1971-93; cons.

Ind. Nat. Network Study, Terre Haute, 1978-79; cons., researcher Nat. Ctr. Edn. Stats., Washington, 1978-79; mem. Ind. State Libr. Adv. Coun., Indpls., 1981-91. Co-author: Public Library Users and Uses, 1988; editor: Cataloging, Processing, Administering AV Materials, 1972; contbr. articles to profl. jours. Pres. West Cen. Ind. chpt. Ind. Civil Liberties Union, 1988-92. Edn. Act fellow U. Wis., Madison, 1967, 68. Mem. ALA, Am. Assn. Sch. Librs., Assn. Ind. Media Educators (pres. 1981-82, Peggy Leach Pfeiffer Svc. award 1987), AAUP. Methodist. Avocations: reading, travel. Home: 376 Keane Ln Terre Haute IN 47803-2010 Office: Ind State U Ctr for Libr Sci Reeve Hall 336 Terre Haute IN 47809

LITTLE, ROBERT EUGENE, mechanical engineering educator, materials behavior researcher, consultant; b. Enfield, Ill., May 24, 1933; s. John Henry and Mary (Stephens) L.; m. Barbara Louina Farrell, Feb. 4, 1961; children: Susan Elizabeth, James Robert, Richard Roy, John William. BSME, U. Mich., 1959; MSME, Ohio State U., 1960; PhDME, U. Mich., 1963. Asst. prof. mech. engring. Okla. State U., Stillwater, 1963-65; assoc. prof. U. Mich., Dearborn, 1965-68, prof., 1968—. Author: Statistical Design of Fatigue Experiments, 1975, Probability and Statistics for Engineers, 1978. Mershon fellow Ohio State U., 1960. Mem. ASTM, Am. Statis. Assn., Rehab. Engring. Soc. N.Am. Home: 3230 Pine Lake Rd West Bloomfield MI 48324-1951 Office: U Mich 4901 Evergreen Rd Dearborn MI 48128-2406

LITTLE, THOMAS MAYER, public relations executive; b. Columbus, Ohio, Dec. 21, 1935; s. John William and Eulalia Josephine (Mayer) L.; m. Susan Mulford, Sept. 29, 1959; children: Carin Andrea, Debora Mayer, Sharon Mulford, Patricia Anne. BS in Journalism, Northwestern U., 1958; postgrad., Bradley U., 1958. Account supr. Philip Lesly Co., Chgo., 1962-77; v.p., account supr. Burson-Marsteller, N.Y.C., 1977; v.p. Foote Cone & Belding, Inc., N.Y.C., 1977-78; pres. FCB Pub. Rels., N.Y.C., 1978-81, Bus. Orgn., Inc. div. Carl Byoir & Assocs., N.Y.C., 1982, Tracy-Locke/BBDO Pub. Rels., Dallas, 1983-85; exec. v.p., gen. mgr. Manning, Selvage & Lee, N.Y.C., 1986; pres. T.J. Ross & Assocs., N.Y.C., 1986-87; pres., gen. mgr. Golin/Harris Communication, N.Y., 1987-91; pub. rels. cons., 1992—. Bd. dirs. Damon Runyon-Walter Winchell Cancer Fund, N.Y.C. Lt. (j.g.) USN, 1959-62. Mem. Am. Mktg. Assn., Pub. Rels. Soc. Am., Publicity Club N.Y.C., Mt. Kisco (N.Y.) Country Club, Sea Pines Country Club (Hilton Head Island), Lotos Club (N.Y.C.), Sigma Alpha Epsilon. Roman Catholic. Home and Office: 2 Newhall Rd Hilton Head Island SC 29928-3112

LITTLE, THOMAS WARREN, broadcast executive; b. Portland, Oreg., June 24, 1939; s. Hollis R. and Bernice (Lesseg) L.; m. Ruth Brady, Aug. 31, 1958; children—Vincent Thomas, Elizabeth Ann. BA and MA in Radio-TV, UCLA. Stage mgr. Sta. KPIX-TV, San Francisco, 1969-61; producer, dir. Sta. KVCR-TV, San Bernadino, Calif., 1963-65; telecommunications prof. San Bernadino Valley Coll., 1965-75; gen. mgr. Sta. KVCR-TV, Sta. KVCR-FM, San Bernadino, 1975-77, dir. radio, TV, 1979—; dir. TV Sta. KVZK-TV, Pago Pago, Am. Samoa, 1977-79. Served with U.S. Army, 1961-63. Mem. Assn. Calif. Pub. TV Stations, Calif. Pub. Radio, Pub. Broadcasting Service, Pacific Mountain Network. Democrat. Office: Sta KVCR-TV 701 S Mount Vernon Ave San Bernardino CA 92410-2705*

LITTLE, W(ILLIA)M A(LFRED), foreign language educator, researcher; b. Boston, July 28, 1929; s. Wm. A. and Myrle A. (Holmes) L. BA, Tufts U., 1951; LTCL, Trinity Coll., London, 1952; MA, Harvard U., 1953, PhD, 1961. Asst. prof. Williams Coll., Williamstown, Mass., 1957-63; assoc. prof., chair Tufts U., Medford, Mass., 1963-66; chair U. Va., Charlottesville, 1966-72, prof., 1966-95, prof. German and music emeritus, 1995—; vis. prof. musicology U. Rochester, N.Y., 1996—. Author: G.A. Bürger, 1974; editor: Mendelssohn-Complete Organ Works, 5 vols., 1987-90; editor The German Quarterly, 1970-78; contbr. articles to profl. jours. Cpl. U.S. Army, 1953-55. Sesquicentennial fellow U. Va., 1972-73, 78-79, 88-89. Mem. MLA (chair comp. lit. 1970-72), Am. Assn. Tchrs. German (nat. exec. coun. 1968-78), Am. Guild Organists (registrar Mass. chpt. 1949-53, dean Charlottesville chpt. 1977-78, registrar, archivist Ctrl. Fla. chpt. 1995—, nat. com. profl. edn. 1993—), Am. Mus. Soc., Orgn. Hist. Soc. Home: 6853 S Atlantic Ave New Smyrna Beach FL 32169

LITTLE, WILLIAM ARTHUR, physicist, educator; b. South Africa, Nov. 17, 1930; came to U.S., 1958, naturalized, 1964; s. William Henry and Margaret (Macleod) L.; m. Annie W. Smith, July 15, 1955; children—Lucy Claire, Linda Susan, Jonathan William. Ph.D., Rhodes U., S. Africa, 1953, Glasgow (Scotland) U., 1957. Faculty Stanford, 1958—, prof. physics, 1965-94; prof. emeritus, 1994—; cons. to industry, 1960—; co-founder, chmn. MMR Techs. Inc., 1980—. Recipient Deans award for disting. teaching Stanford U., 1975-76, Walter J. Gores award for excellence in teaching, Stanford U., 1979, IR-100 award Indsl. Rsch. and Devel., 1981; NRC Can. postdoctoral fellow Vancouver, Can., 1956-58, Sloan Found. fellow, 1959-63, John Simon Guggenheim fellow, 1964-65, NSF sr. postdoctoral fellow, 1970-71. Fellow Am. Phys. Soc. Spl. research low temperature physics, superconductivity, neural network theory cryogenics; holder 14 patents in area of cryogenics and med. instrumentation. Home: 15 Crescent Dr Palo Alto CA 94301-3106 Office: Stanford Univ Dept Physics Stanford CA 94305

LITTLE, WILLIAM CAMPBELL, cardiologist, physiologist; b. Cleve., May 1, 1950; s. Robert Colby and Claire (Means) L.; m. Constance Lydia Loydall, June 9, 1975; children: John Campbell, Elizabeth Loydall. BA in Physics, Oberlin Coll., 1972; MD, Ohio State U., 1975. Diplomate Am. Bd. of Internal Medicine, Am. Bd. Cardiovascular Disease. Intern, then resident in internal medicine U. Va. Hosp., 1975-78; fellow in cardiology Sch. of Medicine U. Ala.; instr. U. Ala. Sch. Medicine, Birmingham, 1980-81; asst. prof. medicine U. Tex. Health Sci. Ctr., San Antonio, 1981-84, assoc. prof. medicine, 1984-86; assoc. prof. medicine Bowman Gray Sch. Medicine, Winston-Salem, N.C., 1986-89, prof. medicine, 1989—, chief cardiology, 1990—; cons. study sec. NIH, Bethesda, Md., 1987—. Co-author: (book) Physiology of the Heart and Circulation, 1989; contbr. over 100 articles on cardiac physiology and clin. cardiology to profl. publs. Recipient Established Investigator award Am. Heart Assn., 1986-91, Young Investigator award So. Sec. Am. Fedn. Clin. Rsch., 1991; grantee NIH, 1985—. Mem. Am. Coll. Cardiology, Am. Physiological Soc. (Lamport award 1987), Am. Soc. Clin. Investigation (Harrison award 1993), Assn. Univ. Cardiologists. Presbyterian. Office: Bowman Gray Sch Medicine Medical Ctr Blvd Winston Salem NC 27157*

LITTLEFIELD, EDMUND WATTIS, mining company executive; b. Ogden, Utah, Apr. 16, 1914; s. Edmond Arthur and Marguerite (Wattis) L.; m. Jeannik Mequet, June 14, 1945; children: Edmund Wattis, Jacques Mequet, Denise Renee. BA with great distinction, Stanford U., 1936, MBA, 1938. With Standard Oil Co. of Calif., 1938-41, Golden State Co., Ltd., 1946-50; v.p., treas. Utah Internat. Inc. (formerly Utah Constrn. & Mining Co.), San Francisco, 1951-56; exec. com., dir. Utah Internat. Inc. (formerly Utah Constrn. & Mining Co.), 1951—, exec. v.p., 1956, gen. mgr., 1958—, pres., 1961—, chmn. bd., 1971—, chief exec. officer, 1971-78, chmn. exec. com., dir., 1978-86; bd. dirs. SRI Internat., FMC Gold. Served as lt. (j.g.) USNR, 1941-43; spl. asst. to dep. adminstr. Petroleum Adminstrn. for War 1943-45. Recipient Ernest C. Arbuckle award Stanford Bus. Sch. Assn., 1970, Golden Beaver award, 1970, Bldg. Industry Achievement award, 1972, Harvard Bus. Statesman award, 1974, Internat. Achievement award World Trade Club, 1986, Lone Sailor award U.S. Naval Found., 1997; named to Nat. Mining Hall of Fame. Mem. San Francisco C. of C. (pres. 1956), Bus. Council (hon. mem., past chmn.), Conf. Bd., Phi Beta Kappa, Chi Psi. Clubs: Burlingame (Calif.) Country; Pacific Union, San Francisco Golf (San Francisco); Augusta National Golf, Eldorado Country; Bohemian, Cypress Point (Pebble Beach, Calif.); Vintage. Office: 550 California St San Francisco CA 94104-1006

LITTLEFIELD, JOHN WALLEY, geneticist, cell biologist, pediatrician; b. Providence, Dec. 3, 1925; s. Ivory and Mary Russell (Walley) L.; m. Elizabeth Lascelles Legge, Nov. 11, 1950; children: Peter P., John W., Elizabeth L. M.D., Harvard U., 1947; MHS, Johns Hopkins U, 1992. Diplomate: Am. Bd. Internal Medicine. Intern Mass. Gen. Hosp., Boston, 1947-48; resident in medicine Mass. Gen. Hosp., 1948-50, staff, 1956-74, chief genetics unit children's service, 1966-73; asso. in medicine Harvard U. Med. Sch., 1956-62, asst. prof. medicine, 1966-66, asst. prof. pediatrics, 1966-69, prof. pediatrics, 1970-73; prof., chmn. dept. pediatrics Johns Hopkins U. Sch. Medicine, Balt., 1974-85; pediatrician-in-chief Johns Hopkins U. Hosp., 1974-85; prof., chmn. dept. physiology Johns Hopkins U. Sch. Medicine, Balt., 1985-92. Author: Variation, Senescence and Neoplasia in Cultured Somatic Cells, 1976. Served with USNR, 1952-54. Guggenheim fellow, 1965-66; Josiah Macy Jr. Found. fellow Oxford U., 1979. Mem. NAS, Am. Acad. Arts and Scis., Am. Soc. Biol. Chemists, Am. Soc. Clin. Investigation, Tissue Culture Assn., Soc. Pediatric Rsch., Am. Soc. Human Genetics, Am. Pediatric Soc., Assn. Am. Physicians, Phi Beta Kappa, Alpha Omega Alpha, Delta Omega. Home: 304 Golf Course Rd Owings Mills MD 21117-4114 Office: Johns Hopkins U Sch Medicine Dept Physiology Baltimore MD 21205

LITTLEFIELD, MARTIN See KLEINWALD, MARTIN

LITTLEFIELD, PAUL DAMON, management consultant; b. Cambridge, Mass., June 8, 1920; s. W. Joseph and Sally Pastorius (Damon) L.; m. Emmy Farnsworth Neiley, June 19, 1943 (dec. Apr. 9, 1982); children: Diane Neiley Littlefield Ritsher, Elizabeth Damon Littlefield Lehman, Paul Damon Jr.; m. Lucy Jean Boyd, Dec. 30, 1983. A.B., Harvard U., 1942, M.B.A. with distinction (Baker scholar), 1948. Assoc., Freeport Minerals Co., N.Y.C., 1948-50, 52-62, treas., 1956-62; v.p. finance, treas. Arthur D. Little, Inc., Cambridge, 1962-73; sr. v.p., chief fin. officer Arthur D. Little, Inc., 1973-85, cons., 1985—; pres. Brynmere Assoc., Inc., 1991-92; asst. to pres. Coty, Inc., 1950-52; hon. bd. mem. Cambridge Trust Co.; mem. investment com. N.E. Health Sys., Inc. Trustee Old Sturbridge Village, ESOP Arthur D. Little, Cambridge. Mem. Fin. Execs. Inst., Harvard Bus. Sch. Assn. Boston (past pres.), Treas.' Club of Boston, Cape Ann Hist. Assn. (bd. mgrs.). Home: 15 Norwood Heights Annisquam Gloucester MA 01930 Office: Acorn Pk Cambridge MA 02140

LITTLEFIELD, ROBERT STEPHEN, communication educator, training consultant; b. Moorhead, Minn., June 21, 1952; s. Harry Jr. and LeVoyne Irene (Berg) L.; m. Kathy Mae Soleim, May 24, 1974; children: Lindsay Jane, Brady Robert. BS in Edn., Moorhead State U., 1974; MA, N.D. State U., 1979; PhD, U. Minn., 1983. Tchr. Barnesville (Minn.) Pub. Schs., 1974-78; teaching asst. N.D. State U., Fargo, 1978-79, lectr., 1979-81; teaching assoc. U. Minn., Mpls., 1981-82; instr. N.D. State U., Fargo, 1982-83, asst. prof., chmn., 1983-89, assoc. prof., chmn., 1989-90, interim dean, 1990-92, assoc. prof., chmn., 1992-94, prof., 1994—; dir. Inst. for Study of Cultural Diversity, 1992—; owner KIDSPEAK Co., Moorhead, 1987—. Author/co-author: (series) KIDSPEAK, 1989-92; lyricist (centennial hymn) Built on a Triangle with Faith in the Triune, 1989; contbr. more than 50 articles to profl. jours. Vol. forensic coach Fargo Cath. Schs. Network, 1992—; mem. N.D. dist. com. Nat. Forensic League, 1995—; advisor to exec. coun. Nat. Jr. Forensic League, 1995—. Recipient Burlington No. award N.D. State U., 1988-89; named Outstanding Speech Educator, Nat. Fedn. High Sch. Activities Assn., 1990-91. Mem. Am. Forensic Assn. (sec. 1990-92), N.D. Speech and Theatre Assn. (historian 1989—, pres. 1985-87, Hall of Fame 1989, Scholar of Yr. 1989), N.D. Multicultural Assn., Speech Comm. Assn., Pi Kappa Delta (nat. coun. 1983—, nat. pres. 1991-93, nat. sec.-treas. 1993—), Fargo Lions Club (pres. 1990-91). Democrat. Lutheran. Office: ND State U 321G Minard Hall Fargo ND 58105

LITTLEFIELD, ROY EVERETT, III, association executive, legal educator; b. Nashua, N.H., Dec. 6, 1952; s. Roy Everett and Mary Ann (Prestipino) L.; m. Amy Root; children: Leah Marie, Roy Everett IV, Christy Louise. BA, Dickinson Coll., 1975; MA, Catholic U. Am., 1976, PhD, 1979. Aide U.S. Senator Thomas McIntyre, Democrat, N.H., 1975-78, Nordy Hoffman, U.S. Senate Sergeant-at-arms, N.H., 1979; dir. govt. rels. Nat. Tire Dealers and Retreaders Assn., Washington, N.H., 1979-84; exec. dir. Svc. Sta. and Automotive Repair Assn., Washington, N.H., 1984—; exec. v.p. Svc. Sta. Dealers of Am., 1994—; cons. Am. Retreaders Assn., 1984; mem. faculty Cath. U. Am., Washington, 1979—. Author: William Randolph Hearst: His Role in American Progressivism, 1980, The Economic Recovery Act, 1982, The Surface: Transportation Assistance Act, 1984; editor Nozzle mag.; contbr. numerous articles to legal jours. Mem. Nat. Dem. Club, 1978—. Mem. Am. Soc. Legal History, Md. Hwy. User's Fedn. (pres.), Nat. Hwy. User's Fedn. (bd. dirs.), Nat. Capitol Area Transp. Fedn. (v.p.), N.H. Hist. Soc., Kansas City C. of C., Capitol Hill Club, Phi Alpha Theta. Roman Catholic. Home: 1707 Pepper Tree Ct Bowie MD 20721-3021 Office: 9420 Annapolis Rd Ste 307 Lanham Seabrook MD 20706-3061

LITTLEFIELD, VIVIAN MOORE, nursing educator, administrator; b. Princeton, Ky., Jan. 24, 1938; children: Darrell, Virginia. B.S. magna cum laude, Tex. Christian U., 1960; M.S., U. Colo., 1964; Ph.D., U. Denver, 1979. Staff nurse USPHS Hosp., Ft. Worth, Tex., 1960-61; instr. nursing Tex. Christian U., Ft. Worth, 1961-62; nursing supr. Colo. Gen. Hosp., Denver, 1964-65, pvt. patient practitioner, 1974-78; asst. prof. nursing U. Colo., Denver, 1965-69, asst. prof., clin. instr., 1971-74, asst. prof., 1974-76, acting asst. dean, assoc. prof. continuing edn., regional perinatal project, 1976-78; assoc. prof., chair dept. women's health care nursing U. Rochester Sch. Nursing, N.Y., 1979-84; clin. chief ob-gyn., nursing U. Rochester Strong Meml. Hosp., N.Y., 1979-84; prof., dean U. Wis. Sch. Nursing, Madison, 1984—; cons. and lectr. in field. Author: Maternity Nursing Today, 1973, 76, Health Education for Women: A guide for Nurses and Other Health Professionals, 1986; mem. editorial bd. Jour. Profl. Nursing; contbr. articles to profl. jours. Bur. Health Professions Fed. trainee, 1963-64; Nat. Sci. Service award, 1976-79. Mem. MAIN, AACN (bd. dirs.), NLN (bd. dirs.), Am. Acad. Nursing, Am. Nurses Assn., Consortium Prime Care Wis. (chair), Health Care for Women Internat., Midwest Nursing Research Soc., Sigma Theta Tau (pres. Beta Eta chpt., co-chair coun nursing practice and edn. 1995). Avocations: golf, biking. Office: U Wis Sch Nursing 600 Highland Ave # H6 150 Madison WI 53792-0001

LITTLEFIELD, WARREN, television executive; m. Theresa Littlefield; 2 children. Student, Am. U., Washington; grad. in psychology, Hobart Coll., Geneva, N.Y. With Westfall Prodns., N.Y.C.; dir. comedy devel. Warner Bros. TV, 1979; mgr. comedy devel. NBC, 1979-81, v.p. current comedy programs, 1981-85; sr. v.p series, spls. and variety programming NBC Entertainment, 1985-87, exec. v.p. prime time programs, 1987-90, pres., 1990—. Office: NBC Entertainment 3000 W Alameda Ave Burbank CA 91523-0001*

LITTLEJOHN, DAVID, journalism educator, writer; b. San Francisco, May 8, 1937; s. George Thomas and Josephine Mildred (Cullen) L.; m. Sheila Beatrice Hageman, June 10, 1963; children: Victoria Schoenke, Gregory David. BA, U. Calif., Berkeley, 1959; MA, Harvard U., 1961, PhD, 1963. Asst. prof. English U. Calif., Berkeley, 1963-69, assoc. prof. journalism, 1969-76, prof., 1976-97, chmn. com. ednl. policy, 1981-82, chmn. senate policy com., vice chmn. acad. senate, 1984-86, assoc. dean Grad. Sch. Journalism, 1974-78, 85-86, 87-89, prof. emeritus, 1997—. Author: Architect: The Life and Work of Charles W. Moore, 1984, The Ultimate Art: Essays around and about Opera, 1992, The Fate of The English Country Houses, 1997, also 9 other books, over 300 articles and 200 TV programs; arts critic Sta. KQED-TV, San Francisco, 1965-75, PBS nationwide, 1971-72; critic and corr. London Times, 1975-89, Architecture mag., 1984-89, Wall St. Jour., 1990—. Fulbright lectr., Montpellier, France, 1966-67; Am. Coun. Learned Socs. rsch. fellow, London, 1972-73; NEH grantee 1976-77. Mem. Arts Club (Berkeley). Democrat. Roman Catholic. Home: 719 Coventry Rd Kensington CA 94707-1403 Office: U Calif Grad Sch Journalism Berkeley CA 94720

LITTLER, GENE ALEC, professional golfer; b. San Diego, Calif., July 21, 1930; s. Stanley Fred and Dorothy (Paul) L.; m. Shirley Mae Warren, Jan. 5, 1951; children: Curt Michael, Suzanne. Student, San Diego State Coll. Mem. U.S. Ryder Cup Team, 61, 63, 65, 67, 69, 71, 75. Served with USN, 1951-54. Winner 29 PGA tour events including Nat. Jr. Championship, 1948, Nat. Amateur Championship, 1953, U.S. Open, 1961, Canadian Open, 1965, Tournament of Champions, 1955, 56, 57, World Series of Golf, 1966, Taheiyo Masters, Japan, 1974, 75, Australian Masters, 15 sr. tour titles and Coca Cola Grand Slam, Japan, 1983, 87.

LITTLE RICHARD (RICHARD WAYNE PENNIMAN), recording artist, pianist, songwriter, minister; b. Macon, Ga., Dec. 5, 1932; s. Bud and Leva Mae Penniman; m. Ernestine Campbell, 1957 (div.). BA, Oakwood Coll. Sem., Huntsville, Ala., 1961. Ordained to ministry Seventh Day Adventist Ch., 1961. Began singing and dancing on streets of Macon, Ga., 1942; won talent shows in Atlanta, 1943 and 1951; toured with Dr. Hudson's Medicine Show and other shows, 1949-51; worked with own band doing dances and clubs, 1951-52, with Tempo Toppers in New Orleans, 1953-54; recording artist Peacock Records, Houston, 1953-54, Splty. Records, 1955-58, 64; toured in Big 10 Package shows, U.S., Australia and Gt. Brit., 1957-58; recording artist Veejay Records, 1964-65. Songs include Long Tall Sally, Tutti Frutti, Slippin' and Slidin', Rip it Up, Ready Teddy, Lucille, Send Me Some Lovin', Jenny, Jenny, Miss Ann, Keep A-Knockin', Good Golly Miss Molly, Baby Face, True Fine Mama, Kansas City, Bama Lama Bama Loo, Freedom Blues, Greenwood Mississippi; albums include Here's Little Richard, 1958, Little Richard 2, 1958, The Fabulous, 1959, Well Alright, 1959, Sings Gospel, 1964, Coming Home, 1964, Sings Freedom Songs, 1964, King of Gospel Songs, 1965, Wild & Frantic, 1965, The Explosive, 1967, The Explosive & Roy Orbison, 1970, The Rill Thing, 1971, King of Rock N Roll, 1971, Second Coming, 1971, All Time Hits, 1972, Rock Hard Rock Heavy, 1972, The Very Best Of, 1975, Georgia Peach, 1980, Get Down With It, 1982, Ooh! My Soul, 1983, Lucile, 1984, Shut Up, 1988, The Specialty Sessions, 1990, Greatest Songs, 1995, Mega-Mix, 1995; film appearances include The Girl Can't Help It, 1956, Don't Knock the Rock, 1957, She's Got It, 1957, Mr. Rock and Roll, 1957, Jimi Plays Berkeley, 1970, Let the Good Times Roll, 1973, Jimi Hendrix, 1973, Down and Out in Beverly Hills, 1985; TV appearances include Tonight Show, Merv Griffin Show, Mike Douglas Show, Smothers Brothers Show, American Bandstand, Glen Campbell Good Time Hour, Tom Jones Show, Midnight Special, Donny & Marie Show; stage appearances include Paramount Theatre, The Felt Forum, Wembley Stadium, Hollywood Paladium. Inducted Rock & Roll Hall of Fame. Office: PO Box 29 Hollywood CA 90078-0029*

LITTLETON, CAROL, film editor. Editor: (films) The Mafu Cage, 1978, French Postcards, 1979, Roadie, 1980, Body Heat, 1981, E.T. The Extra-Terrestrial, 1982 (Academy award nomination best film editing 1982), The Big Chill, 1983, Places in the Heart, 1984, Silverado, 1985, Brighton Beach Memoirs, 1986, Swimming to Cambodia, 1987, The Accidental Tourist, 1988, Vibes, 1988, White Palace, 1990, Grand Canyon, 1991, Benny & Joon, 1993, China Moon, 1994, Wyatt Earp, 1994, Diabolique, 1996, Magic Hour, 1997. Mem. Acad. Motion Picture Arts and Scis. (bd. gov.), Editors Guild (v.p. local 776). Office: care United Talent 9560 Wilshire Blvd Ste 500 Beverly Hills CA 90212

LITTLETON, HARVEY KLINE, artist; b. Corning, N.Y., June 14, 1922; s. Jesse Talbot and Bessie (Cook) L.; m. Bess Toyo Tamura, Sept. 6, 1947; children—Carol Louise Littleton Shay, Thomas Harvey, Kathryn Tamra (dec.), Maurine Bess, John Christopher. Student, U. Mich., 1939-42, B in Design, 1947; MFA, Cranbrook Acad. Art, 1951; DFA, Phila. Coll. Art, R.I. Sch. Design, 1996. Instr. ceramics Toledo Mus. Art, 1949-51; prof. art U. Wis., Madison, 1951-77; chmn. dept. U. Wis., 1964-67, 69-71, prof. emeritus, 1977—. Author: Glass Blowing - A Search for Form, 1971; recent one- and two-man exhbns. include Lee Nordness Galleries, N.Y.C., 1969-70, Maison de Culture, Liege, Belgium, 1974, J & L Lobmeyr, Vienna, 1974, Brooks Meml. Art Gallery, Memphis, 1975, Contemporary Art Glass Gallery, N.Y.C., 1977, 78, 79, Habatat Gallery, Detroit, 1980, 81, Heller Gallery, N.Y.C., 1980, 81, 82, 83, 84, 85, Glasmuseum Ebeltoft, Sweden, 1989, Royal Copenhagen Gallery, 1989, Finnish Glasmusem, Riihimaki, Finland, 1989, Kunsthaus am Mus., Cologne, Germany, 1990, Immenhausen, Germany, 1990, Glasmuseum, Frauenau, Germany, 1992, Yokohama (Japan) Mus. Art, 1995, retrospective exhbn. originated by High Mus. Art, Atlanta, 1984, traveling to the Renwick Gallery, Am. Craft Mus., Iowa State U., Milw. Art Mus. and Portland (Maine) Mus. Art; represented in permanent collections, Victoria and Albert Mus., London, museums in, Germany, Holland, Switzerland, Belgium, Austria and, Czechoslovakia, also, Met. Mus. Art, N.Y.C., Mus. Modern Art, N.Y.C., Am. Craft Mus., N.Y.C., L.A. County Mus. Art., L.A., Corning Mus. of Glass, Toledo Mus. Art, Detroit Art Inst., Milw. Art Center, Smithsonian Instn., Washington, High Mus. Art, Atlanta, Chrysler Mus., Norfolk, Va., U. Mich., U. Ill., Ohio State U., Phila. Mus. Art, The White House, Washington, numerous other pub. and pvt. collections. Bd. dirs. Penland Sch., N.C., pres. bd. dirs., 1986-88; pres., chmn. Littleton Co., Inc., Spruce Pine, N.C., 1981—. With Signal Corps U.S. Army, 1942-45, ETO. Recipient Fine Arts award Gov. of N.C., 1987, Master of Medium award James Renwick Alliance, 1997; Toledo Mus. Art research grantee, 1962; Louis Comfort Tiffany Found. grantee, 1970-71; Corning Glass Works grantee, 1974; U. Wis. research grantee, 1954, 57, 62, 73, 75; Nat. Endowment for Arts grantee, 1978-79; Diploma of Honor, Glass Mus. Frauenau, Fed. Republic Germany. Fellow Am. Crafts Coun. (trustee 1957, 61-64, trustee emeritus, gold medal 1983), Corning Mus. Glass (Rakow award for excellence in art of glass); mem. Nat. Coun. for Edn. in Ceramic Arts (hon.), Glass Art Soc. (hon. life, lifetime achievement award 1993), Am. Ceramic Soc. (hon. life), Nat. Assn. Schs. Art and Designs (Disting. Svc. in Visual Arts citation 1996).

LITTLETON, ISAAC THOMAS, III, retired university library administrator, consultant; b. Hartsville, Tenn., Jan. 28, 1921; s. Isaac Thomas Jr. and Bessie (Lowe) L.; m. Dorothy Etta Young, Aug. 12, 1949; children—Sally Lowe Littleton Phillips, Thomas Young, Elizabeth Ann. B.A., U. N.C., Chapel Hill, 1943; M.A., U. Tenn., Knoxville, 1950; M.S.L.S., U. Ill., Champaign-Urbana, 1951, Ph.D., 1968. Circulation librarian, asst. librarian U. N.C., Chapel Hill, 1951-58; asst. dir. then dir. libraries N.C. State U., Raleigh, 1959-87; emeritus dir. libraries N.C. State U., 1987—; mem. N.C. Libr. Networking Steering Com., Raleigh, 1982-85; bd. dirs. Southeastern Libr. Network, Atlanta, 1973-74, 83-86, chmn., 1985-86; chmn. Assn. Southeastern Rsch. Librs., 1969-71; mem. com. Gov.'s Conf. on Libr. and Info. Svcs., 1990. Author: The Literature of Agricultural Economics, 1969, State Systems of Higher Education and Libraries, 1977, D.H. Hill Library: An Informal Historu, 1993; editor: N.C. Union List of Scientific Serials, 1967. Bd. dirs., treas. Theater in Park, Raleigh, 1982-85, Friends of Wake County Pub. Librs.; sec. N.C. State U. Friends of Libr., Raleigh, 1964-87, bd. dirs., 1990-94; pres. Friends of N.C. Libr. for Blind and Physically Handicapped, 1989-93, bd. dirs. 1993—; v.p. Wake County UN Assn., 1994-95. Lt. (j.g.) USN, 1943-46, PTO. Council on Library Resources fellow, Washington, 1975-76. Mem. Southeastern Library Assn. (exec. bd. 1974-78), N.C. Library Assn. (exec. bd. 1969-71, hon. life). Mem. Community United Ch. of Christ. Club: Torch (pres. Raleigh, N.C. 1974-75). Avocations: theater; reading; concerts. Home: 4813 Brookhaven Dr Raleigh NC 27612-5706

LITTLETON, JESSE TALBOT, III, radiology educator; b. Corning, N.Y., Apr. 27, 1917; s. Jesse Talbot and Bessie (Cook) L.; m. Martha Louise Morrow, Apr. 17, 1943 (dec. 1994); children: Christine, Joanne, James, Robert, Denise; m. Mary Lou Durizch, Mar. 25, 1995. Student, Emory (Va.) and Henry Coll., 1934-35. Johns Hopkins U., 1935-39; MD, Syracuse U., 1939-43. Diplomate Am. Bd. Radiology, Intern Buffalo Gen. Hosp., 1943; resident in medicine, surgery and radiology Robert Packer Hosp., Sayre, Pa., 1946-51, assoc. radiologist, 1951-53, chmn. dept. radiology, 1953-76; prof. radiology U. South Ala., Mobile, 1976-87, prof. emeritus, 1987—; cons. in field. Author textbooks (4); contbr. chpts. to books and articles to profl. jours., sci. exhibits to profl. confs. With U.S. Army MC, 1944-46; Pacific. Fellow Am. Coll. Radiology; mem. AMA, Radiol. Soc. N.Am., Am. Roentgen Ray Soc., Ala. Acad. Radiology, Med. Assn. Ala., French Soc. Neuroradiology, Sigma Xi, Alpha Omega Alpha. Republican. Methodist. Club: Country of Mobile (Ala.). Research on conventional tomography, phys. principles, equipment devel. and testing and clin. applications; transp. and radiology of acutely ill and traumatized patient; devel. patient liter with removeable top leading to placement of backboards in ambulances; devel. dedicated trauma x-ray machine; angiography, devel. first sheet film serialograph; devel. of equipment for sectional radiographic anatomy with Durizch; patented first patient stratcher with removeable top leading to placement of back boards in ambulances. Home: 5504 Churchill Downs St Theodore AL 36582-9601 Office: U South Ala Med Ctr 2451 Fillingim St Mobile AL 36617-2238

LITTLETON, TAYLOR DOWE, humanities educator; b. Birmingham, Ala., Mar. 14, 1930; s. M. Taylor and Florence (Longcrier) L.; m. Lucy Williams, Aug. 7, 1954; children: Dowe, George, Franklin, Mary Wood. B.S., Fla. State U., 1951, M.A., 1952, Ph.D., 1960. Teaching fellow Fla. State U., Tallahassee, 1954-57; from instr. to prof. dept. English Auburn U., Ala., 1957—, dean undergrad. studies, 1968-71, v.p. for acad. affairs, 1972-83, W. Kelly Mosley prof. sci. and humanities, 1983—. Author: Advancing American Art: Painting, Politics, and Cultural Confrontation at

Mid-century, 1989, Athletics and Academe: An Anatomy of Abuses and a Prescription for Reform, 1991; author, editor: To Prove A Villain: The Case of King Richard III, 1964, The Idea of Tragedy, 1965; editor: multi-vol. series The Franklin Lectures in Sci. and Humanities: Approaching the Benign Environment, 1970; The Shape of Likelihood, 1974, A Time To Hear and Answer, 1977, The Rights of Memory, 1985; assoc. editor So. Humanities Rev., 1967-70. Served with U.S. Army, 1952-54. Mem. So. Atlantic MLA, Phi Kappa Phi, Omicron Delta Kappa. Democrat. Episcopalian. Home: 415 Norman Cir Auburn AL 36830-6307 Office: Auburn U Dept English & Humanities Haley 9030 Auburn AL 36830

LITTLEWOOD, DOUGLAS BURDEN, business brokerage executive; b. Buffalo, Sept. 24, 1922; s. Frank and G. Joan (Burden) L.; m. Jevene Hope Baker, July 2, 1949; children—Douglas Baker, Dean Houston, Laurie Littlewood Vogelsang. B.S. in Mech. Engring, Rensselaer Poly. Inst., 1945; M.B.A., Harvard, 1947. Sales engr. Otis Elevator Co., 1948-49; asst. to sec. Nat Gypsum Co., Buffalo, 1949-52; sec. Nat Gypsum Co., 1952-67; investment banker Hornblower & Weeks, 1967-68; pres. Littlewood Assocs., Inc., 1968-95, chmn. bd., 1995—. Past pres. Greater Niagara Frontier coun. Boy Scouts Am.; active Buffalo YMCA, United Fund; bd. dirs. Presbyn. Homes of Western N.Y.; bd. dirs., chmn. emeritus Salvation Army; v.p. N.E. region Boy Scouts Am. Served to lt. (j.g.) USNR, 1943-46. Recipient Silver Beaver, 1965; recipient Silver Antelope, 1978, Disting. Eagle, 1979. Mem. Country Club of Sebring, Buffalo Jr. C. of C. (past dir., chmn. bd.), Am. Soc. Corp. Secs., Buffalo Canoe Club (past commodore), Buffalo Country Club. Home: 1925 SE Lakeview Dr Sebring FL 33870-4938 Office: 22 Dawnbrook Ln Buffalo NY 14221-4930 *If you truly believe you are happy and successful then, and only then, you truly are.*

LITTLEWOOD, THOMAS BENJAMIN, retired journalism educator; b. Flint, Mich., Nov. 30, 1928; s. Thomas Nelson and Louise Engela (Grebenkemper) L.; m. Barbara E. Badger, June 9, 1951; children: Linda S. Johnson, Lisa L. Ratchford, Thomas S., Leah J. Hamrick. Student, DePauw U., 1948-51; BS, Northwestern U., 1952, MS, 1953. Reporter Chgo. Sun-Times, 1953-76, chief Springfield State Capital Bur., 1955-64, corr. Washington Bur., 1965-76; prof. journalism U. Ill., Urbana-Champaign, 1977-96; prof. emeritus, 1996—; head dept. U. Ill., Urbana-Champaign, 1977-87. Author: Bipartisan Coalition in Illinois, 1959, Horner of Illinois, 1969, The Politics of Population Control, 1977, Coals of Fire, 1988, Arch, 1990. John F. Kennedy Inst. Politics Harvard U. fellow, 1975. Mem. Soc. Profl. Journalists (SDX Nat. award 1988), Ill. State Hist. Soc., N.Am. Soc. Sports History, Sigma Delta Chi, Kappa Tau Alpha. Office: Univ Ill Journalism Dept 119 Gregory Urbana IL 61801

LITTMAN, EARL, advertising and public relations executive; b. Bklyn., Jan. 29, 1927; s. David and Cele Littman; m. Natalie Carol Jacobson, Dec. 21, 1948; children: Erica Humphrey, Bonnie Likover, Michael L. Littman. BS, NYU, 1948. With George N. Kahn, N.Y.C., 1948-50, Jones & Brown, Pitts., 1950-52; chmn., CEO Goodwin, Dannenbaum, Littman & Wingfield Inc., Houston, 1952-92; pres. The Advertizing Firm, Inc., 1992Two Nerds and A Suit, Inc., 1994, Chmn. Anti Defamation League, Tex. 1984; bd. dirs. Am. Heart Assn., Houston, Glassell Sch. Sect. Houston Chpt. World Pres. Orgn.; active End Hunger Network, Houston, 1984, active NCCJ. With USN, 1944-45. Recipient Silver medal Am. Advt. Fedn., 1989, Outstanding Vol. award Savvy, 1990, Anti-Defamation League Popkin award, 1990, End Hunger Network award, 1992; Am. Heart Assn. honoree, 1988, John McMahon award Am. Heart Assn., 1996; Heritage award Am. Women in Radio and TV, 1992. Mem. Affiliated Advt. Agys. Internat. (pres. 1979-80), Am. Advt. Agy. Assn. (gov. Houston chpt. 1990, Paul Dudley White award 1991), Houston Advt. Fedn. (Living Legend award 1993), Winedale Hist. Assn. Houston Marathon Assn. (adv. dir.). Jewish.

LITTMAN, HOWARD, chemical engineer, educator; b. Bklyn., Apr. 22, 1927; s. Morris and Gertrude (Goldberg) L.; m. Arline F. Caruso, July 3, 1955; children—Susan Joy, Vicki Kim, Paul William. BChemE, Cornell U., 1951; PhD, Yale U., 1956. Asst., then assoc. prof. Syracuse U., 1955-65; on leave to Brookhaven Nat. Lab., summer 1957, Argonne Nat. Lab., 1957-59; faculty Rensselaer Poly. Inst., Troy, N.Y., 1965—; prof. chem. engring. Rensselaer Poly. Inst., 1967—, chmn. faculty council, 1975-76; vis. prof. Imperial Coll., London, Eng., 1971-72, Chonn'am Nat. U., Kwangju, Korea, 1988; Fulbright lectr. U. Belgrade, Yugoslavia, 1972; pres. Particle Systems Internat. Corp., 1990—. Patentee in field; contbr. articles to profl. jours. A founder Onondaga Hill Free Library, 1961, trustee, 1961-65, pres., 1965; a founder Onondaga Library System, 1962, trustee, 1962-65, v.p., 1965; trustee Capital Dist. Library Council, 1969-75, pres., 1970, 73. Served with USN, 1945-46. IREX grantee U. Belgrade, summer 1973; recipient Disting. Faculty award Rensselaer Poly. Inst., 1988. Mem. Am. Inst. Chem. Engrs., Am. Chem. Soc., Sigma Xi. Home: 7 Tulip Tree Ln Niskayuna NY 12309-1837 Office: Rensselaer Poly Inst Troy NY 12180-3590

LITTMAN, IRVING, forest products company executive; b. Denver, Apr. 21, 1940; s. Maurice Littman and Cecile P. Zohn.; m. Gertrude Pepper, Aug. 16, 1964; children: Margaret R., Michael J., Elizabeth B. BS in Engring. (Applied Math.), U. Colo., 1964; MBA, U. Chgo., 1966. Mgr. corp. sys. Boise (Idaho) Cascade Corp., Idaho, 1966-68, corp. mgr. budgeting, 1968-71, asst. to pres., 1971-73; asst. contr. realty group Boise Cascade Corp., Palo Alto, Calif., 1973-76; dir. investor rels. Boise Cascade Corp., Boise, 1976-84, treas., 1984-86, v.p., treas., 1986—. Bd. dirs. Idaho Humanities Coun., Boise, 1985-88, vice chair, 1987-88; trustee Boise H.S. Band Scholarship Endowment, 1987—, Boise Art Mus., 1996—; referee US Soccer Fedn., 1982—; investment com. Idaho Cmty. Found., 1989—, chmn. investment com., 1991—. With U.S. Army, 1958-59. Mem. Bogus Basin Ski Area Assn. (bd. dirs. 1988—, treas. 1989-94, vice-chmn. 1991-94, chmn. 1994-96), Treas. Club San Francisco, Fin. Execs. Inst., Crane Creek Country Club, Arid Club (Boise). Office: Boise Cascade Corp PO Box 50 Boise ID 83728-0001

LITTMAN, RICHARD ANTON, psychologist, educator; b. N.Y.C., May 8, 1919; s. Joseph and Sarah (Feinberg) L.; m. Isabelle Cohen, Mar. 17, 1941; children—David, Barbara, Daniel, Rebecca. AB, George Washington U., 1943; postgrad., Ind. U., 1943- 44; PhD, Ohio State U., 1948. Faculty U. Oreg., 1948—, prof. psychology, 1959—, chmn. dept., 1963-68, vice provost acad. planning and resources, 1971-73; Vis. scientist Nat. Inst. Mental Health, 1958-59. Contbr. articles to profl. jours. Sr. postdoctoral fellow NSF, U. Paris, 1966-67; sr. fellow Nat. Endowment for Humanities, U. London, 1973-74; Ford Found. fellow, 1952-53; recipient U. Oreg. Charles H. Johnson Meml. award, 1980. Mem. Am., Western, psychol. assns., Soc. Research and Child Devel., Psychonomics Soc., Animal Behavior Soc., Soc. Psychol. Study of Social Issues, Internat. Soc. Developmental Psychobiology, History of Sci. Soc., Am. Philos. Assn., AAUP, Sigma Xi. Home: 3625 Glen Oak Dr Eugene OR 97405-4736 Office: U Oreg Dept Psychology Eugene OR 97403

LITTON, DAPHNE NAPIER RUDHMAN, special education educator; b. Schenectady, July 28, 1952; d. James Napier and Mary (Stathas) Rudhman; m. John Shelby Litton, Oct. 5, 1984; children: Christian Napier, Erin Elizabeth. BS in Elem. Edn., Ind. U., South Bend, 1974, MS in Elem. Edn., 1978, cert. learning disabled, 1978; cert. emotionally disturbed, Ind. U.-Purdue U., Indpls., 1982. Tchr. remedial reading, dir. motor skills, tchr. summer sch. Olive Twp. Elem. Sch., New Carlisle, Ind., 1976; tchr. learning disabled, gifted, remedial reading Ox Bow Elem. Sch., Elkhart, Ind., 1976-85, dir. motor skills, 1976-85; tchr. learning disabled Stafford (Va.) Community Schs., 1985-87; tchr. emotionally disturbed Elvin Hill Elem. Sch., Columbiana, Ala., 1987-88; dir., adminstr. Riverchase Presbyn. Presch./Mother's Day Out, Birmingham, Ala., 1989-90; tchr. learning disabled Yorkshire Elem. Sch., Manassas, Va., 1993-95, Piney Grove Elem. Sch., Kernersville, N.C., 1995—; mem. Ind. State Com. for Svc. Personnel Devel., Elkhart, 1979-85; asst. girl's volleyball coach Ox Bow Elem. Sch., Elkhart, 1985-87; asst. dir. Sports Medicine 10K Run Vols., South Bend, 1986. Active Am. Cancer Soc., South Bend, 1975, Girl Scouts. Mem. Coun. Exceptional Children. Republican. Presbyterian. Avocations: mus. instruments, choir, travel, swimming. Home: 1820 Glen Ridge Dr Kernersville NC 27284

LITTON, ROBERT CLIFTON, marine engineer, consultant; b. Banner Elk, N.C., Jan. 11, 1934; s. Hailey Clifton and Edna (Walsh) L.; m. Michele Louise Gennette, July 1, 1961. B in Mech. Engring., U. Va., 1957; MS in Mech. Engring., Rensselaer Polytech. Inst., 1963. Commd. ensign USN, 1957, advanced through grades to capt., ret., 1984; pvt. practice marine engring. cons. Great Falls, Va., 1985-94; sr. cons. engr. Mech. Tech., Inc., Latham, N.Y., 1988-95; program mgr. Innovative Tech., Inc., McLean, Va., 1988-89, Sachse Engring. Assocs., Inc., San Diego, 1989-90; bus. area mgr. naval engring. RGS Assocs., Arlington, Va., 1994-96; v.p. ops. New Dawn Universal Power Corp., Arlington, 1996—. Mem. Soc. Naval Archs. and Marine Engrs., Am. Soc. Naval Engrs., U.S. Naval Inst., Naval Sub. League. Republican. Avocations: personal computers, audio and video systems, golf. Home and Office: 10334 Eclipse Ln Great Falls VA 22066-1730

LITVACK, SANFORD MARTIN, lawyer; b. Bklyn., Apr. 29, 1936; s. Murray and Lee M. (Korman) L.; m. Judith E. Goldenson, Dec. 30, 1956; children—Mark, Jonathan, Sharon, Daniel. BA, U. Conn., 1956; LLB, Georgetown U., 1959. Bar: N.Y. 1964, D.C. 1979. Trial atty. antitrust div. Dept. Justice, Washington, 1959-61; asst. atty. gen. Dept. Justice, 1980-81; asso. firm Donovan, Leisure, Newton & Irvine, N.Y.C., 1961-69; ptnr. Donovan, Leisure, Newton & Irvine, 1969-80, 81-86, Dewey, Ballantine, Bushby, Palmer & Wood, N.Y.C., 1987-91; sr. exec. v.p., chief of corp. ops., gen. counsel The Walt Disney Co., Burbank, Calif., 1991—, also bd. dirs. Bd. dirs. Bet Tzedek. Fellow Am. Coll. Trial Lawyers; mem. ABA, Fed. Bar Coun., N.Y. State Bar Assn. (sec. antitrust sect. 1974-77, chmn. antitrust sect. 1985-86), Va. Bar Assn. Office: The Walt Disney Co 500 S Buena Vista St Burbank CA 91521-0001

LITWACK, GERALD, biochemistry researcher, educator, administrator; b. Boston, Jan. 11, 1929; s. David and Edith Jean (Berkman) Lytell; m. Patricia Lynn Gorog, Feb., 1956 (div. 1973); 1 child, Claudia; m. Ellen Judith Schatz, Aug. 31, 1973; children: Geoffrey Sandor, Katherine Victoria. BA, Hobart Coll., 1949; MS, U. Wis., 1950, PhD, 1953. Postdoctoral fellow Biochem. Labs. U. Paris, 1953-54; asst. prof. Rutgers U., New Brunswick, N.J., 1954-60; assoc. prof. U. Pa., Phila., 1960-64; Carnell prof., dep. dir. Fels Inst., Sch. of Medicine Temple U., Phila., 1964-91; prof., chair dept. pharmacology Thomas Jefferson U., Phila., 1991-96, also dep. dir. Kimmel Cancer Inst., 1991-97; assoc. dir. for basic sci. Kimmel Cancer Ctr., Phila., 1992-97, chmn. dept. biochemistry and molecular pharmacology, 1996—, dir. Ctr. Apoptosis Rsch., assoc. dean sci. affairs, 1996—; chmn. adv. com. am. Cancer Soc., N.Y.C., 1977-80; mem. adv. panel NSF, Washington, 1980-84; mem. ad hoc panels NIH, Bethesda, 1985, 89, reviewer, 1977, 84, 91, cons. Nat. Inst. Environ. Health Scis., 1982; mem. ad hoc panels Israel Cancer Rsch. fund Sci. Rev. Panel, 1992-93, U.S. Army Breast Cancer Study Sect., 1994; councilor Soc. for Exptl. Biology and Medicine, N.Y.C., 1984-88; cons. Franklin Inst., 1976, Georgetown U., 1980; reviewer Haverford Coll., 1976; evaluator Roswell Park Meml. Inst., 1978; mem. sci. adv. bd. Norris Cotton Cancer Ctr. Dartmouth Med. Sch., 1984—; Jefferson rep. U. Catania, Sicily, 1994—. Author/co-author: Experimental Biochemistry, 1960, Hormones, 1987, 2d edit., 1997; editor: Biochemical Actions of Hormones, Vol. XIV, 1970-87, Receptor Purification, 1990; founder, editor-in-chief Receptor, 1990-96, re-named Receptors and Signal Tranduction, 1996—; editor-in-chief Vitamins and Hormones, 1992—; co-editor Actions of Hormones on Molecular Processes, 1964; mem. editl. bd. Chemtracts, Cancer Comm., Cancer Rsch., Endocrinology, Anticancer Rsch., Oncology Rsch., 1992, Oncology Reports, 1993—, Critical Revs. and Eukaryotic Gene Expression, 1994—, Apoptosis, 1995—. Bd. dirs. Sharpe Found. Bryn Mawr Hosp., 1997—. Recipient Pub. Svc. award Chapel of Four Chaplains, 1977, Faculty Rsch. award Temple U., 1987. Mem. Endocrine Soc. (program com. 1991-93, sci. and edn. com. 1992-93), Am. Assn. Cancer Rsch. (chair task force on endocrinology 1995), Am. Chem. Soc. Achievements include discovery and identification of the glucocorticoid receptor; co-discovery of ligandin (glutathione S-Transferase family) mechanism of glucocorticoid receptor activation, studies in apoptosis, immunophilin signal transduction, basic studies in asthma. Home: 380 E Montgomery Ave Wynnewood PA 19096 Office: Thomas Jefferson U 10th and Locust St Philadelphia PA 19107-3197

LITWACK, LEON FRANK, historian, educator; b. Santa Barbara, Calif., Dec. 2, 1929; s. Julius and Minnie (Nitkin) L.; m. Rhoda Lee Goldberg, July 5, 1952; children: John Michael, Ann Katherine. BA, U. Calif., Berkeley, 1951, MA, 1952, PhD, 1958. Asst. prof., then assoc. prof. history U. Wis., Madison, 1958-65; mem. faculty U. Calif., Berkeley, 1965—, prof. history, 1971—, Alexander F. and May T. Morrison prof. history, 1987—; dir. NDEA Inst. Am. History, summer 1965; vis. prof. U. S.C., 1975, Colo. Coll., Sept. 1974, 79, La. State U., 1985; Fulbright prof. Am. history U. Sydney, Australia, 1991, Moscow (USSR) State U., 1980; vis. lectr. Peking U., (China), 1982; Walter Lynwood Fleming lectr. La. State U., 1983; Wentworth scholar-in-residence U. Fla., Spring 1983; mem. Nat. Afro-Am. History and Culture Comm., 1981-83; mem. screening com. Fulbright Sr. Scholar Awards, 1983-86; bd. acad. advisors The American Experience Sta. WGBH-TV, 1986—, Africans in America, WGBH-TV, 1990—; Ford Found. prof. So. studies U. Miss., 1989; mem. exec. com. of dels. Am. Coun. of Learned Socs., 1993-96. Author: North of Slavery: The Negro in the Free States, 1790-1860, 1961, Been in the Storm So Long: The Aftermath of Slavery, 1979; (film) To Look for America, 1971; co-author: The United States, 1981, rev. edit., 1991; editor: American Labor Movement, 1962; co-editor: Reconstruction, 1969, Black Leaders in the Nineteenth Century, 1988, Harvard Guide to African American History, 1991—. Mem. Bradley Commn. on History in Schs., 1987-90, Schomburg Commn. for the Preservation of Black Culture; trustee Nat. Coun. for History Edn., 1990-96, mem. steering com. 1994 NAEP History Consensus Project. Served with AUS, 1953-55. Recipient Excellence in Teaching award U. Calif., Berkeley, 1967, Disting. Tchg. award, 1971, 95. Mem. Orgn. Am. Historians (chmn. nominations bd. 1975-76, exec. bd. 1983-85, pres. 1986-87), Am. Hist. Assn. (chmn. program com. 1980-81), So. Hist. Assn., Soc. Am. Historians, Am. Acad. Arts and Scis., Am. Antiquarian Soc., U. Calif. Alumni Assn., Am. Studies Assn., PEN Am. Ctr. Office: U Calif Dept History 3229 Dwinelle Hall Berkeley CA 94720-2551

LITWEILER, JOHN BERKEY, writer, editor; b. South Bend, Ind., Feb. 21, 1940; s. John Ernest and Pauline Lucile (Yoder) L. BA, North Cen. Coll., Naperville, Ill., 1962. Indexer-researcher Urban Rsch. Corp., Chgo., 1970-74; editor Maher Publs., Chgo., 1974-75, 79-81; instr. Am. Sch., Chgo., 1975-79; writer, editor Ency. Brittanica, 1992—; free-lance writer, editor, jazz critic Chgo., 1981—; vis. instr. Sch. of Art Inst., Chgo., 1982. Author: The Freedom Principle, 1984, Ornette Coleman: A Harmolodic Life, 1993; contbr. numerous articles to Reader, Chgo. Tribune, N.Y. Times Book Rev., Kulchur, Down Beat, other other publs. Bd. dirs. Jazz Inst. of Chgo., 1977-88; com. mem. DeMichael Jazz Archives, 1977-88, Chgo. Jazz Festival, 1984-88, Jazz Criticism Inst. Music Critics Assn. fellow, 1974, NEH fellow, 1981. Home: 5633 S Kenwood Ave Chicago IL 60637-1738

LITWIN, BURTON HOWARD, lawyer; b. Chgo., July 26, 1944; s. Manuel and Rose (Boehm) L.; m. Nancy Iris Stein, Aug. 25, 1968; children: Robin Meredith, Keith Harris, Jill Stacy. BBA with honors, Roosevelt U., 1966; JD cum laude, Northwestern U., 1970. Bar: Ill. 1970, U.S. Dist. Ct. (no. dist.) Ill. 1970, U.S. Tax Ct. 1971, U.S. Ct. Fed. Claims 1983; CPA, Ill. Ptnr. Hopkins & Sutter, Chgo., 1970—. Author chpts. of books; contbr. articles to profl. jours. Recipient Gold Watch award Fin. Execs. Inst., Chgo., 1965. Mem. ABA (chmn. nonfiler task force for No. Ill. 1992-94), Fed. Bar Assn., Chgo. bar Assn. (chmn. adminstrv. practice subcom., fed. taxation subcom. 1982-83), Rosarian-Am. Rose Soc. (cons.), Legal Club Chgo. Avocations: roses, painting, photography. Office: Hopkins & Sutter 3 First National Plz Chicago IL 60602

LITWIN, MARTIN STANLEY, surgeon; b. Florence, Ala., Jan. 8, 1930; s. Ben and Rose L.; m. Cheryl Denise Mason; children: Anna Marie, Rebecca, Benjamin, Martin. BS, U. Ala., 1951, MD, 1955; Cert. in Med. Mgmt., Tulane U., 1996. Diplomate Am. Bd. Surgery, Am. Bd. Med. Mgmt. Intern Michael Reese Hosp., Chgo., 1955-56; asst. in surgery to chief surg. resident Peter Bent Brigham Hosp., Boston, 1956-65; pvt. practice specializing in surgery New Orleans; asst. prof. to assoc. prof. surgery Tulane Med. Sch., New Orleans, 1966-75; prof. surgery Tulane Med. Sch., 1975—, assoc. dean, med. dir. faculty practice, 1976—, Robert and Viola Lobrano prof. surgery, 1977—; chmn. continuing edn., 1979-93; clin. investigator VA Hosp., West Roxbury, Mass., 1964-66; vis. surgeon Charity Hosp. of La., 1966; active staff Tulane Med. Ctr. Hosp., 1977—; univ. staff Touro Infirmary, 1967—. Contbr. articles to profl. jours.; assoc. editor Emergency Medicine, 1969-84. 1st lt. to col. USAR-MC, 1956-80. Fellow ACS; mem. Assn. Am. Med. Colls. (chmn. steering com. 1994—, Group on Faculty Practice), Am. Coll. Phys. Execs., Am. Burn Assn., Am. Surg. Assn., Am. Assn. Surgery of Trauma, Am. Surg. Assn., Am. Assn. Surgery of Trauma, Soc. Surg. Assn., Soc. Med. Assn., Southeastern Surg. Congress, La. Med. Soc., New Orleans Surg. Soc. (pres. 1989), Orleans Parish Med. Soc. (mem. hosp. com. 1983), Internat. Surg. Soc., Assn. Acad. Surgery, Soc. Surgeons of Alimentary Tract, Soc. Univ. Surgeons, Brigham Sur. Alumni Assn., Tulane Surg. Soc., others. Address: 5591 Bellaire Dr New Orleans LA 70124-1001 Office: Tulane U Med Ctr 1415 Tulane Ave New Orleans LA 70112-2605

LITWINOWICZ, ANTHONY, information specialist, researcher; b. Jelenia Gora, Poland, July 29, 1952; came to U.S., 1978; s. Anthony and Anna (Zdrojewski) L.; m. Catherine Veronica Gajdos, June 30, 1979; children: Catherine, Anthony, John Paul, Peter. MA in History and Philosophy, Lodz U., Poland, 1976; MS in Info. Studies, Drexel U., 1984, postgrad., 1985-90. Cert. in info. mgmt. Sr. info. specialist Laventhol & Horwath CPAs, Phila., 1984-89; instr. info. sci. Delaware Valley Coll., Doylestown, Pa., 1989-91; dir. Info. Ctr. Samsung Electronics, Ridgefield Park, N.J., 1992—. Author: Nazi Occupation of Poland, 1978; contbr. articles to profl. jours. Mem. Am. Soc. for Info. Sci. Republican. Roman Catholic. Avocations: collecting antiques, reading, martial arts. Home: 108 W Pumping Station Rd Quakertown PA 18951-4214 Office: Samsung Electronics Am 105 Challenger Rd Ridgefield Park NJ 07660-2106

LITZ, ARTHUR WALTON, JR., English language educator; b. Nashville, Oct. 31, 1929; s. Arthur Walton and Lucile (Courtney) L.; m. Marian Ann Weiler, Feb. 2, 1958 (div. 1993); children: Katharine, Andrew, Victoria, Emily. AB, Princeton U., 1951; DPhil (Rhodes scholar), Oxford (Eng.) U., 1954. Instr. Princeton U., 1956-58; lectr. Columbia U., 1957-58; mem. faculty Princeton U., 1958—, prof. English lit., 1968—, chmn. English dept., 1974-81; vis. prof. Bryn Mawr Coll., Swarthmore Coll., BreadLoaf Sch. of English, Temple U., Columbia U., U. Pa.; mem. editl. bd. Princeton U. Press, 1967-71. Author: The Art of James Joyce, 1961, Modern American Fiction: Essays in Criticism, 1963, Jane Austen, 1965, James Joyce, 1966, James Joyce's Dubliners, 1969, rev. edit., 1996, The Poetic Development of Wallace Stevens, 1972, Eliot in His Time, 1973, Scribner Quarto of Modern Literature, 1977, Major American Short Stories, 1980, rev. edit., 1994, Ezra Pound and Dorothy Shakespear: Their Letters, 1985, Collected Poems of William Carlos Williams, 1986, Personae: The Shorter Poems of Erza Pound, 1990, James Joyce: Poems and Shorter Writings, 1990, Ezra Pound's Poetry & Prose, 1992. With AUS, 1954-56. Recipient E. Harris Harbison award for gifted teaching Danforth Found., 1972; named Am. Coun. Learned Socs. fellow, 1960-61, NEH sr. fellow, 1974-75, Guggenheim fellow, 1982-83, Eastman prof. U. Oxford, 1989-90. Mem. Am. Philos. Soc. Home: 62 Western Way Princeton NJ 08540-7206

LITZSINGER, PAUL RICHARD, publishing company executive; b. Clayton, Mo., Jan. 8, 1932; s. Melvin Paul and Catherine (Mooney) L.; m. Dona Lucy Follett, July 10, 1954; children: Mark, Robin, Heidi, Shawn, Todd. B.S., U. Mo., 1954. With Follett Corp., Chgo., 1957—; retail stores supr. Follett Corp., 1962-66, pres. retail stores div., 1966-76, pres., chief exec. officer corp., 1977—; bd. dirs. Continental Water Corp., Chgo. Area dir. United Crusade; bd. dirs. Hinsdale Community House. Served With USAF, 1954-57. Mem. Nat. Assn. Coll. Stores (dir. 1971-73), Nat. Assn. Colls. Stores Corp. (pres. 1974-75, trustee), Am. Assn. Pubs., Fla. Assn. Coll. Stores, Nat. Assn. Aux. Enterprise Dirs., Nat. Assn. Bus. Mgrs., Nat. Assn. Coll. and Univ. Bus. Officers, Nat. Assn. Jr. Colls., Mgt. Assn. Ill. (bd. dirs. 1992—). Presbyterian. Club: Knollwood Golf. Home: 1650 Green Bay Rd Lake Bluff IL 60044-2306 Office: Follett Corp 2233 N West St River Grove IL 60171-1817

LIU, ALICE YEE-CHANG, biology educator; b. Hunan, China, July 12, 1948; came to U.S., 1970; d. Tin-Kai and Te-Ming (Young) L.; m. Kuang Yu Chen, Aug. 26, 1978; children: Andrew T-H, Winston T-C. BS, Chinese U., Hong Kong, 1969; PhD, Mount Sinai Sch. Med., 1974. Postdoctoral fellow Yale U. Med. Sch., New Haven, Conn., 1974-77; asst. prof. Harvard Med. Sch., Boston, 1977-84; assoc. prof. Rutgers U., Piscataway, N.J., 1984-89, prof., 1989—; dir. grad. program in cell and devel. biology Rutgers U.-U. Medicine-Dentistry N.J.-R.W. Johnson Med. Sch., 1994—; mem. pharmacological scis. rev. com. NIH, 1984-88; mem. cell biology panel NSF, 1989-93, 94-95; mem. basic rsch. adv. group N.J. Commn. on Cancer Rsch., 1989-93, 94—. Author: Receptors Again, 1985; editorial bd. Biol. Signals, 1991—. Recipient N.Y.C. Bd. of Higher Edn. award, 1972, Am. Cancer Soc. Scholar award, Boston, 1982-85; NIH postdoctoral fellow, 1974-77, Medical Found. fellow, Boston, 1977-79. Mem. Am. Soc. Biochemistry and Molecular Biology, Am. Soc. Pharmacology and Experimental Therapeutics. Home: 4 Silverthorn Ln Belle Mead NJ 08502 Office: Rutgers U PO Box 1059 Nelson Biology Labs Piscataway NJ 08855-1059

LIU, ANDREW TZE CHIU, chemical researcher and developer; b. Hong Kong, July 20, 1929; came to U.S., 1947; s. Yan Tak and Dorothy M. K. (Kwok) L.; m. Helena L. Y. (Chang), Feb. 7, 1956; children: Genevia K. M., Andrea K. Y. BS, Ind. U., 1951; MS, U. Mass., Lowell, 1953; PhD, London U., 1961; DIC, Imperial Coll., London, 1962. Engr. Textile Rsch. Inst., Beijing, 1955-59; tech. officer I.C.I. Ltd., Manchester, Eng., 1961-67; rsch. chemist E.I. du Pont and Nemours & Co., Beaumont, Tex., 1967-71; chief exec. officer LIU Industries, Hong Kong, 1971-77; coord. new ventures Conoco, Inc., Ponca City, Okla., 1977-80; v.p. Continental Overseas Oil, Inc., Houston, 1980-85; chief exec. officer China Ctr. for Tech. Devel., Houston, 1985-88; dir., sr. rsch. scientist Dentsply Internat., York, Pa., 1988-93; spl. projects mgr. Bisco, Inc., Itasca, Ill., 1994—; advisor Ctr. Internat. Bus. Studies Tex. A&M U., College Station, 1986-89. Author: Science and Technology Policy, 1983. Recipient Disting. Svc. award, E. I. du Pont, Wilmington, Del. Mem. ADA (subcom. direct filling working group), Internat. Assn. Dental Rsch., Am. Chem. Soc., Soc. Plastic Engrs., Am. Soc. Materials. Achievements include 15 patents for hydrocarbon conversions, catalyst removal, fuel additives, polyurethanes, hydrocarbon polymers, dental mold fabrication, self lubricating interpenetrating polymer network, medical prosthesis materials. Home: 204 Edgehorne Ave Apex NC 27502-5207

LIU, BEN-CHIEH, economist; b. Chungking, China, Nov. 17, 1938; came to U.S., 1965, naturalized, 1973; s. Pei-juang and Chung-su L.; m. Jill Jyhhuey, Oct. 2, 1965; children—Tina Won-ting, Roger Won-jung, Milton Wonming. B.A., Nat. Taiwan U., 1961; M.A., Meml. U. Nfld., 1965, Washington U., St. Louis, 1968; Ph.D., Washington U., St. Louis, 1971. Economist Chinese Air Force and Central Customs, Taiwan, 1961-63; resource economist Canadian Land Inventory and Forest Services, Nfld., 1963-65; research project dir. St. Louis Regional Indsl. Devel. Corp., 1968-72; prin. econs. Midwest Research Inst., Kansas City, Mo., 1972-80; mgr. Energy and Environ. Systems Div., Argonne (Ill.) Nat. Lab., 1980-81; Fulbright prof., dir. Internat. Enterprises Inst. Nat. Dong-Hwa U., Taiwan, 1997—; prof. econs., assoc. dir. rsch. Oklahoma City U., 1981-82; prof. mgmt., mktg. and info. systems Chgo. State U., 1982—; pres. Liu & Assocs., Inc., 1982—; vis. prof. econs. U. Mo., 1970-78, Nat. Taiwan U., 1991-92; Fulbright prof., dir. Internat. Enterprises Inst., Nat. Dong-Hwa U., Taiwan, 1997—; cons. UN, NSF; mem. Gov. Thompson's Adv. Com. on Agrl. Export, 1985-87, Congressman Fawell's Adv. Com. on Sci. and Tech., 1985—; commr. Nat. Commn. on Librs. and Info. Svcs., 1991-94. Author: Interindustrial Structure Analysis: An Input-Output Study for St. Louis Region, 1968, The Quality of Life in the United States, 1970, Rating, Index and Statistics, 1973, Quality of Life Indicators in U.S. Metropolitan Areas, 1975, Physical and Economic Damage Functions for Air Pollutants by Receptors, 1976, Earthquake Risk and Damage Functions, An Integrated Model, 1981, Income, Energy and Quality of Life: An Information Systems Approach to Decisions, 1988; mem. editorial bd.: Internat. Jour. Math. Social Sci, Am. Jour. Econs. and Sociology, Hong Kong Jour. Bus. Mgmt.; contbr. articles to profl. jours. Recipient rsch. study award Am. Indsl. Devel. Coun., 1969—, Fulbright Scholar awards, 1992, 96, Faculty Meritorious awards Chgo. State U., 1983, 86, 89, 90, Disting. Prof. Advancement Increase awards, 1990, 96; U.S. Econ. Devel. Adminstrn. fellow, 1967-68; Korean Govt. scholar, 1963-65; Fulbright scholar Mgmt. Devel. Inst., Delhi U., 1992. Fellow Am. Statis. Assn. (com. mem.); mem. Am. Econ. Assn. (com. mem.), Econometric Soc., Royal Econ. Soc., Internat. Statis. Instn., Assn. for Social Econs. (com. mem.), Tax Inst. Am., Chinese Acad. and Profl. Assn. (pres. 1984-85), Chinese Econ. Assn. in N.Am. (pres. 1988-90).

Home: 5360 Pennywood Dr Lisle IL 60532-2032 Office: Chgo State U Chicago IL 60628 *The joy of living may temporarily rest on present or past glory, but it is the immersion in planning for the future—the living ahead of one's time—which ensures permanently the flourishing of the joy of life. In a commonwealth society, happiness does not come from doing what we like to do, but from liking what we have to do for the less-well-to-do-ones.*

LIU, BENJAMIN YOUNG-HWAI, engineering educator; b. Shanghai, China, Aug. 15, 1934; s. Wilson Wan-su and Dorothy Pao-ning (Cheng) L.; m. Helen Hai-ling Cheng, June 14, 1958; 1 son, Lawrence A.S. Student, Nat. Taiwan U., 1951-54; B.S. in Mech. Engring., U. Nebr., 1956; Ph.D., U. Minn., 1960; doctorate (hon.), U. Kupio, Finland, 1991. Asso. engr. Honeywell Co., Mpls., 1956; research asst., instr. U. Minn., 1956-60, asst. prof., 1960-67, asso. prof., 1967-69, prof., 1969-93, regent's prof., 1993—, dir. Particle Tech. Lab., 1973-95; dir. Ctr. for Filtration Rsch., 1995—; vis. prof. U. Paris, 1968-69; patentee in field. Contbg. author: Aerosol Science, 1966; editor: Fine Particles, 1976, Application of Solar Energy for Heating and Cooling Buildings, 1977, Aerosols in the Mining and Industrial Work Environment, 1983, Aerosols: Science, Technology and Industrial Application of Airborne Particles, 1984; editor-in-chief: Aerosol Sci. and Tech., 1983-93; contbr. articles to Ency. Chem. Tech., Ency. Applied Physics. Guggenheim fellow, 1968-69; recipient Sr. U.S. Scientist award Alexander von Humboldt Found., 1982-83. Mem. ASME, ASHRAE, Inst. Environ. Scis. (v.p. 1993-95), Air and Waste Mgmt. Assn., Am. Assn. for Aerosol Rsch. (pres. 1986-88), Chinese Am. Assn. Minn. (pres. 1971-72), Nat. Acad. Engring. Home: 1 N Deep Lake Rd North Oaks MN 55127-6504 Office: U Minn Particle Tech Lab 111 Church St SE Minneapolis MN 55455-0150

LIU, BRIAN CHEONG-SENG, urology and oncology educator, researcher; b. Hong Kong, Jan. 15, 1959; came to U.S., 1968; s. Keh Ming and Yin Man (Au) L. BS in Microbiology summa cum laude, UCLA, 1980, PhD in Molecular Biology, 1984; JD, William Howard Taft Law Sch., 1997. Postdoctoral fellow in tumor immunology and tumor biology Sch. Medicine UCLA, 1984-88; instr. dept. urology Mt. Sinai Sch. Medicine, N.Y.C., 1988-89, asst. prof. dept. urology, dir. urologic rsch., 1989—; sr. rsch. fellow Jonsson Comprehensive Cancer Ctr., 1985-88; vis. investigator dept. pathology Henry Ford Hosp., Detroit, 1987-88. Mem. editl. bd. Jour. Urology, 1996—; contbr. articles to profl. jours. Recipient Edwin Beer award N.Y. Acad. Med., 1991-93, New Investigator award Am. Found. Urologic Diseases, 1994—, Cancer of the Prostate Rsch. award Capcure Found., 1995, Merck Young Investigator award in Urology, 1996; Nat. Cancer Inst. grantee, 1991—. Mem. Am. Urologic Assn., Soc. Basic Urologic Rsch. (treas.), Sigma Xi. Office: Mt Sinai Sch Med Dept Urology 1 Gustave L Levy Pl New York NY 10029-6504

LIU, CHUNG LAUNG, computer engineer, educator; b. Canton, China, Oct. 25, 1934; U.S. citizen; married; 1 child. BSc, Cheng Kung U., 1956; SM, MIT, 1960, ScD in Elec. Engring., 1962. From asst. prof. to assoc. prof. elec. engring. MIT, 1962-72; prof. computer sci. U. Ill., Urbana, 1973—. Fellow IEEE (Taylor L. Booth Edn. award Computer Soc. 1992, Edn. medal 1994), Assn. Computing Machinery (Karl V. Karlstron Outstanding Educator award 1990). Office: Univ of Illinois Dept Computer Science 1304 W Springfield Ave Urbana IL 61801-2910

LIU, CHUNG-CHIUN, chemical engineering educator; b. Canton, Kwangtun, China, Oct. 8, 1936; came to U.S., 1961, naturalized, 1972; s. Pay-Yen and Chi-Wei (Chen) L.; m. Mary Lou Rice, Nov. 25, 1967; children: Peter S.H. B.S., Nat. Cheng-Kung U., Taiwan, 1959; M.S., Calif. Inst. Tech., 1962; Ph.D., Case Western Res. U., 1968. Grad. asst. Case Western Res. U., Cleve., 1963-68, postdoctoral fellow, 1968, prof. chem. engring., 1978—; asst. prof. chem. engring. U. Pitts., 1968-72, assoc. prof., 1972-76, prof., 1976-78; prof. chem. engring. Case Western Res. U., Cleve., 1978—; assoc. dir. Case Center for Electrochem. Scis., Cleve., 1982-86; dir. electronics design ctr. Case Center for Electrochem. Scis., 1986-89, Wallace R. Persons prof. sensor tech. and control, 1989—. Contbr. articles in field to profl. jours.; patentee in field. Mem. Electrochem. Soc. (summer fellowship award 1963, 66), Am. Inst. Chem. Engrs. Home: 2917 E Overlook Rd Cleveland OH 44118-2433 Office: Case Western Res U Dept Chem Engr 10900 Euclid Ave Cleveland OH 44106-1712

LIU, DON, ophthalmologist, medical researcher; b. Nanjing, China, July 17, 1947; came to the U.S., 1964; s. Robert Ching Ming and I. Tu Liu; m. Helen Cheng, June 21, 1975; children: David, Grace, Glory, Daniel. BS in Physics, Purdue U., 1969; MS in Physics, U. Mass., 1971; MD, SUNY, Buffalo, 1977. Dir. oculoplastics/orbit. Ford Hosp., Detroit, 1982-90; dir. oculoplastics/orbit. svc. U. So. Calif.-L.A. County Hosp., L.A., 1990—; assoc. dir. tech. transfer U. So. Calif., 1995—; organizer Internat. Conf. U.S.A., China and Hong Kong, Taiwan, 1985, 87, 89, 92, 93, 95; cons. to med. industries, state govt. and the Chinese govt. on health care; sci. referee Ophthalmology, 1990—, Am. Jour. Ophthalmology, 1991—, Ophthalmic, Plastic and Recontructive Surgery, 1991—, Ophthalmic Surgery and Lasers, 1994—; mem. adv. bd. Med. Books for China, Internat., 1985—; vis. prof., lectr. various institutions in U.S., China, Taiwan, Indonesia, England, and Holland. Contbr. numerous book chpts. and articles to textbooks and profl. jours.; mem. editl. bd. numerous jours. Campaign fundraiser Mike Woo for Mayor, L.A., 1993; So. Calif. coord. Bush/Quayle, 1992, L.A.; sponsor San Marino (Calif.) Sch. Dist., 1990—; active Boy Scouts Am., Amnesty Internat., ch. activities. Recipient numerous tchg. awards, hon. degrees and titles from Chinese med. instns. Fellow ACS, Am. Acad. Facial Plastic and Reconstructive Surgery (com. mem. 1992-96), Am. Soc. Ophthalmic, Plastic and Reconstructive Surgery (fellowship dir. 1994—, Outstanding fellow 1981), Am. Acad. Ophthalmology (hon. award 1994), Am. BdOphthalmology (assoc. examiner 1991—); mem. AMA, Chinese Am. Ophthalmologic Soc.(sec.-treas. 1988-92), Internat. Soc. Ocuplastic Surgeons (bd. dirs.), Com. of 100. Office: 1975 Zonal Ave # 516 Los Angeles CA 90033-1039

LIU, ERNEST K. H., international banking executive, international financial consultant; b. Hong Kong, Oct. 4, 1950; came to U.S., 1979; s. Sun-Ip and Mei-Choi (Man) L.; m. Lily Chan, Dec. 5, 1979; children—Aimee On-On, Alvin Lok-Tin. B.Social Sci., Hong Kong U., 1974; M.B.A. in Fin., NYU, 1986. Lending officer Bank of Am. NT and SA, Hong Kong, 1974-76; market officer Hong Kong Trade Devel. Council, Hong Kong, 1976-79; mgr. Hong Kong Trade Devel. Council, N.Y.C., 1979-82; asst. v.p. mktg. Honkong and Shanghi Banking Corp, N.Y.C., 1982-83; sr. account exec. Citibank, N.A., N.Y.C., 1984-88; asst. v.p. Merrill Lynch Internat. Pvt. Client Svcs., N.Y.C., 1988-91; dir. Asia-Pacific Internat. Trade Promotion Ltd., N.Y.C., 1991—.

LIU, GUOSONG, neurobiologist; b. Chengdu, Peoples' Republic China, Jan. 18, 1956; came to U.S., 1985; s. Wanfu Liu and Guizhen Wang; m. Xiaoyun Sun, Aug. 13, 1981; 1 child, Robert S. MD, Chuanbei Med. Sch., Sichuan, China, 1980; PhD, UCLA, 1990. Intern Chuanbei Med. Sch., 1979-80; rsch. assoc. Acad. Traditional Chinese Medicine, Beijing, 1982-85; rsch. fellow U. Ill., Chgo., 1985-86; rsch. fellow UCLA, 1986-90, postgrad. researcher, 1990-93; rsch. fellow Stanford U., 1993-96; asst. prof. MIT, Cambridge, Mass., 1996—. Contbr. to profl. publs. Mem. Soc. Neurosci., Sigma Xi. Achievements include synaptic transmission and plasicity at single synapses, activity dependent synapse formation. Office: MIT E25-435 Dept Brain & Cognitive Sci Cambridge MA 02139

LIU, HAN-SHOU, space scientist, researcher; b. Hunan, China, Mar. 9, 1930; came to U.S., 1960, naturalized, 1972; s. Yu-Tin and Chun-Chen (Yeng) L.; m. Sun-Ling Yang Liu, May 2, 1957; children—Michael Fu-Yen, Peter Fu-Tze. Ph.D., Cornell U., 1963. Research asst. Cornell U., 1962-63; research assoc. Nat. Acad. Sci., Washington, 1963-65; scientist NASA Goddard Space Flight Center, Greenbelt, Md., 1965—; Pres. Mei-Hwa Chinese Sch., 1980-81. Contbr. articles to profl. jours. Fellow AAAS; mem. Am. Astron. Soc., Am. Geophys. Union, Planetary Soc., AIAA. Office: NASA Goddard Space Flight Ctr Code # 921 Greenbelt MD 20771

LIU, HUNG-CHING, medical educator; b. June 18, 1942; arrived in U.S., 1965; d. Chin-Hai and Su-Ein (Chiang) Ou; m. Dar-Biau Liu, Dec. 20, 1969; children: Warrick, Benson. BSc, Taiwan Normal U., 1965; PhD, Wayne State U., 1969. Rsch. assoc. U. Wis., Madison, 1970-73; asst. prof. State Univ. Campinas, Sao Paulo, Brazil, 1973-77; rsch. assoc. N.Y. State U., Stony Brook, N.Y., 1977-83; rsch. asst. prof. Eastern Va. Medical Sch., Norfolk, Va., 1983-88; asst. prof. Cornell Univ. Medical Coll., N.Y., 1988-92, assoc. prof., 1992—; dir. Reproductive Endocrine Lab. Cornell U. Med. Coll., 1988—; cons. Sec. of Dept. Health, Taipei, Taiwan, 1990—; mem. editl. bd. Early Pregnancy Biol. and Med., Cherry Hill, N.J., 1994—; pioneer work in the field of reproductive medicine, in vitro fertilization. Contbr. numerous articles to profl. jours. Recipient first prize for Best Paper award, The Am. Fertility Soc., 1986, Poster Prize award, 1988. Mem. The Soc. Study of Reproduction, The Am. Fertility Soc. Republican. Avocations: music, travel, coin collecting, reading. Office: Cornell U Medical Coll 515 E 71st St Rm S500 New York NY 10021-4871

LIU, KATHERINE CHANG, artist, art educator; b. Kiang-si, China; came to U.S., 1963; d. Ming-fan and Ying (Yuan) Chang; m. Yet-zen Liu; children: Alan S., Laura Y. MS, U. Calif., Berkeley, 1965. Instr. U. Va. Ext., Longwood Coll.; mem. tchg. staff master class Hill Country Arts Found., Tex., 1995, 96, 97; invited mem. L.A. Artcore Reviewing and Curatorial Bd., 1993; invited juror, lectr. over 75 exhbns. and orgns., Alaska, Ga., Tex. and Okla. Watercolor Soc. Anns., 1997; juror, lectr. Ala. Watercolor Soc. Ann., 1996, Midwest Watercolor Soc. Nat. Exhibit, 1996, Watercolor West Nat. Open, 1996. One-woman shows include Harrison Mus., Utah State U., Riverside (Calif.) Art Mus., Ventura (Calif.) Coll., Fla. A&M U., Louis Newman Galleries, L.A., L.A. Artcore, Lung-Men Gallery, Taipei, Republic of China, State of the Arts International Biennial, Parkland Coll. Ill., 1989, 91, 97, Inaugural Exhibit, The Union Ctr. for the Arts, L.A., 1997, Treasures for the Community: The Chrysler Mus. Collects, 1989-96, 97, Watercolor U.S.A. Hon. Soc. Invitational, 1989, 91, 93, 95, Hunter Mus. Art, Tenn., 1993, Bakersfield Art Mus., 1994, Sandra Walters Gallery, Hong Kong, 1994, Horwitch-Newman Gallery, Scottsdale, Ariz., 1995, Hong Kong U. Sci. and Tech. Libr. Art Gallery, 1996, J.J. Brookings Gallery, San Francisco, 1996, John N Joe Gallery, L.A., 1996, Bill Armstrong Gallery, Springfield, Mo., 1996, Chrysler Mus. Fine Art, Norfolk, Va., 1997; Invitational, U. B.C. Art Gallery, 1992, U. Sydney Art Mus., 1992, Ruhr-West Art Mus., Wise, 1992, Macau Art Mus., 1992, Rosenfeld Gallery, Phila., 1994, Mandarin Oriental Fine Arts, Hong Kong, 1994; contbr. works to 21 books and 33 periodicals. Co-curator Taiwan-USA-Australia Watermedia Survey Exhbn., Nat. Taiwan Art Inst., 1994; sole juror San Diego Watermedia Internat., 1993, Triton Mus. Open Competition, 1994, Northern Nat. Art Competition, 1994, Watercolor West Nat., 1993, Tenn., Utah, Hawaii, N.C. Watercolor Socs., North Am. Open, Midwest Southwest and over 30 statewide competitions in watermedia or all-media; co-juror Rocky Mountain Nat., San Diego Internat. and West Fedn. Exhibits. Recipient Rex Brandt award San Diego Watercolor Internat., 1985, Purchase Selection award Watercolor USA and Springfield (Mo.) Art Mus., 1981, Gold medal, 1986, Mary Lou Fitzgerald meml. award Allied Arts Am. Nat. Arts Club, N.Y.C., 1987, Achievement award of Artists Painting in Acrylic Am. Artists Mag., 1993; NEA grantee, 1979-80. Mem. Nat. Watercolor Soc. (life, chmn. jury 1985, pres. 1983, Top award 1984, cash awards 1979, 87), Watercolor U.S.A. Honor Soc., Nat. Soc. Painters in Casein and Acrylic (2nd award 1985), Rocky Mountain Nat. Watermedia Soc. (juror 1984, awards 1978, 80, 86).

LIU, KEH-FEI FRANK, physicist, educator; b. Beijing, Jan. 11, 1947; came to U.S., 1969; s. Hsien-Chang and Juihua (Wang) L.; m. Yao-Chin Ko, Apr. 6, 1974; children: Helen, Alexander. BS, Tunghai U., Taichung, Taiwan, 1968; MS, SUNY, Stony Brook, 1972, PhD, 1975. Vis. scientist C.E.N. Saclay France, Paris, 1974-76; from rsch. assoc. to adj. asst. prof. UCLA, 1976-80; assoc. prof. U. Ky., Lexington, 1980-86, prof. physics, 1986—; vis. prof. SUNY, Stony Brook, 1985-86, 1990; univ. rsch. prof. U. Ky., 1992. Editor: Chiral Solitons, 1987; assoc. editor World Scientific Pub. Co., Singapore, 1985—; contbr. articles to profl. jours. Recipient First Prize in Theoretical Physics Academia Sinica, China, 1987, Grand Challenge award DOE, 1988, 1989, Alexander Von Humboldt Sr. Scientist award Humboldt Found., Germany, 1990. Mem. Am. Phys. Soc., European Phys. Soc., Overseas Chinese Physicists Assn. (coord. 1991—). Office: U Ky Dept Physics & Astronomy Lexington KY 40506

LIU, KHANG-LEE, dentist, educator; b. China, Aug. 5, 1939; came to U.S., 1972, naturalized, 1982; s. T.P. and K.H. (Lu) L.; m. Nancy S.Y. Lee (div.); children: Christine, Helen. B.D.S., Nat. Def. Med. Ctr., Faculty of Dentistry, Taipei, 1964; MA, U. Chgo., 1974. Asst., Nat. Def. Med. Ctr., Taipei, Taiwan, 1964-67; instr. Med. Ctr., Republic of China, 1968-72; asst. prof. U. Chgo., 1972-76; assoc. prof. Nat. Def. Med. Ctr., 1976-77; from asst. prof. to assoc. prof. dentistry Northwestern U., Chgo., 1977—; dir. McCormick Boys and Girls Dental Clin. Pres. midwest chpt. Coun. on Chinese Cultural Renaissance, 1984—. Mem. ADA, Chgo. Dental Soc., Am. Soc. Dentistry for Children, Internat. Assn. Dental Rsch., Am. Acad. Pediatric Dentistry, Chinese Am. Dentist Assn. (charter mem., 1st pres. 1990). Office: 2158 S Archer Ave Chicago IL 60616-1514

LIU, MING-TSAN, computer engineering educator; b. Peikang, Taiwan, Aug. 30, 1934. BSEE, Nat. Cheng Kung U., Tainan, Taiwan, 1957; MSEE, U. Pa., 1961, PhD, 1964. Prof. dept. computer and info. sci. Ohio State U. Recipient Engring. Rsch. award Ohio State U., 1982, Best Paper award Computer Network Symposium 1984, Disting. Achievement award Nat. Cheng Kung U., 1987, Disting. Scholar award Ohio State U., 1991, Ameritech prize for excellence in telecom. Ameritech Found., 1991. Fellow IEEE (chmn. tech. com. on distbtd. processing Computer Soc. 1982-84, editor IEEE Transactions on Computers 1982-86, chmn. Eckert-Mauchly award com. 1984-85, 91-92, bd. govs. Computer Soc. 1984-90, chmn. tutorials com. 1982, program chmn. 1985, gen. chmn. 1986, chmn. steering com. 1989, gen. co-chmn. Internat. Conf. on Distbtd. Computing Sys. 1992, chmn. steering com. Symposium on Reliable Distbtd. Sys. 1986-89, v.p. membership and info. Computer Soc. 1984, mem. editl. bd. 1986-88, editor-in-chief IEEE Transactions on Computers 1986-90, program chmn. IEEE Internat. Conf. on Data Engring. 1990, mem. TAB awards and recognition com. 1990-91, program chmn. Internat. Symposium on Comm. 1991, Internat. Phoenix Conf. on Computers and Comm. 1992, mem. TAB new tech. directions com. 1992-93, gen. co-chmn. Internat. Conf. on Parallel and Distbtd. Sys. 1992, Meritorious Svc. award Computer Soc. 1985, 87, 90, Outstanding Mem. Columbus sect. 1986-87). Office: Ohio State U Computer & Information Sci 2015 Neil Ave Columbus OH 43210-1210*

LIU, RAY HO, forensic science program director, educator; b. Taiwan, Apr. 3, 1942; s. Ku and Tsan (Hwang) L.; m. Hsiu-Lan Lin, Dec. 4, 1965; children: Yu-Ting, Eugene, Hubert. LLB, Cen. Police Coll., Taipei, Taiwan, 1965; PhD, So. Ill. U., 1976. Qualified as lab. dir., N.Y. State Dept. Health. Asst. prof. forensic sci. U. Ill., Chgo., 1976-80; mass spectrometrist Cen. Regional Lab, U.S. EPA, Chgo., 1980-82; ctr. mass spectrometrist Ea. Regional Rsch. Ctr. USDA, Phila., 1982-83; assoc. prof. forensic sci. U. Ala., Birmingham, 1984-89, prof., 1989—, dir. grad. program in forensic sci., 1991—; tech. dir. Environ. Health Rsch. and Testing, Birmingham, Ala., 1987-91, Environ. Chem. Corp., Birmingham, 1992-93; cons. in field; vis. prof. Taiwanese Nat. Sci. Coun., 1981, 1994, 96; insp. Nat. Lab. Certification Program, Research Triangle Park, N.C., 1988—. Author: Approaches to Drug Sample Differentiation, 1982, Elements and Practice in Forensic Drug Urinalysis, 1994, Handbook of Workplace Drug Testing, 1995, Handbook for Drug Analysis - Application in Forensic and Clinical Laboratories, 1997; editor-in-chief Forensic Sci. Rev., 1989—; contbr. numerous articles to profl. jours. Fellow Am. Acad. Forensic Scis., mem. Am. Chem. Soc., Am. Assn. for Clin. Chemistry, Am. Soc. for Mass Spectrometry, Sigma XI. Office: U Ala Dept Criminal Scis Birmingham AL 35294

LIU, RHONDA LOUISE, librarian; b. Honolulu; d. David Yuk Fong Liu and Shirley May Chong. BA, U. Hawaii at Manoa, Honolulu, 1974, MLS, 1991. Outreach libr. Alu Like Native Hawaiian Libr. Project, 1992; libr. II Hawaii State Libr., 1992; fgn. expert Beijing Fgn. Studies U., 1992-93; info. specialist Savs. & Cmty. Bankers of Am., Washington, 1993-94; tech. libr. Md. State Libr. for Blind & Physically Handicapped, Balt., 1995—; info. specialist Savings & Cmty. Bankers of Am.; grad. student intern East-West Ctr. Resource Materials Collection, 1991-92; libr. asst. Legis. Reference Bur. Libr., 1989-90; asst. rschr. Legis. Info. Sys. Office, 1984-85; English-as-second lang. tutor Keimei Gakuen, Tokyo, 1979. Active Friends of Md. State Libr. for Blind and Physically Handicapped, 1994—; v.p., sec. Sch. Libr. and Info. Studies, 1990-91. Alu Like Native Hawaiian Libr. fellow, 1990-91; Kamehameha Schs./Bishop Estate scholar, 1991. Mem. ALA, U. Hawaii Alumni Assn., Kamehameha Schs. Alumni Assn. Avocations: gourmet cooking, multi-cultural activities, overseas travel, hula, ESL tutor. Office: Md State Libr for Blind & Phys Handicapped 415 Park Ave Baltimore MD 21201-3603

LIU, SHI-KAU, microbiologist, research scientist; b. Kaohsiung, Taiwan, Nov. 3, 1962; s. Pao-Hen Liu and Chen-Nuo Yen; m. Thyr-Min Lin; 1 child, Chung-Song. BS, Soochow U., Taiwan, 1984; PhD, Purdue U., U.S.A., 1991. Postdoctoral rsch. fellow Stanford U., Calif., 1991-93; assoc. prof. National Sun Yat-Sen Univ., Kaohsiung, Taiwan, 1993-94; rsch. assoc. U. N.C., Chapel Hill, N.C., 1994-96; staff scientist Maxygen, Inc., Santa Clara, Calif., 1996—. Contbr. to profl. jours. Recipient Excellent Achievement award Republic of China Army, 1986, Outstanding Grad. Rsch. award Purdue U., 1990, Outstanding Researcher award Republic of China Nat. Sci. Coun., 1993. Mem. Am. Soc. Microbiology. Avocations: photography, fishing. Home: 281 Jen-Ai Road, Yung-Ho Taiwan

LIU, SHU QIAN, biomedical engineer, researcher, educator; b. Lian-cheng, China, Dec. 22, 1956; came to U.S., 1985; s. Din-An and Jin-Zhen L.; m. Wu Yu-Hua, Feb. 3, 1983; children: Diana Liu, Charley Liu. BS in Medicine, Med. Sch. of NeiMongu, China, 1980; MS, Med. Sch. of NeiMongu, 1983; PhD, U. Calif., San Diego, 1990. Post doctoral fellow U. Calif., San Diego, 1990-92, asst. rsch. bioengineer, 1992-95, asst. prof., 1995—. Contbr. articles to profl. jours. Recipient Melville medal ASME, 1994, best paper award, 1993, Tobacco Rsch. award State of Calif., 1990-92, Whitaker Rsch. award Whitaker Found., 1993-96. Mem. ASME, AAAS, Biomed. Engring. Soc. Home: 533 Ridge Rd Wilmette IL 60091-2439 Office: Northwestern Univ Biomed Engring Dept 2145 Sheridan Rd Evanston IL 60208-0834

LIU, VI-CHENG, aerospace engineering educator; b. Wu-ching, China, Sept. 1, 1917; came to U.S., 1946, naturalized, 1973; s. Bi-Ching and Shu-Fung (Keng) L.; m. Hsi-Yen Wang, Mar. 1, 1947. B.S., Chiao Tung U., 1940; M.S., U. Mich., 1947, Ph.D., 1951. Instr. Tsing-Hua U., Kunming, 1940-46; research engr. Engring. Research Inst., U. Mich., Ann Arbor, 1951-59; prof. aerospace engring. U. Mich., 1959-89, prof. emeritus, 1989—; vis. prof. Inst. of Mechanics, Chinese Acad. Sci., Peking, 1980—; ministry edn., vis. chair prof. Nanjing Aero. Inst., People's Republic China, 1989-91, hon. prof., 1991—; cons. NASA, 1964-65. Ministry of Edn. China research fellow, 1946-49; NASA research grantee, 1964-80, USAF Geophysical Rsch. grantee, 1958-64. Research and 100 sci. publs. in rarefied gas dynamics, ionospheric physics, space physics, geophys. fluid dynamics. Home: 2104 Vinewood Blvd Ann Arbor MI 48104-2762

LIU, WING KAM, mechanical and civil engineering educator; b. Hong Kong, May 15, 1952; came to U.S., 1973, naturalized, 1990; s. Yin Lam and Siu Lin (Chan) L.; m. Betty Hsia, Dec. 12, 1986; children: Melissa Margaret, Michael Kevin. BSc with highest honors, U. Ill., Chgo., 1976; MSc, Calif. Inst. Tech., 1977, PhD, 1981. Registered profl. engr., Ill. Asst. prof. mech. and civil engring. Northwestern U., Evanston, Ill., 1980-83, assoc. prof., 1983-88, prof., 1988—; prin. cons. reactor analysis and safety div. Argonne (Ill.) Nat. Lab., 1981—. Co-editor: Innovative Methods for Nonlinear Problems, 1984, Impact-Effects of Fasts Transient Loadings, 1988, Computational Mechanics of Probabilistic and Reliability Analysis, 1989. Recipient Thomas J. Jaeger prize Internat. Assn. for Structural Mechanics in Reactor Tech., 1989, Ralph R. Teetor award Soc. Automotive Engrs., 1983; grantee USF, Army Rsch. Office, NASA, AFSOR, ONR, GE, Ford Motor, Chrysler. Fellow ASCE, USACM, ASME (Melville medal 1979, Pi Tau Sigma gold medal 1985, Gustus L. Larson Meml. award 1995), U.S. Assn. Computational Mechanics (pres.-elect); mem. Am. Acad. Mechanics. Office: Northwestern U Dept Mech Engring 2145 Sheridan Rd Evanston IL 60208-0834

LIU, YOSEN, nuclear engineer; b. Wuchang, Hupei, China, Oct. 31, 1935; came to U.S., 1977; s. Henry C. and Chin-Feen (Chou) L.; m. Johanna S. Lui, Sept. 2, 1967; children: Sieglinde, Siegrid, Steve. BS, Naval Coll. Tech., 1958; dipl. engr., Tech. Hochschule, Germany, 1966, D of Engring., 1970. Rsch. scientist Kernforschungsanlage, Juelich, Germany, 1968-70; assoc. prof. Nat. Tsing Hua U., Hsinchu, Taiwan, 1970-75; nuclear engr. Kraftwerk Union, Erlangen, Germany, 1975-77; prin. engr. Combustion Engring. Inc., Windsor, Conn., 1977-80; mgr. bus. devel. Combustion Engring. Inc., Taipei, Taiwan, 1980-87; sr. cons. physicist ABB Combustion Engring. Inc., Windsor, 1987-90; staff engr. Battelle Pacific Northwest Lab., Richland, Wash., 1990—. Mem. Am. Nuclear Soc., Rotary Internat. Roman Catholic. Avocation: golf. Home: 218 Sitka Ct Richland WA 99352-8730 Office: Battelle Pacific NW Lab Battelle Blvd Richland WA 99352

LIU, YOUNG KING, biomedical engineering educator; b. Nanjing, China, May 3, 1934; came to U.S., 1952; s. Yih Ling and Man Fun (Teng) L.; m. Nina Pauline Liu, Sept. 4, 1964 (July, 1986); children—Erik, Tania; m. Anita Beeth, Aug. 14, 1994. BSME, Bradley U., 1955; MSME, U. Wis.-Madison, 1959; PhD, Wayne State U., 1963. Cert. acupuncturist, Calif. Asst. prof. Milw. Sch. of Engring., 1956-59; instr. Wayne State U., Detroit, 1960-63; lectr. then asst. prof. U. Mich., Ann Arbor, 1963-69; assoc. prof. then prof. Tulane U., New Orleans, 1969-78; prof. biomed. engring., dir. dept. U. Iowa, Iowa City, 1978-93; pres. U. No. Calif., Petaluma, 1993—. Contbr. articles to profl. jours., chpts. to books. NIH spl. research fellow, 1968-69; recipient Research Career Devel. award NIH, 1971-76. Mem. Internat. Soc. Lumbar Spine (exec. com., central U.S. rep.), Orthopedic Research Soc., Am. Soc. Engring. Edn., Sigma Xi. Democrat.

LIU, YUAN HSIUNG, drafting and design educator; b. Tainan, Taiwan, Feb. 24, 1938; came to U.S., 1970; s. Chun Chang and Kong (Wong) L.; m. Ho Pe Tung, July 27, 1973; children: Joan Anshen, Joseph Pinyang. BEd, Nat. Taiwan Normal U., Taipei, 1961; MEd, Nat. Chengchi U., Taipei, 1967, U. Alta., Edmonton, 1970; PhD, Iowa State U., 1975. Cert. tchr. Tchr. indsl. arts and math. Nan Ning Jr. High Sch., Tainan, Taiwan, 1961-62, 63-64; tech. math. instr. Chung-Cheng Inst. Tech., Taipei, 1967-68; drafter Sundstrand Hydro-Transmission Corp., Ames, Iowa, 1973-75; assoc. prof. Fairmont (W.Va.) State Coll., 1975-80; per course instr. Sinclair Community Coll., Dayton, Ohio, 1985; assoc. prof. Miami U., Hamilton, Ohio, 1980-85, Southwest Mo. State U., Springfield, 1985—; cons. Monarch Indsl. Precision Co., Springfield, 1986, Gen. Electric Co., Springfield, 1988, Fasco Industries, Inc., Ozark, Mo., 1989, 95, Springfield Remfg. Corp., 1990, 92, Ctrl. States Indsl., Intercont Products, Inc., L&W Industries, Inc., ZERCO Mfg. Co., 1994, 95, Paul Mueller Co., 1996. 2d lt. R.O.C. Army, 1962-63. Recipient Excellent Teaching in Drafting award Charvoz-Carsen Corp., Fairfield, N.J., 1978. Mem. Am. Design Drafting Assn. Avocations: walking, watching TV. Office: SW Mo State U Tech Dept 901 S National Ave Springfield MO 65804-0094

LIUZZI, ROBERT C., chemical company executive; b. Boston, 1944; married. AB, Coll. of Holy Cross, 1965; LLB, U. Va., 1968. V.p., gen. counsel U.S. Fin., Inc., 1969-74; with CF Industries, Long Grove, Ill., 1975—, exec. v.p., chief fin. officer, 1977-80, exec. v.p., operating officer, 1980-84, pres., chief exec. officer, 1985—; chmn. ad hoc com. Domestic Nitrogen Prodrs., Washington; chmn., bd. dirs. Can. Fertilizers Ltd., The Fertilizer Inst., Nat. Coun. Farmer Coops.; bd. dirs. Fla. Phosphate Coun., Tallahassee; mem. Nat. Forum Nonpoint Source Pollution sponsored by Nat. Geographic Soc. and Conservation Fund of Washington. Mem. coun. Internat. Exec. Svc. Corps, Stamford, Conn.; mem. bus. adv. coun. Law Sch. U. Va., Charlottesville. Mem. Ill. Bus. Roundtable, Northwestern U. Assocs., Coun. of 100, Tampa Fla., Internat. Fertilizer Industry Assn. (mem. coun.). Office: CF Industries Inc One Salem Lake Dr Long Grove IL 60047-8402

LIUZZO, JOSEPH ANTHONY, food science educator; b. Tampa, Fla., Dec. 16, 1926; s. Joseph and Annie (Minardi) L.; m. Elaine Grammer, Nov. 30, 1951; children: Paul Arthur, Patricia Joyce, Jolaine Marie. BS, U. Fla., 1950, MS, 1955; postgrad., U. So. Calif., 1952-53; PhD, Mich. State U., 1958. Microbiologist Stokely-Van Camp Co., Tampa, 1950; head divsn. microbiology Nutrilite Products, Inc., Buena Park, Calif., 1951-54; asst. prof. biochemistry La. State U., Baton Rouge, 1958-62, assoc. prof. food sci., 1962-69, prof., 1969-97, faculty chmn. athletics, 1979-83, prof. emeritus, 1997—; Chmn. Am. Legion Baseball Program, 1976-82. Contbr. articles to profl. jours. With U.S. Army, 1945-46. Recipient Outstanding Alumnus award Food Sci. and Human Nutrition, Mich. State U., 1994. Fellow AAAS, Am. Inst. Chemists, Inst. of Food Technologists; mem. Am. Inst. Nutrition, Am. chem. Soc., Kiwanis (pres. 1988-89, div. lt. gov. 1990-91),

Sigma Xi, Phi Tau Sigma, Gamma Sigma Delta, Phi Sigma, Omicron Delta Kappa. Democrat. Mem. Ch. of Christ. Office: La State U Dept Food Science Baton Rouge LA 70803

LIVA, EDWARD LOUIS, eye surgeon; b. Lyndhurst, N.J., Aug. 30, 1925; s. Paul Francis and Lucy Agnes (Andreozzi) L.; m. Dorothea Lucille Carter, Aug. 29, 1946; children: Edward Jr., Bradford, Douglas, Jeffrey, Elaine. SB, Harvard U., 1946, MD, 1950. Diplomate Am. Bd. Ophthalmology. Internship Med. Coll. Va., Richmond, 1950-51; fellowship in eye pathology Mass. Eye and Ear, Boston, 1951; residency Brooklyn Eye and Ear, N.Y., 1952-53; chief ophthalmic examiner Workman's Compensation Bd., N.Y.C., 1957-63; sr. ophthalmic surgeon Hackensack (N.J.) Med. Ctr., 1957—, Valley Hosp., Ridgewood, N.J., 1963—; sr. ophthalmic surgeon, resident instr. oculoplastics Manhatten Eye, Ear and Throat, N.Y.C., 1957-96, emeritus, 1996—; pres. Bergen Surg. Ctr., Paramus, N.J., 1991—, Eye Inst. of N.J., Paramus, 1987—. Author: Advances in Ophthalmic Plastic, 1983. Mem. Rep. Club, Ridgewood, 1960—. Capt. USAF, 1955-57. Fellow AMA, Am. Acad. Ophthalmology, Internat. Coll. of Surgeons, Am. Soc. of Ophtalmic Plastic and Reconstructive Surgery (chartered). Republican. Roman Catholic. Achievements include development new lid flaps oculoplastics, prototype of lid canal laceration repair, major modification of ptosis surgical procedures widely used, disproved Trichromatic theory of color vision in 1952. Home: 225 Sollas Ct Ridgewood NJ 07450-2815 Office: Liva Eye Ctr One West Ridgewood Ave Paramus NJ 07652

LIVAUDAIS, MARCEL, JR., federal judge; b. New Orleans, Mar. 3, 1925; m. Carol Black; children: Julie, Marc, Durel. BA, Tulane U., 1945, JD, 1949. Bar: La. Assoc. Boswell & Loeb, New Orleans, 1949-50, 52-56; ptnr. Boswell Loeb & Livaudais, New Orleans, 1956-60, Loeb & Livaudais, 1960-67, 71-77, Loeb Dillon & Livaudais, 1967-71; U.S. magistrate, 1977-84; judge U.S. Dist. Ct. (ea. dist.) La., New Orleans, 1984—. Mem. Am. Judicature Soc. Office: US Dist Ct C-405 US Courthouse 500 Camp St New Orleans LA 70130-3313*

LIVELY, CAROL A., professional society administrator; b. Chgo., Sept. 2, 1935; d. William Mann and Lillian (Juske) Haycock; m. E. Raymond Platig; children: Richard B., Laura Jean. L.P.N., Los Angeles Sch. Nursing, 1953; student, Columbia U., 1954, Boston U., 1956-57. Program dir. United Fund, Pittsfield, Mass., 1966-71; exec. dir. Western Mass. Health Council, 1971-74; asst. exec. dir. Genesee Health Council, Rochester, N.Y., 1974-76; dir. devel. Shimer Coll., Mt. Carroll, Ill., 1976-77; assoc. dir. Am. Hosp. Assn., Chgo., 1977-80; dir. health div., v.p. Smith Bucklin Assn., Washington, 1980-95, ret., 1995; mem. Achievement Rewards Coll. Scientists, Washington, 1980—; cons. Dept. Health Rep. Haiti, Washington, 1976—. Contbg. author: Politics of Health Planning, 1962; contbr. articles to profl. jours. Bd. dirs. Jacobs Pillow Dance Theatre, Pittsfield, 1968; bd. dirs. Albany Regional Med. Program, N.Y., 1971-74; active Jr. League, Washington, 1965—; mem. Commn. Drug Abuse Council, Boston, 1971-74. Recipient Woman of Yr. award Bus. and Profl. Women, 1971. Mem. New Eng. Pub. Health Assn., Mass. Council on Aging, Am. Soc. Hosp. Planning, Am. Pub. Health Assn. Home: 2138 California St NW Washington DC 20008-1876

LIVELY, EDWIN LESTER, retired oil company executive; b. Bowie, Tex., June 16, 1930; s. L. D. and Lois E. Lively; m. G. Marie Bryan; 1 child, James E. B.B.A., Midwestern State U., Wichita Falls, Tex., 1951; postgrad. in Advanced Mgmt., Emory U., 1967. Adminstr. recruiting Conoco, Inc. (subs. E.I. du Pont de Nemours), Houston, 1967-68; Lake Charles coordinator Conoco, Inc., Lake Charles, La., 1968-75, Gulf Coast coordinator, 1975-79, regional coordinator, 1979-85, v.p. and regional coordinator, so.western areas external affairs, 1985-86; gen. mgr. external affairs dept. State Affairs div. E.I. du Pont de Nemours & Co., 1987-88, retired. Served to sgt., U.S. Army, 1952-54. Avocations: golf; fishing. *Always remember, people are the most important asset in any business venture. Success and good friends are God's reward for following that principle.*

LIVELY, EDWIN LOWE, sociology educator; b. Fairmont, W.Va., Aug. 14, 1920; s. E.L. and Lucy (Ross) L.; m. Virginia Isabelle Reed, Aug. 25, 1940; children: Lynellen, Gerianne (Mrs. Michael Green), Edwin L. II. A.B. in Edn, Fairmont State Coll., 1940; M.A. in Sociology, Ohio State U., 1946, Ph.D., 1959. Tchr. high sch. Farmington, W.Va., 1940-42; instr. Kent State U., 1947-53, asst. prof., 1953-58, assoc. prof., 1958-63; prof. sociology, chmn. dept. Akron U., 1963-68, dean grad. studies and research, 1968-75, prof., 1975-78; lectr. Labor and Edn. Service, Ohio State U., 1966-68; cons. Ohio Youth Commn., Akron Urban Renewal, Akron Community Action Council, Akron Community Relations Commn., Canton (Ohio) Bd. Edn. Contbg. editor: Dynamic Urban Sociology, 1954; guest editor: Sociol. Focus, 1970; co-author: (with V. Lively) Sexual Development of Young Children, 1990. Pres. Greater Akron Area Council Alcoholism, 1969-71; chmn. Akron Commn. Civil Disorders, 1968-69; pres. United Community Council, 1972-74; bd. dirs. Goals for Greater Akron Area, 1974-80. Served with USAAF, 1942-45. Decorated Air medal with five oak leaf clusters.; Swift fellow, 1963; grantee Esso Edn. Found., 1966; grantee div. adult and vocational research Dept. Health, Edn. and Welfare, 1967; grantee Ohio Bd. Regents, 1967; grantee Ohio Dept. Health, 1968. Fellow Am. Sociol. Assn.; mem. Ohio Valley Sociol. Soc. (bd. dirs. 1964-68), Nat. Council Family Relations, Summit County Mental Health Assn. (pres. 1965-67). Club: Mason. Home: 634 Brackenwood Cv West Palm Beach FL 33418-9001

LIVELY, PIERCE, federal judge; b. Louisville, Aug. 17, 1921; s. Henry Thad and Ruby Durrett (Keating) L.; m. Amelia Harrington, May 25, 1946; children: Susan, Katherine, Thad. AB, Centre Coll., Ky., 1943; LL.B., U. Va., 1948. Bar: Ky. 1948. Individual practice law Danville, Ky., 1949-57; mem. firm Lively and Rodes, Danville, 1957-72; judge U.S. Ct. Appeals (6th cir.), Cin., 1972—, chief judge, 1983-88; now sr. judge; Mem. Ky. Commn. on Economy and Efficiency in Govt., 1963-65, Ky. Jud. Advisory Com., 1972. Trustee Centre Coll. Served with USNR, 1943-46. Mem. ABA, Am. Judicature Soc., Order of Coif, Raven Soc., Phi Beta Kappa, Omicron Delta Kappa. Presbyterian. Office: US Ct Appeals PO Box 1226 Danville KY 40423-5226 also: US Courthouse Rm 418 Cincinnati OH 45202

LIVENGOOD, CHARLOTTE LOUISE, employee development specialist; b. L.A., June 18, 1944; d. James Zollie and Zela (Cogburn) L. BS in Secondary Edn., Tex. A & I U., 1968; MEd in Pers. Guidance and Counseling, North Tex. U., 1971. Cert. secondary teaching, Tex.; cert. counselor, Tex. Counselor Gus Grissom H.S., Huntsville, Ala., 1971-72; tchr. West Springfield H.S., Springfield, Va., 1972-73; edn. specialist U.S. Dept. Def., El Paso, Tex., 1975-78; instr. El Paso (Tex.) C.C., 1977-78; employee devel. specialist U.S. Office Pers. Mgmt., Dallas, 1978-79; pers. mgmt. specialist Dept. Vets. Affairs, Houston, 1979-87; labor rels. specialist Dept. Vets. Affairs, VA Med. Ctr., Houston, 1987-89; pers. staffing specialist Dept. Vets. Affairs, Houston, 1989-90; employee devel. specialist, acad. tng. officer HUD, Ft. Worth, 1990-95; assoc. prof. Ariz. State U., 1995—; Bur. of Engraving and Printing univ. tng. officer Dept. Treasury, Ft. Worth, 1995—; EEO investigator Dept. Vet. Affairs, 1984-87, fed. women's program mgr., 1984-85; mem. standing panel for pers. specialists/fed. suprs./mgrs. Merit Systems Protection Bd., 1996—; speaker in field. Editor: (monthly office newspaper) Pipeline, 1980-87. Chairperson, forensics coach Jr. High Sch. Speech Dept., 1968-69; tchr. S. Grand Prairie H.S., 1969-71; mem. Dallas/Ft. Worth Quality Control Coun., Tex. War on Drugs Com., 1990—; hon. mem. Dallas/Ft. Worth Fed. Exec. Bd., 1993-94. Recipient Future Secs. of Am. scholarship, 1962. Mem. ASTD, AAUW, Am. Pers. and Guidance Assn., Assn. for Quality Participation, Internat. Transactional Analysis Assn., Tex. State Tchrs. Assn., Tex. Classroom Tchrs. Assn., Fed. Bus. Assn., VA Employee Assn., Intergovernmental Tng. Assn., Intergovernmental Tng. Coun. (chairperson 1993-94), Federal Women's Program Mgr., Merit Sys. Protection Bd. Standing Panel for Personnel Specialists, Federal Supv., Mgrs. Mem. Church of Christ. Avocations: reading, travel, bridge, fishing, theater. Office: US Dept Treasury Bur Engraving & Printing Western Currency Facility 9000 Blue Mound Rd Fort Worth TX 76131-3304

LIVENGOOD, JOANNE DESLER, healthcare administrator; b. Omaha, Sept. 29, 1936; d. Arthur Frederick and Rosamond Christina (Knudsen) D.; m. Richard Vaughn Livengood, Aug. 11, 1962; children: Linda Renee, John David. BA, W.Va. State Coll.Inst., 1975; Diploma, Swedish Am. Hosp. Sch. Nursing, Rockford, Ill., 1961; MBA, Ea. Ill. U., Charleston, 1984. RN, Ill. W.Va. State Inst.; DON Hoopeston (Ill.) Hosp. and Nursing Home, 1981-84; adminstr. Vermilion Manor Nursing Home, Danville, Ill., 1984-88; asst. adminstr. R.E. Thomason Hosp., El Paso, Tex., 1989-91; adminstr. Horizon Splty. Hosp., El Paso, Tex., 1992-93, Ill. Vets. Home at Anna, 1994—; cons. J.D. Williams Ins. Agy., El Paso, Tex., 1991-92, The Regional Clinic, Carterville, Ill., 1994. Mem. Danville (Ill.) Dist. 118 Sch. Bd., 1976-82. Fellow Am. Coll. Healthcare Execs.; mem. S.W. Healthcare Execs. (treas. 1989-93), Anna-Jonesboro Rotary Club. Home: 1810 Paula Ln Marion IL 62959-1425

LIVENGOOD, VICTORIA ANN, opera singer; b. Thomasville, N.C., Aug. 8, 1959; d. Gerald Winston and Carolyn Ann (Young) L. MusB in Voice, U. N.C., 1983; MusM in Opera, Boston Conservatory, 1985. tchr. master classes Pittsburg U., Kans., 1990, Temple U., Phila., 1993, U. N.C., Chapel Hill, 1994. Appeared as Queen Gertrude in Hamlet, Greater Miami (Fla.) Opera Co., 1987, Beauty in Beauty and the Beast, Opera Theater St. Louis, 1987, Mercy Kirke in Hazel Kirke, Lake George (N.Y.) Opera, 1987, Giulietta in Les Contes d'Hoffmann, Cleve. Opera Co., Charlotte in Werther, Seattle Opera Co., 1989, Carmen in Carmen, Conn. Opera Co., Hartford, 1990, Dalila in Samson and Dalila, Lyric Opera, Kansas City, 1990, Dorabella in Cosi Fan Tutti, Hawaii Opera Theater, 1990, Carmen in Carmen, Oper der Stadt Köln, Cologne, Germany, 1992, 95, Meg Page in Falstaff, Calgary (Can.) Opera Co., 1991, Idamante in Idomeneo, and Sesto in La Clemenza, L'Opera de Nice, France, 1991, Laura in Louisa Miller, Met. Opera Co., N.Y.C., 1991, Mrs. Grose in Turn of the Screw, Edmonton Opera, Can., 1993, Isolier in Il Conte Ory with Charleston's Spoleto Festival, 1993, Maddalena in Rigoletto, Oper der Stadt Köln and Edmonton Opera, 1994, Desideria in the Saint of Bleeker Street, Kansas City Lyric Opera, 1994, Lola in Cavalleria Rusticana, Met. Opera, 1994, Sonetka in Lady Macbeth of Mtsensk, Met. Opera, 1994, Dalila, Balt. Opera, 1995, Carmen, Edmonton Opera, 1995, Can., Giulietta in Les Contes d'Hoffmann, Santiago (Chile) Opera, 1995, girl in Mahogany, Met. Opera Co., 1995, 96, Preziosilla in La Forza Del Destino, 1996, Queen Isabella in The Voyage, Met Opera, 1996, Maddalena, Rigoletta, Met. Opera, 1996, Hippolyta: A Midsummer Night's Dream, Met. Opera, 1996, Waltraute in Die Waklyre, Met Opera, 1997; soloist at J.F. Kennedy Ctr., Washington, 1986; performed with Am. Symphony Orch., Carnegie Hall, N.Y., 1986, N.C. Symphony Orch., Carnegie Hall, 1987, Nat. Symphony Orch., Washington, 1990, Atlanta Symphony Orch., 1991, Honolulu Symphony, 1991, Balt. Symphony Orch., 1991, Cologne Symphony, Germany, 1992, Minn. Symphony, 1992, Columbus Symphony, 1993, Buffalo Philharm., 1994, Northwest Chamber Mus. Soc., Portland, Oreg., 1994, Am. Composers Orch., 1995, San Diego Symphony, 1995, Rochester Philharmonic, 1995, Concerto, Cincinnati May Festival, 1996, Lincoln Ctr. Chamber Music Soc., 1996, others; solo recitalist in numerous locations including Boston, N.Y., N.C., Kans., Mo., Portland, Washington, others; EMI recs. include Oberon (soloist), 1992; subject of article Mus. Am. mag., 1986, Opera News Mag., 1987, 94, 95, Carolina Alumni Rev. Mag., 1997. Min. music Mills Home Bapt. Ch., Thomasville, 1980-81; recitalist Hosp. Guild, Thomasville, 1980-82, 87, 92, Epilepsy Benefit, Kansas City, Mo., 1989, Aids Benefit-Buffalo Philharmonic N.Y., 1994. Recipient Nat. award Met. Opera Auditions, N.Y.C., 1985, Internat. award Rosa Ponselle Competition, N.Y.C., 1987, D'Angelo Competition award, 1987, Recipient of the U. N.C. Disting. Young Alumnus award, 1996, Luciano Pavarotti Competition, Phila., 1988, 1996, Key to City of Thomasville, 1992; grantee Sullivan Found., 1987, Nat. Inst. Music Theater, 1989. Avocations: cross-stitch, swimming, floral arranging, dancing, movies, interior design. Office: ICM Artists Ltd 40 W 57th St New York NY 10019

LIVERGOOD, ROBERT FRANK, prosecutor; b. Akron, Ohio, Dec. 20, 1957; s. Robert Burton and Rita Veronica (Haidnick) L.; m. Sandra Anne Ko, Aug. 5, 1983; children: Robert Santos, Jacob Christopher, Sarah Nicole. BA, St. Louis U., 1981, M in Health Adminstrn., 1983, JD, 1988. Bar: Mo. 1988, Ill. 1989, U.S. Dist. Ct. (ea. dist.) Mo. 1989, U.S. Dist. Ct. (so. dist.) Ill. 1989. Dir. market rsch. St. Joseph's Hosp. Kirkwood, Mo., 1983-85; assoc. Husch & Eppenberger, St. Louis, 1988-90; asst. prosecuting atty. Office of the Prosecutor, Clayton, Mo., 1990—. Editor St. Louis U. Law Jour., 1986-87, mng. editor, 1987-88. Vol. lawyer Voluntary Lawyers Program, St. Louis, 1988-90; spkr. St. Louis (Mo.) County and Mcpl. Police Acad., 1993-94. Mem. ABA, Ill. State Bar Assn., Bar Assn. Met. St. Louis. Avocations: martial arts, amateur radio. Office: Office of the Prosecutor 7900 Carondelet Ave Clayton MO 63105-1720

LIVERIGHT, BETTY FOUCH, actress, director, writer; b. La Grange, Ill., Oct. 20, 1913; d. Squire and Edna Amanda (Wright) Fouch; m. Herman Elsas Liveright, Feb. 1, 1936; children: Beth, Timothy. BA, Temple U., 1963. Actress L'Aiglon, N.Y.C., 1934, White Plains (N.Y.) Comty. Theater, 1947-52; coord., actress TV Tulane U., New Orleans, 1953-56; actress TV Commercials, New Orleans, 1954-56; rschr. Friends Libr. Swarthmore (Pa.) Coll., 1956-69; pub. rels. agt. Highlander Rsch. and Edn. Ctr., Knoxville, Tenn., 1969-71; co-dir. Berkshire Forum, Stephentown, N.Y., 1972-90; rschr., author pvt. practice, Pittsfield Mass., 1990—. Co-coord. This Just In bull. Pres. Yorkville Peace Coun., N.Y.C., 1940-42; bd. dirs. Women's Internat. League for Peace and Freedom, Phila., 1965-85. Home and Office: 103 Bartlett Ave Pittsfield MA 01201-6901

LIVERMORE, JOSEPH MCMASTER, judge; b. Portland, Oreg., Feb. 5, 1937; s. Ernest R. and Frances (McMaster) L.; m. Elaine Dufort, Mar. 18, 1966; 1 son, Caleb. A.B., Dartmouth, 1958; LL.B., Stanford, 1961. Bar: Calif. 1962, Minn. 1968, Ariz. 1974. Assoc. Brobeck, Phleger & Harrison, San Francisco, 1961, 64-65; prof. law U. Minn., Mpls., 1965-73; asst. U.S. atty., Mpls., 1971-72; dean Coll. Law, U. Ariz., Tucson, 1973-77, prof., 1977-85; judge Ariz. Ct. Appeals, 1985-97; ret., 1997; vis. prof. Coll. Law U. Ariz., 1997—. Served with JAG Corps AUS, 1962-63. Mem. ABA, Ariz. Bar Assn., State Bar Calif., Order of Coif, Phi Beta Kappa. Home: 3228 E 3rd St Tucson AZ 85716-4232 Office: Univ Ariz College Law Tucson AZ 85721

LIVERSAGE, RICHARD ALBERT, cell biologist; b. Fitchburg, Mass., July 8, 1925; s. Rodney Marcellus and Hazel Mildred (Huntting) L.; m. June Patricia Krebs, June 19, 1954; children: John Walter, Robert Richard, James Keith, Ross Andrew. B.A., Marlboro Coll., 1951; A.M., Amherst Coll., 1953, Princeton U., 1957; Ph.D., Princeton U., 1958. Fellow Bowdoin Coll., Brunswick, Maine, 1953-54; instr. Amherst Coll., 1954-55, Princeton, 1958-60; mem. faculty U. Toronto, 1960—, prof. zoology, 1969—, grad. sec. dept., 1975-77, asso. chmn. grad. affairs dept., 1978-84, acting chmn., 1980-81; Investigator Huntsman Marine Lab., St. Andrews, N.B., Can., 1968-71. Contbr. over 87 articles on role of nerves and endocrine secretions at cellular-molecular levels in vertebrate appendage regeneration to sci. jours. Served as flight engr. USAAF, 1943-45. Recipient 5 decorations. Mem. Soc. Devel. Biology, Can. Soc. Zoologists, Royal Can. Inst., Wound Healing Soc., Sigma Xi (exec. com., v.p., pres. U. Toronto chpt.). Home: 48 Ferndell Cir, Unionville, ON Canada L3R 3Y8 Office: U Toronto, Ramsay Wright Zool Lab, Toronto, ON Canada M5S 3G5

LIVESAY, THOMAS ANDREW, museum administrator, lecturer; b. Dallas, Feb. 1, 1945; s. Melvin Ewing Clay and Madge Almeda (Hall) L.; m. Jennifer Clark, June 15, 1985 (div.); 1 child, Russell; m. Amanda Haralson, Nov. 12, 1994; children: Heather Marie, Seth Stover. BFA, U. Tex., Austin, 1968, MFA, 1972; postgrad., Harvard U. Inst. Arts Adminstrn., 1978. Curator Elisabet Ney Mus., Austin, 1971-73; dir. Longview (Tex.) Mus. and Arts Center, 1973-75; curator Amarillo (Tex.) Art Center, 1975-77, dir., 1977-80; asst. dir. for adminstrn. Dallas Mus. Fine Arts, 1980-85; dir. Mus. of N.Mex., Santa Fe, 1985—; mem. touring panel Tex. Commn. Arts; mem. panel Nat. Endowment Arts, Inst. Mus. Svcs.; adj. prof. U. Okla., Coll. Liberal Studies, 1992—, U. N.Mex., 1992—; chmn. N.Mex. State Records and Archives Commn., 1986—. Author: Young Texas Artists Series, 1978, Made in Texas, 1979; editor: video tape American Images, 1979, Ruth Abrams, Paintings, 1940-85, NYU Press. Served with U.S. Army, 1969-71. Mem. Am. Assn. Mus. (coun. 1986-89, commn. on ethics 1992—, accreditation commn. 1994—, chmn. accreditation commn. 1997—), Tex. Assn. Mus. (v.p. 1981, pres. 1983), Rotary. Methodist. Office: Mus of New Mexico 113 Lincoln PO Box 2087 Santa Fe NM 87504-2087

LIVESAY, VALORIE ANN, security analyst; b. Greeley, Colo., Sept. 9, 1959; d. John Albert and Mary Magdalene Yurchak. BA in Bus., U. No. Colo., 1981; M in Computer Info. Sys., U. Denver, 1991; AAS in Fashion Mktg., Colo. Inst. Art, 1996. Drafter Computer Graphics, Denver, 1981, Advanced Cable Sys., Inc., Denver, 1981-82, Am. TV Comm. Corp., Englewood, Colo., 1982-83; janitor Rockwell Internat., Golden, Colo., 1983-84, analytical lab tech., 1984-86, metall. operator, 1986-88; nuclear material coord. EG&G Rocky Flats Inc., Golden, 1988-92, lead security analyst, 1992-95. Active Channel 6, Denver, 1985, World Wildlife Fund, Westminster, Colo., 1987, Denver Dumb Friends League, 1987, The Nature Conservancy, Boulder, Colo., 1989. Mem. NAFE, Am. Soc. Insdl. Security. Avocations: scuba diving, mountain biking, skiing, reading, boating. Home: 6344 W 115th Ave Broomfield CO 80020-3034

LIVEZEY, MARK DOUGLAS, physician; b. Columbus, Ohio, June 30, 1951; s. Robert Edward and Dorothy Elizabeth (Hendrickson) L.; m. Rebecca Joan Cabral; children: Allison, Brooke, Adam. BA, U. Mich., 1973; PhD, Wayne State U., 1979, MD, 1983. Diplomate Am. Bd. Internal Medicine, Am. Bd. Allergy and Immunology. Intern, resident in internal medicine William Beaumont Hosp., 1983-86; fellow allergy and immunology Henry Ford Hosp., 1986-88; assoc. Allergy and Asthma Cons., P.C., Atlanta, 1988—. Fellow Am. Coll. Allergy and Immunology; mem. Am. Acad. Allergy and Immunology. Avocations: golf, music.

LIVICK, MALCOLM HARRIS, school administrator; b. Staunton, Va., Apr. 5, 1929; s. Arthur Crawford and Sallie (Harris) L.; m. Linda Moorman Roller, July 21, 1956; children: Malcolm Harris, Charles Roller, Linda Lee, Todd Stephenson, Taylor Crawford (dec.). Student, Hampden Sydney Coll., 1947-48; B.S., U. Va., 1951; M.Ed., Madison Coll., 1965. Instr., coach Augusta Mil. Acad., 1955-56; instr. Norfolk (Va.) pub. schs., 1956-57; underwriter Mutual of N.Y., Norfolk, 1957-58; coach, asst. prin. Augusta Mil. Acad., Ft. Defiance, Va., 1958-66; supt. Augusta Mil. Acad., 1966-83; dir. ednl. devel. Blue Ridge C.C., 1984-85, dir. continuing edn., 1986; dir. Blue Ridge C.C., Harrisonburg, Waynesboro, 1986—. Chmn. Upper Valley Regional Park Authority, 1969-78; Trustee King's Daus. Hosp., Staunton, Massanetta Springs. Served with USAF, 1951-55. Mem. Va. Mil. Schs. League (pres. 1966-68), Va. Assn. Prep. Schs. (exec. com. 1967-73, pres. 1971-72), Nat., Va. assns. secondary sch. prins. Presbyn. (deacon 1963-65, elder 1965—). Lodge: Kiwanis (pres. 1970-71, lt. gov. 1971, gov. 1979-80). Address: PO Box 22 Fort Defiance VA 24437-0022

LIVICK, STEPHEN, fine art photographer; b. Leeds, Yorkshire, Eng., Feb. 11, 1945; arrived in Can., 1947; Student, Sir George Williams U., Montreal, Can., 1963-66. Self employed artist, 1970—. One man shows include Centaur Gallery, Montreal, 1972, London Art Gallery, Ont., 1973, George Eastman House, Rochester, N.Y., 1975, David Mirvish Gallery, Toronto, 1976, 77, Photography Gallery, Bowmanville, Ont., 1976, 77, Balt. Mus. Art, 1978, Lunn Graphics, Washington D.C., 1978, Gallery Graphics, Ottawa, 1978, Jane Corkin Gallery, Toronto, 1979, 80, 81, U. Western Ont., London, 1981, 93, George Dalsheimer Gallery, Balt., 1982, MacDonald Stewart Art Ctr., Guelph, 1983, 94, New Brunswick Craft Sch., Fredericton, 1986, Winnipeg Photographers Group, 1987, Galerie Sequence, Quebec, 1988, U. Sherbrooke, 1990, Can. Mus. Contemporary Photography, Ottawa, 1992, MacKenzie Art Gallery, Regina, 1994, Meml. U. Art Gallery, St. John's, 1994, Beaverbrook Art Gallery, Fredicton, 1995, Art Gallery Windsor, 1995; travelling exhibitions include George Eastman House, 1978-81, London Regional Art Gallery, 1976-77, Nat. Film Bd., 1976-84, Art Gallery Ont., 1980, 81, Can. Mus. Contemporary Photography, 1986, 87; exhibited in group shows at Nat. Art Gallery, Ottawa, 1975, London Pub. Art Gallery, 1976, Nat. Film Bd., Ottawa, Can., 1977, Mendal Art Gallery, Saskatoon, Can., 1977, Neikrug Galleries, N.Y.C., 1978, Banff-London Exchange, Alberta, Can., 1978, Smithsonian Instn., Washington, 1981, Carpenter Ctr. Visual Arts, Cambridge, Mass., 1981, U. Calgary, 1982, Saidy Bronfman Mus., Montreal, 1984, Photographers Gallery, London, Eng., 1984, Presentation House, Vancouver, B.C., 1985, Photo Union Gallery, Hamilton, Ont., 1986, Film In The City, St. Paul, 1989, Corcoran Gallery Art, Washington, 1989, London (Can.) Regional Art Mus., 1990, Can. Mus. Contemporary Photography, Ottowa, 1992, others; represented in permanent collections Nat. Art Gallery Can., Can Mus. Contemporary Photography, Art Gallery Ont., Can. Art Bank, Nat. Archives Can., Mus. Modern Art, N.Y., George Eastman House, Rochester, N.Y., Carnegie Mus. Art, Pitts., Mus. Fine Arts, Houston, Fogg Art Mus., Cambridge, Mass., Balt. Mus. Art, George Washington U., Washington, Norton Gallery Art, West Palm Beach, Fla., Syracuse (N.Y.) U., Middlebury (Vt.) Coll., Hickory (N.C.) Mus. Art, U. Iowa Mus., U. No. Iowa, Art Gallery Hamilton, Can., High Mus. Art, Atlanta, Ga., London Regional Art Gallery, Corcoran Gallery Art, Washington, Queens U., Kingston, Can., Winnipeg (Can.) Art Gallery, Sarnia (Ont.) Art Gallery, U. Western Ont., London, Macdonald Stewart Art Ctr., Guelph, Ont., numerous pvt., corp. collections. B level grantee Can. Coun., Ottawa; sr. grantee Ont. Arts Coun., Toronto. Home and Office: 22A Maitland St Studio, London, ON Canada N6B 3L2

LIVINGOOD, CLARENCE S., dermatologist; b. Elverson, Pa., Aug. 7, 1911; s. Clarence A. and Eliza (Zerr) L.; m. Louise Sinclair Woelpper, Oct. 24, 1947; children: Wilson, Louise S., Clarence, Susan, Elizabeth. B.S., Ursinus Coll., 1932, D.Sc. (hon.), 1982; M.D., U. Pa., 1936. Diplomate Am. Bd. Dermatology (exec. dir. 1968-92, exec. cons. 1993—). Intern, then resident dermatology Hosp. U. Pa., 1936-41; asst. prof. dermatology U. Pa. Med. Sch., 1946-48, U. Pa. Med. Sch. (Grad. Sch.), 1946-49; chief dermatology Children's Hosp. Pa., 1946-48; prof., chmn. dept. dermatology Jefferson Med. Sch., Phila., 1948-49, U. Tex. Sch. Medicine, 1949-53; chmn. dermatology dept. Henry Ford Hosp., Detroit, 1953-76; chmn. emeritus Henry Ford Hosp., 1976—; team physician Detroit Tigers Baseball Club, 1967—; clin. prof. dermatology U. Mich. Sch. Medicine; mem. com. on cutaneous diseases AFEB, 1956-72; chief cons. dermatology VA, 1953-59; sec.-gen. XII Internat. Congress Dermatology, 1962; mem. Am. Bd. Med. Spltys., 1963-92, mem. exec. com., 1974-76, spl. award, 1993; mem. residency rev. com. for dermatology AMA, 1957-67; mem. adv. com. Nat. Disease and Therapeutic Index, 1974—; bd. dirs., treas. Coun. Med. Splty. Socs., 1976-80, mem. liaison com. on grad. med. edn., 1978-83; mem. Accreditation Coun. for Grad. Med. Edn., 1977-83. Author: (with D.M. Pillsbury, M.B. Sulzberger) Manual of Dermatology; contbr. articles to med. jours. Trustee Dermatology Found., 1965-71, ECFMG, 1975-79. Served to lt. col. M.C. AUS, 1942-46. decorated Bronze Star, Legion of Merit; recipient Profl. Achievement award Wayne County Med. Soc., 1993, Dermatology Found. Practitioner of Yr. award, 1993. Fellow Am. Acad. Dermatology (dir., past pres., Gold medal 1975, Masters in Dermatology 1985, Presdl. Citation 1987, C.S. Livingood Ann. Lectureship established 1993), FACP; mem. AMA (ho. of dels., chmn. sect. dermatology 1958, Disting. Svc. award 1990), Soc. Investigative Dermatology (past pres., Stephen Rothman award 1980), Am. Dermatol. Assn. (past pres., dir. 1964-68, named hon. mem. 1981), Am. Bd. Dermatology (diplomate, exec. dir. 1968-92, exec. cons. 1993—), Coll. Physicians Phila., Pacific Dermatol. Soc. (hon. mem.), Phila. Dermatol Soc., Mich. Dermatol. Soc. (past pres.), Mich. Med. Soc. (jud. council, ho. dels. 1974-80), Med. Cons. Soc. World War II, Assn. Mil. Dermatologists, Detroit Acad. Medicine, Assn. Maj. League Team Physicians, Assn. Dermatology Argentina (corr.), N.Y. Acad. Scis. (internat. congress dermatology), Danish Soc. (hon.), Indian Assn. Dermatologists (hon.), Brit. Dermatol. Soc. (hon.), Yugoslavian Dermatol. Soc. (hon.), Israel Dermatol. Soc. (hon.), N.Y. Dermatol. Soc. (hon. 1992), 18th World Congress Dermatology (hon. pres. 1992). Clubs: Grosse Pointe, Witenagemote. Home: 17111 E Jefferson Ave # 4 Grosse Pointe MI 48230 Office: Henry Ford Hosp 2799 W Grand Blvd Detroit MI 48202-2608

LIVINGSTON, ALAN WENDELL, communications executive; b. McDonald, Pa.; s. Maurice H. and Rose L. (Wachtel) L.; m. Nancy Olson, Sept. 1, 1962; children: Peter, Laura, Christopher. BS, U. Pa., 1940. Exec. v.p. Capitol Records, Inc., Hollywood, Calif., 1946-55, pres., chmn., 1960-68; v.p. programming NBC, Burbank, Calif., 1955-60; pres. Mediarts, Inc., Los Angeles, 1968-76; exec. v.p., pres. entertainment group 20th Century Fox Film Corp., Beverly Hills, Calif., 1976-80; pres. Pacific Rim Entertainment, Los Angeles, 1980-95; novelist, cons. Access Fund and Atlantal Investment Fund, Inc., Beverley Hills, 1995—. Creator various children's books, records and Bozo the Clown, 1946—; author: Ronnie Finklehof, Superstar, 1988; writer, producer (animated film) Sparky's Magic Piano, 1988. Bd. dirs. Ctr. Theater Group, Los Angeles. Served to 2d lt. inf. U.S. Army, 1943-46. Mem. ASCAP, Nat. Acad. Rec. Arts and Scis., Acad. TV Arts and Scis., Acad. Motion Picture Arts and Scis.

LIVINGSTON, BARBARA, special education educator. BA in Elem. Edn., Bklyn. Coll., 1955; MA in Early Childhood Edn., Adelphi U., 1975. Cert. elem. edn. tchr., N.Y., early childhood edn., N.Y., spl. edn., N.Y. Reading tchr. P.S. 182, Dist. 19, Bklyn., 1974-76; spl. edn. tchr. self-contained classroom P.S. 13, East N.Y., Bklyn., 1976-81; resource room tchr. P.S. 128, Middle Village, Queens, N.Y., 1981-86; spl. edn. lang. coor./tchr. trainer/staff developer Dist. Office 24Q, Middle Village, N.Y., 1986-90; VAKTS (reading system)/lang. coord. Dist. 24 Queens, Corona, N.Y., 1988-90; resource room tchr., staff developer Intermediate Sch. 61Q, Corona, N.Y., 1990—. Author: VAKTS (Visual Auditory Kinesthet Tactile, Social-emotion)- A Multi-Sensory Approach to Beginning Reading based on OrtonGillingham Method, 1988. Pres. alumni chpt. Children's Centre for Creative Arts, Adelphi U., Garden City, N.Y., 1974-75; bd. dirs. Alumni Assn., Adelphi U., Garden City, 1974-75; group leader Centre for Creative Arts Saturday Morning Program, Adelphi U., Garden City, 1972-75; dir. adult edn. program Temple Judea Howard Beach, 1974-76. Recipient Educator of Yr. award Assn. Tchrs. of N.Y., 1985. Mem. Orton Dyslexia Soc., Coun. for Exceptional Children (Master Tchr. 1987), ASCD, Internat. Reading Assn., United Fedn. Tchrs., Am. Fedn. Tchrs., Jewish Tchrs. Assn., Lincoln Ctr. Inst. (cert.). Home: 15506 86th St Howard Beach NY 11414-2404

LIVINGSTON, DAVID MORSE, biomedical scientist, physician, internist; b. Cambridge, Mass., Mar. 29, 1941; s. Arthur Joshua and Phyllis Freda (Kanters) L.; m. Jacqueline Gutman, June 23, 1963 (div. 1983); m. Emily Rabb, Jan. 25, 1986; children: Catherine Ellen, Julie. AB cum laude, Harvard U., 1961; MD magna cum laude, Tufts U., 1965. Diplomate Nat. Bd. Med. Examiners, Am. Bd. Internal Medicine. Intern, resident Peter Bent Brigham Hosp., Boston, 1965-67; rsch. assoc., sr. staff fellow, sr. investigator NCI-NIH, Bethesda, Md., 1967-69, 71-73; rsch. fellow in biol. chemistry Harvard Med. Sch., Boston, 1969-71, asst. prof. medicine, 1973-76, assoc. prof. medicine, 1976-82, prof. medicine, 1982-92; Emil Frei III prof. medicine Harvard Med. Sch., 1992—; v.p. Dana-Farber Cancer Inst., Boston, 1989-91; dir., physician-in-chief Harvard Med. Sch., Boston, 1991-95, Emil Frei III prof. medicine, 1992—, chmn. res. exec. com., 1995—. Mem. editorial bd. Virology jour., 1989—; editor BBA Revs. on Cancer, 1988—; contbr. articles to profl. jours. Mem. sci. adv. com. Damon Runyan-Walter Winchell Cancer Fund, N.Y.C., 1988-92, chmn. sci. adv. com., 1989-92; bd. dirs. Cancer Rsch. Fund, 1992—, pres. bd., 1997—, mem. exec. com., 1994—; vice chmn. sci. adv. com. Pexcoller Found., Trento, Italy, 1994—; mem. sci. adv. bd. Inst. Cancer Rsch., Fox Chase, Pa., 1991-96, Lineburger Comprehensive Cancer Ctr., U. N.C., Chapel Hill, 1993-95, MIT Cancer Ctr., 1994—, Fred Hutchinson Cancer Ctr., 1992—; chmn. bd. sci. advisors NIC/NIH, 1995—. Comdr. USPHS, 1967-73. Recipient Claire & Richard Morse award for Rsch., Dana-Farber Cancer Inst., 1991. Mem. NAS, Am. Soc. for Clin. Investigation, Assn. Am. Physicians, Am. Soc. Biol. Chemistry and Molecular Biology, Am. Soc. Microbiology, Am. Soc. Virology, Inst. Medicine of NAS, Met. Club Washington, St. Botolph Club, Harvard Club (N.Y.C., Boston), Alpha Omega Alpha. Achievements include discovery of important aspects of the neoplastic transforming process and of the mechanisms governing control of the mammalian cell cycle. Office: Dana-Farber Cancer Inst 44 Binney St Boston MA 02115-6013

LIVINGSTON, DONALD RAY, lawyer; b. Oak Ridge, Tenn., Jan. 11, 1952; s. Tally R. and Pansy L. (Heiskell) L.; m. Anne Davis, May 2, 1992; 1 child, John Tally. AB in Econs., U. Ga., 1974, JD, 1977. Bar: Ga. 1977, U.S. Dist. Ct. (no. dist.) Ga. 1977, U.S. Dist. Ct. (mid. dist.) Ga. 1978, U.S. Dist. Ct. (no. dist.) Calif. 1984, U.S. Dist. Ct. (no. dist.) N.Y. 1994, U.S. Ct. Appeals (5th cir.) 1978, U.S. Ct. Appeals (4th and 11th cirs.) 1981, U.S. Ct. Appeals (6th cir.) 1984, U.S. Supreme Ct. 1983. Assoc. Adair, Goldthwaite, Stanford & Daniel, Atlanta, 1977-79; ptnr. Adair, Goldthwaite & Daniel, Atlanta, 1979-87; exec. asst. to gen. counsel EEOC, Washington, 1987-90, acting gen. counsel, 1990-91, gen. counsel, 1991-93; ptnr. Akin, Gump, Strauss, Hauer & Feld, Washington, 1993—; lectr. seminars on employment law, 1987—. Contbr. articles to profl. jours. Mem. ABA, Ga. Bar Assn. (chair labor law sect. 1985-86), D.C. Bar Assn. Office: Akin Gump Strauss Hauer & Feld 1333 New Hampshire Ave NW Washington DC 20036-1511

LIVINGSTON, DOUGLAS MARK, lawyer; b. Lawton, Okla., Nov. 2, 1945; s. Oscar Calloway and Irene (Norton) L.; m. Vicki Sue Ratts, Dec. 21, 1969; children: Lisa Marie, Stephen Mark, Anna Lee, Micah James. BS, Okla. Christian Coll., 1967; MPH, U. Okla., 1969, JD, 1980; MEd, Wayne State U., 1981. Bar: Okla. 1980, U.S. Dist. Ct. (we. dist.) Okla. 1987, U.S. Army Ct. Mil. Rev. 1989, U.S. Ct. Appeals for Armed Forces 1995, U.S. Ct. Appeals (fed. cir.) 1995, U.S. Supreme Ct. 1997. Intern Cleveland County Dist. Atty., Norman, Okla., 1979-80; gen. counsel Delphi Devel., Ltd., Norman, 1980-81, Pepco Devel., Inc., Norman, 1981-85, Pepco, Inc., Norman, 1981-85; owner, ptnr. Payne, Livingston & Harold, P.C., Oklahoma City, 1985-86, Livingston Law Office, Norman, 1986-92, 93-94; staff atty. U.S. Dept. of Army, Ft. Sill, Okla., 1992-93, labor atty., 1994—; ptnr. Concord Investments, Ltd., Norman, 1982-88; staff judge adv. 4003d U.S. Army Garrison, Ft. Chaffee, Ark., 1993-95, 122nd USAR Command, North Little Rock, Ark., 1995; comdr. 1st Legal Support Orgn., San Antonio, 1995—. Editor coll. newspaper Talon, 1966; note editor Am. Indian Law Rev., 1979-80. Bd. dirs. Big Bros./Big Sisters, Norman, 1983-85, Rock Creek Youth Camp, Norman, 1985-94; Rep. precinct chmn., Oklahoma City, 1971. Capt. U.S. Army, 1973-77; col. USAR. Named one of Outstanding Young Men of Am., 1973. Mem. Okla. Bar Assn., Fed. Bar Assn., Cleveland County Bar Assn., Res. Officers Assn., Assn. U.S. Army., Sr. Army Res. Comdr.'s Assn. Mem. Ch. of Christ. Avocations: family activities, reading, running. Home: 911 S Lahoma Ave Norman OK 73069-4509 Office: Office of Staff Judge Adv Building 462 Fort Sill OK 73503

LIVINGSTON, GROVER D., newspaper publishing executive. V.p. information management The Dallas Morning News, Tex. Office: The Dallas Morning News Communication Ctr 400 S Record St Dallas TX 75202-4841*

LIVINGSTON, JAMES DUANE, physicist, educator; b. Bklyn., June 23, 1930; s. James Duane and Florence (Boullee) L.; m. Nancy Lee Clark, June 27, 1953 (div. 1976); children: Joan, Susan, Barbara; m. Sharon Hood Penney, Mar. 30, 1985. B in Engring. Physics, Cornell U., 1952; PhD in Applied Physics, Harvard U., 1956. Physicist R & D GE, Schenectady, N.Y., 1956-89; sr. lectr. dept. material sci. and engring. MIT, Cambridge, 1989—. Author: Driving Force: The Natural Magic of Magnets, 1996; author, co-author over 100 publications in field. Coolidge Fellow Gen. Electric Corp. R & D, 1987; recipient Disting. Career award Hudson-Mohawk chpt. AIME, 1986. Fellow Am. Soc. Metals, Am. Phys. Co.; mem. Nat. Acad. Engring., IEEE, AAAS, Materials Rsch. Soc., The Minerals, Metals and Materials Soc. Democrat. Unitarian. Achievements include 7 patents; advanced research in superconducting, ferromagnetic, and mechanical properties of materials. Home: 90 Albee Dr Braintree MA 02184-8252 Office: MIT 13 4066 Cambridge MA 02139

LIVINGSTON, JAY HAROLD, composer, lyricist; b. McDonald, Pa., Mar. 28, 1915; s. Maurice and Rose (Wachtel) L.; m. Lynne Gordon, Mar. 19, 1947; m. Shirley Mitchell, May 16, 1992; children from previous marriage: Travilyn, Tammy. B.A., U. Pa., 1937. With Paramount Pictures, 1945-55. Writer songs for over 100 motion pictures; songs, spl. material for Broadway shows Sons O' Fun, Hellzapoppin, also for Bob Hope, 1947-89, 90; scores for Broadway prodns. Oh Captain, 1958, Let It Ride, 1961; 2 songs in Sugar Babies, 1979; TV theme songs including Bonanza, Mister Ed, To Rome With Love; songs To Each His Own, Silver Bells, Tammy, Golden Earrings, Dear Heart, Never Let Me Go. Recipient 3 Acad. Award Oscars for songs Buttons and Bows, Mona Lisa, Que Sera Sera, Star on Hollywood Blvd. Walk of Fame, 1995; named to Songwriters Hall of Fame, 1973. Mem. Acad. TV Arts and Scis., ASCAP, Acad. Motion Picture Arts and Scis. (exec. bd.), Nat. Acad. Rec. Arts and Scis. (gov.), Songwriters Guild (exec. com.), AFTRA, Dramatist's Guild. Office: care ASCAP 1 Lincoln Plz New York NY 10023-7129

LIVINGSTON, JOHNSTON R., manufacturing executive; b. Foochow, China, Dec. 18, 1923; s. Henry Walter V and Alice (Moorehead) L.; m. Caroline Johnson, Aug. 17, 1946 (dec.); children: Henry, Ann, Jane, David; m. Patricia Karolchuck, Sept. 4, 1965. BS in Engring. with honors, Yale U., 1947; MBA with distinction, Harvard U., 1949. With Mpls.-Honeywell Regulator Co., 1949-55; with Whirlpool Corp., 1956-66, v.p., until 1966; v.p. Redman Industries, Dallas, 1966-67; dir. Constrn. Tech., Inc., Dallas, 1967—; pres., chmn. bd. dirs. Constrn. Tech., Inc., Denver, 1974-89; chmn. bd. dirs. Enmark Corp., Denver, 1979—; pres. Marcor Housing Sys., Inc., Denver, 1971-74. Past mem. industry adv. com. Nat. Housing Ctr.; bd. dirs., past pres. Nat. Home Improvement Coun.; pres., chmn. bd. dirs. Denver Symphony Assn., 1977-81; bd. dirs., past chmn. bd. dirs. Rocky Mountain Regional Inst. Internat. Edn.; trustee, v.p. Bonfils-Stanton Found., Denver, 1980—; hon. trustee Inst. Internat. Edn., N.Y. Baker scholar Harvard U., 1949. Mem. Rocky Mountain World Trade Assn. (bd. dirs., past chmn. bd. dirs.), Denver Country Club, Sigma Xi, Tau Beta Pi. Home: 1649 Keystone Ranch Rd Dillon CO 80435-8384 Office: 5070 Oakland St Denver CO 80239-2724

LIVINGSTON, LOUIS BAYER, lawyer; b. N.Y.C., Dec. 12, 1941; s. Norman and Helen (Bayer) L.; m. Mari Livingston, Apr. 6, 1968; children: Diana, Alex, Ann. BA, Yale U., 1963; LLB, Harvard U., 1966. Bar: N.Y. 1967, Oreg. 1971. Atty. NLRB, Memphis, 1967-68, Poletti, Freidin et al., N.Y.C., 1968-71; ptnr. Miller, Nash, Wiener, Hager & Carlsen, Portland, Oreg., 1971—. Office: Miller Nash Wiener Hager & Carlsen 111 SW 5th Ave Portland OR 97204-3604

LIVINGSTON, MARGERY ELSIE, missionary, clinical psychologist; b. Petoskey, Mich., Oct. 29, 1940; d. David Eugene and Beryl Mae (Herrington) L. BS with honors, Taylor U., Upland, Ind., 1962; MA with high honors, Wheaton (Ill.) Coll., 1983; student, U. Paris Sorbonne, 1970. Lic. psychologist, Pa. Tchr. Waterford (Mich.) Sch. Sys., 1962-64; ednl. missionary, county dir. BCM Internat., Union County, N.J., 1965-69; ednl. missionary BCM Internat. and AIM Internat., Albertville and Paris, France, 1969-70; ednl. missionary, technician BCM Internat. and AIM Internat., Watsa, Zaire, 1970-81; counselor, therapist BCM Internat./AIM Internat. Amani Counseling Ctr., Nairobi, Kenya, 1983-84; counselor, cons. BCM Internat., Upper Darby, Pa., 1985—; guest lectr. Bunia (Zaire) Theol. Sem., 1984, Adi (Zaire) Bible Inst., 1978, Aru (Zaire) Bible Inst., 1978, Todro (Zaire) Bible Inst., 1980; organizer/facilitator Missions and Mental Health-East, Mt. Bethel, Pa., 1995—. Editor: Commit Thy Way, 1994; author: (Bible study series) Living in Community, 1980; contbr. articles to profl. jours. Spkr., adj. staff Rockford (Mich.) Bapt. Ch., 1965—, Haven Reformed Ch., Kalamazoo, 1978—, Clinton Hill Bapt. Ch., Union, N.J., 1965—, Silvercrest Bapt. Ch., Waterford, Mich., 1966—, First Congl. Ch., Rockford, 1985—, North Plainfield (N.J.) Bapt. Ch., 1988—. Billy Graham Evangelistic Assn. scholar, 1981-83. Mem. APA (assoc.), Am. Assn. of Christian Counselors, Assn. N.Am. Missions, Christian Therapists Bible Study, Episcopal Bible Study, Greater Phila. Christian Writers Fellowship, Alpha Chi. Baptist. Avocations: poetry, clarinet, walking, aerobic weight-lifting, swimming. Office: BCM Internat 237 Fairfield Ave Upper Darby PA 19082-2206

LIVINGSTON, ROBERT GERALD, university official, political scientist; b. N.Y.C., Nov. 17, 1927; s. Robert Teviot and Geraldine (Gray) L.; m. Jeanne Andrée Nettel, May 12, 1955; children: Catherine Schuyler Livingston Fernandez, Robert Eric. AB, Harvard U., 1953, AM, 1953, PhD, 1959. Fgn. svc. officer U.S. Dept. State, Washington, 1956-74; v.p. German Marshall Fund U.S., Washington, 1974-77, pres., 1977-81; writer Washington, 1981-83; acting dir. Am. Inst. for Contemporary German Studies, Johns Hopkins U., Washington, 1983-87, dir. Am. Inst. for Contemporary German Studies, 1987-94, sr. devel. officer Am. Inst. for Contemporary German Studies, 1994-95, chief devel. officer, 1995-96; sr. vis. fellow German Hist. Inst., Washington, 1997—; commentator Deutschlandfunk, Cologne, 1991—. Co-author, editor: The Federal Republic in the 1980s, 1983, West German Political Parties, 1986; contbr. over 200 articles to polit. jours. and newspapers. Sgt. U.S. Army, 1946-49. Mem. German Studies Assn. U.S., Harvard Grad. Sch. Alumni Assn. Coun., Coun. on Fgn. Rels., N.Y. Soc. Cons. of Cincinnati, Cosmos Club, Chevy Chase Club, Barnstable Yacht Club (Mass.), Phi Beta Kappa. Democrat. Episcopalian. Avocations: hiking, swimming, tennis. Office: Am Inst Contemporary German Studies 1400 16th St NW Ste 420 Washington DC 20036-2216

LIVINGSTON, ROBERT LINLITHGOW, JR. (BOB LIVINGSTON, JR.), congressman; b. Colorado Springs, Colo., Apr. 30, 1943; s. Robert L. and Dorothy (Godwin) L.; m. Bonnie Robichaux, Sept. 13, 1965; children: Robert Linlithgow, III, Richard Godwin, David Barkley; SuShan Alida. BA in Econs., Tulane U., 1967, JD, 1968; postgrad., Loyola Inst. Politics, 1973. Bar: La. 1968. Ptnr. Livingston & Powers, New Orleans, 1976-77; asst. U.S. atty., dep. chief criminals divsn. U.S. Attys. Office, 1970-73; chief spl. prosecutor, chief armed robbery divsn. Orleans Parish Dist. Atty.'s Office, 1974-75; chief prosecutor organized crime unit La. Atty. Gen.'s Office, 1975-76; mem. 95th-105th Congresses from 1st La. Dist., 1977—; chair appropriations com., 1996—; Mem. nat. adv. bd. Young Ams. for Freedom. Mem. nat. adv. bd. Young Ams. for Freedom; bd. suprs. Smithsonian Inst.; bd. dirs. Internat. Rep. Inst. Ctr. for Democracy. Named Outstanding Asst. U.S. Atty., 1973. Mem. ABA, Fed. Bar Assn., La. Bar Assn., New Orleans Bar Assn., Navy League, Am. Legion. Roman Catholic. Home: 111 Veterans Memorial Blvd Metairie LA 70005-3028 Office: US Ho of Reps 2406 Rayburn HOB Washington DC 20515*

LIVINGSTON, STANLEY C., architect. BArch, U. So. Calif., 1961; student, U. Calif., San Diego. Lic. architect Calif., N.Mex., Nev., Ariz., Colo., Ky.; cert. Nat. Coun. Archtl. Registration. Prin. Salerno/Livingston Architects, San Diego; lectr. numerous instns. Archtl. projects include Residence Hall Tower & Multi Purpose Bldg. San Diego State U., Pacific Southwest Airlines Adminstrv. Offices & Hangar Facility, Fujitsu Microelectronics, Inc., Belden Village Low Income Sr. Housing Project, Atkinson Marine Corp. Hdqs. & Ship Repair Facility, Campbell Industries, Islandia Hotel Tower, Marlin Club, Sportfishing Facility and 500 Boat Marina, Branch Libr., Belmont Park Master Plan, Expert Witness Projects; other comml. projects include U.S. Fin. Office Bldg., Lake Murray Office Bldg., San Diego Fed. Branch Bank (5 locations), Nat. U. Office Bldg., Harbor Boat & Yacht Shipyard Renovation, Pacific Southwest Airlines Passenger Lounges & Gates (2 locations), and others. Symposia chmn. "Frank Lloyd Wright-Living in the Wright Century...An Evaluation" San Diego Archtl. Found./San Diego Mus. Art, 1990; mem. design competition adv. panel Balboa Park Organ Pavilion Parking Garage, 1990; mem. urban design com. San Diego Centre City, 1982-86; founder Orchids and Onions Program, 1976, com. chmn. 1984, jury chmn. 1985; chmn. design adv. com. San Diego Center City Devel. Corp., 1980. Fellow AIA (San Diego chpt., past pres. 1978-79, chmn. urban design com. 1978-86, chmn. task force Balboa Pk. master plan); mem. Am. Planning Assn. (mem. bd. dirs. San Diego 1981-82), Soc. Mktg. Profl. Svcs., Am. Arbitration Assn. (mem. panel arbitrators 1988—), Urban Land Inst. (assoc.), Urban Design & Planning Com., Bldg. Industry Assn. (mem. construction quality com.), Community Assn. Inst., San Diego Archtl. Found. (bd. dirs.), SCARAB. Office: Salerno/Livingston Architects 363 5th Ave Fl 3 San Diego CA 92101-6965

LIVINGSTON, WILLIAM SAMUEL, university administrator, political scientist; b. Ironton, Ohio, July 1, 1920; s. Samuel G. and Bata (Elkins) L.; m. Lana Sanor, July 10, 1943; children: Stephen Sanor, David Duncan. B.A., Ohio State U., 1943, M.A., 1943; Ph.D., Yale U., 1950. Asst. prof. U. Tex., Austin, 1949-54; asso. prof. U. Tex., 1954-61, prof. govt., 1961—, chmn. dept. govt., 1965-69, Jo Anne Christian centennial prof. Brit. studies, 1982-95, asst. dean Grad. Sch., 1954-58, chmn. Grad. Assembly, 1965-68, chmn. faculty senate, 1973-79, chmn. comparative studies program, 1978-79; vice chancellor acad. programs U. Tex. System, 1969-71; v.p., dean grad. studies U Tex. Austin, 1979-95; acting pres. U. Tex. Austin, 1992-93; sr. v.p., 1995—; vis. prof. Yale U., 1955-56, Duke U., 1960-61; sec.-treas. Assn. Grad. Schs., 1982-85; bd. dirs. Council Grad. Schs. in U.S., 1983-86. Author: Federalism and Constitutional Change, 1956; contbg. author: World Pressures on American Foreign Policy, 1962, Teaching Political Science, 1965, Federalism: Infinite Variety in Theory and Practice, 1968, Britain at the Polls 1979, 1981; editor: The Presidency and Congress: A Shifting Balance of Power, 1979; co-editor: Australia, New Zealand and the Pacific Islands Since the First World War, 1979; editor, contbr. author: Federalism in the Commonwealth, 1963, A Prospect of Liberal Democracy, 1979, The Legacy of the Constitution: An Assessment for the Third Century, 1987; book rev. editor: Jour. Politics, 1965-68, editor-in-chief, 1968-72; mem. editl. bd. Publius: Jour. of Federalism, 1971-95; mem. bd. editors: P.S, 1976-82, chmn., 1978-82. Served to 1st lt. FA AUS, 1943-45. Decorated Bronze Star, Purple Heart.; Recipient Teaching Excellence award, 1959; Ford Found. fellow, 1952-53; Guggenheim fellow, 1959-60; USIS lectr. in U.K. and India, 1977. Mem. Am. Polit. Sci. Assn. (exec. coun. and adminstrv. com. 1972-74, chmn. nominating com. 1973-74, 78-79), So. Polit. Sci. Assn. (exec. coun. 1964-67, pres. 1974-75), Southwestern Polit. Sci. Assn. (pres. 1973-74), Hansard Soc. (London), Philos. Soc. Tex., Austin Soc. for Pub. Adminstrn. (pres. 1973-74), Southwestern Social Sci. Assn. (pres. 1977-78), Phi Beta Kappa, Omicron Delta Kappa, Phi Gamma Delta, Pi Sigma Alpha (nat. coun. 1976-84, nat. pres. 1980-82). Home: 3203 Greenlee Dr Austin TX 78703-1621 Office: U Tex Office Sr VP Austin TX 78712

LIVINGSTONE, HARRISON EDWARD, writer; b. Urbana, Ill., May 23, 1937; s. Harry E. and Elsie (Harrison) L. BA, Harvard U., 1970; JD, U. Balt., 1963. Pres., owner The Conservatory Press, Balt., 1976—. Author: David Johnson Passed Through Here, 1971, The Wild Rose, 1985, HARVARD, John, 1987, High Treason, 1989 (N.Y. Times Bestseller), High Treason 2, 1992 (N.Y. Times Bestseller), Killing the Truth, 1993, Killing Kennedy, 1995, also numerous poems. Recipient Cert. of Honor, Balt. City Police, 1964; inductee Nat. Police Hall of Fame, 1964. Avocations: model railroading. Office: c/o The Conservatory Press PO Box 7149 Baltimore MD 21218-0149

LIVINGSTONE, JOHN LESLIE, accountant, management consultant, business economist, educator; b. Johannesburg, South Africa, Aug. 29, 1932; m. Trudy Dorothy Zweig, Aug. 7, 1977; children: Roger Miles, Adrienne Jill, Graham Ross, Robert Edward. B in Commerce, U. Witwatersrand, South Africa, 1956; MBA, Stanford U., 1963, PhD, 1966. C.P.A., N.Y., Tex. Budget dir. Edgars Stores Ltd., South Africa, 1958-61; asso. prof. Ohio State U., Columbus, 1966-69; Arthur Young Disting. prof. Ohio State U., 1970-73; Fuller E. Callaway prof. Ga. Inst. Tech., Atlanta, 1973-78; mem. exec. bd. Ga. Inst. Tech., 1976-78; ptnr. Coopers & Lybrand, N.Y.C., 1978-81; prin., v.p. Mgmt. Analysis Center, Inc., Cambridge, Mass., 1975-90; prof., chmn. div. acctg. and law Babson Coll., 1985-89, adj. prof., 1990—; cons. FPC, SEC, HEW, also maj. corps. Author 10 books including Accounting for Changing Prices: Replacement Cost and General Price Level Adjustments, 1976, Management Planning and Control, 1987, The Portable MBA: Finance and Accounting, 1992, 2d edit., 1997; assoc. editor: Decision Scis., 1973-78; mem. editl. bd. The Acctg. Rev., 1969-72, 76-78, Acctg., Orgns. and Socs., 1975-78, Jour. Acctg. and Pub. Policy, 1983-95; contbr. numerous articles to profl. jours. Mem. AICPA, Fla. Inst. CPAs, N.Y. Soc. CPAs, Am. Acctg. Assn., Acad. of Experts, Nat. Assn. for Forensic Econs., Nat. Assn. Bus. Economists, Tex. Soc. CPAs, Am.Arbitration Assn., Palm Beach Nat. Golf and Country Club, Breakers Club (Palm Beach), Govs. Club (Palm Beach). Office: 2300 Palm Beach Lakes Blvd West Palm Beach FL 33409-3303

LIVINGSTONE, SUSAN MORRISEY, nonprofit administrator; b. Carthage, Mo., Jan. 13, 1946; d. Richard John II and Catherine Newell (Carmean) Morrisey; m. Neil C. Livingstone III, Aug. 30, 1968. AB, Coll. William and Mary, 1968; MA, U. Mont., 1973; postgrad., Tufts U., 1973, Fletcher Sch. Law and Diplomacy, 1973—. Rschr. Senator Mark O. Hatfield, Washington, 1969-70; chief legis. and press asst. Congressman Richard H. Ichord, Washington, 1973-75, adminstrv. asst., 1975-81; cons. Congressman Wendell Bailey, Washington, 1981; exec. asst. VA, Washington, 1981-85, assoc. dep. adminstr. logistics and mgmt., 1985-86, sr. procurement exec., 1985-89, assoc. dep. adminstr. logistics, 1986-89; asst. sec. Army U.S. Dept. of Def., Washington, 1989-93; v.p. health and safety svcs. ARC, Washington, 1993—; mem interagy. com. on women's bus. enterprise The White House, 1985-89; mem. Pres.'s Coun. on Mgmt. Improvement, 1985-86. NDEA fellow. Mem. Exec. Women in Govt., Procurement Round Table (bd. dirs. 1994—), Assn. U.S. Army (bd. dirs. 1994-96, mem. coun. trustees 1996—), Women in Internat. Security (mem. adv. bd. 1994-97). Republican. Episcopalian. Office: ARC 8111 Gatehouse Rd Falls Church VA 22042-1203

LIVINGSTONE, TRUDY DOROTHY ZWEIG, dancer, educator; b. N.Y.C., June 9, 1946; d. Joseph and Anna (Feinberg) Zweig; m. John Leslie Livingstone, Aug. 7, 1977; 1 child, Robert Edward. Student, Charles Lowe Studios, N.Y.C., 1950-52, Nina Tinova Studio, N.Y.C., 1953-56, Ballet Russe de Monte Carlo, N.Y.C., 1956-57, Bklyn. Coll., 1964-66; BA in Psychology cum laude, Boston U., 1968, MEd, 1969; postgrad., Serena Studios, Carnegie Hall Ballet Arts, N.Y.C., 1973-74. Tchr. Millis (Mass.) Pub. Schs., 1969-72, Hebrew Acad. Atlanta, 1974-76; profl. dancer various orgns. including Rivermont Country Club, Jewish Community Ctr., Calanwolde Performing Arts Ctr., Atlanta, 1974-84; founder, owner, instr. dance Sasha Studios, Atlanta, 1974-77; owner Trudy Zweig Livingstone Studios, Wellesley, Needham, Mass., 1987-88, Palm Beach, Fla., 1989—; judge dance competition Atlanta Council Run-Offs, 1976. Vol. League Sch., Bklyn., 1965, Kennedy Meml. Hosp., Brighton, Mass., 1969, Nat. Affiliation for Literacy Advances, Santa Monica, Calif., 1982. Mem. Am. Alliance for Health, Phys. Edn., Recreation and Dance, Poets of the Palm Beaches, L.A. Athletic Club, Wellesley Coll. Club, Governor's Club (West Palm Beach). Avocation: writing poetry.

LIVSEY, ROBERT CALLISTER, lawyer; b. Salt Lake City, Aug. 7, 1936; s. Robert Frances and Rosezella Ann (Callister) L.; m. Renate Karla Guertler, Sept. 10, 1962; children: Scott, Rachel, Daniel, Benjamin. BS, U. Utah, 1962, JD, 1965; LLM, NYU, 1967. Bar: Utah 1965, Calif. 1967. Prof. Haile Selassie U., Addis Ababa, Ethiopia, 1965-66; spl. asst. to chief counsel IRS, Washington, 1977-79; assoc., then ptnr. Brobeck, Phleger & Harrison, San Francisco, 1967—; adj. prof. U. San Francisco Law Sch., 1970-77; mem. adv. com. IRS Dist. Dirs., 1986-89; mem. western region liason com IRS (chmn. 1989). Research editor U. Utah Law Rev., 1964-65; editor Tax Law Rev., 1966-67; contbr. articles to profl. jours. Bd. dirs. Gilead Group, 1986-88, East Bay Habitat for Humanity, 1987-88, Morning Song, 1992-94. Mem. ABA (chmn. subcom. real estate syndications 1981-84), State Bar Calif. (chmn. taxation sect. 1984-85), San Francisco Bar Assn. (chmn. taxation sect. 1982), Am. Coll. Tax Counsel, Am. Law Inst., Tax Litigation Club (pres. 1986-87), Order of Coif, Beta Gamma Sigma. Democrat. Mem. Evangelical Covenant Ch. Club: Commonwealth (San Francisco). Home: 128 La Salle Ave Piedmont CA 94610-1233 Office: Brobeck Phleger & Harrison 1 Market Plz San Francisco CA 94105

LIZT, SARA ENID VANEFSKY, lawyer, educator; b. USSR, Mar. 10, 1913; came to U.S., 1921; d. Max and Yocheved (Koval) Vanefsky; widowed. LLB, CUNY, Bklyn., 1941, LLM, 1962. Bar: N.Y. 1946, U.S. Dist. Ct. (so. and ea. dists.) N.Y. 1946. Pvt. practice Bklyn., 1946—; prof. CUNY, Bklyn., 1966-80. Address: 2060 E 19th St Brooklyn NY 11229-3943

LLAMANZARES, MAGDA CAROLINA GO VERA, nurse, clinical child psychologist; b. Manila, Oct. 23, 1940; d. Misael Poblete and Rosalina (Go) Vera; m. Teodoro Paraiso Llamanzares, Apr. 20, 1967; children: Michael Denis, Teodoro Misael Daniel, Rachel Marie Dorothy. B in Liberal Arts, U. Philippines, 1960; BSN, St. Paul Coll. Manila, 1967; M in Child Psychiat. Nursing and Cmty. Health, Wayne State U., 1972; PhD in Clin. Psychology, Ateneo U., The Philippines, 1988. Cert. psychiat. nurse, behavioral medicine specialist, counselor. Reporter Manila Chronicle, 1960-61; grade sch. tchr. Ateneo de Manila, 1961-62; vol. nurse Md. Mental Retardation Sch., Balt., 1972; nursing bd. examiner Profl. Regulation Commn., Manila, 1978-81; dir. child day care The Lamp Ctr., San Juan, Philippines, 1974-94; counselor In Touch Found., Manila, 1982-86; ind. nurse practitioner Makati (Philippines) Med. Ctr., 1974—, clin. child psychiatrist, 1988—; child cons. Internat. Sch., Manila, 1982-86; dir. psychol. svcs. Sulo ng Zonta, San Juan, 1981-90; dir. Holy Angels Day Care, Quezon City, Philippines, 1985-90. Author: Practice of Filial Therapy in The Philippines, 1988; editor Perspective in Mental Health and Psychiat. Nursing Jour., 1974-86; author, chmn. (booklet): Practice on Philippine Psychiatric Nursing Mental Health, 1984. Founding pres. Quezon City Barangay Lioness Club, 1985-86; chmn. Z-Club of Zonta Club of Mandaluyong, San Juan, 1990-92; sec. Zonta Club of Mandaluyong, San Juan, 1980-90; chmn. Cathetical Instrn. U. of The Philippines Cath. Action, 1957-60. Named Most Outstanding UPSCAN, Univ. Philippines Cath. Action, 1960; recipient Mich. State Fund grant Wayne State U., 1970-72, First prize Free Paper category Philippines Pediat. Soc., 1977, 3M Internat. Coun. Nurses Fellowship award, Geneva, 1981-85, Brit. Coun. grant, London, summer, 1982, Cmty. Svc. award Barangay Lions Club, 1986, Philippine Outstanding Women in Nation Svc. in Nursing award Assn. TOWNS, 1986, Svc. award Zonta Club Mandaluyong San Juan, 1991, Mother Madeline

Nursing award St. Paul Coll., Manila, Diamond Yr. Alumni Assn., 1992, Most Disting. Alumna Psychology & Child Devel. award La Consolacion Coll., 1995. Mem. Philippine Nurses Assn. (founder, pres./dir 1982-88, #M Philippines Nat. Nursing award 1981, Founding Pres. award 1983), Postillon Specialist Internat., Inc. (founder, pres. 1988—), Psychiat. Nursing Specialists Found. of Philippines (founder, pres. 1980-83, dir. 1974—), Sigma Theta Tau Lambda. Roman Catholic. Avocation: travel. Office: Makati Med Ctr, 2 Amorsolo St, Manila The Philippines

LLANUSA, STEVEN MICHAEL, elementary education educator; b. Burbank, Calif., Feb. 26, 1960; s. Louis Henry and Margaret Mary (Ferruzza) L.; life ptnr. Glenn Miya; children: Anthony Miya Llanusa. AA, L.A. Valley Coll., Van Nuys, Calif., 1982; BA, UCLA, 1985. Cert. tchr., Calif. Tchr. nursery sch. Child Devel. Ctr., L.A. Valley Coll. Campus, 1979-82; asst. tchr. UCLA Child Devel. Ctr., 1982-85; tchr. L.A. Unified Sch. Dist., Lincoln Heights, Calif., 1987-89, Colton Unified Sch. Dist., Bloomington, Calif., 1989—; curriculum specialist Gerald Smith Sch., Bloomington, 1993—. Chmn. diversity com. UCLA, 1992-94. Recipient cmty. svc. award ARC, 1981; scholar Tau Alpha Epsilon, 1982. Mem. ASCD, San Bernardino Humane Soc., UCLA Alumni Assn. (bd. dirs.-at-large 1992-94, co-chmn. Lambda alumni 1993-94, beginning tchr. support mentor), U. So. Calif. Lambda Alumni Assn. (edn. com. 1993-94), Sigma Phi Epsilon. Roman Catholic. Avocations: computer philanthropy theatre. Home: 2627 San Andres Way Claremont CA 91711-1556 Office: Gerald Smith Sci Magnet Sch 9551 Linden Ave Bloomington CA 92316-1430

LLAURADO, JOSEP G., nuclear medicine physician, scientist; b. Barcelona, Catalonia, Spain, Feb. 6, 1927; s. José and Rosa (Llaurado) García; m. Deirdre Mooney, Nov. 9, 1966; children—Raymund, Wilfred, Mireya; m. Catherine D. Entwistle, June 28, 1958 (dec.); children—Thadd, Oleg, Montserrat. B.S., B.A., Balmes Inst., Barcelona, 1944; M.D., Barcelona U., 1950; Ph.D. in Pharmacology, 1960; M.Sc. Biomed. Engring., Drexel U., 1963. Diplomate: Am. Bd. Nuclear Medicine. Resident Royal Postgrad. Sch. Medicine, Hammersmith Hosp., London, 1952-54; fellow M.D. Anderson Hosp. and Tumor Inst., Houston, 1957-58, U. Utah Med. Coll., Salt Lake City, 1958-59; asst. prof. U. Otago Dunedin, N.Z., 1954-57; sr. endocrinologist Pfizer Med. Research Lab., Groton, Conn., 1959-60; assoc. prof. U. Pa., 1963-67; prof. Med. Coll. Wis., Milw., 1970-82, Marquette U., 1967-82; clin. dir. nuclear medicine service VA Med. Ctr., Milw., 1977-82; chief nuclear medicine service VA Hosp., Loma Linda, Calif., 1983—; prof. dept. radiation scis. Loma Linda U. Sch. Medicine, 1983—; U.S. rep. symposium on dynamic studies with radioisotypes in clin. medicine and research IAEA, Rotterdam, 1970, Knoxville, 1974. Editor: Internat. Jour. Biomed. Computing; dep. editor Environ. Mgmt. and Health; contbr. numerous articles to profl. jours. Merit badge counselor Boy Scouts Am., 1972—; pres. Hales Corners (Wis.) Hist. Soc., 1981-83. Recipient Commendation cert. Boy Scouts Am., 1980. Fellow Am. Coll. Nutrition; mem. Soc. Nuclear Medicine (computer and acad. councils), IEEE (sr.), IEEE in Medicine and Biology Soc. (nat. adminstrv. Com. 1986-89), Biomed. Engring. Soc. (charter), Am. Physiol. Soc., Am. Soc. Pharmacology and Exptl. Therapeutics, Soc. Math. Biology (founding), Endocrine Soc., Royal Soc. Health, Societat Catalana de Biologia, Casal dels Catalans de Calif. (pres. 1989-91), Calif. Med. Assn. (sci. adv. panel nuclear medicine 1983—). Office: VA Hosp Nuclear Med Svc Rm 115 11201 Benton St Loma Linda CA 92357-1000

LL COOL J (JAMES TODD SMITH), rap singer, actor; b. Queens, N.Y., 1968; s. Jimmy Nunya. Albums: Radio, 1984, Bigger and Deffer, 1987, Walking with A Panther, 1989, Mama Said Knock You Out (Grammy award Best Rap Vocal), 1991, Mr. Smith, 1996; actor: (films) Krush Groove, 1984, The Hard Way, 1991, Toys, 1992, The Right to Remain Silent, 1996, Woo, 1997, BAPS, 1997; (TV series) In the House, 1995—; (TV movie) Wildcats, 1986. Grammy nomination (Best Rap Solo, 1994) for "Stand By Your Man". Office: Bad Boy Entertainment Inc 8 W 19th St New York NY 10011-4206*

LLEWELLYN, CHARLES ELROY, JR., psychiatrist; b. Richmond, Va., Jan. 16, 1922; s. Charles Elroy and Pearl Ann (Shield) L.; m. Grace Eldridge, Sept. 25, 1948; children: Charles Elroy III, George E. (dec.), Richard S. BS, Hampden-Sydney Coll., 1943; MD, Med. Coll. Va., 1946; MS in Psychiatry, U. Colo., 1953. Diplomate Am. Bd. Psychiatry and Neurology; lic. marriage and family therapist, N.C. Intern psychiatry Tucker Hosp., Inc., Richmond, 1946-47, asst. to staff, 1948-50; intern gen. medicine Bellevue Hosp., N.Y.C., 1947-48; fellow psychiatry Colo. Psychopathic Hosp. and U. Colo. Med. Ctr., Denver, 1950-53; assoc. dept. psychiatry Duke U., Durham, N.C., 1955-56, asst. prof., 1956-63, assoc. prof., 1963-87; asst. dir. adult psychiat. outpatient clinic Duke U. Med. Ctr., Durham, 1955-56, head adult psychiat. outpatient div., 1956-76, acting head divsn. cmty. and social psychiatry, 1976-81, chief tng. divsn. cmty. and social psychiatry, 1976-85, head divsn. cmty. and social psychiatry, 1985-87; pvt. practice Durham, 1987—; psychiat. cons., supr., seminar dir. pastoral counseling tng. programs Duke U. Med. Ctr., 1965-87, dir. student mental health svc. Duke U., 1959-68; psychiat. cons. N.C. Divsn. Social Svcs., 1955-79, N.C. Medicaid Program, 1971-75, N.C. Med. Peer Rev. Found., Inc., 1975-79; sr. psychiat. cons. Family Cons. Svc., Durham, 1966-87; mem.-at-large N.C. Substance Abuse Profl. Ctr. Bd., 1984-89; part-time cons., med. dir. Durham Substance Abuse Treatment Ctr., 1968-88. Contbr. articles to profl. jours, chpts. to books. Mem. adv. bd. Durham County Drug Counseling and Evaluation Svc., 1972-79; bd. dirs. Family Counseling Svc. Durham, 1973-78, pres., 1975; bd. dirs. United Health Svcs., 1975-84; trustee Epworth United Meth. Ch., 1959-62, dir. cmty. ministries com., 1961-62; cubmaster Boy Scouts Am., 1960-66; mem. ch. campus rels. com. The Meth. Ctr., Duke U., 1964-66. Capt. U.S. Army, 1953-55. Recipient Outstanding Profl. Human Svcs. Am. Acad. Human Svcs., 1974-75; grantee U.S. Inst. Mental Health, 1967-71. Fellow Am. Psychiat. Assn. (life); mem. AMA (life), Am. Group Psychotherapy Assn., Pan Am. Med. Soc. (life), Am. Assn. Marriage and Family Therapy, Carolinas Group Psychotherapy Soc. (treas. 1983-94), N.C. Med. Soc. (life), N.C. Assn. Marriage and Family Therapists, Mental Health Assn. N.C., Durham-Orange County Med. Soc. (life). Avocations: fishing, electronic gadgets, gardening. Office: Ste 110 3308 Durham Chapel Hill Blvd Durham NC 27707-2643

LLEWELLYN, JOHN SCHOFIELD, JR., food company executive; b. Amsterdam, N.Y., Jan. 10, 1935; s. John S. and Dorothea (Breedon) L.; m. Mary Martha Pallotta, June 9, 1962; children: Mary M., John S. III, Robert J., James P., Timothy J. AB, Holy Cross Coll., 1956; MBA, Harvard U., 1961. With mktg. Gen. Foods Corp., White Plains, N.Y., 1961-69, Sunshine Biscuit div. Am. Brands, N.Y.C., 1973-77; exec. v.p. Morton Frozen Foods div. ITT Continental Baking Co., Charlottesville, Va., 1977-79; gen. mgr. Continental Kitchens ITT Continental Baking Co., Rye, 1980-81; sr. v.p. Ocean Spray Cranberries Inc., Plymouth, Mass., 1982-86; exec. v.p., chief operating officer Ocean Spray Cranberries Inc., Plymouth, 1986-87, pres., chief exec. officer, 1988—; bd. dirs. Dean Foods Co. Trustee St. Sebastian's Country Day Sch., Needham, Mass., 1991—; bd. dirs. Mass. Environ. Trust, 1991—. Capt. USMC, 1957-63. Mem. Nat. Food Processors Assn. (bd. dirs., exec. com., chmn. emeritus), Grocery Mfrs. Am. (bd. dirs., fin. com., govt. affairs coun.). Roman Catholic. Home: Steamboat Ln Hingham MA 02043 Office: Ocean Spray Cranberries Inc 1 Ocean Spray Dr Middleboro MA 02349-1000

LLEWELLYN, LEONARD FRANK, real estate broker; b. Harlowton, Mont., Oct. 31, 1933; s. Ralph Emory and Frances Louise (Ewing) L.; m. Patricia Lockrom, Aug. 16, 1951 (div. 1955); m. Corrie J. Spruit, Apr. 21, 1974 (div. 1995). BSEE, Eastern Mont. Coll. Edn., 1955. Enlisted USMC, 1957, advanced through grades to capt., 1960, ret., 1967; owner Capitol Fla. Assn., Inc., Alexandra, Va., 1966-74; pres., owner Fla. Properties, Inc., Balt., 1968-74; chmn. Marco Beach Realty, Inc., Marco Island, Fla., 1975-82, 82—, Cons., Inc. of S.W. Fla., Marco Island, 1982—; served as presdl. pilot for presidents Kennedy and Johnson, 1963-66; bd. dirs. Founders Nat. Bank and Trust Co.; mem. adv. bd. Founding Ptnrs. Capital Mgmt. Co. Author: (manual) Aero-Gunnery Tactics, 1958. Bd. dirs. Collier County Servancy, 1978-83; trustee Naples (Fla.) Cmty. Hosp., 1980-93, Cmty. Found. Collier County, 1990-94. Named Top Gun, USN, USMC, 1958, Citizen of Yr. Marco Island N.Y. Times and Marco Island Eagle, 1982. Mem. Marco Island Bd. Realtors (pres. 1982), Marco Island C. of C. (pres. 1981-82, pres. emeritus 1984), Naples Forum (pres. 1985-86), Nat. Aviation Club, Nat. Assn. Sales Masters, Rotary Club. Republican. Home: PO Box 825 852 Bald Eagle Dr Marco Island FL 34146-0825 Office: Cons Inc of SW Fla Marco Island FL 33937

LLEWELLYN, RALPH ALVIN, physics educator; b. Detroit, June 27, 1933; s. Ralph A. and Mary (Green) L.; m. Laura Diane Alsop, June 12, 1955; children: Mark Jeffrey, Rita Annette, Lisa Suzanne, Eric Matthew. B.S. in Chem. Engring. with high honors, Rose-Hulman Inst. Tech., 1955; Ph.D. in Physics, Purdue U., 1962. Mem. faculty Rose-Hulman Inst. Tech., Terre Haute, Ind., 1961-70, assoc. prof. physics, 1964-68, prof., 1968-70, chmn. dept. physics, 1969-70; prof., chmn. dept. Ind. State U., Terre Haute, 1970-72, 74-80; dean Coll. of Arts and Scis. U. Cen. Fla., Orlando, 1980-84, prof., 1984—; exec. sec. Energy Bd., staff officer environmental Studies Bd. NAS/NRC, Washington, 1972-74; vis. prof. Rensselaer Poly. Inst., Troy, N.Y., 1964; cons. Commn. on Coll. Physics, 1987-89, NSF, 1965-66; mem. Ind. Lt. Gov.'s Sci. Adv. Coun., 1974-80; adv. bd. Ind. Gov.'s Energy Extension Svc., Fla. Solar Energy Ctr., policy coun. Fla. Inst. Govt., Fla. Radon Adv. Coun., 1988—; mem. environ. adv. com. Fla. Inst. Phosphate Rsch.; mem. grievance com. Fla. Bar, nat. adv. coun. Nat. Commn. on Higher Edn. Issues, 1982. Assoc. editor: Phys. Rev. Letters; contbr. articles to profl. jours.; producer instructional films and TV. Trustee Merom (Ind.) Inst. Recipient Tchg. Incentive award Fla. State Univ. Sys., 1994, 97; NSF Coop. fellow, 1959-60, Am. Coun. Edn. Acad. Adminstrn. Internship Program fellow. Fellow Ind. Acad. Sci. (chmn. physics divsn. 1969-70, Spkr. of Yr. award 1975, pres.-elect 1980); mem. AAAS, AAUP, Am. Phys. Soc., Am. Assn. Physics Tchrs. (pres. Ind.), N.Y. Acad. Scis., Fla. Acad. Scis. (endowment com.), Internat. Oceanographic Found., Ind. Acad. Sci., Sigma Xi, Tau Beta Pi. Home: 1463 Palomino Way Oviedo FL 32765-9304 Office: U Cen Fla Dept Physics Orlando FL 32816

LLINÁS, RODOLFO RIASCOS, medical educator, researcher; b. Bogota, Colombia, Dec. 16, 1934; came to U.S., 1959, naturalized, 1973; s. Jorge Enrique (Llinas) and Bertha (Riascos) L.; m. Gillian Kimber, Dec. 24, 1965; children: Rafael Hugo, Alexander Jorge. B.S., Gimnasio Moderno, Bogota, 1952; M.D., U. Javeriana, Bogota, 1959; Ph.D., Australian Nat. U., 1965; M.D. (hon.), U. Salamanca, Spain, 1985; PhD (hon.), U. Barcelona, Spain, 193, U. Nacional Bogota, Colombia, 194. Research fellow Mass. Gen. Hosp.-Harvard U., 1960-61; NIH research fellow in physiology U. Minn., Mpls., 1961-63, assoc. prof., 1965-66; assoc. mem. AMA Inst. Biomed. Research, Chgo., 1966-68, mem., 1970, head neurobiology unit, 1967-70; assoc. prof. neurology and psychiatry Northwestern U., 1967-71; guest prof. physiology Wayne State U., 1967-74; professorial lectr. pharmacology U. Ill.-Chgo., 1967-68, clin. prof., 1968-72; prof. physiology, head neurobiology div. U. Iowa, 1970-76; prof., chmn. physiology and biophysics NYU, N.Y.C., 1976—; Thomas and Suzanne Murphy prof. neurosci. NYU, 1985—; mem. neurol. sci. research tng. com. Nat. Inst. Neurol. Diseases and Stroke, NIH, 1971-73; mem. neurology A study sect. div. research grants NIH, 1974-78; assoc. neurosci. research program MIT, 1974-83; mem. U.S. Nat. Com. for IBRO, 1978-81; acting chmn. U.S. Nat. Com. For IBRO, 1982, chmn., 1983-89, exec. com., 1985—; mem. sci. adv. bd. Max-Planck Inst. for Psychiatry, Munich, 1979-83; professorial lectr. Coll. de France, Paris, 1979, Nat. Poly. Inst., Mexico City, 1981; IBRO internat. lectr., S.Am., 1982; McDowall lectr. King's Coll., London, 1984. Author: (with Hubbard and Quastel) Electrophysiological Analysis of Synaptic Transmission, 1969; editor: Neurobiology of Cerebellar Evolution and Development, 1969, (with W. Precht) Frog Neurobiology: A Handbook, 1976; chief editor: Neurosci., 1974—; mem. editorial bd.: Jour. Neurobiology, 1980—; mem.: Pfluegers Archives, 1981—, Jour. Theoretical Neurobiology, 1981—. Recipient John C. Krantz award U. Md., 1976, Einstein Gold medal UNESCO, 1991, Signoret award in cognition, Fondation Ipsen La Salpâtrière, Paris, 1994. Mem. NAS, Soc. For Neurosci. (council 1974-78), Am. Physiol. Soc. (Bowditch Lectr. 1973), Am. Soc. Cell Biology, Biophys. Soc., Harvey Soc., Internat. Brain Research Orgn., N.Y. Acad. Scis., Alpha Omega Alpha (hon.). Office: NYU Med Ctr 550 1st Ave New York NY 10016-6481*

LLOYD, ALBERT LAWRENCE, JR., German language educator; b. Evanston, Ill., Aug. 10, 1930; married; 1 child. A.B., George Washington U., 1951, M.A., 1954, Ph.D., 1957. Asso. in German, George Washington U., 1954-57; mem. faculty U. Pa., 1957—, prof. German, 1970—, chmn. dept., 1972-80; nat. adv. bd. Jr. Yr. in Munich and Freiburg Program, 1962-82. Author: The Manuscripts and Fragments of Notker's Psalter, 1958, Der Münchener Psalter des 14. Jahrhunderts: Eine Auswahl zusammen mit den entsprechenden Teilen von Notkers Psalter, 1969, Anatomy of the Verb: The Gothic Verb as a Model for a Unified Theory of Aspect, Actional Types, and Verbal Velocity, 1979; co-author: Deutsch und Deutschland heute, 1967, 2d edit., 1981, Etymologisches Wörterbuch des Althochdeutschen, Vol. I, 1988; also articles. Grantee Am. Philos. Soc., 1966; Nat. Endowment for Humanities grantee, 1978—. Mem. Inst. Deutsche Sprache, Linguistic Soc. Am., Am. Assn. Tchrs. of German, Mediaeval Acad. Am., Soc. for Germanic Philology, Phi Beta Kappa. Office: U Pa 745 Williams Hall Philadelphia PA 19104-6305

LLOYD, CECIL RHODES, pediatric dentist; b. Corpus Christi, Tex., Aug. 18, 1930; s. Cecil Rhodes Hilbun and Cidney W. (Linxwiler) Lloyd; m. Donna Mae Thomas, Dec. 31, 1955 (div. 1973); children: James Michael, Leigh Ann, Lisa Kendall; m. Glenda Sue Williams, Dec. 31, 1979; children: Lauren Cecily, Sutton Rhodes. Student, La. State U., 1949, La. Tech. Inst., 1950, Centenary Coll., 1952-54; DDS, Loyola U., New Orleans, 1958. Pediatric dentist Shreveport, La., 1958—; cons. pediatric dentistry Barksdale AFB, La., 1970—. Chmn. Cen. YMCA, Shreveport, 1974, met. bd., 1969, Ind. Bowl Football Classic, Shreveport, 1984, 85, Fellowship Christian Athletes, 1986; bd. dirs. Riverside Hosp., Bossier, La., 1982-84; pres.-elect Sports Found., 1989, pres., 1990; founder Sports Mus. of Champions, Shreveport-Bossier; interim mem. Shreveport City Coun., 1990. With USMC, 1950-52. Named Southwestern Handball Hall of Fame, 1996. NW La. Dental Assn., La. Dental Assn., ADA, Am. Acad. Pediatric Dentistry, La. Bd. Dentistry (pres., 1969-70, 77-78, 83-84), Ark.-La.-Tex. Dental Congress (chmn. 1979-80). Republican. Baptist. Avocation: Theatre. Office: 927 Shreveport Barksdale Hwy Shreveport LA 71105-2205

LLOYD, CHRISTOPHER, television writer and producer. Writer TV series The Golden Girls, 1987-88, Down Home, 1990-91, Wings, 1991-92; exec. prodr. TV series Frasier, 1992— (Emmy award for outstanding comedy series 1995). Office: care Broder Kurland Webb Offner Agy 9242 Beverly Blvd Ste 200 Beverly Hills CA 90210-3710*

LLOYD, DOUGLAS SEWARD, physician, public health administrator; b. Bklyn., Oct. 16, 1939; s. Heber Hughes and Virginia Seward (Chamberlin) L. A.B. in Chemistry, Duke U., 1961, M.D., 1971; postgrad., Old Dominion U., 1965-67; M.P.H. in Health Planning, U. N.C., 1971. Diplomate Am. Bd. Preventive Medicine. Intern in pediatrics Duke U., Durham, N.C., 1971-72; clin. scholar Duke U., 1972, resident in family practice, 1972-73; commr. health Conn. Dept. Health Services, 1973-87; assoc. med. dir. Nat. Med. Rsch. Corp., Hartford, Conn., 1987-89; pres. Doug Lloyd Assocs., Farmington, Conn., 1989-92; assoc. adminstr. Health Resources and Svcs. Adminstrn., Rockville, Md., 1992—; lectr. Yale U., Conn., 1973-87; chmn. bd. Pub. Health Found., 1984-87. Contbr. articles to profl. jours. Served to capt. USNR. Recipient Lange Publ. award, 1971, McCormick award for excellence in pub. health, 1987. Fellow Am. Coll. Preventive Medicine; mem. AMA, Am. Pub. Health Assn., Assn. State and Territorial Health Ofcls. (past pres.). Home: 11410 Stonewood Ln Rockville MD 20852-4543 Office: Health Resources & Svcs Adminstrn 5600 Fishers Ln Rockville MD 20857-0001

LLOYD, EMILY (EMILY LLOYD PACK), actress; b. North London, England, Sept. 29, 1970; d. Roger Lloyd Pack. Grad., Italia Conti Sch. for Performing Arts. Films: Wish You Were Here, 1987, Cookie, 1989, In Country, 1989, Chicago Joe and the Showgirl, 1990, A River Runs Through It, 1992, Les Cent et Une Nuits, 1995, Livers Ain't Cheap, 1995, Under the Hula Moon, 1995, When Saturday Comes, 1995. Office: United Talent Agy 9560 Wilshire Blvd # 500 Beverly Hills CA 90212-2704*

LLOYD, EUGENE WALTER, construction company executive; b. Bklyn., Apr. 9, 1943; s. Walter Vincent and Mary Regina (Conway) L.; m. Julia Ann Bain Menzies, May 6, 1967; children: Deborah Ann, Doreen Marie. AA in Constrn., N.Y. Tech. Coll., 1960-63. Estimator Stephen H. Falk & Assocs., Great Neck, N.Y., 1962-65, Builder's Estimating Service, N.Y.C., 1965-67, Humphreys & Harding, Inc., N.Y.C., 1967-68; chief estimator, corp. sec. Conforti & Eisele, Inc., N.Y.C., 1968-76; exec. v.p. Torcon, Inc., Westfield, N.J., 1976-93; v.p., dir. The Henderson Corp., Raritan, N.J., 1994—. Served with U.S. Army, 1963-69. Republican. Roman Catholic. Avocation: working on old cars. Home: 242 W Central Ave Pearl River NY 10965-2119 Office: The Henderson Corp 575 State Route 28 Raritan NJ 08869-1354

LLOYD, GREGORY LENARD, professional football player; b. Miami, Fla., May 26, 1965. Student, Ft. Valley State Coll. Linebacker Pitts. Steelers, 1987—. Named to Sporting News NFL All-Pro Team, 1994, 95; selected to Pro Bowl, 1991-95. Office: 300 Stadium Cir Pittsburgh PA 15212-5729*

LLOYD, HUGH ADAMS, lawyer; b. Pine Apple, Ala., Oct. 5, 1918; s. James Adams and Kate (Compton) L.; m. Lydia Douglas, Sept. 18, 1942; children: Kathryn Lloyd Allen, Sally Douglas (Mrs. Charles Proctor), Elizabeth Anne (Mrs. Thomas Goodman), Hugh Adams Jr. Student, Oglethorpe U., 1936-37; A.B., U. Ala., 1941, LL.B., 1942. Bar: Ala. 1942, U.S. Supreme Ct 1958. Adjudicator VA, Montgomery, Ala., 1946-47; partner firm Lloyd, Dinning, Boggs & Dinning, Demopolis, Ala., 1947—; chmn. bd. dirs., chief exec. officer Robertson Banking Co., Demopolis, ret., 1995. Active Boy Scouts Am.; chmn. Demopolis Indsl. Devel. Com., 1970; mem. Regional Com. Juvenile Delinquency, 1970; chmn. Marengo County Devel. Bd., 1972-73; mem. Demopolis City Coun., 1974; chmn. Indsl. Devel. Bd. Marengo County, 1980; pres. Marengo County Port Authority, 1987, Demopolis City Schs. Found., 1995—; trustee Judson Coll., Marion, Ala., 1981, vice-chmn. bd., 1989, chmn., 1991. With AUS, 1943-45. Decorated Bronze Star; recipient Silver Beaver award Boy Scouts Am., 1972. Mem. Am. Judicature Soc., ABA, Ala. Bar Assn., 17th Jud. Circuit Bar Assn. (pres.), Marengo County Hist. Soc. (v.p. 1980), Demopolis C. of C. (pres.), Ala. Law Inst. (coun.), Bus. Coun. Ala. (dir. 1995), Ala. Safety Coun. (former dir.), Demopolis Country Club (pres. 1967-68), Kiwanis (dist. gov. 1967, chmn. internat. com. Key clubs 1969, internat. com. on boys and girls work 1972, dist. chmn. laws and regulations com. Ala. dist. 1979). Baptist (past chmn. ch. bd. deacons). Home: 1409 Colony Rd Demopolis AL 36732-3445 Office: PO Drawer Z 501 N Walnut Ave Demopolis AL 36732-2037 also: Robertson Banking Co 216 N Walnut Ave Demopolis AL 36732-2032

LLOYD, JACQUELINE, English language educator; b. N.Y.C., Aug. 21, 1950; d. R.G. and Hortense (Collins) L. BA, Fisk U., 1972; MEd, U. North Fla., 1989. Instr. English, dir. Writing Ctr. Edward Waters Coll., Jacksonville, Fla., 1983, 90—. Mem. Nat. Coun. Tchrs. English. Democrat. Presbyterian. Avocation: movies. Home: 5006 Andrew Robinson Dr Jacksonville FL 32209-1002

LLOYD, JOHN RAYMOND, mechanical engineering educator; b. Mpls., Aug. 1, 1942; s. Raymond Joseph and Wilma Mable (Epple) L.; m. Mary Jane Whiteside, Dec. 20, 1963; children: Jay William, Stephanie Christine. BS in Engring., U. Minn., 1964, MSME, 1966, PhDME, 1971. Devel. engr. Procter & Gamble Co., Cin., 1966-67; prof. mech. engring. U. Notre Dame, South Bend, Ind., 1970-83; Univ. Disting. prof. Mich. State U., East Lansing, 1983-92, chmn. dept. mech. engring., 1983-91, disting. prof., 1991—; cons. LeRoy Troyer & Assocs., Mishawaka, Ind., 1980-90, Azdel Inc., Shelby, N.C., 1987-90; advisor NSF, Washington, 1987-90; mem. Nat. Bur. Standards assessment panel NRC, Washington, 1987-93; mem. sci. coun. Internat. Ctr. Heat and Mass Transfer, Yugoslavia, 1986—; chmn. Midwest Energy Consortium, 1993—; adv. editor McGraw Hill, Inc., 1990—. Adv. editor Internat. Jour. Heat and Fluid Flow, 1985—, Jour. Engring. Physics and Thermodynamics, 1993—; contbr. over 100 articles to profl. jours., chpts. to books. Recipient Outstanding Faculty award U. Notre Dame, 1975, 82, Ralph R. Teetor Ednl. award Soc. Automotive Engrs., 1986, Heat Transfer Mem. award Am. Soc. of Manufacturing Engineers, 1995. Fellow ASME (v.p. rsch. 1995—, mem. nat. bd. comm. 1983-90, mem. rsch. and tech. devel. bd. 1985—, mem. coun. on edn. 1991-93, mem. critical techs. com. 1991—, editor Jour. Heat Transfer 1989-95, Outstanding Paper award 1977, Melville medal 1978, Heat Transfer Meml. award 1995). Office: Mich State Univ Dept Mech Engring East Lansing MI 48824

LLOYD, JOSEPH WESLEY, physicist, researcher; b. N.Mex., Jan. 31, 1914; s. William Washington and Mattie May (Barber) L.; m. Lenora Lucille Hopkins, Jan. 24, 1944 (dec. June 1969); 3 children (dec.); m. Ruth Kathryn Newberry, Nov. 19, 1988; children: Kathryn Ruth Jordan, Mary Evelyn Jordan. Student, Pan Am. Coll., 1942. Plumber Pomona, Calif., 1951-57; plumber, pipefitter Marysville, Calif., 1957-79; ret., 1979; ind. researcher in physics and magnetism, Calif., 1944—. With CAP, 1944-45. Mem. AAAS, N.Y. Acad. Scis. Mem. Ch. of Christ.

LLOYD, LEWIS KEITH, JR., surgery and urology educator; b. Shreveport, La., Sept. 18, 1941; s. Lewis Keith Sr. and Cidney (Linxwiler) L.; m. Karen Hansen, June 9, 1970; children—Kristine Elizabeth, Lewis Keith III, Kevin Hansen. Student, Centenary Coll., 1959-62; M.D., Tulane Med. Sch., 1966. Diplomate Am. Bd. Urology. Intern USPHS Hosp., Norfolk, Va., 1966-67; resident in urology Tulane U. Med. Sch., New Orleans, 1970-74; from asst. to assoc. prof. surgery U. Ala., Birmingham, 1974-77, prof., 1981—; dir. Urol. Rehab. Rsch. Ctr., Birmingham, 1978, dir. urol. divsn., 1995; chmn. exec. com. Univ. Hosp., 1988-90. Adminstrv. bd. Highlands Meth. Ch., Birmingham, 1983-90; trustee Ala. chpt. Multiple Sclerosis Soc., Birmingham, 1984-85, 92—; bd. dirs. Am. Spinal Injury Assn., 1986-92. Lt. comdr. USPHS, 1966-70, Vietnam. Mem. AMA (Billings Gold medal 1978), Am. Urol. Assn. (bd. dirs. Southeastern sect. 1991-94), Am. Spinal Injury Assn., Birmingham Urology Club (pres. 1981-82), Greystone Golf Club. Republican. Clubs: Birmingham Urology (pres. 1981-82); Mountain Brook Swim and Tennis, Summit Club. Office: U Ala Med Sch 606 MEB Birmingham AL 35294

LLOYD, MICHAEL JEFFREY, recording producer; b. N.Y.C., Nov. 3, 1948; s. John and Suzanne (Lloyd) Sutton; m. Patricia Ann Varble, Sept. 6, 1980; children: Michael, Christopher, Jeni, Deborah. Student, U. So. Calif. V.p. artists and repertoire MGM Records, Inc., 1969-73; ind. record producer, 1973—; pres. Heaven Prodns., 1975—, Michael Lloyd Prodns., 1979—, Taines-Lloyd Film Prodns., 1984-85; music dir. TV series Happy Days; music dir. Kidsongs, Living Proof, NBC-TV movie, Kidsongs Videos; prodr. Love Lines, NBC-TV movie Swimsuit; guest lectr. UCLA; judge Am. Song Festival. Composer: (music for feature films) Tough Enough, If You Could See What I Hear, Dirty Dancing, All Dogs Go to Heaven; composer music for 8 Movies of the Week, 12 TV spls., 28 TV series and 34 feature motion pictures. Recipient 50 Gold Album awards, 24 Platinum Album awards, 26 Gold Single awards, 2 Platinum Single awards, 3 Grammy awards, 41 Chart Album awards, 100 Chart Single awards, 10 Broadcast Music Inc. awards, 1 Am. Music award, 1 Dove award, 2 Nat. Assn. of Record Minets. Mem. ASCAP (12 awards), Am. Fedn. Musicians, Screen Actors Guild, Nat. Assn. Rec. Arts and Scis., AFTRA.

LLOYD, MICHAEL STUART, newspaper editor; b. Dickinson, N.D., Aug. 11, 1945; s. James William and Mary Marie (Ripley) L.; m. Judith Ann Baxter, May 24, 1966; children: Matthew James, Kristen Ann. B.Jour., U. Mo., 1967. Reporter Grand Rapids (Mich.) Press, 1967-72, asst. city editor, 1972-74, city editor, 1975-77, editor-in-chief, 1978—. Bd. dirs. Mary Free Bed Hosp., Grand Valley State Coll. Found., Celebration on Grand Com. Mem. Am. Soc. Newspaper Editors. Office: The Grand Rapids Press Booth Newspaper 155 Michigan St NW Grand Rapids MI 49503-2302*

LLOYD, RAY DIX, health physicist, consultant; b. Mar. 10, 1930; s. Ray Ernest and Dixie (Penrose) L.; m. Louise Mortensen, July 10, 1954; children: Thomas R., Janna L. Brady, Alan T., Christopher R., Heather L. Smith. BS, U. Utah, 1954, MS, 1956, PhD, 1974; postgrad., U. Southwestern La., 1959, La. State U., 1960. Diplomate Am. Bd. Health Physics; recert. Rsch. asst. radiobiology divsn. U. Utah, 1961, rsch. assoc. radiobiology divsn., 1961-64, rsch. instr. dept. anatomy, radiobiology divsn., 1964-74, rsch. assoc. prof. dept. pharmacology, radiobiology divsn., 1979-84, rsch. prof. dept. pharmacology, radiobiology divsn., 1984-86, rsch. prof. Sch. Medicine, 1986-92, part-time rsch. prof. Sch. Medicine, 1992—; adj. asst. prof. dept. mechanical engring. U. Utah, 1975-90; adj. prof. U. Utah, 1997—; cons. numerous orgns, health sys., and projects including Hale and

Dorr, attys., Boston, Life Sys., Inc., Cleve., BioTrace, Salt Lake City, Plateau Resources, Ltd., Grand Junction, Colo., Hercules Aerospace, Magna, Utah, Mini-Dose Labs., Golden, Colo., Western Analytical Labs., Salt Lake City, 1979-94, Holy Cross Hosp., Salt Lake City, U.S. Dept. Justice, Nat. Cancer Inst; mem. Nat. Coun. Radiation Protection and Measurements, 1980-86, 86-92, consociate mem., 1992—; mem. radiol. health adv. com. Utah State Divsn. Health. Assoc. editor: (jour.) Health Physics, 1990-92, (book) Delayed Effects of Bone Seeking Radionuclides; reviewer: Radiation Rsch., Health Physics, Radiat. Protection, Internat. Jour. Radiation Biology, others; contbr. numerous articles to jours., chpts. to books, abstracts and tech. papers; patentee radiation detector. M sgt. U.S. Army, 1948-52, Korea, 1951-52. Fellow Health Physics Soc.; mem. Am. Acad. Health Physics, Radiation Rsch. Soc., Health Physics Soc. (Great Salt Lake chpt.), Utah br. Am. Assn. for Lab. Animal Sci., Internat. Radiation Protection Assn., Sigma Xi, Phi Kappa Phi, Gamma Theta Upsilon. Office: U Utah Radiobiology Lab Bldg 586 Salt Lake City UT 84112

LLOYD, ROBERT ANDREW, art educator; b. Boston, Mar. 10, 1934; s. Claude T. and Dorothy (Clarkson) L.; m. Susan M. McIntosh, Jan. 28, 1956; children: Benjamin, Seth, Thomas. BA, Harvard U., 1956, MArch, 1959. Tchr. art Phillips Acad., Andover, Mass., 1962—, dean Visual Studies Inst., 1978-95; mem. accreditation com. Taft Acad., Stoneleigh-Burnham Acad., Deerfield Acad., Baylor Acad., Westminster Schs., coun. acad. affairs The Coll. Bd., 1978-81, steering com. 1996 Nat. Assessment Ednl. Progress Arts Edn. Consensus Project. Author: Images of Survival, 1973. Chmn. bldg. com. Bancroft Sch., Andover, 1965-70, Greater Lawrence (Mass.) Habitat for Humanity, 1991-95; mem. Andover Hist. Commn., 1982-85. Klingenstein fellow Columbia U., N.Y.C., 1981-82. Avocations: singing, writing, land conservation. Home: 49 Highland Rd Andover MA 01810-4147

LLOYD, SUSAN ELAINE, middle school educator; b. Sioux Falls, S.D., Aug. 25, 1942; d. Travis Monroe and Lois Elaine (Herridge) Hetherington; m. Jerry Glynn Lloyd, Mar. 13, 1982; children: Joseph Sanders Rogers III, Melissa Elaine Rogers. BS in Edn., SW Tex. State U., 1965; MA, U. Tex., San Antonio, 1979; AA, Stephens Coll., 1962. Cert. reading specialist, supervisory, art (all levels), secondary English, elem. edn. Art tchr. South Park Ind. Sch. Dist., Beaumont, Tex., 1965-68; reading specialist John Jay High Sch., San Antonio, 1979-84; reading dept. coord. Sul Ross Mid. Sch., Northside Ind. Sch. Dist., San Antonio, 1984—, remedial reading tchr., 1990; developer reading curricula, cons.; advisor Scholastic TAB Book Club, 1992-94. Author: Reading Education in Texas, 1992, 93. Named Sul Ross Middle Sch. Tchr. of Yr., 1993, Trinity U. Disting. Educator, 1993. Mem. ASCD, Internat. Reading Assn. (hon. chmn. 14th ann. SW regional meeting, presenter 19th 1991, 20th 1992), Tex. Reading Coun., Alamo Reading Assn., Assn. Tex. Profl. Educators, San Antonio Watercolor Group. Home: 7614 Tippit Trl San Antonio TX 78240-3627 Office: Sul Ross Mid Sch 3630 Callaghan Rd San Antonio TX 78228-4323

LLOYD, TIMOTHY L., art educator; b. Canton, Ohio, May 31, 1937; s. Donald J. and Wilma A. (Little) L.; m. Susan J. Lloyd, Dec. 19, 1959; children: Timothy Jr., Stephen. BFA, Kent State U., 1960, postgrad, 1960; MFA, Rochester Inst. Tech., 1964. Prof. art Carleton Coll., Northfield, Minn., 1964—; instr. Haystack Mountain Sch. Crafts, Deer Isle, Maine, 1964; vis. artist Duncan of Jordanstone Coll. Art, Dundee, Scotland, 1978-79. One-man shows include Stubhahn Gallery, Salzburg, Austria, 1971, Duncan of Jordanstone Coll., Dundee, Scotland, 1979, Clark Gallery, Lincoln, Mass., 1987, Raymond Ave. Gallery, St. Paul, 1988, 91, others; exhibited in group shows at Canton (Ohio) Art Inst., 1959, Akron (Ohio) Art Inst., 1960, Wichita Art Assn., Kans., 1960, 85, Amerika Hause, Heidelberg, Germany, 1961, Mus. Contemporary Crafts, N.Y.C., 1962, Am. Fedn. Arts. Traveling Exhibit: Young Americans, 1962-63, Everhart Mus., Scranton, Pa., 1967, Brooks Art Gallery, Memphis, Tenn., 1967, Cedar Rapids (Iowa) Art Ctr., 1970, First Nat. Bank, Mpls., 1973, Minn. Mus. Art, St. Paul, 1974, Rochester Art Ctr. Gallery, 1977, U. Wis., River Falls Gallery, 1978, Zaner Gallery, Rochester, N.Y., 1982, Aaron Faber Gallery, 1985, Downey (Calif.) Nus. Art, 1985, Helen Drutt Gallery, Phila., 1985, Smithsonian Inst., Washington, 1986, Esther Saks Gallery, Navy Pier, Chgo., 1986, 87, Javier Puig Decorative Arts, Mpls., 1991, others; represented in permenent collectins including Smithsonian Inst. Nat. Air and Space Mus., Washington, Duncan of Jordanstone Coll. Art, Dundee, CRM Russell Mus., Great Falls, Mont., St. John's Abbey, Collegeville, Minn., Northwestern Nat. Life Inst., Mpls., Maud Hill Family Found., St. Paul, Minn., Carleton Coll., Northfield, Minn.; prin. works include Carleton Centennial Medal, 1966, communion vessels Nidaros Luth. Ch., Ashland Wis., 1966, communion vessels St. Andrew's Luth. Ch., Ames Iowa, 1966, communion vessels, processional cross, 1973, Minn. State Art Ctr. award sculpture, 1969, 73, Pres.'s Medal, St. John's Coll., 1972, gift from city of Northfield to Sidney Rand, Amb. to Norway, 1980, raised sterling vessel, Trustee award, Carleton Coll., 1980, Presdl. medal, 1987, William Carleton medal, 1992. Mem. Soc. N.Am. Goldsmiths, Am. Crafts Coun., Minn. Crafts Coun. (exec. bd. 1986-89, 93-95). Avocations: fly fishing, kayaking, canoeing. Office: Carleton College One N College St Northfield MN 55057-4002

LLOYD, WALT, cinematographer. Cinematographer: (films) Dangerously Close, 1986, Down Twisted, 1987, The Wash, 1988, Sex, Lies, and Videotape, 1989, To Sleep with Anger, 1990, Pump Up the Volume, 1990, Kafka, 1992, Short Cuts, 1992, There Goes the Neighborhood, 1992, Amos & Andrew, 1993, (TV movies) Out On the Edge, 1989, Extreme Close-up, 1990. *

LLOYD, WANDA SMALLS, newspaper editor; b. Columbus, Ohio, July 12, 1949; d. Gloria Walker; m. Willie Burk Lloyd, May 25, 1975; 1 child, Shelby Renee. BA, Spelman Coll., Atlanta, 1971. Copy editor Providence Evening Bull., R.I., 1971-73, Miami Herald, Fla., 1973-74, Atlanta Jour., Ga., 1974-75, Washington Post, 1975-76; instr. program for minority journalists Columbia U., N.Y.C., summer 1972; dep. Washington editor Times-Post News Service, 1976-86; dpt. mng. editor cover stories, USA Today, 1986-87, mng. editor/adminstrn., 1987-88, sr. editor, 1988-96; mng. editor The Greenville News, 1996—; cons. So. Regional Press Inst., Savannah State Coll., Ga., 1973-94; mem. adv. bd. urban journalism workshop Howard U., Washington, 1983-96. Mem., bd. dirs. Nation's Capital council, Girl Scouts U.S., Washington 1985; trustee Spelman Coll., 1988—; mem. adv. com. Alfred Friendly Found., 1992-96; bd. dirs. Dow Jones Newspaper Fund, 1992—. Mem. Washington Assn. Black Journalists, Nat. Assn. Black Journalists, Washington Spelman Alumnae Assn. (v.p. 1984-86; Named Alumna of Yr. 1985), Am. Soc. of Newspaper Editors (bd. dirs. 1997—), Delta Sigma Theta. Baptist. Office: The Greenville News PO Box 1688 Greenville SC 29602

LLOYD, WILLIAM F., lawyer; b. Youngstown, Ohio, Dec. 27, 1947. AB magna cum laude, Brown U., 1969; JD cum laude, U. Chgo., 1975. Bar: Ill. 1975, U.S. Supreme Ct. 1980. Ptnr. Sidley & Austin, Chgo. Mem. ABA (mem. litigation and bus. sects.), Chgo. Bar Assn., Legal Club Chgo. Office: Sidley & Austin 1 First Natl Plz Chicago IL 60603-2003

LLOYD-JONES, DONALD J., transportation executive; b. N.Y.C., May 25, 1931; s. Silas and Esther (McDonald) L.-J.; m. Beverly Louise Miller, June 12, 1954; children: Anne, Lisa, Susan, Donald. BA, Swarthmore Coll., 1952; MBA, Columbia U., 1954, PhD, 1961. Sr. analyst Am. Airlines, N.Y.C., 1957-63, asst. v.p., 1963-66, v.p., 1966-69, chief fin. officer, 1969-72, chief oper. officer, 1972-82; pres. Air Fla., Miami, 1982-84; cons. Western Airlines, L.A., 1984-85, pres., 1985-87; pres. Am. Express Bank-Aviation Svcs., N.Y.C., 1987-95, Am. Geog. Soc., 1996—; dir. SL Industries, Mt. Laurel, N.J., 1972-93. Bd. dirs. Aeronautics and Space Engring. Bd., Washington, 1985, Swarthmore (Pa.) Coll., 1972-84; councilor Am. Geog. Soc., 1992—. Republican. Episcopalian.

LLOYD WEBBER, BARON ANDREW, composer; b. London, Mar. 22, 1948; s. of late William Southcombe and Jean Hermione (Johnstone) Lloyd W.; m. Sarah Jane Tudor Hugill, July 24, 1971 (div. 1983); children: Imogen, Nicholas; m. Sarah Brightman, Mar. 1984 (div. 1990); m. Madeleine Astrid Gurdon, Feb. 1, 1991; children: Alastair Adam, William Richard, Isabella Aurora. Ed., Westminster Sch., Magdalen Coll., Oxford U., Royal Coll. Music. Composer: (with lyrics by Timothy Rice) Joseph and The Amazing Technicolor Dreamcoat, 1968, rev., 73, 81 (Best Score Tony award nominee 1982), 91, Jesus Christ Superstar, 1970 (Drama Desk award 1971, Best Original Score Tony award nominee 1972), (with lyrics by Alan Ayckbourn) Jeeves, 1975, (with lyrics by Timothy Rice) Evita, 1978 (Best Score Tony award 1980, Drama Desk award 1980), (with lyrics by Don Black) Tell Me On A Sunday, 1980, Cats, 1981 (Best Musical and Best ScoreTony awards 1983, Drama Desk award 1983), (with lyrics by Richard Stilgoe) Starlight Express, 1984, (with lyrics by Don Black) Song and Dance, 1985 (Best Score Tony award nominee 1986), (with lyrics by Richard Stilgoe and Charles Hart) The Phantom of the Opera, 1986 (Ivor Novello award 1987, Drama Desk award 1988, Best Score Tony award nominee 1988), (with lyrics by Don Black and Charles Hart) Aspects of Love, 1989, (with lyrics by Don Black and book by Christopher Hampton) Sunset Boulevard, 1993 (Tony award for best score, best musical, 1995); prodr.: Cats, 1981, Daisy Pulls It Off, 1983, The Hired Man, 1984, Starlight Express, 1984, On Your Toes, 1984, Shirley Valentine, 1986, Lend Me A Tenor, 1986, The Resistible Rise of Arturo Vi, 1987, Aspects of Love, 1989, Joseph and the Amazing Technicolor Dreamcoat, 1991, Sunset Boulevard, 1993; co-producer: Jeeves Takes Charge, 1975, Cats, 1981, Song and Dance, 1982, The Phantom of the Opera, 1986, GIE Puccini, 1986, La Bete, 1991; composer film scores: Gumshoe, 1971, The Odessa File, 1974; composer: Variations (based on A Minor Caprice #24 by Paganini), 1977, symphonic version, 1986, Requiem Mass, 1985. Decorated knight Order Brit. Empire; recipient Grammy awards, 1980, 83, 85, Triple Play award ASCAP, 1988, award City and Music Ctr. of L.A., 1991, Praemium Imperiale award for music, 1995, Richard Rodgers award for Contbn. to Musical Theatre, 1996, Bernard Delfont award for Contbn. to Show Bus., 1997; named a Living Legend Grammy, 1989; named to Queen's Birthday List, 1992; named in New Yrs. Honours list as a Life Peer, 1997. Fellow Royal Coll. Music. Avocations: architecture, art. Office: 22 Tower St, London WC2H 9NS, England

LLUBIÉN, JOSEPH HERMAN, psychotherapist, counselor; b. San Juan, PR, July 14, 1943; s. Herman LLubién-Torres and Guilliermina Diaz Asad-LLubién; children: Sanjay Alexander, Jiang Carlos, Jose Lorenzo, Jill Ann Jo Garcia; m. Patricia Deveda, 1995; 1 child, Michael D.; 1 adopted child, Darius Johann. BA in Psychology and English, Fordham U., 1973; MA in Lit. and Creative Writing, CUNY, 1981; PhD, Sch. for Social Rsch., 1984; PhD in Psychology and Human Svcs., Walden U. Inst. for Advanced Studies, Mpls., 1995. Adj. prof. English and poetry Coll. Human Scis., Fordham U. Alumni Fedn., N.Y.C., 1969-70; nat. adminstr., dir. counseling Employment Tng. Adminstrn. U.S. Labor Dept., Washington, 1970-82, nat. dir. counseling and tng. Community Employment Tng. Adminstrn./Employment Tng. Adminstrn., 1971-82; adj. prof. English and poetry Coll. Human Svcs., Washington, 1979-80; adjunct prof. English and Composition Malcolm King Coll., N.Y.C., 1984; substance abuse treatment counselor, psychotherapist Alcohol Drug Addiction Svcs. Adminstrn. D.C. Gen. Hosp., Washington, 1989-90; psychotherapist, crisis counselor, bilingual guidance counselor, clin. mental health specialist JMC Assocs., Inc., Washington, 1990-91; bilingual guidance counselor D.C. Pub. Schs. Bancroft Elem. Sch., Washington, 1991-93; clin. mental health specialist, bilingual Dept. Human Svcs., Commn. on Mental Health, Washington, 1993; psychol. treatment counselor II Nat. Capital Systems, Inc. Methadone Therapy Treatment Ctr., Washington, 1993-95; behav. therapist, activity coord. P.S.I. Assocs., Inc., 1995—; clin. counselor Vesta Found., Inc., 1995—; social worker D.C. Pub. Schs., 1995—; curriculum co-writer (with others) Substance Abuse Prevention Curriculum for pre-kindergarten and primary grades; helped develop a bilingual activity workbook for elem. schs. with U.S. Dept. Justice and Nat. Crime Prevention Coun., 1992; mem. youth coun. U.S. State Dept. Fgn. Desk. Author: (poetry) From the Belly of the Shark, 1978, For Neruda La Luz Que Llega, 1979, Black Yellow Red Indian Songs, 1993, Black Streams, 1993. Vol. counselor Apache reservation in southern Tex., 1986-87, Northern Cheyenne reservation, Lamedeer, Mont.; vol. trainer for guidance counselors Howard U. in substance abuse prevention, 1988-92. With USAF, 1961-67, Vietnam, USAR, 1982—. Doctoral fellow Walden U. Inst. Advanced Studies. Mem. NAACP, ACA, Assn. of Sch. Counselors, La Raza Unida, U.S. Karate Assn., Am. Karate Assn., U.S. Tai Chi Assn., Japan-USA Akeido Fedn., Internat. Kung Fu Assn., All Japan Am. Akeido Fedn., Tai Chi Chinese Fedn., Tae Quan Do Am. Karate Fedn., Kung Fu Am. Fedn. Home: Apt C-401 4660 Martin L King Ave SW Washington DC 20032

LO, ARTHUR WU-NIEN, electrical engineering educator; b. Shanghai, China, May 21, 1916; came to U.S., 1945, naturalized, 1957; s. Liang-Kan and Shou-Pan (Heng) L.; m. Elizabeth H. Shen, Aug. 24, 1950; children: Katherine E., James A. B.S., Yenching U., 1938; M.A., Oberlin Coll., 1946; Ph.D., U. Ill., 1949. Mem. tech. staff RCA Research Labs., 1951-60; mgr. advanced devel., data systems div. IBM Corp., 1960-62, mgr. exploratory devel., components div., 1962-64; prof. elec. engring. Princeton U., 1964-86, prof. emeritus, 1986—; Cons. in field, 1964—, spl. research digital electronics and computer systems. Author: Transistor Electronics, 1955, Introduction to Digital Electronics, 1967; also papers in field. Fellow IEEE; mem. Sigma Xi, Eta Kappa Nu, Pi Mu Epsilon. Patentee in field. Home: 102 Maclean Cir Princeton NJ 08540-5623

LO, KWOK-YUNG, astronomer; b. Nanking, Jiangsu, China, Oct. 19, 1947; came to U.S., 1965; s. Pao-Chi and Ju-Hwa (Hsu) Lu; m. Helen Bo Kwan Chen Lo, Jan. 1, 1973; children: Jan Hsin, Derek. BS in Physics, MIT, 1969, PhD in Physics, 1974. Rsch. fellow Calif. Inst. Tech., Pasadena, 1974-76, sr. rsch. fellow, 1978-80, asst. prof., 1980-86; prof. U. Ill., Urbana, 1986—, assoc. Ctr. for Advanced Study, 1991-92, chmn. astronomy dept., 1995-97; dir., disting. fellow Inst. Astronomy and Astrophysics, Academia Sinica, Taipei, Taiwan, 1997—, disting. rsch. fellow, 1997—; chmn. vis. com. to Haystack Obs., Westford, Mass., 1991-92; mem. adv. panel Academic Sinica Inst. Astronomy and Astrophysics, Taipei, Taiwan, 1993—; mem. AUI vis. com. for Nat. Radio Astrophysics Obs., 1993-97. Recipient Alexander von Humboldt award, 1995; grantee NSF, 1977-96; Miller fellow U. Calif., Berkeley, 1976-78, James Clerk Maxwell telescope fellow U. Hawaii, 1991. Mem. Am. Astron. Soc., Internat. Astron. Union. Achievements include identification of accretion of ionized gas in center of Galaxy, size measurement of compact radio source at Galactic Center, first suggestion of circumnuclear H2O masers in active galaxies, and conditions of star formation in galaxies. Office: U Ill Astronomy Dept 1002 W Green St Urbana IL 61801-3074

LO, SHUI-YIN, physicist; b. Canton, Oct. 20, 1941; came to the U.S., 1959; s. Long tin and Ty-Fong (Chow) L.; m. Angela Kwok-Kie Lau, Dec. 18, 1969; children: Alpha Wei-min, Fiona Ai-ming, Hao-min. BS, U. Ill., 1962; PhD, U. Chgo., 1966. Rsch. assoc. Rutherford High Energy Lab., Chilton, United Kingdom, 1966-69, Glasgow (United Kingdom) U., 1969-72; sr. lectr. U. Melbourne, Australia, 1972-89; pres. Inst. for Boson Studies, Pasadena, Calif., 1986-92; dir. Sinotronic Co., Hong Kong, 1980—; exec. v.p., dir. rsch. Am. Environ. Tech. Group, Monrovia, Calif., 1993—; vis. assoc. Calif. Inst. Tech.; prof. physics Zhong Shan U. Author: Scientific Studies of Chinese Character, 1986; author, editor: Geometrical Picture of Hadron Scattering, 1986; contbr. over 100 articles to profl. jours. Prin. Chinese Sch. of Chinese Fellowship Victoria, Australia, 1977-84. Fellow Australian Inst. Physics; mem. Am. Phys. Soc. Achievements include patents for Chinese computer and BASER, and creator of IE crystals.

LOACH, PAUL ALLEN, biochemist, biophysicist, educator; b. Findlay, Ohio, July 18, 1934; s. Leland Oris and Dorothy Elizabeth (Davis) L.; m. Patricia A. Johnson, Dec. 27, 1957; children: Mark, Eric, Jennifer; m. Pamela Sue Parkes, Apr. 19, 1986; children: Matthew, Sarah, Andrew. B.S., U. Akron, 1957; Ph.D. (NIH fellow), Yale, 1961. Research assoc. Nat. Acad. Scis.-NRC; postdoctoral fellow U. Calif. at Berkeley, 1961-63; asst. prof. chemistry Northwestern U., 1963-68, assoc. prof., 1968-73, prof., 1973-74, prof. biochemistry and molecular biology, and chemistry, 1974—; mem. BBCA study sect. NIH, 1978-82. Assoc. editor: Photochemistry and Photobiology, 1973-80, Biophysics of Structure and Mechanism, 1973-82; Contbr. articles, revs. to profl. jours. Recipient C.P. award U. Akron, 1957, Research Career Devel. award USPHS, 1971-76. Mem. Am. Soc. Biol. Chemists, AAAS, Biophys. Soc., Am. Soc. Photobiology (pres. 1985-86).

LOACH, ROBERT EDWARD, federal agency administrator; b. Worcester, Mass., Aug. 18, 1946; s. Charles Henry and Elizabeth Josephine (Feeney) L.; m. Mary Regina Burke, May 10, 1969; children: Christopher, Matthew, Bethany. BS, Worcester State Coll., 1968; MS, SUNY, 1969; MA, Webster U., 1976. Cert. tchr., Mass. Commd. 2d lt. USAF, 1969, advanced through grades to capt., 1979; missile systems analyst USAF, Tucson, Ariz., 1970-72; comdr. deputy missile combat crew USAF, Jacksonville, Ark., 1972-74, comdr. evaluation missile combat crew, 1974-78; air staff tng. officer USAF, Washington, 1978-79; program analyst U.S. Nuclear Regulatory Commn., Bethesda, Md., 1979-80, sr. program analyst, 1980-86, chief programs analysis br., 1986-88, mgr. human resources info. systems, 1988—; dir. divsn. resource mgmt. and adminstrn. U.S. Nuclear Regulatory Commn., King of Prussia, Pa., 1988; cons. Quest Rsch., Falls Church, Va., 1979-80. Coach soccer Springfield (Va.) Youth Club, 1983-93; coach basketball Cath. Youth Orgn., Springfield, 1988-90; active PTO, Springfield, 1985—. Col. USAFR. Recipient commendation medal USAF, meritorious svc. medal (3 oak leaf clusters). Mem. ASTD, Internat. Pers. Mgmt. Assn., Reserve Officers' Assn., Disabled Am. Vets., Federal Exec. Inst. Alumni Assn., Am. Legion, U.S. Youth Soccer Coaches Assn. Republican. Avocations: reading, coaching. Office: US Nuclear Regulatory Commn Washington DC 20555

LOADER, JAY GORDON, retired utility company executive; b. Plainfield, N.J., Aug. 3, 1923; s. Carl and Madalyn (Wright) L.; m. Joan Merrell, Aug. 19, 1965; children: Patricia Kay, Michael Jay, Sandra Lee, Gigi Ann. B.S., U. Ala., 1951. C.P.A., Ga. Auditor Arthur Andersen & Co., Atlanta, 1951-55; with Fla. Power Corp., St. Petersburg, Fla., 1955-82; asst. sec., asst. treas. Fla. Power Corp., 1960-67, sec.-treas., 1967-82, v.p., 1980-89; v.p., sec. Fla. Progress Corp., St. Petersburg, 1983-89; ret., 1989. Served with AUS, 1943-44. Mem. Soc. CPAs, Am. Soc. Corporate Secs., Fin. Analysts Soc. Central Fla., U. Ala. Alumni Assn., Phi Eta Sigma, Beta Gamma Sigma, Beta Alpha Psi. Clubs: St. Petersburg Yacht; Treasure Island Tennis and Yacht. Home: 13325 108th Ave Largo FL 33774-4649

LOADHOLT, MILES, lawyer; b. Columbia, S.C., Jan. 28, 1943. BS, U. S.C., 1965, JD cum laude, 1968. Bar: S.C. 1968. Ptnr. Ness, Motley, Loadholt, Richardson & Poole P.A., Barnwell, S.C. Mem. ABA, Barnwell County Bar Assn., S.C. Bar Assn., S.C. Trial Lawyers Assn., The Assn. of Trial Lawyers of Am., Phi Delta Phi, Order of the Wig & Robe. Address: Ness Motley Loadholt Richardson & Poole PA PO Box 365 2202 Jackson St Barnwell SC 29812-1579

LOARIE, THOMAS MERRITT, healthcare executive; b. Deerfield, Ill., June 12, 1946; s. Willard John and Lucile Veronica (Finnegan) L.; m. Stephanie Lane Fitts, Aug. 11, 1968 (div. Nov. 1987); children: Thomas M., Kristin Leigh Soule. BSME, U. Notre Dame, 1968; Student, U. Minn., 1969-70, U. Chgo., 1970-71, Columbia U., 1978. Registered profl. engr., Calif. Prodn. engr. Honeywell, Inc., Evanston, Ill., 1968-70; various positions Am. Hosp. Supply Co., Evanston, Ill., 1970-83, pres. Heyer-Schulte divsn., 1979-83; pres. COO Novacor Med. Corp., Oakland, Calif., 1984-85, also bd. dirs.; pres. ABA Bio Mgmt., Danville, Calif., 1985-87; chmn., CEO Keravision, Inc., Fremont, Calif., 1987—; founder, chmn., med. device CEO Roundtable, 1993—; asst. prof. surgery Creighton U. Med. Sch., Omaha, 1986-94; speaker in field. Contbr. articles on med. tech. and pub. policy to Wall St. Jour., others. Bd. dirs. Marymount Sch. Bd., 1981-84; bd. dirs. United Way Santa Barbara, 1981-84, assoc. chairperson, 1982-83, treas., 1983. Named One of 50 Rising Stars: Exec. Leaders for the 80's Industry Week mag., 1983. Mem. Assn. for Rsch. in Vision and Ophthalmology, Contact Lens Assn. Ophthalmology, Health Industry Mfrs. Assn. (spl. rep. bd. dirs. 1993-96, bd. dirs. 1997—), Am. Entrepreneurs for Econ. Growth. Roman Catholic. Avocations: competitive running, snow skiing, backpacking, oil painting, the arts. Office: KeraVision Inc 48630 Milmont Dr Fremont CA 94538-7353

LOBANOV-ROSTOVSKY, OLEG, arts association executive; b. San Francisco, July 12, 1934; s. Andrei and Grace S. (Pope) L-R.; m. Susan Waters, Sept. 8, 1979; 1 child, Alexandra; children by previous marriage: Christopher, Nicholas. BA, U. Mich., 1956. Community concert rep. Columbia Artists Mgmt. Inc., 1958-59; mgr. Columbus (Ohio) Symphony Orch., 1959-62, Hartford (Conn.) Symphony Orch., 1962-65, Balt. Symphony, 1965-69; program officer div. humanities and arts Ford Found., 1969-75; exec. dir. Denver Symphony Orch., 1975-76; mng. dir. Nat. Symphony Orch., Washington, 1977-80; cons. Fed. Coun. on Arts, 1980-81; exec. dir. Del. Ctr. for Performing Arts, 1981-82; exec. v.p., mng. dir. Detroit Symphony Orch., 1982-83, pres., 1983-89; ind. cons., 1989-90; mng. ptnr. Middle Am. div. Jerold Panas, Young & Ptnrs. Inc., Chgo., 1990-91; pres. Calif. Ctr. for the Arts, Escondio, Calif., 1991—.

LOBB, WILLIAM ATKINSON, financial services executive; b. Arlington, Pa., Apr. 21, 1951; s. Anthony William and Annamarie (Hilpert) L.; m. Maureen Veronique O'Hagan, July 7, 1977; children: William Atkinson III, Anthony Hagan. BS, Georgetown U., 1977. Account exec. Johnston Lemon, Washington, 1977-78; sr. account exec. Merrill Lynch, Alexandria, Va., 1979-83; asst. v.p. E.F. Hutton, Washington, 1983-85; mng. dir., ptnr.-in-charge Oppenheimer and Co., Inc., Atlanta, 1985—. Bd. trustees The Howard Sch.; bd. dirs. Atlanta Charity Clays. Mem. Ga. Rep. Found., Nat. Assn. Securities Dealers (bd. arbitrators), Nat. Securities Traders Assn., Ga. Securities Assn., Am. Arbitration Assn., Univ. Club, Army-Navy Club, Setindown Creek Club, Burge Plantation Hunt Club, Piedmont Driving Club. Avocation: squash. Office: Oppenheimer & Co Inc 1200 Monach Plz 3414 Peachtree Rd NE Atlanta GA 30326-1113

LOBBIA, JOHN E., utility company executive; b. 1941; married. BSEE, U. Detroit, 1964. With Detroit Edison Co., 1964—, asst. primary svc. engr. sales dept., 1964-68, acting asst. dist. mgr., dir. svc. planning, 1969-72, project mgr. constrn., 1972-74, dir. generation constrn. dept., 1974-75, mgr. Ann Arbor div., 1975-76, asst. mgr. Detroit div., 1976-78, mgr. Oakland div., 1978-80, asst. vice chmn., 1980-81, asst. v.p., mgr. fuel support, 1981-82, v.p. fin. svcs., 1982-87, exec. v.p., 1987-88, pres., chief operating officer, 1988—, also chmn., chief exec. officer, 1990—, also bd. dirs.; bd. dirs. Nat. Bank of Detroit, NBD Bancorp, Inc. Office: Detroit Edison Co 2000 2nd Ave Detroit MI 48226-1203*

LOBDELL, FRANK, artist; b. Kansas City, Mo., 1921; m. Ann Morency, 1952; children: Frank Saxton, Judson Earle. Studied, St. Paul Sch. Art, 1938-39, Calif. Sch. Fine Arts, 1947-50, Academie de la Grande Chaumiere, Paris, France, 1950-51. Tchr. Calif. Sch. Fine Arts, 1957-65; prof. art, Stanford, 1965—. One man shows, Lucien Labaudt Gallery, 1949, Martha Jackson Gallery, 1958, 60, 63, 72, 74, de Young Meml. Mus., San Francisco, 1959, Ferus Gallery, 1962, Pasadena Art Mus., 1961, San Francisco Mus. Art, 1969, Benador Gallerie, Geneva, Switzerland, 1964, Gallerie Anderson-Mayer, Paris, 1965, Smith-Anderson Gallery, San Francisco, 1982, Oscarsson Hood Gallery, N.Y.C., 1983, 84, 85, John Berggruen Gallery, San Francisco, 1987, Campbell-Thiebaud Gallery, San Francisco, 1988, 90, 92, 95, Stanford Mus. Art, 1988, retrospective show, Pasadena Art Mus. and Stanford Mus., 1966, San Francisco Mus. Modern Art, 1983, Stanford Mus., 1993; exhibited group Shows, Salon du Mai, Paris, 1950, III Sao Paulo Biennial, 1955, Whitney Mus. Am. Art, 1962-63, 72, Guggenheim Mus., N.Y.C., 1964, Van Abbemuseum, Eindhoven, Holland, 1970, Corcoran Gallery Art, Washington, 1971, U. Ill., 1974; represented in permanent collections, San Francisco Mus. Art, Oakland Mus. Art, L.A. County Mus., Nat. Gallery Washington, others. Served with AUS, 1942-46. Recipient Nealie Sullivan award San Francisco Art Inst., 1960, award of merit AAAL, 1988. Home: 2754 Octavia St San Francisco CA 94123-4304

LOBDELL, ROBERT CHARLES, retired newspaper executive; b. Mankato, Minn., Jan. 1, 1926; s. Darwin Norman and Hilda Cecelia (Peterson) L.; m. Nancy Marion Lower, July 12, 1952; children: Teresa M., Robert John, William Scott, James Marston. A.B., Stanford U., 1948, LL.B., 1950. Bar: Calif. 1951, U.S. Supreme Ct 1964. Atty. legal dept. Bank of Am., Los Angeles, 1951-52; atty., corp. officer Youngstown Sheet and Tube Co., 1952-65; asst. gen. counsel, asst. sec. Times Mirror Co., 1965-70, v.p., asst. sec., 1970-86; v.p., gen. counsel Los Angeles Times, 1970-86; bd. dirs. Embarcadero Pub. Co.; former sec., trustee Pfaffinger Found., Los Angeles Times Fund. Trustee, former pres. Long Beach Mus. of Art Found. Mem. Beta Theta Pi. Home: 925 Hillside Dr Long Beach CA 90815-4720

LOBECK, CHARLES CHAMPLIN, JR., pediatrics educator; b. New Rochelle, N.Y., May 20, 1926; s. Charles Champlin and Jeanne (Weiss) L.; m. Isabelle Anne Emerson, Feb. 6, 1954; children: Charles III, Anne, Sarah, Jane. AB, Hobart Coll., 1948; MD, U. Rochester, 1952. Diplomate Am. Bd. Pediatrics. Instr. U. Rochester, N.Y., 1955-58; asst. prof. U. Wis.,

Madison, 1958-62, assoc. prof., 1962-66, chmn. dept. pediatrics, 1964-74, prof., 1966-75; dir. clin. affairs Univ. Hosp., Madison, 1974-75; dean U. Mo. Sch. Medicine, Columbia, 1975-83; assoc. dean U. Wis. Med. Sch., Madison, 1984-91, prof. emeritus, 1991—; mem. study sect. NIH, Bethesda, Md., 1968-72. Author: (with others) Metabolic Basis of Inherited Disease, 2d edit., 1965, 3d edit., 1972. V.P. Cystic Fibrosis Found., Rockville, Md., 1982-83. Sgt. USAAF, 1944-46, ETO. Recipient Rsch. Career Devel. award, NIH, 1962. Fellow Am. Acad. Pediatrics; mem. Soc. for Pediatric Rsch., Am. Pediatric Soc., Am. Coll. Physician Execs., Rotary, Am. Assn. Accreditation Lab Animal Care (chmn. bd. 1984-89, Bennet J. Cohen award 1990). Democrat. Avocations: fly-fishing, biking. Home: 3420 Valley Creek Cir Middleton WI 53562-1990 Office: Programs Health Mgmt 1300 University Ave Madison WI 53706-1510

LOBECK, WILLIAM E., rental company executive; b. 1940. BBA, Old Dominion U., 1963. With Little Creek Leasing Corp., Norfolk, Va., 1963-69; pres. Am. Internat. Rent-A-Car, Inc., Dallas, 1969-81; pres., chmn. bd. Thrifty Rent-A-Car System, Inc., Tulsa, 1981-93, Pentastar Transp. Group, Inc., Tulsa, 1981-93; pres., CEO Nat. Car Rental, Mpls., 1995—. Office: National Car Rental 7700 France Ave S Minneapolis MN 55435-5228

LO BELLO, JOSEPH DAVID, bank executive; b. Northampton, Mass., Feb. 5, 1940; s. Joseph Vincenzo and Marie (Mandella) Lo B.; m. Karen Suzanne Martin, June 21, 1969; children: Mark, Kara, Kimberly. BS, Babson Coll., 1961; MBA, U. Mass., 1963; postgrad., Harvard Bus. Sch., 1987. Loan officer Third Nat. Bank Hampden County, Springfield, Mass., 1963-65, v.p., 1965-75, sr. v.p., 1975-81; exec. v.p. Bank of New Eng. West, N.A., Springfield, 1981-90; regional pres. Bank of New Eng. N.A., Springfield, 1990-92; pres., chief exec. officer Peoples Savs. Bank, Holyoke, Mass., 1992—. Dir. Mass. Indsl. Fin. Agy., Boston, 1987; treas., trustee Basketball Hall of Fame, Springfield, 1985; trustee Springfield Coll., 1984, Baystate Med. Ctr., Springfield, 1983. Mem. Rotary Club, Robert Morris Assn. Avocations: golf, hiking, theatre, travel. Home: 152 Meadowbrook Rd Longmeadow MA 01106-1341

LO BELLO, NINO, author, journalist; b. Bklyn., Sept. 8, 1921; s. Joseph and Rosalie (Moscarelli) Lo B.; m. Irene Helen Rooney, Feb. 22, 1948; children: Susan, Thomas. BA, Queens Coll., 1947; MA, NYU, 1948. Reporter and columnist Ridgewood (N.Y.) Times, 1946-50; instr. sociology U. Kans., 1950-55; Rome corr. Bus. Week mag., 1959-62, N.Y. Jour. Commerce, 1962-64; European editor corr. Opera Is My Hobby Syndicated Radio Show, 1960—; bus. news writer N.Y. Herald Tribune, 1964-66; Vienna corr. 103 U.S. and Can. dailies, 1966—; vis. prof. sociology Denison U., Ohio, spring 1956; vis. prof. journalism U. Alaska, summer 1974; writer in Italy, Austria, Switzerland, France, Germany, Eng. Author: The Vatican Empire (N.Y. Times Best Seller List), 1968, The Vatican's Wealth, 1971, Vatican, U.S.A., 1972, European Detours, 1981, The Vatican Papers, 1982, Guide to Offbeat Europe, 1985, English Well Speeched Here, 1986, Guide to the Vatican, 1987, Der Vatikan, 1988, Vatikan im Zwielicht, 1990, The Danube: Here And There, 1992, Travel Trivia Handbook of Oddball European Sights, 1992, A Catholic's Encyclopedia of Vatican Trivia and Papal Oddities, 1997; contbr. articles to mags. and jours.; editor The New Gazette, Vienna, 1980-81; columnist "From Here to Nostalgia" Times Newsweekly, N.Y.C., 1994—. With USAAF, 1942-46. Recipient Goldener Rathausmann award for Outstanding Fgn. Reporting, Vienna, 1974, Silver decoration (Austria), 1988, Gold plaque Austrian Nat. Tourist Office, 1988; named Alumnus of Yr., Grover Cleveland High Sch., Queens, N.Y., 1977. Mem. Overseas Press Club Am., Am. Soc. Journalists and Authors, Fgn. Press Club Vienna (bd. dirs.). Home: 5706 N 10th Rd Apt 7 Arlington VA 22205-2362 Office: 8 Bankgasse, Vienna 1010, Austria *Work hard, play hard!.*

LOBENHERZ, RICHARD ERNEST, real estate developer; b. Washington, Mar. 29, 1953; s. Ernest P. and Emma J. (Krautheim) L.; m. Kathryne A. Shepard, Feb. 15, 1991; children: Alexandra C., Austen J. BBA, U. Mich., 1975. CCIM, Nat. Assn. Realtors. Sales mgr. Ski & Shore Properties, Charlevoix, Mich., 1978-82, v.p., 1983-87; assoc. broker Vacation Properties Network, Charlevoix, 1988-90, pres., owner, 1991—; pres. Resort Reservations Inc., Gold Coast Properties Inc., Charlevoix, 1989—, Charlevoix Country Club, Inc., Charlevoix, 1987—; pres. Antrim Charlevoix Bd. Realtors, 1981. Trustee, bd. dirs. Little Traverse Conservancy, Harbor Springs, Mich., 1992—. Named Realtor of Yr. Antrim Charlevoix Bd. Realtors, 1981, Top-Producing Agt., 1983-95. Mem. Mich. Assn. Realtors (bd. dirs. 1981-86). Republican. Avocations: skiing, golf, diving. Office: Vacation Properties Network 203 Bridge St Charlevoix MI 49720-1403

LOBENHERZ, WILLIAM ERNEST, association executive, legislative counsel, lawyer; b. Muskegon, Mich., June 22, 1949; s. Ernest Pomeroy and Emajean (Krautheim) L.; m. Andrea Risdon L.; children: Jessica Anne, Rebecca Jean, Christopher William, Andrew William. BBA, U. Mich., 1971; JD cum laude, Wayne State U., 1974. Bar: Mich. 1974. Legal counsel Mich. Legis. Services Bur., Lansing, Mich., 1974-77; legal legis. cons. Mich. Assn. of Sch. Bds., Lansing, 1977, asst. exec. dir. for legal legis. affairs, 1977-79; asst. v.p. state and congl. relations Wayne State U., Detroit, 1979-81, assoc. v.p. state relations, 1981-82, v.p. govtl. affairs, 1982-87; assoc. Dykema Gossett, Lansing, Mich., 1987-89; pres., chief exec. officer Mich. Soft Drink Assn., 1989—; guest lectr. in govtl. affairs, Wayne State U., U. Mich., U. Detroit. Contbr. chpt. Mich. Handbook for School Business Officials, 1979, 2d ed. 1980, articles to profl. jours. and mags. Mem. govtl. affairs com. New Detroit Inc., 1984-87, chmn. state subcom. of govtl. affairs com., 1986-87; chmn. ind. schs. campaign Greater Metro Detroit United Fund Torch Dr., 1979, chmn. Colls. and Univs. campaign, 1980; bd. dirs. Mich. Epilepsy Ctr., 1991—; bd. dirs. Coun. for Mich. Pub. Univs. Recipient Book award Lawyer's Coop. Pub. Co., 1973, Outstanding Svc. award Mich. Assn. for Marriage and Family Therapy, 1992, 95; Silver scholar key Wayne State U. Law Sch., 1974. Mem. Mich. Bar Assn., NAACP, Coun. for Advancement and Support of Edn. (Mindpower citation 1982), Mich. Delta Found. (bd. dirs. 1977—, sec. 1981-84, v.p. 1987-88), Greater Metro Detroit C. of C. (contact interviewer bus. attraction and expansion coun. 1984-86), City Club. Home: 2601 Ricker Richland MI 49083 Office: Mich Soft Drink Assn 634 Michigan Nat Towers Lansing MI 48933

LOBIG, JANIE HOWELL, special education educator; b. Peoria, Ill., June 10, 1945; d. Thomas Edwin and Elizabeth Jane (Higdon) Howell; m. James Frederick Lobig, Aug. 16, 1970; 1 child, Jill Christina. BS in Elem. Edn., So. Ill. U., 1969; MA in Spl. Edn. Severely Handicapped, San Jose State U., 1989. Cert. elem. tchr., Calif., Mo., Ill., handicapped edn., Calif., Mo.; ordained to ministry Presbyn. Ch. as deacon, 1984. Tchr. trainable mentally retarded children Spl. Luth. Sch., St. Louis, 1967-68; tchr. trainable mentally retarded and severly handicapped children Spl. Sch. Dist. St. Louis, 1969-80, head tchr., 1980-83; tchr. severly handicapped children San Jose (calif.) Unifed Sch. Dist., 1983-86; tchr. autistic students Santa Clara County Office Edn., San Jose, 1986—; tchr. Suzanne Dancers, 1991-92. Vol. Am. Cancer Soc., San Jose, 1986-89, 92, St. Louis Reps., 1976-82, Am. Heart Assn., 1985—, Multiple Sclerosis Soc., 1990—; troop leader Camp Fire Girls, San Jose, 1984-85; moderator bd. deacons Evergreen Presbyn. Ch., 1986-89; mem. exec. bd. Norwood Creek Elem. Sch. PTA, 1983-86. Mem. Council for Exceptional Children, Assn. for Severly Handicapped, Nat. Edn. Assn., Calif. Tchrs. Assn. Independent. Avocations: golf, bowling, bridge, needlework. Home: 3131 Creekmore Way San Jose CA 95148-2037 Office: Weller Elem Sch 345 Boulder St Milpitas CA 95035-2869

LOBIONDO, FRANK A., congressman; m. Jan Dwyer; children: Adina, Amy. BA in Bus. Adminstrn., St. Joseph's U., 1968. Ops. mgr. LoBiondo Bros. Motor Express, Inc., Rosenhayn, N.J., 1968-94; mem. Cumberland County Bd. Chosen Freeholders, 1985-88; chmn. Gen. Assembly Econ. and Cmty. Devel., Ar. and Tourism Com., 1992-94; mem. First Legis. Dist. N.J. Gen. Assembly, 1988-94; mem. U.S. House Reps., 1995—. Bd. dirs. YMCA, 1975, 87089, trustee, 1981-84, 90-94, Senate dir., 1995—; pres. Cumberland County Guidance Ctr., 1982-84; founder Cumberland County Environ. Health Task Force, 1987; chmn. Cumberland County chpt. Am. Heart Assn., 1989-90; hon. chmn. ann. fund raising drive Cumberland County Hospice, 1992. Office: US House Reps 222 Cannon Ho Office Bldg Washington DC 20515-3301

LOBITZ, WALTER CHARLES, JR., physician, educator; b. Cin., Dec. 13, 1911; s. Walter Charles and Elsa (Spangenberg) L.; m. Caroline Elizabeth Rockwell, July 11, 1942; children: Walter Charles III, John Rockwell, Susan Hastings. Student, Brown U., 1930-31; B.Sc., U. Cin., 1939, M.B., 1940, M.D., 1941; M.Sc., U. Minn., 1945; M.A. (hon.), Dartmouth, 1958; LL.D., Hokkaido U., 1976. Diplomate Am. Bd. Dermatology (bd. dirs. 1955-64, pres. 1962). Intern Cin. Gen. Hosp., 1940, resident medicine, 1941; fellow Mayo Found., 1942-45; 1st asst. Mayo Clinic, 1945-47; chmn. sect. dermatology Hitchcock Clinic, Hanover, N.H., 1947-59; bd. dirs. Hitchcock Clinic, 1955; faculty Dartmouth Med. Sch., 1947-59, prof. dermatology, 1957-59; prof. dermatology, head div. U. Oreg. Med. Sch., 1959-69, chmn. dept., 1969-77; prof. Oreg. Health Scis. Univ., until 1980; emeritus prof. U. Oreg. Health Scis. Ctr., 1980—; area cons. VA, 1949-59; mem. commn. cutaneous diseases Armed Forces Epidemiologic Bd., 1965-75; cons., mem. gen. med. study sect. USPHS, 1961-65; mem. grant rev. com. United Health Found., 1964-65; cons. dermatology tng. grants com. NIAMD, 1966-70; cons. VA Hosp., U. Oreg. Med. Sch., 1959—; civilian cons. to surgeon gen. USAF, 1969-79; U.S. Air Force-Nat. cons. to Surgeon Gen., 1970-80; Dohi Meml. lectr. Japanese Dermatol. Assn., 1964; lectr. U. Copenhagen, Denmark, 1969, 74. Author numerous articles in field.; Co-editor: The Epidermis; editorial bd.: Jour. Investigative Dermatology, 1958-61, Excerpta of Medicine, 1961-78, Clinics in Dermatology, 1982; mem. editorial bd.: Archives Dermatology, 1960-77, chief editor, 1963-68. Trustee Dermatology Found., Med. Research Found. Oreg., 1972, exec. com., 1977-80, v.p., 1975-76, pres., 1977-78; music adv. com. Oreg. Symphony Orch., 1970-73; mem. Oreg. Ballet Council, 1974; bd. govs. Hitchcock Hosp., 1955; trustee Hitchcock Found., 1958-59, exec. com., 1958-59. Recipient Outstanding Achievement award U. Minn., 1964, Disting. Alumni award U. Cin. Coll. Medicine, 1995; dedication of Lobitz-Jillson Libr., Dartmouth-Hitchcock Med. Ctr., 1992; decorated Japanese Order of the Sacred Treasure, Gold Rays with neck ribbon, Emperor of Japan, 1993. Fellow ACP, Am. Acad. Dermatology (hon., bd. dirs. 1958-61, 66-69, pres. 1969, gold medal 1985, Master in Dermatology 1987), Phila. Coll. Physicians (hon.); mem. AMA, AAAS, Am. Dermatol. Assn. (bd. dirs. 1962-67, pres. 1972, hon. 1982), Soc. Investigative Dermatology (hon., v.p. 1952, bd. dirs. 1953-58, pres. 1957, Stephan Rothman medal for disting. achievement 1989), N.H., Multnomah County, Oreg., med. socs., N.Y. Acad. Scis., Pacific N.W. Dermatol. Assn. (pres. 1971), Pacific Dermatol. Assn., Israel Dermatol. Assn. (hon.), N.W. Soc. Clin. Rsch., Oreg. Dermatol. Soc. (pres. 1969), Portland Acad. Medicine, Am. Fedn. Clin. Rsch., Pacific Interurban Clin. Club (councilor 1971), Internat. Soc. Tropical Dermatology, Assn. Univ. Profs. Dermatology (founder, bd. dirs. 1961-66, pres. 1965-66), Soc. Venezolana de Dermatologia & Leprologia (hon.), French Soc. Dermatology, Brit. Assn. Dermatology, Assn. parala Investigacion Dermatologica (Venezuela), Soc. Dermatol. Danicae, Italian, Japan, Hokkaido, Sapporo derm. socs., Sigma Xi, Pi Kappa Epsilon, alpha Omega Alpha. Presbyn. Home: 2211 SW 1st Ave Portland OR 97201-5057

LOBL, HERBERT MAX, lawyer; b. Vienna, Austria, Jan. 10, 1932; s. Walter Leo and Minnie (Neumann) L.; m. Dorothy Fullerton Hubbard, Sept. 12, 1960; children: Peter Walter, Michelle Alexandra. AB magna cum laude, Harvard U., 1953, LLB cum laude, 1959, Avocat honoraire, 1993. Bar: N.Y. 1960, U.S. Tax Ct. 1963, French Conseil Juridique 1973; French avocat, mem. Paris bar, 1992, avocat hon., 1993. Assoc. Davis, Polk & Wardwell, N.Y.C., 1959-60; assoc. counsel to Gov. Nelson Rockefeller, Albany, N.Y., 1960-62; assoc. Davis, Polk & Wardwell, N.Y. and Paris, 1963-69, ptnr., Paris, 1969-92, sr. counsel, 1993—; lectr. law Columbia U., N.Y.C., 1993-95; supervisory bd. mem. CII-HB Internationale, Amsterdam, Holland, 1977-82. Gov. Am. Hosp. Paris, 1981-83, 88-93; trustee Am. Libr., Paris, 1969-81, Nantucket (Mass.) Cottage Hosp., 1996—. Served to 1st lt. USAF, 1954-56, Berlin. Fulbright scholar U. Bonn, Germany, 1954. Mem. Am. C. of C. (bd. dirs. France 1988-90), Univ. Club, Harvard Club (N.Y., Boston). Address: PO Box 2488 Nantucket MA 02584-2488 Home: 3 Weetamo Rd Nantucket MA 02554 also: 22 Waters Edge Rye NY 10580-3254 also: Davis Polk & Wardwell 450 Lexington Ave New York NY 10017-3911

LOBLEY, ALAN HAIGH, retired lawyer; b. Elkhart, Ind., Aug. 26, 1927; s. Frederick Askew and Eva May (Haigh) L.; m. Kathleen Covert Nolan, Mar. 2, 1957; children: James, Sarah. BSChemE, Purdue U., 1949; JD, Ind. U., 1952. Bar: Ind. 1952, U.S. Dist. Ct. (so. dist.) Ind. 1955, U.S. Ct. Appeals (7th cir.) 1963, U.S. Supreme Ct. 1971, U.S. Ct. Appeals (6th cir.) 1979. From assoc. to ptnr. Ice, Miller, Donadio & Ryan (formerly Ross, McCord, Ice & Miller), Indpls., 1955-97; ret., 1997. 1st lt. USAF, 1952-54. Mem. ABA, Ind. Bar Assn., Indpls. Bar Assn., Indpls. Rowing Ctr. Democrat. Avocations: photography, music, sculling. Home: 4535 N Park Ave Indianapolis IN 46205-1836

LOBO, REBECCA, basketball player; b. Hartford, Conn.. Student, U. Conn. Basketball player USA Women's Nat. Team, N.Y. Liberty, 1997—; mem. 1992 U.S. Olympic Festival East Team, 1992 Jr. World Championship Qualifying Team, 1993 USA Jr. World Championship Team. Recipient Wade trophy and named Nat. Player of Yr., Naismith, U.S. Basketball Writers Assn., 1995, 1994 and 1995 Kodak All-Am. First Team, Big East Conf. Player of Yr., Big East Tournament Most Outstanding Player, 1994 and 1995 Big East Conf. Women's Basketball Scholar Athlete of Yr. Office: NY Liberty Madison Sq Garden 2 Penn Plz 14th Fl New York NY 10121

LOBOSCO, ANNA FRANCES, state development disabilities program planner; b. Binghamton, N.Y., Nov. 13, 1952; d. James H. and Marie A. (Wilcox) Mee; m. Charles M. Lobosco, Apr. 27, 1974; children: Charles Jr., Amanda, Nicholas, Dennis. BA in History, Marist Coll., Poughkeepsie, N.Y., 1974; MS in Edn./Spl. Edn., Coll. St. Rose, Albany, 1978; PhD in Curriculum and Instrn., SUNY, Albany, 1989. Cert. tchr. elem., secondary and spl. edn., N.Y. Diagnostic remedial tchr. Orange County Assn. for Help of Retarded Children, Middletown/Newburgh, N.Y., 1973-78; instr., supr. student tchrs. Mt. St. Mary Coll., Newburgh, 1980-82; rsch. asst., assoc. dir. evaluation consortium SUNY, Albany, 1985-89; devel. disability program planner/prevention specialist N.Y. State Developmental Disabilities Planning Coun., Albany, 1989—; cons. N.Y. State Edn. Dept. Edn., 1987-89, N.Y. State Unified Tchrs., 1988-89, N.Y. State Coun. on Children's Families, 1986-88, N.Y. State Assn. Counties, 1987-88; instr. Coll. St. Rose, Albany, 1989-90. Contbr. articles to profl. jours; exec. producer vieoeos Mary's Choice: The Effects of Prenatal Exposure to Alcohol and Other Drugs, 1992, Its Up to You, 1995. Named Advocate of the Yr., N.Y. Libr. Assn., 1993. Mem. Coun. Exceptional Children, Am. Evaluation Assn., Am. Ednl. Rsch. Assn., Am. Assn. Mental Retardation, Kappa Delta Pi. Avocations: needlework, sports, reading. Office: NYS Devel Disabilities Planning Coun 155 Washington Ave Fl 2 Albany NY 12210-2329

LOBRON, BARBARA L., speech educator, writer, editor, photographer; b. Phila., Mar. 19, 1944; d. Martin Aaron and Elizabeth (Gots) L.; student Pa. State U., 1962-63; B.A. cum laude, Temple U., Phila., 1966; student photography Harold Feinstein, N.Y.C., 1970, 79-80; student art therapy Erika Steinberger, N.Y.C., 1994—. Reporter, writer Camden (N.J.) Courier-Post, 1966-68; editorial asst. Med. Insight mag., N.Y.C., 1970-71; mng. editor Camera 35 mag., N.Y.C., 1971-75, also assoc. editor photog. anns. for U.S. Camera/Camera 35, 1972, 73; freelance editor as Word Woman, N.Y.C., 1975-77, 79—; acct. exec. Bozell & Jacobs, N.Y.C., 1977-79; copy editor Camera Arts mag., N.Y.C., 1981-83; editorial coord. Center mag., Nat. Ctr. Health Edn., 1985; editorial coord. Popular Photography mag., 1986-95; assoc. editor Sony Style, 1995; tchr. speech improvement N.Y.C. Bd. Edn., 1995—; contbg. editor Photograph; participant 3M Editor's Conf. (1st woman), 1972. Photographs: group exhbns. include Internat. Women's Art Festival, N.Y.C., 1975, Rockefeller Ctr., N.Y.C., 1976, Photograph Gallery, N.Y.C., 1981 ; acrylic painting exhbns. at Tchrs. Coll., N.Y.C., 1994, Warwick Hotel, N.Y.C., 1995; represented in collection Library of Calif. Inst. Arts, Valencia. Tchr. Sch. Vol. Program, N.Y.C., 1994—. Recipient 1st pl. honors Dist. 1, Internat. Assn. Bus. Communicators, 1977. Copy editor: The Complete Guide to Cibachrome Printing, 1980, The Popular Photography Question and Answer Book, 1979, The Photography Catalog, 1976, Strand: Sixty Years of Photography, 1976, You and Your Lens, 1975; contbr. articles to comml. publs., chpts. to books. Dist. leader SGI-USA. Buddhist. Avocations: dancing, reading, photography, singing, walking. Home: 85 Hicks St Apt 7 Brooklyn NY 11201-6825

LOBSENZ, HERBERT MUNTER, data base company executive; b. N.Y.C., June 10, 1932; s. Jacob Munter and Marjorie (Roset) L.; m. Viola Pedreira, Sept. 29, 1961 (div. 1975); children: Jonathan, Andrew; m. 2d Sheila Katharine Martin, Dec. 18, 1975; children: James, Elizabeth, Emily, Daniel. B.A., NYU, 1953; acad. diploma, Courtauld Inst. Art, U. London, 1959; cert. Spanish studies, U. Madrid, Spain, 1956; postgrad., U. Perugia, Italy, 1958. Sales promotion mgr. Remington Rand, N.Y.C., 1964-66, product planning mgr., 1966-67; long range planning mgr. Xerox Pub., Stamford, Conn., 1967-69; v.p. Houghton Mifflin, Boston, 1976-81; pres. Market Data Retrieval, Shelton, Conn., 1969—; exec. v.p. Dun & Bradstreet Bus. Mktg. Services, 1987; CEO D&B Receivables Mgmt. Svc., 1991. Author: Vangel Griffin, 1961 (Harper Prize 1961). Chmn. Bd. Edn., Westport, Conn., 1975-85, 89-93. Jewish. Office: Market Data Retrieval 16 Progress Dr Shelton CT 06484-6216

LOBSINGER, THOMAS, bishop; b. Ayton, Ont., Can., Nov. 17, 1927. Ordained priest Roman Cath. Ch., 1954, bishop, 1987. Bishop Whitehorse, Y.T., Can., 1987—. Home: 5119 5th Ave, Whitehorse, YK Canada Y1A 1L5*

LOCALIO, MARCIA JUDITH, medical/surgical nurse; b. Phila., June 14, 1947; d. Herman Julius and Mildred Barbara (Brown) Bandarsky; m. Anthony Bernard Localio, Feb. 25, 1967; children: Jennifer Hope, David Anthony. Diploma in nursing, Bucks County Vocat. Tech. Sch., 1984; ADN, Bucks County Community Coll., 1989; student, Ctr. for Nursing Excellence, Thomas Edison State Coll. RN, N.J., Pa.; cert. EMT, instr. CPR, first aid; cert. phlebotomist Am. Soc. Clin. Pathology. Instr. CPRand EMT State of N.J., Princeton; nurse instr. IV therapy and venipuncture State of N.J., North Princeton Devel. Ctr.; Coord. habilitation plan State of N.J. Recipient Sustained Achievement award N.J. Dept. Human Svcs., 1991-92, Recognition award North Princeton Devel. Ctr., 1986, 95, 10 Yr. Career Svc. award State of N.J.; State of N.J. nursing scholar. Mem. Am. Soc. Clin. Pathologists (assoc.), N.J. Nursing Assn., Intravenous Nurses Soc.

LOCALIO, S. ARTHUR, retired surgeon, educator; b. N.Y.C., Oct. 4, 1911; s. Joseph and Carmella (Franco) L.; m. Ruth Virginia Adkins, July 14, 1945; children: William Hale, Susan Emily, Arthur Russell, David Charles. A.B., Cornell U., 1932; M.D., U. Rochester, 1936; D.Sc., Columbia, 1942. Diplomate Am. Bd. Surgery. Intern pathology N.Y. U. Hosp., 1936-37, intern medicine, 1937-38, asst. resident in surgery, 1938-40, sr. resident, 1940-42, asst. surgeon, 1945-47, asst. attending surgeon, 1947-49, asso. attending surgeon, 1949-52, attending surgeon, 1952—; clin. asst. vis. surgeon 4th surg. div. Bellevue Hosp., N.Y.C., 1945-46; asst. vis. surgeon 4th surg. div. Bellevue Hosp., 1946-48, asso. vis. surgeon, 1948-52, vis. surgeon, 1952—; practice medicine specializing in surgery N.Y.C., 1945—; instr. surgery Columbia Postgrad. Med. Sch., N.Y.C., 1945-48; asst. prof. Columbia Postgrad. Med. Sch., 1948-49; asst. prof. surgery N.Y. U. Schs. Medicine, N.Y.C., 1949-50; asso. prof. N.Y. U. Schs. Medicine, 1950-53, prof., 1953—; Johnson and Johnson Disting. prof. surgery N.Y.U. Schs. Medicine, 1972-92, Johnson and Johnson Disting. prof. surgery emeritus, 1992—; cons. in surgery Riverview Hosp., Red Bank, N.J., 1952—, Monmouth Meml. Hosp., Long Branch, N.J., 1952—, St. Barnabas Hosp., N.Y.C., 1958—, VA Hosp., N.Y.C., Wyckoff Heights Hosp., Bklyn., N.Y. Infirmary, N.Y.C., Booth Meml. Hosp., Flushing, N.Y., Brookhaven Meml. Hosp., Patchogue, N.Y. Contbr. articles to med. jours. Trustee Deerfield (Mass.) Acad. Served from capt. to lt. col. M.C. AUS, 1942-45, PTO. Mem. Am. Gastroent. Assn., N.Y. Gastroent. Assn., ACS, AMA, Am. Assn. for Surgery of Trauma, Soc. for Surgery Alimentary Tract, N.Y. Acad. Medicine (trustee 1971-75), N.Y. Acad. Scis., N.Y. Cancer Soc., N.Y. Soc. Colon and Rectal Surgeons, Pan Am. Med. Soc. (N.Am. chmn. sect. gen. surgery 1972—), N.Y. County Med. Soc., N.Y. State Med. Soc., Sociedad Colombiana de Cirujanos, Société Internationale de Chirurgie, Collegium Internationale Chirurgie Digestivae, Royal Soc. Medicine, N.Y. Surg. Soc., B.C. Surg. Soc., Transplantation Soc., Am. Surg. Assn., Sigma Xi. Home: Mill Village Rd # 147 Deerfield MA 01342-9724 Office: NYU Sch Medicine 530 1st Ave New York NY 10016-6451

LOCASCIO, SALVADORE JOSEPH, horticulturist; b. Hammond, La., Oct. 29, 1933; s. John A. and Mary (Dantone) L.; m. Sybil Olivette Johnson, Nov. 21, 1954 (dec. May 1991); children: John David, Judy Lynn, Paul Anthony; m. Carol Smith Riggall, Dec. 29, 1993; children: Todd, Heather. BS, Southeastern La. Coll., 1955; MS, La. State U., 1956; PhD, Purdue U., 1959. Grad. asst. La. State U., 1955-56, Purdue U., 1956-59; asst. horticulturist U. Fla., Gainesville, 1959-65; assoc. prof. U. Fla., 1965-69, prof., 1969—. Contbr. articles to profl. publs. Recipient Ann. Rsch. award Fla. Fruit and Vegetable Assn., 1993. Fellow Am. Soc. for Hort. Sci.; mem. Fla. State Hort. Soc. (v.p. vegetable sci. 1975-76, pres. 1994, chmn. bd. dirs. 1995, presdl. gold medal 1978), Fla. Weed Sci. Soc. (outstanding weed sci. of yr. 1989, pres.-elect 1989-90, pres. 1990-91). Democrat. Roman Catholic. Achievements include research in efficient use of fertilizer, polyethylene mulch, and water for the production of vegetable crops. Office: U Fla Dept Hort Scis 406 NW 32nd St Gainesville FL 32607-2532

LOCATELLI, PAUL LEO, university president; b. Santa Cruz, Calif., Sept. 16, 1938; s. Vincent Dino and Marie Josephine (Piccone) L. B.S. in Acctg., Santa Clara U., 1961; MDiv, Jesuit Sch. Theology, 1974; DBA, U. So. Calif., 1971. CPA, Calif. Ordained priest Roman Cath. Ch., 1974. Acct., Lautze & Lautze, San Jose, Calif., 1960-61, 1973-74; prof. acctg. Santa Clara (Calif.) U., 1974-86, assoc. dean Bus. Sch. and acad. v.p., 1978-86, pres., 1988—. bd. dirs. chair, Assn. Jesuit Colls. and Univs., Silicon Valley, Tech. Mus.; bd. trustees Inst. of European & Asian Studies; mem. Nat. Cath. Bishops and Pres.' Com., exec. com. Ind. Colls. and Univs. of Calif., adv. couns. Parents Helping Parents and Community Found.; past rector Jesuit Comty. at Loyola Marymount U. Past trustee U. San Francisco, Seattle U., St. Louis U. and Loyola Marymount U., Regis U.; past mem. Sr. Commn. of Western Assn. Schs. and Colls., Acctg. Edn. Change Commn. Mem. AICPA, NCCJ, Calif. Soc. CPAs (Disting. Prof. of the Yr award, 1994), Am. Acctg. Assn., Am. Leadership Forum Silicon Valley (bd. dirs.). Democrat. Office: Santa Clara U 500 El Camino Real Santa Clara CA 95050-4345

LOCHAMY, RICHARD EDWARD, physician; b. Gadsden, Ala., Jan. 28, 1955; s. Edward Harold and Edna Louise (Farrar) L.; m. Marlene Ruth Hebert, June 3, 1978; 1 child, Chelsea Pri. BS, U. Tex., Galveston, 1980; MD, Autonomous Universidad de Guadalajara, Mexico, 1988. Pvt. practice physician Junction City, Kans., 1993—; med. dir. Geary County Diabetes Assn., Junction City, 1995—. Recipient John J. Calabro award for House Officer of the Year St. Vincent's Hosp., 1993. Mem. AMA, Kans. Med. Assn. Office: 1106 Saint Marys Rd Ste 306 Junction City KS 66441-4158

LOCHBIHLER, FREDERICK VINCENT, lawyer; b. Chgo., Jan. 30, 1951; s. Frederick Louis and Marion Helen (Rutkauskas) L.; m. Darlene Gotfryde Wantuch, Nov. 8, 1952; 1 child, Frederick Karlman. AB in Govt. summa cum laude, U. Notre Dame, 1973; JD with honors, U. Chgo., 1976. Bar: Ill. 1976, U.S. Dist. Ct. (no. dist.) Ill. 1977, U.S. Ct. Appeals (7th cir.) 1980, U.S. Ct. Appeals (8th cir.) 1981, U.S. Supreme Ct. 1982, U.S. Dist. Ct. (ctrl. dist.) Ill. 1983, U.S. Dist. Ct. Ariz. 1991. Assoc. Chapman and Cutler, Chgo., 1976-84, ptnr., 1984—. Mem. Phi Beta Kappa, Order of Coif. Avocations: military history, literature, travel. Home: PO Box 72 Golf IL 60029-0072 Office: Chapman and Cutler 111 W Monroe St Chicago IL 60603

LOCHER, RICHARD EARL, editorial cartoonist; b. Dubuque, Iowa, June 4, 1929; s. Joseph John and Lucille (Jungk) L.; m. Mary Therese Cosgrove, June 15, 1957; children: Stephen Robert, John Joseph, Jana Lynne. Student, Loras Coll., 1948, Chgo. Acad. Fine Arts, 1949-51; BFA, Art Center, Los Angeles, 1954, postgrad., 1955-56; DHL (hon.), Ill. Benedictine Coll., 1992. founder, pres. Novamark Corp., Chgo., 1968-72; cons. McDonalds Corp., Oakbrook, Ill.; tchr. art at local high schs. and colls. Asst. writer, artist: Buck Rogers Comic Strip, 1954-57, Dick Tracy Comic Strip, 1957-61, Martin Aerospace co., Denver, 1962-63; art dir. Hansen Co., Chgo., N.Y.C., 1963-68; editorial cartoonist Chgo. Tribune, 1972—; artist Dick Tracy Comic Strip, 1983—; author: Dick Locher Draws Fire, 1980, Send in the Clowns, 1982, Vote for Me, 1988, The Dick Tracy Casebook, 1990, Dick Tracy's Fiendish Foes, 1991, None of the Above, 1992, The Daze of Whine and Neurosis, 1995, (with Michael Kilian) Flying Can Be Fun, 1985; patentee Poker Face device to play poker without cards. Trustee Ill. Benedictine Coll., 1984—. Served with USAF, 1951-53. Recipient Dragonslayer award U.S. Indsl. Coun., 1976, 77, 78, 80, 81, 82, Disting. Health Journalism award, 1981, 82, 83, 84, 85, 92, Overseas Press Club award, 1983, 84,

Pulitizer prize, 1983, Sigma Delta Chi award, 1985, World Population Inst. award, 1986, John Fischetti award, 1987, Peter Lisagor award, 1987, 89, 91; Named Ill. FBI Man of Yr., 1993. Mem. Assn. Am. Editorial Cartoonists. Office: care Mark J Cohen PO Box 1892 Santa Rosa CA 95402-1892*

LOCHMILLER, KURTIS L., real estate entrepreneur; b. Sacramento, Dec. 30, 1952; s. Rodney Glen and Mary Margaret (Frauen) L.; m. Mariye Susan Mizuki, Nov. 9, 1951; children: Margaux Sian, Chase Jordan. BA in Econs. and Fin., U. Denver, 1975. Dist. sales mgr. Hertz Truck Div., Denver, 1975-76; drilling foreman Shell Oil, Alaska, Mont., Colo., 1976-79; pres., owner Kurtex Mortgage & Devel. Co., Denver, 1979—, Kurtex Properties Inc., Denver, 1980-86; pres., chief exec. officer Kurtex Inc., Denver, 1981—, Bankers Pacific Mortgage, Denver, 1980—, Bankers Fin. Escrow Corp., Denver, 1984—, Northwest Title & Escrow, Denver, 1984—; pres., chief exec. officer Steamboat Title, Steamboat Springs, Colo., 1985—, First Escrow, Denver, 1986—, Fidelity-Commonwealth-Continental Escrow, Denver, 1984—; pres. Colonnade Ltd., Denver, 1981-88; pres., bd. dirs. Breckridge (Colo.) Brewery. V.p., founder Colfax on the Hill, Denver, 1984; mediator, arbitrator Arbitrator/Mediation Assn., Denver, 1986; mem. Police Athletic League, Denver, 1988. Recipient Pres. Spl. Achievement/Founder award Colfax on the Hill, Denver, 1984, Spl. Mayor's award, City & County of Denver, 1985. Mem. Nat. Assn.of Real Estate Appraisers, Internat. Brotherhood of Teamsters, Colo. Mortgage Bankers Assn., Mortgage Banking Assn., Denver C. of C., Phi Beta Kappa, Omicron Delta Epsilon. Clubs: U.S. Karate Assn. (Phoenix) (3d degree Black Belt), Ferrari (Portland). Lodge: Internat. Supreme Council Order of Demolay. Avocations: collecting cars, karate, fishing, art collecting. Home: 1 Carriage Ln Littleton CO 80121-2010 Office: Bankers Fin Escrow Corp 9655 E 25th Ave Ste 101 Aurora CO 80010-1056

LOCHNER, PHILIP RAYMOND, JR., lawyer, communications executive; b. New Rochelle, N.Y., Mar. 3, 1943; s. Philip Raymond and Maryl (Browning) L.; m. Sally Soth, June 23, 1973; children: Lauren Soth, John Philip. BA, Yale U., 1964, LLB, 1967; PhD, Stanford U., 1971. Bar: N.Y. 1972, D.C. 1991. Assoc. dean SUNY Law Sch., Amherst, 1971-73; assoc. Cravath, Swaine & Moore, N.Y.C., 1973-78; assoc. gen. counsel Time Inc., N.Y.C., 1978-80, corp. assoc. gen. counsel, 1980-84, sr. v.p., gen. counsel video, 1984-86, v.p., 1986-88, gen. cousel, sec., 1988-90; commr. SEC, Washington, 1990-91; sr. v.p. Time Warner Inc., N.Y.C., 1991—; bd. dirs. Bklyn. Bancorp., N.Y.C., 1993-96 Office: Time Warner Inc 75 Rockefeller Plz New York NY 10019-6908

LOCHRIDGE, LLOYD PAMPELL, JR., lawyer; b. Austin, Tex., Feb. 3, 1918; s. Lloyd Pampell and Franklyn (Blocker) L.; m. Frances Potter, Jan. 23, 1943; children: Anne, Georgia, Lloyd P. III, Patton G., Hope N., Frances P. AB, Princeton U., 1938; LLB, Harvard U., 1941. Bar: D.C. 1942, Tex. 1945, U.S. Ct. Appeals (5th cir.), U.S. Supreme Ct. Assoc. Law Office Vernon Hill, Mission, Tex., 1945-46; ptnr. Hill & Lochridge, Mission, Tex., 1946-49, Hill, Lochridge & King, Mission, Tex., 1949-59, McGinnis, Lochridge & Kilgore, Austin, 1959—. Mem. adv. bd. Salvation Army, Austin, 1962—; mem. vestry Ch. Good Shepherd, Austin, 1968-73; trustee Austin Lyric Opera, 1986—. Comdr. USNR, 1941-46, ETO. Mem. ABA (bd. govs. 1989-92), State Bar Tex. (pres. 1974-75), Travis County Bar Assn. (pres. 1970-71), Hidalgo County Bar Assn. (pres. 1954-55). Episcopalian. Avocations: tennis, squash, sailing. Office: McGinnis Lochridge & Kilgore 1300 Capitol Ctr 919 Congress Ave Austin TX 78701-2444

LOCICERO, DONALD, language educator, writer; b. Bklyn., Nov. 14, 1937; s. Peter and Nancy (Passnante) LoC.; m. Cecelia Molfetto, Aug. 16, 1958; 1 child, Darius. BA, Bklyn. Coll., 1960; MA, PhD, Rutgers U., 1965; post doctoral, U. Tübingen (Germany), 1966. Tech. Zenith Radio Corp., N.Y.C., 1953-58; asst. prof. Cedar Crest Coll., Oneonta, N.Y., 1965-66; prof. German and Russian lang. and lit., creative writing Cedar Crest Coll., Allentown, Pa., 1966—, chair internat. lang. dept., coord. comparative lit., 1990—, dir. honors program, 1991—. Author: (novels) The Twisted Star, 1993, The Superhero, 1993, (textbooks) Scholarly Novellentheorie, 1967, Scholarly Study Humor and Witz, 1993; editor, author:Mafkikker, 1972—; contbr. articles to profl. jours. Nat. Def. fellow U.S. Govt., 1961-64, fellow Rutgers U., 1965, Post Graduate fellow Columbia U., 1965. Mem. MLA. Avocations: tennis, skiing, travel. Office: 2815 W Greenleaf St Allentown PA 18104-3854

LOCIGNO, PAUL ROBERT, public affairs executive; b. Cleve., Sept. 1, 1948; s. Paul Robert and Anna Mae (Zingale) L.; m. Ki Cho Rim; children: Tammy, Robert. AA, Cuyahoga Community Coll., Parma, Ohio, 1974; BA, Case Western Res. U., 1976; postgrad., Cleve. State U., 1977-78. Part-time faculty Cuyahoga Community Coll., 1979-83; vice chmn. Presdl. Inaugural Labor Com., Washington, 1980-81; vice chmn. labor com. Presdl. Inaugural Com., Washington, 1984-85; legis. agt. Internat. Brotherhood of Teamsters, Washington, 1977-90, dir. govt. internat. affairs, 1983-89; dir. Asian/Pacific br. Internat. Brotherhood of Teamsters, Taipei, Taiwan, 1985-88; spl. rep. of chmn. Hill & Knowlton Pub. Affairs Worldwide, Washington, 1989-91; pres., founding ptnr. Rollins Internat. Ltd., Alexandria, Va.; bd. dirs. Nanjing Ya Dong Corp. Mem. Pres.'s Export Coun., 1988-89; mem. Asia adv. com. Bicentennial of U.S. Constitution, 1990; bd. govs. Am. League for Exports and Security Assistance, 1989; mem. Nat. Commn. for Employment Policy, Washington, 1981-86; bd. dirs. Children's Right Coun., Washington, 1997—. With USMC, 1968-70, Vietnam. Republican. Roman Catholic. Avocations: archery, hunting, fishing. Home: 8203 Cherry Ridge Rd Fairfax VA 22039-3011 Office: Rollins Internat Ltd 510 King St Ste 302 Alexandria VA 22314-3132

LOCK, GERALD SEYMOUR HUNTER, retired mechanical engineering educator; b. London, June 30, 1935; arrived in Can., 1962, naturalized, 1973; s. George and Mary (Hunter) L.; m. Edna Burness, Sept. 19, 1959; children: Graeme, Gareth, Grenville. B.Sc. with honors, U. Durham, Eng., 1959, Ph.D., 1962. Asst. prof. mech. engring. U. Alta. (Can.), Edmonton, 1962-64; assoc. prof. U. Alta. (Can.), 1964-70, prof., 1970-93, dean interdisciplinary studies, 1976-81; cons. mech. engr., Edmonton, 1993—; chmn. Internat. Arctic Sci. Commn. Regional Bd., 1993-96. Vice chmn. Alta. Manpower Adv. Coun., 1979-84, chmn., 1984-89; chmn. Salvation Army Red Shield Appeal, 1980-82; bd. govs. Alta. Coll., chmn., 1982-85; founding pres. Alta. Poetry Festival Soc., 1981. Recipient Queen Elizabeth II Silver Jubilee medal, 1977. Fellow Engring. Inst. Can, Can. Soc. Mech. Engring. (pres. 1977-78), ASME; mem. Sci. Coun. Can., Can. Polar Commn. Mem. Progressive Conservative Party. Anglican. Home: 11711 83d Ave, Edmonton, AB Canada T6G 0V2 Office: U Alta, Edmonton, AB Canada T6G 2G3

LOCK, RICHARD WILLIAM, packaging company executive; b. N.Y.C., Oct. 5, 1931; s. Albert and Catherine Dorothy (Magnus) L.; m. Elizabeth Louise Kenney, Nov. 2, 1957; children—Albert William, Dorothy Louise Lock Kuhl, John David. B.S., Rutgers U., 1953; M.B.A., N.Y. U., 1958. Acct. Gen. Electric Co., 1953-54, Union Carbide Co., N.Y.C., 1956-58; div. controller St. Regis Paper Co., Houston, 1959-62; div. controller Owens-Illinois, Inc., Toledo, 1962-64, supr. programmer office methods and data processing, 1964-65, asst. mgr. data processing procedures, 1965-67, mgr. systems analysis and devel., 1967-68, mgr. corp. systems analysis and devel., 1968-70, dir. corp. systems and data processing, 1970-72, gen. mgr. electro/optical display, 1972-75, treas., 1975-80, v.p., dir. corp. planning, 1980-84, v.p., asst. chief fin. officer, treas., 1984-88; mng. dir. Magnus Assocs., 1989—. Mem. adv. bd. Toledo Salvation Army, 1973—, chmn., 1974-77; pres. Toledo Area Govtl. Research Assn., 1978-79; bd. dirs. Riverside Hosp. Found., Toledo, 1982—. Served with USAF, 1954-56. Mem. Fin. Execs. Inst., Am. Soc. Corp. Secs., Phi Beta Kappa. Republican. Lutheran. Club: Toledo. Home: 5831 Monroe St Apt 406 Sylvania OH 43560-2256

LOCKARD, JOHN ALLEN, naval officer; b. Mobile, Ala., July 30, 1944; s. John David and Mary Ethlyn (Wyatt) L.; m. Peggy Lee Cantrell, Apr. 25, 1970; children: Denise, Karen, John, Kelley. BS, U.S. Naval Postgrad. Sch., 1971. Commd. ensign USN, 1966, advanced through grades to vice adm., 1995; commanding officer Attack Squadron 25 USN, Lemoore, Calif., 1980-81, commanding officer Strike Fighter Squadron 125, 1983-84; exec. officer USS Coral Sea USN, Norfolk, Va., 1985-86; program mgr. F/A-18 Naval AIr Systems Command USN, Washington, 1986-90, asst. comdr. for systems engring., 1990-91, program exec. officer to sec. navy staff, 1991-95, commdr. naval air systems command, 1995—; chmn., bd. dirs. Navy Fed. Credit Union, Merrifield, Va., 1991—. Mem. Assn. Naval Aviation. Office: 1421 Jefferson Davis Hwy Arlington VA 22201-1010

LOCKE, CARL EDWIN, JR., academic administrator, engineering educator; b. Palo Pinto County, Tex., Jan. 11, 1936; s. Carl Edwin Sr. and Caroline Jane (Brown) L.; m. Sammie Rhae Batchelor, Aug. 25, 1956; children: Stephen Curtis, Carlene Rhae. BSChemE, U. Tex., 1958, MSChemE, 1960, PhDChemE, 1972. Rsch. engr. Continental Oil Co., Ponca City, Okla., 1959-65; prodn. engr. R.L. Stone Co., Austin, Tex., 1965-66; prodn. rsch. engr. Tracor Inc., Austin, 1966-71; vis. assoc. prof. U. Tex., Austin, 1971-73; from asst. prof. to prof., dir. chem. engring. U. Okla., Norman, 1973-86; dean engring. U. Kans., Lawrence, 1986—; Co-author: Anodic Protection, 1981; contbr. articles to profl. jours. Disting. Engring. grad. U. Tex., 1993. Fellow Am. Inst. Chem. Engrs.; mem. ASTM, Nat. Assn. Corrosion Engrs. (regional chair 1988-89, Eben Junkin award South Cen. region 1990), Am. Soc. Engring. Edn., Lawrence C. of C., Rotary. Democrat. Presbyterian. Office: U Kans Sch of Engring 4010 Learned Hall Lawrence KS 66044-7526*

LOCKE, EDWIN ALLEN, JR., investment banker; b. Boston, June 8, 1910; s. Edwin Allen and Elizabeth (Ferguson) L.; m. Dorothy Q. Clark, June 16, 1934 (div.); children: Elizabeth Eliane, Edwin Allen III, Benjamin Clark; m. Karin Marsh, 1952; 1 son, Jonathan Winston. Grad., Phillips Acad., Exeter, N.H., 1928; A.B. cum laude, Harvard U., 1932. Assoc. Chase Nat. Bank, N.Y.C., 1932-33, assoc. Paris br., 1933-35, assoc. London br., 1935-36, assoc., N.Y.C., 1936-40, v.p., 1947-51; Office Coordinator Purchases, adv. commn. to Council Nat. Def., 1940-41; asst. dep. dir. priorities div. Office Prodn. Mgmt., 1941; dep. chief staff officer Supply Priorities and Allocation Bd., 1941-42; asst. to chmn. WPB, 1942-44; exec. asst. to personal rep. of Pres., 1944-45, personal rep. of, 1945-47; also spl. asst. to pres., 1946-47; spl. rep. Sec. State; ambassador to Near East, 1951-53; exec. asst. to pres. Union Tank Car Co., Chgo., 1953-54, exec. v.p., 1954-55, pres., CEO, dir., 1955-63; pres., CEO Modern Homes Constrn. Co., Valdosta, Ga., 1963-67, Coastal Products Corp., Blountstown, Fla., 1964-67, Am. Paper Inst., N.Y.C., 1967-77, Econ. Club of N.Y., 1977-85; investment banker, 1985—; dir. Alusit Holdings, L.P., 1993—; chmn., dir. Fed. Home Loan Bank of Chgo., 1956-63; overseer Harvard U., 1958-64; trustee Century Power Corp. Ariz., 1989-91. Mem. Presdl. Survey Mission to Liberia and Tunisia, 1963; mem. adv. com. on internat. bus. problems Dept. State, 1962-67; trustee China Med. Bd., 1947-80, Radio Officers Union Benefit Plans, 1988-93. Mem. Racquet and Tennis Club (N.Y.C.), Metropolitan Club (Washington). Home and Office: 935 N Halifax Ave Apt 1009 Daytona Beach FL 32118

LOCKE, EDWIN ALLEN, III, psychologist, educator; b. N.Y.C., May 15, 1938; s. Edwin Allen and Dorothy (Clark) L.; m. Anne Hassard, June 13, 1968. B.A., Harvard U., 1960; M.A., Cornell U., 1962, Ph.D., 1964. Assoc. research scientist Am. Inst. Research, 1964-66, research scientist, 1966-70; asst. prof. psychology U. Md., College Park, 1967-69; assoc. prof. U. Md., 1969-70, assoc. prof. bus., mgmt. and psychology, 1970-73, prof., 1973-96; chmn. faculty mgt. and orgn. Coll. Bus. and Mgmt. U. Md., College Park, 1984-96. Author: A Guide to Effective Study, 1975; co-author: Goal Setting: A Motivational Technique That Works, 1984, A Theory of Goal Setting and Task Performance, 1990, The Essence of Leadership, 1991; editor: Generalizing from Laboratory to Field Settings, 1986; cons. editorial bd. Organizational Behavior and Human Decision Processes, J. Applied Psychology; contbr. articles to profl. jours. Office Naval Research grantee, 1964, 79; NIMH grantee, 1967; Army Rsch. Inst. grantee, 1993. Fellow APA, Acad. Mgmt., Am. Psychol. Soc., Soc. Indsl. and Orgnl. Psychology (Disting Scientific Contbn. award 1993). Home: 30 Old Mill Bottom Rd N Annapolis MD 21401 Office: U Md Coll Bus and Mgmt College Park MD 20742 *The most important literary/philosophical influence in my life has been Ayn Rand. Her philosophy of Objectivism demonstrates that man's highest moral purpose is the achievement of his own happiness and that reason is his only means to achieve it. Her novels, which portray man as an heroic being, are an inspiration to every man to achieve the best within him.*

LOCKE, ELIZABETH HUGHES, foundation administrator; b. Norfolk, Va., June 30, 1939; d. George Morris and Sallie Epps (Moss) Hughes; m. John Rae Locke, Jr., Sept. 13, 1958 (div. 1981); children: John Rae III, Sallie Curtis. BA magna cum laude with honors in English, Duke U., 1964, PhD, 1972; MA, U. N.C., 1966. Instr. English, U. N.C., Chapel Hill, 1970-72; vis. prof. English, Duke U., Durham, N.C., 1972-73, dir. univ. pubs., 1973-79; corp. contbns. officer Bethlehem Steel Corp., Pa., 1979-82; dir. edn. div. and comm. Duke Endowment, Charlotte, N.C., 1982-96, exec. dir., 1996-97; pres., 1997—; past pres. Comm. Philanthropy, Washington; mem. comms. com. Coun. on Founds., Washington, 1995— . Editor: Duke Encounters, 1977, Prospectus for Change: American Private Higher Education, 1985, (mag.) Issues, 1985-96. Pres., Jr. League, Durham, 1976, Hist. Preservation Soc., Durham, 1977, Pub. Rels. Soc. Am., Charlotte chpt., 1988, Charlotte Area Donors Forum; past pres. Sch. of Arts, Charlotte; bd. visitors Davidson Coll., Charlotte Country Day Sch., Duke U., Johnson C. Smith U. Recipient Leadership award Charlotte C. of C., 1984; Danforth fellow, 1972. Mem. Nat. Task Force, English Speaking Union, The Most Venerable Order of St. John of Jerusalem (officer sister), Phi Beta Kappa. Democrat. Episcopalian. Club: Charlotte City. Office: 100 N Tryon St Ste 3500 Charlotte NC 28202-4000

LOCKE, FRANCIS PHILBRICK, retired editorial writer; b. Lincoln, Nebr., May 1, 1912; s. Walter Leonard and Annette Elizabeth (Philbrick) L.; m. Carroll Day, Dec. 31, 1936; children: Margaret Locke Newhouse, Alice Locke Carey, Walter Day. BA, Harvard Coll., 1933; posgrad., Harvard U., 1946-47. Reporter Miami (Fla.) Daily News, 1934-36, editorial writer, 1936-41; editorial writer St. Louis Post-Dispatch, 1941; editor of editorial page Miami Daily News, 1941-46; Nieman fellow Harvard U., Cambridge, Mass., 1946-47; assoc. editor Dayton (Ohio) Daily News, 1947-63; editorial writer Riverside (Calif.) Press-Enterprise, 1963-72. Author: (chpt.) Public Men In & Out of Office, 1943; contbr. articles to profl. jours. Bd. dirs. Mission Inn Found., Riverside, 1987-95; mem. adv. bd. YWCA, Riverside; trustee Miami U., Oxford, Ohio, 1954-63; divsn. chmn. United Way, Dayton, 1956-57. Recipient aviation writing award TWA, 1956. Mem. Nat. Conf. Editorial Writers, Soc. Profl. Journalists (nat. editorial writing prize 1946), Harvard U. Alumni Assn. (S.W. and Pacific regional dir. 1980-86, Harvard medal 1983), Harvard-Radcliffe Club So. Calif. (bd. dirs. 1975-92), Harvard Club Dayton (pres. 1961-63). Democrat. Congregationalist. Avocations: classical music, Gilbert & Sullivan, Civil War military history, baseball, college football. Home: 7368 Westwood Dr Riverside CA 92504-2729

LOCKE, GARY, governor; b. Jan. 21, 1950; s. James and Julie L.; m. Mona Lee Locke, Oct. 15, 1994. BA in Polit. Sci., Yale U., 1972; JD, Boston U., 1975. Dep. prosecuting atty. State of Wash., King County; with Ho. of Reps., Wash., 1982-93; gov. State of Washington; cmty. rels. mgr. U.S. West; chief exec. King County, 1993. Named First in effectiveness among Puget Sound area lawmakers Seattle Times, 1990. Office: Office of the Gov PO Box 40002 Olympia WA 98504*

LOCKE, MICHAEL, zoology educator; b. Nottingham, Eng., Feb. 14, 1929; came to U.S., 1961; s. R.H. and K.N. (Waite) L.; m. J. V. Collins; children by previous marriage, Vanessa , John, Timothy, Marius. B.A., Cambridge U., 1952, M.A., 1955, Ph.D., 1956, Sc.D., 1976. State scholar, found. scholar St. John's Coll., 1949-56; lectr. zoology Univ. Coll. W.I., 1956-61; guest investigator Rockefeller Inst., N.Y.C., 1960; assoc. prof. biology Case Western Res. U., Cleve., 1961-67, prof. biology, 1967-71; prof., chmn. dept. zoology U. Western Ont., London, Can., 1971-85; prof. zoology U. Western Ont., 1985-94; prof. emeritus, 1994—; Raman prof. U. Madras, India, 1969; vis. dir. rsch. Internat. Ctr. Insect Physiology and Ecology, Nairobi, Kenya, 1977-81. Editor Monographs on Ultrastructure, 1970—; mem. editorial bd. Tissue and Cell, 1968—, Jour. Insect Physiology, 1978—, Insect Sci. and Its Applications, 1979-89; former editor: Growth Soc. Symposia; editor, contbr. vols. II a, b, c, Insecta-Microscopic Anatomy of Invertebrate, 1997; contbr. over 200 articles to profl. jours. Served with RAF. Disting. Internat. award in Insect Morphology & Embryology, Gold medal, 1988; Killam fellow, 1988-90. Fellow Royal Soc. Can., AAAS; mem. Am. Soc. Cell Biology. Avocations: lapidary; gemologist. Office: Dept Zoology, U Western Ont, London, ON Canada N6A 5B7

LOCKE, NORTON, hotel management and construction company executive; b. Mpls., May 22, 1927; s. Ben and Harriet (Markus) L.; m. Peggy Jane Smith, Nov. 6, 1959; children: Alexandria, Jonina, Elizabeth, Victoria. B.S., U. Wis., 1951; M.B.A., Mich. State U., 1957, cert. food and beverage exec., 1984, cert. hotel adminstr., 1986, cert. food service profl., 1988. Corp. dir. food and beverage Kahler Corp., Rochester, Minn., 1970; gen. mgr., chief exec. officer Carolando Corp., Orlando, Fla., 1971-74; also dir.; gen. mgr. Radisson Muehlebach Hotel, Kansas City, Radisson Cadillac Hotel, Detroit, 1974-79; v.p., gen. mgr. White Co. Hospitality Div., Merrillville, Ind., 1979-80; dist. dir. I.D.M. Mgmt. Co., Chgo., 1980-83; v.p., gen. mgr. Skirvin Plaza Hotel, Oklahoma City, 1983-87; v.p., dir. ops. SBI Mgmt. Co., Oklahoma City, 1987-91; v.p., gen. mgr. Anaheim (Calif.) Plz. Hotel, 1991-93; corp. dir. Midwest Hospitality Mgmt., Anaheim, Calif., 1993—; faculty Vallencia Coll., 1971-74; adj. prof. Oklahoma City Community Coll., 1983-89; adj. prof. Century Coll., San Diego. Author: Hard Times Cook Book, World Without Milk Cookbook, Land of Milk and Honey, Heritage, A Taste of Tradition. Bd. dirs. U. Minn. Tech. Coll., 1970-75, Am. Hotel and Motel Assn. Sch., 1975-79, Detroit Conv. and Visitors Bur. Served with inf. AUS, 1944-46. Mem. Internat. Food Service Execs. Assn. (dir. 1971-74), Am. Hotel and Motel Assn. (cert.), Am. Chefs Assn., Mich. and Ind. Hotel Assn., Nat. Restaurant Assn., Hotel Sales Mgrs. Assn., Am. Fisheries Inst. (dir. 1970-71), Okla. State Hotel Assn. (Innkeeper of Yr. 1985, Bd. Mem. of Yr. 1986). Republican. Clubs: Masons (Scottish Rite 32 degree), Shriners, Rotary, SKAL Internat, Toastmasters Internat.

LOCKE, VIRGINIA OTIS, freelance writer, editor; b. Tiffin, Ohio, Sept. 4, 1930; d. Charles Otis and Frances Virginia (Sherer) L. BA, Barnard Coll., 1953; MA in Psychology, Duke U., 1972, postgrad. Program officer, asst. corp. sec. Agrl. Devel. Coun., N.Y.C., 1954-66; staff psychologist St. Luke's-Roosevelt Med. Ctr., N.Y.C., 1973-75; freelance writer and editor N.Y.C., 1976-85; writer-editor Cornell U. Med. Coll./N.Y. Hosp. Med. Ctr., N.Y.C., 1986-89; sr. editor humanities and social scis. coll. divsn. Prentice Hall divsn. Simon & Schuster, Upper Saddle River, N.J., 1989-96. Co-author: (coll. textbook) Introduction to Theories of Personality, 1985, The Agricultural Development Council: A History, 1989. Founder Help Our Neighbors Eat Year-Round (H.O.N.E.Y.), Inc., N.Y.C., chmn., 1983-87, vol., 1987—, newsletter editor, 1992—; reader Recording for the Blind, N.Y.C., 1978-84; vol. Reach to Recovery program Am. Cancer Soc., Bergen County, N.J., 1990—. Recipient Our Town Thanks You award, N.Y.C., 1984, Mayor's Vol. Svc. award, N.Y.C., 1986, Cert. of Appreciation for Community Svc. Manhattan Borough, 1986, Jefferson award Am. Ins. Pub. Svc., Washington, 1986. Home and Office: 2140 South St Fort Lee NJ 07024-5009

LOCKE, WILLIAM, endocrinologist; b. Morden, Man., Can., Mar. 16, 1916; s. Corbet and Ruby Louise (Brown) L.; m. Katherine Elizabeth Acer Russell, Sept. 29, 1945 (dec.). MD, U. Man., Winnipeg, 1938; MS in Medicine, U. Minn., 1947. Diplomate Am. Bd. Internal Medicine. Intern Winnipeg (Man., Can.) Gen. Hosp., 1937-38; fellow in medicine Mayo Found., Rochester, Minn., 1938-40, 46-48; rsch. fellow Harvard U., Boston, 1948-50; mem. staff Ochsner Clinic, New Orleans, 1950—, sr. cons., 1987—; clin. prof. medicine Tulane U., New Orleans, 1968-86, prof. emeritus, 1986—; sec. Alton Ochsner Med. Found., New Orleans, 1950—; pres. med. staff Ochsner Found. Hosp., New Orleans, 1954-55, trustee, 1978—. Author, editor: Hypothalmus and Pituitary in Health and Disease, 1972; contbr. numerous chpts. to books and articles to sci. jours. Lt. comdr. RCNVR, 1940-46. NIH grantee, 1958-62. Fellow ACP; mem. Am. Diabetes Assn., Endocrine Soc., Sigma Xi, others. Republican. Episcopalian. Home: 4815 Dryades St New Orleans LA 70115-5533 Office: Ochsner Clinic 1514 Jefferson Hwy New Orleans LA 70121-2429

LOCKER, J. GARY, university official, civil engineering educator; b. Kenora, Ont., Can., Nov. 19, 1937; s. Lorne John and Gladys Sarah (Kirk) L.; m. Elaine June Letawsky, May 25, 1963; children: Laura Lee, Tiffany Dawn. BSCE, U. Man., Winnipeg, Can., 1961; MS, U. Alta., Edmonton, Can., 1963, PhD, 1969. Registered profl engr., Ont. Lectr. dept. civil engring., Royal Mil. Coll., Kingston, Ont., 1963-66, asst. prof., 1968-71; assoc. prof. faculty engring. U. Regina,, Sask., Can., 1971-73; chmn. dept. civil engring. Lakehead U., Thunder Bay, Ont., 1973-76, dir. Sch. Engring., 1976-94; dean Faculty Engring. Lakehead U., Thunder Bay, 1994—; mem., past chmn. Coun. Ont. Deans Engring., Nat. Coun. Deans Engring. and Applied Sci. Fellow Engring. Inst. Can.; mem. Can. Geotech. Inst., Profl. Engrs. Ont. (order of honor), Internat. Soc. Soil Mechanics and Found. Engring., Thunder Bay Fly Fishing Club. Geotech. engring. rsch. in organic soils and clay shales. Avocations: fly fishing and tying, gardening, trailer travel, cross-country skiing. Office: Lakehead U Faculty Engring, Oliver Rd, Thunder Bay, ON Canada P7B 5E1

LOCKER, RAYMOND DUNCAN, editor; b. Dunkirk, N.Y., Apr. 15, 1960; s. Robert Smith and Margaret Ellen (Duncan) L.; m. Debbie Elizabeth Long, July 2, 1988; 1 child, Margaret Katherine. BA in Political Sci., U. Cin., 1982; MS in Journalism, Ohio U., 1984. Reporter Lake Wales Highlander, Lake Wales, Fla., 1982-83, The Montgomery Advertiser, Montgomery, Ala., 1985-87; political reporter The Tampa Tribune, Tampa, Fla., 1987-89, Washington corr., 1989-91, political columnist, 1991-93, night metro editor, 1993-94, political editor, 1994-97, sr. edito, 1997—. Panelist Tampa Bay Week, WEDU-TV, 1993—, Bayside, WTOG-TV, 1994—. Roman Catholic. Office: The Tampa Tribune PO Box 191 Tampa FL 33601-0191

LOCKETT, BARBARA ANN, librarian; b. Northampton, Mass., Feb. 21, 1936; d. William M. and Anna A. (Vachula) Prabulos; m. Richard W. Rice, June 2, 1957 (div. Feb. 1966); 1 child, Annamarie Louise; m. Benjamin B. Lockett, June 7, 1985. BS, U. Mass., 1957; MLS, U. Calif., Berkeley, 1967. Documents librarian Knolls Atomic Power Lab., Schenectady, N.Y., 1968-74; coordinator bibliog. devel. SUNY, Albany, 1974-81; prin. librarian reference services N.Y. State Library, Albany, 1981-85; dir. libraries Rensselaer Poly. Inst., Troy, N.Y., 1985-94, libr. emeritus, 1994—; cons. Office Mgmt. Svcs., Assn. Rsch. Librs., Washington, 1981-86. Contbr. articles on collection devel., mgmt. and info. systems to profl. jours. Mem. ALA (cons. collection mgmt. and devel. com., Resources and Tech. Svcs. div. 1983-87), Assn. Coll. and Rsch. Librs. (chmn. standards and accreditation com. 1988-90), N.Y. State Edn. and Rsch. Network (chmn. info. resources com. 1988-89), N.Y. State Libr./NYSERNet (joint planning team 1991-94, del. N.Y. State Gov.'s Conf. on Librs., 1990), Sigma Xi, Phi Kappa Phi, Beta Phi Mu. Mem. Unitarian Ch. Avocations; tennis, master gardener, accordion. Home: 1772 Calle Poniente Santa Barbara CA 93101-4916

LOCKETT, TYLER CHARLES, state supreme court justice; b. Corpus Christi, Tex., Dec. 7, 1932; s. Tyler Coleman and Evelyn (Lemond) L.; m. Sue W. Lockett, Nov. 3, 1961; children: Charles, Patrick. AB, Washburn U., 1955, JD, 1962. Bar: Kans. 1962. Pvt. practice law Wichita, 1962—; judge Ct. Common Pleas, 1971-77, Kans. Dist. Ct. 18th Dist., 1977-83; justice Supreme Court Kans., Topeka, 1983—. Methodist. Office: Kans Supreme Ct 389 Kans Jud Ctr 301 SW 10th Ave Topeka KS 66612-1502*

LOCKETT-EGAN, MARIAN WORKMAN, advertising executive; b. Murray, Ky., May 5, 1931; d. Otis H. Workman and Myrtle A. (Jones) Jordan; m. Gene Potts, Jan. 6, 1947 (div. Feb. 1962); children: Reed Nasser, Jennifer Anglin, George M., Cynthia Klenk; m. Barker Lockett, Oct. 11, 1963 (div. Dec. 1972); 1 child, Stephen R.W.; m. Douglas S. Egan Jr., Feb. 14, 1981. BA Murray State U., 1962. Asst. media dir. Noble-Dury & Assocs., Nashville, 1963-64; asst. research dir. Triangle Publs. Phila., 1964-66; assoc. media dir. Lewis & Gilman, Phila., 1966-72; v.p. advt. media, Scott Paper Co., Phila., 1972-83; pres. DMS Communications Inc., Ardmore, Pa., 1983—; exec. dir. The Media Sch., N.Y.C., 1983-85, 87—; mem. TV com. Assn. Nat. Advertisers, N.Y.C., 1977-83; guest lectr. Wharton U., Phila., 1981-82, 85, 86, 87; Gannet vis. prof. Sch. Journalism U. Fla., Gainesville, 1982. Guest editor Media Decisions, 1981. Trustee Meth. Hosp. Found., Phila., 1973-87. Mem. Broadcast Pioneers, TV and Radio Advt. Club (pres. 1973, 94-96). Republican. Episcopalian. Avocations: sailing, tennis. Home: 45 Llanfair Cir Ardmore PA 19003-3342

LOCKEY, RICHARD FUNK, allergist, educator; b. Lancaster, Pa., Jan. 15, 1940; s. Stephen Daniel and Anna (Funk) L.; m. Carol Lee Madill, July 3, 1982; children: Brian Christopher, Keith Edward. B.S., Haverford Coll., 1961; M.D., Temple U., 1965; M.S., U. Mich., 1972. Diplomate Am. Bd. Internal Medicine, Am. Bd. Allergy and Immunology. Intern Temple U.

Med. Sch., Phila., 1965-66; asst. resident internal medicine Univ. Hosp. U. Mich., Ann Arbor, 1966-67, resident, 1966-68, fellow in allergy and immunology, 1969-70; asst. prof. medicine U. South Fl. Coll. Medicine, Tampa, 1973-77, assoc. prof. medicine, 1977-83, asst. dir. div. allergy and immunology, 1979-82, dir. allergy and immunology, 1982—, prof. medicine, 1983—, prof. pediats., 1983—, prof. pub. health, 1987—; asst. chief sect. allergy and immunology VA Hosp., Tampa, 1973-82, chief sect. allergy and immunology, 1983—; mem. allergenic adv. com. FDA, 1985-89. Editor: Allergy and Clinical Immunology, 1980; co-editor: (with S.C. Bukantz) Fundamentals of Immunology and Allergy, 1987, (with S.C. Bukantz) Principles of Immunology and Allergy, 1987, JAMA Primer on Allergic and Immunologic Diseases, 1987, (with S. C. Bukantz) Allergen Immunotherapy, 1991, (with M. Levine) Monograph on Insect Allergy, 1995; contbr. articles to profl. jours. and chpts. to books; author monographs. Served to maj. USAF, 1971-73. Named Outstanding Med. Specialist, Town and Country Mag., 1989, Claude P. Brown Meml. lectr. Assn. Clin. Scientists, ADA, 1981, Disting. Visitor Ann. Meeting of Coll. of Medicine, Republic of Costa Rica, 1979, spl. mem. Internat. Sci. Bd. Pharmacia Allergy Rsch. Found., 1992—; recipient Alumni Achievement award Temple U. Sch. of Medicine Alumni Assn., 1990, Outstanding Leadership in Chpt. Devel. and Patient Support, Nat. Asthma and Allergy Found. of Am. award, 1992, Cert. of Appreciation, Fla. Med. Assn., 1992. Fellow ACP, AAAS, AMA, Am. Coll. Chest Physicians, Am. Acad. Allergy and Immunology (chmn. com. on insects 1978-81, chmn. undergrad. and grad. edn. com. 1982-88, com. on occupational lung disease 1982—, chmn. com. on standardization of allergenic extracts 1983-86, exec. com. mem. at large 1986-88, historian 1988-89, sec. 1989-90, treas. 1990-91, pres.-elect 1991-92, pres. 1992-93, Am. Bd. Allergy and Immunology (bd. dirs. 1993—), Soc. Allergy and Immunology of Cordoba, Argentina (hon.), John M. Sheldon U. of Mich. Allergy Soc. (councilor 1977-80, pres. 1980-82), Fla. Allergy and Immunology Soc. (sec.-treas. 1979-80, pres. 1981-82), Southeastern Allergy Assn., Hillsborough County Med. Assn., Joint Coun. Allergy and Immunology, Clin. Immunology Soc., Fla. Thoracic Soc., Univ. Club, Carrollwood Village Club. Avocation: antique cut glass and tools. Home: 3909 Northampton Way Tampa FL 33624-4443 Office: U So Fla VA Hosp 13801 Bruce B Downs Blvd Tampa FL 33612-4745

LOCKHART, AILEENE SIMPSON, retired dance, kinesiology and physical education educator; b. Atlanta, Mar. 18, 1911; d. Thomas Ellis and Aileene Reeves (Simpson) L. B.S., Tex. Woman's U., 1932; M.S., U. Wis., 1937, Ph.D., 1942; D.Sc. (hon.), U. Nebr., 1967. Mem. faculty Mary Hardin Baylor Coll., Belton, Tex., 1937-42, U. Wis., 1941-42; asst. prof., then assoc. prof. phys. edn. and pharmacology U. Nebr., 1942-49; assoc. prof., then prof. U. So. Calif., 1949-73; dean Coll. Health, Phys. Edn., Recreation and Dance Tex. Woman's U., 1973-78, prof. dance and phys. edn., chmn. dept. dance, 1978-83, adj. prof., 1983-88, Rachel Bryant Meml. lectr., 1997; Clare Small lectr. U. Colo., 1975; Ethel Martus Lawther lectr. U. N.C., 1978; Amy Morris Homans lectr., Milw., 1976; Donna Mae Miller Humanities scholar/lectr. , U. Ariz., Tucson, 1989; vis. prof./lectr. Iowa State U., univs., Wash., Oreg., Wis., Mass.; N.H., Calif. State U., Long Beach, Springfield (Mass.) Coll., Smith Coll., Wellesley Coll., U. Maine-Presque Isle, Dunfermline Coll., Edinburgh, Scotland, U. Brazil, Brasilia; cons. editor William C. Brown Publishing Co., Dubuque, Iowa, 1954—. Author or co-author 12 books; contbr. numerous articles profl. jours.; cons. editor or editor over 300 books. Recipient Disting. Alumnae award Tex. Woman's U., 1971, Disting. Alumnae award U. Wis.-Madison, 1981, Cornaro award, 1980, Honor award Ministry Edn., Taiwan, 1981, Minnie Stevens Piper Found. award State of Tex., 1983, Nat. Dance Assn. Heritage award, 1985, Amy Morris Homans fellow, 1961-62; honra ao Merito Ministerio de Educato and Cultura Brazilia, Brazil, 1977; Nat. Dance Assn. scholar, 1986-87; Tex. Assn. Health, Phys. Edn., Recreation and Dance scholar, 1986. Fellow Am. Coll. Sports Medicine, Am. Alliance Health, Phys. Edn., Recreation and Dance (Honor award 1963, Luther Halsey Gulick award 1980), Am. Acad. Phys. Edn. (pres. 1980-81, Hetherington award 1992); mem. Nat. Assn. Girls and Women in Sports (honor award 1991, Rachel Bryant Meml. lectr. 1997), Nat. Dance Assn., So. Assn. Phys. Edn. Coll. Women, Nat. Assn. Phys. Edn. in Higher Edn., Phi Kappa Phi. Presbyterian. *That my students, many now well respected scholars, others eager neophytes in the journey of learning, exemplify some of the goals, ideals and visions, the high standards and high expectancies we have shared together is to me the most meaningful and fulfilling aspect in my life as an educator.*

LOCKHART, GREGORY GORDON, lawyer; b. Dayton, Ohio, Sept. 2, 1946; s. Lloyd Douglas and Evelyn (Gordon) L.; m. Paula Louise Jewett, May 20, 1978; children: David H., Sarah L. BS, Wright State U., 1973; JD, Ohio State U., 1976. Bar: Ohio 1976, U.S. Dist. Ct. (so. dist.) Ohio 1977, U.S. Ct. Appeals (6th cir.) 1988, U.S. Supreme Ct. 1993. Legal advisor Xenia and Fairborn (Ohio) Police Dept., 1977-78; asst. pros. atty. Greene County Prosecutor, Xenia, 1978-87; ptnr. DeWine & Schenck, Xenia, 1978-82, Schenck, Schmidt & Lockhart, Xenia, 1982-85, Ried & Lockhart, Beavercreek, Ohio, 1985-87; asst. U.S. atty. So. Dist. of Ohio, Columbus, 1987-89, Dayton, 1989—; adj. prof. Coll. Law U. Dayton, 1990—, Wright State U., Dayton, 1979—. Co-author: Federal Grand Jury Practice, 1996. Pres. Greene County Young reps., Xenia, 1977-79. With USAF, 1966-70; Vietnam. Mem. Fed. Bar Assn. (chpt. pres. 1994-95), Kiwanis (pres. 1983-84, lt. gov. 1986-87), Jaycees (pres. 1976-79), Am. Inns of Ct. (master of bench). Methodist. Avocations: golf, tennis, hiking, camping. Office: US Attorney 200 W 2d St Rm 602 Federal Bldg Dayton OH 45402

LOCKHART, JAMES BICKNELL, III, company executive; b. White Plains, N.Y., May 13, 1946; s. James Bicknell Jr. and Mary Ann (Riegel) L.; m. Carolyn Strahan Zoephel, June 17, 1972; children: James Bicknell IV, Grace Strahan. BA, Yale U., 1968; MBA, Harvard U., 1974. Asst. treas. Gulf Oil (E.H.), London, 1979-80; fin. dir. Gulf Oil Belgium, Brussels, 1980-81; sr. mgr. Gulf Oil Corp., Pitts., 1981-82, asst. treas., 1982-83; v.p., treas. Alexander and Alexander Services, N.Y.C., 1983-89; exec. dir. Pension Benefit Guaranty Corp., Washington, 1989-93; mng. dir., head pvt. fin. group Smith Barney, Inc., N.Y.C., 1993-95; sr. v.p. fin. Nat. Reins. Corp., 1996; mng. dir., CFO NetRisk, 1997—. Contbr. articles to profl. jours. Treas. Reps. Abroad, London, 1978-80. Served to lt. (j.g.) USNR, 1969-72. Fellow Assn. Corp. Treas. (Eng.); mem. Assn. Pvt. Pension and Welfare Plans (bd. dirs. 1993-95).

LOCKHART, JOHN MALLERY, management consultant; b. Mellen, Wis., May 17, 1911; s. Carl Wright and Gladys (Gale) L.; m. Judith Anne Wood, Feb. 26, 1938 (dec. June 1991); children: Wood Alexander, Gale, Thomas; m. Frances Whittaker, Jan. 7, 1993. BS, Northwestern U., 1931; JD, IIT, 1938. CPA, Ill. Teaching fellow Northwestern U., 1931; asst. v.p. Welsh, Davis & Co. (investment bankers), Chgo., 1935-41; treas. Transcontinental & Western Air, Inc., Kansas City, Mo., 1941-47; exec. v.p., CEO TACA Airways, S.A., 1944-45; v.p., dir. The Kroger Co., 1947-71, exec. v.p., 1961-71; pres. Kroger Family Ctr. Stores, 1969-71, Lockhart Co. (mgmt. cons.), 1971—; v.p. corp. fin. Gradison & Co., 1973-86; chmn. bd. dirs., CEO Ohio Real Estate Investment Co., Ohio Real Estate Equity Corp., 1974-76; bd. dirs. Employers Mut. Cos., Des Moines, Witt Co.; chmn. bd. dirs. Autotronics Systems, Inc., 1976-78; bd. dirs. Vectra Internat., Inc., Hamilton Mut. Ins. Co. Chmn. Hamilton County Hosp. Commn., 1965-84; mem. adv. bd. Greater Cin. Airport, 1961-86. Mem. Comml. Club, Cin. Country Club, Conquistadores del Cielo Club. Home and Office: 2770 Walsh Rd Cincinnati OH 45208-3425

LOCKHART, KEITH ALAN, orchestra conductor, musician, teacher; b. Poughkeepsie, N.Y., Nov. 7, 1959; s. Newton Frederick and Marilyn Jean (Woodyard) L.; m. Ann Louise Heatherington, Aug. 22, 1981 (div. 1983). B.A. summa cum laude in German, Furman U., 1981, Mus.B. summa cum laude in Piano Performance, 1981; M.F.A. in Orch. Conducting, Carnegie-Mellon U., 1983. Mem. condrs. faculty Carnegie-Mellon U., 1983-89; music dir. Pitts. Civic Orch., 1987-90; asst. condr. Akron Symphony Orch., 1988-90, Cin. Symphony Orch., Cin. Pops Orch., 1990-92; assoc. condr., 1992-95; music dir. Cin. Chamber Orch., 1992—; condr. Naples (Fla.) Philharmonic Orch., 1993—, Boston Pops Orch., Boston Symphony Orch. Youth Concerts, 1995—. Guest condr. Chgo. Symphony Orch., Cleve. Orch., L.A. Philharmonic, L.A. Chamber Orch., Toronto Symphony, Mont. Symphony Orch., Indpls. Symphony, Vt. Symphony, Eugene Symphony, Long Island Philharmonic, Orch. Sinfonica de Tucuman (Argentina); mem. adv. bd. Music Educators Nat. Conf.; pres. nat. adv. bd. Brevard Music Ctr., 1996—. Co-editor, arranger performance edition opera John Gay: The Beggars' Opera, 1985; recordings: Telarc, Christmas Songs with Mel Torme, 1992, works by Glabraith, Alonso-Crespo, 1995, New Energy from the Americas with Cin. Chamber Orch., 1996, Runnin Wild, 1996, American Visions, 1997. Mem. Conductors' Guild Am., Symphony Orch. League, Am. Fedn. Musicians. Avocations: reading; cooking; skiing; raquetball; outdoor sports. Office: The Boston Pops Orchestra care Boston Symphony Orchestra Symphony Hall Boston MA 02115

LOCKHART, PATSY MARIE, secondary education educator; b. San Francisco, Nov. 7, 1949; d. Alfred Jr. and Georgia Anna (Walker) Lax; m. Terence C. Lockhart, Apr. 23, 1977 (div. Apr. 1984); children: Dana Nolley, Therese C., Mishua. BA, San Jose State U., 1975, postgrad., 1992—. Tchr. Ravenswood City Sch. Dist., East Palo Alto, Calif., 1975-79, edn. specialist, 1979-80, tchr., 1980-84; tchr. Barnard White Middle Sch., New Haven Unified Sch. Dist., Union City, Calif., 1984—; coord. Urban Sites Writing Network, N.Y.C., 1993-94; cons. Bay Area Writing Project, Berkeley, Calif., 1984—; table leader Calif. Learning Assessment-State of Calif., Sacramento, 1994; writer curriculum devel Calif. Assessment Program Secondary, Sacramento, 1990-92. Mem. choir and Cantateers, Allen Temple Bapt. Ch. Mem. NAACP, Nat. Coun. for Tchrs. of English, Calif. League of Mid. Schs. (adv. bd. 1992—), Calif. Tchr.'s Assn. Minority Caucus. Democrat. Avocations: swimming, sewing, decorating, singing, photography. Home: 4473 Deep Creek Rd Fremont CA 94555-2059 Office: Barnard White Mid Sch 725 Whipple Rd Union City CA 94587-1343

LOCKHEAD, GREGORY ROGER, psychology educator; b. Boston, Aug. 8, 1931; s. John Roger and Ester Mae (Bixby) L.; m. Jeanne Marie Hutchinson, June 9, 1957; children: Diane, Elaine, John. B.S., Tufts U., 1958; Ph.D., Johns Hopkins, 1965. Psychologist research staff IBM Research, Yorktown Heights, N.Y., 1958-61; research assoc., instr. Johns Hopkins U., Balt., 1961-65; asst. prof. psychology Duke U., Durham, N.C., 1965-68; assoc. prof. Duke, 1968-71, prof., 1971-91; chmn. dept. exptl. psychology Duke U., Durham, N.C., 1991—; scholar Stanford U.; research asso. U. Calif., Berkeley, 1971-72; fellow Wolfson Coll., Oxford (Eng.) U., 1980-81; scholar Fla. Atlantic U., 1981; Cons. in human engring. Cons. editor: Perception and Psychophysics, 1972-92; contbr. articles to profl. jours., co-author, editor chpts. in books. Served with USN, 1951-55. NSF grantee, 1966-69, 79-84, USPHS grantee, 1963-69, 70-79, Air Force Office Sci. Rsch., 1983-91. Fellow Am. Psychol. Assn., Am. Psychol. Soc.; mem. Psychonomic Soc., Internat. Soc. Psychophysics, Sigma Xi, Phi Beta Kappa (hon.). Home: 2900 Montgomery St Durham NC 27705-5638 Office: Duke U Dept Exptl Psychology Durham NC 27708

LOCKLAIR, GARY HAMPTON, computer science educator; b. Sacramento, May 1, 1956; s. Oliver Hampton and Frances Eleanor (Snyder) L.; m. Karen Ann Kellar, Aug. 13, 1977; children: Joshua, Sabrina, David, Daniel, Valerie. BA in Chemistry, Calif. State U., Sacramento, 1979, BS in Computer Sci., 1980; MS, U. Idaho, 1986. Programmer, analyst Calif. Dept. Transp., Sacramento, 1977-79; mem. tech. staff Hewlett-Packard Co., Cupertino, Calif., 1980-81; software quality engr. Hewlett-Packard Co., Corvallis, Oreg., 1981-83; software program mgr. Hewlett-Packard Co., Boise, Idaho, 1983-86; asst. prof. Concordia U. Wis., Mequon, 1986—, chair computer sci. dept., 1986—, dir. computer ctr., 1986-93; computing cons., Milw., 1986—. Author: All of the Above, 1992; contbr. articles to profl. jours. Dist. computer cons. Philomath (Oreg.) Sch. Dist., 1981-83. Recipient HP Customer Svc. award Hewlett-Packard and Exxon Corp., 1985. Mem. IEEE, Assn. for computing Machinery. Lutheran. Avocation: photography. Office: Concordia U Wis 12800 N Lake Shore Dr Mequon WI 53097-2418

LOCKLEAR, BRENDA LOUISE, mathematics educator; b. Laurinburg, N.C., Apr. 22, 1950; d. Glassie and Emma Bell (Jones) L.; m. Edward Arnold Locklear, Apr. 29, 1973; children: Glendoria, Margaret Joyce. Early childhood cert., Fayetteville State U., 1987. Tchr. Robeson County Schs., N.C., 1987—. Mem. NEA, N.C. Assn. Educators. Republican. Baptist. Avocations: writing children stories, programming computer student activities, cooking.

LOCKLEAR, HEATHER, actress; b. L.A., Sept. 25, 1961; d. Bill and Diane L.; m. Tommy Lee, 1986 (div. 1994); m. Richie Sambora, 1994. Appeared in (TV series) Dynasty, 1981-89, T.J. Hooker, 1982-87, Going Places, 1990, Melrose Place, 1992—, (films) Firestarter, 1986, Return of the Swamp Thing, 1990, Wayne's World 2, 1993, A Dangerous Woman, 1993, The First Wives Club, 1996; (TV movies) Twil, 1981, City Killer, 1984, Blood Sport, 1986, Rich Men, Single Women, 1990, Fade to Black, 1993, Texas Justice, 1995, Shattered Mind, 1996. Office: William Morris Agy 151 S El Camino Dr Beverly Hills CA 90212-2704

LOCKLIN, WILBERT EDWIN, management consultant; b. Washington, Apr. 2, 1920; s. Wilbert Edwin and Margaret Mae (Franklin) L.; m. Olga Maria Osterwald, June 28, 1947; children: Kenneth, Patricia, Randall. BS, Johns Hopkins U., 1942; LLD, George Williams Coll., 1966; DHum, Springfield Coll., 1994. Vice-pres. Nat. Bur. Pvt. Schs., N.Y.C., 1947-49; account exec. Reuel Estill & Co., N.Y.C., 1949-51; asst. dir. admissions Johns Hopkins, 1945-47, asst. to pres., 1955-65; v.p. Johns Hopkins Fund, 1960-65; pres. Springfield (Mass.) Coll., 1965-85, Locklin Mgmt. Services, 1985—; chmn. bd. dirs., mem. exec. com., salary com., charitable funds com.; chmn. trust com. Bay Bank Valley Trust Co., 1966-91; mem. exec. com. Assn. Ind. Colls. and Univs. in Mass., 1971-83; founding mem. Cooperating Colls. of Greater Springfield.; pres. Cooperating Colls. of Greater Springfield, 1982-83; mem. exec. com., bd. dirs. Business Friends of Arts. Bd. dirs. Springfield Symphony Orch., 1973-83; campaign dir. Elms Coll., 1992-94; sr. advisor Mass. Soc. for Prevention of Cruelty to Animals, 1995—. Served with USAAF, 1942-45. Decorated DFC, Air medal. Home: 225 Prynnwood Rd Longmeadow MA 01106-2754

LOCKMAN, STUART M., lawyer; b. Jersey City, July 18, 1949; s. Albert Korey and Edna Sally (Easton) L.; m. Deena Laurel Young, Dec. 27, 1970; children: Jeffrey, Susan, Karen. BA, U. Mich., 1971, JD, 1974. Bar: Mich. 1974, Fla. 1991; bd. cert. health law specialist, Fla. Ptnr. Honigman Miller Schwartz and Cohn, Detroit, 1974—. Office: Honigman Miller Schwartz & Cohn 2290 1st National Bldg Detroit MI 48226

LOCKMILLER, DAVID ALEXANDER, lawyer, educator; b. Athens, Tenn., Aug. 30, 1906; s. George Franklin and Lotta May (Ulrey) L.; m. Alma Elizabeth Russell, Sept. 23, 1930; children: Franklin Russell, Carlotta Elizabeth Lockmiller Fanari; m. Virginia L. Wilkinson, May 20, 1996. B.Ph., Emory U., 1927, A.M., 1928, LL.D., 1954; J.D., Cumberland U., 1929, LL.D., 1940; Ph.D., U. N.C., 1935; postgrad. summers, Oxford U., Eng., 1937, U. Chgo., 1940, U. Paris, 1952; Litt.D., U. Chattanooga, 1960; L.H.D., Am. U., 1961; EdD, Tenn. Wesleyan Coll., 1962. Bar: Ohio, Mo., Okla., Ark., N.C., Tenn., Supreme Ct. U.S. Practiced in Monett, Mo., 1929-33; research asst. Inst. Research in Social Sci., U. N.C., 1934-35; instr. history and polit. sci. N.C. State U., 1935-36, asst. prof., 1936-38, asso. prof., 1938-41, prof., head dept., 1940-42; pres. U. Chattanooga, 1942-59, Ohio Wesleyan U., 1959-61; exec. dir. Distance Edn. and Tng. Coun., Washington, 1961-72; edn. cons., 1972—; vis. prof. Am. history Emory U., summer 1938, N.C. Coll., Durham, summer 1941; vis. prof. geography Meredith Coll., 1941-42; 1st vice chmn. Am. Council on Edn., 1952-53. Author: Magoon in Cuba, A History of the Second Intervention, 1906-09, 1938, 69, Sir William Blackstone, 1938, 70, History of N.C. State College of Agriculture and Engineering, 1889-1939, 1939, The Consolidation of the University of North Carolina, 1942, General Enoch H. Crowder: Father of Selective Service, 1955, Scholars on Parade: Academic Degrees and Costumes, 1969, 92; contbr. to hist., ednl. jours., encys. Mem. exec. com. N.C. Hist. Highway Markers, 1935-42, Nat. Mental Health Council USPHS; def. adv. com. edn. Armed Forces; mem. Pres.'s Commn. to Argentina Sesquicentennial, 1960; Past mem. U. Senate Meth. Ch. State dept. rep. to colls. and univs. Far East, 1953; hon. trustee U. Chattanooga Found., Rockefeller Found. Recipient Chattanooga Man of Yr. award, 1953, Hon. alumnus award N.C. State U., 1940, NTL Home Study Coun. Man of Yr. award, 1969, Disting. Svc. award United Schs. Bus., 1972, Spl. Achievement award Nat. Assn. Trade and Tech. Schs., 1972, Alumnus medal St. Andrew's Sch., 1980, Honor Leadership award Cleve. Inst. Electronics, 1982, Lifetime Achievement award Samford U., 1994; named to NTL Home Study Coun. Hall of Fame; Travel grantee to Brit. Univs., 1956. Fellow Am. Scandinavian Found.; mem. Assn. Am. Colls. and Univ. (pres. 1960-61), So. Univ. Conf. (exec. sec. 1956-59), Assn. Urban Univs. (past pres.), Internat. Conf. Correspondence Edn., Chattanooga Bar Assn., Chattanooga Exec. Club (ex-pres.), SAR, Am. Hist. Assn., Tenn. Coll. Assn. (pres. 1948-49), So. Assn. Colls. and Secondary Schs. (v.p. 1953), Am. Polit. Sci. Assn., So. Hist. Assn., Bar Assn. Ohio, Am. Mil. Inst., Conf. Latin Am. Studies, State Lit. and Hist. Assn. N.C., Newcomen Soc., Sovereign Order St. John of Jerusalem-Knights of Malta, Phi Beta Kappa, Phi Kappa Phi, Omicron Delta Kappa, Blue Key, Phi Delta Phi, Pi Gamma Mu, Pi Delta Epsilon, Tau Kappa Alpha, Sigma Chi, Alpha Pi Omega, Delta Sigma Rho, Alpha Beta Kappa (founder). Republican. Methodist. Clubs: Masons, KT, Shriners; Rotary (Washington) (past Chattanooga pres., dist. gov.), Kiwanis (Chattanooga) (hon.), Torch International (Washington), Cosmos (Washington). Home: McKendree Towers 4343 Lebanon Rd # 1711 Hermitage TN 37076-1223

LOCKNER, VERA JOANNE, farmer, rancher, legislator; b. St. Lawrence, S.D., May 19, 1937; d. Leonard and Zona R. (Ford) Verdugt; m. Frank O. Lockner, Aug. 7, 1955; children: Dean M., Clifford A. Grad., St. Lawrence (S.D.) High Sch., 1955. Bank teller/bookkeeper First Nat. Bank, Miller, S.D., 1963-66, Bank of Wessington, S.D., 1968-74; farmer/rancher Wessington, 1955—. Sunday sch. tchr. Trinity Luth. Ch., Miller, 1968-72; treas. PTO, Wessington, 1969-70; treas., vice chmn., chmn., state com. woman Hand County Dems., Miller, 1978—. Named one of Outstanding Young Women of Am., Women's Study Club, Wessington, 1970. Mem. Order of Ea. Star (warder, marshall, chaplain 1970—). Avocations: oil painting, crafts, gardening, photography. Home and Office: RR 2 Box 102 Wessington SD 57381-8932

LOCKSHIN, MICHAEL DAN, rheumatologist; b. Columbus, Ohio, Dec. 9, 1937; s. Samuel Dan and Florence (Levin) L.; m. Jane Toby Roberts, Sept. 2, 1965; 1 child, Amanda. AB, Harvard U., 1959, MD, 1963. Diplomate Am. Bd. Internal Medicine. From asst. prof. to prof. Cornell U. Med. Coll., N.Y.C., 1970-89; attending physician Hosp. for Spl. Surgery and N.Y. Hosp., N.Y.C., 1970-89; dir. extramural program Nat. Inst. Arthritis & Musculoskeletal Skin Diseases/NIH, Bethesda, Md., 1989-97, acting dir., 1994-95; dir. Barbara Volcker Ctr. Hosp. for Spl. Surgery, N.Y.C., 1997—; prof. Cornell U. Med. Coll., N.Y.C., 1997—. Contbr. over 150 articles to jours., chpts. to books. Mem. Am. Rheumatism Assn. (2d v.p. 1984-85), La Sociedad Chilena de Reumatologica (hon.), Alpha Omega Alpha. Office: 535 E 70th St Rm 416 Erpb New York NY 10021-4892

LOCKWOOD, DEAN H., physician, pharmaceutical executive; b. Milford, Conn., June 17, 1937; s. Horace Musson and Lucille Ruth (Fengler) L.; m. Carol Hay, June 21, 1958 (div. Mar. 1979); children: Andrew Brooks, Craig Stewart, Wendy Susan; m. Elizabeth East, July 19, 1980. AB, Wesleyan U., 1959; MD, John Hopkin's U., 1963. Intern in medicine Olser Medical Svc., The John Hopkins Hosp., Balt., 1963-64, asst. resident in medicine, 1964-65; staff assoc. sect. of intermediary metabolism Nat. Inst. Arthritis and Metabolic Diseases, NIH, Bethesda, Md., 1965-67; fellow dept pharmacology and experimental therapeutics and of medicine The John Hopkins U., Balt., 1967-69, asst. prof. medicine Sch. Medicine, 1969-74, asst. prof. pharm. and exptl. therapeutics, 1971-76, assoc. prof. medicine, 1974-76; staff physician The John Hopkins Hosp., Balt., 1969-76; dir. Diabetes Mgmt. Clin., The John Hopkins Hosp., Balt., 1971-76; prof. medicine Sch. Medicine U. Rochester, N.Y., 1976-92, head endocrine metabolism unit, dept. medicine, Sch. Medicine, 1976-91; assoc. chair medicine U. Rochester, 1991; v.p. clin. rsch. Warner Lambert Co., Ann Arbor, Mich., 1991-92, 93-94, acting sr. v.p. clin. rsch., 1992-93; staff physician Balt. City Hosp., 1969-76, Strong Meml. Hosp., 1976-91; med. cons. Highland Hospital of Rochester, 1977-91, attending cons. Park Ridge Hosp., 1989-91; assoc. chmn. rsch. dept. medicine U. Rochester, 1991; adj. prof. medicine Sch. Medicine U. Rochester, 1992-93; lectr. in the field. Editorial bd. mem.: Internat. Jour. Obesity, 1975-84, Endocrinology, 1981-85, Am. Jour. Physiology, 1982-88; cons. editor: Jour. Clin. Investigation, 1992-97. Recipient Bordon Undergrad. Rsch. award, 1963, NIH Rsch. Career Devel. award, 1969-74; Henry Strong Denison scholar, 1962-63; Am. Diabetes Assn. grantee, 1986-91, NIH grantee, 1969-92. Mem. Am. Diabetes Assn., Am. Fedn. for Rsch., The Endocrine Soc., Am. Soc. Biol. Chemists, Am. Soc. Clin. Investigation, Sigma Xi, Alpha Omega Alpha, Phi Beta Kappa. Home: 3431 Wagner Woods Ct Ann Arbor MI 48103-2167 Office: Warner Lambert 2800 Plymouth Rd Ann Arbor MI 48105-2430

LOCKWOOD, FRANK JAMES, manufacturing company executive; b. San Bernadino, Calif., Oct. 30, 1931; s. John Ellis and Sarah Grace (Roberts) L.; children from previous marraige: Fay, Frank, Hedy, Jonnie, George, Katherine, Bill, Dena; m. 2d. Crystal Marie Miller, 1986. Student, Southeast City Coll., Chgo., 1955, Ill. Inst. Tech., 1963-64, Bogan Jr. Coll., Chgo., 1966. Foreman Hupp Aviation, Chgo., 1951-60; dept. head UARCO, Inc., Chgo., 1960-68; pres. XACT Machine & Engring., Chgo., 1968—; chmn. bd., pres., bd. dirs. Lockwood Engring., Inc., Chgo.; Ill. Nat. Corp., Chgo., and cons. engr., Chgo. Patentee printing equipment, beverage cans, gasoline pump dispenser "Super Pin", bus. forms equipment. Participant Forest Land Mgmt. Program; mem. Ill. Ambassadors; commr. Econ. Devel. Commn., Mt. Vernon, Ill., 1985; mem. bd. County of Jefferson, Ill., 1992—; mem. exec. com., legis. com. Ill. County Bds. Coun. Named Chgo. Ridge Father of the Yr., 1964. Mem. Ill. Divers' Assn. (pres. 1961-62). Lodge: Masons (32 degree), Shriners (past master 2). Home: RR 1 Texico IL 62889-9801 Office: 7011 W Archer Ave Chicago IL 60638-2201

LOCKWOOD, GARY LEE, lawyer; b. Woodstock, Ill., Dec. 3, 1946; s. Howard and Luella Mae (Behrens) L.; m. Cheryl Lynn Wittrock, Jan. 5, 1967; children: Jennifer, Lee, Cynthia. BA magna cum laude, Iowa Wesleyan Coll., 1969; student, Albert Ludwig U., Freiburg in Breisgau, Fed. Republic Germany, 1968-69; JD, Northwestern U., 1976. Bar: Ill. 1976, U.S. Dist. Ct. (no. dist.) Ill. 1976. Assoc. Lord, Bissell & Brook, Chgo., 1976-85, ptnr., 1985—. Bd. dirs. McHenry Sch. Dist. 15, Ill., 1974-85, pres., 1979-80. Served to sgt. U.S. Army, 1970-72. Mem. ABA (bus. and ins. com. 1985—). Methodist. Avocations: sports. Home: 175 N Harbor Dr Chicago IL 60601-7344 Office: Lord Bissel & Brook 115 S La Salle St Ste 3600 Chicago IL 60603-3801

LOCKWOOD, JOANNE SMITH, mathematician educator; b. Quebec City, Can., Nov. 9, 1946; d. Donald William MacKay and Sylvia Eleanor (Howard) Smith; m. Bryce M. Lockwood Jr., Aug. 10, 1968; children: Daren MacKay, Keith McLellan. BA in English, St. Lawrence U., 1968; MBA, Plymouth State Coll., 1980, BA in Math., 1985. Editor Houghton Mifflin Co., Boston, 1969-86; tchr. New Hampton (N.H.) Sch., 1974-76, 80-81; lectr. Plymouth (N.H.) State Coll., 1988—. Author: (textbooks) Beginning Algebra with Applications, 1989, 92, 96, Intermediate Algebra with Applications, 1989, 92, 96, Business Mathematics, 1988, 94, Introductory Algebra with Basic Mathematics, 1989, 96, Algebra with Trigonometry for College Students, 1991, A Review of Geometry, 1993, Prealgebra, 1994, Algebra for College Students: A Functions Approach, 1994. Mem. Am. Math. Assn. of Two Yr. Colls., Text and Acad. Authors Assn. Home: RR 1 Box 180 New Hampton NH 03256-9717

LOCKWOOD, JOHN LEBARON, plant pathologist; b. Ann Arbor, Mich., May 28, 1924; s. George LeBaron and Mary Bonita (Leininger) L.; m. Jean Elizabeth Springborg, Mar. 21, 1959; children: James L., Laura A. Student, Western Mich. Coll., 1941-43; BA, Mich. State Coll., 1948, MS, 1950; PhD, U. Wis., 1953. Asst. prof. Ohio Agrl. Expt. Sta., Wooster, 1953-55; asst. prof. Mich. State U., East Lansing, 1955-61, assoc. prof., 1961-67, prof., 1967-90, prof. emeritus, 1990—. Served with U.S. Army, 1943-46. NSF research fellow, 1970-71. Fellow Am. Phytopathol. Soc. (pres. 1984-85). Home: 1931 Yuma Trl Okemos MI 48864-2744 Office: Mich State Univ Dept Botany and Pathol East Lansing MI 48824

LOCKWOOD, RHODES GREENE, retired lawyer; b. Buchanan, Va., Nov. 26, 1919; s. Rhodes G. and Violet (Bennett) L.; m. Mary Hitchcock, Jan. 22, 1949 (dec. Feb. 1991); children: Mary Howland, Rhodes G., Faith B., Rebecca Ingersoll; m. Linda Uttaro, Feb. 18, 1994. B.A., Williams Coll., 1941; postgrad, U. Va., 1941-42, Va. Poly. Inst., 1946-47; LL.B., Harvard U., 1949. Bar: Mass. bar 1949. Assoc. firm Choate, Hall & Stewart, Boston, 1949-59; ptnr. Choate, Hall & Stewart, 1959-92—. Trustee Brigham and Women's Hosp.; sec., trustee Univ. Hosp.; vice chmn. Wellesley (Mass.) Sch. Com., 1966, chmn., 1967-69; mem. Wellesley Bd. Health. Served with

USNR, 1942-52. Mem. Boston Bar Assn., Am. Law Inst., Am. Soc. Hosp. Attys., Mass. Hosp. Assn., Harvard U. Law Sch. Alumni Assn. Democrat. Home: 1 Edgewater Dr Wellesley MA 02181-1617 Office: Choate Hall & Stewart 53 State St Exchange Pl Boston MA 02109

LOCKWOOD, RHONDA J., mental health services professional; b. Jacksonville, N.C., Apr. 4, 1960; d. George Barton and Sally Lynn (Hassell) L. BA, Newberry Coll., 1982; MS in Edn., Youngstown State U., 1988. nat. cert. counselor. Corrections/tng. officer Geauga County Sheriff's Dept., Chardon, Ohio, 1982-87; forensic counselor Human Svcs. Ctrs., Inc., New Castle, Pa., 1987-89; dir. children & family svcs. Marion Citrus Mental Health Ctrs., Inc., Ocala, Fla., 1989-96; clin. social worker Fla. Dept. Juvenile Justice, Alachua Halfway House, 1996-97; regional supv. Family Action Program Corner Drug Store, Inc., Gainesville, Fla., 1997—; cofounder Sexual Abuse Intervention Network, Ocala, 1990-96, chair, 1990-92, Family Svcs. Planning Team, 1992-94; cons. Health & Human Svcs. Bd. Dist. 13, 1993-96. Pol. vol. state campaigns Dem. Party, Warren, Ohio, 1978-85; mem. Sexual Abuse Prevention Edn. Network, New Castle, 1987-88; cons. to gov.'s task force Sex Offenders and Their Victims; cons. Mad Dads Orgn., Ocala, 1993; mem. Juvenile Justice Coun., Ocala, 1993-94; children's svc. rep. Fla. Coun. for Cmty. Mental Health, 1995-96. Recipient Outstanding Teen Vol. award Am. Red Cross, 1977. Fellow N. Eastern Ohio Police Benevolent Assn.; mem. Nat. Mus. for Women in the Arts, Nat. Bd. Cert. Counselors, NGLTF, Hamilton Columbia Counties Juvenile Justice Coun., Human Rights Campaign Fund, Chi Sigma Iota, Phi Kappa Phi. Democrat. Avocations: softball, volleyball, golf, fishing. Home: 201 E Main St Archer FL 32618-5517

LOCKWOOD, ROBERT PHILIP, publishing executive; b. Yonkers, N.Y., Dec. 21, 1949; s. Albert Francis and Evelyn (Toburn) L.; m. Christiana Lynn Nowels, July 21, 1973; children—Ryan Robert, Theresa Lynn. B.A. in History, Fairfield U. Assoc. editor Our Sunday Visitor, Huntington, Ind., 1971-77, dir. books, 1982-90, editor, 1977-85, dir., editor in chief, 1985-87, pub., 1987-90, pres., chief exec. officer, 1990—. Author: 70 Years of Our Sunday Visitor, 1982; columnist Catholic Jour.; contbr. articles to profl. jours., numerous periodicals. Chmn. St. Mary's Sch. Bd., Huntington, 1984-85; coach Huntington Cath. H.S. Tennis, 1983-85; bd. dirs. Cath. League for Religious and Civil Rights, 1994—; nat. adv. bd. Cath. Campaign for Am., 1993—. Mem. Cath. Press Assn. (editl. com. 1983—, Best Regular Column 1992, 94). Avocations: writing; tennis. Home: 4919 Long Canon Pl Fort Wayne IN 46804-6534

LOCKWOOD, ROBERT W., management consultant; b. Boise, Idaho, June 11, 1924; s. Walter Thomas and Elizabeth C. (Chamberlain) L.; m. Lois M. Minely, Feb. 19, 1945; children—Linda Kay Lockwood Johnson, Craig H. B.S., U. Calif., Berkeley, 1949, M.B.A., 1950; LL.D. (hon.), Northrop U., 1971. Civilian chief mgmt. Los Angeles procurement dist. U.S. Army, 1955-56; cons. Booz Allen and Hamilton, Los Angeles, 1956-58; v.p. United Calif. Bank, Los Angeles, 1958-75; v.p. acad. affairs Northrop U., 1975-76; asst. to pres. Bradston Hurricane, 1979-80; pres. Diversified Baby Products Internat., West Covina, Calif., 1980—; grad. prof. mgmt. Northrop U., Nat. U., San Diego. Served to 1st lt. USAR, 1942-45. Fellow Am. Inst. Indsl. Engrs. (pres. 1971-72). Club: Masons.

LOCKWOOD, THEODORE DAVIDGE, former academic administrator; b. Hanover, N.H., Dec. 5, 1924; s. Harold John and Elizabeth (Van Campen) L.; m. Elizabeth Anne White, Apr. 13, 1944 (dec. Feb. 1980); children: Tamara Jane Lockwood Quinn, Richard Davidge, Mavis Ferens Borak, Serena Katherine; m. Lucille LaRose Abbot, Sept. 7, 1980. B.A., Trinity Coll., 1948, Litt.D. (hon.), 1981; M.A., Princeton, 1950, Ph.D., 1952; L.H.D., Concord Coll., 1968; LL.D., Union Coll., 1968, U. Hartford, 1969; L.H.D., Wesleyan U., Middletown, Conn., 1970. Instr. great issues Dartmouth, 1952-53; asst. prof. history Juniata Coll., Huntingdon, Pa., 1953-55, Mass. Inst. Tech., 1955-60; dean faculty Concord Coll., Athens, W.Va., 1960-64; provost, dean faculty Union Coll., Schenectady, 1964-68; pres. Trinity Coll., Hartford, Conn., 1968-81, Armand Hammer United World Coll. of Am. West, Montezuma, N.Mex., 1981-93; chmn. Greater Hartford Consortium for Higher Edn., 1972-81. Author: Mountaineers, 1945, Studies in European Socialism, 1960, Our Mutual Concern: The Role of the Independent College, 1968, Dreams and Promises: The Story of the Armand Hammer United World College, 1997. Bd. dirs. Vols. Internat. Tech. Assistance, 1965-85, chmn., 1966-71; Bd. fellows Trinity Coll., 1962-64, trustee, 1964-81; corporator Hartford Hosp., 1978-81, Hartford Pub. Libr., 1969-81; bd. dirs. Inst. for Living, 1969-81, Edn. Commn. of States, 1969-71, Am. Coun. on Edn., 1977-81; trustee Northwood Sch., Lake Placid, N.Y., 1969-78; dir. adv. coun. Audubon Soc. Expdn. Inst., 1978-90; bd. dirs. Harry Frank Guggenheim Found., 1979—, Nepal adv. com. World Wildlife Fund, 1985-95; dir. Ars Publica, 1989-95. With U.S. Army, 1943-45. Belgian-Am. Fellow, 1959. Mem. Assn. Am. Colls. (dir. 1973-78, chmn. 1976-77, mem. project on undergrad. edn. 1981-85), Greater Hartford C. of C. (dir. 1977-81), Phi Beta Kappa, Pi Gamma Mu. Unitarian.

LOCKYER, CHARLES WARREN, JR., corporate executive; b. Phila., Apr. 6, 1944; s. Charles Warren and Mary Alice (Underwood) L.; B.A., Fordham U., 1966; M.A., Princeton U., 1968, Ph.D., 1971, J.D. Georgetown U., 1995; m. Karen A. Damiani, Jan. 22, 1966; children: Charles Warren III, Larissa A., Daphne M. Vice pres. Fidelity Bank, Phila., 1970-79; v.p., chief fin. officer Pubco Corp., Glenn Dale, Md., 1980-82; exec. v.p. Perpetual Savs. Bank, F.S.B., Alexandria, VA, 1982-90; pres. Alleco Inc., Cheverly, Md., 1991-95; assoc. Fred, Frank, Harris, Schriver & Jacobson, Washington, 1996—; dir. Gulfstream Land & Devel. Corp., Plantation, Fla., 1980-86. Trustee Jeanes Hosp., Phila., 1973-87; dir. Foulkeways at Gwynedd (Pa.), 1975-80; mem. adv. com. classics Princeton U., 1978-83. Woodrow Wilson fellow, 1966. Mem. Phi Beta Kappa. Home: 4409 Glenridge St Kensington MD 20895-4255 Office: Fried Frank Harris Schriver & Jacobson 1001 Pennsylvania Ave NW Washington DC 20004-2505

LODDER, ROBERT ANDREW, chemistry and pharmaceutics educator; b. Cin., May 31, 1959. BS, Xavier U., Cin., 1981, MS, 1983; PhD, Ind. U., 1988. Teaching asst. Xavier U., 1981-83; teaching asst. Ind. U., Bloomington, 1983-85, rsch. asst., 1985-87; asst. prof. chemistry and pharmaceutics U. Ky., Lexington, 1988-94, assoc. prof., 1994—. Contbr. articles to profl. jours.; patentee in field. Recipient 100 award R & D mag., 1988, Tomas Hirschfeld award Pitts. Conf., 1988; 1st prize IBM Supercomputing Competition, 1990, NSF New Young Investigator award 1992; Technicon near-infrared analysis rsch. fellow, 1987. Mem. AAAS, ASTM, Coun. for Near-Infrared Spectroscopy (del.-at-large to nat. bd. dirs.), Am. Chem. Soc., Am. Assn. Pharm. Scientists, Am. Pharm. Assn., Ky. Acad. Sci. Office: U Ky Coll Pharmacy Rose St Lexington KY 40536-0082

LODER, VICTORIA KOSIOREK, information broker; b. Batavia, N.Y., May 27, 1945; d. Leon Stanley and Jennie Joann (Amatrano) Kosiorek; m. Ronald Raymond Loder, Nov. 6, 1965. BS in Bus. Mgmt., Roberts-Wesleyan Coll., Rochester, N.Y., 1989; MLS, SUNY, Buffalo, 1992; postgrad. in Religious Study, Liberty U., 1993—. Tech. info. specialist Eastman Kodak Co., Rochester, 1985-92; reference libr. Xerox Corp., Webster, N.Y., 1993-95; mgr. XPS strategy and integration libr. Xerox Corp., Fairport, N.Y., 1995-96, mgr. PSG Strategy and Bus. Info. Resource Ctr., 1997—; v.p., treas. Victron Design Svc. USA, Kent, N.Y., 1988—; pres., owner Alpha Omega Info Source, Kent, N.Y., 1993—. Avocations: clothing design/construction, horticulture/landscape design, floral design.

LODEWICK, PHILIP HUGHES, equipment leasing company executive; b. Bklyn., Dec. 31, 1944; s. Robert John and Louise Mary (Bockhold) L.; m. Christine Helen Lobeck, July 5, 1969; children: Alyssa Erin, Kendra Blythe. BS, U. Conn., 1966, MBA, 1967. With sales dept. IBM Corp., N.Y.C., 1969-71; officer Boothe Fin. Corp., San Francisco, 1971-80; pres. The Tradewell Corp., equipment leasing co., Ridgefield, Conn., 1980—; gen. ptnr. Sierra Assoc. IV, San Francisco, 1981-88; CFO Wicklo's Maple Hill Farm, Ridgefield, 1983—; bd. dirs. Ancora Coffee Roasters Inc., U. Conn. Found.; bd. overseers U. Conn. Bus. Sch. Trustee U. Conn. Found.; bd. dirs. St. Andrew's Luth. Ch., Ridgefield, 1979—; mem. Conn. Refugee Resettlement Commn., 1985-88; bd. dirs., treas. Family Y in Ridgefield, 1985-89; founder, dir. Discovery Ctr., 1986—; founder, pres. A Better Chance in Ridgefield, 1987—. With AUS, 1967-69, Korea. Mem. Computer Lessors and Dealers Assn., Golden Bridge Hounds, L.I. Golden Retreiver Club (pres. 1979-80). Republican. Lutheran. Avocations: golf, tennis, basketball, travel, reading. Home and Office: Tradewell Corp 201 Spring Valley Rd Ridgefield CT 06877-1229

LODGE, ARTHUR SCOTT, mechanical engineering educator; b. Waterloo, Lancashire, Eng., Nov. 20, 1922; s. Wilfred Claude and Jean Dea (Scott) L.; m. Helen Catherine Bannatyne, July 18, 1945; children: Keith Bannatyne, Alison Mary Shambrook, Timothy Patrick. B.A., U. Oxford, 1945, M.A., 1948, D.Phil., 1948. Jr. sci. officer Admiralty, Eng., 1942-45; theoretical physicist NRC, Montreal, Que., Can., 1945-46, Brit. Rayon Research Assn., Manchester, Eng., 1948-60; sr. lectr. Math Inst. Sci. and Tech., U. Manchester, 1961-68; prof. dept. engring. mechanics U. Wis., Madison, 1968-91, Hougen vis. prof., 1991, prof. emeritus, 1991—; v.p. Bannatek Co., Inc., Madison, 1981—. Author: Elastic Liquids, 1964 (citation classics award 1981), Body Tensor Fields..., 1974; contbr. articles to profl. jours.; patentee stressmeter. Recipient Byron Bird award U. Wis.-Madison, 1980; grantee U.S. govt. agys. Fellow Inst. Physics London; mem. NAE, Soc. Rheology (Bingham medal 1971), Brit. Soc. Rheology (Gold medal 1983). Republican. Episcopalian. Avocation: piano playing.

LODGE, EDWARD JAMES, federal judge; b. 1933. BS cum laude, Coll. Idaho, 1957; JD, U. Idaho, 1969. Mem. firm Smith & Miller, 1962-63; probate judge Canyon County, Idaho, 1963-65; judge Idaho State Dist. Ct., 1965-88; U.S. bankruptcy judge State of Idaho, 1988; dist. judge, now chief judge U.S. Dist. Ct. Idaho, 1989—. Recipient Kramer award for excellence in jud. adminstrn.; named three time All-Am., disting. alumnus Coll. Idaho, Boise State U.; named to Hall of Fame Boise State U., Coll. Idaho. Mem. ABA, Idaho Trial Lawyer Assn., Idaho State Bar Assn., U.S. Fed. Judges Assn., Boise State Athletic Assn., Elks Club. Office: US Dist Ct MSC 040 550 W Fort St Fl 6 Boise ID 83724-0101

LODGE, GEORGE C(ABOT), business administration educator; b. Boston, July 7, 1927; s. Henry Cabot Jr. and Emily (Sears) L.; m. Nancy Kunhardt, Apr. 23, 1949; children: Nancy Lodge Burmeister, Emily Lodge Pingeon, Dorothy Lodge Peabody, Henry, George Jr., David. AB cum laude, Harvard U., 1950; hon. doctorate, INCAE, 1994. Polit. reporter, columnist Boston Herald, 1950-54; dir. info. U.S. Dept. Labor, Washington, 1954-58, asst. sec. labor for internat. affairs, 1958-61, U.S. del. to ILO, chmn. governing body, 1960-61; lectr. Grad. Sch. Bus. Adminstr., Harvard U., Boston, 1961-68, assoc. prof., 1968-72, prof. bus. adminstrn., 1972-91, Jaime and Josefina Chua Tiampo prof. bus. adminstrn., 1991—. Author: Spearheads of Democracy: Labor in the Developing Countries, 1962, Engines of Change: United States Interests and Revolution in Latin America, 1970, The New American Ideology, 1975 (Ann. Book award Am. Acad. Mgmt. 1995), The American Disease, 1984, Perestroika for America, 1990, Comparative Business-Government Relations, 1990, Managing Globalization in the Age of Interdependence, 1995; co-author: Ideology and National Competitiveness, 1987; editor: U.S. Competitiveness in the World Economy, 1984. Rep. candidate U.S. Senate, Mass., 1962; vice-chmn. Inter-Am. Found., 1970-77. With USN, 1945-46. Named one of 10 Outstanding Youn Men in U.S., U.S. Jr. C. of C., 1961; recipient Arthur S. Fleming award, 1961, McKinsey award Harvard Bus. Rev., 1970, 74; Lee Kuan Yew fellow Gov. of Singapore, 1991. Mem. Coun. Fgn. Rels., Carnegie Endowment for Internat. Peace (trustee), Robert F. Kennedy Meml. (trustee). Office: Harvard U Bus Sch Soldiers Field Boston MA 02163

LODGE, JAMES ROBERT, dairy science educator; b. Downey, Iowa, July 1, 1925; s. Labon Ferrel Lodge and Margaret Clara (Elliott) Funk; m. Jean Agnes Wessel, June 15, 1947; children—Julie Beth, James Robert. B.S., Iowa State U., 1952, M.S., 1954; Ph.D., Mich. State U., 1957. Research asst. Mich. State U., East Lansing, 1954-57; research asso. U. Ill., Urbana, 1957-60; asst. prof. reproductive physiology U. Ill., 1960-63, asso. prof., 1963-69, prof., 1969-91, prof. emeritus, 1991—. Co-author: Reproductive Physiology and Artificial Insemination of Cattle, 2d edit, 1978; contbr. articles to profl. jours. Asst. coach girls softball Babe Ruth Little League, Urbana, 1972-74. Served with AUS, 1944-46. Recipient Outstanding Instr. award Dairy Club U. Ill., 1969, Alpha Zeta Outstanding Instr. award U. Ill. Coll. Agr., 1981, Campus award for excellence in undergrad. teaching U. Ill., 1984, D.E. Becker award, 1987, Outstanding Advisor award Student Affiliated div. Am. Dairy Sci. Assn., 1988; Alpha Zeta Outstanding Instr. award U. Ill. Coll. Agr., 1991, Karl E. Gardner Outstanding Undergrad. Adviser award, 1991; NIH rsch. fellow, 1969. Fellow Am. Soc. Animal Sci.; mem. Am. Physiol. Soc., AAAS, Soc. Study Reproduction, Am. Dairy Sci. Assn. (student affiliate advisor 1986-88), Am. Soc. Animal Sci., Soc. Cryobiology, N.Y. Acad. Sci., Masons, Sigma Xi, Phi Kappa Phi (chmn. scholarship com. 1973, 77), Gamma Sigma Delta. Mem. commn. edn. Methodist Ch., 1975-78. Home: 1701 S Cottage Grove Ave Urbana IL 61801-5925 Office: U Ill Dept Animal Scis 312 Animal Sci Lab 1207 W Gregory Dr Urbana IL 61801-3838

LODISH, HARVEY FRANKLIN, biologist, educator; b. Cleve., Nov. 16, 1941; s. Nathan H. and Sylvia B. (Friedman) L.; AB, Kenyon Coll., 1962, DSc (hon.), 1982; PhD, Rockefeller U., 1966; m. Pamela Chentow, Dec. 29, 1963; children: Heidi, Martin, Stephanie. Postdoctoral fellow Med. Rsch. Coun. Lab. of Molecular Biology, Cambridge, Eng., 1966-68; asst. prof. biology M.I.T., Cambridge, Mass., 1968-71, assoc. prof., 1971-76, prof., 1976—; vis. scientist Imperial Cancer Rsch. Fund, Lincoln's Inn Fields, London, 1977-78; vis. prof. U. Calif., San Francisco Med. Ctr., 1977, Pa. State U. Med. Ctr., 1977; Staples vis. prof. U. Maine, 1989; Wellcome vis. prof. U. Oreg., 1990; Roering vis. lectr. U. Wash. Med. Sch., 1991; Sackler vis. scholar Tel Aviv U., 1994; Berson Meml. lectr. Internat. Endocrinology Congress, 1992, Presdl. lectr. Internat. Hematology Congress, 1992, McGinnis Meml. lectr., 1994, Sigma Xi lectr., 1994, Harry Eagle Meml. lectr., 1994; cons. scientist medicine Children's Hosp. Med. Ctr., Boston, 1977—; cons. in pediatric oncology Sidney Farber Cancer Inst., 1977—; cons. Ministry Edn. and Rsch., Denmark, 1991-92; mem. Whitehead Inst. Biomed. Rsch.; sci. adv. bd. Damon Biotech., Inc., Fisher Sci. Group, Genzyme, Inc., Arris Pharm. Co., Millennium Corp., Astra AB, Sweden, Cogito, Inc.; pres. Bioinfo. Assocs., Inc.; cons. biotech.; mem. NSF adv. panel in devel. and cellular biology; mem. NIH study sect. of molecular biology and cell biology; adv. bd. Biozentrum, U. Basel, Switzerland, Fred Hutchinson Cancer Ctr., chair, Seattle, Cleve. Clin. Rsch. Found., chair, European Molecular Biology Lab., Heidelberg, Germany, Ctr. for Molecular Biology, Heidelberg; cons. NIH, Am. Cancer Soc. Vice chairperson Gordon Rsch. Conf., 1975, chairperson, 1976, 85, 89. Trustee Kenyon Coll., 1989—. Recipient NIH Career Devel. award, 1971-75, grantee, 1968—, Stadie award and lecture Am. Diabetes Assn., 1989; NSF grantee, 1971—; Am. Cancer Soc. grantee, 1971-76, Guggenheim fellow, 1977-78, Rockefeller fellow, 1962-66. Fellow AAAS, Am. Acad. Microbiology; mem. NAS (mem. editl. bd. proceedings 1996—), Am. Soc. for Microbiology, Am. Soc. of Biol. Chemists (nominating com. 1979, 86), Am. Soc. for Cell Biology (coun. 1983-85), Am. Chem. Soc., European Molecular Biol. Orgn. (assoc. fgn.), Phi Beta Kappa, Sigma Xi. Contbr. numerous articles on biochemistry to profl. jours.; mem. editorial bds. Jour. Biol. Chemistry, 1974-80, 82-87, Jour. Cell Biology, 1974-77, Nucleic Acids Rsch., 1976-88, Jour. Supramolecular Structure, 1978-88, Virology, 1979-84; assoc. editor Molecular and Cellular Biology, 1980-81; editor: Molecular and Cellular Biology, 1982-87; mem. bd. of reviewing editors Science, 1991—. Home: 195 Fisher Ave Brookline MA 02146-5706 Office: Whitehead Inst Biomed Rsch 9 Cambridge Ctr Cambridge MA 02142-1401

LODISH, LEONARD MELVIN, marketing educator, entrepreneur; b. Cleve., Aug. 1, 1943; s. Nathan H. and Sylvia (Friedman) L.; m. Susan Joyce Fischer, July 11, 1965; children: Max, Jacob, Chaim. AB magna cum laude, Kenyon Coll., 1965; PhD, MIT, 1968. Asst. prof. mktg. U. Pa., Phila., 1968-71, assoc. prof., 1971-75, prof. mktg., 1975-87, chmn. mktg. dept., 1991-92., 1984-88, Samuel R. Harrell prof., 1988—; founding dir. Evergreen Health Group, Inc., 1984-91; bd. dirs. Info. Resources, Inc., Chgo., Franklin Electronic Pub. Inc., Mt. Holly, N.J., J&J Snack Foods, Inc., Pennsauken, N.J., Walsh Internat., London, Bogen Comm. Internat., Inc., Ramsey, N.J.; co-founder, prin. Mgmt. Decisions Sys., Inc., Waltham, Mass., 1967-85; co-founder, dir. Shadow Broadcast Svcs., Bala Cynwyd, Pa., 1991—. Author: The Advertising and Promotion Challenge: Vaguely Right or Precisely Wrong?, 1986; mem. editorial bd. Mgmt. Sci., Jour. Mktg. Sci., Mktg. Sci., Jour. Personal Selling and Sales Mgmt.; contbr. articles to profl. jours. Pres. Temple Beth Hillel/Beth El, Wynnewood, Pa., 1983-85, bd. dirs. 1975—. Mem. Inst. Mgmt. Scis. (Franz Edelman award 1987), Ops. Research Soc. Am., Am. Mktg. Assn. (winner 1st Paul E. Green award 1996), Phi Beta Kappa. Jewish. Home: 301 Kent Rd Wynnewood PA 19096-1814 Office: U Pa Wharton Sch Dept Mktg Philadelphia PA 19104

LODWICK, GWILYM SAVAGE, radiologist, educator; b. Mystic, Iowa, Aug. 30, 1917; s. Gwylim S. and Lucy A. (Fuller) L.; m. Maria Antonia De Brito Barata; children by previous marriage: Gwilym Savage III, Philip Galligan, Malcolm Kerr, Terry Ann. Student, Drake U., 1934-35; B.S., State U. Iowa, 1942, M.D., 1943. Resident pathology State U. Iowa, 1947-48, resident radiology, 1948-50; fellow, sr. fellow radiologic and orthopedic pathology Armed Forces Inst. Pathology, 1951; asst., then asso. prof. State U. Iowa Med. Sch., 1951-56; prof. radiology, chmn. dept. U. Mo. at Columbia Med. Sch., 1956-78, research prof. radiology, 1978-83, interim chmn. dept. radiology, 1980-81, chmn. dept. radiology, 1981-83, prof. bioengring., 1969-83, acting dean, 1959, assoc. dean, 1959-64; assoc. radiologist Mass. Gen. Hosp., 1983-88, radiologist, 1988-91; hon. radiologist Mass. Gen. Hosp., Boston, 1991—; vis. prof. dept. radiology Harvard Med. Sch., 1983-93; cons. in field; vis. prof. Keio U. Sch. Medicine, Tokyo, 1974; chmn. sci. program com. Internat. Conf. on Med. Info., Amsterdam, 1983; trustee Am. Registry Radiologic Technologists, 1961-69, pres., 1964-65, 68-69; mem. radiology tng. com. Nat. Inst. Gen. Med. Scis., NIH, 1966-70; com. radiology Nat. Acad. Scis.-NRC, 1970-75; chmn. com. computers Am. Coll. Radiology, 1965, Internat. Commn. Radiol. Edn. and Info., 1969-73; cons. to health care tech. div. Nat. Ctr. for Health Services, Research and Devel., 1971-76; dir. Mid-Am. Bone Tumor Diagnostic Ctr. and Registry, 1971-83; adv. com. mem. NIH Biomed. Image Processing Grant Jet Propulsion Lab., 1969-73; nat. chmn. MUMPS Users Group, 1973-75; mem. radiation study sect. div. research grants NIH, 1976-79, mem. study sect. on diagnostic radiology and nuclear medicine div. research grants, 1979-82, chmn. study sect. on diagnostic radiology div. research grants, 1980-82; mem. bd. sci. counselors Nat. Library of Medicine, 1985, chmn. 1987-89; dir. radiology Spaulding Rehab. Hosp., 1986-92. Adv. editorial bd. Radiology, 1965-86, cons. to editor, 1986-91; adv. editorial bd. Current/Clin. Practice, 1972-88; mem. editorial bd. Jour. Med. Systems, 1976—, Radiol. Sci. Update div. Biomedia, Inc., 1975-83, Critical Revs. in Linguistic Imaging, 1990; mem. cons. editorial bd. Skeletal Radiology, 1977-92, Contemporary Diagnostic Radiology, 1978-80; assoc. editor Jour. Med. Imaging, 1988—. Served to maj. AUS, 1943-46, ETO. Decorated Sakari Mustakallio medal Finland; named Most Disting. Alumnus in Radiology, State U. Ia. Centennial, 1970; recipient Sigma Xi Research award U. Mo., Columbia, 1972, Gold medal XIII Internat. Conf. Radiology, Madrid, 1973, Founder's Gold medal Internat. Skeletal Soc., 1990. Fellow AMA (radiology rev. bd. coun. med. edn., coun. rep. on residency rev. com. for radiology 1969-74), Am. Coll. Radiology (co-chmn. ACR-NEMA standardization com. 1983-90, NEMA Med. Tech. Leadership award 1995); mem. NAS Inst. Medicine, Am. Coll. Med. Informatics (founding), Nat. Acad. Practice in Medicine, Radiol. Soc. N.Am. (3d v.p. 1974-75, chmn. ad hoc com. representing assoc. scis. 1979-87, chmn. assoc. scis. com. 1981-87), Assn. Univ. Radiologists, Mo. Radiol. Soc. (1st pres. 1961-62), Salutis Unitas; hon. mem. Portuguese Soc. Radiology and Nuclear Medicine, Tex. Radiol. Soc., Ind. Roentgen Soc., Phila. Roentgen Ray Soc., Finnish Radio. Soc. (ho.), Rotary, Harvard of Boston Club, Cosmos, Alpha Omega Alpha. Home: 3900 Galt Ocean Dr Apt 307 Fort Lauderdale FL 33308-6622

LÖE, HARALD, dentist, educator, researcher; b. Steinkjer, Norway, July 19, 1926; s. Haakon and Anna (Bruem) L.; m. Inga Johansen, July 3, 1948; children: Haakon, Marianne. DDS, U. Oslo, 1952; D in Odontology, 1961; hon. degree, U. Gothenburg, 1973, Royal Dental Coll., Aarhus, 1980, U. Athens, 1980, Cath. U., Leuven, 1980, U. Lund, 1983, Georgetown U., 1983, U. Bergen, 1985, U. Md., 1986, Med. U. N.J., 1987, Royal Dental Coll., Copenhagen, 1988, U. Toronto, 1989, U. Detroit, 1990, S.C. Med. U., 1990, U. Helsinki, Finland, 1992, Pacific U., 1993, U. Milan, Italy, 1994. Instr. Sch. Dentistry, Oslo U., 1952-55; rsch. assoc. Norwegian Inst. Dental Rsch., 1956-62; Fulbright rsch. fellow, rsch. assoc. dept. oral pathology U. Ill., Chgo., 1957-58; Univ. rsch. fellow Oslo U., 1959-62, asso. prof. dept. periodontology, 1960-61; prof. dentistry, chmn. dept. periodontology Royal Dental Coll., Aarhus, Denmark, 1962-72; asso. dean, dean-elect Royal Dental Coll., 1971-72; prof., dir. Dental Rsch. Inst. U. Mich., Ann Arbor, 1972-74; dean, prof. periodontology Sch. Dental Medicine U. Conn., Farmington, 1974-82; dir. Nat. Inst. Dental Rsch. Nat. Inst. Dental Rsch., Bethesda, Md., 1983-94; univ. prof. Sch. Dental Medicine U. Conn. Health Ctr., Farmington, 1994—; vis. prof. periodontics Hebrew U., Jerusalem, 1966-67; hon. prof. Med. Scis. U. Beijing, 1987; cons. WHO, NIH. Contbr. over 300 articles to sci. publs. With Norwegian Army, 1944-48. Recipient 75th Anniversary award Norwegian Dental Assn., 1958, Aalborg Dental Soc. prize, Denmark, 1965, William J. Gies Periodontology award, 1978, Alfred C. Fores medal, U.S. Surgeon Gen.'s medal and Exemplary award, 1988, Internat. award Swedish Dental Assn., 1989, Harvard medal, 1992, Scandinavian Pub. Health award, 1994; decorated Knight of Danebrog by Queen of Denmark, 1972, Comdr. of Royal Norwegian Order of Merit by King of Norway, 1989. Mem. AAAS, ADA (gold medal 1994, Callahan medal 1995, Spenadel medal 1995), Am. Coll. Dentists, Nat. Acad. Inst. Medicine, Danish Dental Assn., Am. Acad. Periodontology, Am. Assn. Dental Rsch. (hon. mem.), Am. Soc. Preventive Dentistry (internat. award), Mass. Dental Soc. (internat. award), Internat. Assn. Dental Rsch. (award for basic rsch. in periodongology 1969, pres. 1980), Internat. Coll. Dentists, Scandinavian Assn. Dental Rsch. Office: U Conn Health Ctr Sch Dental Medicine Farmington CT 06030-1710

LOEB, BEN FOHL, JR., lawyer, educator; b. Nashville, May 15, 1932; s. Ben Fohl and Frances (Paysinger) L.; m. Anne Nelson, Sept. 23, 1961 (div. 1982); children: Charles Nelson, William Nelson. BA, Vanderbilt U., 1955, JD, 1960. Bar: Tenn. 1960, U.S. Supreme Ct. 1966, N.C. 1975. Assoc. Crownover, Branstetter & Folk, Nashville, 1960-64; asst. dir. Inst. Govt. U. N.C., Chapel Hill, 1964—, prof. pub. law and govt. Inst. Govt., 1972—; counsel to N.C. legis. coms. on motor vehicle law and transp., Raleigh, 1973-83; cons. on alcohol beverage control, 1985-89; cons. on wildlife, natural and scenic areas, 1989-93; mem. U. N.C. Faculty Coun., 1994-97. Author: Traffic Law and Highway Safety, 1970, Alcohol Beverage Control Law, 1971, Motor Vehicle Law, 1975, Legal Aspects of Dental Practice, 1977, Eminent Domain Procedure, 1984; assoc. editor Vanderbilt Law Rev., 1959-60. Served to 1st lt. U.S. Army, 1955-57. Mem. ABA, Tenn. Bar Assn., Phi Beta Kappa, Phi Delta Phi, Pi Kappa Alpha (chpt. pres. 1954-55), Carolina Club (Chapel Hill). Democrat. Baptist. Home: 17 Bluff Trl Chapel Hill NC 27516-1603 Office: U NC Inst Govt Cb 3330 Knapp Bldg Chapel Hill NC 27599

LOEB, G. HAMILTON, lawyer; b. New Orleans, June 22, 1951; s. Ferdinand M. and Margaret (Gibbs) L.; m. Bonnie Schlitz, June 9, 1973; children: Miller Anne, Maxwell Lazard. BA, U. Va., 1973; JD magna cum laude, Harvard U., 1978. Bar: Calif. 1979, D.C. 1980, U.S. Ct. Appeals (9th cir.) 1979, U.S. Ct. Appeals (D.C. cir.) 1980, U.S. Dist. Ct. D.C. 1981. Legis. asst. to Hon. Robert Steele U.S. Ho. Reps., Washington, 1973-74; law clerk to Hon. James Browning U.S. Ct. Appeals, San Francisco, 1978-79; assoc. Wald, Harkrader & Ross, Washington, 1981-82; ptnr. Paul, Hastings, Janofsky & Walker, LLP, Washington, 1982—, mng. ptnr., 1997—. Author, editor: North American Free Trade Agreement, 1993; articles editor Harvard Law Review., 1977-78. Chair, pres. Washington Area Lawyers for the Arts, 1986-92; mem. exec. com. Netherlands Am. Amity Trust, 1987—. Echols scholar U. Va., 1973. Jewish. Home: 3802 Gramercy St NW Washington DC 20016-4226 Office: Paul Hastings Janofsky & Walker Ste 1000 1299 Pennsylvania Ave NW Washington DC 20004-2400

LOEB, JANE RUPLEY, university administrator, educator; b. Chgo., Feb. 22, 1938; d. John Edwards and Virginia Pentland (Marthens) Watkins; m. Peter Albert Loeb, June 14, 1958; children: Eric Peter, Gwendolyn Lisl, Aaron John. BA, Rider Coll., 1961; PhD, U. So. Calif., 1969. Clin. psychology intern Univ. Hosp., Seattle, 1966-67; asst. prof. ednl. psychology U. Ill., Urbana, 1968-69, asst. coord. rsch. and testing, 1968-69, coord. rsch. and testing, 1969-72, asst. to vice chancellor acad. affairs, 1971-72, dir. admissions and records, 1972-81, assoc. prof. ednl. psychology, 1973-82, assoc. vice chancellor acad. affairs, 1981-94, prof. edn. psychology, 1982—. Author: College Board Project: the Future of College Admissions, 1989. Chmn. Coll. Bd. Coun. on Entrance Svcs., 1977-82; bd. govs. Alliance for Undergrad. Edn., 1988-93; active charter com. Coll. Bd. Acad. Assembly, 1992-93. HEW grantee, 1975-76. Mem. APA, Am. Ednl. Rsch. Assn., Nat. Coun. Measurement in Edn., Harvard Inst. Ednl. Mgmt. Avocation: the french horn. Home: 1405 N Coler Ave Urbana IL 61801-1625 Office: U Ill 1310 S 6th St Champaign IL 61820-6925

LOEB, JEROME THOMAS, retail executive; b. St. Louis, Sept. 13, 1940; s. Harry W. and Marjorie T. Loeb; m. Carol Bodenheimer, June 15, 1963; children: Daniel W, Kelly E. BS, Tufts U., 1962; MA, Washington U., St. Louis, 1964. Asst. dir. rsch., dir. EDP, div. v.p., dir. mgmt. info. scvs. Famous-Barr div. May Dept. Stores Co., St. Louis, 1964-74, v.p. mgmt. info. svcs./EDP parent co., 1974-77, sr. v.p., CFO Hecht's div., Washington, 1977-79; exec. v.p. devel. May Dept. Stores Co., St. Louis, 1979-81, exec. v.p., CFO, 1981-86, vice chmn., CFO, 1986-93, pres., 1993—; also bd. dirs. Bd. dirs. Jr. Achievement of Mississippi Valley, 1980—, chmn., 1993-95; bd. dirs. Jr. Achievement Nat. Bd., 1988—; bd. commrs. St. Louis Sci. Ctr., 1991—, chmn., 1995—; bd. dirs. Barnes-Jewish Hosp., 1984—, vice chmn. 1988, bd. dirs. BJC Health Sys., 1992—; mem. pres. cabinet Am. Jewish Com., 1994—. Mem. Westwood Country Club, Boone Valley Golf Club. Office: May Dept Stores Co 611 Olive St Saint Louis MO 63101-1721

LOEB, JOHN LANGELOTH, JR., investment counselor; b. N.Y.C., May 2, 1930; s. John Langeloth and Frances (Lehman) L.; children: Nicholas, Alexandra. Grad., Hotchkiss Sch., 1948; A.B. cum laude, Harvard, 1952, M.B.A., 1954; LL.D. (hon.), Georgetown U. With Loeb, Rhoades & Co., N.Y.C., from 1956; gen. ptnr., mem. mgmt. com. Loeb, Rhoades & Co., 1964-73, mng. ptnr., pres., 1971-73, ltd. ptnr., 1973-84; chmn. bd. Holly Sugar Co., Colo., 1969-71; amb. to Denmark Copenhagen, 1981-83; chmn. John L. Loeb, Jr. Assocs., N.Y.C., 1984—; U.S. del. to 38th session Gen. Assembly of UN; spl. advisor environ. matters to Gov. Nelson A. Rockefeller, 1967-73; chmn. Gov. N.Y. Coun. Environ. Advisors, 1970-75; pres. Winston Churchill Found., 1981—; trustee Ednl. Testing Svc., Princeton, N.J., 1986-93. Trustee Montefiore Hosp. and Med. Ctr. Mus. City N.Y., 1962-94, John and Frances L. Loeb Found., 1957—; mem. Harvard vis. com. Loeb Drama Ctr., 1988-94; mem. N.Y. State Coun. on the Arts, 1996—; bd. dirs. N.Y. State Environ. Facilities Corp., 1997—. Lt. USAF, 1954-56. Decorated Grand Cross of the Order of Dannebrog (Denmark); recipient Lee Max Friedman award Am. Jewish Hist. Soc., Disting. Patriot award SAR; Hon. Comdr. of the Most Excellent Order of the Brit. Empire. Mem. Downtown Assn. (N.Y.C.), City Midday Club, Harvard Club, Century Country Club, Sleepy Hollow Club (Westchester, N.Y.), Buck's Club, Brooks's Club, Hurlingham Club (London), Royal Swedish Yacht Club (Stockholm), Royal Danish Yacht Club (Copenhagen), Lyford Cay Club (Nassau, Bahamas). Home: Ridgeleigh 194 Anderson Hill Rd Purchase NY 10577-2101 Office: Loeb Family Office 375 Park Ave Ste 801 New York NY 10152-0899

LOEB, JOYCE LICHTGARN, interior designer, civic worker; b. Portland, Oreg., May 20, 1936; d. Elias Lichtgarn and Sylvia Amy (Margulies) Freedman; m. Stanley Robinson Loeb, Aug. 14, 1960; children: Carl Eli, Eric Adam. Student U. Calif.-Berkeley, 1954-56; BS, Lewis and Clark Coll., 1958; postgrad. art and architecture, Portland State U., 1976. Tchr. art David Douglas Sch. Dist., Portland, 1958-59, 61-64; tchr., chmn. art dept. Grant Union High Sch. Dist., Sacramento, 1959-60; designer, pres. Joyce Loeb Interior Design, Inc., Portland, 1976—; cons. designer to various developers of health care facilities. Chairperson fundraisers for civic orgns. and Jewish orgns.; mem. women's com. Reed Coll.; bd. dirs., mem. exec. com. Inst. Judaic Studies, 1989-92; bd. dirs. Young Audiences, Inc., Portland, 1970-76, chmn. long range planning, 78-80; bd. dirs. Met. Family Svc., Portland, 1968-71, Portland Opera Assn., 1978-84, Arts Celebration, Inc., Portland, 1984—, Friends of Chamber Music; chmn. Artquake Festival, 1985, Operaball, 1987, Children's Charity Ball Com., 1989, Women's Bd. Jewish Fedn. Portland, 1993-96, pres. 1996—; sec. exec. com., bd. dir. Oreg. Children's Theatre, 1992—; v.p. Beth Israel Sisterhood, 1981-83; bd. dirs., trustee Congregation Beth Israel, 1986-92, chmn. art interior design com.; trustee Robison Home, 1990-96; bd. dirs. Friends of Chamber Music, 1994—, Nat. Found. for Jewish Culture, 1996. Recipient Women of Distinction award in architecture and design Girl Scouts Columbia River Coun., 1994. Mem. Am. Soc. Interior Design (allied, bd. dirs. 1993-95), Multnomah Athletic Club. Democrat. Home: 4371 NW Tamoshanter Way Portland OR 97229-8738

LOEB, MARSHALL ROBERT, journalist; b. Chgo., May 30, 1929; s. Monroe Harrison and Henrietta (Benjamin) L.; m. Elizabeth Peggy Loewe, Aug. 14, 1954; children: Michael, Margaret. BJ, U. Mo., 1950; postgrad., U. Goettingen, Germany, 1950-51. Reporter Garfield News and Austinite, Chgo., 1944-45; reporter, columnist Garfieldian and Austin News, Chgo., 1946-47, 49-51; reporter Columbia Missourian, 1948-50; staff corr. UP, Frankfurt, Germany, 1952-54; reporter St. Louis Globe-Democrat, 1955-56; contbg. editor Time mag., 1956-61, assoc. editor, 1961-65, sr. editor, 1965-80, econs. editor and columnist, 1978-80; mng. editor Money Mag., 1980-84; editor Time Inc. Mag. Devel., 1984-86; mng. editor Fortune, 1986-94, editor-at-large, 1994-95, columnist, 1996; editor Columbia Journalism Rev., 1997—; daily commentator CBS Radio Network; assoc. fellow Yale U., Berkeley Coll., 1977—. Author: (with William Safire) Plunging Into Politics, 1962, Marshall Loeb's Money Guide, 1983, ann. edits., 1985-94, Money Minutes, 1986, Lifetime Financial Strategies, 1996. Recipient INGAA award U. Mo., 1966; Gerald M. Loeb award UCLA Sch. Mgmt., 1974; John Hancock award, 1974; Champion Media award for econ. understanding citation, 1978, first prize, 1981; Dallas Press Club award, 1978; Freedoms Found. award, 1978; N.Y. citation Sigma Delta Chi, 1979; Nat. Assn. Home Builders award, 1984; Great Am. Patriot award Jefferson Barracks Chapel Assn., 1988, Journalism medal U. Mo., 1988, N.Y. award Navy League, 1989, TJFR Bus. Journalism Luminaries award 1990. Mem. World Econ. Forum (Geneva), Nat. Neurofibromatosis Found. (dir.), Econ. Club of N.Y. (dir.), NYU Stern Sch. of Bus. (trustee), Knight-Bagehot Fellowship (chair bd. adv.), Recording for the Blind and Dyslexic (dir.), Coun. Fgn. Rels., Brit.-Am. C. of C. (v.p. 1979-81, dir. 1979-84), Am. Soc. Mag. Editors (v.p. 1986-88, pres. 1988-90), Overseas Press Club Am. (dir. 1963-65, treas. 1964-65). Jewish. Home: 31 Montrose Rd Scarsdale NY 10583-1129 Office: Columbia Journalism Rev 2950 Broadway New York NY 10027-7004

LOEB, NACKEY SCRIPPS, publisher; b. Los Angeles, Feb. 24, 1924; d. Robert Paine and Margaret (Culbertson) Scripps; m. William Loeb, July 15, 1952 (dec. 1981); children—Nackey Loeb Scagliotti, Edith Loeb Tomasko. Student, Scripps Coll. Pub. Union-Leader Corp., Manchester, N.H., 1981—, Neighborhood Pubs., Inc., Goffstown, N.H., 1993—. Republican. Baptist. Home: Paige Hill Rd Goffstown NH 03045 Office: Union Leader Corp 100 William Loeb Dr Manchester NH 03109-5309*

LOEB, PETER KENNETH, money manager; b. N.Y.C., Apr. 8, 1936; s. Carl M. and Lucille H. (Schamberg) L.; m. Jeanette Winter, Nov. 1, 1980; 1 child, Alexander Winter; children by previous marriage: Peter Kenneth Jr., Karen Elizabeth, James Matthew. BA, Yale U., 1958; MBA, Columbia U., 1961. Security analyst Loeb, Rhoades & Co., N.Y.C., 1961-66, syndicate dept. ptnr., 1966-71, with trading/instl. sales sect., 1971-79; mng. dir. corp. fin. Shearson Corp., N.Y.C., 1979-83; mng. dir., portfolio mgr. PaineWebber Inc., N.Y.C., 1983-92; ptnr. Shufro, Rose & Ehrman, N.Y.C., 1992—; mem. com. on securities Am. Stock Exch., 1978-80; mem. del. to Beijing symposium N.Y. Stock Exch., 1986. Coach, games ofcl. Manhattan Spl. Olympics, 1980—; bd. dirs., co-chmn. devel. com. N.Y. Spl. Olympics, 1985-89; chmn. devel. com. Spl. Olympics Internat., 1986—, bd. dirs., 1989—; mem. com. on univ. investments Columbia U., 1977-85, trustee, 1979-85, vice-chmn. alumni adv. bd., 1986-92; fund chmn. Columbia U. Bus. Sch., 1964-66, mem. alumni counseling bd., 1970—, pres. Columbia Bus. Sch. Assocs., 1971-73, mem. bd. overseers, 1976—; dir. City Ctr. Theatre Found.; trustee Allen Stevenson Sch., 1969—, Langeloth Found., 1972-97, trustee emeritus, 1997—; trustee N.Y. Infirmary-Beekman Downtown Hosp., 1978-85; mem. adv. bd. Atoms Track Club Bedford-Stuyvesant, 1970—; cert. track ofcl. USA Track and Field, 1985—; mem. marshals com. Westchester Golf Classic, 1970—; contbg. mem. Mus. Modern Art, Met. Mus. Art; mem. Statue of Liberty/Ellis Island Found., Friends of Kennedy Ctr., Friends of the Philharm., Friends of Carnegie Hall; mem. Wall St. com. N.Y. Urban Coalition, 1969-71; mem. exec. bd. new leadership div. Fedn. Jewish Philanthropies, 1963-64; vice-chmn. Pacesetter com. Greater N.Y. coun. Boy Scouts Am., 1966-67. Recipient Alumni medal for conspicuous service Columbia U., 1975, Alumni medal for disting. service Columbia U. Bus. Sch., 1976. Mem. SAR, Securities Traders Assn. N.Y., Investment Assn. N.Y. (exec. bd. 1969), Securities Industry Assn. (governing council 1977-79, minority capital com. 1980-85, trustee Econ. Edn. Found. 1986—, vice chmn. 1992—), Nat. Assn. Security Dealers (chmn. dist. 12 com. 1981, gov. 1982-85, chmn. corp. fin. com. 1983-86, vice-chmn. fin. 1984, mem. arbitration com. 1986-89, NASDAQ qualifications com. 1989—), N.Y.C. Baseball Fedn. (pres. 1968-91, chmn. 1992—, award for disting. service 1976), Univ. Club, Doubles Club, Bond Club, Century Country Club, Beta Gamma Sigma, Alpha Kappa Psi, Phi Gamma Delta. Office: Shufro Rose & Ehrman 745 5th Ave New York NY 10151

LOEB, RONALD MARVIN, lawyer; b. Denver, Sept. 24, 1932; s. Ellis and Lillian (Mosko) L.; m. Shirley Ross; children: Joshua Ross, Gabriel Ross, Daniel Seth, Jennifer Miriam, Rachel Sarah.. AB with highest honors, UCLA, 1954; LLB cum laude, Harvard U., 1959. Bar: Calif. 1960. Assoc. Irell & Manella, L.L.P, L.A., 1959-64, ptnr., 1964—; bd. dirs. Mattel, Inc., Internat. Transpersonal Ctr.; course presenter The Esalen Inst., 1995-97; instr. corp. governance and social responsibility KVK Raju Internat. Leadership Acad., Hyderabad, India; task force on social cohesion sponsored by Danish Min. Pub. Affairs. Co-editor: Duties and Responsibilities of Outside Directors. Trustee Crossroads Sch. Arts and Scis., Santa Monica, Calif., 1987—; past chmn. Pacific Crest Outward Bound Sch.; founding trustee, dir. World Bus. Acad. Mem. ABA, State Bar Assn. Calif., Los Angeles County Bar Assn., Beverly Hills Bar Assn., Nat. Assn. Securities Dealers (mem. legal adv. bd.). Office: Irell & Manella LLP 1800 Avenue Of The Stars Los Angeles CA 90067-4212

LOEB, VIRGIL, JR., oncologist, hematologist; b. St. Louis, Sept. 21, 1921; s. Virgil and Therese (Meltzer) L.; m. Lenore Harlow, Sept. 8, 1950 (dec. Nov. 1987); children: Katherine Loeb Doumas, Elizabeth Loeb McCane, David, Mark; m. Elizabeth Moore, Dec., 1990. Student, Swarthmore Coll., 1938-41; MD, Washington U., St. Louis, 1944. Diplomate Am. Bd. Internal Medicine. Intern Barnes and Jewish Hosps., St. Louis, 1944-45; resident in internal medicine, research fellow in hematology Barnes Hosp., St. Louis, 1947-52; med. faculty Washington U., St. Louis, 1951—, prof. clin. medicine, 1978-96, prof. emeritus clin. medicine, 1996—; practice medicine specializing in oncology and hematology St. Louis, 1956-96; cons., clin. researcher; dir. Cen. Diagnostic Labs., Barnes Hosp., 1952-68; staff numerous hosps., 1951-96; cons. Nat. Cancer Inst., 1966-96, chmn. cancer clin. investigation rev. com., 1966-69, mem. diagnostic research adv. com., 1972-75, bd. sci. counselors, DCPC, 1983-87; mem. oncology merit rev. bd. VA, 1971-75. Contbr. author books, articles to profl. jours. Bd. dirs. Am. Cancer Soc., mem. nat. adv. com., 1969—, pres. Mo. div., 1983-85, nat. pres., 1986-87; bd. dirs. St. Louis Blue Cross and Blue Shield, Bi-State Red Cross; trustee John Burroughs Sch., 1966-69. Served with M.C. AUS, 1945-47. Fellow ACP; mem. Cen. Soc. Clin. Research, Inst. Medicine of Nat. Acad. Sci., Am. Assn. Cancer Research, Internat. Soc. Hematology, Am. Soc. Hematology, St. Louis Soc. Internal Medicine (pres. 1974), Am. Soc. Clin. Oncology, Am. Assn. for Cancer Edn., St. Louis Met. Med. Soc. (hon.), Sigma Xi, Alpha Omega Alpha. Home: 24 Deerfield Rd Saint Louis MO 63124-1412 Office: Barnes Hosp 1 Barnes Hospital Plz Saint Louis MO 63110

LOEBLICH, HELEN NINA TAPPAN, paleontologist, educator; b. Norman, Okla., Oct. 12, 1917; d. Frank Girard and Mary (Jenks) Tappan; m. Alfred Richard Loeblich, Jr., June 18, 1939; children: Alfred Richard III, Karen Elizabeth Loeblich, Judith Anne Loeblich Covey, Daryl Louise Loeblich Valenzuela. BS, U. Okla., 1937, MS, 1939; PhD, U. Chgo., 1942. Instr. geology Tulane U., New Orleans, 1942-43; geologist U.S. Geol. Survey, Washington, 1943-45, 47-59; mem. faculty UCLA, 1958—, prof. geology, 1966-84, prof. emeritus, 1985—, vice chmn. dept. geology, 1973-75; research assoc. Smithsonian Instn., 1954-57; assoc. editor Cushman Found. Foraminiferal Research, 1950-51, incorporator, hon. dir., 1950—. Author: (with A.R. Loeblich Jr.) Treatise on Invertebrate Paleontology, part C, Protista 2, Foraminiferida, 2 vols., 1964, Foraminiferal Genera and Their Classification, 2 vols., 1987, Foraminifera of the Sahul Shelf and Timor Sea, 1994; author: The Paleobiology of Plant Protists, 1980; mem. editl. bd. Palaeoecology, 1972-82, Paleobiology, 1975-81; contbr. articles to profl. jours., govt. publs. and encys. Recipient Joseph A. Cushman award Cushman Found., 1982; named Woman of Yr. in Sci. Palm Springs Desert Mus., 1987; Guggenheim fellow, 1953-54. Fellow Geol. Soc. Am. (sr., councilor 1979-81); mem. Paleontol. Soc. (pres. 1984-85, patron 1987, medal 1982), Soc. Sedimentary Geology (councilor 1975-77, hon. mem. 1978, Raymond C. Moore medal 1984), UCLA Med. Ctr. Aux. (Woman of Yr. medal), AAUP, Internat. Paleontological Assn., Paleontol. Rsch. Inst., Am. Microscopical Soc., Am. Inst. Biol. Scis., Phi Beta Kappa, Sigma Xi. Home: 1556 W Crone Ave Anaheim CA 92802-1303

LOEDDING, PETER ALFRED, trade association executive; b. Sewickly, Pa., July 29, 1934; s. Peter Herbert and Alice Regina (Bourne) L.; m. Mary Ellen Cahalan, June 28, 1958; children—Peter, Joseph, Jeffrey. BSBA, Youngstown U., 1967; Grad. Inst. for Orgn. Mgmt., 1988. Credit mgr. Gen. Foods Corp., Newark, Del., 1962-64; v.p. John Blackson Assn., New Castle, Pa., 1964-70, Modulage Homes Co., Niles, Ohio, 1970-72; exec. dir. Redevel. Auth. Authority, Sharon, Pa., 1972-76, Shenango Valley C. of C., Pa., 1980-85; free-lance cons., Sharon, 1976-80; adminstr. Mercer County Devel. Corp., Sharon, 1980-85; exec. dir. Shenango Valley Indsl. Devel. Corp., 1980-85, Mercer County Indsl. Devel. Authority, 1982-85, Mercer County PTA, 1978-85; pres. Capital Region Econ. Devel. Corp., Camp Hill, Pa., 1993—. Bd. dirs. Shenango Valley Campus, Pa. State U., 1972-84, Shenango Valley Urban League, 1984—; pres. Susquehanna Alliance, 1995—. Mem. Am. Inst. Cert. Planners, Am. Planning Assn. (pres. Pitts. region 1972-73), Pa. Assn. Redevel. Ofcls. (v.p. 1976), Williamsport-Lycoming C. of C. (pres. 1985-94). Home: 2312 Valley Rd Harrisburg PA 17104-1432 also: Capital Region Econ Devel Corp 214 Senate Ave Ste 605 Camp Hill PA 17011-2336

LOEFFEL, BRUCE, software company executive, consultant; b. Bklyn., Aug. 13, 1943; s. Samuel and Loretta (Bleiweiss) L.; children: Alisa, Joshua. BBA, Pace U., 1966; MBA, St. John's U., 1971. Certified data processor. Mgr. fin. systems Gibbs & Hill Inc., N.Y.C., 1973-76; mgr. sales, tech. support Mgmt. Sci. Am. Inc., Fort Lee, N.J., 1976-81; dir. mktg. Info. Scis., Inc., Montvale, N.J., 1981-82; dir. bus. devel. Cullinet Software, Inc., Westwood, Mass., 1982-85; exec. v.p. strategic planning Online Data Base Software Inc., Pearl River, N.Y., 1985-88; pres. Corp. Application Software, Inc., Nyack, N.Y., 1988-94; sr. dir. IMRS, Inc., Stamford, Conn., 1994—, Hyperion Software, Inc., 1994-96; pres. Corp. Application Software, Inc., Congers, N.Y., 1996—. With U.S. Army, 1966-71. Mem. Inst. Cert. Computer Profls. Democrat. Jewish. Avocations: sports, electronics. Home: 107 High Ave Apt 308 Nyack NY 10960-2500 Office: 777 Long Ridge Rd Stamford CT 06902-1247

LOEFFLER, FRANK JOSEPH, physicist, educator; b. Ballston Spa, N.Y., Sept. 5, 1928; s. Frank Joseph and Florence (Farrell) L.; m. Eleanor Jane Chisholm, Sept. 8, 1951; children: Peter, James, Margaret, Anne Marie. B.S. in Engring. Physics, Cornell U., 1951, Ph.D. in Physics, 1957. Research asso. Princeton U., 1957-58; mem. faculty Purdue U., Lafayette, Ind., 1958—; prof. physics Purdue U., 1962—; vis. prof. Hamburg U., Germany, 1963-64, Heidelberg U., Germany, CERN, Switzerland, 1971, Stanford U. Linear Accelerator Ctr., 1980-83; trustee, mem. exec. com., chmn. high energy com. Argonne Univs. Assn., 1972-76, 78-79, mem. com. on fusion programs, 1979-80; vis. prof. U. Hawaii, 1985-86. Contbr. to profl. publs. Recipient Antarctic Svc. medal NSF/USN, 1990, Ruth and Joel Spira award for outstanding tchg., 1992. Fellow Am. Phys. Soc., Sigma Xi, Tau Beta Pi. Exptl. research in astrophysics, high energy gamma ray astronomy, high energy particle interactions using counter-wire chamber techniques, prodn. resonant state from strong and electromagnetic interactions and on-line data acquisition-processing systems, cold fusion research. Established gamma ray astronomy lab. at South Pole, Antarctica, 1989, 91, 92. Home: 437 Maple St West Lafayette IN 47906-3016 Office: Purdue U Dept Physics Lafayette IN 47907

LOEFFLER, JAMES JOSEPH, lawyer; b. Evanston, Ill., Mar. 7, 1931; s. Charles Adolph and Margaret Bowe L.; m. Margo M. Loeffler, May 26, 1962; children—Charlotte Bowe, James J. B.S., Loyola U.; J.D., Northwestern U. Bar: Ill. 1956, Tex. 1956. Assoc. Fulbright & Jaworski, Houston, 1956-69, ptnr., 1969-86, sr. ptnr., 1986; sr. ptnr. Chamberlain, Hrdlicka, White, Johnson & Williams, Houston, 1986-90; pvt. practice law Houston, 1990—. Mem. ABA, Ill. Bar Assn., Tex. Bar Assn., Houston Bar Assn., Houston Country Club. Office: 808 Travis 1616 Niels Esperson Bldg Houston TX 77002

LOEFFLER, RICHARD HARLAN, retail and technology company executive; b. Kansas City, Mo., Sept. 15, 1936; s. Sidney A. and Lily (Cowell) L.; m. Sheila Kay Gilligan, July 7, 1984; children: Kimberly Anne, Melissa Anne; stepchildren: Patrick K. Gilligan, Todd M. Gilligan. Student, U. Mo.; M.B.A., Pepperdine U., 1975. Ptnr. Foristall & Co., L.A., 1960-65; pres. Beverly Hills Film Corp., Calif., 1962-65; v.p. Buttes Gas and Oil Corp., Oakland, Calif., 1965-66; exec. v.p. TRE Corp., Beverly Hills, Calif., 1966-72; chmn., pres. Simplex Industries, Adrian, Mich., 1972-76; pres., chief oper. officer TRE Corp., L.A., 1976-86; chmn., CEO, MemTech Corp., Beverly Hills, 1987-91; chmn. Am. Builders Hardware Corp., Beverly Hills, Calif., 1991—; chmn., CEO RHL Mgmt. Group, Inc., Beverly Hills, Calif., 1992—; pres., COO, bd. dirs. Standard Brands Paint Co., Torrance, Calif., 1992-93; bd. dirs. Future Flow Sys. Inc., Newbury Park, Calif., Lorus Corp., Beverly Hills, Calif.; chmn., CEO Hawaiian Grocery Stores Ltd., 1996—. Mem. bus. coun. Nat. Democratic Com., Washington, 1983—; trustee Internat. Assn. for Shipboard Edn.; bd. dirs. U. So. Calif. Cancer Rsch. Assocs. Mem. Hawaii Food Industry Assn. (bd. dirs.), Hawaii Food Industry Shipping and Transp. Assn. Office: 2915 Kaihikapu St Honolulu HI 96819-2013

LOEFFLER, ROBERT HUGH, lawyer; b. Chgo., May 27, 1943; s. Julius and Faye (Fink) L.; m. Jane Canter, Sept. 6, 1970; children: James Benjamin, Charles Edward. AB magna cum laude, Harvard Coll., 1965; JD cum laude, Columbia U., 1968. Bar: N.Y. 1969, U.S. Ct. Appeals (2d cir.) 1969, D.C. 1970, U.S. Ct. Appeals (D.C. cir.) 1972, U.S. Supreme Ct. 1976, U.S. Ct. Appeals (9th cir.) 1981, U.S. Ct. Appeals (Fed. cir.) 1992. Law clk. to Hon. Harold R. Medina U.S. Ct. Appeals, 1968-69; assoc. Covington & Burling, Washington, 1969-76; assoc., ptnr. Isham, Lincoln & Beale, Washington, 1976-79; mng. ptnr. Morrison & Foerster, Washington, 1980-89, sr. ptnr., 1990—. Chmn. consumer com. Muskie presdl. campaign, 1972. Mem. ABA (vice chmn. energy law com. adminstrv. law sect. 1980-85), Am. Intellectual Property Law Assn., Fed. Energy Bar Assn. (chmn. oil pipeline regulation), Columbia Law Sch. Assn. Washington (pres. 1993, nat. v.p. 1994—), Univ. Club, Std. Club, Harvard Club (N.Y.C.). Home: 2607 36th Pl NW Washington DC 20007-1414 Office: Morrison & Foerster Ste 5500 2000 Pennsylvania Ave NW Washington DC 20006-1831

LOEFFLER, WILLIAM GEORGE, JR., advertising executive; b. Washington, Feb. 23, 1939; s. William George and Sara Mae (Henderson) L.; children: William Douglas, Sara Cantillon, Michael Christopher; m. Christine Sinclair Tomberlin, Apr. 19, 1991. BA, Washington and Lee U., 1960. Pub. rels. specialist Gen. Electric Co., Schenectady, N.Y. and Winston-Salem, N.C., 1965-68; v.p., account supr. Cargill, Wilson & Acree, Charlotte, N.C., 1968-74; exec. v.p. McConnell and Assocs., Charlotte, 1974-81; pres. Loeffler Ketchum Mountjoy, Charlotte, 1981-90, chmn. 1990—; bd. dirs. First Commerce Bank; mem. Advt. Rev. Bd., Charlotte, 1983-87; chmn. Nat. Advt. Agy. Network, 1988-89; judge advt. awards competitions. Bd. dirs. Better Bus. Bur., Charlotte, 1980-81, 89-93; v.p. Play Units for the Severely Handicapped, Charlotte, 1977-84; active Win with Charlotte Com., 1984, Charlotte Basketball Com., 1978-95, pres. 1987; mem. adv. bd. United Carolina Bank, 1995-97; bd. dirs. acad. guidance com. Charlotte Christian Sch., 1974-75; bd. dirs. Matthews Athletic Assn., N.C., 1979; comm. chmn. fund drive Arts and Sci. Coun., 1988, bd. dirs. 1991-96; mem. bd. visitors mktg. dept. U. N.C., Charlotte. Served to lt. USMCR, 1962-65. Mem. Advt. Club of Charlotte (pres. 1980-81, Silver medal 1984), Bus. and Profl. Advt. Assn., Charlotte Sales and Mktg. Execs., Am. Mktg. Assn., Charlotte C. of C. (bd. advisors 1989-97), River Run Country Club (bd. advisors). Republican. Home: 18830 River Wind Ln Davidson NC 28036-8878 Office: Loeffler Ketchum Mountjoy 2101 Rexford Rd Ste 200 E Charlotte NC 28211-3477

LOEFFLER, WILLIAM ROBERT, quality productivity specialist, engineering educator; b. Cleve., Aug. 31, 1949; s. Harry T. and Frances R. (Pearson) L.; children: Kelly Lynn, Robert Jason. BA, Wittenberg U., 1971; MA, SUNY-Stony Brook, 1972; Ed. Specialist, U. Toledo, 1979; PhD, U. Mich., 1984. Dir. alt. learning ctr. Lucas County Schs., Toledo, 1977-79; dir. chem. and metall. svcs. Toledo Testing Lab., 1979-82; pres. Chem. Resources, Lambertville, Mich., 1982-83; v.p. Benchmark Techs., Toledo, 1983-86; pres. Loeffler Group, Inc., 1986—; pres. Tech. Soc. Toledo, 1985-86; conf. chmn. Am. Soc. Quality Control. Deming Conf., Toledo, 1984; mem. Nat. Task Force ALARA Atomic Indsl. Forum, Washington; congl. sci. counselor PACCOS, Ohio; Ford Motor Co. prof., endowed chair Statis. Quality Studies Eastern Mich. U., 1986; examiner, trainer Malcolm Baldrige Nat. Quality Award, 1988-90. Editor Jour. Toledo Tech. Topics 1982-92; asst. editor Jour. English Quarterly, 1976-77. Contbr. articles to profl. jours. Vice chmn. Pvt. Industry Coun., Monroe County, Mich., 1983, 84; chmn. Bus.-Industry-Edn. Day Toledo & Detroit C. of C., 1984, 85; trustee Bedford Pub. Schs., Mich., 1982-85; chmn. Robotics Internat., 1985; bd. dirs., trustee Wittenberg U., 1991-95, Franciscan Health Systems, 1991-94, Riverside Health Group, 1993—, North Coast Health Systems, 1994—, Corp. for Effective Government, 1995—. Recipient Harvard Book award, 1967, internat. man of yr. award for total quality mgmt. Cambridge Centre, Eng., 1992; fellow SUNY-Stony Brook 1975-76, Cambridge U. 1976-77. Fellow Am. Psychol. Soc.; mem. Am. Chem. Soc. (chmn. Toledo chapt. 1984), Am. Soc. Non-Destructive Testing, Phi Delta Kappa, Phi Kappa Phi. Methodist. Club: U. Mich. (Toledo). Lodge: Rotary. Office: Loeffler Group Inc 4230 N Holland Sylvania Rd Toledo OH 43623-2506

LOEH, CORINNE GENEVIEVE, artist; b. Livingston, Ill., Apr. 6, 1918; d. Tipmer Charles and Mae Leona (Batemon) Rachow; m. Hugo William Loeh (dec.); children: Sandra Mae Blaeser, Danna Clare Koschkee (dec.). Grad., Blackburn Coll., 1937; BS in Edn., Greenville Coll., 1950; MS in Art Edn., So. Ill. U., 1958. Tchr. pub. schs., Ill., 1937-52; art supr. Unit Dist. #1, Carlyle, Ill., 1952-55; tchr. art high sch., supr. K-9 Unit Dist. #2, Greenville, Ill., 1955-65, title one author, dir., 1965-69; prof. art Greenville Coll., 1956-65; art dir. Unit Dist. #46, Elgin, Ill., 1969-77; freelance artist Oro Valley, Ariz., 1982—; art collector CLO Art Gallery, Oro Valley, 1982—; cons. in field. Author: Prescription for Titans, 1971; editor: Ill. Art Edn. Assn. News, 1972, 77; one-woman shows include Judson Coll., Elgin, 1979, Western Gallery, Tucson, Ariz., 1985, 87. Mem. AAUW, Ill. Art Edn. Assn., Nat. Mus. Women in Arts, Surface Designers, Fibert Arts Internat., Tucson Art Mus., Met. Mus. Art Internat., Nat. Art Edn. Assn. Republican. Home and office: 151 E Carolwood Dr Oro Valley AZ 85737

LOEHLE, BETTY BARNES, artist, painter; b. Montgomery, Ala., Mar. 21, 1923; d. Harry McGuinn and Elizabeth (Fowler) B.; m. Richard E. Loehle, Aug. 16, 1947; children—Craig Edward, Alan David, Bruce Barnes, Lynn Elizabeth. Student Auburn U., Harris Sch. Art, Nashville, 1942-46, Evanston Art Ctr., 1964-68. Layout artist Atlanta Art Studios, 1970-75; free lance designer, painter, Atlanta, 1975-80; full time painter, Atlanta, 1980—; dir., publicity chmn., exhibition chmn. Ga. Watercolor Soc., 1981-85; pres. Artists Assocs. Gallery, Atlanta, 1977-79, sec., 1985—. Represented by SOHO Myriad Gallery, Atlanta, Little House on Linden Gallery, Birmingham, Ala., Little Art Gallery, Raleigh, N.C. Entries judge Arts Festival of Atlanta, 1974; chmn. Unitarian Ch. Art Com., Atlanta, 1973-76. Recipient Purchase award Decatur Sesquicentennial, Ga., 1974, Hunter Mus. of Art, Chattanooga, 1977, Ga. Council for the Arts, Atlanta, 1977, 1980. Mem. DeKalb Council for the Arts, Ga. Watercolor Soc. (signature mem.; merit awards 1980, 82, 83, 87, 88), So. Watercolor Soc. (signature mem.; silver award 1979, merit award 1980), Ky. Watercolor Soc. (artist mem.), Atlanta Artist Club (exhbn. chmn. 1972-74). Home: 2608 River Oak Dr Decatur GA 30033-2805

LOEHLIN, JOHN CLINTON, psychologist, educator; b. Ferozepore, India, Jan. 13, 1926; s. Clinton Herbert and Eunice (Cleland) L.; m. Marjorie Leafdale, Jan. 2, 1962; children—Jennifer Ann, James Norris. AB, Harvard U., 1947; PhD, U. Calif., Berkeley, 1957. With rsch dept. McCann-Erickson, Inc., Cleve., 1947-49; instr. to asst. prof. psychology U. Nebr., Lincoln, 1957-64; mem. faculty U. Tex., Austin, 1964—, prof. psychology and computer scis., 1969-92, prof. emeritus, 1992—. Author: Computer Models of Personality, 1968, Latent Variable Models, 1987, Genes and Environment in Personality Development, 1992; co-author: Race Differences in Intelligence, 1975, Heredity, Environment and Personality, 1976, Introduction to Theories of Personality, 1985. With USNR, 1945-47, 51-53. Fellow Ctr. Advanced Study Behavioral Scis., 1971-72. Fellow Am. Psychol. Soc.; mem. Behavior Genetics Assn., Soc. Multivariate Exptl. Psychology. Home: 304 Almarion Dr Austin TX 78746-5644 Office: U Tex Dept Psychology Austin TX 78712

LOEHR, ARTHUR WILLIAM, JR., healthcare executive, nurse; b. Cleve., July 26, 1948; s. Arthur William and Margaret Osborne (Robison) L.; m. Carol Lynn Hiatt; children: Brett Lawrence, Melissa Margaret, Joshua Hiatt. Diploma, Jackson Meml. Hosp., 1971; BS in Health Sci., Fla. Internat. U., 1975, M of Healthcare Adminstrn., 1977. RN, Fla. Psychiat. nurse Jackson Meml. Hosp., Miami, Fla., 1971, nurse cons., 1972, adminstr. pediats., 1973-74, hosp. planner, 1975-77; hosp. planner Duke U. Med. Ctr., Durham, N.C., 1977-80; v.p. planning N.C. Hosp. Assn., Raleigh, 1980-84, Catawba Meml. Hosp., Hickory, N.C., 1984—; preceptor U. N.C., Chapel Hill, N.C., 1988—. V.p., pres. Hospice of Catawba Valley, Hickory, 1985-90, Rape Crisis Ctr., Hickory, 1987-92; mem. Catawba County United Way Bd., 1991—, Family Care Ctr. of Catawba County, bd. dirs., 1992—. Scholar B'nai Brith, Miami, 1971. Fellow Am. Coll. Healthcare Execs.; mem. Rotary Internat. (bd. dirs. 1990-93). Presbyterian. Avocations: golf, fishing, snow skiing. Home: 4322 3rd Street Pl NW Hickory NC 28601-9033 Office: Catawba Memorial Hospital 810 Fairgrove Church Rd Hickory NC 28602-9617

LOEHR, MARLA, spiritual care coordinator; b. Cleve., Oct. 7, 1937; d. Joseph Richard and Eleanore Edith (Rothschuh) L. BS, Notre Dame Coll., South Euclid, Ohio, 1960; MAT, Ind. U., 1969; PhD, Boston Coll., 1988; Degree (hon.), Notre Dame Coll. Ohio, 1995. Joined Sisters of Notre Dame, Roman Cath. Ch., 1956; cert. high sch. tchr., counselor, Ohio. Mem. faculty Notre Dame Acad., Cleve., 1960-64, John F. Kennedy High Sch., Warren, Ohio, 1964-66; adminstrn. asst., dir. residence halls Notre Dame Acad., Chardon, Ohio, 1966-72; dean students Notre Dame Coll., South Euclid, Ohio, 1972-85, acting acad. dean, 1988, pres., 1988-95; spiritual care coord. Hospice of Western Res., Cleve., 1995—; facilitator Coun. for Ind. Colls., Washington, 1980-84. Author: Mentor Handbook, 1985; co-author: Notre Dame College Model for Student Development, 1980. Hon. mem. Segund Montes Solidarity City Campaign; Leadership Cleve. Class of 1990; vol. Hospice of Western Res.; bd. trustees S.J. Wellness Ctr. Recipient Career Woman of Achievement award YWCA, 1992; named One of 100 Cleve.'s Most Powerful Women, New Cleve. Woman. Mem. Pax Christi, Alpha Sigma Nu, Kappa Gamma Pi. Avocations: photography, hiking, reading, sports. Office: Hospice Western Res U 300 E 185th St Cleveland OH 44119-1330

LOEHWING, RUDI CHARLES, JR., publicist, marketing, advertising, internet, commerce, radio broadcasting executive, journalist, broadcast journalist; b. Newark, July 26, 1957; s. Rudy Charles Sr. and Joan Marie (Bell) L.; m. Claire Popham, Sept. 4, 1987; children: Aspasia Joyce, Tesia Victoria, Rudi Douglas, Anna Marie, Samantha Diane, Ian Ryan. Student, Biscayne U., 1975, Seton Hall U., 1977, Hubbard Acad., 1980. Announcer radio sta. WHBI FM, N.Y.C., 1970-72; producer Am. Culture Entertainment, Belleville, N.J., 1973-74; exec. producer Am. Culture Entertainment, Hollywood, Calif., 1988-94; CEO Broadcaster's Network Internat., Hollywood, U.K., also U.K., 1989—, Broadcaster's Network Internat., Ltd., Hollywood, also U.K.; v.p. pub. rels. The Dohring Co.; bd. dirs. First Break, Hollywood, also U.K., 1988—. Author: Growing Pains, 1970; exec. producer TV documentaries and comml. advertisements, 1983; patentee in field. Devel. dir. Tricentennial Found., Washington, 1989-90; bd. dirs. Civic Ligh Opera of South Bay Cities, Just Say No to Drugs, L.A., 1989, Hands Across the Atlantic, Internat. Country Top 10, The Rock of Russia, Job Search, Hollywood, U.K. and Russia. Named Youngest Comml. Radio Producer and Announcer for State of N.Y., Broadcaster's Network Internat., 1972. Mem. Broadcasters Network Assn. (bd. dirs. 1977—), Profl. Bus. Comms. Assn. (founder 1989), BNI News Bur. (chmn. 1991—), Civic Light Opera of South Bay Cities (bd. dirs. 1996—). Avocations: flying, music, writing, photography, martial arts. Office: Broadcasters Network Internat Ltd 2624 Medlow Ave Ste B Los Angeles CA 90065-4617

LOENGARD, JOHN BORG, photographer, editor; b. N.Y.C., Sept. 5, 1934; s. Richard Otto and Margery (Borg) L.; m. Eleanor Sturgis, Aug. 25, 1963 (div. 1987); children: Charles, Jennifer, Anna. B.A., Harvard Coll., 1956. Staff photographer Life mag., N.Y.C., 1961-72, picture editor, 1973-87; freelance photographer, 1987—; columnist Popular Photography mag., N.Y.C., 1987, Am. Photographer, N.Y.C., 1988—. Author: Pictures Under Discussion, 1987, Life Classic Photographs: A Personal Interpretation by John Loengard, 1988, Life Faces: Commentary by John Loengard, 1991, Celebrating the Negative, 1994, Georgia O'Keeffe at Ghost Ranch, 1995; essays in Life mag., The Shakers, 1967, Georgia O'Keeffe, 1968, Vanishing Cowboys, 1970, Photographers Over 80, 1982, Henry Moore, 1983, Interstate 80, 1989. Recipient Ansel Adams award Am. Soc. Mag. Photographers, 1987, Lifetime Achievement award Photographic Adminstrs., Inc., 1996. Home: 20 W 86th St New York NY 10024-3604 Office: Time & Life Bldg Rm 2841 New York NY 10020

LOENGARD, RICHARD OTTO, JR., lawyer; b. N.Y.C, Jan. 28, 1932; s. Richard Otto and Margery (Borg) L.; m. Janet Sara Senderowitz, Apr. 11, 1964; children: Maranda C., Philippa S.M. AB, Harvard U., 1953, LLB, 1956. Bar: N.Y. 1956, U.S. Dist. Ct. (so. dist.) N.Y. 1958. Assoc. Fried, Frank, Harris, Shriver & Jacobson, predecessor firms, N.Y.C., 1956-64, ptnr., 1967-97; of counsel Fried, Frank, Harris, Shriver & Jacobson, N.Y.C., 1997—; dep. tax legis. counsel, spl. asst. internat. tax affairs U.S. Dept. Treasury, Washington, 1964-67; mem. Commerce Clearing House, Riverwoods, Ill. Editl. bd. Tax Transaction Libr., 1982-94; contbr. articles to profl. publs. Fellow Am. Coll. Tax Counsel; mem. ABA, N.Y. State Bar Assn. (exec. com. tax sect. 1984—, sec. 1994-95, vice chair 1995-97, chair 1997—), Assn. Bar City N.Y. Office: Fried Frank Harris Shriver & Jacobson 1 New York Plz New York NY 10004

LOEPER, F. JOSEPH, state senator; b. Dec. 23, 1944; m. Joann M. Loeper; children: F. Joseph III, James H., Joanne M. BS in Edn., West Chester U., 1966; MEd, Temple U., 1970; D of Law (hon.), Widener U., 1992. Tchr. social studies, asst. basketball coach, advisor sch. paper Aldan Sch. Dist., 1966-67; tchr. social studies, football coach Drexel Hill Jr. High Sch. Upper Darby Sch. Dist., 1967-68; dir. leisure svcs. Upper Darby Sch. Dist. Upper Darby Twp., 1968-78; instr. Pub. Svc. Inst. Millersville, Kutztown and West Chester U., 1972; mem. Rep. State Com. 26th Senatorial Dist., 1972-74; co-adj. instr. Delaware County Community Coll., 1973-74; mem. Upper Darby Gov. Study Commn., 1973-74; treas. Upper Darby Sch. Dist., 1973-78; senator Pa. Senate, 1978—, senate majority caucus sec., 1980-83, senate majority whip, 1984-87, senate majority leader, 1988-92, 94—, minority whip, 1992-93; chmn. Rules and Exec. Nominations com.; mem. Appropriations Com., Banking and Ins. Com., law and justice com.; bd. govs. State Systems of Higher Edn. com. Past chmn. Eastern Delaware County Br. ARC, past bd. dirs. southeastern Pa. chpt.; past bd. dirs. Delaware County Assn. for Retarded Citizens; past pres. Garrettford-Drexel Hill Fire Co., Upper Darby Twp. Fireman's Relief Assn. Recipient Delaware County Citizen of Yr. award, 1990, West Chester Univ. Disting. Alumni award, 1989, Presdl. award Delaware County Fed. Sr. Svcs., 1988, Legis. award Fraternal Order Police, 1985, Legion Honor award Chapel Four Chaplains, 1982, St. Charles Cath. Youth Assn. award, Delaware County Saving League award, YMCA Youth in Gov. award, Citizen of Yr. award Del. C. of C., 1992, Pres. medal West Chester U., 1994. Mem. Pa. Recreation and Park Soc. (Governmental svc. award, 1982), Nat. Edn. Assn. (life), Upper Darby Assn. Suprs. and Adminstrators, Nat. Rep. Legislators Assn. (Legislator of Yr. 1988), Senate Rep. Campaign Com. (treas.). Office: Rm 362 Main Capitol Bldg Harrisburg PA 17120 also: 403 Burmont Rd Drexel Hill PA 19026-3003

LOEPP, HERMAN ALBERT, subrogation examiner; b. Wichita, Kans., Sept. 30, 1953; s. Edward and Mary (Dennis) L.; m. Kerri Louise Huss, May 26, 1979; 1 child, Jonathan Aaron. AA, Hutchinson (Kans.) C.C., 1973; BS, Emporia State U., 1975; JD, Washburn U., 1981. Bar: Kans. 1982, U.S. Dist. Ct. Kans. 1982. Atty. Anderson County Kans., Garnett, Kans., 1982-88; claims atty. Associated Aviation Underwriters, Overland Park, Kans., 1988-94; claims mgr. Associated Aviation Underwriters, Atlanta, 1994-95; subrogation examiner Am. Family Ins., 1996—. Mem. Lawyers Pilots Bar Assn., Rotary Internat. (pres. 1987). Republican. Avocations: golf, softball. Home and Office: 12210 Bradshaw St Overland Park KS 66213-4812

LOERKE, WILLIAM CARL, art history educator; b. Toledo, Aug. 13, 1920; s. William Carl and Anna Louisa (Stallbaum) L.; m. Helen Trautmann, 1944; children—Anna Hurd, Timothy, Eric, Alison, Lisa Huff, Ellen, Martha. B.A., Oberlin Coll., 1942; M.F.A., Princeton U., 1948, Ph.D., 1957. Acad. positions history of art Brown U., 1949-59; assoc. prof. Bryn Mawr Coll., 1959-64; prof. art history U. Pitts., 1964-71, chmn. fine arts dept., 1964-69; prof. Byzantine art Harvard U., Dumbarton Oaks Research Library, 1971-88, prof. emeritus, 1988—; dir. studies Ctr. Byzantine Studies, 1971-77; vis. prof. Cath. U. Am., 1978-88; vis. prof. U. Md., 1988-92; mem. adv. bd. Ctr. for Advanced Study in Visual Arts, Nat. Gallery Art, Washington, 1979-82, 89-92; bd. dirs. Internat. Ctr. Medieval Art, 1973-91; mem. mng. com. Am. Sch. Classical Studies, 1973-93. Co-author: The Place of Book Illumination in Byzantine Art, Princeton, 1975, Monasticism and the Arts, 1984, Codex Rossanensis, Commentarium, Rome, 1987, Architecture: Fundamental Issues, N.Y., 1990; contbr. Byzantine East, Latin West: Art Historical Studies in Honor of Kurt Weitzman, 1995; contbr. articles to profl. jours.; contbr. Dictionary of Byzantium, 1991. Served with USNR, 1943-46. Jr. fellow Princeton U., 1946-48, Dumbarton Oaks Harvard U., 1948-49, Danforth Tchr. fellow, 1956-57; Fulbright Rsch. scholar Am. Acad. Rome, 1952-53; recipient A.K. Porter prize Coll. Art Assn., 1961. Mem. Coll. Art Assn., Medieval Acad. Am., Soc. Fellows, Am. Acad. at Rome, Internat. Ctr. Med. Art. Home: 227 Gralan Rd Catonsville MD 21228-4835

LOESCH, HAROLD C., retired marine biologist, consultant; b. Osage, Tex., Oct. 3, 1926; s. Eldor E. and Martha (Niemeier) L.; m. Mabel Treichler, Oct. 19, 1945; children: Stephen C., Gretchen Drinkard, Jonathan, Frederick. BS in Fisheries, Tex. A&M Univ., 1951; postgrad., Univ. Tex., Port Aransas, 1951, 52; MS in Biol. Oceanography, Tex. A&M Univ., 1954, PhD in Biol. Oceanography, 1962. Prin. marine biologist, acting lab. dir. Dept. Conservation, Bayou la Batre, Ala., 1952-57; teaching asst. Tex. A&M Univ., College Station, 1957-58; assoc. rsch. scientist Tex. A&M Rsch. Found., College Station, 1958-60; shrimp biologist Food & Agrl. Orgn. of UN, Guatamala, 1960-62; fisheries biologist Food & Agrl. Orgn. of UN, Ecuador, 1962-66; fisheries officer Food & Agrl. Orgn. of UN, La Ceiba, Honduras, 1967-68; prof. zoology La. State U., Baton Rouge, 1968-69; prof. marine scis. La. State U., 1970-75; expert marine biologist United Nat. Edn. Social and Cultural Orgn., Guaymas, Sonora, Mex., 1976-79; sr. resource assessment surveyor, project mgr. FAO, UN, Dhaka, Bangladesh, 1981-85; cons. Pensacola, Fla., 1985—; vis. prof. Orgn. Am. States, Guayaquil, Ecuador, 1972, Sch. for Field Study, Beverly, Mass., S. Caicos Isl, BWI, 1990; cons. Univ. Mex. U. N. Ed. Soc. & Cult Orgn., 1979-80. Contbr. articles to profl. jours. With USAF, 1945-46. Mem. AAAS (life), Am. Fisheries Soc., Internat. Acad. Fisheries Sci., Tex. Acad. Sci. (life), World Mariculture Soc., Am. Soc. Ichthyologists and Herpetologists (life), Sigma Xi. Democrat. Lutheran. Avocations: canoeing, wilderness camping, photography, traveling. Home: 2140 E Scott St Pensacola FL 32503-4957

LOESCH, KATHARINE TAYLOR (MRS. JOHN GEORGE LOESCH), communication and theatre educator; b. Berkeley, Calif., Apr. 13, 1922; d. Paul Schuster and Katharine (Whiteside) Taylor; student Swarthmore Coll., 1939-41, U. Wash., 1942; BA, Columbia U., 1944, MA, 1949; grad. Neighborhood Playhouse Sch. of Theatre, 1946; postgrad. Ind. U., 1953; PhD, Northwestern U., 1961; m. John George Loesch, Aug. 28, 1948; 1 child, William Ross. Instr. speech Wellesley (Mass.) Coll., 1949-52, Loyola U., Chgo., 1956; asst. prof. English and speech Roosevelt U., Chgo., 1957, 62-65; assoc. prof. communication and theatre U. Ill. at Chgo., 1968—; assoc. prof. emerita speech in communication and theater, U. Ill., Chgo., 1987—. Contbr. writings to profl. jours.; poetry performances. Active ERA, Ill., 1975-76. Am. Philos. Soc. grantee, 1970; U. Ill., Chgo., grantee, 1970. Mem. MLA, Speech Communication Assn. (Golden Anniversary prize award 1969, chmn. interpretation div. 1979-80), Celtic Studies Assn. N.Am., Pi Beta Phi. Episcopalian. Home: 2129 N Sedgwick St Chicago IL 60614-4619 Office: U Ill Dept Performing Arts M/C 255 1040 W Harrison St Chicago IL 60607-7129

LOESCH, MABEL LORRAINE, social worker; b. Annandale, Minn., July 1, 1925; d. Rudolph and Hedwig (Zeidler) Treichler; m. Harold Carl Loesch, Oct. 19, 1945; children: Stephen, Gretchen, Jonathan, Frederick. BS, La. State U., 1972, MSW, 1974. Cert. Acad. Cert. Social Worker, bd. cert. diplomate. Tchr. Am. schs. Tegucigalpa, Honduras, 1960-61, Guayaquil, Ecuador, 1962-66, La Ceiba, Honduras, 1966-67; supr. clin. svc. Blundon Home, Baton Rouge, 1974-81; social worker, cons. Dhaka, Bangladesh, 1981-85; social worker Manna Food Bank, Pensacola, Fla., 1986—; adj. instr. social work dept. Southern U., Baton Rouge, 1976-81. Author: Generations in Germany and America, 1995; editor: Making Do, 1989, Making Do II, 1994. Mem. adv. com. Luth. Ministries of Fla., 1993—. Mem. NASW, Mensa (local sec. 1986-90, chair scholarships com.), Phi Kappa Phi. Democrat. Lutheran. Avocation: genealogy. Home: 2140 E Scott St Pensacola FL 32503-4957

LOESCHER, GILBURT DAMIAN, international relations educator; b. San Francisco, Mar. 7, 1945; s. Burt Garfield and Helen (Aachen) L.; m. Ann Gordon Dull, Sept. 25, 1971; children: Margaret Madeline, Claire Helen. BA, St. Mary's Coll. of Calif., 1967; MA, Monterey Inst. Internat. Study, 1969; PhD, London Sch. Econs./Polit. Sci., 1975. Asst. prof. U. Notre Dame, Ind., 1975-84, assoc. prof., 1984-90, prof., 1990—, asst. dean., 1977-79; vis. fellow London Sch. Econs., 1978-79, Princeton (N.J.) U., 1982-83; rsch. cons. U.S. Select Commn. on Immigration and Refugee Policy, Washington, 1989; sr. rsch. fellow Queen Elizabeth House, Oxford (Eng.) U., 1986-89; rsch. assoc. Internat. Inst. for Strategic Studies, London, 1990-91. Author: Refugee Movements and International Security, 1992, Beyond Charity: International Cooperation and the Global Refugee Problem, 1993; co-author: Calculated Kindness: Refugees and America's Half-Open Door, 1985 (Gustavas Meyers award 1986). Mem. exec. bd. Ind. Consortium for Internat. Programs, 1976-80; bd. dirs. Amnesty Internat., N.Y., 1980-82; chair adv. com. on internat. experts UN Commn. for Refugees, Geneva, 1992—; advisor UN High Commnr. for Refugees, 1996. Grantee Ford Found., 1982-84, 92-93, 96, Twentieth Century Fund, 1987-89, MacArthur Found., 1990-91. Mem. Internat. Studies Assn., Am. Polit. Sci. Assn., Royal Inst. Internat. Affairs, Internat. Inst. for Strategic Studies, Academic Coun. of UN Sys. Democrat. Roman Catholic. Avocations: basketball, walking, theater. Office: U Notre Dame Notre Dame IN 46556

LOESCHER, RICHARD ALVIN, gastroenterologist; b. Brockton, Mass., Feb. 6, 1940; s. Vernon Alvin and Anna Marie (Good) L.; m. Linda Rockwell Clifford Loescher, June 5, 1965 (div. Jan. 1982); children: Steven Clifford Loescher, Laura May Loescher. BA, De Pauw U., 1961; MD cum laude, Harvard U., 1965. Diplomate Am. Bd. Internal Medicine, 1972, Am. Bd. Gastroenterology, 1973. Chief Med. Svc. U.S. Pub. Health Svc. Hosp., Lawton, Okla., 1967-69; chief Med. Staff, 1968-69, svc. unit dir., 1969; attending physician Seattle, 1970-71, U. Hosp., Seattle, 1970-71; active staff Sacred Heart Med. Ctr., Eugene, Oreg., 1973—, Eugene (Oreg.) Hosp., 1972-88; courtesy staff McKenzie-Williamette Hosp., Springfield, Oreg., 1982—. Recipient Rector scholarship DePauw U., 1957-61, Maimonides award Harvard Med. Sch., 1965. Mem. AMA, Lane County Med. Soc., Oreg. Med. Assn., Oreg. Soc. Internal Medicine, Am. Soc. Internal Medicine, Am. Soc. for Gastrointestinal Endoscopy, Am. Acad. Med. Acupuncture, Alpha Omega Alpha, Phi Beta Kappa. Democrat. Unitarian. Avocations: physical fitness, personal growth, magic, outdoor activities. Home: 2345 Patterson St Apt 34 Eugene OR 97405-2974 Office: 1162 Willamette St Eugene OR 97401-3568

LOESER, HANS FERDINAND, lawyer; b. Kassel, Germany, Sept. 28, 1920; s. Max and Cecilia H. (Erlanger) L.; m. Herta Lewent, Dec. 14, 1944; children—Helen, Harris M., H. Thomas. Student CCNY, 1940-42, U. Pa., 1942-43; LL.B. magna cum laude, Harvard U., 1950. Bar: Mass. 1950, U.S. Supreme Ct. 1968. Asso. firm Foley, Hoag & Eliot, Boston, 1950-55, ptnr., 1956—; hon. consul-gen. Republic of Senegal; mem. Mass. Bd. Bar Overseers; trustee Vineyard Open Land Found., Martha's Vineyard, Mass.; mem. exec. com. and nat. bd. Lawyers' Com. for Civil Rights Under Law, steering com. and past chmn. Lawyer's Com. for Civil Rights Under Law of Boston Bar Assn.; incorporator Univ. Hosp., Boston, Mt. Auburn Hosp., Cambridge, Mass. Served to capt. U.S. Army, 1942-46. Decorated Bronze Star, Purple Heart; hon. fellow U. Pa. Law Sch., 1978-79, commencement speaker, 1978. Fellow Am. Bar Found., Mass. Bar Found.; mem. ABA, Mass. Bar Assn., Boston Bar Assn. Clubs: Union, Harvard, Cambridge. Office: Foley Hoag & Eliot 1 Post Office Sq Boston MA 02109

LOESER, JOHN DAVID, neurosurgeon, educator; b. Newark, Dec. 14, 1935; s. Lewis Henry and Rhoda Sophie (Levy) L.; m. Susan Winifred Becker, June 11, 1961 (div. 1974); children: Sally Ann, Thomas Eric, Derek William; m. Karen Winslow, Dec. 29, 1977; 1 child, David Winslow. BA, Harvard U., 1957; MD, NYU, 1961. Diplomate Am. Bd. Neurol. Surgery; cert. Nat. Bd. Med. Examiners.; lic. neurosurgeon, Wash. Intern dept. surgery U. Calif., San Francisco, 1961-62; resident neurol. surgery U. Wash., Seattle, 1962-67; asst. prof. neurosurgery U. Calif., Irvine, 1967-68; asst. prof. neurol. surgery U. Wash., Seattle, 1969-75, assoc. prof., 1975-80, prof., 1980—, dir. Multidisciplinary Pain Clinic, 1983-97; chief div. of neurosurgery Children's Hosp. & Med. Ctr., 1987-93; Fulbright sr. scholar, Australia, 1989-90. Contbr. articles to profl. jours.; editor profl. books. Served as maj. U.S. Army, 1968-70. Fellow AAAS; mem. Internat. Assn. Study of Pain (sec. 1984-90, pres. 1993-96), Am. Pain Soc. (treas. 1980-85, pres. 1986-87), Am. Assn. Neurol. Surgeons, North Pacific Soc. Neurology and Psychiatry, Wash. Assn. Neurosurgery, Western Neurosurg. Soc., Am. Acad. Pain Medicine, King County Med. Soc., Conf. Neurol. Surgeons, Phi Beta Kappa, Alpha Omega Alpha. Avocations: skiing, woodcarving. Office: U Wash Dept Neurol Surgery Box 356470 Seattle WA 98195

LOESS, HENRY BERNARD, psychology educator; b. Chgo., June 24, 1924; s. Henry William and Alice Cecilia (Mansfield) L.; m. Frances Mary Van Horn, May 26, 1951; children—Kurt, Karin, Andrew, Alan. BS, Northwestern U., 1949, MS, 1950; PhD, U. Iowa, 1952. Prof. psychology, chmn. dept. Lake Forest (Ill.) Coll., 1952-58; Prof. psychology, chmn. dept. Wooster (Ohio) Coll., 1958-88, prof. emeritus, 1988—; vis. lectr. Ohio State U., 1958-63; vis. research scholar U. Calif. at Berkeley, 1963-64, Cambridge (Eng.) U., 1968-69, U. Mich., 1973-74, Yale U., 1980-81; vis. scientist Ohio Acad. Sci., 1962-92; regional coord. Am. Inst. Rsch. Project Talent, 1961-69; assoc. North Ctrl. Assn. Colls. and Secondary Schs., 1970-86; bd. dirs. Habitat for Humanity, Wayne County, 1989—, Hospice of Wayne County, 1990—, Wayne County Bd. Mental Retardation and Devel. Disabiliies, 1978-86, 93—. Author articles in field; cons. editor: Memory and Cognition, 1971-85. Served with USAAF, 1943-46. Mem. Am., Midwestern, Eastern psychol. assns., Psychonomic Soc., AAAS, Am. Assn. U. Profs., Sigma Xi. Home: 5410 Lehr Rd Wooster OH 44691-9288

LOETE, STEVEN DONALD, pilot; b. Tacoma, Aug. 21, 1959; s. Donald Kenneth and Ida Lorraine (Buck) L.; 1 child, Samantha. BA, Pacific Luth. U., 1984. Pilot contracting office USAF, Williams AFB, Ariz., 1985; flight instr. Clover Park Tech. Coll., Tacoma, 1986; charter pilot Stellar Exec., Chandler, Ariz., 1986-87; pilot, airline capt. Maui Airlines, Guam, 1987; airline capt., checkairman Westair Airlines, Fresno, Calif., 1987—. Contbr. Save the Children, 1988-90; mem. Angel Flight, U. Puget Sound, 1981-83; bd. dirs. aviation adv. com. Clover Park Tech. Coll., 1991—. 1st lt. USAF, 1983-93. Mem. Airline Pilots Assn. (chmn. organizing com. 1989, chmn. coun. 1989-91). Republican. Methodist. Avocations: racquetball, fishing. Home and Office: PO Box 57 Spanaway WA 98387

LOEUP, KONG, cultural organization administrator; b. Battambang, Cambodia, May 26, 1944; s. Kong Niem and Chhit Roeun; m. Ly Keo Thim, Aug. 1968; children: Kong Bandaul, Kong Panlauk. Diploma in edn., U. Phnom Penh, 1965; BA, Antioch U., 1983; MA, U. Colo., Denver, 1987; PhD, Columbia Pacific U., 1987. Tchr. Ministry Edn., Phnom Penh, 1964; counselor, community case worker Internat. Refugee Ctr., Denver, 1983; refugee program coord./counselor Refugee Camps, Thailand; cons. Cambodian Buddhist Soc. of Colo., Denver; counselor Cambodian Community Colo., Denver; pres. Cambodian Cultural Ctr., Denver, 1992—. Pres. Cambodian Fine Arts Preservation Group Colo.; mem. Asian Edn. Adv. Coun., Rep. Presdl. Task Force, 1986. Mem. ASCD. Home and Office: 1804 S Eliot St Denver CO 80219-4904

LOEVINGER, LEE, lawyer, science writer; b. St. Paul, Apr. 24, 1913; s. Gustavus and Millie (Strouse) L.; m. Ruth Howe, Mar. 4, 1950; children: Barbara L., Eric H., Peter H. BA summa cum laude, U. Minn., 1933, JD, 1936. Bar: Minn. 1936, Mo. 1937, D.C. 1966, U.S. Supreme Ct., 1941. Assoc. Watson, Ess, Groner, Barnett & Whittaker, Kansas City, Mo., 1936-37; atty., regional atty. NLRB, 1937-41; with antitrust div. Dept. Justice, 1941-46; ptnr. Larson, Loevinger, Lindquist & Fraser, Mpls., 1946-60; assoc. justice Minn. Supreme Ct., 1960-61; asst. U.S. atty. gen. charge antitrust div. Dept. Justice, 1961-63; commr. FCC, 1963-68; ptnr. Hogan & Hartson, Washington, 1968-85; of counsel Hogan & Hartson, 1986—; v.p., dir. Craig-Hallum Corp., Mpls., 1968-73; dir. Petrolite Corp., St. Louis, 1978-83; U.S. rep. com. on restrictive bus. practices Orgn. for Econ. Coop. and Devel., 1961-64; spl. asst. to U.S. atty. gen., 1963-64; spl. counsel com. small bus. U.S. Senate, 1951-52; lectr. U. Minn., 1953-60; vis. prof. jurisprudence U. Minn. (Law Sch.), 1961; professorial lectr. Am. U., 1968-70; chmn. Minn. Atomic Devel. Problems Com., 1957-59; mem. Adminstrv. Conf. U.S., 1972-74; del. White House Conf. on Inflation, 1974; U.S. del. UNESCO Conf. on Mass Media, 1975, Internat. Telecomms. Conf. on Radio Frequencies, 1964, 66. Author: The Law of Free Enterprise, 1949, An Introduction to Legal Logic, 1952, Defending Antitrust Lawsuits, 1977, Science As Evidence, 1995; author first article to use term: jurimetrics, 1949; contbr. articles to profl. and sci. jours.; editor, contbr.: Basic Data on Atomic Devel. Problems in Minnesota, 1958; adv. bd. Antitrust Bull., Jurimetrics Jour. Served to lt. comdr. USNR, 1942-45. Recipient Outstanding Achievement award U. Minn., 1968; Freedoms Found. award, 1977, 84. Fellow Am. Acad. Appellate Lawyers; mem. ABA (del. of sci. and tech. sect. to Ho. of Dels. 1974-80, del. to joint conf. with AAAS 1974-76, co-chair 1990-93, liaison 1984-90, 93—, chmn. sci. and tech. sect. 1982-83, coun. 1986-89, standing com. on nat. conf. groups 1984-90), AAAS, Minn. Bar Assn., Hennepin County Bar Assn., N.Y. Acad. Sci., D.C. Bar Assn., FCC Bar Assn., Broadcast Pioneers, U.S. C. of C. (antitrust coun. 1980-94), Am. Arbitration Assn. (comml. panel), Atlantic Legal Found. (adv. coun.), Cosmos Club (pres. 1990), City Club (Washington), Phi Beta Kappa, Sigma Xi, Delta Sigma Rho, Sigma Delta Chi, Phi Delta Gamma, Tau Kappa Alpha, Alpha Epsilon Rho. Home: 5600 Wisconsin Ave Apt 17D Chevy Chase MD 20815-4414 Office: Hogan & Hartson 555 13th St NW Washington DC 20004-1109 *With age I come increasingly to believe that life is, and should be,a learning experience. This involves a peculiar paradox: Ignorance increases faster than knowledge, as each new fact or principle opens new frontiers for intellectual exploration. Thus, with greater learning comes intellectual humility and skepticism. So, after reaching 75 I am less certain of anything than at 25 I was of everything.*

LOEW, FRANKLIN MARTIN, medical and biological scientist, business entrepreneur; b. Syracuse, N.Y., Sept. 8, 1939; s. David Franklin and Sarah (Adelaide) L.; children: Timothy, Andrew. B.S., Cornell U., 1961, D.V.M., 1965; Ph.D., U. Sask., 1971. Lic. veterinarian; diplomate Am. Coll. Lab. Animal Medicine. Research asst. R.J. Reynolds Co., Winston-Salem, N.C., 1965-66; research asst. Tulane U., New Orleans, 1966-67; prof. U. Sask., Saskatoon, Can., 1967-77; dir. comparative medicine Johns Hopkins U., Balt., 1977-82; dean Sch. Vet. Medicine, Tufts U., Boston, 1982-95, Henry and Lois Foster prof. comparative medicine, 1985-95; v.p. Tufts U. Devel. Corp. Inc., Boston, 1991-95; pres. Tufts Biotech. Corp., Boston, 1993-95; dean Coll. Vet. Medicine Cornell U., Ithaca, N.Y., 1995-97; pres., CEO Med. Foods, Inc., Cambridge, Mass., 1997—; cons. Can. Coun. Animal Care, Ottawa, Ont., 1969-84; mem. life scis. com. Nat. Acad. Sci., Washington, 1981-88, chmn. Inst. Lab. Animal Resources, 1981-87; mem. FDA Commn. on Sr. Biomed. Rsch. Svc. Credentials, 1995—; N.B. lectr. Am. Soc. Microbiology; mem. nat. adv. bd. Ctr. on Bioethics Lit., Kennedy Inst. Georgetown U., 1986—; Schofield lectr. U. Guelph, Can.; Smith lectr. U. Sask.; Schalm lectr. U. Calif.; univ. lectr. Tex. A&M U.; bd. dirs. Mass. Biotech. Rsch. Inst., Commonwealth BioVentures, Inc.; mem. sci. adv. com. Harvard Primate Rsch. Ctr., 1988—, Mass. Health Resources Inst.; sci. and tech. adv. com. State of Mass., 1988-92; mem. USDA Sec.'s Adv. Com. Nat. Rsch. Initiative, 1992—; pres. Tufts Biotech. Corp., 1993-95; bd. trustees Marine Biol. Lab., 1990-94, New Eng. Aquarium, 1991-95, Guys Drug Rsch. Unit, U.K., 1993-94; mem. panel animal health Nat. Rsch. Coun., 1992—. Author: Vet in the Saddle, 1978; editor: Laboratory Animal Medicine, 1984; contbr. numerous articles to profl. jours. Chmn. bd. trustees Boston Zool. Soc., 1984-88; trustee Worcester Acad. 1984-90; mem. Nat. Ctr. Rsch.

Resources adv. coun. NIH, 1988-92, Blue Ribbon adv. coun. USDA, 1987-91; bd. dirs. Ea. States Exhbn,m 1988-85; bd. dirs. Mass. SPCA, 1996—;mem. bus. bd. Pharmacia & Upjohn, 1996—. Decorated Queen Elizabeth II Jubilee medal Gov.-Gen. Can., 1977; Med. Rsch. Coun. Can. fellow, 1969-71; recipient Charles River prize Am. Vet. Med. Assn., 1988, named Vet. of Yr., 1989; recipient Disting. Svc. award Mass. Vet. Med. Assn., 1992. Mem. NAS/Inst. Medicine, AAAS, Am. Inst. Nutrition, Soc. Toxicology, Assn. Am. Vet. Med. Colls. (pres. 1985-86), Am. Coll. Lab. Medicine (bd. dirs. 1979-82), Nat. Acads. Practice, Fedn. Am. Socs. for Exptl. Biology, Am. Antiquarian Soc., Mass. Agrl. Club. Office: Med Foods Inc 201 Broadway Cambridge MA 02139-1955

LOEW, GILDA HARRIS, research biophysicist, biology research executive; b. N.Y.C.; 4 children. BA, NYU, 1951; MA, Columbia U., 1952; PhD in Chem. Physics, U. Calif., Berkeley, 1957. Rsch. physicist Lawrence Radiation Lab., U. Calif., Berkeley, 1957-62, Lockheed Missiles and Space Co., 1962-64; assoc. quantum biophysics Biophys. Lab., Stanford U., 1964-66; from asst. prof. to assoc. prof. physics Pomona coll., 1966-69; rsch. biophysicist, instr. biophysics Stanford U. Med. Sch., 1969-79; adj. prof. genetics Stanford U. Med. Ctr., 1974-79; program dir. molecular theory Life Sci. divsn. Stanford Rsch. Inst., 1979—; adj. prof. Rockefeller U., 1979—. Grantee NSF, 1966—, NASA, 1969—, NIH, 1974—. Fellow Am. Phys. Soc.; mem. Biophys. Soc., Internat. Soc. Magnetic Resonance. Achievements include research in molecular orbital and crystal field quantum chemical calculations; models for protein active sites; mechanisms and requirements for specific drug action; theoretical studies related to chemical evolution of life. Office: Molecular Rsch Inst 845 Page Mill Rd Palo Alto CA 94304-1011*

LOEWEN, ERWIN G., precision engineer, educator, consultant; b. Frankfurt, Germany, Apr. 12, 1921; came to U.S., 1937; s. Franz L. and Gladys M. (Marx) L.; m. Joanna M. Wills, Sept. 5, 1952; children: Oliver F., Heidi R. BMechE, NYU, 1941; MS, MIT, 1949, MMechE, 1950, ScD, 1952. Tech. dir. Taft-Pierce Mfg. Co., Woonsocket, R.I., 1952-60; dir. gratings and metrology Bausch & Lomb, Rochester, N.Y., 1960-85; v.p. R&D Milton Roy Co., Rochester, 1985-87, emeritus, 1987—; prof. optics U. Rochester, 1988-97. Author: Diffraction, Gratings and Applications, 1997; contbr. numerous articles on metal cutting, precision engring., and diffraction grating to profl. jours., chpt. to book. Staff sgt. U.S. Army, 1944-46, PTO. Fellow ASME (v.p. standardization), Optical Soc. Am. (David Richardson medal, 1984, Robert M. Burley prize 1993, Fraunhofer medal 1993), Soc. Mfg. Engrs.; mem. Am. Soc. Precision Engrs. (hon.), Soc. Photoinstrumentation Engrs., Internat. Instn. Prodn. Engring. Rsch., Sigma Xi. Avocations: photography, skiing, swimming. Home: 34A Brookhill Ln Rochester NY 14625-2212 Office: Spectronics Instruments Inc 820 Linden Ave Rochester NY 14625-2710

LOEWENBERG, GERHARD, political science educator; b. Berlin, Germany, Oct. 2, 1928; came to U.S., 1936, naturalized, 1943; s. Walter and Anne Marie (Cassirer) L.; m. Ina Perlstein, Aug. 22, 1950; children: Deborah, Michael. A.B., Cornell U., 1949, A.M., 1950, Ph.D., 1955. Mem. faculty Mount Holyoke Coll., 1953-69, chmn. dept. polit. sci., 1963-69, acting academic dean, 1968-69; prof. polit. sci. U. Iowa, Iowa City, 1970—, chmn. dept., 1982-84, dean Coll. Liberal Arts, 1984-92, dir. Comparative Legis. Research Center, 1971-82, 92—; vice chair East-West Parliamentary Practice Project, 1990—; vis. assoc. prof. Columbia, UCLA, 1966, U. Mass. summer session at Bologna, Italy, 1967, Cornell U., 1968; mem. council Inter-Univ. Consortium for Polit. Research, 1971-74, chmn., 1973-74. Author: Parliament in the German Political System, 1967, Parlamentarismus im politischen System der Bundesrepublik Deutschland, 1969, Modern Parliaments: Change or Decline, 1971; co-author: Comparing Legislatures, 1979; co-editor: Handbook of Legislative Research, 1985; co-editor: Legis. Studies Quar.; contbr. articles to profl. jours. Trustee Mt. Holyoke Coll., 1971-84, chmn., 1979-84. Fulbright fellow, 1957-58; Rockefeller fellow, 1961-62; Social Sci. Research Council faculty research fellow, 1964-65; Guggenheim fellow, 1969-70. Mem. Am. Polit. Sci. Assn. (coun. 1971-73, v.p. 1990-91), Midwest Polit. Sci. Assn., Phi Beta Kappa, Phi Kappa Phi, Pi Sigma Alpha. Office: U Iowa 336 Schaeffer Hall Iowa City IA 52242-1409

LOEWENSTEIN, BENJAMIN STEINBERG, lawyer; b. Atlantic City, Aug. 22, 1912; s. Sidney and Cecilia (Steinberg) L.; m. Eleanor Lax Schieren, June 14, 1966; children: Sally L. (Mrs. David S. Well, Jr.), P. Edward: stepchildren: Susan (Mrs. Stanton A. Moss, dec.), Julie (Mrs. Robert Dreidink). A.B., Haverford Coll., 1934; J.D., U. Pa., 1937. Bar: Pa. 1937. Practiced in Phila., 1937—; sr. partner Abrahams & Loewenstein, 1937-87, of counsel, 1988—; Sec., dir. Rojess Corp., Gen. Syndicate Corp., Jonns Inc., Engelside Realty Corp., Sherill Corp., Oak Blvd. Inc., Kahn's Inc., Atlas Rug Cleaners, Inc.; Counsel Diamond Coun. Am., Phila. County Dental Soc.; Del. White House Conf. on Aging; chmn. Task Force on Aging, Pa. Comprehensive Health Plan, Regional Comprehensive Health Planning Delaware Valley, Pa., 1968; mem. Pa. Human Relations Commn., 1974-87. Hon. chmn. bd. Jewish Occupational Coun., 1971—; pres. Jewish Employment and Vocat. Service, 1954-59, hon. pres. 1976—; pres. So. Home for Children, 1968-69, Health and Welfare Coun. Phila., 1969-71; pres. Jewish Community Rels. Coun. Phila., 1974-77, hon. pres., 1978—; mem. bd. govs. Am. Jewish Com., 1968—, hon. chmn. Phila. chpt.; trustee Community Svcs. Pa., 1968-78; bd. mgrs. Haverford Coll., 1970—; bd. dirs. Vocat. Rsch. Inst., 1960—, United Way of Phila., Fedn. Jewish Agys., Phila., Pa. Law and Justice Inst., 1971-76, Fellowship Commn. Phila., 1972-86, Phila. Anti-Poverty Action Commn., 1976-87, Nat. Inst. on the Holocaust, 1977-82; treas. Interfaith Council on the Holocaust, 1986—; bd. dirs. Quadrangle Retirement Community, 1977-96, Martins Run Retirement Community, 1981—. Recipient Community Service award Allied Jewish Appeal Phila., 1956, certificate of appreciation Phila. County Med. Soc., 1961, certificate appreciation Fedn. Jewish Agys., 1972, Phila. Commn. Human Relations award, 1974; certificate Merit Am. Cancer Soc., 1974; Samuel Greenberg Meml. award Nat. Assn. Jewish Vocat. Services, 1980; Human Relations award Am. Jewish Com., 1981; Legion of Honor Chapel of Four Chaplains, 1980. Mem. Am., Pa., Phila. bar assns., Lawyers Club Phila., Socialegal Club Phila., Haverford Coll. Alumni Assn. (pres. 1956-57), Am. Arbitration Assn. (nat. panel arbitrators). Home: 2804 Kennedy House 1901 John F Kennedy Blvd Philadelphia PA 19103-1502 Home: 198 NW 67th St Apt 306 Boca Raton FL 33487-8306 Office: 1650 Market St Ste 3100 Philadelphia PA 19103-7301

LOEWENSTEIN, WALTER BERNARD, nuclear power technologist; b. Gensungen, Hesse, Germany, Dec. 23, 1926; came to U.S., 1938; s. Louis and Johanna ((Katz) L.; m. Lenore C. Pearlman, June 21, 1959; children: Mark Victor, Marcia Beth. BS, U. Puget Sound, 1949; postgrad., U. Wash., 1949-50; PhD, Ohio State U., 1954. Registered profl. engr., Calif. Rsch. asst., fellow Ohio State U., Columbus, 1951-54; rsch. asst. Los Alamos Nat. Lab., 1952-54; sr. physicist, divsn. dir. Argonne (Ill.) Nat. Lab., 1954-73; dept. dir., dep. divsn. dir. Electric Power Rsch. Inst., Palo Alto, Calif., 1973-89, profl. cons., 1989—, mem. large aerosol containment experiment project bd., 1983-87; mem. Marviksen project bd. Studsvik Rsch. Ctr., Stockholm, 1978-85; mem. LOFT project bd. Nuclear Energy Agy., Paris, 1982-89; mem. tech. adv. nuclear safety Ontario Hydro Corp., 1990—; mem. nuclear engring. dept. adv. com. Brookhaven Nat. Lab., 1992-96. With USNR, 1945-46. Recipient Alumnus Cum Laude award U. Puget Sound, 1976. Fellow Am. Phys. Soc., Am. Nuclear Soc. (v.p., pres. 1988-90); mem. Am. Assn. Engring. Socs. (sec., treas. 1990), Nat. Acad. Engring. Jewish. Avocations: history, golf. Home and Office: 515 Jefferson Dr Palo Alto CA 94303

LOEWENSTEIN, WERNER RANDOLPH, physiologist, biophysicist, educator; b. Spangenberg, Germany, Feb. 14, 1926; came to U.S., 1957; naturalized, 1965.; s. Siegfried and Adele (Muller) von Loewenstein; m. Birgit Rose, Oct. 7, 1971; children: Claudia, Patricia, Harriett, Stewart. BS, U. Chile, 1945, PhD, 1950. Instr. physiology U. Chile, Santiago, 1951-53, assoc. prof., 1955-57; fellow in residence Wilmer Inst., Johns Hopkins U., Balt., 1953-54; rsch. zoologist UCLA, 1954-55; asst. prof. physiology Columbia U. Coll. Physicians and Surgeons, N.Y.C., 1957-59, assoc. prof., 1959-66, prof., 1966-71, dir. cell physics lab., 1963-71; prof. physiology and biophysics, chmn. dept. U. Miami (Fla.) Sch. Medicine, 1971-95, prof., chmn. emeritus, 1995—; dir. lab. cell comm. Marine Biol. Lab., Woods Hole, 1995—; Block lectr. U. Chgo., 1960; lectr. Royal Swedish Acad. Sci., 1966; Max Planck lectr., 1967, Claude Bernard lectr., Coll. de France, 1970; Fulbright disting. prof., 1970, USSR Acad. Sci. lectr., Leningrad, 1975; Humboldt lectr., 1988, Humbolt lectr., Munich, 1988, Lauger lectr., Konstanz, 1991, Hillarp lectr., Munich, 1993; mem. Pres. Ford's Biomed. Rsch. Adv. Panel, 1975-77, USAF Sci. Adv. Panel, 1982-86. Author, editor several books; editor Biochimica et Biophysica Acta, 1967-74; editor in chief Jour. Membrane Biology, 1969—; editor Handbook of Sensory Physiology, 51 vols., 1971-77; contbr. numerous articles on membrane biophysics, physiology of intercellular communication, neurophysiolog and cancer rsch. to profl. jours. Kellogg internat. fellow in physiology, 1953-55; Commonwealth Fund internat. fellow, 1967; NSF, NIH Rsch. grantee. Mem. N.Y. Acad. Scis.; mem. Am. Physiol. Soc., Biophys. Soc., Soc. Gen. Physiologists, The Harvey Society, Soc. Neuroscience, Marine Biol. Lab. Woods Hole (corp. mem.), Quisset Yacht Club, Coconut Grove Sailing Club, Royal Key Biscayne Tennis and Racquet Club. Office: Marine Biol Lab Lab Cell Comm 7 M B L St Woods Hole MA 02543-1015

LOEWENTHAL, NESSA PARKER, communications educator; b. Chgo., Oct. 13, 1930; d. Abner and Frances (Ness) Parker; m. Martin Moshe Loewenthal, July 7, 1951 (dec. Aug. 1973); children: Dann Marcus, Ronn Carl, Deena Miriam; m. Gerson B. Selk, Apr. 17, 1982 (dec. June 1987). BA in Edn. and Psychology, Stanford U., 1952. Faculty Stanford Inst. for Intercultural Communication, Palo Alto, Calif., 1973-87; dir. Trans Cultural Svcs., San Francisco, 1981-86, Portland, Oreg., 1986—; dir. dependent svcs. and internat. edn. Bechtel Group, San Francisco, 1973-81, internat. edn. cons., 1981-84; mem. adv. com. dept. internat. studies Lesley Coll., Cambridge, Mass., 1986—; mem. Oreg. Ethics Commns., 1990—; mem. Bay Area Ethics Consortium, Berkeley, 1985-90; chmn. ethics com. Sietar Internat., Washington, 1987—, mem. governing bd., 1992-95; mem. faculty Summer Inst. for Internat. Comms., Portland, Oreg., 1987—; core faculty Oreg. Gov.'s Sch. Svc. Leadership, Salem, 1995—. Author: Professional Integration, 1987, Update: Federal Republic of Germany, 1990, Update: Great Britain, 1987; author, editor book series Your International Assignment, 1973-81; contbr. articles to profl. jours. Mem. equal opportunity and social justice task force Nat. Jewish Rels. Adv. Coun.; bd. dirs. Kids on the Block, Portland, Portland Jewish Acad., 1996—, Portland Ashkalon Sister City Assn., Soc. Humanistic Judaism, 1996—; mem. Lafayette (Calif.) Traffic Commn., 1974-80; bd. dirs. Ctr. for Ethics and Social Policy, 1988-91; mem. exec. bd. and planning com. Temple Isaiah, Lafayette, 1978-82; bd. dirs. Calif. Symphony, Orinda, 1988-90; mem. exec. com. overseas schs. adv. com. U.S. Dept. State, 1976-82; mem. cmty. rels. com. Portland Jewish Fedn.; mem. Nat. Jewish Cmty. Rels. Task Force Social Justice and Econ. Opportunity, 1995—. Named Sr. Interculturalist, Sietar Internat., 1986. Mem. ASTD (exec. bd. internat. profl. performance area 1993—), Soc. for Intercultural Edn. Tng. and Rsch. (chmn. 1986-87, nomination com. 1984-86, co-chmn. 1989-90, chmn. ethics com. 1989—, governing bd. 1992-95), World Affairs Coun., Am. Women for Internat. Understanding, Portland City Club. Democrat. Avocations: photography, swimming. Office: TransCultural Svcs 712 NW Westover Ter Portland OR 97210-3136

LOEWY, ROBERT GUSTAV, engineering educator, aeronautical engineering executive; b. Phila., Feb. 12, 1926; s. Samuel N. and Esther (Silverstein) L.; m. Lila Myrna Spinner, Jan. 16, 1955; children: David G., Esther Elizabeth, Joanne Victoria, Raymond Matthew. B in Aero. Engring., Rensselaer Poly. Inst., 1947; MS, MIT, 1948; PhD, U. Pa., 1962. Sr. vibrations engr. Martin Co., Balt., 1948-49; assoc. research engr. Cornell Aero. Lab., Buffalo, 1949-52, prin. engr., 1953-55; staff stress engr. Piasecki Helicopter Co., Morton, Pa., 1952-53; chief dynamics engr., then chief tech. engr. Vertol divsn. Boeing Co., Essington, Pa., 1955-62; from assoc. prof. to prof. mech. and aerospace scis. U. Rochester, 1962-73, dean Coll. Engring. and Applied Sci., 1967-74; dir. Space Sci. Center, 1966-71; v.p., provost Rensselaer Poly. Inst., Troy, N.Y., 1974-78, Inst. prof., 1978-93; dir. Rotorcraft Tech. Ctr., 1982-93; chmn. sch. aerospace engring. Ga. Inst. Tech., 1993—; chief scientist USAF, 1965-66; cons. govt. and industry, 1959—; mem. aircraft panel Pres.'s Sci. Adv. Coun., 1968-72; mem. Air Force Sci. Adv. Bd., 1966-75, 78-85, vice chmn., 1971, chmn., 1972-75, chmn. aero. systems div. adv. group, 1978-84; mem. Post Office Rsch. and Engring. Adv. Coun., 1966-68; mem. rsch. and tech. adv. com. on aeros. NASA, 1970-71, mem. rsch. and tech. adv. coun., 1976-77, chmn. aero. adv. com., 1978-83; mem. aerospace engring. bd. NRC, 1972-78, 1988-93, mem. bd. on army sci. and tech., 1986-90; mem. naval studies bd. NAS, 1979-82; chmn. tech. adv. com. FAA, 1976-77; bd. dirs. Vertical Flight Found. Contbr. articles to profl. jours. Served with USNR, 1944-46. Recipient NASA disting. pub. service award, 1983; Gotshall-Powell scholar Rensselaer Poly. Inst.; USAF Exceptional Civilian Service awards, 1966, 75, 85, Spirit of St. Louis medal ASME, 1996. Fellow AAAS; hon. fellow AIAA (Lawrence Sperry award 1958), Am. Helicopter Soc. (tech. dir. 1963-64); mem. Am. Soc. Engring. Edn., Nat. Acad. Engring., Sigma Xi, Sigma Gamma Tau, Tau Beta Pi. Achievements include research on unsteady rotor aerodynamics first showing it to be fundamentally different from fixed wing. Home: 3420 Wood Valley Rd NW Atlanta GA 30327-1518 Office: Ga Inst Tech Sch Aerospace Engring Atlanta GA 30332-0150 *Looking back, I was fortunate to have known somehow, from an early age, that I would be an aeronautical engineer. That profession, through positions in industry, research and education, has provided challenge, satisfaction and valued associations.*

LOEWY, STEVEN A., lawyer; b. N.Y.C., Dec. 21, 1952; s. Samuel Alexander and Irene Dorothy (Aber) L.; children: Tamar, David. BA, Washington U., St. Louis, 1974; JD, Yeshiva U., 1979. Bar: Md. 1980, U.S. Supreme Ct. 1983. Assoc. Gordon, Feinblatt, Rothman, Hoffberger & Hollander, Balt., 1980-81, Constable, Alexander, Daneker & Skeen, Balt., 1981-85, Weinberg & Green, Balt., 1985-87; ptnr. Ober, Kaler, Grimes & Shriver, Balt., 1987-92; pvt. practice Rockville, 1993—; lectr. in law U. Balt., 1981-84; mem. edn. appeal bd. U.S. Dept. Edn., Washington, 1985-90. Research grantee U.S. Dept. Housing and Devel., 1979. Mem. ABA (chmn. title ins. com. 1992-95, com. on coms. 1995-96, real property sect.), Md. Bar Assn. (real property sect.). Republican. Jewish. Office: 12016 Shagbark Dr N Bethesda MD 20852-4147

LOFGREN, CHARLES AUGUSTIN, legal and constitutional historian, history educator; b. Missoula, Mont., Sept. 8, 1939; s. Cornelius Willard and Helen Mary (Augustin) L.; m. Jennifer Jenkins Wood, Aug. 6, 1986. AB with great distinction, Stanford U., 1961, AM, 1962, PhD, 1966. Instr. history San Jose State Coll., 1965-66; asst. prof. Claremont McKenna Coll., 1966-71, assoc. prof., 1971-76, prof., 1976—, Roy P. Crocker prof. Am. history and politics, 1976—. Served with USAR, 1957-63. Mem. Am. Soc. Legal History, Orgn. Am. Historians, Am. Hist. Assn. Republican. Roman Catholic. Author: Government from Reflection and Choice, 1986, The Plessy Case, 1988, Claremont Pioneers, 1996; contbr. articles to profl. jours. Office: Claremont McKenna Coll Dept History 850 Columbia Ave Claremont CA 91711-3901

LOFGREN, DONNA LEE, geneticist; b. Bay Shore, N.Y., Apr. 13, 1957; d. Carl Oscar and Esther Louise (Kustes) L. BS, Cornell U., 1979; MS, Va. Polytech. Inst. and State U., 1981, PhD, 1984. Postdoctoral rsch. assoc. Dept. Animal Scis. Purdue U., West Lafayette, Ind., 1985-90; profl. assoc. in animal breeding Dept. Animal Scis. Purdue U., 1990—. Mem. Am. Soc. Animal Sci., Am. Dairy Sci. Assn., Sigma Xi (rsch. award 1985). Office: Dept Animal Sci Purdue U 1151 Lilly Hall West Lafayette IN 47907-1151

LOFGREN, KARL ADOLPH, surgeon; b. Killeberg, Sweden, Apr. 1, 1915; s. Hokan Albin and Teckla Elizabeth (Carlsson) L.; m. Jean Frances Taylor, Sept. 12, 1942; children: Karl Edward, Anne Elizabeth. Student, Northwestern U., 1934-37; M.D., Harvard U., 1941; M.S. in Surgery, U. Minn., 1947. Diplomate Am. Bd. Surgery. Intern U. Minn. Hosps., Mpls., 1941-42; Mayo Found. fellow in surgery, 1942-44, 46-48; asst. surgeon Royal Acad. Hosp., Uppsala, Sweden, 1949; asst. to surg. staff Mayo Clinic, Rochester, Minn., 1949-50; cons. sect. peripheral vein surgery Mayo Clinic, 1950-81; instr. in surgery Mayo Grad. Sch. Medicine, 1951-60, asst. prof. surgery, 1960-74; comdg. officer USNR Med. Co. Mayo Clinic, 1963-67, head sect. peripheral vein surgery, dept. surgery, 1966-79, sr. cons., 1980-81; assoc. prof. surgery Mayo Med. Sch., 1974-79, prof., 1979-81, emeritus prof., 1982—; cons. surg. staff Rochester Meth. Hosp., St. Mary's Hosp. Contbr. chpts. to textbooks, articles to profl. jours. Mem. adv. bd. Salvation Army, Rochester, 1959-81, 82—, pres., 1962-63. Served to capt. M.C. USNR, 1944-46. Decorated Bronze Star. Fellow ACS; mem. Soc. Vascular Surgery, Midwestern Vascular Surgery Soc., Internat. Cardiovascular Soc., Minn. Surg. Soc., Swedish Surg. Soc. (hon.), Swiss Soc. Phlebology (co-worker), So. Minn. Med. Assn. (pres. 1972-73), Scandinavian Soc. Phlebology (hon.), Am. Venous Forum, Rotary Club, Sigma Xi. Baptist. Home: 1001 7th Ave NE Rochester MN 55906-7074 Office: Mayo Clin Rochester MN 55905

LOFGREN, ZOE, congresswoman; b. San Mateo, Calif., Dec. 21, 1947; d. Milton R. and Mary Violet L.; m. John Marshall Collins, Oct. 22, 1978; children: Sheila Zoe Lofgren Collins, John Charles Lofgren Collins. BA in Polit. Sci., Stanford U., 1970; JD cum laude, U. Santa Clara, 1975. Bar: Calif., 1975. D.C. Adminstrv. asst. to Congressman Don Edwards, San Jose, Calif., 1970-79; ptnr. Webber and Lofgren, San Jose, 1979-81; mem. Santa Clara County Bd. Suprs., 1981-94; congresswoman 104th U.S. Congress, Calif. 16th Dist., 1995—; part-time prof. Law, U. Santa Clara, 1978-80; jud. com., judiciary subcom. on comml. and adminstrv. law, subcom. on crime, sci. com. subcoms. on basic rsch. & tech.; house com. on sci., subcommittee on tech., basic rsch. Exec. dir. Community Housing Developers, Inc., 1979-80; trustee San Jose Community Coll. Dist., 1979-81; bd. dirs. Community Legal Svcs., 1978-81, San Jose Housing Svc. Ctr., 1978-79; mem. steering com. sr. citizens housing referendum, 1978; del. Calif. State Bar Conv., 1979-82, Dem. Nat. Conv., 1976; active Assn. Immigration and Nationality Lawyers, 1976-82, Calif. State Dem. Cen. Com., 1975-78, Santa Clara County Dem. Cen. Com., 1974-78, Notre Dame High Sch. Blue Ribbon Com., 1981-84, Victim-Witness Adv. Bd., 1981-94. Recipient Bancroft-Whitney award for Excellence in Criminal Procedure, 1973. Mem. Santa Clara County Bar Assn. (trustee 1979—), Santa Clara County Women Lawyers Com. (exec. bd. 1979-80), Santa Clara Law Sch. Alumni Assn. (v.p. 1977, pres. 1978), Nat. Women's Polit. Caucus, Assn. of Bay Area Govts. (exec. bd. 1981-86). Office: US House Reps 318 Cannon Bldg Ofc Bldg Washington DC 20515-0516 also: 635 N 1st St Ste B San Jose CA 95112-5110*

LOFLAND, GARY KENNETH, cardiac surgeon; b. Milford, Del., Mar. 5, 1951; s. Joseph Sudler and Doris Louise (Peters) L.; m. Janice Marie Show, Feb. 3, 1979; children: Kiernan Sudler, Glennis Kathleen. BA cum laude, Boston U., 1969, MD cum laude, 1975. Diplomate Am. Bd. Surgery, Am. Bd. Thoracic Surgery; lic. physician, Va., N.Y., Mont., N.C. Intern, jr. asst. resident in surgery Duke U. Med. Ctr., Durham, N.C., 1975-81; rsch. fellow dept. surgery Duke U. Med. Ctr., Durham, 1979-81, sr. asst. resident in surgery, 1981-84, chief resident in surgery, 1984-85, teaching scholar in cardiac surgery, 1985-86; sr. registrar in cardiothoracic surgery Hosp. for Sick Children, London, 1986-87; dir. cardiovascular surgery Children's Hosp. of Buffalo, 1987-88; asst. prof. surgery SUNY, Buffalo, 1987-88; assoc. prof. surgery/pediatrics, Med. Coll. Va., Richmond, 1988-94, dir. pediatric cardiac surgery/med. dir. cardiac surgery ICU, 1988-94; clin. prof. surgery Georgetown U., Washington, 1994-97; dir. Columbia/HCA Ctr. Congenital Heart Disease, Richmond, 1994-97; dir. cardiovascular surgery Children's Mercy Hosp., Kansas City, Mo., 1997—; clin. prof. surgery U. Mo. Kansas City Sch. Medicine, 1997—. Editorial rev. bd. Progress in Pediatric Cardiology, Year Book of Thoracic Surgery; contbr. articles to profl. jours. Pres. Am. Heart Assn., Richmond; mem. bd. trustees Transplant Found. Lt. comdr. USPHS, 1977-79. Recipient Univ. Hosp. Trustees award, Boston, 1975; HEW/USPHS commendation medal, 1979. Mem. AMA, Am. Heart Assn., Assn. for Acad. Surgery, Internat. Soc. for Heart Transplantation, Med. Soc. Va., Richmond Acad. Medicine, Richmond Surg. Soc., So. Thoracic Surg. Assn., Soc. for Thoracic Surgeons, Congenital Heart Surgeons Soc., , Alpha Omega Alpha. Home: 740 Lee Rd PO Box 126 Crozier VA 23039 Office: Children's Mercy Hosp Divsn Cardiovascular Surgery Div Cardiovascular Surgery 2406 Gillham Rd Kansas City MO 64108

LOFLAND, JOHN FRANKLIN, sociologist, educator; b. Milford, Del., Mar. 4, 1936; s. John Purnell and Juanita (Jobe) L.; m. Lyn Hebert, Jan. 2, 1965. B.A., Swarthmore Coll., 1958; M.A., Columbia U., 1960; Ph.D., U. Calif., Berkeley, 1964. Asst. prof. sociology U. Mich., 1964-68; assoc. prof. sociology Calif. State U., Sonoma, 1968-70; asso. prof. sociology U. Calif., Davis, 1970-74; prof. U. Calif., 1974-94; prof. emeritus U. Calif., Davis, 1994—. Author: Doomsday Cult, 1966, 77, Analyzing Social Settings, 1971, 3d edit., (with L. H. Lofland) 1995, Protest, 1985, Polite Protestors, 1993, Social Movement Organizations, 1996, 6 other books; founding editor Jour. Contemporary Ethnography, 1970-74; contbr. articles and revs. to profl. lit. Mem. Am. Sociol. Assn. (chair sect. on collective behavior and social movements 1980-81, chair sect. on sociology of peace and war 1989-90, Outstanding Scholarship award 1987), Pacific Sociol. Assn. (pres. 1980-81), Soc. Study Symbolic Interaction (pres. 1986-87, G.H. Mead award for outstanding career contbns. 1995). Home: 523 E St Davis CA 95616-3816 Office: U Calif Sociology Dept Davis CA 95616

LOFLAND, LYN HEBERT, sociology educator; b. Everett, Wash., Dec. 2, 1937; d. Lisle Francis and Estelle Mae (Hogan) Hebert; m. Stuart A. Jones, Dec. 28, 1958 (div. 1964); m. John Franklin Lofland, Jan. 2, 1965. BA, Antioch Coll., Yellow Springs, Ohio, 1960; MA, U. Mich., 1966; PhD, U. Calif., San Francisco, 1971. Asst. prof. sociology U. Calif., Davis, 1971-77, assoc. prof., 1977-85, prof., 1985—, vice chair dept., 1986-89, chair dept., 1986—, acad. dir. Women's Resource and Rsch. Ctr., 1976-78. Author: A World of Strangers, 1973, The Craft of Dying, 1978; co-author: Analyzing Social Settings, 1984, 95; editor: Toward a Sociology of Death and Dying, 1976; co-editor: The Community of the Streets, 1994. Mem. Am. Sociol. Assn. (chair comty. and urban sociology sect. 1986-88, Robert and Helen Lynd award comty. and urban sociology sect. 1995), Pacific Sociol. Assn. (pres. 1989-90), Soc. for Study Symbolic Interaction (pres. 1980-81), Davis Faculty Assn. (chair 1988-89). Democratic Socialist. Avocations: reading, puzzles, indoor gardening. Home: 523 E St Davis CA 95616-3816 Office: U Calif Dept Sociology Davis CA 95616

LÖFSTEDT, BENGT TORKEL MAGNUS, classics educator; b. Lund, Sweden, Nov. 14, 1931; came to U.S., 1967; s. Ernst Martin Hugo and Sigrid (Johanson) L.; m. Maija-Leena Kekomäki, Oct. 15, 1961; children: Ragnar, Torsten, Ritva, Ingvar. M.A., U. Uppsala, Sweden, 1954, Fil. Lic. (Ph.D.), 1957, Fil. doktor, 1961. Asst. prof. Latin U. Uppsala, 1962-67; asso. prof. Mediaeval Latin U. Calif. at Los Angeles, 1967-68, prof., 1968—; contbr. Swedish newspapers Fria Ord, Vägen Framåt. Author: Studien Über die Sprache der langobardischen Gesetze, 1961, Der hibernolateinische Grammatiker Malsachanus, 1965, Zenonis Veronensis Tractatus, 1971, Ars Laureshamensis, 1977, Sedulius Scottus: In Donati artem minorem, in Priscianum, in Eutychem, 1977, Ars Ambrosiana, 1982, Beatus Liebanensis: Adversus Elipandum, 1984 (with G.J. Gebauer) Bonifatius Ars Grammatica, 1980, (with L. Holtz and A. Kibre) Smaragdus: Liber in Partibus Donati, 1986, Sedulius Scottus: Kommentar zum Evangelium nach Matthäus 11,2 bis Schluss, 1991, (with B. Bischoff) Anonymus ad Cuimnanum, 1992, Vier Juvenal-Kommentare aus dem 12. Jh., 1995; contbr. articles to profl. jours. Served to lt. Swedish Army, 1959-60. Alexander von Humboldt-Stiftung fellow Munich, 1961-62; Humanities Inst., U. Calif. grantee, 1968, 71; Am. Philos. Soc. grantee, 1971, 74; Am. Council Learned Socs. grantee, 1972, 75. Lutheran. Office: UCLA Dept Classics 405 Hilgard Ave Los Angeles CA 90095-9000

LOFSTROM, MARK D., lawyer, educator, communications executive; b. Mpls., May 11, 1953; s. Dennis E. and Dorothy Dee (Schreiber) L. BA in Art History, Carleton Coll., 1979; MBA, Columbia U., 1989; JD, U. Hawaii, 1992. Bar: Hawaii 1992, Minn. 1995. Pub. rels. asst. Honolulu Acad. Arts, 1979, pub. rels. rep., 1980-84, pub. rels. officer, 1984-87; law clk. Kiefer Oshima Chun Fong and Chung, 1990-91; assoc. Cades Schutte Fleming & Wright, 1991-95; sole proprietor Law Offices of Mark D. Lofstrom, 1995—; instr. internat. bus. law/bus. law for accts. U. Hawaii Coll. Bus., 1995-96; instr. art law U. Hawaii summer session, 1995-96; organizer artists and writers exhbn., 1981; coord. rep. program Carleton Coll. Alumni Assn., Hawaii, 1984-87; co-editor and mktg. assoc. Pacific Telecomms. Coun., 1988-92, intern East-West Ctr., 1992. Editor mag. on preservation; exec. editor U. Hawaii Law Rev., 1991-92; co-editor: (newsletter) Pacific Comm. Coun. Procs., 1990-92; bd. editors Hawaii Bar Jour., 1992—; contbr. articles on current exhbns., intellectual property, art, and internat. law. Sec., bd. dirs. Arts Coun. Hawaii, 1985-86, chmn. ways and means com., 1986-87, pres. bd. dirs.; bd. dirs. Hawaii Alliance for Arts Edn., 1994-95, chair-elect, 1995—. Recipient NCR Stakeholders award, 1988, legal rsch. and writing award Hawaii State Bar Assn. Young Lawyers Div., 1991. Mem. ABA, Hawaii State Bar Assn. (sec. internat. law sect. 1994, chair internat. law sect. 1995-

96), Minn. Bar Assn. Office: PO Box 3506 Minneapolis MN 55403-0506 also: PO Box 3605 Minneapolis MN 55403-0605

LOFT, BERNARD IRWIN, education educator, consultant. BS, West Chester (Pa.) U., 1939; MA in Edn., U. Fla., 1949; Directorate in Health and Safety, Ind. U., 1956, D of Health and Safety, 1957. Ednl. advisor Civilian Conservation Corps, Branchville, N.J., 1940-42; dir. phys. edn., coach Lower Paxton Twp. High Sch., Harrisburg, Pa., 1942; field rep. in safety svcs. ARC, Atlanta, 1946; instr. in biology and phys. edn., coach Andrew Jackson High Sch., Jacksonville, Fla., 1946-48; chmn. safety edn. program, instr. phys. edn., faculty, coach U. Fla., Gainesville, 1948-51; asst. prof. edn. and continuing edn. Mich. State U., East Lansing, 1951-55; prof. Sch. of Health, Phys. Edn. and Recreation, dir. health and safety Ind.U., Bloomington, 1956—, assoc. prof. health and safety, 1957-65; fgn. assignment Cultural Exchange Program Americans Abroad Dept. State, Cambodia, 1961-62; dir. Ctr. fo Safety Studies, prof. health safety edn. Ind.U., Bloomington, 1962-63, prof. emeritus Applied Health Sci., dir., 1981; emeritus prof. health and safety Ind. U., Bloomington, 1981—; ednl. cons. Am. Automobile Assn., Washington, Am. Trucking Assn., Washington; vis. lectr. U. Md., U. N.C., U. Ga., Syracuse (N.Y.) U., Kent (Ohio) State U., U. Miami, Fla. State U., S.C. A&M Coll., Purdue U.; faculty advisor doctoral studies and PhD and EdD degrees, chair health svcs. track Walden U., acad. policies bd.; participant The White House Conf. on Health, 1965, White House Conf. on Occupational Safety, 1956; participant cultural exch. program to Phnom Penh, Cambodia, U.S. Dept. State, Voice of Am. Author: How to Prevent Accidents in the Motor Home, 1978; contbr. articles to profl. jours. Head counselor Camp Ridgedale, Sumneytown, Pa., waterfront dir., counselor; athletic dir. Camp Arthur, Zieglersville, Pa.; waterfront dir. Pocono Highland Camp, Marshall's Creek, Pa., Blue Mountain Camps, East Stroudsburg, Pa., Kitatinny Camps, Dingman's Ferry, Pa., head counselor. Lt. comdr. USN, 1942-46, USNR, 1946-65, World War II, ret., 1965. Recipient Cert. of Appreciation, Ind. U. Student Found., 40 Yr. Svc. Pin, ARC; decorated Cheva'Lier de L'Order du Monisaraphon (Cambodian Govt.). Fellow AAHPERD, Am. Acad. Safety Edn. (charter, pres.), Am. Sch. Health Assn.; mem. NEA, Ind. Mobile Home Assn. (hon. Cert. of Appreciation 1966), Nat. Safety Coun. (gen. chmn. higher edn. sect. 1960-61 Plaque), Ind. Assn. for Health, Phys. Edn. and Recreation (v.p.), Am. Sch. Health Assn. (chmn. sch. safety edn. com., and others), Ind. Coll. Health Assn. (pres. 1958-59), Ind. Tchr.'s Assn., Am. Acad. Safety Edn. (pres., v.p., chmn. membership com., pres. 1967-68), Mid-Am. Coll. Health Assn., Ind. Assn. Health Educator. Avocations: soccer, football, swimming, boxing, Lacrosse. Office: Walden Univ Liaison Rep to Ind Univ 801 Anchor Rode Dr Naples FL 34103-2751

LOFTFIELD, ROBERT BERNER, biochemistry educator; b. Detroit, Dec. 15, 1919; s. Sigurd and Katherine (Roller) L.; m. Ella Bradford, Aug. 24, 1946 (dec. Dec. 1990); children: Lore Loftfield DeBower, Eric, Linda, Norman, Bjòrn, Curtis, Katherine, Earl, Allison, Ella-Kari. BS, Harvard U., 1941, MA, 1942, PhD, 1946. Research assoc. MIT, Cambridge, 1946-48; research assoc. to sr. research assoc. Mass. Gen. Hosp., Boston, 1948-64; asst. to assoc. prof. biochemistry Harvard U. Sch. Medicine, Boston, 1948-64; prof. biochemistry Sch. Medicine U. N.Mex., Albuquerque, 1964-90, chmn. dept. biochemistry, 1964-71, 78-90, prof. emeritus, 1990—. Contbr. articles on protein biosynthesis and enzymology to profl. jours. Served as corp. U.S. Army, 1945-46. Fellow Damon Runyon Fund, 1952-53, Guggenheim Found., 1961-62; Fulbright fellow, 1977, 83; sr. fellow NIH, 1971-72. Mem. AAAS, Am. Soc. Biol. Chemists, Am. Chem. Soc., Am. Assn. Cancer Research, Biophys. Soc., Marine Biol. Lab. Lutheran. Avocations: sailing, hiking, camping, skiing. Home: 707 Fairway Rd NW Albuquerque NM 87107-5718 Office: Univ NMex Sch of Medicine Dept of Biochemistry Albuquerque NM 87131

LOFTIN, MARION THEO, sociologist, educator; b. Coushatta, La., Sept. 10, 1915; s. John Griffin and Ida Estella (Huckaby) L. B.A., Northwestern La. State Coll., 1936; M.A., La. State U., 1941; Ph.D., Vanderbilt U., 1952. Tchr. pub. high schs. Red River Parish, La., 1935-40; asso. prof. Southeastern La. State Coll., 1946-47; faculty Miss. State U., 1949—, Thomas L. Bailey prof. sociology and anthropology, head dept., 1961-67; assoc. dean Miss. State U. (Grad. Sch.), 1965-77, dean, 1977-79, v.p. grad. studies and research, 1980-85, prof. sociology, v.p. grad. studies and research emeritus, 1986—. Served with AUS, 1941-45. Mem. Am. Sociol. Assn., Rural Sociol. Soc., So. Sociol. Soc., Phi Kappa Phi, Omicron Delta Kappa. Home: 1214 Hillcrest Cir Starkville MS 39759-9306

LOFTIN, SISTER MARY FRANCES, religious organization administrator; b. Atlanta, Mar. 25, 1928. B, Marquette U., 1955; M, George Washington U., 1970. Various positions, 1955-66; dir. nursing svcs. Seton Med. Ctr., Austin, 1966-68; adminstrv. resident Med. Ctr. East, Birmingham, Ala., 1969-70, asst. adminstr., 1970-71; asst. adminstr. St. Joseph Hosp. & Health Care Ctr., Chgo., 1971-74; adminstr. St. Thomas Hosp., Nashville, 1974-81; pres. Daus. of Charity Health Sys., Evansville, Ind., 1981-87; pres., CEO Daus. of Charity Nat. Health Sys., St. Louis, 1992-94; chancellor Diocese of Birmingham, Ala., 1995—. Home: St Vincent's Residence 2724 Hanover Cir S Birmingham AL 35205-1706 Office: Chancellor's Office Diocese of Birmingham PO Box 12047 Birmingham AL 35202-2047

LOFTIS, JACK D., newspaper editor, newspaper executive. Exec. v.p., editor Houston Chronicle. Office: Houston Chronicle Pub Co 801 Texas St Houston TX 77002-2906*

LOFTIS, JOHN (CLYDE), JR., English language educator; b. Atlanta, May 16, 1919; s. John Clyde and Marbeth (Brown) L.; m. Anne Nevins, June 29, 1946; children: Mary, Laura, Lucy. BA, Emory U., 1940; MA, Princeton U., 1942, PhD, 1948. Instr. English Princeton, 1946-48; instr., then asst. prof. English UCLA, 1948-52; faculty Stanford U., 1952-81, prof. English, 1958-81, Bailey prof. English, 1977-81, Bailey prof. emeritus, 1981—, chmn. dept., 1973-76. Author: Steele at Drury Lane, 1952, Comedy and Society from Congreve to Fielding, 1959, La Independencia de la Literatura Norteamericana, 1961, The Politics of Drama in Augustan England, 1963, The Spanish Plays of Neoclassical England, 1973, (with others) The Revels History of Drama in English, Vol. V, 1976, Sheridan and the Drama of Georgian England, 1977, Renaissance Drama in England and Spain: Topical Allusion and History Plays, 1987; editor: (Steele) The Theatre, 1962, Restoration Drama: Modern Essays in Criticism, 1966, (with V.A. Dearing) The Works of John Dryden, Vol. IX, 1966, (Sheridan) The School for Scandal, 1966, (Nathaniel Lee) Lucius Junius Brutus, 1967, (Addison) Essays in Criticism and Literary Theory, 1975, The Memoirs of Anne, Lady Halkett and Ann, Lady Fanshawe, 1979, (with D.S. Rodes and V.A. Dearing) The Works of John Dryden, Vol. XI, 1978, (with P.H. Hardacre) Colonel Bampfield's Apology, 1993; co-editor Augustan Reprint Society, 1949-1952, English Literature, 1660-1800: A Current Bibliography, 1951-56; gen. editor: Regents Restoration Drama Series, 35 vols, 1962-81; mem. editorial bd.: Studies in English Literature, 1966-76, Huntington Library Quar., 1968-76, Wesleyan Edit. Works Henry Fielding, 1970-83 , Augustan Reprint Soc., 1985-90. Served with USNR, 1942-46, PTO. Fellow Fund Advancement Edn., 1955-56; Fulbright lectr. Am. studies Peru, 1959-60; Guggenheim fellow, 1966-67; fellow Folger Shakespeare Library, 1967; NEH fellow, 1978-79. Mem. MLA, Phi Beta Kappa, Kappa Alpha. Home: 7 Arastradero Rd Portola Valley CA 94028-8012 Office: Stanford Univ Dept English Stanford CA 94305

LOFTIS, REBECCA HOPE, psychotherapist; b. Ferndale, Mich., Aug. 19, 1958; d. Harold Lewis and Virginia (Warren) L.; m. Leonard H. Chyet, Oct. 8, 1988. BA, Salem (Mass.) State Coll., 1985; MA, U. Hartford, Conn., 1987, PhD, Mass. Sch. Profl. Psychology, 1997. Psychotherapist Lynn (Mass.) Youth Resource Bur., 1988-92; practicum Atlantic Care Mental Health Ctr., Lynn, 1992-93, Lynn Youth Resource Bur., 1993-94; intern Teuksbury Hosp., 1994-96; clin. dir. Westboro Secure Treatment Program, 1997—. Avocations: equestrienne, bonsai collecting, cooking. Office: Lynn Youth Resource Bureau 19 Sutton St Lynn MA 01901-1008

LOFTNESS, MARVIN O., electrical engineer; b. Altacortes, Wash., Feb. 20, 1920. BA in Chemistry, Pacific Luth. U., 1957. Owner, engr. Loftness Engring. Fellow IEEE (co-organizer/instr. tutorial on power-line EMI), Power Engring. Soc. (corona and field effects subcom.). Office: Loftness Engineering 115 W 20th Olympia WA 98501

LOFTNESS, VIVIAN ELLEN, architecture educator. BS, MIT, 1974, MArch, 1975; postgrad., Harvard U. Instr. MIT, 1976; asst. prof. SUNY, Buffalo, 1977-78; prof., head dept. arch. Carnegie Mellon U., Pitts., 1981—; bldg. rsch. bd., com. mem. Nat. Acad. Scis., 1986-89, bd. applied climatology, 1983-85, adv. bd. for built environment, 1982-84; vis. critic dept. arch. U. Pa., 1985; coun. mem. Nat. Inst. Bldg. Scis., 1983-85; rsch. project mgr. Housing Urban Devel. Office Policy Devel. and Rsch.; spkr. and cons. in field. Author: (with others) The Office of the Future: The Japanese Approach to Tomorrows Workplace, 1992; co-author: (with others) Evaluating and Predicting Design Performance, 1992, Occupational Medicine: Building-Associated Illness, 1989, Building Evaluation, 1989, The Handbook of Climatology, 1987, Intelligent Buildings: Applications of IT and Building Automation to High Technology Construction Projects, 1988, The Ergonomic Payoff: Designing the Electronic Office, 1986, The Building Systems Integration Handbook, 1985; contbr. articles to profl. jours. Grantee NSF, 1988—, U.S. Army Constrn. Engring. Labs., 1993-94, State Pa. Energy Office, Nat. Endowment for the Arts, 1986-87; Rotary fellow, 1975-76, Grunsfeld Found. fellow, 1973; recipient N.Y. State Passive Solar Residential Design award, 1979. Mem. AIA, ASTM, ASHRAE, Pa. Soc. Arch., Internat. Facility Mgmt. Assn., Internat. Solar Energy Soc., Am. Solar Energy Soc., Ctr. Internat. Batiment. Office: Carnegie Mellon Univ Sch of Architecture Rm 201 Coll Fine Arts Pittsburgh PA 15213-3890*

LOFTON, KENNETH, professional baseball player; b. East Chicago, Ind., May 31, 1967. Student, U. Ariz. Baseball player Houston Astros, 1988-91, Cleveland Indians, 1991-96, Atlanta Braves, 1996—. Ranked 1st in Am. League for stolen bases, 1992; recipient Am. League Gold Glove award, 1993-96; named to All-Star Team, 1994-96. Office: Cleveland Indians 2401 Ontario St Cleveland OH 44115-4003

LOFTON, KEVIN EUGENE, medical facility administrator; b. Beaumont, Tex., Sept. 29, 1954. BS, Boston U., 1976; M Health Care Adminstrn., Ga. State U., 1979. Adminstrv. resident Meml. Med. Ctr., Corpus Christi, Tex., 1978-79; adminstr. emergency svcs. Univ. Hosp., Jacksonville, Fla., 1979-80, adminstr. material mgmt., 1980-81, asst. exec. dir. ambulatory care, 1981-82, asst. v.p. ambulatory svcs., 1982-83, v.p. profl. svcs., 1983-86; exec. v.p. Univ. Med. Ctr., Jacksonville, 1986-90; exec. dir. Howard Univ. Hosp., Washington, 1990-93, U. Ala. Hosp., Birmingham, 1993—. Contbr. articles to profl. publs. Fellow Am. Coll. Health Care Execs. (R.S. Hudgens award 1993); mem. Am. Hosp. Assn., Nat. Assn. Health Svcs. Execs. (pres.). Home: 2112 Lake Heather Way Hoover AL 35242 Office: U Ala Hosp 619 19th St S Rm 246/ohb Birmingham AL 35233-1924

LOFTON, THOMAS MILTON, lawyer; b. Indpls., May 12, 1929; s. Milton Alexander and Jane (Routzong) L.; m. Betty Louise Blades, June 20, 1954; children: Stephanie Louise, Melissa Jane. BS, Ind. U., 1951, JD, 1954. Bar: Ind. 1954, U.S. Ct. Appeals (7th cir.) 1959, U.S. Supreme Ct. 1958. Law clk. to justice U.S. Supreme Ct., Washington, 1954-55; ptnr. Baker & Daniels, Indpls., 1958-91; dir. Ind. U. Found., Bloomington, 1978-91, Clowes Fund, 1980—, Bank One Indpls., 1993—; chmn. bd. Lilly Endowment, Indpls., 1991—; mem. bd. visitors Ind. U. Law, Bloomington, 1976—. Editor-in-chief Ind. Law Jour., 1953. Trustee Earlham Coll., 1988-91. 1st lt. U.S. Army, 1955-58. Recipient Peck award Wabash Coll., 1982. Mem. Order of Coif, Masons, Beta Gamma Sigma. Republican. Presbyterian. Home: 9060 Pickwick Dr Indianapolis IN 46260-1714 Office: Lilly Endowment 2800 N Meridian St Indianapolis IN 46208-4713

LOFTUS, THOMAS ADOLPH, ambassador; b. Stoughton, Wis., Apr. 24, 1945; s. Adolph Olean and Margaret Elaine (Nielson) L.; m. Barbara Carolyn Schasse, Aug. 23, 1969; children: Alec Kristian, Karl Edward. B.S., U. Wis.-Whitewater, 1970; M.A., U. Wis.-Madison, 1971. Analyst Wis. Assembly Dem. Caucus, Madison, 1974-75; adminstrv. asst. to speaker Wis. Assembly, Madison, 1975-76; mem. Wis. Assembly, 1977-91, majority leader, 1981-82, speaker, 1983-91; dir. WisKids Count Wis. Coun. Children and Families, 1991-93; amb. to Norway, Oslo, 1993—; adj. prof. polit. sci. U. Wis.-Whitewater; lectr. Edgewood Coll.; vis. prof. Rutgers U., Eagleton Inst. Author: The Art of Legislative Politics, 1994. Del. Dem. Nat. Conf., 1976, 82, 88, 92; mem. Dem. Nat. Com., 1989-91; Dem. nominee for Gov. of Wis., 1990. Served with U.S. Army, 1965-67. Fellow John F. Kennedy Sch. Govt. Harvard U. Democrat. Lutheran. Home and Office: Am Embassy Oslo PSC 69 Box 1000 APO AE 09707

LOFTUS, THOMAS DANIEL, lawyer; b. Seattle, Nov. 8, 1930; s. Glendon Francis and Martha Helen (Wall) L. BA, U. Wash., 1952, JD, 1957. Bar: Wash. 1958, U.S. Ct. Appeals (9th cir.) 1958, U.S. Dist. Ct. Wash. 1958, U.S. Ct. Mil. Appeals 1964, U.S. Supreme Ct. 1964. Trial atty. Northwestern Mut. Ins. Co., Seattle, 1958-62; sr. trial atty. Unigard Security Ins. Co., Seattle, 1962-68, asst. gen. counsel, 1969-83, govt. rels. counsel, 1983-89; of counsel Groshong, LeHet & Thornton, 1990—; mem. Wash. Commn. on Jud. Conduct (formerly Jud. Qualifications Commn.), 1982-88, vice-chmn., 1987-88; judge pro tem Seattle Mcpl. Ct., 1973-81; mem. nat. panel of mediators Arbitration Forums, Inc., 1990—. Sec., treas. Seattle Opera Assn., 1980-91; pres., bd. dirs. Vis. Nurse Svcs., 1979-88; pres., v.p. Salvation Army Adult Rehab. Ctr., 1979-86; nat. committeeman Wash. Young Rep. Fedn., 1961-63, vice chmn., 1963-65; pres. Young Reps. King County, 1962-63; bd. dirs. Seattle Seafair, Inc., 1975; bd. dirs., gen. counsel Wash. Ins. Coun., 1984-86, sec., 1986-88, v.p., 1988-90, Am. Mediation Panel of Mediators, 1990-96; bd. dirs. Arson Alarm Found., 1987-90; bd. visitors law sch. U. Wash., 1993—. 1st lt. U.S. Army, 1952-54, col. Res., 1954-85. Fellow Am. Bar Found.; mem. Am. Arbitration Assn. (nat. panel arbitrators 1965—), Am. Arbitration Forums, Inc. (nat. panel arbitrators 1992), Nat. Assn. Security Dealers (bd. arbitrators 1997—), Am. Mediation Panel, Wash. Bar Assn. (gov. 1981-84), Seattle King County Bar Assn. (sec., trustee 1977-82), ABA (ho. of dels. 1984-90), Internat. Assn. Ins. Counsel, U.S. People to People (del. Moscow internat. law-econ. conf. 1990), Def. Rsch. Inst., Wash. Def. Trial Lawyers Assn., Wash. State Trial Lawyers Assn., Am. Judicature Soc., Res. Officers Assn., Judge Advocate General's Assn., Assn. Wash. Gens., U. Wash. Alumni Assn., Coll. Club Seattle, Wash. Athletic Club, Masons, Shriners, Ranier Club, Pi Sigma Alpha, Delta Sigma Rho, Phi Delta Phi, Theta Delta Chi. Republican. Presbyterian. Home: 3515 Magnolia Blvd W Seattle WA 98199-1841 Office: 2133 3rd Ave Seattle WA 98121-2321

LOGA, SANDA, physicist, educator; b. Bucharest, Romania, June 13, 1932; came to U.S., 1968; d. Stelian and Georgeta (Popescu) L.; m. Karl Heinz Werther, Mar. 1968 (div. 1970); m. Radu Zaciu, 1996. MS in Physics, U. Bucharest, 1955; PhD in Biophysics, U. Pitts., 1978. Asst. prof. faculty medicine and pharmacy Bucharest, 1963-67; rsch. asst. Presbyn./St. Luke's Hosp., Chgo., 1968-69; assoc. rsch. scientist Miles Labs., Elkhart, Ind., 1969-70; rsch. asst. U. Pitts., 1971-78; rsch. assoc. Carnegie-Mellon U., Pitts., 1978-80; health physicist VA Med. Ctr., Westside, Chgo., 1980; med. physicist, VA Med. Ctr. N. Chgo, 1980-97; assoc. prof. Chgo. Med. Sch., N. Chgo., 1985—. Mem. Am. Assn. Physicists in Medicine, Health Physics Soc. Office: Chgo Med Sch U Health Scis 3333 Green Bay Rd North Chicago IL 60064-3037

LOGAN, DAVID BRUCE, health care administrator; b. Grand Rapids, Mich., Jan. 30, 1942; s. Wesley Goldsmith and Ernestine (Sovereen) L.; m. Joann Fern Jordan, Nov. 5, 1961; children: Jennifer, Julie, Jeanine, David II, Douglas, Dean. MusB, U. Mich., 1964; B Zoology with honors, Mich. State U., 1970; MBA, U. Ill., 1978. Tchr. sci. Flint (Mich.) Pub. Schs., 1970-71; health care adminstr. USAF, Mpls., 1971-75; asst. chief, med. adminstrn. svc. trainee VA, Mpls., 1975-76; asst. chief med. adminstrn. svc. VA, Danville, Ill., 1976-78; asst. med. dist. coord. VA Med. Dist. 15, Indpls., 1978-80; med. dist. coord. VA Med. Dist. 8, Durham, N.C., 1980-87; nat. disaster med. system mgr. VA, Salisbury, N.C., 1987—. Dir. choir Kirk of Kildaire Presbyn. Ch., 1981-85; asst. scoutmaster, scoutmaster Boy Scouts Am., 1978-94. Capt. USAF, 1964-68, lt. col. Res. ret. Fellow Am. Coll. Healthcare Execs., Soc. Air Force Res. Med. Officers, Air Force Assn., Res. Officers Assn. (bd. dirs. Minn. 1973-74, jr. v.p. for air 1974-75). Office: Dept VA Med Ctr 1601 Brenner Ave Salisbury NC 28144-2515

LOGAN, DOUGLAS GEORGE, service company executive; b. Glenridge, N.J., May 11, 1943; s. Douglas Haig and Isabel (Mendoza) L.; m. Catherine Ann Vigilante, Dec. 27, 1965 (div. 1975); children: Douglas, Caroline; m. Ann E. Brooks, May 3, 1980; children: Carter, Philip. Student, Manhattan Coll., 1961-64, U. Balt., 1969-73. Project mgr. Raymond Internat., N.Y.C., 1967-68; v.p. Green Assocs., Towson, Md., 1968-74, Atec Assocs., Indpls., 1974-75; project mgr. Continental Drilling Co., Los Angeles, 1975-77; project coordinator City of Rockford (Ill.), 1977-78; gen. mgr. Metro Ctr., Rockford, 1978-86, The Lighting (Continental Basketball Assn.), Rockford, 1986; sr. v.p. Ogden Entertainment Svcs., N.Y.C., 1986—; commr., pres., CEO Maj. League Soccer, N.Y.C., 1995—; cons. Ft. Lauderdale (Fla.) Performing Arts Ctr., 1980, Performing Arts Ctr., Springfield, Mo., 1982, Seattle Ctr., 1986, Profl. Hockey Team, Ft. Wayne, Ind., 1985; regent, lectr. Facility Mgmt. Sch., 1987. Editor law rev. Univ. Balt., 1972. Founder, bd. dirs. Rockford Local Devel. Corp., 1980-84; commr. Rockford Pub. Works, 1981; mem. exec. com. Greater Rockford Alliance for Strategic Planning, 1985-87. Served to 1st lt. U.S. Army, 1964-67, Vietnam. Decorated Bronze Star with bronze oak leaf clusters: recipient Disting. Service award Rockford Park Dist., 1986, Top of Ill. award Rockford C. of C., 1987. Mem. Internat. Assn. Auditorium Mgrs. (chmn. gov. affairs com. 1985-87), Country Music Buyers Assn., Friars of N.Y.C., Rockford Country Club. Democrat. Club: City (Rockford). Avocations: running, reading. Office: Ogden Entertainment Svcs 2 Penn Plz New York NY 10121 also: Maj League Soccer 110 E 42d St 10 Fl New York NY 10017*

LOGAN, FRANCIS DUMMER, lawyer; b. Evanston, Ill., May 23, 1931; s. Simon Rae and Frances (Dummer) L.; m. Claude Riviere, Apr. 13, 1957; children: Carolyn Gisele, Francis Dummer. B.A., U. Chgo., 1950; B.A. Juris, Oxford U., 1954; LL.B., Harvard U., 1955. Bar: N.Y. 1956, Calif. 1989. Assoc. Milbank, Tweed, Hadley & McCloy, N.Y.C., 1955-64; ptnr. Milbank, Tweed, Hadley & McCloy, N.Y.C. and L.A., 1965-96, chmn., 1992-96. Mem. Calif. State Bar, Coun. on Fgn. Rels., Am. Law Inst. Home: 1726 Linda Vista Ave Pasadena CA 91103 Office: Milbank Tweed et al 601 S Figueroa St Los Angeles CA 90017-5704

LOGAN, HENRY VINCENT, transportation executive; b. Phila., Nov. 7, 1942; s. Edward Roger and Alberta (Gross) L.; m. Mary Genzano, Sept. 28, 1963; children: Michele Leah, Maureen Laura, Monica Lynn. BS in Commerce, DePaul U., 1975; M in Mgmt., Northwestern U., 1984. Successively supr. corp. acctg., asst. mgr. gen. acctg., mgr. gen. acctg., dir. corp. acctg. and taxes TTX Co., Chgo., 1962-70, controller, 1970-78, dir. fin. planning, 1978-83, mng. dir., fin. adminstr., 1983-85, v.p., chief fin. officer, 1985-88, sr. v.p. fleet mgmt., 1988—; bd. dirs. Calpro, Co., Mira Loma, Calif., RailGon Co., Chgo.; bd. dirs., fin. com. Railway Supply Assn. Treas. TTX Co. Polit. Action Com., Chgo., 1980; vol Sch. Dist. 87 Task Force, Glen Ellyn, Ill., 1986. Mem. Nat. Freight Transp. Assn., Intermodal Assn. N.Am. (chmn. legis. com. 1992-94), Union League Club (reception com. 1987-92, fin. com. 1993-95), Medinah (Ill.) Country Club. Republican. Roman Catholic. Avocations: golf, music, reading, bicycling. Home: 812 Abbey Dr Glen Ellyn IL 60137-6130

LOGAN, J. MURRAY, investment manager; b. Balt., Mar. 15, 1935; s. Lloyd and Helen Mildred (Gilbert) L.; m. Mary Page Cole, June 19, 1987 (dec. Sept. 1993); 1 child by previous marriage, Maria Charlotte. BA, Johns Hopkins U., 1959. Securities analyst Merrill Lynch Pierce Fenner & Smith, N.Y.C., 1959-62; ptnr. Wood Struthers & Winthrop, N.Y.C., 1962-70; v.p. EFC Mgmt. Corp., L.A., 1970-73, Faulkner, Dawkins & Sullivan, Inc., N.Y.C., 1973-75; chmn. investment policy com. Rockefeller & Co., Inc., N.Y.C., 1975—; bd. dirs. Europe Fund, N.Y.C., World Trust Fund, Luxembourg, Berkshire Opera Co., Camphill Found., U.K. Fund, N.Y.C., Camphill Village, U.S.A. Trustee Johns Hopkins U., Balt., 1984-91; bd. dirs. United Kingdom Fund, N.Y.C., Camphill Village USA. With USCG, 1954-56. Mem. Racquet and Tennis Club, The Leash. Office: Rockefeller & Co Inc 30 Rockefeller Plz # 5425 New York NY 10112

LOGAN, J. PATRICK, lawyer; b. Buffalo, Oct. 4, 1950. BA, Coll. Holy Cross, 1972; JD, Temple U., 1976. Bar: Pa. 1977, Ala. 1977. With Burr & Forman, Birmingham, Ala. Mem. ABA, Ala. State Bar (chmn. labor and employment law sect. 1989-90), Birmingham Bar Assn. Office: Burr & Forman 3000 S Trust Twr 420 20th St N Birmingham AL 35203-3204

LOGAN, JAMES KENNETH, federal judge; b. Quenemo, Kans., Aug. 21, 1929; s. John Lysle and Esther Maurine (Price) L.; m. Beverly Jo Jennings, June 8, 1952; children: Daniel Jennings, Amy Logan Sliva, Sarah Logan Sherard, Samuel Price. A.B., U. Kans., 1952; LL.B. magna cum laude, Harvard, 1955. Bar: Kans. 1955, Calif. 1956. Law clk. U.S. Cir. Judge Huxman, 1955-56; with firm Gibson, Dunn & Crutcher, L.A., 1956-57; asst. prof. law U. Kans., 1957-61, prof., dean Law Sch., 1961-68; ptnr. Payne and Jones, Olathe, Kans., 1968-77; judge U.S. Ct. Appeals (10th cir.), 1977—; Ezra Ripley Thayer tchg. fellow Harvard Law Sch., 1961-62; vis. prof. U. Tex., 1964, Stanford U., 1969, U. Mich., 1976; sr. lectr. Duke U., 1987, 91, 93; commr. U.S. Dist. Ct., 1964-67. Author: (with W.B. Leach) Future Interests and Estate Planning, 1961, Kansas Estate Administration, 5th edit., 1986, (with A.R. Martin) Kansas Corporate Law and Practice, 2d edit., 1979, The Federal Courts of the Tenth Circuit: A History, 1992; also articles. Candidate for U.S. Senate, 1968. Served with AUS, 1947-48. Rhodes scholar, 1952; recipient Disting. Service citation U. Kans., 1986. Mem. Am., Kans. bar assns., Phi Beta Kappa, Order of Coif, Beta Gamma Sigma, Omicron Delta Kappa, Pi Sigma Alpha, Alpha Kappa Psi, Phi Delta Phi. Democrat. Presbyterian.

LOGAN, JAMES SCOTT, SR., federal agency administrator, emergency analyst; b. Stanford, Ky., June 18, 1948; s. James M.H. and Lillian Elizabeth (Givens) L.; m. Rose Marie Helm, Aug. 31, 1968; children: James Matthew, Tasha Marie. AA, Columbia (Mo.) Coll., 1990, BS/BA cum laude, 1992; postgrad., U. Colo., 1992—. Unit adminstr. USAR, Lakewood, Colo., 1972-82; continuity of govt. planner Fed. Emergency Mgmt. Agy. Region VIII, Lakewood, 1983-90, tech. hazards program specialist, 1991-92, sr. tech. hazards program specialist, 1992-95; team leader state and local programs Fed. Emergency Mgmt. Agy. Region VIII, Lakewood, Colo., 1995—; emergency analyst Office of Regional Dir., Denver, 1995—; bd. dirs. Rocky Mountain Human Svcs. Coalition, 1995—. Mem. NAACP, Denver, 1992; mem. NCOA NCO Assn., Denver, 1979—; mem. citizen's adv. com. polit. sci. dept. U. Colo., Denver. With U.S. Army, 1968-71, Vietnam, USAR, 1972. Decorated Legion of Merit. Mem. VFW, Am. Legion, Pi Sigma Alpha. Democrat. Baptist. Avocations: reading, computers, political science. Home: 16952 E Bates Ave Aurora CO 80013-2243 Office: FEMA Region VIII PO Box 25267 Bldg 710 Denver CO 80225-0267

LOGAN, JOHN ARTHUR, JR., retired foundation executive; b. Chgo., Dec. 8, 1923; s. John Arthur and Dorothea (Halstead) L.; m. Ann Orr deForest, Aug. 30, 1960. Grad., Taft Sch., Watertown, Conn., 1942; B.A., Yale, 1949, M.A., 1951, Ph.D., 1954; LL.D., Western Md. Coll.; L.H.D., Hollins Coll. Faculty Yale, 1949-61, asst. prof. history, 1958-61; pres. Hollins Coll., 1961-75, Inst. Coll. Funds Am., N.Y.C., 1975-86; vis. lectr. Salzburg Seminar in Am. Studies, 1961. Author: No Transfer: An American Security Principle, 1961. Served to capt. AUS, 1942-46. Fellow Saybrook Coll., Yale, 1950—. Mem. Phi Beta Kappa. Clubs: Elizabethan (New Haven); Century Assn. (N.Y.C.), Yale (N.Y.C.). Home: 88 Notch Hill Rd Apt 353 North Branford CT 06471-1853

LOGAN, JOHN FRANCIS, electronics company executive, management consultant; b. Norristown, Pa., Apr. 10, 1938; s. Francis Michael and Elizabeth V. L. BS in Bus. Adminstrn., Drexel U., 1961. CPA, N.Y. Auditor Hurdman and Cranston CPA's (merger KPMG Peat Warwick), N.Y.C., 1961-69; v.p. fin., chief fin. officer, treas. Aero Flow Dynamics, Inc., N.Y.C., 1969-84; v.p. fin. and adminstrn., chief fin. officer, treas. Codenoll Tech. Corp., Yonkers, N.Y., 1985-90; v.p. fin., chief fin. officer, treas. VTX Electronics Corp., Farmingdale, N.Y., 1991-92; mgmt. cons. Comtex Info. Systems, Inc./KLMB Group Inc., N.Y.C., 1992-95; v.p. fin., CFO, treas. M-Power Corp., N.Y.C., 1995—. With U.S. Army, 1962-64. Mem. AICPAs, N.Y. State Soc. CPA's, Pa. Soc.

LOGAN, JOSEPH GRANVILLE, JR., physicist; b. Washington, June 8, 1920; s. Joseph Granville and Lula (Briggs) L.; m. Esther Taylor, June 30, 1944; children—Joseph Michael, Eileen Cecile. B.S., D.C. Tchrs. Coll., 1941; Ph.D. in Physics, U. Buffalo, 1955. Physicist Nat. Bur. Standards, 1944-47, Cornell Aero. Lab., 1947-58; head propulsion research dept. Space Tech. Labs., 1958-61; dir. aerodynamics and propulsion research lab. Aerospace Corp., 1961-67; spl. asst. to dir. research and devel. McDonnell Douglas Astronautics Co., Santa Monica, Calif., 1967-69; mgr. vulnerability and hardening, devel. engring. McDonnell Douglas Astronautics Co., 1969-74; pres. Applied Energy Scis., Inc., Los Angeles, 1974—; v.p. rsch. and devel. Advent Resources, Inc., Torrance, Calif., 1994—; mem. faculty dept. physics Calif. Poly. U., Pomona, 1977-78; bus. devel. specialist Urban U. Center, U. So. Calif., Los Angeles, 1978-79, assoc. dir., 1979-80, dir., 1980-88. Mem. Am. Phys. Soc., AIAA, Soc. Info. Display, N.Y. Acad. Scis. Home: 3652 Olympiad Dr Los Angeles CA 90043-1144 Office: Applied Engery Scis Consulting Svcs PO Box 36583 Los Angeles CA 90043

LOGAN, JOSEPH PRESCOTT, lawyer; b. Topeka, Jan. 21, 1921; s. Joseph Glenn and Corinne (Ripley) L.; m. Yvonne Marie Westrate, July 17, 1943; children: John Daniel, Kathleen Elisabeth, Laurie Prescott. AB, Dartmouth Coll., 1942; LLB, Harvard U., 1948. Bar: Mo. 1948, U.S. Dist. Ct. Mo. 1948. Ptnr. Thompson Coburn, St. Louis, 1958—. Pres., chmn. bd. Ranken Jordan Home for Covalescent Crippled Children, St. Louis, 1968-93. Lt. USNR, 1942-46. Mem. ACLU (bd. mem. 1988, civil liberties award 1982), Noonday Club. Democrat. Congregationalist. Avocations: hiking, mountain climbing, sailing. Home: 36 S Gore Ave Saint Louis MO 63119-2910 Office: Thompson Coburn 1 Mercantile Ctr Ste 3300 Saint Louis MO 63101-1643

LOGAN, JOYCE POLLEY, education educator; b. Providence, Ky., Sept. 18, 1935; d. Vernon and Hattie Alice Polley; m. Jewell Wyatt Logan (dec.), June 4, 1956; 1 child, James Edward. BS, Murray State U., 1956, MA, 1960; EdD, Vanderbilt U., 1988. Cert. bus. tchr., vocat. adminstrn. Student sec. Murray (Ky.) State U., 1954-56; bus. tchr. Hopkins County Schs., Madisonville, Ky., 1956-68; regional coord. Vocational Region 2 Ky. Dept. Edn., Madisonville, 1968-83; prin. Health Occupations Sch., Madisonville, 1983-88; voc., tech. administr. Ky. Dept. Edn., Frankfort, 1988-90; asst. prof. dept. adminstrn. and supervision Coll. Edn. U. Ky., Lexington, 1991—; state dir. Ky. Com. for Secondary and Middle Schs. Southern Assn. Colls. and Schs., 1995—; evaluator Distance Edn. Training Coun., Washington, 1981—; field coord. military evaluations, Am. Coun. on Edn., Washington, 1984—. Author: (with A.C. Krizan) Basics of Writing, 1993. Mem. alumni bd. Murray (Ky.) State U. Coll. Bus., 1988—; fundraiser Ky. Spl. Olympics, Madisonville, 1983, YMCA, Madisonville, 1984; mem. edn. com. Greater Leadership Program Madisonville, Ky. C. of C., 1987-88. Named FFA Hon. State Farmer, Ky. FFA., 1979, Woman of the Year, Lion's Club, Madisonville, Ky., 1987, Outstanding Teacher Educator, 1992. Mem. Nat. Bus. Edn. Assn., Am. Vocat. Assn., Ky. Vocat. Assn., Southern Assn. of Colls. and Schs. (trustee 1973, 1976-78, chmn. Commn on Occupational Ednl. Insts. 1973), Ky. Assn. for Sch. Adminstrs., Assn. for Supervision and Curriculum Devel., Phi Delta Kappa, Omicron Delta Kappa (hon.). Avocations: jogging, tennis, reading, piano playing. Home: 2956 Tabor Oaks Lane Lexington KY 40502-2898 Office: U Ky 111 Dickey Hall Coll of Edn Lexington KY 40506

LOGAN, LOX ALBERT, JR., museum director; b. Rutherfordton, N.C., Feb. 7, 1954; s. Lox Albert Sr. and Grace (Hawkins) L.; m. Bernadette Wall, May 6, 1978; children: Mark Thomas, Garrett Michael, Sean Timothy. BS, U.S. Mil. Acad., 1976; MA in History Mus. Studies, SUNY, Cooperstown, 1982; postgrad. Am. History, Marquette U., 1988-89. Exec. dir. Wyo. Hist. and Geol. Soc., Wilkes-Barre, Pa., 1983-86; dir. Manitowoc (Wis.) Maritime Mus., 1986-95; exec. dir. USS Constitution Mus., Boston, 1995—; field reviewer Inst. Mus. Svcs., Washington, 1986—; mem. exec. com. Pa. Fedn. Hist. Socs., Harrisburg, 1983-85. Author: (with others) Maritime America, 1988; contbr. to profl. jour. Bd. dirs. Manitowoc-Two Rivers YMCA, 1989-93, scholarship selection com., 1991-95; Pa. rep. admissions to U.S. Mil. Acad., 1984-85; coord. N.E. Pa. Records Coop., Wilkes-Barre, 1983-86; active Com. Econ. Growth, Wilkes-Barre, 1983-85, Govs. Commn. on USS Wis., 1988; rec. sec. adv. com. underwater archaeology State Hist. Soc. Wis., 1988; cabinet Manitowoc United Way Campaign, 1990-92; chmn. Mishabago dist. Boy Scouts Am., 1990-92; bd. dirs., pres. Riverwalk Festival, 1989-95. Nat. Mus. Act. fellow Smithsonian Instn., 1982; recipient award Hugenot Soc. N.Y., 1982. Mem. Am. Assn. Mus. (cons. mus. assessment program 1988—), Am. Assn. State and Local History, Wis. Fedn. Mus. (adv. com. 1988-89, treas. 1989-92, exec. com. 1989-93), Assn. Gt. Lakes Maritime History (bd. dirs. 1986-95), sec. 1986-89, pres. 1989-93), Coun. Am. Maritime Mus. (bd. dirs. 1989, v.p. 1991-93, pres. 1993-95), Presbyn. Hist. Assn. (adv. com. 1989-95, moderator 1991-95). Presbyterian. Avocations: gardening, running, canoeing. Office: USS Constitution Mus PO Box 1812 Boston MA 02129

LOGAN, LYNDA DIANNE, elementary education educator; b. Detroit, June 22, 1952; d. Horatio Bernard and Ruby (Newsom) Graham; m. Keith L. Logan, Aug. 16, 1980; 1 child, Lauren Nicole. BS, Ea. Mich. U., 1974, MA, 1980. Cert. tng. program quality rev., Calif.; cert. tchr., Calif., Miss., Mich.; cert. Lang. Devel. Specialist (CLAD), 1996; lic. guidance counselor basic related edn., Miss.; cert. counselor pupil pers. svc. credential, Mich., Calif. Substitute tchr. Detroit Pub. Schs., 1974-76; mid. sch. tchr. Inkster (Mich.) Pub. Schs., 1976-80; CETA vocat. counselor Golden Triangle Vocat.-Tech. Ctr., Mayhew, Miss., 1980-82, basic related educator, 1980-82; elem. tchr. Inglewood (Calif.) Unified Sch. Dist., 1982-93, resource tchr., 1993-96; tchr. Crozier Mid. Sch., Inglewood, Calif., 1996—; mem. forecast adv. bd. COED Mag., N.Y.C., 1979-80; advisor/founder Newspaper Club Fellrath Mid. Sch., Inkster, 1979-80; mem. interviewing com. Golden Triangle Vocat.-Tech. Ctr., Mayhew, 1980-82, evaluation and follow-up com., 1980-82; pronouncer spelling bee Inglewood Unified Sch. Dist., 1991, 94; organizer student body team meetings Worthington Sch., Inglewood, 1993-96, coord. reading program, 1993-96; mem. interviewing com., 1987-95; co-chair yearbook com., 1993-94, prin. adv. bd., 1987-92, ct.-liaison and child welfare attendance rep. L.A. County Edn., 1995-96, supt. adv. coun., 1995-96, reading is fundamental coord., 1993-96, mem. team earthquake preparedness com., 1994-96. youth co-chairperson March of Dimes, Detroit, 1976-80; com. mem. Nat. Coun. Negro Women, L.A. chpt., 1982-84; com. mem. Cmty. Action Program, Eternal Promise Bapt. Ch., L.A., 1991, pres. choir, 1991, v.p. hospitality com., 1987-88; co-chmn. women's com., 1990; mem. parent adv. com. Knox Presbyn. Ch. Nursery Sch., L.A., 1988-89. Mem. ASCD, AAUW, NAFE, Black Women's Forum, Ladies Aux. Knights of St. Peter Claver, Ea. Mich. U. Alumni Assn., Phi Gamma Nu. Avocations: bike riding, community organizational activities, travel, movies, theater. Office: Crozier Middle School 151 N Grevillea Ave Inglewood CA 90301-1705

LOGAN, MARIE-ROSE VAN STYNVOORT, literature educator, editor; b. Brussels, Belgium, May 26, 1944; d. Jean Stevo and Marie-Rose (Mabille) Van Stynvoort; m. John Frederick Logan, Sept. 7, 1968; 1 child, Franklin. Licence, U. Brussels, 1966; MA, Yale U., 1970; MPhil, 1972, PhD, 1974. Instr. Yale U., New Haven, Conn., 1972-74; asst. prof. Columbia U., N.Y.C., 1974-83; assoc. prof. Rice U., Houston, 1983-93, Goucher Coll., Balt., 1993-96; assoc. prof. dept. English Temple U., Phila., 1996—; gen. editor Annals of Scholarship Quar. in Humanities and Social Scvs., 1994—; assoc. editor Columbia Dictionary in European Lit., N.Y., 1978-81. Editor: Contending Kingdoms, 1992, Gerard Genette Figures of Literary Discourse, 1981; author: Michel de Ghelderode, 1996; contbr. over 50 articles to profl. jours. Recipient Chevalier de l'Ordre des Palmes Academiques Govt. of France, 1980; Nat. Endowment of Humanities fellow, 1981-88, Harvard U. fellow, 1975-76, Inst. for Advanced Study in Humanities fellow U. Edinburgh, 1989. Mem. Soc. Fellows in Humanities Columbia U., Elizabethan Club Yale U. Home: 4041 Ridge Ave #4-416 Philadelphia PA 19129 Office: Temple U Coll Arts and Scis Dept English Philadelphia PA 19129

LOGAN, MATHEW KUYKENDALL, journalist; b. Norman, Okla., Aug. 19, 1933; s. Leonard Marion and Floy-Elise (Duke) L.; m. Linda Dianne Elderkin, Dec. 31, 1964. B.A. in Journalism, U. Okla., 1955. Reporter UPI, 1957-58; city editor Daily Oklahoman, 1958-69; asst. mng. editor Houston Post, 1969-76, mng. editor, 1976-83; mng. editor Sta. KHOU-TV, Houston, 1984-87; asst. dean for community affairs Med. Sch. U. Tex., Houston, 1987-92; v.p. pub. affairs and mktg. Hermann Hosp., Houston, 1992—. Served with AUS, 1957. Mem. UPI Editors Tex. (pres. 1977), Tex. AP Mng. Editors Assn. (pres. 1983), Sigma Chi. Methodist. Home: 24 Sunlit Forest Dr The Woodlands TX 77381-2986 Address: 6411 Fannin Administration Houston TX 77030*

LOGAN, NANCY ALLEN, library media specialist; b. Rochester, N.Y., Mar. 27, 1933; d. Warren William and Dorothea Amelia (Pund) Allen; m. Joseph Skinner Logan, Dec. 29, 1952; children: Jennifer Martha, Joseph Skinner Jr., Susan Logan Huber, Annette Logan Miller. Student, Middlebury Coll., 1951-52; BA, Cornell U., 1955; MLS, SUNY, Albany, 1967; cert. legal asst., Marist Coll., 1983. Cert. libr. media specialist, tchr., social studies tchr., N.Y. Libr. media specialist Hyde Park (N.Y.) Sch. Dist., 1971-93. Editor: Dear Friends, 1989; editor newsletter Sch. Libr. Media Specialists, 1984-85; contbr. articles to profl. publs. Arts chmn. Jr. League, Poughkeepsie, N.Y., 1967-69, dir. Jr. Arts Ctr., 1967-69, edn. chmn., 1970-71; sec. bd. dirs. Poughkeepsie (N.Y.) Tennis Club, 1973-79; indexer periodicals Dutchess County Hist. Soc., Poughkeepsie, 1979-93; county rep. Sch. Libr. Media Specialists, S.E. N.Y., 1982, exhibits chmn. ann. meeting, 1983, 84; vol. libr., indexer Jamestown (R.I.) Philomenian Libr., 1993—; bd. dirs. Friends of Jamestown Philomenian Libr., 1994—. Mem. Newport Hist. Soc., Beavertail Lighthouse Assn. (bd. dirs. 1994—), New Eng. Hist. Geneal. Soc. (bd. dirs. 1994-96), Phi Delta Kappa. Avocations: reading, sailing, swimming, travel, bicycling. Home: 149 Seaside Dr Jamestown RI 02835-3117

LOGAN, RALPH ANDRE, physicist; b. Cornwall, Ont., Sept. 22, 1926; s. Joseph A. and Lucy T. (Carter) L.; m. Aug. 26, 1950; children: Howard, Mary, Marguerite, Anthony, Enid, Alisa, Ruth, John, Thomas. BSc, McGill U., Montreal, 1947, MSc, 1948; PhD, Columbia U., N.Y.C., 1952. Tech. staff mem. AT&T Bell Labs Research Div., Murray Hill, N.J., 1952-94. Author: numerous tech. pubs.; patentee in field. Fellow IEEE, Am. Physics Soc.; mem. NAE, Optical Soc. Home: 7 Cindy Dr Manahawkin NJ 08050-4230

LOGAN, RODMAN EMMASON, retired jurist; b. West Saint John, N.B., Can., Sept. 7, 1922; s. Gilbert Earle and Emma Zela (Irwin) L.; m. Evelyn Pearl DeWitt, June 19, 1948; children: John Bruce DeWitt, Ian David Alexander, Mary Jane Irwin, Bruce Rodman Hans. BA, U. N.B., 1949, BCL, 1951, DCL (hon.), 1988; DCL, St. Thomas U., Fredericton, N.B., 1974. Bar: N.B. 1951, created Queen's Counsel 1972. Partner firm Logan, Bell and Church, Saint John, N.B., 1951-70; elected to Legis. Assembly, 1963, 67, 70, 74, 78; minister of labor and provincial sec. Province of N.B., 1970-77; atty.-gen. and minister of justice, 1977-82; justice Ct. of Queen's Bench, 1982-96. Served with Can. Armed Forces, 1942-45, U.K., N.W. Europe and Ctrl. Mediterranean Forces; hon. col. Royal N.B. Regt. Mem. Royal Commonwealth Soc., St. Andrew's Soc. Anglican. Clubs: Royal Can. Legion, Carleton and York Regtl. Home: RR 2, 273 Nerepis Rd, Westfield, NB Canada E0G 3J0

LOGAN, VICKI, advertising executive; b. Oakland, Calif., Aug. 3, 1954; d. Robert Lee and Freida Elizabeth (Luckett) L. BS in Bus. Adminstrn. magna cum laude, Pepperdine U., 1976; M in Internat. Mgmt. with honors, Am. Grad. Sch. Internat. Mgmt., 1979. Asst. to dep. dir. HUD, Washington, 1978; account exec. Doyle Dane Bernbach Advt., Inc., N.Y.C., 1979-81; sr. v.p., creative dir. Jordan, McGrath, Case, Taylor & McGrath Advt., N.Y.C., 1981-96, exec. v.p., 1996. Office: Jordan McGrath Case & Taylor Inc 445 Park Ave New York NY 10022-2606

LOGANBILL, G. BRUCE, logopedic pathologist; b. Newton, Kans., Sept. 6, 1938; s. Oscar and Warrene (Rose) L. B.A., Bethel Coll., Kans., 1956; M.A., U. Kans., 1958; Ph.D., Mich. State U., 1961; postdoctoral fellow, Inst. Logopedics, 1965-66. Mem. faculty Kalamazoo Coll., 1961-63; mem. faculty Fresno (Calif.) State U., 1966-68; mem. faculty Calif. State U., Long Beach, 1968—, prof., 1975—; lectr. on speech communication and pathologies, Argentina, Denmark, France, Japan, Can., India, Scotland, Czechoslovakia, USSR, Germany, People's Republic of China; U.S. rep. 2d Internat. Congress de Melodie-Therapie du Language en accord Nat. Coll. Psychiatry, Paris, 1990. Author: The Bases of Voice, Articulation and Pronunciation, 1974, 5th edit., 1992; contbr. more than 30 articles to profl. jours. Mem. Speech Comm. Assn., Western Speech Comm. Assn., Am. Speech and Hearing Assn., Calif. Speech and Hearing Assn., Internat. Assn. Logopedics and Phoniatrics, Internat. Phonetics Assn., Internat. Assn. Art Therapy (v.p. 1996—), Assn. Calif. State U. Profs. (univ. chpt. pres. 1985, Calif. del. NEA/Calif. Tchrs. Assn. 1990), others. Republican. Episcopalian. Office: Calif State U Long Beach 1250 N Bellflower Blvd Long Beach CA 90840-0006

LOGEMANN, JERILYN ANN, speech pathologist, educator; b. Berwyn, Ill., May 21, 1942; d. Warren F. and Natalie M. (Killmer) L.; BS, Northwestern U., 1963; MA, 1964, PhD, 1968. Grad. asst. dept. communicative disorders Northwestern U., 1963-68; instr. speech and audiology DePaul U., 1964-65; instr. dept. communicative disorders Mundelein Coll., 1967-71; research assoc. depts. neurology and otolaryngology and maxillofacial surgery Northwestern U. Med. Sch., Chgo., 1970-74, asst. prof., 1974-78, dir. clin. and research activities of speech and lang., 1975—, assoc. prof. depts. neurology, otolaryngology and comm. scis. and disorders, 1978-83, prof., 1983, chmn. dept. communication scis. and disorders, 1982—, Ralph and Jean Sundin Prof. of Comm. Scis. and Disorders, 1995—; mem. assoc. staff Northwestern Meml. Hosp., 1976—, N. Chgo. VA Hosp., 1983—, Evanston (Ill.) Hosp., 1988—, Children's Meml. Hosp., Chgo., 1988—; cons. in field; assoc. dir. cancer control. Ill. Comprehensive Cancer Council, Chgo., 1980-82. Mem. rehab. com. Ill. div. Am. Cancer Soc., 1975-79, chmn., 1979—; mem. upper aerodigestive tract organ site com. Nat. Cancer Inst., 1986-89. Postdoctoral fellow Nat. Inst. Neurologic Disease, Communicative Disorders and Stroke, Northwestern U., 1966-70; fellow Inst. Medicine Chgo., 1981—; grantee Nat. Cancer Inst., 1975—, Am. Cancer Soc. , 1981-82; Honors award Conn. Speech Lang. Hearing Assn., 1995, Appreciation award Coun. Grad. Programs in Comms. Scis. and Disorders, 1995, Cellular One award Vanderbilt U. Fellow Am. Speech, Lang. and Hearing Assn. (pres.-elect 1993, pres. 1994, past pres. 1995), Inst. Medicine; mem. Internat. Assn. Logopedics and Phoniatrics, AAUP, Acoustic Soc. Am. (program com. Chgo. regional chpt.), Linguistic Soc. Am., Speech Comm. Assn., Am. Cleft Palate Assn., Ill. Speech and Hearing Assn. (DiCarlo award 1988), Chgo. Heart Assn., Chgo. Speech Therapy and Auditory Soc. Author: The Fisher-Logemann Test of Articulation Competence, 1971, Evaluation and Treatment of Swallowing Disorders, 1983; Manual for the Videofluorographic Evaluation of Swallowing, 1985, 93; assoc. editor Jour. Speech and Hearing Disorders, Jour. Head Trauma Rehab., Dysphagia jour., 1978-82. Office: Northwestern U Med Sch 303 E Chicago Ave Chicago IL 60611-3008 also: Dept Comm Sci & Disorder 2299 Sheridan Rd Evanston IL 60208-0837

LOGGIA, ROBERT, actor; b. S.I., N.Y., Jan. 3, 1930; s. Benjamin and Elena (Blandino) L.; m. Audrey O'Brien; children: Tracey, John, Kristina, Cynthia. Student, Wagner Coll., S.I., 1947-49; B. Journalism, U. Mo., Columbia, 1951. Appeared in Broadway prodns. Toys in the Attic, 1961, Three Sisters, 1964, Boom Boom Room, 1973-74; TV series T.H.E. Cat, 1968-69, The Nine Lives of Elfego Baca, 1958-59, Mancuso F.B.I., 1989-90 (Emmy Best Actor award nominee), Sunday Dinner, 1991; films include Somebody Up There Likes Me, 1956, The Garment Jungle, 1957, Cop Hater, The Lost Missile, 1958, Cattle King, 1963, Greatest Story Ever Told, 1965, Che!, 1969, First Love, 1977, Speed Trap, Revenge of the Pink Panther, 1978, The Ninth Configuration (Twinkle Twinkle Little Kane), S.O.B., 1981, An Officer and a Gentleman, 1982, Trail of the Pink Panther, 1982, Scarface, 1983, Psycho II, 1983, Curse of the Pink Panther, 1983, Prizzi's Honor, 1985, Jagged Edge, 1985 (Acad. Best Supporting Actor award nominee 1986), Armed and Dangerous, 1986, Over the Top, 1986, Hot Pursuit, 1986, That's Life, 1986, The Believers, Big, 1988, Oliver & Company (voice), 1988, Triumph of the Spirit, 1989, Gaby, 1989, Marrying Man, 1990, Opportunity Knocks, 1990, Necessary Roughness, 1991, Gladiator, 1992, Innocent Blood, 1992, Bad Girls, 1994, I Love Trouble, 1994, Independence Day, 1996, Lost Highway, 1996, Mistrial, 1996, Wide Awake, 1996, Smille's Sense of Snow, 1996, Shakespeare's Sister, 1997; TV miniseries Echoes in the Darkness, Favorite Son, 1989, Wild Palms, 1993; TV appearances include Chicago Conspiracy Trial, 1988 (Ace Best Actor award nominee), Afterburn, 1992, Merry Christmas Baby, 1992, Nurses on the Line, 1993, Mercy Mission, 1993, White Mile, 1994, Lifepod, 1993, Between Love & Honor, 1995, Jake Lassiter, 1995, Pandora's Clock. With U.S. Army, 1951-53. Office: Creative Artists Agy 9830 Wilshire Blvd Beverly Hills CA 90212-1804 *Pursue excellence.**

LOGGIE, JENNIFER MARY HILDRETH, medical educator, physician; b. Lusaka, Zambia, Feb. 4, 1936; came to U.S., 1964, naturalized, 1972; d. John and Jenny (Beattie) L. M.B., B.Ch., U. Witwatersrand, Johannesburg, South Africa, 1959. Intern Harare Hosp., Salisbury, Rhodesia, 1960-61; gen. practice medicine Lusaka, 1961-62; sr. pediatric house officer Derby Children's Hosp., also St. John's Hosp., Chelmsford, Eng., 1962-64; resident in pediatrics Children's Hosp., Louisville, 1964, Cin., 1964-65; fellow clin. pharmacology Cin. Coll. Medicine, 1965-67; mem. faculty U. Cin. Med. Sch., 1967—, prof. pediatrics, 1975, asso. prof. pharmacology, 1972-77. Contbr. articles to med. publs.; editor Pediatric and Adolescent Hypertension, 1991. Grantee Am. Heart Assn., 1970-72, 89-90. Mem. Am. Pediatric Soc. (elected, Founder's award 1996), Midwest Soc. Pediatric Research. Episcopalian. Home: 1133 Herschel Ave Cincinnati OH 45208-3112 Office: Children's Hosp Med Ctr Children's Hosp Rsch Found 3300 Burnet Ave Cincinnati OH 45229-3021

LOGGINS, KENNY (KENNETH CLARKE LOGGINS), singer, songwriter; b. Everett, Wash., Jan. 17, 1947; s. Robert George and Lina Clelia (Massie) L.; m. Julia Cooper. Student, Pasadena City Coll. Mem. groups, Second Helping, Loggins & Messina, Electric Prunes, rec. artist, Columbia Records and Sony Wonder Records; songwriter, Milk Money and Gnossos Music Pub. Co.; solo albums include: Celebrate Me Home, 1977, Nightwatch, 1978, Keep the Fire, 1979, Alive, 1980, Footloose, 1984, Vox Humana, 1985, Back to Avalon, 1988, Leap of Faith, 1991, Outside From the Redwoods, 1993, Return to Pooh Corner, 1994; albums with Messina include: Sittin' In, 1971, Loggins & Messina, 1972, Full Sail, 1973, On Stage, 1974, Motherlode, 1975, So Fine, 1975, Native Sons, 1976, Best of Friends, 1977, Finale, 1978, Best of Loggins and Messina, 1980; other albums: stage: Kenny Loggins on Broadway, 1988; composed and performed theme for This Island Earth (The Disney Channel), 1993 (Cable Ace award, Best Original Song, Emmy award). Adv. bd. Earthtrust. Recipient Rock 'n Roll Sports Classic Gold medal, Grammy award for What A Fool Believes, 1980, Grammy award for This is It, 1981, Harry Chapin award We Are the World. Mem. ASCAP, Nat. Assn. Rec. Arts and Scis. Office: care William Morris Agy 151 S El Camino Dr Beverly Hills CA 90212-2704 also: Columbia Records 550 Madison Ave New York NY 10019*

LOGHRY, RICHARD M., architecture and engineering services executive. CEO Mason & Harger Engring., now pres. Office: Mason & Hanger Corp 2355 Harrodsburg Rd Lexington KY 40504-3307*

LOGIE, JOHN HOULT, mayor, lawyer; b. Ann Arbor, Mich., Aug. 11, 1939; s. James Wallace and Elizabeth (Hoult) L.; m. Susan G. Duerr, Aug. 15, 1964; children: John Hoult Jr., Susannah, Margaret Elizabeth. Student Williams Coll., 1957-59; BA, U. Mich., 1961, JD, 1968; MS, George Washington U., 1966. Bar: Mich. 1969, U.S. Dist. Ct. (we. and ea. dists. 1969) Mich., U.S. Ct. Appeals (6th cir. 1987). Assoc. Warner, Norcross & Judd, Grand Rapids, Mich., 1969-74, ptnr., 1974—; mayor City of Grand Rapids, 1992—; chmn. civil justice adv. group U.S. Dist. Ct. (we. dist.) Mich., 1995—. program coord. condemnation law sect. Inst. Continuing Legal Edn.; guest lectr. Grand Rapids C.C., Grand Valley State U., Western Mich. U., Mich. State U.; bd. visitors Sch. Bus & Pub. Mgmt., George Washington U., 1995—; legal counsel to 15 West Mich. hosps.; instr. U.S. Naval Acad., 1964-66. Pres. Grand Rapids PTA Council, 1971-73, Heritage Hill Assn., 1976, sec., trustee 1971-84; chmn. Grand Rapids Urban Homesteading Commn., 1975-80, Grand Rapids Hist. Commn., 1985-90, Grand Rapids/Kent County Sesquicentennial Com., 1986-88; MEM. Headlee Blue Ribbon Commn., 1993-94; v.p. bd. dirs. Goodwill Industries, Grand Rapids, 1973-79, Am. Cancer Soc., Grand Rapids, 1970-81; pres., trustee Hist. Soc. Mich., 1984-90. Lt. USN, 1961-66. Mem. ABA (forum com. on health law 1980—), Mich. Bar Assn. (chmn. condemnation com. real property sect. 1985-88), Grand Rapids Bar Assn. (dir. young lawyers sect. 1970), Am. Acad. Hosp. Attys., Mich. Soc. Hosp. Attys. (pres. 1976-77), Nat. Health Lawyers Assn., Univ. Club (dir. 1979-82, pres. 1980-82), Peninsular Club, Williams Club (NYC). Avocations: sailing, hunting, fishing. Home: 601 Cherry St SE Grand Rapids MI 49503-4726 Office: Warner Norcross and Judd 900 Old Kent Bldg Grand Rapids MI 49503 also: Office of Mayor 300 Monroe Ave NW Grand Rapids MI 49503-2206

LOGUE, DENNIS EMHARDT, financial economics educator, consultant; b. Bklyn., Mar. 28, 1944; s. Joseph Paul and Helen Rose (Emhardt) L.; m. Marcella Julia Watson, June 11, 1966; children: Dennis E. Jr., Patrick G. A.B., Fordham U., 1964; M.B.A., Rutgers U., 1966; Ph.D., Cornell U., 1971. Asst. prof. Ind. U., Bloomington, 1971-73; sr. economist U.S. Treasury, Washington, 1973-74; prof. bus. Tuck Sch., Dartmouth Coll., Hanover, N.H., 1974—, now Steven Roth prof. mgr., former assoc. dean; founding bd. dirs. Ledyard Nat. Bank. Author: Legislative Influence on Corporate Pension Plans, 1979, The Investment Performance of Corporate Pension Plans, 1988, Managing Pension Plans, 1997; editor: Handbook of Modern Finance, 1993; co-editor Fin. Mgmt., 1978-81. Served to 1st lt. U.S. Army, 1966-68. Mem. Am. Econ. Assn., Am. Fin. Assn. (bd. dirs. 1981-84), Fin. Mgmt. Assn. (bd. dirs., pres. 1995—), Knights of Malta, Order Holy Sepulchre, N.Y. Athletic Club, Rotary, Beta Gamma Sigma. Republican. Roman Catholic. Home: 1 River Ridge Rd Hanover NH 03755-1910 Office: Dartmouth Coll Amos Tuch Sch Bus Admin Hanover NH 03755

LOGUE, EDWARD JOSEPH, development company executive; b. Phila., Feb. 7, 1921; s. Edward J. and Resina (Fay) L.; m. Margaret DeVane, June 7, 1947; children: Katherine, William DeVane. B.A., Yale U., 1942, LL.B., 1947. Bar: Pa. 1948, Conn. 1950. Practiced in Phila., 1948; legal sec. Gov. Chester Bowles, Hartford, Conn., 1949-51; spl. asst. to ambassador Chester Bowles, New Delhi, 1952-53; devel. adminstr. City of New Haven, 1954-60, City of Boston, 1961-67; vis. Maxwell prof. govt. Boston U., 1967-68; pres., chief exec. officer N.Y. State Urban Devel. Corp., 1968-75; pres. Roosevelt Island Devel. Corp., 1969-75, Logue Devel. Co., Inc., 1976—, South Bronx Devel. Orgn., Inc., 1978-85; chief exec. officer Logue Boston, 1987-1994; Thomas Jefferson prof. Sch. Architecture, U. Va., spring 1985; sr. lectr. Sch. Architecture and Planning, MIT, 1985-89; prin. devel. cons. to Ft. Lincoln New Town, Washington, 1968; vis. lectr. Yale Sch. Law, 1957-77; chmn. Task Force on Housing and Neighborhood Improvement, N.Y.C., 1966; mem. Critical Choices Commn., 1973-76; founder Vineyard Open Land Found., 1970; mem. vis. com. Harvard U. Sch. Design, 1969-75; mem. resource team Mayor's Inst. on City Design. Chmn. Dukes County Charter Commn., 1991-92; advisor to Mayor Jackson and Corp. for Olympic Devel., Atlanta, 1993. With USAAF, 1943-45. Decorated Air medal with clusters. Fellow Am. Acad. Arts and Scis.; mem. AIA (hon. mem.), Tavern Club (Boston), Century Club (N.Y.C.), Saturday (Boston), Yale Club (N.Y.C.), Harvard Club, Phi Beta Kappa (hon.). Democrat. Home and Office: Scotchman's Bridge Ln West Tisbury MA 02575

LOGUE, FRANK, arbitrator, mediator, urban consultant, former mayor New Haven; b. Phila., Aug. 18, 1924; s. Edward J. and Resina (Fay) L.; m. Mary Ann Willson, June 10, 1950; children: Nancy, Jennifer, Jonathan. BA, Yale U., 1948, JD, 1951. Bar: Conn. 1951. Practiced in Bridgeport and Trumbull, Conn., 1951-64; dir. Community Action Inst., OEO Regional Tng. Center, New Haven, 1965-69, Nat. Urban Fellows, New Haven, 1969-75; alderman City of New Haven, 1972-75; mayor, 1976-79; prosecutor Town of Trumbull, 1955-57; town atty., 1957-61; regional cons. U.S. Civil Rights Commn., 1961-63; lectr. New Haven Police Acad., 1965-70; vis. asst. prof. So. Conn. State Coll., 1968-69; assoc. fellow Morse Coll., Yale U., 1968—; mem. adv. bd. Yale U. Sch. Mgmt., 1976-80, mem. faculty, 1980-81; vice chmn. Inst. Pub. Mgmt., 1975-82; chmn. task force on arts Nat. League Cities, 1977-79; mem. adv. bd. U.S. Conf. Mayors, 1977-79; panelist pub. programs div. Nat. Endowment for Humanities, 1974-78; mem. Pres.'s Adv. Commn. on the Holocaust; chmn. bd. dirs. Internat. Inst. Public Mgmt., 1979-82; mem. Conn. Adv. Com. Intergovtl. Relations, 1984-86; pub. interest arbitrator Conn. Dept. Edn., 1985—; pub. mem. alt. panel Conn. Bd. Mediation and Arbitration, 1986-89. Author: Who Administers—Access to Leadership Positions in the Administration of Government, 1972. Served with inf. AUS, 1944-45, ETO. Mem. Am. Arbitration Assn. (labor panel 1987—), Conn. Bar Assn. (exec. com. labor and employment law sect. 1989—). Home and Office: 173 Livingston St New Haven CT 06511-2209

LOGUE, GERALD L., hematologist; b. Parker, Pa., July 22, 1941; s. Charles Albert and Wiloven (Bashline) L.; m. Joelle Bronstein, Dec. 11, 1942; children: Christopher, Timothy, Nicolas. BS, Pa. State U., 1962; MD,

U. Pitts., 1966. Lic. physician, N.Y., Pa., N.C. Chief staff Dept. Vets. Affairs Med. Ctr., Buffalo, 1986—; prof. medicine SUNY, Buffalo, 1982—, chief hematology dept. medicine, 1982—, co-chair Ctr. Clin. Ethics and Humanities in Health Care, 1994—; pres. Buffalo Inst. Med. Rsch., 1992—; mem. Nat. VA Rsch. Eligibility Com., 1991—. Bd. dirs. Western N.Y. Hemophilia Ctr., Buffalo. Lt. comdr. USN, 1972-74. Lt. comdr. USN, 1972-74. Recipient Spl. Citation for exceptional vol. svc. Nat. Red Cross, 1994. Mem. ACP, Am. Soc. Hematology. Home: 327 N Forest Rd Williamsville NY 14221 Office: Buffalo VA Med Ctr 3495 Bailey Ave Buffalo NY 14215-1129

LOGUE, JAMES NICHOLAS, epidemiologist; b. Duryea, Pa., June 18, 1946; s. James and Lucille (Polen) L.; m. Mary Frances Carey, Nov. 25, 1972; children: Melissa, Jimmy, Jeffrey. BS, Kings Coll., 1968; MPH, U. Mich., 1971; DrPH, Columbia U., 1978. Statistician Warner Lambert Co., Morris Plains, N.J., 1969-70, 71-73; sr. med. biostatistician Ciba-Geigy Co., Summit, N.J., 1973-78; epidemiologist GEOMET Technologies, Inc., Rockville, Md., 1978-80; supervisory epidemiologist US FDA, Rockville, 1980-82; dir. divsn. environ. health assessment Pa. Dept. Health, Harrisburg, 1982—. Office: Pa Dept of Health PO Box 90 Harrisburg PA 17120

LOGUE, JOHN J(OSEPH), psychologist; b. Phila., Nov. 16, 1929; s. Edwin J. and Ellen V. (Mallon) L.; m. Evelyn Bortnick, Apr. 24, 1954; 1 child, Eileen Logue Handel. BS, Temple U., 1954, MEd, 1958, EdD, 1966. Lic. psychologist Pa., Md., N.J., Del. Ptnr., sr. cons. RHR Internat., Phila., 1966-88; mgmt. psychologist pvt. practice Phila, 1988—. With U.S. Army, 1954-56. Mem. APA (indsl., orgn., cons., counseling, edn. divsns.), Quaker City Yacht Club. Home: 1942 Greymont St Philadelphia PA 19116-3926 Office: 205 Keith Valley Rd Horsham PA 19044-1408

LOGUE, JOSEPH CARL, electronics engineer, consultant; b. Phila., Dec. 20, 1920; s. Percival J. and Mathilda (Moser) L.; m. Jeanne Martha Neubecker, Mar. 28, 1943; children: Raymond, Marilyn, Paul. BEE, Cornell U., 1944, MEE, 1949. Instr. Cornell U., Ithaca, N.Y., 1944-49, asst. prof., 1949-51; engr. IBM, Poughkeepsie, N.Y., 1951-86; dir. rsch. divsn. IBM, Yorktown Heights, N.Y., 1986; cons. Lorex Industries Inc., Poughkeepsie, 1986—. 30 patents in field; contbr. papers to profl. publs. IBM fellow. Fellow IEEE, AAAS; mem. NAE, Rsch. Soc. Am. Avocations: scuba diving, photography. Home: 52 Boardman Rd Poughkeepsie NY 12603-4228

LOGUE-KINDER, JOAN, alcoholic beverages company executive; b. Richmond, Va., Oct. 26, 1943; d. John T. and Helen (Harvey) Logue; m. Lowell A. Henry Jr., Oct. 6, 1963 (div. Sept. 1981); children: Lowell A. Henry III, Catherine D. Henry, Christopher Logue Henry; m. Randolph S. Kinder, Dec. 13, 1986 (div. Nov. 1995). Student, Wheaton Coll., 1959-62; BA in Sociology, Adelphi U., 1964; cert. in edn., Mercy Coll., Dobbs Ferry, N.Y., 1971; postgrad., NYU, 1973; cert. in edn., St. John's U., 1974. Asst. to dist. mgr. U.S. Census Bur., N.Y.C., 1970; tchr. and adminstr. social studies Yonkers (N.Y.) Bd. Edn., 1971-75; dir. pub. rels. Nat. Black Network, N.Y.C., 1976-83; corp. v.p. NBN Broadcasting (formerly Nat. Black Network), N.Y.C., 1984-90; sr. v.p. The Mingo Group/Plus, N.Y.C., 1990-91; v.p. Edelman Pub. Rels. Worldwide, N.Y.C., 1991-93; dep. asst. sec. pub. affairs U.S. Dept. Treasury, Washington, 1993-94, asst. sec. pub. affairs, 1994-95; dir. corp. comm. programs The Seagram Co., N.Y.C., 1995-96; v.p. Save the Children, Westport, Conn., 1997—; cons. in field. Mem. alumnae recruitment coun. Wheaton Coll.; mem. Nigerian-Am. Friendship Soc., 1978-81; bd. dirs. Westchester Civil Liberties Union, 1974-77, Greater N.Y. coun. Girl Scouts U.S.A., 1985-93, Operation PUSH, 1985-93; del. White House Conf. on Small Bus.; active polit. campaigns, including Morris Udall for U.S. Pres., Howard Samuels for Gov.; sr. black media advisor Dukakis/Bentsen presdl. campaign, 1988; conv. del. N.Y. State Women's Polit. Caucus, 1975, pres. black caucus, 1976-77. Recipient Excellence in Media award Inst. New Cinema Artists, 1984. Mem. World Inst. Black Comm. (bd. dirs. 1983-91). Home: 1800 7th Ave Apt 9B New York NY 10026 Office: Save the Children 54 Wilton Rd Westport CT 06880-3108

LOH, ARTHUR TSUNG YUAN, finance company executive; b. Shanghai, People's Republic of China, Dec. 2, 1923; came to U.S., 1948; s. Chengor and Kwei N. (Wang) L.; m. Monica K.L. Chen, Apr. 16, 1955; children: Stephanie T.L., Pamela T.K. BA, St. John's U., Shanghai, 1945; MS, U. Ill., 1949, PhD, 1952. V.p., co-owner R.W. Pressprich & Co., N.Y.C., 1952-69; exec. v.p. fin. GAC Corp., Allentown, Pa., 1970-71; v.p., co-owner N.Y. Securities Co., N.Y.C., 1972-74; sr. v.p., chief fin. officer Govt. Employees Ins. Co., Criterion Ins. Co., Washington, 1974-80; chief fin. officer Rotary Internat., Evanston, Ill., 1981-88; founder, chmn. Loh Assocs., Greenwich, Conn., 1988—; chmn. bd. GAC Securities Co., Ft. Lauderdale, Fla., 1973-74. Chmn. devel. com. Travelers Aid Soc., N.Y.C.; active Rep. Nat. Com., Washington, Heritage Found. Mem. Internat. Soc. Security Analysts, Am. Econ. Assn., Fin. Execs. Inst., Inst. Chartered Fin. Analysts (chartered), N.Y. Soc. Security Analysts, Wall Street Club, Bankers Club Am., Windmill Club, Rotary, Downtown Assn. (N.Y.C.), City Midday Club (N.Y.C.). Methodist. Avocations: tennis, swimming, skiing, travel. Home: 9 North Ln Armonk NY 10504-2238 Office: Loh Assocs 30 Milbank Ave Greenwich CT 06830-5730

LOH, EUGENE C., physicist, educator; b. Soochow, China, Oct. 1, 1933; 3 children. BS, Va. Polytech. U., 1955; PhD, MIT, 1961. Rsch. assoc. in physics MIT, Cambridge, Mass., 1961-64; asst. prof. MIT, Cambridge, 1964-65; sr. rsch. assoc. in nuc. studies Cornell U., Ithaca, N.Y., 1965-75; assoc. prof physics U. Utah, Salt Lake City, 1975-77, prof., chmn. dept. physics, 1977-90, Disting. prof. physics, 1995, dir. High Energy Astrophysics Inst., 1993—; vis. sci. Stanford Linear Accelerator Ctr., 1980-81. Fellow Am. Physics Soc.; mem. Sigma Xi. Office: U Utah 201 James Fletcher Bldg Salt Lake City UT 84112-1195*

LOH, HORACE H., pharmacology educator; b. Canton, Republic China, May 28, 1936. BS, Nat. Taiwan U., Taipei, Republic China, 1958; PhD, U. Iowa, 1965. Lectr. dept. pharmacology U. Calif. Sch. Medicine, San Francisco, 1967; assoc. prof. biochem. Wayne State U., Detroit, 1968-70; lectr., rsch. assoc. depts. psychiatry, pharmacology Langley Porter Neuropsychiatric Inst. U. Calif. Sch. Medicine, San Francisco, 1970-72, assoc. prof. depts. psychiatry, pharmacology Langley Porter Neuropsychiatric Inst., 1972-75, prof. depts. psychiatry, pharmacology Langley Porter Neuropsychiatric Inst., 1975-88; prof., head dept. pharmacology U. Minn. Med. Sch., Mpls., 1989—, Frederick and Alice Stark prof., head dept. pharmacology, 1990—; chmn. annual meeting theme com. on receptors Fedn. Am. Socs. for Exptl. Biology, 1984; mem. exec. com. Internat. Narcotic Rsch. Conf., 1984-87, chair sci. program annual meeting, 1986; mem. adv. com. Nat. Tsing Hua U. Inst. Life Scis., Taiwan, Republic China, 1985-89; mem. exec. com. Com. on Problems of Drug Dependence, Inc., 1985-88; mem. sci. adv. coun. Nat. Found. for Addicitive Diseases, 1987—; cons. U.S. Army R & D Dept. Defense, 1980-84. Mem. editorial adv. bd. Life Scis., 1978—, Substance and Alcohol Abuse, 1980—, Neurochemistry Internat., 1980-88, Neuropharmacology, 1982—, Neurosci. Series, 1982-83, Annual Rev. Pharmacology and Toxicology, 1984-89, Jour. Pharmacology and Exptl. Therapeutics, 1987—; assoc. editor Annual Rev. Pharmacology and Toxicology, 1990-95, CRC Critical Rev. in Pharmacological Scis., 1987-88; author 56 book chpts; editor 1 book; contbr. 300 articles to profl. jours. Recipient Career Devel. award USPHS, 1973-78, 78-83, Rsch. Scientist award, 1983-88, 1989-94, Humboldt award for sr. U.S. scientists (Fed. Republic Germany), 1977. Mem. Am. Coll. Neuropsychopharmacology (honorific awards com. 1988—), Am. Soc. Pharmacology and Exptl. Therapeutics (program com. 1976-86, trustee bd. publs. 1987-93, com. on confs. 1990-93), Soc. Chinese Bioscientists in Am. (pres. 1985-86), Western Pharmacology Soc. (councilor 1980-83, pres. 1984-85). Office: U Minn Med Sch Dept Pharmacology 3 249 Millard Hall Minneapolis MN 55455

LOH, ROBERT N. K., academic administrator, engineering educator; b. Lumut, Malaysia; arrived in Can., 1962, came to U.S., 1968; m. Annie Loh; children: John, Peter, Jennifer. BSc in Engring., Nat. Taiwan U., Taipei, 1961; MSc in Engring., U. Waterloo, Ont., Can., 1964, PhD, 1968. Asst. prof. U. Iowa, Iowa City, 1968-72, assoc. prof., 1973-78; prof. Oakland U., Rochester, Mich., 1978—, John F. Dodge prof., 1984—, assoc. dean, 1985—, dir. Ctr. for Robotics and Advanced Automation, 1984—. Mem. editorial bd. Info. Systems, 1975—, Jour. of Intelligent and Robotic Systems, 1987—, Asia-Pacific Engring. Jour., 1990—; contbr. over 190 jour. publs. and tech. reports. Recipient numerous research grants and contracts from Dept. Def., NSF and pvt. industry. Mem. IEEE, Soc. Machine Intelligence (bd. dirs. 1985—), Assn. Unmanned Vehicle Systems, 1987—, Sigma Xi, Tau Beta Pi. Office: Oakland U Ctr for Robotics and Advanced Automation Dodge Hall Engring Rochester MI 48309-4401

LOHF, KENNETH A., librarian, writer; b. Milw., Jan. 14, 1925; s. Herman A. and Louise (Krause) L. AB, Northwestern U., 1949; AM, Columbia U., 1950, MS in Library Sci., 1952. Asst. librarian spl. collections Columbia U., N.Y.C., 1957-67; librarian rare books and manuscripts Columbia U., 1967-92. Author: Thirty Poems, 1966, Conrad at Mid-Century: Editions and Studies, 1957, The Achievement of Marianne Moore: A Bibliography, 1958, Yvor Winters: A Bibliography, 1959, Frank Norris: A Bibliography, 1959, Sherwood Anderson: A Bibliography, 1960, An Index to The Little Review, 1914-1929, 1961, The Collection of Books, Manuscripts and Autograph Letters in the Library of Jean and Donald Stralem, 1962, Indices to Little Magazines, 1953-64, The Literary Manuscripts of Hart Crane, 1967, The Jack Harris Samuels Library, 1974, The Centenary of John Masefield's Birth, 1978; (poems) Seasons, 1981, Arrivals, 1987, Fictions, 1990, Passages, 1991, Places, 1992, Endings/Beginnings, 1994; editor: Hart Crane, Seven Lyrics, 1966, Collections and Treasures of the Rare Book and Manuscript Library of Columbia University, 1985, Poets in a War, 1995, Hours, 1996, Moon and Sun, 1997; editor Columbia Library Columns, 1981-92; contbr. prefaces, afterwards, essays and articles to profl. publs. Sec.-treas. Friends of Columbia U. Librs., 1973-92; mem. coun. Am. Mus. Britain. 1st lt. USAAF, 1943-46. Mem. Knickerbocker Club, Century Club, Grolier Club (coun., sec. 1987-90, pres. 1990-94), Coun. Fellows Pierpont Morgan Libr., Order of St. John of Jerusalem. Episcopalian. Home: 560 Riverside Dr Apt 21B New York NY 10027-3236

LOHMAN, GORDON R., manufacturing executive; b. 1934. BS, MIT, 1955. Rsch. metallurgist, project engr. Amsted Industries, Inc., Chgo., 1958-61; project engr. Amstead Rsch. Labs. Amsted Rsch. Labs., Chgo., 1961-67; dir. rsch. Amstead Industries, Inc., Chgo., 1967-68, pres. rsch., 1968-76, pres. MacWhyte divsn., 1976-78, v.p., 1978-87, exec. v.p., then pres., 1987-88, pres., COO, 1988-90, pres., CEO, 1990—; trustee Ill. Inst. Tech.; bd. dirs. Am. Brands, Inc., CIPSCO. Lt. USAF, 1955-58. Office: Amsted Industries Inc 205 N Michigan Ave Chicago IL 60601*

LOHMAN, JOHN FREDERICK, editor; b. Bismarck, N.D., Oct. 29, 1935; s. William Ernest and Viola (Paulson) L.; m. Dorothy Louise Stolp, July 13, 1962; children—Sheryl, Susan, Timothy, Jeffrey. B.S. in Engring., N.D. State U., 1960. Copy boy The Forum, Fargo, N.D., 1952-56, reporter, 1957-68, night editor, 1969-71, city editor, 1972-76, mng. editor, 1977-86, assoc. editor, 1987—; outdoor editor, 1988—. Mem. AP Mng. Editors Assn., Eagles. Avocations: hunting; fishing. Home: 2029 33rd Ave S Fargo ND 58104-6563

LOHMAN, WALTER REARICK, banker; b. Ashland, Ill., Nov. 14, 1917; s. Harry Joseph and Annette (Rearick) L.; m. Carol L. Coultas, June 26, 1948; children: Marian Carol, Roberta Baxter. B.S., Ill. Wesleyan U., 1939. Accountant U.S. Dept. Agr., 1939-41; with Pleasant Plains State Bank, Ill., 1941-42; dir. Pleasant Plains State Bank, 1951-76; with State Bank of Ashland, Ill., 1946-62, pres., 1957-62; exec. v.p. 1st Nat. Bank of Springfield, Ill., 1962-67; pres. 1st Nat. Bank of Springfield, 1967-81, chmn. bd., 1977-85; pres. First Bank of Ill. Co., Springfield, 1972-83, chmn. bd., 1983-87; bd. dirs. State Bank of Ashland, 1st Nat. Bank Springfield, First Bank of Ill. Co. and subs., MII Inc., Lincoln, Ill. Pres. Meml. Med. Ctr., 1983, 84, 85; chmn. bd. Meml. Med. Ctr. Found., 1989-91; bd. dirs. Ill. Indsl. Devel. Authority; trustee Ill. Wesleyan U. 1st lt. AUS, 1942-46, PTO. Recipient Distinguished Alumni award Ill. Wesleyan U., 1971; Distinguished Eagle Scout award Boy Scouts Am., 1973. Mem. Assn. for Modern Banking in Ill. (chmn. 1981-83), Ill. C. of C. (v.p., dir.), Springfield C. of C. (pres. 1969, 76-82). Clubs: Mason (Springfield) (Shriner), Illini Country (Springfield), Sangamo (Springfield). Home: 38 Oakmont Dr Springfield IL 62704-6207 Office: Firstbank Ill Co 205 S 5th St Apt 900 Springfield IL 62701-1406

LOHMANN, GEORGE YOUNG, JR., neurosurgeon, hospital executive; b. Scranton, Pa., Aug. 9, 1947; s. George Young Lohmann and Elizabeth (Nichols) Frantzen; m. Joette Calabrese, May 15, 1973 (div. 1981); m. Rosemary Ei-Ling Ma, Sept. 24, 1988; 1 child, Norelle Christa Victoria. AB in Chemistry with honors, Hobart Coll., 1968; MD, SUNY, Buffalo, 1972. Diplomate Am. Bd. Neurol. Surgeons, Am. Acad. Pain Specialists, Am. Bd. Forensic Medicine. Resident gen. surgery Wesley Meml. Hosp., Chgo., 1972-73; asst. med. dir. West Side Orgn., Chgo., 1973-74; emergency physician St. James Hosp., Chicago Heights, Ill., 1973-74; from jr. resident to chief resident neurosurgery Georgetown U. Hosp., Washington, Ill., 1975-79; chief resident neurosurgery Washington Vets. Hosp., 1978; pvt. practice Baton Rouge, 1979-81, 81-84; dir. dept. neurosurgery Brookdale Hosp. Med. Ctr., Bklyn., 1984-93; pres. Bklyn. Neurosurg. Svcs., Inc., 1985—; pvt. practice Midland, Tex., 1994-96; mem. Med. Dir. Com., Risk Mgmt. Com., Exec. Quality Assurance Com., 1987-93; mem. Med. Bd. Com., 1985-93, Exec. Bd. Com., 1984-93, Pain Mgmt. Com., 1988-91. Patentee in field; contbr. articles to profl. jours. Mem. adv. bd. Ctr. Latin Affairs, Baton Rouge, 1982-84; mem. Senatorial Inner Cir., 1988; bd. trustees Christian Victory Ctr., Hempstead, N.Y., 1986-88; fellow Am. Coll. Pain Mgmt. Named to Compton-Connolly Guide to Best Physicians in the N.Y. Met. Area; selected by peers as one of Best Doctors in America Ctrl. Region, 1996-97. Fellow ACS, Am. Coll. Forensic Examiners; mem. AMA, AANS (sect. intensive care), Christian Med. and Dental Soc., Am. Assn. Neurologic Surgeons, N.Y. State Neurosurg. Soc., N.Y. Soc. Neurosurgery, Congress Neurologic Surgeons (spine sect., sect. on trauma, sect. on intensive care), Tex. State Med. Soc., So. Med. Soc. Presdl. Roundtable, Shanhai Tiffin Club, Donyin Sister City Assn., Senatorial Inner Circle, Midland C. of C., Midland-Odessa Symphony and Choral Soc., Christian Med.-Dental Soc. Avocations: skiing, painting, poetry, music, cooking. Office: 2205 W Tennessee Ave Midland TX 79701-5953

LOHMILLER, JOHN M. (CHIP LOHMILLER), professional football player; b. Woodbury, Minn., July 16, 1966. Student, U. Minn. Placekicker Washington Redskins, 1988-94, New Orleans Saints, 1995, St. Louis Rams, 1996—. Named kicker The Sporting News NFL All-Pro team, 1991. Played in Pro Bowl, 1991. Office: St Louis Rams 1 Rams Way Bridgeton MO 63045*

LOHMULLER, MARTIN NICHOLAS, bishop; b. Phila., Aug. 21, 1919; s. Martin Nicholas and Mary Frances (Doser) L. B.A., St. Charles Borromeo Sem., Phila., 1942; D.Canon Law, Catholic U. Am., 1947. Ordained priest Roman Catholic Ch., 1944; officialis Diocese Harrisburg, Pa., 1948-63; vicar for religious Diocese of Harrisburg, 1958-70; pastor Our Lady of Good Counsel parish, Marysville, Pa., 1954-64, St. Catherine Laboure Parish, Harrisburg, 1964-68; consecrated Bishop of Ramsbury, 1970; vicar gen. Archdiocese Phila., 1970-94; aux. bishop of Phila., 1970-94; pastor Old St. Mary's Parish, Phila., 1976-89, Holy Trinity Parish, Phila., 1976-89.

LOHNES, WALTER F. W., German language and literature educator; b. Frankfurt, Germany, Feb. 8, 1925; came to U.S., 1948, naturalized, 1954; s. Hans and Dina (Koch) L.; m. Claire Shane, 1950; children: Kristen, Peter, Claudia. Student, U. Frankfurt, 1945-48, Ohio Wesleyan U., 1948-49, U. Mo., 1949-50; PhD, Harvard U., 1961. Asst., Inst. German Folklore, U. Frankfurt, 1947-48; instr. German U. Mo., 1949-50; head dept. German, Phillips Acad., Andover, Mass., 1951-61; asst. prof. Stanford (Calif.) U., 1961-65, assoc. prof., 1965-68, prof., 1969-95, prof. emeritus, 1995—, dir. NDEA Inst. Advanced Study, 1961-68, chmn. dept. German studies, 1973-79, dir. Inst. Basic German, 1975-95, prin. investigator NEH grant, 1978-80; vis. prof. Woehler-Gymnasium, Frankfurt, 1956-57, Middlebury Coll., 1959, U. N.Mex., 1980, 81, 86, U. Vienna, 1990, Coll. de France, Paris, 1992; mem., chmn. various coms. of examiners Ednl. Testing Svc. and Coll. Bd.; chmn. German Grad. Record Exam. Author: (with V. Nollendorfs) German Studies in the United States, 1976, (with F. W. Strothmann) German: A Structural Approach, 1968, 4th rev. edit., 1988; (with E.A. Hopkins) Contrastive Grammar of English and German, 1982, (with Martha Woodmansee) Erkennen und Deuten, 1983, (with J.A. Pfeffer) Grunddeutsch, Texte zur gesprochenen deutschen Gegenwartssprache, 3 vols., 1984, (with D. Benseler and V. Nollendorfs) Teaching German in America: Prolegomena to a History, 1988; contbr. numerous articles to profl. jours.; editor: Unterrichtspraxis, 1971-74. Bd. dirs. Calif. Youth Symphony, 1977-78, Oakland (Calif.) Symphony Youth Orch., 1978-80. Decorated Fed. Order of Merit (Germany); Medal of Honor in Gold (Austria); German Govt. grantee, 1975, 76, 78. Mem. MLA, Am. Assn. Tchrs. German (v.p. 1961-62, 70-71, Outstanding Educator award; hon. 1995), Am. Assn. Applied Linguistics, Am. Coun. on Teaching Fgn. Langs., German Studies Assn., Internat. Vereinigung Germanische Sprach und Literaturwissenschaft. Home: 733 Covington Rd Los Altos CA 94024-4903 Office: Stanford U Dept German Studies Stanford CA 94305-2030

LOHR, HAROLD RUSSELL, bishop; b. Gary, S.D., Aug. 31, 1922; s. Lester ALbert and Nora Helena (Fossum) L.; m. Theola Marie Kottke, June 21, 1947 (div. Dec. 1973); children: Philip Kyle, David Scott, Michael John; m. Edith Mary Morgan, Dec. 31, 1973. BS summa cum laude, S.D. State U., 1947; PhD, U. Calif.-Berkeley, 1950; MDiv summa cum laude, Augustana Theol. Sem., Rock Island, Ill., 1958. Ordained to ministry Augustana Luth. Ch., 1958; installed as bishop, 1980. Research chemist Argonne Nat. lab., Lemont, Ill., 1950-54; pastor Luth. Ch. of Ascension, Northfield, Ill., 1958-70; assoc. exec. Bd. Coll. Edn., N.Y.C., 1970-73; dir. research Div. Profl. Leadership, Phila., 1973-77, assoc. exec., 1977-80; synodical bishop Luth. Ch. in Am., Fargo, N.D., 1980-87; synodical bishop Evang. Luth. Ch. in Am., Moorhead, Minn., 1988-91, ret., 1991; mem. exec. council Luth. Ch. in Am., N.Y.C., 1982-87; mem. commn. of peace and war, 1983-85. Contbg. author: Growth in Ministry, 1980; also articles to sci. jours. Bd. dirs. Gustavus Adolphus Coll., 1980-87, Luther Northwestern Sem., St. Paul, 1980-87, Concordia Coll., Moorhead, Minn., 1988-91; mem. ch. coun. Evang. Luth. Ch. in Am., Chgo., 1990-91, disciplinary hearing officer, 1992-97, interim dir. synodical rels., 1993-94; mem. bd. govs. Chgo. Ctr. Religion and Sci., 1987—; mem. Summit on Environ., Joint Appeal in Religion and Sci., Washington, 1992; mem. adv. bd. Ctr. for Faith and Sci. Exch., Concord, Mass., 1995—. Recipient Suomi award Suomi Coll., 1983. Mem. Phi Kappa Phi. Democrat. Home: 154 Woodridge Rd Marlborough MA 01752-3327

LOHR, WALTER GEORGE, JR., lawyer; b. Balt., Mar. 3, 1944; s. Walter George and Janet Louise (Cartee) L.; children: Lila Meredith, Walter George III, Frederick Boyce. AB, Princeton U., 1966; LLB, Yale U., 1969. Bar: Md. 1969. Law clk.to Hon. Harrison L. Winter U.S. Cir. Ct., Richmond, Va., 1969-70; assoc. Piper & Marbury, Balt., 1970-74, ptnr., 1977-88; ptnr. Hogan & Hartson, Washington, 1992—; asst. atty. gen. State of Md., Balt., 1974-76; prin. Walter G. Lohr Jr., Balt., 1988-92; bd. dirs. Danaher Corp., Washington, Cmty. of Sci., Inc., Balt., Diginet Comm., Inc., Rockville, Md., Sky Alland Rsch., Inc., Laurel, Md.; mem. adv. bd. prudential Venture Ptnrs., N.Y.C., 1985-93. Trustee Balt. Mus. Art, Gilman Sch. Office: Hogan & Hartson 111 S Calvert St Ste 1600 Baltimore MD 21202-6106

LOHRER, RICHARD BAKER, investment consultant; b. Boston, Nov. 30, 1932; s. Leo and Elizabeth Louise (Kaiser) L.; m. Ruth Willa Gutekunst, Feb. 15, 1958; children: Richard Baker, William L., Elizabeth G., Andrew M. AB, Harvard U., 1954; MBA, NYU, 1961. Asst. sec. comml. lending Irving Trust Co. (now Bank of N.Y.), N.Y.C., 1957-64; asst. to v.p. fin. and treas. Nat. Dairy Products Corp. (now Kraft Foods Divsn. of Philip Morris, Inc.), N.Y.C., 1964-71; asst. treas. Martin Marietta Corp. (now Lockheed Martin Corp.), N.Y.C., 1971-74; with Northrop Corp. (now Northrop Grumman Corp.), Los Angeles, 1974-90; treas. Northrop Corp. (now Northrop Grumman Corp.), 1977-87, v.p. trust investments, 1987-90; prin., pres. R.B. Lohrer Assocs., Inc., Palos Verdes Estates, Calif., 1990—. Bd. dirs., pres. Cmty. Helpline, Inc., 1992—; bd. dirs., vice chmn. Presbyn. Ch. (U.S.A.) Investment and Loan Program, Inc., 1995—; bd. dirs., chmn. endowment fund trustees Palos Verdes Comty. Art Assn., 1996—. Mem. L.A. Treas. Club (pres. 1981), Boston Latin Sch. West Coast Alumni Assn. (bd. dirs., pres. 1982-84), Fin. Exec. Inst., Harvard Club of So. Calif., Palos Verdes Country Club, Masons. Republican. Presbyterian.

LOHSE, AUSTIN WEBB, banker; b. N.Y.C., Jan. 22, 1926; s. Henry Vincent and Gertrude (Schroeder) L.; m. Virginia Meyer Butler, May 14, 1949; children: Constance Butler, John Daniel. B.A., Dartmouth Coll., 1947. Credit analyst Irving Trust Co., N.Y.C., 1947-52; with Am. Express Internat. Banking Corp., N.Y.C., 1952-73; asst. v.p. Am. Express Internat. Banking Corp., 1958-61, v.p., 1961-68, sr. v.p., 1968-73; v.p. Charterhouse Group Internat. Inc., N.Y.C., 1973-78, R.T. Madden & Co. Inc., N.Y.C., 1978-81; pres. A.W. Lohse & Co. Inc., N.Y.C., 1981-96; former dir. Am. Express Bank G.M.B.H., Frankfurt, Germany, Am. Express Bank S.P.A., Rome, Am. Express Securities S.A., Paris, LB/Amex Ltd., London, Eng. Mem. Casque and Gauntlet Soc., Beta Theta Pi. Republican. Episcopalian. Clubs: Short Hills (N.J.); Knickerbocker (N.Y.C.). Home: 7 Taylor Rd Short Hills NJ 07078-2225 Office: PO Box 234 Short Hills NJ 07078-0234

LOIELLO, JOHN PETER, public affairs executive, consultant; b. Oceanside, N.Y., Aug. 16, 1943; s. Rosario Paul and Mary Agnes (Butler) L.; m. Elaine Margaret Robinson, June 14, 1944. BA in History, Fordham U., 1965; MA in History, SUNY, Buffalo, 1973; PhD in African History, U. London, 1980. Tchr. history The Gow Sch., South Wales, N.Y., 1967-71; instr. U. Md. (U.K.), London, 1976-78; exec. dir. Dem. Party Com. Abroad, Washington and London, 1978-80; sr. cons. Assn. Am. Chambers of Commerce in Latin Am., Washington, 1980; spl. asst. to chmn. NEH, Washington, 1978-82; assoc. dir. Democracy Prog., Washington, 1982-83; founding exec. dir. Nat. Dem. Inst. for Internat. Affairs, Washington, 1983-85; pres. Gowran Internat., Washington, 1985-93; assoc. dir. ednl. and cultural affairs U.S. Info. Agy., Washington, 1994—; pres. Alcide de Gaspari Found. (USA), Washington, 1987-89. Contbr. articles to profl. jours. Commr. Commn. on Platform Accountability, Dem. Nat. Com., Washington, 1981-85, chmn. fgn. policy subcom., 1980, platform com., 1980; sec. Tax Equity for Ams. Abroad, London, 1977-79; sec. Dems. Abroad, London, 1976-79. African Studies scholar, U. London, 1974-78, grantee, 1975. Mem. Nat. Italian Am. Found., Royal African Soc. Democrat. Roman Catholic. Avocations: travel, racquetball, swimming.

LOIN, E. LINNEA, social work administrator; b. Middletown, Conn., Nov. 20, 1942; d. Alfred William Skinner and Ada Patricia Moore; m. Peter Michael Loin, Sept. 16, 1972. BA, U. Conn., 1965. Social worker State of Conn., Middletown and Hartford, 1964-69; case supr. State of Conn., Hartford, 1969-74; program supr. State of Conn., Hartford, Manchester and, Rockville, Hartford, 1984-90, Willimantic, 1990—; state liaison Nat. Ctr. for Child Abuse and Neglect, Washington, 1985-90. Editor: Connecticut's Children, 1985, Common Ground, 1987-89. Town rep. Charter Cable Adv. Bd. Avocations: swimming, walking, reading, travel, water sports. Home: 29 Cowles Rd West Willington CT 06279-1705 Office: DCYS Region 6 1320 Main St Willimantic CT 06226-1940

LOIS, GEORGE, advertising agency executive; b. N.Y.C., June 26, 1931; s. Harry and Vasilike (Thanasoulis) L.; m. Rosemary Lewandowski, Aug. 27, 1951; children: Harry (dec.), Luke. Student, Pratt Inst., 1949-51, D.F.A. (hon.), 1982. Designer Reba Sochis, 1951; designer CBS-TV, 1954-56; art dir. Sudler & Hennessey, 1956-57, Doyle, Dane, Bernbach, 1958-59; partner, creative dir. Papert, Koenig, Lois, Inc., N.Y.C., 1960-67; chmn. bd., chief exec. officer Lois Holland Callaway Inc., N.Y.C., 1967-78; chmn. bd., creative dir. Lois/EJL, N.Y.C., 1978—. Author: George, Be Careful, 1972, The Art of Advertising, George Lois on Mass Communication, 1977, What's the Big Idea?, 1991, Covering The 60's/George Lois, The Esquire Era, 1996. Served with AUS, 1952-54, Korea. Elected to Art Dirs. Hall of Fame, 1978, Creative Hall of Fame, 1980. Mem. N.Y. Art Dirs. Club (pres. 1971-73). Office: Lois/EJL 40 W 57th St New York NY 10019-4001

LOIUDICE, THOMAS ANTHONY, gastroenterologist, researcher; b. Wilmington, Del., Dec. 3, 1942; s. Dominick and Carmela (Vignola) LoI.; m. Jean Anne Lang, June 20, 1970; children: Christopher, Mark. BS, St. Joseph's U., 1966; DO, Chgo. Coll., 1972. Diplomate Am. Bd. Family Practice, Am. Bd. Internal Medicine, Am. Bd. Nutrition; lic. physician Tenn., Pa., Ind., Ohio, N.Y., Fla. Intern U. Health Ctr. Pitts. Hosp., 1972-73, jr. asst. resident in inernal medicine, 1973-74, sr. asst. resident in internal medicine, 1974, fellow cardiology, 1975; fellow gastroenterology and clin. nutrition Union U., Albany, N.Y., 1975-77; pres. Akron (Ohio) Gastroenterology Assocs., Inc., 1978—; instr. Northeastern Ohio U., Akron, 1977-83, asst. prof., assoc. prof. gastroenterology, 1983-91, prof., 1991—, head subsect. nutrition, 1986—; sec.-treas. Tri-County Emergency Med. Svc., Inc., 1983—; clin. rsch. assoc. Smith, Kline & French Labs., 1983—; mem. sr. teaching staff St. Thomas Med. Ctr., Akron, chief nutrition, head nutritional support team, 1989—; mem. courtesy staff Barberton Citizens Hosp., Barberton, Ohio, Cuyahoga Falls (Ohio) Gen. Hosp.; mem. jr. staff Akron Gen. Med. Ctr.; mem. staff Akron City Hosp.; speaker in field. Contbr. numerous articles to So. Med. Jour., Gastroenterology, Ob/Gyn., Am. Jour. Gastroenterology, Am. Jour. Digestive Diseases, Am. Jour. Clin. Nutrition, N.Y. Jour. Medicine, and other. Grantee William H. Rorer, Smith Kline and French, Ortho Pharm. Corp., Glaxo Pharm. Fellow ACP, Am. Coll. Angiology, Am. Coll. Gastroenterology, Am. Coll. Nutrition, Royal Soc. Medicine (Eng., affiliate); mem. AMA, AAAS, Am. Coll. Emergency Physicians, Am.Soc. Contemporary Medicine and Surgery, Am. Soc. Internal Medicine, Am. Gastroenterology Assn., Am. Assn. for Study Liver Disease, Am. Soc. Gastrointestinal Endoscopy, Am. Fedn. Clin. Rsch., Ohio Med. Assn., Ohio Soc. Internal Medicine, Northeastern Ohio Soc. Gastrointestinal Endoscopy, Summit County Med. Soc. Roman Catholic. Achievements include research in treatment of radiation enteritis with nutritional support and steroids; in zinc and radiation enterities; in tagamet prophylasic in the prevention of gastric ulcers produced by non-steroidal anti-inflamatory agents.

LOKEN, JAMES BURTON, federal judge; b. Madison, Wis., May 21, 1940; s. Burton Dwight and Anita (Nelson) L.; m. Caroline Brevard Hester, July 30, 1966; children: Kathryn Brevard, Kristina Ayres. BS, U. Wis., 1962; LLB magna cum laude, Harvard U., 1965. Law clk. to chief judge Lumbard U.S. Ct. Appeals (2d Cir.), N.Y.C., 1965-66; law clk. to assoc. justice Byron White U.S. Supreme Ct., Washington, 1966-67; assoc. atty. Faegre & Benson, Mpls., 1967-70, ptnr., 1973-90; gen. counsel Pres.'s Com. on Consumer Interests, Office of Pres. of U.S., Washington, 1970; staff asst. Office of Pres. of U.S., Washington, 1970-72; judge U.S. Ct. Appeals (8th cir.), St. Paul, 1991—. Editor Harvard Law Rev., 1964-65. Mem. Minn. State Bar Assn., Phi Beta Kappa, Phi Kappa Phi. Avocations: golf, running. Home: PO Box 75848 Saint Paul MN 55175-0848 Office: Cir Cts Appeals 8th Cir 510 Federal Bldg 316N Robert St Saint Paul MN 55101-1423*

LOKER, ELIZABETH ST. JOHN, newspaper executive; b. Leonardtown, Md., Jan. 1, 1948; d. William Meverell and June Whiting (Farner) L.; m. Donald Scott Rice, Sept. 11, 1980. B.A., George Washington U., 1969. Analyst Met. Washington Council Govt., 1973-74; analyst, programmer Washington Post, 1974-75, mgr. systems research, 1976, dir. data processing, 1976-78, asst. to pub., 1979, v.p. advanced systems, 1979—, v.p. sys. and engring., 1992—. Contbr. chpt. to book. Trustee Greater Washington Research Ctr., also mem. exec. com.; mem. bus. coun. Washington Opera; bd. dirs. Washington Chamber Symphony. Mem. Newspaper Systems Group (past pres.), Assn. for Computing Machinery, Soc. Info. Mgmt., Ops. Research Soc. Am., Inst. Mgmt. Sci. Avocations: antiques; gardening; historic preservation. Office: Washington Post Co 1150 15th St NW Washington DC 20071-0001

LOKEY, FRANK MARION, JR., broadcast executive, consultant; b. Ft. Worth, Oct. 15, 1924; s. Frank Marion Sr. and Corinne (Whaley) L. Student, Smith-Hughes Evening Coll., 1955-59. Announcer, newscaster, disc jockey, morning personality Radio Stas. WAPI, WBRC and WSGN, Birmingham, Ala., 1941-52; pres. WRDW-TV, Augusta, Ga., 1952-55; asst. gen. mgr., mgr. sales, news anchor Sta. WLW-A TV (now named WXIA-TV), Atlanta, 1955-66; co-owner, gen. mgr. Sta. WAIA, Atlanta, 1960-62; S.E. news corr., talk show host CBS News N.Y., N.Y.C., 1960-66; asst. to owner, gen. mgr. Sta. WBIE-AM-FM, Atlanta, 1962-64; asst. to pres., gen. mgr. Stas. KXAB-TV, KXJB-TV, KXMB-TV, Aberdeen, Fargo, Bismarck, S.D., N.D., 1966-67; exec. v.p., gen. mgr. St. WEMT-TV, Bangor, Maine, 1967-70; pres., gen. mgr. Stas. KMOM-TV, KWAB-TV, Odessa-Midland, Big Spring, Tex., 1970-75; exec. v.p., gen. mgr. Sta. KMUV-TV (now named KRBK-TV), Sacramento, Calif., 1975-77; CEO Lokey Enterprises, Inc., Sacramento, L.A., El Centro, Calif., 1977—, also chmn. bd. dirs.; cons., troubleshooter 16 TV stas. nationwide, 1977—; cons., actor 5 movie prodn. cos., Hollywood, Calif., 1980—; cons., outside dir. Anderson Cons., Manhattan, L.I., N.Y., 1981—; network talk show host/news corr. for 7 news orgns. worldwide, 1984—; bd. dirs. Broadcast Audience Behavior Rsch., Manhattan, 1986—, mem. inner circle, 1986—; owner/franchiser The Party Place. Creator, originator approach to real estate mktg. Hon. mem. Imperial County Bd. Suprs., El Centro, 1986—, El Centro City Coun., 1987—. Mem. Am. Legion. Baptist. Avocations: producer big bands parties, movie acting, ancient history, tracing family tree. Home: 2709 Hwy 111 Imperial CA 92251-9772 Office: Lokey Enterprises Inc 626 W Main St El Centro CA 92243-2920

LOKMER, STEPHANIE ANN, public relations counselor; b. Wheeling, W.Va., Nov. 14, 1957; d. Joseph Steven and Mary Ann (Mozney) L. BA in Comm., Bethany Coll., 1980; cert., U. Tübingen, Germany, 1980, Sprach Inst. Tübingen, 1980. V.p., Wheeling Coffee and Spice, W.Va., 1981—; pres. Lokmer & Assocs., Inc., McLean, Va., 1986—. Mem. Pub. Rels. Soc. Am. (accredited), Pub. Rels. Soc. Am. Internat., Counselors Acad., Zeta Tau Alpha. Republican. Roman Catholic. Avocations: flying, sailing, tennis, reading.

LOKYS, LINDA J., dermatologist; b. Poughkeepsie, N.Y., July 30, 1954. BA, Vassar Coll., 1972; MS, Columbia U., 1982; MD, Albany Med. Coll., 1987. Diplomate Am. Bd. Dermatology. Dermatologist Diagnostic Clinic, Clearwater, Fla., 1991—. Office: Diagnostic Clinic 3131 N Mcmullen Booth Rd Clearwater FL 33761-2008

LOLLAR, KATHERINE LOUISE, social worker, therapist; b. Cin., Nov. 1, 1944; d. Robert Miller and Dorothy Marie L.; div.; 2 children. BA, U. Kans., 1966; MSW, Loyola U., 1971. Lic. clin. social worker, Oreg.; cert. social worker, Wash.; bd. cert. diplomate clin. social work. Head activity therapy dept. Fox Children's Ctr., Dwight, Ill., 1966-68; child care worker Madden Mental Health Ctr., Hines, Ill., 1968-69, social worker, 1971-74; pvt. practice therapy Wheaton and Oakbrook, Ill., 1977-82; intern Monticello Care Unit alcohol and drug treatment program, 1983; cons. Residential Facility for Developmentally Disabled Adults, Battle Ground, Wash., 1983-85; therapist Cath. Community Svcs., Vancouver, Wash., 1983-88; outsta. mgr. Wash. Div. Devel. Disabilities, Vancouver, 1987—; pvt. practice therapy Vancouver, 1988—. Troop cons. Columbia River coun. Girl Scouts Am., 1984-86, internat. trip leader, 1993, 96-97, alt. leader, 1995-96, life mem.; mem. Friends of Sangam INternat. Com., 1994-97; mem. Internat. Field Selection Team, 1994-96; mem. Unity of Vancouver. Mem. NASW (sec. Vancouver chpt. 1982-84, co-chair 1985-87, unit rep. Wash. state unit 1990-92), Singles on Sat. Sq. Dance Club, Recycles Sq. Dance Club (pres. 1995-97). Avocations: travel, reading, camping, dancing, hiking, rafting. Office: 650 Officers Row Vancouver WA 98661-3836

LOLLEY, WILLIAM RANDALL, minister; b. Troy, Ala., June 2, 1931; s. Roscoe Lee and Mary Sara (Nunnelee) L.; m. Clara Lou Jacobs, Aug. 28, 1952; children: Charlotte, Pam. AB, Samford U., 1952, DD (hon.), 1980; BD, Southeastern Sem., 1957, ThM, 1958; ThD, Southwestern Sem., 1962; DD (hon.), Wake Forest U., 1971, U. Richmond, 1984; LLD (hon.), Campbell U., 1986; LittD (hon.), Mercer U., 1988. Ordained to ministry So. Bapt. Conv., 1951; pastor First Bapt. Ch., Winston-Salem, N.C., 1962-74; pres. Southeastern Bapt. Theol. Sem., Wake Forest, N.C., 1974-88; pastor First Bapt. Ch., Raleigh, N.C., 1988-90; pastor First Bapt. Ch., Greensboro, N.C., 1990-96, ret., 1996. Author: Crises in Morality, 1963, Bold Preaching of Christ, 1979, Servant Songs, 1994. Democrat. Club: Rotary. Home: 3200 W Market St Greensboro NC 27403-1456

LOLLI, ANDREW RALPH, industrial engineer, former army officer; b. Seatonville, Ill., Oct. 15, 1907; s. Joseph Fredrick and Adolfa (Fiocchi) L. Student Armed Forces Staff Coll., 1950, Nat. War Coll., 1957, N.Y. Inst. Fin., 1971; BS, Dickinson Coll., 1952; postgrad. Fordham U., 1952. Enlisted in U.S. Army, 1940, advanced through grades to maj. gen., 1960; chief plans and priorities Allied Forces So. Europe, 1952-56; comdr. Air Def. units, N.Y. and San Francisco, 1957-60; comdr. XX U.S.A. Corps, 1961-62, XV, 1962-63, comdr. Western NORD Region, Hamilton AFB, Calif., 1963-66; ret., 1966; exec. asst. Hughes Aircraft Co., Fullerton, Calif., 1967; dir. gen. services State of Calif., Sacramento, 1967-70; v.p. Sigmatics, Newport Beach, Calif., 1970-73, Intercoast Investments Co., Sacramento, 1975-76; pres. Andrew R. Lolli Assocs. Inc., San Francisco, 1973—, Lolman Inc., San Francisco, 1976—; commr. Small Bus. Adv. Commn., San Francisco, 1989-93; pres. bd. trustees Commonwealth Equity Trust, 1974-80; vice chmn. Calif. Pub. Works bd., 1967-69; mem. adv. panel Nat. Acad. Scis. and Engring. in Research, Washington, 1968-70; mem. fed., state and local govt. adv. panel Fed. Gen. Services, Washington, 1968-69. Bd. dirs. Columbia Boys Park Club, San Francisco, Lab. for Survival, San Francisco; mem. Presido of San Francisco Restoration Adv. Bd., 1994. Decorated D.S.M., Legion of Merit with oak leaf cluster, Bronze Star with oak leaf cluster; named Man of Year, Italian Sons of Am., 1964. Mem. Nat. Assn. Uniformed Services, Assn. U.S. Army, Ret. Officers Assn. Roman Catholic. Developed short notice inspection system for army air def. missiles, 1960. Home: 1050 N Point St San Francisco CA 94109-8302 Office: 286 Jefferson St San Francisco CA 94133-1126

LOMAN, MARY LAVERNE, retired mathematics educator; b. Stratford, Okla., June 10, 1928; d. Thomas D. and Mary Ellen (Goodwin) Glass; m. Coy E. Loman, Dec. 23, 1944; 1 child, Sandra Leigh Loman Easton. BS, U. Okla., 1956, MA, 1957, PhD, 1961. Grad. asst., then instr. U. Okla., Norman, 1956-61; asst. prof. math. U. Ctrl. Okla., Edmond, 1961-62; assoc. prof. U. Cen. Okla., Edmond, 1962-66, prof., 1966-93; prof. emeritus U. Ctrl. Okla., Edmond, 1993—; ret., 1993. NSF fellow, 1965-67. Mem. Math. Assn. Am., Nat. Coun. Tchrs. Math., Okla. Coun. Tchrs. Math. (v.p. 1972-76), Higher Edn Alumni Coun. Okla., VFW Aux., Delta Kappa Gamma. Home: 2201 Tall Oaks Trl Edmond OK 73003-2325 *Strive to do each task to the best of your ability. Then don't look back, saying "If only I had ...", but look forward to the next with the comfort of knowing you gave your very best effort.*

LOMAS, BERNARD TAGG, college president emeritus; b. Mackinaw City, Mich., Aug. 14, 1924; s. Percy L. and Eva (Tagg) L.; m. Barbara Jean West, June 21, 1947; children: Paul Neil, David Mark. AB, Albion Coll., 1946, DD, 1965; BD, Oberlin Grad. Sch. Theology, 1948; MDiv., Vanderbilt U., 1967; LLD, Adrian U., 1983. Ordained minister Meth. Ch., 1948. Minister William St. Meth. Ch., Delaware, Ohio, 1950-54; counsellor to students Ohio Wesleyan U., 1950-54; sr. minister Trinity Meth. Ch., Portsmouth, Ohio, 1954-60; sr. minister heading staff of five ministers Epworth-Euclid Ch., Univ. Circle, Cleve., 1960-70; pres. Albion (Mich.) Coll., 1970-83, chancellor, 1983-88, pres. emeritus, 1988—; cons. Am. Enterprise Inst., Washington, 1980-81; pers. and human rels. cons. to U.S. and fgn. bus. Author 5 books; contbr. numerous articles to edn. and religious jours. Organizer, head Citizens Com. for Law Enforcement, Portsmouth, 1957-58; founding mem. pres. Christian Residences Found.; bd. dirs. Goodwill Industries Cleve., 1964-70; trustee St. Lukes Hosp., Cleve., 1965-70; bd. govs. Greater Mich. Found., 1978-83; bd. dirs. Christian Children's Fund, 1978-81; counselor Heritage Found., Washington, 1984—, Bd. Inst. Am. Univs., Aix En Provence-France, 1988—. Mem. Masons, Shriners, Rotary.

LOMAS, ERIC JAMES, investment banker; b. N.Y.C., Mar. 12, 1947; s. James and Florence (Marletti) L.; m. Florence Jean Mauchant, Jan. 18, 1992. BS cum laude, L.I. U., 1970; MBA, NYU, 1972. Cert. CFA. Analyst Troster, Singer & Co., N.Y.C., 1972-76; cons. Deloitte Haskins & Sells, N.Y.C., 1976-85; mng. dir. Gruntal & Co., N.Y.C., 1985-89; pres. Hill Thompson Group, Ltd., N.Y.C., 1989—; chmn. Rexel, Inc., Coral Gables; dir. Goodland Foods, Inc. Mem. adv. bd. L.I. U., grad. sch. bus. NYU. With USNR, Vietnam. Mem. N.Y. Athletic Club. Avocations: skiing, sailing, biking, photography. Office: Hill Thompson Group Ltd 437 Madison Ave New York NY 10022-7001

LOMAS, LYLE WAYNE, agricultural research administrator, educator; b. Monett, Mo., June 8, 1953; s. John Junior and Helen Irene Lomas; m. Connie Gail Frey, Sept. 4, 1976; children: Amy Lynn, Eric Wayne. BS, U. Mo., 1975, MS, 1976; PhD, Mich. State U., 1979. Asst. prof., animal scientist S.E. Agrl. Rsch. Ctr., Kans. State U., Parsons, 1979-85, assoc. prof., 1985-92, prof., 1992—, head, 1985—. Contbr. articles to refereed sci. jours. Mem. Am. Soc. Animal Sci., Am. Registry Profl. Animal Scientists, Am. Forage and Grassland Coun., Rsch. Ctr. Adminstrs. Soc. (bd. dirs. 1993—), Rotary (bd. dirs. Parsons 1992—, v.p. 1994-95, pres. 1995-96), Phi Kappa Phi, Gamma Sigma Delta. Presbyterian. Achievements include research in ruminant nutrition, forage utilization by grazing stocker cattle. Home: 24052 Douglas Rd Dennis KS 67341-9014 Office: Kans State U SE Agrl Rsch Ctr PO Box 316 Parsons KS 67357-0316

LOMAX, DONALD HENRY, physician; b. Davison County, N.C., Dec. 30, 1921; s. William Henry and Bessie Idalia (Young) L.; m. Marie Smith, Dec. 14, 1947; children: Susan, Don, Melissa, Sally, Ann, Laurie, John. BS, Wake Forest U., 1948, MD, 1951. Diplomate Am. Bd. Family Practice. Intern Letterman Gen. Hosp., San Francisco, 1951-52, Mather AFB Hosp., 1952-53; attending physician Rowan Regional Med. Ctr., 1953—, chief of staff, trustee; pvt. practice Salisbury, N.C., 1953—. Past med. dir. N.C. Cerebral Palsy Assn. Capt. USAF, 1942-46, 51-53. Fellow Am. Acad. Family Physicians; mem. AMA, N.C. Acad. Family Physicians (past dir., past chmn. sci. com.), N.C. Med. Soc., So. Med. Assn. Office: 1710 W Innes St Salisbury NC 28144-2508

LOMAX, JOHN H., financial service company executive; b. Macon, Ga., Mar. 28, 1924; s. John H. and Regis (Garrity) L.; m. Ann E. Davis, Dec. 30, 1947; children: J. Harvey, Jan (Mrs. Ben Teal). BBA, U. Ga., 1948; student, U. N.C., 1962. Exec. v.p. Am. Credit Corp., Charlotte, N.C., 1958-76; exec. v.p. Assocs. Corp. of N.Am., Dallas, 1976-87; dir. Gulf Coast Consol. Office Resolution Trust Corp., Houston, 1989-91, dir. north ctrl. region, 1991-92; v.p. S.W. region Resolution Trust Corp., Dallas, 1992-94; chmn., CEO Policy Funding Corp., Dallas, 1994-95; chmn. Utility Gen. Corp., Dallas, 1997—. Bd. dirs. Dallas Summer Musicals. Capt. USAF, 1942-46. Home: 4215 Glenaire Dr Dallas TX 75229-4140 Office: Utility General Corp 16901 Dallas Pkwy Dallas TX 75248-1933

LOMAX, KENNETH MITCHELL, agricultural engineering educator; b. Wilmington, Del., Nov. 4, 1947; s. Ernest S. and Martha W. (Mitchell) L.; m. Nancy R. Beltz, Oct. 16, 1971. BS in Chem. Engring., Lafayette Coll., Easton, Pa., 1969; MS in Entomology, U Del., Newark, 1971; PhD in Agrl. Engring., U. Md., College Park, 1976. Registered profl. engr., Del. Asst. prof. Horn Point Environ. Labs. U. Md., Cambridge, 1976-80; asst. prof. agrl. engring. U. Del., Newark, 1980-85, assoc. prof. agrl. engring., 1985—; pres. faculty senate U. Del., 1992-93. Contbr. articles to profl. jours. Recipient Excellence In Teaching award U. Del. and Lindbach Found., 1988; named Faculty Mem. of Yr., Panhellenic Coun., 1993. Mem. Am. Soc. Agrl. Engrs. (assoc.), Am. Mushroom Inst. (dir. 1987-90). Avocation: outdoor activities. Office: U Del Bio Resources Engring Dept Newark DE 19717

LOMBARD, ARTHUR J., judge; b. N.Y.C., Nov. 30, 1941; s. Maurice and Martha (Simons) L.; m. Frederica Koller, Aug. 18, 1968; children: David, Lisa. BS in Acctg. magna cum laude, Columbia U., 1961; JD, Harvard U., 1964. Bar: N.Y. 1964, U.S. Ct. Appeals (2d cir.) 1965, U.S. Supreme Ct. 1970, U.S. Ct. Appeals (6th cir.) 1972, Mich. 1976. Law clk. to J. Edward Lumbard chief judge U.S. Ct. Appeals (2d cir.), N.Y.C., 1964-65; teaching fellow law sch. Harvard U., Cambridge, Mass., 1965-66; instr. Orientation Program in Am. Law, Assn. Am. Law Schs., Princeton, N.J., 1966; prof. law Wayne State U., Detroit, 1966-87, assoc. dean law, 1978-85; prof. Detroit Coll. Law, 1987-94, dean, chief adminstrv. officer, 1987-93; judge Wayne County (Mich.) Cir. Ct., 1994—; chmn. revision of Mich. class action rule com. Mich. Supreme Ct., 1980-83; reporter rules com. U.S. Dist. Ct. (ea. dist.) Mich., 1978-94. Contbr. articles to profl. jours. Mem. Mich. Civil Rights Commn., 1991-94, co-chmn., 1992-93, chmn. 1993-94. Office: 1913 City County Bldg Detroit MI 48226

LOMBARD, DAVID NORMAN, lawyer; b. Seattle, Dec. 6, 1949; s. John Cutler and Dororthy Marie (Brandt) L.; m. Susan Elliott, Oct. 22, 1983; children: Matthew, Jeffrey, Megan. BA, U. Wash., 1973; JD, U. Puget Sound, Tacoma, 1976. Bar: Wash. 1976, U.S. Dist. Ct. (we. dist.) Wash. 1976, U.S. Dist. Ct. (ea. dist.) Wash. 1983, U.S. Ct. Appeals (9th cir.) 1976. Law clk. Wash. State Supreme Ct., Olympia, 1976-77; assoc. Schwabe, Williamson, Ferguson & Burdell, Seattle, 1977-82, ptnr., 1983-93; Jameson Babbitt Stites & Lombard Seattle, 1994—. Mem. Wash. Athletic Club. Presbyterian. Office: Jameson Babbitt Stites & Lombard 999 3rd Ave Ste 1900 Seattle WA 98104-4001

LOMBARD, JOHN JAMES, JR., lawyer; b. Phila., Dec. 27, 1934; s. John James and Mary R. (O'Donnell) L.; m. Barbara Mallon, May 9, 1964; children: John James, William M., James G., Laura K., Barbara E. BA cum laude, LaSalle Coll., Phila., 1956; JD, U. Pa., 1959. Bar: Pa. 1960. Assoc., Obermayer, Rebmann, Maxwell & Hippel, Phila., 1960-65, ptnr., 1966-84, fin. ptnr., 1980-84; ptnr. Morgan, Lewis & Bockius, LLP, Phila., 1985—, mgr. personal law sect., 1986-90, vice chair personal law sect., 1990-92, chair, 1992—; sec., dir. Airline Hydraulics Corp., Phila., 1969—; mem. adv. com. on decedents estates laws Joint State Govt. Commn., 1992—, mem. subcom. on powers of atty., 1993—; co-chair So. Jersey Ethics Alliance, 1993—. Bd. dirs. Redevel. Authority Montgomery County, Pa., 1980-87, Gwynedd-Mercy Coll., Gwynedd Valley, Pa., 1980-89, LaSalle College High Sch., Wyndmoor, Pa., 1991—. Recipient Treat award Nat. Coll. Probate Judges, 1992. Mem. ABA (chmn. com. simplification security transfers 1972-76, chmn. membership com. 1972-82, mem. council real property, probate and trust law sect. 1979-85, sec. 1985-87, div. dir. probate div. 1987-89, chair elect 1989-90, chair 1990-91, co-chair Nat. Conf. Lawyers & Corp. Fiduciaries), Pa. Bar Assn. (ho. of dels. 1979-81), Phila. Bar Assn. (chmn. probate sect. 1972), Am. Coll. Trust and Estate Counsel (editor Probate Notes 1983, bd. regents 1986-91, mem. exec. com. 1988-91, elder law com. 1993—), Internat. Acad. Estate and Trust Law (exec. com. 1984-88, 90—), Am. Bar Found., Internat. Fish and Game Assn. Clubs: Union League (Phila.); Ocean City (N.J.) Marlin and Tuna, Ocean City Yacht. Co-author: Durable Power of Attorney and Health Care Derectives 1984, 3d edit. 1994; contbr. articles to profl. jours. Office: Morgan Lewis & Bockius LLP 2000 One Logan Sq Philadelphia PA 19103

LOMBARD, JUDITH MARIE, human resource policy specialist; b. Harmony, Maine, June 7, 1944; d. Clayton Selden and Helen Mae (Wentworth) L. BA, U. Maine, 1966; MPA, U. So. Calif., 1982, D of Pub. Adminstrn., 1987. Psychodramatist HEW, Washington, 1966-68; creative arts therapist U.S. Health and Human Svcs., Washington, 1968-87; sr. therapist Mental Health Svcs., Washington, 1987-88; tng. officer USDA, Washington, 1988-92; mem. adj. faculty U. So. Calif., L.A., 1988—; employee devel. specialist U.S. Office Personnel Mgmt., Washington, 1992—; pvt. cons., Alexandria, Va., 1988—; speaker on fed. law at nat. confs. and meetings. Author (book chpt.) How Public Organizations Work, 1991, (handbook) Supervisor's Guide, 1993, U.S. Training Policy Handbook, 1996; contbr. articles to profl. jours. Active Maine State Soc., Washington, 1980—; mem. fundraising bd. doctorial assn. U. So. Calif., Washington, 1986—; active Del Ray Citizens Assn., Alexandria, 1982—. Recipient Dorothy Dix award St. Elizabeth's Hosp., Washington, 1982. Mem. Am. Soc. Pub. Adminstrn., Am. Soc. Tng. and Devel., Nat. Therapeutic Recreation Soc., Am. Therapeutic Recreation Assn. (pres. Washington chpt. 1990), Med. Soc. Washington (pres. 1990), Nat. Recreation and Parks Assn. (elections chair 1990, 91), D.C. Jungian Soc. Office: US Office Personnel Mgmt 1900 E St NW Washington DC 20415-0001

LOMBARD, RICHARD SPENCER, lawyer; b. Panama Canal Zone, Jan. 28, 1928; s. Eugene C. and Alice R. (Quinn) L.; m. Arlene Olson, Dec. 27, 1952; children: Anne, James. AB, Harvard U., 1949, JD, 1952. Bar: N.Y. 1953, Tex. 1971. Assoc. Haight, Gardner, Poor & Havens, N.Y.C., 1952-55; mem. law dept. Creole Petroleum Corp., Caracas, Venezuela, 1955-65, mgr., 1963-65; gen. counsel Esso Chem. Co., N.Y.C., 1966-69; assoc. gen. counsel Humble Oil & Refining Co., Houston, 1969-71; asst. gen. counsel Exxon Corp., N.Y.C., 1971-72, assoc. gen. counsel, 1972-73, gen. counsel, 1973-93, v.p., 1980-93; counsel Baker & Botts, Dallas, 1993-96; trustee Parker Sch. Fgn. and Comparative Law, Columbia U., 1977—, Southwestern Legal Found., 1978, Practicing Law Inst., 1980. Author: American-Venezuelan Private International Law, 1965. Served with AC AUS, 1946-47. Fellow Am. Bar Found.; mem. Am. Law Inst., Am. Arbitration Assn. (bd. dirs., chmn. bd. 1983-86), N.Y. State Bar Assn., Assn. Bar City of N.Y., State Bar of Tex., Dallas Bar Assn., Univ. Club (N.Y.C.). Address: 3227 McKinney Ave Apt 8 G Dallas TX 75204 Address: 7401 N Cobblestone Rd Tucson AZ 85718 also: 108 Eastbank Ct N Hudson WI 54016

LOMBARDI, CORNELIUS ENNIS, JR., lawyer; b. Portland, Oreg., Feb. 12, 1926; s. Cornelius Ennis and Adele (Volk) L.; m. Ann Vivian Foster, Nov. 24, 1954; children—Cornelius Ennis, Gregg Foster, Matthew Volk. B.A., Yale, 1949; J.D., U. Mich., 1952. Bar: Mo. bar. Since practiced in Kansas City, Mo.; mem. firm Blackwell, Sanders, Matheny, Weary & Lombardi, 1957-92, of counsel. Former pres. Kansas City Mus. Assn., Estate Planning Coun. of Kansas City; trustee Pembroke Country Day Sch.; chmn. soc. of fellows Nelson Gallery Found. Served with USMCR, 1944-46. Mem. Order of Coif, Phi Alpha Delta, Kansas City Country Club. Home: 5049 Wornall Rd Kansas City MO 64112-2423 Office: 2 Pershing Sq 2300 Main St Ste 1100 Kansas City MO 64108-2415

LOMBARDI, DENNIS M., lawyer; b. L.A., May 15, 1951; s. Peter Joseph and Jean (Nelson) L.; m. Suan Choo Lim, Jan. 9, 1993; children: Alexis Jeanne, Erin Kalani. BA, U. Hawaii, 1974; JD summa cum laude, U. Santa Clara, 1977. Bar: Calif. 1977, U.S. Dist. Ct. Hawaii, 1981. Assoc. Frandzel & Share, Beverly Hills, Calif., 1977-79; pvt. practice Capistrano Beach, Calif., 1979-81; ptnr. Case, Bigelow & Lombardi, Honolulu, 1982—. Office: Case Bigelow & Lombardi 737 Bishop St Fl 26 Honolulu HI 96813-3201

LOMBARDI, EUGENE PATSY, orchestra conductor, violinist, educator, recording artist; b. North Braddock, Pa., July 7, 1923; s. Nunzio C. and Mary (Roberto) L.; m. Jacqueline Sue Davis, Mar. 1955; children: Robert, Genanne. BA, Westminster Coll., 1948; MA, Columbia U., 1948; Edn. Specialist, George Peabody Coll., 1972; MusD, Westminster Coll., 1981. Band dir. Lincoln High Sch., Midland, Pa., 1948-49; orch. dir. Male High Sch., Louisville, 1949-50, Phoenix Union High Sch., 1950-57; orch. dir., prof. Ariz. State U., Tempe, 1957-89. Condr. Phoenix Symphonette, 1954-61, 70-73, Phoenix Symphony Youth Orch., 1956-66, Phoenix Pops Orch., 1971-83, Fine Arts String Orch., 1995-97. Condr. fine arts strings, Phoenix, 1995—. With USAAF, 1943-46. Decorated Bronze Star; named Outstanding Grad. Westminster Coll., 1948; recipient Alumni Achievement award, 1976, gold medal Nat. Soc. Arts and Letters, 1973, Disting. Tchr. award Ariz. State U. Alumni, 1974, Phoenix Appreciation award, 1983. Mem. Music Educators Nat. Conf., Am. String Tchrs. Assn. (pres. Ariz. unit 1965-67), Am. Fedn. Musicians, Ariz. Music Educators Assn. (pres. higher edn. sect. 1973-75, Excellence in Teaching Music award 1989), Ind. Order Foresters, Phi Delta Kappa, Phi Mu Alpha, Alpha Sigma Phi. Republican. Presbyterian. Home: 920 E Manhatton Dr Tempe AZ 85282-5520

LOMBARDI, FREDERICK MCKEAN, lawyer; b. Akron, Ohio, Apr. 1, 1937; s. Leonard Anthony and Dorothy (McKean) L.; m. Margaret J. Gessler, Mar. 31, 1962; children: Marcus M., David G., John A., Joseph F. BA, U. Akron, 1960; LLB, Case Western Res., 1962. Bar: Ohio 1962, U.S. Dist. Ct. (no. dist.) Ohio 1964, U.S. Ct. Appeals (6th cir.) 1966. Prin., shareholder Buckingham, Doolittle & Burroughs, Akron, 1962—, chmn. comml. law and litigation dept., 1989—. Bd. editors Western Res. Law Rev., 1961-62. Trustee, mem. exec. com., v.p. Ohio Ballet, 1985-93; trustee Walsh Jesuit H.S., 1987-90, Akron Golf Charitise, Summa Health Sys. Found., Downtown Akron Partnership; chmn. formation com., 1st pres. St. Hilary Parish Coun., trustee, 1976-78; past chmn. World Series of Golf. Mem. Ohio State Bar Assn. (coun. of dels. 1995—), Akron Bar Assn. (trustee 1991-94), Case Western Res. U. Law Alumni Assn. (soc. of benchers 1989, bd. govs. 1995-98), Soc. Benchers, Fairlawn Swim and Tennis Club (past pres.), Portage Country Club (fin. com.), Akron City Club, Rotary (fin. com. Akron), Pi Sigma Alpha. Democrat. Roman Catholic. Office: Buckingham Doolittle & Burroughs 50 S Main St Akron OH 44308-1828

LOMBARDI, JOHN BARBA-LINARDO, broadcasting executive; b. Toronto, Ont., Can., Dec. 4, 1915; s. Léonardo and Teresa L.; m. Antonia Lena Crisologo, July 4, 1949; children: Leonard, Theresa Maria, Donina Antonia. Grad. high sch., Toronto; student, Toronto Cen. Tech. Sch. Trumpet player Benny Palmer's Band, London, Ont., 1930-42; with Lombardi Grocery; later pres. Lombardi Italian Foods Ltd.; producer Italian radio programs Stas. CHUM, CKFH, from 1946; founder, pres., mng. dir. CHIN Radio/TV Internat. (multilingual broadcasting), 1966—; pres. Bravo Records & Music Co. Ltd., Carpejon Investments Ltd., Italian Shows Ltd.; chmn., pres. Radio 1540 Ltd. Originator ann. Johnny Lombardi Talent and Song Festival. Originator CHIN Internat. Picnic, free ann. festival ethnocultural music, song, dance; mem. Toronto Gen. Hosp Found.;

founding dir., gov. Villa Colombo; founding officer Italian Immigrant Aid Soc.; trustee Nat. Arts Centre Corp., 1982-85; patron Ont. Mus. Arts Ctre, 1989—; founder, host Italian Spring Festival, 1988; bd. dirs. Can. Coun. Christian and Jews, 1990; supporting mem. numerous civic organs., hosps. univs. and schs. including Easter Seal Soc., Boys/Girls Clubs Can., Kidney Found. Can., Cath. Charities, Hebrew Culture Orgn. Can., Can. Citizenship Found., Can. Opera Co., United Way; supporter elimination of apartheid in South Africa, eliminatin of anti-semitism, 1992; founding mem. Met. Toronto Police Community Projects Found., 1990. Sgt. Can. Army, 1942-46, ETO. Recipient Ethnic Entrepreneur of Yr. award, 1994, Fed. Citation of Citizenship, 1994, Silver medal for Elimination of Racial Discrimination, 1995, Communicator of Yr. award, 1997; named Officer Brother-Order of St. John, 1994. Mem. Broadcast Execs. Soc., Can. Assn. Ethnic (Radio) Broadcasters (pres. 1981), Toronto Musicians Assn. Can., Can. Italian Bus. and Profl. Assn., Toronto, Soc. for Recognition of Can. Talent Inc., Ont. Multicultural Assn. (patron), Can. Coun., Nat. Coun. Boy Scouts Can. (hon.), Can./Holland 1945 Liberation Soc., Order of Can., Order of Ontario, Variety Club (award 1985). Office: CHIN, 622 College St, Toronto, ON Canada M6G 1B6

LOMBARDI, JOHN V., university administrator, historian; b. Los Angeles, Aug. 19, 1942; s. John and Janice P. Lombardi; m. Cathryn Lee; children: John Lee, Mary Ann. B.A., Pomona Coll., 1963; M.A., Columbia U., 1964, Ph.D., 1968. Prof. contratado Escuela de Historia, Universidad Central de Venezuela, Caracas, 1967; lectr. history Ind. U. S.E., Jeffersonville, 1967-68; asst. prof. Ind. U. S.E., 1968-69; vis. asst. prof. Ind. U., Bloomington, 1968-69; asst. prof. history Ind. U., 1969-71, assoc. prof., 1971-77, prof., 1977-87, dir. Latin Am. studies program, 1971-74, dean Internat. Programs, 1978-85, dean Coll. Arts and Scis., 1985-87; prof. history Johns Hopkins U., 1987-89, provost, vp. for acad. affairs, 1987-89; pres. U. Fla., Gainesville, 1989—. Author: (with others) Venezuelan History: A Comprehensive Working Bibliography, 1977, People and Places in Colonial Venezuela, 1976, Venezuela: Search for Order, Dream of Progress, 1982; Mem. editorial bd.: (with others) UCLA Statis. Abstracts Latin Am, 1977—; contbr. (with others) articles to profl. jours. Fulbright-Hayes research fellow, 1965-66. Mem. Am. Hist. Assn., Latin Am. Studies Assn., Pan Am. Inst. Geography and History, Academia Nacional de la Historia (corr. mem .). Office: U Fla Office of Pres Gainesville FL 32611*

LOMBARDI, KENT BAILEY, insurance company administrator; b. Keene, N.H., Nov. 24, 1955; s. Louis Richard Lombardi and Jean (Thurston) Tacy; m. June M. Havas, Aug. 12, 1978; children: Marina, Anthony. BS in Mktg. & Mgmt., Siena Coll., 1977. CPCU. Claims adjuster Crawford & Co., Poughkeepsie, N.Y., 1977-78; adjuster-in-charge Crawford & Co., Middletown, N.Y., 1978-82, 83-85; adjuster Ft. Orange Claims, Clifton Park, N.Y., 1982-83; claims examiner Frontier Ins. Co., Monticello, N.Y., 1985-87, asst. claims mgr. property & casualty, 1987-92; asst. claims mgr. med./dental malpractice Frontier Ins. Co., Monticello & Rock Hill, N.Y., 1992-94; v.p., claims mgr. med./dental malpractice Frontier Ins. Co., Rock Hill, N.Y., 1993-96, v.p. med./dental malpractice, 1996—. Mem. Mid Hudson Claims Assn. Avocations: skiing, golf, music. Office: Frontier Ins Co Lake Louise Marie Rd Rock Hill NY 12775

LOMBARDINI, CAROL ANN, lawyer; b. Framingham, Mass., Dec. 29, 1954; d. Harry and Sarah (Scarano) L. m. William L. Cole, Apr. 23, 1983; children: Kevin Daniel, Kristin Elizabeth. BA, U. Chgo., 1976; JD, Stanford U., 1979. Bar: Calif. 1979. Assoc. Meserve, Mumper & Hughes, L.A., 1979-80, Proskauer Rose Goetz & Mendelsohn, L.A., 1980-82; from counsel to sr. v.p. legal and bus. affairs Alliance of Motion Picture and TV Prodrs., Encino, Calif., 1982—; trustee Dirs. Guild Contract Adminstrn., Encino, 1982—, Prodr.-Writers Guild Pension & Health Plans, Burbank, Calif., 1983—, SAG-Prodr. Pension & Health Plans, Burbank, 1986—, Dirs. Guild-Prodr. Pension & Health Plans, L.A., 1987—. Avocations: hiking, cooking. Office: Alliance Motion Picture & TV Prodrs 15503 Ventura Blvd Encino CA 91436-3103

LOMBARDO, GAETANO (GUY LOMBARDO), venture capitalist; b. Salemi, Italy, Feb. 4, 1940; came to U.S., 1947; s. Salvatore and Anna Maria L.; Sc.B. with honors, Brown U., 1962; Ph.D. in Physics, Cornell U., 1971; m. Nancy B. Emerson, Sept. 2, 1967 (div. 1993); children: Nicholas Emerson, Maryanne Chilton. Sr. staff Arthur D. Little Inc., Cambridge, Mass., 1967-77; v.p. logistics Morton Salt Co., Chgo., 1977-78; dir. logistics and distbn. Gould Inc., Chgo., 1978-80; corp. dir. Bendix Corp., Southfield, Mich., 1980-82; group v.p. Bendix Indsl. Group, 1982-84; founder, pres., chief exec. officer Comau Productivity Systems, 1984-86; pres. Nelmar Corp., 1983-90; chmn., chief exec. officer Courtesy Mfg. Co., Elk Grove, Ill., 1988—; pres. Poplar Industries, Inc., 1989—; vis. prof. ops. mgmt. Boston U., 1973. Contbr. articles on physics and bus. mgmt. to profl. jours. Office: Courtesy Mfg Co 1300 Pratt Blvd Elk Grove Village IL 60007-5711

LOMBARDO, JOSEPH SAMUEL, acoustical engineer; b. Chgo., Aug. 16, 1946; s. Joseph and Frances Lombardo; m. Maureen Frick, May 25, 1974; children: Christopher, Jennifer. BS in Elec. Engring., U. Ill., 1969; MS in Elec. Engring., Johns Hopkins U., 1974. Registered profl. engr., Ill. Instrumentation specialist Johns Hopkins U./Applied Physics Lab., Laurel, Md., 1970-78, sect. supr. acoustics group, 1978-84, program mgr. Navy undersea rsch., 1984—, program mgr. for info. tech. devel., 1996—; com. mem. Adv. Group to Asst. Sec. of Navy, Washington, 1990. Contbr. articles to profl. jours. Bd. govs. Cape St. Claire (Md.) Improvement Assn., 1985. Mem. IEEE, Nat. Security Indsl. Assn. (com. 1992-95), Cape St. Claire Yacht Club (commodore 1984-86), Eta Kappa Nu, Tau Beta Pi, Sigma Tau. Achievements include patents for vibration sensor, large aperture element location sys., towing configuration hardware for geophys. exploration sys.; avocation: sailing. Office: Johns Hopkins U Applied Physics Lab Johns Hopkins Rd Laurel MD 20723

LOMBARDO, MICHAEL JOHN, lawyer, educator; b. Willimantic, Conn., Mar. 25, 1927; s. Frank Paul and Mary Margaret (Longo) L.; children: Nancy C., Claire M. BS, U. Conn., 1951, MS, 1961, JD, 1973. Bar: Conn. 1974, U.S. Dist. Ct. Conn. 1975, U.S. Supreme Ct. 1979, U.S. Ct. Appeals (2d cir.) 1980. Div. controller Jones & Laughlin Steel Corp., Willimantic, 1956-67; adminstrv. officer health ctr. U. Conn., Hartford, 1968-69; dir. adminstrv. svcs. South Central Community Coll., New Haven, 1969-70; asst. dir. adminstrn. Norwich (Conn.) Hosp., 1970-77; asst. atty. gen. State of Conn., Hartford, 1977-92; pvt. practice, Willimantic, 1992—; adj. asst. prof. U. Hartford, 1961-70; adj. prof. bus. Old Dominion U., 1973-81; adj. lectr. in law and bus. Ea. Conn. State U., 1973—, disting. adj. faculty, 1990. Vol. Windham Ctr. (Conn.) Fire Dept. Sgt. U.S. Army, 1945-46, 1st lt. USAFR, 1951-53, col. USAFR, 1953-87, col. USAF ret., 1987. Named Disting. Mil. Grad., U. Conn., 1951. Mem. AAUP, VFW, Internat. Platform Assn., Retired Officers Assn., Conn. Bar Assn., Windham County Bar Assn., Mensa Internat., Am. Legion, Lions (bd. dirs. Willimantic chpt. 1960-64). Home: 35 Oakwood Dr Windham CT 06280-1520 Office: 6 Storrs Rd Ste 2 Willimantic CT 06226-4006

LOMBARDO, PHILIP JOSEPH, broadcasting company executive; b. Chgo., June 13, 1935; s. Joseph Pete and Josephine (Franco) L.; m. Marilyn Ann Tellefsen, June 22, 1963; children: Dean, Jeffrey. Student, U. Ill., 1953-55; BA in Speech, Journalism and Radio/TV, U. Mo., 1958, postgrad. speech, 1958; grad. advanced mgmt. program, Harvard U., 1976. Account exec. Sta. WWCA, Ind., 1959-60; producer-dir. Sta. WBBM-TV, Chgo., 1960-65; program mgr., acting gen. mgr. Sta. WLWT, Cin., 1965-67; v.p., gen. mgr. Sta. WGHP-TV, N.C., 1968-73; pres., chief exec. officer Corinthian Broadcasting Corp., N.Y.C., 1973-82; chmn., pres., chief exec. officer Champlain Communications Corp., N.Y.C., 1982-84; mng. gen. ptnr. Citadel Communications Co. Ltd., N.Y.C., 1982—; chmn., pres., chief exec. officer Citadel Communications, Co. Ltd., C.C.C. Communications Corp., Lombardo Communications II, Inc., P.J.L. Investments, Inc., N.Y.C., 1984—; mng. gen. ptnr., nat. sales rep. U.S. and Can. TV stas. Can. Communications Co., Toronto, 1985—; mng. gen. ptnr. Coronet Communications Co., N.Y.C., 1985—, Capital Comm. Co., Inc., 1994—, Citadel Comm., LLC, 1995—; bd. dirs. The Gabelli Group, The Lynch Corp., N.Y.C. Mem. adv. bd. Salvation Army; com. budget, bd. dirs. United Fund; mem. com. High Point (N.C.) United Schs.; 1st vice chmn. Central Carolina chpt. Nat. Multiple Sclerosis Soc., 1968-73; bd. dirs. High Point Arts Council, 1968-73. Served with AUS, 1959, 62. Recipient Disting. Svc. award Freedom Found., Am. Legion, High Point (N.C.) Youth Coun. Mem. Dirs. Guild Am., Internat. Radio and TV Soc. (bd. govs.). Clubs: Winged Foot Golf, Marco Polo, Board Room, Bronxville Field, Chgo. Press. Lodges: Rotary, Kiwanis. Home: 24 Masterton Rd Bronxville NY 10708-4804 Office: Citadel Comm Co 130 Pondfield Rd Ste 1 Bronxville NY 10708-4002

LOMBARDO, TONY, film editor. Editor: (films) A Wedding, 1978, A Perfect Couple, 1979, Cheech & Chong's Nice Dreams, 1981, Blame It on the Night, 1984, Reckless, 1984, P.K. and the Kid, 1987, (with Thomas Stanford) Born to Race, 1988, Man Outside, 1988, Uncle Buck, 1989, (with Frank Morriss) The Hard Way, 1991, (with Barry B. Leirer) The Distinguished Gentleman, 1992, My Cousin Vinny, 1992, Greedy, 1994, (TV movie) By Dawn's early Light, 1989. Office: The Gersh Agency 232 N Canon Dr Beverly Hills CA 90210-5302*

LOMICKA, WILLIAM HENRY, investor; b. Irwin, Pa., Mar. 9, 1937; s. William and Carabel L.; m. Carol L. Williams, Feb. 14, 1979; 1 son, Edward W. B.A., Coll. Wooster, Ohio, 1959; M.B.A., U. Pa., 1962. Sr. securities analyst Guardian Life Ins. Co., N.Y.C., 1962-65; treasury svcs. mgr. L.B. Foster Co., Pitts., 1966-68, Welch Foods Co., Westfield, N.Y., 1969-70; asst. treas. Ashland Oil, Inc., Ky., 1970-75; sr. v.p. fin. Humana Inc., Louisville, 1975-85; pres., fin. cons. Old South Life Ins. Co., Louisville, 1985-87; sec. econ. devel. Commonwealth of Ky., 1987-88; acting pres. Citizens Security Life Ins. Co., Louisville, 1988-89; pres. Mayfair Capital, Inc., Louisville, 1988—; bd. dirs. Vencor, Inc., Regal Cinemas, Inc., Sabratek, Inc. Trustee Bellarmine Coll. Served with USAR, 1962-63. Home: 402 Mockingbird Valley Rd Louisville KY 40207-1322 Office: Capital Holding Ctr 400 W Market St Ste 2510 Louisville KY 40202-3376

LOMON, EARLE LEONARD, physicist, educator, consultant; b. Montreal, Nov. 15, 1930; came to U.S., 1951, naturalized, 1965; s. Harry and Etta (Rappaport) L.; m. Ruth Margaret Jones, Aug. 4, 1951; children: Martha Glynis, Christopher Dylan, Deirdre Naomi. B.Sc., McGill U., Montreal, 1951; Ph.D., MIT, 1954. NRC Can. overseas research fellow Inst. Theoretical Physics, Copenhagen, 1954-55; fellow Weizmann Inst., Rehovoth, Israel, 1955-56; research assoc. lab. nuclear studies Cornell U., Ithaca, N.Y., 1956-57; assoc. prof. theoretical physics McGill U., Montreal, 1957-60; assoc. prof. physics MIT, Cambridge, 1960-70, prof., 1970—; vis. staff mem. Los Alamos Nat. Lab., 1968—; project dir. Unified Scis. and Math. for Elem. Schs., Cambridge, 1970-77; adj. prof. U. Louvain-la-Neuve, Belgium, 1980; vis. prof. U. Paris, 1979-80, 86-87, UCLA, 1983, U. Wash., 1985; vis. rschr. Kernforschungsanlage Jülich, 1986-92, U. Geneva, 1993, CERN, Geneva, 1994, IPN, Orsay, 1994; Lady Davis vis. prof. Hebrew U., Jerusalem, 1993-94. Contbr. articles to profl. jours. Guggenheim Meml. Found. fellow CERN, Geneva, 1965-66; Dupont fellow, 1952-53; Ossabaw Island Project fellow (Ga.), 1978; Sci. Research Council fellow U. London, 1980. Fellow Am. Phys. Soc.; mem. Can. Assn. Physicists. Office: MIT 6-304 77 Massachusetts Ave Cambridge MA 02139-4301

LOMONOSOFF, JAMES MARC, marketing executive; b. Van Nuys, Calif., Apr. 29, 1951; s. Boris Marc and Eileen Fairfax (Thomson) L.; m. Elisabeth Maas, June 12, 1982; children; Marc Frederik, James Forrest. BA in Econs., Colgate U., 1973; MBA in Gen. Mgmt., U. Va., 1975. With Saatchi and Saatchi Advt., N.Y.C., 1975-93, v.p., account supr., 1975-85, sr. v.p., mgmt. supr., 1986-87, exec. v.p., mgmt. dir., 1987—, pres. Collateral Plus div., 1987-90; pres., chief exec. officer Saatchi & Saatchi Specialized Communications, 1991-92; account dir. VDB/Compton B.V., Amsterdam, The Netherlands, 1980-83; acct. dir. Saatchi and Saatchi Compton S.A., Madrid, 1983-84; regional acct. dir. Saatchi and Saatchi Compton Worldwide, London, 1984-86; mng. dir., CEO BSB/Saatchi and Saatchi, Prague, 1992-93; v.p. internat. mktg. Walt Disney Attractions Inc., Lake Buena Vista, Fla., 1994—. Mem. Beta Theta Pi. Republican. Home: 10905 Bayshore Dr Windermere FL 34786-7801 Office: Walt Disney Attractions Inc PO Box 10000 Lake Buena Vista FL 32830-1000

LONBORG, JAMES REYNOLD, dentist, former professional baseball player; b. Santa Maria, Calif., Apr. 16, 1942; s. Reynold H. and Ada (Ryan) L.; m. Rosemary Irene Feeney, Nov. 21, 1970; children: Phoebe Lea, Claire Elizabeth, Nicholas James, Nora Kathleen, John Bartholomew, Jordon Michael. B.A., Stanford U., 1964; D.M.D., Tufts U. Dental Sch., 1983. Baseball player Boston Red Sox, 1965-71, Milw. Brewers, 1972; pitcher Phila. Phillies, 1973-79; gen. dentist; asst. to adminstr. New Eng. Rehab. Clinic, Woburn, Mass., 1972-74. Mem. sports medicine com. U.S. Olympic Com., 1997. Recipient Cy Young award, 1967. Recorded 1000th maj. league strikeout, Aug. 19, 1973; career record 157 wins, 137 losses. Home: 498 First Parish Rd Scituate MA 02066-3201 Office: 105 Webster St Hanover MA 02339-1227

LONCOSKY, WALTER BEUGGER, real estate manager; b. Gowanda, N.Y., Nov. 12, 1935; s. Walter Herman and Ida B. (Beugger) L.; m. Anita Lucile Thorp, June 27, 1964; 1 child, Helga B. BA in Journalism and Pub. Adminstrn., Columbia Pacific U., 1984, MA in Journalism and Pub. Adminstrn., 1985; diploma Gen. Bible, Liberty U., 1985. Lic. real estate broker, Pa.; cert. conservationist, Pa., erosion and sediment control inspector, Pa.; ordained to ministry Bapt. Ch., 1984. Sports editor Danville (Pa.) News, 1956-58; performance specialist U.S. Agr. Stabilization & Cons. Dept., Danville, 1961-68; info. specialist Pa. Dept. Agr., Harrisburg, 1968-70; editor, owner Montour News Svc., Danville, 1971-80; pres., owner Skyco, Inc., Bloomsburg, Pa., 1981—; chmn., dir. Conservation Dist., Montour County, Pa., 1967-80; mem. adv. bd. County Planning Commn., Danville, 1969-80; chmn. Environ. Adv. Coun., Derry Twp., Pa., 1971-78; panel mem. Pa. Rural Studies Program, Danville, 1975. Author: Preservation of Agricultural Land, 1969, Columbia-Pacific Press, 1984. Bd. mem. Area Agy. on Aging, Danville, 1972-80; chmn. Home Rule Task Force, Danville, 1973; constable Derry Twp., Pa., 1976-82; bd. mem. County Dem. Com., Montour County, 1976-80. With U.S. Army, 1958-60. Named Hon. Chpt. Farmer Future Farmers Am., Turbotville, Pa., 1971; W.K. Kellogg Found. fellow, 1973; recipient award of merit World of Poetry, 1987. Mem. Pa. Assn. Environ. Profls., Rainbow Morgan Horse Assn., Masons, Elks. Democrat. Avocations: gardening, hiking, political science, soccer. Office: Skyco Inc 150 E 9th St Bloomsburg PA 17815-2708

LOND, HARLEY WELDON, editor, publisher; b. Chgo., Feb. 5, 1946; s. Henry Sidney and Dorothy (Shaps) L.; m. Marilyn Moss, Aug. 20, 1981; 1 child Elizabeth. BA in Journalism, Calif. State U., L.A., 1972. Adminstrv. dir. Century City Ednl. Arts Project, L.A., 1972-76, hon. dir., 1982—; founder, editor Intermedia mag., L.A., 1974-80; prodn. mgr. FilmRow Publs., L.A., 1981; assoc. editor Box Office mag., Hollywood, Calif., 1981-84, editor, assoc. pub., 1984-94; dir. publs. Entertainment Data, Inc., 1994-95; pres. CyberPod Prodns., 1995—; chief copy editor The Hollywood Reporter, 1995—; syndicated columnist Continental Features, Washington, Tel-Aire Publs., Dallas, 1986—; hon dir. Monterey (Calif.) Film Festival, 1987; mem. media adv. bd. Cinetex Internat. Film Festival, 1988; cons. Take 3 Info. Svc.; web architect-master, OnVideo website, 1995—. Editor: Entertainment Media Electronic Info. Svc.; contbr. articles to profl. publs. Calif. Arts Council grantee, 1975, Nat. Endowment for Arts grantee, 1976-77. Mem. MLA, Soc. Profl. Journalists, Assn. for Edn. in Journalism and Mass Communication, Speech Communication Assn., Soc. for Cinema Studies. Home and Office: PO Box 17377 Beverly Hills CA 90209-3377

LONDON, ANDREW BARRY, film editor; b. Bronx, N.Y., Jan. 1, 1949; s. Max Edward and Nellie (Steiner) L. BA in Cinema magna cum laude, U. So. Calif., 1970. Represented by Mont. Artists, Santa Monica, Calif. Prin. works include: (features) The Meteor Man, 1993, F/X 2, 1991, Rambo III, 1988, Planes, Trains and Automobiles, 1987, Link, 1986, Cloak & Dagger, 1984, Psycho II, 1983, The True Story of Eskimo Nell, 1975, (TV shows) Before He Wakes, 1997, Perfect Crime, 1997, Divided By Hate, 1997, The Crying Child, 1996, Evil Has a Face, 1996, Don't Talk to Strangers, 1994, Day of Reckoning, 1993, Mortal Sins, 1992, Running Delilah, 1992, True Tales, 1992, Sweet Poison, 1991, Tales from the Crypt, 1989-90, Beauty and the Beast pilot, 1987, The Christmas Star, 1986; sound editor: Wolfen (MPSE Golden Reel award 1982), Hammett, Roadgames, Psycho II, I'm Dancing As Fast As I Can, Perfect, Protocol, Coal Miner's Daughter, The Long Riders, others. Mem. Acad. Motion Picture Arts and Scis., Motion Picture Sound Editors (Golden Reel award 1982), Phi Beta Kappa. Office: 2622 Armstrong Ave Los Angeles CA 90039-2613

LONDON, CHARLOTTE ISABELLA, secondary education educator, reading specialist; b. Guyana, S.Am., June 11, 1946; came to U.S., 1966, naturalized, 1980; d. Samuel Alphonso and Diana Dallett (Daniels) Edwards; m. David Timothy London, May 26, 1968 (div. May 1983); children: David Tshombe, Douglas Tshaka. BS, Fort Hays State U., 1971; MS, Pa. State U., 1974, PhD, 1977. Elem. sch. tch., Guyana, 1962-66, secondary sch. tchr., 1971-72; instr. lang. arts Pa. State U., University Park, 1973-74; reading specialist/ednl. cons. N.Y.C. Community Coll., 1975; dir. skills acquisition and devel. center Stockton (N.J.) State Coll., 1975-77; reading specialist Pleasantville (N.J.) Public Schs., 1977—; ind. specialist United Nations Devel. Programme , Guyana, 1988—; v.p. Atlantic County PTA, 1980-82; del. N.J. Gov.'s Conf. Future Edn. N.J., 1981; founder, pres. Guyana Assn. Reading and Lang. Devel., 1987. Sec. Atlantic County Minority Polit. Women's Caucus. Mem. Internat. Reading Assn., Nat. Council Tchrs. English, Assn. Supervision and Curriculum Devel., NEA, N.J. Ednl. Assn., AAUW, Pi Lambda Theta, Phi Delta Kappa (sec.). Mem. African Methodist Episcopal Ch. Home: 6319 Crocus St Mays Landing NJ 08330-1107 Office: Pleasantville Pub Schs W Decatur Ave Pleasantville NJ 08232

LONDON, GARY WAYNE, neurologist; b. Alexandria, La., Sept. 21, 1943; s. Arthur Jack and Aileen Ida (Friedman) L.; m. Susan Tolkan, June 19, 1965; children: David, Jeremy, Benjamin. BSM, Northwestern U., 1965, MD, 1968. Diplomate Nat. Bd. Med. Examiners, Am. Bd. Psychiatry and Neurology, Am. Bd. Electrodiagnostic Medicine; lic. Md., D.C., Va., Calif., Bur. Narcotic and Dangerous Drugs. Intern U. Calif. Affiliated Hosps., L.A., 1968-69; resident in neurology U. Mich., Ann Arbor, 1969-70; resident in neurology dept. neurosci. U. Calif. San Diego, 1972-74; neurologist in pvt. graoup practice Drs. Mayle, London & Einbinder, LLC, Bethesda, Md., 1974—; affiliated with hosps. including Montgomery (Md.) Gen. Hosp., Holy Cross Hosp., Suburban Hosp., Shady Grove Adventist Hosp., Potomac Ridge Med. Ctr., Montgomery County, Md., Sibley Meml. Hosp., George Washington U. Hosp., Washington; clin. instr. neuroscis. U. Calif., San Diego, 1973-74; adj. asst. clin. prof. neurology George Washington U. Sch. Medicine and Health Scis., 1985—. Contbr. articles to profl. jours., chpt. to book. Mem. steering com. Washington chpt. of Weissmann Inst., 1993—; v.p. Hebrew Home of Greater Washington, Rockville, Md., 1993—. Fellow Am. Acad. Neurology, Royal Soc. Medicine; mem. AMA, ACP, Am. Assn. Electrodiagnostic Medicine (liason to Nat. Coalition for Rsch. in Neurolog. and Comm. Disorders 1984-94), Am. Med. Electroencephalographic Assn., Am. Acad. Clin. Neuropsychology, Am. Soc. Clin. Evoked Potentials, Am. Epilepsy Soc., Am. Soc. Neurol. Rehab., Am. Soc. Neuroimaging, N.Y. Acad. Scis., Russell W. DeJong Soc., Md. Neurol. Soc., Md. State Med. Soc., Jacobi Soc. Washington, Phi Delta Epsilon (pres. Washington grad. club 1982-83), Phi Eta Sigma. Republican. Jewish. Avocations: golf, mysteries, wine, modern art, motorcycles. Office: Camalier Bldg 10215 Fernwood Rd Ste 301 Bethesda MD 20817-1106

LONDON, HERBERT IRA, humanities educator; b. N.Y.C., Mar. 6, 1939; s. Jack and Esta (Epstein) L.; m. Joy Weinman, Oct. 13, 1942 (div. 1974); children: Staci, Nancy; m. Vicki Pops, Nov. 18, 1950; 1 child, Jaclyn. BA, Columbia U., 1960, MA, 1961; PhD, N.Y. U., 1966; DL, U. Aix.-Marseille, Aix-en-Provence, France, 1982, Grove City Coll., 1993. Teaching fellow N.Y. U., N.Y.C., 1963-64, instr., 1964-65, asst. prof., 1967-68, univ. ombudsman, 1968-69, assoc. prof., 1969-73, prof., 1973—, dean Gallatin div., 1972-92, John M. Olin U. Prof. Humanities, 1992—; instr. New Sch. for Social Research, N.Y.C., 1964-65; research scholar Australian Nat. U., Canberra, Australia, 1966-67; bd. overseers Ctr. for Naval Analysis, Washington, 1983—; trustee Hudson Inst., Indpls., 1979—, research fellow 1974—; sr. fellow Nat. Strategy Info. Ctr. Created TV programs: Myths That Rule America, The American Character; contbr. numerous articles to profl. jours. Bd. dirs., chmn. Nat. Assn. Scholars, N.Y.C., 1986; bd. advisors Coalition for Strategic Def. Initiative, Washington, 1986; candidate for mayor of N.Y.C., 1989; conservative candidate for gov., N.Y., 1990, 94; candidate for comptroller of N.Y. State, 1994. Recipient Def. Sci. award Def. Sci. Jour., 1985, Fulbright award U.S. Govt., 1966-67, Anderson award NYU, 1965, Martin Luther King award Congress of Racial Equality, 1995, Peter Shaw Meml. award Exemplary Writing Nat. Assn. Scholars, 1996, Jacques Maritain Humanitarian award Am. Maritain Assn., 1996; named Danforth Assoc. Danforth Found., 1971. Mem. Freedom House, Am. Hist. Assn., Edn. Excellence Network, Heritage Found (assoc. scholar 1983—), Ethics and Pub. Policy Ctr. (assoc. scholar 1985—), Nat. Strategy Info. Ctr., N.Y.C., 1984. Republican. Jewish. Avocations: writing, tennis. Home: 2 Washington Square Vlg New York NY 10012-1732 Office: NYU 113 University Pl New York NY 10003-4527

LONDON, IRVING MYER, physician, educator; b. Malden, Mass., July 24, 1918; s. Jacob A. and Rose (Goldstein) L.; m. Huguette Piedzicki, Feb. 27, 1955; children: Robert L.J., David T. AB summa cum laude, Harvard U., 1939, MD, 1943; DSc (hon.), U. Chgo., 1966. Sheldon Traveling fellow Harvard U., 1939-41, Delamar research fellow med. sch., 1940-41; intern Presbyn. Hosp., N.Y.C., 1943; asst. resident Presbyn. Hosp., 1946-47, asst. physician, 1946-52, assoc. attending physician, 1954-55; Rockefeller fellow in medicine Coll. Physicians and Surgeons, Columbia U., 1946-47; instr. Columbia U., 1947-49; asso. in medicine Coll. Phys. and Surg., Columbia U., 1949-51; asst. prof. Coll. Phys. and Surg., Columbia, 1951-54, assoc. prof., 1954-55; prof., chmn. dept. medicine Albert Einstein Coll. Medicine, N.Y.C., 1955-70; vis. prof. medicine Albert Einstein Coll. Medicine, 1970—; prof. biology MIT, 1969-89, prof. emeritus, 1989—; vis. prof. medicine Harvard Med. Sch., 1969-72, prof. medicine, 1972-89, prof. emeritus, 1989—; dir. div. health scis. and tech. Harvard and MIT, 1969-85, prof. medicine, 1972—, Grover M. Hermann prof. health scis. and tech., 1977-89, prof. emeritus, 1989—; dir. Whitaker Coll. Health Scis., Tech. and Mgmt., MIT, 1978-83; dir. med. service Bronx Mcpl. Hosp. Center, 1955-70; Phi Delta Epsilon lectr. U. Colo., 1962, Harvey lectr., 1961; Jacobaeus lectr., Stockholm, Sweden, 1964; vis. scientist Pasteur Inst., Paris, 1962-63; Commonwealth Fund fellow, 1962-63; Alpha Omega Alpha lectr. Yale, Boston U., Columbia, SUNY Downstate Med. Center, U. Chgo.; Harry L. Alexander vis. prof. Washington U., St. Louis, 1968; Alpha Omega Alpha vis. prof. Johns Hopkins U., 1970; Eugene A. Stead Jr. vis. lectr. Duke Med. Center, 1970; Cons. to Surgeon Gen., AUS, 1957-60; chmn. metabolism study sect. USPHS, 1961-63; Med. fellowship bd. Nat. Acad. Scis., NRC, 1955-64; mem. bd. sci. cons. Sloan Kettering Inst., 1960-72; bd. sci. counselors Nat. Heart Inst., 1964-68; exec. com. Health Research Council, City N.Y., 1958-63; mem. sci. adv. council Pub. Health Research Inst., N.Y.C., 1958-63; mem. adv. com. to dir. NIH, 1966-70, nat. cancer adv. bd., 1972-76; physician Brigham and Women's Hosp., 1972-83, sr. physician 1983—; chmn. research group Nat. Commn. on Arthritis, 1975-76; chmn. adv. com. Div. Health Scis., Inst. Medicine, 1979-82; mem. Bd. Sci. Counselors, NIADDK, 1979-83; bd. dirs., cons. Johnson and Johnson, 1982-89; founder Genetix Pharms., 1996. Asso. editor: Jour. Clin. Investigation, 1952-57; mem. editorial bd.: Am. Jour. Medicine, 1965-79. Bd. dirs. Philippe Found. Capt. AUS, 1944-46. Recipient Theobald Smith award in med. scis. AAAS, 1953; Bloomfield medal and lectr., Lady Davis Inst., 1986. Fellow Am. Acad. Arts and Scis.; mem. Am. Soc. Biol. Chemists, Am. Soc. Clin. Investigation (pres. 1963-64), Nat. Acad. Scis. (mem. bd. medicine 1967-70, founding mem. Inst. Medicine 1970), Internat. Soc. Hematology, Soc. Exptl. Biology and Medicine, Assn. Am. Physicians, Nat. Acad. Scis., Phi Beta Kappa, Alpha Omega Alpha. Office: Harvard U-MIT Div Health Scis and Tech 77 Massachusetts Ave Cambridge MA 02139-4301

LONDON, WILLIAM LORD, pediatrician; b. Durham, N.C., Nov. 1, 1930. BS in Medicine, U. N.C., 1952, MD, 1955. Diplomate Am. Bd. Pediatrics. (sec., treas. 1996). Intern Children's Med. Ctr., Boston, 1955-56, resident, 1956-57, 59-60, fellow in pediatric hematology, 1960-61; mem. staff Durham (N.C.) Gen. Hosp.; clin. assoc. prof. Duke U., Durham. Fellow Am. Acad. Pediatrics; mem. AMA (pres. Durham Pediatrics 1961—). Office: 2609 N Duke St Ste 801 Durham NC 27704-3048

LONDRÉ, FELICIA MAE HARDISON, theater educator; b. Ft. Lewis, Wash., Apr. 1, 1941; d. Felix M. and Priscilla Mae (Graham) Hardison; m. Venne-Richard Londré, Dec. 16, 1967; children: Tristan Graham, Georgianna Rose. BA with high honors, U. Mont., 1962; MA, U. Wash., 1964; PhD, U. Wis., 1969. Asst. prof. U. Wis. at Rock County, Janesville, 1969-75; asst. prof., head theatre program U. Tex. at Dallas, Richardson, 1975-78; assoc. prof. U. Mo., Kansas City, 1978-82, prof. theatre, 1982-87, curators' prof., 1987—; women's chair in humanistic studies Marquette U., 1995; dramaturg Mo. Repertory Theatre, Kansas City, 1978—, Nebr. Shakespeare

Festival, 1990—; guest dramaturg Gt. Lakes Theater Festival, 1988; mem. archives task force Folly Theatre, 1982-83; artistic advisor New Directions Theatre Co., 1983-90; hon. lectr. Mid.-Am. State Univs. Assn., 1986-87; mem. U.S.-U.S.S.R. Joint Commn. on Theatre Historiography, 1989; mem.adv. bd. Contemporary World Writers, 1991—; lectr. univs. Budapest, Pecs, Debrecen, Hungary, 1992; vis. prof. Hosei U., Tokyo, 1993. Author: Tennessee Williams, 1979, Tom Stoppard, 1981, Federico Garcia Lorca, 1984, (play) Miss Millay Was Right, 1982 (John Gassner Meml. Playwriting award 1982), The History of the World Theatre: From the English Restoration to the Present, 1991 (Choice Outstanding Acad. Book award 1991), Chow Chow Pizza, 1995 (Kansas City Gorilla Theatre First Prize, winner Stages '95 Competition, Dallas), (book) Love's Labour's Lost: Critical Studies, 1997; (opera libretto) Duse and D'Annunzio, 1987; co-editor: Shakespeare Companies and Festivals: An International Guide, 1995; book rev. editor: Theatre Jour., 1984-86; assoc. editor: Shakespeare Around the Globe: A Guide to Notable Postwar Revivals; mem. editl. bd. Theatre History Studies, 1981-87, 89—, Studies in Am. Drama, 1945 to the present, 1984—, 19th Century Theatre Jour., 1984-95, Bookmark Press, Tennessee Williams Rev., 1985-87, (jours.) Dramatic Theory and Criticism, 1986—, On-Stage Studies, The Elizabethan Rev., 1992—, Theatre Symposium, 1994—; contbr. articles and book and theatre revs. to profl. publs. Hon. co-founder, bd. dirs. Heart of Am. Shakespeare Festival, 1991—; bd. dirs. Edgar Snow Meml. Fund, 1993—. Fulbright grantee U. Caen, Normandy, France, 1962-63, faculty rsch. grantee U. Mo., 1985, 86, 90, 91, tchr. seminar grantee Mo. Humanities Coun., 1993, 96; grad. fellow U. Wis., 1966-67, Trustees fellow U. Kansas City, 1987-88. Mem. MLA, Am. Soc. Theatre Rsch. (mem. exec. com. 1984-90, program chair 1995), Shakespeare Theatre Assn. Am. (sec. 1991-93), Internat. Fedn. for Theatre Rsch. (del. gen. assembly 1985), Am. Theatre Assn. (commn. on theatre rsch. 1981-87, chmn. 1984-86), Theatre Libr. Assn., Dramatists Guild, Literary Mgrs. and Dramaturgs Am., Shakespeare Oxford So., Mid.-Am. Theatre Conf. (chair grad. rsch. paper competition 1985), Am. Theatre and Drama Soc. (v.p. 1995—). Roman Catholic. Avocations: travel, theatre, continental cuisine. Home: 528 E 56th St Kansas City MO 64110-2769 Office: Mo Repertory Theatre 4949 Cherry St Kansas City MO 64110-2229

LONEGAN, THOMAS LEE, retired restaurant corporation executive; b. Kansas City, Mo., July 4, 1932; s. Thomas F. and Edna L. (Payton) L.; m. Donna F. Ednie, Apr. 11, 1958; children: Timothy L., John M. BSME, Gen. Motors Inst., 1955; MS in Mgmt., USN Post Grad Sch., 1963; grad., Indsl. Coll. Armed Forces, Washington, 1970; postgrad., Calif. State U., Long Beach, 1979-83; grad., Coll. for Fin. Planning, Denver, 1984. Registered profl. engr.; CFP. Commd. ensign USN, 1956, advanced through grades to comdr., 1978; dir. pub. works Naval Weapons Sta., Seal Beach, Calif., 1974-78; ret., 1978; dir. cen. staff McAthco Enterprises, Inc., Camarillo, Calif., 1985, exec. v.p., CFO, 1986-90, pres., CEO,, 1991-93, exec. v.p., CFO, 1994-95; ret. Author: Analysis and Attenuation of Air Borne Noise in Industrial Plants, 1955, Formalized Training of Maintenance Personnel, 1963. Vol. various couns. Boy Scouts Am., 1968-74. Decorated Bronze Star with combat device, Meritorious Svc. medal, Jt. Svcs. Commendation medal, Navy Achievement medal; recipient Order of Chamoro Govt.of Guam; named Sr. Engr./Arch. Yr. Naval Facilities Engr. Command, 1972. Fellow Soc. Am. Mil. Engrs., Ret. Officers Assn., GM Inst. Robots Honor Soc.; mem. Beta Gamma Sigma. Avocations: reading, theater, music, foreign travel. Home: 8578 Amazon River Cir Fountain Valley CA 92708-5510

LONERGAN, WALLACE GUNN, economics educator, management consultant; b. Potlatch, Idaho, Mar. 18, 1928; s. Willis Gerald and Lois (Gunn) L.; m. Joan Laurie Penoyer, June 1, 1952; children: Steven Mark, Kevin James. BA, Coll. Idaho, 1950; MBA, U. Chgo., 1955, PhD, 1960. Asst. dir., asst. prof. bus. Indsl. Relations Ctr. U. Chgo., 1960-70, assoc. dir., assoc. prof., 1970-74, dir., prof., 1974-84; vis. prof. Rikkyo U., Tokyo, 1985; vis. fellow Merton Coll. Oxford (Eng.) U., 1986; chair, prof. bus., econs. divsn. Albertson Coll. Idaho, Caldwell, 1987—; v.p. Human Resources Research Cons., Chgo., 1980-87. Author: Leadership and Morale, 1960, Group Leadership, 1974, Performance Appriasal, 1978, Leadership and Management, 1979. Chmn. Episcopal Commn. on Higher Edn., Chgo., 1970-80, mgmt. com. United Way Chgo., 1982-85. 1st lt. U.S. Army, 1950-53, Korea. Named Disting. Alumni Coll. Idaho, 1962; vis. scholar Internat. Anglican Exchange, N.Y.C., 1976, Tokyo, 1986. Mem. Internat. House Japan, Internat. Indsl. Relations Research Assn., Acad. Mgmt., Rotary. Avocations: power walking, hiking. Home: 812 E Linden St Caldwell ID 83605-5335 Office: Albertson Coll Idaho Bus Econs Divsn 2112 Cleveland Blvd Caldwell ID 83605-4432

LONEY, GLENN MEREDITH, drama educator; b. Sacramento, Dec. 24, 1928; s. David Merton and Marion Gladys (Busher) L. BA, U. Calif., Berkeley, 1950; MA, U. Wis., 1951; PhD, Stanford U., 1953. Teaching asst. U. Calif., Berkeley, 1949-50, Stanford U., Calif., 1952-53; instr. San Francisco State U., 1955-56, U. Nev., Las Vegas, 1956; prof. U. Md., Europe, N. Africa, Middle East, 1956-59; instr. Hofstra U., Hempstead, N.Y., 1959-61, Adelphi U., Garden City, N.Y., 1959-61; prof. speech and theater Bklyn. Coll. and City U. Grad. Ctr., 1961-71, prof. theater, 1971—. Author: Briefing and Conference Techniques, 1959, Peter Brook Midsummer Night's Dream, 1974, The Shakespeare Complex, 1974, Young Vic Scapino, 1980, The House of Mirth-The Play of the Novel, 1981, Twentieth Century Theatre, 1983, California Gold Rush Drama, Musical Theatre in America, 1984, Unsung Genius, 1984, Creating Careers in Music Theatre, 1988, Staging Shakespeare, 1990, Peter Brook: Oxford to Orghast, 1997; editor: The Modernist; chief correspondent N.Y. Theatre wire and N.Y. Mus. Wire, Curator's Choice on Internet, 1996—. Served with AUS, 1953-55. Fellow Am. Scandinavian Found.; mem. AAUP, Am. Theatre Critics Assn., Outer Critics Circle (sec.), Am. Music Critics Assn., Am. Soc. Theatre Research, Internat. Fedn. Theatre Research, Theatre Library Assn., Theatre Hist. Soc., Phi Beta Kappa, Alpha Mu Gamma, Phi Eta Sigma, Phi Delta Phi. Democrat. Office: CUNY Grad Ctr Theater 33 W 42nd St New York NY 10036-8003

LONEY, MARY ROSE, airport administrator. Dir. aviation Phila. Internat. Airport; commr. Chgo. Dept. Aviation. Office: Chgo Dpt Aviation Chgo O'Hare Internat Terminal 2 Mezzanine PO Box 66142 AMF Ohare IL 60666*

LONG, ALFRED B., former oil company executive, consultant; b. Galveston, Tex., Aug. 4, 1909; s. Jessie A. and Ada (Beckwith) L.; student S. Park Jr. Coll., 1928-29, Lamar State Coll. Tech., 1947-56, U. Tex., 1941; grad. Citizens Police Acad.; m. Sylvia V. Thomas, Oct. 29, 1932; 1 child, Kathleen Sylvia (Mrs. E.A. Pearson, II). With Sun Oil Co., Beaumont, Tex., 1931-69, driller geophys. dept., surveyor engring. dept., engr. operating dept., engr. prodn. lab., 1931-59, regional supr., 1960-69, cons., 1969—. Sr.'s bd. dirs. Bapt. Hosp., Beaumont, Tex.; chaplain sr.'s vols. bd. dirs., S.E. Tex. Rehab. Hosp., Beaumont, Seniors-Lawmen Coun.; chaplain; Jefferson County Program Planning Com., 1964; mem. tech. adv. group Oil Well Drilling Inst., Lamar U., Beaumont. Mem. IEEE, Soc. Petroleum Engrs., Am. Petroleum Inst., Am. Assn. Petroleum Geologists, Houston Geol. Soc., Gulf Coast Engring. and Sci. Soc. (treas. 1962-65), U.S. Power Squadron, Soc. Wireless Pioneers, Citizen Police Acad. Recipient Nat. Jefferson award for Outstanding Pub. Svc. Am. Inst. for Pub. Svc., 1992, Community Svc. award Quarter Century Wireless Assn., 1994, Sensational Seniors of the U.S. honor CBS TV, 1994, Hometown Heroes Sta. CH6TV, 1995, Olympic torch bearer, 1996. Inventor oil well devices. Office: PO Box 7266 Beaumont TX 77726-7266

LONG, ALVIN WILLIAM, title insurance company executive; b. Steubenville, Ohio, Oct. 9, 1923; s. Roger H. and Emma (Reilley) L.; m. Ethelle Sherman, Jan. 1, 1944; children—Roger H., Sherry Long McBain. J.D., John Marshall Law Sch., 1949, LL.D., 1977; M.B.A., U. Chgo., 1955. Bar: Ill. 1950. V.p. Chgo. Title & Trust Co., 1960-63, sr. v.p., 1966-69, pres., chief adminstrv. officer, 1969-71, pres., chief exec. officer, 1971—, chmn., 1981, hon. chmn. ret., 1982—, also dir.; sr. v.p. Chgo. Title Ins. Co., 1963-66, pres., 1967—, chmn. bd., 1981-82, hon. chmn. ret., 1982—, also dir. Bd. dirs. Bradner Central Co.; pres. Chgo. Central Area Com., 1980-82; trustee John Marshall Law Sch.; bd. dirs. Ill. Childrens Home and Aid Soc., pres., 1975-77; mem. citizens bd. and alumni council U. Chgo. Served to 1st lt. USAAF, 1943-45. Recipient Distinguished Alumni citation John Marshall Law Sch., 1968. Mem. Ill., Bar Assn., Am. Land Title Assn. (pres. 1970-71), Law Club Chgo., Comml. Club Chgo., Chgo. Club, Flossmoor (Ill.) Country Club, Quail Ridge Country Club (Fla.).

LONG, ANTHONY ARTHUR, classics educator; b. Manchester, Eng., Aug. 17, 1937; came to U.S. 1983; s. Tom Arthur and Phyllis Joan (LeGrice) L.; m. Janice Calloway, Dec. 30, 1960 (div. 1969); 1 child, Stephen Arthur; m. Mary Kay Flavell, May 25, 1970 (div. 1990); 1 child, Rebecca Jane; m. Monique Marie-Jeanne Elias, Mar. 22, 1997. B.A., U. Coll. London, 1960; Ph.D., U. London, 1964. Lectr. classics U. Otago, Dunedin, N.Z., 1961-64; lectr. classics U. Nottingham, Eng., 1964-66; lectr. Greek and Latin U. Coll. London, 1966-71; reader in Greek and Latin U. London, 1971-73; Gladstone prof. Greek U. Liverpool, Eng., 1973-83; prof. classics U. Calif., Berkeley, 1982—; pub. orator U. Liverpool, Eng., 1981-83; Irving Stone prof. lit. U. Calif., Berkeley, 1991—, chmn. dept. classics, 1986-90; mem. Inst. Advanced Study, Princeton, N.J., 1970, 79; vis. prof. U. Munich, 1973, Ecole Normale Supérieure, Paris, 1993; Cardinal Mercier prof. philosophy U. Louvain, Belgium, 1991; mem. Mellon Fellowships Selection Com., 1984-90; mem. selection com. Stanford U. Humanities Coun., 1985-86. Author: Language and Thought in Sophocles, 1968 (Cromer Greek prize 1968), Problems in Stoicism, 1971, 96, Hellenistic Philosophy, 1974, 2d edit., 1986, (with Fortenbaugh and Huby) Theophrastus of Eresus, 1985, (with Sedley) The Hellenistic Philosophers, 1987, (with Dillon) The Question of Eclecticism, 1988, 96, (with Bastianini) Hierocles, 1992, (with others) Images and Ideologies, 1993, Stoic Studies, 1996; editor: Classical Quar., 1975-81, Classical Antiquity, 1987-90; gen. editor: (with Barnes) Clarendon Later Ancient Philosophers, 1987—. Served to lt. Royal Arty., Eng., 1955-57. Named hon. citizen City of Rhodes, Greece; sr. fellow humanities coun. Princeton U., 1978, Bye fellow Robinson Coll., Cambridge, 1982, Guggenheim fellow, 1986-87, sr. fellow Ctr. for Hellenic Studies, 1988-93, fellow NEH, 1990-91, Wissenschaftskolleg fellow, Berlin, 1991-92, William Evans fellow U. Otago, New Zealand, 1995. Fellow Am. Acad. Arts and Scis., Brit. Acad. (corr.); mem. Classical Assn., Aristotelian Soc., Am. Philol. Assn., Phi Beta Kappa (hon.). Avocations: music, walking, travel, bridge. Home: 1088 Tevlin St Albany CA 94706-2467 Office: U Calif Dept Classics Berkeley CA 94720

LONG, BERT LOUIS, JR., artist; b. Houston, Sept. 27, 1940; s. Bertran Louis and Tennessee (Morris) L.; m. Connie Dianne Kelly, Aug. 15, 1964; children: Deborah Denise Foster, John Alan, Bertran Louis III. Class A tchg. credential adult edn., UCLA, 1972. Tchr. adult edn. L.A. (Calif.) Unified Sch. Dist., 1972-75; owner, exec. chef Berts Gourmet Restaurant, Klamath Falls, Oreg., 1975-76; sous chef Hilton Hotels, Las Vegas, Nev., 1976; exec. sous chef Ritz Carlton Hotels, Chgo., 1976-77, Hyatt Regency Hotel, Houston, 1977-78; exec. chef Holiday Inn, Houston, 1978-79; chmn. Artists in Action, 1979-83; visual arts panelist allocations com. Cultural Arts Coun., visual arts sub-panelist selection com., 1988; adv. panel appointee Task Force Midtown Arts Ctr.; exec. com. mem. Houston Arts Alliance; panelist visual arts Tex. Commn. on the Arts, 1990; presenter in field. One-man shows include Butler Gallery, Houston, 1988, Art Mus. S.E. Tex., Beaumont, 1987-88, Dallas (Tex.) Mus. Art, 1988, Tex. A&M Meml. Student Ctr., College Station, 1989, Barry Whistler Gallery, Dallas, 1989, Allan Stone Gallery, N.Y.C., 1990, Lew Allen Gallery, Santa Fe, 1991, Contemporary Arts Mus., Houston, 1991, Lyons Matrix Gallery, Austin, 1992, The Fabric Workshop Mus., Phila., 1993, complejo Cultural San Francisco, Spain, 1996, San Francisco/Ctr. de Expericiones San Jorge de Caceres, others; exhibited in group shows at Dallas (Tex.) Mus. Art, 1990, Calif. Afro-Am. Mus., L.A., 1990, Duke U. Mus. Art, Durham, N.C., 1990, Studio Mus. in Harlem, N.Y.C., 1990, Palm Springs (Fla.) Desert Mus., 1990, Alternative Mus., N.Y.C., 1991, Contemporary Arts Mus., Houston, 1991, Barry Whistler Gallery, Dallas, 1991, Sala 1, Rome, 1991, Am. Acad. in Rome, Italy, 1991, Lewallen Gallery, Santa Fe, 1991, Dishman Art Gallery, Beaumont, 1991, The Painted Bride Gallery, Phila., 1993, Lyons Matrix Gallery, Dallas, 1993, Mus. Fine Arts, Houston, 1993, The Galveston (Tex.) Arts Ctr., 1993, Amazing Space, Cleveland, Tex., 1994, First Interstate Bank, 1994, Irving Arts Ctr., Tex., 1996, others; represented in permanent collections including Huntington Art Gallery, U. Tex., Mus. Fine Arts, Houston, Dallas (Tex.) Mus. Art, Bell Telephone, Met. Mus. Art, Dinos of Calif., Spikes Pers., Erenwert Produce, Pfeffer Interests, Fleming Prodns., Craig Washington Law Firm, Highland Distributing, Mus. Contemporary Art, Chgo. Libr., Ajuntamiento Berzocana, Fabric Workshop Mus., Mus. S.E. Tex., Inst. Mario Roso de Luna, Spain; pub. Houston ArtScene, 1979-88; performances include Fire/Falla Installations Canermero, Cáceres, Spain, 1994-96; contbr. articles to profl. jours. With USMC, 1959-64. Recipient proclamation State of Tex., Tex. Senate, 1990; named Outstanding Texan, State of Tex. Ho. of Reps., 1991. Fellow Soc. Fellows Am. Acad. in Room; mem. Tex. Fine Art Assn. (internat. bd. dirs. 1992—). Avocations: traveling, reading, gardening, photography, writing. Home: PO Box 1254 Houston TX 77033 Home and Office: c/o Pilar S/N, 10129 Berzocana, Caceres Spain*

LONG, BEVERLY GLENN, lawyer; b. Omaha, Mar. 1, 1923; d. Max Edgar and Allise Katherine Dorothea (Nielsen) Glenn; m. Jacob Emery Long, May 6, 1950. AB in Econs., U. Chgo., 1944; LLB, Columbia U., 1947. Bar: N.Y. 1948, R.I. 1951, U.S. Dist. Ct. (so. dist.) N.Y. 1949, U.S. Tax Ct. 1949, U.S. Dist. Ct. R.I. 1951, U.S. Ct. Appeals (2d cir.) 1949, U.S. Ct. Appeals (1st cir.) 1958, U.S. Ct. Claims 1960, U.S. Supreme Ct. 1960. Assoc. Edwards & Angell, Providence, 1950-59, ptnr., 1959-86, of counsel, 1986—. Adv. com. child welfare svcs. R.I. Dept. Social Welfare, 1959-66; pers. com. Big Bros. R.I., 1964-67; mem. Gov.'s Com. on Status of Women, 1965; chmn. R.I. Children's Code Commn., 1967-74; fundraiser Columbia U. Sch. Law, 1947-88, R.I. area for U. Chgo., 1951—; bd. dirs. Child Welfare League of Am., Inc., 1975-80, Children's Friend and Svc., Inc., 1966-75, 77-79, Providence chpt. ARC, 1967-72; bd. dirs. St. Mary's Home for Children, 1966-80, v.p., 1978-80; bd. dirs. R.I. Conf. Social Work, 1961-66, Coun. Cmty. Svcs., Inc., 1957-64; task force evaluation of criminal justice program LEAA, 1974-78; active United Way Southeastern New Eng., Inc., 1951-81, ad hoc adv. com., exec. budget com., 1971-78, bd. dirs., 1973-74, ABA sr. lawyers divsn. coun., 1986-91, sec., 1991-95. Recipient citation for pub. service U. Chgo., 1959. Fellow Am. Bar Found., R.I. Bar Found.; mem. ABA (Outstanding State Membership Chmn. award 1984), R.I. Bar Assn. (ho. dels., exec. com., pres., Merit award 1990), New Eng. Bar Assn. (bd. dirs. 1982-85), Fed. Bar Assn., Am. Law Inst., Am. Judicature Soc. (bd. dirs. 1988-90), U.S. Supreme Ct. Hist. Soc., U. Club R.I. Republican. Home: 200 Elmgrove Ave Providence RI 02906-4233

LONG, CARL FERDINAND, engineering educator; b. N.Y.C., Aug. 6, 1928; s. Carl and Marie Victoria (Wellnitz) L.; m. Joanna Margarida Tavares, July 23, 1955; children: Carl Ferdinand, Barbara Anne. S.B., MIT, 1950, S.M., 1952; D.Eng., Yale U., 1964; A.M. (hon.), Dartmouth Coll., 1971. Registered profl. engr., N.H. Instr. Thayer Sch. Engring., Dartmouth Coll., Hanover, N.H., 1954-57; asst. prof. Thayer Sch. Engring., Dartmouth Coll., 1957-64, assoc. prof., 1964-70, prof., 1970-94, assoc. dean, 1970, dean, 1972-84, dean emeritus, 1984—; prof. emeritus, 1994—; dir. Cook Design Ctr. Thayer Sch. Engring., Dartmouth Coll., 1984-94; engr. Western Electric Co., Alaska, 1956-57; v.p. ops., dir. Controlled Enivronment, 1975-81; pres., dir. Q-S Oxygern Processes, Inc., 1979-84; N.H. Water Supply and Pollution Control Com., U.S. Army Small Arms Systems Agy.; mem. New Eng. Constrn. Edn. Adv. Coun., 1971-74; mem. adv. com. U.S. Patenta and Trademark Office, 1975-79; mem. ad hoc vis. com. Engrs. Coun. for Profl. Devel., 1973-81; pres., dir. Roan of Thayer, Inc., 1986-93; bd. dirs. Micro Tool Co., Inc., Micro Weighing Systems, Inc., 1986-91, Roan Ventures, Inc., 1987-91; pres., dir. Hanover Water Works Co., 1989-97. Mem. Hanover Town Planning Bd., 1963-75, chmn., 1966-74; trustee Mt. Washington Obs., 1975-92; bd. dirs. Eastman Community Assn., 1977-80; mem. corp. Mary Hitchcock Meml. Hosp., 1974—. NSF Sci. Faculty fellow, 1961-62; recipient Robert Fletcher award Thayer Sch. of Engring., 1985, Fellow Members awd., Am. Soc. for Engineering Education, 1992. Fellow AAAS, ASCE, Am. Soc. Engring. Edn. (chmn. New Eng. sect. 1977-78, chmn. council of sects. Zone 1, dir. 1981-83); mem. Sigma Xi, Chi Epsilon, Tau Beta Pi. Republican. Baptist. Home: 25 Reservoir Rd Hanover NH 03755-1311

LONG, CEDRIC WILLIAM, health research facility executive; b. Mpls., Mar. 4, 1937; s. Tracy Steven and Clarice Cecilia (Robertson) L. BA, UCLA, 1960, MA, 1962; PhD, Princeton U., 1966. Postdoctoral fellow U. Calif., Berkeley, 1966-68; instr. NYU Med. Sch., N.Y.C., 1969-70; lab. chief Flow Labs., Rockville, Md., 1968-70, Litton Industries, Frederick, Md., 1976-80; preclin. chief NIH, Nat. Cancer Inst., DCT, Bethesda, Md., 1980-86; gen. mgr. Nat. Cancer Inst.- Frederick Cancer R&D Ctr., 1986-97; spl. asst. to dir. Nat. Cancer Inst. - Divsn. Extramural Activities, 1997—. Home: 2 Basildon Cir Rockville MD 20850-2724

LONG, CHARLES FRANKLIN, corporate communications executive; b. Norman, Okla., Jan. 19, 1938; s. James Franklin and Mary Katherine (Nemecek) L.; m. Joan Hampton, Sept. 16, 1961; children: Charles Franklin, David Hampton, Stephen Andrew. B.A., U. Okla., 1961. Sports writer San Angelo (Tex.) Standard-Times, 1961-62; news reporter Norman Transcript, 1962-63; asso. editor Sooner mag., U. Okla., 1963-66; news editor Quill mag., Chgo., 1967-71; editor Quill mag., 1971-80; sr. editor Cahners Pub. Co., Des Plaines, Ill., 1981-83; mgr. internal communications Beatrice Cos., Inc., Chgo., 1983-86, dir. communications, 1986-88; dir. corp. communications Tellabs Ops., Inc., Lisle, Ill., 1989—. Author: With Optimism for the Morrow, 1965. Bd. dirs. Wheaton (Ill.) Youth Outreach, 1988-94, Western DuPage Spl. Recreation Assn. Found., 1994— (Vol. of Yr. 1994). Named to Okla. Journalism Hall of Fame, 1979. Mem. Pub. Relations Soc. Am., Internat. Assn. Bus. Communicators (Spectra Excellence award Chgo.), Am. Mktg. Assn., Soc. Profl. Journalists-Sigma Delta Chi, Beta Theta Pi. United Methodist. Home: 1106 N Washington St Wheaton IL 60187-3860 Office: Tellabs Ops Inc 1000 Remington Blvd Bolingbrook IL 60440-4955 *My parents, through gentle persuasion and by their own example, taught their sons to be curious and conscientious. I suppose it was those principles which eventually led me into a career in journalism and to come to realize that the supreme test of any good journalism is the measure of its public service—to serve the truth; to subscribe to ethical standards; to enlighten the public as to the nature and meaning of journalistic pursuits, especially in how those efforts support the American people's stake in their First Amendment to the Constitution.*

LONG, CHARLES THOMAS, lawyer; b. Denver, Dec. 19, 1942; s. Charles Joseph and Jessie Elizabeth (Squire) L.; m. Susan Rae Kircheis, Aug. 9, 1967; children: Brian Christopher, Lara Elizabeth, Kevin Charles. BA, Dartmouth Coll., 1965; JD cum laude, Harvard U., 1970. Bar: Calif. 1971, U.S. Dist. Ct. (cen. dist.) Calif. 1971, U.S. Ct. Appeals (9th cir.) 1975, D.C. 1980, U.S. Dist. Ct. D.C. 1981, U.S. Ct. Claims 1995. Assoc. Gibson, Dunn & Crutcher, Los Angeles, 1970-77, ptnr., 1977-79; ptnr. Gibson, Dunn & Crutcher, Washington, 1979-83; dep. gen. counsel Fed. Home Loan Bank Bd., Washington, 1984-85; ptnr. Jones, Day, Reavis & Pogue, Washington, 1985—; Bar: Calif. 1971, U.S. Dist. Ct. (ctrl. dist.) Calif. 1971, U.S. Ct. Appeals (9th cir.) 1975, D.C. 1980, U.S. Dist. Ct. 1981, U.S. Ct. Fed. Claims 1995. Contbr. articles to profl. jours. Pres. Leigh Mill Meadows Assn., Great Falls, Va., 1980. Served to lt. USNR, 1965-67. Mem. ABA, Calif. Bar Assn., D.C. Bar Assn., Coun. for Excellence in Govt., Women in Housing and Fin., Herrington Harbour Sailing Assn. (sec.-treas. 1996), Westwood Country Club (Vienna, Va.). Republican. Methodist. Avocations: sailing, photography. Office: Jones Day Reavis & Pogue Met Sq 1450 G St NW Ste 600 Washington DC 20005-2001

LONG, CHARLES WILLIAM, child and adolescent psychiatrist; b. Helena, Ark., Sept. 22, 1947; s. Benjamin Asa and Laura Jo (Underwood) L.; m. Heather Barbara Murray, Sept. 19, 1987; children: Charles William 2d, Lindsay Catherine. BS in Biology and Chemistry, Ark. State U., 1969; MD, U. Ark., Little Rock, 1976. Diplomate in gen. psychiatry and child and adolescent psychiatry Am. Bd. Psychiatry and Neurology. Chief resident in psychiatry William S. Hall Psychiat. Inst., Columbia, S.C., 1978-79; from instr. to asst. prof. dept. neuropsychiatry U. S.C. Sch. Medicine, Columbia, 1978-80, asst. clin. prof., 1980-82; chief child and adolescent psychiatry WSHPI, Columbia, 1978-80; pvt. practice Columbia, 1982-88; from vice chief to chief psychiatry Bapt. Med. Ctr., Columbia, 1983-87; med. dir. Psychiat. Health Svcs., Columbia, 1987-88; pvt. practice Charter Hosp. Charleston, S.C., 1988-95, assoc. med. dir., 1994-95; assoc. med. dir. Charter Hosp., Charleston, S.C., 1993-95; pres. med. staff Charter Hosp. Charleston, 1993-95; med. dir. Charter Behavior Health Sys., Charleston, 1995, Behavior Resources, Greenville, S.C., 1995; psychiat. cons. Univ. Devel. Disability, Columbia, 1982-83. Mem. Am. Psychiat. Assn., Am. Acad. Child Psychiatry, Am. Soc. Adolescent Psychiatry, S.C. Med. Assn., Greenville Med. Soc. Avocations: physical fitness, Tae Kwon Do (black belt), wildlife rehab.

LONG, CLARENCE DICKINSON, III, lawyer; b. Princeton, N.J., Feb. 7, 1943; s. Clarence Dickinson and Susanna Eckings (Larter) L.; m. Clothilde Camille Jacxsens, June 24, 1972; children: Clarence IV, Andrew, Amanda, Victoria, Stephen. BA, Johns Hopkins U., 1965; JD, U. Md., 1971; postgrad. Judge Adv. Gen.'s Sch., 1979-80. Bar: Ct. Appeals Md. 1972, U.S. Dist. Ct. D.C. 1972, U.S. Ct. Mil. Appeals 1975, U.S. Supreme Ct. 1976, N.C. 1978, U.S. Ct. Claims 1982, U.S. Ct. Appeals (fed. cir.) 1990. Asst. state's atty., Balt., 1973-74; trial atty., trial team chief Office Chief Trial Atty. Contract Appeals div., U.S. Army, Washington, 1980-84; chief atty. Def. Supply Svc., Washington, 1984-87; trial team chief contract appeals divsn. U.S. Army, 1987-92. Lt. col. U.S. Army. Decorated Silver Star, Soldier's medal, Bronze Star, Purple Heart (2), Meritorious Svc. medal (2), Army Commendation medal (2), Cross of Gallantry with gold star, Combat Infantryman's badge, Legion of Merit. Mem. ABA, D.C. Bar Assn., N.C. Bar Assn. Home: 119 N Fairfax St Falls Church VA 22046-3528 Office: Sec of Air Force Office of Gen Counsel Pentagon Washington DC 20330-1740

LONG, CLARENCE WILLIAM, accountant; b. Hartford City, Ind., Apr. 17, 1917; s. Adam and Alice (Weschke) L.; m. Mildred Bernhardt, Aug. 8, 1940; children: William Randall, David John, Bruce Allen. B.S., Ind. U., 1939. With Ernst & Young, Indpls., 1939—, ptnr., 1953—; mem. econ. exec. com. Gov. Ind., 1968-73. Mem. nat. budget and consultation com. United Way of Am., 1968-70; bd. dirs. United Fund Greater Indpls., 1966—, treas., 1968—; bd. dirs. Jr. Achievement, Ind., 1966-67; mem. exec. com. Nat. Jr. Achievement, 1966-67; mem. fin. com. Indpls. Hosp. Devel. Assn., 1966-67; trustee Ind. U., 1975-84; trustee Art Assn. Indpls., pres., 1977-86; mem. adv. com. to dir. NIH, 1986-92. Mem. Am. Inst. C.P.A.'s (council 1959-62), Ind. Assn. C.P.A.'s, Nat. Assn. Accountants, Ind. C. of C. (dir.), Delta Chi, Beta Alpha Psi, Alpha Kappa Psi. Republican. Lutheran. Clubs: Woodstock (Indpls.) (dir. 1958-60), Columbia (Indpls.) (dir. 1971-77, pres. 1976), Royal Poinciana Golf Club (Naples, Fla.). Home: 607 Somerset Dr W Indianapolis IN 46260-2924 Office: 1 Indiana Sq Indianapolis IN 46204-2004

LONG, DAVID L., magazine publisher. Publisher Sports Illustrated, N.Y.C. Office: c/o Sports Illustrated Time Inc. 1271 Avenue Of The Americas New York NY 10020-1300*

LONG, DAVID MICHAEL, JR., biomedical researcher, cardiothoracic surgeon; b. Shamokin, Pa., Feb. 26, 1929; s. David Michael and Elva (Christ) L.; m. Donna Rae Long, Feb. 26, 1954; children: Kurt, Raymond, Carl, Grace, Carolyn, Ruth. BS magna cum laude, Muhlenberg Coll., Allentown, Pa., 1951; MS, Hahnemann U., Phila., 1954, MD, 1956; PhD, U. Minn., 1965. Lic. physician, Ariz., Calif., Colo., Ill., Md., Minn., Pa., Tex.; diplomate Nat. Bd. Med. Examiners, Am. Bd. Surgery, Am. Bd. Thoracic Surgery; cert. trauma provider, advanced life support; advanced cardiac life support. Intern Hahnemann U. Hosp., Phila., 1956-57; resident in surgery U. Minn., Mpls., 1957-65, fellow in surgery, 1957-61, 63-65, fellow in physiology, 1959-61; pres., chmn. bd. Long Labs., San Diego, 1984-85; chmn., dir. rsch. Fluoromed Pharm., Inc., San Diego, 1985-89; chmn., dir. sci. Alliance Pharm. Corp., La Jolla, Calif., 1989-91; pres., chmn. Abel Labs., Inc., Spring Valley, Calif., 1991—; mem. faculty Hahnemann U., 1953-54, U. Calif., San Diego, 1973-92, U. Minn., 1959-61, 63-64, Naval Med. Sch., 1962, Chgo. Med. Sch., 1965-67, Cook County Grad. Sch. Medicine, 1965-73, U. Ill., 1967-73; cons. Chgo. State Tuberculosis Sanitarium, 1967-72; asst. dir. dept. surg. rsch. Hektoen Inst. for Med. Rsch. of Cook County Hosp., 1965-68, dir., 1968-73, assoc. attending staff, 1965-73; attending staff West Side VA Hosp., 1966-73, U. Ill. Hosp., 1967-73, Villa View Hosp., 1973-85, AMI Valley Med. Ctr., 1973-85, Grossman Dist. Hosp., 1973-85, Alvarado Cmty. Hosp., 1973-85, Sharp Meml. Hosp., 1973-84; head divsn. cardiovasc. and thoracic surgery U. Ill., 1967-73; cons. continuing med. edn. com. Grossmont Dist. Hosp., 1985—; mem. continuing med. edn. com. Sharp Healthcare Sys., 1994—; cons. Docent Corp., 1975-76; com. mem. consensus devel. com. Thrombolytic Therapy in Thrombosis, NIH/FDA, 1980. Contbr. numerous articles and abstracts to profl. jours., chpts. to books; editl. bd. Current Surgery, 1967-89; co-editor Hematrix, 1982-85. Bd. dirs. Rsch. Assocs. of Point Loma Nazarene coll., San Diego, chmn., 1984-85; bd.

trustees Muhlenberg Coll., Allentown, Pa., 1992—, chmn., 1994—; bd. dirs. Grossmont Hosp. Found., Grossmont Hosp., La Mesa, Calif., 1992—; co-chmn. Calif. divsn. of campaign of Muhlenberg Coll., 1992-93; chmn. Campaign of Grossmont Hosp. Found. for David and Donna Long Cancer Treatment Ctr. and Cardiac Diagnosis Ctr., 1992-94; co-chmn. Campaign for Health Ctr., Point Loma Nazarene Coll., San Diego, 1992-94. Rsch. fellow Heart Assn. Southeastern Pa., 1953-54, Student Senate of Hahnemann U., 1955; trainee Nat. Cancer Inst., 1957-58, Nat. Heart Inst., 1958-60, 63-64; spl. rsch. fellow Nat. Heart Inst., 1960-61; established investigator Minn. Heart Assn, 1964-65; Muhlenberg Coll. scholar, 1947-51, Hahnemann U. scholar, 1952-55, Luth. Brotherhood Leadership scholar, 1951. Fellow ACS, Am. Coll. Chest Physicians (sec. cardiovascular surgery com. 1976-78), Am. Coll. Cardiology; mem. AAAS, AMA, Am. Assn. Thoracic Surgery, Am. Assn. Anatomists, Internat. Cardiovascular Surgery Soc., Internat. Soc. for Artificial Cells and Immobilization Biotechnology, Am. Heart Assn., Am. Physiol. Soc., Am. Thoracic Soc., Assn. for Advancement of Med. Instrumentation, Cajal Soc. Neuroanatomy, Calif. Med. Assn., Internat. Soc. Surgery, Internat. Soc. Hemorheology (founding mem.), N.Y. Acad. Sci., San Diego County Med. Soc., Soc. Thoracic Surgeons, Soc. Univ. Surgeons, Warren H. Cole Soc., Western Thoracic Surg. Soc. Lutheran. Achievements include 17 U.S. patents and 11 fgn. patents. Avocations: hiking, gardening, philanthropic programs, books on Winston Churchill. Office: Abel Laboratories Inc 2737 Via Orange Way Ste 108 Spring Valley CA 91978-1750

LONG, DONLIN MARTIN, surgeon, educator; b. Rolla, Mo., Apr. 14, 1934; s. Donlin M. and Davene E. (Johnson) L.; m. Harriett Page, June 13, 1959; children: Kimberley Page, Elisabeth Merchant, David Bradford. Student, Jefferson City Jr. Coll., 1951-52; M.D., U. Mo., 1959; Ph.D., U. Minn., 1964. Diplomate: Am. Bd. Surgery. Intern U. Minn. Hosps., Mpls., 1959-60; resident U. Minn. Hosps., 1960-64; resident in neurosurgery Peter Bent Brigham and Children's Hosp. Med. Center, Boston, 1965; practice medicine specializing in neurosurgery Balt., 1973—; asst. prof. dept. neurosurgery U. Minn. Hosps., 1967-70, neurosurgeon, 1967-73, asso. prof., 1970-73; neurosurgeon-in-chief dept. neurosurgery Johns Hopkins Hosp., 1973—; prof. and chmn. dept. neurosurgery Johns Hopkins U., 1973—; mem. prin. staff Applied Physics Lab., 1976—; cons. neurosurgery Mpls. VA Hosp., 1967-73, John F. Kennedy Inst., 1977, Balt. City Hosp., 1973—. Contbr. numerous articles on neuropathology and surgery to profl. jours.; contbr. to book chpts. in field. Served with USPHS, 1965-67. Mem. Soc. Neurosci., Am. Assn. Neuropathologists, Soc. Neurol. Surgeons, AAAS, AMA, Balt. Neurol. Soc., Internat. Assn. Study of Pain, Internat. Soc. Pediatric Neurosurgery, William T. Peyton Soc., Congress Neurol. Surgeons, Johns Hopkins Med. and Surg. Assn., Electron Microscopy Soc. Am., Md. Neurosurg. Soc., Am. Acad. Neurosurgery, Am. Assn. Neurol. Surgery, Neurol. Soc. Am., Cajal Club, Sigma Xi, Omicron Delta Kappa, Alpha Omega Alpha, Phi Eta Sigma, Pi Mu Epsilon, Mystical 7. Home: 9 Blythewood Rd Baltimore MD 21210-2401 Office: Johns Hopkins Hosp Dept Neurosurgery Meyer 7-109 600 N Wolfe St Baltimore MD 21205-2110

LONG, DOUGLAS CLARK, philosophy educator; b. Ann Arbor, Mich., May 25, 1932; s. Dwight Clark and Marjorie Isabel (Grant) L.; m. Annie Nicole Groven, Aug. 21, 1961; children—Matthew Groven, Jonathan Wilson. B.A., U. Mich., 1954; M.A., Harvard U., 1955, Ph.D., 1963; postgrad., Oxford U., Eng., 1958-59. Instr. UCLA, 1960-62, asst. prof., 1962-67; vis. asst. prof. U. Wash., Seattle, 1965; assoc. prof. U. N.C., Chapel Hill, 1967-79; vis. assoc. prof. Brown U., Providence, 1969; prof. U. N.C., 1979-; asst. chair dept. Brown U., Providence, 1979-82, 91-92; dept. chair U. N.C., Chapel Hill, 1996—. Contbr. articles to profl. jours. Woodrow Wilson fellow, 1954; grantee NSF, 1967, NEH, 1976-77. Mem. Am. Philos. Assn., Phi Beta Kappa. Home: 419 Granville Rd Chapel Hill NC 27514-2723 Office: U NC CB 3125 Dept Philosophy Chapel Hill NC 27599-3125

LONG, EARLINE DAVIS, elementary education educator; b. Chgo., Mar. 31, 1944; d. Augustus (step father) and Eddie Virginia (Long) Grant; children: Tommie A. Grant, Virginia C. Sears. BS in Edn., Chgo. State U., 1971, MA in Adminstrn., 1983. Cert. tchr., adminstr., Ill. Electronic order writer Spiegels, Chgo., 1962-65; sr. clk. Chgo. Police Dept., 1966-72; tchr. Chgo. Bd. Edn., 1972—; consulting tchr. Teachers' Union, Chgo., 1990-92; continuing edn. courses in computer literacy, alcohol and drug edn., improving tchr. effectiveness, immersion week-end in Spanish. Home: 9608 S Eggleston Ave Chicago IL 60628-1106

LONG, EDWARD ARLO, business consultant, retired manufacturing company executive; b. Detroit, May 5, 1927; s. Arlo Russell and Florence Viola (Magown) L.; m. Lorraine Ruth Nordin, May 21, 1947; children: Karin Louise Long Schelke, Marian Elizabeth Long Benton. B.S., Wayne State U., 1956, MBA, 1964. Mfg. mgr. Ex-Cell-O Corp., Detroit, 1950-68; v.p. mktg. Colonial Broach & Machine, Warren, Mich., 1968-70; group v.p. Blue Bird Body Co., Fort Valley, Ga., 1970-75; pres. tool equipment div. Chgo. Pneumatic Tool, Franklin, Pa., 1975-77; group v.p. Joy Mfg. Co., Pine Bluff, Ark., 1977-87; v.p., gen. mgr. Wheeling Machine Products Co./Cooper Industries, Pine Bluff, 1987-94; ret., 1994; dir. Security Nat. Bank, Wheeling, W.Va. Bd. dirs. Franklin Hosp., 1976-76, Oglebay Inst., Wheeling, 1981-83, Ohio Valley Hosp. Trust, Wheeling, 1982-83, Ark. Ind. Colls., 1984, Jefferson County Indsl. Found., 1985, Pine Bluff Fifty for the Future, 1985, Pine Bluff Symphony Orch., 1987, Leadership Pine Bluff, 1990; apptd. zoning commr., Pine Bluff, 1995. Served with USCG, 1945-46. Scholar Nat. Office Mgmt. Assn., 1952, Beta Gamma, Detroit, 1953. Mem. AIME, Am. Petroleum Inst., Duquesne (Pitts.) Club, Rotary, Alpha Kappa Psi, Psi Chi, Sigma Iota Epsilon. Democrat. Roman Catholic. Home and Office: 7409 S Laurel St Pine Bluff AR 71603-8121

LONG, EDWIN TUTT, surgeon, data base company executive; b. St. Louis, July 23, 1925; s. Forrest Edwin and Hazel (Tutt) L.; m. Mary M. Hull, Apr. 16, 1955; children: Jennifer Ann, Laura Ann, Peter Edwin. AB, Columbia U., 1944, M.D., 1947. Diplomate Am. Bd. Surgery, Am. Bd. Thoracic Surgery. Rotating intern Meth. Hosp., Bklyn., 1947-78; surg. intern U. Chgo. Clinics, 1948-49, resident in gen. surgery, 1952-55, resident in thoracic surgery, 1955-57; asst. prof. surgery U. Chgo., 1957-59; thoracic and cardiovascular surgeon, chief surgery dept. Watson Clinic, Lakeland, Fla., 1960-69; asso. prof. surgery U. Pa., Phila., 1970-73; thoracic and cardiovascular surgeon Allegheny Cardiovascular Surg. Assocs., Pitts, 1973-88; exec. v.p. Mailings Clearing Ho. and Roxbury Press, Inc., 1988-90, pres., 1990—, chmn., bd. dir., 1991—; chmn. Watson Clinic Rsch. Found., 1965-69; bd. dirs. Roxbury Press, Inc., Cardiac Telecom, Inc., Pitts. Pressure Vectorography Rsch. grantee Alfred P. Sloan Found., 1963; patentee gas sterilizer, 1969. Capt. USAF, 1950-52. Mem. ACS, Am. Coll. Cardiology, Internat. Soc. for Cardiovascular Surg., Allegheny Vascular Soc. (pres. 1987), Ea. Vascular Soc. (founding mem.), Soc. Thoracic Surgery (founding mem.), Direct Mktg. Assn., Midwest Bioethics Ctr., Woodside Club, Rotary, Sigma Xi, Beta Theta Pi. Home: 4550 Warwick Blvd # 1204 Kansas City MO 64111-7725 Office: Roxbury Press Inc 4520 Main St Kansas City MO 64111 also: Roxbury Press Inc 601 E Marshall St Sweet Springs MO 65351-0295 *The important things in life are: Your health, your education, your spouse and family, your service. With these in order your life is a success.*

LONG, ELIZABETH VALK, magazine publisher; b. Winston-Salem, N.C., Apr. 29, 1950; d. Henry Lewis and Elizabeth (Fuller) V. BA, Hollins Coll., 1972; MBA, Harvard Bus. Sch., 1979. Clin. adminstr. Mass. Gen. Hosp., Boston, 1973-77; asst. to circulation dir. Time Mag.-Time Inc., N.Y.C., 1979-80, 81-82; circulation dir. Fortune Mag.-Time Inc., N.Y.C., 1982-84, Sports Illustrated-Time Inc., N.Y.C., 1984-85, Time Mag.-Time Inc., N.Y.C., 1985-86; publisher Life Mag.-Time Inc., N.Y.C., 1987-93; pres. Time Mag., 1993-95; exec. v.p. Time Inc., N.Y.C., 1995. Trustee Hollins Coll., 1987—; mem. bus. com. Mus. Modern Art, N.Y.C.; mem. bd. visitors Wake Forest U., Winston-Salem, N.C.; bd. dirs. Hanover Direct, Inc., Weehawken, N.J.; mem. Com. of 200. Recipient Matrix award N.Y. Women in Comms., 1992, Silver Medal award Am. Advt. Fedn., 1993. Mem. Phi Beta Kappa. Avocations: golf, gardening. Office: Time Inc Time & Life Bldg 1271 Avenue Of The Americas New York NY 10020-1300

LONG, EUGENE THOMAS, III, philosophy educator, administrator; b. Richmond, Va., Mar. 16, 1935; s. Eugene Thomas and Emily Joyce (Barker) L.; m. Carolyn Macleod, June 25, 1960; children: Scott, Kathryn. BA, Randolph-Macon Coll., Ashland, Va., 1957; BD, Duke U., 1960; PhD, U. Glasgow (Scotland), 1964. Asst. prof. philosophy Randolph-Macon Coll., 1964-67, assoc. prof., 1967-70; assoc. prof., U. S.C., Columbia, 1970-73, prof., 1973—, chmn. dept., 1972-87. Mem. S.C. Com. for Humanities, 1980-85; mem. adv. bd. The Franklin J. Matchette Found., 1992—. Recipient Research award NEH, 1968, Duke U./U. N.C. Coop. Program in Humanities, 1968-69. Mem. Soc. Philosophy in Religion (pres. 1980-81), Metaphys. Soc. Am. (sec. treas. 1977-81, exec. coun. 1991-94, v.p./pres.- elect 1996-97, pres. 1997-98), So. Soc. Philosophy and Psychology (exe. council 1976-79), Am. Philos. Assn. (sec. treas. eastern div. 1985-94). Author: Jaspers and Bultmann, 1968; Existence, Being and God, 1985; contbr., editor: God, Secularization & History, 1974, Experience, Reason and God, 1980; contbr., editor Prospects for Natural Theology, 1992; editor in chief Internat. Jourl for Philosophy of religion, 1990—; assoc. editor Internat. Jour. Philosophy of Religion, 1975-90, So. Jour. Philosophy, 1978-93; contbr., co-editor: God and Temporality, 1984, Being and Truth, 1986; mem. adv. editorial bd. The Works of William James, 1974-88, The Correspondence of William James, 1988—; contbg. editor: God, Reason and Religions, 1995; contbr. articles to profl. jours. Office: U SC Dept Philosophy Columbia SC 29208

LONG, FRANCIS MARK, retired electrical engineer, educator; b. Iowa City, Nov. 10, 1929; s. Frank B. and Hilda B. (Rohret) L.; m. Mary Ann Coyne, June 8, 1964 (dec. Apr. 1994); children: Ann Brett, Mary Bronwyn, Thomas Martin Carver, Caitlin Frances. B.S., U. Iowa, 1953, M.S., 1956; Ph.D., Iowa State U., 1961; NIH fellow, Stanford U. and Lawrence Livermore Lab, 1972-73. With Collins Radio Co., Cedar Rapids, Iowa, summers 1952, 55, Douglas Aircraft Co., Santa Monica, Calif., summer 1953, USNAMTC, Point Mugu, Calif., summer 1956, Good All Electric Co., Ogallala, Nebr., summer 1957, Lawrence Radiation Lab., Livermore, Calif., summer 1967, Globe Union Co., Milw., summer 1975, Naval Rsch Lab., Washington, 1988, 89, 91; instr. U. Wyo., Laramie, 1956-58; prof. elec. engring. U. Wyo., 1960-95; prof. emeritus U. Wyo., Laramie, 1995—; head elec. engring. dept. U. Wyo., 1977-87; instr. Iowa State U., 1958-60; dir. Wyo. Biotelemetry, Inc., Rocky Mountain Bioengring. Symposium; pres. Alliance for Engring. in Medicine and Biology, 1983, 84, mem. exec. com., 1979-89; conf. chmn., procs. editor 1st, 2d, 3d and 5th Internat. Conf. on Wildlife Biotelemetry; adj. prof. Univ. Denver, 1996—, Colo. Tech. Univ., 1997—. Author: (with E.M. Lonsdale) Introductory Electrical Concepts, 1967, rev. edit., 1977; co-author: (with R.G. Jacquot) Introduction to Engineering Systems, 1988. Trustee St. Paul's Newman Center Parish, 1969-72; mem. City of Laramie Planning Commn., 1970-72. Served with C.E. U.S. Army, 1953-55. Decorated citation Republic of Korea Army C.E.; recipient G.D. Humphrey Outstanding Faculty award U. Wyo., 1973, Western Electric Fund award for engring. teaching, 1978. Mem. IEEE (life, edn. activities com. chmn. Denver sect. 1997), Am. Soc. Engring. Edn. (v.p., dir., 1st Outstanding Biomed. Engring. Educator award biomed. engring. divsn. 1981, chmn. Elec. Engring. divsn. 1986-87), Internat. Soc. for Hybrid Microelectronics (v.p. Rocky Mountain chpt. 1996-97), Sigma Xi. Republican. Home: 1888 S Jackson St Apt 701 Denver CO 80210

LONG, FRANK WESLEY, JR., chemist; b. Springfield, Ill., Aug. 26, 1925; s. Frank Wesley and Elizabeth Margaret (Franke) L.; m. Thelma Elizabeth Keil Long, Nov. 17, 1951; children: Stephen Wesley, William Douglas, Valerie Elizabeth Long Feiss. BS, U. Ill., 1946; PhD in Organic Chemistry, State U. Iowa, 1950. Grad. asst. State U. Iowa, Iowa City, 1946-50; lab. chemist 3M Co., Mpls., summer 1948, Ethyl Corp., Ferndale, Mich., summer 1949, GAF Corp., Easton, Pa., 1950-52; project mgr. textile dyeing and finishing U.S. Army Quartermaster, Phila., 1952-53; sec. mgr. sales devel. Hooker Electrochem. Co., Niagara Falls, N.Y., 1953-64; dir. product devel. Princeton (N.J.) Chem. Rsch. Inc., 1964-67; product dir. ARCO Chem. Co. (subsidiary of Atlantic Richfield Co.), Phila., 1967-83; owner Riverside Assocs., Princeton, 1983—; dir. bus. devel. Princeton Advanced Tech., Princeton, 1991—; expert witness in field. Contbr. chpts. to books: Chemicals in Plastics, 1967, U.S. Petrochemical Industry, 1974, Fundamentals of the U.S. Petroleum Industry, 1980. Pres. elem. sch. PTA, Niagara Falls, 1963. Mem. Comml. Devel. Assn. (bd. dirs. 1976-78, Golden C award 1991), Am. Chem. Soc. (bd. dirs. chem. mktg. divsn. 1974-76), Am. Assn. Textile Chemists and Colorists, Chemist's Club. Achievements include development of flame retardant chemicals and plastics, heat resistant plastics, petrochemicals. Avocations: hunting, fishing, coins, Indian artifacts. Home and Office: Riverside Assocs 292 Riverside Dr Princeton NJ 08540-5432

LONG, FRANKLIN ASBURY, chemistry educator; b. Great Falls, Mont., July 27, 1910; s. F.A. and Ethel (Beck) L.; m. Marion Thomas, 1937; children: Franklin, Elizabeth. A.B., U. Mont., 1931, M.A., 1932; Ph.D., U. Calif., 1935. Instr. chemistry U. Calif., 1935-36, U. Chgo., 1936-37; instr. chemistry Cornell U., 1937-38, prof., 1939-79, prof. emeritus, 1979—, chmn. dept., 1950-60, v.p. research and advanced studies, 1963-69, Henry Luce prof. sci. and society, 1969-79, dir. program on sci., tech. and society, 1969-73, dir. peace studies program, 1976-79; adj. prof. U. Calif., Irvine, 1988—; dir. United Tech. Corp., Exxon Corp., 1969-81, cons., 1970-82; Mem. President's Sci. Adv. Com., 1961-66; asst. dir. U.S. Arms Control and Disarmament Agy., 1962-63, cons., 1963-73, 77-79 dir. Arms Control Assn., 1971-76; mem. adv. com. for planning and instnl. affairs NSF, chmn., 1973-74, mem. adv. panel for policy research analysis, 1976-80; co-chmn. Am. Pugwash Steering Com., 1974-79; mem. Indo-U.S. subcom. for ednl. and cultural affairs, 1974-82, co-chmn., 1977-82; bd. dirs. Assoc. Univs., Inc., 1947-74, hon. bd. dirs., 1975—; bd. dirs. Albert Einstein Peace Prize Found., 1979—, Fund for Peace, 1981—. Mem. editorial bd.: Am. Scientist, 1974-81, Bulletin of the Atomic Scientists, 1986—; Contbr. articles on chemistry, sci. policy and pub. affairs and arms control and disarmament to books, jours., encys. and reference works. Faculty Trustee Cornell U., 1956-57, Alfred P. Sloan Found., 1970-83, Fund for Peace, 1981—. Recipient U.S. Medal of Merit, 1948; (Korea) Dongbaeg medal, 1975; Guggenheim fellow, 1970. Fellow AAAS (v.p. 1976-80, Abelson prize 1989); mem. NAS, Coun. on Fgn. Rels., Am. Chem. Soc. (Charles Lathrop Parsons award 1985). Home: 311 N Mountain Claremont CA 91711-4530

LONG, GREGORY ALAN, lawyer; b. San Francisco, Aug. 28, 1948; s. William F. and Ellen L. (Webber) L.; m. Jane H. Barrett, Sept. 30, 1983; children: Matthew, Brian, Michael, Gregory. BA, magna cum laude, Claremont Men's Coll., Calif., 1970; JD cum laude, Harvard U., 1973. Bar: Calif. 1973, U.S. Dist. Ct. (cen. dist.) Calif. 1973, U.S. Ct. Appeals (9th cir.) 1976, U.S. Supreme Ct. 1977, U.S. Ct. Appeals (fed. cir.) 1984. Assoc. Overton, Lyman & Prince, L.A., 1973-78, ptnr., 1978-87; ptnr. Sheppard, Mullin, Richter & Hampton, 1987—; arbitrator L.A. Superior Ct. Fellow Am. Bar Found.; mem. ABA (young lawyers div. exec. coun. 1974-88, chmn. 1984-85, ho. of dels. 1983-89, exec. coun. litigation sect. 1981-83), Calif. Bar Assn. (del. 1976-82, 87-88), L.A. County Bar Assn. (exec. com. 1979-82, trustee 1979-82, barristers sect. exec. coun. 1976-82, pres. 1981-82, exec. council trial lawyers sect. 1984-88, chair amicus briefs com. 1989-92). Office: Sheppard Mullin Richter & Hampton 333 S Hope St Bldg 48 Los Angeles CA 90071-1406

LONG, H. OWEN, retired economics educator, fiction writer; b. Decatur, Tenn., Mar. 6, 1921; s. Thomas Frank and Mattie Lena (Powers) L.; m. Mary Virginia Patrick, Dec. 20, 1951; children: Belinda Jane Long Stevens, John Owen Long. BA, Maryville (Tenn.) Coll., 1943; MS, U. Tenn., 1947; PhD, Vanderbilt U., 1952. Asst. prof. econs. Carson-Newman Coll., Jefferson City, Tenn., 1947-48; assoc. prof. Maryville Coll., 1948-50; prof., dean, registrar, co-founder Ky. Wesleyan Coll., Owensboro, 1951-60; prof., registrar, dean admissions, scholarship officer Evansville (Ind.) U., 1960-62; prof., head dept. bus. and econs. Pensacola (Fla.) Jr. Coll., 1962-86; ret., 1986, writer fiction, history and econs., 1986—. Author: Long-Told Tales, 1990, The Long Path to the Western Waters, 1991, Tales of the Gulf Coast, 1992, Tales of Pleasant Grove, 1992, Tales with a Smile, 1992, A Medley of Tales, 1992, Tales de Guerre, 1993, Get Three Out..Unto a Land (History of Kentucky Wesleyan College), 1994, Tales of Father Gander, 1994, Outline of the Principles of the Science of Economics: Macro-Economics and Micro-Economics, 1994, More Tales of the Gulf Coast, 1994, Tales of the River Country, 1995, Tales of the 50 States and the D.C., 1996. Named Hon. Order Ky. Cols., 1958. Mem. Am. Econ. Assn. (life), Alpha Beta Gamma (life). Home: Long White House 1712 N Whaley Ave Pensacola FL 32503-5733

LONG, HELEN HALTER, author, educator; b. St. Louis; d. Charles C. and Ida (May) Halter; m. Forrest E. Long, June 22, 1944. A.B., Washington U., St. Louis, 1927, A.M., 1928; Ph.D., N.Y. U., 1937. Grad. fellow Washington U., 1927-28; tchr. social studies Venice, Ill., 1928-30; asst. prof. social sci. N.Y. State Coll. for Tchrs., Albany, 1930-38; tchr. pub. schs. Mamaroneck, N.Y., 1938-42; prin. elem. and jr. high schs., 1942-54, asst. supt. schs., 1954-61; dir. Inst. Instructional Improvement, N.Y.C., 1962-88; pres. Books of World, Sweet Springs, Mo., 1962-73; bd. dirs. Roxbury Press, Sweet Springs, Mo., 1963—; teaching fellow, instr. Sch. Edn. NYU, 1936-43; assoc. editor Clearing House, 1935-55. Author: Society in Action, 1936, National Safety Council Lesson Units, 1944-52, (with Forrest E. Long) Social Studies Skills, 8th edit, 1976 (with Forrest E. Long); assoc. editor Clearing House, 1935-55. Mem. Phi Beta Kappa, Pi Gamma Mu, Kappa Delta Pi, Alpha Xi Delta (Diamond Jubilee Outstanding Women award 1968). Home: The Gatesworth One McKnight Pl Saint Louis MO 63124 Office: 107 Medallion Dr PO Box 295 Sweet Springs MO 65351-0295

LONG, HOWARD CHARLES, physics educator emeritus; b. Seizholtzville, Pa., Dec. 12, 1918; s. Howard William and Isabella Geneva (Reese) L.; m. Frances Monroe Hoke, Apr. 16, 1945; children—Howard Charles, David William, Carol Joyce. B.A., Northwestern U., 1941, postgrad., 1941-42; Ph.D., Ohio State U., 1948. Asst. prof. physics Washington and Jefferson Coll., 1948-51; head Electromagnetism Influence Fields sec., U.S. Naval Ordnance Lab., 1951-52; assoc. prof., dept. chmn. physics Am. U., 1952-53; prof. physics, chmn. dept. Gettysburg Coll., 1953-59; prof. physics Dickinson Coll., 1959-81, chmn. dept., 1963-75, Joseph Priestley Chair of Natural Philosophy, 1973, prof. emeritus, 1981—; cons. physicist Naval Ordnance Lab., White Oak, Md., 1952-73, McCoy Electronics Co., Mt. Holly Springs, Pa., 1958-59. Contbr. articles to ednl. jours. Active Boy Scouts Am. Served with USNR, 1944-45. Mem. Am. Assn. Physics Tchrs. (sec.-treas. Central Pa. sect. 1958-59, v.p. 1959-60, pres. 1960-61), A.A.U.P. (sec.-treas. Dickinson chpt. 1963-64, v.p. 1964-65, pres. 1965-66), A.A.A.S., Am. Phys. Soc., Cumberland Conservancy. Methodist (chmn. adminstrn. bd. 1961-62, chmn. ofcl. bd. 1957-59, mem. conf. bd. edn. 1971-73). Home: 240 Belvedere St Carlisle PA 17013-3501 Office: Dickinson Coll Carlisle PA 17013

LONG, JAN MICHAEL, judge; b. Pomeroy, Ohio, May 31, 1952; s. Lewis Franklin and Dorothy (Clatworthy) L.; m. Susan Louise Custer, May 12, 1978; children: John D., Justin M., Jason M. BA, Ohio State U., 1974; JD, Capital U., 1979. Adminstrv. asst. Congressman Doug Applegate, Washington, 1974-77; asst. prosecuting atty. Pickaway County, Circleville, Ohio, 1979-80; mem. Ohio State Senate, Columbus, 1987-97; asst. minority whip Ohio Senate, Columbus, 1995-97; juvenile/probate judge for Pickaway County Circleville, Ohio, 1997—. Named one of Outstanding Young Men Am. U.S. Jaycees, 1987. Mem. Pickaway County Bar Assn. (treas. 1985-86, sec. 1986-87). Democrat. Home: 522 Glenmont Dr Circleville OH 43113-1523 Office: Juvenile Ct Rm 134 Courthouse Circleville OH 43113

LONG, JEANINE HUNDLEY, state legislator; b. Provo, Utah, Sept. 21, 1928; d. Ralph Conrad and Hazel Laurine (Snow) Hundley; m. McKay W. Christensen, Oct. 28, 1949 (div. 1967); children: Cathy Schuyler, Julie Schulleri, Kelly M. Christensen, C. Brett Christensen, Harold A. Christensen; m. Kenneth D. Long, Sept. 6, 1968. AA, Shoreline C.C., Seattle, 1975; BA in Psychology, U. Wash., 1977. Mem. Wash. Ho. of Reps., 1983-87, 93-94, mem. bd. joint com. pension policy, Inst. Pub. Policy; mem. Wash. Senate, 1995—; chair Human Svcs. and Corr. com., Wash. Senate, vice chair Sen. Rep. Caucus. Mayor protem, mem. city coun. City of Brier, Wash., 1977-80. Republican. Office: PO Box 40482 Olympia WA 98504-0482

LONG, JOHN BROADDUS, JR., economist, educator; b. Bklyn., Feb. 28, 1944; s. John Broaddus and Katherine Lumpkin (Wicker) L.; m. Carol Elaine Stephens, Aug. 6, 1966; children—Jennifer Tipton, Owen Rosser, John McCauley. B.A., Rice U., 1966; Ph.D., Carnegie-Mellon U., 1971. Asst. prof. U. Rochester, N.Y., 1969-74, assoc. prof., 1974-84, prof., 1984—. Editor Jour. Fin. Econs., 1982-96, adv. editor, 1996—; contbr. articles to profl. jours. Office: U Rochester William E Simon Grad Sch Bus Adminstrn Wilson Blvd Rochester NY 14627

LONG, JOHN D., retired insurance educator; b. Earlington, Ky., July 21, 1920; s. John Boyd and Effie (Yates) L.; m. Hazel Elinor Schnyder; children: Douglas P., Martha S. Caughey, Elinor J. Badanes. BS, U. Ky., 1942; MBA, Harvard U., 1947; D. Bus. Adminstrn., Indiana U., 1954. CLU, CPCU. Instr. De Pauw U., Greencastle, Ind., 1947; instr. Indiana U., Bloomington, 1947—, asst. prof., 1954-56, assoc. prof., 1956-59, prof., 1959-90, acting dean sch. bus., 1983-84, Arthur M. Weimer prof. bus., 1985-90, Arthur M. Weimer prof. bus. emeritus, 1990—; bd. dirs. Meridian Ins. Cos., Indpls., 1975—; property-liability ins. cons. and expert witness. Author: Ethics, Morality, and Insurance, 1971; co-editor: Property and Liability Insurance Handbook, 1965; editor: Issues in Insurance, 1978; author numerous ins. related monographs; contbr. articles to profl. jours. Served to capt. U.S. Army, 1943-46, 51-52. Mem. Soc. CPCUs, Am. Risk and Ins. Assn. (pres. 1966-67, Elizur Wright award 1975), Am. Inst. Property and Liability Underwriters (trustee 1978-89). Republican. Office: Ind U Sch of Bus 447 Bloomington IN 47405

LONG, JOHN MALOY, university dean; b. Guntersville, Ala., Dec. 28, 1925; s. Sam James and Lillian (Letson) L.; m. Mary Lynn Adams, July 7, 1950; children: John Maloy, Deborra Lynn. B.S., Jacksonville State U., 1949, LL.D., 1971; M.A., U. Ala., 1956. Dir. bands Oneonta (Ala.) High Sch., 1949-50; dir. bands. Ft. Payne (Ala.) High Sch., 1950-55; dir. bands Robert Lee High Sch., Montgomery, Ala., 1955-65; dir. bands. Troy (Ala.) State U., 1965—, chmn. music dept., 1969, dean Sch. Fine Arts, 1971, dean Coll. Arts and Scis., 1972—. Contbr. articles to mags. Pres. Troy City Sch. Bd., 1977; mem. Ala. Hist. Commn., 1976—. Served with AUS, 1944-46. Recipient citation fo excellence Nat. Band Assn., 1972, Disting. Citizens Service award City of Montogomery, 1964, Cert. Appreciation State of Ala., 1964, Algernon Sydney Sullivan award, 1989, Sudler Order of Merit, 1994; named one of top 10 band dirs. in U.S. Sch. Musician Mag., 1969, to Bandmasters Hall of Fame, 1977; named Ala. Outstanding Educator, Ala. Music Educators Assn., 1984; new music bldg.l named in honor Troy State U., 1975, named Disting. prof., 1989. Mem. Am. Bandmaster Assn. (pres. 1987-88), Am. Sch. Band Dirs. Assn. (state pres. 1968-72), Coll. Band Dirs. Nat. Assn. (state pres.), Nat. Band Assn. (named to Hall of Fame, chmn. bd. Hall of Fame), Omicron Delta Kappa Phi, Mu Alpha, Pi Beta Mu, Phi Delta Kappa, Kappa Kappa Psi (Nat. Disting. Svc. to Music award 1979), Delta Chi. Democrat. Methodist. Lodges: Masons; Shriners; Rotary (past pres.). Office: Troy State U John M Long Hall Troy AL 36082

LONG, JOHN PAUL, pharmacologist, educator; b. Albia, Iowa, Oct. 4, 1926; s. John Edward and Bessie May L.; m. Marilyn Joy Stookesberry, June 11, 1950; children: Jeff, John, Jane. B.S., U. Iowa, 1950, M.S., 1952, Ph.D., 1954. Research scientist Sterling Winthrop Co., Albany, N.Y., 1954-56; asst. prof. U. Iowa, Iowa City, 1956-58, asso. prof., 1958-63, prof. pharmacology, 1963—, head dept., 1970-83. Author 315 research publs. in field. Served with U.S. Army, 1945-46. Recipient Abel award Am. Pharm. Assn., 1958; Ebert award Pharmacology Soc., 1962. Mem. Am. Soc. Pharm. Exptl. Therapy, Soc. Exptl. Biol. Medicine. Republican. Home: 1817 Kathlin Dr Iowa City IA 52246-4617 Office: U Iowa Coll Medicine Dept Pharmacology Iowa City IA 52242

LONG, LELAND TIMOTHY, geophysics educator, seismologist; b. Auburn, N.Y., Sept. 6, 1940; s. Walter K. and Carmalita Rose Long; m. Sarah Alice Blackard, Mar. 1970; children: Sarah Alice, Katherine Rose, Amy Virginia. BS in Geology, U. Rochester, 1962; MS in Geophysics, N.Mex. Inst. Mining and Tech., 1964; PhD in Geophysics, Oreg. State U., 1968. Registered profl. geologist, Ga. From asst. to assoc. prof. Sch. Earth and Atmosphere Scis. Ga. Inst. Tech., Atlanta, 1968-81, prof., 1981; cons. in seismology, near-surface seismic imaging, seismic road vibrations and gravity data analysis. Contbr. articles to profl. jours. Office: Ga Inst Tech Earth and Atmospheric Scis Atlanta GA 30332

LONG, MADELEINE J., mathematics and science educator; b. N.Y.C.; d. Harry L. and Irma (Silverman) L. B.A., Queens Coll., 1960; M.Ed., Harvard U., 1963; Ed.D., Columbia U., 1967. Tchr. Westbury (N.Y.) Sch. System, 1960-61; teaching fellow Harvard U., 1962-63; prof. edn. L.I. U., asst. to dean, 1967-69, chmn. dept., 1969-76, dir. div. edn., dir. grad.

programs at Westchester br. campus, 1977-83, dir. Inst. Advancement Math. and Sci., 1983-91; program officer (on leave from L.I. U.) NSF, Washington, 1993—, mem. Presdl. awards program, 1991-92; v.p. The Implementation Group, 1996—; vis. scientist, spl. asst. comprehensive design planning NSF, 1992-93, sr. program officer Urban Systemic Initiative, 1993-96, reader, 1973, 77, 79, 85, 88, 90, career access panelist and chair, 1988; dir. summer tng. programs N.Y.C. Bd. Edn., 1978, 79, 81; reader Fund for Imporvement Postsecondary Edn., 1984, 85, 87, N.J. Bd. Higher Edn., Minority Instns. Sci. Improvement Program; cons. to various univs. and sch. sys.; lectr. in field; apptd. coun. on excellence and equity in math. and sci. edn. N.Y. State, 1986-91; v.p. The Implementation Group, 1996—. Mem. editorial bd. Jour. Coll. Sci. Teaching, 1986-89; contbr. articles to profl. jours. Mem. edn. subcom. Mayor's Commn. on Sci. and Tech., 1989-91. Columbia U. fellow, 1963-64, grantee NSF, 1972, 78, 79, 80, 81, 84-87, 87-91, 91-94, Career Edn., 1975, Fund for Improvement Postsecondary Edn., 1983-87, Title II Edn. for Econ. Security Act N.Y. State. Fellow Philosophy of Edn. Soc.; mem. AAAS (chair sect. Q, Sci. Edn., chmn. edn. section) Assn. Supervision and Curriculum Devel., N.Y. Acad. Sci., Nat. Sci. Tchrs. Assn., Nat. Coun. Tchrs. Math., Am. Ednl. Rsch. Assn., Kappa Delta Pi. Office: NSF 4201 Wilson Blvd Arlington VA 22201

LONG, MARY LOUISE, retired government official; b. Macon, Ga., Aug. 25, 1922; d. Willie and Sarah (Sparks) Tyson; A.B., Morris Brown Coll., Atlanta, 1946; m. Samuel F. Long, Apr. 14, 1962. Supervisory procurement clk. Dept. Def., N.Y., 1954-62, purchasing agt. Phila. Procurement Dist., 1962-64, Army Electronic Command, Phila., 1964-66, Med. Directorate, Def. Personnel Support Center, Phila., 1966-75, contracting officer, 1975-80, sect. chief/contracting officer, 1980-83. Active NAACP, YMCA; established Mary Louise Tyson Long Scholarship Fund, Morris Brown Coll., 1986; mem. Phila Inter-alumni coun. United Negro Coll. Fund. Named Alumna of Yr. Morris Brown Coll., 1987, 50th Reunion Cert., 1997. Mem. Beta Omicron, Iota Phi Lambda. Congregationalist. Home: 617 E Mt Airy Ave Philadelphia PA 19119-1147

LONG, MAURICE WAYNE, physicist, electrical engineer, radar consultant; b. Madisonville, Ky., Apr. 20, 1925; s. Maurice K. and Martha Ann (Nourse) L.; m. Patricia Lee Holmes, Feb. 25, 1950 (dec. Aug. 1961); children: Anne Catherine Long Key, Jane Elizabeth Long Rice; m. Beverly Ann Benson, Jan. 1, 1963; stepchildren: Theodore Douglas Downing, Beverly Patricia Downing. BEE, Ga. Inst. Tech., 1946, MS in Physics, 1957, PhD, 1959; MSEE, U. Ky., 1948. Registered profl. engr., Ga. Rsch. asst. Ga. Inst. Tech., Atlanta, 1946-47, rsch. engr., then spl. rsch. engr., asst. rsch. prof., prin. rsch. physicist, 1950-68, prof. elec. engring., 1968-73, head radar devel. br., 1955-60, chief div. electronics, 1959-68, dir. Engring. Expt. Sta. (now Ga. Tech. Rsch. Inst.), 1968-75; dir. rsch., sec., asst. treas. Ga. Tech. Rsch. Corp., 1968-75; liaison scientist U.S. Office Naval Rsch. London Br., 1966-67; bd. dirs. Ga. Tech. Rsch. Inst., 1968-82; mem. com. on remote sensing programs for earth resources surveys NAS, 1977, space applications adv. com., subcom. on remote sensing NASA, 1983-86; mem. Acad. Electromagnetics, MIT, 1990; mem. various coms. on radar U.S. Army, Navy, Air Force, NASA, 1967—. Author: Radar Reflectivity of Land and Sea, 1975, 2d edit., 1983; editor, contbg. author: Airborne Early Warning System Concepts, 1992; contbr. numerous articles to profl. jours., chpts. to books; patentee in field. Mem. Ga. Gov.'s Sci. Adv. Coun., 1972-74, chmn. ad hoc com. on tech. growth in Ga., 1974. Fellow IEEE (life); mem. Acad. Electromagnetics, Internat. Union Radio Sci. (commn. F.), Assn. Old Crows, Sigma Xi. Avocations: sailing, traveling. Home: 1036 Somerset Dr NW Atlanta GA 30327-3736

LONG, MAXINE MASTER, lawyer; b. Pensacola, Fla., Oct. 20, 1943; d. Maxwell L. and Claudine E. (Smith) M.; m. Anthony Byrd Long, Aug. 27, 1966; children: Deborah E., David M. AB, Bryn Mawr Coll., 1965; MS, Georgetown U., 1971; JD, U. Miami, 1979. Bar: Fla. 1979, U.S. Ct. Appeals (5th cir.) 1980, U.S. Dist. Ct. (so. dist.) Fla. 1980, U.S. Ct. Appeals (11th cir.) 1981, U.S. Dist. Ct. (mid. and no. dists.) Fla. 1987. Law clk. to U.S. dist. judge U.S. Dist. Ct. (so. dist.) Fla., Miami, 1979-80; assoc. Shutts & Bowen, Miami, 1980-90, of counsel, 1990-92, ptnr., 1992—. Mem. Fla. Bar Assn. (vice chair bus. litigation cert. com. 1996—, past chair bus. litigation com., exec. coun. bus. law sect.), Dade County Bar Assn. (mem. fed. cts. com., recipient pro bono award/Vol. Lawyers for the Arts 1989). Office: Shutts & Bowen 201 S Biscayne Blvd Miami FL 33131-4332

LONG, MICHAEL THOMAS, lawyer, manufacturing company executive; b. Hartford, Conn., Feb. 22, 1942; s. Michael Joseph and Mary Fagan (Maguire) L.; m. Ann Marie O'Connell, Sept. 9, 1967; children: Michael, Maura, Deirdre. BBA, U. Notre Dame, 1964; JD, U. Conn., 1967, postgrad., 1968. Bar: Conn. 1967. Law clk. U.S. Bankruptcy Ct., U.S. Dist. Ct., Hartford, 1966-68; supr. indsl. rels. Ensign-Bickford Industries, Inc., Simsbury, Conn., 1968-72, contract adminstr., 1972-74, div. controller, 1974-79, mgr. govt. and legal affairs, 1978-81, gen. counsel, sec., 1981-83, v.p., gen. counsel, sec., 1983—; bd. dirs. Ensign-Bickford Co.; pres., chief exec. officer, Ensign-Bickford Haz-Pros Inc., 1989—; U. Notre Dame Alumni Clubs of Greater Hartford scholarship chmn., 1990—. Chmn. Dem. Town Com., Simsbury, 1971-81, Dem. State Ctrl. Com. of Conn., 1992—, Bradley Internat. Airport Commn., Windsor Locks, Conn., 1983—; mem. pub. bldg. com. Town of Simsbury, 1981-85, mem. cultural, parks and recreation com., 1986-87, mem. fin. bd., 1987—; mem. Simsbury Jr. Achievement, 1970-74; pres. parish council St. Mary's Ch., Simsbury, 1982-85; chmn. Bradley Internat. Airport Commn., 1983-91. Named Home Town Hero Town of Simsbury, 1987; recipient Man of Yr. award U. Notre Dame Alumni Clubs of Greater Hartford, 1995. Mem. ABA, Conn. Bar Assn., Hartford County Bar Assn., Inst. Makers of Explosives (bd. govs. 1987—, chmn. legal affairs com. 1986-93, 95—), Am. Corp. Counsel Assn. (bd. dirs. Hartford chpt. 1988—), Greater Harford C. of C. (bd. dirs. 1991-94), Internat. Soc. Explosive Engrs., Simsbury Farms Men's Club (founder 1972), Hop Meadow Country Club. Democrat. Roman Catholic. Home: 9 Metacom Dr Simsbury CT 06070-1851 Office: Ensign-Bickford Industries Inc 10 Mill Pond Ln PO Box 7 Simsbury CT 06070-0007

LONG, PATRICIA GAVIGAN, elementary education educator, English language educator; b. Bryn Mawr, Pa., Mar. 5, 1942; d. Thomas and Martha Mary Gavigan; m. James Robert III, Nov. 22, 1978; children: Jon Rhys Long, Martha Lucille Long. AA, AssumptionColl., Mendham, N.J., 1964; BS in Elem. Edn., St. Joseph's Coll., Phila., 1970; MEd, Pa. State U., 1975. Cert. Tchr. grades 1-7, mid. sch., 6-8. Reading Specialist, K-12, Pa., Va. Grade 2 tchr. St. Nicholas Elem. Sch., Jersey City, N.J., 1962-64; grade 1 and 2 tchr. St. Lawrence Elem. Sch., Harrisburg, Pa., 1964-66, Holy Trinity Elem. Sch., Hazelton, Pa., 1966-68; grade 3 tchr. St. Margaret's Elem. Sch., Narberth, Pa., 1968-75; reading resource tchr. K-5 Arrowhead Elem. Sch., Virginia Beach, Va., 1975-84; reading tchr. grade 8-9 Stonewall Jackson Jr. High, Mechanicsville, Va., 1984-89; grade 6 tchr., chair English dept. Stonewall Jackson Middle Sch., Mechanicsville, Va., 1989—. Named Reading Tchr. of Yr. Arrowhead Elem. Sch., Virginia Beach, Va., 1978, Stonewall Jackson/Richmond Area Reading Coun., Richmond, Va., 1992. Mem. PTA Stonewall Jackson Middle Sch. (reflection chair), Richmond Area reading Coun., Va. State Reading Coun., Hanover Edn. Assn. Va. Edn. Assn., NEA, Richmond Area English Coun., Va. Area Tchr. of English, Arrowhead PTA Bd. (life.). Republican. Roman Catholic. Avocations: reading, walking, wallpapering, painting, helping others. Office: Stonewall Jackson Mid Sch Lee Davis Rd Mechanicsville VA 23111-4699

LONG, PHILIP LEE, information systems executive; b. Cleve., Jan. 24, 1943; s. Philip Joseph and Anne Catherine (Woodward) L.; BEE, Ohio State U., 1968, MSc, 1970; m. LeAnn Boyack Edvalson, Apr. 22, 1982; children: Sarah J., Caitlin T.; children by previous marriage: Philip Imants, Michael Oskar; Assoc. dir. Ohio Coll. Libr. Ctr., 1969-73; asso. for computer systems devel. SUNY, Albany, 1974-75; pres. Philip Long Assos., Inc., Salt Lake City, 1975-81; v.p. Novell Data Systems, 1981-82; v.p. Telerate Systems, Inc., 1983-93; pres. Philip Long Assocs., Ltd., South Orange, N.J., 1993—; instr. computer sci. Ohio State Univ., libr. sci. SUNY, Catholic U. Am.; cons. to UNESCO, Bibliotheque National de France, Lib. Congress, Nat. Comm. Library and Info. Sci. Grantee, Nat. Rsch. Coun., Nat. Acad. Sci., 1971. Mem. Am. Soc. Info. Sci., IEEE, ALA, Assn. Computing Machinery, Am. Nat. Stds. Inst. Contbr. articles to profl. jours. Office: 397 Thornden St South Orange NJ 07079-1423

LONG, PHILLIP CLIFFORD, museum director; b. Tucson, Oct. 11, 1942; s. Hugh-Blair Grigsby and Phyllis Margaret (Clay) L.; m. Martha Whitney Rowe, Aug. 26, 1972; children—Elisha Whitney, Charlotte Clay, Elliot Sherlock. B.A., Tulane U., 1965. Sec. Fifth Third Bancorp, Cin., 1974-94; sr. v.p., sec. Fifth Third Bank, Cin., 1988-94; dir. Taft Mus., Cin., 1994—. Trustee Contemporary Arts Ctr., 1974-84, Art Acad. Cin., 1980-94, Cin. Symphony Orch., 1981-87, Cin. Nature Ctr., 1982-88, Taft Mus., 1987-94, Cin. Country Day Sch., 1991—; trustee, treas. Cin. Music Hall, 1981-92, Convalescent Hosp. for Children, 1989—, Cin. Assn. for Arts, 1992—. Mem. The Camargo Club, Queen City Club. Home: 4795 Burley Hills Dr Cincinnati OH 45243-4007 Office: Taft Mus 316 Pike St Cincinnati OH 45202-4214

LONG, RALPH STEWART, clinical psychologist; b. Pitts., Feb. 23, 1926; s. Ralph S. and Virginia (Hawk) L.; m. Vera Lazorchak, June 16, 1951; children: Karen Virginia, Brian Reed, Lauri Michelle. BS, Lock Haven U., 1950; MEd, Pa. State U., 1951; PhD, Washington U., St. Louis, 1965. Lic. psychologist, Tex. Commd. 2d lt. USAF, 1951, advanced through grades to lt. col., 1968; psychologist various hosps. USAF, U.S. and Europe, 1951-71; ret., 1971; dir. psychol. svcs. Community Ctr. Mental Health, Mental Retardation, Wichita Falls, Tex., 1971-72; psychol. cons. Family Counseling Ctr., Wichita Falls, 1972-74; dir. psychol. svcs. Nueces County Mental Health-Mental Retardation Community Ctr, 1974-77; dir. Corpus Christi Counseling Ctr./Physicians-Surgeons Hosp., Tex., 1977-79, Psychol. Cons., Corpus Christi, 1979-82; exec. dir. Personal Dynamics Inst., Corpus Christi, 1982—, dir., 1988—; instr. dept. psychology McKendree Coll., Lebanon, Ill., 1962-63; instr. So. Ill. U., 1962-64; adj. prof. human rels. Webster U., Webster Groves, Mo., 1976-79, 88-93; adj. prof. psychology Del Mar Coll., Corpus Christi, 1977-83, adj. prof. bus. adminstrn., 1991-93; cons. Tex. Dept. Corrections, 1988-90; bd. dirs. Ctr. Creative Living, 1986—; cons., trainer Crisis Svcs., 1980—; profl. adv. bd. North Tex. Regional Coun. Alcoholism, 1971-74, Mental Health Assn. Coastal Bend, 1974-83, Wichita Mental Health Assn., 1965-67, 70-74; adj. prof. Embry-Riddle U., Corpus Christi, 1991-93; consulting psychologist Nueces County Juvenile Justice Ctr., Corpus Christi, 1992—, Warm Springs Rehab. Ctr., Corpus Christi, 1992—, MCC Managed Behavioral Care, Inc., Eden Prairie, Minn., 1992—, Champus Provider, 1972—; bd. dirs. Consumer Credit Counseling Svc. South Tex., 1983-92, emeritus, 1993—. Contbr. to profl. jours.; presenter in field. Active Tex. chpt. ARC. With USN, 1944-51. Named Am. Man Sci., 1962. Fellow Soc. Air Force Clin. Psychologists; mem. APA, DAV, VFW, Am. Inst. Hypnosis, U.S. Holocaust Meml. Mus. (charter), Libr. of Congress Assocs. (charter), Tex. Assn. Mental Health (exec. com. 1980-83), Air Force Assn., Nat. Register Health Svc. Providers in Psychology, Smithsonian, Sierra Club, Am. Assn. Ret. Persons, Ret. Officers Assn., Am. Legion, Common Cause, United Srs. Assn., Theosophical Soc. Am., Nat. Wildlife Fedn., F.D. Roosevelt Meml. (founding), Am. Air Mus. in Britain (charter), Masons, Shriners, Sigma Xi. Avocations: painting, writing, travel, camping, fishing. Office: Personal Dynamics Inst 1819 S Brownlee Blvd Corpus Christi TX 78404-2901

LONG, RICHARD PAUL, civil engineering educator, geotechnical engineering consultant; b. Allentown, Pa., Nov. 29, 1934; s. Peter Anthony and Matilda (Stier) L.; m. Mary Elizabeth Doyle, Aug. 29, 1964; children: Marybeth, Christopher. BCE, U. Cin., 1957; MCE, Rensselaer Poly. Inst., 1963, PhD, 1966. Registered profl. engr., Conn. NSF postdoctoral fellow Rensselaer Poly. Inst., Troy, N.Y., 1966-67; from asst. to assoc. prof. civil engring. U. Conn., Storrs, 1967-77, prof., 1978—, head dept., 1977-90; com. mem. Transp. Research Bd., Washington, 1971—. Contbr. articles to profl. jours.; co-inventor, patentee prefabricated subsurface drain, stress laminated timber bridges. Pres. Mansfield Middle Sch. Assn., Storrs, 1977-79; commr. Mansfield Housing Authority, Storrs, 1987—, chmn., 1988-93. 1st lt. U.S. Army, 1958-61. Recipient T.A. Bedford prize Rensselaer Poly. Inst., 1966, AT&T Found. award for Teaching Excellence, 1988, Recognition award Conn. Soc. Profl. Engrs., 1989. Fellow ASCE; mem. Conn. Soc. Civil Engrs. (sec. 1986-88, pres.-elect 1988-89, pres. 1989-90), Am. Soc. Engring. Edn. Roman Catholic. Avocations: jogging, travel. Home: 31 Westgate Ln Storrs Mansfield CT 06268-1506 Office: Univ Conn U-37 Dept Civil Engring Storrs CT 06269-2037

LONG, ROBERT EMMET, author; b. Oswego, N.Y., June 7, 1934; s. Robert Emmet and Verda (Lindsley) L. BA, Columbia Coll., 1956; MA, Syracuse U., 1964; PhD, Columbia U., 1968. Instr. SUNY, Cortland, 1962-64; asst. prof. Queens Coll., CUNY, N.Y.C., 1968-71; writer, 1971—. Author: The Great Succession: Henry James and the Legacy of Hawthorne, 1979, The Achieving of the Great Gatsby, 1979, Henry James: The Early Years, 1983, John O'Hara, 1983, Nathanael West, 1985, Barbara Pym, 1986, James Thurber, 1988, James Fenimore Cooper, 1990, The Films of Merchant Ivory, 1991, Ingmar Bergman: Film and Stage, 1994, The Films of Merchant Ivory: Newly Updated Edition, 1997; editor numerous books; contbr. articles to profl. jours. and popular mags. Democrat. Episcopalian. Avocations: films, theater, ballet, jazz, travel. Address: 254 S 3rd St Fulton NY 13069-2356

LONG, ROBERT EUGENE, banker; b. Yankton, S.D., Dec. 5, 1931; s. George Joseph and Malinda Ann (Hanson) L.; m. Patricia Louise Glass, June 19, 1959; children: Malinda Ann, Robert Eugene, Jennifer Lynn, Michael Joseph. B.S. in Acctg., U. S.D., 1956; M.B.A., U. Mich., 1965; grad., Madison Grad. Sch. Banking, 1973, Nat. Comml. Lending Grad. Sch., U. Okla., 1977. Cert. comml. lender. Financial analyst Chrysler Corp., 1958-59; supr. finance Ford Motor Co., 1966-67; with First Wis. Bankshares Corp., Milw., 1967—; v.p. fin. First Wis. Bankshares Corp., 1973—; exec. v.p. 1st Wis. Fond du Lac, 1978—; dir. 1st Wis. Nat. Bank of, Southgate, Waukesha and Fond du Lac; exec. v.p., dir. West Allis State Bank, 1979-81, pres., dir., 1981—, chief exec. officer, 1983—; sr. v.p. adminstrn. Park Banks, 1987—; speaker/chmn. banking seminars Am. Mgmt. Assn., 1970—. Pres. local br. Aid Assn. Luth., 1970—, corp. bd. dirs., 1982—, vice chmn. bd., 1989—; pres. Mt. Carmel Luth. Ch., Milw., 1972; team capt. Re-elect Nixon campaign, 1972; bd. dirs. Luth. Social Svcs. of Wis. and Upper Mich., 1978—, chmn. bd., 1983—; bd. dirs. Luther Manor, 1981, Luther Manor Found., 1984, pres. bd. dirs. United Luth. Program for Aging, 1986—; bd. dirs. Wis. Inst. Family Medicine, 1985, pres., 1992—; vice chmn. adv. coun. West Allis Meml. Hosp., 1993—, elected corp. adv. coun., 1996. With USAF, 1951-52. Recipient Good Citizenship award Am. Legion, 1948. Mem. Wis. Assn. Family Practice (bd. dirs. 1992—), Wauwatosa C. of C. (bd. dirs. 1992—), Alpha Tau Omega. Lutheran. Clubs: Western Racquet (Elm Grove, Wis.) (dir. 1976—); Bluemound Golf and Country; Elmbrook Swim (pres. 1977-78). Lodges: Masons, Shriners, Jesters. Home: N21w24052 Dorchester Dr Unit D Pewaukee WI 53072-4692 Office: Park Banks 330 E Kilbourn Ave Milwaukee WI 53202

LONG, ROBERT LIVINGSTON, retired photographic equipment executive; b. Abbeville, S.C., Jan. 3, 1937; s. Clarance Blakely and Amy (Wolff) L.; m. Phyllis Jo Crews, May 30, 1959; children: J. Blake, Brynn Diane, Brant Wolff. BSCE, U. S.C., 1959; grad. in Indsl. Mgmt. Program, U. Tenn., 1967. Chem. engr. Tenn. div. Eastman Kodak Co., Kingsport, 1959-66, gen. mgmt. staff tech. Tenn. div., 1966-74, mgr. licensing chemicals div., 1974-80, dir. mfg. staff Tenn. div., 1980-83, v.p., dir. planning div., chemicals div., 1983-86; v.p., dir. corp. planning Eastman Kodak Co., Rochester, N.Y., 1986-92, sr. v.p., 1989; cons., Melbourne Beach, Fla., 1992—; bd. dirs. Sun Microsystems Inc., Mt. View, Calif., Broadband Comms. Products, Melbourne, Fla., 1995—. Participant Tenn. Exec. Devel. Program, Knoxville, 1974; multiple adv. bd. City of Kingsport, 1978-86; bd. dirs. Boy's Club Greater Kingsport, 1965-81, chmn., 1973-75; bd. dirs. Holston Valley Hosp. and Med. Ctr., Kingsport, 1983-86, Rochester Gen. Hosp., 1988-92. Sgt. U.S. Army N.G., 1955-63. Recipient Medallion, Boys Club Am., 1976, Bronze Keyston award Boys Club Am., 1985. Mem. Am. Inst. Chem. Engrs., Soc. for Info. Mgmt., Acad. Natural Scis. (bd. dirs. environ. assocs. 1982-85), Sigma Alpha Epsilon. Episcopalian. Lodge: Rotary (chmn. coms. Kingsport 1975-86).

LONG, ROBERT LYMAN JOHN, naval officer; b. Kansas City, Mo., May 29, 1920; s. Trigg A. and Margaret (Franklin) L.; m. Sara Helms, Aug. 28, 1944; children: Charles Allen, William Trigg, Robert Helms. BS, U.S. Naval Acad., 1943; grad., Naval War Coll., 1954. Commd. ensign USN, 1943, advanced through grades to adm., 1977; assigned PTO; comdr. two nuclear polaris submarines, 1966-68; comdr. service force for 7th fleet, 1968-69; dep. comdr. Naval Ship Systems Command, 1969-72; comdr. submarine force U.S. Atlantic Fleet, 1972-74; dep. chief naval ops. for submarine warfare Washington, 1974-77; vice chief naval ops., 1977-79; comdr.-in-chief U.S. Forces Pacific, 1979-83. Decorated D.S.M. (two), Legion of Merit (three), Bronze Star. Club: Cosmos. Home: 247 Heamans Way Annapolis MD 21401-6303

LONG, ROBERT M., newspaper publishing executive; m. June Long; children: Shannon, Bob. BBA, Dyke Coll. CPA, Ohio. From acct. to treas. and contr. Plain Dealer Pub. Co., Cleve., 1965-92, exec. v.p., 1992—; v.p. Plain Dealer Charities, Inc., Delcom, Inc. Trustee Dyke Coll., Cleve. Ballet, St. Vincent Quadrangle, Inc.; bd. dirs. Jr. Achievement; active Leadership Cleve., 1993. Mem. Internat. Newspaper Fin. Execs. (bd. dirs.), Ohio Soc. CPAs, Cleve. Treas. Club. Office: The Plain Dealer Pub Co 1801 Superior Ave E Cleveland OH 44114-2107*

LONG, ROBERT MERRILL, retail drug company executive; b. Oakland, Calif., May 19, 1938; s. Joseph Milton and Vera Mai (Skaggs) L.; m. Eliane Quilloux, Dec. 13, 1969. Student, Brown U., 1956-58; BA, Claremont Men's Coll., 1960. With Longs Drug Stores Inc., Walnut Creek, Calif., 1960—, dist. mgr., 1970-72, exec. v.p., 1972-75, pres., 1975-77, pres., chief exec. officer, 1977-91; chmn., chief exec. officer Longs Drug Stores, Walnut Creek, Calif., 1991—. Mem. Nat. Assn. Chain Drug Stores (dir.). Office: Longs Drug Stores Corp PO Box 5222 141 N Civic Dr Walnut Creek CA 94596-3858

LONG, ROBERT RADCLIFFE, fluid mechanics educator; b. Glen Ridge, N.J., Oct. 24, 1919; s. Clarence D. and Gertrude (Cooper) L.; m. Cristina Nersing, 1962; children: John Radcliffe, Robert W. AB in Econs, Princeton, 1941; MS in Meteorology, U. Chgo., 1949, PhD, 1950. Meteorologist U.S. Weather Bur., Paris, France, 1946-47; asst. prof. Johns Hopkins U., Balt., 1951-56, assoc. prof., 1956-59, prof. fluid mechanics, 1959-88, prof. emeritus, 1988—, dir. hydrodynamics lab., 1951-88; assoc. dept. aero. and mech. engring. Ariz. State U. Author: Mechanics of Solids and Fluids, 1960, Engineering Science Mechanics, 1964; also articles in field. Home: PO Box 10381 Sarasota FL 34278-0381

LONG, RONALD ALEX, real estate and financial consultant, educator; b. Scranton, Pa., Dec. 9, 1948; s. Anthony James and Dorothy Agnas (Posgay) L.; m. Geraldine Sinneway, July 17, 1976; 1 child, Elizabeth Dorothy. BA, Bethany Coll., Lindsburg, Kans., 1971; MAT, Trenton (N.J.) State Coll., 1973; BS, Spring Garden Coll., 1980; MBA, St. Joseph's U., Phila., 1985; JD, Widener U., 1996; cert. new home sales profl., Grad. Realtor Inst., 1990. Cert. real estate instr. Substitute tchr. Hackettstown and Roxbury (N.J.) Sch. Bds., 1971-72; prof., chmn. bus. adminstrn. dept. Spring Garden Coll., Phila., 1973-92; sales assoc. Red Carpet Real Estate, Doylestown, Pa., 1980—; cons. real estate Doylestown, 1980—; cons. mgmt. Budd Wheel Corp., Phila., 1978-82; pres., prin. Aladdin Fin. Svcs., Inc.; prin. Loan Finders, Inc.; dir. Met. Real Estate Sch., Doylestown, 1991-95; cons. The Princeton Group Telecom. Specialist, 1993-96; adj. prof. Pa. State U., Thomas Edison Coll. Co-author: Explorations in Macroeconomics, 1988, Explorations in Microeconomics, 1989; contbr. articles to area newspapers. Site dir. ARC Blood Mobile, 1975-91; bd. dirs Buckingham (Pa.) PTA, 1984-88. Recipient Legion Honor award Chapel of the 4 Chaplains, Phila., 1984. Mem. Nat. Assn. Realtors, Pa. Assn. Realtors, Bucks County Assn. Realtors, U.S. Power Squadrons, U.S. Coast Guard Aux., Profl. Assn. Diving Instrs. (cert.), Moe Levine Trial Advocacy Honor Soc. (cert. achievement land transactions, ocean and coastal law, alcohol, vehicle and the law), Alcohol, Vehicle and the Law, Bus. Club (treas. 1969-71, pres. 1970-71), Alpha Chi, Pi Sigma Chi, Eta Beta Phi, Delta Theta Phi. Republican. Avocations: scuba diving, karate, surface and underwater photography, running. Home: 2698 Cranberry Rd Doylestown PA 18901-1770

LONG, RUSSELL CHARLES, academic administrator; b. Alpine, Tex., Oct. 9, 1942; s. Roy Joel and Lovis Lorene (Graham) L.; m. Elaine Gresham, May 8, 1964 (div. Jan. 1986); 1 child, Mark Roy; m. Natrelle Hedrick, Mar. 28, 1986. BS, Sul Ross State U., Alpine, 1965; MA, N.Mex. State U., 1967; PhD, Tex. A&M U., 1977. Assoc. prof. Schreiner Coll., Kerrville, Tex., 1967-69; instr. Tarleton State U., Stephenville, Tex., 1969-72, asst. prof., 1972-77, assoc. prof., 1977-85, prof., 1985-92, asst. v.p. acad. adminstrn., 1987-90, chair dept. English and Lang., 1990-92; provost and v.p. acad. adminstrn. West Tex. A&M U., Canyon, 1992-94, interim pres., 1994-95, pres., 1995—. Office: West Texas A&M Univ WT Sta 2501 4th Ave Canyon TX 79016

LONG, SARAH ANN, librarian; b. Atlanta, May 20, 1943; d. Jones Lloyd and Lelia Maria (Mitchell) Sanders; m. James Allen Long, 1961 (div. 1985); children: Andrew C., James Allen IV; m. Donald J. Sager, May 23, 1987. BA, Oglethorpe U., 1966; M in Librarianship, Emory U., 1967. Asst. libr. Coll. of St. Matthias, Bristol, Eng., 1970-74; cons. State Libr. of Ohio, Columbus, 1975-77; coord. Pub. Libr. of Columbus and Franklin County, Columbus, 1977-79, dir. Fairfield County Dist. Libr., Lancaster, Ohio, 1979-82, Dauphin County Libr. System, Harrisburg, Pa., 1982-85, Multnomah County Libr., Portland, Oreg., 1985-89; system dir. North Suburban Libr. System, Wheeling, Ill., 1989—; chmn. Portland State U. Libr. Adv. Coun., 1987-89. Contbr. articles to profl. jours. Bd. dirs. Dauphin County Hist. Soc., Harrisburg, 1983-85, ARC, Harrisburg, 1984-85; pres. Lancaster-Fairfield County YWCA, Lancaster, 1981-82; vice-chmn. govt. and edn. div. Lancaster-Fairfield County United Way, Lancaster, 1981-82; sec. Fairfield County Arts Coun., 1981-82; adv. bd. Portland State U., 1987-89; mentor Ohio Libr. Leadership Inst., 1993, 95. Recipient Dir.'s award Ohio Program in Humanities, Columbus, 1982; Sarah Long Day established in her honor Fairfield County, Lancaster, Bd. Commrs., 1982. Mem. ALA (elected coun. 1993—), Pub. Libr. Assn. (pres. 1989-90, chair legis. com. 1991-95, chair 1998 nat. conf. com. 1995—), Ill. Libr. Assn. (pub. policy com. 1991—). Office: N Suburban Libr Systems 200 W Dundee Rd Wheeling IL 60090-4750

LONG, SARAH ELIZABETH BRACKNEY, physician; b. Sidney, Ohio, Dec. 5, 1926; d. Robert LeRoy and Caroline Josephine (Shue) Brackney; m. John Frederick Long, June 15, 1948; children: George Lynas, Helen Lucille Corcoran, Harold Roy, Clara Alice Lawrence, Nancy Carol Sieber. BA, Ohio State U., 1948, MD, 1952. Intern Grant Hosp., Columbus, Ohio, 1952-53; resident internal medicine Mt. Carmel Med. Ctr., Columbus, 1966-69, chief resident internal medicine, 1968-69; med. cons. Ohio Bur. Disability Determination, Columbus, 1970—; physician student health Ohio State U., Columbus, 1970-73; sch. physician Bexley (Ohio) City Schs., 1973-83; physician advisor to peer rev. Mt. Carmel East Hosp., Columbus, 1979-86, med. dir. employee health, 1981-96; physician cons. Fed. Black Lung program U.S. Dept. Labor, Columbus, 1979—. Mem. AMA, Gerontol. Soc. Am., Ohio Hist. Soc., Ohio State Med. Assn., Franklin County Acad. Medicine, Alpha Epsilon Delta, Phi Beta Kappa. Home: 2765 Bexley Park Rd Columbus OH 43209-2231

LONG, SARAH S., pediatrician, educator; b. Portland, Oreg., Oct. 31, 1944. MD, Jefferson Med. Coll., 1970. Diplomate Am. Bd. Pediatrics. Intern St. Christopher Hosp. for Children, Phila., 1970-71, resident, 1971-73; fellow pediatric and infant depts. Temple U. Sch. Medicine, Phila., 1973-75; staff St. Christopher Hosp. for Children, Phila., 1975—; prof. Temple U. Sch. Medicine, 1975—. Chief editor: Principles and Practice of Pediatric Infectious Diseases, 1997; contbr. over 90 articles to med. jours. Mem. Am. Acad. Pediatrics, Soc. for Pediat. Rsch., Am. Pediat. Soc. Office: St Christopher Child Hosp Erie Ave at Front St Philadelphia PA 19134

LONG, SHARON RUGEL, molecular biologist, plant biology educator; b. San Marcos, Tex., Mar. 2, 1951; d. Harold Eugene and Florence Jean (Rugel) Long; m. Harold James McGee, July 7, 1979; 2 children. BS, Calif. Inst. Tech., 1973; PhD, Yale U., 1979. Rsch. fellow Harvard U., Cambridge, Mass., 1979-81; asst. prof. molecular biology Stanford U., Palo Alto, Calif., 1982-87, assoc. prof., 1987-92, prof., 1992—; investigator Howard Hughes Med. Inst., 1994—; bd. dirs. Ann. Revs. Inc. Assoc. editor (jour.) Plant Physiology, 1992—; editor Jour. Bacteriology; mem. editl. bd. Devel. Biology; editl. com. Ann. Review Cell Biology. Bd. scientific advisors Jane Coffin Childs Meml. Fund. Recipient postdoctoral award NSF, 1979, NIH, 1980, Shell Rsch. Found. award 1985, Presdl. Young Investigator award

NSF, 1984-89, Faculty awards for women, 1991; rsch. grantee NIH, Dept. Energy, NSF; MacArthur fellow, 1992-97. Fellow AAAS, Am. Acad. Arts and Scis., Am. Acad. Microbiology, Noble Found.; mem. NAS, Genetics Soc. Am., Am. Soc. Plant Physiology (Charles Albert Shull award 1989), Am. Soc. Microbiology, Soc. Devel. Biology. Office: Stanford U Dept Biol Scis Stanford CA 94305-5020

LONG, SHELLEY, actress; b. Fort Wayne, Ind., Aug. 23, 1949; m. Bruce Tyson; 1 child, Juliana. Student, Northwestern U. Writer, assoc. prodr., co-host Chgo. TV program Sorting It Out, 1970s (3 local Emmys 1970); mem. Second City, Chgo.; guest TV appearances various shows including M.A.S.H., Love Boat, Family, Frasier; regular TV series Cheers, 1982-87, Good Advice, 1993-94; motion pictures include A Small Circle of Friends, 1980, Caveman, 1981, Night Shift, 1982, Losin' It, 1983, Irreconcilible Differences, 1984, The Money Pit, 1986, Outrageous Fortune, 1987, Hello Again, 1987, Troop Beverly Hills, 1989, Don't Tell Her It's Me, 1990, Frozen Assets, 1992, The Brady Bunch Movie, 1995, A Very Brady Sequel, 1996; TV films include The Cracker Factory, 1979, The Promise of Love, 1980, The Princess and the Cabbie, 1981, Memory of a Murder, 1992, A Message from Holly, 1992, The Women of Spring Break, 1995, Freaky Friday, 1995; TV mini-series, Voices Within: The Lives of Trudy Chase, 1990. Recipient Emmy award Outstanding Actress in a Comedy Series for Cheers, 1983. Office: Creative Artists Agy Ron Meyer 9830 Wilshire Blvd Beverly Hills CA 90212-1804

LONG, THAD GLADDEN, lawyer; b. Dothan, Ala., Mar. 9, 1938; s. Lindon Alexander and Della Gladys (Pilcher) L.; m. Carolyn Wilson, Aug. 13, 1966; children: Louisa Frances, Wilson Alexander. AB, Columbia U., 1960; JD, U. Va., 1963. Bar: Ala. 1963, U.S. Dist. Ct. (no. dist., so. dist., mid. dist.) Ala., U.S. Ct. Appeals (11th cir., 5th cir.), U.S. Supreme Ct. Assoc. atty. Bradley, Arant, Rose & White, Birmingham, Ala., 1963-70; ptnr. Bradley, Arant, Rose & White, Birmingham, 1970—; adj. prof. U. Ala., Tuscaloosa, 1988—. Co-author: Unfair Competition Under Alabama Law, 1990, Protecting Intellectual Property, 1990; mem. editl. bd. The Trademark Reporter; contbr. articles to profl. jours. chmn. Columbia U. Secondary Schs. Com. Ala. Area, 1975—, Greater Birmingham Arts Alliance, 1977-79; trustee, treas. Birmingham Music Club; trustee Oscar Wells Trust for Mus. Art, Birmingham, 1983—, Canterbury Meth. Found., 1993—, sec., 1993—; chmn. Entrepreneurship Inst. Birmingham, 1989; vice chmn., trustee Sons Revolution Found., Ala., 1994—; pres. Birmingham-Jefferson Hist. Soc., 1995-97; trustee Birmingham Music Club Endowment, 1995—; mem. Birmingham Com. Fgn. Rels. Mem. U.S. Patent Bar, Internat. Trademark Assn., Am. Law Inst., Ala. Law Inst., Birmingham Legal Aid Soc., Ala. Bar Assn. (chmn., founder bus. torts and antitrust sect.), U. Va. Law Alumni (chmn. Birmingham chpt. 1984-89), S.R. (pres. 1994-95), Gen. Soc. S.R. (gen. solicitor 1994—), Am. Arbitration Assn., Order of the Coif, Omicron Delta Kappa. Republican. Methodist. Avocations: travel, writing, table tennis. Home: 2880 Balmoral Rd Birmingham AL 35223-1236 Office: Bradley Arant Rose & White 2001 Park Pl Birmingham AL 35203-2735

LONG, THOMAS LESLIE, lawyer; b. Mansfield, Ohio, May 30, 1951; s. Ralph Waldo and Rose Ann (Cloud) L.; m. Peggy L. Bryant, Apr. 24, 1982. AB in Govt., U. Notre Dame, 1973; JD, Ohio State U., 1976. Bar: Ohio 1976, U.S. Dist. Ct. (so. dist.) Ohio 1976, U.S. Dist. Ct. (no. dist.) Ohio 1977, U.S. Ct. Appeals (6th cir.) 1978. Assoc. Alexander, Ebinger, Fisher, McAlister & Lawrence, Columbus, Ohio, 1976-82, ptnr., 1982-85; ptnr. Baker & Hostetler, Columbus, 1985—. Mem. ABA, Ohio Bar Assn., Columbus Bar Assn., Fed. Bar Assn., Assn. Trial Lawyer Am. Democrat. Roman Catholic. Club: Capitol (Columbus). Home: 2565 Leeds Rd Columbus OH 43221-3613 Office: Baker & Hostetler 65 E State St Columbus OH 43215-4213

LONG, TIMOTHY SCOTT, chemist, consultant; b. Racine, Wis., Dec. 20, 1937; s. Leslie Alexander and Esther (Sand) L.; m. Karen M. Koniarski, July 13, 1985; children by previous marriage: Corinne, Christine. BS in Chemistry, Winona State U., 1975. Staff chemist IBM, Rochester, Minn., 1962-77; adv. chemist IBM, Harrison, N.Y., 1977-80, IBM Instruments, Inc., Danbury, Conn., 1980-81; mgr. Midwest Instrument Ctr. IBM Instruments, Inc., Chgo., 1981-85; mgr. corp. environ. engring. IBM, Stamford, Conn., 1985-89; industry cons. IBM, White Plains, N.Y., 1989-92; environ. cons. Geraghty & Miller, Inc., Rochelle Park, N.J., 1992-94, Indpls., 1994—; mem. World Environ. Ctr., N.Y.C., 1985-89; adv. bd. Coop. Ctr. Rsch. in Hazardous and Toxic Substances, Newark, 1985-89. Autohr: Testing for Prediction of Material Performance, 1972, Methods for Emissions Spectrochemical Analysis, 1977, 2d edit., 1982; contbr. articles to Applied Spectroscopy, Plating, Polymer Engring. and Sci. Mem. ASTM (com. emission spectroscopy), Soc. Applied Spectroscopy (chmn. Minn. sect. 1976-77), Assn. Am. Indian Affairs, Soc. Plastics Engrs. (bd. reviewers 1975-76). Achievements include demonstration of world's first application using ion chromatography in the analysis of indsl. waste water. Home: 559 Lord St Indianapolis IN 46202-4014

LONG, WALTER EDWARD, international trade company executive, consultant; b. Little Rock, Nov. 11, 1935; s. James Edward and Daisy Mae (Cooper) L. BA summa cum laude, Philander Smith Coll., 1957; MA in Psychology, U. Pa., 1960. Mgr. indsl. and psychol. testing Richton Co. Inc., Newark, 1960-63; pres. Best Resume Co., Inc., N.Y.C., 1963-65; pres., chief exec. officer PHAT Advt. Cons., Inc., N.Y.C., 1965-74; chmn. Nubian Internationale, Ltd. PHAT Advt. Cons., Inc., 1973-78; sr. v.p. internat. trade Daniels & Cartwright, Inc., 1978-80; pres., chief exec. officer Epic Internat. Trade, Ltd., 1980—, Am. Gas & Energy Corp., 1988—; v.p. internat. trade Swiss Bullion Internat. Corp., 1988-91; CEO GlobalArk Internat. Trade Ltd., Little Rock, 1991—; pres. Walter Long Assocs., 1991—; v.p. internat. trade World Trade Ctr., Memphis, 1993-94; spl. trade and fin. devel. cons., Namabia, S. Africa, 1993—; sr. cons./coord. World Econ. Developers Unlimited, N.Y.C., 1995—; dir. Pepsi-Cola, Mali, West Africa, 1995—; bd. dirs. Harlem br. N.Y. Urban Coalition, N.Y.C., 1972-74; condr. internat. trade seminars Queens (N.Y.) Coll., 1968. With U.S. Army, 1958-60. N.Y. Film Inst. grantee, 1973. Mem. Am. Psychol. Assn., Masons. Democrat. African Methodist Episcopalian. Avocations: golf, chess, writing, video-sound buff, travel. Office: GlobalArk Internat Trade 7500 Azalea Dr Little Rock AR 72209-4417

LONG, WILLIAM ALLAN, retired forest products company executive; b. Columbus, Ohio, Aug. 25, 1928; s. Allan C. and Dorothy (Crates) L.; m. Ann Cors, Aug. 27, 1954; children: Leslie, David, Steven, Jeffrey. B.A., Ohio Wesleyan U., 1951. Vice pres. Diamond Internat., N.Y.C., 1951-70; exec. v.p. Overhead Door Corp., Dallas, 1970-75; v.p. St. Regis Paper Co., N.Y.C., 1975-79; group v.p. Inland Container Corp., Indpls., 1979-93; ret., 1993. Sgt. U.S. Army, 1946-47. Republican. Presbyterian. Home: 5010 Plantation Dr Indianapolis IN 46250-1639

LONG, WILLIAM D., retail company executive; b. Watertown, Wis., Nov. 30, 1937; s. William D. and Olive (Piper) L.; m. Doreen Loveall, Sept. 23, 1967; children—Angela, Scott, Irene, Jeffrey, William, Jennifer. Student U. Wis.-Madison. Store mgr. Safeway, Salt Lake City, 1961-68; pres., chief exec. officer Waremart Inc., Boise, Idaho, 1968—. Served to cpl. U.S. Army, 1957-60. Office: Waremart Inc PO Box 5756 Boise ID 83705-0756*

LONG, WILLIAM EVERETT, retired utility executive; b. Oklahoma City, Sept. 3, 1919; s. William Everett and Hazel Kathleen (Stafford) L.; m. Frances Jeanne Baum, Aug. 7, 1942; children: Susan Jeanne, Nancy Lee. Student, U. Colo., 1937-39, Northwestern U., 1940. With Houston Natural Gas Corp., 1949-84, sr. v.p., gen. mgr. distbn. div., 1971-78, sr. v.p., chief adminstrv. officer, 1981-84. Served with USAAF, 1941-46; Served with USAF, 1951-53; mem. Res. (ret.). Mem. Christian Ch. (Disciples of Christ). Clubs: Lakeside Country, Masons. Home: 9585 Longmont Dr Houston TX 77063-1026 *I am blessed with parents who, when I was a youth, instilled in me a good sense of social, moral and civic values. They prepared me to seek opportunity, accept responsibility and respect my fellow man.*

LONG, WILLIAM JOSEPH, software engineer; b. Kokomo, Ind., Feb. 1, 1956; s. George Alexander and Rebecca Bethina (Burgan) L. BA, Harvard U., 1979; cert. in project mgmt., U. Calif., Berkeley, 1994. Cons. Bechtel Corp., San Francisco, 1982-85; assoc. prof. Dalian (Liaoning, China) Inst. Tech., 1985-86; software engr. Bechtel Corp., San Francisco, 1986-92; EDI project mgr. Pacific Gas & Electric Co., San Francisco, 1992-94; software engr. Am. Pres. Lines, Oakland, Calif., 1994-95; mem. adv. bd. Synetics, Inc., San Francisco, 1987—; owner William J. Long and Assocs., Oakland, Calif., 1990—. Vol. English tutor, Oakland, Calif., 1983—. Rsch. grantee Smithsonian Astrophys. Obs., Cambridge, Mass., 1976. Mem. IEEE, Assn. Computing Machinery, Am. Assn. Artificial Intelligence, Math. Assn. Am. Avocations: languages, photography, playing hammer dulcimer, jogging. Home and Office: William J Long and Assocs 2225 7th Ave #33 Oakland CA 94606-1969

LONG, WILLIS FRANKLIN, electrical engineering educator, researcher; b. Lima, Ohio, Jan. 30, 1934; s. Jesse Raymond and Cerelda Elizabeth (Stepleton) L.; m. Ginger Carol Miller; children: Andrew Mark, Kristin Kay, David Franklin. BS in Engring. Physics, U. Toledo, 1957, MSEE, 1962; PhD, U. Wis., 1970. Registered profl. engr., Wis. Project engr. Doehler Jarvis div. Nat. Lead Co., Toledo, Ohio, 1957, 59-60; instr. U. Toledo, 1962-66; mem. tech. staff Hughes Rsch. Labs., Malibu, Calif., 1969-73; asst., then assoc. prof. depts. extension engring. and elec. engring. U. Wis., Madison, 1973-80, prof., chair dept. extension engring., 1980-83, prof. depts. engring., profl devel. and elec. and computer engring., 1985—; dir. ASEA Power System Ctr., New Berlin, Wis., 1983-85; prin. Long Assocs., Madison, 1973—; cons. Dept. Energy, Washington, 1978—, ABB Power Systems, Raleigh, N.C., 1985—. Editor EMTP Rev., 1987-91; contbr. articles to profl. jours.; patentee power switching. Mem. adv. com. energy conservation Wis. Dept. Labor, Industry and Human Rels., Maidson, 1976-77; chmn. Wis. chpt. Sierra Club, 1977; pres. bd. dirs. Madison Urban Ministries, 1993-95. 2d lt. Signal Corps., U.S. Army, 1958. Recipient Disting. Engring. Alumnus award U. Toledo, 1983, award of excellence U. Wis.-Extension, 1987; Sci. Faculty fellow NSF, 1966. Fellow IEEE (Meritorious Achievement in Continuing Edn. award 1991); mem. Internat. Conf. on Large High Voltage Electric Systems (expert advisor 1979—). Mem. United Ch. of Christ. Avocation: canoeing. Home: 1444 E Skyline Dr Madison WI 53705-1133 Office: U Wis 432 N Lake St Madison WI 53706-1415

LONGAKER, NANCY, elementary school principal. Prin. Templeton Elem. Sch., Tigard, Oreg. Recipient Elem. Sch. Recognition award U.S. Dept. Edn., 1989-90. Office: Templeton Elem Sch 9500 SW Murdock St Tigard OR 97224-5707

LONGAKER, RICHARD PANCOAST, political science educator emeritus; b. Phila., July 1, 1924; s. Edwin P. and Emily (Downs) L.; m. Mollie M. Katz, Jan. 25, 1964; children—Richard Pancoast II, Stephen Edwin, Sarah Ellen, Rachel Elise. B.A. in Polit. Sci, Swarthmore Coll., 1949; M.A. in Am. History, U. Wis., 1950; Ph.D. in Govt, Cornell U., 1953. Teaching asst. Cornell U., 1950-53, vis. asso. prof., 1960-61; asst. prof. Kenyon Coll., 1953-54, asso. prof., 1955-60; asst. prof. U. Calif., Riverside, 1954-55; faculty U. Calif., Los Angeles, 1961-76, chmn. dept. polit. sci., 1963-67, prof., 1965-76, dean acad. affairs grad. div., 1970-71; prof. Johns Hopkins U., Balt., 1976-87, provost and v.p. for acad. affairs, 1976-87; prof. emeritus, cons. western states office Johns Hopkins U., Santa Monica, Calif., 1987—. Author: The Presidency and Individual Liberties, 1961; co-author: The Supreme Court and the Commander in Chief, 1976, also articles, revs. Served with AUS, 1943-45. Mem. Am. Polit. Sci. Assn. Office: 16550 Chalet Ter Pacific Palisades CA 90272-2344

LONGAN, GEORGE BAKER, III, real estate executive; b. Kansas City, Mo., Apr. 20, 1934; s. Benjamin Hyde and Georgette Longan O'Brien; divorced; 1 child, Nancy Ann Longan LaPoff. BSBA, U. Ariz., 1956; post-grad., U. Kans., 1956-57. Cert. real estate broker. Sr. v.p., gen. mgr. Paul Hamilton Co., Kansas City, 1963-84; pres. Eugene D. Brown Co., Kansas City, 1984-93; v.p. J.C. Nichols Real Estate, 1993-94; bd. dirs. Genesis Relocation Network, N.J. Served to staff sgt. USAF, 1958-62. Mem. Nat. Real Estate Assn. (bd. dirs. 1991-94), Mo. Real Estate Assn. (bd. dirs. 1987-90), Real Estate Bd. Kansas City (bd. dirs. 1987-90), Met. Kansas City Real Estate Bd. (pres. 1992), Beta Sigma Psi, Sigma Chi. Episcopal. Avocations: antique collecting, tennis. Home: 2701 E Camino Pablo Tucson AZ 85718-6625 Office: Long Realty Co 5683 N Swan Rd Tucson AZ 85718-4565

LONGANECKER, DAVID A., federal official. BA in Sociology, Wash. State U., 1968; MA in Student Personnel Work, George Washington U., 1971; EdD in Adminstrn. and Policy Analysis in Higher Edn., Stanford U., 1978. With student affairs and residence life dept. George Washington U., Washington; with Congl. Budget Office, Washington, 1977-81; with Minn. Higher Edn. Coordinating Bd., 1981-84, exec. dir., 1984-88; exec. dir., exec. dir. dept. higher edn., officer Gov. Roy Romer's cabinet Colo. Commn. Higher Edn., 1988-93; asst. sec. postsecondary edn. U.S. Dept. Edn., Washington, 1993—; past. pres. State Higher Edn. Exec. Officers orgn.; commr. We. Interstate Commn. Higher Edn.; mem. postsecondary edn. and tng. for workplace com. Nat. Acad. Scis., commn. on ednl. credit and credentials Am. Coun. Edn.; mem. various bds. and coms. including Exec. Com. Minority Edn. Coalition Colo., Gov.'s Commn. Families and Children, Math., Sci. and Tech. Commn. Office: Dept Edn Post Secondary Edn Office 7th and D Sts SW Washington DC 20202-5100*

LONGBERG, DEBRA LYNN, dietitian, nutrition consultant; b. Queens, N.Y., May 2, 1960; d. Seymour Longberg and Gail Toby (Funk) Borock; m. Stuart Soycher, Aug. 18, 1991; 1 child, Nikki Samantha. BS in Dietetics, U. Del., 1982; MS in Dietetics, N.Y. Inst. Tech., 1987. Registered dietitian, N.Y.; cert. dietitian/nutritionist N.Y. Clin. dietitian A. Holly Patterson Nursing Home, Uniondale, N.Y., 1984-85; dir. dietary Grace Plaza Nursing Home, Gt. Neck, N.Y., 1986-89; asst. dir. dietary Beth Israel Nursing Home, White Plains, N.Y., 1989-91; chief clin. dietitian New Rochelle (N.Y.) Hosp., 1991-93; adminstrv. dietitian Ramapo Manor Nursing Ctr., Suffern, N.Y., 1993—; counselor Sharon Saka Assocs., Suffern, 1991—; nutrition cons. Metro Mosaic segment, NBC-TV, N.Y.C., 1992; nutrition cons. Sta. WVOX, Westchester, N.Y., 1991-93. Mem. T.O.U.C.H., AIDS orgn., Rockland, N.Y., 1994—; mem. subcom. on health issues Spl. Com. on Women's Issues, Clarkstown Legislature, N.Y., 1995. Mem. NOW, Am. Dietetic Assn., Westchester-Rockland Dietetic Assn., Planned Parenthood. Democrat. Jewish. Avocations: walking, listening to music, people watching. Home: 201 Richard Ct Pomona NY 10970 Office: Ramapo Manor Nursing Ctr 30 Cragmere Rd Suffern NY 10901-7520

LONGENECKER, HERBERT EUGENE, biochemist, former university president; b. Lititz, Pa., May 6, 1912; s. Abraham S. and Mary Ellen (Herr) L.; m. Marjorie Jane Segar, June 18, 1936; children: Herbert Eugene, Marjorie Segar Longenecker White, Geoffrey Herr, Stanton Lee. B.S., Pa. State U., 1933, M.S., 1934, Ph.D., 1936; D.Sc., Duquesne U., 1951; LL.D., Loyola U., 1962; Litt.D., U. Miami, 1972; D.Sc., U. Ill., 1976, Loyola U. of South, 1976. Instr. biochemistry Pa. State U., 1935-36; NRC fellow univs. Liverpool (Eng.), Cologne (Germany), Queen's, Kingston, Can., 1936-38; sr. research fellow and lectr. in chemistry U. Pitts., 1938-41, asst. research prof. chemistry, 1941-42; prof. chemistry and dir. Buhl Found. Research Project, 1942-44; dean research in natural scis. U. Pitts., 1944-55; dean U. Pitts. (Grad. Sch.), 1946-55; v.p. U. Ill. Med. Center, 1955-60; pres. Tulane U., 1960-75, pres. emeritus, 1975—; mng. dir. World Trade Ctr., New Orleans, 1976-79; dir. Equitable Life Ins. Soc. U.S., 1968-84, cons. dir., 1984-92; dir. CPC Internat., 1966-85; mem. food and nutrition bd. NRC, 1943-53, chmn. com. on food protection, 1948-53; mem. com. on chem. warfare R & D Bd., 1949-53; mem. rsch. coun. Chem. Corps. Adv. Bd., 1949-65; pres. Nat. Commn. on Accrediting, 1964-66; mem. coun. Nat. Inst. Gen. Med. Scis., 1963-66; mem. site selection panel for high energy accelerators NAS, 1964-66; mem. nat. selection com. Fulbright Student awards, 1953-55; chmn. West Europe sect. Fulbright Student Awards, 1954-55; mem. coun. Nat. Inst. Environ. Health Scis., 1970-71; mem. panel on sci. and tech. Ho. of Reps. Com. on Sci. and Astronautics, 1970-76; mem. adv. panel on ROTC affairs Office Sec. Def., 1961-75, chmn., 1968-75; mem. Commn. on Pvt. Philanthropy and Pub. Needs, 1973-77. Pres. Pitts. Housing Assn., 1948-51; bd. govs. Inst. Medicine Chgo., 1957-60; trustee Council of So. Univs., 1960-75, pres., 1964-65; pres. Univs. Research Assn., 1971-72; trustee Inst. Def. Analyses, 1959-88, vice chmn., 1984-88; chmn. acad. adv. bd. U.S. Naval Acad., 1966-72; trustee Nat. Med. Fellowships, Inc., 1965-72; bd. dirs. Council Fin. Aid to Edn., 1964-71; trustee Inst. Service to Edn., Inc., 1965-71; trustee Am. Univs. Field Staff, 1960-74, pres., 1962-63; sec.-treas. Assn. Am. Univs., 1969-72, pres., 1972-73; trustee S.W. Research Inst., 1960-69; bd. dirs. World Trade Ctr., New Orleans, 1961—, Nat. Merit Scholarship Corp., 1969-75; trustee Sloan Found., 1970-84, Inst. for Future, 1975-76, La. Expo. Inc., 1976-82, United Student Aid Funds, 1971-85, Pacific Tropical Bot. Garden, 1974-77, Council of the Ams., 1976-79; trustee Nutrition Found., 1961-85, chmn., 1965-72; mem. bd. Indian Springs Sch., 1987-88. Recipient Army and Navy Cert. for service during World War II, USN Disting. Pub. Service award; Disting. Alumni award Pa. State U., 1960; Papal award Bene Merenti, 1977. Fellow Am. Public Health Assn., Am. Inst. Nutrition, Am. Inst. Chemists; mem. Am. Chem. Soc. (chmn. Pitts. sect. 1946-47), Am. Soc. Biol. Chemists, Am. Council Edn. (chmn. commn. on fed. relations 1963-65, coordinating com. 1972-74), Am. Oil Chemists Soc. (v.p. 1946-47), Nat. League Nursing, Sigma Xi (exec. com. 1965-70, pres. 1980-81), Phi Delta Kappa, Sigma Pi. Club: Boston (New Orleans). Home: 2717 Highland Ave S Apt 1002 Birmingham AL 35205-1730

LONGENECKER, MARK HERSHEY, JR., lawyer; b. Akron, Ohio, Feb. 16, 1951; s. Mark Hershey and Katrina (Hetzner) L.; m. Ruth Rounding, June 17, 1978; children: Emily Irene, Mark Hershey III. BA, Denison U., 1973; JD, Harvard U., 1976. Bar: Ill. 1976, Ohio 1979. Atty. Lord, Bissell & Brook, Chgo., 1976-79; ptnr. Frost & Jacobs, Cin., 1979—, chmn. bus.-corp. dept., 1996—. Bd. govs. Ohio Fair Plan Underwriting Assn., Columbus, 1989-92; dir. Seven Hills Neighborhood Houses, Cin., 1990—. Mem. Cin. Country Club, Queen City Club, Gyro Club, Harvard Club (Cin. pres. 1993-94). Office: Frost & Jacobs 2500 PNC Ct 201 E 5th St Cincinnati OH 45202-4117

LONGERBONE, DOUG, hotel executive. BBA, Ohio State U., 1971. Regional dir. ops. Red Roof Inns, 1981, divsn. v.p., group v.p. ops., exec. v.p. ops., 1996—. With U.S. Army Res., 1967-73. Office: Red Roof Inns Inc 4355 Davidson Rd Hilliard OH 43026-2436

LONGEST, BEAUFORT BROWN, health services administration educator, research director; b. Rose Hill, N.C., Oct. 22, 1942; s. Beaufort Brown and Mary (Faircloth) L.; m. Carolyn Hepler, Jan 23, 1965; children: Brant, Courtland. BS, Davidson Coll., 1965; MHA, Ga. State U., 1969, PhD in Bus. Adminstrn., 1972. Instr. health adminstrn. Coll. Bus. Adminstrn., Ga. State U., 1969-72, asst. prof. health adminstrn., 1972-75; clin. asst. prof. preventive medicine and community health Sch. Medicine, Emory U., 1974-75; asst. prof. hosp. and health svcs. mgmt. J.L. Kellogg Grad. Sch. Mgmt., Northwestern U., 1975-78, faculty assoc. Ctr. Health Svcs. and Policy Rsch., 1978-79, assoc. prof. hosp. and health svcs. mgmt., 1979; prof. health svcs. adminstrn. Grad. Sch. Pub. Health and Joseph M. Katz Grad. Sch. Bus., U. Pitts., 1980—, prof. bus. adminstrn., 1987—, dir. Health Policy Inst., 1980—, dir. Health Adminstrn. Program, 1984-91, faculty assoc. Ctr. Med. Ethics, 1987—; lectr. in field, 1976—; condr. seminars including Am. Assn. Clin. Chemists, Am. Soc. Woman Accts., Am. Soc. Med. Tech., Ga. Hosp. Assn., Hosp. Assn. Pa., Gov.'s Policy Group, Pa., Ohio Hosp. Assn., Ontario Hosp. Assn., VA, many others; mem. coms. U. Pitts.; dir. Midland-Colt Retiree Med. Plan, Media Info. Svc. Adv. Bd., Biomed. Tech. Devel. Corp. Adv. Bd.; cons. Am. Soc. Med. Tech., 1972-74, Fetter Family Health Ctr., Charleston, S.C., 1974-75, Hosp. Fin. Mgmt. Assn., 1974-75, Am. Acad. Pediatrics, 1977, DuPage County Health Systems Agy., 1978, Health Care Fin. Adminstrn., 1989, U.S. Agy. Internat. Devel., Kingston, Jamaica, Gov.' s Policy Group, Pa., 1989, Sec. Health, Pa., 1990-91, Mfrs. Assn. Northwest Pa., 1992, Pan Am. Health Orgn., 1992. Author: Principles of Hospital Business Office Management, 1975, Management Practices for the Health Professional, 1976, 4th edit., 1990, (with others) Hospital Cost Containment Programs, A Policy Analysis, 1978, (with J.S. Rakich and T.R. O'Donovan) Managing Health Care Organizations, 1977, (with J.S. Rakich and K. Darr) Cases in Health Services Management, 1983, 3d edit., 1992, Managing Health Services Organizations, 2d edit., 1985; contbr. numerous articles, book chpts. papers to anthologies, profl. jours.; author rsch. monograph; book reviewer in field; editorial cons. Harper and Row, Inc., Health Professions Press, Little, Brown Pub. Co., Nat. Health Pub., Reston Pub. Co., Inc., W.B. Saunders Co. Dir. The Grove Sch., 1978-80; Hosp. Utilization Project, 1985-87; mem. adv. bd. work-study program minority students Chgo. Hosp. Coun., 1978-79, rsch. adv. com. Hosp. Utilization Project, 1982-83, steering com. Pitts. Program Affordable Health Care, 1984-88, com. health policy and planning Hosp. Coun. Western Pa., 1986—, health care and human svcs. Task Force, Leadership Pitts., 1985, 87, community problem solving com. United Way Allegheny County, 1986-89, chmn. community problem solving com. on frail elderly and disabled, 1989-92, mem. resource panel health and human svcs. Allegheny County 2001 Project, 1992, steering com. HSR&D devel. grant VA Med. Ctr., 1992-93; external examiner U. West Indies, Kingston, Jamaica, 1985-89. W.K. Kellogg Found. fellow, 1977-78. Fellow Am. Coll. Healthcare Execs. (ad hoc com. univ. program faculty 1982, regent's advisor 1985-89, com. book of yr. 1985-88, chmn. com. book of yr. 1988, com. awards and testimonials 1988, membership com. subcom. recruitement 1991-92, chmn. membership com. subcom. recruitement 1991-92); mem. Acad. Mgmt. (1st place rsch proposal award 1976), Am. Hosp. Assn., Am. Pub. Health Assn., Assn. Health Svcs. Rsch., Assn. Pub. Policy Analysis and Mgmt., Assn. Univ. Programs Health Adminstrn. (nom. com. bd. dirs. 1987, 88, adv. panel clin. edn. health adminstrn. 1986), Beta Gamma Sigma. Avocation: gardening. Office: U Pitts Health Pol Inst Grad Sch Pub Health 130 Desoto St Pittsburgh PA 15213-2535

LONGFELLOW, LAYNE ALLEN, psychologist, educator, author, musician; b. Jackson, Ohio, Oct. 23, 1937; s. Hershel Herman and Opal Edna (Pursley) L. BA in Psychology magna cum laude with honors, Ohio U., 1959; MA, U. Mich., 1961, PhD, 1967. Asst. prof. psychology Reed Coll., Portland, Oreg., 1967-68; postdoctoral fellow Dr. Carl Rogers, La Jolla, Calif., 1968-70; asst. prof. psychology Prescott (Ariz.) Coll., 1970-71, chmn. dept., 1971-72, acad. v.p., 1972-74; dir. exec. seminars Menninger Found., Topeka, 1975-78; dir. wilderness exec. seminars Banff Ctr., Alta., Can., 1978-86; pres. Lecture Theatre, Inc., Prescott, Ariz., 1981—; dir. Inst. for Human Skills, 1985—; internat. lectr., cons. in field; adj. faculty Union Grad. Sch. and Humanistic Psychology Inst., 1974-84. Composer: Ten Songs, 1969, Uncommon Festival of Christmas, 1974; creator Body Talk, 1970, The Feel Wheel, 1972, The Mountain Waits, 1983 (Gold medal N.Y. Festival of TV); video producer, author: Generations of Excellence, 1992, Beyond Success, 1993, Sustainable Growth, 1994, Healty, Wealthy and Wise, 1994; author: (with W.M. Hubbard) Visual Feast, 1995, Imaginary Menagerie, 1997. Active Alliance for Democracy. Woodrow Wilson fellow, NSF fellow, NIMH fellow. Mem. APA, Nat. Speakers Assn., Nature Conservancy, Phi Beta Kappa. Office: Lecture Theatre Inc PO Box 4317 Prescott AZ 86302-4317 *Through much of the life cycle, activity substitutes for meaning. The gentler pace of maturity allows life's meaning to be faced directly, without the filter of frenzied ambition.*

LONGFIELD, WILLIAM HERMAN, health care company executive; b. Chgo., Aug. 8, 1938; s. William A. and Elizabeth (Beringer) L.; m. Nancy Shofstall, June 10, 1961; children: William, Scott. BS, Drake U., 1960; grad. bus. mgmt. program, Northwestern U., 1972. Pres. Convertors div. Am. Hosp. Supply, Evanston, Ill., 1961-82; exec. v.p., dir. Lifemark, Inc., Houston, 1982-83; pres., chief exec. officer Cambridge Group, Inc., Dallas, 1983-89; chmn., CEO C.R. Bard, Inc., Murray Hill, N.J., 1989—, also bd. dirs.; bd. dirs. United Dental Care, Dallas, Atlantic Health Sys., Manor Care Inc., Balt., Centenary Coll., Health Industry Mfrs. Assn., The West Co., Pa., Horizon Mental Health Mgmt., Dallas; exec. resident U. Colo., 1980-82; chmn. bd. Internat. Non-Wovens Assn., N.Y.C., 1975-82. Chmn., dir. Deerfield (Ill.) Youth Orgn., 1975-80. Recipient Pres.' award Nat. Nurse Cons. Assn., 1980. Mem. Baltrusol Golf Club, Echo Lake Country Club, Metedeconk Country Club. Republican. Presbyterian. Avocations: golf, tennis. Office: C R Bard Inc 730 Central Ave New Providence NJ 07974-1139

LONGHOFER, RONALD STEPHEN, lawyer; b. Junction City, Kans., Aug. 30, 1946; s. Oscar William and Anna Mathilda (Krause) L.; m. Elizabeth Norma McKenna; children: Adam, Nathan, Stefanie. BMus, U. Mich., 1968; JD, 1975. Bar: Mich. 1975, U.S. Dist. Ct. (ea. dist.) Mich., U.S. Ct. Appeals (6th cir.) 1975, U.S. Supreme Ct. Law clk. to judge U.S. Dist. Ct. (ea. dist.) Mich., Detroit, 1975-76; ptnr. Honigman, Miller, Schwartz & Cohn, Detroit, 1976—, chmn. litigation dept., 1993-96. Co-author: Mich. Court Rules Practice-Evidence, 1996, Courtroom Handbook on Michigan Evidence, 1997; editor Mich. Law Rev., 1974-75. Served with U.S. Army, 1968-72. Mem. ABA, Detroit Bar Assn., Fed. Bar Assn., Detroit Club, Detroit Econ.

Club, U. Mich. Pres. Club, Order of Coif, Phi Beta Kappa, Phi Kappa Phi, Pi Kappa Lambda. Home: 46401 W Main St Northville MI 48167-3035 Office: Honigman Miller Schwartz & Cohn 2290 1st National Bldg Detroit MI 48226

LONGIN, THOMAS CHARLES, education association administrator; b. Lewistown, Mont., Nov. 17, 1939; s. Charles Otto and Anne Dorothy (Vavrovsky) L.; m. Nancy Tillinghast; children: Kevin C., Teresa L., Karl T., Anne M. BA in History, Carroll Coll., 1962; MA in History, Creighton U., 1965; PhD in Am. History, U. Nebr., 1970. Instr. Carroll Coll., Helena, Mont., 1965-67; asst. prof. Va. Poly. Inst. and State U., Blacksburg, 1970-73; asst. prof., then assoc. prof. Ithaca (N.Y.) Coll., 1973-82, dean humanities and scis., 1976-82, provost, 1985-96; v.p. acad. affairs Seattle U., 1982-85; v.p. programs and rsch. Assn. of Governing Bds., Washington, 1997—. Office: Assn of Governing Bds 1 Dupont Cir NW Ste 400 Washington DC 20036-1136

LONGLEY, BERNIQUE, artist, painter, sculptor; b. Moline, Ill., Sept. 27, 1923; d. Eli James and Effie Marie (Coen) Wilderson; 1 child, Bernique Maria Glidden. Grad., Art Inst. Chgo., 1945. One-woman shows at Mus. N.Mex., 1947, 50, 52, Appleman Gallery, Denver, 1950, Van Dieman-Lilienfield Galleries, N.Y.C., 1953, Knopp-Hunter Gallery, Santa Fe, 1954, 57, 58, Gallery Five, Santa Fe, 1964, 65, Coll. Santa Fe, 1967, Sanger-Harris, Dallas, 1968, Lars Laine Gallery, Palm Springs, Calif., 1969, Canyon Rd. Gallery, Santa Fe, 1972, Summer Gallery, Santa Fe, 1973, 74, 75, 76, Cushing Galleries, Dallas, 1977, Gov.'s Gallery, N.Mex. State Capitol, 1978, Santa Fe East, Austin, Tex., 1979, Santa Fe East Gallery, 1985, 86, 88, Leslie Levy Gallery, 1985-86; Artists of Am. exhbn., Denver, 1993-94, Contemporary Southwest Gallery, 1997, St. John's Coll., Santa Fe, 1997; group shows include Denver Art Mus., 1948, N.Mex. Highlands U., 1957, Lars Laine Gallery, 1961, 63, Santa Fe Festival of Arts, 1977, 78, 79, 80, Leslie Levy Gallery, Scottsdale, Ariz., 1985-86, Santa Fe East, 1985-86, 88, Invitational Mask Exhbn., Bank of Santa Fe, 1987, Hickory (N.C.) Mus., 1989, El Trado Gallery, 1989-94, Contemporary Southwest Gallery, 1995—, El Prado Gallery, 1989-94, Contemporary Southwest Gallery, 1995—, Craighead-Green Gallery, Dallas, 1996, many others; retrospective exhbn. Santa Fe East Gallery, 1982; represented in permanent collections Mus. N.Mex., Fine Arts Ctr., Colorado Springs, Colo., Coll. Santa Fe; collection of Oprah Winfrey, 1987, other pvt. collections; subject of book Bernique Longley- A Retrospective, 1982. Bryan Lathrop Fgn. Travelling fellow, 1945. Mem. Art Inst. Chgo. Alumni Assn., Artists Equity Assn. Home and. Home and Studio: 427 Camino Del Monte Sol Santa Fe NM 87501-2825

LONGLEY, GLENN, biology educator, research director; b. Del Rio, Tex., June 2, 1942; s. Glenn L. and Cleo M. (Tipton) L.; m. Francis Van Winkle, Aug. 5, 1961; children: Kelly Francis, Kristy Lee, Katherine Camille, Glenn C. BS in Biology, S.W. Tex. State U., 1964; MS in Zoology and Entomology, U. Utah, 1966, PhD in Environ. Biology, 1969. Lectr. U. Utah, 1968-69; from lectr. to prof. S.W. Tex. State U., San Marcos, 1969-79, prof. aquatic biology, dir. Edward Aquifer Rsch. Ctr., 1979—. Contbr. 138 papers to profl. jours. or meetings. Recipient more than 50 grants or contracts for water related studies; named Emminent Tex. Hydrologist, Am. Inst. Hydrology and Am. Water Resource Assn., Tex. sects., 1993. Fellow Tex. Acad. Sci. (past. pres.); mem. Am. Water Resource Assn., Tex. Orgn. for Endangered Species (past pres.), Tex. Water Conservation Assn., Tex. Water Pollution Control Assn. (past pres.), Assn. Groundwater Scientists and Engrs., Water Environment Fedn., Sigma Xi (life), Phi Sigma (former chpt. pres.). Achievements include research on redescription and assignment to the new Lircelous of the Texas troglobitic water slater, Asellus smithii, the larva of a new subterranean water beetle, Haideoporus texanus, watchlist of endangered, threatened and peripheral vertebrates of Texas, the generic status and distribution of Monodella texana Maguire, the only known North American Thermosbaeneacean, the Edwards Aquifer, Hadoceras taylori, a new genus and species of phreatic Hydrobiidae from South-Central Texas, Phreatoceras, a new name for Hadoceras Hershler and Longley, Phreatodrobia coronae, a new species of cavesnail from southwestern Texas, reproductive patterns of the subterranean shrimp Palaemonetes antrorum Benedict from Cental Texa, population size, distribution, and life history of Eurycea nana in the San Marcos River. Home: 814 Palomino Ln San Marcos TX 78666-1130 Office: SW Tex State U Edwards Aquifer Rsch Ctr San Marcos TX 78666

LONGLEY, MARJORIE WATTERS, newspaper executive; b. Lockport, N.Y., Nov. 2, 1925; d. J. Randolph and Florence Lucille (Craine) Watters; m. Ralph R. Longley, Oct. 1, 1949 (dec.). B.A. in English with highest honors cum laude, St. Lawrence U., 1947. Sports editor, feature writer Lockport Union Sun and Jour., 1945; with N.Y. Times, N.Y.C., 1948-88, asst. to v.p. consumer mktg., 1975-78, circulation sales mgr., 1978-79, sales dir., 1979-81, dir. pub. affairs, 1981-88; pres. Gramercy Internat., Inc. (mktg. and pub. rels.), N.Y.C., 1988—; assoc. pub. The Earth Times, N.Y.C., 1996—; dir. pub. affairs and pub. info., N.Y.C. Off-Track Betting Corp., 1990-94; mem. Nat. Newspapers' Readership Coun., 1979-82; mem. adv. coun. API, 1980-85. Author: America's Taste, 1960. Trustee St. Lawrence U., 1969-75, 77—; chmn. bd. dirs. Am. Forum for Global Edn., 1977—; pres. N.Y. City Adult Edn. Coun., 1974-77; mem. N.Y. State Adv. Coun. for Vocat. Edn., 1976-81, postsecondary edn., 1978-81, Mayor's Coun. Environment of N.Y.C., 1983-96; bd. dirs. Nat. Charities Info. Bur., 1983-96, Literacy Ptnrs., Inc., 1996—; chmn. 42d St. Edn., Theatre, Culture, 1984-88, chmn. emeritus, 1988—. Mem. Nat. Inst. Social Scis., Am. Mgmt. Assn. (nat. mktg. coun. 1972-89, bd. dirs. 1986-88), Nat. Arts Club, Overseas Press Club, Phi Beta Kappa. Democrat. Baptist. Office: Gramercy Internat Inc 34 Gramercy Park E New York NY 10003-1731

LONGMAN, ANNE STRICKLAND, special education educator, consultant; b. Metuchen, N.J., Sept. 17, 1924; d. Charles Hodges and Grace Anna (Moss) Eldridge; m. Henry Richard Strickland, June 22, 1946 (dec. 1960); m. Donald Rufus Longman, Jan. 20, 1979 (dec. 1987); children: James C., Robert H. BA in Bus. Adminstrn., Mich. State U., 1945; teaching credentials, U. Calif., Berkeley, 1959; postgrad., Stanford U., 1959-60; MA in Learning Hand, Santa Clara U., 1974. Lic. educator. Exptl. test engr. Pratt & Whitney Aircraft, East Hartford, Conn., 1945-47; indsl. engr. Marchant Calculators, Emeryville, Calif., 1957-58; with pub. rels. Homesmith, Palo Alto, Calif., 1959-62; cons. Right to Read Program, Calif., 1978-79; monitor, reviewer State of Calif., Sacramento, 1976-79; tchr. diagnosis edn. Cabrillo Coll., Aptos, Calif., 1970-79; lectr. edn. U. Calif., Santa Cruz, 1970-79; cons. Santa Cruz Bd. Edn., 1970-79; reading rschr. Gorilla Found., Woodside, Calif., 1982—; bd. mem. Western Inst. Alcoholic Studies, L.A., 1972-73; chmn. Evaluation Com., Tri-County, Calif., 1974; speaker Internat. Congress Learning Disabilities, Seattle, 1974; ednl. cons. rsch. on allergies, 1993—. Author: Word Patterns in English, 1974-92, Cramming 3D Kids, 1975—, 50 books for migrant students, 1970-79; contbr. articles on stress and alcoholism and TV crime prevention for police, 1960-79. Founder Literacy Ctr., Santa Cruz, 1968-092; leader Girl Scouts U.S.A., San Francisco, 1947-50; vol. Thursday's Child, Santa Cruz, 1976-79, Golden Gate Kindergarten, San Francisco, 1947-57. Recipient Fellowships Pratt & Whitney Aircraft, 1944, Stanford U., 1959. Mem. Internat. Reading Assn. (pres. Santa Cruz 1975), Santa Clara Valley Watercolor Soc., Los Altos Art Club (v.p. 1992), Eichler Swim and Tennis Club. Republican. Episcopalian. Avocations: watercolor painting, travel, drama. Home and Office: 153 Del Mesa Carmel Carmel CA 93923-7950

LONGMAN, GARY LEE, accountant; b. Kewanee, Ill., Apr. 25, 1948; s. Howard L. and Dorothy (Wenk) L.; m. Ruth Ann Biesboer; children: Gregory, Rebecca. AA, Joliet (Ill.) Jr. Coll., 1968; BS in Acctg., No. Ill. U., 1970. CPA, Ill. Staff acct. KPMG Peat Marwick, Chgo., 1970-72, sr. acct., 1972-74, mgr., 1974-80, ptnr., 1980-91, ptnr.-in-charge Chgo. office mfg. practice, 1991—, ptnr.-in-charge Chgo. audit dept., 1991-93, midwest ptnr.-in-charge info., comm. & entertainment, 1993-96, midwest ptnr.-in-charge mfg., retailing, and distbn., 1996—. Bus. adv. coun. Dept. Commerce, DePaul U., 1991—; bd. dirs. Jr. Achievement, Chgo. Mem. AICPAs, Ill. Soc. CPAs, LaGrange Country Club. Office: KPMG Peat Marwick 303 E Wacker Dr Chicago IL 60601-5212

LONGMIRE, WILLIAM POLK, JR., physician, surgeon; b. Sapulpa, Okla., Sept. 14, 1913; s. William Polk and Grace May (Weeks) L.; m. Jane Jarvis Cornelius, Oct. 28, 1939; children—William Polk III (dec.), Gill, Sarah Jane. A.B., U. Okla., 1934; M.D., Johns Hopkins, 1938; M.D. hon. degrees, U. Athens, Greece, 1972, Northwestern U., 1976, U. Lund, Sweden, 1976; M.D. (h.c.), U. Heidelberg, Germany, 1974. Diplomate Am. Bd. Surgery (chmn. 1961-62). Intern surgery Johns Hopkins Hosp., Balt., 1938-39, resident surgery, 1944, surgeon in charge plastic out-patient clinic, 1946-48, surgeon, 1947-48; Harvey Cushing fellow exptl. surgery Johns Hopkins, 1939-40, Halsted fellow surg. pathology, 1940, successively instr., asst. prof. assoc. prof. surgery, 1943-48; prof. surgery UCLA, 1948-81, prof. emeritus, 1981—, chmn. dept., 1948-76; cons. surgery Wadsworth VA Hosp., Los Angeles County Harbor Hosp., 1945-76, VA disting. physician, 1982-87; guest prof. spl. surgery Free U. Berlin, Fed. Republic Germany, 1952-54; vis. prof. surgery Mayo Grad. Sch. Medicine, 1968, Royal Coll. Physicians and Surgeons of Can., 1968; chmn. surgery study sect. NIH, USPHS, 1961-64; mem. Conf. Com. on Grad. Edn. in Surgery, 1959-66, chmn., 1964-66; mem. spl. med. adv. group to med. dir. VA, 1963-68, vice chmn., 1967-68; chmn. surgery tng. com. NIH, 1969-70; mem. pres.' cancer panel Nat. Cancer Inst., 1982-91; Wade vis. prof. Royal Coll. Surgeons Edinburgh, 1972; nat. civilian cons. surgery Air Surgeon USAF; surg. cons. Surgeon Gen. U.S. Army, 1961-88; commr. Joint Commn. on Accreditation of Hosps., 1975-80. Editor: Advances in Surgery, 1975-76; editorial bd.: Annals of Surgery, 1965—. Served as maj. USAF, 1952-54; spl. cons. Air Surgeon Gen.'s Office. Recipient hon. certificate for advancement cardiovascular surgery Free U. of Berlin, 1954, certificate for high profl. achievement USAF, 1954, Gold medal UCLA, 1980, prize Societe Internationale De Chirurgie, 1987; inducted into Okla. Hall of Fame, 1980. Fellow ACS (chmn. forum com. fundamental surg. problems 1961-62, regent 1962-71, chmn. bd. regents 1969-71, pres. 1971-73, Sheen award N.J. chpt. 1987); hon. fellow Assn. Surgeons Great Britain and Ireland, Royal Coll. Surgeons Ireland, Royal Coll. Surgeons Edinburgh, Royal Coll. Surgeons Eng., Italian Surg. Soc., Association Française de Chirurgie, Japan Surg. Soc.; mem. AMA (mem. council on med. edn. 1964-69), Soc. Scholars of Johns Hopkins U., Soc. Clin. Surgeons, Am. Surg. Assn. (pres. 1967-68), Pacific Coast Surg. Assn., Western Surg. Assn., So. Surg. Assn., Soc. U. Surgeons, Internat. Soc. Surgery, Internat. Fedn. Surg. Colls. (pres. 1984-87), Internat. Surgical Group, (pres. 1993), Am. Assn. Thoracic Surgery, Pan-Pacific Surg. Assn., Los Angeles Surg. Soc. (pres. 1956), Bay Dist. Surg. Soc., Soc. Surgery Alimentary Tract (pres. 1975-76), Calif. Med. Assn. (sec. surg. sect. 1950-51, chmn. sci. bd. 1966-67, Golden Apple award 1990), James IV Assn. Surgeons (pres. 1981), Soc. Surg. Chairmen (pres. 1970-72), Sociédad Argentina di Cirugia Digestiva (hon.), Italian Surg. Soc. (hon.), Phi Beta Kappa, Alpha Omega Alpha; corr. mem. Deutsche Gesellschaft fur Chirugie. Home: 10102 Empyrean Way Bldg 8 Unit 203 Los Angeles CA 90067 Office: U Calif Med Ctr Los Angeles CA 90024

LONGNECKER, DAVID EUGENE, anesthesiologist, educator; b. Kendallville, Ind., 1939. MD, Ind. U., 1964, MA in Anesthesiology, 1968. Diplomate Am. Bd. Anesthesiology. Intern Blodgett Meml. Hosp., Grand Rapids, Mich., 1964-65; resident in anesthesiology U. Ind., 1965-69; asst. prof. dept. anesthesiology U. Mo., 1970-73; assoc. prof. dept. anesthesiology U. Va., Charlottesville, 1974-78, prof., 1978-88; Robert D. Dripps prof., chmn. dept. anesthesia U. Pa., Phila., 1988—. With USPHS, 1968-70. Mem. Am. Soc. Anesthesiology, Inst. Medicine. Office: U Pa Health Sys Dept Anesthesia 3400 Spruce St Philadelphia PA 19104

LONGO, DANIEL ROBERT, health services researcher, medical educator; b. Jersey City, N.J., Feb. 20, 1952; s. Frank and Rose (Liguori) L.; m. Karen Ann Ludy, Sept. 4, 1976; children: Gregory Seton, Alexis Seton. BS cum laude, Villanova U., 1974; M of Hosp. Adminstrn., George Washington U., 1976; ScD in Health Policy Mgmt., Johns Hopkins U., 1982. Cons. Am. Hosp. Assn. Hosp., Chgo., 1980-82; dir., multi-hosp. systems project Joint Commn. Healthcare Orgns., Chgo., 1982-85; dir. rsch. Joint Commn. Healthcare Orgns., 1984-86; asst. exec. dir. quality mgmt. Ancilla Systems Inc., Chgo. Applied Healthcare Group, 1986-87; v.p. quality assurance Hosp. Assn. N.Y. State, Albany, 1987-89; pres. Hosp. Rsch. Ednl. Trust, Chgo., 1989-92; assoc. prof. family and community medicine U. Mo. Sch. Medicine, Columbia, 1992—; bd. dirs. Inst. on Quality of Care and Patterns of Practice, 1991-92, Assn. Health Svcs. Rsch., Washington, 1990-92; adv. com., Quality Improvement Task Force, Chgo., 1988-92; liaison com., Inst. Medicine, Washington, 1990-91; adj. faculty Columbia U.; vis. scholar Northwestern U., Evanston, Ill., Johns Hopkins U., Balt., 1991-93; quality of care advisor Mo. Dept. Health, 1993—. Author: Integrated Qaulity Assessment, 1989, Inventory of External Data, 1990; editor: Quantative Methods in Quality Assurance, 1990; contbr. articles to profl. jours. Lt. USNR, 1975-79. Rsch. fellow Sisters Mercy Health Corp., 1983-87. Mem. Am. Pub. Health Assn. (program chmn. 1987), Assn. Health Svcs. Rsch. (bd. dirs. 1990-93), Soc. Tchrs. Family Medicine (Best Rsch. Paper Yr. award 1997). Home: Ridley Wood Columbia MO 65203 Office: U Mo Sch Medicine Health Sci Ctr MA306 Columbia MO 65212

LONGO, KATHRYN MILANI, pension consultant; b. Jersey City, N.J., July 22, 1946; d. Joseph John Baptiste and Kathryn (Sacco) Milani; BA, Adelphi U., 1969; postgrad. N.Y. U., 1968-69, Hunter Coll., 1969-70; m. John Carmine Longo, Mar. 15, 1970 (div. June 1984). Pension cons. Laiken, Siegel & Co., N.Y.C., 1967-84, ptnr., 1977-84; mng. ptnr. Laventhol & Horwath Retirement and Employee Benefit Cons. Div., 1984-88; pres. Pension Alternatives Inc., 1988—, mgmt. cons. Creative Pension Systems, Inc., 1988—. cons., 1988—; pres., creative cons. Pinch-Hitters, Inc., North Bergen, N.J., 1978-82; Teaneck Econ. Devel. Corp., 1993-96. Co-founder, cochmn. Greater N.Y. Pension Cons. Workshop, 1974-96; jazz dance tchr. Kay Marie Sch. Dance Arts, Hammonton, N.J., 1976-83; guest choreographer Regis Drama Soc., Regis High Sch., N.Y.C., 1978-79; choreographer The Garage Theater, Tenafly, N.J., 1993—. Bd. dirs. Phila. Chamber Orch., 1988, Cmty. Arts Acad. of Bergen County, Englewood, N.J., 1994—. Adelphi U. scholar, 1964-68. Mem. Am. Soc. Pension Actuaries (assoc.), N.J. Network of Bus. and Profl. Women, Women Entrepreneurs of N.J., Women Bus. Ownership Ednl. Coalition, Inc. (bd. dirs. 1988), Ft. Lee C. of C., Teaneck C. of C. (pres. 1993-94). Roman Catholic.

LONGO, LAWRENCE DANIEL, physiologist, obstetrician-gynecologist; b. Los Angeles, Oct. 11, 1926; s. Frank Albert and Florine Azelia (Hall) L.; m. Betty Jeanne Mundall, Sept. 9, 1948; children: April Celeste, Lawrence Anthony, Elisabeth Lynn, Camilla Giselle. BA, Pacific Union Coll., 1949; MD, Coll. Med. Evangelists, Loma Linda, Calif., 1954. Diplomate: Am. Bd. Ob-Gyn. Intern Los Angeles County Gen. Hosp., 1954-55, resident, 1955-58; asst. prof. ob-gyn UCLA, 1962-64; assoc. prof. physiology and ob-gyn U. Pa., 1964-68; prof. physiology and ob-gyn Loma Linda U., 1968—; dir. ctr. for perinatal biology Loma Linda U. Sch. Medicine, 1974—; mem. perinatal biology com. Nat. Inst. Child Health, NIH, 1973-77; co-chmn. reprodn. scientist devel. program NIH; NATO prof. Consiglio Nat. delle Richerche, Italian Govt. Editor: Respiratory Gas Exchange and Blood Flow in the Placenta, 1972, Fetal and Newborn Cardiovascular Physiology, 1978, Charles White and A Treatise on the Management of Pregnant and Lying-in Women, 1987; co-editor: Landmarks in Perinatology, 1975-76, Classics in Obstetrics Gynecology, 1993; editor classic pages in ob-gyn. Am. Jour. Ob-Gyn.; contbr. articles to profl. jours. Served with AUS, 1945-47. Founder Frank A. and Florine A. Longo lectureship in faith, knowledge, and human values Pacific Union Coll., 1993. Fellow Royal Coll. Ob-Gyns., Am. Coll. Ob-Gyns.; mem. Am. Assn. History Medicine (coun.), Am. Osler Soc. (bd. govs., sec.-treas.), Am. Physiol. Soc., Assn. Profs. Ob-Gyn., Perinatal Rsch. Soc., Soc. Gynecologic Investigation (past pres.), Neurosci. Soc., Royal Soc. Medicine. Adventist. Office: Loma Linda U Sch Medicine Ctr Perinatal Biology Loma Linda CA 92350

LONGOBARDI, JOSEPH J., federal judge; b. 1930; m. Maud L.; 2 children: Joseph J. Longobardi III, Cynthia Jean Hermann. BA, Washington Coll., 1952; LLB, Temple U., 1957. Deputy atty. Gen. State Del., Wilmington, 1959-61, tax appeal bd., 1973-74; ptnr. Longobardi & Schwartz, Wilmington, 1964-72, Murdoch, Longobardi, Schwartz & Walsh, Wilmington, 1972-74; judge Superior Ct. State of Del., Wilmington, 1974-82; vice chancellor Ct. Chancery, State Del., Wilmington, 1982-84; federal judge U.S. Dist. Ct. Del., Wilmington, 1984—, chief judge, 1989-96; assoc. editor Temple Law Rev. Recipient Paul C. Reardon award Nat. Ctr. for State Cts., 1981, S.S. Shull Meml. awrd for excellence in legal rsch. and writing. Office: US Dist Ct 844 N King St # 40 Wilmington DE 19801-3519

LONGOBARDO, ANNA KAZANJIAN, engineering executive; b. N.Y.C.; d. Aram Michael and Zarouhy (Yazejian) Kazanjian; m. Guy S. Longobardo, July 12, 1952; children: Guy A., Alicia. Student, Barnard Coll., 1947; BSME, Columbia U., 1949, MSME, 1952. Sr. systems engr. Am. Bosch Arma Corp., Garden City, N.Y., 1950-65; rsch. sect. head gyroscope Sperry Rand Corp., Gt. Neck, N.Y., 1965-68, rsch. sect. head systems mgmt., 1968-73; mgr. engring. personnel, utilization dir. hdqrs. Sperry Corp., Gt. Neck, 1973-77, mgr. systems mgmt. program planning, 1977-81, mgr. planning systems mgmt. group, 1981-82; dir. tech. svc. Systems Devel., Unisys Corp., Gt. Neck, 1982-89, dir. field engring., 1989-93, dir. strategic initiatives, 1993-95;, 1993-95, ret., 1995; mem. bd. dirs. Woodward Clyde Graves; bd. dirs. and chmn. exec. compensation com. Woodward-Clyde Group, Denver. Contbr. articles to profl. publs. Trustee Columbia U., N.Y.C., 1990—, chmn. engring. coun., 1987-91; mem. Bronxville (N.Y.) Planning Bd.; chmn. Bronxville Design Rev. Com. Recipient hon. citation Wilson Coll. Centennial, 1970, Alumni medal for conspicuous svc. Columbia U., 1980, Egleston medal for disting. engring. achievement Columbia U., 1997; named One of 100 N.Y. Women of Influence, New York Woman mag., 1986. Fellow Soc. Women Engrs. (founder, pioneer); mem. AIAA (sr.), Columbia U. Engring. Alunni Assn. (pres. 1977-81), Columbia U. Alumni Fedn. (pres. 1981-85), Bronxville Field Club.

LONGONE, DANIEL THOMAS, chemistry educator; b. Worcester, Mass., Sept. 16, 1932; s. Daniel Edward and Anne (Novick) L.; m. Janice B. Bluestein, June 13, 1954. B.S., Worcester Poly. Inst., 1954; Ph.D., Cornell U., 1958. Research fellow chemistry U. Ill., Urbana, 1958-59; mem. faculty dept. chemistry U. Mich., Ann Arbor, 1959—, assoc. prof., 1966-71, prof., 1971—; cons. Gen. Motors Research Co., 1965-77. Am. Chem. Soc.-Petroleum Research Fund internat. fellow, 1967-68; Fulbright scholar, 1970-71. Mem. Am. Chem. Soc., Sigma Xi, Tau Beta Pi, Phi Lambda Upsilon. Home: 1207 W Madison St Ann Arbor MI 48103-4729 Office: U Mich 3537 Chemistry Ann Arbor MI 48109

LONGSTAFF, RONALD E., federal judge; b. 1941. BA, Kans. State Coll., 1962; JD, U. Iowa, 1965. Law clk. to Hon. Roy L. Stephenson U.S. Dist. Ct. (so. dist.) Iowa, 1965-67, clk. of ct., 1968-76, U.S. magistrate judge, 1976-91; fed. judge U.S. Dist. Ct. (so. dist.) Iowa, Des Moines, 1991—; assoc. McWilliams, Gross and Kirtley, Des Moines, 1967-68; adj. prof. law Drake U., 1973-76. Mem. Iowa State Bar Assn. (chmn. spl. commn. to revise Iowa exemption law 1968-70, mem. adv. com. 8th cir. ct. appeals 1988—). Office: US Dist Ct 422 US Courthouse Des Moines IA 50309

LONGSTREET, HARRY STEPHEN, television producer, director, scriptwriter; b. Bklyn., Feb. 24, 1940; s. Stephen and Ethel Muriel (Godoff) L.; m. Diana Gail Bodlander, Nov. 25, 1962 (div. Jan. 1977); children: Stacy Robyn, Gregory Stephen; m. Renee Myrna Schonfeld, Jan. 9, 1977. Student, U. So. Calif., 1962-64. Producer Voyagers, 1983, Trauma Center, 1983, Misfits of Science, 1986; supervising producer Hot Pursuit, 1984, Shadow Chasers, 1985; exec. producer TV show Fame, 1986-87, Rags to Riches, 1987—. Scriptwriter: (TV shows) Quincy, Father Murphy, Jack & Mike, Magnum PI, Designing Women, (TV films) The Gathering Part II, 1979, The Promise of Love, 1980, The Sky's No Limit, 1984, Gunsmoke: One Man's Justice, 1993, Alien Nation: Body and Soul, 1995, Alien Nation: The Udara Legacy, 1996, (feature films) Wounded, 1996; exec. prodr., scriptwriter: Night Walk, 1989; dir.: Identity Crisis, 1984, The Big Contract, 1987, The Jenifer Graham Story, 1989, Alien Nation, 1989-90, The Perfect Daughter, 1996; exec. prodr. With A Vengeance, 1992; writer, dir.: Sex, Love and Cold Hard Cash, 1993, A Vow to Kill, 1995. Served with USAR, 1960-67. Mem. NATAS, Writers Guild Am. (Outstanding Script nominee 1984, 90, Genesis award 1989, Humanitas nominee 1990), Dirs. Guild Am.

LONGSTREET, STEPHEN (CHAUNCEY LONGSTREET), author, painter; b. N.Y.C., Apr. 18, 1907; m. Ethel Joan Godoff, Apr. 22, 1932; children: Joan, Harry. Student, Rutgers Coll., Harvard U.; grad., N.Y. Sch. Fine and Applied Art, 1929; student in Rome, Paris. Ind. artist, writer, 1930—; staff lectr. Los Angeles Art Assn., 1954, UCLA, 1955, 58-59, lectr. Los Angeles County Mus., 1958-59; staff mem. arts and humanities dept. UCLA, 1965—; prof. art, dir. dept. Viewpoints Inst. of Gen. Semantics, Los Angeles, 1965; prof. modern writing U. So. Calif., Los Angeles, 1975-80. Began as painter; contbr. to French, Am. and English mags.; also cartoonist; radio writer for NBC, CBS, and other networks, writer shows for Rudy Vallee, Deems Taylor, John Barrymore, Bob Hope, Ellery Queen; writer popular series detective stories for Lippincott and Morrow under pen name Paul Haggrad, 1936; film critic Saturday Rev., 1941; mem. editorial staff Time mag., 1942, Screenwriters mag., 1947-48; critic L.A. Daily News, Book Pages, 1948; assoc. producer Civil War series The Blue and Gray, NBC, 1959—; author: All or Nothing, 1983, Delilah's Fortune, 1984, Our Father's House, 1985; painting exhibited: L.A., 1946, 48, N.Y., 1946, London, 1947; one-man shows include Padlia Galleries, L.A., 1970, Memphis Mus., 1979, Erie Mus., 1981, Coll. of Libr. of Congress, 1980, Jazz Age Revisited, 1983, Smithsonian Nat. Portrait Gallery, 1983, Sr. Eye Gallery, Long Beach, Calif., 1990, Columbus (Ohio) Mus. Art, 1992, tour of Japan, 1994; retrospective show Longstreet the Mature Years, L.A., 1983, Jazz-The Chgo. Scene, Regenstein Libr. U. Chgo., 1989, Columbus (Ohio) Mus. Fine Arts; author: The Pedlocks, 1951, The Beach House, 1952, The World Revisited, 1953, A Century of Studebaker on Wheels, 1953, The Lion at Morning, 1954, The Boy in the Model-T, 1956, Real Jazz, 1956, The Promoters, 1957, The Bill Pearson Story, 1957, (in French), Complete Dictionary of Jazz, 1957, Man of Montmartre, 1958, The Burning Man, 1958, The Politician, 1959, The Crime, 1959, Geisha, 1960, Gettysburg, 1960, A Treasury of the World's Great Prints, 1961, Eagles Where I Walk, 1961, The Flesh Peddler, 1962, A Few Painted Feathers, 1963, War In Golden Weather, 1965, Pedlock & Sons, 1965, The Wilder Shore: San Francisco '49 to '06, 1968, A Salute to American Cooking, (with Ethel Longstreet), 1968, War Cries on Horseback, An Indian History, 1970, The Canvas Falcons, 1970, Chicago: 1860-1920; a history, 1973, The General, 1974, (with Ethel Longstreet) World Cookbook, 1973, Win or Lose, 1977, The Queen Bees, 1979, Storm Watch, 1979, Pembroke Colors, 1981, From Storyville to Harlem - 50 years of the Jazz Scene, 1987, Magic Trumpets--The Young Peoples Story of Jazz, 1989, (poems) Jazz Solos, 1990, My Three Nobel Prizes; Life with Faulkner, Hemingway and Sinclair Lewis, 1994, Up River-The Jazz of Kansas City and Chicago, 1997; editor, illustrator: The Memoirs of W.W. Windstaff Lower Than Angels, 1993; writer screen plays including Uncle Harry, 1943, Rider on a Dead Horse, The Imposter, First Travelling Saleslady, Stallion Road, 1946, The Jolson Story, 1947, Helen Morgan Story, 1956, plays including High Button Shoes, 1947, Gauguin, 1948, All Star Cast, Los Angeles, A History, 1977, (TV series) Playhouse 90, TV writer for Readers Digest Theatre, 1955; contbr. dialogue for films Greatest Show on Earth, Duel In the Sun. Pres. Los Angeles Art Assn., 1973-90. Recipient Stafford medal London, 1946, Bowman prize, 1948, Photo-Play mag. Gold medal for The Jolson Story, 1948, Billboard-Donaldson Gold medal for High Button Shoes, 1948. Mem. Motion Picture Acad. Arts and Letters, Writers Guild Am. (bd. dirs. 1948), Phi Sigma (charter mem.). Clubs: Sketch, Daguerreotype Society, Winadu Players. *I seem to have stumbled into the most dangerous world history since the fall of Rome. This time little of civilization may survive. The vulgarization of the culture by TV and lack of an American greatness in the White House can bring Orwell's world into being. But mankind will most likely remain in some form in his polluted planet, recalling what was the past. Man will always remain an undomesticated animal; rather kill than think.*

LONGSTREET, VICTOR MENDELL, government official; b. Louisville, Jan. 1, 1907; s. Joseph Emens and Allan Bemus (McKinley) L.; m. Mary Margaret Landry, 1930 (dec.); 1 child, Katherine Allan. BS magna cum laude, Harvard U., 1930. Economist AT&T, 1930-31; sr. economist Fed. Res. Bd., 1931-43; assoc. chief div. econ. devel. Dept. State, 1945-48; program rev. officer ECA U.S. Spl. Mission to Netherlands, The Hague, 1948-49; dep. U.S. sr. rep. Fin. Com., NATO, 1950-51; dep. dir. Office Trade and Fin., Econ. Coop. Adminstrn., Paris, 1951-52; v.p., mgr. Louisville br. Fed. Res. Bank, St. Louis, 1953-57; dir. mgmt. rsch. Schering Corp., 1957-62; asst. sec. Dept. Navy, 1962-65; assoc. dir. Internat. Mgmt. Group of Boston, 1966-69; chmn. The Boston Group, Inc., 1970-79; bd. dirs. N.Am. Fund Mgmt. Corp. Author: Financial Control in Multi-National Companies, 1971. Served from capt. to lt. col. AC, U.S. Army, 1943-45. Mem. Harvard Club (N.Y.C.), Phi Beta Kappa. Address: 4000 Cathedral Ave NW Washington DC 20016-5249

LONGSTRETH, BEVIS, lawyer; b. N.Y.C., Jan. 29, 1934; s. Alfred Bevis and Mary Agnes (Shiras) L.; m. Clara St. John, Aug. 10, 1963; children: Katherine Shiras, Thomas Day, Benjamin Hoyt. B.S. cum laude, Princeton U., 1956; LL.M., Harvard U., 1961. Bar: N.Y. 1962. Assoc. Debevoise & Plimpton, N.Y.C., 1962-70, ptnr., 1970-81; commr. SEC, Washington, 1981-84; ptnr. Debevoise & Plimpton, 1984—; lectr. Columbia U. Law Sch., N.Y.C., 1975-81, adj. prof., 1994—; cons. Ford Found., 1971-72; cons. to Comptroller Gen. of U.S.; mem. pension fin. com. World Bank, 1987-95; bd. govs. Am. Stock Exch., 1992—; bd. dirs. AMVESCO, plc, Capstead Mortgage Co., Coll. Ret. Equities Fund. Author books, numerous articles on investment, securities and law. Bd. dirs. Symphony Space Inc.; trustee Nathan Cummings Found., 1991—, trustee, 1993—; New Sch. for Social Rsch., 1987—; chmn. fin. com. Rockefeller Family Fund, 1986—. Lt. USMC, 1956-58. Mem. Am. Law Inst., Assn. of Bar of City of N.Y., Coun. Fgn. Rels. Democrat. Home: 322 Central Park W New York NY 10025-7629 Office: Debevoise & Plimpton 875 3rd Ave New York NY 10022-6225

LONGSWORTH, CHARLES R., foundation administrator; b. Fort Wayne, Ind., Aug. 21, 1929; s. Maurice A. and Marjorie K. L.; m. Polly Ormsby, June 30, 1956; children: Amy Porter, Elizabeth King, Laura Cramer, Anne Graybill. B.A., Amherst Coll., 1951; M.B.A., Harvard U., 1953. Mktg. trainee Campbell Soup Co., Camden, N.J., 1955-58; account exec. Ogilvy & Mather, Inc., N.Y.C., 1958-60; asst. to pres. Amherst (Mass.) Coll., 1960-65; chmn. edn. trust Hampshire Coll., Amherst, 1966, v.p., sec., 1966-71, pres., 1971-77, pres. emeritus, 1992; pres., chief operating officer Colonial Williamsburg Found., Va., 1977-79, pres., CEO, 1979-92; chmn. Colonial Williamsburg Found., 1991-94, chmn. emeritus, 1994—; dir. Houghton Mifflin Co., Crestar Fin. Corp., Caliber Sys. Inc., Saul Ctrs. Inc., Pub. Radio Internat., Va. Ea. Shore Corp. Author: (with others) The Making of a College, 1966, Five Colleges: Five Histories, 1993; contbr. articles to profl. jours. Chmn. bd. trustees Amherst Coll.; trustee Colonial Williamsburg Found., 1977-94, Emeritus Nat. Trust Hist. Preservation; bd. dirs. Ctr. for Pub. Resources, bd. advisors, trustee of reservations. Lt. USMC, 1953-55. Mem. Am. Philos. Soc., Am. Antiquarian Soc., Phi Beta Kappa, Univ. Club (N.Y.C.), Century Assn. Club (N.Y.C.), Commonwealth Club (Richmond, Va.). Home: Davis Hill Farm Davis Hill Rd Royalston MA 01368 Office: Colonial Williamsburg PO Box C Williamsburg VA 23187-3707

LONGSWORTH, ELLEN LOUISE, art historian, consultant; b. Auburn, Ind., Aug. 21, 1949; d. Robert Smith and Alice Louise (Whitten) L.; m. Frederic Sanderson Stott, Sept. 1, 1973 (div. 1981); m. Joseph Nicholas Teta, June 15, 1991. BA, Mt. Holyoke Coll., 1971; MA, U. Chgo., 1976; PhD, Boston U., 1987. Trainer, designer Polaris Enterprises Corp., Quincy, Mass., 1981-82, asst. v.p., 1982-84, cons., 1989-93; from asst. prof. to assoc. prof. Merrimack Coll., N. Andover, Mass., 1985-95, prof., 1995—, chmn. dept., 1993—; adj. instr. art and art history Bradford Coll., Haverhill, Mass., 1975-80; vis. lectr. art history Lowell (Mass.) U., 1981-82, Boston U., 1982-86, 88, 91, Babson Coll., Wellesley, Mass., 1984-85. Mem. Merrimack Valley Coun. on the Arts and Humanities, Haverhill, 1975-78, Friends of Kimball Tavern, Bradford Coll., Haverhill, 1975-80; bd. dirs. Winnekenni Found., Haverhill, 1990—; mem. Haverhill Arts Commn., 1996—. Grantee Faculty Devel., Merrimack Coll., 1989-90, 92-93, 95, 97, Kress Summer Travel, Boston U., summers 1980, 86; fellowship Boston U., 1980-82, 85; recipient internship Isabella Stewart Gardner Mus., Boston, 1979-80. Mem. AAUW, Coll. Art Assn., South-Ctrl. Renaissance Conf., Am. Assn. Italian Studies, Italian Art Soc., Renaissance Soc. Am. Republican. Methodist. Avocations: reading, playing the piano, painting and drawing, weight training, swimming. Home: 649 Main St Haverhill MA 01830-2647 Office: Merrimack Coll North Andover MA 01845

LONGSWORTH, ROBERT MORROW, college professor; b. Canton, Ohio, Feb. 15, 1937; s. Robert H. and Margaret Elizabeth (Morrow) L.; m. Carol Herndon, Aug. 16, 1958; children—Eric D., Margaret W., Ann E. A.B., Duke U., 1958; M.A., Harvard U., 1960, Ph.D., 1965. Asst. prof. Oberlin Coll., 1964-70, assoc. prof., 1970-75, prof. English, 1975—, dean Coll. Arts and Scis., 1974-84. Author: The Cornish Ordinalia, 1967, The Design of Drama, 1972. Contbr. articles to profl. jours. Danforth Found. fellow. Fellow Am. Council Learned Socs., Nat. Humanities Ctr.; mem. MLA, Medieval Acad. Am., Cornwall Archaeol. Soc., Phi Beta Kappa.

LONGUEMARE, R. NOEL, JR., federal official; b. El Paso, Tex., Mar. 26, 1932; s. Robert Noel Sr. and Lorenza (Escajeda) L.; m. Julianna Josephine Isdebski, June 6, 1959; 1 child, Maria Christine. BSEE, U. Tex., El Paso, 1952; MSE, Johns Hopkins U., 1958. Corp. v.p., gen. mgr. electronic sys. group Westinghouse Electric, Balt., 1952-93; prin. dep. under sec. of def. acquisition and tech. Dept. Def., Washington, 1993—; cons. Def. Sci. Bd., Washington, 1988-91, mem., 1991-93; mem. Air Force Sci. Adv. Bd., Washington, 1990-93. Recipient Greer award Nat. Security Indsl. Assn., 1993, Excellence in Mfg. award, 1995. Fellow IEEE; mem. AAAS, AIAA (sr.). Democrat. Roman Catholic. Achievements include 8 patents. Avocation: piano. Office: Dept of Defense 3015 Defense Pentagon Washington DC 20301-3015

LONGWELL, H.J., petroleum engineer; b. 1941. Degree in petroleum engring., La. State U. Drilling engr. Exxon, New Orleans, 1963-95, sr. v.p., 1995—. Office: Exxon Corp 225 E John W Carpenter Fwy Irving TX 75062-2298

LONGWELL, JOHN PLOEGER, chemical engineering educator; b. Denver, Apr. 27, 1918; s. John Stalker and Martha Dorothea (Ploeger) L.; m. Marion Reed Valleau, Dec. 11, 1945; children: Martha Reed, Elizabeth Ann, John Dorney. BSME, U. Calif., Berkeley, 1940; ScD in Chem. Engring, MIT, 1943. With Exxon Rsch. & Engring. Co., Linden, N.J., 1943-77; dir. Exxon Rsch. & Engring. Co. Central Basic Rsch. Lab., 1960-69, sr. sci. adv., 1969-77; prof. chem. engring. MIT, Cambridge, 1977—. Contbr. articles to profl. jours. Recipient Sir Alfred Egerton medal for contbns. to combustion Nat. Acad. Engring., 1976. Mem. Am. Chem. Soc., Combustion Inst. (past pres.), Am. Inst. Chem. Engrs. (award 1979), Sigma Xi, Tau Beta Pi. Republican. Patentee in field. Home: 22 Follen St Cambridge MA 02138-4534 Office: MIT Rm 66-456 Cambridge MA 02139

LONGWORTH, RICHARD COLE, journalist; b. Des Moines, Mar. 13, 1935; s. Wallace Harlan and Helen (Cole) L.; m. Barbara Bem, July 19, 1958; children: Peter, Susan. BJ, Northwestern U., 1957; postgrad., Harvard U., 1968-69. Reporter UPI, Chgo., 1958-60; parliamentary corr. UPI, London, 1960-65; corr. UPI, Moscow, 1965-68, Vienna, 1969-72; diplomatic corr. UPI, Brussels, 1972-76; econ. and internat. affairs reporter Chgo. Tribune, 1976-86, bus. editor, econ. columnist, 1987-88, chief European corr., 1988-91, sr. writer, 1991—; internat. affairs commentator Sta. WBEZ-FM, Chgo., 1984—. Served with U.S. Army, 1957-58. Nieman fellow, 1968-69; recipient award for econ. reporting U. Mo., 1978, 80, John Hancock award for econ. reporting, 1978, 79, 82, Gerald Loeb award for econ. reporting, 1979, Media award for econ. understanding Dartmouth Coll., 1979, award Inter-Am. Press Assn., 1979, Peter Lisagor award Sigma Delta Chi, 1979, Sidney Hillman award, 1985, Lowell Thomas award for travel writing, 1985, Beck award for fgn. corr., 1986, Domestic Reporting award, 1987, Overseas Press Club award, 1994, 97. Mem. Chgo. Com. of Council Fgn. Rels., Assn. Am. Corrs. in London, Internat. Music Found. (dir.). Office: Chicago Tribune 435 N Michigan Ave Chicago IL 60611

LONNEBOTN, TRYGVE, battery company executive; b. Bergen, Norway, Oct. 4, 1937; came to U.S., 1965; s. Trygve and Nora Gertrude (Hoyland) L.; m. Aud Amalie Engesaeter, Sept. 28, 1963 (div.); children: Anne V., Paal T. MChemE, Tech. U. Norway, 1963. With Rayovac Corp., Madison, Wis., 1965—, project engr., then. project mgr., 1965-74, materials mgr., 1974-75, plant mgr., 1975-77, dir. ops., 1977-79, v.p. tech., 1979-82, v.p. ops., 1982-86, sr. v.p. ops., 1986-95, exec. v.p. ops., 1995—; apptd. hon. Norwegian consul, 1996. Served to sgt. Norwegian Army, 1957-58. Mem. Norges Ingenior Forening (Norwegian Engring. Soc.), Torskeklubben Club (Madison). Lutheran. Avocations: hiking, soccer, music. Office: Rayovac Corp 601 Ray O Vac Dr # 4960 Madison WI 53711-2460

LONNEKE, MICHAEL DEAN, radio and television marketing executive; b. Wichita, Kans., Jan. 15, 1943; s. John Henry and Lillian Eleanor (Millspaugh) L.; m. Charlene Bertha Wilson, Apr. 10, 1975; children: Rebecca, Marietta, Alison. Student, Wichita State U., 1962-63, Friends U., 1961-66. Ops. mgr. Sta. KCMO, Kansas City, Mo., 1968-80; program dir. Sta. WCAU/CBS, Phila., 1980-81; v.p., gen. mgr. Sta. WGSO, New Orleans, 1981-83, Sta. KRNT/KRNQ-FM, Des Moines, 1983-85, Sta. KHOW, Denver, 1985-86, Sta. WMAQ/WKQX-FM (NBC Inc.), Chgo., 1986-89; pres. broadcast divsn. TransAm. Mktg. Svcs., Inc., Washington, 1989-94; v.p., gen. mgr. Metromedia Internat., Moscow, Russia, 1994-96, Budapest, Hungary, 1996—. Bd. dirs. Youth Symphony of DuPage (Ill.); pres. Loudoun Symphony Orch. Mem. Radio-TV News Dirs. Assn. (bd. dirs. 1970-72), Nat. Assn. Broadcasters, Am. Radio Relay League, Quarter Century Wireless Assn., U.S. Yacht Club, Masons. Republican. Episcopalian.

LONNGREN, KARL ERIK, electrical and computer engineering educator; b. Milw., Aug. 8, 1938; s. Bruno Leonard and Edith Irene (Osterlund) L.; m. Vicki Anne Mason, Feb. 16, 1963; children: Sondra Lyn, Jon Erik. B.S. in Elec. Engring., U. Wis., 1960, M.S., 1962, Ph.D., 1964. Postdoctoral appointment Royal Inst. Tech., Stockholm, 1964-65; asst. prof. elec. engring. U. Iowa, Iowa City, 1965-67; assoc. prof. U. Iowa, 1967-72, prof., 1972—; vis. scientist Danish Atomic Energy, Riso, 1982, Inst. Space and Astron. Sci., Tokyo, 1981, Los Alamos Sci. Labs. (N.M.), 1979, 80, Math. Research Ctr., Madison, 1976, Inst. Plasma Physics, Nagoya, Japan, 1972, others. Author: Introduction to Physical Electronics, 1988; co-author: Introduction to Wave Phenomena, 1985; co-editor: Solitons in Action, 1978. Recipient Disting. Svc. citation U. Wisc. Madison, 1992. Fellow Am. Phys. Soc., IEEE. Presbyterian. Home: 21 Prospect Pl Iowa City IA 52246-1932 Office: U Iowa Dept Elec & Computer Engring Iowa City IA 52242

LONNQUIST, GEORGE ERIC, lawyer; b. Lincoln, Nebr., Mar. 29, 1946; s. John Hall and Elizabeth Claire (Hanson) L.; m. Sandra Lynn Wise, May 7, 1971; children: Alethea, Courtenay, Barrett. BS, U. Tenn., 1968; JD, U. Nebr., 1971; LLM, NYU, 1974. Bar: Calif. 1983, Oreg. 1972, Nebr. 1971. Law clerk Oreg. Supreme Ct., Salem, 1971-72; dep. legis. counsel Oreg. Legislature, Salem, 1972-73; ptnr. Meysing & Lonnquist, Portland, 1974-78; v.p., assoc. gen. counsel Amfac, Inc., Portland and San Francisco, 1978-84; sr. v.p., gen. counsel Homestead Fin. Corp., Millbrae, Calif., 1984-91, Homestead Savs., Millbrae, 1984-93; pvt. practice, San Francisco, 1993—. Democrat. Roman Catholic. Avocation: woodcarving. Home: 846 E Greenwich Pl Palo Alto CA 94303-3416 Office: 1855 Gateway Blvd Concord CA 94520-3200

LOO, BEVERLY JANE, publishing company executive; b. L.A.; d. Richard Y. and Bessie E. Sue Loo. B.A., U. Calif., Berkeley. Dir. subs. rights Prentice-Hall, Inc., N.Y.C., 1957-59; fiction editor McCall's mag., 1959-62; exec. editor and dir. subs. rights, gen. books div. McGraw-Hill Book Co., N.Y.C., 1962-82; pres. Beverly Jane Loo Assocs., Inc., N.Y.C., 1982-85; sr. editor, dir. subs. rights World Almanac Pharos Books, N.Y.C., 1985-88; dir. mktg. and subs. rights Paragon House, N.Y.C., 1988-91; dir. mktg. and sales Thomasson-Grant, Charlottesville, Va., 1991-93; dir. pub. and comm. programs U. Va. Div. Continuing Edn., Charlottesville, 1993—. Clubs: Arts (London); Overseas Press (N.Y.C.); Va. Writers. Home: Lewis & Clark Sq # 701 250 W Main St Charlottesville VA 22902-5079 Office: Univ Va Zehmer Hall 104 Midmont Ln Charlottesville VA 22903-2449

LOO, MARCUS H., physician, educator; b. N.Y.C., Aug. 12, 1955; s. David Wei and Patricia (Pai) L.; m. Donna C. Wingshee, Oct. 3, 1987; children: Christopher, Courtney. BSEE with distinction, Cornell U., 1977, MD, 1981. Diplomate Am. Bd. Urology. Asst. attending urologist N.Y. Hosp. Med. Ctr., N.Y.C., 1988—; clin. asst. prof. urology Cornell U. Med. Ctr., N.Y.C., 1994—. Fellow Am. Coll. Surgeons; mem. AMA, IEEE, Am. Assn. Clin. Urologists, Am. Urol. Soc., Societé Internationale Urologie, Cornell Alumni Assn., Chinese Am. Med. Soc. (pres., bd. dirs. 1990-97), Fedn. Chinese Am. and Chinese Can. Med. Socs. (bd. dirs.), Tau Beta Pi, Eta Kappa Nu, Phi Tau Phi. Office: 53 E 70th St New York NY 10021-4941

LOO, MARITTA LOUISE, military officer, nurse; b. Denver, Feb. 6, 1945; d. William Del Rio and Audrey Elaine (Fromholz) Dugan; m. Albert W.S. Loo, June 26, 1971 (div. Apr. 1976). Diploma, St. Mary's, Kansas City, Mo., 1966; BS in Health Svcs. Adminstrn., Calif. U., Navato, 1986; student, Army War Coll., 1986-87. RN, Tex. From staff to head nurse Kansas City Gen. Hosp., Mo., 1966-69; shift charge, emergency nurse St. Mary's Hosp., Kansas City, 1969-71; research nurse office of Dr. J. Willoughby, Kansas City, 1970-71; dir. critical care Dallas-Ft. Worth Med. Ctr., Grand Prairie, Tex., 1974-86; rev. supr. Tex. Med. Found., 1988-92; dir. home health Dallas-Ft. Worth Med. Ctr., Grand Prairie, 1993—; freelance leadership trainer, mgmt. cons., 1985-93; owner, mgr. Masavic Properties, Inc., Ft. Worth, 1979—; co-chmn. Tex. Adj. Gen.'s adv. coun., Austin, 1985-86; spl. advisor Am. Security Coun., Washington, 1985, nat. advisor, 1985-87; rep. Partnership For Peace program, Prague, 1995; mem. Congl. Bd. for candidate selection Annapolis Acad., 1995—; comdr. med. unit Tex. Air N.G., 1996—; rep. Partnership for Peace Program, Prague, 1995; mem. Cong. Bd. for Candidate Selection for Sr. Mil. Acads., 1995—; motivational spkr., 1994—. Contbr. articles to mags., 1984—. Resource coord. ARC, Carlisle, Pa., 1986-87; mem. Cath. Adults, Arlington, Tex. Served to capt. USAF, 1971-74; col. Air N.G., 1975—, Desert Shield, 1990, Desert Storm, 1990-91; comdr. Tex. Air Nat. Guard, 1995—; mem. humanitarian mission Joint-Forces BRAVO to Honduras, Ctrl. Am. Recipient honored vol. award ARC, 1982, Profl. Devel. award Tex. Adj. Gen.'s Adv. Coun., 1986, Rare Joint Forces award, 1995; named one of Notable Women of Tex., 1985. Mem. ANA, DAV (bronze leader comdrs. club), AACN (bd. advisors 1983, office Ft. Worth chpt. 1984-86), N.G. Assn. (del. 1984—), Air Force Assn., Am. Legion, Soroptomist. Republican. Roman Catholic. Avocations: theater, music. Home: 2433 Parkwood Grand Prairie TX 75050-1727

LOO, THOMAS S., lawyer; b. 1943. BS, U. So. Calif., JD. Bar: Calif. 1969. Ptnr. Bryan Cave LLP, Santa Monica, Calif. Office: Bryan Cave LLP 120 Broadway Ste 500 Santa Monica CA 90401-2386

LOOGES, PETER JOHN, systems engineer, architect; b. East Orange, N.J., Mar. 4, 1963; s. Edwin John and Ida Claire (Jacobus) L.; m. Heather Marta Evans, Apr. 6, 1989 (dec.); 1 child, Adrian. BS in Computer Sci., Rensselaer Poly. Inst., 1985; MS in Computer Sci., Old Dominion U., 1991, PhD in Computer Sci., 1992. Commd. ensign USN, 1985, advanced through grades to lt., resigned, 1992; researcher, adj. prof. Old Dominion U., Norfolk, Va., 1992-93; adj. computer sci. prof. Old Dominion U., Norfolk, 1993—; chief engr., asst. v.p. Sci. Applications Internat. Corp., Hampton, Va., 1993—. Contbr. articles to profl. jours. Mem. IEEE, Assn. for Computing Machinery, Software Engring. Inst. Avocations: scuba, sky diving, raquetball. Office: Sci Applications Internat Corp 22 Enterprise Pky Ste 200 Hampton VA 23666-5844

LOOI, LAI-MENG, pathology educator; b. Bentong, Pahang, Malaysia, July 28, 1950; d. Choong-Foon Looi and Lin-Kiew Chai; m. Kwong-Choong Chang, June 13, 1981. MB BS, U. Singapore, 1975; M in Pathology, U. Malaya, Malaysia, 1979; MD, U. Malaya, 1987. Lectr. U. Malaya, Kuala Lumpur, Malaysia, 1979-85; assoc. prof. U. Malaya, Kuala Lumpur, 1985-86, prof., 1986—; dir. pathology U. Hosp., Kuala Lumpur, 1984—, sr. cons. pathologist, 1986—; external examiner U. Singapore, 1988-97; vis. prof. Harvard Med. Sch., Mass., 1991-92; external assesor U. Aberdeen, U.K., 1993; vis. fellow U. Tasmania, 1997. Editor Malaysian Jour. Pathology, 1986—; mem. editl. adv. bd. Histopathology, 1994—, Human Pathology, 1995—, Jour. Pathology, 1996—; contbr. articles to profl. jours. Coord. Brit. Coun. Edn. Projects Malaysia-U.K., 1984-95; senate mem. U. Malaya, Malaysia, 1984—; elected mem. Med. Ctr. Rsch. Com., U. Malaya, 1992—; cons. Ofcl. Secrets Act Project, Malaysia, 1994. Found. fellow Acad. Scis. Malaysia, 1995; Hon. fellow U. Tasmania, 1997. Fellow Royal Coll. Pathologists U.K. (examiner 1988—), Royal Coll. Pathologists Australasia (Malaysian rep. 1988—), Royal Soc. Medicine; mem. Malaysian Soc. Pathologists (pres. 1990-91, 93—), Acad. Medicine Malaysia (mem. coun. 1993-95), Internat. Acad. Cytology, Internat. Acad. Pathology, Malaysian Med. Coun. (councillor 1986—), N.Y. Acad. Scis., Royal Microscopical Soc. U.K., Assn. Clin. Pathologists, Arthur Purdy Stout Soc. Surg. Pathologists. Avocations: swimming, music, poetry. Office: Dept Pathology, Univ Malaya, Kuala Lumpur 50603, Malaysia

LOOK, DONA JEAN, artist; b. Port Washington, Wis., Mar. 30, 1948; m. Kenneth W. Loeber. BA, U. Wis., Oshkosh, 1970. Art tchr. Dept. Edn., NSW, Australia, 1976-78; ptnr. Look and Heaney Studio, Byron Bay, NSW, 1978-80; studio artist Algoma, Wis., 1980—. One person shows include Perimeter Gallery, Chgo., 1991; exhibited in group shows Perimeter Gallery, Chgo., 1983, 93, 94, Phila. Mus. Art, 1984, Civic Fine Arts Mus., Sioux Falls, S.D., 1985, Dacotah Prairie Mus., Aberdeen, S.D., 1985, Bergstrom-Mahler Mus., Neenah, Wis., 1985, Lawton Gallery, U. Wis.-Green Bay, 1985, J. B. Speed Art Mus., Louisville, 1986, Laguna (Calif.) Art Mus., Am. Craft Mus., N.Y.C., 1985, 86, 87, 89, Ark. Arts Ctr. Decorative Arts Mus., Little Rock, 1987, Cultural Ctr., Chgo., 1988, Erie (Pa.) Art Mus., 1988, Maine Crafts Assn., Colby Coll. Mus. Art, 1989, Ft. Wayne (Ind.) Mus. Art, 1989, The Forum, St. Louis, 1990, Palo Alto (Calif.) Cultural Ctr., 1990, Neville Pub. Mus., Green Bay, Wis., 1992, Waterloo (Iowa) Mus. Art, 1993, Sybaris Gallery, Royal Oak, Mich., 1993, 95, Sun Valley Ctr. for Arts and Humanities, Ketchum, Idaho, 1995, Nat. Mus. Am. Art, Smithsonian Instn., Washington, 1995; represented in permanent collections The White House Collection, Phila. Mus. Art, MCI Telecomms. Corp., Inc., Washington, Am. Craft Mus., N.Y.C., Ark. Arts Ctr., Little Rock, C. A. Wustum Mus. Fine Arts, Racine, Erie Art Mus.; works included in publs. The White House Collection of American Crafts, 1995, Craft Today: Poetry of the Physical, 1986, International Crafts, 1991, FIBERARTS Design Book Four, 1991, The Tactile Vessel, 1989, Creative Ideas for Living, 1988, The Basketmaker's Art: Contemporary Baskets and Their Makers, 1986. Recipient 1st prize award Phila. Craft Show, 1984, 2d prize award, 1985, Design award Am. Craft Mus., 1985, Craftsmen's award Phila. Craft Show, 1986; Nat. Endowment for Arts/Arts Midwest fellow, 1987, Nat. Endowment for Arts Fellowship grantee, 1988. Office: Perimeter Gallery 750 N Orleans St Chicago IL 60610-3598*

LOOK, JANET K., psychologist; b. Bklyn., Mar. 11, 1944; d. Harry and Isabelle (Chernoff) Kaplan; divorced; children: Howard, Erika (dec.). AB, NYU, 1964; EdM, Rutgers U., 1967, EdD, 1976. Lic. psychologist; cert. sch. psychologist. Asst. examiner Ednl. Testing Svc., Princeton, N.J., 1964-66; instr. Rutgers U., New Brunswick, N.J., 1968-69; psychologist Seattle Pub. Schs., 1991—; pvt. practice Kirkland, Wash., 1993—; adj. instr. U. Conn., Waterbury, 1973-91; appearances on various TV and radio shows including the Today Show; interviews include Litchfield County Times, 1987, Waterbury Rep.-Am., 1983-87, Manchester Jour. Inquirer, 1986, Danbury News-Times, 1985; presenter APA, San Francisco, 1991, Nation's Concern and Its Response, U. Wis., Milw., 1991, Nat. Assn. Sch. Psychologists, Dallas, 1991, Divorce Issues Inst., So. Conn. State U., New Haven, 1989. Author: (with others) The Troubled Adolescent, 1991; contbr. articles to newspapers, including N.Y. Times. Mem. APA, Wash. State Psychol. Assn., Nat. Assn. Sch. Psychologists, Wash. State Assn. Sch. Psychologists (area rep., bd. dirs. 1991-93). Avocations: writing, reading, dance, film, running. Office: 1104 Market St Kirkland WA 98033-5441

LOOMAN, JAMES R., lawyer; b. Vallejo, Calif., June 5, 1952; s. Alfred R. and Jane M. (Halter) L.; m. Donna G. Craven, Dec. 18, 1976; children: Alison Marie, Mark Andrew, Zachary Michael. BA, Valparaiso U., 1974; JD, U. Chgo., 1978. Bar: Ill, 1978, U.S. Dist. Ct. (no dist.) Ill. 1978, U.S. Claims Ct. 1979. Assoc. Isham, Lincoln & Beale, Chgo., 1978-83; assoc. Sidley & Austin, Chgo., 1983-86, ptnr., 1986—. Fellow Am. Coll. Comml. Fin. Lawyers; mem. ABA, Chgo. Bar Assn., Chgo. Athletic Assn., Skokie Country Club. Lutheran. Office: Sidley & Austin 1 First Natl Plz Chicago IL 60603-2003

LOOMIS, CAROL J., journalist; b. Marshfield, Mo., June 25, 1929; d. Harold and Mildred (Case) Junge; m. John R. Loomis, Mar. 19, 1960; children: Barbara, Mark. Student, Drury Coll., 1947-49; B in Journalism, U. Mo., 1951. Editor Maytag News, Maytag Co., Newton, Iowa, 1951-54; rsch. assoc. Fortune mag., N.Y.C., 1954-58, assoc. editor, 1958-68, mem. bd. editors, 1968—. Office: Fortune Mag 1271 Avenue Of The Americas New York NY 10020-1300

LOOMIS, EARL ALFRED, JR., psychiatrist; b. Mpls., May 21, 1921; s. Earl Alfred and Amy Louise (Shore) L.; m. Victoria Malkerson, June 2, 1944 (div.); children: Rebecca Marie Keith, Kathleen Victoria, Jennifer Lee; m. Lucile Meyer, July 1, 1962 (dec. 1967); 1 child, Amy Windeler; m. Anita Muriel Peabody, Mar. 22, 1969. MD, U. Minn., 1945. Diplomate Am. Bd. Psychiatry and Neurology, Am. Bd. Adult and Child Psychiatry; cert. Am. Soc. Addiction Medicine. Intern in internal medicine, pediatrics Univ. Hosp., Boston, 1945-46; resident Western Psychiat. Hosp., Pitts., 1946-48, Hosp. U. Pa., Phila., 1948-50; assoc. prof. child psychiatry U. Pitts. Sch. Medicine, 1952-56; prof. psychiatry and religion Union Theol. Sem., N.Y.C., 1956-63; chief div. child psychiatry St. Luke's Hosp., N.Y.C., 1956-62; rsch. fellow U. Geneva (Switzerland) Inst. Jean-Jacques Rousseau, 1962-63; med. dir. Blueberry Treatment Ctr./Severly Emotionally Ill Children, Bklyn., 1963-81; prof. psychiatry Med. Coll. Ga., Augusta, 1980-90; pvt. practice, cons. Vet. Hosp., Charter Hosp. of Augusta, 1985-95; cons. U.S. VA Hosp., Augusta, 1985-95; cons. Gracewood Sch. and Hosp., Augusta, 1983-89, Eisenhower Army Med. Ctr., Augusta, 1983-96. Author: The Self in Pilgrimage, 1960; contbr. articles to profl. jours. Lt. (j.g.) USNR, 1950-52. Rsch. grant NIMH, 1956-63, travel grant, 1962-63, U.S. Info. Svcs., 1963. Fellow Am. Psychiat. Assn. (chair psychiatry and religion 1955-60); Group for the Advancement of Psychiatry (chair psychiatry and religion 1959-62), Am. Psychoanalytic Assn., Psychoanalytic Study Group of S.C. (founder, pres. 1981-88). Achievements include development of techniques for studying ego functions in psychotic, retarded and normal children via play pattern observations. Home and Office: 1002 Katherine St Apt 6 Augusta GA 30904-6141 also: PO Box 697 125 Cove Cir Greenport NY 11944

LOOMIS, HENRY, former broadcasting company executive, former government official; b. Tuxedo Park, N.Y., Apr. 19, 1919; s. Alfred Lee and Ellen Holman (Farnsworth) L.; m. Mary Paul Macleod, May 18, 1946 (div. Jan. 1974); children—Henry, Mary, Lucy, Gordon; m. Jacqueline C. Williams, Jan. 19, 1974; stepchildren—Charles Judson Williams, John Chalmers Williams, David Finley Williams, Robert Wood Williams. A.B., Harvard, 1941; ed., U. Calif., 1946. With radiation lab. U. Calif., 1945-47; asst. to pres. MIT, 1947-50; asst. to chmn. research and devel. bd. Dept. Def., 1950-51; cons. Psychol. Strategy Bd., Washington, 1951-52; staff Pres.'s Com. Internat. Info., 1953; chief Office Research and Intelligence, USIA, 1954-57; staff to Spl. Asst. to Pres. for Sci. and Tech., 1957-58; dir. broadcasting service Voice of Am. USIA, 1958-65; dep. commr. edn. HEW, 1965-66; ptnr. St. Vincents Island Co., N.Y.C., 1966-69; dep. dir. USIA, 1969-72; pres. Corp. for Pub. Broadcasting, Washington, 1972-78; trustee, vice chmn. bd. dirs. Mitre Corp., 1967-69, 78-91. Vice chmn. bd. dirs. Nat. Mus. Natural History, Smithsonian Instn., 1991-92, trustee, 1992-95; trustee Mus. Sci. and History, Jacksonville, 1991-96; bd. dirs., hon. mem. Jacksonville Zool. Soc., 1991-96. Recipient Rockefeller Pub. Service award for fgn. affairs, 1963. Home: 4661 Ortega Island Dr Jacksonville FL 32210-7500

LOOMIS, HOWARD KREY, banker; b. Omaha, Apr. 9, 1927; s. Arthur L. and Genevieve (Krey) L.; AB, Cornell U., 1949, MBA, 1950; m. Florence Porter, Apr. 24, 1954; children: Arthur L. II, Frederick S., Howard Krey, John Porter. Mgmt. trainee Hallmark Cards, Inc., Kansas City, Mo., 1953-56; sec., controller, dir. Mine Svc. Co., Inc., Ft. Smith, Ark., 1956-59; controller, dir. Electra Mfg. Co., Independence, Kans., 1959-63; v.p., dir. The Peoples Bank, Pratt, Kans., 1963-65, pres., 1966—; pres., dir. Gt. Plains Leasing, Inc., Pratt, 1966-80, Central States Inc., Pratt, 1970-76, Krey Co. Ltd., Pratt, 1978—; fin. chmn. Econ. Lifelines, Topeka; bd. dirs. All Ins., Inc., Pratt, Kans. Devel. Credit Corp., Topeka, Kans. Wildscape Found.; past dir. Fed. Reserve Bank of Kansas City, Mo.; past pres. Pratt County United Fund. Past chmn. Cannonball Trail chpt. ARC; bd. dirs., past comdg. gen. Kans. Cavalry; past pres. Investment Com., Kanza coun. Boy Scouts Am. With AUS, 1950-52. Mem. Kans. C. of C. and Industry (past transp. chmn., dir., v.p.), Pratt Area C. of C. (past pres., dir.), Kans. Bankers Assn. (past dir.), Fin. Execs. Inst. (Wichita chpt.), Sigma Delta Chi, Chi Psi. Republican. Presbyterian. Club: Park Hills Country (past pres.). Lodges: Elks, Rotary. Home: 502 Welton St Pratt KS 67124-1357 Office: The Peoples Bank 222 S Main St Pratt KS 67124-2713

LOOMIS, NORMA IRENE, marriage and family therapist; b. Dunlap, Ind., May 6, 1941; d. Edwin Clifford and Lucille DeVere (Hall) Dick; m. Edwin Dale Loomis; children: William Dale, James Vernon. BS in Edn., Western Mich. U., 1973, MA in Edn., 1976; PhD in Christian Counseling, Rocky Mountin Inc., 1990. Cert. marriage and family therapist. Tchr.

Cassopolis (Mich.) Schs., 1973—; counseling Christian Counseling Svcs., Goshen, Ind., 1985—; presenter Elkhart (Ind.) Pub. Schs., 1992-95, Middlebury (Ind.) Pub. Schs., 1992-94, Elkhart Ct., 1995—; pres. Champion Reality Inc., Elkhart, 1983—. Contbr. articles to profl. publs.; author tchg. materials Hot Shots Prodns. Mem. Cmty. Corrections Adv. Bd., Elkhart County, 1994—; pres. Juniper Beach Assn., Mears, Mich., 1985—, Women in Action, Elkhart, 1985-94. Mem. ACA, Am. Mental Health Counselors Assn., Ind. Counselors Assn. for Alcohol and Drug Abuse, Am. Assn. Christian Counselors, Christian Assn. Psychol. Studies. Republican. Mem. Bretheran Ch. Avocations: swimming, boating, bowling, crafts. Home: 22650 Lake Shore Dr Elkhart IN 46514-9570 Office: Christian Counseling Svcs 333 E Madison St Goshen IN 46526-3429

LOOMIS, PHILIP CLARK, investment executive; b. Plainville, Conn., Sept. 24, 1926; s. Winfield Hathaway and Lucy Erma (Clark) L.; m. Jean Ann Slater, 1950 (div. 1970); children: Philip Clark Jr., Leslie Jean, Martha Lynn; m. Greta Elaine Gustafson, 1970. BA in Econs., Yale U., 1949; MBA in Fin. with distinction, Wharton Sch. U. Pa., 1950. CFA. Trust investment specialist No. Trust Co., Chgo., 1950-54; investment analyst, portfolio mgr. Hartford (Conn.) Ins. Group, 1954-61; ptnr./dir. of rsch. Eastman, Dillon Union Securities, N.Y.C., 1961-66; ptnr.-in-charge, rsch. svcs. divsn. Francis I. duPont & Co., N.Y.C., 1967-70; v.p. rsch. Dean Witter & Co., N.Y.C., 1971-73; v.p., dir. rsch. Reynolds Securities, Inc., N.Y.C., 1974-78; dir. Office of Securities Markets Policy, Dept. Treasury, Washington, 1978-81; freelance cons. N.Y.C., 1981-86; v.p. Crispi Wagner & Co., N.Y.C., 1987-89; ind. cons. and money mgr., 1989—. Mem. N.Y. Soc. Security Analysts, Assn. for Investment Mgmt. and Rsch. Avocations: music, opera, ballet, do-it-yourself projects, travel. Home and office: 130 E End Ave New York NY 10028-7553

LOOMIS, ROBERT DUANE, publishing company executive, author; b. Conneaut, Ohio, Aug. 24, 1926; s. Kline C. and Louise C. (Chapman) L.; m. Gloria Colliani, Apr. 12, 1956 (div.); 1 dau., Diana Rachel; m. Hilary Paterson Mills, Sept. 18, 1983; 1 child, Robert Miles. B.A., Duke U., 1950. Assoc. editor Rinehart & Co., N.Y.C., 1956-58; v.p., exec. editor Random House, Inc., N.Y.C., 1958—. Author: Story of the U.S. Air Force, 1959, Great American Fighter Pilots, 1961, All About Aviation, 1964. Served with USAF, 1945. Recipient Roger Klein award for creative editing, 1977. Home: 68 W 11th St New York NY 10011-8673 Office: Random House Inc 201 E 50th St New York NY 10022-7703

LOOMIS, SALORA DALE, psychiatrist; b. Peru, Ind., Oct. 21, 1930; s. S. Dale Sr. and Rhea Pearl (Davis) L.; m. Carol Marie Davis, Jan 3, 1959; children: Stephen Dale, Patricia Marie. AB in Zoology, Ind. U., 1953, MS in Human Anatomy, 1955, MD, 1958. Diplomate Am. Bd. Psychiatry and Neurology. Intern Cook County Hosp., Chgo., 1958-59; resident in psychiatry Logansport (Ind.) State Hosp., 1959-60, Ill. State Psychiat. Inst., Chgo., 1960-62; staff psychiatrist Katharine Wright Psychiat. Clinic, Chgo., 1962-65, dir., 1965-92; cons. Ill. Youth Commn. 1962-64; instr. psychiatry Northwestern U. Med. Sch., Chgo., 1962-64, assoc. 1964-67; asst. dir. Northwestern U. Psychiat. Clinics, Chgo., 1963-65; attending psychiatrist St. Joseph Hosp., Chgo., 1964—; lectr. psychiatry and neurology Loyola U. Med. Sch. Chgo., 1964-65, assoc. 1965, asst. prof. 1965-73, lect. 1980-89, clin. assoc. prof., 1989—; psychiat. cons. Ill. Dept. Pub. Health, 1967—; sr. attending psychiatrist, chmn. dept. psychiatry Ill. Masonic Med. Ctr., Chgo. 1970-92, chmn. emeritus, 1992—; assoc. prof. psychiatry U. Ill. Coll. Medicine, Chgo., 1973—. Fellow Am. Coll. Psychiatrists, Am. Psychiat. Assn. (life), Acad. Psychosomatic Medicine; mem. AMA, Ill. State Med. Soc. (chmn. council on mental health and addiction 1974-75, chmn. joint peer rev. com. 1975-76), Ill. Psychiat. Soc. (chmn. ethics com. 1974-75, chmn. peer rev. com. 1976-78), Chgo. Med. Socs. Office: 8 S Michigan Ave Chicago IL 60603-3357

LOOMIS, WESLEY HORACE, III, former publishing company executive; b. Kansas City, Mo., July 29, 1913; s. Wesley Horace, Jr. and Mary (Gary) L.; m. Mary Bradford Paine, Apr. 17, 1937; children: Mary Elizabeth (Mrs. R.M. Norton), Jonathan Lee (dec.), Frederick Pierson. Grad., Hackley Sch., Tarrytown, N.Y., 1931; B.S. in Engring. and Bus. Adminstrn, MIT, 1935. Indsl. engr. Automatic Elec. Co., Chgo., 1935-42; pres. Loomis Advt. Co., 1946-55, Gen. Telephone Directory Co., Des Plaines, Ill., 1956-78; v.p. Dominion Directory Co., Vancouver, B.C., 1956-64; pres. Dominion Directory Co., 1964-78, Courtnay Pty., Ltd., Adelaide, Courtnay Pty., Ltd. S.A. Australia, Directories (Australia) Pty., Ltd., Melbourne, Australia, Gen. Telephone Directory Co. C por A, Santo Domingo, 1971-78, Directorio Telefonico Centroamericano, S.A., 1972-78; dir. Directorio Telefonico de El Salvador (SA). Pres. Episc. Charities 1969-70, dir., 1962-83, now life trustee; trustee emeritus U.S. Naval Acad. Found., Annapolis, Md.; bd. dirs. Traveler Aid Soc. Met. Chgo./Immigrants' Service League, 1957-80, pres., 1960-61; chmn. Travelers Aid Internat., Social Service Am., 1973-77; bd. dirs. Travelers Aid Assn. Am., 1977-82, pres., 1978-80; pres. Ind. Telephone Hist. Found., 1967-81, trustee, 1981—; trustee emeritus Colby-Sawyer Coll., New London, N.H., sec., 1976-81; mem. corp. devel. com. M.I.T., 1979-81; trustee Ill. Bus. Hall of Fame, 1981-83; bd. dirs., trustee, chmn. planning com. Mote Marine Lab., Sarasota, Fla., 1983—. Served to lt. col., Ordnance AUS, 1942-46. Decorated hon. mil. mem. Order Brit. Empire; laureate Am. Nat. Bus. Hall of Fame, 1980; elected to Ind. Telephone Hall of Fame, 1981, Calif. chpt., 1990. Mem. Ind. Telephone Pioneers Assn. (pres. 1964-66), Racquet Club (Chgo.), Field and Bird Key Yacht (Sarasota), Longboat Key Club, Masons (32 deg.), Phi Gamma Delta. Republican. Episcopalian (warden). Home: 700 John Ringling Blvd Apt 305 Sarasota FL 34236

LOOMSTEIN, ARTHUR, real estate company executive; b. St. Louis, July 27, 1939; s. Meyer and Ann (Mariam) L.; m. Kay Diane Oppenheim, Aug. 22, 1975; children: David Jay, Debi, Debra Ann. BSBA, Washington U., St. Louis, 1961, JD, 1964. Pres. Centerco Properties Inc., St. Louis, 1961—. Recipient Disting. Citizen Citation, St. Louis Regional Commerce and Growth Assn., 1973. Mem. Bldg. Owners and Mgrs. Assn. Met. St. Louis (bd. dirs. 1969-75, treas. 1971-72, pres. 1973-74), Soc. Real Property Adminstrs. (founding mem.). Clubs: Meadowbrook Country. Avocations: swimming, golfing, thoroughbred racing. Home: 13032 Pembrooke Valley Ct Saint Louis MO 63141 Office: Centerco Properties Inc 7730 Carondelet Ave Saint Louis MO 63105-3314

LOONEY, CLAUDIA ARLENE, academic administrator; b. Fullerton, Calif., June 13, 1946; d. Donald F. and Mildred B. (Gage) Schneider; m. James K. Looney, Oct. 8, 1967; 1 child, Christopher K. BA, Calif. State U., 1969. Dir. youth YWCA No. Orange County, Fullerton, Calif., 1967-70; dir. dist. Camp Fire Girls, San Francisco, 1971-73; asst. exec. dir. Camp Fire Girls, Los Angeles, 1973-77; asst. dir. community resources Childrens Hosp., Los Angeles, 1977-80; dir. community devel. Orthopaedic Hosp., Los Angeles, 1980-82; sr. v.p. Saddleback Meml. Found./Saddleback Meml. Med. Ctr., Laguna Hills, Calif., 1982-92; v.p. planning and advancement Calif. Inst. Arts, Santa Clarita, Calif., 1992-96; pres. Northwestern Meml. Found., Chicago, Ill., 1996—; instr. U. Calif., Irvine, Univ. Irvine; mem. steering com. U. Irvine. Mem. steering com. United Way, Los Angeles, 1984-86. Fellow Assn. Healthcare Philanthropy (nat. chair-elect, chmn. program Nat. Edn. Conf. 1986, regional dir. 1985-89, fin. com. 1988—, pres., com. chn. 1987—, Give To Life com. chmn. 1987-91, Orange County Fund Raiser of Yr. 1992, L.A. County fund raiser of yr. 1996); mem. Nat. Soc. Fund Raising Execs. Found. (cert., vice chmn. 1985-90, chair 1993—), So. Calif. Assn. Hosp. Devel. (past pres., bd. dirs.), Profl. Ptnrs. (chmn. 1986, instr. 1988—), Philanthropic Edni. Orgn. (past pres.). Avocations: swimming, sailing, photography. Office: Calif Inst of the Arts 24700 Mcbean Pky Valencia CA 91355-2340

LOONEY, GERALD LEE, medical educator, administrator; b. Bradshaw, W.Va., Nov. 22, 1937; s. Noah Webster and Anna Belle (Burris) L.; m. Linda Louise Pluebell, Oct. 19, 1962 (div. Apr. 1975); children: Deborah Lynn, Catherine Ann, Karen Marie, Kelli Rachelle; m. Patricia Marie Terrazas, Dec. 22, 1987. AB, Johns Hopkins U., 1959, MD, 1963; MPH, Harvard U., 1968. Diplomate Am. Bd. Preventive Medicine, Am. Bd. Pediatrics. Resident pediatrics Tufts-New Eng. Med. Ctr., Boston, 1965-67; physician-in-chief Kennedy Meml. Hosp., Boston, 1969-71; asst. prof. family and cmty. medicine U. Ariz. Coll. Medicine, Tucson, 1971-72; asst. prof. emergency medicine U. So. Calif. Sch. Medicine, L.A., 1972-77; assoc. clin. prof. medicine U. Calif., Irvine, 1991—; emergency dept. dir. Glendale (Calif.) Adventist Med. Ctr., 1978-84; edn. dir. Orthopaedic Hosp., L.A., 1985-88; urgent care dir. Bay Shore Med. Group, Torrance, Calif., 1988-93; med. dir. Surecare and LAX Clinics Centinela Hosp., Inglewood, Calif., 1993-95; dir. med. svc. McDonnell Douglas Aerospace, Long Beach, Calif., 1996—; bd. dirs. Beach Cities Health Dist., Redondo Beach, Calif., 1992-93. Avocation: history. Office: McDonnell Douglas MTA C-17 Program PAC 174-11 2401 E Wardlow Rd Long Beach CA 90807-5309

LOONEY, JOHN G., mental health services administrator; b. La Grange, Tex., Oct. 4, 1941; s. Gene Guy and Rowena Totten (Darter) L.; m. Susan Kathleen Boyd, June 7, 1969; children: Matthew H., Colin G., Christopher B. BA, Cornell U., 1964; BMS, Dartmouth Med. Sch., 1966; MD, U. Tex., 1969; MBA, So. Meth. U., 1986. Bd. cert. in psychiatry, child psychiatry, adolescent psychiatry, adminstrv. psychiatry, addiction psychiatry. Head of health care sys. br. Naval Health Rsch. Ctr., San Diego, 1974-76; staff psychiatrist, dir. child and adolescent psychiatry Timberlawn Hosp., Dallas, 1976-86; dir. child and adolescent psychiatry Duke Med. Ctr., Durham, N.C., 1986-92, dir. campus alcohol initiative, 1992—; adminstrv. cons. to numerous health care ogns., 1987—. Author: The Long Struggle, Chronic Mental Illness in Children; co-editor: Adolescent Psychiatry, Vols. VIII-XIV, 1980-93; contbr. articles to profl. jours. Lt. comdr. USN, 1974-76. Fellow ACP, Am. Acad. of Child and Adolescent Psychiatry, Am. Psychiat. Assn.; mem. Am. Soc. Adolescent Psychiatry (pres. 1985), Rotary Club Durham. Episcopalian. Avocation: fly fishing.

LOONEY, NORMAN EARL, pomologist, plant physiologist; b. Adrian, Oreg., May 31, 1938; came to Can., 1966; s. Gaynor Parks and Lois Delilah (Francis) L.; m. Arlene Mae Willis, Oct. 4, 1957 (div. 1982); children: Pamela June, Patricia Lorene, Steven Paul; m. Norah Christine Keating, July 16, 1983. BSc in Agr. Edn., Washington State U., 1960, PhD in Horticulture, 1966. Rsch. scientist Agr. Can., Summerland, B.C., 1966-71, scientist, sect. head, 1972-81, sr. scientist, 1982-87, sr. scientist, sect. head, 1987-90, prin. scientist, sect. head, 1991-95; prin. scientist, 1995—; vis. scientist food rsch. divsn. CSIRO, Sydney, Australia, 1971-72, East Malling Rsch. Sta., Maidstone, Kent, 1981-82, Dept. Horticulture Lincoln U., Christchurch, New Zealand, 1990-91; sec. Expert Com. on Horticulture, Ottawa, Ont., Can., 1986-90; chmn. Agrl. Can. Tree Fruit Rsch. Network, 1993—; chmn. working group on growth regulators in fruit prodn. Internat. Soc. Hort. Sci., Leuven, Belgium, 1987-94, chmn. fruit sect., 1994—. Author textbook on cherries, 1995; contbr. numerous articles and chpts. to sci. publs. Fellow Am. Soc. Hort. Sci.; mem. Can. Soc. for Hort. Sci. (pres. 1997—). Achievements include patent for Promotion of Flowering in Fruit Trees (U.S. and foreign). Office: Agr Can Rsch Sta, Summerland, BC Canada V0H 1Z0

LOONEY, RICHARD CARL, bishop; b. Hillsville, Va., Feb. 14, 1934; s. Carl and Ruth (Bourne) L.; m. Carolyn Adele McKeithen, Sept. 3, 1957; children: Teresa, David, Jonathan. BA, Emory and Henry Coll., 1954; postgrad., Edinburg (Scotland U.), 1956; BD, Emory U., 1957; postgrad., Union Theol. Sem., Richmond, Va. Ordained to ministry United Meth. Ch. as deacon, 1955, as elder, 1959. Pastor Rising Faawn (Ga.) Cir., 1957-61, Pleasant View-Wyndale Charge, Abington, Va., 1961-65, Pleasant View, Abington, Va., 1965-67, White Oak United Meth. Ch., Chattanooga, 1968-71, Broad St. United Meth. Ch., Cleveland, Tenn., 1972-75; dist. supt. Chattanooga Dist., 1976-78; pastor Munsey Meml. United Meth. Ch., Johnson City, Tenn., 1979-86, Church St. United Meth. Ch., Knoxville, Tenn., 1987-88; elected bishop Southeastern Jurisdiction, United Meth. Ch., Macon, Ga., 1988—. Office: The United Meth Ctr PO Box 13616 Macon GA 31208-3616*

LOONEY, WILLIAM FRANCIS, JR., lawyer; b. Boston, Sept. 20, 1931; s. William Francis Sr. and Ursula Mary (Ryan) L.; m. Constance Mary O'Callaghan, Dec. 28, 1957; children: Willam F. III, Thomas M., Karen D., Martha A. AB, Harvard U., JD. Bar: Mass. 1958, D.C. 1972, U.S. Supreme Ct. 1972, U.S. Dist. Ct. (ea. dist.) Mich. 1986. Law clk. to presiding justice Mass. Supreme Jud. Ct., 1958-59; assoc. Goodwin, Procter & Hoar, Boston, 1959-62; chief civil div. U.S. Attys. Office, 1964-65; ptnr. Looney & Grossman, Boston, 1965-94, sr. counsel, 1995—; asst. U.S. atty. Dist. Mass., 1962-65; spl. hearing officer U.S. Dept. Justice, 1965-68; mem. Mass. Bd. Bar Overseers, 1985-91, vice chmn., 1990-91; corp. mem. Greater Boston Legal Svcs., Inc., 1994—. Mem. Zoning Bd. of Appeals, Dedham, Mass., 1971-74; bd. dirs. Boston Latin Sch. Found., 1981-85, pres. 1981-84, chmn. bd. dirs., 1984-86; trustee Social Law Libr., 1994—. Fellow Am. Coll. Trial Lawyers (state com. 1996—); mem. Mass. Bar Assn. (co-chmn. standing com. lawyers responsibility for pub. svc. 1987-88), Boston Bar Assn. (pres. 1984-85, coun. mem. 1985-90, chmn. sr. lawyers sect. 1992-94, Maguire award for professionalism 1995), Nat. Assn. Bar Pres.'s, Boston Latin Sch. Assn. (pres. 1980-82, life trustee 1982—, man of yr. 1985), USCG Found. (bd. dirs. 1987—), Norfolk Golf Club, Harvard Club, New Seabury Golf Club. Democrat. Roman Catholic. Home: 43 Coronation Dr Dedham MA 02026-6230 Office: 101 Arch St 9th Fl Boston MA 02110-1112

LOOPER, GEORGE KIRK, religious society executive; b. Gould, Okla., Feb. 18, 1943; s. Ishmel Guy and Edna Mae (Burge) L.; m. Vivian Kay Swanson, Dec. 13, 1963; children: Michael Edward, Steven Allen, Jodell Lin. BS in Sci., Northeastern Okla. Tchrs. Coll, 1966; MS in Physics, U. Wyo., 1973; MS in Elem. Edn., Western Carolina U., 1968. Exec. dir. Seventh Day Bapt. Missionary Soc., Westerly, R.I. Republican. Seventh Day Baptist. Home: 7 State St Westerly RI 02891-3101

LOORY, STUART HUGH, journalist; b. Wilson, Pa., May 22, 1932; s. Harry and Eva (Holland) L.; m. Marjorie Helene Dretel, June 19, 1955 (div. July 1995); children: Joshua Alan, Adam Edward, Miriam Beth; m. Nina Nikolaevna Kudriavtseva, Aug. 17, 1995. B.A., Cornell U., 1954; M.S. with honors, Columbia U., 1958; postgrad., U. Vienna, Austria, 1958. Reporter Newark News, 1955-58; Reporter N.Y. Herald Tribune, 1959-61, sci. writer, 1961-63, Washington corr., 1963-64; fgn. corr. N.Y. Herald Tribune, Moscow, 1964-66; sci. editor Metromedia Radio Stas., 1962-64, Moscow corr., 1964-66; sci. writer N.Y. Times, 1966; White House corr. Los Angeles Times, 1967-71; fellow Woodrow Wilson Internat. Center for Scholars, Washington, 1971-72; exec. editor WNBC-TV News, 1973; Kiplinger prof. pub. affairs reporting Ohio State U., Columbus, 1973-75; assoc. editor Chgo. Sun-Times, 1975-76, mng. editor, 1976-80; v.p., mng. editor Washington bur. Cable News Network, 1980-82, Moscow bur. chief, 1983-86, sr. correspondent, 1986, exec. producer, 1987-90; exec. dir. internat. rels. Turner Broadcasting System, Inc., Atlanta, 1988—; editor-in-chief CNN World Report, 1990-91; v.p. CNN, 1990-95; exec. v.p. Turner Internat. Broadcasting, Russia, 1993—; v.p., supervising prodr. Turner Original Prodns., 1995; lectr. in field. Author: (with David Kraslow) The Secret Search for Peace in Vietnam, 1968, Defeated: Inside America's Military Machine, 1973, (with Ann Imse) Seven Days That Shook the World: The Collapse of Soviet Communism, 1991; contbr. articles mags. and encys. Recipient citation Overseas Press Club, 1966; Raymond Clapper award Congl. Press Gallery, 1968; George Polk award L.I.U., 1968; Du Mont award U. Calif. at, Los Angeles, 1968; Distinguished Alumni award Columbia, 1969; 50th Anniversary medal Columbia Sch. Journalism, 1963; Edwin Hood award for diplomatic corr. Nat. Press Club, 1987; Pulitzer traveling scholar, 1958. Jewish. Office: CNN Moscow Box 26 Post International Inc 666 5th Ave Ste 572 New York NY 10103-0001

LOOS, RANDOLPH MEADE, financial planner; b. Warren, Ohio, May 22, 1954; s. Donald Ambert and Kathleen Jean (Woods) L.; m. Jolene Lora Turkoc, Aug. 3, 1985. BSBA, U. Fla., 1977. CFP. Rsch. cons. Fla. State U., Tallahassee, 1977-78; exec. sec. Chi Phi Fraternity, Atlanta, 1978-79, nat. dir., 1979-80; systems rep. Burroughs Corp., Chgo., 1980-81, sr. systems rep., 1981-82; account exec. Prudential-Bache Securities, Charlotte, N.C., 1982-84; investment broker A. G. Edwards & Sons, Clearwater, Fla., 1984—, sr. investment broker, 1991-92, v.p. investments, 1992—, trust specialist, 1995—. Musical dir. Toast of Tampa Show Chorus, 1986-97, internat. champions 1994. Mem. Inst. CFP. Republican. Avocations: golf, barbershop harmony, wine collecting. Office: A G Edwards & Sons Inc 28100 Us Highway 19 N Ste 500 Clearwater FL 33761-2686

LOOSBROCK, CAROL MARIE, information management professional; b. Dubuque, Iowa, Aug. 21, 1936; d. Julius Carl and Elizabeth Cecilia (Kurz) L. BA, Clarke Coll., 1958; postgrad., Art Inst. Chgo., 1959-63; MS, Am. U., 1979. With Dept. Def., Washington, 1968—, specialist, 1979—. Mem. AAAS, Assn. Computing Machinery (Washington D.C. symposium steering coms. 1980-81, exec. coun. 1981-84); N.Y. Acad. Scis. (life), Am. Mgmt. Assn., Am. Security Coun. Found. (U.S. congl. adv. bd. 1984—, coalition for peace through strength leadership award, coalition for Desert Storm, coalition for internat. security), Am. Mus. Natural History. Republican. Home: 4514 Connecticut Ave NW Washington DC 20008 Office: The Pentagon Washington DC 20310

LOOSE, VICKY DIANNE, special education educator; b. Bethesda, Md., Dec. 22, 1953; d. Josiah Arthur and Frances Maxine (Richeson) L. BS in Health and Phys. Edn., East Carolina U., 1977, MEd in Adapted Phys. Edn., 1983, MEd in Spl. Edn., 1985. Cert. tchr., N.C. Tchr. health, phys. edn. Craven County Schs., Havelock, N.C., 1978-80; adapted phys. edn. specialist O'Berry Ctr. Mentally Retarded/Devel. Disabled Facility, Goldsboro, N.C., 1980-82, asst. coord. therapeutic recreation, 1982-84, outreach svc. specialist, 1984-85; rsdl. srs. coord. Wake County Mentally Retarded/Devel. Disabled Svcs., Raleigh, 1985-88; devel. disabled specialist Wilson-Green Mentally Retarded/Devel. Disabled Svcs., N.C., 1988-89; crisis tchr. Wilson County Schs., 1989-90, tchr. behavioral emotionally handicapped, 1990-92; program dir. Adolescent Partial Hosp. Program, Wilson, 1992—; tchr. behavioral emotional handicapped Johnston County Schs., 1994-95; program svcs. dir. QDDP/QMAP Health Svcs. Personnel, 1995-97; edni. cons. Nash-Wilson-Wake-Green county schs., 1988—; faculty Wake-Nash-Wilson Tech. Coll., 1988—; tutor Wilson County schs., 1990—; cons. Health Svcs. Personnel. Author counseling game: Word Up, 1989. Named Tchr. of the Yr. Wilson County Schs., 1991. Mem. NCABA, CEC, NCCCBD, Phi Kappa Phi. Avocations: running, biking, camping, hiking, reading. Home: 4514 Virginia Rd Wilson NC 27893-8541 Office: North Johnston Mid Sch Micro NC 27555

LOPACH, JAMES JOSEPH, political science educator; b. Great Falls, Mont., June 23, 1942; s. John Ernest and Alma Marie (Schapman) L.; divorced, Dec. 10, 1991; children: Christine, Paul. AB in Philosophy, Carroll Coll., 1964; MA in Am. Studies, U. Notre Dame, 1967, MAT in English Edn., 1968, PhD in Govt., 1973. Mgr. Pacific Telephone, Palo Alto, Calif., 1968-69; adminstr. City of South Bend, Ind., 1971-73; prof. U. Mont., Missoula, 1973—, chmn. dept. polit. sci., 1977-87, assoc. dean Coll. Arts and Scis., 1987-88, acting dir. Mansfield Ctr., 1984-85, spl. asst. to the univ. pres., 1988-92, assoc. provost, 1992-95; spl. asst. to provost Mansfield Ctr., 1995-96; cons. local govts., state agys., 1973—. Author, editor: We the People of Montana, 1983, Tribal Government Today, 1990, Planning Small Town America, 1990; contbr. articles to profl. jours. Roman Catholic. Office: U Mont Dept Polit Sci Missoula MT 59812

LOPATA, HELENA ZNANIECKA, sociologist, researcher, educator; b. Poznan, Poland, Oct. 1, 1925; d. Florian Witold and Eileen (Markley) Znaniecki; m. Richard Stefan Lopata, Feb. 8, 1946 (wid. July 1994); children: Theodora Karen Lopata-Menasco, Stefan Richard. B.A., U. Ill., 1946, M.A., 1947; Ph.D., U. Chgo., 1954; DSc (hon.), Guelph U., Can., 1995. Lectr. U. Va. Extension, Langley AFB, 1951-52, DePaul U., 1956-60; lectr. Roosevelt U., 1960-64, asst. prof. sociology, 1964-67, assoc. prof., 1967-69; prof. sociology Loyola U., Chgo., 1969—; chmn. dept. sociology Loyola U., 1970-72, dir. Center for Comparative Study of Social Roles, 1972—; mem. NIMH Rev. Bd., 1977-79; mem. Mayor's Council Manpower and Econ. Devel., 1974-79; mem. adv. com., chair tech. com. White House Conf. on Aging, 1979-81; adv. council Nat. Inst. Aging, 1978-83. Author: Occupation: Housewife, 1971, Widowhood in an American City, 1973, Polish Americans: Status Competition in an Ethnic Community, 1976, (with Debra Barnewolt and Cheryl Miller) City Women: Work, Jobs, Occupations, Careers, Vol. I, America, 1984, Vol. II, Chicago, 1985, City Women in America, 1986, (with Henry Brehm) Widows and Dependent Wives: From Social Problem to Federal Policy, 1986, Polish Americans, 1994, Circles and Settings: Role Changes of American Women, 1994, Current Widowhood: Myths and Realities, 1996; adv. editor: Sociologist Quar., 1969-72, Jour. Marriage and Family, 1978-82, Symbolic Interaction, 1989—, Sociol. Inquiry, 1996—; mem. editl. bd. Am. Sociologist, 1996; editor: Marriages and Families, 1973, (with Nona Glazer and Judith Wittner) Research on the Interweave of Social Roles: vol. I, Women and Men, 1980, (with David Maines) vol. 2, Friendship, 1981, (with Joseph Pleck) vol. 3, Families and Jobs, 1983, vol. 4, Current Research on Occupations and Professions, 1987, vol. 5, 1987, Widows: The Middle East, Asia and the Pacific, 1987, Widows: North America, 1987, (with Anne Figert) Current Research on Occupations and Professions: Vol. 9: Getting Down to Business, 1996, (with David Maines) Friendship in Context, 1990; adv. bd. Symbolic Interaction, 1977-89, 92—; contbr. articles to profl. jours. Bd. overseers Wellesley Ctr. of Rsch. and Women, 1979-84. Recipient Research award Radcliffe Coll., 1982; grantee Chgo. Tribune, 1956, Midwest Coun. Social Research on Aging, 1964-65, Adminstrn. on Aging, 1967-69, 68-71, Social Security Adminstrn., 1971-75, also 1975-79, Indo-Am. Fellowship Program: Coun. for Internat. Exchange Scholars, 1987-88, Rsch. Stimulation grantee Loyola U. Chgo., 1988, 92, Am. Coun. Learned Soc. travel grant, 1995, Internat. Rsch. Exchange Bd. short term travel grant, 1995; named Faculty Mem. of Yr., Loyola U., 1975. Fellow Midwest Coun. for Social Rsch. on Aging (pres. 1969-70, 91-92, postdoctoral tng. dir. 1971-77), Ill. Sociol. Assn. (pres. 1969-70), Gerontol. Soc. Am. (chmn. social and behavioral sci. sect. 1980-81, Mentoring award 1995), Internat. Gerontol. Assn.; mem. Soc. for Study Social Problems (chmn. spl. problems com. 1971, v.p. 1975, coun. 1978-80, pres. 1983, Disting. Scholar award family div. 1989), Am. Sociol. Assn. (coun. 1978-81, chmn. sect. family 1976, chmn. sect. sex roles 1975, Sorokin awwards com. 1970-73, publs. com. 1972-73, nominations com. 1977, chmn. sect. on aging 1982-83 (Disting. Career award, 1992 Section on Aging), Cooley-Blumer awards com., 1984, Jessie Bernard awards com. 1984-86, disting. scholarly publ. awards selection com. 1988-89, awards policy com. 1990-92, co-chair com. on internat. sociology, 1992-95), Soc. for the Study of Symbolic Interaction (mem 1977—, Mead award for Life Time Achievement, 1993), Internat. Sociol. Soc. (com. on family rsch., bd. dirs. 1991-94, com. on work 1972—, rsch. com. on aging 1990—), Midwest Sociol. Assn. (state dir. 1972-74, pres. 1975-76, chair 1994—, publs. com. 1993-95), Nat. Coun. Family Rels. (Burgess award 1990, chair internat. sect. 1991-93), Polish Inst. of Arts and Scis. in Am. (dir. 1976-82, with Zbigniew Brzezinski, Bronislaw Malinowski award in social scis. 1995), Polish Welfare Assn. (bd. dirs. 1988-91), Internat. Inst. Sociology, 1994—, Sociologists for Women in Society (mem. task force alternative work patterns, pres. 1993-94, adv. editor Gender and Soc. 1993-94). Home: 5815 N Sheridan Rd Apt 917 Chicago IL 60660-3829 Office: Loyola Univ Dept Sociology 6525 N Sheridan Rd Chicago IL 60626-5311

LOPATIN, ALAN G., lawyer; b. New Haven, Conn., May 25, 1956; s. Paul and Ruth (Rosen) L.; m. Debra Jo Engler, May 17, 1981; children: Jonah Adam, Asa Louis. BA, Yale U., 1978; JD, Am. U., 1981. Bar: D.C. 1981, U.S. Supreme Ct. 1985. Law clk. Fed. Maritime Commn., Washington, 1980-81; counsel com. on post office and civil service U.S. Ho. of Reps., Washington, 1981-82, counsel com. on budget, 1982-86, dep. chief counsel, 1986-87, counsel Temporary Joint Com. on Deficit Reduction, 1986, dep. gen. counsel Com. on P.O. and Civil Service, 1987-90; gen. counsel Com. on Edn. & Labor, Washington, 1991-94; pres. Ledge Counsel, Inc., Washington, 1994—; exec. dir. Nat. and Cmty. Svc. Coalition, 1995—; mem. presdl. task force Health Care Reform, Washington, 1993. Mem. ABA, D.C. Bar Assn., Nat. Dem. Club, Yale Club. Democratic. Jewish. Home: 4958 Butterworth Pl NW Washington DC 20016-4354 Office: Ledge Counsel Inc PO Box 40097 Washington DC 20016

LOPATIN, DENNIS EDWARD, immunologist, educator; b. Chgo., Oct. 26, 1948; s. Leonard Harold and Cynthia (Shifrin) L.; m. Marie S. Ludmer, June 6, 1971 (div. 1983); 1 child, Jeremy; m. Constance Maxine McLeod, July 24, 1983. BS, U. Ill., 1970, MS, 1972, PhD, 1974. Postdoctoral fellow Northwestern U. Med. Sch., Chgo., 1974-75; rsch. scientist U. Mich., Ann Arbor, 1976-90, prof., 1982—. Contbr. articles to sci. jours. Mem. Am. Assn. Immunologists, Am. Soc. Microbiology, Internat. Assn. Dental Rsch., Sigma Xi. Office: U Mich Sch Dentistry Ann Arbor MI 48109-1078

LOPATKA, SUSANA BEAIRD, maternal, child health nurse consultant; b. White Plains, N.Y., May 1, 1937; d. Paul J. and Dorothy V.L. (Jewell) Grueninger; m. John Rudolph Lopatka, Sept. 6, 1975. AB in Polit. Sci., Duke U., 1959; BSN, Columbia U., N.Y.C., 1962; MA in Parent/Child Nursing, NYU, N.Y.C., 1975. RN, Ill. Staff nurse Columbia-Presbyn. Med.

Ctr., N.Y.C., 1962; pub. health nurse Dept. of Health, City of N.Y., 1962-66; pub. health nurse high-risk maternal and infant care project N.Y. Med. Coll., N.Y.C., 1966-67; nursing coord. Brownsville East N.Y. Ctr. Maternal and Infant Care Project City of N.Y., 1967-69; asst. supr. ambulatory care Mt. Sinai Med. Ctr., N.Y.C., 1969-70, sr. supr. ambulatory care, 1970-72, asst. DON ambulatory care, 1972-75; clin. specialist in maternity Chgo. Lying-In Hosp., U. Chgo. Med. Ctr., 1976-80, DON, 1980-86; maternal/child health nurse cons. Ill. Dept. Pub. Health, Chgo., 1986—; mem. perinatal nursing adv. coun. Greater Ill. chpt. March of Dimes, Chgo., 1979—. Founding pres., bd. dirs. Am. Scandinavian Assn. Ill., Chgo., 1983-95; active Chgo. Coun. Fgn. Rels., 1976—, Chgo. Hist. Soc., 1994—. Recipient Nurses Recognition award Greater Ill. chpt. March of Dimes, 1993. Mem. ANA, APHA, Ill. Nurses Assn., Chgo. Nurses Assn. (dist. 1), Ill. Pub. Health Assn. (chairperson maternal/child health sect. 1992-94, asst. chairperson 1990-92), Ill. Assn. Maternal/Child Health (pres. 1992-94, bd. dirs. 1989-96), Sigma Theta Tau, Pi Sigma Alpha. Avocations: hiking, bicycling, classical music. Office: Ill Dept Pub Health 33 E Congress Pky Chicago IL 60605-1223

LOPER, CARL RICHARD, JR., metallurgical engineer, educator; b. Wauwatosa, Wis., July 3, 1932; s. Carl Richard S. and Valberg (Sundby) L.; m. Jane Louise Loehning, June 30, 1956; children: Cynthia Louise Loper Koch, Anne Elizabeth. BS in Metall. Engring., U. Wis., 1955, MS in Metall. Engring., 1958, PhD in Metall. Engring., 1961; postgrad., U. Mich., 1960. Metall. engr. Pelton Steel Casting Co., Milw., 1955-56; instr., rsch. assoc. U. Wis., Madison, 1956-61, asst. prof., 1961-64, assoc. prof., 1964-68, prof. metall. engring., 1968-88, prof. materials sci. and engring., 1988—; assoc. chmn. dept. metall. and mineral engring. U. Wis., 1979-82; rsch. metallurgist Allis Chalmers, Milw., 1961; cons., lectr. in field. Author: Principles of Metal Casting, 1965; contbr. over 400 articles to profl. jours. Chmn. 25th Anniversary of Ductile Iron Symposium, Montreal, 1973; pres. Ygdrasil Lit. Soc., 1989-90. Foundry Ednl. Found. fellow, 1953-55; Wheelabrator Corp. fellow, 1960; Ford Found. fellow, 1960; recipient Adams Meml. award Am. Welding Soc., 1963, Howard F. Taylor award, 1967, Service citation, 1969, 72, others; recipient Silver medal award of Sci. Merit Portuguese Foundry Assn., 1978, medal Chinese Foundrymen's Assn., 1989. Fellow Am. Soc. Metals (chmn. 1969-70), AIM; mem. Am. Foundrymen's Soc. (bd. dirs. 1967-70, 76-79, best paper award 1966, 67, 85, John A. Penton gold medal 1972, Hoyt Meml. lectr. 1992, aluminum divsn. award of sci. merit 1995, Foundry Ednl. Found. dirs. award 1994), Am. Welding Soc., Foundry Ednl. Found., Torske Klubben (bd. dirs., co-founder 1978—), Blackhawk Country Club, Sigma Xi, Gamma Alpha, Alpha Sigma Mu, Tau Beta Pi. Lutheran. Achievements include significant contributions to understanding the solidification and metallurgy of ferrous and non-ferrous alloys; recognized authority on solidificaton and cast iron metallurgy, and on education in metallurgy and materials science. Office: U Wis Cast Metals Lab 1509 University Ave Madison WI 53706-1538

LOPER, D. ROGER, retired oil company executive; b. Mpls., Dec. 14, 1920; s. Donald Rust and Agnes (Yerxa) L.; m. Sylvia Lee Brainard, Aug. 16, 1946 (dec. Apr. 1973); children: Ann Kathleen, Michael Brainard, Joyce Elizabeth, Nancy Jean Loper Woods; m. Genevieve Jean Kusles, May 4, 1974. BSMetE, Carnegie Tech. Inst., 1947. Registered chem. engr., Calif. Div. supr. Standard Oil of Calif., San Francisco, 1958-64, asst. chief engr., 1964-74; gen. mgr. Chevron Petroleum, London, 1974-80; pres. Chevron Shale Oil Co., Denver, 1980-82; v.p. Chevron Overseas Petroleum, San Francisco, 1982-85; cons. Loper Assocs., Carmel, Calif., 1985—. Inventor hydrocracking reactor, remote inspection device. Pres. Our Saviour Luth. Ch., Lafayette, Calif., 1971-72. Maj. U.S. Army, 1942-46. Republican. Home and Office: 2804 Pradera Rd Carmel CA 93923-9717

LOPER, DAVID ERIC, mathematics educator, geophysics educator; b. Oswego, N.Y., Feb. 14, 1940; married, 1966; 4 children. BS, Carnegie Inst. Tech., 1961; MS, Case Inst. Tech., 1964, PhD in Mech. Engring., 1965. Sr. scientist Douglas Aircraft Corp., 1965-68; from asst. prof. to assoc. prof. Fla. State U., Tallahassee, 1968-77, prof. math., 1977—; dir. Geophysical Fluid Dynamics Inst., 1994—; sr. vis. fellow U. Newcastle-upon-Tyne, Eng., 1974-75. Nat. Ctr. Atmospheric Rsch. fellow, 1967-68, sr. vis. fellow U. Newcastle-upon-Tyne, Eng., 1974-75, Cambridge U., Eng., 1990; H.C. Webster fellow U. Queensland, Australia, 1983. Mem. Am. Phys. Soc., Am. Geophys. Union, Soc. Indsl. and Applied Math, Sigma Xi. Achievements include research on boundary layers in rotating, stably stratified, electrically conducting fluids; evolution of the earth's core including stratification, heat transfer, solidification and particle precipitation. Address: Florida State U Dept Math Tallahassee FL 32306 Office: Fla State U Geophys Fluid Dynamics Inst 18 Keen Bldg Tallahassee FL 32306

LOPER, GEORGE WILSON, JR., physical education educator; b. Phila., Sept. 1, 1927; s. George Wilson Sr. and Emma Margaretta (Davis) L.; m. Eleanor Ruth Shell, mar. 10, 1951 (div. Aug. 1967); children: George Wilson III, Carol Ann Loper Cloud; m. Jeanne Ann Lodeski, Aug. 12, 1967; children: Lynn Jeanne Loper Sakers, Anne Marie Loper Todd, John Vincent. BS, W. Chester State U., 1954; MEd, Temple U., 1957. Cert. tchr. Fla. Tchr., coach Media (Pa.) Pub. Schs., 1954-63, Duval County Sch. System, Jacksonville, Fla., 1963-67; tchr., dept. chmn., coach Bradford County Sch. System, Starke, Fla., 1967—. Dir. March Dimes Walkathon, Starke, 1970; coord. Spl. Olympics, Starke, 1970-89; chmn. Adminstrv. Bd. First Meth. Ch., Starke, 1970; co-chmn. Toys for Tots USMC, Starke, 1976, 78. With USMC Res., 1945-87. Named Coach of Yr. Fla. Times Union, 1966, 67, Coach of Yr. Cross Country Gainesville Sun, 1985, 86. Mem. AAHPERD (life), NEA, Nat. Health Assn. (life), Nat. High Sch. Coaches Assn., Fla. Athletic Coaches Assn. (state vice chmn. 1972—, Meritorious Svc. awrd 1988, Nat. Boys Track Coach of Yr. 1991, Life Membership award 1992), The Athletic Congress (lead instr. 1987—, internat. level track official 1983—, Track Hall of Fame 1987), Fla. Officials Assn. (high sch. games com. 1964—, state vice chmn. track 1972—), Bradford Edn. Assn. (v.p. 1977-79). Democrat. Methodist. Avocations: reading, music, art, swimming and track officiating. Home: RR 2 Box 1674 Starke FL 32091-9539 Office: Bradford High Sch 581 N Temple Ave Starke FL 32091-2609

LOPER, JAMES LEADERS, broadcasting executive; b. Phoenix, Sept. 4, 1931; s. John D. and Ellen Helen (Leaders) L.; m. Mary Louise Brion, Sept. 1, 1955; children: Elizabeth Margaret Sehran (Mrs. Michael K. Sehran), James Leaders Jr. BA, Ariz. State U., 1953; MA, U. Denver, 1957; PhD, U. So. Calif., 1967; DHL (hon.), Columbia Coll., 1973; LLD (hon.), Pepperdine U., 1978. Asst. dir. bur. broadcasting Ariz. State U., Tempe, 1953-59; news editor, announcer Sta. KTAR, Phoenix, 1955-56; dir. ednl. TV, Calif. State U., Los Angeles, 1960-64; v.p. Community TV So. Calif., Los Angeles, 1962-63; asst. to pres. Sta. KCET-Pub. TV, Los Angeles, 1963-65, sec., 1965-66, dir. ednl. services, 1964-65, asst. gen. mgr., 1965-66, v.p., gen. mgr., 1966-69, exec. v.p., gen. mgr., 1969-71, pres., gen. mgr., 1971-76, pres., CEO, 1976-82; exec. dir. Acad. TV Arts and Scis., 1983—; bd. dirs., chmn. audit com. Western Fed. Savs. and Loan Assn., L.A., 1979-93; bd. dirs. Global View, Washington; bd. dirs. Tennessee Ernie Ford Enterprises, 1994—; chmn. bd. Pub. Broadcasting Service, Washington, 1969-72; dir. Calif. Arts Coun., 1991—; adj. prof. Sch. Cinema and TV U. So. Calif., 1984—; sr. lectr. U. So. Calif., Los Angeles, 1969-70; pres. Western Ednl. Network, 1968-70; mem. Gov.'s Ednl. TV and Radio Adv. Com., Calif., 1968-74; U.S. rep. CENTO Conf. Radio and TV, Turkey, 1978, trustee Internat. Council Nat. Acad. TV Arts and Scis., 1988—. Contbr. articles to profl. jours; contbr. to ETV: The Farther Vision, 1967, Broadcasting and Bargaining: Labor Relations in Radio and Television, 1970. Mem. adv. bd. Jr. League of Los Angeles, 1970-76, Jr. League of Pasadena, 1972-75, Los Angeles Jr. Arts Ctr., 1968-72; exec. v.p. Assocs. of Otis Art Inst., 1971-77, pres., 1975-77; chmn., dir. The Performing Tree, Los Angeles; bd. dirs. Sears-Roebuck Found., 1976-79; chmn. bd. visitors Annenburg Sch. Communications, U. So. Calif., 1975-80; trustee Poly. Sch., Pasadena; mem. Calif. State Arts Commn., 1991. Recipient Disting. Alumnus award Ariz. State U., 1972; Alumni award of Merit, U. So. Calif., 1975; Gov's. award Hollywood chpt. Nat. Acad. TV Arts and Scis., 1975; Alumni Achievement award Phi Sigma Kappa, 1975; named Centennial Alumnus Nat. Assn. of State Univs. and Land Grant Colls., 1988. Named to Hall of Fame Walter Cronkite Sch. Comms., Ariz. State U., 1994 Mem. Acad. TV Arts and Scis. (past gov., v.p. Hollywood chpt., trustee nat. acad.), TV Acad. Found., Hollywood Radio and TV Soc. (treas., dir.), Western Ednl. Soc. Telecommunications (past pres.), Assn. Calif. Pub. TV Stas. (past pres.), Young Pres.'s Orgn., Phi Sigma Kappa, Pi Delta Epsilon, Alpha Delta Sigma, Sigma Delta Chi. Presbyterian (chmn. Mass Media Task Force So. Calif. synod 1969-75). Clubs: Valley Hunt (Pasadena), Bel-Air Bay, California, Los Angeles, 100 of Los Angeles, Calif. (Los Angeles), Twilight Pasadena, Lincoln Club, L.A. Office: Acad TV Arts and Scis PO Box 7344 North Hollywood CA 91603-7344

LOPER, LINDA SUE, learning resources center director; b. Wakefield, R.I., Jan. 28, 1945; d. Delmas Field and Dora Belle (Hanna) Sneed; children: Matthew Lee Mathany, Amanda Virginia Mathany Van Der Heyden, Morgan Lynnclare Loper. BA, Peabody Coll., Nashville, 1966, MLS, 1979; EdD in Ednl. Adminstrn., Vanderbilt U., Nashville, 1988. Tchr. Parkway Sch., Chesterfield, Mo., 1966-68, Charlotte Mecklenburg Schs., Charlotte, N.C., 1968-71; dir. city libr. Jackson George Regional Libr. System, Pascagoula, Miss., 1979-82; media ctr. specialist Pascagoula Mcpl. Sch. Dist., 1982-83, Moore County Sch. System, Lynchburg, Tenn., 1983-91; ref. libr. Motlow State Community Coll., Tullahoma, Tenn., 1983-85; dir. learning resource ctr. Columbia (Tenn.) State C.C., 1991-96; exec. dir. Tenn. Bd. Regents Media Consortium, 1993-96; pres., CEO Grant Seekers, Inc., 1996—; presenter TLA Ann. Conv., Knoxville, Tenn., LEAP State Dept. Edn. Conf. for Libr., Chattanooga; career ladder participant Tenn. Edn. Dept. Level II; TIM trainer Dept. Edn., Nashville; exec. dir. Tenn. Bd. of Regents Media Consortium, 1993-96. Author: Bibliography for Tennessee Commission on Status of Women, 1979; contbr. article to profl jour. Pres. Moore County Friends of Libr., Lynchburg, Tenn., 1991; bd. dirs. Moore County Hist. and Geneal. Soc., Lynchburg, 1991; mem. Tenn. Bicentennial Com., Giles County; co-dir. So. Tapestry, a Bicentennial oral history project; sec., mem. exec. bd. Hope House Domestic Violence Shelter, 1993-96, mem. adv. bd., 1996—; mem. steering com. Bus., Industry, Edn. Partnership. Recipient Gov.'s Acad. award State Dept. of Edn., U. Tenn., 1988, Inst. for Writing Tenn. History, U. Tenn., 1990, Gov.'s Conf. on Info. Sci., Nashville, 1990. Mem. ASCD, ALA, S.E. Libr. Assn., Tenn. Libr. Assn., Moore County Edn. Assn. (treas., chair tchrs. study coun., chair polit. action commn. 1989-91), Giles County Edn. Found. UDC, (historian), DAR, Phi Delta Kappa, Beta Phi Mu, Delta Kappa Gamma. Democrat. Methodist. Avocations: French hand sewing, crosstitch, sewing, reading, gardening. Office: Columbia State Cmty Coll PO Box 1315 Columbia TN 38402-1315

LOPER, ROBERT BRUCE, theater director, educator; b. Olathe, Colo., June 30, 1925; s. Roy Major and Charlotte (Matthews) L.; m. Shirley McClurg, Aug. 28, 1948; children—William, Matthew. B.A., U. Colo., 1948, M.A., 1951; Ph.D. in Elizabethan Lit. (Fulbright scholar Stratford-on-Avon 1951-53), Birmingham (Eng.) U., 1957. Actor, also documentary film writer N.Y.C., 1948-49; radio writer and newscaster Tacoma, 1949-50; faculty Stanford, 1953-68; prof., 1962-68, head dept. drama, 1963-68; founder Stanford Repertory Theatre, 1965; prof. drama U. Wash., 1968—; mem. San Franciso Actor's Workshop, 1960-64; dir., actor Oreg. Shakespeare Festival, Ashland, 1955—; vis. dir. Brecht's Caucasian Chalk Circle at Vancouver (Can.) Internat. Festival, 1959, Seattle Repertory Theatre, 1967; actor, dir. Contemporary Theatre, Empty Space Theatre, 1968—; dir. Joe Egg, The Price; guest dir. Talbot Theatre Centre, London, Ont., 1970. Actor, dir. Oedipus Rex, Death of a Salesman, Member of the Wedding, 1987, Seattle Repertory Theatre, 1967, Awake and Sing, Joe Egg, And Miss Reardon Drinks a Little, The Prize, 1987, A Contemporary Theatre, 1968—; dir. Billy Bishop, Old Times, Otherwise Engaged, Duet for One, 1985, Empty Space Theatre, 1975, Wozzeck; actor Fool for Love, 1984, Intiman Theatre, Waterworks, Kennedy Ctr., 1988; featured actor Bergen Internat. Festival, Norway, 1969; premiere Centralia (Pritchard), Stand Still (Arlin); producer (stage works) Am. premiere Dallapiccola's opera Night Flight, 1962, Alchemist, 1960. Mem. Phi Beta Kappa, Tau Kappa Delta. Home: 2641 E Helen St Seattle WA 98112-3619 *The theatre has been my obsession and my religion. Directing a play is a kind of communion, the sharing of a fictional struggle which illuminates the more chaotic struggles and obsessions of our day-to-day lives. In making us more civilized, less lonely, the theatre can be teaching at its best.*

LOPES, MARIA FERNANDINA, commissioner; b. Ganda, Angola, Portugal, Dec. 12, 1934; came to U.S., 1963; d. Rodrigo do Carmo and Maria Jose Fernandes (Mendes) Marques; m. Fernandes Esteves Lopes, Aug. 11, 1962; children: Lisa Maria Lopes Moss, Mark Esteves. Student, Lisbon (Portugal) Comml. Inst., 1953, Massasoit Community Coll., Brockton, Mass., 1988. With archives dept. Portuguese Govt., Lisbon, 1958-62; congl. aide Congresswoman Margaret M. Heckler, Fall River, Taunton, Mass., 1972-74; mem. Taunton (Mass.) Sch. Com., 1976-93; commr., chairperson Bristol County, Mass., 1991—. Founder Day of Portugal, 1974. Avocations: traveling, politics, antiques, music. Home: 28 Worcester St Taunton MA 02780-2041 Office: Office County Commissioners Superior Courthouse Nine Court St PO Box 208 Taunton MA 02780

LOPEZ, A. RUBEN, lawyer; b. San Juan, P.R., Oct. 1, 1955; s. Angel and Elizabeth (Hernandez) L.; m. Magaly Retamar, Oct. 17, 1993. BA in Psychology, SUNY, Buffalo, 1979; JD, U. Toledo, 1982. Bar: Ohio 1992. Instnl. care asst. Dept. Anti-Addiction Svcs., San Juan, 1984; instnl. social worker Dept. Social Svcs., San Juan, 1984-86; supr. location Child Support Enforcement Program, San Juan, 1986-88; chief of benefits Bur. Social Security for Chauffeurs, San Juan, 1988-90; pvt. practice Cleve., 1992-93; atty. Legal Aid Soc. of Columbus, Ohio, 1993-95; asst. state pub. defender Ohio Pub. Defender Office, Columbus, 1995—. Bd. trustees Ct. Apptd. Spl. Advocates of Franklin County, 1994-96, sec. 1995. Mem. Ohio State Bar Assn. SDA. Avocations: camping, jogging. Office: Asst State Pub Defender 8 E Long St Fl 11 Columbus OH 43215-2914

LOPEZ, ALFONSO RAMON, retired baseball player; b. Tampa, Fla., Aug. 20, 1908. Baseball player Bklyn. Dodgers, 1928-35, Boston Braves, 1936-40, Pitts. Pirates, 1941-46; baseball player Cleve. Indians, 1947, mgr., 1951-56; mgr. Chgo. White Sox, 1957-69. Named to Baseball Hall of Fame, 1977. Office: c/o Nat Baseball Hall Fame PO Box 590 Cooperstown NY 13326-0590

LOPEZ, ANDY, university athletic coach. Head coach Pepperdine U. Waves, 1989-94, U. Florida, 1994—. NCAA Divsn. 1A Champions, 1992. Office: U Florida P O Box 14485 Gainesville FL 32604*

LOPEZ, ANTONIO VINCENT, education educator; b. Montgomery, Ala., Apr. 24, 1938; s. Joseph Charles and Eva Mae (Hall) Maschi. BS in Pharmacy, Auburn U., 1959, MS, 1961; PhD, U. Miss., 1966. Asst. prof. Mercer U. Sch. Pharmacy, Atlanta, 1966-68, assoc. prof., 1968-74, prof., 1974-96, assoc. dean for student affairs, 1994-96, prof. emeritus, 1996—, dept. chmn. Sch. Pharmacy, 1967-78, asst. dean, 1978-80, assoc. dean, 1980-85, dir. student affairs, 1985-94. Author: Exploring Mental Health, 1974. Pres. Met. Coun. on Alcohol and Drugs, Atlanta, 1985-86; bd. dirs. Families in Action, Atlanta, 1981-86; active Ga. Alcohol and Drug Abuse Adv. Coun., 1978-83; treas. Ga. Opera Co., Atlanta, 1976. Recipient Cert. of Recognition Ga. Citizens Coun. on Alcoholism, 1986, Cert. of Appreciation State of Ga., 1984, Lederle Labs. Faculty Rsch. award, 1967, 72. Mem. Phi Lambda Sigma, Rho Chi, Kappa Psi (Tchr. of Yr. 1976-89), Kappa Epsilon, Phi Delta Chi. Republican. Roman Catholic. Office: Mercer U 3001 Mercer University Dr Atlanta GA 30341-4115

LOPEZ, BARRY HOLSTUN, writer; b. Port Chester, N.Y., Jan. 6, 1945; s. Adrian Bernard and Mary Frances (Holstun) L.; m. Sandra Jean Landers, June 10, 1967. BA, U. Notre Dame, 1966, MA in Teaching, 1968; postgrad., U. Oreg., 1968-69; LHD (hon.), Whittier Coll., 1988, U. Portland, 1994. Free-lance writer, 1970—; assoc. Media Studies Ctr. at Columbia Univ., N.Y.C., 1985—; mem. U.S. Cultural Delegation to China, 1988. Author: Desert Notes, 1976, Giving Birth to Thunder, 1978, Of Wolves and Men, 1978 (John Burroughs Soc. medal 1979, Christophers of N.Y. medal 1979, Pacific Northwest Booksellers award in nonfiction 1979), River Notes, 1979, Winter Count, 1981 (Disting. Recognition award Friends Am. Writers in Chgo. 1982), Arctic Dreams, 1986 (Nat. Book award in nonfiction Nat. Book Found. 1986, Christopher medal 1987, Pacific Northwest Booksellers award 1987, Frances Fuller Victor award in nonfiction Oreg. Inst. Literary Arts 1987), Crossing Open Ground, 1988, Crow and Weasel, 1990 (Parents Choice Found. award), The Rediscovery of North America, 1991, Field Notes, 1994 (Pacific Northwest Booksellers award in fiction 1995, Critics' Choice award 1996); also numerous articles, essays and short stories; contbg. editor Harper's mag., 1981-82, 84—, N.Am. Rev., 1977—; works translated into Japanese, Swedish, German, Dutch, Italian, French, Norwegian, Chinese, Finnish, Spanish. Recipient award in Lit., Am. Acad. Arts and Letters, 1986, Gov.'s award for Arts, 1990, Lannan Found. award, 1990, Antarctic Svc. medal USN/NSF, 1989; John Simon Guggenheim Found. fellow, 1987. Mem. PEN Am. Ctr., Authors Guild, Poets and Writers.

LOPEZ, DAVID TIBURCIO, lawyer, educator, arbitrator, mediator; b. Laredo, Tex., July 17, 1939; s. Tiburcio and Dora (Davila) L.; m. Romelia G. Guerra, Nov. 20, 1965; 1 child, Vianei López Robinson. Student, Laredo Jr. Coll., 1956-58; BJ, U. Tex., 1962; JD summa cum laude, South Tex. Coll. Law, 1971. Bar: Tex. 1971, U.S. Dist. Ct. (so. dist.) Tex. 1972, U.S. Ct. Appeals (5th cir.) 1973, U.S. Dist. Ct. (we. dist.) Tex. 1975, U.S. Ct. Claims 1975, U.S. Ct. Appeals (fed. cir.) 1975, U.S. Supreme Ct. 1976, U.S. Dist. Ct. (ea. dist.) Tex. 1978, U.S. Ct. Appeals (11th cir.) 1981, U.S. Ct. Appeals (9th cir.) 1984; cert. internat. com. arbitrator Internat. Ctr. for Arbitration; mediator tng. Atty.-Mediator Inst. Reporter Laredo Times, 1958-59; cons. Mexican Nat. Coll. Mag., Mexico City, 1961-62; reporter Corpus Christi (Tex.) Caller-Times, 1962-64; state capitol corr. Long News Svc., Austin, Tex., 1964-65; publs. dir. Interam. Regional Orgn. of Workers, Mexico City, 1965-67; nat. field rep. AFL-CIO, Washington, 1967-71, publs. dir. Tex. chpt., Austin, 1971-72; pvt. practice, Houston, 1971—; adj. prof. U. Houston, 1972-74, Thurgood Marshall Sch. Law, Houston, 1975-76; mem. adv. com. nat. Hispanic ednl. rsch. project One Million and Counting Tomas Rivera Ctr., 1989-91; mem. adv. bd. Inst. Transnat. Arbitration; charter mem. Resolution Forum Inc.; mem. adv. bd. South Tex. Ctr. Profl. Responsibility; mem. nat. panel of neutrals JAMS/ENDISPUTE, 1996—. Bd. dirs. Pacifica Found., N.Y.C., 1970-72, Houston Community Coll., 1972-75; mem. bd. edn. Houston Ind. Sch. Dist., 1972-75. With U.S. Army. Mem. ABA (chair sub-com. atty. fees in appeals), FBA, ATLA, Tex. Bar Assn. (dir. State Bar Coll., task force on rules of civil procedures), Houston Bar Assn., Internat. Bar Assn., Interam. Bar Assn., Bar of U.S. Fed. Cir., Mex.-Am. Bar Assn., Inter-Pacific Bar Assn., Tex.-Mex. Bar Assn. (chair labor com.), Hispanic Bar Assn., World Assn. Lawyers (chair com. on law and the handicapped), Am. Judicature Soc., Indsl. Rels. Rsch. Assn., Kappa Tau Alpha, Phi Theta Kappa, Sigma Delta Chi, Phi Alpha Delta. Democrat. Roman Catholic. Home: 28 Farnham Ct Houston TX 77024 Office: 3900 Montrose Blvd Houston TX 77006-4908

LOPEZ, FRANCISCA UY, elementary education educator; b. Leyte, The Philippines, Mar. 9, 1925; d. Juan and Perpetua (Loyola) Uy; m. Elias Espiritu Lopez, Apr. 10, 1955; 1 child, Maria Elisa Lopez Stevens. BSE, Philippine Normal Coll., Manila, Philippines, 1952; MEd, Pa. State U., 1961; MA, Nat. Tchr. Coll., Manila, 1955. Cert. life standard tchr., Calif., tchr. (life cert.), Tex. Instructional resource tchr. El Tejon Union Sch. Dist., Mettler, Calif.; reading specialist Saudi Arabia Internat. Sch., Dhahran; facilitator staff devel. unit, instr. indsl. tng. ctr. Arabian Am. Oil Co., Dhahran; tchr. Dallas Ind. Sch. Dist. Leader Girl Scouts U.S. Fulbright Smith-Mundt grantee, 1960-61. Mem. NEA, Classroom Tchrs. Dallas (sch. rep., Tex. State Tchrs. Assn. Home: 1816 Tawakoni Ln Plano TX 75075-6732 Office: Dallas Ind Sch Dist 4200 Met Ave Dallas TX 75210

LOPEZ, FRANCISCO, IV, health care administrator; b. San Jose, Costa Rica, Costa Rica, Aug. 31, 1956; s. Francisco III and Myriam (Bolanos) L.; m. Marie Jeanne de Lassus; children: Matthew Chase, Kathryn Louise, Elizabeth Myriam Jane, James Austin. BS, La. State U., 1976; MHA, Tulane U., 1980. Adminstrv. asst. Mercy Hosp. of New Orleans, 1980-81, asst. v.p., 1981-82, v.p., 1982-85, exec. v.p., 1985-86, chief operating officer, 1986—; exec. v.p. Mercy Health Sys., 1995—; pres. St. Mary's/Mercy Hosp., 1995—; bd. cons. St. John's Place, New Orleans, 1986—. Bd. dirs. Enid Beautiful; trustee Enid Telecomms. Authority; v.p. Calhoun/Palmer Neighborhood Assn., New Orleans, 1984-85; bd. dirs. Holy Name of Jesus Sch., New Orleans, 1985, United Cerebral Palsy, New Orleans, 1986, Mount St. Mary H.S., Okla. Cath. Health Care Assn., bd. dirs. YMCA, Rotary Club; trustee Vance Devel. Authority, Phillips U., YMCA. Recipient Associated U. Programs in Health Adminstrn. scholarship, 1979, Nat. Hispanic scholarship, 1980. Fellow Am. Coll. Health Care Execs. (Foster G. McGaw scholarship 1979); mem. Am. Hosp. Assn., Fedn. Am. Hosps., New Health Care Mgrs., Enid C. of C. (trustee), So. Yacht Club (New Orleans), Greens Country Club (Oklahoma City), Oakwood Country Club. Clubs: So. Yacht (new Orleans); Greens Country (Oklahoma City). Avocations: tennis, travel, swimming. Home: 2029 Oak Leaf Cir Enid OK 73703 Office: St Mary's Mercy Hosp PO Box 232 Enid OK 73702

LOPEZ, JENNIFER, actress, dancer. Appeared in films Money Train, 1995, Jack, 1996, Blood and Wine, 1996, Anaconda, 1997, Selena, 1997. Office: United Talent Agy 9560 Wilshire Blvd 5th Fl Beverly Hills CA 90212*

LOPEZ, JOSEPH JACK, oil company executive, consultant; b. N.Y.C., July 26, 1932; s. Florentino Estrada and Leah (Bodner) L.; m. June Elliott, June 20, 1953; children: Karen Marie Lopez Romino, Debra Jo Lopez, Laura Jean Lopez Berrell. Student, CCNY, 1955-59. Project estimator Chem. Constrn.-Engrs., N.Y.C., 1960-64, Dorr Oliver-Engrs., Stamford, Conn., 1964-66; chief estimator R.M. Parsons-Engrs., Frankfurt, Germany, 1966-74; mgr. project svcs. A.G. McKee-Engrs., Berkley Heights, N.J., 1974-76; mgr. tech. svcs. Rsch. Cottrell Corp., Sommerville, N.J., 1976-78; cons. Booz Allen & Hamilton, Abu Dhabi, United Arab Emirates, 1978-84; v.p. XL Tech. Corp., N.Y.C., 1984-87; cons. Qatar Gen. Pete Corp., Doha, 1987-90; pres. J. Lopez Cons., Babylon, N.Y., 1990—; estimator Combustion Engring. Co., N.Y.C., 1955-60. With USAF, 1950-54. Mem. Am. Assn. Cost Engrs., Project Mgmt. Inst. Republican. Roman Catholic. Home and Office: 15 Hinton Ave Babylon NY 11702-1407

LOPEZ, LOURDES, ballerina; b. Havana, Cuba, 1958; came to U.S., 1959; Studied with, Alexander Nigodoff and Martha Mahr, Miami, Perry Brunson; attended, Sch. of Am. Ballet, N.Y.C. Mem. corps de ballet N.Y.C. Ballet, 1974-80, soloist, 1980-84, prin., 1984—. Created roles in Peter Martins' Sonate di Scarlatti and Rejouissance; other repertory includes: La Sonnambula, Divertimento No. 15, Serenade, Stars and Stripes, Apollo, Kammermusik No. 2, Firebird, The Four Seasons, The Goldberg Variations, Moves, Violin Concerto, Concerto Barocco, Theme and Variations, N.Y.C. Ballet's Balanchine Celebration, 1993, Cortège Hongrois, others; appeared in PBS series Dance in Am. Office: care NYC Ballet Inc NY State Theater Lincoln Ctr Plz New York NY 10023*

LOPEZ, MANUEL, immunology and allergy educator; b. Bucaramanga, Colombia, Sept. 30, 1939; came to U.S., 1971.; married; 4 children. BS, Colegio San Pedro Claver, Bucaramanga, 1956; MD, Univ. Javeriana, Bogota, Colombia, 1963. Diplomate Am. Bd. Allergy and Immunology, Am. Bd. Diagnostic Lab. Immunology. Intern Hosp. San Juan De Dios, Bucaramanga, 1962-63, resident, 1963-64, med. dir., 1969-71; clin. and rsch. fellow dept. medicine allergy unit Harvard U. and Harvard Med. Sch. at Mass. Gen. Hosp., Boston, 1964-68; dir. med. rsch. Univ. Indsl. De Santander, Bucaramanga, 1968-69; dir. immunology svc. lab. La. State Med. Ctr., New Orleans, 1971-74; asst. prof. medicine med. ctr. La. State U., New Orleans, 1971-74; from clin. asst. prof. to assoc. prof. med. sch. Tulane U., New Orleans, 1974-89, prof., 1989—, dir. immunology diagnostic lab. med. sch., 1974-83, dir. clin. immunology labs., 1983—, program dir. allergy and immunology tng. program, 1990—, acting chief sect. allergy and clin. immunology, 1990-91, chief, 1991—; mem. med.-sci. adv. com. Asthma and Allergy Found. Am., 1986-89; ad hoc mem. immunological sci. study sect. NIH, 1987, allergy and clin. immunology spl. reviewer immunology and transplantation rsch. com., 1988, mem. gen. clin. rsch. ctrs. com., 1993—; reviewer merit rev. grants VA, 1988, 89, 90; grant program reviewer Ctrs. of Excellence, Dept. Health and Human Svcs., 1991; mem. allergic products adv. com. FDA, 1993—; mem. spl. rev. com. Nat. Inst. Allergy and Infectious Diseases, 1993; presenter in field. Mem. editl. bd. Jour. Allergy and Clin. Immunology, 1986-94, reviewer, 1987-88; contbr. articles to profl. jours. and chpts. to books. Fellow John Simmon Guggenheim Meml. Found., 1964-66. Fellow Am. Acad. Allergy and Clin. Immunology (mem. internat. com. 1986-89, mem. immunotherapy of asthma com. 1987—, mem. Latin Ctrl. and South Am. com. 1987—, chmn. internat. grant aids 1988-89, mem. continuing med. edn. com. 1992-94), Am. Coll. Chest Physicians; mem. Am. Assn. Immunologists, Am. Fedn. Clin. Rsch., Am. Thoracic Soc., U.S.-Colombian Med. Assn. (pres. IX Congress 1989), La. Allergy Soc., N.Y. Acad. Scis., Southeastern Allergy Assn., Assn. Med. Lab. Immunologists, Internat. Assn. Aerobiology, Cordoba Allergy Soc. (hon.), Sigma Xi. Office: Tulane U Med Sch Clin Immunology Sect 1700 Perdido St Fl 3 New Orleans LA 70112-1210

LOPEZ, NANCY, professional golfer; b. Torrance, Calif., Jan. 6, 1957; d. Domingo and Marina (Griego) L.; m. Ray Knight, Oct. 25, 1982; children: Ashley Marie, Erinn Shea, Torri Heather. Student, U. Tulsa, 1976-78. Author: The Education of a Woman Golfer, 1979. First victory at Bent Tree Classic, Sarasota, Fla., 1978; named AP Athlete for 1978; admitted to Ladies Profl. Golf Assn. Hall of Fame, 1987, to PGA World Golf Hall of Fame, 1989. Mem. Ladies Profl. Golf Assn. (Player and Rookie of Yr. 1978). Republican. Baptist. Wiiner 33 LPGA Tour events, 2 maj. championships. Office: care Internat Mgmt Group 1 Erieview Plz Ste 1300 Cleveland OH 44114-1715*

LOPEZ, RAMON, recording industry executive. Now chmn. bd. dirs. WEA Internat. Inc., N.Y.C. Office: WEA Internat Inc 75 Rockefeller Plz Fl 20 New York NY 10019-6908*

LOPEZ, RICARDO, professional boxer; b. Mexico City, July 25, 1967. Named Strawweight Champion WBC. Achievements include record of 42 wins and no losses with 32 knock-outs. Office: c/o Consejo Mundia de Boxeo, Genova 33 Oespacho # 503, 06600 Mexico City Mexico

LOPEZ-COBOS, JESUS, conductor; b. Toro, Spain, Feb. 25, 1940; m. Alicia Ferrer, May 15, 1987; 3 children. PhD in philosophy and music, U. Madrid, 1964; diploma composition, Madrid Conservatory, 1966; diploma conducting, Vienna (Austria) Acad., 1969. Gen. music dir. Deutsche Oper Berlin, 1981-90; prin. guest condr. London Philharm., 1981-86; prin. condr., artistic dir. Spanish Nat. Orch., 1984-89; music dir. Cin. Orch., 1986—; music dir. Orchestre de Chambre de Lausanne, Switzerland, 1990, condr.; also condr. concerts Edinburgh Festival, London Symphony, Royal Philharm., N.Y. Philharm., L.A. Philharm., Chgo. Symphony, Cleve. Orch., Phila. Orch., Berlin Philharm., Berlin Radio Orch., Amsterdam Concertgebouw, Vienna Philharm., Swiss Romande, Muncih Philarharm., Hamburg NDR, Oslo Philharm., Zurich Tonhalle, Israel Philharm., opera prodns. at Royal Opera House, Covent Garden, London, La Scala, Milan, Italy, Met. Opera, N.Y.C., Paris Opera, others; recs. include Lucia di Lammermoor New Philham. Orch., Otello, recital and operatic disc with José Carrera and London Symphony Orch., Liszt's Dante Symphony with Swiss Romande, Falla's Three-Cornered Hat, R-K Capricio Espangnole, Chiabrier's Espana with L.A. Philharm., others. Recipient 1st prize Besancon Internat. Condr.'s Competition, 1969, Prince of Astrurias award Spanish Govt., 1981, 1st Class Disting. Svc. medal Fed. Republic of Germany, 1989. Office: Cin Symphony Orch 1241 Elm St Cincinnati OH 45210-2231 also: Orchestre de Chambre de Lausanne, Chemin de devin 72, CH-1012 Lausanne Switzerland*

LÓPEZ DE MENDEZ, ANNETTE GISELDA, education educator; b. Santurce, P.R., July 13, 1949; d. Frank and Ana Maria (Vale) López; m. Héctor Méndez, Feb. 15, 1971; 1 child, Nannette. BA in Humanities, U. P.R., Rio Piedras, 1970; MA in Early Childhood Edn., NYU, 1978; EdD, Harvard U., 1994. Rsch. asst. Mt. Sinai Hosp., N.Y.C., 1972-73; founder, elem. educator Humacao (P.R.) Montessori Sch., 1973-76; dir., tchr. Montessori Sch. P.R., San Juan, 1976-78; supr., trainer Head Start Invsc. Program, U. P.R., Rio Piedras, 1978-80; assoc. prof. Coll. Edn. U. P.R., Rio Piedras, 1980-85, 87—; teaching fellow Harvard U., Cambridge, Mass., 1985-86; dir. ednl. rsch. U. P.R., 1992—; cons. Gen. Coun. Edn., San Juan, 1992-95, Commn. Women's Affairs, San Juan, 1990-92; dir. Edn. Rsch. Ctr. U. P.R., 1992—; mem. Educators' Forum Harvard U., 1990—; mem. systemwide ednl. reform com. Dept. Edn., P.R., 1992-94; mem. Action Rsch. for Ednl. Change Com., 1993—. Pres. Isla Verde Residence Assn., P.R., 1992-95. Mem. ASCD, Am. Montessori Soc., Assn. Childhood Edn. Internat., Nat. Assn. Edn. Young Children, N.Am. Montessori Soc., Montessori Internat. Assn., Am. Ednl. Rsch. Assn. Democrat. Roman Catholic. Avocations: swimming, travel. Office: Univ PR Sch Edn PO Box 23304 Rio Piedras PR 00931-3304

LOPEZ-NAKAZONO, BENITO, chemical and industrial engineer; b. Nuevo Laredo, Tam., Mex., Oct. 26, 1946; came to U.S., 1968; s. Benito and Ayko (Nakazono) Lopez-Ramos; m. Anastacia Espinoza, June 22, 1981; children: Benito Keizo, Martin Key, Tanzy Keiko, Mayeli, Aiko Michelle. BSc in Chem. Engrng. & Indsl. Engrng., ITESM, Monterrey, Mexico, 1968; MS in Chem. Engrng., U. Houston, 1971. Prof. chem. engring. ITESM, Monterrey, 1971-72; vessel analytical design engr./process engr. M.W. Kellogg, Houston, 1973-79, 81; product mgr. Ind. Del Alcali, Monterrey, 1980-81; sr. process engr. Haldor Topsoe, Inc., Houston, 1982—. Pres. adminstrv. coun. United Meth. Ch., Houston, 1990-92, lay leader, 96. ITESM fellow, 1963, U. Houston fellow, 1968. Mem. Tex. Soc. Profl. Engrs., Am. Inst. Chem. Engrs., Sigma Xi. Achievements include development and design of hydrogen, ammonia, methanol, formaldehyde and SNOx/WSA plants, start-up, commissioning and supervision of ammonia plants in Mexico, U.S., Canada., Russia, Somalia, India and Bangladesh. Home: 1805 Lanier Dr League City TX 77573-4720 Office: Haldor Topsoe Inc Ste 302 17629 El Camino Real Houston TX 77058-3051

LOPEZ-NAVARRO, EDUARDO LUIS, family therapist; b. Santiago de Cuba, Oriente, Cuba, June 29, 1959; came to U.S, 1970; s. Eduardo Regino and Alicia Del Pilar (Navarro) Lopez. BA, UCLA, 1982; MS in Psychology with honors, Calif. State U., L.A., 1991. Counselor L.A. Unified Sch. Dist., 1982-90; family therapist Family Counseling Svcs., San Gabriel, Calif., 1990-93; program coord. El Centro del Pueblo, L.A., 1993—; family therapist Hillsides Home for Children, Pasadena, Calif., 1992—, El Centro Del Pueblo, L.A., 1993—; dir. North Ctrl. L.A. Family Preservation Project; cons. (counselor) UCLA/Valley Alternative Magnet Sch., Ban Nuys, 1990; rsch. asst. UCLA/Fernald Sch., 1981; lectr. in field; expert presenter and cons. various TV programs including Univision and Telemundo Networks, L.A., 1993—. Author: Voces: Aprendiendo a escuchar mas alla de las palabras, 1997; contbr. articles to profl. jours.; author video: The World of Perpetual Night: Insights into the Psychology of Street Prostitution, 1990. Counselor Hollywood Sunset Cmty. Clinic, L.A., 1986-89; family counselor St. Matthias Ch.; mem. san Gabriel Valley Child Abuse Coun.; dir. Latino Family Preservation, L.A., 1994. Am. Assn. for Marriage and Family Therapy Minority fellow, 1981; recipient Counseling Dept. Spl. Recognition award Hollywood Sunset Cmty. Clinic, 1988, Exito Internat. award. Mem. Calif. Assn. Marriage and Family Therapists, Am. Assn. Marriage and Family Therapists. Roman Catholic. Avocations: writing poetry, photography, video science. Office: El Centro Del Pueblo 1157 Lemoyne St Los Angeles CA 90026-3206

LOPICCOLO, JOSEPH, psychologist, educator, author; b. L.A., Sept. 13, 1943; s. Joseph E. and Adeline C. (Russo) Lo P.; m. Leslie Joan Matlen, June 20, 1964 (div. 1978); 1 child, Joseph Townsend; m. Cathryn Gail Pridal, Dec. 20, 1980; 1 child, Michael James. BA with highest honors, UCLA, 1965; MS, Yale U., 1968, PhD, 1969. Lic. psychologist, Mo. Asst. prof. U. Oreg., Eugene, 1969-73; assoc. prof. U. Houston, 1973-74; prof. SUNY, Stony Brook, 1974-84, Tex. A&M U., College Station, 1984-87; prof. psychology U. Mo., Columbia, 1987—, chmn. dept., 1987-90; vis. scholar Cambridge (Eng.) U., 1991. Author: Becoming Orgasmic, 1976, 2d edit., 1988, also book chpts.; editor: Handbook of Sex Therapy, 1978; contbr. numerous articles to profl. jours. Woodrow Wilson Found. fellow; NIH rsch. grantee, 1973-84. Fellow Am. Psychol. Assn.; mem. Internat. Acad. Sex Rsch., Soc. for Sci. Study of Sex (pres. 1983-84, Alfred Kinsey Meml. Rsch. award), Soc. for Sex Therapy and Rsch. (Masters and Johnson Rsch. award 1997), Phi Beta Kappa, Sigma Xi. Office: U Mo Dept Psychology 210 McAlester Hall Columbia MO 65211

LOPINA, LAWRENCE THOMAS, retired manufacturing executive; b. Chgo., Nov. 9, 1930; s. Thomas F. and Augustine A. (Schwantes) L.; PhB, U. Notre Dame, 1952; MBA, DePaul U., 1953; MBA, U. Chgo., 1963; m. Marion T. Toomey, Nov. 5, 1955; children: Joseph D., Lawrence M., Mary E., Celeste N., James P. Jr. CPA, Wis.; cert. mgmt. acct. Acct. Haskins & Sells, CPA's, Chgo., 1952-53; acctg. positions with Motorola, Inc., Chgo., 1953-63; div. contr. then v.p. fin. fluid power group Applied Power, Inc., Milw., 1963-74; sr. v.p. fin. Broan Mfg Co., Inc., Hartford, Wis., 1974-96, former dir., ret., 1996. With AUS, 1953-55. Mem. AICPA, Inst. Mgmt. Accts. (treas. Milw. chpt.), Fin. Execs. Inst. (past pres. Milw. chpt.), Wis. Inst. CPA's, Catholic League (past Wis. chpt. treas.), Beta Gamma Sigma. Club: KC.

LOPKER, ANITA MAE, psychiatrist; b. San Diego, May 25, 1955; d. Louis Donald and Betty Jean (Sayman-Campbell) L. BA magna cum laude, U. Calif., San Diego, 1978; MD, U. Rochester, 1982. Diplomate Nat. Bd. Med. Examiners, Am. Bd. Forensic Examiners, Am. Bd. Forensic Medicine. Intern in internal medicine Yale U. Sch. Medicine-Greenwich Hosp., 1982-83; resident in psychiatry Yale U. Sch. of Medicine, 1983-86; postdoctoral fellow Yale U. Sch. Medicine, New Haven, Conn., 1982-86; clin. instr. Yale U. Sch. Medicine, New Haven, 1986-88; pvt. practice specializing eating disorders and Lyme disease Westport, Conn., 1987—; cons. psychiatrist Yale-New Haven Hosp Lyme Disease Study Clinic, 1987-94, Yale U. Lyme Disease Rsch. Project, 1986—, Alcoholism and Drug Dependency Coun., Inc., 1989-90; internat. lectr. on Lyme psychiat. syndrome; nat. lectr. on eating disorders, substance abuse. Contbr. articles to profl. jours. Founding mem. Nat. Mus. for Women in the Arts, Washington, 1986; patron Menninger Found.; bd. dirs. The Fairfield Orch., 1993-96. Recipient Benjamin Rush prize in psychiatry U. Rochester Sch. Medicine, 1982. Mem. AAAS, Am. Psychiat. Assn., Conn. Psychiat. Soc., World Fedn. Mental Health (life), N.Y. Acad. Scis., Menninger Found., Alpha Omega Alpha, Phi Beta Kappa. Achievements include discovery of preventable neuropsychiatric disorders associated with Lyme disease. Avocation: classical dressage. Home: 27 Strathmore Ln Westport CT 06880-4700 Office: 7 Whitney Street Ext Westport CT 06880-3761

LOPPNOW, MILO ALVIN, clergyman, former church official; b. St. Charles, Minn., Jan. 13, 1914; s. William and Doretta (Penz) L.; m. Gertrude Stoltz, Feb. 6, 1942; children—Donald, Bruce, David. B.A., Moravian Coll., 1937; M.Div., Moravian Theol. Sem., 1940, D.D., 1970. Ordained to ministry Moravian Ch. in Am., 1940; pastor congregations nr. Wisconsin Rapids, Wis., 1940-41, Waconia, Minn., 1941-53; pastor congregations nr. Lakeview Ch., Madison, Wis., 1953-64; dist. pres. Western Dist. Moravian Ch., Madison, 1965-78; elected bishop, 1970. Chmn. Youth Commn., Madison, 1957-63; Trustee Moravian Coll., 1954-78, Moravian Theol. Sem., Bethlehem, Pa.; former chaplain, dir. devel. Marquardt Meml. Manor, Watertown, Wis.

LOPREATO, JOSEPH, sociology educator, author; b. Stefanaconi, Italy, July 13, 1928; came to U.S., 1951; s. Frank and Marianna (Pavone) L.; m. Carolyn H. Prestopino, July 18, 1954; (div. 1971); children: Gregory F., Marisa S. Schmidt; m. Sally A. Cook, Aug. 24, 1972 (div. 1978). BA in Sociology, U. Conn., 1956; MA in Sociology, Yale U., 1957, PhD in Sociology, 1960. Asst. prof. sociology U. Mass., Amherst, 1960-62; vis. lectr. U. Rome, 1962-64; assoc. prof. U. Conn., Storrs, 1964-66; prof. sociology U. Tex., Austin, 1968—; chmn. dept. sociology U. Tex., 1969-72; vis. prof. U. Catania, Italy, 1974, U. Calabria, Italy, 1980; mem. steering com. Council European Studies, Columbia U., 1977-80; chmn. sociology com. Council for Internat. Exchange of Scholars, 1977-79; mem. Internat. Com. Mezzogiorno, 1986—; Calabria Internat. Com., 1988—. Author: Italian Made Simple, 1959, Vilfredo Pareto, 1965, Peasants No More, 1967, Italian Americans, 1970, Class, Conflict and Mobility, 1972, Social Stratification, 1974, The Sociology of Vilfredo Pareto, 1975, La Stratificazione Sociale negli Stati Uniti, 1945-1975, 1977, Human Nature and Biocultural Evolution, 1984, Evoluzione e Natura Umana, 1990, Mai Più Contadini, 1990, Sociology Against Darwin, 1998; contbr. articles to profl. jours. Mem. Nat. Italian-Am. Com. for U.S.A. Bicentennial; mem. exec. com. Congress Italian Politics, 1977-80. Served to cpl. U.S. Army, 1952-54. Fulbright faculty research fellow, 1962-64, 73-74; Social Sci. Research Council faculty research fellow, 1963-64; NSF faculty research fellow, 1965-68; U. Tex. Austin research fellow, 1973-74, spring 1985, spring 1993; Guido Dorso award for U.S.A., Italy, 1992. Mem. AAAS (behavioral sci. rsch. prize com. 1992-94), Internat. Sociol. Assn., Am. Sociol. Assn., European Sociobiolog. Soc., Evolution and Behavior Soc., So. Sociol. Soc. (assoc. editor Am. Sociol. Rev. 1970-72, Social Forces 1987-90, Jour. Polit. and Mil. Sociology 1980—), Internat. Soc. Human Ethology. Catholic-Episcopalian. Office: Univ of Tex Dept Sociology Austin TX 78712

LOPRETE, JAMES HUGH, lawyer; b. Detroit, Sept. 17, 1929; s. James Victor and Effie Hannah (Brown) LoP.; m. Marion Ann Garrison, Sept. 11, 1952; children: James Scott, Kimberly Anne, Kent Garrison, Robert Drew. AB, U. Mich., 1951, JD with Distinction, 1953. Bar: Mich. 1954. Practiced law Detroit, 1953—; atty. Chrysler Corp., Detroit, 1953; assoc. firm Monaghan, LoPrete, McDonald, Yakima & Grenke, P.C. and predecessor firms, Detroit, from 1954; mem. firm Monaghan, LoPrete, McDonald, Yakima & Grenke, P.C. and predecessor firms, 1966—, pres., 1979—; bd. dirs. Drake's Batter Mix Co., Orsco Inc.; instr. legal writing Wayne State U., Detroit, 1955-57. Trustee U. Mich. Club of Detroit Scholarship Fund, 1967, pres., 1982—, Samuel Westerman Found., 1971—, pres., 1984, John R. & M. Margrite Davis Found. Fellow Am. Coll. Trust and Estate Counsel, Internat. Acad. Estate and Trust Law; mem. ABA, Oakland County bar assns., State Bar Mich., Detroit Athletic Club (dir. 1983-88, sec. 1986-88), Orchard Lake Country Club, U. Mich. of Greater Detroit (pres. 1966). Home: 2829 Warner Dr Orchard Lake MI 48324-2449 Office: Monaghan LoPrete McDonald et al 1700 N Woodward Ave Ste A Bloomfield Hills MI 48304-2249

LORAN, ERLE, artist; b. Mpls., Oct. 3, 1905; m. Clyta Sisson, May 8, 1937 (dec. Mar. 1982); m. Ruth Schorer, July 22, 1993. Student, U. Minn., 1922-23; grad., Mpls. Sch. Art, 1926; M.F.A. (hon.), 1968. Travelled and painted in Europe, 1926-30; prof. art U. Calif., Berkeley; now prof. emeritus. U. Calif.; participant Cezanne, the Lateworks Symposium Mus. Modern Art, 1977. Represented in permanent collections of Denver Art Mus., San Francisco Mus. Art, U. Minn., Santa Barbara Mus. Art, San Diego Mus. Art, Krannert Art Mus. of U. Ill., 1965, Art. Mus. U. Calif. Berkeley, Oakland (Calif.) Mus., Smithsonian Instn., Washington, also numerous pvt. collections; U.S. Treasury Dept. purchases Great Shipyards and Last Year's Swamplands; works in large exhbns. in U.S. since 1933, numerous one-man shows, 1934—, including Oakland Mus., 1981, San Francisco Gallery, Paula Anglim, Bergruen Gallery, 1989, Univ. Art Mus., Berkeley, Calif., 1990, DeYoung Mus., San Francisco, 1994, Richmond (Calif.) Art Ctr., 1996; invited nat. exhbns. Mus. Modern Art, 1935, Whitney Mus. Am. Art, 1943, 44, 46, 48, Carnegie Inst., 1942, Pa. Acad., 1945, Met. Mus. Art, 1950, 51, 53, Richmond, Calif. Art Ctr., 1996, also 9 other nat. mus.; author: Cezanne's Composition, 1943, 45, 46, 47, 63, 70, 77, 81, paperback edit., 1985; also author numerous critical essays on art; chpts. on Cezanne in Les Peintres Celebres (Lucien Mazenod), Paris, 1948. Recipient numerous prizes and awards.; Awarded Paris prize ($6,000) by John Armstrong Chaloner Found., N.Y.C., 1926. Club: Arts (Berkeley). Home: 10 Kenilworth Ct Kensington CA 94707-1320

LORANCE, ELMER DONALD, organic chemistry educator; b. Tupelo, Okla., Jan. 18, 1940; s. Elmer Dewey and Imogene (Triplett) L.; m. Phyllis Ilene Miller, Aug. 20, 1969; children: Edward Donald, Jonathan Andrew. BA, Okla. State U., 1962; MS, Kansas State U., 1967; PhD, U. Okla., 1977. NIH research trainee Okla. U., Norman, 1966-70; asst. prof. organic chemistry So. Calif. Coll., Costa Mesa, 1970-73, assoc. prof., 1973-80, prof., 1980—, chmn. div. natural scis. and math., 1985-89, chmn. chemistry dept., 1990-93, chmn. divsn. natural scis. and math., 1993—. Contbr. articles to profl. jours. Mem. AAAS, Am. Chem. Soc., Internat. Union Pure and Applied Chemistry (assoc.), Am. Inst. Chemists, Am. Sci. Affiliation, Phi Lambda Upsilon. Republican. Mem. Ch. Assembly of God. Avocations: reading, gardening, music. Office: So Calif Coll 55 Fair Dr Costa Mesa CA 92626-6520

LORBER, BARBARA HEYMAN, communications executive; b. N.Y.C.; d. David Benjamin and Gertrude (Meyer) Heyman; divorced. AB in Polit. Sci., Skidmore Coll., 1966; MA, Columbia U., 1973, postgrad., 1973-76. Asst. dir. young citizens divsn. Dem. Party, 1966-68; exec. asst. to dean Albert Einstein Coll. Medicine, Bronx, N.Y., 1968-72; exec. asst. to v.p. devel. Vanderbilt U., Nashville, 1976-77; spl. projects dir. Am. Acad. in Rome, N.Y.C., 1977-78; pub. affairs dir., assoc. devel. dir. Met. Opera, N.Y.C., 1978-84; sr. v.p. Hill and Knowlton, N.Y.C., 1985-88; pres. Lorber Group, Ltd., N.Y.C., 1989-95; v.p. comms. and planning N.Y.C. Partnership and C. of C., 1996—; guest lectr. Arts and Bus. Coun., N.Y.C., Internat. Soc. Performing Arts Adminstrs., N.Y.C., NYU Sch. Continuing Edn., Nat. Media Conf., Nat. Soc. Fund Raising Execs., N.Y.C.; exec. prodr., prodr., writer N.Y. Internat. Festival Arts, N.Y.C., 1988. Author chpts. to book; contbr. articles to profl. jours. Office: NYC Partnership and C of C One Battery Pk Plz New York NY 10004

LORBER, MORTIMER, physiology educator; b. N.Y.C., Aug. 30, 1926; s. Albert and Frieda (Levin) L.; m. Eileen Segal, May 20, 1956; children: Kenneth, Stephanie. BS, NYU, 1945; DMD cum laude, Harvard U., 1950, MD cum laude, 1952. Diplomate Nat. Bd. Med. Examiners. Rotating intern A.M. Billings Hosp., 1952-53; resident in hematology Mt. Sinai Hosp., N.Y.C., 1953-54, asst. resident in medicine, 1957; asst. resident medicine Georgetown U. Hosp., Washington, 1958; instr., asst. prof. dept. physiology and biophysics Georgetown U., Washington, 1959-68, assoc. prof., 1968; lectr. physiology U.S. Naval Dental Sch., Bethesda, Md., 1962-70, Walter Reed Army Inst. Dental Rsch., Washington, 1963-70; guest scientist Naval Med. Rsch. Inst., Bethesda, 1978-83. Contbr.: The Merck Manual, 14th, 15th and 16th edit., 1982, 87, 92; contbr. articles to profl. jours. Lt. USNR, 1954-56. Recipient Lederle Med. Faculty award Lederle Co., Pearl River, N.Y., 1960-63, USPHS Rsch. Career Devel. award Nat. Inst. Dental Rsch., Bethesda, 1963-70; grantee Am. Cancer Soc., USPHS. Mem. Am. Physiol. Soc., Am. Soc. Hematology, Assn. Rsch. in Vision and Ophthalmology, Internat. Assn. Dental Rsch. Jewish. Achievements include discovery that the ground substance is masked but not lost in calcification, removal of spleen is followed by a reticulocytosis that is permanent in dogs, dogs have many more young reticulocytes in their blood than man, stretching of skin increases mitoses in the rat showing physical factors can modulate DNA and cell division, adult Gaucher cells contain iron secondary to erythrophagocytosis, the spleen protects against insecticide-induced hematoxicity, biological armature provides internal stability to exocrine glands, rat lacrimal glands are stretched by their attachments, mastication reflexly increases gastroduodenal motility. Home: 5823 Osceola Rd Bethesda MD 20816-2032 Office: Georgetown U Sch Medicine 3900 Reservoir Rd NW Washington DC 20007-2195

LORCH, ERNEST HENRY, lawyer; b. Frankfurt, Germany, Oct. 11, 1932; came to U.S., 1940; s. Alexander and Kate (Freundt) L. AB, Middlebury Coll., 1954; JD, U. Va., 1957; LLD (hon.), Fairfield U., 1987. Bar: N.Y. 1958. Assoc. Olwine, Connelly, Chase, O'Donnell & Weyher, N.Y.C., 1957-65, ptnr., 1965-84; pres., chief oper. officer Dyson-Kissner-Moran Corp., N.Y.C., 1984-90, pres., chief exec. officer, 1990-91; chmn., chief exec. officer, 1991-92, ret., 1992; of counsel Whitman, Breed, Abbott & Morgan, N.Y.C., 1992—; chmn. bd. dirs. Varlen Corp., Chgo.; bd. dirs. Tyler Corp., Dorsey Trailers, Inc. Dir. various inner city athletic assns., N.Y.C., 1959—; The DYSM Found., N.Y.C., 1985-92; trustee, officer, dir. The Riverside Ch., N.Y.C., 1961—; treas., dir. Wheelchair Charities Inc., Religion in American Life, 1993-96. Mem. ABA, N.Y. State Bar Assn. Office: Whitman Breed Abbott & Morgan 200 Park Ave New York NY 10166-0005

LORCH, GEORGE A., manufacturing company executive; b. Glenridge, N.J., 1941. BS, Va. Poly. Inst. & State U., 1963. With Armstrong World Industries, Inc., 1963—, v.p. mktg. E&B div., 1974-76, mktg. mgr., 1976-78, gen. sales mgr., 1978-83, then group v.p. carpet ops., from 1983, past exec. v.p., now chmn. bd., CEO, dir. Office: Armstrong World Industries Inc 313 W Liberty St Lancaster PA 17603-2717*

LORCH, KENNETH F., lawyer; b. Indpls., July 24, 1951. BSBA, Washington U., 1973; JD, John Marshall Sch. Law, 1976. Bar: Ill. 1976, U.S. Dist. Ct. (no. dist.) Ill. 1977; CPA, Ill. Ptnr. Holleb & Coff, Chgo. Mem. planned giving adv. coun. Chgo. Symphony Orch.; mem. planned giving com. Am. Technion Soc.; mem. planned giving steering com. City of Hope. Mem. Chgo. Bar Assn. (exec. com., Cook County Probate Ct. rules and forms com., mem. legis. com., mem. probate practice com. 1991, mem. trust law com., chmn. estate planning com., mem. young lawyers sect. 1983-85), Chgo. Estate Planning Coun., Com.-Agy./Ct. Sr. Citizen Issues, Jewish Fedn. Chgo. (chair profl. adv. com.). Office: Holleb & Coff 55 E Monroe St Ste 4100 Chicago IL 60603-5803

LORCH, MARISTELLA DE PANIZZA (MRS. INAMA VON BRUNNENWALD), Romance languages educator, writer, lecturer; b. Bolzano, Italy, Dec. 8, 1919; came to U.S., 1947, naturalized, 1951; d. Gino and Giuseppina (Cristoforetti) de Panizza Tuama von Brunnenwald; m. Claude Bové, Feb. 10, 1944 (div. 1955); 1 child, Claudia; m. Edgar R. Lorch, Mar. 25, 1956; children: Lavinia Edgarda, Donatella Livia. Ed., Liceo Classico, Merano, 1929-37; Dott. in Lettere e Filosofia, U. Rome, 1942; DHL (hon.), Lehman Coll., CUNY, 1993. Prof. Latin and Greek Liceo Virgilio, Rome, 1941-44; assoc. prof. Italian and German Coll. St. Elizabeth, Convent Station, N.J., 1947-51; faculty Barnard Coll., 1951-90, prof., 1967—, chmn. dept., 1951—, chmn. medieval and renaissance program, 1972-86; founder, dir. Ctr. for Internat. Scholarly Exch., Barnard Coll., 1980-90; dir. Casa Italiana, Columbia U., 1969-76, chmn. exec. com. Italian studies, 1980-90, founding dir. Italian Acad. Advanced Studies in Am., 1991-96, dir. emerita, 1996—. Author: Critical edit. L. Valla, De vero falsoque bono, Bari, 1970, (with W. Ludwig) critical edit. Michaelida, (with K. Hieatt), 1976, On Pleasure, 1981, A Defense of Life: L. Valla's Theory of Pleasure, 1985, (with E. Grassi) Folly and Insanity in Renaissance Literature, 1986, (with F. Colombo, M. Spaziani, Sinisca) All' America, 1990; editor: Il Teatro Italiano del Renascimento, 1981, Humanism in Rome, 1983, La Scuola, New York, 1987; mem. editorial bd. Italian jour. Romanic Review; also articles on Renaissance lit. and theater. Chmn. Am. Ariosto Centennial Celebration, 1974; chmn. bd. trustees La Scuola N.Y., 1986-91; trustee Lycée Française de N.Y., 1986—. Decorated Cavaliere della Repubblica Italiana, 1973, Commendatore della Repubblica Italiana, 1988, Grande Ulfale della Repubblican Italiana, 1996; recipient AMITA award for Woman of Yr. in Italian Lit., 1973, Columbus '92 Countdown prize of excellence in humanities, 1990, Elen Cornaro award Sons of Italy Woman of Yr., 1990, Father Ford award, 1994. Mem. Medieval Acad. Am., Renaissance Soc. Am., Am. Assn. Tchrs. Italian, Am. Assn. Italian Studies (hon. pres. 1990-91), Internat. Assn. for Study of Italian Lit. (Am. rep., assoc. pres. 8th Congress 1973), Acad. Polit. Sci. (life), Pirandello Soc. (pres. 1972-78), Arcadia Acad. (Asteria Aretusa 1976). Home: 445 Riverside Dr New York NY 10027-6842

LORD, EVELYN MARLIN, former mayor; b. Melrose, Mass., Dec. 8, 1926; d. John Joseph and Mary Janette (Nourse) Marlin; m. Samuel Smith Lord Jr., Feb. 28, 1948; children: Steven Arthur, Jonathan Peter, Nathaniel Edward, Victoria Marlin, William Kenneth. BA, Boston U., 1948; MA, U. Del., 1956; JD, U. Louisville, 1969. Bar: Ky. 1969, U.S. Supreme Ct. 1973. Exec. dir. Block Blight Inc., Wilmington, Del., 1956-60; mem. Del. Senate, Dover, 1960-62; administrv. asst. county judge Jefferson County, Louisville, 1968-71; corr. No. Ireland News Jour. Co., Wilmington, 1972-74; legal adminstr. Orgain, Bell & Tucker, Beaumont, Tex., 1978-83; v.p. Tex. Commerce Bank, Beaumont, 1983-84; councilman City of Beaumont, 1980-82, mayor pro tem, 1982-84, mayor, 1990-94; tourism chmn. U.S. Conf. Mayors, 1994, mem. adv. bd., chmn. arts, culture and recreation, 1992-94; bd. dirs. Tex. Commerce Bank. Bd. dirs. Symphony Soc. S.E. Tex., 1990—, Beaumont Cmty. Found., 1990—, Lincoln Inst. Land Policy, Beaumont Pub. Schs. Found., Cmtys. in Schs.; trustee, pres. United Way, Beaumont, 1995, 97; exec. bd. Boy Scouts Am., Three Rivers, 1978-84, 89—; pres. Girl Scouts Am., Louisville, 1966-70, Tex. Energy Mus., 1996—; active Sister City Commn.; chmn. Ptnrs. for Children, Child Protective Svcs. Recipient Silver Beaver award Boy Scouts Am., Beaumont, 1979, Disting. Alumni award Boston U., 1983, Disting. Leadership award Nat. Assn. Leadership Orgns., Indpls., 1991, Labor-Mgmt. Pub. Sector award, 1991, Disting. Grad. award Leadership Beaumont, 1993, Rotary Svc. Above Self award, 1994; named Citizen of Yr., Sales and Mktg. Assn., 1990, Beaumont "Man of Yr.", 1993. Mem. LWV (Del. state pres. 1960-62, bd. dirs. Tex. 1978-80), Bus. and Profl. Women Assns. (Woman of Yr. 1983), 100 Club (pres. 1995—), Girl Scouts Am. (life), Rotary (hon.), Sigma Kappa (life), Phi Kappa Phi, Delta Kappa Gamma (hon.), Sigma Iota Epsilon (hon.). Avocations: writing, reading, African violets, genealogy. Home: 1240 Nottingham Ln Beaumont TX 77706-4316 *Basically - I believe in "blooming where you're planted". Life with my husband has taken me all over the world but we've always managed to be "at home" wherever we've been able to give a bit of ourselves.*

LORD, GEORGE DEFOREST, English educator; b. N.Y.C., Dec. 2, 1919; s. George deForest and Hazen (Symington) L.; m. Ruth Ellen du Pont, Mar.

22, 1947 (div. 1978); children: Pauline, George deForest Jr., Edith (dec.), Henry; m. Louise Robins Hendrix, 1978 (div. 1992); m. Marcia Adkisson Babbidge, 1993. BA, Yale U., 1942, PhD, 1951. Instr. English Yale U., New Haven, 1947-66, prof., 1966—; master Trumbull Coll., 1963-66, dir. directed studies, 1968-70, assoc. chmn. English dept., 1983-86; dir. Fiduciary Trust, N.Y., 1969-91; cons. PBS TV program Transformations of Myth Through Time, 1982-90; lectr. in field. Author: Homeric Renaissance: the "Odyssey" of George Chapman, 1956, Poems on Affairs of State, 1963, Andrew Mavell, Complete Poetry, 1968, rev. edit., 1985, Andrew Marvell: A Collection of Critical Essays, 1968, Anthology of Poems on Affairs of State, 1975, Heroic Mockery: Variations on Epic Themes from Homer to Joyce, 1977, Trials of the Self: Heroic Ordeals in the Epic Tradition, 1983, Classical Presences in Seventeenth-Century English Poetry, 1987 (Outstanding acad. book 1987 Choice mag.); gen. editor Poems on Affairs of State: Augustan Satirical Verse: 1660-1714, 7 vols., 1963-75; contbr. articles, revs. to acad. jours. Trustee Winterthur Mus., 1952-80, Mary Holmes Coll., West Point, Miss., 1971-80, Fair Haven Housing, 1972-78; trustee, advisor Outward Bound USA, 1977—; vestryman Calvary Episcopal Ch., Stonington, Conn., 1986-89. Morse fellow 1954-55, NEH sr. fellow, 1982. Mem. MLA, English Inst., Renaissance Soc. Am., Am. Acad. in Rome, The Century Assn. Home: 3 Diving St Stonington CT 06378-1405 Office: Yale U Dept English New Haven CT 06520

LORD, HAROLD WILBUR, electrical engineer, electronics consultant; b. Eureka, Calif., Aug. 20, 1905; s. Charles Wilbur and Rossina Camilla (Hansen) L.; B.S., Calif. Inst. Tech., 1926; m. Doris Shirley Huff, July 25, 1928; children—Joann Shirley (Mrs. Carl Cook Disbrow), Alan Wilbur, Nancy Louise (Mrs. Leslie Crandall), Harold Wayne. With GE, Schenectady, 1926-66, electronics engr., 1960-66; pvt. cons. engr., Mill Valley, Calif., 1966-90. Coffin Found. award Gen. Electric Co., 1933, GE Inventors award, 1966. Fellow IEEE (life, tech. v.p. 1962, Centennial medal 1984, IEEE Magnetics Soc. 1984 Achievement award). Contbr. articles to profl. jours. Patentee in field. Home: 1565 Golf Course Dr Rohnert Park CA 94928-5638

LORD, JERE JOHNS, retired physics educator; b. Portland, Oreg., Jan. 3, 1922; s. Percy Samuel and Hazel Marie (Worstel) L.; m. Miriam E. Hart, Dec. 30, 1947; children—David, Roger, Douglas. Physicist U. Calif. Radiation Lab., Berkeley, 1942-46; research asso. U. Chgo., 1950-52; asst. prof. physics U. Wash., Seattle, 1952-57; assoc. prof. U. Wash., 1957-62, prof., 1962-92, prof. emeritus, 1992—. Fellow AAAS, Am. Phys. Soc.; mem. Am. Assn. Physics Tchrs. Home: 720 Seneca St Apt 1004 Seattle WA 98101-2761 Office: U Wash Dept Physics Box 351560 Seattle WA 98195-1560

LORD, JERE WILLIAMS, JR., retired surgeon; b. Balt., Oct. 12, 1910; s. Jere Williams and Evelyn (Pope) L.; m. June Harrah, Dec. 6, 1941; children: Harrah, Jere W. III, Lonna; m. Margaret Humphreys Graham, Feb. 13, 1971. A.B., Princeton U., 1933; M.D., Johns Hopkins U., 1937. Diplomate Am. Bd. of Surgery. Intern Surgery N.Y. Hosp., Cornell U. Med. Coll., 1937-38, intern pathology, 1938-39, asst. resident surgeon, 1939-44, resident surgeon, 1944; vis. surgeon. 4th Div., Bellevue Hosp.; cons. surgeon U. Hosp.; prof. clin. surgery N.Y.U.; instr. surgery and surgeon to out-patients N.Y. Hosp., Cornell U. Med. Coll., 1944-45; mem. med. bd. Doctors Hosp.; attending surgeon Manhattan State Hosp., 1945-48; cons. surgeon Greenwich (Conn.) Hosp., Hackensack Hosp., Paterson Gen. Hospital, Elizabeth Horton Meml. Hosp., Middletown., N.Y., Norwalk Hosp., Conn., Central Suffolk Hosp., Riverhead, N.Y., Arden Hill Hosp., Goshen, N.Y., St. Agnes Hosp., White Plains, N.Y., St. Luke's Hosp., Newburgh, N.Y., Putnam Community Hosp., Carmel, N.Y.; chief vascular surgery Columbus Hosp., N.Y.C. Awarded 3d essay prize; Am. Urol. Assn., 1942. Fellow ACS; mem. N.Y. Gastroent. Assn. (pres. 1956), Am. Assn. Surgery of Trauma, Soc. for Vascular Surgery, N.Y. Soc. for Cardiovascular Surgery (pres. 1957-59), N.Y. Soc. for Thoracic Surgery (pres. 1961-62), N.Y. Heart Assn. (pres. 1957-59), N.Y. Surg. Soc., Eastern Surg. Soc. (pres. 1982), Am., Pan-Pacific, So. surg. assns., Internat. Cardiovascular Soc., James IV Assn. Surgeons (sec. 1967-75). Democrat. Episcopalian. Clubs: Ivy (Princeton); Pithotomy (Johns Hopkins); Bedford Golf and Tennis. Home: Greenwich Rd Bedford NY 10506

LORD, JEROME EDMUND, education administrator, writer, businessman; b. Waterbury, Conn., Dec. 24, 1935; s. James Andrew and Mary Frances (Hayes) L.; m. Eleanor Louise Collins, Apr. 22, 1967; children: Hayes Alexander FitzWarin, Stavely Hampston deHodnet, Savile Collins de Montenay, Dorian Warfield d'Amours, Wallis Jennings dePantulf. BA, Georgetown U., 1957; MA, Boston Coll., 1962, Columbia U., 1963; PhD, Columbia U., 1969; diploma (hon.), U. Madrid, 1962. Tchr. The Taft Sch. Peekskill Mil. Acad., 1957-60; editor, lang. recs. supr. Allyn and Bacon Inc., Boston, 1961-62; adminstrv. assoc. internat. programs and services Tchrs. Coll. Columbia U., N.Y.C., 1963-65, assoc. in higher edn., 1965-66; asst. prof. edn., exec. asst. to dean acad. devel. CUNY, 1965-67, assoc. prof. edn., exec. asst. to vice chancellor exec. office, 1967-69; dir. rsch. Ford and Carnegie Study of Fed. Politics of Edn. Brookings Instn., Washington, 1969-70; program officer Nat. Ctr. for Ednl. Tech., U.S. Dept. Edn., Washington, 1971-73; sr. assoc. Nat. Inst. Edn., Washington, 1973-86, Office Ednl. Rsch. and Improvement, Dept. Edn., Washington, 1986—; pres. Jerome Lord Enterprises, Inc., Washington; advisor to vol. edn. policy group Office Dir. Def. Edn., U.S. Dept. Def., 1975-76; chmn. Fed. Interagy. Panel for Rsch. on Adulthood; mem. World Affairs Coun., Washington, other various nat. panels and coms.; cons. in field; lectr. in field. Playwright: Teresa, 1971, The Election, 1972, Audition!, 1973, Decent Exposure, 1979, Amazing Grace, 1987, Heads You Win, 1991, Making Believe, 1996, An Only Child, 1997; author: Perfectly Proper, 1993, Teacher Training Abroad: New Realities, 1993, Adult Literacy Programs: Guidelines for Effectiveness, 1995; contbr. articles to profl. jours. Trustee St. John's Child Devel. Ctr., Washington, 1978-83; mem. nat. bd. sponsors Protestant and Orthodox Ctr., N.Y. World's Fair, 1964; mem. adv. bd. N.Y.C. Urban Corps, 1965-69, others; mem. coun. of friends Folger Shakespeare Libr.; sponsor Nat. Symphony Orch.; mem., donor reception rooms Dept. State. Named Coakley scholar, 1953-57, M.T. Runyan scholar, 1967-68; fellow W.T. Kellogg Found., 1968-69, Rinehart Found., 1970-71, others. Mem. Pilgrim Soc., Soc. Friends St. George's and Desc. Knights of Garter, Friends of Blair House, Pilgrims of the U.S., World Affairs Coun., City Tavern Club, Met. Club, Kappa Delta Pi, Phi Delta Pi, Eta Sigma Phi. Episcopalian. Avocations: writing, historic preservation, music, art history, architecture. Office: 555 New Jersey Ave NW Washington DC 20208-0001

LORD, KATHLEEN VIRGINIA, fundraising executive; b. Lakewood, Ohio, Feb. 11, 1934; d. Wallace Matthew and Ernestine (McNutt) Anderson; m. Donald Charles Lord, Feb. 9, 1954 (div. June 1978); children: Marita Beth, Sean Christopher. Student, Oberlin Coll., 1951-52; BS in Theater and Music with honors, Tex. Woman's U., 1972, MA in English and Drama, 1974; postgrad., Ohio U., 77, 78, 79, 80. Advt. supr. Cleve. Plain Dealer, 1954-61; devel. dir. Denton (Tex.) Christian Pre-Sch., 1970-73; asst. prof. Unity (Maine) Coll., 1973-80; dir. alumni rels. and ann. fund Ashland (Ohio) U., 1980-85; dir. devel. Pa. Stage Co., Allentown, 1985-86; dir. devel. and pub. rels. Singing City Choir, Phila., 1986-88; pvt. practice cons. for philanthropy and pub. rels. Phila., 1988-92; dir. major gifts/planned giving Luther Care, Lititz, Pa., 1992—; contralto Dallas Opera Co., 1964-73. Author: (drama) Once There Was A Camelot, 1973. Pres. Cen. Pa. Luth. Devel. Consortium, 1995-97; bd. dirs., pres. Opera Outreach, Harrisburg, Pa., 1997—. Coun. Advancement and Support of Edn. scholar, 1981. Mem. Nat. Soc. Fund Raising Execs. (cert., Franklin Form com., membership com. presenter 1986-97), Ohio Conf. Women in Minorities in Higher Edn. (exec. com. 1983-84, adv. com.), Ind. Coll. Adminstrs. Assn. of Ohio (bd. dirs., exec. com. 1982-83), Coun. Advancement and Support Edn. (presenter, moderator 1982-83). Lutheran. Avocation: singing. Office: Luther Care East Region 600 E Main St Lititz PA 17543-2202

LORD, M. G., writer; b. La Jolla, Calif., Nov. 18; d. Charles Carroll and Mary (Pfister) L.; m. Glenn Horowitz, May 19, 1985. BA, Yale U., 1977. Reporter N.Y. Bur. Wall St. Jour., N.Y.C., summer 1976; editl. artist Chgo. Tribune, 1977-78; editl. cartoonist, columnist Newsday, N.Y.C., 1978-94; cartoons syndicated L.A. Times Syndicate, 1984-89; column syndicated Copley News Svc., 1989-94. Author: Mean Sheets, 1982, Prig Tales, 1990, Forever Barbie: The Unauthorized Biography of a Real Doll, 1994. Resident humanities fellow U. Mich., 1986-87. Office: care Eric Simonoff Janklow & Nesbit Assoc 598 Madison Ave New York NY 10022

LORD, MARION MANNS, retired academic director; b. Fort Huachuca, Ariz., Dec. 17, 1914; d. George Wiley and Annie May (Pellett) Manns; children: Caroline L. Gross (dec.), Polly Steadman, Jane Chapin Humphries. BS, Northwestern U., 1936; MEd, Harvard U., 1962; MA, U. Wis., 1968, PhD, 1968. Columnist, exec. sec. Boston Am., 1936-38; dean women, dir. counseling Henniker, N.H., 1962-64; psychology tchr. Cen. Mich. U., Washington, 1975-79; higher edn. adminstr. U.S. Office Edn., Washington, 1968-75; dean faculty Borough of Manhattan Community Coll., CUNY, 1975-79, Cottey Coll., Nevada, Mo., 1979-80; English tchr. high sch., 1982-84, realtor, 1984-90; asst. dir. Franklin Pierce Coll., Concord, N.H., 1992; mem. faculty N.H. Coll., 1994-95; ednl. cons. N.H. Coll. and Univ. Coun., 1974-80, David W. Smith & Assocs., Washington, U.S. Office Edn., 1975-80. Editor, contbr.: A Survey of Women's Experiences and Perceptions Concerning Barriers to Their Continuing Education, Review of the Literature. State rep. Gen. Ct. N.H., 1957-62; active various polit. campaigns; active in past numerous civic orgns. E.B. Fred fellow, 1964-68; Breadloaf Coll. scholar, 1936, Northwestern U. scholar, 1933-36. Mem. Am. Psychol. Assn., Pi Lambda Theta. Republican. Avocations: gardening, hiking, writing, reading. Home: 169 Havenwood Concord NH 03301 Office: 33 Christian Ave Ste 410 Concord NH 03301

LORD, MARVIN, apparel company executive; b. N.Y.C., Sept. 22, 1937; s. Harry and Irene (Taub) L.; m. Joan Simon, Aug. 5, 1961; children—Elisa Anne, Michael Harris. B.S., Long Island U., Bklyn., 1959. Mdse. mgr. Oxford Industries, Inc., N.Y.C., 1964-66, gen. mdse. mgr., 1966-70, v.p., gen. mgr., 1970-73; pres. Holbrook Co., Inc. Div Oxford Industries, Inc., N.Y.C., 1970-85; pres., chief exec. officer Crystal Brands, Inc.-Youthwear Group, N.Y.C., 1985—; pres. Cluett Shirtmakers, N.Y.C., 1988—, M.L. Enterprises, Roslyn Heights, N.Y., 1990—; pres., chief oper. officer Sanyo Fashion House, N.Y.C., 1991—; pres., CEO MAternity Resources Inc., N.Y.C., 1994—; exec. v.p. E.A. Hughes & Co., N.Y.C., 1996—. Chmn. Fathers Day Coun., N.Y.C., 1984—. Recipient Disting. Alumni award L.I. U., 1987. Mem. Mens Fashion Assn., Young Menswear Assn. Jewish. Avocation: tennis. Home: 53 Parkway Dr Roslyn Heights NY 11577-2705 Office: E A Hughes & Co 146 E 37th St New York NY 10016-3108

LORD, ROY ALVIN, retired publisher; b. Middletown, Ohio, July 2, 1918; s. Arthur Edwin and Mary Marie (Bell) L.; m. Elizabeth Frances Powell, Nov. 1, 1941; children—Thomas A., Frances A., William F. B.A., Ohio Wesleyan U., 1941; postgrad., Harvard U. Bus. Sch., 1962. With advt. sales Time Inc., N.Y.C. and Chgo., 1946-55; upper midwest mgr. advt. sales Time Inc., Mpls., 1955-62; nat. advt. sales mgr. Time Inc., N.Y.C., 1963-68; pres. ML&A Inc., N.Y.C., 1968-73; v.p. In-Store Publs., N.Y.C., 1973-74; pres. The Weekend Co., Inc., 1974-76; pub. A.D. Publs., Inc., N.Y.C., from 1976. Bd. dirs. Minn. Orchestral Assn., 1957-62; Minn. state chmn. Crusade for Freedom, 1960-62. Served with AC U.S. Army, 1942-45. Presbyterian.

LORD, WALTER, author; b. Balt., Oct. 8, 1917; s. John Walter and Henrietta Mactier (Hoffman) L. B.A., Princeton U., 1939; LL.B., Yale U., 1946. Editor bus. information services, 1946-53, engaged in advt., 1953-56, civilian aide to sec. army for So. N.Y. area, 1964-66. Author: A Night to Remember, 1955, Day of Infamy, 1957, The Good Years, 1960, A Time to Stand, 1961, Peary at the Pole, 1963, The Past That Would Not Die, 1965, Incredible Victory, 1967, The Dawn's Early Light, 1972, Lonely Vigil, 1977, The Miracle of Dunkirk, 1982, The Night Lives On, 1986; editor: The Fremantle Diary, 1954. Bd. dirs. Union Settlement, N.Y.C., 1959—, chmn., 1962-64; bd. dirs. Mcpl. Art Soc., N.Y.C., 1958-67; trustee N.Y. Soc. Library, 1963—, Mus. City N.Y., 1964-72, N.Y. Hist. Soc., 1965—; trustee Soc. Am. Historians, 1972—, pres., 1981-84; trustee Gilman Sch., Balt., 1962-80, Council Authors Guild, Inc., 1966-72, Coun. Authors League, 1972-83, sec., 1975-80; trustee N.Y. State Maritime Mus., 1968-79, South St. Seaport Mus., 1980—, Ocean Liner Mus., 1982—; mem. adv. bd. Protect Historic Am. Mem. Soc. Am. Historians, Authors Guild, ASCAP. Clubs: 14 W. Hamilton St. (Balt.); Century Assn. (N.Y.C.); Metropolitan (Washington).

LORD, WILLIAM GROGAN, financial holding company executive; b. Hearne, Tex., Oct. 21, 1914; s. Otis G. and Erminee G. Lord; m. Dorothy Nell Manning, Dec. 28, 1938 (dec.); children: Roger Griffin, Sharon Lord Caskey; m. Betty Fowler Hendrick, May 24, 1986. L.H.D. (hon.), Southwestern U., Georgetown, Tex., 1967. Sr. chmn. bd. dirs. TCC Industries, Inc. (formerly TeleCom Corp.), Austin, 1958—; sr. chmn. First Tex. Bancorp, Inc., Georgetown, 1971—; bd. dirs. Frozen Food Express Industries, Inc., Dallas; sr. chmn. bd. 1st Tex. Bancorp, Inc., Georgetown; mem., chmn. State Securities Bd., 1971-83. Trustee, mem. exec. com., vice chmn. bd. Southwestern U., 1958. Served to 1st lt. F.A. AUS, World War II. Decorated Purple Heart, Air medal with 4 oak leaf clusters; named Most Worthy Citizen Georgetown C. of C., 1971. Mem. Nat. Assn. Small Bus. Investment Cos. (past pres.), Regional Assn. Small Bus. Investment Cos, Tex. Research League, Tex. Philosophical Soc. Republican. Methodist. Clubs: River Oaks Country (Houston); (Austin, Tex.), Headliners (Austin, Tex.); St. Anthony (San Antonio). Office: PO Box 649 Georgetown TX 78627-0649

LORDO, PHILLIP JAMES, telecommunications professional; b. Berea, Ohio, July 6, 1959; s. Albert B. and Rose M. (Mazzei) L. BBA, Cleve. State U., 1983, M of Computer and Info. Sci., 1991. Staff Def. Investigative Svc., Dept. Def., Cleve., 1978-80; tech. sales support mgr. Kanex U.S.A., Cleve., 1984-86; proces control engr. Allen-Bradley, Highland Heights, Ohio, 1986; data processing cons. Std. Oil, Cleve., 1986; tech. cons. AT&T, Cleve., 1986-88; tech. instr. AT&T Gen. Bus. Systems, Cin., 1988-91; complex support mgr. AT&T Ohio Franchise, Columbus, 1991-93, AT&T Nat. Info. Infrastructure, Holmdel, N.J., 1993-96; product mgr. AT&T Electronic Commerce Svcs., Lincroft, N.J., 1996—. Del. People to People Internat., Peoples Republic of China, 1992, Berlin, Germany, 1994. Mem. IEEE, Assn. for Computing Machinery, Inst. of Mgmt. Sci./Ops. Rsch. Soc. Am. Avocations: scuba, photography, aquarology.

LORD OF CURSONS See RAWL, ARTHUR JULIAN

LORD ROSENTHAL, SHIRLEY, cosmetics magazine executive, novelist; b. London, Aug. 28; came to U.S., 1971; d. Francis J. and Mabel Florence (Williamson) Stringer; m. Cyril Lord; m. David Anderson; m. A.M. Rosenthal, June 10, 1987; children: Mark, Richard. Matriculation, S.W. Essex Coll., London, 1948. Reporter London Daily Mirror; fiction editor Woman's Own, 1950-53; features editor Good Taste mag., 1953-56; features, fiction editor Woman and Beauty, 1956-59; women's editor Star Evening newspaper, 1959-60, London Evening Standard, 1960-63, London Evening News, 1963-68; beauty editor Harper's Bazaar, London, 1963-71, N.Y.C., 1971-73; beauty, health editor Vogue mag., Condé Nast Publs., N.Y.C., 1973-75; v.p. corp. rels. Helena Rubinstein, N.Y.C., 1975-80; beauty dir. Vogue mag., 1980-94, contbg. editor, 1994—; chairwoman media coun. The Am. Acad. Dermatology, 1995—. Syndicated Field columnist on beauty, health; author 3 beauty books; also novels: Golden Hill, 1982; One of My Very Best Friends, (Lit. Guild Selection), 1985; Faces, 1989; My Sister's Keeper, 1993. City commr. Craigavon City, No. Ireland, 1963-68. Office: 140 E 45th St Fl 38 New York NY 10017-3144

LORE, MARTIN MAXWELL, lawyer; b. Milw., June 13, 1914; s. Michael and Jean (Dinerstein) L.; m. Doris Silver, Mar. 19, 1944; children: Amy L. Kovner, Dr. Cathy Jo. BA, U. Wis., 1934, LLB, 1936; LLM, Harvard, 1937; BCS, Strayer Coll. Accountancy, 1939. Bar: Wis. 1936, N.Y. 1946, D.C. 1947, Fla. 1977, U.S. Supreme Ct. 1939; CPA, D.C. Assoc. Rubin, Zabel & Ruppa, Milw., 1936-37; with Office Undersec. Treasury, 1937-38; spl. atty. office chief counsel, bur. IRS, 1938-40; trial counsel IRS (New Eng. div. tech. staff), 1940-42, IRS (N.Y. div.), 1945-47; tax counsel S.J. Foosaner, Newark, 1947-48; pvt. law practice N.Y.C., 1948-72; mem. firm Zissu Lore Halper & Robson, N.Y.C., 1972-76; counsel Zissu Lore Halper & Robson, 1976-80; ptnr. Lore & Levy, N.Y.C., 1981—; pres. bd. Fed. Tax Forum, Inc.; lectr. Tax Workshop, 1953-55, law sch. St. John's U., 1954, Fairleigh Dickinson U., 1955-56; specialist fed. tax matters, lectr. taxation NYU, 1946-50, 65, Practising Law Inst., 1947-48, Tax Inst., 1948, Pa. State Coll., 1949-50, U. W.Va., U. San Francisco, 1951, SUNY, Stony Brook, 1978-79; tax cons. Med. Econs.; pres., dir. Estate Planning Coun. N.Y.C.; part-time employee Melnik & Karan, Milw., 1933-36. Author: The Administration of The Federal Income Tax Through the United States Board of Tax Appeals, 1937, How to Win a Tax Case, 1955, Thin Capitalization, 1958; co-editor: Jour. of Taxation; chmn. bd. editors: How To Work with the Internal Revenue Code of 1954; contbr. articles to legal and accounting jours. Lt. comdr. Office Gen. Counsel, USNR, 1942-44. Mem. ABA (com. income taxation estates and trusts), N.Y. State Bar Assn., Assn. Bar City of N.Y. (taxation com., com. on trusts, estates and surrogate's cts.), FBA (chmn. com. fed. taxation), AICPA (sec. fed. tax lawyers com.), D.C. Accts., County Lawyers Assn. (taxation com.), Seawane Club (bd. govs.), Lawyers Club (N.Y.C.), Harvard Club (N.Y.C.), Barristers (Washington). Home: 46 Broome Ave Atlantic Beach NY 11509-1214 Office: Lore & Levy 1 Madison Ave New York NY 10010-3603

LORELL, MONTE, newspaper editor. Managing editor Sports, USA Today, Arlington, Va. Office: USA Today 1000 Wilson Blvd Arlington VA 22209-3901

LORELLI, MICHAEL KEVIN, consumer products and services executive; b. N.Y.C., Apr. 17, 1951; s. Domenic and Effie (Stankevich) L.; m. Judith Bryant; children: Karen, Elizabeth. BE, NYU, 1972, MBA in Mktg., 1973. Dir. mktg. Clairol Co., N.Y.C., 1973-81, v.p., gen. mgr. divsn. Almay cosmetics, 1983-84; v.p., gen. mgr. internat. div. Playtex, Stamford, Conn., 1981-84; v.p. mktg. Apple Computer, Cupertino, Calif., 1984-85; exec. v.p. Pepsi-Cola Co., Somers, N.Y., 1985-88; pres. Pepsi-Cola East, Somers, N.Y., 1989-92, Pizza Hut Internat., 1993-95; pres. America's divsn. Tambrands, Inc., White Plains, N.Y., 1995-96; pres, CEO MobileComm, Ridgefield Park, N.J., 1996—. Author: (children's book) Traveling Again, Dad?. Bd. dirs. MobileMedia Corp., Trident Internat., Inc., Closure Inc., Keep Am. Beautiful, Rosenbluth Travel, Am. Health Found.; trustee Sarah Lawrence Coll., Madison Sq. Boys and Girls Club. Republican. Roman Catholic. Avocations: flying, golf, running. Office: MobileComm 65 Challenger Rd Ridgefield Park NJ 07660-2104

LOREN, DONALD PATRICK, naval officer; b. N.Y.C., Mar. 17, 1952; s. Nicholas A. and Helen T. (Carrado) L.; m. Maureen M. Lynch, Jan. 12, 1991. BS in Ops. Analysis, U.S. Naval Acad., 1974; MS in Edn., Old Dominion U., 1983; postgrad., Harvard U., 1993-94, MIT, 1994-95. Commd. ens. USN, 1974, advanced through grades to capt., 1994, combat sys. officer, Destroyer Squadron Thirty-One, 1978; ops. officer USS Peterson, 1979-80; ops. and readiness officer Destroyer Squadron Two Staff, 1981-82; asst. chief of staff for comms. Cruiser Destroyer Group Eight Staff, 1983-85; exec. officer USS John Hancock, 1985-86; flag sec. to comdr. in chief U.S. Naval Forces, Europe, 1986-88; NATO policy officer Strategic Plans and Policy Directory, Joint Staff, 1989-91; comdg. officer USS Elrod FFG-55, 1991-93; doctrine devel. officer Naval Doctrine Command, 1993; fed. exec. fellow Ctr. for Internat. Affairs Harvard U., Cambridge, Mass., 1993-94; profl. staff mem. Ind. Commn. on Roles and Missions of Armed Forces, 1993-94; comdr. Destroyer Squadron Twenty-eight, Norfolk, Va., 1995-97; dep. dir. strategy and policy divsn. Office the the Chief of Naval Ops., 1997—. Author: Shape Up! A Shipboard Program for Physical Fitness, 1981; contbr. articles to profl. publs. Mem. Phi Kappa Phi, Sigma Iota Epsilon. Avocations: jogging, weight training, classical music, ballet, opera. Home: 6201 Littlethorpe Ln Alexandria VA 22315 Office: Dep Dir Strategy and Policy Divsn Office of the Chief of Naval Ops Washington DC 20350-2000

LOREN, MARY ROONEY, controller; b. Monaghan, Ireland, Nov. 18, 1939; came to U.S., 1957; d. Peter Paul and Mary Alice (McKenna) Rooney; m. Thomas Leroy Loren, Aug. 22, 1959; children: Mary Teresa, Aileen Frances, Susan Marie. AAS in Acctg., Adirondack C.C., 1976; BS in Bus., Skidmore Coll., 1979; postgrad., SUNY, Plattsburgh, 1995—. Acctg. supr. Neles-Jamesbury, Glens Falls, N.Y., 1979-88; contr. Queensbury Hotel, Glens Falls, 1988-89; mgmt. acct. Ahlstrom Screen Pl., Glens Falls, 1989-92; mill contr. Hollingsworth & Vose, Greenwich, N.Y., 1993—; owner Heritage Heirlooms. Treas. Every Woman's Coun., Glens Falls, 1985—; lectr., eucharistic min. St. Michael's Roman Cath. Ch., South Glens Falls, 1980—. Mem. Inst. Mgmt. Accts. (corp., acad. dir. 1993-94, pres. 1992-93, Achievement award 1992-93, Cmty. Svc. award 1993). Republican. Avocations: golf, hiking, genealogical research, travel.

LOREN, SOPHIA, actress; b. Rome, Sept. 20, 1934; d. Riccardo Scicolone and Romilda Villani; m. Carlo Ponti, Apr. 12, 1967; children: Carlo Ponti, Edoardo. Student, Scuole Magistrali Superiori. Films include E Arrivato l'Accordatore, 1951, Africa sotto i Mari, La Favorita, La Tratta Delle Bianche, 1952, Aida, Tempi Nostri, Ci Troviamo in Gellera, La Domenica Della Buona Genti, Il Paese dei Campanelli, Un Giorno in Pretura, Due Notti con Cleopatra, Pelegrini d'Amore, Attila, Carosello Napoletano, 1953, Miseria e Nobilta, Gold of Naples, Woman of the River, Too Bad She's Bad (Best Actress award Buenos Aires Festival), 1954, Lucky To Be A Woman, Sign of Venus, The Millers Wife, Scandal in Sorrento, 1955, Pride and Passion, Boy on a Dolphin, Legend of The Lost, 1957, Desire Under the Elms, Houseboat, The Key (Best Actress award Japan), 1958, That Kind of Woman, Black Orchid, 1959 (Best Actress Venice Festival, David Di Donatello award Italy, Victoire Popularity award France), Heller in Pink Tights (Best Actress Rapallo Festival Italy), It Started in Naples, A Breath of Scandal, The Millionaires, 1960, Two Women, (11 Best Actress awards including Oscar, Hollywood, Di Donatello award, Cannes Film Festival, N.Y. Critics, Golden Globe, Brit. Film Acad., others from Ireland, Japan, Belgium, Spain, France, W. Ger., also other awards), El Cid, Madame, Bocaccio 70, 1961, The Condemned of Altona, Five Miles to Midnight, 1962, Yesterday, Today and Tomorrow, (Best Actress Di Donatello award, Golden Globe award), 1963, The Fall of the Roman Empire, Marriage Italian Style, 1964 (Best Actress Di Donatello award, Golden Globe award, Alexander Korda award Brit. Film Inst., others), Operation Crossbow, Lady L, Judith, 1965, Arabesque, A Countess From Hong Kong, 1966, Happily Ever After, Ghosts, Italian Style (Best Fgn. Actress Diploma USSR), 1967, More Than A Miracle, (Ramo d'Oro award Italy, other awards), 1968, Sunflower (Best Actress Di Donatello award), 1969, The Priest's Wife, 1970, Lady Liberty, White Sister, 1971, Man of La Mancha, 1972, The Voyage (Di Donatello award), 1973, Brief Encounter, The Verdict, 1974, The Cassandra Crossing, A Special Day, 1977, Firepower, 1978, Brass Target, 1979, Blood Feud, 1981, Grumpier Old Men, 1995, Messages, 1996; TV film appearances include Sophia Loren: Her Own Story, 1980, Angela, 1982, Aurora, 1985, Mother Courage, 1986, The Fortunate Pilgrim (Best Actress of Yr. for TV mini-series), 1987, La Ciociara, 1989, Ready to Wear (Prêt-à-Porter), 1994. Recipient numerous awards including Nastro d'Argento, Italy, 14 Bambi and Bravo Popularity awards, Fed. Republic Germany, 3 Prix Uilenspigoel Fiamingo award, Belgium, Popularity awards Am. Legion, Tex. Cinema Exhibitors, 4 Snosiki Popularity awards, Finland, 2 Best Actress awards Bengal Film Journalists Assn., India, Box-Office Favourite Medal, Italy, Helene Curtis award, U.S.A., Simpatia Popularity award, Italy, Rudolph Valentino Screen Svcs. award, Italy, Best Actress award Moscow Film Festival, Hon. Acad. award, 1990; named Most Popular Actress in Italy. Office: Via di Villa Ada 10, Rome I-00199, Italy*

LORENTZ, WILLIAM BEALL, pediatrician; b. Glenville, W.Va., July 8, 1937; s. William Beall and Mary Gay (Garrett) L.; m. Anne Lynne Hickman, June 20, 1960 (div. Aug. 30, 1977); children: Pamela Lynne, Lisa Anne, William Chad; m. Suzy Vernice Gibson, Sept. 5, 1977. BA, W.Va. U., 1959; MD, Jefferson Med. Coll., 1963. Diplomate Am. Bd. Pediatrics, Sub-board of Pediatric Nephrology. Internship Harrisburg (Pa.) Polyclinic Hosp., 1963-64, resident in pediatrics, 1964-65; resident in pediatrics U. Tex. Med. Br., Galveston, Tex., 1965-67; med. corp USN, Quantico (Va.) Naval Hosp., 1967-69; fellow in renal physiology U. N.C. Sch. of Medicine, Chapel Hill, 1969-71; asst. prof. pediatrics U. Tex. Med. Br., Galveston, 1971-74, Bowman Gray Sch. Medicine, Winston-Salem, N.C., 1974-75; assoc. prof. pediatrics Bowman Gray Sch. Medicine, Winston-Salem, 1975-81; prof. pediatrics Bowman Grey Sch. Medicine, Winston-Salem, 1981—; assoc. chief staff N.C. Bapt. Hosp., 1991—; med. dir. Medcost, Winston-Salem, 1989—; cons. physician Allegheny Regional Hosp., Low Moor, Va., 1988; pres. Piedmont Med. Found., Winston-Salem, 1983-88. Contbr. articles to profl. jours. Lt. comdr. USN, 1966-69. Mem. Soc. for Pediatric Rsch., Am. Pediatric Soc., Am. Acad. Pediatrics, Am. Soc. Nephrology, Am. Soc. for Pediatric Nephrology. Democrat. Presbyterian. Avocation: running. Office: Bowman Gray Sch Medicine 300 S Hawthorne Rd Winston Salem NC 27157-0002

LORENZ, ANNE PARTEE, special education educator, consultant; b. Nashville, Aug. 6, 1943; d. McCullough and Mary Elizabeth (Shemwell) Partee; m. Philip Jack Lorenz, Jr., Nov. 26, 1970; stepchildren: Brenna Ellen, Philip Jack III. Student, Rhodes Coll., 1961-63, 64; BS, George Peabody Coll., 1966; postgrad., Ga. State U., 1967-68; MS, George Peabody Coll., 1969. Clerk Tenn. State Libr. Archives, Nashville, 1963-64; tchr. learning disabilities Howard Sch., Atlanta, 1966-68; prin., tchr. learning disabilities Sewanee (Tenn.) Learning Ctr., 1969-78; tchr. learning disabilities Clark Meml. Sch., Winchester, Tenn., 1978-79; tutor, cons. learning disabilities Anne Partee Lorenz Tutoring Consultation Svc., Sewanee, 1979—; psychol. cons. U. of South, 1974-78; cons. St. Andrew's-Sewanee Sch., Tenn., 1980—; vol. presenter Effective Adv. for Citizens With Handicaps, Inc. workshop, 1986. Active Coun. for Exceptional Children, 1968-79; treas. Franklin County Dem. Party; sec. Sewanee Precinct Dem. Party, 1974-76; del. dist. and state Dem. Conf.; judge John M. Templeton Laws of Life Essay Contest, 1995; vol. Cordelle-Lorenz Obs., U. of the South, 19706; bd. dirs. Franklin County Adult Activities Ctr., 1979-82; vol. presenter E.A.C.H., Inc. (Effective Advocacy for Citizens with Handicaps), 1986. Recipient letter of commendation Gov. Tenn., 1974. Mem. Tenn. LWV (pres., bd. dirs.), Franklin County LWV (pres.), Learning Disabilities Assn. Tenn. (1st Tchr. Yr. 1975), Children and Adults with Attention Deficit Disorders. Avocations: wild flowers, bird and wild animal watching, walking, reading, crocheting. Home and Office: 390 Onteora Ln Sewanee TN 37375-2639

LORENZ, HUGO ALBERT, retired insurance executive, consultant; b. Elmhurst, Ill., July 5, 1926; s. Hugo E. and Linda T. (Trampel) L. B.S., Northwestern U., 1949; LL.B., Harvard U., 1952. Bar: Ill. 1954. Mem. patent staff Bell Telephone Labs., Murray Hill, N.J., 1952-53; atty. First Nat. Bank Chgo., 1954-58; gen. counsel N.Am. Life Ins. Co. of Chgo., 1958-73; dir., v.p., gen. counsel, sec. Globe Life Ins. Co., Chgo., 1973-95; v.p. Union Fidelity Life Ins. Co., Chgo., 1993-96; sec. Gt. Equity Life Ins. Co., Chgo., 1977-80, Pat Ryan & Assos. Inc., Va. Surety Co., Chgo., 1977-96. Bd. dirs. Sr. Ctrs. Met. Chgo., 1977-93, pres., 1983-85; trustee Hull House Assn., 1983-88. With USNR, 1944-46. Mem. ABA, Assn. Life Ins. Counsel, Connoisseurs Internat (bd. dirs. 1972—, pres. 1980-95), Internat. Wine and Food Soc. Chgo. (gov. and oenologist 1980—). Unitarian. Home: 950 A N Clark St Chicago IL 60610 Office: Aon Corp 123 N Wacker Dr Chicago IL 60606-1700

LORENZ, JOHN DOUGLAS, college official; b. Talmage, Nebr., July 2, 1942; s. Orville George and Twila Lucille (Larson) L.; m. Alice Louise Hentzen, Aug. 26, 1967; 1 child, Christian Douglas. BS, U. Nebr., 1965, MS, 1967, PhD, 1973. Systems analyst U. Nebr., Lincoln, 1967-73; asst. prof. GMI Engring. and Mgmt. Inst., Flint, Mich., 1973-74, assoc. prof., 1974-78, prof., 1978—, dept. head, 1984-87, asst. dean, 1986-88, provost, dean faculty, 1988-92, Richard L. Terrell prof. acad. leadership, 1990—, v.p. for acad. affairs, provost, 1992—; cons. GM, Detroit, 1973-82, various orgns. Contbr. articles to profl. jours. Judge Internat. Sci. and Engring. Fair, various locations, 1989—. Mem. NSPE, Soc. Mfg. Engrs. (sr.), So. Automotive Engrs., Bd. for Engring. and Tech., Am. Soc. Engring. Edn., Triangle Fraternity Edn. Found., Antique Auto Racing Assn., Model Engine Collectors Assn., Antique Model Race Car Club. Home: 8165 Shady Brook Ln Flushing MI 48433-3007 Office: GMI Engring and Mgmt Inst 1700 W 3rd Ave Flint MI 48504-4832

LORENZ, JOHN GEORGE, librarian, consultant; b. N.Y.C., Sept. 28, 1915; s. John W. and Theresa T. (Wurtz) L.; m. Josephine R. Trumbull, Oct. 1, 1944; children: Laurence T., Janice R. B.S. (Library fellow), CCNY, 1939; B.S. in L.S, Columbia U., 1940; M.S. in Pub. Adminstrn., Mich. State U., 1952. With Queens Borough (N.Y.) Library, then Schenectady Pub. Library, 1940-44; chief reference div. Grand Rapids Pub. Library, 1944-46; asst. librarian Mich. State Library, 1946-56; with U.S. Office Edn., 1957-65, dir. div. library services and ednl. facilities, 1964-65; dep. librarian of congress Library of Congress, Washington, 1965-76; exec. dir. Assn. Research Libraries, 1976-80; library cons., 1980—; interim dir. libraries Cath. U. Am., 1982-83; liaison mem. com. sci. and tech. info. exec. office, 1966-73; interim dir. CAPCON, 1985; spl. asst. to librarian Georgetown U. Library, 1985-87; interim dir. Washington Research Library Consortium, 1987-88; coord. libr. stats. program Nat. Commn. on Librs. and Inf. Sci., 1988—; exec. com. Nat. Book Com., 1968-74. Author numerous articles in field; contbr. to books. Presdl. appointee Nat. Hist. Publs. and Records Commn., 1979-83. Recipient Superior Svc. award HEW. Mem. ALA (coun. 1960-64, 69-73, chmn. panel UNESCO 1965-70, exec. bd. 1970-75, Lippincott award 1993), D.C. Libr. Assn., Internat. Fedn. Libr. Assn. (mem. program devel. group 1974-78), Am. Nat. Stds. Inst. (treas. libr. stds. com. 1980-88), Cosmos Club, Kenwood Golf and Country Club. Home: 5629 Newington Rd Bethesda MD 20816-3321 Office: US Nat Commn on Librs Info Sci 1110 Vermont Ave NW Washington DC 20005-3522

LORENZ, KATHERINE MARY, banker; b. Barrington, Ill., May 1, 1946; d. David George and Mary (Hogan) L. BA cum laude, Trinity Coll., 1968; MBA, Northwestern U., 1971; grad., Grad. Sch. for Bank Adminstrn., 1977. Ops. analyst Continental Bank, Chgo., 1968-69, supr. ops. analysis, 1969-71, asst. mgr. customer profitability analysis, 1971-73, acctg. officer, mgr. customer profitability analysis, 1973-77, 2d v.p., 1976, asst. gen. mgr. contr.'s dept., 1977-80, v.p., 1980, contr. ops. and mgmt. svcs. dept., 1981-84, v.p., sector contr. retail banking, corp. staff and ops. depts., 1984-88, v.p., sr. sector contr. pvt. banking, centralized ops. and corp. staff, 1988-90, v.p., sr. sector contr. bus. analysis group/mgmt. acctg., 1990-94, mgr. contrs. dept. adminstrn. and tng., 1990-94; v.p., chief of staff to chief adminstrv. officer Bank of Am. Ill., Chgo., 1994-96, sr. v.p., mgr. adminstrv. svcs., 1996—. Mem. Execs. Club Chgo. Office: Bank of Am Ill 231 S La Salle St Rm 1320 Chicago IL 60604-1407

LORENZ, LATISHA JAY, elementary education educator; b. Uniontown, Pa., June 16, 1967; d. Lou Jean Lorenz and Mary Lou (Sesler) Rupp; m. Donald Raye Shetley, May 25, 1991 (div. Oct. 1993). AA, U. S.C., Union, 1987; BS in Edn., Lander U., 1989. Cert. elem. edn. 6th grade tchr. Union (S.C.) Acad., 1990-93; 7th grade lang. arts tchr. Sims Jr. H.S., Union, 1993—. Mem. S.C. State Coun. of the Internat. Reading Assn., Union Jr. Charity League. Republican. Baptist. Avocations: cats, reading Stephen King, watching the Buffalo Bills, going to movies. Office: Sims Jr High 200 Sims Dr Union SC 29379-7319

LORENZ, LEE SHARP, cartoonist; b. Hackensack, N.J., Oct. 17, 1932; s. Alfred Lloyd and Martha (Castagnetta) L.; m. Jill Allison Runcie, Sept., 1986; children: Christopher, Matthew, Martha, Ava. Student, Carnegie Inst. Tech., 1950-51; BFA, Pratt Inst., 1954. Staff cartoonist New Yorker mag., 1958—, art editor, 1973—; profl. cornetist, 1955—. Cartoonist: Here it Comes, 1968; author, illustrator: Scornful Simkin, 1980; collection Npw Look What You've Done, 1977; illustrator: Real Men Don't Eat Quiche, 1982, A Bridge Bestiary, 1986, Collection the Golden Age of Trash, 1987; author, illustrator: A Weekend in the Country, 1985; author: The Art of the New Yorker, 1995. Trustee Swann Coll. of Cartoon and Caricature, 1978—; dir. Mus. for African Art. Mem. Century Club. Home: PO Box 117 Easton CT 06612-0117 Office: 20 W 43rd St New York NY 10036-7400

LORENZ, LORETTA ROSE, English language educator; b. Chgo., Apr. 14, 1931; arrived in Japan, 1961; d. Karl Adolph and Juliana (Grunauer) L. BS in Humanities, Loyola U., Chgo., 1953; postgrad., U. Chgo., 1954-55, Am. Acad. Art, Chgo., 1956, Am. U., Washington, 1958-59. Part-time editl. asst. Poetry: A Mag. of Verse, Chgo., 1952-58; advt. copywriter Spiegel, Inc., Chgo., 1954-56; publicity and promotions writer Chgo. Ednl. TV Assn., Sta. WTTW, 1956-58; editl. asst. Cath. U. of Am. Press, Washington, 1959; copywriter, layout designer D.C. Health and Co., Boston, 1959-60; tchr., contbr. to books and tapes Seido Lang. Inst., Ashiya City, Japan, 1961-80; tchr. English Shimogamo Acad., Kyoto, Japan, 1964-86; lectr. Kyoto U. Fgn. Studies, 1964-86; prof. Nagasaki (Japan) Jr. Coll. Fgn. Langs., 1986—; lectr. various cmty. ctrs. Japan, 1986—. Contbg. author, cons.: (textbook series) Modern English: An Oral Approach, 1965-80, Modern English, Cycle Two, 1965-80; contbr. articles to profl. jours.; contbg. author: Guide to English and American Literature, 1996, EPT: English Proficiency Tests for Practice, 1996. Office: Nagasaki Jr Coll Fgn Langs, College Hill Togitsu-machi, Nagasaki 851-12, Japan

LORENZEN, ROBERT FREDERICK, ophthalmologist; b. Toledo, Ohio, Mar. 20, 1924; s. Martin Robert and Pearl Adeline (Bush) L.; m. Lucy Logsdon, Feb. 14, 1970; children: Roberta Jo, Richard Martin, Elizabeth Anne. BS, Duke, 1948, MD, 1948; MS, Tulane U., 1953. Intern, Presbyn. Hosp., Chgo., 1948-49; resident Duke Med. Center, 1949-51, Tulane U. Grad. Sch., 1951-53; practice medicine specializing in ophthalmology, Phoenix, 1953—; mem. staff St. Joseph's Hosp., St. Luke's Hosp., Good Samaritan Hosp., Surg. Eye Ctr. of Ariz. Pres. Ophthalmic Scis. Found., 1970-73; chmn. bd. trustees Rockefeller and Abbe Prentice Eye Inst. of St. Luke's Hosp., 1975—. Recipient Gold Headed Cane award, 1974; named to Honorable Order of Ky. Cols. Fellow ACS, Internat. Coll. Surgeons, Am. Acad. Ophthalmology and Otolaryngology, Pan Am. Assn. Ophthalmology, Soc. Eye Surgeons; mem. Am. Assn. Ophthalmology (sec. of ho. of dels. 1972-73, trustee 1973-76), Ariz. Ophthal. Soc. (pres. 1966-67), Ariz. Med. Assn. (bd. dirs. 1963-66, 69-70), Royal Soc. Medicine, Rotary (pres. Phoenix 1984-85). Republican. Editor in chief Ariz. Medicine, 1963-66, 69-70. Office: 367 E Virginia Ave Phoenix AZ 85004-1202

LORENZETTI, OLE JOHN, pharmaceutical research executive, ophthalmic research and development executive; b. Chgo., Oct. 25, 1936; s. Natale and Quintilia (Bertochinni) L.; m. Lorna Joyce Bailey, June 20, 1961; children: Elizabeth Anne, Maria Anne, Dario. BS, U. Ill., Chgo., 1958; MS, Ohio State U., 1963, PhD, 1965; MBA (hon.), MIT, 1989. Rsch. fellow Ohio State U., Columbus, 1964-65; scientist Miles Labs., Elkhardt, Ind., 1965-67; sr. scientist Dome Labs. div. Miles Labs., Elkhardt, 1967-69; sr. scientist R&D Alcon Labs., Ft. Worth, 1969-72, mgr. R&D div. pre clin. sci., 1972-75, assoc. dir. R&D div. dermatology, 1975-80, dir. ophthal. R&D, 1980-83, sr. dir. surg. R&D, 1983-92, sr. dir. therapeutic rsch./licensing, 1992-94; v.p. therapeutic rsch./licensing, 1994—; asst. prof. pharmacology Health Scis. Ctr. U. Tex., Dallas, 1970-90; clin. prof. dermatology Health Scis. Ctr., U. Tex., Dallas, 1974-80; adj. prof. Tex. Christian U., 1972-82; J.J. Able lectr. pharmacology Ohio No. U., 1965, 69; Kaufman-Lattimer lectr. Ohio State U., 1967, 70, 73, 78; vis. lectr. in therapeutic and drug rsch. U. Ill., 1973-80; vis. lectr. U. Tex. Med. Schs., 1990-95. Mem. editorial bd. Jour. Pharm. Sci., 1974-84, Cutis, 1977-89, Jour. Sci. Investigative Dermatology, 1978-82, Current Eye Rsch., 1990-94; contbr. articles to profl. jours., book chpts., govt. reports. Am. Heart Assn. fellow Ohio State U., 1964. Fellow Acad. Pharm. Scis. (pharmacology-toxicology sect.), Am. Acad. Clin. Toxicology, Soc. for Exptl. Biology and Medicine; mem. AAAS, Am. Pharm. Assn., N.Y. Acad. Sci., Am. Chem. Soc., Soc. Investigative Dermatology, Drug Metabolism Group, Am. Soc. Pharmacology and Exptl. Therapeutics, Western Pharmacology and Exptl. Therapeutics, Western Pharmacology Soc., Am. Coll. Toxicology, Inflammation Rsch. Assn., Am. Soc. Clin. Pharmacology, Am. Acad. Ophthalmology, Assn. for Rsch. and Vision and Ophthalmology, Drug Info. Assn., Rotary (pres. 1990), Sigma Xi. Avocations: ranching, horses, sailing, photography, marathon running. Office: Vice Pres Ther Rsch & Devel Alcon Labs Inc 6201 South Fwy Fort Worth TX 76134-2001

LORENZO, ALBERT L., academic administrator. BS, U. Detroit, 1965, MBA, 1966; LLD (hon.), Walsh Coll. Accountancy and Bus. Adminstrn., 1987. Asst. dir. housing U. Detroit, 1964-65; staff acct. McManus, McGraw and Co., Detroit, 1964-66; asst. prof. acctg. Macomb Community Coll., Warren, Mich., 1966-68, bus. mgr., 1968-74, contr., 1974-75, v.p. bus., 1975-79, pres., 1979—; lectr., pub. speaker, presenter in field. Dir. rsch. SBA, 1966; mem. Mayor's Adv. Com. Small Bus., Detroit, 1967-70, base-community coun. Selfridge Air NG, 1978-86, steering com. March of Dimes, 1980-86, adv. coun. Met. Affairs Corp., 1982—, Mich. Competitive Enterprise Task Force, 1988-90, adv. bd. Nat. Inst. Leadership Devel., 1988—, Community Growth Alliance Macomb County, 1982—, selection panel Heart of Gold ann. awards Southeastern Mich. United Way, 1990; chair div. II United Found., 1981; apptd. commr. State Mich. High Edn. Facilties Authority, 1988-90; bd. dirs. N.E. Guidance Community Mental Health Ctr., 1976-79, Mich. Nat. Bank Macomb, 1981-87, Indsl. Tech. Inst., 1982—; trustee Nat. Commn. Coop. Edn., 1985—; trustee St. Joseph Hosp., 1984-87, sec. 1985-87, mem. adv. bd. 1981-83. Recipient Resolution of Tribute Mich. State Senate, 1979, Italian-Am. Citizen Recognition award, 1980, Volkswagen Am. Recognition award, 1982, Excellence in Speech Writing award Internat. Assn. Bus. Communicators, 1988, Nat. Leadership award U. Tex., 1989, Thomas J. Peters Nat. Leadership award, 1989; named Pres. of Yr. Am. Assn. Women in Community and Jr. Colls., 1985. Mem. Am. Assn. Community and Jr. Colls., World Future Soc., Met. Mus. Art, Mich. Community Coll. Assn., Econ. Club Detroit. Office: Macomb Community Coll 14500 E 12 Mile Rd Warren MI 48093-3870*

LORENZO, MICHAEL, engineer, government official, real estate broker; b. Newton, N.J., 1920; m. Anastasia Hackett; 5 children. BS in Chemistry and Physics, Pa. State U., 1947; MEA, George Washington U., 1956, postgrad., 1975-78; postgrad., USDA Grad. Sch. Registered profl. engr., D.C., Md.; cert. Internat. Property Specialist (CIPS), FIPC. Field instrumentation engr. Fischer and Porter Co., Harboro, Pa., 1947-52; aerospace engr. Dept. Def., 1952-65; with Westinghouse Electric Corp., Friendship, Md., 1965-81; mgr. Air Resources Westinghouse Mgmt. Services, Inc., 1966-70, dir. environ. quality control, 1970-73; founder, pres. Tech. Protection Engring. Co., 1982—; dep. under-sec. def. Washington, 1981-82; founder, prin. broker First Lady Realty Corp., 1986—. Author: (with others) Chemical Equipment Costs, 1950; assoc. editor: Missile and Rockets, 1958-61; contbr. articles to profl. jours.; patentee stall surge sonic sensor. Rear Admiral AC USN, World War II, Korea. Decorated D.S.M., D.F.C. (2), Air medals (7). Mem. Profl. Tennis Registry. Office: First Lady Realty Corp 3126 Shadeland Dr Falls Church VA 22044-1726 *Healthy mind requires healthy body and vice versa. Per Winston Churchill "A Democracy is the worst form of Government that was ever invented except for all the others." It's my time in life to give back. You don't get a second chance to make a good first impression.*

LORENZO, NICHOLAS FRANCIS, JR., lawyer; b. Norfolk, Va., Nov. 22, 1942; s. Nicholas and Jean W. L.; m. Patricia C. Connare, Sept. 7, 1968; children: Nicholas Michael, Matthew Christopher. B.A., St. Francis Coll., 1964; J.D., Duquesne U., 1968. Bar: Pa. 1968, U.S. Dist. Ct. (we. dist.) Pa. 1969, U.S. Supreme Ct. 1976, U.S. Dist. Ct. (mid. dist.) Pa. 1977, U.S. Ct. Appeals (3d cir.) 1983. Pres. Lorenzo and Lundy, P.C., Punxsutawney, 1979-81, Nicholas F. Lorenzo, Jr. P.C., Punxsutawney, 1981-90, Lorenzo & Kulakowski, P.C., 1990—; instr. Sch. Continuing Edn., Pa. State U., 1969-73. Bd. dirs. Punxsutawney Area Hosp., 1972-74; mem. parish council S.S.C.D. Roman Cath. Ch., 1978-84, pres., 1979-84; bd. dirs. dist. Council Boy Scouts Am., 1982-84. Mem. ABA, Jefferson County Bar Assn. (v.p. 1980-82, pres. 1982-84), Pa. Bar Assn., Pa. Bar Inst. (bd. dirs. 1988-94), Pa. Trial Lawyers Assn. (bd. govs), West Pa. Trial Lawyers Assn., Assn. Trial Lawyers Am., Nat. Bd. Trial Advocacy (civil cert.). Republican. Club: Punxsutawney Country. Lodges: K.C., Elks, Eagles, Rotary (pres. Punxsutawney 1973). Home: 180 Monticello Dr Punxsutawney PA 15767-2614 Office: 410 W Mahoning St Punxsutawney PA 15767-1908

LORENZO FRANCO, JOSÉ RAMÓN, Mexican government official; b. Apizaco, Tlaxcala, Mexico, Jan. 2, 1935. Student, Naval Staff Sch., Mexico, Navy War Coll., U.S. Joined Mexican Navy, 1952, adj., chief tech. dept. naval edn., chief of staff naval zone, dir. gen. Ctr. of Navy Capacities, dir. Ctr. for Higher Naval Studies, comdr. of Naval Region, insp., comptr. gen.; Sec. of the Navy Govt. of Mexico, 1995—.

LORIA, CHRISTOPHER JOSEPH, marine officer; b. Newton, Mass., July 9, 1960; s. Robert Louis and Joan (Novitski) L.; m. Sandra Lee Sullivan, July 5, 1986; children: Taylor Elizabeth Michelle, Madison Isabelle. BS, U.S. Naval Avad., 1983. Commd. 2d lt. USMC, 1983, advanced through grades to major, 1989; staff officer Marine Aviation Tng. Support Group USMC, NAS Pensacola, Fla., 1984-86; F/A-18 transition pilot VFA-125 COMSTKFITWGPAC USMC, NAS Lemoore Field, Calif., 1988-89; quality assurance officer VMFA-314 MAG-11 3d MAW USMC, MCAS El Toro, Calif., 1989-91, asst. maintenance officer VMFA-314 MAG-11 3d MAW, 1991-92, F/A-18 instr. pilot VMFAT-101 MAG-11 3d MAW, 1992; test pilot strike aircraft directorate USMC, NAS Patuxent River, Md., 1994; cons. Los Alamos (N.Mex.) Nat. Lab./DARPA, 1991. Mem. Rep. Nat. Com. Mem. NRA (life), U.S. Naval Acad. Alumni Assn. (life), Marine Corps Aviation Assn. (life), Ducks Unltd. Roman Catholic. Avocations: sailing, soaring, hiking, fishing, camping. Home: 102 Sea Mist Dr League City TX 77573 Office: NASA Johnson Space Ctr Mail Code: CB Houston TX 77058

LORIAUX, MAURICE LUCIEN, artist, ecclesiologist; b. Chanute, Kans., Aug. 27, 1909; s. Amour Joseph and Eva (Goosens) L.; m. Susan Bowman, Oct. 17, 1935; children: Donald Lynn, Michael Maurice. B.A., U. Tulsa, 1931; M.A., Northwestern U., 1933; pvt. student, Berger Sandzen, Laura Requa, George Serraz. Dir. string dept. U. Tulsa, 1933-38; exec. dir. Santa Fe (N.Mex.) Studios of Church Art, 1947-66; pres. Art Horizons, 1961—; founder, pres. Southwest Art League Seminars; dir. Georgia O'Keeffe Country Workshops. Designer over 300 church interiors, Am. and abroad; condr. annual seminars art, Santa Fe; works include mural Healing, Tex. Med. Ctr., Houston, 1967; restoration of Old Mission, Santa Barbara, Calif., 1964, The Cabrini Shrine, Denver, 1956, Las Supper mural (1st distinctive award achievement Am. Assn. Arts), the Junipero Serra monument, Sacramento. Recipient First award of merit Church Property Adminstrn., 1966; Okla. Art and Humanities award of distinction in sculpture and arts, 1978; award of distinction Sierra Clubs Am. Fellow Stained Glass Assn. Am.; mem. Am. Internat. Stained Glass Inst. (founder, pres.), Artes Italia, Community Entertainment Assn. (pres. 1940-44). Home and Office: 812 Camino Acoma Santa Fe NM 87505-4932

LORIE, JAMES HIRSCH, business administration educator; b. Kansas City, Feb. 23, 1922; s. Alvin J. and Adele (Hirsch) L.; m. Sally Rosen, June 16, 1948 (div. 1953); 1 child Susan; m. Nancy A. Wexler, June 19, 1958 (dec. 1966); stepchildren: Katherine Wexler, Jeffrey Wexler; m. Vanna Metzenberg Lautman, Aug. 27, 1967; stepchildren: Erika Lautman, Victoria Lautman, Karl Lautman. A.B., Cornell U., 1942, A.M., 1945; Ph.D., U. Chgo., 1947. Research asst. Cornell U., Ithaca, N.Y., 1944-45; mem. staff seminar Am. civilization Salzburg, Austria, 1947; mem. faculty U. Chgo. Grad. Sch. Bus., 1947-92, prof. bus. adminstrn., asso. dean, 1956-61; dir. Center Research in Security Prices, 1960-75; cons. divsn. rsch. and statistics bd. govs. Fed. Res. Sys., 1950-52; cons. U.S. Treas. Dept., 1973-74; bd. dirs. Acorn Fund, N.Y.C., Thornburg Mortgage Asset Co., Inc., Ardco Inc., Chgo.; mem. Nat. Market Adv. Bd., 1975-77. Author: (with Harry V. Roberts) Basic Methods of Marketing Research, 1951, (with Richard A. Brealey) Modern Developments in Investment Management, 1972, (with Mary T. Hamilton) The Stock Market: Theories and Evidence, 1973; Contbr. articles to profl. jours. Served with USCGR, 1942-44. Mem. Am. Econ. Assn., Mont Pelerin Soc., Nat. Assn. Securities Dealers (dir. 1972-75), Phi Beta Kappa. Clubs: Arts (Chgo.); Quadrangle (U. Chgo.). Home: 2314 N Lincoln Park W Chicago IL 60614-3454

LORIMER, LINDA KOCH, university educator; m. Ernest McFaul Lorimer; children: Katharine Elizabeth, Peter Brailler. AB, Hollins Coll., 1974; JD, Yale U., 1977; DHL, Green Mountain Coll., 1981, Washington Coll., 1992, Randolph-Macon Coll., 1992. Bar: N.Y. 1978, Conn. 1982. Assoc. Davis Polk and Wardwell, N.Y.C., 1977-78; asst. gen. counsel Yale U., New Haven, 1978-79, assoc. gen. counsel, 1979-84, assoc. provost, 1983-87, acting assoc. v.p. human resources, 1984-85; prof. law, pres. Randolph-Macon Woman's Coll., Lynchburg, Va., 1987-93; v.p., sec. Yale Univ., New Haven, 1993—; lectr. Yale Coll. Undergrad. Seminars, 1980, 83; bd. dirs. Spring, McGraw Hill; past pres., mem. exec. com. Women's Coll. Coalition; mem. corp. Yale U., 1990-93, chair Virginia Rhodes scholarship com., 1991-93. Chair editorial bd. Jour. Coll. and Univ. Law, 1983-87. Former trustee Hollins Coll., Berkeley Div. Sch.; mem. com. on responsible conduct rsch. Inst. Medicine, NAS, 1988; bd. dirs. Norfolk Acad.; cabinet mem. United Way of Greater New Haven. Mem. Nat. Assn. Coll. and Univ. Attys. (exec. bd. 1981-84), Nat. Assn. Schs. and Colls. of United Meth. Ch. (1st v.p.), Assn. Am. Colls.,(pres. bd. dirs., chmn. bd.), Am. Assn. Theol. Schs. (bd. dirs.), Mory's Assn., Phi Beta Kappa. Episcopalian. Home: 87 Trumbull St New Haven CT 06511-3723 Office: Woodbridge Hall Yale Univ New Haven CT 06520-9999

LORING, ARTHUR, lawyer, financial services company executive; b. N.Y.C., Oct. 13, 1947; s. Murray and Mildred (Rogers) L.; m. Vicki Hootstein, June 4, 1978. BS in Commerce, Washington and Lee U., 1969; JD cum laude, Boston U., 1972. Bar: Mass. 1972. Atty. Fidelity Mgmt. & Research Co., Boston, 1972; sr. legal counsel Fidelity Mgmt. & Research Co., 1980-82, v.p., gen. counsel, 1984-93; sr. v.p., gen. counsel, 1993—; v.p.-legal FMR Corp., Boston, 1982—; sec. Fidelity Group of Funds, Boston, 1982—; dir. Fidelity Capital Publs. Inc., 1991—; v.p. Fidelity Distbr. Corp., Boston, 1984—; sr. v.p., gen. counsel Fidelity Investments Instnl. Svcs., Inc., 1994—; bd. govs. Investment Co. Inst., 1988-90; chmn. ICI SEC Rules Com., 1990-95; adv. bd. Fund Directions, 1993—. Case editor Boston U. Law Rev., 1971-72. Mem. adv. bd. sch. of commerce Washington and Lee Univ., 1996—. Mem. ABA (securities regulation com.), Boston Bar Assn., Cavendish Club (dir. 1981-84), Boston Chess Club (pres. Brookline, Mass. 1981-83), Pine Brook Country Club, Polo Club of Boca Raton, Palm Beach Cuntry Club. Republican. Jewish. Avocations: golf, bridge, exercise. Home: 300 Boylston St Apt 803 Boston MA 02116-3923 Office: Fidelity Mgmt & Rsch Co 82 Devonshire St Boston MA 02109-3605

LORING, CALEB, JR., investment company executive; b. Boston, Feb. 5, 1921; s. Caleb and Suzanne (Bailey) L.; m. Rosemary Merrill, Feb. 12, 1943; children—Caleb, David, Rosemary, Keith. A.B., Harvard U., 1943, LL.B., 1948. Bar: Mass. 1948, U.S. Dist. Ct. Mass. 1948. Asso., then partner firm Gaston, Snow, Motley & Holt, Boston, 1948-70; dir., trustee Loring, Wolcott and Coolidge Office-Fiduciary Services, Boston, 1948-86; gen. counsel Fidelity Mgmt. and Rsch. Co., 1964-74; v.p., dir. Puritan Fund, Inc., and all other funds in Fidelity Group of Funds, Boston, 1973-86; treas. Fidelity Mgmt. & Research Co., Boston, 1977-86, ret., 1986; dir. Fidelity Mgmt. & Research Co., 1959-86; mng. dir. FMR Corp. (parent co. Fidelity Mgmt. & Rsch. Co.), Boston, 1986—; dir. Fidelity Investments, Boston, 1974—. Served with USNR, 1943-46. Mem. Am. Bar Assn., Mass. Bar Assn., Boston Bar Assn. Office: Fidelity Investments 82 Devonshire St Ste 8sa Boston MA 02109-3605

LORING, GLORIA JEAN, singer, actress; b. N.Y.C., Dec. 10, 1946; d. Gerald Louis and Dorothy Ann (Tobin) Goff; m. Alan Willis Thicke, Aug. 22, 1970 (div. 1986); children: Brennan Todd, Robin Alan; m. Christopher Beaumont, June 18, 1988 (div. 1993); m. René Lagler, Dec. 20, 1994. Grad. high sch. Owner Glitz Records, L.A., 1984—; pres. Only Silk Prodns., L.A., 1985-90; owner Silk Purse Prodns., 1992—. Began profl. singing, Miami Beach, 1965; appeared in numerous TV shows; featured singer: Bob Hope's Ann. Armed Forces Christmas Tour, 1970; featured several record albums; featured actress: Days of Our Lives, 1980-86; composer: TV themes Facts of Life, 1979, Diff'rent Strokes, 1978; author: Days of Our Lives Celebrity Cookbook, 1981, Vol. II, 1983, Living the Days of Our Lives, 1984, Kids, Food and Diabetes, 1986, Parenting a Diabetic Child, 1991, The Kids Food and Diabetes Family Cookbook, 1991. Celebrity chmn. Juvenile Diabetes Found. Recipient Humanitarian of Yr. award Juvenile Diabetes Found., 1982, 88, Parents of Yr. award, 1984, Woman of Yr. award Jeweler's Assn. Am., 1986. Mem. Nat. Acad. Songwriters (gold mem.). *I feel the most important element in any life is to continue reaching out, growing, and learning. Don't be afraid to ask. Don't be afraid to challenge. Don't be afraid.*

LORING, HONEY, small business owner; b. Phila.. BA in Psychology, U. Md., 1970; MEd, Wash. U., St. Louis, 1971. Lic. psychologist-master Vt.; directress cert. Assn. Montessori Internat. Counselor Gardenville Diagnostic Ctr., St. Louis, 1971-72; tchr. Early Learning Pre-Sch., St. Louis, 1972-74; music dir., cabin counselor Follow Through Day Camp, Brattleboro, Vt., 1972-74; tchr. Montessori Sch., Dublin, 1974-75; ednl. cons. children's books Left Bank Books, St. Louis, 1975-76; program dir. day camp Brattleboro Child Devel., 1975-79; behavioral therapist Behavioral Medicine Unit, Dartmouth Med. Sch., 1979-84; pvt. therapist Brattleboro, Vt., 1984-85; founder, pres. Gone to the Dogs, Inc., Putney, Vt., 1984—; dog groomer, 1979-92; founder, dir. Camp Come to the Dogs., 1990—; mfr. dog collars, 1984-96; founder Tails Up Inn, 1995—; took wolves around U.S. to do ednl. environ. programs with the Clem and Jethro Lectr. Svc., 1974-76. Author: (with Jeremy Birch) You're On. . .Teaching Communication Skills, 1984, The Big Good Wolf; contbr. articles to profl. jours. Leader 4-H Dog Club; helper Riding for the Physically Handicapped, St. Louis, 1974. Home and Office: RR 1 Box 958 Putney VT 05346-9748

LORING, JOHN ROBBINS, artist; b. Chgo., Nov. 23, 1939; s. Edward D'Arcy and China Robbins (Logeman) L. B.A., Yale U., 1960; postgrad., Ecole Beaux Arts, Paris, 1960-63; Dr. Arts (hon.), Pratt Inst., 1996. Disting. vis. prof. U. Calif., Davis, 1977; bur. chief Archtl. Digest mag., N.Y.C., 1977-78; assoc. dir. Tiffany and Co., N.Y.C., 1979—, exec. v.p., design dir., 1981-84, sr. v.p. design and merchandising, 1984—; mem. acquisitions com. dept. prints and illustrated books Mus. Modern Art, N.Y.C., 1990—. Contbg. editor: Arts mag., 1973—; books include: The New Tiffany Tablesettings, 1981, Tiffany Taste, 1986, Tiffany's 150 Years, 1987, The Tiffany Wedding, 1988, Tiffany Parties, 1989, The Tiffany Gourmet, 1992, A Tiffany Christmas, 1996, Tiffany's 20th Century, 1997; one-man exhbns. include Balt. Mus. Art, 1972, Hundred Acres Gallery, N.Y., 1972, Pace Edits., 1973, 77, Long Beach Mus. Art, 1975, A.D.I. Gallery, San Francisco, 1976; group exhbns. include Phila. Mus. Art, 1971, N.Y. Cultural Ctr., 1972, Biennale graphic Art, Ljubljana, Yugoslavia, 1973, 77, Intergrafia 74, Krakow, Poland, 1974, Bklyn. Mus. Nat. Print Exhbn., 1974, Art Inst. Chgo., 1975, R.I. Sch. Design, 1976; represented in permanent collections Mus. Modern Art, N.Y.C., Whitney Mus. Am. Art, Chgo. Art Inst., Boston Mus. Fine Arts, R.I. Sch. Design, Balt. Mus. Art, Yale U. Art Gallery; commd. by U.S. Customhouse, N.Y.C., Prudential Ins. Co. Am. Eastern Home Office, Woodbridge, N.J., City of Scranton, Pa., Western Savs., Phila. Recipient Edith Wharton award Design & Art Soc., 1988. Office: Tiffany & Co 727 5th Ave New York NY 10022-2503 also: Doubleday 1540 Broadway New York NY 10036 *I look on whatever talents I may have as natural resources to be given freely wherever needed. A lot has been given out; a lot has come in.*

LORO, LAUREN MARGUERITE, secondary education educator; b. New Haven, Mar. 14, 1948; d. Anthony S. and Marguerite (Belviso) L. BS, Western Conn. State Coll., Danbury, 1970; MS, U. Bridgeport (Conn.), 1977. Instrumental music dir. Sleeping Giant Jr. High, Hamden, Conn., 1970-77, Hamden High Sch., 1977—; flute with New Haven Symphony Orch., 1971, 72; music dir. Hamden H.S. Concert Band, Orch., Marching Band, 1977—, Hamden H.S. Dance Band, 1982—, Theatre Dept., 1972—, Hamden Summer Theatre, 1974—, Michael J. Whalen Theatre Dept., 1975-84, Sleeping Giant Jr. High, Hamden, 1972-83, Quinnipiac Coll., Hamden, 1980, dist. so. region CMEA All Mid. Sch. Band, 1994; profl. devel. chairperson Hamden H.S.; profl. devel. co-chair Town of Hamden. Mem. Hamden Edn. Assn., Conn. Music Educators Assn. Avocations: photography, French gourmet cooking. Office: Hamden High Music Dept 2040 Dixwell Ave Hamden CT 06514-2404

LORSUNG, THOMAS NICHOLAS, news service editor; b. Milw., June 9, 1938; s. Nicholas A. and Margaret (Senger) L.; m. Mary Jelen, Aug. 27, 1960; children: Kristin Lorsung Shulder, Anne K., Erin Lorsung Krauss. BJ, Marquette U., 1960. Reporter Journal-Times, Racine, Wis., 1961-63; reporter, photographer, news editor Cath. Rev., Balt., 1963-69; photo, copy editor The Sentinel, Milw., 1969-72; photo editor Nat. Cath. News Svc., Washington, 1972-75, news editor, 1975-76, mng. editor, 1976-89; dir., editor-in-chief Cath. News Svc. (formerly Nat. Cath. News Svc.), Washington, 1989—; chmn. bd. dirs. Carroll Pub., Washington, 1993-95; cons. Pontifical Coun. for Social Comms., 1995—. Recipient By-Line award Marquette U., 1997. Mem. Cath. Press Assn. (bd. dirs. 1991—, St. Francis de Sales award 1995), Internat. Cath. Union of the Press, Fed. Cath. News Agys. (v.p. 1992). Avocations: photography, biking, choral singing. Home: 5367 Iron Pen Pl Columbia MD 21044 Office: Catholic News Svc 3211 4th St NE Washington DC 20017-1106

LORTEL, LUCILLE, theatrical producer; b. N.Y.C., Dec. 16, 1905; d. Harry and Anna (Moes) Wadler; m. Louis Schweitzer, Mar. 23, 1931 (dec.). Student, Adelphi Coll., 1920, Am. Acad. Dramatic Arts, 1920-21, abroad; DFA (hon.), U. Bridgeport, 1985. Established White Barn Theatre, Westport, Conn., 1947—; owner, producer Lucille Lortel Theatre (originally Lucille Lortel's Theatre de Lys), N.Y.C., 1955—; artistic dir. ANTA Matinee Series, N.Y.C., 1956—; founder Am. Shakespeare Festival Theatre, Stratford, Conn., 1955. Appeared in various stage plays including: Caesar and Cleopatra, 1925; The Dove, 1925; One Man's Woman, 1926; radio appearances, 1935; producer various stage plays, including Three Penny Opera, 1955, I Knock at the Door, 1957, Cock a Doodle Dandy, 1958, The Balcony, 1960, The Blood Knot, 1964, A Streetcar Named Desire, 1973; coproducer plays including Angels Fall, 1983 (Tony nomination), As Is, 1984 (Tony nomination), Blood Knot, 1985 (Tony nomination), numerous others. V.p. exec. com. bd. dirs. Friends of Theatre Collection of Mus. City of N.Y.; mem. adv. bd. Nat. Theatre of Deaf, Chester, Conn.; trustee Goodspeed Opera House, East Haddam, Conn. Recipient 2 awards Greater N.Y. chpt. ANTA, 1958, Off-Broadway award, 1956, 58, 60, 84, Margo Jones award, 1962, award Nat. ANTA, 1962, Villager award, 1979, Cert. Merit City of N.Y., 1980, Arnold Weissberger award Theatre Hall Fame, 1982, Spl. citation N.Y. Drama Critics, 1983, Lee Strasberg Lifetime Achievement in Theatre award, 1985, Spl. Theatre World award, 1985, Exceptional Achievement award Women's Project Am. Pl. Theatre, 1986, George M. Cohan award Cath. Actors Guild Am., 1986, 1st citation Mus. Am. Theatre, New Haven, 1986, numerous others. Office: Lucille Lortel Theatre 121 Christopher St New York NY 10014-4204*

LORTON, LEWIS, dentist, researcher, computer scientist; b. N.Y.C., Nov. 3, 1939; s. Frederick S. and Rosell (Engel) L.; divorced; children: Elizabeth, Mark, Michael S.; m. Jacqueline Carol Andor, Aug. 3, 1982; children: Michael E., Erin. BA, Brandeis U., 1960; DDS, U. Pa., 1964; MSD, Ind. U., 1978. Pvt. practice West Medway, Mass., 1964-66; commd. lt. U.S. Army, 1966, advanced through grades to col., 1983, researcher, tchr., 1976—; cons. Armed Forces Inst. Pathology, Washington, 1986—; chief info. mgr. Henry M. Jackson Found., 1989-91; v.p. Klemm Analysis Group, Inc., 1991-92; pres. Lorton Assoc., 1992-94; exec. dir. Health Care Open Systems & Trials, Inc., 1994—. Contbr. numerous articles to profl. jours. Recipient Carl Schlack award Assn. Mil. Surgeons U.S., 1988. Fellow Am. Forensic Soc.; mem. Internat. Assn. Dental Rsch., Am. Assn. Dental Rsch., Am. Soc. Forensic Odontology, Soc. for Clin. Trials. Avocations: statistics, computers, fly fishing, squash. Home: 10096 Hatbrim Ter Columbia MD 21046-1318 Office: 200 Hall of the States 444 N Capitol St NW Washington DC 20001-1512

LORY, LORAN STEVEN, lawyer; b. Phoenix, July 11, 1961; s. Marvin and Lee (Shain) L.; m. Diane Tabachman, Aug. 4, 1984. JD, Thomas Jefferson Sch. Law, 1984. Bar: Calif., U.S. Dist. Ct. (so. dist.) Calif., U.S. Dist. Ct. Ariz. Legal documentation coord. Ernest W. Hahn Co., Inc., San Diego, 1984-86; pvt. practice San Diego, 1986—. Mem. Juvenile Justice Bar Assn. Avocations: golf, tennis, boating. Office: 1515 2nd Ave Ste 110 San Diego CA 92101-3051

LOS, MARINUS, retired agrochemical researcher; b. Ridderkerk, The Netherlands, Sept. 18, 1933; came to U.S., 1960; s. Cornelis and Neeltje (Zoutewelle) L.; m. Lorraine Betty Lowe, May 11, 1957; children: Simon, Sija, Michael, Martin (dec.). BS, Edinburgh U., Scotland, 1955, PhD, 1957. Sr. rsch. chemist Am. Cyanamid Co., Princeton, N.J., 1960-71, group leader, 1971-84, sr. group leader, 1984-86, mgr. crop protection chems., 1986-88, assoc. dir. crop scis., 1988-92, rsch. dir. crop scis., 1992-96; ret., 1996. Recipient Disting. Inventor of 1990 award Intellectual Property Owners, Inc., Washington, 1990, Thomas Alva Edison Patent award R&D Coun. of N.J., 1991, Nat. Medal of Tech. NSF, 1993, Achievement award Indsl. Rsch. Inst. Inc., 1994. Mem. AAAS, Am. Chem. Soc. (Perkin medal, 1994, Creative Invention award, 1995), Plant Growth Regulator Soc. Achievements include 53 patents.

LOSCALZO, JOSEPH, cardiologist, biochemist; b. Camden, N.J., Oct. 26, 1951; s. Joseph and Dolores Rita (Ventura) L.; m. Anita Beth Sendrow, Mar. 10, 1974; children: Julia, Alexander. AB summa cum laude, U. Pa., 1972, MD and PhD, 1978. Diplomate Am. Bd Internal Medicine; cert. in cardiovascular disease. Postdoctoral fellow U. Pa., Phila., 1978; resident in internal medicine Brigham and Women's Hosp., Boston, 1978-81, clin. fellow cardiology, 1981-83, chief med. resident, 1983-84, instr. medicine, 1983-85; clin. fellow medicine Harvard Med. Sch., Boston, 1978-81, asst. prof. medicine, 1985-88, assoc. prof., 1989-93; chief cardiol. sect. Brockton West Roxbury VA Med. Ctr., Boston, 1989-93; disting. prof. medicine, prof. biochemistry Boston U., 1994—, dir. Whitaker Cardiovasc. Inst., Sch. Medicine, 1994—, vice chmn. dept. medicine, chief cardiovasc. medicine, 1994-96, Wade prof., chmn. dept. medicine, 1997—; mem. rsch. rev. com. Am. Heart Assn., 1988—; rsch. rev. cons. Nat. Heart, Lung and Blood Inst., Bethesda, Md., 1990—. Author: (with others) books on vascular biology and medicine, thrombosis and hemostasis; assoc. editor New England Jour. of Medicine; contbr. mem. editorial bd.: Circulation, Circulation Rsch., Jour. Thrombosis and Thrombolysis, Jour. Vascular Medicine Biology, Am. Jour. of Cardiology; contbr. over 250 articles to profl. jours. Recipient Med. Scientist Tng. award NIH, 1972-77, Rsch. Career Devel. award, 1989-94, Clin. Scientist award Am. Heart Assn., 1983-88. Fellow ACP, Am. Coll. Cardiology (mem. editl. bd. jour.); mem. Am. Fedn. Clin. Rsch., Am. Soc. Clin. Investigation, Assn. Univ. Cardiologists, Am. Soc. Biol. Chemistry, Phi Beta Kappa, Alpha Omega Alpha. Achievements include ten patents related to nitric oxide congeners. Office: Boston U Sch Medicine Whitaker Cardiovasc Inst 700 Albany St Boston MA 02118-2518

LOSCAVIO, ELIZABETH, dancer; b. Jacksonville, Fla.. Student, Contra Costa Ballet Sch., Pacific N.W. Ballet Sch., San Francisco Ballet Sch. Co. apprentice San Francisco Ballet, 1986, mem. corps de ballet, 1986-88, soloist, 1988-90, prin. dancer, 1990—. Performances include Romeo and Juliet, The Sleeping Beauty, Swan Lake, Sonata, Tuning Game, Quartette, Nanna's Lied, Haffner Symphony, Con Brio, Handel-a Celebration, Menuetto, Contradanses, Ballet D'Isoline, Intimate Voices, The Lesson, Maninyas, La Fille mal gardée, Ballo della Regina, Tchaikovsky Pas de Deux, Theme and Variations, Who Cares?, Symphony in C, Tarantella, Rubies, Stars and Stripes, The Four Temperaments, A Midsummer Night's Dream, Rodeo, Maelstrom, La Pavane Rouge, Dark Elegies, Grand Pas de Deux, Flower Festival at Genzano, Rodin, Connotations, Le Corsaire Pas de Deux, Sunset, In the Night, Interplay In G Major, The End, The Comfort Zone, Dreams of Harmony, The Wanderer Fantasy, The Sons of Horus, The Dance House, Nutcracker, Divertissemet d'Auber, Vivaldi Concerto Grosso, New Sleep, La Sylphide. Recipient Isadora Duncan award, 1991. Office: San Francisco Ballet 455 Franklin St San Francisco CA 94102-4438

LO SCHIAVO, JOHN JOSEPH, university executive; b. San Francisco, Feb. 25, 1925; s. Joseph and Anne (Re) Lo S. A.B., Gonzaga U., 1948, Ph.L. and M.A., 1949; S.T.L., Alma Coll., 1962. Joined S.J., Roman Catholic Ch., 1942; tchr. St. Ignatius High Sch., San Francisco, 1949-50; instr. philosophy and theology U. San Francisco, 1950-52, 56-57, 61-62, v.p. for student affairs, dean of students, 1962-68, pres., 1977-91, chancellor, 1991—; pres. Bellarmine Coll. Prep. Sch., San Jose, 1968-75. Bd. dirs. Sch. of Sacred Heart, St. Mary's Hosp., 1990-96. Mem. Olympic Club, Bohemian Club, Univ. Club. Office: U San Francisco 2130 Fulton St San Francisco CA 94117-1080

LOSCHIAVO, LINDA BOSCO, library director; b. Rockville Ctr., N.Y., Aug. 31, 1950; d. Joseph and Jennie (DelRegno) Bosco; m. Joseph A. LoSchiavo, Sept. 7, 1974. BA, Fordham U., 1972, MA, 1990; MLS, Pratt Inst., 1974. Picture cataloguer Frick Art Reference Libr., N.Y.C., 1972-75; sr. cataloguer Fordham U. Libr., Bronx, N.Y., 1975-87, head of retrospective conversion, 1987-90, systems libr., 1990-91, dir. libr. at Lincoln Ctr., 1991—; libr. cons. Mus. Am. Folk Art Libr., N.Y.C., 1985-90; indexer Arco Books, N.Y.C., 1974. Editor: Macbeth, 1990, Julius Ceasar, 1990, Romeo and Juliet, 1990. Mng. producer Vineyard Opera, N.Y.C., 1981-88. Mem. ALA, N.Y. Tech. Svcs. Librs., Beta Phi Mu, Alpha Sigma Nu. Home: 317 Collins Ave Mount Vernon NY 10552-1601 Office: Fordham Univ Library 113 W 60th St New York NY 10023-7404

LOSEE, THOMAS PENNY, JR., publisher; b. Mineola, N.Y., Dec. 9, 1940; s. Thomas Penny and Jeanne Hubbell (Grandeman) L.; m. Muriel Frances Hahn, Apt. 25, 1964; children: Thomas Penny III, Kendall Louise; m. Clark Edward Graebner Jr., Aug. 28, 1993. A.B., Duke U., 1963. Advt. salesman Look mag., 1964-71; advt. dir. House Beautiful, 1971-72; pub. Harper's Bazaar, N.Y.C., 1972-76, House Beautiful, 1976—; v.p., asst. to gen. mgr. Hearst Mag. div., 1981—; v.p., pub. Sci. Digest mag., 1983—, Archtl. Digest mag., 1989-91; sr. v.p., pub. dir. Knapp Communications, 1991—; pub. Archtl. Digest mag. CondÉ Nast Publs., 1993—. Mem. editorial bd. Duke Mag. Trustee Taft Sch., Heckscher Mus. With USAR, 1963-69. Mem. Univ. Club, Creek Club, Country Club Fla., Cold Spring Harbor Beach Club, Coral Beach Club (Bermuda), Gulf Stream Bath and Tennis Club, Lawrence Beach Club, Beta Theta Pi. Republican. Episcopalian. Home: PO Box 471 Cold Spring Harbor NY 11724-0471 Office: 350 Madison Ave New York NY 10017-3704

LOSER, JOSEPH CARLTON, JR., dean, retired judge; b. Nashville, June 16, 1932; s. Joseph Carlton and Pearl Dean (Gupton) L.; m. Mildred Louise Nichols, May 25, 1972; 1 child, Joseph Carlton III. Student, U. Tenn., 1950-51, Vanderbilt U., 1952-55; LLB, Nashville YMCA Night Law Sch., 1959. Bar: Tenn. 1959. Pvt. practice, 1959-66; judge Gen. Sessions Ct., Davidson County, Tenn., 1966-69, Cir. Ct. 20th Jud. Dist. Tenn., 1969-86; dean Nashville Sch. Law, 1986—. Mem. ABA, Tenn. Bar Assn., Nashville Bar Assn., Am. Legion, Masons, Shriners, Sigma Delta Kappa, Kappa Sigma, Rotary.

LOSEY, MICHAEL ROBERT, professional society administrator; b. Cin., Nov. 10, 1938; s. Clyde William And Hilda C. (Ploom) L.; m. Ann J. Liparoto, Aug. 27, 1960; children: Debra Lynn, Scott Douglas, Robert Michael. BBA, U. Mich., 1961, MBA, 1962. Labor relations assoc. Ford Motor Co., Ypsilanti, Mich., 1962-64; personnel mgr. Sperry New Holland, Lancaster, Pa., 1964-66, Grand Island, Nebr., 1966-69; dir. plant & field personnel Sperry New Holland, New Holland, Pa., 1969-72; dir. personnel relations Sperry New Holland, 1972-74, v.p. human resources, 1974-83; staff v.p. compensation & benefits Sperry Corp., N.Y.C., 1983-84, Sperry Corp. (now Unisys Corp.), 1984-86; v.p. human resources Unisys Corp., Blue Bell, Pa., 1986-90; pres., CEO Soc. for Human Resource Mgmt., Alexandria, Va., 1990—; speaker in field. Contbr. articles to profl. jours. Pres. United Way, Grand Island, Nebr., 1968; campaign chmn., mem. various coms. United Way, N.Y., Pa. and Nebr. Recipient Equal Employment Opportunity award City of Lancaster, Pa., 1983. Avocations: boating, golf, fishing. Office: Soc Human Resource Mgmt 606 N Washington St Alexandria VA 22314-1943*

LOSH, SAMUEL JOHNSTON, engineering administrator; b. Hershey, Pa., Nov. 11, 1932; s. Charles Seibert and Esther Dora (Johnston) L.; m. Llewellyn Mathews Hall, Sept. 26, 1964 (div. Oct., 1994); children: Elizabeth Mathews, Stephen Johnston. BSME, MIT, 1954; postgrad., Syracuse U., Utica, 1956-57, UCLA, 1968-74, U. So. Calif., 1975-81. Cert. profl. mgr. Inst. Cert. Profl. Mgrs. Engr. RCA, Camden, N.J., 1954-55; instr. Syracuse U., Utica, 1956; mem. tech. staff TRW, L.A., 1957-59; systems engr. Hoffman Electronics, L.A, 1959-62; spacecraft systems engr. Lockheed Calif. Co., Burbank, 1962-64; sr. systems specialist Xerox Spl. Info. Systems, Pasadena, Calif., 1964-87; sr. systems engr. Datametrics Corp., Chatsworth, Calif., 1987-89; pres. Milner Street, Inc., Pasadena, 1980—; sec. Regina Properties, Inc., Pasadena, 1981-92. Chmn. L.A. chpt. MIT Ednl. Coun., 1978—; facilitator Math. Standards Program, L.A. Unified Sch. Dist., 1994. Recipient George Morgan award MIT Ednl.Coun., 1987; named Silver Knight of Mgmt., Nat. Mgmt. Assn., 1980. Mem. IEEE, AIAA, MIT Alumni Assn. (bd. dirs. 1981-83). Republican. Unitarian. Avocations; skiing, travel, apt. mgmt. Home and Office: PO Box 50368 Pasadena CA 91115-0368

LOSI, MAXIM JOHN, medical communications executive; b. Jersey City, Dec. 27, 1939; s. Maxim Fortune and Carrie (Rivoli) L.; m. Mary Ann De Grandis, May 30, 1968; children: Christopher, Benjamin. AB, Princeton U., 1960; postgrad. N.Y. Med. Coll., 1960-61, Albert Einstein Coll. Medicine, 1961-62, PhD in English, NYU, 1972. Lectr. English C.W. Post Coll. L.I.U., Greenvale, N.Y., 1965-67; instr. English, Centenary Coll. for Women, Hackettstown, N.J., 1967-71, chmn. dept., 1970-71; med. abstractor/indexer Coun. for Tobacco Rsch., N.Y.C., 1972-73; freelance med. writer, 1973-74; sr. clin. info. scientist Squibb Inst. Med. Rsch., Princeton, N.J., 1974-77, project team leader, 1975-77; chief med. writer ICI Ams., Wilmington, Del., 1977-79; dir. biomed. communications Revlon Health Care Group, Tuckahoe, N.Y., 1979-86; pres. Max Losi Assocs. Biomed. Writers, Trenton, N.J., 1986-87; exec. dir. documentation mgmt. and regulatory submissions Covance Clin. and Peri-Approval Svcs. Inc., Princeton, N.J., 1987-97; v.p. regulatory affairs Scirex Corp., Blue Bell, Pa., 1997—; FDA cons. Microbiol. Assocs., Bethesda, Md., 1973; mgmt. cons. Robert S. First Assocs., N.Y.C., 1974; vis. lectr. med. writing techniques St. George U. Med. Sch., Grenada, W.I., 1977. Mem. Am. Med. Writers Assn. (N.Y. chpt. pres. 1984-85, nat. pres. 1987-88), Drug Info. Assn., Soc. Tech. Communication. Roman Catholic. Home: 1194 Parkside Ave Trenton NJ 08618-2626

LOSOS, JOSEPH ZBIGNIEW, epidemiologist; b. Kolhapur, Valivade, India, Dec. 12, 1943; arrived in Canada, 1951; s. Marian and Wladyslawa (Cieklinska) L.; m. Joanne Cameron Carr, July 24, 1977; children: Andrew, Michelle, Craig. MD, U. Toronto, Ont., 1968, Diploma Epidemiology, Cmty. Health, 1975. Physician Can. Univ. Svc. Overseas, Uganda, 1969-71; clin. tchr. U. Toronto, 1971-73; project officer Internat. Devel. Rsch. Ctr., Ottawa, Ont., 1973-75; resident U. Toronto, 1976-77; cons. epidemiologist WHO, Ndola, Zambia, 1977-79; dir. infection control Lab. Ctr. for Disease Control, Ottawa, 1980-84, dir. epidemiology, 1985-86, dir. gen., 1987—. Coauthor: Traveling with Children; contbr. articles to profl. jours. Soccer coach Can. Coaches Assn., Ottawa, 1989-93. Sub-lt. Can. Navy, 1964. Fellow Royal Coll. Physicians and surgeons, Am. Coll. Preventive Medicine; mem. Can. Soc. Tropical Medicine (pres. 1987-89). Avocations: athletics, classical music, drawing/sketching. Home: 175 Rothwell Dr, Gloucester, ON Canada K1J 7G7 Office: Laboratory Ctr for Disease Control, Tunneys Pasture, Ottawa, ON Canada K1A 0L2

LOSS, JOHN C., architect, retired educator; b. Muskegon, Mich., Mar. 6, 1931; s. Alton A. and Dorothy Ann (DeMars) Forward; m. LaMyrna Lois Draggoo, June 7, 1958. B.Arch., U. Mich., 1954, M.Arch., 1960. Registered architect, Md., Mich. Architect Eero Saarinen & Assocs., Bloomfield Hills, Mich., 1956-57; owner John Loss & Assocs, Detroit, 1960-75; prof., acting dean Sch. Architecture, U. Detroit, 1960-75; prof., head dept. architecture N.C. State U., Raleigh, 1975-79; assoc. dean. Sch. Architecture U. Md., College Park, 1981-83, prof. architecture, 1979-93, prof. emeritus architecture, 1993—; dir. Architecture and Engring. Performance Info. Ctr., 1982-93; pvt. practice, Annapolis, College Park, 1979-93, Whitehall, Mich., 1993—; mem. com. NRC-NAS, 1982-93; mem. bldg. diagnostics com. Adv. Bd. on Build Environ., 1983-93; mem. com. on earthquake engring. NRC, 1983-93; leader survey team for tornado damage in Pa. and Ohio, 1985. Author: Building Design for Natural Hazards in Eastern United States, 1981, Identification of Performance Failures in Large Structures and Buildings, 1987, Analysis of Performance Failures in Civil Structures and Large Buildings, 1990, Performance Failures in Buildings and Civil Works, 1991; works include med. clinic, N.C.; Aldersgate Multi Family Housing, Oscoda, Mich. Advisor Interfaith Housing Inc., Detroit, 1966-74; advisor Detroit Mayor's Office, 1967-69, Interim Housing Com. Mich. State Housing Devel. Authority, Lansing, 1969-71, Takoma Park Citizens for Schs. (Md.), 1981-82; advisor, cons. Hist. Preservation Commn., Prince George's County, Md.; mem. planning commn. Blue Lake Twp., Mich., 1994—; apptd. to art and environ. commn. Grand Rapids Diocese of Cath. Ch., 1996—. With U.S. Army, 1954-56. NSF grantee, 1978-81, 1982-84, 86-87, 88-90; named one of Men of Yr., Engring. News Record, 1984. Fellow AIA. Democrat. Roman Catholic. *To participate, as an architect, in the continuing saga of the creation of the built environment and, as a teacher, in the continuing rebirth of our intellectual and spiritual lives remains a very special honor. I feel a sincere debt of gratitude to my mother who read to me when I was a very small child and who launched me on a life of reading and service. Happiness is a spiritual thing - not a physical thing! Success (our happiness) begins with what we aspire to be - not what we have or want.*

LOSS, LOUIS, lawyer, retired educator; b. Lancaster, Pa., June 11, 1914; s. Zelig and Elizabeth (Wenger) L.; m. Bernice Segaloff, June 19, 1938; children: Margaret Ruth, Robert Stanley. B.S., U. Pa., 1934; LL.B., Yale U., 1937; A.M. (hon.), Harvard U., 1953. Bar: D.C. 1937, Mass. 1952, U.S. Supreme Ct. 1953. Atty. SEC, 1937-44, chief counsel div. trading and exchanges, 1944-48, assoc. gen. counsel, 1948-52; lectr. law Cath. U. Am., 1941-42; vis. lectr. law Yale U., 1947-52; professorial lectr. law George Washington U., 1949-52; prof. law Harvard U., 1952-62, William Nelson Cromwell prof. law, 1962-84, prof. emeritus, 1984—, dir. program instrn. for lawyers, 1976-84; prof. Faculté Internationale de Droit Comparé, Luxembourg, summer 1958, U. Witwatersrand, summer 1962, Salzburg (Austria) Seminar in Am. Studies, summers 1968, 77, Australian Nat. U., summer 1973; Ford prof. Inst. Advanced Legal Studies, U. London, 1969; Turner Meml. lectr. U. Tasmania, Australia, 1973; Kimber fellow U. Toronto, 1978; Taylor lectr. U. Lagos, Nigeria, 1981; vis. prof. U. Pa., 1989; scholar-in-residence, U. Ga., 1985, draftsman Uniform Securities Act, 1954-56; cons. Internat. Bank, 1963-65, various fgn. govts. Author: Securities Regulation, 1951, supplememt, 1955, 2d edit., 1961, supplement 1969 (6 vols.), 3d edit. (with Joel Seligman) 11 vols., 1988-93, Commentary on the Uniform Securities Act, 1976, Fundamentals of Securities Regulation, 1983, 2d edit., 1988, supplements, 1989-92, Japanese translation, 1989; co-author: Blue Sky Law, 1958; editor: Multinational Approaches-Corporate Insiders, 1976; sr. co-editor: Japanese Securities Regulation, 1983; reporter: Am. Law Inst.'s Fed. Securities Code, 1969-78. Vice chmn. bd., gen. counsel Harvard Coop. Soc., 1961-89, N.Y. Stock Exch. Legal Adv. Com., chmn., 1987-89. Fellow AAAS, Am. Bar Found. (ann. research award 1979); mem. ABA (coun. bus. law 1966-69, 1974-75), Am. Law Inst., Assn. Bar City N.Y. (assoc.), Soc. Pub. Tchrs. Law (assoc.)(Britain), Cosmos Club (Washington), Phi Beta Kappa (hon. Alpha chpt.-Harvard). Home: 39 Meadow Way Cambridge MA 02138-4635 Office: Harvard U Sch Law Cambridge MA 02138

LOSS, MARGARET RUTH, lawyer; b. Phila., June 17, 1946; d. Louis and Bernice Rose (Segaloff) L.; m. Harry Clark Johnson, 1986; 1 child, Elizabeth Loss Johnson. B.A., Radcliffe Coll., 1967; LL.B., Yale U., 1970. Bar: Conn. 1970, N.Y. 1973. Assoc. Sullivan & Cromwell, N.Y.C., 1971-77; with Equitable Life Assurance Soc. U.S., N.Y.C., 1977-88, asst. gen. counsel, 1979-85, v.p. and counsel, 1985-88; counsel LeBoeuf, Lamb, Greene & MacRae, N.Y.C., 1988—; dir. Yale Law Sch. Fund. Mem. ABA, Am. Law Inst., Conn. Bar Assn., Assn. of Bar of City N.Y. Office: LeBoeuf Lamb Greene & MacRae 125 W 55th St New York NY 10019-5369

LOSS, STUART HAROLD, financial executive; b. Lancaster, Pa., June 15, 1946; s. Nathan and Natalie M. (Koenigsberg) L.; m. Rachelle Smithline; children: Jessica Lauren, David Jonathan, Andrew Jordan. BS in Acctg., Syracuse U.; MBA in Fin., NYU. CPA, N.Y. With KPMG Peat Marwick, N.Y.C., 1971-77; exec. v.p., CFO TBWA Chiat/Day Inc.-East, N.Y.C., 1977-96; sec. TBWA Chiat/Day Inc.; exec. v.p., CFO Manning Selvage & Lee, Inc., N.Y.C., 1996—. Mem. AICPA, N.Y. State Soc. CPAs, N.Y. Credit and Fin. Mgmt. Assn., Treas. Club. Office: Manning Salvage & Lee Inc 79 Madison Ave New York NY 10016-7802

LOSSE, CATHERINE ANN, pediatric nurse, critical care nurse, educator, clinical nurse specialist, family nurse practitioner; b. Mount Holly, N.J., Mar. 12, 1959; d. David C. and Bernice (Lewis) L. Diploma, Helene Fuld Sch. Nursing, 1980; BSN magna cum laude, Thomas Jefferson U., 1986; MSN, U. Pa., 1989; cert. family nurse practitioner, Widener U., 1995-97. RN, N.J., Pa., Del.; cert. pediatric nurse, cert. pediatric critical care nurse; cert. PALS provider, BLS instr.; cert. clin. nurse specialist, N.J.; pediat. clin. nurse specialist, Del. Staff nurse adult med.-surg. Meml. Hosp. Burlington County, Mount Holly, N.J., 1980-81; staff nurse pediatric home care Newborn Nurses, Moorestown, N.J., 1986-87; clin. nurse II surg. intensive care Deborah Heart & Lung Ctr., Browns Mills, N.J., 1986-87, clin. nurse III pediatric cardiology, 1981-86, 87—; ednl. nurse specialist critical care The Children's Hosp., Phila., 1992-94; instr. nursing of families, maternal-child health, pediat., geriatrics Burlington County Coll., 1994-96; staff nurse pediatric home care Bayada Nurses, Burlington, N.J., 1995—; clin. instr. pediatrics Thomas Jefferson U., 1990; clin. instr. adult med. surg. Burlington County Coll., 1991. Mem. ANA, AACN (CCRN, pediat. spl. interest cons. 1995-96), Nat. Assn. Pediat. Nurse Assocs. and Practitioners, Am. Acad. Nurse Practitioners, N.J. State Nurses Assn. (cabinet on continuing edn. rev. team III 1992-96, advanced practice forum 1994—), Am. Heart Assn. (cert. instr. BLS, PALS provider, bd. dirs. Burlington County divsn. 1995—, vice chmn. cmty. site com. 1995—), Sigma Theta Tau. Home: 253 Spout Spring Ave Mount Holly NJ 08060-2041

LOSSE, JOHN WILLIAM, JR., mining company executive; b. St. Louis, Mar. 16, 1916; s. John William and Claire (Schmedtje) L.; m. Marjorie West Penney, Mar. 7, 1942; children: John William IV, Georgia Shane, Barbara Stevens, Mary Coulter, Penney Gregersen, Jane Momberger. BS, Washington U., St. Louis, 1937; MBA, Harvard U., 1939. Sec.-treas. J.W. Losse Tailoring Co., St. Louis, 1939-41, 45-55; treas., controller, asst. sec. Uranium

Reduction Co., Salt Lake City, 1955-62; v.p. finance Atlas Minerals div. Atlas Corp., Salt Lake City, 1962-64; asst. v.p., asst. treas. Am. Zinc Co., St. Louis, 1965-66; v.p. finance, treas. Am. Zinc Co., 1966-70; v.p. finance Conrad, Inc., St. Louis, 1970-71; v.p. finance, sec., dir. Fed. Resources Corp., Salt Lake City, 1971-82, pres., chief exec. officer, dir., 1982-84, 85-86, chief fin. officer, dir., 1986-88, v.p., treas., 1988—, also bd. dirs., 1988-89; sec.-treas. Madawaska Mines Ltd., Bancroft, Ont., Can., 1976-82, pres., bd. dirs., 1983—; pres. Camp Bird Colo., Inc., Ouray, 1983-92; Pres. Utah Natural Resources Council, 1964; tax com. and fin. adv. com. Am. Mining Congress, 1965-84; bd. dirs. Episcopal Mgmt. Corp., Salt Lake City. Bd. dirs. St. Mark's Hosp., Salt Lake City, 1987-88, Arthritis Found., Salt Lake City, 1988-97; vice chmn., bd. dirs. St. Mark's Charities, Salt Lake City, 1987-92; mem. investment com. Corp. of the Bishop, Salt Lake City, 1989-96; mem. investment adv. com. Perpetual Trust of St. Peter and St. Paul, 1995-96. Lt. comdr. USNR, 1941-45. Mem. Utah Mining Assn. (bd. dirs., legis. and tax coms. 1971-91), Country Club of Salt Lake City, Alta Club of Salt Lake City, Phi Delta Theta. Republican. Episcopalian. Office: Fed Resources Corp PO Box 806 Salt Lake City UT 84110-0806

LOSSING, FREDERICK PETTIT, retired chemist; b. Norwich, Ont., Can., Aug. 4, 1915; s. Frank Edgar and Evelyn (Pettit) L.; m. Frances Isabella Glazier; children—Wilda, Patricia, Catherine. B.A., U. Western Ont., London, 1938, M.A., 1940; Ph.D., McGill U., Montreal, Que., Can., 1942. Research chemist Shawinigan Chems. Ltd., Shawinigan Falls, Que., 1942-46; research officer Nat. Research Council Can., Ottawa, Ont., 1946-80; asso. dir. div. chemistry Nat. Research Council Can., 1969-77, prin. research officer, 1977-80; rsch. scientist dept. chemistry U. Ottawa, 1980-94. Fellow Royal Soc. Can., Chem. Inst. Can.; mem. Am. Soc. Mass. Spectrometry, Royal Astron. Soc. Can. Home: 95 Dorothea Dr, Ottawa, ON Canada K1V 7C6

LOSTEN, BASIL HARRY, bishop; b. Chesapeake City, Md., May 11, 1930; s. John and Julia (Petryshyn) L. BA, St. Basil's Coll., 1953; STL, Cath. U., Washington, 1957. Ordained priest Ukranian Cath. Ch., 1957. Personal sec. to archbishop, 1962-66; contr. Archdiocese, 1966-75; apptd. monsignor, 1968; apptd. titular bishop of Arcadiopolis and aux. bishop Ukrainian Cath. Archeparchy of Phila., 1971-77; vicar gen., 1971, apostolic adminstr., 1976-77; bishop of Stamford, Conn., 1977—. Pres. Ascension Manor. Club: Union League (Phila.). *

LOSTER, GARY LEE, personnel director; b. Birmingham, Ala., Aug. 8, 1946; s. Sylvester and Leola (Madison) L.; m. Allene Shells, Dec. 14, 1969; children: Jennifer, Jacqueline. Assoc. in Law Enforcement, Delta Coll., Bay City, Mich., 1977; BA, Saginaw Valley State U., 1988. Lic. pvt. investigator, Mich. Assembler GM, Saginaw, Mich., 1968-69, spl. investigator, 1978-83, security supr., 1984-85; supr. to assoc. adminstr. fire, security, vehicle adminstrn. Delphi Saginaw Steering Sys. GM Corp., Saginaw, Mich., 1985—; chief of police Buena Vista Twp. (Mich.) Police Dept., 1970-78; speaker law enforcement subjects to various ednl., govt., religious orgns. Council mem. Saginaw City Council, 1988; bd. dirs. Am. Heart Assn., Saginaw County Info. Ctr. on Alcoholism, Saginaw Bay County Substance Abuse Com. Sgt. USMC, 1964-68. Recipient numerous awards, certs. of appreciation from law enforcement agencies,schs., govt. agencies. Mem. Nat. Fire Protection Assn., Nat. Crime Prevention Assn., Am. Soc. for Indsl. Security, Law Enforcement Adv. Council Delta Coll., Citizen Band Assn. Saginaw County. Seventh Day Adventist. Avocations: weightlifting, swimming, scuba diving, youth work. Office: Delphi Saginaw Steering Sys GM Corp 3900 E Holland Rd Saginaw MI 48601-9494

LOSTY, BARBARA PAUL, college official; b. Norwich, N.Y., June 16, 1942; d. Henry Edward and Mary Frances (Crowell) Paul; m. Thomas August Losty, Nov. 27, 1965; children: Ellen Christine, Amanda Elizabeth. BA, Wellesley Coll., 1964; MA, U. Conn., 1969, PhD, 1971. Asst. prof. psychology Westminster Coll., Fulton, Mo., 1971-73; asst. prof. psychology Stephens Coll., Columbia, Mo., 1973-75, assoc. dir. sch. liberal and profl. studies, 1975-79, assoc. dean of faculty, 1979-85; dean U. Wis. Ctr.-Sheboygan County, Sheboygan, 1985-91; coord. human svcs. degrees Thomas Edison State Coll., Trenton, N.J., 1992-94, assoc. dean human svcs. degrees, 1994-96; pres. Waycross (Ga.) Coll., 1996—. Home: 922 Wood Valley Dr Waycross GA 31503 Office: Waycross Coll 2001 S Ga Pky Waycross GA 31503

LO SURDO, ANTONIO, physical chemist, educator; b. Spadafora, Italy, Jan. 1, 1943; came to U.S., 1955, naturalized, 1961; s. Salvatore Giuseppe and Marianna (La Macchia) Lo S.; m. Claudia Piva, Nov. 26, 1988. B.A., Syracuse U., 1965, Ph.D., 1970. Postdoctoral fellow, instr. chemistry Rutgers U., New Brunswick, N.J., 1969-71; vis. faculty Syracuse U., N.Y., 1971-72; research assoc. U. Conn., Storrs, 1972; vis. research assoc., lectr. Ohio State U., Columbus, 1972-74; research assoc. Clark U., Worcester, Mass., 1974-75; chief chemist Cambridge Instrument Co., Inc., Ossining, N.Y., 1975-76; research asst. prof. Rosenstiel Sch. Marine and Atmospheric Sci., U. Miami, Fla., 1977-79, research assoc. prof., 1979-82; chief chemist O'Brien & Gere Engrs., Syracuse, 1982-87; sect. chief, lab. dir. Roy F. Weston/REAC Project, 1988—. Contbr. articles to profl. jours. NSF fellow, 1965-66, 74-76; NIH fellow, 1969-70; Syracuse U. grantee, 1966-69. Mem. AAAS, Am. Chem. Soc., N.Y. Acad. Scis., Sigma Xi, Phi Lambda Upsilon. Home: 6 Chestnut Hill Rd Howell NJ 07731-1708 Office: GSA Raritan Depot 2890 Woodbridge Ave Bldg 209 Edison NJ 08837-3602

LOTAS, JUDITH PATTON, advertising executive; b. Iowa City, Apr. 23, 1942; d. John Henry and Jane (Vandike) Patton; children: Amanda Bell, Alexandra Vandike. BA, Fla. State U., 1964. Copywriter Liller, Neal, Battle and Lindsey Advt., Atlanta, 1964-67, Grey Advt., N.Y.C., 1967-72; creative group head SSC&B Advt., N.Y.C., 1972-74, asso. creative dir., 1974-79, v.p., 1975-79, sr. v.p., 1979-82, exec. creative dir., 1982-86; founding ptnr. Lotas Minard Patton McIver, Inc., N.Y.C., 1986—. Active scholarship fund raising; bd. dirs. Samuel Eaxman Cancer Rsch., Found., N.Y.C., 1981-88; fundraiser Nat. Coalition for the Homeless, N.Y.C., 1986—. Recipient Clio award, Venice Film Festival award, Graphics award Am. Inst. Graphic Artists, 1970, Effie award, Grad. of Distinction award Fla. State U., 1993; named Woman of Achievement, YWCA, One of Advt. Agys. 100 Best Women Ad Age, 1989. Mem. Advt. Women N.Y. (1st v.p. 1984-87, bd. dirs. 1981-87, Advt. Woman of Yr. 1993), The Ad Coun. (mem. creative rev. bd. 1994—, bd. dirs. 1995—), Women's Venture Fund (bd. dirs. 1995—), Kappa Alpha Theta. Democrat. Home: 45 E 89th St New York NY 10128-1251

LOTEYRO, CORAZON BIGATA, physician; b. Manila, Apr. 9, 1951; came to U.S., 1979; d. Victor G. Loteyro and Emilia Bigata; 1 child, Elizabeth. BS, Mindanao State U., Marawi City, The Philippines, 1972; MD, U. of East, Manila, 1976. Diplomate Am. Bd. Family Physicians. Physician Humana Medfirst, Peoria, Ill., 1984-85, Family Health Plan, Elm Grove, Wis., 1985-96, Covenant Health, Pewaukee, Wis., 1996—. Vol. Salvation Army, Milw., 1993. Fellow Am. Acad. Family Physicians; mem. Filipino-Am. Med. Assn. (pres. 1994-95), U. of East Alumni Assn. Midwest (treas. 1990-94). Republican. Roman Catholic. Avocations: skiing, traveling, movies, reading, music. Home: 16965 Beverly Dr Brookfield WI 53005-2754 Office: Covenant Health Care Pewaukee WI 53072

LOTHROP, KRISTIN CURTIS, sculptor; b. Tucson, Feb. 8, 1930; d. Thomas and Elizabeth (Longfellow) Curtis; m. Francis B. Lothrop, Jr., Dec. 27, 1951; children—Robin B., Thornton K. and Jonathan C. (twins). B.A., Bennington Coll., 1951. Exhbns. include: Nat. Sculpture Soc., 1967-71, NAD, 1968-71, Hudson Valley Art Assn., 1968, Allied Artists Am., 1969, Concord Art Assn., 1970; represented in permanent collection, Brookgreen Gardens, S.C. Recipient Mrs. Louis Bennett award Nat. Sculpture Soc., 1967; Thomas R. Procter award N.A.D., 1968; Dessie Greer award, 1969; Daniel Chester French medal, 1970; hon. mention Hudson Valley Art Assn., 1968; 1st prize Concord Art Assn., 1970, 83; 1st prize Manchester Arts Assn., 1975; 1st prize Hamilton-Wenham Art Show, 1980; Liskin purchase prize Nat. Sculpture Soc., 1986. Mem. Nat. Sculpture Soc., New Eng. Sculptors Assn. (1st prize 1987), The Copley Soc. of Boston (Copley master). Address: 71 Bridge St Manchester MA 01944-1412

LOTITO, MICHAEL JOSEPH, lawyer; b. Carbondale, Pa., July 22, 1948; s. Dominic Joseph and Margaret Mary (Miller) L.; m. Luanne R. McMaster, Nov. 9, 1985; 1 child, Kelly C. AB, Villanova U., 1970, JD, 1974. Bar: Pa. 1974, Calif. 1983; lic. sr. profl. human resources. Assoc. Barley, Snyder, Cooper & Barber, Lancaster, Pa., 1974-76, Jackson, Lewis, Schnitzler & Krupman, N.Y.C., 1976-81; mng. ptnr. Jackson, Lewis, Schnitzler & Krupman, San Francisco, 1982—; bd. dirs. No. Calif. Human Resource Coun., San Francisco. Co-author: Making the ADA Work for You, 1992, What Managers and Supervisors Need to Know About the ADA, 1992, The Americans With Disabilities Act: A Comprehensive Guide to Title I, 1992, Minding Your Business: Legal Issues and Practical Answers for Managing Workplace Privacy, 1997; contbr. articles to profl. jours. Mem. ABA, Calif. Bar Assn., Soc. for Human Resource Mgmt. (chmn. legis. affairs com. 1988-90, nat. employment law com. 1981-86, legal adv. bd. 1988—, bd. dirs. 1991—, chair edn. task force 1990-92, edn. com. 1993-94, vol. counsel to bd. dirs. 1993—), Calif. C. of C. (labor com. 1986-88). Republican. Roman Catholic. Home: 95 Deer Park Ave San Rafael CA 94901-2310 Office: Jackson Lewis Schnitzler & Krupman 525 Market St Ste 3400 San Francisco CA 94105-2742

LOTMAN, HERBERT, food processing executive; b. Phila., Oct. 9, 1933; s. Samuel Meyer and Gertrude L.; m. Karen Levin, Apr. 6, 1957; children: Shelly Hope, Jeffrey Mark. Pres., chmn. bd. Keystone Foods Corp., Bryn Mawr, Pa., 1951; pres. Keystone Foods Corp., 1960, chmn. bd., CEO, 1960—. Bd. dirs. Nat. Juvenile Diabetes Found. Served with U.S. Army, 1952-54. Mem. Young Pres. Orgn. Office: Keystone Foods Corp 401 City Ave # 800 Bala Cynwyd PA 19004-1122*

LOTOCKY, INNOCENT HILARIUS, bishop; b. Petlykivci Stari, Buchach, Ukraine, Nov. 3, 1915; came to U.S., 1946; s. Stefan and Maria (Tytyn) L. Student at various religious insts., Ukraine, Czechoslovakia; Ph.D. in Sacred Theology, U. Vienna, Austria, 1994. Ordained priest Ukrainian Catholic Ch., 1944, consecrated bishop, 1981; cert. tchr., Mich. Superior-novice master Order St. Basil, Dawson, Pa., 1946-51; provincial superior U.S. province Order St. Basil, N.Y., 1951-53; novice master Order St. Basil, Glen Cove, N.Y., 1958-60; pastor-superior St. George Ch., N.Y.C., 1953-58; pastor St. Nicholas Ch., Chgo., 1960-62; pastor-superior Immaculate Conception Ch., Hamtramck, Mich., 1962-81, also tchr., 1962-81; bishop Diocese St. Nicholas, Chgo., 1981-93, ret., 1993; provincial counselor U.S. province Order St. Basil, 1962-80, del. to gen. chpt. Rome, 1963. Active numerous civic orgns. Mem. Nat. Council Cath. Bishops. Home and Office: Diocese St Nicholas 2245 W Rice St Chicago IL 60622-4858*

LOTRICK, JOSEPH, aeronautical engineer; b. Plymouth, Pa.; s. Stephen and Catherine (Turpak) L.; m. Barbara Sue Vining; 1 child, Pegge Jo. Student, U. Pa., 1943; BS in Aero. Engring., Northrop U., 1962. Sr. engr. flight test N.Am. Aviation, L.A., 1952-86; project engr. Rockwell Internat., L.A., 1986—. With USN, 1943-46. Mem. AAAS, AIAA (mem. nat. tech. com. flight test 1984-86), Assn. Naval Aviation, Aircraft Owners and Pilots Assn., Elks. Republican. Achievements include flight testing of exotic airborne R&D avionics systems and sensors. Home: 2531 Highcliff Dr Torrance CA 90505-7305 Office: Rockwell Internat 201 N Douglas St # 21 El Segundo CA 90245-4637

LOTSCH, RICHARD CHARLES, osteopath; b. Waverly, Pa., Oct. 3, 1961; s. Charles Francis and Doris Emily (Shuster) L.; m. June Pamela Dennis, Sept. 21, 1985. BS, Hahnemann U., 1985; DO, Phila. Coll. Osteo. Medicine, 1996. Cert. physician asst. Emergency paramedic Lower Providence Ambulance, Eagleville, Pa., 1985-87; staff physician asst. Mont. County Emergency Svc., Norristown, Pa., 1985-87, 92-95; med. physician asst. USAF, 1987-92; emergency medicine resident Albert Einstein Med. Ctr., Phila., 1996—. Troop com. chmn. Boy Scouts Am., Cannon AFB, N.Mex., 1991-92, asst. scoutmaster, 1988-91; vol. paramedic Lower Providence Ambulance, Eagleville, 1982-85, asst. ambulance chief, 1982. Capt. USAF, 1987-92. Decorated Air Force Commendation medal, USAF, Air Force Health Professions scholar, 1992. Mem. Am. Coll. Emergency Physicians (student mem.), Assn. Mil. Osteo. Physicians and Surgeons (student mem.), Am. Osteo. Assn., Am. Acad. Family Physicians (student mem.), Am. Coll. Osteo. Family Physicians (student mem.). Avocations: snowskiing, sailing, computers, furniture building, hiking. Office: Albert Einstein Med Ctr 5501 Old York Rd Philadelphia PA 19141-3001

LOTSPEICH, ELLIN SUE, art specialist, educator; b. Spring Valley, Ill., July 2, 1952; d. Donald Robert and Mary Rita (Smith) Mason; m. Thomas Grant Weaver, Jan. 26, 1974 (dec. July 1989); children: Jennifer, Michelle, Patrick; m. Micheal Charles Lotspeich, Apr. 9, 1994; children: Michael Charles II, Charles David. BS, Western Ill. U., 1974, M Ednl. Adminstrn., 1995. Unit art specialist Winola Unit Dist., Viola, Ill., 1974-84, Al Wood Unit Dist., Woodhull, Ill., 1984—; discipline based art cons. Getty Ctr. for Edn. in Arts, 1989—; exec. bd. Commn. on Edn. Diocese of Peoria, Ill., 1993—, exec. chmn. Religious Edn. Com., 1994—. Mem. Nat. Art Edn. Assn., Ill. Art Edn. Assn. (exec. bd. 1980—, state youth art chmn. 1990-93), Ill. Rembrandt State Assn. (editor newsletter 1987-90, bd. dirs.), Ill. Alliance for Arts, Henry Stark H.S. Art Tchrs. (pres. 1984-96). Home: 4220 34th Ave Pl Moline IL 61265 Office: Al Wood Unit Dist 301 W 5th Ave Woodhull IL 61490-9589

LOTT, IRA TOTZ, pediatric neurologist; b. Cin., Apr. 15, 1941; s. Maxwell and Jeneda (Totz) L.; m. Ruth J. Weiss, June 21, 1964; children: Lisa, David I. BA cum laude, Brandeis U., 1963; MD cum laude, Ohio State U., 1967. Intern Mass. Gen. Hosp., Boston, 1967, resident in pediatrics, 1967-69, resident in child neurology, 1971-74; clin. assoc. NIH, Bethesda, Md., 1969-71; from clin. rsch. fellow to asst. prof. Harvard Med. Sch., Boston, 1971-82; clin. dir. Eunice Kennedy Shriver Ctr. for Mental Retardation, Waltham, Mass., 1974-82; assoc. prof. U. Calif., Irvine, 1983-91, prof., 1992—; chmn. dept. pediatrics U. Calif., Irvine, 1992—, dir. pediatric neurology, 1983—; pres. Prof. Child Neurology, Mpls., 1992—. Editor: Down Syndrome-Medical Advances, 1991; contbr. articles to profl. jours. Sec., treas. Child Neurology Soc., Mpls., 1987-90. Lt. comdr. USPHS, 1969-71. NIH grantee, 1974—; recipient Career Devel. award Kennedy Found., 1976. Fellow Am. Acad. Neurology; mem. Am. Pediatric Soc., Am. Neurol. Assn., Nat. Down Syndrome Soc. (sci. acad. bd. 1985—), Western Soc. for Pediatric Rsch. (councillor 1989-91). Achievements include research in relationship of Down Syndrome to Alzheimer's disease, neurometabolic disease, extracorporeal membrane oxygenation in infants. Office: U Calif Irvine Med Ctr Dept Pediatrics 101 The City Dr S # 27 Orange CA 92868-3201

LOTT, LESLIE JEAN, lawyer; b. Louisville, Nov. 12, 1950; d. Emmett Russell Jr. and Allene (Barbee) L.; m. Michael T. Moore, Dec. 28, 1977; children: Michael T. Jr., Emmett Russell Lott. BA, U. Fla., 1972, JD, 1974; postgrad., Escuela Libre de Derecho, Mexico City, 1973. Bar: Fla. 1974, D.C. 1975, U.S. Ct. Appeals (fed. cir.) 1975, N.Y. 1977, U.S. Dist. Ct. (so. dist.) Fla. 1981, U.S. Dist. Ct. (so. dist.) Trial Bar 1981, U.S. Dist. Ct. (mid. dist.) Fla. 1995. Trademark examiner U.S. Patent and Trademark Office, Arlington, Va., 1974-76; assoc. Pennie & Edmonds, N.Y.C., 1976-80, Hassan Mahassni/Burlingham, Underwood & Lord, Jeddah, Saudi Arabia, 1978-79, Floyd, Pearson, Stewart, Richman, Greer, Weil & Zack, Miami, Fla., 1981-83; pvt. practice Leslie J. Lott & Assocs., P.A., Coral Gables, Fla., 1983-94, Lott & Friedland, P.A., Coral Gables, 1994—; judge Moot Ct., Trial Advocacy U. Miami, 1981, 82, 84, 85, 87; lectr. continuing legal edn., 1987—. Editor So. Dist. Digest, 1981-84; contbr. articles to profl. jours. Recipient Am. Jurisprudence Book Award in Fed. Practice, 1973. Mem. Internat. Trademark Assn. (chmn. com. 1986-88, 97—, bd. dirs. 1993-94), Am. Intellectual Property Law Assn., Fla. Bar Assn. (chmn. 1983—), Exec. Coun. Bus. Law Sec., 1991-93, South Fla. Patent Law Assn., mem. CPR/INTA Panel of Distinguished neutrals for the Resolution of Trademark Disputes, 1994—. Office: Lott & Friedland PA 255 Alhambra Cir Ste 555 Coral Gables FL 33134-7404

LOTT, RONNIE (RONALD MANDEL LOTT), professional football player; b. Albuquerque, May 8, 1959. BS in Pub. Adminstrn., U. So. Calif., 1981. With San Francisco 49ers, 1981-90, L.A. Raiders, 1991-93, N.Y. Jets, 1993-94, Kansas City Chiefs, 1994-95; analyst NFL Fox Broadcasting Co., Beverly Hills, Calif., 1996—. founder, All Stars Helping Kids, 1989. Named to Sporting News Coll. All-Am. team, 1980, Pro Bowl team, 1981-84, 86-91, Sporting News All-Pro team, 1981, 87, 90. Office: Fox Broadcasting Co PO Box 900 Beverly Hills CA 90213*

LOTT, TRENT, senator; b. Grenada, Miss., Oct. 9, 1941; s. Chester P. and Iona (Watson) L.; m. Patricia E. Thompson, Dec. 27, 1964; children—Chester T., Jr., Tyler Elizabeth. B.P.A., U. Miss., 1963, J.D., 1967. Bar: Miss. 1967. Assoc. Bryan & Gordon, Pascagoula, Miss., 1967; adminstrv. asst. to Congressman William M. Colmer, 1968-72; mem. 93d-100th Congresses from 5th Miss. dist., 1973-89; Rep. whip 97th-100th Congresses from 5th Miss. dist., mem. Ho. Rules com.; U.S. senator from Miss., 1989—, Senate armed svcs. com., budget com., energy, natural resources com., mem. commerce, sci. and transp. com., fin./rules and adminstrn. com., Senate Rep. policy com., 102d Congress, sec. Senate Rep. Conf., 103d Congress, majority whip 104th Congress; field rep. for U. Miss., 1963-65; acting alumni sec. Ole Miss Alumni Assn., 1966-67; named as observer from House to Geneva Arms Control talks; chmn. Commerce, Sci. & Transp. subcom. on surface transp. & merchant marine; mem. Senate Republican Policy Com. Recipient Golden Bulldog award, Guardian of Small Bus. award. Mem. ABA, Jackson County Bar Assn., Sigma Nu, Phi Alpha Delta. Republican. Baptist. Lodge: Mason. Office: 487 Russell Senate Office Bldg Washington DC 20510*

LOTT, WAYNE THOMAS, systems engineer; b. Pitts., Mar. 20, 1959; s. Wayne Thomas Lott Sr. and Patricia Julia (Malanowski) Lott Martin; m. Diane Mary Phillips, Sept. 11, 1982; children: Sarah Marie, Justin Thomas. AS in Computer Sci., C.C. Allegheny County, Pitts., 1984; BSBA in Info. Sys., Robert Morris Coll., 1986. Intern, programmer Thrift Drug Co., Pitts., 1986; contract programmer Comsource Tech. Svcs., Pitts., 1986-87; programmer Tippins Inc., Pitts., 1987; initial designer tng. ATT, Herndon, Va., 1988; tech. tester ATT, Herndon, 1988-89; sys. analyst ATT, Herndon, Va., 1989-92; sys. engr. ATT Bell Labs., Herndon, 1992-94, ATT, Herndon, 1995—. Mem. IEEE. Roman Catholic. Home: 12779 Misty Creek Ln Fairfax VA 22033-3102

LOTTES, PATRICIA JOETTE HICKS, foundation administrator, retired nurse; b. Balt., Aug. 18, 1955; d. James Thomas and Linda Belle (Cadd) Hicks; m. Jeffrey Grant Gross, Aug. 18, 1979 (div. 1981); m. William Melamet Lottes, Sept. 10, 1983. Diploma in practical nursing, Union Meml. Hosp., 1978. Staff nurse Union Meml. Hosp., Balt., 1978-79, critical care nurse, 1979-81; vis. critical care nurse Balt., 1981-84; head nurse Pharmakinetics, Inc., Balt., 1984-85; dir. Arachnoiditis Info. and Support Network, Inc., Ballwin, Mo., 1991—, dir. nat. support groups, 1992—; nat. support group leader Arachnoid, 1993—. Sec., treas. O'Fallon (Mo.) Elks Ladies Aux., 1989-91, treas., 1991-92, incorporator, 1991, bd. dirs., 1991-94; co-chairperson 303d Field Hosp., U.S. Army Family Support Group, St. Louis, 1990-94. Mem. Nat. Disaster Med. Systems (assoc.), Elks Benevolent Trust, Elks Nat. Home Perpetual Trust. Republican. Baptist. Avocation: quilting. Home: 606 Barbara Dr O'Fallon MO 63366-1306

LOTTMAN, EVAN, film editor. Editor: (films) Puzzle of a Downfall Child, 1970, Panic in Needle Park, 1971, Scarecrow, 1973, The Effects of Gamma Rays on Man-in-the-Moon Marigolds, 1973, (with others) The Exorcist, 1973 (Academy award nomination best film editing 1973), (with Richard Fetterman) Sweet Revenge, 1976, The Seduction of Joe Tynan, 1979, (with Aram Avakian, Norman Gay, and Marc Laub) Honeysuckle Rose, 1980, Rollover, 1981, The Pilot, 1981, Sophie's Choice, 1982, The Muppets Take Manhattan, 1984, The Protector, 1985, Maximum Overdrive, 1986, On the Yard, 1987, Orphans, 1987, See You in the Morning, 1989, Presumed Innocent, 1990, Beyond Innocence, 1992, The Public Eye, 1992, Missing Pieces, 1992, Guilty as Sin, 1993, (TV movies) Gotham, 1988. Home: 15 W 72nd St New York NY 10023-3402 Office: The Gersh Agency 232 N Canon Dr Beverly Hills CA 90210-5302*

LOTWIN, STANFORD GERALD, lawyer; b. N.Y.C., June 23, 1930; s. Herman and Rita (Saltzman) L.; m. Judy Scott, Oct. 15, 1994; children: Lori Hope, David. BS, Bklyn. Coll., 1951, LLB, 1954, LLM, 1957. Bar: N.Y. 1954, U.S. Supreme Ct. 1961, Pa. 1986. Ptnr. Tenzer, Greenblatt LLP, N.Y.C., 1987—; of counsel Frankfurt, Garbus, Klein & Selz, N.Y.C., 1983-87. Served with U.S. Army, 1954-56. Fellow Am. Acad. Matrimonial Lawyers (bd. of mgrs. 1984—); mem. N.Y. State Bar Assn. (family law sect.), N.Y. County Trial Lawyers (lectr. 1980—), Internat. Acad. Matrimonial Attys. Office: 405 Lexington Ave New York NY 10174-0002

LOTZ, DENTON, minister, church official; b. Flushing, N.Y., Jan. 18, 1939; s. John Milton and Adeline Helen (Kettell) L.; m. Janice Robinson, Mar. 15, 1970; children: John-Paul, Alena, Carsten. BA, U. N.C., 1961; STB, Harvard Div. Sch., 1966; ThD, U. Hamburg, Fed. Republic Germany, 1970; DD (hon.), Campbell U., 1982, Ea. Bapt. Sem., 1991, Alderson-Broadus, 1995. Prof. mission Bapt. Sem., Ruschlikon, Switzerland, 1972-80; dir. evangelism Bapt. World Alliance, McLean, Va., 1980-88, gen. sec., 1988—; fraternal rep. Am. Bapt. Internat. Ministries To Ea. Europe, Valley Forge, Pa., 1970-80. Author, editor: Baptists in the USSR, 1987; editor: Spring Has Returned to China, 1987. V.p. CARE, N.Y.C., 1981. 1st lt. USMC, 1961-63. Mem. Internat. Religious Liberty Assn. (pres. 1990-91, 96-97). Office: Bapt World Alliance 6733 Curran St Mc Lean VA 22101-3804

LOTZE, BARBARA, physicist; b. Mezokovesd, Hungary, Jan. 4, 1924; d. Matyas and Borbala (Toth) Kalo; came to U.S., 1961, naturalized, 1967; Applied Mathematician Diploma with honors, Eotvos Lorand U. Scis., Budapest, Hungary, 1956; PhD, Innsbruck (Austria) U., 1961; m. Dieter P. Lotze, Oct. 6, 1958. Mathematician, Hungarian Cen. Statis. Bur., Budapest, 1955-56; tchr. math., Iselsberg, Austria, 1959-60; asst. prof. physics Allegheny Coll., 1963-69, assoc. prof., 1969-77, prof., 1977-90, prof. emeritus, 1990—, chmn. dept., 1981-84; lectr. in history of physics; speaker to civic groups. Mem. Am. Phys. Soc. (mem. com. internat. freedom of scientists 1993-95), Am. Inst. Physics (mem. adv. com. history of physics 1994-97), Am. Assn. Physics Tchrs. (coun., sect. rep. Western Pa., chmn. nat. com. on women in physics 1983-84, com. internat. physics edn. 1991-93, com. history and philosophy of physics 1996—, Disting. Svc. award 1986, cert. of appreciation 1988), AAUW, N.Y. Acad. Scis., Am. Hungarian Educators Assn. (pres. 1980-82), Wilhelm Busch Gesellschaft (Hanover). Editor: Making Contributions: An Historical Overview of Women's Role in Physics, 1984; co-editor The First War Between Socialist States: The Hungarian Revolution of 1956 and Its Impact, 1984; contbr. articles to profl. jours. Home: 462 Hartz Ave Meadville PA 16335-1325 Office: Allegheny Coll Dept Physics Meadville PA 16335

LOTZE, MICHAEL THOMAS, surgeon; b. Altadena, Calif., July 11, 1952; s. Thomas Hilary and Joanne Bernice (Bellas) L.; m. Joan Harvey, June 25, 1977; children: Thomas, Anna, Michael, Jenette. BA, Northwestern U., 1973, MD with hons., 1974. Diplomate Am. Bd. Surgery, Nat. Bd. Med. Examiners; lic. N.Y., Minn., Md., Pa. Jr. fellow in surgery M.D. Anderson Tumor Inst., Houston, Tex., 1975; intern, resident Stong Meml. Hosp., Rochester, N.Y., 1975-76; asst. resident in surgery Stong Meml. Hosp., Rochester, 1976-77; fellow surgery br. Nat. Cancer Inst., Bethesda, Md., 1978-80; sr. and chief resident surgery, instr. U. Rochester, N.Y., 1980-82; asst. prof. surgery Uniformed Svcs. U. of Health Scis., Bethesda, Md., 1983-88; assoc. prof. surgery Uniformed Svcs. U. of Health Scis., Bethesda, 1988-90; prof. surgery, molecular genetics and biochemistry chief sect. surgical oncology U. Pitts., 1990—; co-dir. human gene therapy program Pitts. Genetics Inst., 1991—; co-dir. divsn. biol. therapeutics Pitts. Cancer Inst., 1992—; mem. numerous groups involved in rsch. on melanoma and other cancers including: coord. NIH Melanoma Working Group, 1985-87, Rev. Bd. United Cancer Coun., Inc., Rochester, 1985-87, chmn. spl. study sect. Exptl. Immunology NIH, 1990, mem. planning com. NIH Consensus Devel. Conf. on Diagnosis and Treatment of Early Melanoma, 1991, mem. search com. Chair U. Pitts. Med. Ctr. dir. radiation oncology, 1992, Mellon Dickson Prize com. U. Pitt. Sch. Medicine, 1993-95; vis. prof. Duke Univ, Durham, N.C., 1987, Acad. Sinica/Veteran's Gen. Hosp, Tapei, Taiwan, 1993; co-organizer Keystone Symposium on Cellular Inunity and the Immunotherapy of Cancer, Park City, Utah, 1990, Keystone Symposium on Melanoma and Biology of the Neural Crest, Taos, N. Mex., 1992. on Cellular Immunity and the Immunotherapy of CancerII, Taos, 1993; organizer 2d Internat. Congress on Biol. Response Modifiers, San Diego, 1993. Contbr. over 280 articles to profl. jours. including Jour. Am. Med. Assn. New Eng. Jour Medicine, Immunology, Exptl. Immunology and others; presenter at about 200 sci. workshops, confs., symposiums.; editor: (with others) (books) Cellular Immunity and the Immunotherapy of Cancer, 1990, Current Cancer Therapy, 1994, Regional Therapy of Advanced Cancer,

1996; producer films on Ultrasound Imaging, Laser surgery and other Spectacular Problems in Surgery, 1986, Immunotherapy Vidoe Handbook, 1992, Resection of a Giant Lipoma, 1995; assoc. editor The Cancer Jour., 1995; mem. edtl. bd. European Cytokine Jour., 1988, Jour. Immunotherapy, 1990, Jour. Immunology, 1990-95, Contemporary Oncology, 1990-94, Gen. Surgery and Laparoscopy News, 1991, Melanoma Rsch., 1991, Therapeutic Immunology, 1993, Gene Therapy (Nature), 1995 and others. Med. Officer, Nat. Health Svc. Corps, 1977-78. Named Ann. Edith Hamilton Cancer Lectr., Genesee Hosp., Wasyl Pluta Cancer Ctr., Rochester, N.Y., 1986; Virginia Mason Rsch. Ctr. Disting. Lectr., Seattle, 1990, Ann. John Palmer Lectr., U. Toronto, Can., 1991, 10th Hinshaw Lectr. U. Rochester, 1991, Sommer Meml. Lectr. Portland, Oreg., 1994, El Tabah Lectr., McGill U., Montreal, Can., 1995, 1st Peter Fink Lectr., Meml. Sloan Kettering, 1995; grantee: NIH, 1992-96, 92-94, 94-99, 95, 95-99 and others, VA RAG, 1991-93. Fellow Am. Coll. Surgeons; mem. AMA, Am. Assn. Cancer Rsch. (program com. 1991), Am. Assn. Immunology (program com. 1990, 92), Am. Soc. Clin. Oncology, Assn. Acad. Surgery, Cell Transplant Soc., Clin. Immunological Soc. (program com. 1993),Soc. for Analytical Cytology, Soc. for Surgical Oncology (program com. 1992, 93, clin. affairs com. 1991-93), Soc. Univ. Surgeons, Soc. for Biologic Therapy (program com. 1991-93), World Assn. Hepato-Pancreatico-Biliary Surgery. Office: Univ Pitts 200 Lothrop St Pittsburgh PA 15201

LOTZENHISER, GEORGE WILLIAM, music educator, university administrator, composer; b. Spokane, Wash., May 16, 1923; married; 1 child. BA cum laude, Ea. Wash. U., 1946, BEd in Social Sci., 1947; MusM, U. Mich., 1948; EdD, U. Oreg., 1956. Prof. music U. Ariz., Tucson, 1948-60; prof. Ea. Wash. U., Cheney, 1960-83, dir. H.S. creative arts summer series, 1960-83; dean Ea. Wash. U. Sch. Fine Arts, Cheney, 1960-83, dean emeritus, 1983—; cons. and lectr. in field; tchg. fellow U. Mich., 1947-48. Author: A Study of Faculty Loads in Member Schools of the National Association of Schools of Music, 1963, A Study of the Selection Process of Administrators of the Fine Arts in Colleges and Universities in the U.S., 1970, Music 200: A Programmed Music Theory Text; numerous solo and ensemble compositions; contbr. articles to profl. jours.; profl. condr./trombonist symphony, opera, musical theatre, ballet, circus, etc. Mem. Wash. State Music Adv. Com., 1967-83, exec. com. Alliance for Arts Edn., 1972-83; mem. Spokane Riverfront Festival of the Arts, 1976-78, Allied Arts of Wash. State, 1977-83. Served to rear adm. USNR, 1942-82. Decorated Legion of Merit, 1982. Mem. ASCAP, Nat. Assn. Schs. Music (accreditation com. chmn. 1960—), Nat. Music Educators Research Council, N.W. Assn. Accreditation Com., Western Assn. Schs. and Colls. Com., Eastern Wash. Music Educators. Congregationalist. Home: PO Box 1528 Coupeville WA 98239-1528

LOU, ZHENG (DAVID), mechanical engineer, biomedical engineer; b. Changshu, Jiangsu, Peoples Republic China; came to U.S., 1982; s. Gui-Xin and Pei-Ling Lou; m. Min Yu, 1984; children: Katherine, Paul, Craig. BE, Zhejiang U., Hangzhou, China, 1982; PhD, U. Mich., 1990. Asst. rsch. scientist Transp. Rsch. Inst. U. Mich., Ann Arbor, 1990-93; tech. specialist Ford Motor Co., Ypsilanti, Mich., 1993—. Contbr. articles to Jour. Rheology, Jour. Biomechanics, others. Grantee NASA, 1992-94, U.S. Army, 1992-94. Mem. ASME, SAE, N.Y. Acad. Scis., SME, Tau Beta Pi, Sigma Xi. Achievements include research in nonlinear dynamic interaction between an electrorheological fluid and a viscometer, dynamics of electrorheological valves and dampers, heat transfer model in hyperthermia as a tumor therapy. Home: 1613 Old Salem St Plymouth MI 48170-1026 Office: Ford Motor Co EFHD PO Box 922 McKean and Textile Rds Ypsilanti MI 48197

LOUARGAND, MARC ANDREW, real estate executive, financial consultant; b. San Francisco, July 3, 1945; s. Andrew Louargand and Edna Antoinette McNeil (dec.); m. Elizabeth A. Warner, June 18, 1966 (div. Oct. 1978); m. J. R. McDaniel, Feb. 14, 1986. BA, U. Calif., Santa Barbara, 1967; MBA, U. Calif., L.A., 1974, PhD, 1982. Asst. prof. Calif. State Polytech. U., Pomona, 1975-77; assoc. prof. Calif. State U., Northridge, 1977-83, U. Mass., Boston, 1983-88; sr. lectr. Ctr. for Real Estate Devel. MIT, Cambridge, 1986-93; 2d v.p., sr. officer Mass. Mut. Life Ins. Co., Springfield, Mass., 1993-94; mng. dir. Cornerstone Real Estate Advisors, 1993—; chmn. Mile Square Farm Inc., Vt. Only of Mile Square Farm; cons. in field. Author: CRE2000: Managing the Fifth Strategic Resource, Study Guide to Financial Management, 1986, (with others) Principles and Techniques of Appraisal Review, 1980, Handbook of Real Estate Portfolio Management; assoc. editor Jour. Real Estate Lit., Jour. Real Estate Portfolio Management; contbr. articles to profl. jours. Bd. dirs. Beverly Glen Assn., Bel Air, Calif., 1973-77, Citronia Homeowners Assn., Northridge, Calif., 1978-83; chmn. Carlisle (Mass.) Bd. Assessors, 1985-93. Mem. Nat. Coun. Real Estate Investment Fiduciaries (chair portfolio strategy com.), Am. Real Estate Soc. Republican. Avocations: tree farming, skiing, building restoration. Home: 32 Longmeadow St Longmeadow MA 01106-1015

LOUBE, SAMUEL DENNIS, physician; b. Rumania, Aug. 26, 1921; came to U.S., 1922, naturalized, 1927; s. Harry and Rebecca (Pollack) L.; m. Emily Wallace, Apr. 14, 1976; children—Julian M., Jonathan B., Susan C., Karen E., Patricia A., Pamela B., Brian R. A.B., George Washington U., 1941, M.D. cum laude, 1943. Diplomate: Am. Bd. Internal Medicine. Intern, then resident in medicine Gallinger Municipal Hosp., Washington, 1943-46; physician USPHS, 1946-48; postdoctoral fellow NIH, 1948-50; research fellow in endocrinology Michael Reese Hosp., Chgo., 1948-49; research fellow in metabolism and endocrinology May Inst. Jewish Hosp., Cin., 1949-50; mem. faculty George Washington U. Med. Sch., 1950-89, clin. prof. medicine, 1975-89, prof. emeritus, 1989; practice medicine specializing in endocrinology and metabolic diseases, Washington, 1950-88, mem. Washington Internal Medicine Group, 1965-88; former chmn. dept. medicine, chief sect. endocrinology Sibley Meml. Hosp. Contbr. articles to med. jours. Fellow ACP; mem. AMA, Am. Diabetes Assn., Endocrine Soc., Am. Soc. Internal Medicine, Diabetes Assn. D.C. (past pres.), Jacobi Med. Soc. (past pres.). Jewish.

LOUBET, JEFFREY W., lawyer; b. Mt. Vernon, N.Y., May 12, 1943; s. Nathaniel R. and Joan (Fleischer) L.; m. Susan Maria Thom, Aug. 29, 1972; 1 child, Thom Carlyle. BA, Colgate U., 1965; JD, St. John's U., 1968; LLM in Taxation, N.Y. U., 1970. Bar: N.Y. 1968, U.S. Tax Ct. 1969, U.S. Dist. Ct. (so. dist.) N.Y. 1969, N.Mex. 1976, U.S. Dist. Ct. N.Mex. 1977. Assoc. Poletti, Freidin, Prashker, Feldman & Gartner, N.Y.C., 1969-76; ptnr. Modrall, Sperling, Roehl, Harris & Sisk, Albuquerque, 1976-94; counsel Rodey, Dickason, Sloan, Akin & Robb, Albuquerque, 1994—; lectr. N.Mex. Estate Roundtable, Albuquerque, 1979—; vis. prof. Estate and Gift Tax U. N.Mex., Albuquerque, 1988-89. Contbr. articles to profl. jours. Mem. Lovelace Inst. Estate Planning Adv. Coun., 1993—; mem. adv. bd. on charitable giving Albuquerque Cmty. Found., 1995—. Masters World Record Holder, high hurdles and decathlon. Fellow Am. Coll. Trust and Estate Counsel (mem. estate and gift com.); mem. N.Mex. Estate Planning Coun., Greater Albuquerque C. of C. (chair tax task force, 1992, chair state govt. com., 1993), YMCA (mem. bd. dirs.). Avocations: track & field, skiing, fly fishing. Home: PO Box 3754 Albuquerque NM 87190 Office: Rodey Dickason Sloan Akin & Robb PO Box 1888 Albuquerque NM 87103-1888

LOUCK, LISA ANN, lawyer; b. Davenport, Iowa, July 16, 1963; d. Richard Lane and Jo Ann (Frerkes) L. BSBA, Iowa State U., 1985; JD, South Tex. Coll. Law, 1991. Bar: Tex. 1992. Atty. Woodard, Hall & Primm, Houston, 1994—; mediator Tex. Registry Alt. Dispute Resolution Profls., 1992—. Recipient Am. Jurisprudence award Lawyers Coop. Pub., 1991. Mem. ABA, State Bar Tex., Houston Bar Assn., Houston Young Lawyers Assn., Phi Alpha Delta. Office: Woodard Hall & Primm PC 7100 Texas Commerce Tower Houston TX 77002

LOUCK, LORI ANN, speech-language pathologist; b. Davenport, Iowa, Sept. 5, 1965; d. Richard Lane and JoAnn (Frerkes) L.; m. John Joseph Jenkus III, July 10, 1993. BS in Edn., U. Houston, 1990; MS in Speech Pathology, Nova Southeastern U., 1995. Tchr. Broward County Schs., Hollywood, Fla., 1990-95; speech pathologist Dade County Pub. Schs., Miami, Fla., 1996—; interview com. Dade County Schs., 1996—, child study team, 1996—. Col. Humane Soc.-Broward, Ft. Lauderdale, 1995—, Coconut Grove Arts Festival, Miami, 1996. Mem. Am. Speech-Lang.-Hearing Assn. (cert. clin. competency 1996). Home: 501 El Dorado Pky Plantation FL 33317

LOUCKS, DANIEL PETER, environmental systems engineer; b. Chambersburg, Pa., June 4, 1932; s. Emerson Hunsberger and Eleanor Wright (Johnson) L.; m. Marjorie Ann Grant, June 24, 1967; children: Jennifer Lee, Susan Louise. B.S., Pa. State U., 1954; M.S., Yale U., 1955; Ph.D., Cornell U., 1965. Asst. prof. environ. engrng. Cornell U., Ithaca, N.Y., 1965-70; assoc. prof. Cornell U., 1970-74, prof., 1974—, chmn. dept., 1974-80; assoc. dean research and grad. studies Cornell U. (Coll. Engring.), 1980-81; rsch. fellow Harvard U., Cambridge, Mass., 1968; economist IBRD, Washington, 1972-73; vis. prof. MIT, Cambridge, 1977-78; rsch. scholar Internat. Inst. for Applied Sys. Analysis, 1981-82; vis. disting. prof. U. Colo., 1992, U. Adelaide, 1992, Tech. U. Aachen, Germany, 1993, U. Tech., Delft, The Netherlands, 1995; cons. NATO, UN, WHO, FAO, UNESCO, IRBD on water resources and regional devel. projects in Asia, Western and EAstern Europe, Africa and L.Am., 1970—, EPA on water quality planning USSR, 1975-77; vis. prof. Internat. Inst. Hydraulic and Environ. Engring., Delft, 1976-80, 86—; environ. adv. bd. U.S. Army Corps Engrs., 1994—, chmn. 1996—; dir. NATO Advanced Rsch. Workshops, 1990, 95. Contbr. articles to jours. and books on math. models. for mng. water resources systems and environ. quality. Bd. dirs. Wilderness Corp., Plymouth, Vt., 1968-96, treas., 1987-96; pres. Cmty. Improvement Assn., Ithaca, 1976-77. Capt., aviator USNR, 1956-81. Recipient U.S. Sr. Rsch. award Alexander von Humboldt Found., 1992, Joy Wyatt Challenge (EDUCOM) award, 1991, Disting. Lecture award Nat. Rsch. Coun. Taiwan, 1990; Fulbright-Hayes fellow Yugoslavia, 1975. Fellow ASCE (Walter Huber rsch. award 1970, Julian Hinds award 1986); mem. AAAS, NAE, Am. Geophys. Union, Inst. Mgmt. Scis., Internat. Water Resources Assn., Am. Water Resources Assn., Internat. Assn. Hydraulic Rsch., Internat. Assn. Hydrologic Scis., Sigma Xi. Home: 116 Crest Ln Ithaca NY 14850-2704 Office: Cornell U Hollister Hall Ithaca NY 14853

LOUCKS, RALPH BRUCE, JR., investment company executive; b. St. Louis, Dec. 10, 1924; s. Ralph Bruce and Dola (Blake) L.; m. Lois Holloway, June 4, 1949 (dec. Sept. 1983); children: Elizabeth, Mary Jane; m. Mary Sutliffe Stahl, June 2, 1984. BA, Lake Forest Coll., 1949; postgrad. U. Chgo., 1950-52. Registered prin. Nat. Assn. Securities Dealers. Investment fund mgr. No. Trust Co., Chgo., 1950-53, Brown Bros. Harriman & Co., Chgo., 1953-55; investment counsel, pres. Tilden, Loucks & Grannis, Chgo., 1955-80; sr. v.p. Bacon, Whipple & Co., 1981-88; sr. v.p. Roberts, Loucks & Co., 1988—. Served with 11th Armored Div., AUS, 1943-45. Decorated Bronze Star medal, Purple Heart. Mem. Investment Analysts Soc., Investment Counsel Assn. Am., Huguenot Soc. Ill. (pres. 1960-61), Nat. Assn. Security Dealers (registered prin.), Soc. Colonial Wars. Clubs: Economic, Racquet, Chgo. Yacht (Chgo.). Office: 250 S Wacker Dr Chicago IL 60606-6313

LOUCKS, VERNON R., JR., medical technologies executive; b. Evanston, Ill., Oct. 24, 1934; s. Vernon Reece and Sue (Burton) L.; m. Linda Kay Olson, May 12, 1972; 6 children. B.A. in History, Yale U., 1957; M.B.A., Harvard U., 1963. Sr. mgmt. cons. George Fry & Assos., Chgo., 1963-65; with Baxter Travenol Labs., Inc. (now Baxter Internat. Inc.), Deerfield, Ill., 1966—, exec. v.p., 1976, also bd. dirs., pres., chief oper. officer, 1980, chief exec. officer, chmn., 1987—; bd. dirs. Dun & Bradstreet Corp., Emerson Electric Co., Quaker Oats Co., Anheuser-Busch Cos.; bd. advisors Nestlé U.S.A. Trustee Rush-Presbyn.-St. Luke's Med. Ctr.; assoc. Northwestern U. 1st lt. USMC, 1957-60. Recipient Citizen Fellowship award Chgo. Inst. Medicine, 1982, Nat. Health Care award B'nai B'rith Youth Svcs., 1986, William McCormick Blair award Yale U., 1989, Yale medal, 1997, Semper Fidelis award USMC, 1989, Disting. Humanitarian award St. Barnabas Found., 1992, Alexis de Tocqueville award for community svc. United Way Lake County, 1993, Industrialist of Yr. award Am. Israel C. of C., 1996; named 1983's Outstanding Exec. Officer in the healthcare industry Fin. World; elected to Chgo.'s Bus. Hall of Fame, Jr. Achievement, 1987. Mem. Health Industry Mfrs. Assn. (chmn. 1983), Bus. Roundtable (conf. bd., mem. policy com.), Bus. Coun. Clubs: Chgo. Commonwealth, Commercial, Mid-America. Office: Baxter Healthcare Corp One Baxter Pkwy Deerfield IL 60015

LOUD, WARREN SIMMS, mathematician; b. Boston, Sept. 13, 1921; s. Roger Perkins and Esther (Nickerson) L.; m. Mary Louise Strasburg, Dec. 27, 1947; children: Margaret Loud McCamant, Elizabeth Ann Loud Liebman, John Alden. S.B., Mass. Inst. Tech., 1942, Ph.D., 1946. Asst. prof. U. Minn., 1947-56, assoc. prof., 1956-59, prof. math., 1959-92, prof. emeritus, 1992—; vis. prof. Math. Rsch. Ctr., U. Wis., 1959-60, Technische Hochschule Darmstadt, Germany, 1964-65, Kyoto U., Japan, 1974-75, U. Florence, 1981-82, U. Trento, 1982, 83; vis. lectr. Math. Assn. Am., 1965—. Mem. Am. Math. Soc., Math. Assn. Am. (bd. govs. 1960-62, 77-80), Soc. Indsl. and Applied Math. (editor Rev. 1961-66, Jour. Applied Math. 1966-75, mem. editorial bd. 1975-79), AAAS. Congregationalist. Achievements include research, publs. in nonlinear ordinary differential equations. Home: 1235 Yale Pl Apt 504 Minneapolis MN 55403-1944 Office: U Minn Sch of Math 206 Church St SE Minneapolis MN 55455-0488

LOUDERBACK, KEVIN WAYNE, business owner; b. Mt. Vernon, Ill., Mar. 10, 1971; s. Richard Lynn and Wilberta Maxine (Anderson) L. Draftsman, civil engr. Finley Engrng. Co., Inc., Lamar, Mo., 1988-91; civil engr. GTE North, Sun Prairie, Wis., 1991-92; with Empiregas Corp., Lebanon, Mo., 1992-93; EMT-A Breech Paramedics Ambulance Svc., Lebanon, Mo., 1993-94; EMT Lake of the Ozarks Ambulance Svc., 1994—; owner, chmn., pres. Ozark Jerky Co., Inc., Conway, 1992—; v.p., CFO J&K Enterprises, Inc., 1997—; vol. EMT-P Conway Rescue Group, 1993-95, EMT-P Dallas County Rescue, 1995—. Vol. fireman Barton County Alert Squad, Lamar, 1989-92; mem. Barton County Disaster Team, 1989-92, Barton County Haz-Mat Squad, 1988-92, Mo. Emergency Preparedness Assn., 1989-92; dir. Dallas County First Responders, 1995—. Baptist. Avocations: flying private planes, golf, photography, travel. Home: 612 West Benton Buffalo MO 65622 Office: RR 3 Box 132E Buffalo MO 65622-9112

LOUDERMILK, PEGGY JOYCE, pediatrics nurse, public health nurse; b. Mar. 1, 1944; d. Marshall Brown and Esther Rebecca (Gaines) Fisher; m. George E. Loudermilk, Dec. 21, 1968; children: Darrell Wayne, Donna Lynn. ADN, Dabney S. Lancaster C.C., 1985. Nursing asst. Alleghany Regional Hosp., Low Moor, Va., 1980-84, nursing extern, 1984-85, staff nurse med./surg., 1985-87, staff nurse ICU, 1987-92; nurse pediatrics Alleghany County/Covington (Va.) Health Dept., 1992—; CPR instr. ARC, Covington, 1984-92. Mem. sch. adv. bd. Alleghany County Sch. System, 1994; local interagency coun. (State Mandated Orgn.), Clifton Forge, Va., 1993—. Nursing grantee Alleghany Regional Hosp., 1983-85. Fellow Nursing Coun. Alleghany Dist. Republican. Baptist. Avocations: reading, sewing, cross stitch, sports, hiking. Home: 2700 Sugar Maple Dr PO Box 52 Low Moor VA 24457

LOUDON, DONALD HOOVER, lawyer; b. Kansas City, Kans., Nov. 20, 1937; s. Donald Charles and Berenice (Hoover) L.; m. W. Sue Cantrell, Aug. 17, 1958; children: Donald H. Jr., Kurt William. BJ, U. Mo., 1959; LLB, U. Kans., 1962. Bar: Mo. 1962, U.S. Supreme Ct. 1977. Reporter Kansas City Times, 1959; assoc. Blackmar, Swanson & Midgley, Kansas City, Mo., 1962-65; asst. gen. counsel Commerce Bank of Kansas City (Mo.), 1965-68; dir., shareholder Morris, King, Stamper & Bold, Kansas City, Mo., 1968-87, Shughart, Thomson & Kilroy, P.C., Kansas City, Mo., 1987—. Elder, Presbyn. Ch. Mem. ABA, Met. Bar Assn. Kansas City, Lawyers Assn. Kansas City, Delta Tau Delta (pres., bd. dirs. Columbia, Mo. chpt.). Office: Shughart Thomson & Kilroy 12 Wyandotte Plz 120 W 12th St Kansas City MO 64105-1917

LOUDON, DOROTHY, actress; b. Boston, Sept. 17, 1933; d. James E. and Dorothy Helen (Shaw) L.; m. Norman Paris, Dec. 18, 1971 (dec.). Student, Syracuse U., 1950-51, Emerson Coll., summers 1950, 51, Alviene Sch. Dramatic Art, 1952, 53, The Am. Acad. Dramatic Art. Appeared in nat. repertory cos. of The Effect of Gamma Rays on Man in the Moon Marigolds, 1970, Plaza Suite, 1971, Luv, 1965, Anything Goes, 1967; appeared in Broadway prodns. Nowhere to Go But Up, 1962 (Theatre World award), Sweet Potato, 1968, Fig Leaves Are Falling, 1969 (Tony nominee), Three Men on a Horse, 1969 (Drama Desk award), The Women, 1973, Annie (Tony award, Drama Desk award, Outer Critics Circle award), 1976 (Dance Educators Am. award), Ballroom, 1979 (Tony nominee), Sweeney Todd, 1980, West Side Waltz, 1981 (Sarah Siddons award), Noises Off, 1983 (Tony nomination), Jerry's Girls, 1985 (Tony nomination), Driving Miss Daisy, 1988, Annie 2, 1990, Comedy Tonight, 1994, Love Letters, 1995, Showboat, 1996, N.Y. Encore series, 1997; appeared in film Garbo Talks, 1984; numerous appearances on TV variety and talk shows; latest TV appearances In Performance at the White House, A Salute to Stephen Sondheim at Carnegie Hall, 1992; star TV show Dorothy, 1979; appeared in supper clubs The Blue Angel, Le Ruban Bleu, Persian Room; rec.: (CDs) Saloon, Broadway Baby. Mem. Actors Equity, Screen Actors Guild, AFTRA. Office: Lionel Larner Ltd 119 W 57th St Ste 1412 New York NY 10019-2401 *I have no "thoughts on my life" that do not include my late husband, Norman Paris. He loved the theatre, as do I, and was my reason for being and my constant inspiration to persevere. That perserverance brought me the coveted Tony award for Miss Hannigan in "Annie." My husband lived to share that glorious moment with me. The award is small consolation, indeed-but the letters of love and encouragement from people all over the country is wondrous. It is a tribute to my husband as well as to me. I will devote my life to the justification of the faith he had in me-and to the faith of all those everywhere who love the theatre.*

LOUDON, KAREN LEE, physical therapist; b. Kansas City, Mo., July 25, 1958; d. Walter Raymond and Clarice Frances (Washburn) L. BS in edn., U. Kans., 1980; BS in physical therapy, U. Kans. Medical Ctr., 1985; MS in edn., U. Kans., 1987. Registered physical therapist, Kans., Mo. Physical therapist Watkins Ctr. Univ. Kans., Lawrence, Kans., 1985—; adv. Pre Physical Therapy Club/Students, Lawrence, 1985—; mem./presenter Kans. City Orthopaeic Study Group, Kans. City, 1987—; athletic trainer, Sunflower State Games, Lawrence, 1990-92; clinical instr. Univ. of Kans. Medical Ctr., Lawrence, 1987—. Contbr. articles to profl. jours. Mem. Am. Phys. Therapy Assn. (Kans. leg. com. 1983-84, Kans. Disting. Clin. Svc. award 1995), Nat. Athletic Trainer Assn., Am. Coll. Sports Medicine, Phi Kappa Phi. Avocations: golfing, biking, softball, hiking. Office: Watkins Health Ctr U Kans Lawrence KS 66045

LOUGANIS, GREG E., former Olympic athlete, actor; b. San Diego, Jan. 29, 1960; s. Peter E. and Frances I. (Scott) L. Student, U. Miami, Fla., 1978-80; B.A. in Drama, U. Calif., Irvine, 1983. Mem. U.S. Nat. Diving Team, 1976—. Author: Breaking The Surface, 1995. Recipient Silver medal Olympic Games, 1976, 2 Olympic Gold medals, 1984, 2 Olympic Gold medals, 1988; James E. Sullivan award, Olympic Games, 1984; inducted into Olympic Hall of Fame, 1985; winner 48 U.S. nat. diving titles; World Diving Champion (platform and springboard) 1986, Jesse Owens award, 1987, Pan Am Gold medal, 1979, 83, 87; Gold medalist (platform and springboard) Seoul Olympics, 1988. Home: PO Box 4130 Malibu CA 90264-4130

LOUGH, RICK LEO, sales and marketing professional; b. Belleville, Ont., Can., Sept. 15, 1948; came to U.S., 1990; s. Leslie Robert and Jessie Pearl (Logue) L. BA, U. Western Ont., London, Can., 1971; BS with honors, U. Guelph, Ont., 1972, DVM, 1976. Toxicologist Bio Rsch. Labs. Ltd., Montreal, Que., Can., 1976-78, head gen. toxicology, 1978-81, head gen. toxicology and animal health, 1981-83, assoc. dir. toxicology, 1983-84, dir. mktg., 1984-87, sr. dir. pacific rim bus. Devel., 1987-90; v.p. internat. sales and mktg. Internat. Rsch. and Devel. Corp., Mattawan, Mich., 1991-95; cons. environ. toxicology specialist Calif. State Pub. Health, L.A., 1984-87; cons. in regulatory toxicology Consultra Internat. Ltd., Tokyo, 1990-91. Hastings County Vet. scholarship Ont. Vet. Assn., 1972. Mem. Soc. of Toxicology of Can., European Soc. of Toxicology, Occupational Hygiene Assn. of Ont. (pub. rels. com. 1985-87), Am. Mgmt. Assn., Ont. Vet. Assn. Avocations: photography, philately, languages. Home: 631 Carrington Ct Kalamazoo MI 49009-2463 Office: Internat Rsch & Devel 500 N Main Mattawan MI 49071

LOUGHEAD, JEFFREY LEE, physician; b. Mystic, Conn., May 11, 1957; s. Lawrence L. and Alice M. L.; m. Melinda K., Apr. 29, 1995; children: Brittany, Molly. BA, Miami U., 1979; MD, U. Cin., 1983. Intern Children's Hosp. Med. Ctr., Cin., 1983-84, resident, 1984-86, chief resident, 1986-87; fellow in neonatal-perinatal medicine U. Cin., 1987-90; med. dir. spl. care unit Good Samaritan Hosp., Dayton, 1991-95; dir. quality assurance Children's MEd. Ctr., Dayton, 1991-97, physician advisor nursing rsch. com., 1993-97, clin. dir., 1995-97. Author: (chpts.) Principles of Perinatal and Neonatal Metabolism, 1991, 2d edit., 1997, Current Pediatric Therapy, 1996. Fellow Am. Coll. Nutrition (Young Investigator award 1988), Am. Acad. Pediatrics (diplomate pediatrics, neonatal perinatal medicine). Avocation: amateur and profl. auto racing driver. Office: 1430 Nature Ct Dayton OH 45440

LOUGHEED, PETER, lawyer, former Canadian official; b. Calgary, Alta., Can., July 26, 1928; s. Edgar Donald and Edna (Bauld) L.; m. Jeanne Estelle Rogers, June 21, 1952; children—Stephen, Andrea, Pamela, Joseph. B.A., U. Alta., 1950, LL.B., 1952; M.B.A., Harvard U., 1954. Bar: Alta 1955. With firm Fenerty, Fenerty, McGillivray & Robertson, Calgary, 1955-56; sec. Mannix Co., Ltd., 1956-58, gen. counsel, 1958-62, v.p., 1959-62, dir., 1960-62; individual practice law, from 1962; formerly mem. Alta. Legislature for Calgary West; formerly leader Progressive Conservative Party of Alta., 1965-85; premier of Alta., 1971-85; ptnr. Bennett Jones Verchere, Calgary, 1986—. Office: Bennett Jones Verchere, 4500 Bankers Hall E 855 2d St SW, Calgary, AB Canada T2P 4K7

LOUGHLIN, MARY ANNE ELIZABETH, television news anchor; b. Biddeford, Maine, July 30, 1956; d. John Francis and Jacqueline Anne (LaLonde) L.; BS, Fla. State U., 1977. Reporter, Sta. WFSU-FM, Tallahassee, 1976; news anchor/producer Sta. WECA-TV, Tallahassee, 1977-81; producer/show host Sta. WTBS-TV, Atlanta, 1981-84; news anchor, producer Cable News Network, Atlanta, 1983-91; anchor Time Man of the Year specials, 1988-90 (Silver award Houston Film Festival); anchor Dem. and Rep. Nat. Conv., 1988; freelance journalist, 1991-95; news anchor News 12 Conn., 1995—. Recipient Woman at Work Broadcast award Nat. Commn. on Working Women, 1982, Grad. Made Good award, Fla. State U., 1987, Archbishop Fulton J. Sheen Angel award Archdiocese of St. Petersburg, 1988. Mem. Women in Cable, Women in Communications, Am. Women in Radio and TV (Woman of Achievement award 1982, 84). Roman Catholic.

LOUGHLIN, WILLIAM JOSEPH, priest, religious organization administrator; b. Wharton, N.J., Mar. 3, 1927; s. William Joseph and Theresa Catherine (May) L. AB, Seton Hall U., 1954, AM, 1957; MDiv, Pope John XXIII Sem., Weston, Mass., 1969; postgrad., Rutgers U., 1959. Ordained priest Roman Cath. Ch., 1969. Deacon St. Mary's Ch., Greenwich, Conn., summer 1968, parochial vicar, 1980-82, 90-92; parochial vicar St. Rose Ch., Newtown, Conn., 1969-70, Assumption Ch., Westport, Conn., 1970-73; defender of the bond Diocesan Marriage Tribunal, Bridgeport, Conn., 1973-82; parochial vicar St. Philip Ch., Norwalk, Conn., 1973-78, St. Augustine Cathedral, Bridgeport, Conn., 1978-80; pastor St. Joseph Ch., Shelton, Conn., 1982-90; dir. pilgrimages Diocese of Bridgeport, 1982—; parochial vicar St. Luke Ch., Westport, 1992-95, St. Thomas Aquinas Ch., Fairfield, Conn., 1995—; chaplain to His Holiness Pope John Paul II, Rome, 1988—. Mem. Am. Pers. and Guidance Assn. (evaluation com. Cath. counselors Phila. 1960, Denver 1961), Nat. Vocat. Guidance Assn., KC (Lafayette coun. Dover, N.J. 1947—, Walter J. Barrett Gen. Assembly 1950—). Avocations: collecting Hummel figurines, travel. Home: 16 Walnut St Wharton NJ 07885-2516

LOUGHMAN, BARBARA ELLEN, immunologist researcher; b. Frankfurt, Ind., Oct. 26, 1940; d. Jimmie Jewel and Ruth Eileen (Hoyer) Evers; m. Terry B. Loughman, June 28, 1962 (dec.); children: Lance Evers Loughman, Chad Elliott Loughman. BS, U. Ill., 1962; PhD, Notre Dame U., 1972. Rsch. scientist Ames Research Labs., Elkhart, Ind., 1962-72; staff fellow NIH, Balt., 1972-74; from research assoc. to research mgr. The Upjohn Co., Kalamazoo, Mich., 1974-84; dir. immunology research Monsanto Co., St. Louis, 1984-85; sr. dir. immunology diseases research G.D. Searle/Monsanto Co., St. Louis, 1986-88; dir. project mgmt. Rorer Cen. Research, Horsham, Pa., 1988-91; dir. internat. drug regulating affairs Marion Merrell Dow, Kansas City, Mo., 1991-95; v.p. devel. svcs. Internat. Med. Tech. Cons., Inc.,

Lenexa, Kans., 1995-97, Pharm. Rsch. Assoc., Inc., Lenexa, 1997—. Contbr. over 20 articles to profl. jours. 1. Mem. AAAS, Am. Acad. Asthma Allergy and Immunology, Am. Assn. Immunology. Avocations: singing, golf. Office: Pharm Rsch Assoc Inc 16400 College Blvd Lenexa KS 66219

LOUGHNANE, DAVID J., lawyer; b. Chgo., Sept. 3, 1947. BA, U. Wis., 1969; student, U. So. Calif.; JD, Loyola U., 1972. Bar: Ill. 1972, Wis. 1972, U.S. Dist. Ct. (no. dist.) Ill., 1972. With Price, Tunney, Loughnane, Reiter & Bruton, P.C., Chgo. Author: Institutional Negligence, 1989. Mem. Am. Acad. Hosp. Attys., Def. Rsch. Inst. Office: Price Tunney Loughnane Reiter & Bruton PC 100 S Wacker Dr Ste 800 Chicago IL 60606-4002

LOUGHNANE, LEE DAVID, trumpeter; b. Chgo., Oct. 21, 1946; s. Philip Louis and Juanita (Wall) L. Student, DePaul U., Chgo., 1964-66, Chgo. Conservatory Music, 1966-67. Mem. musical group The Big Thing, 1967, Chicago, 1967—; v.p. Chgo. Music, Inc. Rec. artist: Columbia Records; albums include Greatest Hits 1982-89, Chicago 19, 1988, Live in Toronto, 1996, (with others) Night and Day. Named Entertainer of Yr., People's Choice Awards, 1974, Best Instrumental Band, Playboy mag., 1971-75; recipient 3 Grammy awards, 1977. Mem. AFTRA, Nat. Acad. Recording Arts and Scis., Screen Actors Guild, Psi Mu Alpha Sinfonia. Address: care Howard Rose Agy 8900 Wilshire Blvd # 320 Beverly Hills CA 90211-1906 also: Reprise 3300 Warner Blvd Burbank CA 91505*

LOUGHRAN, JAMES NEWMAN, philosophy educator, college president; b. Bklyn., Mar. 22, 1940; s. John Farley and Ethel Margaret (Newman) L. A.B., Fordham U., 1964, M.A., 1965, Ph.D. in Philosophy, 1975; Ph.D. (hon.), Loyola Coll., Balt., 1985. Joined S.J., 1958; ordained priest Roman Catholic Ch., 1970. Instr. philosophy St. Peter's Coll., Jersey City, 1965-67; asst. dean Fordham U., Bronx, N.Y., 1970-73; tchr. philosophy Fordham U., Bronx, 1974-79, 82-84, dean, 1979-82; pres. Loyola Marymount U., L.A., 1984-91; acting pres. Bklyn. Coll., 1992; Miller Prof. Philosophy John Carroll U., Cleve., 1992-93; interim pres. Mount St. Mary's Coll., Emmitsburg, Md., 1993-94; interim acad. v.p., Fordham U., Bronx, N.Y., 1994-95; pres. St. Peter's Coll., 1995—. Contbr. numerous articles and revs. to popular and scholarly jours. Trustee St. Peter's Coll., Jersey City, 1972-78, 94—, Xavier U., Cin., 1981-84, Canisius Coll., Buffalo, 1994—. Mem. Am. Philos. Assn. Avocation: tennis.

LOUGHREY, CAROL ELAINE ASHFIELD, government official; b. Fredericton, N.B., Can., July 13, 1948; d. Vincent Evans and Marion Loretta (Thomas) Ashfield; m. Ronald Loughrey, 1970; children: Margaret, Katherine. BBA, U. N.B., 1970; MBA, U. Maine, 1982. From asst. to assoc. prof., asst. grad. dean U. N.B., Fredericton, 1977-88; comptroller Province of N.B., Fredericton, 1988-96, dep. minister of edn., 1996—; cons. in field. Contbr. articles to profl. jours.; adv. bd. F.M.I. Jour. Pres. Muriel McQueen Fergusson Found., 1991-93; vice chmn. N.B. Law Found., 1981-88, YM-YWCA Endowment Fund, Fredericton, 1991-92, co-founder Breast Cancer Support Svcs., Fredericton, 1993—, N.B. Breast Cancer Network, 1995; sec.-treas. Can. Women's Found., 1996—. Recipient Pres.'s Merit award four outstanding contbn. in tchg., rsch. and univ. svc. U. N.B., 1987, Faculty of Adminstrn. Cert. of Achievement, 1992. Fellow Inst. Chartered Accts., Inst. Chartered Accts. of Ont.; mem. Can. Inst. Chartered Accts. (bd. govs. 1985-87, 92-95, chmn., CEO 1994-95), Ont. Inst. Chartered Accts., Fin. Mgmt. Inst. Can., Inst. Pub. Adminstrs. Can., N.B. Inst. Chartered Accts. (pres. 1986-87). Avocations: aerobics, walking, snowshoeing. Home: 28 Eagle Ct, Fredericton, NB Canada E3B 5&3 Office: PO Box 6000, Fredericton, NB Canada E3B 5H1

LOUGHRIN, JAY RICHARDSON, mass communications educator, consultant; b. Mankato, Minn., Oct. 21, 1943; s. J. Richardson and Jane Aileen (Smith) L.; m. Helen Marie Struyk, Aug. 8, 1964 (div. Sept. 1985); children: Jennifer, Amy; m. Yolanda Christina Ramos, July 17, 1986; children: Tawny, Heather. BA in Drama, Calif. State U., Los Angeles, 1968; postgrad., San Diego State U., 1968-69, UCLA, 1970-71, U. Redlands, Calif., 1983-84, Fla. State U., 1990; MA, Whittier (Calif.) Coll., 1992. Prodn. asst. Andrews-Yagemann Prodns., Hollywood, Calif., 1961-63; with merchandising, sales Sta. KTTV-TV, Hollywood, 1963-64; assoc. producer Born Losers Am. Internat. Pictures, Hollywood, 1964; assoc. producer V.P.I. Prodns., Hollywood, 1964, Ralph Andrews Prodns., North Hollywood, Calif., 1965; producer Stein Erikson Ski Films, North Hollywood, 1965, F.K. Rocket Films, North Hollywood, 1966-68; dir. promotion and publicity Sta. KCST-TV, San Diego, 1968-69; prof. mass communication Rio Hondo Coll., Whittier, 1969—; sales mgr. Warren Miller Films, Hermosa Beach, Calif., 1984-85, cons., 1985-86; exec. producer Echo Prodns., Hollywood, 1985-87; cons. Radio Concepts, Los Angeles, 1978-80, Tom Cole Prodns., Los Angeles, 1985-87, Chuck Richards Whitewater, Lake Isabella, Calif., 1984-86; media relations cons. Police Officers Standards and Training, Sacramento, 1986—; venue mgr. Los Angeles Olympic Organizing Com., Long Beach, Calif., 1984. Winter sports writer Kern Valley Sun; contbr. articles to Review Publs., Orange Coast mag., Jet Am. mag., Ted Randall Report. Pres. Rue Le Charlene Homeowners Assn., Palos Verdes, Calif., 1984, Hilltop Homeowners Assn., Walnut, Calif., 1989-90; v.p. West Walnut Homeowners Assn., 1988-89. Recipient Pub. Service Programming award Advt. Council, N.Y.C., 1982; named Adviser of Yr., U. So. Calif.'s 50th Annual Journalism Awards, Los Angeles, 1985. Mem. Acad. TV Arts and Scis., Rio Hondo Coll. Faculty Assn. (pres. 1978), So. Calif. Broadcasters Assn. (Pub. Service award 1978), N.Am. Snowsport Journalists Assn. Republican. Avocations: sailing, skiing, whitewater rafting, motorcycling, bicycling. Office: Rio Hondo Coll 3600 Workman Mill Rd Whittier CA 90601-1616

LOUI, ALEXANDER CHAN PONG, electrical engineer, researcher; b. San Fernando, Trinidad and Tobago, Feb. 20, 1961; came to U.S., 1990; s. John Sue-Tang and Mary Loui; m. Jessie S.B. Chong, May 25, 1991. BSc in Elec. Engring., U. Toronto, 1983, MSc in Elec. Engring., 1986, PhD in Elec. Engring., 1990. Rsch. asst. Atomic Energy of Can. Ltd., Chalk River, Ont., 1982; teaching asst. dept. elec. engring. U. Toronto, Ont., 1983-89; rsch. assoc. signal processing lab. U. Toronto, 1985-90; mem. tech. staff applied rsch. Bellcore, Red Bank, N.J., 1990-94; rsch. scientist Applied Rsch., Bellcore, Red Bank, N.J., 1995-96; rsch. assoc. Networked Imaging Tech. Ctr. Eastman Kodak Co., Rochester, N.Y., 1996—. Contbr. articles to profl. jours. Founding mem., past pres. Jarvis Multicultural Soc., Toronto, 1988-90. Wallbery Undergrad scholar, 1981-82, NSERC postgrad. scholar, 1983-87. Mem. IEEE, (mem. tech. com. Internat. Conf. on Image Processing 1994—), Soc. Motion Picture and TV Engrs. Baptist. Avocations: table tennis, skating, reading, hi-fi systems, travel. Office: Eastman Kodak Co Mail Code 37102 1447 St Paul St Rochester NY 14653

LOUIS, BARBRA SCHANTZ, dean; b. Dover, N.J., Nov. 26, 1940; d. Henry Albert and Priscilla Ruth (Schantz) L.; m. Roger Donald Coss, Sept. 1957 (div. 1973); children: Candee Lee Coss Spizzirri, Lynn Ellen Coss Brandimarte, Amber Mary Coss Gillespie. AA, County Coll. of Morris, Dover, N.J., 1971; BA, Montclair State Coll., 1973, MA, 1973; DEd, Rutgers U., 1985. Cert. secondary tchr. Counselor, adminstr. Bergen C.C., Paramus, N.J., 1974-77; exec. asst. to exec. dir. Bergen County Cmty. Action Program, Hackensack, N.J., 1977-80; cons. Nat. Multiple Sclerosis Soc., Teaneck, N.J., 1984-85; dir. devel. Passaic County C.C., Paterson, N.J., 1985-90; dean for continuing edn. Santa Barbara (Calif.) City Coll., 1990—. Bd. dirs. Edwin Gould Svcs. for Children, N.Y.C., 1980-90, Planned Parenthood of Passaic County, Paterson, N.J., 1989-90, Santa Barbara, Ventura Counties, Calif.; bd. mem. Passaic County Cultural and Heritage Coun., Paterson, 1987-90, Found. for Santa Barbara City Coll., 1992—. Mem. The Hamilton Club (bd. govs. 1988-90). Democrat. Unitarian. Avocations: travel, antique collecting. Home: 126 San Clemente St Santa Barbara CA 93109-2130 Office: Santa Barbara City Coll Schott Ctr 310 W Padre St Santa Barbara CA 93105-4309

LOUIS, LESTER See BROWN, LES

LOUIS, MURRAY, dancer, choreographer, dance teacher; b. N.Y.C., Nov. 4, 1926; s. Aaron and Rose (Mintzer) Fuchs. B.S., N.Y. U., 1951. Principal dancer Nikolais Dance Theatre, 1950-59; assoc. dir. dance div., Henry St. Playhouse, N.Y.C., 1953-70; artistic dir. Nikolais/Louis Found. Dance, N.Y.C., 1970—, Murray Louis Dance Co., 1953—; co-dir. Choreoarts, 1973—; choreographer numerous works, 1953—, including Porcelain Dialogues, 1974, Moments, 1975, Catalogue, 1975, Cleopatra, 1976, Ceremony, 1976, Deja Vu, 1976, Glances, 1976, Schubert, 1977, The Canarsie Venus, 1978, Figura, 1978, A Suite for Erik, 1979, Afternoon, 1979, The City, 1980, November Dances, 1980, Aperitif, 1982, A Stravinsky Montage, 1982, Repertoire, 1982, The After Boat, 1983, Frail Demons, 1984, Four Brubeck Pieces (with Dave Brubeck Quartet), 1984, Pug's Land, 1984, The Station, 1985, Revels, 1986, The Disenchantment of Pierrot, 1986, Black and White, 1987, Return to Go, 1987, Horizons, 1994, Alone, 1994; choreographer: By George (music by George Gershwin for Cleve. Ballet), 1987, Act I (with Dave Brubeck Quartet), 1987, Bach II, 1987, Asides, 1987; TV projects include Repertoire Workshop, CBS, N.Y.C., 1965, Proximities, Calligraph for Matyrs, ZDF-TV, Munich, 1974, Soundstage (with Dave Brubeck) PBS, Chgo., 1977, Studio Two, Polish Nat. TV, Warsaw, 1978, Murray Louis Dance Co., TeleFrance 1, Paris, 1982, video AT&T (with Dave Brubeck Quartet), 1988; 5 part film series Dance as an Art Form, 1974; choreographer for 23d, 27th Annual Coty Am. Fashion Critics awards; author: Inside Dance, Letters to Nik from India; Nik and Murray (film by Christian Blackwood), 1986, Murray Louis on Dance, 1992. Chmn. U.S. chpt. Conseil Internat. de la Danse (UNESCO). Served with USNR, 1945-46. Guggenheim fellow, 1969, 73; grantee Rockefeller Found., 1974; Nat. Endowment Arts, 1968, 70, 72, 74-78, Mellon Found., 1976; recipient Critics award Internat. Festival Weisbaden, Ger., 1972, Dance Mag. award, 1977, Grand Medaille de la Ville de Paris, 1979; decorated knight Order of Arts and Letters, France, 1984. Mem. Am. Guild Mus. Artists, Assn. Am. Dance Cos., Asso. Council Arts, Dance Notation Bur. Jewish. Office: Nikolais/Louis Found 611 Broadway Rm 221 New York NY 10012-2608 *I think, to discover the intuitive force within oneself, and then know how to utilize and trust its judgment, is essential for the creative artist. My aesthetics were achieved by this intuitive judgment.*

LOUIS, PAUL ADOLPH, lawyer; b. Key West, Fla., Oct. 22, 1922; s. Louis and Rose Leah (Weinstein) L.; m. Nancy Ann Lapof, Dec. 28, 1971; children: Louis Benson, IV, Connor Cristina and Marshall Dore (twins). B.A., Va. Mil. Inst., Lexington, 1947; LL.B., U. Miami, Fla., 1950, J.D., 1967. Bar: Fla. 1950, U.S. Dist. Ct. (so. dist.) Fla. Asst. state atty., 1955-57; atty. Beverage Dept. Fla., 1957-60; spl. asst. atty. gen. State of Fla., 1970-71; partner firm Sinclair, Louis, Heath, Nussbaum & Zavertnik (P.A.), Miami, 1960—; mem. Fed. Jud. Nominating Commn., 1977-80; mem. peer rev. com. U.S. Dist. Ct. for So. Dist. Fla., 1983-85. Author: Defamation, How Far Can You Go, Trial and Tort Trends, 1969; contbr.: chpts. to Fla. Family Law, 1967, 72. Founder mem. Palm Springs Gen. Hosp. Scholarship Com., 1968; mem. Dade County Health Facilities Authority, 1979—; trustee Fla. Supreme Ct. Hist. Soc., 1994—. Served to maj. USAAF, 1943-45, ETO. Decorated Air medal with five oak leaf clusters, Bronze Star (7), Purple Heart. Mem. ABA, Fla. Bar (bd. cert. civil trial lawyer and marital and family law, bd. govs. 1970-74), Dade County Bar Assn. (dir. 1954-55, 66-69), Assn. Trial Lawyers Am., Am. Judicature Soc., Va. Mil. Inst. Alumni Assn. Democrat. Jewish. Club: Miami, Bath. Home: 4411 Palm Ln Miami FL 33137-3346 Office: 1125 A I duPont Bldg 169 E Flagler St Miami FL 33131-1210

LOUIS, WILLIAM ROGER, historian, educator, editor; b. Detroit, May 8, 1936; s. Henry Edward and Bena May (Flood) L.; m. Dagmar Cecilia Friedrich; children: Antony Andrew, Catherine Ann. BA, U. Okla., 1959; MA, Harvard U., 1960; PhD, Oxford U., 1962, DLitt, 1979. Asst. prof., then assoc. prof. history Yale U., 1962-70; prof. history, curator hist. collections Humanities Research Center U. Tex., Austin, 1970-85, dir. Brit. Studies, 1975—, Kerr chair English history and culture, 1985—; supernumerary fellow St. Antony's Coll., U. Oxford, Eng., 1986-96, hon. fellow, 1996—; corr. fellow Brit. Acad., 1993—; Chichele lectr. All Souls Coll., U. Oxford, Eng., 1990; Disting. lectr. London Sch. Econs., 1992; Cust lectr. Nottingham (Eng.) U., 1995; Brit. Acad. Elie Kedorie Meml. lectr., 1996; dir. summer seminars NEH, 1985, 88, 90, 91, 96. Author: Ruanda-Urundi, 1963, Germany's Lost Colonies, 1967, (with Jean Stengers)The Congo Reform Movement, 1968, British Strategy in the Far East, 1919-1939, 1971, Imperialism at Bay, 1977 (History Book Club), British Empire in the Middle East, 1984 (George Louis Beer prize Am. Hist. Assn. and Tex. Inst. Letters award), In The Name of the God Go! Leo Amery and the British Empire in the Age of Churchill, 1992; editor British Documents on the End of Empire, 1988—; editor-in-chief Oxford History of the British Empire, 1993—; editor: (with P. Gifford) Britain and Germany in Africa, 1967, France and Britain in Africa, 1971, The Origins of the Second World War: A.J.P. Taylor and his Critics, 1972, National Security and International Trusteeship in the Pacific, 1972, Imperialism: The Robinson and Gallagher Controversy, 1976, (with William S. Livingston) Australia, New Zealand and the Pacific Islands since the First World War, 1979, (with P. Gifford) The Transfer of Power in Africa, 1982, (with R. Stookey) End of the Palestine Mandate, 1986, (with H. Bull) The Special Relationship: Anglo-American Relations Since 1945, 1986, (with P. Gifford) Decolonization and African Independence, 1988, (with James Bill) Musaddiq, Iranian Nationalism, and Oil, 1988, (with Roger Owen) Suez 1956: The Crisis and Its Consequences, 1989, (with Robert A. Fernea) The Iraqi Revolution of 1958, 1991, (with Robert Blake) Churchill, 1993, Adventures with Britannia, 1995. Woodrow Wilson fellow Harvard U., 1959-60, Marshall scholar Oxford U., 1960-62, NEH fellow, Am. Inst. Indian Studies fellow, Guggenheim fellow, vis. fellow All Souls Coll., U. Oxford, overseas fellow Churchill Coll., U. Cambridge, Eng., fellow Woodrow Wilson Internat. Ctr.; guest scholar Brookings Instn. Fellow Royal Hist. Soc.; mem. Am. Hist. Assn. (life), Coun. on Fgn. Rels. (N.Y.C.), Tex. Inst. Letters, Reform Club (London), Century (N.Y.C.), Met. Club (Washington). Democrat. Office: U Texas Dept History Austin TX 78712

LOUIS-COTTON D'ENGLESQUEVILLE, FRANCOIS PIERRE, automobile company executive; b. Neuilly Seine, France, Sept. 4, 1929; came to U.S., 1955; s. Georges Auguste and Paule Marie Cotton (d'Englesqueville) L.; m. Martine Combaluzier, Apr. 30, 1965 (div.); 1 child, Veronique; m. Mary Elizabeth Thames, June 14, 1986; children: George, Timothy, Jennifer, Mary Beth. BEE, Ecole Brequet, Paris, 1952. Engr. Demarais Freres, Paris, 1954-55, Cadillac Motor Cars div. GM, Detroit, 1955-58; nat. svc. mgr. Peugeot, S.A., N.Y.C., 1958-60; engr. Michelin Tire Group, Woodside, N.Y., 1960-61, Port Authority N.Y. and N.J., N.Y.C., 1962-68; dir. Renault USA, Inc., Washington, 1968-94; cons. Garden City, N.Y., 1994—. Mem. Conseiller du Commerce Exterieur de la France, Soc. Automotive Engrs., Assn. Internat. Automobile Mfrs. (bd. dirs. 1974-94), The European Inst. (Washington, D.C.), Cercle Militaire Paris, Army and Navy Club (Washington), Cherry Valley Club. Avocations: photography, travel, cooking. Office: 101 3rd St Garden City NY 11530-5931

LOUIS-DREYFUS, JULIA, actress. TV appearances include Saturday Night Live, 1982-85, Day by Day, 1986-89, Seinfield, 1990— (Emmy nomination Supporting Actress-Comedy, 1993, 94); films include Soul Man, 1986, Troll, 1986, Hannah and Her Sisters, 1986, National Lampoon's Christmas Vacation, 1989, Jack the Bear, 1993, North, 1994. Emmy nominations 1992, 93, 94, 95. Office: TPEG Mgmt 9150 Wilshire Blvd Ste 205 Beverly Hills CA 90212-3429

LOUISON, DEBORAH FINLEY, public affairs consultant; b. Aberdeen, S.D., Sept. 20, 1951; d. Donald S. and Barbara F. (Lowenstein) Finley; 1 child, Stacey Renee. BA, Nat. Coll. Edn., 1987. Asst. to sec. Dept. Edn. & Cultural Affairs State of S.D., Pierre, 1973-77; program dir. forestry div. State of S.D., Pierre, 1978-81; legisl. dir. Congressman Clint Roberts, Washington, 1981-83, Congresswoman Barbara Vucanovich, Washington, 1983-84; assoc. dir. fed. affairs Nat. Conf. State Legisl., Washington, 1984-89; dir. govt. affairs Nat. Conf. State Legisl., 1989; dept. asst. sec. U.S. Dept. of Energy, 1989-93; sr. v.p. APCO Assocs., Washington, 1993—. Contbr. articles to profl. jours. Planning and devel. com. Pierre C. of C., 1974-76; campaign asst. Clint Roberts for Congress, 1979-80; coordinator for state legisl. Bush/Quayle Campaign, Washington, 1988. Mem. NAFE, Women in Govt. Relations (com. chair), Am. Soc. Assn. Execs. Republican. Roman Catholic. Avocations: golf, running.

LOUNSBERRY, ROBERT HORACE, former state government administrator; b. Carlisle, Iowa, June 22, 1918; s. Horace Charles and Alice Mae (Elmore) L.; m. Muriel Dirks, Aug. 2, 1942; children: William, Beth, Janet, Paul, Steven. BA, Luther Coll., 1940; postgrad., U. Iowa, 1940-42. Farmer McCallsburg, Iowa, 1946-69; dep. sec. agr. Iowa Dept. Agr., Des Moines, 1969-72, sec. agr., 1973-87. Chmn. Story County Bd. Edn., 1950-69; bd. dirs. Iowa Assn. Sch. Bds., 1961-68, Des Moines Area Community Coll., 1964-70; clk. Richland Twp., 1952-64; chmn. Story County Rep. Party, 1964-68, chmn. 5th Rep. Dist., 1968-70; dir Am. Legion Boys State, 1957-88; active Iowa Arboretum, Iowans Right to Work Com.; active Gov's. Conf. for Aging; elected to Older Iowa Legislature (spkr. of house 1989); nat. dir. Comm. for Agriculture (sr. citizens adv. com.); active Iowa Aging Coalition, Retired Sr. Vol. Program. With USAAF, 1942-45. Decorated D.F.C., Air medal with 4 oak leaf clusters. Mem. Nat. Assn. Depts. Agr., Am. Assn. Retired Persons, Midwest Assn. State Depts. Agr., Mid-Am. Internat. Agri-Trade Coun., Greater Des Moines C. of C., Davis County Sheeps Producers, Iowa Cattlemen's Assn., Story County Cattlemen's Assn., Res. Officers Assn., Am. Legion (mem. nat. exec. com. 1965-70, state comdr. 1953-54), Lions, Masons, Shriners. Home: RR Mc Callsburg IA 50154

LOUNSBURY, HELEN MARIE, education educator, consultant; b. Dumont, N.J., Mar. 14, 1939; d. Joseph Anthony Sr. and Helen Teresa Golden; m. Patrick Lounsbury Sr., Jan. 30, 1960; children: Patrick Jr., Elaine Teresa, Amy Jo. BS with distinction, SUNY, 1960; MA in Lit., Vt. Coll., 1993. Tchr. Mohanasen Ctrl. Sch., Rotterdam, N.Y., 1960-62, Berne-Knox-Westerlo Ctrl. Sch., Berne, N.Y., 1962-96; clin. edn. regional supr. SUNY, Oneonta, 1996—; instr. Coll. St. Rose, Albany, N.Y., 1996—; presenter in field; cons. U.S. Dept. Edn.; bd. dirs. Albany County Reading Assn.; bd. edn. Berne-Knox-Westerlo Ctrl. Sch. Dist. Co-author: DeBeers, A Factory Family, 1985, Chances Are: Investigations in Probability, 1995. Bd. dirs. Hilltown Cmty. Rsch. Ctr., Berne, 1982-94, Albany County (N.Y.) Rural Housing Alliance, 1984—, Albany City Reading Coun.; coord. Arts Connection Learning Partnership, Albany, 1992-95; active PTA. Named N.Y. Tchr. of Excellence, 1993; NEH Masterworks Study grantee, 1995, N.Y. Found. of the Arts grantee, 1993, 94, Pioneering Partnership grantee, 1996. Mem. ASCD, PTA (hon. life, Disting. Svc. award 1996)), N.Y. State Reading Assn., N.Y. State Math. Assn., Internat. Reading Assn., Assn. Math. Tchrs. N.Y. State, N.Y. State English Tchrs., Hodge Podge Soc., Civil War Roundtable, Kiwanis, Kappa Delta Pi. Avocations: travel, reading. Office: Berne-Knox-Westerlo Ctr Sch 1738 Helderberg Trl Berne NY 12023-2926

LOUNSBURY, JOHN FREDERICK, geographer, educator; b. Perham, Minn., Oct. 26, 1918; s. Charles Edwin and Maude (Knight) L.; m. Dorothea Frances Eggers, Oct. 3, 1943; children—John Frederick, Craig Lawrence, James Gordon. B.S., U. Ill., 1942, M.S., 1946; Ph.D., Northwestern U., 1951. Asst. dir. rural land classification program Insular Govt., P.R., 1949-52; cons., research analyst Dayton Met. Studies, Inc., Ohio, 1957-60; chmn. dept. earth scis., prof. geography Antioch Coll., 1951-61; prof. geography, head dept. geography and geology Eastern Mich. U., 1961-69; chmn. dept. geography Ariz. State U., 1969-77; dir. Ctr. for Environ. Studies, 1977-80; prof. emeritus Ariz. State U., 1987—; project dir. Geography in Liberal Edn. Project, Assn. Am. Geographers, NSF, 1963-65, project dir. commn. on coll. geography, 1965-74; dir. environment based edn. project US. Office Edn., 1974-75; dir. spatial analysis of land use project NSF, 1975-85. Author articles, workbooks, textbooks. Mem. Yellow Springs Planning Commn., Ohio, dir. research, 1957-60; mem. Ypsilanti Planning Commn., 1961-66; research com. Washtenaw County Planning Commn., 1961-69; mem. cons. Ypsilanti Indsl. Devel. Corp., 1961-63. Served with AUS, 1942-46, ETO. Named Man of Yr., Yellow Springs C. of C., 1956-57. Fellow Ariz.-Nev. Acad. Sci.; mem. Assn. Am. Geographers (chmn. East Lakes div. 1959-61, mem. nat. exec. council 1961-64, chmn. liberal edn. com. 1961-65), Nat. Council Geog. Edn. (chmn. earth sci. com. 1961-68, regional coord. 1961-63, mem. exec. bd. 1968-71, 77-83, v.p. 1977-78, pres. 1979-80, Disting. Svc. award 1988, Disting. Mentor award 1990), Mich. Acad. Sci. Arts and Letters (chmn. pub. relations com. 1964-69, past chmn. geography sect.), Ohio Acad. Sci. (past exec. v.p.), Mich. Acad. Sci., Ariz. Acad. Sci., Am. Geog. Soc., AAAS, Sigma Xi, Delta Kappa Epsilon, Gamma Theta Upsilon. Home: 7850 E Vista Dr Scottsdale AZ 85250-7641 Office: Ariz State U Dept Geography Tempe AZ 85281

LOUNSBURY, STEVEN RICHARD, lawyer; b. Evanston, Ill., July 26, 1950; s. James Richard and Reba Janette (Smith) L.; m. Dianne Louise Daley, Apr. 16, 1983; children: Jimson, Cody, Richard. BA, U. Calif., Santa Barbara, 1973; JD, U. West L.A., 1977. Bar: Calif. 1979, U.S. Dist. Ct. (cen. dist.) Calif. 1979, Oreg. 1997. Pvt. practice L.A., 1979-83; contract atty. FAA, L.A., 1981; trial atty. Hertz Corp., L.A., 1983-86; mng. counsel 20th Century Ins. Co., Woodland Hills, Calif., 1986-94; mng. atty. Lounsbury and Assocs., Brea, Calif., 1986-94; sr. trial atty. Bollington, Lounsbury and Chase, Brea, 1994—; arbitrator Orange County Superior Ct., Santa Ana, Calif., 1992—. Dir. internat. rels. Rotary Internat., Venice-Marina Club, Calif., 1980-81; dir. L.A. Jr. C. of C., 1981-82. Mem. Calif. Bar Assn., Oreg. Bar Assn., Calif. House Counsel (bd. dirs., chmn. membership 1993-94). Avocations: snow skiing, music, travel. Office: Bollington Lounsbury and Chase 1800 E Imperial Hwy Ste 101 Brea CA 92821-6012

LOURENCO, RUY VALENTIM, physician, educator; b. Lisbon, Portugal, Mar. 25, 1929; came to U.S., 1959, naturalized, 1966; s. Raul Valentim and Maria Amalia (Gomes-Rosa) L.; children: Peter Edward, Margaret Philippa. M.D., U. Lisbon, 1951. Intern Lisbon City Hosps., 1951-53, resident internal medicine, 1953-55; instr. U. Lisbon, 1955-59; fellow dept. medicine Columbia U.-Presbyn. Med. Ctr., N.Y.C., 1959-63; asst. prof. medicine N.J. Coll. Medicine, 1963-66, assoc. prof., 1966-67; practice medicine specializing in pulmonary medicine, 1967—; assoc. prof. medicine and physiology U. Ill. Coll. Medicine, Chgo., 1967-69, prof., 1969-89, Foley prof. medicine, 1978-89, chmn. dept. medicine, 1977-89, exec. head dept. medicine, 1983-89; dir. respiratory rsch. lab. Hektoen Inst., Chgo., 1967-71; dir. pulmonary medicine Cook County Hosp., Chgo., 1969-70; attending physician U. Ill. Med. Ctr., Chgo., 1967-89; dir. pulmonary sect. and labs U. Ill. Med. Ctr., 1970-77, physician-in-chief, 1977-89, pres. med. staff, 1980-81; prof. medicine and physiology, dean N.J. Med. Sch. U. Medicine and Dentistry N.J., Newark, 1989—; cons. task force on rsch. in respiratory diseases NIH, 1972, mem. pathology study sect., 1972-76; mem. rev. bd. Spl. Ctrs. of Rsch. program, 1974; cons. career devel. program VA, 1972-90; mem. nat. com. Rev. Sci. Basis of Respiratory Therapy, 1973-74; pres. exec. com. U. Hosp., Newark, 1989—; mem. bd. govs. Hackensack U. Hosp., 1993—; mem. step II USMLE and fin. com. Nat. Bd. Med. Examiners, 1994—; mem. bd. trustees Bergen Pines County Hosp., 1994—. Editorial bd. Jour. Lab. and Clin. Medicine, 1973-77, 84-91, Am. Rev. Respiratory Diseases, 1985-91; contbr. numerous articles on pulmonary diseases, respiratory physiology and biochemistry to med. jours. Fellow AAAS, Am. Coll. Chest Physicians, ACP (pres. Ill. chpt. 1974-75, vice chmn. com. on environ. health 1981-82, gov. 1988-90, 93-95); mem. Assn. Am. Med. Colls. (coun. of deans 1989—, exec. com. project 3000 by 2000), Am. Fedn. Clin. Rsch., Am. Heart Assn., Am. Physiol. Soc., Am. Soc. Clin. Investigation, Am. Thoracic Soc. (chmn. sci. assembly 1974-75, bd. dirs. 1987-90, chmn. com. on internat. rels. 1989-91), Am. Soc. Internal Medicine, Chgo. Soc. Internal Medicine (pres. 1988-89), Am. Lung Assn. (com. smoking and health 1981-84), Internat. Acad. Chest Physicians and Surgeons (chmn. nominating com. 1984-90), Chgo. Lung Assn. (bd. dirs. and mem. exec. com. 1974-82), Soc. Exptl. Biology and Medicine, Sigma Xi, Alpha Omega Alpha, Phi Kappa Phi. Office: NJ Med Sch 185 S Orange Ave Rm C671 Newark NJ 07103-2714

LOURIE, ALAN DAVID, federal judge; b. Boston, Mass., Jan. 13, 1935. AB, Harvard U., 1956; MS, U. Wis., 1958; PhD, U. Pa., 1965; JD, Temple U., 1970. Bar: Pa. 1970. Chemist Monsanto Co., St. Louis, 1957-59; lit. scientist, chemist, patent agt. Wyeth Labs., Radnor, Pa., 1959-64; counsel Smith Kline Beecham Corp., Phila., 1964-90, successively as patent agt., atty., dir. corp. patents, asst. gen. counsel, v.p. corp. patents; cir. judge U.S. Ct. Appeals (fed. cir.), Washington, 1990—; mem. Judicial Conf. Com. on Financial Disclosure, 1990—; mem. U.S. del. to Diplomatic Conf. on Revision of Paris Conv. for Protection of Indsl. Property, 1982, 84; vice chmn. industry functional adv. com. to U.S. Trade Rep. and Dept. Commerce, 1987-90; chmn. U.S. group of U.S.-Japan Bus. Coun. Task Force on Patents. Bd. visitors Law Sch., Temple U. Mem. ABA, Phila. Patent Law Assn. (pres. 1984-85), Am. Intellectual Property Law Assn. (bd. dirs. 1982-85), Assn. Corp. Patent Counsel (treas. 1987-89), Pharm. Mfrs. Assn. (chmn. patent com. 1981-86), Am. Chem. Soc., Cosmos Club, Harvard Club Washington. Office: US Ct Appeals Fed Cir 717 Madison Pl NW Washington DC 20439-0002

LOURIE, NORMAN VICTOR, government official, social worker; b. N.Y.C., Feb. 1, 1912; s. Inte and Elsie (Horowitz) L.; m. Betty Pokrassa, Dec. 31, 1945 (dec. 1975); children: Richard, Iven, Mary Ann, Susan, Sara; m. Dorothy Maxey, Sept. 1, 1991; stepchildren: Lynn Zimmerman, Karen Biondi, Matthew Maxey, Margaret Calnon. Student, Cornell U., 1932-35; BS, NYU, 1936; diploma, N.Y. Sch. Social Work; MSW, Columbia U., 1938; DHL, Adelphi U., 1976. Rsch. assoc. Russell Sage Found. Greater N.Y. Fund, N.Y.C. Health and Welfare Coun., 1937-39; asst. dir. Bronx House Settlement, N.Y.C., 1939- 41; dir. Madison Settlement House, 1941-43, Hawthorne Cedar Knoll Sch., 1946-51; DHL, PhD Adelphi Coll. Grad. Sch. Social Work, 1948-51; dir. Assn. Jewish Children, Phila., 1951-55; exec. dep. sec., and sec. Pa. Dept. Pub. Welfare, 1955-80; policy adv. Inst. Econ. Devel., Washington, 1979-82; cons. Pa. Dept. Public Welfare, 1980-81; vis. prof. U. Pa. Sch. Social Work; prof. Norman Lourie Archives, U. Pa. Van Pelt and Grad. Sch. Social Work Libraries, 1975, Philippine Women's U., 1982; sr. policy advisor Nat. Immigration, Refugee and Citizenship Forum, 1982-90; sr. policy advisor Schirm Assocs.-Head Injury, 1987-93; chmn. Nat. Task Force on Definition of Developmental Disabilities, 1977; mem. Vietnamese Children's Resettlement Adv. Com., 1976; chmn. Nat. Coalition for Refugee Resettlement, 1978-82; cons. NIMH, Office Econ. Opportunity, Nat. Commn. on Marijuana and Drug Abuse, Social Rehab. Service, Health and Human Services; speaker White House Conf. on Children and Youth, 1950, 60, 70, White House Conf. on Aging, 1960; welfare cons. Fels Inst., Wharton Sch., U. Pa., 1953-55; mem. bd. Joint Commn. Mental Health of Children, 1965-67, chmn. com. on studies, exec. com., 1965-67; adv. council Pres.'s Com. on Juvenile Delinquency and Youth; chmn. bd. trustees Community Mental Health and Family Services, Refugee Camps, Southeast Asia, 1982-84, emeritus, 1984-94; instr. part-time Grad. Sch. U. Pa., Pitts., Columbia U. Author books in field; chmn. editorial bd.: Jour. Jewish Communal Service, 1952-58, Child Welfare, 1962-64; editorial bd.: Social Casework, 1969-72, Jour. Social Work Edn, 1970-72, Jour. Adminstrn. and Social Work; contbr. to encys., jours. Bd. dirs. Am. Child Guidance Found., Indochinese Community Ctr., Washington, 1986-94, Inst. Child Mental Health, Nat. Accreditation Council for Blind; adv. com. Bryn. Mawr Sch. Social Work.; bd. dirs. Alan Gutmacher Inst., 1976-80, Soc. for Study Traumatic Stress Studies, 1985-87, Indochinese Cultural Ctr., Washington, 1985-89; mem. adv. bd. Indochinese Refugee Action Ctr., 1985-94; life sr. advisor Tri-County Planned Parenthood, Harrisburg, Pa., 1988-94; bd. dirs. Sr. Citizen's Ctr., Harrisburg, 1988-94. 1st lt., inf., Med. Service Corps, AUS, 1943-46; acting chief psychiat. social worker USAR, Pentagon, 1946-51. Recipient Man of Yr. award Am. Soc. Pub. Adminstrn., 1963, Heritage and Social Svcs. award Gov. of Pa., 1991. Fellow Am. Orthopsychiat. Assn. (chmn. legis. com. 1956-60, pres. 1966-67, Ortho Lourie Family award), Am. Psychiat. Assn. (hon.); mem. NASW (pres. 1961-63, chmn. commn. on social policy and action 1958-60, chmn. poverty com. 1964-66, Lifetime Svc. award Pa. chpt. 1990), Am. Pub. Welfare Assn. (dir., 1st v.p. 1965-66, chmn. fed. policy com., W.S. Terry Meml. merit award 1971), Nat. Council State Adminstrs. (exec. com. 1972-79, emeritus 1979-94, chmn. health com. 1974-75, chmn. supplementary security income liaison com. 1976-79), Child Welfare League Am. (dir. 1960-62, chmn. editorial bd.), Nat. Rehab. Assn., Internat. Child Welfare Union, Internat. Council Social Welfare (chmn. U.S. com. 1971-75, exec. com. 1975-79), Nat. Conf. Social Welfare (dir. 1971-75, v.p. 1972-73, pres. 1975-76), Alumni Assn. Columbia Sch. Social Work, Internat. Assn. Workers for Maladjusted Children (Am. br. chmn. 1972-79, permanent rep. to UN 1973-79), Nat. Inst. Pub. Mgmt. (bd. dirs. 1977-79), Soc. Traumatic Stress Studies (bd. dirs. 1986-86), Cosmos Club (Washington). Home: 5740 Union Deposit Rd Harrisburg PA 17111-4708 *Literature is full of solutions to the anger and violence which continue to characterize the current society. My current experience, in retirement, with refugee programs in Southeast Asia and other parts of the world, leads me to conclude that our glorious civilization of knowledge and science is still too much marred with hate and inequality. Our protestations of religion are suspect because of our behavior. Poverty and violence are our greatest sins, as is inequality. Only when we act out that each person is a holy place and we learn to love our children and our species more than we hate and fight, will we have the right to say we are civilized. We are good at rescue, but very poor at prevention. We should respect that every person is a holy place.*

LOUX, GORDON DALE, organization executive; b. Souderton, Pa., June 21, 1938; s. Curtis L. and Ruth (Derstine) L.; m. Elizabeth Ann Nordland, June 18, 1960; children: Mark, Alan, Jonathan. Diploma, Moody Bible Inst., Chgo., 1960; BA, Gordon Coll., Wenham, Mass., 1962; BD, No. Bapt. Sem., Oak Brook, Ill., 1965, MDiv, 1971; MS, Nat. Coll. Edn., Evanston,Ill., 1974; LHD (hon.), Sioux Falls Coll., 1985. Ordained to ministry, Bapt. Ch., 1965. Assoc. pastor Forest Park (Ill.) Bapt. Ch., 1962-65; alumni field dir. Moody Bible Inst., Chgo., 1965-66, dir. pub. rels., 1972-76; dir. devel. Phila. Coll. Bible, 1966-69; pres. Stewardship Svcs., Wheaton, Ill., 1969-72; exec. v.p. Prison Fellowship Ministries, Washington, 1976-84, pres., CEO, 1984-88; pres., CEO Prison Fellowship Internat., Washington, 1979-87; pres. Internat. Students, Inc., Colorado Springs, Colo., 1988-93, Stewardship Svcs. Group, Colorado Springs, 1994—, Trinity Cmty. Found., 1996—. Author: Uncommon Courage, 1987, You Can Be a Point of Light, 1991; contbg. author: Money for Ministries, 1989, Dictionary of Christianity in America, 1989. Bd. dirs. Evang. Coun. for Fin. Accountability, Washington, 1979-92, vice chmn., 1981-84, 86-87, chmn., 1987-89; vice chmn. Billy Graham Greater Washington Crusade, 1985-85; bd. dirs. Evang. Fellowship of Mission Agys., 1991-94. Named Alumnus of Yr., Gordon Coll., 1986. Mem. Broadmoor Golf Club (Colo. Springs). Republican. Home: 740 Bear Paw Ln Colorado Springs CO 80906-3215 Office: PO Box 38898 Colorado Springs CO 80937-8898

LOUX, NORMAN LANDIS, psychiatrist; b. Souderton, Pa., June 27, 1919; s. Abram Clemmer and Martha Wasser (Landis) L.; m. Esther Elizabeth Brunk, June 4, 1941; children—Philip Michael, Elizabeth Ann, Peter David. Student, Eastern Mennonite Coll., 1940-42; B.A., Goshen Coll., 1943; M.D., Hahnemann Med. Coll., 1946; postgrad., Yale, 1950-51. Intern Hahnemann Hosp., Phila., 1947; gen. practice medicine Souderton, 1947-48; psychiat. resident Butler Hosp., Providence, 1949-50; chief service, clin. dir., asst. supt. Butler Hosp., 1951-55; founder Penn Found. Mental Health, Inc., Sellersville, Pa., 1955; med. dir. Penn Found. Mental Health, Inc., 1955-80; chief Psychiat. Svc. Grand View Hosp., Sellersville, 1955-80; pres. med. staff Grand View Hosp., 1963-64; exec. com., joint conf. com. Mem. Gov.'s Adv. Com. for Mental Health and Mental Retardation, 1955-80; mem. Pa. State Bd. Pub. Welfare, 1971-85. Bd. dirs. Dock Woods Retirement Community, 1989—, Adult Communities Total Svcs. Inc., 1990—. Co-recipient Earl D. Bond award, 1964; recipient Achievement award Souderton Lions Cub, 1963, Community Svc. award B'nai B'rith, 1976, citation for achievements Mennonite Med. Assn., 1978; dept. of psychiatry Grand View Hosp. rededicated in his name, 1992. Fellow Am. Psychiat. Assn., A.C.P., Pa. Psychiat. Soc., Am. Coll. Psychiatrists; mem. AMA, Pa., Bucks County med. socs., Group for Advancement Psychiatry, Southeastern Mental Health Assn., Acad. Religion and Mental Health. Mem. Mennonite Ch. Home: 138 Cowpath Rd Souderton PA 18964-2007 Office: Penn Found Mental Health Inc PO Box 32 Sellersville PA 18960-0032

LOUX, PETER CHARLES, anesthesiologist; b. Phila., Feb. 1, 1949; s. Theodore Clewell and Agnes Elva (Eichelman) L.; m. Jean Alyce McCluskey, Sept. 27, 1975; children: Tara Jean, Kimberly Marie. Student, Ea. Bapt. Coll., St. David's, Pa., 1967-68; BS in Biology, Widener Coll., Chester, P., 1971; DO, Phila. Coll. Osteo. Medicine, 1975. Diplomate Am. Bd. Anesthesiology. Resident USPHS, Staten Island (N.Y.C.), 1975-78; fellowship Milton S. Hershey Med. Ctr. Pa State U., Hershey, 1978-79, asst. prof. Anesthesiology Milton S. Hershey Med. Ctr., 1979-83; pvt. practice Huntsville, Ala., 1983-95; ptnr. Comprehensive Anesthesia Svcs., Huntsville, 1995—; clin. assoc. prof. Anesthesiology and Surgery U. Ala. Sch. Medicine, Huntsville, 1993—; co-med. dir. Surgery Ctr. of Huntsville, 1985-86; chief divsn. of Anesthesiology Huntsville Hosp., 1986-87. Contbr. articles to profl. jours. Mem. St. Mark's Luth. Ch. (constitution com., 1987, long-range planning com., 1989, fellowship com., 1986). Lt. cmdr. USPHS, 1975-78. Mem. AMA, Am. Soc. Anesthesiologists, Ala. State Soc. Anesthesiologists (pres. 1993-95, alt. del. to Am. Soc. Anesthesiologists 1989, 91, del. 1990, 92), Madison County Med. Soc. (anesthesiology rep. to exec. bd. 1987-92, dist. 5 rep. to Ala. State Soc. Anesthesiologists 1987-92). Soc. Critical Care Medicine, Am. Soc. Regional Anesthesia. Avocations: sailing, water sports, golf, tennis. Home: 1606 Drake Ave SE Huntsville AL 35802-1057 Office: Comprehensive Anesthesia Svcs 2006 Franklin St Ste 300 Huntsville AL 35801

LOVAS, SÁNDOR, chemist, researcher, educator; b. Kunmadaras, Hungary, Apr. 28, 1958; came to the U.S., 1990; s. Sándor and Mária (Diószegi) L.; m. Éva Ács, Apr. 19, 1980; 1 child, Veronika Éva. MS in Chemistry, József Attila U., Szeged, Hungary, 1982, PhD in Organic Chemistry, 1985. Rsch. asst. Biol. Rsch. Ctr., Szeged, 1982-85, rsch. fellow, 1985-90; postdoctoral fellow Creighton U., Omaha, 1990-93, asst. prof., 1994—. Contbr. articles to profl. jours. Grantee State of Nebr., 1991. Mem. Am. Chem. Soc., Am. Peptide Soc., Hungarian Chem. Soc., World Assn. Theoretically Oriented Chemists. Achievements include patent for specific anticancer activity of GNRH-III analogs; research in conformationally constrained peptides and molecular dynamics simulations of peptides. Office: Creighton Univ Dept Biomed Sci 2500 California Plaza Omaha NE 68178

LOVE, AMY DUNDON, business executive, marketing and sales executive; b. Atlanta, Mar. 6, 1966; d. David Milton and Jo Ann (Pleak) L. BBA in Mktg., BBA in Mgmt., Tex. Tech. U., Lubbock, 1988; MBA, Harvard U., Boston, 1993. Unit mgr. Procter & Gamble, Cin., 1988-91; asst. to pres. SLT Environ. Inc., Conroe, Tex., 1992; sr. assoc. Booz, Allen & Hamilton, San Francisco, 1993-95; v.p. sales and mktg. Navigation Technologies, Sunnyvale, Calif., 1995—. Founder Tex. State Student Govt. Pres. Coun., Austin, Tex., 1987; exec. adv. Jr. Achievement, Houston, 1989; mem. exec. bd. Taft/HBS Partnership, Boston, 1989. Mem. Stanford Fast Break Club, Harvard Alumni Club. Democrat. Avocations: basketball, biking, hiking, tennis, reading, entrepreneurial activities. Home: 712 Partridge Ave Menlo Park CA 94025-5214

LOVE, BEN HOWARD, retired organization executive; b. Trenton, Tenn., Sept. 26, 1930; s. Ben Drane and Virginia (Whitehead); m. Ann Claire Hugo, Mar. 4, 1933; children: Ben H. Jr., Phillip H., Leigh Ann, Mark E. BS, Lambuth Coll., 1955, HHD (hon.), 1986; Dr. Philanthropy (hon.), Pepperdine U., 1987; LHD (hon.), Montclair State U., 1991. With Boy Scouts Am., 1955—; dist. exec. Boy Scouts Am., Jackson, Tenn., 1955-60; scout exec. Delta area council, Boy Scouts Am., Clarksdale, Miss., 1960-64; dir. Nat. council, Boy Scouts Am., North Brunswick, N.J., 1964-68; scout exec. Longhorn council, Boy Scouts Am., Ft. Worth, 1968-71; scout exec. Sam Houston council, Boy Scouts Am., Houston, 1971-73; dir. Northeast region, Boy Scouts Am., Dayton, N.J., 1973-85; chief scout exec. Nat. council, Boy Scouts Am., Irving, Tex., 1985-93; bd. dirs. Am. Gen. Series Portfolio Co., Mid.-Am. Waste Sys. Inc. Served with U.S. Army, 1951-52. Recipient Gold medal SAR, Bronze Wolf award World Scout Orgn. Mem. La Cima Club (bd. dirs. Irving chpt. 1985—), Diamond Oaks Country Club. Republican. Presbyterian. Avocations: tennis, golf, swimming, reading, spectator sports. Office: 4407 Eaton Cir Colleyville TX 76034-4653

LOVE, COURTNEY, singer, actress; b. San Francisco, July 9, 1964; d. Hank Harrison and Linda Carroll; m. Kurt Cobain, Feb. 1992 (dec.); 1 child, Frances Bean. Singer, writer, musician Hole. Albums include Pretty on the Inside, 1991, Live Through This, 1994; appeared in film Sid and Nancy, 1986, Feeling Minnesota, 1996, The People vs. Larry Flynt, 1996, Basquiate, 1996, Life, 1997; television appearance on MTV Unplugged, 1995. Office: care David Geffen Co 9130 W Sunset Blvd Los Angeles CA 90069-3110*

LOVE, DANIEL JOSEPH, consulting engineer; b. Fall River, Mass., Sept. 27, 1926; s. Henry Aloysius and Mary Ellen (Harrington) L.; m. Henrietta Maurisse Popper, June 10, 1950 (dec. Mar. 1986); children: Amy, Timothy, Terence, Kevin; m. Adeline Aponte Esquivel, Feb. 11, 1989; stepchildren: Eric, Brian, Jason. BSEE, Ill. Inst. Tech., 1951, MSEE, 1956; MBA, Calif. State U., Long Beach, 1973. registered profl. engr., Calif., Ariz., Ill., La.; cert. fire protection, Calif. Test engr. Internat. Harvester Co., Chgo., 1951-52; designer Pioneer Svc. & Engrng. Co., Chgo., 1952-53; project engr., ops. mgr. Panellit Co., Skokie, Ill., 1953-60; mktg. mgr. Control Data Co., Mpls., 1961-62; mktg. mgr., asst. to pres. Emerson Electric Co., Pasadena, Calif., 1963-65; pres., gen. mgr. McKee Automation Co., North Hollywood, Calif., 1965-68; engrng. specialist Bechtel Co., Vernon and Norwalk, Calif., 1968-80; chief elec. engr. Bechtel Co., Madrid, 1980-83; engrng. specialist Bechtel Co., Norwalk, Calif., 1983-87; cons. engr. Hacienda Heights, Calif., 1987—. Contbr. articles to jours. in field. Pres. Wilson High Sch. Band Boosters, Hacienda Heights, 1971-73. With USN, 1944-46. Named Outstanding Engr., Inst. for Advancement Engrng., 1986; recipient 3d place prize paper award Industry Application Soc., 1995. Fellow IEEE (disting. lectr., chmn. Met. L.A. sect. 1973-74, chmn. L.A. coun. 1977-78, chmn. protection com. 1990-91, Richard Harold Kaufmann award 1994, Ralph H. Lee prize paper award 1995); mem. NSPE, Nat. Acad. Forensic Engrs., Instrument Soc. Am. (sr.), Soc. Fire Protection Engrs. Republican. Roman Catholic. Avocations: duplicate bridge, travel, walking, writing. Home: 16300 Soriano Dr Hacienda Heights CA 91745-4863

LOVE, DAVIS, III, professional golfer. Mem. Ryder Cup Team, 1993; winner Buick Invitational Calif., 1996. Winner The Internat., 1990, MCI Heritage Classic Champion, 1991, 92, Tournament Players Championship, 1992, 93, Greater Greensboro Open, 1992. Address: care PGA Tour 112 TPC Blvd Ponte Vedra Beach FL 32082-3046*

LOVE, DUVAL LEE, professional football player; b. L.A., June 24, 1963. Student, UCLA. Guard L.A. Rams, 1985-91, Pitts. Steelers, 1992-94, Ariz. Cardinals, 1995—. Named to NFL Pro Bowl Team, 1994. Address: 17 Meadow Wood Dr Coto De Caza CA 92679-4737 Office: Ariz Cardinals PO Box 888 Phoenix AZ 85001-0888*

LOVE, FRANKLIN SADLER, retired trade association executive; b. Rock Hill, S.C., Nov. 9, 1915; s. Franklin Sadler and Edna (Hull) L.; m. Jessie Huggins, Apr. 10, 1943; children: Judith (Mrs. J. Lindsay Freeman), Beverly (Mrs. Ronald Sparrow), Franklin Sadler III, Glenn. A.B., Presbyn. Coll., Clinton, S.C., 1937. Sec. Cotton Mfrs. Assn. S.C., Clinton, 1937-42, Am. Cotton Mfrs. Assn., Charlotte, N.C., 1946-49; sec. treas. Am. Textile Mfrs. Inst., 1949-79, v.p., 1979-80, ret., 1980; speaker numerous civic and bus. groups; Adviser Internat. Cotton Adv. Com., 1958. Former mem. adv. bd. Charlotte Salvation Army; former bd. dirs. Charlotte Council on Alcoholism. Capt. Ordnance dept. AUS, 1942-46. Recipient Alumni citation for outstanding achievement Presbyn. Coll., 1955; certificate of merit Ala. Textile Mfrs. Assn., 1972. Mem. Def. Supply Assn. (pres. Carolinas chpt. 1952), Phi Psi, Rotary (pres. Charlotte chpt.), Goodfellows Club (Charlotte), Charlotte Execs. Club (former sec.). Presbyterian. Home: Cottage 136 5100 Sharon Rd Charlotte NC 28210-4799

LOVE, GAYLE MAGALENE, special education educator, adult education educator; b. New Orleans, July 25, 1953; d. Lowell F. Sr. and Nathalie Mae (Adams) L.; children: Nathanael Dillard, Raphael. BMEd, Loyola U., New Orleans, 1975, MMEd, 1981; postgrad., Nova Southeastern U. Cert. learning disabled, emotionally disturbed, gifted-talented, adult edn., mild-moderate, elem.-secondary vocal music, prin., spl. sch. prin., parish/city sch. supr. instrn., supervision of student tchg., supr. adult edn. & spl. edn., child search coord. Prin., dean student svcs. Jefferson Parish Sch. Bd., Harvey, La., chmn. spl. edn. dept., 1990-93; adult educator instr.; chmn. Sch. Bldg. Level Com., 1994-96; presenter St. Joseph the Worker Cath. Ch., 1988, Very Spl. Arts Week Jefferson Parish Pub. Sch. Sys., 1989, 90, 91, 92, 93, 94, 95, 96; mem. spl. edn. alternative curriculum com., 1990—, Urban Ctr. Tchrs. Devel. com. U. New Orleans, 1990-91. Mem. NAFE, ASCD, Coun. Exceptional Children (workshop presenter 1990), La. Assn. Prins., Nat. Assn. Secondary Sch. Prins., Jefferson Assn. Pub. Sch. Adminstrs., East Bank Jefferson Parish Parent Adv. Coun., New Orleans C. of C. (com. Alliance for Quality, small bus. improvement team), Jefferson Chamber Leadership Inst., La. Assn. Sch. Execs., Phi Beta, Kappa Delta Pi, Alpha Kappa Alpha. Home: 1740 Burnley Dr Marrero LA 70072-4522

LOVE, GORDON LEE, pathologist, researcher; b. Concord, Calif., Dec. 11, 1951; s. Curtis and Violet (Cota) L.; m. Margaret Fuller, Jan. 12, 1985. B.S., La. Tech. U., 1973; M.D., Tulane Med. Sch., 1978. Diplomate Am. Bd. Pathology, Anatomic and Clin. Pathology, Am. Bd. Med. Microbiology, Mycology; spl. qualification in med. microbiology, cytopathology. Resident in pathology Charity Hosp., New Orleans, 1978-83, vis. pathologist, 1984-93; staff pathologist VA Hosp., New Orleans, 1983-93; instr. pathology La. State U. Med. Sch., New Orleans, 1984-86; asst. prof., 1986-92, assoc. prof., 1992-93; dir. labs. VA No. Calif. Health Care Sys. Clinics, Martinez, 1993—; clin. assoc. prof. U. Calif., Davis, 1994—. Contbr. articles to profl. jours. Fellow Coll. Am. Pathologists; mem. Internat. Acad. Pathologists, Am. Soc. for Microbiologist. Democrat. Lutheran. Avocation: computing. Home: 1300 Bonita Bahia Benicia CA 94510-2406 Office: VA Clin 150 Muir Rd Martinez CA 94553-4612

LOVE, JEFFREY BENTON, lawyer; b. Houston, Oct. 4, 1949; s. Benton Fooshee and Margaret (McKean) L.; m. Katherine Brownlee, Dec. 30, 1972; children: Benton Fooshee III, Elizabeth Houston. BA, Vanderbilt U., 1971; JD, U. Tex., 1976. Bar: Tex. 1976. Assoc. Liddell, Sapp, Zivley, Hill & LaBoon, L.L.P., Houston, 1976-81, ptnr., 1982—, adv. dir., 1990—, vice chmn. bd. dirs. nominating com. 1992—; dir. Tex. Commerce Bank-Houston regional adv. bd., Kinark Corp., 1985-88, St. Luke's Episc. Hosp., 1989-96; hon. consul gen. Sweden in Tex., 1983-89, U. Tex. Devel. Bd., 1991—; mem. com. for Tex. campaign U. Tex., 1992—; assoc. mem. bd. visitors U. Tex. M. D. Anderson Cancer Ctr., 1991—; chmn. Harris County Fin. Com. Re-Election Campaign, Tex. Supreme Ct. Justice Tom Phillips, 1995-96; dir. exec. com. Houston Grand Opera. Pres. Sunrisers Houston Breakfast Assn., Houston, 1979; dir. exec. com. Houston Grand Opera Assn., Houston, 1979-86; dir., chmn. Children's Fund, Inc., Houston, 1981-82; bd. dirs. Tex. Bus. Hall of Fame Found., 1985—, chmn. bd. dirs., 1987, awards com. 1992—; bd. dirs. March of Dimes, Houston, 1989—, chmn. 1989, bd. nominations com. 1992—; adv. dir. Eileen McMillin Blood Ctr., Meth. Hosp.; bd. govs., exec. com., sec. The Forum Club, 1987-92, The Hospice Tex. Med. Ctr. Cap. Campaign, 1991, St. John Divine Episcopal Ch. Cap. Campaign, 1992; bd. dirs., exec. com. Nat. Conf. Christians and Jews, Inc., 1987-90; mem. devel. council Tex. Children's Hosp., 1987—; mem. adv. bd. Covenant House Tex., 1988—; Houston Internat. Festival: co-chmn., Mayor's Gala, 1993, mem. underwriters com. Houston Ballet Ball, 1992; bd. dirs., mem. exec. com. Houston Youth Symphony & Ballet, 1990—, pres., 1992-93, chmn., emcee 1993 Cultural Leader of Yr. Dinner; hon. chair Lupus Disease Benefit, 1992. Recipient Outstanding Young Texas Ex award U. Tex. Ex Students Assn., 1988, 5 Outstanding Young Houstonian awards Houston Jr. C. of C., 1988, 5 Outstanding Young Texan awards Tex. Jaycees, 1988; named one of Outstanding Young Men in Am., U.S. Jaycees, 1980, 81; decorated Knighthood of Royal Order of North Star King Carl XVI Gustaf of Sweden, 1989, Hon. Family of Yr., Child Advocates, Inc., 1991. Mem. ABA, Houston C. of C., Houston Bar Assn., Tex. Bar Assn., Swedish Am. Trade Assn. (bd. dirs. 1983—), Swedish Am. C. of C., U. Tex. Law Alumni Assn. (bd. dirs. 1981—, nat. pres., chmn. exec. com. 1986-87), Phi Delta Theta Alumni Assn. Episcopalian. Clubs: River Oaks, Allegro, Houston. Home: 3744 Inwood Dr Houston TX 77019-3002 Office: Liddell Sapp Zivley Hill & LaBoon LLP 600 Travis St 3400 Texas Commerce Tower Houston TX 77002-3095

LOVE, JOSEPH L., history educator, cultural studies center administrator; b. Austin, Tex., Feb. 28, 1938; s. Joseph L. Sr. and Virginia (Ellis) L.; m. Laurie Reynolds, Dec. 23, 1978; children: Catherine R., David A.; children from previous marriage: James A., Stephen N. AB in Econs. with honors, Harvard U., 1960; MA in History, Stanford U., 1963; PhD in History with distinction, Columbia U., 1967. From instr. to prof. U. Ill., Urbana-Champaign, 1966—, dir. ctr. Latin Am. and Caribbean studies, 1993—; rsch. assoc. St. Antony's Coll. Oxford U.; vis. prof. Pontifical Cath. U., Rio de Janeiro, 1987; presenter in field. Author: Rio Grande do Sul and Brazilian Regionalism, 1882-1930, 1971, Sao Paulo in the Brazilian Federation, 1889-1937, 1980, Crafting the Third World: Theorizing Underdevelopment in Rumania and Brazil, 1996; editor: (with Robert S. Byars) Quantitative Social Science Research on Latin America, 1973, (with Nils Jacobsen) Guiding the Invisible Hand: Economic Liberalism and the State in Latin American History, 1988; bd. editors Latin Am. Rsch. Rev., 1974-78, Hispanic Am. Hist. Rev., 1984-89, The Americas, 1995—; contbr. articles to profl. jours. Fulbright-Hays Rsch. grantee; fellow Social Sci. Rsch. Coun., IREX, Guggenheim; vis. fellow U. São Paulo, Inst. Ortega y Gasset, Madrid; sr. rsch. fellow NEH, others; sr. univ. scholar U. Ill., 1993-96. Mem. Am. Hist. Assn., Conf. Latin Am. History (chair Brazilian studies com. 1973, mem. gen. com. 1983, Conf. prize 1971), Latin Am. Studies Assn. Unitarian. Office: U Ill Ctr Latin Am and Caribbean Studies 910 S 5th St Rm 201 Champaign IL 61820-6216

LOVE, KENNETH EDWARD, real estate, investment and business consultant; b. Bamberg, S.C., Dec. 8, 1941; s. Murray Eugene and Mozelle (Bodiford) L.; widowed; children: Kenneth E. II, Karen C., Kimberly Ann. Student, So. Meth. U., 1960, Columbia Coll., 1961; BS in History, U. S.C., 1963. Magistrate State of S.C., Columbia, 1970-73; real estate broker Crown KEL, Inc., Columbia, 1973-87; exec. v.p. McDaniels So. Chems., Columbia, 1984—; pres. Crown KEL, Inc. Pub. Co., Columbia, 1986—, Comput-MED, Inc., 1987—; Owner Antiques Inc., Columbia, 1978—. Trustee Allen U., Columbia, 1973; mem. exec. com. S.C. Dem. Party, Columbia, 1962-74, chmn. 1971—; mem. U.S. Fgn. Affairs Panel, 1986—; chmn. So. East Dem. Regional Dist., 1994; mem. White Ho. Com. Policies; exec. dir. S.C. Citizens and Merchants' Assn., 1992—; chmn., CEO Carolina Hist. Found. Soc., Inc., 1996—. Served to sgt. U.S. Army, 1957-59. Named Outstanding Young Man Columbia City, 1972, Outstanding Dem. Nat. Dem. Party, 1992. Mem. S.C. Citizens and Merchants Assn. (pres. 1994—, exec. dir. 1995—), Greater Columbia Assn., Carolina Hist. Found. Soc. Inc. (chmn. bd. 1996—). Avocations: woodworking, medical research reading, politics. Home: 500 Northwood Rd Lexington SC 29072-2128 Office: Ken Love and Assoc 609 Columbia Ave Lexington SC 29072-2619

LOVE, MICHAEL KENNETH, lawyer; b. Richmond Height, Mo., Oct. 2, 1951; s. Clarence Kenneth and Helen (Schlapper) L.; m. Gloria Pia Miccioli, Sept. 8, 1979; children: Claire Pia, Patrick Kenneth. BS in Forestry, U. Mo., 1974; JD, George Washington U., 1977. Bar: Va. 1977, D.C. 1978, Md. 1981. Asst. dir. model procurement code project ABA, Washington, 1977-80; assoc. Wickwire, Gavin & Gibbs, P.C., Vienna, Va., 1980-84; ptnr. Wickwire, Gavin & Gibbs, P.C., Vienna, 1984-86, Smith, Pachter, McWhorter & D'Ambrosio, Vienna, 1986-94; corp. counsel Info. Sys. and Networks, Inc., Bethesda, 1994-95; sr. atty. Epstein, Becker & Green, Washington, 1995—. Contbr. articles to prof. publs. Vice chair D.C. Procurement Reform Task Force. Mem. ABA (chmn. subcontracting and constrn. com. pub. contract law sect. 1984-92, constrn. com. 1990-91, chair constrn. divsn. 1993-94, mem. coun. 1994-97), Nat. Contract Mgmt. Assn., Nat. Security Indsl. Assn., Va. Bar Assn. Office: Epstein Becker & Green 1227 25th St NW Washington DC 20037-1156

LOVE, MIRON ANDERSON, retired judge; b. Houston, Oct. 25, 1920; s. Robert William and Josephine (Moody) L.; m. Marjorie Skiles, Dec. 21, 1948; children: Ross, Mark. BA, So. Meth. U., 1948; LLB, So. Tex. Law Sch., 1951. Bar: Tex. 1951, U.S. Dist. Ct. Tex. 1952, U.S. Supreme Ct. 1967. Asst. dist. atty. Harris County (Tex.) Dist. Atty.'s Office, Houston, 1951-53; pvt. practice Houston, 1953-58; adminstrv. judge 177th Dist. Ct., Harris County, Houston, 1958-95; ret., 1995. Pres. Nat. Conf. Met. Cts. 1st lt. USAF, 1944-46, PTO. Mem. Internat. Acad. Trial Judges (mem. bd. regents). Democrat. Unitarian.

LOVE, RICHARD EMERSON, equipment manufacturing company executive; b. N.Y.C., Dec. 15, 1926; s. Emerson C. and Ruth A. (Mealley) L.; m. Margaret A. Lloyd, June 24, 1950; children—Mary Ann, Nancy, Jane, Thomas. Grad., N.Y. State Maritime Coll., 1946; AAS, Hofstra Coll., 1955. Group v.p. Crane Co., N.Y.C., 1967-72, U.S. Filter Co., N.Y.C., 1972-75; group pres. Peabody Internat. Corp., Stamford, Conn., 1975-77; exec. v.p. Peabody Internat. Corp., Stamford, 1978-85; group v.p. Pullman Co. (merged with Peabody Internat. Corp.), Stamford, 1985-87; v.p. ops. Hosokowa Micron Internat. Inc., N.Y.C., 1987-93; dir., cons. Hosokawa Micron Internat., N.Y.C., 1993-95; ret., 1995; pres. Internat. Area Mgmt., Hilton Head, S.C., 1995—. Served with USN, 1948-49. Mem. ASME, Instruments Soc. Am. Office: Internat Area Mgmt 16 Old Fort Dr Hilton Head Island SC 29926-2698

LOVE, ROBERT LYMAN, educational consulting company executive; b. Oswego, N.Y., July 28, 1925; s. Robert Barnum and Marion Alberta (Peavy) L.; m. Janet May Fuller, June 26, 1948; children: Robert H., Andrew L., Charles D., Cynthia S. Student, U. Rochester, 1943-44; A.B., Syracuse U., 1945, postgrad. in medicine, 1946-48, M.Ed., 1949; postgrad., Cornell U., 1963-64. Sci. tchr. Middlesex Valley Central Sch., Rushville, N.Y., 1949-53; mem. faculty Agrl. and Tech. Coll., SUNY-Alfred, 1953-81; prof., dean Agrl. and Tech. Coll., SUNY (Sch. Allied Health Techs.), until 1981, dean emeritus, 1981—; pres. Edn. Cons. Services, Alfred Station, N.Y., 1981—; former mem. bd. dirs. Nat. Tech. Inst. Deaf Med. Records program; program evaluation steering com. AMA; allied health reviewer HEW; mem. health sub-com. 39th Congl. Dist. Author: He and She, An Introduction to Human Sexuality and Birth Control, 1970; editor: Upward Mobility for Lab Personnel, 1970. Fin. sec., mem. adminstrv. bd. Alfred United Meth. Ch.; mem. Roving Vols. in Christ's Svc., 1982-91, bd. dirs. 1984-86, 89-91, chmn. bd. dirs., 1989-90; mem. Selected Vols. in Christ's Svc., 1987-88; litercy vol.; pres., bd. dirs. Genesee Valley Habitat for Humanity, Inc., 1993-95; treas. 1995—; Allegany County Office for Aging Handyman's Svc. Fellow Sci. Tchrs. Assn. N.Y. State, Am. Soc. Allied Health Professions; mem. Gideons Internat. (past pres. Hornell Camp), Literacy Vols. Am. (bd. dirs. Allegany County chpt. 1990-93), Masons, Order Eastern Star. Republican. Office: Edn Cons Svc 5366 Jericho Hill Rd Alfred Station NY 14803-9736 *Having had the opportunity to work with young people has kept me young and knowing the Lord has saved me.*

LOVE, ROBERT WILLIAM, JR., retired physician, government administrator; b. Springfield, Mo., June 28, 1929; s. Robert William and Ruby Gladys (Teel) L.; m. Barbara Joyce Few, July 5, 1974; children—Robert William, III, Curry Maria, Rebecca Anne. A.B., Drury Coll., 1950; M.D., St. Louis U., 1954. Intern Kansas City (Mo.) Gen. Hosp., 1954-55, resident in surgery, 1955-59; staff surgeon VA Hosp., Asheville, N.C., 1961-62; chief gen. surgery VA Hosp., 1962-72, asst. chief surg. service, 1962-72; chief of staff VA Hosp., Mountain Home, Tenn., 1972-74; dir. field ops. VA Central Office, Washington, 1974-75, dir. ops. rev. and analysis, 1975-79; med. dir., evaluation and analysis office VA Central Office, 1979-85; dir. VA Outpatient Clinic, Pensacola, Fla., 1985-90; asst. clin. prof. surgery Duke U., 1967-72. Served to capt. M.C. USNR, 1959-61. Recipient dirs. commendation VA Hosp., Mountain Home, 1974, Adminstrs. commendation, VACO, 1985. Mem. A.C.S., Assn. VA Surgeons, Naval Res. Assn., Res. Officers Assn., Assn. Mil. Surgeons U.S., Escambia County Med. Soc., Alpha Omega Alpha. Research in magnification lymphangiographic radiography, Tb and gastric ulcer, med. treatment of spinal Tb. Home: 8774 Thunderbird Dr Pensacola FL 32514-5659

LOVE, SHARON IRENE, elementary education educator; b. Pontiac, Mich., July 27, 1950; d. James and Ethlyn (Cole) M.; married; 1 child, Sheralyn Reneé. BS, Western Mich. U., 1964; postgrad., Oakland U., Rochester, Mich. Cert. elem. educator, early childhood educator, Mich. Tchr. kindergarten Pontiac Bd. Edn., 1964-69, 76-83, 87—, tchr. 1st grade, 1965-66, tchr. 4th grade, 1983-84, tchr. 2d grade, 1984-87; tchr. trainer triple I.E. classroom instruction Emerson Elem. Sch., Pontiac, 1988-89; trainer Math Their Way, Pontiac Sch. Sys., 1989, leadership, 1990; trainer Mich. Health Model Oakland Schs., Waterford, 1987; co-chair com. for developing and writing new Fine Arts curriculum for Pontiac Sch. Dist., 1993-94; chmn. coordinating coun. Webster Elem. Sch., 1994-95; head tchr. kindergarten pilot Bethune Elem. Sch., 1995-96. Chair coord. coun. Walt Whitman Elem. Schs., Pontiac, 1987-91; mem. PTA, 1970-90; chair coord. coun. Webster Elem. Sch., 1993-94. Creative Art grantee Pontiac PTA, 1965; recipient cert. Appreciation Pontiac Blue Ribbon Com., 1991, cert. for outstanding educatorMich. Gov. Engler, 1991. Mem. NAACP, Mich. Edn. Assn., Pontiac Edn. Assn. (del. 1965-66). Avocations: art, writing poetry, sewing. Office: Pontiac Bd Edn 350 Wide Track Dr E Pontiac MI 48342-2243

LOVE, WILLIAM EDWARD, lawyer; b. Eugene, Oreg., Mar. 13, 1926; s. William Stewart and Ola A. (Kingsbury) L.; m. Sylvia Kathryn Jaureguy, Aug. 6, 1955; children: Kathryn Love Petersen, Jeffrey, Douglas, Gregory. B.S., U. Notre Dame, 1946; M.A. in Journalism, U. Oreg., 1950, J.D., 1952. Bar: Oreg., 1952. Newspaper reporter Eugene Register Guard, 1943-44, 47-52; asst. prof. law, asst. dean Sch. Law U. Wash., Seattle, 1952-56; ptnr. Cake, Jaureguy, Hardy, Buttler & McEwen, Portland, Oreg., 1956-69; pres., chmn., chief exec. officer Equitable Savs. & Loan, Portland, 1969-82; sr. ptnr. Schwabe, Williamson & Wyatt, Portland, 1983—; chmn. Oreg. Savs. League, 1976; dir. Portland Gen. Electric, 1976-83, Fed. Home Loan Bank of Seattle, 1976-79, 85-96, adv. council Fed. Nat. Mortgage Assn., Washington, 1978-80; exec. dir. Health, Housing, Ednl. & Cultural Facilities Authority, 1990—. Author: (with Jaureguy) Oregon Probate Law and Practice, 2 vols., 1958. Contbr. articles to profl. jours. Commr., past chmn. Oreg. Racing Commn., 1963-79; pres. Nat. Assn. State Racing Commrs., 1977-78; commr. Port of Portland, 1979-86, pres., 1983; referee Pac-10 football, 1960-81, Rose Bowl, 1981; active United Way, Boy Scouts Am., Portland Rose Festival, polit. campaigns; mem. adv. coun. Jockeys' Guild, Inc., 1990—. Served to lt. (j.g.), USN, 1944-47. Mem. Oreg. Bar Assn., Multnomah County Bar Assn. Republican. Clubs: Arlington, Multnomah Athletic, Golf (Portland). Home: 10225 SW Melnore St Portland OR 97225-4356 Office: Schwabe Williamson & Wyatt 1211 SW 5th Ave Ste 1700 Portland OR 97204-3717

LOVE, WILLIAM JENKINS, sales and marketing executive; b. Atlanta, June 12, 1962; s. James Erskine Jr. and Gay (McLawhorn) L.; m. Helen Elizabeth Brumley, Aug. 6, 1988. BS, Duke U., 1984, MBA, 1992. Comml. appraiser Coldwell Banker, Atlanta, 1985-88; mktg. specialist Printpack Inc., Atlanta, 1988-90, also bd. dirs., sales rep., 1992-96, account mgr., 1996—. Vol. Atlanta Symphony Assocs., 1987-90, Project READ, 1995—; elder Trinity Presbyn. Ch., 1996—. Mem. Duke U. Alumni Assn. (trustee 1996—). Avocations: photography, travel, tennis, golf, softball. Office: Printpack Inc 4335 Wendell Dr SW Atlanta GA 30336-1622

LOVEJOY, ALLEN FRASER, retired lawyer; b. Janesville, Wis., Oct. 9, 1919; s. Henry Stow and Mary Fraser (Beaton) L.; m. Betty Foote, Dec. 20, 1944; children: Jennifer Lovejoy Craddock, Charles F., Allen P. BA, Yale U., 1941, LLB, 1948. Bar: N.Y. 1949, U.S. Ct. Appeals (2d cir.) 1975. Assoc. Breed, Abbott & Morgan, N.Y.C., 1948-58, ptnr., 1958-87. Served with U.S. Army, 1941-46; ETO. Decorated Purple Heart with oak leaf cluster; recipient Frank M. Patterson award Yale U., 1941. Fellow Am. Numis. Soc. (life, councillor 1988—, 1st v.p. 1990—), Am. Numis. Assn. Republican. Episcopalian. Clubs: Pilgrims (N.Y.C.); Mid Ocean (Bermuda); Stanwich (Greenwich, Conn.); Riverside (Conn.) Yacht. Author: La Follette and the Establishment of the Direct Primary in Wisconsin, 1890-1904, 1941; co-author: Early United States Dimes, 1796-1837, 1984; contbr. articles to numismatic publs. Home: 100 Club Rd Riverside CT 06878-2032

LOVEJOY, ANN LOUISE, organizational development consultant; b. Baker, Oreg., Aug. 18, 1949; d. Victor and Norma (Peters) Lovejoy; m. Pierre Ventur, June 9, 1975 (div. 1997); 1 child, Conrad Ventur. Bachelors, U. Wash., 1971, Masters, 1975. Bot. field asst. (grant) Yale U., San Luis, Guatemala, 1975-77; editorial asst., micro personal computer trainer Yale U., New Haven, Conn., 1977-86; tech. trainer Bunker Ramo/Allied Signal, Shelton, Conn., 1984-86; sr. training specialist Bank of Boston, Springfield, Mass., 1986-87, MassMutual Life Ins., Springfield, Mass., 1987-96, CIGNA, Hartford, Conn., 1996—. Mem. bd. corporators Springfield Metro YMCA, 1994—. Mem. ASTD (bd. dirs. Pioneer Valley 1986-91), Assn. for Computing Machinery. Office: CIGNA Health Care 900 Cottage Grove Rd # A145 Hartford CT 06152-0001

LOVEJOY, BARBARA CAMPBELL, sculptor, architectural designer; b. Detroit, Oct. 31, 1919; d. Robert Bruce and Mona (Goodwin) Campbell; m. William Edward Gibson, Oct. 27, 1941 (dec. Aug. 1969); children: Linda Dean Gibson Stoner, William Kent; m. John Marshall Lovejoy, Jan. 27, 1971 (dec. Nov. 1994). B of Design, Tulane U., 1941; studied sculpture with Lothar Kestenbaum; also studied with Yuri Hollosy, New Orleans. Archtl. designer Aurora Devel. Co., New Orleans, 1950-60; pvt. practice archtl. design New Orleans, 1960-70; chief designer D.H. Holmes Store Planning, New Orleans, 1970-78; dir. store planning and interior design Wray Williams Display Co., New Orleans, 1978-86. One-woman shows include D.H. Homes Canal St. Window Exhbn., New Orleans, 1981, Kaplan'a Art Exhibit, Alexandria, La., 1983, 85, Ea. Art Assoc., Fairhope, Ala., 1985; exhibited in group shows at Salon de Refuses, New Orleans, 1967, Edgewater Mall, 1980, New Orleans Commodity Exchange, 1982, Palm Beach (Fla.) Art Galleries, 1984, (Patron's award in sculpture 1983), Peyton Meml. Arts Festival, Alexandria, 1983-85, 91, 93 (Patron's award 1983, Spl. Purchase award 1984), U. New Orleans Gallery, 1983-84, St. Tammany Art Assn., Covington, La., 1984, 90, New Orleans Women's Caucus for Art, 1985, New Orleans Acad. Art Summer Group Show, 1985, New Orleans Ctr. Contemporary Art, 1984-86, Grand Festival Art at Grand Hotel, Point Clear, La., 1985, 87, La. Women Artists, Baton Rouge, 1987, 5th Juried Exhbn. for La. Artists, 1987-88, Decatur Arts Alliance, 1990, Memphis Arts Festival, 1990 (Patron's award in sculpture), Mystic Conn. Art Gallery, 1991, Artist in Still Zinsel Gallery, New Orleans, 1988-91, Miriam Walmsley Gallery, 1992, Masur Mus. Art, Monroe, La., 1992, 95, La. Competition, Baton Rouge, 1993, 95, Art for Advocacy, La., 1993, 95, Carol Robinson Gallery, 1994-97, La. Arts & Sci. Ctr., Baton Rouge, 1996. Recipient 1st pl. Painting award Chevron Art Exhbn., 1965, 66, 1st pl. Sculpture award Nat. Art Appreciation Soc., 1984, other awards New Orleans Mus. Art, 1985, Art for Advocacy, 1993, Slidell Art League, 1995, Masur Mus. Art (Monroe, La.), 1995, Ben Weiner Found. (permanent display in Wilson Ctr., Tulane U.), 1995. Mem. Am. Soc. Interior Designers (prof.), Women's Caucus for Art, Southeastern Women's Caucus for Art. Presbyterian. Home and Studio: 100 Finland Pl New Orleans LA 70131-3904

LOVEJOY, GEORGE MONTGOMERY, JR., real estate executive; b. Newton, Mass., Apr. 15, 1930; s. George Montgomery and Margaret (King) L.; m. Ellen West Childs, June 30, 1956; children: George Montgomery III, Edward R., Philip W., Henry W. BA, Harvard U., 1951. V.p. Minot, DeBlois & Maddison, Boston, 1955-72; exec. v.p. Meredith & Grew, Inc., Boston, 1972-78, pres., 1978-88, chmn., 1988-95; chmn. Fifty Assocs., Boston, 1988-94, pres., 1994—; trustee Scudder Cash Investment Trust, Scudder GNMA Fund, Scudder Investment Trust, Scudder Portfolio Trust, Scudder Mcpl. Trust, Scudder Tax Free Money Fund, Scudder U.S. Treas. Money Fund; bd. dirs. MGI Properties, L.Am. Dollar Income Fund, Scudder World Income Fund. Mem. Weston (Mass.) Planning Bd., 1961-68, chmn., 1965-67; mem. Bd. Selectmen, 1968-71, chmn., 1970-71; bd. dirs. Boston Mcpl. Rsch. Bur., 1966—, chmn., 1982-84; mem. com. Fund for Preservation Wildlife and Natural Areas, 1985-94, chmn., 1992-94; trustee New Eng. Aquarium, 1969—, pres. 1992-94, chmn. 1994; trustee Radcliffe Coll., 1987-95; mem. Corp. Northeastern U. Mem. Am. Soc. Real Estate Counselors (past pres., bd. dirs.), Greater Boston Bldg. Owners and Mgrs. Assn. (past pres.), Internat. Coun. Shopping Ctrs., Inst. Real Estate Mgmt. (past pres. New Eng. chpt.), Greater Boston Real Estate Bd. (past pres.), Mass. Assn. Realtors, Nat. Assn. Realtors, Nature Conservancy (chmn. Mass. adv. bd.), Harvard Club Boston (past pres.). Avocations: outdoor activities, land conservation. Home: 54 Beacon St Boston MA 02108 Office: Fifty Assoc 50 Congress St Boston MA 02109-4002

LOVEJOY, JENNIFER CAROLE, medical educator; b. Seattle, Mar. 30, 1961; d. Roland William and Deborah (Daniels) L.; m. Robert M. Straughn, Sept. 24, 1995; 1 child, Teresa S. BS in Zoology magna cum laude, Duke U., 1982; MA in Psychobiology, Emory U., 1986, PhD in Psychobiology, 1988. Rsch. tech. pediatric virology Duke U. Med. Ctr., Durham, N.C., 1982-83; grad. fellow psychobiology dept. psychology Yerkes Primate Rsch. Ctr., Atlanta, 1983-88; rsch. fellow endocrinology and metabolism, dept. medicine Emory U. Sch. Medicine, Atlanta, 1988-89, instr. in medicine dept. medicine, 1989-91; asst. prof. obesity, diabetes and metabolism sect. Pennington Biomed. Rsch. Ctr., La. State U., Baton Rouge, 1991—; clin. asst. prof. rsch. dept. ob-gyn. La. State U., Sch. Medicine, New Orleans, 1993—; lab. specialist glycolipid biochemistry dept. pathology U. Va. Med. Ctr., Charlottesville, 1985; introductory psychology lectr. Oglethorp U., Atlanta, 1990; lectr. and seminar leader in field. Contbr. chpts. to books and articles to profl. jours. Recipient Nat. Rsch. Svc. award NIH-Nat. Inst. Diabetes, Digestive & Kidney Diseases, 1989-91, New Populations award The Obesity Found., 1990. Mem. Am. Diabetes Assn. (coun. mem. nutritional sci. and metabolism, Frances O. Hazzard award 1992, Career Devel. award 1993—, clin. rsch. grantee 1996), Am. Inst. Nutrition, Am. Soc. for Clin. Nutrition, Assn. for Women in Sci., N.Am. Assn. for the Study of Obesity, Internat. Assn. for the Study of Obesity, Soc. for the Study Ingestive Behavior, Sigma Xi. Office: Pennington Biomed Rsch Ctr 6400 Perkins Rd Baton Rouge LA 70808-4124

LOVEJOY, RAY, film editor. Editor: (films) 2001: A Space Odyssey, 1968, The Ruling Class, 1972, A Day in the Death of Joe Egg, 1972, Fear Is the Key, 1973, Little Malcolm and His Struggle Against the Eunuchs, 1974, Ghost in the Noonday Sun, 1974, The Shining, 1980, Krull, 1983, The Dresser, 1983, Sheena, 1984, Eleni, 1985, Aliens, 1986, Suspect, 1987, The House on Carroll Street, 1988, Batman, 1989, Homeboy, 1989, Mr. Frost, 1990, Year of the Comet, 1992, A Far Off Place, 1993. Office: Sandra Marsh Mgt 9150 Wilshire Blvd Ste 220 Beverly Hills CA 90212-3429*

LOVELACE, ALAN MATHIESON, aerospace company executive; b. St. Petersburg, Fla., Sept. 4, 1929; married; 2 children. BA, U. Fla., 1951, MA, 1952, PhD in Chemistry, 1954. Staff mem. Air Force Materials Lab., Wright-Paterson AFB, 1954-72; dir. sci. and tech. Andrews AFB, Washington, 1972-73; prin. dep. asst. sec., dept. R & D USAF, 1973-74; assoc. adminstr. Aerospace Tech. Office, 1974-76; dep. NASA Aerospace Tech. Office, 1976-81; v.p. sci. and engring., space systems div. Gen. Dynamics Corp., San Diego, 1981-82, corp. v.p. quality assurance and productivity, 1982-85, corp. v.p., gen. mgr., 1985—; chmn. Nat. Acad. Engr., Washington, 1996—. Fellow AIAA (Goddard Astronautics award 1989, George M. Low Space Transp. award 1992); mem. NAE, Air Force Assn., Sigma Xi. *

LOVELACE, BYRON KEITH, lawyer, management consultant; b. Vernon, Tex., Feb. 15, 1935; s. Joseph Edward and Hattie Pearl (Brians) L.; m. Sandra Alene Daniel, June 17, 1961; children: Kirk Daniel, Bethany Alene, Amy Kathleen. BS in Chem. Engring., U. Tex., 1958, MS, 1961, PhD, 1973; JD, South Tex. Coll. Law, 1978. Bar: Tex. 1978. R & D engr. Core Labs., Dallas, 1960-61; with Tex. Instruments, Inc., Dallas and Houston, 1961-78, mgr. process control for advanced tech., 1969-70, reliability mgr. metal oxide semicondr. (MOS) div., 1971-75, MOS reliability dir., 1975-78; pres. P-V-T Inc., Houston, 1978-80, Mgmt. Resources Internat., Houston, 1980—; pvt. practice Law Offices of Keith Lovelace, Houston, 1980—. Contbr. articles to profl. jours.; patentee in field. Mem. Houston Clean City Commn., 1991-94, Greater Southwest Houston C. of C. (bd. dirs. 1996—, vice chmn. 1996—). With U.S. Army, 1953. Tex. Instruments fellow, 1965-68; FMC Corp. fellow, 1958-60; Eastern States Petroleum and Chem. scholar, 1957-58; Ethyl Corp. scholar, 1956-57. Mem. ABA, AIChE, Am. Chem. Soc. (award 1958), Soc. Petroleum Engrs. (vice chmn. reservior group 1979-80), State Bar Tex., Trial Lawyers Am., S.W. Houston C. of C. (bd. dirs. 1988-91, pres. 1990-91), Greater S.W. Houston C. of C. (bd. dirs. 1996—, vice chmn. 1996—), Tau Beta Pi (chpt. v.p. 1958-59), Omega Chi Epsilon. Office: 7322 Southwest Fwy Ste 1480 Houston TX 77074-2000

LOVELACE, ELDRIDGE HIRST, retired landscape architect, city planner; b. Kansas City, Kans., Mar. 16, 1913; s. Charles Wilson and Eva (Hirst) L.; m. Marjorie Van Evera, May 15, 1937; children: Jean (Mrs. William C. Stinchcombe), Richard. B.F.A. in Landscape Architecture, U. Ill., 1935. Registered profl. engr., Mo. With Harland Bartholomew & Assocs., Inc., St. Louis, 1935—81; mem. firm Harland Bartholomew & Assocs., Inc., 1943-79, chmn. bd., 1979—81; cons., 1981—; prepared comprehensive city plans numerous cities including Toledo, Baton Rouge, Oklahoma City, Vancouver, Waco, Lincoln, Washington; master plans for naval facilities Hawaiian Islands and P.I.; also plans parks, subdivs., housing projects.; Vice pres. Internat. Fedn. Landscape Architects, 1975-77, sec. gen., 1980—81. Author: Harland Bartholomew: His Contributions to American Urban Planning. Mem. bd. commrs. Tower Grove Park, 1971—, pres. 1986-94. Fellow Am. Soc. Landscape Architects (past sec.), ASCE; mem. Am. Inst. Cert. Planners. Clubs: Mo. Athletic (St. Louis). Home: 5 Brookside Ln Saint Louis MO 63124-1814

LOVELACE, JULIANNE, library director; b. Jackson, Miss., July 30, 1941; d. Benjamin Travis and Julia Elizabeth (Knight) Robinson; m. William Frank Lovelance, July 6, 1963 (div. Mar. 17, 1972); 1 child, Julie Lynn. BA in History, So. Meth. U., 1963; MLS, U. North Tex., 1970. Clk. Dallas Pub. Libr., 1963-64, children's libr. asst., 1964-66, children's libr., 1966-69; libr. Richardson (Tex.) Pub. Libr., 1971-72, supr. pub. svcs., 1972-87, dir., 1987—. Mem. exec. bd. Youth Svcs. Coun., Richardson Adult Literacy Ctr.; mem. Altrusa Internat., Inc. Richardson, Leadership Richardson Alumni Assn., Friends of the Richardson Pub. Libr.; mem. Women's Adv. Coun. Baylor/Richardson Med. Ctr. Mem. ALA, Tex. Libr. Assn., Pub. Libr. Adminstrs. North Tex. Avocations: horse racing, blackjack. Office: Richardson Pub Libr 900 Civic Center Dr Richardson TX 75080-5210

LOVELACE, ROBERT FRANK, health facility administrator, researcher; b. Elizabethton, Tenn., Oct. 7, 1950; s. Douglas Clayton and Doris Ivalee (Guy) L.; m. Diane Marie Wamsley, June 3, 1972; children: Jason Robert, Geoffrey Mark. BS, Phila. Coll. Bible, 1972; MA, Ea. Sem., Phila., 1974; PhD, Temple U., 1988. Lic. nursing home adminstr. Adminstr. research The Franklin Inst., Phila., 1974-79, adminstr. contracts, 1979-81; dir. research adminstrn. The Grad. Hosp., Phila., 1981-88; adminstr. Elm Terr. Gardens, Lansdale, Pa., 1988-95, pres., 1995—; adj. lectr. Temple U., Phila., 1983-86, Wilkes Coll., 1986-90, Rutgers U., 1989-93, St. Joseph's U., 1993—; exec. dir., sec.-treas. Gradtech, Phila., 1985-88. Contbr. articles to profl. jours. V.p., bd. dirs. Elm Terr. Gardens, Lansdale, 1986-88; dir. bd. Christian edn. 1st Bapt. Ch., Lansdale, 1985-88, 90-96, chmn. program com., 1987-90, chmn. worship svcs. com., 1992, chmn. search com., 1995. Fellow Am. Coll. Health Care Adminstrs.; mem. Am. Assn. Homes and Svcs. for the Aging, Pa. Assn. Non-profit Homes for the Aging, Rsch. and Devel. Mgmt. Assn., Am. Soc. on Aging. Republican. Home: 553 Millers Way Lansdale PA 19446-4059 Office: Elm Terr Gardens 660 N Broad St Lansdale PA 19446-2361

LOVELAND, DONALD WILLIAM, computer science educator; b. Rochester, N.Y., Dec. 26, 1934; s. Roger Platt and Dorothy (Dobbin) L.; m. Amy Straw, May 21, 1966; children: Robert Philip, Douglas Roger. AB, Oberlin Coll., 1956; SM, MIT, 1958; PhD, NYU, 1964. Mathematician, programmer IBM, Yorktown Heights, N.Y., 1958-59; asst. prof. math. NYU, 1964-67; asst. prof., then assoc. prof. math. and computer sci. Carnegie-Mellon U., Pitts., 1967-73; prof., chmn. dept. computer sci. Duke U., Durham, N.C., 1973-78, 91-92, prof. computer sci., 1973—; disting. faculty visitor IBM Rsch. Ctr., Yorktown Heights, 1979-80; program chmn., editor procs. 6th Conf. on Automated Deduction, 1982, trustee corp. controls, 1994-97. Author: Automated Theorem Proving: A Logical Basis, 1978; co-editor: (with W.W. Bledsoe) Automated Theorem Proving: After 25 Years, 1984; mng. editor book series Artificial Intelligence, 1983-92; editorial bd. Artificial Intelligence, 1983-93, Jour. Automated Reasoning. Grantee NSF, 1970-73, 75-77, 88-92, 92-96, Air Force Office Sci. Rsch., 1981-86, Army Rsch. Office, 1984-91. Mem. Assn. for Computing Machinery, Assn. for Symbolic Logic, Am. Assn. for Artificial Intelligence (elected fellow 1993), AAAS. Home: 3417 Cambridge Dr Durham NC 27707-4507 Office: Duke Univ Box 90129 Durham NC 27708-0129

LOVELAND, EUGENE FRANKLIN, petroleum executive; b. Anderson, Ind., Sept. 11, 1920; s. Irving Eugene and Clare (McFarlane) L.; m. Joan King, Aug. 4, 1944; children: Jeffrey, David C. and Peter F. (twins), Mark, Laurie E. B.A., Wesleyan U., Middletown, Conn. With Shell Oil Co., 1946-80, v.p. central mktg. region, 1968-71; v.p. oil products Shell Oil Co., Houston, 1972-80; pres. Transworld Oil USA, Inc. (formerly T.W. Oil Inc.), Houston, 1981—; chmn., chief exec. officer T.W. Oil Inc., 1983-89, ret., 1989; bd. dirs. Transworld Oil Ltd., Bermuda. Bd. dirs. Lyric Theatre, Houston, Am. Dance Cos.; chmn. Houston Ballet Found., Combined Arts Corp., Campaign, Houston, Greater Houston Skating Coun., vice chmn. Better Bus. Bur., Houston; hon. counsul gen. Republic of Malta in Tex.; dir. Cultural Arts Coun. Houston, 1989-93; chmn. Greater Houston Ice Skating Coun., 1989—; mem. exec. com. Houston Internat. Festival, 1992; chmn. devel. commn. Fay Sch., 1992. With USNR, 1943-45. Decorated D.F.C., Air medal (2); recipient Disting. Alumnus award Wesleyan U., 1993. Mem. Mil. and Hospitaller Order St. Lazarus Jerusalem. Office: Transworld Oil USA Inc 910 Travis St Ste 800 Houston TX 77002

LOVELESS, EDWARD EUGENE, education educator, musician; b. Lafayette, Ind., July 29, 1919; s. Benjamin Moses and Belva Lucille (Bowles) L.; m. Jean Evelyn Skinner, May 18, 1941; children: Linda Louise Loveless Reeder, Kathleen Beal Loveless Bodine, Stephen Edward, Melissa Jane Loveless Campbell, Benjamin Warwick. B.S., Purdue U., 1940, M.S., 1941; Ed.D., Stanford U., 1960. Tchr., prin., supt. public schs. Ind., 1941-57; asst. Stanford U., 1957-60; prin. public schs. Palo Alto, Calif., 1961-65; asst. prof. sch. adminstrn. San Francisco State Coll. and assoc. prof. San Jose State Coll., 1960-65; assoc. prof. U. Nev., Reno, 1965-72; prof. U. Nev., 1972-85, prof. emeritus, 1986—; vis. prof. Purdue U., summers 1965, 68, 75; prof. exec. devel. program USAF, Crete, spring 1973. Author: (with Frank Krajewski) The Teacher and School Law: Cases and Materials in the Legal Foundations of Education, 1974, (with J. Clark Davis) The Administrator and Educational Facilities, 1982; contbr. over 70 articles to profl. jours.; editor: Who's Who in Northern Nevada Education, 1976; spkr. on sch. vandalism; clarinetist, saxaphonist, vocalist Jean and Ed (musical duo), 1984—; musical tours Ms World Discoverer, Singapore, The South Seas, New Guinea, Western Samoa, Tonga, Fiji, Tahiti, others, 1984-85; performance South Pacific Coll., Stanford U. Alumni Assn., 1985; royal command performance King Tauf-ahau Tupou IV, Tonga, 1985; commd. performance Trident submarine USS Nev., 1986; concert U.S. Embassy, Geneva, 1987; recs. include Songs of the 30's and 40's, The Gershwin Bros., The Best of Irving Berlin, Jerome Kern Favorites, Hoagy & Benny Revisited, An Evening with Cole Porter, We Like Rodgers & Hart, The Genius of Duke Ellington, Easy Listening, Songs of Jule Styne, A Tribute to Jimmy Van Heussen, Rodgers and Hammerstein Music, 1989, cassette tape series for Wickenburg (Ariz.) Hist. Mus., 1989, Golden Anniversary performance Purdue U., 1990, 74th Birthdays Cassette, 1993, Nat King Cole Songs, 1996. Performer, concert artist for retirement homes and hosps., Palo Alto, Calif., 1990—. Recipient Commendations for providing benefit concerts and performances Sierra Health Care Ctr., 1985, Salvation Army Family Emergency, 1986, VA Hosp., 1988, Daus. of Norway, 1988, Westwood Retirement Home, 1989, State of Nev. Employees Assn., 1989; recipient Certs. of Appreciation Riverside Hosp., 1986, Carson Convalescent Ctr., 1987, Reno Lions Club, 1987, Thank-U-Gram Physicians Hosp., 1988, Manor at Lakeside, 1988, award Washoe County Sr. Citizens Ctr., 1989, Sharon Heights Convalescent Hosp., Palo Alto, Calif., 1993. Mem. NEA, Nev. Edn. Assn., Internat. Soc. Gen. Semantics, Nat. Soc. Profs., Navy League, Kappa Sigma, Phi Delta Kappa (cert. for disting. service 1974, placque of appreciation Gamma Psi chpt. 1976). Democrat. Presbyterian (elder). Home: 2170 Princeton St Palo Alto CA 94306-1325 *Providing musical entertainment for retired and/or hospitalized people has a therapeutic effect that medicine cannot provide. Wynton Marsalis says that "music washes away the dust of everyday life from your feet".*

LOVELESS, GEORGE GROUP, lawyer; b. Baldwinsville, N.Y., Sept. 16, 1940; s. Frank Donald and Mayme (Lont) L.; m. Shirley Morrison, Nov. 27, 1965; children: Michael, Peter. BS, Cornell U., 1962, MBA, 1963; JD, U. Md., 1968. Bar: Pa. 1969, U.S. Dist. Ct. (ea. dist.) Pa., U.S. Ct. Appeals (3d cir.). Ptnr. Morgan, Lewis & Bockius, Phila., 1968—. With USAFR, 1963-68. Republican. Presbyterian. Home: 11 Rose Valley Rd Media PA 19063-4217 Office: Morgan Lewis & Bockius 2000 One Logan Sq Philadelphia PA 19103

LOVELESS, KATHY LYNNE, client services executive; b. Corsicana, Tex., Mar. 7, 1961; d. Vernon Ray and Barbara Alice (Brown) L. BA, Baylor U., 1983. Adminstrv. asst. InterFirst Bank, Dallas, 1983-85; adminstrv. asst. Chaparral Steel Co., Midlothian, Tex., 1985-89, audio/visual coord., 1989-93; freelance computer instr. Duncanville, Tex., 1993-94; tng. specialist U. Tex. Southwestern Med. Ctr., Dallas, 1994-95, supr. client svcs. ctr., 1995—. Pres., v.p. Midlothian Cmty. Theatre, 1990-93, mem., 1987-94; v.p. Lovers Ln. United Meth. Ch. Choir, Dallas, 1994, 95, Adminstrv. Bd., 1995-96; chmn. worship and mem. care com. Elmwood United Meth. Ch., 1990, 91; bd. dirs. Trinity River Mission, Dallas, 1994, 95, 96. Mem. NAFE, AAUW, USA Film Festival, Am. Film Inst. Avocations: sports, films, music, books, theatre. Home: 8903 San Benito Way Dallas TX 75218

LOVELESS, PATTY (PATTY RAMEY), country music singer; b. Pikeville, Ky., Jan. 4, 1957; m. Terry Lovelace (div.); m. Emory Gordy, Jr., Feb. 1989. Recording artist MCA, 1985-93, Sony Music, 1993—. Albums: Patty Loveless, 1987, If My Heart Had Windows, 1988, Honky Tonk Angel, 1988 (gold), On Down the Line, 1990, Up Against My Heart, 1991, Only What I Feel, 1993, Greatest Hits, 1993, When Fallen Angels Fly, 1994, The Trouble With the Truth; # 1 hit singles Timber, I'm Falling in Love, Chains. Named Favorite New Country Artist by Am. Music Awards, 1989; recipient TNN Music City News Country Award, Female Artist, 1990, Country Music Awards' Album of the Yr.; inductee Grand Ole Opry, 1988. Office: Sony Music/Epic Records 550 Madison Ave New York NY 10022*

LOVELESS, PEGGY ANN, social work administrator; b. Decatur, Ill., June 9, 1952; d. William Walter and Rose Marie (Sheppard) L. Student, Ill. State U., 1970-72; BA, U. Ill., 1974, MSW, 1976. Cert. lic. clin. social worker; cert. in health care ethics; diplomate Am. Bd. Examiners in Clin. Social Work. Social worker Met.-Police Social Svcs., Urbana, Ill., 1976-80; clin. supr. Ctr. Children's Svcs., Danville, Ill., 1980-84; med. social worker Sarah Bush Lincoln Health Ctr., Mattoon, Ill., 1984-86, Portland (Oreg.) Adventist Med. Ctr., 1986-88; dept. supr., social worker Oreg. Health Scis. U., Portland, 1988-92, interim dir. social work, 1992-93, asst. dir. social work Ctr. Ethics, 1993-96, mem. ethics consulting svc., 1991-96; behavioral health case mgr. PacifiCare Behavioral Health, 1996—. Vol. Goose Hollow Family Homeless Shelter, Portland, 1993-94, vol. supr., 1994-95, bd. dirs., 1996-97. Mem. Soc. Social Work Adminstrs. Health Care (com. nominations 1995-96, chair, pres. meeting planning com. 1994, com. mem. devel. 1997), Oreg. Soc. Social Work Adminstrs. Health Care (pres. elect 1993, pres. 1994, chair/conf. com. 1995). Avocations: reading, walking, skiing, travel. Office: PacifiCare Behavioral Health 5 Centerpointe Dr Ste 270 Lake Oswego OR 97035-8652

LOVELL, CHARLES C., federal judge; b. 1929; m. Ariliah Carter. BS, U. Mont., 1952, JD, 1959. Assoc. Church, Harris, Johnson & Williams, Great Falls, Mont., 1959-85; judge U.S. Dist. Ct. Mont., Helena, 1985—; chief counsel Mont. Atty Gen.'s Office, Helena, 1969-72. Served to capt. USAF, 1952-54. Mem. ABA, Am. Judicature Soc., Assn. Trial Lawyers Am. Office: US Dist Ct PO Drawer 10112 301 S Park Ave Rm 504 Helena MT 59626

LOVELL, EDWARD GEORGE, mechanical engineering educator; b. Windsor, Ont., Can., May 25, 1939; s. George Andrew and Julia Anne (Kopacz) L.; children: Elise, Ethan. B.S., Wayne State U., 1960, M.S., 1961; Ph.D., U. Mich., 1967. Registered profl. engr., Wis. Project engr. Bur. Naval Weapons, Washington, 1959, Boeing Co., Seattle, 1962; test engr. Ford Motor Co., Troy, Mich., 1960; instr. U. Mich., Ann Arbor, 1963-67; design engr. United Tech., Hartford, Conn., 1970; prof. engring. U. Wis., Madison, 1968—, chmn. dept. engring. mechanics and astronautics, 1992-95; cons. structural engring. to govt. labs., indsl. orgns., maj. textbook pubs., 1968—. Contbr. numerous articles to profl. jours. Postdoctoral research fellow Nat. Acad. Sci., 1967; NATO Sci. fellow, 1973; NSF fellow, 1961. Mem. Wis. Fusion Tech. Inst., Wis. Ctr. for Applied Microelectronics, Sigma Xi, Tau Beta Pi, Phi Kappa Phi. Office: U Wis Dept Mech Engring Dept Mech Engring 1513 University Ave Madison WI 53706-1539

LOVELL, FRANCIS JOSEPH, investment company executive; b. Boston, Mar. 21, 1949; s. Frank J. and Patricia Anna (Donnellan) L. BBA, Nichols Coll., 1971. With Brown Bros. Harriman & Co., Boston, 1971—, deputy mgr., 1990—. alumni dir. St. Columbkille Sch., Brighton, Mass. Mem. New Eng. Hist. Gen. Soc., Union Club of Boston. Republican. Home: 25 Pomfret St West Roxbury MA 02132-1809 also (summer): 48 Hidden Village Rd West Falmouth MA 02574 Office: 40 Water St Boston MA 02109-3604

LOVELL, GLENN MICHAEL, film critic; b. Bishop Stortford, Eng., Sept. 21, 1948; came to U.S., 1952; s. Lester Eugene and Audrey Mary (Caton) L.; divorced; 1 child, Andrew Hurst Lovell. BA cum laude, Lycoming Coll., 1970; MA, Pa. State U., 1972. TV-film-book critic Hollywood Reporter, L.A., 1972; entertainment editor Richmond (Va.) Mercury, 1973, Miami Beach Sun-Reporter, 1974, Fort Lauderdale (Fla.) Sun-Sentinel, 1976-80; theater critic San Jose (Calif.) Mercury News, 1980-82, film critic, 1982-96; Nat. Arts Journalism fellow U. So. Calif., 1995-96; film critic Sta. KARA-FM, San Jose, 1985-86, Sta. KOME-FM, San Jose, 1985-86; instr. film San Jose State U., 1984-87, 97, San Francisco State U., 1997, Cogswell Coll., Sunnyvale, Calif., 1997; instr. De Anza Coll., Cupertino, Calif., 1989, 94; film commentary Sta. KGO, San Francisco, 1985—; judge Palo Alto (Calif.) Film Festival, 1983; panel moderator Screenwriter's Workshop, San Francisco, 1991, Cinequest panel, San Jose, 1994-97; profl.-in-residence journalism dept. U. Iowa, 1996. Revs. pub. in numerous newspapers, including Atlanta Constn., Boston Globe, Chgo. Tribune, Cin. Enquirer, Des Moines Register, Detroit Free Press, L.A. Daily News, Miami Herald, N.Y. Daily News, Phila. Inquirer, San Francisco Chronicle, Washington Post, others; also freelance work in L.A. Times, Columbia Journalism Rev., Miami Herald, Toronto Star, Aquarian Weekly, Calif. Theatre Ann., Cinefantistique Mag., Hollywood Reporter, L.A. Free Press.; co-writer (short film) Night Ride, Miami Film Festival, 1977. Union rep. Newspaper Guild, Bay Area, San Jose, 1991, 94. Nominee, Nat. Soc. Film Critics, 1995. Democrat. Avocations: running, scuba, skiing. Home: 975 Terra Bella Ave San Jose CA 95125-2656 Office: San Jose Mercury News 750 Ridder Park Dr San Jose CA 95131-2432

LOVELL, MALCOLM READ, JR., public policy institute executive, educator, former government official, former trade association executive; b. Greenwich, Conn., Jan. 1, 1921; s. Malcolm Read and Emily (Monihan) L.; m. Celia Coghlan, 1978; children by previous marriage: Lucie, Sara. Annette, Caroline. Grad., Lawrenceville Sch., 1939; student, Brown U., 1939-42; I.A., Harvard U., 1943; M.B.A., Harvard, 1946. With Ford Motor Co., Dearborn, Mich., 1946-58; mgr. employee services Am. Motors Corp., Detroit, 1958-61; chmn. State Labor Mediation Bd., Detroit, 1963; dir. Mich. Office Econ. Opportunity, 1964, Mich. Employment Security Commn., Detroit, 1965-69; exec. asso. Manpower, Urban Coalition, 1969; dep. asst. sec. of labor and manpower adminstr., 1969-70, asst. sec. of labor for manpower, 1970-73; pres. Rubber Mfrs. Assn., 1973-81; asst. dir. Office Policy Coordination and Econ. Affairs, Office Pres.-Elect, 1980; undersec. Dept. Labor, Washington, 1981-83; vis. scholar Brookings Instn., Washington, 1983-85; disting. vis. prof. govt. and dir. Labor Mgmt. Inst. George Washington U., 1985-92; pres. Nat. Planning Assn., 1992—; sr. fellow Hudson Inst., 1985-88; mem. Nat. Adv. Coun. on Vocat. Edn., 1975-79, Nat. Commn. for Manpower Policy, 1977-79; chmn. sec. labor Task Force on Econ. Adjustment and Worker Dislocation, 1985-86. Vice pres. Birmingham (Mich.) Sch. Bd., 1956-60; bd. dirs. Nat. Alliance Bus., 1984—; bd. dirs. Travelers Aid of Washington, 1983—, pres., 1985-86; Served to lt. USNR, 1943-46. Mem. City Tavern Club (Washington), Clean Plate (Washington), Cosmos Club (Washington), Alpha Delta Phi. Quaker. Office: Nat Planning Assn 1424 16th St NW Washington DC 20036-2211

LOVELL, ROBERT MARLOW, JR., retired investment company executive; b. Orange, N.J., June 24, 1930; s. Robert Marlow and Agnes Whipple (Keen) L.; m. Barbara Jane Cronin, Jan. 16, 1960; children—Kimberley, Kerry, Anthony, Matthew. B.A. with honors in History, Princeton U., N.J., 1952. Trainee Halsey, Stuart & Co., N.Y.C., 1955-57; assoc. Lehman Bros., N.Y.C., 1957-64, assoc. dir., investment adv. service, 1965-67; v.p. New Court Securities Corp., N.Y.C., 1968-70; fin. v.p. Crum & Forster, Morristown, N.J., 1970-73, sr. v.p. fin., 1973-85; pres. First Quadrant Corp., 1985-88, chmn. bd., 1988-96, ret., 1996; trustee Coll. Retirement Equities Fund. Contbr. articles to profl. jours. Former chmn. fin. com. Morristown Meml. Hosp. Served to lt. (j.g.) USNR, 1952-55. Republican. Club: Princeton Quadrangle. Office: First Quadrant Corp PO Box 939 100 Park Ave Florham Park NJ 07932-1004

LOVELL, ROBERT R(OLAND), engineering executive; b. Gladwin, Mich., Feb. 22, 1937. BS, U. Mich., MS. Various tech. and tech. mgmt. positions Lewis Rsch. Ctr. NASA, Cleve., 1962-80; dir. satellite comm., advanced R & D programs NASA, 1980-87; corp. v.p., pres., gen. mgr. Orbital Sci. Corp., Fairfax, Va., 1987-95; Jerome C. Hunsaker prof. Aeronatics and Astronautics MIT, 1995—. Author over 50 tech. publs. Recipient Nat. Medal Tech. U.S. Dept. Commerce Tech. Adminstrn., 1991, Yuri Gagarin medal USSR Acad. Cosmonautics, NASA Outstanding Leadership medal; named to Space Tech. Hall of Fame, U.S. Space Found., 1997. mem. Am. Inst. Aeronautics and Astronautics. Achievements include development of unmanned spacecraft technology, communications systems and research in rocket propulsion. Home: Orbital Science Corp Divsn Space Systems 162 Wilton Creek Rd Hartfield VA 23071

LOVELL, THEODORE, electrical engineer, consultant; b. Paterson, N.J., May 10, 1928; s. George Whiting and Ethel Carol (Berner) L.; m. Wilma Syperda, May 8, 1948 (div. Oct. 1961); m. Joyce Smelik, July 15, 1962; children: Laurie, Dorothy Jane, Valerie, Cynthia, Karen, Barbara. BEE, Newark Coll. Engring., 1948; postgrad., Canadian Inst. Tech., 1950. Exec. dir. Lovell Electric Co., Franklin Lakes, N.J., 1955-82; ptnr., exec. dir. Lovell Design Services, Swedesboro, N.J., 1982—. Author engring. computer software, 1982. Bd. dirs., treas. Contact "Help" of Salem County, 1991-93; pres. Bloomingdale Bd. Edn., N.J., 1970-82; mem. Mcpl. Planning Bd., Bloomingdale, 1980-82, Swedesboro/Woolwich Bd. Edn., 1987-94, v.p., 1990-92, pres. 1993-94; mayoral candidate Borough of Bloomingdale, 1982; v.p. Woolwich Twp. Rep. Club, 1996—. Recipient Outstanding Service award Lake Iosco Co., Bloomingdale, 1985, 20 Yr. Svc. award N.J. Sch. Bd. Assn., 1994. Mem. Am. Soc. Engring. Technicians, Radio Club Am., Dickinson Theater Organ Soc. Presbyterian. Avocations: Lincoln history, theatre organ music. Home: 502 Liberty Ct Woolwich Township NJ 08085-9416 Office: Lovell Design Svcs PO Box 366 Swedesboro NJ 08085-0366 *It has become apparent to me, slowly perhaps that as I progress through life, the things that bring lasting joy and satisfaction are not personal achievements, but those things that help others.*

LOVELL, WALTER BENJAMIN, secondary education educator; b. Cottonwood, Ariz., Jan. 7, 1947; s. Walter William Lovell and Mary Katherine (MacDonald) Bruce; m. Patsy Nichols, July 16, 1965 (div. Nov. 1986); children: Katherine Vi, Walter Kenneth, Karen Jennifer, Kristin Diane; m. Karen Lynn Bird, Mar. 3, 1990. AA, Ea. Ariz. Coll., 1966; B of Music Edn., No. Ariz. U., 1969, MusM, 1975. Dir. of bands Kingman (Ariz.) High Sch., 1968-70; asst. dir. bands Phoenix Union High Sch., 1970-71; dir. bands Carl Hayden High Sch., Phoenix, 1971-73, Mohave High Sch., Bullhead City, Ariz., 1973-78, Elko (Nev.) High Sch., 1978—; condr. numerous winning, competitive performances with Elko H.S. Band, including Grand Champions Holiday Bowl Parade, Field and Jazz competition, 1994, pregame performance and field show, Nat. Freedom Bowl, Anaheim, Calif., 1988, 90, Disneyland Parade, Anaheim, 1990, pre-game and half-time performances Weber State U., Ogden, Utah, 1990, 91, 92, 93, 94, 95, U. Utah, 1995, Concert Band Festival, Boise (Idaho) State U., 1990, U. Nev.-Las Vegas Band Competition, 1988, Fiesta Bowl Parade, Phoenix, 1985, Tournament of Roses Parade, Pasadena, 1983, 95, Presdl. Inaugural Parade, Washington, 1981. Composer: (concert band compositions) Suite For Band, 1975, Tranquility, 1988, (jazz band compositions) Maybe Tuesday, 1974, Sunday Afternoon, 1987. Recipient Gubernatorial Proclamation for Elko H.S. Band, 1981, 83, 86, 88, 90, 92, 94, 96, Proclaimed The Pride of Nev., 1995, 96; Gubernatorial Proclamation No. Nev. Youth Band, 1982, Nat. Sch. Band Schievement awards, 1981, 82; recipient Disting. Svc. award U. Nev.-Reno Bands, 1986, Citation of Excellence Nat. Band Assn., Nev. State Bd. Edn., 1983, Disting. Bandmaster of Am. award, 1981, Nev. State Marching Band Champion award, 1983, 84, 85, 86, 92, 93, 94, Holiday Bowl Jazz Festival Grand Champion award, 1992; condr. No. Nev. Youth Band Tour of Great Britain, 1982; assoc. dir. All-Ariz. Bi-Centennial Band, 1976; runner-up Ariz. State Young Educator of Yr., 1970. Mem. Nat. Band Assn. (citation of Excellence 1987), Am. Sch. Band Dirs. Assn., Nev. Music Educators Assn., Music Educators Nat. Conf., Ariz. Band and Orchestra Dir.'s Assn., Nat. Assn. Jazz Educators, Ariz. Music Educators Assn. Office: Elko High Sch 987 College Ave Elko NV 89801-3419

LOVELL, WALTER CARL, engineer, inventor; b. Springfield, Vt., May 7, 1934; s. John Vincent and Sophia Victoria (Klementowicz) L.; m. Patricia Ann Lawrence, May 6, 1951; children: Donna, Linda, Carol, Patricia, Diane, Walter Jr. B of Engring., Hillyer Coll., Hartford, Conn., 1959. Project engr. Hartford Machine Screw Co., Windsor, Conn., 1954-59; design engr. DeBell and Richardson Labs., Enfield, Conn., 1960-62; cons. engr. Longmeadow, Mass., 1962—; freelance inventor Wilbraham, Mass., 1965—. Numerous patents include Egg-Stir mixer, crown closure sealing gasket, circular unleakable bottle cap, sonic wave ram jet engine, solid state heating tapes, card key lock; composer over 50 country-and-Western songs. Achievements include patents for sonic wave ram jet engine, solid state heat and resistor tape, card key lock, security lock system, heat producing paints and ceramics; innovations include discovery of monothermal electric effect and micro-inductive film that replaces ballast in fluorescent lights.

LOVELLETTE, CLYDE, retired basketball player; b. Petersburg, Ind., Sept. 7, 1929. Grad., Helms Coll. Basketball player Mpls. Lakers, Cin. Royals, St. Louis Hawks, Boston Celtics. Named to Basketball Hall of Fame, 1988, Helms Coll. Player of Yr.; selected NCAA All-Am. Team, NBA All-Star Team; mem. NBA Championship Team, 1954, 63, 64, U.S. Olympic Gold Medal Team, 1952. Office: c/o Basketball Hall Fame PO Box 179 Springfield MA 01101-0179

LOVELY, THOMAS DIXON, banker; b. N.Y.C., Apr. 2, 1930; s. Thomas John and Margaret Mary (Browne) L.; AB, Adelphi U., 1954, MA, 1956, MBA, 1958; m. Erna Susan Fritz, June 16, 1956; children: Thomas John Hall, Richard Robert. Treas., Pepsi Cola Bottling Co., Garden City, N.Y., 1957-60; assoc. prof. mgmt. and communications CUNY, 1958-77; dist. adminstr. Lido Beach (N.Y.) Pub. Schs., 1971-80; chmn. bd., pres. Fidelity Fed. Savs. and Loan Assn., Floral Park, N.Y., 1980-82, chmn. bd., pres. Fidelity N.Y., 1982—; v.p., dir. N.Y. Enterprise Co. Trustee, SUNY, 1992, chmn. bd. SUNY Old Westbury Coll. Found., 1989—, vice chmn. bd. trustees Adelphi U., 1967-91, chmn. bd. govs. Univ. Sch. Banking and Money Mgmt., 1975—; trustee Nassau County (N.Y.) Med. Center, 1982—; exec. v.p., treas. Nassau County coun. Boy Scouts Am., 1986—, pres., 1989-92; regional chmn. campaign U.S. Treasury Savs. Bonds Sales, Long Island, 1987—; pres., trustee Meadowbrook Med. Edn. Found., Inc., 1987—. Mem. SAR, L.I. Insured Savs. Group (v.p.). Clubs: Pinehurst Country (N.C.), Cherry Valley Country (Garden City). Home: 52 Locust St Garden City NY 11530-6329 Office: Fidelity NY Fed Savs Bank 1000 Franklin Ave Garden City NY 11530-2910

LOVEN, ANDREW WITHERSPOON, environmental engineering company executive; b. Crossnore, N.C., Jan. 31, 1935; s. Andrew Witherspoon Loven and Annie Laura (Crowell) Stewart; m. Elizabeth Joann DeGroot, June 20, 1959 (dec.); children: Laura Elizabeth, James Edward. BS, Maryville Coll., 1957; PhD, U. N.C., 1962. Registered profl. engr., Va., Ga., Md., N.C., S.C., D.C., Ohio, Fla., Mich. Rsch. assoc. U. N.C., Chapel Hill, 1962-63; sr. rsch. chemist Westvaco Corp., Charleston, S.C., 1963-66; mgr. carbon devel. Westvaco Corp., Charleston, 1966-71, mgr. Westvaco Wastewater Cons. Service, 1967-71; mgr. engring. concepts Engring.-Sci. Inc., McLean, Va., 1971-74; v.p., regional mgr. Engring.-Sci. Inc., Atlanta, 1974-80, group v.p., 1980-86; pres., chief exec. officer Engring. Sci. Inc., Pasadena, Calif., 1986-95, also chmn. bd. dirs.; exec. v.p. Parsons Engring. Sci. Inc., Pasadena, Calif., 1995; pres., CEO Millennium Sci. & Engring., Inc., McLean, Va., 1995—. Contbr. articles to profl. jours. NSF grantee, 1958-59; recipient Maryville Coll. Alumni Citation award, 1992. Mem. AIChE, NSPE, Am. Acad. Environ. Engrs. (diplomate, membership com. 1985—), Water Pollution Control Fedn., Am. Water Works Assn., Am. Pub. Works Assn., Constrn. Industry Pres. Forum, Country Club Roswell, Sigma Xi, Alpha Gamma Sigma. Avocations: golf, hiking. Home: 7720 Tremayne Pl #703 McLean VA 22102 Office: Millennium Sci & Engring Inc 1364 Beverly Rd Ste 302 Mc Lean VA 22101-3627

LOVENTHAL, MILTON, writer, playwright, lyricist; b. Atlantic City; s. Harry and Clara (Feldman) L.; m. Jennifer McDowell, July 2, 1973. BA, U. Calif., Berkeley, 1950, MLS, 1958; MA in Sociology, San Jose State U., 1969. Researcher Hoover Instn., Stanford, Calif., 1952-53, spl. asst. to Slavic Curator, 1955-57; librarian San Diego Pub. Library, 1957-59; librarian, bibliographer San Jose (Calif.) State U., 1959-92; tchr. writing workshops, poetry readings, 1969-73; co-producer lit. and culture radio show Sta. KALX, Berkeley, 1971-72; editor, pub. Merlin Press, San Jose, 1973—. Author: Books on the USSR, 1951-57, 57, Black Politics, 1971 (featured at Smithsonian Inst. Special Event, 1992), A Bibliography of Material Relating to the Chicano, 1971, Autobiographies of Women, 1946-70, 72, Blacks in America, 1972, The Survivors, 1972, Contemporary Women Poets an Anthology, 1977, Ronnie Goose Rhymes for Grown-Ups, 1984; co-author: (Off-Off-Broadway plays) The Estrogen Party to End War, 1986, Mack the Knife, Your Friendly Dentist, 1986, Betsy & Phyllis, 1986, The Oatmeal Party Comes to Order, 1986, (plays) Betsy Meets the Wacky Iraqi, 1991, Bella and Phyllis, 1994; co-writer (mus. comedy) Russia's Secret Plot to Take Back Alaska, 1988. Recipient Bill Casey Award in Letters, 1980; grantee San Jose State U., 1962-63, 84. Mem. Assn. Calif. State Profs., Calif. Alumni Assn., Calif. Theatre Coun. Office: PO Box 5602 San Jose CA 95150-5602

LOVERDE, PAUL S., bishop; b. Framingham, Mass., Sept. 3, 1940. Grad., St. Thomas Sem., Bloomfield, Conn., 1960; B.A. summa cum laude, St. Bernard Sem., Rochester, N.Y.; Licentiate in Sacred Theology, Gregorian U., Rome, Italy, 1966; Licentiate in Canon Law, Cath. U., Washington, D.C., 1982. Ordained priest, Dec. 18, 1965. Asst. pastor St. Sebastian Church, Middletown, CT, 1966-69; Catholic chaplain Wesleyan U., Middletown, CT, 1966-68; chaplain, Religion instructor & chmn. of Religious Studies Dept. St. Bernard Girls' Sch., New London, CT, 1969-72; Religion instructor & chmn. Religious Studies Dept. St. Bernard HS, Montville, CT, 1972-73; assoc. defender of the Bond Diocesan Tribunal of Norwich, 1970-81; Catholic chaplain Conn. Coll., New London, CT, 1970-79; dir. of Campus Ministry Diocese of Norwich, 1973-79; campus min. Eastern Conn. State Coll., Willimantic, CT, 1973-76; mem. bd. of dirs. Conn. Catholic Conf., 1973-78; vicar for priests Wyndham Co., 1974-75; chmn. bd. of vicars for priests, Diocese of Norwich, 1975-79; vice-officialis Diocesan Tribunal, 1981-88; chmn. bd. of conciliation/arbitration for priests, 1982-85; exec. coord. bd. of conciliation & arbitration, 1983-89; mem. Presbyteral Council, 1983-90, chmn., 1985-89; priests' rep. Diocesan Pastoral Council, 1984-88, vice-chmn., 1984-87; Bishop's del. for clergy, 1985-88; mem. Coll. of Consulters, 1985-90; reg. rep. U.S. Catholic Bishop's Nat. Adv. Council, 1986-90; appointed titular bishop of Ottabia, 1988; aux. bishop Diocese of Hartford, 1988-94; bishop Diocese of Ogdensburg, 1994—; mem. Continuing Edn. for the Clergy Comm. for Diocese of Norwich, 1967-71; mem. Clergy Assn. of Middletown, 1966-69; bd. of dirs., Conn. Project Equality, 1968-73; vocation promoter Middletown area, 1968-69; Diocese of Norwich rep., Task Force on Race & Ministry with Minorities, 1970; mem. Senate of Priests of Norwich Diocese, 1971-75 (v.p. 1971-72, pres. 1972-75); v.p. Church Vocations Task Group, 1973-79; temp. admin., Holy Trinity Church, Pomfret, CT, 1981; temp. admin. St. Catherine of Siena Church, Preston, CT, 1982, 85-86. contributor of articles to The Priest, Pastoral Life, and Today's Parish. 1st Hon. Brother, Altruism House, New London, CT, 1970. Address: Bishops Residence 624 Washington St Ogdensburg NY 13669*

LOVETT, CLARA MARIA, university administrator, historian; b. Trieste, Italy, Aug. 4, 1939; came to U.S., 1962; m. Benjamin F. Brown. BA equivalent, U. Trieste, 1962; MA, U. Tex.-Austin, 1967, PhD, 1970. Prof. history Baruch Coll., CUNY, N.Y.C., 1971-82, asst. provost, 1980-82; chief European div. Library of Congress, Washington, 1982-84; dean Coll. Arts and Scis., George Washington U., Washington, 1984-88; provost, v.p. academic affairs, George Mason U., Fairfax, Va., 1988-93; on leave from George Mason U.; dir. Forum on Faculty Roles and Rewards Am. Assn. for Higher Edn., 1993-94; pres. No. Ariz. U., Flagstaff, 1994—; vis. lectr. Fgn. Service Inst., Washington, 1979-85; bd. dirs. Assn. Am. Colls. and Univs., 1990-93, Blue Cross Blue Shield Ariz., 1995—; trustee Western Govs. U., 1996—. Author: The Democratic Movement in Italy 1830-1876, 1982 (H.R. Marraro Prize, Soc. Italian Hist. Studies); Giuseppe Ferrari and the Italian Revolution, 1979 (Phi Alpha Theta book award); Carlo Cattaneo and the Politics of Risorgimento, 1972 (Soc. for Italian Hist. Studies Dissertation award), (bibliography) Contemporary Italy, 1985; co-editor: Women, War, and Revolution, 1980, (essays) State of Western European Studies, 1984; contbr. sects. to publs. U.S., Italy. Organizer Dem. clubs Bklyn., 1972-76; exec. com. Palisades Citizens Assn., Washington, 1985-87; vestry mem. St. David's Episc. Ch., Washington, 1986-89. Fellow Guggenheim Found., 1978-79, Woodrow Wilson Internat. Ctr. for Scholars, 1979 (adv. bd. West European program), Am. Council Learned Socs., 1976, Bunting Inst. of Radcliffe Coll., 1975-76, others. Named Educator of Yr., Va. Fedn. of Bus. and Profl. Women, 1992. Mem. Am. Hist. Assn. (officer 1984-87), Am. Assn. Higher Edn. (cons. 1979—), Council for European Studies, Soc. for Italian Hist. Studies, Conf. Group on Italian Politics, Ariz. C. of C. (bd. dirs. 1996—), others. Avocations: choral singing, swimming. Office: No Ariz U Office of Pres PO Box 4092 Flagstaff AZ 86011

LOVETT, JOHN ROBERT, retired chemical company executive; b. Norristown, Pa., June 17, 1931; s. James and Margaret (Creighton) L.; m. Sandra Miller, May 26, 1956; children: Judy, Jackie, John Robert Jr. BS, Ursinus Coll., 1953; MS, U. Del., 1955, PhD, 1957. Rsch. chemist Exxon Rsch., Linden, N.J., 1957-64; lab. dir. Exxon Rsch./Exxon Chem., Linden, 1964-70; v.p. Paramins Exxon Chem., Houston, 1970-74; tech. mgr. Exxon Chem., Linden, 1974-76; v.p. rsch. Air Products and Chems., Inc., Allentown, Pa., 1976-81; pres. Europe Air Products and Chems., Inc., Hersham, Eng., 1981-88; group v.p. chems. Air Products and Chems., Inc., Allentown, 1988-92, exec. v.p. gases & equipment, 1992-93, exec. v.p. strategic planning and tech., 1993-96. Mem. AICE, Chem. Mfrs. Assn. (bd. dirs. 1990-95), Am. Chem. Soc., Soc. Chem. Industry.

LOVETT, MILLER CURRIER, management educator, clergyman; b. Lynn, Mass., Mar. 18, 1923; s. Charles William and Phoebe Frances (Miller) L.; m. Dorothy Johnsen, Feb. 14, 1946 (div.); children: Anne E., Celeste M., Peter W., Rebecca J.; m. Virginia Lavelli, May 26, 1979. BSBA, Boston U., 1944, STB, 1946, PhD, 1964; postgrad., MIT, 1970-72. Pastor Wesley United Meth. Ch., Medford, Mass., 1946-52; sr. pastor United Meth. Ch., Ellensburg, Wash., 1952-62, Congl. Ch., Laconia, N.H., 1965-70; assoc. prof. bus. adminstrn. Belknap Coll., Center Harbor, N.H., 1970-73; prof. bus. adminstrn. Bunker Hill Community Coll., Charlestown, Mass., 1973-77; assoc. prof. mgmt. Boston State Coll., 1977-82, U. Mass., Boston, 1982—; founder and exec. dir. Social Ventures Trust, Lexington, Mass., 1985—; mem. cmty. econ. devel. projects, Peru, USA, 1985—, Boston, 1990—, N.H., 1995—. Contbr. articles to profl. jours. Lt. col. CAP USAF, 1955—. Recipient Disting. Svc. award Ellensburg Jr. C. of C., 1956. Mem. Mass. Tchrs. Assn., Assn. Enterprise Opportunity, Masons. Avocations: stamp and coin collecting. Home: PO Box 1669 25 Spindle Point Rd Meredith NH 03253-1669 Office: U Mass Coll Pub & Community Svc Boston MA 02125-3393

LOVETT, RADFORD DOW, real estate and investment company executive; b. Jacksonville, Fla., Sept. 6, 1933; s. William Radford and Agnes (Dow) L.; AB, Harvard U., 1955; m. Katharine Rutledge Howe, June 25, 1955 (dec. Jan. 1991); children: Katharine, William Radford, Philip, Lauren; m. Susan Wylie Rogers, June 15, 1995; children: Nick, Peter, Teddy Rogers. With Merrill Lynch, Pierce, Fenner & Smith Inc., N.Y.C., 1958-78; mng. dir. Capital Markets Group, 1975-78; pres. Piggly Wiggly Corp., Jacksonville, 1978-82; chmn. bd. Commodores Point Terminal Corp., Jacksonville, 1978—; chmn. Southcoast Capital Mgmt. Corp., Jacksonville, 1995—; dir. First Union Corp., Fla. Rock Industries Inc., FRP Properties, Inc., Am. Heritage Life Investment Corp., Winn-Dixie Stores, Inc. Trustee, Drew U., 1976-79, St. Vincent's Found., Jacksonville Zool. Soc. Lt., F.A., U.S. Army, 1955-57. Mem. Coastal Conservation Assn. Fla. Episcopalian. Office: 1600 Independent Sq Jacksonville FL 32202-5009

LOVETT, WENDELL HARPER, architect; b. Seattle, Apr. 2, 1922; s. Wallace Herman and Pearl (Harper) L.; m. Eileen Whitson, Sept. 3, 1947; children: Corrie, Clare. Student, Pasadena Jr. Coll., 1943-44; B.Arch., U. Wash., 1947; M.Arch., Mass. Inst. Tech., 1948. Architect, designer Naramore, Bain, Brady & Johanson, Seattle, 1948; architect, assoc. Bassetti & Morse, Seattle, 1948-51; pvt. practice architect Seattle, 1951—; instr. architecture U. Wash., 1948-51, asst. prof., 1951-60, assoc. prof., 1960-65, prof., 1965-83, prof. emeritus, 1983—; lectr. Technische Hochschule, Stuttgart, 1959-60. Prin. works include nuclear reactor bldg. U. Wash., 1960, Villa Simonyi, Medina, Wash., 1989. Pres. Citizen's Planning Council, Seattle, 1968-71. Served with AUS, 1943-46. Recipient 2d prize Progressive Architecture U.S. Jr. C. of C., 1949; Internat. design award Decima Triennale di Milano, 1954; Arch. Record Homes awards, 1969, 72, 74; Interiors award, 1973; Sunset-AIA awards, 1959, 62, 69, 71; Fulbright grantee, 1959; AIA fellow, 1978. Mem. AIA (sec. Wash. chpt. 1953-54, bd. dirs. Found. Seattle chpt. 1991-92, Seattle chpt. medal 1993, pres. sr. coun. 1991-92), Plestcheeff Inst. (bd. dirs. 1992). Patentee in field. Home and Office: 420 34th Ave Seattle WA 98122-6408

LOVETT, WILLIAM ANTHONY, law and economics educator; b. Milw., Sept. 2, 1934. AB, Wabash Coll., 1956; JD, NYU, 1959; PhD in Econs., Mich. State U., 1969. Bar: N.Y. 1960. Atty. U.S. Dept. Justice, Washington, 1962; economist FTC, Washington, 1963-69; prof. Tulane U., New Orleans, 1969—, dir. internat. law, trade and fin. program, 1985—; Joseph Merrick Jones prof. law and econs., 1991—. Author: Inflation and Politics, 1982, Banking and Financial Institutions Law, 1984, 88, 92, 97, World Trade Rivalry, 1987, U.S. Shipping Policies and the World Market, 1996. Root-Tilden scholar, 1956-59. Mem. ABA, Am. Econs. Assn., Am. Soc. Internat. Law, Phi Beta Kappa. Office: Tulane Law Sch New Orleans LA 70118

LOVETT, WILLIAM LEE, physician; b. Natchez, Miss., June 12, 1941; s. Frank Lee and Lucille (Mullen) L.; m. Martha Lynn Gray, Aug. 15, 1964; children: Shelby Elizabeth Lovett Cuevas, Heather Lee, Michael Gray. BA, U. Miss., Oxford, 1963; MD, U. Miss., Jackson, 1967. Diplomate Am. Bd. Surgery, Am. Bd. Hand Surgery. Intern in surgery U. Va. Med. Ctr., Charlottesville, 1967-68, jr. asst. resident in surgery, 1968-69, sr. asst. resident in surgery, 1970-72, co-chief resident in surgery, 1972-73; fellow surg. rsch. dept. surgery U. Va., Charlottesville, 1969-70; physician S.W. Hand Surgeons Ltd., Phoenix, 1983—; vice chief of staff St. Joseph's Hosp., Phoenix, 1990-93, rep. orthopedic surgery com., 1990—, vice chair dept. orthopedics, 1991-92, chief of staff, 1996—; physician S.W. Hand Surgeons Ltd., Phoenix; mem. sports medicine adv. team Ariz. State U., 1991-95; presenter in field. Contbr. articles to profl. jours. Mem. Sch. Bd. Xavier High Sch., 1983-87, v.p., 1985-86, pres., 1986-87; chief Webelos den Roosevelt coun. Boy Scouts Am., Phoenix, 1992-93, asst. scoutmaster, 1993—. Comdr. USN, 1974-76. Fellow ACS (pres. Ariz. chpt. 1983-84); mem. AMA, Am. Soc. for Surgery of the Hand, Ariz. Med. Assn. (del. 1985), Phoenix Surg. Soc. (pres. 1985-86), Muller Surg. Soc. Avocations: horseback riding, fly fishing, bird hunting, canoeing. Home: 6049 N 5th Pl Phoenix AZ 85012 Office: SW Hand Surgeons Ltd 2610 N 3rd St Phoenix AZ 85004-1102

LOVIN, KEITH HAROLD, university administrator, philosophy educator; b. Clayton, N.Mex., Apr. 1, 1943; s. Buddie and Wanda (Smith) L.; m. Marsha Kay Gunn, June 11, 1966; children—Camille Jenay, Lauren Kay. B.A., Baylor U., 1965; postgrad., Yale U., 1965-66; Ph.D., Rice U., 1971. Prof. philosophy Southwest Tex. State U., San Marcos, 1970-77, chmn. dept. philosophy, 1977-78; dean liberal arts Southwest Tex. State U., 1978-81; provost, v.p. acad. affairs Millersville U., Pa., 1981-86; provost, v.p. acad. and student affairs U. So. Colo., Pueblo, 1986-92; pres. Maryville U. St. Louis, 1992—. Contbr. articles on philosophy of law, philosophy of religion to profl. publs.; mem. adv. bd. Southwest Studies in Philosophy, 1981-90. Bd. dirs. St. Louis Symphony Orch., Boys Hope, Jr. Achievement Mississippi Valley, Inc., United Way, St. Luke's Hosp., Nat. Coun. Alcohol and Drug Abuse Adv. Bd., St. Louis Intercollegiate Athletic Conf., Ind. Colls. and Univs. of Mo., Higher Edn. Coun. Mem. Chesterfield C. of C., Univ. Club (bd. dirs.), Media Club. Avocation: fly fishing. Home: 13664 Conway Rd Saint Louis MO 63141-7234 Office: Maryville U 13550 Conway Rd Saint Louis MO 63141-7232

LOVING, GEORGE GILMER, JR., retired air force officer; b. Roanoke, Va., Aug. 7, 1923; s. George Gilmer and Ora Page (Carr) L.; m. Mary Ambler Thomasson, Jan. 15, 1945; children—Cary Ambler, Betty Page Behler. Student, Lynchburg Coll., 1941; B.A., U. Ala., 1960; M.A. in Internat. Affairs, George Washington U., 1965; grad., Air War Coll., 1965. Commd. 2d lt. U.S. Army Air Force, 1943; advanced through grades to lt. gen. U.S. Air Force, 1975; fighter pilot, test pilot, operations officer, fighter squadron comdr., 1943-55; U.S. adviser (Nat. War Coll.), Republic of China, 1960-62; staff planner Hdqrs. U.S. Air Force, Washington, 1965-69; comdr. Air Command and Staff Coll., 1970-73; dir. plans Hdqrs. U.S. Air Force, Washington, 1973-75; Joint Chiefs Staff rep. for mut. and balanced force reductions Washington, 1975; comdr. 6th Allied Tactical Air Force Izmir, Turkey, 1975-77; comdr. U.S. forces Japan; comdr. 5th Air Force Yokota Air Base, Japan, 1977-79; ret., 1979; cons. RAND Corp., 1979-80; exec. dir. Marie Selby Bot. Gardens, Sarasota, Fla, 1981-88. Decorated D.S.M. with 2 oak leaf clusters, Silver Star medal, Legion of Merit, D.F.C. with oak leaf cluster, Meritorious Service medal, Air Force Commendation medal, Air medal with 25 oak leaf clusters.; N.Y.C. Council on Fgn. Relations fellow, 1969-70. Mem. Am. Fighter Aces Assn. Episcopalian. Club: Sarasota Yacht. Home: 508 Whitfield Ave Sarasota FL 34243-1603

LOVING, SUSAN B., lawyer, former state official; m. Dan Loving; children: Lindsay, Andrew, Kendall. BA with distinction, U. Okla., 1972, JD, 1979. Asst. atty. gen. Office of Atty. Gen., 1983-87, first asst. atty. gen., 1987-91; atty. gen. State of Okla., Oklahoma City, 1991-94; ptnr.; Master Ruth Bader Ginsburg Inn of Ct., 1995; bd. dirs. Bd. for Freedom of Info., Okla., Inc., Partnership for Drug Free Okla., 1993—; adv. bd. Law and You Found. Vice chmn. Pardon and Parole Bd., 1995; mem. Gov.'s Commn. on Tobacco and Youth, 1995-96; bd. dirs. Bd. for Freedom of Info., Okla. Inc., Boy Scouts Am., Legal Aid of West Okla., Okla. Com. for Prevention of Child Abuse; mem. med. steering com. Partnership for Drug Free Okla., Inst. for Child Advocacy, 1996—; mem. adv. bd. Law and You Found. Recipient Nat. Red Ribbon Leadership award Nat. Fedn. Parents, Headliner award, By-liner award Okla. City and Tulsa Women in Comm., First Friend of Freedom award, Freedom of Info., Okla., Dir. award Okla. Dist. Attys. Assn. Mem. Okla. Bar Assn. (past chmn. adminstrv. law sect., mem. ho. dels. 1996—, mem. adminstrn. of justice com., mem. profl. responsibility commn.), Phi Beta Kappa. Office: Lester Loving & Davies PLLC 1505 Renaissance Blvd Edmond OK 73013-3018

LOVING, WILLIAM RUSH, JR., public relations company executive, consultant; b. Norfolk, Va., Sept. 14, 1934; s. William Rush and Margaret Elizabeth (Billups) L.; m. Jane Parker, July 1963 (div. Dec. 1987); children: Katharine G., Margaret Borden, Leslie R.; m. Marsha Thaler, June 30, 1989 (div. June 1994). BA, U. Richmond, 1956. Lt. U.S. Army, 1957-59; reporter Richmond (Va.) Times-Dispatch, 1959-62, bus. editor, 1965-69; reporter The Virginian-Pilot, Norfolk, 1962-63; info. coord. Va. Mus. Fine Arts, Richmond, 1963-65; assoc. editor Fortune mag., N.Y.C., 1969-79; asst. dir. U.S. Office Mgmt. and Budget, Washington, 1979-80; pres. Loving Asssocs. Ltd., New Hope, Pa., 1980—, Loving Assocs. Ltd. Va., Alexandria, 1989—; dir. Railway Svc. Corp., Alfred I. duPont Found.; trustee Loving Assocs. Pension and Profit Sharing Funds, New Hope, Pa.; bd. dirs. Alfred I. duPont Found. Editor: How To Protect What's Yours, 1983; contbr. numerous articles to Fortune mag. Mem. Old Town Civic Assn., Alexandria, 1986—, The Torpedo Factory, Alexandria, 1986—. Mem. Nat. Press Club, R.R. Pub. Rels. Assn., Bucks County C. of C., Va. Hist. Soc. Avocations: photography, painting. Home: 1917 Windsor Rd Alexandria VA 22307 Office: 519 Oronoco St Alexandria VA 22314-2305

LOVINGER, SOPHIE LEHNER, child psychologist; b. N.Y.C., Jan. 15, 1932; d. Nathaniel Harris and Anne (Rosen) Lehner; m. Robert Jay Lovinger, June 18, 1957; children: David Fredrick, Mark Andrew. BA, Bklyn. Coll., 1954; MS, City Coll., N.Y.C., 1959; PhD, NYU, 1967. Sr. clin. psychologist Bklyn. State Hosp., 1960-61; grad. fellow NYU, N.Y.C., 1961-67; psychotherapy trainee Jamaica (N.Y.) Ctr., 1964-67; asst. prof. Hofstra U., Hempstead, N.Y., 1967-70; prof. Cen. Mich. U., Mt. Pleasant, 1970—; psychotherapist, psychoanalyst N.Y.C. and Mt. Pleasant, Mich., 1964—. Author: Learning Disabilities and Games, 1978, Language-Learning Disabilities, 1991; contbr. articles to profl. jours. Fellow Am. Orthopsychiat. Assn.; mem. Am. Psychol. Assn., Nat. Register Health Svc. Providers. Office: 405 S Main St Mount Pleasant MI 48858-2522

LOVINGER, WARREN CONRAD, emeritus university president; b. Big Sandy, Mont., July 29, 1915; s. Wilbur George and Ruth Katherine (Hokanson) L.; m. Dorothy Blackburn, Aug. 14, 1937; children—Patricia Mae, Jeanie, Warren Conrad. B.A., U. Mont., 1942, M.A., 1944; Ed.D., Columbia U., 1947. Tchr., prin. Pub. Schs. Mont., 1937-43; instr. history U. Mont., Missoula, 1943-44; pres. No. State Coll., Aberdeen, S.D., 1951-56; pres. Central Mo. State U., Warrensburg, 1956-79, pres. emeritus, 1979—; exec. sec. Am. Assn. Colls. for Tchr. Edn., 1947-51, nat. pres., 1963-64; nat. pres. Am. Assn. State Colls. and Univs., 1974-75; mem. del. to study effects of Marshall Plan on Western Europe, 1950; leader study of tchr. edn. in Fed. Republic of Germany, 1964; leader del. People's Republic of China, 1975; mem. comparative study tour of Republic of China, 1976. Author: General Education in Teachers Colleges, 1948; contbr. articles to profl. jours. Served as lt. USNR, 1944-46, ETO. Recipient Silver Beaver award Boys Scouts Am., 1970; Outstanding Civilian Service award Dept. Army, 1979. Mem. Mo. Tchrs. Assn., Am. Assn. Sch. Adminstrs., Mo. Assn. Sch. Adminstrs., Columbia U. Alumni Assn., Stover C. of C., Am. Legion, Gideons Internat., Phi Kappa Phi, Phi Delta Kappa, Kappa Delta Pi,. Baptist. Lodges: Masons, Shriners, Rotary, Lions. Avocations: travelling; writing; fishing; farming.

LOVINS, AMORY BLOCH, physicist, energy consultant; b. Washington, Nov. 13, 1947; s. Gerald Hershel and Miriam (Bloch) L.; m. L. Hunter Sheldon, Sept. 6, 1979. Student, Harvard U., 1964-65, 66-67, Magdalen Coll., Oxford, Eng., 1967-69; MA, Oxford U., Oxford, 1971; DSc (hon.), Bates Coll., 1979, Williams Coll., 1981, Kalamazoo Coll., 1983, U. Maine, 1985; LLD (hon.), Ball State U., 1983; D of Environ. Sci. (hon.), Unity Coll., 1992. Jr. research fellow Merton Coll., Oxford, England, 1969-71; Brit. rep., policy advisor Friends of the Earth, San Francisco, 1971-84; regent's lectr. U. Calif., Berkeley and Riverside, 1978, 81; v.p., dir. research Rocky Mountain Inst., Old Snowmass, Colo., 1982—; govt. and indsl. energy cons., 1971—; vis. prof. Dartmouth Coll., 1982; disting. vis. prof. U. Colo., 1982; prin. tech. cons. E Source, 1989—; prin. The Lovins Group, 1994—. Author: (also layout artist and co-photographer) Eryri, The Mountains of Longing, 1971, The Stockholm Conference: Only One Earth, 1972, Openpit Mining, 1973, World Energy Strategies: Facts, Issues, and Options, 1975, Soft Energy Paths: Toward a Durable Peace, 1977; co-author: (with J. Price) Non-Nuclear Futures: The Case: The Case for an Ethical Energy Strategy, 1975, (with L.H. Lovins) Energy/War: Breaking the Nuclear Link, 1980, Brittle Power: Energy Strategy for National Security, 1982, (with L.H. Lovins, F. Krause, and W. Bach) Least-Cost Energy: Solving the CO2 Problem, 1982, 89 (with P. O'heffernan, sr. author and L.H. Lovins) The First Nuclear World War, 1983, (with L.H. Lovins, sr. author and S. Zuckerman) Energy Unbound: A Fable for America's Future, 1986, (hardware reports) The State of the Art: Lighting, 1988, The State of the Art: Drivepower, 1989, The State of the Art: Appliances, 1990, The State of the Art: Water Heating, 1991, The State of the Art: Space Cooling and Air Handling, 1992, (with Ernst von Weizsaecker, sr. author and L.H. Lovins) Faktor Vier, 1995, Factor Four, 1997, (with M.M. Brylawski, D.R. Cramer, T.C. Moore) Hypercars: Materials, Manufacturing, and Policy Implications, 1995; co-photographer (book) At Home in the Wild: New England's White Mountains, 1978; author numerous poems; contbr. articles to profl. jours., reports to tech. jours.; patentee in field. Recipient Right Livelihood award Right Livelihood Found., 1983, Sprout award Internat. Studies Assn., 1977, Pub. Edn. award Nat. Energy Resources Orgn., 1978, Pub. Svc. award Nat. Assn. Environ. Edn., 1980; Mitchell prize Mitchell Energy Found., 1982, Delphi prize Onassis Found., 1989, Nissan prize Internat. Symposium Automotive Tech. and Automation, 1993, Award of Distinction, Rocky Mountain chpt. AIA, 1994; MacArthur fellow John D. and Catherine T. MacArthur Found., Chgo., 1993. Fellow AAAS, World Acad. Art and Sci., Lindisfarne Assn; mem. Fedn. Am. Scientists, Am. Phys. Soc., Soc. Automotive Engrng., Am. Solar Energy Soc., Internat. Assn. Energy Economists. Avocations: mountaineering, photography, music. Home and Office: 1739 Snowmass Creek Rd Snowmass CO 81654-9199 *Personal philosophy: Devotion to efficient and sustainable use of resources as a path to global security, with emphasis on how advanced technologies, market economics, and Jeffersonian politics can provide new solutions to old problems, or better still, avoid them altogether.*

LOVINS, L. HUNTER, public policy institute executive; b. Middlebury, Vt., Feb. 26, 1950; d. Paul Millard and Farley (Hunter) Sheldon; m. Amory Bloch Lovins, Sept. 6, 1979; 1 child, Nanuq. BA in Sociology, Pitzer Coll., 1972, BA in Polit. Sci., 1972; JD, Loyola U., L.A., 1975; LHD, U. Maine, 1982. Bar: Calif. 1975. Asst. dir. Calif. Conservation Project, L.A., 1973-79; exec. dir., co-founder Rocky Mountain Inst., Snowmass, Colo., 1982—; vis. prof. U. Colo., Boulder, 1982; Henry R. Luce vis. prof. Dartmouth Coll., Hanover, N.H., 1982; pres. Nighthawk Horse Co., 1993, Lovins Group, 1994. Co-author: Brittle Power, 1982, Energy Unbound, 1986, Least-Cost Energy Solving the CO2 Problem, 2d edit., 1989. Bd. dirs. Renew Am., Basalt and Rural Fire Protection Dist., E Source, Roaring Fork Polocrosse Assn.; vol. EMT and firefighter. Recipient Mitchell prize Woodlands Inst., 1982, Right Livelihood Found. award, 1983, Best of the New Generation award Esquire Mag., 1984. Mem. Calif. Bar Assn., Am. Quarter Horse Assn., Am. Polocrosse Assn. Avocations: rodeo, fire rescue, polocrosse. Office: Rocky Mountain Inst 1739 Snowmass Creek Rd Snowmass CO 81654-9115

LOVITT, GEORGE HAROLD, advertising executive; b. Bridgeport, Conn., June 7, 1922; s. Leon H. and Sarah (Lubetkin) L.; m. Nancy Posner, Nov. 27, 1947 (dec. Apr. 1995); children: Alison Lovitt Reinfeld, Charles, Robert, Patricia Barrier; m. Judith Bronston, Dec. 8, 1996. BA, NYU, 1944. Asst. to publicity dir. Prentice-Hall, Inc., N.Y.C., 1946-48; advt. and publicity dir. John Wiley & Sons, Inc., N.Y.C., 1948-52; successively account exec., v.p., pres., chmn. Franklin Spier, Inc., N.Y.C., 1952-82; pres. Keynote Mktg., Inc., N.Y.C., 1982-84; adj. prof. English dept. Hofstra U., 1986. Trustee Baldwin Pub. Library, 1971-76, 77-78. Served with inf. AUS, 1943-46. Decorated Purple Heart. Home: 44 Ginger Ct Princeton NJ 08540-9421

LOW, ANTHONY, English language educator; b. San Francisco, May 31, 1935; s. Emerson and Clio (Caroli) L.; m. Pauline Iselin Mills, Dec. 28, 1961; children: Louise, Christopher, Georgianna, Elizabeth, Peter, Catherine, Nicholas, Alexandra, Michael, Frances, Jessica, Edward, Charlotte. A.B., Harvard U., 1957, M.A., 1959, Ph.D., 1965. Mem. faculty Seattle U., 1965-68; mem. faculty NYU, N.Y.C., 1968—; prof. English lit., 1978—, chmn. dept. English, 1989-95; vis. scholar Jesus Coll., Cambridge, Eng., 1974-75. Author: Augustine Baker, 1970, The Blaze of Noon, 1974, Love's Architecture, 1978, The Georgic Revolution, 1985, The Reinvention of Love, 1993; editor: Urbane Milton, 1984. Pres. Conf. on Christianity and Lit., 1996-97. Pew Evangelical fellow, 1995; Milton scholar, 1996. Mem. Milton Soc., Donne Soc., MLA, Renaissance Soc., Phi Beta Kappa. Home: 7 Christopher Rd Ridgefield CT 06877-2407 Office: NYU Dept English 19 University Pl New York NY 10003-4556

LOW, BARBARA WHARTON, biochemist, biophysicist; b. Lancaster, Eng., Mar. 23, 1920; came to U.S., 1946, naturalized, 1956; d. Matthew and Mary Jane (Wharton) L.; m. Metchie J.E. Budka, July 13, 1950 (dec. 1995). B.A. (Coll. scholar), Somerville Coll., Oxford (Eng.) U., 1942, M.A., 1946, DPhil, 1948. Research fellow Calif. Inst. Tech., 1946-47; research assoc. in phys. chemistry Harvard U. Med. Sch., 1948, assoc. in phys. chemistry, 1948-50; assoc. mem. Univ. Lab. Phys. Chemistry Related to Medicine and Public Health, 1950-54; asst. prof. phys. chemistry Harvard U., 1950-56; assoc. prof. biochemistry Columbia U. Coll. Physicians and Surgeons, 1956-66, prof., 1966-90, prof. emeritus, 1990—; cons. USPHS; mem. biophysics and biophys. chemistry study sect. div. rsch. grants NIH, 1961, spl. study sect., 1966-69, 1988, 90; rsch. coun. Pub. Health Rsch. Inst. City N.Y., 1973-78, bd. dirs., 1974-78; assoc. prof. U. Strasbourg, France, 1965; vis. prof. Japan Soc. Promotion Sci., Tohoku U., Sendai, Japan, 1975; invited lectr. Chinese Acad. Scis. 1981, Soviet Acad. Scis., 1988; mem. seminar on archaeology of Ea. Mediterranean, Ea. Europe and near East, Columbia U. Contbr. articles to chem., biochem., biophys., and crystallographic jours., also chpts. in books. Recipient Career Devel. award NIH, 1963-68; NIH sr. research fellow, 1959-63. Fellow Am. Acad. Arts and Scis.; mem. AAAS, Am. Crystallographic Assn., Am. Inst. Physics, Am. Soc. Biol. Chemists, Biophys. Soc., Royal Soc. Chemistry, Harvey Soc., Internat. Soc. Toxinology, Protein Soc., Soc. Neurosci. Achievements include determination of three dimensional structure of penicillin; structure determination of protein implicated in neurological block; discovery of pi helix; co-developer use of heavy atoms in protein crystal structure determination; introduction of low temperature studies for protein data collection and of polaroid photography of protein X-ray diffraction patterns; established probable binding site of snake venom neurotoxins to Acetylcholine receptor. Office: Columbia U Dept Biochem & Mo Bio 630 W 168th St New York NY 10032-3702

LOW, BOON CHYE, physicist; b. Singapore, Feb. 13, 1946; came to U.S., 1968; s. Kuei Huat and Ah Tow (Tee) Lau; m. Daphne Nai-Ling Yip, Mar. 31, 1971; 1 child, Yi-Kai. BSc, U. London, Eng., 1968; PhD, U. Chgo., 1972. Scientist High Altitude Observatory Nat. Ctr. for Atmospheric Rsch., Boulder, Colo., 1981-87, sect. head, 1987-90, 97—, acting dir., 1989-90, sr. scientist, 1987—; mem. mission operation working group for solar physics NASA, 1992-94. Mem. editl. bd. Solar Physics, 1991—. Named Fellow Japan Soc. for Promotion of Sci., U. Tokyo, 1978, Sr. Rsch. Assoc., NASA Marshall Space Flight Ctr., 1980. Mem. Am. Physical Soc., Am. Astron. Soc., Am. Geophysical Union. Office: Nat Ctr for Atmosph Rsch PO Box 3000 Boulder CO 80307-3000

LOW, DONALD GOTTLOB, retired veterinary medicine educator; b. Cheyenne Wells, Colo., May 14, 1925; s. John Louis and Marie (Gabriel) L.; m. Jeanette Maxine Reedy, Dec. 4, 1948 (div. Feb. 1972); children: Ronald, Raymond, Richard, Christine, Cheryl; m. Jane M. Herschler, May 12, 1973. D.V.M., Kans. State U., 1947; Ph.D., U. Minn., 1956. Pvt. practice vet. medicine, 1947-49; dist. veterinarian U.S. Dept. Agr., 1949-50; instr. U. Minn., 1950-53, 55-56, asso. prof., 1956-60, prof., 1960-65, head dept. vet. hosps., 1965-70; prof., head dept. clin. scis. Colo. State U., 1971-74; prof. vet. medicine, dir. teaching hosp. U. Calif.-Davis, 1974-80, assoc. dean instrn., 1982-83, assoc. dean pub. programs, 1983-93; ret., 1993. Author: (with Osborne, Finco) Small Animal Urology, 1972; Contbr. articles to tech. jours. Active Boy Scouts Am., PTA; established Don Low/Calif. Vet. Med. Assn. Practitioner Fellowship, 1995. Served with AUS, 1943-44; as capt. 1953-55. Recipient Disting. Teaching award U. Minn., 1965, Disting. Svc. award, 1990, 91, Robert W. Kirk award for Disting. Svc., Am. Coll. Vet. Internal Medicine, Disting. Alumnus award Kans. State U. and the Vet. Med. Alumni Assn., 1994. Mem. AVMA, Am. Coll. Vet. Internists (founder), Colo. Vet. Med. Assn., Am. Animal Hosp. Assn. (Veterinarian of Yr. award 1970), Nat. Acad. Practice-Vet. Medicine, Calif. Vet. Med. Assn. (pres. award 1988), Calif. Acad. Vet. Medicine (excellence in Continuing Edn. award 1989, disting. svc. award Wild West Vet. Conf. 1995), Phi Zeta. Methodist. Home: 26778 County Road 34 Winters CA 95694-9064

LOW, EMMET FRANCIS, JR., mathematics educator; b. Peoria, Ill., June 10, 1922; s. Charles Walter and Nettie Alys (Baker) Davis; m. Lana Carmen Wiles, Nov. 23, 1974. B.S. cum laude, Stetson U., 1948; M.S., U. Fla., 1950, Ph.D., 1953. Instr. physics U. Fla., 1950-54; aero. research scientist NACA, Langley Field, Va., 1954-55; asst. prof. math. U. Miami, Coral Gables, Fla., 1955-60; assoc. prof. U. Miami, 1960-67, prof., 1967-72, chmn. dept. math., 1961-66; acting dean U. Miami (Coll. Arts and Scis.), 1966-67, assoc. dean, 1967-68, assoc. dean faculties, 1968-72; prof. math. Clinch Valley Coll., U. Va., 1972-89, dean, 1972-86, chmn. dept. math. scis., 1986-89; emeritus prof. math., 1989—; vis. research scientist Courant Inst. Math. Scis., NYU, 1959-60. Contbr. articles to profl. jours. Mem. Wise County Indsl. Devel. Authority, 1992—, chmn., 1996—. Served with USAAF, 1942-46. Recipient award for excellence in tchg. Clinch Valley Coll., 1988; hon. Ky. Col. Mem. Am. Math. Soc., Math. Assn. Am., Soc. Indsl. and Applied Math., Nat. Council Tchrs. of Math., Southwest Va. Council Tchrs. of Math., AAUP, AAAS, Sigma Xi, Delta Theta Mu, Phi Delta Kappa, Phi Kappa Phi. Clubs: Univ. Yacht (Miami, Fla.); Kiwanis.

LOW, FRANCIS EUGENE, physics educator; b. N.Y.C., Oct. 27, 1921; s. Bela and Eugenia (Ingerman) L.; m. Natalie Sadigur, June 25, 1948; children—Julie, Peter, Margaret. B.S., Harvard U., 1942; M.A., Columbia U., 1947, Ph.D., 1949. Mem. Inst. Advanced Study, 1950-52; asst. prof. U. Ill., Urbana, 1952-55, asso. prof., 1955-56; prof. physics MIT, Cambridge, 1957-67, Karl Taylor Compton prof., 1968-85, Inst. prof., 1985-92, Inst. prof. emeritus, 1992—, dir. Center for Theoretical Physics, 1973-76, dir. Lab. for Nuclear Scis., 1979-80, provost, 1980-85; cons. in field; mem. high energy physics adv. panel Dept. Energy, 1972-76, chmn., 1987-90. Contbr. articles to profl. jours. Served with USAAF, 1942-43; Served with AUS, 1944-46. Mem. NAS (nat. coun. 1986-89), Am. Phys. Soc. (chmn. divsn. particles and fields 1974, councillor-at-large 1979-82), Fedn. Am. Scientists (nat. coun. 1973-77), Am. Acad. Arts and Scis., Internat. Union of Pure and Applied Physics (commn. on particles and fields 1976-82). Home: 28 Adams St Belmont MA 02178-3525 Office: MIT Rm 6-301 Cambridge MA 02139

LOW, FRANK NORMAN, anatomist, educator; b. Bklyn., Feb. 9, 1911; s. William Wans and Hilda (Nelson) L. BA, Cornell U., 1932, PhD, 1936; DSc (hon.), U. N.D., 1983. Postdoctoral Charlton fellow Sch. Medicine Tufts Coll., Boston, 1936-37; instr. to asst. prof. U. N.C., Chapel Hill, 1937-45; assoc. Sch. Medicine U. Md., Balt., 1945-46; assoc. prof. U. W.Va., Morgantown, 1946; asst. prof. Johns Hopkins Med. Sch., Balt., 1946-49; assoc. prof. to prof. anatomy Sch. Medicine La. State U., New Orleans, 1949-64, vis. prof., 1981—; rsch. prof. anatomy U. N.D., Grand Forks, 1964-81, emeritus, 1981—, Chester Fritz Disting. prof., 1975-77; mem. regional rev. bd. Am. Heart Assn., Grand Forks, 1971-74. Author: (with J.A. Freeman) Electron Microscopic Atlas of Normal and Leukemic Human Blood, 1958; assoc. editor Am. Jour. Anatomy, 1971-91; contbr. over 100 rsch. articles to profl. jours. Participant People's Republic China-U.S. exchange program, People to People; citizen amb. Soviet Union, 1991; del. Anniversary Caravan '91, People to People Internat., Russia, Uzbekistan. Mem. Am. Assn. Anatomists (exec. com. 1976-80, Henry Gray award 1989), Am. Soc. Cell Biology, La. Soc. Electron Microscopy (chmn. 1962), Am. Assn. History of Medicine, World Trade Ctr. (New Orleans), Sigma Xi (pres. U. N.D. chpt. 1977). Avocation: travel, history of medicine. Office: La State Med Ctr Dental Sch 1100 Florida Ave New Orleans LA 70119-2714

LOW, HARRY WILLIAM, judge; b. Oakdale, Calif., Mar. 12, 1931; s. Tong J. and Ying G. (Gong) L.; m. May Ling, Aug. 24, 1952; children: Larry, Kathy, Allan. AA, Modesto Jr. Coll., 1950; AB Polit. Sci. with honors, U. Calif., Berkeley, 1952, JD, 1955. Bar: Calif. 1955, U.S. Ct. Appeals (9th cir.) 1955. Commr. Workmen's Compensation Commn., 1966; teaching assoc. Boalt Hall, 1955-56; dep. atty. gen. Calif. Dept. Justice, 1956-66; judge Mcpl. Ct., San Francisco, 1966-74; presiding judge Mcpl. Ct., 1972-73; judge Superior Ct., San Francisco, 1974-82; presiding justice Calif. Ct. Appeals, 1st dist., 1982-92; pres. San Francisco Police Commn., 1992-96; mem. Jud. Arbitration and Mediation Svcs., 1992—, Commn. on Future of Cts., 1991-94, Commn. on Future of Legal Profession, 1993-95. Contbr. articles to profl. jours. Chmn. bd. Edn. Ctr. for Chinese, 1969—, Chinese-Am. Bilingual Sch.; bd. visitors U.S. Mil. Acad., 1980-83; bd. dirs. Friends of Recreation and Parks, Salesian Boys Club, World Affairs Coun., 1979-85, NCCJ, San Francisco chpt. St. Vincent's Boys Home, Coro Found., 1970-76, San Francisco Zool. Trust, 1987, Union Bank, 1993—; pres. San Francisco City Coll. Found., 1977-87, Inst. Chinese Western History U. San Francisco, 1987-89. Mem. ABA (chmn. appellate judges conf. 1990-91, commr. on minorities), San Francisco Bar Assn., Chinese Am. Citizens Alliance (pres. San Francisco chpt. 1976-77, nat. pres. 1989-93), Calif. Judges Assn. (pres. 1978-79), Calif. Jud. Coun., State Bar Calif. (rsch. editor publs. 1958-76, pub. affairs com. 1987-90, exec. bd. 1992-94), Calif. Conf. Judges (editor jour. cts. commentary 1973-76), Calif. Judges Assn. (exec. bd. 1976-79), Asian Bus. League (dir. 1986-93), Nat. Ctr. State Cts. (bd. dirs. 1986-91), San Francisco Bench Bar Media Commn. (chmn. bd. dirs. 1987-92), Phi Alpha Delta. *Try to enjoy whatever task you are doing and enjoy the good company of those with whom you associate. Be an active part of the community and try to improve it. Keep busy and try to understand and respect others.*

LOW, JAMES A., physician; b. Toronto, Ont., Can., Sept. 22, 1925; s. Donald M. and Doris V. (Van Duzer) L.; m. Margery Una, Oct. 5, 1952; children: Donald E., Margeret P., Norman I. M.D., U. Toronto, 1949. Intern Toronto Gen. Hosp., 1949-50; resident in ob-gyn U. Toronto, 1950-54, clin. instr. dept. ob-gyn, 1955-65; fellow ob/gyn Duke U., 1955; prof. and chmn. dept. ob-gyn Queens U., Kingston, Ont., Can., 1965-85; prof. Queens U., 1985—; bd. dirs. Obstet. Health Care Eastern Ontario. Mem. editorial bd. Ob-Gyn., 1986-89, Am. Jour. Ob-Gyn., 1995—. Served with Can. Navy, 1943-45. Fellow Royal Coll. Physicians and Surgeons Can. (chmn. splty. com. 1976-82, chmn. manpower com. 1984-92); mem. Assn. Profs. Ob-Gyn Can. (sec.-treas. 1972-80, pres. 1983-84), Am. Gynecol. and Obstet. Soc., Soc. Gynecol. Investigation, Soc. Obstetricians and Gynecologists of Can., Can. Soc. Clin. Investigation, Am. Acad. Cerebral Palsy, Internat. Incontinence Soc. Home: 185 Fairway Hills, Kingston, ON Canada K7M 2B5 Office: Queens U, Dept Ob Gyn, Kingston, ON Canada K7L 3N6

LOW, JOHN WAYLAND, lawyer; b. Denver, Aug. 7, 1923; s. Oscar Wayland and Rachel E. (Stander) L.; m. Merry C. Mullan, July 8, 1979; children: Lucinda A., Jan W. BA, Nebr. Wesleyan U., 1947; JD cum laude, U. Denver, 1951. Bar: Colo. 1951, U.S. Dist. Ct. (Colo. dist.) 1951, U.S. Ct. Appeals (10th cir.), U.S. Supreme Ct. 1960. Ptnr. Sherman & Howard LLC, Denver, 1951-93, counsel, 1993—. Trustee U. Denver, 1987—; chmn. bd. Denver Symphony Assn., 1989-90; vice chmn. Colo. Symphony Assn., 1990-96; chmn. Colo. Alliance of Bus., Denver, 1983-87. 1st lt. U.S. Army, 1942-46, CBI. Recipient Learned Hand award Am. Jewish Com., 1989, Outstanding Alumni award U. Denver, 1994. Mem. ABA, Colo. Bar Assn., Denver Bar Assn., University Club of Denver, Garden of Gods Club (Colorado Springs). Republican. Mem. United Ch. of Christ. Office: Sherman & Howard 633 17th St Ste 3000 Denver CO 80202-3660

LOW, JOSEPH, artist; b. Coraopolis, Pa., Aug. 11, 1911; s. John Routh and Stella (Rent) L.; m. Ruth Hull, Oct. 21, 1940; children: Damaris, Jennifer. Student, U. Ill., 1930-32, Art Students League N.Y., 1935. founder,

1959; since propr. Eden Hill Press. Engaged in printmaking and graphic arts, 1943—; exhbns. include, Princeton, Dartmouth, Williams, U. Ill., Phila. Mus. Art, Brandeis U., Grinnell Coll., Carnegie Inst. Tech., Herron Art Inst., Indpls., U. Ky., others; rep. permanent collections, Princeton, Dartmouth, U. Ky., State Dept., Library of Congress, Chapin Library at Williams Coll., U. Ill., Wesleyan U., Middletown, Conn., Va. Mus. Fine Arts, San Francisco Pub. Library, Boston Atheneum, Boston Mus. Fine Arts, Harvard Coll. Library, Pratt Inst., U. Okla., Newberry Library, Chgo., Met. Mus. Art, Ohio State U., Bodleian Library, Oxford U., pvt. collections. Home: RFD 278 Chilmark MA 02535

LOW, MARY LOUISE (MOLLY LOW), documentary photographer; b. Quakertown, Pa., Jan. 3, 1926; d. James Harry and Dorothy Collyer (Krewson) Thomas; m. Antoine Francois Gagné, Nov. 3, 1945 (div.); children: James L., David W., Stephen J., Jeannie Wolff-Gagné; m. Paul Low, July 11, 1969 (dec. July 1991). Student, Oberlin Conservatory of Music, 1943-44, Oberlin Coll., 1944; cert., Katharine Gibbs Sec. Sch., 1945; degree in psychiat. rehab. work, Einstein Coll. Medicine, 1968-70. Sec. Dept. Store, N.Y.C., 1945; sec., treas. Gagné Assocs., Consulting Engrs., Binghamton, N.Y., 1951-66; psychiat. rsch. asst. Jacobi Hosp., Bronx, 1969-70; asst. to head of sch. Brearley Sch., N.Y.C., 1976-78; pvt. practice documentary photographer San Diego, 1984—. Contbr. articles to profl. jours. Pres., bd. trustees Unitarian-Universalist Ch. Recipient Dir.'s award for excellence Area Agy. on Aging, San Diego, 1993, Citizen Recognition award County of San Diego, Calif., 1993. Avocations: singing, directing church choir, traveling. Office: Molly Low Photography 5576 Caminito Herminia La Jolla CA 92037-7222

LOW, MORTON DAVID, physician, educator; b. Lethbridge, Alta., Can., Mar. 25, 1935; s. Solon Earl and Alice Fern (Litchfield) L.; m. Cecilia Margaret Comba, Aug. 22, 1959 (div. 1983); children—Cecilia Alice, Sarah Elizabeth, Peter Jon Eric; m. Barbara Joan McLeod, Aug. 25, 1984; 1 child, Kelsey Alexandra. M.D., C.M., Queen's U., 1960, M.Sc. in Medicine, 1962; Ph.D. with honors, Baylor U., 1966. From instr. to asst. prof. Baylor Coll. Medicine, Houston, 1965-68; assoc. prof. medicine U. B.C., Vancouver, Can., 1968-78, prof. medicine, 1978-89, clin. assoc. dean, 1974-76, assoc. dean rsch. and grad. studies, 1977-78, coord. health scis., 1985-89; creator Health Policy Rsch. Unit U. B.C., Vancouver, 1987; Alkek-Williams Disting. Prof. and pres. U. Tex. Health Sci. Ctr., Houston, 1989—, prof. neural scis. Grad. Sch. Biomed. Scis., 1989—, dir. Health Policy Inst., 1990—; prof. neurology U. Tex. Med. Sch., Houston, 1989—; prof. health policy and mgmt. Sch. Pub. Health U. Tex., 1989—; cons. in neurology U. Hosp. Shaughnessy site, Vancouver, 1971-89, U. B.C. site, Vancouver, 1970-89; dir. dept. diagnostic neurophysiology Vancouver Gen. Hosp., 1968-87; cons. in EEG, 1987-89; exec. dir. Rsch. Inst., 1981-86; mem. med. sci. adv. com. USIA, 1991-93. Mem. editorial bd. numerous jours.; contbr. articles to profl. jours. Bd. dirs. Greater Houston Ptnrship., 1994—, Episcopal Health Charities Found., 1997—; mem. governing bd. Houston Mus. Natural Sci., 1991—; trustee Kinkaid Sch., Houston, 1991—. Med. Rsch. Coun. Can. grantee, 1968-80; recipient Tree of Life award Jewish Nat. Fund, 1995, Caring Spirit award Inst. Religion, 1995. Fellow Am. EEG Soc., Royal Coll. Physicians (Can.), Royal Soc. Medicine (London); mem. AMA, Tex. Med. Assn. (coun. on med. edn. 1990—), Can. Soc. Clin. Neurophysiology, Internat. Fedn. Socs. for EEG and Clin. Neurophysiology (rules com. 1977-81, sec. 1981-85), Assn. Acad. Health Ctrs. (task force on access to care and orgn. health svcs. 1988—, chmn. 1992, task force on instnl. values 1989—), Harris County Med. Soc., Am. Coun. Edn., Forum Club of Houston (governing bd. 1991—). Avocations: sailing instructing, photography, youth soccer coach, vol. ski-patrol, flying. Office: U Tex-Houston Health Sci PO Box 20036 Houston TX 77225-0036

LOW, RANDALL, internist, cardiologist; b. San Francisco, June 24, 1949; s. Huet Hee and Betty Tai (Quan) L.; m. Dorothy Fung, May 4, 1975; children: Audrey, Madeleine, Jennifer. AA, City Coll., San Francisco, 1969; BA, U. Calif., Berkeley, 1971; MD, U. Calif., Davis, 1975. Diplomate Am. Bd. Internal Medicine, Nat. Bd. Med. Examiners, Am. Bd. Cardiovascular Diseases. Intern Hosp. of Good Samaritan, L.A., 1975-76, resident, 1976-77, chief med. resident, 1977-78; mem. staff St. Francis Meml. Hosp., San Francisco, 1981—, chmn. dept. cardiology, 1995—; pvt. practice internal medicine and cardiology San Francisco, 1981—; mem. staff Chinese Hosp., San Francisco, 1981—, chief of medicine, 1991-92; asst. clin. prof. U. Calif., San Francisco, 1994—; mem. courtesy staff St. Mary's Hosp., San Francisco, 1981—, Calif. Pacific Med. Ctr., San Francisco, 1990—; cardiology cons. Laguna Honda Hosp., San Francisco, 1981—. Mem. home health quality assurance com. Self Help for Elderly, San Francisco, 1991—; bd. dirs. Youth Advocates, San Francisco, 1992—. Recipient Hearst Pub. Svc. award U. Calif.-Berkeley, 1970, 6th ann. homecare recognition award Self Help for Elderly, 1993. Mem. ACP, Am. Soc. Internal Medicine, Am. Coll. Cardiology, Am. Heart Assn. (bd. govs. 1983-90), Calif. Acad. Medicine, Calif. Med. Soc., San Francisco Med. Soc., Assn. Chinese Cmty. Physicians (sec.-treas. 1986-89), Chinese Cmty. Health Care Assn. (pres. 1991-96). Office: 909 Hyde St Ste 501 San Francisco CA 94109-4833

LOW, RICHARD H., broadcasting executive, producer; b. Union City, N.J., Feb. 20, 1927; s. Irving and Regina (Krieger) L.; 1 dau., Jennifer Alixe. Student, U. Mich., 1947-49; J.D., Columbia U., 1952. With CBS News, 1952-56; with CBS-TV Network, 1956-62, dir. contracts, facilities and program sales, 1959-62; with Young & Rubicam, 1962-84, v.p. TV-radio dept., 1970-72, v.p. programming, 1972-73, sr. v.p., 1973-81, responsible for network TV programming and purchasing, 1973-84, includes cable TV, 1980-84, exec. v.p., dir. broadcast programming and purchasing, 1981-84; pres. Manticore Prodns., Inc. 1985—; pres. Universal Holding Co.; advisor LWV presdl. TV debates, 1980; judge N.Y. World TV Festival, 1979-80, Internat. Emmy awards, 1981-83; panelist Nat. Assn. TV Programming Execs. Conf., 1981; keynote spkr. 25th Anniversary seminar Broadcasters Promotion Assn., 1981; presenter S.I. Newhouse Sch. Pub. Comm., 1981; discussant Ctr. for Comm., 1982; mem. Task Force on Pub. Broadcasting, 1983. Mem. media task force Nat. Coun. Arts, 1977, Aspen Inst., 1973; v.p., trustee Am. Mus. Immigration; trustee Town Hall Found.; bd. dirs. U.S. Organizing Com. 1983 Bicentennial of Air and Space. With U.S. Army, 1945-46. Mem. NATAS (gov. N.Y. 1979-83). Office: 1056 Fifth Ave New York NY 10028-0112 *In the beginner's mind, there are many possibilities.*

LOW, RON ALBERT, professional hockey coach; b. Birtle, Man., Can., June 21, 1950. Profl. hockey player Toronto Maple Leaves, Can., 1970-74, Washington Capitals, 1974-77, Detroit Red Wings, 1977-78, Quebec Nordiques, Can., 1979-80, Edmonton Oilers, Can., 1980-83, N.J. Devils, 1983-85; player Nova Scotia Oilers, Can., 1985-86, asst. coach, 1985-87; asst. coach Edmonton Oilers, 1989-96, head coach, 1996—. Recipient Tommy Ivan trophy, 1978-79; named to CHL All-Star 2d team, 1973-74, All Star 1st team, 1978-79. Office: Edmonton Oilers Coliseum, Edmonton, AB Canada T5B 4M9*

LOW, STEPHEN, foundation executive, educator, former diplomat; b. Cin., Dec. 2, 1927; s. Martin and Margaret (Friend) L.; m. Helen Sue Carpenter, Oct. 9, 1954; children: Diego, Rodman, Jesse. B.A., Yale U., 1950; M.A., Fletcher Sch. Law and Diplomacy, Tufts U., 1951, Ph.D., 1956. With Dept. State, various locations, 1956-74; sr. staff mem. NSC, 1974-76; U.S. ambassador to Zambia, 1976-79, U.S. ambassador to Nigeria, 1979-81; dir. Fgn. Service Inst. Dept. State, 1982-87; dir. Bologna (Italy) Ctr. Sch. Advanced Internat. Studies Johns Hopkins U., 1987-92; pres. Assn. Diplomatic Studies and Tng., 1992—. Served with AUS, 1946-47. Address: 2855 Tilden St NW Washington DC 20008-3820

LOWD, JUDSON DEAN, oil and gas processing equipment manufacturing executive; b. Chelsea, Mass., June 8, 1918; s. Dana Joseph and Olive Wanda (Dean) L.; m. Alice Carroll, Sept. 6, 1975; 1 dau., Dana. BS in Mech. Engring. with honors, Worcester Poly. Inst., Mass., 1940. Mgr. oil field equipment divsn. Parkersburg Rig & Reel Co., W.Va., 1948-56; exec. v.p. internat. mktg. ops. C-E Natco, Tulsa, 1957-73, pres., 1973-82; chmn. C-E Randall, 1980-84; bd. dirs. Ocean Corp., Houston; pres. Nat. Tank France, Paris; vice chmn. Williams TEch., Inc.1985-90. Trustee U. Tulsa, 1977-87, Goodland Children's Home, Hugo, Okla., 1976-82, Lebanese Am. U., Beirut, 1973-87, dir. and overseer acads.; bd. dirs. Jr. Achievement, Tulsa, 1978-81, Tulsa United Way, 1975-80; elder Presbyn. Ch., 1954—; mem. Tu lsa Execs. Svc. Corps, 1985-96, chmn. 1990. Officer AUS, 1941-48, ETO. Decorated Bronze Star; named Marketer of Year, Am. Mktg. Assn., 1974. Mem. ASME (life), Inst. Petroleum (U.K.), Tulsa C. of C. (dir.), Sigma Xi, Tau Beta Pi. Republican. Clubs: So. Hills Country, Tulsa, Tulsa So. Tennis (Tulsa); Lost Hound Hunt (Edmond, Okla.). Office: 427 S Boston Ave Ste 815 Tulsa OK 74103-4113

LOWDEN, JOHN L., retired corporate executive; b. Yakima, Wash., Oct. 29, 1921; s. Roy Ruben and Hildegarde Annie (Grommesch) L.; m. Janet Katherine Langan, Jan. 21, 1961; children: Susan Elizabeth, Jonathan Roy, Andrew Matthias. B.A., U. Nev., 1949. Account supr. Campbell-Ewald Advt., 1951-57, Erwin, Wasey Advt., 1957-59; advt. dir. Gen. Dynamics Corp., 1959-61; account supr. Foote, Cone & Belding, 1961-63; with ITT Corp., 1963-84, v.p. corp. rels. and advt., 1977-84. Author: Silent Wings at War, 1992. Served with USAAF, 1941-45. Decorated Air Medal with Oak Leaf Cluster and Order of William by the Queen of The Netherlands; seven unit battle stars. Roman Catholic.

LOWE, ANGELA MARIA, small business owner; b. Newark, Nov. 15, 1963; d. Eleanor Gugliocciello; m. Thomas Edward Lowe, Nov. 1, 1986; children: Matthew Richard, Bethany Elena. BSCE, Pa. State U., 1985; MBA, Rutgers U., 1994. Registered profl. engr., N.J. Engr. Greenhorne & O'Mara, Inc., Greenbelt, Md., 1985-86; structural engr. Goodkind & O'Dea, Inc., Rutherford, N.J., 1986-88; civil engr. Charles Mackie Assocs., Inc., Barnegat, N.J., 1988-90; planning engr. Naval Weapons Sta. Earle, Colts Neck, N.J., 1992-93; co-owner, co-founder, v.p., CFO Compro Techs. Inc., computer telephone value added resellers, Barnegat, 1993—. Lt. Civil Engring. Corps, USNR, 1990—. Mem. Pa. State Alumni Assn., Naval Res. Assn. Home: 28 Deer Run Dr S Barnegat NJ 08005-2216

LOWE, CLAYTON KENT, visual imagery, cinema, and video educator; b. Endicott, N.Y., July 10, 1936; s. Clayton Edwin and Loretta Arlene (Terry) L.; m. Janet E. Snider, 1957 (div. 1977); children: Steven Scott, Kim Ann Parker, David William, Rebecca Michelle Sobel; m. Robin S. McKell, 1980 (div. 1993). BA, Bethany Coll., 1958; MS, Butler U., 1967; PhD, Ohio State U., 1970; BD, Christian Theol. Sem., Indpls., 1962. Pastor Bellaire (Ohio) Christian Ch., 1957-58, Beallsville (Ohio) Christian Ch., 1958, Russellville (Ind.) Christian Ch., 1958-60, Montclair (Ind.) Christian Ch., 1960-61; youth dir. St. Paul United Ch. of Christ, Columbus, 1967-70; asst. prof. journalism U. Ga., 1970-72; asst. prof. comm. Ohio State U., Columbus, 1972-73, asst. prof. photography and cinema, 1973-74, assoc. prof., 1974—, chairperson photography and cinema, 1974-78, dir. grad. studies photography and cinema, 1989-92; assoc. prof. emeritus Ohio State U., 1992—; comml. TV prodr., dir., writer Stas. WISH-TV, 1960-66, WLWI-TV, 1966-67, WOSU-TV, 1967-70; moderator World Film Classics, Educable TV-25, 1991—, also bd. dirs.; exec. prodr. World Film Classics, 1996—; Ednl. Resources Info. Ctr. (U.S.) evaluator-film theory, 1973-78; juror Columbus Internat. Film and TV Festival, 1993, 94. Book reviewer The Arts Edn. Rev. of Books; editor: The Movies on Media Catalog, 1995; co-host Columbus Mus. of Art film series, 1995, 96, 97, Drexel Theatre Talk Cinema film series, 1997. Mem. bd. Columbus Friends of the Libr.; trustee Met. Libr., 1997. Eli Lilly Found. grantee, 1961-63, Ohio State U. Devel. of Media on Media Study Collection grantee, 1985, Ohio Humanities Coun. grantee 1996-97; recipient Casper award for A Thing Called Hope, Sta. WOSU-TV, 1966, Regional Emmy for A Tribute to Dr. King, 1968, Regional Emmy nominee Lucasville, 1970, High Street, 1975, Leadership award Ohio State U. Outstanding Alumni Soc., 1997. Mem. NATAS (bd. govs. Ohio chpt. 1973-74), Univ. Film and Video Assn., Ohio State U. Dept. Photography and Cinema Alumni Assn. (pres. 1994-95, bd. dirs. 1994—), Kiwanis. Home: 68 Walhalla Rd Columbus OH 43202-1441 *If these were my last words, I would write of the beauty that has filled me and that I in turn have filled. I would look past the darkness and pain, toward those radiant spots of light when family and friends were most open and life was at its wondrous best.*

LOWE, DONALD CAMERON, corporate executive; b. Oshawa, Ont., Can., Jan. 29, 1932; s. Samuel John and Carales Isobel (Cox) L.; m. Susan Margaret Plunkett, July 22, 1955; children: Michelle, Jeffrey, Steven. B of Applied Sci., U. Toronto, 1954; MS (Athlone fellow), U. Birmingham, Eng., 1957; grad. internat. sr. mgrs. seminar, Harvard U., 1975. With Gen. Motors Can. Ltd., 1957-71; from asst. gen. mgr. to gen. mgr. Gen. Motors Can. Ltd., St. Therese, Que., 1969-71; dir. mfg. Vauxhall Motors Ltd., Luton, Eng., 1971-75; pres., CEO Pratt & Whitney Aircraft Ltd., Can., 1975-80; also chmn. bd.; pres. comml. products divsn. Pratt & Whitney Aircraft Group, East Hartford, Conn., 1980-82; chmn., CEO Allied Can. Inc., 1982-83; pres., CEO Kidd Creek Mines Ltd., 1983-86, Canadair, Montreal, 1986-90; dep. chmn. Bombardier, Inc., Montreal, 1990-92; pres., CEO Fleet Aerospace Corp./Magellan Aerospace Corp., Toronto, 1993-96, vice-chmn., 1996—; bd. dirs. Algoods, Trilon Fin., Can. Tire Corp., Devtek Corp., Magellan Aerospace Corp.; chmn. Sedgwick Ltd., Bombardier, Inc., Ingersoll-Rand Can., Haley Industries, Exal Aluminum Inc., Strong Equipment Co. Bd. govs. U. Montreal; hon. dir. Can. Aviation Hall of Fame. Mem. Aerospace Industries Assn. Can., Conf. Bd. Can., Les Ambassadeurs Club (London), Muskoka Lakes Golf and Country Club (Port Carling), Donalda Club, Granite Club, Cambridge Club (Toronto). Office: Sedgwick Ltd, PO Box 439 Toronto Dominion Ctr, Toronto, ON Canada M5K 1M3

LOWE, E(DWIN) NOBLES, lawyer; b. Minturn, Ark., Oct. 4, 1912; s. James A. and Ether (Nobles) L.; m. Catherine McDonald, June 9, 1934 (div. 1959); children: Nancy, Edwin N.; m. Margaret Breece, Dec. 1, 1961; 1 son, James W. A.B., U. Ark., 1932, LL.B., 1934; postgrad., Harvard U. Bus. Sch. Advanced Mgmt. Program, 1950; JD, U. Ark., 1976. Bar: Ark. 1934, N.Y. 1936, U.S. Ct. Appeals (2d cir.) 1938, D.C. 1975, U.S. Ct. Internat. Trade 1979, U.S. Supreme Ct. 1942. Mem. staff Ark. Bond Refunding Bd., 1934; with legal dept. Electric Bond & Share Co., N.Y.C., 1934-35; assoc. mng. atty., ptnr. Reid & Priest, 1935-43; gen. counsel Westvaco Corp. (formerly W.Va. Pulp & Paper), N.Y.C., 1943-77; dir. pub. rels. Westvaco Corp., 1944-48, dir. govt. affairs, 1944-76, sec., 1947-66, v.p., 1966-77; spl. ptnr. Gadsby & Hannah, N.Y.C., 1978-79; mem. firm Lowe & Knapp, N.Y.C., 1979-84; sole practice N.Y.C., 1985-86, Carmel, N.Y., 1986—; sec., dir. Fund for Modern Cts., N.Y., 1974—; counsel, dir. Photographic Adminstrs., Inc., 1995—. Trustee Clinton Hall Assn., 1956—, pres., 1966-69, 85-90, Found. Merc. Libr.; dir. Putnam County Alliance, counsel dir., 1990—; dir. Putnam County Arts Coun., 1992—. Recipient Am. Law Inst.-ABA Continuing Legal Edn. Spl. award, 1985. Mem. ABA (sr. lawyers divsn. coun. 1992—, book pub. com. 1990-95, chmn. 1991-95, Experience mag. 1990—, chmn. 1995-97), Am. Law Inst. (life, bus. law sect. emeritus & co-founder corp. gen. counsel com. 1979—), N.Y. State Bar Assn., Gen. Counsel Assn., Dutch Treat Club. (gov., sec. 1992—), Univ. Club (v.p. coun., chmn. club activities, charter revision com.), Sigma Nu. Methodist. Home and Office: The Knoll Gypsy Trail Rd Carmel NY 10512

LOWE, HARRY, museum director; b. Opelika, Ala., Apr. 9, 1922; s. Harry Foster and Lois (Fletcher) L. B.F.A., Auburn U., 1943, M.F.A., 1949; student, Cranbrook Acad., 1951, 53. Prof. art, dir. Art Gallery, Auburn U., 1957-59; dir. Tenn. Fine Arts Center, Nashville, 1959-64; curator exhibits Nat. Mus. Am. Art (formerly Nat. Collection Fine Arts), Smithsonian Instn., 1964-72, dep. commr. U.S. Exhbn. at Venice Biennale, 1966, asst. dir. for ops., 1972-74, asst. dir., 1974-81, acting dir., 1981-82, dep. dir., 1983-84, dep. dir. emeritus, 1985—; 1st pres. Tenn. Assn. Museums, 1960. Served with F.A. AUS, World War II, ETO. Home: 802 A St SE Washington DC 20003-1340 Office: Nat Mus Am Art Smithsonian Instn Washington DC 20560

LOWE, JOHN, III, consulting civil engineer; b. N.Y.C., Mar. 14, 1916; s. John and Rose Marie (Jahoda) L.; m. Jeanne Wright, June 19, 1943; children: Jonathan Alan, Barbara Jean, Heather Ellen. B.S. in Engring., CCNY; M.S.C.E., MIT. Registered profl. engr., N.Y., La., PR., Calif. Instr. U. Md., College Park, 1937-40, MIT, Cambridge, Mass., 1941-44; physicist David Taylor Model Basin, Carderock, Md., 1945; chief soils engr. Tippetts-Abbett-McCarthy-Stratton, N.Y.C., 1945-55, assoc. ptnr., 1956-62, ptnr., 1962-83; pvt. practice geotech. and dam engring., 1984—; adj. assoc. prof. NYU, 1949-51; lectr. soil mechanics CCNY, 1953-60; 8th Terzaghi lectr., 1971, 4th Nabor Carrillo lectr., 1978, 2d U.S. Com. on Large Dams lectr., 1982, Marty Kapp lectr., 1986; keynote address Roller Compacted Concrete II, 1988; cons. Corps. Engrs., Washington, 1962-80. Contbr. chpts. to 4 books, 38 articles in field to profl. jours. Decorated comdr. Order of Alouites (Morocco); recipient Townsend Harris medal Alumni CCNY, 1982. Fellow ASCE; mem. NAE, U.S. Com. Large Dam (chmn. 1977-78), Nat. Com. Soil Mechanics and Found. Engring., Moles, Univ. Club, Bronxville Field Club.

LOWE, JOHN BURTON, molecular biology educator, pathologist; b. Sheridan, Wyo., June 13, 1953; s. Burton G. and Eunice D. Lowe. BA, U. Wyo., 1976; MD, U. Utah, 1980. Diplomate Am. Bd. Pathology. Asst. med. dir. Barnes Hosp. Blood Bank, St. Louis, 1985-86; instr. Sch. of Medicine Washington U., St. Louis, 1985, asst. prof. Sch. of Medicine, 1985-86; asst. investigator Howard Hughes Med. Inst., Ann Arbor, Mich., 1986-92, assoc. investigator, 1992-96, investigator, 1997—; asst. prof. Med. Sch. U. Mich., Ann Arbor, 1986-91, assoc. prof. Med. Sch., 1991-95, prof. Med. Sch., 1995—. Dep. editor Jour. Clin. Investigation, 1997—; contbr. articles to Jour. Biol. Chemistry, Genes and Devel., Nature, Cell. Office: U Mich Howard Hughes Med 1150 W Medical Center Dr Ann Arbor MI 48109-0726

LOWE, JOHN STANLEY, lawyer, educator; b. Marion, Ohio, May 11, 1941; s. John Floyd and Florence (Andrews) L.; m. Jacquelyn Taft, Jan. 15, 1968; children: Sarah Staley, John Taft. BA, Denison U., 1963; LLB, Harvard U., 1966. Bar: Ohio 1966, Okla. 1980, U.S. Supreme Ct. 1972, Tex. 1989. Adminstrv. officer Govt. of Malawi, Limbe, 1966-69; assoc. Emens, Hurd, Kegler & Ritter, Columbus, Ohio, 1970-75; assoc. prof. law U. Toledo, Ohio, 1975-78; prof. law U. Tulsa, 1978-87, So. Meth. U., Dallas, 1987—; vis. prof. U. Tex., Austin, 1983; disting. vis. prof. natural resources law U. Denver, 1987; disting. vis. prof. U. N.Mex., 1996. Author: Oil and Gas Law in a Nutshell, 1983, 3d edit., 1995; editor: Cases and Materials on Oil and Gas Law, 1986, 2d edit., 1993; editor Internat. Petroleum Transactions, 1993. Trustee Rocky Mountain Mineral Law Found., mem. exec. com., 1985-87. Recipient Outstanding Law Rev. Article award Tex. Bar Found., 1988, 96. Mem. ABA (chair natural resources, energy and environ. law 1992-93). Episcopalian. Avocation: sailing. Home: 3526 Greenbrier Dr Dallas TX 75225-5003 Office: So Meth U 3315 Daniel Ave Dallas TX 75205-1439

LOWE, KEVIN HUGH, professional hockey player; b. Apr. 15, 1959; m. Karen Percy. Hockey player Edmonton Oilers, 1979-92, capt., 1991-92; hockey player N.Y. Rangers, 1992—. Played in NHL All-Star game 1984-86, 88-90, 93; winner Clancy Meml. Trophy, 1989-90; named Budweiser/NHL Man of Yr., 1989-90. Office: care NY Rangers 4 Pennsylvania Plz New York NY 10001

LOWE, MARVIN, artist; b. Bklyn., May 19, 1922; m. Juel Watkins, Apr. 1, 1949; 1 dau., Melissa. Student, Julliard Sch. Music, 1952-54; BA, Bklyn. Coll., 1956; MFA, U. Iowa, 1961. Prof. fine arts Ind. U., Bloomington, 1968-92, prof. emeritus, 1992—; vis. artist-lectr., 1970-91. Exhibited in 62 one-person shows; over 200 group and invitational exhbns.; participated in U.S. info. exhbns. in Latin Am., Japan, USSR, and most European countries; represented in 84 permanent collections including Phila. Mus. Art, Bklyn. Mus., Smithsonian Instn., Brit. Mus., Japan Print Assn., N.Y.C. Pub. Libr., Calif. Palace Legion of Honor, San Francidso, Boston Pub. Libr., Columbia U., Libr. of Congress, Indpls. Mus. Art, Ringling Mus., Honolulu Acad. Art, Ft. Wayne Mus. Art, Purdue U. Mus. Fine Art, Springfield, Mass. Served with USNR, 1942-45. Fellow Nat. Endowment for Arts, 1975; fellow Ford Found., 1979, Ind. Arts Commn., 1987; recipient numerous Purchase awards, 1960—. Office: Ind U Sch Fine Arts Bloomington IN 47405 *As a visual artist, I have tried to refrain from making public statements about my work which ultimately must speak for itself.*

LOWE, MARY FRANCES, federal government official; b. Ft. Meade, Md., Apr. 15, 1952; d. Benno Powers and Peggy Catherine (Moore) L. B.A., Coll. William and Mary, 1972; M.A., Fletcher Sch. Law and Diplomacy, 1974, M.A. Law and Diplomacy in, 1975; diplome, Grad. Inst. Internat. Studies U. Geneva, Switzerland, 1975; M.P.H. in epidemiology, Johns Hopkins Sch. Hygiene and Pub. Health, 1986. External collaborator ILO, Geneva, 1974; legis. asst. to U.S. Senator Richard S. Schweiker Washington, 1975-76; profl. staff mem. health and sci. rsch. subcom. U.S. Senate Com. Labor and Human Resources, Washington, 1976-81; exec. sec. U.S. Dept. HHS, Washington, 1981-85; sr. asst. to commr. program policy FDA, 1985-89; sr. asst. pesticide programs EPA, 1989-96; Pesticide Ch Comms., 1996—; rep. U.S. delegations 34th and 35th World Health Assemblies, Geneva, 1981, 82, NAFTA and WTO Coms., 1995—; alt. trustee Woodrow Wilson Internat. Ctr. Scholars. Mem. Soc. for Epidemiologic Rsch., Am. Assn. World Health, Exec. Women in Govt., Soc. Risk Analysis, Washington World Affairs Coun., Delta Omega. Home: 7920 Spotswood Dr Alexandria VA 22308-1125 Office: EPA 401 M St SW Washington DC 20460-0001

LOWE, MARY JOHNSON, federal judge; b. N.Y.C., June 10, 1924; m. Ivan A. Michael, Nov. 4, 1961; children: Edward H. Lowe, Leslie H. Lowe, Bess J. Michael. BA, Hunter Coll., 1952; LLB, Bklyn. Law Sch., 1954; LLM, Columbia U., 1955; LLD, CUNY, 1990. Bar: N.Y. 1955. Pvt. practice law N.Y.C., 1955-71; judge N.Y.C. Criminal Ct., 1971-72; acting justice N.Y. State Supreme Ct., 1972-74; judge Bronx County Supreme Ct., 1974; justice N.Y. State Supreme Ct., 1977, 1st Jud. Dist., 1978; judge U.S. Dist. Ct. (so. dist.) N.Y., 1978-91, sr. judge, 1991—. Recipient award for outstanding service to criminal justice system Bronx County Criminal Cts. Bar Assn., 1974, award for work on narcotics cases Asst. Dist. Attys., 1974. Mem. Women in Criminal Justice, Harlem Lawyers Assn., Bronx Criminal Lawyers Assn., N.Y. County Lawyers Assn., Bronx County Bar Assn., N.Y. State Bar Assn. (award for outstanding jud. contbn. to criminal justice Sect. Criminal Justice 1978), NAACP, Nat. Urban League, Nat. Council Negro Women, NOW. Office: US Dist Ct 40 Foley Sq New York NY 10007-1502*

LOWE, PETER STEPHEN, non-profit company executive; b. Lahore, Pakistan, Oct. 23, 1958; s. Eric and Margaret Winnifred (Bradshaw) L.; m. Tamara Angela Forte, May 9, 1987. BA, Carleton U., Ottawa, Ont., Can., 1986. Pres. Lifemasters Tng. Co., Vancouver, B.C., Can., 1981-87, Global Achievers, New Orleans, 1987-90; pres., chief exec. officer Peter Lowe Internat., Inc., Tampa, Fla., 1990—. Mem. Nat. Speakers Assn., Nat. Christian Speakers Assn. (founder), Internat. Platform Assn. Office: 8405A Benjamin Rd Tampa FL 33634

LOWE, RALPH EDWARD, lawyer; b. Hinsdale, Ill., Nov. 24, 1931; s. Charles Russell and Eva Eleanor (Schroeder) L.; m. Patricia E. Eichhorst, Aug. 23, 1952; children: John Stuart, Michael Kevin, Timothy Edward. BA, Depauw U., 1953; LLB, U. Ill., 1956. Bar: Ill. 1956, U.S. Dist. Ct. (no. dist.) Ill. 1957, Ga. 1974, U.S. Dist. Ct. (no. dist.) Ga. 1980, S.C. 1990. Assoc. Ruddy & Brown, Aurora, Ill., 1956-58; ptnr. Lowe & Richards, Aurora, 1959-62, Vincent, Lowe & Richards, Aurora, 1963-71; pvt. practice Aurora, 1972-74, Aurora and Atlanta, 1974-85; prin. Lowe & Steinmetz, Ltd., Aurora and Atlanta, 1985-91; chmn. Inter-Am. Devel. Corp., Ill., 1965-67. Office: 407 W Galena Blvd Aurora IL 60506-3946

LOWE, RANDALL BRIAN, lawyer; b. Englewood, N.J., Nov. 20, 1948. BA, U. R.I., 1970; JD, Washington U., 1973. Bar: Ill. 1973, Conn. 1975, D.C. 1976, U.S. Ct. Appeals (2d and D.C. cirs.) 1976, N.J. 1977, U.S. Dist. Ct. N.J. 1977, U.S. Ct. Appeals (3d cir.) 1977, U.S. Ct. Appeals (9th cir.) 1979, N.Y. 1980, U.S. Dist. Ct. (ea. and so. dists.) N.Y. 1980. Atty. Callis & Filcoff, Granite City, Ill., 1973-75, AT&T, Washington and N.Y.C., 1975-78, ITT Corp, 1978-83, Surrey & Morse, Washington, 1983-86; ptnr. Jones, Day, Reavis & Pogue, Washington, 1986-94, Piper & Marbury, Washington, 1994—. Office: Piper & Marbury 1200 19th St NW Washington DC 20036-2412

LOWE, RICHARD GERALD, JR., computer programming manager; b. Travis AFB, Calif., Nov. 8, 1960; s. Richard Gerald and Valerie Jean (Hoeffer) L.; m. Claudia Maria Arevalo, 1993; 1 child, Alvaro Arevalo. Student, San Bernardino Valley Coll., 1978-80. Microsoft cert. sys. engr. Tech. specialist Software Techniques Inc., Los Alamitos, Calif., 1980-82, sr. tech. specialist, 1982-84, mgr. tech. services, 1984-85; mgr. cons. services Software Techniques Inc., Cypress, Calif., 1985-86; sr. programmer BIF Accutel, Camarillo, Calif., 1986-87; systems analyst BIF Accutel, Camarillo, 1987-88; mgr. project Beck Computer Systems, Long Beach, Calif., 1988-91, v.p. devel., 1991-93; dir. tech. svcs. Trader Joe's Co., S. Pasadena, Calif., 1994—. Author: The Autobiography of Richard G. Lowe, Jr., 1991, The Lowe

Family and Their Relatives, 1992; contbr. articles to profl. jours. Vol. min., field staff mem. L.A. Found. Ch. of Scientology, 1993—; active Concerned Citizens for Human Rights. Mem. Assn. Computing Machinery, Digital Equipment Corp. Users Group, UniData Users Group, Internat. Assn. Scientologists. Avocations: reading and writing science fiction, collecting movies, battlefield simulations, painting fantasy miniatures, collecting stamps. Office: Trader Joe's Co 538 Mission St South Pasadena CA 91030-3036

LOWE, ROBERT CHARLES, lawyer; b. New Orleans, July 3, 1949; s. Carl Randall and Antonia (Morgan) L.; m. Theresa Louise Acree, Feb. 4, 1978. 1 child, Nicholas Stafford. BA, U. New Orleans, 1971; JD, La. State U., 1975. Bar: La. 1975, U.S. Dist. Ct. (ea. dist.) La. 1975, U.S. Ct. Appeals (5th cir.) 1980, U.S. Dist. Ct. (we. dist.) La. 1978, U.S. Supreme Ct. 1982. Assoc. Sessions, Fishman, Rosenson, Boisfontaine, and Nathan, New Orleans, 1975-80, ptnr., 1980-87; ptnr. Lowe, Stein, Hoffman, Allweiss and Hauver, 1987—. Author: Louisiana Divorce, 1984; mem. La. Law Rev., 1974-75; contbr. articles to profl. jours. Mem. ABA, La. State Bar Assn. (chmn. family law sect. 1984-85), La. Assn. Def. Counsel, New Orleans Bar Assn. (chmn. family law sect. 1991-92), La. State Law Inst., La. Trial Lawyers Assn., Order of Coif, Phi Kappa Phi. Republican. Home: 9625 Garden Oak Ln River Ridge LA 70123 Office: 701 Poydras St Ste 3600 New Orleans LA 70139-7735

LOWE, ROBERT CHARLES, lawyer, banker; b. Seattle, Jan. 15, 1927; s. Martin M. and Helen (Yaster) L.; m. Hope Lucille Sperstad, Mar. 21, 1952; children: Karen, Karlton, Nelson, Inez. B.A., U. Wash., 1953; LL.B., U. Denver, 1959. Bar: Alaska 1961. Accountant Haskins & Sells (C.P.A.s), Los Angeles, 1953-54; agt. Internal Revenue Service, 1954-57; atty. State Alaska, 1960; mem. firm Hughes, Thorsness, Lowe, Gantz & Clark, Anchorage, 1960-75; pres. Safeco Title Agy., Inc., Anchorage, 1975-79; chmn. bd. Peoples Bank & Trust Co., Anchorage. Served with USNR, 1944-46. Mem. Am., Alaska, Anchorage bar assns., Anchorage Estate Planning Council (pres. 1970), Rotary. Home: 2765 S Saint Andrews Dr Sierra Vista AZ 85635-5221

LOWE, ROBERT EDWARD, financial company executive; b. Winnipeg, Man., Can., Oct. 31, 1940; s. Mark Currie and Florence Irene L. Lowe; m. Isabella Love Hunter Liddell, Oct. 1, 1965; children: Susan Patricia, Donna Jane, Mark William. MBA, York U., Toronto, 1975. Chartered acct. Ptnr. Coopers & Lybrand, Toronto, 1971; pres. Coopers & Lybrand Ltd., Toronto, 1975-80, chmn. corp. reorgn. and bankruptcy, 1980-96. Lt. Can. Army Res., 1958-61. Mem. Insolvency Inst. Can., Toronto Golf Club, Can. Club, Nat. Club. Mem. Conservative Party. Presbyterian. Avocations: golf, sailing. Office: Coopers & Lybrand, 145 King St W Ste 2300, Toronto, ON Canada M5H 1V8

LOWE, ROBERT STANLEY, lawyer; b. Herman, Nebr., Apr. 23, 1923; s. Stanley Robert and Ann Marguerite (Feese) L.; m. Anne Kirtland Selden, Dec. 19, 1959; children: Robert James, Margaret Anne. AB, U. Nebr., 1947, JD, 1949. Bar: Wyo. 1949. Ptnr. McAvoy & Lowe, Newcastle, 1949-51, Hickey & Lowe, Rawlins, 1951-55; county and pros. atty. Rawlins, 1955-59, pvt. practice, 1959-67; assoc. dir. Am. Judicature Soc., Chgo., 1967-74; counsel True Oil Co. and affiliates, 1974—; bd. dirs. Hilltop Nat. Bank, Casper, sec., 1981—; legal adv. divsn. Nat. Ski Patrol Sys., 1975-88; city atty. City of Rawlins, 1963-65; atty., asst. sec. Casper Mountain Ski Patrol, 1988—. Mem. Wyo. Ho. of Reps., 1952-54; bd. dirs. Vols. in Probation, 1969-82; leader lawyer del. to China, People to People, 1986; mem. Wyo. Vets. Affairs Coun. 1994—, chmn., 1996—; mem. legis. com. United Vets. Coun. Wyo., 1993—; trustee Troopers Found., Inc., 1994—, pres., 1994—; pres. Caspter WWII Commemorative Assn., 1995-96. Recipient Dedicated Community Worker award Rawlins Jr. C. of C., 1967, Yellow merit star award Nat. Ski Patrol System, 1982, 85, 87, 88. Fellow Am. Bar Found. (life); mem. VFW (life mem.; post adv. 1991-96, nat. aide-de-camp 1993-94, judge adv. dist. 3 Dept. Wyo., 1994—, mil. order of cootie grand judge adv. 1994—), ABA (sec. jud. adminstrn. divsn. lawyers conf., exec. com. 1975-76, chmn. 1977-78, chmn. judicial qualification and selection com. 1986-93, coun. jud. adminstrn. divsn. 1977-78, mem. com. to implement jud. adminstrn. stds. 1978-83, Ho. of Dels. state bar del. 1978-79, 86-87, state del. 1987-93, Assembly del. 1980-83), Am. Judicature Soc. (dir. 1961-67, 85-89, bd. editors 1975-77, Herbert Harley award 1974), Wyo. State Bar (chmn. com. on cts. 1961-67, 77-87), Nebr. State Bar Assn., Ill. State Bar Assn., D.C. Bar, Inter-Am. Bar Assn., Selden Soc., Inst. Jud. Adminstrn., Rocky Mountain Oil and Gas Assn. (legal com. 1976—, chmn. 1979-82, 90-91), Rocky Mountain Mineral Law Found. (trustee 1980-94), Am. Law Inst., Order of Coif, Delta Theta Phi (dist. chancellor 1982-83, chief justice 1983-93, assoc. justice 1993—; Percy J. Power Meml. award 1983, Gold Medallion award 1990), Casper Rotary Club (pres. 1985-86), Casper Rotary Found. (dir., sec. 1990—). Mem. Ch. of Christ, Scientist. Home: 97 Primrose Casper WY 82604-4018 Office: 895 River Cross Rd Casper WY 82601-1758

LOWE, WILLIAM DANIEL, automotive company research executive, consultant; b. Oklahoma City, Dec. 23, 1949; s. Daniel Potter and Nova Jene (Werrell) L.; children: Kellie Christine, William Matthew. BA, Baylor U., 1972; MS, Cen. Mich. U., 1991; PhD, Walden U., 1994. Asst. office mgr. Oldsmobile Divsn., GMC, L.A., 1972-74; dist. mgr. Oldsmobile Divsn. GM, Mpls., L.A., Houston, 1975-83; office mgr. Oldsmobile Divsn., GMC, Kansas City, 1984-88; field mktg. mgr. Oldsmobile divsn. GMC, Lansing, Mich., 1989-90; mktg. mgr. Oldsmobile divsn GMC, Washington, 1991; consumer rsch. mgr. GMC, Lansing, 1992-95, rsch. mgr. Oldsmobile Divsn., 1996—. Republican. Baptist. Avocations: classical music, tennis. Home: 3033 Ingersoll Rd Lansing MI 48906-9152 Office: Oldsmobile Divsn GMC 920 Townsend St Lansing MI 48921-0001

LOWELL, HOWARD PARSONS, government records administrator; b. Rockland, Maine, May 10, 1945; s. Chauncey Vernon Lowell and Delia Coffin (Parsons) Morey; m. Marcia Barrell, Feb. 15, 1969 (div. 1980); m. Charlesa Ann Gatson, July 27, 1985, 1 stepson, Garrett Timmons. BA, U. Me., Orono, 1967; MS, Simmons Coll., 1974. Adminstrn. svcs. officer Maine state archives, Augusta, 1968-72; ednl. specialist Mass. bur libr. ext., Boston, 1974-75; dir. Revere (Mass.) Pub. Libr., 1975-76; freelance cons. Salem, Oreg., 1976-81, Denver, 1976-81; adminstr. Okla. resources br. Okla. Dept. Librs., Oklahoma City, 1981-89; archivist and records administrator State of Del., 1990—; acting dir. N.E. Document Conservation Ctr., Andover, Mass., 1978. Commr. Nat. Hist. Publs. and Records Commn., 1997—. Mem. Acad. Cert. Archivists, Nat. Assn. Govt. Archives and Records Adminstrs. (bd. dirs. 1985-87, 1995-96, pres. 1992-94), Phi Beta Kappa, Phi Kappa Phi, Phi Alpha Theta, Beta Phi Mu. Democrat. Mem. Unitarian Ch. Office: Del Pub Archives Hall of Records PO Box 1401 Dover DE 19903

LOWELL, JULIET, author; b. N.Y.C., Aug. 7, 1901; d. Max and Helen (Kohut) Loewenthal; m. Leo E. Lowell, Aug. 17, 1922 (dec.); children—Margot, Ross; m. Ben Lowell, 1945. A.M., Vassar Coll., 1922. lectr. Vassar Coll., June 1987. Writer, from 1920, newspaper columnist, lectr.; writer comedy script; appeared on radio programs Underwood Typewriter, Ford Motor Co., Sanka Coffee, also TV shows throughout U.S., Can.; made films for Fox, Warner Bros. motion picture cos., 30 shorts for RKO.; author: Dumb-Belles Lettres, 1933, Dear Sir, 1944, Dear Sir or Madam, 1946, Dear Mr. Congressman, 1948, Dear Hollywood, 1950, Dear Doctor, 1955, 68, Dear Justice, A Book for the Just, the Unjust, and Those Who Just Like to Laugh, 1958, Dear Folks, 1960, Dear Man of Affairs, 1961, Dear VIP, 1963, It Strikes Me Funny, 1964, Boners in the News, 1967, Humor U.S.A, 1968, Dear Candidate, 1968, Racy Tales For Adults and Adultresses, 1969; contbr. article on war humor to Ency. Brit, 1947, articles to nat. mags.; author weekly column Juliet Lowell's Celebrity Letters, Sunday supplement Family Weekly, from 1972. Chmn. book com. N.Y.-Tokyo Sister City Affiliation.; Mem. bd. Hecksher Found. for Children, ID II. Mem. Authors League Am., Internat. Platform Assn., Vassar Alumnae Assn. Clubs: Woman's Press, Overseas Press. Home: Chestnut Hill Mass. *Doing what I like to do has provided me with a living and kept me content, sharing my fun with others. I have been able to find a bright spot in most situations. Naturally there have been problems and sorrows. The only way to entirely circumvent them is to be stillborn. I prefer to have been born alive and lively. Born on a train, lower berth. Date of birth August 7, date of death as yet undetermined.*

LOWEN, GERARD GUNTHER, mechanical engineering educator; b. Munich, Germany, Oct. 25, 1921; came to U.S., 1939; s. Charles and Stefanie (Frank) L.; m. Doris Julie Wolff, July 2, 1952; children: Deborah Lowen-Klein, Nicole Vianna, Daniel. BSME, CCNY, 1954; M of Mech. Engring., Columbia U., 1958; D of Engring., Tech. U. Munich, 1963. Registered profl. engr., N.Y. Machinist, tool and diemaker Germany and the U.S., 1938-54; lectr. mech. engring. CCNY, 1954-59, asst. prof., 1959-64, assoc. prof., 1964-69, prof., 1969—, Herbert Kayser prof., 1987—, chmn. mech. engring. dept., 1987-90; assoc. dean grad. studies, engring., 1990—; cons. in field. Contbr. articles to profl. jours.; patentee in field. Named Outstanding Tchr., CCNY, 1984; NSF grantee, 1968-89. Fellow ASME (machine design award 1987); mem. AAAS, Am. Soc. Engring. Edn., Verein Deutscher Ingenieure (corr.), Soc. Mfg. Engrs., N.Y. Acad. Scis. Jewish. Avocations: reading, history, hiking. Home: 484 Eisenhower Ct Wyckoff NJ 07481-2206 Office: CCNY Grad Engring Office Convent Ave New York NY 10031-2604

LOWEN, WALTER, mechanical engineering educator; b. Cologne, Germany, May 17, 1921; came to U.S., 1936, naturalized, 1945; m. Sylvia Lowen, May 22, 1943; children: Robert Gary, John Gordon. B.S. in Mech. Engring, N.C. State Coll., 1943, M.S., 1947; student, Oak Ridge Sch. Reactor Tech., 1955; D.Sc., Swiss Fed. Inst. Tech., 1963. Instr. N.C. State Coll., 1943-47; faculty Union Coll., Schenectady, 1947-68; prof. mech. engring. Union Coll., 1956-68, chmn. div. engring., 1956-60, 66-67, acting chmn. mech. engring. dept., 1959-60, chmn. dept., 1966-67; prof., dir. Sch. Advanced Tech. SUNY, Binghamton, 1967-68, dean Sch. Advanced Tech., 1968-77, prof. systems sci., 1968-90, Thomas J. Watson sch. prof. emeritus, 1991—; cons. Oak Ridge Nat. Lab., Knolls Atomic Power Lab., Alco Products, Inst. Applied Tech. of Nat. Bur. Standards.; adj. faculty IBM Systems Research Inst., 1979-89; vice chmn. Niskayuna Sch. Centralization Bldg. Com., 1954; co-founder Vols. for Internat. Tech. Assistance, Inc., 1960—. Author: Dichotomies of the Mind, 1982. NSF fellow to Switzerland, 1961-62. Mem. ASME (sect. vice-chmn. local chpt. 1959-60), Am. Soc. Engring. Edn., Sigma Xi, Tau Beta Pi, Pi Tau Sigma, Phi Kappa Phi. Home: 152 Moore Ave Binghamton NY 13903-3124

LOWENFELD, ANDREAS FRANK, law educator, arbitrator; b. Berlin, May 30, 1930; s. Henry and Yela (Herschkowitsch) L.; m. Elena Machado, Aug. 11, 1962; children: Julian, Marianna. AB magna cum laude, Harvard U., 1951, LLB magna cum laude, 1955. Bar: N.Y. 1955, U.S. Supreme Ct. 1961. Assoc. Hyde and de Vries, N.Y.C., 1957-61; spl. asst. to legal adv. U.S. Dept. State, 1961-63; asst. legal adviser for econ. affairs, 1963-65, dep. legal adviser, 1965-66; fellow John F. Kennedy Inst. Politics, Harvard U., Cambridge, Mass., 1966-67; prof. law Sch. Law, NYU, N.Y.C., 1967—, Charles L. Denison prof. law, 1981-94, Herbert and Rose Rubin prof. internat. law, 1994—; arbitrator internat. comml. panels ICC. Mem. ABA, Assn. of Bar of City of N.Y., Am. Soc. Internat. Law, Am. Arbitration Assn. (arbitrator), Coun. Fgn. Rels., Inst. de Droit Internat. Author: (with Abram Chayes and Thomas Ehrlich) International Legal Process, 1968-69; Aviation Law, Cases and Materials, 1972, 2d edit., 1981; International Economic Law, vol. I, 1975, 3d edit., 1996, vol. II, 1976, 2d edit., 1982, vol. III, 1977, 2d edit., 1983, vol. IV, 1977, 2d edit., 1984, vol. VI, 1979, 2d edit., 1983, Conflict of Laws, Federal, State and International Perspectives, 1986, International Litigation and Arbitration, 1993, International Litigation: The Quest for Reasonableness, 1996; editor, co-author: Expropriation in the Americas: A Comparative Law Study, 1971; assoc. reporter Am. Law Inst. Restatement on Foreign Relations Law; contbr. articles and book revs. on pub. internat. law, internat. econ. law, air law, conflict of laws, arbitration, history and politics to profl. jours. Mem. Gray's Inn (assoc.). Home: 5776 Palisade Ave Bronx NY 10471-1212 Office: NYU Sch Law 40 Washington Sq S New York NY 10012-1005

LOWENFELS, FRED M., lawyer; b. Richmond, Va., Mar. 22, 1944; s. Fred C. and Joan (Weber) L.; m. Joan Roberta Brafman, June 10, 1974; children: Erica Anne, Helene Beth. AB, Harvard U., 1965, JD, 1968; postgrad., Univ. Libre de Bruxelles, 1968-69. Bar: N.Y. 1969. Assoc. Wolf, Haldenstein, Adler, Freeman & Herz, N.Y.C., 1970-74; sr. v.p., gen. counsel Transammonia Inc., N.Y.C., 1974—. Trustee Jewish Home and Hosp. for the Aged, N.Y.C., 1974—. Mem. Assn. Bar. City of N.Y., Am. Corp. Counsel Assn., Harvard Club N.Y.C. Office: Transammonia Inc 350 Park Ave New York NY 10022-6022

LOWENFELS, LEWIS DAVID, lawyer; b. N.Y.C., June 9, 1935; s. Seymour and Jane (Phillips) L.; m. Fern Gelford, Aug. 15, 1965; children: Joshua, Jacqueline. BA magna cum laude, Harvard U., 1957, LLB, 1961. Bar: N.Y. 1961; lic. corp. and securities atty. Ptnr. Tolins & Lowenfels, N.Y.C., 1967—; adj. prof. law Seton Hall U. Law Sch; lectr. law Practicing Law Inst., Southwestern Legal Found., U. Minn. Fed. Bar Assn., 1972; pub. gov. Am. Stock Exch., 1993-96. Co-author: Securities Fraud and Commodities Fraud, 6 vols., 1996; contbr. articles to profl. jours. With USAR, 1957-63. Mem. ABA (fed. regulation of securities com. 1978—, lectr.), N.Y. County Lawyers Assn. (securities and exchanges com. 1974—), Phi Beta Kappa, Harvard Club. Avocations: reading, writing, athletics. Office: Tolins & Lowenfels 12 E 49th St New York NY 10017-1028

LOWENHAUPT, CHARLES ABRAHAM, lawyer; b. St. Louis, May 19, 1947; s. Henry Cronbach and Cecile (Koven) L.; m. Rosalyn Lee Sussman, Dec. 28, 1969; children: Elizabeth Anne, Rebecca Jane. BA cum laude, Harvard U., 1969; JD magna cum laude, U. Mich., 1973. Bar: Mo. 1973, U.S. Dist. Ct. (ea. dist.) Mo. 1975, U.S. Ct. Appeals (8th cir.) 1975, U.S. Tax Ct. 1975, U.S. Ct. Claims 1975, U.S. Supreme Ct. 1987. Law clk. to presiding justice U.S. Tax Ct., Washington, 1973-75; ptnr. Lowenhaupt, Chasnoff, Armstrong & Mellitz, St. Louis, 1977-94; advisor Inst. for Pvt. Investors, 1991-93; mem. Lowenhaupt & Chasnoff, LLC, St. Louis, 1994—; speaker Nat. Assn. Ind. Schs., St. Louis Assn. Legal Assts., Washington U. Bus. Sch., Inst. for Pvt. Investors, numerous others; mem. adv. bd. dirs. Cottonwood Gulch Found., Thoreau, N.Mex., Textile Mus., Washington. Bd. dirs. Ctrl. West End Assn., Inc., St. Louis, 1976-80, Temple Emanuel, St. Louis, 1982-89, Craft Alliance St. Louis, 1987-90, Helicon Found., San Diego, 1989—, St. Louis Met. Assn. for Philanthropy, 1997—; bd. dirs. St. Louis Regional Med. Ctr. Found., 1993—, chmn. bd. dirs., 1995—; bd. dirs. St. Louis Zoo Found., 1993—, sec., 1995—; mem. What Works com. St. Louis Bus. Jour., 1994—; sec. Gladys & Henry Crown Ctr. for Sr. Living, 1996—; bd. govs. Clements Libr. Assocs., U. Mich., 1997—. Mem. ABA (tax section, estate and gift section, real property section, probate and trust law, task force legal financial planning, chmn. generation-skipping transfer tax subcom., estate and gift tax com. tax sect. 1995—), Mo. Bar Assn. (tax section, probate and trust section), Bar Assn. of Met. St. Louis (tax section, real property and development sect.), Order of the Coif, St. Louis Estate Planning Coun., Mo. Athletic Club, Harvard Club of N.Y.C., Noonday Club. Home: 58 Kingsbury Pl Saint Louis MO 63112-1859 Office: Lowenhaupt & Chasnoff LLC 10 S Broadway Ste 600 Saint Louis MO 63102-1733

LOWENSTEIN, ALAN VICTOR, lawyer; b. Newark, Aug. 30, 1913; s. Isaac and Florence (Cohen) L.; m. Amy Lieberman, Nov. 23, 1938; children: John, Roger, Jane Lowenstein Forsyth. A.B., U. Mich., 1933; M.A., U. Chgo., 1935; LL.B., Harvard U., 1936. Bar: N.J. 1936. Practiced in Newark and Roseland, 1936—; sr. partner Lowenstein, Sandler, Kohl, Fisher & Boylan, 1961—; assoc. atty. Temporary Nat. Econ. Com., 1938-39; asst. prof. Rutgers U. Law Sch., 1951-57; chmn. N.J. Corp. Law Revision Commn., 1959-72; spl. hearing officer Dept. Justice, 1961-65; chmn. bd. United Steel & Aluminum Corp., 1976-96. Pres. Jewish Community Council Essex County, 1950-53, United Way Essex and West Hudson, 1953-55; chmn. Newark Charter Commn., 1953, Newark Citizens Com. Mcpl. Govt., 1954-58, Newark Community Survey, 1959-60; v.p. Council Jewish Fedns., 1965-68, assoc. treas., 1981; pres. N.J. Symphony Orch., 1971-73, chmn. bd., 1973-76; mem. adv. council Rutgers U. Sch. Social Work, 1955-64; vice chmn. Liberty State Park Devel. Corp., 1984—; bd. overseers Rutgers U. Found., 1994—. Recipient Brotherhood award Nat. Conf. Christians and Jews, 1972, Trustees award for Disting. Community Service, N.J. Inst. Tech., 1984, Equal Justice award Legal Services N.J./N.J. State Bar Assn., 1988. Mem. ABA, N.J. Bar Assn., Essex County Bar Assn. (Pro-Bono Achievement award 1994), Am. Judicature Soc., Order of Coif, Phi Beta Kappa (v.p. N.J. 1951-52), Phi Kappa Phi, Tau Kappa Alpha. Home: 285 N Ridgewood Rd South Orange NJ 07079-1503 also: RR 3 Box 3892 Vergennes VT 05491-8601 Office: Lowenstein Sandler et al 65 Livingston Ave Roseland NJ 07068-1725

LOWENSTEIN, DEREK IRVING, physicist; b. Hampton Court, Eng., Apr. 26, 1943; came to U.S., 1946; s. Siegfried and Ilse (Mildenberg) L.; m. Elaine Hartmann, July 6, 1968; children: Jessica R., Peter D. BS, CCNY, 1964; MS, U. Pa., 1965, PhD, 1969. Postdoctoral fellow U. Pa., Phila., 1969-70; research assoc. U. Pitts., 1970-73; asst. physicist Brookhaven Nat. Lab., Upton, N.Y., 1973-75; assoc. physicist Brookhaven Nat. Lab., 1975-77, physicist, 1977-83, sr. physicist, 1983—, head Exptl. Planning and Support div., 1977-84, dep. chmn. accelerator dept., 1981-84, chmn. Alternating Gradient Synchrotron dept., 1984—; assoc. mem. U.S.-Russia Joint Coordinating Commn. on Fundamental Properties of Matter, 1983—, U.S.-Japan Commn. on High Energy Physics, 1984—; mem. Dept. of Energy High Energy Physics Adv. Panel, 1993-96. Contbr. articles on particle and accelerator physics to profl. jours. Fellow Am. Phys. Soc.; mem. AAAS, N.Y. Acad. Scis., Sigma Xi. Office: Brookhaven Nat Lab AGS Dept Upton NY 11973

LOWENSTEIN, JAMES GORDON, former diplomat, international consultant; b. Long Branch, N.J., Aug. 6, 1927; s. Melvyn Gordon and Katherine Price (Goldsmith) L.; m. Dora Laurinda Richardson, June 11, 1955 (div. 1977); children: Laurinda Vinson, Price Gordon; m. Anne Cornely de la Selle, July 4, 1981. Grad., Loomis Sch., 1945; B.A., Yale U., 1949; postgrad., Harvard Law Sch., 1955-56. With Office Spl. Rep. in Europe, Econ. Cooperation Adminstrn., Paris, 1950-51; mem. U.S. Spl. Mission to Yugoslavia, Sarajevo, 1951; fgn. svc. officer Bur. European Affairs Dept. State, 1957-58; fgn. service officer Am. Embassy, Colombo, Ceylon, 1959-61, Belgrade, Yugoslavia, 1961-64; cons. Fgn. Relations Com., U.S. Senate, Washington, 1965-74; prin. dep. asst. sec. state for European affairs Washington, 1974-77; ambassador to Luxembourg, 1977-81; with Bur. European Affairs, Dept. State, 1981-82; ptnr. IRC Group, Washington, 1982-87; sr. cons. APCO Assocs., Washington, 1988—; mem. internat. observer group Sri Lanka elections, 1993, 94, sr. elections adv. Osce Mission to Bosnia, 1996, 97; vice chmn. U.S. Bus. Coun. for Southeastern Europe: chmn. bd. Baltic Investments, S.A., Luxembourg; bd. dirs. AIS Worldwide Fund Ltd.; past sec. bd. Emerging Eastern European Fund; co-founder, bd. dirs. French-Am. Found.; bd. dirs. Washington Found. for European Studies, Refugees Internat.; past mem. adv. coun. Sch. Advanced Internat. Studies and Bologna (Italy) Ctr. Johns Hopkins U. Lt. (j.g.) USNR, 1952-55. Decorated chevalier Légion d'Honneur (France); Grand Croix de la Couronne de Chene (Luxembourg). Mem. Coun. Fgn. Rels., Internat. Inst. Strategic Studies (London). Clubs: Metropolitan (Washington); Army-Navy Country (Arlington, Va.); Century Assn., Knickerbocker (N.Y.C.); Harbor (Seal Harbor, Maine); Travellers, Racing (Paris). Home: 3139 O St NW Washington DC 20007-3117 also: 32 Rue de Verneuil, 75007 Paris France Office: 1615 L St NW Ste 900 Washington DC 20036-5623

LOWENSTEIN, LOUIS, legal educator; b. N.Y.C., June 13, 1925; s. Louis and Ralphina (Steinhardt) L.; m. Helen Libby Udell, Feb. 12, 1953; children: Roger Spector, Jane Ruth, Barbara Ann. B.S., Columbia, 1947, LL.B., 1953; M.F.S., U. Md., 1951. Bar: N.Y. 1953. Pvt. practice law N.Y.C., 1954-78; Assoc. Judge Stanley H. Fuld, N.Y. Ct. Appeals, 1953-54; assoc., then partner Hays, Sklar & Herzberg, 1954-68; partner Nickerson, Kramer, Lowenstein, Nessen, Kamin & Soll, 1968-78; Simon H. Rifkind prof. emeritus law and fin. Columbia U. Law Sch., 1980—, project dir. Instl. Investor Project, 1988-94; pres. Supermarkets Gen. Corp., Woodbridge, N.J., 1978-79; bd. dirs. Liz Claiborne, Inc. 1988-96. Author: What's Wrong with Wall Street, 1988, Sense and Nonsense in Corporate Finance, 1991; contbr., co-editor: Knights, Raiders and Targets, 1988; editor in chief Columbia Law Rev., 1951-53. Vice pres., mem. exec. com. Fedn. Jewish Philanthropies N.Y.; pres. Jewish Bd. Family and Children's Services N.Y., 1974-78; trustee Beth Israel Med. Center, N.Y.C., 1975-81; dir. Goddard-Riverside Cmty. Ctr., 1996—. Served to lt. (j.g.) USNR, 1943-46. Mem. Am. Bar Assn., Assn. of Bar of City of N.Y., Am. Law Inst. Home: 1 Fountain Sq Larchmont NY 10538-4105 Office: Columbia U Law Sch 435 W 116th St New York NY 10027-7201

LOWENSTEIN, PETER DAVID, lawyer; b. N.Y.C., Dec. 31, 1935; s. Melvyn Gordon and Katherine Price (Goldsmith) L.; m. Constance Cohen; children from previous marriage: Anthony, Kate E., Christopher. BA, Trinity Coll., 1958; LLB, Georgetown U., 1961. Bar: Conn. 1962, N.Y. 1963. With SEC, Washington, 1961-63; assoc. Whitman & Ransom, N.Y.C., 1963-70, ptnr., 1970-83; sec., gen. counsel Value Line, Inc., N.Y.C., 1983-87; v.p., sec., gen. counsel Service Am. Corp., Stamford, Conn., 1988-90; ptnr. O'Connor, Morris & Jones, Greenwich, Conn., 1990-92, pvt. practice, 1992—; legal counsel Value Line Mutual Funds. Bd. dirs. Grand St. Settlement, N.Y.C., 1970-92, Greenwich Health Assn., Conn., 1978-85; bd. dirs. Greenwich chpt. ARC, 1989-94, vice chmn., 1991-93. Mem. Nantucket Yacht Club, Greenwich Field Club. Home: 496 Valley Rd Cos Cob CT 06807-1627 Office: Two Greenwich Plz Ste 100 Greenwich CT 06830-5436

LOWENSTEIN, RALPH LYNN, university dean emeritus; b. Danville, Va., Mar. 8, 1930; s. Henry and Rachel (Berman) L.; m. Bronia Grace Levenson, Feb. 6, 1955; children: Joan, Henry. BA, Columbia U., 1951, MS in Journalism, 1952; PhD in Journalism, U. Mo., 1967. Reporter Danville (Va.) Register, 1952, El Paso Times, 1954-57; asst. prof. journalism U. Tex. at El Paso, 1956-62, assoc. prof., 1962-65; publs. editor Freedom of Info. Ctr., Columbia, Mo., 1965-67; vis. prof., head journalistic studies Tel Aviv U., 1967-68; assoc. prof. Sch. Journalism, U. Mo., Columbia, 1968-70; prof. Sch. Journalism, U. Mo., 1970-76, chmn. news-editorial dept., 1975-76; press critic CBS Morning News, 1975-76; dean Coll. Journalism and Communications, U. Fla., Gainesville, 1976-94. Author: Bring My Sons from Far, 1966; (with John C. Merrill) Media, Messages and Men, 2nd edit., 1979, Macromedia, 1990, Pragmatic Fund-Raising, 1997; editor: (with Paul Fisher) Race and the News Media, 1967. Served with Israeli Army, 1948-49; AUS, 1952-54. Recipient Research in Journalism award Sigma Delta Chi, 1971, Disting. Svc. award Columbia Journalism Alumni, 1957, 30th Anniversary award State of Israel, 1978, Freedom Forum Journalism Adminstr. of Yr. award, 1994. Mem. Assn. Edn. in Journalism and Mass Comm. (pres. 1990-91), Kappa Tau Alpha. Home: 1705 NW 22nd Dr Gainesville FL 32605-3953

LOWENSTINE, MAURICE RICHARD, JR., retired steel executive; b. Valparaiso, Ind., Feb. 28, 1910; s. Maurice Richard and Etta (Hamburger) L.; m. Miriam Jean Richards, Nov. 9, 1940; children: Martha Jean, Linda Jane, Mark Richards. Student, U. Mich., 1928-29, U. Ariz., 1929-30. With Central Steel & Wire Co., Chgo., 1932-71, exec. v.p., treas., dir., 1942-71; Chmn. exec. com. Steel Service Center Inst., 1962-64. Chmn. bd. Greater Hinsdale Cmty. Chest, 1960; bd. dirs. Chgo. area coun. Boy Scouts Am., 1957-97, Hinsdale Cmty. House, 1961-64; vice commodore Chgo. Sea Explorer Scouts, 1973-97. Episcopalian. Clubs: Chgo. Yacht; Ruth Lake Country. Address: 407 E 3rd St Hinsdale IL 60521-4224

LOWENTHAL, ABRAHAM FREDERIC, international relations educator; b. Hyannis, Mass., Apr. 6, 1941; s. Eric Isaac and Suzanne (Moos) L.; m. Janet Wyzanski, June 24, 1962 (div. 1983); children: Linda Claudina, Michael Francis; m. Jane S. Jaquette, Jan. 20, 1991. A.B., Harvard U., 1961, M.P.A., 1964, Ph.D., 1971; postgrad., Harvard Law Sch., 1961-62. Tng. assoc. Ford Found., Dominican Republic, 1962-64; asst. rep. Ford Found., Lima, Peru, 1969-72; asst. dir., then dir. of studies Coun. Fgn. Rels., N.Y.C., 1974-76; dir. Latin Am. program Woodrow Wilson Internat. Ctr. for Scholars, Washington, 1977-83; exec. dir. Inter-Am. Dialogue, Washington, 1982-92; prof. Sch. Internat. Rels., U. So. Calif., Los Angeles, 1984—; dir., ctr. internat. studies U. So. Calif., 1992—; pres. Pacific Coun. Internat. Policy, L.A., 1995—; vis. fellow, rsch. assoc. Ctr. Internat. Studies, Princeton U., 1972-74; vis. lectr. polit. sci. Cath. U. Santiago, Dominican Republic, 1966; lectr. Princeton U., 1974; spl. cons. Commn. U.S.-L.Am. rels., N.Y.C., 1974-76; mem. internat. adv. bd. Ctr. U.S.-Mex. Rels., U. Calif.-San Diego, 1981-94; mem. internat. adv. bd. Helen Kellogg Inst., 1984-95; cons. Ford Found., 1974-90. Author: The Dominican Intervention, 1972, 2nd edit., 1995, Partners in Conflict: The United States and Latin America in 1990s, 1991; editor, contbg. author: The Peruvian Experiment: Continuity and Change Under Military Rule, 1975, Armies and Politics in Latin America, 1976, Exporting Democracy: The United States and Latin America, 1991; co-editor, contbg. author: The Peruvian Experiment Reconsidered, 1983, The California-Mexico Connection, 1993; editor Latin Am. and Caribbean Record, vol. IV, 1985-86, vol. V, 1986-87, Latin America in a New World, 1994, Constructing Democratic Governance: Latin America, 1996; mem. editorial bd. Jour. Inter-Am. Studies and World Affairs, Hemisphere, Internat. Security, 1977-85, Wilson Quar., 1977-83; contbr. articles to profl. jours. Mem. nat. adv. coun. Amnesty Internat., 1977-83, Ctr. for Nat. Policy, 1986—. Mem. Internat. Inst. Strategic Studies, Am. Polit. Sci. Assn. (coun. 1979-81), Latin Am. Studies (exec. coun. 1979-81), Coun. Fgn. Rels., Overseas Devel. Coun., Human Rights Watch, Calif. com. Democrat. Jewish. Home: 903 Stanford St Santa Monica CA 90403-2223 Office: Pacific Coun Internat Policy Los Angeles CA 90089-0035

LOWENTHAL, CONSTANCE, art historian; b. N.Y.C., Aug. 29, 1945; d. Jesse and Helen (Oberstein) L. BA cum laude, Brandeis U., 1967; AM, Inst. Fine Arts, NYU, 1969; PhD, Inst. Fine Arts, NYU, N.Y.C., 1976. Mem. faculty Sarah Lawrence Coll., Bronxville, N.Y., 1975-78; asst. mus. educator Met. Mus. Art, N.Y.C., 1978-85; exec. dir. Internat. Found. Art Research, N.Y.C., 1985—; bd. dirs. Ctr. for Edn. Studies, Inc. Regular contbr. Art Crime Update column Wall Street Jour., 1988—; mem. editl. bd.: The Spoils of War, World War II and Its Aftermath: The Loss, Reappearance and Recovery of Cultural Property, 1997; contbr. articles to Mus. News and other profl. publs. Office: Intl Found for Art 500 5th Ave New York NY 10110

LOWENTHAL, HENRY, retired greeting card company executive; b. Frankfurt, Germany, Oct. 26, 1931; came to U.S., 1940, naturalized, 1945; s. Adolf and Kella (Suss) L.; m. Miriam Katzenstein, June 29, 1958; children—Sandra, Jeffry, Joan Chana, Benjamin, Avi. B.B.A. cum laude, City U. N.Y., 1952, M.B.A., 1953; J.D., N.Y. U., 1962. CPA. Lectr. acctg. Baruch Coll., N.Y.C., 1952-53; auditor Price Waterhouse & Co., N.Y.C., 1955-62; v.p., controller Am. Greetings Corp., Cleve., 1962-68, controller, 1966-68, sr. v.p., chief fin. officer, 1977-95, sr. v.p., 1995-97; v.p. fin., treas. Tremco Inc., Cleve., 1968-77; mem. adv. bd. Case Western Res. U. Dept. Accountancy, 1986-97. Chmn. bd. dirs. Rabbinical Coll. Telshe, 1974-77, v.p., 1977-90; v.p. Hebrew Acad. Cleve., 1977-97; pres. Agudath Israel of Cleve., 1978-95, treas., 1995-97; v.p. Agudath Israel Am., 1989—, chmn. regional v.p.s, 1996—; bd. dirs. Jewish Cmty. Fedn., Cleve., 1979-88, 90-95, chmn. audit com., 1992-95; trustee Mt. Sinai Med. Ctr., Cleve., 1992-96; chmn. citizens rev. com. Cleveland Heights-Univ. Heights Sch., 1972-73, mem. lay fin. com., 1974-79; mem. Cleveland Heights Citizens Adv. Com. for Cmty. Devel., 1976-79. With AUS, 1953-55. Mem. AICPA, Assn. of Publicly Traded Cos. (budget & fin. com. 1986-97, bd. dirs. 1987-97, treas. 1990-97), Fin. Execs. Inst. (sec. N.E. Ohio chpt. 1979-80), Ohio Soc. CPA's, Greater Cleve. Growth Assn., Beta Gamma Sigma, Beta Alpha Psi. Home: 6115 Biltmore Ave Baltimore MD 21215

LOWENTHAL, JACOB, finance executive; b. Frankfurt, Germany, July 27, 1938; came to U.S., 1941; s. Adolf and Kella (Suss) L.; m. Fanny Z. Rothschild, Aug. 27, 1960; children: Joyce Lowenthal Meisner, David, Evelyn Weisz Lowenthal, Leon A. BBA, CCNY, 1959. CPA, N.Y. Jr. acct. Skydell & Shatz CPAs, N.Y.C., 1959-60; mgr. George Funaro & Co. CPAs, N.Y.C., 1960-68; contr., asst. sec. Advanced Computer Tech, N.Y.C., 1968-76; contr. AGS Computers Inc., Mountainside, N.J., 1976-80, Software Design Assocs., N.Y.C., 1980-83; v.p. fin. and adminstrn. Vista Concepts Inc. subs. NYNEX, N.Y.C., 1983-94; computer cons. N.Y.C., 1994—. EMT Hatzalah, N.Y.C., 1980—; treas. Congregation Khal-Adath Jeshurun, N.Y.C., 1977—. Mem. AICPA, N.Y. State Soc. CPAs, Cheshbonot. Home: 100 Bennett Ave New York NY 10033-3000

LOWENTROUT, PETER MURRAY, religious studies educator; b. Salinas, Calif., Mar. 14, 1948; m. Christine Ione, Sept. 30, 1980; children: Mary, Brandon. AB, U. Calif., Riverside, 1973; PhD, U. So. Calif., L.A., 1983. Prof. religious studies Calif. State U., Long Beach, 1981—. Contbr. articles to profl. jours. Capt. Orange County Fire Dept., Orange, Calif., 1977-94. Mem. Am. Acad. Religion (regional pres. 1989-90), Ctr. for Theology and Lit. U. Durham (Eng.), Sci. Fi. Rsch. Assoc. (pres. 1991, 92). Office: Calif State U Dept Religious Studies 1250 N Bellflower Blvd Long Beach CA 90840-0006 *Though it is the hatred in life that seems most quickly to catch our attention, there is far more love in the world. Learning to see that love and helping others to do so is life's best work.*

LOWER, JOYCE Q., lawyer; b. Milford, Mass., July 15, 1943; d. Raymond Joseph and Marion (Little) Quenneville; m. Michael Rhodes Lower, Aug. 7, 1965; children: Anthony Miles, Courtney Anne. BA, Wellesley Coll., 1965; JD, U. Mich., 1967. Pvt. practice Bloomfield Hills, Mich., 1968—. Co-author: Michigan Estate Planning, Drafting and Estate Administration, 1989. Pres. YMCA Met. Detroit, 1984-86; trustee Roeper City and Country Sch., Bloomfield Hills, Mich., 1981-86, Fin. and Estate Planning Coun., Detroit, Oakland County Estate Planning Coun.; bd. dirs. United Cmty. Svcs., Detroit, 1990-95, United Way Cmty. Svcs., 1995—, Alzheimers Assn., Detroit, 1990-92. Mem. ABA, DAR, Mich. Bar Assn., Oakland County Bar Assn., Village Club, Soc. Mayflower Descendants Mich. (state historian). Office: Suite 100-A 1500 Woodward Ave Ste 100-a Bloomfield Hills MI 48304-3973

LOWER, ROBERT CASSEL, lawyer, educator; b. Oak Park, Ill., Jan. 8, 1947; s. Paul Elton and Doris Thatcher (Heaton) L.; m. Jean Louise Lower, Aug. 24, 1968 (dec. Aug. 1985); children: David Elton, Andrew Bennett, James Philip Thatcher; m. Cheryl Bray, July 26, 1986. A.B. magna cum laude with highest honors, Harvard U., 1969, J.D., 1972. Bar: Ga. 1972. Assoc. Alston & Bird, Atlanta, 1972-78, ptnr., 1978—; adj. prof. Emory U., 1978-85, 92. Contbr. articles to law jours. Co-founder, pres. Ga. Vol. Lawyers for the Arts, Inc., 1975-79; chmn. Fulton County (Ga.) Arts Council, 1979-87; trustee Woodruff Arts Ctr., 1988-95, Piedmont Coll., Ga. Found. Ind. Colls. Mem. Ga. Bar Assn., Atlanta Bar Assn., Midtown Bus. Assn. (bd. dirs. 1988-90), Author's Ct., Harvard Club (Ga.), Ansley Golf Club, Phi Beta Kappa. Presbyterian. Avocations: running, music, bonsai. Home: 935 Plymouth Rd NE Atlanta GA 30306-3009 Office: Alston & Bird One Atlantic Ctr 1201 W Peachtree St NW Atlanta GA 30309-3400

LOWERY, CHARLES DOUGLAS, history educator, academic administrator; b. Greenville, Ala., May 8, 1937; s. Reuben F. and Frances Louise (Jordan) L.; m. Sara Bradford, June 24, 1961; children: Thomas Bradford, Douglas Trenton, Charles Daniel. BA, Huntingdon Coll., 1959; MA, Fla. State U., 1961; PhD, U. Va., 1966. Asst. prof. history Ball State U., Muncie, Ind., 1964-66; from asst. prof. to prof. Miss. State U., Starkville, 1966—, head dept. history, 1985—, asst. dean Coll. Arts and Scis., 1971-74, assoc. dean, 1974-81, dir. Inst. for Humanities, 1981-85. Author: James Barbour: The Biography of A Jeffersonian Republican, 1984, (with others) America: The Middle Period, 1973; Encyclopedia of African-American Civil Rights: From Emancipation to the Present, 1992; contbr. articles to profl. jours. Mem. Citizen's Adv. Coun., Starkville, 1971; mem. Miss. Com. for Humanities, Jackson, 1986-88; vice chmn. Miss. Humanities Coun., Jackson, 1988-89. Grantee NEH, 1980, 81, 84, Miss. Humanities Coun., 1983, 84, 88. Mem. Orgn. Am. Historians, Soc. Historians of Early Am. Rep., So. Hist. Soc., Miss. Hist. Soc. (com. chmn. 1989-90). Democrat. Presbyterian. Avocations: camping, travel, fishing, historical preservation. Home: 609 Sherwood Rd Starkville MS 39759-4009 Office: Miss State U Dept History Drawer H Mississippi State MS 39762

LOWERY, DOMINIC GERALD (NICK), professional football player; b. Munich, Germany, May 27, 1956. BA, government, Dartmouth U., 1978. Place kicker New England Patriots, 1978, Kansas City Chiefs, 1980-94, N.Y. Jets, 1994-96. Played in Pro Bowls 1981, 90, 92; NFL All-Pro team kicker, The Sporting News, 1990. NFL record for most seasons (11) with 100 or more points, 19 team records with the Kansas City Chiefs including ALL-Time Leading Scorer. Most accurate kicker in NFL history. 2nd most field goals in NFL history.

LOWERY, LEE LEON, JR., civil engineer; b. Corpus Christi, Tex., Dec. 26, 1938; s. Lee Leon and Blanche (Dietrich) L.; children: Kelli Lane, Christianne Lindsey. B.S. in Civil Engring, Tex. A&M U., 1960, M.E., 1961, Ph.D., 1965. Prof. dept. civil engring. Tex. A&M U., 1960; rsch. engr. Tex. A&M Rsch. Found., 1962—; pres. Pile Dynamics Found. Engring., Inc., Bryan, Tex., 1962—; pres. Tex. Measurements, Inc., College Station, 1965—; pres. Interface Engring. Assos., Inc., College Station, 1969—; dir. Braver Corp. Bd. dirs. Deep Found. Inst. Recipient Faculty Disting. Achievement Teaching award Tex. A&M U., 1979, Zachary Teaching award, 1989, 91, award of merit Tex. A&M Hon. Soc., 1991; NDEA fellow, 1960-63. Mem. ASCE, NSPE, Tex. Soc. Profl. Engrs., Sigma Xi, Phi Kappa Phi, Tau Beta Pi. Baptist. Achievements include patents in field. Home: 2905 S College Ave Bryan TX 77801-2510 Office: Tex A&M U Dept Civil Engring College Station TX 77843

LOWERY, WILLA DEAN, obstetrician-gynecologist; b. Caryville, Fla., Apr. 16, 1927; d. Ernest and Nadine (Fowler) L. BS in Chemistry, Stetson U., 1948; MS in Microbiology, U. Fla., 1952; MD, U. Miami, 1959; MPH, U. Pitts., 1963; MDiv in Theology, Pitt. Theol. Sem., 1995. Diplomate Am. Bd. Ob-Gyn.; ordained to ministry Presbyn. Ch. Microbiologist Fla. Dept. Pub. Health, Jacksonville, 1948-52, pub. health officer, 1959-65; microbiologist U. S. Operation Mission to Brazil, Belém, 1952-55; rotating intern Jackson Meml. Hosp., Miami, Fla., 1959-60; resident in ob-gyn. Magee Women's Hosp., Pitts., 1965-68; asst. prof. ob-gyn. Sch. Medicine, U. Pitts., 1968-69; pvt. practice Pitts., 1970-88; cons. Med. Mission in Brazil, Teresina, 1986-89. Contbr. articles to profl. jours. Mem. AMA, ACOG, Pa. State Med. Soc., Allegheny County Med. Soc. Home: 119 Sunnyhill Dr Pittsburgh PA 15237-3666

LOWERY, WILLIAM HERBERT, lawyer; b. Toledo, June 8, 1925; s. Kenneth Alden and Drusilla (Pfanner) L.; m. Carolyn Broadwell, June 27, 1947; children: Kenneth Latham, Marcia Mitchell. PhB, U. Chgo., 1947; JD, U. Mich., 1950. Bar: Pa. 1951, U.S. Supreme Ct. 1955. Assoc. Dechert Price & Rhoads, Phila., 1950-58, ptnr., 1958-89, mng. ptnr., 1970-72; mem. policy com., chmn. litigation dept., 1962-68, 81-84; of counsel Dechert Price & Rhoads, Phila., 1989—; counsel S.S. Huebner Found. Ins. Edn., Phila., 1970-89; faculty Am. Conf. of Legal Execs., Pa. Bar Inst.; permanent mem. com. of visitors U. Mich. Law Sch. Author: Insurance Litigation Problems, 1972, Insurance Litigation Disputes, 1977. Pres. Stafford Civic Assn., 1958; chmn. Tredyffrin Twp. Zoning Bd., Chester County, Pa., 1959-75; bd. dirs. Paoli (Pa.) Meml. Hosp., 1964-89, chmn., 1972-75; bd. dirs. Main Line Health, Radnor, Pa., 1984-89; permanent mem. Jud. Conf. 3d Cir. Ct. Served to 2d lt. USAF, 1943-46. Mem. ABA (chmn. life ins. com. 1984-85, chmn. Nat. Conf. Lawyers and Life Ins. Cos. 1984-88), Order of the Coif, Royal Poinciana Golf Club, Phi Gamma Delta, Phi Delta Phi. Home: 2777 Gulf Shore Blvd N Apt S-4 Naples FL 34103-4386 Office: Dechert Price & Rhoads 4000 Bell Atlantic Tower 1717 Arch St Philadelphia PA 19103-2713

LOWEY, NITA M., congresswoman; b. N.Y., July 5, 1937; m. Stephen Lowey, 1961; children: Dona, Jacqueline, Douglas. BS, Mt. Holyoke Coll., 1959. Community activist, prior to 1975; asst. sec. state State of N.Y., 1975-87; former mem. 101st-102nd Congresses from 20th N.Y. dist., 1989-92; mem. 103rd-105th Congresses from 18th N.Y. dist., 1993—; mem. appropriations com., 1993—. Democrat. Office: US Ho of Reps 2421 Rayburn HOB Washington DC 20515*

LOWI, THEODORE J(AY), political science educator; b. Gadsden, Ala., July 9, 1931; s. Alvin R. and Janice (Haas) L.; m. Angele M. Daniel, May 11, 1963; children: Anna Amelie, Jason Daniel. BA, Mich. State U., 1954; MA, Yale U., 1955, PhD, 1961; HLD (hon.), Oakland U., 1972; LittD (hon.), SUNY, Stony Brook, 1988; Docteur honoris causa, Fondation Nationale des, Sciences Politiques, Paris, 1992. Mem. faculty dept. govt. Cornell U., 1959-65, 72—, asst. prof., 1961-65, John L. Senior prof. Am. instns., 1972—; assoc. prof. U. Chgo., 1965-69, prof., 1969-72; Gannett disting. prof. Rochester Inst. Tech., 1986-87, 90-91; fellow Ctr. Advanced Study in Behavioral Scis., 1977-78; chair Am. civilization U. Paris, 1981-82. Author: At the Pleasure of the Mayor, 1964, (with Robert Kennedy) The Pursuit of Justice, 1964, The End of Liberalism, 1969, 2d edit., 1979, Japanese edit., 1981, French edit., 1987, The Politics of Disorder, 1971, Poliscide, 1976, (with others) Nationalizing Government: Public Policies in America, 1978, Incomplete Conquest: Governing America, 1981, The Personal President: Power Invested, Promise Unfulfilled, 1985, Spanish edit., 1994, (with B. Ginsberg) American Government: Freedom and Power, 1990, 4th edit., 1996, (with B. Ginsberg) Embattled Democracy, 1995, The End of the Republican Era, 1995; (with B. Ginsberg and M. Weir) We the People, 1997; anthologies: Private Life and Public Order, 1968, Legislative Politics U.S.A., 3d edit., 1973. Recipient J. Kimbrough Owen award Am. Polit. Sci. Assn., 1962, French-Am. Found. award, 1981-82, Fulbright award, 1981-82, Harold Lasswell award Policy Studies Orgn., 1986, Richard Neustadt award for Best Book on Presidency, 1986; Social Sci. Rsch. Coun. fellow, 1963-64; Guggenheim Found. fellow, 1967-68; Nat. Endowment for Humanities fellow, 1977-78; Ford Found. fellow, 1977-78; Fulbright 40th Anniversary Disting. fellow, 1987. Mem. Am. Polit. Sci. Assn. (v.p. 1985-86, pres. 1991), Am. Acad. Arts and Sci., Policy Studies Orgn. (pres. 1977), Internat. Polit. Sci. Assn. (1st v.p. 1994—). Home: 101 Delaware Ave Ithaca NY 14850-4707 *If there is a how-to of success it is this: a passion for work, an ethic of workmanship, and an idea of what, in the end, is a good product.*

LOWITT, RICHARD, history educator; b. N.Y.C., Feb. 25, 1922; s. Eugene and Eleanor (Lebowitz) L.; m. Suzanne Catharine Carson, Sept., 1953; children: Peter Carson, Pamela Carson. B.S.S., CCNY, 1943; M.A., Columbia U., 1945, Ph.D., 1950. Instr. U. Md., College Park, 1948-52; asst. prof. U. R.I., Kingston, 1952-53; faculty mem. Conn. Coll., New London, 1953-66, prof. history, 1966; prof. history Fla. State U., Tallahassee, 1966-68, U. Ky., Lexington, 1968-77; prof., chmn. dept. history Iowa State U., Ames, 1977-87, prof., 1987-89; prof. U. Okla., Norman, 1990-97; mem. Iowa Humanities Bd., 1987-89; mem. Okla. Humanities Bd., 1995—; vis. prof. U. Colo., summer 1953, Yale U., 1961-62, Brown U., 1965-66, U. Chattanooga, summer 1965, Emory U., Atlanta; Sutton vis. prof. U. Okla., 1989-90. Author: A Merchant Prince of the 19th Century, 1954, George W. Norris, 3 vols., 1963, 71, 78; editor: Nils Olsen and the Bureau of Agricultural Economics, 1980; co-editor: One Third of a Nation-Lorena Hickok Reports on the Great Depression, 1981, The New Deal and the West, 1984, Letters From An American Farmer: The Eastern European and Russian Correspondence by Roswell Garst, 1987, Henry A. Wallace's Irrigation Frontier: On the Trail of the Cornbelt Farmer, 1990, Bronson M. Cutting, Progressive Politican, 1992, Politics in the Postwar American West, 1995. Trustee Pub. Library, Lexington, 1973-77. NEH sr. fellow, 1974, John Simon Guggenheim Found. fellow, 1957; grantee Social Sci. Rsch. Coun., 1958, Am. Coun. Learned Socs., 1962, Am. Philos. Soc., 1964, Huntington Libr., 1986; recipient Gaspar Perez de Villagra award Hist. Soc. N.Mex., 1993, Muriel H. Wright award Hist. Soc. Okla., 1995. Mem. Am. Hist. Assn., So. Hist. Assn. (membership com. 1973, Ramsdell p rize com. 1975, program com. 1983, nominating com. 1990), Western History Assn. (bd. editors 1986-88, program com. 1995, merit award 1992), Orgn. Am. Historians (nominating com. 1970, Turner prize com. 1972-76, bd. editors 1985-87), Agrl. History Soc. (exec. com. 1973-75, pres. 1991-92). Democrat. Office: Univ Okla Dept History Norman OK 73019

LOWMAN, GEORGE FREDERICK, lawyer; b. N.Y.C., Oct. 29, 1916; s. William H. and Mary (Canty) L.; m. Mary Farrell, Oct. 4, 1947; children—John F., Peter H., Patricia A. A.B., Harvard U., 1938, J.D., 1942. Bar: Conn. 1946. Since practiced in Stamford; assoc. Cummings & Lockwood, 1946-52, ptnr., 1952—; chmn. bd. dirs., chmn. exec. com. Farrell Lines, Inc.; bd. dirs. S.S. Owners Mutual Protection and Indemnity Assn., Inc.; bd. govs. Nat. Maritime Coun.; bd. mgrs. Am. Bur. Shipping, 1980-86. Chmn. Darien YMCA-YWCA fund campaign, 1956; chmn. fund campaign Darien ARC, 1953-54, bd. dirs., 1953-59; mem. exec. com. Alfred W. Dater council Boy Scouts Am., 1956; chmn. Darien Cancer Fund, 1959-60; pres., bd. dirs. Silvermine Guild Artists, 1967-77; bd. dirs., trustee King Sch., Stamford; trustee Low-Heywood Sch.; advisory com. U. Bridgeport Law Sch.; pres. B/G India House, N.Y.C., 1980—; trustee Am. Merchant Marine Mus., 1997—. Lt. col. AUS, 1942-46. Decorated Legion of Merit, Bronze Star. Fellow Am. Coll. Trial Lawyers, Internat. Acad. Trial Lawyers, Am. Bar Found.; mem. ABA, Conn. Bar Assn. (past pres.), Stamford Bar Assn. (past pres., Conn. state trial referee 1983-96), Harvard U. Alumni Assn. (v.p.), Marine Soc. N.Y.C. (hon.), St. Andrew's Soc., Conn. Srs. Golf Assn., Delta Upsilon. Home: 40 Allwood Rd Darien CT 06820-2416 Office: 10 Stamford Forum Stamford CT 06901-3240

LOWMAN, ROBERT PAUL, psychology educator, academic administrator; b. Lynwood, Calif., Jan. 23, 1947; s. Hubert Alden and Martha Guynn (Howard) L.; m. Kathleen Marie Drew, June 25, 1972; children: Sarah Guynn, Amy Katherine. AB, U. So. Calif., 1967; MA, Claremont U., 1969, PhD, 1973. Asst. prof. U. Wis., Milw., 1972-76; adminstrv. officer APA, Washington, 1976-81; asst. dean Kans. State U., Manhattan, 1981-86, assoc. dean grad. sch., 1986-90, assoc. vice provost, 1990-91; dir. rsch. svcs. and adj. assoc. prof. psychology U. N.C., Chapel Hill, 1991—, assoc. vice chancellor for rsch., 1994-96, assoc. vice provost for rsch., 1996—. Editor: APA's Guide to Rsch. Support, 1981; contbr. over 30 articles to profl. jours. Recipient numerous grants. Mem. APA (sec. bd. sci. affairs 1976-81, sec. com. on internat. rels. in psychology 1978-81), AAAS, Am. Psychol. Soc., Soc. for Psychologists in Mgmt. (newsletter editor 1994-96, bd. dirs. 1996—), Nat. Coun. Univ. Rsch. Adminstrs., Soc. Rsch. Adminstrs., Phi Beta Kappa, Phi Kappa Phi, Phi Eta Sigma, Psi Chi. Democrat. Methodist. Home: 104 Chesley Ln Chapel Hill NC 27514-1459 Office: Univ NC Office Rsch Svcs CB# 4100 Chapel Hill NC 27599-4100

LOWN, BERNARD, cardiologist, educator; b. Utena, Lithuania, June 7, 1921; came to U.S., 1935; s. Nisson and Bella (Grossbard) L.; m. Louise Charlotte Lown, Dec. 29, 1946; children—Anne Lown Green, Frederick, Naomi Lown Lewiton. BS summa cum laude, U. Maine, 1942, DS (hon.), 1982; MD, Johns Hopkins U., 1945; DSc (hon.), Worcester State Coll., 1983, Charles U., Prague, 1987, Bowdoin Coll., 1988, SUNY, Syracuse, 1988, Columbia Coll., Chgo., 1989; LLD (hon.), Bates Coll., Lewiston, Maine, 1983, Queen's U., Kingston, Ont., Can., 1985; LHD (hon.), Colby Coll., 1986, Thomas Jefferson U., 1988; PhD (hon.), U. Buenos Aires, 1986; D honoris causa, Autonomous U. Barcelona, Spain, 1989; D Univ. (hon.), Hiroshima (Japan) Shudo U., 1989. Asst. in pathology Yale U.-New Haven Hosp., 1945-46; intern in medicine Jewish Hosp., N.Y.C., 1947-48; asst. resident in medicine Montefiore Hosp., N.Y.C., 1948-50; research fellow in cardiology Peter Bent Brigham Hosp., Boston, 1950-53, asst. in medicine, 1955-56, dir. Samuel A. Levine Cardiovascular Research Lab., 1956-58, jr. assoc. in medicine, 1956-62, research assoc. in medicine, 1958-59, assoc. in medicine, 1962-63, sr. assoc. in medicine, 1963-70, dir. Samuel A. Levine Coronary Care Unit, 1965-74, physician, 1973-81, sr. physician, 1982—; asst. in medicine Harvard U., Boston, 1955-58, asst. prof. medicine dept. nutrition Sch. Pub. Health, 1961-67, assoc. prof. cardiology, 1967-73, prof. cardiology, 1974—, dir. cardiovascular research lab. Sch. Pub. Health, 1961—; cons. in cardiology Newton-Wellesley Hosp., Mass., 1963-77, Beth Israel Hosp., Boston, 1963-94, Children's Hosp. Med. Ctr., Boston, 1964-82; spl. cons. WHO, Copenhagen, 1971; coordinator U.S.-USSR Coop. Study, 1973-81; mem. lipid metabolism adv. com. NIH, Bethesda, Md., 1975-79; vis. prof., lectr., guest speaker numerous univs., hosps., orgns. Author: (with Samuel A. Levine) Current Advances in Digitalis Therapy, 1954; (with Harold D. Levine) Atrial Arrhythmias, Digitalis and Potassium, 1958, (with A. Malliani) Neural Mechanisms and Cardiovascular Disease, 1986, The Lost Art of Healing, 1996; mem. editorial bd. Circulation, Coeur et Medecine Interne, Jour. Electrocardiology; mem. editorial adv. bd. Jour. Soviet Research in Cardiovascular Diseases; contbr. numerous articles to profl. jours.; mem. internat. adv. bd. Internat. Med. Tribune, 1987—; inventor cardioverter; introduced Lidocaine as antiarrythmic drug. Founder, chmn. SatelLife, 1985—. Recipient Modern Medicine award, 1972, Ray C. Fish award and Silver medal Tex. Heart Inst., Houston, 1978, A. Ross McIntyre award and Gold medal U. Nebr. Med. Ctr., Omaha, 1979, Richard and Hinda Rosenthal award Am. Heart Assn., 1980, George W. Thorn award Brigham and Women's Hosp., 1982, 1st Cardinal Medeiros Peace medallion, 1982, Nikolay Burdenko medal Acad. Med. Scis. USSR, 1983; co-recipient Peace Edn. award UN Edn., Sci. and Cultural Orgn., 1984, Beyond War award, 1984, Nobel Peace prize, 1985, Ghandi Peace award, 1985, New Priorities award, 1986, Andres Bello medal 1st class Ministry Edn. and Ministry Sci., Venezuela, 1986, Gold Shield, U. Havana, Cuba, 1986, Dr. Tomas Romay y Cahcon Medallion Acad. Sci., Havana, 1986, George F. Kennan award, 1986, Fritz Gietzelt Medaille Council of Medico-Sci. Socs. of German Democratic Republic, 1987; named hon. citizen City of New Orleans, 1978, Pasteur award Pasteur Inst., Leningrad, USSR, 1987, Alumni Humanitarian award U. Maine, Orono, 1988, Internat. Peace and Culture award Soka Gokkai, Tokyo, 1989, Golden Door award Internat. Inst. Boston, 1989; named Disting. Citizen and recipient Key to City Buenos Aires, 1986. Fellow Am. Coll. Cardiology; mem. Am. Soc. for Clin. Investigation, Am. Heart Assn., Assn. Am. Physicians, AAAS, Physicians for Social Responsibility (founder, 1st pres. 1960-70), U.S.-China Physicians Friendship Assn. (pres. 1974-78), Internat. Physicians for Prevention Nuclear War (pres. 1980-93); mem. Brit. Cardiac Soc. (corr.), Cardiac Soc. Australia and New Zealand, Swiss Soc. Cardiology, Belgian Royal Acad. Medicine, Acad. Medicine of Columbia (hon.), Harvard Club (Boston), Nat. Acad. Scis. (sr. mem. inst. medicine), Phi Beta Kappa, Alpha Omega Alpha. Club: Harvard (Boston). Avocations: photography; music; philosophy; bicycling. Office: Lown Cardiovascular Group PC 21 Longwood Ave Brookline MA 02146-5239

LOWNDES, JANINE MARIE HERBERT, journalist; b. Albany, N.Y., May 15, 1958; d. Bernard and Wanda E. (Ahrens) H.; m. Jeffrey D. Lowndes; children: Nicholas, Grant, Victoria, Jeffrey Lee (dec.). BS in Adminstrn. of Justice, MacMurray Coll., 1984. Pvt. investigator Springfield, Ill., 1984-85; ins. claims investigator Tulsa, 1985; self-employed paralegal investigator Springfield, Ill. and Norfolk, Va., 1985-90; pvt. investigator Dayton, Ohio, 1990-91; freelance author, investigative reporter, journalist, 1976—. Author: Crystal Images (poetry), 1976; contbr. articles to newspaper, poetry to anthology; editor coll. newspaper: Spectator, 1982. Vol. chmn. Mental Health Assn., Springfield, 1969-76; pres. World Dem. Family Club Internat., 1979—. Recipient Golden Poets award, 1989-95. Mem. Maine Writers and Publishers Alliance. Avocations: piano, snowmobiling, travel, environ. issues, antique collecting. Home: Writer's Garret Box 2475 Brunswick ME 04011

LOWNSDALE, GARY RICHARD, mechanical engineer; b. Poplar Bluff, Mo., Nov. 2, 1946; s. Edward Lee and Margie Lee (Tesreau) L.; m. Paulette Ann Wermuth, Nov. 30, 1968; children: Charles Edgar, Larissa Renee. BSME, U. Cin., 1970. Registered profl. engr., Mich. Trainee engring. mgmt. Chrysler Corp., Highland Park, Mich., 1965-69; contact engr. Chrysler Corp., Hamtramck, Mich., 1970-71; prin. design engr. Ford Morot Co., Dearborn, Mich., 1971-82; exec. dir. advance programs Schlegel Corp., Madison heights, Mich., 1982-86; mgr. automotive design ctr. GE, Pittsfield, Mass., 1986-87; mgr. strategic projects GE, Southfield, Mich., 1990; v.p. design and engring. Autopolymer Design inc., Auburn Hills, Mich., 1987-88; chief engr. polymer body Saturn corp., Troy, Mich., 1988-90; industry dir. Hercules Incorp., Troy, Mich., 1990-92; dir. mktg. automotive systems group Johnson Controls, Inc., Plymouth, Mich., 1992; dir. comml. bus. APX Internat., Madison Heights, Mich., 1993-94; v.p., COO TRANS 2 Corp., Livonia, Mich., 1994-96; pres. Mastercraft Boat Co., Vonore, Tenn., 1996—. Presenter internat. and tech. papers; patentee in field. Sec. Coventry Gardens Homeowners Assn., Livonia, Mich., 1976-86; dist. leader Boy Scouts Am., Livonia, 1977—; pres. PTA, Livonia, 1982-84. Mem. ASME (sr.), Am. Soc. Body Engrs., Engring. Soc. Detroit (vice chmn. 1972-82), Soc. Plastics Engrs., Soc. Automotive Engrs. (co-chmn. com. 1991-92), Elfen Soc., Hadley Hills Homeowners Assn. (pres. 1990—), Sports Car Club Am. (solo chmn. 1972-76, Solo Nat. Champion award 1974). Avocations: classic car racing and restoration, horse ranching. Home: 4221 Meadow Pond Ln Metamora MI 48455-9751 Office: Mastercraft Boat Co 100 Cherokee Cove Dr Vonore TN 37885-2129

LOWREY, ANNIE TSUNEE, retired cultural organization administrator; b. Osaka, Japan, Mar. 3, 1929; naturalized U.S. citizen, 1963; d. Shigeru Takahata and Kuniko Takahata Takahashi; m. Lawrence K. Lowrey, Mar. 17, 1953; children: Kristine K. Ricci, Jay. BS in Lit., Wakayama (Japan) Shin-Ai, 1949; BS in Art Edn., Kans. State U., 1967; MA in Indsl. Tech., Wichita State U., 1976. Cert. instr. Wichita-Tchr. Assessment and Assistance Program, 1987. Tchr. Minoshima Elem. Sch., Wakayama, Japan, 1945-46, Wakayama Jr. H.S., 1948-49, Truesdell Jr. H.S., Wichita, Kans., 1967-69; tchr., coord. dept. fine arts Wichita H.S. East, 1969-92, instr. Japanese, 1991-92; lectr. dept. art and indsl. tech. Wichita State U., 1974-88, instr. computer applications in industry, 1990-91; tchr. Woodman Elem. Sch., Wichita, summer 1987; instr. art appreciation Butler County C.C., McConnell and Wichita, 1988-92; dir. edn. and exhbn. Wichita Ctr. for Arts, 1992-95; ret., 1995; asst. to fine arts photographer Charles Phillips, Wichita, spring 1989; judge Sister City Art Contest, 1991, Wichita Botanica Photography Competition, painting competition Wichita Painter's Guild, design competition Kans. Aviation Mus., 1991-92; instr. art instrnl. strategy to elem. and secondary art tchrs. Ft. Collins and Loveland, Colo. sch. dists., 1989; presenter many profl. confs. and workshops, most Nat. Art Edn.

Conf., Phoenix, 1992, Kans. Accessible Arts, 1994, Kans. State U., 1994. Chairperson writing team for Kans. Plan for Indsl. Edn.-TV, 1974-75; co-author tech. edn. curriculum Kans. State Bd. Regents, 1989. Judge Miss Asia contest 10th Ann. Asian Festival, Wichita, 1990; pres. pub. art adv. bd. City of Wichita, 1991—. Carnegie grantee for development of inter-disciplinary program on cultural literacy, 1984, Matsushita Electronic Co. grantee for curriculum devel., 1986; inductee Kans. Tchrs. Hall of Fame, 1994. Mem. NEA (presenter nat. conv. 1985), ASCD, Nat. Art Edn. Assn.Western Region Secondary Outstanding Educator of Yr. 1988), Kans. Alliance for Arts Edn. (bd. dirs. 1987-89), Phi Delta Kappa (pres. Wichita State U. chpt. 1983-84), Delta Phi Delta. Home: 2727 S Linden St Wichita KS 67210-2423

LOWRIE, JEAN ELIZABETH, librarian, educator; b. Northville, N.Y., Oct. 11, 1918; d. A. Sydney and Edith (Roos) L. A.B., Keuka Coll., 1940, LLD (hon.), 1973; B.L.S., Western Res. U., 1941, Ph.D., 1959; M.A., Western Mich. U., 1956. Childrens librarian Toledo Pub. Library, 1941-44; librarian Elementary Sch., Oak Ridge, Tenn., 1944-51; exhange tchr., librarian Nottingham, Eng., 1948-49; campus sch. librarian Western Mich. U., Kalamazoo, 1951-56; asso. prof. Western Mich. U. (Sch. Librarianship), 1958-61, prof., 1962-83, dir. sch., 1963-81; mem. faculty U. Ky., summer 1951, U . Calif., Berkeley, summer 1958; chmn. Internat. Steering Com. for Devel. Sch. Librs.; also del. World Conf. Orgns. Tchg. Profn., meetings, Paris, 1964, Vancouver, 1967, Dublin, 1968, Abidjan, 1969, Sydney, 1970; pres. Internat. Assn. Sch. Librarianship, 1971-77, exec. sec., 1978-96; mem. exec. bd. Internat. Fedn. Libr. Assns. and Instns., 1979-83. Author: Elementary School Libraries, rev. edit., 1970, School Libraries: International Developments, 1972, 2d edit., 1991, also articles.; adviser: filmstrip Using the Library, 1962. Recipient Dutton-Macrae award ALA, 1957, Profl. Achievement award Keuka Coll. Alumni, 1963. Mem. ALA (pres. 1973-74), Mich. Library Assn., Assn. Libr. & Info. Sci. Educators, Am. Assn. Sch. Librarians (dir., past pres., 1st President's award 1978), Altrusa Club (Kalamazoo), Delta Kappa Gamma, Beta Phi Mu. Home: 1235 NE Ocean View Circle Jensen Beach FL 34957

LOWRIE, WALTER OLIN, management consultant; b. North Braddock, Pa., Apr. 7, 1924; s. Robert Newell and Laura Rae (Essick) L.; m. Dorothy Ann Williams, Aug. 28, 1948; children: Susan, Allison, James. B.S. in Aero. Engring., MIT, 1948; Dr. Engring. (hon.), U. Central Fla., 1985. With Martin Marietta, 1948-86; v.p., program dir. Viking Program Martin Marietta, Denver, 1972-77; v.p., program dir. Peacekeeper Martin Marietta, 1977-78, v.p. tech. ops. Denver divsn., 1978-80, v.p., gen. mgr. space and electronics, 1980-82; pres. Martin Marietta Orlando, Fla., 1982-86; pvt. practice mgmt. cons. Maitland, Fla., 1986—. Bd. dirs. U. Ctrl. Fla. Found., Orlando, 1983-91; gen. chmn. 42d Internat. Sci. and Engring. Fair, 1991; mayor City of Bow-Mar, Colo., 1964-68; mem. Colo. Gov.'s Adv. Commn. on Corrs., 1979-80; bd. dirs. Indsl. Devel. Commn. Mid-Fla. Inc., Orlando, 1983; chmn. Met. Transp. Authority of Greater Orlando, 1985-86; trustee Orlando Sci. Ctr., 1986—, chmn. bd. trustees, 1994-95. 1st lt. USAAF, 1943-45, ETO. Decorated DFC; decorated Air medal with 6 oak leaf clusters; recipient Disting. Pub. Service award NASA, 1977. Fellow Am. Astronaut. Soc.; assoc. fellow AIAA (Space Systems Engr. of Yr. award 1977). Republican. Presbyterian.

LOWRIE, WILLIAM G., oil company executive; b. Painesville, Ohio, Nov. 17, 1943; s. Kenneth W. and Florence H. (Strickler) L.; m. Ernestine R. Rogers, Feb. 1, 1969; children: Kristen, Kimberly. BChemE, Ohio State U., 1966. Engr. Amoco Prodn. Co. subs. Standard Oil Co. (Ind.), New Orleans, 1966-74, area supt., Lake Charles, La., 1974-75, div. engr., Denver, 1975-78, div. prodn. mgr., Denver, 1978-79, v.p. prodn., Chgo., 1979-83; v.p. supply and marine transp. Standard Oil Co. (Ind.), Chgo., 1983-85; pres., Amoco Can., 1985-86; sr. v.p. prodn., Amoco Prodn. Co., 1986-87, exec. v.p. USA, 1987-88; exec. v.p. Amoco Oil Co., Chgo., 1989-90, pres., 1990-92; pres. Amoco Prodn. Co., 1992-94; exec. v.p. E&P sector Amoco Corp., 1994-95, pres. 1996—. Bd. dirs. Jr. Achievement, Northwestern Meml. Corp.; trustee, bd. dirs. Nat. 4-H Coun. Named Outstanding Engring. Alumnus, Ohio State U., 1979, Disting. Alumnis Ohio State U., 1985. Mem. Am. Petroleum Inst., Soc. Petroleum Engrs., Mid-Am. Club (Chgo.). Republican. Presbyterian. Office: Amoco Corp PO Box 87703 Chicago IL 60680-0703

LOWRY, A. ROBERT, federal government railroad arbitrator; b. Salem, Oreg., Jan. 16, 1919; s. Archie R. and Emaline (Hyland) L.; m. Nancy Jo Srb, May 3, 1975. Student, Albion (Idaho) Normal Coll., 1938. With U.P. R.R., 1937-53; local chmn., then asst. to pres. Order R.R. Telegraphers, 1949-64; v.p., then pres. Transp.-Communications Employees Union, 1964-68; pres. TC div., internat. v.p. Brotherhood Ry. and Airline Clks., 1969-72; supt. ops. Amtrak, 1972-73, dir., top labor rels. officer, 1973-75, asst. v.p., top labor rels. officer, 1975-79; now neutral arbitrator for fed. govt. and R.R. industry San Antonio. Served to lt. col. AUS, 1941-46, USAR, 1946-65, ret. Lodge: Mason, Shriners. Home and Office: 13919 Bluff Wind San Antonio TX 78216-7923

LOWRY, BATES, art historian, museum director; b. Cin., June 21, 1923; s. Bates and Eleanor (Meyer) L.; m. Isabel Barrett, Dec. 7, 1946; children: Anne, Patricia. PhB, U. Chgo., 1944, MA, 1952, PhD, 1955. Asst. prof. U. Calif., Riverside, 1954-57, Inst. Fin. Arts NYU, 1957-59; prof., chmn. dept. art Pomona Coll., Claremont, 1959-63, Brown U., Providence, 1963-68; dir. Mus. Modern Art, N.Y.C., 1968-69; prof., chmn. dept. art U. Mass., Boston, 1971-80; dir. Nat. Bldg. Mus., Washington, 1980-87; cons. dept. photography Getty Mus., 1992; disting. vis. prof. U. Del. Newark, 1988-89; founder, pres. Com. to Rescue Italian Art, 1966-76; mem. arts coun. MIT, 1974-80. Author: Visual Experience, 1961, Renaissance Architecture, 1962, Muse or Ego, 1963, Building a National Image, 1985, Looking for Leonardo, 1993; editor: College Art Association Monograph Series, 1957-59, 65-68, Architecture of Washington, D.C., 1977-79, Art Bull., 1965-68; mem. editorial bd. Smithsonian Instn. Press, 1981-87. Mem. bd. cons. NEH, 1975-81. With U.S. Army, 1943-46. Decorated Grand Officer of Order of Star of Solidarity, Italy, 1967; recipient Gov.'s award for contbn. to art, R.I., 1967; fellow Guggenheim Found., 1972, Inst. for Advanced Study, 1971. Mem. Coll. Art Assn. (bd. dirs. 1962-65), Soc. Archtl. Historians (bd. dirs. 1959-61, 63-65), Dunlap Soc. (pres. 1974-92), Academia del Disegno (hon. mem. Italy). Home: 255 Massachusetts Ave Boston MA 02115-3505

LOWRY, BRUCE ROY, lawyer; b. Lima, Ohio, Mar. 4, 1952; s. Lewis Roy and Gloria May (Rekers) L.; m. Kathleen Ann Sherman, Sept. 1, 1973; children: Bruce Benjamin, Tyler Sherman. BA cum laude, Ohio State U., 1974, JD cum laude, 1977. Bar: Ohio 1977. Tax intern Coopers & Lybrand, CPAs, Columbus, Ohio, 1976-77; assoc. Smith & Schnacke, LPA, Dayton, Ohio, 1977-84; chmn. tax dept. Smith & Schnacke, LPA, 1984-89; tax ptnr. Thompson, Hine and Flory, Dayton, 1989-96; internat. tax ptnr. Deloitte & Touche, LLP, 1996—; discussion leader Ohio Soc. CPAs, Cleve., 1980-97; adj. prof. U. Dayton Coll. Law, 1981-82; mem. faculty Ohio Continuing Legal Edn. Inst., 1987-97, mem. tax curriculum com.; mem. faculty Banff (Alta., Can.), Ctr. for Mgmt.-Internat. Tax, 1991; mem. faculty, program chair Coun. Internat. Tax Edn., 1995-97. Contbr. articles to profl. jours. Nat. swimming ofcl. YMCA, S.W. Ohio, 1990-93; chmn. Miami County Planning Commn., Troy, Ohio, 1991-97; bd. dirs. Miami Valley coun. Boy Scouts Am., Dayton, 1988-97. Recipient award of merit Ohio Legal Ctr. Inst., 1987, Golden Rule award, 1991, Up and Comer in Dayton award, 1991. Mem. Internat. Bar Assn., Internat. Fiscal Assn., Ctr. for Internat. Legal Studies (Vienna, Austria), Fgn. Activities of U.S. Taxpayers Com. of ABA, Tipp City C. of C. (chmn. econ. devel. com. 1989-91), Rotary Club Tipp City (pres.). Avocations: tennis, golf. Office: Deloitte & Touche LLP 155 E Broad St Columbus OH 43215-3609

LOWRY, CHARLES WESLEY, clergyman, lecturer; b. Checotah, Okla., Mar. 31, 1905; s. Charles Wesley and Sue (Price) L.; m. Edith Clark, June 14, 1930; children: Harriet Richards Lowry King, Charles Wesley, Atherton Clark, James Meredith Price; m. Kate Rowe Holland, Jan. 11, 1960. BA, Washington and Lee U., 1926, DD, 1959; MA, Harvard U., 1927; BD, Episcopal Theol. Sch., 1930; DPhil, Oxford (Eng.) U., 1933. Ordain deacon Episcopal Ch., 1930. Priest Episcopal Ch., 1931; traveling fellow Episc. Theol. Sch., 1930-32; Episc. chaplain U. Calif., 1933-34; prof. systematic theology Va. Theol. Sem., 1934-43; rector All Saints' Ch., Chevy Chase, Md., 1943-53; lectr. theology Seabury Western Theol. Sem., 1947, Phila. Div. Sch. (Bohlen lectr.), 1947, 49-50, Gen. Theol. Sem., 1951-52; chmn. Bd. Examining Chaplains, Diocese of Washington, 1945-53, sec., standing com., 1945-51; ofcl. del. from U.S. Internat. Conv. on Peace and Christian Civilization, Florence, Italy, 1952; chmn., exec. dir. Found. for Religious Action in Social and Civil Order, 1953-59, pres., 1960—, project research dir. on morals revolution, 1973-75; cons. FCDA, 1953-55; cons. Air War Coll., 1953, lectr., 1953-54; lectr. Naval War Coll., 1955, Nat. War Coll., 1957, 59-61, Command and Staff Coll., 1961-62, Indsl. Coll. Armed Forces, 1963, Inst. Lifetime Learning, 1964-66, Campbell Coll. Sch. Law, 1979, 80; also lectr. various seminars; lectr. philosophy and polit. sci. Sandhills Community Coll., 1967-69, 71, 89; spl. lectr. Oxford (Eng.) Poly. Coll., 1974; spl. lectr. Washington and Lee U., 1977, baccalaureate preacher, 1984; dir. Nat. Conf. on Spiritual Founds. Am. Democracy, Washington, 1954-55, 57, 59; minister The Village Chapel, Pinehurst, N.C., 1966-73; mem. faculty Wallace O'Neal Day Sch., Southern Pines, N.C., 1976—; columnist Pinehurst Outlook, 1977-78, Moore County News, 1978-79, The Pilot, 1979—; priest assoc. Emmanuel Epis. Ch., Southern Pines, 1981—. Author: The Trinity and Christian Devotion, 1946, Christianity and Materialism (Hale Sermon), 1948, Communism and Christ, rev. edit, 1962 (Brit. edit. 1954), Conflicting Faiths, 1953, The Ideology of Freedom vs. The Ideology of Communism, 1958, To Pray or Not to Pray, rev. edit, 1968, The Kingdom of Influence, 1969, William Temple: An Archbishop for All Seasons, 1982, The First Theologians, 1986, Constitution Commentary, 1989; (with others) Anglican Evangelicalism, 1943, Encyclopaedia of Religion, 1945, The Anglican Pulpit To-Day, 1953; editor: Blessings of Liberty, 1956-90; contbr. articles to profl. publs. Chmn. Nat. Jefferson Davis Hall of Fame Co., 1960, 64-65; candidate for U.S. Congress 10th Dist. Va., 1962; mem. N.C. Bicentennial Constn. Conv., 1985-89. Recipient George Washington medal Freedoms Found., 1955, 59, 61, 68, other award, 1953, 81. Mem. Am. Peace Soc. (past pres.), Am. Polit. Sci. Assn., Internat. Platform Assn., Am. Theol. Soc. (treas. 1955-70, 72, past v.p.), Cum Laude Soc. (pres. O'Neal chpt.), World Conf. Faith and Order, Phi Beta Kappa, Omicron Delta Kappa, Delta Sigma Rho, Sigma Upsilon. Clubs: Achilles (Oxford and Cambridge); Rotary (dist. gov. 1970-71), Chevy Chase, Pinehurst Country, Nat. Press. Address: 160 Longleaf Rd Southern Pines NC 28387-2832 *A religious view of life is not an easy optimism. The serious person knows the force of moral evil or sin. But when in the great religions we meet a Power that transforms, we see with new eyes. We are saved by hope and by faith and love.*

LOWRY, DENNIS MARTIN, communications executive; b. Cleve., Dec. 13, 1953; s. Martin Patrick and Phyllis Ann (Bova) L.; m. Mary Cullinan, Aug. 8, 1973 (div. 1978); 1 child, Matthew Christopher; m. Sylvia Susanne Patterson, Nov. 3, 1979; children: Kevin Thomas, Caitlin Ilene, Danielle Amanda. Student, Cleve. State U., 1971-78. Sr. technician Union Carbide Corp., Cleve., 1973-78; applications analyst Davy McKee Co., Independence, Ohio, 1978-79; sr. systems programmer Cuyahoga County Hosp., Cleve., 1979-83; regional support specialist Commex Ltd., Rocky River, Ohio, 1987-88; nat. tech. support mgr. Commex Maintenance Ltd., Rocky River, 1987-89; mgr. divsn. tng. Cap Gemini Am., Beachwood, Ohio, 1989—. Avocations: theater directing, locksmith. Home: 21144 Mastick Rd Cleveland OH 44126-3056

LOWRY, DONALD MICHAEL, lawyer; b. Milw., 1929. LLB, Marquette U., 1953, PhB. Bar: Wis. 1953, Ill. 1961. Underwriter CNA Lloyd's of Tex.; sr. v.p., gen. counsel Am. Casualty Co., Reading, Pa., CNA Life & Annuity Co., Continental Assurance Co., Nat. Fire Ins. Co., Hartford, Conn., Transcontinental Ins., Transportation Ins. Co., Valley Forge Ins. Co., Valley Forge Life Ins. Co., Continental Casualty Co. Inc.; v.p., sec. CNA Fin. Corp., 1958—. Office: Continental Casualty Co CNA Plaza Chicago IL 60685

LOWRY, EDWARD FRANCIS, JR., lawyer; b. L.A., Aug. 13, 1930; s. Edward Francis and Mary Anita (Woodcock) L.; m. Patricia Ann Palmer, Feb. 16, 1963; children: Edward Palmer, Rachael Louise. Student, Ohio State U., 1948-50; A.B., Stanford, 1952, J.D., 1954. Bar: Ariz. 1955, D.C. 1970, U.S. Supreme Ct. 1969. Camp dir. Quarter Circle V Bar Ranch, 1954; tchr. Orme Sch., Mayer, Ariz., 1954-56; trust rep. Valley Nat. Bank Ariz., 1958-60; pvt. practice, Phoenix, 1960—; assoc. atty. Cunningham, Carson & Messinger, 1960-64; ptnr. Carson, Messinger, Elliott, Laughlin & Ragan, 1964-69, 70-80, Gray, Plant, Mooty, Mooty & Bennett, 1981-84, Eaton, Lazarus, Dodge & Lowry Ltd., 1985-86; exec. v.p., gen. counsel Bus. Realty Ariz., 1986-93; pvt. practice, Scottsdale, Ariz., 1986-88; ptnr. Lowry & Froeb, Scottsdale, 1988-89, Lowry, Froeb & Clements, P.C., Scottsdale, 1989-90, Lowry & Clements P.C., Scottsdale, 1990, Lowry, Clements & Powell, P.C., Scottsdale, 1991—; asst. legis. counsel Dept. Interior, Washington, 1969-70; mem. Ariz. Commn. Uniform Laws, 1972—, chmn., 1976-88; judge pro tem Ariz. State Ct. Appeals, 1986, 92-94. Chmn. Council of Stanford Law Socs., 1968; vice chmn. bd. trustees Orme Sch., 1972-74, treas., 1981-83; bd. trustees Heard Mus., 1965-91, life trustee, 1991—, pres., 1974-75; bd. visitors Stanford Sch. Law; magistrate Town of Paradise Valley, Ariz., 1976-83; juvenile ct. referee Maricopa County, 1978-83. Served to capt. USAF, 1956-58. Fellow Ariz. Bar Found. (founder); mem. ABA, Maricopa County Bar Assn., State Bar Ariz. (chmn. com. uniform laws 1979-85), Stanford Law Soc. Ariz. (past pres.), Scottsdale Bar Assn. (bd. dirs. 1991—, v.p. 1991, pres. 1992-95), Ariz. State U. Law Soc. (bd. dirs.), Nat. Conf. Commrs. Uniform State Laws, Delta Sigma Rho, Alpha Tau Omega, Phi Delta Phi. Home: 7600 N Moonlight Ln Paradise Valley AZ 85253-2938 Office: Lowry Clements & Powell PC 2901 N Central Ave Ste 1120 Phoenix AZ 85012-2731 also: Ste 1040 6900 E Camelback Rd Scottsdale AZ 85251

LOWRY, GLENN DAVID, art museum director; b. N.Y.C.; s. Warren and Laure (Lynn) L.; m. Susan Chambers, Aug. 24, 1974; children: Nicholas, Alexis, William. BA, Williams Coll., 1976; MA, Harvard U., 1978, PhD, 1982. Asst. curator Fogg Art Mus., Harvard U., Cambridge, Mass., 1978-80; rsch. asst. Archeol. Survey of Mediterranean Town of Amalfi, Italy, 1980; curator Oriental art Mus. Art, R.I. Sch. Design, Providence, 1981-82; dir. Joseph and Margaret Muscarelle Mus. Art, Williamsburg, Va., 1982-84; curator Nr. Ea. art Arthur M. Sackler and the Freer Gallery Art, Smithsonian Instn., Washington, 1984-90, curatorial coord., 1987-89; dir. Art Gallery Ont., Toronto, Can., 1990-95, Mus. Modern Art, N.Y.C., 1995—; mem. adv. coun. dept. art history and archaeology Columbia U. Co-author: Fatehpur-Sikri: A Source Book, 1985, From Concept to Context: Approaches to Asian and Islamic Calligraphy, 1986, An Annotated Checklist of the Vever Collection, 1988, A Jeweler's Eye: Art of the Book from the Vever Collection, 1988, Timur and the Princely Vision: Persian Art and Culture in the Fifteenth Century, 1989, Europe and the Arts of Islam: The Politics of Taste, 1991. Trustee Metro Toronto Conv. and Visitors Assn. Recipient Inst. Turkish Studies Travel award Smithsonian Instn., 1980, Spl. Exhbns. award, 1987, Scholarly Studies award, 1990. Mem. Assn. Am. Art Mus. Dirs., Coll. Art Assn. Office: Mus Modern Art 11 W 53rd St New York NY 10019-5401

LOWRY, LARRY LORN, management consulting company executive; b. Lima, Ohio, Apr. 12, 1947; s. Frank William and Viola Marie L.; m. Jean Carroll Greenbaum, June 23, 1973; 1 child, Alexandra Kristin. BSEE, MIT, 1969, MSEE, 1970; MBA, Harvard U., 1972. Mgr. Boston Consulting Group, Menlo Park, Calif., 1972-80; sr. v.p., mng. ptnr. Booz, Allen & Hamilton Inc, San Francisco, 1980—. Western Electric fellow, 1969, NASA fellow, 1970. Mem. Sigma Xi, Tau Beta Pi, Eta Kappa Nu. Presbyterian. Home: 137 Stockbridge Ave Atherton CA 94027-3942

LOWRY, LOIS (HAMMERSBERG), author; b. 1937. Author: A Summer to Die, 1977, Find A Stranger, Say Goodbye, 1978, Anastasia Krupnik, 1979, Autumn Street, 1980, Anastasia Again, 1981, Anastasia at Your Service, 1982, The One Hundredth Thing About Caroline, 1983, Taking Care of Terrific, 1983, Anastasia, Ask Your Analyst, 1984, Us and Uncle Fraud, 1984, Anastasia on Her Own, 1985, Switcharound, 1985, Anastasia Has the Answers, 1986, Anastasia's Chosen Career, 1987, Rabbie Starkey, 1987, All About Sam, 1988, Number the Stars, 1989 (John Newbery medal 1990), Your Move, J.P.!, 1990, Anastasia at This Address, 1991, Attaboy, Sam!, 1992, The Giver, 1993 (John Newbery medal 1994), Anastasia Absolutely, 1995, See You Around, Sam!, 1996, Stay! Keeper's Story, 1997. Address: 205 Brattle St Cambridge MA 02138-3345 Office: care Houghton Mifflin 222 Berkeley St Boston MA 02116-3748

LOWRY, MIKE, former governor, former congressman; b. St. John, Wash., Mar. 8, 1939; s. Robert M. and Helen (White) L.; m. Mary Carlson, Apr. 6, 1968; 1 child, Diane. B.A., Wash. State U., Pullman, 1962. Chief fiscal analyst, staff dir. ways and means com. Wash. State Senate, 1969-73; govtl. affairs dir. Group Health Coop. Puget Sound, 1974-75; mem. council King County Govt., 1975-78, chmn., 1977; mem. 96th-100th congresses from 7th dist. Wash., 1979-1989; governor State of Wash., 1993-96. Chmn. King County Housing and Community Devel. Block Grant Program, 1977; pres. Wash. Assn. Counties, 1978. Democrat. Address: PO Box 4246 Seattle WA 98104*

LOWRY, WILLIAM KETCHIN, JR., insurance company executive; b. Columbia, S.C., Oct. 4, 1951; s. William Ketchin and Beverly Hubbard (Frazee) L.; m. Elaine Diana Kent, June 22, 1984; children: Jennifer Lyn, Julia Ann, Samuel Ketchin. BSBA, U. S.C., 1972, M in Acctg., 1973. CPA, S.C. Supr. Ernst & Whinney, Columbia, 1973-81; sr. mgr. Price Waterhouse, Hartford, Conn., 1981-83, Phila., 1983-84; dir. corp. sys. devel. and analysis Am. Can Co., Greenwich, Conn., 1984-86; v.p., treas., CFO Phoenix Re Corp. and Reins. Co., N.Y.C., 1986-90, sr. v.p., treas., CFO, 1990; v.p., treas. Transnat. Ins. Co., N.Y.C., 1989-90; bd. dirs., v.p., treas. Nat. Bus. Brokers, Inc., Greenlawn, N.Y., 1989-90; sr. v.p., CFO SCOR U.S. Corp., SCOR Reins. Co. Gen. Security Assurance Corp., N.Y.C., 1990-93, Constn. Reins Corp., 1993-96; exec. v.p. CFO Constn. Reins. Corp., 1996—, 1996—; bd. dirs. Constn. Reins Corp., 1994—, Constn. Reins. Corp. Sirius Reins. Corp., 1993—; pres. CRC Corsair Inc, 1995—. Pres., bd. dirs. Groves Homes Assn., Columbia, 1980-81; diaconate West Side Presbyn. Ch., Ridgewood, N.J., 1989-91. Fellow Life Mgmt. Inst.; mem. AICPA, Am. Soc. CLUs, Fin. Execs. Inst., Soc. Ins. Rsch., Soc. Fin. Examiners, Inst. Mgmt. Accts., S.C. Assn. CPAs, City Midday Drug and Chem. Club, Forest Lake Club, Saddle River Valley Swim and Tennis Club, Beta Gamma Sigma, Omicron Delta Kappa, Beta Alpha Psi, Omicron Delta Epsilon, Sigma Phi Epsilon. Presbyterian. Avocations: horseback riding, golf. Home: 22 Autumn Ct Saddle River NJ 07458 Office: Constn Reins Corp 110 William St New York NY 10038-3901

LOWRY, WILLIAM RANDALL, executive recruiter; b. Columbus, Ohio, Nov. 15, 1947; s. William Ralph and Joyce Naomi (Videto) L.; m. JoAnne Theresa Toth, Sept. 6, 1969; children: Gregory William, David Scott. BA, Ohio State U., 1969. Dealer rep. Shell Oil Co., Columbus, Dayton, Ohio, 1969-72; sales rep. Xerox Corp., Cin., 1972-73; area dir. sales devel. Greyhound Lines, Inc., Cin., 1973-75, N.Y.C., 1975-77; dept. mgr. Salesworld, Inc., Houston, 1977-79; sr. assoc. Korn/Ferry Internat., Houston, 1979-81, mng. assoc., 1981-83, v.p., ptnr., 1983-85; ptnr. Barton Raben, Inc., Houston, 1985-95; founding ptnr. Raben Freud Lowry, Houston, 1995; ptnr. Ray & Berndtson, Houston, 1996—. Chmn. Lombardi award for Coll. Football Lineman of Yr., Houston, 1986; bd. dirs. Episcopal H.S. Dad's Club; mem. Houston Met. Racquet Club. Mem. Petroleum Club Houston, Cypresswood Country Club (pres. 1985-87), Rotary (Houston bd. dirs. 1987-90). Home: 4649 Spruce St Bellaire TX 77401 Office: Ray & Berndtson 500 Dallas St Ste 3010 Houston TX 77002-4708

LOWRY-JOHNSON, JUNIE, casting director. Films include Summer Heat, 1987, La Bamba, 1987, Born in East L.A., 1987, Powwow Highway, 1989, Blind Fury, 1990, Little Vegas, 1990, The Hand That Rocks the Cradle, 1992; TV series includes N.Y.P.D. Blue (Emmy award for outstanding individual achievement in casting 1995). Mem. Casting Soc. Am. Office: 20th Century Fox Bochco Bldg Rm 232 Los Angeles CA 90035*

LOWTHER, FRANK EUGENE, research physicist; b. Orrville, Ohio, Feb. 3, 1929; s. John Finger and Mary Elizabeth (Mackey) L.; m. Elizabeth E. Koons, Apr. 21, 1951; children: Cynthia E., Victoria J., James A., Frank Eugene. Grad. Ohio State U., Columbus, 1952. Scientist missile systems div. Raytheon Corp., Boston, 1952-57, GE, Syracuse, N.Y., and Daytona Beach, Fla., 1957-65; chief sci. Purification Sci., Inc., 1965-72; mgr. ozone rsch. and devel. W.R. Grace Co., Curtis Bay, Md., 1972-75; sr. engring. assoc. Linde div. Union Carbide Corp., Tonawanda, N.Y., 1975-80; chief sci., Atlantic Richfield-Energy Conversion and Materials Lab, 1980-83; prin. sci. Atlantic Richfield-Corp. Tech., 1983-85, sci. advisor, 1985-88, rsch. advisor, 1988-93, cons. tech. advisor, 1993—; advisor Energy Sci., Inc., Canandaigua, N.Y., 1993—, Custom Tech. Creations, Inc., Buffalo, N.Y., 1993—. Recipient Inventor of Yr. award Patent Law Assn. and Tech. Socs. Council, 1976, Gen. Elec. Gen. Mgr.'s award 1962, Tech. Achievements awards ARCO, 1990, 92. Assoc. fellow AIAA; mem. IEEE (sr.), AAAS, N.Y. Acad. Scis., Masons. Patentee in field of ozone tech., plasma generators, solid state power devices, internal combustion engines, electro-desorption, thermoelectrics, virus and bacteria disinfection systems, oil field technology, electric power distribution, nuclear fusion, chemical and physical reactors, exploding bridge wires, weapons. Home and Office: 2578 Glen Echo Dr Columbus OH 43202

LOWTHER, GERALD HALBERT, lawyer; b. Slagle, La., Feb. 18, 1924; s. Fred B. and Beatrice (Halbert) L.; children by previous marriage: Teresa, Craig, Natalie, Lisa. A.B., Pepperdine Coll., 1951; J.D., U. Mo., 1951. Bar: Mo. 1951. Since practiced in Springfield; ptnr. firm Lowther, Johnson, Joyner, Lowther, Cully & Housley; Mem. Savs. and Loan Commn. Mo., 1965-68, Commerce and Indsl. Commn. Mo., 1967-73; lectr. U. Tex., 1955-57, Crested Butte, Colo., 1958-59. Contbr. articles law jours. Past pres. Ozarks Regional Heart Assn.; Del., mem. rules com. Democratic Nat. Conv., 1968; treas. Dem. Party Mo., 1968-72, mem. platform com., 1965, 67, mem. bi-partisan commn. to reapportion Mo. senate, 1966; Bd. dirs. Greene County Guidance Clinic, Ozark Christian Counseling Service, Greene County, Mo.; past pres. Cox Med. Center. Served with AUS, 1946-47; Col. staff of Gov. Hearnes 1964, 68, Mo. Mem. ABA, Mo. Bar Assn., Greene County Bar Assn., Def. Orientation Conf. Assn., Internat. Assn. Ins. Counsel, Def. Rsch. Inst., Springfield C. of C. Clubs: Kiwanian (pres. 1962), Quarterback (pres. 1958), Tip Off (pres. 1960). Home: 2320 Englewood Springfield MO 65806 Office: 901 E Saint Louis St Fl 20 Springfield MO 65806-2505

LOWTHERT, WILLIAM HUGHES, III, utility company executive; b. Pottsville, Pa., Sept. 9, 1948; s. William Hughes and Jane (Burke) L.; m. Thelma May Gorman, Oct. 17, 1970; children—William, Brian, Rebecca. BS in Technology Mgmt. magna cum laude, U. Md., 1978; MS in Vocat. Edn., Pa. State U., 1984, PhD in Workforce Devel., 1996; postgrad. in bus. mgmt. Bloomsburg U., 1984—. Lic. reactor operator Nuclear Regulatory Commn. Nuclear reactor operator Balt. Gas & Electric, Lusby, Md., 1974-78; nuclear instr. Pa. Power & Light Co., Berwick, Pa., 1978-79, tng. supr., 1979-83, supr. nuclear instrn., 1983-86; mgr. nuclear tng., 1986—; adv. faculty U. State N.Y., Albany, 1983—; adj. instr. nuclear tech. Luzerne County C.C., 1986—; part time instr. in edn. Pa. State U., 1990—. Lay moderator First English Bapt. Ch., Bloomsburg, Pa., 1992—. Served with USN, 1968-74. Mem. Internat. Soc. Performance Improvement, Phi Kappa Phi, Pi Lambda Theta, Alpha Sigma Lambda. Republican. Baptist. Home: 34 Willow Ln Bloomsburg PA 17815-3375 Office: Pa Power & Light Co 34 Willow Ln Bloomsburg PA 17815-3375

LOWY, FREDERICK HANS, university president, psychiatrist; b. Grosspetersdorf, Austria, Jan. 1, 1933; arrived in Can., 1944; s. Eugen and Maria (Braun) L.; m. Anne Louise Cloudsley, June 25, 1965 (dec. 1973); children: David, Eric, Adam; m. Mary Kathleen O'Neil, June 1, 1975; 1 dau., Sarah. BA, McGill U., Montreal, Que., Can., 1955, MD, 1959. Intern, resident in internal medicine Royal Victoria Hosp., Montreal, Que., Can.; resident in psychiatry U. Cin. Hosp., Cin. VA Hosp.; psychoanalytic tng. Montreal Psychoanalytic Inst.; psychiatrist Allan Meml. Inst.-Royal Victoria Hosp., Montreal-McGill U. Faculty Medicine, 1965-70; psychiatrist-in-chief Ottawa Civic Hosp.; also prof. dept. psychiatry U. Ottawa Faculty Medicine, 1971-74; prof. psychiatry, chmn. dept. U. Toronto Faculty Medicine; also dir. Clarke Inst. Psychiatry U. Toronto, 1974-80, dean Sch. Medicine, 1980-87, dir. Ctr. for Bioethics, 1989-95; rector, vice chancellor Concordia U., Montreal, 1995—. Author numerous papers in field; co-editor: A Method of Psychiatry, 1980, Alzheimer's Disease Research, 1991. Fellow Royal Coll. Physicians and Surgeons, Am. Coll. Psychiatrists; mem. Internat. Psychoanalytic Assn., Can. Psychiat. Assn. (editor jour. 1972-76), Am. Psychiat. Assn., Am. Coll. Psychoanalysts. Office: Concordia U Office Rector, 1455 de Maisonneuve Blvd W, Montreal, PQ Canada H3G 1M8

LOWY, GEORGE THEODORE, lawyer; b. N.Y.C., Oct. 6, 1931; s. Eugene and Elizabeth Lowy; m. Pier M. Foucault, Sept. 7, 1957. BA cum laude,

LLB cum laude, NYU. Bar: N.Y. 1955, U.S. Dist. Ct. (so. dist.) N.Y. 1958, U.S. Supreme Ct. 1972, U.S. Ct Appeals (2d cir.) 1975. Assoc. Cravath, Swaine and Moore, N.Y.C., 1957-65, ptnr., 1965—; trustee NYU Law Ctr. Found.; bd. dirs. Equitable Life Assurance Soc. U.S., Eramet, Paris; adj. prof. NYU Law Sch., 1983—. Fellow ABA; mem. Am. Law Inst., Assn. of Bar of City of N.Y., Internat. Bar Assn., Union Internat. des Avocats, Cercle Interallie Paris. Home: 580 Park Ave New York NY 10021-7313 Office: Cravath Swaine & Moore World Wide Pla 825 8th Ave New York NY 10019-7416

LOWY, JAY STANTON, music industry executive; b. Chgo., Nov. 22, 1935; s. Joseph Alfred and Minnie Lowy; m. Diane Friedland, Oct. 10, 1959 (div.); children—Dana Kim, Jeffrey Mark; m. Brenda Belle Orloff, Mar. 22, 1982; 1 child, Jason Louis. Student, UCLA, 1954-58. Gen. mgr. Robbins Feist & Miller Music Pub. Cos., 1959-67, Famous Music Corp., 1967-69; v.p. Dot and Paramount Records, 1969-71; pres., chief operating officer Capitol-EMI Music Pub. Cos., 1971-73; v.p., gen. mgr. Jobete Music Co., Inc. (Motown Industries), Hollywood, Calif., 1976-86; cons., personal mgr., 1986—. Served with AUS, 1958. Named one of Top 200 Music Execs. Billboard Mag., 1976, Old Master Purdue U., 1979. Mem. Nat. Acad. Recording ARts and Scis. (nat. pres. and chmn. bd. trustees 1979-81), Calif. Copyright Conf. (pres. 1977-78), Tau Epsilon Phi. Democrat. Jewish. Home: 1350 N Laurel Ave Unit 13 West Hollywood CA 90046-4623

LOY, FRANK ERNEST, conservation organization executive; b. Nuremberg, Germany, Dec. 25, 1928; came to U.S., 1939; s. Alfred Loewi and Elizabeth (Loeffler) L.; m. Dale Haven, 1963; children: Lisel, Eric Anthony. BA, UCLA, 1950; LLB, Harvard U., 1953. Bar: D.C. 1953, Calif. 1954. With O'Melveny & Myers, L.A., 1954-65; spl. asst. to adminstr. FAA, 1961-63; spl. cons. to adminstr. AID, 1963-64; dep. asst. sec. state for econ. affairs, 1965-70; sr. v.p. Pan Am. World Airways, Inc., N.Y.C., 1970-73; pres. Pennsylvania Co., Washington, 1974-79, Penn Ctrl. Corp., 1978-79; dir. Bur. Refugee Programs, Dept. State, Washington, 1980-81; pres. German Marshall Fund of U.S., 1981-95; chmn. League Conservation Voters, Washington, 1993—, pres., 1995-96; instr. corp. fin. Grad. Sch. Commerce, U. So. Calif., 1959-61; vis. lectr. Yale Law Sch., 1996; dir. Pharm. Product Devel., Inc. Chmn. bd. trustees Goddard Coll., Vt., 1976-78, Environ. Def. Fund, 1983-90, Washington Ballet, 1991-94; U.S. mem. Bd. Regional Environ. Ctr. for Ctrl. and Ea. Europe, Budapest, Hungary. With U.S. Army, 1953-55. Home: 3230 Reservoir Rd NW Washington DC 20007-2955 Office: League Conservation Voters 1707 L St NW Washington DC 20036-4201

LOY, RICHARD FRANKLIN, civil engineer; b. Dubuque, Iowa, July 6, 1950; s. Wayne Richard and Evelyn Mae (Dikeman) L.; m. Monica Lou Roberts, Sept. 2, 1972 (div.); children: Taneha Eve, Spencer Charles. BSCE, U. Wis., Platteville, 1973. Registered profl. engr., Wis., Ohio. Engr. aid Wis. Dept. of Transp., Superior, 1969; asst. assayer Am. Lead & Zinc Co., Shullsburg, Wis., 1970; asst. grade foreman Radandt Construction Co., Eau Claire, Wis., 1970; air quality technician U. Wis., Platteville, 1972-73; asst. city engr. City of Kaukauna, Wis., 1973-77; asst. city engr. City of Fairborn, Ohio, 1977-89, city engr., 1989-93; pub. works dir. City of Fairborn, 1993—. Bd. dirs. YMCA Fairborn, 1990-95; mem. coun. Trinity United Ch. of Christ, Fairborn, 1989—; chmn. Chillicothe dist. Tecumseh coun. Boy Scouts Am., 1991-93. Recipient Blue Coat award, 1983; named to Exec. Hall of Fame, N.Y., 1990. Mem. ASCE, NSPE, Am. Pub. Works Assn., Am. Water Works Assn., Inst. Transp. Engrs.

LOYND, RICHARD BIRKETT, consumer products company executive; b. Norristown, Pa., Dec. 1, 1927; s. James B. and Elizabeth (Geigus) L.; m. Jacqueline Ann Seubert, Feb. 3, 1951; children: Constance, John, Cynthia, William, James, Michael. B.S. in Elec. Engring., Cornell U., 1950. Sales engr. Lincoln Electric Co., Cleve., 1950-55; with Emerson Electric Co., St. Louis, 1955-68; pres. Builder Products div. Emerson Electric Co., 1965-68, v.p. Electronics and Space div., 1961-65; v.p. ops. Gould, Inc., Chgo., 1968-71; exec. v.p. Eltra Corp., N.Y.C., 1971-74; pres. Eltra Corp., 1974-81; chmn. Converse, Inc., 1982-88; CEO Furniture Brands Internat., Inc (formerly Interco Inc.), St. Louis, 1989-96; chmn. Interco Inc., St. Louis, 1989—. Home: 19 Randall Dr Short Hills NJ 07078-1957 Office: Furniture Brands Internat Inc 101 S Hanley Rd Saint Louis MO 63105-3406

LOZANO, JOSE, nephrologist; b. San Vicente, El Salvador, Feb. 11, 1941; came to U.S., 1968; s. Jose E. and Transito Maria (Mendez) L.; m. Hilda Berganza, Jan. 27, 1965; children: Jose E., Claudia Maria. MD, U. El Salvador, 1965. Diplomate Am. Bd. Internal Medicine, Am. Bd. Nephrology. Rotating intern Nat. Med. Ctr., San Salvador, El Salvador, 1963-64; asst. resident in internal medicine Rosales Hosp., San Salvador, 1965-66, resident in internal medicine, 1966-67, chief resident in internal medicine, 1967-68; resident in internal medicine Baylor U. Affiliated Hosps., Houston, 1968-70, fellow in nephrology, 1970-71, 73-74; asst. prof. medicine U. El Salvador, 1971-72; internist and nephrologist Social Security Hosp., San Salvador, 1971-72; instr. in medicine Baylor Coll. Medicine, Houston, 1974-75, asst. prof. medicine in nephrology, 1975-76, clin. asst. prof. medicine, 1976-80; mem. staff internal medicine St. Elizabeth Hosp., Beaumont Med./Surg. Hosp., Bapt. Hosp., Beaumont, Tex., 1976; med. dir. Golden Triangle Dialysis Ctr., Beaumont, 1977—, BMA Jasper, Jasper, Tex., 1986, BMA Orange, Orange, Tex., 1987-90; med. dir. Golden Triangle Dialysis Ctr., Beaumont, 1977; med. dir. BMA Jasper, Tex., 1986, Orange, Tex., 1987-90; mem. Kidney Health Care Adv. Com., 1981-82; pesenter in field. Contbr. articles to profl. publs. Mem. AMA, ACP, Am. Soc. Nephrology, Internat. Soc. Nephrology, Tex. Med. Assn., Harris County Med. Soc., Jefferson County Med. Soc., Am. Coll. Physicians Execs., Physicians for A Nat. Health Plan. Avocations: study of socioeconomic factors in healthcare in U.S., Catholic theologies. Home: 4655 Ashdown St Beaumont TX 77706-7723 Office: Beaumont Nephrology Assocs 3282 College St Beaumont TX 77701-4610 *In terms of health care we need a system that provides easy, uncomplicated access to primary care services. We urgently need a health care system that provides universal and comprehensive access to health care without considerations given to the ability to pay, race, gender, religion or sexual orientation. We need a system that is independent of employment, in which people with existing conditions are not restricted from free and adequate access to health care. The creation of a universal health care system is in the best interests of all citizens of this country.*

LOZANO, RUDOLPHO, federal judge; b. 1942. BS in Bus., Ind. U., 1963, LLB, 1966. Mem. firm Spangler, Jennings, Spangler & Dougherty. P.C., Merrillville, Ind., 1966-88; judge U.S. Dist. Ct. (no. dist.) Ind., Hammond, 1988—. With USAR, 1966-73. Mem. ABA, Ind. State Bar Assn., Def. Rsch. Inst. Office: US Dist Ct 205 Fed Bldg 507 State St Hammond IN 46320-1503*

LOZANSKY, EDWARD DMITRY, physicist, author, consultant; b. Kiev, Ukraine, Feb. 10, 1941; came to U.S., 1977; s. Dmitry R. and Dina M. (Chizhik) L.; m. Tatiana I. Yershov, Feb. 27, 1971; 1 child, Tania. MS, Moscow Phys. Engring. Inst., 1966; PhD, Inst. Atomic Energy, Moscow, 1969; LHD, Waynesburg Coll., 1995. Asst. prof. Moscow State U., 1969-71; assoc. prof. Mil. Tank Acad., Moscow, 1971-75; prof. U. Rochester, N.Y., 1977-80, Am. U., Washington, 1981-83, L.I. U., Bklyn., 1983-87; pres. Independent U., Washington, 1987-91; exec. dir. Andrei Sakharov Inst., Washington, 1981-86; pres. Russia House, Inc., 1991—, Am. U. in Moscow, 1992—, Am. Univs. in Russia, Ukraine and New Independent States, 1994—. Author: Theory of the Spark, 1976, For Tatiana, 1984, Andrei Sakharov, 1986, Mathematical Competitions, 1988, Democracy: USA-Russia, 1994, Winning Solutions, 1996. Mem. Russian Acad. Soc. Scis. Avocations: skiing, chess, lecturing on Russia. Office: Russia House 1800 Connecticut Ave NW Washington DC 20009-5731

LOZEAU, DONNALEE M., state legislator; b. Nashua, N.H., Sept. 15, 1960; m. David Lozeau; 3 children. Attended, Rivier Coll. Mem. N.H. Ho. of Reps., former vice chair corrections and criminal justice com., vice chair rules com., legis. adminstrn. com., dep. spkr. Former chair ward five Rep. City Com.; commr. Nashua Airport Authority. Avocations: reading, outdoor sports, travel. Home: 125 Shore Dr Nashua NH 03062-1339 Office: NH Ho of Reps State Capitol Concord NH 03301

LOZITO, DEBORAH ANN, osteopathic internist; b. Paterson, N.J., Jan. 20, 1960; d. Joseph Anthony and Geraldine Anita (Note) L. BS, Montclair State U., 1982; DO, Phila. Coll. Osteo. Medicine, 1987. Diplomate Am. Bd. Osteo. Internists. Physician-in-tng. Union (N.J.) Hosp., 1987-91; physician Hawthorne (N.J.) Med. Assocs., 1991—. Mem. AMA, Am. Osteo. Assn., N.J. Assn. Osteo. Physicians and Surgeons, Am. Coll. Osteo. Internists. Office: Hawthorne Med Assocs 484 Lafayette Ave Hawthorne NJ 07506-2522

LOZNER, EUGENE LEONARD, internal medicine educator, consultant; b. Stamford, N.Y., Apr. 29, 1915; s. Samuel and Rebecca (Barnhard) L.; m. Jean MacPherson Culver, July 3, 1942; 1 child: Eugene Culver. BA, Columbia Coll., 1933; MD, Cornell U., 1937. Diplomate Am. Bd. Internal Medicine. Intern Albany (N.Y.) Hosp., 1937-38; resident Boston City Hosp., 1938-41; assoc. in pathology George Washington U., Washington, 1942-46; instr. medicine Harvard Med. Sch., Cambridge, Mass., 1946-47; assoc. prof. medicine Syracuse (N.Y.) U., 1947-50; assoc. prof. medicine SUNY, Syracuse, 1950-56, prof. medicine, 1956-75, emeritus prof., 1975—; prof. internal med. U. So. Fla., Tampa, 1976—; attending physician Univ. Hosp., Syracuse, 1948-75, Vet.'s Affairs Hosp., Tampa, 1980—; dir. clin. labs. Univ. Hosp., Syracuse, 1948-65; staff physician Vet.'s Affairs Hosp., Tampa, 1975-79. Contbr. over 80 articles to profl. jours. Chmn. Syracuse Regional Bd. Program, 1952; bd. dirs. Am. Cancer Soc., 1970; mem. nat. med. com. Planned Parenthood Fedn. Am., 1970-75; chmn. Syracuse and Onondaga County chpts. ARC, 1972-73. Comdr. USNR, 1941-47. Fellow Am. Coll. Physicians, Am. Soc. Hematology, Internat. Soc. Hematology; mem. Am. Soc. Clin. Investigation, Am. Fed. Clin. Rsch. (councillor 1941-47, pres. 1946-47), Phi Beta Kappa, Alpha Omega Alpha, Sigma Xi. Avocation: kite flying. Home and Office: 10364 Carrollwood Ln Apt 223 Tampa FL 33618-4728

LOZOFF, BETSY, pediatrician; b. Milw., Dec. 19, 1943; d. Milton and Marjorie (Morse) L.; 1 child, Claudia Brittenham. BA, Radcliffe Coll., 1965; MD, Case Western Res. U., 1971, MS, 1981. Diplomate Am. Bd. Pediat. From asst. prof. to prof. pediatrics Case Western Res. U., Cleve., 1974-93; prof. pediatrics U. Mich., Ann Arbor, 1993—, dir. Ctr. for Human Growth and Devel., 1993—. Recipient Rsch. Career Devel. award Nat. Inst. Child Health and Human Devel., 1984-88. Fellow Am. Acad. Pediatrics; mem. Soc. for Pediatric Rsch., Soc. Rsch. in Child Devel. (program com. 1988—), Soc. Behavioral Pediatrics (exec. com. 1985-88), Ambulatory Pediatric Soc. Office: Univ Mich Ctr Human Growth and Devel 300 N Ingalls St Ann Arbor MI 48109-2007

LOZOFF, BO, nonprofit organization administrator; b. Miami, Fla., Jan. 10, 1947; s. Eli Saul and Molly (Rubitzky) L.; m. Sita Linda Shrager, Sept. 25, 1966; 1 child, Joshua Elias Bo. Student, Tulane U., 1963-64, U. Fla., 1967. Rsch. assoc. Psychical Rsch. Found., Durham, N.C., 1972-74; mgr. Sunshine Farms Yoga Ashram, Durham, 1973-77; dir. Prison-Ashram Project, Durham, 1973—, Human Kindness Found., Durham, 1973—, Kindness House, Mebane, N.C., 1994—; cons. in field. Author: We're All Doing Time, 1984, Lineage and Other Stories, 1987, Inner Corrections, 1989, Just Another Spiritual Book, 1990. Recipient Quetlalcotyl award Xat Medicine Soc., 1986, Temple Award for Creative Altruism, Inst. of Noetic Scis., 1994. Office: Human Kindness Foundation RR 1 Box 201-n Durham NC 27705-9801*

LOZYNIAK, ANDREW, manufacturing company executive; b. N.Y.C., July 28, 1931; s. Stephen and Helen (Pupchek) L.; m. Florence Slovitski, Nov. 24, 1955; children: Cynthia, Andrew, Richard, Wendy, Cathy. Grad., U. Conn., 1954. Pres. Fermont div. Dynamics Corp. Am., 1968-70; group v.p. Dynamics Corp. Am., Greenwich, Conn., 1970; exec. v.p. Dynamics Corp. Am., 1970, pres., 1970—, chmn. bd., 1978—, also dir.; bd. dirs. CTS Corp., Elkhart, Ind., Physicians Health Svcs., Trumbull, Conn. Mem. Patterson, Indian Harbor Yacht Club. Office: Dynamics Corp Am 475 Steamboat Rd Greenwich CT 06830-7144

LU, BAI, neurobiologist; b. Shanghai, China; s. Shi Chang and Tian Zheng (Li) L.; m. Liya Shen, July 25, 1985; 1 child, Benjamin. BS, East China Normal U., Shanghai, 1982; PhD, Cornell U., 1990. Asst. mem. Rochech Inst. Molecular Biology, Nutley, N.J., 1993-95; adj. asst. prof. Columbia U., N.Y.C., 1994, Robert Wood Johnson Med. Coll., Piscataway, N.Y., 1995; unit chief Nat. Inst. Child and Human Devel., NIH, Bethesda, Md., 1996—. Contbr. articles to profl. jours. Mem. AAAS, Soc. for Neurosci. Achievements include research in role of nitric oxide in synapse development and plasticity; role of neurotrophic factors in synapse development and plasticity; role of calcium binding proteins in synapse development and plasticity. Office: NICHD NIH 49 Convent Dr MSC 4480 Bethesda MD 20892-4480

LU, DAN, systems analyst, mathematician, consultant; b. Beijing, Jan. 22, 1960; came to U.S., 1981; s. Yingzhong Lu and Huaiqing Chen; m. Hong Lou, Sept. 28, 1994; 1 child, Katherine H. BS in Physics, Beijing U., 1981; MS in Physics, U. Wash., 1983, PhD in Theoretical Physics, 1986. Tchg., rsch. asst. U. Wash., Seattle, 1981-86; postdoctoral rsch. assoc. Washington U., St. Louis, 1986-88; R&D mgr. Yu Feng Internat. Ltd., Hong Kong, 1988-90; sys. cons. Summit Computer Svcs., Charlotte, N.C., 1991-93; sr. sys. cons. Criterion Group, Charlotte, 1993-94; bus. sys. analyst, mathematician INMAR Enterprise, Inc. Info. Tech. (formerly CMS, Inc.), Winston-Salem, N.C., 1994—. Contbr. articles to profl. publs. China-U.S. Physics Examination and Application fellow, 1981. Mem. Am. Phys. Soc. Achievements include development of model for market promotion, forecasting system for coupon redemption, set of subroutines to calculate EXAFS electron energy losses. Home: 325 Craver Pointe Dr Clemmons NC 27012 Office: INMAR Enterprises Inc Info Tech 2650 Pilgrim Ct Winston Salem NC 27106-5238

LU, DAVID JOHN, history educator, writer; b. Keelung, Taiwan, Sept. 28, 1928; came to U.S., 1950, naturalized, 1960; s. Ming and Yeh (Lai) L.; m. Annabelle Compton, May 29, 1954; children: David John, Daniel Mark, Cynthia King, Stephen Paul. B.A. in Econs, Nat. Taiwan U., 1950; postgrad., Westminster Theol. Sem., Phila., 1950-52; M. Internat. Affairs, Columbia, 1954; certificate, East Asian Inst., 1954, Ph.D., 1960. Editor Prentice-Hall, Inc., 1956-60; instr. Rutgers U., 1959; asst. prof. history Bucknell U., Lewisburg, Pa., 1960-64; assoc. prof. Bucknell U., 1964-69, prof., 1969-94, prof. emeritus, 1994—, dir. Ctr. for Japanese Studies, 1965-94; cons. on global edn. Pa. Dept. Edn., 1961-62, 78, U.S. Dept. Edn., 1973-85; resident dir. associated Kyoto program Doshisha U., 1987-88. Author: From the Marco Polo Bridge to Pearl Harbor, 1961, (Japanese edit.) Taiheiyo Senso e no Dotei, 1967, Sources of Japanese History, 2 vols., 1974, Bicentennial History of the United States (in Japanese), 1976, The Life and Times of Matsuoka Yosuke, 1880-1946, 1981, Inside Corporte Japan: The Art of Fumble-free Management, 1987, Japan: A Documentary History, 1997; translator: The China Quagmire, 1983, What Is Total Quality Control? The Japanese Way, 1985, Kanban, Just-in-Time at Toyota, 1986, Total Quality Control for Management: Strategies and Techniques from Toyota and Toyoda Gosei, 1987 TQC (Total Quality Control), The Wisdom of Japan, 1988; contbr. Sekai to Nippon, weekly, Tokyo. Fulbright-Hays scholar Japan, 1966-67. Presbyterian. Home: 1303 Mazeland Dr Bel Air MD 21015-6358

LU, GUIYANG, electrical engineer; b. Guiyang, China, May 10, 1946; came to U.S., 1982; s. Wen and Yunqiu Deng; m. Jing Du; 1 child, Jia. Degree in elec. engring., Tsing Hua U., Beijing, 1970; postgrad., South China U. Tech., Guangzhou, 1980-81; MA in Math., Calif. State U., Fresno, 1984; MSEE, Poly. U., N.Y.C., 1986. Instr. in elec. engring. South China U. Tech., Guangzhou, 1973-80; v.p. engring. Kawahara Corp., N.Y.C., 1986-88; H.S. math. tchr. N.Y.C. Bd. Edn., 1988-90; sr. R&D engr. Avid Inc., Norco, Calif., 1991—. Mem. IEEE. Home: 1718 Eastgate Ave Upland CA 91784-9210 Office: Avid Inc 3179 Hamner Ave Norco CA 91760-1983

LU, HUIZHU, computer scientist, educator; m. Yin Ming Wang; children: Serkuang, Qiang. BS in Physics, Fudan U., Shanghai, 1961; MS in Computer Science, U. Okla., 1983, PhD in Computer Science, 1988. Lectr. Shanghai U. Technology, Shanghai, China, 1961-80; visiting research associate, scientist U. Okla., Norman, 1981-85; asst. prof. Okla. State U., Stillwater, 1985-92, assoc. prof., 1992—; prin. investigator of projects Okla. Dept. Health, Okla. Dept. Environ. Quality, others. Co-author: Digital Measurement Techniques, 1980; contbr. numerous rsch. articles to profl. jours. Recipient numerous rsch. grants. Mem. Assn. for Computing Machinery, IEEE Computer Soc., Sigma Xi. Office: Oklahoma State U 213 Mathematical Sci Bldg Stillwater OK 74078

LU, PAUL HAIHSING, mining engineer, geotechnical consultant; b. Hsinchu, Taiwan, Apr. 6, 1921; came to U.S., 1962; m. Sylvia Chin-Pi Liu, May 5, 1951; children: Emily, Flora. BS in Mining Engring., Hokkaido U., Sapporo, Japan, 1945; PhD in Mining Engring., U. Ill., 1967. Sr. mining engr., br. chief Mining Dept. Taiwan Provincial Govt., Taipei, 1946-56; sr. indsl. specialist mining and geology U.S. State Dept./Agy. for Internat. Devel., Taipei, 1956-62; rsch. mining engr. Denver Rsch. Ctr. Bur. of Mines, U.S. Dept. Interior, 1967-90; geotech. cons. Lakewood, Colo., 1991—. Contbr. over 60 articles to profl. jours. Rsch. fellow Hokkaido U., 1945-46, Ill. Mining Inst., 1966-67. Mem. Internat. Soc. for Rock Mechanics, Am. Rock Mechanics Assn., Mining and Materials Processing Inst. Japan, Chinese Inst. of Mining and Metall. Engrs. (dir., mining com. chair 1960-62, Tech. Achievement award 1962, merit award 1996). Achievements include development of prestressed concrete mine supports; invention of new technologies of rock stress measurement with hydraulic borehole pressure cells and measurement of geomechanical properties of rock masses with borehole pressure cells; invention of integrity factor approach to mine structure design. Home and Office: 1001 S Foothill Dr Lakewood CO 80228-3404

LU, PONZY, molecular biology educator; b. Shanghai, China, Oct. 7, 1942; came to U.S., 1949, naturalized, 1963; s. Abraham and Beth (Chou) L.; m. Heidi Fahl, Jan. 13, 1975; 1 child, Kristina. B.S., Calif. Inst. Tech., 1964; Ph.D., MIT, 1970. Arthritis Found. postdoctoral fellow Max Planck Inst., Goettingen, Fed. Republic Germany, 1970-73; asst. prof. dept. chemistry U. Pa., Phila., 1973-78; assoc. prof. U. Pa., 1978-82, prof., 1982—; mem. study sect. NIH, 1982-86, 92-96; mem. Univ. Space Reseach Assn./NASA Biotechnology Discipline Working Group, microgravity sci. and applications div., 1986-91. Recipient Career Devel. award NIH, 1977-82. Mem. Am. Soc. Biochemistry, Molecular Biology, Biophys. Soc., Sigma Xi. Office: Univ Pa Dept Chemistry Philadelphia PA 19104

LU, SHIH-PENG, history educator; b. Kao-Yu, Chiang-Su, China, Sept. 16, 1928; s. Ch'un-Tai and Chu-Yin (Chia) L.; m. Wei-Chun Julia Lee; children: Ting Ting, Shin. BA, Nat. Taiwan U., Taipei, 1952. Cert. full prof., Ministry of Edn., Taiwan. Tchg. asst. Taiwan U., Taipei, 1953-55; rsch. asst. Acad. Sinica, Taipei, 1955-58; lectr. Tunghai U., Taichung, Taiwan, 1958-63, assoc. prof., 1963-67, prof., 1967—; vis. scholar Harvard U., Cambridge, Mass., 1961-63; rsch. fellow Yale U., New Haven, 1980-81; dir. evening divsn. Tunghai U., 1972-81, chmn. dept. history, 1981-87, dean Coll. Arts, 1988-94; dir. Chinese Culture Monthly, Taichung, 1988—. Author: Vietnam During the Period of Chinese Rule, 1964 (Nat. Sci. Coun. Publ. award 1965), The Modern History of China, 1979 (World Books Co. Authors award 1979), The Contemporary History of China, 1991 (Ministry of Edn. Outstanding Textbook award 1992); editor Chinese Culture Monthly, 1979— (Ministry of Edn. Best Jour. award 1991). 2nd lt. ROTC, Chinese Mil., 1952-53. Named Outstanding Youth, China Youth Corps, Taiwan, 1952, Outstanding Prof., Ministry of Edn., 1992. Mem. Assn. Modern History (chairperson bd. overseers 1994-96), Chinese Hist. Assn. (bd. dirs. 1983-94), Taiwan U. Alumni Assn. (chmn. 1987-89), Assn. for Ming Studies (exec. dir. 1995—). Avocations: reading, classical music, table tennis, jogging, Chinese opera. Home: 49 Tunghai Rd, 407 Taichung Taiwan Office: Tunghai Univ, Dept History, 407 Taichung Taiwan

LUBACHIVSKY, MYROSLAV IVAN CARDINAL, archbishop; b. Dolyna, West Ukraine, June 24, 1914; came to U.S., 1947, naturalized, 1952; s. Eustahi and Anna (Oliynik) L. Student, Theol. Acad. Lviv; Grad., Faculty of Theology, U. Innsbruk, 1939, S.T.D., 1942; M. in Biblical Studies, Papal Biblical Inst., 1943; M.Phil., Gregorian U., Rome, 1945; student in medicine U. Rome, before 1947. Ordained priest Cath. Ch. of the Ukranian Rite, 1938. Began pastoral career in U.S., 1947, apptd. archbishop of Ukranian-rite archeparchy of Phila., 1979; coadjutor archbishop of Lviv of the Ukranians, 1980; archbishop of Lviv and major archbishop of Ukranians, 1984, created cardinal, 1985; titular ch., St. Sofia. Office: Sobor Sviatoho Jura, Plosha Bohduna Khmelnyckoho 5, 290000 Lviv Ukraine

LUBAR, JEFFREY STUART, journalist, trade association executive; b. Rockville Centre, N.Y., Apr. 15, 1947; s. Sidney and Rose (Grupsmith) L.; m. Barbara Ruth Bigelman; children—Debra, Adam, Rachel. B.A., Am. U., 1969. Dir. Washington News Bur., Susquehanna Broadcasting Co., 1969-86; v.p. pub. affairs Nat. Assn. Realtors, Washington, 1987-96, v.p. comm., 1997—; Mem. exec. com. of corrs. Radio-TV Assn. (U.S. Congress), 1974-75. Served with AUS, 1969-75. Mem. Burke Racquet Club, Nat. Press Club. Jewish. Home: 6307 Karmich St Fairfax VA 22039-1622 Office: 700 11th St NW Washington DC 20001-4507

LUBATTI, HENRY JOSEPH, physicist, educator; b. Oakland, Calif., Mar. 16, 1937; s. John and Pauline (Massimino) L.; m. Catherine Jeanne Berthe Ledoux, June 29, 1968; children: Karen E., Henry J., Stephen J.C. AA, U. Calif., Berkeley, 1957, AB, 1960; PhD, U. Calif., 1966; MS, U. Ill., 1963. Research assoc. Faculty Scis. U. Paris, Orsay, France, 1966-68; asst. prof. physics MIT, 1968-69; assoc. prof., sci. dir. visual techniques lab. U. Wash., 1969-74, prof., sci. dir. visual Techniques lab., 1974—; vis. lectr. Internat. Sch. Physics, Erice, Sicily, 1968, Herceg-Novi, Yugoslavia Internat. Sch., 1969, XII Cracow Sch. Theoretical Physics, Zapokane, Poland, 1972; vis. scientist CERN, Geneva, 1980-81; vis. staff Los Alamos Nat. Lab., 1983-86; guest scientist SSC Lab., 1991-93; mem. physics editorial adv. com. World Sci. Pub. Co. Ltd., 1982-93. Editor: Physics at Fermilab in the 1990's, 1990; contbr. numerous articles on high energy physics to profl. jours. Alfred P. Sloan research fellow, 1971-75. Fellow AAAS, Am. Phys. Soc.; mem. Sigma Xi, Tau Beta Pi. Office: U Wash Visual Techniques Lab Physics Box 351560 Seattle WA 98195-1560

LUBAWSKI, JAMES LAWRENCE, health care consultant; b. Chgo., June 4, 1946; s. Harry James and Stella Agnes (Pokorny) L.; m. Kathleen Felicity Donnellan, June 1, 1974; children: Kathleen N., James Lawrence, Kevin D., Edward H. BA, Northwestern U., 1968, MBA, 1969, MA, 1980. Asst. prof. U. Northern Iowa, Cedar Falls, 1969-72; instr. Loyola U., Chgo., 1974-76; dir., market planning Midwest Stock Exchange, Chgo., 1976-77; dir. mktg. Gambro Inc., Barrington, Ill., 1977-79; mktg. mgr. Travenol Labs., Deerfield, Ill., 1979-82; dir. mktg. Hollister Inc., Libertyville, Ill., 1982-84; pres., chief exec. officer Neomedica Inc., Chgo., 1984-86; v.p. bus. devel. Evangl. Health Svcs., Oak Brook, Ill., 1986-87; pres., chief exec. officer Cath. Health Alliance Met. Chgo., 1987-95; mng. dir. Ward Howell Internat., Chgo., 1995—. Author: Food and Man, 1974, Food and People, 1979; co-editor: Consumer Behavior in Theory and in Action, 1970. Am. Assn. Advt. Acys. Faculty fellow, 1973. Mem. Evanston Golf Club, Equestrian Order of Knights of Holy Sepulchre. Avocation: golf, fishing. Office: Ward Howell Internat 300 S Wacker Dr Ste 2940 Chicago IL 60606-6703

LUBBERS, AREND DONSELAAR, academic administrator; b. Milw., July 23, 1931; s. Irwin Jacob and Margaret (Van Donselaar) L.; m. Eunice L. Mayo, June 19, 1953 (div.); children—Arend Donselaar, John Irwin Darrow, Mary Elizabeth; m. Nancy Vanderpol, Dec. 21, 1968; children—Robert Andrew, Caroline Jayne. AB, Hope Coll., 1953; AM, Rutgers U., 1956; LittD, Central Coll., 1977; DSc, U. Sarajevo, Yugoslavia, 1987; LHD, Hope Coll., 1988; DSc, Akademia Ekonomiczna, Krakow, Poland, 1989, U. Kingston Univ., Eng., 1995. Research asst. Rutgers U., 1954-55; research fellow Reformed Ch. in Am., 1955-56; instr. history and polit. sci. Wittenberg U., 1956-58; v.p. devel. Central Coll., Iowa, 1959-60; pres. Central Coll., 1960-69, Grand Valley State U., Allendale, Mich., 1969—; mem. Am. Assn. State Colls. and Univs. seminar in India, 1971, Fed. Commn. Orgn. Govt. for Conduct Fgn. Policy, 1972; USIA insp., Netherlands, 1976; mem. pres.'s commn. NCAA, 1984-87, 89—, pres. com., 1989-95; bd. dirs. Grand Bank, Grand Rapids, Mich. Sutdent Cmty. amb. from Holland (Mich.) to Yugoslavia, 1951; bd. dirs. Grand Rapids Symphony, 1976-82, Butterworth Hosp., 1988; chmn. divsn. II NCAA Pres.'s Commn., 1992-95. Recipient Golden Plate award San Diego Acad. Achievement, 1962, Golden-Emblem Order of Merit Polish Peoples Republic, 1988; named 1 of top 100 young men in U.S. Life mag., 1962. Mem. Mich. Coun. State Univs. Pres. (chmn. 1988), Grand Rapids World Affairs Council (pres. 1971-73), Phi Alpha Theta, Pi Kappa Delta, Pi Kappa Phi. Home: 801 Plymouth Ave SE Grand Rapids MI

49506-6555 Office: Grand Valley State U Coll Landing 1 Campus Dr Allendale MI 49401-9401*

LUBCHENCO, JANE, marine biologist, educator; b. Denver, Dec. 4, 1947; married; 2 children. BA, Colo. Coll., 1969; MS, U. Wash., 1971; PhD in Ecology, Harvard U., 1975. Asst. prof. ecology Harvard U., Cambridge, Mass., 1975-77; from asst. prof. to assoc. prof. Oreg. State U., Corvallis, 1978-88, prof. zoology, 1988—; rsch. assoc. Smithsonian Inst., 1978—; prin. investigator NSF, 1976—; adv. panel long term ecol. rsch. programs, 1977; vis. asst. prof. Discovery Bay Marine Lab., 1976; sci. adv. Ocean Trust Found., 1978-84, West Quoddy Marine Sta., 1981-88; vis. assoc. prof. U. Antofagasta, Chile, 1985, Inst. Oceanography, Qingdao, China, 1987. Fellow John D. and Katherine T. MacArthur Found., 1993. Mem. Ecol. Soc. Am. (George Mercer award 1979, mem. coun. 1982-84, chair awards com. 1983-86, nominating com. 1986), Phycological Soc. Am. (nat. lectr. 1987-89), Am. Soc. Naturalists, Am. Soc. Zoologists, Am. Inst. Biol. Sci. Achievements include research in population and community ecology, plant-herbivore and predator-prey interactions, competition, marine ecology, algal ecology, algal life histories, biogeography and chemical ecology. Office: OR State U Dept Of Zoology Corvallis OR 97331

LUBECK, MARVIN JAY, ophthalmologist; b. Cleve., Mar. 20, 1929; s. Charles D. and Lillian (Jay) L. A.B., U. Mich., 1951, M.D., 1955, M.S., 1959. Diplomate Am. Bd. Opthamology; m. Arlene Sue Bitman, Dec. 28, 1955; children: David Mark, Daniel Jay, Robert Charles. Intern, U. Mich. Med. Ctr., 1955-56, resident ophthalmology, 1956-58, jr. clin. instr. ophthalmology, 1958-59; pvt. practice medicine, specializing in ophthalmology, Denver, 1961—; mem. staff Rose Hosp., Porter Hosp., Presbyn. Hosp., St. Luke's Hosp.; assoc. clin. prof. U. Colo. Med. Ctr. With U.S. Army, 1959-61. Fellow ACS; mem. Am. Acad. Ophthalmology, Denver Med. Soc., Colo. Ophthalmol. Soc. Home: 590 S Harrison Ln Denver CO 80209-3517 Office: 3600 E Alameda Ave Denver CO 80209-3111

LUBELL, HAROLD, economic consultant; b. N.Y.C., Mar. 29, 1925; s. Morris and Fannie (Bell) L.; m. Claudie Marchaut, 1962; children: Martin, Diane. BA, Bard Coll., 1944; MPA, Harvard U., 1947, MA in Econs., 1948, PhD in Econs., 1953. Economist Fed. Res. Bd., Washington, 1944-45, ECA/MSA, Paris, 1949-53; Economist AID, Ankara, Turkey, 1965-68, New Delhi, 1969-71, Washington, 1978-82, Cairo, 1982-85, Dakar, 1985-89; economist Falk Project for Econ. Research, Jerusalem, 1954-57, Rand Corp., Santa Monica, Calif., 1957-62; with Ford Found., Saigon, Vietnam, Kuala Lumpur, Malaysia, 1963-64; economist World Employment Program, ILO, Geneva, 1971-78; econ. cons. 1989—. Author: Middle East Oil Crises and Western Europe's Energy Supplies, 1963, Urban Development and Employment: the Prospects for Calcutta, 1974, The Informal Sector in the 1980s and the 1990s, 1990. Office: 25 Rue de Lille, Paris 75007, France

LUBENSKY, EARL HENRY, diplomat, anthropologist; b. Marshall, Mo., Mar. 31, 1921; s. Henry Carl and Adele Gertrud (Biesemeyer) L.; m. Anita Ruth Price, June 27, 1942 (dec. July 1992); children: Tom, Gerald, John Christopher; m. Margot Truman Patterson, Mar. 26, 1994. BA, Mo. Valley Coll., 1948, LLD (hon.), 1968; BS, Georgetown U., 1949; MS, George Washington U., 1967; MA, U. Mo., 1983, PhD, 1991. Mgr. Tavern Supply Co., Marshall, Mo., 1938-42; real estate salesman Mitchell Quick Realtor, Silver Spring, Md., 1948; rsch. analyst Georgetown U., Washington, 1949; reference asst. Libr. of Congress, Washington, 1949; fgn. svc. officer Dept. of State, Washington, 1949-79; served in Germany, Philippines, Spain, Ecuador, Colombia and El Salvador; diplomat-in-residence, Olivet, Albion and Adrian Colls., Mich.; mem. staff internat. affairs Coun. on Environ. Quality, Washington. Contbr. articles to profl. jours. With Mo. N.G. 1937-40. 2d lt. U.S. Army, 1942-45, lt. col. USAR, 1945-81. Eagle Scout Boy Scouts Am., 1939. Mem. Mo. Archaeol. Soc. (charter, trustee, Appreciation award 1991), Soc. for Am. Archaeology (Presdl. Recognition award 1991), Inst. Andean Studies, Fgn. Svc. Assn., Diplomatic and Consular Officrs Retired, Boone County Hist. Soc., others. Democrat. Avocations: genealogy, gardening, music, ham radio, philately. Home: 1408 Bradford Dr Columbia MO 65203-2302 Office: Dept Anthropology Univ Mo Columbia MO 65211

LUBER, THOMAS J(ULIAN), lawyer; b. Louisville, Feb. 16, 1949; s. John J. and Martha E. (Cotton) L.; m. Dorothy Ann Carter, Dec. 19, 1975; children: Katharine Ann, Allison Julia. BS in Acctg., U. Louisville, 1972, JD with honors, 1976; LLM in Taxation, NYU, 1977. Bar: Ky. 1976. Agt. IRS, Louisville, 1972-73; assoc. Fahey & Gray, Louisville, 1977-79; from assoc. to ptnr. Wyatt, Tarrant & Combs and predecessor firms, Louisville, 1979—, chmn. tax sect., 1983—; lectr. U. Louisville, 1978-80; speaker in field; bd. advisors Jour. Multistate Taxation. Contbr. articles to profl. jours. Bd. dirs. Univ. Pediatrics Found., Louisville, Univ. Ob-gyn. Found., Louisville, Assumption High Sch., Louisville. With USAF, 1967-69. Mem. ABA, Ky. Bar Assn. (chmn. tax sect. 1983-84), Louisville Bar Assn., Ky. Inst. Fed. Taxation (mem. planning com. 1981—, chmn. 1984—), Jefferson Club, Big Spring Country Club. Democrat. Roman Catholic. Avocations: hiking, working out. Home: 2324 Saratoga Dr Louisville KY 40205-2021 Office: Wyatt Tarrant & Combs 2800 Citizens Plz Louisville KY 40202-2898

LUBERDA, GEORGE JOSEPH, lawyer, educator; b. N.Y.C., Apr. 27, 1930; s. Joseph George and Mary Loretta (Koslowski) L.; m. Beverly Louis Carey, Feb. 13, 1954; children: Margaret, Joseph, Eileen, Ann Marie, Julie. Bar: D.C. 1959, U.S. Ct. Appeals (D.C. cir.) 1959, Mich. 1970, Mo. 1973. Washington rep. Ford Motor Co., Washington, 1955-59; atty. FTC, Washington, 1960-64; trial atty. Antitrust Div. Dept. Justice, Washington, 1965-69; sr. atty. Bendix Corp., Mich., 1970-71; assoc. Butzel, Long, Gust, Klein & Van Zile, Detroit, 1972; antitrust counsel Monsanto Co., St. Louis, 1973-88; assoc. Herzog, Crebs and McGhee, 1988-93; ptnr. Luberda & Carp, St. Louis, 1993—; adj. prof. St. Louis U., 1985—. Mem. Mo. Bar Assn., Bar Assn. Met. St. Louis. Republican. Roman Catholic. Home: 716 Ridgeview Circle Ln Ballwin MO 63021-7810 Office: Luberda & Carp 225 S Meramec Ave Ste 325 Saint Louis MO 63105-3511

LUBETSKI, EDITH ESTHER, librarian; b. Bklyn., July 16, 1940; d. David and Leah (Aronson) Slomowitz; m. Meir Lubetski, Dec. 23, 1968; children: Shaul, Uriel, Leah. BA, Bklyn. Coll., 1962; MS in L.S., Columbia U., 1965; MA in Jewish Studies, Yeshiva U., 1968. Judaica librarian Stern Coll., N.Y.C., 1965-66, acquisitions librarian, 1966-69, head librarian, 1969—; Author: (with Meir Lubetski) Building a Judaica Library Collection, 1983; contbr. articles to profl. jours. Mem. ALA, Assn. Jewish Libraries (corr. sec. 1980-84, pres. N.Y. chpt. 1984-86, nat. v.p. 1984-86, nat. pres. 1986-88, Fanny Goldstein Merit award 1993), N.Y. Library Assn. Home: 1219 E 27th St Brooklyn NY 11210-4622 Office: Yeshiva U Hedi Steinberg Libr 245 Lexington Ave New York NY 10016-4605

LUBIC, ROBERT BENNETT, lawyer, arbitrator, law educator; b. Pitts., Mar. 9, 1929; s. H. Murray and Rose M. (Schwartz) L.; m. Benita Joan Alk, May 18, 1959; children—Wendy, Bret, Robin. AB, U. Pitts., 1950, JD, 1953; LLM in Patent Law, Georgetown U., 1959. Bar: Pa. 1953, U.S. Supreme Ct. 1958, U.S. Ct. Appeals (D.C. cir.) 1958, U.S. Patent Office, 1959, U.S. Dist. Ct. D.C. 1964. Atty., adviser FCC, Washington, 1957-59; sole practice, Pitts., 1959-63; asst. prof. law Duquesne U. Law Sch., Pitts., 1963-65; prof. law Am. U. Law Sch., Washington, 1965—, assoc. dean, 1970-71; cons. to Embassy Rep. of Georgia; pres. Stas. WRGI and WRGI-FM, Naples and Marco Island, Fla., 1974-77; vis. prof. U. P.R. Law Sch., 1993, Internat. Christian U., Tokyo, 1988-89, East China U. Politics and Law, 1994, U. Warsaw, Poland, 1995, U. Torino, Italy, 1997—; permanent panel arbitrator U.S. Postal System, Washington, 1978—, U.S. Dept. Labor, Washington, 1982-87; arbitrator Pub. Employee Relations Bd. D.C., Washington, 1984—, Pub. Employee Rels. Bd. V.I., 1982—; dir. Labor Disputes Resolution Seminar, Hamilton, Bermuda, 1982, 83, Nassau, Bahamas, 1983, labor cons. Govt. of Bermuda, 1985; creator, dir. Eastern European Summer Law Program, Moscow and Warsaw, 1979-81, Chinese Am. Summer Law Program, Peking, Shanghai and Hong Kong, 1984-86; co-dir. Middle East Summer Law Program, Jerusalem, 1976, 78. Served as cpl. U.S. Army, 1953-55. Recipient Outstanding Tchr. award Am. U. Student Bar Assn., 1981. Mem. ABA, Fed. Comm. Bar Assn., D.C. Bar Assn., Am. Arbitration Assn. Democrat. Jewish. Home: 2813 Mckinley Pl NW Washington DC 20015-1104 Office: Am U Sch Law 4801 Massachusetts Ave NW Washington DC 20016-8180

LUBIC, RUTH WATSON, association executive, nurse midwife; b. Bucks County, Pa., Jan. 18, 1927; d. John Russell and Lillian (Kraft) Watson; m. William James Lubic, May 28, 1955; 1 son, Douglas Watson. Diploma, Sch. Nursing Hosp. U. Pa., 1955; BS, Columbia U., 1959, MA, 1961, EdD in Applied Anthropology, 1979; Cert. in Nurse Midwifery, SUNY, Bklyn., 1962; LLD (hon.), U. Pa., 1985; DSc (hon.), U. Medicine and Dentistry, N.J., 1986; LHD (hon.), Coll. New Rochelle, 1992; DSc (hon.), SUNY, Bklyn., 1993; LHD (hon.), Pace U., 1994. RN, Pa. Mem. faculty Sch. Nursing, N.Y. Med. Coll.; mem. faculty Maternity Ctr. Assn., SUNY Sch. Nurse-Midwifery, Downstate Med. Ctr.; staff nurse through head nurse Meml. Hosp. for Cancer and Allied Disease, N.Y.C., 1955-58; clin. assoc. Grad. Sch. Nursing N.Y. Med. Coll., N.Y.C., 1962-63; parent educator, cons. Maternity Ctr. Assn., N.Y.C., 1963-67, gen. dir., 1970-95; dir. clin. projects., 1995—; cons. in midwifery, nursing and maternal and child health Office of Pub. Health and Sci. HHS, 1995—; adj. prof. divsn. nursing, NYU, 1995—; bd. dirs., v.p. Am. Assn. for World Health U.S. Com. for WHO, 1975-94, pres. 1980-81; mem. bd. maternal child and family health NRC, 1974-80; mem. Commn. on Grads. Fgn. Nursing Schs., 1979-83, v.p. 1980-91, treas., 1982-83; bd. govs. Frontier Nursing Svc., 1982-92; bd. dirs. Pan Am. Health Edn. Found., pres. 1987-88; vis. prof. King Edward Meml. Hosp., Perth, Australia, 1991; Kate Hanna Harvey vis. prof. cmty. health nursing Frances Payne Bolton Sch. Nursing Case Western Res., 1991; Lansdowne lectr. U. Victoria, B.C., Can., 1992. Author: (with Gene Hawes) Childbearing: A Book of Choices, 1987; contbr. articles to profl. jours. Recipient Letitia White award, Florence Nightingale medal, 1955, Rockefeller Pub. Svc. award, 1981, Hattie Hemschemeyer award, 1983, Alumnae award Sch. Nursing U. Pa., 1986, Tchrs. Coll. Columbia U., 1992, Disting. Svc. award Francis Payne Bolton Sch. Nursing, 1993, MacArthur Fellowship award, 1993, Hon. Recognition N.Y. State Nurses Assn., 1993, Nurse-Midwifery Faculty award Columbia U., 1993, Spirit of Nursing award Vis. Nurses Svc. N.Y., 1994, Maes-MacInnes award Divsn. Nursing NYU, 1994, Hon. recognition ANA, 1994, Carola Warburg Rothschild award Maternity Ctr. Assn., 1997; named Maternal-Child Health Nurse of Yr., ANA, 1985. Fellow AAAS, Am. Acad. Nursing, N.Y. Acad. Medicine, Soc. for Applied Anthropology, Am. Coll. of Nurse Midwives; mem. APHA (mem. com. on internat. health, sec. maternal and child health coun. 1982, mem. governing coun. 1986-89, mem. nominating com. 1987, mem. action bd. 1988-90), Am. Coll. Nurse-Midwives (v.p. 1964-66, pres.-elect 1969-70), Soc. Applied Anthropology, Inst. Medicine of NAS, Nat. Assn. Childbearing Ctrs. (pres. 1983-91), Herman Biggs Soc. (sec., treas. 1989-90), Cosmopolitan Club, Sigma Theta Tau. *As a professional nurse-midwife and public health scientist, the guiding principles of my professional life are to listen carefully to the families to be served and to combine their needs with proven scientific knowledge in constructing models for care. It is my belief that the primary purpose of maternal and child health programs is to assist families to achieve a sense of self-confidence about their ability to bring forth and rear offspring in conjunction with, but not dependent upon, professional guidance.*

LUBICK, DONALD CYRIL, lawyer; b. Buffalo, Apr. 29, 1926; s. Louis and Minna D. (Nabith) L.; m. Susan F. Cohen, June 5, 1960; children:Jonathan, Caroline, Lisa. BA summa cum laude, U. Buffalo, 1945; JD magna cum laude, Harvard U., 1949. Bar: N.Y. 1950, Fla. 1974, D.C. 1981; lic. fgn. law cons. Ont., 1989. Teaching fellow Harvard U. Law Sch., 1949-50; lectr. law U. Buffalo, 1950-61; assoc., then ptnr. Hodgson, Russ, Andrews, Woods & Goodyear, Buffalo and Washington, 1950-61, 64-77, 81-94; tax legis. counsel Treasury Dept., Washington, 1961-64; asst. sec. for tax policy Treasury Dept., 1977-81; dir. tax adv. program for countries of Ctrl. and Ea. Europe and former Soviet Union Treasury Dept., Paris, 1994—; acting asst. sec. for tax policy Treasury Dept., 1996—. Author: (with Hussey) Basic World Tax Code and Commentary, 1992, 95. Chmn. Tax Revision Com., City of Buffalo, 1958; mem. adv. com. to select Com. on Election Reform, N.Y. State Legislature, 1974, mem. adv. group to commr. internal revenue, 1976. Served with USAAF, 1945-46. Harvard Internat. Tax Program sr. fellow, 1991—. Mem. ABA, Am. Law Inst., Am. Bar Found., N.Y. State Bar Assn., Fla. Bar Assn., Erie County Bar Assn. Democrat. Jewish. Office: Main Treasury 15th & Pennsylvania Ave NW Washington DC 20220

LUBICK, SONNY, college football coach; b. Mar. 12, 1937; m. Carol Jo Lubick; children: Matthew, Michelle, Mark. BS, Western Mont. Coll., 1960; MS in Phys. Edn., Mont. State U., 1978. Head football coach Tutte (Mont.) H.S., 1963-69; asst. football coach Mont. State U., Bozeman, 1970-77, head coach, 1977-81; asst. coach Stanford U., Palo Alto, Calif., 1985-88; defensive coord. U. Miami, Fla., 1989-92; offensive coord. Colo. State U., Ft. Collins, 1982-84, head football coach, 1992—. Named Football Coach of Yr., State of Mont., 1968, Western Athletic Conf., 1994, Sports Illustrated, 1994, Nat. Coach of Yr., 1995. Office: Colo State U Football Dept Fort Collins CO 80523*

LUBIN, BERNARD, psychologist, educator; b. Washington, Oct. 15, 1923; s. Israel Harry and Anne (Cohen) L.; m. Alice Weisbord, Aug. 5, 1957. B.A., George Washington U., 1952, M.A., 1953; Ph.D., Pa. State U., 1958. Diplomate: Am. Bd. Profl. Psychology, Am. Bd. Psychol. Hypnosis; lic. psychologist, Mo., Tex. Intern St. Elizabeths Hosp., 1952-53, Roanoke (Va.) VA Hosp., 1954-55, Wilkes-Barre (Pa.) VA Hosp., 1955; USPHS postdoctoral fellow, postdoctoral residency in psychotherapy U. Wis. Sch. Medicine, 1957-58; staff psychologist, instr. dept. psychiatry Ind. U. Sch. Medicine, Indpls., 1958-59; chief psychologist adult outpatient service Ind. U. Sch. Medicine, 1960-62, assoc. prof., 1964-67; dir. psychol. services Dept. Mental Health, Indpls., 1962-63; dir. div. research and tng. Dept. Mental Health, 1963-67; dir. div. psychology Greater Kansas City (Mo.) Mental Health Center, 1967-74; prof. dept. psychiatry U. Mo. Sch. Medicine, Kansas City, 1967-74, 76—; prof., dir. clin. tng. program dept. psychology U. Houston, 1974-76; prof., chmn. dept. psychology U. Mo. at Kansas City, 1976-83, Curators' prof., 1988; trustees' faculty fellow, 1994; cons. Am. Nurses Assn., Panhandle Eastern Pipeline Co., Eli Lilly Pharm. Co., U.S. Sprint, Inst. Psychiat. Research, Ind. U. Med. Center, Ind. U. Sch. Dentistry, Goodwill Industries, USPHS Bur. Health Services, mental retardation div., (univ.-affiliated facilities br.), U.S. VA, Baylor U. Med. Sch., U. Tex. Health Scis. Center, Houston, 1974-76; Mem. tng. staff Nat. Tng. Labs. Inst.; dean or faculty mem. numerous confs., 1960—; exec. sec. Ind. Assn. for Advancement Mental Health Research and Edn., 1962-67. Author: (with M. Zuckerman) Multiple Affect Adjective Check List: Manual, 1965, 2d edit., 1985, (with E.E. Levitt) The Clinical Psychologist: Background, Roles and Functions, 1967, Depression: Concepts, Controversies, and Some New Facts, 1975, 2d edit., 1983, Depression Adjective Check Lists: Manual, 1967, rev. edit., 1994, (with L.D. Goodstein and A.W. Lubin) Organizational Development Sourcebooks I and II, 1979; (with W.A. O'Connor) Ecological Approaches to Clinical and Community Psychology, 1984, (with D.C. Martin and R.A. Blanc) Study Guide and Readings for Abnormal Psychology, 1984, (with Alice W. Lubin) Comprehensive Index to the Group Psychotherapy Literature: 1906-1980, 1987, (with A.W. Lubin) Family Therapy: A Bibliography, 1937-86, 1988, (with R. Gist) Psychosocial Aspects of Disaster, 1989 (with R.V. Whitlock) Homelessness in America: A Bibliography with Selective Annotations, 1894-1994, (with D. Wilson, S. Petren and A. Polk) Research on Group Methods of Treatment: 1970-1996, (with D. Wilson) Annotated Bibliography on Organizational Consultation, (with P. G. Hanson) Answers to the Most Frequently Asked Questions About Organization Development, also articles; editorial bd. Jour. Community Psychology; mem. editorial bd. Internat. Jour. Group Psychotherapy, Profl. Psychology: Research and Practice; cons. reader, bd. dirs. Jour. Cons. and Clin. Psychology. pres. Midwest Group for Human Resources, Inc., 1965-69, trustee, 1965. Recipient N.T. Veatch award for disting. rsch. and creative activity, 1983; faculty fellow U. Kansas City, 1994. Mem. APA (chmn. sponsor approval com., exec. bd. dirs. cons. psychology, coun. rep., Disting. Sr. Contbr. to Counseling Psychology award 1995, Harry Levinson award for excellence in consultation 1996), AAAS, Mo. Psychol. Assn. (exec. bd., Richard Wilkinson Lifetime Achievement award 1997), Am. Group Psychotherapy Assn. (edit. com.); mem. Midwestern Psychol. Assn., Ind. Psychol. Assn. (pres. 1967), World Fedn. for Mental Health, Conf. Psychologist Dirs. and cons. in State, Fed. and Territorial Mental Health Programs (editor conf. procs. 1966-68, Perspective 1966-68, mem. exec. com. 1946-68), Inter-Am. Congress Psychology, Cert. Cons. Internat. (charter), NTL Inst. (bd. dirs. 1986-92), Sigma Xi, Phi Kappa Phi, Psi Chi (v.p. for midwest, mem. nat. coun. 1986-90, pres.-elect 1991-92, pres. 1992-93, past pres. 1993-94). Office: U Mo Kansas City Dept Psychology 5307 Holmes St Kansas City MO 64110-2437

LUBIN, DONALD G., lawyer; b. N.Y.C., Jan. 10, 1934; s. Harry and Edith (Tannenbaum) L.; m. Amy Schwartz, Feb. 2, 1956; children: Peter, Richard, Thomas, Alice Lubin Spahr. BS in Econs., U. Pa., 1954; LLB, Harvard U., 1957. Bar: Ill. 1957. Ptnr., chmn. exec. com. Sonnenschein Nath & Rosenthal, Chgo., 1957—; bd. dirs., mem. exec. com. McDonald's Corp.; bd. dirs. Molex, Inc., Daubert Industries Inc., Charles Levy Co., Tennis Corp. Am., Arcade Holdings, Inc.; former v.p., dir. San Diego Nat. League Baseball Club, Inc.; former dir., mem. exec. com. First Nat. Bank of Highland Park; former mem. Spl. Commn. on Adminstrn. of Justice in Cook County, Chgo. Former mem. Navy Pier Redevel. Corp., Highland Park Cultural Arts Commn.; life trustee, former chmn. bd. Highland Park Hosp., Ravinia Festival Assn.; trustee, mem. exec. com. Rush-Presbyn.-St. Luke's Med. Ctr.; life trustee Orchestral Assn. Chgo.; bd. dirs., v.p. and sec. Ronald McDonald House, Inc., Chgo. Found. for Edn., Smithsonian Inst., Washington; pres., bd. dir. The Barr Fund; former bd. dirs., v.p., sec. Ragdale Found.; bd. govs. Art Inst. Chgo., Chgo. Lighthouse for the Blind; mem. citizens bd. U. Chgo.; mem. coun. Children's Meml. Hosp.; former bd. overseers Coll. Arts and Sci., U. Pa. Woodrow Wilson vis. fellow. Fellow Am. Bar Found., Ill. Bar Found., Chgo. Bar Found.; mem. ABA, Ill. Bar Assn., Chgo. Bar Assn., Law Club Chgo., Chgo. Hort. Soc. (past bd. dirs.), Econ. Club, Comml. Club (former sec. civic com.), Chgo. Club, Std. Club, Lakeshore Club, Beta Gamma Sigma. Home: 2269 Egandale Rd Highland Park IL 60035-2501 Office: Sonnenschein Nath & Rosenthal 233 S Wacker Dr Ste 8000 Chicago IL 60606-6342

LUBIN, MARTIN, cell physiologist educator; b. N.Y.C., Mar. 30, 1923; m. Dorothy Alpern, Sept. 5, 1942; children—Peter, Adam, Thomas, John Caleb. B.A., Harvard U., 1942, M.D., 1945; Ph.D. in Biophysics, MIT, 1954. Research assoc. biology MIT, 1953-54; assoc. pharmacology then asst. prof. pharmacology Harvard U. Med. Sch., 1957-68; prof. microbiology Dartmouth Med. Sch., 1968—. Served with AUS, 1946-48. USPHS fellow, 1949-51; Childs Meml. Fund med. research fellow, 1951-53; Guggenheim fellow and Commonwealth Fund fellow Lab. Molecular Biology, Cambridge, Eng., 1965-67. Home: 21 Lyme Rd Hanover NH 03755-1406

LUBIN, MICHAEL FREDERICK, physician, educator; b. Phila., Mar. 20, 1947; s. Leonard and Ethel Sybil (Stern) L. BA, Johns Hopkins U., 1969, MD, 1973. Resident Emory U. Affiliated Hosp., Atlanta, 1973-76; asst. prof. medicine Emory U. Sch. Medicine, Atlanta, 1976-82, assoc. prof. medicine, 1982—, dir. div. gen. medicine, 1989-95; dir. preoperative clinic Grady Hosp., Atlanta, 1995—; chmn. housestaff evaluation com. Dept. medicine Emory U. Sch. Medicine; chmn. pharmacy and therapeutics com. Grady Hosp. Editor: Medical Management of the Surgical Patient, 1982, 3d rev. edit., 1995, Med. Rounds, 1988-90; mem. editl. bd. I-M: Internal Medicine, 1992-95; contbr. to Med. Knowledge Self Assessment Program X, 1994. Mem. alumni coun. Johns Hopkins U., 1995—; mem. Cmty. Supporters of the Atlanta Symphony Orch., 1996—, bd. dirs. 1996-97. Hartford scholar in Geriatrics UCLA, 1984-85. Fellow ACP; mem. Am. Geriatrics Soc., Soc. Gen. Internal Medicine, Phi Lambda Upsilon, Phi Beta Kappa (bd. dirs. Met. Atlanta chpt. 1996—). Office: Emory U Sch Medicine 69 Butler St SE Atlanta GA 30303-3033

LUBIN, STEVEN, concert pianist, musicologist; b. N.Y.C., Feb. 22, 1942; s. Jack and Sophie (Auslander) L.; m. Wendy Lubin, June 2, 1974; children: Benjamin, Nathaniel. AB in Philosophy, Harvard U., 1963; MS in Piano, Juilliard Sch. Music, 1965; PhD in Musicology, NYU, 1974. Mem. faculty Juilliard Sch. Music, N.Y.C., 1964-65, Aspen (Colo.) Music Sch., 1965; Mem. faculty Vassar Coll., Poughkeepsie, N.Y., 1970-71; coordinator grad. music theory program Cornell U., Ithaca, N.Y., 1971-75; adj. prof. Sch. Arts, SUNY, Purchase, 1975—; founding mem. The Mozartean Players, 1978—. Mem., NYU Electronic Composers Workshop, 1967-68; concert pianist tours in U.S. and Europe, 1976—; appeared as fortepiano soloist and condr. in Authentic-Instrument concert series, N.Y.C., 1981—; rec. artist Decca, Arabesque Records, Harmonia Mundi; filmed solo performances for Brit. documentary TV in London and Vienna, 1986; soloist in complete Beethoven piano concertos for London/Decca Records, 1987; performed complete cycle Beethoven concertos, London, 1987; solo recordings (new series) Decca including Beethoven Sonatas, 1991; contbr. articles to N.Y. Times, Keyboard Classics, others. Martha Baird Rockefeller grantee, 1968. Mem. Am. Mus. Soc., Soc. Music Theory.

LUBINSKY, MENACHEM YECHIEL, communications executive; b. Hanover, Germany, Apr. 13, 1949; arrived in country 1950; s. Chaim P. and Pesa (Lubinsky) L.; m. Hindy Deborah Fink, Jan. 14, 1973; children: Tziporah, Meiri, Tzviya. BBA, CUNY, 1975, MBA, 1982. Asst. to pres. Agudath Israel of Am., N.Y.C., 1971-72; dir. Boro Park Sr. Citizens Ctr., Bklyn., 1973-74, Project COPE, N.Y.C., 1975-80; dir. gov., pub. affairs Agudath Israel of Am., N.Y.C., 1981-84; pres. Lubinsky, Schild Assocs., N.Y.C., 1985-86, Lubicom, 1987-90, Integrated Mktg. & Comm. Inc., N.Y.C., 1990—; v.p. Agudath Israel of Am., Inc.; pres. Integrated Mktg. and Comm. Author: Op-Ed-Page, New York Times, 1984, Struggle and Splendor. Bd. dirs. Ohel Children's Home, Jewish Com. Rels. Coun., 1986; pres. Met. N.Y. Coordinating Coun. on Jewish Poverty; v.p. Agudath Israel of Am.; mem. domestic affairs com. United Jewish Appeal, 1992—; mem. Pvt. Industry Coun. City of N.Y. Mem. Pub. Rels. Soc. Am., League of Advt., N.Y.S. Procurement Coun. Avocation: tennis.

LUBKIN, GLORIA BECKER, physicist; b. Phila., May 16, 1933; d. Samuel Albert and Anne (Gorrin) B.; m. Yale Jay Lubkin, June 14, 1953 (div. Apr. 1968); children: David Craig, Sharon Rebecca. AB, Temple U., 1953; MA, Boston U., 1957; postgrad., Harvard U., 1974-75. Mathematician Fairchild Stratos Co., Hagerstown, Md., 1954, Letterkenny Ordnance Depot, Chambersburg, Pa., 1955-56; physicist TRG Inc., N.Y.C., 1956-58; acting chmn. dept. physics Sarah Lawrence Coll., Bronxville, N.Y., 1961-62; v.p. Lubkin Assocs., electronic cons., Port Washington, N.Y., 1962-68; assoc. editor Physics Today Am. Inst. Physics, N.Y.C., 1963-69; sr. editor Physics Today Am. Inst. Physics, 1970-84, editor, 1985-94, editl. dir., 1994—; cons. in field; mem. Nieman adv. com. Harvard U., 1978-82; co-chmn. search/adv. com. Theoretical Physics Inst., U. Minn., 1987-89, co-chmn. oversight com. 1989—; mem. mng. com. Westinghouse Sci. Writing Prizes, 1988-91; mem. selection com. Knight Fellowships, 1990. Contbr. articles to profl. publs. Gloria Becker Lubkin Professorship of Theoretical Physics established in her honor U. Minn., 1990; Nieman fellow, 1974-75. Fellow AAAS (mem. nominating com. for sect. B phusics 1987-89, chair 1989), Am. Phys. Soc. (founding mem. com. on the status of women in physics 1971-72, exec. com. history of physics divsn. 1983-86, 92-95, exec. com. forum on physics and soc. 1977-78); mem. N.Y. Acad. Scis. (chair The Scis. pub. com. 1992-93), Nat. assn. Sci. Writers, D.C. Science Writers Assn., Sigma Pi Sigma. Jewish. Office: Am Inst Physics One Physics Ellipse College Park MD 20740

LUBKIN, VIRGINIA LEILA, ophthalmologist; b. N.Y.C., Oct. 26, 1914; d. Joseph and Anna Fredericka (Stern) L.; m. Arnold Malkan, June 6, 1944 (div. 1949); m. Martin Bernstein, Aug. 28, 1949; children: Ellen Henrietta, James Ernst, Roger Joel, John Conrad. BS summa cum laude, NYU, 1933; MD, Columbia U., 1937. Diplomate Am. Bd. Ophthalmology. Intern Harlem Hosp., N.Y.C., 1938-40; asst. resident neurology Montefiore Hosp., N.Y.C., 1940, asst. resident pathology, 1940-41, fellow in ophthalmology, 1941-42; resident ophthalmology Kings County Hosp., Bklyn., 1942-43, Mt. Sinai Hosp., N.Y.C., 1943-44; attending ophthalmologist, assoc. clin. prof. emeritus Mt. Sinai Sch. Medicine, 1944—; also sr. attending surgeon N.Y. Eye and Ear Infirmary, Mt. Sinai Sch. Medicine; pvt. practice N.Y.C., 1945-90; surgeon, now sr. surgeon N.Y. Eye and Ear Infirmary, 1945—; rsch. prof. N.Y. Med. Coll., 1986—; co-creator, now chief of rsch. bioengineering lab. N.Y. Eye and Ear Infirmary (name now The Aborn), N.Y.C., 1978—; creator first grad. course in oculoplastics and bi-yearly symposia in devel. dyslexia Mt. Sinai Sch. Medicine; educator courses in psychosomatic ophthalmology Am. Acad. Ophthalmology, 1950-60, educator course in complications of blepharoplasty, 1980-90; bd. dirs. Jewish Guild for the Blind; tchr. surg. ophthalmology in French Cameroon, Presbyn. Mission, 1951; lectr. in numerous countries including India, 1976, 92, Pakistan, 1976, 84, China, 1978, Sri Lanka, 1979, South Africa, 1982, Singapore, 1984, Thailand, 1984, Argentina, 1986, Peru, 1987. Author: (with others) Ophthalmic Plastic and Reconstructive Surgery, 1989; contbr. articles to profl. jours. Bd. dirs. Ctr. fo Environ. Therapeutics, 1995. Grantee Intraocular Lens Implant Mfrs., 1989. Fellow AMA, AAAS, Am. Soc. Ophthalmic Plastic and Reconstructive Surgery (founding), Am. Coll.

Surgeons, N.Y. Acad. Medicine, N.Y. Acad. Scis., Am. Acad. Ophthalmology, Am. Soc. Cataract and Refractive Surgery, PanAm. Soc. Ophthalmology, N.Y. Soc. Clin. Ophthalmology (pres. 1975), Soc. Light Treatment and Biol. Rhythms, Phi Beta Kappa, Alpha Omega Alpha. Home: 1 Blackstone Pl Bronx NY 10471-3607 Office: NY Eye and Ear Infirmary 310 E 14th St New York NY 10003-4201

LUBLINSKI, MICHAEL, lawyer; b. Eskilstuna, Sweden, Sept. 11, 1951; came to U.S., 1956; s. Walter and Dora L. BA magna cum laude, CCNY, 1972; JD, Georgetown U., 1975. Bar: N.Y. 1976, Calif. 1980, Ct. Internat. Trade 1981, U.S. Dist. Ct. (cen. dist.) Calif. 1981, U.S. Dist. Ct. (so. dist.) N.Y. 1981, U.S. Ct. Appeals (D.C. cir.) 1982. Atty. U.S. Customs Service, Washington, 1975-79, U.S. Dept. Commerce, Washington, 1980; assoc. Mori & Ota, Los Angeles, 1980-84; assoc. Kelley Drye & Warren, Los Angeles, 1984-85, ptnr., 1986—. Panel moderator Calif. continuing edn. of bar Competitive Bus. Practices Inst., Los Angeles and San Francisco, 1984. Mem. ABA, Calif. Bar Assn., Los Angeles County Bar Assn. (arbitrator 1981-82, chmn. customs law sect. 1986). Avocations: travel, photography, movies. Home: 2609 Creston Dr Los Angeles CA 90068-2207 Office: Kelley Drye & Warren 515 S Flower St Los Angeles CA 90071-2201

LUBORSKY, FRED EVERETT, research physicist; b. Phila., May 14, 1923; s. Meyer and Cecelia (Miller) L.; m. Florence R. Glass, Aug. 25, 1946; children—Judith, Mark, Rhoda. B.S., U. Pa., 1947; Ph.D., Ill. Inst. Tech., 1952. Teaching-research asst. Ill. Inst. Tech., Chgo., 1947-51; research assoc. Gen. Elec. Co., Schenectady, 1951-52, West Lynn, Mass., 1952-58; research physicist Gen. Elec. Co., Schenectady, 1958-92; gen. chmn. 2d Joint Internat. Magnetism and Magnetic Materials Conf., 1979; chmn. adv. com. Conf. on Magnetism and Magnetic Materials, 1980. Editor: Amorphous Metallic Alloys, 1984; mem. editorial bd. Internat. Jour. Rapid Solidification, 1984—; mem. editorial adv. bd. Internat. Jour. Magnetism, 1972—; contbr. articles to profl. jours.; patentee in field. Served with USN, 1944-46. Recipient citation achievement in indsl. sci. AAAS, 1956; Brit. Sci. Research Council fellow, 1977; Coolidge fellow in research and devel. Gen. Elec. Corp., 1978. Fellow IEEE (editorial bd. Transactions on Magnetics jour. 1968—, editor-in-chief 1972-75, editorial bd. Spectrum jour. 1972-73, Centennial medal 1984, mem. Fellows com. 1993—), Am. Inst. Chemists, N.Y. Acad. Scis.; mem. Nat. Acad. Engring., Magnetics Soc. of IEEE (pres. 1975-77, named disting. lectr. 1979, achievement award 1981), Am. Chem. Soc., Materials Research Soc. Home: 1162 Lowell Rd Schenectady NY 12308-2512

LUBOVITCH, LAR, dancer, choreographer; b. Chgo.. Student, Art Inst. Chgo., U. Iowa, Juilliard Sch. Music, Am. Ballet Theatre Sch., Martha Graham, Anthony Tudor. Debut with Pearl Lang Dance Co., 1962; danced with modern cos. Glen Tetley, John Butler, Sophie Maslow and Donald McKayle; also with Manhattan Festival Ballet, Santa Fe Opera and Harkness Ballet; formed Lar Lubovitch Dance Co., 1968, choreographer, 1968—, guest choreographer, Bat-Dor Dance Co., Gulbenkian Ballet, Dutch Nat. Ballet, Ballet Rambert, Pa. Ballet, Am. Ballet Theatre, Royal Danish Ballet, Bejart Ballet XX Century, Alvin Ailey Am. Dance Theater, John Curry Ice Dancing Co., Les Grandes Ballets Canadiens, Stuttgart Ballet, N.Y.C. Ballet, Pacific N.W. Ballet, Paris Opera Ballet, White Oak Dance Project; ballets choreographed include Blue, 1968, Freddie's Bag, 1968, Journey Back, 1968, Greeting Sampler, 1969, Whirligogs, 1969, Unremembered Time-Forgotten Place, 1969, Variations and Theme, 1970, Ecstasy, 1970, Sam Nearlydeadman, 1970, The Teaching, 1970, Some of the Reactions,1970, The Time Before, 1971, Clear Lake, 1971, Air, 1972, Joy of Man's Desiring, 1972, Chariot Light Night, 1973, Scherzo for Massah Jack, 1973, Three Essays, 1974, Zig Zag, 1974, Avalanche, 1975, Rapid Transit, 1975, Session, 1975, Eight Easy Pieces, 1975, Girl on Fire, 1975, Marimba, 1976, Les Noces, 1976, Scriabin Dances, 1977, Exultate Jubilate, 1977, North Star, 1978, Valley, 1978, Tiltawhirl, 1979, Up Jump, 1979, Mistral, 1980, Cavalcade, 1980, American Gesture, 1981, Beau Danube, 1981, Big Shoulders, 1983, Tabernacle, 1983, Adagio and Rondo, 1984, A Brahms Symphony, 1985, Concerto Six Twenty-Two, 1986, Blood, 1986, Of My Soul, 1987, Musette, 1988, Rhapsody in Blue, 1988, Fandango, 1989, Just Before Jupiter, 1990, Hautbois, 1990, Sinfonia Concertante, 1991, Waiting for the Sunrise, 1991, American Gesture, 1992, So In Love, 1994, Touch Me, 1996, Bach Adagio, 1996, Gershwin Variations, 1996, I'll Be Seeing You, 1996, Othello, 1997, Orthello, 1997, others; choreographer Sleeping Beauty (WGBH-TV), 1987, Into the Woods (Broadway), 1987, Salome, (Broadway), 1992, The Red Shoes (Broadway), 1993, The Planets (A&E-TV), 1995, The King and I (Broadway), 1996. Guggenheim fellow; CAPS grantee, NEA grantee; nominee Tony award, 1988, Astaire award, 1993-94. Address: care Lubovitch Dance Co 625 Broadway Ste 11-h New York NY 10012-2611

LUBRECHT, HEINZ D., publishing company executive, antiquarian book expert, appraiser; b. Reutlingen, Fed. Republic Germany, Dec. 2, 1908; came to U.S., 1928, naturalized, 1935; s. Adolf Carl and Amelia Sophie (Gueninger) L.; m. Anne M. Ficke, Oct. 2, 1937; children: Peter Thomas, Charles Frederick. Student pub. schs., Stuttgart, Fed. Republic Germany. Vice pres. Hafner Pub. Co., N.Y.C., 1928-69; v.p., editor Macmillan Pub. Co., N.Y.C., 1969-74; pres. Lubrecht & Cramer, Ltd., Forestburgh, N.Y., 1974, Monticello, N.Y., 1974—. Co-author: Early American Botanical Works, 1967. Mem. N.Y. Bot. Garden, Old Book Table, N.Am. Mycological Assn. (Svc. award 1991), Sullivan County C. of C. (award 1994), Antiquarian Booksellers Assn. Republican. Lutheran. Home: 38 County Road 48 Forestburgh NY 12777-6400 Office: 18 Mini Ln Monticello NY 12701-4402

LUBY, THOMAS STEWART, lawyer; b. Meriden, Conn., Jan. 12, 1952; s. Robert M. and Ruth (McGee) L.; m. Paula P. Falcigno, July 19, 1985; children: Elizabeth, Caroline, Katherine. BA, Yale U., 1974; JD, U. Conn., 1977. Bar: Conn., U.S. Dist. Ct. Conn., U.S. Ct. Appeals (2d cir). Law clk. to Hon. T. F. Gilroy Daly U.S. Dist. Ct., Bridgeport, Conn., 1977-78; asst. U.S. atty. New Haven, Conn., 1978-81; ptnr. Luby, Olson, Mango & Gaffney, Meriden, 1981—; mem. grievance com. U.S. Dist. Ct. Conn., 1985-90, chmn., 1990-91; mem. U.S. Magistrate SelectionCom., 1996. Rep. Conn. Gen. Assembly, 1987-92, house majority leader, 1993-94; co-chair Conn. Task Force on Groundwater Strategy, 1987-89, chmn. commerce com., 1991-92. Recipient Spl. Achievement award U.S. Dept. Justice, 1980, Outstanding Pub. Service award United Way, 1986; named Legis. Leader of Yr., Greater Hartford C. of C., 1990, Person of Yr., Gov.'s Tourism Council, 1991, team Conn. award Conn. Dept. Econ. and Cmty. Devel., 1996, legis. advocacy award Coalition for Children, 1993. Mem. Conn. Bar Assn. Democrat. Roman Catholic. Home: 32 Westfield Rd Meriden CT 06450-2426

LUCANDER, HENRY, investment banker; b. Helsingfors, Finland, Dec. 21, 1940; came to U.S., 1965, naturalized, 1974; student Gronesche Handelsschule, Hamburg, W.Ger., 1961-62, Pontificia Universidade Católica, Rio de Janeiro, 1963-64; diploma Brazilian Coffee Inst., Rio de Janeiro, 1965; M.B.A., Columbia U., 1968; m. Karen-Jean Olson, Aug. 22, 1981. With Schenkers Internat. Forwarders, Inc., N.Y.C., 1965-66; coffee merchandizer Anderson Clayton & Co., Inc., N.Y.C., 1966-68; with Smith Barney & Co., Inc., N.Y.C., 1968-69, Kidder Peabody & Co., Inc., N.Y.C., 1969-70; with Lucander & Co., Inc., Investment Bankers, 1970—, pres., 1972—. Served to lt. Finnish Army, 1960-61. Home: 333 Pearl St New York NY 10038-1609

LUCAS, ALEXANDER RALPH, child psychiatrist, educator; b. Vienna, Austria, July 30, 1931; came to U.S., 1940, naturalized, 1945; s. Eugene Hans and Margaret Ann (Weiss) L.; m. Margaret Alice Thompson, July 6, 1956; children: Thomas Alexander, Nancy Elizabeth Watson, Alexander Eugene, Peter Clayton. B.S., Mich. State U., 1953; M.D., U. Mich., 1957. Diplomate Am. Bd. Psychiatry and Neurology. Intern U. Mich. Hosp., 1957-58; resident in child psychiatry Hawthorn Ctr., Northville, Mich., 1958-59, 61-62, staff psychiatrist, 1963-65, sr. psychiatrist, 1965-67; resident in psychiatry Lafayette Clinic, Detroit, 1959-61, rsch. child psychiatrist, 1967-71, rsch. coord., 1969-71; asst. prof. psychiatry Wayne State U., 1967-69, assoc. prof., 1969-71; cons. child and adolescent psychiatry Mayo Clinic, 1971—; assoc. prof. Mayo Med Sch., 1973-76, prof., 1976—; head sect. child and adolescent psychiatry Mayo Clinic, Rochester, Minn., 1971-80; dir. com. on certification in child and adolescent psychiatry Am. Bd. Psychiatry and Neurology, 1997—. Author: (with C. R. Shaw) The Psychiatric Disorders of Childhood, 1970. Fellow Am. Acad. Child and Adolescent Psychiatry (editl. bd. jour. 1976-82), Am. Orthopsychiat. Assn. (life), Am. Psychiat. Assn. (life); mem. Minn. Soc. Child and Adolescent Psychiatry (pres. 1993-95), Soc. Biol. Psychiatry, Soc. Profs. Child and Adolescent Psychiatry, Sigma Xi. Research in biol. aspects of child psychiatry, psychopathology, psychopharmacology, eating disorders, psychiat. treatment of children, adolescents, and young adults. Office: Mayo Clinic 200 1st St SW Rochester MN 55902-3008

LUCAS, AUBREY KEITH, university president; b. State Line, Miss., July 12, 1934; s. Keith Caldwell and Audelle Margaret (Robertson) L.; m. Ella Frances Ginn, Dec. 18, 1955; children: Margaret Frances, Keith Godbold (dec.), Martha Carol, Alan Douglas, Mark Christopher. BS, U. So. Miss., 1955, MA, 1956; PhD, Fla. State U., 1966. Instr. Hinds Jr. Coll., Raymond, Miss., 1956-57; pres. Delta State U., Cleveland, Miss., 1971-75; asst. dir. reading clinic U. So. Miss., Hattiesburg, 1955-56, dir. admissions, 1957-61, registrar, 1963-69, dean Grad. Sch., 1969-71, pres., 1975-96, pres. emeritus, prof. higher edn., 1997—. Author: The Mississippi Legislature and Mississippi Public Higher Education, 1890-1960; contbg. author: A History of Mississippi, 1973. Bd. dirs. Pine Burr Area coun. Boy Scouts Am., Miss. Inst. Tech. Devel., Miss. Power Co., Miss. Assn. Coll., 1979-80, Miss. Arts Commn., 1977-87, Salvation Army, Pine Burr; mem. gen. bd. Global Ministries, United Meth. Ch., 1984-92, mem. gen. bd. higher edn. and ministry, 1992—; chmn. Miss. Arts Commn., 1983-85; campaign chmn. Forest United Way, 1979, So. U. Conf., 1995—; state chmn. Am. Cancer Soc., 1978; mem. Commn. on Nat. Devel. Postsecondary Edn., 97th Congress; pres. Miss. Econ. Coun., 1982-83; lay leader Miss. Meth. Conf., 1980-88, mem. adminstrv. bd., 1989-92; bd. visitors Air U., 1990-94, chmn., 1991-92; mem. exec. bd. Commn. on Colls. of So. Assn. Colls. and Schs., 1990-93. Mem. So. Assn. Colls. and Schs. (mem. exec. bd. commn. on colls. 1990-93, v.p. commn. on colls. 1993, mem. exec. coun.), Hattiesburg C. of C., Miss. Forestry Assn., Newcomen Soc. N.Am., Am. Assn. State Colls. and Univs. (bd. dirs. 1982-86, chmn. 1984-85), Am. Coun. Edn. (bd. dirs. 1984-86), Miss. Inst. Arts and Letters, Red Red Rose Club, Sigma Phi Epsilon, Omicron Delta Kappa, Phi Kappa Phi, Pi Gamma Mu, Pi Tau Chi, Kappa Delta Pi, Phi Delta Kappa, Kappa Pi. Home: 3701 Jamestown Rd Hattiesburg MS 39402-2336 Office: U So Miss PO Box 5001 Hattiesburg MS 39406-5001

LUCAS, BETH ANNE, television producer; b. Grand Rapids, Mich., Sept. 15, 1960; d. Gordon Patrick and Phyllis (Sablack) Galka; m. Mark Fordham, Mar. 19, 1982 (div. 1985); m. Gus Lucas, June 3, 1991. BA in Psychology, Antioch U., 1995. Segment producer Breakaway, Metromedia TV, Hollywood, Calif., 1983; asst. dir. Anything for Money, Paramount TV, Hollywood, 1984; post prodn. supr. Heathcliff DIC, Hollywood, 1984; post prodn. supr. Beauty and the Beast, Witt-Thomas Prodns., Hollywood, 1986-88; assoc. producer Anything But Love, 20th Century Fox, Hollywood, 1989; assoc. producer Easy Street Viacom Prodns., Hollywood, 1984-85; mgr. post prodn. Matlock, Perry Mason, Father Dowling, Jack and the Fatman, Hollywood, 1990-91; project coord. Teen Dating Violence Prevention Team, Haven Hills, Inc. Vol. Children Are Our Future, Haven Hills Battered Woman's Shelter; mem. AIDS Project, L.A., L.A. Mission, Children Def. Fund. Mem. NASW, APA, NOW, Amnesty Internat., Am. Profl. Soc. on the Abuse of Children, Calif. Profl. Soc. on the Abuse of Children, Nature Conservancy, Nat. Parks and Conservation Assn., Feminist Majority, Nat. Abortion Rights Action League, Greenpeace, Smithsonian Assocs., Mus. Contemporary Art, Los Angeles County Mus., Sta. KCET, UCLA Alumni Assn., Child Help USA, Childreach, Mus. of Tolerance. Avocations: world travel, skiing, writing, wine tasting, cooking.

LUCAS, C. PAYNE, development organization executive; b. Spring Hope, N.C., Sept. 14, 1933; s. James Russell and Minnie (Hendricks) L; m. Freddie Emily Myra Hill, Aug. 29, 1964; children: Therese Raymonde, C. Payne Jr., Hillary Hendricks. BA in History, U. Md.; LLD (hon.), U. Md., 1975; MA in Govt., Am. U. Asst. dir. Peace Corps, Togo, 1964; dir. Peace Corps, Niger, 1965-67; dir. Africa region Peace Corps, 1967-71; pres. Africare, Washington, 1971—; lectr. in field. Author: (with Kevin Lowther) Keeping Kennedy's Promise--The Peace Corps: Unmet Promise of the New Frontier, 1978; contbr. articles to profl. publs. Bd. dirs. Coun. Fgn. Rels., Overseas Devel. Coun. World Resources Inst., InterAction, Population Action Internat., Kagiso Trust USA, Nat. Planning Assn.; bd. dirs., chmn. Reach & Teach USA; bd. dirs., founding mem. Corp. Coun. on Africa. Recipient Disting. Fed. Svc. award Pres. Lyndon B. Johnson, Presdl. Hunger award for Outstanding Achievement, Pres. Ronald Reagan, 1984, Aggrey medal Phelps-Stokes Fund, 1986, Order of Disting. Svc. award Pres. Kenneth Kaunda of Zambia, 1986, Recognition awards Nat. Order of Rep. Niger, 1988, Zambia, Cote D'Iroire, Senegal, Benin, Disting. Bicentennial award Land Grant Coll., 1990, Hubert H. Humphrey Pub. Svc. award APSA, 1991. Mem. Cosmos Club, Omega Psi Phi. Office: Africare 440 R St NW Washington DC 20001-1935*

LUCAS, CAROL LEE, biomedical engineer; b. Aberdeen, S.D., Feb. 13, 1940; d. Howard Cleveland and Sarah Ivy (Easterby) Nogle; B.A., Dakota Wesleyan U., 1961; M.S., U. Ariz., 1967; Ph.D., U. N.C., 1973; m. Richard Albert Lucas, Feb. 26, 1961; children—Wendy Lee, Sean Richard. Tchr. Spanish, Mitchell (S.D.) High Sch., 1960-61; tchr. math, English, sci. U.S. Army, Furth, Ger., 1961-62; systems analyst Cargill Inc., Mpls., 1962-65; research assoc. U. N.C., Chapel Hill, 1973-76, lectr., 1976-77, asst. prof. curriculum in biomed. engring. and math, 1977-84, assoc. prof. dept. surgery, 1984-89, prof. dept. surgery, 1989—, acting chmn. curriculum biomed. engring. and math., 1990-92, chmn. biomed. engring., 1992—; NIH trainee, 1968-73. Mem. IEEE, Am. Heart Assn., N.C. Heart Assn., Biomed. Engring. Soc., Cardiovascular System Dynamics Soc., Am. Inst. Biol. and Med. Engrs. Democrat. Methodist. Contbr. articles to profl. jours. Home: 2421 Sedgefield Dr Chapel Hill NC 27514-6810 Office: U NC Sch Medicine Dept Biomed Engring 152 Macnider Hall Chapel Hill NC 27599-7575

LUCAS, CHRISTOPHER, artist; b. Durham, N.C., Nov. 13, 1958; s. M.S.P. and Marie L. Student, Yale Summer Sch. Music and Art, 1979; BA, U. Kans., 1980. Tchr. extended day program kindergarten N.Y. St. Grade Sch., Lawrence, Kans., 1981-83; vis. artist lectr. Carnegie-Mellon, Pitts., 1985, 87; tchr. Nat. Mus. Contemporary Art, Kwachon-Si, Republic of Korea, 1990-91. One-man shows include Jack Tilton Gallery, N.Y.C., 1984, John Good Gallery, N.Y.C., 1986-87, 89, 92, Paolo Baldacci Gallery, N.Y.C., 1995; exhibited in group shows at Anderson Theatre Gallery, N.Y.C., 1983, Barbara Braathen Gallery, N.Y.C., 1984, Patrick Fox Gallery, N.Y.C., 1984, Anne Plumb Gallery, N.Y.C., 1985, Simard, Halm and Shee Gallery, L.A., 1986, Jan Turner Gallery, L.A., 1987, Carnegie Mus. Art, Pitts., 1988, Gilbert Brownstone Gallery, Paris, 1988, Gabrielle Bryers Gallery, N.Y.C., 1988, Greenberg Gallery, St. Louis, 1988, Michael Maloney Gallery, 1988, John Good Gallery, 1985, 87, 88, 89, 90, Luise Ross Gallery, N.Y.C., 1989, Karl Bornstein Gallery, Santa Monica, Calif., 1990, Nicole Klagsbrun Gallery, N.Y.C., 1990, Leopold-Hoesch Mus., Duren, Germany, 1990, Duke U. Mus. Art, Durham, N.C., 1991, Mario Diacono Gallery, Boston, 1992, Galleria Planta, Rome, 1992, Galleria Nazionale d'Arte, Moderna, San Marino, 1993, Mario Diacomo Gallery, Boston, 1997, Paolo Baldacci Gallery, 1997 ; represented in permanent collections at High Mus. Art, Atlanta, Carnegie Mus. Art, Pitts., New Sch., N.Y.C. Recipient Nat. Endowment Arts fellowship, 1987, award Pollock-Krasner Found.; Fulbright profl. rsch. grantee USIS, South Korea, 1990-91. Home: PO Box 20308 New York NY 10011-0007

LUCAS, CYNTHIA, ballet mistress, dancer; b. San Rafael, Calif.. Studies with, Leona Norman. Formerly with Royal Winnipeg Ballet, Joffrey II Co.; mem. corps de ballet Nat. Ballet Can., Toronto, Ont., 1972-76, 2nd soloist, 1976-78, 1st solist, 1978-89, ballet mistress, 1989—. Created roles including Farmer's Daughter in Apples at the Shaw Festival, The Chic Couple in The Party for CBC-TV, Sweet Young Thing in La Ronde; performances include Isabelle-Marie in Mad Shadows, Catherine Sloper in Washington Square; leading role in Kudelka's The Rape of Lucerne, 1980, The Merry Widow, 1986; dancer in Toronto Internat. Festival premiere Onegin, 1984. Office: National Ballet of Canada, 470 Queens Quay W, Toronto, ON Canada M5V 3K4*

LUCAS, DEAN HADDEN, retired educator; b. Avera, Ga., June 2, 1931; d. Thomas Clayton and Lonice Ethyl (Williams) Hadden; m. Ben F. Lucas, June 27, 1953 (dec. Mar. 1992); children: Jon Gregory, Barry Hadden, Angela d'Arcy; m. Ray Ninche Renbarger, Sept. 10, 1994. Student, U. Ga., 1951; BS in Home Econs. Edn., Berry Coll., 1952; MAT in Home Econs. Edn., Winthrop Coll., 1969; postgrad., Clem. U., 1976-77, U. S.C., 1977, 80, 81, 88, S.C. State Coll., 1985, 87. Asst. home demonstration agt. Ga. Extension Svc., Calhoun, 1952; home demonstration agt. Ga. Extension Svc., Alma, 1952-53; 1st grade tchr. Tenn. Edn. Dept., East Ridge, 1953-54; 4th grade tchr. Kershaw County Sch. Dist., Camden, S.C., 1954-55, home econs. tchr., 1955-57; asst. home dem. agt. Clemson Extension Svc., Camden, 1958-61, home dem. agt., 1963-69, assoc. home economist, 1970-74; assoc. county extension leader Clemson Extension Svc., Sumter, S.C., 1974-76; home econs. instr. Kershaw County Sch., Camden, 1976-93, ret., 1993. Writer curriculum guides for home econs. courses. Mem. adv. bd. Dist. Home Econs., Kershaw County, S.C., 1985-92, Supt. Adv. Coun., Camden, 1989-90, Teen Coalition, Camden, 1989-92, Teen Pregnancy Prevention, Kershaw County, 1985-89; mem. Kershaw County Jr. Welfare League, Camden, 1959-92; co-sponsor, organizer SADD Chpt. at North Central, Kershaw, 1988; Clemson U. del. Nat. 4-H Conf., Chgo., 1974, Home Econs. Educators Citizens Amb. Program, Russia, Hungary, 1992; tchr. Sunday sch. Bapt. Ch. Named for Nat. Disting. Svc., Nat. Extension Home Econs. Assn., 1973, S.C. Home Econs. Tchr. of Yr., S.C. Home Econ. Assn., 1990. Mem. NEA, Am. Vocat. Assn. (del. to policy seminar), S.C. Vocat. Assn. (v.p. 1989-90, 92), S.C. Assn. Home Econs. Tchrs. (pres. 1989-90), Am. Home Econs. Assn. (legis. contact 1988-91, Vocat. Home Econs. Tchr. of Yr. 1993, Vocat. Tchr. of Yr. 1993), S.C. Edn. Assn. Cert. Home Economists. Avocations: running, workouts, boating, cooking, traveling. Home: 1136 Brookgreen Ct Camden SC 29020-3716 Office: North Cen High Sch 3000 Lockhart Rd Kershaw SC 29067-9661

LUCAS, DONALD LEO, private investor; b. Upland, Calif., Mar. 18, 1930; s. Leo J. and Mary G. (Schwamm) L.; BA, Stanford U., 1951, MBA, 1953; m. Lygia de Soto Harrison, July 15, 1961; children: Nancy Maria Lucas Thibodeau, Alexandra Maria Lucas Ertola, Donald Alexander Lucas. Assoc. corp. fin. dept. Smith, Barney & Co., N.Y.C., 1956-59; gen., ltd. ptnr. Draper, Gaither & Anderson, Palo Alto, Calif., 1959-66; pvt. investor, Menlo Park, Calif., 1966—; bd. dirs. Cadence Design Systems, San Jose, Calif., Coulter Pharm., Inc., Palo Alto, Amati Comm., Corp., San Jose, Oracle Corp., Redwood Shores, Calif., Racotek, Inc., Mpls., Macromedia, San Francisco, TriCord Systems, Inc., Plymouth, Minn., Transcend Svcs., Inc., Atlanta, Coulter Pharms., Palo Alto, Calif.; Mem. bd. regents Bellarmine Coll. Prep., 1977—; regent emeritus U. Santa Clara, 1980—. 1st lt. AUS, 1953-55. Mem. Am. Coun. Capital Formation (dir.), Stanford U. Alumni Assn., Stanford Grad. Sch. Bus. Alumni Assn., Order of Malta, Stanford Buck Club, Vintage Club (Indian Wells, Calif.), Menlo Country Club (Woodside, Calif.), Menlo Circus Club (Atherton, Calif.), Jackson Hole Golf and Tennis Club, Teton Pines Club, Zeta Psi. Home: 224 Park Ln Atherton CA 94027-5411 Office: 3000 Sand Hill Rd # 3-210 Menlo Park CA 94025-7116

LUCAS, FRANK D., congressman; b. Cheyenne, Okla., Jan. 6, 1960; m. Lynda L. Bradshaw, 1988. BS, Okla. State U., 1982. Mem. Okla. Ho. of Reps., 1989-94, 103rd to 105th Congresses from 6th Okla. Dist., 1994—. Baptist. Office: US Ho of Reps 107 Cannon Bldg Washington DC 20515-3609 Home: Rte 2 Box 136A Cheyenne OK 73628*

LUCAS, FRANK EDWARD, architect; b. Charleston, S.C., Oct. 31, 1934; m. Edith R. Dority; children: Susan R. Lucas Tezza, Kelly E., Julie C. Lucas Rodenberg. BArch, Clemson U., 1959. Registered architect, S.C., Fla., N.C., W.Va., Ala., Ga., Va., Ky. Founder, architect (now LS3P Architects Ltd.) Lucas and Stubbs Assocs., Charleston, S.C., 1964—; chmn. bd. dirs. LS3P Architects Ltd. Mem. Charleston County Bd. Rev., Bldg. and Elec. Codes, 1972-85; mem. St. Philip's Episcopal Ch., former vestryman, sr. warden, lay reader St. James Episcopal Ch.; trustee Cities in Schs., Charleston, 1990-94; past pres. nine county region Girl Scouts Am., 1988-90; affiliate S.C. Sch. Bds. Assn.; bd. dirs. Charleston World Trade Ctr., S.C. Golf Expo; hon. chmn. March of Dimes Walkathon, 1991; pres. adv. coun. Clemson U.; mem. Am. Cancer Soc., Trident Tech. Coll. Found., Coll. Charleston Found.; mem. S.C. State Commn. on Def. Base Devel.; bd. dirs. S.C. Athletic Hall of Fame. Recipient Elizabeth O'Neill Verner award S.C. Arts Commn., 1990; featured in exhibit at Gibbes Art Gallery titled 20 Yrs. of Design Excellence, 1988. Fellow AIA; mem. S.C. AIA (pres. 1970), S.C. Econ. Developers Assn., Soc. Am. Mil. Engrs., Charleston Trident C. of C. (pres. 1990-91, Jos. P. Riley Leadership award 1996), Preservation Soc. Charleston, S.C. Hist. Soc., Carolina Art Assn., S.C. Arts Found. (bd. dirs.), Executives Assn. Greater Charleston (pres. 1983), Greater Charleston Real Estate Bd., Clemson Archtl. Found. (bd. dirs. 1967-73, 77-81, 86—, pres. 1975, 81, 89), Hibernian Soc. (mng. com. 1984-96), Hibernian Soc. Found. (v.p. 1990-92, pres. 1992-94), Country Club of Charleston (bd. dirs. 1976-79, exec. com. 1991), S.C. State C. of C. (bd. dirs. 1989-98, com. to reorganize state govt. 1990, exec. com. 1992), S.C. Arts Commn. (bus. and arts awards adv. com.), Assn. of Citadel Men, IPTAY Clemson U., Clemson Alumni Assn., Clemson Low Country Assn., Palmetto State Tchrs. Assn. (affiliate), Carolina Yacht Club, Rotary (N. Charleston chpt., Paul Harris fellow), Country Club Charleston (bd. dirs. 1973-76), Health Scis. Found. (bd. dirs.), The Harbor Club (Charleston, founding dir.). Home: 607 North Shore Dr Charleston SC 29412 Office: 24 N Market St Ste 300 Charleston SC 29401-2640

LUCAS, FRED VANCE, pathology educator, university administrator; b. Grand Junction, Colo., Feb. 7, 1922; s. Lee H. and Katherine W. (Vance) L.; m. Rebecca Ross Dudley, Dec. 21, 1948; children: Fred Vance, Katherine Dudley Lucas Volk. A.B., U. Calif.-Berkeley, 1942; M.D., U. Rochester, 1950. Am. Bd. Patholgy. Intern, postgrad. fellow in pathology U. Rochester, 1950-51, asst. in pathology, 1951-53, Lilliy fellow, 1952-53, Gleason fellow, 1953-54, instr., 1953-54, asst. prof., 1954-55; chief resident in pathology Strong Meml. Hosp., 1953-54; practice medicine specializing in pathology; assoc. prof. Coll. Physicians and Surgeons, Columbia U., 1955-60; assoc. attending pathologist Presbyn. Hosp., N.Y.C., 1955-60; prof., chmn. pathology U. Mo.-Columbia Sch. Medicine, 1960-77; research assoc. Space Sci. Research Ctr., 1964-70; prof. pathology Vanderbilt U., 1977-89, dir. program planning, dir. med. services, 1977-79, acting assoc. v.p. med. affairs, 1979, assoc. v.p. med. affairs, 1979-81, acting exec. dir. hosp., assoc. v.p. med. affairs, 1981-82, assoc. vice-chancellor med. affairs, 1982-89; cons. in field. Contbr. numerous articles to med. jours. Del WHO, Geneva, 1971; bd. dirs. Univs. Assoc. Research and Edn. in Pathology; commr. for Mo. and Ark. Coll. Am. Pathologists, 1975-77. Served in U.S. Army, 1942-46. Recipient Lederle Faculty award, 1954-56; recipient Disting. Service award Columbia U., 1967, Edn. and Social Affairs medal U. Mo.-Columbia, 1975, Student exec. com. service award U. Mo.-Columbia, 1975. Fellow Coll. Am. Pathologists, Am. Soc. Clin. Pathologists; mem. Am. Pathology Assn., Internat. Acad. Pathology, Harvey Soc., Sigma Xi, Alpha Omega Alpha (lectr. 1977). Democrat. Roman Catholic. Home: 333 Lee Dr Apt G12 Baton Rouge LA 70808-4985

LUCAS, GEORGE W., JR., film director, producer, screenwriter; b. Modesto, Calif., May 14, 1944. Student, Modesto Jr. Coll.; BA, U. So. Calif., 1966. Chmn. Lucasfilm Ltd., San Rafael, Calif. Creator short film THX-1138 (Grand prize Nat. Student Film Festival, 1967); asst. to Francis Ford Coppola on The Rain People; dir. Filmmaker (documentary on making of The Rain People); dir., co-writer THX-1138, 1970, American Graffiti, 1973; dir., author screenplay Star Wars, 1977; exec. producer More American Graffiti, 1979, The Empire Strikes Back, 1980, Raiders of the Lost Ark, 1981, Indiana Jones and the Temple of Doom, 1984, Labyrinth, 1986, Howard the Duck, 1986, Willow, 1988, Tucker, 1988, Radioland Murders, 1994; exec. producer, co-author screenplay Return of the Jedi, 1983; co-exec. producer Mishima, 1985; co-author, co-exec. producer Indiana Jones and the Last Crusade, 1989; exec. producer (TV series) The Young Indiana Jones Chronicles, 1992-93. Office: Lucasfilm Ltd PO Box 2009 San Rafael CA 94912-2009

LUCAS, GEORGES, physicist, researcher; b. Marosvasarhely, Transylvania, Rumania, Dec. 11, 1914; arrived in France, 1933; s. Emeric and Hermine (Grun) Lukacs; m. Irene Weingrow, Jan. 10, 1948. Degree in Chem. Engring., U. Strasbourg, France, 1938; postgrad., Ecole Normale Superieure, Paris, 1938-40; PhD, U. Paris, Sorbonne, 1955. Rsch. assoc. astrophysics Centre Nat. de la Recherche Scientifique Observatory, Meudon, France, 1953-55; with rsch. dept. Tidewater Oil Co., Avon, Calif., 1956-65; with rsch. dept. Elf-Aquitaine, Paris, 1965-77, ret., 1977. Author: Transfer Theory for Trapped Electromagnetic Energy, 1983; contbr. articles to profl. jours., abstracts to profl. proceedings; patentee in field. Mem. Am. Phys. Soc., Am. Soc. Photobiology, European Photochemistry Assn., European Soc. Photobiology, N.Y. Acad. Scis. Avocation: drawing. Home: 83-85 rue Saint Charles, 75015 Paris France

LUCAS, HENRY CAMERON, JR., information systems educator, writer, consultant; b. Omaha, Sept. 4, 1944; s. Henry Cameron and Lois (Himes) L.; m. Ellen Kuhbach, June 8, 1968; children: Scott C., Jonathan G. B.S. in Indsl. Adminstrn. magna cum laude, Yale U., 1966; M.S., MIT, 1968, Ph.D., 1970. Cons. Arthur D. Little, Inc., Cambridge, Mass., 1966-70; asst. prof. computer and info. systems Stanford U., Calif., 1970-74; assoc. prof. computer applications and info. systems NYU, 1974-78, prof., chmn. dept. info. systems, 1978-84; on leave IBM European Systems Research Inst., Belgium, 1981; INSEAD Fontainebleau, France, 1985; prof. info. systems NYU, 1985—. Author: The T-Form Organization, 1996 Computer-Based Information Systems in Organizations, 1973, The Information Systems Environment, 1980 (with F. Land, T. Lincoln and K. Supper) Casebook for Management Information Systems, 3d edit., 1985, The Analysis, Design and Implementation of Information Systems, 4th edit., 1992, Information Technology for Management 6th edit., 1997, Coping with Computers: A Manager's Guide to Controlling Information Processing, 1982, Introduction to Computers and Information Systems, 1986, Managing Information Services, 1989; editor Indsl. Mgmt., 1967-68; mem. editorial bd. Sloan Mgmt., Rev., 1975-91; assoc. editor MIS Quar., 1977-83; editor in chief Systems, Objectives, Solutions, 1980—; contbr. articles to profl. jours. Recipient award for excellence in teaching NYU Sch. Bus., 1982. Mem. IEEE, Publs. Assn. for Info. Sys. (v.p. 1995—), Assn. Computing Machinery, Inst. Mgmt. Scis., Phi Beta Kappa, Tau Beta Pi. Home: 18 Portland Rd Summit NJ 07901-3044 Office: NYU 44 W 4th St # 9 67 New York NY 10012-1106

LUCAS, J. RICHARD, retired mining engineering educator; b. Scottdale, Pa., May 3, 1929; s. J.W. and Mary (Hirka) L.; m. Joan H. Hathaway, Aug. 30, 1952; children: Eric Scott, Jay Hathaway. Student, Pa. State U., 1947-48; B.S. in Math. and Physics, Waynesburg Coll., 1951; B.S. in Mining Engring, W.Va. U., 1952; M.S. in Mining Engring, U. Pitts., 1954; Ph.D., Columbia, 1965. Registered profl. engr., Va., Ohio, W.Va. Miner Crucible Steel Co., 1947-52; field engr. Joy Mfg. Co., 1952-54; mem. faculty Ohio State U., Columbus, 1954-61; head dept. mining engring. Va. Poly. Inst. and State U., Blacksburg, 1961-71, head div. minerals engring., 1971-76, head dept. mining and minerals engring., 1976-87, Massey prof. mining and minerals engring., 1987-92; dir. mining systems design and ground control Generic Mineral Tech. Ctr.; ret., 1992; chmn. exec. com. Ann. Inst. on Coal-Mining Health, Safety and Rsch., 1969-87. Mem. Am. Inst. Mining, Metall. and Petroleum Engrs., AAAS, Coal Mining Inst., W.Va. Coal Mining Inst., AAUP, Nat., Va. socs. profl. engrs., Am. Soc. Engring. Edn., Va. Acad. Sci., Soc. Mining Engrs. (bd. dirs., chmn. coal div.). Home: 408 Hemlock Dr Blacksburg VA 24060-5232

LUCAS, JAMES E(VANS), operatic director; b. San Antonio, Mar. 15, 1933; s. Mason Harley and Nora Norton (Evans) L. B.A., Hiram Coll., 1951; postgrad., Stanford U., 1951-52, Juilliard Sch. Music, 1952-53. mem. faculty Temple U., 1965-71, Mannes Coll. Music, 1964-70, Manhattan Sch. Music, 1970-78, Carnegie-Mellon U., 1977-79; prof. music, stage dir. Ind. U., 1987-94; vis. prof. Seoul Nat. U., 1996, Dartmouth Coll., 1997. Free-lance operatic stage dir.; worked for numerous opera cos. in U.S., Can., including, Met. Opera, San Francisco Opera, N.Y.C. Opera, Can. Opera Co.; dir. for various summer festivals. Mem. Am. Guild Musical Artists, Am. Fedn. Musicians, Can. Actors Equity. Home and Office: 201 W 85th St New York NY 10024-3917

LUCAS, JAMES WALTER, federal government official; b. Frankfort, Ind., Oct. 20, 1940; s. Walter Kenneth and Hester (Kesterson) L.; m. Sara Sue Stewart, Feb. 17, 1962; 1 dau., Catherine Anne. BS, Ball State U., 1963, MA, 1964; postgrad., Am. U., 1977, Harvard U., 1990; DA, George Mason U., 1995. Asst. dir. intelligence coordination Nat. Security Council, Washington, 1975-76; exec. asst. to dep. dir. CIA, Washington, 1976-77, dep. exec. sec., 1977-79; CIA program budget officer Intelligence Community Staff, 1979-81; dep. asst. sec. U.S. Dept. Air Force, 1981-82, prin. dep. asst. sec., 1982-83; dir. crisis mgmt. planning staff Nat. Security Council, 1983-85; Disting. prof., dean Def. Intelligence Coll., Washington, 1985-93; assoc. dir. liaison Def. Intelligence Agy., 1993-96; dep. dir. Open Source Info., CIA, 1996-97; prof. Nat. Def. U., Washington, 1997—; adj. prof. U. Md.-Far East div., 1970-71, Def. Intelligence Coll., 1974-83; guest lectr. Am. U., Washington, 1971-77; cons. Pres.'s Fgn. Intelligence Adv. Bd. Author: Intelligence and National Security in the Nixon Administration, 1972, Simulation and Strategic Intelligence Analysis, 1973, Information Needs of Presidents, 1989, Organizing the Presidency: The Role of the Director of Central Intelligence, 1995. Pres. Muncie Young Republican's Club, Ind., 1959-64; pres. Muncie Students for Goldwater, 1964; mem. Rep. Nat. Com., Reston Rep. Assn. With USAF, 1965-77, brig. gen. Res., 1977-96. Decorated Legion of Merit, Bronze Star medal, Meritorious Svc. medal, Republic of Vietnam Gallantry Cross with palm. Mem. Am. Polit. Sci. Assn., Internat. Studies Assn., Air Force Assn., Nat. Mil. Intelligence Assn., Res. Officers Assn., Pi Sigma Alpha, Phi Gamma Mu, Sigma Chi. Lodge: Masons. Office: CIA Nat Def Univ Washington DC 20319-6000

LUCAS, JERRY, retired basketball player; b. Middletown, Ohio, Mar. 30, 1940. Grad., Ohio State U., 1962. Basketball player Cin. Royals, 1963-70, San Francisco Warriors, 1970-71, N.Y. Knicks, 1971-73. Named to Basketball Hall of Fame, 1979; Coll. Player of Yr. Sporting News, 1961, 62, All-Am. 1st Team, 1960, 61, 62; recipient Rookie of Yr. award, 1964; selected All-NBA 1st Team, 1965, 66, 68, All-NBA 2d Team, 1964, 67, NBA All-Rookie Team, 1964; mem. NCAA Championship Team, 1973, U.S. Olympic Gold Medal Team, 1960, NBA Championship Team, 1973, MVP NBA All-Star Team, 1965. Office: c/o Basketball Hall Fame PO Box 179 Springfield MA 01101-0179

LUCAS, JOHN KENNETH, lawyer; b. Chgo., July 9, 1946; s. John and Catherine (Sykes) L.; m. Mary Ellen McElligott, Oct. 14, 1972; 1 child, John Patrick. BS with distinction, Ill. Inst. Tech., 1968; JD, DePaul U., 1972. Bar: Ill. 1972. Shareholder Brinks, Hofer, Gilson & Lione, Chgo.; hearing officer Ill. Pollution Control Bd., 1981-86; adj. prof. De Paul U. Coll. of Law, 1986-93. Mem. ABA, Ill. Bar Assn., Chgo. Bar Assn., Fed. Cir. Bar Assn., Bar Assn. of 7th Fed. Cir., Am. Intellectual Property Law Assn., Patent Law Assn. Chgo., Lic. Execs. Soc., Internat. Assn. Protection Indsl. Property, Legal Club of Chgo., Phi Alpha Delta, Tau Beta Pi, Eta Kappa Nu. Office: Brinks Hofer et al 455 N Cityfront Plaza Dr Chicago IL 60611-5503

LUCAS, LINDA LUCILLE, dean; b. Stockton, Calif., Apr. 22, 1940; d. Leslie Harold Lucas and Amy Elizabeth (Callow) Farnsworth. BA, San Jose State Coll., 1961, MA, 1969; EdD, U. San Francisco, 1982. Dist. libr. Livermore (Calif.) Elem. Schs., 1962-64; libr. Mission San Jose High Sch., Fremont, Calif., 1964-69; media reference libr. Chabot Coll., Hayward, Calif., 1969-75; asst. dean instrn. Chabot-Las Positas Coll., Livermore, 1975-91; assoc. dean instrn. Las Positas Coll., Livermore, 1991-94, dean acad. svcs., 1994—; participant Nat. Inst. for Leadership Devel., 1991. Bd. dirs. Tri-Valley Community TV, Livermore, 1991—, Valley Choral Soc., 1993—, Chabot-Las Positas Colls. Found., Pleasanton, Calif., 1991-94; mem. needs assessment com Performing Arts Coun., Pleasanton. Mem. ALA, Coun. Chief Librs., Assn. Calif. Community Coll. Adminstrs., Calif. Libr. Assn. Avocations: choral music, photography. Office: Las Positas Coll 3033 Collier Canyon Rd Livermore CA 94550-9797

LUCAS, MELINDA ANN, pediatrician, educator; b. Maryville, Tenn., June 27, 1953; d. Arthur Baldwin and Dorthy (Shields) L. BA, Maryville Coll., 1975; MS, U. Tenn., 1976, MD, 1981; postgrad., U. Tenn. Law Sch., 1992-93. Diplomate Am. Bd. Pediatrics; lic. dr. N.Y., Tenn. Intern in pediatrics U. Rochester, N.Y., 1981-82, resident in pediatrics, 1982-84; pvt. practice, Maryville, 1984-85; emergency room pediatrician U. Tenn. Med. Ctr., Knoxville, 1985-90, dir. child abuse clinic, 1987-90, pediatric intensivist, 1987—, acting dir. pediatric ICU, 1990-92, mem. faculty, 1988—; fellow in pediatric critical care U. Mich., Ann Arbor, 1995-96; mem. Pediatric Cons., Inc. Knoxville; physician rep. Project Search Working Symposium, 1990—. Contbr. articles to profl. jours. Mem. Blount County Foster Care Rev. Bd., Maryville, Tenn., 1985-93, Blount County Exec. Bd. Maryville Coll. Alumni Assn., 1988-92. Fellow U. Tenn. Genetics Ctr., 1988-89, pediatric critical care fellow U. Mich., 1995-96; scholar United Presbyn. Ch., 1971, Mary Lou Braly scholar, 1971-74; grantee AAP-NHTSA for Safe Ride Program. Fellow Am. Acad. Pediatrics; mem. AMA (Physician Recognition award 1984-87, 88-91, 91-94, 94-97), Am. Profl. Soc. on Abuse of Children, Tenn. Pediatric Soc. (co-chmn. accident and injury prevention com. 1993-95, 1996—), Knoxville Area Pediatric Soc., Soc. Critical Care Medicine (abstract reviewer 1991, 92, 93, 94). Methodist. Avocations: basketball, tennis, piano. Home: 1608 Mcilvaine Dr Maryville TN 37803-6230

LUCAS, PANOLA, elementary education educator; b. Pikeville, Ky., Nov. 18, 1932; d. Robert Lee and Trulie Ann (Pinson) Fields; m. Kenneth R. Lucas, Dec. 7, 1956 (div. Apr. 1984); 1 child, Nathan Wade. BS in Vocat. Home Econs., Marshall U., 1971; elem. teaching cert., W.Va. State Coll., 1976; cert. prin., W.Va. Coll. Grad. Studies, elem., mid., jr. and sr. high sch. prin., supt., supr. gen. instrn., vocat. admnstr., 1986. Tchr. Buffalo (W.Va.) High Sch., 1972; tchr. homebound Putnam County Bd. Edn., Winfield, W.Va., 1972-86; tchr. Poca (W.Va.) Elem. Sch., 1986-91, Scott Teays Elem. Sch., Scott Depot, W.Va., 1991—. Mem. W.Va. Profl. Educators, Kappa Delta Pi. Democrat. Baptist. Avocations: reading, travel, gardening, bowling, dancing. Home: 205 Hillside Dr # B Nitro WV 25143-2327

LUCAS, PATRICIA LYNN, financial executive; b. Memphis, Apr. 22, 1962; d. James Devoughn Harrington and Joyce Marie Horn Raiolo; m. Robert Warren Lucas, May 4, 1957; children: Matthew Robert, Lauren Ashley. Student, DePaul U., 1987. Lic. broker, Ill. Asst. mgr. McDonald's, South Chicago Heights, Ill., 1981, Taco Bell, Chgo., 1982, Brown's Chicken, Chicago Heights, Ill., 1983; customer svc. rep. Am. Nat. Bank, Chgo., 1983-85; bank mktg. rep. Kemper Fin. Svcs., Inc., Chgo., 1985-88; investment exec. Pathway Fin., Chicago Heights, 1988-90; mgr. INVEST Fin. Corp. Calumet Fed. Savs. & Loan, Dolton, Ill., 1990—. Vice pres., treas. Cedarwood Coop., Inc., Park Forest, 1990-92. DePaul U. scholar, 1982-86. Mem. Kemper Exec. Coun., Moose, Fortis Castle Club. Avocations: boating, reading, volleyball. Home: 3501 Dale Dr Crete IL 60417-1354 Office: Calumet Fed Savs & Loan 1350 E Sibley Blvd Dolton IL 60419-2965

LUCAS, RHETT ROY, artist, lawyer, chemical engineer; b. Columbia, S.C., Nov. 27, 1941; s. Spurgeon LeRoy and Elizabeth (Wells) L.; m. Uta Henkel, Apr. 12, 1967 (div. 1973). BSChemE, U. S.C., 1963; JD, NYU, 1967; postgrad., U. Glasgow, Scotland, 1965-66. Bar: U.S. Supreme Ct., Calif., D.C. Rsch. assoc. Twentieth Century Fund, N.Y.C., 1968-69; gen. counsel James Madison Inst., N.Y.C., 1969-72, Population Law Ctr., San Francisco, 1972-75; prin. Lucas & Assocs., Washington, 1972-84; artist Beverly Hills (Calif.) Fine Arts, 1984-86, The Rhett Lucas Collection, Santa Fe, and Scottsdale, Ariz., 1988-94. Prin. author U.S. Supreme Ct. briefs in Roe v. Wade, 1972, U.S. vs. Vuitch, 1971, Doe vs. Bolton, 1972 (ACOG amicus), others; contbr. articles to profl jours.; painter approx. 200 nat. and state parks; exhbns. include Oxford U., 1988, Banff Ctr., 1989, Grand Canyon Nat. Park, Ariz., 1991, 92, Capital Reef Nat. Park, Canyonlands Nat. Park, Cumberland Gap Hist. Nat. Park, Death Valley Nat. Pk., John Wesley Powell Meml. Mus., 1992, Powell River History Mus., 1992-93, O'Laurie (Canyonlands) Mus.; also exhbns. in Santa Fe, New Masters Gallery, Taos, N.M., Scottsdale, Fuller Lodge, Los Alamos, N. Mex., Petroglyph Nat. Monument, Casa Grande Art Mus., Hubbell's Trading Post Nat. Hist. Pk. Co-founder NARAL, N.Y.C., 1969. Root-Tilden scholar NYU Law Sch., 1963-67; Richard Found. fellow U. Glasgow, 1965-66; population rsch. grantee Rockefeller Found., 1972-74. Mem. ABA (litigation sect.), AIChE, Am. Soc. Marine Artists, Am. Inst. Conservation, Coll. Art Assn., Scottsdale Artist's League, Rockport (Mass.) Art Assn. (life), Wilderness Soc., Can. Alpine Club, Zero Population Growth, Sierra Club (life), Nat. Geog. Soc. (life), Rotary, Order of Coif, Mensa, Nat. Health Lawyers Assn., Am. Trial Lawyers Assn., Materials Info. Soc., Soc. Plastics Industry, Am. Chem. Soc., Phi Beta Kappa, Tau Beta Pi, Blue Key (pres.). Avocations: travel, photography, art collecting.

LUCAS, ROBERT ELMER, soil scientist; b. Malolos, The Philippines, June 27, 1916; (parents Am. citizens); s. Charles Edmund and Harriet Grace (Deardorff) L.; m. Norma Emma Schultz, Apr. 27, 1941; children: Raymond and Richard (twins), Milton, Keith, Charles. BSA, Purdue U., 1939, MS, 1941; PhD, Mich. State U., 1947. Research asst. Va. Agrl. Research Sta., Norfolk, 1941-43; farmer Culver, Ind., 1943-44; grad. asst. Mich. State U., East Lansing, 1945, assoc. prof. soil sci., 1951-57, prof., 1957-77, prof. emeritus, 1977—; agronomist William Gehring, Inc., Rensselaer, Ind., 1946-50, 77-78; vis. prof. Everglades Research Sta. U. Fla., Belle Glade, 1979-80. Author chpts. in books, research reports. Leader Boy Scouts Am., Lansing, Mich., 1961-72, dist. chmn. Chief Okemos (Mich.) Coun. Boy Scouts Am., 1965-66; pres. Okemos Cmty. Sr. citizens, 1987-88, pres. Lansing Area Farmers Agrl. Club, 1992, sec.-treas., 1994-96. Named Outstanding Specialist Mich. Coop. Extension Specialist Assn., 1967. Fellow Soil Sci. Soc. Am., Am. Soc. Agronomy (contbr. articles to jour.); mem. Internat. Peat Soc. (del. 1963—), U.S. Peat Soc., Mich. Onion Growers Assn. (sec. 1953-72), Mich. Muck Farmers Assn. (sec. 1953-72, Assoc. Master-Farmers award 1966), Mich. Mint Growers Assn. (sec. 1953-60). Republican. Lutheran. Avocations: traveling, gardening, sports, genealogy. Home: 3827 Dobie Rd Okemos MI 48864-3703 Office: Mich State Univ Dept Of Crop & Soil Sci East Lansing MI 48824

LUCAS, ROY EDWARD, JR., minister; b. Shawnee, Okla., Dec. 19, 1955; s. Roy Edward Sr. and Shirley Ann (Padgett) L.; m. Roberta Lee Duncan, Feb. 28, 1975; children: Jonathon Edward, Jerebeth Glenae. BA, Okla. Bapt. U., 1978, BA in Edn., 1979; MDiv, Southwestern Bapt. Theol. Sem., Ft. Worth, 1984, MRE, 1985, PhD, 1993. Ordained to ministry So. Bapt. Conv., 1978; cert. elem. tchr., Okla. Assoc. pastor Temple Bapt. Ch., Shawnee, 1975, Calvary Bapt. Ch., Shawnee, 1975-79; pastor Brandon (Tex.) Bapt. Ch., 1982-85, Fox (Okla.) Bapt. Ch., 1985-90, Union Hill Bapt. Ch., Purcell, Okla., 1990—; instr. Sem. Ext.-Enon Assn., Ardmore, Okla., 1986-89; teaching fellow Southwestern Bapt. Sem., 1989; adj. prof. Ministry Tng. Inst. Okla. Bapt. U., 1996-97. Home: 612 N 6th Ave Purcell OK 73080-2202 Office: Union Hill Bapt Ch RR 2 Box 80 Purcell OK 73080-9630

LUCAS, STANLEY JEROME, radiologist, physician; b. Cin., Mar. 23, 1929; s. Morris and Ruby (Schaen) L.; m. Judith Esther Schulzinger, May 14, 1953; children—Barbara Ellen, Daniel Nathan, Betsy Diane, Marvin Howard, Ronna Sue. B.S., U. Cin., 1948, M.D., 1951. Diplomate Am. Bd. Radiology. Intern Cin. Gen Hosp., 1951-52, resident, 1952-53, 55-57; practice medicine specializing in radiology Cin., 1957—; mem. staff William Booth Meml. Hosp., 1957-61, Speer Meml. Hosp., 1957-61, Jewish Hosp., Cin., 1961-94; past chmn. bd. Iona, Inc. Chmn. med. div. United Appeal, 1978, Jewish Welfare Fund, 1980; bd. dirs., treas. Midwest Found. Med. Care; founder Choicecare, Inc., 1978-86; mem. policy devel. com. Local Health Planning Agy., 1978-82. Capt. USAF, 1953-55. Honoree, Jewish Nat. Fund, 1994. Fellow Am. Coll. Radiology; mem. Radiol. Soc. N.Am., AMA (alt. del. 1982-87, del. 1987—), Ohio Med. Assn. (del. 1975-85, 94—, 1st dist. councilor 1985-90, pres.-elect 1991, pres. 1992-93), Cin. Acad. Medicine (pres. 1976-77, co-chmn. 140th anniversary 1997), Radiol. Soc. Cin. (pres. 1967), Am. Roentgen Ray Soc., Phi Beta Kappa, Phi Eta Sigma. Club: Losantiville Country. Jewish. Home: 6760 E Beechlands Dr Cincinnati OH 45237-3728 Office: 2905 Burnet Ave Cincinnati OH 45219-2403

LUCAS, STEVEN MITCHELL, lawyer; b. Ada, Okla., Jan. 19, 1948; s. John Dalton and Cherrye (Smith) L.; m. Lori E. Seeberger; children: Steven Turner, Brooke Elizabeth, Sarah Grace. BA, Yale U., 1970; JD, Vanderbilt U., 1973. Bar: D.C. 1973, U.S. Ct. Mil. Appeals 1974, U.S. Dist. Ct. D.C. 1979, U.S. Ct. Appeals (D.C.) 1979, U.S. Supreme Ct. 1979. Assoc. Shaw, Pittman, Potts & Trowbridge, Washington, 1978-82, ptnr., 1983-92; ptnr., head fin. instns. practice Wiley, Rein & Fielding, Washington, 1992-93, Winston & Strawn, Washington, 1993-97; pvt. practice Washington, 1997—; cons. on internat. rels., Rockefeller Found., N.Y.C., 1978, mem. negotiating team Panama Canal Treaty, Washington, 1975-77, legal adviser Dept. Def. Panama Canal negotiations working group. Editor in chief Vanderbilt U. Jour. Transnational Law, 1972-73. Capt. JAGC, U.S. Army, 1974-77. Mem. ABA, FBA (chmn. internat. law com. 1978-80, Outstanding Com. Chmn. award 1979), Inter-Am. Bar Assn., Am. Soc. Internat. Law, Army-Navy Country Club (Arlington, Va.), Yale Club (N.Y.C.), Army and Navy Club (Washington). Republican. Episcopalian. Home: 1696 Dunstable Green Annapolis MD 21401-6424 Office: 1730 K St NW Ste 304 Washington DC 20006

LUCAS, WILLIAM MAX, JR., structural engineer, university dean; b. Lamar, Mo., July 23, 1934; s. William Max and Margaret (Jones) L.; children—Jennifer Lynn Lucas Wyatt, Sarah Frances Lucas Whittington, Amy Johanne. B.S., U. Kans., 1956, M.S., 1962; Ph.D., Okla. State U., 1970. Registered profl. engr., Kans., Mo. Structural engr. Finney & Turnipseed, Topeka, 1960-62; prof. structural engring. U. Kans., Lawrence, 1962-74, 78-80, dir. facilities planning, 1974-78, dean Sch. Architecture and Urban Design, 1980-94; prof. arch. and archtl. engring., 1962—; owner W.M. Lucas, Engr., Lawrence, 1964—. Author: Matrix Analysis for Structural Engineers, 1968, Structural Analysis for Engineers, 1978; contbr. articles to profl. jours. Mem. Lawrence Bd. Bldg. Code Appeals, 1967-73, Kans. Bldg. Commn., 1982-84; pres. bd. dirs. United Fund, Lawrence, 1976; chmn. Lawrence/Douglas County Planning Commn., 1977-79; mem. consultative coun. Nat. Inst. Bldg. Scis., 1993—. Mem. Am. Soc. for Engring. Edn., Assn. Collegiate Schs. Architecture, Nat. Soc. Archtl. Engrs., Sigma Xi, Tau Beta Pi, Tau Sigma Delta. Club: Lawrence Country. Home: 2629 Bardith Ct Lawrence KS 66046-4536 Office: U Kans Sch Architecture & Urban Design Lawrence KS 66045

LUCAS, WILLIAM RAY, aerospace consultant; b. Newbern, Tenn., Mar. 1, 1922; married 1948; 3 children. B.S., Memphis State U., 1943; M.S., Vanderbilt U., 1950, Ph.D. in Chem. Metallurgy, 1952; L.H.D. (hon.), Mobile Coll., 1977; D.Sc. (hon.), Southeastern Inst. Tech., 1980, U. Ala., Huntsville, 1981. Instr. chemistry Memphis State U., 1946-48; chemist guided missile devel. div. Redstone Arsenal, 1952-54, chief chem. sect., 1954-55; chief engr. material sect. Army Ballistic Missile Agy., 1955-56, chief engr. material br., 1956-60; with Marshall Space Flight Center, NASA, 1960—, material div., 1963-66, dir. propulsion and vehicle engring. lab., 1966-68, dir. program devel., 1968-71, dep. dir., 1971-74, dir., 1974-86; pvt. practice aerospace cons. Hunstville, Ala., 1986—. Served as lt. USNR, 1943-46. Recipient Exceptional Sci. Achievement medal NASA, 1964, 2 Exceptional Service medals, 1969, Disting. Service medal, 1972, Disting. Service award, 1981, 86; Presdl. rank Disting. Exec., 1980; Roger W. Jones award for outstanding exec. leadership Am. U., 1981; Space award for outstanding contbns. in field of space VFW, 1983; Disting. Alumni award Memphis State U., 1984; Aubrey D. Green award Lions Club Ala., 1986; named one of Tenn. Outstanding Scientists and Engrs., Tenn. Tech. Found., 1986; named to Ala. Engring. Hall of Fame, 1990. Fellow Am. Soc. Metals, Am. Astronautical Soc. (Space Flight award 1982), AIAA (Oberth award 1965, Holger N. Toftoy award 1976, Elmer A. Sperry group award 1986); mem. Nat. Acad. Engring., Am. Chem. Soc., Sigma Xi, Tau Beta Pi. Research in materials engring. metallurgy, inorganic chemistry, environ. effects on materials, especially space environ. effects.

LUCCA, JOHN JAMES, retired dental educator; b. Bklyn., July 12, 1921; s. Thomas and Marie (Ciancia) L.; m. Mary A. Pascarell, June 22, 1946; children—Diane, Eileen, Denise, Nancy, John, William. A.B., NYU, 1941; D.D.S., Columbia, 1947. Diplomate: Am. Bd. Prosthodontics. Research fellow prosthetics Columbia Dental Sch., 1949-52, asst. prof., 1952-57, assoc. prof., 1957-64, head clin. prosthodontics; and postgrad. instr. 1st, 10th Dist. dental socs., 1954-87, prof. dentistry, 1964-87, dir. div. prosthodontics; prof. emeritus Columbia U., 1987—; cons. Westchester County Med. Ctr.; attending emeritus Presbyn. Hosp.; cons., lectr. U.S. Naval Dental Sch.; mem. examination com. N.E. Regional Bd. Dental Examiners; mem. med. staff Valley Hosp. Contbr. to dental jours., chpts. to various textbooks. Extraordinary minister of the Eucharist, 1974—; mem. parish council Mt. Carmel Ch., 1985—; hon. police surgeon N.Y.C. Police Dept., 1964—. Served with AUS, 1943-44. Recipient Ella M. Ewell medal Columbia, 1947. Fellow N.Y. Acad. Dentistry, Internat. Coll. Dentists Am. Coll. Dentists, Greater N.Y. Acad. Prosthodontics (pres. 1968), Internat. Coll. Prosthodontists, Am. Acad. Osseo Integration, Am. Coll. Prosthodontics (charter, pres. N.J. state sect. 1979-81); mem. Am. Equilibration Soc., First Dist. Dental Soc. (chmn. prosthodontia sect. 1971), Am. Prosthodontics Soc., William Jarvie Rsch. Soc., Chgo. Acad. Dental Rsch., Knight of Malta, Omicron Kappa Upsilon (pres. Epsilon Epsilon chpt. 1967). Home: 524 Eastgate Rd Ridgewood NJ 07450-2204

LUCCA, MARIA, advertising executive; married; two children. Sr. ptnr. creative supr. Ogilvy & Mather Direct, 1981—. Recipient numerous industry awards for art direction and direct mktg. Avocations: skiing, swimming, sailing, shopping. Office: Ogilvy & Mather Direct 309 W 49th St New York NY 10019-7316

LUCCHETTI, LYNN L., career officer; b. San Francisco, Calif., Aug. 21, 1939; d. Dante and Lillian (Bergeron) L. AB, San Jose State U., 1961; MS, San Francisco State U., 1967; grad. U.S. Army Basic Officer's Course, 1971, U.S. Army Advanced Officer Course, 1976, grad. U.S. Air Force Command and Staff Coll., 1982, U.S. Air Force War Coll., 1983, Sr. Pub. Affairs Officer Course, 1984. Media buyer Batten, Barton, Durstine & Osborn, Inc., San Francisco, 1961-67; producer-dir. Sta. KTVA-TV, Anchorage, 1967-68; media supr. Bennett, Luke and Teawell Advt., Phoenix, 1968-71; commd. 1st lt. U.S. Army, 1971; advanced through ranks to lt. col., 1985, col., 1989, brig. gen. nom. 1993; officer U.S. Army, 1971-74, D.C. N.G., , 1974-78, U.S. Air Force Res., 1978—, program advt. mgr. U.S. Navy Recruiting Command, 1974-76; exec. coordinator for the Joint Advt. Dirs. of Recruiting (JADOR), 1976-79; dir. U.S. Armed Forces Joint Recruiting Advt. Program (JRAP), Dept. Def., Washington, 1979-91; resources mgr. Exec. Leadership Devel. Program Dept. Def., Washington, 1991-94. Author: Broadcasting in Alaska, 1924-1966. Decorated U.S. Army Meritorious Svc. medal, Nat. Def. medal, U.S. Air Force Longevity Ribbon, U.S. Navy Meritorious Unit Commendation, Dept. Def. Joint Achievement medal, 1984. Sigma Delta Chi journalism scholar, 1960. Mem. Women in Def., Sr. Profl. Womens Assn. Home: 11401 Malaguena Ln NE Albuquerque NM 87111-6899

LUCE, CHARLES FRANKLIN, former utilities executive, lawyer; b. Platteville, Wis., Aug. 29, 1917; s. James Oliver and Wilma Fisher (Grindell) L.; m. Helen G. Oden, Oct. 24, 1942; children: James O., Christine Mary, Barbara Anne, Charles Franklin. B.A., LL.B., U. Wis., 1941; Sterling fellow, Yale U., 1941-42. Bar: Wis. 1941, Wash. 1946, Oreg. 1945, N.Y. 1981. Law clk. Justice Hugo L. Black, U.S. Supreme Ct., 1943-44; gen. practice law Walla Walla, Wash., 1946-61; adminstr. Bonneville Power Adminstrn., Dept. Interior, Portland, Oreg., 1961-66; under sec. interior Washington, 1966-67; chmn. bd. Consol. Edison Co. of N.Y., Inc., 1967-82, chief exec. officer, 1967-81, chmn. emeritus, 1982—; ptnr. Preston, Thorgrimson, Ellis & Holman, Portland, Oreg., 1982-86; spl. counsel Met. Life Ins. Co., 1987-94; dir. emeritus UAL and Met. Life Ins. Co.; trustee Hudson River Found., Henry M. Jackson Found.; trustee emeritus Columbia U., N.Y.C. Mem. N.Y., Wash., Wis. bar assns., Phi Beta Kappa, Order of Coif. Episcopalian. Office: Consol Edison 4 Irving Pl New York NY 10003-3502

LUCE, GREGORY M., lawyer. Bar: D.C., Va., Md. With Jones, Day, Reavis & Pogue, Washington. Mem. ABA, Nat. Health Lawyers Assn. (bd. dirs. 1996—), Am. Acad. Hosp. Attys., Va. State Bar (past chair, mem. bd. govs. health law sect.). Office: Jones Day Reavis & Pogue 1450 G St NW Washington DC 20005-2001

LUCE, HENRY, III, foundation executive; b. N.Y.C., Apr. 28, 1925; s. Henry Robinson and Lila Hotz (Tyng) L.; m. Patricia Potter, June 27, 1947 (div. 1954); children: Lila Frances, Henry Christopher; m. Claire McGill, Aug. 6, 1960 (dec. June 1971); stepchildren: Kenneth, William, James; m. Nancy Bryan Cassiday, Aug. 15, 1975 (dec. Mar. 1987); stepchildren: Richard, Bryan (dec.); m. Leila Eliott Burton Hadley, Jan. 5, 1990; stepchildren: Arthur T. Hadley III, Victoria Smitter Barlow, Matthew Smitter Eliott, Caroline Smitter Nicholson. BA, Yale U., 1945; L.H.D. (hon.), St. Michael's, 1973; student, L.I. U., 1986; L.H.D., Pratt Inst., 1991; LLD (hon.), Coll. of Wooster, 1994. Commr.'s asst. Hoover Commn. on Orgn. Exec. Br. of Govt., 1948-49; reporter Cleve. Press, 1949-51; Washington corr. Time Inc., 1951-53, Time writer, 1953-55, head new bldg. dept., 1956-60, asst. to pub., 1960-61; circulation dir. Fortune and Archtl. Forum, 1961-64, House & Home, 1962-64; v.p. Time Inc., 1964-80, chief London bur., 1966-68; pub. Fortune, 1968-69; pub. Time, 1969-72, dir. corp. planning, 1972-80; dir. Time, Inc., 1967-89, Time Warner Inc., 1989-96; pres., chmn., CEO Henry Luce Found., Inc., 1958—; pres. The New Mus. Contemporary Art,

1977—; chmn. Am. Security Systems Inc. Trustee Princeton Theol. Sem., Coll. Wooster, Eisenhower Exch. Fellowships, Ctr. Theol. Inquiry, Christian Ministry in Nat. Pks., N.Y. Hist. Soc.; mem. Am. Coun. UN Univ.; pres. Assn. Am. Corrs. in London, 1968; dir. Nat. Com. on U.S. China Rels., Fishers Island Devel. Co.; trustee, china Inst. in Am., 1975-78, chmn. Am. Russian Youth Orch. Lt. (j.g.) USNR, 1943-46. 2nd Ann. recipient medal for disting. philanthropy Am. Assn. Museums, 1994, Ann. award Assn. N.Y. State Arts Coun., 1995, Frederick Law Olmstead medal Central Park Conservancy, 1996. Mem. Univ. Club (coun. mem.), Pilgrims Club U.S.), Explorers Club, Fishers Island Club, Hay Harbor Club. Presbyterian (elder). Office: 720 5th Ave Ste 1500 New York NY 10019-4107 also: Mill Hill Rd Mill Neck NY 11765

LUCE, R(OBERT) DUNCAN, psychology educator; b. Scranton, Pa., May 16, 1925; s. Robert Rennselaer and Ruth Lillian (Downer) L.; m. Gay Gaer, June 6, 1950 (div.); m. Cynthia Newby, Oct. 5, 1968 (div.); m. Carolyn A. Scheer, Feb. 27, 1988; 1 child, Aurora Newby. BS, MIT, 1945, PhD, 1950; MA (hon.), Harvard U., 1976. Mem. staff research lab electronics MIT, 1950-53; asst. prof. Columbia U., 1953-57; lectr. social relations Harvard U., 1957-59; prof. psychology U. Pa., Phila., 1959-69; vis. prof. Inst. Advanced Study, Princeton, 1969-72; prof. Sch. Social Scis., U. Calif., Irvine, 1972-75; Alfred North Whitehead prof. psychology Harvard U., Cambridge, Mass., 1976-81, prof., 1981-83, Victor S. Thomas prof. psychology, 1983-88, Victor S. Thomas prof. emeritus, 1988; chmn. Harvard U., 1988-94; disting. prof. cognitive sci. U. Calif., Irvine, 1988-94, dir. Irvine Rsch. Unit in math. behavioral sci., 1988-92, disting. rsch. prof. cognitive sci. and rsch. prof. econs., 1994—; dir. Inst. for Math. Behavioral Sci., 1992—; chmn. assembly behavioral and social scis. NRC, 1976-79. Author: (with H. Raiffa) Games and Decisions, 1957, Individual Choice Behavior, 1959, (with others) Foundations of Measurement, I, 1971, II, 1989, III, 1990, Response Times, 1986, (with others) Stevens Handbook of Experimental Psychology, I and II, 1988, Sound & Hearing, 1993. Served with USNR, 1943-46. Ctr. Advanced Study in Behavioral Scis. fellow, 1954-55, 66-67, 87-88, NSF Sr. Postdoctoral fellow, 1966-67, Guggenheim fellow, 1980-81; recipient Disting. award for Rsch. U. Calif., Irvine, 1994. Fellow AAAS, APA (disting. sci. contbn. award 1970, bd. sci. affairs 1993-95), Am. Psychol. Soc. (bd. dirs. 1989-91); mem. Am. Acad. Arts and Scis., Am. Philos. Soc., Nat. Acad. Scis. (chmn. sect. psychology 1980-83, class behavioral and social scis. 1983-86), Am. Math. Soc., Math. assn. Am., Fedn. Behavioral Psychol. and Cognitive Scis. (pres. 1988-90), Psychometric Soc. (pres. 1976-77), Psychonomic Soc., Soc. Math. Psychology (pres. 1979), Sigma Xi, Phi Beta Kappa, Tau Beta Pi. Home: 20 Whitman Ct Irvine CA 92612-4057 Office: U Calif Social Sci Plz Irvine CA 92697-5100

LUCEK, DONALD WALTER, surgeon; b. Rockford, Ill., Jan. 26, 1945; s. Walter Joseph and Magdalen Mary (Kazunas) L.; m. Mary Philomena Keany, July 6, 1968; children: Patricia, Donald Jr., Michael, Stephen. BA, U. Ill., 1970, MD, 1974. Diplomate Am. Bd. Surgery. Intern, resident in surgery Boston U., 1974-79, clin. instr. surgery, 1980-87, asst. clin. prof. surgery, 1987—; surgeon Milton (Mass.) Hosp., 1979—, pres. med. staff, 1993, chief of surgery, 1993-95, chmn. tissue and transfusion, 1987-93, chmn. operating rm. com., 1993-94; chief of staff, pres. med. staff, chmn. trauma com. Mobridge Regional Hosp., S.D., 1996—. Pres. Milton Office Condo Assn., 1990-94; med. examiner Commonwealth of Mass., Norfolk County, 1989—. Fellow ACS, Mass. Med. Soc.; mem. AMA, Boston Surg. Soc., Mass. Medicolegal Soc., S.D. State Med. Assn. Office: 100 Highland St Milton MA 02186-3802

LUCENKO, LEONARD KONSTANTYN, sport, recreation management, and safety educator, coach, consultant; b. Ukraine, Aug. 2, 1937; came to U.S., 1949; s. Konstantyn and Pauline Lucenko; m. Larissa Rohowsky, June 7, 1963; children: Leonard Jr., Kristina. BA, Temple U., 1961; MA, NYU, 1962; PhD, U. Utah, 1972. Instr. Lehman Coll., N.Y.C., 1962-62; athletic dir. Eron Prep Sch., N.Y.C., 1962-65; coach, trainer Pratt Inst., Bklyn., 1965; prof. sport, recreation mgmt., and safety, coach, administrator Montclair (N.J.) State Coll., 1966—; mem. com. N.J. Vol. Coaches Com., Trenton, 1988-91; cons. soccer Pres.'s Coun. Phys. Fitness, Washington; bd. dirs. All Am. Soccer Camp, South Orange, N.J., 1966—, Montclair State Coaching Acad., 1980—. Author: (with others) U.S. Soccer Federation Official Book, 1982; contbr. articles to profl. jours. Named Coach of Yr. Met. Conf., N.Y., 1971, N.J. State Athletic Conf. Mem. Ea. N.Y. Soccer Assn. (bd. dirs. coaching sch. 1972—, Most Valuable Player 1983). Office: Montclair State Coll Normal Rd Montclair NJ 07043

LUCENTE, ROSEMARY DOLORES, educational administrator; b. Renton, Wash., Jan. 11, 1935; d. Joseph Anthony and Erminia Antoinette (Argano) Lucente; BA, Mt. St. Mary's Coll., 1956, MS, 1963. Tchr. pub. schs., Los Angeles, 1956-65, supr. tchr., 1958-65, asst. prin., 1965-69, prin. elem. sch., 1969-85, 86—, dir. instrn., 1985-86, 1986—; nat. cons., lectr. Dr. William Glasser's Educator Tng. Ctr., 1968—; nat. workshop leader Nat. Acad. for Sch. Execs.-Am. Assn. Sch. Adminstrs., 1980; L.A. Unified Sch. Dist. rep. for nat. pilot of Getty Inst. for Visual Arts, 1983-85, 92—, site coord., 1983-86, team leader, mem. supt.'s adv. cabinet, 1987—. Recipient Golden Apple award Stanford Ave. Sch. PTA, Faculty and Community Adv. Council, 1976, resolution for outstanding service South Gate City Council, 1976, named Woman of Yr., Calif. State Senate, 1997. Mem. Nat. Assn. Elem. Sch. Prins., L.A. Elem. Prins. Orgn. (v.p. 1979-80), Assn. Calif. Sch. Adminstrs. (charter mem.), Assn. Elem. Sch. Adminstrs. (vice-chmn. chpt. 1972-75, city-wide exec. bd., steering com. 1972-75, 79-80), Asso. Adminstrs. Los Angeles (charter), Pi Theta Mu, Kappa Delta Pi (v.p. 1982-84), Delta Kappa Gamma. Democrat. Roman Catholic. Home: 6501 Lindenhurst Ave Los Angeles CA 90048-4733 Office: Figueroa St Sch 510 W 111th St Los Angeles CA 90044-4231

LUCERO, CARLOS, federal judge; b. Antonito, Colo., Nov. 23, 1940; m. Dorothy Stuart; 1 child, Carla. BA, Adams State Coll.; JD, George Washington U., 1964. Law clk. to Judge William E. Doyle U.S. Dist. Ct., Colo., 1964-65; pvt. practice Alamosa, Colo.; sr. ptnr. Lucero, Lester & Sigmund, Alamosa, Colo.; judge U.S. Ct. Appeals (10th cir.), 1995—; mem. Pres. Carter's Presdl. Panel on Western State Water Policy. Bd. dirs. Colo. Hist. Soc., Santa Fe Opera Assn. of N.Mex. Recipient Outstanding Young Man of Colo. award Colo. Jaycees, Disting. Alumnus award George Washington U.; Paul Harris fellow Rotary Found. Fellow Am. Coll. Trial Lawyers, Am. Bar Found., Colo. Bar Found. (pres.), Internat. Acad. Trial Lawyers, Internat. Soc. Barristers; mem. ABA (mem. action com. to reduce ct. cost and delay, mem adv. bd. ABA jour., mem. com. on the availability of legal svcs.), Colo. Bar Assn. (pres. 1977-78, mem. ethics com.), San Luis Valley Bar Assn. (pres.), Nat. Hispanic Bar Assn., Colo. Hispanic Bar Assn. (profl. svc. award), Colo. Rural Legal Svcs. (bd. dirs.), Order of the Coif. Office: US Ct Appeals 1823 Stout St Denver CO 80257-1823*

LUCERO, MICHAEL, sculptor; b. Tracy, Calif., Apr. 1, 1953. BA, Humboldt State U., 1975; MFA, U. Wash., 1978. instr. NYU, 1979-80, Parsons Sch. Design, 1981-82; guest lectr. RISD, Providence, 1979; Richard R. Koopman chair visual arts U. Hartford, 1995. One-man shows include Charles Cowles Gallery, Inc., N.Y., 1981, 83, 84, 86, Linda Farris Gallery, Seattle, 1982, 87, Hokin Kaufman Gallery, Chgo., 1983, 86, Fuller Goldeen Gallery, San Francisco, 1985, ACA Contemp, N.Y., 1988, Contemp ARts Ctr., Cin., 1990, Contemp Cutouts, Whitney Mus. Am. Art, N.Y., 1988, Ceramic Tradition: Figuration, Palo Alto Cultural Arts Ctr., Calif., 1989; two-man shows Reese Bullen Gallery, Humboldt State U., Arcata, Calif., 1989, Explorations-The Aesthetics of Excess, Am. Craft Mus., N.Y., 1990, Natural Image, Stanford Mus. and Nature Ctr., Conn., 1990, Seattle Art Mus., Nat. Mus. Contemporary Art, Seoul, Corcoran Gallery Art, Washington, Mus. Fine Arts, Boston; Michael Lucero Sculpture 1976-1995 show organized by Mint Mus. Art, Am. Craft Mus., Kemper Mus., Renwick Mus., Carnegie Mus. Art, 1996. Recipient award Nat. Endowment Arts, 1979, 81, 84; Creative Artists Pub. Svc. Program fellow, 1981, Nettie Marie Jones fellow Ctr. Music, Drama & Art, Lake Placid, N.Y., 1983. Office: c/o Fay Gold Gallery 247 Buckhead Ave NE Atlanta GA 30305-2237

LUCERO, SCOTT ALAN, special education educator; b. Denver, Mar. 23, 1968; s. Raymond Lucero and Barbara Jean (McElliott) Gonzales; m. Deborah Ann Cole, Nov. 24, 1989; children: Lori Lynn, Kimberly Ann. Cert. welding, Warren Occupational, Golden, Colo., 1986; student, Arapahoe C.C., Littleton, Colo., 1992-94; grad., U. Denver, 1997. Cert. nurse, Colo. Self-employed welder Denver, 1986-88; care mgr. for developmentally disabled Arvada, Colo., 1988—; residential coord. Dungaruin Inc.; guest lectr. physics and chemistry to elem. schs. Vol. Polit.-Wyo. Gov., 1985. Honors scholar Denver U. Mem. Honors Inst., Phi Theta Kappa (officer), Alpha Epsilon Delta, Theta Chi (Gamma Lambda chpt.). Democrat. Avocations: fishing, coaching disabled and planning activities for developmentally disabled, car restoration. Home: 9135 W Maplewood Littleton CO 80123

LUCEY, JEROLD FRANCIS, pediatrician; b. Holyoke, Mass., Mar. 26, 1926; s. Jeremiah F. and Pauline A. (Lally) L.; m. Ingela Barth, Oct. 7, 1972; 1 child, Patrick; children by previous marriage: Colleen, Cathy, David. AB, Dartmouth Coll., 1948; MD, NYU, 1952. Intern Bellevue Hosp., N.Y.C., 1952-53; resident in pediat. Columbia-Presbyn. Med. Ctr., 1953-55; rsch. fellow Harvard-Children's Hosp., 1955-56; rsch. fellow in biochemistry U. Vt., 1956-60, from asst. prof. to prof. pediat., 1961-74, prof., 1974—; rsch. fellow in biol. chemistry Harvard Coll., 1960-61; cons. NIH; vis. prof. Royal Soc. Medicine, Eng., 1980; Wallace prof. neonatology, 1995. Editor Pediatrics, 1974—; contbr. articles on neonatology, phototherapy and transcutaneous oxygen to profl. jours. With USNR, 1944-46. Recipient Humbolt Sr. Scientist award, 1978, United Cerebral Palsy Rsch. award, 1984, McDonald prize, 1991, Apgar award, 1993; Markel scholar, 1960-65, Humbolt scholar, 1978, Univ. scholar, 1991, Columbia Alumnus of the Year award, 1995. Fellow Am. Acad. Pediat. (Grulee award 1988); mem. Royal Soc. Medicine, World congress on Perinatal Medicine (pres. 1993), Indian Pediat. Soc. (hon., Gold medal 1994). Home: 52 Overlake Park Burlington VT 05401-4012 Office: Mary Fletcher Hosp McClure Rm 718 111 Colchester Ave Burlington VT 05401-1473

LUCEY, JOHN DAVID, JR., lawyer; b. Phila., May 4, 1930; s. John David and Eleanor (Gallagher) L.; m. Carol Ann Henderson, Oct. 29, 1955; children—John David, Michael Dakin, Timothy Gallagher, Carol Anne. A.B., U. Pa., 1953, LL.B., 1956. Bar: Pa. 1957. Mem. firm LaBrum and Doak, Phila., 1957—; instr. estate counselling Temple U. Sch. Law, 1977-86; course planner, author, lectr. Pa. Bar Inst., 1967—. Mem. Phila. Bar Assn. (chmn. sect. probate and trust law 1976), Pa. Bar Assn., ABA, Am. Coll. Trust & Estate Counsel. Republican. Roman Catholic. Club: Union League of Phila. Home: 1237 Hagys Ford Rd Narberth PA 19072-1103 Office: LaBrum & Doak 1818 Market St Ste 2900 Philadelphia PA 19103-3602

LUCHE, THOMAS CLIFFORD, foreign service officer; b. Bklyn., Jan. 24, 1934; s. Theodore Paul Albert and Jennie Kristine (Thompsen) L.; m. Winifred Jean Bogardus, May 26, 1959; children: Stephen Edward, Jenna Elizabeth, Sarah Hope. BS in Gen. Forestry, SUNY, Syracuse, 1955; student employment tng. program, Scandinavian Am. Found., Denmark and Finland, 1955-56. Various positions USAID, Saigon, Vietnam, 1957-63; rural devel. officer Joseph Z. Taylor Assocs., Chiang Mai, Thailand, 1967-70, USAID, Upper Volta, 1975-79; area coord. USAID, Arusha, Tanzania, 1979-81; grants officer USAID, Washington, 1981-83; gen. devel. officer USAID, Accra, Ghana, 1983-85; spl. projects officer USAID, Washington, 1985-87; rep. USAID, Praia, Cape Verde, 1987-92; rep. USAID, Burkina Faso, 1992-94, ret., 1994. Recipient Vietnam Civilian Service medal, 1968, HRH The Princess Mother's Memorial medal, Thailand, 1969. Mem. Am. Fgn. Svc. Assn., Sr. Fgn. Svc. of the USA, Soc. Am. Foresters. Democrat. Episcopalian. Avocations: fishing, hunting, water sports, opera, ballet.

LUCHETTE, FREDERICK A., surgeon; b. Sharon, Pa., Aug. 9, 1954; s. Albert and Rosemary (Songer) L.; m. Barbara Ann O'Brien, Aug. 31, 1985; children: Richard, Matthew, Claire, Katherine. BA, Thiel Coll., 1976; MS, U. Louisville, 1978, MD, 1981. Diplomate Am. Bd. Surgery. From clin. instr. to asst. prof. surgery SUNY, Buffalo, 1981-93; assoc. prof. surgery U. Cin., 1994—. Fellow Am. Coll. Surgeons; mem. Am. Assn. Surgery of Trauma, Am. Trauma Soc., Eastern Assn. Surgery of Trauma, Soc. Critical Care Medicine, Surgical Infection Soc. Roman Catholic.9. Avocations: jogging, reading, traveling. Office: U Cin Med Ctr 231 Bethesda Ave # 0558 Cincinnati OH 45229-2827

LUCHT, JOHN CHARLES, management consultant, executive recruiter, writer; b. Reedsburg, Wis., June 1, 1933; s. Carl H. and Ruth A. (Shultis) L.; m. Catherine Ann Seyler, Dec. 11, 1965 (div. 1982). BS, U. Wis., 1955, LLB, 1960. News dir. Sta. WISC-AM/FM, Madison, Wis., 1952-55; merchandising dir. The Bartell Group (radio and TV stas.), Milw., 1955-56; instr. U. Wis. Law Sch., 1959-60; TV contracts exec., account exec. J. Walter Thompson Co., N.Y.C., 1960-64; product mgr., new products supr., dir. new product mktg. Bristol-Myers Co., N.Y.C., 1964-69; dir. mktg. W.A. Sheaffer Pen Co., Ft. Madison, Iowa, 1969-70; gen. mgr. Tetley Tea div. Squibb Beech-Nut Inc., N.Y.C., 1970-71; v.p. Heidrick & Struggles, N.Y.C., 1971-77; pres. The John Lucht Consultancy, Inc., N.Y.C., 1977—, The Viceroy Press Inc., 1987—; Lectr. in field. Author: Rites of Passage at $100,000 Plus, The Insider's Guide to Executive Job-Changing, Executive Job-Changing Workbook. Mem. Soc. Am. Bus. Editors and Writers, Internat. Assn. Corp. and Profl. Recruiters, State Bar Wis., N.Y. Bd. Trade, Assn. Exec. Search Cons., Nat. Assn. Corp. Profl. Recruiters, N.Y. Acad. Scis., Overseas Press Club, Met. Club, Can. Club, Phi Beta Kappa, Phi Eta Sigma, Phi Kappa Phi, Phi Delta Phi, Sigma Alpha Epsilon. Office: Olympic Tower 641 5th Ave New York NY 10022-5908

LUCHTERHAND, RALPH EDWARD, financial advisor; b. Portland, Oreg., Feb. 9, 1952; s. Otto Charles II and Evelyn Alice (Isaac) L.; children: Anne Michelle, Eric Alexander, Nicholas Andrew. BS, Portland State U., 1974, MBA, 1986. Registered profl. engr., Oreg.; gen. securities broker NYSE/NASD, CFP. Mech. engr. Hyster Co., Portland, 1971-75, svc. engr., 1975-76; project engr. Lumber Systems Inc., Portland, 1976-79; prin. engr. Moore Internat., Portland, 1979-81, chief product engr., 1981-83; project engr. Irvington-Moore, Portland, 1983, chief engr., 1983-86; ind. cons. engr., 1986; engring. program mgr. Precision Castparts Corp., Portland, 1986-87; personal fin. adv., Am. Express Fin. Advs., Clackamas, Oreg., 1987-94, sr. fin. adv., 1994—; ptnr. Bacon, Luchterhand Wilmot & Assocs. Divsn. of Am. Express Fin. Advisors, Clackamas, Oreg., 1996—; apptd. to Silver Team, 1991, Gold Team, 1994. Treas. Village Bapt. Ch., Beaverton, Oreg., 1988-91; bd. dirs. Carus Community Planning Orgn., Oregon City, Oreg., 1993—; active Rolling Hills Cmty. Ch., Tualatin, Oreg., 1995—. Republican. Home: 24440 S Eldorado Rd Mulino OR 97042-9629 Office: Bacon Luchterhand Wilmot & Assocs Am Express Fin Advisors 8800 SE Sunnyside Rd Ste 300 Clackamas OR 97015-9786

LUCIA, DON, head coach men's ice hockey; married; 4 children. Grad., U. Notre Dame, 1981. Asst. coach U. Alaska, Fairbanks, 1981-85, Anchorage, 1985-87; head coach Colorado Coll., Colorado Springs, 1987—; head coach Team West U.S. Olympic Festival, Denver. Recipient Spencer Penrose award Nat. Coach of Yr. Am. Hockey Coaches Assn.; named Coach of Yr. WCHA. Office: Colorado Coll Ice Hockey Dept 14E Cache La Poudre Colorado Springs CO 80903

LUCIA, MARILYN REED, physician; b. Boston; m. Salvatore P. Lucia, 1959 (dec. 1984); m. C. Robert Russell; children: Elizabeth, Walter, Salvatore, Darryl. MD, U. Calif., San Francisco, 1956. Intern Stanford U. Hosps., 1956-57; NIMH fellow, resident in psychiatry Langley Porter, U. Calif., San Francisco, 1957-60; NIMH fellow, resident in child psychiatry Mt. Zion Hosp., San Francisco, 1964-66; NIMH fellow, resident in community psychiatry U. Calif., San Francisco, 1966-68, clin. prof. psychiatry, 1982—; founder, cons. Marilyn Reed Lucia Child Care Study Ctr., U. Calif., San Francisco; cons. Cranio-facial Ctr., U. Calif., San Francisco, No. Calif. Diagnostic Sch. for Neurologically Handicapped Children; dir. children's psychiat. svcs. Contra Costa County Hosp., Martinez. Fellow Am. Psychiat. Assn., Am. Acad. Child Psychiatry; mem. Am. Cleft Palate Assn. Office: 350 Parnassus Ave Ste 602 San Francisco CA 94117-3608

LUCIANO, GWENDOLYN KAYE, planning specialist, utility rates administrator; b. Cleve., Feb. 26, 1954; d. Charles Wayne and Lila (Cole) Rhodes. BA in Math. and Mktg., Lake Erie Coll., 1975, MBA, 1988. cert. project mgmt. profl. Scheduling engr. A.G. McKee & Co., Independence, Ohio, 1975-78; project scheduling supr. Perry Nuclear Plant Raymond Kaiser Engrs., Perry, Ohio, 1978-85; maintenance planning supr. Cleve. Electric Illuminating Co., 1985-89; mgmt. cons. Liberty Cons. Group, Balt., 1989-91; outage planning coord. Cleve. Electric Illuminating, 1991-94; mgr. fed. regulation Centerior Energy Corp., Independence, Ohio, 1994-96, mgr. fed. reg. and pricing, 1996—; instr. Inst. Nuclear Power Ops., Atlanta, 1993-94; bd. dirs. Learning About Bus.; bd. trustees Lake Erie Coll., 1996—. Trustee Lake Erie (Pa.) Coll. Recipient Woman Profl. Excellence award YMCA, 1997. Mem. Am. Assn. Cost Engrs., Project Mgmt. Inst., Lake Erie Coll. Nat. Alumni Assn. (pres. 1996—). Republican. Episcopalian. Avocations: gourmet cooking, golf, tennis. Office: Centerior Energy Corp 6200 Oak Tree Blvd Independence OH 44131-2510

LUCIANO, PETER JOSEPH, professional society administrator; b. Washington, Dec. 10, 1946; s. Samuel Gabriel and Eleanor Claire Luciano. AB, Boston Coll., 1968; MA, Brown U., 1970. Sr. economist U.S. Dept. Commerce, 1970-76; dir. of policy devel. Transp. Inst., 1976-80, exec. dir., 1980-88; exec. dir. Nat. Bus. Travel Assn., 1988-90; v.p. APEX Property Mgmt., Inc., 1990-91; CEO Nat. Alliance of Sr. Citizens, 1991—; sec. and dir. NASC Clinkscales Found., 1992—; dir. Seniorcare Ins. Svcs., Washington, 1992—. Capt. USAR, 1964-78. Mem. Univ. Club, Nay League of the U.S. (life). Roman Catholic. Office: Nat Alliance of Sr Citizens 1744 Riggs Pl NW Fl 3 Washington DC 20009-6113*

LUCIANO, ROBERT PETER, pharmaceutical company executive; b. N.Y.C., Oct. 9, 1933; s. Peter and Jennie (Mastro) L.; m. Barbara Ann Schiavone, June 21, 1953; children: Susan Ann, Richard Peter. BBA, CCNY, 1954; JD, U. Mich., 1958. Sr. tax assoc. Royall Koegel & Rogers (now Rogers & Wells), N.Y.C., 1958-66; atty. CIBA Corp., Summit, N.J., 1966-68, asst. sec., 1968-70; asst. gen. counsel, dir. pub. affairs CIBA Pharm. Co., Summit, 1970-71, v.p. mktg., 1973-75; v.p. planning and adminstrn. pharm. div. CIBA-GEIGY Corp., Summit, 1971-73, pres. pharm. div., 1975-77; pres. Lederle Labs. div. Am. Cyanamid Co., Pearl River, N.Y., 1977-78; sr. v.p. adminstrn. Schering-Plough Corp., Kenilworth, N.J., 1978-79, exec. v.p. pharm. ops., 1979-80, pres., COO, 1980-82, pres., CEO, 1982-84, chmn. bd., pres., CEO, 1984-86, chmn. bd., CEO, 1986-96, also chmn. bd. dirs.; bd. dirs. C.R. Bard Inc., Murray Hill, N.J., Bank of N.Y. Co. Inc., N.Y.C. Asst. editor: U. Mich. Law Rev., 1957-58. Served with U.S. Army, 1954-56. Mem. ABA, N.Y. Bar Assn., Nat. Assn. Mfrs. (bd. dirs. 1982—), N.J. State C. of C. (bd. dirs. 1986—). Republican. Clubs: Union League, Sky, Econ. (N.Y.C.). Office: Schering-Plough Corp PO Box 1000 1 Giralda Farms Madison NJ 07940-1027*

LUCIANO, ROSELLE PATRICIA, advertising executive, editor; b. Bklyn., Feb. 10, 1921; d. Giacomo Roberto and Francesca Rosa (Ruvolo) Rubino; m. Anthony Vincenzo Luciano, Nov. 24, 1946; 1 child, Nino Vincenzo Luciano. Attended, NYU. College shop mgr. Abraham & Straus, Bklyn., 1939-41, advtg. copywriter, 1941-44; fashion editor Syndicated MB Reports, N.Y.C., 1945-48; advtg. mgr., fashions copywriter Macy's 34th St., N.Y.C., 1949-54; publicist, adminstr. Fun With Prodns., N.Y.C., 1959-69; chair, adminstr. U.U. Plandome Forum, Manhasset, N.Y., 1970-78, UU Veatch Found., Manhasset, N.Y., 1979-84; dir. devel. IALRW Literacy For Women Program, Great Britain and India, 1984—; coord. numerous workshops in field for various orgns.; served as spkr., editor, writer, publicist, 1984—. Operator political booth Democratic Party, Garden City, 1984, 88, 92; founder R.P.L. Literacy Fund for Women, 1996—. Recipient Best Advtg. Ad of the Yr. award Women's Wear Daily, 1954, Citizen of the Yr. award Carle Place Schs., 1965, award for outstanding leadership and encouragement for working women Women-On-the-Job, Inc., N.Y., 1987, Susan B. Anthony award U. U. Women;s Fedn., 1997. Unitarian Universalist. Avocations: reading, opera, ballet, theater, travelling.

LUCID, ROBERT FRANCIS, English educator; b. Seattle, June 25, 1930; s. Philip Joseph and Nora May (Gorman) L.; m. Joanne K. Tharalson, Sept. 18, 1954; 1 son, John Michael. B.A., U. Wash., 1954; M.A., U. Chgo., 1955, Ph.D., 1958. Faculty U. Chgo., 1957-59, Wesleyan U., Middletown, Conn., 1959-64; mem. faculty U. Pa., Phila., 1964-97, prof. English, 1975-96, emeritus, 1996—, chmn. dept. English, 1980-85, 90-91, chmn. faculty senate, 1976-77, master Hill Coll. House, 1979-96. Editor: Journal of Richard Henry Dana, 1968, The Long Patrol, 1971, Norman Mailer, the Man and His Work, 1971. Served with USAF, 1951-53. Recipient Lindback award U. Pa., 1975, Abrams award, 1986; Yaddo fellow, 1970. Mem. MLA, AAUP, PEN (exec. bd. 1987-93), Am. Studies Assn. (exec. sec. 1964-69), Princeton Club (N.Y.C.), Penn Club (N.Y.C.). Office: U Pa Dept English Philadelphia PA 19104

LUCID, SHANNON W., biochemist, astronaut; b. Shanghai, China, Jan. 14, 1943; d. Joseph Oscar and Mary Wells; m. Michael F. Lucid, 1968; children: Kawai Dawn, Shandara Michelle, Michael Kermit. BS in Chemistry, U. Okla., 1963, MS in Biochemistry, 1970, PhD in Biochemistry, 1973. Sr. lab. technician Okla. Med. Rsch. Found., 1964-66, rsch. assoc., from 1974; chemist Kerr-McGee, Oklahoma City, 1966-68; astronaut NASA Lyndon B. Johnson Space Ctr., Houston, 1979—; mission specialist flights STS-51G and STS-34 NASA Lyndon B. Johnson Space Ctr., mission specialist on Shuttle Atlantis Flight, 1991; mission specialist flight STS-58 NASA, 1993, mission specialist flight STS 76 & 79, 1996; mission specialist stationed on Space Station Mir, 1996. First woman to fly on the shuttle three times; remained aloft 188 days in shuttle Mir. Address: NASA Johnson Space Ctr CB-Astronaut Office Houston TX 77058

LUCIDO, CHESTER CHARLES, JR., educational consultant; b. Pitts., Dec. 5, 1939; s. Chester C. and Alma (Dolence) L.; m. Linda G. Firrell, June 16, 1962; children: Chester C. III, Bradley J., Kristen L. BS in Mgmt., Pa. State U., 1961. Sales rep. Prentice-Hall, Englewood Cliffs, N.J., 1962-63, supr. sales, 1963-66, dist. mgr., 1966-69, editor, 1969-71, mgr. regional sales, 1971-72, exec. editor, 1972; pub., v.p. Glencoe Press, Encino, Calif., 1972-77; v.p. Little, Brown & Co., Boston, 1977-86, sr. v.p., 1986-88; pres., chief exec. officer Van Nostrand Reinhold, N.Y.C., 1988-89, South-Western Pub. Co., Cin., 1990-93; COO Encore Mktg. Internat., Inc., Lanham, Md., 1994-95; mgmt. cons., 1996; AVP regional mgr. ACT, 1996—. With U.S. Army, 1961-62. Mem. Assn. Am. Pubs. (exec. coun. higher edn. 1977-87, chmn. 1987, profl. and scholarly exec. coun. 1988-89, sch. exec. coun. 1990-91). Republican. Episcopalian. Avocation: reading, running. Home: 290 Grapevine Run Atlanta GA 30350-4438 Home and Office: ACT 3350 Lenox Rd NE Ste 320 Atlanta GA 30326

LUCIER, GREGORY THOMAS, manufacturing executive; b. Plainfield, N.J., May 9, 1964; s. Thomas Edward and Ann (Rivinius) L.; m. Marilena Cieri, June 4, 1988; children: Ross Edward, Grant Michael, Allana Marie. BS in Indsl. Engring., Pa. State U., 1986; MBA, Harvard U., 1990. Product mgr. Internat. Paper Co., Memphis, 1986-88; asst. to the pres. Morrison Knudsen Corp., Boise, Idaho, 1990-91, mfg. mgr., 1991-92, dir. ops., 1992-94, sr. v.p. ops., 1994-95; gen. mgr. bus. devel. GE, 1995; pres., CEO GE-Harris Rlwy. Electronics, 1996—; cons. in field. Fundraising organizer Arthritis Found., Boise, 1992; instr. Jr. Achievement, Memphis, 1986-88; vol. Project Outreach, Boston, 1989-90. Mem. Inst. Indsl. Engrs., Railway Suppliers Assn., Idaho Total Quality Mgmt. Inst., Harvard Club of Idaho, Tau Beta Pi. Republican. Roman Catholic. Avocations: golf, tennis, skiing. Home: 709 Oak Park Dr Melbourne FL 32940-1858 Office: GE Harris Rlwy Electronics PO Box 8900 Melbourne FL 32902

LUCIER, JAMES ALFRED, advertising executive; b. Grand Forks, N.D., Feb. 5, 1920; s. Alfred Joseph and Mildred Perry (Fahar) L.; BA, U. Minn., 1946; postgrad. U. So. Methodist, 1965; m. Juliann K. Dunlap, July 26, 1991; children: Edward, Kelley, John, Jane, Teddi, James. Sales exec. Times, Ft. Smith, Ark., 1946-47; sales mgr. KRKN, Ft. Smith, 1947-48; dir. advt. Times, Fayetteville, Ark., 1948-51; sales exec. Express, San Antonio, 1952-53; mgr. Sunday mag. Times, Dallas, 1953-65; dir. advt. and advt. and pub. rels. Home Furniture Co., Dallas, 1965-81; advt. mgr. Smith Furniture Co., Dallas, 1981-85; v.p. Home Furnishings Internat. Assn., 1985—; owner Lucier Assocs. Advt., Dallas, 1965—. Editor Home Furnishings Rev., 1986-97. Unit chmn. United Way, 1965-81; precinct chmn. Democratic Party, 1974-85; mem. bd. Dem. Forum, 1974-75; pres. bd. dirs. Dallas coun. USO; mem. orgns. com. Greater Dallas Sesquicentennial Com., 1983-86. Served with inf., AUS, 1942-44, USAAF, 1944-45, USAF, 1951-52. Decorated Air medal with 2 oak leaf clusters. Mem. Retail Furniture Assn. Greater Dallas (pres. 1971-72, pres. 1983-84, dir. 1972-85), Exch. Club (pres. East Dallas chpt. 1967, pres. Tex. dist. 1969-70, nat. dir. 1970-72, chmn. nat. edn. com. 1974-76, fin. com. 1976-80), U. Minn. Alumni (past pres.), Vagabond Club, Dallas Magic Cir. Club (past pres.), Greater Dallas Ret. Officer Assn. (sec.

1991—), Sigma Delta Chi, Theta Chi. Episcopalian. Home: 4345 Meadowdale Ln Dallas TX 75229-5339 Office: Home Furnishings Internat Assn 110 World Trade Ctr Dallas TX 75258

LUCIER, P. JEFFREY, publishing and computer company executive; b. Manchester, N.H., June 20, 1941; s. Paul A. and Elaine (Wilson) Fraser L.; m. Judith Margaret Akers, Dec. 21, 1963 (div. 1975); children—Kathryn Elizabeth, Amy Wilson; m. Velma Lee Frye, Nov. 27, 1976 (div. 1981); m. Susan Elizabeth Hess, May 25, 1985; children: Madalyn Antonette, Caitlin Elaine. B.A., Union Coll., N.Y., 1963; M.A., U. Chgo., 1964. Instr. English Northwestern U., Evanston and Chgo., Ill., 1967-69; registered rep. Paine Webber, Akron, Ohio, 1969-71; asst. to pres. Banks-Baldwin Law Pub., Cleve., 1971-74, v.p. editorial, 1974-76, exec. v.p., 1977-78, pres., editor-in-chief, 1978-96; CEO Pegasus Technologies, Ltd., Painesville, Ohio, 1996—, All-Stater Pub. LLC, Rocky River, Ohio, 1997—; mem. adv. bd. Cleve. Collaborative for Math. Edn.; pres. The Banks-Baldwin Found. Trustee Horizon Montessori Sch.; pres. Cleve. chpt. Juvenile Diabetes Found. Internat. Democrat. Roman Catholic. Club: Cleve. City, Cleve. Playhouse. Office: Pegasus Technologies Ltd 1100 Mentor Ave Painesville OH 44077 Office: All State Publishing LLC 315 Falmouth Dr Rocky Road OH 44116

LUCK, DAVID JONATHAN LEWIS, biologist, educator; b. Milw., Jan. 7, 1929; s. Max. and Sarah (Plonsker) L. S.B., U. Chgo., 1949; M.D., Harvard, 1953; Ph.D., Rockefeller U., 1962. House officer Mass. Gen. Hosp., Boston, 1953-54; resident physician Mass. Gen. Hosp., 1957-58; research asso. Rockefeller U., 1962—, mem. faculty, 1964—, prof. biology, 1968—; v.p. acad. affairs, 1994. Editor: Jour. Cell Biology, 1968-74. Served to capt. USAF, 1955-57. Decorated Commendation medal with oak leaf cluster. Mem. Am. Soc. Biol. Chemists, Am. Soc. Cell Biologists, Nat. Acad. Sci. Club: University (N.Y.C.). Home: 205 E 78th St New York NY 10021-1243

LUCK, EDWARD CARMICHAEL, professional society administrator; b. Urbana, Ill., Oct. 17, 1948; s. David Johnston and Adele Suzanne (Kanter) L.; m. Dana Dee Zaret, June 19, 1971; 1 dau., Jessica Robin. B.A. cum laude with high distinction in Internat. Relations, Dartmouth Coll., 1970; M.I.A., Columbia U., 1972, M.A., 1973, M.Ph., 1974. Project dir. conventional arms control UN Assn. of U.S.A., N.Y.C., 1974-77, dep. dir., dep. v.p. for policy studies, 1977-82, v.p. policy studies, 1982-83, exec. v.p., 1983-84, pres., 1984-94, pres. emeritus, sr. policy advisor, 1994—; cons. UN, 1995—; cons. book project 20th Century Fund, 1995—; cons. social sci. dept. Rand Corp., Santa Monica, Calif., 1973-76, U.N., 1995—. Co-editor, contbr. On The Endings of War, 1980; editor, contbr. Arms Control: The Multilateral Alternative, 1983; contbr. articles to profl. publs. Herbert H. Lehman fellow and Internat. fellow Columbia U., 1970-73; jr. fellow, cert. Russian Inst., Columbia U, 1973-74. Mem. Coun. Fgn. Rels., Century Assn. Democrat. Home: 136 Elm Rd Briarcliff Manor NY 10510-2225

LUCK, GEORG HANS BHAWANI, classics educator; b. Bern, Switzerland, Feb. 17, 1926; came to U.S., 1951; s. Hans and Hanna (Von Ow) L.; m. Harriet Richards Greenough, June 15, 1957; children: Annina, Hans, Stephanie. Student, U. Bern, 1945-49, 50-51, Ph.D., 1953; student, U. Paris, 1949-50; A.M. (Smith-Mundt fellow), Harvard, 1952. Instr. classics Yale U., 1952-53; instr. classics Brown U., 1953-55, vis. prof., 1969; instr. classics Harvard U., 1955-58; vis. prof. Summer Sch., 1968; lectr. classics U. Mainz, 1958-62; prof. classics U. Bonn, 1962-71; vis. prof. Johns Hopkins U., 1970-71, prof. classics, 1971-90; prof. emeritus, 1990—; chmn. dept. classics Johns Hopkins U., 1973-75; vis. prof. classics UCLA, 1974, U. Fribourg, 1989; lectr. Smithsonian Instutions, 1992. Author: Der Akademiker Antiochos, 1953, The Latin Love Elegy, 1959, 2d edit., 1969 (German edit. 1961, Spanish edit. 1995), Über einige Interjektionen, d. lat. Umgangssprache, 1964, Ovid, Tristia, text, transl. and commentary, 2 vols., 1967-77, Untersuchungen zur Textgeschichte Ovids, 1969, Eine Schweizerreise: Aus dem Tagebuch des Alfred Meill von Salisbury, 1981, Arcana Mundi: Magic and the Occult in the Greek and Roman World, 1985 (Spanish and Italian edits. 1994), Lucan, Der Bürgerkrieg, 1985, Der Dichter in der Kutsche, 1986; editor: Tibullus, Carmina, 1987, Magie und andere Geheimwissenschaften der Antike, 1990, Properz und Tibull, Elegien, 1996, Collected Essays on Ancient Religion, Magic and Philosophy, 1997; editor-in-chief Am. Jour. Philology, 1971-81, 86-89; editor Noctes Romanae, 1975—; contbr. articles to profl. jours. Guggenheim fellow, 1958-59; Swiss Nat. Research Council grantee, 1976-77. Mem. Johns Hopkins Club. Episcopalian. Avocations: gardening, hiking, classical guitar. Home: 1108 Bryn Mawr Rd Baltimore MD 21210-1213 Office: Johns Hopkins U Classics Dept Baltimore MD 21218 *I am not sure I know what success really means, but I do know today that the rewards for your work or your dedication or your experience and skill do not come from outside; they must be found within you, as a gift from God.*

LUCK, JAMES I., foundation executive; b. Akron, Ohio, Aug. 28, 1945; s. Milton William and Gertrude (Winer) L.; children: Andrew Brewer, Edward Aldrich, L. BA, Ohio State U., 1967; MA, U. Ga., 1970. Caseworker Franklin County Welfare Dept., Columbus, Ohio, 1967-69; dir. forensics Tex. Christian U., Ft. Worth, 1970-74; assoc. dir. Bicentennial Youth Debates, Washington, 1974-76; exec. dir. Nat. Congress on Volunteerism and Citizenship, Washington, 1976-77; fellow Acad. Contemporary Problems, Columbus, Ohio, 1977-79; exec. dir. Battelle Meml. Inst. Found., Columbus, 1980-82; pres. Columbus Found., 1981—; exec. dir. Columbus Youth Found. and Ingram-White Castle Funds, 1981—; bd. dirs. Cardinal Group of Funds.; co-chmn. Task Force on Citizen Edn., Washington, 1977; mediator Negotiated Investment Strategy, Columbus, 1979; chmn. Ohio Founds. Conf., 1985; cons. HEW, Peace Corps., U. Va.; bd. vis. McGregor Sch., Antioch U. Author: Ohio-The Next 25 Years, 1978, Bicentennial Issue Analysis, 1975; editor: Proceedings of the Nat. Conf. on Argumentation, 1973; contbr. articles to profl. jours. Trustee Godman Guild Settlement House, Columbus, 1979-81, Am. Diabetes Assn., Ohio, 1984-88; chmn. spl. com. on displacement Columbus City Coun., 1978-80; bd. dirs. Commn. on the Future of the Professions in Soc., 1979. Mem. Donors Forum Ohio. Clubs: Capital, Columbus Club, Columbus Met., Kit-Kat. Lodge: Rotary. Avocations: travel, reading. Home: 1318 Hickory Ridge Ln Columbus OH 43235-1131 Office: The Columbus Found 1234 E Broad St Columbus OH 43205-1405

LUCKE, ROBERT VITO, merger and acquisition executive; b. Kingston, Pa., July 26, 1930; s. Vito Frank and Edith Ann (Adders) L.; m. Jane Ann Rushin, Aug. 16, 1952; children: Thomas, Mark, Carl. BS in Chemistry, Pa. State U., 1952; MS in Mgmt., Rensselaer Polytech Inst., 1960. Polymer chemist Uniroyal Naugatuck (Conn.) Chem. Div., 1954-60; comml. devel. engr. Exxon Enjay Div., Elizabeth, N.J., 1960-66; gen. mgr. Celanese Advanced Composites, Summit, N.J., 1966-70; bus. mgr. polymer div. Hooker Chem., Burlington, N.J., 1970-74; gen. mgr. Oxy Metal Industries Environ. Equipment. Divs., Warren, Mich., 1974-79; v.p., gen. mgr. Hoover Universal Plastic Machinery Divs., Manchester, Mich., 1979-84; pres. Egan Machinery, Somerville, N.J., 1984-87; pres., chief exec. officer Krauss Maffei Corp., Cin., 1987-93; pres. Dubuc, Lucke, Koring Co., Inc., Cin., 1990—; instr., Chem. Market Rsch. Assn., 1974. Author: (with others) Plastics Handbook, 1972; inventor, patentee in field. 1st lt. Corp Engrs., 1952-54, Korea. Senatorial scholar, Pa. State U., 1948-52. Mem. Am. Chem. Soc., Soc. Plastics Engrs. (sect. engr. STDS com. 1969), Tech. Assn. Pulp Paper Industry, Comml. Devel. Assn., Assn. Corp. Growth. Avocations: golf, skiing, travel, gardening. Office: Dubuc Lucke & Co Ste 1005 120 W 5th St Cincinnati OH 45202-2710

LUCKER, JAY K., library education educator; b. N.Y.C., Feb. 23, 1930; s. Joseph Jerome and Ella (Schwartz) L.; m. Marjorie Stern, Aug. 17, 1952; children—Amy Ellen, Nancy Judith. A.B., Bklyn. Coll., City U. N.Y., 1951; M.S., Columbia, 1952; postgrad., N.Y. U., 1955-57. Head procurement br., acquisition div. New York Pub. Library, 1954-57, first asst., acting chief, sci. and tech. div., 1957-59; asst. univ. librarian for sci. and tech., asso. prof. Princeton U. Library, 1959-68, asso. univ. librarian, prof., 1968-75; dir. librs. MIT, Cambridge, 1975-95; vis. prof. Grad. Sch. Libr. and Info. Sci. Simmons Coll., Boston, 1995—; chmn. bd. dirs. Captain Libr. Svcs. Corp., 1972-75; vis. lectr. Drexel U. Grad. Sch. Libr. Svc., 1962-67; vice chmn. New Eng. Libr. Info. Network, 1978-79, chmn., 1980-82. Bd. dirs. Boston Libr. Consortium; mem. adv. coms. Brown U., Tufts U., Washington U., St. Louis, Libr. Congress, Engring. Info. Inc. Served with Signal Corps U.S. Army, 1952-54. Council on Library Resources fellow, 1970-71. Mem. ALA (council 1978-82), AAAS, Am. Soc. Info. Sci., N.J. Library Assn. (Distinguished Service award coll. and univ. sect. 1975), Assn. Research Libraries (chmn. interlibrary loan com. 1976-80, dir. 1977-80, pres. 1980-81), Spl. Libraries Assn., Phi Beta Kappa, Alpha Phi Omega, Beta Phi Mu. Office: Simmons Coll Grad Sch Libr & Info Sci Boston MA 02115

LUCKER, RAYMOND ALPHONSE, bishop; b. St. Paul, Feb. 24, 1927; s. Alphonse and Josephine (Schiltgen) L. B.A., St. Paul Sem., 1948, M.A., 1952; S.T.L., U. St. Thomas, Rome, 1965, S.T.D., 1966; Ph.D., U. Minn., 1969; LHD honoris causa, Coll. St. Catherine, 1993. Ordained priest Roman Cath. Ch., 1952, bishop, 1971. Asst. dir. Confrat. of Christian Doctrine, Archdiocese of St. Paul, 1952-58, dir., 1958-68; prof. catechetics St. Paul Sem., 1957-68; dir. dept. edn. U.S. Cath. Conf., Washington, 1969-71; consecrated bishop, 1971; aux. bishop of St. Paul and Mpls., 1971-76; bishop of New Ulm, Minn., 1976—. Author: Aims of Religious Education, 1966, Some Presuppositions on Released Time, 1969, My Experience: Reflections on Pastoring, 1988; editor: The People's Catechism, 1995; contbg. author: Catholic Social Thought, 1990, The Universal Catechism Reader, 1990, Living the Vision, 1992. Recipient Nat. Catechetical award, 1991. Home: 1400 6th St N New Ulm MN 56073-2057 Office: Catholic Pastoral Ctr 1400 6th St N New Ulm MN 56073-2057

LUCKETT, BYRON EDWARD, JR., air force chaplain; b. Mineral Wells, Tex., Feb. 2, 1951; s. Byron Edward and Helen Alma (Hart) L.; m. Kathryn Louise Lambertson, Dec. 30, 1979; children: Florence Louise, Byron Edward III, Barbara Elizabeth, Stephanie Hart. BS, U.S. Mil. Acad., 1973; MDiv, Princeton Theol. Sem., 1982; MA, Claremont Grad. Sch., 1987. Commd. 2d lt. U.S. Army, 1973, advanced through grades to maj.; stationed at Camp Edwards, Korea, 1974-75; bn. supply officer 563rd Engr. Bn., Kornwestheim, Germany, 1975-76; platoon leader, exec. officer 275th Engr. Co., Ludwigsburg, Germany, 1976-77; boy scout project officer Hdqrs., VII Corps, Stuttgart, Germany, 1977-78; student intern Moshannon Valley Larger Parish, Winburne, Penn., 1980-81; Protestant chaplain Philmont Scout Ranch, Cimarron, N.Mex., 1982; asst. pastor Immanuel Presbyn. Ch., Albuquerque, 1982-83, assoc. pastor, 1983-84; tchr. Claremont High Sch., 1985-86; Protestant chaplain 92nd Combat Support Group, Fairchild AFB, Wash., 1986-90; installation staff chaplain Pirinclik Air Station, Turkey, 1990-91; protestant chaplain Davis-Monthan AFB, Ariz., 1991-95; dir. readiness ministries Offutt AFB, Nebr., 1995, sr. protestant chaplain, 1996; mem. intern program coun. Claremont (Calif.) Grad. Sch. Contbr. articles to profl. jours. Bd. dirs. Parentcraft, Inc., Albuquerque, 1984, United Campus Ministries, Albuquerque, 1984, Proclaim Liberty, Inc., Spokane, 1987-90; bd. dirs. western region Nat. Assn. Presbyn. Scouters, Irving, Tex., 1986-89, chaplain, 1991-93; mem. N.Mex. Employer Co, in Support of the Guard and Reserve, Albuquerque, 1984, Old Baldy coun. Boy Scouts Am., 1986; chmn. Fairchild Parent Coop., Fairchild AFB, 1986-87; pres. Co. Grade Officers Coun., Fairchild AFB, 1987-88. Capt. U.S. Army Reserve; chaplain USAF Reserve 1983-86, maj. 1990—. Recipient Dist. Award of Merit for Disting. Svc. Boy Scouts Am., 1977. Mem. Soc. Cin. Md., Mil. Order Fgn. Wars U.S., Civil Affairs Assn. Presbyterian. Home: 12909 S 29th Ave Bellevue NE 68123-1929 Office: 55 WG/HC 301 Lincoln Hwy Offutt AFB NE 68113

LUCKETT, JOHN MILLS, III, construction company financial executive; b. Henderson, Ky., Dec. 9, 1948; s. John Mills and Margaret (Burns) L.; m. Doris Jeanelle Vaught, June 3, 1989; children: John Mills IV, Christopher Patrick, Brian J. Garrand. AS, U. Ky., 1969; BS, U. Evansville, 1972. CPA. Ky., Ind., Ill. Ptnr. Gaither Koewler Rohlfer Luckett, Evansville, Ind., 1970-90; v.p. fin., CFO Indsl. Contractors Inc., Evansville, 1991—. Treas. Evansville Freedom Festival Found., 1988-97, Vision 2000, Evansville, 1991-94; mem. acctg. and audit com. Ky. Soc. CPA's, Louisville, 1981; mem. Hosp. Fin. Mgmt. Assn., Indpls., 1974-90; treas. S.W. Ind. United Way, 1996-97. Mem. Nat. Assn. Accts., Ind. Soc. CPA's, Ind. Soc. of Chgo., Evansville Country Club. Republican. Methodist. Avocations: golf, photography, scuba diving. Office: Indsl Contractors Inc 401 NW 1st St Evansville IN 47708-1001

LUCKETT, PAUL HERBERT, III, manufacturing executive; b. El Paso, Tex., Feb. 6, 1935; s. Paul Herbert Jr. and Maxine (Mooney) L.; m. Caroline Foisie, Oct. 6, 1956 (div. Mar. 1991); children: Elizabeth Winkler, Christopher Lloyd; m. Cheryl Elaine Kanoff, June 15, 1991. BSChemE, MIT, 1956. Various positions El Paso Products Co., El Paso Co., 1956-69; exec. v.p. Beaunit Corp., El Paso Co., Raleigh, N.C. and N.Y.C., 1969-77; pres. Penn Athletic Co., Gencorp., Monroesville, Pa., 1977-82; pres. wallcovering divsn. Gencorp., Hanckensack, N.J., 1982-89; COO Insilco, Midland, Tex., 1989-91; dir. bus. devel. Wagner & Brown, Midland, 1991—; pres., CEO Flamecoat Systems, Inc., 1991-94; assoc. Bariston, Inc., West Palm Beach, Fla., 1994—; pres., co-owner Market Allies, Inc., Beaverton, Oreg., 1997—. 2d lt. U.S. Army, 1957. Mem. Union League Club (N.Y.C.), Racquet Club (Midland), Delta Kappa Epsilon. Roman Catholic. Avocations: bicycling, hiking, snorkeling, tennis. Office: Bariston (USA) Inc 400 N Congress Ave West Palm Beach FL 33401-2902

LUCKEY, ALWYN HALL, lawyer; b. Biloxi, Miss., Oct. 3, 1960; s. Toxie Hall and Joy Evelyn (Smith) L.; m. Jeanne Elaine Carter, Aug. 4, 1984; children: Laurel McKay, Taylor Leah. BA in Zoology, U. Miss., 1982, JD, 1985. Bar: Miss. 1985, U.S. Dist. Ct. (so. and no. dist.) Miss. 1985, U.S. Ct. Appeals (5th cir.) 1985. Assoc. Richard F. Scruggs, Pascagoula, Miss., 1985-88; shareholder Richard F. Scruggs, Pascagoula, 1988—, Asbestos Group P.A., 1988-93; prin. Alwyn H. Luckey, Atty. at Law, Ocean Springs, Miss., 1993—; v.p., bd. dirs. Marine Mgmt., Inc., Ocean Springs, Miss., 1987—. Author: Mississippi Landlord Tenant Law, 1985. Deacon First Presbyn. Ch., Ocean Springs, 1989; chmn. Dole for Pres. com., Jackson County, 1988. Mem. Am. Trial Lawyers Assn., Miss. Bar Assn., Miss. Trial Lawyers Assn., Jackson County Bar Assn., Jackson County Young Lawyers Assn. (v.p.), Ocean Springs Yacht Club, Bienville Club, Treasure Oak Country Club. Avocations: tennis, boating, traveling. Office: 705 Washington Ave Ocean Springs MS 39564-4635

LUCKEY, DORIS WARING, civic volunteer; b. Union City, N.J., Sept. 17, 1929; d. Jay Deloss and Edna May (Ware) Waring; m. George William Luckey, Mar. 29, 1958; children: G. Robert, Jana Elizabeth, John Andrew. AB, U. Rochester, 1950; CLU, Am. Coll., Bryn Mawr, Pa., 1957. With pers. dept., supr. life dept. Travelers Ins. Co., Rochester, N.Y., 1952-58; agt. asst. life underwriting Mass. Mut. Ins. Co., Rochester, 1958. Chairperson, various past offices Bd. Coop. Ednl. Svcs. and State Edn. Dept., Vocat. Tech. Adv. Com., Rochester and Albany, 1975—, pres. Rochester, 1975-85, Monroe County Sch. Bds. Assn., Rochester, 1980-81; v.p. Penfield (N.Y.) Schs., 1978-81; various fin. ednl. and speaking engagements LWV, 1983—; pres. ch. coun., chair ch. and min. com., co-chair United Ch. Christ denomination, Genesee Valley; pres. William Warfield Scholarship Fund Bd.; former adv. to bd. St. John's Home for Aging, now mem. fin. and pension and pers. com., bd. dirs.; vol. numerous other civic, cultural, ch. and artistic orgns. Mem. AAUW (past pres., past bd. dirs., dist. 1 state rep.). Republican.

LUCKEY, ROBERT REUEL RAPHAEL, retired academic administrator; b. Houghton, N.Y., Nov. 19, 1917; s. James Seymour and Edith Bedell (Curtis) L.; m. Ruth Ida Brooks, Aug. 25, 1945; children: James, John, Linda, Peter, Daniel (dec.), Thomas. BS, BA, Houghton Coll., 1937; MA, N.Y. U., 1939; PhD, Cornell U., 1942; LittD, Houghton Coll., 1980; LLD, Marion Coll., 1987. Secondary tchr. Wilson (N.Y.) Cen. Sch., 1937-39; math. & physics instr. Houghton Coll., 1942, assoc. prof., prof. math. and physics, alumni dir., 1954, dir. devel., v.p. in devel.; pres. Marion (Ind.) Coll., 1976-84, 1986-87. Pres. Seneca Council Boy Scouts Am., Olean, N.Y., 1964-65; assessor Township of Caneadea, N.Y., 1951-76. Recipient Silver Beaver award Boy Scouts Am., 1965; named Alumnus of Yr. Houghton Coll., 1976, Disting. Alumnus Houghton Coll., 1984, Sagamore of the Wabash by Gov. of Ind., 1980. Mem. Grant County C. of C. (bd. dirs. 1981-84). Republican. Wesleyan. Avocations: golfing, personal computers. Home: 7363 Campus Heights Houghton NY 14744-9718

LUCKING, PETER STEPHEN, marketing consultant, industrial engineer; b. Kalamazoo, Oct. 11, 1945; s. Henry William, Sr., and Mary (Lynn) L.; m. Marilyn Barbara Jensen, Dec. 18, 1971. BA, Western Mich. U., 1968; BS in Indsl. Engring., 1973. Indsl. engr. Motorola, Phoenix, 1974, Revlon, Inc., Phoenix, 1974-75; indsl. engr. Hooker Chem. and Plastics Co., Niagara Falls, N.Y., 1975-76, sr. corp. indsl. engr., 1976-77; indsl. engr. Carborundum Co., Niagara Falls, 1977-78; cons. H.B. Maynard and Co., Pitts., 1978-85; mgr. indsl. engring. Carrier, Tyler, Tex., 1985-88; cons. H.B. Maynard and Co., Pitts., 1988-92; pres., mktg. cons. MARPET Systems, Inc., 1992—; lectr. in field, 1989. Advisor, Jr. Achievement, Niagara Falls, 1977. Author chpts. to books. Served with U.S. Army, 1969-70, Vietnam. Mem. Inst. Indsl. Engrs. (sr. mem., region v.p. 1983-85), Inst. Indsl. Engrs. (pres. Niagara Frontier chpt. 1977-78, paper presented fall conf.). Democrat. Roman Catholic. Home: 12826 Weatherstone Dr Florissant MO 63033-4045 Office: MARPET Systems Inc 11220 W Flossant Ste 141 Saint Louis MO 63033

LUCKMAN, CHARLES, architect; b. Kansas City, Mo., May 16, 1909; m. Harriet McElroy, 1931; children: Charles, James M., Stephen A. Grad. magna cum laude, U. Ill., 1931; LLD, U. Miami, Fla., 1950; AFD (hon.), Calif. Coll. Arts and Crafts, 1958; DFA (hon.), Adelphi U., 1986; LLD (hon.), Pepperdine U., 1989. Lic. architect, 1931 Registered architect, 48 states and D.C. sr. registration Nat. Archtl. Registration Bds. Employed in architect's office for license qualifications, 2 years; joined Colgate- Palmolive-Peet Co. as retail salesman, 1931, Chgo. sales supr., 1933; mgr. Colgate-Palmolive-Peet Co. as retail salesman (Wis. dist.), 1934; divisional mgr. Colgate- Palmolive-Peet Co. as retail salesman (Cin. hdqrs.), 1935; with Pepsodent Co. (later Pepsodent Div. of Lever Bros. Co.), 1935-50, sales promotion mgr., sales mgr., 1935-36, v.p. in charge sales, 1936, in charge sales and advt., 1937, v.p., gen. mgr., 1938, exec. v.p., 1942-43, pres., 1943-46; exec. v.p. Lever Bros., Jan.-July 1946, pres., 1946-50; pres., partner Pereira & Luckman, Los Angeles, 1950-58; founder, ptnr. The Luckman Partnership, Inc., 1958—; chmn. bd., chief exec. officer Ogden Devel. Corp., 1968-74, Luckman Mgmt. Co., 1973—; dir. Hollywood Bowl. Maj. projects include Madison Sq. Garden, N.Y.C., Conv. and Exhbn. Center, Los Angeles, U.S. World's Fair Pavilion, N.Y.C., Los Angeles World Zoo, U. Calif. at Santa Barbara, Civic Plaza, Phoenix, Prudential Center, Boston, State Office Bldg, Madison, Wis., Phoenix Civic Plaza, Los Angeles Internat. Airport, First Nat. Bank of Ariz, Phoenix, Broadway Plaza, Los Angeles, United Calif. Bank, Los Angeles, U. Del. Student Living Center, La Jolla VA Hosp, Aloha Stadium, Honolulu, 9200 Sunset Tower, Los Angeles, Manned Space Craft Center, Houston, VA Hosp, West Los Angeles, Calif., Hoover Library and Linear Accelerator Center, Stanford U., 1st Natl Bank of Oreg, Portland, Forum, Inglewood, Calif., Ralph M. Parsons Co. hdqrs, Pasadena, Calif., Nat. Security and Resources Study Center, Los Alamos, Hyatt Regency Hotels, Dearborn, Mich., The Harriet & Charles Luckman Fine Arts Complex, L.A., The Harriet & Charles Luckman Child Guidance Clin., L.A., Phoenix, City Hall and Police Bldg., Inglewood, Xerox Corp. hdqrs., Stamford, Conn., Warner Bros. Office Bldg., Burbank, Calif., Orange County Conv./Civic Ctr., Orlando, Fla.; also numerous other pub. bldgs; author: (autobiography) Twice in a Lifetime, 1988. Pres., chmn. bd. Los Angeles Orchestral Soc., 1962; v.p., dir. So. Calif. Symphony Assn.; mem. bd. assocs., pres. council George Pepperdine Found., Los Angeles; trustee Calif. State Colls.; chmn. bd. trustees, 1963-65; bd. govs. Library Presdl. Papers; trustee Nat. Art Mus. Sport; mem. U. Ill. Found.; Calif. mem. Ednl. Commn. of States; mem. bd. Am. Nat. Red Cross, YMCA; bd. dirs., past pres. AID-United Givers.; Mem. Pres.'s Commn. on Equality of Treatment and Opportunity in Armed Services and Civil Rights, Gov.'s Commn. Met. Area Problems; dir. Advt. Council; trustee Adelphi U.; chmn. Citizens Food Com., 1947; mem. Commerce and Industry Assn. N.Y.C., Los Angeles World Affairs Council, Com. Econ. Devel., Council U.S. Assocs. of Internat. C. of C.; bd. dirs. Nat. Adv. Council Community Chest, Am. Heritage Found.; bd. assocs. Northwestern U., Calif. Inst. Tech.; chmn. Nat. Council Trustees of Freedoms Found. at Valley Forge, 1986. Decorated Star of Solidarity Republic of Italy; chevalier Nat. Order Legion of Honor France; Order of St. John; recipient Horatio Alger award Am. Schs. and Colls. Assn., George Washington Honor medal Freedom's Found., 1964, 67, 68, Make Am. Beautiful award Nat. Assn. Realty Bds.; named Outstanding Mgmt. Exec. N.Y. Mgmt. Club, Man of Year Constrn. Industries, 1974; Disting. Achievement award U. Ill., 1970; Henry Laurence Gantt medal Am. Mgmt. Assn. and ASMF, 1981. Mem. AIA (Fellowship award 1963), Ill. Soc. Architects, U.S. Jr. C. of C. (One of Outstanding Young Men 1945, dir.), Tau Beta Pi, Theta Tau, Gargoyle. Home and Office: The Luckman Management Co 9220 W Sunset Blvd West Hollywood CA 90069-3501

LUCKNER, HERMAN RICHARD, III, interior designer; b. Newark, Ohio, Mar. 14, 1933; s. Herman Richard and Helen (Friednour) L. BS, U. Cin., 1957. Cert. interior designer and appraiser. Interior designer Greiwe Inc., Cin., 1957-64; owner, internat. designer Designers Loft Interiors, Cin., 1964—; owner Designer Accents, Cin., 1991—. Mem. bd. adv. Ohio Valley Organ Procurement Ctr., Cin., 1987—, U. Cin. Fine Arts Collection and Hist. Southwest Ohio, 1987-97; bd. dirs. Cin. Travelers Club, 1997—. Mem. Am. Soc. Interior Designers, Appraisers Assn. Am., Metropolitan Club, Cin. Club Travelers (bd. dirs. 1997—). Republican. Avocations: needlepoint, collecting 18th century Chinese porcelain. Home and Office: 555 Compton Rd Cincinnati OH 45231-5005

LUCORE, CHARLES LEE, cardiologist; b. Southington, Conn., Apr. 30, 1957; s. Charles Earl and Eleanor Christina Lucore; m. Paula F. Sorensen, Sept. 25, 1982; children: Alexander Charles, Jordan Mari. AB, Colgate U., 1979; MD, Duke U., 1983. Diplomate Am. Bd. Internal Medicine, Am. Bd. Cardiovasc. Diseases. Intern N.Y. Hosp.-Cornell Med. Ctr., N.Y.C., 1983-84, resident, 1984-86; cardiovasc. postdoctoral rsch. fellow Sch. Medicine Wash. U., St. Louis, 1986-88, clin. cardiology fellow, 1988-89, invasive cardiology fellow, 1989-90, asst. prof. medicine and interventional cardiology, 1990-92; interventional cardiologist Prairie Cardiovasc. Cons., Ltd., Springfield, Ill., 1992—; co-dir. cardiac catherization lab. St. John's Hosp., Springfield, Ill., 1992—, chmn. dept. cardiology, 1994—, mem. exec. com. Prairie Cardiovasc. Consultants, Ltd., 1995—; asst. clin. prof. medicine So. Ill. U., Springfield, Ill., 1992—; exec. com. St. Johns Hosp., Springfield, 1996—, prairie edn. and rsch. coop. coord., 1995—. Recipient Rsch. award Corvas Internat., 1991. Fellow Am. Coll. Cardiology; mem. ACP, Am. Heart Assn. (thrombosis coun. 1989—, coun. on cardiology 1994—, grantee 1992-93), Phi Beta Kappa, Beta Beta Beta. Avocation: golf. Office: Prairie Cardiovasc Cons Ltd 301 N 8th St Ste 3b-301 Springfield IL 62701-1041

LUCOW, MILTON, lawyer; b. Detroit, Oct. 4, 1924; s. Louis and Dora (Schupps) L.; m. Audrey B. Kline, Mar. 30, 1947; children: Celia (Mrs. James Stegman), Michael B. LLD, Wayne State U., 1948. Bar: Mich. bar 1948. Since practiced in Detroit; ptnr., pres. firm Garan, Lucow, Miller, Seward & Cooper (P.C.), Detroit, 1948-95; of counsel, 1995—; lectr. in field; mediator Wayne Circuit Ct. Mich., 1973—. Pres. Detroit Svc. Group, 1983-87; bd. dirs. Jewish Welfare Fedn. Detroit; pres. Temple Emanu-El, 1960-62; chmn. Madrasha Coll. Jewish Learning, 1977-80, United Found., atty.'s sec., 1985; pres. United Hebrew Schs. Detroit, 1974-77. Sgt. U.S. Army, 1943-45, ETO. Decorated Purple Heart, Metz medal, Bronze Star. Mem. ABA, Am. Arbitration Assn. (arbitrator), Detroit Bar Assn., Mich. Bar Assn. (mem. del. assembly 1979-80), Def. Rsch. Inst. Tam-O-Shanter Club (pres. 1971-72), Longboat Key Club. Avocations: golf, tennis, squash. Home: 3040 Grand Bay Blvd Apt 246 Longboat Key FL 34228 Office: Garan Lucow Miller & Seward 1000 Woodbridge St Detroit MI 48207-3108 Home: Apt 246 3040 Grand Bay Blvd Longboat Key FL 34228-3219

LUCY, DENNIS DURWOOD, JR., neurologist; b. Little Rock, July 3, 1934; s. Dennis Durwood and Ann Louise (Besiegel) L.; m. Patricia Wilch, Nov. 26, 1958; children: Stephen H., Vincent A., Denise D., David D. B.S., U. Ark., 1959, M.D., 1959. Diplomate: Am. Bd. Psychiatry and Neurology. Intern U. Ark. Med. Scis., 1959-60, resident in internal medicine, 1960-62, resident in psychiatry, 1962-63; resident in neurology U. Iowa Hosp., 1963-64, 65-66; instr., acting head dept. neurology U. Ark., 1964-65, prof., 1974—, chmn. dept. neurology, 1966-94; mem. exec. com. U. Ark. Coll. Medicine, 1979-83, chmn. council Departmental Chairmen, 1980-81; chief of staff Univ. Hosp., 1973-76. Bd. dirs. Ark. chpt. Multiple Sclerosis Soc., 1965-78; mem. Ark. Council Devel. Disabilities, 1971-74; bd. dirs. Ark. chpt. Epilepsy Soc., 1972-76; bd. dirs. Holy Souls Cath. Sch., 1974-77, pres. bd., 1976-77. Recipient Golden Apple award U. Ark., 1968-69. Mem. Am. Acad. Neurology, Alpha Omega Alpha. Roman Catholic. Home: 17 Robinwood Little Rock AR 72227-2241 Office: 4301 W Markham St Little Rock AR 72205-7101

LUCY, ROBERT MEREDITH, lawyer; b. Poplar Bluff, Mo., Apr. 16, 1926; s. James Raymond and Lucile Hargrove (Meredith) L.; m. Mary White George, June 10, 1947; children—Meredith Lucy Knight, Celia Lucy Denton, John Rackley, Robert Meredith Jr. BS, U.S. Naval Acad., 1947; JD, George Washington U., 1954, MS in Internat. Affairs, 1968. Bar: Mo. 1954, D.C. 1954. Commd. 2d lt. USMC, 1947; advanced through grades to col., 1969; student Air War Coll. Maxwell AFB, Montgomery, Ala., 1967-68; staff judge adv. 1st Marine Div., Danang, Vietnam, 1969-70; asst. for legal affairs Office Asst. Sec. Navy for Manpower and Res. Affairs, Washington, 1970-71; legal advisor, legis. asst. to chmn. Joint Chiefs of Staff, Washington, 1971-74; ret., 1974; ptnr. Bryan Cave, St. Louis, 1974—; chmn. litigation dept. Bryan, Cave, St. Louis, 1992-94, vice chmn., 1994-95. Dir. St. Andrew's Episcopal Presbyn. Found., 1995—. Decorated Bronze Star, Legion of Merit (3). Mem. ABA (litigation sect.), TechLaw Group, Inc. (pres. 1994-95), Childrens Home Soc. of Mo. (trustee 1989—). Presbyterian. Home: 38 Picardy Ln Saint Louis MO 63124-1628 Office: Bryan Cave 1 Metropolitan Sq Saint Louis MO 63102-2733

LUDDEN, JOHN FRANKLIN, retired financial economist; b. Michigan City, Ind., May 6, 1930. BS in Econs., U. Wis., 1952, MS in Econs., 1955; postgrad., U. Mich., 1955-59. Wage and hour investigator U.S. Dept. Labor, 1960, mgmt. intern, 1960-61, labor economist, 1963; economist, instr. U.S. Bur. of Labor Statis., 1961-63; economist Office of Internat. Ops. IRS, 1963-68, fin. economist Audit div., 1968-86, fin. economist Office of the Asst. Commr. Internat., 1986-95; ret. Office of the Asst. Commr. Internat., 1995. With U.S. Army, 1952-54. Recipient spl. svc. award U.S. Dept. Treasury, 1967, 68, 87, spl. achievement award, 1984, Spl. Act award, 1990, Albert Gallatin award, 1995. Mem. Am. Econ. Assn.

LUDDINGTON, BETTY WALLES, library media specialist; b. Tampa, Fla., May 11, 1936; d. Edward Alvin and Ruby Mae (Hiott) L.; m. Robert Morris Schmidt, Sept. 20, 1957 (div. Dec. 1981); children: Irene Schmidt-Losat, Daniel Carl Schmidt. AA, U. South Fla., 1979, BA in Am. Studies and History, 1980, MA in Libr., Media and Info. Studies, 1982, EdS in Gifted Edn., 1986. Cert. tchr. media and gifted edn., Fla. Media intern Witter Elem. Sch., spring 1982; media specialist Twin Lakes Elem. Sch., 1982-84, Just Elem. Sch., 1984-87, Blake Jr. H.S., 1987-88, Dowdell Jr. H.S. (now Dowdell Mid. Sch.), 1988—; educator Saturday enrichment program for gifted children U. South Fla., springs 1980, 84, 85; participant pilot summer program in reading and visual arts Just Elem. Sch., 1987; educator gifted edn. program in visual and performing arts Kingswood Elem. Sch., summers 1985, 86, gifted edn. program in video camera Apollo Beach Elem. Sch., summer 1989. Author: (book of poetry) Aaron Tippin: A Hillbilly Knight, 1993; contbr. articles and poems to various books and periodical publs., 1986—. Parent vol. media ctr. Witter Elem. Sch., 1976-78; tchr. sponsor Storytelling Club, Dowdell Jr. H.S., 1994-95; news media liaison, tchr. vol. Dowdell Jr. H.S., 1993-96. Recipient Student Affairs Golden Signet award U. South Fla., 1980, Parent award for continuing support of Fla. chpt. # 39 Am. Indsl. Arts Student Assn., 1987-88, Editor's Choice awards for outstanding achievement in poetry Nat. Libr. of Poetry, 1996; nominee Tchr. of Month, Sta. WTSP-TV, 1994; recognized for contbn. of motivational activity for Sunshine State Young Reader's Award program Fla. Assn. for Media in Edn., Inc., 1985; named to Internat. Poetry Hall of Fame, 1996. Mem. Internat. Soc. Poets (Disting. mem. 1995), Hillsborough Classrm. Tchrs. Assn. (grantee 1988, 90), Hillsborough Assn. Sch. Libr. Media Specialists, Clan Wallace Soc. (life), Phi Kappa Phi, Kappa Delta Pi, Phi Alpha Theta (pres., v.p., rep. to honors coun. 1980, 81, Outstanding Student award), Omicron Delta Kappa (treas., chairperson, del., mem. selection com. 1981, Leslie Lynn Walbolt book award), Pi Gamma Mu. Episcopalian. Avocations: poetry, books, cats, country music. Home: 1032 E Robson St Tampa FL 33604

LUDERS, ADAM, ballet dancer; b. Copenhagen, Feb. 16, 1950; came to U.S., 1975; s. Sten Otto and Hanne Marie (Jansen) L. Student, Royal Danish Ballet Sch. Balletmaster, prin. tchr. Royal Danish Ballet, 1995—. Mem., Royal Danish Ballet Co., 1968-72, prin. dancer, London Festival Ballet Co., 1972-75, N.Y.C. Ballet Co., 1975-94; TV appearance in Choreography by Balanchine; guest artist TV appearance in, Paris Opera Ballet Co., Royal Danish Ballet Co., tour of, Japan, 1979, appearance at, White House, 1978. Office: NYC Ballet Co NY State Theater Lincoln Ctr Plz New York NY 10023 *Although the road to becoming a successful dancer is hard and never ending, I have been fortunate in many respects: I have the Bournonville tradition in teaching and performing as a sound basis for my technique, and the choreography of George Balanchine.*

LUDGIN, CHESTER HALL, baritone, actor; b. N.Y.C., May 20, 1925; s. Michael and Dora Josephine L. Student, Lafayette Coll., 1943, Am. Theatre Wing Profl. Tng. Program, 1948-50. Premiere leading baritone roles in: The Crucible, 1961, The Golem, 1962, Angle of Repose, 1976, A Quiet Place, 1983; appeared in major opera houses throughout the world, including San Francisco Opera Co., N.Y.C. Opera Co., Netherlands Opera, La Scala Opera, Vienna State Opera; singing actor in: musical comedies including Kismet, summer 1972, Most Happy Fella, summer 1977, Shenandoah, summer, 1978, Student Prince, summer 1980, South Pacific, summer 1981, Fanny, summer 1986. Co-chmn. exec. com. Norman Treigle Meml. Fund, 1975—. Served with inf. U.S. Army, 1943-46. Mem. Am. Guild Musical Artists, Actors Equity, AGVA, AFTRA. Home: 205 W End Ave New York NY 10023-4804 Office: care Thea Dispeker Artists Rep 59 E 54th St New York NY 10022-4211 *In observing many of my colleagues in the performing arts as well as those in other walks of life, I long ago came to the conclusion that it is wiser and more personally fulfilling to avoid compromising one's principles in the hope of advancing one's career. If there is truly a talent present, the act of quietly going about one's business with maximum efficiency makes the ultimate statement. Awareness by others of that talent inevitably follows.*

LUDGUS, NANCY LUCKE, lawyer; b. Palo Alto, Calif., Oct. 28, 1953; d. Winston Slover and Betty Jean (Brilhart) Lucke; m. Lawrence John Ludgus, Apr. 8, 1983. BA in Polit. Sci. with highest honors, U. Calif., Berkeley, 1975; JD, U. Calif., Davis, 1978. Bar: Calif. 1978, U.S. Dist. Ct. (no. dist.) Calif. 1978. Staff atty. Crown Zellerbach Corp., San Francisco, 1978-80, Clorox Co., Oakland, Calif., 1980-82; staff atty. Nat. Semiconductor Corp., Santa Clara, Calif., 1982-85, corp. counsel, 1985-92, sr. corp. counsel, asst. sec., 1992—. Mem. ABA, Am. Corp. Counsel Assn., Calif. State Bar Assn., Phi Beta Kappa. Democrat. Avocations: travel, jogging, opera. Office: Nat Semiconductor Corp 1090 Kifer Rd #16135 Sunnyvale CA 94086-5301

LUDINGTON, CHARLES TOWNSEND, JR., English and American studies educator; b. Bryn Mawr, Pa., Jan. 31, 1936; s. Charles Townsend and Constance (Cameron) L.; m. Jane Ross, Feb. 22, 1958; children: David, Charles, James, Sarah. BA, Yale U., 1957; MA, Duke U., 1964; PhD, Duke U, 1967. Tchr. English Ransom Sch., Miami, Fla., 1960-62; from asst. prof. to prof. English U. N.C., Chapel Hill, 1967-78, Cary C. Boshamer prof. English and Am. Studies, 1982—, chair Am. studies curriculum, 1986—; part-time instr. Duke U., 1963-66; resident scholar U.S. Internat. Communication Agy., 1980-81; vis. prof. U.S. Mil. Acad., West Point, N.Y., 1988-89. Author: John Dos Passos, 1980 (Mayflower award 1981), Marsden Hartley, 1992; editor: The Fourteenth Chronicle, 1973. Capt. USMCR, 1957-60. Recipient Outstanding Svc. medal U.S. Army, 1988-89; Fulbright fellow, 1971-72, Nat. Humanities Ctr. fellow, 1985-86. Mem. Am. Studies Assn., South Atlantic MLA, PEN. Democrat. Avocations: golf, reading. Office: U NC Curriculum in Am Studies Greenlaw Hall CB# 3520 Chapel Hill NC 27599-3520

LUDLAM, HEATHER JO, veterinarian; b. Detroit, Dec. 17, 1965; d. H. Bernard and Joan Mabel (Reetz) Spafford; m. Michael Joseph Ludlam, July 22, 1989; 1 child, Samantha Jo. BS, Mich. State U., 1989, DVM, 1991. Lic. vet. State Mich. Bd. Vet. Medicine. Vet. intern Laurel East Vet. Svc., Laurel, Mont., 1991; assoc. vet. Allegan Vet. Clinic, Allegan, Mich., 1991-94; vet., owner, mgr. Monterey Vet. Ctr., Hopkins, Mich., 1994—; assoc. mem. Midwest Police Canine Assn., Mich., Ind., Ill. (1989-1991). Vol. conservation officer, Mich. Dept. Natural Resources, Allegan County, Mich., 1992—. Mem. AVMA, Am. Assn. Bovine Practitioners Assn., Am. Assn. Equine Practitioners, Assn. Women Veterinarians, Wester Mich. Vet. Med. Assn., Mich. Vet. Med. Assn. Avocations: drawing and painting, cross-country skiing, equine sports, camping, livestock farming. Home and Office: 3051 130th Ave Hopkins MI 49328-9749

LUDLAM, JAMES EDWARD, III, insurance company executive; b. L.A., Jan. 9, 1943; s. James Edward and Jane Bramen (Hyde) L.; m. Mary Patricia McVee, Apr. 12, 1969; children—Jay, Erin. B.A. in Econs., Claremont McKenna Coll., 1965. M.B.A. U. So. Calif. 1967. Vice pres. group pensions Prudential Ins. Co., Florham Park, N.J., 1968-82; sr. v.p. Home Life Ins. Co., N.Y.C., 1982-90; v.p. employer sponsored plans Security Life of Denver, Denver, 1991-93; pres., CEO First ING Life of N.Y., 1993-94; pres., COO Rocky Mountain Life Ins. Co., Denver, 1994—. Mem. corp. United Way, Morris County, N.J., 1980-91; campaign exec. United Way, Denver, 1991—, bd. dirs. Mile High United Way, 1995—. Democrat. Presbyterian. Avocations: reading; investing; golf; rafting.

LUDLUM, DAVID BLODGETT, pharmacologist, educator; b. N.Y.C., Sept. 30, 1929; s. C. Daniel and Elsie B. (Blodgett) L.; B.A., Cornell U., 1951; Ph.D., U. Wis., 1954; M.D., N.Y.U., 1962; m. Carlene L. Dyke, Dec. 23, 1952; children: Valerie Jean Ludlum Wright, Kenneth David. Research scientist Dupont Co., Wilmington, Del., 1954-58; intern Bellevue Hosp., N.Y.C., 1962-63; asst. prof. pharmacology Yale U., 1963-68; assoc. prof. U. Md., 1968-70, prof., 1970-76; prof. pharmacology Albany (N.Y.) Med. Coll., 1976-86 , chmn. dept. pharmacology, 1976-80, prof. medicine, 1980-86, dir. oncology research, 1980-86; prof. pharmacology and medicine U. Mass. Med. Sch., 1986—; affiliate prof. chemistry Clark U., Worcester, Mass., 1996—; adj. prof. chemistry Rensselaer Poly. Inst., Troy, N.Y., 1977-80; vis. prof. oncology Johns Hopkins U., 1973-76; vis. prof. Courtauld Inst., London, 1970. WARF fellow, 1951-52; NSF fellow, 1952-54; Am. Heart Assn. fellow, 1960-62; recipient NIH Research Career Devel. award 1968; Markle scholar in acad. medicine, 1967-72; lic. physician, N.Y., Conn., Md. Mem. Am. Soc. Pharmacology and Exptl. Therapeutics, Am. Soc. Clin. Pharmacology and Therapeutics, Am. Assn. Cancer Research, Am. Soc. Biochem. and Molecular Biology, Am. Chem. Soc., Phi Beta Kappa, Sigma Xi, Phi Kappa Phi, Alpha Omega Alpha. Assoc. editor Cancer Rsch., 1980-87, 89—; contbr. articles to profl. jours.; patentee in field; grantee in field. Home: 24 Linda Ct Delmar NY 12054-3512 Office: U Mass Med Sch Worcester MA 01655-0126

LUDLUM, ROBERT, author; b. N.Y.C., May 25, 1927; s. George Hartford and Margaret (Wadsworth) L.; m. Mary Ryducha, March 31, 1951; children: Michael R., Jonathan C., Glynis J. BA with distinction, Wesleyan U., 1951. Actor Broadway, TV, 1952-60; prodr. No. Jersey Playhouse, Ft. Lee, 1957-60, N.Y.C., 1960-69, Playhouse-on-the-Mall, Paramus, N.J., 1960-70; novelist, 1969—. Author: The Scarlatti Inheritance, 1971, The Osterman Weekend, 1972, The Matlock Paper, 1973, Trevayne, 1973, The Cry of the Halidon, 1974, The Rhinemann Exchange, 1974, The Road to Gandolfo, 1975, The Gemini Contenders, 1976, The Chancellor Manuscript, 1977, The Holcroft Covenant, 1978, The Matarese Circle, 1979, The Bourne Identity, 1980, The Parsifal Mosaic, 1982, The Aquitaine Progression, 1984, The Bourne Supremacy, 1986, The Icarus Agenda, 1988, The Bourne Ultimatum, 1990, The Road to Omaha, 1992, The Scorpio Illusion, 1993, The Apocalypse Watch, 1995. Served with USMC, World War II. Recipient Scroll of Achievement Am. Nat. Theatre and Acad., 1960. Mem. Authors Guild. Office: care Henry Morrison Inc PO Box 235 Bedford Hills NY 10507-0235*

LUDOVICE, PETER JOHN, chemical engineer; b. Des Plaines, Ill., Apr. 1, 1962; s. William Peter and Mary Jane (Unger) L.; m. Jennifer Davis Clair, May 29, 1993; 1 child, Miranda Claire. BSChemE, U. Ill., 1984; PhDChemE, MIT, 1989. Rsch. assoc. ETH-Zurich, Switzerland, 1988-89; vis. scientist IBM Almaden Rsch. Ctr., San Jose, Calif., 1989-91, NASA Ames Lab., Moffett Field, Calif., 1989-91; polymer product mgr. Polygen Inc., Waltham, Mass., 1991-92, Molecular Simulations Inc., Burlington, Mass., 1992-93; asst. prof. Ga. Inst. Tech., Atlanta, 1993—; tech. cons. Molecular Simulations, Inc., Burlington, Mass., 1992—; faculty mem. Polymer Edn. Rsch. Ctr., Atlanta, 1993—, Ga. Tech Bioengrng. Program, Atlanta, 1994—. Mem. editorial bd. Chem. Design Automation News, N.Y.C., 1992—. Mem. AIChE, Am. Chem. Soc. (Sherwin Williams award 1988). Office: Ga Inst of Technology Sch of Chem Engrng Atlanta GA 30332-0100

LUDTKE, JAMES BUREN, business and finance educator; b. Waterloo, Iowa, Mar. 4, 1924; s. Henry George and Eteska (Buren) L.; m. Jean Seaver Edwards, Sept. 8, 1948; children—Melissa, Leslie, Mark, Betty, Rebecca. Student, Iowa Tchrs. Coll., 1942-43, N.W. Mo. State Tchrs. Coll., 1943-44; B.A., State U. Iowa, 1947, M.A., 1948, Ph.D., 1951. Instr. econs. U. Iowa, 1947-51; mem. faculty U. Mass., Amherst, 1951-86, prof. fin., 1960-86, chmn. dept. gen. bus. and fin., 1958-70. Author: The American Financial System: Markets and Institutions, 2d edit, 1967. Served with USNR, 1943-46. Sloan fellow Mass. Inst. Tech., 1961-62; Ford Found. faculty fellow Harvard U., summers 1961, 66. Mem. Fin. Mgmt. Assn., AAUP (pres. Mass. state conf. 1977-80, treas. Assembly of State Confs. 1980-82). Home: 30 Wachusett Hyannis Port MA 02647-9999

LUDWIG, ALLAN IRA, photographer, author; b. N.Y.C., June 9, 1933; s. Daniel and Honey (Fox) L.; m. Janine Lowell, Aug., 1955 (div. 1991); children: Katherine Arabella, Pamela Vanessa, Adam Lowell; m. Gwendolyn Akin, 1992; children: Allan B. Ludwig Jr., Alison Ludwig. BFA, Yale U., 1956, MA, 1962, PhD, 1964. Instr., R.I. Sch. Design, 1956-58; asst. instr. Yale U., 1958-64; asst. prof. Dickinson Coll., 1964-65; assoc. prof., 1965-68; assoc. prof. Syracuse U., 1968-69; pres. Automated Communications, Inc., Verona, N.J., 1969-75; dir. Ludwig Portfolios, 1975-90; co-dir. Akin/Ludwig, 1990-97; mem. exec. bd. Alternative Mus. N.Y.C., 1978-88, chmn. bd. dirs., 1982-83; cons. presses U. Mass., U. Ga., Boston Mus. Fine Arts, Smithsonian Instn. Author: Graven Images: New England Stonecarving and its Symbols, 1966; author exhbn. catalogues; one-person shows include: Silvermine (Conn.) Guild of Art, 1955, Davison Art Ctr., Wesleyan U., Middletown, Conn., 1961, Portland Mus. of Art, Portland, 1962, Met. Mus. and Art Ctrs., Miami, Fla., 1976, Jorgenson Art Gallery, U. Conn., Storrs, 1976, Alternative Mus., N.Y.C., 1977, Watson Art Gallery, Norton, Mass., 1978, Alonzo Gallery, N.Y.C., 1978, 79, Cayman Gallery, N.Y.C., 1980, IL Diaframma, Milan, Italy, 1981, Simon Gallery, Montclair, N.J., 1983, art gallery Farleigh Dickinson U., Madison, N.J., 1984, Ctr. for Creative Photography, Tucson, 1986, The Twining Gallery, N.Y.C., 1986, Cepa Gallery, Buffalo, 1986, The Shadai Gallery, Tokyo Inst. of Tech, Tokyo, 1987, White Columns, N.Y.C., 1988, O'Kane Gallery, Houston, 1988, Farideh Cadot Gallery, N.Y.C., 1988, XYZ Gallery, Ghent, Belgium, 1989, Northlight Gallery, 1990, Ariz. State U., Tempe, 1990, Galerie Farideh Cadot, Paris, 1990, Pamela Auchincloss Gallery, N.Y.C., 1991, 92, 94, Gallery 954, Chgo., 1994, Gallery at 777, L.A., 1994, Houston Ctr. for Photography, 1995, Hudson River Mus. Westchester, Yonkers, N.Y., 1995—, The Chrysler Mus., Norfolk, Va., 1995, CEPA Gallery, Buffalo, 1995, The Kemper Mus. Contemporary Art, Kansas City, Mo., 1997; exhibited in group shows at Bannister Art Gallery, Providence, 1979, Westmoreland County (Pa.) Mus. Art, 1979, Ind. Am. Photography exhbn., Warsaw, Cracow, Katowice, Gdynia, Poland, 1980, Alonzo Gallery, N.Y.C., 1980, Alternative Mus., N.Y.C., 1981, Floating Found. for Photography, N.Y.C., 1981, World Photographic Archive, Parma, Italy, 1984, Diverse Works, Houston, 1985, The State Mus., Trenton, N.J., 1985, San Francisco Mus. Modern Art, 1986, Mus. Photog. Arts, San Diego, 1987, Public Image Gallery, N.Y.C., 1985; Alternative Mus., N.Y.C., 1986, Internat. Ctr. for Photography, N.Y.C., 1987, Farideh Cadot Gallery, N.Y.C., 1987, 88, Farideh Cadot Gallery, Paris, 1988, de Cordova and Dana Mus., Lincoln, Mass., 1988, Musee d'Art Moderne de la Ville de Paris, 1988, Musee d'Art et Histoire, Fribourg, Switzerland, 1988, Nat. Muse. of Am. Art, Washington, 1988, Security Pacific Corp., Gallery At The Plaza, L.A., 1988, Houston Ctr. for Photography, 1988, Catherine Edelman Gallery, Chgo., 1989, Musee fur Minerologie und Geologie, Leiden, Holland, 1989, The Friends of Photography, Ansel Adams Ctr., San Francisco, 1989, Alternative Mus., N.Y.C., 1989, Mus. of Contemporary Art, Chgo., 1989, The Walker Art Ctr., Mpla., 1990, Musee Zool. U. Louis Pasteur, Strasbourg, France, 1990, Akin Gallery, Boston, 1990, Monserrat Gallery, Beverly, Mass., 1990, Hallwalls, Buffalo, 1990, Natur Mus. Seckenberg Forshungsinstitut, Frankfort, Germany, 1990, Art 21-90, Basel, Switzerland, 1990, The Walker Art Ctr., Mpls., 1990, Lights Works, St. Paul, 1990, The Boston Athenaeum, 1990, Arts Festival Braga, Portugal, 1991, Nat. Mus. Am. Art, Washington, 1991, Addison Gallery Am. Art, Andover, Mass., 1991, The New Mus., N.Y.C., 1991, Mus. Fine Arts, Houston, 1992, Ctr. for Photography-Mid-Town, N.Y.C., 1992, Univ. Gallery, Clark U., Worcester, Mass., 1992, Long Beach (Calif.) Mus. Art, 1992, Preservation House, B.C., Can., 1992, Henry Art Gallery, U. Wash., Seattle, 1992, Akin Gallery, Boston, 1992, Internat. Mus. Photography George Eastman House, Rochester, N.Y., 1993, Wadsworth Athanaeum, Hartford, Conn., 1993, The New Museum, N.Y.C., 1993, Akin Gallery, Boston, 1993, Ctr. for Photography at Woodstock, 1993, Montage, Rochester, N.Y., 1993, Gallery 954 Chgo., 1993, Parko Gallery, Tokyo, 1993, Addison Gallery Am. Art, Andover, Mass., 1994, New Mus., N.Y.C., 1994, Mus. Photographic Arts, San Diego, 1995, Mus. Contemporary Art, Chgo., 1995, The New Orleans Mus. Art, 1995, The Mercury Gallery, Boston, 1995, Thread Waxing Space, N.Y.C., 1995, Calif. Ctr. for the Arts Mus., Escondido, 1996, Univ. Art Mus., San Diego State U., 1997, Fullerton Mus. Ctr., 1997, The Mus. Modern Art, Oxford, Eng., 1997, The Julie Dermansky Gallery, N.Y.C., 1997; represented in permanent collections: Mus. Modern Art, N.Y.C., Library of Congress, Washington, Smithsonian Instn., Washington, Archives Am. Art, Washington, Snite Mus. Art, Notre Dame, Ind., Walker Art Ctr., Mpls., Mus. Photog. Art, San Diego, N.Y.C., Polaroid Found. Collection, Cambridge, Mass., Yale U. Art Gallery, New Haven, Conn., San Francisco Mus. Modern Art, Ctr. for Creative Photography Collection, Tucson, Shadai Gallery, Tokyo, Maison Europeenne de la Photographie, L.A. County Mus. of Art, Mus. Fine Arts, Houston, Metropolitan Mus. Art, N.Y.C., The State Mus., Trenton, N.J, The Chrysler Mus., Norfolk, Va., The New Orleans Mus. Art, Kiyosato (Japan) Mus., Mus. Photographic Arts, San Diego. Regional chmn. Campaign for Yale Art Sch. Div., Met. N.Y.C. area, 1975-76. Bollingen Found. fellow, 1961-63; Am. Philos. Soc. fellow, 1964-66; Am. Coun. Learned Socs. fellow, 1967-68; NEH fellow, 1967; recipient USIS Merit award, 1966; Merit award Assn. State and Local History, 1967-68; Harriette Merrifield Forbes award Assn. Gravestone Studies, U. Conn., Storrs, 1981; Polaroid Found. grantee, 1987-88, Arts grantee N.J. State Coun., 1990, Agfa Corp. grantee, 1990, NEA grantee, 1990-91. Democrat.

LUDWIG, CHARLES T., technical company executive; b. Peoria, Ill., Dec. 2, 1947; s. Homer Charles and Mary Ellen (Turner) L.; m. Annette Ludwig, Sept. 9, 1972; children: Michelle S., Kristina A. BS in Chemistry, Purdue U., West Lafayette, Ind., 1970, MS in Indsl. Adminstrn., 1971. Program mgr. General Electric-Plastics Divsn., Pittsfield, Mass., 1971-79; v.p. specialty chemicals Great Lakes Chemical Co., West Lafayette, 1979-94; pres. Glasteel Indsl. Laminates, Collierville, Tenn., 1994—; alumni adv. bd. Purdue U. Sch. Science, West Lafayette, 1991-93; dean's adv. Purdue U. Sch. Science, West Lafayette, 1993—; dir. Ag Day Corp., Lafayette, Ind., 1992-96, The Alpha Corp. of Tenn., Collierville, 1996—. Mem. TPC. Avocations: golf, snow skiing, fishing. Home: 9489 Fox Hill Circle N Germantown TN 38139 Office: GIL 175 Commerce St Collierville TN 38017-9016

LUDWIG, CHRISTA, mezzo-soprano; b. Berlin; d. Anton and Eugenie (Besalla) L.; m. Walter Berry, Sept. 29, 1957 (div. 1970); 1 son, Wolfgang; m. Paul-Emile Deiber, Mar. 3, 1972. Ed. German schs. Prof. H.S. Berlin, 1995; hon. mem. Vienna Philharm., 1995. Appeared at Staedtische Buehnenm, Frankfurt, W. Ger., 1946-52, Landestheatre, Darmstadt, W. Ger., 1952-54, Hannover, W. Ger., 1954-55, Vienna (Austria) State Opera, 1955—, Medaille, Ville de Paris, 1993, Shibuya-Price, Japan, 1993, others, U.S. appearances include Avery Fisher Hall, N.Y.C., 1978, Lyric Opera, Chgo., 1959-60, 70-71, 73-74, Philharmonic Hall, N.Y.C., 1968, 69, 72, 74, others; guest artist London, Buenos Aires, Munich, Berlin, Tokyo, Salzburg Festival, Athens Festival, Saratoga Festival, Hunter Coll., Met. Mus., Scala Milano, Expo 67, Montreal, and others; rec. artist. Decorated Commdr. des Arts et des Lettres, France, 1988, Goldenes Ehren Zeichen Stadt, Salzburg, 1988, Goldene Ehrennadel Stadt und Land, Wien, Austria, 1988; chevalier Legion d'Honneur, France, 1989; recipient Mozart medal, Mahler medal, Hugo Wolf medal, Fidelio medal Opera Wien, 1991, Shibuya prize Japan, 1993, Medaille ville Paris, 1993, Medaille Ville de Dijon, 1993, Echo Deutscher Preis, 1994, Karajan preis, Berliner Bär, 1994, Grosses Ehrenzeichen Osterreich, 1994, Ehrenmitglied der Wiener Philharm., Silver Rose, Vienna Philharm., Golden Ring, Vienna Staatsoper, Musician of Yr. award Musical Am., 1994; named Kammersaengerin, Govt. of Austria, 1962. Mem. NARAS.

LUDWIG, EDMUND VINCENT, federal judge; b. Phila., May 20, 1928; s. Henry and Ruth (Viner) L.; children: Edmund Jr., John, Sarah, David. AB, Harvard U., 1949, LLB, 1952. Assoc. Duane, Morris & Heckscher, Phila., 1956-59; ptnr. Barnes, Biester & Ludwig, Doylestown, Pa., 1959-68; judge Common Pleas Ct., Bucks County, Pa., 1968-85, U.S. Dist. Ct. (ea. dist.), Phila., 1985—; mem. faculty Pa. Coll. of the Judiciary, 1974-85; presenter Villanova (Pa.) U. Law Sch., 1975-80, lectr., 1984—; vis. lectr. Temple Law Sch., 1977-80; clin. assoc. prof. Hahnemann U., Phila., 1977-85; mem. Pa. Juvenile Ct. Judge's Commn., 1978-85; chmn. Pa. Chief Justice's Ednl. Com., 1984-85; pres. Pa. Conf. State Trial Judges, 1981-82; mem. 3rd Cir. Ct. of Appeals Task Force on Equal Treatment in the Cts., 1994—. Contbr. articles to profl. jours. Chmn. Children and Youth Adv. Com., Bucks County, 1978-83; mem. Pa. Adv. Com. on Mental Health and Mental Retardation, 1980-85; founder, bd. dirs. Today, Inc., Newtown, Pa., 1971-85, Probation Vols., Bucks County, 1971-81; bd. dirs. New Directions for Women, Del. Valley, 1988—; mem. Pa. Joint Coun. Criminal Justice, Inc., 1979-80; mem. Joint Family Law Council Pa., 1979-85; vice chmn. Human Services Council Bucks County, 1979-81; mem. Com. to Study Unified Jud. System Pa., 1980-82, Pa. Legislative Task Force on Mental Health Laws, 1986-87; chmn. Juvenile Justice Alliance, Phila., 1992—; co-chmn. Doylestown (Pa.) Revitalization Bd., 1993—; mem. 3d cir. task force on equal treatment in the cts., 1995—. Recipient Disting. Svc. award Bucks County Corrections Assn., 1978, Spl. Svc. award Big. Bros., 1989, Humanitarian award United Way Bucks County, 1980, Founder's award Vol. Svcs., 1982, Spl. award Bucks County Juvenile Ct., 1985, Humanitarian award Ctrl. Bucks County C. of C., 1994; Wasserstein Pub. Interest fellowship Harvard Law Sch., 1996-97. Mem. ABA, Pa. Bar Assn. (chmn. com. legal svcs. to disabled 1990-92), Fed. Bar Assn. (hon.), Harvard Club (N.Y.C. and Phila., v.p. 1979-80), Harvard Law Sch. Assn. (mem. exec. com. 1993—). Office: 12614 US Courthouse Independence Mall W 601 Market St Philadelphia PA 19106-1713

LUDWIG, EUGENE ALLAN, United States comptroller of the currency, lawyer; b. Bklyn., Apr. 11, 1946; s. Jacob and Louise (Rabiner) L.; m. Carol Lynn Friedman, Mar. 11, 1978; children: Abigail Sarah, Elizabeth Madelaine Cathleen, David Maxwell. BA magna cum laude, Haverford Coll., 1968; BA, MA, Oxford U., Eng., 1970; LLB, Yale U., 1973. Bar: D.C. 1973. Assoc. Covington & Burling, Washington, 1973-81, ptnr., 1981-93; comptr. of the currency Dept. of the Treasury, Washington, 1993—; pres. Yale Legis. Svcs., 1972-73; guest lectr. Harvard U., Georgetown U., 1974-77, 79, Yale U., 1989. Editor Yale Law Jour., 1972-73; mem. editorial bd., Jour. Internat. Banking Law, 1989; contbr. articles to profl. jours. Office: Comptroller of the Currency Independence Sq 250 E St SW Washington DC 20024-3202

LUDWIG, GEORGE HARRY, physicist; b. Johnson County, Iowa, Nov. 13, 1927; s. George McKinley and Alice (Heim) L.; m. Rosalie F. Vickers, July 21, 1950; children: Barbara Rose, Sharon Lee, George Vickers, Kathy Ann Ramsay. BA in Physics cum laude, U. Iowa, 1956, MS, 1959, PhD in Elec. Engring., 1960. Head fields and particles instrumentation sect. Goddard Space Flight Center, NASA, 1960-65, chief info. processing div., 1965-71, assoc. dir. for data ops., 1971-72; dir. systems integration Nat. Environ. Satellite Service, NOAA, 1972-75, dir. ops., 1975-80, tech. dir., 1980; sr. scientist Environ. Rsch. Labs. NOAA, Boulder, Colo., 1980-81; dir. Environ. Rsch. Labs. NOAA, 1981-83; asst. to chief scientist NASA, 1983-84 ret., ind. cons. data mgmt. and space sta. design, 1983-92; sr. rsch. assoc. Lab. for Atmospheric and Space Physics U. Colo., 1985-91; vis. sr. scientist NASA hdqrs., Calif. Inst. Tech., 1989-91; prin. designer radiation detection instrumentation for numerous sci. spacecraft including Explorer I, 1956-65; co-discoverer Van Allen radiation belts; expert on NASA sci. and applications research data processing; oversaw devel. and operation U.S. Nat. Environ. Satellite System, 1972-80; oversaw environ. research program Nat. Oceanic and Atmospheric Adminstrn., 1981-83. Served from pvt. to capt. USAF, 1946-52. Van Allen scholar, 1958; research fellow U.S. Steel Found., 1958-60; recipient Exceptional Service medal NASA, 1969, Program Adminstrn. and Mgmt. award NOAA, 1977, Exceptional Sci. Achievement medal NASA, 1984. Mem. IEEE (sr.), Am. Geophys. Union (life), Phi Beta Kappa, Sigma Xi, Phi Eta Sigma, Eta Kappa Nu. Home: 215 Aspen Trl Winchester VA 22602-1404

LUDWIG, KARL DAVID, psychiatrist; b. Johnstown, Pa., June 9, 1930; s. Karl Döring and Kathryn Bride (Palmer) L.; m. Darlene Ann Fisher, July 9, 1959; children: John D., Karl David Jr., Elizabeth Ann Craig, Mark D., Michael D. BA in Biology, St. Vincent Coll., 1952; postgrad., Pa. State U., 1952-53, St. Mary's Sem. & Univ., Balt., 1953-54; MD, U. Pitts., 1960. Intern U.S. Naval Hosp., Phila., 1960-61; resident psychiatry Ea. Pa. Psychiat. Inst., Phila., 1961-64; fellow psychiat. rsch. and teaching Jefferson Med. Coll., Phila., 1964-66; rsch. psychiatrist, dir alcoholism program Friends Hosp., Phila., 1966-73; staff psychiatrist Haverford State Hosp., Haverford, Pa., 1964-71; cons. in psychiatry VA Hosp., Coatesville, Pa., 1968-70; chief outpatient svcs. Northeast Community Mental Health Ctr., Phila., 1973; clin. dir. Northeast Community Mental Health Ctr., 1973-80; supt. Dixmont State Hosp., Sewickley, Pa., 1980-81; dir. inpatient psychiatry Sewickley Valley Hosp., Sewickley, 1981-95; asst. med. dir. Staunton Clin., 1990-95; pres. med. staff Friends Hosp., Phila., 1969-71, Northeast Community Mental Health Ctr., Phila., 1974-75. Pres. Phila. Navy chpt. Res. Officers Assn. of U.S., 1976-77, dept. Pa., 1978-79; bd. trustees Valley Care Assn., Sewickley, 1983-93; bd. dirs. Valley Care Nursing Home, Sewickley, 1983-93. Capt. med. corps USNR, ret. Fellow Am. Psychiat. Assn., Psychiat. Physicians Pa. (pres. 1990-91); mem. AMA, Pitts. Psychiat. soc. (pres. 1985-86), Pa. Med. Soc., Allegheny County Med. Soc., Res. Officers Assn. of U.S. (life), Naval Res. Assn. (life), Am. Legion (life), Assn. Mil. Surgeons U.S. (life), Navy League U.S. (life), Mil. Order World Wars. (perpetual). Republican. Roman Catholic. Home and Office: 2168A Reis Run Rd Pittsburgh PA 15237-1425

LUDWIG, RICHARD JOSEPH, ski resort executive; b. Lakewood, Ohio, July 28, 1937; s. Mathew Joseph and Catherine Elizabeth (Sepich) L.; m. Emily Kathleen Popovich, Dec. 2, 1961 (div. Feb. 1967); 1 dau., Susan Kay; m. Erleen Catherine Halambeck Ramus, July 22, 1977; children: Charleen, Tracey, Charles. Cassandra. Student, Ohio State U., 1955-59; BBA Fenn Coll., Cleve. State U, 1963. C.P.A., Ohio. Sr. acct. Ernst & Whinney, Cleve., 1964-66; supervising acct. Ernst & Young, 1966-70; asst. treas. Midland Ross Corp., Cleve., 1970-71; treas. Midland Ross Corp., 1971-76; v.p. fin., treas. U.S. Realty Investments, 1976-78, v.p.-fin., chief fin. officer, 1978-79; owner Boston Mills Ski Resort, Inc., Peninsula, Ohio, 1979—, Brandywine Ski Resort, Inc., Sagamore Hills, Ohio, 1990—. Mem. Firestone Country Club (Akron, Ohio), Saddlebrook Club (Wesley Chapel, Fla.), Black Diamond Ranch Club (Lecanto, Fla.), Walden Country Club (Aurora, Ohio). Home: 5106 Pinelake Rd Wesley Chapel FL 33543-4459 Office: PO Box 175 7100 Riverview Rd Peninsula OH 44264

LUDWIG, RICHARD MILTON, English literature educator, librarian; b. Reading, Pa., Nov. 24, 1920; s. Ralph O. and Millie (Smeltzer) L. A.B., U. Mich., 1942; A.M., Harvard U., 1943, Ph.D., 1950. Mem. faculty Princeton U., 1950-86, prof. English, 1968-86, dir. spl. program humanities, 1956-64; dir. Am. civilization program, 1969-71, assoc. univ. librarian for rare books and spl. collections, 1974-85; teaching fellow Harvard, 1946-50, mem. faculty summer sch., 1951, 52. Editor Princeton U. Library Chronicle, 1977-85; editor: Aspects of American Poetry, 1963, Letters of Ford Madox Ford, 1965, Dr. Panofsky & Mr. Tarkington, 1974; co-editor: Major American Writers, 1952, Nine Short Novels, 1952, Guide to American Literature and Its Backgrounds, Since 1890, 1972, Literary History of the United States, 1974, Advanced Composition, 1977, Annals of American Literature, 1986, 89. Served with AUS, 1944-46. Dexter traveling fellow Harvard, 1950; Jonathan Edwards preceptor Princeton, 1954-57; McCosh Faculty fellow, 1967-68. Mem. MLA, Am. Studies Assn. Home: 143 Hartley Ave Princeton NJ 08540-5613

LUDWIKOWSKI, RETT RYSZARD, law educator, researcher; b. Skawina, Cracow, Poland, Nov. 6, 1943; came to U.S., 1982; s. Ryszard and Maria Ludwikowski; m. Anna Ludwikowski; children: Mark, Agnes. MA, Jagiellonian U., Poland, 1966, PhD in Law, 1971, D in Legal/Polit. Ideas, 1976. Bar: D.C. 1987; cert. legal counselor, 1973. Chmn. modern polit. movement/ideas Jagiellonian U., Cracow, 1976-82, chmn. div. bus., 1976-81, chmn. div. law, 1980-81; sr. fellow Marguerite Eyer Wilbur Found., Santa Barbara, Calif., 1981-82; vis. prof. politics Elizabethtown (Pa.) Coll., 1983; vis. scholar Hoover Inst., Stanford (Calif.) U., 1983; vis. prof. politics Alfred U., N.Y.C., 1983; vis. prof. politics Cath. U. Am., Washington, 1984, prof. law, 1985—, dir. comparative and internat. law inst., 1992—; vis. scholar Max Planck Inst., Hamburg, Fed. Republic of Germany, 1990. Author: Conservatism of Kingdom of Poland, 1976 (Ministry of Sci. award 1977), Black Radicalism in USA, 1976 (Pres. of Univ. award), Main Currents of Polish Political Thought, 1982, The Crisis of Communism, 1986 (grants and awards of Wilbur Found., Hoover Inst., Stanford U.), Continuity and Change in Poland, 1991, (with W.F. Fox) The Beginning of the Constitutional Era, 1993, Constitution-Making in the Region of Former Soviet Dominance, 1996, Regulations of International Trade and Business, 1996, others; contbr. articles to profl. jours. 2d lt. Polish Army. Recipient Vis. Prof. award Earhart Found., 1982—, award of Wilbur Found.; Disting. scholar; Heritage Found. grantee, 1981-82; grantee Hoover Inst., Stanford U., Bradley Found., 1992, Earhart Found., 1992-94, Max Planck Inst. grantee, 1990. Mem. ABA, The Smithsonian Assocs., Polish Inst. Arts and Scis., Wilson Ctr. Assocs. (charter mem.). Avocations: tourism.

LUEBKE, NEIL ROBERT, philosophy educator; b. Pierce, Nebr., Sept. 15, 1936; s. Robert Carl and Cinderetta Amelia (Guthmann) L.; m. Phyllis Jean Madsen, June 15, 1957; children: Anne Elizabeth, Karen Marie. B.A., Midland Coll., 1958; M.A., Johns Hopkins U., 1962, Ph.D., 1968. Asst., assoc. then prof. philosophy Okla. State U., Stillwater, 1961—, head philosophy dept., 1979-85, 89-96, Regents Svc. prof., 1997—; dir. Exxon Critical Thinking Project, 1971-74. Contbr. articles to profl. jours. Woodrow Wilson nat. fellow, 1958-59. Mem. Am. Philos. Assn., Soc. Bus. Ethics, Mountain-Plains Philos. Conf. (chmn. 1971-72, 80-81), Southwestern Philos. Soc. (pres. 1981-82), Phi Kappa Phi (nat. pres.-elect 1995—). Democrat. Lutheran. Home: 616 W Harned Ave Stillwater OK 74075-1303 Office: Okla State U Dept Philosophy 226 Hanner Stillwater OK 74078-5063

LUECKE, ELEANOR VIRGINIA ROHRBACHER, civic volunteer; b. St. Paul, Mar. 10, 1918; d. Adolph and Bertha (Lehman) Rohrbacher; m. Richard William Luecke, Nov. 1, 1941; children: Glenn Richard, Joan Eleanor Ratliff, Ruth Ann. Student, Macalester Coll., St. Paul, 1936-38, St. Paul Bus. U., 1938-40. Author lit. candidate and ballot issues, 1970—; producer TV local issues, 1981—; contbr. articles to profl. jours. Founder, officer, dir., pres. Liaison for Inter-Neighborhood Coop., Okemos, Mich., 1972—; chair countrywide special edn. millage proposals, 1958, 1969; trustee, v.p., pres. Ingham Intermediate Bd. Edn., 1959-83; sec., dir. Tri-County Cmty. Mental Health Bd., Lansing, 1964-72; founder, treas., pres. Concerned Citizens for Meridian Twp., Okemos, 1970-86; mental health rep. Partners of the Americas, Belize, Brit. Honduras, 1971; trustee Capital Area Comprehensive Health Planning, 1973-76; v.p., dir. Assn. Retarded Citizens Greater Lansing, 1973-83; chair, mem. Cmty. Svcs. for Developmentally Disabled Adv. Coun., 1973—; dir., founder, treas. Tacoma Hills Homeowners Assn., Okemos, 1985—; facilitator of mergers Lansing Child Guidance Clinic, Clinton and Easton counties Tri-County Cmty. Mental Health Bd., Lansing Adult Mental Health Clinic, founder. Recipient Greater Lansing Cmty. Svcs. Coun. "Oscar," United Way, 1955, state grant Mich. Devel. Disabilities Coun., Lansing, 1983, Disting. award Mich. Assn. Sch. Bds., Lansing, 1983, Pub. Svc. award C.A.R.E.ing, Okemos, 1988, Earth Angel award WKAR-TV 23, Mich. State U., East Lansing, 1990, Cert. for Cmty. Betterment People for Meridian, Okemos, 1990, 2nd pl. video competition East Lansing/Meridian Twp. Cable Comm. Commn., 1990, 1st pl. award video competition, 1992; Ingham Med. Hosp. Commons Area named in her honor, Lansing, 1971. Mem. Advocacy Orgn. for Patients and Providers (dir. 1994—). Avocations: reading, interior design, landscaping, gardening. Home: 1893 Birchwood Dr Okemos MI 48864-2766

LUECKE, RICHARD WILLIAM, biochemist; b. St. Paul, July 12, 1917; s. Frederick William and Susan (Trautz) L.; m. Eleanor Virginia Rohrbacher, Nov. 1, 1941; children—Glenn R., Joan E., Ruth A. B.A., Macalester Coll., 1939, M.S., 1941; Ph.D., U. Minn., 1943. Assoc. prof. A&M U., Tex., 1943-45; assoc. prof. biochemistry Mich. State U., East Lansing, 1945-49; prof. Mich. State U., 1949-87, prof. emeritus, 1987—; cons. Merck Sharpe & Dohme Labs., 1963-76; mem. nutrition bd. FAO. Contbr. articles to profl. jours.; mem. editorial bd.: Jour. Nutrition, 1974-78. Mem. Am. Assn. Animal Sci. (Research award 1956), Am. Chem. Soc., AAAS, Am. Inst. Nutrition, Brit. Nutrition Soc., Am. Soc. Biol. Chemists, N.Y. Acad. Sci., Soc. Exptl. Biology and Medicine. Home: 1893 Birchwood Dr Okemos MI 48864-2766 Office: Dept Biochemistry Mich State U East Lansing MI 48824

LUEDECKE, WILLIAM HENRY, mechanical engineer; b. Pittsburg, Tex., Apr. 5, 1918; s. Henry Herman and Lula May (Abernathy) L.; B.S., U. Tex., 1940; m. Mary Anne Copeland, June 3, 1939; children—William Henry, John Copeland. Mech. engr. Columbian Gasoline Corp., Monroe, La., 1940-41; supr. shipbldg., mech. engr. USN, Orange, Tex., 1941-42; gen. supr. factory mgrs. N. Am. Aviation Co., Dallas, 1944-46; mech. engr., charge Chrysler Airtemp. div. Chrysler Corp., Los Angeles, 1946-50; owner Luedecke Engring. Co., Austin, Tex., 1950—, also Luedecke Investment Co.; chmn. bd. dirs. Mut. Savs. Instn., Austin; dir. City Nat. Bank, Austin, 1st Tex. Fin. Corp., Dallas. Bd. dirs. Travis County Heart Fund, Austin YMCA. Named Man of Year, Tex. Barbed Wire Collectors Assn.; registered profl. engr., Tex. Mem. Am. Soc. Heating, Refrigerating and Air Conditioning Engrs. (dir., pres. Austin chpt.), Tex., Nat. socs. profl. engrs., C. of C., Econ. Devel. Council, Better Bus. Bur., Nat. Fedn. Ind. Bus. (nat. adv. council). Lutheran. Clubs: Rotary, Austin, Westwood Country (treas., dir.). Home: 15 Woodstone Sq Austin TX 78703-1159 Office: 1007 W 34th St Austin TX 78705-2008

LUEDER, DIANNE CAROL, library director; b. Racine, Wis., Aug. 5, 1944; d. James Richard and Margaret Ann (Eick) Helland; m. Roland Herman Lueder, Aug. 29, 1981 (dec. July 1993); children: Daniel Lee Bertelsen, Barbara Marie Bertelsen. BA, U. Wis.-Parkside, Kenosha, 1972; MLS, U. Wis., Milw., 1979. Ref./outreach libr. Elk Grove Village (Ill.) Libr., 1979-80; dir. Bartlett (Ill.) Pub. Libr., 1980-84; asst. exec. dir. DuPage Libr. Sys., Geneva, Ill., 1984-88; pres. Lueder Enterprises, Inc., Wauconda, Ill., 1988—; exec. dir. Roselle (Ill.) Pub. Libr., 1990—. Author: Administrator's Guide to Library Building Maintenance, 1992. Vice pres. Roselle Pub. Libr. Found., 1994-96. Mem. NAFE, ALA, AAUW, Ill. Libr. Assn., Libr. Admisntrs. Coun. No. Ill. Roselle C. of C. (program dir. 1994-95). Lutheran. Avocations: flying, travel, learning Norwegian language. Home: 27798 N Forest Garden Rd Wauconda IL 60084-2829 Office: Roselle Pub Libr Dist 40 S Park St Roselle IL 60172-2020

LUEDERS, EDWARD GEORGE, author, poet, educator, editor; b. Chgo., Feb. 14, 1923; s. Carl G. and Vera (Simpson) L.; m. Julia Demaree, June 5, 1946 (div. Apr. 1991); children: Kurt D., Joel E., Julia Anne; m. Deborah Keniston, Aug. 11, 1992. A.B., Hanover Coll., 1947; M.A., Northwestern U., 1948; Ph.D., U. N.Mex., 1952. Instr. U. N.Mex., 1948-52, asst. prof. English and speech, 1952-57; asso. prof. English Long Beach State Coll., 1957-61; prof., chmn. dept. English Hanover Coll., 1961-66; prof. English U. Utah, Salt Lake City, 1966—; chmn. dept. U. Utah, 1969-71, dir. creative writing, 1980-83, univ. prof., 1987-88, prof. emeritus, 1988—; mem. faculty Bread Loaf Sch. English, 1990—; editorial chmn. Coll. and Adult Reading List of Books in Lit. and Fine Arts, 1962; dir. Seminar Am. Poetry, Am. Studies Rsch. Ctr., Hyderabad, India, 1971; writer-in-residence Sch. of Ozarks, 1971, Behrend campus Pa. State U., 1972, sch. arts, U. Wis., Madison, 1987, Deep Springs Coll., 1989. Author: Carl Van Vechten and the Twenties, 1955, Carl Van Vechten, 1965, Images and Impressions: Poems by Brewster Ghiselin, Edward Lueders and Clarice Short, 1969, The Gang from Percy's Hotel and Other Poems, 1971, The Clam Lake Papers, A Winter in the North Woods, 1977, 2d edit., 1996, The Wake of the General Bliss, 1989; editor: (with others) Reflections on a Gift of Watermelon Pickle and Other Modern Verse, 1966, 2d edit., 1995, Some Haystacks Don't Even Have Any Needle and Other Complete Modern Poems, 1969, (with Primus St. John), Zero Makes Me Hungry, 1976, Writing Natural History: Dialogues with Authors, 1989, co-translator (with Naoshi Koriyama) Like Underground Water, The Poetry of Mid-20th Century Japan, 1995, Western Humanities Rev., 1969-72; gen. editor Peregrine Smith Literary Naturalists Series, 1989-92, U. Utah Press Nature and Environmental Studies, 1993—. Bd. dirs. Ucross Found., 1989—, The Mesa, 1996—. Served with USAAF, 1943-46, CBI. Recipient Poetry prize Utah Inst. Fine Arts Creative Writing Competition, 1969, Disting. Alumni award Hanover Coll., 1972, Nat. Endowment Arts Creative Writing fellow, 1983, Utah Humanities Coun. Gov.'s award in the Humanities, 1992. Home: 958 Windsor St Salt Lake City UT 84105-1308

LUEDERS, WAYNE RICHARD, lawyer; b. Milw., Sept. 23, 1947; s. Warren E. and Marjorie L. (Schramek) L.; m. Patricia L. Rasmus, Aug. 1, 1970 (div. Nov. 1990); children: Laurel, Daniel, Kristin. BBA with honors, U. Wis., 1969; JD, Yale U., 1973; Yale Law Sch. Bar: Wis. 1973. Acct. Arthur Andersen & Co., Milw., 1969-70; atty. Foley & Lardner, Milw., 1973-80, ptnr., 1980—; bd. dirs. numerous cos. Bd. dirs. Riveridge Nature Ctr., Milw., 1983-92, 96—, Milw. Pro Soccer, 1986—, Milw. Art Mus., 1992—, Child abuse Prevention Fund, Milw., 1989—, Michael Fields Agrl. Inst., 1991—; mem. adv. bd. Florentine Opera Co., 1992—; class agt. Yale Law Sch., 1978—. With U.S. Army, 1969-75. Mem. ABA, AICPA (Wisc.), Wis. Bar Assn., Milw. Bar Assn., Estate Counselors Forum, Univ. Club (Milw.), Phi Kappa Phi. Avocations: theater, racquetball, violin. Office: Foley & Lardner 777 E Wisconsin Ave Milwaukee WI 53202-5302

LUEDTKE, ROLAND ALFRED, lawyer; b. Lincoln, Nebr., Jan. 4, 1924; s. Alfred C. and Caroline (Senne) L.; m. Helen Snyder, Dec. 1, 1951; children: Larry O., David A. B.S., U. Nebr., 1949, J.D., 1951. Bar: Nebr. 1951. Since practiced in Lincoln, 1951—; mem. Luedtke, Radcliffe & Evans (and predecessor), 1973-79; dep. sec. state State of Nebr., 1953-60; spl. legis. liaison Nebr. Dept. State, 1953-60; corps and elections counsel to sec. of state State of Nebr., 1960-65; senator Nebr. Unicameral Legislature, 1967-78, speaker, 1977-78; lt. gov. State of Nebr., 1979-83; mayor City of Lincoln, 1983-87; of counsel McHenry, Haszard, Hansen & Roth, Lincoln, 1987—; exec. sec. Gov. Nebr. Com. Refugee Relief, 1954-58; del., conferee nat. confs. Past pres. Lancaster County Cancer Soc.; crusade chmn. Nebr. div. Am. Cancer Soc., 1981-82; past dist. v.p., fin. chmn. Boy Scouts Am.; treas. Nebr. Young Republicans, 1953-54; jr. pres. Founders Day, Nebr. Rep. Com., 1958-59; chmn. Lancaster County Rep. Com., 1962-64; bd. dirs. Concordia Coll. Assn., Seward, Nebr., 1962-66, pres., 1965-66; bd. dirs. Lincoln Lutheran Sch. Assn., 1961-65, pres., 1964-65; bd. dirs. Immanuel Health Ctr. Omaha; Tabitha Found., Lincoln, 1986—, v.p., 1990-97; bd. dirs. Nebraskaland Found., Lincoln, 1980-94; pres. 1990-93; bd. dirs. Coords. for Adult Literacy, Nebr., 1984-95, v.p., 1990-92. Served with AUS, 1943-45, ETO. Decorated Bronze Star, Purple Heart; recipient Disting. Service award Concordia Tchrs. Coll., 1965, Disting. Alumni award Lincoln High Sch., 1983. Mem. Am. Bar Assn., Nat. Conf. State Legislators (chmn. criminal justice task force 1975-77, chmn. consumers affairs com. 1975-77, exec. com. 1977-78), Nat. Conf. Lt. Govs. (exec. com. 1981-83), U.S. Conf. Mayors (chmn. human devel. com.), Nat. Conf. Cities (bd. dirs., bd. advisor human devel. com. NLC), Nat. League Cities (bd. dirs.), Nebr. Bar Assn., Lincoln Bar Assn., Am. Legion, DAV, VFW, Lincoln C. of C., Lincoln Gateway Sertoma Club (pres. 1962-63, chmn. bd. 1963-64), Delta Theta Phi. Lutheran. Office: McHenry Haszard Hansen & Roth Ste 870 NBC Ctr Lincoln NE 68508

LUEKE, DONNA MAE, national retail company manager; b. Toledo, Sept. 18, 1946; d. Herbert Henry and Margery Alberta (Welsh) L. BA, Adrian Coll., 1968. Tchr. Anchor Bay Schs., New Baltimore, Mich., 1968-74; salesperson Jacobson's, Birmingham, Mich., 1974-76; sales rep. Stark & Co., Detroit, 1976-80; regional retail supr. Norwich-Eaton Consumer Pharms., Louisville, 1980-83; territory rep. Procter & Gamble, Louisville, 1983-84; dir. Progressive Retail, Raleigh, N.C., 1984-89; nat. retail mgr. CIBA Consumer Pharms. and CIBA Vision Corp., Wayne, Pa., 1989-92. Student govt. v.p. Adrian Coll., 1966, 67. Mem. Nature Conservancy, Sierra Club. Avocations: travel, creative writing, photography.

LUELLEN, CHARLES J., retired oil company executive; b. Greenville, S.C., Oct. 18, 1929; s. John B. and Dorothy C. (Bell) L.; m. Jo S. Riddle, July 11, 1953; children: Margaret L. Briggs, Nancy L. Bissell. B.S., Ind. U., 1952. Sales rep. Ashland Oil, Inc., Ky., 1952-70, v.p. sales, 1970-72, group v.p. sales, 1972-80, pres., chief operating officer, 1986-92; also dir. emeritus Emeriti-Ashland, Inc., Ky.; pres. Ashland Petroleum Co., 1980-86; bd. dirs. Tosco Corp., Stamford, Conn. Bd. dirs. Kings Daus. Hosp., Ashland, 1981-87, Ashland Area YMCA, 1980-92, Nat. Chamber Found., Washington, 1987-92; trustee Centre Coll., Danville, Ky., 1988, Joint Coun. for Econ. Edn., N.Y.C. Mem. Beta Gamma Sigma. Home: 3409 Monte Vista Dr Austin TX 78731-5722 Office: Ashland Inc PO Box 391 Ashland KY 41105-0391 also: Ashland Inc 1000 Ashland Dr Russell KY 41169-1829

LUENING, ROBERT ADAMI, agricultural economics educator emeritus; b. Milw., Apr. 20, 1924; s. Edwin Garfield and Irma Barbara (Adami) L.; m. Dorothy Ellen Hodgskiss, Aug. 27, 1966. B.S., U. Wis., 1961, M.S., 1968. Dairy farmer Hartland, Wis., 1942-58; fieldman Waukesha County Dairy Herd Improvement Assn., Waukesha, Wis., 1958; adult agr. instr. Blair Sch. Dist., Wis., 1961-63; extension farm mgmt. agt. U. Wis.-Racine, 1963-69; extension farm record specialist Dept. Agrl. Econs. U. Wis.-Madison, 1969-88; free-lance work, 1988—. Author: (with others) The Farm Management Handbook, 1972, 7th edit., 1991, Teacher's Manual, 1991, Managing Your Financial Future Farm Record Book Series, 1980, 4th edit., 1987, USDA Yearbook of Agriculture, 1989, Beef, Sheep and Forage Production in Northern Wisconsin, 1992, Dairy Farm Business Management, 1996; writer mag. column: Agri-Vision, 1970-88. Founder, exec. pres. Lüning Family Orgns. U.S.A., Inc.; bd. dirs. Friends of the Max Kade Inst. for German-Am. Studies. Recipient John S. Donald Excellence in Teaching award U. Wis.-Madison, 1980; recipient Wis. State Farmer award Vocat. Agr. Inst. Wis., 1980, Second Mile award Wis. County Agts. Assn., 1980, Outstanding Svc. to Wis. Agr. award Farm and Industry Short Course, 1989. em. Am. Soc. Farm Mgrs. and Rural Appraisers (coll. v.p. 1976, chmn. editorial com. 1978-80, sec.-treas. 1968-80, pres. Wis. chpt. 1982, Silver Plow award 1988), Epsilon Sigma Phi (Disting. Service award 1988), Alpha Gamma Rho, Kiwanis. Presbyterian. Lodge: Masons. Home: 5313 Fairway Dr Madison WI 53711-1038 Office: U Wis Dept Agrl and Applied Econs 427 Lorch St Rm 216 Madison WI 53706-1513

LUEPKE, GRETCHEN, geologist; b. Tucson, Nov. 10, 1943; d. Gordon Maas and Janice (Campbell) Luepke; B.S., U. Ariz., 1965, M.S., 1967; U. Colo., summer, 1962. Geol. field asst. U.S. Geol. Survey, Flagstaff, Ariz., 1964; with U.S. Geol. Survey, Menlo Park, Calif., 1967—, geologist, Pacific Br. of Marine Geology, 1976—. Registered geologist, Ore. Mem. U.S. Congress Office Tech. Assessment Workshop, Mining and Processing Placers of EEZ, 1986. Fellow Geol. Soc. Am. (Interdisciplinary Perspectives on the Hist. Earth Scis., Penrose Conf. 1994); mem. Soc. Econ. Paleontologists and Mineralogists (chmn. com. libraries in developing countries 1988-91), Ariz. Geol. Soc., Peninsula Geol. Soc., Bay Area Mineralogists (chmn. 1979-80), History of the Earth Scis. Soc., Internat. Assn. Sedimentologists, Internat. Marine Minerals Soc. (charter), Geospeakers Toastmasters Club (charter, Competent Toastmaster 1995), Sigma Xi. Editor: Stability of Heavy Minerals in Sediments; Econ. Analysis of Heavy Minerals in Sediments; editor book rev. Earth Scis. History, 1989—. Contbr. articles on heavy-mineral analysis to profl. jours. Office: 345 Middlefield Rd Menlo Park CA 94025-3561

LUEPKER, RUSSELL VINCENT, epidemiology educator; b. Chgo., Oct. 1, 1942; s. Fred Joeseph and Anita Louise (Thornton) L.; m. Ellen Louise Thompson, Dec. 22, 1966; children: Ian, Carl. BA, Grinnell Coll., 1964; MD with distinction, U. Rochester, 1969; MS, Harvard U., 1976; PhD (hon.), U. Lund, Sweden, 1996. Intern U. Calif., San Diego, 1969-70; resident Peter Bent Brigham Hosp., Boston, 1973-74; cardiology fellow Peter Bent Brigham Hosp./Med., Boston, 1974-76; asst. prof. divsn. epidemiology med. lab. physiol. hygiene U. Minn., Mpls., 1976-80, assoc. prof., 1980-87, prof. divsn. epidemiology and medicine, 1987—, dir. divsn. epidemiology, 1991—; cons. NIH, Bethesda, Md., 1980—, U. So. Calif., L.A., 1985—, Armed Forces Epidemiology Bd., 1993—; vis. prof. U. Goteborg, Sweden, 1986, Ninewells Med. Sch., Dundee, Scotland, 1995. Lt. comdr. USPHS, 1970-73. Harvard U. fellow, 1974-76, Bush Leadership fellow, 1990; recipient Prize for Med. Rsch. Am. Coll. Chest Physicians, 1970, Nat. Rsch. Svc. award Nat. Heart, Lung and Blood Inst., Bethesda, 1975-77, Disting. Alumni award Grinnell Coll., 1989. Fellow ACP, Am. Coll. Cardiology, Am. Heart Assn. Coun. on Epidemiology (chmn. 1992-94), Am. Heart Assn. Sci. Sessions (program com. chair 1995—), Am. Coll. Epidemiology; mem. Am. Epidemiol. Soc., Delta Omega Soc. (Nat. Merit award 1988). Office: Univ Minn Sch Pub Health Div Epidemiology 1300 S 2nd St Ste 300 Minneapolis MN 55454-1087

LUEPNITZ, ROY ROBERT, psychologist, consultant, small business owner, entrepreneur; b. Ft. McClellan, Ala., June 3, 1955; s. Carl A. and Helen Elizabeth (Brown) L.; m. Mary Kinloch Bush, Dec. 18, 1981; 1 child, Noel. BA cum laude, Southwestern U., 1979; MS in Counseling Psychology, U. So. Miss., 1981; PhD in Counseling Psychology, Tex. A & M U., 1985. Diplomate Am. Bd. Forensic Examiners; cert. health svc. provider in psychology, Tex.; cert. travel agt.; registered treator of sex offenders; bd. cert. forensic examiner; lic. marital and family therapist. Intern, vol. Austin (Tex.) State Hosp., 1978-79; counselor Univ. Counseling Psychology Clinic, Hattiesburg, Miss., 1980; master level psychologist Pine Belt Mental Health Ctr., Hattiesburg, 1981, Tex. Rehab. Commn., Bryan, 1981-82; grad. tchr. Tex. A & M Univ., College Station, 1982-83; psychologist Brazos Valley MHMR Authority, Bryan, 1983-84; mental health dir. Brazos Valley MHMR Authority, Bryan, 1984-86; pvt. practice psychologist College Station, 1987—; cons. Dept. Human Svcs., Bryan, 1987—, Brazos Valley MHRA, Bryan, 1987—, Sandstone Psychiatry, College Station, 1990—, HCA Greenleaf Hosp., College Station, 1991—, various chs., schs., govt. agys., 1983—; Noel's Wonderful World of Travel, Village Square Office Park. Sec. Miss. APGA, 1979-81; active sex offender's assessment/treatment program. Mem. Assn. Treatment of Sexual Abuses, Am. Assn. Christian Counselors, Nat. Register Health Svc. Providers in Psychology, Tex. Psychol. Assn., Brazos Valley Psychol. Assn. Republican. Methodist. Avocations: coaching little league, baseball, basketball, softball. Home: 1200 Noel Ct College Station TX 77845-3803 Office: Brazos Valley Christian Counseling 2748 Longmire Dr College Station TX 77845-5424

LUERS, WILLIAM HENRY, art museum administrator; b. Springfield, Ill., May 15, 1929; s. Carl U. and Ann L. (Lynd) L.; m. Wendy Woods Turnbull, Oct. 18, 1979; children by previous marriage: Mark B., David L., William F., Amy L. AB, Hamilton Coll., 1951, LLD, 1984; MA, Columbia U., 1958; postgrad., Northwestern U., 1951-52. Commd. fgn. service officer Dept. State, 1957; vice consul Naples, Italy, 1957-59; 2d sec. Am. Embassy, Moscow, 1963-65; polit. counselor Am. Embassy, Caracas, Venezuela, 1969-73; dep. exec. sec. Dept. State, 1973-75; dep. asst. sec. for inter Am. affairs, Washington, 1975-77; dep. asst. sec. European affairs (Soviet-Eastern Europe), 1977-78; ambassador to Venezuela, Caracas, 1978-82, Czechoslovakia, Prague, 1983-86; pres. Met. Mus. Art, N.Y.C., 1986—; bd. dirs. Wickes Lumber Co., Vernon Hills, Ill., IDEX Corp., Northbook, Ill., Scudder New Europe Fund, N.Y., Scudder Global/Internat. Funds, StoryFirst Corp., San Francisco; dir.'s visitor Inst. Advanced Study, Princeton, N.J., 1982-83; vis. lectr. Woodrow Wilson Sch., Princeton U., 1983; trustee Rockefeller Bros. Fund, N.Y.C., Eurasia Found., Washington. Mem. adv. bd. Trust for Mut. Understanding, N.Y.C.; trustee adv. coun. Appeal of Conscience Found., N.Y.C.; bd. dirs. Inst. for East West Studies, N.Y.C., Am. Acad. Diplomacy, Washington; trustee Eurasia Found., Washington. Fellow Am. Acad. Arts and Scis.; mem. Coun. Fgn. Rels., Econ. Club N.Y. (bd. dirs.). Episcopalian. Office: Met Mus Art 1000 5th Ave New York NY 10028-0113

LUERSSEN, FRANK WONSON, retired steel company executive; b. Reading, Pa., Aug. 14, 1927; s. George V. and Mary Ann (Swoyer) L.; m. Joan M. Schlosser, June 17, 1950; children: Thomas, Mary Ellen, Catherine, Susan, Ann. BS in Physics, Pa., State U., 1950; MSMetE, Lehigh U., 1951; LLD (hon.), Calumet Coll.; DPS (hon.), Xavier U. Metallurgist research and devel. div. Inland Steel Co., East Chicago, Ind., 1952-54; mgr. various positions Inland Steel Co., 1954-64, mgr. research, 1964-68, v.p. research, 1968-77, v.p. steel mfg., 1977-78, pres., 1978-85, chmn., 1983-92; bd. dirs. Morton Internat., Inc. Contbr. articles on steelmaking tech. to various publs. Trustee Northwestern U., 1980—; trustee, sec., treas. Munster Sch. Bd., 1957-66. With USNR, 1945-47. Named disting. alumnus Pa. State U. Fellow Am. Soc. Metals; mem. AIME (Disting. life mem., B.F. Fairless award, Howe meml. lectr. 1988-91), Am. Iron and Steel Inst. (Gary medal, chmn. 1989-90), Nat. Acad. Eng. Home and Office: 8226 Parkview Ave Munster IN 46321-1419

LUETKEHOELTER, GOTTLIEB WERNER (LEE), retired bishop, clergyman; b. Wheatwyn, Sask., Can., Nov. 16, 1929; s. Henry William and Marie Louise (Schlepper) L.; m. Betty Edwards, July 25, 1959; children—David Lee, Jonathan Richard. B.A., U. Sask., 1952; B.D., Lutheran

Coll. and Sem., Saskatoon, Sask., 1955; S.T.M., Vancouver Sch. Theology, 1975; DD, St. John's Coll., U. Manitoba, 1990. Ordained to ministry United Luth. Ch. in Am., 1955. Pastor Markinch-Wheatwyn-Cupar Parish, 1955-57; pastor St. Mark's Luth. Ch., Regina, Sask., 1957-61, Erloeser Luth. Ch., Phila., 1961-63, Faith Luth. Ch., Burnaby, B.C., Can., 1963-69, Trinity Luth. Ch., Edmonton, Alta., Can., 1969-76; bishop Central Can. Synod, Luth. Ch. in Am., Winnipeg, Man., Can., 1976-85; bishop Man./Northwestern Ont. Synod, Evang. Luth. Ch. in Can., Winnipeg, Man., 1985-94; ret., 1994; mem. exec. coun. Luth. Ch. in Am., N.Y.C., 1978-85, Anglican-Luth. Dialogue, Can., 1983-95; dir. Can. Luth. World Relief, 1989—. Bd. govs. Luth. Theol. Sem., Saskatoon, 1976-94, Schmieder resident, 1994-95, lectr. Luth. Theol. Sem., 1995-96. With Royal Can. Navy, 1952-54. Avocations: golf; swimming, writing.

LUFFSEY, WALTER STITH, transportation executive; b. Richmond, Va., Mar. 15, 1934; s. Roland Emmit and Bernice Irene (Hall) L.; m. Louise Arlington Hicks, Dec. 19, 1956; children: Dennis Glenn, Melinda Denise. Student, U. Richmond, 1952-55, Agrl. Dept. Grad. Sch., 1963-65. With FAA, 1957—; supervisory air traffic control specialist FAA, Atlantic City, 1960-63; air traffic control specialist research FAA, 1963-65, sr. air traffic control analyst systems research and devel. service, 1965-71; chief program analysis and reports br. FAA, Washington, 1971-72; asst. chief program mgmt. staff FAA, 1972-73, spl. asst., assoc. adminstr. for engring. and devel., 1973-74, chief program mgmt. staff system research and devel. service, 1974-75, tech. asst., assoc. adminstr. policy devel. and rev., 1975-78, tech. asst., assoc. adminstr. policy and internat. aviation affairs, tech. asst. to the assoc. adminstr. for aviation standards, 1978-79, dep. assoc. adminstr. for aviation standards, 1979-80, assoc. adminstr. for aviation standards, 1980-85, assoc. adminstr. for air traffic, 1985-86, dir. advanced aviation system design team, 1986-89; sr. v.p. ops. and planning Tech. and Mgmt. Assistance, Washington, 1989-90, exec. v.p., 1990—; pres. WSL Enterprises, Arlington, 1989—. Author: Air Traffic Control: How to Become an FAA Air Traffic Controller, 1990; contbr. articles to profl. jours. Served with USAF, 1955-58. Recipient Meritorious Achievement award Air Traffic Control Assn., 1965; recipient Spl. Achievement award FAA, 1970, 78, 85, Disting. Service award Aviation Week and Space Tech.-Flight Safety Found., 1982; Sec.'s award for outstanding achievement, 1982; Meritorious Exec. award-Presdl. Rank, 1983; Adminstr.'s Superior Achievement award for excellence in equal employment opportunity, 1985, numerous others. Mem. AIAA (mem. aero. policy com.), Soc. Sr. Aerospace Execs., Nat. Aero. Assn., Exptl. Aircraft Assn., Aircraft Owners and Pilots Assn., Profl. Women Contrs. Assn., Air Traffic Control Assn. (hon. mem. award 1986, chair publs. com.), John Marshall Cadet Alumni Assn., Soc. Airway Pioneers, Va. Aero. Hist. Soc., Order of Quiet Birdmen, Aero Club, Nat. Aviation Club (past pres., gov. emeritus), Kiwanis (past pres. Crystal City club). Home: 1805 Crystal Dr #713-S Crystal Park Arlington VA 22202 Office: Tech & Mgmt Assistance 600 Maryland Ave SW Ste 420 Washington DC 20024-2520 also: WSL Enterprises PO Box 16223 Arlington VA 22215-1223

LUFT, HAROLD S., health economist; b. Newark, N.J., Jan. 6, 1947; s. George and Kay (Grossman) L.; m. Lorraine Ellin Levinson, May 24, 1970; children: Shira Levinson, Jana Levinson. A.B., Harvard U., 1968, AM, 1970, Ph.D., 1973. Systems analyst, rsch. asst. Harvard Transport Rsch., Cambridge, Mass., 1965-68; systems analyst Harvard Econ. Rsch. Project, Cambridge, Mass., 1968-72; instr. econs. Tufts U., Medford, Mass., 1972-73; postdoctoral fellow Harvard Ctr. Community Health, Boston, 1972-73; asst. prof. health econs. Stanford U., Calif., 1973-78; prof. health econs., acting dir. Inst. Health Policy Studies, U. Calif., San Francisco, 1978-93; dir. Inst. Health Policy Studies U. Calif., San Francisco, 1993—; cons. Applied Mgmt. Scis., Silver Spring, Md., 1979—, Robert Wood Johnson Found., Princeton, N.J., 1982—; study sect. Nat. Ctr. Health Svcs., Rockville, Md., 1981-83; mem. coun. Agy. for Health Care Policy and Rsch. Author: Poverty and Health, 1978, Health Maintenance Organizations, 1981, 2d edit., 1988, (with Deborah Garnick, David mark, Stephen McPhee) Hospital Volume, Physician Volume, and Patient Outcomes, 1990, HMOs and the Elderly, 1994; contbr. chpts. to books, articles to profl. jours. Advisor, fin. planning com. Mid-Peninsula Health Service, Palo Alto, Calif., 1984—. NSF fellow, Carnegie Found. fellow, Grad. Prize fellow Harvard U., 1968-72, fellow Ctr. for Advanced Study in Behavioral Scis., 1988-89. Mem. Am. Pub. Health Assn., Am. Econ. Assn., Inst. Medicine, Western Econ. Assn., Assn. for Health Svcs. Rsch. (bd. dirs.). Home: 1020 Ramona St Palo Alto CA 94301-2443 Office: U Calif Inst for Health Policy Studies 1388 Sutter St Fl 11 San Francisco CA 94109-5427*

LUFT, RENE WILFRED, civil engineer; b. Santiago, Chile, Sept. 21, 1943; came to U.S., 1968; s. David and Malwina (Kelmy) L.; m. Monica Acevedo, Aug. 24, 1970; children: Deborah Elaine, Daniel Eduardo. CE, U. Chile, 1967; MS, MIT, 1969, DSc, 1971. Registered profl. engr., Alaska, Calif., Wash., Mass., N.H., R.I., Republic of Chile; registered structural engr., Vt. Asst. prof. civil engring. U. Chile, 1967-68; research asst. MIT, Cambridge, Mass., 1969-71, vis. lectr., 1983-84; staff engr. Simpson, Gumpertz & Heger Inc., Arlington, Mass., 1971-74, sr. staff engr., 1975-78, assoc., 1978-83, sr. assoc., 1984-90; prin. Simpson, Gumpertz & Heger Inc., San Francisco, 1990-91; head design div. Simpson, Gumpertz & Heger Inc., 1991-95; sec. seismic adv. com. Mass. Bldg. Code Commn., 1978-80, chmn., 1981-82; mem. Boston seismic instrumentation com. U.S. Geol. Survey; mem. slabs on ground com. Post-Tensioning Inst., 1994—. Contbr. articles to profl. jours. Mem. design overview com., bldg. seismic safety coun. Earthquake Hazards Reduction Program, 1983-91, chmn. rsch. com. 1987-88. Mem. ASCE, Boston Soc. Civil Engrs. (chmn. seismic design adv. com. 1981-86, Clemens Herschel award for tech. paper 1980, pres.'s award for leadership in earthquake engring. 1984), Am. Concrete Inst., Earthquake Engring. Research Inst., Structural Engrs. Assn. Calif., NSPE (Young Engr. of Yr., 1979), Sigma Xi, Chi Epsilon. Home: 107 Glendon Way Petaluma CA 94952 Office: 221 Main St Ste 1500 San Francisco CA 94105-1934

LUFTGLASS, MURRAY ARNOLD, manufacturing company executive; b. Bklyn., Jan. 2, 1931; s. Harry and Pauline (Yaged) L.; children by previous marriage: Paula Jean, Bryan Keith, Robert Andrew, Richard Eric; m. Christine L. Novick, May 29, 1988; 1 child, Andrew William. BS, Ill. Inst. Tech., 1952; MS, U. So. Calif., 1959; MBA, U. Conn., 1972.With Shell Chem. Co., Torrance, Calif., 1955-60, N.Y.C., 1960-61, Wallingford, Conn., 1961-64, Torrance, 1964-66, N.Y.C., 1966-69; asst. gen. mgr. Westchester Plastics div. Ametek, Inc., Mamaroneck, N.Y., 1969-75; dir. corp. devel. Ametek, Inc., N.Y.C., 1975-76, v.p., 1976-83, sr. v.p. corp. devel., 1984-96; mng. dir. M&A London, LLC, N.Y.C., 1996—. Served to lt. (j.g.) USN, 1952-55. Mem. NAM, Soc. Plastics Industry, Assn. Corp. Growth, Soc. Plastics Engrs., Tau Beta Pi, Beta Gamma Sigma, Phi Lambda Upsilon. Club: University (N.Y.C.). Contbr. articles to profl. jours., publs. Patentee in field. Office: M&A London LLC 99 Park Ave New York NY 10016-1601

LUFTIG, STEPHEN D., federal agency administrator. B in Chem. Engring. magna cum laude, CUNY; M in Civil Engring., NYU. Lic. profl. engr. With EPA, Arlingont, VA, 1972—; dir. emergency response visn. EPA, Arlingont, dir. region II emergency remedial respnose divsn., dir. office emergency remedial response; cons. Phillippine Govt.; U.S. rep. Internat. Working Group Contaminated Land; with Exxon Corp., Allied Chem. Corp. Mem. Tau Beta Pi. Office: Office Emergency Remedial Response EPA Crystal Gateway 1 1235 Jefferson Davis Hwy Arlington VA 22202-3283

LUGAR, RICHARD GREEN, senator; b. Indpls., Apr. 4, 1932; s. Marvin L. and Bertha (Green) L.; m. Charlene Smeltzer, Sept. 8, 1956; children: Mark, Robert, John, David. B.A., Denison U., 1954; B.A., M.A. (Rhodes scholar), Oxford (Eng.) U., 1956. Mayor Indpls., 1968-75; vis. prof. polit. sci. U. Indpls., 1976; mem. from Ind. U.S. Senate, 1977—, chmn. com. fgn. relations, 1985-86, chmn. com. on agr.nut. and forestry, 1995—; chmn. Nat. Rep. Senatorial Com., 1983-84; Treas. Lugar Stock Farm, Inc.; mem. Indpls. Sch. Bd., 1964-67, v.p., 1965-66; vice chmn. Adv. Commn. on Intergovtl. Relations, 1969-75; pres. Nat. League of Cities, 1970-71; mem. Nat. Commn. Standards and Goals of Criminal Justice System, 1971-73; Del., mem. resolutions com. Republican Nat. Conv., 1968, del., mem. resolutions com., 1992, Keynote speaker, 1972, del., speaker, 1980. Author: Letters to the Next President, 1988. Trustee Denison U., U. Indpls.; bd. dirs. Nat. Endowment for Democracy, Am. Running and Fitness Assn. Served to lt. (j.g.) USNR, 1957-60. Pembroke Coll., Oxford U. hon. fellow. Mem. Blue Key, Phi Beta Kappa, Omicron Delta Kappa, Pi Delta Epsilon, Pi Sigma Alpha, Beta Theta Pi. Methodist. Club: Rotary. Office: US Senate 306 Hart Senate Bldg Washington DC 20510

LUGENBEEL, EDWARD ELMER, publisher; b. Balt., June 6, 1932; s. Nimrod Augustus and Victoria Elizabeth (Shilling) L.; m. Alice Marie Smith, June 12, 1953; children: Craig Edward, Susan Elizabeth, Douglas Paul, Leslie Jean. B.S., U. Md., 1954. With Prentice-Hall, Inc., N.J., 1957-76; exec. editor, asst. v.p. Prentice-Hall, Inc., 1972-76; pres. D. Van Nostrand Co., div. Litton Ednl. Pub., Inc. (pubs. coll. textbooks), N.Y.C., 1976-81; v.p. Lynne Palmer Exec. Recruitment, Inc., N.Y.C., 1981-83; v.p., editorial dir. W.B. Saunders Med. Pubs., Phila., 1983-85; exec. editor Columbia U. Press, N.Y.C., 1985—. Served as 1st lt. USAF, 1954-57. Mem. AAAS, Am. Inst. Biol. Scis., Am. Geophys. Union, Soc. Vertebrate Paleontology, Internat. Assn. Landscape Ecology, Soc. Conservation Biology, Delta Sigma Pi. Office: 136 S Broadway Irvington NY 10533-2500

LUGER, DONALD R., engineering company executive; b. Elizabeth, N.J., May 12, 1938; s. George A. and Elizabeth M. Luger; m. Pat Sanders, Feb. 17, 1968 (dec. 1982); m. Sharon L. Luger, May 14, 1983; children: Christopher Daniel, Morgan Kathleen. BCE, Auburn U., 1962, MSCE, Auburn U., 1964, exec. program Stanford U., 1979. Registered profl. engr., N.C., Ga., Mich., Va., N.Y. Structural engr. NASA, Huntsville, Ala., summer 1962; area engr. E.I. DuPont Co., Nashville, 1964; structural engr. Hayes Internat. Corp., Huntsville, 1964-65; resident engr. Fibers Industries, Inc., Shelby, N.C. and Greenville, S.C., 1965-66; project mgr. Lockwood Greene Engrs., Inc., Atlanta, 1967-71, sr. project mgr., 1971-74, v.p., corp. dir., 1974-78, sr. v.p., corp. dir., 1978-82, pres., 1982—, chief exec. officer, 1983—, chmn. 1989. Mem. ASCE, NSPE, Ga. Soc. Profl. Engrs., So. Ctr. for Internat. Studies, Auburn U. Alumni Assn., Auburn Alumni Engring. Coun., Stanford Alumni Assn., Constrn. Industry Pres. Forum, Commerce Club, Atlanta Athletic Club.

LUGT, HANS JOSEF, physicist; b. Bonn, Germany, Sept. 12, 1930; came to U.S., 1960; s. Josef and Elisabeth (Pütz) L.; m. Anneliese W. Scheller, Nov. 22, 1957; children: Christian H., Brigitte M. Prae Diploma, Bonn U., Fed. Republic of Germany, 1952; diploma, Aachen U., Fed. Republic of Germany, 1954; PhD, Stuttgart U., Fed. Republic of Germany, 1960. Asst., physics lab. Ruhrgas Co., Essen, Fed. Republic of Germany, 1954-57, head, physics lab., 1957-60; rsch. physicist U.S. Naval Weapons Lab., Dahlgren, Va., 1960-66; sci. cons. David Taylor Rsch. Ctr., Bethesda, Md., 1967-74, div. head, 1974-78, sr. rsch. physicist, 1978-95. Author: Vortex Flow in Nature and Technology, 1983, reprint, 1995, Introduction to Vortex Theory, 1996; also over 110 articles to profl. jours. and govt. reports. Recipient Humboldt award Fed. Republic of Germany, 1981, Disting. Civilian Svc. award USN, 1982. Fellow Am. Physical Soc., Washington Acad. Scis.; mem. Am. Hist. Soc., Am. Goethe Soc. (pres. 1985-87), German Soc. for Applied Math. and Mechanics, Sigma Xi. Achievements include discovery of vortex breakdown in pipes; explanation of autorotating plates, Navier-Stokes computer simulations.

LUHN, ROBERT KENT, writer, magazine editor; b. Oakland, Calif., Nov. 23, 1953; s. Joel Adrian and Norma Jeanne (Arnold) L.; m. Marla Mieko Miyashiro, Sept. 14, 1992; 1 child, Pudge. Student, U. Calif., Davis, 1972-76. Freelance writer, 1968—; broadcaster, 1979-82; sr. editor PC World mag., San Francisco, 1983-90, contbg. editor, 1990-94; contbg. editor Calif. Republic mag., San Francisco, 1990-94, editor in chief Computer Currents Mag., 1994—. Author: The Swedish Catfish & Other Tales, 1979, Collected Works, Vol. 3, 1985, Going West, 1988, The Wit is Out, 1993; contbr. fiction, features and poetry to numerous publs., including Harper's, Mother Jones, Omni, Am. Film, Hudson Rev., Nantucket Rev., Christian Sci. Monitor, San Francisco Chronicle, Chgo. Tribune, Phila. Inquirer, PC mag., Computerworld, The Oregonian, Exec. Update, Grapevine Weekly; columnist Computer Currents, 1993—. Adv. bd. mem. Baykeeper, San Francisco, 1994-96. Mem. ACLU, Amnesty Internat., Greenpeace, Environ. Defense Fund. Avocations: tennis, quoits, writing.

LUHRS, CARO ELISE, internal medicine physician, administrator, educator; b. Dover, N.J., Jan. 21, 1935; d. Albert Weigand and Ethel Adelaide (Voss) L. BA, Swarthmore Coll., 1956; MD, Harvard U., 1960. Diplomate Am. Bd. Internal Medicine; cert. personal fitness trainer, fitness instr., strength and conditioning specialist. Instr., asst. prof. medicine, dir. hematology labs. Georgetown Univ. Hosp., Washington, 1964-68; White House fellow USDA, Washington, 1968-69, spl. asst. to Sec. of Agr., 1969-73; dir. health and med. divsn. Booz, Allen & Hamilton, Washington, 1973-77; v.p., med. dir. EHE/Nat. Health Svcs., Washington, 1977-78; physician Washington, 1978—; med. dir. Hummer Cos., Washington, 1989—; clin. prof. family medicine Georgetown U., Washington, 1991—. Trustee Swarthmore (Pa.) Coll., 1975-79; bd. dirs. USDA Grad. Sch., Washington, 1970-74, The Pillsbury Co., 1973-89, White House Fellow Found., Washington, 1979; bd. regents Uniformed Svcs. U. of Health Scis., Bethesda, Md., 1980-85; cons. Office Sci. and Tech. Policy, The White House, 1977-80; with D.C. Mayor's Adv. Com. on Emergency Med. Svcs., 1980-84; mem. adv. com. hazardous materials EPA, 1970-76. Recipient Disting. Svc. award Uniformed Svcs. U. Health Scis., 1985. Fellow ACP, Royal Soc. Medicine; mem. AMA, Am. Coll. Sports Medicine, Med. Soc. D.C., Cosmos Club. Office: Caro Luhrs Assocs 1100 Connecticut Ave NW Ste 720 Washington DC 20036-4116

LUHRS, H. RIC, toy manufacturing company executive; b. Chambersburg, Pa., Mar. 22, 1931; s. Henry E. and Pearl (Beistle) L.; m. Grace B. Walke, June 12, 1973; children by previous marriage: Stephen Frederick, Christine Michelle, Terriann, Patricia Denise. BA, Gettysburg Coll., 1953. With The Beistle Co., Shippensburg, Pa., 1948-53, 1959—; pres., gen. mgr. Beistle Co., 1962-90, chmn. bd., 1978—; pres. Lakeside Holding Co. Inc., Boca Raton, Fla., 1996—; bd. dirs. First Nat. Bank of Shippensburg, 1964-80, Commonwealth Nat. Bank, 1980-81, Mellon Bank Commonwealth region, 1991—; vice chmn. CompuPix Tech. Inc.; pres., 1986-88, gemologist, 1977—; owner Luhrs Gem Testing Lab., 1977—, Luhrs Jewelry, 1976—, Allied Leasing Co., Shippensburg, 1968; pres. South Lac Devel. Co., 1986-92; owner Gun Depot, Shippensburg, 1992; chmn. The Walking Quail, Sports Goods Store, Shippensburg, 1994—, Lakeside Holding Co., Inc. 1996—. Pres. Shippensburg Public Library, 1964-66, 1970-72, 76-78, bd. dirs., 1963-82; pres. Community Chest, 1965, bd. dir., 1963-72; pres. Shippensburg Area Devel. Corp., 1966-72; bd. dirs., trustee Carlisle (Pa.) Hosp., 1967-71, Chambersburg Hosp., 1969-75; mem. consumer adv. coun. Capital Blue Cross, 1976-78; bd. dirs. Fla. Atlantic U. Found., 1988-91, Shippensburg U. Found., 1991—. Capt. USAF, 1953-59. Mem. SAR (life), Shippensburg Hist. Soc. (life, bd. dirs. 1968), Shippensburg C. of C. (pres. 1965, bd. dirs. 1964-65), Toy Mfrs. Assn. (bd. dirs. 1969-71), Nat. Sml. Businessmen's Assn., NRA (life, benefactor), NRA Whittington Ctr. Founder's Club, NRA Golden Eagles, Shippensburg Fish and Game Assn. (life, pres. 1963), Carlisle Fish and Game Assn. (life), Am. Legion (life) VFW (life), Cumberland Valley Indsl. Mgmt. Club, York Printing House Craftsmen, Masons (32 deg.), Shriners, Tall Cedars of Lebanon. Lutheran. Office: 1 Beistle Plz Shippensburg PA 17257

LUICK, ROBERT BURNS, lawyer; b. Belmond, Iowa, Aug. 6, 1911; s. Albert Lee and Estella Margaret (Burns) L.; m. Evelyn Pelletier, Nov. 21, 1942 (dec.); children: Elisabeth, Susan, Sarah, Nancy. AB, U. Minn., 1933, LLB, 1936; MBA cum laude, Harvard U., 1939. Bar: Mass. 1941. Atty. New Eng. Mut. Life Ins. Co., Boston, 1939-43; ptnr. Sullivan & Worcester, Boston, 1943-93, of counsel, 1993; bd. dirs. Ionics, Inc., Watertown, Mass., Setra Systems, Inc., Acton, Mass. and others; pres. and dir. Boston Investment Co. Mem. ABA, Boston Bar Assn., Knights of Malta, Union Club, Longwood Cricket Club. Avocations: tennis, painting, music. Home: 51 Rutledge Rd Belmont MA 02178-3322

LUIGS, CHARLES RUSSELL, gas and oil drilling industry executive; b. Evansville, Ind., Apr. 4, 1933; s. Charles Anthony and Agnes A. (Russell) L.; m. Mary M. McClaine, Sept. 7, 1957; children: Charles Edwin, James Russell, Carol Lynn, Susan Nadine, Michael Alan. B.S. in Petroleum Engring., U. Tex., 1957; student, St. Edwards U., 1951-52. With U.S. Industries, various locations, 1957-76; v.p. U.S. Industries, 1969-71, exec. v.p., 1971-74, pres., 1974-76; dir. U.S. Industries, 1971-76; pres., chief exec. officer, dir. Global Marine, Inc., 1977—, chmn. bd., 1982—. Mem. NSPE, AIME, Internat. Assn. Drilling Contractors (dir.), Houstonian Club, Houston Club, Westlake Club. Home: PO Box 4577 Houston TX 77210-4577 Office: Global Marine Inc 777 N Eldridge Pky Houston TX 77079-4425

LUIKART, FORDYCE WHITNEY, management consultant; b. Cleve., Aug. 17, 1910; s. Louis Edward and Grace (Latham) L.; m. Margaret Clark, Sept. 7, 1935; children—Clark W., James L., John F. A.B. cum laude, Ohio Wesleyan U., 1933, teaching certificate, 1934. Teaching fellow, asst. Maxwell Grad. Sch. Citizenship and Pub. Affairs, Syracuse U., 1934-37; instr. social sci. State Tchrs. Coll., Brockport, N.Y., 1937-39; mgr. br. office U.S. CSC, Cleve., 1942-44; chief investigations div. U.S. CSC, Washington, 1944-45; chief orgn. and methods staff U.S. CSC, 1945-46, chief inspection div., 1947-50, dir. exec. devel. program, 1950-51, exec. vice chmn. fed. personnel council, 1951, chief examining and placement div., 1951-53; dep. dir. adminstrn. HEW, 1953-54, dir. adminstrn., 1954; vis. lectr. pub. personnel adminstrn. Maxwell Grad. Sch., 1946-62; sr. staff mem. Brookings Instn., 1962-76, cons., 1976—; pvt. cons. on govt. orgn. and mgmt., exec. devel. and tng., 1976—; cons. on govt. orgn. with Cresap, McCormick & Paget (mgmt. cons.), 1955-57; cons., staff dir. Pres.'s Com. on Career Exec. Service, Sept. 1957; dir. Fed. Aviation Orgn. Study, White House Staff, 1957-58; asst. adminstr. personnel and tng. FAA, 1958-62; lectr. Eisenhower Exchange Fellowship Inc. Program, 1979—. Author pub. personnel adminstrn. articles profl. jours. Pres. Group Health Assn., Inc.; trustee Community Group Health Found., Washington.; Spl. adv. asst. to mem. Commn. Orgn. of Exec. Br. (Hoover Commn.), 1948-49; spl. adv. personnel and civil service to Greek Govt., E.C.A. mission, 1949-50. Mem. Pub. Personnel Assn., Soc. Personnel Adminstrn. (pres. 1952-53), Phi Beta Kappa, Omicron Delta Kappa, Sigma Chi. Methodist. Home: 3257 Beech St NW Washington DC 20015-2207 Office: Brookings Instn Washington DC 20036

LUIKART, JOHN FORD, investment banker; b. Washington, Apr. 9, 1949; s. Fordyce Whitney and Margaret Lucille (Clark) L.; m. Lorry Adele Haycock, June 2, 1973; children: Erin Kristine, James Benjamin, John Thomas. BA, Ohio Weslyan U., 1971. Ptnr. Prescott Ball and Turben, Cleve., 1977, sr. v.p., mgr. fixed income, 1982-86, exec. v.p., also bd. dirs., 1986-88; pres. Sutro & Co. Inc., San Francisco, 1989—, CEO, 1995—; bd. dirs. John Hancock Freedom Securities, San Francisco; pres. Selected Money Mkt. Fund, Chgo., 1986, 1331 Advisors, Cleve., 1986; mgr. Ohio Bond Fund, Cleve., 1983—; chmn. NASD Dist. Bus. Conduct Com., 1994; bd. dirs. Freedom Securities, Freedom Capital Mgmt. Chmn. Ohio Mcpl. Adv. Council, Cleve., 1978-79. Mem. Cleve. Bond Club (pres. 1980). Methodist. Avocations: sports, reading. Office: Sutro & Co 201 California St San Francisco CA 94111-5002

LUING, GARY ALAN, financial management educator; b. Collins, Iowa, Apr. 24, 1937; s. Dwight Orn and Marjorie Mae (Clemons) L.; m. Sherry Lea Gates, Dec. 19, 1954; 1 child, Heather Sherry-Anne. B.S. cum laude, Stetson U., 1960; M.A., U. Ill., 1961; Dr. Adminstrn. (hon.), Canadian Sch. Mgmt. Auditor Arthur Andersen & Co., Chgo., 1963; prof. Fla. Atlantic U., Boca Raton, 1965—, dean Sch. Bus., 1970-87; cons. U.S. Treasury; expert witness on valuing closely held corps., 1972—, lectr., U.S., various fgn. countries; dir. Fla. Liquid Assets, Templeton Trust Co.; mem. faculty Internat. Assn. Fin. Planners. Editor Fla. C.P.A., 1974; assoc. editor Intelect, 1975-79; tax editor Quick Print, 1988—; contbr. articles to profl. jours. Chmn. Palm Beach County Transp. Com., 1972-75. Served to 1st lt. U.S. Army, 1961-63. Recipient Disting. Service Fla. Accountants Assn., 1971. Hon. fellow Internat. Soc. Preventive Medicine, Canadian Sch. Mgmt.; mem. AICPA, Am. Acctg. Assn., Acctg. Rsch. Assn., Beta Gamma Sigma, Beta Alpha Psi, Phi Beta Phi (pres. 1974), Phi Kappa Phi. Baptist. Home: 9550 NW 42nd Ct Coral Springs FL 33065-1576 *In the professions, as in life, so much is owed to those who have gone before.*

LUIZZI, RONALD, wholesale distribution executive; b. Neptune, N.J., Apr. 7, 1953; s. Alfredo Luizzi and Mary Kay (Mumford) Figart; m. Kim T. Richardson, May 14, 1994. BA in Psychology, Trenton State Coll., 1975. Pres., chief exec. officer Profl. Divers, Inc., Neptune, 1975-78; nat. dir. projects Nat. Assn. Scuba Diving Schs., Long Beach, Calif., 1978-81; sales mgr. TW Systems, Inc., Honolulu, 1981-85; gen. mgr. TW Systems, Ltd.-Kona, Kailua-Kona, Hawaii, 1985—; East coast regional dir. Nat. Assn. Scuba Diving Schs., Neptune, 1977-78. Contbg. author: (tng. manual) Gold Book, 1977, Safe Scuba, 1977. Scuba advisor YMCA-Kona, Kailua-Kona, 1985—. Mem. Nat. Assn. Instnl. Laundry Mgrs. (cert.), Hawaii Assn. Instnl. Laundry Mgrs. (allied), Nat. Exec. House Keepers Assn. (allied), Hawaii Hotel Assn. (allied), Rotary (sec. 1988-89, v.p. 1989-90, pres. 1990-91), Kona-Kohala C. of C. Avocations: scuba diving, sport fishing, racquetball, jogging, exotic bird collector. Home: 76-6303 Kaheiau St Kailua Kona HI 96740-2275 Office: TW Systems Ltd-Kona 74-5622 Alapa St Kailua Kona HI 96740-3108

LUJAN, ROSA EMMA, bilingual specialist, trainer, consultant; b. El Paso, Tex., May 17, 1949; d. Rosendo G. and Petra (Rubalcava) López; m. Daniel Lujan, Feb. 21, 1976; children: Lorena Janel, Daniel Omar, Carina Viani, Crystal Rose. BA in Elem. Edn., U. Tex. El Paso, 1972, MS in Edn., 1978, postgrad., 1988; postgrad., N.Mex. State U. Tchr. Ysleta Ind. Sch. Dist., El Paso, 1972-74, bilingual tchr., 1974-90, immigrant tchr., 1990-94; cons. Internat. Acad. Coop. Learning, 1994; mem. Tex. Task Force on Profl. Preparation and Profl. Devel.; nat. bd. dirs. profl. tchg. stds. com. English as a New Lang., 1994; cooperating tchr. U. Tex. El Paso, 1978—; tchr. tnr. Ysleta Ind. Sch. Dist., 1980—; rschr. tnr. Johns Hopkins, U. Tex. El Paso, Haifa U., Israel, 1988—; mentor tchr. U. Tex. El Paso, El Salvador C.A., Boise, Idaho, 1990—; bd. dirs. Nat. Bd. for Profl. Tchg. Stds. Editor: (bilingual newsletter) El Chisme Bilingüe, 1986—. Pres. Ysleta Assn. Bilingual Edn., 1975-76, SW Assn. Bilingual Edn., El Paso, 1990-91; mem. Mt. Carmel Sch. Bd., El Paso, 1991-94, Tex. Com. Student Learning, Austin, 1992—. Named Tex. Tchr. of Yr., Tex. Edn. Agy., 1991-92, Tex. Elem. Tchr. of Yr., 1991-92. Mem. NEA, AAUW, ASCD, Nat. Assn. Bilingual Edn., Tex. Assn. Bilingual Edn., Tex. State Tchrs. Assn., Delta Kappa Gamma, Kappa Delta Pi. Democrat. Roman Catholic. Avocations: reading, sewing, traveling, dancing. Home: 1933 Sea Gull Dr El Paso TX 79936-3602 Office: Ysleta Ind Sch Dist 9600 Sims Dr El Paso TX 79925-7200

LUKAC, GEORGE JOSEPH, fundraising executive; b. Garfield, N.J., Mar. 6, 1937; s. Michael and Elizabeth (Gall) L.; m. Alice Louise Osborn, Nov. 8, 1958; children: Mark Robert (dec.), Amy Elizabeth. BA in Polit. Sci., Rutgers U., 1958. Trainee, systems reviewer Prudential Ins. Co., Newark, 1958-59; asst. editor comm. dept. Johnson & Johnson, New Brunswick, N.J., 1959-61; editor Rutgers Alumni Monthly Rutgers U., New Brunswick, 1961-66, asst. dir. alumni rels. and devel., 1966-77; exec. dir. Sangamon State U. Found., Springfield, Ill., 1977-81; dir. devel. and pub. rels. Mo. Hist. Soc., St. Louis, 1981-84; v.p. devel. Rio Grande (Ohio) U., 1984-86; exec. dir. St. Luke's Hosps. Meritcare Found., Fargo, N.D., 1986-90; pres., CEO Venice (Fla.) Hosp. Found., 1990-92; pres. Lehigh Valley Hosp. Trust Fund, Allentown, Pa., 1992-96; exec. dir. Meml. Devel. Found. Rockford (Ill.) Health Sys., 1996—; vol. cons. Presbyn. chs., Fargo, Ballwin, Mo. and Venice, Fla., 1978-92, social welfare groups, Fargo, Ballwin, Venice and Allentown, 1978—; ofcl. cons. Ohio Arts Coun., Columbus, Ohio, 1986; instr., adviser, speaker univs., groups, confs., 1978—; jury mem. 1982 CASE Nat. Awards Contest. Editor: Aloud to Alma Mater, 1966, Copyright-The Librarian and the Law, 1972 (Citation N.J. Writers Conf. 1974); contbr.: Big Gifts, 1990; contbr. articles to mags. and profl. jours. Loaned exec. United Way, Fargo, 1987-88, capt., com. mem., 1988-90; bd. dirs. Red. River Dance Co., Fargo, 1989-90; v.p. bd. dirs. Ronald McDonald House, Fargo, 1987-90; mem. Indsl. Devel. Corp. of Lehigh Valley, 1992-96; Rep. nat. com. Chmn.'s Campaign Adv. Panel, 1994—. Recipient Citation N.J. Writers Conf., 1974, Ashmead award Rutgers Fund, 1968,76, Spl. Recognition award CASE Nat. Alumni Mag. Competition, 1966, award Rutgers Fund, 1961. Mem. Nat. Soc. Fund Raising Execs. (cert., found. bd. dirs.), Inst. on Philanthropy U. Ind. (charter assoc.), Assn. Hosp. Philanthropy, Nat. Conf. Nonprofit Bds. Republican. Presbyterian. Avocations: writing, volunteer consulting, nature, music. Home: 4114 Verde Ln Rockford IL 61114 Office: Rockford Meml Devel Found 2340 Glenwood Ave Rockford IL 61103-3633

LUKACS, JOHN ADALBERT, historian, retired educator; b. Budapest, Hungary, Jan. 31, 1924; came to U.S., 1946, naturalized, 1953; s. Paul and Magdalena Maria L.; m. Helen Schofield, May 29, 1953 (dec. 1970); children: Paul, Annemarie; m. Stephanie Harvey, May 18, 1974. Ph.D., Palatine

Joseph U., Budapest, 1946. Prof. history Chestnut Hill Coll., 1947-94, Chmn. dept. history, 1947-74, ret., 1994; vis. prof. history La Salle Coll., 1949-82, Columbia U., 1954-55, U. Toulouse, France, 1964-65, U. Pa., 1964, 67, 68, Johns Hopkins U., 1970-71, Fletcher Sch. Law, Diplomacy, 1971-72, Princeton U., 1988; vis. prof. U. Budapest, 1991, U. Pa., 1995—. Author books, including: The Great Powers and Eastern Europe, 1953, A History of the Cold War, 1961, Decline and Rise of Europe, 1965, The Passing of the Modern Age, 1970, Historical Consciousness, 1968, 2d edit., 1985, The Last European War, 1939-41, 1976; 1945, Year Zero, 1978, Philadelphia: Patricians and Philistines, 1900-1950, 1981, Outgrowing Democracy: A historical interpretation of the U.S. in the 20th Century, 1984, Budapest 1900, 1988, Confessions of an Original Sinner, 1990, The Duel (Hitler vs. Churchill 10 May-31 August 1940), 1991, the End of the 20th Century (and the End of the Modern Age), 1993, Destinations Past, 1994, The Hitler of History, 1997; contbr. numerous articles, essays, revs. to hist. and lit. jours. Mem. Schuylkill Twp. (Pa.) Planning Commn. Recipient Ingersoll prize, 1991, Order of Merit, Republic of Hungary, 1994. Fellow Soc. Am. Historians; mem. Am. Catholic Hist. Assn. (pres. 1977). Home: Valley Park Rd Phoenixville PA 19460

LUKAS, JOSEPH FRANK, paralegal; b. Bronx, N.Y., Mar. 24, 1952; s. Francis Joseph and Theresa (Beaumont) L.; m. Jane Elizabeth Roberts, Dec. 23, 1989; 1 child, Matthew Joseph. AA, Fulton-Montgomery C.C., Johnstown, N.Y., 1972; BA, L.I. U., Southampton, N.Y., 1974, Miss. U. for Women and Men, Columbus, 1993. Cert. Miss. Assn. Legal Assts. Paralegal Webb, McLaurin & O'Neal, Tupelo, Miss., 1990-94; ind. paralegal Thorne & Assocs., Tupelo, 1994-96; paralegal Roger M. Tubbs, Atty. at Law, 1996—. Mayoral candidate Guntown, Miss., 1992; justice ct. judge candidate No. Dist. Lee County, Miss. Mem. ATLA (paralegal divsn.), Nat. Assn. Legal Assts. Republican. Avocations: photography, reading, swimming, landscaping. Home: PO Box 444 Tupelo MS 38802-0444 Office: Thorne & Assocs 210 W Main St Tupelo MS 38801-3954

LUKASIK, STEPHEN JOSEPH, information technology executive; b. S.I., N.Y., Mar. 19, 1931; s. Stephen Joseph and Mildred Florence (Tynan) L.; m. Marilyn Bertha Trappiel, Jan. 31, 1953 (div. 1982); children: Carol J., Gregory C., Elizabeth A., Jeffrey P.; m. Virginia Dogan Armstrong, Feb. 11, 1983; stepchildren: Elizabeth L., Alan D. B.S., Rensselaer Poly. Inst., 1951; M.S., MIT, 1953, Ph.D., 1956. Dir. Advanced Research Project Agy., Washington, 1966-74; v.p. Xerox Corp., Rochester, N.Y., 1974-76; chief scientist and sr. v.p. Rand Corp., Santa Monica, Calif., 1977-79; chief scientist FCC, Washington, 1979-82; v.p. and mgr. Northrop Research and Tech. Ctr., Palos Verdes, Calif., 1982-85, corp. v.p. for tech., 1985-90; v.p. for tech. TRW Space and Def. Sector, Redondo Beach, Calif., 1990-92; asst. to the CEO SAIC, San Diego, Calif., 1992—; dir. Face to Face Game Co., Calabasas, Calif., 1991—; cons. numerous gov. orgns. Assoc. editor: The Info. Soc. Trustee Stevens Inst. Tech., Hoboken, N.J., 1975-92; trustee Harvey Mudd Coll., Claremont, Calif., 1987—. Served to capt. USAR. Recipient Sec. Def. Disting. Civilian Service medal, 1973, 74. Mem. Am. Phys. Soc., AAAS. Club: Cosmos, D.C., Regency, Los Angeles. Home: 1714 Stone Canyon Rd Los Angeles CA 90077-1915 Office: Face to Face Game Co 3820 N Orchid Ln Los Angeles CA 90043

LUKE, DAVID LINCOLN, III, retired paper company executive; b. Tyrone, Pa., July 25, 1923; s. David Lincoln and Priscilla Warren (Silver) L.; m. Fanny R. Curtis, June 11, 1955. AB, Yale U., 1945; LLD (hon.), Juniata Coll., 1967, Lawrence U., 1976, Salem Coll., 1983, W. Va. U., 1984. V.p., dir. Westvaco Corp., N.Y.C., 1953-57, exec. v.p., dir., 1957-62, pres., bd. dirs., 1962-80, chief exec. officer, 1963-88, chmn. bd. dirs., 1980-96. Chmn. bd. trustees Cold Spring Harbor Lab.; bd. dirs. Josiah Macy Jr. Found.; past chmn., trustee emeritus Hotchkiss Sch. Served from aviation cadet to capt. USMCR., 1942-45. Mem. The River Club, Piping Rock Club, Megantic Fish and Game Corp.

LUKE, DOUGLAS SIGLER, business executive; b. Middletown, N.Y., Oct. 1, 1941; s. Douglas Sigler Luke and Joanne (Benton) Cowles; m. Anne Sturgis Roosevelt, June 20, 1964 (div. Sept. 1976); m. Sarah Chappell Mullen, Mar. 23, 1991; children: Haven Roosevelt, David Russell, Lindsay Hall. Student, Mexico City Coll., 1961; BA Fgn. Affairs, U. Va., 1964; MBA, The Darden Sch., Charlottesville, Va., 1966. Mem. staff, chem. div. WestVaco Corp., Covington, Va., 1966-69; dir. corp. planning SCOA Industries, Columbus, Ohio, 1969-71; v.p. fin. Multicon Prop. div. Bethlehem Steel Corp., Columbus, 1971-72; gen. ptnr., chief exec. officer Personal Investments, Columbus, 1972-79; v.p. Rothschild, Inc. (formerly New Court Securities), N.Y.C., 1979-83, sr. v.p., 1984-87, mng. dir., 1987-90; pres, chief exec. officer WLD Enterprises, Inc., Ft. Lauderdale, Fla., 1991—; bd. dirs. Westvaco Corp., N.Y.C., Regency Realty Corp., Jacksonville, Fla., Orbital Scis. Corp., Fairfax, Va. Founding donor Adopt-a-Class, N.Y.C., 1988;mem. space adv. bd. U. Colo., 1985-89; bd. dirs. condrs. com. Columbus Symphony Orch., 1972-75; trustee The Columbus Acad., Gahanna, Ohio, 1973-77, Girl Scouts U.S., Piedmont Region, Roanoke, Va., 1967-69; high tech. com. working group N.Y.C. Partnership Inc., 1988-90. Mem. Ausable Club (St. Huberts, N.Y.), Adirondack Mountain Reserve (St. Huberts, trustee 1985-94, pres. 1988-91, chmn. 1991-94), The Brook (N.Y.C.), Mashomack Fish and Game Preserve (Pine Plains, N.Y.), The Ocean Reef Club (Key Largo, Fla.). Avocations: running, skiing, fly fishing.

LUKE, JAMES PHILLIP, manufacturing executive; b. Bklyn., Nov. 11, 1942; s. Edmon George and Gertrude Caroline (Sanial) L.; A.B., Princeton U., 1965; M.B.A., Columbia U., 1968; m. Elizabeth Joanne Hooke, Sept. 21, 1968; children—James Phillip, Karin Margaret, Shelby Elizabeth, Thomas Edmon. Exec. trainee WestPoint Pepperell, Inc., N.Y.C., 1968-69, salesman, Atlanta, 1969-70; venture devel. mgr. Internat. Paper Co., Inc., N.Y.C., 1970-71, dist. mgr. Formed Fabrics div., Atlanta, 1971-72, div. controller, Lewisburg, Pa., 1972-75; dir. planning Blessings Corp., Inc., N.Y.C., 1975-77, v.p. fin., Piscataway, N.J., 1977—, also sec.-treas., 1984-88, exec. v.p., CFO, 1988—. Served to lt. USNR, 1965-67. Roman Catholic. Mem. Am. Soc. Corp. Secs. Clubs: Princeton of N.Y., Two Rivers Country. Home: 3012 Hearthstone Rd Williamsburg VA 23185-7523 Office: Blessings Corp 200 Enterprise Dr Newport News VA 23603-1300

LUKE, JOHN A., JR., paper, packaging and chemical company executive; b. Nov. 24, 1948; s. John Anderson Sr. and Joy (Carter) L.; m. Kathleen Allen, June 30, 1984; children: Lindsay Allen, Elizabeth Carter, John A. III. BA, Lawrence U., 1971; MBA, U. Pa., 1979. Unit sales mgr. Procter & Gamble, 1974-77; corp. assoc. Westvaco Corp., N.Y.C., 1979-81, sr. fin. analyst, 1981-82, asst. treas., 1982-83, treas., 1983-86, v.p., treas., 1986, 1986-87, sr. v.p. mktg., internat. and Brazilian subsidiary, 1987-90, exec. v.p., 1990-92, pres., CEO, 1992—, chmn., 1996—; bd. dirs. Arkwright Ins. Boston, Bank of N.Y., The Tinker Found., Americas Soc., Coun. of Ams., Bank of N.Y.; bd. trustees Lawrence U.; mem. Coun. on Fgn. Rels. Bd. govs. NCASI; dir. United Negro Coll. Fund. Mem. Am. Forest and Paper Assn. (dir., exec. com.), Univ. Club, The Links, The Commonwealth Club. Office: Westvaco Corp 299 Park Ave New York NY 10171

LUKE, RANDALL DAN, retired tire and rubber company executive, lawyer; b. New Castle, Pa., June 4, 1935; s. Randall Beamer and Blanche Wilhelmina (Fisher) L.; m. Patricia Arlene Moody, Aug. 4, 1962 (div. Jan. 1977); children: Lisa Elin, Randall Sargent; m. Saralee Frances Krow, Mar. 1, 1979; 1 stepchild, Stephanie Sogg. BA in Econs. with honors, U. Pa., 1957, JD, 1960. Bar: Ohio 1960, Calif. 1962, Ill. 1989. Assoc., ptnr. Daus, Schwenger & Kottler, Cleve., 1965-70; ptnr. Kottler & Danzig, Cleve., 1970-75, Hahn, Loeser, Freedheim, Dean & Wellman, Cleve., 1975-81; assoc. gen. counsel The Firestone Tire & Rubber Co., Akron, Ohio, 1981-82, v.p., assoc. gen. counsel and sec., 1982-88; v.p., assoc. gen. counsel and sec. Bridgestone/Firestone, Inc., Akron, 1988-91; of counsel Hahn Loeser & Parks, Cleve., 1991—. Trustee, Akron Art Mus., 1982-87, Akron Symphony Orch., 1986-87, Cleve. Opera League, 1992—. Served to Capt. USNR, 1960-81; ret. 1981. Mem. ABA, Assn. Corp. Secs., Calif. Bar Assn., Ohio Bar Assn., Ill. Bar Assn. Republican. Clubs: Cleve. Skating (Shaker Heights, Ohio); Union (Cleve.). Avocations: tennis, jogging, skiing, swimming. Home: 13901 Shaker Blvd Cleveland OH 44120-1582 Office: Hahn Loeser & Parks 200 Public Sq Cleveland OH 44114-2301

LUKEHART, CHARLES MARTIN, chemistry educator; b. DuBois, Pa., Dec. 21, 1946; s. David Blair and Grace Dorothy (Lundgren) L.; m. Marilyn Orleana McKinney, Aug. 4, 1973; children: Mark, Brian, Laura. BS in Chemistry, Pa. State U., 1968; PhD in Inorganic Chemistry, MIT, 1972. Postdoctoral assoc. Tex. A&M U., College Sta., 1972-73; asst. prof. chemistry Vanderbilt U., Nashville, 1973-77, assoc. prof. chemistry, 1977-82, prof., 1982—. Author: Fundamental Transition Metal Organometallic Chemistry, 1985. Rsch. fellow Alfred P. Sloan Found., 1979-81. Mem. Am. Chem. Soc. (chmn. Nashville sect. 1979, 92), Materials Rsch. Soc. Office: Vanderbilt U Dept Chemistry Box 1822 Sta B Nashville TN 37235

LUKENBILL, GREGG, sports promoter, real estate developer; b. Sacramento, Aug. 15, 1954; s. Frank and Leona L.; children: Jake, Molly, Ben. BS in Bus. Adminstrn., Calif. State U., 1995, MBA, 1997. Owner, developer/builder Lukenbill Enterprises, Sacramento Valley Region; mng. gen. ptnr. Sacramento Kings Profl. Basketball/NBA, 1983-92, ARCO Arena, 1985-93; pres. Hyatt Regency, Sacramento, 1986-92; owner Sky King Inc.; pilot. Office: Lukenbill Enterprises 3600 Power Inn Rd Sacramento CA 95826-3826

LUKENS, ALAN WOOD, retired ambassador and foreign service officer; b. Phila., Feb. 12, 1924; s. Edward Clark and Frances (Day) L.; m. Susan Atkinson, Dec. 29, 1962; children: Lewis Alan, Susan Lukens Stone, Frances Lukens Bennett, Timothy Eric. AB, Princeton U., 1948; postgrad., U. Sorbonne, Paris, 1948, U. Madrid, 1948, Georgetown U., 1951; LLD (hon.), St. Lawrence U., 1987. Tchr. St. Albans Sch., Washington, 1950-51; joined U.S. Fgn. Svc., 1951; vice consul Ankara, Turkey, 1952, Istanbul, Turkey, 1953; pub. affairs officer Martinique, 1954-56; with news divsn. State Dept., 1956-57; U.S. del. 12th UN Gen. Assembly, 1957; mem. internat. staff NATO, Paris, 1958-60; consul Brazzaville, 1960; U.S. rep. to Independence of Congo, Brazzaville, Chad, Gabon, Central African Republic, 1961; charge d'affaires Am. Embassy, Bangui, Central African Republic, 1961, Paris, 1961-63, Rabat, Morocco, 1963-65; chief personnel Bur. African Affairs, State Dept., 1965-67; dep. chief mission, counselor embassy Dakar, 1967-70, Nairobi, 1970-72; chief jr. officer div. personnel State Dept., 1973-75; dir. Office Iberian Affairs, 1974-75; counselor, dep. chief mission Am. Embassy, Copenhagen, 1975-78; with Bur. African Affairs, Dept. State, Washington, 1978-79; consul gen. Cape Town, South Africa, 1979-82; dir. office analysis for Western Europe, Bur. Intelligence and Research, Dept. State, Washington, 1982-84; A.E.& P. People's Republic of Congo, 1984-87; cons. on internat. affairs and crisis mgmt. Dept. of State, 1987-93; lectr. on Africa. Co-chair, Peace Commn. Washington Nat. Cathedral. With AUS, 1943-46. Recipient Commendable Service award State Dept., 1961. Mem. Washington Inst. Fgn. Affairs (bd. sec. DACOR, Diplomatic and Consular Officers Ret.), Rotary, Princeton Club N.Y.C., Washington Club, Nairobi (pres. Paris chpt. 1961-63), Princeton U. Alumni Coun. (mem. exec. com., pres. Class of 1946), Explorers Club Washington (bd. dirs.), Chevy Chase Club (gov.). Episcopalian. Home: 18 Grafton St Chevy Chase MD 20815-3428

LUKER, KRISTIN, sociology educator; b. San Francisco, Aug. 5, 1946; d. James Wester and Bess (Littlefield) L. BA, U. Calif., Berkeley, 1968; PhD, Yale U., 1974. Postdoctoral fellow U. Calif., Berkeley, 1974-75, asst. prof. sociology, San Diego, 1975-81, assoc. prof., 1981-85, prof., 1985-86, co-dir. women's studies program, 1984-85, prof. jurisprudence and social policy, sociology, Berkeley, 1986—; Doris Stevens prof. women's studies, prof. sociology Princeton (N.J.) U., 1993-95. Author: Taking Chances: Abortion and the Decision Not to Contracept, 1976 (hon. mention Jessie Bernard award), Abortion and the Politics of Motherhood, 1984 (Charles Horton Cooley award 1985). Bd. dirs. Ctr. for Women's Studies and Services, San Diego, Ctr. for Population Options, Washington. Recipient Disting. Teaching award U. Calif., San Diego, 1984; Guggenheim Found. grantee, 1985. Mem. Am. Sociol. Assn., Sociologists for Women in Soc. Office: U Calif Berkeley Jurisprudence & Social Policy 2240 Piedmont Ave Berkeley CA 94720-2151

LUKEY, JOAN A., lawyer; b. Malden, Mass., Dec. 28, 1949; d. Philip Edward and Ada Joan (Roberti) L.; m. Philip Davis Stevenson. BA magna cum laude, Smith Coll., 1971; JD cum laude, Boston Coll., 1974. Bar: Mass. 1974, U.S. Dist. Ct. Mass. 1975, U.S. Ct. Appeals (1st cir.) 1976, U.S. Supreme Ct. 1985. Assoc. Hale & Dorr, Boston, 1974-79, jr. ptnr., 1979-83, sr. ptnr., 1983—. Mem. Joint Bar Com. on Judicial Appointments, Mass., 1985-87, steering com. Lawyers' Com. for Civil Rights Under the Law, Boston, 1987-90. Fellow Am. Coll. Trial Lawyers; mem. ABA, Mass. Bar Assn., Boston Bar Assn. (chair litigation sect. 1990-92, mem. coun. 1987-90), Women's Bar Assn. Mass., Boston Club. Office: Hale & Dorr 60 State St Boston MA 02109-1800

LUKS, ALLAN BARRY, executive director; b. N.Y.C., June 27, 1941; s. Joseph Moses and Evelyn (Gropper) L.; m. Karen Greenbaum, Feb. 22, 1969; children: Rachel, David. BA, U. N.C., 1963; JD, Georgetown Law Sch., 1966. Bar: N.Y. Vol. U.S. Peace Corps, Maracay, Venezuela, 1967-69; legal dir. Children's Aid Soc. East Harlem, N.Y.C., 1970-72; asst. dir. Life Ins. Industry Urban Investment Program, N.Y.C., 1972-75; sec.-treas. N.Y.C. Rand Inst., 1975-78; exec. dir. Alcoholism Coun. of Greater N.Y., N.Y.C., 1978-88, Inst. for the Advancement of Health, N.Y.C., 1988-90, Big Bros./Big Sisters of N.Y., N.Y.C., 1990—; author N.Y.C. law, warning posters on drinking during pregnancy, 1983; adj. prof. Fordham U. Grad. Sch. Social Svc., N.Y.C., 1979-88; chmn. legal sect. Internat. Coun. on Alcohol and Addictions, Lausanne, Switzerland, 1980-88; mem. NGO-Crime Prevention and Criminal Justice, UN, N.Y.C., 1982-90. Author: Will America Sober Up?, 1983, The Healing Power of Doing Good, 1991; co-author: You Are What You Drink, 1989; editor Having Been There, 1979. Pres. Cadman Towers Housing, Bklyn., 1971-75; sch. bd. mem. N.Y.C. Sch. Bd. #13, Bklyn., 1975-80; v.p. Brooklyn Heights Assn., N.Y.C., 1982-86; adv. coun. mem. Jr. League N.Y., N.Y.C., 1984-88. Recipient Vol. Leadership award Mayor of N.Y., N.Y.C., 1987, Pub. Svc. award Crains N.Y. Bus. Mag., N.Y.C., 1994. Office: Big Bros/Big Sisters NYC 223 E 30th St New York NY 10016-8203*

LUKSHA, ROSEMARY DOROTHY, art educator; b. Wilkes-Barre, Pa., Jan. 5, 1952; d. William Peter and Julia Catherine (Zavislak) L.; 1 child, Mary Rose. BS in Art Edn., Kutztown (Pa.) U., 1973, MEd, 1991; postgrad., Skidmore Coll., 1978, Marywood Coll., 1975, Wilkes U. Cert. instrnl. II art K-12. Art educator Wyoming Valley West Sch. Dist., Kingston, Pa., 1973-84; co. dancer Wilkes-Barre (Pa.) Ballet Theatre, 1973-80; dance instr. Coll. Misericordia, Dallas, Pa., 1980-81; art educator N.W. Area Sch. Dist., Shickshinny, Pa., 1988—; co. dancer Scranton (Pa.) Ballet Theatre, 1980-84; art cons. Wilkes U. Polish Rm. Com., Wilkes-Barre, 1976-92; mem. planning com. Wilkes-Barre Fine Arts Fiesta, 1980-82; illustrator Wilkes-Barre Ballet Theatre, N.E. Ballet, 1977-85, Wyo. Valley Oratorio, Wilkes-Barre, 1979. Choreographer: (dance work) Continue the Balance We Hold, Sisters, Young Choreographer's Performance inN.E. Regional Ballet Festival, 1979. Recipient Dance Scholarship N.E. Regional Ballet Festival, Melissa Hayden Ballet Sch., N.Y.C., 1979. Mem. N.W. Area Edn. Assn., Pa. Edn. Assn., Osterhout Libr. Soc., PTO State St. Sch. Republican. Roman Catholic. Avocations: reading, gardening, travel, bicycling, calligraphy. Office: NW Area Jr/Sr HS RR 2 Box 2271 Shickshinny PA 18655-9201

LULL, WILLIAM PAUL, engineering consultant; b. Indpls., Nov. 5, 1954; s. William Roger and Florence Elizabeth (Morris) L.; m. Mary Ann Garrison, Dec. 22, 1989. Student, Ind. State U., 1973-75; BS in Arts & Design, MIT, 1978. Systems designer James Assocs., Architects, Engrs., Indpls., 1978-79; architect TVA, Knoxville, Tenn., 1980; mgr. energy mgmt. div. Dubin-Bloome, Engrs., N.Y.C., 1981; asst. chief of design Syska & Hennessy, Engrs., N.Y.C., 1982-83; prin. Garrison/Lull Inc., Princeton Junction, N.J., 1984—; adj. assoc. prof. NYU, 1983—; lectr., presenter cons. environ. field. Author: Conservation Environment Guidelines for Libraries and Archives, 1990; co-author: Criteria for Storage of Paper-Based Archival Records, 1984; contbr. articles to profl. publs. Mem. ASHRAE (affiliate, conf. presenter 1983), Illuminating Engring. Soc. N.Am., Am. Inst. Conservation of Historic and Artistic Works (assoc.), Sigma Pi Sigma. Achievements include pioneering discipline of consulting on conservation environments for preservation of museum and archival collections. Home: 7 High St Allentown NJ 08501-1914 Office: Garrison/Lull Inc PO Box 337 Princeton Junction NJ 08550-0337

LUM, JEAN LOUI JIN, nurse educator; b. Honolulu, Sept. 5, 1938; d. Yee Nung and Pui Ki (Young) L. BS, U. Hawaii, Manoa, 1960; MS in Nursing, U. Calif., San Francisco, 1961; MA, U. Wash., 1969, PhD in Sociology, 1972. Registered nurse, Hawaii. From instr. to prof. Sch. Nursing U. Hawaii Manoa, Honolulu, 1961-95, acting dean, 1982, dean, 1982-89, prof. emeritus, 1995—; project coordinator Analysis and Planning Personnel Svcs., Western Interstate Commn. Higher Edn., 1977; extramural assoc. div. Rsch. Grants NIH, 1978-79; mem. mgmt. adv. com. Honolulu County Hosp., 1982-96; mem. exec. bd. Pacific Health Rsch. Inst., 1980-88; mem. health planning com. East Honolulu, 1978-81; mem. rsch. grants adv. coun. Hawaii Med. Svcs. Assn. Found., Nat. Adv. Coun. for Nursing Rsch., 1990-93. Contbr. articles to profl. jours. Trustee Straub Pacific Health Found., Honolulu; bd. dirs. Friends of the Nat. Inst. of Nursing Rsch., 1994—. Recipient Nurse of Yr. award Hawaii Nurses Assn., 1982; named Disting. Practitioner in Nursing, Nat. Acads. of Practice, 1986; USPHS grantee, 1967-72. Fellow Am. Acad. Nursing; mem. Am. Nurses Assn., Am. Pacific Nursing Leaders Conf. (pres. 1983-87), Council Nurse Researchers, Nat. League for Nursing (bd. rev. 1981-87), Western Council Higher Edn. for Nurses (chmn. 1984-85), Western Soc. for Research in Nursing, Am. Sociol. Assn., Pacific Sociol. Assn., Assn. for Women in Sci., Hawaii Pub. Health Assn., Hawaii Med. Services Assn. (bd. dirs. 1985-92), Western Inst. Nursing, Mortar Bd., Phi Kappa Phi, Sigma Theta Tau, Alpha Kappa Delta, Delta Kappa Gamma. Episcopalian. Office: U Hawaii-Manoa Sch Nursing Webster 409 2528 The Mall Honolulu HI 96822

LUM, JODY MAE KAM QUON, real property appraiser; b. Honolulu, Sept. 15, 1961; d. Joseph Tai and Alice Moi (Lau) L. BA, U. Hawaii, 1983. Cert. residential appraiser. Asst. appraiser Hanamura Appraisal Co., Honolulu, 1986-87; real estate staff appraiser Am. Savs. Bank, Honolulu, 1987-89; real property appraiser III City and County of Honolulu, Hawaii, 1989-90; real property appraiser IV City and County of Honolulu, 1990—. Active, profl. yound adult co-leader Kalihi Union Ch., 1993—. Named Outstanding Woman of Yr., 1991. Mem. Honolulu Chinese Jaycees (rec. sec. 1989-90, mem. devel. v.p. 1990-91, community devel. v.p. 1991-92, Woman of Yr. 1989-90, Outstanding Community Devel. v.p. 1991-92). Avocations: aerobics, reading Christian psychology. Office: City and County Honolulu 842 Bethel St Honolulu HI 96813-4320

LUMB, WILLIAM VALJEAN, veterinarian; b. Sioux City, Iowa, Nov. 26, 1921; m. Lilly Carlson, 1949; 1 child, John W. DVM, Kans. State U., 1943; MS, Tex. A&M U., 1953; PhD in Vet. Medicine, U. Minn., 1957. Intern, resident Angell Meml. Animal Hosp., Boston, 1946-48; from instr. to assoc. prof. medicine and surgery Tex. A&M U., 1949-52; asst. prof. clin. surgery Colo. State U., 1954-58; assoc. prof. surgery and medicine Mich. State U., 1958-60; assoc. prof. medicine Coll. Vet. Medicine, Colo. State U., Ft. Collins, 1960-63, dir. surg. lab., 1963-79, prof. surgery, 1963-81, emeritus prof., 1981—. Mem. AVMA, AAAS, Am. Coll. Vet. Anesthesiologists, Am. Coll. Vet. Surgeons, Nat. Acad. Sci., N.Y. Acad. Sci., Am. Assn. Vet. Clinicians, Nat. Acads. of Practice. Address: 1905 Mohawk Fort Collins CO 80525-1501

LUMBARD, ELIOT HOWLAND, lawyer, educator; b. Fairhaven, Mass., May 6, 1925; s. Ralph E. and Constance Y. L.; m. Jean Ashmore, June 21, 1947 (div.); m. Kirsten Dehner, June 28, 1981 (div.); children: Susan, John, Ann, Joshua Abel, Marah Abel. BS in Marine Transp., U.S. Mcht. Marine Acad., 1943-46; BS in Econs., U. Pa., 1949; JD, Columbia U., 1952. Bar: N.Y. 1953, U.S. Supreme Ct. 1959, Pa. 1983. Assoc. Breed, Abbott and Morgan, N.Y.C., 1952-53; asst. U.S. atty. So. Dist. N.Y., 1953-56; assoc. Chadbourne, Parke, Whiteside & Wolff, N.Y.C., 1956-58; ptnr. Townsend & Lewis, N.Y.C., 1961-70; ptnr. Spear and Hill, N.Y.C., 1970-75; ptnr. Lumbard and Phelan, P.C., N.Y.C., 1977-82, Saul, Ewing, Remick & Saul, N.Y.C., 1982-84; pvt. practice law, N.Y.C., 1984-86; ptnr. Haight, Gardner, Poor & Havens, N.Y.C., 1986-88; pvt. practice law, N.Y.C., 1988-92, ret.; chief counsel N.Y. State Commn. Investigation, 1958-61; spl. asst. counsel for law enforcement to Gov. N.Y., 1961-67; organizer N.Y. State Identification and Intelligence Sys., 1963-67; chair Oyster Bay Conf. on Organized Crime, 1962-67; criminal justice cons. to Gov. Fla. and other states, 1967; chief criminal justice cons. to N.J. Legis., 1968-69; chmn. com. on organized crime N.Y.C. Criminal Justice Coordinating Coun., 1971-74; organizer schs. of criminal justice at SUNY Albany and Rutgers, Newark; mem. departmental disciplinary com. First Dept., N.Y. Supreme Ct., 1982-88; trustee bankruptcy Universal Money Order Co., Inc., 1977-82, Meritum Corp., 1983-89; spl. master in admiralty Hellenic Lines Ltd., 1984-86; chmn. Palisades Life Ins. Co. (former Equity Funding subs. 1974-75); bd. dir. RMC Industries Corp.; dir. Am. Maritime History Inst., Kings Point, N.Y., 1996—; lectr. trial practice NYU Law Sch., 1963-65; mem. vis. com. Sch. Criminal Justice, SUNY-Albany, 1968-75; adj. prof. law and criminal justice John Jay Coll. Criminal Justice, CUNY, 1975-86; arbitrator Am. Arbitration Assn. and N.Y. Civil Ct.-Small Claims Part, N.Y. County; mem. Vol. Master Program U.S. Dist. Ct. (so. dist.) N.Y. Contbr. articles to profl. jours. Bd. dirs. Citizens Crime Commn. N.Y.C., Inc.; Big Bros. Movement, Am. Maritime Hist. Project, 1996—, Citizens Union; trustee Trinity Sch, 1964-78, N.Y.C. Police Found., Inc., 1971-92, chmn., 1971-74, emeritus. Lt. j.g. USNR, 1943-52. Recipient First Disting. Svc. award Sch. Criminal Justice, SUNY-Albany, 1976. Mem. Assn. Bar City N.Y., N.Y. County Lawyers Assn., ABA, N.Y. State Bar Assn., Maritime Law Assn., Down Town Assn. Club. Republican. Home: 39B Apple Ln Hollis NH 03049-6311

LUMBARD, JOSEPH EDWARD, JR., federal judge; b. N.Y.C., Aug. 18, 1901; s. Joseph Edward and Martha Louise (Meier) L.; m. Polly Poindexter, Sept. 4, 1929; children: Abigail, Thomas. A.B. cum laude, Harvard U., 1922, LL.B., 1925, LL.D., 1970; LL.D., William Mitchell Coll., U. Bridgeport, Northwestern U., N.Y. Law Sch., Columbia U.; S.J.D. (hon.), Suffolk U. Asst. U.S. atty. So. Dist. N.Y., 1925-27; spl. asst. atty. gen. N.Y. State, in Queens Sewer investigation and prosecution of Maurice E. Connelly, 1928-29; mem. firm Fogarty, Lumbard & Quel, 1929-31; asst. to William J. Donovan in bankruptcy inquiry conducted by Assn. Bar City N.Y. and others, 1929; asst. U.S. atty. charge criminal div. So. Dist. N.Y., 1931-33; mem. firm Donovan, Leisure, Newton, Lumbard & Irvine (and predecessor firms), 1934-53; spl. asst. atty. gen. N.Y. State, in Drukman murder prosecutions, 1936; def. counsel U.S. vs. Standard Oil and 23 oil cos., 1937-38; spl. asst. atty. gen. N.Y. State charge Election Frauds Bur., 1943; justice Supreme Ct. N.Y. State, June-Dec. 1947; U.S. atty. So. Dist. N.Y., 1953-55; U.S. circuit judge 2d Circuit, 1955—; chief judge U.S. Court Appeals, 2d Circuit, 1959-71. Contbr. to law jours. Bd. overseers Harvard, 1959-65; trustee William Nelson Cromwell Found. Jud. fellow Am. Coll. Trial Lawyers; mem. ABA (chmn. spl. com. minimum standards for criminal justice 1964-68, Gold medal 1968), N.Y. State Bar Assn. (Gold medal 1969), Assn. Bar City N.Y., S.R. Republican. Unitarian. Clubs: Country (Fairfield); Harvard, Century (N.Y.C.). Home: 490 Hillside Rd Fairfield CT 06430-2140

LUMENG, LAWRENCE, physician, educator; b. Manila, Aug. 10, 1939; came to U.S., 1958; s. Ming and Lucia (Lim) Lu; m. Pauline Lumeng, Nov. 26, 1966; children: Carey, Emily. AB, Ind. U., 1960, MD, 1964, MS, 1969. Intern U. Chgo., 1964-65; resident Ind. U. Hosps., Indpls., 1965-67, fellow, 1967-69, asst. prof. Sch. of Medicine, 1971-73, assoc. prof. Sch. of Medicine, 1974-79, prof. Sch. of Medicine, 1979—, dir. div. gastroenterology and hepatology Sch. of Medieine, 1984—; chief gastroenterology sect. VA Med. Ctr., Indpls., 1979—; mem. merit rev. bd. VA. Cen. Office, Washington, 1981-84; mem. alcohol biomed. res. rev. com. NIAAA, Washington, 1982-86; mem. grant rev. panel USDA, Washington, 1985—. Contbr. articles to profl. jours. Maj. U.S. Army, 1969-71. Fellow ACP; mem. Am. Soc. Clin. Investigation, Am. Soc. Biol. Chemists, Rsch. Soc. on Alcoholism (treas. 1985-87, sec. 1987-89), Am. Gastroenterological Assn., Am. Assn. for the Study of Liver Diseases. Avocations: painting, music. Office: Ind U Med Ctr 975 W Walnut St Indianapolis IN 46202-5181*

LUMET, SIDNEY, film director; b. Phila., June 25, 1924; s. Baruch and Eugenia (Wermus) L.; m. Rita Gam (div.); m. Gloria Vanderbilt, Aug. 27, 1956 (div. 1963); m. Gail Jones, Nov. 23, 1963 (div. 1978); m. Mary Gimbel, Oct. 1980; children: Amy, Jenny. Ed., Profl. Children's Sch.; student, Columbia. Tchr. acting High Sch. of Profl. Arts. Author: (with Alfred A. Knopf) Making Movies, 1995; appeared as child actor in several plays including Dead End, 1935, George Washington Slept Here, 1940-41, My Heart's in the Highlands, 1939; dir. summer stock, 1947-49; assoc. dir., CBS,

1950, dir., 1951-57; TV shows include Omnibus; films including Twelve Angry Men, 1957, Stage Struck, 1958, That Kind of Woman, 1959, The Fugitive Kind, 1960, A View from the Bridge, 1961, Long Days Journey into Night, 1962, Fail Safe, 1964, The Pawnbroker, 1965, The Hill, 1965, The Group, 1966, The Deadly Affair, 1967, The Sea Gull, 1968, Bye, Bye Braverman, 1968, The Appointment, 1969, (with Joseph L. Mankiewicz) King: A Filmed Record, 1969, Last of the Mobile Hot Shots, 1970, The Anderson Tapes, 1971, Child's Play, 1972, the Offence, 1973, Serpico, 1974, Lovin' Molly, 1974, Murder on the Orient Express, 1974, Dog Day Afternoon, 1975, Network, 1976, Equus, 1977, The Wiz, 1978, Just Tell Me What You Want, 1979, Prince of the City, 1981, Deathtrap, 1981, The Verdict, 1982, Daniel, 1983, Garbo Talks, 1984, Power, 1985, The Morning After, 1986, Running on Empty, 1988, Family Business, 1989, Q & A, 1990, A Stranger Among Us, 1992, Guilty As Sin, 1993, Night Falls on Manhattan, 1997, Critical Care, 1997; over 200 plays for, TV Playhouse 90, Kraft TV Theatre, Studio One; staged: play Caligula, 1960. Recipient D.W. Griffith Lifetime Achievement award, 1993. Mem. Dirs. Guild Am. (hon. life).

LUMIA, FRANCIS JAMES, internist; b. Trenton, N.J., Apr. 24, 1941; s. Joseph and Rose (Amodio) L.; m. Carolyn King, May 2, 1970; children: Margaret E., Joseph J. BA, U. Chgo., 1963, MD, 1967. Diplomate Am. Bd. Internal Medicine, Am. Bd. Quality Assurance and Utilization Rev. Intern and resident in medicine George Washington U. Hosp., Washington, 1967-70, fellow in cardiology, 1970-72; attending physician Northport VAH, L.I., N.Y., 1972-77; asst. prof. medicine SUNY, Stony Brook, 1972-77; attending physician Deborah Heart and Lung Ctr., Browns Mills, N.J., 1977—, co-dir. sect. of Nac medicine, 1990—, asst. chair cardiology, 1991—; physician advisor Peer Rev. Orgn. of N.J., East Brunswick, N.J., 1985—, sanctions com., 1994—; governing coun. Med. Soc. of N.J., Lawrenceville, 1987—. Contbr. articles to profl. jours. Recipient Washington Spl. Clin. fellow Heart Assn., 1971-72. Fellow ACP, Am. Coll. Cardiology, Acad. of Medicine of N.J., Am. Coll. Med. Quality, Am. Coll. of Angiology; mem. Am. Coll. Physician Execs. Roman Catholic. Avocations: painting, theatre. Office: Deborah Heart & Lung Ctr 200 Trenton Rd Browns Mills NJ 08015-1705

LUMLEY, JOHN LEASK, physicist, educator; b. Detroit, Nov. 4, 1930; s. Charles S. and Jane Anderson Campbell (Leask) L.; m. Jane French, June 20, 1953; children: Katherine Leask, Jennifer French, John Christopher. B.A., Harvard, 1952; M.S. in Engring, Johns Hopkins, 1954, Ph.D., 1957; Haute Distinction Honoris Causa, Ecole Central de Lyon, France, 1987. Postdoctoral fellow Johns Hopkins, 1957-59; mem. faculty Pa. State U., 1959-77, prof. aerospace engring., 1963-74, Evan Pugh prof. aerospace engring., 1974-77; Willis H. Carrier prof. engring. Cornell U., 1977—; prof. d'echange U. d'Aix-Marseille, France, 1966-67; Fulbright sr. lectr. U. Liege; vis. prof. U. Louvain-La-Neuve, Belgium; Guggenheim fellow U. Provence and Ecole Centrale de Lyon, France, 1973-74. Author: (with H.A. Panofsky) Structure of Atmospheric Turbulence, 1964, Stochastic Tools for Turbulence, 1970, (with H. Tennekes) A First Course in Turbulence, 1971, (with P. Holmes and G. Berkooz) Turbulence, Coherent Structures, Dynamical Systems and Symmetry, 1996; also articles; editor: (with A. Acrivos, L.G. Leal and S. Leibovich) Research Trends in Fluid Dynamics, 1996; tech. editor: Statistical Fluid Mechanics, 1971, 75, Variability of the Oceans, 1977; assoc. editor: Physics of Fluids, 1971-73; assoc. editor Ann. Rev. of Fluid Mechanics, 1976-85, co-editor, 1986—; chmn. tech. editorial bd.: Izvestiya: Atmospheric and Oceanic Physics, 1971—; editorial bd.: Fluid Mechanics: Soviet Research, 1972-94; editor Theoretical and Computational Fluid Dynamics, 1989—; prin.: films Deformation of Continuous Media, 1963, Eulerian and Lagrangian Frames in Fluid Mechanics, 1968. Recipient medallion U. Liege, Belgium, 1971, Timoshenko medal ASME, 1993, Hugh LDryden lectureship Am. Inst. of Aeronautics and Astronautics, 1996. Fellow Am. Acad. Arts and Scis., Am. Acad. Mechanics, Am. Phys. Soc. (exec. com. divsn. fluid dynamics 1972-75, 81-84, chmn. exec. com. divsn. fluid dynamics 1982, 87-89, Fluid Dynamics prize 1990), AIAA (fluid and plasma dynamics award 1982, Hugh L. Dryden rsch. lectureship 1996); mem. NAE, AAAS, N.Y. Acad. Sci., Soc. Natural Philosophy, Am. Geophys. Union, Johns Hopkins Soc. Scholars (charter), Sigma Xi. Home: 743 Snyder Hill Rd Ithaca NY 14850-8708 Office: Cornell U 238 Upson Hall Ithaca NY 14853-7501

LUMPE, SHEILA, state legislator; b. Apr. 17, 1935; m. Gustav H. Lumpe, 1958. AB, Ind. U.; postgrad., Johns Hopkins U.; MA, U. Mo. Mem. Mo. Ho. of Reps. Trustee Mo. Consol. Health Care Plan; active Civil Liberties Union; bd. dirs. People to People. Democrat. Home: 6908 Amherst Ave Saint Louis MO 63130-3124 Office: Mo Ho of Reps State Capitol Building Jefferson City MO 65101-1556

LUMPKIN, JOHN HENDERSON, retired banker; b. Fairbanks, Alaska, Jan. 28, 1916; s. Hope Henry and Mary Isobel (Henderson) L.; m. Caroline Sparrow Dalton, Apr. 8, 1942; children: John Henderson, Caroline Dalton (Mrs. Sozzi). BA, U. S.C., 1937, doctorate (hon.); LLB, Harvard U., 1940; doctorate (hon.), Columbia Coll., Coker Coll., Benedict Coll. Bar: N.Y. 1940. With firm White & Case, N.Y.C., 1940-41, Boyd, Bruton & Lumpkin, Columbia, S.C., 1946-64; sr. exec. v.p. S.C. Nat. Bank, Columbia, 1964-65, pres., 1965-70, chief exec. officer, 1965-81, chmn. bd., 1970-81; ret., 1981, hon. chmn. bd.; of counsel The McNair Firm, P.A., 1983-92; trustee Fed. Res. Bank of Richmond, 1976-79; bd. dirs. CSX Corp., SCANA Corp. Chmn., trustee S.C. Found. Ind. Colls.; trustee Brookgreen Gardens (chmn. exec. com.). Lt. comdr. USNR, 1941-46. Decorated Commendation medal. Recipient Algernon Sydney Sullivan award U. S.C., 1963; inductee S.C. Bus. Hall of Fame, 1991. Mem. 4th Circuit Jud. Conv., S.C. C. of C. (pres. 1971-72), Columbia C. of C. (pres. 1953-54), ABA, S.C. Bar Assn., Richland County Bar Assn., S.C. Bankers Assn. (pres. 1974-75). Office: NCNB Tower PO Box 11390 Fl Columbia SC 29211-1390

LUMPKIN, LEE ROY, dermatologist, educator; b. Oklahoma City, Sept. 6, 1925; s. Lee R. and Martha L. (Lockard) L.; m. Mona F. Long, Jan. 28, 1953; children: Lee Roy III, Patricia J., Megan E., Julie A., William S. BA, U. Okla., 1949, MD, 1953. Intern Tripler Gen. Hosp., Honolulu, 1953-54; gen. practice medicine San Francisco, 1955-57; commd. capt. U.S. Air Force, 1957, advanced through grades to col., 1968; resident in dermatology Walter Reed Gen. Hosp., Washington, 1958-61; chief of dermatology Madrid, Spain, 1961-64; fellow in dermatopathology Armed Forces Inst. Pathology, Washington, 1964-65; chief USAF Regional Center, Carswell AFB, Tex., 1964-67; chief dermatology USAF Med Center, Lackland AFB, San Antonio, 1967-72; assoc. clin. prof. dermatology U. Tex. Sch. Medicine, San Antonio, 1969-72; ret. U. Tex. Sch. Medicine, 1972; clin. prof. dermatology Albany (N.Y.) Med. Center, 1972-92; ret. Editor: Bull. Assn. Mil. Dermatologists, 1968-71; mem. editorial bd. Mil. Medicine, 1968-76; contbr. articles to med. jours. Decorated Bronze Star medal, Air Force Commendation medal with oak leaf cluster, Meritorious Service medal; recipient James Clarke White award, 1971. Fellow Am. Acad. Dermatology, ACP, Am. Coll. Cryosurgery; mem. Assn. Profs. Dermatology, Dermatology Found., Internat. Soc. Pediatric Dermatology, N.Am. Clin. Dermatology Soc., Internat. Soc. Tropical Dermatology, Soc. Air Force Physicians (pres.-elect), New Eng. Dermatol. Soc., Central N.Y. Dermatol. Soc., N.Y. State Soc. Dermatology (bd. govs. 1980-83, pres. 1981-83). Episcopalian. Home: 223 Lancaster St Albany NY 12210-1131

LUMRY, RUFUS WORTH, II, chemist, educator; b. Bismarck, N.D., Nov. 3, 1920; s. Rufus Worth and Mabel (Will) L.; m. Gayle Kelly, Mar. 27, 1943 (div. Aug. 1973); children—Rufus Worth III, Ann Eliza, Stephen Ellis. A.B., Harvard U., 1942, M.S., 1948, Ph.D., 1948. Research chemist div. 8 Nat. Def. Research Council, 1942-45; NRC fellow Harvard U., 1946-48; Merck fellow nat. scis. U. Utah, 1948-51, asst. prof. chemistry and biochemistry, 1951-53; mem. faculty U. Minn., 1953—, prof. chemistry, 1956-91, prof. emeritus, 1991—; vis. prof. Inst. Protein Research, Osaka, Japan, 1961, U. Rome, Italy, 1964, U. Calif., San Diego, 1977, U. Va., 1978, U. Granada, Spain, 1985; cons. in field, 1948—. Author: (with W. Reynolds) Mechanisms of Electron Transfer, 1966, (with R. Gregory) The Fluctuating Enzyme, 1986; also articles. NSF sr. postdoctoral fellow Carlsberg (Denmark) Lab., 1959-60. Mem. Am. Chem. Soc., Am. Inst. Biol. Scis., Am. Biophysics Soc., Am. Soc. Biol. Chemists, Sigma Xi. Democrat. Home: 940 Franklin Ter Minneapolis MN 55406-1153

LUMRY, WILLIAM RAYMOND, physician, allergist; b. Coronado, Calif., Feb. 17, 1951; s. Raymond Harley and Evelyn (Bamson) L.; m. Rozalia Nadel, May 18, 1980; children: Ariel Martina, Randall Bamson. BS, Tex. A&M U., 1973; MD, U. Tex., Galveston, 1977. Diplomate Am. Bd. Internal Medicine, Am. Bd. Allergy and Immunology. Intern Jewish Hosp., St. Louis, 1977-78, resident in internal medicine, 1978-80; fellow in allergy/immunology Scripps Clinic and Rsch. Found., La Jolla, Calif., 1980-82; physician Dallas Allergy Clinic, 1982-96; assoc. clin. prof. Southwestern Med. Sch., U. Tex., Dallas, 1982—; med. dir. Children's Lung Disease, Dallas, 1985—, Better Breathing Club, Med. City, Dallas, 1985—. Contbr. articles to profl. jours. Recipient Alcoa award Alcoa Found., 1976. Fellow Am. Coll. Physicians, Am. Coll. Allergists, Am. Acad. Allergy and Immunology. Republican. Methodist. Avocations: tennis, skiing, photography, sailing. Office: Allergy & Asthma Spec Dallas 9900 N Central Expy Ste 525 Dallas TX 75231-3304

LUMSDEN, IAN GORDON, art gallery director; b. Montreal, Que., Can., June 8, 1945; s. Andrew Mark and Isobel Dallas (Wilson) L.; m. Katherine Elizabeth Carson, July 28, 1979; 1 child, Craig Ian. B.A., McGill U., 1968; postgrad., Mus. Mgmt. Inst., U. Calif., Berkeley, 1991. Curator art dept. N.B. Mus., Saint John, 1969; curator Beaverbrook Art Gallery, Fredericton, N.B., 1969-83, dir., 1983—; bd. dirs. ArtsAtlantic; mem. Cultural Property Export Rev. Bd., 1982-85; mem. program com. 49th Parallel Ctr. for Contemporary Can. Art., 1990-92. Author exhbn. catalogues; contbr. numerous articles to Can. art periodicals. Mem. Can. Museums Assn. (sec.-treas. 1973-75), Can. Art Mus. Dirs. Orgn. (1st v.p. 1977-83, pres. 1983-85), Atlantic Provinces Art Gallery Assn. (chmn. 1970-72), Am. Assn. Museums, Union Club (St. John, N.B.). Mem. Anglican Ch. of Can. Home: 725 George St, Fredericton, NB Canada E3B 1K6

LUMSDEN, LYNNE ANN, publishing company executive; b. Battle Creek, Mich., July 30, 1947; d. Arthur James and Ruth Julia (Pandy) L.; m. Jon B. Harden, May 3, 1986; 1 child, Heather Lynne. Student, U. Paris, 1967-69; BA, Sarah Lawrence Coll., 1969; postgrad., City Grad. Ctr., 1979-81, NYU, 1970-71; cert. of mgmt., Am. Mgmt. Assn., 1982. Copy editor Harcourt, Brace, Jovanovich, N.Y.C., 1970-71; editor Appleton-Century Crofts, N.Y.C., 1971-73, Coll. div. Prentice-Hall, Englewood Cliffs, N.J., 1974-78; sr. editor Coll. div. Prentice-Hall, 1978-81; asst. v.p., editor-in chief Spectrum Books, 1981-82; v.p. editorial dir., gen. pub. div., 1982-85; exec. v.p., publ., co-owner Dodd, Mead & Co., Inc., N.Y.C., 1985-89; owner, chmn. JBH Communications Inc., Hartford, Conn., 1989—; pub. Hartford News and Southside Media, 1989—. Bd. dirs. Greater Hartford Architecture Conservancy; pres.-elect Friends of Mark Twain House. Mem. Jr. League of Hartford, Women Connect (bd. dirs.), Hartford Club, Pub. Lunch Club, N.Y.C. Sandbar Club, Town and County Club, Hartford Golf Club. Episcopalian. Office: 191 Franklin Ave Hartford CT 06114-1373

LUNA, BARBARA CAROLE, expert witness, accountant, appraiser; b. N.Y.C., July 23, 1950; d. Edwin A. and Irma S. (Schub) Schlang; m. Dennis Rex Luna, Sept. 1, 1974; children: John S., Katherine E. BA, Wellesley Coll., 1971; MS in Applied Math. and Fin. Analysis, Harvard U., 1973, PhD in Applied Math. and Fin. Analysis, 1975. CPA, cert. gen. real estate appraiser, accredited sr. appraiser, cert. valuation analyst, cert. fraud examiner, cert. mgmt. cons. Investment banker Warburg Paribas Becker, L.A., 1975-77; cons./mgr. Price Waterhouse, L.A., 1977-83; sr. mgr. litigation Pannell Kerr Forster, L.A., 1983-86; nat. dir. litigation cons. Kenneth Leventhal & Co., L.A., 1986-88; ptnr. litigation svcs. Coopers & Lybrand, L.A., 1988-93; sr. ptnr. litigation svcs. White, Zuckerman, Warsavsky & Luna, Sherman Oaks, Calif., 1993—. Wellesley scholar, 1971. Mem. AICPA, Assn. Bus. Trial Lawyers (com. on experts), Am. Soc. Appraisers, Nat. Assn. Cert. Valuation Analysts, Assn. Cert. Real Estate Appraisers, Assn. Cert. Fraud Examiners, Assn. Insolvency Accts., Inst. Mgmt. Cons., Calif. Soc. CPAs (steering com. L.A. litigation svcs. com. econ. damages Common Interest Mem. Svcs. com., fraud Common Interest Mem. Svcs. com., bus. valuation Common Interest Mem. Svcs. com.), Am. Bd. Forensic Examiners. Avocations: golf, swimming. Home: 18026 Rodarte Way Encino CA 91316-4370 Office: White Zuckerman Warsavsky & Luna PO Box 56359 Sherman Oaks CA 91413-1359

LUNA, CHARALINE, superintendent of schools; b. Feb. 7, 1955; d. Earle Russell and Edith (Gibbs) Vaughan; m. Robert E. Luna; children: Elizabeth, Michele, Gabrielle. AA in Early Childhood Adminstrn., Santa Ana (Calif.) Coll., 1977; BA in Liberal Studies and Elem. Edn., Calif. State U., L.A., 1985; MSEd in Adminstrn., Pacific We. U., L.A., 1991, EdD, 1992. Cert. tchr., Calif., Fla. Tchr.'s aide Page Pvt. Schs., L.A., 1970-72, team kindergarten tchr., 1972-75, pre-sch. tchr., 1976-78, dir., prin., 1978-86; dir. Page Pvt. Schs., Sanford, Fla., 1986; supr. Page Pvt. Schs., Fla., 1988—. Mem. Fla. Tri-County Prekindergarten Interagy. Coun., 1994-97; mem. Seminole County health Start Coalition, 1994—; mem. Seminole County Health Adv. Bd., 1995—; mem. adv. county Seminole County DARE, 1996—; mem. Gov.'s Children's Summit, 1996-97. Recipient Pres.'s award Page Pvt. Sch., 1990, Appreciation award Desert Storm Support Group, 1992, Outstanding Svc. award Assn. Ind. Schs. of Fla., 1995. Mem. DAR (regent 1991-92), Assn. Ind. Schs. of Fla. (bd. dirs. 1990—, rep. to Nat. Coun. Pvt. Sch. Accreditation 1994—), Cen. Fla. Assn. Non-Pub. Schs. (sec. 1988-89), Sanford C. of C. (edn. com. 1987-93), Sanford Woman's Club, Zeta Tau Alpha (collegiate pres. 1974). Office: Page Pvt Schs 650 E Airport Blvd Sanford FL 32773-8020

LUND, BERT OSCAR, JR., publisher; b. Stillwater, Minn., Nov. 8, 1920; s. Bert O. and Mary O. (Vordal) L.; m. Katherine Kingsley, July 31, 1943; children—Katherine Lund Cohen, Julie Lund Everett, Bert Oscar. B.B.A., U. Minn., 1942; postgrad., Harvard U., 1943. Advt. salesman Webb Co., St. Paul, 1946-54; advt. mgr. Webb Co., 1954-61; pub. Farmer Mag., 1961—, v.p. pub., 1963—, also dir.; v.p. pub. Pub. Cons., 1985—; dir. Audit Bur. Circulations, Gt. No. Ins. Co.; pres. Midwest unit Farm Papers, Inc., 1971; dir. Gt. No. Ins. Co., 1980—. Vice pres. Indianhead Council, Boy Scouts Am., 1974, Minn. Agrl. Soc., 1981; chmn. ops. com. St. Paul Civic Center Authority, 1972; bd. dirs. Minn. Council on Econ. Edn., 1969, Cath. Digest, 1980; chmn., trustee Dunwoody Inst., 1980, Hill Reference Library, 1984; trustee Minn. Med. Found. Served to lt. USNR, 1943-46. Mem. Agrl. Pubs. Assn. (past pres., dir.), State Farm Mag. Bur. (past pres., dir.), Advt. Club Minn (past pres.), U. Minn. Alumni Assn. (treas.), Sigma Alpha Epsilon. Republican. Episcopalian. Clubs: Minnesota, Royal Poinciana Country Club, Hole-in-Wall Golf, Somerset Country. Home: 2151 Upper St Dennis Rd Saint Paul MN 55116-2823

LUND, SISTER CANDIDA, college chancellor; b. Chgo.; d. Fred S. Lund and Katharine (Murray) Lund Heck. BA, Rosary Coll., River Forest, Ill.; MA, Catholic U. Am.; PhD, U. Chgo., 1963; DLitt (hon.), Lincoln Coll., 1968; LLD (hon.), John Marshall Law Sch., 1979; LHD honoris causa, Marymount Coll., 1979; LittD (hon.), St. Mary-of-the Woods Coll., 1994. Pres. Rosary Coll., 1964-81, chancellor, 1981—. Editor: Moments to Remember, 1980, The Days and the Nights: Prayers for Today's Woman, In Joy and in Sorrow, 1984, Coming of Age, 1992, Nunsuch, 1982, God and Me, 1988, Praymates, 1993; author, editor: If I Were Pope, 1987; contbr.: Why Catholic. Mem. women's bd. U. Chgo., 1984—; bd. dirs. The Chgo. Network, 1983-86, The Park Ridge Ctr., 1987-93, Gottlieb Hosp., 1991—. Recipient Profl. Achievement award U. Chgo. Alumni, 1974, U.S. Catholic award, 1984. Fellow Royal Soc. Arts; mem. Thomas More Assn. (bd. dirs. 1975—), The Arts Club (bd. dirs. 1987—). Home and Office: Dominican Univ 7900 Division St River Forest IL 60305-1066

LUND, DARYL BERT, food science educator; b. San Bernardino, Calif., Nov. 4, 1941; married June 15, 1963; children: Kristine, Eric. BS in Math., U. Wis., 1963, MS in food Sci., 1965, PhD in Food Sci., 1968. Rsch. asst. in food sci. U. Wis., Madison, 1963-67, instr., 1967-68, asst. prof., 1968-72, assoc. prof., 1972-77, prof. food sci., 1977-87, chmn. dept. food sci., 1984-87; chmn. dept. food sci., assoc. dir. agrl. experiment sta. Rutgers, the State U., New Brunswick, 1988-89; interim exec. dean agr. and natural resources Rutgers, the State U., New Brunswick, N.J., 1989-91; exec. dean agr./natural resources Rutgers, the State U., New Brunswick, 1991-95, exec. dir. N.J. Agrl. Experiment Sta., dean Cook Coll., 1991-95; Ronald P. Lynch dean of agr. and life scis. Cornell U., Ithaca, N.Y., 1995—; vis. engr. Western Regional Rsch. Lab., Berkeley, Calif., 1970-71; advisor for evaluation of food tech. dept. Inst. Agr., Bogor, Indonesia, 1973; mem. four-man evaluation team to review grad. edn. programs Brazilian univs., 1976; vis. prof. food process engring. Agrl. U., Wageningen, The Netherlands, 1979; invited vis. prof. food process engring. Univ. Coll., Dublin, 1982; invited advisor Inter-Univ. Ctr. on Food Sci. and Nutrition, Bogor, 1991; advisor Agrl. U., Bogor, 1992; lectr. in field. Contbr. over 150 articles to profl. jours.; editor 5 books; co-author text book. Recipient Food Engring. award Dairy and Food Industries Supply Assn. and Am. Soc. Agrl. Engring., 1987. Fellow Inst. Food Technologists (Wis. sect. 1968-87, N.Y. sect. 1988—, Travel award as promising young scientist to Interatn. Congress on Food Sci. and tech., Madrid 1974, pres. 1990-91, Internat. award 1995); mem. AIChE, Am. Inst. Nutrition, Am. Soc. Agrl. Engrs., Sigma Xi, Gamma Sigma Delta, Phi Tau Sigma. Avocations: golf, travel, wood working. Home: 56 Teeter Rd Ithaca NY 14850-8507

LUND, DAVID NATHAN, artist; b. N.Y.C., Oct. 16, 1925; s. Isidore and Mollie (Hirschfield) Lifshitz; m. Sally Harriet Amster, June 17, 1961 (dec. Feb. 1988); children: Andrew Ethan, Giuliana Elizabeth; m. Judith Manelis. BA, Queens Coll., 1948; postgrad., NYU, 1948-50. Adj. asst. prof. painting, drawing, design Cooper Union Art Sch., 1955-57, 59-66, 67-74; instr. painting Cummington (Mass.) Sch. Arts, 1963; instr. in painting Haystack Sch., Deer Isle, Maine, 1963; instr. in drawing and painting Parsons Sch. Design, 1963-66, 67-69; lectr. in drawing Queens Coll., 1964-66; vis. prof. painting Washington U., St. Louis, 1966-67, 85; asst. prof. painting and drawing Columbia U., 1969-82; vis. prof. painting Boston U., 1975-76; vis. critic; lectr. in field; juror Nat. Selection Com., Fulbright Grants In Art; cons. in painting Creative Artists Public Service, 1979-81; vis. artist Winston-Salem Arts Council and Associated Artists of Winston-Salem, 1975. One-man shows include Grand Central Moderns Gallery, N.Y.C., 1954, Galleria Trastevere, Rome, 1959, Grace Borgenicht Gallery, N.Y.C., 1960, 63, 66, 67, 69, 76, 78, 80, 83, 86, Martin Schweig Gallery, St. Louis, 1966, Kirkland Coll., 1971, Arts Council Winston-Salem, N.C., 1975, Creiger-Seson Gallery, Boston, 1981, Meredith Contemporary Art Gallery, Balt., 1982, U. Alaska, Fairbanks, 1983, Washington U., St. Louis, 1985, Allport Gallery, San Francisco, 1984, A.J. Laderman Fine Arts, Hoboken, N.J., 1990; group shows include Whitney Mus., N.Y.C., 1958, 60, 61, 62, 77, Galleria Schneider, Rome, 1959, Palazzo Venezia, Rome, 1959, Galleria San Marco, Rome, 1959, Washington Gallery Art, 1963, Am. embassy, Athens, Greece, 1966-67, White House, Washington, 1966-67, 67-68, 68-69, Nat. Collection Fine Arts, Washington, 1972-73; represented in permanent collections Whitney Mus., Balt. Mus., Toronto (Ont., Can.) Gallery Art, Art Gallery Ont., Toronto, Corcoran Gallery Art, Washington, Ft. Worth Art Center, U. Mass., Montclair (N.J.) Mus., Haas Gallery at Bloomsburg State Coll., Kranert Art Gallery, Champagne, Ill., also other public and pvt. collections. Fulbright grantee Rome, 1957-59. Mem. Nat. Acad. Design, Artists Equity. Jewish. Subject of numerous profl. publs.

LUND, DORIS HIBBS, retired dietitian; b. Des Moines, Nov. 10, 1923; d. Loyal Burchard and Catharine Mae (McClymond) Hibbs; m. Richard Bodholdt Lund, Nov. 9, 1946; children: Laurel Anne, Richard Douglas, Kristi Jane Lund Lozier. Student, Duchesne Coll., Omaha, 1941-42; BS, Iowa State U., 1946; postgrad., Grand View Coll., Des Moines, 1965; MS, Iowa State U., 1968. Registered dietitian, lic. dietitian. Clk. Russell Stover Candies, Omaha, 1940-42; chemist Martin Bomber Plant, Omaha, 1942-43; dietitian Grand Lake (Colo.) Lodge, 1946; tailoring instr. Ottumwa Pub. Schs., 1952-53; cookery instr. Des Moines Pub. Schs., 1958-62; dietitian Calvin Manor, Des Moines, 1963; home economist Am. Wool Coun./Am. Lamb Coun., Denver, 1963-65, The Merchandising Group of N.Y., 1965-68, Thomas Wolff, Pub. Rels., 1968-70; home economist weekly TV program Iowa Power Co., 1968-70; cons. in child nutrition programs Iowa Dept. Edn., Des Moines, 1970-95; ret. Nutritioneering, Ltd., 1995; Mem. Iowa Home Economists in Bus. (pres. 1962-63), PEO, Pi Beta Phi (Iowa Gamma chpt. pres. 1945-46). Pres. Callanan Jr. H.S. PTA, 1964, Roosevelt H.S. PTA, 1966; pres., mem. Ctrl. Presbyn. Mariners, Des Moines; ruling elder, clk. of session Ctrl. Presbyn. Session, Des Moines, 1972-78; bd. dirs. Ctrl. Found., 1996; amb. Friendship Force Internat., 1982—. Duchesne Coll. 4 yr. scholar. Mem. Iowa Home Economists in Bus. (pres. 1962-63), PEO, Pi Beta Phi (pres. 1945-46). Republican. Avocations: international travel, writing, sailing, sewing, cooking. Home: 105 34th St Des Moines IA 50312-4526

LUND, GEORGE EDWARD, retired electrical engineer; b. Phila., Feb. 17, 1925; s. Harold White and Hannah (Lawford) L.; m. Shirley Bolton Stevens, Sept. 24, 1960; 1 child, Gretchen Lund (Mrs. Kevin J. Collette); step-children: Marsha Stevens (Mrs. Donald Barnett), Roger Stevens, Sharon Stevens (Mrs. David Bailey). BEE, Drexel U., 1952; MEE, U. Pa., 1959; postgrad. in computer sci., Villanova U., 1981-83. Project engr. Burroughs Corp., Paoli, Pa., 1952-86; project engr. UNISYS Corp., Paoli, 1986-90, ret., 1990. Assoc. editor, contbr.: Digital Applications of Magnetic Devices, 1960; patentee in field. With USN, 1943-46, ETO. Mem. IEEE (sr.), Eta Kappa Nu. Republican. Methodist. Avocations: photography, amateur radio. Home: 923 Pinecroft Rd Berwyn PA 19312-2123

LUND, LOIS A., retired food science and human nutrition educator; b. Thief River Falls, Minn., Aug. 9, 1927; d. Robert J. and E. Luella (Tosdal) L. BS, U. Minn., 1949, MS, 1954, PhD, 1966. Instr. foods U. Iowa, 1951-55, U. Minn., 1955-63; assoc. prof., dir. core studies program, asst. dir. Sch. Home Econs., 1966-68; research fellow U.S. Dept. Agrl., 1963-66; assoc. dean, dir. Sch. Home Econs. Ohio State U., 1969-72; dean Coll. Human Ecology Mich. State U., East Lansing, 1973-85, prof. food sci. and human nutrition, 1985-96; ret., 1997; bd. dirs. Consumers Power Co., Jackson, Mich., CMS Energy, Dearborn, Mich. Contbr. articles to profl. jours. Recipient Betty award for excellence in teaching U. Minn., 1958, 63, 68, Hon. Alumni award Mich. State U., 1977, Outstanding Achievement award U. Minn. Alumni Assn., 1977. Mem. Am. Coun. on Consumer Interest, Am. Assn. Cereal Chemists, Inst. Food Technologists, Am. Agrl. Econs. Assn., Soc. for Nutrition Edn., Pi Lambda Theta, Phi Kappa Phi, Phi Upsilon Omicron, Omicron Nu (nat. treas. 1971-74, 84-86), Sigma Delta Epsilon. Lutheran. Avocation: gardening. Home: 5927 Shadowlawn Dr East Lansing MI 48823-2379

LUND, PETER ANTHONY, broadcast executive; b. Mpls., Jan. 12, 1941; s. Arthur Harold and Elizabeth (Rohan) L.; m. Theresa Mary Kessel, Sept. 3, 1960; children: Mark, Timothy. Ed., St. Thomas Coll., 1958-62. Announcer, sales rep. Sta. KCCR, Pierce, S.D., 1961-62; sales rep. Sta. KELO-TV, Sioux Falls, S.D., 1962-64; sales rep., sales mgr. Sta. WTTC, Mpls., 1964-66; gen. sales mgr. Westinghouse Broadcasting Co., 1966-71; v.p., gen. mgr. Sta. KSDO, San Diego, Calif., 1972-75, Sta. WTOP, Washington, 1975-77; v.p. CBS owned AM Stas., N.Y.C., 1977-80; v.p., gen. mgr. WBBM-TV, Chgo., 1980-83, WCBS-TV, N.Y.C., 1983-84; exec. v.p. CBS Sports, N.Y.C., 1984-85, pres., 1985-87; pres. Multimedia Entertainment, N.Y.C., 1987-90; exec. v.p., pres. CBS, 1990-94; exec. v.p., pres. CBS TV Network, N.Y.C., 1994-95; pres. CBS Broadcast Group, N.Y.C., 1995—; pres., CEO CBS Inc., 1995-97, CBS TV and Cable, 1997—. Office: CBS 51 W 52nd St New York NY 10019-6119

LUND, RITA POLLARD, aerospace consultant; b. Vallscreek, W.Va., Aug. 28, 1950; d. Willard Garfield and Faye Ethel (Perry) Pollard; m. James William Lund, Dec. 30, 1969. Student, Alexandria Sch. Nursing, 1969-70, Columbia Pacific U., 1989-91. Confidential asst. U.S. Ho. of Reps., Washington, 1975-76; exec. asst. White House Domestic Policy Staff, Washington, 1977-82; exec. asst. to dep. sci. advisor to pres. White House Sci. Office, Washington, 1982-83; asst. to pres. Telecom Futures Inc., Washington, 1983-84, v.p. for adminstrn., 1985-86; internat. accounts mgr. TFI Ltd., McLean, Va., 1987-89; ind. cons. telecom. Washington, 1989-90, aerospace cons., 1990—; rep. Scott Sci. & Tech., Washington, 1992—; cons. Vanguard Space Corp., Washington, 1992—; exec. dir. Puckett Bros. Co., Washington, 1995—; sec. ELS Corp., 1992; Washington rep. Scott Sci. & Tech., 1992—; cons. Vanguard Space Corp., 1992—; exec. dir. Puckett Brothers Corp., 1995—. Mem. AIAA, NAFE, Women in Aerospace, Am. Space Transp. Assn., Competitive Alliance Space Enterprise. Republican. Methodist. Avocations: tennis, traveling, genealogy, reading. Home: 9020 Patton Blvd Alexandria VA 22309-3334

LUND, VICTOR L., retail food company executive; b. Salt Lake City, 1947; married. BA, U. Utah, 1969, MBA, 1972. Audit mgr. Ernst and Whinney, Salt Lake City, 1972-77; sr. v.p. Skaggs Cos. Inc., from 1977; v.p., contr.

Am. Stores Co., 1980-83, sr. v.p., contr., from 1983, exec. v.p., co-chief exec. officer, vice-chmn., chief fin. and adminstrv. officer, pres., CEO, dir., 1992-95, now chmn., CEO, dir., 1995—. Office: Am Stores Co PO Box 27447 Salt Lake City UT 84127-0447 also: Am Stores Co 709 E South Temple Salt Lake City UT 84102-1205

LUND, VIRGINIA LLEGO, museum director, curator, chemistry educator; b. Dagupan, Philippines, Jan. 23, 1939; came to U.S., 1981; d. Moises Permolan and Cristina Rosario (Bautista) Llego; m. Dennis Wayne Lund, Feb. 21, 1979; 1 child, Tina Ruth. BS in Chemsitry, Silliman U., Dumaguete, Philippines, 1970; MS in Food Chemsitry, U. Philippines, 1977. Analyst, cosmetics dept. FDA, Manila, Philippines, 1971-72; instr. chemistry Foundation U., Dumaguete, 1972-77; acting chair dept. chemistry Foundation U., 1977-79; dir., curator The Frank House, U. Nebr., Kearney, 1990—; tech. cons. Pap Food Products, Manila, 1971-72; dir. cultural affairs Found. U., 1976-77; chem. lab. supr. U. Nebr., Kearney, 92-94. Bd. dirs. Buffalo County ARC, Kearney, 1990-93, vol. ARC, 1988—. Named Vol. of Yr., AMI Westpark Community Hosp., Hammond, La., 1987. Mem. Nat. Trust Historic Preservation, Victorian Soc. of Am., Buffalo County Hist. Soc., Nebr. Mus. Assn., Kearney Hospitality Group., Kearney C. of C., Am. Assn. of Mus. Avocations: collecting antiques, visiting historic homes, cooking. Home: 2010 W 24th St Kearney NE 68847-4908 Office: Frank House 905 W 25th St Kearney NE 68847-4238

LUND, WENDELL LUTHER, lawyer; b. Prentice, Wis., Dec. 31, 1905; s. Rev. Carl A. and Bertha Elizabeth L.; m. Anne Catherine Greve, Nov. 8, 1934 (dec.); children: Judith (Mrs. Barton Biggs), Carole (Mrs. John A. Benning), Mary Wendell; m. Marian Alice Hope, 1981. A.B., Augustana Coll., Rock Island, Ill., 1927, D.H.L., 1968; A.M., Columbia U., 1930; J.D., Georgetown U., 1938; Ph.D., Princeton U., 1933. Checker C.&N.W. R.R. (iron ore docks), Escanaba, Mich., 1922-23; worked in tie yard and iron ore docks C.&N.W. R.R. (iron ore docks), summers 1924-27; tchr. Upsala Coll., E. Orange, N.J., 1927-29; asso. prof. English Augustana Coll., 1930-31, exec. sec., 1933-34; exec. sec. Upper Monongahela Valley Com., Washington, 1934; mem. Taylor Act Com., Dept. Interior, 1934; sec. Mich Adminstrv. Bd., Lansing, 1941; exec. dir. Mich. Unemployment Compensation Com., 1941-42; dir. labor prodn. div. WPB, also mem. War Manpower Comm., 1942-43; spl. asst. to chmn. WPB, 1943; practicing atty., mem. firm Lund & O'Brien & predecessor firms, Washington, 1943—; chmn., CEO Schonstedt Instrument Co., 1993; Del. World Council of Chs., Evanston, 1954, Uppsala, Sweden, 1968; mem. Bd. Pensions, Lutheran Ch. in Am., 1963-67, 70-79, pres., 1967-68, 74-79; Democratic nominee for Congress, 11th Mich. Dist., 1940; presdl. elector, 1944. Contbr. articles to profl. jours. Bd. dirs. Augustana Coll., 1974-88. Mem. ABA, Bar Assn. D.C., Congl. Country Club (Washington), Burning Tree (Washington), Met. Club (Washington). Home: 1255 N Gulfstream Ave Sarasota FL 34236-8920

LUNDBACK, STAFFAN BENGT GUNNAR, lawyer; b. Stockholm, Sweden, Mar. 23, 1947; came to U.S., 1965; s. B. Holger and Ingrid (Fjellstrom) L.; m. Lee Craig, June 14,1969; children: Hadley Elizabeth, Erik Burchfield. Student, U. Stockholm, 1966-67; BA, U. Rochester, 1970; JD, Boston U., 1974. Bar: N.Y. 1975, Fla. 1983. Assoc. Nixon, Hargrave, Devans & Doyle, Rochester, N.Y., 1974-83; ptnr. Nixon, Hargrave, Devans & Doyle, Rochester, 1983—; bd. dirs. Scandinavian Seminar, Amherst, Mass.; chmn. Scanamerican Properties, Inc., Atlanta, 1989—. Mem. Swedish-Am. C. of C. (sec., bd. dirs. 1994—), Genesee Valley Club, Phi Beta Kappa. Avocations: music, literature, sports, current events, photography. Office: Nixon Hargrave Devans & Doyle PO Box 1051 Clinton First Sq Rochester NY 14603

LUNDBERG, GEORGE DAVID, II, medical editor, pathologist; b. Pensacola, Fla., Mar. 21, 1933; s. George David and Esther Louise (Johnson) L.; m. Nancy Ware Sharp, Aug. 18, 1956 (div.); children: George David III, Charles William, Carol Jean; m. Patricia Blacklidge Lorimer, Mar. 6, 1983; children: Christopher Leif, Melinda Suzanne. AA, North Park Coll., Chgo., 1950; BS, U. Ala., Tuscaloosa, 1952; MS, Baylor U., Waco, Tex., 1963; MD, Med. Coll. Ala., Birmingham, 1957; ScD (hon.), SUNY, Syracuse, 1988, Thomas Jefferson U., 1993, U. Ala., Birmingham, 1994, Med. Coll. Ohio, 1995. Intern Tripler Hosp., Hawaii; resident Brooke Hosp., San Antonio; assoc. prof. pathology U. So. Calif., Los Angeles, 1967-72, prof., 1972-77; assoc. dir. labs. Los Angeles County-U. So. Calif. Med. Ctr., 1968-77; prof., chmn. dept. pathology U. Calif.-Davis, Sacramento, 1977-82; v.p. scientific info., editor Jour. AMA, Chgo., 1982—, editor in chief scientific publ., 1991-95; editor in chief AMA Sci. Info. and Multimedia, Chgo., 1995—; vis. prof. U. London, 1976, Lund U., Sweden, 1976; prof. clin. pathology Northwestern U., Chgo., 1982—; adj. prof. health policy Harvard U., Boston, 1993—; vis. prof. pathology, 1994-96. Author, editor: Managing the Patient Focused Laboratory, 1975, Using the Clinical Laboratory in Medical Decision Making, 1983, 51 Landmark Articles in Medicine, 1984, AIDS From the Beginning, 1986, Caring the the Uninsured and Underinsured, 1991, Violence, 1992, 100 Years of JAMA Landmark Articles, 1997; contbr. articles to profl. jours. Served to lt. col. M.C., U.S. Army, 1956-67. Fellow Am. Soc. Clin. Pathologists (past pres.), Am. Acad. Forensic Sci.; mem. N.Y. Acad. Scis., Inst. Medicine, Alpha Omega Alpha. Democrat. Episcopalian. Office: JAMA 515 N State St Chicago IL 60610-4325

LUNDBLAD, ROGER LAUREN, research director; b. San Francisco, Oct. 31, 1939; s. Lauren Alfred and Doris Ruth (Peterson) L.; m. Susan Hawly Taylor, Oct. 15, 1966 (div. 1985); children: Christina Susan, Cynthia Karin. BSc, Pacific Luth. U., 1961; PhD, U. Wash., 1965. Rsch. assoc. U. Wash., Seattle, 1965-66, Rockefeller U., N.Y.C., 1966-68; asst. prof. U. N.C., Chapel Hill, 1968-71, assoc. prof., 1971-77, prof. pathology and biochemistry, 1977-91; adj. prof., 1991—; dir. sci. tech. devel. Baxter-Biotech, Duarte, Calif., 1991—; vis. scientist Hyland div. Baxter Healthcare, Glendale, Calif., 1988-89. Author: Chemical Reagents for Protein Modification, 1984, 2d edit., 1990; editor: Chemistry and Biology of Thrombin, 1977, Chemistry and Biology of Heparin, 1980, Techniques in Protein Modification, 1994; editor-in-chief: Biotechnology and Applied Biochemistry, 1996—; contbr. articles to profl. jours. Recipient Career Achievement award U. N.C., 1986. Mem. Am. Soc. Biochem. Molecular Biology, Am. Soc. Microbiology, Am. Heart Assn., Sigma Xi. Office: Baxter Biotech Hyland Divsn 1720 Flower Ave Duarte CA 91010-2923

LUNDE, ASBJORN RUDOLPH, lawyer; b. S.I., N.Y., July 17, 1927; s. Karl and Elisa (Andenes) L.; AB, Columbia U., 1947, LLB, 1949. Bar: N.Y. 1949. Since practiced in N.Y.C.; with firm Kramer, Marx, Greenlee & Backus, and predecessors, 1950-68, mem., 1958-68; individual practice law, 1968—; bd. dirs., v.p. Orchestra da Camera, Inc., 1964—; bd. dirs. Sara Roby Found., 1971—, The Drawing Soc., 1977—. Mem. ABA, N.Y. State Bar Assn., Assn. Bar City N.Y., Met. Opera Club, East India Club (London); life fellow Met. Mus. Art, N.Y.C. Art collector, donor paintings and sculptures to Met. Mus. Art, N.Y.C., Nat. Gallery Art, Washington, Mus. Fine Arts, Boston, Clark Art Inst., Williamstown, Mass., others. Home and Office: 135 LaBranche Rd Hillsdale NY 12529-5713

LUNDE, HAROLD IRVING, management educator; b. Austin, Minn., Apr. 18, 1929; s. Peter Oliver and Emma (Stoa) L.; m. Sarah Jeanette Lysne, June 25, 1955; children: Paul, James, John, Thomas. B.A., St. Olaf Coll., 1952; M.A., U. Minn., 1954, Ph.D., 1966. Assoc. prof. econs. Macalester Coll., St. Paul, 1957-64; fin. staff economist Gen. Motors Corp., N.Y.C., 1965-67; corp. sec. Dayton Hudson Corp., Mpls., 1967-70; mgr. planning and gen. research May Dept. Stores Co., St. Louis, 1970-72; v.p. planning and research May Dept. Stores Co., 1972-78; exec. v.p. adminstrn. Kobacker Stores, Inc., Columbus, Ohio, 1979; prof. mgmt. Bowling Green (Ohio) State U., 1980—. Mem. Acad. Internat. Bus., Acad. Mgmt., Am. Econ. Assn., Nat. Assn. Bus. Economists, Planning Forum, Case Research Assn., Decision Scis. Inst., Phi Beta Kappa, Phi Kappa Phi, Omicron Delta Kappa, Beta Gamma Sigma. Home: 880 Country Club Dr Bowling Green OH 43402-1602 Office: Bowling Green State U Dept Mgmt Bowling Green OH 43403

LUNDE, KATHERINE LAMONTAGNE, educational consultant; b. Kankakee, Ill., May 3, 1947; d. James Armond and Frances Elizabeth (Maas) LaMontagne; m. Walter A. Lunde Jr., June 15,1969; children: Lisa Christine, Walter James. BS, No. Ill. U., 1969; postgrad., Jacksonville (Fla.) U., 1972. Cert. elem., secondary and early childhood educator. Tchr. 1st grade Kenwood Elem. Sch., Ft. Walton Beach, Fla.; kindergarten tchr., supr. Orange Park (Fla.) Kindergarten; asst. dir. Stoneway Sch., Stoneway Pvt. Sch., Plano, Tex.; former dir. Westminster Preschool and Kindergarten, Dallas; exec. dir. edn. TLC Child Devel. Ctr., Legacy, Tex.; dep. gov. Am. Biog. Rsch. Inst. (life); internat. motivational spkr. spkr.'s bur. Assn. Childhood Edn. Internat.; exec. dir. TLC Child Devel. Ctr., Legacy. Track coach Spl. Olympics, 1981-83; learning disabilities tutor, 1978-85; bd. dirs. Mi Escuelita Preschs., Inc., 1985-90, v.p. bd. dirs., 1989-90. Grantee Sewell Fund, Lard Trust; recipient Christa McAuliffe Outstanding Educator award, 1994. Mem. ASCD, Nat. Assn. Edn. Young Children (life), Dallas Assn. Edn. Young Children, Kappa Delta Pi.

LUNDEBERG, PHILIP KARL BORAAS, curator; b. Mpls., June 14, 1923; s. Olav Knutson and Vivian Juliet (Boraas) L.; m. Eleanore Lillian Berntson, July 18, 1953; 1 son, Karl Fredrik. BA summa cum laude, Duke U., 1944, MA, 1947; PhD, Harvard U., 1954. Asst. to historian U.S. Naval Ops. in World War II, Navy Dept., 1950-53; asst. prof. history St. Olaf Coll., 1953-55, U.S. Naval Acad., 1955-59; assoc. curator naval history Nat. Mus. History and Tech., Smithsonian Instn., 1959-61, curator of naval history, 1961-84, curator emeritus, 1984—; v.p. Am. Mil. Inst., 1968-71, pres., 1971-73; chmn. Internat. Congress Maritime Museums, 1972-75; v.p. U.S. Commn. on Mil. History, 1975-79, pres., 1980-83; sec. Internat. Commn. Mus. Security, 1975-79; pres. Coun. Am. Maritime Museums, 1976-78. Author: The Continental Gunboat Philadelphia, 1966, 2d edit., 1995, Samuel Colt's Submarine Battery, 1974; co-author: Sea Power: A Naval History, 1960, 81; contbg. author: Guide to the Sources of U.S. Military History, 1975, 93, Seafaring and Society, 1987, To Die Gallantly, 1994, The Battle of the Atlantic (1939-1945), 1994; editor: Bibliographie de L'Histoire des Grandes Routes Maritimes: États-Unis D'Amèrique, 1970; exhibits: Armed Forces of U.S., 1961, By Sea and by Land, 1981. With USNR, 1943-83, 89, comdr. Res. ret., 1992. Decorated Bronze Star, Purple Heart; recipient Bronze medal Internat. Commn. Mil. History, 1975; Austin fellow Harvard U., 1949. Fellow Am. Mil. Inst. (Moncado prize 1964); mem. Coun. Am. Maritime Mus. (hon.), N.Am. Soc. for Oceanic History, Naval Hist. Found., Naval Order of U.S., Internat. Congress Maritime Mus. (life mem.), Soc. for Mil. History, Phi Beta Kappa. Home: 1107 Croton Dr Alexandria VA 22308-2009

LUNDELIUS, ERNEST LUTHER, JR., vertebrate paleontologist, educator; b. Austin, Tex., Dec. 2, 1927; s. Ernest Luther and Hazel (Halton) L.; m. Judith Weiser, Sept. 28, 1953; children—Jennifer, Rolf Eric. B.S. in Geology, U. Tex., 1950; Ph.D. in Paleozoology, U. Chgo., 1954. Postdoctoral Fulbright scholar to Western Australia, 1954-55; postdoctoral research fellow Calif. Inst. Tech., 1956-57; mem. faculty U. Tex., Austin, 1957—; prof. vertebrate paleontology U. Tex., 1969; John Andrew Wilson prof. vertebrate paleontology, 1978—. Served with AUS, 1946-47. Fulbright sr. scholar to Australia, 1976. Home: 7310 Running Rope Austin TX 78731-2132 Office: U Tex Dept Geol Scis Austin TX 78712

LUNDEN, JOAN, television personality; b. Fair Oaks, CA, Sept. 19, 1950; d. Erle Murray and Gladyce Lorraine (Somervill) Blunden; children: Jamie Beryl, Lindsay Leigh, Sarah Emily. Student, Universidad de Las Americas, Mexico City, U. Calif., Calif. State U., Am. River Coll., Sacramento, Calif. Began broadcasting career as co-anchor and prodr. at Sta. KCRA-TV and Radio, Sacramento, 1973-75; with Sta. WABC-TV, N.Y.C., 1975—, co-anchor, 1976-80; co-host Good Morning America, ABC-TV, 1980—; host spl. report for Whittle Comm.; host Everyday with Joan Lunden, 1989; (TV spl.) Behind Closed Doors With Joan Lunden, 1994, 95; film appearances include: Macho Callahan, 1970, What About Bob?, 1991; co-author: (with Andy Friedburg) Good Morning, I'm Joan Lunden, 1986, (with Michael Krauss) Joan Lunden's Mother's Minutes, 1986, Your Newborn Baby, Healthy Cooking For Your Family With Joan Lunden; syndicated columnist: Parent's Notes. Recipient Outstanding Mother of Yr. award, Nat. Mother's Day Com., 1982; Albert Einstein Coll. of Yeshiva U. Spirit of Achievement award; Nat. Women's Polit. Caucus award; NJ Divsn. of Civil Rights award; Baylor U. Outstanding Woman of the Year award. Office: Good Morning Am 147 Columbus Ave New York NY 10023-5900*

LUNDERGAN, BARBARA KEOUGH, lawyer; b. Chgo., Nov. 6, 1938; d. Edward E. and Eleanor A. (Erickson) Keough; m. James A. Lundergan, Dec. 29, 1962; children—Matthew K., Mary Alice. B.A., U. Ill., 1960; J.D., Loyola U., Chgo., 1964. Bar: Ill. 1964, U.S. Dist. Ct. (no. dist.) Ill. 1964, U.S. Tax Ct. 1974. With Seyfarth, Shaw, Fairweather & Geraldson, Chgo., 1964—, ptnr., 1971—. Fellow Am. Coll. Trust and Estate Counsel; mem. ABA (com. on fed. taxation), Ill. Bar Assn. (coun. sect. on fed. taxation 1983-91, chair 1989, coun. sect. on trusts and estates sect. coun. 1992—, sec. 1996—, editl. bd. Ill. Bar Jour. 1993-96), Chgo. Bar Assn. (chmn. trust law com. 1982-83, com. on fed. taxation). Office: Seyfarth Shaw Fairweather & Geraldson 55 E Monroe St Chicago IL 60603-5701

LUNDGREN, CARL WILLIAM, JR., physicist; b. Columbus, Sept. 17, 1933; s. Carl William and Anne Katherine (Kuntz) L.; BEE, U. Cin., 1957, MS, 1959, PhD, 1961; m. Virginia Anne Cullis, Dec. 7, 1963; children: David John, Janet Marie. Coop. undergrad. engr. Govt. Products div. Avco Corp., Cin. and Evendale, Ohio, 1953-56; asst. supr., research fellow Basic Sci. Research Lab., U. Cin., 1959-61; mem. tech. staff Bell Telephone Labs., Murray Hill, N.J., 1961-66, Holmdel, N.J., 1966-84; dist. mgr. advanced fiber optics planning Bell Communications Rsch. Inc., Red Bank, N.J., 1984-92; dir. transmission systems engring. Bellcore, Morristown and Red Bank, 1992-95; dist. mgr., tech. cons. local access architecture AT&T, Holmdel, N.J., 1996—. Capt., Signal Corps, U.S. Army, 1961-63. Mem. AAAS, IEEE, N.Y. Acad. Sci., Optical Soc. Am., Nat. Spectrum Mgrs. Assn., Gideons Internat., Sierra Club, Delta Tau Delta, Tau Beta Pi, Eta Kappa Nu, Phi Eta Sigma, Omicron Delta Kappa. Republican. Episcopalian. Contbr. articles to profl. jours.; patentee in field. Home: 60 Woodhollow Rd Colts Neck NJ 07722-1323 Office: AT&T 101 Crawfords Rd Holmdel NJ 07733

LUNDGREN, LEONARD, III, retired secondary education educator; b. San Francisco, June 22, 1933; s. Leonard II and Betty (Bosold) L.; m. Jane Gates, June 12, 1976. AA, City Coll. San Francisco, 1952; AB, San Francisco State U., 1954, MA, 1958, postgrad., 1958-71. Cert. tchr., Calif. Phys. edn. tchr., athletic coach Pelton Jr. High Sch., San Francisco, 1958-59; social studies tchr., dept. chair, phys. edn. tchr., athletic coach Luther Burbank Jr. High Sch., San Francisco, 1959-78; history, govt. econs., geography tchr. George Washington High Sch., San Francisco, 1978-93; water safety instr. ARC, San Francisco, 1946-61; mem. Calif. Quality Teaching Ctr. Conf. Bd., 1965-67. Author: Guide for Films and Filmstrips, 1966, Teacher's Handbook for Social Studies, 1966, Guide for Minority Studies, 1968. V.p. Lakeside Property Owners Assn., San Francisco, 1986-88, legis. advocate, 1988-95; v.p. West of Twin Peaks Coun., San Francisco, 1986-87; pub. affairs polit. econ. cons., Calif., 1993—. With USN, 1954-56. Fulbright scholar, Greece, 1963; recipient Svc. Pin, ARC, 1961. Mem. NEA (life, del. 1970, 72-76), Calif. Tchrs. Assn. (state coun. rep. 1963-74), Nat. Coun. Social Studies, Calif. Coun. Social Studies (v.p. San Francisco chpt. 1969-70), San Francisco Classroom Tchrs. Assn. (pres. 1972-73, Gavel award 1973), PTA (sch. v.p. 1980-81), Calif. Ret. Tchrs. Assn. (life, legislation chmn. San Francisco divsn. 1995—), Am. Assn. Ret. Persons (cmty. coord. San Francisco 1996—), San Francisco State U. Alumni Assn. (life, treas. 1959), Calif. Assn. Health, Phys. Edn., Recreation and Dance (life, treas. San Francisco chpt. 1959-60), Nat. Geog. Soc. (life), Phi Delta Kappa (life, pres. chpt. 1965-66). Avocations: travel, swimming, gardening, research, service. *A career in education for me is my life from learning to teaching over and over again. History, government, geography and economics are my major subjects. World travel gives me the chance to see the places I studied and taught.*

LUNDIN, BRUCE THEODORE, engineering and management consultant; b. Alameda, Calif., Dec. 28, 1919; s. Oscar Linus and Elizabeth Ellen (Erickson) L.; m. Barbara Ann Bliss, July 27, 1946 (wid. Feb. 1981); children: Dianne, Robert, Nancy; m. Jean Ann Oberlin, Mar. 22, 1982. BSME, U. Calif.-Berkeley, 1942; D of Engring. (hon.), U. Toledo, 1975. Chief engine research NASA Lewis Ctr., Cleve., 1952-58, asst. dir., 1958-61, assoc. dir., 1961-68, dir., 1969-77; dep. assoc. adminstrn. NASA, Washington, 1968-69; adv. U.S. Air Force Sci. Adv. Bd., Washington, 1961-77; mem. Aerospace Safety Adv. Bd., Washington, 1961-72; staff dir. Pres.'s Commn. on the Accident at Three Mile Island, 1981; mem. TM1-2 Safety Adv. Bd., 1981-89; chmn. Rockwell Internat. Safety Oversight Panel, 1988-89. Pres. Westshore Unitarian Ch., Rocky River, Ohio, 1967-68; trustee Southwest Gen. Hosp., Berea, Ohio, 1970-75. Recipient Outstanding Leadership medal NASA, 1965, Pub. Service award NASA, 1971, 75, Disting. Service medal NASA, 1971, 77, Engineer of the Year award Nat. Space Club, 1975. Fellow AIAA; mem. Nat. Acad. Engring. Avocations: woodworking; gardening; reading; travel. Home: 5859 Columbia Rd North Olmsted OH 44070-4611

LUNDIN, RICHARD ALLEN, career military officer, federal government administrator, educator; b. Holyoke, Mass., Feb. 19, 1937; s. Gustav Regner and Frances (Gaston) L.; m. Dolores Segovia, Nov. 19, 1962; children: Valerie Frances, Joanie Elizabeth, Dana James. AA, Am. River Jr. Coll., 1970; BA, Golden Gate U., 1973, MBA, 1976; EdD, LaSalle U., 1997; diploma, Command and Gen. Staff Coll. U.S. Army, 1985, Air War Coll., 1989. Cert. tchr., Calif.; instr. cert. U.S. Army. Commd. USAF, 1954, advanced through grades to lt. col., 1977; with res. USAR, Calif., 1962—; with Gen. Services Adminstrn. USN, USAF, Tex. and Calif.; col. Calif. NG, 1993; instr. USAR, 1985—; adj. profl. Golden Gate U., San Francisco, 1978—; cons. contracts, mktg., edn.; adminstr. Chapman Coll., 1994. Asst. chmn. Waterfront Planning Commn., Benicia, Calif. 1982-84; mem. Utility User Tax Com., Benicia, 1984; Sister Cities Com., Benecia, 1982-86; active Calif. Rep. Assembly; Solano County Parole Commr., 1992-95; mem. WWII Commemorative Com. Calif., 1995; rep. ctrl. com.; Solano County U.S. Savings Bond rep., 1995-96; registrar Selective Svc., 1997. Recipient Sister Cities Com. Appreciation award Mayor of Tula, Hidalgo, Mex., 1985, Benicia City Appreciation award, Mayor of Benicia, 1984. Mem. Res. Officers Assn. U.S. Army (pres.), Nat. Contracts Mgmt. Assn. (mem. chmn.), Golden Gate U. Alumni Assn., Benicia C. of C., VFW, AUSA, Am. Legion. Republican. Roman Catholic. Club: Yacht (Benicia). Lodge: K.C., Knights Templar.

LUNDING, CHRISTOPHER HANNA, lawyer; b. Evanston, Ill., June 15, 1946; s. Franklin J. and Virginia (Hanna) L.; children: Elizabeth, Nelson, Alexander, Andrew, Kirsten; m. Barbara J. Fontana, Aug. 19, 1989. BA, Harvard U., 1968; JD, Yale U., 1971. Bar: N.Y. 1972, Fla. 1972, U.S. Supreme Ct. 1975. Law clk. to judge 2d Cir. U.S. Ct. Appeals, N.Y.C., 1971-72; assoc. Cleary, Gottlieb, Steen & Hamilton, N.Y.C., 1973-79, ptnr., 1980—; chmn. Legal Svcs. N.Y.C., 1987-94. Chmn. Belle Haven Tax Dist., Greenwich, Conn., 1986-96. Fellow Am. Bar Found.; mem. N.Y. County Lawyers Assn. (bd. dirs. 1988-94). Episcopalian. Office: Cleary Gottlieb Steen & Hamilton Ste 4300 1 Liberty Plz Rm 4300 New York NY 10006-1404

LUNDQUIST, CHARLES ARTHUR, university official; b. Webster, S.D., Mar. 26, 1928; s. Arthur Reynald and Olive Esther (Parks) L.; m. Patricia Jean Richardson, Nov. 28, 1951; children: Clara Lee, Dawn Elizabeth, Frances Johanna, Eric Arthur, Gary Lars. BS, S.D. State U., 1949, DSc, 1979; PhD, U. Kans., 1953. Asst. prof. engring. research Pa. State U., 1953-54; sect. chief U.S. Army Ballistic Missile Agy., Huntsville, Ala., 1956-60; br. chief (NASA-Marshall Space Flight Center), Huntsville, 1960-62; dir. Space Scis. Lab., 1973-81; asst. dir. sci. Smithsonian Astrophys. Obs., Cambridge, Mass., 1962-73; assoc. Harvard Coll. Obs., 1962-73; dir. rsch. U. Ala., Huntsville, 1982-90, assoc. v.p. for rsch., 1990-96, dir. consortium for materials devel. in space, 1985—. Editor: (with G. Veis) Smithsonian Institution Standard Earth, 1966, The Physics and Astronomy of Space Science, 1966, Skylab's Astronomy and Space Sciences, 1979. Served with U.S. Army, 1954-56. Recipient Exceptional Sci. Achievement medal NASA, 1971; Hermann Oberth award AIAA, 1978. Mem. AAAS, Am. Grophys. Union, Am. Astron. Soc., Am. Phys. Soc., Nat. Speleological Soc. Home: 214 Jones Valley Dr SW Huntsville AL 35802-1724 Office: U Ala Research Instit Rm M-65 Huntsville AL 35899

LUNDQUIST, DANA R., health insurance executive; b. Mpls., Sept. 12, 1941; s. R. Dana and Mary Jane (Norton) L.; children: Brenda A., Sheila R. BA, Valparaiso U., 1963; postgrad., U. Hawaii, 1963-64, U. Colo., 1963; MBA, U. Chgo., 1966. Adminstrv. asst. U. Chgo. Hosps. and Clinics, 1966-67, asst. supt., 1967-68, asst. dir., 1968-70; officer, bd. dirs. affiliates Hamot Health Systems, Inc., Erie, Pa., 1970-92, pres. parent co., 1981-92, cons. to bd., 1993—; cons. Highmark Blue Cross Blue Shield, 1992-93, sr. v.p.,1993-96; lectr. grad. program in hosp. adminstrn. U. Chgo., 1967-70; mem. Erie County Hosp. Coun., 1978-92, pres., 1982; bd. dirs. Hosp. Coun. Western Pa., 1978-92, vice chmn.; exec. com. Pa. Coun. Teaching Hosps., 1986-90; adv. coun. risk mgmt. Pa. Hosp. Ins. Co., 1982-90, bd. dirs. Vol. Hosps. Am. of Pa., 1985-92, chmn. bd.; bd. visitors The Behrend Coll., Pa. State U., 1990-92; bd. dirs. Pa. Med. Coll., 1991-92, Hardware Hawaii, 1989—. Mem. Erie Conf. on Community Devel., 1981-92, bd. dirs., 1988-92; bd. dirs. N.W. Pa. Buy Right Coun., 1986-92, United Way Erie County, 1983-92; mem. pres.'s coun. Villa Maria Coll., Erie, 1981-90, bd. incorporators Gannon U., Erie, 1981-92; mem. governing bd. St. Paul's Luth. Ch., Erie, 1973-78, v.p., 1974-78; mem. Erie Down Town Coalition Steering Com., 1990-92, chmn., 1991-92, numerous other activities. Mem. Am. Coll. Healthcare Execs. (former regents adv. coun. Pa.); mem. Am. Hosp. Assn. (governing coun. sect. met. hosps. 1987, alt. ho. of dels. 1988), Hosp. Assn. Pa. (polit. action com. 1981-92), Pa. C. of C., U. Chgo. Hosp. Alumni Assn. (exec. com. 1967-70, 87-92, sec.-treas. 1988, pres. 1990-91), Downtown Athletic Club, Rotary. Lutheran. Office: PO Box 22130 Pittsburgh PA 15222-0130

LUNDQUIST, GENE ALAN, cotton company executive; b. Bakersfield, Calif., Feb. 25, 1943; s. Felix Waldemar and Elsia Geneva (Bartlett) L.; m. Linda Fern Smotherman, June 17, 1966; 1 child, Nels Eric. B.S., Colo. State U., 1964. Info. specialist Calcot Ltd., Bakersfield, 1969-71, field rep., 1971-74, asst. v.p., 1974-77, asst. v.p., corp. sec., 1977-80, v.p., corp. sec., 1980—; bd. dirs. Calif. Farm Water Coalition, Water Assn. Kern County; apptd. Calif. Gov.'s Agrl. Summit. Bd. dirs. Kern County Water Agy., Bakersfield, 1975-91, dir., 1996—; bd. dirs. Bakersfield Salvation Army, 1985-88. Served with U.S. Army, 1965-67. Decorated Army Commendation medal; Calif. Agr. Leadership Found. fellow, 1973. Mem. Cotton Bd. (alt. dir. 1984—), Nat. Cotton Council Am. (del. 1984—), Calif. Cotton Growers Assn. (adv. com. 1976—), Calif. Planting Cotton Seed Distbrs. (adv. com. 1976—). Republican. Mem. Mennonite Brethren Ch. Avocations: golf; tennis; running; landscaping; reading. Office: Calcot Ltd 1601 E Brundage Ln PO Box 259 Bakersfield CA 93302

LUNDQUIST, JOHN MILTON, librarian, author, travel writer, photographer; b. Twin Falls, Idaho, Sept. 22, 1938; s. Milton Rocine and Mildred (Toolson) L.; m. Suzanne Evertsen, Sept. 6, 1966 (div. July 1985); children: Jennifer, Lila, Eric, Margaret, John, Jack. BA in History, Portland State U., 1970; MLS, Brigham Young U., 1972; MA in Near Eastern Studies, U. Mich., 1974, PhD in Near Eastern Studies, 1983. Instr. anthropology and religious instrn. Brigham Young U., Provo, Utah, 1979-83, asst. prof. anthropology and religious instrn., 1983-85; mem. faculty New Sch. for Social Rsch., N.Y.C., 1986-88; Susan and Douglas chief libr. Oriental divsn. N.Y. Pub. Libr., N.Y.C., 1985—; rschr. Archive for Rsch. in Archetypal Symbolism, N.Y.C., 1987—; lectr. Inst. for Asian Studies, Inc., N.Y.C., C.G. Jung Found., N.Y.; adj. assoc. prof. art history and archaeology Columbia U., N.Y.C., 1987-89; adj. assoc. prof. Near Eastern langs. and lit. NYU, 1987; adj. instr. grad. studies divsn. Fashion Inst. Tech., N.Y.C., 1966—; spkr., lectr. in field; dir. excavation Am. Sch. Oriental Rsch., Tell Quarqur, Syria, 1981-85, field archaeologist, Syria, 1979-82; area supr. Am. Expedition to Tell Hadidi, Syria, summers 1974-76; extensive travel, rsch., field work China, Tibet, Japan, Hong Kong, Taiwan, India, Indonesia, others; guest scholar Japan Ctr. for Area Studies, Nat. Mus. Ethnology, Osaka, Mar. 1996. Author: The Temple: Meeting Place of Heaven and Earth, 1993, Japanese edit., 1994, Babylon in European Writing and Art Civilizations of the Ancient Near East, 1995; contbr. articles to The N.Y. Times, United Airlines Hemispheres, and other publs.; translator langs. and lang. behavior abstracts. Bd. advisors The Asian Classics Inst., 1995—. Mem. Internat. Assn. Orientalist Librs., Am. Inst. Archaeology (bd. govs. N.Y.C. chpt.), Am. Schs. Oriental Rsch. (corp. instnl. rep. 1985—), Oriental Club N.Y.C. (pres. 1992-95), East Side Conservative Club, Phi Kappa Phi. Republican. Mormon. Avocation: marathon running. Home: 881 7th Ave # 1001 New York NY 10019-3210 Office: NY Pub Libr Oriental Divsn Fifth Ave and 42d St New York NY 10018

LUNDQUIST, WEYMAN IVAN, lawyer; b. Worcester, Mass., July 27, 1930; s. Hilding Ivan and Florence Cecilia (Westerholm) L.; m. Joan Durrell,

Sept. 15, 1956 (div. July 1977); children—Weyman, Erica, Jettora, Kirk; m. Kathryn E. Taylor, Dec. 28, 1978; 1 child, Derek. BA magna cum laude, Dartmouth Coll., 1952; LLB, Harvard U., 1955. Bar: Mass. 1955, Alaska 1961, Calif. 1963, Vt. 1994. Assoc. Thayer, Smith & Gaskill, Worcester, 1957-60; atty. U.S. Attys. Office, Mass. and Alaska, 1960-62; assoc. Heller, Ehrman, White & McAuliffe, San Francisco, 1963-65, ptnr., 1967—; counsel, v.p. State Mut. Life Ins. Co., Worcester, 1965-67; vis. prof. environ. studies Dartmouth Coll., Hanover, N.H., 1980, 84, bus. sch., 1997, vis. scholar, 1994-97; vis. scholar Dickey Ctr. for Internat. Understanding, 1994—; program chmn. 1990 Moscow Conf. on Law and Bilateral Econs. Rels.; mem. U.S. adv. com. Alaska/Can./Soviet No. Justice Conf., 1993-94, N.Y., San Francisco Cutting Edge Lawyer Liability Programs, 1989; adv. bd. U. Press New England, 1997; dir. West Coast Magnetics, Stockton, Calif. Author: (fiction) The Promised Land, 1987; contbr. articles to profl. jours. Trustee Natural Resources Def. Coun., 1982-91. Recipient CPR Significant Achievement award, 1987. Fellow ABA (founder and chmn. litigation sect. 1978-79, chmn. Soviet Bar Assn. liaison com. 1986, co-chmn. spl. com. for study discovery abuse 1976-83, spl. com. on tort liability sys. 1981-84, superfund 301e study group advisor to U.S. Congress, 1983), Am. Coll. Trial Lawyers; mem. Dartmouth Lawyer's Assn. (founding mem.), Am. Antiquarian Soc. (councillor), Fgn. Rels. Coun., Assn. Life Ins. Coun., U.S. Supreme Ct. Hist. Soc., No. Dist. Hist. Soc., Dartmouth Lawyers Assn., Swedish Am. C. of C. (pres., bd. dirs. western area U.S. 1982-89). Avocations: squash, skiing, writing. Home: 16 Occum Rdg Hanover NH 03755-1410 Office: Heller Ehrman White & McAuliffe 333 Bush St San Francisco CA 94104-2806 also: PO Box 200 Norwich VT 05055-0200

LUNDSTEDT, SVEN BERTIL, behavioral and social scientist, educator; b. N.Y.C., May 6, 1926; s. Sven David and Edith Maria L.; m. Jean Elizabeth Sanford, June 16, 1951; children: Margaret, Peter, Janet. AB, U. Chgo., 1952, PhD, 1955; SM, Harvard U., 1960. Lic. in psychology, N.Y., Ohio; cert. Council for Nat. Register of Health Services. Asst. dir. Found. for Research on Human Behavior, 1960-62; asst. prof. Case-Western Res. U., Cleve., 1962-64, assoc. prof., 1964-68; assoc. prof. adminstrv. sci. Ohio State U., Columbus, 1968-69, prof. pub. policy and mgmt., 1969—, Ameritech Research prof., 1987-89, prof. internat. bus. and pub. policy, 1988—; prof. mgmt. and human resources, 1990—; affiliate scientist Battelle PNL, 1994—; chmn. Battelle endowment program for tech. and human affairs, 1976-80, mem. Univ. Senate; dir. project on edn. of chief exec. officer Aspen Inst., 1978-80; advisor Task Force on Innovation, U.S. Ho. of Reps., 1983-84, Citizens Network for Fgn. Affairs, 1988—; mem. Am. Com. on U.S. Soviet Relations, 1985—, chair trade and negotiation project; cons. E.I. duPont de Nemours & Co., B.F. Goodrich Co., Bell Telephone Labs., Battelle Meml. Inst., Nat. Fulbright Award Com.; invited speaker Royal Swedish Acad. Scis., 1989. Author: Higher Education in Social Psychology, 1968; co-author: Managing Innovation, 1982, Managing Innovation and Change, 1989; author, editor: Telecommunications, Values and the Public Interest, 1990; contbr. articles to profl. jours. Pres., Cleve. Mental Health Assn., 1966-68; mem. Ohio Citizen's Task Force on Corrections, 1971-72. Served with U.S. Army, 1944-46. Harvard U. fellow, 1960; grantee Bell Telephone Labs., 1964-65, NSF, 1965-67, Kettering Found., 1978-80, Atlantic Richfield Found., 1980-82, German Marshall Fund of U.S. to conduct internat. ednl. joint ventures on econ. negotiations, Budapest, Hungary, 1990; recipient Ohio Ho. of Reps. award, 1986. Mem. Am. Psychol. Assn., Internat. Inst. for Applied Systems Analysis (innovation task force, nat. adv. com. project internat. negotiation with Am. Acad. Arts and Scis., founder, chmn. U.S. Midwest Assn. for IIASA 1986—, sr. social sci. advisor 1994—), Am. Acad. Arts and Scis. (chmn. PIN com. on east/west trade negotiation), Am. Soc. for Pub. Adminstrn. (pres. Central Ohio chpt. 1975-77, founder, chmn. com. on bus. govt. relations, 1977-79, editorial bd. Pub. Adminstrn. Rev., 1978-82), Internat. Soc. Panetics (sec. bd. govs., founding mem.). Unitarian. Home: 197 Riverview Park Dr Columbus OH 43214-2023 Office: Ohio State U Sch Pub Policy and Mgmt 1775 S College Rd Columbus OH 43210-1309

LUNDSTROM, GILBERT GENE, banker, lawyer; b. Gothenburg, Nebr., Sept. 27, 1941; s. Vernon G. and Imogene (Jackett) L.; m. Joyce Elaine Ronin, June 26, 1965; children: Trevor A., Gregory G. BS, U. Nebr., 1964, JD, 1969; MBA, Wayne State U., 1966. Bar: U.S. Dist. Ct. (1st dist.) Nebr. 1969, Nebr. 1969, U.S. Ct. Appeals (5th cir.) 1970, U.S. Ct. Appeals (10th cir.) 1971, U.S. Ct. Appeals (8th cir.) 1974, U.S. Ct. Appeals (3d cir.) 1986. Ptnr. Woods & Aitken, Lincoln, Nebr., 1969-93; pres., CEO First Fed. Lincoln Bank, 1994—; part-time faculty law sch. U. Nebr.-Lincoln, 1970-74; dir. First Fed. Lincoln Bank, TMS Corp. of Ams., First Fin. Corp.; bd. dirs. Sahara Enterprises, Inc., Sahara Coal Co., Chgo.; dir., vice chmn. Fed. Home Loan Bank Topeka. Bd. dirs. Folsom Children's Zoo, Lincoln, 1979-83, St. Elizabeth Hosp. Found.; dir. Nat. Coun. Fed. Home Loan Banks. Fellow Nebr. State Bar Assn.; mem. ABA, ATLA, Lincoln Bar Assn., Nebr. Bar Assn., Newcomer Soc. U.S., Nat. Coun. Fed. Home Loan Banks (bd. dirs.). Republican. Methodist. Club: Country Club of Lincoln. Lodge: Masons, Scottish Rite (33 degree). Home: 7441 N Hampton Rd Lincoln NE 68506-1633 Office: First Fed Lincoln 1235 N St Lincoln NE 68508-2008

LUNDSTROM, MARJIE, newspaper editor. Grad., U. Nebr. Columnist, editor, nat. corr. The Denver Post, 1981-89; with The Sacramento Bee, 1989-90, 91—; nat. corr. Gannett News Svc., Washington, 1990-91. Recipient Pulitzer Prize for nat. reporting, 1991. Office: The Sacramento Bee 2100 Q St PO Box 15779 Sacramento CA 95852

LUNDSTROM, THOMAS JOHN, lawyer; b. Ashland, Dec. 21, 1954; s. Martti Albert and Shirley Dorothy (Carlson) L. BS, U. Wis., 1978; JD, Ohio No. U., 1981; LLM in Environ. Law, U. San Diego, 1996. Bar: Ohio, Va., U.S. Dist. Ct. (ea. dist.) Va., U.S. Ct. Appeals (4th cir.). Commd. ensign USN, 1983, advanced through grades to lt. comdr., 1988; staff comdr. naval surface Atlantic fleet USN, Norfolk, Va., 1983-84, staff judge adv. U.S. forces Lebanon, 1983-84, legal svc. office Norfolk def. counsel, 1984-86; staff judge adv. comdr. U.S. forces Caribbean USN, Key West, Fla., 1986-87; staff judge adv. USS Coral Sea USN, 1987-89; def. counsel Va. State Pub. Defender, Portsmouth, 1989-91; asst. counsel Office of Gen. Counsel of Navy, Norfolk, 1991-93; counsel Marine Corps Logistics Base, Barstow, Calif., 1993—; wine steward Williamsburg (Va.) Inn, 1990-93. Big brother Big Bros. Am., Norfolk, 1989-92; tchr., tutor Op. Read & Write, Norfolk, 1989-91. Avocations: golf, sailing, camping, cooking, wines. Office: Marine Corps Logistics Base Office Gen Counsel Box 110100 Barstow CA 92311

LUNDY, AUDIE LEE, JR., lawyer; b. Columbus, Ga., Mar. 10, 1943; s. Audie Lee and Mary Blanche (Snipes) L.; m. Ann Porter, June 11, 1966; children: Travis Stuart, Katherine Porter. BA, Yale U., 1965; LLB magna cum laude, Columbia U., 1968. Bar: N.Y. 1968, D.C. 1976, Pa., 1988, Md. 1990. Assoc. firm White & Case, N.Y.C., 1968-71, 74-75, London, 1971-74, Washington, 1975-78; asst. gen. counsel Campbell Soup Co., Camden, N.J., 1978, gen. counsel, 1979-88, v.p., gen. counsel, 1988-89; ptnr. Tydings & Rosenberg LLP, Balt., 1989—. Bd. mgrs. St. Christopher's Hosp. for Children, Phila., 1980-89, vice-chmn. 1986-89; trustee Food and Drug Law Inst., Washington, 1982-91, The Children's Guild, Inc., Balt., 1992—, chmn. 1997—. Mem. ABA, Am. Soc. Internat. Law, Assn. Gen. Counsel (emeritus). Republican. Presbyterian. Clus: Merion Cricket. Home: 203 Goodwood Gdns Baltimore MD 21210-2531 Office: Tydings & Rosenberg LLP 100 E Pratt St Baltimore MD 21202-1009

LUNDY, JOSEPH E., lawyer; b. Phila., Dec. 30, 1942; s. Martin L. and Adele E. (Zion) L.; m. Bonnie Verbit, Aug. 30, 1966; children: Seth Harris, Nancy Elizabeth. BS in Econs., U. Pa., 1965; JD, Temple U., 1968; LLM in Taxation, N.Y. U., 1969. Bar: Fla. 1968, Pa. 1969. Assoc. MacCoy, Evans & Lewis, Phila., 1969-73, ptnr., 1974-76; ptnr. Montgomery, McCracken, Walker & Rhodes, Phila., 1976-88, Ballard, Spahr, Andrews & Ingersoll, Phila., 1988-97, Coopers & Lybrand, 1997—; adj. prof. law Temple U., 1974—. Editor-in-Chief Jour. Taxation of Exempt Orgns. Trustee Pa. Coll. Podiatric Medicine, Phila.; assoc. trustee U. Pa., Phila.; bd. overseers U. Pa. Univ. Mus., Phila. Fellow Am. Coll. Tax Counsel; mem. ABA (exempt orgn. com., com. govt. subcoms.), Am. Acad. Hosp. Attys., Phila. Bar Assn. (vice chair tax sect. 1988-90, chair 1990-92). Office: Ballard Spahr Andrews & Ingersoll 1735 Market St Ste 51 Philadelphia PA 19103-7501

LUNDY, J(OSEPH) EDWARD, retired automobile company executive; b. Iowa, Jan. 6, 1915; s. Vern E. and Mary L. (Chambers) L. B.A., State U. Iowa, 1936. Fellow Princeton U., 1936-39, mem. econs. faculty, 1940-42, beginning as planning ofcl.; with Ford Motor Co., Dearborn, Mich., 1946-85, successively dir. fin. planning and analysis, gen. asst. contr., 1946-57, treas., 1957-61, v.p., contr., 1961-62, v.p. fin., 1962-67, exec. v.p., 1967-79, dir. and vice-chmn. fin. com., 1979-85; dir. research and analysis Office Statis. Control, Hdqrs. USAAF, 1945. Served from pvt. to maj. USAAF, 1943-45. Decorated Legion of Merit. Mem. Phi Beta Kappa, Delta Upsilon. Roman Catholic. Clubs: Detroit Princeton, Detroit. Home: 7 Brookwood Ln Dearborn MI 48120-1302

LUNDY, SHERMAN PERRY, secondary school educator; b. Kansas City, Mo., July 26, 1939; s. Loren F. and O. Metta (Brown) L.; m. Beverly J., Feb. 25, 1960; children: Paul, Carolyn. BA, U. Okla., 1963; MA, So. Meth. U., 1966; EdS, U. Iowa, 1975. Cert. tchr., Iowa. Tchr. Platte Canyon High Sch., Bailey, Colo., 1964-65, Lone Grove (Okla.) High Sch., 1966-68, Ardmore (Okla.) High Sch., 1968-69; tchr., sci. dept. chair Burlington (Iowa) High Sch., 1969—; geologist Basic Materials Corp., Waterloo, Iowa, 1983—, Raid Quarries, Burlington, 1975-80. Contbr. articles to profl. jours.; author curriculum guide: Environmental Activities, 1975. Mem., commr. Regional Solid Waste Commn., Des Moines County, 1990—; mem., pres. Conservation Bd., Des Moines County, 1978-88; bd. dirs. Iowa Conservation Bd. Assn., 1984-85; mem. Civil Rights Commn., City of Burlington, 1970-76. With USMC, 1960-64. Recipient Silver Beaver Boy Scouts Am., 1975, Service Recognition, Des Moines County Conservation Bd., 1988, Project ESTEEM agt., Harvard/Smithsonian, 1992. Mem. Geol. Soc. Am. (North Cen. edn. com. 1989—), Iowa Acad. Sci. (edn. com. 1990-91, chair earth sci. tchrs. sect. 1993-94, exec. bd. 1992-94), Nat. Assn. Geology Tchrs. (Outstanding Earth Sci. Tchr. 1992, v.p. ctrl. sect. 1994-95), Soc. Econ. and Sedimentary Geology, Geol. Soc. Iowa, Am. Chem. Soc., Unitarian Fellowship, Sons of Confederate Vets., SE Iowa Civil War Round Table (chair 1992-94). Unitarian. Avocations: civil war, stamp collecting, fossil collecting. Home: RR 1 Burlington IA 52601-9801*

LUNDY, VICTOR ALFRED, architect, educator; b. N.Y.C., Feb. 1, 1923; s. Alfred Henry and Rachel Lundy; m. Shirley Corwin, 1947 (div. 1959); children: Christopher Mark, Jennifer Alison; m. Anstis Manton Burwell, Sept. 19, 1960; 1 child, Nicholas Burwell. BArch, Harvard U., 1947, MArch, 1948. Registered architect, Tex., N.Y., Calif. Pvt. practice architecture Sarasota, Fla., 1951-59, N.Y.C., 1960-75; prin. Victor A. Lundy & Assocs., Inc., Houston, 1976-84; design. prin., v.p. HKS Inc., Dallas, 1984—; vis. prof. Grad. Sch. Design, Harvard U., Sch. Architecture, Yale U., Columbia U., U. Calif., Berkeley, Calif. Poly. State U. San Luis Obispo, U. Houston, U. Rome, others; U.S. specialist-architect in U.S.I.A. exhibit, USSR, 1965. Responsible for design St. Paul's Luth. Ch., Sarasota, 1959, new sanctuary, 1970, 1st Unitarian Ch. of Fairfield County, Westport, Conn., 1961, 1st Unitarian Congl. Soc., Hartford, Conn., 1964, Ch. of Resurrection, East Harlem Protestant Parish, N.Y.C., 1966, exhbn. bldg. and exhibit for AEC in S.Am. (Buenos Aires, Rio de Janeiro, Bogota, Santiago), 1967 (Silver medal for exhbn. Archtl. League N.Y. 1965), recreation shelters for Nat. Mus. History and tech., Smithsonian Instn., Washington, 1967, U.S. States Tax Ct. bldg. and pla., Washington, 1976, U.S. Embassy, Colombo, Sri Lanka, for Office of Fgn. Bldgs., Dept. State, 1983 (U.S. Presdl. Design Awards Program 1988, Fed. Design Achievement award), Austin Centre-Omni Hotel, Austin, Tex., 1984, One Congress Pla., Austin, Tex., 1984, Walnut Glen Tower, Dallas, 1985, Mack Ctr. II, Tampa, Fla., 1990, Greyhound Corp. Ctr., Phoenix, 1991, GTE Telephone Ops. World Hdqrs., Irving, Tex., 1991, others; archtl. work represented in Berlin Internat. Archtl. Exposition, 1957, Sao Paulo Internat. Biennial Exposition, 1957, 5th Congress Union Internat. Des Architectes, Moscow, 1958, Expo '70 Exhbn., Osaka, Japan, 1970, travelling exhbn. of architecture in S.Am. Sgt. inf. U.S. Army, 1943-46, ETO. Decorated Purple Heart; recipient Gold medal award Buenos Aires Sesquicentennial Internat. Exhbn., 1960, Gold medal award Buenos Aires Sesquicentennial Internt.Exhbn., 1960; Silver medal Archtl. League N.Y., 1965; Charles Hayden Meml. Scholastic scholar, 1939-43, Edward H. Kendall scholar Harvard U., 1947-48, Rotch travelling scholar Boston Soc. Architects, 1948-50; travelling fellow Harvard U., 1948-50; Dept. State grantee, 1965. Fellow AIA. Avocations: painting, sculpture. Home: 701 Mulberry Ln Bellaire TX 77401-3805 Office: HKS Inc 1111 Pla of the Americas N Ste LB 307 Dallas TX 75201

LUNDY, WALKER, newspaper editor; b. St. Petersburg, Fla.; m. Saralyn Lundy; 2 children. BSJ, U. Fla. Reporter Atlanta Jour.-Constitution; reporter, city editor Detroit Free Press; mng. editor, exec. editor Tallahassee Democrat; mng. editor Ft. Worth Star-Telegram; editor Arkansas Gazette, Little Rock; gen. editor, sr. v.p. St. Paul Pioneer Press, 1990—, exec. editor, sr. v.p., 1990—. Office: Northwest Publs Inc 345 Cedar St Saint Paul MN 55101-1014*

LUNEV, ALEKSANDR (SASHA), dancer; b. Leningrad, 1965. Grad., Choreographic Inst., 1983. Dancer Kirov, 1983; prin. dancer Boston Ballet; now premiere danseur, artistic advisor Tulsa Ballet Theatre, Tulsa, OK. Performed throughout the USSR, France, Italy, Germany, U.S., Can. and Japan; tour with Kirov to London and Paris; major dance roles include Giselle, Swan Lake, Sleeping Beauty, Chopiniana, La Sylphide, Les Sylphides, Fountain of Bakchisarai, Corsaire; debut in the U.S. with the Boston Ballet. Office: Tulsa Ballet Theatre 4512 S Peoria Ave Tulsa OK 74105-4563*

LUNEY, PERCY ROBERT, JR., law educator, dean, lawyer, consultant; b. Hopkinsville, Ky., Jan. 13, 1949; s. Percy Robert and Alice Charline (Woodson) L.; m. Gwynn Teresa Swinson, Feb. 18, 1979; children: Jamille, Robyn. AB, Hamilton Coll., 1970; JD, Harvard U., 1974. Bar: D.C. 1975, Tenn. 1977, U.S. Supreme Ct. 1979, U.S. Dist. Ct. Tenn., U.S. Dist. Ct. D.C., U.S. Ct. Claims, U.S. Ct. Appeals (6th, 9th and D.C. cirs.). Asst. prof. econ., geology Cornell U., Ithaca, N.Y., 1974-75; atty., advisor office of solicitor U.S. Dept. of Interior, Washington, 1975-77; legal counsel, spl. asst. to pres. Fisk U., Nashville, 1977-79; assoc. Birch, Horton, Bittner, Monroe, Pestinger & Anderson, Washington, 1979-80; asst. dean, asst. prof. N.C. Cen. U., Durham, 1980-85, assoc. prof. law, 1985-90, prof. law, 1990—, dean, 1994—; sr. lectr. Duke U. Sch. Law, 1985-87, vis. prof. law, 1987—; Fulbright lectr. Kobe U., Japan, 1991-92. Producer, dir., editor: (videotape) Practicing Law in N.C., 1985; contbr. articles to profl. jours. Mem. adv. panel Z. Smith Reynolds Found., Winston-Salem, N.C., 1983-86; bd. dirs. Research Triangle Park (N.C.) Internat. Visitors Ctr., 1983-88, N.C. Coastal Fedn., Raleigh, 1983-85; trustee Environ. Def. Fund, 1987-96, Hamilton Coll., 1993-97. Thomas J. Watson research fellow, 1971-72; vis. research scholar U. Tokyo, 1983; Fulbright research scholar U. Tokyo, 1986; Martha Price research fellow Duke U. Sch. Law, 1985-87. Fellow ABA; mem. FBA, N.C. Bar Assn., Tenn. Bar Assn., D.C. Bar Assn., Delta Upsilon. Club: Harvard (N.C.). Home: 1401 Brooks Ave Raleigh NC 27607 Office: NC Ctrl U Law Sch Durham NC 27707

LUNGER, IRVIN EUGENE, university president emeritus, clergyman; b. Williamsport, Pa., June 28, 1912; s. George Lee and Mabel Clara (Griggs) L.; m. Eleanor Jeanne Zink, Feb. 10, 1939 (dec. Aug. 1955); children: Susan Ann (Mrs. Lee C. Brown) (dec.), Kathryn Elizabeth (Mrs. Bob Willis) (dec.); m. Kay Walsh Ritchey, June 19, 1957; foster son, Owsley Ritchey. A.B. magna cum laude, Bethany Coll., 1934, Litt.D. (hon.), 1959; B.D., U. Chgo., 1935, A.M., 1936, Ph.D., 1938; postgrad., U. Munich, Germany, 1936-37; L.H.D. (hon.), U. Ala., 1965, Transylvania U., 1980; Litt.D. (hon.), Eastern Ky. U., 1974. Ordained to ministry Disciples of Christ Ch., 1932; minister Christian Ch., Morristown, 1930-34, University Ch. Disciples of Christ, Chgo., 1939-55; prof. religion, dean Morrison Chapel, Transylvania U., Lexington, Ky., 1955-56, acad. dean, 1956-57, pres., 1957-76, pres. emeritus, 1976—, interim pres., 1981-82; dir., pres., Bd. Higher Edn., Disciples of Christ, 1963-64; interim minister Christian Ch., Frankfort, Ky., 1980, Christian Ch., Danville, Ky., 1985. Contbr. to: Faith of the Free, 1940. Pres. bd. dirs. Henry Clay Found., Lexington, 1968-87 ; chmn. exec. com. Ky. Ind. Coll. Found., 1967-68, Ky. chmn. Rhodes Scholarship Selection Com., 1960-67; mem. Gov.'s Commn. Higher Edn., Ky., 1964-69; chmn. bd. dirs. Living Arts and Sci. Center, Inc., 1968-69; bd. dirs. Ednl. Adv. and Reference Corp., N.Y.C; bd. dirs. United Fund, 1959-65, pres., 1962-64; chmn. bd. dirs. Lexington Pub. Library, 1966-70; bd. dirs. Fund for Advancement of Edn. and Research, U. Ky. Med. Center, 1974-87 . Named Ky. col., 1959. Mem. Council Ind. Ky. Colls. and Univs. (pres. 1966, 68), Conf. Ch.-Related Colls. of South (pres. 1970), Omicron Delta Kappa, Tau Kappa Alpha, Beta Theta Pi. Democrat. Home: 461 Herrington Woods Harrodsburg KY 40330-9717

LUNGREN, DANIEL EDWARD, state attorney general; b. Long Beach, Calif., Sept. 22, 1946; s. John Charles and Lorain Kathleen (Youngberg) L.; m. Barbara Kolls, Aug. 2, 1969; children: Jeffrey Edward, Kelly Christine, Kathleen Marie. A.B. cum laude, Notre Dame U., 1968; postgrad., U. So. Calif. Law Sch., 1968-69; J.D., Georgetown U., 1971. Bar: Calif. 1972. Staff asst. Sen. George Murphy, Sen. William Brock, 1969-71; spl. asst. to co-chmn. Rep. Nat. Com., dir. spl. programs, 1971-72; assoc., selected as ptnr. Ball, Hunt, Hart, Brown & Baerwitz, Long Beach, 1973-78; mem. 96th-97th Congresses from 34th, 98th-100th Congresses from 42d Calif. Dist., 1979-1989, Rep. State Cen. Com. Calif., 1974-89; ptnr. Diepenbrock, Wulff, Plant & Hannegan, Sacramento, 1989-90; atty. gen. State of Calif., Sacramento, 1991—. Bd. dirs. Long Beach chpt. ARC, Boy's Club, 1976-88; committeeman Rep. Nat. Com., Calif., 1988-96. Recipient Good Samaritan award Los Angeles Council Mormon Chs., 1976. Republican. Roman Catholic. Office: Office of the Atty Gen 1300 I St Sacramento CA 95814-2919

LUNGSTRUM, JOHN W., federal judge; b. Topeka, Kans., Nov. 2, 1945; s. Jack Edward and Helen Alice (Watson) L.; m. Linda Eileen Ewing, June 21, 1969; children: Justin Matthew, Jordan Elizabeth, Alison Paige. BA magna cum laude, Yale Coll., 1967; JD, U. Kans., 1970. Bar: Kans. 1970, Calif. 1970, U.S. Dist. Ct. (ctrl. dist.) Calif., U.S. Ct. Appeals (10th crct.). Assoc. Latham & Watkins, L.A., 1970-71; ptnr. Stevens, Brand, Lungstrum, Golden & Winter, Lawrence, Kans., 1972-91; U.S. Dist. judge Dist. of Kans., Kansas City, Kans., 1991—; lectr. law U. Kans. Law Sch., 1973—; mem. faculty Kans. Bar Assn. Coll. Advocacy , Trial Tactics and Techniques Inst., 1983-86; chmn. Douglas County Rep. Ctrl. Com., 1975-81; mem. Rep. State Com.; del. State Rep. Convention, 1968, 76, 80. Chmn. bd. dirs. Lawrence C. of C., 1990-91; pres. Lawrence United Fund, 1979; pres. Independence Days Lawrence, Inc., 1984, 85, Seem-to-be-Players, Inc., Lawrence Rotary Club, 1978-79; bd. dirs. Lawrence Soc. Chamber Music, Swarthout Soc. (corp. fund-raising chmn.); mem. Lawrence Art Commn., Williams Scholarship Fund, Lawrence League Women Voters, Douglas County Hist. Soc.; bd. trustees, stewardship chmn. Plymouth Congl. Ch.; pres. Lawrence Round Ball Club; coach Lawrence Summertime Basketball; Vice chmn. U. Kans. Disciplinary Bd.; bd. govs. Kans Sch. Religion; bd. dirs. Kans. Day Club, 1980, 81. National Merit scholar, Yale Nat. scholar. Fellow Am. Bar Found.; mem. ABA (past mem. litigation and ins. sect.), Douglas County Bar Assn., Johnson County Bar Assn., Wyandotte County Bar Assn., Kans. Bar Assn. (vice chair legislative com., subcom. litigation, mem. continuing legal edn. com.), U Kans. Alumni Assn. (life), Phi Beta Kappa, Phi Gamma Delta, Phi Delta Phi. Avocations: basketball, hiking, skiing. Office: US Courthouse 500 State Ave Kansas City KS 66101-2403

LUNIN, JOSEPH, lawyer; b. Jersey City, Oct. 30, 1940; s. Benjamin Lunin and Ethel Ranz; m. Diana Sussman, Aug. 13, 1967; children: Jennifer, Benjamin. BA, Rutgers U., 1963, LLB, 1966; LLM, NYU, 1973. Bar: N.J. 1966. Legal sec. to judge appellate div. N.J. Superior Ct., 1966-67; assoc. Pitney, Hardin, Kipp & Szuch, Morristown, N.J., 1970-73, ptnr., 1974—; adj. faculty Rutgers U. Grad. Sch. Bus., Newark, 1972-77, adj. prof. Law Sch., 1988-93; cons. N.J. Corp. Law Revision Commn., 1970-73. Author: Forms for Practice Under the New Jersey Nonprofit Corporation Act, 1983, rev. edit., 1991, Forms for Practice Under the New Jersey Business Corporation Act, 1991; editor: Rutgers Law Rev., 1965-66, Organization and Sale of Small Business, 1968-70. Served to capt. U.S. Army, 1968-70, Vietnam, 1969. Mem. ABA, N.J. Bar Assn. (chmn. nonprofit law revision com. 1975—, chmn. corp. and bus. law sect. 1982-84), Morristown Club. Unitarian. Office: Pitney Hardin Kipp & Szuch PO Box 1945 Park Ave at Morris County Morristown NJ 07962-1945

LUNINE, JONATHAN IRVING, planetary scientist, educator; b. N.Y.C., June 26, 1959. BS magna cum laude, U. Rochester, 1980; MS, Calif. Inst. Tech., 1983, PhD, 1985. Rsch. assoc. U. Ariz., Tucson, 1984-86, asst. prof. planetary scis., 1986-90; vis. asst. prof. UCLA, 1986, assoc. prof., 1990-95, prof., 1995—, faculty mem. program in applied math., 1992—; interdisciplinary scientist on joint U.S.-European Cassini mission to Saturn; mem. com. planetary and lunar exploration space sci. bd. NAS, 1986-90; chmn. NASA Solar Sys. Exploration subcom., 1990-95; chmn. Pluto Express Sci. Definition Team, 1995; disting. vis. scientist Jet Propulsion Lab., 1997-99. Contbr. articles to profl. jours.; co-editor: Protostars and Planets III, 1993. Mem. Internat. Mars Exploration Adv. Panel NASA, 1993-94, space sci. adv. com., 1990-95. Recipient Cospar Zeldovich prize Soviet Intercosmos and Inst. for Space Rsch., 1990. 1 of the 50 emerging leaders Time Mag., 1994; Co-Recipient James B. Macelwane Young Investigator medal Am. Geophysical Union, 1995. Fellow Am. Geophys. Union (Macelwane medal 1995); mem. Am. Astron. Soc. (Harold C. Urey prize 1988), Internat. Acad. Astronautics (corr. mem.), Internat. Coun. Sci. Unions, European Geophys. Soc., Sigma Xi. Avocation: hiking. Office: U Ariz Dept Planetary Scis PO Box 210092 Lunar & Planetary Lab Tucson AZ 85721-0092

LUNING, THOMAS P., lawyer; b. St. Louis, Oct. 11, 1942. AB magna cum laude, Xavier U., 1964; JD, Georgetown U., 1967. Bar: D.C. 1968, Ill. 1968. Law clk. to Hon. Spottswood W. Robinson III and to ct. U.S. Ct. Appeals (D.C. cir.), 1967-68; atty. Schiff Hardin & Waite, Chgo. Mng. editor Georgetown Law Jour., 1966-67. Mem. ABA, Chgo. Bar Assn., 7th Cir. Bar Assn., Chgo. Coun. Lawyers. Office: Schiff Hardin & Waite 7200 Sears Tower Chicago IL 60606-6327

LUNN, JANET LOUISE SWOBODA, writer; b. Dallas, Dec. 28, 1928; naturalized Can. citizen, 1950; m. Richard Lunn, 1950; children: Eric, Jeffrey, Alexander, Katherine, John. Student, Queen's U., Kingston, Ont., Can., 1947-50; LLD (hon.), Queen's U., 1992; hon. diploma, Loyalist Coll. Applied Arts, 1993. Author: (with Richard Lunn) The County, 1967, Double Spell, 1968, Larger Than Life, 1979, The Twelve Dancing Princesses, 1979 (IODE Children's Book award 1979, one of 10 best children's Can. Libr. Assn.), The Root Cellar, 1981 (Ruth Schwartz Children's Book of Yr. 1981, Children's Book of Yr., Can. Libr. Assn. 1982, Tchr.'s Choice for 1983, Internat. Bd. of Books for Young People honors list 1984, Am. Nat. Coun. Tchrs. English, Young Reader medal 1988, Reviewers' Choice Booklist), Shadow in Hawthorn Bay, 1986 (Honor list Internat. Bd. Books for Young People 1986, Young Adult Book of Yr. award Sask. Libr. Assn. 1986, Book of Yr. IDOE 1986, Can. Libr. Assn. Children's Lit. award, Can. Coun. Children's Book of Yr., Book of Yr. Internat. Children's Libr. Munich, Germany 1986), Amos's Sweater, 1988 (Ruth Schwartz award Can. Booksellers' Assn. 1989), Duck Cake for Sale, 1989, One Hundred Shining Candles: A Christmas Story, 1990, (with Christopher Moore) The Story of Canada, 1992 (Info. Book award Children's Lit. Round Tables fo Can. 1993, Mr. Christie Book award 1993, IODE 1993); editor: The Unseen, 1994. Recipient Vicki Metcalk award for body of work for children Can. Author's Assn., 1981. Mem. Can. Children's Book Ctr. (bd. dirs. 1989, v.p. 1990); IBBY Can. (bd. dirs. 1989), Writer's Union of Can. (2d vice chair 1979-80, 1st vice chair 1983-84, chair 1984-85), Can. Soc. Children's Authors, Illustrators and Performers, PEN Internat. Home and Office: RR #2, Hillier, ON Canada K0K 2J0

LUNSFORD, JULIUS R(ODGERS), JR., lawyer; b. Weston, Ga., Jan. 22, 1915; s. Julius Rodgers and Mary (Robinson) L.; m. Mary Eugenia Vann, Aug. 24, 1941; children: J. Rodgers III, Clark V., Alan H. BA, Mercer U., 1935; JD, U. Ga., 1936. Bar: Ga. 1936, U.S. Ct. Customs and Patent Appeals 1953-82, U.S. Ct. Mil. Appeals 1955, U.S. Supreme Ct. 1955, U.S. Ct. Appeals (5th cir.) 1975, D.C. 1975, U.S. Ct. Appeals (11th cir.) 1981, U.S. Ct. Appeals for Fed. Cit. 1982. With legal dept. The Coca-Cola Co., 1936-75; asst. v.p., mgr. trademarks and unfair competition dept., 1972-75; ptnr. Beveridge, DeGrandi, Kline & Lunsford, Atlanta, 1975-79; sr. ptnr. Hurt, Richardson, Garner, Todd & Cadenhead, Atlanta, 1980-87; ptnr. Jones, Askew & Lunsford, Atlanta, 1987-92; cons., presenter expert testimony, 1992—; mem. law faculty Mercer U. Law Sch. 1990-95; lectr. in field. Contbr. numerous articles to profl. jours.; contbg. author: The Trademark Reporter, 1949—. Trustee, bd. dirs. Mercer U., Macon, Ga., 1988-93. Capt. USNR, 1942-75. Mem. ABA (chmn. state trademark rights and statues com. 1968-69), U.S. Trademark Assn. (pres. 1971-72, bd. dirs. 1969-66, 67-72, 74-77), Am. Intellectual Property Law Assn., Corp. Bar Assn., Atlanta Bar Assn., Lawyers Club Atlanta, Kiwanis, Phi Delta Phi,

Kappa Alpha. Democrat. Baptist. Avocations: sports fan and spectator. Home: 4187 Conway Valley Rd NW Atlanta GA 30327-3607

LUNSFORD, MARVIN CARL, chemical company executive; b. Winston-Salem, N.C., Jan. 15, 1947; s. Marvin Carl and Claudia Bunn (Simpson) L.; m. Christian Elizabeth Lunsford, June 27, 1965; children: John Marvin, James Lacy. BS in Engring., N.C. State U., 1970. Lic. profl. engr., Tenn. Process systems engr. Tenn. Eastman Co., Kingsport, 1970-73, project engr., 1973-77, asst. to engring. supt., 1977-79, govt. rels. supt., 1979-81, head dept. mech. engring., 1981-84, asst. to v.p. facilities, 1984-87; mgr. bus. devel. and licensing Eastman Chem. Co., Kingsport, 1987-90; v.p. Eastman Coatings Specialties Inc., Kingsport, Tenn., 1990-94, Exergy Power Inc., Hayward, Calif., 1994—; pres., dir. Wescon, Inc., 1994—; dir. Texet Inc. Editor: Quality First, 1986; contbr. articles to profl. publs.; patentee in field. Bd. dirs. Indsl. Productivity Initiative, Washington, 1986-90, Kingsport Area United Way, 1987-90; trustee TPAC, Nashville, 1986-92; mem. Rep. Nat. Com., Washington, 1980-95. Recipient Engr. of Yr. award Tenn. Soc. Profl. Engrs., 1976, Steinman Coun. Nat. Engring. Ednl. Found., 1990. Fellow Am. Acad. Mechanics; mem. ASME (chmn. 1975-76, Svc. award 1977), Am. Quality and Productivity Inst. (bd. dirs. 1989-94), Nat. Soc. Profl. Engrs. (v.p. bd. dirs. 1988-90, Outstanding Svc. award 1991), Nat. Inst. Engring. Mgmt. (chmn. bd. dirs. 1990-92), Nat. Cmty. Quality Coalition (bd. dirs. 1990-94), Am. Soc. Quality Control, Appalachian Quality Coun. (pres. 1987-89), Licensing Execs. Soc., Ridgefields Country Club, Sertoma Internat. (life, pres. 1979-80, GEM award 1974). Republican. Episcopalian. Avocations: golf, tennis, swimming. Home: 2112 Heatherly Rd Kingsport TN 37660-3415 Office: Wescon Inc 440 E Sullivan St Kingsport TN 37660-4406

LUNT, HARRY EDWARD, metallurgist, consultant; b. N.Y.C., Apr. 30, 1924; m. Carmela (Tamburri) Lunt, June 19, 1950; children: Teresa, Alan, Diana, Linda, Steven. AB, Syracuse U., 1948, postgrad., 1948-50; MS, Iowa State U., 1953. Registered profl. engr., Del., Calif. Rsch. asst. Ames (Iowa) Lab., U.S. AEC, 1950-53; devel. metallurgist U.S. Steel Corp. Applied Rsch. Labs., Monroeville and Homestead, Pa., 1953-63; sr. engr. Westinghouse Rsch. Labs., Churchill, Pa., 1963-66; corp. metallurgist Worthington Corp., Harrison, N.J., 1967-74; corp. cons. engr. Burns & Roe Enterprises, Inc., Oradell, N.J., 1974-94; cons. metallurgist Mendham, N.J., 1995—; mem. tech. adv. com. Materials Properties Coun., N.Y.C., 1980—. Author tech. papers and conf. proceedings in field. Fellow ASTM (chmn. com. on steel, stainless steel and related alloys 1986-92, bd. dirs. 1990-92, Merit award 1981), Standards Engring. Soc. (Robert J. Painter Meml. award 1989), Am. Soc. Metals (life; chmn. N.J. chpt. 1976-77); mem. Am. Welding Soc., Nat. Assn. Corrosion Engrs. (accredited corrosion specialist), Phi Beta Kappa. Home and Office: 13 Brockden Dr Mendham NJ 07945-3010

LUNT, HORACE GRAY, linguist, educator; b. Colorado Springs, Colo., Sept. 12, 1918; s. Horace Fletcher and Irene (Jewett) L.; m. Sally Herman, June 2, 1963; children: Elizabeth, Catherine. A.B., Harvard U., 1941; M.A., U. Calif., Berkeley, 1942; postgrad., Charles U., Prague, Czechoslovakia, 1946-47; Ph.D. (Rockefeller fellow), Columbia U., 1950. Lectr. in Serbo-Croatian Columbia U., 1948-49; asst. prof. Slavic langs. and lit. Harvard U., 1949-54, asso. prof., 1954-60, prof., 1960—, Samuel H. Cross prof. Slavic langs. and lits., 1965-89, Samuel H. Cross prof. Slavic langs. and lits., emeritus, 1989—, chmn. dept. Slavic langs. and lits., 1959-73, 75-76, 82-83; chmn. Slavic and East European Lang. and Area Ctr., 1983-89; mem. exec. com. Russian Rsch. Ctr., 1970-91, fellow, 1991—; mem. exec. com. Harvard Ukrainian Research Inst., 1974-91, fellow, 1991—. Author: Grammar of the Macedonian Literary Language, 1952, Old Church Slavonic Grammar, 1955, 6th, rev. edit., 1974, Fundamentals of Russian, 1958, 2d rev. edit., 1968, Progressive Palatalization of Common Slavic, 1981; editor: Harvard Slavic Studies, 1953-70. Served with U.S. Army, 1942-45. Guggenheim fellow, 1960-61. Mem. Macedonian Acad. Arts and Scis. (corr.). Home: 75 Bradford Rd Weston MA 02193-2142 Office: Harvard U Boylston 301 Cambridge MA 02138

LUNT, JACK, lawyer; b. Hartford, Conn., Oct. 19, 1944. BS magna cum laude, U. Utah, 1966, JD, 1969. Bar: Utah 1969. Assoc. Jones, Waldo, Holbrook & McDonough, Salt Lake City, 1969-73, ptnr., 1974-89; pres., exec. v.p. law and adminstrn. Am. Stores Properties, Inc., Salt Lake City, 1989—; sr. v.p., asst. gen. counsel, corp. sec. Am. Stores Co., Salt Lake City, 1993—. Mem. Salt Lake County Bar Assn., Utah Bar Assn. Office: Am Stores Co 709 E South Temple Salt Lake City UT 84102-1205

LUNT, JENNIFER LEE, lawyer; b. Big Springs, Tex., July 18, 1965; d. John Daleton and Karen Adele (Olson) L. BS, Auburn U., 1986; JD, U. Ala., 1989, MLS, 1990. Bar: Ala. 1989, U.S. Ct. Appeals (11th cir.) 1990, U.S. Dist. Ct. (mid. dist.) Ala. 1991, U.S. Dist. Ct. (no. dist.) Ala. 1993, U.S. Supreme Ct. 1997. Rsch. asst. Supreme Ct. Ala., Tuscaloosa, 1988-90; cons. Gorham, Waldrep, Stewart, Kendrick & Bryant P.C., Birmingham, 1990; pvt. practice Montgomery, Ala., 1991—; legal asst. adv. bd. Auburn U., Montgomery, 1994—. Rsch. editor: Law and Psychology Rev., 1988-89. Mem. ABA (Young Lawyers Divsn. law practice mgmt. com. planning bd. 1996—), Ala. State Bar (com. on small firms and solo practitioners 1995—), Montgomery County Bar Assn. (com. on continuing legal edn. 1995—). Office: 207 Montgomery St Ste 224 Montgomery AL 36104-3528

LUNTZ, MAURICE HAROLD, ophthalmologist; b. Capetown, South Africa, July 27, 1930; came to U.S. 1978; s. Montague Bernard and Sarah Marian (Friedman) L.; m. Angela June Myerson, June 21, 1956; children—Melvyn Howard, Caryn Susan, David Sean. M.B., Ch.B., Capetown U., 1952; M.D., U. Witwatersrand, Johannesburg, S. Africa, 1964. Diplomate Am. Bd. Ophthalmology. Lectr. ophthalmology Oxford U. (Eng.), 1960-62; prof., chmn. ophthalmology Witwatersrand U., 1964-78; dir. ophthalmology Beth Israel Med. Ctr., N.Y.C., 1978—; chief glaucoma svc. Manhattan Eye, Ear & Throat Hosp., 1989-92, pres., bd. surgeon dirs., 1992—; prof. Mt. Sinai Sch. Medicine, N.Y.C., 1978-82; cons. Merck, Sharp & Dohme, N.J., 1980-82. Author: Uveitis, 1983; Glaucoma Surgery, 1984 second edition, 1995; editorial bd. Highlight Ophthalmology, Panama, 1970—; contbr. articles to profl. jours.; producer movie Glaucoma Surveys, 1970. Fellow Royal Coll. Surgeons (Edinburgh). Mem. Academia Ophthalmologica Internationalis. Office: 121 E 60th St New York NY 10022-1102

LUO, JESSICA CHAOYING, actuary; b. Guangzhou, China, Jan. 31, 1958; came to U.S., 1984; d. Xiang-Guang Luo and Xiu-Juan Qi; m. Yu Wang, Aug. 21, 1991; children: Amanda Mei, Lauren Shuyan, Alexander Shufeng. BS in Mechanics with honors, Zhongshan U., 1982; MS in Stats., U. Toledo, 1986. Actuarial analyst Towers Perrin, Denver, 1986-91; dir. actuarial support Lynchval Systems Inc., Reston, Va., 1991; chief actuary DCP Adminstrs., Inc., Bethesda, Md., 1991-95; actuarial cons. Towers Perrin, Rosslyn, Md., 1995—. Mem. Am. Acad. Actuaries, Soc. Actuaries. Avocations: reading, music, travel. Home: 14209 Amberleigh Terr Silver Spring MD 20905

LUONGO, C. PAUL, public relations executive; b. Winchester, Mass., Dec. 31, 1930; s. Carmine and Carmela (Gilberti) L. Grad., Cambridge Sch. Radio-TV, 1955; diploma, Bentley Coll., 1951; BSBA, Suffolk U., 1955; MBA, Babson Coll., 1956; AAS (hon.), Grahm Jr. Coll., 1970. Jr. exec. Raytheon Co., Lexington, Mass., 1956-59; account exec. Young & Rubicam, Inc., 1959-62; v.p. Copley Advt. Agy., Boston, 1962-64; pres. C. Paul Luongo Co., Boston, 1964—. Guest appearances include: (TV programs) Today Show, NBC-TV, 1984-89, Tomorrow Show, NBC-TV; TV-radio programs, Can.; author: America's Best!, 1980; contbr. syndicated newspaper-mag. features to Pub. Rels. Today; contbg. editor Travel Smart, N.Y., mo. newsletter. Pub. rels. dir. Anthony Spinazzola Meml. Scholarship Found., Boston U., 1986-88; vol. U.S.S. Constn. Mus., Boston, Sta. WGBH-TV, Boston, TV Auctions, 1991—; mem. Boston Ctr. for Internat. Visitors, French Libr., Boston, Mus. Fine Arts, Black Ships Festival, Inc., Newport, R.I.; chmn. centennial ba.. Belcourt Castle, Newport, 1994. With AUS, 1952-54. Mem. Bostonian Soc., Boston Stockbrokers Club, Newcomen Soc. N.Am., Internat. Food, Wine and Travel Writers Assn., Am. Inst. Wine and Food, Japan-Am. Soc. R.I., Neighborhood Assn. of Back Bay, Inc., Back Bay Assn., Suffolk U. Gen. Alumni Assn. (bd. dirs. 1994—). Office: 441 Stuart St Boston MA 02116-5019 *I believe in the work ethic, integrity and the maximum utilization of time for work and recreational activities. I loathe prejudice in any form, dishonesty and indolent people.*

LUPBERGER, EDWIN ADOLPH, utility executive; b. Atlanta, June 5, 1936; s. Adolph and Esma L.; m. Mary Jane McAlister Redmon, Jan. 6, 1989; children by previous marriage: David Todd, Edward Townsend. A.B. in Econs, Davidson (N.C.) Coll., 1958; M.B.A., Emory U., 1963. Asst. v.p. Southern Co. Services, Inc., Atlanta, 1963-69; v.p., treas. Gulf Power Co., Pensacola, Fla., 1969-77; sr. v.p. fin. Indpls. Power & Light Co., 1977-79; sr. v.p., chief fin. officer Middle South Utilities, Inc., New Orleans, 1979-85; chmn., CEO Entergy Corp., New Orleans, 1985—. Ensign USN, 1960. Mem. Edison Electric Inst., Univ. Club, Met. Club. Presbyterian.

LUPERT, LESLIE ALLAN, lawyer; b. Syracuse, N.Y., May 24, 1946; s. Reuben and Miriam (Kaufman) L.; m. Roberta Gail Fellner, May 19, 1968; children: Jocelyn, Rachel, Susannah. BA, U. Buffalo, 1967; JD, Columbia U., 1971. Bar: N.Y. 1971. Ptnr. Orans Elsen & Lupert, N.Y.C., 1971—. Contbr. articles to profl. jours. Mem. ABA, N.Y. State Bar Assn. (trial lawyers sect.), Assn. of Bar of City of N.Y. (com. fed. legislation 1977-80, profl. and jud. ethics com. 1983-86, com. on fed. cts. 1986-89, 95-96), Phi Beta Kappa. Office: Orans Elsen & Lupert 1 Rockefeller Plz New York NY 10020-2102

LUPIA, DAVID THOMAS, corporate financial advisor, management consultant; b. Flandreau, S.D., Mar. 18, 1950; s. Archy L. and Carol L. (Cherney) L; children: Allison, Nathan. AB, Rutgers Coll., New Brunswick, N.J., 1972; MBA, U. Pa., 1974. Cert. mgmt. cons. Fin. analyst Exxon Corp., N.Y.C., 1974-76; sr. fin. analyst Esso Inter-Am., Inc., Coral Gables, Fla., 1976-78; treas. Esso Caribbean, Coral Gables, 1978-80; fin. mgr. Esso Australia, Ltd., Sydney, 1980-83; sr. fin. advisor Exxon Co., U.S.A., Houston, 1983-85, Exxon Corp., N.Y.C., 1985-87; sr. v.p. Lehman Bros., N.Y.C., 1987-92; prin. David T. Lupia, Inc., Corp. Fin. Svcs., 1992—. Mem. Phi Beta Kappa, Omicron Delta Epsilon, Beta Gamma Sigma. Home: 19 Northridge Rd Old Greenwich CT 06870-1115 Office: David T Lupia Inc 1117 E Putnam Ave Ste 252 Riverside CT 06878-1333

LUPIANI, DONALD ANTHONY, psychologist; b. N.Y.C., June 7, 1946; s. Louis and Josephine (Boccia) L.; m. Linda Moyik, June 20, 1970; 1 child, Jennifer. BA, Iona Coll., 1968; MA, Columbia U., 1971, PhD, 1973; postdoctoral, Behavior Therapy Inst., White Plains, N.Y., 1976. Lic. psychologist, N.Y.; diplomat Am. Bd. Profl. Psychology, Am. Bd. Psychotherapy, Am. Acad. Behavioral Medicine, Intenat. Acad. Behavioral Medicine, Internat. Acad. Behavioral Medicine. Clin. assoc. Columbia U., N.Y.C., 1974-85, Fordham U., Bronx, N.Y., 1979-81; dir. psychology and spl. edn. svcs. Riverdale Country Sch., Bronx, 1973-87; chief psychologist Franciscan Order of Priests, N.Y.C., 1983—; pvt. practice Yonkers, N.Y., 1975—; dir. spl. svcs. Riverdale Country Sch., Bronx., 1973-87; bd. dirs. St. Ursula Learning Ctr., Mt. Vernon, N.Y. Contbr. articles to profl. jours. Bd. dirs., mem. The St. Ursula Learning Ctr. Fellow Am. Orthopsychiat. Assn., Am. Coll. Psychology, Am. Acad. Sch. Psychology; mem. APA, N.Y. State Psychol. Assn., Westchester County Psychol. Assn. (chmn. ethics com. 1980-87). Roman Catholic. Avocations: woodworking, painting, drawing. Home and Office: 227 Mile Square Rd Yonkers NY 10701-5369

LUPIENT, JAMES, automotive executive; b. 1934. With Iten Chevrolet, Mpls., 1964-69; pres. Lupient Oldsmobile Co., Inc., Mpls., 1969—; CEO Lupient Automotive Group, Mpls. Office: Lupient Automotive Group 750 Pennsylvania Ave S Minneapolis MN 55426-1603*

LUPIN, ELLIS RALPH, physician, lawyer, coroner; b. New Orleans, Apr. 1, 1931; s. Albert I. and Yetta (Linneck) L.; m. Freda Merlin, Mar. 18, 1951; 1 child, Jay Stephen. BS in Pharmacy, Loyola U., New Orleans, 1952, PharmD, 1983; JD, Loyola U. South, New Orleans, 1988; MD, La. State U., 1956. Diplomate Am. Bd. Ob-Gyn. Bar: La. Practice medicine specializing in ob-gyn. Tenet Physician Svcs., New Orleans, 1962—; atty. Middleberg, Riddle & Gianna; chief dep. coroner City of New Orleans, 1974-86, asst. dist. atty., 1997—; pvt. med.-legal practice; cons. Tenet Corp., E.R. Lupin, Ltd., 1984—; med. legal cons. Surgeon Gen., U.S. Army; mem. vis. com. Loyola Sch. Law. Bd. dirs. ARC, New Orleans, 1965-90, St. Charles Gen. Hosp., 1972-92, U. New Orleans Found., 1990-92, City of New Orleans Vieux Carre Commn., 1995—; trustee New Orleans Symphony, 1982-90, Lupin Found., 1980—, Children's Hosp. of New Orleans, 1984-95, Jewish Welfare Fedn. of New Orleans, 1972, 80, 84, Jewish Family and Children Svcs., 1972-76, New Orleans Mus. Art, 1993—; chmn. bd. dirs. La. State Mus., 1984-88, 92—; chmn. Upper Pontabla Commn., 1982-90; mem. adv. bd. Ladies Luekemia League, 1980—, Sophie Gumbel Guild, 1980—, others. With USAF, 1958-60, col. La. N.G. Fellow Am. Coll. Legal Medicine; mem. Jefferson Parish Med. So., Gyecology Laser So., Royal Soc. Medicine, New Orleans Ob-Gyn Soc., La. State Bar Assn. Jewish. Lodge: Masons. Avocation: collecting antiques. Home: 1021 Chartres St New Orleans LA 70116-3239 Office: Zoller Lupin Levinson Cohen & Castillo 515 Westbank Expy Gretna LA 70053-5644

LUPKE, DUANE EUGENE, insurance company executive; b. Ft. Wayne, Ind., July 17, 1930; s. Walter Herman and Lucy (Bell) L.; married, Sept. 14, 1957; children: Diane Carol, Mark Duane, David Burgess, Andrea Lucy. BS, Ind. U., 1952. CPCU. With Lupke Rice Clancy Assocs., Ft. Wayne, Ind., 1954—, pres., 1969—. Bd. dirs. Concordia Ednl. Found., Ft. Wayne, Luth. Found. Inc., 1995; trustee YWCA. Lt. U.S. Army, 1952-54. Lutheran. Home: 1407 Hawthorne Rd Fort Wayne IN 46802-4957 Office: Lupke Rice Clancy Assocs PO Box 11309 Fort Wayne IN 46857-1309

LUPKIN, STANLEY NEIL, lawyer; b. Bklyn., Mar. 27, 1941; s. David B. and Sylvia (Strassman) L.; m. Anne Rachel Fischler, June 3, 1962; children: Jonathan Daniel, Deborah Eve. BA, Columbia Coll., 1962; LLB, NYU, 1966. Bar: N.Y. 1966, U.S. Dist. Ct. (so. and ea. dists.) N.Y. 1970, U.S. Ct. Appeals (2d cir.) 1970, U.S. Supreme Ct. 1971. Asst. dist. atty., sr. trial atty., chief indictment bur. N.Y. County Dist. Atty.'s Office, N.Y.C., 1966-71; asst. commr. City of N.Y., 1966-71; 1st dep. commr., commr. Dept. Investigation, N.Y.C., 1978-82; ptnr. Litman, Asche, Lupkin, Gioiella & Bassin, N.Y.C., 1982-96; sr. v.p. and deputy gen. counsel Fairfax Group Ltd, New York, 1996—; mem. faculty Nat. Coll. Dist. Attys., Houston, 1974-75, FBI Nat. Acad., Quantico, Va., 1980-82; chmn. com. on criminal justice ops. Assn. of Bar of City of N.Y., 1982-85. Co-author book: Anatomy of A Municipal Franchise: N.Y.C. Bus Shelter Program, 1973-79, 4 vols., 1981. Trustee, counsel Solomon Schechter Sch. of Queens, Flushing, N.Y., 1974—; mem. secondary schs. com. admissions office Columbia Coll., N.Y.C., 1987—. With USAR, 1963-69. Mem. N.Y. State Bar Assn. (chmn. com. on def. 1985—, chmn. com. on prosecution 1977-85, exec. com. criminal justice sect. 1977—, Prosecutor of Yr. 1981), N.Y. State Assn. Criminal Def. Lawyers, Nat. Assn. Criminal Def. Lawyers, N.Y. Criminal Bar Assn., Soc. Columbia Grads. (v.p. 1989—). Avocations: classical music, Talmudic law. Office: Fairfax Group Ltd 505 Park Ave New York NY 10022-1106

LUPO, RAPHAEL V., lawyer; b. Washington, Oct. 15, 1941. BSEE, George Washington U., 1963, JD, 1968. Bar: Va. 1968, D.C. 1968, U.S. Dist. Ct. D.C. 1968, U.S. Dist. Ct. (ea. dist.) Va. 1969, U.S. Patent and Trademark Office, U.S. Claims Ct. 1969, U.S. Ct. Appeals ((D.C. cir.) 1968, U.S. Ct. Appeals (4th cir.) 1969, U.S. Ct. Appeals (Fed. cir.) 1982, U.S. Ct. Customs and Patent Appeals 1969, U.S. Supreme Ct. 1969. Assoc. solicitor U.S. Patent and Trademark Office, 1969-77; dep. asst. gen. counsel for patents Dept. Energy, 1977-80; atty. Spencer & Kaye, Washington, 1980-82, Lupo Lipman & Lever, Washington, 1982-89, Willian Brinks Olds Hofer Gilson & Lione, P.C., Washington; adj. prof. George Washington U. Law Sch., 1992—; speaker 6th Annual Jud. Conf. U.S. Ct. Appeals (Fed. cir.), 1988. Mem. ABA (amicus com.), D.C. Bar, Va. State Bar, Am. Intellectual Property Law Assn. Office: McDermott Will & Emery 1850 K St NW 5th Fl Washington DC 20006

LUPO, ROBERT EDWARD SMITH, real estate developer and investor; b. New Orleans, May 27, 1953; s. Thomas Joseph and Alvena Florence (Smith) L.; m. Mary Lynn Puissegur, June 16, 1980; children: Robert Thomas Smith, Francesca Marfese Smith. BArch, Tulane U., 1977. Owner Robert Edward Smith Lupo Properties, New Orleans, 1976—; cons. various firms, New Orleans, 1977—; COO Commodore Thomas J. Lupo Enterprises, Williams-Lupo, Smith-Lupo, New Orleans, 1981—; pres. Hedwig, Inc., Zephyr, Inc., Noroaltom Devel. Co., Inc., New Orleans, 1981—; cons. Mrs. Thomas J. Lupo properties. Grad. Met. Area Leadership Forum, New Orleans, 1980; bd. dirs., pres. New Orleans Mcpl. Yacht Harbor, 1989-93; life mem. Friends Audubon Zoo, 1983—; bd. dirs. New Orleans Met. Area Com., 1985-90, Orleans Levee Dist. Commn.; guardian mem. Boy Scouts Am., 1991—; mem. capital projects oversight com. Orleans Parish Sch. Bd., 1995—; mem. bd. commrs. Orleans Levee Dist., 1996—. Recipient Gov.'s award State of La., 1980, Tulane Assocs. award Tulane U., 1986; named One of 10 Best Dress Men, Men of Fashion, 1983, named to Hall of Fame, 1991. Mem. Aquarium Ams. (life), Assn. Naval Aviation (charter), Sigma Alpha Epsilon (founding). Republican. Roman Catholic. Club: Semreh. Office: 145 Robert E Lee Blvd New Orleans LA 70124-2552

LUPONE, PATTI, actress; b. Northport, L.I., N.Y., Apr. 21, 1949; d. Orlando Joseph and Angela Louise (Patti) LuP.; m. Matt Johnston; 1 child, Joshua Luke. BFA, The Juilliard Sch., 1972. Off-Broadway prodns. include: The Woods, School for Scandal, The Lower Depths, Stage Directions; appeared in Broadway prodns.: Next Time I'll Sing to You, The Time of Your Life, The Three Sisters, The Robber Bridegroom (Tony award nominee), The Water Engine, The Beggar's Opera, Edward II, The Baker's Wife, 1976, The Woods, 1977, Working, 1978, Catchpenny Twist, 1978, As You Like It, 1982, The Cradle Will Rock, 1983, Stars of Broadway, 1983, Edmond, 1982, Oliver, 1984; star Broadway musicals Evita, 1979 (Best Actress in Musical Tony award 1980), Anything Goes, 1987, Pal Joey, 1995; London prodns. Les Miserables, 1985, Sunset Boulevard, 1993; films include: King of the Gypsies, 1978, 1941, 1979, Fighting Back, 1982, Witness, 1985, Wise Guys, 1986, Driving Miss Daisy, 1989; TV appearances include: Kitty, The Time of Your Life, Lady Bird in LBJ, 1987, The Water Engine, 1992, Family Prayers, 1993, The Song Spinner, 1995, Her Last Chance, 1996; TV series, Life Goes On, 1989-93. Office: ICM 40 W 57th St New York NY 10019-4001

LUPU, RADU, pianist; b. Galati, Romania, Nov. 30, 1945; s. Meyer and Ana (Gabor) L. Attended Conservatoire, Moscow, USSR, 1961-69. London debut, 1969, Berlin, 1972, U.S. debut with Cleve. Orch. in N.Y.C., appearances with worldwide maj. orchs., including Berlin Philharmonic, Vienna Philharmonic, Israel Philharmonic, Orch. de Paris, Concertgebouw, N.Y. Philharmonic, Phila. Symphony Orch., Chgo. Symphony Orch., Cleve. Symphony Orch.; recs. include Beethoven cycle with Israel Philharmonic and Zubin Mehta, Schubert Sonatas, Beethoven Sonatas, Mozart Sonatas for Violin and Piano with Szymon Goldberg, Schubert Lieder with Barbara Hendricks, Mozart and Schubert duets and Mozart Concerto for 2 pianos, both with Murray Perahia, Brahms Piano Concerto #1 Mozart and Beethoven Quintets in E Flat, Schubert Piano Duets with Daniel Barenboim. Recipient 1st prize Van Cliburn Internat. Piano Competition, 1966, Enescu Competition, 1967, Leeds Internat. Piano Competition, 1969, Edison award, 1995, Grammy award for Best Instrumental Record of Yr. for Schumann Kinderszenen and Kreisleriana record, 1995, Best Instrumental Record of Yr. award for Schubert Sonatas D960 and D664, 1996.

LUPULESCU, AUREL PETER, medical educator, researcher, physician; b. Manastiur, Banat, Romania, Jan. 1, 1923; came to U.S., 1967, naturalized, 1973; s. Peter Vichentie and Maria Ann (Dragan) L. MD magna cum laude, Sch. Medicine, Bucharest, Romania, 1950; MS in Endocrinology, U. Bucharest, 1965; PhD in Biology, Faculty of Scis., U. Windsor, Ont., Can. Diplomate Am. Bd. Internal Medicine. Chief Lab. Investigations, Inst. Endocrinology, Bucharest, 1950-67; research assoc. SUNY Downstate Med. Ctr., 1968-69; asst. prof. medicine Wayne State U., 1969-72; assoc. prof., 1973—; vis. prof. Inst. Med. Pathology, Rome, 1967; cons. VA Hosp., Allen Park, Mich., 1971-73. Author: Steroid Hormones, 1958, Advances in Endocrinology and Metabolism, 1962, Experimental Pathophysiology of Thyroid Gland, 1963, Ultrastructure of Thyroid Gland, 1968, Hormones and Carcinogenesis, 1983, Hormones and Vitamins in Cancer Treatment, 1990; reviewer for various sci. jours.; contbr. chpts., numerous articles to profl. publs.; research on hormones and tumor biology; studies regarding role of hormones and vitamins in carcinogenesis. Fellow Fedn. Am. Socs. for Exptl. Biology; mem. Electron Microscopy Soc. Am., Soc. for Investigative Dermatology, N.Y. Acad. Sci., AMA (physician's recognition award 1983, 86), Am. Soc. Cell Biology, Soc. Exptl. Biology and Medicine, AAAS. Republican. Home: 21480 Mahon Dr Southfield MI 48075-7525 Office: Wayne State U Sch Medicine 540 E Canfield St Detroit MI 48201-1928

LURAIN, JOHN ROBERT, III, gynecologic oncologist; b. Princeton, Ill., Oct. 27, 1946; s. John Robert Jr. and Elizabeth Helen (Grampp) L.; m. Nell Lee Snavely, June 14, 1969; children: Alice Elizabeth, Kathryn Anne. BA, Oberlin Coll., 1968; MD, U. N.C., 1972. Diplomate Am. Bd. Ob-Gyn., Am. Bd. Gynecologic Oncology. Resident in ob-gyn. U. Pitts./Magee-Women's Hosp., 1972-75; fellow in gynecologic oncology Roswell Park Cancer Inst., Buffalo, 1977-79; prof. ob-gyn. Northwestern U. Med. Sch., Chgo., 1979—, John and Ruth Brewer prof. gynecology and cancer rsch., 1985—; head sect. gynecol. oncology, chief gynecologic oncology svc. Northwestern Meml. Hosp./Prentice Women's Hosp., Chgo., 1985—. Contbr. chpts. to books, more than 100 articles to profl. jours. Lt. comdr. USN, 1975-77. Fellow Am. Coll. Ob-Gyn.; mem. Soc. Gynecologic Oncologists, Am. Soc. Clin. Oncology, Ctrl. Assn. Ob-Gyn., Am. Soc. for Colposcopy and Cervical Pathology, Chgo. Gynecol. Soc. Avocations: golf, tennis. Office: Northwestern U Med Sch 333 E Superior St Chicago IL 60611-3056

LURENSKY, MARCIA ADELE, lawyer; b. Newton, Mass., May 4, 1948. BA magna cum laude, Wheaton Coll., 1970; JD, Boston Coll. Law Sch., 1973. Bar: Mass. 1973, D.C. 1990, U.S. Dist. Ct. (we. dist.) Wis. 1978, U.S. Dist. Ct. Mass. 1974, U.S. Ct. Appeals (1st cir.) 1974, U.S. Ct. Appeals (3d cir.) 1982, U.S. Ct. Appeals (4th cir.) 1984, U.S. Ct. Appeals (5th cir.) 1995, U.S. Ct. Appeals (8th cir.) 1985, U.S. Ct. Appeals (9th cir.) 1976, U.S. Ct. Appeals (10th cir.) 1995, U.S. Ct. Appeals (11th cir.) 1982, U.S. Ct. Appeals (fed. cir.) 1989, U.S. Claims Ct. 1989, U.S. Supreme Ct. 1979. Atty. U.S. Dept. Labor, Washington, 1974-90, Fed. Energy Regulatory Commn., U.S. Dept. Energy, Washington, 1990—. Mem. Phi Beta Kappa. Office: Fed Energy Regulatory Commn 888 1st St NE Washington DC 20426-0001

LUREY, ALFRED SAUL, lawyer; b. Greenville, S.C., Oct. 17, 1942; s. Meyer and Pearl Sarah (Zaglin) L.; m. Betsy Ann Bennett, June 13, 1982; children: Mollie K., Allison A.; 1 stepchild, Amy E. Startari. AB, Duke U., 1964; LLB, Harvard U., 1967. Bar: Calif. 1967, U.S. Ct. Appeals (4th cir.) 1968, Ga. 1970, U.S. Dist. Ct. (no. dist.) Ga. 1971, U.S. Ct. Claims 1972, U.S. Ct. Appeals (5th cir.) 1976, U.S. Ct. Appeals (11th cir.) 1982. Law clk. to chief justice U.S. Ct. Appeals (4th cir.), Richmond, Va., 1967-69; assoc. Kilpatrick Stockton LLP, Atlanta, 1969-75; ptnr. Kilpatrick & Cody, Atlanta, 1975—; adj. prof. law Emory U., 1989. With USAR, 1968-74. Am. Coll. of Bankruptcy fellow; Angier B. Duke Meml. scholar Duke U., 1960. Mem. Am. Bankruptcy Inst., Calif. Bar Assn., Ga. Bar Assn., Phi Beta Kappa, Phi Eta Sigma. Jewish. Avocations: physical fitness, tennis, reading. Home: 5115 Jett Forest Trl NW Atlanta GA 30327-4559 Office: Kilpatrick Stockton LLP 1100 Peachtree St NE Ste 2800 Atlanta GA 30309-4528

LURIA, MARY MERCER, lawyer; b. Boston, Dec. 29, 1942; d. Albert and Mabel (Jacomb) Mercer; m. Nelson J. Luria, June 19, 1967. AB, Radcliffe Coll., 1964; LLB, Yale U., 1967. Bar: N.Y. 1968. Assoc. Simpson, Thacher & Bartlett, N.Y.C., 1967-68, Hale & Dorr, Boston, 1968-69; assoc. Satterlee & Stephens, N.Y.C., 1969-74, ptnr., 1974-86; ptnr. Patterson, Belknap, Webb & Tyler, N.Y.C., 1986-97, Davis & Gilbert, N.Y.C., 1997—. Mem. ABA, N.Y. State Bar Assn., Assn. of Bar of City of N.Y., Metropolitan Club. Avocations: gardening, photography. Office: Davis & Gilbert 1740 Broadway New York NY 10019-4315

LURIA, ZELLA HURWITZ, psychology educator; b. N.Y.C., Feb. 18, 1924; d. Hyman Hurwitz and Dora (Garbarsky) H.; m. Salvador Edward Luria, Apr. 18, 1945; 1 child, Daniel David. BA, Bklyn., 1944; MA, Ind. U., 1947, PhD, 1951. lic. clin. psychologist, Mass. Ford Found. postdoctoral fellow U. Ill., Urbana, 1951-53, Russell Sage found. fellow, 1953-56, clin. researcher, 1954-58; asst. prof. psychology Tufts U., Medford, Mass., 1958-62, assoc. prof., 1962-70, prof., 1970—; psychiatry lectr. Mass. Gen. Hosp., Boston, 1970-79; vis. scholar Stanford U., 1977, 83; vis. prof. UCLA, 1992, 94, U. Mich., 1993. Sr. author: Psychology of Human Sexuality, 1979, Human Sexuality, 1987. Postdoctoral fellow USPHS, Paris, 1963-64, Bunting fellow Radcliffe Coll., 1989-90; Mellon Found. Faculty grantee Wellesley Coll., 1979-80. Mem. Tufts U. Am. Assn. Univ. Profs. (pres. 1986-87). Office: Tufts Univ Dept Of Psychology Medford MA 02155

LURIE, ALISON, author; b. Chgo., Sept. 3, 1926; children: John, Jeremy, Joshua. AB, Radcliffe Coll., 1947. Lectr. English Cornell U., 1969-73; adj. assoc. prof. English Cornell U., Ithaca, N.Y., 1973-76, assoc. prof., 1976-79, prof., 1979—. Author: V.R. Lang: A Memoir, 1959, Love and Friendship, 1962, The Nowhere City, 1965, Imaginary Friends, 1967, Real People, 1969, The War Between the Tates, 1974, Only Children, 1979, The Language of Clothes, 1981, Foreign Affairs, 1984, The Truth About Lorin Jones, 1988, Don't Tell the Grownups, 1990, Women and Ghosts, 1994. Recipient award in lit. Am. Acad. Arts and Letters, 1978, Pulitzer prize in fiction, 1985; fellow Yaddo Found., 1963-64, 66, Guggenheim Found., 1965, Rockefeller Found., 1967. Office: Cornell U Dept English Ithaca NY 14853

LURIE, ALVIN DAVID, lawyer; b. N.Y.C., Apr. 16, 1923; s. Samuel and Rose L.; m. Marian Weinberg, Aug. 21, 1944; children: James, Jeanne, Margery, Jonathan. AB, Cornell U., 1943, LLB, 1944. Bar: N.Y. 1944, D.C. 1978. Ptnr. various N.Y.C. law firms, 1944-74, including Lurie & Rubin, 1961-68, Aranow, Brodsky, Bohlinger & Einhorn, 1968-74; asst. commr. for employee plans and exempt orgns. IRS, Washington, 1974-78; ptnr. Chadbourne, Parke, Whiteside & Wolff, N.Y.C., 1978-80; counsel Chadbourne, Parke, Whiteside & Wolff, 1980-84; ptnr. Meyers, Tersigni, Lurie, Feldman & Gray, N.Y.C., 1984-91; counsel Meyers, Tersigni, Lurie, Feldman & Gray, 1992-94; pvt. practice N.Y.C., 1994-95; ptnr. Lurie & Gelband, 1996; pvt. practice, 1996—; mem. adv. bd. NYU Tax Inst., 1978-90, Tax Mgmt. adv. bd., 1978—. Author: Lurie's Commentaries on Pension Design, 1980, Lurie's Guide to VEBAs, 1983, Collected Commentaries on Pensions, 1984, ESOPs Made Easy, 1985. Contbr. articles to law revs., tax jours. Mem. ABA, N.Y. State Bar Assn. (chmn. spl. com. pension simplification 1986—), Assn. Bar City N.Y., Am. Coll. Tax Counsel, N.Y. Bar Found. Office: 1890 Palmer Ave Larchmont NY 10538-3059 *Hard work, in intensive spurts, is my formula. The work must be varied, permitting application of different skills in constantly changing, creative ways. But one thing more is needed: carpe diem.*

LURIE, HAROLD, engineer, lawyer; b. Durban, South Africa, Mar. 28, 1919; came to U.S., 1946, naturalized, 1952; s. Samuel Isaac and Dora (Mitchell) L.; m. Patricia Elkin, Mar. 26, 1959 (div. 1978); children—Diana Isabel, David Andrew. BS, U. Natal, South Africa, 1940, MS, 1946; PhD, Calif. Inst. Tech., 1950; JD, Northeastern U., 1989. Bar: Mass. 1989, D.C. 1991, U.S. Supreme Ct. 1993. Lectr. aeros. Calif. Inst. Tech., 1948-50, asst. prof. applied mechanics, 1953-56, assoc. prof., 1956-64, prof. engrng. sci., 1964-70, assoc. dean grad. studies, 1964-70, prof. emeritus, 1997—; dir. research and devel. New Eng. Electric System, 1971-79; dean engrng. Poly. Inst. N.Y., Bklyn., 1979-81; dean Coll. Engrng. Northeastern U., Boston, 1981-86; acting dir. advanced systems dept. Electric Power Rsch. Inst., 1974-75; cons. Yankee Atomic Electric Co., 1970-71; head weapons effectiveness group RAND Corp., 1950-52l sr. devel. engr. Oak Ridge Nat. Lab., 1956-57; vis. scholar U. Wash. Law Sch., 1990-91; assoc. dir. Calif. Coun. on Sci. and Tech., 1992-96; exec. dir. program for technical workshops with industry Calif. Inst. Tech., 1997—. Home: 8811 Pacific Coast Hwy # 189 Laguna Beach CA 92651

LURIE, HUGH JAMES, psychiatrist, educator; b. Chgo., May 22, 1935; s. Harold Hiram and Gertrude (Geitner) L.; m. Edythe Bruce Hammond, Oct. 7, 1961; children: Nicholas Hubbard, Jessica Stevens, Hugh Sterling. AB, Harvard U., 1955; MD, Yale U., 1961. Diplomate Am. Bd. Psychiatry and Neurology, Am. Bd. Child Psychiatry, Am. Gd. Geriatric Psychiatry. Resident in pediatrics Johns Hopkins U., Balt., 1961-63; resident in gen. psychiatry McLean Hosp.-Harvard U., Belmont, Mass., 1965-67; resident in child psychiatry Children's Hosp., Judge Baker Clinic, Harvard U., Boston, 1967-69; med. dir. Child Guidance Clinic, Tacoma, 1969-80; chief psychiatrist Good Samaritan Mental Health Ctr., Puyallup, Wash., 1980—; clin. asst. prof. psychiatry U. Wash. Sch. Medicine, Seattle, 1969-72, clin. assoc. prof., 1972-75, clin. prof., 1975—; coord. behavioral scis. Medex, physician asst. program, 1975—. Author: Clinical Psychiatry for the Primary Physician, 1985; writer, prod. about 85 ednl. videotapes for Am. Psychiat. Assn., U. Wash., Assn. Am. Med. Colls., Am. Acad. Family Practice, 1976—; exec. prodr. ednl. video Time Mirror, 1979 (bronze medal N.Y. Film and Video Festival 1979). Bd. dirs. Sta. KVOW, pub. radio, Seattle, 1988-94. Lt. M.C., USN, 1963-65. Recipient hon. mention Assn. for Acad. Psychiatry, 1990. Fellow Am. Psychiat. Assn. (mem., chmn. video subcom. 1978-95), Am. Acad. Child and Adolescent Psychiatry; mem. Group for Advancement Psychiatry (social issues com. 1992—), Wash. State Psychiat. Assn. (co-chmn. geriatrics com. 1992—), Wash. State Coun. Child and Adolescent Psychiatry. Avocations: playing chamber music (violin, viola), etching. Home: 1417 E Aloha St Seattle WA 98112-3931 Office: Good Samaritan Mental Health Ctr 325 E Pioneer Ave Puyallup WA 98372-3265

LURIE, JEFFREY, professional sports team executive; b. Sept. 8, 1951; married; 2 children. BA, Clark U.; MS in Psychology, Boston U.; PhD in Social Policy, Brandeis U. Pres., CEO Chestnut Hills Prodn., L.A.; pvt. practice, internat. publishing, specialty retailing; owner Phila. Eagles, 1994—; mem. NFL expansion com. Former trustee Clark U.; dir. Autism Rsch. Found., Boston; active local charitable cmty., Phila. Mem. Phila. C. of C. (exec. com.). Office: Philadelphia Eagles 3501 S Broad St Philadelphia PA 19148-5249*

LURIE, PAUL MICHAEL, lawyer; b. Chgo., Apr. 9, 1941; s. Haskell and Fay (Weinstein) L.; m. Margaret Berman, Aug. 2, 1966; children: Alexander, Rachel, Daniel, Matthew. BA, U. Mich., 1962, JD, 1965. Bar: Ill. 1965, U.S. Dist. Ct. (no. dist.) Ill., U.S. Ct. Appeals (7th cir.), U.S. Supreme Ct. Assoc. Fischel & Kahn, Chgo., 1967-68; ptnr. Fohrman, Lurie, Sklar & Simon, Ltd., Chgo., 1968-86, Neal, Gerber, Eisenberg & Lurie, Chgo., 1987-89, Schiff, Hardin & Waite, Chgo., 1989—; adj. prof. U. Ill. Coll. Art, Architecture and Urban Scis.; cons. Australian Law Reform Commn.; founder, gen. counsel, bd. dirs. Chgo. Architecture Found., 1966-76; counsel, bd. dirs. Chgo. Archtl. Assistance Ctr., 1979-89. Mem. editorial bd. Fed. Publs., Inc., constrn. adv. bd.; contbr. articles to profl. jours. Fellow Am. Coll. Constrn. Lawyers; mem. ABA (forum com. on constrn. industry, tort and ins. practice sect., design and constrn. com.), ASCE (hon. affiliate mem.), AIA (hon. mem. Chgo. chpt.), Internat. Bar Assn., Ill. Bar Assn., Chgo. Bar Assn. (former chmn. and founder land devel. and constrn. com.), Chgo. Coun. Lawyers, Nat. Inst. Bldg. Sci. (consultive coun.), Am. Consulting Engrs. Counsel (gen. counsel's forum), Am. Arbitration Assn. (chmn. constrn. adv. coun. Chgo. region, constrn. industry arbitrator), Internat. Constrn. Contracts Com., Cliff Dwellers Club, Std. Club. Jewish. Office: Schiff Hardin & Waite 7200 Sears Tower Chicago IL 60606-6327

LURIE, RANAN RAYMOND, political analyst, political cartoonist, artist, lecturer; b. Port Said, Egypt, May 26, 1932; came to U.S., 1968, naturalized, 1974; s. Joseph and Rose (Sam) L. (parents Israeli citizens); m. Tamar Fletcher, Feb. 25, 1958; children: Rod, Barry, Daphne, Danielle. Student, Herzelia High Sch., Tel Aviv, Israel, 1949; student, Jerusalem Art Coll., 1951. Corr. Maariv Daily, 1950-52; features editor Hador Daily, 1953-54; editor-in-chief Tevel mag., 1954-55; staff polit. cartoonist Yedioth Aharonot Daily, 1955-66, Honolulu Advertiser, 1979; lectr. polit. cartooning U. Hawaii; univ. lectr. in fine arts, polit. cartoon and polit. analysis Am. Program Bur., Boston.; polit. cartoonist Time Internat. mag., 1994-97; inventor 1st electronically syndicated bus.-news cartoon Lurie's Business World; 101 million reads of 1,-98 newspapers in 102 countries; 1996-97 Guiness Book of World Records; chief judge Internat. Cartoon Comp., Seoul, Korea, 1996. Author: Among the Suns, 1952, Lurie's Best Cartoons, 1961, Nixon Rated Cartoons, 1973, Pardon Me, Mr. President, 1974, Lurie's Worlds, 1980, So sieht es Lurie, 1981, Fed. Republic Germany, Lurie's Almanac (U.K.), 1982, (U.S.A.), 1983, Taro's International Politics, Japan, 1984, Lurie's Middle East, Israel, 1986; creator: The Expandable Painting, 1969; Cartoons used as guidelines in several encys., polit. sci. books.; 22 shows, Israel, Can., U.S., 1960-75, including, Expo 67, Can., Dominion Gallery, Montreal, Que., Can., Lim Gallery, Tel Aviv, 1965, Overseas Press Club, N.Y.C., 1962, 64, 75, U.S. Senate, Washington, Honolulu Acad. Fine Arts, 1979; represented by Circle Gallery, 1988-93, Genesis Gallery, Greenwich, 1996—; exhibited numerous group shows including, Smithsonian Instn., 1972, Circle Gallery, Washington, 1989; creator Japan's nat. cartoon symbol Taro-San, Taiwan's nat. cartoon symbol Cousin Lee; polit. cartoonist, Life Mag., N.Y.C., 1968-73, polit. cartoonist, interviewer, Die Welt, Bonn, W. Ger., 1980-81; contbr.: N.Y. Times, 1970—; contbg. editor, polit. cartoonist, Newsweek Internat., 1974-76, editor, polit. cartoonist, Vision Mag. of South Am., 1974-76, syndicated, United Features Syndicate, 1971-73; syndicated nationally by Los Angeles Times, also internationally by, N.Y. Times to over 260 newspapers, 1973-75, internationally by Editors Press Syndicate (345 newspapers), King Features Syndicate, 1975-83; syndicated in U.S. by Universal Press Syndicate, 1982-86, Cartoonews Internat. Syndicat, 1986—; polit. cartoonist, The Times of London, 1981-83, ABC's Nightline, 1991—, World News Show, 1993; sr. polit. analyst, editorial cartoonist Asahi Shimbun, Japan's largest daily newspaper, 1983-84; sr. analyst and polit. cartoonist U.S. News & World Report, 1984-85; chief editorial dir. Editors Press Service, 1985; joined staff MacNeil/Lehrer News Hour (PBS) as daily polit. cartoonist, analyst; editl. bd. Mid. East Quarterly, 1994—; creator, editor-in-chief Cartoon News, 1996. Chief judge Seoul (Republic of Korea) Internat. Cartoon Competition, 1996. Served as maj. Combat Paratroop, Israeli Army Res., 1950-67. Recipient highest Israeli journalism award, 1954; U.S. Headliners award, 1972; named Outstanding Editorial Cartoonist of Nat. Cartoonist Soc., 1971-78; Salon award Montreal Cartoon, 1971; N.Y. Front Page award, 1972, 74, 77; cert. merit U.S. Publ. Designers, 1974; award Overseas Press Club, 1979; John Fischetti polit. cartoon award, 1982, 86; sr. adj. fellow Ctr. Strategic Internat. Studies, Washington; Ranan R. Lurie Internat. Polit. Cartoon ann. award created in his honor by Nat. Fedn. Hispanic Owned Newspapers, 1994, RananR. Lurie Internat. award for Polit. Cartooning created by U.N. Soc. of Writers, 1995; recip. 1996 Hubert Humphrey 1st Amendment and Freedom of the Press Award, 1996. Mem. Soc. Profl. Journalists, Nat. Cartoonists Soc. Am., Assn. Editorial Cartoonists, Mensa, Overseas Press Club, Friars Club. Inventor 1st electronically animated TV news cartoon; creator 1st syndicated bus.-news cartoon Lurie's Business World; 104 million readers of 1,105 newspapers in 104 countries; 1997 Guiness Book of World Records. Office: Cartoonews Inc 9 Mountain Laurel Dr Greenwich CT 06831-2741 *The moment of truth will come when the cartoonist gauges the margin of time from the day he drew the cartoon. Then he can see how clearly or unclearly he has evaluated the situation through his work. Eventually, the simple facts and reality always win. Then it becomes apparent that wishful thinking is meaningless and the capacity to evaluate the project and even predict the events that are happening will eventually cement the professional status and integrity of the cartoonist.*

LURIE, ROD, film critic, writer, film director; b. Tel Aviv, May 15, 1962; came to U.S., 1966; s. Ranan R. and Tamar R. (Fletcher) L.; m. Gretchen Bean, June 24, 1989; children: Hunter Fletcher, Paige Clark. BS, U.S. Mil. Acad., West Point, N.Y., 1984. Film critic Greenwich (Conn.) News, 1986-89; entertainment reporter N.Y. Daily News, N.Y.C., 1988-89; contbg. editor L.A. Mag., 1990—, film critic, 1991—; American editor Empire Mag., L.A., 1991—; TV commentator Paramount TV, L.A., 1994—. Author: Once Upon A Time in Hollywood, 1995; talk show host Sta. KMPC, L.A., 1994—. Capt. U.S. Army, 1980-88. Mem. Broadcast Film Critic's Assn. (pres. 1995-96). Achievements include 1st Israeli born grad of West Point; profiled on Sixty Minutes. Office: 3815 W Olive Ave Ste 201 Burbank CA 91505-4648

LURIX, PAUL LESLIE, JR., chemist; b. Bridgeport, Conn., Apr. 6, 1949; s. Paul Leslie and Shirley Laurel (Ludwig) L.; m. Cynthia Ann Owens, May 30, 1970; children: Paul Christopher, Alexander Tristan, Einar Gabrielson. BA, Drew U., 1971; MS, Purdue U., 1973; postgrad., 1973—. Tech. dir. Analysts, Inc., Linden, N.J., 1976-77; chief chemist Caleb Brett USA, Inc., Linden, 1977-80; v.p. Tex. Labs., Inc., Houston, 1980-82; pres. Lurix Corp., Fulshear, Tex., 1982—; cons. LanData, Inc., Houston, 1980-88, Nat. Cellulose Corp., Houston, 1981-88, Met. Transit Authority, Houston, 1981—, Phillips 66, Houston, 1986—, Conoco, Inc., Houston, 1988—, Caronia Corp., Houston, 1988—, Compaq Computer, 1996—, M&H Engrng., 1994—, WBC Holdings, Inc., 1989-96; dir. research and devel. Stockbridge Software, Inc., Houston, 1986-88; v.p. Diesel King Corp., Houston, 1980-82. Contbr. articles to profl. jour. Patentee distillate fuel additives. Fellow Am. Inst. Chemists; mem. Am. Chem. Soc., ASTM, AAAS, Soc. Applied Spectroscopy, N.Y. Acad. Sci., Phi Kappa Phi, Phi Lambda Upsilon, Sigma Pi Sigma. Republican. Methodist. Lodge: Kiwanis (pres., 1970-71). Current work: Infrared spectroscopy; data base programming for science and industrial applications. Subspecialties: Infrared spectroscopy; Information systems, storage, and retrieval (computer science). Avocations: tennis, golf, piano.

LURTON, HORACE VANDEVENTER, brokerage house executive; b. Washington, Oct. 16, 1941; s. Horace Harmon III and Eleaner (Pentz) L.; m. Nancy Taylor Mackall, Aug. 30, 1964 (dec. 1992); children: Bowie VanDeventer, Sallie Taylor. Student, Gettysburg U., 1962; BS, Am. U., 1965. Registered prin. SEC. Stockbroker Thomson, McKinnon & Auchincloss, Washington, 1966-76, Dean Witter Reynolds, Chevy Chase, Md., 1977-79; stockbroker, branch mgr., dir. Johnston, Lemon & Co., Inc., Bethesda, Md., 1979-89; stockbroker, br. mgr., dir. Johnston, Lemon & Co., Inc., Washington, 1989-90; v.p., branch mgr. Janney, Montgomery, Scott, Washington, 1990—. Active various orgns. and charities, Washington, Md. Episcopalian. Avocation: biking. Home: 5004 Scarsdale Rd Bethesda MD 20816-2438 Office: Janney Montgomery Scott 1225 23rd St NW Washington DC 20037-1102

LURVEY, IRA HAROLD, lawyer; b. Chgo., Apr. 6, 1935; s. Louis and Faye (Grey) L.; m. Barbara Ann Sirvint, June 24, 1962; children: Nathana, Lawrence, Jennifer, Jonathan, David, Robert. BS, U. Ill., 1956; MS, Northwestern U., 1961; JD, U. Calif., Berkeley, 1965. Bar: Calif. 1965, Nev. 1966, U.S. Dist. Ct. (cen. dist.) Calif. 1966, U.S. Tax Ct. 1966, U.S. Ct. Appeals (9th cir.) 1966, U.S. Supreme Ct. 1975. Law clk. to hon. justices Nev. Supreme Ct., Carson City, 1965-66; from assoc. to ptnr. Pacht, Ross, Warne, Bernhard & Sears, Inc., 1966-84; predecessor firm Shea & Gould, L.A.; founding ptnr. Lurvey & Shapiro, L.A., 1984—; lectr. legal edn. programs; mem. Chief Justice's Commns. on Ct. Reform, Weighted Caseloads; mediator family law L.A. Superior Ct. Editor Community Property Jour., 1979-80, Primary Consultant CFL 2d, 1994; columnist Calif. Family Law Monthly; contbr. articles to profl. jours. Former chmn. L.A. Jr. Arts Ctr.; past pres. Cheviot Hills Homeowners Assn.; exec. v.p., counsel Hillel Acad. Sch., Beverly Hills, Calif., 1977—. With U.S. Army, 1957-58. Fellow Am. Acad. Matrimonial Lawyers (pres. So. Calif. chpt. 1991-92, mem. nat. bd. govs. 1992-94), Internat. Acad. Matrimonial Lawyers; mem. ABA (chair family law sect. 1996-97, exec. com. 1991-97, governing coun. 1986—, fin. officer 1991-92, chmn. support com., chmn. CLE, chmn. policy and issues com., vice chmn. com. arbitration and mediation, bd. of editors Family Adv. mag.), Calif. Bar Assn. (editor jour. 1982-85, chmn. family law sect. 1986-87, exec. com. family law sect. 1982-88, specialization adv. bd. family law 1979-82), L.A. County Bar Assn. (chmn. family law sect. 1981-82, exec. com. family law 1989-92), Beverly Hills Bar Assn. (chmn. family law sect. 1976-77). Home: 2729 Motor Ave Los Angeles CA 90064-3441 Office: Lurvey & Shapiro Ste 1550 2121 Avenue Of The Stars Los Angeles CA 90067-5010

LUSAS, EDMUND WILLIAM, food processing research executive; b. Woodbury, Conn., Nov. 25, 1931; s. Anton Frank and Damicele Nellie (Kasputis) L.; m. Jeannine Marie Muller, Feb. 2, 1957; children—Daniel, Ann, Paul. B.S., U. Conn., 1954; M.S., Iowa State U., 1955; Ph.D., U. Wis., 1958; M.B.A., U. Chgo., 1972. Project leader Quaker Oats Research Labs., Barrington, Ill., 1958-61, mgr. canned pet foods research, 1961-67, mgr. pet foods research, 1967-72, mgr. sci. services, 1972-77; assoc. dir. Food Protein R & D Ctr., Tex. A&M U., College Station, 1977-78, dir., 1978-93, head fats, oils and extrusion programs, 1993-97; pres. Ed Lusas, Problem Solvers, Inc., Bryan, Tex., 1997—. Author over 125 publs.; patentee in field. Assoc. editor Jour. Am. Oil Chem. Soc., 1980-88. Fund raiser YMCA, Crystal Lake, Ill., 1970-77, chmn. fin. com., 1977. Recipient F.N. Peters research award Quaker Oats Co., 1968. Mem. Am. Oil Chemists Soc., Inst. Food Technologists (Gen. Foods research fellow 1956, 57), Am. Chem. Soc., Am. Assn. Cereal Chemists, Am. Soc. Agrl. Engrs., R&D Assocs., Guayule Soc. Am., Sigma Xi, Phi Tau Sigma. Avocation: fishing. Home and Office: 3604 Old Oaks Dr Bryan TX 77802-4743

LUSBY, GRACE IRENE, infection control nurse practitioner; b. Huntington Park, Calif., Aug. 20, 1935; d. Fletcher Homer and Charlotte Ione (Hayden) L. BS in Nursing, U. Calif., San Francisco, 1964, MS, 1968; cert. program in epidemiology, U. Calif., San Diego, 1981. RN, pub. health nurse, psychiat. nurse. Staff nurse, head nurse cancer rsch. unit U. Calif., San Francisco, 1964-66; pvt. duty nurse open heart surgery Profl. Registry, San Francisco, 1966-68; infection control coord. San Francisco Gen. Hosp., 1969-92; infection control cons. Oakland, Calif., 1992—; infection control rep. Calif. Task Force on AIDS, Sacramento, 1983-87, U.S. AIDS Task Force, San Francisco, 1983-92; co-establisher 1st infection control program for AIDS, San Francisco Gen. Hosp., 1983; mem. infection control-adv. coms. Svc. Employees Internat. Union, Calif. Nurses Assn., Mayor's Homeless Com., CAL-OSHA, also others, San Francisco, 1985—; infection control cons. emergency, home care, skill nursing, psychiatry, San Francisco, 1985—. Contbr. chpts. to books. Recipient Founder's award U. Calif.-San Francisco AIDS/ARC Update, 1988. Mem. Assn. Practitioners Infection Control (past treas., rec. sec., chmn. AIDS resource group), Women's AIDS Network (charter), PEO (rec. sec., corr. sec.), Sigma Theta Tau. Avocations: hiking, genealogy, weaving. Home and Office: 5966 Chabolyn Ter Oakland CA 94618-1914

LUSCH, CHARLES JACK, physician; b. Lehighton, Pa., Feb. 15, 1936; s. Charles Norman and Loretta (Gaumer) L.; m. Carole Faye Eckart, Aug. 17, 1957; children: Marjorie, Susan, Stephen, Robert. AB in Biology magna cum laude, Lafayette Coll., Easton, Pa., 1957; MD, Temple U., 1961. Diplomate in med. oncology, hematology, internal medicine, forensic medicine; diplomate Am. Bd. Forensic Medicine. Pres. Berks Hematology-Oncology Assocs., Reading, Pa., 1968—; chief sect. of med. oncology & hematology Reading Hosp. & Med. Ctr., Reading, 1970—; dir. Pa. State Hemophilia Ctr., Reading Hosp. & Med. Ctr., 1973—; v.p. Lusch Motor Parts, Lehighton, Pa., 1975—; chief sect. med. oncology & hematology Community Gen. Hosp., Reading, 1980—; asst. chief medicine Reading Hosp. and Med. Ctr., 1986—; med. dir. Pocono Internat. Raceway, 1980-85; chmn. institutional rev. bd. Reading Hosp. and Med. Ctr., 1986—, dir. continuing med. edn., 1987—; med. dir. Berks County Hospice, Berks County Vis. Nurse Assn., Reading, 1987—; dir. oncology svcs. Reading Hosp. and Med. Ctr., 1990—; med. adv. com. Pa. Blue Shield, Camp Hill, Pa., 1987—; bd. dirs. Berks Home Health Car, Reading Cancer Ctr., Reading Hosp.; malpractice cons. Med. Protective Ins. Co., Ft. Wayne, Ind., 1985—; cons. in hematology and oncology Pottsville (Pa.) Hosp. and Good Samaritan Hosp., 1975—; clin. asst. prof. medicine Pa. Med. Sch., 1984—, Pa. State Med. Sch., 1981—, Temple U. Med. Sch., clin. assoc. prof. 1990; sr. clin. instr. Mahnemann U. Med. Sch., 1968—; prin. investigator Ea. Coop Oncology Group, 1975-90, Nat. Surg. Adj. & Breast Project, 1986—. Contbr. articles to profl. jours.; editor The Med. Record (regional med. jour.), 1970-71. Advisor Future Physicians Am., Reading, 1965; bd. dirs. Berks County unit Am. Cancer Soc., Reading, 1968-78, Keystone Cmty. Blood Bank, Reading, 1970-80; adv. com. The Women's Ctr., Reading Hosp., 1987-88; mem. bd. divsn. ch. soc. Evang. Luth. Ch. Am., Chgo.; pres. ch. coun. Atonement Luth. Ch., Wyomissing, Pa. Lt. comdr. USPHS, 1965-67. Fellow ACP; mem. Pa. Soc. Hematology-Oncology (sec.-treas. 1986-87), Am. Soc. Clin. Oncology, Am. Soc. Hematology, Am. Fedn. Clin. Rsch., Acad. Hospice Physicians (publs. com. 1989—), U.S. Amateur Ballroom Dance Assn. (past pres. Reading chpt.), Sports Car Club Am., Phi Beta Kappa, Alpha Omega Alpha. Republican. Lutheran. Avocations: competition ballroom dancing, tennis, motor racing. Home: 1617 Meadowlark Rd Wyomissing PA 19611 Office: Berks County Oncology Assoc 301 S 7th Ave Reading PA 19611-1410

LUSCOMBE, HERBERT ALFRED, physician, educator; b. Johnstown, Pa., Aug. 9, 1916; s. Herbert O. and Clara C. (Geiselhart) L.; m. Sally T. McHugh; children: Herbert J., Susan M., Jill A. B.S., St. Vincent Coll., 1936, M.D., Jefferson Med. Coll., 1940. Diplomate: Am. Bd. Dermatology. Intern Jefferson Hosp., Phila., 1940-42, resident, 1946-48; resident U. Pa., 1948-49; mem. faculty Jefferson Med. Coll. Thomas Jefferson U., Phila., 1949—, prof., chmn. dept. dermatology, 1959-86; chief attending dermatologist Thomas Jefferson U. Hosp., 1959—, prof. emeritus of dermatology, 1987—, sr. attending dermatologist, 1987—; cons. dermatology Wills Eye Hosp., Lankenau Hosp., Herbert A. Luscombe lectr. in dermatology, 1984—. Contbr. articles to profl. jours. Recipient Clark Finneraud award Dermatology Found., 1981. Fellow AMA, Soc. Investgative Dermatology, Am. Acad. Dermatologists, Sigma Xi; mem. Phila. Dermatologic Soc. (pres. 1963-64), Alpha Omega Alpha. Roman Catholic. Club: Aronimink Golf. Home: 600 Old Gulph Rd Narberth PA 19072-1622 Office: Jefferson Med Coll 111 S 11th St Philadelphia PA 19107-4824

LUSHER, JEANNE MARIE, pediatric hematologist, educator; b. Toledo, June 9, 1935; d. Arnold Christian and Violet Cecilia (French) L. BS summa cum laude, U. Cin., 1956, MD, 1960. Lic. physician, Mich.; cert. in pediat. and hematology/oncology, Am. Bd. Pediat. Resident in pediat. Tulane divsn. Charity Hosp. La., New Orleans, 1961-64; fellow in pediat. hematology-oncology Child Rsch. Ctr. Mich., Detroit, 1964-65, St. Louis Children's Hosp./Washington U., 1965-66; instr. pediat. Washington U., St. Louis, 1965-66; from instr. to assoc. prof. Sch. Medicine Wayne State U., Detroit, 1966-74, prof., 1974—; dir. divsn. hematology-oncology Children's Hosp. Mich., Detroit, 1976—; Marion I. Barnhart prof. hemostasis rsch. Sch. Medicine Wayne State U., Detroit, 1989—; med. dir. Nat. Hemophilia Found., N.Y.C., 1987-94, chmn. med. and sci. adv. coun., 1994—. Author, editor: Treatment of Bleeding Disorders with Blood Components, 1980, Sickle Cell, 1974, 76, 81, Hemophilia and von Willebrand Disease in the 1990's, 1991, Acquired Bleeding Disorder in Children, 1981, F VIII/von Willebrand Factor and Platelets in Health and Disease, 1987, Inhibitors to Factor VIII, 1994, Blood Coagulation Inhibitors, 1996. Mem. Citizens Info. Com., Pontiac Township, Mich., 1980-82; apptd. mem. Hazardous Waste Incinerator Commn., Oakland County, Mich., 1981. Recipient Disting. Alumnus award U. Cin. Alumni Assn., 1990. Mem. Am. Bd. Pediat. (chmn. sub-bd. on hematology-oncology 1988-90), Am. Soc. Hematology (chmn. sci. com. pediat. 1991-92), Am. Pediat. Soc., Soc. Pediat. Rsch., Internat. Soc. Thrombosis-Hemostasis (chmn. factor VIII/IX subcom. 1985-90, chmn. sci. and standardization com. 1996-98), Mich. Humane Soc. Avocations: nature, wildlife, hiking, gardening. Office: Children's Hosp Mich 3901 Beaubien Blvd Detroit MI 48201-2119

LUSHT, KENNETH MICHAEL, business administration educator; b. N.Y.C., Dec. 22, 1942; m. Elizabeth Enloe Hall; children: Elizabeth, Alexander. BBA, Emory U., 1964; PhD, Ga. State U., 1973. Prof. bus. adminstrn. Pa. State U., University Park, 1973—, acad. program dir. continuing edn., 1983—, dir. inst. for real estate studies, 1986—, chmn. dept. ins. and real estate, 1989—, assoc. dean for rsch., 1995—; pres. Kenneth M. Lusht Cons., State College, 1983—. Author 3 textbooks; editorial bd. Jour. of the Am. Real Estate And Urban Econs. Assn., 1986-92, Jour. of Property Rsch., 1990—, Appraisal Jour., 1991—, Jour. of Real Estate Fin., 1993—; contbr. articles to profl. jours. Vis. fellow RMIT, 1989, 95, 97, Vis. Rsch. fellow U. West Sydney, 1993, U. Hong Kong, 1994, 95; recipient Wagner award Am. Inst. of Real Estate Appraisers, 1986. Mem. Am. Real Estate and Urban Econs. Assn. (pres. 1987, bd. dirs. 1982-84, 88-90), Am. Real Estate Soc. Office: Coll Bus Pa State U 409 Bab University Park PA 16802

LUSK, HARLAN GILBERT, national park superintendent; b. Jersey City, June 22, 1943; s. Harlan H. and Mary M. (Kuhl) L.; m. Catherine L. Rutherford, Oct. 11, 1986. BA in History, Gettysburg Coll., 1965. Supervisory historian Cape Hatteras Nat. Seashore, Manteo, N.C., 1968; historian Nat. Pk. Svc., Washington, 1968-69; programs specialist So. Utah Group, Cedar City, 1968-70; pk. supt. Wolf Trap Farm Pk., Vienna, Va., 1970-72; supervisory pk. ranger Blue Ridge Pkwy., Roanoke, Va., 1972-74; pk. supt. Appomattox (Va.) Courthouse, Nat. Hist. Pk., 1974-76, Valley Forge (Pa.), Nat. Hist. Pk., 1976-81, Big Bend (Tex.) Nat. Pk., 1981-86, Glacier Nat. Pk., West Glacier, Mont., 1986-94; pk. supt. Albright Tng. Ctr. Grand Canyon Nat. Pk., Ariz., 1994-95; chief, Divsn. Tng. and Employee Nat. Park Svc., Washington, 1995-97; chmn. Gil Lusk Assocs., 1997—; group mgr. The Cholla Group, 1997—; organizer 1st regional conf. Rio Grande Border, States on Pks. and Wildlife, Laredo, Tex., 1985. Bd. dirs. Tech. Com. on Pks. & Recreation Cen. Va. Planning Dist., 1972-74, Fed. Exec. Assn. Roanoke Valley, 1972-74, Flathead Basin Commn., 1986-94, Flathead Conv. & Visitor Assn., 1986-94, Sonoran Inst., 1995—; prin. founder, 1st pres., Appomattox County Hist. Soc., 1974-76; trustee Sci. Mus. Assn. Roanoke Valley, 1972-74, Nature Conservancy Mont., 1994—; ex-officio Friends of Valley Forge, 1977-81; founder, ex-officio, bd. dirs. Valley Forge Pk. Interpretive Assn., 1977-81; founder Big Bend Area Travel Assn., chmn., 1984-86. Recipient Meritorious Svc. award Dept. Interior, 1986. Mem. Glacier Natural History Assn. (ex officio 1986-94), Glacier Nat. Pk. Assocs. (founder, ex-officio 1989-94), George Wright Soc., Lions, Rotary.

Avocations: golf, antiques, computers, collecting artwork, hiking. Office: Grand Canyon Nat Pk 3665 E Windy Point Dr Tucson AZ 85718-1422

LUSK, WILLIAM EDWARD, real estate, oil company executive; b. Medicine Lodge, Kans., May 16, 1916; s. William Edward and Teresa (Rhoades) L.; m. Anita Ballard, Feb. 1, 1942; children—William Edward, Janet Kathryn and James Raymond (twins). B.S. in Edn; A.B. in Econs, Ft. Hays State Coll., 1939; student, Washburn U., 1936; postgrad., Kans. U., 1940-41. Tchr. Protection (Kans.) High Sch., 1939-41; mgr. real estate dept. Wheeler, Kelly & Hagny Investment Co., Wichita, Kans., 1946-63; co-founder, exec. v.p., treas., dir. Clinton Oil Co., Wichita, 1963-73; pres. Lusk Real Estate Co., 1963—, Lusk Investment Co., 1973—; Pres. Wichita Real Estate Bd., 1961. Founder Lusk Found., 1968, William E. Lusk Scholarship, Ft. Hays State Coll., 1969; bd. dirs. Jr. Achievement Wichita. Served with USNR, 1942-46; comdr. Res. Named Kans. Realtor of Year Kans. Assn. Real Estate Bds., 1962; recipient Alumni Achievement award Ft. Hays Kan. State Coll., 1971. Mem. VFW, Sojourners, Res. Officers Assn., Naval Res. Officers Assn., Navy League, Phi Alpha Delta, Alpha Kappa Psi (hon.). Methodist (bd. dirs. 1965-70, fin. chmn. 1969—). Clubs: Wichita Country, Wichita (bd. dirs. 1969-72, pres. 1972), McConnell AFB Officers. Lodge: Masons (32 degree). Home: 6 W Parkway N Wichita KS 67206 Office: 1608 E Lewis St Wichita KS 67211-1823 *In business and personal relationships I have found strength in times of adversity and self-control in times of success by forming the habit of calling to mind this guideline: Things are never as good as they seem to be on the day they look good-nor are things as bad as they seem to be on the day they appear bad.*

LUSKY, LOUIS, legal educator; b. Columbus, Ohio, May 15, 1915; s. Leonard Morris and Amy (Kleeman) L.; m. Ruth Agnes Anderson, Aug. 31, 1946; children: Mary Hibbard Friedman, John Anderson; 1 child by previous marriage, Peter Joris. BA, U. Louisville, 1935; LLB, Columbia, 1937. Bar: N.Y. 1938, Ky. 1947. Law clk. to Supreme Ct. Justice Harlan F. Stone, 1937-38; assoc. Root, Clark, Buckner & Ballantine, N.Y.C., 1938-42, 44-45; civilian mem. ops. analysis sect. 8th Air Force, 1943-44; with legal div. U.S. Mil. Govt., Germany, 1945-46; ptnr. Wyatt & Grafton, Louisville, 1947-51; sole practice Louisville, 1952-63; prof. law Columbia Law Sch., 1963-85, Betts prof. law, 1979-85, prof. emeritus, 1985—. Author: (with others) Southern Justice, 1965, By What Right?, 1975, Our Nine Tribunes, 1993. Mem. ABA, ACLU (nat. com. 1963-67, nat. bd. 1967-70), Am. Law Inst. Home: 623 Eastbrook Rd Ridgewood NJ 07450-2114 Office: 435 W 116th St New York NY 10027-7201 also: 1250 E Ridgewood Ave Ridgewood NJ 07450-3930

LUSS, DAN, chemical engineering educator; b. Tel Aviv, Israel, May 5, 1938; came to U.S., 1963, naturalized, 1973; s. Manfred and Gertrude (Weinstein) L.; m. Amalia Rubin, Sept. 4, 1966; children: Noya, Limor. BS, Technion Inst. Tech., Haifa, Israel, 1960, MSc, 1963; PhD, U. Minn., 1966. Registered profl. engr., Tex. Asst. prof. chem. engring. U. Minn., Mpls., 1966-67; asst. prof. chem. engring. U. Houston, 1967-69, asso. prof., 1969-72, prof., 1972—, chmn. dept., 1975-95; assoc. dir. Tex. Ctr. for Superconductivity, 1988-92; cons. to several chem. cos. Editor: Revs. in Chem. Engring.; mem. editorial bd. Sci. and Engring, Catalysis Rev. Fellow Am. Inst. Chem. Engrs. (Allan P. Colburn award 1973, Profl. Progress award 1979, Wilhelm award 1986, chmn. awards com., former mem. editorial bd. jour.,former dir.), Am. Chem. Soc. (Honor scroll award of Indsl. Engring. Chemistry div. 1967); mem. NAE, Am. Soc. Engring. Edn. (Curtis McGraw award 1977 3M-Chem. Engring. lectureship award 1985). Home: 6242 Paisley St Houston TX 77096-3727 Office: U Houston Dept Chem Engring Houston TX 77204-4792

LUSSEN, JOHN FREDERICK, pharmaceutical laboratory executive; b. N.Y.C., Jan. 5, 1942; s. Frederick Maurice and Kathleen (Herlihy) L.; m. Kathleen Elizabeth Sheppard; children: Tara, Eric, Gregory. BS in Fin., Fordham U., 1963, JD, 1967; LLM in Tax, NYU, 1971. Bar: N.Y. 1967. Tax atty. Pfizer Inc., N.Y.C., 1971-74; mgr. taxes SCM Corp., N.Y.C., 1974-79; v.p. taxes Abbott Labs., Abbott Park, Ill., 1979—. Capt. U.S. Army, 1968-70. Mem. ABA, Tax Execs. Inst., Bus. Roundtable (mem. tax subcom.), P.R. USA Found. (pres.). Avocations: tennis, golf. Home: 1055 Westleigh Rd Lake Forest IL 60045 Office: Abbott Labs D367 AP6D 100 Abbott Park Rd Abbott Park IL 60064-3502

LUSSIER, JEAN-PAUL, dentistry educator; b. Montreal, Sept. 17, 1917; s. Eugene and Parmelia (Gauthier) L.; m. Juliette Laurin, May 4, 1943; children: Louis, Renee Lussier Brecknock, Josee, Anne Lussier Morin, Pierre, Helene Lussier Black, Andre. BA, U. Montreal, 1938, DDS, 1942, MS, 1952; PhD, U. Calif., San Francisco, 1959; DSc (hon.), McGill U., 1972, Laval U., 1995. Mem. U. Montreal faculty medicine, dept. physiology, 1946-52, 54-57, mem. faculty dentistry, 1957-62, 79-83, prof. emeritus, 1983—, dean, 1962-79, chmn. health scis. coordinating com., 1979-83; rsch. fellow U. Calif.-San Francisco, 1952-54; cons. WHO, 1972—. Recipient award Am. Acad. Dental Medicine, 1958, award Alpha Omega, 1962. Fellow Am. Coll. Dentists, Internat. Coll. Dentists, Acad. Dentistry Internat. (hon.), Royal Coll. Dentists, Academie dentaire du Quebec; mem. Fedn. Dentaire Internationale, Can. Dental Assn. (hon.). Home: Apt 415, 4800 de Maisonneuve Blvd W, Westmount, PQ Canada H3Z 1M2

LUST, BARBARA C., psychology and linguistics educator; d. John Benedict and Virginia (Sleth) L. BA in English Lit., Manhattanville Coll., 1963; postgrad., Fairleigh Dickinson, 1965, The New Sch. for Social Rsch., 1965-66, U. Geneva, 1968-69; MA in English Lit., Fordham U., 1971; PhD Devel. Psychology, CUNY, 1975. Postdoctoral fellow dept. linguistics and philosophy MIT, Cambridge, 1974-76; from asst. prof. to prof. dept. human development and family studies Cornell U., Ithaca, N.Y., 1976—, field rep. cognitive studies program, 1987—, co-dir., 1992—, prof. modern langs. and linguistics, 1990—; vis. prof. SUNY, Binghamton, 1977; vis. scientist MIT, 1984, 90, 96-97; vis. scholar Kelaniya U., Sri Lanka, 1984, U.S. Edml. Found., 1984; cons. in field, lectr. various colls. and univs. Author: Studies in the Acquisition of Anaphora (vol I 1986, II 1987); co-editor, author: Syntactic Theory & First Language Acquisition, 1994 (vol. I and II); co-author: Studies in the Cognitive Basis of Language Development, 1975; contbr. articles to prof. jours., chpts. to books. Grantee NIMH, 1976; fellow NIH, 1990; Smithsonian grant Am. Inst. Indian Studies, 1980-81; recipient Travel award Lingustistic Soc. Am. and NSF, 1982, James McKeen Cattell award, 1992-93, N.Y. State Coll. Human Ecology award, 1976-79, 83; grantee NSF, 1979-88, 92-93, 95, fellow, 1989-91, Rsch. award, 1988-89, Vis. Professorship for Women award, 1996-97, UFE award, 1997. Fellow AAAS (chair linguistics and the lang. scis. 1993-94); mem. APA, Linguistic Soc. Am. (del. to AAAS psychology and linguistics sects. 1988—), Am. Psychol. Soc., Internat. Assn. Study Child Language, Soc. Rsch. Child Devel., Internat. Soc. Woman in Cognitive Neurosci., Internat. Soc. Korean Linguistics, New England Child Lang. Assn., N.Y. Acad. Scis., Soc. Philosophy and Psychology, Linguistic Assn. Great Britian, Piaget Soc. Democrat. Office: Cornell U Human Devel & Family Studies Ng 28 Marth Van Rensse Ithaca NY 14853

LUST, HERBERT COHNFELDT, II, finance executive; b. Chgo., Oct. 31, 1926; s. Herbert Cohnfeldt and Jennie (Friedman) L.; m. Virginia Wertheimer; children: Herbert Cohnfeldt III, Conrad. MA, U. Chgo., 1948. Pres. Pvt. Water Supply, Inc. Greenwich Assocs., N.Y.C., 1961—, co-owner, dir. Gallery Bernard, 1969-87; dir. First Va. Real Estate Trust, Washington, 1981-83; chmn. bd. BRT, Great Neck, N.Y., 1983-85; chmn. United Mchts. & Mfg., Teaneck, N.J., 1991-93; owner Herbert Lust Gallery, N.Y.C., 1995—; lectr. comparative lit. U. Chgo., 1956-59; bd. dirs. Prime Hospitality, BRT. Author: 12 Principals of Art Investment, 1969, Alberto Giacometti, 1970, Enrico Baj, 1972, Violence and Defiance, 1983. Served in USN, 1944-46. Named Fulbright scholar, 1949-51. Jewish. Office: 1356 Madison Ave New York NY 10128-0826

LUSTE, JOSEPH FRANCIS, JR., land use, environmental transportation and planning specialist; b. Troy, N.Y., Dec. 7, 1940; s. Joseph Francis and Catherine (Coler) L.; m. Migdalia Malissa Gallardo, Jan. 31, 1970; children: Kimberly, Jonathan. AAS in Engring., Hudson Valley Community Coll., 1960; BA in Planning, Rutgers U., 1979; M in Aviation Mgmt., Embry-Riddle Aero. U., 1985; PhD in Property Mgmt., Western States U., 1987. Lic. profl. planner; cert. environ. specialist; cert. instr. Jr. engr. Tallamy Assocs., Inc., Washington, 1965-71; staff engr., planner Barrett & Hale, Inc., Hato Rey, P.R., 1971-73; sr. engr., planner T&M Assocs., Inc., Middletown, N.J., 1973-80; dir. planning and devel. Twp. of Middletown, 1980-82; head planning, engring. and devel. County of Atlantic, Atlantic City, 1982-84; prin. planner, office mgr. Edwards and Kelcey, Inc., Atlantic City, 1984-86; dir. planning, assoc. Pennoni Assocs., Inc., Haddon Heights, N.J., 1986-90; exec. dir., chief exec. officer Cross County Connection Transp. Mgmt. Assn., Marlton, N.J., 1990-92; pres, CEO Phoenix Group Consulting Svcs., Cherry Hill, N.J., 1992—. Author planning, environ., housing and transp. reports. Dir. aerospace edn. USAF, CAP, McGuire AFB, N.J., 1984; exec. com. Cross Country Transp. Mgmt. Assn., Burlington County, N.J., 1989-90, trustee, 1989-90; chmn. N.J. Transit Corp. Bus. Transit Adv. Bd., 1994—. Recipient Assistance award Sr. Citizens Council, 1981., Cert. Appreciation Atlantic County Pvt. Industry Council, 1983. Mem. Am. Planning Assn. (charter, exec. com. N.J. chpt. 1982), Urban Land Inst., Met. Assn. Urban Designers and Environ. Planners, Internat. Real Estate Inst., Greater Atlantic City C. of C. (chmn. transp. com. 1986-91), South Jersey C. of C. (transp. com. 1986—), Greater Mainland C. of C. (bd. dirs.), Nat. Coun. Urban Devel. (planning and devel. com. N.J. chpt. 1989—), Internat. Platform Assn., World Affairs Coun., Assn. Commuter Transp., U.S. Nature Conservancy, Inst. Transp. Engrs., Environ. Assessment Assn., Libr. of Congress (assoc.), Nat. Trust for Hist. Preservation, U.S. Dept. Def. Excellent Installations Team. Democrat. Seventh Day Adventist. Avocations: camping, remodeling, reading, youth programs. Office: The Phoenix Group 515 Grove St Ste 3Ca Haddon Heights NJ 08035-1756

LUSTENBERGER, LOUIS CHARLES, JR., lawyer; b. Chgo., Mar. 13, 1936; s. Louis Charles and Virginia (Chesrown) L.; m. Anita T. Anderson, June 17, 1961; children: Louis, Gwyn. BA, Williams Coll., 1959; LLB, Harvard U., 1962. Bar: N.Y. 1963, U.S. Dist. Ct. (so. and ea. dist.) N.Y. 1964, U.S. Dist. Ct. (we. dist.) N.Y. 1986, U.S. Ct. Appeals (2d cir.) 1964, U.S. Ct. Appeals (3d cir.) 1989, U.S. Ct. Appeals (5th cir.) 1980, U.S. Supreme Ct. 1978, U.S. Ct. Appeals (10th cir.) 1993, U.S. Dist Ct. (we. dist.) Mich., 1996, U.S. Ct. Appeals (6th cir.) 1996, U.S. Dist. Ct. (so. dist.) Tex., 1997. Assoc. Donovan, Leisure, Newton & Irvine, N.Y.C., 1962-71, ptnr., 1971—. Sr. warden St. Barnabas Ch., Irvington, N.Y., 1980-82; chmn. Irvington Zoning Bd., 1989—. Fellow Am. Coll. Trial Lawyers; mem. Assn. of Bar of City of N.Y., N.Y. State Bar Assn., N.Y. County Lawyers Assn., Phi Beta Kappa. Republican. Presbyterian. Home: 86 Fargo Ln Irvington NY 10533-1202 Office: Donovan Leisure Newton & Irvine 30 Rockefeller Plz New York NY 10112

LUSTER, GEORGE ORCHARD, professional society administrator; b. Pitts., Mar. 20, 1921; s. James W. and Gertrude (Orchard) L.; m. Edith A. Townsend, May 3, 1946 (dec. May 1989); children: Thomas, Carolea, Patricia; m. Mary Jane Herbolich, Oct. 1990. BS with honors, U. Pitts., 1949. CPA, Pa. Acct., Am. Inst. Rsch., Pitts., 1948-49; mgr. Price Waterhouse (CPAs), Pitts., 1949-59; treas., asst. sec. Mellon Inst., Pitts., 1959-67; treas. Carnegie-Mellon U., 1967-80; asst. sec., asst. treas., supervising com. Bellefield Boiler Plant, Pitts., 1962-71; treas., asst. sec. MPC Corp., Pitts., 1963-80; dir. adminstrn. Fin. Execs. Inst., 1980-86; instr. Robert Morris Sch., 1955-59, U. Pitts., 1959. Bd. dirs. Ctrl. Blood Bank, Pitts., 1973-80. With USAAF, 1943-46. Mem. AICPA, Fin. Execs. Inst., Air and Waste Mgmt. Assn. (treas. 1966-95), Pa. Inst. CPAs, River Bend Golf Club, Alpha Kappa Psi, Beta Gamma Sigma. Republican. Methodist. Home: 9238 SE Deerberry Pl Tequesta FL 33469-1804 *Individual success is relative to the challenges that one meets through life and how one perceives them as opportunities to learn, to be creative, and to be innovative in defining and planning actions to achieve one's goals.*

LUSTGARTEN, IRA HOWARD, lawyer; b. N.Y.C., July 31, 1929; s. Louis and Florine Josephine (Van Mindeno) L.; m. Rhoda Manne, Oct. 24, 1954; children: Lise Anne, Nancy Ellen. AB, NYU, 1950; LLB, Columbia U., 1958. Bar: N.Y. 1958, Fla. 1978, U.S. Dist. Ct. (so. dist.) N.Y. 1959, U.S. Ct. Claims 1985, U.S. Ct. Appeals (fed. cir.) 1986. Assoc. Proskauer Rose Goetz Mendelsohn, N.Y.C., 1958-68, ptnr., 1968-79; ptnr. Willkie Farr & Gallagher, N.Y.C., 1979—; former lectr. law Columbia U. Served to lt. USNR, 1951-55. Mem. ABA, Am. Law Inst., Am. Coll. Probate Counsel Found. (past pres.), Am. Coll. Probate Counsel, N.Y. Bar Assn. (past chmn. trusts and estates law sect.), Assn. of Bar of City of N.Y. (former chmn. trusts, estates, and surrogate cts.), Pub. Adminstrs. N.Y. (adm. bd. oversee), Fla. Bar Assn., Internat. Acad. Estate and Trust Law, N.Y. (legis. adv. com. to rev. law of trusts and estates). Office: Willkie Farr & Gallagher 1 Citicorp Ctr 153 E 53rd St New York NY 10022-4611

LUSTIG, JOANNE, librarian; b. Newark, July 22, 1952; d. Melvin and Grace Ann (Kertsmar) L.; m. Glenn Seggel, Mar. 26, 1988. BA summa cum laude, Montclair State Coll., 1975; MLS, Rutgers U., 1978. Asst. libr. Sterling Drug Inc., N.Y.C., 1979-80, sr. editor, 1980; info. specialist Knoll Pharms., Whippany, N.J., 1980-82, sr. info. specialist, 1982-84, mgr. med. and sci. info., 1984-96, assoc. dir. med. and sci. info., 1996—; bd. dirs. Highlands Regional Libr. Coop., Chester, N.J., 1990-94, pres. 1991-92; mem. N.J. Libr. Network Strategic Planning Com., 1990-91. Mem. NAFE, Spl. Librs. Assn. (N.J. chpt. pres. 1987-88, v.p. 1986-87, editor bull. 1984-86, Pharm. Divsn. archivist 1989-90, chair regional program planning com. 1985-86), Soc. for Competitive Intelligence Profls., Drug Info. Assn. Jewish. Office: Knoll Pharms 3000 Continental Dr N Budd Lake NJ 07828-1202

LUSTIG, NORA CLAUDIA, researcher; b. Buenos Aires, Argentina, Jan. 13, 1951; came to U.S., 1989; d. Xavier Friedrich and Anna (Tenenbaum) L.; m. Antonio Carlos Martin-Del-Campo, Mar. 22, 1975; children: Carlos Javier, Liliana. BA in Econs., U. Calif., Berkeley, 1972, MA in Econs., 1974, PhD in Econs., 1979. Prof. econ. studies ctr. El Colegio de Mex., Mex., Mex., 1975-91; acad. coord. El Colegio de Mex., Mex., 1975-76, 86-88; vis. scholar econs. dept. MIT, Cambridge, 1982; vis. prof. dept. natural resources and agrl. econs. Inst. of Internat. Studies U. Calif., Berkeley, 1984; sr. fellow Fgn. Policy Studies program The Brookings Inst., 1989—; cons. Office of Econ. and Social Planning, Ministry of Budget and Programming, Mexico City, Mexican Food System, Office of Advisors to the Pres., Mexico City, UN Econ. Commn. for Latin Am., Mexico City, 1984-85, World Bank and Inter-American Devel. Bank; editorial bd. Economia Mexicand Neuva Epoca, Ctr. US-Mexican Studies, Latin American Rsch. Review. Author: Mexico: The Remaking of an Economy, 1992; co-editor: North America Free Trade Assessing the Impact, 1992; editor: Coping with Austerity, Poverty and Inequality in Latin America, 1994; contbr. numerous articles to profl. jours. Mem. Internat. Food Policy Rsch. Inst. (bd. dirs.). Office: Brookings Instn 1775 Massachusetts Ave NW Washington DC 20036-2188

LUSTMAN, PATRICK J., psychiatrist. Recipient Am. Diabetes Clin. Rsch. grantee, 1996. Office: Washington U Sch Med 660 S Euclid Ave Saint Louis MO 63110-1010

LUSZTIG, PETER ALFRED, university dean, educator; b. Budapest, Hungary, May 12, 1930; s. Alfred Peter and Susan (Szabo) L.; m. Penny Bicknell, Aug. 26, 1961; children: Michael, Cameron, Carrie. B in Com., U. B.C., Vancouver, Can., 1954; MBA, U. Western Ont., London, Can., 1955; PhD, Stanford U., 1964. Asst. to comptroller B.C. Electric, Vancouver, 1955-57; instr. fin. U. B.C., 1957-60, asst. prof. fin., 1962-64, assoc. prof., 1968-95, Killam sr. research fellow, 1968-69, prof., 1965-68, dean faculty commerce, 1977-91, dean emeritus, 1995—; bd. trustees BC Health Benefit Trust; bd. dirs. Canfor Corp., Royal Ins. (Can.) Western Assurance, Roins Holding Co.; fed. commr. BC Treaty Commn., 1995—; vis. prof. IMEDE, Switzerland, 1973-74, London Grad. Sch. Bur. Studies, 1968-69, Pacific Coast Banking Sch., 1977—; sr. advisor B.C. Ministry of Econ. Devel., Small Bus. and Trade, 1991. Author: Report of the Royal Commission on Automobile Insurance, 2 vols., 1968, Financial Management in a Canadian Setting, 5th rev. edit., 1993, Report of the Commission on the B.C. Tree Fruit Industry, 1990. Ford Found. faculty dissertation fellow, Stanford U., 1964. Mem. Am. Fin. Assn., Fin. Mgmt. Assn. Lutheran. Office: Dept Commerce & Bus Admin, Vancouver, BC Canada V6T 1Z2

LUTALI, A. P., governor of American Samoa; b. Aunu'u, American Samoa, Dec. 24, 1919; married. Gov. Am. Samoa, 1985-89, 93—; spkr. of the House Senate, Am. Samoa, 1956-57, pres., 1965-67, v.p., 1988—; chair Constnl. Conv., 1966. Mem. Am. Samoa Bar Assn. (founder 1972). Office: Governor's Office Pago Pago AS 96799

LUTER, JOHN, news correspondent, educator; b. Knoxville, Tenn., Jan. 17, 1919; s. John Thomas and Bertha Mae (Carver) L.; m. Mary Hickey, 1948 (dec.); 1 child, Linda; m. Yvonne Spiegelberg, 1966 (div. 1971); m. Nan Hoyt Lawrence, 1974 (dec. 1996). BA, St. Mary's U., Tex., 1939, postgrad., 1939-42; fellow Time Inc., Sch. Advanced Internat. Studies, Washington, 1945. Reporter San Antonio Light, 1939-42, Washington Star, 1942-44; Wash. corr. Time mag., 1944-45; war corr. Time mag., Pacific, 1945; fgn. corr. Time and Life mags., Southeast Asia, 1945-46, Japan, 1946-47, Israel, 1948-49, Italy, 1949-54; asst. editor internat. edit. Life mag., 1954-56; reporter, writer CBS News, 1957-58; asso. editor Newsweek mag., 1958-61; radio news commentator Stas. WQXR and QXR-FM Network, 1960-61; coord. advanced internat. reporting program Columbia Grad. Sch. Journalism, 1961-72; dir. Maria Moors Cabot Prize Program, 1961-74; mem. profl. staff Bank St. Coll. Edn., N.Y.C., 1973-74; prof., dir. journalism U. Hawaii, Honolulu, from 1974, prof. and chmn. journalism dept., 1982-92, prof. journalism, 1992-94; prof emeritus, 1994—. Adv. editor: Columbia Journalism Rev., 1961-72. Chmn. internat. rels. com. N.Y.C. Protestant Coun., 1968-71; chmn. adv. screening com. communications Sr. Fulbright Program, 1970-73; trustee Overseas Press Club Found., 1962-72, chmn., 1964-65; bd. dirs. UN Assn. N.Y.C., 1973-74; chmn. Honolulu Community Media Coun., 1982-84. Mem. Assn. Edn. Journalism and Mass Comm., Assn. Schs. Journalism and Mass Comm., Honolulu com. Fgn. Rels. and Pacific and Asian Affairs Coun., World Affairs Coun., San Antonio, Soc. Profl. Journalists (exec. coun. chpt. 1966-69, 89-90), Japan Am. Soc., Overseas Press Club (pres. N.Y.C. 1960-62), Outrigger Canoe Club. Home: 340 Alta Ave San Antonio TX 78209-4513

LUTES, DONALD HENRY, architect; b. San Diego, Mar. 7, 1926; s. Charles McKinley and Helen (Bjoraker) L.; m. Donnie Wageman, Aug. 14, 1949; children: Laura Jo, Gail Eileen, Dana Charles. B.Arch., U. Oreg., 1950. Pvt. archtl. practice Springfield, Oreg., 1956-58; ptnr. John Amundson, Springfield, 1958-70; pres. Lutes & Amundson, Springfield, 1970-72; ptnr. Lutes/Sanetel, 1973-86; adj. assoc. prof. architecture U. Oreg., 1964-66, 89—; chmn. Springfield Planning Comm., 1954-65, 93—, Urban Design and Devel. Corp., 1968-70, Eugene Non-Profit Housing, Inc., 1970. Architect: Springfield Pub. Library, 1957, Mt. Hood Community Coll, 1965-79, Shoppers Paradise Expt. in Downtown Revitalization, 1957. Chmn. Springfield United Appeal, 1959. Served to 1st lt. AUS, 1943-46, 51-52. Decorate Bronze Star; named Jr. 1st Citizen, Springfield C. of C., 1957, 1st Citizen, 1968, Disting. Citizen, 1995. Fellow AIA (bd. dirs. 1987-90, v.p. 1991); mem. Rotary, Theta Chi. Home and Office: 778 Crest Ln Springfield OR 97477-3601

LUTGEN, ROBERT RAYMOND, newspaper editor; b. Fairmont, Minn., Oct. 27, 1949; s. William J. and Barbara Estella (Sanger) L.; m. Teresa L. Palm, July 17, 1971; children: Mark, Kyle, Laura. BA, Ctrl. Wash. State Coll., 1971. Reporter, asst. city editor Yakima (Wash.) Herald Republic, 1970-77; city editor Bryan (Tex.) Eagle, 1977-81; city editor Texarkana (Tex.) Gazette, 1981-83, mng. editor, 1983-87; asst. mng. editor Ark. Dem., 1987-91; mng. editor Ark. Dem.-Gazette, 1991—. Recipient Best News Story award, Editorial Writing award, Headline Writing award AP Mng. Editors Assn., 1985. Mem. Ark. AP (pres. 1989-90), Mng. Editors Assn. (bd. dirs. 1986-91). Avocations: travel, golf, reading. Home: 5 Nicole Ct North Little Rock AR 72118 Office: Ark Democrat Gazette 121 E Capitol Ave Little Rock AR 72201-3819

LUTGENS, HARRY GERARDUS, food company executive; b. Geleen, The Netherlands; s. Hubertus and Antoinetta (Ramakers) L.; m. Denyse Richard; children: Louise, Carolyn. Cert. Administrv. Mgr., U. Toronto, Ont., Can., 1969, Cert. Gen. Acct., 1971. From acct. to mgr. fin. planning analysis Miracle Food Mart div. Steinberg Inc., Rexdale, Ont., 1963-74, regional mgr., 1974-78; various mgmt. positions to pres., gen. mgr. Valdi Foods Inc., Rexdale, 1978-93; ret., 1993. Mem. Cert. Gen. Accts. Assn., Cert. Adminstrv. Mgrs. Assn. Avocations: traveling, golf, home repair. Home: 20 Inverary Cres, Agincourt, ON Canada M1T 2W5

LUTH, WILLIAM CLAIR, retired research manager; b. Winterset, IA, June 28, 1934; s. William Henry Luth and Ora Anna (Klingaman) Sorenson; m. Betty L. Heubrock, Aug. 23, 1953; children: Linda Diane, Robert William, Sharon Jean. BA in Geology, U. of Iowa, 1958, MS in Geology, 1960; PhD in Geochemistry, Penn State U., 1963. Research assoc. in geochemistry Pa. State U., University Park, Pa., 1963-65; asst. prof. geochemistry MIT, Cambridge, Mass., 1965-68; assoc. prof. geology Stanford U., 1968-77, prof. of geology, 1977-79; supr. geophysics div. Sandia Nat. Labs, Albuquerque, N. Mex., 1979-82; mgr. geosciences dept. Sandia Nat. Labs, Albuquerque, 1982-90; mgr. geoscis. rsch. program U.S. Dept. Energy, Washington, 1990-95, acting dir. divsn. engring. & geosci., 1994-95, dir. divsn. engring and geosci., 1996; ret., 1996; geoscientist US ERDA/DOE Washington, 1976-78; faculty sabbatical Sandia Laboratories, Albuquerque, N. Mex., 1975, visiting staff mem. Los Alamos Nat. Lab, 1978. Contbr. articles to profl. jours. Served with U.S. Army, 1953-56. Grantee NSF, 1964-78. Avocations: photography, shooting. Home: 6532 E June St Mesa AZ 85205

LUTHER, DARLENE, state legislator; b. 1947; m. Bill Luther; 2 children. BA, U. St. Thomas. Mem. Minn. Ho. of Reps., 1993—. Home: 6809 Shingle Creek Dr Brooklyn Park MN 55445-2647 Office: Minn Ho of Reps State Capital Building Saint Paul MN 55155-1606

LUTHER, DAVID BYRON, glass company executive; b. Utica, N.Y., May 26, 1936; s. Everett David and Mary (Brown) L.; m. Geraldine Frost; children: Leslie, Gregory, Valorie. B.S., Syracuse U., 1958, M.B.A., 1961. Dir. pers. resources Corning Glass Works, N.Y., 1974-76, asst. corp. contr., 1976-78, dir. corp. planning, 1978-79, dir. info. svcs., 1979-80, v.p. pers., 1980-83, v.p. quality, 1983-85, sr. v.p., corp. dir. quality, 1985-94, ret., 1994; founder, prin. Luther Quality Assocs., 1994—; mem. Human Resource Roundtable, N.Y.C., 1981-83; judge Malcolm Baldrige Nat. Quality Award, 1988-91; co-chair exec. com. N.Y. State Excelsior Quality Award; exec. in residence sch. mgmt. Syracuse U., mem. adv. bd.; chmn. Excelsion Inc., 1992-95; mem. steering com. Conf. Bd. Total Quality Mgmt. Ctr.; mem. adv. bd. ABS Quality Evaluations, Inc. Bd. dirs. Southeastern Steuben County United Way, Corning, 1975-77; advisor Donovan Acad., Corning, 1980-82; trustee Corning C.C., 1980-83, Coll. Ctr. of Finger Lakes, Corning, 1981-91, chmn. bd. trustees, 1988-90; nat. chmn. Koalaty Kid; adv. coun. Transformations to Quality Orgns. NSF, 1995—. Served to 1st lt. U.S. Army, 1958-60. Mem. Conf. Bd. Quality Coun. (co-founder 1985), Am. Execs. for Mfg. Excellence, Am. Soc. Quality Control (treas. 1992-93, pres.-elect 1993-94, pres. 1994-95, chmn. 1995-96), Archaeol. Inst. Am., Internat. Acad. Quality. Roman Catholic. Home: 22 Overbrook Rd Painted Post NY 14870-9339 Office: 85 E Market St Corning NY 14830-2708

LUTHER, GEORGE ALBERT, truck brokerage executive; b. Pulaski, N.Y., Feb. 16, 1926; s. Leslie Leon and Bertha Adelaide (Kind) L.; m. Lucile Pauline Lane, May 26, 1945; children: John Paul, Roger Lane. Grad., Ithaca (N.Y.) High Sch., 1943. Driver Mayflower Van Lines, Ithaca, 1946-47, Red Star Express, Auburn, N.Y., 1947-52; owner, operator B&L Trucking, Locke, N.Y., 1952-56; transport broker Cross Country Truck Svc. Inc., Lakeland, Fla., 1956-61, Horne Distbrs., Inc., Sanford, Fla., 1961-62; office mgr., broker Cross Country Truck Svc., Inc., Lakeland, 1962-67; office mgr., broker Haines City (Fla.) Truck Brokers, Inc., 1967-84, co-owner, 1984-88; pres. Nat. Agrl. Transp. League, Tavares and Leesburg, Fla., 1966-67, 75-77; v.p. Fla. Watermelon Growers & Distbrs. Assn., Lakeland, 1972-74, Nat. Watermelon Growers & Distbrs. Assn., Morven, Ga., 1974-75. Editor, writer Luther Family newsletter, 1986—; pub. Luther Family in Am., 1976; contbr. articles to mags. Sec., chief exec. officer, genealogist Luther Family Assn., Lakeland, 1986—. Avocations: history, genealogy. Home: 2027 Spyglass Ct Lakeland FL 33810-6737

LUTHER, GEORGE AUBREY, orthopedic surgeon; b. Keokuk, Iowa, Dec. 11, 1933; s. George August and Leda (Galbraith) L.; m. Dorothy Gould Luther, Aug. 18, 1956; children: Melinda, George Bradley. AB, Cen Meth. U., 1955; MD, Vanderbilt U., 1959. Diplomate Am. Bd. Orthopaedic Surgery. Intern Vanderbilt U. Hosp., Nashville, 1959-60, resident, 1961-64, instr., 1964; resident St. Louis City Hosp., 1960-61; pres. St. Louis Orthopedic Inst., 1965—; pres. med. staff St. Joseph Hosp., St. Louis, 1982-83; trustee St. Joseph Hosp., 1981-84. Contbr. article profl. jours. Served to maj. U.S. Army, 1967-69. Fellow Am. Acad. Orthopedic Surgery, ACS (admissions com. 1982—); mem. AMA, Mo. Orthopedic Soc. (v.p. 1985-86, pres. 1986-87), St. Louis Metro. Med. Soc. (counselor 1983-85), Vanderbilt Orthopedic Soc. (pres. 1981-82), Tenn. Soc. of St. Louis. Republican. Methodist. Club: Bellerive Country. Avocations: music, sports. Home: 177 Ladue Oaks Ct Saint Louis MO 63141-8128 *I have been most fortunate to be associated with the most important people in my life - great parents, a wonderful wife, and terrific friends. With the support and guidance of these individuals, one could not help but succeed in any and all endeavors.*

LUTHER, THOMAS WILLIAM, physician; b. Milw., Feb. 27, 1925; s. Elmer Charles and Ida Martha (Sohrweide) L.; children: Brian Thomas, Siri Karen Luther Witt. BS, U. Wis., 1947, MD, 1950. Diplomat Am. Bd. Dermatology. Intern West Suburban Hosp., Oak Park, Ill., 1950-51; resident VA Hosps., 1951-52, 55-56, U. Pa., 1954-55. Bd. dirs. Tri-Cmtys. Crime Reduction Coalition, Meenah-Menasha, Wis., 1994-96. Lt. USN, 1943-54. Fellow Am. Acad. Dermatology; mem. AMA, Wis. Med. Soc., Wis. Dermatologic Soc., Appleton Rotary. Avocations: archaeology, genealogy. Home: 1936 Palisades Dr Appleton WI 54915-1023

LUTHER, WILLIAM LEE, construction company executive; b. Philipsburg, Pa., Dec. 10, 1952; s. William Denis and Edna Patricia (Culp) L.; m. Carolyn Jane Shadburn, May 27, 1976 (div. June 1983). BS, Pa. State U., 1975. Tchr. Huntingdon (Pa.) Sch. Dist., 1977-79; carpenter Zimmerman Homes, Inc., State College, Pa., 1981-83, sales mgr., 1983-86, dir. sales, 1986—; bd. dirs. Zimmerman Homes, Inc., State College; owner, ptnr. Housewrights, Inc., State College, 1991—. Mem. Pa. Builders Assn., Nat. Assn. Home Builders, Nat. Inst. Residential Mtkg. Republican. Roman Catholic. Avocations: golf, reading, weight training. Home: 1019 Tanney St Bellefonte PA 16823-2417 Office: Housewrights Inc 2790 W College Ave State College PA 16801-2600

LUTHER, WILLIAM P., congressman; b. Fergus Falls, Minn., June 27, 1945; s. Leonard and Eleanor L.; m. Darlene Luther, Dec. 16, 1967; children: Alexander, Alicia. BS in Elec. Engring. with high distinction, U. Minn., 1967; JD cum laude, U. Minn. Law Sch., 1970. Judicial clerkship 8th cir. U.S. Ct. Appeals, 1970-71; atty. Dorsey & Whitney Law Firm, Mpls., 1971-74, William P. Luther Law Office, Mpls., 1974-83; founder, sr. ptnr. Luther, Ballenthin & Carruthers Law Firm, Mpls., 1983-92; state sen. 47th dist. State of Minn., 1977-94, asst. maj. leader, 1983-94; mem. 104th-105th Congresses from 6th Minn. Dist., 1995—. Home: 6375 Saint Croix Trl N Apt 147 Stillwater MN 55082-6932 Office: US House Reps 117 Cannon Washington DC 20515 also: 1811 Weir Dr Ste 150 Woodbury MN 55125-2254*

LUTHER-LEMMON, CAROL LEN, middle school educator; b. Waverly, N.Y., May 8, 1955; d. Carl Ross and Mary Edith (Auge) Luther; m. Mark Kevin Lemmon, June 21, 1986; children: Matthew C., Cathryn M. BS, Ithaca Coll., 1976; MS in Edn., Elmira Coll., 1982. Cert. elem. and secondary tchr., Pa., N.Y. Reading aide Waverly (N.Y.) Central Schs., 1978-80; tchr. reading N.Y. State Div. for Youth, Lansing, 1981-82; tchr. title I reading, mem. student assistance program and instructional support team Rowe Mid. Sch., Athens (Pa.) Area Sch. Dist., 1982-94; tchr. Title I reading Lynch Elem. Sch., 1995—. Basketball coach Youth Activities Dept., Athens, 1982-85, asst. softball coach, 1990-91; mem. ad hoc com. Waverly Sch. Dist., 1990-91; mem. Goal G parents & edn. Mid. Sch. Implementation Team for WINGS-Waverly in a Global Soc. for Waverly Ctr. Sch. Dist. Strategic Plan; bd. dirs. SACC, 1995-96, Waverly Cmty. Ch., 1976-78; active Girls' Softball League Waverly, 1978-80, commr., 1980; choir mem. Meth. Ch., Wverly, 1976-90, adminstrv. bd., trustee, chmn. bd. trustees, 1995, 96; mem. Valley Chorus, Pa. and N.Y., 1983-86. With USAR, 1977-83. Mem. ASCD, AAUW (v.p. Waverly br. 1982-83, pres. Waverly br. 1992-97), Am. Legion Aux. (girl's state rep. 1972, girl's state chmn. 1976-80 Waverly post, counselor 1977), Chemung Area Reading Coun., N.Y. State Reading Assn. Republican. Home: 490 Waverly St Waverly NY 14892-1102 Office: Athens Area Sch Dist Pennsylvania Ave Athens PA 18810-1440

LUTHEY, GRAYDON DEAN, JR., lawyer; b. Topeka, Sept. 18, 1955; s. Graydon Dean Sr. and S. Anne (Murphy) L.; m. Deborah Denise McCullough, May 26, 1979; children: Sarah Elizabeth, Katherine Alexandra. BA in Letters with highest honors, U. Okla., 1976, JD, 1979; Fellow in Theology, Oxford (Eng.) U., 1976. Bar: Okla. 1979, U.S. Ct. Appeals (10th cir.) 1979, U.S. Dist. Ct. (no., we. and ea. dists.) Okla. 1980, U.S. Supreme Ct. 1982. Assoc. Jones, Givens, Gotcher, Bogan & Hilborne, Tulsa, 1979-84, ptnr., 1984-92, also bd. dirs.; ptnr. Hall, Estill, Hardwick, Gable, Golden & Nelson, Tulsa, 1992—, also bd. dirs.; adj. assoc. prof. U. Tulsa, 1985-87, adj. prof., 1987—; vis. fellow in theology Keble Coll., Oxford (Eng.) U., 1976; presiding judge Okla. Temporary Ct. Appeals, 1992-93; mem. Okla. Supreme Ct. Rules Com., 1992—. bd. dirs. Tulsa Ballet, 1987—; chmn. Tulsa Pub. facilties Authority, 1990-93; trustee Episcopal Theol. Sem. of S.W., 1991—, exec. com., 1992—; vice chmn. Univ. Hosps. Authority, 1993-94, chmn. 1994—. Nat. Merit scholar U. Okla., 1973. Fellow Am. Bar Found.; mem. ABA, Okla. Bar Assn. (chmn. continuing legal edn. com. 1989-91), Tulsa County Bar Assn. (bd. dirs. 1983-89, Disting. Svc. award 1988), Am. Inns of Ct. (barrister), Summit Club, Golf Club Okla., Beta Theta Pi, Phi Beta Kappa, Omicron Delta Kappa. Office: Hall Estill Hardwick Gable Golden & Nelson 320 S Boston Ave Ste 400 Tulsa OK 74103-3704

LUTHRINGSHAUSER, DANIEL RENE, manufacturing company executive; b. Fontainebleau, France, July 23, 1935; came to U.S., 1937; s. Ernest Henri and Jeanne (Guerville) L.; m. Carol King; children: Mark Ernest, Heidi Elizabeth. BS, NYU, 1956, MBA, 1970. With exec. tng. program, internat. pub. relations Merck & Co. Inc., Rahway, N.J. and N.Y.C., 1962-65; dep. mktg. dir. Merck Sharp & Dohme Internat., Brussels, 1965-66; mktg. service dir. Paris, 1966-69; gen. mgr. Merck Sharp & Dohme/Chibret, Paris, 1970-74; v.p. mktg. Merrell (France), Paris, 1974-78; v.p. gen. mgr. Revlon Devel. Corp., Paris, 1978-82, Medtronic Europe, Paris, Africa, Middle East, 1982-86; v.p. internat. Medtronic Inc., Mpls., 1986—; bd. dirs. Medtronic Found., Mpls., 1986-91; chmn. Internat. Assn. of Prosthesis Mfrs., Paris, 1983-85. Bd. dirs. Am. Hosp. Paris, 1983-86, 94-95, Minn. Internat. Ctr., 1990—; mem. Am. Club Paris, 1970-80, Medtronic Found., Mpls., 1986-91. Served to capt. USAF, 1956-62. Recipient Gold medal Am. Mktg. Assn., 1956. Club: Ausable (Keene Valley, N.Y.). Avocations: gardening, golf, squash, skiing. Home: 480 Peavey Rd Wayzata MN 55391-1529 Office: Medtronic Inc 7000 Central Ave NE Minneapolis MN 55432-3568

LUTHY, JOHN FREDERICK, management consultant; b. Kansas City, Mo., Dec. 12, 1947; s. Walter Frederick Luthy and Loraine Florence Tramill; children: Roslyn, Bryan, John Paul. BA, Baker U., 1969; MS, U. Mo., 1973; MPA, Boise State U., 1978; EdD, U. Idaho, 1991. Mgr. State Com. Disease Edn., Topeka, 1973; dir. Divsn. Health Edn., Johnson County, Kans., 1973-75; state dir. Bur. Health Edn., Boise, Idaho, 1975-80; dir. Gen. Svcs. Adminstrn., Boise, 1980-84; dir. bus. devel. Morrison Knudsen Tech. Inc., Boise, 1984-86; pres. The Futures Corp., Boise, 1986—; pres. Exec. Mgmt. Devel. Inst., Boise, 1991—; del. to China People to People, 1994. Author: (manual) Grantsmanship--A Time of Plenty, 1988; contbr. articles to profl. jours. Staff sgt. USAR, 1969-75. Recipient Nat. Early Career award APHA, 1978; named one of Outstanding Young Men of Am., U.S. Jaycees, 1977. Mem. ASTD, Am. Mgmt. Assn., U.S. Powerlifting Fedn. (exec. bd. dirs., regional chmn. 1981-86), Phi Delta Kappa. Avocations: mountain biking, power lifting, backpacking. Office: The Futures Corp 1109 Main St Ste 299A Boise ID 83702-5642

LUTHY, RICHARD GODFREY, environmental engineering educator; b. June 11, 1945; s. Robert Godfrey Luthy and Marian Ruth (Ireland) Haines; m. Mary Frances Sullivan, Nov. 22, 1967; children: Matthew Robert, Mara Catherine, Jessica Bethlin. BSChemE, U. Calif., Berkeley, 1967; MS in Ocean Engring., U. Hawaii, 1969; MSCE, U. Calif., Berkeley, 1974, PhDCE, 1976. Registered profl. engr., Pa.; diplomate Am. Acad. Environ. Engrs. Rsch. asst. dept. civil engring. U. Hawaii, Honolulu, 1968-69; rsch. asst. div. san. and hydraulic engring. U. Calif., Berkeley, 1973-75; asst. prof. civil engring. Carnegie Mellon U., Pitts., 1975-80, assoc. prof., 1980-83, prof., 1983—, assoc. dean Carnegie Inst. Tech., 1986-89, head dept. civil and environ. engring., 1989-96, Lord prof. environ. engring., 1996—; Shimizu Corp. vis. prof. dept. civil engring. Stanford U., 1996-97; cons. sci. adv. bd. U.S. EPA, 1983—, Bioremediation Action com., 1990-92; cons. U.S. Dept. Energy, 1978—, various pvt. industries; del. water sci. and tech. bd. NAE, Washington and Beijing, 1988; mem. tech. adv. bd. Remediation Techs., Inc., Concord, Mass., 1989-94, Fostin Capital, Pitts., 1991-94, Balt. Gas & Elec., 1992-95, Pa. Dept. Environ. Protection, 1994—; mem. sci. adv. com. Hazardous Substance Rsch. Ctr. Stanford U., 1994—; chair Gordon Rsch. Conf. Environ. Scis., 1994, Nat. Rsch. Coun. Commn. on Innovative Remediation Tech. Contbr. articles to tech. and sci. jours. Chmn. NSF/AEEP Conf. on Fundamental Rsch. Directions in Environ. Engring, Washington, 1988. Lt. C.E. Corps, USN, 1969-72. Recipient George Tallman Ladd award Carnegie Inst. Tech., 1977. Mem. ASCE (Pitts. sect. Prof. of Yr. award 1987), Assn. Environ. Engring. Profs. (pres. 1987-88, Nalco award 1978, 82, Engring. Sci. award 1988), Water Environ. Fedn. (rsch. com. 1982-86, awards com. 1981-84, 89-94, std. methods com. 1977—, groundwater com. 1989-90, editor jour. 1989-92, Eddy medal 1980), Internat. Assn. on Water Quality (Founders award U.S. Nat. Com. 1986, 93, orgnl. com. 16th Biennial Conf. Washington 1992), Am. Chem. Soc. (divsn. environ. chemistry, mem. editl. adv. bd. Environ. Sci. Tech. 1992-95). Presbyterian. Home: 620 S Linden Ave Pittsburgh PA 15208-2813 Office: Carnegie Mellon U Dept Civil & Environ Engring Pittsburgh PA 15213-3890

LUTI, WILLIAM JOSEPH, career officer; b. Boston, Nov. 13, 1953; s. William Vincent and Marjorie Louise (Barnes) L.; m. Donna Margaret King, Dec. 13, 1990; children: Lauren Marie, Natalie Rose. BA in History, The Citadel, 1975; MA in Nat. Security Affairs, U.S. Naval War Coll., 1986; MA in Internat. Rels., Salve Regina Coll., 1986; MA in Law and Diplomacy, PhD in Internat. Rels., Tufts U., 1990. Commd. ensign USN, 1975, advanced through grades to capt., 1997; flight student Naval Air Station, Pensacola, Fla., 1975-76; div. officer VQ-1 (EA-3B aircraft), Agana, Guam, 1976-79; asst. dept. head VAQ-131 (EA-6B aircraft), Oak Harbor, Wash., 1979-82; dept. head VAQ-135 (EA-6B), Oak Harbor, 1986-88; commanding officer VAQ-130 (EA-6B squadron) USN, Oak Harbor, 1991-93; admiral's aide U.S. Naval Acad., Annapolis, Md., 1982-85; dep. dir. Chief of Navel Ops. Exec. Panel, Alexandria, Va., 1993-96; congl. fellow Office of Spkr. of the House Hon. Newt Gingrich, Washington, 1996—; panelist Persian Gulf War Symposium, Naval Inst., Pensacola, 1992. Tchr.'s aide Hillcrest Elem. Sch., Oak Harbor, 1991-92. Decorated with Air medal U.S. Navy, Iraq, 1991. Mem. U.S. Naval Inst. (contbr. editor), Assn. of Naval Aviation, Phi Alpha Theta. Roman Catholic. Avocations: writing, golf, swimming. Office: Office of Spkr of House 232 E Capitol St NE Rm H Washington DC 20003-1036

LUTRINGER, RICHARD EMIL, lawyer; b. N.Y.C., Feb. 4, 1943; s. Emil Vincent Lutringer and Alice Rich Danser; m. Dagmar Bonitz, May 1, 1970 (div. 1980); m. Clarinda Higgins, Oct. 11, 1980; children: Emily, Eric. AB, Coll. of William and Mary, 1964; JD in Internat. Affairs, Cornell U., 1967; MCL, U. Chgo., 1969. Bar: N.Y. 1972, U.S. Dist. Ct. (so. dist.) N.Y. 1972. Assoc. Whitman & Ransom, N.Y.C., 1971-80, ptnr., 1980-94; ptnr. Morgan, Lewis & Bockius, N.Y.C., 1994—. Vice pres. N.Y.-N.J. Trail Conf., N.Y.C., 1976-80. Mem. ABA, Internat. Bar Assn., Assn. of Bar of City of N.Y. (chmn. com. fgn. and comparative law 1990-93), Am. Fgn. Law Assn. (pres. 1989-93, treas. 1986-89), European-Am. C. of C. (vice chair trade com. 1992—). Avocations: sailing, hiking, skiing. Home: 2 Owenoke Park Westport CT 06880-6851 Office: Morgan Lewis & Bockius 101 Park Ave New York NY 10178

LUTTER, PAUL ALLEN, lawyer; b. Chgo., Feb. 28, 1946; s. Herbert W. and Lois (Muller) L. BA, Carleton Coll., 1968; JD, Yale U., 1971. Bar: Ill. 1971, U.S. Tax Ct. 1986. Assoc. Ross & Hardies, Chgo., 1971-77, ptnr., 1978—. Co-author: Illinois Estate Administration, 1993. Dir. ACLU of Ill.; pres., dir. Howard Brown Health Ctr.; chmn.'s coun. DIFFA Chgo. Mem. ABA, Chgo. Bar Assn. Home: 2214 N Magnolia Ave Chicago IL 60614-3104 Office: Ross & Hardies 150 N Michigan Ave Ste 2500 Chicago IL 60601-7524

LUTTIG, J. MICHAEL, federal judge; b. 1954. BA, Washington and Lee U., 1976; JD, U. Va., 1981. Asst. counsel The White House, 1981-82; law clk. to Judge Antonin Scalia U.S. Ct. of Appeals D.C. Cir., 1982-83; law clerk to chief justice Warren Burger Supreme Ct. of U.S., 1983-84, spl. asst. to chief justice Warren Burger, 1984-85; assoc. Davis Polk & Wardwell, 1985-89; prin. dep. asst. atty. gen., office of legal counsel U.S. Dept. of Justice, 1989-90, asst. atty. gen., office of legal counsel, counselor to atty. gen., 1990-91; judge U.S. Cir. Ct. (4th cir.), McLean, Va., 1991—. Mem. Nat. Adv. Com. of Lawyers for Bush, 1988, Lawyers for Bush Com., 1988. Mem. ABA, Va. Bar Assn., D.C. Bar Assn. Office: Circuit Ct 8280 Greensboro Dr Ste 780 Mc Lean VA 22102-3807*

LUTTNER, EDWARD F., consulting company executive; b. Cleve., Feb. 16, 1942; s. John J. and Angela (Haberbosch) L.; m. Nancy E., July 15, 1977; children: Amy, Mark. BA, Loyola U., 1966, MDiv, 1974; MA, U. Detroit, 1970. Cert. NASD. Dir. standards-devel. Bernard Haldane Assocs., Boston, Internat. Career Consulting Corp., Waltham, Mass.; v.p. career mgmt. svcs. Bernard Haldane Assocs., Cleve.; dir. profl. svcs. Right Assocs., Phila.; pres. Elby Career Group, Inc., Cleve. V.p. Rotary, Fairview Park, 1988-89. Mem. AACD, Nat. Career Devel. Assn.

LUTTRULL, SHIRLEY JOANN, protective services official; b. Fordland, Mo., Feb. 26, 1937; d. Thomas Marion and Pauline (Sherrow) Pirtle; m. Leslie Allen Luttrull, June 3, 1956 (div. May 1978); children: Vicki Lynn, Ricki Allen; m. Orben Lowell Clark, Dec. 31, 1982 (div. Oct. 1987); m. Barry Mabe, June 1992 (div. Oct. 1994). Student, Southwest Mo. State U., 1979. Checker Lea's Market, Fordland, Mo., 1955-56; plant supr. Mellers Photo Lab., Springfield, Mo., 1968-82; shopper Hopper and Hawkins, Dallas, 1982-83; crew leader Sentinal Security, Okla. City; from crew leader to sales mgr. Shrink Control Corp., Houston, 1984-88; owner Internal Theft Control, Springfield, 1988—. Mem. Mo. Retail Grocers Assn., Pilot Internat., Springfield C. of C. Republican. Avocations: water skiing, scuba diving, ballroom dancing. Home and Office: 1347 S Airwood Dr Springfield MO 65804-0520

LUTTS, RALPH HERBERT, museum administrator, scholar, educator; b. Quincy, Mass., Jan. 7, 1944; s. Herbert Warren Lutts and Jean May (MacKenzie) Easton. BA in Biology, Trinity U., San Antonio, 1967; EdD, U. Mass., 1978. Curator, educator Mus. Sci., Boston, 1967-73; naturalist Hampshire Coll., Amherst, Mass., 1973-80; natural sci. faculty Hampshire Coll., 1976-84; dir. Blue Hills Trailside Mus., Mass. Audubon Soc., Milton, 1980-90; dir. edn. Va. Mus. Natural History, Martinsville, 1990-92, dir. outreach div., 1992-94, rsch. assoc., 1994—; assoc.faculty Goddard Coll., Plainfield, Vt., 1995—; adj. faculty Univ. Va., 1995—; pres. Alliance for Environ. Edn., 1988-89; founding pres. New Eng. Environ. Edn. Alliance, 1980-84; assoc. Ctr. for Animals and Pub. Policy, Tufts U. Sch. Vet. Medicine, North Grafton, Mass., 1989-90; dept. dir. mid-atlantic region Global Network of Environ. Edn. Ctrs., 1993-95, bd. dirs., 1994-96. Author: The Nature Fakers: Wildlife, Science and Sentiment, 1990; founding editor New Eng. Jour. Environ. Edn., 1985-88; editor: The Wild Animal Story: Tales, Controversies and Interpretations, 1997; contbr. articles to profl. jours. Pres. Hitchcock Ctr. for Environ., Amherst, Mass., 1977-79; treas. Mass. Environ. Edn. Soc., 1982-84; mem. Blue Hills citizens' adv. com. Met. Dist. Commn., 1988-89, mgmt. adv. com., 1989-90; mem. sec.'s adv. group on environ. edn. Mass. Exec. Office for Environ. Affairs, 1989-90. Recipient New Eng. Regional awrd for achievement New Eng. Environ. Edn. Alliance, 1989; Paul Harris fellow Rotary Internat. Mem. AAAS, Am. Soc. Environ. History, Assn. for Study of Lit. and Environ., Internat. Soc. Environ. Ethics, Forest History Soc. (Ralph W. Hidy award 1993), N.Am. Assn. Environ. Edn., Am. Nature Study Soc. (bd. dirs. 1990—, pres. 1995-97), Authors Guild, Popular Culture Assn. (area chair 1993-95), Nat. Writers Union. Avocations: natural history, book collecting.

LUTTWAK, EDWARD NICOLAE, academic, writer policy and business consultant; b. Arad, Transylvania, Nov. 4, 1942; came to U.S., 1972, naturalized, 1981; s. Josif Menashe and Clara (Baruch) L.; m. Dalya Iaari, Dec. 14, 1970; children: Yael Rachel, Joseph Emmanuel. B.Sc. with honors, London Sch. Econs., 1964; Ph.D. (Univ. fellow), Johns Hopkins U., 1975. Vis. prof. polit. sci. Johns Hopkins U., 1973-78; sr. fellow Georgetown U. Center Strategic and Internat. Studies, 1978-87, research prof. internat. security affairs, 1978-82, Burke chair in strategy, 1987—, dir. geo-econs., 1991-94, sr. fellow, 1994—; sr. fellow in preventive diplomacy Office of Sec. of Def., Nat. Security Coun. and Dept. State; cons. Office of Sec. of Def., Nat. Security Coun., Dept. of Def. Army, Navy and U.S. Air Force, Fgn. (allied) Govs. and U.S., overseas bus. entities. Author: Coup d'Etat, 19 edits. including 12 for lang. translations, 1968-79, Dictionary of Modern War, 1971 (also Spanish edit.), The Political Uses of Sea Power, 1975 (also Japanese edit.), The Israeli Army, 1975, 85, (also Chinese edit.), The Grand Strategy of the Roman Empire, 1976 (also Hebrew, Italian and French edits.), Strategy and Politics: Collected Essays, 1980, The Grand Strategy of the Soviet Union, 1983 (also Italian and French edits.),The Pentagon and the Art of War: The Question of Military Reform, 1985 (also Italian, Japanese and Korean edits.), Strategy and History: Collected Essays, On the Meaning of Victory, 1986 (also Italian edit.), Strategy: The Logic of War and Peace, 1987 (also Chinese, French and Italian edits.), (with Stuart Koehl) Dictionary of Modern War, 1991 (also Italian edit.), The Endangered American Dream, 1993 (also French, Italian, German and Japanese edits.), (with G. Tremonti, Carlo Palanda) Il Fantasma della Poverta, 1995, (with Susanna Creperio) Cose e Davvero La Democrazia, 1996; contbr. articles to Fgn. Affairs, London Rev. of Books, Times Lit. Supplement. Republican. Jewish. Office: CSIS 1800 K St NW Washington DC 20006-2202

LUTU, AFOA MOEGA, legislator, lawyer; b. Leulumoega-Fou, W.S., Feb. 24, 1947; s. Solofa Suesue and Vaituutuu (Leotaleuluaiali) L.; m. Etenauga Lam Yuen, Sept. 23, 1972; 10 children. BA in Polit. Sci., U. Hawaii, 1971; JD, Valparaiso U., 1974. Asst. law clk. High Ct. of Am. Samoa, Utulei, Pago Pago, 1972; rep. from 7th dist. Legislature of Am. Samoa, Utulei, 1993—, spl. counsel to senate, 1989-93; pvt. practice law Utulei, 1976-84; atty. gen. Govt. of Am. Samoa, Utulei, 1985-89; chmn. econ. devel. authority Govt. of Am. Samoa, 1986, legal counsel constnl. convention, 1986; chmn. judiciary com. Ho. of Reps., Am. Samoa, 1993—; chmn. Real Property Mgmt. Bd. and Indsl. Park Commn., Am. Samoa, 1985-89; chmn. adv. panel Western Pacific Regional Fishery Coun., Am. Samoa; chmn. 1st bond issue Am. Samoa Econ. Devel. Authority, 1987. Chief Afoafouvale, Fagatogo-Utulei Village Coun., 1990. Mem. ABA, Am. Samoa Bar Assn. (treas.), U.S. Supreme Ct. Bar Assn., Tautai-O-Samoa Fishing Assn. (pres.). Avocations: deep sea fishing, golf. Office: Fono PO Box 1029 Pago Pago AS 96799-1029

LUTVAK, MARK ALLEN, computer company executive; b. Chgo., Feb. 9, 1939; s. Joseph Issac and Jeanette Nettie (Pollock) L.; BS in Elec. Engring., U. Mich., 1962; MBA, Wayne State U., Detroit, 1969; m. Gayle Helene Rotofsky, May 24, 1964; children: Jeffrey, Eric. Sales rep. IBM Corp., 1962-64; successively sales rep., product mktg. mgr., corp. product mgr. Burroughs Corp., Detroit, 1964-76; mgr. product mktg. Memorex Corp., Santa Clara, Calif., 1976-80, product program gen. mgr., 1980-81; dir. product mktg. Personal Computer div. Atari, Inc., Sunnyvale, Calif., 1981-83; dir. mktg., v.p. Durango Systems, San Jose, Calif., 1983-85; dir. mktg. ITTQUME Corp., San Jose, 1985-87; v.p. mktg. Optimem, Mountain View, Calif., 1987-88; dir. mktg. Priam Corp., San Jose, 1988-91; dir. Memorex, Santa Clara, Calif. 1991-94; pres. Synergistic Mktg., 1994—; prof. Applied Mgmt. Center, Wayne State U., 1967-72, Walsh U., Troy, Mich., 1974-76, West Valley Coll., Saratoga, Calif., 1977-78. Trustee, pres. brotherhood Temple Emanuel, San Jose, Calif., 1979-80. Mem. IEEE, Soc. Applied Math., Alpha Epsilon Pi. Home: 899 Balboa Ln Foster City CA 94404

LUTZ, CARL FREIHEIT, academic administrator; b. Lansing, Mich., Dec. 8, 1934; s. Paul and Edmunda (Freiheit) L.; m. Vivian Ericson; m. Aug. 18, 1959; children—Timothy Paul, Elizabeth. B.S. in Metallurgy, Mich. State U., 1956; M.S., Carnegie Inst. Tech., 1957, Ph.D., 1959; postgrad. student, Max Planck Inst. Physics, 1959-60. Asst. prof. USAF Acad., 1960-63; sr. engr. Rockwell-Standard Corp., Detroit, 1963-66, Kaiser Aluminum Co., Spokane, 1966-67; v.p., dean engring. S.D. Sch. Mines and Tech., Rapid City, 1967-74; dep. commr. higher edn. State of Ind., Indpls., 1974-79; chancellor Ivy Tech. State Coll., South Bend and others, 1979—. Served with USAF, 1960-63. Mem. Am. Soc. Engring. Edn., Am. Inst. Mining, Metall. and Petroleum Engrs., Am. Soc. Metals, Soc. Research Adminstrs., Sigma Xi, Delta Sigma Phi.

LUTZ, FRANCIS CHARLES, university dean, civil engineering educator; b. Pottsville, Pa., Apr. 5, 1944; s. Charles Henry and Pauline Anna (Weislo) L.; m. Evelyn Florence Zommer, Apr. 29, 1972; 1 child, Stephanie Diane. BSCE, N.J. Inst. Tech., 1966; MSCE, NYU, 1967, PhD, 1971. Assoc. M. Disko Assocs., West Orange, N.J., 1970-72; asst. prof. civil engring. Worcester Poly. Inst., Mass., 1972-76; prof. Worcester Poly. Inst., 1980-96, assoc. dean, 1980-90, dean undergrad. studies, 1990-95; dean sch. sci., tech. & engring. Monmouth U., West Long Branch, N.J., 1996—; cons. Council on Environ. Quality, Washington, 1974-75; reviewer NSF. Co-editor: Studies in Science, Technology and Culture, Worcester Poly. Inst.; contbr. articles to profl. jours. Trustee Worcester Ctr. for Crafts, 1992—; mem. Boston Fed. Exec. Bd., 1972-74, Cen. Mass. Regional Planning Commn., Worcester, 1975-77. Am. Council on Edn. fellow, 1988-89; honors scholar NYU. Mem. ASCE, Am. Soc. Engring. Edn., Boynton Assn. (pres. 1982, 83), Sigma Xi, Chi Epsilon. Office: Monmouth U Office of Dean Sch Sci Tech & Engring West Long Branch NJ 07764-1898

LUTZ, FRANK WENZEL, education administration educator; b. St. Louis, Sept. 24, 1928; s. Vincent J. and Helen M. (Scrivens) L.; m. Susan Virginia Bleikamp, July 12, 1958; children: Paul E., Andrew C., Lynn S. AA, Harris Tchrs. Coll., 1948; BS, Washington U., 1950, MS, 1954, EdD, 1962. Instr. Washington U., St. Louis, 1961-62; from asst. to assoc. prof. NYU, N.Y.C., 1964-68; dir. div. policy studies Pa. State U., State College, 1968-73; prof. edn. adminstrn. Pa. State U., 1974-80; dean Sch. Edn. Eastern Ill. U., 1980-82, asst. to v.p., 1982-83; prof., dir. Ctr. Policy Studies Tex. A&M (formerly East State U.), Commerce, Tex., 1983-91, prof. edn. adminstrn., 1983—; sr. nat. lectr. Nova S.W. U., 1991—; mem., pres. Pattonville (Mo.) Sch. Bd., 1960-62; mem. adv. com. Opportunities Acad. Mgmt. Tng., Phila., 1975-90. Author seven books, numerous book chpts. in field; contbr. over 100 articles to profl. jours. Deacon 1st Presbyn. Ch., Commerce, Tex., 1989-91. Doctoral fellow Washington U., 1960-61; grantee U.S. Office Edn., OEO. Mem. Am. Ednl. Rsch. Assn. (sec. Div. 1970-72, dir. rsch. pre-session 1969, program com. 1970), Commerce Rotary (pres. 1991-92, chair internat. svc. 1994-96), Phi Delta Kappa (life, pres. Washington U. chpt. 1960, 1st v.p. East Tex. State U. chpt. 1985, Lafferty Faculty Senate Disting. scholarship award 1996). Avocations: appaloosa horses, opera, classical music. Home: PO Box 51 Nederland CO 80466-0051 Office: Tex A&M U Edn North Building Rm 214 Commerce TX 75428

LUTZ, GRETCHEN KAY, English language educator; b. Ft. Worth, Tex., Jan. 6, 1948. BA, Tex. Christian U., 1970; MA, U. Houston, 1974, Rice U., 1995; postgrad., Dartmouth Coll., 1994; MA, Rice U., 1995. High sch. and mid. sch. tchr. English Galveston and Deer Park (Tex.) Sch. Dists., 1970-77; instr. ESL and English Schreiner Coll., Kerrville, Tex., 1979-80; instr. English San Jacinto Coll. Ctr., Pasadena, Tex., 1981—; tchr. English Sch. of the Talented and Gifted Magnet High Sch., Dallas. Contbr. articles to profl. jours. Mem. MLA, Nat. Symposium for Coherence in Liberal Arts, C.C. Humanities Assn., Am. Culture and Popular Culture Assn., U.S. European Command Mil. to Mil. Program Conf., Am. Studies Assn. Tex., South Ctrl. MLA, Conf. Coll. Tchrs. English (exec. coun.), S.W. Conf. Christianity and Lit., Western Soc. 18th Century Studies, Tex. Folklore Soc., S.W. Regional Conf. English in Two-Year Colls., Tex. Voices Sesquicentennial Series, Rice English Symposium, San Jacinto Coll. Faculty Symposium. Home: 3946 Sherwood Forest #135E Dallas TX 75220

LUTZ, JAMES GURNEY, lawyer; b. Cin., Sept. 18, 1933; s. Arthur Harold and Frances (Gurney) L.; children: Monica, Susan. JD, U. Cin., 1960. Bar: Ohio 1960, U.S. Dist. Ct. (so. dist.) Ohio 1961, U.S. Ct. Appeals (6th cir.) 1961, U.S. Tax Ct. 1975, U.S. Supreme Ct. 1975. Ptnr. Barbour, Kinpel & Allen, Cin., 1960-68; chief counsel E.C. Industries Inc., Cin., 1968-71; sr. ptnr. Lutz Cornetet & Albrinck, Cin., 1971—; pres., mem. bd. dirs. Motivation Dynamics Inc., Cin., 1978-85. Advisor, staff Hamilton County Vocat. Schs., Cin., 1968; advisor U. Cin. Coll., 1970-75; mem. adv. counsel Wyoming (Ohio) Bd. Edn., 1972-75; mem. bd. Ohio Pvt. Industry Coun., Columbus, 1975; gen. counsel S.W. Ohio Autistic Assn., Cin., 1980—. Mem. ABA, Am. Trial Lawyers Assn., Ohio State Bar Assn., Cin. Bar Assn. Avocations: psychology, computer science. Office: Lutz Cornetet & Albrinck 130 Tri County Pkwy Cincinnati OH 45246-3289

LUTZ, JOHN SHAFROTH, lawyer; b. San Francisco, Sept. 10, 1943; s. Frederick Henry and Helena Morrison (Shafroth) L.; m. Elizabeth Boschen,

Dec. 14, 1968; children: John Shafroth, Victoria. BA, Brown U., 1965; JD, U. Denver, 1971. Bar: Colo. 1971, U.S. Dist. Ct. Colo. 1971, U.S. Ct. Appeals (2d cir.) 1975, D.C. 1976, U.S. Supreme Ct. 1976, U.S. Dist. Ct. (so. dist.) N.Y. 1977, U.S. Tax Ct. 1977, U.S. Ct. Appeals (10th cir.) 1979, N.Y. 1984, U.S. Ct. Appeals (9th cir.) 1990, U.S. Dist. Ct. (no. dist.) Calif. 1993. Trial atty. Denver regional office U.S. SEC, 1971-74; spl. atty. organized crime, racketeering sect. U.S. Dept. Justice, So. Dist. N.Y., 1974-77; atty. Kelly, Stansfield and O'Donnell, Denver, 1977-78; gen. counsel Boettcher & Co., Denver, 1978-87, Kelly, Stansfield and O'Donnel, Denver, 1987; spl. counsel, 1987-88, ptnr., 1988-93; of counsel LeBoeuf, Lamb, Greene and Mac Rae, L.L.P., 1993-94, ptnr. 1995—; spkr. on broker, dealer, securities law and arbitration issues to various profl. orgns. Contbr. articles to profl. jours. Bd. dirs. Cherry Creek Improvement Assn., 1980-84, Spalding Rehab. Hosp., 1986-89; chmn., vice-chmn. securities sub sect. Bus. Law Sect. of Colo. Bar, 1990, chmn., 1990-91. Lt. (j.g.), USNR, 1965-67. Mem. ABA, Colo. Bar Assn., Denver Bar Assn., Am. Law Inst., Securities Industry Assn. (state regulations com. 1982-86), Nat. Assn. Securities Dealers, Inc. (nat. arbitration com. 1987-91), St. Nicholas Soc. N.Y.C., Denver Law Club, Denver Country Club, Denver Athletic Club (dir. 1990-93), Rocky Mountain Brown Club (founder, past pres.), Racquet and Tennis Club. Republican. Episcopalian. Office: LeBoeuf Lamb Greene Et Al 633 17th St Ste 2000 Denver CO 80202-3660

LUTZ, JULIE HAYNES, astronomy and mathematics educator; b. Mt. Vernon, Ohio, Dec. 17, 1944; d. Willard Damon and Julia Awilda (Way) Haynes; m. Thomas Edward Lutz, July 8, 1967 (dec. 1995); children: Melissa, Clea. BS, San Diego State U., 1965; MS, U. Ill., 1968, PhD, 1971. Asst. prof. astronomy Wash. State U., Pullman, 1972-78, asst. dean sci., 1978-79, assoc. prof., 1978-84, assoc. provost, 1981-82, prof., 1984—, chair math. and astronomy dept., 1992-96; rsch. fellow Univ. Coll. London, England, 1976-77, 82-83; vis. resident astronomer Cerro Tololo Inter-Am. Obs., 1988-89; dir. div. astron. scis. NSF, 1990-92. Contbr. articles on astron. research to profl. jours. Fellow AAAS (mem. com. 1982-85, mem. nominating com. 1992-94, chair sect. D 1993-95, program com. 1997—), Royal Astron. Soc.; mem. Am. Astron., Soc. (chair publs. bd. 1986-88), Astron. Soc. Pacific (bd. dirs. 1988—, v.p. 1989, pres. 1990-92), Internat. Astron. Union. Avocations: cooking, backpacking, fishing. Home: 1200 NE Mcgee St Pullman WA 99163-3818 Office: Wash State U Program in Astronomy Pullman WA 99164-3113

LUTZ, LAWRENCE JOSEPH, family practice physician; b. Detroit, Dec. 16, 1949; s. Stephen A. and Eva B. (Groh) L.; m. Joan Regedanz, Dec. 27 (div. 1986); m. Ruthanne Rocki Ramsey, Apr. 29, 1989; 1 child, Alex Joseph. BS in Computer Sci., U. Mich., 1972; MD, Wayne State U., 1976; MSPH, U. Utah, 1982. Resident Saginaw Coop. Hosp., 1976-79; Robert Wood Johnson fellowship U. Utah, 1979-81; mem. faculty, divsn. dir. U. Utah, Salt Lake City, 1981-89; mem. faculty U. Colo., Denver, 1989-93; mem. faculty, chair family medicine and preventive medicine Emory U., Atlanta, 1993—. *

LUTZ, MATTHEW CHARLES, geologist, oil company executive; b. Bunkie, La., Mar. 28, 1934; s. John Matthew and Maxie Mae (Andrus) L.; m. Patricia Dawnn Feazel, Apr. 11, 1953; children: Matt, Jr., Cyndy, Tracey, Clay. BS, U. Southwestern La., 1956. Various geol. profl. positions Tidewater-Getty Oil Co., 1956-71; asst. dist. geologist Getty Oil Co., Houston, 1971-73, dist. geologist, Midland, Tex., 1973-78, central div. geologist, Tulsa, 1978-80, offshore dist. exploration mgr., Houston, 1980, so. div. exploration mgr., Houston, 1980-82, gen. mgr. offshore exploration and prodn., Houston, 1982-83, exploration mgr. so. div., Houston, 1983-84; sr. v.p. exploration Enserch Exploration Inc., Dallas, 1984-92, also dir.; vice chmn. & bus. devel. mgr. Hunter Resources, Inc., Irving, Tex., 1993-95, also bd. dirs.; vice chmn. exploration and bus. devel. mgr. Magnum Hunter Resources, Inc., Irving, Tex., 1995-97, chmn., exec. v.p. exploration and bus. devel., 1997—. Mem. Am. Assn. Petroleum Geologists, Houston Geol. Soc., Dallas Geol. Soc., Mid-Continent Oil Gas Assn., Am. Petroleum Inst., Independent Petroleum Assn. Am. Republican. Baptist. Clubs: Dallas Petroleum, Las Colinas Sports. Avocations: travel, golf, hunting. Office: Magnum Hunter Resources Inc 600 Las Colinas Blvd E Ste 1200 Irving TX 75039-5611

LUTZ, MYRON HOWARD, obstetrician, gynecologist, surgeon, educator; b. N.Y.C., June 26, 1938; s. Morris David and Rose (Greenblatt) L.; m. Judy Cohen, Aug. 6, 1963; children: Mark Steven, Sheri Lutz Barnett, Kenneth Ian. BA, Columbia U., 1960; MD, NYU, 1964. Diplomate Am. Bd. Ob-Gyn., Am. Bd. Gynecologic Oncology. Intern Phila., Gen. Hosp., 1964-65; resident in ob-gyn. Albert Einstein Coll. Medicine, Bronx, N.Y., 1965-69; fellow M.D. Anderson Hosp., Houston, 1971-72, U. Miami (Fla.) Sch. Medicine, 1972-73; asst. prof. ob-gyn. Med. U. S.C., Charleston, 1973-76, codir. gynecology oncology, 1973-77, clin. assoc. prof. ob-gyn., 1977—, clin. assoc. prof. surgery, 1986—; pvt. practice, Charleston, 1973—; mem. cancer adv. bd. Roper Hosp., Charleston, 1993—; star TV mid-day talk show, 1990—. Author pub. svc. ednl. tapes on gynec. problems; mem. editl. bd. House Calls mag., 1992—. Bd. dirs. Am. Cancer Soc., Charleston, 1974-75, v.p., 1975-76, pres., 1976-78; bd. dirs. Trident Acad., Charleston, 1982-86, Hospice, Charleston, 1984-86. Maj. M.C., U.S. Army, 1969-71. Fellow ACOG, ACS; mem. AMA, Am. Radium Soc., Am. Soc. Clin. Oncology, Soc. Gynecologic Oncologists, Felix Rutledge Soc., S.C. Med. Soc., S.C. Oncology Soc., Charleston Med. Soc. Avocations: water and snow skiing, archery, biking. Home: 55 Chadwick Dr Charleston SC 29407 Office: 1606 Ashley River Rd Charleston SC 29407-5902

LUTZ, RAYMOND PRICE, industrial engineer, educator; b. Oak Park, Ill., Feb. 27, 1935; s. Raymond Price and Sibyl Elizabeth (Haralson) L.; m. Nancy Marie Cole, Aug. 23, 1958. BSME, U. N.Mex., 1958, MBA, 1962; PhD, Iowa State U., 1964. Registered profl. engr., N.Mex., Okla. With Sandia Corp., Albuquerque, summers 1958-63; instr. mech. engring. U. N.Mex., 1958-62; from asst. to assoc. prof. indsl. engring. N.Mex. State U., 1964-68; prof. head indsl. engring. U. Okla., 1968-73; prof., acting dean U. Tex. Sch. Mgmt., Dallas, 1973-76, dean, 1976-78, exec. dean grad. studies and rsch., 1979-92, prof. ops. mgmt., 1992—; cons. Bell Telephone Labs., Tex. Instruments, Kennecott Corp., Bath Iron Works, City of Dallas, Oklahoma City; cons. U.S. Army, USAF, U.S. Dept. Transp., Los Angeles and Seattle public schs.; mem. shipbldg. productivity panel NRC. Editor: The Engring. Economist, 1973-77, Indsl. Mgmt., 1983-87. Pres., bd. dirs. United Cerebral Palsy, Dallas, 1978, treas., 1984-88; bd. dirs., treas. Amigos Bibliographic Network, Dallas, 1984-90; chmn., bd. dirs. S.W. Police Inst., Dallas, 1980—; v.p., bd. dirs. Santa Fe Opera, 1988—; bdl dirs. Dallas Opera, 1989—, Santa Fe Opera Found., 1993—. Fellow AAAS, Am. Inst. Indsl. Engrs. (v.p. industry and mgmt. divsns., trustee, dir. engring. economy divsn., systems engring. group); mem. Am. Soc. Engring. Edn. (chmn. engring. economy divsn., Eugene L. Grant award 1972), INFORMS, Dallas Classic Guitar Soc. (bd. dirs. 1993-96, v.p. 1994-96), Ops. Mgmt. Assn. (bd. dirs. 1994—), Sigma Xi (bd. dirs. 1990—, chmn. capital campaign 1992—, exec. com. 1992-95). Avocation: jogging. Home: 10275 Hollow Way Dallas TX 75229 Office: U Tex at Dallas PO Box 830688 Richardson TX 75083-0688

LUTZ, ROBERT ANTHONY, automotive company executive; b. Zurich, Switzerland, Feb. 12, 1932; came to U.S., 1939; s. Robert H. and Marguerite (Schmid) L.; m. Betty D. Lutz, Dec. 12, 1956 (div. 1979); children: Jacqueline, Carolyn, Catherine, Alexandra; m. Heide Marie Schmid, Mar. 3, 1980 (div. Dec. 1993); m. Denise Ford, Apr. 17, 1994; 2 stepchildren. BS in Prodn. Mgmt., U. Calif., Berkeley, 1961, MBA in Mktg. with highest honors, 1962; LLD, Boston U., 1985. Research assoc., sr. analyst IMEDE, Lausanne, Switzerland, 1962-63; sr. analyst forward planning GM, N.Y.C., 1963-65; mgr. vehicle div. GM, Paris, 1966-69; staff asst., mng. dir. Adam Opel, Russelsheim, Germany, 1965-66, asst. mgr. domestic sales, 1969, dir. sales Vorstand, 1969-70; v.p. Vorstand BMW, Munich, 1972-74; gen. mgr. Ford of Germany, Cologne, Germany, 1974-76; v.p. truck ops Ford of Germany, Brentwood, Eng., 1976-77; pres. Ford of Europe, Brentwood, Eng., 1977-79, chmn., 1979-82, also bd. dirs.; exec. v.p. Ford Internat., Dearborn, Mich., 1982-84, Chrysler Motors Corp., Highland Park, Mich., 1986-88; pres. ops., pres., COO Chrysler Corp., Highland Park, Mich., 1988--96; also chmn. bd. dirs. Chrysler Corp., Highland Park; bd. dirs. Silicon Graphics; adv. bd. Creditanstalt Bank, Vienna, Austria; bd. dirs. ASCOM, Switzerland; mem., former chmn. Hwy. Users Fedn. for Safety and Mobiligy. Trustee Mich. Cancer Found.; bd. dirs. United Way of Southeastern Mich.; bd. dirs. USMC Command and Staff Coll. Found.; adv. bd. Walter A. Haas Sch. Bus., U. Calif., Berkeley, 1979—. Capt. USMC, 1954-59. Named Alumnus of Yr., Sch. Bus., U. Calif., 1983; Kaiser Found. grantee 1962. Mem. NAM (exec. com.), Phi Beta Kappa. Republican. Avocations: skiing, motorcycling, bicycling, helicopter flying. Office: Chrysler Corp 1000 Chrysler Dr Auburn Hills MI 48326-2766

LUTZ, WILLIAM LAN, lawyer; b. Chgo., May 18, 1944; s. Raymond Price and Sibyl (McCright) L.; m. Jeanne M. McAlister, Dec. 27, 1969; children: William Lan, David Price. BS, U. Tex., 1965, JD, 1969. Bar: Tex. 1969, N.Mex. 1970. Assoc. Martin, Lutz, Cresswell & Hubert and predecessor firms, Las Cruces, N.Mex., 1969-82; former U.S. atty. dist. N.Mex. U.S. Dept. Justice, Albuquerque, 1982-91; ptnr. Martin, Lutz & Brower, P.C., Las Cruces, 1991—. Mem. ABA, N.Mex. Bar Assn. (mem. bd. bar commrs. 1995—); Aggie Sports Assn. (bd.dirs.) N.Mex. State U. Methodist. Office: Martin Lutz & Brower PO Drawer 1837 2100 N Main St Ste 3 Las Cruces NM 88004-1837

LUTZE, RUTH LOUISE, retired textbook editor, public relations executive; b. Boston, Apr. 19, 1917; d. Frederick Clemons and Louise (Rausch) L. BA with honors, Radcliffe Coll., 1938; postgrad., Boston U., 1938-39. Tchr. Winthrop (Mass.) Pub. Schs., 1938-39; with pub. rels. dept. Boston City Club, 1939-42; sr. projects editor D.C. Heath & Co., Lexington, Mass., 1942-82; book reviewer, lectr., cons. on pub. rels., lectr. textbook publ. Bd. dirs. Winthrop Improvement and Hist. Assn., 1980—; vol. tchr. Boston Pub. Schs., 1967-77; mem. Winthrop Rep. Town Com., 1970—; v.p. 1st Luth. Ch. Boston, 1986, deacon, 1980—. Recipient cert. appreciation for vol. in edn., Kiwanis Club of East Boston, 1972. Mem. Radcliffe Club Boston. Avocations: vol. work, theatre, birdwatching, reading, art exhibits. Home: 110 Circuit Rd Winthrop MA 02152-2819

LUTZER, DAVID JOHN, mathematics professor; b. Sioux Falls, S.D., Mar. 27, 1943; s. Alois John and Marcia Estelle (Nelsen) L.; m. Victoria DeFilippo, Feb. 6, 1982; children: Jacob, Carl, Lisa, Joseph. BS, Creighton U., 1964; Diploma in Advanced Mathematics, Oxford U., England, 1966; PhD, U. Wash., 1970. Asst. prof. math. U. of Pitts., 1970-75, assoc. prof., 1975-78; vis. prof. Tex. Tech U., Lubbock, 1976-77, assoc. prof., 1977-78, prof., 1978-82; prof., chmn. dept. Miami U., Oxford, Ohio, 1982-87; dean, prof. Coll. William and Mary, Williamsburg, Va., 1987—. Contbr. articles to profl. jours. NSF fellow, 1964, 66; Rhodes scholar, 1964. Mem. Am. Math. Soc. (editor Proceedings 1976-83), Math. Assn. Am., Soc. Indsl. and Applied Math. Office: Coll William and Mary Sch Arts and Scis Williamsburg VA 23187

LUU, JANE, astronomer. With Astronomy Dept. Harvard U., Cambridge, Mass. Recipient Annie Jump Cannon award Am. Astron. Soc., 1991. Office: Harvard U Astronomy Dept 60 Garden St # 15 Cambridge MA 02138-1516

LUVISI, LEE, concert pianist; b. Louisville, Dec. 12, 1937; m. Nina Hussey, June 20, 1959; 1 son, Brian. Student, Curtis Inst. Music, 1952-57. Mem. faculty Curtis Inst. Music, 1957-62; artist in residence U. Louisville Sch. Music. Artist-mem., Chamber Music soc. Lincoln Ctr. Office: U Louisville Sch Of Music Louisville KY 40292 also: Michal Schmidt Artists Int 59 E 54th St New York NY 10022-4211

LUXEMBURG, WILHELMUS ANTHONIUS JOSEPHUS, mathematics educator; b. Delft, Netherlands, Apr. 11, 1929; s. Everardus H. and Digna (Van Kranendonk) L.; m. Geetruida Zappeij, Aug. 2, 1955; children—Ronald P., Jacqueline T. B.A., U. Leiden, Netherlands, 1950, M.A., 1953; Ph.D., Delft Inst. Tech., 1955. Postdoctoral fellow NRC, Can., 1955-56; mem. faculty U. Toronto, 1956-58; faculty Calif. Inst. Tech., Pasadena, 1958—; prof. math. Calif. Inst. Tech., 1962—, exec. dir. for math., 1970-85; cons. Burroughs Corp., Pasadena, 1963-64. Mem. Am., Dutch math. socs., Math. Assn. Am., Canadian Math. Congress, Soc. for Indsl. and Applied Math., Royal Acad. Scis. Amsterdam (Humboldt award 1980). Research and publs. on theory of integration, spaces of measurable functions, ordinary differential equations, numerical analysis, topological linear spaces, Boolean algebras, axiomatic set theory, theory of Riesz spaces, non-standard analysis. Home: 817 S El Molino Ave Pasadena CA 91106-4411

LUXENBERG, MALCOLM NEUWAHL, ophthalmologist, educator; b. Philipsburg, Pa., July 29, 1935; s. Maurice and Henrietta (Neuwahl) L.; m. Sandra Diane Rosen, June 16, 1957; children: Steven Neuwahl, Cathy Ann. Student, Tulane U., 1953-56; M.D., U. Miami, Fla., 1960. Diplomate: Am. Bd. Ophthalmology. Intern Cin. Gen. Hosp., 1960-61; resident in neurology U. Vt. Affiliated Hosps., Burlington, 1961-63; resident in ophthalmology Bascom Palmer Eye Inst., U. Miami-Jackson Meml. Hosp., Miami, Fla., 1963-66; asst. prof. ophthalmology Coll. Medicine, U. Iowa, Iowa City, 1968-70; chief ophthalmology service VA Hosp., Iowa City, 1968-70; practice medicine specializing in ophthalmology West Palm Beach, Fla., 1970-72; clin. asst. prof. ophthalmology Bascom Palmer Eye Inst., Sch. Medicine, U. Miami, 1971-72; prof., chmn. dept. ophthalmology Med. Coll. Ga., Augusta, 1972—; cons. ophthalmology VA Hosp., Augusta, 1972—; sr. surgeon USPHS, 1966-68. Mem. editl. bd.: Archives of Ophthalmology, 1986-94. Recipient Outstanding Civilian Service Medal Dept. of Army, 1986. Mem. AMA, Am. Acad. Ophthalmology (hon. award 1986), Am. Ophthalmol. Soc., Assn. Univ. Profs. in Ophthalmology (pres. 1982-83), Ga. Soc. Ophthalmology, Med. Assn. Ga., Richmond County Med. Soc. Home: 512 Scotts Way Augusta GA 30909-3238 Office: Med Coll Ga Dept Ophthalmology Augusta GA 30912

LUXENBERG, STEVEN MARC, newspaper editor; b. Detroit, July 25, 1952; s. Julius Sam and Beth (Cohen) L.; m. Mary Jo Kirschman, June 28, 1981; children: Joshua K., Jill K. AB magna cum laude, Harvard U., 1974. Reporter Balt. Sun, 1974-79, 81-82, city editor, 1979-81, met. editor, 1982-84; dep. asst. mng. editor The Washington Post, 1985-91, asst. mng. editor investigative news/spl. projects, 1991-96; asst. mng. editor Outlook, 1996—. Recipient Outstanding News Reporting award Nat. Headliners, 1975, award for state govt. reporting Md.-Del.-D.C. Press Assn., 1982, Feature Writing award, 1988. Office: Washington Post 1150 15th St NW Washington DC 20071-0001

LUXMOORE, ROBERT JOHN, soil and plant scientist; b. Adelaide, South Australia, Australia, Nov. 7, 1940; came to U.S., 1966; s. John Alexander and Mary Elinor (Martin) L.; Annetta Paule Watson, Oct. 18, 1975. B Agrl. Sci., U. Adelaide, 1962, B. Agrl. Sci. with honours, 1963; PhD, U. Calif., Riverside, 1969. Cert. profl. soil scientist. Agronomist Dept. Agr., Adelaide, 1963-66; rsch. assoc. U. Ill., Champaign-Urbana, 1969-70; soil physicist U. Calif., Riverside, 1970-71; rsch. assoc. U. Wis., Madison, 1971-72; rsch. scientist Oak Ridge (Tenn.) Nat. Lab., 1973-86, sr. rsch. scientist, 1986—; cons. Ctr. for Law and Social Policy, Washington, 1979; com. mem. NRC, Washington, 1989-90. Editor: Coupling of Carbon, Water and Nutrient, 1986; contbr. articles to profl. jours. and chpts. to books. Com. mem. Rural Abandoned Mines Program, Morgan County, Tenn., 1979-81; bd. dirs. Tenn. Citizens for Wilderness Planning, Oak Ridge, 1988-91; bd. dirs. Save Our Cumberland Mountains, Lake City, Tenn., 1995—. Recipient Tech. Achievement award Martin Marietta Energy Systems, 1987; Australian Cattle & Beef Rsch. scholar, 1962. Fellow AAAS, Soil Sci. Soc. Am. (tech. editor 1988-90, editor-in-chief 1991-93, bd. dirs. 1994—); mem. Internat. Union Forestry Rsch. Orgns. (chmn. working party 1983-90, coord. dep. subject group 1991-95, exec. bd. 1996—), Am. Geophys. Union. Home: 295 Solomon Hollow Rd Harriman TN 37748-3634 Office: Oak Ridge Nat Lab PO Box 2008 Oak Ridge TN 37831-6038

LUYENDYK, BRUCE PETER, geophysicist, educator, institution administrator; b. Freeport, N.Y., Feb. 23, 1943; s. Pieter Johannes and Frances Marie (Blakeney) L.; m. Linda Kay Taylor, Sept. 7, 1967 (div. 1979); 1 child, Loren Taylor Luyendyk; m. Jaye Ellen UpDeGraff, Oct. 12, 1984 (div. 1987). BS Geophysics, San Diego State Coll., 1965; PhD Marine Geophysics, Scripps Inst. Oceanography, 1969. Registered geophysicist, Calif. Geophysicist Arctic Sci. and Tech. Lab. USN Electronics Lab. Ctr., 1965; lectr. San Diego State Coll., 1967-68; rsch. geologist Scripps Inst. Oceanography, 1969; postdoctoral fellow dept. geology and geophysics Woods Hole Oceanographic Instn., 1969-70, asst. scientist dept. geology and geophysics, 1970-73; asst. prof. U. Calif., Santa Barbara, 1973-75, assoc. prof., 1975-81, prof. dept. geol. scis., 1981—, acting dir. Inst. Crustal Studies, 1987-88, dir. Inst. Crustal Studies, 1988—; com. marine geophysical formats NASCO, 1971; working group problems mid-Atlantic ridge NAS NRC, 1972; working group Inter-Union commn. Geodynamics; participant, chief sci. oceanographic cruises, geol. expeditions. Editorial bd. Geology, 1975-79, Marine Geophysical Rschs., 1976-92, Jour. Geophysical Rsch., 1982-84, Tectonophysics, 1988-92, Pageoph, 1988—; contbr. articles to profl. jours., chpts. to books, encys. Recipient Newcomb Cleveland prize AAAS, 1980, Antarctic Svc. medal U.S. NSF, Dept. Navy, 1990, numerous rsch. grants, 1971—. Fellow Geol. Soc. Am.; mem. Am. Geophysical Union, Soc. Exploration Geophysics. Office: Univ of Calif Santa Barbara Inst for Crustal Studies 140 Girvetz Hall U Calif Santa Barbara CA 93106

LUZA, RADOMIR VACLAV, historian, educator; b. Prague, Czechoslovakia, Oct. 17, 1922; s. Vojtech V. and Milada (Vecera) L.; m. Libuse Ladislava Podhrazska, Feb. 5, 1949; children: Radomir V., Sabrina. JuDr, U. Brno, Czechoslovakia, 1948; MA, NYU, 1958, PhD, 1959. Assoc. prof. modern European history La. State U., New Orleans, 1966-67; prof. history Tulane U., New Orleans, 1967—; scholar-in-residence Rockefeller Found., Bellagio Study Ctr., 1988; prof. gen. history Masaryk U., Brno, 1993—. Author: The Transfer of the Sudeten Germans, 1964, History of the International Socialist Youth Movement, 1970, (with V. Mamatey) A History of the Czechoslovak Republic, 1918-1948, 1973, Austro-German Relations in the Anschluss Era, 1975, Österreich und die Grossdeutsche Idee in der NS-Zeit, 1977, Geschichte der Tschechoslowakischen Republik 1918-1948, 1980, A History of the Resistance in Austria, 1938-1945, 1984, Der Widerstand in Österreich, 1938-1945, 1985, La Rèpublique Tchècoslovaque 1918-1948, 1987; mem. editl. bd. East European Quar., Contemporary Austrian Studies. With Czechoslovak Resistance, 1939-45. Recipient all Czechoslovak mil. decorations; prize Theodor Körner Found., Vienna, 1965, J. Hlavka Hon. medal Czechoslovak Acad. Arts and Scis., 1992, Masaryk medal Pres. of Czech Rep., 1996, T.G. Masaryk medal of honor, 1996, Austrian Cross of Honor Sci. and Art I. Class, 1997; grantee Social Rsch. Coun., Am. Philos. Soc., Coun. Learned Socs., Fulbright Com., NEH. Mem. Am. Hist. Assn., Czechoslovak History Conf., So. Conf. Slavic Studies, Am. Assn. Advancement Slavic Studies, Am. Com. to Promote Studies of Habsburg Monarchy. Home: 18 Golf Club Dr Langhorne PA 19047-2163 Office: Tulane U Dept History New Orleans LA 70118

LUZKOW, JACK LAWRENCE, history educator, writer, consultant; b. Detroit, Dec. 18, 1941; s. Irving and Sally (Eagle) Farber; m. Susan Frankel, Mar. 27, 1964 (div. Dec. 1973); 1 child, Catherine Alexis; m. Virginia Ann Trieglaff, May 15, 1976; 1 child, Frank Jason. BA, Wayne State Univ., 1966; MA, St. Louis Univ., 1975, PhD, 1981. Bibliographic specialist Southern Ill. Univ., Carbondale, 1979-81; history prof. Union Coll., Barbourville, Ky., 1981-84, Marycrest Coll., Davenport, Iowa, 1984-90, Teikyo-Marycrest Univ., Davenport, Iowa, 1990—; pres. Cons. Global Learning, Davenport, 1992—; v.p. Lonetree Enterprises, Davenport, 1991—; v.p. Marycrest Acad. Senate, Davenport, 1990-91; past pres. Inst. Ednl. Seninars, Davenport, 1988; speaker Vis. Artists Series, Davenport, 1985. Contbr. articles to profl. jours. V.p. Latin Am. Human Rights Action Ctr., Iowa City, Iowa, 1988-90. Recipient Mellon-James Still fellowship, Univ. Ky., 1982, 84, rsch. grant Ky. Humanities Coun., Barbourville, 1984, dean's grant Marycrest Coll., 1986, 89, 90, Teikyo Marycrest Univ., 1991. Mem. Nat. Soc. Sci. Assn. (nat. governing & edn. bd. 1990—), European Studies Assn., Radical Historians of Am., Mo. Valley Hist. Assn., Western Ill. Humanities Coun. Office: Teikyo Marycrest Internat U 1607 W 12th St Davenport IA 52804-4034 Home: 1804 Pershing Ave Davenport IA 52803-4327

LYALL, KATHARINE C(ULBERT), academic administrator, economics educator; b. Lancaster, Pa., Apr. 26, 1941; d. John D. and Eleanor G. Lyall. BA in Econs., Cornell U., 1963, PhD in Econs., 1969; MBA, NYU, 1965. Economist Chase Manhattan Bank, N.Y.C., 1963-65; asst. prof. econs. Syracuse U., 1969-72; prof. econs. Johns Hopkins U., Balt., 1972-77; dir. grad. program in public policy Johns Hopkins U., 1979-81; dep. asst. sec. for econs. Office Econ. Affairs, HUD, Washington, 1977-79; v.p. acad. affairs U. Wis. System, 1981-85; prof. of econ. U. Wis., Madison, 1982—; acting pres. U. Wis. System, Madison, 1985-86, 91-92, exec. v.p., 1986-91, pres., 1992—; bd. dirs. Kemper Ins. Cos.; mem. bd. Carnegie Found. for Advancement of Teaching. Author: Reforming Public Welfare, 1976, Microeconomic Issues of the 70s, 1978. Mem. Mcpl. Securities Rulemaking Bd., Washington, 1990-93. Mem. Am. Econ. Assn., Assn. Am. Univs., Phi Beta Kappa. Home: 6021 S Highlands Ave Madison WI 53705-1110 Office: U Wis System Office of Pres 1720 Van Hise Hall 1220 Linden Dr Madison WI 53706-1525

LYASHENKO, NIKOLAI NIKOLAEVICH, mathematician, educator; b. Leningrad, Russia, Jan. 19, 1946; came to U.S., 1990; s. Nikolai Makarovich and Rufina Stepanovna (Poshekhonova) L.; m. Tatiana Vasilievna Giga, June 21, 1969; 1 child, Anna Nikolaevna. BS, Leningrad U., 1966, MS, 1969, PhD in Physics and Math. Scis., 1974, D in Phys. Math. Scis., 1986. Assoc. prof. Leningrad Elec. Engring. Inst., 1975-85; prof. Leningrad Poly. Inst., 1986-88; dir. info. processing lab. Leningrad Inst. Informatics and Automation, 1988-90; vis. prof. George Mason U., Fairfax, Va., 1991—; pres. Knowledge Extraction Tools, Inc., L.A. Contbr. numerous articles to profl. jours.; patentee in field. Avocation: playing piano. Home: 4614 W 131st St Hawthorne CA 90250-5107 Office: 801 S Grand Ave Fl 10 Los Angeles CA 90017-4613

LYBARGER, JEFFREY ALLEN, epidemiology research administrator; b. Granite, Ill., 1951. MD, So. Ill. U., 1976. Diplomate Am. Bd. Preventive Medicine in Pub. Health, Preventive Medicine and Occupl. Medicine. Intern in pediat. St. Louis U. Glennon Hosp., 1976-77; resident in occupl. medicine U. Cin., 1979-81; resident in pub. health, pub. medicine Ctrs. for Disease Control, Atlanta, 1982-84; dir. divsn. health studies Agy. for Toxic Substances and Disease Registry, Atlanta, 1989—. Mem. Soc. for Epidemiol. Rsch., Soc. for Occupl. and Environ. Health, Internat. Soc. for Environ. Epidemiology. Office: Agy Toxic Subs/Disease Reg Divsn Health Studies 1600 Clifton Rd NE Stop E31 Atlanta GA 30329-4018

LYBARGER, JOHN STEVEN, business development consultant, trainer; b. Yuba City, Calif., June 13, 1956; s. Rodger Lee and Phyllis Ruth (Roseman) L.; m. Marjorie Kathryn Den Uyl, Aug. 22, 1981; children: Ashley Ann, Ryan Christopher. AA, Yuba Community Coll., 1977; BS in Christian Edn., Biola U., La Mirada, Calif., 1980; MS in Counseling, Calif. State U., Fullerton, 1984; PhD in Psychology, Calif. Coast U., 1985. Lic. marriage family and child counselor; cert. alternative dispute resolution educator/practitioner. Assoc. dir. Concept 7 Family Svcs., Tustin, Calif., 1981-85; exec. dir. Family Life Ctr., Tustin, 1984-86; pres. Marriage & Family Counseling, La Habra, Calif., 1985-89; clin. dir. New Life Treatment Ctrs., Inc., Laguna Beach, Calif., 1988-89; faculty Loma Linda (Calif.) U. Sch. Medicine, 1990—; dir. partial hospitalization programs CPC Brea Canyon Hosp., 1991-93; clin. dir. Oasis Counseling Ctr., Denver, 1993-95; dir. Oasis Counseling Ctr., Denver; tng. cons. Dale Carnegie Tng., Denver; pres., CEO Nat. Coun. on Sexual Addiction, Atlanta, 1990-94. Mem. Am. Assn. for Marriage and Family Therapy (clin.). Republican. Avocations: skiing, tennis, racquetball. Home: 8489 W 95th Dr Westminster CO 80021 Office: 9975 Wadsworth Pky Ste K2-414 Broomfield CO 80021

LYBECKER, MARTIN EARL, lawyer; b. Lincoln, Nebr., Feb. 11, 1945; s. Earl Edward and Jeanette Frances (Kiefer) L.; m. Andrea Kristine Tollefson, Dec. 27, 1969; children: Carl Martin, Neil Anders. BBA, U. Wash., 1967, JD, 1970; LLM in Taxation, NYU, 1971; LLM, U. Pa., 1973. Bar: Wash. 1970, D.C. 1972, Pa. 1982. Atty. investment mgmt. div. SEC, Washington, 1972-75, assoc. dir. div., 1978-81; assoc. prof. SUNY, Buffalo, 1975-78; ptnr. Drinker Biddle & Reath, Washington, 1981-87, Ropes & Gray, Washington, 1987—; adj. prof. Georgetown U., Washington, 1974-75, 80-81; vis. assoc. prof. Duke U., Durham, N.C., 1977-78. Contbr. articles to law revs. Fellow U. Pa. Ctr. for Study of Fin. Instns., 1971-72. Mem. ABA (mem. subcom. on investment cos. and investment advisers, mem. subcom. on securities activities of banks, mem. com. on fed. regulation of securities bus. law sect., chairperson com. on devels. in investment svcs. bus. law sect., chairperson subcom. on bank holding co. activities and subcom. on fiduciary svcs. of com. of banking bus. law sect.), Univ. Club Washington. Home: 2806

Daniel Rd Bethesda MD 20815-3149 Office: Ropes & Gray 1301 K St NW Ste 800 E Washington DC 20005-3317

LYDOLPH, PAUL EDWARD, geography educator; b. Bonaparte, Iowa, Jan. 4, 1924; s. Guy W. and Pauline (Ruschke) L.; m. Mary J. Klahn, Dec. 17, 1966; children by previous marriage—Edward, Donald, Paul, Thomas, Andrew. B.A., U. Iowa, 1948; M.S., U. Wis., 1951, Ph.D., 1955; student, Harvard U., 1944, MIT, 1945, UCLA, 1956, U. Calif. at Berkeley, 1956-57. Tchr. math. Pisgah (Iowa) Pub. Sch., 1946-47, Packwood (Iowa) Pub. Sch., 1947-49; asst. prof., then asso. prof. Los Angeles State Coll., 1952-59; mem. faculty U. Wis. at Milw., 1959—, prof. geography, 1962-92, emeritus, 1992—, chmn. dept., 1963-69, 71-72; Lectr. U. Hawaii, summer 1965, Oxford U., Stockholm Sch. Econs., 1970; C.I.C. Exchange prof. U. Mich., Ann Arbor, 1977, U. Iowa, Iowa City, 1978; Smithsonian Instn. tour dir. to, USSR, 1976, 77, 78, 79. Author: Geography of the USSR, 5th edit., 1990, Climates of the USSR, vol. 7, World Survey of Climatology, 1977, Weather and Climate, 1985, The Climate of the Earth, 1985, also articles; Festschrift written by colleagues in his honor: Soviet Geography Studies in Our Time, 1987. Served with USAAF, 1943-47. Ford Found. fellow, 1956-57. Home: N8328 Snake Rd Elkhart Lake WI 53020-2011 Office: U Wis Dept Geography Milwaukee WI 53201

LYDON, THOMAS J., federal judge; b. Portland, Maine, June 3, 1927. B.A., U. Maine, 1952; LL.B., Georgetown U., 1955, LL.M., 1957. Bars: Maine, D.C. Trial atty. civil div. Dept. Justice, Washington, 1955-67, chief Ct. Claims sect. civil div., 1967-72; sr. judge U.S. Ct. Clms., Washington, 1972—. Office: US Claims Ct 717 Madison Pl NW Washington DC 20005-1011*

LYE, WILLIAM FRANK, history educator; b. Kimberley, B.C., Can., Feb. 19, 1930; came to U.S., 1955, naturalized, 1981; s. Arthur Percy and Jessie Loretta (Prince) L.; m. Velda Campbell, Oct. 16, 1953; children: William Mark, Matthew Campbell, David Arthur, Victoria, Regina. Student Ricks Coll., 1953-55, Duke U., 1963; BS, Utah State U., 1959; MA, U. Calif.-Berkeley, 1959; PhD, UCLA, 1969. Instr. polit. sci. Ricks Coll., Rexburg, Idaho, 1959-63, 67-68, head dept. polit. sci., 1959-63; teaching asst. dept. history UCLA, 1964-65; asst. prof. Utah State U., Logan, 1968-69, acting head dept. history and geography, 1969-70, assoc. prof., head dept. history and geography, 1970-73, prof., head dept. history and geography, 1973-76, dean Coll. Humanities, Arts and Social Scis., 1976-83, v.p. for univ. relations, prof. dept. history and geography, 1983-91, prof. history, 1991-95, emeritus, 1996—; vis. lectr. dept. history Brigham Young U., Provo, Utah, 1970; temporary lectr. dept. history U. Cape Town, Republic of South Africa, 1974; social cons. for project design teams in land conservation, U.S. Agy. for Internat. Devel. Khartoum, Sudan, 1978, Maseru, Lesotho, 1979; mem. higher edn. taskforce on telecommunications, Utah, 1977-82; chmn. State of Utah Telecommunications Coop., 1987, Regents' Com. on Credit by Exam., Utah, 1976; mem. adv. com. Sta. KULC-TV, State Ednl. Telecommunications Operating Ctr., 1986-90; bd. dirs., exec. com. Children's Aid Soc. Utah, 1985-89, pres., 1990-91; mem. Utah Statehood Centennial Commn., 1989-96, Utah Christopher Columbus Quincentenary Commn., 1990-91. Author: (with Colin Murray) Transformations on the Highveld: The Tswana and Southern Sotho, 1980, paperback edit., 1985; editor: Andrew Smith's Journal of His Expedition into the Interior of South Africa, 1834-36, 1975. Producer (TV series) Out of Africa, 1977, The God Seekers, 1978; contbr. articles and book revs. to profl. publs. Chmn. State Day celebration, Logan, Utah, 1973, univ. drive for new Logan Regional Hosp; bishop LDS Ch., 1993-96; chair bd. Nora Eccles Harrison Mus. of Art, 1996—; pres. Friends of USU Librs., 1997—. Recipient Leadership award Standard of Calif., 1957, Idea of Yr. award Utah State U., 1971, Faculty Service award Associated Students, Utah State U., 1977-78, Nicholas and Mary Kay Leone Leadership award, 1991; Woodrow Wilson Nat. fellow 1958, Foreign Area fellow Social Sci. Research Council, Republic of South Africa, England, 1966-67, 67-68; faculty devel. grantee Utah State U., 1972, Human Sci. Research Council of South Africa publ. grantee, 1975, Mauerberger Trust grantee, 1976. Mem. African Studies Assn., Royal African Soc., Western Assn. Africanists (program chmn. 1972-74, pres. 1974-76), Am. Soc. Landscape Architects (accreditation bd. 1967-93), Phi Kappa Phi, Phi Alpha Theta. Home: 60 Raymond Ct Logan UT 84321-4259 Office: Utah State U Dept History 650 N 1100 E Logan UT 84322-0710 *Personal philosophy: I support education for everyone as the means by which we make our fullest contribution to society, and it is by service to others that we earn our place on earth.*

LYERLY, ELAINE MYRICK, advertising executive; b. Charlotte, N.C., Nov. 26, 1951; d. J.M. and Annie Mary (Myrick) L.; m. Marc Rauch, Jan. 17, 1987. AA in Advt. and Comml. Design, Cen. Piedmont Community Coll., 1972. Freelance designer Sta. WBTV, Charlotte, N.C., 1972; fashion illustrator Matthews Belk, Gastonia, N.C., 1972-73; designer Monte Curry Mktg. and Communication Svcs., Charlotte, 1973-74, exec. v.p., 1974-77; pres. Repro/Graphics, Charlotte, 1975-77, Lyerly Agy. Inc., Charlotte, 1977—; bd. dirs. SouthTrust Bank. Illustrator: Mister Cookie Breakfast Cookbook, 1985. Chmn. regional blood com. ARC, chmn. Greater Carolinas chpt., 1990-93, mem. nat. implementation com., 1991; bd. dirs. United Way, Child Care Resources, Inc., YMCA. Named Bus. Woman of Yr., Shearson Lehman Hutton/Queens Coll., 1989, N.C. Young Careerist Bus. and Profl. Women's Club, 1981; recipient ACE award Women in Comms., 1993, CPCC Hagemeyer award, 1996. Mem. Women Execs. (bd. dirs.), Women Bus. Owners (adv. coun., Leadership award 1990, Woman Bus. Owner of Yr. award 1994), Pub. Rels. Soc. Am. (Counselors Acad. 1985—), Charlotte C. of C. (bd. dirs., diversity coun., long-range planning com., Bus. Woman of Yr. award 1985), Hadassah. Republican. Jewish. Office: Lyerly Agy Inc 4819 Park Rd Charlotte NC 28209-3274

LYERLY, HERBERT KIM, surgical oncology educator, researcher; b. San Diego, Aug. 26, 1958; s. Albert Elliot and Mitsu (Kinoshita) L. BS, U. Calif., Riverside, 1980; MD, UCLA, 1983. Diplomate Am. Bd. Surgery. Intern Duke U., Durham, N.C., 1983, resident in surgery, 1990-94, from asst. prof. to assoc. prof. surgery, 1990-97, asst. prof. pathology, 1991—, clin. dir. molecular therapeutics, 1993—, asst. prof. immunology, 1995—, prof. surgery, 1997—, clin. dir. Ctr. for Molecular and Cellular Therapy, 1997—. Editor: Surgical Intensive Care, 2d edit., 1989, co-editor: Surgical Intensive Care, 3d edit., 1991, Companion Textbook of Surgery, 1992, Essentials of Surgery, 1994; co-editor Textbook of Surgery, 15th edit., 1997, Companion Textbook of Surgery, 2d edit., 1997. Mem. Assn. Acad. Surgery, Soc. Surg. Oncology, Soc. Univ. Surgeons, Am. Coll. Surgeons. Office: Duke U Hosp Box 2606 Durham NC 27710

LYFORD, CABOT, sculptor; b. Sayre, Pa., May 22, 1925; s. Frederic Eugene and Eleanor (Cabot) L.; m. Joan Ardyth Richmond, June 22, 1953; children: Matthew, Julia, Thaddeus. BFA, Cornell U., 1950. Exec. trainee NBC, N.Y.C., 1952-54; producer and dir. J. Walter Thompson, N.Y.C., 1954-57, Sta. WGBH-TV, Boston, 1957-59; program mgr. Sta. WENH-TV, Durham, N.H., 1959-63; chmn. Dept. Art The Phillips Exeter (N.H.) Acad., 1963-86. Prin. sculptures include pub. monuments in Portland, Maine and Portsmouth, N.H., Berwick, Maine; represented in permanent collections at Portland Mus., Chattanooga Mus., Indpls. Mus., Wichita (Kans.) Mus., Ogunquit (Maine) Mus., Currier Gallery, Manchester, N.H., Addison Gallery, Andover, Mass. With inf. U.S. Army, 1943-46, PTO. Recipient Sculpture prize Nat. Design Acad., 1990. Home and Studio: PO Box 104 HC 62 New Harbor ME 04554-9005

LYJAK CHORAZY, ANNA JULIA, pediatrician, medical administrator, educator; b. Braddock, Pa., Feb. 25, 1936; d. Walter and Cecilia (Swiatkowski) Lyjak; m. Chester John Chorazy, May 6, 1961; children: Paula Ann Chorazy, Mary Ellen Chorazy-Cuccaro, Mark Edward Chorazy. BS, Waynesburg Coll., 1958; MD, Women's Med. Coll. Pa., 1960. Diplomate Am. Bd. Pediats. Intern St. Francis Gen. Hosp., Pitts., 1960-61; resident in pediats., tchg. fellow Children's Hosp. of Pitts., 1961-63, pediatrician, devel. clinic, 1966-75; pediat. house physician Western Pa. Hosp., Pitts., 1963-66; med. dir. Rehab. Instn. Pitts., 1975-94; clin. asst. prof. pediats. Children's Hosp. Pitts. and U. Pitts. Sch. Medicine, 1971-94, clin. assoc. prof. pediats., 1994—; pediat. cons. Children's Home Pitts., 1985—. Author chpts. to books. Co-chmn. EACH Joint Planning and Assessment, Pitts., 1980-85; mem. adv. com. 10th Nat. Conf. on Child Abuse, Pitts., 1993. Recipient Miracle Maker award Children's Miracle Network, 1995. Fellow Am. Acad. Pediats.; mem. Pitts. Pediat. Soc. Avocations: reading, comedy, theatre, music, opera. Home: 131 Washington Rd Pittsburgh PA 15221-4437 Office: Rehab Inst Pitts 6301 Northumberland St Pittsburgh PA 15217-1360

LYKES, JOSEPH T., III, shipping company executive; b. Galveston, Tex., Mar. 6, 1948. BA, Washington and Lee U., 1970. Sr. v.p. Lykes Bros. Steamship Co., Tampa. Office: 111 E Madison St Tampa FL 33602-4712

LYKINS, MARSHALL HERBERT, insurance company executive; b. Cin., Mar. 5, 1944; s. Herbert Cooper and Hilda Freda (Krall) L.; m. Betty Foushee Sweaney, June 27, 1970; 1 child, Elizabeth Foushee. BS, U. Chgo., 1966; M in Actuarial Sci., U. Mich., 1968. Actuarial student New Eng. Mut. Life Ins. Co., Boston, 1970-72, asst. actuary, 1972-75, assoc. actuary, 1975-78, 2d v.p. and actuary, 1978-85, v.p. and actuary, 1986—. Active Beacon Hill Civic Assn., Boston, 1970—, Byron St. Assn., Boston, 1982—; treas. King's Chapel, 1995—. Served with USPHS, 1968-70. Fellow Soc. Actuaries; mem. Chartered Life Underwriters, Am. Council of Life Ins. (com. on N.Y. expense limitations 1982—), Life Office Mgmt. Assn. (com. on profitability studies 1985—), Actuaries Club of Boston (treas. 1979—), U. Chgo. Alumni of Boston, U. Mich. Alumni of Boston, Phi Kappa Phi, Beta Gamma Sigma. Unitarian. Club: U. Club (Boston). Avocations: skiing, jogging, bridge. Home: 14 Byron St Boston MA 02108-3401 Office: New Eng Mut Life Ins Co 501 Boylston St Boston MA 02116-3706

LYLE, JAMES ARTHUR, real estate broker; b. Charlottesville, Va., Mar. 9, 1945; s. James Aaron and Sallie (Tuthill) Lyle; m. Martha Lee Gale, Jan. 28, 1978; children: Cory Jackson, Martha Jessica. BS in Indsl. Mgmt., Ga. Inst. Tech., 1968. Cert. comml. investment mem. Mktg. rep. IBM, Atlanta, 1970-71; investment cons. La Salle Ptnrs., El Paso, Tex., 1971-76; owner James Arthur Lyle and Assocs., El Paso, 1976—; v.p., bd. dirs. Hueco Mountain Estates, Inc., 1983-94; bd. dirs. Vista Hills Townhomes, 1977-78; bd. dirs. Southwestern Savs., 1984-86. Chmn., vice-chmn. El Paso City Plan Commn., 1978-82; vice-chmn. Internat. Airport Bd., 1982; adv. bd. El Paso Bikeway, 1986-88; active El Paso County Planning Commn., 1986-96; bd. dirs. NCCJ, 1978-82, Southwestern Gen. Hosp., 1979-83, El Paso Econ. Devel. Bd., 1980-82; bd. dirs. Am. Heart Assn., 1989-93. 1st lt. U.S. Army, 1968-70. Named Bus. Assoc. of Yr., Am. Bus. Womens Assn., 1984, S.W. Challenge Series Champion, 1991-96, Ironman World Triathlon Championship, 1992; I.T.U. World Long Course Triathlon Championsip, Nice, France, 1997. Mem. SAR (dist. v.p., Bronze Good Citizenship medal, Cert. of Disting. Svc.), Nat. Assn. Realtors, Realtors Nat. Mktg. Inst., Nat. Assn. Indsl. and Office Parks, Tex. Property Exchangors (Best Exch. 1979), Tex. Assn. Realtors, Tex. Real Estate Polit. Action Com. (life), El Paso Bd. Realtors (bd. dirs. 1975-88, cert. comml. investment mem. 1975—, El Paso-West Tex. cert. comml. investment mem., pres., sec.-treas. 1975—, comml.-investment real estate coun. 1971—), El Paso Indsl. Devel. Bd., El Paso Investment Exch. Svc., Sons Confederate Vets, Sunturians (life), Half Fast Track Club (v.p. multisports), USA Triathlon (bd. dirs. 1995-96), Team El Paso. Republican. Episcopalian. Avocation: triathlons. Home: 626 Blacker Ave El Paso TX 79902-2711 Office: James Arthur Lyle & Assocs 6028 Surety Dr Ste 204 El Paso TX 79905-2024

LYLE, JOHN TILLMAN, landscape architecture educator; b. Houston, Aug. 10, 1934; s. Leo Tillman and Martha Ellen (Rawlins) L.; m. Harriett Laverna Fancher, Dec. 28, 1967; children: Alexander Tillman, Cybele Katsura. BArch, Tulane U., 1957; postgrad., Royal Acad. of Fine Arts, Copenhagen, 1965-67; M of Landscape Architecture, U. Calif., Berkeley, 1966. Registered architect, Calif. Architect Stanford (Calif.) U., 1959-62; urban designer John Carl Warnecke & Assocs., San Francisco, 1963-65; prof. Calif. State Poly. U., Pomona, 1968—; vis. prof. Liubliana (Yugoslavia) U., 1982, Instituto Universitario Di Architectura, Venice, Italy, 1988, U. Sao Paulo, Brazil, 1989, Kyushu Inst. Design, Fukuoka, Japan, 1990; dir. design bldg. and landscape Ctr. for Regenerative Studies, 1984—. Author: Design for Human Ecosystems, 1985 (award Assn. Am. Pubs. 1985, Am. Soc. Landscape Architects 1986), Regenerative Design for Sustainable Development, 1994; contbr. articles to profl. jours. Mem. bd. govs. Desert Studies Consortium, Mojave Desert, 1984-88. Recipient Honor award Calif. Coun. Landscape Architects, 1988, Disting. Educator award Coun. Educators in Landscape Architecture, 1989; named Fulbright Disting. prof. U.S. Dept. State, 1982. Fellow Am. Soc. Landscape Archs. (ASLA medal 1996). Democrat. Avocations: hiking, skiing. Home: 580 N Hermosa Ave Sierra Madre CA 91024-1117 Office: Calif State Poly U 3801 W Temple Ave Pomona CA 91768-2557

LYLE, JOHN WILLIAM, JR., former state senator, lawyer, social sciences educator, secondary school principal; b. Providence, May 19, 1950; s. John William and Lois (Smith) L.; m. Lori A. Lyle, Feb. 16, 1992. BA, Barrington Coll., 1973; MEd, Providence Coll., 1978; JD, Suffolk U., 1992 Tchr. Lincoln (R.I.) Sch. Dept., 1974-95, adminstr., 1995—; senator State of R.I., Dist. 34, 1981-86, 91-94, minority whip, 1993-94; asst. prin. Lincoln H.S.; mem. adj. faculty R.I. Coll., Providence, 1990—, C.C. R.I., Lincoln, 1991—. Contbr. articles to profl. jour. Trustee Cumb-Line Boys and Girls Club, Cumberland, R.I., 1982; Rep. candidate for Sec. of State of R.I., 1986; tennis umpire USTA, N.Y.C., 1985-95; 1st v.p. New Eng. Tennis Umpires Assn.; Robert A. Taft Inst. fellow, 1975, 79; recipient Outstanding Alumnus award Barrington Coll., 1982, Disting. Alumnus award, 1984; Appreciation award No. R.I. Sr. Services, 1983, John E. Fogarty award, 1995, Johns Hopkins U. Close Up fellow. Mem. R.I. Bar Assn., R.I. Assn. Social Studies Tchrs., Lincoln Fraternal Order Police, R.I. Assn. Secondary Sch. Prins., Lincoln Tchrs. Assn. (exec. bd. 1987-90).Avocations: travel, reading, running, tennis. Office: Lincoln HS 135 Old River Rd Lincoln RI 02865-1336

LYLE, ROBERT EDWARD, chemist; b. Atlanta, Jan. 26, 1926; s. Robert Edward and Adaline (Cason) L.; m. Gloria Gilbert, Aug. 28, 1947. B.A., Emory U., 1945, M.S., 1946; Ph.D., U. Wis.-Madison, 1949. Asst. prof. Oberlin Coll., Ohio, 1949-51; asst. prof. U. N.H., Durham, 1951-53; assoc. prof. U. N.H., 1953-57, prof., 1957-76; prof., chmn. dept. chemistry U. North Tex., Denton, 1977-79; v.p. chemistry, chem. engr. S.W Rsch. Inst., San Antonio, 1979-91; v.p. GRL Cons., San Antonio, 1992—; vis. prof. U. Va., Charlottesville, 1973-74, U. Grenoble, France, 1976; adj. prof. Bowdoin Coll., Brunswick, Maine, 1975-79, U. Tex., San Antonio, 1985—. Mem. editorial bd. Index Chemicus, 1976—. USPHS fellow Oxford U., Eng., 1965; recipient honor scroll award Mass. chpt. Am. Inst. Chemistry, 1971; Harry and Carol Mosher awardee, 1986. Fellow AAAS; mem. Am. Chem. Soc. (councilor 1965-84, 86-92, medicinal chemistry divsn.), Royal Soc. Chemistry, Alpha Chi Sigma (editor Hexagon 1992—). Methodist. Office: GRL Cons 12814 Kings Forest St San Antonio TX 78230-1511

LYLES, MARK BRADLEY, advanced technology company executive, dentist; b. Paducah, Ky., Dec. 3, 1957; s. Kendall Smith Lyles and Charlotte Dean (Ruley) Martell; m. Catherine Lynn Gregg, Mar. 17, 1984 (div. 1995); children: Austin Bradley, Dahlon Patrick. AS, BS, BA in Biology and Chemistry, Murray (Ky.) State U., 1978, MS, EdS, 1981; DMD, U. Louisville, 1986; postgrad., U. Tex., San Antonio, 1991—. Resident in oral and maxillofacial surgery U. Tex. Health Sci. Ctr., 1991—; founder, chief exec. officer, pres. Talis Techs., Inc., San Antonio, 1992—; founder, pres., chief sci. officer Materials Evolution and Devel. U.S.A., Inc. (M.E.D. USA), San Antonio, 1993—; presenter in field. Contbr. articles to profl. jours.; inventor use of ultra-low density fused fibrous ceramics for indsl. applications, use of fused fibrous ceramics in dental materials, implantable sys. for cell growth control, filters for polynuclear aromatic hydrocarbon containing smoke. Lt. comdr. USNR, 1983—. Recipient Dentist-Scientist award Nat. Inst. Dental Rsch., 1991—; Dept. Chemistry and Bd. Regents scholar Murray State U., 1975-77; Grad. Coop. Edn. fellow Nat. Ctr. Toxicol. Rsch., EPA, FDA, 1979-80, Grad. fellow U. Louisville, 1981-82. Mem. Am. Coll. Oral and Maxillofacial Surgeons (Walter Lorenz Residents Rsch. award 1994), Acad. Osseointegration, Acad. Gen. Dentistry, Navy Inst., Assn. Mil. Surgeons U.S., Hon. Order Ky. Cols., Naval Res. Officers Assn., Phi Delta Kappa. Republican. Avocations: rifle and pistol marksmanship, weight training, sailing, travel, convertibles. Office: Materials Evolution & Devel USA Inc 8535 Wurzbach Rd Ste 104 San Antonio TX 78240-1263

LYMAN, ARTHUR JOSEPH, financial executive; b. Evergreen Park, Ill., May 18, 1953; s. Arthur Edward and Margaret (O'Conner) L.; m. Janet Lee Wenzel, Sept. 9, 1984; children: Christina Lee, Alissa Mary, Arthur Joseph Jr. BA, Knox Coll., 1975; M in Mgmt., Northwestern U., 1977. CPA, Ill.; CFP. Audit supr. Arthur Andersen & Co., Chgo., 1977-83; fin. planning analyst Montgomery Ward & Co., Chgo., 1983-84; dir. fin. and adminstrn. ctrl. region Coopers & Lybrand, Chgo., 1984-88, CFO Midwest region, 1989-93, nat. dir. fin. field ops., 1993—. Nation chief YMCA Indian Guides, 1994, 95, 96, fedn. chief, 1997. Mem. AICPA, Fin. Execs. Inst. (bd. dirs. Chgo. chpt. 1992—, pres. 1997—), Ill. Inst. CPA's, Pi Sigma Alpha, Tau Kappa Epsilon (honor award 1988, chmn. bd. trustees 1988-93). Roman Catholic. Home: 3 Cornell Dr Lincolnshire IL 60069-3222 Office: Coopers & Lybrand 203 N La Salle St Chicago IL 60601-1210

LYMAN, CHARLES PEIRSON, comparative physiologist; b. Brookline, Mass., Sept. 23, 1912; s. Henry and Elizabeth (Cabot) L.; m. Jane Hunnewell Cheever, June 21, 1941; children—Charles Peirson, Jane Sargent, Theodore, David Russell, Elizabeth Anne. A.B., Harvard U., 1936, A.M., 1939, Ph.D., 1942. Asst. curator mammals Mus. Comparative Zoology, Harvard U., Cambridge, Mass., 1945-51; assoc. curator mammals Mus. Comparative Zoology, Harvard U., 1951-56, research assoc., 1956-58, curator in mammalogy, 1968-82; curator Warren Anat. Mus., Harvard Med. Sch., Boston, 1970-82; assoc. Harvard Med. Sch., 1949-60, asst. prof. anatomy, 1960-67, assoc. prof. anatomy, 1967-76, prof. biology, 1976-82; mem. NIH Study Sect., 1965-69; mem. nat. adv. bd. Biotron, 1965-75; mem. standing com. Trustees Public Reservations; trustee Mass. Soc. Promoting Agr. Contbr. articles, mostly on hibernation in mammals and reactions of mammals to environ. extremes, to profl. jours. Served to maj. USAF, 1942-45. NSF grantee, 1960-82; NIH grantee, 1955-76. Fellow AAAS; mem. Am. Zool. Soc., Am. Physiol. Soc., Am. Acad. Arts and Sci., Sigma Xi. Republican. Unitarian. Clubs: Harvard, Tavern, Dedham Country and Polo. Home: 105 Elm St Canton MA 02021-1255

LYMAN, DAVID, lawyer; b. Washington, Sept. 25, 1936; s. Albert Moses and Freda (Ring) L.; m. Yubol Pumsathit, Nov. 10, 1979. BS in Elec. Engring., Duke U., 1958; cert. U.S. Naval Officers Submarine Sch., 1960; JD, U. Calif.-San Francisco, 1965; postgrad. in fgn. and comparative law Columbia U., 1974. Bar: Calif. 1966; registered elec. engr., Thailand. Active minesweepers and submarine force U.S. Navy, 1958-62; assoc. Fitzsimmons & Petris, Oakland, Calif., 1965-66; Lempres & Seyranian, Oakland, 1966-67; Tilleke & Gibbins, R.O.P., Advocates and Solicitors, Bangkok, assoc. ptnr. 1967-84, sr. ptnr., 1984—; dir. Goodyear (Thailand) Ltd., Triumph Internat. (Thailand) Ltd.; founding mem. Prime Minister Thailand's Fgn. Investment Adv. Council, 1975, chmn. Fgn. C. of C. in Thailand Law Change Proj for the Prime Minister, 1992; mem. USAID Adv. Com. on U.S.-Thai Trade and Investment, 1988; founder, mem. steering com. tech. cooperation office U.S. Asian Environ. Partnership Program. 1994. Contbr. articles to profl. publs. Chmn. King Bhumiphol Rama IX Park U.S. Geodesic Dome Pavillion Com., 1987; founding mem. Thailand Bus. Coun. Sustainable Devel., 1993—; founder Davos Group World Economic Forum on Anti-Corruption Standards for Global Businesss, 1995—, co-founder, advisor Cmty. Svcs. Bangkok, 1985; mem. Internat. C. of C. Standing Com. Extortion and Bribery, 1997; sec.-gen. Thailand Soc. Prevention of Cruelty to Animals, 1996—. Served with U.S. Navy, 1958-68; lt. comdr. Res. Recipient U.S. Naval Inst. prize, 1958, Am. Jurisprudence prize, 1965, U.S. Dept. Commerce cert., 1987; Paul Harris fellow, 1987, Thai Prime Minister's Cert. of Achievement 1990, 92, Am. C. of C. Disting. Svc. Award, 1990. Mem. Am. C. of C. in Thailand (bd. govs. 1973—, v.p. 1974, 83-85, pres. 1975, 86), Asia-Pacific Coun. of Am. C. of C. (vice chmn. 1975-77, 85-89, 92-93, bd. dirs. 1975, 86), AmCham Environ. Coun. (founder, 1992), Environ. Bus. Exchange (creator 1993), Thai Bd. Trade (bd. dirs. 1975, 86), Fgn. Chambers of Commerce Working Group (sec. 1982-87, chmn. 1987-90), Thailand bd. of Investment Environ. Study Adv. Com., 1993, World Econ. Forum (program fellow Europe/East Asia Econ. Forum 1992-94), Lex Mundi (bd. dirs. 1989-91), ABA, Calif. Bar Assn., LAWASIA, U.S. Naval Inst. (life), Naval Submarine League (life), Internat. Oceanographic Found. (life), Thailand Bus. Coalition AIDS Assn. (founder, 1994), 999 Wildlife Trust, Wildlife Fund Thailand, Chaine Des Rotisseurs (charge de mission), Jewish Assn. Thailand, Tau Epsilon Phi, Phi Alpha Delta, Beta Gamma Sigma (hon.). Republican. Jewish. Clubs: Royal Bangkok Sports, Heritage (founder Gov. 1985—), Fgn. Corrs. of Thailand (life). Lodge: Rotary (1969-89, sec. 1982-83, v.p. Bangkok 1984-85), Community Services of Bangkok (founder, acting pres. 1986, v.p. 1986-87, bd. dirs. 1985-88). Avocations: scuba diving, swimming, outdoor photography. Home: 39/221 Moo 3 Nichada Thani Soi 11, Tambol Bangtalad Amphur Pakkred, Nonthaburi 11120, Thailand Office: Tilleke and Gibbins ROP, 64/1 Soi Tonson, Ploenchit Rd, Bangkok 10330, Thailand

LYMAN, GARY HERBERT, epidemiologist, cancer researcher, educator; b. Buffalo, Feb. 24, 1946; s. Leonard Samuel and Beatrice Louise L.; children: Stephen Leonard, Christopher Henry. BA, SUNY-Buffalo, 1968, MD, 1972; MPH, Harvard U., 1982. Diplomate: Am. Bd. Internal Medicine (med. oncology, hematology). Resident in medicine U. N.C.-Chapel Hill, 1972-74; fellow in oncology Roswell Park Meml. Inst., Buffalo, 1974-77; rsch. instr. medicine SUNY Med. Sch.-Buffalo, 1974-77; mem. faculty U. South Fla. Coll. Medicine, Tampa, 1977—, assoc. prof. medicine, 1980-86, prof. medicine, 1986—, dir. div. med. oncology, 1979-93, chief medicine H. Lee Moffitt Cancer Ctr. and Rsch. Inst., prof. epidemiology and biostats., 1988—. Co-author: Geriatric Oncology, 1992, Comprehensive Geriatric Oncology, 1997; contbr. articles to profl. jours., chpts. to books. Spl. fellow Leukemia Soc. Am., 1976-77; postdoctoral fellow biostats. Harvard U., 1981-82; spl. clin. fellow Roswell Park Meml. Inst., Buffalo, 1975-76. Fellow ACP, Am. Coll. Preventive Medicine, Am. Coll. Clin. Pharm.; mem. Am. Soc. Clin. Oncology. Current work: Cancer clinical trials, biostatistics, epidemiology, clinical decision analysis. Office: 12902 Magnolia Dr Tampa FL 33612-9416

LYMAN, HENRY, retired publisher, marine fisheries consultant; b. Boston, Oct. 30, 1915; s. Henry and Elizabeth (Cabot) L.; m. Marjorie Borum, June 27, 1953 (dec. Mar. 1996). AB cum laude, Harvard Coll., 1937. Reporter Cape Cod Colonial, Hyannis, Mass., 1937-38; reporter Athol Daily News, Mass., 1938-40; editor Open Road Pub. Co., Boston, 1946-48; publisher Salt Water Sportsman, Boston, 1948-85, pub. emeritus, 1985—; advisor Internat. Conv. Conservation of Atlantic Tunas, Washington, 1976-86, New England Fishery Mgmt. Coun., Saugus, Mass., 1980—; bd. dirs. Atlantic Salmon Fedn., N.Y.C., Nat. Coalition for Marine Conservation, Savannah, Ga., Environ. League Mass., Boston; mem. U.S. sect. North Atlantic Salmon Conservation Orgn., Edinburgh, Scotland, 1983-92. Author: Bluefishing, 1953, rev. edit., 1987, Successful Bluefishing, 1974, (with others) The Complete Book of Striped Bass Fishing, 1954, The Complete Book of Weakfishing, 1959, Tackle Talk, 1971, Bottom Fishing, 1984; contbr. articles on marine fisheries matters. Trustee New England Aquarium, Boston, 1973-88, life trustee, 1988—; founding. trustee Coldwater Conservation Fund, Vienna, Va., 1993—; trustee Manomet Obs., Mass., 1978-90, hon. trustee, 1990—; bd. dirs. Samual Cabot, Inc., Boston, 1974-91, Fund for Preservation of Wildlife and Natural Areas, Boston, 1979-89; incorporator Harvard Mag., Cambridge, Mass., 1979—. Comdr. USNR, 1940-46, 52-53. Mem. Nat. Wildlife Fedn. (bd. dirs. 1983-89), New England Outdoor Writers Assn. (life., bd. dirs. 1960-62), Outdoor Writers Assn. Am., Tavern Club (sec. 1980-83, pres. 1983-84), Harvard Club, Phi Beta Kappa. Avocations: angling; hunting. Home: 10 Longwood Dr Westwood MA 02090-1123 Office: Salt Water Sportsman 77 Franklin St Boston MA 02110-1510

LYMAN, JOHN, psychology and engineering educator; b. Santa Barbara, Calif., May 29, 1921; s. Oren Lee and Clara Augusta (Young) L. A.B. in Psychology and Math., UCLA, 1943, M.S., 1950, Ph.D. in Psychology, 1951. Research technician Lockheed Aircraft Corp., Burbank, Calif., 1940-43; mathematician Lockheed Aircraft Corp., 1943-44; with dept. psychology UCLA, 1947—, assoc. prof., 1957-63, prof., 1963—, from instr. to assoc. prof. Sch. Engring. and Applied Sci., 1950-63, prof. Sch. Engring. and Applied Sci., 1963—, chmn. engring. systems dept., 1978-84, head Biotech. Lab., 1958-80, head Human-Machine-Environment Engring. Lab., 1981-96; prof. materials sci. and engring., 1984-91; prof. emeritus Sch. Engring. and Applied Sci. UCLA, 1991—; research engr. Inst. Traffic and Transp., 1967-73; vis. prof. bioengring. Technol. Inst., Delft, Netherlands, 1965; spl. cons. Nat. Acad. Scis., Washington, 1973; cons. VA, Los Angeles, 1962-66, 67-76, NIH, 1963-66, 68-73, med. devices div. FDA, 1976-78, Perceptronics, Inc., Woodland Hills, Calif., 1978—, other agys. and cos.; bd. dirs. Perceptronics, Inc., MegaGraphics, Inc., also chmn. bd. Author chpts. in books, articles in profl. jours.; editor in field. Served to lt. (j.g.) U.S. Navy, 1944-46. Recipient Japanese Govt. Research award for Fgn. Specialists (Robotics), 1985, also numerous fellowships and grants. Fellow APA, Am. Psychol.

Soc., Soc. Engring. Psychologists, AAAS, Human Factors and Ergonomics Soc. (Paul Fitts award 1971, pres. 1967-68, pres. disting. svc. award 1991); mem. Biomed. Engring. Soc. (pres. 1980-81), IEEE, Am. Soc. Engring. Edn., Am. Assn. Artificial Intelligence, Robotics Internat., Robotics Soc. Japan, Soc. Mfg. Engrs., Sigma Xi, Tau Beta Pi. Office: UCLA 6732 Boelter Hall Los Angeles CA 90024

LYMAN, PEGGY, dancer, choreographer, educator; b. Cin., June 28, 1950; d. James Louis and Anne Earlene (Weeks) Morner; m. David Stanley Lyman, Aug. 29, 1970 (div. 1979); m. Timothy Scott Lynch, June 21, 1982 (div. 1987); 1 child, Kevin Kynch. Grad. high sch., Cin. Solo dancer Cin. Ballet Co., 1964-68, Contemporary Dance Theater, 1970-71; chorus dancer N.Y.C. Opera, 1969-70; Radio City Music Hall Ballet Co., 1970; chorus singer and dancer Sugar, Broadway musical, N.Y.C., 1971-73; prin. dancer Martha Graham Dance Co., N.Y.C., 1973-88, rehersal dir., 1989-90; artistic dir. Martha Graham Ensemble, N.Y.C., 1990-91; faculty Martha Graham Sch., 1975—; head dance div. No. Ky. U., 1977-78; artistic dir. Peggy Lyman Dance Co., N.Y.C., 1978-89; asst. prof. dance, guest choreographer Fla. State U., Tallahassee, 1982-89; guest choreographer So. Meth. U., Dallas, 1986; adjudicator Nat. Coll. Dance Festival Assn., 1983—; co-host To Make a Dance, QUBE cable TV, 1979; mem. guest faculty Am. Dance Festival, Durham, N.C., 1984; site adjudicator Nat. Endowment for Arts, 1982-84; tchr. Hartford Ballet Sch., 1992—, East Conn. Concert Ballet, 1992—; guest faculty Wesleyan U., Middletown, Conn., 1992; guest artist Conn. Coll., 1993; chair dance dept. Hartt sch. U. Hartford, Conn., 1994—; freelance master tch. internat. univs. Prin. dancer Dance in America, TV spls., 1976, 79, 84; guest with Rudolph Nureyev, Invitation to the Dance, CBS-TV, 1980; guest artist Theatre Choregraphique Rennes, Paris, 1981, Rennes, France, 1983, Adelaide U., 1991; site dir. Martha Graham's Diversion of Angels for student concert U. Mich., 1992, Martha Graham's Panorama, U. Ill., Champaign-Urbana, 1993, Panorama, Towson State U., 1997, Martha Graham's Diversion of Angels for Dutch Nat. Ballet, 1995; choregrapher: Conundrum (solo), 1982, Mantid (group), 1984, Roll, Spin, Draw, or Fold (group), 1984, Chope Dance (Solo), 1985, Mirror's Edge (group), 1986, No Gavotte Bach (group), 1995, Interior Landscapes (group), 1997. Founding mem. Cin. Arts Coun., 1976-78. Mem. Am. Guild Mus. Artists. Office: Hartford Ballet 224 Farmington Ave Hartford CT 06105-3501

LYMAN, PRINCETON NATHAN, ambassador; b. San Francisco, Nov. 20, 1935; s. Arthur and Gertrude (Kramer) L.; m. Helen Carolyn Ermann, July 7, 1957; children: Cindy, Sheri, Lori. B.A., U. Calif., Berkeley, 1957; M.A., Harvard U., 1959, Ph.D., 1961. Program officer U.S. Aid Mission, Seoul, Korea, 1964-67; research assoc. Harvard U., Cambridge, Mass., 1967-68; dir. civic participation div. AID, Washington, 1968-71, equal employment counselor, 1969-71, dir. devel. resources for Africa, 1971-76; dir. U.S. Aid Mission, Addis Ababa, Ethiopia, 1976-78; dep. asst. sec. Africa Bur. U.S. Dept. State, Washington, 1981-86, U.S. amb. to Nigeria, 1986-89, dir. Bur. Refugee Programs, 1989-92, U.S. amb. to South Africa, 1992-95; asst. sec. Bureau of Int'l Org., 1995—; professorial lectr. Johns Hopkins U., Washington, 1980-86. Contbr. articles and book chpts. to profl. publs. Recipient AID Meritorious Honor award, 1966, Superior Honor award, 1970, 86, President's Meritorious Svc. award, 1989, 91; President's Disting. Svc. award, 1993. Mem. Am. Fgn. Service Assn. (v.p. 1969-70, bd. dirs.), Coun. Fgn. Rels. Office: Bureau of Intl Org 2201 C St NW Washington DC 20520-0001*

LYMAN, RICHARD WALL, foundation and university executive, historian; b. Phila., Oct. 18, 1923; s. Charles M. and Aglae (Wall) L.; m. Elizabeth D. Schauffler, Aug. 20, 1947; children: Jennifer P., Holly Lyman Antolini, Christopher M., Timothy R. BA, Swarthmore Coll., 1947, LLD (hon.), 1974; MA, Harvard U., 1948, PhD, 1954, LLD (hon.), 1980; LLD (hon.), Washington U., St. Louis, 1971, Mills Coll., 1972, Yale U., 1975; LHD (hon.), U. Rochester, 1975, Coll. of Idaho, 1989. Teaching fellow, tutor Harvard U., 1949-51; instr. Swarthmore Coll., 1952-53; instr., then asst. prof. Washington U., St. Louis, 1953-58; mem. faculty Stanford U., 1958-80, 88-91, prof. history, 1962-80, 88-91, Sterling prof., 1980-91, assoc. dean Sch Humanities and Scis., 1964-66, v.p., provost, 1967-70, pres., 1970-80, pres. emeritus, 1980—, dir. Inst. Internat. Studies, 1988-91; pres. Rockefeller Found., 1980-88; spl. corr. The Economist, London, 1953-66; bd. dirs. Coun. on Founds., 1982-88, Independent Sector, 1980-88, chair, 1983-86, Nat. Com. on U.S.-China Rels., 1986-92; dir. IBM, 1978-92, Chase Manhattan Corp., 1981-91. Author: The First Labour Government, 1957; editor: (with Lewis W. Spitz) Major Crises in Western Civilization, 1965, (with Virginia A. Hodgkinson) The Future of the Nonprofit Sector, 1989; editorial bd. Jour. Modern History, 1958-61. Mem. Nat. Coun. on Humanities, 1976-82, vice chmn., 1980-82; chmn. Commn. on Humanities, 1978-80; trustee Rockefeller Found., 1976-88, Carnegie Found. Advancement of Tchg., 1976-82, World Affairs Coun. of No. Calif., 1992—; bd. dirs. Nat. Assn. Ind. Colls. and Univs., 1976-77, Assn. of Governing Bds. of Univs. and Colls., 1994-97, Am. Alliance for Rights and Responsiblities, 1993—; chmn. Assn. Am. Univs., 1978-79. With USAAF, 1943-46. Decorated officier Legion of Honor; Fulbright fellow London Sch. Econs., 1951-52, hon. fellow, 1978—; Guggenheim fellow, 1959-60. Fellow Royal Hist. Soc.; mem. Am. Acad. Arts and Scis., Am. Hist. Assn., Council on Fgn. Relations, Conf. Brit. Studies, Phi Beta Kappa. Office: Stanford U Sch Edn Stanford CA 94305

LYMAN, ROBERT HOWARD, veterans association executive; b. Long Beach, Calif., Sept. 2, 1949; s. Herbert Stewart and Eleanor Louise (McConnell) L.; m. Carol Ann Rybik, Oct. 24, 1981; 1 stepchild, Brian Orman. BA in History, Asbury Coll., 1971; MS in Sys. Mgmt., U. So. Calif., 1984. With USMC, 1971-91, commd. 2d lt., 1973, advanced through grades to maj., 1983, ret., 1991; exec. dir. Naval Enlisted Res. Assn., Falls Church, Va., 1991—. Mem. Ret. Officers Assn., Exch. Club of Capitol Hill. Republican. Roman Catholic. Avocation: golf. Office: NERA 6703 Farragut Ave Falls Church VA 22042-2115

LYMAN, RUTH ANN, psychologist; b. Nashville, Ark., Feb. 2, 1948; d. Oren Ernest and Frances Emeline (Urban) Frerking. BS, U. Ala., 1969, MA, 1972, PhD, 1974, MPA, 1986. Lic. psychologist, Ala. Cons. Ohio Coun. Community Mental Health Ctrs., Columbus, 1983, Ellard-Harper Found., Birmingham, Ala., 1983; resource cons. Ala. State Legis. Task Force on Child Abuse & Neglect, Montgomery, 1984-86; chief mental health sect., clin. psychologist U. Ala., Tuscaloosa, 1973-75; exec. dir. Western Mental Health Ctr., Birmingham, 1975-87; pvt. practice clin. psychologist Birmingham, 1988-95; founding ptnr. Ala. Psychotherapy & Wellness Ctr., P.C., Birmingham, 1995—; bd. dirs. Med. Bus. Mgmt., Inc.; mem. dept. psychiatry steering com. Brookwood HOsp., Birmingham, 1990—; adj. clin. prof. dept. psychology U. Ala., 1973-75, 77—. Author: (with others) Behavior Modification in Children: Case Studies and Illustrations from a Summer Camp, 1974, Outpatient Psychiatry: Progress, Treatment, Prevention, 1985, Administrative Discretion and the Implementation of Public Policy, 1986; contbr. articles to profl. jours. Treas., exec. com. Alcoholism Recovery Svcs., Inc., 1978-87; mem. adv. com. Nat. Alliance for the Mentally Ill., Birmingham, 1986-87, Pers. Bd. Jefferson County, 1978-82, chair, 1982, legis. com. chair, 1980-81; mem. Group Home Adv. Com., 1976-83; bd. dirs. Ala. NCCJ, 1979-82; mem. task force Birmingham Regional Health Systems Agy., Inc., 1977-79, mental health subcom., com. chair, 1979; chair by-laws com. Head Start Policy Coun., Birmingham, 1976-78; v.p. Ala. Coun. Community Health, 1987, stds. com., 1982, planning com., 1980-81, 83-85, sec., treas. and exec. com., 1978-79; bd. dirs., program co-chair Women's Network Birmingham, 1986; adv. com. Mental Health Assn. of Jefferson County, 1976-87. Named Birmingham Career Woman of the Yr., 1981. Mem. APA, NAFE, Southeastern Psychol. Assn., Ala. Psychol. Assn. (chair ad hoc com. for psychologists in pub. agys. 1985-86, chair ethics com. 1990, sec. 1990-92, pres. 1996), Birmingham Regional Assn. Lic. Psychologists (co-chair steering com. and cmty. edn. com. 1989-90, pres. 1991), Assn. for Advancement of Psychology, Assn. Lic. Psychologists in Ala., Women's Network of Birmingham (bd. dirs., co-chair program 1986), Zonta Internat. Avocation: classical music.

LYMAN, WILLIAM WELLES, JR., retired architect; b. New London, Conn., Aug. 31, 1916; s. William Welles and Gladys Estelle (Latimer) L.; m. Margaret Helen Whittemore, July 12, 1941 (div. Sept. 1970); children: Cheryl, Steven, Philip, Susan, Donna, Patricia; m. Joan Evelyn Dalrymple, Sept. 26, 1970. BArch, U. Mich., 1939; MArch, Harvard U., 1940. Architect various orgns., Boston, 1941-42; pvt. practice Cambridge, Mass., 1947-53; chief designer Smith, Hinchman & Grylls, Detroit, 1953-56; architect Swanson Assocs., Bloomfield Hills, Mich., 1956-59, Smith & Smith Assocs., Royal Oak, Mich., 1959-62; architect Jickling Lyman & Powell Assocs., Inc., Birmingham, Mich., 1962-81, ret., 1981; mem. faculty Harvard U., Cambridge, Mass., 1947-53; lectr. on early Am. furniture, 1975—. Pres. Cambridge Coun. PTAs, 1950-52, Harlan Sch. PTA, 1960-61; treas. Mass. Coun. for Better Schs., 1950-52; chmn. Citizens Elem. Curriculum Study Birmingham Pub. Schs., 1962-63; bd. dirs. South Oakland Symphony Soc., 1960-63, Birmingham Teen. Ctr., 1965-67, Birmingham Community House, 1967-70, Profl. Skills Alliance, Detroit, 1973-75, Birmingham Hist. Bd., 1969-73, chmn., 1972-73; chmn. Birmingham Hist. Dist. Study Com., 1975-77, Community Devel. Svcs., Portsmouth, N.H., 1993-96; pres. Birmingham Hist. Soc., 1980-81, bd. dirs. 1967-70; chmn. acquisitions com. John W. Hunter House, 1974-82; bd. govs. Warner House Assn., Portsmouth, N.H., 1983-91, chmn., 1986-88. U.S. Coast Guard, 1942-46. Fellow AIA; mem. Mich. Soc. Architects (pres. 1970). Unitarian. Home: 171 Gates St Portsmouth NH 03801-4607

LYNCH, BENJAMIN LEO, oral surgeon educator; b. Omaha, Dec. 29, 1923; s. William Patrick and Mary (Rauber) L.; m. Colleen D. Cook, Nov. 10, 1956; children: Kathleen Ann, Mary Elizabeth, Patrick, George, Martha, Estelle. BSD, Creighton U., 1945, DDS, 1947, MA, 1953; fellow, U. Tex., 1947-48; MSD, Northwestern U., 1954. Diplomate Am. Bd. Oral and Maxillofacial Surgery. Asst. instr. oral surgery Creighton U., 1948-50, instr., 1950-52, asst. prof., 1952-53; dean Creighton U. (Sch. Dentistry), 1954-61, assoc. prof. oral surgery, 1954-55, prof. oral surgery, 1957-86, prof. emeritus, 1986—, dir. oral surgery dept., 1954-67; also coordinator grad. and postgrad. programs; chief oral surgeon Douglas County Hosp., Omaha, 1951-63; pres. dental staff Children's Meml. Hosp., Omaha, 1952, 59; co-founder cleft palate team Children's Meml. Hosp., 1959; chmn. dept. dentistry Bergan-Mercy Hosp., Omaha, 1963-68; mem. exec. com., head dental staff Luth. Hosp., 1963-66; bd. dirs. Nebr. Dental Service Corp., 1972-78, pres., 1974-78; treas. Children's Meml. Hosp. Med.-dental staff, 1979-81; guest lectr. Walter Reed Grad. Sch. Medicine, 1957-58. Mem. Omaha-Douglas County Health Bd., 1966-68, v.p., 1967, pres., 1968; exec. com. Nebr. divsn. Am. Cancer Soc., 1963-67; bd. dirs. Nebr. Blue Cross, 1968-89, Creighton U. Alumni Coun., Omaha chpt., 1989-91; trustee United Cath. Social Svcs., 1989-95; adv. bd. to dean Creighton U. Dental Sch., 1984—, vice chmn., 1992-93, chmn., 1993-94; pres. Creighton U. Graybackers, 1991-94. Served at Walter Reed U.S. Army Med. Ctr., 1955-57. Recipient Alumni merit award Creighton U., 1978; named one of Ten Outstanding Young Omahans, 1952, 53, 58; inducted into Nebr. Dental Hall of Fame, 1981. Fellow Am. Coll. Dentists (pres. Nebr. chpt. 1973-74); mem. Am. Soc. Oral Surgeons, Midwest Soc. Oral Surgeons, Nebr. Soc. Oral Surgeons (founder 1957, pres. 1961), Nebr. Dental Soc. (trustee 1964-66), Omaha Dist. Dent Soc. (pres. 1963-64), Am. Coll. Oral-Maxillofacial Surgeons (founding mem.), Nebr. Soc. Dental Anesthesiology (founder, 1st pres.), Alpha Sigma Nu, Omicron Kappa Epsilon, Delta Sigma Delta. Home: 509 S Happy Hollow Blvd Omaha NE 68106-1224

LYNCH, BEVERLY PFEIFER, education and information studies educator; b. Moorhead, Minn., Dec. 27, 1935; d. Joseph B. and Nellie K. (Bailey) Pfeifer; m. John A. Lynch, Aug. 24, 1968. B.S., N.D. State U., 1957, L.H.D. (hon.); M.S., U. Ill., 1959; Ph.D., U. Wis., 1972. Librarian Marquette U., 1959-60, 62-63; exchange librarian Plymouth (Eng.) Pub. Library, 1960-61; asst. head serials div. Yale U. Library, 1963-65, head, 1965-68; vis. lectr. U. Wis., Madison, 1970-71, U. Chgo., 1975; exec. sec. Assn. Coll. and Research Libraries, 1972-76; univ. librarian U. Ill.-Chgo., 1977-89; dean Grad. Sch. Libr. and Info. Sci. UCLA, 1989-94, prof. Grad. Sch. Edn. and Info. Studies, 1989—. Author: (with Thomas J. Galvin) Priorities for Academic Libraries, 1982, Management Strategies for Libraries, 1985, Academic Library in Transition, 1989, Information Technology and the Remaking of the University Library, 1995. Named Acad. Libr. of Yr., 1982, one of top sixteen libr. leaders in Am., 1990; fellow Indo-U.S. Subcommn. on Edn. and Culture, 1992-93. Mem. ALA (pres. 1985-86), Nat. Info. Stds. Orgn. (bd. dirs. 1996—), Acad. Mgmt., Am. Sociol. Assn., Assn. for the Study of Higher Edn., Bibliog. Soc. Am., Caxton Club, The Chicago Network, Grolier Club, Arts Club Chgo., Book Club Calif., Phi Kappa Phi. Office: UCLA Grad Sch Edn and Info Mailbox 951521 Los Angeles CA 90095-1521

LYNCH, CATHERINE GORES, social work administrator; b. Waynesboro, Pa., Nov. 23, 1943; d. Landis and Pamela (Whitmarsh) Gores; BA magna cum laude and honors, Bryn Mawr Coll., 1965; Fulbright scholar, Universidad Central de Venezuela, Caracas, 1965-66; postgrad. (Lehman fellow), Cornell U., 1966-67; m. Joseph C. Keefe, Nov. 29, 1981; children: Shannon Maria, Lisa Alison, Gregory T. Keefe, Michael D. Keefe. Mayor's intern, Human Resources Adminstrn., N.Y.C., 1967; rsch. asst. Orgn. for Social and Tech. Innovation, Cambridge, Mass., 1967-69; cons. Ford Found., Bogota, Colombia, 1970; staff Nat. Housing Census, Nat. Bur. Statistics, Bogota, 1971; evaluator Foster Parent Plan, Bogota, 1973; rsch. staff FEDESARROLLO, Bogota, 1973-74; dir. Dade County Advocates for Victims, Miami, Fla., 1974-86; asst. to dep. dir. Dept. Human Resources, Miami, 1986-87, computer liaison, 1987-88, asst. adminstr. placement svcs. program, 1988-89; exec. dir. Health Crisis Network, 1989-96; liaison HIV cmty. svc. State of Fla. Health and Rehab. Svcs., 1996—; guest lectr. local univs. Participant, co-chmn. various task forces rape, child abuse, incest, family violence, elderly victims of crime, nat., state, local levels, 1974-86; developer workshops in field; participant, chair, co-chair task forces on HIV/AIDS impact, long term care, children and AIDS, AIDS orgnl. issues, 1991-96; mem. gov.'s task force on victims and witnesses, gov.'s task force on sex offenders and their victims, gov.'s Red Ribbon panel on AIDS, 1992-93, gov.'s interdepartmental work group, 1993—; mem. ednl. review com. Am. Found. AIDS Rsch., 1991-96; vice chair Metro-Dade HIV Svcs. Planning Council, 1991-93; active Fla. HIV Svcs. Adv. Coun., 1991-94; review panel Fed. Spl. Projects of Nat. Significance; adv. coun. Metro Dade Social Svcs., 1995-96; cert. expert witness on battered women syndrome in civil and criminal cts. Recipient various public svc. awards including WINZ Citizen of Day, 1979, Outstanding Achievement award Fla. Network Victim Witness Svcs., 1982, Pioneer award Metro-Dade Women's Assn., 1989; cert. police instr. Mem. Nat. Orgn. of Victim Assistance Programs (bd. dirs. 1977-83; Outstanding Program award 1984). Fla. Network of Victim/Witness Programs (bd. dirs., treas., 1980-81), Nat. Assn. Social Workers, Am. Soc. Public Adminstrs., Dade County Fedn. Health and Welfare Workers, Fla. Assn. Health and Social Svcs. (Dade County chpt., treas., 1979-80), LWV (bd. dirs. Dade County chpt. 1989-92). Contbr. writings in field to publs. Office: Fla HRS Office Dist Administr N-1007 401 NW 2nd Ave Miami FL 33128-1740

LYNCH, CHARLES ALLEN, investment executive, corporate director; b. Denver, Sept. 7, 1927; s. Laurence J. and Louanna (Robertson) L.; divorced; children: Charles A., Tara O'Hara, Casey Alexander; m. Justine Bailey, Dec. 27, 1992. BS, Yale U., 1950. With E.I. duPont de Nemours & Co., Inc., Wilmington, Del., 1950-69, dir. mktg., 1965-69; corp. v.p. SCOA Industries, Columbus, Ohio, 1969-72; corp. exec. v.p., also mem. rotating bd. W.R. Grace & Co., N.Y.C., 1972-78; chmn. bd., chief exec. officer Saga Corp., Menlo Park, Calif., 1978-86, also dir.; chmn., chief exec. officer DHL Airways, Inc., Redwood City, Calif., 1986-88; also dir.; pres., chief exec. officer Levolor Corp., 1988-89, also bd. dir., chmn. exec. com. of bd., 1989-90; chmn. Market Value Ptnrs. Co., Menlo Park, Calif., 1990-95; chmn., dir. Fresh Choice, Inc., Santa Clara, Calif., 1995—, chmn., 1995—; also bd. dirs.; bd. dirs. Pacific Mut. Life Inst. Co., Nordstrom, Inc., PST Vans, Inc., SRI Internat., Palo Alto Med. Found., Age Wave, Inc.; chmn. BJ Holdings, Inc., La Salsa Franchise, Inc. Bd. dirs. United Way, 1990-92, past chmn. Bay Area campaign, 1987; chmn., dir. Bay Area Coun.; past chmn. Calif. Bus. Roundtable; mem. adv. bd. U. Calif.-Berkeley Bus. Sch., Governance Bd. Mem. Yale Club (N.Y.C.), Internat. Lawn Tennis Club, Menlo Country Club (Calif.), Pacific Union Club (San Francisco), Coral Beach and Tennis Club (Bermuda), Vintage Club (Indian Wells, Calif.), Menlo Circus Club. Republican. Home: 96 Ridge View Dr Atherton CA 94027-6464 Office: 2901 Tasman Dr Ste 109 Santa Clara CA 95054-1137

LYNCH, CHARLES ANDREW, chemical industry consultant; b. Bklyn., Jan. 6, 1935; s. Charles Andrew and Mary Martina (McEvoy) L.; m. Marilyn Anne Monaco, July 30, 1960; children: Nancy Callan, Cara Martina. BS, Manhattan Coll., 1956; PhD, U. Notre Dame, 1960. Rsch. chemist Esso Rsch. & Engring. Co., Linden, N.J., 1960-65; rsch. supr. FMC Corp., Organic Chem. Div., Balt., 1965-72; rsch. mgr. FMC Corp., Indsl. Chem. Div., Princeton, N.J., 1972-74; exec. v.p. Am. Oil & Supply Co., Newark, 1974-80; tech. dir., dir. sales & mktg., dir. rsch. & bus. devel., v.p. tech. Hatco Corp., Fords, N.J., 1981-95; with Calivera Cons., 1995—. Contbr. articles to profl. jours.; patentee in field (U.S. and foreign). Mem. Am. Chem. Soc., Am. Oil Chemists Soc., Soc. AutomotiveEngrs., Soc. Tribologists and Lubrication Engrs. (chmn. N.Y. sect. 1980-81, 97—), Ind. Lubricant Mfrs. Assn. (bd. dirs. 1985-88).

LYNCH, CHARLES THEODORE, SR., materials science engineering researcher, consultant, educator; b. Lima, Ohio, May 17, 1932; s. John Richard and Helen (Dunn) L.; m. Betty Ann Korkolis, Feb. 3, 1956; children: Karen Elaine Ostdiek, Charles Theodore Jr., Richard Anthony, Thomas Edward. BS, George Washington U., 1955; MS, U. Ill., 1957, PhD in Analytical Chemistry, 1960. Group leader ceramics div. Air Force Materials Lab., Wright-Patterson AFB, Ohio, 1962-66; lectr. in chemistry Wright State U., Dayton, Ohio, 1964-66; chief advanced metall. studies br. Air Force Materials Lab., Wright-Patterson AFB, Ohio, 1966-74, sr. scientist, 1974-81; head materials div. Office of Naval Rsch., Arlington, Va., 1981-85; pvt. practice cons. Washington, 1985-88; sr. engr. space ops. Vitro Corp., Washington, 1988-95, 96—; cons. Burke, Va., 1996—; USAF liaison mem. NMAB Panels on Solids Processing, Ion Implantation and Environ. Cracking, Washington, 1965-68, 78, 81; U.S. rep. AGARD structures and materials panel NATO, 1983-85. Co-author: Metal Matrix Composites, 1972; editor, author: Practical Handbook of Materials Science, 1989; editor: (series) Handbook of Materials Science, vol. I, 1974, vol. II, 1975, vol. III, 1975; vice chmn. editorial bd. Vitro Corp. Tech. Jour., 1989-92, chmn., 1993; contbr. articles to profl. jours. including Jour. Am. Ceramics Soc., Analytical Chemistry, Sci., Transactions AIME, Corr. Jour., Jour. Inorganic Chemistry, SAMPE, Jour. Less Common Metals. Mem., soloist George Washington U. Traveling Troubadours, Washington, 1950-55; choir dir. Trinity United Ch. of Christ, Fairborn, Ohio, 1966-81, Univ. Bapt. Ch., Champaign, Ill., 1957-60, Chapel II, Wright-Patterson AFB, Ohio, 1960-64; pres. Pub. Sch. PTO, 1967-69. 1st lt. USAF, 1960-62. Bailey scholar U. Ill., 1958-60; recipient Commendation medal USAF, 1962, Outstanding Achievement cert. NASA, 1992, award Soc. for Tech. Comm. Publ., 1993. Mem. Am. Chem. Soc. (treas. 1966-67, chmn. audit sect. 1967-68), ASM Internat. (sec. oxidation and corrosion com. 1980-81, chmn. 1981-82). Presbyterian. Achievements include patents for new corrosion inhibitors including encapsulated types, and for alkoxides and oxides; co-development of the refractory ceramic Zyttrite, the first high density translucent zirconia made from thermal or hydrolytic decomposition of mixed alkoxides followed by hot pressing; pioneered general approach of organometallic compounds as precursors of high purity, fine particulate, materials. Home and Office: 5629 Kemp Ln Burke VA 22015-2041

LYNCH, CHARLOTTE ANDREWS, communications executive; b. Fall River, Mass., Mar. 25, 1928; d. Alan Hall and Florence (Worthen) Andrews; m. Francis Bradley Lynch, June 7, 1952; children: Sarah, Richard, Stephen, William. AB in Philosophy, Radcliffe Coll., 1950; postgrad., U. Bridgeport, 1969-71. Adminstrv. asst. Mass. Congl. Confs. and Missionary Soc., Boston, 1951, 52; journalist Town Crier newspaper, Westport, Conn., 1968; asst. dir. devel. Cape Cod Hosp., Hyannis, Mass., 1975-76; parish adminstr. S. Congl. Ch., Centerville, Mass., 1976-83; cons. to ethnic advt. agy. Loiminchay, Inc., N.Y.C., 1992—. Mem. Radcliffe Club Cape Cod (v.p. 1990-97, pres. 1997—, exec. com. 1990—). Republican. Roman Catholic. Avocation: travel.

LYNCH, DAVID WILLIAM, physicist, educator; b. Rochester, N.Y., July 14, 1932; s. William J. and Eleanor (Fouratt) L.; m. Joan N. Hill, Aug. 29, 1954 (dec. Nov. 1989); children: Jean Louise, Richard William, David Allan; m. Glenys R. Bittick, Nov. 14, 1992. BS, Rensselaer Poly. Inst., 1954; MS, U. Ill., 1955, PhD, 1958. Asst. prof. physics Iowa State U., 1959-63, assoc. prof., 1963-66, prof., 1966—, chmn. dept., 1985-90, disting. prof. liberal arts and scis., 1985—; on leave at U. Hamburg, Germany; and U. Rome, Italy, 1968-69; sr. physicist Ames Lab. of Dept. of Energy; acting assoc. dir. Synchrotron Radiation Ctr., Stoughton, Wis., 1984; vis. prof. U. Hamburg, summer 1974; dir. Microelectronics Rsch. Ctr., Iowa State U., 1995—. Fulbright scholar U. Pavia, Italy, 1958-59. Fellow Am. Phys. Soc.; mem. AAAS, Optical Soc. Am. Achievements include research on solid state physics. Home: 3315 Ross Rd Ames IA 50014-3959

LYNCH, EDWARD FRANCIS, professional sports team executive; b. Bklyn., Feb. 25, 1956; m. Kristin Kacer; children: Meghan, James. BA in Fin., U. S.C., 1977; JD, U. Miami, 1990. Pitcher Chgo. Cubs, 1977-80, 86-87, gen. mgr., 1995—; spl. asst. to exec. v.p. baseball ops. N.Y. Mets, 1980-86; dir. minor leagues San Diego Padres, 1990-93; pitcher Tex. Rangers, 1977-79, N.Y. Mets, 1980-86. Office: Chicago Cubs 1060 W Addison St Chicago IL 60613-4305

LYNCH, EUGENE F., federal judge; b. 1931. B.S., U. Santa Clara, 1953; LL.B., U. Calif., 1958. Assoc. O'Connor, Moran, Cohn & Lynch, San Francisco, 1959-64, ptnr., 1964-71; judge Mcpl. Ct., San Francisco, 1971-74; justice Superior Ct. City and County San Francisco, 1974-82; judge U.S. Dist. Ct. (no. dist.) Calif., San Francisco, 1982—. Office: US Dist Ct PO Box 36060 450 Golden Gate Ave San Francisco CA 94102*

LYNCH, FRANCIS CHARLES, lawyer; b. Pittsfield, Mass., Nov. 4, 1944; s. Frank Charles and Elizabeth Ellen (Dowd) L.; m. Sally Mapp Walker, June 24, 1972; children: William Mapp, Edward Walker, Katherine Francis. Student, London Sch. Econs., 1964-65; BS summa cum laude, Boston Coll., 1966; LLB, Yale U., 1969. Bar: S.D. 1969, Rosebud Sioux Tribal Ct. 1969, Oglala Sioux Tribal Ct. 1970, U.S. Dist. Ct. S.D. 1970, U.S. Dist. Ct. Mass. 1971, U.S. Ct. Appeals (1st cir.) 1973, U.S. Supreme Ct. 1980. Reginald Haber Smith fellow Rosebud Legal Svcs., Rosebud, S.D., 1969-70; assoc. Featherston, Homans & Klubock, Boston, 1971-73, Goodwin, Procter & Hoar, Boston, 1973-76; ptnr. Lynch & Walker, Boston, 1976; assoc. Newman & Meserve, Boston, 1977-78; assoc. Palmer & Dodge, Boston, 1978-79, ptnr., 1980—; asst. bar counsel Bd. Bar Overseers, Boston, 1976-77; commr. Mass. Com. Against Discrimination, Boston, 1973; lectr. profl. seminars. Contbr. articles to profl. jours. Trustee Bank Five for Savs., Arlington, Mass., 1980-87. Mem. Boston Bar Assn. (chair com. on fed. appointment of counsel/indigents plaintiffs in civil cases 1982-89). Democrat. Avocations: squash, tennis, golf. Home: 44 Woodland Rd Newton MA 02166-2322 Office: Palmer & Dodge 1 Beacon St Boston MA 02108-3107

LYNCH, GEORGE MICHAEL, family practice physician; b. Seneca Falls, N.Y., June 20, 1952; s. Victor Kamerer and Jane (Sutherland) L.; m. Kathryn Louise Lavrich, Feb. 24, 1979; children: Matthew Michael, Michelle Louise, Meredith Morgan. BS in Psychology, Pa. State U., 1974; MD, Jefferson Med. Coll., 1978. Diplomate Am. Bd. Family Practice. Pvt. practice family physician Herndon, Va., 1981—; 1st vice chmn. Physicians' Care Health Plan, Arlington, Va., 1984-89; chmn. med. audit com. Fair Oaks Hosp., Fairfax, Va. , 1984-86, chmn. bylaws com, 1996—; med. dir., chmn. of the bd. Reston Nursing Assn., 1985; chmn. Reston Hosp. Dept. Family Practice, 1994-96. Fellow Am. Acad. Family Physicians; mem. Fairfax County Med. Assn. Office: 13350 Franklin Farm Rd Ste 340 Herndon VA 20171-4087

LYNCH, GERALD WELDON, academic administrator, psychologist; b. N.Y.C., Mar. 24, 1937; s. Edward Dewey and Alice Margaret (Weldon) L.; m. Eleanor Gay Sherry, Dec. 5, 1970; children: Timothy, Elizabeth. B.S., Fordham Coll., 1958; Ph.D., N.Y. U., 1968. Tech. employment rep. Bell Telephone Labs., N.Y.C., 1958-63; psychologist VA Hosp., N.Y., Palo Alto, Calif., 1964-68; asst. prof. psychology John Jay Coll. Criminal Justice, N.Y.C., 1967-71; dir. student activities John Jay Coll. Criminal Justice, 1968-70, asso. prof., 1971-74, prof., 1974—, dean students, 1968-71, v.p., 1971-76, pres., 1976—; chmn. Use of Force in Jails, N.Y.C., 1987—. Contbr. articles to profl. jours. Chmn. N.Y.C. Police Found., 1979-92; chmn. N.Y. State Casino Gambling Study Panel, 1979, N.Y. State Fire Fighting Pers. Edn. and Stds. Com., 1980—, Westchester County Spl. Task Force on Dept. Pub. Safety Svcs.; mem. N.Y. State Fire Safety Task Force, 1981, N.Y. State Crime Control Planning Bd., 1979-86; chmn. bd. advisors Channel 13, 1984-87; chmn. N.Y.C. Fire Safety Found., 1984—; vice chmn. U.S. Marshals

Found., 1987—; pres. Cath. Interracial Coun., 1990—; chmn. Mayoral Search Com. for Police and Fire Commn. Recipient Criminal Justice award N.Y. State Bar Assn., 1977; Disting. Alumni award in edn. Fordham Coll. Alumni Assn., 1978; Brotherhood award NCCJ, 1985; named Person of Yr., N.Y.C. chpt. Indsl. Security Soc., 1987, N.Y.C. Police Dept. Patrolwomen's Endowment Assn., 1987, Man of Yr., Police Self Support Group, 1989. Mem. Acad. Criminal Justice Scis., Am. Soc. Criminology, Am. Assn. State Colls. and Univs., AAAS, Am. Psychol. Assn. Democrat. Roman Catholic. Office: CUNY John Jay Coll Criminal Justice 899 10th Ave New York NY 10019-1029

LYNCH, GERARD E., law educator; b. N.Y.C., Sept. 4, 1951; s. Gerard Norman and Marjorie Ann (Werner) L.; m. Karen Marisak, June 10, 1972; 1 child, Christopher Marisak Lynch. BA, Columbia U., 1972, JD, 1975. Bar: N.Y. 1976, U.S. Supreme Ct., U.S. Ct. Appeals (2d, 4th and D.C. cirs.). Law clk. U.S. Ct. Appeals, N.Y.C., 1975-76, U.S. Supreme Ct., Washington, 1976-77; asst. U.S. atty. So. Dist. N.Y., N.Y.C., 1980-83; chief criminal div. U.S. Dist. Ct. (so. dist.) N.Y., N.Y.C., 1990-92; assoc. independent counsel Iran/Contra, 1988-90; asst. prof. Columbia U., N.Y.C., 1977-80, assoc. prof., 1980-87, prof. law, 1987—, vice dean, 1992-97; of counsel Howard, Darby & Levin, N.Y.C., 1992—. Office: Columbia U Sch Law 435 W 116th St New York NY 10027-7201

LYNCH, HARRY JAMES, biologist; b. Glenfield, Pa., Jan. 18, 1929; s. Harry James and Rachel (McComb) L.; m. Pokum Lee Lynch. BS, Geneva Coll., Beaver Falls, Pa., 1957; PhD, U. Pitts., 1971; postgrad. Bio-Space Tech. Tng. Program, NASA and U. Va., 1970. Clin. chemist West Penn Hosp., Pitts., 1955-56; grad. teaching asst. U. Pitts., 1966-71, sr. teaching fellow, 1971; postdoctoral fellow MIT, Cambridge, 1973-75, rsch. assoc. dept. nutrition, lab. neuroendocrine regulation, 1973-75, lectr., 1976-81, rsch. scientist dept. brain and cognitive sci., 1982-92; cons. Ctr. for Brain Scis. and Metabolism Charitable Trust, 1992—. Contbr. more than 60 articles on the pineal gland to profl. jours. and books; patentee on implantable programmed microinfusion apparatus, 1981. With USN, 1950-54. NIH postdoctoral fellow 1971-73. Mem. Soc. Light Treatment and Biol. Rhythms. Democrat. Avocation: study of animal behavior. Office: MIT E25-615 77 Massachusetts Ave Cambridge MA 02139-4301

LYNCH, JAIR, Olympic athlete; b. Amherst, Mass., Oct. 2, 1971. BS in Civil Engring., BA in Urban Design, Stanford U., 1994. Mem. Sr. Nat. Team, 1991-92, 92-93, 93-94, 94-95, 95-96; mem. U.S. Olympic Team, Barcelona, Spain, 1992, Atlanta, 1996; mem. World Championships Team, 1995; with Silicon Graphics, Inc. Bd. dirs. Omega Youth Club Peninsula chpt.; active Friends for youth, Big Brother/Big Sister Vol. Program. 3rd place in all around, 1st place in floor exercise and vault Nat. Boys Invitational, Allentown, Pa., 1988, 3rd place in all around, 1st place in vault J.O. Nats., Albuquerque, 1988, 1st place in jr. all-around U.S. Gymnastics Championships, Denver, 1990, 3rd place in NCAA Championships, University Park, Pa., 1991, 1st place in all-around, pommel horse, parallel bars, and high bar, 2d place in floor exercise U.S. Olympic Festival, L.A., 1991, 1st place in team and high bar NCAA Championships, Lincoln, Neb., 1992, 1st place parallel bars and high bar U.S. Gymnastics Championships, Columbus, 1992, 1st place in team and parallel bars NCAA Championships, Albuquerque, 1993, 2nd place in all-around, pommel horse, and high bar, 1st place in floor exercise and parallel bars Malarcupen, Stockholm, 1988, Internat. Tournament of France, Paris, 1989, 3rd place in team and parallel bars World U. Games, Buffalo, 1993, silver medal parallel bars Olympic Games, Atlanta, 1996; selected mem. All Pac-10 Acad. Team; recipient Stanford Black Cmty. Svc. award, 1991, 92. Avocations: reading non-fiction, writing, visiting museums, viewing exhibits and films. Office: care USA Gymnastics Pan Am Plz Ste 300 201 S Capitol Ave Indianapolis IN 46225-1000

LYNCH, JAMES WALTER, mathematician, educator; b. Cornelia, Ga., Mar. 28, 1930; s. Ulysses Samuel and Ida Dell (Woodall) L.; m. Monika Antonie Fehrmann, May 2, 1959; children: Steve, David, Judith. AB, U. Ga., 1952, MA, 1956. Math. statistician Proving Ground, Aberdeen, Md., 1956-61; asst. prof. math. Ga. So. U., Statesboro, 1961-92, prof. emeritus math., 1992—. Contbr. articles to profl. jours.; author/contbr.: Crux Mathematicorum, 1982-92. NSF grantee, 1964. Mem. Ga. Coun. Tchrs. Math. (life), Ga. Coalition for Excellence in Teaching Math., Can. Math. Soc., Math. Assn. Am., Sigma Xi. Lutheran. Achievements include discovery that American Indians designed their projectile points to conform to the golden section ratio. Avocations: coin collecting, gardening, shooting. Home and Office: 172 Thornhill Dr Athens GA 30607

LYNCH, JOHN A., lawyer, state senator; b. New Brunswick, N.J., Oct. 21, 1938; s. John A. Lynch; m. Deborah A. Lynch; children: Patricia, John P., Matthew J. L. Grad. Holy Cross Coll., 1960; LLB, Georgetown U., 1963. Bar: N.J. 1963; ptnr. Lynch, Martin, Philibosian, Chansky, Fitzgerald & Kane, North Brunswick, Brielle and Somerville; pres. N.J. Senate, 1990-92, minority leader, 1992—; mayor City of New Brunswick, 1979-91. Mem. Gov.'s Commn. on Sci. and Tech. Mem. Middlesex County Trial Lawyers Assn. (past pres.). Home: 11 Cotter Dr New Brunswick NJ 08901-1506 Office: 100 Bayard St New Brunswick NJ 08901-2165 also: NJ State Senate Trenton NJ 08625

LYNCH, JOHN BROWN, plastic surgeon, educator; b. Akron, Ohio, Feb. 5, 1929; s. John A. and Eloise L.; student Vanderbilt U., 1946-49; M.D., U. Tenn., 1952; children: John Brown, Margaret Frances Lynch Callihan; m. Mary Joyce Burrus, Dec. 1, 1994. Rotating intern John Gaston Hosp., Memphis, Tenn., 1953-54; resident in gen. surgery U. Tex. Med. Br., Galveston, 1956-59, resident in plastic surgery, 1959-62, instr., 1962, asst. prof. surgery, 1962-67, asso. prof., 1967-72, prof., 1972-73; prof., plastic surgery, chmn. dept. plastic surgery Vanderbilt U. Med. Center, 1973—. Served as capt. USAF, 1954-56. Diplomate Am. Bd. Plastic Surgery (chmn.). Fellow ACS; mem. Singleton Surg. Soc. (pres. 1982-83), AMA, Am. Soc. Plastic and Reconstructive Surgeons (pres. 1983-84), Am. Assn. Plastic Surgeons, Plastic Surgery Research Council, Am. Cleft Palate Assn., Am. Burn Assn., Soc. Head and Neck Surgeons, Internat. Burn Assn., Pan Am. Med. Assn., Am. Cancer Soc. (pres. Galveston County, Tex., Chpt. 1968), So. Med. Assn. (pres.-elect 1983-84), Tenn. med. Assn., Nashville Acad. Medicine, Tenn. Soc. Plastic Surgeons, Southeastern Soc. Plastic Surgeons, Southeastern Surg. Soc., H. William Scott, Jr. Soc., Nashville Surg. Soc., Am. Soc. Maxillofacial Surgeons, So. Surg. Assn., Am. Surg. Assn., Sigma Xi. Contbr. numerous articles to med. publs.; editor: (with S.R. Lewis) Symposium on the Treatment of Burns, 1973. Home: 5810 Hillsboro Pike Nashville TN 37215-4602 Office: Vanderbilt Hospital Nashville TN 37232

LYNCH, JOHN DANIEL, educator; b. Butte, Mont., Sept. 17, 1947; s. Leo and Queenie Veronica Lynch; m. Shannon Christine Crawford, May 7, 1983; 2 children: Kaitlin, Jennifer. B.S., West Mont. Coll.; M.S. No. Mont. Coll. Tchr. Butte High Sch., Mont., 1970-78, Butte Vo-Tech, 1978-89, Adult Basic Edn., 1989—; mem. Mont. State Legis., Helena, 1971-79, state senator, 1982—. Democrat. Roman Catholic. Lodge: KC.

LYNCH, JOHN EDWARD, JR., lawyer; b. Lansing, Mich., May 3, 1952; s. John Edward and Miriam Ann (Hyland) L.; m. Brenda Jayne Clark, Nov. 16, 1984; children: John E. III, Robert C., David B., Patrick D., Jacqueline E. AB, Hamilton Coll., 1974; JD, Case Western Res. U., 1977. Bar: Conn. 1978, Ohio 1980, U.S. Dist. Ct. (no. dist.) Ohio 1980, U.S. Ct. Appeals (6th cir.) 1980. Assoc. Thompson, Weir & Barclay, 1977-78; law clk. U.S. Dist. Judge, Cleve., 1978-80; assoc. Squire, Sanders and Dempsey, Cleve., 1980-86, ptnr., 1986-96; v.p., gen. counsel, sec. Caliber System, Inc., Akron, Ohio, 1996—; master bencher Am. Inns of Ct. Found., 1987—; mem. civil justice reform act adv. group U.S. Dist. Ct. (no. dist.) Ohio. Del. Hamilton Coll. Alumni Coun., 1992—, regional chair alumni admissions, 1993—; trustee The Cath. Charities Corp., 1995—; mem. Cuyahoga County Rep. Exec. Com., Cleve., 1984—; mem. Seton Soc. St. Vincent Hosp. Fund. Roman Catholic. Avocations: golf, jogging. Home: 6075 Deepwood Dr Chagrin Falls OH 44022-2569 Office: Caliber System Inc 3925 Embassy Pkwy PO Box 5459 Akron OH 44334-0459

LYNCH, JOHN JAMES, lawyer; b. Evergreen Park, Ill., Aug. 22, 1945; s. John J. and Agnes (Daly) L.; m. Kathleen Russell, Aug. 15, 1970; children: Kerry, Elizabeth, Erin. BA, St. Mary of the Lake Sem., 1967; MA in Philosophy, DePaul U., 1970, JD, 1973. Bar: Ill. 1973, U.S. Dist. Ct. (no. dist.) Ill. 1973, U.S. Ct. Appeals (7th cir.) 1976. Assoc. McKenna, Storer, Rowe, White & Haskell, Chgo., 1973-75; ptnr. Haskell & Perrin, Chgo., 1975—. Mem. ABA, Ill. State Bar Assn., Chgo. Bar Assn., Fedn. Ins. & Corp. Counsel. Office: Haskell & Perrin 200 W Adams St Chicago IL 60606-5208

LYNCH, JOHN PETER, lawyer; b. Chgo., June 5, 1942; s. Charles Joseph and Anne Mae (Loughlin) L.; m. Judy Godvin, Sept. 21, 1968; children: Julie, Jennifer. AB, Marquette U., 1964; JD, Northwestern U., 1967. Bar: Ill. 1967, U.S. Ct. Appeals (7th cir.) 1979, U.S. Ct. Appeals (5th cir.) 1976, U.S. Supreme Ct. 1979. Ptnr. Kirkland & Ellis, Chgo., 1973-76, Hedlund, Hunter & Lynch, Chgo., 1976-82, Latham, Watkins, Hedlund, Hunter & Lynch, Chgo., 1982-85, Latham & Watkins, Chgo., 1985—. Mem. vis. com. Northwestern U. Law Sch. Served as lt. USN, 1968-71. Mem. ABA, Ill. Bar Assn., Assn. Trial Lawyers Am., Order of Coif, City Club, Exec. Club, Met. Club. Notes and Comments editor Northwestern U. Law Rev., 1967. Home: 439 Sheridan Rd Kenilworth IL 60043-1220 Office: Latham & Watkins Ste 5800 Sears Tower Chicago IL 60606

LYNCH, JOHN T., management consultant; b. 1948. With Towers Perrin, N.Y.C., 1969—, pres., 1990-96; now chmn., CEO Towers Perrin, Stamford, Conn. Office: Towers Perrin 695 Main St Stamford CT 06901-2141*

LYNCH, JOHN THOMAS, science foundation administrator, physicist; b. Washington, Mar. 21, 1938; s. John Thomas and Mary Ellen (Kaye) L.; m. Leslie Gray, June 22, 1959 (div. June 1972); children: John Thomas III, Michael Gray; m. Carol Rollins, July 5, 1980. BS in Physics, Va. Poly. Inst., 1963; MS in Physics, U. Wis., 1965, PhD, 1972. Lab. technician Nat. Bur. Standards, Washington, 1957-60; rsch. scientist U. Wis., Madison, 1965-78; staff mem. Los Alamos (N.Mex.) Nat. Labs., 1978-81; program scientist NASA Hdqs., Washington, 1981-85; program dir. aeronomy and astrophysics Polar programs NSF, Washington, 1985—. Contbr. articles to sci. jours. Recipient Antarctic svc. medal USN, 1986. Mem. AAAS, Am. Geophys. Union, Astron. Soc. Pacific. Avocation: sailing. Office: NSF Polar Programs 4201 Wilson Blvd Arlington VA 22230-0001

LYNCH, KEVIN, publishing executive. BA in English and Comm., Kean Coll. Sales rep. McCall, 1981-83; sales rep. So. Living, 1983-86, ea. regional mgr., 1986, nat. sales mgr., 1992, nat. advt. dir., 1994-95, v.p., pub., 1995—. Office: So Living 2100 Lakeshore Dr Birmingham AL 35209

LYNCH, MARK BRADLEY, electrical engineer, biomechanical researcher; b. Ft. Worth, Apr. 29, 1959; s. James Almon and Dolores (Heuring) L.; m. Amy Jo Fleming, Oct. 15, 1988; children: Abigail, Anthony, Emily. BSEE, U. Mo., Rolla, 1981, MS in Computer Sci., 1985; M of Engring. Mgmt., Washington U., St. Louis, 1989; PhD in Engring. Mgmt., U. Mo., Rolla, 1992. Registered profl. engr., Mo. Sr. design engr. Emerson Electric, St. Louis, 1981-85, Cencit Inc., St. Louis, 1985-89; project engr. Mark Andy Inc., St. Louis, 1989-90; univ. faculty La. Tech. U., Ruston, 1992-94; owner Beyond Inc., St. Louis, 1994—; rschr. Inst. for Micromanufacturing, Ruston, 1992-94; grad. rsch. asst. Intelligent Sys. Ctr., Rolla, 1991-92. Author: (book chpt.) Intelligent Systems in Design and Manufacturing, 1995. Grantee State of La., 1992; summer fellow U.S. Army, 1992. Mem. IEEE, Soc. Mfg. Engrs., Tau Beta Pi. Roman Catholic. Avocations: outdoor activities, sports. Home: 1058 Mission Hills Dr O'Fallon MO 63366-5915 Office: Beyond Inc 102 Trade Center Dr Saint Peters MO 63376-1100

LYNCH, MARTIN ANDREW, retail company executive; b. Chgo., Oct. 5, 1937; s. George Irwin and Cecilia Veronica (Corley) L.; children: Kathleen Marie, Kevin Michael, Karen Ann, Daniel Patrick, Michelle Eileen. BSc, DePaul U., 1962. CPA, Ill., Calif. Audit mgr. Price Waterhouse & Co., Chgo., 1962-69; asst. to pres. Scot Lad Foods, Chgo., 1969-70; v.p. fin. N.Am. Car Corp., Chgo., 1970-76; sr. v.p. fin. Tiger Internat. Inc., L.A., 1976-83; exec. v.p., chief fin. officer Duty Free Shoppers Group Ltd., San Francisco, 1983-89, Casino USA Inc., Santa Barbara, Calif., 1989—, Smart & Final Inc., Santa Barbara, 1989—. Mem. AICPA, Calif. CPA Soc., Fin. Execs. Inst., Nat. Assn. Whole Grogery, Inst. Food Distbn. Assn., Bel Air Country Club (L.A.). Roman Catholic. Avocations: jogging, swimming, skiing, golf. Office: Smart & Final Inc 4700 S Boyle Ave Vernon CA 90058-3021

LYNCH, MICHAEL EDWARD, medical facility administrator; b. Rye, N.Y., Apr. 15, 1938; s. Michael Joseph and Josephine Agatha (Reilly) L. BA, Thomas A. Edison State Coll., 1982. Radiol. tech. Alexian Brothers Hosp., Elizabeth, N.J., 1956-88; nuclear medicine tech. Elizabeth Gen. Med. Ctr., 1988-89; supervisor nuclear medicine St. Elizabeth Hosp., 1990—. Served in U.S. Navy, 1960-62. Mem. Am. Soc. Radiol. Techs., Soc. Nuclear Medicine.

LYNCH, MILTON TERRENCE, retired advertising agency executive; b. Denver, Feb. 27, 1931; s. Thomas Lillis and Pauline Regina (Yaeger) L.; m. Katherine Marie Stamey, July 19, 1958; children—Carrie Elizabeth, Michael Thomas, Brian Wilson. B.F.A., Washington State U., Pullman, 1953. Promotion mgr. Gen. Mills, Inc., Palo Alto, Calif., 1956-62; v.p. Robert Ebey Co., Palo Alto, Calif., 1962-66; exec. v.p. Steedman, Cooper & Busse, San Francisco, 1966-74; owner, prin. Lynch & Assocs., San Francisco, 1974-78; exec. v.p. Lynch & Rockey Advt., San Francisco, 1978-84; pres., chief exec. officer Evans/Lynch Rockey, Inc., San Francisco, 1984-87; chmn., chief exec. officer Evans/San Francisco, 1987-90; dir. Evans Communications, Salt Lake City. Served to capt. Inf. U.S. Army, 1953-55. Mem. San Francisco Advt. Golf Assn. (pres. 1982-83). Republican. Roman Catholic. Avocations: golf; tennis; gardening. Home: 12779 Homes Dr Saratoga CA 95070-4016

LYNCH, NANCY ANN, computer scientist, educator; b. Bklyn., Jan. 19, 1948; d. Roland David and Marie Catherine (Adinolfi) Evraets; m. Dennis Christopher Lynch, June 14, 1969; children: Patrick, Kathleen (dec.), Mary. BS, Bklyn. Coll., 1968; PhD, MIT, 1972. Asst. prof. math. Tufts U., Medford, Mass., 1972-73, U. So. Calif., Los Angeles, 1973-76, Fla. Internat. U., Miami, 1976-77; assoc. prof. computer sci. Ga. Tech. U., Atlanta, 1977-82; assoc. prof. computer sci. MIT, Cambridge, 1982-86, prof. computer sci., 1986—, NEC prof. software sci. and engring., 1996—; Ellen Swallow Richards chair MIT, 1982-87, Cecil H. Green chair, 1994-96. Contbr. numerous articles to profl. jours. Fellow Assn. Computing Machinery. Roman Catholic. Office: MIT NE43-525 Dept Computer Sci Cambridge MA 02139

LYNCH, NITA MARIE SMITH, vocational curriculum developer; b. Portland, Oreg., Aug. 11, 1952; d. Jay Harvey Jr. and Harriet Smith; m. Paul Michael Lynch. AAS, C.C. of Air Force, 1987, C.C. of Air Force, 1989; BS with highest honors, U. So. Miss., 1991, MS, 1992, postgrad., 1992—. Cert. tchr., Miss. Enlisted USAF, 1979; tech. tng. instr. USAF, Keesler AFB, Miss., 1985-89; curriculum developer USAF, Keesler AFB, 1989-95; ret. USAF, 1995; ednl. cons., 1995—. Contbr. articles to profl. jours. Mem. Fed. Women's Program, 1992-95. Mem. Am. Vocat. Assn., Nat. Computer Security Assn., Fed. Info. Sys. Security Edn. Assn., Soc. Applied Learning Tech., Info. Sys. Security Assn., Phi Kappa Phi. Home and Office: 7815 SE Carlton St Portland OR 97206

LYNCH, PATRICIA GATES, broadcasting organization executive consultant, former ambassador; b. Newark, Apr. 20, 1926; d. William Charles and Mary Frances Lawrence; m. Mahlon Eugene Gates, Dec. 19, 1942 (div. 1972); children: Pamela Townley Gates Sprague, Lawrence Alan; m. William Dennis Lynch. Student, Dartmouth Inst., 1975. Broadcaster Sta. WFAX-Radio, Falls Ch., Va., 1958-68; pub. TV host Sta. WETA, Washington, 1967-68; broadcaster NBC-Radio, Europe, Iran, USSR, 1960-61; internat. broadcaster, producer Voice of Am., Washington, 1962-69; staff asst. to First Lady The White House, Washington, 1969-70; host Voice of Am. Breakfast Show, Morning show, 1970-86; U.S. ambassador to Madagascar and the Comoros, 1986-89; dir. corp. affairs Radio Free Europe/Radio Liberty, Washington, 1989-94; worldwide lectr., 1968-86; adv. com. Ind. Fed. Savs. and Loan Assn., Washington, 1970-86. Author stories on Am. for English teaching dept. Radio Sweden, 1967-68, others on internat. broadcasting. Chair internat. svc. com. Washington chpt. ARC, 1979-86; bd. visitors Duke U. Primate Ctr., Durham, N.C. Grantee USIA, 1983; recipient Pub. Service award U.S. Army, 1960. Mem. Coun. Am. Ambs., (bd. dirs., v.p.), Assn. Diplomatic Studies and Tng. Dept. State (bd. dirs.), Am. Women in Radio and TV (Washington chpt. pres. 1966-67), Am. News Women's Club, Washington Inst. Fgn. Affairs (bd. dirs.). Republican. Episcopalian. Avocations: travelling, reading, volunteer work, wildlife conservation.

LYNCH, PATRICK, lawyer; b. Pitts., Nov. 11, 1941; s. Thomas Patrick and Helen Mary (Grimes) L.; m. M. Linda Maturo, June 20, 1964; children: Megan, Kevin, Colin, Brendan, Erin, Brian, Liam, Eamonn, Kilian, Caitlin, Ryan, Declan, Cristin, Mairin, Sean. BA in Philosophy, Loyola U., Los Angeles, 1964, LLB, 1966. Bar: Calif. 1967, U.S. Dist. Ct. (cen., so., no. and ea. dists.) Calif., U.S. Ct. Appeals (9th cir.), U.S. Supreme Ct. Ptnr. O'Melveny & Myers, Los Angeles, 1966—; panelist PLI Annual Antitrust Law Inst., 1982-93. Bd. editors Matthew Bender Fed. Litigation Guide Reporter. Fellow Am. Coll. Trial Lawyers; mem. L.A. County Bar Assn. Office: O'Melveny & Myers 400 S Hope St Los Angeles CA 90071-2801

LYNCH, PAUL VINCENT, safety engineer, consultant; b. Bklyn., Apr. 11, 1932; s. John Andrew and Mary Catherine L.; m. Nancy Gates; children: David, Marianne. BA, St. Anselm's Coll., Manchester, N.H., 1954; postgrad. Fordham U., 1958-59, U. N.H., 1969-71. Registered profl. engr. in safety engring., Calif. Corp. ins. specialist Allied Chem. Corp., 1959-66; asst. to dir. risk mgmt. Am. Metal Climax, Inc., N.Y.C., 1966-68; lectr. risk mgmt., adminstr. safety U. N.H., Durham, 1969-71; assoc. prof. safety N.H. Vocat.-Tech. Coll., 1971-75; pres. Lynch Assocs., Inc., cons., Pittsfield, N.H., 1972-75; regional safety officer GSA, 1976-79; safety mgr. Calif., Bur. Land Mgmt., U.S. Dept. of Interior, Sacramento, 1979-86, bur. def. liaison officer and dep. dept. def. liaison officer Region IX Fed. Emergency Mgmt. Agy., 1979-86, emergency preparedness and disaster planning coord., 1979-86, chief safety mgmt. Bur. Land Mgmt. U.S. Dept. Interior, Washington, 1986-94, ret., 1994; guest lectr. in risk mgmt. Am. Mgmt. Assn., 1959-68; justice peace, Pittsfield, N.H., 1970-75; v.p. N.H. Safety Coun., 1972-74; mem. Vt. Roundtable for Fire and Bldg. Safety, 1972-75, Vt. Adv. Coun. on Fire Safety, 1972-75; advisor Vt. Occupl. Safety and Health Rev. Bd., 1972-75; instr. safety mgmt. Am. River Coll., Sacramento, 1975-76; pvt. cons., 1994-96. Prodr., host Around Town, Hingham (Mass.) Cmty. TV, 1994-96; weekly columnist for Hingham Times, 1995—. Active Boy Scouts Am., 1962—, dist. vice chmn. Nat. Capitol Area coun., 1987-92, membership chmn., mem. exec. bd. Golden Empire Coun., 1978-86, dist. chmn., 1984-85; pres. Deer Park PTA, 1961-62, George Washington Elem. Sch. PTA, 1961-62. With U.S. Army, 1955-57. Recipient Silver Beaver award Boy Scouts Am., 1977, Disting. Svc. award U.S. Dept. Interior, 1994, Disting. Svc. award Dept. Interior Safety and Health Coun., 1994. Mem. Am. Soc. Safety Engrs. (pres. Sacramento chpt. 1981-82; regional v.p., nat. long range planning com., chmn. legis. affairs com., adminstr. pub. sector divsn., named divsns. Safety Profl. of Yr. 1986, named pub. sector divsn. safety profl. of yr. 1986, Sacramento chpt. Safety Profl. Yr. 1986, chmn. sch. safety task force Nat. Safety Coun. 1988-91), Nat. Constructors Assn. (mem. ins. com. 1959-66), Am. Indsl. Hygiene Assn., Vets of Safety (pres. Sacramento chpt. 1984-85), Rotary (sec. Pittsfield club 1970-73, vice-chmn. Hingham commn. on disability issues 1995-96). Author, editor govt. publs. and books. Home: 6328 Buenos Aires Pl NW Albuquerque NM 87120

LYNCH, PETER, biology educator; b. Cambridge, Mass., Jan. 10, 1957; s. Kevin Andrew and Anne (Borders) L.; m. Jessica Maria Jansen, June 16, 1984; children: Ian Jacob, Micah William. BS in Zoology with honors, U. N.C., 1981; postgrad, U. Md., 1981; MS in Zoology, U. R.I., 1985; EdM in Curriculum and Instrn., U. Lowell, 1986. Spl. seminar tchr. biology Cambridge (Mass.) Friends Sch., 1975-76; grad. lab. instr. gen. biology U. Md., College Park, 1981; chemistry & algebra tchr., ice hockey coach, dormitory dir. Concord (Mass.) Acad., 1983; dir. Living Word Summer Program Beauvoir Elem. Sch., Washington, 1983; grad. lab. instr. U. R.I., Kingston, 1983-84; sci. tchr. Haverhill (Mass.) H.S., 1986-88, Fair Haven (Vt.) Union High Sch., 1988-95; math/sci. dept. chair, 1995-96; sci. dept. chair The Gailer Sch. at Middlebury, Vt., 1996—; technician dept. environ. medicine NYU, Sterling Forest, 1976; summer tchr. Beauvoir Elem. Sch., 1976-80, 82; co-chair Joint Tchrs. Assn./Sch. Bd. com. to investigate health ins. alternatives Fair Haven Union H.S., 1989-90, chair Tchrs. Assn. contract negotiation team, 1990-91, mem. search com. for vice prin., 1991, mem. search com. for prin., 1995; founder, chmn. Undergrad. Zoology Colloquium, U. N.C., Chapel Hill; seminar presenter. Recipient Coker award for excellence in undergrad. rsch. U. N.C., 1981, award for excellence in teaching Addison-Rutland Supervisory Union Bd., 1994. Mem. NSTA, Tanglefoot Cloggers (Winchester, Mass.), Cub Hill Cloggers (Balt.), Cane Creek Cloggers (Carrboro, N.C.), Stony Creek Cloggers (Durham, N.C.), The Christmas Revels (chorus mem.), Pi Lambda Theta. Office: The Gailer School at Middlebury 19 Shannon St Middlebury VT 05753-1008

LYNCH, PETER GEORGE, artist; b. Aug. 5, 1932. BFA, Pratt Inst., Bklyn., 1954; postgrad., CCNY. pub.: Limited Editions Prints (11 eds.), News-n-viewsletter, Concerns-Artists and Art Marketing and the Environment, The Catalog of Art, Fine Crafts and Home Accessories. Exhibitions include: (internat. and nat.) The Art Gallery of La Merced, Maracaibo, Venezuela, Nephente Mundi Internat. Competition, Allied Artist Am., Nat. Arts Club, Chautauqua Instn., Acad. Artist Assn. Nat. Exhibition, Internat. Festival of The Arts, Mexico-Douglas, Wiesner Gallery Intertnat., Global Visions, Fed. Pla., Gallery Cozumel, Yergeau Mus. Internat. d'Art, Montreal, Que. (Named One of Best Am. Painters, One of Best Am. Printmakers, 1991, Deuxieme prix Ann. Ctr. P.R.D. Montreal Exhbn., 1992), and numerous others; (regional and local) Arsenal Gallery, Coler Meml., Vega Fine Arts, Casino Gallery, Fulton Gallery, Artifax Galleries, Cabrini Gallery, Ten Talents Gallery, Inroads Multimedia Ctr. among others; author: (dossiers), Collaborative Photolithographic Prints: Publishing Your Own, 1990, Direct Marketing: Survival Factors and the Artist, 1990, Succeeding as a Fine Artist: Professionalism in a Difficult Environment, 1991, Artist's Eye vs. Photographers Eye: Shooting Your Art Right, 1991, Overused and Underexplored: The Paradox of Print Media: Effective Advertising for Creative People, 1991, Direct-Contact Marketing: Art Fairs and Festivals, 1991, The Video Portfolio: A New User-Friendly Marketing Tool, 1991, Survival Factors and The Artist; Keeping Up or Dropping Out, 1994, Creativity-What On Earth Is It? Where Can We Get Some?, 1994. With U.S. Army, 1956-58. Recipient Citation for Superior Competence, U.S. Army Air Def. Command, 1958, Hon. Mention Nat. Exhibition at Bakersfield, 1985, Second Place Assn. Artist Nat. Exhibition, 1985, Cert. of Merit, Academic Artist Assn. Annual Nat. Exhibition, 1986, First Place Nephente Mundi Internat. Art Competition, 1987, Watson-Guptill award Lake Worth Silver Anniversary Exhbn., 1991.

LYNCH, PETER JOHN, dermatologist; b. Mpls., Oct. 22, 1936; s. Francis Watson and Viola Adeline (White) L.; m. Barbara Ann Lanzi, Jan. 18, 1964; children: Deborah, Timothy. Student, St. Thomas Coll., 1954-57; BS, U. Minn., 1958, MD, 1961. Intern U. Mich. Med. Ctr., 1961-62, resident in dermatology, 1962-65, asst. prof., then assoc. prof. dermatology, 1968-73; clin. instr. U. Minn., 1965; chief dermatology and venereal disease Martin Army Hosp., Columbus, Ga., 1966-68; asso. prof. to prof. dermatology U. Ariz., Tucson, 1973-86; chief sect. dermatology U. Ariz., 1973-86, asso. head dept. internal medicine, 1977-86; prof., head dermatology U. Minn. Med. Sch., Mpls., 1986-95; med. dir. ambulatory care U. Minn. Health Sys., 1993-95; prof., chmn. dept. dermatology U. Calif., Davis, 1995—. Author: (with S. Epstein) Burckhardt's Atlas and Manual of Dermatology and Venereology, 1977, Dermatology for the House Officer, 1982, 3rd edit., 1994, (with W.M. Sams) Principles and Practice of Dermatology, 1992, 2nd edit., 1996, (with I.E. Edwards) Genital Dermatology, 1994. With AUS, 1966-68. Decorated Army Commendation Medal; recipient Disting. Service award for faculty U. Mich., 1970, Disting. Faculty award U. Ariz., 1981. Mem. Am. Acad. Dermatology (bd. dirs. 1974-78, v.p. 1991-92), Assn. Profs. Dermatology (bd. dirs. 1976-80, pres. 1994-96), Internat. Soc. Study of Vulvar Disease (bd. dirs. 1976-79, pres. 1983), Soc. Investigative Dermatology, Am. Bd. Dermatology (bd. dirs. 1984-89), Gougerot Soc. (Bronze medal award), Alpha Omega Alpha. Democrat. Roman Catholic. Home: 332 Sandpiper Dr Davis CA 95616-7536 Office: U Calif Dept Dermatology 1605 Alhambra Blvd # 2300 Sacramento CA 95816-7051

LYNCH, PHYLLIS ANNE, stockbroker; b. Lakeville, Minn., Aug. 9, 1944; d. Eugene and Helen mary (Brown) L.; children from previous marriage:

Evan Astrowsky, Amy Astrowsky. BS in Mktg., Fairfield U., 1983. Lic. securities broker, N.Y. Account exec. Blythe Eastman Dillon, N.Y.C., 1976-79, Great Western Fin., L.A., 1979-91, Smith Barney, L.A., 1991-92; fin. rep. Fidelity Investments, L.A., 1992-96; investment broker A.G. Edwards & Sons, Inc., Coral Gables, Fla., 1996—. Treas. L.A. Children's Hosp. Aux., Conejo Valley, Calif., 1988-90; bd. mem. L.A. County H.S. for the Arts, L.A., 1989-91. Recipient Parent of the Yr. award L.A. County Bd. Edn., 1991. Mem. Women's Polit. Action, Miami Project to Cure Paralysis. Avocations: tennis, golf.

LYNCH, PRISCILLA A., nursing educator, therapist; b. Joliet, Ill., Jan. 8, 1949; d. LaVerne L. and Ann M. (Zamkovitz) L. BS, U. Wyo., 1973; MS, St. Xavier Coll., Coll., 1981. RN, Ill. Staff nurse Rush-Presby.-St. Luke's Med. Ctr., Chgo., 1977-81, psychiat.-liaison cons., 1981-83, asst. prof. nursing, unit leader, 1985—; mgr. and therapist Oakside Clinic, Kankakee, Ill., 1987—; mem. adv. bd. Depressive and Manic Depression Assn., Chgo., 1986—; mem. consultation and mental health unit Riverside Med. Ctr., Kankakee, 1987—; speaker numerous nat. orgns. Contbr. numerous abstracts to profl. jours., chpts. to books. Bd. dirs. Cornerstone Svcs. Recipient total quality mgmt. award Rush-Presby.-St. Luke's Med. Ctr., 1991. Mem. ANA, Ill. Nurses Assn. (coms.), Coun. Clin. Nurse Specialists, Profl. Nursing Staff (sec. 1985-87, mem. coms.). Presbyterian. Home: 606 Darcy Ave Joliet IL 60436-1673

LYNCH, ROBERT EMMETT, mathematics educator; b. Chgo., Feb. 5, 1932; s. Joseph Burke and Mildred Cecilia (Bildhauser) L.; m. Martha Bolling Hacker, Oct. 8, 1955; children: Barbara Ann, William Robert, Pamela Elizabeth. B Engring. Physics, Cornell U., 1954; MS, Harvard, 1959, PhD, 1963. Sr. rsch. mathematician Gen. Motors Rsch. Lab., Warren, Mich, 1961-64; assoc. prof. computer sci. and math. U. Tex., Austin, 1964-67; assoc. prof. computer sci. and math. Purdue U., West Lafayette, Ind., 1967-85, prof., 1985—. Author: (with Garrett Birkhoff) Numerical Solution of Elliptic Problems, 1984; (with John R. Rice) Computers, Their Impact and Use/with Basic, 1975, Computers, Their Impact and Use/With Fortran, 1977, Computers, Their Impact and Use/with PL/1, 1978. Lt. USAF, 1955-57. Office: Purdue Univ Computer Sci Dept West Lafayette IN 47907

LYNCH, ROBERT L., art association administrator. Former exec. dir. arts ext. svc. divsn. continuing edn. U. Mass., Amherst; former pres., CEO Nat. Assembly Local Arts Agys.; pres., CEO Ams. for Arts, Washington; spkr., trainer in field. Past bd. dirs. Ireland Am. Arts Exchange, Craft Emergency Relief Fund, State Arts Advocacy League Am., Kennedy Ctr.'s Alliance Arts Edn., edn. adv. coun. Nat. Endowment Arts, Nat. Coalition Edn. and Arts; founding mem., bd. dirs. Nat. Cultural Alliance; past vice chmn. advocacy team Mass. State Arts Coun.; original sponsor Humanities Month. Recipient 4 Top Innovative Programming awards in continuing edn. Nat. U. Continuing Edn. Assn. Office: Ams for Arts 927 15th St NW 12th Fl Washington DC 20005*

LYNCH, ROBERT MARTIN, lawyer, educator; b. St. Louis, Mar. 28, 1950; s. Raymond Burns and Nancy Winn (Roeder) L.; m. Cynthia Kay Allmeyer, June 7, 1974; children: Christopher, Kelly, Stephanie. AB, St. Louis U., 1972, JD, 1975. Bar: Mo. 1975, D.C. 1985, Tex. 1992. Law clk. to presiding justice Mo. Ct. Appeals, St. Louis, 1975-76; atty. Southwestern Bell Telephone Corp., St. Louis, 1976-79, atty. network, 1979-83, gen. atty., 1983-88, v.p., asst. gen. counsel, 1988-91; v.p., gen. counsel Tex. office Southwestern Bell Telephone Co., Dallas, 1991-93; v.p., gen. counsel external affairs Southwestern Bell Telephone Co., San Antonio, 1993—; instr. paralegal studies St. Louis Community Coll., 1977—. Mem. ABA, Tex. Bar, Dallas Bar Assn., Mo. Bar Assn. (adminstrv. law com. coun.), St. Louis Bar Assn. (chmn. adminstrv. law com. 1981-82), Am. Corp. Counsel Assn. (chmn. communications com. St. Louis chpt.). Republican. Avocations: racquetball, writing. Office: Southwestern Bell 175 E Houston St San Antonio TX 78205-2233

LYNCH, SANDRA LEA, federal judge; b. Oak Park, Ill., July 31, 1946; d. Bernard Francis and Eugenia Tyus (Shepherd) L.; 1 child, Stephen Lynch Bowman. AB, Wellesley Coll., 1968; JD, Boston U., 1971. Bar: Mass. 1971, U.S. Dist. Ct. Mass. 1973, U.S. Dist. Ct. R.I., U.S. Ct. Appeals (1st cir.) 1974, U.S. Supreme Ct. 1974. Law clk. U.S. Dist. Ct., Providence, 1971-72; asst. atty. gen. Mass. Atty. Gen.'s Office, Boston, 1972-73; gen. counsel Mass. Dept. Edn., Boston, 1973-78; assoc. Foley, Hoag & Eliot, Boston, 1978-81, ptnr., 1981-95; apptd. U.S. cir. ct. judge U.S. Ct. of Appeals (1st cir.), Boston, 1995—; spl. counsel Jud. Conduct Commn., 1990-92. Contbr. articles to legal jours. Recipient Disting. Service award Planned Parenthood League of Mass., 1981, Boston U. Law Sch. Disting. Alumni award., 1996, Alumnae Achievement award Wellesley Coll., 1997. Mem. ABA (com. on partnership, ho. of dels. 1993-95), Boston Bar Assn. (pres. 1992-93, bd. bar overseers 1982-86, joint bar com. 1986). Office: US Ct Appeals 1st Cir 1617 US PO & CH Boston MA 02109

LYNCH, THOMAS FRANCIS, archeologist, educator; b. Mpls., Feb. 25, 1938; s. Francis Watson and Viola Eugenia (Le Blanc) L.; m. Barbara Amy Deutsch, Feb. 4, 1961 (div. 1989); children: Elizabeth Ann, Jean Margaret, Julia Frances; m. Jane Ellen Flaherty, Oct. 7, 1989; children: Clare Viola, William Finn, Patrick Thomas. B.A., Cornell U., 1960; M.A., U. Chgo., 1962, Ph.D., 1967. Archeologist Idaho State U. Mus., Pocatello, 1963-64; instr. to prof. and chmn. anthropology dept. Cornell U., Ithaca, N.Y., 1964-93; dir. Cornell Intercollege Program in Archeology, 1971-74, 75-82; rsch. prof. Universidad Catolica del Norte, Antofagasta, Chile, 1976-77, rsch. assoc., 1983—, adj. prof., 1994—; adj. prof. Tex. A&M U.; dir. Brazos Valley Mus. Natural History, 1995—. Author: Guitarrero Cave: Early Man in the Andes, 1980; assoc. editor Am. Antiquity, 1986-90; mem. editorial bd. Latin Am. Antiquity, Andean Past, Chungara, Estudios Atacameños; contbr. articles to profl. jours. Recipient NSF, Nat. Geographic Soc., and other research grants for archeol. excavations in Peru, Chile and Ecuador, 1964—. Fellow AAAS; mem. Soc. for Am. Archeology, Tex. Archeol. Soc., Archeol. Inst. Am., Am. Quaternary Assn., Inst. Andean Rsch. (dir. 1976-79), N.Y. Archeology Coun., Am. Assn. Mus., Soc. for History Discoveries, Ctr. for Study First Ams. (sci. coun.), Inst. Andean Studies, Assn. Cornell U. Emeritus Profs., Centro de Estudios Andinos Cuzco (cons. mem.), Soc. Chilena de Arqueologia, Phi Beta Kappa. Office: Brazos Valley Mus of Nat Hist 3232 Briarcrest Dr Bryan TX 77802-3015

LYNCH, THOMAS JOSEPH, museum manager; b. Omaha, Nebr., Feb. 15, 1960; s. James Humphery and Patricia Mae (Gaughan) L. BA in History, U. Nebr., 1984. Grad. tchng. asst. U. Nebr., 1984-86; mus. asst. Father Flanagan's Boys' Home, Boys Town, Nebr., 1986-88; mus. assoc. Father Flanagan's Boys' Home, Boys Town, 1988-93, mus. mgr., 1993—. Contbr. Boys Town: a Photographic History, 1992, Letters form the Front: Boys Town on the Battlefield from Pearl Harbor to the Persian Gulf, 1995. Vol. Omaha Metro Arts, 1988, Bot. Gardens, 1997; adv. bd. Metro Area History Day, Omaha, 1997. Named Most Valuable Player Father Flanagan's Boys' Home, 1992. Mem. Am. Assn. for State and Local History, Am. Mus. Assn., Nebr. Mus. Assn. Office: Boys Town Hall of History 14057 Flanagan Blvd Boys Town NE 68010-7509

LYNCH, THOMAS PETER, securities executive; b. N.Y.C., May 3, 1924; s. Michael Joseph and Margaret Mary (Fitzgerald) L.; m. Madeleine D'Eufemia, June 3, 1950; children: Francie, Richard. Student, Syracuse U., 1943-44; B.B.A., Baruch Coll., 1947. Acct. Deloitte, Haskins & Sells, N.Y.C., 1947-56; partner Bache & Co., N.Y.C., 1956-61; v.p. E.F. Hutton Co. Inc., N.Y.C., 1962-67; sr. v.p. E.F. Hutton Group Inc., 1967-72, exec. v.p., 1972-83, pres., dir., 1983-85; ret., 1985; pres., dir. Cash Res. Mgmt. Inc., 1976-85. Served with U.S. Army, 1943-46. Decorated Bronze Star. Mem. AICPA, Fin. Execs. Inst., India House, Canoe Brook Country Club, Baltusrol Golf Club, Johns Island Club, Morris County Golf Club.

LYNCH, THOMAS WIMP, lawyer; b. Monmouth, Ill., Mar. 5, 1930; s. William Brennan and Mildred Maurine (Wimp) L.; m. Elizabeth J. McDonald, July 30, 1952; children: Deborah, Michael, Maureen, Karen, Kathleen. BS in Geology, U. Ill., 1955, MS in Geology, 1958, JD, 1959. Bar: Ill. 1960, Okla. 1960, U.S. Supreme Ct. 1971, Tex. 1978. Staff atty. Amerada Hess Corp., Tulsa, 1959-72, asst. gen. counsel, 1972-75; mem. Hall, Estill, Hardwick, Gable, Collingsworth & Nelson, Tulsa, 1975; v.p., gen. counsel Tex. Pacific Oil Co., Inc., Dallas, 1975-80, Oryx Energy Co., Dallas, 1980-94; ret., 1994; adj. prof. law U. Tulsa, 1974; trustee Southwestern Legal Found., chmn., lectr. ann. Oil and Gas Short course, 1976-92; adv. bd. Oil and Gas Edn. Ctr.; chmn. Oil, Gas and Mineral Law Coun. of State Bar of Tex., 1995-96. Served with USN, 1948-49, U.S. Army, 1951-53. Mem. ABA, Tex. Bar Assn. (chmn. oil, gas and mineral law sect.), Dallas County Bar Assn. Roman Catholic.

LYNCH, TIMOTHY JEREMIAH-MAHONEY, lawyer, educator, theologian, realtor, writer; b. June 10, 1952; s. Joseph David and Margaret Mary (Mahoney) L. *Grandparents Jeremiah and Suzanne McKeen Mahoney are descended from old pioneer lineage in California from a ranching and construction family who settled in California prior to the Gold Rush. Family ancestors date back to to hard Scandanavian viking warlords whose crest is the same that belongs presently to the royal family of Denmark and Sweden. In our family, whose lives can be traced to Anglo-Norman Lords in present Ireland and also claims several British aristocrats; one Simon Lynch, who was Archbishop of Canterbury and served in the House of Lords. Another was Jeremy Lynch, who was Deacon of Canterbury who also became 1st Lord Justice of England under King George III and was a Canon lawyer and theologian and not a barrister.* MS, JD in Taxation, Golden Gate U., 1981; MA, PhD in Modern European History, U. San Francisco, 1983; Licentiate, Inter-Am. Acad., Rio de Janeiro, 1988; PhD in Classics and Divinity/Theology, Harvard U., 1988; JSD in Constl. Law, Hastings Law Ctr., 1990. Bar: D.C. 1989, Calif., U.S. Ct. Appeals (2d cir.) 1989, U.S. Ct. Appeals (4th cir.) 1990; mem. Bar/Outer Temple/Comml. Bar of U.K.; European Econ. Ct. of 1st Instance. Legal bus., tax, counsel Lynch Real Estate, San Francisco, 1981-85; researcher, writer Kolb, Roche & Sullivan, San Francisco, 1986-88; chmn. internat. law dept. Timothy J.M. Lynch & Assocs., San Francisco, 1987-88, chmn., mng. dir. law dept., 1988—; chmn., pres., CEO Lynch Real Estate Investment Corp., San Francisco, 1989—; ptnr. Lynch Investment Corp.; bd. lawyer/arbitrators Pacific Coast Stock Exch., NASD, 1994—; chmn. bd. Lynch Holdings Corp. Group; corp. counsel, sr. ptnr. L.A. Ctr. Internat. Comml. Arbitration, 1991—; vis. fellow classics, Inst. of Classical Studies, U. London; rsch. prof. Canon law and ecumenical ch. history grad. Theological Union U. Calif. Berkeley, 1992—; vis. scholar Patristic theology and classical philosophy of ecumenical doctrines, U. Laval, Quebec, Can., 1993—; vis. scholar Medieval ch. history U. Leeds, Eng., 1993-95; del. lectr. 24th Internat. Congress Arts Comms., Kreble Coll., Oxford U., 1997; arbitrator Iran-U.S. Claims Tribunal, The Hague, 1993; mem. internat. corp. adv. bd. J.P. Morgan and Co., N.Y.C.; bd. dirs. Morgan-Stanley Corp., N.Y.C.; chmn. Latin Am., African and Middle East Corp. Groups J.P. Morgan Internat., Corp.; adv. bd. Morgan Stanley Corp., N.Y.C.; mem. Orgn. Econ. Cooperation and Devel., mem. adv. com. Internat. Labor Orgn.; participant Forum/A Group of Internat. Leaders, Calif., 1995, mem. adv. bd. U.S.-Saudi Arabia Bus. Coun., OECD on Industry and Fin., Paris, 1995, others; apptd. U.S. amb. Spl. Del. to Commn. Security/Coop. in Europe on Econ. and Pub. Reforms in Russian Republics; participant World Outlook Conf. on 21st Century, 1995; mem. Nat. Planning Assns., Washington, Brit.-North Am. Com. on Econ. and Pub. Policy Planning, Global Econ. Coun.; mem. adv. bd. Nat. Bus. Leadership Coun., Washington; mem. Arbitration Tribunal, Geneva; judge World Intellectual Property Orgns.; selected arbitrator, mem. tribunal; mem. arbitration bd., panel of arbitrators NAFTA Trade Policy; mem. adv. com. on private internat. law U.S. State Dept., Washington. Author: (10 vol. manuscript) History of Ecumenical Doctrines and Canon Law of Church; editorial bd. Internat. Tax Jour., 1993; author: Publishers National Endowment for Arts and Humanities Classical Translations: Latin, Greek, and Byzantine Literary Texts for Modern Theological-Philosophical Analysis of Social Issues; Essays on Issues of Religious Ethics and Social, Public Policy Issues, 1995, 96, others; editorial bd. Internat. Tax Jour., 1993, Melrose Press: Internat. Firm; contbr. articles to profl. jours. Dir., vice chmn. Downtown Assn. San Francisco; councillor, dir. Atlantic Coun. U.S., 1984—; corp. counsel, chmn. spl. arbitrator's tribunal on U.S.-Brazil trade, fin. and banking rels. Inter-Am. Comml. Arbitration Commn., Washington; chmn. nat. adv. com. U.S.-Mid. East rels. U.S. Mid. East Policy Coun., U.S. State Dept., Washington, 1989—; mem. Pres. Bush's Adv. Commn. on Econ. and Public Policy Priorities, Washington, 1989; mem. conf. bd. Mid. East Policy Coun., U.S. State Dept., Washington, 1994—; elected mem. Coun. of Scholars U.S. Libr. Congress, Washington; bd. dirs. Internat. Diplomacy Coun., San Francisco Opera, Ballet, Symphony Assns. Recipient Cmty. Svc. honors Mayor Dianne Feinstein, San Francisco, 1987, Leadership awards St. Ignatius Coll. Prep., 1984, Calif.'s Gold State award, 1990, AU-ABA Achievement award, 1990, Medal of Honor Order Internat. Ambs. Com. U.S. State Dept. and Foreign Svc. Inst., Washington D.C., World Lifetime Achievement award Am. Acad. Achievement, 1997, Internat. Cultural award, 1997, Presdl. Seal Honor, 1997, Decree Internat. Cultural Letters, 1997; named Civic Leader of Yr., Nat. Trust for Hist. Preservation, 1988, 89; named to Presdl. Order of Merit, 1991.. Fellow World Jurist Assn., World Assn. Judges (Washington); mem. ATLA, Internat. Bar Assn. (various coms., internat. litigation, taxation, labor issue), Am. Arbitration Assn. (panelist, internat. decree), Am. Fgn. Law Assn. (various coms.), Am. Soc. Ch. History, Am. Inst. Archaeology (Boston), Pontifical Inst. Medieval Studies (Toronto, Can.), Am. Hist. Assn., Am. Philol. Assn., Inst. European Law, Medieval Acad. Am., U.S. Supreme Ct. Hist. Soc. (presdl. seal of honor, cultural diploma honor), J Canon Law Soc. U.S., Nat. Planning Assn., Nat. Assn. Scholars (Eminent Scholar of Yr. 1993), Netherlands Arbitration Inst. (mem. Gen. Panels of Arbitrators, mem. Permanent Ct. Arbitration), Calif. Coun. Internat. Trade (GATT com., tax com., legis. com.), Practicing Law Inst., Am. Fgn. Law Assn. (mem. editl. bd. Working Groups on Rsch. Jour. for Legal systems of Africa, Mid. East, Latin Am., EEC and Soviet Union), U.S.-China Bus. Coun. (export com., GATT com., banking and fin. com., import com.), Bay Area Coun. (corp. mem.), Nat. Acad. Conciliators (Spl. award), Internat. Bar (mem. U.S. Group on Model on Insolvency Corp. Acts), Ctr. Internat. Comml. Arbitration, Comml. Club (various positions), Am. Venture Capital Assn., Pacific Venture Capital Assn., Am. Soc. Internat. Law, Washington Fgn. Law Soc., Asia-Pacific Lawyers Assn., Soc. Profls. in Dispute Resolution, British Inst. Internat. and Comparative Law, Internat. Law Assn. (U.S. br.), Commercial Bar Assn. of United Kingdom (London), Inter-Pacific Bar Assn. (Tokyo; mem. arbitration intellectual property, consitutional taxation, labor, legal groups), Inst. European Law Faculty of Laws (United Kingdom), Urban Land Inst. Internat., Mid. East Inst. (Am.-Arab Affairs Coun.), Inter-Am. Bar Assn., 1987—, Calif. Trial Lawyers Assn., Ctr. Reformation Rsch. (co-chmn. Calif. State Com. on U.S-Mid. East Econ. and Polit. Rels.), Soc. Biblical Lit., Am. Acad. Arts and Letters, Am. Acad. Religion, World Lit. Acad., Coun. Scholars, Am. Com. on U.S.-Japan Rels., Japan Soc. No. Calif., Pan-Am. Assn. San Francisco, Soc. Indsl./Office Realtors, Assn. Entertainment Lawyers London, Royal Chartered Inst. Arbitrators (London), Soc. Indsl. and Office Realtors, Urban Land Inst., San Francisco Realtors Assn., Calif. Realtors Assn., Coun. Fgn. Rels., Chgo. Coun. Fgn. Rels., Conf. Bd., San Francisco Urban and Planning Assn., U.S. Trade Facilitation Coun., Asia Soc., Am. Petroleum Inst., Internat. Platform Assn., San Francisco C. of C. (bus. policy com., pub. policy com., co-chmn. congl. issues study group), Am. Inst. Diplomacy, Overseas Devel. Coun. (Mid. East, Russian Republics, Latin Am. studies group), Internat. Vis. Ctr. (adv. bd.), Fin. Execs. Inst., Nat. Assn. Corp. Dirs., Heritage Found. (bd. dirs.), Archaeological Inst. Am. (fellow coun. near east studies, Egyptology), Am. Literature Judicature Soc., Soc. of Biblical, Nat. Assn. Indsl. and Office Properties, World Literary Acad. (Cambridge, Eng.), Am. Acad. Arts & Letters, Am. Acad. Religion, Pres. Club, Nat. Assn. Bus. Economists, Villa Taverna Club, Palm Beach Yacht Club, Pebble Beach Tennis Club, Calif. Yacht Club, Commonwealth Club, City Club San Francisco, British Bankers Club, London, San Diego Track Club (registered athlete), Crow Canyon Country Club (bd. dirs.), Western Venture Capital Assn., Am. Venture Capital Assn., Authors Guild, Internat. Pen Soc. Republican. Roman Catholic; Clubs: Crow Canyon Country Club, The Players. Avocations: theater, social entertainment events, opera, ballet, fine arts. Home: 501 Forest Ave Palo Alto CA 94301-2631 Office: 540 Jones St Ste 201 San Francisco CA 94102-2008 *Over twenty years as a top-notch commercial industrial real estate investor, manager, broker and developer. Major achievements include financing venture capital, large scale investments and developments in hotel shopping center markets and through use of applying long-range capital through refinancing of existing mortgages principals net yields. Leading consultant and speaker on business and economic issues that are influenced by Federal Government policies. Also leading expert on corporate governance and speaker issues affecting coporate directors and shareholders.*

LYNCH, VIRGINIA ANNE (VIRGINIA A. RED HAWK), forensic nurse, educator, consultant; b. Weatherford, Tex., Jan. 27, 1941; m. Z. G. Standing Bear, Mar. 22, 1988; children from previous marriage: Kristi Lynch Hulme, Keri Lynch Kembel, Angela Lynch Thompson. AA, Weatherford Coll., 1979; BSN, Tex. Christian U., 1982; MSN, U. Tex., Arlington, 1990. RN, Tex., Ga.; cert. coroner, Ga.; cert. profl. instr. in forensic sci.; cert. sexual assault nurse examiner; cert. ARC disaster nurse; diplomate Am. Bd. Forensic Examiners. Asst. head nurse surgery All Saints Hosp., Ft. Worth, 1982-83; RN emergency surgery Campbell Meml. Hosp., Weatherford, Tex., 1983-84; med. investigator Tarrant-Parker Med. Examiners Dist., Ft. Worth, 1984-90; forensic clin. nurse specialist, addiction and forensic mental health substance abuse program psychiat. nurse Ga. Dept. Mental Health, Valdosta, 1990-91; dep. coroner Echols County, Ga., 1990-95; exec. dir. Forensic Nurse Cons., Valdosta, 1990-95, Ft. Collins, Colo., 1995—; tng. specialist Parker County Rape Crisis Program, Weatherford, 1982-88; facilitator in group therapy for sexual abuse, awareness tng., and in-svc. tng. for tchrs., 1984-85; mem. Tarrant County Multidisciplinary Inst. for Child Sexual Abuse, Intervention and Treatment, 1988-90; mem. curriculum devel. com. Nurse Sexual Assault Examiner Program John Peter Smith Hosp., Ft. Worth, 1989-90; instr. in rape crisis counseling dept. sociology, anthropology and criminal justice Valdosta (Ga.) State Coll., 1990; instr. in emergency dept. sexual assault protocol, hosp. instrn. Women's Health Ctr., Albany, Ga., 1990; mem. organizing com. for rape crisis ctr. Victim-Witness Assistance Program Valdosta-Lowndes County, Ga., 1990-92; nurse educator, forensic sci. cons. Barbara Clark Mims Assocs., Lewisville, Tex., 1991-94, Bearhawk Consulting Group, Valdosta, Ga., 1988-95, Fort Collins, Colo., 1995—; cons. Ga. Dept. Mental Health. 1991-95; adj. faculty Beth El Coll. Nursing, Colorado Springs, Colo., 1995—; presenter, lectr. in field. Editl. bd. Jour. Psychosocial Nursing & Mental Health Svcs., 1996—; editl. bd., cons. Jour. Trauma Nursing; internat. editl. bd. Jour. CLin. Forensic Medicine, 1994—; contbr. articles to profl. jours. Fellow Am. Acad. Forensic Scis. (program chair gen. sect. 1988-90, 95-96); mem. ANA, ASTM (co-coord. task group to devel. stds. for sexual assault protocol, mem. subcom. forensic scis.), Tex. Nursing Assn., Internat. Assn. Bloodstain Pattern Analysts, Am. Soc. Criminology, Am. Bd. Forensic Examiners (cert. forensic examiner, mem. exec. bd.), Am. Profl. Soc. on Abuse of Children, Internat. Assn. Forensic Nurses (founding mem., mem. exec. bd., pres. 1993-96, Virginia A. Lynch Pioneer award 1994), Internat. Homicide Investigators, Nurses Network on Violence Against Women.

LYNCH, WILLIAM DENNIS, JR., broadcast journalist; b. Salina, Kans., Sept. 11, 1945; s. William Dennis and Jean (Donelan) L.; children—Brendan Merrick, Patrick Hoctor. Student, U. Kans., 1963-66. Reporter, anchorman WTOP-AM-TV, Washington, 1968-70; newscaster WNEW-AM, N.Y.C., 1970-71; reporter WCBS Radio, N.Y.C., 1971-75, asst. news dir., 1975-76; corr. NBC News, N.Y.C. and Washington, 1977-81, CBS News, N.Y.C. and Washington, 1981—; anchor CBS World News Roundup, N.Y.C., 1985—; adj. prof. Sch. Journalism, Fordham U., N.Y.C., 1973-75. Served with U.S. Army, 1966-68. Recipient Rube Goldberg award N.Y. Sigma Delta Chi, 1973, N.Y. State AP Broadcasters' award, 1973, Champion-Tuck award 1985; inducted Radio Hall of Fame, 1995. Mem. AFTRA (N.Y. local bd. 1988-94), Mus. of Broadcasting (mem. creative coun. 1988—). Office: CBS News 524 W 57th St New York NY 10019-2902

LYNCH, WILLIAM FRANCIS, JR., secondary mathematics educator; b. Sharon Hill, Pa., July 9, 1956; s. William Francis Sr. and Patricia Claire Marie (Kilpatrick) L.; m. Marian Grace Geiger, Nov. 11, 1985. BS in Social Studies Edn., Temple U., 1978, postgrad., 1980-81; MA in Edn. in Math., Beaver Coll., 1984; postgrad., U. of the Arts, Phila., 1992-93. Social studies tchr. Ben Franklin H.S., Phila., 1978-79; math., English, reading, TV tchr. William Penn H.S., Phila., 1979; math., English, reading, social studies tchr. Stetson Jr. H.S., Phila., 1980-84; secondary sch. math. tchr. CAPA, Phila., 1984-85, Phila. H.S. for Girls, 1985, Kensington H.S., Phila., 1985, Edison H.S., Phila., 1985-86; math., sci., reading tchr. Jones Mid. Sch., Phila., 1986-90; math. tchr., head dept. LaBrum Mid. Sch., Phila., 1990-96, Phila. H.S. Girls, 1996—; acad. tutor, student advisor Phila. Sch. Dist., 1978—. Author curriculum in field. Mem. Phila. Fedn. Tchrs. Avocations: woodwork, music, sports, art, reading. Office: Phila HS Girls Broad St and Olney Ave Philadelphia PA 19141

LYNCH, WILLIAM REDINGTON, lawyer; b. N.Y.C., Nov. 17, 1928; s. Francis Russell Vincent and Helen Adams (Barrett) L.; m. Mary Pomeroy Grant, Aug. 22, 1958; children: Melissa L. Woolford, Elizabeth Barrett, Cynthia Pomeroy, Kimberly Townsend, Sarah Phillips. Student, Phillips Exeter Acad., 1944-47; BA, Yale U., 1951; JD, Columbia U., 1958. Bar: N.Y. 1959, Conn. 1963. Assoc. Milbank Tweed Hadley & McCloy, N.Y.C., 1958-62; assoc. Cummings & Lockwood, Stamford, Conn., 1962-66, ptnr., 1966—, ptnr. in charge Greenwich office, 1978-88; bd. dirs. Greenwich Plaza Inc., 1970-74, Harrison & Ellis Inc., Cairo, Ga., 1985-87, Greenwich News Inc., 1986-90; chmn. ADM Mgmt. Corp., 1989-91. Chmn. Pub. Works Com., Greenwich, 1974-77, Greenwich United Way Campaign, 1975-76; vice chmn. Greenwich Bd. Edn., 1977-81, Rep. Town Meeting, 1967-77, dir., sec. Forum World Affairs, 1992-95. Lt. USNR, 1952-56. Mem. ABA, Conn. Bar Assn., Greenwich Bar Assn. (pres. 1979-80), Greenwich Field Club (pres. 1973-75), Round Hill Club (dir., sec. 1993-96). Congregationalist. Home: 100 Bedford Rd Greenwich CT 06831-2535 Office: Cummings & Lockwood 2 Greenwich Plz Greenwich CT 06830-6353

LYNCH, WILLIAM THOMAS, JR., advertising agency executive; b. Evergreen Park, Ill., Dec. 3, 1942; s. William T. and Loretta J. L.; m. Virginia Louise Venteicher, Aug. 21, 1965; children: Kelly, Maureen, Kim, Meagan, Molly. BA, Loras Coll., 1964; MBA, U. Iowa, 1966. Media trainee Leo Burnett Co. Inc., chgo., 1966-68, asst. account exec., 1968-76, v.p., 1976-79, sr. v.p., 1979-82, exec. v.p., 1981-85; vice chmn. Leo Burnett USA, chgo., 1985-89; chmn., CEO Leo Burnett USA, Chgo., 1987-91; pres. Leo Burnett Co., Inc., Chgo., 1992-93; pres., CEO Leo Burnett Worldwide, Chgo., 1993; CEO, pres. Leo Burnett Worldwide, Leo Burnett Co. Inc., Chgo., 1993-97; exec. cons. Leo Burnett Co., Inc., Chgo., 1997—. Mem. coun. U. Chgo. Grad. Sch. Bus.; bd. dirs. Chgo. United, Northwestern Meml. Hosp., Chgo. Mem. Econ. Club Chgo. Roman Catholic. Avocations: tennis, running, skiing, gardening, antiques. Office: Leo Burnett Co Inc 35 W Wacker Dr Chicago IL 60601-1614*

LYNCH, WILLIAM WALKER, savings and loan association executive; b. Washington, Sept. 18, 1926; s. Talbott and Gertrude (Farrell) L.; m. Barbara Van Sant, Apr. 21, 1951; children: John S., William Walker, Franklin P., Mark F. BA, George Washington U., 1950. Vice pres., treas., dir. Met. Mortgage Co., Washington, 1950-55; dir., mem. exec. com. Prog. Fed. Savs. & Loan Assn., Washington, 1953-58; v.p., treas., dir. Anderson & Co., Inc., Washington, 1953-59; with First Bank of Fla., West Palm Beach, Fla., 1959—, exec. v.p., 1966-89, pres., chief exec. officer, 1989-94, chmn. bd., 1994—; chmn. 1st Palm Beach Bancorp., 1994—; mem. tournament com. 53d PGA Championship, 1971; mem. tournament com. 19th World Cup, Internat. Golf Assn., 1971, 69th PGA Championship, 1987; dist. dir. Fla. League Fin. Instns., 1991; dir. Fed. Home Loan Bank of Atlanta, 1991-94; bd. dirs. Fla. Bankers Assn., 1994. Treas. Herbert Hoover Dike Dedication com., 1960; Asst. treas. Fla. Kennedy-Johnson campaign, 1960; bd. dirs. Am. Cancer Soc., 1967-69, 79—, hon. life dir. local United Way, 1962-64. With USNR, 1944-46. Recipient Free Enterprise Companion medal Palm Beach Atlantic Coll., 1989. Mem. West Palm Beach C. of C. (bd. dirs. 1970), Old Guard Soc. of Palm Beach Golfers, Kiwanis (bd. dirs. West Palm Beach club 1961, v.p. 1970-71, pres. 1971-72), City Club, No. Palm Beach Country Club, Bonnette Hunt Club, Pi Kappa Alpha. Republican. Roman Catholic. Office: First Bank of Fla 450 S Australian Ave West Palm Beach FL 33401-5008 Home: 1032 Country Club Dr North Palm Beach FL 33408-3716

LYNCH, WILLIAM WRIGHT, JR., investment executive, engineer; b. Dallas, Aug. 26, 1936; s. William Wright Sr. and Alma Martha (Hirsch) L.; m. June 11, 1960; children: Mary Margaret, Katherine. BSEE, U. Ariz., 1959; MBA, Stanford U., 1962. Pres. Ins. Bldg. Corp., Dallas, 1965-84; ptnr. Estacado Ptnrs., Dallas, 1985—, Encino Co., Dallas, 1970—, Cimarron Properties Co., Tucson, 1972-83; pres., bd. dirs. Argus Realty Corp., Dallas, 1972—; bd. dirs. Lynch Properties Inc., Dallas, Lynch Investment Co., Dallas, G.P. Bourrous Trucking Co., Inc., Dallas, Tex. Metal Works, Inc., Beaumont, Tex.; adv. dir. Sun Valley Fruit Co., Albuquerque, Patent Smith

Tech., LTD, Enersyst Devel. Ctr., Inc., Dallas, 1995—. Bd. dirs. Dallas Symphony Orch., 1966-74, Dallas Civic Music, 1970-77, Ednl. Opportunities Inc., Dallas, 1973-90, Dallas Coun. World Affairs, 1990—; trustee W. W. Lynch Found., Dallas, 1968—. Capt. U.S. Army, 1959-60. Mem. Brook Hollow Club, Verandah Club, M.O. Club (Tuscon). Republican. Episcopalian. Office: Lynch Investment Co 1845 Woodall Rodgers Fwy Dallas TX 75201-2287

LYNCH-STAUNTON, JOHN, Canadian senator; b. Montreal, Quebec, Canada, June 19, 1930. Student, Stanislas Coll., John de Brébeuf Coll., Georgetown U.; BSc, Queen's U. Councilman City of Montreal, 1960-74; Can. senator from Québéc, 1990—; now leader of opposition Can. Senate; dep. leader govt. in senate, 1991; vice-chair exec. com. Montreal CityCoun., 1970-74; chmn. bd., CEO Soc. de Kuyper Can., Inc. Co-chair United Way Campaign, 1991. Mem. Canadian Club of Montreal (pres. 1976-77), Montreal Bd. Trade (pres. 1985-86). Office: Senate Bldg, S Ctr Block Rm 375, Ottawa, ON Canada K1A 0A4*

LYNDEN, FREDERICK CHARLES, librarian; b. San Jose, Calif., Jan. 20, 1939; s. John Ross Jr. and Madeleine Lawton (Speik) L.; m. Deborah Reid Oehler, July 7, 1964; 1 child,Madeleine Scandrett. BA in Internat. Rels., Stanford U., 1960, MA in Am. History, 1961; MA in LS, U. Minn., 1963. Reference libr. Bancroft Libr., U. Calif., Berkeley, 1964-66, Meyer Libr., Stanford U., 1966-67; order libr., asst. chief acquisition dept. Stanford U. Libr., 1968-77; assoc. univ. libr. Brown U. Libr., Providence, 1977—. Assoc. editor Advances in Librarianship, 1991—, Pub. Rsch. Quar., 1985-94. Treas. Friends of Barrington (R.I.) Pub. Libr., 1984-86. Coun. on Libr. Resources fellow, 1977-78; Martinus Nijhoff Internat. travel grantee, The Hague, 1986; Blackwell N.Am. scholar, 1989. Mem. ALA (mem. coun.), Assn. Coll. and Rsch. Librs. (pres. New England chpt. 1990-91), Internat. Fedn. Libr. Assns. (mem. standing com. on stats 1991-95, editor calendar Internat. Leads 1996—), Brown Faculty Club (sec. 1991—). Episcopalian. Avocations: tennis, gardening. Office: Brown Univ Libr Rockefeller Libr Box A Providence RI 02912

LYNDRUP, PEGGY B., lawyer; b. Winnipeg, Can., Mar. 27, 1949. BS in Edn. magna cum laude, U. N.D., 1969; MEd, Kent State U., 1971; JD summan cum laude, U. Louisville, 1979. Bar: Ky. 1979, U.S. Dist. Ct. (we. dist.) Ky. 1979, U.S. Dist. Ct. (ea. dist.) Ky. 1981. Atty. Greenebaum Doll & McDonald, PLLC, Louisville. Recipient Disting. Alumnus award U. Louisville Sch. Law, 1989; Brandeis scholar. Mem. ABA, Louisville Bar Assn. (pres. 1989), Phi Kappa Phi, Delta Theta Phi. Office: Greenbaum Doll & McDonald PLLC 3300 National City Tower Louisville KY 40202

LYNDS, BEVERLY TURNER, retired astronomer; b. Shreveport, La., Aug. 19, 1929; d. Homer Emory and Nettie Lee (Robertson) Turner; m. Clarence Roger Lynds, June 19, 1954 (div. Oct. 1986); 1 dau., Susan Elizabeth; m. Leo Goldberg, Jan. 2, 1987 (dec. Nov. 1987). B.S., Centenary Coll., 1949; postgrad., Tulane U., 1949-50; Ph.D., U. Calif., Berkeley, 1955. Research assoc. U. Calif., 1955-58, Nat. Radio Astronomy Obs., Green Bank, W.Va., 1959-60; asst. prof. astronomy U. Ariz., 1961-65, assoc. prof., 1965-71; assoc. astronomer, asst. to dir. Kitt Peak Nat. Obs., Tucson, 1971-75; astronomer, asst. dir. Kitt Peak Nat. Obs., 1976-77, astronomer, 1977-86; cons. Assn. Univs. for Rsch. in Astronomy, 1986-87; assoc. Ctr. for Astrophysics and Space Astronomy U. Colo., Boulder, 1987—; edn. program coord. Unidata, UCAR, 1991—. Author: (with others) Elementary Astronomy, 1959; editor: (with others) Dark Nebulae, 1971. Mem. AAAS (chmn. sect. D), Internat. Astron. Union, Am. Astron. Soc. (councillor), Am. Meteorol. Soc., Am. Indian Sci. and Engring. Soc. *Knowing that there are many ways of making a contribution to the world we live in and choosing to use the opportunities available can result in a personal satisfaction which is the best form of success.*

LYNE, ADRIAN, director; b. Peterborough, Eng., Mar. 4, 1941. Dir. feature films: Foxes, 1980, Flashdance, 1983, 9 1/2 Weeks, 1986, Fatal Attraction, 1987 (Acad. award nomination), Jacob's Ladder, 1990, Indecent Proposal, 1993, Lolita, 1996. Mem. Dirs. Guild Am. Office: ICM 8942 Wilshire Blvd Beverly Hills CA 90211-1934

LYNE, AUSTIN FRANCIS, sporting goods business executive; b. Newton, Mass., Jan. 7, 1927; s. Daniel Joseph and Susan Markham O'Brien L.; m. Ann Blair, Nov. 27, 1954; children: Austin Francis, Jane Markham, Elizabeth Morgan, James Blair, Michael Davitt, Stephen Christopher. B.A., Harvard U., 1948; postgrad., U. Geneva, Switzerland, 1948-49. Store clk. 1st Nat. Stores Inc., Somerville, Mass., 1949-50, mgmt. trainee, 1950, warehouse supr., 1950, buyer, 1950-64, sales promotion mgr., 1964-67, advt. mgr., 1967, v.p. sales devel., 1968-73, sr. v.p. services, 1973-76, mgmt. cons., 1976-77; pres., treas. The Good Sport, Inc., Cohasset, Mass., 1977—. Coach Belmont Youth Hockey Assn., 1963-78; mem. Concord (Mass.) Rep. Town Com., 1964—, treas., 1967-74; dirs. Internat. Friendship League, Elizabeth Peabody Settlement House, 1961-67, Concord-Carlisle Cmty. Chest, 1983-89; trustee Fenn Sch., 1972-78, Belmont Hill Sch., 1972-73, corporator, 1973—, Robert B. Brigham Hosp., 1971—. Served with USNR, 1945-46. Mem. Sorrento Village Improvement Assn. Clubs: Harvard in Concord (pres. 1965-67), Concord Country, Megunticook Rod and Gun, Harvard Varsity. Home: 68 Sudbury Rd Concord MA 01742-2420 Office: 166 Cushing Hwy Cohasset MA 02025

LYNE, DOROTHY-ARDEN, educator; b. Orangeburg, N.Y., Mar. 9, 1928; d. William Henry and Janet More (Freston) Dean; m. Thomas Delmar Lyne, Aug. 16, 1952 (div. June 1982); children: James Delmar, Peter Freston, Jennifer Dean. BA, Ursinus Coll., 1949; MA, Fletcher Sch. Law and Diplomacy, 1950. Assoc. editor World Peace Found., Boston, 1950-51; editorial assoc. Carnegie Endowment Internat. Peace, N.Y.C., 1951-52; dir. Assoc. of Internat. Rels. Clubs, N.Y.C., 1952-53; editor The Town Crier, Westport, Conn., 1966-68; editorial assoc. Machinery Allied Products Inst., Wash., 1959-63; tchr. Helen Keller Mid. Sch., Easton, Conn., 1967-89; vice chmn. Cooperative Ednl. Svcs., Fairfield, 1983-85. Editor: Documents in American Foreign Rels., 1950, Current Rsch. in Internat. Affairs, 1951. Chmn. Westport Zoning Bd. of Appeals, 1976-80, Westport Bd. of Edn., 1985-87; vice chmn. Westport Bd. of Edn., 1980-85; mem. Westport Charter Revision Commn., 1966-67. Republican. Episcopalian.

LYNES, JAMES WILLIAM, SR., communications company executive; b. Waverly, Iowa, July 26, 1928; s. James Kendall and Lenore Clara (Kuethe) L.; m. Opal Marie Kerdus, Aug. 24, 1954; 1 child, James William Jr. Student, U.S. Mil. Acad., 1946-47; BA in History, Wartburg Coll., 1950. Rural letter carrier U.S. Postal Svc., Plainfield, Iowa, 1951-86; corp. sec. Butler-Bremer Mut. Telephone Co., Plainfield, Iowa, 1962—, also bd. dirs.; pres. Iowa Rural Letter Carriers Assn., 1981-83, v.p., 1979-81, state bd. dirs. 1976-83. Vice chmn. Bremer County Bd. Health, Waverly, Iowa, 1969-84, Waverly-Shell Rock Hospice, 1989-93, pres., 1992-93; fin. chmn. Bremer County Rep. Ctrl. Com., Waverly, 1987-92; mayor pro-tem City of Plainfield, Iowa, 1985-89, 91-94, mayor, 1994—, coun. mem., 1983-94; pres. Bremer County Hist. Soc., 1966—. With U.S. Army, 1951-53. Named Lion of Yr. Waverly Lions Club, 1988; Melvin Jones fellow, 1994. Mem. Plainfield Lions (sec. Plainfield chpt. 1971-72, pres. Waverly chpt. 1982-83, editor bulletin 1978—), Kopper Klowns (pres. 1980-81), Waterloo German-Am. (v.p., 1979-80), A.F. & A.M., Shriners. Lutheran. Home: PO Box 218 219 Main St Plainfield IA 50666-0218

LYNETT, GEORGE VINCENT, newspaper publisher; b. Scranton, Pa., Dec. 1, 1943; s. Edward James and Jean Marie (O'Hara) L.; m. Patricia Brady, June 4, 1966; children—Sheila Ellen, George Vincent, James Brady, Sharon Elizabeth. A.B. in English, Coll. of Holy Cross, 1965; M.B.A., U. Scranton, 1971; J.D., Georgetown U., 1978. Co-pub. Scranton Times and Sunday Times, 1967—; assoc. Haggerty, McDonnell, O'Brien & Wright, Scranton, 1978—; dir. 3d Nat. Bank and Trust Co., Scranton. Co-chmn. United Way of Lackawanna County, 1972; chmn. Lackawanna County Cancer Crusade, 1969; pres. Allied Services for Handicapped, 1973-75; trustee U. Scranton, 1970-76. Served with USNR, 1965-67. Mem. Lackawanna Bar Assn., Pa. Bar Assn., Pa. Newspaper Pubs. Assn., Am. Newspaper Pubs. Assn. Democrat. Roman Catholic. Club: Scranton Country. Office: The Scranton Times 147 Penn Ave Scranton PA 18503-2015*

LYNETT, LAWRENCE WILSON, electronics company executive; b. N.Y.C., Sept. 11, 1921; s. James Degge and Lillian (Lonquist) L.; 1 dau., Michele. B.B.A., Manhattan Coll., 1943. With IBM Corp., 1946—, dir. adminstrv. rsch., 1966—; assoc. adminstrv. mgmt. Simmons Coll., 1966—; Mem. Nat. Adv. Com. for Bus. Edn. Curriculum Devel., 1973—. Chmn. editorial bd.: Impact, 1977—; mem. editorial bd. Adminstrv. Mgmt. Mag., 1983—. Chmn. bd. trustees AMS Rsch. Found. Lt. comdr. USNR, WWII, PTO. Decorated Navy Commendation ribbon; Presdl. Commendation for devel. adminstrv. mgmt. program for U.S. Govt. Mgrs., 1966. Mem. Adminstrv. Mgmt. Soc. (internat. pres. 1966-67, bd. dirs. 1980-83, Diamond Mgmt. key 1963, Internat. Mgmt. award 1967, Internat. Ambassador award 1985, Silver medal for mgmt. achievements 1988), Office Execs. Assn. N.Y. (pres. 1960-61, Leadership award 1961), Am. Mgmt. Assn. (v.p. gen. svcs. dir., bd. dirs. 1975-87). Home: 11 Purchase Hills Dr Purchase NY 10577-1615 Office: IBM Corp Old Orchard Rd Armonk NY 10504 *The most effective way to cope with change is to help create it.*

LYNETT, WILLIAM RUDDY, publishing, broadcasting company executive; b. Scranton, Pa., Jan. 18, 1947; s. Edward James and Jean O'Hara L.; children: Scott, Jennifer, Christopher P. B.S., U. Scranton, 1972. Pub. Scranton Times, 1966—; pres., chief exec. officer Shamrock Communications, Inc., 1971—; pres. Towanda Daily Rev., 1977-81, Owego Pennysaver Press, Inc., 1977-81; owner, Pres. Mgmt. Program, Harvard U., 1990. Bd. dirs. Community Med. Ctr., Scanton, 1974-96; chmn. Mayor's Libr. Fund Drive, 1974; chmn. spl. gifts divsn. Heart Fund, 1975; bd. govs. Scranton Area Found., chmn., 1996-97; trustee U. Scranton, 1990-96; chmn. Steamtown Nat. Pk. Grand Opening com. Mem. Nat. Assn. Broadcasters, Pa. Assn. Broadcasters, Am. Newspaper Pubs. Assn., Pa. Newspaper Pubs. Assn., Greater Scranton C. of C. (chmn. membership drive 1980-81). Democrat. Roman Catholic. Clubs: Scranton Country, Elks, K.C. Office: 149 Penn Ave Scranton PA 18503-2022

LYNG, RICHARD EDMUND, former secretary of agriculture; b. San Francisco, June 29, 1918; s. Edmund John and Sarah Cecilia (McGrath) L.; m. Bethyl Ball, June 25, 1944; children: Jeanette (Mrs. Gary Robinson), Marilyn (Mrs. Daniel O'Connell). Ph.B. cum laude, U. Notre Dame, 1940; PhD (hon.), Carroll Coll., 1988. With Ed J. Lyng Co., Modesto, Calif., 1945-66, pres., 1949-66; dir. Calif. Dept. Agr., 1967-69; asst. sec. Dept. Agr., Washington, 1969-73, dep. sec., 1981-85; vice chmn. Commodity Credit Corp., 1981-85; pres. Lyng & Lesher, Inc., Washington, 1985-86; Sec. of Agr. Dept. Agr., Washington, 1986-89; pres. Am. Meat Inst., Washington, 1973-79; pvt. cons., 1980; dir. Commodity Credit Corp., 1969-73, Nat. Livestock and Meat Bd., 1973-76, Tri-Valley Growers, 1975-81; bd. govs. Refrigeration Rsch. Found., 1974-77, Chgo. Merc. Exch.; chmn. food industry trade adv. com. Commerce Dept.; chmn. U.S. Child Nutrition Adv. Com., 1971-73; mem. animal health com. NAS; sr. rsch. fellow Harvard U. Sch. Bus. Adminstrn., 1989-91; chmn. export adv. com. Nat. Dairy Bd., 1989—; bd. dirs. Ecosci., Corp, 1991—; trustee Internat. Life Sci. Inst., 1990—. Chmn. Stanislaus County (Calif.) Republican Central Com., 1961-62; dir. agr. div. Pres. Ford Com., 1976; co-dir. farm and food div. Reagan-Bush Campaign, 1980. Served with AUS, 1941-45. Mem. Washington Golf and Country Club, Del Rio Country Club (hon.). Roman Catholic.

LYNGBYE, JØRGEN, hospital administrator, researcher; b. Andst, Denmark, July 23, 1929; arrived in Norway, 1988; s. Knud and Estrid Marie Schou (Nielsen) L.; m. Ulla von Holstein, July 15, 1967 (div. 1982); 1 child, Rie; m. Jintana Detwilaiphong, Jan. 3, 1994. MD, U. Copenhagen, 1956; PhD, U. Arhus, Denmark, 1969. Asst. U. Arhus, 1957-65; asst. prof. U. Copenhagen, 1966-72; sr. cons. Regional Hosp., Frederiksborg, Denmark, 1973-83, Førde, Norway, 1984; assoc. prof. molecular biology U.S., 1985-86; prof. U. Thailand, 1986-88; dir. Regional Hosp., Molde, Norway, 1988—. Author: Clinical Biochemistry, 1986, Twins--A Unique World Scenario, 1995; contbr. numerous articles to sci. and popular sci. jours. and newspapers. Sec. Danish Polit. Orgn., Copenhagen, 1977-81. Lt. Danish Army, 1951-66. Decorated WEO Order (Thailand); recipient prize Danish Sci. Soc., 1978, Prix Scientifique, France, 1980, prize Danish Soc. for Protection of Animals, 1987, Applied Physics award, 1993. Fellow N.Y. Acad. Scis.; mem. Danish Med. Assn. (rep. 1978-83). Avocations: world ecology, philosophy, mathematics, nuclear physics, music.

LYNHAM, C(HARLES) RICHARD, foundry company executive; b. Easton, Md., Feb. 24, 1942; s. John Cameron and Anna Louise (Lynch) L.; m. Elizabeth Joy Card, Sept. 19, 1964; children: Jennifer Beth, Thomas Richard. BME, Cornell U., 1965; MBA with distinction, Harvard U., 1969. Sales mgr. Nat. Carbide Die Co., McKeesport, Pa., 1969-71; v.p. sales Sinter-Met Corp., North Brunswick, N.J., 1971-72; sr. mgmt. analyst Am. Cyanamid Co., Wayne, N.J., 1972-74; gen. mgr. ceramics and additives div. Foseco Inc., Cleve., 1974-77, dir. mktg. steel mill products group, 1977-79; pres., chief exec. officer Exomet, Inc. subs. Foseco, Inc., Conneaut, Ohio, 1979-81, Fosbel Inc. subs. Foseco, Inc., Cleve., 1981-82; gen. mgr. splty. ceramics group Ferro Corp., Cleve., 1982-84, group v.p. splty. ceramics, 1984-92; owner, pres. Harbor Castings, Inc., North Canton, Ohio, 1992—; bd. dirs. Chick Master Incubator Inc., Corrpro Cos., Inc. Patentee foundry casting ladle, desulphurization of metals. V.p. bd. trustees Hospice of Medina County; pres. bd. trustees Bridges Home Health Care. Capt. C.E., U.S. Army, 1965-67. Decorated Bronze Star with one oak leaf cluster. Mem. Am. Foundrymen's Soc., Cornell U. Alumni Coun., Cornell U. Alumni Class 1963 (past v.p., past pres.), Cornell U. Alumni Fedn. (past pres., bd. dirs., past v.p.), Chippewa Yacht Club (commodore 1982), Cornell Club of N.E. Ohio (past pres., bd. dirs.). Republican. Congregationalist. Avocations: sailing, genealogy. Home: 970 Hickory Grove Ave Medina OH 44256-1616 Office: Harbor Castings Inc 4321 Strausser St NW North Canton OH 44720-7144

LYNKER, JOHN PAUL, newscaster; b. Bklyn., Aug. 30, 1927; s. Paul Warren and Evelyn Foland (Briggs) L.; m. Linda Ann Cairrao, Sept. 26, 1992; children: Roger John, Denise Suzanne Lynker Duclos, John Paul Jr., Whitney Ellen Lynker Trifiletti. Student, Steven's Inst. Tech., 1944, 46, Columbia U., 1946-49. News anchor WPAT Radio, Paterson, N.J., 1951-52, Sta. WVNJ, Newark, 1952-56, WWJ Radio, Detroit, 1960-65, KGO Radio (ABC), San Francisco, 1971-75, WEEI Radio (CBS), Boston, 1975-80, WTOP Radio, Washington, 1980—; pres., gen. mgr. WSKN (now WQHQ), Kingston, N.Y., 1956-60; freelance newscaster N.Y.C., 1965-71; pres. The Programmers, N.Y.C., 1965-71. Bd. dirs. Arthritis Found., Washington and Atlanta; pres. Res. Officers' Assn., Boston, 1973, Washington, 1982; deacon Reformed Ch. of Am. Capt. USCGR, 1959-85. Recipient Legend award Washington Area Broadcasters Assn., 1992. Mem. VFW, Washington Automotive Press Assn. (pres. 1990-91), Internat. Motor Press Assn., Aircraft Owner and Pilots Assn., Radio and TV Corrs. Assn. Avocations: flying, boating, old cars. Home: 39 N Highland St Arlington VA 22201 Office: WTOP Radio 3400 Idaho Ave NW Washington DC 20016-3046

LYNN, ARTHUR DELLERT, JR., economist, educator; b. Portsmouth, Ohio, Nov. 12, 1921; s. Arthur Dellert and Helen B. (Willis) L.; m. Pauline Judith Wardlow, Dec. 29, 1943; children: Pamela Wardlow, Constance Karen, Deborah Joanne, Patricia Diane. Student, Va. Mil. Inst., 1938-39, U.S. Naval Acad., 1939; BA, Ohio State U., 1941, MA in Econs., 1943, JD, 1948, PhD in Econs., 1951; postgrad. in law, U. Mich., 1968-70. Bar: Ohio 1948, U.S. Supreme Ct. 1966. Upper Ohio Valley corr. Cin. Enquirer, 1937-38; ptnr. Lynn & Lynn, Portsmouth, 1949-50; chief clk. to dir. Ohio Dept. Hwys., 1957; mem. faculty Ohio State U., Columbus, 1941-86, prof. econs., 1961-86, asst. dean, 1959-62, assoc. dean Coll. Commerce and Adminstrn., 1962-65, assoc. dean faculties, assoc. provost, 1965-70, assoc. dean Coll. Adminstrv. Sci., 1984-86, assoc. dean emeritus Coll. Bus., 1986—, lectr. Coll. Law, 1961-67, adj. prof. law, 1967-86, prof. pub. adminstrn., 1969-86, prof. emeritus pub. policy and mgmt., 1986—, lectr. exec. devel. program, 1958-71, acting dir. divsn. pub. adminstrn., summers 1973, 74, acting dir. Sch. Pub. Adminstrn., summer 1975, 84-86; vis. prof. econs. Ohio Wesleyan U., 1958-59, U. Calif., Berkeley, summer 1972; vis. lectr. USAF Inst. Tech., Wright-Patterson AFB, Ohio, 1959-60; mem. Ohio Gov.'s Econ. Rsch. Coun., 1966-70; mem. assoc. faculty Lincoln Inst. Land Policy, Cambridge, Mass., 1989—. Author: Building the House: The Ohio State University School of Public Administration, 1969-89; editor: The Property Tax and Its Administration, 1970, Property Taxation, Land Use and Public Policy, 1976, Land Value Taxation, 1982; editorial adv. bd.: Tax Bramble Bush, 1959-70; assoc. editor: Nat. Tax Jour., 1971-88; bd. editors: Am. Jour. Econs. and Sociology, 1981—. Trustee Griffith Meml. Found. Ins. Edn.; chmn. external econs. adv. com. Marietta Coll., 1975-79; assoc. Nat. Regulatory Rsch. Inst., 1980—; mem. Alcohol, Drug Addiction and Mental Health Svcs. Bd., Franklin County, Ohio, 1990—; bd. dirs. Ohio Alliance for Mentally Ill, 1992-95, hon., 1995—; bd. dirs. Metro Behavioral Health Care Network, 1996—. 1st lt. F.A. AUS, 1942-46, PTO and Japan. Rsch. fellow Ohio Dept. Mental Health, 1991-92. Mem. ABA (chmn. com. state and local taxes sect. taxation 1961-63), Ohio Bar Assn., Columbus Bar Assn., Am. Econ. Assn., Royal Econ. Assn., Nat. Tax Assn. (chmn. com. model property tax assessment and equalization methods and procedures 1961-65, mem. exec. com. 1965-73, v.p., pres. 1969-70), Tax Inst. (adv. coun. 1960-63), Nat. Tax Assn.-Tax Inst. Am. (sec. 1975-84, treas. 1984-88, bd. dirs. 1975-88, counselor 1988—, hon. 1988—), Am. Arbitration Assn. (nat. panel), Ohio Coun. Econ. Edn. (bd. dirs. 1964-74), Com. on Taxation, Resources, and Econ. Devel. (co-chmn. 1979-87), Internat. Fiscal Assn., Internat. Assn. Assessing Officers (edn. adv. com.), Torch Club, Faculty Club, Rotary, Omicron Delta Epsilon, Beta Theta Pi, Phi Delta Phi, Beta Gamma Sigma, Pi Sigma Alpha, Pi Alpha Alpha. Republican. Episcopalian. Home: 2679 Wexford Rd Columbus OH 43221-3217 Office: 1775 S College Rd Columbus OH 43210-1309

LYNN, BARRY WILLIAM, religious organization executive; b. Harrisburg, Pa., July 20, 1948; s. Harold William and Edith Christine (Fairchild) L.; m. Dorcas Joanne Harley, June 6, 1970; children: Christina Dorcas, Nicholas Guy. BA summa cum laude, Dickinson Coll., 1970; ThM magna cum laude, Boston U., 1973; JD, Georgetown U., 1978. Bar: D.C.; ordained United Church of Christ. Tchr. religious studies dept. Cardinal Cushing Ctrl. H.S., South Boston, Mass., 1971-74; dir. To Heal A Nation program United Ch. of Christ, Washington, 1974-76, assoc. for emerging issues Ctr. for Social Action, 1976-77, legis. counsel Office for Ch. in Soc., 1978-80; pres. Draft Action, Inc., Washington, 1981-83; dir. Nat. Security Dissent Project William O. Douglas Inquiry into the State of Ind. Freedom, Washington, 1983; legis. counsel ACLU, Washington, 1984-91; exec. dir. Ams. United for Separation of Ch. and State, Washington, 1992—; cons. Ctr. for the Evaluative Clin. Scis., Hanover, N.H., 1992. Editor-in-chief Mil. Law Reporter, 1981-83; co-author: The Right to Religious Liberty: The Basic American Civil Liberties Union Guide to Religious Rights, 1994; co-host Battleline Radio Show, Washington, 1989-93, Pat Buchanan & Co. Radio Show, Washington, 1993-95; commentator on religion UPI Radio, Washington, 1993—; contbr. articles to profl. jours. Recipient Hugh Hefner First Amendment award Playboy Found., Chgo., 1986-87. Avocation; film. Home: 1406 Ingeborg Ct Mc Lean VA 22101 Office: Ams United for Sep Ch & State 1816 Jefferson Pl NW Washington DC 20036-2505

LYNN, D. JOANNE, physician, ethicist, health services researcher; b. Oakland, Md., July 2, 1951; d. John B. and Mary Dorcas (Clark) Harley; m. Barry W. Lynn; children: Christina, Nicholas. BS summa cum laude, Dickinson Coll., 1970; MD cum laude, Boston U., 1974; MA in Philosophy and Social Policy, George Washington U., 1981; MS Clin. Evaluative Scis., Dartmouth Coll., 1995. Diplomate Am. Bd. Internal Medicine. Resident internal Medicine The George Washington U. Med. Ctr., 1974-77; emergency rm. physician, triage physician Washington VA Hosp., 1977-78; faculty assoc. for medicine and humanities divsn. experimental programs George Washington U., Washington, 1978-81, dir. divsn. aging studies, 1988-92, prof. health care scis. and medicine, 1991-92, assoc. chairperson dept. health care scis., 1990-92; dir of the Ctr. to Improve the Care of the Dying George Washington U., 1995—; prof. medicine, cmty. and family medicine, sr. assoc. Ctr. Evaluative Clin. Scis. Dartmouth-Hitchcock Med. Ctr., Hanover, N.H., 1992-95, assoc. dir. Ctr. for Aging, 1992-95; Robert Wood Johnson clin. scholar George Washington U., 1977-78, sr. fellow Ctr. Health Policy Rsch., 1991-92; asst. dir. med. studies The Pres. Commn. for Study of Ethical Problems in Medicine and Biomed. and Behavioral Rsch., 1981-83; med. dir. The Washington Home, 1983-89, Hospice of Washington, 1979-91, George Washington Cancer Home Care Program and Home Health Svcs. of The Washington Home, 1990-92, staff physician, 1979-92; fellow Hastings Ctr., 1984—; mem. working group on guidelines for care of terminally ill, 1985-87, rsch. project on ethical issues in care and treatment of chronically ill, 1985-87, working group on new physician-patient relationship, 1991-94, v.p., 1987, chair fellows nominating com., 1991; mem. coordinating coun. on life-sustaining med. treatment decision making by cts. Nat. Ctr. State Cts., 1989-93; fellow Kennedy Inst., 1991; mem. geriat. and gerontology adv. com. Dept. Vet. Affairs, 1991—; mem. bioethics com. Vets. Health Adminstrn., 1991-93; active Washington Area Seminar on Sci., Tech., and Ethics, 1982-92, Nat. Clin. Panel on High-Cost Hospice Care, Washington, 1991; presenter in field. Author chpts. to books; mem. editl. bd. The Ency. of Bioethics, 1994-95; mem. adv. editl. bd. Biolaw, 1983, The Hospice Jour., 1984—, Med. Ethics for the Physician, 1985-92, Med. Humanities Rev., 1986—, Cambridge Quar., 1991-95; contbr. articles, revs. to profl. jours. Peter Jeffries and Jeanne Arnold scholar, 1973; recipient Wellington Parlin Sci. Scholarship award, 1979, Dr. Bertha Curtis prize Boston U. Med. Sch., 1974, Nat. Bd. award Med. Coll. Pa., 1992. Fellow ACP (mem. subcom. on aging 1986-91), Am. Geriatrics Soc. (mem. com. public policy 1983—, mem. ethics com. 1988, chair subcom. on ethics and policy 1986, chair ethics com. 1991—, bd. dirs. 1991—); mem. AAAS, APHA, Am. Fedn. Clin. Rsch., Am. Health Care Assn. (mem. task force on AIDS 1987-89), Am. Hosp. Assn. (mem. spl. com. on biomedical ethics 1983-85, 89-94), Am. Med. Dirs. Assn., Am. Soc. Law and Medicine, Am. Coll. Health Care Adminstrs. (mem. nat. adv. com. wandering patients 1987-88), Nat. Inst. on Aging (mem. senile dementia of Alzheimer's type, mem. rsch. ethics task force 1981-82, Am. Geriatrics Soc. rep. 1984-86), Soc. Health and Human Values (mem. gov. coun. 1981-84), Inst. Medicine (mem. com. on future issues in med. tech. devel. 1992-94), N.H. Med. Soc., Soc. Health and Human Values (mem. gov. coun. 1981-84), Internat. Hospice Inst. (mem. physician's adv. com. 1984-86), Med. Soc. D.C. (mem. legis. affairs com. 1985-92, vice chairperson 1991-92), Soc. Gen. Internal Medicine (mem. editl. adv. bd. Jour. 1988-91). Office: Ctr Improve Care Dying George Washington Univ 1001 22nd St NW # 3820 Washington DC 20037-1803

LYNN, EUGENE MATTHEW, insurance company executive; b. Kansas City, Mo., Nov. 6, 1918; s. Eugene M. and Marthield (Ellis) L.; m. Mary E. Spoors, Mar. 12, 1947 (dec.); 1 dau., Diane E.; m. Christine E. Koppl, Jan. 19, 1980. Student John B. Stetson U., 1937-39. Pilot Trans World Airlines, 1944-47; v.p. U.S. Epperson Underwriting Co., Boca Raton, Fla., 1949-55, pres., 1955—; pres. LIG Ins. Agy., Inc., Boca Raton, 1978—; v.p. Universal Underwriters Ins. Co., Kansas City, 1949-55, pres., 1955-82. Hon. chmn. bd., trustee Boca Raton Community Hosp.; trustee Lynn U. Boca Raton. Clubs: Boca Raton Hotel and Club, Royal Palm Yacht and Country (Boca Raton, Fla.), Delray Beach (Fla.), Ocean Reef (Key Largo, Fla.), Indian Creek Country, (Miami Beach), Fisher Island Surf (Miami Beach). Home: 565 Alexander Palm Rd Boca Raton FL 33432-7986 Office: Lumbermens Undwrt Aliance 2501 N Military Trl Boca Raton FL 33431-6356

LYNN, GWENDOLYN RENAYE, educator; b. Monticello, Fla., Nov. 12, 1958; d. Elder Joe Gray and Beatrice W. Lynn-Gray. BS, Fla. A&M U., 1980, MEd, 1984. Cert. profl. educator, Fla. Playground dir. Tallahassee Parks & Recreation Dept., 1978-84, instr. and recreation leader, 1978-82; tchr. phys. edn. Leon County Schs., Tallahassee, 1984-89, tchr. health edn., 1990—; team leader Griffin Mid. Sch., Tallahassee, 1993-95, sch.-based mgmt. mem., 1995, Newton/learner profile trainer, 1994—. Bd. dirs., treas. New Hope New Faith Ministries, Tallahassee, 1993—; co-sponsor Fellowship of Christian Athletes, Tallahassee, 1994—. Mem. NEA, Fla. Alliance Health, Phys. Edn., Recreation, Dance. Avocations: reading, writing, public speaking. Office: Griffin Middle School 800 Alabama St Tallahassee FL 32304-2211

LYNN, JAMES DOUGAL, newspaper editor, journalist; b. Houlton, Maine, June 14, 1934; s. Charles Edward and Ethel Florence (Cripe) L.; m. Nancy Deborah Solomon, Jan. 30, 1965 (div. July 1979); children: Nina Vanessa, Nora Melissa. AB, Princeton U., 1955. Reporter L.I. Star-Jour., 1955-61; writer Newsweek, N.Y.C., 1961-63; copy editor, city hall reporter, state capital bur. chief N.Y. Herald Tribune, 1963-66; info. officer Temp. State Commn., N.Y.C., 1966-67; editorial dir. Sta. WABC-TV and Radio, N.Y.C., 1967-69; pub. affairs dir. Sta. WMCA-Radio, N.Y.C., 1969-72; editorial writer, dep. editorial page editor, opinion pages editor Newsday, L.I., 1972—. Jefferson fellow East-West Ctr., Honolulu, 1983. Office: Newsday Inc 235 Pinelawn Rd Melville NY 11747-4226

LYNN, JAMES THOMAS, investment banker, insurance company executive, government executive, lawyer; b. Cleve., Feb. 27, 1927. BA, Western Res. U., 1948; LLB, Harvard U., 1951. Bar: Ohio 1951, D.C. 1977. Gen. counsel U.S. Dept. Commerce, 1969-71, under sec., 1971-73; sec. HUD, 1973-75; dir. Office Mgmt. and Budget, 1975-77; asst. Pres. U.S., 1975-77; with Jones Day Reavis & Pogue, Cleve., 1951-69; with Jones Day Reavis & Pogue, Washington, 1977-84, ptnr., 1960-69, mng. ptnr., 1977-84; with Aetna Life & Casualty Co., Hartford, Conn., 1984, vice chmn., 1984, chmn., CEO, 1984-92, also bd. dirs.; sr. advisor Lazard Frères & Co., L.L.C., N.Y.C., 1992—; bd. dirs. TRW Inc. Case editor Harvard Law Rev., 1950-51. Served with USNR, 1945-46. Mem. Phi Beta Kappa. Office: Lazard Frères & Co LLC 5335 Wisconsin Ave NW Ste 440 Washington DC 20015-2030

LYNN, LARRY (VERNE LAURISTON LYNN), engineering executive; b. Seattle, Sept. 5, 1930; s. Eldin Verne and Irma (Tuell) Lynn; m. Emily Jean Badger, Oct. 4, 1952 (div. 1988); m. Shirley Marie Pieczynski, Sept. 27, 1988. BS in Physics, Tufts U., 1951. Assoc. divsn. head, mem. steering com. Lincoln Lab. M.I.T., Lexington, Mass., 1953-79; dir. defensive systems Office of the Undersecretary of Defense, Washington, 1979-81; dep. dir. Adv. Rsch. Project Agy., Washington, 1981-85; v.p., COO Atlantic Aerospace Electronics, Greenbelt, Md., 1985-93; dep. under sec. defense Office Sec. Defense, Washington, 1993-95, dir. def. adv. rsch. project agy., 1995—. contbr. numerous articles to profl. jours. Lt. JG USNR, 1951-53. Mem. IEEE (life). Home: 1117 N Utah Arlington VA 22201 Office: DARPA 3701 Fairfax Dr Arlington VA 22203-1700

LYNN, LAURENCE EDWIN, JR., university administrator, educator; b. Long Beach, Calif., June 10, 1937; s. Laurence Edwin and Marjorie Louise (Hart) L.; m. Patricia Ramsey Lynn; 1 dau., Katherine Bell; children from previous marriage—Stephen Louis, Daniel Laurence, Diana Jane, Julia Suzanne. A.B., U. Calif., 1959; Ph.D. (Ford Found. fellow), Yale, 1966. Dir., dep. asst. sec. def. (OASD/SA) Dept. Def., Washington, 1965-69; asst. for program analysis NSC, Washington, 1969-70; assoc. prof. bus. Grad. Sch. Bus., Stanford (Calif.) U., 1970-71, vis. prof. pub. policy, 1982-83; asst. sec. planning and evaluation HEW, Washington, 1971-73; asst. sec. program devel. and budget U.S. Dept. Interior, Washington, 1973-74; sr. fellow Brookings Instn., 1974-75; prof. pub. policy John Fitzgerald Kennedy Sch. Govt. Harvard U., Cambridge, Mass., 1975-83; dean Sch. Social Service Adminstrn. U. Chgo., 1983-88, prof., sch. of social svc. adminstrn. and Harris grad. sch. pub. policy studies, 1983—, dir. Ctr. for Urban Rsch. and Policy Studies, 1986—; dir. Mgmt. Inst., 1992—. Author: Designing Public Policy, 1980, The State and Human Services, 1980, Managing the Public's Business, 1981, Managing Public Policy, 1987, Public Management as Art, Science and Profession, 1996; co-author: The President as Policymaker, 1981; contbr. articles to profl. jours. Bd. dirs. Chgo. Met. Planning Coun., 1984-89, Leadership Greater Chgo., 1989-92; mem. coun. of scholars Libr. of Congress, 1989-93. 1st lt. AUS, 1963-65. Recipient Sec. Def. Meritorious Civilian Svc. medal, Presdl. Cert. of Disting. Achievment, Vernon prize. Fellow Nat. Acad. Public Adminstrn.; mem. U. Calif. Alumni Assn., Council on Fgn. Relations, Assn. Pub. Policy Analysis and Mgmt. (past pres.), Phi Beta Kappa. Home: 5000 S Cornell Ave Chicago IL 60615-3041 Office: Univ Chgo 969 E 60th St Chicago IL 60637-2640

LYNN, LORETTA WEBB (MRS. OLIVER LYNN, JR.), singer; b. Butcher Hollow, Ky., Apr. 14, 1935; d. Ted and Clara (Butcher) Webb; m. Oliver V. Lynn, Jr., Jan. 10, 1948; children—Betty Sue Lynn Markworth, Jack Benny (dec.), Clara Lynn Lyell, Ernest Ray, Peggy, Patsy. Student pub. schs. Sec.-treas. Loretta Lynn Enterprises; v.p. United Talent, Inc.; hon. chmn. bd. Loretta Lynn Western Stores. Country vocalist with MCA records, 1961—(numerous gold albums); most recent album Just a Woman, 1985, (with Conway Twitty) Making Believe, 1988, Greatest Hits Live, 1992, The Country Music Hall of Fame, 1991, Country's Favorite Daughter (reissue), 1993. Author: Coal Miner's Daughter, 1976; appearance (TV movie) Loretta Lynn: The Seasons of My Life, 1992, Big Dreams and Broken Hears: The Dottie West Story, 1995. Hon. rep. United Giver's Fund, 1971. Named Country Music Assn. Female Vocalist of Year 1967, 72, 73, Entertainer of Year, 1972, named Top Duet of 1972, 73, 74, 75; recipient Grammy award 1971, Am. Music award 1978, named Entertainer of Decade, Acad. Country Music 1980; inducted into Country Music Hall of Fame, 1988; first country female vocalist to record certified Gold album. Office: care MCA Records Inc 70 Universal City Plz Universal Cty CA 91608-1011*

LYNN, MARK WAYNE, secondary school educator, assistant principal; b. Daytona Beach, Fla., Dec. 14, 1965; s. Richard Patrick and Marie Joan (Amodio) L. BA, St. John's U., Jamaica, N.Y., 1986, MA, 1988. Tchr. Xavier High Sch., N.Y.C., 1986-91, chmn. dept., 1989-91; prin. Our Lady Queen of Martyrs Sch., Ft. Lauderdale, Fla., 1991-93; tchr., chmn. dept. Father Lopez High Sch., Daytona Beach, Fla., 1993—, asst. prin., 1996—. Mem. ASCD, NAESP, Nat. Cath. Edn. Assn., K.C., Theta Alpha Kappa.

LYNN, NAOMI B., academic administrator; b. N.Y.C., Apr. 16, 1933; d. Carmelo Burgos and Maria (Lebron) Berly; m. Robert A. Lynn, Aug. 28, 1954; children: Mary Louise, Nancy, Judy Lynn Chance, Jo-An. BA, Maryville (Tenn.) Coll., 1954; MA, U. Ill., 1958; PhD, U. Kans., 1970. Instr. polit. sci. Cen. Mo. State Coll., Warrensburg, Mo., 1966-68; asst. prof. Kans. State U., Manhattan, 1970-75, assoc. prof., 1975-80, acting dept. head, prof., 1980-81, head polit. sci. dept., prof., 1982-84; dean Coll. Pub. and Urban Affairs, prof. Ga. State U., Atlanta, 1984-91; chancellor U. Ill., Springfield, 1991—; cons. fed., state and local govts., Manhattan, Topeka, Altanta, 1981-91; bd. dirs. Bank One Springfield. Author: The Fulbright Premise, 1973; editor: Public Administration, The State of Discipline, 1990, Women, Politics and the Constitution, 1990; contbr. articles and textbook chpts. to profl. pubs. Bd. dirs. United Way of Sangamon County, 1991—, Ill. Symphony Orch., 1992-95; bd. dirs. Urban League, 1993—. Recipient Disting. Alumni award Maryville Coll., 1986; fellow Nat. Acad. Pub. Adminstrn. Mem. Nat. Assn. Schs. Pub. Affairs and Adminstrn. (nat. pres.), Am. Soc. Pub. Adminstrn. (nat. pres. 1985-86), Am. Polit. Sci. Assn. (mem. exec. coun. 1981-83, trustee 1993—), Am. Assn. State Colls. and Univs. (bd. dirs.), Midwest Polit. Sci. Assn. (mem. exec. coun. 1976-79), Women's Caucus Polit. Sci. (pres. 1975-76), Greater Springfield C. of C. (bd. dirs. 1991—, accreditation task force 1992), Pi Sigma Alpha (nat. pres.). Presbyterian. Office: U Ill at Springfield Office of Chancellor Springfield IL 62794-9243*

LYNN, OTIS CLYDE, former army officer; b. nr. Flynn's Lick, Tenn., Feb. 14, 1927; s. Dillard A. and Jennie Sue (Pruett) L.; m. Jacque Gilbert, Mar. 17, 1946; children: Clyde Gilbert, Gary Jackson. Student, Vanderbilt U., 1944-45; B.G.E., U. Omaha, 1963; M.S., George Washington U., 1968. Commd. 2d lt. U.S. Army, 1946, advanced through grades to maj. gen., 1972; chief of staff 2d Div., Korea, 1970; comdr. 1st Brigade 2d div., Korea, 1971; asst. div. comdr. 101st Div., Fort Campbell, Ky., 1974; chief of staff XVIII Airborne Corps, Fort Bragg, N.C., 1975, U.S. Forces, Japan, 1975-78; comdg. gen. 25th Inf. Div., Schofield Barracks, Hawaii, 1978-80; chief staff U.S. Army in Europe, Heidelberg, Fed. Republic Germany, 1980-82; ret., 1982, ret. real estate broker. Decorated Silver Star with two oak leaf clusters, Def. Superior Service medal, Legion of Merit (with two oak leaf clusters), Bronze Star, Air Medal, D.S.M., Purple Heart. Mem. Assn. of U.S. Army, Rotary. Mem. Ch. of Christ. Home: 140 Arborvitae Dr Pine Knoll Shores NC 28512-6200

LYNN, PHYLLIS JEAN, entrepreneur; b. Harrisburg, Ill., Feb. 14, 1936; d. Waldo Houston Basham and Ruth Pearl Irvin; m. Vincent Paul Kaduk, Feb. 21, 1958 (div. 1970); children: Kimberly, Tamara, Christopher; m. John M. Lynn, Oct. 8, 1982. AD in Psychology, George Williams Coll., Downers Grove, Ill., 1973. Lic. real estate salesperson. Real estate owner Birdsong Builders, Inc., Downers Grove, 1965-72; owner Charmills Restaurant & Bar, Clearwater, Fla., 1977-82, On Target Co., Indian Head Park, Ill., 1983-92; adminstrv. asst. J.S. James Co., Burr Ridge, Ill.; part owner Atocha Silver Mine, CoChBomba, Bolivia, 1980-81, Cleaves/Lynn, Inc., Western Springs, Ill., 1993—. Lobbyist for ERA, NOW, 1972-73. Avocations: oil painting, interior decorating, collecting antiques, boating. Home: 6418 Blackhawk Trl La Grange IL 60525-4316 Office: Cleaves/Lynn Inc PO Box 229 Western Springs IL 60558-0229

LYNN, ROBERT PATRICK, JR., lawyer; b. N.Y.C., Nov. 17, 1943; s. Robert P. and Marie (Madeo) L.; m. Maria T. Zeccola, Nov. 18, 1967; children—Robert P. III, Stephanie M., Kerry Elizabeth. B.A., Villanova U., 1965; J.D., St. John's U., Bklyn., 1968. Bar: N.Y. 1969, U.S. Dist. Ct. (ea. dist.) N.Y. 1975, U.S. Ct. Appeals (1st cir.) 1978, U.S. Ct. Appeals (2d cir.) 1975, U.S. Supreme Ct. 1978. Clk., then assoc. Leboeuf, Lamb & Leiby, N.Y.C., 1966-69; dep. town atty. Town of North Hempstead, Manhasset, N.Y., 1969-71; assoc. Sprague Dwyer Aspland & Tobin, Mineola, N.Y., 1971-75, ptnr., 1975-76; ptnr. Lynn & Ledwith, Garden City, N.Y., 1976-92; spl. prosecutor Inc. Village of Bayville, 1975-76. Bd. dirs. Cath. Charities, 1971-89, chmn., 1982; vice chmn. Diocese of Rockville Centre Family Life Ctr., 1978-82. Mem. Nassau County Bar Assn., Suffolk County Bar Assn., N.Y. State Bar Assn. Roman Catholic. Clubs: Wheatley Hills Golf Club (East Williston, N.Y.); Lloyd Neck Bath (Lloyd Harbor, N.Y.), La Romana Country Club (Dominican Rep.). Home: 10 Seaforth Ln Huntington NY 11743 Office: 330 Old Country Rd Ste 103 Mineola NY 11501-4143 also: GV269 Casade Campo La Romana Dominican Republic

LYNN, ROBERT WOOD, theologian, educator, dean; b. Wheatland, Wyo., Apr. 3, 1925; s. William McGregor and Janet (Reid) L.; m. Katharine Mitchell Wuerth, Mar. 8, 1952; children—Thomas Taylor, Janet MacGregor, Elizabeth Mitchell, Sarah McKee. A.B., Princeton U., 1948; B.D., Yale U., 1952; Th.D., Union Theol. Sem., N.Y.C., 1962. Ordained to ministry Presbyn. Ch., 1952; asst. minister Montview Presbyn. Ch., Denver, 1952-59; mem. faculty Union Theol. Sem., N.Y.C., 1959-75, dean Auburn program, 1960—, prof., 1965-75; v.p. Lilly Endowment, Inc., 1976-84, sr. v.p., 1985-89; vis. prof. Drew U., Andover Newton Theol. Sch., Fordham U., Tchrs. Coll., Columbia U.; scholar in residence Bangor Theol. Sem., 1989—. Author: Protestant Strategies in Education; co-author: The Big Little School; also articles. Trustee Louisville Sem., 1990-95, Yale U., 1991-95. Serve with AUS, 1943-44. Woodrow Wilson fellow, 1948-49; Presbyn. Grad. fellow, 1959-60. Home: PO Box 3290 Leeds ME 04263

LYNN, SHEILAH ANN, service executive, consultant; b. Anderson, Ind., Jan. 28, 1947; d. John Benton and Kathleen (Taylor) Bussabarger; m. John Hoftyzer, Dec. 21, 1968 (div. June 1982); children: Melanie Kay, John Theo; m. Guy C. Lynn, May 20, 1984. BS, Ind. U., 1969; postgrad., U. N.C., Greensboro, 1970, Webster U., 1994; diploma, Data Processing Inst., Tampa, Fla., 1983; MS, Ctrl. Mich. U., 1993. Bookkeeper John Hancock Life Ins. Co., Greensboro, 1970-72; freelance seminar leader and devel. Dhahran, Saudi Arabia, 1978-82; dir. programming Fla. Tech. Inst., Jacksonville, 1983-84, instr. in computer sci., 1984-85; real estate sales assoc. Fla. Recreational Ranches, Gainesville, 1985; instrnl. program coord., workforce tng. coord. Fla. C.C., Jacksonville, 1986—; handwriting analyst, cons. Sheilah A. Lynn & Assocs., Jacksonville, 1989—; cons. programmer, analyst Postmasters Co., Jacksonville, 1986—; pres. Options Cons., Jacksonville, 1986-89, Sheilah A. Lynn & Assocs., Jacksonville, 1989—; 6L cons. assocs. Dacum facilitator and curriculum developer. Mem. Jacksonville Community Council, Inc., 1986-87, Fla. Literacy Coalition, 1986-87. Mem. NAFE, ASTD, Fla. Assn. Ednl. Data Systems, Bus. and Profl. Women, Jacksonville C. of C. (bd. dirs. south coun. 1987, sec. 1989, treas. 1990, v.p. 1991, pres. 1992). Democrat. Avocations: duplicate bridge, reading, fishing, bowling.

LYNN, THEODORE STANLEY, lawyer; b. N.Y.C., Aug. 2, 1937; s. Irving and Sydell (Gorlie) L.; m. Linda Isabel Freeman, July 21, 1968; children: Jessica, Douglas. AB, Columbia U., 1958; LLB, Harvard U., 1961; LLM, NYU, 1962; SJD, George Washington U., 1972. Law clerk to Hon. Bruce M. Forrester, U.S. Tax Ct., Washington, 1962-64; teaching fellow in law George Washington U., Washington, 1963-64; ptnr. Webster & Sheffield, N.Y.C., 1964-90; ptnr. Stroock & Stroock & Lavan, N.Y.C., 1991—; cons. Adminstrv. Conf. U.S., Washington, 1974-75; founding counsel Pension Real Estate Assn., Washington, 1981-84 . Author: Real Estate Limited Partnerships, 3d edit., 1991, Real Estate Investment Trusts, 2d edit., 1994, supplement 1995; contbr. articles to profl. jours.; Spl. asst. Mayor John V. Lindsay, N.Y.C. 1966-69; sec. Manhattan Sch. of Dance, 1974-93; trustee Birch Wathen Lenox Sch., N.Y.C., 1975-93; bd. dirs. Manhattan Community Bd. #6, N.Y.C., 1977—, chair nominating com., 1992-94; bd. dirs. Citizens Union, 1991—, exec. com., 1995—, dir., Sutton Area Cmty., Inc., 1995—. Mem. ABA, Fed. Bar Council, Assn. of Bar of City of N.Y., Univ. Club, Inwood C. of C., Harvard Club. Office: Stroock & Stroock & Lavan 180 Maiden Ln New York NY 10038-4925

LYNN, THOMAS NEIL, JR., retired medical center administrator, physician; b. Ft. Worth, Feb. 14, 1930; s. Thomas Neil and Florence Van Zandt (Jennings) L.; m. Virginia Carolyn Harsh, July 26, 1952; children: Thomas Neil, Leslie Elizabeth, Kathryn Barry. B.S., U. Okla., 1951, M.D., 1955. Diplomate: Am. Bd. Internal Medicine, Am. Bd. Preventive Medicine. Intern Barnes Hosp., St. Louis, 1955-56; resident Barnes Hosp., 1956-57; clin. asso Nat. Heart Inst. NIH, Bethesda, Md., 1957-59; chief resident medicine U. Okla. Hosps., 1959-61; med. staff U. Hosps. and Clinics, 1970-72; staff Okla. Children's Meml. Hosp., Presbyn. Hosp., VA Hosp., Oklahoma City; instr. asst. prof. community health Okla. Med. Center, 1961-63, asso. prof., 1963-67, prof., chmn. dept., 1970-76; acting dean U. Okla. Coll. Medicine, 1974-76, dean, 1976-80; v.p. for med. staff affairs Bapt. Med. Ctr., Oklahoma City, 1980-95; mem. governing bd. Okla. Physician Manpower Tng. Commn., 1974-80, Ambulatory Health Care Consortium, Inc., 1977-78, Integris Mental Health Corp., 1996—, T.N. Lynn Inst. for Healthcare Rsch., 1996—; mem. Okla. Bd. Medicolegal Examiners. Contbr. articles to profl. jours. Bd. dirs. Okla. Arthritis Found., 1978-82, v.p., 1981-82; bd. dirs. North Care Mental Health Ctr., 1981-87, pres., 1986-87, Oklahoma City Community Coun., 1982-90; med. dir. Okla. Organ Sharing Network, 1989-90; mem. Bd. Health Oklahoma City-County Health Dept., 1983-85; bd. dirs. Okla. chpt. Am. Heart Assn., 1984-86; mem. Nat. Commn. on Cert. Physician Assts., 1987-90. Fellow Am. Coll. Preventive Medicine; mem. AMA, Okla. Med. Assn. (trustee 1981-87, chmn. bd. trustees 1986-87), Oklahoma County Med. Soc. (trustee), Am. Acad. Family Physicians, Okla. Acad. Family Physicians, Sigma Xi, Alpha Omega Alpha, Phi Sigma, Alpha Tau Omega. Presbyn. Home: 3136 Pine Ridge Rd Oklahoma City OK 73120-5918 *Individuals should live their life and conduct their affairs such that all succeeding generations will be benefitted and be glad that these people lived.*

LYNN, TONY LEE, import company executive; b. Burke City, N.C., Oct. 13, 1939; s. Craig and Marie (Lowman) L.; m. Cindy Robson; 1 child, Gretchen. Student, Lenoir Rhyne Coll., 1958-62, N.C. Sch. Banking, 1972, Sch. Banking of South, Baton Rouge, 1972-75, Am. Inst. Banking, 1976. Dist. mgr. Am. Credit Co., Atlanta, 1961-66; v.p. First Nat. Bank Catawba County, Hickory, N.C., 1966-76; exec. v.p. Dixie Boat Works, Newton, N.C., 1976-82; founder, pres. Friitala Am., Hickory, 1982—. Named one of Outstanding Young Men of Am., 1975. Mem. Am. Inst. Banking (past bd. dirs., pres. Hickory unit), Nat. Ski Patrol Alumni Assn. (lifetime mem., tng. officer, sr. profl.), Catawba County C. of C. (lifetime hon. mem.). Home: 5670 37th St NE Hickory NC 28601-9703 Office: Friitala Am 231 10th St NW Hickory NC 28601-4857

LYNN, WALTER ROYAL, civil engineering educator, university administrator; b. N.Y.C., Oct. 1, 1928; s. Norman and Gussie (Gdalin) L.; m. Barbara Lee Campbell, June 3, 1960; children: Michael Drew. B.S., U. Miami, 1950; M.S., U. N.C., 1955; Ph.D., Northwestern U., 1963. Registered profl. engr., N.Y. State registered land surveyor, Fla. Land surveyor Ehly Constrn. Co., Miami, Fla., 1950-51; chief party Rader Engrng. Co., Miami, 1951; supt. sewage treatment, lectr. civil engring. U. Miami, 1951-53, asst. prof. mech. engring., 1954-55, asst. prof. civil engring., 1955-57, research asst. prof. marine lab., 1957-58, assoc. prof. civil and indsl. engring., 1959-61; dir. research Ralph B. Carter Co., 1957-58; assoc. prof. san. engring. Cornell U., Ithaca, N.Y., 1961-64; prof. civil and environ. engring. Cornell U., 1964—, dir. Center Environ. Quality Mgmt., 1966-76, dir. Sch. Civil and Environ. Engring., 1970-78, dir. Program on Sci., Tech. and Society, 1980, dean univ. faculty, 1988-93; sr. fellow Ctr. for the Environ., 1992—, dir., 1996—; adj. prof. pub. health Med. Coll. Cornell U., 1971-80; mem. spl. adv. commn. on solid wastes NRC, 1968-76, mem. com. to rev. Washington met. water supply, 1976-84, chmn., 1980-84, mem. bd. water sci. and tech., 1982-86, chmn., 1982-85, mem. com. on water resources rsch., 1987-90, chmn., 1988-90; mem. U.S. Nat. Com. for the Decade on Nat. Disaster Reduction, 1991—, chmn., 1991—; cons. WHO, 1969—, Rockefeller Found., 1976-81, SEARO, 1978; chmn. N.Y. State Water Resources Planning Coun., 1986—, NRC Bd. on Nat. Disasters, 1992— (chmn. 1992-96). Editor: (with A. Charnes) Mathematical Analysis of Decision Problems in Ecology, 1975; assoc. editor: Jour. Ops. Research, 1968-76, Jour. Environ. Econs. and Mgmt, 1972-88; contbr.: chpt. to Human Ecology and Public Health, 1969; author articles. Chmn. Ithaca Mayor's Citizens Adv. Com., 1964-65, Ithaca Urban Renewal Agy., 1965-68; trustee Cornell U., 1980-85; bd. dirs. Cornell Research Found., 1978-96. Served with AUS, 1946-48. Recipient Disting. Alumnus award U. Miami, 1985, Pub. Svc. award Universities Coun. on Water Resources, 1991, Conservation Svc. award U.S. Dept. Interior, 1994. Fellow ASCE (life), AAAS; mem. Nat. Acad. Engrs. Mex. (corr.), Sigma Xi, Phi Kappa Phi., Chi Epsilon. Home: 102 Iroquois Pl Ithaca NY 14850-2221

LYNN, WILLIAM J., III, federal agency administrator. BA, Dartmouth Coll., 1976; MA in Public Affairs, Princeton U., 1982; JD, Cornell Law Sch., 1980. Exec. dir. defense orgn. project Ctr. for Strategic and Internat. Studies, 1982-85; sr. fellow Strategic Devel. Ctr. Nat. Defense U., 1986-87; mem. staff Sen. Edward M. Kennedy, 1987-93; dir. Program Analysis and Evaluation Office of the Sec. of Def., 1993—. Author: (book) Toward A More Effective Defense, 1985; contbr. articles to profl. jours. Office: Office Sec Defense Rm 3E 836 The Pentagon Washington DC 20301

LYNNE, GILLIAN BARBARA, choreographer, dancer, actress, director; b. Bromley, Eng., Feb. 20, 1926; d. Leslie and Barbara (Hart) Pyrke; m. Peter Land, May 17, 1980. Ed., Baston Sch., Bromley; Arts Ednl. Sch. Leading soloist Sadler's Wells Ballet, 1944-51; star dancer London Palladium, 1951-53. Dancing debut with Royal Ballet; soloist roles included: The Black Queen (Checkmate), The Lilac Fairy (Sleeping Beauty), The Queen of the Wilis (Giselle) and The Black Ballerina (Ballet Imperial, Symphonic Variations); role in film, Master of Ballantrae, 1952; lead in Can-Can, Coliseum, 1954-55; Becky Sharp in Vanity Fair, Windsor Theatre, 1956; guest principal dancer: Samson and Delilah, Sadler's Wells Ballet, 1957, Aida, and Tannhauser, Covent Garden, 1957, Puck in A Midsummer Night's Dream, BBC TV, 1958; star dancer in Chelsea at Nine (featured dance segments), Granada TV, 1958; lead in New Cranks, Lyric and Hammersmith Theatres, 1959; roles in Wanda, Rose Marie, Cinderella, Out of My Mind, and lead in revue, 1960-61; leading lady, 5 Past Eight Show, Edinburgh, 1962, Queen of Cats, London, 1962-63; conceived, directed, choreographed, and starred in Collages, Edinburgh Festival, 1963, Royal Variety Performance Simple Man Extract, 1989; staged: England Our England, Revue, Princes Theatre, 1961; choreographer: The Owl and the Pussycat (1st ballet), Western Theatre Ballet, 1962, Queen of the Cats, London Palladium, 1962-63, Wonderful Life (1st film), 1963-64, Every Day's a Holiday, and Three Hats for Lisa (musical films), 1964, The Roar of the Greasepaint, and Pickwick, Broadway, 1965, The Flying Dutchman, Covent Garden, 1966, Half a Sixpence (film), 1966-67, How Now Dow Jones, Broadway, 1967, Midsummer Marriage, Covent Garden, 1968, The Trojans, Covent Garden, 1969, 1977, Breakaway (ballet), Scottish Theatre Ballet, 1969, Phil the Fluter, Palace Theatre, 1969, Ambassador Theatre, Her Majesty's Theatre, 1971, Man of La Mancha (film), 1972, The Card, Queen's, 1973, Hans Andersen, London Palladium, 1975, The Way of The World, Aldwych, 1978; My Fair Lady, nat. tour and Adelphi, 1979, Parsifal, Covent Garden, 1979, (also assoc. dir.) Cats, New London Theatre, 1981 (Olivier award 1981), Broadway 1982, nat. tour, 1983, dir. and choreographer prodn. in Vienna, 1983 (Silver Order of Merit, Austria, 1984), L.A., Sydney, 1985, East Berlin, 1987, also Can., Japan, Australia, Moscow, 1989, Paris, 1989 (Molière award Best Musical), Amsterdam, 1990, Café Soir (ballet), Houston Ballet Co., 1985, Cabaret, Strand, 1986, The Phantom of the Opera, Her Majesty's Theatre, 1986, Broadway, Japan, Vienna, 1989, Stockholm, Chgo., Hamburg, Australia, 1990, Canada, 1991, Amsterdam, 1993, Manchester, Eng., 1993, A Simple Man (ballet), Sadler's Wells, 1988, Aspects of Love, Prince of Wales Theatre, 1989, Broadway, 1990, The Brontës (ballet), Northern Ballet Theatre, 1995; choreographer, dir.: The Match Girls, Globe Theatre, 1966; Bluebeard, Sadlers Wells Opera, 1966, new prodn., Coliseum, 1969), Love on the Dole (musical), Nottingham Playhouse, 1970; Liberty Ranch, Greenwich, 1972, Once Upon a Time, Duke of York's, 1972, Jasperina, Amsterdam, 1978, Valentine's Day, Chichester, 1991, Globe, 1992, A Simple Man (BBC-TV) (Brit. Acad. award for conception, direction and choreography 1988); dir. Round Leicester Square, Prince Charles Theatre, 1963, Tonight at Eight, Hampstead, 1970, Fortune, 1971, Lillywhite Lies, Nottingham, 1971, A Midsummer Night's Dream, Stratford, 1977, Tomfoolery, Criterion, 1980, Jeeves Takes Charge, Fortune, 1980, off-Broadway, 1983, L.A., 1985, To Those Born Late, New End Theatre, 1981, La Ronde, RSC, Aldwych, 1982, (also appeared in) Alone Plus One, Newcastle, 1982, The Rehearsal, Yvonne Arnaud, Guildford and tour, 1983, Cabaret, Strand, 1986; staged: England Our England (revue), Princes, 1961, 200 Motels (pop-opera film), 1971, musical nos. in Quilp (film), 1974, A Comedy of Errors, Stratford, 1976 (Oliver award 1977), TV musical, 1977, As You Like It (musical), Stratford, 1977, Songbook, Globe Theatre, 1979, Once in a Lifetime, Aldwych Theatre, 1979 (Oliver award for best play 1978), new stage act for Tommy Steele, 1979, wedding sequence in Yentl (film), 1982, European Vacation II (film), Pirelli Calendar, 1988, Pickwick, Chichester and Sadler's Wells, 1993; conceived, directed dance for Life Gala, Her Majesty's Theatre, 1991; choreographer and staging: (films) Mr. Love, Under Milkwood, Quilp; choreographer for TV: Peter and the Wolf (narrated and mimed all 9 parts), 1958, At the Hawk's Well (ballet), 1975, There Was a Girl, 1975, The Fool on the Hill (1st Colour Spl. for ABC; Best Musical, Best Prodn. awards in Australia 1977), with Australian Ballet and Sydney Symphony Orch., staged Sydney Opera House, 1975, Muppet Show series, 1976-80 (Golden Rose Montreux award 1977); (also musical staging) Alice in Wonderland, 1985, shows and specials for Val Doonican, Perry Como, Petula Clark, Nana Mouskouri, John Curry, Harry Secombe, Ray Charles, and Mike Burstein, also produced and devised Noel Coward and Cleo Laine spls.; directed for TV: Mrs. F's Friends, 1981, Easy Money, 1982, Le Morte d'Arthur, 1983, A Simple Man, 1987 (BAFTA award), Gilliam Lynne and Friends Chichester Festival Theatre, 1994, The V.E. Day Gala Coliseum, 1995, (ballet in three acts) The Brontes, 1995; for internat. TV in various capacities as producer, deviser, stager, choreographer and dir.: 1989 Royal Variety Performance (Andrew Lloyd Webber segment), The Look of Love, BBC North West, (BBC) A Simple Man, The Morte D'Arthur, Easy Money, The Various Ends of Mrs. F.'s Friends, The Look of Love, Pickwick, It's Topol, Val Doonican, Nana Mouskouri, Soccer Dance, Tiptoes, There Was a Girl, A World of Music, The Great American Songbook; (ABC) The Fool on the Hill; (LTW) Marvellous Party, Tickertape Children's series, Cleo Laine Sings; (CBS/USA) Alice in Wonderland; (ATV) The Muppet Show, Marty Feldman Show; (VARA/Holland) The Mike Burstyn Show; (Thames) Comedy Tonight, The Royal Variety Show, 1991, 93, Sadlers Wells Theatre, 1993, Pickwick Chichester Festival Theatre, 1993; dir. AVOW, 1996; conceiver, dir., choreographer Anyone Who Had a Heart, 1997; pub. contbr. to Cats, The Book of the Musical; articles in Dancing Times. Mem. Pickwick Club. Address: care Lean Two Prodns Ltd, 18 Rutland St Knightsbridge, London SW7 IEF, England

LYNNE, JEFF, rock musician, composer; b. Birmingham, Eng., Dec. 30, 1942. Musician with The Nightriders, Eng., The Move, also The Electric Light Orch.; albums include No Answer, 1971, ELO, II, 1973, On the Third Day, 1973, Eldorado, 1974, Face the Music, 1975, Ole ELO, 1976, A New World Record, 1976, The Light Shines On, 1977, 3 Light Years, 1978, ELO, 1978, Out of the Blue, 1978, Discovery, 1979, The Light Shines On, Vol. 2, 1979, Greatest Hits, 1979, Xanadu, 1980, Box of Their Best, 1980, Secret Messages, 1984, Balance of Power, 1986, Afterglow, 1990, ELO Part II, 1991, (with Traveling Wilburys) Traveling Wilburys, 1988, Traveling Wilburys Vol. 3, 1990, (solo) Armchair Theatre, 1990, Beatles Anthology, 1995; producer various artists including Dave Edmunds, George Harrison, Daryl Hall. Recipient Grammy award (with Traveling Wilburys), 1990. *

LYNNE, SEYBOURN HARRIS, federal judge; b. Decatur, Ala., July 25, 1907; s. Seybourn Arthur and Annie Leigh (Harris) L.; m. Katherine Donaldson Brandau, June 16, 1937 (dec. Mar. 1997); 1 dau., Katherine Roberta (dec. Nov. 1988). BS, Ala. Poly. Inst., 1927; LLB, U. Ala., 1930, LLD, 1973. Bar: Ala. 1930. Pvt. practice law Decatur, Ala., 1930-34; judge Morgan (Ala.) County Ct., 1934-41, 8th Jud. Cir. Ct. Ala., 1941-42; judge U.S. Dist. Ct. (no. dist.) Ala., 1946—, chief judge, 1953-73, sr. judge, 1973—. Lt. col., JAGC, U.S. Army, 1942-46. Decorated Bronze Star; named to Ala. Acad. Honor, 1978. Mem. Ala. Bar Assn. (Award of Merit 1989), ABA, Blue Key, Scabbard and Blade, Pi Kappa Alpha, Phi Kappa Phi, Phi Delta Phi, Omicron Delta Kappa, Alpha Phi Epsilon. Democrat. Baptist. Clubs: Kiwanian (dist. gov. Ala. dist. 1938), Birmingham Country,

Univ. of Ala. A. Office: US Dist Ct 419 US Courthouse 1729 5th Ave N Birmingham AL 35203-2000

LYNNES, R. MILTON, advertising executive; b. Chgo., Apr. 16, 1934; s. Roy Milton and Ethel (Wolfe) L.; m. Carol Rinehart, Aug. 30, 1958; children: Christopher, Katherine, Jeffrey, Jennifer. BS, Iowa State U., 1957. Advt. sales promotion supr. Interlake Steel, Chgo., 1961-62; copywriter Garfield-Linn, Chgo., 1963; account exec. Biddle Co., Appleton, Wis., 1964-66; exec. v.p. Marsteller HCM, Chgo., 1966-84; bd. dirs. Marsteller HCM, 1978-84; prin. Grant, Jacoby Inc., Chgo., 1985-89, pres., 1989-94, chmn. CEO, 1994—; bd. dirs. Worldwide Ptnrs., Denver, chmn. N.Am. region, 1996-97. bd. dirs. MTW/WWP Media Venture, 1995, Better Bus. Bur., Chgo., 1984-87. Mem. Am. Assn. Advt. Agys. (vice chmn. ctrl. region, bd. dirs. 1981-82), Chgo. Advt. Club (bd. dirs. 1985-86), Exmoor Country Club, Bob O Link Golf Club, Pelican Bay Golf Club, Econs. Club, Tavern Club, Chicago Club. Republican. Congregationalist. Office: Grant/Jacoby Inc 737 N Michigan Ave Chicago IL 60611-2615

LYNTON, ERNEST ALBERT, physicist, educator, former university official; b. Berlin, Germany, July 17, 1926; came to U.S., 1941, naturalized, 1945; s. Arthur J. and Lizzie (Kiefe) Lowenstein; m. Carla Ellen Kaufmann, Aug. 4, 1953; children—David Michael, Eric Daniel. B.S., Carnegie Inst. Tech., 1947, M.S., 1948; Ph.D., Yale, 1951. AEC postdoctoral fellow U. Leiden, Holland, 1951-52; faculty Rutgers U., 1952-74, prof. physics, 1962-74; dean Rutgers U. (Livingston Coll.), 1965-73; Commonwealth prof. U. Mass., Boston, 1974-95, sr. v.p. acad. affairs, 1974-80, sr. assoc. N.E. Resource Ctr. for Higher Edn.; vis. prof., Fulbright fellow U. Grenoble, France, 1959-60; cons. NSF, 1965-70, Ford Found., 1973, 80-82, Spelman Coll., 1980—, Cambridge Coll., 1982-83, OECD, 1981-93, Coun. of Europe, 1982-83, Carnegie Found., 1992—, Am. Assn. Higher Edn., 1992—; mem. Commn. on Higher Edn. Mid. States Assn., 1972-74; adv. bd. Princeton Sch. Architecture, 1971-80; chmn. Mass. Commn. Telecoms., 1981-83. Author: Superconductivity, 3d edit., 1968 (translated into French, Russian, German), Missing Connection Between Business and the Universities, 1984, (with Sandra Elman) New Priorities for the University, 1987, Making the Case for Professional Service, 1995; exec. editor Met. Univs., 1988—; contbr. articles to profl. jours. Pres. Princeton (N.J.) Jewish Ctr., 1964-66; bd. dirs. Princeton Assn. Human Rights, 1962-65, Mercer County chpt. ACLU, 1966-70; trustee Marlboro Music, 1982—. With AUS, 1944-46. Fellow Am. Phys. Soc. Home: 14 Allerton St Brookline MA 02146-7727

LYNTON, HAROLD STEPHEN, lawyer; b. N.Y.C., Nov. 2, 1909; widowed, Mar. 12, 1990; children: Stephen Jonathan, Richard David, Andrew Edward; m. Hattie Gruenstein Kalish, Jan. 27, 1991. AB magna cum laude, Yale U., 1929; JD cum laude, Harvard U., 1932. Bar: N.Y. 1933, U.S. Supreme Ct. 1947. Ptnr. Kaufman, Gallop, Gould, Climenko & Lynton, N.Y.C., 1934-51, Lynton & Klein and predecessors, N.Y.C., 1951-80; ptnr. Shea & Gould, N.Y.C., 1980-91, counsel, 1992-94; counsel Dornbush Mensch Mandelstam & Schaeffer, N.Y.C., 1994—; gen. counsel, trustee, mem. adv. bd. Barron Collier Cos., Naples, Fla., 1945—; also bd. dirs. Barron Collier Cos. and predecessors, Naples, Fla. Capt. AUS, 1943-45. Mem. ABA, N.Y. State Bar Assn., Assn. of Bar of City of N.Y., N.Y. County Lawyers Assn., Yale Club N.Y., Sunningdale Country Club, Phi Beta Kappa. Avocations: travel, theatre, tennis, swimming. Home: 870 UN Plz New York NY 10017-1807 Office: Dornbush Mensch et al 747 3rd Ave New York NY 10017-2803

LYON, ANDREW BENNET, economics educator; b. Elmhurst, Ill., June 6, 1958; s. Richard M. and Rhee Lyon; m. Jennifer A. Sour, May 1987; 1 child. AB, Stanford U., 1980; PhD, Princeton U., 1986. Economist Jt. Com. on Taxation, U.S. Congress, Washington, 1985-87; asst. prof., dept. econ. U. Md., College Park, 1987-93, assoc. prof., dept. econ., 1993—; vis. fellow Brookings Inst., 1994-95; cons. and expert witness, 1987—; dir. Unisys Credit Corp., Detroit, 1991-92; sr. econ. Coun. Econ. Advisers, 1992-93. Author: Cracking the Code: Making Sense of the Corporate Alternative Minimum Tax, 1997; contbr. numerous articles to profl. jours. Nat. Bur. Econs. fellow, 1987-94. Mem. Am. Econ. Assn., Nat. Tax Assn. (Outstanding Doctoral Dissertation award 1986, Fed. Tax Com. 1991), Phi Beta Kappa. Office: U Md Dept Econs College Park MD 20742

LYON, BRYCE DALE, historian, educator; b. Bellevue, Ohio, Apr. 22, 1920; s. E. Paul and Florence (Gundrum) L.; m. Mary Elizabeth Lewis, June 3, 1944; children—Geoffrey P., Jacqueline M. AB, Baldwin-Wallace Coll., 1942; PhD, Cornell U., 1949; PdD (hon.), 1972; LittD (hon.), U. Ghent, 1988. Asst. prof. history U. Colo., 1949-51, Harvard U., 1951-56; assoc. prof. U. Ill. at Urbana, 1956-59; prof. U. Calif. at Berkeley, 1959-65; Barnaby and Mary Critchfield Keeney prof. history emeritus Brown U., 1965-86, chmn. history dept., 1968-75. Author: Medieval Institutions, 1954, From Fief to Indenture, 1957, A History of the World, 1960, Constitutional and Legal History of Medieval England, 1960, Medieval History, 4th rev. edit., 1962, The High Middle Ages, 1964, The Middle Ages in Recent Historical Thought, 2d edit., 1965, Medieval Finance, 1967, The Origins of the Middle Ages, 1971, Henri Pirenne: A Biographical and Intellectual Study, 1974, The Journal de Querre of Henri Pirenne, 1976, Studies of West European Medieval Institutions, 1978, The Wardrobe Book of William de Norwell (1338-1340), 1983, The Birth of Annales History: The Letters of Lucien Febvre and Marc Bloch to Henri Pirenne (1921-1935), 1991, Réflexions d'un solitaire by Henri Pirenne, 1994. Served with AUS and USAAF, 1942-46. Fellow Royal Hist. Soc., Am. Acad. Arts and Scis., Medieval Acad. Am., Belgian Royal Acad.; mem. Econ. History Assn., Am. Hist. Assn., Conf. Brit. Studies. Home: HC 63 Box 108 Alstead NH 03602-7720

LYON, CARL FRANCIS, JR., lawyer; b. Sumter, S.C., May 9, 1943; s. Carl Francis and Sophie (Goldstrum) L.; m. Maryann Mercier; children—Barbara Ruth, Sarah Frances, Carl Francis, III. A.B., Duke U., 1965, J.D. with honors, 1968. Bar: N.Y. 1969, D.C. 1977. Assoc., then ptnr. Mudge Rose Guthrie Alexander & Ferdon, N.Y.C., 1968-95, mem. exec. com., 1986-87, 94-95; ptnr. Orrick Herrington & Sutcliffe, N.Y.C., 1995—. Contbr. articles to profl. publs. Mem. ABA (vice-chmn. spl. com. on energy fin. 1988-91), N.Y. State Bar Assn., D.C. Bar Assns., Am. Pub. Power Assn., Duke U. Law Alumni Coun., Order of Coif, Phi Alpha Delta. Office: Orrick Herrington Sutcliffe 666 5th Ave New York NY 10103-0001

LYON, ISOLDA YVETTE, dietitian; b. Managua, Nicaragua, Nov. 10, 1954; came to U.S., 1982; naturalized citizen 1989; d. Lauriston Edmund and Teresa del Carmen (Rodriguez) Burey; m. Ward Burton Lyon, Mar. 25, 1983; children: Jessica Yvette, Angelica Isolda. BS in Nutrition and Dietetics, U. San Carlos, Guatemala, 1978. Registered dietitian; lic. dietitian; cert. food and beverage mgr., correctional officer. Nutritionist Health Ministry, Managua, Nicaragua, 1975-77; cons. Welfare Ministry and Health Ministry, Managua, Nicaragua, 1978-79; prof. faculty Ctrl. Am. U., Managua, Nicaragua, 1981; dietitian Nestle Co., Managua, Nicaragua, 1979-82; nutritionist Harris County Hosp. Dist., Houston, 1983-85; food svc. dir. Carnegie Gardens Nursing, Melbourne, Fla., 1985-86; food svc. supr. Wuesthoff Hosp., Rockledge, Fla., 1986-87; sgt., food svc. mgr. Tex. Dept. of Corrections, Rosharon, Tex., 1987-88; dir. dietary svcs. Washington Sq. Devel. Svcs. Inc., Titusville, Fla., 1988-96; sr. clin. dietitian Holmes Regional Med. Ctr./Health First, Melbourne, Fla., 1996—; item writer Commn. Dietetic Registration Am. Dietetic Assn., 1997. Mem. Dem. Party, Managua, 1981-82. Named Employee of Yr., Carnegie Gardens, 1985, Intelligent Employee of the Yr., Devel. Svcs., 1992. Mem. Am. Dietetic Assn., Dietetics in Devel. and Psychiat. Disorders, Clin. Nutrition Mgmt., Dietetics in Phys. Medicine and Rehab., Space Coast Dietetic Assn. (pres. 1995-96, chair nominating com. 1996-97), Nicaraguan Nutritionist and Dietetic Assn. (treas. 1979-82), Ctrl. Am. and Panama Nutritionist Dieticians Assn. Republican. Roman Catholic. Avocations: church, dancing, reading. Home: 847 Tiffany Pl Rockledge FL 32955 Office: Washington Sq Devel Svcs 1350 S Hickory St Melbourne FL 32901-3276

LYON, JAMES BURROUGHS, lawyer; b. N.Y.C., May 11, 1930; s. Francis Murray and Edith May (Strong) L. BA, Amherst Coll., 1952; LLB, Yale U., 1955. Bar: Conn. 1955, U.S. Tax Ct. 1970. Asst. football coach Yale U., 1953-55; assoc. Murtha, Cullina, Richter and Pinney (and predecessor), Hartford, Conn., 1956-61, ptnr., 1961-96, counsel, 1996—; mem. adv. com., lectr. and session leader NYU Inst. on Fed. Taxation, 1973-86; mem. IRS Northeast Key Dist.'s Exempt Orgns. Liaison Group, Bklyn., 1993—. Mem. editl. bd. Conn. Law Tribune, 1988—. Chmn. 13th Conf. Charitable Orgn. NYU on Fed. Taxation, 1982; mem. adv. bd. Charitable Giving, Trusts & Estates Mag., 1996—; trustee Kingswood-Oxford Sch., West Hartford, Conn., 1961-91, hon. trustee, 1991—, chmn. bd. trustees, 1975-78; mem. exec. com., chmn. Amherst Coll. Alumni Coun., 1963-69; trustee Old Sturbridge Village, Mass., 1974, chmn. bd. trustees, 1991-93; trustee Ella Burr McManus Trust, Hartford, 1980—, Ellen Battell Stoeckel Trust, Norfolk, Conn., 1994—, Hartford YMCA, 1985—, St. Francis Found., 1991—, Watkinson Libr., 1990—; trustee Wadsworth Atheneum, Hartford, 1968—, pres., 1981-84, hon. trustee, 1993—; sec. bd. trustees Horace Bushnell Meml. Hall, Hartford, 1993—, trustee, 1994—; corporator Inst. Living, 1981—, Hartford Hosp., 1975-96, St. Francis Hosp., Hartford, 1976—, Hartford Pub. Libr., 1979—, Hartford Sem., 1991; bd. dirs. Conn. Policy and Econ. Com., Inc., 1991—; mem. Conn. adv. com. New Eng. Legal Found., 1991—; bd. vis. Hartford Art Sch., 1995—. Recipient Eminent Svc. medal Amherst Coll., 1967, Nathan Hale award Yale Club Hartford, 1982, Disting. Am. award No. Conn. chpt. Nat. Football Found. Hall of Fame, 1983, Community Svc. award United Way of the Capital Area, 1986. Fellow ABA (mem. exempt orgn. com., co-chairperson subcom. on mus. and other cultural orgns. sect. of taxation 1988—), Am. Coll. Tax Counsel; mem. Am. Law Inst., Hartford Golf Club, Yale Club, Union Club N.Y.C., Dauntless Club (Essex, Conn.), Wianno Club (Osterville, Mass.), Mory's Assn. (New Haven), Yale Golf Club, Phi Beta Kappa. Office: 185 Asylum St Hartford CT 06103-3402

LYON, JAMES CYRIL, chemical society executive; b. Eldorado, Ill., May 14, 1937; s. James S. and Helen D. (Podrasky) L.; m. Sandra K. Lasseter, June 14, 1958; children: Lori Anne, Lisa J. BS, So. Ill. U., Carbondale, 1959; MS, No. Ill. U., DeKalb, 1967. Tchr. English, coach Bremen High Sch., Midlothian, Ill., 1959-61, Maine Twp. High Sch. East, Park Ridge, Ill., 1961-64; bus. mgr., treas. Nat. Coun. Tchrs. of English, Urbana, Ill., 1964-71; exec. dir. Am. Oil Chemists' Soc., Champaign, Ill., 1971—, Internat. Soc. for Fat Rsch., 1992—. Bd. dirs. Champaign-Urbana Conv. and Visitors Bur., 1987-95, chmn., 1988-92; bd. dirs. Champaign County Hist. Mus., 1975-81, pres. 1980; bd. dirs., vice-chairperson Champaign County Econ Devel. Partnership, 1995—. Mem. Am. Soc. Assn. Execs., Ill. Soc. Assn. Execs., Found. for Internat. Meetings (bd. dirs. 1982), Champaign Country Club, Rotary, Phi Delta Kappa, Kappa Delta Pi. Republican. Avocations: travel, reading, golf. Home: 24 Field East Champaign IL 61821-6535 Office: Am Oil Chemists Soc PO Box 3489 Champaign IL 61826-3489

LYON, JAMES HUGH, educational rights specialist, legislative consultant, political strategist; b. Clarksburg, W.Va., Apr. 17, 1936; s. James M. and Mildred E. Lyon; m. Marilyn Jean Lyon. BA in English, Salem Coll., 1960; MA, W.Va. U., 1967. Cert. English tchr., Ohio. Tchr. coll. preparatory English Harrison County (W.Va.) Schs., 1960-64, Urbana (Ohio) City Schs., 1964-70; edn. cons., lobbyist Ohio Edn. Assn., Columbus, 1970-93; edn. cons. Lyon Assocs., Canton, Ohio, 1993—. Mem. Nat. Assn. Lobbyists for Sch. Employees, Ohio Edn. Assn. (tchr. rights specialist in Ohio state legislature 1981-93, Outstanding Svc. award 1986), Elks. Home and Office: 6627 Avalon St NW Canton OH 44708-1084

LYON, JAMES KARL, German language educator; b. Rotterdam, Holland, Feb. 17, 1934; came to U.S., 1937; s. T. Edgar and Hermana (Forsberg) L.; m. Dorothy Ann Burton, Dec. 22, 1959; children: James, John, Elizabeth, Sarah, Christina, Rebecca, Matthew, Melissa. BA, U. Utah, 1958, MA, 1959; PhD, Harvard U., 1963. Instr. German Harvard U., Cambridge, Mass., 1962-63, asst. prof., 1966-71; assoc. prof. U. Fla., Gainesville, 1971-74; prof. U. Calif. San Diego, La Jolla, 1974-94, provost Fifth Coll., 1987-94; prof. dept. Germanic and Slavic langs. Brigham Young U., Provo, Utah, 1994—; vis. prof. U. Augsburg, Germany, 1993. Author: Konkordanz zur Lyrik Gottfried Benns, 1971, Bertolt Brecht and Rudyard Kipling, 1975, Brecht's American Cicerone, 1978, Bertolt Brecht in America, 1980, Brecht in den USA, 1994. Capt. M.I., U.S. Army, 1963-66. NEH fellow, 1970, Guggenheim Found. fellow, 1974; Ford Found. grantee, 1988, 91. Mem. MLA, Am. Assn. Tchrs. German, Internat. Brecht. Soc., Phi Beta Kappa. Democrat. Mormon. Avocations: back-packing, fishing. Office: BYU Dept Germanic & Slavic Lang 4094 Jesse Knight Human Bld Provo UT 84602-6120

LYON, JEFFREY, journalist, author; b. Chgo., Nov. 28, 1943; s. Herbert Theodore and Lyle (Hoffenberg) L.; m. Bonita S. Brodt, June, 20, 1981; children: Lindsay, Derek. BS in Journalism, Northwestern U., 1965. Reporter Miami (Fla.) Herald, 1964-66, Chgo. Today, 1966-74; reporter Chgo. Tribune, 1974-76, columnist, 1976-80, 94—, feature writer specializing in sci., 1980—; creative writing adj. prof.; coord. joint sci. and journalism programs Columbia Coll., Chgo., 1987—, dir., 1988—. Author: Playing God in the Nursery, 1985, Altered Fates: Gene Therapy and the Retooling of Human Life, 1995; also newspaper series Altered Fates, 1986 (Pulitzer Prize 1987). Mem. State of Ill. Perinatal Adv. Com., Springfield, 1986-90; mem. pediat. ethics com. U. Chgo. Hosps., 1985-90; bd. dirs. Shore Cmty. Svcs. to Retarded Citizens, Evanston, Ill., 1985-90; mem. bd. Little City, Palatine, Ill., 1979—. Recipient Nat. Headliner award Atlantic City Press Club, 1984, Citizen Fellow award Inst. Medicine of Chgo., 1987, Peter Lisagor award, 1990. Office: The Chgo Tribune 435 N Michigan Ave Chicago IL 60611

LYON, PATTY, advertising executive; m. Jon Lyon; 1 child, Samantha. BA in Latin Am. Studies, Denison U., 1975; MA, U. do Victoria, Brazil. Account exec. Ogilvy & Mather, 1980-85; mgmt. supr. Ogilvy & Mather Direct, 1985, account dir. ETC Group, head pers. and worldwide tng., 1988—. Vol. Children's Mus.; bd. dirs. Clinton Cmty. Assn.; vol. fireman. Avocations: scuba diving, salt water fishing. Office: Ogilvy & Mather Direct 309 W 49th St New York NY 10019-7316

LYON, PHILIP K(IRKLAND), lawyer; b. Warren, Ark., Jan. 19, 1944; s. Leroy and Maxine (Campbell) L.; children by previous marriage: Bradford F., Lucinda H., Bruce P., Suzette P., John P., Martin K., Meredith J.; m. Jayne Carol Jack, Aug. 12, 1982. JD with honors, U. Ark., 1967. Bar: Ark. 1967, U.S. Supreme Ct. 1970, Tenn. 1989. Sr. ptnr., dir. ops. House, Wallace, Nelson & Jewell, P.A., Little Rock, 1967-86; pres. Jack, Lyon & Jones, P.A, Little Rock & Nashville, 1986—; instr. bus. law, labor law, govt. bus. and collective bargaining U. Ark., Little Rock, 1969-72, lectr. practice skills and labor law, U. Ark. Law Sch., 1979-80; bd. dirs. Southwestern Legal Found., 1978—; editorial bd. dirs. Entertainment Law & Fin., 1993—. Co-author: Schlei and Grossman Employment Discrimination Law, 2d edit., 1982; editor-in-chief: Ark. Law Rev., 1966-67, bd. dirs., 1978-93, v.p., 1990-92; editor: Ark. Employment Law Letter, 1995. Inaugural fellow Coll. Labor and Employment Lawyers, 1996; mem. ABA (select com. liason office fed. contract compliance programs 1982—, select com. liason EEOC 1984—, select com. immigration law, forum com. entertainment and sports industries), Ark. State C. of C. (bd. dirs. 1984-88), Greater Little Rock C. of C. (chmn. community affairs com. 1982-84, minority bus. affairs 1985-89), Ark. Bar Assn. (chmn. labor law com. 1977-78, chmn. labor law sect. 1978-79, chmn. lawyers helping lawyers com. 1988-94), Tenn. Bar Assn. (labor sect., lawyers helping lawyers com. 1989—), Nashville Bar Assn. (entertainment law com., lawyers concerned for lawyers com., editor Ark. Employment Law Letter 1995—), Pulaski County Bar Assn., Country Music Assn., Acad. of Country Music, Nashville Entertainment Assn., Nashville Songwriters Assn. Internat., Copyright Soc. of South, Coll. Labor and Employment Lawyers (original class fellow 1996—), Capitol Club. Recipient Golden Gavel award Ark. Bar Assn., 1978, Writing Excellence award Ark. Bar Found., 1980. Home: 350 Ardsley Pl Nashville TN 37215-3247 also: 17 Heritage Park Cir North Little Rock AR 72116-8528 Office: Jack Lyon & Jones PA 11 Music Cir S Nashville TN 37203-4335 also: Jack Lyon & Jones PA 425 W Capitol 3400 TCBY Tower Little Rock AR 72201 *One of the true secrets of success is to concentrate your efforts—for if you apply these efforts everywhere at once then you will accomplish very little anywhere.*

LYON, RICHARD, mayor, retired naval officer; b. Pasadena, Calif., July 14, 1923; s. Norman Morais and Ruth (Hollis) L.; m. Cynthia Gisslin, Aug. 8, 1975; children: Patricia, Michael, Sean; children by previous marriage: Mary, Edward, Sally, Kathryn, Patrick (dec.), Susan. B.E., Yale U., 1944; M.B.A., Stanford U., 1953. Commd. ensign USN, 1944; advanced through grades to rear adm. SEAL, 1974; served in Pacific and China, World War II; with Underwater Demolition Team Korea; recalled to active duty as dep. chief Naval Res. New Orleans, 1978-81; mem. Chief Naval Ops. Res. Affairs Adv. Bd., 1978-81; exec. v.p. Nat. Assn. Employee Benefits, Newport Beach, Calif., 1981-90; mem. Bd. Control, U.S. Naval Inst., 1978-81; pres. Civil Svc. Commn., San Diego County, 1990—, Oceanside Unified Sch. Bd., 1991; mayor City of Oceanside, 1992-96. Pres. bd. trustees Children's Hosp. Orange County, 1965, 72. Decorated Legion of Merit. Mem. Nat. Assn. Securities Dealers (registered prin.), Newport Harbor Yacht Club, Oceanside Yacht Club, Rotary (Anaheim, Calif. pres. 1966). Republican. Episcopalian. Home: 4464 Inverness Dr Oceanside CA 92057-5052

LYON, RICHARD HAROLD, physicist educator,; b. Evansville, Ind., Aug. 24, 1929; s. Chester Clyde and Gertrude Lyon; m. Jean Wheaton; children: Katherine Ruth, Geoffrey Cleveland, Suzanne Marie. A.B., Evansville Coll., 1952; Ph.D. in Physics (Owens-Corning fellow), Mass. Inst. Tech., 1955; D.Eng., U. Evansville, 1976. Asst. prof. elec. engring. U. Minn., Mpls., 1956-59; Mem. research staff Mass. Inst. Tech., 1955-56, lectr. mech. engring., 1963-69, prof. mech. engring., 1970-95, prof. emeritus, 1995—, head mechanics and materials div., 1981-86; NSF postdoctoral fellow U. Manchester, Eng., 1959-60; sr. scientist Bolt Beranek & Newman, Cambridge, 1960-66, v.p., 1966-70; chmn. Cambridge Collaborative, Inc., 1972-90; v.p. Grozier Pub., Inc., 1972; pres. Grozier Tech. Systems, 1976-82, RH Lyon Corp., 1976—. Author: Transportation Noise, 1974, Theory and Applications of Statistical Energy Analysis, 1975, 2d edit. (with R. DeJong), 1994, Machinery Noise and Diagnostics, 1987. Bd. dirs. Boston Light Opera, Ltd., 1975; mem. alumni bd. U. Evansville, 1988-94, bd. trustees, 1995—, chmn. ann. fund, 1996-97. Recipient Rayleigh medal Brit. Inst. Acoustics, 1995, Nat. Acad. Engring. award 1995, Disting. Alumni award U. Evansville, 1997. Fellow AAAS, Acoustical Soc. Am. (assoc. editor jour. 1967-74, exec. coun. 1976-79, v.p. 1989-90, pres. 1993-94); mem. Sigma Xi, Sigma Pi Sigma, Nat. Acad. Engring., Brit. Inst. Acoustics (Rayleigh medal 1995). Research, publs. in fields of nonlinear random oscillations, energy transfer in complex structures, sound transmission in marine and aerospace vehicles, building acoustics, environmental noise, machinery diagnostics, home theater audio systems. Home: 60 Prentiss Ln Belmont MA 02178-2021 Office: RH Lyon Corp 691 Concord Ave Cambridge MA 02138-1002

LYON, RONALD EDWARD, management consultant, computer consultant; b. Kansas City, Kans., Apr. 13, 1936; s. William Edward and Lillian (Gee) L.; m. Josette Paula Larré, July 24, 1959; children: Michael Alan, Mark Alexander, Matthew Adam, Collette Allison. Owner Hansler Outboard & Austin Aqua Sports, Austin, Tex., 1959-63; gen. mgr. Wayne Green Ent.-73 Mag., Peterboro, N.H., 1963-65; with Computer Control Corp., Peterboro, N.H., 1965-71; sales person Radio Shack (Tandy) & Sterling Elec. Co., Maine, N.H., Vt. areas, 1971-82; sales engr. Pall Corp./Russell Assocs., Inc., Watertown, Mass., 1982-87; mgr. eastern region Fansteel/Wellman Dynamics, 1984-87; CEO, COO Laryon Assocs., Inc., Keene, N.H., 1987—. With USAF, 1955-59. Mem. U.S. Power Squadron, Soc. for Preservation and Encouragement of Barber Shop Quartet Singing in Am. Avocations: sailing, ham radio, computers, skiing, square dancing. Home: Mcintire Rd Munsonville NH 03457 Office: Laryon Assocs Inc 187D Main St Keene NH 03431-3739

LYON, STERLING RUFUS WEBSTER, justice; b. Windsor, Ont., Can., Jan. 30, 1927; s. David Rufus and Ella Mae (Cuthbert) L.; m. Barbara Jean Mayers, Sept. 26, 1953; children: Nancy, Andrea, Peter, Jennifer, Jonathan. B.A., U. Winnipeg, 1948; LL.B., U. Man., 1953. Bar: Man. 1953, created Queen's Counsel 1960. Crown atty., atty. gen. Man., 1953-57; mem. Man. Legis. Assembly, 1958-69, 76-86; atty. gen. Man., 1958-63, 66-69; minister of mcpl. affairs, 1960-61, of pub. utilities, 1961-63, of mines and natural resources, 1963-66, of tourism and recreation, 1966-68, commr. No. affairs, 1966-68; leader Man. Progressive Conservative Party, 1975-83; premier of Man., 1977-81; leader of the opposition, 1976-77, 81-83; mem. Her Majesty's Privy Council for Can., 1982; apptd. justice Man. Ct. of Appeal, Winnipeg, 1986—; chmn. 1st Can. Conf. on Pollution, Montreal, 1966, Can. Premier's Conf., 1980-81; pres. Can. Coun. Resource Ministers, 1965-66. Former trustee Ducks Unltd., Delta Waterfowl Found.; bd. regents U. Winnipeg, 1972-76; dir. Can. Royal Heritage Trust. With RCAF Res., 1950-53. Recipient U. Winnipeg Alumni Assn. Jubilee award, 1973; U. Man. scholar, 1945. Office: Law Cts, 408 York Ave, Winnipeg, MB Canada R3C 0P9

LYON, THOMAS L., agricultural organization administrator; b. Toledo, Iowa, Sept. 12, 1940; m. Barbara Lyon; children: Jeff, Melissa, Scott. BS in Dairy Sci., Iowa State U., 1962. Exec. sec. Iowa State Dairy Assn.; with 21st Century Genetics, gen. mgr., 1976-93; pres. Coop. Resources Internat., Shawano, Wis., 1993—. Bd. dirs. Am. Farmland Trust, Coop. Bus. Internat., Coop. Devel. Found.; chmn. Nat. Coop. Bus. Assn.; mem. Nat. Rural Devel. Task Force & Coop. 2000 com., Dairy Shrine Club, steering com. Wis. Dairy Inititative 2020, Kellogg Found. Food Systems; bd. advisors U. Wis., Eau Claire; bd. visitors U. Wis., Madison; trustee Grad. Inst. Coop. Leadership, Coop. Found.; cons. U. Wis. Bus. Schs. Review. Recipient Friend of Extension award U. Wis., 1981, Wis. Friend of County Agents award, 1984, Dairy Industry Person of Yr. award World Dairy Expo, 1985, Nat. Coop. Pub. Svc. award, 1991, Disting. Citizen Shawano award, 1993, Agribus. award Iowa State U. Coll. Agr. Alumni Soc., 1995. Office: Coop Resources Internat 100 MBC Dr Shawano WI 54166

LYON, WILFORD CHARLES, JR., insurance executive; b. Blackfoot, Idaho, June 1, 1935; s. Wilford Charles and Nellie Anna (Estenson) L.; m. Eleanor Perkins, Aug. 23, 1957; children: Katherine Ann, Wilford Charles III. BS, Ga. Inst. Tech., 1958; MA in Actuarial Sci., Ga. State Coll., 1962. Asst. v.p. Ind. Life and Accident Ins. Co., Jacksonville, Fla., 1963-69, asst. v.p., dir. methods and planning dept., 1969-70, v.p., home office coordinator, 1970-79, pres., chief adminstrv. officer, 1979-84, chmn. bd., chief exec. officer, 1984-96; trustee, mem. exec. com. Edward Waters Coll., Jacksonville, 1983-96, chmn., bd. visitors, 1993-96. Trustee Gator Bowl Assn., Jacksonville, 1981—, pres., 1981; pres. Jacksonville C. of C., 1984; trustee community TV, Inc., Jacksonville, 1980-93, chmn., 1991-92; trustee Univ. Hosp., Jacksonville, Inc., 1985-86; bd. dirs. YMCA Fla.'s First Coast, 1985—, sec., 1986, vice chmn., 1987, chmn., 1988 (Svc. to Youth award 1991); chmn. 1991 Nat. Vol. Week, Vol. Jacksonville, Inc. Recipient Disting Svc. award Jacksonville Jaycees, 1972, Jack Donnell award Outstanding Businessman of the Year, 1983, Dick Hutchinson award Sertoma Club South Jacksonville, 1972, Svc. to Mankind award, 1972, Boss of Yr. award Profl. Secs. Internat., 1972-73, Victory Crusade award Fla. Cancer Soc., 1969, Ins. Industry Community Svc. award Jacksonville Assn. Life Underwriters, 1986, C.G. Snead Meml. award Jacksonville Assn. of Life Underwriters, 1991, Top Mgmt. award Sales and Mktg. Execs. of Jacksonville, 1990, Clanzel T. Brown award Jacksonville Urban League, 1991, Svc. to Youth award YMCA of Fla.'s First Coast, 1991, Humanitarian award NCCJ, 1994. Mem. Life Insurers Conf. (exec. com. 1981-91, chmn. membership com. 1981-86, sec. 1984-85, vice chmn. 1985-86, chmn. 1986-87), Am. Coun. Life Ins. (Fla. state v.p. 1981-96, bd. dirs. 1987-88, bd. dirs. Polit. Action Com. 1988-94), Southeastern Actuaries Club, Rotary Club Jacksonville (pres. Mandarin club 1977-78, Paul Harris fellow, dist. gov. 697 1985-86), Masons, York Rite, Scottish Rite Bodies, Shriners (potentate Morocco Temple 1973). Republican. Presbyterian. Home: 1129 Mapleton Rd Jacksonville FL 32207-5342

LYON, WILLIAM CARL, sports columnist; b. Carmi, Ill., Feb. 10, 1938; s. Clyde William and Harriet Kathryn (Murphy) L.; m. Ethel Gay Slade, Nov. 6, 1964; children—James Charles, John William. Student, Western Mil. Acad., Alton, Ill., 1956; B.S. in Liberal Arts, U. Ill., Champaign, 1961. Feature writer, sports writer, police reporter Champaign-Urbana News-Gazette, 1956-66; sports writer, gen. columnist Evansville (Ind.) Courier & Press, 1966-69; mng. editor East St. Louis (Ill.) Metro-East Jour., 1969-71, Champaign-Urbana News-Gazette, 1971-72; bus. editor Phila. Inquirer, 1972-73, sports writer, syndicated columnist, 1973—; Author: It's All in the Game, We Owed You One; contbr. numerous articles to mags. in U.S. and Can.; TV commentary twice weekly. Served with inf. U.S. Army, 1961. Named Sportswriter of the Yr., State of Pa., 1977, 79-85; recipient 73 state and nat. awards for writing, Best Newspaper Writing award Am. Soc. Newspaper Editors, 1980, Nat. Headliner award, 1988; inducted into Pa. Sports Hall of Fame, 1989. Mem. Baseball Writers Am., Profl. Hockey Writers Assn., Football Writers Assn. Am., Sigma Delta Chi. Methodist. Home: 89 Cherry Hill Ln Broomall PA 19008-1508 Office: Phila Inquirer 400 N Broad St Philadelphia PA 19130-4015

LYONS, BRIAN WESLEY, marketing professional; b. Houston, Oct. 6, 1950; s. Alva Lyons Jr. and Alice Elaine (Jones) Reitz; m. Rita Perrin, July 10, 1976; children: Ashley, Brooke, Caitlin. AA, U. Houston, 1972. Sales rep. Burke Concrete Assoc., Houston, 1972-75, Vallen Corp. Safety Equipment, Houston, 1975-76; gen. sales mgr. Vallen Safety Corp./Encon Mfg. Div., Houston, 1976-79; gen. mgr. Delta Safety & Supply, Houston, 1979-81; gen. mgr., CEO Tex. Firefighters and Safety Equipment, New Braunfels, Tex., 1981-88; v.p. sales and mktg. Std. Safety Equipment Co., Palatine, Ill., 1991-93; dir. N.Am. Sales Kappler Safety Group, Guntersville, Ala., 1993—; cons. Houston, 1988-90; cons., mfg. rep. Hale Fire Pump/Tex. Fire Rescue, Houston,, 1987-89; mem. Scott Aviation Dist. Adv. Coun., 1992—; instr. Tex. A&M Indsl. Fire Sch., College Station, 1976—. Mem. Wurstfest Assn., New Braunfels, 1983-88; chmn. Ducks Unltd., New Braunfels, 1985; officer Am. Heart Assn., New Braunfels, 1985-87. Mem. ASSE, Nat. Fire Protection Assn. (voting mem. com. on chem. protection clothing stds. 1992—), Indsl. Safety Equipment Assn. (chmn. task force developing indsl. stds. chem. protective clothing, Internat. Fire Instrs. Assn., Rotary. Roman Catholic. Avocations: golf, hunting, fishing, reading, snow skiing. Home: 5505 Cedar Mill Dr Guntersville AL 35976-2961 Office: Kappler Safety Group 18 Grimes Dr Guntersville AL 35976-9380

LYONS, CHAMP, JR., lawyer; b. Boston, Dec. 6, 1940; m. Emily Lee Oswalt, 1967; children—Emily Olive, Champ III. A.B., Harvard U., 1962; LL.B., U. Ala., 1965. Bar: Ala. 1965, U.S. Supreme Ct. 1973. Law clk. U.S. Dist. Ct., Mobile, Ala., 1965-67; assoc. Capell, Howard, Knabe & Cobbs, Montgomery, Ala., 1967-70; ptnr. Capell, Howard, Knabe & Cobbs, 1970-76, Helmsing, Lyons, Sims & Leach, Mobile, 1976—; mem. adv. commn. on civil procedure Ala. Supreme Ct., 1971—, chmn., 1985—. Author: Alabama Practice, 1973, 3d edit., 1996; contbr. articles to law jours. Mem. ABA, Ala. Bar Assn., Mobile Bar Assn. (pres. 1991), Am. Law Inst., Ala. Law Inst., Farrah Law Soc., Harvard U. Alumni Assn. (S.E. regional dir. 1988-91, v.p.-at-large 1992-94, 1st v.p. 1994-95, pres. 1995-96). Home: PO Box 1033 Point Clear AL 36564-1033 Office: Helmsing Lyons Sims & Leach 200 LaClede Bldg PO Box 2767 Mobile AL 36652-2767

LYONS, CHARLES, professional hockey team executive. Gov., pres. Colo. Avalanche, Denver. Office: Colorado Avalanche 1635 Clay St Denver CO 80204-1743*

LYONS, CHARLES R., drama educator and critic; b. Glendale, Calif., Apr. 27, 1933; s. James Grey and Daphne Mae (Burlingham) L.; m. Leila B. Phee, Dec. 22, 1956; children: John Christopher, James Charles. AB, Stanford U., 1955, AM, 1956, PhD, 1964. Asst. prof. Principia Coll., Elsah, Ill., 1964-68; assoc. prof. U. Calif., Berkeley, 1968-72, prof., assoc. dean, 1972-73; prof., chmn. Stanford (Calif.) U., 1973-85, Margery Bailey prof. english and dramatic lit., 1985—, chmn. grad. studies in drama, 1985-95, chmn. dept. drama, 1995—, chmn. Arts and Tech. Initiative, 1994—; vis. prof. Washington U., St. Louis, 1966. Author: Brecht: Despair and Polemic, 1968, Shakespeare and the Ambiguity of Love's Triumph, 1971, Ibsen: the Divided Consciousness, 1972, Samuel Beckett, 1983; editor: Critical Essays on Henrik Ibsen, 1987, Hedda Gabler: Gender, Role, and World, 1990; editorial bd. Comparative Drama, Kalamazoo, Mich., 1977—, Jour. Dramatic, Lit. and Theory, Lawrence, Kans, 1986—. Bd. dirs. San Francisco Archives for Performing Arts, 1985—. Served to lt. USNR, 1956-60. Recipient Younger Scholar award NEH, 1968; Guggenheim Found. fellow, 1977. Mem. Modern Language Assn., Samuel Beckett Soc. Democrat. Home: 728 Tolman Dr Palo Alto CA 94305-1045 Office: Stanford U Dept Drama Mail Code MC 5010 Stanford CA 94305*

LYONS, DAVID BARRY, philosophy and law educator; b. N.Y.C., Feb. 6, 1935; s. Joseph and Betty (Janower) L.; m. Sandra Yetta Nemiroff, Dec. 18, 1955; children—Matthew, Emily, Jeremy. Student, Cooper Union, 1952-54, 56-57; B.A., Bklyn. Coll., 1960; M.A. (Gen. Electric Found. fellow), Harvard U., 1963, Ph.D. (Woodrow Wilson dissertation fellow), 1963; postgrad., Oxford (Eng.) U., 1963-64. Asst. prof. philosophy Cornell U., Ithaca, N.Y., 1964-67; asso. prof. Cornell U., 1967-71, prof. philosophy, 1971-90, Susan Linn Sage prof. philosophy, 1990-95; chmn. dept. philosophy, 1978-84; prof. law, 1979-95, Boston U., 1995—. Author: Forms and Limits of Utilitarianism, 1965, In the Interest of the Governed, 1973, Ethics and the Rule of Law, 1984, Moral Aspects of Legal Theory, 1993, Rights, Welfare, and Mill's Moral Theory, 1994; editor: Philos Rev., 1968-70, 73-75. Recipient Clark award Cornell U., 1976; Woodrow Wilson hon. fellow, 1960-61, Knox travelling fellow, 1963-64; Guggenheim fellow, 1970-71, Soc. for Humanities fellow, 1972-73, Nat. Endowment for Humanities fellow, 1977-78, 84-85, 93-94. Mem. Am. Philos. Assn., Am. Soc. Polit. and Legal Philosophy, Soc. Philosophy and Pub. Affairs. Office: Boston U Law Sch 765 Commonwealth Ave Boston MA 02215-1401

LYONS, DENNIS GERALD, lawyer; b. Passaic, N.J., Nov. 20, 1931; s. Denis A.G. and Agnes C. (Dyt) L.; m. Anna Maria Nuñez, 1983; 1 child, Alexandra; children by previous marriage: Andrew, Sarah, Tessa. A.B., Holy Cross Coll., 1952; J.D., Harvard U., 1955. Bar: D.C. 1955, N.Y. 1956, U.S. Supreme Ct 1960. Law clk. U.S. Supreme Ct., Washington, 1958-60; assoc. firm Arnold & Porter, Washington, 1960-62; ptnr. Arnold & Porter, 1963—; v.p., gen. counsel, dir. Gulf United Corp., Jacksonville, Fla., 1968-80; asst. sec. Braniff Airways, Dallas, 1966-77; trustee GMR Properties, Boston, 1971-81; dir. Gulf Broadcast Co., Dallas, 1983-86; vis. prof. law U. Va., Charlottesville, 1982-83; Pres. Harvard Law Rev., 1954-55. Served with USAF, 1955-58. Mem. ABA, Am. Law Inst. Office: Arnold & Porter 555 12th St NW Washington DC 20004-1200

LYONS, ELLIS, retired lawyer; b. Scranton, Pa., Mar. 24, 1915; s. Charles and Anna (Abrams) L.; m. Anita Chester, June 12, 1952; children: Charles, Cathy. Student, U. Scranton, 1933-34; A.B. (Coll. scholar), Oberlin Coll., 1936; J.D. (Univ. fellow), Northwestern U., 1939; LL.D. hon., Pa. Coll. Optometry, 1983. Bar: D.C. 1939, U.S. Supreme Ct 1946. Atty. Dept. Justice, 1940-43; spl. asst. to U.S. Atty. Gen., 1945-50; chief legal cons. U.S. Dept. Justice, 1950-53; acting asst. atty. gen. U.S., 1952-53; partner firm Perlman, Lyons and Emmerglick (and predecessors), Washington, 1953-65, Volpe, Boskey and Lyons, Washington, 1965-96; of counsel, 1995-96; instr. bus. law Am. U., 1963-66; gen. counsel Am. Optometric Assn., 1968-94; gen. counsel, sec. Am. Automotive Leasing Assn., 1960-93, Equipment Leasing Assn. Am., 1961-94. Served to lt. USCG, 1943-45. Mem. D.C. Bar, Bar Assn. D.C., Fed. Bar Assn., Am. Bar Assn., Am. Law Inst., Phi Beta Kappa, Tau Epsilon Rho. Home: 4101 Blackthorn St Chevy Chase MD 20815-5053

LYONS, GENE MARTIN, political scientist, educator; b. Revere, Mass., Feb. 29, 1924; s. Abraham M. and Mary (Karger) L.; m. Micheline Pohl, Sept. 5, 1951; children—Catherine Anne, Daniel Eugene, Mark Lucien. B.A., Tufts Coll., 1947; license en Scis. Politiques, Grad. Inst. Internat. Studies, Geneva, Switzerland, 1949; Ph.D., Columbia, 1958. Mgmt. officer Internat. Refugee Orgn., Geneva, 1948-52; budget and adminstrv. officer UN Korean Reconstrn. Agy., 1952-56; mem. faculty Dartmouth Coll., 1957-94, prof. govt., 1965-94, dir. Pub. Affairs Center, 1961-66, 73-75, asso. dean faculty social scis., 1974-78; rsch. fellow Dickey Ctr. Dartmouth Coll., Hanover, N.H., 1994—; vis. lectr. Sch. Mgmt. MIT, 1961-70; exec. sec. adv. com. govt. program behavioral scis. Nat. Acad. Scis., 1966-68; dir. dept. social scis. UNESCO, 1970-72; mem. U.S. Nat. Commn. for UNESCO, 1975-80, vice chmn., 1977-78; adv. U.S. del. UNESCO 19th Gen. Conf., 1976, 20th Gen. Conf., 1978; U.S. rep. to UNESCO European Conf., 1977; prof. associé U. Paris I, 1986; exec. dir. acad. council on the UN system, 1987-92. Author: Military Policy and Economic Aid: The Korean Case, 1961; co-author: (with J.W. Masland) Education and Military Leadership, 1959, (with L. Morton) Schools for Strategy, 1965, The Uneasy Partnership, 1969; Editor: Social Research and Public Policies, 1975; editor, contbr. America: Purpose and Power, 1965, Social Science and the Federal Government, 1971; co-editor, contbr. Beyond Westphalia?, 1995, The United Nations System: The Policies of Member States, 1995. Served with AUS, 1943-46. Mem. Acad. Coun. on UN System, Internat. Studies Assn., Coun. on Fgn. Rels. Home: Main St Norwich VT 05055 Office: Dartmouth Coll Dickey Ctr Hanover NH 03755

LYONS, GEORGE SAGE, lawyer, oil industry executive, former state legislator; b. Mobile, Ala., Oct. 1, 1936; s. Mark, Jr. and Ruth (Kelly) L.; m. Elsie Crain, Feb. 5, 1960; children: George Sage, Amelia C. B.A. in Econs, Washington and Lee U., Lexington, Va., 1958; LL.B., U. Ala., 1960. Bar: Ala. 1960. Assoc. Lyons, Pipes & Cook, Mobile, 1963-66; ptnr. Lyons, Pipes & Cook, 1966-82, sr. ptnr., 1982-87; pres. Lyons, Pipes & Cook, P.C., 1987-95, LPC Oil Co., Inc., 1988—, Amelia Land Co., Inc., 1978—; chmn., dir. Crain Oil Co., Inc., Guntersville, Ala., 1975—; commr. Ala. Dept. Rev., 1996; dir., CFO Ala. Dept. Finance, 1996—; dir. Jordan Industries, Inc., State Docks; mem. exec. com. Ala. Petroleum Coun.; mem. Tenn.-Tombigbee Waterway Devel. Authority, 1966-70, 91-95; chmn. Ala. Commn. on Higher Edn., 1971-78. Trustee 11th cir. Hist. Soc. Served to capt., JAGC U.S. Army, 1960-62. Decorated Army Commendation medal. Fellow Am. Bar Found., Nat. Assn. Bond Lawyers, Coun. Ala. Law Inst., Farrah Law Soc. (trustee); mem. Am., Ala., Mobile County bar assns., Mid-Continent Oil and Gas Assn. (dir. Ala.-Miss. div.), Maritime Law Assn. U.S., Omicron Delta Kappa, Phi Delta Phi. Episcopalian. Home: 107 Carmel Dr E Mobile AL 36608-2479 Office: 5 Itacon St Mobile AL 36670-0414

LYONS, HARVEY ISAAC, mechanical engineering educator; b. N.Y.C., Sept. 26, 1931; s. Joseph and Betty (Janower) L.; m. Rebecca Anne Szeman, June 10, 1978; children: Neal Joshua, Leslie Eve. Cert. in indsl. design, Pratt Inst., 1952; BSME, The Cooper Union, 1962, ME in Mech. Engring., 1971; PhD in Mech. Engring., Ohio State U., 1978. Registered profl. engr., N.Y. From design engr. to sr. mech. engr. various orgns., N.Y.C., 1962-72; assoc. prof. mech. engring. Mont. State U., Bozeman, 1978-79, U. Wis.-Parkside, Kenosha, 1979-81, U. N.H., Durham, 1981-84, Seattle U., 1984-85; chmn. dept. mech. engring. Alfred (N.Y.) U., 1985-88; chair dept. mech. engring. Union Coll., Schenectady, 1988-92, Ind. Inst. Tech., Ft. Wayne, 1992-95; cons. engr. in pvt. practice Ft. Wayne, Ind., 1995—. Contbr. articles to profl. jours. Sgt. U.S. Army, 1952-54, Korea. Mem. ASME, NSPE, Am. Soc. Engring. Edn., Soc. Mfg. Engrs. Achievements include development of methods to investigate tribological phenomenon of Fretting-Wear in-situ, towards development of failure prediction criteria, development of mechanical engineering departments in industry and academe. Avocations: skiing, flying, karate, tennis, backpacking. Home and Office: 6303 Alvarez Dr Fort Wayne IN 46815-7001

LYONS, J. ROLLAND, civil engineer; b. Cedar Rapids, Iowa, Apr. 27, 1909; s. Neen T. and Goldie N. (Hill) L.; BS, U. Iowa, 1933; m. Mary Jane Doht, June 10, 1924; children: Marlene R. Sparks, Sharon K. Hutson, Mary Lynn Lyons. Jr. hwy. engr. Works Projects Adminstrn. field engr. Dept. Transp., State Ill., Peoria, 1930-31, civil engr. I-IV Cen. Office, Springfield, 1934-53, civil engr. V, 1953-66, municipal sect. chief, civil engr. VI, 1966-72. Civil Def. radio officer Springfield and Sangamon County (Ill.) Civil Def. Agy., 1952—. Recipient Meritorious Service award Am. Assn. State Hwy. Ofcls., 1968, 25 Yr. Career Service award State Ill., 1966, Cert. Appreciation Ill. Mcpl. League, 1971. Registered profl. engr., Ill.; registered land surveyor, Ill. Mem. NSPE, Nat. Soc. Profl. Engrs., Ill. Soc. Profl. Engrs., Ill. Assn. State Hwy. Engrs., State Ill. Employees Assn., Am. Pub. Works Assn., Am. Assn. State Hwy. Ofcls., Amateur Trapshooters Assn., Sangamon Valley Radio Club, Lakewood Golf and Country Club, KC, Abe Lincoln Gun Club, South Fork Conservation Club (Ill.). Address: 3642 Lancaster Rd Springfield IL 62703-5022

LYONS, JAMES EDWARD, publishing executive; b. N.Y.C., Feb. 7, 1952; s. James Vincent and Audrey Lucille (Garbers) L.; m. Blythe Mitchell Jones, June 6, 1981; children: James Edward Jr., Michael Davidson. BA cum laude, Bowdoin Coll., 1974. Advanceman and legis. asst. to Congressman William S. Cohen of Maine Washington, 1972-75; pub. Univ. Press Am., Lanham, Md., 1975—, also dir.; pres. Madison Books, Inc., 1986—, Univ. Pub. Assocs. Inc., 1986—, Rowman and Littlefield Pubs., Inc., 1988—, Barnes and Noble Books, 1988—, Littlefield, Adams Quality Paperbacks, 1988—, Nat. Book Network, Inc., 1986—, Scarecrow Press, Inc., 1995—; mem. nat. adv. com. to sec. HEW, 1974; panelist U.S. Dept. Edn., 1986-87; mem. USIA book and libr. adv. com., 1981-93. Mem. Statue of Liberty-Ellis Island Centennial Commn., 1986-89; Presdl. appointee Nat. Commn. on Librs. and Info. Sci., 1991-93; trustee Georgetown U. Libr., 1981-92. Mem. Assn. Am. Pubs. (exec. coun. profl. and scholarly pub. div. 1990-93, coll. div. faculty rels. com.), Soc. Scholarly Pubs. (chmn. publs. com. 1979-80), Coun. on Fgn. Rels., Young Pres. Orgn. (bd. dirs 1994—), Rolling Rock Club (Ligonier, Pa.), Psi Upsilon. Presbyterian. Home: 4812 Tilden St NW Washington DC 20016-2330 Office: Univ Press Am Inc 4720 Boston Way Lanham Seabrook MD 20706-4310

LYONS, JAMES ROBERT, federal official. BS in Forest and Wildlife Mgmt. with high honors, Rutgers U., 1977; M in Forestry, Yale U., 1979. Program analyst U.S. Fish and Wildlife Svc. Dept. Interior, 1979-82; dir. resource policy Soc. Am. Foresters, Bethesda, Md., 1982-86; staff dir. sub-com. forests, family farms, engergy Com. Agriculture, 1986, staff asst. com. agr., 1987-93; asst. sec. agr. natural resources and environ. USDA, Washington, 1993—, under sec. natural resources and environment; agrl. advisor Cong. Leon Panetta, 1989-91. Office: USDA Natural Resources & Environment 14th & Independence Ave SW Washington DC 20250-0002

LYONS, JERRY LEE, mechanical engineer; b. St. Louis, Apr. 2, 1939; s. Ferd H. and Edna T. Lyons. Diploma in Mech. Engring., Okla. Inst. Tech., 1964; MSME, S.W. U., 1983; PhD in Engring. Mgmt., Southwest U., 1984. Registered profl. engr., Calif. Project engr. Harris Mfg. Co., St. Louis, 1965-70, Essex Cryogenics Industries, St. Louis, 1963-65, 70-73; mgr. engring. rsch. Chemetron Corp., St. Louis, 1973-77; cons. fluid controls Wis. U., 1977—; pres., chief exec. Yankee Ingenuity, Inc., St. Louis, 1974—; v.p., gen. mgr. engring. R & D Essex Fluid Controls divsn. Essex Industries, Inc., St. Louis, 1977-90; pres. Lyons Pub. Co., St. Louis, 1983—; pres., CEO Innovative Controls subs. Yankee Ingenuity, Inc., Ft. Wayne, Ind., 1991—; chmn. exec. bd. continuing engring. edn. in St. Louis for U. Mo., Columbia, 1980-81; bd. dirs. Intertech., Inc., Houston; cons. fluid power dept. Bradley U., Peoria, 1977-84. Author: Home Study Series Course on Actuators and Accessories, 1977, The Valve Designers Handbook, 1983, The Lyons' Encyclopedia of Valves, 1975, 93, The Designers Handbook of Pressure Sensing Devices, 1980, Special Process Applications, 1980; co-author: Handbook of Product Liability, 1991; contbr. articles to profl. jours.; patentee in field. With USAF, 1957-62. Recipient Winston Churchill medal, 1988, Dwight D. Eisenhower Achievement award of honor, 1990; named Businessman of Week (KEZK radio), Eminent Churchill fellow Winston Churchill Wisdom Soc. Fellow ASME; mem. N.Y. Acad. Scis., Soc. Mfg. Engrs. (cert. product design, chmn. Mo. registration com. 1975-90, chmn. St. Louis chpt. 1979-80, internat. dir. 1982-84, 85-87, engr. of yr. 1984, internat. award of merit 1985), Nat. Soc. Profl. Engrs., Mo. Soc. Profl. Engrs., St. Louis Soc. Mfg. Engrs. (chmn. profl. devel., registration and cert. com. 1975-79), Instrument Soc. Am. (control valve stability com. 1978-84), Computer and Automated Sys. Assn. (1st chmn. St. Louis chpt. 1980-81), St. Louis Engrs. Club (award of merit 1977, wisdom award of honor 1987, Wisdom Hall of Fame 1987), Am. Security Coun. (committeeman 1976—), Nat. Fluid Power Assn. (com. on pressure ratings 1975-77), Am. Legion. Lutheran. Achievements include patentee in field. Home and Office: 2607 Northgate Blvd Fort Wayne IN 46835-2986

LYONS, JOHN DAVID, French, Italian and comparative literature educator; b. Springfield, Mass., Oct. 14, 1946; s. John Joseph and Loretta Francis (Feighery) L.; m. Patricia Stuart, July 31, 1971; 1 dau., Jennifer Catherine. A.B., Brown U., 1967; M.A., Yale U., 1968, Ph.D., 1972. Asst. prof. French, Italian and comparative lit. Dartmouth Coll., Hanover, N.H., 1972-78, assoc. prof., 1978-82, prof., 1982-87, chmn. comparative lit. program, 1981-84, chmn., prof. dept. French and Italian, 1987; dir. Am. Univ. Ctr. for Film and Critical Studies, Paris, 1984-85; prof. French U. Va., Charlottesville, 1987-92, Commonwealth prof. French, 1993—, chmn. dept., 1989-92. Author: A Theatre of Disguise, 1978, The Listening Voice, 1982, Exemplum, 1989, The Tragedy of Origins, 1996; co-editor: Mimesis: Mirror to Method, 1982, Dialectic of Discovery, 1983, Critical Tales, 1993; editor: Art, Architecture, Text: The Late Renaissance, 1985; assoc. editor Continuum, 1987-93; editor Academe, 1994-97; editl. adv. bd. Philosophy and Literature. Recipient Robert Fish award for teaching Dartmouth Coll., 1978, Outstanding Tchr. award U. Va., 1996; Woodrow Wilson fellow, 1967, ACLS study fellow, 1978, NEH fellow, 1985-89, 92-93, Ctr. for Advanced Studies U. Va. fellow, 1987-89. Office: U Va Dept French Lang & Lit Charlottesville VA 22903

LYONS, JOHN MATTHEW, telecommunications executive, broadcasting executive; b. N.Y.C., Nov. 5, 1948; s. Matthew Joseph and Anna (Coroneos) L.; m. Natalia Astakhova, Apr. 12, 1992; 1 child, Matthew. BSEE, Roosevelt U., Chgo., 1970, MSEE, 1976; BSE, Century U., L.A., 1981, MBA in Engring. Mgmt., 1982; PhD in Communications, Loyola U., Chgo., 1979; PhD in Broadcasting (hon.), Sicluna U. Found., 1987. Registered profl. engr. Engr., producer Sta. WRFM, N.Y.C., 1965-69; sr. facilities planning and project engr. Sta. WWRL-Radio, N.Y.C., 1969-76; sr. facilities planning, project engr. Sta. WWRL/WRVR, N.Y.C., 1976-78; asst. chief engr. Sta. WOR, Inc., N.Y.C., 1978-80; chief engr. Sta. WRKS-FM, N.Y.C., 1980-90; sr. project mgr. DSI Communications, Kenilworth, N.J., (now known as DSI RF Systems Inc., Somerset, N.J.), 1990-94; sr. project mgr., Vista Engring. Corp., N.Y.C., 1994—; pvt. cons., 1994—; dir. Raritan Ctr. Internat. Teleport, N.J., 1992-94; chief engr. Sta. WLTW/WAXQ, 1996—; ind. broadcasting cons., 1994—; pres. Lyon Records, N.Y., 1971—, Short Lines Co., N.Y., 1980—; chmn. master antenna com. Empire State Bldg., N.Y., 1980-88; bd. dirs. The Document Ctr., N.Y.; cons. broadcasting and telecommunications; ofcl. photographer U.S. Imperial Soc. Tchrs. of Dance, 1991—, Blackpool Dance Festival, 1992—; dir. Raritan Ctr. Internat. Teleport, 1994. Producer: (radio broadcast) The Cuban Missile Crisis, 1962 (Peabody award 1963); exec. producer: (broadcast series) Radio: The First 50 Years, 1970, Sta. WOR 60th Anniversary Program, 1982 (Armstrong award 1983, Internat. Radio Festival award 1983), Sta. WOR 65th Anniversary Program, 1987; photography editor Amateur Dancers mag., Ability Mag.; contbg. photographer to Dance Scene mag., Dance News, Eng.; photographer Dance Beat, U.S.A., Australian Dance Rev., Dance Action, U.S.A., Japan Dance News, U.S. Imperial Soc. Tchrs. of Dance, 1991—. Chmn. media curriculum com. Westchester Community Coll., N.Y., 1987—; v.p. U.S. Amateur Ballroom Dancers Assn., 1987-89. With USAF, 1967-70. Fellow Soc. Broadcast Engrs. (sr., cert., bd. dirs. 1974-78), Internat. Biog. Assn.; mem. Nat. Assn. Radio and Telecommunications Engrs. (cert.), Broadcast Music, Inc., Audio Engring. Soc., IEEE, Internat. Radio and TV Soc., VA Hosp. Radio and TV Guild (v.p. 1976-82, 84—, pres. 1982-84, chmn. exec. com. 1984—, Bennie award 1981), Broadcast Pioneers, Am. Soc. Composers, Authors, and Pubs., Broadcast Music, Am. Inst. Plant Engrs., U.S. Amateur Ballroom Dancers Assn. (regional v.p. 1987-89, dir. for internat. liaison 1989—), Knights of Malta, 1986. Avocation: competitive ballroom dancing, photography. Home: 305 E 86th St New York NY 10028-4702 Office: WLTW/WAXQ 1515 Broadway New York NY 10036

LYONS, JOHN W(INSHIP), government official, chemist; b. Reading, Mass., Nov. 5, 1930. A.B. in Chemistry, Harvard U., 1952; A.M. in Phys. Chemistry, Washington U., St. Louis, 1963, Ph.D. in Phys. Chemistry, 1964. With Monsanto Co., 1955-73, group leader, sect. mgr. research dept., inorganic chems. div., 1962-69, mgr. comml. devel., head fire safety center, 1969-73; mem. ad hoc panel on fire research Nat. Bur. Standards, Washington, 1971-73; dir. Center for Fire Research, 1973-77, Inst. Applied Tech., 1977-78, Nat. Engring. Lab., 1978-89; acting dep. dir. Nat. Bur. Standards, 1983; dir. Nat. Inst. Standards and Tech., Gaithersburg, Md., 1990-93, Army Rsch. Lab., Adelphi, Md., 1993—; chmn. Products Rsch. Com. (trust which adminstrs. fire rsch. fund), 1974-79; vis. lectr. various univs.; co-chmn. U.S.-Japan Natural Resources Panel on Fire Rsch., 1975-78; mem. adv. com. on engring NSF, 1981-90; mem. bd. visitors U. Md. Coll. Engring., 1980-90; mem. adv. com. Naval Rsch. Lab., 1985; mem. com. on fed. labs. Office Sci. and Tech. Policy. Author: Viscosity and Flow Measurement, 1963, The Chemistry and Uses of Fire Retardants, 1970; Fire, 1985; contbr. numerous articles to profl. publs. Chmn. blue ribbon com. on rsch. and pub. svc. U. Md., 1993. Recipient gold medal Dept. Commerce, 1977, President's Mgmt. Improvement award White House, 1977, President's Disting. Exec. Rank award, 1981, E.U. Condon award, 1986; Disting. Svc. award U. Md. Coll. Engring., 1990, Centennial medal, 1994; 1st ann. Outstanding Achievement award Fire Retardant Chem. Assn., 1994. Fellow AAAS, Washington Acad. Sci.; mem. Am. Chem. Soc. (chmn. St. Louis sect. 1971-72), Nat. Fire Protection Assn. (bd. dirs. 1978-84), ASTM (bd. dirs. 1985-87), Nat. Acad. Engring., Sigma Xi. Office: Army Rsch Lab 2800 Powder Mill Rd Adelphi MD 20783-1145

LYONS, LAURENCE, securities executive; b. Jersey City, Aug. 11, 1911; s. Louis and Teresa (Serge) L.; m. Gertrude Starr, Sept. 1, 1945 (dec.); 1 son, Jonathan. BS, NYU, 1934, postgrad., 1935. Securities analyst Allen & Co., N.Y.C., 1935-52; with Allen Co., Inc., N.Y.C., 1952—, sr. v.p., 1989—. Mem. Soc. Security Analysts. Home: 1 Kensington Gate Apt 221 Great Neck NY 11021-1229 Office: Allen & Co Inc 711 5th Ave New York NY 10022-3111

LYONS, NATALIE BELLER, family counselor; b. Habana, Cuba, Apr. 3, 1926; d. Herman Lawrence and Jennie (Engler) B.; widowed, Apr. 18, 1986; children: Anne, Sara. BS, degree in surveying/land Appraising, Inst. Vedado, Habana, Cuba, 1943; BA, U. Mich., 1946; MEd, U. Miami, Fla., 1967. Family counselor, mem. staff furniture design and mfg. co. George B. Bent Co., Gardner, Mass., 1953-58; tchr. H.S., Winchendon, Mass., Hollywood, Fla., 1962; tchr. parochial sch., Ft. Lauderdale, Fla., 1963-64; family counselor Miami, 1967—; project dir. Cen. Am. fisheries program Peace Corps, 1972-74; counselor Svc. Corp. of Ret. Execs., Miami, 1993, bd. dirs., 1994—; bd. dirs., mem. Com. for Accuracy in Mid East Reporting, 1990—. Pres. Miami region Hadassah, 1989-91; bd. dirs. Greater Miami Jewish Fedn., 1985—, mem. women's divsn., mem. cmty. rels. coun., 1985—; bd. dirs. Miami Civic Music Assn., Fedn.'s Cmty. Rels. Coun., 1985—; mem. nat. bd. dirs. nat. women's divsn. Am. Soc. for Technion, 1991—; co-chair Pro-Israel Rally, Tri County, 1991, Joint Action Com., Miami, 1989-91; tng. dir. Los Amigos de las Ams., 1975—; founder, dir. Cmty. Inst. Jewish Studies, Hollywood, Fla., 1962-64. Recipient Leadership award Hadassah, 1987, honoree Am. Soc. for Technion Scholarship Fund, 1991; named Woman of Yr., Hadassah, 1991. Mem. Israel Inst. Tech. (pres. so. region 1996—). Democrat. Avocations: travel, reading, antiques, family, performing arts.

LYONS, PAUL MICHAEL, producer, film; b. Washington, Aug. 21, 1932; s. Thomas William and Nora (Bagley) L.; m. Bernadette Marie O'Rourke, Oct. 24, 1953; children—Stephen W., Loretta N., Sharon D. Student, Georgetown U., 1950-52. V.p. Charlie Papa Prodns., Rockville, Md., 1972-79; v.p., gen. mgr. Capital Film Labs., Washington, 1979-81; pres., chief exec. officer Am. Bus. Media Council, Inc., Washington, 1982-83; v.p., owner Images and Ideas, Vienna, Va., 1967—; exec. dir. Occupational Safety and Health Rev. Commn., Washington, 1984-90; dir. mktg. Nat. Empowerment TV, Washington, 1993—. Film editor Treasures of King Tut, 1977 (nominated Academy award); prodn. mgr. (film) Carry the Fire, Olympic Torch Relay, 1984. Mem. Vienna Town Council, 1968-76; chmn. Bicentennial Commn., Vienna, 1971-76; mem. Fairfax County Rep. Com., Va., 1978-84. Recipient Disting. Service award Jaycees of Vienna, 1965; named Citizen of the Yr. Vienna C. of C., 1976. Mem. Council on Internat. Nontheatrical Events (mem. adv. bd. 1979-92), Council on Nat. Policy (bd. govs. 1982—), Soc. Motion Picture & TV Engrs. (bd. mgrs.), White House News Photographers Assn. (pres. 1990-92), Washington Film Council (pres. 1982-83). Roman Catholic. Home: 603 Upham Pl NW Vienna VA 22180-4128*

LYONS, PAUL VINCENT, lawyer; b. Boston, July 19, 1939; s. Joseph Vincent and Doris Irene (Griffin) L.; m. Elaine Marie Hurley, July 13, 1968; children: Judith Marie, Maureen Patricia, Paula Anne, Joseph Hurley. BS cum laude, Boston Coll., 1960; MBA, NYU, 1962; JD, Suffolk U., Boston, 1968. Bar: Mass. 1968, U.S. Ct. Ct. (1st cir.) 1969, U.S. Supreme Ct. 1991. Div. adminstrn. mgr. Pepsi-Cola Co., N.Y.C., 1962-64; mem. bus. faculty Burdett Coll., Boston, 1964-68; atty. NLRB, Boston, 1968-73; assoc. Foley, Hoag & Eliot, Boston, 1973-77, ptnr., 1978—; mem. faculty Boston U., 1972-74. Mem. Town Meeting, Milton, Mass., 1986—, mem. pers. bd., 1994—. Lt. U.S. Army, 1960-62. Mem. ABA, Mass. Bar Assn., Boston Bar Assn. Office: Foley Hoag & Eliot 1 Post Office Sq Boston MA 02109

LYONS, THOMAS PATRICK, economics educator; b. Groton, Conn., Sept. 8, 1953. BA in Asian Studies, Cornell U., 1979, MA in Econs., 1982, PhD in Econs., 1983. Asst. prof. econs. Dartmouth Coll., Hanover, N.H., 1983-87; vis. asst. prof. Cornell U., Ithaca, N.Y., 1986-88, asst. prof., 1988-91; assoc. prof., 1991—; dir. East Asia program Cornell U., Ithaca, N.Y., 1991-94; dir. undergrad. studies, econs., 1995—. Author: Economic Integration and Planning in Maoist China, 1987, China's War on Poverty, 1992, Economic Geography of Fujian: A Sourcebook, 1995; contbr.

numerous articles to profl. jours. With USN, 1972-76. Rsch. grantee Ford Found., 1987. Mem. Am. Econ. Assn., Assn. for Asian Studies. Office: Cornell U Dept Econs Uris Hall Ithaca NY 14853-7601

LYONS, WILLIAM CLAYPOOL, engineering educator and consultant; b. Bronxville, N.Y., Nov. 26, 1937; s. Thomas Edward and Lucile (Marks) L.; m. Alahna Carter Weller, Feb. 25, 1961 (div. July 1980); children: Andrew W., Terrence W., Dale W. BS in Geol. Engring., U. Kans., Lawrence, 1961, MS in Engring. Mechanics, 1962, PhD, 1965. Registered profl. engr., N.Mex. Jr. engr. Phillips Petroleum Co., Bartlesville, Okla., 1961-62; instr. U. Kans., Lawrence, 1962-64; postdoctoral fellow Northwestern U., Evanston, Ill., 1964-65; staff mem. Sandia Nat. Lab., Albuquerque, 1965-69; asst. group leader Los Alamos (N.Mex.) Nat. Lab., 1969-76; tech. asst. to dir. U.S. ERDA/Fuel Cycle, Germantown, Md., 1976-77; pres. Rift Pneumatics Inc., Farmington, N.Mex., 1977-80; prof. N.Mex. Inst. Mining Tech., Socorro, 1977—; adj. prof. U. N.Mex., Albuquerque, 1966-68; rsch. fellow Polish Acad. Sci., Warsaw, 1963-64; Disting. vis. prof. U.S. Air Force Acad., Colorado Springs, 1993-94. Author: Air and Gas Drilling Manual, 1984; author, editor: Standard Handbook of Petroleum and Natural Gas Engineering, 1996. Soccer referee NCAA, 1975-85. With USMCR, 1955-61. Recipient Energy Innovation award U.S. Dept. Energy, 1988. Mem. ASCE, NSPE, Soc. Petroleum Engrs., Am. Soc. Engring. Edn. Achievements include patents for drilling devices. Avocations: fishing, skiing, writing. Home: 1008 Rocky Rd Socorro NM 87801-4484 Office: NMex Inst Mining Tech Dept Petroleum Engring MSEC Bldg Rm 300 Socorro NM 87801

LYSHAK-STELZER, FRANCIE, artist; b. Detroit, June 3, 1948; d. Peter Paul and Frances Ellen (Harrington) Lyshak; m. Stephen Stelzer, Oct. 10, 1994. BFA, Wayne State U., 1970; MPS, Pratt Inst., 1978. Art therapist Creative Women's Collective, N.Y.C., 1978-79; asst. activities dir., dir. art therapy internship tng. Bronx Children's Psychiat. Ctr., 1979—. One woman shows include La Mama La Galleria, N.Y.C., 1993, 96, Pvt. Exhibn., N.Y.C., 1990, Claire Dunphy's Studio, N.Y.C., 1985, Wow Theatre/Gallery, N.Y.C., 1983, Bill Rice Studio, N.Y.C., 1984, 88; group shows include Art Quest 86, L.A., Mus. of the Hudson Highlands, N.Y., 1985, Interart de St. Armand Gallery, 1983, Park Ave. Atrium, 1984, Cash/Newhouse Gallery, 1985, Marymount Manhattan Coll. Gallery, 1989, La Mama La Galleria, N.Y.C., 1985, 86, 92, Denise Bibro Fine Art, N.Y.C., 1996; co-author: Expressive Therapy: A Creative Arts Approach to Depth-Oriented Treatment, 1980, Psychoanalytic Review The Creative Act as a Means of Overcoming Resistance in Treatment; author: The Secret, 1994. Mem. Am. Art Therapy Assn., A.T.R.

LYSTAD, MARY HANEMANN (MRS. ROBERT LYSTAD), sociologist, author, consultant; b. New Orleans, Apr. 11, 1928; d. James and Mary (Douglass) Hanemann; m. Robert Lystad, June 20, 1953; children: Lisa Douglass, Anne Hanemann, Mary Lunde, Robert Douglass, James Hanemann. A.B. cum laude, Newcomb Coll., 1949; M.A., Columbia U., 1951; Ph.D., Tulane U., 1955. Postdoctoral fellow social psychology S.E. La. Hosp., Mandeville, 1955-57; field rsch. social psychology Ghana, 1957-58, South Africa and Swaziland, 1968, Peoples Republic of China, 1986; chief sociologist Collaborative Child Devel. Project, Charity Hosp. La., New Orleans, 1958-61; feature writer African div. Voice Am., Washington, 1964-73; program analyst NIMH, Washington, 1968-78; asso. dir. for planning and coordination div. spl. mental health programs NIMH, 1978-80; chief Nat. Ctr. for Prevention and Control of Rape, 1980-83, Ctr. Mental Health Studies of Emergencies, 1983-89; pvt. cons. specializing on mental health implications social and econ. problems Bethesda, Md., 1990—; cons. on youth Nat. Goals Research Staff, White House, Washington, 1969-70. Author: Millicent the Monster, 1968, Social Aspects of Alienation, 1969, Jennifer Takes Over P.S. 94, 1972, James the Jaguar, 1972, As They See It: Changing Values of College Youth, 1972, That New Boy, 1973, Halloween Parade, 1973, Violence at Home, 1974, A Child's World As Seen in His Stories and Drawings, 1974, From Dr. Mather to Dr. Seuss: 200 Years of American Books for Children, 1980, At Home in America, 1983, Play Ball, 1997; editor: Innovations in Mental Health Services to Disaster Victims, 1985, Violence in the Home: Interdisciplinary Perspectives, 1986, Mental Health Response to Mass Emergencies: Theory and Practice, 1988. Recipient Spl. Recognition award USPHS, 1983, Alumna Centennial award Newcomb Coll., 1986. Home and Office: 4900 Scarsdale Rd Bethesda MD 20816-2440

LYSTAD, ROBERT ARTHUR LUNDE, retired university dean, educator; b. Milw., Aug. 10, 1920; s. Arthur Frederick and Lulu Marion (Lunde) L.; m. Anita E. Firing, June 11, 1945 (dec. 1952); m. Mary Agnes Hanemann, June 20, 1953; children: Lisa Douglass, Anne Hanemann, Mary Lunde, Robert Douglass, James Hanemann. B.A., U. Wis., 1941; B.D., Drew Theol. Sem., 1944; Ph.D. in Anthropology, Northwestern U., 1951. Prof. anthropology Tulane U., 1951-61, head dept. sociology and anthropology Newcomb Coll., 1959-61; asso. prof. African studies Sch. Advanced Internat. Studies, Johns Hopkins U., 1961-64, prof., 1964-91, assoc. dean for acad. affairs, 1980-91; acting assoc. dean, 1992; cons. Voice of Am., various depts. U.S. govt., 1961-86, various ednl. and rsch. instns. in Japan, Korea, People's Republic of China, Taiwan, 1981. Author: The Ashanti: A Proud People, 1958; also articles in field.; editor: The African World: A Survey of Social Research, 1965. Mem. Ohio Conf. Methodist Ch., 1944-73. Recipient Founder's award Sch. Advanced Internat. Studies, 1991; fellow Social Sci. Research Council Gold Coast and Ivory Coast, 1949-50; grantee Carnegie Corp., Ghana, 1957-58. Home: 4900 Scarsdale Rd Bethesda MD 20816-2440

LYSYK, KENNETH MARTIN, judge; b. Weyburn, Sask., Can., July 1, 1934; s. Michael and Anna (Maradyn) L.; m. Patricia Kinnon, Oct. 2, 1959; children: Joanne, Karen (dec.), Stephanie. B.A., McGill U., 1954; LL.B., U. Sask., 1957; B.C.L., Oxford U., 1960. Bar: Sask., B.C., Yukon, apptd. Queen's counsel 1973. Lectr. U. B.C., 1960-62, asst. prof., 1962-65, assoc. prof., 1965-68, prof., 1968-69; adviser Constl. Rev. sect. Privy Council Office, Govt. of Can., Ottawa, 1969-70; prof. Faculty of Law U. Toronto, 1970-72; dep. atty. gen. Govt. of Sask., Regina, 1972-76; dean Law Sch., U. B.C., Vancouver, 1976-82; judge Supreme Ct. of B.C., Vancouver, 1983—; dep. judge Supreme Ct. Yukon, 1991—, N.W. Territories, 1991—; judge ct. Martial Appeal Ct. Can., 1995—; assoc. dir. Nat. Jud. Inst., 1996—; chmn. Alaska Hwy. Pipeline Inquiry, 1977; sole commr. Yukon Electoral Boundaries Commn., 1991. Mem. Can. Bar Assn., Internat. Commn. Jurists (Can. sect.; v.p. for B.C. 1992—), Can. Inst. for Adminstrn. of Justice (pres. 1989-91). Office: Law Ct, 800 Smithe St, Vancouver, BC Canada V6Z 2E1

LYTHCOTT, MARCIA A., newspaper editor. Op-ed editor Chicago Tribune, Ill. Office: Chicago Tribune 435 N Michigan Ave Chicago IL 60611

LYTLE, GUY FITCH, III, priest, educator, dean; b. Birmingham, Ala., Oct. 14, 1944; s. Guy Fitch and Nelle (Stewart) L.; m. Maria Rasco, Dec. 30, 1978; children: Elizabeth Eva Maria, Ashley Alexandra Gabriella. BA in History magna cum laude, Princeton U., 1966, MA in History, 1969, PhD in History, 1976; Marshall Scholar, U. Oxford, Eng., 1967-70. Ordained priest in Episcopalian Church, 1986. From instr. to asst. prof. history and medieval studies Cath. Univ. of Am., Washington, 1971-77; asst. prof. history, U. Tex., Austin, 1977-84; assoc. prof. of church history The Church Divinity Sch. of the Pacific, Berkeley, Calif., 1984-89; prof. of church history and hist. theology The Church Divinity Sch. of the Pacific, Berkeley, 1989-91; doctoral prof. of history Grad. Theol. Union, Berkeley, Calif., 1984-91; dean, prof. Anglican studies Sch. of Theology, Univ. of the South, Sewanee, Tenn., 1991—, Juhan prof. divinity, 1992—; from asst. to rector All Souls Episcopal Ch., Berkeley, Calif., 1985; chaplain Merrithew Meml. Hosp., Martinez, Calif., 1986-87; assoc. rector Episcopal Ch. of St. John the Evangelist, San Francisco, 1987-90, rector, 1990; lectr. in history of sci. and medicine U. Ala., 1967; rsch. fellow, mem. sr. common rm., Corpus Christi Coll., 1971-73; vis. prof. Oxford U., Eng., 1980, 85, The Folger Shakespeare Libr., 1975-76, Australian Nat. Univ., 1983, Episcopal Sem. of the S.W., 1983-84; mem. Gen. Bd. Examining Chaplains, 1991—; pres. Conf. of Anglican Theologians, 1989-90, exec. com., 1990-95; mem. and theol. cons. Bishop's Commn. on Evangelism and Church Growth, Diocese of Calif., 1990-91; convenor Conf. of Anglican Ch. Historians, 1987-89; exec. bd. Coun. for Devel. of Min., 1994—; mem. Internat. Anglican-Meth. Ecumenical Commn., 1992—. Author: A Bishop's Household in Late Medieval England: an edition of the account roll of William of Wykeham, Bishop of Winchester for 1393, 1976, rev. edit., 1996, Reform and Authority in the Medieval and Reformation Church, 1981, paperback edit., 1987, Theological Education for the Future, 1988, Lambeth Conferences Past and Present, 1989, (with Stephen Orgel) Patronage in the Renaissance, 1981, paperback edit., 1982; mem. editl. bd. Anglican and Episcopal History, 1986—. Mem. Mayor's Task Force of Religious Leaders and Cmty. Problems, San Francisco, 1990. Avocations: tennis, rare books, music. Home: 484 Roarks Cove Rd Sewanee TN 37375-3024 Office: Univ of the South Sch of Theology 335 Tennessee Ave Sewanee TN 37383-1000*

LYTLE, L(ARRY) BEN, insurance company executive, lawyer; b. Greenville, Tex., Sept. 30, 1946; children: Hugh, Larry. BS in Mgmt. Sci. and Indsl. Psychology, East Tex. State U., 1970; JD, Ind. U., 1980. Computer operator/programmer U.S. Govt., Ft. Smith, Ark., 1962-63; customer engr. Olivetti Corp., San Antonio, 1963-64; mgr. computer ops. and computer software LTV Electrosystems, Greenville, 1964-69; project mgr. electronic fin. system, dir. systems planning Assocs. Corp. N.Am., South Bend, Ind., 1969-74; asst. v.p. systems Am. Fletcher Nat. Bank, Indpls., 1974-76; with Assoc. Ins. Cos., Inc., Indpls., 1976—, pres., 1987—, COO, 1987-89, CEO, 1989—; now pres., CEO Anthem Ins. Cos., Inc., Indpls.; CEO, chmn. bd. dirs. Anthem Cos., Inc., Acordia, Inc.; chmn. bd. dirs. AdminaStar, Inc., Health Networks Am., Inc., Novalis, Inc., Robinson-Conner Nev., Inc.; bd. dirs. The Shelby Ins. Group, Raffensperger, Hughes & Co., Inc., Acordia Benefits, Inc., Indpls. Power and Light Co., Indpls. Power and Light Co. Enterprises; mem. adv. bd. CID Venture Ptnrs., Ltd. Partnership; rschr., cons. state and fed. govt. orgns., including, Adv. Coun. on Social Security, Pepper Commn. of U.S. Congress, others. Chmn. health policy commn. State of Ind., Indpls., 1990-92; bd. dirs., mem. exec. com. Community Leaders Allied for Superior Schs.; bd. dirs. Indpls. Convention and Visitors Bur., Indpls. Symphony Orch.; mem. Corp. Community Coun.; active various civic orgns., including United Negro Coll. Fund, Indpls. Mus. Art. Mem. ABA, Ind. Bar Assn., Indpls. Bar Assn., Ind. State C. of C. (bd. dirs.), Indpls. C. of C. (bd. dirs.). Home: 426 E Vermont St Indianapolis IN 46202-3680 Office: Anthem Ins Cos Inc 120 Monument Cir Indianapolis IN 46204-4906*

LYTTLE, DOUGLAS ALFRED, photographer, educator; b. Three Rivers,, Mich., July 7, 1919; s. Stephen Henry and Ruth (Marshall) L.; m. Vivian M. Quell, October 12, 1991; children: Judith Ann Lyttle Nelson, Janet Ruth Lyttle Chobanian, Marsha Jane Lyttle Pidek. B.S. cum laude, U. Mich., 1941. Organic research chemist Merck and Co., Rahway, N.J., 1941-45, Upjohn Co., Kalamazoo, Mich., 1945-60; prin. Douglas Lyttle Photographer, Kalamazoo, 1961-69; mem. faculty Sch. Photog. Arts and Scis., Rochester (N.Y.) Inst. Tech., 1969-83, prof. emeritus, 1983—; freelance photographer. Exhibitor photographs; presenter audio-visual programs based on travels; contbr. photographs to mags. Mem. Profl. Photographers Am., Am. Soc. Photographers, Phi Beta Kappa. Office: 10 Downing Dr Pittsford NY 14534-3612 *The Christian faith, its morality, spirit and theology as active fellowship with God in Christ, is the basis for a life in which people are most important. Honesty with self and others, caring, commitment and a continuing reach for excellence and growth have been keystones for every endeavour. If there has been 'success' it has been a gift and a result.*

LYTTON, ROBERT LEONARD, civil engineer, educator; b. Port Arthur, Tex., Oct. 23, 1937; s. Robert Odell and Nora Mae (Verrett) L.; m. Eleanor Marilyn Anderson, Sept. 9, 1961; children: Lynn Elizabeth, Robert Douglas, John Kirby. BSCE, U. Tex., 1960, MSCE, 1961, PhD, 1967. Registered profl. engr., Tex., La.; registered land surveyor, La. Assoc. Dannenbaum and Assocs., Cons. Engrs., Houston, 1963-65; U.S. NSF fellow U. Tex., Austin, 1965-67, asst. prof., 1967-68; NSF postdoctoral fellow Australian Commonwealth Sci. & Indsl. Rsch. Orgn., Melbourne, Australia, 1969-70; assoc. prof. Tex. A&M U., College Station, 1971-76, prof., 1976-90, Wiley chair prof., 1990-95, dir. ctr. for infrastructure engring., 1991—, Benson chair prof., 1995—; divsn. head Tex. Transp. Inst., 1982-91, head infrastructure and transp. divsn. civil engring. dept., 1993-95; bd. dirs. MLA Labs., Inc., Austin, Trans-tec, Inc., Austin, Lyric Tech., Llc., Houston; v.p. bd. dirs. MLAW Cons., Inc., Austin, 1980—, ERES Cons., Inc., Champaign, Ill., 1981-95; prin. investigator strategic hwy. rsch. program A005 rsch. project, 1990-93. Patentee for sys. identification and analysis of subsurface radar signals. Mem. St. Vincent de Paul Soc., Houston, 1963-65, Redemptorist Lay Mission Soc., Melbourne, Australia, 1969-70. Capt. U.S. Army, 1961-63. Recipient SAR medal of honor St. Mary's U., 1957, Soc. Am. Mil. Engrs. Outstanding Sr. cadet U. Tex., 1959, Disting. Mil. grad. award, 1960, Hamilton Watch award Coll. Engring., 1960, Disting. Achievement award Tex. A&M U. Assn. Former Students, 1996, Zachry sr. rschr. award Tex. Transportation Inst., 1996. Fellow ASCE; mem. NSPE, Transp. Rsch. Bd. (chmn. com. A2LO6 1987-93), Internat. Soc. for Soil Mechanics & Found. Engring. (U.S. rep. tech. com. TC-6 1987—, keynote address 7th internat. conf. on expansive soils 1992, keynote address 1st internat. conf. on unsaturated soils 1995), Assn. Asphalt Paving Technologists, Post-Tensioning Inst. (adv. bd.), Tex. Soc. Profl. Engrs., Internat. Soc. Asphalt Pavements, Sigma Xi, Phi Kappa Delta, Chi Epsilon, Tau Beta Pi, Phi Kappa Phi. Roman Catholic. Office: Tex A&M U 508G CE/TTI Bldg College Station TX 77843

LYU, SEUNG WON, metallurgical engineer, environmental scientist; b. Seoul, Korea, May 15, 1934; came to U.S., 1958; s. Yohan and Kyun Shin (Kim) L.; m. Yun O. Chung; children: John A., Lori K. BS in Chem. Engring., Ind. Inst. Tech., Ft. Wayne, 1961; BS in Metall. Engring., Ill. Inst. Tech., Chgo., 1975; MAS in Environ. Sci., Governors State U., University Park, Ill., 1981. Registered profl. engr. Ill., Calif.; cert. ind. wastewater treatment operator, Ill. Metallurgist Verson Allsteel Press Co., Chgo., 1962-65; metall. engr. Am. Std.-ARI, Franklin Park, Ill., 1965-67; sr. rsch. metallurgist Continental Group, Oak Brook, Ill., 1967-70; sr. prin. engr. Am. Nat. Can Co., Chgo., 1970-83; asst. prof. Ill. Inst. Tech., Glen Ellyn, Ill., 1983-88; pres., chief engr. Prospect Testing Labs., Des Plaines, Ill., 1985—; tech. cons. Korean Small and Medium Indsl. Promotion Corp., Seoul, 1983; metall. cons. Verson Allsteel Press Co., Chgo., 1985—. Bd. dirs. Korean-Am. Cmty. Svc., Chgo., 1989—, Niles (Ill.) Korean Sch., 1990—. Mem. ASTM. Republican. Presbyterian. Achievements include 6 patents in metallurgy, tooling and container application; method of making tin-layered stock material; die and method of assembly and application; split punch design and wall/bottom profile for containers. Home: 824 Shibley Ave Park Ridge IL 60068-2352 Office: Prospect Testing Labs Inc 1245 E Forest Ave Des Plaines IL 60018-1564

MA, ALAN WAI-CHUEN, lawyer; b. Hong Kong, Apr. 20, 1951; s. Pak Ping and Oi Quon (Hung) M.; m. Carrie Pak, Mar. 17, 1993. BBA, U. Hawaii, 1975; MBA, Chaminade U., 1981; JD, Golden Gate U., 1983. Bar: Hawaii 1984, U.S. Dist. Ct. Hawaii 1984, U.S. Ct. Appeals (9th cir.) 1986, U.S. Supreme Ct. 1989. Ptnr. Oldenberg & Ma, Honolulu, 1984-90; prin. Law Offices Alan W.C. Ma, Honolulu, 1990-95; counsel Goodsill Anderson Quinn & Stifel, Honolulu, 1995—; adj. prof. law U. Hawaii, Honolulu, 1988—. Co-editor: New Waves for Foreign Investors, 1990. Recipient Outstanding Vol. award Hawaii Cmty. Svc. Coun., 1990. Mem. ABA, Am. Immigration Lawyers Assn. (chpt. chair 1993-94), Internat. Bar Assn., Inter-Pacific Bar Assn., U.S. Japan Vols. Assn. (bd. dirs. 1989—), Overseas Chinese Am. Assn. (bd. dirs. 1993-94). Avocation: tennis. Office: Goodsill Anderson et al 1800 Alii Pl 1099 Alakea St Honolulu HI 96813-4500

MA, FENGCHOW CLARENCE, agricultural engineering consultant; b. Kaifeng, Honan, China, Sept. 4, 1919; came to U.S., 1972; s. Chao-Hsiang and Wen-Chieh (Yang) Ma; m. Fanny Luisa Corvera-Achá, Jan. 20, 1963; 1 child, Fernando. BS in Agr., Nat. Chekiang U., Maytan, Kweichow, China, 1942; postgrad., Iowa State U., 1945-46. Cert. profl. agronomist, Republic of China, 1944; registered profl. agrl. engr., Calif. Chief dept. ops. Agrl. Machinery Operation and Mgmt. Office, Shanghai, China, 1946-49; sr. farm machinery specialist Sino-Am. Joint Commn. on Rural Reconstrn., Taipei, Taiwan, Republic of China, 1950-62; agrl. engring. adviser in Bolivia, Peru, Chile, Ecuador, Liberia, Honduras, Grenada, Bangladesh FAO, Rome, 1962-80; consulting agrl. engr. to USAID projects in Guyana & Peru IRI Rsch. Inst., Inc., Stamford, Conn., 1981-82, 83, 85; chief adviser Com. Internat. Tech. Coop., Taipei, 1984-85; pres. FCM Assocs., Inc., 1962—; short consulting missions to Paraguay, Saudi Arabia, Indonesia, Malawi, Swaziland, Barbados, Dominica, Ivory Coast, Vietnam, Philippines, Nicaragua and others. Author papers, studies; contbr. articles to profl. publs. Mem. Am. Soc. Agrl. Engrs. Avocations: reading, stamp and coin collecting. Home: 1004 Azalea Dr Sunnyvale CA 94086-6747 Office: PO Box 70096 Sunnyvale CA 94086-0096

MA, HONG, plant molecular biologist, educator; b. Shanghai, People's Republic of China, Oct. 19, 1960; came to U.S., 1980; s. Zhe and Linsun (Hu) M.; m. Yi Hu, Aug. 10, 1987; 1 child, Jason J. BA summa cum laude, Temple U., 1983; PhD, MIT, 1988. Teaching asst. MIT, Cambridge, 1983-84, rsch. asst., 1984-88; postdoctoral fellow Calif. Inst. Tech., Pasadena, 1988-90; staff investigator Cold Spring Harbor (N.Y.) Lab., 1990-91, sr. staff investigator, 1992-96, assoc. investigator, 1996—; adj. faculty SUNY, Stony Brook, 1991—; mem. faculty SUNY-Cold Spring Harbor Lab.-Brookhaven Joint, 1991—; adviser undergrad. rsch. program Cold Spring Harbor Lab., 1991—; mem. panel NIH Biol. Study Sect., 1995; spkr. in field; competitive grants review panelist USDA, 1997. Assoc. editor for Plant Molecular Biology, 1996; reviewer articles for Genetics, Molecular Cellular Biology, Molecular Gen. Genetics, Plant Cell, Plant Jour., Plant Molecular Biology; contbr. articles to profl. jours. Mem. selection com. Ptnrs. for Future High Sch. Students, Cold Spring Harbor Lab., N.Y., 1991—; mentor high sch. student rsch. project Westinghouse Talent Competition, 1993. MIT fellow, 1983, Helen H. Whitney Found. fellow, 1988; NSF rsch. grantee, 1990, 91, 94, USDA rsch. grantee, 1991, 92, 94, 95, 96, Am. Cancer Soc. rsch. grantee, 1995; Am. Cancer Soc. jr. faculty rsch. awardee, 1994. Mem. AAAS, Genetic Soc. Am., Am. Soc. Microbiology, Internat. Soc. Plant Molecular Biologists, Assn. Chinese Students and Scholars in Life Scis., Soc. Chinese Bioscientists Am., N.Y. Acad. Scis. Avocations: reading, stamp collecting, gardening. Office: Cold Spring Harbor Lab 1 Bungtown Rd Cold Spring Harbor NY 11724-2209

MA, TAI-LOI, library curator, Chinese studies specialist; b. Canton, China, Oct. 14, 1945; came to U.S., 1970; s. James Chun-Woon and Mary (Wong) M. BA, U. Hong Kong, 1969; MA, U. Chgo., 1972, PhD, 1987. Cataloger East Asian Libr., U. Chgo., 1972-78, head cataloger, 1978-87, curator, 1987—; cons. Chinese collection Kinsey Inst. Rsch., Bloomington, Ind., 1983; fellowship panelist NEH, Washington, 1988—; mem. internat. adv. com. Chinese rare books project Rsch. Librs. Group, Mountain View, Calif., 1988-96; mem. adv. bd. East Asian Libr. Jour., Princeton, N.J., 1990—; cons. Chinese collection Libr. Congress, 1995. Translator: Traditional Chinese Stories, 1978; contbr. articles to profl. publs. Fellow, scholar U. Chgo., 1970-73; Mellon Found. fellow Princeton U., summer 1980; conf. travel grantee Am. Coun. Learned Socs., Canton, 1983, Com. on Scholarly Comm. with China, Beijing, 1993. Mem. ALA, Assn. for Asian Studies (com. on East Asian librs. exec. group 1989-92, subcom. chmn. 1993-96, pres. coun. on East Asian librs. 1997—). Office: U Chgo East Asian Collection Regenstein Libr 1100 E 57th St Fl 5 Chicago IL 60637-1502

MA, TSO-PING, electrical engineering educator, researcher, consultant; b. Lan-Tsou, Gan-Su, China, Nov. 13, 1945; came to U.S., 1969; s. Liang-Kway and Zwey-Yueen (Liu) Ma; m. Pin-fang Lin, June 10, 1972; children: Mahau, Jasmine. BS, Nat. Taiwan U., 1968; MS, Yale U., 1972, PhD, 1974. Teaching asst. Yale U., New Haven, 1971-74, asst. prof. elec. engring., 1977-80, assoc. prof., 1980-85, prof., 1985—, chmn. dept. elec. engring., 1991-95, acting chmn. dept. elec. engring., 1988, vis. lectr., 1976-77, advisor Yale Chinese Student Svc., 1977—, Yale Mainland-Taiwan Soc.; staff engr. IBM, Hopewell Junction, N.Y., 1974-77; GE Whitney Symposium lectr., 1985; cons. in field. Contbr. articles to profl. jours. Patentee in field. Bd. dirs. New Haven Chinese Sch., 1982—. Grantee Rsch. Corp., 1978, Mobil Found., 1981-84, G.E. Found., 1984; recipient Conn. Yankee Ingenuity award, 1991, B.F. Goodrich Nat. Collegiate Inventor's Advisor award, 1993. Fellow IEEE (chmn. various coms. 1986—, officer semiconductor interface specialists conf. 1986-88); mem. Materials Rsch. Soc., Am. Phys. Soc., Orgn. of Chinese Ams. (pres. New Haven chpt. 1988-90, bd. dirs. 1990—), Electrochem. Soc., Conn. Acad. Sci. and Engring., Yale Figure Skating Club (v.p. 1991-93), Yale Sci. and Engring. Assn., Sigma Xi (v.p. Yale chpt. 1986, pres. 1987-88). Avocations: music, violin, skating. Home: 169 Northford Rd Branford CT 06405-2823 Office: Yale Univ Dept Elec Engring 15 Prospect St New Haven CT 06511-6816

MA, YO-YO, cellist; b. Paris, 1955; m. Jill; children: Nicholas, Emily. Studied with Janos Scholz; studied with Leonard Rose, Juilliard Sch. Music, N.Y.C., 1962; AB, Harvard U., 1976, MusD (hon.), 1991. Debut at age 9, Carnegie Hall, N.Y.C.; appeared with Pablo Casals, Isaac Stern, Leonard Bernstein, Emanuel Ax, Jaime Laredo, performs throughout world with maj. orchs.; rec. artist Sony Classical; recs. include Portrait of Yo-Yo Ma, China and Japan: Japanese Melodies, Anything Goes (with Stephanie Grapelli), Hush (with Bobby McFerrin), Yo-Yo Ma at Tanglewood, The New York Album. Recipient Avery Fisher prize, 1978, Ten-time Grammy award winning artist. Office: ICM Artists 40 W 57th St New York NY 10019-4001 also: Harold Holt Ltd, 31 Sinclair Rd, London WI4 0NS, England*

MA, YUANXI, Chinese and English language and literature educator, translator; b. Shanghai, China, Feb. 18, 1933; came to U.S., 1985; d. Shu Yuan and Jingxing Ma; m. Zailiang Zhang, Feb. 16, 1958 (div. 1981); children: Xiaodan, Jia. BA, Beijing Fgn. Studies U., China, 1953, MA, 1956; MA, SUNY, Buffalo, 1988, PhD, 1992. Assoc. prof. Beijing Fgn. Studies U., 1953-82; assoc. prof., vice-chair English dept. Inst. Internat. Rels., Beijing, 1982-85; assoc. dir. Sch. Chinese Studies, China Inst., N.Y.C., 1989-95; dir. translation Baker & McKenzie Law Firm, Chgo., 1995—; adj. prof. NYU, 1990-95, The New Sch. for Social Rsch., 1991; interpreter, translator Conf. Internat. Coop. Alliance, Washington, 1985, interpreter, Am.-Chinese Friendship Group traveling in China, 1975. Author: College English, 1983, English, I-V, 1978, 79, TV English, I-III, 1980, English Textbooks, I, II, 1962; translator of lit. works; contbr. to profl. jours. and textbooks; numerous presentations in field. Mem. U.S.-China Friendship Assn., Chinese Lang. Tchr. Assn., Nat. Assn. Women's Studies, Assn. Asian Studies. Home: 405 N Wabash Ave #4005 Chicago IL 60611-3034 Office: Baker & McKenzie Law Firm One Prudential Plz 130 E Randolph Dr Chicago IL 60601

MAAG, URS RICHARD, statistics educator; b. Winterthur, Switzerland, Jan. 20, 1938; m. Tannis Yvonne Arbuckle, July 31, 1965; children: Liane, Karin, Eric. Diploma in Math, Swiss Fed. Inst. Tech., Zurich, 1961; M.Sc., U. Toronto, Can., 1962, Ph.D., 1965. Asst. prof. U. Montreal, Que., Can., 1965-72; assoc. prof. U. Montreal, Can., 1972-78, prof., 1978—. Contbr. articles to profl. jours. Mem. Statis. Soc. Can. (sec. 1973-77, pres. 1980), Am. Statis. Assn. (pres. Montreal chpt. 1975-77), Internat. Statis. Inst., Can. Assn. Rd. Safety Profls., Inst. Math. Stats. Home: 3484 Marlowe Ave, Montreal, PQ Canada H4A 3L7 Office: U Montreal Dept Math and Stats, CP 6128 Succ Centre-ville, Montreal, PQ Canada H3C 3J7

MAAHS, KENNETH HENRY, SR., religion educator; b. Peoria, Ill., June 19, 1940; s. Silas Henry Maahs and Lydia Nettie (Heinold) Blessman; m. Vivian Louise Dawn Englert, Sept. 1, 1962; children: Kirsten Allison Dawn, Kenneth Henry Jr. BA in Philosophy/Theology magna cum laude, Simpson Coll., 1962; MDiv, Fuller Theol. Sem., Pasadena, Calif., 1965; ThM in N.T. Studies, Princeton Theol. Sem., 1966; PhD in Old Testament Studies, So. Bapt. Theol. Sem., Louisville, 1972. Ordained to ministry Missionary Ch./Am. Bapt. Conv., 1968. Instr. Nyack (N.Y.) Coll., 1966-67, Bethel Coll., Mishawaka, Ind., 1968; prof. Bibl. studies Ea. Coll., St. Davids, Pa., 1972—, Abram Clemens chair, 1986—, chmn. dept. religion-philosophy, 1985-88, chmn. humanities div., 1988-92, 95; faculty mem. The Jerusalem Ctr. for Biblical Studies, 1994—; interim pastor Columbus (N.J.) Bapt. Ch., 1975-76, Roxborough Bapt. Ch., Phila., 1980-81, Bapt. Temple, Blue Bell, Pa., 1981-83, Willowgrove (Pa.) Bapt. Ch., 1988, Belmont Bapt. Ch., Broomall, Pa., 1989, Lower Merion Bapt. Ch., Bryn Mawr, Pa., 1989-90, 2d Bapt. Ch. Germantown, Pa., 1990-92, Roxborough Bapt. Ch., Phila., 1992-93, No. Wales (Pa.) Bapt. Ch., 1994-96, Springfield (Pa.) Bapt. Ch., 1996-97; adj. prof. Ea. Bapt. Theol. Sem., 1980, 83, 85, 89, Lay Acad. of Phila. Bapt. Assn., 1984-86, 88, 90, 94, Fuller Theol. Sem./Young Life's Inst. Youth Ministries, 1986-87, 89,; keynote speaker Am. Bapt. Women's Regional Conf., 1983; feature lectr. Am. Bapt. Commn. on Continuing Edn., 1985; featured theologian Common Ground conf., ABC of N.J., 1997. Recipient Legion of Honor award Chapel of Four Chaplains, 1983, Lindback award Ea. Coll., 1984; named Prof. of Yr. Ea. Coll., 1983-84. Mem. Bibl.

Archaeology Soc., Soc. Bibl. Lit. Delta Epsilon Chi. Republican. Home: 346 E Valley Forge Rd King Of Prussa PA 19406-2035 Office: Eastern Coll Dept Bibl Studies Saint Davids PA 19087

MAAR, ROSINA, medical organization executive. BS, Ga. Inst. Tech., 1984; MD, Morehouse Sch. Medicine, 1988. Bd. cert. in internal medicine; lic. Ga., N.C. Intern and resident in internal medicine Emory U. Sch. Medicine, Atlanta, 1991; physics lab. instr. Ga. Inst. Tech., Atlanta, 1981-84; rsch. asst. Emory U., Atlanta, 1985-86; med. evaluator maternal and infant project Grady Meml. Hosp., Atlanta, 1987-88; contract physician Wesley Woods Geriatric Hosp., Atlanta, 1989-90; contract physician, program dir. Piedmont Hosp./Spinal Shepard Ctr., Atlanta, 1989-91; med. dir. Cellcor, Inc., Atlanta, 1991-92; corp. med. dir. Cellcor, Inc., Newton, Mass., 1992-93; med. scientist med./regulatory svcs. Quintiles, Inc., Research Triangle Park, N.C., 1993-94, dir. med. svcs., 1994-95, v.p. clin. ops., 1995—. Contbr. articles and abstracts to med. jours. Mem. ACP, AMA, Am. Bd. Internal Medicine (diplomate). Office: Quintiles Inc PO Box 13979 Research Triangle Park NC 27709

MAARBJERG, MARY PENZOLD, office equipment company executive; b. Norfolk, Va., Oct. 2, 1943; d. Edmund Theodore and Lucy Adelaide (Singleton) Penzold; m. John Peder Maarbjerg, Oct. 20, 1966; 1 son, Martin Peder. A.B., Hollins Coll., 1965; M.B.A., Wharton Sch., Pa., 1969. Cons. bus. and fin., Stamford, Conn., 1977-78; corp. staff analyst Pitney Bowes, Inc., Stamford, Conn., 1978-80, mgr. pension and benefit fin. 1980-81, dir. investor relations, 1981-85; v.p. planning and devel. Pitney Bowes Credit Corp., Norwalk, Conn., 1985-86; treas., v.p. planning Pitney Bowes Credit Corp., 1986-94; v.p. mkt. devel. and mng. dir. Asia Pacific Bowes Fin. Svcs., 1994-95, v.p. ops. and mng. dir., 1995—. Mem. adv. com. City of Stamford Mcpl. Employees Retirement Fund, 1980-85; mem. fin. adv. com. YWCA, Stamford, 1982-86; bd. dirs. Stamford Symphony, 1985-95, Vis. Nurses Assn., 1984-86, Am. Recorder Soc., 1986—. Fellow Royal Statis. Soc.; mem. Fin. Execs. Inst., Phi Beta Kappa. Congregationalist. Office: Pitney Bowes Credit Corp 201 Merritt Seven Norwalk CT 06856

MAAS, ANTHONY ERNST, pathologist; b. Utrecht, The Netherlands, May 6, 1926; came to U.S., 1959; s. Willem A. and Tono Clara (Bonebakker) M.; m. Julia Margaret Lampley, July 7, 1962; children: Willem Fulton, Julie Estelle, Anthony Ernst Jr. BS, U. Utrecht, 1948, MD, 1953. MD, Pa.; cert. anatomical and clin. pathologist. Asst. pathologist United Hosp., Port Chester, N.Y., 1965-66; assoc. pathologist Polyclinic Hosp., Harrisburg, Pa., 1966-74; assoc. pathologist Holy Spirit Hosp., Camp Hill, Pa., 1974-90, dir. labs., 1990—; dir. labs. Harrisburg State Hosp., Harrisburg, 1990-96. Contbr. articles to profl. jours. Fellow Coll. Am. Pathologists, Am. Soc. Clin. Pathologists; mem. AMA, Pa. Med. Soc., Dauphin County Med. Soc., Torch Club of Harrisburg (pres. 1983). Republican. Presbyn. Avocations: reading, traveling, gardening, walking.

MAAS, DUANE HARRIS, distilling company executive; b. Tilleda, Wis., Aug. 26, 1927; s. John William and Adela (Giessel) M.; m. Sonja Johnson, Mar. 11, 1950; children: Jon Kermit, Duane Arthur, Thomas Ervin. B.S., U. Wis., 1951. With Shell Chem. Corp., 1951-59; plant mgr. Fleischmann Distilling Corp., Owensboro, Ky., 1959-63, Plainfield, Ill., 1963-65; asst. to v.p. Barton Distilling Co., Chgo., 1965-68; exec. asst. to pres. Barton Distilling Co., 1968, v.p. adminstrn., 1968; v.p., gen. mgr. Barton Brands, Inc., Chgo., 1968—72; pres. Leaf Confectionery div. W.R. Grace, Chgo., 1972-74; v.p., gen. mgr. Romano Bros., Chgo., 1974-79; v.p., sec.-treas. Marketing Directions Inc., Chgo., 1974-77; pres. Associated Wine Producers, Inc., 1979-80; exec. v.p., chief exec. officer Mohawk Liqueur, Detroit, 1980-86; v.p. McKesson Wine & Spirits Group of N.Y., Detroit, 1982-86; pres. Mgmt. Cons. Services Co., Chgo., 1986-96, U.S. Distilled Products Co., Princeton, Minn., 1996—; past pres. Barton Distilling (Can.), Ltd.; past mng. dir. Barton Distilling (Scotland), Ltd.; past dir. Barton Distillers Europe, Barton Internat., Ltd. Sec.-treas. Plainfield Twp. Park Dist., 1967-70; chmn. Plainfield Planning and Zoning Commn., 1965-70. Served with USAAF, 1945-47. Mem. Wis. Alumni Assn. Lutheran. Home: 13264 W Highway 29 Bowler WI 54416 Office: 1607 12th St S Princeton MN 55371-2300

MAAS, JANE BROWN, advertising executive; b. Jersey City; d. Charles E. and Margaret (Beck) Brown; m. Michael Maas, Aug. 30, 1957; children: Katherine, Jennifer. BA, Bucknell U., 1953; postgrad., U. Dijon, France, 1954; MA, Cornell U., 1955; LittD, Ramapo Coll., 1986, St. John's U., 1988. Assoc. producer Name That Tune TV Program, N.Y.C., 1957-64; v.p. Ogilvy and Mather Inc., N.Y.C., 1964-76; sr. v.p. Wells, Rich, Greene, Inc., N.Y.C., 1976-82; pres. Muller Jordan Weiss Inc., N.Y.C., 1982-89; pres. Earle Palmer Brown Cos., N.Y.C., 1989-92, chmn., 1992-94, chmn. emeritus, 1994—. Co-author: How to Advertise, 1975, Better Brochures, 1981, Adventures of a Advertising Woman, 1986, The New How to Advertise, 1992, Christmas in Wales: a Homecoming, 1994. Trustee Bucknell U., Lewisburg, 1976-86, Fordham U., N.Y., 1983-91; bd. govs. com. Scholastic Achievement, 1985-92; active Girl Scouts U.S. Greater N.Y., 1970-76; mem. adv. bd. William E. Simon Grad. Sch. Bus. U. Rochester, 1989—, pub. dir. AIA, 1993-95. Recipient Matrix award Women in Communications, 1980, N.Y. Advt. Woman of Yr., 1986. Mem. AIA (hon.), Am. Archtl. Found. (regent 1993—), Am. Assn. Advt. Agys. (bd. govs.), Phi Beta Kappa. Avocations: creative writing, jogging. Home: PO Box 1109 Westhampton Beach NY 11978-7109

MAAS, JOE (MELVIN JOSEPH MAAS), retired federal agency administrator; b. Washington, Feb. 29, 1940; s. Melvin Joseph and Katherine (Endress) M.; m. Constance Mary Haile, June 13, 1965; children: Christine, Michael, Kevin. BS, U. Md., 1965; postgrad., Stanford U., 1972-73. Dir. career edn. U.S. Dept. Labor, Washington, 1969-73; dep. dir. pers. SBA, Washington, 1973-76, dir. pers., 1976-82, asst. adminstr., 1982-95; mem. Internat. Pers. Assn., 1981-83, chairperson, 1982. Bd. dirs., treas. Snowden Mill Assn., Silver Spring, Md., 1991; Wash. rep. Ind. Charities of Am., 1995-96. With USMCR, 1957-64. Mem. Fed. Exec. Adminstrs. Assn., Sr. Exec. Assn., Pub. Employee Roundtable (bd. dirs. 1994—, chair Pub. Svc. Freelance awards 1996—), Coun. Former Fed. Execs. (v.p., bd. dirs. 1995—), Nat. Assn. Ret. Fed. Employees (chpt. pres. 1996—, state tng. officer 1997—), Fed. Exec. Inst. Assn. (co-chair Challenge After Pub. Svc. com.), Volkswagen Club (pres. Washington club 1988-95). Roman Catholic. Home: 2213 Aventurine Way Silver Spring MD 20904-5253

MAAS, PETER, writer; b. N.Y.C., June 27, 1929; s. Carl and Madeleine (Fellheimer) M.; m. Audrey Gellen, Apr. 4, 1962 (dec. July 1975); 1 child, John-Michael; m. Suzanne Jones, Feb. 1, 1986; 1 child, Terrence. B.A., Duke U., 1949; postgrad., The Sorbonne, Paris, 1950. Reporter N.Y. Herald Tribune, Paris, 1950-52; assoc. editor Collier's mag., 1954-56; sr. editor Look mag., 1959-61; contbg. writer Sat. Evening Post, 1961-66; cons. Curtis Pub. Co., 1966-67; contbg. editor New York mag., 1968-71. Free lance contbr. to nat. mags., newspapers, 1954—; author: The Rescuer, 1967, The Valachi Papers, 1969, Serpico, 1973, King of the Gypsies, 1975, Made in America, 1979, Marie: A True Story, 1983, Manhunt, 1986, Father and Son, 1989, In A Child's Name, 1990, China White, 1994, Killer Spy, 1995, Underboss, 1997; works included in anthology. Served with USNR, 1952-54. Mem. PEN Am. Center, Author's Guild. Roman Catholic. Office: care Internat Creative Mgmt 40 W 57th St New York NY 10019-4001

MAAS, WERNER KARL, microbiology educator; b. Kaiserslautern, Germany, Apr. 27, 1921; came to U.S., 1936, naturalized, 1945; s. Albert and Esther (Meyer) M.; m. Renata Diringer, Oct. 15, 1960; children—Peter, Andrew, Helen. AB, Harvard U., 1943; PhD, Columbia U., 1948. Postdoctoral fellow Calif. Inst. Tech., Pasadena, 1946-48; commd. officer USPHS, Tb Research Lab., Cornell U. Sch., N.Y.C., 1948-54; asst. prof. pharmacology NYU, 1954-57, assoc. prof. microbiology, 1957-63, prof., 1963-94, prof. emeritus, 1994—, chmn. dept. basic med. scis., 1974-81. Career grantee USPHS, 1962-94. Mem. Am. Soc. Biol. Chemists, Genetics Soc. Am., Am. Soc. Microbiology. Home: 86 Villard Ave Hastings on Hudson NY 10706-1821 Office: 550 1st Ave New York NY 10016-6481

MAASS, ARTHUR, political science and environmental studies educator; b. Balt., July 24, 1917; s. Arthur Leopold and Selma (Rosenheim) M. A.B., Johns Hopkins, 1939; M.P.A., Harvard, 1941, Ph.D., 1949. Adminstrv. asst. Bur. Budget, 1939-40; intern Nat. Inst. Pub. Affairs, 1939-40; research technician Nat. Resources Planning Bd., 1941-42; budget analyst Dept. Navy, 1946; water resources analyst Natural Resources Task Force, Hoover Commn., 1948; faculty Harvard, 1949—, prof. govt., 1959-67, Frank G. Thomson prof. govt., 1967-84, prof. emeritus, 1984—, chmn. dept., 1963-67; cons. Office Dir. Budget, 1949, Office Sec. Interior, 1950-52, Pres.'s Materials Policy Commn., 1951-52, TVA, 1952, C.E., 1961—, Bur. Reclamation, 1971, Ministry Water Conservancy, People's Republic China, 1980—; vis. prof. polit. sci. U. Calif. at Berkeley, 1951, U. P.R., 1955, El Colegio de México, 1986, U. Internat. Menendez y Pelayo, Valencia, Spain, 1990. Author: Muddy Waters, The Army Engineers and the Nation's Rivers, 1951, Congress and the Common Good, 1983, Water Law and Institutions in the Western U.S.: Comparisons with Early Developments in California and Australia, Contemporary Developments in Australia and Recent Legislation Worldwide, 1990; co-author: Area and Power, 1959, Design of Water-Resource Systems: New Techniques for Relating Economic Objectives, Engineering Analysis and Governmental Planning, 1962, A Simulation of Irrigation Systems, 1971, rev., 1974, 78, 87, Chinese edit., 1980, . . . and the Desert Shall Rejoice: Conflict, Growth and Justice in Arid Environments, 1978, rev. edit., 1986, Un Modelo de Simulacion Para Sistemas de Regadio, 1985; contbr. articles to profl. jours. Served to lt. comdr. USNR, 1942-46. Guggenheim fellow, 1955; Fulbright research fellow Spain, 1960-61; Faculty research fellow Social Sci. Research Council, 1961. Club: Harvard (N.Y.C.). Home: 63 Atlantic Ave Boston MA 02110-3722 Office: Harvard U Littauer Ctr Cambridge MA 02138

MAATMAN, GERALD LEONARD, insurance company executive; b. Chgo., Mar. 11, 1930; s. Leonard Raymond and Cora Mae (Van Der Laag) M.; children: Gerald L. Jr., Mary Ellen; m. Bernice Catherine Brummer, June 3, 1971. BS, Ill. Inst. Tech., 1951. Asst. chief engineer Ill. Inspection & Rating Bur., Chgo., 1951-58; prof., dept. chmn. Ill. Inst. Tech., Chgo., 1959-65; v.p. engring. Kemper Group, Chgo., 1966-68, pres. Nat. Loss Control Svc. Corp., 1969-74; v.p. corp. planning Kemper Group, Long Grove, Ill., 1974-79, sr. v.p. info. svcs. group, 1979-85, exec. v.p. ins. ops., 1985-87; pres. Kemper Nat. Ins. Co., Long Grove, Ill., 1987-92, CEO, 1989-95, also bd. dirs., chmn. bd. dirs., 1991-95. Bd. dirs. Advs. for Auto and Hwy. Safety, 1992—, Nat. Down Syndrome Soc.; chmn. bd. trustees Underwriters Labs., 1991—. Lt. (j.g.) USCGR, 1952-54. Mem. Wynstone Golf Club, Tau Beta Pi. Republican. Roman Catholic.

MAATSCH, DEBORAH JOAN, paralegal, tax specialist, tax advisor, controller; b. Lincoln, Nebr., Mar. 26, 1950; d. Leon F. Forst and Jarolyn J. Hoffman Forst Conrad; m. Gordon F. Maatsch, Mar. 14, 1969; children: Jason, Diana. BS, U. Nebr., 1976; MBA, U. Phoenix, 1997. Acct., supr. U.S. Civil Svc., Heidelberg, Ger., 1971-73; paralegal Mattson Rickets Davies et al, Lincoln, Nebr., 1976-87; tax cons. Lincoln and Denver, 1981—; pres. DGJD Inc.-Bleachers, 1993—; paralegal Wade Ash Woods & Hill, P.C., Denver, 1986-94; sr. trust adminstr. Investment Trust Co., Denver, 1994-96; compliance officer Nelson, Benson and Zellmer, Inc., 1995-96; controller Arena Devel., Inc., 1996—; mem. Denver Trust Officers Assocs., bus. adv. bd. Ponderosa H.S., 1994—; spkr., coord. Nebr. Continuing Legal Edn. Seminars, 1976-86. Contbr. articles to profl. jours. Mem. Doane Coll. Alumni Assn. (dir. 1989-93), Rocky Mt. Legal Assts. (dir., sect. chair 1990-94), Am. Soc. Women Accts. (officer, dir.), Nebr. Assn. Legal Assts. (officer, dir. 1976-87), Colo. Bar Assn. (computer probate sect.), Phi Chi Theta (treas. 1988-89). Avocations: travel, snow skiing, outdoor activities, motorcycles, home decorating. Office: DGJD Inc PO Box 267 Jefferson CO 80456 Address: 753 Windford St Parker CO 80134

MAAZEL, LORIN, conductor, composer, violinist; b. Neuilly, France, Mar. 6, 1930; s. Lincoln and Marie (Varencove) M.; m. Dietlinde Turban, 1986; 3 children; 4 children from previous marriages. Studies with, Vladimir Bakaleinikoff; student, U. Pitts., Mus. D. (hon.), 1968; H.H.D., Beaver Coll., 1973. Debut as condr., 1938; condr. Am. symphony orchs., 1939—; violin recitalist; European debut, 1953; festivals include Bayreuth, Salzburg, Edinburgh; tours include S.Am., Australia, USSR, Japan, Korea, People's Republic China; artistic dir. Deutsche Opera Berlin, 1965-71; assoc. prin. condr. New Philharm. Orch., London, 1970-72; dir. Cleve. Orch., 1972-82, condr. emeritus, 1982-86; dir. Vienna State Opera, 1982-84; music dir. Pitts. Symphony Orch., 1988-96, Orchestre Nat. de France, 1988-90, Bavarian Radio Symphony Orch., Munich, 1993—. Decorated officer Legion d'Honneur 1981; Finnish Commdr. of the Lion; Portuguese Commdr.; Bundesverdienstkreuz, Germany.

MABBS, EDWARD CARL, retired management consultant; b. St. Louis, Sept. 8, 1921; s. Ralph I. and Anna (Renner) M.; m. Margaret E. von Paulsen, Oct. 16, 1943; children: Susan, Carl, Kenneth, Meg. BS in Mech. Engring., Cornell U., 1943. Registered profl. engr. With Linde div. Union Carbide Corp., Newark, Essington, Pa., Tonawanda, N.Y., 1946-55; plant mgr. Wright Hoist div., York, Pa., 1955-62; group v.p. Am. Chain & Cable Co., Bridgeport, Conn., 1962-68, exec. v.p., dir., 1968-71; pres., CEO, dir. Esterline Corp., N.Y.C., 1971-72; pres. Indsl. Components group Rockwell Internat. Corp., Pitts., 1972-75; pres., CEO, dir. Incom Internat. Inc., Pitts., 1975-81; mgmt. cons. Tavernier, Fla., 1981-84; chmn., CEO, dir. L.B. Foster Co., Pitts., 1984-86; past dir. Cross & Trecker Corp., Signode Industries, Arnold Corp., SPD Techs., Inc. Trustee emeritus Point Park Coll.; v.p. Pomperaug coun. Boy Scouts Am.; past dir. Friends of Islamorada Area State Parks. Served to capt. U.S. Army, 1943-46, ETO. Mem. Internat. Materials Mgmt. Soc. (past dir.), Am. Prodn. and Inventory Control Soc. (past dir.), Bridgeport (Conn., York, Pa.) C. of C. (past dir.), Material Handling Inst. (past pres.). Home: PO Box 679 Tavernier FL 33070-0679

MABE, HUGH PRESCOTT, III, prosecutor; b. San Antonio, Sept. 28, 1945; s. Hugh Prescott and Maxine (Edwards) M.; m. Suzanne Marie White, Dec. 18, 1982. B.B.A., U. Okla., 1967; J.D., U. Tex., 1970. Trial atty. Dept. Justice, Washington, 1971-78; asst. U.S. atty. Office U.S. Atty. Dept. Justice, St. Thomas, V.I., 1978-82, U.S. atty., 1982-83, asst. U.S. atty., 1983-93, 94—; U.S. atty. U.S. Dept. of Justice, St. Thomas, V.I., 1993—. Served to Capt. U.S. Army, 1970. Recipient Spl. Achievement award Atty. Gen., 1982. Mem. Tex. Bar Assn., V.I. Bar Assn. Episcopalian. Office: US Attys Office Fed Bldg Rm 260 5500 Veterans Dr Saint Thomas VI 00802-6424

MABEE, CARLETON, historian, educator; b. Shanghai, China, Dec. 25, 1914; s. Fred Carleton and Miriam (Bentley) M.; m. Norma Dierking, Dec. 20, 1945; children: Timothy I., Susan (Mrs. Paul Newhouse). A.B., Bates Coll., 1936; M.A. (Perkins scholar), Columbia U., 1938, Ph.D., 1942. With Civilian Pub. Svc., 1941-45; Instr. history Swarthmore (Pa.) Coll., 1944; tutor Olivet (Mich.) Coll., 1947-49; asst. prof. liberal studies Clarkson Coll. Tech., Potsdam, N.Y., 1949-51; asso. prof. Clarkson Coll. Tech., 1951-55; prof., 1955-61; dir. social studies div. Delta Coll., University Center, Mich., 1961-64; prof., chmn. dept. humanities and social scis. Rose Poly. Inst., Terre Haute, Ind., 1964-65; prof. history State U. Coll. at New Paltz, N.Y., 1965-80; prof. emeritus State U. Coll. at New Paltz, 1980—; participant in projects for Am. Friends Service Com., 1941-47, 53, 63; Fulbright prof. Keio U., Tokyo, 1953-54. Author: The American Leonardo, A Life of Samuel F.B. Morse, 1943, The Seaway Story, 1961, Black Freedom: The Nonviolent Abolitionists from 1830 through the Civil War, 1970, Black Education in New York State: From Colonial to Modern Times, 1979; author: (with Susan Mabee Newhouse) Sojourner Truth: Slave, Prophet, Legend, 1993; Listen to the Whistle: An Ancedotal History of the Wallkill Valley Railroad in Ulster and Orange Counties, N.Y., 1995; also articles: editor: (With James A. Fletcher) A Quaker Speaks from the Black Experience: The Life and Selected Writings of Barrington Dunbar, 1979. Trustee Young-Morse Hist. Site, Poughkeepsie, N.Y.; bd. dirs. Wallkill Valley Land Trust, New Paltz, N.Y. Recipient Pulitzer prize in biography, 1944, Bergstein award for excellence in teaching Delta Coll., 1963, Anisfield-Wolf award race rels., 1971, Gustavus Myers award for outstanding book on human rights, 1994; rsch. grantee Rsch. Found. SUNY, 1965, 67, 68, 80, Am. Philos. Soc., 1970, Nat. Inst. Edn., 1973-76, NSF, 1982-83. Mem. N.Y. State Hist. Assn., Phi Beta Kappa, Delta Sigma Rho. Methodist. Home: 2121 Route 44-55 Gardiner NY 12525-5808

MABEE, JOHN RICHARD, physician assistant, educator; b. San Francisco, Sept. 18, 1956; s. Robert John and Mary Sachiko (Nose) M.; m. Cheryl Ann Saxton, June 24, 1978 (div. Aug. 1995); children: Jonathan, Alan; m. Carol Mendez, 1998. BS, Regents Coll., 1981; MS, Calif. State U., L.A., 1991; postgrad., Union Inst., Cin., 1994—. Cert. physician asst., Nat. Commn. Cert. Physician Assts. Physician asst. resident dept. emergency medicine LA County/U. So. Calif. Med. Ctr., 1984-85, emergency medicine physician asst., 1985—; rsch. asst. dept. biology Calif. State U., L.A., 1987-88, lectr., 1988-91, physician asst., 1992; rsch. physician asst. U. So. Calif. Emergency Medicine Assocs., L.A., 1993-95, clin. instr. dept. emergency medicine, 1994—, conscious sedation adv. com., 1995—, lectr. sch. medicine, 1995—. Contbr. articles to profl. jours. Named Alumnus of Yr., Emergency Medicine Physician Asst. Residency, 1994. Fellow Am. Acad. Physician Assts.; mem. Soc. Emergency Medicine Physician Assts. (founding, election com., 1988—). Democrat. Avocations: reading, watching videos, horseback riding, chess, cooking, tae kwon do. Home: 717 S Almansor St # A Alhambra CA 91801-4508 Office: LAC-USC Med Ctr 1200 N State St Rm 1060 Los Angeles CA 90033-4525

MABEY, RALPH R., lawyer; b. Salt Lake City, May 20, 1944; s. Rendell Noel and Rachel (Wilson) M.; m. Sylvia States, June 5, 1968; children: Rachel, Elizabeth, Emily, Sara. BA, U. Utah, 1968; JD, Columbia U., 1972. Bar: Utah 1972, U.S. Dist. Ct. Utah 1972, U.S. Ct. Appeals (10th cir.) 1976, N.Y. 1985, U.S. Supreme Ct. 1988, U.S. Ct. Appeals (4th cir.) 1988, U.S. Ct. Appeals (3d cir.) 1993. Law clk. Atty. Gen., Salt Lake City, 1970, U.S. Dist. Ct., Salt Lake City, 1972-73; ptnr. Irvine, Smith & Mabey, Salt Lake City, 1973-79; U.S. bankruptcy judge U.S. Ct., Salt Lake City, 1979-83; ptnr. LeBoeuf, Lamb, Greene & MacRae, Salt Lake City and N.Y.C., 1983—; adj. prof. Brigham Young U. Sch. Law, Provo, Utah, 1983—, U. Utah Coll. Law, Salt Lake City, 1983-85. Mng. editor Norton Bankruptcy Law Adviser, 1983-85; contbg. author: Collier Bankruptcy Manual, 1986—, Collier on Bankruptcy, 15th Edition. With USAR, 1968-74. Mem. ABA (bus. bankruptcy com., joint task force bankruptcy court structure and insolvency processes), Nat. Bankruptcy Conf., Am. Bankruptcy Inst., Am. Coll. Bankruptcy (bd. dirs.). Republican. Mormon. Avocation: running. Home: 253 S 1550 E Bountiful UT 84010-1350 Office: LeBoeuf Lamb Greene & MacRae 1000 Kearns Bldg 136 S Main St Salt Lake City UT 84101-1601 also: 125 W 55th St New York NY 10019-5369

MABIE, SUSAN (SUSSE), secondary education educator; b. Rockville Centre, N.Y., Nov. 13, 1946; d. James Spencer and Marjorie Janet (Van Fleet) Rothston; m. Howard Evon Mabie, June 22, 1968; 1 child, Robin Marie Boyette. AAS in Graphic Arts, SUNY, Farmingdale, 1966; BS in Art Edn., SUNY, Buffalo, 1969; MEd in Art Edn., U. Ctrl. Fla., 1972. Artist, account exec. Graphics III, Inc., N.Y.C., 1966-67; tchr. art Lyman High Sch., Longwood, Fla., 1970-85; tchr. photography and graphic arts, yearbook advisor Oviedo (Fla.) High Sch., 1985-997; sales and svc. rep. Taylor Pub. Co., Dallas, 1997—; instr. seminars Taylor Pub. Co., 1988—, Sunshine Journalism Workshop, 1991-94. Mem. Fla. Scholastic Press Assn. (coord. state conv. spkrs. 1991, pres. 1995-97, Fla. Journalism Tchr. of Yr. award 1992), Seminole County Art Edn. Assn. (sec. 1991-93), So. Interscholastic Press Assn. (spkr.), Columbia Scholastic Press Assn. (judge), Journalism Edn. Assn., Nat. Scholastic Press Assn. Republican. Home and Office: 1697 Sparkling Water Circle Ocoee FL 34761

MABLEY, JACK, newspaper columnist, communications consultant; b. Binghamton, N.Y., Oct. 26, 1915; s. Clarence Ware and Mabelle (Howe) M.; m. Frances Habeck, Aug. 29, 1940; children: Mike, Jill, Ann, Pat, Robert. B.S., U. Ill., 1938. With Chgo. Daily News, 1938-61, reporter, writer, columnist, 1957-61; columnist Chgo.'s Am., 1961-69, asst. mng. editor, 1966-69; asso. editor Chgo. Today, 1969-73; columnist Chgo. Today, Chgo. Tribune, 1973-74, Chgo. Tribune, 1974-82; pres. Mabley & Assocs., Corp. Communications, Glenview, Ill., 1982; columnist Daily Herald, Arlington Heights, Ill., 1987—; Lectr. journalism Northwestern U., 1949-50. Pres. Village of Glenview, Ill., 1957-61, Skokie Valley Community Hosp., Skokie, Ill., 1977-79. Served from ensign to lt. USNR, 1941-45. Recipient Media award Nat. Assn. for Retarded Citizens, 1977. Home and Office: 2275 Winnetka Rd Glenview IL 60025-1825

MABRY, DONALD JOSEPH, university administrator, history educator; b. Atlanta, Apr. 21, 1941; s. Jerry Leon and Eunice Leigh (Harris) M.; m. Susan Strong Johnston, July 28, 1962 (div. Oct. 1986); children: Scott, Mark; m. Paula Ann Crockett, Dec. 18, 1992. BA, Kenyon Coll., Gambier, Ohio, 1963; MEd, Bowling Green State U., 1964; PhD, Syracuse U., 1970. Instr. St. Johns River Community Coll., Palatka, Fla., 1964-67; rsch. asst. fin. aid Syracuse (N.Y.) U., 1967-68, teaching fellow in history, 1968-69, Maxwell fellow, 1969-70, vis. lectr. dept. history, 1969, 70; asst. to chancellor U. Kans., Lawrence, 1978-79; from. asst. prof. to prof. dept. history Miss. State U., Mississippi State, 1970—, asst. to pres., 1979-81, assoc. dean for budget and rsch., 1991—; now dir., assoc. dean Biol. Physical Sciences Rsch. Inst., Mississippi State, Miss.; sr. fellow Ctr. for Internat. Security and Strategic Studies, Miss. State U., 1981—. Author: Mexico's Accion Nacional, 1973, The Mexican University and the State, 1982, (with others) Neighbors--Mexico and the United States, 1981; editor: The Latin American Narcotics Trade and U.S. National Security, 1989; contbr. articles to profl. jours. Mem. Am. Coun. on Edn. (exec. com. Coun. of Fellows 1980-83), South Ea. Coun. on Latin Am. Studies. Avocation: computer telecommunications. Home: 206 Hiwassee Dr Starkville MS 39759-2117 Office: Mississippi State U College of Arts & Sciences Box AS Mississippi State MS 39762

MABSON, ROBERT LANGLEY, clergyman, librarian; b. New Orleans, Apr. 17, 1931; s. Eugene Beall and Eva Louise (Lea) M.; m. Minnie Augusta Lewis, Dec. 22, 1953; children: Lewis, Susan Jane, Laura Lea. BA, Tulane U., 1952; postgrad., Union Theol. Sem., 1952-55; M. of Religious Edn., Pres. Sch. Christian Edn., 1955; MS, La. State U., 1964. Ordained to ministry Presbyn. Ch., 1955. Pastor, Mt. Pleasant Presbyn. Ch., Sinks Grove, W.Va., 1955-57; dir., Christian edn. Barbee Larger Parish 1957-59; pastor, 1st Presbyn. Ch., Perry (Mo.), 1957-59; pastor, 1st Presbyn. Ch., Talihina, Okla., 1959-63, Eastland Presbyn. Ch., Memphis, 1966-78, Ebenezer Presbyn. Ch., Strong, Ark., 1983-84, Sulphur Springs Cumberland Presbyn. Ch., Louann, Ark., 1984-88; chaplain USPHS Hosp., Talikina, Okla., 1959-63, Calvary Colony Alcoholic Rehab. Ctr., also Kings Daus. and Sons Home, Memphis, 1979-83; head librarian, prof. Meth. Coll., Fayetteville, N.C., 1964-66; asst. libr. Memphis Theol. Sem., 1967-74; active Presbyn. Coun. Evangelism, 1959-63, Covenant Presbytery, 1973-84, stated clk., 1973-75, moderator, 1976, Mound Prairie Presbytery, 1984-88, Ark. Presbytery, 1989. Author: Presbyterian Missionary Labors in Kiamichi Valley, Oklahoma, 1850-1960. Recipient Congl. Cmty. Svc. award, 1978. Mem. ALA (life). Address: PO Box 92 Mount Holly AR 71758-0092 *My purpose has been to help others, and to encourage all to be good listeners—there is too much talking by too many ministers.*

MACADAM, WALTER KAVANAGH, consulting engineering executive; b. N.Y.C., Nov. 16, 1913; s. John Moore and Mary (Kavanagh) MacA.; m. Rilla Reed, Jan. 30, 1941; children: Ann (Mrs. Richard vonHoorn), Marie (Mrs. Paul Hoffman), Clair (Mrs. Bruno Aimi), Daniel, David, Barbara. B.S. and M.S. in Elec. Engring, Mass. Inst. Tech., 1937. With AT&T, 1937-68, with long lines dept., 1951-53, 54-56; supt. engring Distant Early Warning radar installation in Arctic for Western Electric Co., 1953-54; transmission engr. AT&T, 1956-59, bldg. and equipment engr., 1959, asst. chief engr., 1959-60, v.p. def., 1960-68; v.p. engring. N.Y. Telephone Co., 1968-73; cons. engr., 1973—. Bd. dirs. United Engring. Trustees, 1965-73, pres., 1971; mem. N.H. Legis. Acad. Sci. and Tech., 1980-82, N.H. Adv. Panel on Pub. Utility Legis., 1985-86. Recipient Vail medal AT&T, 1937. Fellow IEEE (dir. 1963-68, pres. 1967 Centennial medal); mem. ASME, Nat. Soc. Profl. Engrs., Sigma Xi, Tau Beta Pi, Eta Kappa Nu. Club: K.C. (4 deg.). Home: 9 Pinewood Vlg West Lebanon NH 03784-3120

MACAFEE, SUSAN DIANE, reporter; b. Feb. 1944. Attended, Foothill Coll. Disc jockey with news, pub. affairs; engr., editor, prodr. Sta. KZSU-Stanford U., Calif., 1975-80; freelance reporter, broadcast journalist, 1975—. Writer, prodr., engr. editor, narrator 25 original nationwide news stories and furnished story material for numerous radio stas. and networks, TV stas. including NPR, Pacifica, ABC, NBC and CBS networks, BBC radio and TV, Channel 9 Australia, numerous newspapers and magazines; rschr., documentor and author: Agent Orange Pilot Nutritional Detox Program, 1986, (5-part series) Food-Diet-Crime, Behavior and Learning Disability Connection, 1986; author, prodr., engr., editor and narrator: Treatment of Refractory Eosinophillia Myalgia Syndrome Associated with the Injestion of L-Tryptophan Containing Products, Parts I and II, 1990; interviewer, recorder, transcriber: A Historical Prospective of Vitamin C With Linus Pauling, 1991; researcher, documentor, writer Postscipt: Interactions of Glutathione, Ascorbic Acid HIV and AIDS, 1992, Neural Tube Defects and Folic Acid, 1995, Chromiun - A New Treatment for Adult Type II (Maturity Onset) Diabetes, 1996. V.p. Calif. Coll. Young Reps., 1967; sec., asst. to Nat. Field Dir. Coll. Young Reps., Rep. Nat. Com., Washington, 1968; dir. precinct orgn. Calif. State Assembly Campaign, San Francisco Rep. Ctrl. Com., 1968. Recipient 3 Nat. awards Young Rep. Nat. Com., 1967-68. Home and Office: PO Box 4644 Rockville MD 20849-4644

MACAIS, TELLO MANUEL, diplomat; s. Manuel Tello and Guadalupe Macías Viadero. Amb. to Gt. Britain Govt. of Mexico, London, 1977-79, under-sec. fgn. affairs, 1979-82; permanent rep. internat. orgns. Govt. of Mexico, Geneva, 1983-89; amb. to France Govt. of Mexico, 1989-92; sec. fgn. rels. Govt. of Mexico, Mexico City, 1994-95; now permanent rep. of Mexico to UN N.Y.C. Office: Permanent Mission of Mexico 2 United Nations Plz Fl 28 New York NY 10017-4403

MACALISTER, ROBERT STUART, oil company executive; b. L.A., May 22, 1924; s. Robert Stuart and Iris Grace (Doman) MacA.; m. Catherine Vera Willby, Nov. 15, 1947 (dec. 1994); children: Rodney James, Sara Marjorie Pfirrmann; m. Grace V. LeClerc, Dec. 2, 1995. Student, Brighton Coll., Sussex, Eng., 1945; BSME, Calif. Inst. Tech., 1947. Registered profl. engr., Tex. Petroleum engr. Shell Oil Co., 1947-56; mgmt. trainee Royal Dutch Shell, The Hague, Netherlands, 1956-57; with exec. staff, mgr. Shell Oil Co., U.S.A., 1957-68; v.p., ops. mgr. Occidental Petroleum Corp., Tripoli, Libya, 1968-71; mng. dir.various subs. London, 1971-76; mng. dir., pres. Occidental Internat. Oil, Inc., London, 1976-78; pres., chmn. bd. Can. Occidental Petroleum Ltd., Calgary Alberta, 1978-81; mng. dir. Australian Occidental Petroleum Ltd., Sydney, 1982-83, Hamilton Bros. Oil & Gas Ltd., London, 1983-86; petroleum cons. Camarillo, Calif., 1986—; exec. U.K. Offshore Operators, London, 1972-78, 83-86. Cubmaster Boy Scouts Am., Larchmont, N.Y., 1964-65, scoutmaster, Houston, 1965-68. Sgt. U.S. Army, 1944-45, ETO. Mem. Am. Assn. Petroleum Geologists, Soc. Petroleum Engrs., Can. Petroleum Assn. (bd. govs. 1978-81), Las Posas Country Club, Gold Coast Srs. Republican. Episcopalian. Avocations: carpentry, crafts, watercolor painting, golfing, gardening. Home and Office: 78 Lopaco Ct Camarillo CA 93010-8846

MACALUSO, FRANK AUGUSTUS, oil company executive; b. Cheyenne, Wyo., May 27, 1931; s. Frank R. and Thelma Elizabeth (Speight) M.; m. Margaret Ann Lynch, Oct. 14, 1950; children: Anne Marie Macaluso Foust, Elizabeth Mary Macaluso Nance, Margaret Mary Macaluso Walters, Teresa Marie Macaluso Fleming, Frank A. Jr. ABBA, Regis Coll., 1950. Asst. cashier Merchants Bank, Gallup, N.Mex., 1950-52, Citizens Bank, Aztec, N.Mex., 1952-56; v.p. 1st Nat. Bank, Farmington, N.Mex., 1957-59; founder, chmn., CEO Macaluso Oil Co., Farmington, 1959—; dir. Four Corners Savings Bank, Farmington, 1969-85; organizer, chmn. bd. dirs. Sunwest Bank, Farmington, 1974—; dir. Sunwest Fin. Svcs., Albuquerque, 1988-92; pres., chmn. bd. dirs. Amigo Petroleum Co., Albuquerque, 1988—; chmn. Texaco Wholesale Coun., 1994; pres., dir. Star Mktg. Acceptance Corp., Starmac Acceptance Corp., Star Merketers Acct. Corp., Houston, 1994-97. Mem. Gov's. Bus. Adv. Coun., N.Mex. State Bd. Fin., Santa Fe, 1970-82, 91-95, N.Mex. Engery Conversation Comm., N.Mex. 1st, Albuquerque, 1986—; bd. dirs. U. N.Mex. Found., Albuquerque, 1988—. Named Boss of Yr. by Jaycees, 1971. Mem. N.Mex. Petroleum Marketers Assn. (pres. 1974-75), N.Mex. Amigos, San Juan Country Club (pres. 1980-82), Farmington C. of C., KC, Elks. Democrat. Roman Catholic. Avocation: golf. Office: PO Box 90 2501 E Main St Farmington NM 87499-0090

MACAN, WILLIAM ALEXANDER, IV, lawyer; b. Boston, Nov. 21, 1942; s. William A. and Carol (Whitten) M.; m. Jane Mitchell Ahern, Sept. 3, 1965; children: Sandra Jane, William Andrew. BS, Haverford Coll., 1964; LLB, U. Pa., 1967. Bar: Pa. 1968, U.S. Tax Ct. 1970. Law clk. to judge U.S. Tax Ct., Washington, 1967-69; assoc. firm Morgan, Lewis & Bockius, Phila., 1969-76; ptnr. Morgan, Lewis & Bockius L.L.P., 1976—; lectr. legal instns., seminars. Author publs. on tax-oriented equipment leasing, other tax subjects. Mem. ABA, Pa. Bar Assn., Phila. Bar Assn. Republican. Presbyterian. Office: Morgan Lewis & Bockius LLP 101 Park Ave New York NY 10178 also: 2000 One Logan Sq Philadelphia PA 19103

MACARIO, ALBERTO JUAN LORENZO, physician; b. Naschel, Argentina, Dec. 1, 1935; came to U.S., 1974, naturalized, 1980; s. Alberto Carlos and Maria Elena (Giraudi) M.; MD, Nat. U. Buenos Aires, 1961; m. Everly Conway, Mar. 16, 1963; children: Alex, Everly. Intern, Ramos Mejia Hosp., Buenos Aires, 1958-60, resident 1960; resident Rivadavia Hosp., Buenos Aires, 1961-62, physician-hematologist, 1962-64; fellow NRC Argentina, Buenos Aires, 1964-69; head dept. radioactive isotopes Inst. Hematological Investigations, Nat. Acad. Medicine Argentina, Buenos Aires, 1967-69; Eleanor Roosevelt fellow Internat. Union Against Cancer, Dept. Tumorbiology, Karolinska Inst., Stockholm, 1969-71; mem. sci. staff Lab. Cell Biology, NRC Italy, Rome, 1971-73; head Lab. Immunology, Internat. Agy. Rsch. on Cancer, WHO, Lyons, France, 1973-74; research scientist Brown U., Providence, 1974-76, Div. Labs. and Rsch., N.Y. State Dept. Health, Albany, 1976-79; chief hematology Clin. Lab. Center, N.Y. State Dept. Health, Albany, 1979-81, dir. clin. and exptl. immunology sect. Lab. Medicine Inst., 1981-83; rsch. physician, 1981—, Wadsworth Ctr. N.Y. State Dept. of Health; prof. Dept. Biomed. Scis. Sch. Pub. Health U. at Albany, 1985—, mem. senate at SUNY Albany, N.Y., 1989-94; adj. prof. pathology and lab. medicine Albany Med. Coll., 1991—; mem. structural and cell biology program Albany Univs. and Colls.; grant reviewer for nat. and internat. agys.; manuscript reviewer for sci. jours. Recipient Diploma de Honor prize Nat. U. Buenos Aires, 1961, Bernardino Rivadavia prize Nat. Acad. Medicine Argentina, 1967, Ciencia e Investigation prize Argentinian Soc. Advancement Sci., 1967; Ford Found.-NAS travel fellow, 1968, Eleanor Roosevelt fellow, 1969. Mem. Scandinavian Soc. Immunology, Italian Assn. Immunologists, French Soc. Immunology, Am. Assn. Immunologists, Am. Soc. Microbiology (sect. editor Manual of Clin. Lab. Immunology 5th edit. 1994—), Am. Soc. Investigative Pathology. Achievements include patents in field; discovered primary myeloperoxydase deficiency in leucocytes, and oscillations of antibody affinity during maturation of immune responses; developed method for immunologic identification of bacteria that produce methane gas; discovered antigenic diversity of these bacteria in natural and manufactured ecosystems; described structural topography of methanogenic bacteria and population dynamics in granular microbial consortia; found novel multicellular forms of archaebacteria; isolated for the first time the genes in the dnaK locus from an archaebacterium; devised and constructed the first integration vector for genetically engineering a methanogen useful for waste bioconversion. Editor multivol. treatise Monoclonal Antibodies Against Bacteria and treatise Gene Probes for Bacteria; contbr. articles to profl. jours., chpts. to books. Office: Empire State Pla Dept Health Wadsworth Ctr PO Box 509 Albany NY 12201-0509 *I am capable to walk alone, but with my wife by me I fly. We can both ascend toward the sky and together we reach the stars. Separately, alone, who knows, we might never have been able to rise above the mountains, perhaps not even the hills, we have conquered flapping our wings in unison.*

MACARTHUR, CAROL JEANNE, pediatric otolaryngology educator; b. Glendale, Calif., Aug. 23, 1957; d. Seth Gerald and Barbara Jeanne (Shaw) MacA.; m. Geoffrey Buncke, Dec. 14, 1990; children: Keith Davis, Michelle Jeanne. BS, Occidental Coll., 1979; MD, UCLA, 1984. Diplomate Am. Bd. Otolaryngology. Intern U. Calif., Davis, 1984-85, resident in otolaryngology, 1985-90; fellow in pediatric otolaryngology Boston Children's Hosp., 1990-91; instr. dept. otolaryngology U. Calif.-Davis, Sacramento, 1989-90; clin. fellow in otology and laryngology Harvard U. Med. Sch., Boston, 1990-91; asst. prof. U. Calif., Irvine, 1991—, asst. prof. dept. pediatrics, 1993—, program dir. dept. otolaryngology-head and neck surgery, 1992-95. Recipient investigator devel. award Am. Acad. Facial Plastic and Reconstructive Surgery, 1993. Fellow ACS, Am. Acad. Pediatrics; mem. Am. Soc. Pediat. Otolaryngology, Soc. for Ear, Nose and Throat Advances in Children, Am. Cleft Palate Craniofacial Assn., Am. Acad. Otorhinolaryngology-Head and Neck Surgery, Alpha Omega Alpha. Office: 302 W La Veta Ave Ste 201 Orange CA 92866-2607

MACARTHUR, ROBERT S., foundation administrator, Episcopalian priest; M. Peggy MacArthur; children: Colin, Bronwen, Stuart, Hillary. BA, Dartmouth Coll.; MDiv, Yale U. Dir. outward bound ctr. Dartmouth Coll.; pres. Am. Youth Found., St. Louis, 1985—. Office: Am Youth Found Saint Louis MO 63100

MACAULAY, DAVID (ALEXANDER), author, illustrator; b. Burton-on-Trent, Eng., Dec. 2, 1946; s. James and Joan (Lowe) M.; m. Janice Elizabeth Michel, 1970 (div.); 1 child, Elizabeth Alexandra; m. Ruth Marris, 1978 (div.); 1 child, Charlotte Valerie; m. Ruth Ellen Murray, 1997. BArch, R.I. Sch. Design, 1969. Instr. interior design R.I. Sch. Design, Providence, 1969-73, instr. two-dimensional design, 1974-76, adj. faculty dept. illustration, 1977-79; tchr. art Central Falls (R.I.) Pub. Schs., 1969-70, Newton, Mass., 1972-74; designer Morris Nathanson Design, 1969-72. Author, illustrator: Cathedral: The Story of Its Construction, 1973 (Caldecott Honor book 1973), City, 1974, Pyramid, 1975 (Christopher medal 1975), Underground, 1976, Castle, 1977 (Caldecott Honor book 1977), Great Moments in Architecture, 1978, Motel of the Mysteries, 1979, Unbuilding, 1980, Mill, 1983, Baaa, 1985, Why the Chicken Crossed the Road, 1987, The Way Things Work, 1988, Black and White, 1990 (Caldecott medal 1991), Ship, 1993, Shortcut, 1995; illustrator: Help! Let Me Out!, 1982, Electricity, 1983, The Amazing Brain, 1984; cons., presenter various TV projects. Recipient Wash. Children's Book Guild award, 1977, AIA medal, 1978, Bradford Washburn meda. Boston Mus. Sci., 1993, Charles Frankel prize NEH, 1995, Chevalier of Order of Arts and Letters, France, 1995.

MACAULAY, LAWRENCE A., Canadian government official; b. St. Peters Bay, Sept. 9, 1946; s. Archibald and Bernadette MacAulay; m. Frances Elaine O'Connell, Aug. 16, 1972; children: Carolyn, Rita, Lynn. Mem. House of Commons, 1988—, apptd. assoc. critic for fisheries and oceans, 1989, apptd. critic for srs. and assoc. critic for fisheries, 1990; sec. of state for vets. Govt. of Can., 1993—; mem. standing com. on forestry and fisheries, caucus com. on health and social devel.; acclaimed chair Atlantic Caucus, 1992. Roman Catholic. Office: Veterans Affairs Can, 161 Grafton St PO Box 7700, Charlottetown, PE Canada C1A 8M9*

MACAULAY, RONALD KERR STEVEN, linguistics educator, former college dean; b. West Kilbride, Ayrshire, Scotland, Nov. 3, 1927; came to U.S., 1965; s. Robert Wilson and Mary Robb (McDermid) M.; m. Janet Grey, July 25, 1956; children: Harvey, Anna. M.A., U. St. Andrews, 1955; Ph.D., UCLA, 1971. Lectr. Brit. Inst., Lisbon, Portugal, 1955-60, Brit Council, Buenos Aires, Argentina, 1960-64; asst. prof. linguistics Pitzer Coll., Claremont, Calif., 1965-67; assoc. prof. Pitzer Coll., 1967-73, prof., 1973—, dean faculty, 1980-86. Author: Language, Social Class and Education, 1977, Generally Speaking: How Children Learn Language, 1980, Locating Dialect in Disourse: The Language of Honest Men and Bonnie Lasses in Ayr, 1991, The Social Art: Language and Its Uses, 1994, Standards and Variation in Urban Speech: Some Examples From Lowland Scots, 1997; editor: (with R.P. Stockwell) Linguistic Change and Generative Theory, 1972, (with D. Brenneis) The Matrix of Language: Contemporary Linguistic Anthropology, 1996. Home: 317 W 7th St Claremont CA 91711-4312 Office: Pitzer Coll 1050 N Mills Ave Claremont CA 91711-3908

MACAULEY, EDWARD C., company executive; b. St. Louis, Mar. 22, 1928; s. Charles J. and Josephine (Durkin) M.; m. Jacqueline Combs, July 12, 1952; children: Mary Ann, Robert, Teresa, Michael, Kathleen, Margaret. BS, St. Louis U., 1949. Basketball player Boston Celtics, 1950-56; basketball player St. Louis Hawks, 1957-58, coach, 1959-60; sports dir. Stas. KTVI-TV and KSDK-TV, St. Louis, 1960-70; stockbroker A.G. Edwards-Shearson Lehman, St. Louis, 1970-81; pres. Macauley Kremjet, St. Louis, 1981—, Eagle Communications, St. Louis, 1982-86; bd. dirs. Color Art Printing Co., St. Louis. Trustee Basketball Hall of Fame, Springfield, Mass., 1980—, Mo. Basketball Hall of Fame, Columbia, 1988—, Marianist Apostolic Ctr., St. Louis, 1988—; mem. St. Liborius Food Pantry, St. Louis, 1988-89; organizer St. Nicholas Food Pantry, St. Louis, 1989; ordained deacon Archdiocese of St. Louis, Roman Cath. Ch., 1989—. Named to All Am. Basketball Team, AP, UP, Life, Colliers mag., 1948, 49, All Pro Team, NBA, 1951, 52, 53; inducted into Basketball Hall of Fame, 1961. Avocations: golf, travel, preaching. Home and Office: 1455 Reauville Dr Saint Louis MO 63122-1441

MACAVOY, PAUL WEBSTER, economics, management educator, university dean; b. Haverhill, Mass., Apr. 21, 1934; s. Paul Everett and Louise Madeline (Webster) MacA.; m. Katherine Ann Manning, June 13, 1955; children: Libby, Matthew. A.B., Bates Coll., 1955, LL.D., 1976; M.A., Yale, 1956, Ph.D., 1960. Asst. to full prof. MIT, Cambridge, Mass., 1963-74, Henry R. Luce prof. pub. policy, 1974-75; mem. Pres.'s Coun. Econ. Advisers, 1975-76; prof. econs. and mgmt. Yale U., 1976-81, Beinecke prof. econs., 1981-83; dean W.E. Simon Grad. Sch. Bus. Admin. U. Rochester, 1983-91; Williams Bros. prof. Yale Sch. Mgmt. Yale U., 1991—, dean Yale Sch. Mgmt., 1992-94; bd. dirs. Alumax Inc., Lafarge Corp. Author: Price Formation in Natural Gas Fields, 1962, (with Stephen Breyer) Energy Regulation by the Federal Power Commission, 1974, (with R. Pindyck) The Economics of the Natural Gas Shortage, 1975, The Regulated Industries and the Economy, 1979, World Crude Oil Prices, 1981, Energy Policy, 1983, Explaining Metals Prices, 1988, Industry Regulation and the Performance of the American Economy, 1992, The Failure of Antitrust and Regulation to Establish Competition in Long Distance Telephone Service Markets, 1996; editor: Ford Administration Papers on Regulatory Reform, 8 vols., 1977-78, Privatization and State-Owned Enterprise: Assessment for the United Kingdom, Canada and the United States, 1988. Home: 420 Humphrey St New Haven CT 06511-3711 Office: Yale Sch Mgmt PO Box 208200 New Haven CT 06520-8200

MACAVOY, THOMAS COLEMAN, glass manufacturing executive, educator; b. Jamaica, N.Y., Apr. 24, 1928; s. Joseph V. and Edna M. Mac A.; m. Margaret M. Walsh, Dec. 27, 1952; children: Moira Mac Avoy Brown, Ellen Mac Avoy Jennings, Christopher, Neil. B.S. in Chemistry, Queens Coll., 1950; M.S. in Chemistry, St. John's U., 1952, D.Sc. (hon.), 1973; Ph.D. in Chemistry, U. Cin., 1952. Chemist, Charles Pfizer & Co., Bklyn., 1957-60; mgr. electronics research Corning Glass Works, N.Y., 1960-64; dir. phys. research Corning Glass Works, 1964-66, v.p. electronic products div., 1966-69, v.p. tech. products div., 1969-71, pres., 1971-83, vice-chmn., 1983-87; prof. mgmt. grad. sch. U. Va., 1988—; bd. dirs. Quaker Oats Co., Chubb Corp. Patentee in field; contbr. articles to tech. jours. Trustee Corning Mus. Glass; past pres. Boy Scouts Am. With USN, 1946; with USAF, 1952-53. Recipient Silver Antelope award Boy Scouts Am., 1976, Silver Beaver award, 1975, Silver Buffalo award, 1982, Bronze Wolf award, 1988. Roman Catholic. Office: U Va Darden Grad Sch Bus Admin Charlottesville VA 22096

MACBAIN, WILLIAM HALLEY, minister, theology educator, seminary chancellor; b. Cambridge, Ont., Can., Aug. 12, 1916; s. George Alexander and Grace Ann (Wilkins) MacB.; m. Mary Ann Munday, Aug. 20, 1941; children: Grace Elizabeth MacBain Silvester, Constance Marilyn MacBain Parker. Licentiate in Theology, Toronto Baptist Sem., Ont., 1939; DD (hon.), Cen. Bapt. Sem., Toronto, 1962. Ordained to ministry Bapt. Ch., 1940. Pastor, founder Temple Bapt. Ch., Sarnia, Ont., 1937-64; pastor Forward Bapt. Ch., Toronto, 1964-73; dir., gen. sec. Fellowship Fgn. Missions, Toronto, 1973-81; chancellor Cen. Bapt. Sem., 1981-93, Heritage Bapt. Bible Coll. and Theol. Sem., Cambridge, Ont., Can., 1993—; pastor emeritus Forward Bapt. Ch., Toronto, 1994—; chmn. Can. Bd. Greater Europe Mission, 1963-73. Mem. Fellowship Evang. Bapt. Chs. in Can. (pres. 1953-54, 83-84). Conservative. Home: 35 Wynford Heights Cres Apt 2603, Don Mills, ON Canada M3C 1L1 Office: Heritage Bapt Bible Coll and Theol Sem, 175 Holiday Inn Dr, Cambridge, ON Canada N3C 3T2

MACBETH, ANGUS, lawyer; b. L.A., May 9, 1942. BA, Yale U., 1964, LLB, 1969. Bar: N.Y. 1970, D.C. 1981. Law clk. to Hon. Harold R. Tyler, Jr. U.S. Dist. Ct. (so. dist.) N.Y., 1969-70, asst. U.S. atty. criminal divsn., 1975-77; chief pollution control sect. Land and Natural Resources Divsn., U.S. Dept. Justice, 1977-79, dep. asst. atty. gen., 1979-81; ptnr. Sidley & Austin, Washington; adj. prof. law N.Y. Law Sch., 1985—; spl. counsel Wartime Relocation and Internment Civilians Commn., 1981-83. Mem. D.C. Bar (steering com. energy and natural resources divsn. 1982-84), N.Y. State Bar Assn. (exec. com. sect. environ. law 1981—), Phi Beta Kappa. Office: Sidley & Austin 1722 I St NW Washington DC 20006-3705

MACBRIDE, THOMAS JAMISON, federal judge; b. Sacramento, Mar. 25, 1914; s. Frank and Lotta Kirtley (Little) MacB.; m. Martha Harrold, Nov. 7, 1947; children—Peter, Thomas Jamison, David, Laurie. A.B., U. Calif. at Berkeley, 1936, J.D., 1940. Bar: Calif. 1940. Dep. atty. gen. Calif., 1941-42; pvt. practice Sacramento, 1946-61; U.S. dist. judge Eastern Dist. Calif., Sacramento, 1961-67; chief judge Eastern Dist. Calif., 1967-79, sr. judge, 1979-96; mem. U.S. Temporary Emergency Ct. Appeals, 1982-87; mem. Criminal Justice Act Com., U.S. Jud. Conf., 1969-88; mem. U.S. Jud. Conf., 1975-78; chmn. Criminal Justice Act Com. of U.S. Jud. Conf., 1979-88; mem. U.S. Fgn. Intelligence Surveillance Ct., 1979-80. Pres. Town Hall, Sacramento, 1952, N.E. area YMCA, 1960; mem. Calif. Legislature from Sacramento County, 1955-60 mem. Nat. Commn. on Reform Fed. Criminal Laws, 1967-71; bd. dirs. Sacramento YMCA; trustee U. Calif., San Francisco Found., 1982-96; bd. dirs. Sacramento Regional Found., 1988-96; founding dir. League to Save Lake Tahoe, 1965. Lt. USNR., 1942-46. Mem. ABA, U. Calif. Alumni Assn. (v.p. 1955, 60), Mason (33 deg., Shriner, Jester), Rotarian (pres. 1966-67), Sutter Club, Univ. (pres. 1951-52), Comstock (pres. 1975-76), Senator Outing (sec.-treas.), Kappa Sigma, Phi Delta Phi. Democrat. Office: US Dist Ct US Courthouse 650 Capitol Mall Sacramento CA 95814

MACCARTHY, TALBOT LELAND, civic volunteer; b. St. Louis, Jan. 28, 1936; d. Austin Porter Leland and Dorothy (Lund) Follansbee; m. John Peters MacCarthy, June 21, 1958; children: John Leland MacCarthy, Talbot MacCarthy Payne. BA, Vassar Coll., 1958. Sec., treas. Station List Pub. Co., St. Louis, 1975-85, pres., 1985-90. Trustee Robert E. Lee Meml. Assn., Arts and Edn. Coun. Greater St. Louis, pres., 1978-80, emerita; trustee St. Louis Art Mus.; past trsutee St. Louis Mercantile Libr. Assn., Family & Children's Svc. Greater St. Louis, Health and Welfare Coun., Greater St. Louis, Jr. Kindergarten St. Louis Page Park YMCA, Scholarship Found. St. Louis, Friends St. Louis Art Mus. Bd., Ch. St. Michael and St. George Sch. Bd., Mid-Am. Arts Alliance; chmn. Mo. Arts Coun., 1980-85; past chmn. Vol. Action Ctr. Greater St. Louis; past vice chmn. bd. dirs. Mary Inst.; past pres. Jr. League St. Louis; mem. Nat. Coun. Arts, 1985-91; vestry mem. Ch. of St. Michael and St. George. Recipient Woman of Achievement citation St. Louis Globe Democrat, 1979, Mo. Citizens for Arts/Arts Advocacy award, 1987, Mo. Arts Award, 1993. Mem. Vassar Club St. Louis (past pres.), Mary Inst. Alumnae Assn. (past pres.), Colonial Dames Am., Garden Club St. Louis. Republican. Episcopalian. Avocations: tennis, visual arts, performing arts.

MACCARTHY, TERENCE FRANCIS, lawyer; b. Chgo., Feb. 5, 1934; s. Frank E. and Catherine (McIntyre) MacC.; m. Marian Fulton, Nov. 25, 1961; children—Daniel Fulton, Sean Patrick, Terence Fulton, Megan Catherine. B.A. in Philosophy, St. Jospeh's Coll., 1955; J.D., DePaul U., 1960. Bar: Ill. 1960, U.S. Dist. Ct. (no. dist.) Ill. 1961, U.S. Ct. Appeals (7th cir.) 1961, U.S. Supreme Ct. 1966. Assoc. prof. law Chase Coll. Law, Cin., 1960-61; law clk. to chief judge U.S. Dist. Ct., 1961-66; spl. asst. atty. gen. Ill., 1965-67; exec. dir. Fed. Defender Program, U.S. Dist. Ct. (no. dist.) Ill., Chgo., 1966—; mem. nat. adv. com. on criminal rules; 7th cir. criminal jury instrn. com.; chmn. Nat. Defender Com.; chmn. bd. regents Nat. Coll. Criminal Def.; faculty Fed. Jud. Ctr., Nat. Coll. Criminal Def., Nat. Inst. Trial Advocacy, U. Va. Trial Advocacy Inst., Harvard Law Sch. Trial Advocacy Program, Western Trial Advocacy Inst., Northwestern U., U. Ill. Defender Trial Advocacy course, Loyola U. Trial Advocacy Program; lectr. in field. Contbr. articles on criminal law to profl. jours. Bd. dirs. U.S.O. Served as 1st lt. USMC, 1955-57. Recipient Nat. Legal Aid and Defender Assn./ABA Reginald Heber Smith award, 1986, Alumni Merit award St. Joseph Coll., 1970, Cert. of Distinction USO, 1977, Harrison Tweed Spl. Merit award Am. Law Inst./ABA, 1987, Bill of Rights award Ga. chpt. ACLU, 1986, William J. Brennan award U. Va., 1989, Alumni Svc. award DePaul U. Coll. Law, 1994, Ann. Significant Contbns. award Calif. Attys. for Criminal Justice; named to Outstanding Young Men of Am., 1970. Mem. ABA (past chmn. criminal justice sect., ho. of dels.), Ill. Bar Assn., Chgo. Bar Assn., 7th Cir. Bar Assn., Nat. Assn. Criminal Def. Lawyers (Disting. Svc. award 1993), Nat. Legal Aid and Defender Assn., Nat. coll. Criminal Def. (chair), Union League of Chgo. (pres.). Democrat. Roman Catholic. Office: US Dist Ct No Dist Ill 55 E Monroe St Ste 2800 Chicago IL 60603-5802

MACCARTY, COLLIN STEWART, neurosurgeon; b. Rochester, Minn., Sept. 20, 1915; s. W.C. MacCarty; married; 3 children. AB, Dartmouth Coll., 1937; MD, Johns Hopkins U., Balt., 1940; MS in Neurosurgery, U. Minn., 1944. Diplomate Am. Bd. Neurol. Surgery. Surg. house officer Johns Hopkins Hosp., Balt., 1940-41; fellow in neurosurgery Mayo Found., Rochester, 1944; instr. neurol. surgery on grad. faculty U. Minn., Rochester, 1947-53, asst. prof., 1953-57, assoc. prof., 1957-61, prof., 1961-73; prof. Mayo Med. Sch./U. Minn., Rochester, 1973-80, assoc. dir. grad. edn., 1975-77, dir., 1977-80, prof. emeritus, 1980—; mem. neurosurg. staff Mayo Clinic, Rochester, 1946-75, sr. cons., 1975, chmn. med. staff, 1965-66; sec. for congress affairs World Fedn. Neurosurg. Socs., 1965-69, chmn. program com., mem. liaison com., mem. adminstrv. coun.; adv. com. to dean Dartmouth Med. Sch., 1968-72, bd. overseers, 1973—, chmn. bd., 1977-79; adv. bd. Bur. of Medicine and Surgery, Dept. of Navy, 1970; nat. cons. in neurosurgery Air Force, Wilford Hall Hosp., Lackland AFB, Tex., 1971; cons. in neursurgery to Surgeon Gen., USN, 1977-80; vis. prof. neurosurgery Western Res. U., Cleve., 1966, Johns Hopkins U., 1969, U. Okla., 1971, Ohio State U., 1977, U. Tex., 1979; Caldwell lectr. Am. Roentgen Ray Soc., 1974; Elsberg lectr. N.Y. Soc. Neurol. Surgery, 1981. Author: (monograph) The Surgical Treatment of Intracranial Meningiomas, 1961; co-author: Primary Intramedullary Tumors of the Spinal Cord and Filum Terminale, 1964; contbr. over 158 articles to various med. jours. With USN, 1944-46. Mem. AMA (residency rev. com., sect. on med. edn. 1967-72), ACS, Am. Assn. Neurol. Surgeons (v.p. 1965, pres. 1970, bd. dirs. 1965-73, del. to World Fedn. 1973-77), Neurosurg. Soc. of Am. (v.p. 1954, pres. 1959, rep. to AANS bd. dirs. 1965-69), Minn. Med. Assn., Zumbro Valley Med. Soc., Minn. Soc. Neurol. Scis., Soc. Neurol. Surgeons, So. Minn. Med. Assn., Minn. Neurosurg. Soc., Found. for Internat. Edn. in Neurol. Surgery, Inc., Societa Italiana de Neurochirurgia (corr. mem.), Egyptian Soc. Neurol. Surgeons (hon.), Japan Soc. Neurol. Surgeons (hon.), Internat. Travellers Club, Neurosurg. Travel Club, Sigma Xi (chpt. pres. 1979-80). Home: HC 60 Box 71A Cable WI 54821-9510

MACCAULEY, HUGH BOURNONVILLE, banker; b. Mt. Vernon, N.Y., Mar. 12, 1922; s. Morris Baker and Alma (Gardiner) MacC.; m. Rachael Gleaton, Aug. 30, 1943 (div. May 1980); m. Felice Cooper, Dec. 2, 1980. Student, Rutgers U., 1939-41, Tex. Christian U., 1948-50, U. Omaha, 1957-59. With 102nd Cavalry, Essex Troop N.J. Nat. Guard, 1940-42; commd. 2d lt. U.S. Army, 1943; advanced through grades to col. U.S. Army, USAF, Washington, 1943-73; v.p. Great Am. Securities, San Bernardino, Calif., 1979-94; founder., chmn. bd. Desert Cmty. Bank, Victorville, Calif., 1980-95, chmn. emeritus, 1995; account exec. Gorian Thornes, Inc., San Bernardino, Calif., 1995-96. bd. dirs. Air Force Village West, 1986-88; chmn. bd. and CEO Gen. and Mrs. Curtis E. Lemay Found., 1987—. Decorated Air medal, Legion of Merit. Mem. Daedalian Soc., Rotary, Internat. Platform Soc., Balboa Bay Club. Republican. Presbyterian. Avocation: golf. Home: 214 Golden West St Huntington Beach CA 92648 *Personal philosophy: Whatever the game play by the rules.*

MACCHIAROLA, FRANK JOSEPH, academic administrator; b. N.Y.C., Apr. 7, 1941; s. Joseph John and Lucy (Bernardo) M.; m. Mary Teresa Collins, June 13, 1970; children: Joseph John, Michael Collins, Frank Joseph. B.A., St. Francis Coll., 1962, L.H.D. (hon.), 1981; LL.B., Columbia U., 1965, Ph.D., 1970; L.H.D. (hon.), Coll. S.I., 1983; LL.D. (hon.), Dominican Coll., 1983, Manhattan Coll., 1983. From fellow to prof. polit. sci. CUNY, 1964-83, v.p., 1977-78; asst. v.p. Columbia U., N.Y.C., 1973-74; dep. dir. N.Y. State Emergency Fin. Control Bd. for N.Y.C., 1976-77; chancellor of schs. N.Y.C. Public Sch. System, 1978-83; pres., chief exec. officer N.Y.C. Partnership, Inc., 1983-87; pres. Acad. of Polit. Sci., 1987-91; prof. bus. Columbia U., N.Y.C., 1987-91; dean Benjamin N. Cardozo Sch. of Law, Yeshiva U., N.Y.C., 1991-96; of counsel Newman, Tannenbaum, Helpern, Syracuse and Hirschtritt, N.Y.C., 1991—; pres. St. Francis Coll., N.Y., 1996—; bd. dirs. Jeffries Group Inc., Schuller; trustee Manville Personal Injury Settlement Trust. Mem., pres. Community Sch. Bd. 22, N.Y.C., 1973-78; mem., vice chmn. bd. trustees St. Joseph's Coll., 1977—. Decorated cavalieri Order of Merit Italy; recipient cert. of merit Dirigible Soc. Am.,

1976. Democrat. Roman Catholic. Office: 900 3rd Ave New York NY 10022-4728 also: 180 Remsen St Brooklyn NY 11201

MACCINI, LOUIS JOHN, economic educator; b. Cambridge, Mass., Aug. 3, 1942; s. Joseph and Jennie (Leccacorvi) M.; m. Carol Monterisi, June 25, 1965; children: Michael S., Sharon L. BS in Economics, Boston Coll., 1965; PhD in Economics, Northwestern U., 1970. From asst. prof. to assoc. prof. economics The Johns Hopkins U., Balt., 1969-86, prof., 1986—, chair, 1992—; ad hoc com. mem. graduate fin. aid, Johns Hopkins U., editorial bd., public interest investment adv. com., law sch. com., med. sch. com., and other coms.; mem. recruting chair dept. grad. student advisor dept., and other depts. Referee Am. Econ. Review, Jour. Econ. Dynamics and Control, Oxford Econ. Papers, and others; contbr. articles to profl. jours. Grantee NSF. Mem. Am. Econ. Assn., The Econometric Soc., Internat Soc. Inventory Rsch. Office: Johns Hopkins U 3400 N Charles St Baltimore MD 21218-2608

MACCLEAN, WALTER LEE, dentist; b. Sheridan, Wyo., July 10, 1935; s. Edward Satterlee and Eleanor Elizabeth (Weir) Mac.; m. Nancy Lee Strale, Sept. 4, 1965 (div. 1975); children: David Satterlee, Carrie Lynn. BS with honors, U. Wyo., 1957, postgrad., 1958; DMD, U. Oreg., Portland, 1962. Mil. dental adv. Korean Mil. Adv. Group, Wonju, 1962-63; chief dental svc. Dugway Chem. Testing Ctr., Utah, 1965-68; pvt. dental practice Cheyenne, Wyo., 1968-70; assoc. prof. Sheridan Coll., Wyo., 1970-76; staff dentist VA Hosp. Med. Ctr., Ft. Meade, S.D., 1976-93; ret., 1993; cons., lectr. Health Edn. Program Svc., Ft. Meade, 1984-93. With U.S. Army 1962-68. Mem. ADA. Episcopalian. Home: PO Box 450 Hardin MT 59034-0450 also: Highbourne House, 13-15 Marylebone High St, London W1M 3PE, England

MACCLUGGAGE, REID, newspaper editor, publisher; b. Norwich, Conn., Oct. 18, 1938; s. Everett Reid and Edith Kathryn (Bowen) MacC.; m. Joellen Thompson, Mar. 29, 1965 (div. 1980); children: Stewart Reid, Scot Thompson; m. Linda Howell, May 30, 1981; 1 child, Katherine Elizabeth. BA, U. Hartford, 1962. Asst. state editor Hartford (Conn.) Courant, 1965-69, state editor, 1969-74, asst. mng. editor, 1974-82, mng. editor, 1982-84; editor, pub. New London (Conn.) Day, 1984—; bd. dirs. Day Pub. Co.; juror Pulitzer Prize. Trustee Day Trust, Dr. Martin Luther King Meml. Scholarship Trust Fund; founder Bodenwein Fellowship for Minorities, Garde Arts Ctr.; incorporator Lawrence and Meml. Hosp. Recipient Disting. Alumnus award U. Hartford, 1983. Mem. AP Mng. Editors Assn. (v.p.). Office: The Day Pub Co 47 Eugene O'Neil Dr PO Box 1231 New London CT 06320

MACCOBY, ELEANOR EMMONS, psychology educator; b. Tacoma, May 15, 1917; d. Harry Eugene and Viva May (Johnson) Emmons; m. Nathan Maccoby, Sept. 16, 1938 (dec. Apr. 1992); children: Janice Maccoby Carmichael, Sarah Maccoby Bellina, Mark. BS, U Wash., 1939; MA, U. Mich., 1949, PhD, 1950. Study dir. div. program surveys USDA, Washington, 1942-46; study dir. Survey Rsch. Ctr. U. Mich., Ann Arbor, 1946-48; lectr., rsch. assoc. dept. social rels. Harvard U., Cambridge, Mass., 1950-58; from assoc. to full prof. Stanford (Calif.) U., 1958-87, chmn. dept. psychology, 1973-76, prof. emeritus, 1987—. Author: (with R. Sears and H. Levin) Patterns of Child-Rearing, 1957, (with Carol Jacklin) Psychology of Sex Differences, 1974, Social Development, 1980, (with R.H. Mnookin) Dividing the Child: Social and Legal Dilemmas of Custody, 1992, (with Buchanan and Dombusch) Adolescents after Divorce, 1996; editor: (with Newcomb and Hartley) Readings in Social Psychology, 1957, The Development of Sex Differences, 1966. Recipient Gores award for Excellence in Teaching Stanford U., 1981, Disting. Contbn. to Ednl. Research award Am. Ednl. Research Assn., 1984, Disting. Sci. Contbn. to Child Devel. award Soc. for Research in Child Devel., 1987, Disting. Sci. Contbns. award Am. Psychol. Assn., 1988; named to Barbara Kimball Browning professorship Stanford U., 1979—. Fellow APA (pres. Divsn. 7, 1971-72, G. Stanley Hall award 1982), Soc. for Rsch. in Child Devel. (pres. 1981-83, mem. governing coun. 1963-66, Am. Psychol. Soc.; mem. NAS, Am. Acad. Arts and Scis., Inst. Medicine, Western Psychol. Assn. (pres. 1974-75), Inst. for Rsch. on Women and Gender, Social Sci. Rsch. Coun. (chmn. 1984-85), Consortium of Social Sci. Assns. (pres. 1997—), Am. Psychol. Found. (Life Achievement award). Democrat. Home: 729 Mayfield Ave Palo Alto CA 94305-1016 Office: Stanford U Dept Psychology Stanford CA 94305-2130

MACCOMBIE, BRUCE FRANKLIN, composer, college administrator; b. Providence, Dec. 5, 1943; s. Franklin S. and Florence (Corbishley) MacC.; m. Frances Holliday, Sept. 4, 1965 (div. 1970); m. Turi Gundersen, Mar. 10, 1979; 1 child, Juliana. BA, U. Mass., 1967, M of Music, 1968, DFA (hon.), 1986; PhD, U. Iowa, 1971. Assoc. prof. Yale U., New Haven, 1975-80; v.p. G. Schirmer Mus. Publs., N.Y.C., 1980-85; dean, provost The Juilliard Sch., N.Y.C., 1986-92; dean Sch. for Arts Boston U., 1992—. Composer numerous musical works. Recipient Goddard Lieberson award Am. Acad. Inst. Arts and Letters, N.Y.C., 1979. Mem. Coll. Music Soc., Charles Ives Soc. (bd. dirs.). Office: Boston U Sch for Arts 855 Commonwealth Ave Boston MA 02215-1303

MACCONKEY, DOROTHY I., academic administrator; b. New Brunswick, N.J.; d. Donald Thurston and Dorothy Bennett (Hill) Ingling; m. Joseph W. MacConkey, June 19, 1949 (dec. Aug. 1975); children: Donald Franklin, Diane Margaret, Dorothy Frances; m. Karl Schmeidler, May 26, 1994. BA, Beaver Coll., 1947; MA, Wichita State U., 1953; PhD, U. Md., 1974; LLD (hon.), Beaver Coll., 1988. Lectr. Wichita (Kans.) State U., 1950-51; rsch.-campaign assoc. United Fund and Council, Wichita, 1951-62; rsch.- com. coordination Health and Welfare Council of Nat. Capital Area, Washington, 1963-65; exec. dir. multi-program agy. Prince Georges County Assn. for Retarded Children, Hyattsville, Md., 1965-66; prof. George Mason U., Fairfax, Va., 1966-76, asst. vice pres., acting dean, 1976-82; v.p., dean of coll. Hiram (Ohio) Coll., 1982-85; pres. Davis & Elkins (W.Va.) Coll., 1985—; bd. dirs. Davis Trust Co., Elkins, 1987—; adv. bd. George Mason U. Found., Fairfax, 1976-95; trustee Beaver Coll., Glenside, Pa., 1971-87; cons., evaluator North Cen. Assn., Chgo., 1985—, commr., 1993—, chmn., 1995—; mem. exec. com., pres. Assn. Presbyn. Colls. and Univs.; mem. bd. Svc. Opportunity Colls., Presbyn. Found., trustee, 1993—; chmn. North Area Cen. Com.; treas. Coun. of Ind. Colls. Pres. County Chasers of Am., 1985—. Recipient Citizen award for service to handicapped, Fairfax County, 1981, Woman of Yr. in Edn. award W.Va. Fedn. Women's Clubs, 1986. Mem. Coun. of Pres.', Nat. Assn. Intercollegiate Athletics, Coun. Ind. Colls. (bd. dirs.). Office: Davis and Elkins Coll Office of Pres 100 Campus Dr Elkins WV 26241-3971

MACCRACKEN, PETER JAMES, marketing executive, communications executive; b. Trieste, Italy, Dec. 27, 1952; came to U.S., 1956; s. James and Kirsten (Koch) MacC.; divorced. BA summa cum laude, Albion Coll., 1975; MA, U. Calif., Santa Barbara, 1978. Asst. mgr. GranTree Furniture Rental, San Leandro, Calif., 1979-81; freelance writer San Diego, 1981-82; corp. editor Scripps Meml. Hosps., La Jolla, Calif., 1982-84; sr. v.p. Berkman & Daniels Mktg., San Diego, 1984-89; v.p. Stoorza Ziegaus & Metzger, Inc., San Diego, 1989-90; pres. MacCracken & McGaugh, San Diego, 1990—. Contbr. over 500 articles, photographs to numerous publs. Bd. dirs. Downtown San Diego Partnershpi, 1997—. Recipient 30 bus. comm. awards. Mem. Pub. Rels. Soc. Am. (bd. dirs. 1992-96, pres. San Diego chpt. 1996), Internat. Assn. Bus. Communicators (pres. San Diego chpt. 1985), Am. Inst. Wine and Food (bd. dirs. 1990-95, sec. San Diego chpt. 1995), Phi Beta Kappa. Democrat. Avocations: photography, writing, wines, science fiction, fiction, music. Office: 750 B St Ste 1950 San Diego CA 92101-8122

MACCRINDLE, ROBERT ALEXANDER, lawyer; b. Glasgow, Scotland, Jan. 27, 1928; s. Fergus Robertson and Jean (Hill) MacC.; m. Pauline Dilys, Aug. 18, 1959; children: Guy Stephen, Claire. LLB, U. London, 1948; LLM, U. Cambridge, 1952. Called to Bar Eng. and Wales, 1952; created Queen's Counsel, 1963; bar: Hong Kong 1965; conseil juridique France, 1978-91. Barrister Temple, London, 1952-76; Bencher Gray's Inn, London, 1969—; ptnr. Shearman & Sterling, N.Y.C., 1976-94, of counsel, 1995—; Avocat au Barreau de Paris, 1991—. Flight lt. RAF, 1948-50. Fellow Am. Coll. Trial Lawyers. Club: University (N.Y.C.). Avocation: golf. Home: 41 Ave Bosquet, Paris 75007, France also: Shearman & Sterling 599 Lexington Ave & 53d St New York NY 10022

MACCUBBIN, ROBERT PURKS, literature and culture educator; b. Balt., Oct. 30, 1939; s. Walter Aubrey and Mary Anna (Purks) M.; 1 child, Gwyneth Marie; m. Martha J. Hamilton-Phillips, Sept., 1986; children: Charles Aubrey Phillips, Glencora Alison. BA in Biology, Johns Hopkins U., 1961; MA in English, U. Ill., 1962, PhD in English, 1968. From asst. prof. to prof. Coll. William and Mary, Williamsburg, Va., 1964-95; fellow Thomas Reid Inst. for Rsch. in Cultural Studies and the Humanities, Aberdeen (Scotland) U., 1995. Author: The Age of William III and Mary II: Power, Politics and Patronage, 1688-1702, 1989; editor: " 'Tis Nature's Fault": Unauthorized Sexuality During the Enlightenment, 1987, Science and Technology and Their Cultural Contexts, 1982, British Literature and Culture, 1986, English Culture at the End of the 17th Century, 1988, Manners of Reading, 1992, The Art and Architecture of Versailles, 1993, The South Pacific in the Eighteenth Century, 1994; editor: Eighteenth-Century Life, 1983— (Best Spl. Issue award Conf. Editors Learned Jours. 1984, 95); contbr. articles to profl. jours. NEH grantee, 1988-89. Mem. MLA, FHC Soc., Am. Soc. 18th-Century Studies (exec. bd. east ctrl. chpt. 1983—, Clifford prize 1986, 87, Best Article award southeast chpt. 1987, 92), Soc. for Theatre Rsch., Pvt. Librs. Assn., Grolier Club. Avocations: gardening, acting, baseball. Office: Coll William & Mary English Dept Williamsburg VA 23185

MACCURDY, RAYMOND RALPH, JR., modern language educator; b. Oklahoma City, May 12, 1916; s. Raymond R. and Ada May (Eastl) MacC.; m. Blanche Hermine Wolf, June 2, 1939; children—George Grant II, William Douglas. B.A., La. State U., 1939; M.A., 1941; Ph.D., U. N.C., 1948. Assoc. prof. modern langs. U. Ga., 1948-49; Assoc. prof. modern langs. U. N.Mex., Albuquerque, 1949-53, prof., 1953—, chmn. dept. modern and classical langs., 1963-68; Nat. Def. Edn. Act. coordinator lang. Programs Am. Assn. Tchrs. Spanish and Portuguese, 1958-59. Author: The Spanish Dialect in St. Bernard Parish, Louisiana, 1950, Francisco de Rojas Zorrilla and the Tragedy, 1958, Francisco de Rojas Zorilla, 1969; Editor: La Vida en el Ataud, 1961, Lucrecia y Tarquino, 1963, Numancia Cercada y Numancia destruida, 1977, Tirso de Molina, El Burlador de Sevilla, 1965, Del rey abajo, ninguno, 1970, Spanish Drama of the Golden Age-Twelve Plays, 1971, The Tragic Fall: Don Alvaro de Luna and Other Favorites in Spanish Golden Age Drama, 1978, Caesar of Sante Fe, 1990. Served to maj. AUS, World War II, CBI. Julius Rosenwald fellow, 1941, 46; Fund for Advancement Edn. fellow, 1954-55; Fulbright research scholar Spain, 1960-61. Mem. Rocky Mountain Modern Lang. Assn. (pres. 1957), Hispanic Soc. Am. Home: 1804 Newton Pl NE Albuquerque NM 87106-2527

MAC DIARMID, WILLIAM DONALD, physician; b. Arcola, Sask., Can., June 22, 1926; s. John Angus and Evaline (Reed) MacD.; m. Bette Nell Brown, May 16, 1953; children—John A., Margaret A., Donald G., Andrew L. B.A., U. Sask., 1947; M.D., U. Toronto, 1949. Intern Pasqua Hosp., Regina, Sask., 1949-50; family physician, mem. med. staff Pasqua Hosp. and Regina Gen. Hosp., 1950-53; mem. staff Shaunavon (Sask.) Union Hosp., 1953-58; resident in internal medicine, fellow in endocrinology and metabolism U. Utah Affiliated Hosps., Salt Lake City, 1958-62; research asst. in human genetics Univ. Coll. Hosp. Med. Sch., London, 1962-64; mem. faculty U. Utah Med. Sch., 1964-69; prof. medicine U. Man. Med. Sch., Winnipeg, 1969-75, 79-91, chmn. dept., 1979-85; physician-in-chief St. Boniface Gen. Hosp., 1969-75, St. John's Gen. Hosp. and Health Sci. Ctr., 1975-79, Health Sci. Ctr. of Winnipeg, 1979-85; health svcs. cons., 1986-91; prof., chmn. dept. medicine Meml. U. Nfld. Med. Sch., 1975-79; pres. Swift Current and Dist. Med. Soc., 1956-57; mem. bd. Com. for Accreditation of Can. Med. Schs., 1985-91, chmn., 1988-91. Vol. Can. Cancer Soc., 1992—; bd. dirs. Man. Med. Svcs. found., 1986-91, Winnipeg Mcpl. Hosps., 1986-89; chmn. bd. Man. Cancer Treatment and Rsch. Found., 1987-88; v.p. Man. Med. Coll. Found., 1988-91. Fellow ACP, Royal Coll. Physicians and Surgeons Can., Can. Coll. Med. Geneticists; mem. Am. Soc. Human Genetics, Can. Med. Assn. (com. on ethics 1987-91, coun. on med. edn. 1988-91), Man. Med. Assn. (dir. 1981-83, 87—, chmn. bd. 1982-83, hon. sec. 1988-89, hon. treas. 1989-90, chmn. com. on ethics 1987-91). Home and Office: 4142 Cortez Pl, Victoria, BC Canada V8N 4R8

MACDONALD, ALAN HUGH, librarian, university administrator; b. Ottawa, Ont., Can., Mar. 3, 1943; s. Vincent C. and Hilda C. (Durney) MacD.; m. Elizabeth Whalen; children—Eric Paul Henry, Nigel Alan Christopher. B.A., Dalhousie U., Halifax N.S., 1963; B.L.S., U. Toronto, Ont., 1964. With Dalhousie U., 1964-78, law librarian, 1965-67, 69-71, asst. univ. librarian, 1970-72, health sci. librarian, 1972-78; lectr. Sch. Library Services, 1969-78; dir. info. svcs. U. Calgary, Alta., 1988—; dir. libraries U. Calgary, Alta., Can., 1979-92, univ. orator, 1989—; dir. U. Calgary Press, 1984-90; chmn. Alta. Library Network, 1981-89; librarian N.S. Barristers Soc., 1969-74; mem. adv. bd. Nat. Libr. Can., 1972-76, Health Scis. Resource Ctr., Can. Inst. Sci. and Tech. Info., 1977-79; mem. Coun. of Prairie Univ. Librs., 1979-92, chair, 1984-85, 89, 91; Bassam lectr. U. Toronto Faculty Info. Studies, 1994, Lorne MacRae lectr. Libr. Assn. Alta., 1996. Mem. editorial bd. America: History and Life (ABC-CLIO), 1985-93. Pres. TELED Cmty. Media Access Orgn., Halifax, N.S., 1972-74; mem. Minister's Com. on Univ. Affairs, Alta., 1979-83; bd. dirs. Alta. Found. for Can. Music Ctr., 1985-92, Can. Inst. for Hist. Microreprodn., 1990—, pres., 1996—. Council Library Resources fellow, 1975; exec. fellow Univ. Microfilms Internat., 1986; recipient Disting. Acad. Librarian award Can. Assn. of Coll. and Univ. Libraries, 1988. Mem. Can. Libr. Assn. (treas. 1977-79, pres. 1980-81), Atlantic Provinces Libr. Assn. (pres. 1977-78), Libr. Assn. Alta. (v.p. 1988-89, Pres.'s award 1992), Can. Health Libr. Assn. (treas. 1977-79), Australian Libr. and Info. Assn. (assoc. 1977), N.Z. Libr. & Info. Assn., Bibliog. Soc. Can., Foothills Libr. Assn., Can. Assn. Info. Sci. (pres. 1979-80), Can. Assn. Rsch. Librs. (bd. dirs. 1981-86, v.p. 1985-86), Calgary Free-Net Soc. (bd. dirs. 1994—, chair 1996—). Office: U Calgary, 2500 University Dr NW A100, Calgary, AB Canada T2N 1N4

MACDONALD, ANDREW, manufacturing company executive; b. Waterbury, Conn., Apr. 14, 1958; s. James and Martha Rose (Siebert) M.; m. Diane Marie Nodine, Dec. 29, 1989; children: Duncan Andrew, Cameron Lewis, Gavin John. BA in Econ., Drew U., 1980; postgrad., Heriot-Watt U., 1996. Internal auditor, mgmt. cons. Insilco Corp., Meriden, Conn., 1982-85; product mgr., asst. contr. Stewart Stamping Corp., Yonkers, N.Y., 1985-87; dir. mktg. Stewart Connector Systems, Glen Rock, Pa., 1987-89, dir. european ops., 1993-95, v.p., 1996—; mng. dir. Stewart Connector Systems, Konigstein, Germany, 1990-96; v.p. European ops. Stewart Connector Sytems, 1996-97; pres. Intelcap Resources, Inc., Newtown Square, Pa., 1997—. Avocations: writing, tennis, skiing, travel, astronomy. Home: 627 Evergreen Dr York PA 17402-8843

MACDONALD, ANDREW STEPHEN, management consulting firm executive; b. Fairbanks, Alaska, July 15, 1953; s. Bernard L. and Rosemary (Unger) MacD.; m. Josephine A. Joanne, Aug. 4, 1972; children: Peter, Stephen, Charles. BA in Acctg., Seattle U., 1974. CPA, cert. mgmt. cons. Acct. Boeing Aerospace, Seattle, 1976-79; owner, pres. Triak Corp., Seattle, 1977—; pres. Exec. Cons. Group, Inc., Seattle, 1979—. Mem. AICPA, Inst. Mgmt. Cons., Wash. Soc. CPAs, Columbia Tower Club. Home: 10030 Lake Shore Blvd NE Seattle WA 98125-8158 Office: Exec Cons Group Inc 1111 3rd Ave Ste 2700 Seattle WA 98101-3201

MACDONALD, BRIAN SCOTT, management consultant; b. Sudbury, Ont., Can., June 6, 1939; s. David William and Katherine Lillian (McKinnon) MacD.; m. Margaret Louise Young, Aug. 11, 1962 (dec. Apr. 1985); children—Heather Anne, David Colin, Michael Alexander. B.A. with honors, Royal Mil. Coll., Kingston, Ont., 1961; M.B.A. cum laude, York U., Toronto, Ont., 1980; postgrad., U. Toronto, 1980—. Tchr., cons. Bd. Edn., Ont., Can., 1966-80; exec. dir. Can. Inst. Strategic Studies, Toronto, Ont., Can., 1982-89; pres. Strategic Insight Planning and Communications, 1989—. Author: Military Spending in Developing Countries: How Much is Too Much, 1997; editor: Parliament and Defence Policy, 1982, War in the 80's: Men Against High Tech, 1983, Canada's Strategies for Space, 1984, The Grand Strategy of the Soviet Union, 1984, Defence and the Canadian Economy, 1984, Canada's Strategies for the Pacific Rim, 1985, High Tech and the High Seas, 1985, Canada, the Caribbean, and Central Am., 1986, Terror, 1986, Tactics and Technology, 1987, A Grand Strategy for the United States?, 1988, Airwar 2000, 1989, Canadian Strategic Forecast 1989, 1989, Space Strategy: Three Dimensions, 1989; contbg. editor Def. Policy Rev., 1994—. Pres. Royal Can. Arty. Assn., Toronto, 1976; vice chmn. Conf. Def. Assns., Ottawa, Ont., 1975; gov. Can. Corps of Commissionaires, Toronto, 1984-86; hon. aide de camp to Gov. Gen. Can., Ottawa, 1984-86; comdr. Toronto Militia Dist., 1984-86; bd. dirs. Atlantic Coun. Can., 1986—, sr. v.p., 1991; bd dirs. Royal Can. Mil. Inst., 1986-87. Served to col. Can. Army, 1957-86. Marsh-McLennan scholar, 1977, Dept. Nat. Def. scholar, 1981-82. Mem. Toronto Bd. Trade, Can. Ops. Rsch. Soc. Home: 169 Newton Dr, Willowdale, ON Canada M2M 2N6

MACDONALD, CAROLYN HELMS, gifted education educator; b. Leesburg, Va., Oct. 15, 1941; d. Edmund Davis and Mary Irene (Peters) Helms; m. John Mount MacDonald, July 27, 1963 (div. Dec. 1984); children: Christina Hope, Heather Laurel, Katherine Anne. BS, East Tenn. State U., 1964; MS, Nova U., 1979. Cert. elem. tchr., jr. coll. tchr., gifted tchr., Fla. Elem. tchr. Shoemaker Elem. Sch., Gate City, Va., 1964-65, Bakersfield Elem. Sch., Aberdeen, Md., 1965-66, Brookview Elem. Sch., Jacksonville, Fla., 1966-68, Holiday Hill Elem. Sch., Jacksonville, Fla., 1968-69, Arlington Annex 5th Grade Ctr., Jacksonville, 1972-73; elem. tchr., social studies, lang. arts specialist Loretto Elem. Sch., Jacksonville, 1973-81, tchr. gifted, 1981—; mem. steering com. for gifted edn. Duval County Sch. Bd., 1982-85; del to Murmansk, USSR, 1991, ESOL trainer, 1995—. Pres. Mandarin Cmty. Club, Jacksonville, 1980; mem. Panel on Sewage Treatment Problems, 1979, Neighborhood Cancer Drive Com., 1979-84, Com. to Assess Cmty. Recreation Needs, Jacksonville, 1981-82; sponsor ARC. Recipient placque Mandarin Community Club, Jacksonville, 1974-77; named Outstanding Safety Patrol Sponsor North Fla., 1993. Mem. Fla. Jr. Coll. Woman's Club (v.p. 1969-71, pres. 1971-72, Outstanding Young Woman Am. 1971), Southside Jr. Woman's Club (v.p. 1970-73), Phi Mu Alumnae (v.p. 1989-90), Delta Kappa Gamma. Democrat. Methodist. Avocations: reading, traveling, decorating, walking, the arts. Home: 9439 San Jose Blvd Apt 228 Jacksonville FL 32257 Office: Loretto Elem Sch # 30 3900 Loretto Rd Jacksonville FL 32223-2055

MACDONALD, DAVID RICHARD, industrial psychologist; b. Dowagiac, Mich., May 20, 1953; s. Jerrold Brewster and Shirley Ann (Shaffer) MacD.; m. Mary Elizabeth Olson, Dec. 20, 1975 (div. Sept. 5, 1995); 1 child, Sarah Ann; m. Cathleen Jean Carlson, July 25, 1996. AS, Southwestern Mich. Coll., 1973; BBA, Western Mich. U., 1975, MA, 1976, EdS, 1979; PhD, Mich. State U., 1986. Announcer, boardman WDOW AM/FM, Dowagiac, Mich., 1969-72; mgmt. devel. specialist Interstate Motor Freight System, Grand Rapids, Mich., 1977-79; sr. mgmt. tng. instr. GTE Gen. Telephone Co. Mich., Muskegon, 1979-82; cons. human resources devel. Steelcase, Inc., Grand Rapids, 1982-86, mgr. performance devel., 1986-96, mgr. assessment process, 1996—; cons., speaker in field; facilitator, program dir. Devel. Dimensions Internat., Pitts., 1981; facilitator Alamo Learning Systems, Southfield, Mich., 1983, 86, Wilson Learning Corp., Eden Prairie, Minn., 1983; job analysis program mgr. Barry M. Cohen & Assocs., Largo, Fla., 1985; asst. prof. grad. mgmt. Aquinas Coll., Grand Rapids, 1983—; pres. Plectrum, 1997. Co-chair United Way Steelcase campaign, Grand Rapids, 1986. Mem. ASTD (sec. W. Mich. chpt. 1977-79), Soc. Indsl.-Orgnl. Psychology, Am. Psychol. Assn., Nat. Soc. for Performance and Instrn., Mensa, Phi Kappa Phi. Republican. Avocations: building harpsichords, stained glass, brewing, gardening, early music. Home: 2306 Prospect Ave SE Grand Rapids MI 49507-3159 Office: PO Box 1967 Grand Rapids MI 49501-1967

MACDONALD, DAVID ROBERT, lawyer, fund administrator; b. Chgo., Nov. 1, 1930; s. James Wear and Frances Esther (Wine) M.; m. Verna Joy Odell, Feb. 17, 1962; children: Martha, Emily, David, Rachel, Rebecca. B.S., Cornell U., 1952; J.D., U. Mich., 1955. Bar: Ill. 1955, Mich. 1955, D.C. 1983. Practiced in Chgo., 1957-74; mem. firm Kirkland, Ellis, Hodson, Chaffetz & Masters, Chgo., 1957-62, ptnr., 1962; ptnr. Baker & McKenzie, Chgo., 1962-74, 77-81; asst. sec. of Treasury for enforcement, ops. and tariff affairs Dept. Treasury, Washington, 1974-76; undersec. of Navy, 1976-77; dep. U.S. Trade Rep., 1981-83; bd. dirs. Chgo. City Bank and Trust Co., Mestek, Inc. (N.Y. Stock Exch.). Pres. David R. Macdonald Found., 1996—. Mem. ABA, Chgo. Bar Assn., D.C. Bar Assn., Chgo. Assn. Commerce and Industry (bd. dirs. 1977-81), Order of Coif, Econ. Club (Chgo.), Cosmos Club (Washington). Home: 6605 Radnor Rd Bethesda MD 20817-6324 Office: 815 Connecticut Ave NW Washington DC 20006-4004

MACDONALD, DIGBY DONALD, scientist, science administrator; b. Thames, New Zealand, Dec. 7, 1943; came to U.S., 1977; s. Leslie Graham and Francis Helena (Verry) M.; m. Cynthia Lynch, 1969; m. Mirna Urquidi, July 6, 1985; children: Leigh Vanessa, Matthew Digby, Duncan Paul, Nahline. BS in Chemistry, U. Auckland, New Zealand, 1965; MS in Chemistry with honors, U. Auckland, 1966; PhD, U. Calgary, Alta., Can., 1969. Asst. research officer Atomic Energy of Can., Pinawa, Man., Can., 1969-72; lectr. Victoria U., Wellington, New Zealand, 1972-75; sr. research assoc., assoc prof. Alta. Sulfur Research U. Calgary, 1975-77; sr. metallurgist SRI Internat., Menlo Park, Calif., 1977-79; prof. metall. engring. Ohio State U., Columbus, Ohio, 1979-84; lab dir., dep. dir. phys. scis. divsn. SRI Internat., Menlo Park, 1984-91; prof. material sci. engring., dir. Ctr. Advanced Materials Pa. State U., 1991—; adj. prof. Ohio Stae U., 1984; W.B. Lewis Meml. lectr. Atomic Energy Can., 1993; mem. USAF Sci. Adv. Bd., 1994—; cons. in field; A.B. Lewis lectr. Atomic Energy Can., Ltd., 1993. Author: Transient Techniques in Electrochemistry, 1977; contbr. numerous articles to profl. jours.; patentee in field. Nat. Research Council scholar, Ottawa, Can., 1967-69; recipient Research award Ohio State U., 1983. Fellow Nat. Assn. Corrosion Engrs. Internat. (pub. com. 1982-85, Whitney award), Electrochem. Soc. (divsn. editor 1982-84, C. Wagner Meml. award 1991), Royal Soc. Can. Avocations: sailing, flying. Home: 1010 Greenbriar Dr State College PA 16801-6935 Office: Pa State U Ctr Advanced Materials 517 Deike Bldg University Park PA 16802-2714

MACDONALD, DONALD ARTHUR, publishing executive; b. Union City, N.J., Nov. 30, 1919; s. Richard A. and Marie (McDonald) M.; m. Ruth Moran, Dec. 21, 1942; children: Ronald A., Martha J., Marie C., Donald A., Charles A. BS cum laude, NYU, 1948, MBA, 1950. Advt. sales rep. Wall St. Jour., Dow Jones & Co., Inc., N.Y.C., 1953-55, mgr. New Eng. and Can. ter., 1955-58, ea. advt. mgr., 1958-61, exec. advt. mgr., 1961-63, advt. dir. sales promotion and prodn. depts., 1963-67, v.p. advt. sales, 1970-74, sr. v.p., 1974—, also dir.; vice chmn. Dow Jones & Co. Inc., N.Y.C., 1979—; also dir. Dow Jones & Co. Inc.; dir. Far Ea. Econ. Rev., Hong Kong; chmn. coun. judges Advt. Hall of Fame, 1972-78. Author: An Arrow for Your Quiver, 1994. Capt. AUS, 1942-46, World War II. Named to Advt. Hall of Fame, 1985. Mem. Am. Advt. Fedn. (dir. 1962—, past chmn., Barton A. Cummings Gold Medal award, 1995), Advt. Fedn. Am. (past gov. 2d dist., past chmn. joint commn., past chmn.), Advt. Council (dir.), N.Y. Advt. Club (past dir., Silver medal award 1965), Beta Gamma Sigma. Clubs: Downtown Athletic (N.Y.C.), Yale (N.Y.C.); Rumson Country (N.J.). Home: 15 Buttonwood Ln Rumson NJ 07760-1045

MACDONALD, DONALD STOVEL, lawyer; b. Ottawa, Ont., Can., Mar. 1, 1932; s. Donald Angus and Marjorie (Stovel) M.; m. Ruth Hutchison, Mar. 4, 1961 (dec.); children: Leigh, Nikki, Althea, Sonja; m. Adrian Merchant Lang, Sept. 10, 1988; stepchildren: Maria (dec.), Timothy, Gregory, Andrew, Elisabeth, Amanda, Adrian. Student, Ashbury Coll., Ottawa; BA, U. Toronto, Ont., 1951; LLB, Osgoode Hall Law Sch., 1955; LLM, Harvard, 1956; diploma internat. law, Cambridge U., 1957; LLD, St. Lawrence U., U N.B. Saint John, 1990; DEng, Colo. Sch. Mines. Bar: Called to Ont. bar 1955. Assoc. McCarthy & McCarthy, Toronto, 1957-62; M.P. for Toronto-Rosedale, 1962; reelected, 1963, 65, 68, 72, 74; parliamentary sec. to Min. of Justice, 1963-65, to Min. of Finance, 1965, to Sec. of State for External Affairs, 1966-68, to Min. of Industry, 1968; pres. Privy Coun. and Govt. House Leader, 1968; min. of nat. def., 1970-72, min. energy, mines and resources, 1972-75, min. of fin., 1975-77; ptnr. firm McCarthy & McCarthy, Toronto, 1977-88; high commr. for Can. to U.K., 1988-91; counsel McCarthy Tétrault, Toronto, 1991—; spl. lectr. U. Toronto Law Sch.; chmn. Royal Commn. on Econ. Union and Devel. Prospects for Can., 1982-85; chmn. adv. com. competition Ont. Electricity Sys., 1995-96; chmn. Inst. for Rsch. on Pub. Policy, Montreal, 1991-97, Siemens Electric Ltd., 1991—; bd. dirs. Alta Energy Co. Ltd., Boise (Idaho) Cascade Corp., Celanese Can. Inc., chmn.; bd. dirs. Hambros Can. Inc., Banister Found. Inc., Slough Estates Can., Sun Life Assurance Co. Can., TransCan. Pipelines Ltd.; trustee The Clan Donald Lands Trust, Skye, Scotland, 1991—. Named Freeman of the City of London, 1990, hon. fellow Trinity Hall, Cambridge

U., 1994, Companion of the Order of Can., 1994. Mem. Queen's Privy Coun. Can., Delta Kappa Epsilon. Liberal. Baptist. Office: McCarthy Tétrault PO Box 48, Toronto-Dominion Twr Ste 4700, Toronto, ON Canada M5K 1E6

MACDONALD, DONALD WILLIAM, architect; b. Calgary, Alta., Can., May 7, 1935; came to U.S., 1957; s. Wallace Harold and Dorothy Louise (DeFaye) MacD.; m. Kerstin Maria Lindberg, July 22, 1965 (div. 1979); children: Pia, Ian, Denise. BArch, U. Okla., 1962; MS, Columbia U., 1963. Registered architect, Calif., Nev., N.Mex., Colo. Archtl. draftsman Bell and McCulloch Architects, Edmonton, Alta., 1955-57; archtl. designer Anshen and Allen Architects, San Francisco, 1965-67; prin. Donald MacDonald Architects, San Francisco, 1967—; assoc. prof. U. Calif.-Berkeley, 1965-66; prof. advisor Cogswell Coll., San Francisco, 1979-81, U. Okla., Norman, 1982—; lectr. archtl. sch. Idaho State U., Pocatello, 1974, Posnan (Poland) Inst. Art and Architecture, 1974, Portsmouth Inst. Tech., Eng., 1974, U. Okla., Norman, 1982, Tex. Tech U., Lubbock, 1984, Auburn (Ala.) U., 1986, Tulane U., New Orleans, 1987, Moscow Inst. Architecture, 1987, U. Calif. Berkeley, 1987, Mich. State U., Lansing, 1988, Ga. Inst. Tech., 1993, San Francisco Inst. Architecture, 1992—, U. Okla. Coll. Architecture, 1992, Archtl. Inst. B.C. Vancouver, 1991, McGill U., 1991, U. Cin., 1991, Woodbury U., Burbank, 1993, Boston Archtl. Sch., 1993, San Jose State U., 1994, San Francisco Inst. Architecture, 1994, 95, U. Wis., 1995, U. Calif., Berkeley, 1995, 96, U. N.C., 1996, N.C. State U., 1996, U. N.Mex., 1997; lectr. in field; jury mem. Nat. Competition of Plywood Structures, Seattle, 1972, La. AIA Archtl. Design Competition, 1988, Miss. AIA Archtl. Competition, 1988, McGill U., 1991, Northern Calif. Home and Garden, 1991, City Boston Pub. Facilities Dept., 1992, San Diego Housing Commn., 1992, Meccano Erector Contest, 1993, Internat. Making Cities Livable Conf. Urban Spaces Competition, 1995, San Francisco Planning and Urban Rsch. Assn., 1997; mem. juror panel in field; mem. San Francisco Civil Service Archtl. Selection Com., 1974; examiner Calif. Archtl. Registration Bd., 1979; prof. Calif. Coll. Arts and Crafts, San Francisco, 1988; faculty design studio San Francisco Inst. Architecture, fall 1990, Alberta Assn. Architects, 1994; jury chmn. N.C. AIA Archtl. Design Competition, 1988, Alta. Assn. Archs. U. Calgary, 1994, panel mem. 1994; East-West advisor energy conservation in housing Greenpeace, U.S.A.; presenter 9th Ann. Monterey Design Conf., 1989. Author: Democratic Architecture, 1996, (with Bruce Goff) Toward Absolute Architecture, 1988; guest editor: Architecture and Urbanism, 1978; contbr. articles to profl. and consumer jours., U.S., Eng., Germany, Can., Poland, Russia, China, Italy, Japan. Received recognition through the media ABC, CNN, NBC, Time, People, Internat. Herald Tribune, Der Spiegel, London Observer, etc. for the invention of the City Sleeper, an exptl. environment for the homeless, studio house, and earthquake bed, 1987-91; exhbns. of architectural designs include Royal Inst. British Architects, London, 1985, 92, Contract Design Ctr., San Francisco, 1989, Calif. Coll. Arts and Crafts, San Francisco, 1989, Contemporary Realist Gallery, San Francisco, 1989, San Francisco chpt. AIA, 1989, Calif. Sch. Bd. Assn., San Jose, Calif., 1989, Philippe Bonnafont Archtl. Drawings, San Francisco, 1990, Columbia U., N.Y.C., 1991, Mill Valley (Calif.) City Hall, 1991, San Mateo (Calif.) County Fair, 1991, Randolph Street Gallery, Chgo., 1991, Portland (Oreg.) chpt. AIA, 1993, San Francisco Examiner Home Buyers and Sellers Fair, 1993, San Francisco Embarcadero Waterfront Competition Exhibit, 1993. Recipient Regolo d'Or award Domas Milan, Italy, 1966, Okla. U. Regent's Disting. Alumni award, 1988, Honor award Calif. Coun. AIA, 1987, Commendation award for Golden Gate Toll Plaza in San Francisco Calif. Counc. AIA, 1987, also for toll booth award of excellence in archtl. conservation Found. for San Francisco Archtl. Heritage, 1989, Community Assistance award for innovative housing Calif. Coun. AIA, 1989, selected projects award Rolex Awards for Excellence, 1990, Fed. Design Achievement award, Presdl. Design awards, Nat. Endowment for Arts, 1991, World Habitat awards, grand prize Bldg. and Social Housing Foundation World Habitat awards, 1990, Gold Nugget awards, Grand award, Merit award Pacific Coast Builders and Sun/Coast ArchitectBuilder mag., 1991, SF mag. and Showplace Sq. Group Designers on Parade award, 1991, Maxwell award of excellence Fannie Mae, 1992, Oakland Orchids award AIA and Oakland Design Advocates, 1992, WorldDesign 92 award City and County of San Francisco, 1992, Cert. of Spl. Congressional Recognition for Outstanding Creative Leadership, 1996, HUD award for Building Innovation in Home Ownership, 1996, 97, Internat. Making Cities Livable, City of Vision award, 1997; winner Hon. Mention Am. Plywood Assn., 1986, first place Housing Cost Reduction Co., Mich. State Housing Authority, 1987, No. Calif. Home and Garden mag. DIFFA Design Competition, 1990. Fellow AIA (honor awards San Francisco chpt. 1983, jury mem. San Mateo (Calif.) design awards program 1990, Colo. ann. design awards 1995, Oakland Design awards 1995, Archtl. Photography Spl. Commendation award 1993); mem. Constrn. Specification Inst., McIntosh Archtl. Soc. Scotland, Columbia Archtl. League N.Y., Archtl. Assn. London. Clubs: St. Andrews Soc. (San Francisco); Chelsea Art (London); Columbia N.Y. Home: 743 Northpoint St San Francisco CA 94109-1316 Office: 91 S Van Ness Ave San Francisco CA 94103-1226

MACDONALD, FLORA ISABEL, Canadian government official; b. North Sydney, N.S., Can., June 3, 1926; d. George Frederick and Mary Isabel (Royle) MacD. Attended Empire Bus. Coll.; grad., Nat. Def. Coll., 1972; DHL (hon.), Mt. St. Vincent U., 1979, various univs., U.S. and U.K. Exec. dir. Progressive Conservative Party Hdqs., Ottawa, Ont., Can., 1957-66; adminstrv. officer, tutor dept. polit. studies Queen's U., 1966-72; mem. Can. Parliament for Kingston and the Islands, Ont., 1972-88; Progressive Conservative spokesman for Indian affairs and no. devel. Can. Parliament, 1972; for housing and urban devel., 1974; chmn. Progressive Conservative Caucus Com. on Fed.-Provincial Relations, 1976; sec. of state for external affairs, 1979-80, minister employment and immigration, 1984-86, min. comms., 1986-89; chairperson Internat. Developmental Rsch. Ctr., 1992-97; spl. adv. Commonwealth of Learning, 1990-91; nat. sec. Progressive Conservative Assn. of Can., 1966-69; exec. dir. Com. for Ind. Can., 1971; pres. Elizabeth Fry Soc. of Kingston, 1968-70; vis. fellow Ctr. for Can. Studies, U. Edinburgh, 1989; host T.V. series North South Vision T.V., 1990-94. Bd. dirs. Carnegie Commn. Re-preventing Deadly Conflict, Ctr. for Refugee Studies York U., Friends of the Nat. Libr., Queen's U. Coun., Refugee Policy Group, Washington, Shashtri Indo-Can. Inst.; program advisor CARE Can.; chairperson Capital Fundraising Campaign Mt. St. Vincent U., Halifax, 1990-94, Future Generations, Franklin, W.Va., Helpage Internat., London, Partnership Africa-Can., Ottawa, Can. Decorated Officer Order of Can., 1993, Order of Ont., 1995. Mem. Can. Inst. Fgn. Affairs (dir. 1969-73), Can. Polit. Sci. Assn. (dir. 1972-75), Can. Inst. Internat. Affairs, Can. Civil Liberties Assn. (bd. dirs. 1990-95), Commonwealth Human Rights Initiative, Nat. Mus. Scotland (hon. patron Can.), UN (Eminent Persons to study Trans-Nat. Corps. in South Africa 1989). Mem. United Ch. of Canada. Office: #1103-350 Queen Elizabeth, Ottawa, ON Canada K1S 3N1

MACDONALD, GEORGE FREDERICK, anthropologist, Canadian museum director; b. Cambridge, Ont., Can., July 4, 1938; s. George and Jane (Gorton) MacD.; m. Joanne Elizabeth Rice, Sept. 9, 1961; children: Christine, Grant. BA, U. Toronto, 1961; PhD, Yale U., 1966. Joined archaeol. divsn. Nat. Mus. Can., 1964-66, with west coast archaeol., 1966-68, head west Can. sect., 1968-69, chief archaeol. divsn., 1969-72, chief archaeol. survey Can., 1972-78; rsch. fellow Mus. Fur Volkerkunde, Basel, Switzerland, 1977-78; sr. archaeologist Nat. Mus. Can., 1978-82; rsch. fellow Fla. State Mus., Gainesville, 1980-81; head new accomodation task force Nat. Mus. Can., 1982; exec. dir. Can. Mus. Civilization, 1982—; pres. Can. Mus. Civilization Corp., 1995—; vis. fellow Mus. Anthropology U. B.C., 1981; lectr. Trent U., U. Ottawa, Carleton U., Simon Fraser U.; bd. dirs. Nat. Hist. Sites & Monuments, Can., Can. Mus. Construction Corp. Author: Ninstints: Haida World Heritage Site, 1983, Haida Monumental Art, 1983, Museum for the Global Village, 1989, Haida Art, 1996; contbr. articles to profl. jours. Mem. Can. del. drafting com. UNESCO Conv. on World Heritage, Paris, 1972; Can. del. Commn. Experts, Mohenjo, Daro, Pakistan, 1973; mem. hon. com. Nat. Mus. Am. Indian Nat. campaign, Washington, 1991—. Recipient James award Victoria Coll. U. Toronto, 1961; Wenner Gren fellow Yale U., 1964-65; mem. Can. Coun. Govt. Can., Yale, 1962-63. Mem. Can. Archeol. Assn. (pres. 1968). Home: 29 Lynott St, Cantley, PQ Canada J0X 1L0 Office: Can Mus Civilization Sta B, 100 Laurier St PO Box 3100, Hull, PQ Canada J8X 4H2

MACDONALD, GORDON CHALMERS, management consultant; b. Boston, Sept. 27, 1928; s. Frank C. and Anna E. (MacLean) MacD.; m. Eileen T. Harkins, May 25, 1952; children: Brian P., Peter G., Keith A., Audrey A. AA, Boston U., 1950, BBA, 1952; grad. advanced mgmt. program, Harvard U., 1979. Grad. tng. program Westinghouse Electric Corp., Pitts., 1952-64, regional/zone mgr., 1953-60; nat. mdse. mgr. Westinghouse Electric Corp., Metuchen, N.J., 1960-64; asst. to v.p. sales mgr. Magnavox Co., N.Y.C., 1964-68; v.p. mktg. GTE Corp., Batavia, N.Y., 1968-69; dir. mktg. Mitsubishi Internat. Corp., Lincolnwood, Ill., 1969-75; v.p. Mitsubishi Internat. Corp., N.Y.C., 1975-88, sec., 1984-88; advisor Mitsubishi Internat. Corp., 1989-91; bd. dirs. Mitsubishi Internat. Corp., N.Y.C., 1976-88; prin., mgmt. cons. G.C. MacDonald & Assocs., Greenwich, Conn., 1988—. Chmn. Sea Explorers com. Boy Scouts Am., Greenwich, 1976-81. With U.S. Army, 1946-48. Club: U.S. Power Squadron (comdr. 1981-82, exec. com. 1987—) (Greenwich). Avocations: sailing, skiing, bridge. Home: 42 Birchwood Dr Greenwich CT 06831-3354

MACDONALD, GORDON JAMES FRASER, geophysicist; b. Mexico City, July 30, 1929; s. Gordon and Josephine (Bennett) MacD.; m. Marceline Kuglen (dec.); children: Gordon James, Maureen, Michael; m. Betty Ann Kipniss; 1 son, Bruce; m. Margaret Stone Jennings. A.B. summa cum laude, Harvard U., 1950, A.M., 1952, Ph.D., 1954. Asst. prof. geology, geophysics Mass. Inst. Tech., 1954-55, assoc. prof. geology, geophysics, 1955-58; staff assoc. geophysics lab. Carnegie Inst. Washington, 1955-58; cons. U.S. Geol. Survey, 1955-60; prof. geophysics UCLA, 1958-68; dir. atmospheric rsch. lab., 1960-66, assoc. dir. UCLA (Inst. Geophysics and Planetary Physics), 1960-68; v.p. rsch. Inst. for Def. Analyses, 1966-67, exec. v.p., 1967-68, trustee, 1966-70; vice chancellor for rsch. and grad. affairs U. Calif. at Santa Barbara, 1968-70, prof. physics and geophysics, 1968-70; mem. coun. on Environ. Quality Washington, 1970-72; Henry R. Luce prof. environ. studies and policy, dir. environ. studies program Dartmouth Coll., 1972-79; trustee The MITRE Corp., McLean, Va., 1968-70, 72-77, exec. com., 1972-77; disting. vis. scholar The MITRE Corp., 1977-79, chief scientist, 1979-83, v.p., chief scientist, 1983-90; prof. internat. rels., rsch. dir. U. Calif., San Diego, 1990-96; dir. Internat. Inst. for Applied Sys. Analysis, Laxenburg, Austria, 1996—; cons. NASA, 1960-70, mem. lunar and planetary missions bd., 1967; mem. Def. Sci. Bd., Dept. Def., 1966-70; cons. Dept. State, 1967-70; mem. Pres.'s Sci. Adv. Com., 1965-69; adv. panel on nuclear effects Office Tech. Assessment, 1975-77. Author: The Rotation of the Earth, 1960; co-author: Sound and Light Phenomena: A Study of Historical and Modern Occurrences, 1978, The Long-Term Impacts of Increasing Atmospheric Carbon Dioxide Levels, 1982, Global Climate and Ecosystem Change, 1990; contbr. articles to sci., tech. jours. Fellow AAAS, Am. Mineral. Soc., Am. Meteorol. Soc., Geol. Soc. Am., Am. Geophys. Union, Am. Acad. Arts and Scis., Am. Philos. Soc.; mem. Am. Math. Soc., Nat. Acad. Scis. (chmn. environ. studies bd. 1970, 72-73, chmn. commn. on natural resources 1973-77), Royal Astron. Soc. (fgn. assoc.), Geochem. Soc. Am., Seismol. Soc. Am., Soc. Indsl. and Applied Math., Coun. Fgn. Rels., Cosmos Club, Sigma Xi. Office: Internat Inst Applied Sys Analysis, A-2361 Laxenburg Austria

MACDONALD, HUGH IAN, university president emeritus, economist, educator; b. Toronto, Ont., Can., June 27, 1929; s. Hugh and Winnifred (Mitchell) M.; m. Dorothy Marion Vernon, June 4, 1960; 5 children. B.Com., U. Toronto, 1952; M.A. (Rhodes scholar), Oxford (Eng.) U., 1954, B.Phil., 1955; LLD (hon.), U. Toronto, 1974. Lectr. U. Toronto, 1955-62, asst. prof., 1962-65; dean of men U. Toronto (Univ. Coll.), 1956-65; chief economist Govt. Ont., Toronto, 1965-67; dep. treas. Govt. Ont., 1967, dep. treas., dep. minister econs., 1968, dep. treas., dep. minister econs. and intergovtl. affairs, 1972; pres. York U., North York, Ont., 1974-84; prof., dir. York Internat., 1984-94, prof., pres. emeritus, 1984—; past pres. World U., Univ. Svc. Can.; chmn. Hockey Can., The Commonwealth of Learning. Recipient Can. Centennial medal, 1967, Queen's Silver Jubilee medal, 1977, Officer, Order Can., 1977, Commemorative medal 125th Anniv. Can. Confederation, 1992. Office: York U, 4700 Keele St, North York, ON Canada M3J 1P3

MACDONALD, JAMES ROSS, physicist, educator; b. Savannah, Ga., Feb. 27, 1923; s. John Elwood and Antonina Jones (Hansell) M.; m. Margaret Milward Taylor, Aug. 3, 1946; children: Antonina Hansell, James Ross IV, William Taylor. B.A., Williams Coll., 1944; S.B., Mass. Inst. Tech., 1944, S.M., 1947; D.Phil. (Rhodes scholar), Oxford (Eng.) U., 1950, D.Sc., 1967. Mem. staff Digital Computer Lab., Mass. Inst. Tech., 1946-47; physicist Armour Research Found., Chgo., 1950-52; asso. physicist Argonne Nat. Lab., 1952-53; with Tex. Instruments Inc., Dallas, 1953-74; v.p. corporate research and engring. Tex. Instruments Inc., 1968-73, v.p. corporate research and devel., 1973-74; cons., 1974—; dir. Simmonds Precision Products Inc., 1979-83; William Rand Kenan Jr. prof. physics U. N.C., Chapel Hill, 1974-91, prof. emeritus, 1991—; mem. editorial bd. Jour. Applied Physics, 1984-86; adj. prof. biophysics U. Tex. Med. Sch., Dallas, 1954-74; mem. solid state scis. panel NRC, 1965-73; mem. adv. com. for sci. edn. NSF, 1971-73; mem. vis. com. physics Mass. Inst. Tech., 1971-74; mem. external adv. com. Engring. Expt. Sta., Ga. Inst. Tech., 1976-79. Editor, contbr.: Impedance Spectroscopy-Emphasizing Solid Materials and Systems, 1987; contbr. more than 200 articles to profl. jours. Mem. Dallas Radio Commn., 1967-71; mem. sci. adv. coun. Callier Hearing and Speech Ctr., Dallas, 1974-78; bd. dirs. League for Ednl. Advancement in Dallas, 1965-70; mem. adv. com. Weber Rsch. Inst., 1985-90. Fellow Am. Phys. Soc. (com. on edn. 1973-75, com. on applications of physics 1975-78, George E. Pake prize 1985), IEEE (awards 1962, 74, assoc. editor Transactions of Profl. Group on Audio 1961-66, Transactions on Audio and Electroacoustics 1966-73, recipient Edison Gold medal 1988), AAAS; mem. Nat. Acad. Engring. (exec. com. assembly of engring. 1975-78, coun. 1971-74), Nat. Acad. Scis. (chmn. numerical data adv. bd. 1970-74, mem. com. on motor vehicle emissions 1971-74, chmn. com. on motor vehicle emissions 1973-74, mem. com. on satellite power systems 1979-81, mem. com. on sci., engring., and pub. policy 1981-83, mem. commn. on phys. scis., math., and applications 1985-88, mem. report rev. com. 1990—), Am. Inst. Physics (governing bd. 1975-78, chmn. com. on profl. concerns 1976-78), Electrochem. Soc., Audio Engring. Soc., Phi Beta Kappa, Sigma Xi, Tau Beta Pi. Achievements include 10 patents in field. Office: Univ NC Dept Physics and Astronomy Chapel Hill NC 27599-3255

MACDONALD, JOHN BARFOOT, research foundation executive; b. Toronto, Feb. 23, 1918; s. Arthur Albert and Gladys Lillian (Barfoot) M.; m. Liba Bockova, July 10, 1967; children—Kaaren, Grant, Scott, Vivian, Linda. D.D.S. with honors, U. Toronto, 1942; M.S. in Bacteriology, U. Ill., 1948; Ph.D. in Bacteriology, Columbia U., 1953; A.M. (hon.), Harvard U., 1956; LL.D. (hon.), U. Man., 1962, Simon Fraser U., 1965, Wilfrid Laurier U., 1976, Brock U., 1976, U. Western Ont., 1977; D.Sc. (hon.), U. B.C., 1967, U. Windsor, 1977. Chmn. div. dental research U. Toronto, 1953-56, prof. bacteriology, 1956; dir. Forsyth Dental Infirmary, Boston, 1956-62; prof. microbiology Harvard U. Sch. Dental Medicine, 1956-62; pres. U. B.C., 1962-67; exec. dir. Council Ont. Univs., 1968-76; pres. Addiction Research Found., Toronto, 1976-81; chmn. Addiction Research Found., 1981-87; chmn. commn. pharm. services Can. Pharm. Assn., 1967; rev. officer unicameral expt. U. Toronto, 1977; bd. dirs. Donwood Found., 1966-79, chmn., 1972-75; bd. dirs. Banff Sch. Advanced Mgmt., 1962-67, chmn., 1966-67; vice chmn. Ont. Council Health, 1981-84; cons. in field. Served with Dental Corps Can. Army, 1944-46. Decorated officer Order of Can. Home: 30 Metropolitan Cres, Keswick, ON Canada L4P 1L5

MACDONALD, JOHN STEPHEN, oncologist, educator; b. Bklyn., June 2, 1943; s. John Stephen and Margaret (Martin) M.; m. Mary Suzanne Stock, July 11, 1964; children: Margaret Wilson, John Stephen, Kathleen Lenore, Frederick Stock. A.B., Dartmouth Coll., 1965, B.M.S., 1967; M.D., Harvard U., 1969. Diplomate Am. Bd. Internal Medicine (mem. med. oncology com. 1989-93, chmn. med. oncology self edn. process com. 1993-95). Intern and resident in medicine Beth Israel Hosp., Boston, 1969-71; clin. assoc. immunology and med. oncology Nat. Cancer Inst., Bethesda, Md., 1971-74; assoc. dir. cancer therapy evaluation program, div. cancer treatment Nat. Cancer Inst., 1979-82, med. oncologist Washington Clin., 1982-84; instr., asst. prof., then assoc. prof. medicine Georgetown U., Washington, 1974-79; clin. assoc. prof. Georgetown U., 1979-84, George Washington U., 1980-84; prof. medicine, chief div. hematology-oncology U. Ky., Lexington, 1984-89, assoc. dir. Markey Cancer Center, 1984-89; prof. medicine, chief sect. med. oncology, dir. cancer ctr. Temple U., Phila., 1989—; chmn. gastrointestinal cancer com. S.W. Oncology Group, 1985—. Editor-in-chief: Cancer Treatment Reports, 1979-82; co-editor: Gastrointestinal Oncology, 1992; mem. editorial bd. Jour. Clin. Oncology, 1988-91; contbr. over 180 articles to med. jours. Bd. mgmt. YMCA, 1979-84; bd. dirs. CYO, 1979-84. Served with USPHS, 1971-74. Jr. faculty clin. fellow Am. Cancer Soc., 1974-76. Fellow ACP; mem. Am. Fedn. Clin. Research, Am. Soc. Clin. Oncology, Am. Assn. for Cancer Research, Am. Cancer Soc. (bd. dirs. Phila. chpt. 1994—). Roman Catholic. Home: 522 Ridgeview Ln Villanova PA 19085-1715 Office: Temple U PO Box 38346 3322 N Broad St Philadelphia PA 19140-5102

MACDONALD, JOHN THOMAS, educational administrator; b. Utica, N.Y., Nov. 21, 1932; s. Gerald Clement and Mildred (Hayes) MacD.; m. Marcia Sprague Gallup; children: Terrence (dec.), Anthony, Elizabeth, Michele, Elise, Denise. BS, Northeastern U., 1958, MEd, 1960; PhD, U. Conn., 1970. Cert. elem. and secondary sch. tchr., prin., supt., Mass., Conn. Supervising prin. Noank, Ft. Hill. and Poquonnock Elem. Schs., Groton, Conn., 1962-66, Robert E. Fitch Jr. High Sch., Groton, 1966-70; rsch. asst. Ednl. Resources and Devel. Ctr. U. Conn., Storrs, 1969-70; supt. schs. Wallingford (Conn.) Pub. Schs., 1970-73, Walpole (Mass.) Pub. Schs., 1973-78, Dartmouth (Mass.) Pub. Schs., 1978-86; commr. edn. State Dept. Edn., Concord, N.H., 1986-90; asst. sec. for elem. and secondary edn. U.S. Dept. Edn., Washington, 1990-93; dir. state leadership ctr. Coun. of Chief State Sch. Officers, Washington, 1993—; mem. Postsecondary Edn. Commn., Concord, 1986-90, Coun. for Tchr. Edn., Concord, 1986-90, Profl. Standards Bd., Concord, 1986-90; trustee Univ. System of N.H., Durham, 1986-90; mem. Surgeon Gen's Task Force, 1990-93; mem. White House Conf. on Indian Edn., 1990-93; mem. Interagy. Com. on Sch. Health, 1990-93, others. Contbr. articles to profl. jours. Co-chmn. Emergency Sch.-Aide Proposals, U.S. Office Edn., 1973-75; mem. Mass. Adv. Commn. for Ednl. TV, 1983-86; mem. N.H. Task Force on Child Abuse, 1987-90; mem. nat. adv. coun. Northeastern U., 1990—; mem. Galaxy Classroom Nat. Adv. Coun. Galaxy Inst. for Edn., 1992—; mem. sch. health policy initiative Ctr. for Population & Family Health Columbia U., 1992—; mem. Packard roundtable to children Ctr. for Health Policy George Washington U., 1992—; mem. adv. com. external program rev. CDC, 1992—. Recipient Sears B. Condit award, 1958, Alumni award Northwestern U., 1973, Recognition award Coun. of Chief State Sch. Officers, 1990. Fellow Phi Delta Kappa, Phi Alpha Theta; mem. N.H. Sch. Bldg. Authority, Mass. Assn. Sch. Supts. (pres. 1985-86). Office: Coun Chief State Sch 1 Massachusetts Ave NW Washington DC 20001-1401

MACDONALD, KEN CRAIG, geophysicist; b. San Francisco, Oct. 14, 1947; m. Rachel Haymon, 1984. BS in Engring. Physics, U. Calif. Berkeley, 1970; PhD in Marine Geophysics, MIT/Woods Hole, 1975. Cecil H. and Ida Green postdoctoral scholar Scripps Instn. of Oceanography, 1975-76, asst. rsch. geophysicist, lectr., 1976-80; assoc. prof. U. Calif., Santa Barbara, 1980-83; prof. U. Calif., 1983—; chief scientist on over 30 deep sea expeditions; prin. ALVIN diver on over 40 dives to the mid-ocean ridge. Assoc. editor Jour. of Geophys. Rsch., 1979-82, Earth and Planetary Sci. Letters, 1978-88; mem. editorial bd. Marine Sci. Revs., 1986—; editor Marine Geophys. Rschs., 1986-90; contbr. over 100 articles to profl. jours. Mem. ALVIN Rev. Com., 1979-82; mem. Ocean Sci. Bd. of NAS, 1980-83, Lithosphere Panel Advanced Ocean Drilling Project, 1983-85, Ocean Scis. Panel, NSF, 1984-86, COSOD II planning com.; mem. various RIDGE coms., RIDGE steering com., 1987-90; mem. NSF Ocean Scis. Strategic Plan for Rsch. and Edn. Com., 1993-94. Regents scholar U. Calif., Berkeley, 1966-70, Mineral Tech. scholar, 1967-70, Cecil H. and Ida Green scholar Inst. Geophysics and Planetary Physics/U. Calif., San Diego, 1975-76; NSF Grad. fellow, 1970-73;recipient AAAS Newcomb-Cleveland prize, 1980, Robert L. and Bettie P. Cody prize and medal Scripps Instn. Oceanography, 1994; named U. Hawaii SOEST Disting. lectr., 1990. Fellow Am. Geophys. Union, Geol. Soc. Am. Avocations: windsurfing, fly fishing. Office: U Calif Santa Barbara Dept Geol Sci Santa Barbara CA 93106

MACDONALD, KENNETH, journalist, former editor; b. Jefferson, Iowa, Sept. 3, 1905; s. William Arthur and Mabel (Swearingen) McD.; m. Helen Inman, June 17, 1929; 1 child, Stephen. A.B., U. Iowa, 1926. With Des Moines Register and Tribune, 1926-86, successively reporter, copyreader, telegraph editor, city editor, mng. editor, exec. editor, v.p., 1946-76, editor, 1953-76, editorial chmn., 1976-77, pub., 1960-70, dir., 1940-86; Bd. dirs. A.P., 1956-65, 1st v.p., 1963-65; adv. bd. Pulitzer prizes, 1958-70. Co-author: Drink Thy Wine With a Merry Heart, 1983. Trustee Simpson Coll., chmn. bd., 1957-59. Served as air combat intelligence officer USNR, World War II, PTO. Mem. Am. Soc. Newspaper Editors (dir. 1950-56, pres. 1955), Sigma Delta Chi. Mem. Episcopal Ch. Club: Des Moines. Home: 3412 Southern Hills Dr Des Moines IA 50321-1319

MACDONALD, LENNA RUTH, lawyer; b. Providence, July 16, 1962; d. Arthur Robert and Laina Ruth (Weake) M.; m. Robert Christopher Carew, Sept. 18, 1993. BA, Brown U., 1984; postgrad., London Sch. Econs., 1984-85; JD, Emory U., 1988. Bar: Ohio 1988, R.I., 1989, Mass. 1992, Ky. 1996. With Erikson Internat. Biog. Database, Providence, 1983-86; assoc. Smith & Schnacke, Dayton, Ohio, 1988-89, Edwards & Angell, Providence, 1989-91, McDermott, Will & Emery, Boston, 1991-93; asst. gen. counsel, group mgr. Banc One N.H. Asset Mgmt. Corp., Manchester, 1993-96, Banc One Corp., Bank One, Ky., NA, Louisville, 1996—. mem. Mass. Bar Assn., R.I. Bar Assn., Ky. Bar Assn., Am. Friends London Sch. Econs., Phi Alpha Delta. Republican. Episcopalian. Avocations: sailing, pottery. Home: 1721 Devondale Dr Louisville KY 40222-4153 Office: Bank One Ky NA Legal Dept PO Box 32500 KY1-2508 Louisville KY 40232-2500

MAC DONALD, MALCOLM MURDOCH, editor, publisher; b. Uniontown, Pa., June 15, 1935; s. Morgan Bowman and Ruth (Newcomb) Greene Mac D.; m. Constance Emily Marsh, June 13, 1959; children—Randall Malcolm, Alison Margaret, Ellen Marsh. B.A., Trinity Coll., Conn., 1957. Coll. rep. Midwest D. Van Nostrand Co. Inc., Princeton, N.J., 1958-62, assoc. sci. editor, 1962, sci. editor, 1963-68; sci. editor Van Nostrand Reinhold Co., N.Y.C., 1968-70; editor Pa. State U. Press, State College, 1970-72; chief editor U. N.C. Press, Chapel Hill, 1972-76, asst. dir., 1975-76; asst. dir., editor U. Ga. Press, Athens, 1976-78; dir. U. Ala. Press, 1978-96, 1996—; acting dir. U. Ala. Library, 1980-81; cons. in field. Author: (With Cecil E. Johnson) Society and the Environment, 1971, (with Robert E. Davis) Chemistry and Society, 1972. Mem. Assn. Am. Univ. Presses (bd. dirs. 1982-84), Omicron Delta Kappa. Office: U Ala Press Box 870380 Tuscaloosa AL 35487

MACDONALD, MAURICE MARCUS, economics educator; b. Bozeman, Mont., Sept. 20, 1947; s. Bernard Marcus and Alice Mildred (Dira) MacD.; m. Jeanne Frances Reece, June 13, 1969; children: Nicole, Dantia, Anton, Micah, Jasper, Gabriel, Chester, Maurice Jr. AB in Econs., U. Calif., Santa Cruz, 1969; PhD in Econs., U. Mich., 1974. Project assoc. Inst. for Rsch. on Poverty U Wis., Madison, 1973-75, prof. consumer sci. Sch. Family Resources, 1975-95; chair human devel and family studies Iowa State U. Coll. Family and Consumer Scis., Ames, 1995—; mem. acad. adv. bd. Rockford (Ill.) Inst., 1989-95; cons. in field. Author: Food, Stamps and Income Maintenance, 1977. Adult edn. chair on Bishop's pastoral letter on economy. Blessed Sacrament Parish, Madison, 1986. NIH grantee, 1978-79, 90-94. Mem. KC. Roman Catholic. Office: Coll Family and Consumer Scis 1086 LeBaron Hall Ames IA 50011

MACDONALD, PAUL EDWARD, electrical engineer; b. Syracuse, N.Y., Nov. 2, 1954; s. Cornelius J. and Virginia F. (Vassallo) MacD.; m. Linda Marie Fredrick, Aug. 20, 1983; children: Maeghen Leigh, Charles Fredrick. B Archtl. Engring., Pa. State U., 1977. Registered profl. engr., Va., Md., D.C., Conn., W.Va., Del., Ill. Engring. in tng. Syska & Hennessy, Washington, 1977-78, jr. engr., 1978-79, project engr., 1979-80; project engr. Meta Engrs. P.C., Washington, 1980-82, dir. elec. engring., 1982-88, chief elec. engring., 1988-91, v.p., chief elec. engring., 1991—. Den leader cub scouts, Boy Scouts Am., Alexandria, Va., 1994—. Mem. NSPE, Nat. Soc. Archtl. Engrs., D.C. Soc. Profl. Engrs. (pres. 1991-92, bd. dirs. 1986—, Outstanding Svc. award 1987, 88), Sierra Club. Roman Catholic. Avocations: woodworking, making stringed musical instruments, playing guitar, banjo and dulcimer, hiking. Home: 8801 Lukens Ln Alexandria VA 22309-4105 Office: Meta Engrs PC 1220 L St NW Washington DC 20005-4018

MACDONALD, ROBERT ALAN, language educator; b. Salamanca, N.Y., Mar. 25, 1927; s. Guy E. and Hildur V. (Helene) MacD. B.A., U. Buffalo, 1948; M.A., U. Wis., 1949, Ph.D., 1958. Asst. prof. U. Richmond, Va., 1955-61, assoc. prof., 1961-67, prof. Spanish, 1967-95, prof. emeritus, 1995; ofcl.

project reviewer NEH, Washington, 1977-95, Social Sci. and Humanities Research Council, Ottawa, Ont., Can., 1981-95. Author: Espéculo, texto jurídico atribuído a Alfonso X, 1990, Alfonso X, Libro de las Tahurerías, 1995; editor Bull. of Fgn. Lang. Assn. Va., 1962-67, 72-86; contbr. articles to profl. jours. Served with U.S. Army, 1946-47, 51-53. A.L. Markham traveling fellow U. Wis., 1958-59; Am. Council Learned Socs. fellow, 1976; fellow and grantee U. Richmond, 1958-94; named Cultural Laureate of Va., 1977; recipient Disting. Service award Fgn. Lang. Assn. Va., 1981. Mem. Acad. Am. Rsch. Historians on Medieval Spain, Am. Assn. Tchrs. of Spanish and Portuguese (past pres. state chpt.), AAUP (past pres. local chpt.), Am. Council on Teaching Fgn. Langs., Medieval Acad. Am., MLA. Club: Torch (Richmond).

MACDONALD, ROBERT RIGG, JR., museum director; b. Pitts., May 11, 1942; s. Robert Rigg and Ruth (Johnson) M.; m. Catherine Ronan, Nov. 27, 1965; children: Matthew, Robert, Catherine. B.A., U. Notre Dame, 1964, M.A., 1965; M.A., U. Pa., 1970. Asst. curator Smithsonian Instn., Washington, 1965; curator Mercer Mus., Doylestown, Pa., 1966-70; dir. New Haven Colony Hist. Soc., 1970-74, La. State Mus., New Orleans, 1974-85, Mus. of City of N.Y., 1985—; adj. prof. mus. studies NYU, 1989—; mem. Commn. on Mus. for a New Century. Editor: New Haven Colony Furniture, 1973, Louisiana Images 1880-1920, 1975, Louisiana Black Heritage, 1977 Louisiana Portraitures, 1979, Louisiana Legal Heritage, 1981, The Sun King: Louis XIV and the New World, On Being Homeless in New York, 1987, Broadway! 125 Years of Musical Theater, Hives of Sickness: Public Health and Epidemics in New York City, 1995, Our Town: Images and Stories from the Museum of the City of New York, 1997. Active Nat. Endowment for Humanities. Decorated chevalier de l'Ordre des Arts et des Lettres (France), cruz de Caballero de la Order de Isabel La Catolica (Spain); assoc. fellow Berkeley Coll., Yale U., 1978; Hagley fellow U. Del., 1970-71; Univ. scholar U. Notre Dame, 1964-65. Mem. Am. Assn. State and Local History (coun.), Am. Assn. Mus. (pres. 1985-88, chmn. ethics task force 1988-91), Century Assn. Roman Catholic. Home: 35 Edgewood Ln Bronxville NY 10708-1946 Office: Mus NYC 1220 5th Ave New York NY 10029-5221

MACDONALD, ROBERT TAYLOR, newspaper executive; b. Mt. Vernon, N.Y., Oct. 25, 1930; s. Joseph Taylor and Mary Gertrude (Broderick) MacD.; m. Christiana Barbara Besch, June 25, 1960 (div. 1977); children: Gregory, Michael, Jennifer; m. Gillian S. Tripier, 1978. B.S., Yale, 1952; M.B.A., Wharton Sch. of U. Pa., 1958. Pub. Mariner (monthly trade mag.), 1956; bus. mgmt. cons., 1958-61; v.p., adminstrn., dir. N.Y. Herald Tribune, Inc., 1961-63, exec. v.p., 1963-66; pub. N.Y. Herald Tribune-Washington Post Internat., 1966-67, Internat. Herald Tribune, 1967-77; chmn. Hudson Research Europe, Ltd., 1977-87; mng. dir. MacDonald & Co., 1980—; v.p. internat. ops. Washington Post Co., 1966-70, asst. to chmn., 1968-70. Bd. govs. Am. Hosp. of Paris. Served as lt. USNR, 1953-56. Mem. Fgn. Policy Assn., Am. C. of C. in Paris (dir.), Phi Gamma Delta. Clubs: Yale (N.Y.C.), Wharton MBA (N.Y.C.) (dir., past pres.); Apawamis (Rye, N.Y.); Travelers (Paris). Office: Ste 701 9393 Midnight Pass Rd Sarasota FL 34242-2959

MACDONALD, R(ONALD ANGUS) NEIL, physician, educator; b. Calgary, Alta., Can., Jan. 6, 1935; s. Angus Neil and Florence Mary (Macdonald) MacD.; m. Mary Jane Whiting, June 30, 1962; children: Cynthia, David, James, Gavin. BA, U. Toronto, 1955; MD, CM, McGill U., Montreal, 1959. Demonstrator, lectr. McGill U., 1965-67, assoc. dean, faculty of medicine, 1967-70; assoc. dir., dir. Oncology Day Ctr., Royal Victoria Hosp., Montreal, 1967-71; exec. dir. Provincial Cancer Hosps. Bd., Edmonton, Alta., Can., 1971-75; prof. medicine U. Alta., Edmonton, 1971-94; dir. Cross Cancer Inst., Edmonton, 1975-80, 1981-87; assoc. dir., prof. palliative care Royal Victoria Hosp., Montreal, 1980-81; prof. palliative medicine Alta. Cancer Found., Edmonton, 1987-94; dir. cancer ethics program Inst. Recherches Cliniques Montreal, 1994—; prof. oncology McGill U., 1994—; mem. cancer expert adv. panel WHO, Geneva, 1986—, Can. rep. Cancer Pain project, 1983—. Co-editor: Oxford Textbook of Palliative Medicine, 1993; contbr. articles on treatment of cancer pain and other topics to profl. jours. Recipient Queen's Jubilee medal, 1977, Alta. Achievement award, 1980, Blair award Nat. Cancer Inst., 1980, Edmonton Achievement award, 1994. Fellow Coll. Physicians and Surgeons Can., Royal Coll. Physicians Edinburgh (hon.); mem. Order of Can., Can. Cancer Soc. (nat. bd. dirs. 1981-87), Can. Oncology Soc. (pres. 1977-78), Am. Soc. Clin. Oncology (sec.-treas. 1980-82), Can. Soc. Palliative Care Physicians (pres. 1993-94). Roman Catholic. Avocations: squash, history. Office: Inst Clin Rsch, 110 Pine Ave W, Montreal, PQ Canada H2W 1R7

MACDONALD, SHEILA DE MARILLAC, transaction management company executive; b. Santa Monica, Calif., Jan. 17; d. William Alan and M. Jane (Crotty) M. BS, Stanford U.; BA, U. San Francisco; MBA, Harvard U. Prin. Tex. Transaction Mgmt. Co., Houston, 1990—. Mem. Harvard Club N.Y., Met. Club, Petroleum Club.

MACDONALD, THOMAS COOK, JR., lawyer; b. Atlanta, Oct. 11, 1929; s. Thomas Cook and Mary (Morgan) MacD.; m. Gay Anne Everiss, June 30, 1956; children: Margaret Anne, Thomas William. B.S. with high honors, U. Fla., 1951, LL.B. with high honors, 1953. Bar: Fla. 1953; cert. mediator Supreme Ct. Fla. and U.S. Dist. Ct. (mid. dist.) Fla. Practice law Tampa, 1953—; mem. firm Shackleford, Farrior, Stallings & Evans, 1953—; spl. counsel Gov. of Fla., 1963, U. Fla., 1972—; del. 5th cir. Jud. Conf., 1970-81; mem. adv. com. U.S. Ct. Appeals (5th cir.), 1975-78, (11th cir.), 1988-93; mem. Fla. Jud. Qualifications Commn., 1983-88, vice chmn., 1987, chmn., 1988, gen. counsel, 1997—; mem. judicial nominating com. Fla. Supreme Ct., 1995—. Mem. Fla. Student Scholarship and Loan Commn., 1963-67; bd. dirs. Univ. Cmty. Hosp., Tampa, 1968-78, Fla. West Coast Sports Assn., 1965-80, Hall of Fame Bowl Assn., 1989-93, Jim Walter Corp., 1979-87; mem. Hillsborough County Pub. Edn. Study Commn., 1965; lic. lay eucharistic min. Episcopal Ch., 1961—; chancellor Episcopal Diocese of S.W. Fla., 1990-93; bd. dirs. U. Fla. Found., 1978-86, Shands Tchg. Hosp., U. Fla., 1981-95; counsel Tampa Sports Authority, 1983-94. Maj. USAFR, 1950-65. Recipient Disting. Alumnus award U. Fla., 1976, George C. Carr award Fed. Bar Assn., 1991, Fla. Bar Presdl. award of Merit, 1995, Goldburg award Hillsborough County Bar Assn. Trial Lawyers, 1995. Fellow Am. Coll. Trial Lawyers (chmn. state com. 1990-91), Am. Bar Found., Fla. Bar (chmn. com. profl. ethics 1966-70, bd. govs. 1970-74, bar mem. Supreme Ct. com. on stds. conduct governing judges 1976, Fla. bd. cert. appellate lawyer); mem. ABA (com. on ethics and profl. responsibility 1970-76), Am. Law Inst. (life), 11th Cir. Hist. Soc. (trustee 1982-95, pres. 1989-95), U. Fla. Nat. Alumni Assn. (pres. 1973), Phi Kappa Phi, Phi Delta Phi, Fla. Blue Key, Kappa Alpha. Episcopalian. Home: 1904 S Holly Ln Tampa FL 33629-7004 Office: PO Box 3324 Tampa FL 33601-3324

MACDONALD, TIMOTHY LEE, chemistry educator; b. Long Beach, Calif., Mar. 12, 1948; m. Deborah L. Patrick; children: Kate, Alice. BS with honors, UCLA, 1971; PhD, Columbia U., 1975. Asst. prof. chemistry Vanderbilt U., Nashville, 1977-82; assoc. prof. chemistry U. Va., Charlottesville, 1982-89, prof. chemistry, 1989—. Contbr. articles to profl. publs.; patentee in field. Office: U Va Dept Chemistry Mccormick Rd Charlottesville VA 22904

MACDONALD, WAYNE DOUGLAS, publisher; b. Port Elgin, Ont., Can., Sept. 20, 1940; s. John Murdock and Irene Juliana (Lunow) MacD.; m. Marjorie Anne Farwell, Apr. 28, 1968; children: Scott, Ryan. Journalist Kitchener (Ont.)-Waterloo Record, 1964-75, mgn. editor, 1975-79, dir. resource and devel., 1985-88, editor, 1988-90, pub., 1990—; assignment editor Toronto Star, 1979-82; comm. dir. Ministry of Consumer Affairs, Toronto, Canada, 1982-84, Ministry of Health, Toronto, Canada, 1984-85; bd. dirs. Can. Press, Toronto, 1992-93; mem. adv. coun. U. Western Ont. Sch. Journalism, London, Ont., 1993. Mem. Rotary of Kitchener-Waterloo (com. for ednl. excellence), Westmount Golf and Country Club, Univ. Club. Office: Kitchener-Waterloo Record, 225 Fairway Rd S, Kitchener, ON Canada N2G 4E5*

MACDONALD, WILLIAM LLOYD, architectural historian; b. Putnam, Conn., July 12, 1921; s. William Lloyd and Susan Elisabeth (Elrod) MacD.; children: Noel, Nicholas. AB, Harvard U., 1949, AM, 1953, PhD, 1956. Instr. Boston Archtl. Ctr., Mass., 1950-54; from asst. prof. to assoc. prof. Yale U., 1956-65; A.P. Brown prof. Smith Coll., Northampton, Mass., 1965-80; archtl. historian, Washington, 1980—; exec. sec. Byzantine Inst., Boston, 1950-54. Author: Early Christian and Byzantine Architecture, 1962, Northampton Massachusetts Architecture and Buildings, 1976, Piranesi's Carceri: Sources of Invention, 1976, Architecture of the Roman Empire I, 1982, II, 1986 (Alice Davis Hitchcock prize, Kevin Lynch award Dept. Urban Studies MIT); The Pantheon, 1976, (with J.A. Pinto) Hadrian's Villa and its Legacy, 1995 (Alice Davis Hitchcock prize, George Wittenborn Meml. award, Book of Yr. award, Am. Inst. of Architects). Lt. USAAF, 1942-45. Recipient Emerton, Shaw fellow Harvard U., Cambridge, Mass., 1949, 50, Vets. Nat. scholar, 1948; J. Paul Getty Ctr. scholar, Santa Monica, 1985-86. Fellow Am. Acad. Arts and Scis., Am. Acad. Rome (Prize fellow 1954-56); mem. AIA (life), Soc. Archtl. Historians (bd. dirs.), Soc. for Promotion of Roman Studies (life). Home: 3811 39th St NW Washington DC 20016-2835

MACDOUGAL, GARY EDWARD, corporate director, foundation trustee; b. Chgo., July 3, 1936; s. Thomas William and Lorna Lee (McDougall) MacD.; children: Gary Edward, Michael Scott; m. Charlene Gehm, June 15, 1992. BS in Engring., UCLA, 1958; MBA with distinction, Harvard U., 1962. Cons. McKinsey & Co., L.A., 1963-68, ptnr., 1968-69; chmn. bd., chief exec. officer Mark Controls Corp. (formerly Clayton Mark & Co.), Evanston, Ill., 1969-87; gen. dir. N.Y.C. Ballet, 1993-94; chmn. Gov. Task Force on Human Svcs. Reform State of Ill., 1993—; sr. advisor and asst. campaign mgr. George Bush for Pres., Washington, 1988; chmn. Bulgarian-Am. Enterprise Fund, Chgo. and Sophia, Bulgaria, 1991-93, bd. dirs., 1991—; apptd. to U.S. Commn. on Effectiveness of UN, 1992-93; bd. dirs. United Parcel Svc. Am., Inc., Atlanta; bd. dirs. Union Camp Corp., Wayne, N.J.; adv. dir. Saratoga Ptnrs., N.Y.; instr. UCLA, 1969. Contbr. articles to profl. jours., chpts. to books. Trustee, mem. exec. com. Annie E. Casey Found., UCLA Found., 1973-79, W.T. Grant Found., 1992-94, Russell Sage Found., 1981-91, chair, 1987-90; apptd. by Pres. Bush as pub. del., alt. rep., U.S. Del. UN 44th Gen. Assembly, 1989-90; commr. Sec. Labor's Commn. on Workforce Quality and Productivity, Washington, 1988-89. Lt. USN, 1958-61. Mem. Coun. Fgn. Rels., Harvard Club, Econ. Club, Kappa Sigma. Episcopalian. Home: 505 N Lake Shore Dr Ste 2711 Chicago IL 60611

MACDOUGALL, HARTLAND MOLSON, corporate director, retired bank executive; b. Montreal, Que., Can., Jan. 28, 1931; s. Hartland Campbell and Dorothy (Molson) MacD.; m. Eve Gordon, Oct. 29, 1954; children: Cynthia, Wendy, Keith, Willa, Tania. Ed., LeRosey, Switzerland, 1947-48, McGill U., 1949-53, Advanced Mgmt. Program, Harvard U., 1976. With Bank Montreal, various locations, 1953-84; dir. Bank Montreal, 1974, vice chmn., 1981; chmn., dir. Royal Trustco Ltd., Toronto, 1984-93; dep. chmn. London Ins. Group, Inc., London Life Ins. Co., London Ins. Co.; bd. dirs. Internat. Murex Technols. Corp., The Bermudiana Found. of Can. Founding chmn. Heritage Can., St. Michael's Hosp. Found., The Japan Soc., chmn., adv. com. Can.-Japan Bus. Com.; gov., past chmn. Coun. Can. Unity; dir. Friends of the Youth Awards Inc., U.S.; hon. pres. Royal Agrl. Winter Fair; mem. Internat. Coun. Music Ctr. L.A., Adv. Coun. U. B.C.; gov. Olympic Trust; bd. dirs. Can. Soc. for Weismann Inst., Empire Club Found.; sen. Stratford Shakespearean Found.; former chmn. The Duke of Edinburgh Awards Internat. Coun. Decorated Order of Can., 1981, Comdr. Royal Victorian Order, 1989; recipient Order of the Rising Sun, Gold and Silver Star, Govt. of Japan, 1995. Avocations: golf, gardening, skiing, tennis, farming. Home: 16978 Shaws Creek Rd, Belfountain, ON Canada L0N 1B0 Office: 70 York St Ste 1110, Toronto, ON Canada M5J 1S9

MACDOUGALL, JOHN DOUGLAS, earth science educator; b. Toronto, Ont., Can., Mar. 9, 1944; s. Lorn Graham and Grace A. (Virtue) MacD.; m. Shiela Dawn Ward, June 8, 1968; children: Christopher David, Katherine Heather. BS, U. Toronto, 1967; MS, McMaster U., 1968; PhD, U. Calif.-San Diego, 1972. Asst. research geologist U. Calif., Berkeley, 1972-74; prof. earth scis. Scripps Inst. Oceanography U Calif.-San Diego, La Jolla, 1974—, chmn. geol. research div., 1985-89. Contbr. articles to profl. jours. Fellow Meteoritical Soc. ;mem. AAAS, Geochem. Soc., Am. Geophys. Union. Home: 534 Bonair St La Jolla CA 92037-6112 Office: Scripps Inst Oceanography # 0220 La Jolla CA 92093

MACDOUGALL, JOHN DUNCAN, surgeon; b. Indpls., Mar. 4, 1925; s. Duncan Campbell and Beulah Stewart (Ward) MacD.; m. Inga Margaretha Tranberg, Oct. 6, 1951 (div. Oct. 1990); children: Duncan Campbell, Stewart Andrew, Eric Matthew, Victoria Suzanne MacDougall Korb; m. Barbara Lee Mayse, Nov. 1, 1990; children: Katherine Jane, James William. BS, Ind. U., 1948; MD, Ind. U., Indpl., 1951. Diplomate Am. Bd. Surgery, Am. Bd. Thoracic Surgery. Pvt. practice Indpls., 1957-93; pres. med. staff St. Francis Hosp., Beech Grove, Ind., 1975, pres. adv. bd., 1993-95, chmn. governing bd. trustees, 1995—; chmn. bd. dirs. Physician's Ins. Co. of Ind., Indpls., 1987—. Mem. adv. com. Ind. U. Sch. Medicine, Indpls., 1989—, pres. dean's coun., 1992-95; mem. Ind. Govs. Task Force on Organ Transplantation, Indpls., 1986-89; pres. Ind. Med. Polit. Action Com., Indpls., 1992—; bd. dirs. Ind. Med. History Mus., 1989—; mem. Ind. Hist. Soc., Indpls. Mus. Art. With U.S. Army, 1943-46; ETO. Decorated Bronze Star medal. Fellow ACS; mem. AMA (del., chmn. Ind. delegation), Ind. State Med. Assn. (pres. 1987-88), Indpls. Med. Soc. (pres. 1978-79), Orgn. State Med. Assn. Pres. (pres. 1994-95), Nat. Med. Vets. Assn. (bd. dirs. 1992—), Masons, Indpls. Lit. Club, Contemporary Club, Meridian Hills Country Club. Republican. Episcopalian. Avocations: woodworking, golf, fishing. Home: 7202 Dean Rd Indianapolis IN 46240-3628 Office: Physicians Ins Co of Ind Ste 300 8425 Woodfield Crossing Blvd Indianapolis IN 46240-2495

MACDOUGALL, PETER, lawyer; b. Boston, Sept. 22, 1937; s. Duncan Peck and Hildegard (Moebius) MacD. AB, Harvard U., 1958, LLB, 1963. Assoc. Ropes & Gray, Boston, 1964-73, ptnr., 1973—. Sheldon fellow Harvard U., 1963-64. Club: Harvard (Boston). Avocations: concert and opera going, gardening, reading, travel. Office: Ropes & Gray 1 International Pl Boston MA 02110-2602

MACDOUGALL, PRISCILLA RUTH, lawyer; b. Evanston, Ill., Jan. 20, 1944; d. Curtis Daniel and Genevieve Maurine (Rockwood) MacDougall; m. Lester H. Brownlee, July 5, 1987. BA, Barnard Coll., 1965; grad. with honors, U. Paris, 1967; JD, U. Mich., 1970. Bar: Wis. 1970, Ill. 1970. Asst. atty. gen. State of Wis., 1970-74; instr. Law Sch. and undergrad. campuses U. Wis., 1973-75; staff counsel Wis. Edn. Assn. Council, Madison, 1975—; instr. Columbia Coll., Chgo., 1988—; litigator, writer, speaker, educator women's and children's names and women's rights and labor issues. Mem. ABA, Wis. State Bar (founder sect. on individual rights and responsibilities, chairperson, 1973-75, 78-79), Legal Assn. Women Wis. (co-founder). Author: Married Women's Common Law Right to Their Own Surnames, 1972, (with Terri P. Tepper) Booklet for Women Who Wish to Determine Their Own Names After Marriage, 1974, supplement, 1975, The Right of Women to Name Their Children, 1985; contbr. articles to profl. jours. Home: 502 Engelhart Dr Madison WI 53713-4742 Office: 33 Nob Hill Dr Madison WI 53713-2198

MACDOUGALL, WILLIAM LOWELL, magazine editor; b. Des Moines, July 24, 1931; s. David Gregory and Elizabeth Jeanette (Dugan) MacD. A.B., Willamette U., Salem, Oreg., 1952; M.J. in Journalism (Pulitzer scholar 1953-54), Columbia U., 1953. Reporter Washington Star, 1958-62; corr. Los Angeles Times, 1962-63; asso. editor, then London corr. U.S. News & World Report, 1964-68; asst. mng. editor U.S. News & World Report, Washington, 1978-86; mng. editor Artsreview mag. NEA, 1987-8; pres. Atlantic Media Co., Arlington, Va., 1989. Author: American Revolutionary: A Biography of General Alexander McDougall, 1977. Served with USAF, 1954-57. Recipient George Washington medal Freedoms Found., 1978, citation U.S. Bicentennial Commn., 1976. Methodist. Office: Atlantic Media Co 5000 37th St N Arlington VA 22207-1823

MAC DOWELL, SAMUEL WALLACE, physics educator; b. Camaragibe, Brazil, Mar. 24, 1929; came to U.S., 1963; s. Samuel Wallace and Maria Anita (Amazonas) Mac D.; m. Myriam Ramos Da Silva, Feb. 2, 1953; children: Ana Myriam, Samuel Wallace, Maria Dolores. BSc in Engring., U. Pernambuco, Brazil, 1951; PhD in Math. Physics, Birmingham (Eng.) U., 1958. Rsch. assoc. Princeton (N.J.) U., 1959-60; assoc. prof. Centro Brasileiro De Fisicas Pesquisas, Rio de Janeiro, 1960-63; fellow Inst. for Advanced Study, Princeton, 1963-65; assoc. prof. Yale U., New Haven, 1965-67, prof., 1968—. Fellow Am. Phys. Soc.; mem. Brazilian Acad. Scis. Roman Catholic. Office: Yale U Sloane Physics Lab PO Box 6666 New Haven CT 06511-8167

MACE, JOHN WELDON, pediatrician; b. Buena Vista, Va., July 9, 1938; s. John Henry and Gladys Elizabeth (Edwards) M.; m. Janice Mace, Jan. 28, 1962; children: Karin E., John E., James E. B.A., Columbia Union Coll., 1960; M.D., Loma Linda U., 1964. Diplomate: Am. Bd. Pediatrics, Sub-bd. Pediatric Endocrinology. Intern U.S. Naval Hosp., San Diego, 1964-65, resident in pediatrics, 1966-68; fellow in endocrinology and metabolism U. Colo., 1970-72; asst. prof. pediatrics Loma Linda (Calif.) U. Med. Center, 1972-75, prof., chmn. dept., 1975—; med. dir. Loma Linda U. Children's Hosp., 1990-92, physician-in-chief, 1992—. Contbr. articles to profl. jours. Treas. Found. for Med. Care San Bernardino County, 1979-80, pres., 1980-82; mem. Congl. Adv. Bd., 1984-87; pres. So. Calif. affiliate Am. Diabetes Assn., 1985-86, dir., 1987-89; chmn. adv. bd. State Calif. Children's Svcs., 1986—; bd. dirs. So. Calif. Children's Cancer Svcs., 1993-94, Loma Linda Ronald McDonald House, 1991—, Aetna Health Plans of Calif., 1993-95; bd. dirs. Loma Linda U. Health Care, 1995—. Named Alumnist of Yr., Loma Linda U. Sch. Medicine, 1994. Mem. AAAS, N.Y. Acad. Sci., Calif. Med. Soc. (adv. panel genetic diseases State Calif., 1975—), Western Soc. Pediatric Rsch., Lawson Wilkens Pediatric Endocrine Soc., Assn. Med. Pediatric Dept. Chmn., Am. Acad. Pediatrics, Sigma Xi, Alpha Omega Alpha. Office: Loma Linda U Children's Hosp 11234 Anderson St Loma Linda CA 92354-2804

MACEACHEN, ALLAN JOSEPH, retired senator; b. Inverness, N.S., Can., July 6, 1921; s. Angus and Annie (Gillis) M. BA, St. Francis Xavier U., 1944, hon. degree, 1973; MA, U. Toronto, 1946; postgrad., U. Chgo., MIT, 1951; hon. degree, Acadia U., 1973, Loyola Coll., Balt., 1973, St. Marys U., 1973, Dalhousie U., 1974, Sir Wilfrid Laurier U., 1976. Prof. econs. St. Francis Xavier U., 1946-48, head dept. econs. and social scis., 1948-51; M.P. from Inverness-Richmond dist. Can. Ho. of Commons, 1953-57, 62-68, M.P. from Cape Breton-Highlands-Canso dist., 1968-84, minister labor, 1963-65, minister of nat. health and welfare, 1965-68, govt. house leader, 1967-68, minister of manpower and immigration, 1968-70; pres. Privy Council, 1970-74, 76-79, govt. house leader, 1967-68, 70-74, sec. state for external affairs, 1974-76, dep. prime minister, 1977-79, dep. leader of opposition, opposition house leader, 1979, dep. prime minister, minister of fin., 1980-82, dep. prime minister, sec. state for external affairs, 1982-84; govt. leader of Senate Can. Govt., Ottawa, 1984-96, leader of opposition of Senate, 1984-91; parliamentary observer 10th Gen. Assembly UN, 1955; alternate del. 22d session UN Econ. and Social Coun., Geneva, 1956; leader Can. delegation Commonwealth Parliamentary Conf., London, 1973; co-chmn. Conf. Internat. Econ. Cooperation, from 1975; chmn. Internat. Monetary Fund Group of Ten, 1980-81; chmn. interim com. IMF, 1980-81; chmn. GATT, 1982; chmn. adv. coun. Bank of Montreal, 1986-91. Chmn. Can.-Germany Conf., 1984—, Adv. Coun. Internat. Ocean Inst., 1996—; bd. govs. St. Francis Xavier; bd. dirs. North-South Inst., 1996—, Internat. Crisis Group, 1995—. Recipient Order of Merit Pres. of Fed. Republic Germany, 1993. Office: 140 Wellington St Rm 804, Ottawa, ON Canada K1A 0A4

MACEK, ANNA MICHAELLA, cosmetics executive; b. Lancashire, Eng., Aug. 10, 1950; came to U.S., 1974; d. Wasyl and Maria (Litynska) Flaszczak; m. Frank Macek, Aug. 18, 1977. MA, U. Manchester, Eng., 1973; grad., Ecole des Esthеticiennes Inst. de Beaute, Geneva, 1974. Asst. to pres., chief exec. officer Reed-Ingram Corp., N.Y.C., 1974-77; coordinator corp. pub. relations Northrop Corp., Los Angeles, 1978-82; pres. Annastasia Cosmetics, Gardena, Calif., 1983—. Contbr. articles to profl. jours. Mem. Beauty and Barber Supply Inst. Avocations: tennis, gardening. *Personal philosophy: Express the limitless power of soul in anything you take up. Every position you hold in life will be the stepping stone to a higher one if you strive to climb upward.*

MACER, DAN JOHNSTONE, retired hospital administrator; b. Evansville, Ind., May 25, 1917; s. Clarence Guy and Ann (Johnstone) M.; m. Eugenia Loretta Andrews, June 1, 1943; children: Eugenia Ann, Dan James. B.S., Northwestern U., 1939, M.S. in Hosp. Adminstrn. with distinction, 1959. Chief hosp. ops. VA br. office, St. Paul, 1947-50; asst. mgr. VA hosps., Ft. Wayne, Ind., 1951, Kerrville, Tex., 1952, Augusta, Ga., 1952-56; mgr. VA Hosp., Sunmount, N.Y., 1956-58; dir. Va Research Hosp., Chgo., 1958-62; mem. hosp. adminstrn. faculty Northwestern U., 1959-61; dir. VA Hosps., Pitts., 1962-67; asst. vice chancellor health professions U. Pitts., 1968-71; prof. med. and hosp. adminstrn. U. Pitts. Grad. Sch. Pub. Health, 1962-71; prof. Coll. Health and Coll. Medicine, U. Okla., 1971-89, retired, 1989; dir. VA Hosps. and Clinics, Oklahoma City, 1971-76, VA Med. Dist. 20 (Okla.-Ark.), 1971-76; lectr. George Washington U., 1961-71; v.p. Hosp. Casualty Co., Oklahoma City, 1978-89; pres. Dan J. Macer & Assos., Inc.; cons. to health field; cons. nat. health profl. assns., indsl. corps., archtl. corps, health planners; cons. Health Services and Mental Health Adminstrn., HEW, 1968. Mem. editorial bd.: Nursing and Health Care, 1980-88; author articles in field. Coordinator civil def. and disaster planning all hosps., Chgo. nr. North Side, 1961; chmn. welfare and planning council Savannah River Community Chest, Augusta, 1954-56; chmn. group 17 fed. sect., govt. div. United Fund Allegheny County, 1964-65; mem. Fed. Interagy. Bd. Dirs., 1964-68; sec. U. Pitts. Health Center, 1969-71; chmn. health com. Health and Welfare Assn. Alleghany County, 1970-71; chmn. devel. com. Northwestern U. Alumni Program in Hosp. Adminstrn., 1962-63; chmn. adv. com. Regional Med. Program Western Pa., 1966-71; mem. steering com. Comprehensive Health Planning Western Pa.; dir. Am. States Regional Conf., 1971; vice chmn. procedures com., mem.-at-large exec. com. Okla. Regional Med. Program, 1971-78; mem. Gov's Adv. Com. Comprehensive Health Planning, 1971-80, Gov's Com. Employment of Handicapped, 1972, Pres.'s Com. Employment of Handicapped, 1962; chmn. VA chief med. dir.'s com. for evaluation and reorgn. VA health care delivery services, 1974-76; chmn. planning com. for constrn. New Children's Meml. Hosp., 1974-78; chmn. Gov.'s Ad Hoc Com on Fed.-State Planning, 1973-78; mem. Gov.'s Health Scis. Center planning and adv. com., 1973-78, State Health Planning Council, 1973-78; chmn. Okla. Health Goals and Planning Priorities Com., 1973-80; bd. dirs. Comprehensive Health Planning Agy., Western Pa.; bd. dirs. Health Services Corp., 1969-71, Okla. affiliate Am. Heart Assn., 1980-89; trustee Okla. Council Health Careers and Manpower, 1976-80; examiner Am. Coll. Hosp. Adminstrs. Lt. col. Med. Adminstrv. Corps, AUS, 1941-46. Decorated Bronze Star, Purple Heart; recipient citations VFW, 1959, citations Am. Legion, 1956, 58, citations DAV, 1964, citations Okla. Regional Med. Program, 1976, citations Okla. Gov.'s Office Health Planning, 1976, Laura G. Jackson award in recognition exceptional service in field of hosp. adminstrn., 1971, Disting. Service award Coll. Pub. Health U. Okla., 1987, Disting. Dedicated Service award Okla. Hosp. Assn., 1987; Leadership programs established in his honor Coll. Pub. Health, U. Okla. Fellow Am. Pub. Health Assn., Am. Coll. Health Care Execs. (life); mem. Am. Hosp. Assn. (life, mem. council med. edn. 1976-79), Hosp. Assn. Pa. (vice chmn. med. relations 1965-66, chmn. rehab. com. 1965-66, vice chmn. council on profl. practices, dir.), Hosp. Council Western Pa., Assn. Am. Med. Colls. (exec. com. council teaching hosps.), Oklahoma City C. of C. (vice chmn. research and edn. div. 1975-80), Northwestern U. Alumni Assn. (pres. Acacia chpt. 1961, hosp. adminstrn. chpt. 1962). Clubs: Kiwanian (Chgo.), University (Pitts.), Petroleum, Twin Hills Golf and Country (Oklahoma City), Faculty House (Oklahoma City). Home: 2925 Pelham Dr Oklahoma City OK 73120-4348

MACER, GEORGE ARMEN, JR., orthopedic hand surgeon; b. Pasadena, Calif., Oct. 17, 1948; s. George A. and Nevart Akullian M.; m. Celeste Angelle Lyons, Mar. 26, 1983; children: Christiana Marilu, Marina Lynn, Emily Sue. BA, U. So. Calif., 1971, MD, 1976. Diplomate Am. Bd. Med. Examiners, Am. Bd. Orthop. Surgery; cert. in surgery of hand. Intern Meml. Hosp. Med. Ctr., Long Beach, Calif., 1976; resident Orthop. Hosp./U. So. Calif., 1977-81; pvt. practice hand surgery Long Beach, 1983—; asst. clin. prof. orthops. U. So. Calif., Long Beach, 1983-89, 90—; cons. hand surgery svc. Rancho Los Amigos Hosp. Downey, 1990—; cons. Harbor UCLA Med. Ctr., Torrance, 1983—. Joseph Boyes Hand fellow, 1982; mem. AMA, Calif. Med. Assn., Los Angeles County Med. Assn., Western Orthop. Assn., Am. Soc. for Surgery of Hand, Am. Acad. Orthop. Surgery. Republican. Avocations: boating, skiing, scuba diving, carpentry. Office: 3550 Linden Ave Ste 2 Long Beach CA 90807-4577

MACERA, SALVATORE, industrial executive; b. Cambridge, Mass., May 3, 1931; s. Benedetto and Anna (DeVellis) M.; m. Josephine Guarnaccia (div.); children: Michael, Richard, Michelle; m. Daphne Lee. B.B.A., Northeastern U., 1960; grad., MIT Sloan Sr. Exec. Program, 1967. Financial analyst Ford Motor Co., 1955-58; v.p. finance and adminstrn. LFE Electronics div. Lab. for Electronics, Boston, 1958-63; v.p., chief financial officer Itek Corp., 1963-73, exec. v.p., 1973-82, also dir.; pres. Itek Electronics and Optical Industries, 1980-82; chmn., chief exec. officer Camelot Ind., 1981-82; chmn. Bristol Med. Elec., Boston; pres. R.V. Whitehall; chmn. The Fin. Adv. Ctre., Ltd.; bd. dirs. Harbor Nat. Bank, Boston., Fossella Assocs., Patriot Bancorp., Infinite Corp., Saxby Computer Corp., Baker & Lander, Internat. Ins. Corp., Whitman Group Inc., Conifer Group, David Banash and Co., Steinroe Variable Annuity Trust, Steinroe Variable Annuity Fund; advisor R&P, Inc., Great Bay Tool. Mem. budget com. Fin. Inst.; trustee Bentley Coll., Colonial Variable Annuity Fund; bd. dirs. Assoc. Industries Mass.; mem. bd. advisors N.Am. Corp. With AUS. Home: 20 Rowes Wharf Boston MA 02110

MACERO, TEO, composer, conductor; b. Glens Falls, N.Y., Oct. 30, 1925; s. Daniel and Angeline (De Fabio) M.; m. Jeanne Marie Crawley; 1 child, Suzanne E. BS, Juilliard Sch. Music, 1951, MS, 1953. Condr., composer, performer with N.Y. Philharm., Kansas City (Mo.) Symphony Orch., Buffalo Symphony, Santa Clara (Calif.) Symphony Orch.; composer with Pa. Ballet Co., Robert Joffrey Ballet Co., Anna Sokolow Ballet Co., Winnipeg (Can.) Ballet Co.; producer with various artists including Miles Davis, Dave Brubeck, Duke Ellington, Count Basie, Leonard Bernstein, Mahalia Jackson; lectr. Contemporary Am. music and jazz. Producer 20 Gold Records including Chorus Line (original cast album), Bitches Brew (Miles Davis), Sun Goddess (Ramsey Lewis), The Graduate (Simon & Garfunkel), Time Out (Dave Brubeck), Robert Palmer, Wallace Roney, Geni Allen; composer, condr.: (TV films) Sgt. Matlovich vs. U.S. Army Air Corp, Top Secret, Teddy Kennedy Jr. Story, 1986, Special Friendships, 1987; (films) Cassius Clay, Skill, Brains & Guts, Jack Johnson, End of the Road, Virus; (documentary) The Body Human; (TV series) Lifeline, Omni; composer: Time Plus Seven, Acoustic Suspension, Christmas Tree; (ballet) Everything Goes, 1982; (opera) Once A Slave. Served with USN, 1943-47, PTO. Club: Metropolitan (N.Y.C.). Home: 320 E 46th St New York NY 10017-3042

MACER-STORY, EUGENIA ANN, writer, artist; b. Mpls., Jan. 20, 1945; d. Dan Johnstone and Eugenia Loretta (Andrews) Macer; divorced; 1 child, Ezra Arthur Story. BS in Speech, Northwestern U., 1965; MFA, Columbia U., 1968. Writing instr. Polyarts, Boston, 1970-72; theater instr. Joy of Movement, Boston, 1972-75; artistic dir. Magik Mirror, Salem, Mass., 1975-76, Magick Mirror Comm., 1977—. Author: Congratulations: The UFO Reality, 1978, Angels of Time, 1982, Project Midas, 1986, Dr. Fu Man Chu Meets the Lonesome Cowboy: Sorcery and the UFO Experience, 1991, 3d edit., 1994, Gypsy Fair, 1991, The Strawberry Man, 1991, Sea Condor/Dusty Sun, 1994, Awakening to the Light-After the Longest Night, 1995; (short stories) Battles with Dragons: Certain Tales of Political Yoga, 1993, 2d edit., 1994, Legacy of Daedulus, 1995, The Dark Frontier, 1997; (plays) Fetching the Tree, Archaeological Politics, Strange Inquiries, Divine Appliance, 1989, The Zig Zag Wall, 1990, The Only Qualified Huntress, 1990, Telephone Taps Written Up for Tabloids, 1991, Wars With Pigeons, 1992, Conquest of the Asteroids, 1993, Commander Galacticon, 1993, Meister Hemmelin, 1994, Six Way Time Play, 1994, Radish, 1996, Setting Up for the World Trade Centaur, 1996, Mister Shooting Star, 1997, others; philosophy writer; contbr. articles to profl. jours.; author poetry in Woodstock Times, Lamia Ink!, Manhattan Poetry Rev., Sensations, Kore, others; feature writer Borderlands Mag., 1995; editor Magick Mirror Newsletter; personal appearance as profl. clairvoyant (TV documentary) Haunted Houses, 1996, UFO Desk, Sta. WBAI radio shows, 1996-97. Shubert fellow, 1968. Mem. Dramatists Guild, U.S. Psychotronics Assn., Internat. Guild of Occult Scis. Democrat. Avocations: swimming, outdoor activities, hiking. Office: Magick Mirror Comm PO Box 741 New York NY 10116-0741

MACEWAN, BARBARA ANN, middle school educator; b. Adams, Mass., Apr. 22, 1938; d. Thomas Lawrence and Vera (Ziemba) Gaskalka; m. George Louie MacEwan, Feb. 16, 1963; children: Rebecca, Debra. BS in Edn. cum laude, North Adams State Coll., 1959; MEd with honors, Plymouth State Coll., 1994. Cert. K-8, secondary social studies tchr., sch. libr., Mass. Tchr. Town of Valatie, N.Y., 1959-61, 62-63, Dept. Def., Aachefensburg, Germany, 1961-62, Town of East Longmeadow, Mass., 1964; asst. children's libr. Springfield (Mass.) Libr., 1964; tchr. history Southwick (Mass.)-Tolland Regional Schs., 1971—, tchr. history, curriculum coord. mid. sch., 1995—; state coord. Nat. History Day, 1989-92. Author: The Old Cemetery: Southwick, 1977, Shays Rebellion, 1987, The Princess, 1995. Sec. Southwick Hist. Soc., 1976-79, treas., 1979-86, pres., 1986-94; trustee Moore House, Southwick, 1989—; chair Southwick Hist. Commn., 1994—; active Mass. Curriculum Framework Focus Group, 1994-96. Recipient recognition New Eng. League Mid. Schs., 1991; Horace Mann grantee Southwick Sch. Com., 1982, Southwest Regional Alliance grantee. Mem. ASCD, NEA, Mass. Tchrs. Assn., New Eng. Oral History Assn., New Eng. Hisotry Tchrs. Assn., Nat. Coun. for Social Studies, Mass. Coun. Social Studies (recognition 1992), Western Mass. Coun. for Social Studies (bd. dirs. 1987-95), Mass. Assn. Ednl. Media, Nat. Mus. Am. Indian, New Eng. Native Am. Inst., Pioneer Valley Reading Coun., Historic Mass., Nat. Women's Hall Fame, Nat. Trust Historic Preservation, Phi Delta Kappa. Roman Catholic. Avocations: gardening, walking, reading, travel. Office: Powder Mill Mid Sch 94 Powder Mill Rd Southwick MA 01077-9324

MACEWAN, NIGEL SAVAGE, merchant banker; b. Balt., Mar. 21, 1933; s. Nigel Savage and Ellen (Wharton) MacE.; children: Alison, Nigel, Pamela, Elizabeth. BA, Yale U., 1955; MBA, Harvard U., 1959. Assoc. Morgan Stanley & Co., N.Y.C., 1959-62, White, Weld & Co., N.Y.C., 1962-63; v.p. R.S. Dickson & Co., Charlotte, N.C., 1963-68; chmn. Fin. Cons. Internat. Ltd., Brussels, 1965-68; successively gen. ptnr., exec. v.p., pres., dir. White, Weld & Co., N.Y.C., 1968-78; sr. v.p., dir. Merrill Lynch, Pierce, Fenner & Smith, N.Y.C., 1978-87; chmn. Merrill Lynch Capital Ptnrs., N.Y.C., 1985-87; pres., CEO Kleinwort Benson, N.Am. Inc., N.Y.C., 1987-93, also bd. dirs.; chmn. Kleinwort Benson North Am., Inc., Kleinworth Benson Holdings, Inc., Alex Brown Kleinwort Benson Realty Advs.; bd. dirs. Kleinwort Benson Group plc, Kleinwort Benson Ltd., 1987-93, Kleinworth Benson Australian Income Fund, 1992—; adj. prof. bus. adminstrn. NYU, 1973-75. Pres. Tokeneke Tax Dist., Darien, 1978-80, later treas. Served with USN, 1955-57. Mem. Securities Industry Assn. (chmn. N.Y. group 1975-76), N.Y. Yacht Club, Yale Club N.Y., Wee Burn Country Club, Tokeneke Club, Tarrantine Club (Dark Harbor, Maine). Republican. Episcopalian. Home: 153 Oenoke Ln New Canaan CT 06840-4518

MAC EWEN, GEORGE DEAN, physician, medical institute executive; b. Metcalfe, Ont., Can., Nov. 10, 1927; s. George W. and Catherine (Grant) MacE.; m. Marilyn Ruth Heidelberger, May 29, 1954; children: Kathryn, Jane, Nancy, David, John. MD, CM, Queen's U., Kingston, Ont., Can., 1953. Diplomate: Am. Bd. Orthopaedic Surgery (examiner 1971-93). Intern D.C. Gen. Hosp., Washington, 1953-54; resident in gen. surgery Emergency Hosp., Washington, 1954-55; fellow in orthopaedic surgery Campbell Clinic, Memphis, 1955-58; asst. med. dir. Alfred I. duPont Inst., Wilmington, Del., 1958-68; surgeon-in-chief Alfred I. duPont Inst., 1961-79, med. dir., 1969-87; chmn. pediatric orthopaedic surgery Children's Hosp., New Orleans, 1987-93; sr. cons. Orthopedic Ctr. for Children St. Christopher's Hosp. for Children, Phila., 1995—; prof. orthopaedic surgery Med. Coll. Pa. and Hahnemann U. Sch. Medicine, 1995—; chief orthopaedic svc. VA Hosp., Wilmington, 1960-66, cons. in orthopaedics, The Med. Ctr. Del., 1961—; cons. in orthopaedics surgery St. Francis Hosp. Wilmington, 1961-86; cons. in orthopaedic surgery Surgeon Gen. U.S. Navy, 1964-72, USAF Hosp., Dover, Del.; med. cons. John G. Leach Sch., Wilmington; cons. USAF Base, Dover, Del., 1961-86, Evan G. Shortlidge Sch., Wilmington, 1961-70, Pocono Med. Svcs., 1973-74, Walter Reed Army Hosp., Washington, 1978-86; med. adv. com. Del. Systems for Exceptional Children, 1973-86; cons. Surgeon Gen. U.S., 1982-86; emeritus in orthopaedic surgery St. Francis Hosp., Med. Ctr. Del., 1987—; prof. orthopaedic surgery Jefferson Med. Coll., Thomas Jefferson U., Phila., 1970-76, prof., 1976-86; clin. prof. U. Del., Newark, 1977-80; lectr. U.S. Naval Hosp., Phila., 1964-80; exec. com. Del. sch. health adv. com., 1966-86; med. adv. com. VA Hosp., 1965-79; mem. U. Del. Research Found., 1976-79; mem. subcom. Ctr. for Disease Control, 1990-93. Editor Orthopedic Resident, 1990-92; mem. editorial bd. Del. Med. Jour., 1991—; contbr. articles to books, jours. Bd. trustees Wilmington Coll., 1980—; bd. dirs. Arthritis Found., 1974-77; bd. dirs. Blood Bank of Del., 1969-78, exec. com., 1976-78, hon. mem., 1979—; editorial bd. of Evaluation and Health Professions, 1985—. Fellow Am. Acad. Cerebral Palsy; mem. Acad. of Medicine (Wilmington), Academia Mexicana de Cirugia (hon.), Am. Acad. Orthopaedic Surgeons (chmn., mem. various coms.), Am. Acad. Pediatrics (orthopaedic surg. fellow 1977—), ACS, AMA (ho. of dels. 1982-86), Am. Orthopaedic Assn. (traveling fellow 1967, pres. 1980-81, various coms.), Brit. Orthopaedic Assn. (corr.), Brazilian Orthopaedic Soc. (hon.), Campbell Club (pres. 1979), Can. Orthopaedic Assn. (trustee 1969-75), Coll. of Physicians (Phila.), Cosmos Club, Del. State Med. Soc., Eastern Orthopedic Assn., Fla. Orthopaedic Assn. (hon.), New Castle County Med. Soc. (del. 1970-72), Nat. Assn. Children's Hosps. and Related Instns. (bd. trustees 1980—), N.J. Orthopaedic Soc. (hon.), Del. Soc. Orthopedic Surgeons (charter), Orthopaedic Forum Club, Orthopaedic Rsch. Soc., Pan Am. Orthopedic Orgn., Pediatric Orthopaedic Soc. N.Am. (pres. 1972-73), Pa. Orthopaedic Soc. (hon.), Phila. Orthopaedic Soc. (pres. 1968-69), Scoliosis Rsch. Soc. (founding, exec. com. 1969-74, pres. 1971-73), Societe de Scoliose du Quebec (hon.), Societe Internationale de Chirurgie Orthopedique et de Traumatologie (exec com. 1979-86, SICOT Found. bd. dirs. 1979—), S. African Orthopaedic Assn. (hon.), Tex. Orthopaedic Assn. (hon.), Nat. Neurofibromatosis Found. (med. adv. bd. 1981—), German Orthopaedic Assn. (hon.), Costa Rican Orthopaedic Soc. (hon.), Mexican Orthopaedic Soc. (hon.), Japanese Orthopaedic Assn. (hon.), Twentieth Century Orthopaedic Assn., Houston Orthopaedic Soc., La. Orthopaedic Assn., La. State Med. Soc., Mid-Am. Orthopaedic Assn. (hon.), Orleans Parish Med. Soc., So. Med. Assn., So. Orthopaedic Assn., Sociedad Mexicana de Ortopedia (hon.). Office: St Christophers Hosp for children Erie Ave at Front St Philadelphia PA 19134-1095

MACEY, JONATHAN R., law educator; b. 1955. BA, Harvard U., 1977; JD, Yale U., 1982; PhD (hon.), Stockholm Sch. Econs., 1996. Bar: Ga. 1986. Law clk. to Hon. Henry J. Friendly U.S. Ct. Appeals (2nd cir.), N.Y.C., 1982-83; asst. prof. Emory U., 1983-86, assoc. prof., 1986-87; vis. assoc. prof. U. Va., 1986-87; prof. Cornell U., 1987-90; vis. prof. U. Chgo., fall 1989, prof., 1990-92; J. Dupratt White prof. law Cornell U., Ithaca, N.Y., 1993—; dir. John McOlin program in law and econs. Cornell U. Law Sch., Ithaca, N.Y., 1992—. Mem. ABA (com. on corp. laws), Nat. Assn. Security Dealers (bd. arbitrators). Office: Cornell U Law Sch Myron Taylor Hall Ithaca NY 14853

MACEY, MORRIS WILLIAM, lawyer; b. Camilla, Ga., Dec. 25, 1922; s. Isadore and Freda (Berman) M.; m. Dora Rosenfield, Dec. 28, 1950; children: Morris William, Jonathan Rosenfield, Rex Philip. A.B., U. Ga., 1946, LL.B., 1943; LL.M., Harvard, 1947. Bar: Ga. 1943, D.C. 1980. Practiced in Atlanta, 1947—; ptnr. Macey, Wilensky, Cohen, Wittner & Kessler; formerly adj. prof. Emory U. Law Sch., U. Ga. Law Sch.; Pres. Comml. Law League Am., 1966-67. Vice chmn., asso. editor: Comml. Law Jour. Chmn. bd. Associated Credit Union; former chmn. Southeastern Bankruptcy Law Inst.; former pres. Consumer Credit Counseling Svc.; former trustee Fisk U.; trustee Temple Sinai, 1969-70. Served with AUS, 1943-46. Mem. ABA (chmn. ad hoc com. on partnerships in bankruptcy, bus. law sect.), Internat. Bar Assn., Ga. Bar Assn., Atlanta Bar Assn., Nat. Bankruptcy Conf., Nat. Conf. Commrs. on Uniform State Laws, Nat. Assn. Comml. Fin. Attys., Am. Law Inst., Am. Coll. Bankruptcy, Am. Bankruptcy Inst., Nat. Conf. Lawyers and CPAs, Lawyers Club, Harvard Club, Std. Club, Commerce Club, Masons, Shriners, Phi Beta Kappa, Omicron Delta Kappa. Jewish. Home: 75 14th St NE 4420 The Grand Atlanta GA 30309 Office: 600 Marquis Two Tower 285 Peachtree Center Ave NE Atlanta GA 30303-1229

MACEY, WILLIAM BLACKMORE, oil company executive; b. Buffalo, Aug. 1, 1920; s. Richard Charles and Doris (Bourne) M.; m. Jean Olive Mullins, Oct. 6, 1945; 1 dau., Barbara Jean. B.S. in Petroleum Engring, N.Mex. Sch. Mines, 1942; D.Engring. (hon.), N.Mex. Inst. Mining and Tech., 1984. Dist. engr. N.Mex. Oil Conservation Commn., 1946-48; dist. supt. Am. Republics Corp., 1948-52; chief engr. N.Mex. Oil Conservation Commn., 1952-54, state geologist, dir., 1954-56; v.p. Internat. Oil & Gas Corp. (and predecessor co., developers mineral properties), Denver, 1956-60; then pres. Internat. Oil & Gas Corp. (and predecessor co., developers mineral properties), 1960-67; pres. Nielson Enterprises Inc., oil and gas prodn. and pipelines, livestock ranching, 1967-74; v.p., dir. Y-Tex Corp. (mfr. livestock identification tags), 1972-73; pres. GEN Oil Inc. (oil and gas prodn.), 1972-75, Col. Cody Inn (real estate and golf course devel.), 1970-73; pres., dir. Macey & Mershon Oil, Inc., 1974-93; dir. Juniper Oil and Gas Corp., Denver, 1981-83, Ruidoso (N.Mex.) State Bank Holding Co., 1987—; pres. The Macey Corp., Denver, 1985—; chmn. Pres.'s N.Mex. Inst. Mines and Tech., 1980-82; mem. adv. bd. U. Ariz. Heart Ctr., 1997—; mem. Pres.'s U. Ariz. Found. Served from 2d lt. to capt. USAAF, 1942-45. Mem. N.Mex. Oil and Gas Assn. (exec. com. 1949-52, 60-61), Garden of the Gods, Skyline Country Club (Tuscon) (dir., treas. 1980-82, pres. 1982-83), Altolakes Golf and Country Club, Tuscon Country Club, Ruidoso, N.Mex. Jockey Club (bd. dirs. 1985-88, 91-93, pres. 1993). Republican. Home: 7010 N Javelina Dr Tucson AZ 85718-1850 also: PO Box 360 Alto NM 88312-0360 Office: PO Box 2210 Denver CO 80201-2210

MACFARLAND, CRAIG GEORGE, natural resource management professional; b. Great Falls, Mont., July 17, 1943; s. Paul Stanley and Jean Elizabeth (Graham) MacF.; m. Janice Lee Bennett, Dec. 23, 1963 (div. 1987); children: Bennett, Francisco; m. Marilyn Ann Swanson, Mar. 19, 1988; stepchildren: Alyssa, Krista, Sara. BA magna cum laude, Austin Coll., 1965; MA, U. Wis., Madison, 1969, PhD in Zoology, 1993; DSc (hon.), Austin Coll., 1978. Dir. Charles Darwin Rsch. Sta., Galapagos Islands, Ecuador, 1974-78; head Wildlands and watershed mgmt. program C.Am. Centro Agronomico Tropical de Investigacion Enseñanza, Turrialba, Costa Rica, 1978-85; pres. Charles Darwin Found. for Galapagos Islands, Ecuador, 1985-96; cons. natural resources and sustainable use in L.Am. Moscow, Idaho, 1985—; affiliate faculty dept. Resource, Recreation and Tourism, U. Idaho, Moscow, 1988—; affiliate faculty dept. natural resource recreation and tourism Colo. State U., Ft. Collins, 1992. Contbr. to numerous profl. publs. Recipient Internat. Conservation medal Zool. Soc. San Diego, 1978, Order of Golden Ark for internat. conservation, Prince Bernhard of Netherlands, 1984. Mem. Ecol. Soc. Am., Internat. Soc. Tropical Foresters, Assn. Tropical Biology, Soc. Conservation Biology, Nature Conservancy, World Wildlife Fund, Greenpeace. Avocations: cross-country skiing, hiking, camping, skiing. Home and Office: 1117 Sunnyview Ln Brookings SD 57006-4284

MACFARLAND, MIRIAM KATHERINE (MIMI), computer science consultant, writer; b. Trenton, N.J., June 21, 1949; d. James and Merrianne (Collins) MacF.; children: Bridget Lorraine MacFarland, Chloe Merrianne Griffin. Student in computer scis., Rutgers U., 1976-78; student in lit., U. Pa., 1981-83, U. Okla., 1986-88; student in computer scis., Oxford U., Eng., 1988. Programmer-analyst Naval Air Devel. Ctr., Warminster, Pa., 1977-81; programmer, analyst NASA/Ames Rsch. Ctr., Moffett Field, Calif., 1978; writer BancTec, Inc., Oklahoma City and Dallas, 1983-95; cons. engr., writer MCI Comm. Internat., Rye Brook, N.Y., 1984-86; cons. engr. Western Union Internat., N.Y.C., 1984, RCA Global Comm., Fort Lee, N.J., 1985; cons. engr., writer Siemens Med. Sys., Iselin, N.J., 1988—; guest spkr. Okla. State U., Edmond, 1994. Author numerous lit. revs., CONTACT/II Lit. Rev., 1989-92; The Bloomsbury Rev., 1993—; contbr. articles to jours., books and mags. Democrat. Protestant. Avocations: swimming, travel, history, current events. Office: 2323 Blue Creek Ct Norman OK 73071

MACFARLAND, RICHARD B., lawyer; b. N.Y.C., June 21, 1946. BA, Syracuse U., 1968, JD, 1971. Bar: N.Y. 1972, U.S. Dist. Ct. (no. dist.) N.Y. 1975, U.S. Supreme Ct. 1978, Fla. 1980. Mem., chmn. real estate group Broad and Cassel, Boca Raton, Fla. Mem. editorial bd. Syracuse Law Rev., 1970-71. Mem. N.Y. State Bar Assn. (asst. sec. young lawyers sect. 1978, vice chair 1979, chmn. 1980), Fla. Bar, South Palm Beach County Bar Assn., Justinian Soc., Rotary Club Boca Raton (pres. Sunrise chpt. 1994-95), Phi Kappa Phi. Office: Broad and Cassel Corporate Ctr at Boca Raton 7777 Glades Rd Ste 300 Boca Raton FL 33434-4150

MACFARLANE, ALASTAIR IAIN ROBERT, business executive; b. Sydney, Australia, Mar. 7, 1940; came to U.S., 1978; s. Alexander Dunbar and Margaret Elizabeth (Swan) M.; m. Madge McCleary, Sept. 24, 1966; children: Douglas, Dennis, Robert, Jeffrey. B in Econs. with honours, U. Sydney, 1961; MBA, U. Hawaii, 1964; postgrad., Columbia U., 1964; AMP, Harvard U., 1977. Comml. cadet B.H.P. Ltd., Australia, 1958-62; product mgr. H.J. Heinz Co., Pitts., 1965-66; gen. mgr. new products div. H.J. Heinz Co., Melbourne, Australia, 1967-72; ptnr., dir., gen. mgr. Singleton, Palmer & Strauss McAllan Pty. Ltd., Sydney, 1972-73; dir., gen. mgr. successor co. Doyle Dane Bernbach Internat. Inc., Sydney, 1973-77; group sr. v.p. Doyle Dane Bernbach Internat. Inc., N.Y.C., 1978-84; pres., chief exec. officer PowerBase Systems, Inc., 1984-85, Productivity Software Internat. L.P., N.Y.C., 1985-86; div. pres., pub. Whittle Comm. L.P., Knoxville, Tenn., 1987-88; chmn., CEO Phyton Techs. Inc., Knoxville, 1988-94; pres., CEO Knox Internat. Corp., Knoxville, 1988-94; chmn., CEO Mich. Bulb Co., Grand Rapids, 1988-94; chmn., CEO Lansinoh Labs., Inc., Oak Ridge, Tenn., 1994-96; lectr. Monash U., Melbourne, 1970-71; ind. mgmt. cons., Melbourne, 1970-72; dir. Univ. of Sydney USA Found., 1994-97, pres. Cowles Creative Publ. Inc., Minnetonka, Minn., 1997—. Author papers in field. V.p. Waverley Dist. Cricket Club, 1975-77. East-West Ctr. fellow, 1962-64; Australian Commonwealth scholar, Australian Steel Industry scholar, 1961. Fellow Australian Inst. Mgmt. (assoc.); mem. Australian Soc. Accts. (assoc.), Harvard Club N.Y.C., Cherokee Country Club. Home: 2720 Gale Rd Wayzata MN 55391 Office: 5900 Green Oak Dr Minnetonka MN 55343-9607

MACFARLANE, ANDREW WALKER, media specialist, educator; b. Toronto, Ont., Can., Feb. 18, 1928; s. Joseph Arthur and Marguerite (Walker) MacF.; m. Betty Doris Wright Seldon; 1 stepchild, Elizabeth Seldon; children by previous marriage: Jeanie Andreas, Catriona Flora. Student, U. Sask., Can., 1945-46; B.A., U. Toronto, 1949; M.L.S., U. Western Ont., 1977. With Canadian Press, Toronto, 1949; reporter Halifax (N.S., Can.) Chronicle Herald, 1949-51, Scottish Daily Express, Glasgow, 1951-53; subeditor London Evening Standard, 1953-55; copy editor, night editor, feature editor, gen. reporter, daily columnist, asst. to pub. Telegram, Toronto, 1955-64; mng. editor, corporate dir. Telegram, 1964-69, dir. research and devel., 1969-71, exec. editor, 1971—; dir. Citizen's Inquiry br. Ministry Govt. Services, Province of Ont., 1971-72; chmn. dept., dean Grad. Sch. Journalism, U. Western Ont., 1973-80, prof., 1981-93; prof. emeritus U. Western Ont., 1993—; chair mass media studies, dir. Ctr. in Mass Media Studies Grad. Sch. Journalism, U. Western Ont., 1990-93; co-chmn. Ont.-Que. Journalist Exchange. Author: The Neverland of the Neglected Child, 1957, It Seemed Like a Good Idea at the Time, 1983, Local Flavor, 1990; editor: Byline, 1983, Byline Canada, 1984. Bd. dirs. Canadian Medic-Alert, 1959; past bd. dirs. Met. Toronto Children's Aid Soc.; chmn. advisory council Province of Ont. Medal Good Citizenship. Recipient Bowater award, 1960, Nat. Newspaper award, 1958, 59, Nat. Teaching award Poynter Inst. for Media Studies, 1987, Province Ont. Bicentennial medal; Southam fellow, 1961. Mem. Assn. for Edn. in Journalism and Mass Comm., Can. Comm. Assn., Commonwealth Assn. for Edn. in Journalism and Comm. (founding pres.), Toronto Press Club.

MACFARLANE, JOHN ALEXANDER, former federal housing agency administrator; b. Winnipeg, Man., Can., Sept. 6, 1916; s. John MacKay and Annie Catherine (Smith) MacF.; m. Gladys Valda Church, Dec. 20, 1941; children: John Lane, Elizabeth Ann, Janet Christine. BA with honours, U. Man., Winnipeg, 1939. With stats. br. Wartime Prices and Trade Bd., Ottawa, Ont., Can., 1940-46; supr. stats. dept. Cn. Mortgage and Housing Corp., Ottawa, 1946-65, asst. dir. econs. and stats. div., 1965-69, asst. dir. secretariat div., 1969-78; ret., 1978; treas. Caribbean and N.Am. area coun. World Alliance Ref. Chs., Ottawa, 1984—. Treas. Ottawa Valley Cricket Coun., 1946-70, 73-80, pres., 1970-73, 83-88; moderator Presbytery of Ottawa, Presbyn. Ch. Can., 1994-96. Recipient Long Svc. medal Boy Scouts Assn., 1945, Centennial medal Govt. of Can., 1967, spl. achievement award for amateur sport Govt. of Ont., 1991; mem. choir St. Andrew's Presbyn. Ch. Mem. Def. Cricket Club (sec.-treas. 1944-46, pres. 1951-76, 78-92). Avocation: stamp collecting. Address: 99 Acacia Ave, Ottawa, ON Canada K1M 0P8 *I have touched many people as the years have passed; if I have helped one for the better I shall rest content.*

MACFARLANE, JOHN CHARLES, utility company executive; b. Hallock, Minn., Nov. 8, 1939; s. Ernest Edward and Mary Bell (Yates) MacF.; m. Eunice Darlene Axvig, Apr. 13, 1963; children: Charles, James, William. BSEE, U. N.D., 1961. Staff engr. Otter Tail Power Co., Fergus Falls, Mn., 1961-64; div. engr. Otter Tail Power Co., Jamestown, N.D., 1964-71; div. mgr. Otter Tail Power Co., Langdon, N.D., 1972-78; v.p. planning and control Otter Tail Power Co., Fergus Falls, 1978-80, exec. v.p., 1981-82, pres. and chief exec. officer, 1982—, also bd. dirs., now chmn.; bd. dirs. Northwest Bank, Fergus Falls, Pioneer Mut. Ins. Co. Pres. Langdon City Commn., 1974-78; chmn. Fergus Falls Port Authority, 1985-86; bd. dirs. Minn. Assn. Commerce and Industry, Minn. Safety Coun., Edison Electric Inst.; chmn. bd. dirs. U. N.D. Energy Rsch. Adv. Coun. Served with U.S. Army, 1962-64. Mem. Am. Mgmt. Assn., IEEE (chmn. Red River chpt.), U. N.D. Alumni Assn., Fergus Falls C. of C. Republican. Presbyterian. Lodges: Rotary, Masons. Office: Otter Tail Power Co 215 S Cascade St Fergus Falls MN 56537-2801

MACFARLANE, MALCOLM HARRIS, physics educator; b. Brechin, Scotland, May 22, 1933; came to U.S., 1956; s. Malcolm P. and Mary (Harris) M.; m. Eleanor Carman, May 30, 1957; children: Douglas, Kenneth, Sheila, Christine. M.A., U. Edinburgh, Scotland, 1955; Ph.D., U. Rochester, 1960. Research asso. Argonne (Ill.) Nat. Lab., 1959-60; asst. prof. physics U. Rochester, 1960-61; asso. physicist Argonne Nat. Lab., 1961-68, sr. physicist, 1968-80; prof. physics U. Chgo., 1968-80, Ind. U., Bloomington, 1980—; vis. fellow All Souls Coll., Oxford (Eng.) U., 1966-67; mem. nuclear scis. adv. com. Dept. Energy-NSF, 1983-87; cons. Ency. Brit. Contbr. articles of theoretical nuclear physics to profl. jours. Guggenheim fellow physics, 1966-67; Alexander von Humboldt Found. sr. scientist award, 1985. Fellow Am. Phys. Soc.; mem. Nuclear Physics sect. Am. Phys. Soc. (mem. exec. com. 1969-71). Home: 3510 E Brownstead Dr Bloomington IN 47401-4217 Office: Dept Physics Indiana U Bloomington IN 47405

MACFARLANE, MAUREEN ANNE, lawyer; b. Boston, May 19, 1965; d. Joseph Alexander and Lorraine Anne (Walsh) MacF. BA magna cum laude, Boston Coll., 1986; JD, Boston U., 1989, BS in Journalism, 1990. Bar: Mass. 1989, U.S. Dist. Ct. Mass. 1990, U.S. Ct. Appeals (D.C. and 1st cirs.) 1990, U.S. Supreme Ct. 1993. Law clk. to presiding justice Mass. Ct. Appeals, Boston, 1989-90; assoc. Widett Slater & Goldman P.C., Boston, 1990-92, Hutchins, Wheeler & Dittmar, P.C., Boston, 1992-95; atty. Lucash, Gesmer & Updegrove, LLP, Boston, 1995—. Writer Mass. Lawyers Weekly, Boston, 1988-89. Sec. Boston Liturgical Dance Ensemble, Chestnut Hill, Mass., 1989—; leader Boston Mayor's Youth Leadership Corp., Boston, 1991-92; exec. com. Boston U. Sch. Law Alumni, 1993—. Mem. ABA, Mass. Bar Assn., Boston Bar Assn. (YLS steering com. 1991-94). Office: Lucash Gesmer & Updegrove LLP 40 Broad St Boston MA 02109-4307

MACGILLIVRAY, FREDERICK RICHARD, executive; b. Nova Scotia, Can., July 14, 1945; s. Frederick Joseph and Mary Agnes (Dunford) MacG.; m. Susan Lorraine Sullivan, June 10, 1967; children: Elizabeth Diane, Kara Lee, Frederick Edward. LLD, St. Thomas U., 1993. Exec. Domonion Stonvi, Can., 1960-83; pres., CEO Lumsdon Bros., Ltd., Brunswick, Toronto, Can., 1983-88; pres., gen. mgr. Bolanos, Ltd., Halifax, Can., 1988-94; pres., CEO Trade Ctr. Ltd., Halifax, Can., 1994—; chmn. Nova Scotia Rehab. Hosp., Halifax, 1993—; bd. govs. St. Mary's U., Halifax, 1990—; dir. Kidsi & Elp, Halifax, 1990—, Hotel Assn. Nova Scotia, 1994—. Mem. Can. Tourism Commn. (dir.), Halifax Meeting & Conv. Bur. (vice chair). Roman Catholic. Avocations: volunteering, movies, theatre, sports, walking. Office: Trade Ctr Ltd, PO Box 955 1800 Argyle St, Halifax, NS Canada B3J 2V9

MACGILLIVRAY, LOIS ANN, organization executive; b. Phila., July 8, 1937; d. Alexander and Mary Ethel (Crosby) MacG. BA in History, Holy Names Coll., 1966; MA in Sociology, U. N.C., 1971, PhD in Sociology, 1973. Joined Sisters of Holy Names of Jesus and Mary, 1955. Research asst. U. N.C., Chapel Hill, 1969-70, 71-72, instr. sociology, 1970-71; sociologist Rsch. Triangle Inst., Durham, N.C., 1973-75, sr. sociologist, 1975-81; dir. Ctr. for Population and Urban-Rural Studies, Research Triangle Inst., Durham, 1976-81; pres. Holy Names Coll., Oakland, Calif., 1982-92; mem. steering com. Symposium for Bus. Leaders Holy Names Coll., 1982-92; prin. owner Svc. Orgns.: Planning and Evaluation, Chapel Hill, 1994—; vis. scholar dept. sociology U. N.C., Chapel Hill, 1992-94; mem. policy bd. U.

Oakland Met. Forum, co-convenor panel on edn. and youth. Bd. dirs. Oakland Coun. Econ. Devel., 1984-86; bd. dirs. Bay Area Biosci. Ctr., 1990-92, mem. adv. com., 1992-94. Mem. Am. Sociol. Assn., Assn. Ind. Calif. Colls. and Univs. (exec. com. 1985-92, vice chmn. 1989-92), Regional Assn. East Bay Colls. and Univs. (past pres., bd. dirs. 1982-92). Avocation: birding. Home and Office: 101 N Hamilton Rd Chapel Hill NC 27514-5627

MACGINITIE, WALTER HAROLD, psychologist; b. Carmel, Calif., Aug. 14, 1928; s. George Eber and Nettie Lorene (Murray) MacG.; m. Ruth Olive Kilpatrick, Sept. 2, 1950; children: Mary Catherine, Laura Anne. B.A., UCLA, 1949; A.M., Stanford U., 1950; Ph.D., Columbia U., 1960. Tchr. Long Beach (Calif.) Unified Sch. Dist., 1950, 1955-56; mem. faculty Columbia U. Tchrs. Coll., 1959-80, prof. psychology and edn., 1970-80; Lansdowne scholar, prof. edn. U. Victoria, B.C., Can., 1980-84; research assoc. Lexington Sch. Deaf, N.Y.C., 1963-69; mem. sci. adv. bd. Ctr. for Study of Reading, 1977-80, chmn. 1979-80. Co-author: Gates-MacGinitie Reading Tests, 1965, 78, 89, Psychological Foundations of Education, 1968; Editor: Assessment Problems in Reading, 1972; co-editor: Verbal Behavior of the Deaf Child, 1969. Life mem. Calif. PTA. Served with USAF, 1950-54. Fellow APA, AAAS, Am. Psychol. Soc., Nat. Conf. on Rsch. on Language and Literacy, N.Y. Acad. Scis.; mem. Internat. Reading Assn. (pres. 1976-77, Spl. Svc. award 1981), Reading Hall of Fame (pres. 1989-90). Home and Office: PO Box 1789 Friday Harbor WA 98250-1789

MACGOWAN, CHARLES FREDERIC, retired chemical company executive; b. Rock Island, Ill., Nov. 24, 1918; s. Charles John and Clara (Ohge) MacG.; m. Shirley Esther Sutherland, Feb. 22, 1941; children: Lynn Merle, Charles John II. Student, Wright Jr. Coll., Chgo., 1936-37, North Park Coll., Chgo., 1938-39, Harvard, 1955-56. Partner C.B. Isett Co., Chgo., 1946-49; indsl. engr. Graver Tank & Mfg. Co., East Chicago, Ind., 1949-50; asst. bus. mgr. Boilermakers Local 374 State Ind., 1950-54; internat. rep. Internat. Brotherhood Boilermakers, 1954-60; dir. Office Saline Water, U.S. Dept Interior, Washington, 1961-65; spl. asst. to sec. Office Saline Water, U.S. Dept Interior, 1965-66; coordinator intergovtl. relations Fed. Water Pollution Control Adminstrn., 1966-67; govt. relations mgr. Dow Chem. Co., Washington, from 1967; cons. nuclear desalting Internat. Atomic Energy Agy., Vienna, Austria; tech. cons. AFL-CIO.; Chmn. Ind. Boiler and Pressure Vessel Bd., 1960-61. Contbr. articles to profl. jours. Mem. Am. Water Works Assn., Aircraft Owners and Pilots Assn., Md. Acad. Sci. Democrat. Methodist. Club: Mason. Home: 10113 Nedra Dr Great Falls VA 22066-2836

MACGOWAN, MARY EUGENIA, lawyer; b. Turlock, Calif., Aug. 4, 1928; d. William Ray and Mary Bolling (Gilbert) Kern; m. Gordon Scott Millar, Jan. 2, 1970; 1 dau., Heather Mary. A.B., U. Calif., Berkeley, 1950; J.D., U. Calif., San Francisco, 1953. Bar: Calif. 1953; cert. family law specialist Calif. State Bar Bd. Legal Specialization. Research atty. Supreme Ct. Calif., 1954, Calif. Ct. Appeals, 1955; partner firm MacGowan & MacGowan, Calif., 1956-68; pvt. practice, San Francisco, 1968—. Bd. dirs. San Francisco Speech and Hearing Center, San Francisco Legal Aid Soc., J.A.C.K.I.E. Mem. Am., Calif., San Francisco bar assns., Queen's Bench. Clubs: San Francisco Lawyers, Forest Hill Garden. Office: 1 Sansome St Ste 1900 San Francisco CA 94104-4432

MACGOWAN, SANDRA FIRELLI, publishing executive, publishing educator; b. Phila., Nov. 9, 1951; d. William Firelli and Barbara (Gimbel) Kapalcik. BS in Biology, BA in English, Pa. State U., 1973, MA in English Lit., 1978. Cert. supervisory analyst N.Y. Stock Exchange. Editor McGraw-Hill Pub. Co., N.Y.C., 1979-81; sr. acquisitions editor Harcourt Brace Jovanovich, Inc., N.Y.C., 1981-82; sr. editor The Coll. Bd., N.Y.C., 1982-88; v.p., head editorial CS First Boston Corp., N.Y.C., 1988-94; v.p. supervisory analyst internat. rsch. SBC Warburg, N.Y.C., 1994-96; v.p., supervisory analyst internat. rsch. Arnhold and S. Bleichroeder, N.Y.C., 1996—; part time assoc. prof. pub. NYU Sch. Continuing Edn., N.Y.C., 1985—. Author: 50 College Admission Directors Speak to Parents, 1988. Democrat. Avocations: art, reading, travel. Office: Arnhold & S Bleichroeder 1345 Avenue Of The Americas New York NY 10105-0302

MACGREGOR, DAVID LEE, lawyer; b. Cedar Rapids, Iowa, Sept. 17, 1932; s. John H. and Beulah A. (Morris) MacG.; m. Helen Jean Kolberg, Aug. 7, 1954; children—Scott J., William M., Brian K., Thomas D. B.B.A., U. Wis., 1954, LL.B., 1956. Assoc. Quarles & Brady and predecessor firms, Milw., 1959-64, ptnr., 1964—; pres. Milw. Estate Planning Council, 1972-73; mem. adv. bd. CCH Fin. and Estate Planning, N.Y.C., 1982-87. Fellow Am. Coll. Trust and Estate Counsel; mem. ABA, Milw. Bar Assn., State Bar Wis. (chmn. taxation sect. 1977-78), Nat. Assn. Estate Planning Councils (pres. 1979-80). Home: 929 N Astor St Unit 1608 Milwaukee WI 53202-3486 Office: Quarles & Brady 411 E Wisconsin Ave Milwaukee WI 53202-4409

MACGREGOR, GEORGE LESCHER, JR., freelance writer; b. Dallas, Sept. 15, 1936; s. George Lescher and Jean (Edge) MacG.; divorced; children: George Lescher III, Michael Fordtran. B.B.A., U. Tex., 1958. Asst. cashier First Nat. Bank in Dallas, 1960-64, asst. v.p., 1964-68; v.p. Nat. Bank of Commerce of Dallas, 1968-70, sr. v.p., 1970-73, exec. v.p., 1973-74; pres., chief exec. officer Mountain Banks Ltd., Colorado Springs, 1974-77; chief exec. officer Highfield Fin. (U.S.A.) Ltd., 1978-83; chmn. bd., chief exec. officer, dir. Dominion Nat. Bank, Denver, 1981-84; chmn. bd., chief exec. officer Royal Dominion Ltd., Denver; chmn. bd., chief exec. officer, dir. Market Bank of Denver, 1983-84; vice chmn., dir. Bank of Aurora, Denver, 1983-84; chmn., pres., chief exec. officer Alamosa Bancorp. of Colo., Denver, 1983-84; pres., chief exec. officer Am. Interstate Bancorp., 1984-88; pres. Banco, Inc., 1984-89; sr. mng. ptnr. Scotland Co., Denver, London, 1988-91; free-lance writer, 1992—. Served with M.C. AUS, 1958-60. Mem. Am. Inst. Banking (hon.), Young Pres.'s Orgn., Koon Kreek Club, Broadmoore Golf Club, Oxford Club, Phi Gamma Delta. Anglican Catholic. Home and Office: 1736 Blake St Denver CO 80202-1226

MACGREGOR, JAMES THOMAS, toxicologist; b. N.Y.C., Jan. 14, 1944; s. James and Phyllis (Bowman) MacG.; m. Judith Anne Anello, July 12, 1969; 1 child, Jennifer Lee. BS in Chemistry, Union Coll., Schenectady, N.Y., 1965; PhD in Toxicology, U. Rochester, 1970. Diplomate Am. Bd. Toxicology. Postdoctoral fellow U. Calif., San Francisco, 1970-72; dir. food safety rsch. USDA, Berkeley, Calif., 1972-88; assoc. prof. U. Calif., Berkeley, 1978-88; pres. Toxicology Consulting Svcs., Danville, Calif., 1988-90; dir. toxicology and metabolism lab. SRI Internat., Menlo Park, Calif., 1990-97; dir. Office of Testing and Rsch. FDA Ctr. for Drug Evaluation and Rsch., Rockville, Md., 1997—; mem. numerous nat. and internat. profl. coms. and working groups. Mem. editorial bd.: Environ. Molecular Mutagenesis, N.Y.C., 1986-88, Mutation Res., Amsterdam, 1989-91, 97—, Mutagenesis, Oxford, 1989-93. Recipient Alexander Hollender award, 1995. Mem. Am. Assn. Cancer Rsch., Soc. Toxicology, Environ. Mutagen Soc. (treas. 1986-89, pres. 1992-93), Genetic Environ. Toxicology Assn. No. Calif. (pres. 1982). Office: SRI Internat 333 Ravenswood Ave Menlo Park CA 94025-3453

MACGUIGAN, MARK RUDOLPH, judge; b. Charlottetown, P.E.I., Can., Feb. 17, 1931; s. Mark Rudolph and Agnes Violet (Trainor) MacG.; m. Patricia Alice Dougherty, Dec. 26, 1987; children from previous marriage: Ellen, Mark, Thomas, Beth, Buddy. BA summa cum laude, St. Dunstan's U., Charlottetown, 1951; MA, U. Toronto, 1953, PhD, 1957; LLB, York U., Toronto, 1958; LLM, Columbia U., 1959, JSD, 1961; LLD (hon.), U. Prince Edward Island, Charlottetown, 1971, St. Thomas U., Fredericton, N.B., Can., 1981, U. Windsor, Ont., 1983, Law Soc. of Upper Can., Toronto, 1983, York U., 1996. Bar: Ont., Prince Edward Island, Newfoundland, Queen's Counsel-Ont. Asst. prof. law U. Toronto, 1960-63, assoc. prof. law, 1963-66; prof. law Osgoode Hall Law Sch., York U., Toronto, 1966-67; dean of law U. Windsor, Ont., 1967-68; mem. parliament for Windsor-Walkervidge House of Commons Can., Ottawa, 1968-84; joint chmn. spl. joint commn. on constn. of Can. Parliament of Can., Ottawa, 1970-72, 78; parliamentary sec. Min. of Manpower and Immigration, Ottawa, 1972-74, Min. of Labor, Ottawa, 1974-75; vis. assoc. prof. law NYU, N.Y.C., summer 1966; chmn. Justice Com., Ottawa, 1975-79, Sub-Com. on Penitentiaries, Ottawa, 1976-77; critic solicitor-gen., 1979; Sec. State for External Affairs, Govt. of Can., Ottawa, 1980-82, min. of justice and atty. gen., 1982-84; judge, Fd. Ct. Appeal, Ottawa, 1984—; founding dir. Can. Civil Liberties Assn., Toronto, 1996, chair, 1966-67; pres. Can. Sect.-Internat. Commn. of Jurists, 1988-90; founding dir. Parliamentarians for World Order, 1977. Author: (law casebooks) Jurisprudence: Readings and Cases, 2d edit., 1966, Cases and materials on Creditors' Rights, 2d edit., 1967, (monograph) Abortion, Conscience and Democracy, 1994. Recipient Tarnopolsky medal for human rights Internat. Commn. of Jurists-Can. Sect., 1995. Mem. Internat. Law Assn., Can. Inst. for the Adminstrn. of Justice, Can. Judges' Conf., Can. Bar Assn., Cercle Universitaire. Roman Catholic. Avocations: walking, bridge. Office: Fed Ct of Appeals, Ottawa, ON Canada K1A OH9

MACGUINNESS, ROSEMARY ANNE, lawyer; b. Newry, County Down, No. Ireland, June 26, 1957; came to U.S., 1981.; d. Micahel Gerald and Maureen Rosemary (Leavy) MacG.; m. Philip Martin Bellber, Dec. 5, 1987; children: Sam Martin Bellber, Rhys Patrick Bellber, Mason Philip Bellber. B in Civil Law, U. Coll. Dublin, 1978, diploma in European Law, 1979; MS in Criminal Justice, Northeastern U., 1982. Bar: Ireland 1981, Calif. 1994. Legal asst. Bronson, Bronson & McKinnon, San Francisco, 1983; atty. McInerney & Dillon, Oakland, Calif., 1984-87; sr. counsel Pacific Stock Exch., San Francisco, 1987-90, sr. counsel, dir. arbitration, 1990—. Mem. Queen's Bench. Office: Pacific Stock Exch 301 Pine St San Francisco CA 94104-3301

MACH, KENNETH, advertising executive. Sr. ptnr., treas. Tatham Euro RSCG, Chgo. Office: Tatham Euro RSCG 980 N Michigan Ave Chicago IL 60611-4501

MACHALE, JOSEPH P., financial executive; b. Aug. 17, 1951. BA with hons., Oxford U., 1973. With Price Waterhouse, London, 1973-78; mng. dir. J.P. Morgan Co., N.Y.C., 1979—. Office: JP Morgan & Co Inc, 60 Victoria Embankment, London ECH YOJP, England

MACHASKEE, ALEX, newspaper publishing company executive; b. Warren, Ohio; m. Carol Machaskee. LHD (hon.), Cleve. State U., 1995. Sports reporter The Warren (Ohio) Tribune; promotion dir., asst. to pub., dir. pers., v.p., gen. mgr. The Plain Dealer, Cleve., 1985-90, pres., pub., 1990—. V.p. Mus. Arts Assn. (Cleve. Orch.); distbn. com. Cleve. Found.; bd. dirs. Ohio Arts Coun., Greater Cleve. Roundtable, Univ. Cir. Inc., Greater Cleve. Growth Assn., Cleve. Tomorrow Nat. Conf., Gt. Lakes Sci. Mus., United Way Svcs., Cleve. Initiative for Edn., Rock and Roll Hall of Fame and Mus., Mus. Coun. of Cleve. Mus. Art, Cleve. State U. Found., and St. Vladimir's Orthodox Theol. Sem.; vis. com. Weatherhead Sch. Mgmt., Case Western Res. U.; adv. com. Newspaper Mgmt. Ctr., Northwestern U. Mem. Newspaper Assn. Am. (mem. labor rels. subcom.), mem. The Am. Soc. Newspaper Editors. Office: Plain Dealer Pub Co 1801 Superior Ave E Cleveland OH 44114-2107

MACHATZKE, HEINZ WILHELM, dean, science administrator; b. Freiburg, West Germany, Oct. 26, 1932; came to U.S., 1968; s. Friedrich W. and Helene W. (Maluschke) M.; m. Gertraud Zimmermann, Apr. 22, 1962; children: Jorg, Jens. BS, U. Freiburg (West Germany), 1955, MS, 1958, DSci., 1960. Rsch. chemist Bayer AG, Germany, 1962-68; chief chemist Mobay Chem. Corp., Union, N.J., 1968-70, asst. to pres., 1971-72, v.p., 1972-74, gen. mgr. dyes and pigment divsn., 1974-86, group v.p. human resources and quality programs, 1986-89; industry advisor, adj. prof. Duquesne U., Pitts., 1989—, dean Sch. Natural and Environ. Scis., 1994—; rsch. fellow U. Mich., 1960-62. Contbr. articles to profl. jours.; patentee in field. Mem. Am. Chem. Soc. Home: Scaife Rd Sewickley PA 15143 Office: Duquesne U Dean's Office Pittsburgh PA 15282

MACHIDA, CURTIS A., research molecular neurobiologist; b. San Francisco, Apr. 1, 1954. AB, U. Calif., Berkeley, 1976; PhD, Oreg. Health Scis. U., 1982. Postdoctoral scientist Oreg. Health Scis. U., Portland, 1982-88; asst. scientist div. neurosci. Oreg. Regional Primate Research Ctr., Beaverton, 1988-95, assoc. scientist divsn. neuroscience, 1995—; rsch. asst. prof. biochemistry and molecular biology Oreg. Health Scis. U., 1989-95, mem. faculty neurosci. and molecular and cell biology grad. programs, 1989—, adj. assoc. prof. biochemistry and molecular biology, mem. grad. faculty biochemistry and biophysics, 1997—. Editorial cons. Oreg. Health Scis. U. News, 1984-87; ad-hoc reviewer Endocrinology, Molecular Pharmacology, NSF; contbr. articles to profl. jours. Established investigator Am. Heart Assn., 1994—. Recipient Leukemia Assn. award, 1981, Tartar award Med. Rsch. Found. Oreg., 1980; NIH fellow, 1980-82, 85-87, grantee, 1989, 95. Mem. AAAS, ASBMB, Am. Soc. Microbiology, Soc. Neurosci., AHA Basic Scis. Coun. Achievements include patent on dopamine receptor and genes; cloning of several adrenergic receptor genes and simian retroviral infectious genomes.

MACHIN, BARBARA E., lawyer; b. Kansas City, Mo., Mar. 26, 1947; d. Roger H. and Doris D. (Dunkel) Elliott; m. Peter A. Machin, June 1, 1969; 1 child, Andrew D. BS in Sec. Edn., U. Kans., 1969, MA in Curriculum Devel./Anthropology, 1973; JD, U. Toledo Coll., 1978. Bar: Ohio 1978, U.S. Dist. Ct. (no. dist.) Ohio 1978, U.S. Ct. Appeals (6th cir.) 1981, U.S. Supreme Ct. 1987. Instr. rsch. and writing U. Toledo Coll. of Law, 1978-79; law clerk Lucas County Ct. of Common Pleas, Toledo, 1979-80; assoc., ptnr. Doyle, Lewis & Warner, Toledo, 1980-87; assoc. Shumaker, Loop & Kendrick, Toledo, 1987-92; gen. counsel U. Toledo, 1993—; pres., v.p., mem. bd. trustees Toledo Legal Aid Soc., 1983—; pres. Toledo Civil Trial Attys., 1990-93. Contbr. articles to profl. jours. Mem. house corp. bd. Gamma Phi Beta Sorority, 1985—; mem. bd. trustees Epworth Found., 1993—, St. Luke's Hosp., 1994—. Mem. Ohio State Bar Assn., Toledo Bar Assn., Toledo Women's Bar Assn., Toledo Civil Trial Attys. (pres. 1983-92). Home: 5034 W Dauber Dr Toledo OH 43615-2172 Office: U of Toledo Office of the Gen Counsel 3620 University Hall 2801 W Bancroft Toledo OH 43606

MACHIZ, LEON, electronic equipment manufacturing executive; b. Bklyn., June 23, 1924; s. Isadore and Fanny (Klonsky) M.; m. Lorraine Block, Mar. 31, 1951; children: Marc, Linda, Gary. Grad., Cooper Union. Salesman Sun Radio Co., 1942-52; founder Time Electro Sales Co. (merged with Avnet, Inc. 1952-68), Electro Air of Ga. (merged with Avnet, Inc. 1968), 1957-68, Electro Air of Fla., 1960-68; sr. v.p., dir. Avnet Inc., N.Y.C., 1968-80, pres., dir., 1980-86, vice chmn., chief exec. officer, from 1986, dir., chmn., chief exec. officer, 1988—. Trustee North Shore Univ. Hosp., Boys' Brotherhood Republic. Office: Avnet Inc 80 Cuttermill Rd Great Neck NY 11021-3108*

MACHLE, EDWARD JOHNSTONE, emeritus educator; b. Canton, China, Sept. 29, 1918; s. Edward Charles and Jean (Mawson) M.; m. Neva Hull, Aug. 29, 1942; children—Stewart, Douglas, Kathi; m. Mary Lou Reynolds, Dec. 15, 1970; 1 child, Michelle; stepchildren—Rebecca, Richard, Harvey, Robin. Student, Pacific Lutheran Jr. Coll., 1937; B.A., Whitworth Coll., 1939; B.D., San Francisco Theol. Sem., 1942, M.A., 1944; Ph.D., Columbia U., 1952. Ordained to ministry Presbyn. Ch., 1942; minister in Concrete, Wash., 1942-43; asst. minister San Francisco, 1943-44, Mineola, N.Y., 1944-46; instr. Columbia, 1946-47; asst. prof. U. Colo., 1947-53, assoc. prof., 1953-63, prof., 1963-80, emeritus, 1981—, chmn. dept., 1951-52, 56-58, 66-69; vis. lectr. U. Alta., summer 1960, Iliff Sch. Theology, 1962, Evergreen State, 1981, Peninsula Coll., 1986—; in-parish research dir. San Francisco Theol. Sem.; dir. music St. Andrew Presbyn. Ch., Boulder, Colo., 1961-70; guest lectr. ch. music U. Colo. Sch. Music, 1950-65; disting. faculty fellow Sheldon Jackson Coll., 1986-88. Author: Nature and Heaven in the Xunzi, 1993. Mem. Am. Phil. Assn., Soc. Asian and Comparative Philosophy, Acad. Religion. Presbyterian. Home: 2703 Wolff Dr Arlington TX 76015-1020 *Faith is largely willingness to learn of what can destroy us. Idolatry feeds on our fear of having faith. Research methods spring from the soil of our cultured idolatries. Thus, to learn, faith must at times be a traitor to "learning."*

MACHLIN, EUGENE SOLOMON, metallurgy educator, consultant; b. N.Y.C., Dec. 29, 1920; s. Gershon and Rose (Kaplan) M.; m. Edda Servi, May 21, 1960; children: Rona Susan, Argia Debora; m. Gertrude Green, Oct. 15, 1943 (dec. May 1959); 1 child, Chester Elia. BME, CCNY, 1942; MS, Case Inst. Tech., 1948; ScD, MIT, 1950. Aero. rsch. scientist Nat. Adv. Commn. Aeronautics, Cleve., 1942-48; rsch. assoc., asst. prof. MIT, Cambridge, 1948-50, 50-51; asst. prof. Columbia U., N.Y.C., 1951-54, assoc. prof., 1954-58, prof. metallurgy, 1958-89, Howe prof., 1989-91, Howe prof. emeritus, 1991—; cons. Spl. Metals Corp., Utica, N.Y., 1951-76; cons., dir. UV Industries, N.Y.C., 1966-79; summer faculty fellow IBM T.J. Watson Res. Lab., 1984-90. Author: An Introduction to Aspects of Thermodynamics and Kinetics Relevant to Materials Science, 1990, Materials Science in Microelectronics—The Relationships Between Thin Film Processing and Structure, 1995, Materials Science in Microelectronics—The Relationships Between Thin Film Structure and Properties, 1997; editor: Synthesis of Metastable Phases, 1980; inventor Udimet 700, 1960. Chmn. solid state scis. adv. com. Office Sci. Rsch. USAF, Washington, 1954-59. Recipient C.H. Mathewson Gold medal AIME, 1954; Guggenheim fellow, 1965. Fellow AIME; mem. Am. Soc. Metals (Achievement award 1961, Edn. award 1974). Democrat. Jewish. Office: Columbia U 500 W 120th St New York NY 10027-6623

MACHLIN, LAWRENCE J., nutritionist, biochemist, educator; b. N.Y.C., June 24, 1927; s. Morris Louis and Lilly (Manevitz) M.; m. Ruth Beerman, May 30, 1953; children: Marc, Steven, Paul. BS, Cornell U., 1948, M in Nutritional Sci., 1949; PhD, Georgetown U., 1953. Nutritional biochemist USDA, AEC, Beltsville, Md., 1949-56; group chief Monsanto Co., St. Louis, 1956-73; sr. group chief Hoffman-La Roche Inc., Nutley, N.J., 1973-85, dir., 1985-92; pres. Nutrition Rsch. and Info. Inc., Livingston, N.J., 1993—; lectr. in nutrition Washington U., St. Louis, 1969-72; adj. prof. nutrition NYU, 1977-82; adj. assoc. prof. nutrition in medicine Cornell U., 1979—; Samuel Brody lectr. U. Mo., Columbia, 1988; Gladys Emerson Vis. prof. UCLA, 1990. Editor: Vitamin E, 1980, Handbook of Vitamins, 1984, rev. edit. 1991; co-editor: Vitamin Intake & Health, 1991; contbr. over 150 articles to profl. jours. Mem. Am. Inst. Nutrition, Am. Soc. Clin. Nutrition, N.Y. Acad. Scis., N.Y. Lipid Club, Soc. for Exptl. Biology and Medicine. Achievements include 4 patents in field; first to demonstrate that growth hormone stimulates milk production in the dairy cow and lean meat production in the pig; demonstrated that vitamin E functioned as in vivo antioxidant and popularized the concept that antioxidant vitamins are important to human health. Home and Office: 18 Locust Pl Livingston NJ 07039-1213

MACHLIN, MILTON ROBERT, magazine editor, writer; b. N.Y.C., June 26, 1924; s. Morris Lewis and Lillie (Manevetz) M.; 1 foster son, Jason Sheckley; m. Margaret Ryan, 1988. AB, Brown U., 1948; Degre Avance, U. Paris-Sorbonne, 1949. Reporter, columnist Clifton (N.J.) Morning Leader, 1950-52; editor Service Americain AFP (news wire service), 1952, Magazine House, 1953-55, Hillman Periodicals, 1955-57; mng. editor Argosy mag., 1960—, editor, 1969—, dir. film div.; creative dir. Pelican Prodns., 1974; regional v.p. Council Writers Orgns., 1986. Author: Ninth Life, 1961, Private Hell of Hemingway, 1962, MacArthur—A Fighting Man, 1965, The Search for Michael Rockefeller, 1972, The Family Man, 1974, French Connection II, 1975, The Setup, 1975, Pipeline, 1976, Atlanta, 1979, The Complete UFO Book, 1979, Libby, 1980, Complete UFO Catalogue, 1980, The Gossip Wars, 1980, The Worldshakers, 1984, Strangers in the Land, 1985, Minsky's Burlesque, 1985, Joshua's Altar, 1990. With AUS, 1942-45. Recipient Mystery Writers spl. award, 1976, Porgie award, 1977. Mem. Mystery Writers Am. Club: Explorers. Home: 27 Washington Sq N New York NY 10011-9177

MACHOVER, CARL, computer graphics consultant; b. Bklyn., Mar. 26, 1927; s. John Herman and Rose (Alter) M.; m. Wilma Doris Simon, June 18, 1950; children: Tod, Julie, Linda. BEE, Rensselaer Poly. Inst., 1951; postgrad., NYU, 1953-56. Mgr. applied engring. Norden div. United A/C Corp., 1951-59; mgr. sales Skiatron Electronics & TV, N.Y.C., 1959-60; v.p. mktg., dir. Info. Displays, Inc. Info. Displays, Inc., Mount Kisco, N.Y., 1960-73; v.p., gen. mgr., Info. Displays, Inc., Mount Kisco, 1973-76; pres. Machover Assocs. Corp., White Plains, N.Y., 1976—; adj. prof. Rensselaer Poly. Inst. Author: Gyro Primer, 1957, Basics of Gyroscopes, 1958; mem. editorial bd. IEEE Computer Graphics and Applications, Computers and Graphics, Spectrum; editor C4 Handbook, 1989, 2d edit., 1995, The CAD/CAM Handbook, 1996; co-editor Computer Graphics Rev.; contbr. articles to profl. jours. Mem. adv. bd. Pratt Ctr. for Computer Graphics in Design. With USNR, 1945-46. Recipient Frank Oppenheimer award Am. Soc. for Engring. Edn., 1971, Orthagonal award N.C. State U., 1988, Vanguard award Nat. Comp. Graphics Assn., 1993; named to Computer Graphics Hall of Fame Fine Arts Mus. of L.I., Hempstead, N.Y., 1988. Fellow Soc. for Info. Display (pres. 1968-70), mem. IEEE, Assn. for Computing Machinery, Am. Inst. Design and Drafting, Nat. Soc. Profl. Engrs., Nat. Computer Graphics Assn. (bd. dir., pres. 1989-90), Computer Graphics Pioneer, Art and Sci. Collaborators Inc. (pres. 1995—), Sigma Xi, Tau Beta Pi, Eta Kappa Nu. Home: 152 Longview Ave White Plains NY 10605-2314 Office: Machover Assocs Corp PO Box 308 152A Longview Ave White Plains NY 10605-2314

MACHTEI, ELI E., periodontist; b. Petaq-Tikva, Israel, June 6, 1952; s. Ahron and Nechama (Langer) M.; m. Orna Samov, Mar. 24, 1974; children: Avner, Ayelet, Itay. DMD, Hebrew U., 1979. Sr. clin. lectr. Hebrew U., Jerusalem, 1982-93; clin. assoc. prof. SUNY, Buffalo, 1989—. Maj. Israeli Def. Force, 1970-73. Mem. Am. Acad. Periodontology (editorial bd. jour. 1993—, Earl Robinson award for regenerative rsch. 1995), Internat. Assn. Dental Rsch., Internat. Team Oral Implantologists, Internat. Acad. Periodontology (editorial bd. jour. 1992—). Home: 14 Gordon St, Hod-Hasharon Israel 45203 Office: SUNY Dept Oral Biology 3435 Main St Buffalo NY 14214-3001 also: Rambam U Hosp, Periodontal Unit, Haifa Israel

MACHULAK, EDWARD LEON, real estate, mining and financial corporation executive; b. Milw., July 14, 1926; s. Frank and Mary (Sokolowski) M.; BS in Accounting, U. Wis., 1949; student spl. courses various univs.; m. Sylvia Mary Jablonski, Sept. 2, 1950; children: Edward A., John E., Lauren A., Christine M., Paul E. Chmn. bd., pres., Commerce Group Corp., Milw., 1962—, San Luis Estates, Inc., 1973—, Homespan Realty Co., Inc., 1974—, Universal Developers, Inc., 1972—, Picadilly Advt. Agy., Inc., 1974—; chmn. bd., chief exec. officer, Gen. Lumber & Supply Co., Inc., 1949—; bd. dirs., v.p., San Sebastian Gold Mines, Inc., 1969-73, chmn. bd., pres., 1973—; bd. dirs. sec., LandPak, Inc., 1985—; bd. dirs. Edjo Ltd., 1974—, sec., 1976—; ptnr., Weem Assocs., 1974—; bd. dirs., designee Comseb Joint Venture Woodcreek Devel. Corp., 1987. Mem. nat. adv. coun. SBA, 1972-74, co-chmn. 1973, 74. Recipient Recognition award U.S. SBA, 1975, N.W. Festival Corp., 25 Yr. Recognition award San Sebastian Community, Santa Rosa de Lima, El Salvador, 1991, San Sebastian Community El Salvador award, 1992, El Salvador Ministry Edn. award, 1992. Edward L. Machulak Day proclaimed by students of Canton San Sebastian, El Salvador, May 9, 1992; recipient recognition award for valuable consideration of support and svc. to San Sebastian Community, 1992, Cmty. Recognition award Santa Rosa De Lima, 1994. Mem. Nat. Assn. Small Bus. Investment Co's (nat. chmn. legis. com. 1968-73, bd. govts. 1970-74, exec. com. 1971-74, sec. 1972-74, Disting. Service award to Am. Small Bus. 1970), Midwest Regional Assn. Small Bus. Investment Cos. (bd. dirs. 1968-74, v.p. 1970-71, pres. 1971-72, Outstanding Services award 1972), State of Wis. Council on Small Bus. Investment (chmn. 1973-74), Wis. Bd. Realtors (various coms. 1955-88), Milw. Bd. Realtors (various coms. 1955-88). Pres.' Council Marmion Mil. Acad., Aurora, Ill., 1966-79, lay life trustee, 1972, fin. advisor 1967-71, chmn. spl. fund raising com. 1966-67, planning com. 1972-79; chmn. adv. bd. Jesuit Retreat House, Oshkosh, Wis., 1966-68; chmn., bd. dirs. Spencarian Coll. of Bus., 1973-74; chmn. St. John Cathedral Symphony Concert Com., Milw., 1978; sustaining mem. Met. Mus. Art, 1974—. Served with AUS, 1945-46. Recognized bus. leader in Congl. Record, 1976; named Hon. Life Mem., Mid-Continental Railway, 1963. Clubs: Tripoli Golf (Milw.); Lodge: KC (4th degree 1971—, recognition award 1989, 3rd degree hon. life 1996, 4th degree hon. life 1996). Home: 903 W Green Tree Rd Milwaukee WI 53217-3716 Office: 6001 N 91st St Milwaukee WI 53225-1721

MACIAS, EDWARD S., chemistry educator, university official and dean; b. Milw., Feb. 21, 1944; s. Arturo C. Macias and Minette (Schwenger) Wiederhold; m. Paula Wiederhold, June 17, 1967; children: Matthew Edward, Julia Katherine. AB, Colgate U., 1966; PhD, MIT, 1970. Asst. prof. Washington U., St. Louis, 1970-76, assoc. prof., 1976-84, prof. chemistry, 1984—, chmn. dept., 1984-88, provost, 1988-95, interim dean Faculty Arts and Scis., 1994-95, exec. vice chancellor and dean Faculty Arts and Scis., 1995—; cons. Meteorology Rsch., Inc., Altadina, Calif., 1978-81, Salt River Project, Phoenix, 1980-83, Santa Fe Rsch., Bloomington, Minn., 1985-88, AeroVironment, Inc., Monrovia, Calif., 1986-88. Author: Nuclear and Radiochemistry, 1981; editor: Atmospheric Aerosol, 1981; contbr. numerous articles to profl. jours. Bd. dirs. Mark Twain Summer Inst., St. Louis, 1984-87, 88-90, The Coll. Sch., St. Louis, 1984-88. Grantee NSF, EPA, Electric Power Rsch. Inst., So. Calif. Edison Co., Dept. Energy, AEC. Mem. Am. Chem. Soc., Am. Assn. Aerosol Rsch. (editorial bd.), Am. Phys. Soc., AAAS. Home: 6907 Waterman Ave Saint Louis MO 63130-4333 Office: Washington U Campus Box 1094 One Brookings Dr Saint Louis MO 63130

MACILVAINE, CHALMERS ACHESON, retired financial executive, former association executive; b. Bklyn., Oct. 25, 1921; s. James Andrew and Helen Marie (Acheson) MacI.; m. Elizabeth Jean Babcock, Mar. 26, 1943; children: Judith Anne, Joseph Chad, Martha Elizabeth. A.B., Stanford U., 1943. With Kaiser Steel Corp., 1946-73, asst. controller, 1953-62, treas., 1962-70, v.p., 1967-70, v.p. finance and planning, 1970-73; also v.p., dir. subsidiaries; v.p. project financing group Bank of Am., San Francisco, 1973-74; sr. v.p., dep. head Asia div. Bank of Am., 1974-77; sr. v.p.-fin. Peabody Coal Co., St. Louis, 1978-80; sr. v.p., dir. Stifel, Nicolaus & Co., Inc., St. Louis, 1980-83; exec. dir. Japan Am. Soc. of St. Louis, 1983-85; pres. Bamerical Internat. Fin. Corp., 1973-74. Served to lt. (j.g.) USNR, 1943-46. Mem. Phi Beta Kappa, Sigma Chi. Club: Tokyo Lawn Tennis, Burns Club of St. Louis. Home: Martin Point Rd PO Box 332 Friendship ME 04547-0332

MACILWINEN, WILLIAM LEE, JR., executive search consultant; b. Abadan, Iran, Sept. 18, 1958; arrived in U.S., 1961; s. William Lee and Jean (Theabaut) MacI.; m. Teri Jo Teer, Aug. 15, 1981; children: Catherine, Brian. Student, U. Seville, Spain, 1979, U. Santiago, Santiago de Compostela, Spain, 1980-81; BA, U. N.C., 1980; M in Internat. Bus., U. S.C., 1983. Adv. mktg. rep. IBM Corp., Hamden, Conn., Blythewood, S.C., 1983-90; dir. M in Internat. Bus. Studies program U. S.C., Columbia, 1990-94; pres. The MacIlwinen Co., Inc., 1995—; mng. dir. World Trade Ctr. U. S.C., 1995—; ptnr. Solomon Industries, Inc., 1995-97; v.p., assoc. Robison & Assocs., Charlotte, N.C., 1996-97; founding bd. dirs. Columbia World Affairs Coun., 1992-93, pres., 1993, mem. exec. com., 1992-96; bd. dirs. S.C. Internat. Trade and Econ. Devel. Coun. Advisor S.C. World Class Partnership, Columbia, 1993; del. mem. S.C.-Israel Exch., Columbia, 1993; bd. dirs., treas. MIBS Alumni Partnership Orgn. 1995—; mem. planning com. S.C. State Mus. Found., 1996; pres. Parent-Tchr. fellowship Ben Lippen Elem. Sch., 1996-97; deacon First Presbyn. Ch. Mem. Columbia C. of C. (mem. internat. com. 1990-93). Avocations: tennis, golf, cycling. Home: 6 Williamstown Ct Columbia SC 29212-8645 Office: PO Box 11536 Columbia SC 29211-1536

MACINNIS, AL, professional hockey player; b. Inverness, N.S., Can., July 11, 1963. Hockey player Calgary (Can.) Flames, 1981-94, St. Louis Blues, 1994—. Recipient Max Kaminsky trophy, 1982-83, Conn Smythe trophy, 1988-89; played in NHL All-Star Game, 1985, 88, 90-92, 94; named to The Sporting News All-Star first team, 1989-90, 90-91, NHL All-Star first team, 1989-90, 90-91, Stanley Cup championship team, 1989. Office: care St Louis Blues 1401 Clark Ave Saint Louis MO 63103-2700

MACINTOSH, CHARLES WILLIAM, property development company executive; b. Halifax, N.S., Can., Nov. 4, 1928; s. Charles William and Jessie Lenore (Lawrence) MacI.; m. Geraldine Ethel Lawrence, May 15, 1964; children: C.W. Alexander, Constance E.S., Donald S.L. BA, Dalhousie U., Halifax, 1950, LLB, 1952. Barrister and solicitor, N.S. News and ct. reporter Halifax Mail Star, 1950-53; legal practitioner C.W. MacIntosh, Halifax, 1953-61; ptnr. law firm Pace, MacIntosh & Donahoe, Halifax, 1961-74; legal cons. to AG Provincial Govts. of N.S., N.B. and P.E.I., 1974-75; dir. legal svcs. Coun. Maritime Premiers, Halifax, 1975-80; dir. land titles and legal svcs. div. Land Registration and Info. Svc., Halifax, 1980-90; gen. counsel, corp. sec., bd. dirs. The Armour Group Ltd., Halifax, 1990—; mem. drafting com. Joint Land Titles Act, 1990. Author: Intro. to Real Property in the Maritime Provinces, 1980, N.S. Real Property Practice Manual, 1988; author legal articles and papers on Cadastral sci. Pub. rels. officer Progressive Conservative Assn. N.S., Halifax, 1956-57; v.p. Halifax South Progressive Conservative Assn., 1973-74; mem. Halifax Ct. House Commn., 1963-65; bd. dirs. N.S. Adv. Coun. on Heritage Property, 1980-86; gov. MacDonald Barr Meml. Found., Washington, 1988-90. Named Queen's Counsel, N.S., 1968. Mem. Can. Bar Assn. (mem. coun., com. chair), N.S. Barristers Soc. (mem. coun. 1963-66, 80-90, hon. pres. 1993-94), The Halifax Club, The Comml. Club of Halifax (pres. 1966), Clan Chattan Assn., Clan Chattan Soc. of N.S. (pres. 1980-83), Cape Breton Bar Soc. (hon. mem.). Progressive Conservative. Home: 854 Greenwood Ave, Halifax, NS Canada B3H 3K8 Office: The Armour Group Ltd, 1701 Hollis St Ste 1001, Halifax, NS Canada B3J 3M8

MAC INTYRE, DONALD JOHN, college president; b. Detroit, Aug. 19, 1939; s. Donald MacLellan and Ellen (McGrath) MacI.; m. Antoinette Shen, June 2, 1979; children by previous marriage: Honey, Michele, James, John. A.B., U. Detroit, 1961; M.A., U. Iowa, 1963, Ph.D., 1966. Prof. U. Pacific, Stockton, Calif., 1966-73; acad. dean/pres. St. Francis Coll., Biddeford, Maine, 1973-75; acad. v.p. U. San Francisco, 1975-79; pres. Metro. State Coll., Denver, 1979-81, Canada Coll., Redwood City, Calif., 1981-83, Skyline Coll., San Bruno, Calif., 1983-85, John F. Kennedy U., Orinda, Calif., 1985-89, Patricia Montandon & Assocs., San Francisco, 1989-91, Tie Tone, Inc., Mill Valley, Calif., 1991-92, The Fielding Inst., Santa Barbara, Calif., 1993—; cons. Indsl. Rels. Workshops Seminars, Inc., 1978-81, State Bd. Agr. Colo., 1979; assoc. John A. Scalone & Assocs., Orinda, Calif., 1977-85; chmn. adv. com. office adult learning svcs. Coll. Entrance and Exam. Bd., 1980-81; evaluator Women's Equity in Edn. Act Program, 1981. Contbr. articles to profl. jours. Chmn. edn. div. Mile High United Way, Denver, 1980-81; bd. dirs. Nat. Hispanic Center for Advanced Studies and Policy Analysis, 1981-86, Nat. Hispanic U., 1982-86, Chinese Culture Found., 1983-89; chmn. Children As the Peacemakers Found. Recipient award for Commendable Service U. San Francisco, 1979, Henry Clay Hall award, 1976; Disting. Teaching award U. Pacific, 1971; U. Pacific grantee, 1969-71; Don Quixote award Nat. Hispanic U., 1983; hon. mem. World Trade Ctr. Club, Nanjing, Republic of China, 1985—. Mem. Assn. Public Coll. and Univ. Pres.'s (co-chmn. Colo. 1980-81), Internat. Cultural Soc. Korea,. Democrat. Roman Catholic. Club: World Trade Ctr. (hon.) (Nanjing, China). Office: 2112 Santa Barbara St Santa Barbara CA 93105-3544

MACIOCE, FRANK MICHAEL, lawyer, financial services company executive; b. N.Y.C., Oct. 3, 1945; s. Frank Michael and Sylvia Maria (Morea) M.; children: Michael Peter, Lauren Decker, Theodore Kenneth; m. Helen Latourette Duffin, July 9, 1988. BS, Purdue U., 1967; JD, Vanderbilt U., 1972. Bar: N.Y. 1973, U.S. Dist. Ct. (so. dist.) N.Y. 1973, U.S. Ct. Appeals (2d cir.) 1975, U.S. Supreme Ct. 1976. Mem. law dept. Merrill Lynch, Pierce, Fenner & Smith Inc., N.Y.C., 1972-80, v.p., 1978-88, 1st v.p., 1988— ; mgr. corp. law dept. Merrill Lynch & Co., Inc., N.Y.C., 1980-93, asst. gen. counsel, 1982—; gen. counsel investment banking group, 1993-95, ops., svcs. and tech. counsel, 1995—, sec. of audit, compensation and nominating coms. bd. dirs., 1978-83, sec. exec. com., 1981-83; mng. dir. Merrill Lynch Overseas Capital, N.V., Netherlands Antilles, 1980-85; sec., dir. Merrill Lynch Employees Fed. Credit Union, N.Y.C., 1978-82; dir. Merrill Lynch Pvt. Capital Inc., N.Y.C., 1981-87, Enhance Fin. Services Inc, N.Y.C., 1988-92; mem. fin. planning adv. bd. Purdue U., 1996—. Served with U.S. Army, 1969-70. Mem. ABA, Assn. of Bar of City of N.Y. (computer law com.). Home: 22 Essex Rd Summit NJ 07901-2802 Office: Merrill Lynch & Co Inc N Tower World Fin Ctr New York NY 10281-1334

MACIOCH, JAMES EDWARD, investment consultant, financial planner; b. Cleve., Mar. 30, 1947. Cert. fin. planner, Coll. for Fin. Planning, Denver, 1992; BS, U. Dayton, 1969; MBA, Olivet Nazarene U., 1997. Lic. series 7, Nat. Assn. Securities Dealers. Registered floor broker Mid-Am. Commodity Exch., 1988-90; registered floor broker, mem. Chgo. Bd. Trade, 1990—; investment cons. Montano Securities Corp., Chgo., 1993-94, Dickinson & Co., Rosemont, Ill., 1995-96, Rosemont Investment Corp., 1996—. Mem. Internat. Soc. for Fin. Planning. Office: Rosemont Investment Corp 5600 N River Rd Ste 180 Rosemont IL 60018-5184

MACIUSZKO, KATHLEEN LYNN, librarian, educator; b. Nogales, Ariz., Apr. 8, 1947; d. Thomas and Stephanie (Horowski) Mart; m. Jerzy Janusz Maciuszko, Dec. 11, 1976; 1 child, Christinia Alexsandra. BA, Ea. Mich. U., 1969; MLS, Kent State U., 1974; PhD, Case Western Res. U., 1987. Reference libr. Baldwin-Wallace Coll. Libr., Berea, Ohio, 1974-77, dir. Conservatory of Music Libr., 1977-85; dir. bus. info. svcs. Harcourt Brace Jovanovich, Inc., Cleve., 1985-89; staff asst. to exec. dir. Cuyahoga County Pub. Libr., Cleve., 1989-90; dir. Cleve. Area Met. Library System, Beachwood, Ohio, 1990; media specialist Cleve. Pub. Schs., 1991-93, Berea (Ohio) City Sch. Dist., 1993—. Author: OCLC: A Decade of Development, 1967-77, 1984; contbr. articles to profl. jours. Named Plenum Pub. scholar, 1986. Mem. Spl. Librs. Assn. (pres. Cleve. chpt. 1989-90, v.p. 1988-89, editor newsletter 1988-89), Baldwin-Wallace Coll. Faculty Women's Club (pres. 1975),. Avocation: piano. Office: Midpark HS 7000 Paula Dr Middleburg Heights OH 44130

MACIVER, JOHN KENNETH, lawyer; b. Milw., Mar. 22, 1931; s. Wallace and Elizabeth (MacRae) MacI.; m. Margaret J. Vail, Sept. 4, 1954; children: Douglas B., Carolyn V., Kenneth D., Laura E. BS, U. Wisc., 1953, LLB, 1955. Bar: Wisc. 1955. Sr. ptnr. Michael, Best & Friedrich, Milw., 1955—; mem. various bds. dirs. Chmn. Thompson for Gov. steering coms., 1986, 90, 94; state chmn. Wisc. Bush for Pres. coms., 1980, 88, 92; chmn. Wisc. Nixon for Pres. com., 1968, 72, Olson for Gov. com., 1970; vice chmn. Knowles for Gov. com., 1964, 66; bd. dirs. Milw. Symphony Orch., 1968-96, pres. 1981-82; trustee Milw. Symphony Endowment Trust, 1988—; chmn. exec. com., bd. govs. East-West Ctr., 1970-76 (Disting. svc. award Honolulu 1976); pres., chmn. bd. dirs. Nat. Coun. Alcoholism, 1974-77, bd. dirs. 1968-78 (Silver Key award N.Y. 1975); pres., campaign co-chmn. United Performing Arts Fund Greater Milw., 1974-76 (Stiemke award Arts 1988); bd. dirs., exec. com. Greater Milw. Edn. Trust, 1988—, Project New Hope, 1991—; sec., gen. counsel Wisc. Mfrs. and Commerce, 1980—; regent, sec., gen. counsel Milw. Sch. Engring., 1987—; bd. dirs., sec. Pettit Nat. Ice Tng. Ctr., 1992—; bd. dirs. Milw. Nat. Heart Project; bd. dirs., exec. com., founding mem., sec. Competitive Wisc. Inc., 1982—; bd. dirs., vice-chair Met. Milw. Assn. Commerce, 1987—; mem. Greater Milw. Com. 1985—; trustee Milw. County Pub. Mus., 1989-92. Recipient Wisc. Gov's. awards in Support of Arts, 1989, cmty. svc. award Assoc. Gen. Contractors of Greater Milw. Mem. Wis. Bar Assn. (chmn. commn. litigation costs and delay, past chmn. labor law sect., commn. on jud. elections and ethics), Milw. Bar Assn. (chmn. jud. selection and qualifications com.), Milw. Club, Town Club. Republican. Avocations: Am. history, tennis, charities, politics. Home: 959 E Circle Dr Milwaukee WI 53217-5362 Office: Michael Best & Friedich 100 E Wisconsin Ave Milwaukee WI 53202-4107

MACIVER, LOREN, artist; b. N.Y.C., Feb. 2, 1909; d. Charles Augustus Paul and Julia (MacIver) Newman; m. Lloyd Frankenberg. Student, Art Students League, 1919. One-man shows East River Gallery, N.Y.C., 1938, Pierre Matisse Gallery, N.Y.C., 1940-44, 49, 56, 61, 66, 70, Mus. Modern Art Traveling Exhbn., 1941, Vassar Art Gallery, 1950, Wellesley Coll., 1951, Whitney Mus., 1953, Dallas Mus. Fine Arts, 1953, Venice Biennale, 1967, Musée des Beaux Arts, Lyons, France, 1968, Musée de l'Art Moderne de la Ville de Paris, 1968, Pierre Matisse Gallery, N.Y.C., 1981, Rutgers Art Gallery, 1982, U. Md. Art Gallery, 1982, Musée des Ponchettes, Nice, France, 1968, 50-yr. retrospective Newport Harbor Art Mus., Newport Beach, Calif., 1985, Pierre Matisse Gallery, 1987, Mus. Modern Art, 1991, Terry Dintenfass Gallery, 1993; works exhibited Mus. of Modern Art include Federal Art, 1937, Fantastic Art, Dada, Surrealism, 1938, Art In Our Time, 1939, Fourteen Americans, 1946; work in exhbns. Am. art, Jeu de Paume, Paris, 1938, St. Louis Mus., Whitney Mus., Bklyn. Mus., Corcoran Art Gallery, State Dept. exhbn. sent to Europe, 1946, Tolouse Mus. Fine Arts, 1967, Met. Mus. Art, N.Y.C., 1991; represented in permanent collections Mus. Modern Art, Met. Mus., Detroit Inst., Los Angeles, San Francisco, Newark museums, Addison Gallery, Whitney Mus., Wadsworth Atheneum, Smith Coll. Mus., Phillips Collection, Washington, Joseph Hirshhorn Collection, Washington, Williams Coll., Elliott Collection, others. Guggenheim fellow, 1976; recipient 1st prize Corcoran Art Gallery, 1957, 1st prize Art Inst. Chgo., 1961, purchase prize Kranner Art Mus. of U. Ill., 1963, Mark Rothko Found. award, 1972, Lee Krasner award, 1991; Ford Found. grantee, 1960. Mem. Nat. Inst. Arts and Letters. Office: Terry Dintenfass Gallery 50 W 57th St New York NY 10019-3914*

MACK, CHARLES DANIEL, III, labor union executive; b. Oakland, Calif., Apr. 16, 1942; m. Marlene Helen Fagundes, Oct. 15, 1960; children: Tammy, Kelly, Kerry, Shannon. B.A., San Francisco State Coll., 1964. Truck driver Garrett Freight Lines, Emeryville, Calif., 1962-66; bus. agt. Teamsters Local No. 70, Oakland, 1966-70, sec.-treas., 1972—; legis. rep. Calif. Teamsters Pub. Affairs Council, Sacramento, 1970-71; trustee Western Conf. Teamsters Pension Trust Fund, 1980—, pres. Teamsters' Joint Council 7, San Francisco, 1982—; mem. Calif. Inst. for Fed. Policy Rsch., 1993—. Bd. dirs. Econ. Devel. Corp. of Oakland, 1980-90, Calif. Compensation Ins. Fund, San Francisco, 1980-86, Calif. Coun. Econ. and Environ. Balance, The Calif. Found. on Environ. and the Economy.

MACK, CLIFFORD GLENN, investment banker, management consultant; b. Pitts., Feb. 23, 1927; s. Jay Ord and Willa June (Shupe) M.; m. Judith McClain; children: Jeffrey, Cynthia, Marcia. B.B.A., U. Pitts., 1952; M.B.A., Temple U., 1955. Asst. treas. Air Products & Chems., Inc., Allentown, Pa., 1957-69; dir. internat. fin., asst. treas. Harris Corp., Cleve., 1969-75; treas. A.B. Dick Co., Chgo., 1975-83; pres. A.B. Dick Realty Corp., 1978-80, C.G. Mack Assocs. Ltd., Cons., 1983—; ptnr. AVM Fin. Group, Chgo., 1985-93. Contbg. author: Credit Management Handbook, 1955; also articles. Served with AUS, 1945-48. Home: 5100 Trent Woods Dr New Bern NC 28562-6726

MACK, CONNIE, III (CORNELIUS MACK), senator; b. Phila., Oct. 29, 1940; s. Cornelius Mack and Susan (Sheppard) McGillicuddy; children: Debra Lynn, Cornelius Harvey. Degree in bus., U. Fla., 1966. Mgmt. tng. Sun Bank, Cape Coral, Fla., 1966-68; v.p. bus. devel. First Nat. Bank, Ft. Myers, 1968-71; sr. v.p., dir. Sun Bank, Cape Coral, Fla., 1971-75; pres., dir. Fla. Nat. Bank, Cape Coral, 1975-82; mem. U.S. Ho. of Reps. from 13th Dist. Fla., Washington, 1983-89; U.S. Senator from Fla., 1989—, Rep. conf. chmn. 105th Congress. Bd. dirs., chmn. Palmer Drug Abuse Program, Cape Coral; bd. dirs. Cape Coral Hosp. Mem. Met. Ft. Myers C. of C., Cape Coral C. of C. Republican. Roman Catholic. Office: US Senate 517 Senate Hart Bldg Washington DC 20510

MACK, DANIEL RICHARD, furniture designer; b. Rochester, N.Y., Dec. 23, 1947; s. Richard Cornelius and Virginia Anne (Brayer) M.; m. Theresa Marie Husted, May 31, 1969; children: Kendra, Jessica, Eliza. BA, U. Toronto, Ont., Can., 1969; MA, New Sch. for Social Rsch., 1975. Journalist Sta. WRVR-FM, N.Y.C., 1971-73; spl. journalist NBC Radio, N.Y.C., 1973-75; journalist NBC TV, N.Y.C., 1981-83; asst. prof. Fordham U., Bronx, N.Y., 1975-81; pres. Daniel Mack Rustic Furnishings, Inc., Warwick, N.Y., 1983—; treework cons. Centerbrook Architects, Essex, Conn., 1990-91. Author: Making Rustic Furniture, 1992, The Rustic Furniture Companion, 1996; represented in permanent collections at Cooper Hewitt Mus., Mus. of Fine Arts, Houston, Mus. of Fine Arts, Boston, , Am. Craft Mus., The Hechinger Collection. Fellow N.Y. Found. for Arts, 1985-86, 90-91, Mid-Atlantic Arts Found., 1989-90. Home and Studio: 14 Welling Ave Warwick NY 10990-1514

MACK, DENNIS WAYNE, lawyer; b. Chgo., Sept. 11, 1943; s. Walter Andrew and Betty Jane (Klimek) M. B.A., Yale U., 1965; J.D., Harvard U., 1969. Bar: N.Y. 1970. Assoc. firm Curtis Mallet-Prevost Colt & Mosle, N.Y.C. and Paris, 1969-78; sec., gen. counsel Dominion Textile (USA) Inc., N.Y.C., 1978-91, v.p., 1986-91; pvt. practice N.Y.C., 1991—; alt. rep. Internat. Lesbian and Gay Assn. at ECOSOC of UN, 1994. Mem. dept. fin. Presbytery N.Y., 1978-83. Mem. ABA, N.Y. State Bar Assn., Bar Assn. City N.Y. Home: 180 Riverside Dr New York NY 10024-1021

MACK, EDWARD GIBSON, retired business executive; b. Toronto, Ont., Can., Dec. 4, 1917; s. Edward Gibson and Marion Margaret (Ward) M.; m. Ruth Harriet Davies, Aug. 3, 1940 (dec.); children: Edward Davies Mack, Carol Mack Fuller, Susan Mack Vassel; m. Isolde Maderson, Sept. 30, 1978. Grad., Pickering Coll., 1938; student, Syracuse U., 1938-40, U. Pa., 1945-46. Investment analyst trust dept. Syracuse (N.Y.) Trust Co., 1939-43; acct. Hurdman & Cranstoun CPA's, Syracuse, 1943-44; from dist. sales mgr. to dir. mktg. and product research Easy Washing Machine Corp., Syracuse, 1948-55; dir. research Avco Corp., Connersville, Ind., 1955-58; exec. sec. planning and policy bd. Aeronca Mfg. Corp., Middletown, Ohio, 1958-60; pres. E.D.I., State College, Pa., 1960-62; pres., dir. Sherman Indsl. Electronics Inc., Eutectics Inc.; exec. Richards Musical Instruments, Inc., Elkhart, Ind., 1962-65; mgr. supply and distbn. plastic products Union Carbide Ltd., Lindsay, Ont., 1965-68; corp. sec. Dominion Dairies Ltd., Toronto, 1968-73; v.p., sec. Dominion Dairies Ltd., 1973-81; sec., dir. Sealtest (Can.) Ltd., 1968-81. Bd. mgmt. Pickering Coll. Served with U.S. Army, World War II. Mem. Inst. Chartered Secs. and Adminstrs. (assoc.), Am. Legion, Elks, Sigma Chi. Democrat. Home: 217-5 Selby Ranch Rd American River Dr Sacramento CA 95864-5826

MACK, J. CURTIS, II, civic organization administrator; b. Los Angeles, Dec. 22, 1944; s. James Curtis and Ahli Christina (Youngren) M.; m. Tamara Jo Kriner, Jan. 23, 1988; children: James Curtis III, Robert Lee. BA cum laude, U. So. Calif., 1967, M in Pub. Adminstrn., 1969, MA, 1976. Asst. to regional dir. VA, Los Angeles, 1973-79; exec. dir. Citizens for the Republic, Santa Monica, Calif., 1979-85; asst. sec. oceans and atmosphere U.S. Dept. Commerce, Washington, 1985-88; pres. Los Angeles World Affairs Council, 1988—; bd. dirs. Brentwood Bank of Calif. Mem. Pres.'s Commn. on White House Fellowships, 1984-85. Col. USAFR, 1969—. Mem. Nat. Space Club (bd. dirs. 1987-88). Republican. Episcopalian. Avocation: philatelist. Office: Los Angeles World Affairs Coun 911 Wilshire Blvd Ste 1730 Los Angeles CA 90017-3446

MACK, JOHN EDWARD, III, utility company executive; b. Poughkeepsie, N.Y., Feb. 20, 1934; s. John Edward Jr. and Agnes D. (Albrecht) M.; m. Maureen Whitworth, Sept. 12, 1970; children: John, Todd, Ellen, David. BS, Siena Coll., 1956, LHD (hon.), 1966, MBA, 1966; LHD, Mt. St. Mary Coll., 1994. With Ctrl. Hudson Gas & Electric Corp., Poughkeepsie, 1958—, v.p. corp. svcs., 1974-76, v.p. customer svcs., 1976-79, exec. v.p., 1979-82, pres., 1982—, CEO, 1986—, also chmn. bd. dirs.; pres. Empire State Electric Energy Rsch. Corp.; bd. dirs. Mid Hudson Med. Ctr.; chmn. exec. com. N.Y. Power Pool. Pres. Hudson Valley coun. Boy Scouts Am.; bd. dirs. Astor Home for Children, Rhineback, N.Y., Marist Coll., N.Y. Bus. Devel. Corp. With U.S. Army, 1956-58. Recipient Alexis de Tocqueville Volunteerism award United Way, Poughkeepsie, 1988, Americanism award Anti Defamation League, 1988, Citizenship award Hudson-Del. Boy Scouts, 1987, Disting. Citizen award Dutchess County Boy Scouts Am. Mem. Am. Gas Assn., Edison Electric Inst. (bd. dirs.), Energy Assn. N.Y. State (chmn.). Roman Catholic. Office: Cen Hudson Gas & Electric 284 South Ave Poughkeepsie NY 12601-4838

MACK, JOHN J., investment company executive; b. 1944. Mng. dir. Morgan Stanley & Co., N.Y.C., 1979-87; mng. dir. Morgan Stanley Group, N.Y.C., 1987-92, mem. exec. com., 1987—, COO, 1992—, also pres., 1993—. Office: Morgan Stanley Group 1251 Avenue Of The Americas New York NY 10020-1104

MACK, JULIA COOPER, judge; b. Fayetteville, N.C., July 17, 1920; d. Dallas L. and Emily (McKay) Perry; m. Jerry S. Cooper, July 30, 1943; 1 dau., Cheryl; m. Clifford S. Mack, Nov. 21, 1957. B.S., Hampton Inst., 1940; LL.B., Howard U., 1951. Bar: D.C. 1952. Legal cons. OPS, Washington, 1952-53; atty.-advisor office gen. counsel Gen. Svcs. Adminstrn., Washington, 1953-54; trial appellate atty. criminal div. Dept. Justice, Washington, 1954-68; civil rights atty. Office Gen. Counsel, Equal Employment Opportunity Commn., Washington, 1968-75; assoc. judge Ct. Appeals, Washington, 1975-89; sr. judge, 1989—. Mem. Am., Fed., Washington, Nat. Bar Assns., Nat. Assn. Women Judges. Home: 1610 Varnum St NW Washington DC 20011-4206 Office: DC Ct Appeals 500 Indiana Ave NW Ste 6 Washington DC 20001-2131

MACK, RAYMOND FRANCIS, newspaper executive; b. Aitkin, Minn., Sept. 5, 1912; s. Raymond Frederick and Bertha (Tuller) M.; m. Betty Habes, Oct. 17, 1941; children—Patricia, Douglas. Student pub. schs., Va., Minn. Country circulation mgr. Duluth (Minn.) Herald News Tribune, 1930-40, St. Paul Dispatch Pioneer Press, 1940-42; circulation mgr. Washington Daily News, 1942-58, advt. dir., 1958-59, bus. mgr., 1959-72, pres., 1960-72; asst. gen. bus. mgr. Scripps-Howard Newspapers, 1972-79, exec. cons., 1979—; spl. adviser to pres. Washington Star-News, 1972-75. Past mem. exec. bd. Nat. Capitol council Boy Scouts Am.; past bd. dirs. Nat. Capital Com., YMCA Davis Meml. Goodwill Industries; bd. dirs. Washington area chpt. Nat. Multiple Sclerosis Soc. Mem. Inter-State Circulation Mgrs. Assn. (past pres.), Internat. Circulation Mgrs. Assn. (past dir.), Washington Bd. Trade (past dir.), Washington Conv. and Visitor's Bur. (past dir.). Clubs: Washington (Washington), Advertising (Washington), Nat. Press (Washington), Columbia Country (Washington), Kiwanis (Washington). Home: 3706 Leland St Chevy Chase MD 20815-4904 Office: Scripps Howard 1090 Vermont Ave NW Washington DC 20005-4905

MACK, ROBERT EMMET, hospital administrator; b. Morris, Ill., 1924. M.D., St. Louis U., 1948. Diplomate: Am. Bd. Internal Medicine. Intern St. Marys Hosp. Group, 1948-49; asst. physician; asst. resident, then resident internal medicine St. Louis U., 1949-52; asst. chief radioisope clinic Walter Reed Army Med. Center, 1954-56; chief med. service, chief radioisotope service St. Louis VA Hosp., 1956-61; vis. physician St. Louis City Hosp., 1957-61; chmn. dept. medicine Womans Hosp., Detroit, 1961-66; dir. Hutzel Hosp., Detroit, 1966-71; pres. Hutzel Hosp., 1971-80; v.p. for academic affairs Detroit Med. Center Corp., 1980-96; asst. prof. medicine St. Louis U., 1957-61; assoc. prof. medicine, Wayne State U., Detroit, 1961-66, prof., 1966-96, emeritus prof. internal medicine, 1996—, dir. admissions, 1978-81, assoc. dean Med. Ctr. Rels., 1981-96. Fellow ACP, Am. Coll. Hosp. Adminstrs., Soc. Med. Adminstrs. (pres. 1987-89); mem. AMA, Am. Fedn. Clin. Rsch., Cen. Soc. Clin. Rsch., Am. Endocrine Soc., Am. Physiol. Soc. Home: 3020 S Westview Ct Bloomfield Hills MI 48304-2472 Office: Detroit Medical Ctr 4201 Saint Antoine St Detroit MI 48201-2153

MACK, ROBERT WHITING, computer consultant; b. Cambridge, Mass., June 7, 1949; s. Robert Anthony and Caroline Mack. BA, Harvard U., 1971, JD, 1974. Bar: Mass. 1974. Assoc. Hale and Dorr, Boston, 1974-79, jr. ptnr., 1979-83, sr. ptnr., 1983-88, of counsel, 1988-89; computer cons., 1990—; bd. dirs. Cambridge Cmty. Television, Inc. Mem. Conservation Commn., Lincoln, Mass., 1981-91; bd. dirs. Harvard Gay and Lesbian Rev., 1994-97; bd. dirs. Lincoln Homes Corp., 1991-95, pres., 1992-94; bd. dirs. Greater Boston coun. Am. Youth Hostels, 1990-92, pres., 1991-92. Mem. Chiltern Mountain Club (bd. dirs. 1992-95, co-chair 1993-95), Harvard Gay and Lesbian Caucus (bd. dirs. 1994—, co-chair 1994—). Home: 10 Magazine St Apt 805 Cambridge MA 02139-3319

MACK, ROBERT WILLIAM, secondary school educator; b. Elizabeth, N.J., Oct. 25, 1941; s. Edward A. and Genevieve Emma (Kollar) M.; m. D. Nadine Hixson, June 25, 1966; children: Timothy Robert, Gregory Dennis, Katherine Ann. AA, Union Jr. Coll., Cranford, N.J., 1961; BA, Rutgers U., Newark, 1963; MEd, Rutgers U., New Brunswick, N.J., 1970. Cert. tchr. secondary sch. history, English. Tchr. Readington (N.J.) Twp. Pub. Schs., 1963-70; tchr. social studies Bridgewater-Raritan (N.J.) Pub. Schs., 1970—, asst. wrestling coach, 1975-78; ESL GED instr. Somerville Adult Sch., 1968-82. Mem. Hillsborough Twp. (N.J.) Bd. Edn., 1994—; com. mem. Hillsborough Dem. Party, 1975-82. NDEA Inst. grantee in econs. Colo. State U., 1969, in urban studies San Diego State U., 1970, East-West Inst. grantee, 1972, NEH Summer Seminar grantee, 1994. Mem. NEA, N.J. Edn. Assn., Somerset County Edn. Assn., Bridgewater Edn. Assn., Nat. Coun. Social Studies, N.J. Coun. Social Studies. Democrat. Roman Catholic. Avocations: reading, computers, photography. Home: 100 Flanders Dr Somerville NJ 08876-4616 Office: Bridgewater-Raritan Bd Edn 836 Newmans Ln Bridgewater NJ 08807

MACK, RONALD J., park superintendent; b. Ithaca, N.Y., Aug. 13, 1952; s. Voyce Joron and Margaret (Rogers) M.; m. Virlean Hill, Jan. 4, 1955; children: Terrence, Marquisha. BA, Syracuse U., 1973; postgrad., Fed. Law Enforcement Tng. Ctr., Glynco, Ga., 1981. Recreation specialist D.C. Pks. and Recreation, Washington, 1973-74; pk. ranger Nat. Pk. Svc., Washington, 1974-77, Bklyn., 1977-79, S.I., N.Y., 1979-80; supr. pk. ranger Nat. Pk. Svc., Sandy Hook, N.J., 1980-87; chief ranger activities Nat. Pk. Svc., Bklyn., 1987-88; supt. Nat. Pk. Svc., Hardy, Va., 1988-90, Independence, Mo., 1990-95; chief interpretation and edn. Nat. Pk. Svc., Washington, 1995—. Contbr. articles to profl. jours. Mem. City of Independence Heritage, 1990-95, Spl. Events Com., Independence, 1990-95. Mem. Dept. Interior fed. Credit

Union, Cmty. of Concerned Citizens, Roundtable, Employee and Alumni Assn. Nat. Pk. Svc., Syracuse U. Alumni Assn. Avocations: swimming, historic preservation, recreation activities. Office: Nat Park Svc Nat Capital Area 1100 Ohio Dr SW Washington DC 20242-0001

MACK, SANDRA LEE, secondary school educator; b. Charleston, S.C., Feb. 8, 1953; d. Arthur and Lucille (Brown) M. BS in Edn., Knoxville Coll., 1976; MA in Edn., Western Ky. U., Bowling Green, 1977. Cert. tchr., Va. Tchr. Richmond (Va.) Public Schs., 1977—. 4-H vol. Va. Coop. Ext. Svcs., Richmond, 1984—, svc. award, 1990; spl. event coord. West End Svc. unit Commonwealth Girl Scout Coun. of Va., Inc., 1994—, svc. award, 1990, vol. of yr. award, 1995; pres. new mem. com. Trinity Bapt. Ch., Richmond, 1984; head judge Miss Black Am. Richmond pageant, 1990, 91; mem. local PTA; vol. Black History instr. Minority Youth Appreciation Soc., Inc. Learning Ctr., Richmond. Recipient Creighton Ct.'s Youth Sponsor award Richmond Redevel. and Housing Authority, 1990, Cmty. Svc. award, 1994, Vol. of Yr. Gardner-Robinson Youth Svc. award, 1994, Outstanding Vol. award Girl Scout Coun. Va., Inc., 1991, J.C. Penney Golden Rule award for Vol. Excellence in Edn., 1994. Mem. NEA (Va. and Richmond chpts.), Va. Geographic Soc., Va. Socal Studies Coun. (Tchr. of Yr. award 1988), Alpha Kappa Mu. Avocations: stage and set designer, arts and crafts exhibitor, singing, reading.

MACK, THEODORE, lawyer; b. Ft. Worth, Mar. 5, 1936; s. Henry and Norma (Harris) M.; m. Ellen Feinknopf, June 19, 1960; children: Katherine Norma, Elizabeth Ellen, Alexandra. AB cum laude, Harvard U., 1958, JD, 1961. Bar: Tex. 1961, U.S. Sup. Ct. 1971, U.S. Ct. Apls. (5th cir.) 1967, U.S. Ct. Apls. (11th cir.) 1981, U.S. Dist. Ct. (no. dist.) Tex. 1961, U.S. Dist. Ct. (we. dist.) Tex. 1968, U.S. Dist. Ct. (so. dist.) Tex. 1968. Assoc., Mack & Mack, Ft. Worth, 1961-62, ptnr., 1963-70; dir., pres., v.p., treas., ptnr. Renfro, Mack, Hudman, P.C., and predecessors, Ft. Worth, 1970-93; spl. counsel McLean & Sanders A Profl. Corp., Ft. Worth, 1993—. Trustee Ft. Worth Country Day Sch., 1976-82; bd. dirs. Beth-El Congregation, 1964-73, 75-78, pres., 1975-77; bd. dirs. Jewish Fedn. Ft. Worth, 1965-72; mem. Leadership Ft. Worth, 1973-74; bd. dirs. Sr. Citizens Ctrs., Inc., 1969-81, Family and Individual Svcs., 1981-84, Presbyn. Night Shelter Tarrant County, Inc., 1992—; pres. Harvard Law Sch. Assn. Tex., 1976-77. Fellow Tex. Bar Found. (life); mem. Tex. Bar Assn., ABA, Tarrant County Bar Assn., Bar Assn. 5th Cir. Ct., Colonial Country Club, Ft. Worth Club, City Club, Harvard Club (N.Y.C., Boston). Democrat. Jewish. Home: 2817 Harlanwood Dr Fort Worth TX 76109-1226 Office: 100 Main St Fort Worth TX 76102-3009

MACK, WAYNE A., lawyer; b. Chambersburg, Pa., Jan. 31, 1961; s. Wayne A. and Carol (Irwin) M.; m. L. Suzanne Forbis; children; Courtney L., Stephanie E., Ashley C., Audrey G. BS magna cum laude, Temple U., 1982; JD cum laude, U. Pa., 1986. Bar: Pa. 1986, U.S. Dist. Ct. (ea. dist.) Pa. 1986, U.S. Ct. Appeals (3d cir.) 1986, U.S. Supreme Ct. 1995. Assoc. Duane, Morris & Heckscher, Phila., 1986-94, ptnr., 1995—. Mem. ABA (forum com. on franchising, sect. bus. law, com. on bus. and corp. litigation), Pa. Bar Assn., Phila. Bar Assn., Nat. Health Lawyers Assn., Order of Coif. Home: 346 Pelham Rd Philadelphia PA 19119-3110 Office: Duane Morris & Heckscher One Liberty Pl Philadelphia PA 19103

MACKALL, LAIDLER BOWIE, lawyer; b. Washington, Aug. 8, 1916; s. Laidler and Evelyn (Bowie) M.; m. Nancy M. Taylor, Aug. 28, 1942; children: Nancy Taylor Mackall Lurton (dec.), Christie Beall Mackall Connard, Susan Somervell Mackall Smythe, Bruce Bowie Mackall Sloan; m. Prudence Robertson Colbert, July 26, 1978. A.B., Princeton U., 1938; postgrad., Georgetown U., 1938-40, J.D., 1946. Bar: D.C. bar 1947, ICC bar 1951, U.S. Supreme Ct. bar 1958. Law clk. to chief judge of predecessor to D.C. Ct. Appeals, 1946-47; assoc. Minor, Gatley & Drury, Washington, 1947-49, Steptoe & Johnson, Washington, 1949-51; ptnr. Steptoe & Johnson, 1952-86, of counsel, 1986—; mem. D.C. Ct. Appeals Com. on Admissions, 1974-78, D.C. Circuit Jud. Conf., 1983, 85, 86; bd. mgrs. Nat. Conf. Bar Examiners, 1974-77. Served to col. USAAF, 1940-46, 51. Decorated Silver Star, 2 D.F.C.s, 6 Air medals, 3 Presdl. unit citations. Fellow Am. Coll. Trial Lawyers (emeritus); mem. ABA (past vice chmn. standing com. aviation ins. law), D.C. Bar, Bar Assn. D.C. (past chmn. com. on negligence, motor vehicle and compensation law), Barristers Club (v.p. 1964), Chevy Chase Country Club, Met. Club, Wilderness Country Club of Fla., Hawk's Nest Golf Club of Fla. Episcopalian. Home: 151 Passage Island Vero Beach FL 32963-4292 summer: 6400 Brookville Rd Chevy Chase MD 20815-3339 Office: 6400 Brookville Rd Chevy Chase MD 20815-3339

MACKANESS, GEORGE BELLAMY, retired pharmaceutical company executive; b. Sydney, Australia, Aug. 20, 1922; came to U.S., 1965, naturalized, 1978; s. James Vincent and Eleanor Frances (Bellamy) M.; m. Gwynneth Patterson, May 5, 1945; 1 son, Miles Philip. M.B. B.S. with honors, U. Sydney, 1945; D.C.P., London U., 1949; M.A. with honors, U. Oxford, 1949, D.Phil., 1953. Demonstrator, tutor in pathology Sir William Dunn Sch. Pathology, Oxford, 1949-53; sr. fellow Australian Nat. U., 1954-58, asso. prof., 1958-60, professorial fellow, 1960-63; prof. microbiology U. Adelaide, 1963-65; dir. Trudeau Inst., 1965-76; pres. The Squibb Inst. for Med. Research, Princeton, N.J., 1976-88; clin. prof. dept. medicine Coll. of Medicine and Dentistry of N.J.; adj. prof. pathology N.Y. U. Author articles in field. Recipient Paul Ehrlich-Ludwig Darmstaedter prize, 1975. Fellow Royal Soc. London. Home: 2783 Little Creek Rd Johns Island SC 29455-6022

MACKAY, ALFRED F., dean, philosophy educator; b. Ocala, Fla., Oct. 1, 1938; s. Kenneth Hood and Julia Horsey (Farnum) MacK.; m. Ann Nadine Wilson, Feb. 4, 1962; children: Douglas Kevin, Robert Wilson. AB, Davidson Coll., 1960; PhD, U. N.C., 1967. Prof. philosophy Oberlin (Ohio) Coll., 1967—, dean Coll. Arts and Scis., 1984-95, acting pres., 1991; vis. asst. prof. philosophy dept. U. Ill., Urbana/Champaign, 1970-71; vis. prof. philosophy dept. Wayne State U., Detroit, 1983. Author: Arrow's Theorem: The Paradox of Social Choice, 1980; editor: Society: Revolution and Reform, 1971, Issues in the Philosophy of Language, 1976. Campaign cons. Buddy MacKay for U.S. Senate, Fla., 1988. 1st lt. U.S. Army, Airborne, 1961-63. Fellow Woodrow Wilson Found., 1963-66, Am. Coun. of Learned Socs., 1973, Humanities fellow Rockefeller Found., 1981. Democrat. Avocations: choral singing, automobiles. Office: Oberlin Coll Dept Philosophy King Bldg Oberlin OH 44074

MACKAY, EDWARD, engineer; b. Kilmarnock, Ayrshire, Scotland, Feb. 29, 1936; s. Edward and Gertrude (Black) M.; widowed. Higher Nat. Cert., Glasgow Tech. Coll., Scotland, 1957. Layout engr. Stanley Works, New Britain, Conn., 1957-58; project engr. Grumman Olson, Athens, N.Y., 1961-69, asst. chief engr., 1969-74; chief engr. Grumman Olson, Sturgis, Mich., 1974-78, v.p. engring., 1978-95; cons. engr. Dundonald Enterprise, Three Rivers, Mich., 1995—. With U.S. Army, 1959-61. Presbyterian. Avocation: sheep and highland cattle farming. Office: Dundonald Enterprise 19085 Hoshel Rd Three Rivers MI 49093-9316

MACKAY, HAROLD HUGH, lawyer; b. Regina, Sask., Can., Aug. 1, 1940; s. John Royden and Grace Madeliene (Irwin) MacK.; m. Jean Elizabeth Hutchison, Dec. 27, 1963; children: Carol, Donald. BA, U. Sask., 1960; LLB, Dalhousie U., Halifax, N.S., 1963. Bar: Sask. 1964, Queen's Counsel 1981. Assoc. MacPherson Leslie & Tyerman, Regina, 1963-69, ptnr., 1969-75, 76—, mng. ptnr., 1989-96, chmn., 1997—; bd. dirs. Ipsco Inc., Bank of Can., Weyerhauser Can. Ltd., IMC Global Inc. Trustee Found. for Legal Rsch. Mem. Internat. Bar Assn., Can. Bar Assn., Law Soc. Sask. Mem. United Ch. Office: 1500-1874 Scarth St, Regina, SK Canada S4P 4E9

MACKAY, JACK WHITING, civil engineer; b. Asheville, N.C., Jan. 24, 1910; s. Daniel MacNeill and Emily Whiting (Walters) M.; m. Gweneth Moxley, Sept. 24, 1938; children: Jack W., Marian MacKay Pfeiffer, Richard MacNeill. BS in aeronautical engr., U. Ala., 1935, BS in civil engr., 1936, Profl. Degree Civil Engring., 1956. Registered profl. engr., Ala. Instr. U. Ala., Tuscaloosa, 1933-36, Birmingham, Ala., 1936-45; engr. trainee Am. Cast Iron Pipe Co., Birmingham, Ala., 1936-40, sales engr., 1947-50, asst. southern sales mgr., 1951-53, asst. gen. sales mgr., 1953-56, v.p., gen. sales mgr., 1956-75, bd. mgmt., 1956-75, bd. mgmt., sec., 1956-75; chmn. pub. rels. com. Cast Iron Pipe Rsch. Assn., Chgo., 1965-75; pres. Alloy Cast Inst., N.Y., 1960-61; cons. engr. Caldwell MacKay Co., Birmingham, 1983-95. Author: American Pipe Manual, 1951; contbr. articles to profl. jours. Pres. Anti-Tuberculosis Soc., 1957-58. Named Birmingham Civil Engr. Yr., Ala. Soc. Am. Soc. Civil Engrs., 1969. Fellow ASCE (life, chmn. pub. com. pipe 1973); mem. Am. Water Works Assn. (Nat. Distribution award, 1956, life), Ala. Soc. Profl. Engrs., St. Andrews Soc. Sons of Revolution, Birmingham Kiwanis Club (chmn. coms.), Birmingham Country Club, Tau Beta Pi. Presbyterian. Achievements include invention of fastite pipe joint; co-inventor pipejoint conductive gasket and boltless river crossing pipe joint; led company as first U.S. producer of Ductile Iron Pipe and acquisition of steel pipe mill and valve and hydrant business. Home: 3740 Country Club Dr Birmingham AL 35213-2816

MAC KAY, JAMES ROBERT, psychiatric social worker, mayor; b. Medford, Mass., May 8, 1930; s. James Alexander and Julia (MacNaught) Mac K.; BA, Tufts U., 1952, MA, 1954; MS in Social Work, Boston U., 1958; PhD Union U., 1987. Social worker Peter Bent Brigham Hosp., Boston, 1958-60; dir. alcoholism N.H. Dept. Health and Welfare, Concord, 1960-63; dir. community mental health State of N.H., Concord, 1963-64; pvt. practice psychotherapy, Concord, 1964—; assoc. prof. U. N.H., 1995—; mem. bd. examiners mental health practice State of N.H., 1995—; mayor City of Concord, N.H., 1986-88, 90-91; sr. lectr. psychotherapy Franklin Pierce Law Center, Concord, 1978; lectr. U. Conn. Grad. Sch. Social Work, 1981-88; chmn. N.H. Council Aging, 1969-83; pres. N.H. Social Welfare Council; chmn. N.H. del. to White House Conf. Aging, 1974, 80; chmn. N.H. Com. Older Am. Act, 1968-69; mem. Concord City Council, 1980-91; chmn. Concord Pub. Transp. Adv. Bd., 1982-86; del. N.H. Republican Conv., 1982; del. N.H. Constl. Conv., 1984; N.H. state rep., 1995-96. Recipient Ann. award N.H. Social Welfare Council, 1970; Vaughan award Activities in Aging, N.H., 1974. Mem. Nat. League Cities (human devel. policy com. 1986), Am. Assn. Univ. Profs, Nat. Assn. Social Workers (pres. N.H. chpt. 1995-97). Contbr. articles on alcoholism, addiction and juvenile delinquency to profl. jours. Office: 139 N State St Concord NH 03301-6414

MACKAY, JOHN ROBERT, II, lawyer; b. Passaic, N.J., Aug. 17, 1934; s. John R. and Janice Faith (Miller) M.; m. Susan Kellett, July 4, 1959 (div. 1985); children: J. Scott, Lauren A., Amanda F.; m. Patricia Margitan, Feb. 14, 1987; 1 child, Paige Elizabeth. AB, Bowdoin Coll., 1956; LLB, Rutgers U., 1965. Bar: N.J. 1965, U.S. Dist. Ct. N.J., 1965. Tech. writer, editor ITT Communication System, Paramus, N.J., 1960-62; law sec. to Chief Justice Weintraub N.J. Supreme Ct., Newark, N.J., 1965-66; atty. Lowenstein Sandler, Roseland, N.J., 1966-70, ptnr., 1970—; chmn. N.J. Corp. Law Revision Com., 1977-88, sec., 1970-73; adj. faculty Seton Hall sch. Law, 1973-75, Rutgers Sch. Law, 1978-81, 95. Author: New Jersey Business Corporations: Law and Practice, 1992, 2d. edit., 1996; editor in chief Rutgers Law Review, 1964-65; contbr. articles to profl. jours. Trustee Newark Day Ctr., 1972-82, pres. 1975-77; exec. com., pres. Rutgers Law Alumni Assn., Newark, 1980-81; chmn. fin. com. ARC (Nutley chpt.), 1978-86; exec. com., sec. Williams Ctr. Performing Arts, Rutherford, N.J., 1986-92; trustee United Way Essex, West Hudson, 1979-86. Lt. USN 1956-60 PTO. Mem. ABA (commn. corp. laws 1979-87, com. negotiated acquisitions 1986—), N.J. Bar Assn., Essex County Bar Assn. Office: Lowenstein Sandler 65 Livingston Ave Roseland NJ 07068-1725

MACKAY, KENNETH HOOD, JR. (BUDDY MACKAY), state official, former congressman; b. Ocala, Fl, Mar. 22, 1933; m. Anne Selph; children: Ken, John, Ben, Andy. B.S., B.A., U. Fla., 1954, LL.B. with honors, 1961. Bar: Fla. 1961. Mem. Fla. Ho. of Reps. state of Fla., 1968-74; mem. Fla. State Senate, 1974-80, mem. U.S. Ho. Reps. from 6th dist. Fla., 1985-89; lt. gov. State of Fla., 1990—. Elder Ft. King Presbyn. Ch. With USAF 1955-58. Recipient Nat. Legis. Leadership award, 1976; named Most Valuable Legislator St. Petersburg Times, 7 times; recipient Allen Morris award. Mem. ABA, Kiwanis. Democrat. Office: Office of Lt Gov The Capitol PL05 Tallahassee FL 32399-0001

MACKAY, MALCOLM, executive search consultant; b. Bklyn., Nov. 6, 1940; s. John F. and Helen (Pflug) MacK.; m. Cynthia Johnson, Aug. 29, 1964; children: Robert Livingston, Hope Winthrop. A.B. Cum laude, Princeton U., 1963; J.D., Harvard U., 1966. Bar: N.Y. 1967. Assoc. Milbank, Tweed, Hadley and McCloy, N.Y.C., 1966-69; dep. supt. N.Y. State Ins. Dept., N.Y.C., 1969-71; 1st dep. supt. N.Y. State Ins. Dept., 1971-73; vice chancellor L.I. U., Greenvale, N.Y., 1973-75; sr. v.p. Blue Cross & Blue Shield of Greater New York, 1975-77, N.Y. Life Ins. Co., N.Y.C., 1977-89; mng. dir. Russell Reynolds Assocs., N.Y.C., 1989—; bd. dirs. Independence Savs. Bank, Bklyn., Empire Fidelity Investments Life Ins. Co. Trustee Hayden Found., Pratt Inst. Mem. Century Assn., Piping Rock Club. Home: 2 Montague Ter Brooklyn NY 11201-7102 Office: Russell Reynolds Assocs 200 Park Ave New York NY 10166-0005

MACKAY, NEIL DUNCAN, plastics company executive; b. Chelsea, Mass., Nov. 5, 1931; s. Allan Foster and Helen May (Smith) MacK.; m. Marcia Ann McCarthy, Aug. 22, 1953 (dec. 1979); children: Duncan, Jerry, Alan, Neil, Bonnie; m. Beverly J. Burke, May 31, 1991. BS, BA, Northeastern U., Boston, 1954. Gen. mgr. Plastic Molding Corp., Newtown, Conn., 1954-67; market specialist Chem. div. Uniroyal, N.Y.C., 1967-70; project mgr. Colt Ind. Korean Project, N.Y.C., 1970-76; pres. Automatic Injection Molding Corp., Berkeley Heights, N.J., 1976-87, Diamond Mgmt. Cons., Inc., Winchester, N.H., 1988—; bd. dirs. Frazier & Son, Inc., Clifton, N.J., 1987—, Lor-Tech Plastics, Inc., Berkeley Heights, N.J. Author: Korean Plastics, 1973. Mem. Rep. Nat. Com., Washington, 1986-92. Recipient Outstanding Performance award Ministry Nat. Def. Republic of Korea, 1974. Mem. Am. Profl. Capt.'s Assn., Soc. Plastics Engrs. (sec. 1963-70, treas. 1983-86), Scottish-Am. Cultural Soc., St. Andrews Soc. N.Y., Plastic Pioneers Assn., Stuyvesant Yacht Club, Am. Yacht Club. Republican. Presbyterian. Avocation: sailing. Home: 19 Lovely Ln Winchester NH 03470-2916 Office: Diamond Mgmt Cons Inc PO Box 40 Winchester NH 03470-0040

MACKAY, PATRICIA MCINTOSH, counselor; b. San Francisco, Sept. 12, 1922; d. William Carroll and Louise Edgerton (Keen) McIntosh; AB in Psychology, U. Calif., Berkeley, 1944, elem. teaching credential, 1951; MA in Psychology, John F. Kennedy U., Orinda, Calif., 1979; PhD in Nutrition, Donsbach U., Huntington Beach, Calif., 1981; m. Alden Thorndike Mackay, Dec. 15, 1945; children—Patricia Louise, James McIntosh, Donald Sage. Cert. marriage, family and child counselor. Elem. tchr. Mt. Diablo Unified Sch. Dist., Concord, Calif., 1950-60; exec. supr. No. Calif. Welcome Wagon Internat., 1960-67; wedding cons. Mackay Creative Svcs., Walnut Creek, Calif., 1969-70; co-owner Courtesy Calls, Greeters and Concord Welcoming Svcs., Walnut Creek, 1971-94; marriage, family and child counselor, nutrition cons., Walnut Creek, 1979—; coord. Alameda and Contra Costa County chpts. Parents United, 1985—, pres. region 2; bd. dirs. New Directions Counseling Ctr., Inc., 1975-81, founder, pres. aux., 1977-79. Bd. dirs. Ministry in the Marketplace, Inc.; founder, dir. Turning Point Counseling; active Walnut Creek Presbyn. Ch.; bd. dirs. counseling dir. Shepherd's Gate-shelter for homeless women and children, 1985-92, Contra Costa County Child Care Coun., 1993, 94, 95. Recipient Individual award New Directions Counseling Ctr., 1978, awards Neo-Life Co. Am. Prestige Club, yearly, 1977-86, Cmty. Svc. award Child Abuse Prevention Coun., 1990, 92, 94. Mem. Assn. Marriage and Family Therapists, Parents United Internat. (pres. region 2, bd. dirs. 1992), U. Calif. Berkeley Alumni (sec. 1979-94), C. of C., Prytanean Alumnae, Delta Gamma. Republican. Club: Soroptimist (dir. 1976, 86) (Walnut Creek). Home: 1101 Scots Ln Walnut Creek CA 94596-5432 Office: 1399 Ygnacio Valley Rd Ste 34 Walnut Creek CA 94598-2815

MACKAY, RAYMOND ARTHUR, chemist; b. N.Y.C., Oct. 30, 1939; s. Theodore Henry and Helen Marie (Cusack) M.; m. Mary Dilberian, Aug. 13, 1966; 1 child, Chelsea Christine; children by previous marriage: Brett, Edward. BS in Chemistry, Rensselaer Poly. Inst., 1961; PhD in Chemistry, SUNY-Stony Brook, 1966. Rsch. assoc. Brookhaven Nat. Lab., Upton, N.Y., 1966-67; prof. Drexel U., Phila., 1969-83; chief chem. div. Chem. Research and Devel. Ctr., Aberdeen Proving Ground, Md., 1983-91; prof. chemistry, dir. ctr. advanced materials processing Clarkson U., Potsdam, N.Y., 1991—. Contbr. articles to profl. jours. Served to capt. U.S. Army, 1967-69. Grantee U.S. Army, Dept. Energy, Army Rsch. Office, NSF, Acad. Applied Scis., 1972-83, 95—, NATO, 1982-86, NYSSTF, 1991—. Mem. Am. Chem. Soc., Am. Oil Chemists Soc. (assoc. editor), Sigma Xi. Office: Clarkson U PO Box 5665 Potsdam NY 13699-5665

MACKAY, ROBERT BATTIN, museum director; b. Bklyn., Jan. 24, 1945; s. John French and Helen (Pflug) MacK.; m. Anna V.; 1 child, Hale V. B.S., Boston U., 1968, Ph.D. in Am. Studies, 1980; M.Ed., Harvard U., 1972. With Archtl. Heritage, Inc., Boston, 1967-71; dir. So. Preservation of L.I. Antiquities, Setauket, N.Y., 1974—; chmn. N.Y. State Bd. Hist. Preservation; active N.Y. State Coun. Parks, N.Y. State Heritage Assn.; mem. adv. com. N.Y. State Historic Maritime Assn.; mem. curatorial com. Mystic Seaport Mus., Conn. Editor: Between Ocean and Empire: An Illustrated History of Long Island, 1985, AIA Architectural Guide of L.I., L.I. Country Houses and Their Architects, 1997. Trustee Theodore Roosevelt Assn., St. Giles Found. For Crippled Children. With U.S. Army, 1969-70, Vietnam. Club: N.Y. Yacht (chmn. fine arts com.). Home: PO Box 292 East Setauket NY 11733-0292 Office: Soc Preservation of LI Antiquities 93 N Country Rd Setauket NY 11733-1347

MACKAY, WILLIAM ANDREW, judge; b. Halifax, N.S., Can., Mar. 20, 1929; s. Robert Alexander and Mary Kathleen (Junkin) MacK.; m. Alexa Eaton Wright, July 7, 1954; 1 dau., Margaret Kathleen. B.A., Dalhousie U., 1950, LL.B., 1953, LL.M., 1954; LL.M., Harvard U., 1970; LL.D. (hon.), Meml. U. Nfld., St. F.X. Univ., N.S. Bar: N.S.; Named queen's counsel. Fgn. service officer Dept. External Affairs, Ottawa, Ont., Can., 1954-57; asst. sec. Royal Com., Ottawa, 1955-57; sucessively asst. prof., assoc. prof., prof. law, dean Faculty of law Dalhousie U. (Halifax), N.S., Can., 1957-69, v.p., 1969-80, pres., vice-chancellor, 1980-86; ombudsman N.S., 1986-88; judge Fed. Ct. Can., trial div., Ottawa, Ont., Can., 1988—; chmn. Assn. Atlantic Univs., Halifax, 1981-83; v.p.. Assn. Univs. and Colls. Can., 1982-83, pres., 1983-85; pres. Conf. Gov. Bodies Legal Profession Can., 1968-69, Assn. Can. Law Tchrs., 1964-65. Chmn. N.S. Human Rights Com., Halifax, 1967-86; chmn. N.S. Commns. on Salary and Allowances of Elected Provincial Ofcls., 1974, 78, 81, 83, 84, 85; chmn. N.S. Task Force on AIDS, 1987-88. Mem. Can. Bar Assn. Home: 401-21 Durham Priv, Ottawa, ON Canada K1M 2H8 Office: Fed Ct of Canada, Ottawa, ON Canada K1A 0H9

MACKELLAR, KEITH ROBERT, hospital administrator; b. Chgo., Dec. 26, 1943; s. Duncan Harvey and Julie Marie MacK.; m. Deborah Marie Boone, Aug. 26, 1967; children: Andrea Kathleen, Bethany Kristine. AA, Morton Coll., 1969; B in Orgnl. Behavior, Northwestern U., 1978; M in Human Resources, Loyola U. Chgo., 1987. Dir. Ill. Masonic Med. Ctr., Chgo., 1967-74, Northwestern Meml. Hosp., Chgo., 1974-80; div. dir. AMA, Chgo., 1980-89; dir. human resources Physicians & Surgeons Hosp., Shreveport, La., 1989-91; v.p. resource mgmt. Eastern N.Mex. Med. Ctr., Roswell, 1991—; past chmn. N.Mex. Hosp. Workers Compensation Bd. Sec. Sch. Bd. Dist. #88, Bellwood, Ill., 1980-83. Sgt. USMC, 1962-66, Vietnam. Mem. Am. Coll. Healthcare Execs., Am. Soc. Healthcare Human Resources Assn., Am. Mgmt. Assn., Soc. Human Resources Mgmt., N.Mex. Healthcare Human Resources Assn. (pres. 1997), Rotary Internat., Leadership Roswell Alumni Assn. (past pres.). Baptist. Avocations: hiking, camping, softball. Home: 808 La Paloma Roswell NM 88201 Office: Eastern NMex Med Ctr 405 W Country Club Rd Roswell NM 88201-5209

MACKENBACH, FREDERICK W., welding products manufacturing company executive; b. St. Marys, Ohio, Mar. 10, 1931; s. Frederick Jacob and Mabel (Tangeman) M.; m. Jo Ann Dietrich, Oct. 21, 1953; children: John Frederick, David Dietrich. BS in Econs., Wharton Sch. Fin. & Commerce, 1953. Various sales engr. positions The Lincoln Electric Co., Indpls., Ft. Wayne, L.A., 1956-64; asst. dist. mgr. The Lincoln Electric Co., L.A., 1973-76, dist. mgr., 1976-88; pres. Lincoln Electric Mexicana, 1988-91, Lincoln Electric Latin Am., 1991-92; pres., COO The Lincoln Electric Co., Cleve., 1992-96, ret., 1996; mem. Com. on Fgn. Rels.; bd. dirs. The Lincoln Electric Co., Vols. of Am. With U.S. Army 1953-55. Mem. Nat. Elec. Mfrs. Assn., Econ. Roundtable in L.A., Am. Welding Soc., 50 Club of Cleve. Office: The Lincoln Electric Co 732 Via Somonte Palos Verdes Estates CA 90274-1629

MACKENDRICK, PAUL LACHLAN, classics educator; b. Taunton, Mass., Feb. 11, 1914; s. Ralph Fulton and Sarah (Harvey) MacK.; m. Dorothy Grace Lau, Mar. 17, 1945; children: Andrew Lachlan, Sarah Ann. A.B. summa cum laude, Harvard U., 1934, A.M., 1937, Ph.D., 1938; postgrad., Balliol Coll., Oxford, 1934-36. Instr. Phillips Acad., 1938-41, Harvard U., 1946; asst. prof. U. Wis., 1946-48, assoc. prof., 1948-52, prof., 1952-75, Lily Ross Taylor prof., 1975-84, prof. emeritus, 1984—; prof. charge Sch. Classical Studies, Am. Acad. Rome, summers 1956-59; vis. prof. U. Colo., summer 1964; mem. Inst. for Advanced Study, Princeton, 1964-65; vis. prof. U. Ibadan, Nigeria, 1965-66, cons., 1990; prof. charge Intercoll. Ctr. for Classical Studies, Rome, 1973-74; Rockefeller scholar-in-residence Bellagio Center, Italy, 1977; vis. fellow Churchill Coll., Cambridge U., 1977-78; scholar-in-residence Fondation Hardt, Geneva, 1983; Phi Beta Kappa nat. lectr., 1970-71; Sec., dir. Am. Council Learned Socs., 1956-57, dir., 1960-63; vis. lectr. U. Canterbury; N.Z., 1985, Macquarie U., Australia, 1985, Universidade Fed. de Rio de Janeiro, 1987, Universidade de Coimbra, 1989; external examiner U. Tasmania, 1990. Author: (with Herbert M. Howe) Classics in Translation, 1952, (with V.M. Scramuzza) The Ancient World, 1958, The Roman Mind at Work, 1958, The Mute Stones Speak, 1960, 2d edit., 1983, The Greek Stones Speak, 1962, 2d edit., 1981, Western Civilization, 1968, The Athenian Aristocracy, 399-31 B.C, 1969, The Iberian Stones Speak, 1969, Romans on the Rhine, 1970, Roman France, 1972, Dacian Stones Speak, 1975, North African Stones Speak, 1980, The Philosophical Books of Cicero, 1989, Cicero's Speeches: Context, Law, Rhetoric, 1995. Trustee Am. Acad. in Rome, 1966-72; bd. dirs. Nat. Humanities Faculty, 1968-71, chmn., 1969-70. Served to lt. USNR, 1941-45. Fulbright fellow, 1950; Guggenheim fellow, 1957-58; Am. Philos. Soc. grantee, 1981. Mem. Classical Assn. Middle West and South (pres. 1969-70), Am. Philol. Assn. (sec.-treas. 1954-56), Archeol. Inst. Am. Madison Soc. (pres. 1963), Phi Beta Kappa (pres. Wis. 1965-66). Home: 208 Bordner Dr Madison WI 53705-2513

MACKENZIE, CHARLES SHERRARD, academic administrator; b. Quincy, Mass., Aug. 21, 1924; s. Charles Sherrard and Dorothy (Eaton) MacK.; m. Florence Evelyn Phelps Meyer, Aug. 28, 1964 (dec. 1981); 1 child, Robert Walter Meyer; m. Lavonne Rudolph Gaiser, Mar. 30, 1985. B.A., Gordon Coll., 1946; M.Div., Princeton Theol. Sem., 1949, Ph.D., 1955; student, Boston U., 1942-43, U. Paris, 1953. Ordained to ministry Congl. Christian Ch., 1949. Pastor Carversville (Pa.) Christian Ch., 1948-51; fellow faculty Princeton Theol. Sem., 1949-51, 53-54, Princeton U., 1954-64; pastor First Presbyn. Ch., Avenel, N.J., 1954-64, Broadway Presbyn. Ch., N.Y.C., 1964-67, First Presbyn. Ch., San Mateo, Calif., 1967-71; pres. Grove City (Pa.) Coll., 1971-91, chancellor, 1991-92; advisor to pres., prof. philosphy Reformed Seminary, Orlando, Fla., 1992—; sr. min. Eastminster Presbyn. Ch., Wichita, Kans., 1993; bd. dirs. Covenant Life Ins. Co., C.S. Lewis Inst.; cons. Oxford Project, 1992—, Provident Mutual Ins. Co.; lectr. Oxford U., 1965, U. Hamburg, 1968, Columbia U., 1964-67, Stanford U., 1967-71, U. Pitts., 1990-93; adv. Provident Mutual Ins. Co. Author: The Anguish and Joy of Pascal, 1973, Freedom, Equality, Justice, 1980, The Trinity and Culture, 1985. Bd. dirs. Knox Fellowship; mem. Human Relations Commn., San Mateo, 1968-70; mem. Indsl. Devel. Council, Grove City, 1972-75. Served with USAF, 1951-53. Mem. Presbyn. Coll. Union, Am. Assn. Pres.'s Ind. Colls. and Univs. (dir., pres.), Nat. Assn. Ind. Colls. and Univs. (mem. secretariat 1985-91), Freedoms Found. (nat. jury), Soc. Christian Philosphers, Duquesne Club (Pitts.), Univ. Club Boston, Citrus Club (Orlando), Evangelical initiative Notre Dame U., Rockford Inst. Main St. com. Republican. Address: PO Box 945120 Maitland FL 32794-5120

MACKENZIE, DONALD MURRAY, hospital administrator; b. Toronto, Ont., Can., June 5, 1947; s. Donald Alexander and June Cameron MacKenzie; m. Marilyn Adele McNaughton, Jan. 3, 1970; children: Jennifer, Katherine, Kenneth. BA in Econs., U. Toronto, 1968, MA in Polit. Sci., 1970, D Health Adminstr., 1974. Exec. asst. Mt. Sinai Hosp., Toronto, 1974-76, successively asst. exec. dir., assoc. exec. dir., v.p., 1974-89; pres. North York Gen. Hosp., Toronto, 1989—; asst. prof. U. Toronto, 1989—. Editor: History of Canadian Hospitals, 1972; contbr. articles to profl. jours. Bd. dirs. Ont. Cancer Treatment & Rsch. Found., Ont. Cancer Inst. Mem. Can. Coll. Health Svc. Execs. (cert., various coms.), Can. Cancer Soc. (hon. life, pres. Ont. div. 1989-91, award of merit 1988), Ont. Hosp. Assn. (bd. dirs.), Toronto Bd. Trade, Parkview Golf Club (bd. dirs.). Anglican. Avocations: golf, tennis, canoe tripping. Office: North York Gen Hosp, 4001 Leslie St, North York, ON Canada M2K 1E1

MACKENZIE, GEORGE ALLAN, diversified company executive; b. Kingston, Jamaica, Dec. 15, 1931; s. George Adam and Annette Louise (Maduro) MacK.; m. Valerie Ann Marchand, June 30, 1971; children from previous marriage: Richard Michael, Barbara Wynne. Student, Jamaica Coll., Kingston, 1944-48. Commd. flying officer Canadian Air Force, 1951, advanced through grades to lt. gen., 1978; comdr. Canadian Forces Air Command, Winnipeg, Man., 1978-80; resigned Canadian Forces Air Command, 1980; exec. v.p., COO Gendis Inc., 1980-89, pres., COO, 1989—, also bd. dirs.; bd. dirs. Sony of Can. Ltd., Willowdale, Ont., Can.; pres. Gendis Bus. Svcs.; chmn. exec. com. Saan Stores Ltd.; bd. dirs. Tundra Oil and Gas Ltd., Chauvco Resources Ltd., Gendis Inc., bd. dirs.; pres. COO Met. Stores of Can. Ltd. Bd. dirs. St. Boniface Gen. Hosp. Rsch. Found.; coun. mem. Duke of Edinburgh's Award in Can.; mem. regional adv. bd. Carleton U.; mem. jud. coun. Province of Manitoba. Decorated comdr. Order of Mil. Merit, Order St. Johns, Can. Decoration, Knight of St. Lazarus of Jerusalem. Mem. United Services Inst. Can. (hon. v.p.), Canadian Corps Commissionaires (gov.), Police Chiefs Research Found. (co-chmn.), Pan Am. Games Soc. (hon.), Lakewood Country Club (Delta), Manitoba Club, St. Charles Golf and Country Club. Clubs: Lakewood Country (Delta); Manitoba; St. Charles Golf and Country. Home: Box 9, 383 Christie Rd, St Germain, MB Canada R0G 2A0 Office: Gendis Inc, 1370 Sony Pl, Winnipeg, MB Canada R3T 1N5

MACKENZIE, JOHN, retired oil industry executive; b. 1919. B.S., N.Y. U., 1948. Accountant S.Am. Devel. Co., N.Y.C., 1938-41; financial comptroller French Oil Ind. Agy.-Groupment D'Achat des Carburants, N.Y., 1946-53; v.p., treas. George Hall Corp., 1954-56; asst. treas. Am. Petrofina, Inc., 1956-61, sec., 1961-64, v.p., sec., 1964-68, sr. v.p., sec., 1968-84; ret., 1984. Decorated comdr. Order of Crown (Belgium). Address: 1304 Pagewynne Dr Plano TX 75093-2630

MACKENZIE, JOHN DOUGLAS, engineering educator; b. Hong Kong, Feb. 18, 1926; came to U.S., 1954, naturalized, 1963; s. John and Hannah (Wong) MacK.; m. Jennifer Russell, Oct. 2, 1954; children—Timothy John, Andrea Louise, Peter Neil. BS, U. London, 1952, PhD, 1954. Research asst., lectr. Princeton U., 1954-56; ICI fellow Cambridge (Eng.) U., 1956-57; research scientist Gen. Electric Research Ctr., N.Y.C., 1957-63; prof. materials sci. Rensselaer Poly. Inst., 1963-69; prof. engrng. U. Calif., Los Angeles, 1969—; U.S. rep. Internat. Glass Commn., 1964-71. Author books in field (6); editor: Jour. Non-Crystalline Solids, 1968—; contbr. articles to profl. jours. Fellow Am. Ceramic Soc., Royal Inst. Chemistry; mem. Nat. Acad. Engrng., Am. Phys. Soc., Electrochem. Soc., ASTM, Am. Chem. Soc., Soc. Glass Tech. Patentee in field. Office: 5732 Boelter Hall Univ of Calif Los Angeles CA 90024

MACKENZIE, JOHN PETTIBONE, journalist; b. Glen Ellyn, Ill., July 19, 1930; s. John W. P. and Elizabeth (Andersen) MacK.; m. Amanda Fisk, Oct. 24, 1959 (div. 1977); children—Bradley John, Alice Fisk, Douglas Bain. B.A. in Am. Studies cum laude, Amherst Coll., 1952; postgrad., Harvard U. Law Sch., 1964-65. Staff writer Washington Post, 1956-77, Supreme Ct. reporter, 1965-77; Walter E. Meyer vis. research prof. law N.Y. U., 1977-78; lectr. law SUNY Buffalo Law Sch., 1979; spl. contbr. to editorial page N.Y. Times, N.Y.C., 1977-79; editorial bd. N.Y. Times, 1980-97; vis. scholar N.Y. Univ. Sch. of Law, 1997—. Author: The Appearance of Justice, 1974; contbr. articles to mags., law books, law revs. Served to lt. (j.g.) USN, 1952-55. Home: 250 W 89th St New York NY 10024-1700

MACKENZIE, KENNETH DONALD, management consultant, educator; b. Salem, Oreg., Dec. 20, 1937; s. Kenneth Victor and Dorothy Vernon (Minaker) M.; m. Sally Jane McHenry, June 16, 1957; children: Dorothy Jane Rivette, Carolyn M. McFarland, Susan M. Treber, Nancy M. Kalb. AB in Math, U. Calif., Berkeley, 1960, PhD in Bus. Adminstrn, 1964. Cert. mgmt. cons. Asst. prof. indsl. adminstrn. Carnegie Mellon U., 1964-67; assoc. prof. industry Wharton Sch. U. Pa., 1967-71; prof. mgmt. scis. U. Waterloo, Ont., 1969-72; Edmund P. Learned disting. prof. Sch. Bus. U. Kans., Lawrence, 1971—; pres. Organizational Systems, Inc., Lawrence, 1976-84; founder, pres. Mackenzie and Co. Inc., Lawrence, 1983—. Author: An Introduction to Continuous Probability, 1969, A Theory of Group Structures, 2 vols., 1976, Basic Theory, 1976, A Theory of Group Structures, vol. II: Empirical Tests, 1976, Organizational Structures, 1978, Organizational Design: The Organizational Audit and Analysis Technology, 1986, The Organizational Hologram: The Effective Management of Organizational Change, 1991, Practitioner's Guide for Improving an Organization, 1995; editor: Organizations Behavior series; mem. editorial bd. of profl. jours. Served with USMCR, 1957-60, with Army N.G., 1960-64. Fellow AAAS; mem. APA, Am. Mgmt. Assn., Acad. Mgmt., Inst. Mgmt. Scis. (chmn. coll. on orgns. 1983-93), Inst. Mgmt. Cons., Western Acad. Mgmt., Assn. Mgmt. Orgnl. Design, Meso Orgnl. Studies Group. Republican. Home: 502 Millstone Rd Lawrence KS 66049-2350 Office: Mackenzie & Co Inc 700 Massachusetts St Ste 301 Lawrence KS 66044-6604 also: U Kans Sch Bus Lawrence KS 66045 *While the pursuit of a better theory of organizations has led me from the classroom to the laboratory and then into the boardrooms of corporations, the thrust of all these many activities has been to develop the science of organizations.*

MACKENZIE, LEWIS WHARTON, military officer; b. Truro, N.S., Can., Apr. 30, 1940; s. Eugene Murdock and Shirley Helena (Wharton) MacK.; m. Dora Rosalie McKinnon; 1 child, Kimm Katheryn. Student, NATO Def. Coll., Rome, 1977; BA in Polit. Sci., U. Manitoba, Winnipeg, Can., 1988; Phd (hon.), St. Francis Xavier U., 1993; LLB (hon.), St. Mary's U., 1993, Acadia U., 1993. Commd. 2d lt. Can. Armed Forces, 1972, advanced through grades to major gen., 1987; teamsite comdr. Internat. Commn. Control and Supervision, Vietnam, 1972; co. comdr. UN Emergency Peace Keeping Force, Cairo, 1973; exec. asst. to comdr. Can. Forces Europe, Lahr, Fed. Republic Germany, 1974-77; comdr. Nicosia dist. UN Peacekeeping Force, Cyprus, 1978; commdg. officer 1st bn. Princess Patricia's Can. Light Infantry, Calgary, 1977-79; faculty mem. Can. Forces Staff Coll., Toronto, 1979-82; dep. chief staff for tng. Can. Army, Montreal, 1983-85; dir. pers. careers officers Can. Armed Forces, Ottawa, 1985-87; dir. Combar Related Employment of Women, Ottawa, 1987-88; comdr. combat tng. ctr. Can. Armed Forces, Gagetown Can. Forces Base, N.B., 1988—; comdr. UN Peacekeeping Force, Ctrl. Am., 1990-91, chief staff Unprotection force, Yugoslavia, 1992, comdr. UN forces to open Sarajevo airport for humanitarian relief, 1992; host TV documentary "A Soldier's Peace." Author: Peacekeeper, Road to Sarajevo, 1993. Bd. adv. Can. Fedn. for AIDS Rsch., Can. Spl. Olympics; bd. dirs. Pacific Body Armour; chair bd. adv. Can. Abuse Prevention Found.; nat. spokesman Parkinson's Superwalk. Decorated Meritorious Svc. Cross (2) (Can.); recipient Birks gold medal Xavier Jr. Coll., Sydney, N.S., Can., 1960, Vimy award, 1993; Internat. fellow U.S. Army War Coll., 1982-83; Nat. Sports Car champion, 1981; Nat. Formula Ford B Class champion, 1995, 96; named to McLean's Honor Roll., 1993. Avocation: motor racing. Home and Office: RR 2, Bracebridge, ON Canada P1L 1WP

MACKENZIE, MALCOLM LEWIS, marketing executive, museum executive; b. El Paso, Tex., Jan. 19, 1926; s. William Forbes and Grace Meldon (Lewis) M.; m. Barbara Lee Webb, Apr. 4, 1952; children: David, Ellen; m. Marianne Eckerstrom, Nov. 22, 1980; stepchildren: Ann-Marie, Vicki, Adam, Lars. Graduate Maine Maritime Acad., 1946; student R.I. Sch. Design, 1948-51; B.A., Brown U., 1951. 3d mate Am. Export Lines, Jersey City, Pacific Tankers, San Francisco, 1946-48; 2d mate Sun Oil Co., Marcus Hook, Pa., 1948; plans dir., account exec. N. W. Ayer & Son, Phila., 1951-63; plans dir., head mktg. dept. Grey & Rogers Advt., Phila., 1963-64; v.p. Daily Svc., Phila., 1964-65; owner, pres. mktg. svcs. Malcolm L. Mackenzie & Assocs., Wilmington, Del., 1966—; dir., pres., curator Kalmar Nyckel Mus. Inst., 1990—; pres. Christina Marina, Inc., 1992-95; dir., sec., treas. Fort Christina Marina, Inc., 1994-97; incorporator, reg. agent Digital Design Group, Ltd., 1994—; dir., v.p. Wilmington Shipbuilding Co., Inc., 1993—; adminstrv. mgr. Kalmar Nyckel Found., 1986-91; sec.-treas. North Star Charters Inc., Wilmington, 1984-97, Kalmar Marine Supplies Ltd., 1992-96, Lenape Corp., 1992-96; pres. Delmarva Safe Sailing Assocs., Inc., Wilmington, 1977—, pres., bd. dirs., Beta Centaur Holding Co., 1992-96; dir. devel., pres. Am. Pr stige Arts, Inc., Wilmington, 1970-72; dir. Composite Structures, Inc., Wilmington, 1974-76; dir. Cutter Mohawk Corp., Wilmington, 1981-95; mgr., dir. Market Penetration, Wilmington, 1970—; cons. Del. Waterfront 2020; v.p. Landmark Properties, Inc., 1986-92; incorporator, registered agt. Peace Please, Inc., Del. Fin. Accts., Inc., 1993—; pres. Active Young Reps., Brandywine Hundred, 1966, Windybush Civic Assn., Wilmington, Del., 1962-66; pres., dir. Coun. of Civic Orgns. of Brandywine Hundred, 1965; bd. dirs. Del. Safety Coun., 1965-73, 74-75, Wilmington Sister Cities, 1980—, Del. Maritime Ctr., 1989-95; mem. New Castle County Rev. Bd., 1976-78; mem. CPAC Hwy. Dept. Adv. Bd., Dover, Del., 1979-82; vice chmn. No. New Castle County Land Use Study Group, 1990-95. With U.S. Mcht. Svc., 1944-48. Recipient Order of Merit, Boy Scouts Am., 1977, Order of the Arrow, 1974, Woodbadge, 1974; Commodore, Ships on the Shoreline, Inc., Del. Tall Ships Salute, 1982. Mem. Advt. Club Del., Colonial Period Ship Assn. (founding 1987), Swedish Colonial Soc. (councilor, recording sec.), Wilmington Sailboat Show (mgr., owner 1981-89), Nat. Mariner Awards (mgr. 1982—), Cutter Mohawk (capt., 1982-85), coord. Creative Grandparenting, 1995— Republican. Lutheran., coun. Holy Trinity Lutheran Church, Laison, "Love to Learn Tutoring Program, Clubs: Brown U. of Phila. (pres. 1958-61), Brown U. of Del. (pres. 1974-84).

MAC KENZIE, NORMAN HUGH, retired English educator, writer; b. Salisbury, Rhodesia, Mar. 8, 1915; s. Thomas Hugh and Ruth Blanche (Huskisson) MacK.; m. Rita Mavis Hofmann, Aug. 14, 1948; children: Catherine, Ronald. B.A., Rhodes U., South Africa, 1934, M.A., 1935, Diploma in Edn., 1936; Ph.D. (Union scholar), U. London, 1940; DLitt (hon.), St. Joseph's U., Phila., 1989. Lectr. in English Rhodes U., South Africa, 1937, U. Hong Kong, 1940-41, U. Melbourne, Australia, 1946-48; sr. lectr.-in-charge U. Natal, Durban, 1949-55; prof., head English dept. U. Coll., Rhodesia, 1955-65; dean Faculty Arts and Edn. U. Coll., 1957-60, 63-64; prof., head English dept. Laurentian U., Ont., Can., 1965-66; prof. English Queen's U., Kingston, Ont., 1966-80; emeritus prof. Queen's U., 1980—, dir. grad. studies in English, 1967-73, chmn. council grad. studies, 1971-73, chmn. editorial bd. Yeats Studies, 1972-74; Exec. Central Africa Drama League, 1959-65; mem. exec. com. Can. Assn. Irish Studies, 1968-73. Author: South African Travel Literature in the 17th Century, 1955, The Outlook for English in Central Africa, 1960, Hopkins, 1968, A Reader's Guide to G.M. Hopkins, 1981; editor: (with W.H. Gardner) The Poems of Gerard Manley Hopkins, 1967, rev. edit., 1970; Poems by Hopkins, 1974, U. Natal Gazette, 1954-55, The Early Poetic Manuscripts and Notebooks of Gerard Manley Hopkins in Facsimile, 1989, The Poetical Works of Gerard Manley Hopkins, 1990, rev. 1992, The Later Poetic Manuscripts of G.M. Hopkins in Facsimile, 1991; contbr.: chpts. to Testing the English Proficiency of Foreign Students, 1961, English Studies Today-Third Series, 1963, Sphere History of English Literature, Vol. VI, 1970, rev. edit., 1987, Readings of the Wreck of the Deutschland, 1976, Festschrift for E.R. Seary, 1975, British and American Literature 1880-1920, 1976, Myth and Reality in Irish Literature, 1977; articles to Internat. Rev. Edn., Bull. Inst. Hist. Research, Times Lit. Supplement, Modern Lang. Quar., Queen's Quar., others. Served with Hong Kong Vol. Def. Corps, 1940-45; prisoner of war, China and Japan 1941-45. Brit. Council scholar, 1954; Killam sr. fellow, 1979-81; Martin D'Arcy lectr. Oxford U., 1988-89. Fellow Royal Soc. Can.; mem. English Assn. Rhodesia (pres. 1957-65), So. Rhodesia Drama Assn. (vice chmn. 1957-65), Hopkins Soc. (pres. 1972-75), Yeats Soc. (life), MLA (life), Internat. Hopkins Assn. (bd. scholars 1979—). Home: 416 Windward Pl, Kingston, ON Canada K7M 4E4

MACKENZIE, PETER SEAN, instructional designer; b. L.A., Aug. 25, 1954; s. William Duncan and Patricia Ann (Kronschnabel) Mack; m. Carin Willette, Dec. 28, 1983; 1 child, Liam Reynolds. BA, Western Wash. U., 1976. Bus. editor Skagit Valley Herald, Mount Vernon, Wash., 1976-79; mng. editor Stanwood (Wash.)-Camano News, 1979-84; graphic artist Pacific Media Group, Seattle, 1985-90, editor, 1990-94; instnl. designer Mosaix, Inc. (formerly Digital Systems Internat.), Redmond, Wash., 1994—; instr. U. Wash. Exptl. Coll., Seattle, 1990-91, 96-97. Author: Jumper, 1989; rec. artist LP KEZX Album Project, 1987, Victory Music Vol. # 2, 1988; speaker Viacom Cable Pub. Access TV, Seattle, 1990. V.p. Stanwood, Wash. C. of C., 1983. Recipient 1st place newswriting award Wash. Newspaper Pubs. Assn., 1981, 82, 2d place award for comprehensive coverage, 1982, 3d place awards in newswriting, features and spot news, 1983. Mem. Internat. Soc. PErformance Improvement (Pugot Sound chpt.). Avocations: photography, music, political research, philosophy. Home: 316 NW 86th St Seattle WA 98117-3125 Office: Mosaix Inc 6464 185th Ave NE Redmond WA 98052-5032

MACKENZIE, RONALD ALEXANDER, anesthesiologist; b. Detroit, Mar. 31, 1938; s. James and Elizabeth (McIvor) M.; m. Nancy Lee Vogan, Aug. 25, 1962; children: Margaret, James. BS, Alma Coll., 1961; DO, Kansas City Coll., 1967. Diplomate Am. Bd. Anesthesiology. Resident in anesthesiology Detroit Osteo. Hosp., 1970-72, Cleve. Clinic, 1972-73; resident in anesthesiology Mayo Clinic, Rochester, Minn., 1973-74, cons. in anesthesia, 1974—; vice-chmn. dept. anesthesiology Mayo Clinic, 1988—. Pres. Minn. Orch., Rochester, 1987-89. Fellow Am. Coll. Anesthesiologists; mem. Am. Soc. Anesthesiologists (bd. dirs. 1983-87, sec. 1991—), Sigma Xi. Avocations: sailing, photography. Office: Mayo Clinic 200 1st St SW Rochester MN 55902-3008

MACKENZIE, ROSS, newspaper editor; b. Evanston, Ill., Aug. 25, 1941; s. Henry Wallace Dundas and Marion Elizabeth (Gillies) M.; m. Virginia de Bruyn Kops; children: Alexander Ross, Ross Hale. Diploma, Phillips Exeter Acad., 1959; BA in History, Yale U., 1963; MA in Polit. Philosophy, U. Chgo., 1969. Editor editl. pages Richmond (Va.) News Leader, 1969-92, Richmond Times-Dispatch, 1992—; mem. adv. bd. Lincoln Rev., 1972—, Inst. for Polit. Journalism, 1993—. Author: Brief Points: An Almanac for Parents and Friends of the U.S. Naval Academy, 1993, revised, 1996; editor: Eyewitness: Writings From the Ordeal of Communism, 1993. Mem. adv. bd. Massey Cancer Ctr., 1992—. Recipient Eugene Pulliam fellow Sigma Delta Chi, 1978; runner-up Pulitzer Prize for Commentary, 1982. Mem. Am. Soc. Newspaper Editors (past mem. writing awards com.), Phila. Soc. (charter mem.), Nat. Press Club, Commonwealth Club (pres. 1985-87), Country Club of Va., Deep Run Hunt Club. Avocations: one-wall handball, tennis, amateur radio, nature. Office: Richmond Times-Dispatch 333 E Grace St Richmond VA 23293-1000

MACKENZIE-WOOD, MELODY, entrepreneur; b. Portsmouth, Va., Dec. 13, 1955; d. Herbert Marion and Carolyn (Tarkenton) Criswell; m. David Mackenzie-Wood. BS in English & Speech Edn. with honors, U. Tenn., 1977. Pub. rels. Reliance Group Holdings, N.Y.C., 1981-85; human rels./ employee rels. Broad Inc./SunAmerica, L.A., 1985-92; CEO, founder, coach, entrepreneur, corp. trainer, spkr. Lifeworks Resources; motivational spkr., tchr. in field. Office: Lifeworks Resources 645 N Beau Chene Dr Apt 14 Mandeville LA 70471-7108

MACKERODT, FRED, public relations specialist; b. Bklyn., Sept. 17, 1938; s. Leroy and Margaret (Murphy) M.; m. Christy Woods, June 7, 1987. Student, NYU, 1958-59. Freelance writer, photographer N.Y.C. and Barcelona, Spain, 1968-73; editor Cars Mag., Popular Publs. Inc., N.Y.C., 1973-76; pres. Fred Mackerodt, Inc. (pub. relations and publicity), N.Y.C., 1976—. Contbr. articles to popular mags.; contbg. editor, sci. and tech.: Popular Mechanics, 1987—. Spl. Dep. Sheriff, Indian River County, Fla., 1994—. Mem. Aviation and Space Writers Am., Internat. Motor Press Assn., Publicity Club N.Y., Wings Club, N.Y. Zool. Soc. (aquarium field assoc. 1971—). Home: Ste 901 209 W 86th St New York NY 10024 Office: 110 Summit Ave Montvale NJ 07645-1712

MACKERRAS, SIR (ALAN) CHARLES (MACLAURIN), conductor; b. Schenectady, N.Y. (parents Australian citizens), Nov. 17, 1925; s. Alan Patrick and Catherine M.; m. Helena Judith Wilkins, 1947; 2 children. Student with Vaclav Talich, Prague Acad. Music, 1947-48; DMus (hon.) Hull U., 1990, Nottingham U., 1991, U. Brno, Czech Republic, 1994, York (Eng.) U., 1994, Griffith U., Brisbane, 1994, Oxford U., 1997. Prin. oboist Sydney Symphony Orch., Australia, 1943-46; staff condr. English Nat. Opera (formerly Sadler's Wells Opera), London, 1949-53, musical dir., 1970-77; prin. condr. BBC Concert Orch., 1954-56; freelance condr. with most Brit. and many continental orchs., concert tours USSR, S. Africa, N. Am., Australia, 1957-66, U.S. coast-to-coast, 1983; first condr. Hamburg State Opera, 1966-69; chief guest condr. BBC Symphony Orch., 1976-79; chief condr. Sydney Symphony Orch., Australian Broadcasting Commn., 1982-85; prin. guest condr. Royal Liverpool Philharmonic Orch., 1986-88, Scottish Chamber Orch., 1992-95, condr. laureate, 1995—, San Francisco Opera, 1993-96, Royal Philharmonic Orch., 1993-96, Czech Philharmonic Orchestra, 1997—; mus. dir. Welsh Nat. Opera, 1987-92, condr. emeritus, 1993—; appearances many internat. festivals and opera houses; frequent radio and TV broadcasts; many comml. recordings, notably Handel series for DGG and Janacek operas for Decca, Mozart series for Telarc. Published ballet arrangements Pineapple Poll (Sullivan), Lady and the Fool (Verdi), reconstrn. Sullivan's lost Cello Concerto. Contbr. appendices (book) A Musicians' Musician, articles to Opera Mag., Music and Musicians, other jours. Recipient Evening Standard award for opera 1977, Janacek medal, 1978, Gramophone Record of Yr. award, 1977, 80, Grammy award for best opera recording, 1981; prix Fondation Jacques Ibert, 1983, Record of Yr. award Stereo Rev., 1983, Gramophone Operatic Record of Yr. award, 1983-84, Gramophone Choral Recording of Yr., 1986, Gramophone Best Opera Recording award, 1994; decorated comdr. Order Brit. Empire, 1974; created Knight, 1979; recipient Medal of Merit, Czech Republic, 1996; created Companion, Order of Australia, 1997; Brit. Council scholar, 1947-48. Fellow Royal Coll. of Music (hon.), L.R.A.M. (hon.). Office: c/o Robert Rattray, Lies Askonas Ltd, 6 Henrietta St, London WC2E 8LA, England

MACKEY, JEFFREY ALLEN, minister; b. Kingston, N.Y., July 12, 1952; s. Allen William and Vivian Mathilda (Hornbeck) M.; m. Martha LaVonne Webster, Dec. 18, 1971; children: Guy Linwood, Kenyon Paul, Geoffrey Joel. BS, Nyack Coll., 1974; D of Sacred Lit., Ridgedale Theol. Sem., 1975; M Ministry, Trinity Coll., Andover, N.Y., 1976; D Ministry, Mansfield Sch. Div., 1985, Grad. Theol. Found., 1990; cert. of theol. studies, Gen. Theol. Sem., 1993; postgrad., Grad. Theol. Found., 1997—. Ordained to ministry Congl. Christian Ch., 1974; ordained priest Episcopal Ch., 1993. Min. music Neversink Valley Bapt. Ch., Huguenot, N.Y., 1969-70; pastor Ponckhockie Congl. Ch., Kingston, 1971-74, The Alliance Ch., Andover, 1974-76; acad. dean Macon (Ga.) Bible Inst., 1976-78; min. Oak Grove Gospel Tabernacle, Williamsport, Pa., 1977-80, 69th St. Alliance Ch., Phila., 1980-83; sr. min. Vestavia Alliance Ch., Birmingham, Ala., 1983-87, Hope Alliance Ch., New Hartford, N.Y., 1987-91; assoc. rector Grace Ch., Utica, N.Y, 1991-96; vicar Grace Ch., Waterville, N.Y., 1995-96; rector Trinity Episcopal Ch., DeRidder, La., 1996—; vicar Polk Meml. Episcopal Ch., Leesville, La., 1996—. Author: A Worship Manifesto, 1986, Indicatives and Imperatives, 1987, Christ's Centripetal Cross, 1990; contbr. numerous articles to profl. jours. Mem. Alcohol and Drug Abuse Prevention Treatment Program, Birmingham, 1987-88. Mem. Am. Assn. Christian Schs., Fellowship Christian Sch. Adminstrs., Evang. Theol. Soc., Am. Assn. Sch. Adminstrs., Am. Guild Organists, Anglican Assn. of Biblical Scholars, Kiwanis. Republican. Avocations: organ and piano playing, collecting art and statues, hymn writing, walking, restoring antique automobiles. Home: 1104 Meadowbrook Dr Deridder LA 70634 Office: Trinity Ch 625 N Texas St Deridder LA 70634-3330

MACKEY, LEONARD BRUCE, lawyer, former diversified manufacturing corporation executive; b. Washington, Aug. 31, 1925; s. Stuart J. and Margaret B. (Browne) M.; m. Britta Beckhaus, Mar. 2, 1974; children—Leonard B., Cathleen C., Wendy F. B.E.E., Rensselaer Poly. Inst., 1945; J.D., George Washington U., 1950. Bar: D.C. 1951, N.Y. 1954. Instr. elec. engring. Rensselaer Poly. Inst., Troy, N.Y., 1946-47; patent examiner U.S. Patent Office, Washington, 1947-50; atty. Gen. Electric Co., Schenectady and N.Y.C., 1953-60; dir. licensing, asst. sec. ITT, N.Y.C., 1960-73; v.p., gen. patent counsel, dir. licensing ITT, 1973-90; of counsel Davis Hoxie Faithfull & Hapgood, N.Y.C., 1990-93; cons. licensing and tech. transfer Sarasota, Fla., 1994—. Mem. Recreation Commn., Rye, N.Y., 1966-67; mem. Planning Commn., 1967-70, 72-75, city councilman, 1970-71. Served with USNR, 1943-45; to lt. 1951-53. Mem. ABA (coun. mem., intellectual property law sect. 1989-93), Am. Intellectual Property Law Assn. (bd. mgrs. 1968-70, pres. 1982-83), Licensing Execs. Soc. U.S.A. (pres. 1978), Licensing Execs. Soc. Internat. (pres. 1986), Eta Kappa Nu, Am. Yacht Club (sec. 1968-70), N.Y. Yacht Club, Masons, Apawamis. Republican. Presbyterian. Office: 219 S Orange Ave Sarasota FL 34236-6801

MACKEY, LOUIS HENRY, philosophy educator; b. Sidney, Ohio, Sept. 24, 1926; s. Louis Henry and Clara Emma (Maurer) M.; children: Stephen Louis, Thomas Adam, Jacob Louis, Eva Maria. B.A., Capital U., 1948; student, Duke, 1948-50; M.A., Yale, 1953, Ph.D., 1954. Instr. philosophy Yale U., 1953-55, asst. prof., Morse fellow, 1955-59; assoc. prof. philosophy Rice U., Houston, 1959-65, prof., 1965-67; prof. U. Tex., Austin, 1967—. Author: Kierkegaard: A Kind of Poet, 1971, Points of View: Readings of Kierkegaard, 1986, Fact, Fiction, and Representation, 1997; contbr. articles to profl. jours. Recipient Harry Ransom award for Tchng. Excellence, 1987, Pres.'s Assocs. award for Tchng. Excellence, 1991, Grad. Tchng. award 1994; NEH fellow, 1976-77. Episcopalian. Home: 4105 Victory Dr Apt A108 Austin TX 78704-7552 Office: Univ Texas 316 WAG Austin TX 78712

MACKEY, MAURICE CECIL, university president, economist, lawyer; b. Montgomery, Ala., Jan. 23, 1929; s. M. Cecil and Annie Laurie (Kimrey) M.; m. Clare Siewert, Aug. 29, 1953; children: Carol, John, Ann. B.A., U. Ala., 1949, M.A., 1953, LL.B., 1958; Ph.D., U. Ill., 1955; postgrad., Harvard U., 1958-59. Bar: Ala. 1958. Asst. prof. econs. U. Ill., 1955-56; assoc. prof. econs. U.S. Air Force Acad., 1956-57; asst. prof. law U. Ala., 1959-62; with FAA, 1963-65, U.S. Dept. Commerce, 1965-67; asst. sec. U.S. Dept. Transp., 1967-69; exec. v.p., prof. law Fla. State U., Tallahassee, 1969-71; pres. U. South Fla., Tampa, 1971-76; pres., prof. law Tex. Tech U., Lubbock, 1976-79; pres., prof. econs. Mich. State U., East Lansing, 1979-85, prof. econs., 1985—; asst. counsel Subcom. on Antitrust and Monopoly, U.S. Senate, 1962-63; bd. dirs. Community First Bank, Lansing, Mich.; mem. adv. com. U.S. Coast Guard Acad., 1969-71; chmn. Fla. Gov.'s Adv. Com. on Transp., 1975, Nat. Boating Safety Adv. Council, 1975—; mem. adv. council NSF, 1978-81; assoc. China Council, 1979—; Disting. vis. prof. United Arab Emirates U., 1990, 91, 92, 93; bd. dirs. Summit Holding Corp., Lansing. Bd. dirs. Gulf Ridge council Boy Scouts Am.; pres. Chief Okemos council, 1981-82; bd. dirs. Tampa United Fund, Lubbock United Way; chmn., bd. dirs. Debt for Devel. Coalition, 1989—. Served with USAF, 1956-57. Recipient Arthur S. Flemming award Washington Jaycees, 1967. Mem. Fla. Council 100, Tampa C. of C. (bd. govs.), Am. Assn. State Colls. and Univs. (pres., dir.), Artus, Phi Kappa Phi, Chi Alpha Phi. Office: Mich State U Marshall Hall East Lansing MI 48824

MACKEY, PATRICIA ELAINE, librarian; b. Balt., July 29, 1941; d. Timothy and Hazel Mozelle (Davis) M. BA in Anthropology, CUNY, 1978; MLS, Columbia U., 1981. Asst. libr. I, European Exch. Sys., Mainz-Kastel, Germany, 1966-68; interlibr. loan asst. Poly. U., Bklyn., 1968-72; interlibr. loan asst. Rockefeller U., N.Y.C., 1972-73, sr. libr. asst., 1974-80, libr., 1981-91, head libr., 1991—; mem. various libr. coms., N.Y.C., 1991—. Mentor pub. svc. scholars program for srs. Hunter Coll., CUNY, 1992—. Mem. ALA, N.Y. State Libr. Assn., Assn. Coll. and Rsch. Librs. Democrat. Roman Catholic. Avocations: reading, chess, gardening. Office: Rockefeller U Libr RU Box 263 1230 York Ave New York NY 10021-6307

MACKEY, ROBERT JOSEPH, business executive; b. Detroit, Apr. 28, 1946; s. Robert and Bridget (Degnan) M.; m. Regina E. Richmond, July 27, 1968; children: Robert, Scott. BS in Indsl. Mgmt., Lawrence U., Southfield, Mich., 1971; MBA, Wayne State U., 1979. Dir. bus. affairs Harper Grace Hosp., Detroit, 1975-79; v.p. Nat. Health Corp., Southfield, 1979-83; v.p., founder Health Resources Mgmt., Southfield, 1983-86; pres., founder Medview, Inc., Farmington Hills, Mich., 1986-91, CompPro, Inc., Farmington Hills, Mich., 1986-91, CompPro Calif., Inc., Long Beach, 1986-91; founder, owner Regulation Enterprises, Inc., Southfield, 1991—; founder, dir., officer Laser Eye Ctrs. of N.Am., 1994—, Image Sculpting Inc., 1996. Bd. dirs. Am. Cancer Soc., Southfield, 1986-91, Dad's Club, Cath. Cen. High Sch., Redford, 1987-93; mem. Gov.'s Task Force on Health Care Cost Containment, Mich., 1989, 90. Mem. Am. Assn. Profl. Providers, Detroit Econ. Club, Marina City Club. Avocations: skiing, racquetball, golf. Home: 33905 Schulte St Farmington MI 48335-4162 Office: Laser Eye Ctrs NAm 28530 Orchard Lake Rd Ste 106 Farmingtn Hls MI 48334-2987

MACKEY, SHELDON ELIAS, minister; b. Bethlehem, Pa., Nov. 20, 1913; s. Elias and Pearl Elizabeth (Cunningham) M.; m. Marie Louise Dillinger, Sept. 20, 1939; children—Peter David, John Harry, Mary Susan, Timothy

Andrew, Philip James. AB, Moravian Coll., 1936; BD, Lancaster Theol. Sem., 1939; DD, Franklin and Marshall Coll., 1954; LLD, Ursinus Coll., 1958. Ordained to ministry Evang. and Reformed Ch., 1939; pastor Pa. congregations, 1939-54; adminstrv. asst. to pres. Evang. and Reformed Ch., 1954-57, sec., 1957-78; also editor Yearbook, dir. correlation and sec. gen. council Gen. Synod; ret.; co-sec. United Ch. of Christ, also sec. exec. coun., adminstrv. com., 1957-61, mem. fin. and budget com., exec. sec. stewardship coun., 1961-79. Contbr. articles to religious publs. Bd. dirs. Ursinus Coll.; trustee emeritus Lancaster Theol. Sem. Mem. Nat. Council Chs. in U.S.A. Club: Phi Alpha Clergy. Home: 30 Schuylkill Dr Wernersville PA 19565-2011 *Life has a dimension which lies beyond the visible or physical. I believe that this dimension which lies at the heart of my faith is also revealed in art, music and literature. We need to reach out into this dimension which makes life most real.*

MACKEY, WAYNE ALLISON, electrical engineer; b. Pitts., Sept. 22, 1955; s. George Allison and Dorothy Jayne (Ross) M.; m. Mary Lou Herbers, Nov. 16, 1984; children: Benjamin Paul, Craig Thomas. BSEE and Econs., Carnegie Mellon U., 1977; MS in Engring., Loyola Marymount U., L.A., 1982. Engr. space and info. systems Raytheon Co., Sudbury, Mass., 1977-78; mem. tech. staff Hughes Aircraft Co., El Segundo, Calif., 1978-84, head tech. sect., 1984-87, sr. scientist, engr., 1987-90, div. sr. scientist, 1990—, team leader event based concurrent engring., 1991—, team leader estimating process improvement, 1992, team leader customer focused quality and orgn. metrics system, 1993, team leader 6 Sigma quality, 1994, team leader RCS supplier devel., 1995; prin. cons., founder CCC Solutions, El Segundo, Calif., 1997—; team leader 6 Sigma quality, 1994; exec. advisor to Mgmt. Roundtable Inc., 1995, material ops. mgr., 1995; conf. chmn., spkr. Metrics for Product Devel. and Project Mgmt., 1996; team leader best practices supplier cert., 1996; team leader Nat. Metrics Task Force, 1997; mem. Stanford Integrated Mfg. Assn., Stanford Global Supply Chain Forum, MIT Lean Aircraft Initiative, MIT Supplier Sys. and Relationships Focus Group. Inventor automated environ. tester, universal FLIR tester, automatic bid/spread sheet, four steps metric process. Fellow Hughes Corp. Edn. Coun., 1980. Mem. Am. Soc. Quality Control, Assn. Proposal Mgmt. Profls., Tau Beta Pi. Avocations: high end audio equipment, music, skiing, guitar. Home: 1315 10th St Manhattan Beach CA 90266-6035 Office: Hughes Aircraft Co PO Box 902 E180 El Segundo CA 90245 Office:

MACKEY, WILLIAM ARTHUR GODFREY, computer software company executive; b. Glasgow, Scotland, Mar. 23, 1946; came to U.S., 1970; s. William Arthur and Joan Margaret (Sykes) M.; m. Bianca Ann Dell'Isola, June 9, 1973 (dec. Nov. 1993). BSc in Engring., U. London, 1968, MSc in Engring., 1970; MBA, Harvard U., 1972. Prodn. engr. Rolls-Royce PLC, Glasgow, 1969-70; securities analyst Tucker, Anthony & R.L. Day, Inc., Boston, 1972-74; sr. project engr. Fafnir Bearing divsn. Textron Inc., New Britain, Conn., 1974-76; mfg. contr. Loctite Corp., Newington, Conn., 1976-78, mgr. ops. and mktg. divisional, 1978-80, mgr. corp. productivity improvement, 1980-83; worldwide product mgr. Otis Elevator Co., Farmington, Conn., 1985-87; pres., CEO Signum Microsystems, Inc., Bloomfield, Conn., 1982—; bd. dirs. Signum Microsystems, Inc., Bloomfield; sr. cons. Coopers & Lybrand, L.L.P., Hartford, Conn., 1988-91. Vice chmn. Conn. Com. Newcomen Soc. in U.S., Exton, Pa., 1980—; mem. Wadsworth Ahteneum, Hartford, 1975—, coun., 1994—; mem. World Affairs Coun., Hartford, Conn., 1984—, bd. dirs., 1992—; chief staff City fo New Haven Blue Ribbon Commn., 1990. Rolls Royce scholar, 1964-69, 70-72. Mem. ASME, ACLU, Soc. Mfg. Engrs. (vice chmn. Hartford chpt. 1991-95, chmn. 1996—, Pres.'s award 1991-92), Conn. Bus. and Industry Assn., Greater Hartford C. of C., MIT Enterprise Forum Conn., Concord Coalition, Harvard Bus. Sch. Club No. Conn. (bd. dirs. 1991—), U.S. Amateur Ballroom Dancers Assn., Royal Scottish Automobile Club (Glasgow), Masons (Wyllys-St. John's lodge 4). Republican. Congregationalist. Avocations: economics and current affairs, 20th century music, special-interest automobiles and motorcycles. Home: 244 Steele Rd West Hartford CT 06117-2742 Office: Signum Microsystems Inc 11 Mountain Ave Bloomfield CT 06002-2343

MACKEY, WILLIAM STURGES, JR., investor, consultant; b. St. Louis, May 27, 1921; s. William Sturges and Dorothy Francis (Allison) M.; m. Margaret Powell, Dec. 10, 1943; children: Dorothy Mackey Lurie, John Powell, James Wescott; m. Barbara Drozdowski, May 26, 1988. B.A., Rice U., 1943; M.B.A., U. Tex., 1950. Assoc. prof. acctg. Rice U., 1946-62; v.p., treas. Mandrel Industries, 1962-66; v.p. fin. Tex. Internat. Airlines, 1966-69; chmn., chief exec. officer Lifemark Corp., 1969-84; cons. Whole Foods Market, Inc. Served to 1st lt. USAAF, 1943-46. Recipient Disting. Alumni award Rice U., 1997. AICPA, Houston Philos. Soc., The Houston Forum, Rice U. Assocs., Lakeside Country Club, Houston City Club. Unitarian. Home: 6333 Buffalo Speedway Houston TX 77005-3309 Office: PO Box 273202 Houston TX 77277-3202

MACKIE, DONALD JOHN, JR., real estate developer; b. Ashland, Wis., July 29, 1944; s. Donald John and Mary Eleanor (Berglund) M.; m. Sara Nelle Lowrey, Apr. 6, 1974; children: Anna Kathleen, Douglas Lowrey. BBA in Urban Land Econs., U. Wis., 1969. Project mgr. Bliss & Laughlin Industries, Oak Brook, Ill., 1969-72; pres. Green Mark, Inc. subs. Gerald D. Hines, Houston, 1972-78; mng. ptnr. Mill Creek Golf & Country Club, Salado, Tex., 1978—, Mill Creek Properties, Salado, 1978—; pres. Salado Water Supply Corp., 1993—. Sponsor, dir. Cen. Tex. Area Mus., Salado, 1980—, Bell County Rehab Tournament, Salado, 1984—, Table Rock Festival, Salado, 1985—. Served to 1st lt. U.S. Army, 1962-66. Recipient Environ. award, City of Houston, 1977, Design award, Am. Inst. Architects, 1976. Mem. Urban Land Inst. (residential, recreation, indsl., office couns. 1970-87), Nat. Assn. Indsl. and Office Parks, Nat. Assn. Home Builders (Profl. Mktg. award 1976), Nat. Golf Course Owners Assn. Episcopalian. Lodge: Lions. Avocations: golf, skiing, sailing. Home: 806 Hilltop Salado TX 76571-9566 Office: Mill Creek Golf & Country Club PO Box 67 Salado TX 76571-0067

MACKIE, FREDERICK DAVID, retired utility executive; b. Ashland, Wis., Aug. 3, 1910; s. David and Johanna (Zilisch) M.; m. Ruth Elizabeth Babcock, Aug. 27, 1937; children—Marilyn Ruth, Frederick D. B.S. in Elec. Engring, U. Wis., 1933. With Madison Gas & Electric Co., Wis., 1934—; exec. v.p. Madison Gas & Electric Co., 1964-66, pres., gen. mgr., 1966-78, chmn. bd., 1976-78, also dir. Recipient Disting. Service citation Coll. Engring., U. Wis., 1969. Mem. IEEE (life), Nat. Soc. Profl. Engrs., Wis. Soc. Profl. Engrs., Madison Tech. Club, Kiwanis, Madison Club. Lutheran. Home: 58 Golf Course Rd Madison WI 53704-1423

MAC'KIE, PAMELA S., lawyer; b. Jackson, Miss., Jan. 2, 1956; d. Charles Edward and Betty Jo (Moore) Spell; children: John Greene IV, Ann Katherine. BS, Delta State U., Cleveland, Miss., 1978; JD, U. Miss., Oxford, 1984. Bar: Miss. 1984, Fla. 1986. Assoc. Cummings & Lockwood, Naples, Fla., 1985-93; prin. Pamela S. Mac'Kie, P.A., Naples, 1993-95, pres., 1995—. Pres. Naples Better Govt., 1992-95; pres.-elect Women's Rep. Club, Naples, 1994; county commr. Collier County Bd., Naples, 1994—; dir. Youth Haven, 1992, YMCA, 1993, Collier County Women's Polit. Caucus, 1992—. Recipient Pro Bono award Fla. Bar, 1990, Leadership Collier C. of C., Naples, 1991. Recipient Pro Bono award Fla. Bar, 1990; grad. Leadership Collier, Naples, 1991, Leadership S.W. Fla., 1995. Republican. Episcopalian. Office: 4001 Tamiami Trl N Ste 320 Naples FL 34103-3591

MACKIE, ROBERT GORDON, costume and fashion designer; b. Monterey Park, Calif., Mar. 24, 1940; s. Charles Robert and Mildred Agnes (Smith) M.; m. Marianne Wolford, Mar. 14, 1960 (div.); 1 son, Robin Gordon. Student, Chouinard Art Inst., 1958-61. Sketch for Jean Louis, 1962-63; mem. staff Edith Head, 1962-63; pres. ptnr. Bob Mackie Originals, N.Y.C.; costume designer: (films) Brigadoon, 1954, Divorce, American Style, 1967, ...All the Marbles, 1981, Pennies from Heaven, 1981 (Academy award nomination best costume design 1981), Max Dugan Returns, 1983, (TV movies) Fresno, 1986, (TV series) The Carol Burnett Show, 1967-78, The Sonny and Cher Comedy Hour, 1971-74, Cher, 1975-76, The Diahann Carroll Show, 1976, The Sonny and Cher Show, 1976-77, Donny and Marie, 1976-79, Mama's Family, 1983-85, (TV spls.) Alice Through the Looking Glass, 1967, Carousel, 1967, Kismet, 1967, Fred Astaire Show, 1968, Diana Ross and the Supremes, 1969, Of Thee I Sing, 1972, Once Upon a Mattress, 1973, (theatrical prodns.) The Best Little Whorehouse Goes Public, 1994; co-costume designer: (films) Lady Sings the Blues, 1972 (Academy award nomination best costume design 1972), Funny Lady, 1975 (Academy award nomination best costume design 1975), The Villain, 1979, Butterfly, 1981, ... All the Marbles, 1983, Staying Alive, 1983, Brenda Starr, 1987, (theatrical prodns.) On the Town, 1971, Lorelei, 1972; author: Dressing for Glamour, 1969; appeared on Broadway and in TV prodn. Night of 100 Stars II, 1985. Recipient Emmy awards for outstanding costume design, 1966, 67, 69, 70, 76, 78, 84, 88, 95, Emmy award nominations for outstanding costume design, 1972, 74, 75, 76, 77, 79, 80, 83, 86, 87, Costume Designers Guild award, 1968, Fashion Achievement award Otis/Parsons Sch. Design, 1987; named most creative fashion designer in Am. US mag., 1982, 83; honored by Costume Inst. Fine Arts, Houston, 1987, AIDS Project L.A., 1989. Democrat. Address: Bob Mackie Ltd 530 7th Ave 3rd Flr New York NY 10018-3103*

MACKIEWICZ, EDWARD ROBERT, lawyer; b. Jersey City, July 2, 1951; s. Edward John and Irene Helen (Rakowicz) H. BA, Yale U., 1973; JD, Columbia U., 1976. Bar: N.J. 1976, U.S. Dist. Ct. N.J. 1976, N.Y. 1977, U.S. Dist. Ct. (so. and ea. dist.) N.Y. 1977, D.C. 1978, U.S. Dist. Ct. D.C. 1978, U.S. Ct. Appeals (D.C. cir.) 1978, U.S. Ct. Appeals (3d cir.) 1980, U.S. Supreme Ct. 1980, Md. 1984, U.S. Ct. Claims 1984, U.S. Ct. Appeals (4th cir.) 1986, U.S. Dist. Ct. Md. 1990. Assoc. Carter, Ledyard & Milburn, N.Y.C., 1976-77, Covington & Burling, Washington, 1977-82; counsel for civil rights litigation solicitor's office U.S. Dept. Labor, Washington, 1982-83; sr. assoc. Jones, Day, Reavis & Pogue, Washington, 1983-85; gen. counsel Pension Benefit Guaranty Corp., Washington, 1985-87; of counsel Pierson, Ball & Dowd, Washington, 1987-89; ptnr. Reed Smith Shaw & McClay, Washington, 1989; gen. counsel Masters, Mates & Pilots Benefit Plans, Linthicum Heights, Md., 1989-92; of counsel Steptoe & Johnson, Washington, 1992—; mem. adv. coun. Sec. of Labor's ERISA, 1991-93; profl. lectr. in law Nat. Law Ctr., George Washington U., 1993—. Mem. Am. Coun. Young Polit. Leaders (del. to Australia 1985), Univ. Club, Yale Club. Home: 3001 Veazey Ter NW Apt 1032 Washington DC 20008-5406 Office: 1330 Connecticut Ave NW Washington DC 20036-1704

MACKIN, COOPER RICHERSON, university chancellor; b. Selma, Ala., Apr. 26, 1933; s. Thomas R. and Muriel (Green) M.; m. Catherine Barragy, Feb. 15, 1958 (dec.); children: Michele, Patrick, Daniel; m. Mary Kathryn Ruetten, Dec. 14, 1985. B.A., Troy State Coll., 1956; M.A., Tulane U., 1958; Ph.D., Rice U., 1962. Instr. Tex. So. U., 1958-59; asst. prof. N. Tex. State U., Denton, 1962-63; asst. prof. U. New Orleans, 1963-66, assoc. prof., 1966-70, prof. English, 1970—, chmn. dept., 1966-69, dean Coll. Liberal Arts, 1969-80, vice chancellor for acad. affairs, 1980-83, acting chancellor, 1983-84, chancellor, 1984-87, chancellor emeritus, 1987—. Author: William Styron, 1969; Contbr. articles on 17th century English lit. to profl. jours. Bd. dirs. New Orleans chpt. NCCJ, 1969-79, Air U., 1986-88. Served with AUS, 1953-55. Mem. Milton Soc. Am., South Central MLA. Home: 18 Charlotte Dr New Orleans LA 70122-2532 Office: U New Orleans English Dept New Orleans LA 70148*

MAC KINNEY, ARCHIE ALLEN, JR., physician; b. St. Paul, Aug. 16, 1929; s. Archie Allen and Doris (Hoops) MacK.; m. Shirley Schaefer, Apr. 9, 1955; children—Julianne, Theodore, John. B.A., Wheaton (Ill.) Coll., 1951; M.D., U. Rochester, 1955. Intern, resident in medicine U. Wis. Hosp., 1955-59; clin. assoc. NIH, 1959-61; clin. investigator VA, 1961-64; asst. prof. medicine U. Wis., Madison, 1964-68; assoc. prof. U. Wis., 1968-74, prof., 1974—, med. alumni prof., 1987; chief hematology VA Hosp., Madison, 1964—, chief nuclear medicine, 1964-73, 78-79. Author, editor Pathophysiology of Blood, 1984. Contbr. articles to med. jours. Trustee Intervarsity Christian Fellowship, 1985-88. Served with USPHS, 1959-61. Danforth asso., 1962. Mem. Am. Soc. Hematology, Am. Fedn. Clin. Research, Central Soc. Clin. Research. Republican. Baptist. Home: 190 N Prospect Ave Madison WI 53705-4071 Office: 2500 Overlook Ter Madison WI 53705-2254

MACKINNEY, ARTHUR CLINTON, JR., retired university official, psychologist; b. Kansas City, Mo., Oct. 16, 1928; s. Arthur Clinton and Doris (Long) MacK.; m. Lois Elizabeth Lineberry, Sept. 5, 1953; children: Arthur Clinton III, Gordon L., Nada L. B.A., William Jewell Coll., 1951; M.A., U. Minn., 1953, Ph.D., 1955. Instr. U. Minn., 1953-55, Macalester Coll., 1955; cons. psychologist R.N. McMurry & Co., Chgo., 1953; research psychologist Gen. Motors Corp., 1955-57; asst. prof. to prof., head dept. psychology Iowa State U., 1957-70; dean grad. studies and Research Wright State U., Dayton, Ohio, 1971-76; vice chancellor for acad. affairs U. Mo.-St. Louis, 1976-86, interim chancellor, 1986; pres. and chief exec. officer U. Ctr. Tulsa, 1986-91, pres. emeritus, 1992-93; vis. disting. prof. U. Tulsa, 1992-94; vis. prof. U. Minn., 1960, U. Calif., 1962-63, 66; mem. Commn. on Instns. Higher Edn., North Cen. Assn., 1980-84; cons. to industry. Contbr. articles to profl. jours. Bd. dirs. Tulsa Edn. Fund. Served with AUS, 1946-47, 51. Fellow Am. Psychol. Assn. (Cattell research design award 1968, pres. div. indsl. and orgnl. psychology 1981-82); mem. Midwestern Psychol. Assn., Mo. Psychol. Assn. (sec. 1981, pres. 1983-84), Iowa Psychol. Assn. (pres. 1966), Sigma Xi, Psi Chi (nat. historian 1983—, nat. council 1983—, Midwestern regional v.p. 1984-85, pres. 1987-88), Kappa Alpha, Phi Kappa Phi. Unitarian. Research on long-term devel. complex human performance. Home: PO Box 105 Ellison Bay WI 54210-0105

MACKINNON, CATHARINE A., lawyer, law educator, legal scholar, writer; d. George E. and Elizabeth V. (Davis) MacKinnon. BA in Govt. magna cum laude with distinction, Smith Coll., 1969; JD, Yale U., 1977, PhD in Polit. Sci., 1987. Vis. prof. U Chgo., Harvard U., Stanford U, Yale U., others, Osgoode Hall, York U., Canada; prof. of law U. Mich., 1990—. Author: Sexual Harassment of Working Women, 1979, Feminism Unmodified, 1987, Toward a Feminist Theory of the State, 1989, Only Words, 1993; co-author: In Harm's Way, 1997. Office: U Michigan Law School Ann Arbor MI 48109-1215

MACKINNON, JOHN ALEXANDER, lawyer; b. Glen Ridge, N.J., Feb. 5, 1949; s. John and Carol McNeir (Cox) M.; m. Anne Rider Patterson, Aug. 19, 1972; children: Lindsay Rider, John William. BA, Williams Coll., 1971; JD, U. Va., Charlottesville, 1974. Assoc. Brown & Wood, N.Y.C., 1974-82, ptnr., 1983—. Trustee, Tuxedo Park Libr., N.Y., 1982-89; mem. chmn., bd. zoning appeals, Tuxedo Park, 1987-89. Mem. The Tuxedo Club. Home: Mtn Farm Rd Tuxedo Park NY 10987 Office: Brown & Wood 1 World Trade Ctr New York NY 10048-0202

MACKINNON, MALCOLM D(AVID), retired insurance company executive, information systems executive; b. Guelph, Ont., Can., Mar. 9, 1931; came to U.S., 1955; s. A.L. and Jean (Butchart) Mack.; m. Betty Campbell, June 18, 1955; children: Sandra, Katherine, Donald. BA, U. Toronto, 1953. CLU; chartered fin. analyst. With Prudential Ins. Co., 1954-94, v.p., Newark, 1979-81, sr. v.p., 1981-82, sr. v.p., Roseland, N.J., 1982-94; retired 1994; commentator pub. radio, 1995—. Trustee Kean Coll., Union, N.J., 1990-93, Millburn Free Pub. Libr., 1996—; chmn. Milburn Short Hills Chpt. Am. Red Cross, 1992-94; pres. Millburn Free Pub. Libr., 1997—. Fellow Soc. Actuaries. Club: Canoe Brook Country (Summit, N.J.). Home: 23 Grosvenor Rd Short Hills NJ 07078-1639

MACKINNON, PEGGY LOUISE, public relations executive; b. Florence, Ariz., June 18, 1945; d. Lacy Donald Gay and Goldie Louise (Trotter) Martin; m. Ian Dixon Mackinnon, Oct. 20, 1973. BA, San Jose State U., 1967, postgrad., 1968. Cert. secondary tchr., Calif. Tchr. Las Lomas High Sch., Walnut Creek, Calif., 1968-69; edn. officer Ormond Sch., Sydney, Australia, 1970-72; tchr. Belconnen High Sch., Canberra, Australia, 1972-73; temp. exec. sec. various orgns., London, 1973-75; mktg. mgr. Roadtown Wholesale, Tortola, British Virgin Islands, 1975-80; sr. v.p., gen. mgr. Hill & Knowlton Inc., Denver, 1981-96; pres. Peggy Mackinnon Inc., Denver, 1996—. Bd. dirs. Rocky Mountain Poison and Drug Found., Denver, 1984-87, Denver C. of C., Boy Scouts Am., Denver coun. Mem. Pub. Relations Soc. Am. (accredited). Avocations: tennis, skiing, fishing, travel. Home and Office: Apt 21 9200 Cherry Creek South Dr Denver CO 80231-4018

MACKINNON, ROGER ALAN, psychiatrist, educator; b. Attleboro, Mass., Feb. 13, 1927; s. Irville Herbert and Helen (Junk) MacK.; m. Florence Lundgren, Apr. 8, 1949 (div. 1970); children: Carol Louise, Stuart Alan; m. Nadine Trasenster, May 28, 1971. Student, Princeton U., 1944-46; MD, Columbia U., 1950, cert. in psycoanalytic medicine, 1957. Diplomate Am. Bd. Psychiatry and Neurology. Intern E.W. Sparrow Hosp., Lansing, Mich., 1950-51; resident in psychiatry N.Y. State Psychiatric Inst., N.Y.C., 1951-52, 52-54; chief psychiatry Vanderbilt Clinic, Presbyn. Hosp., N.Y.C., 1959-77; prof. clin. psychiatry Coll. Physicians & Surgeons, Columbia U., N.Y.C., 1986—; tng., supervising analyst Columbia U. Psychoanalytic Ctr., 1970—, asst. dir. for selection, 1981-91, dir., 1991-97; attending psychiatrist Presbyn. Hosp., N.Y.C., 1972—, N.Y. State Psychiatric Inst., N.Y.C., 1972—; asst. examiner Am. Bd. Psychiatry and Neurology, 1960-70; lectr. in field. Co-author textbook: The Psychiatric Interview, 1971, The Psychiatric Evaluation, 1986; contbr. articles to profl. jours., chpts. to books. Lt. USNR, 1952-54. Recipient George E. Daniels Merit award Assn. for Psychoanalytic Medicine, 1995, Centennial award N.Y. State Psychiat. Inst., 1996. Fellow Am. Psychiat. Assn. (life), N.Y. Acad. Medicine; mem. Am. Psychoanalytic Assn., N.Y. Psychiat. Soc. (pres. 1987-88). Avocations: woodworking, boating, hiking. Home: 11 Edgewood St Tenafly NJ 07670-2909 Office: 11 E 87th St New York NY 10128-0527 also: Columbia U Ctr Psychoanalytic Tng Rsch 722 W 168th St New York NY 10032-2603

MACKINNON, SALLY ANNE, retired fast food company executive; b. Chgo., Apr. 20, 1938; d. Eugene and Anne Elizabeth (Jones) MacK. B.A., Smith Coll., 1960; postgrad., U. Ark., 1961-62. Brand mgr. Speidel div. of Textron, Providence, 1967-70; mktg. mgr. Candy Corp. Am., Bklyn., 1970-72; v.p. account service William Esty Advt., N.Y.C., 1972-76; mktg. mgr. R.J. Reynolds Tobacco, Winston-Salem, N.C., 1976-84, v.p. new brands, 1984-86; v.p. new products mktg. Ky. Fried Chicken, Louisville, 1986-88; ret., 1988. Democrat. Episcopalian. Avocation: travel. Home: 321 Lamplighter Cir Winston Salem NC 27104-3420

MACKINNON, STEPHEN R., Asian studies administrator, educator; b. Columbus, Nebr., Dec. 2, 1940; s. Cyrus Leland and Helen (Wigglesworth) MacK.; m. Janice Carolyn Rachie, July 15, 1967; children: Rebecca, Cyrus R. BA, Yale U., 1963, MA, 1964; PhD, U. Calif., Davis, 1971. Acting instr. Chinese U., Hong Kong, 1968-69; dir. Asian Studies, prof. history Ariz. State U., Tempe, 1971—; vis. assoc. Chinese Acad. Social Sci., Beijing, 1979-81, 85; mem. U.S. State Dept. Selection Bd., Washington, 1991, Nat. Com. on U.S.-China Rels., N.Y.C., 1991—; cons. PBS film documentary "Dragon and Eagle" on U.S.-China rels., San Francisco, 1986—. Author: (book) Power/Politics China, 1980; co-author: (books) Agnes Smedley, 1988, China Reporting, 1987; co-editor: (book) Chinese Women Revolution, 1976 (ALA notable book 1976); lectr. on China to local orgns. and TV, 1981—. Commr. Phoenix Sister Cities, 1986-91; treas. Com. on Fgn. Rels., Phoenix, 1988-96; bd. dirs. Marshall Fund Ariz., 1995—. Rsch. fellow Am. Coun. Learned Socs., Hong Kong, 1978, Fulbright Found., India, 1977-78; rsch. sr. Com. on Scholarly Com. People's Republic China, Washington-Beijing, 1992. Mem. Assn. Asian Studies (bd. dirs. 1990-91), Am. Hist. Assn. (program com. 1990-91). Avocations: tennis, hiking, jazz. Office: Ariz State U History Dept Ctr for Asian Studies Tempe AZ 85287-2501

MACKINTOSH, CAMERON, musical theater producer; b. Enfield, Middlesex, Eng., Oct. 17, 1946; s. Ian Robert and Diana Gladys (Tonna) M. Student, Prior Pk. Coll., Somerset, Eng., Cen. Sch. for Speech and Drama. Asst. stage mgr. Oliver! tour, British cities, 1965; N.Y. debut as producer, deviser Tomfoolery, Top of the Gate, 1981; London debut producer Little Women, Jeanetta Cochrane, 1967; producer, deviser musicals Anything Goes, Saville, London, 1969, Trelawney, Sadler Wells, Prince of Wales, 1972, The Card, Queens, 1973, Winnie the Pooh, Phoenix, 1974, 75, Owl and the Pussycat Went To See, Westminster, 1975, Side By Side By Sondheim, Wyndhams and Garrick, 1976, Oliver!, Albery, 1977-80, Aldwych, 1983, Godspell, Phoenix, 1975, Her Majesty's P.O.W., Shaftsbury, 1977, Duke of York, 1978, Diary of a Madam, Phoenix, 1977, After Shave, Apollo, 1977, Out On a Limb, Vaudeville, 1977, Gingerbread Man, Old Vic, 1978, 79, Royalty, 1980, Westminster, 1981, My Fair Lady, Adelphi, 1979, Tomfoolery, Criterion, 1980, Jeeves Takes Charge, Fortune, 1981, Cats, New London, 1981, Song and Dance, Palace, 1982, Blondel, Old Vic, Aldwych, 1983, Little Shop of Horrors, Comedy, 1983, Abbacadabra, Lyric Hammersmith, 1983, The Boyfriend, Old Vic and Albery, 1985, Les Misérables, 1985, The Phantom of the Opera, 1987, Follies, 1989, Miss Saigon, 1989, Five Guys Named Moe, 1990, Moby Dick: Putting It Together, 1992, Carousel, 1993 (Tony award, 1994), Oliver!, 1994, Martin Guerre, 1996; major tours in Britian include Little Women, 1967, Murder at the Vicarage, 1969, Rebecca, 1969, At Home with the Dales, 1970, Salad Days, 1972, Butley, 1973, Winnie the Pooh, 1973-74, Time and Time Again, 1974, Godspell, 1974-80, The Owl and The Pussycat Went To See, 1974, 75, 76, Relativeley Speaking, 1974-75, An Inspector Calls, 1974, Private Lives, 1974, Bell, Book and Candle, 1974, A Merry Whiff of Windsor, 1975, So Who Needs Marriage. 1975, John, Paul, George and Ringo, 1975-76, Rock Nativity, 1975-76, Touch of Spring, 1976, Virginia Woolf, 1976, Lauder, 1976, Oliver!, 1977, 83, Side By Side By Sondheim, 1978-79, My Fair Lady, 1978, 81-82, Rocky Horror Show, 1979-80, Gingerbread Man, 1979, Oklahoma, 1980; also tours various shows to Can., Republic S. Africa, Ireland, Scandinavia, Australia, U.S.A. Decorated knight of the Brit. Empire. Fellow St. Catherine's Coll. (hon., Oxford); mem. Soc. West End Theatres (exec. officer), Dramatists League, League Am. Theaters, Am. Dramatists Guild. Address: 1 Bedford Sq, London England WC1B 3RA also: 1650 Broadway Ste 800 New York NY 10019

MACKINTOSH, FREDERICK ROY, oncologist; b. Miami, Fla., Oct. 4, 1943; s. John Harris and Mary Carlotta (King) MacK.; m. Judith Jane Parnell, Oct. 2, 1961 (div. Aug. 1977); children: Lisa Lynn, Wendy Sue; m. Claudia Lizanne Flournoy, Jan. 7, 1984; 1 child, Gregory Warren. BS, MIT, 1964, PhD, 1968; MD, U. Miami, 1976. Intern then resident in gen. medicine Stanford (Calif.) U., 1976-78, fellow in oncology, 1978-81; asst. prof. med. U. Nev., Reno, 1981-85, assoc. prof., 1985-92, prof. medicine, 1992—. Contbr. articles to profl. jours. Fellow ACP; mem. Am. Soc. Clin. Oncology, Am. Cancer Soc. (pres. Nev. chpt. 1987-89, Washoe chpt. 1988-90), No. Nev. Cancer Coun. (bd. dirs. 1981-92), No. Calif. Cancer Program (bd. dirs. alt. 1983-87, bd. dirs. 1987-91). Avocation: bicycling. Office: Nev Med Group 781 Mill St Reno NV 89502-1320

MACKIW, VLADIMIR NICHOLAUS, metallurgical consultant; b. Stanislawiw, Western Ukraine, Sept. 4, 1923; came to Can., 1948, naturalized, 1953; s. Timothy and Irene (Iwanyckyj) M.; m. Bohdanna Irene Kebuz, Nov. 24, 1951. Dipl. Chemist, Univs. Breslau and Erlangen, Germany, 1946; postgrad., U. Louvain, Belgium, 1948; DSc (hon.), U. Alta., Edmonton, 1976. Chemist Lingman Lake Gold Mines, Winnipeg, Man., Can., 1948; with Man. Provincial Bur. Mines, 1949; research chemist Sherritt Gordon Mines Ltd., Toronto, Ont., Can., 1949, dir. research, 1952, dir. research and devel. div., 1955-68, dir., 1964, v.p., 1967, v.p. tech. and corp. devel., 1968-72, exec. v.p., 1972-88; cons. Toronto, 1988—; chmn. Nickel Devel. Inst., Toronto, 1984-86; mem. Nat. Research Council Can., 1971-77; former mem. Nat. Adv. Com. on Mining and Metall. Research; mem. adv. com. to minister energy, mines and resources, 1972-79, co-chmn., 1975-79; presented tech. papers and lectures Federal Republic of Germany, Belgium, Japan, Peoples Republic of China, Australia, Canada, Ukraine, U.S.; participated in fed. gov. tech. missions to USSR, Belgium, Peoples Republic of China. Contbr. articles to profl. jours.; patentee in field. Recipient Jules Garnier prize Metall. Soc. France, 1966, Gold medal Instn. Mining and Metallurty, London, 1977, fellow award TMS, 1994. Fellow Can. Acad. Engring. (life), Can. Inst. Mining and Metallurgy (Inco Platinum medal 1966, Airey award 1972), Chem. Inst. Can. (R.S. Jane Meml. award 1967); mem. AIME (James Douglas Gold medal 1991), Can. Rsch. Mgmt. Assn. (R&D Mgmt. award 1990, Shevchenko Gold medal Ukranian Can. Congress), Am. Powder Metallurgy Inst., Am. Soc. Metallurgy Internat. (lectr. Can. chpts. 1990-91), Assn. Profl. Engrs. Alta., Soc. Chem. Industry (Can. sect.), Shevchenco Sci. Soc. Can. (pres.), Ont. Club. Ukrainian Catholic. Home: 9 Blair Athol Crescent, Toronto, ON Canada M9A 1X6

MACKLEM, MICHAEL KIRKPATRICK, publisher; b. Toronto, Ont., Can., July 12, 1928; s. Hedley Clark and Mary Eileen (Kirkpatrick) M.; m. Anne Woodburne Hardy, Dec. 30, 1950; children—Timothy Street, Nicholas Hardy. B.A., U. Toronto, 1950; A.M. (Charles Scribner fellow), Princeton U., 1952, Ph.D. (Porter Ogden Jacobus fellow, Royal Soc. Can. fellow), 1954. Instr., English Yale U., New Haven, 1954-55; staff editor Ency. Canadiana, 1955-58; asst. to dir. Humanities Research Council of Can., 1958-60; gen. mgr. Oberon Press, Ottawa, Ont., 1966-85; pres. Michael, Hardy, Ltd., Ottawa, 1972—. Author: The Anatomy of the World: Relations Between Natural and Moral Law from Donne to Pope, 1958, God Have Mercy: The Life of John Fisher of Rochester, 1967, Cinderella, 1969,

Voyages to New France 1615-1618, 1970, Voyages to New France 1599-1603, 1971, The Sleeping Beauty, 1973, Jacques the Woodcutter, 1977, Liberty and the Holy City, 1978. Can. Council fellow, 1964-65. Home: 555 Maple Ln, Ottawa, ON Canada K1M 0N7 Office: Oberon Press, 400-350 Sparks St, Ottawa, ON Canada K1R 7S8

MACKLER, TINA, artist; b. London; d. Leon and Ethel Mackler; 1 dau., Leonore Bloom. Student, Arts Students League, N.Y.C., Indsl. Sch. Design, N.Y.C., New Sch., N.Y.C. Tchr. art Nat. Acad. Ballet, N.Y.C., 1966-69; tchr. adults West Side YMCA, N.Y.C.; asst. studio instr. Met. Mus. Art, N.Y.C., vol. program, 1990—. Illustrator: Informal Dictionary of Ballet, co-author, illustrator: To Dance, To Live; pub. Dance Horizons, 1977; one-person exhbns. Alfred Valente Gallery, N.Y.C., 1967, Mus. Performing Arts, Lincoln Ctr., N.Y.C., 1973, Adelphi U., L.I., N.Y., 1975, Phila. Art Alliance, 1976, Jackson (Miss.) Mus. Art, 1978, Northeastern U., Boston, 1980; exhibited in group shows Alfredo Gallery, N.Y.C., 1964, 1966, Dutchess Hall Gallery, Poughkeepsie, N.Y., 1969, Wright/Hepburn/Webster Gallery, N.Y.C., 1960, 70, N.Y. Pub. Library, 1973, O'Keefe Centre, Ont., Can., 1974, Ball State U., 1974, N.A.D. annual, 1974, Audubon Artists Annual, 1975, Nat. Pastel Show, 1975, Commedia Dell Art Adelphi U., 1974, Guild Gallery, N.Y.C., 1978, Dance Collections, Lincoln Ctr., N.Y.C., 1991, Jackson Miss. Mus., 1994; works represented in permanent collections Nat. Collection Fine Prints, Smithsonian Instn., Washington, Israel Mus., Jerusalem, La Jolla (Calif.) Mus., U. Wis. Mus., Circus World Mus., Baraboo, Wis., Fairleigh Dickinson U., Circus Hall of Fame Mus., Sarasota, Fla., Adelphi U., Creative Dance Found. For Negro Arts, Tuskegee, Ala., Mus. Performing Arts Lincoln Center, N.Y.C., Jackson (Miss.) Mus. Art, Original Print Collectors Group Ltd., Northeastern U., also notable pvt. collections, Am. and abroad; completed series of studies on Spanish dance and impressions of Spain for Spanish Ministry Info. and Tourism, 1976, 88; represented in original stone lithographs of Rudolf Nureyev, Marcel Marceau, Margot Fonteyn and numerous dance soloists, N.Y. Times Mag., also nat. mags., 1975-78; History of International Art, Accademia Italia; works profiled Joe Franklin TV Show, 1979; represented in Works shown on TV NBC-TV preview, Mus. Performing Arts, Lincoln Center, 1973, Channel 13 TV Art Auction, 1978, 79, 80, 81, 82, 83; Meml. for Dame Margot Fonteyn oil painting; portrait of Margot Fonteyn & Rudolf Nureyev exhibited Lincoln Ctr. for Performing Arts, 1991; exhbn. ballet art with USA Internat. Ballet Competition, Jackson, Miss., 1994. Mem. Woman's Fedn. for World Peace, 1995—, artist Christmas card. Prints selected for promotional use Texaco, 1979; named to nat. Mus. Women in Arts, 1996. Home: 25 Central Park W New York NY 10023-7253 *I have long felt the influence which the arts exert on the minds and hearts of mankind. Believing, as I do, that the world today stands in need of spiritual truths, ideals and moral standards, it is my desire to reach out and set before the public some of the beauty and grandeur which reside in the human soul and expresses itself through that most primal art - the dance.*

MACKLIN, CROFFORD JOHNSON, JR., lawyer; b. Columbus, Ohio, Sept. 10, 1947; s. Crofford Johnson, Sr. and Dorothy Ann (Stevens) M.; m. Mary Carole Ward, July 5, 1969; children—Carrie E., David J. B.A., Ohio State U., 1969; B.A. summa cum laude, U. West Fla., 1974; J.D. cum laude, Ohio State U., 1976. Bar: Ohio 1977, U.S. Tax Ct. 1978. Acct., Touche Ross, Columbus, 1976-77; assoc. Smith & Schnacke, Dayton, 1977-81; ptnr. Porter, Wright, Morris & Arthur, Dayton, 1983-88; shareholder Smith & Schnacke, 1988-89; ptnr. Thompson, Hine & Flory, 1989—; sole practice, Dayton, 1981-82; adj. faculty Franklin U., 1977; adj. prof. U. Dayton Law Sch., 1981. Contbr. articles to profl. jours. Bd. dirs. Great Lakes Nat. Bank Ohio, 1997—, Easter Seals, 1984-86. Served to capt. USMCR, 1969-74. Fellow Am. Coll. Trust and Estate Counsel; Emem. Dayton Bar Assn. (chmn. probate com. 1981-83), Dayton Trust & Estate Planning (pres. 1983-84), Ohio Bar Assn., ABA. Presbyterian. Home: 3 Forest Pl Glendale OH 45246-4407 Office: Thompson Hine & Flory 2000 Courthouse Pla NE PO Box 8801 Dayton OH 45401-8801

MACKLIN, F. DOUGLAS, bishop. Bishop Ch. of God in Christ, Memphis. Office: Ch of God in Christ 938 Mason St Memphis TN 38126-5219*

MACKLIN, PHILIP ALAN, physics educator; b. Richmond Hill, N.Y., Apr. 13, 1925; s. Egbert Chalmer and Margaret Griswold (Collins) M.; m. Cora Baldwin Galindo, Sept. 5, 1953; children: Susan, Steven, Peter. B.S. cum laude, Yale U., 1944; M.A., Columbia U., 1949, Ph.D., 1956. Physicist Carbide & Carbon Chems. Corp., Oak Ridge, 1946-47; research scientist AEC, Columbia U., 1949-51; instr. physics Middlebury Coll., Vt., 1951-54; acting chmn. dept. Middlebury Coll., 1953-54; mem. faculty Miami U., Oxford, Ohio, 1954—; prof. physics Miami U., 1961-93, chmn. dept., 1972-85, prof. emeritus, 1993—; research scientist Armco Steel Co., summers 1955-56; vis. prof. U. N.Mex., summers 1957-68, Boston U., fall 1985-86; physicist Los Alamos Sci. Labs., summers 1960-62; participant NSF summer insts., 1970-71; vis. scientist MIT, 1985-86. Author publs. in field. Vestryman Holy Trinity Episcopal Ch., Oxford , 1959-61, 67, 71-73, 75-77, mem. fin. com., chmn. blood assurance program, 1980—, lector, 1989—. With USN, 1944-46. Mem. AAAS, AAUP, LWV of Oxford (treas. 1986-88), Am. Phys. soc., Forum Physics and Soc., Am. Assn. Physics Tchrs., Kiwanis (bd. dirs. 1994—), Torch Club of Butler County (pres. 1982-83, 96-97), 1809 Club (pres. 1964-65), Campus Ministry Ctr. (trustee 1994—), Union of Concerned Scientists, Ctr. for Voting and Democracy (charter), Phi Beta Kappa, Sigma Xi, Sigma Pi Sigma, Omicron Delta Kappa. Democrat. Achievements include patents in field. Home: 211 Oakhill Dr Oxford OH 45056-2710 Office: 117 Culler Hall Miami Univ Oxford OH 45056

MACKLIN, RUTH, bioethics educator; b. Newark, Mar. 27, 1938; d . Hyman and Frieda (Yaruss) Chimacoff; m. Martin Macklin, Sept. 1, 1957 (div. June 1969): children: Meryl, Shelley Macklin Taylor. BA with distinction, Cornell U., 1958; MA in Philosophy, Case Western Res. U., 1966, PhD in Philosophy, 1968. Instr. in philosophy Case Western Res. U., Cleve., 1967-68, asst. prof., 1968-71, assoc. prof., 1971-76; assoc. for behavioral studies The Hastings Ctr., Hastings-on-Hudson, N.Y., 1976-80; vis. assoc. prof. Albert Einstein Coll. Medicine, Bronx, N.Y., 1977-78, assoc. prof., 1978-84, prof. dept. epidemiology and social medicine, 1984—; cons. NIH, 1986—; advisor WHO, Geneva, 1989—; mem. White House Adv. Com. on Human Radiation Experiments, Washington, 1994-96. Author: Man, Mind and Morality, 1982, Mortal Choices, 1987, Enemies of Patients, 1993, Surrogates and Other Mothers, 1994; contbr. articles to ethics, law and med. jours. Fellow The Hastings Ctr., Inst. Medicine of NAS, Am. Philos. Assn. (life), Am. Pub. Health Assn., Am. Soc. Law, Medicine and Ethics; mem. Internat. Assn. Bioethics (bd. dirs.), Am. Assn. Bioethics (bd. dirs.), Phi Beta Kappa. Democrat. Office: A Einstein Coll Medicine Dept Epidemiology & Social Medicine 1300 Morris Park Ave Bronx NY 10461-1926

MACKNIGHT, WILLIAM JOHN, chemist, educator; b. N.Y.C., May 5, 1936; s. William John and Margaret Ann (Stuart) M.; m. Carol Marie Bernier, Aug. 19, 1967. B.S., Rochester U., N.Y., 1958; M.A., Princeton U., N.J., 1963, Ph.D., 1964. Research assoc. Princeton U., N.J., 1964-65; asst. prof. chemistry U. Mass., Amherst, 1965-69, assoc. prof. chemistry, 1969-74, prof. chemistry, 1974-76, dept. head polymer sci., 1976-85, prof. polymer sci. and engring., 1985-88, 95-96, head dept. polymer sci. & engring., 1988-95, disting. univ. prof., 1996—; mem. sci. and tech. adv. bd. Alcoa, Pitts., 1984-86, Diversitech Gen., Akron, Ohio, 1985—; mem. panel for materials sci. Nat. Bur. Standards, Washington, 1983-89. Author: Polymeric Sulfur and Related Polymers, 1965; Introduction to Polymer Viscoelasticity, 2d edit., 1983. Served to lt. USN, 1958-61. Recipient Ford prize in high polymer physics Am. Phys. Soc., 1984; Guggenheim fellow, 1985. Fellow AAAS, Am. Phys. Soc. (exec. com. 1975-76); mem. Am. Chem. Soc. (award in polymer chemistry 1997), Am. Soc. Rheology, Cosmos Club. Avocations: music, sports. Home: 127 Sunset Ave Amherst MA 01002-2019 Office: U Mass Polymer Sci & Engring Dept Conte Bldg Amherst MA 01003

MACKOVIC, JOHN, college football coach, athletic director; b. Barberton, Ohio, Oct. 1, 1943; m. Arlene Francis; children: Aimee, John. BA in Spanish, Wake Forest U., 1965; MEd in Secondary Sch. Adminstrn., Miami U., Oxford, Ohio, 1966. Various coaching positions, 1965-72; offensive backfield coach U. Ariz., Tucson, 1973-74; offensive coord. U. Ariz., 1974-75, asst. head coach, 1976; asst. head coach, offensive coord. Purdue U., West Lafayette, Ind., 1976-78; head football coach Wake Forest U., Winston-Salem, N.C., 1978-81; asst. football coach Dallas Cowboys, 1981-83; head football coach Kansas City (Mo.) Chiefs, 1983-87; head football coach U. Ill., 1988-92, dir. of athletics, 1988-92; head coach football U. Tex., Austin, 1992—. Address: PO Box 7399 Austin TX 78713-7399*

MACKOWSKI, JOHN JOSEPH, retired insurance company executive; b. Westport, Mass., Feb. 1, 1926; s. John J. and Victoria K. (Skript) Mieczkowski; m. Ruth Williams, Feb. 3, 1951; children: Martha, John Matthew, Daniel, Joan. AB, Duke U., 1948; student, Harvard Advanced Mgmt. Program, 1970, 71. With Ins. Co. of N.Am., Boston, Phila., Chgo., 1948-51; with Atlantic Mut. Ins. Co., N.Y.C., 1951-88, chmn., CEO, to 1988; bd. dirs. F.W. Woolworth Co., No. Trust Co. Conn., Transatlantic Holdings, Inc. Bd. dirs. Seamen's Ch. Inst. N.Y. and N.J. 1st lt. USMCR, 1943-46. Mem. Sawgrass Club (Ponte Vedra Beach, Fla.), Acoaxet Country Club (Westport Harbor, Mass.), Spindle Rock Yacht Club, Sigma Chi, Beta Lambda. Episcopalian. Home: 33 Widgeon Ln Little Compton RI 02837-1960 Other Home: 1506 Birkdale Ln Ponte Vedra Beach FL 32082-3500

MACLACHLAN, DOUGLAS LEE, marketing educator; b. Hollywood, Calif., Aug. 27, 1940; s. Alexander D. and Patricia E. (Culver) MacL.; m. Natalie Bowditch Knauth, July 23, 1966; children: Heather Bowditch, Trevor Douglas. A.B. in Physics, U. Calif., Berkeley, 1962, M.B.A., 1965, M.A. in Stats., 1970, Ph.D. in Bus. Adminstrn, 1971; student, Hastings Sch. Law, 1965-66. Instr. bus. adminstrn. U. Calif., Berkeley, 1969-70; v.p. Hartec Corp., Newport Beach, Calif., 1965-70; acting asst. prof. U. Wash., Seattle, 1970-71, asst. prof., 1971-74, assoc. prof., 1974-78, prof., chmn. dept. mktg. and internat. bus., 1978-86, prof., acting chair dept. mktg. and internat. bus., 1993-94, Affiliate Program Disting. prof. mktg. and internat. bus., 1986-88, Nordstrom prof. retail mktg., 1988-89, Ford Motor Co. prof. mktg., 1989-90, assoc. dean, 1995—; vis. prof. bus. adminstrn. U. Calif., Berkeley, summer 1974; vis. prof. Institu Européen des Affaires, Fontainebleau, France, 1982-83, Cath. U. Leuven, Belgium, 1991-92; dir. Univ. Book Store, 1985—. Contbr. articles profl. jours.; editorial bd.: Jour. Mktg. Research, 1975-81. Mem. Am. Mktg. Assn. (dir. Puget Sound chpt. 1975-77, 90-91, pres. 1978-79), Inst. Mgmt. Scis., Am. Statis. Assn., Am. Inst. Decision Scis., Assn. Consumer Research, Alpha Kappa Psi, Kappa Delta Rho. Home: 16305 Inglewood Rd NE Bothell WA 98011-3908 Office: Box 353200 University Of Washington Seattle WA 98195-3200

MACLACHLAN, GORDON ALISTAIR, biology educator, researcher; b. Saskatoon, Sask., Can., June 30, 1930; s. Hector Ross and Nellie (Glass) M.; m. Sarah Dangerfield, June 26, 1959; children: Mary, Anna. B.A., U. Sask., 1952, M.A., 1954; Ph.D., U. Man., 1956. NRC postdoctoral fellow Imperial Coll., London, 1956-59; asst. prof. U. Alta., Edmonton, 1960-62; assoc. prof. biology McGill U., Montreal, 1962-69, prof., 1970—, chmn. dept., 1970-75, 95, dean. grad. studies, vice prin. rsch., 1980-90. Assoc. editor Can. Jour. Botany, 1980-86; editor Jour. Plant Molecular Biology, 1988-90. Commonwealth prof. Australia, 1975. Mem. Can. Soc. Plant Physiologists (pres. 1973). Home: 561 Argyle Ave, Westmount, PQ Canada H3Y 3B8 Office: McGill U Biology Dept, 1205 Penfield Ave, Montreal, PQ Canada H3A 1B1

MACLACHLAN, PATRICIA, author; b. Cheyenne, Wyo., Mar. 3, 1938; d. Philo and Madonna (Moss) Pritzkau; m. Robert MacLachlan, Apr. 14, 1962; children: John, Jamie, Emily. BA, U. Conn., 1962. Tchr. English Bennett Jr. High Sch., Manchester, Conn., 1963-79; vis. lectr. Smith Coll., Northampton, Mass., 1986—. Author: The Sick Day, 1979, Arthur, for the Very First Time, 1980 (Golden Kite award Soc. Children's Book Writers 1980), Moon, Stars, Frogs, and Friends, 1980, Through Grandpa's Eyes, 1980, Cassie Binegar, 1982, Mama One, Mama Two, 1982, Tomorrow's Wizard, 1982, Seven Kisses in a Row, 1983, Unclaimed Treasures, 1984 (Boston Globe/Horn Book award 1984), Sarah, Plain and Tall, 1985 (Golden Kite award 1985, Scott O'Dell Historical Fiction award 1985, John Newbery medal 1986, Jefferson Cup award Va. Libr. Assn. 1986, Christopher award 1986, Garden State Children's Book award N.J. Libr. Assn. 1988), The Facts and Fictions of Minna Pratt, 1988 (Parent's Choice award Parent's Choice Found. 1988), Three Names, 1991, Journey, 1991, All the Places to Love, 1993, Baby, 1993, Skylark, 1994. Bd. dirs. Children's Aid Family Svc. Agency, 1970-80. recipient numerous awards for children's fiction. *

MACLAGAN, JOHN LYALL, retired petroleum company executive; b. Lethbridge, Alta., Can., Oct. 26, 1929; s. Frederick Alexander Lyall and Dora Ellen (Dean) M.; m. Joan Lily Prince, July 15, 1965; 1 dau., Susan. B.Commerce, U. Alta., 1952. Chartered accountant, Alta. Staff auditor Price Waterhouse & Co., Calgary, 1952-56; accountant Union Oil Co. of Calif., Alta., 1956-61; mgr. accounting Union Oil Co. of Can., Ltd., Calgary, 1961-72; treas., comptroller Union Oil Co. of Can., Ltd., 1972-75, v.p. fin., treas., 1975-82; v.p. fin. Omega Hydrocarbons Ltd., Calgary, 1982-94; ret., 1994. Mem. Can. Inst. Chartered Accts. Club: Calgary Petroleum. Home: 308 Roxborough Rd SW, Calgary, AB Canada T2S 0R4

MACLAINE, ALLAN HUGH, English language educator; b. Montreal, Can., Oct. 24, 1924. B.A., McGill U., 1945; Ph.D. in English, Brown U., 1951. Instr. English McGill U., 1946-47, Brown U., 1947-50, U. Mass., 1951-54; from asst. prof. to prof. Tex. Christian U., 1954-62; prof. English U. R.I., 1962—, also dean div. univ. extension, 1967-71. Author: Student's Comprehensive Guide to the Canterbury Tales, 1964, Robert Fergusson, 1965, Allan Ramsay, 1985, The Christis Kirk Tradition: Scots Poems of Folk Festivity, 1996; also articles. Mem. Coll. English Assn. (pres. 1965, dir. 1961-66), Assn. for Scottish Literary Studies. Office: U Rhode Island Dept English Kingston RI 02881

MACLAINE, SHIRLEY, actress; b. Richmond, Va., Apr. 24, 1934; d. Ira O. and Kathlyn (MacLean) Beatty; m. Steve Parker, Sept. 17, 1954 (div.); 1 child, Stephanie Sachiko. Ed. high sch. Appearances include (Broadway plays) Me and Juliet, 1953, Pajama Game, 1954, (films) The Trouble With Harry, 1954, Artists and Models, 1954, Around the World in 80 Days, 1955-56, Hot Spell, 1957, The Matchmaker, 1957, The Sheepman, 1957, Some Came Running, 1958 (Fgn. Press award 1959), Ask Any Girl, 1959 (Silver Bear award as best actress Internat. Berlin Film Festival), Career, 1959, Can-Can, 1959, The Apartment, 1959 (Best Actress prize Venice Film Festival), Children's Hour, 1960, The Apartment, 1960, Two for the Seesaw, 1962, Irma La Douce, 1963, What A Way to Go, The Yellow Rolls Royce, 1964, John Goldfarb Please Come Home, 1965, Gambit and Woman Times Seven, 1967, The Bliss of Mrs. Blossom, Sweet Charity, 1969, Two Mules for Sister Sara, 1969, Desperate Characters, 1971, The Possession of Joel Delaney, 1972, The Other Half of the Sky: A China Memoir, 1975, The Turning Point, 1977, Being There, 1979, A Change of Seasons, 1980, Loving Couples, 1980, Terms of Endearment, 1983 (Acad. award 1984, Golden Globe-Best Actress), Cannonball Run II, 1984, Madame Sousatzka, 1988 (Best Actress Venice Film Festival, Golden Globe-Best Actress), Steel Magnolias, 1989, Waiting For the Light, 1990, Postcards From the Edge, 1990, Defending Your Life, 1991, Used People, 1992, Wrestling Ernest Hemingway, 1993, Guarding Tess, 1994, Evening Star, 1995, Mrs. Winterbourne, 1996; (TV shows) Shirley's World, 1971-72, Shirley MacLaine: If They Could See Me Now, 1974-75, Gypsy in My Soul, 1975-76, Where Do We Go From Here?, 1976-77, Shirley MacLaine at the Lido, 1979, Shirley MacLaine...Every Little Movement, 1980 (Emmy award 1980), (TV movie) Out On A Limb, 1987; prodr., co-dir. documentary: China The Other Half of the Sky; star U.S. tour stage musical Out There Tonight, 1990; author: Don't Fall Off the Mountain, 1970, The New Celebrity Cookbook, 1973, You Can Get There From Here, 1975, Out on a Limb, 1983, Dancing in the Light, 1985, It's All in the Playing, 1987, Going Within: A Guide for Inner Transformation, 1989, Dance While You Can, 1991; editor: McGovern: The Man and His Beliefs, 1972. *

MACLANE, SAUNDERS, mathematician, educator; b. Taftville, Conn., Aug. 4, 1909; s. Donald Bradford and Winifred (Saunders) MacL.; m. Dorothy M. Jones, July 21, 1933. (dec. Feb. 1985); children: Margaret Ferguson, Cynthia M. Hay; m. Osa Skotting Segal, Aug. 16, 1986. PhB, Yale U., 1930; AM, U. Chgo., 1931; DPhil, Goettingen, Fed. Republic Germany, 1934; DSc (hon.), Purdue U., 1965, Yale U., 1969, Coe Coll., 1973, U. Pa., 1977, Union Coll., 1990; LLD (hon.), Glasgow U., Scotland, 1971. Sterling Research fellow Yale U., 1933-34; Benjamin Peirce instr. Harvard U., 1934-36; instr. Cornell U., 1936-37, U. Chgo., 1937-38; asst. prof. Harvard U., 1938-41, assoc. prof., 1941-46, prof., 1946-47; prof. math. U. Chgo., 1947-63, chmn. dept., 1952-58, Max Mason Disting. Service prof. of math., 1963-82, prof. emeritus, 1982—; exec. com. mem. Internat. Math. Union, 1954-58; research mathematician Applied Math. Group, Columbia, 1943-44, dir., 1944-45; Mem. Nat. Sci. Bd., 1974-80. Author: (with Garrett Birkhoff) Survey of Modern Algebra, 1942, Homology, 1963, Algebra, 1967, Categories for the Working Mathematician, 1971, Mathematics: Form and Function, 1985, (with I. Moerdijk) Sheaves in Geometry and Logic, A First Introduction to Topos Theory, 1992; editor: Bull. Am. Math. Soc., 1943-46, mng. editor, 1946-47; editor: Trans. Am. Math. Soc., 1949-54; chmn. editorial com., editor Carus Math. Monographs, 1940-45; contbr. articles to Annals Math., other jours. Recipient Nat. Medal of Sci. Nat. Sci. Found., 1989; John Simon Guggenheim fellow, 1947-48, 72-73. Mem. Am. Math. Soc. (coun. mem. 1939-41, v.p. 1946-47, pres. 1973-74, Leroy P. Steele prize 1986), Math. Assn. Am. (v.p. 1948-49, pres. 1950-52, Chauvenet prize for math. expn. 1941, Disting. Svc. award 1975, Proctor prize 1979), Nat. Acad. Sci. (coun. mem. 1958-61, 69-72, v.p. 1973-81, chmn. editorial bd. procs. 1960-68), Royal Danish Acad. Scis. (fgn. mem.), Am. Philos. Soc. (mem. council 1960-63, v.p. 1968-71), Akademie der Wissenschaften (Heidelberg), Royal Soc. Edinburgh, Assn. for Symbolic Logic (exec. com. 1945-47), Am. Acad. Arts and Sci. (coun. mem. 1981-85), Phi Beta Kappa, Sigma Xi. Congregationalist. Home: 5712 S Dorchester Ave Chicago IL 60637-1727

MAC LAREN, DAVID SERGEANT, manufacturing corporation executive, inventor; b. Cleve., Jan. 4, 1941; s. Albert Sergeant and Theadora Beidler (Potter) MacL.; children: Alison, Catherine, Carolyn. AB in Econs., Miami U., Oxford, Ohio, 1964. Chmn. bd., pres., Jet Inc., Cleve., 1967—; founder, chmn. bd., pres. Air Injector Corp., Cleve., 1966-78; founder, pres., chmn. bd. Fluid Equipment, Inc., Cleve., 1966-72; founder, chmn. bd., pres. T&M Co., Cleve., 1966-71, Alison Realty Co., Cleve., 1966—; chmn. bd., pres. Sergeant Realty, Inc., 1979-86; bd. dirs. Gilmore Industries, Cleve., 1975-77, MWL Systems, L.A., 1979-85; mem. tech. com. Nat. Sanitation Found., Ann Arbor, Mich., 1967-90. Patentee in field. Mem. Rep. State Cen. Com., 1968-72; bd. dirs. Cleve. State U. Found., 1986-90. Served with arty. AUS, 1964-66. Fellow Royal Soc. Health (London); mem. Nat. Environ. Health Assn., Am. Pub. Health Assn., Nat. Water Pollution Control Fedn., Cen. Taekwondo Assn. (2d Dan), Jiu-Jitsu/Karati Black Belt Fedn. (black belt instr.), Mercedes Benz Club N.Am. (pres. 1968), H.B. Leadership Soc. (sch. headmaster soc., devel. com. 1976-78), SAR, Soc. Mayflower Descendants, Delta Kappa Epsilon (nat. bd. dirs. 1974-86, dir. Kappa chpt. 1969—), Mentor Harbor Yachting Club, The Country Club, Cotillion Soc., Union League Club (N.Y.C.), Yale Club (N.Y.C.), Deke Club (N.Y.C.), N.Y. Acad. Scis. Home: West Hill Dr Gates Mills OH 44040 Office: Jet Inc 750 Alpha Dr Cleveland OH 44143-2125

MACLAREN, NOEL KEITH, pathologist, pediatrician, educator; b. New Zealand, July 28, 1939; naturalized U.S. citizen, 1986; MD, U. Otago. Resident Cook Hosp., Gisborne; resident Wellington (New Zealand) Hosp., from sr. resident to sr. registrar medicine and pediatrics, 1965-68; resident med. officer Queen Elizabeth Hosp. for Sick Children, London, 1969; cons. in pediatrics and internal medicine Gulf Oil Co., Kuwait, 1970-72; fellow in pediatric endocrinology and metabolism U. Md. Sch. Medicine and John's Hopkins Hosp., Balt., 1972-73; asst. prof. pediatric endocrinology and metabolism U. Md. Sch. Medicine, 1973-74, assoc. prof. pediatrics, dir. endocrinology and metabolism, 1975-78; dir. clin. chemistry Shands Tchg. Hosp., Gainesville, Fla., 1978-86; prof. pathology and pediatrics U. Fla. Coll. Medicine, Gainesville, 1978-97, chmn. dept. pathology, 1988-96; prof. comparative and experimental pathology U. Fla. Coll. Vet. Medicine, Gainesville, 1990-97; dir. Rsch. Inst. for Children, Children's Hosp., New Orleans, 1997—; prof. pediatrics La. State U. Sch. of Medicine, 1997—. Mem. editl. bd. Diabetes Care, 1986-89, Regional Immunology, 1987—, Autoimmunology, 1987—; reviewer numerous jours.; patentee in field; contbr. over 300 articles to jours. and books in field. Mem. med. adv. bd. Juvenile Diabetes Found., 1977-80, 95—; mem. sci. adv. bd. Nat. Coalition on Immune System Disorders, 1986-95; mem. immunobiology study sect. NIH, 1988-94; mem. Internat. Diabetes Found., 1989—; pres. Internat. Diabetes Immunotherapy Group, 1990-94. Recipient Mary Jane Kugel award for Diabetes Rsch., Juvenile Diabetes Assn., 1990, David Rumbaugh award, 1995, Connaught Novo Nordisk award Internat. Canadian Diabetes Assn., 1994, Rsch. Recognition award Am. Diabetes Assn., 1995. Mem. AMA, AAAS, Am. Acad. Pediatrics, Am. Diabetes Assn. (mem. sci. adv. bd. 1986-89), Am. Endocrine Soc., Am. Pediatric Soc., Am. Soc. Clin. Pathologists, Am. Soc. Histocompatibility and Immunogenetics, Am. Soc. Pathology, Internat. Assn. Pathologists, Acad. Clin. Lab. Physicians and Scientists, Assn. Pathology Chairs, Clin. Immunology Soc., Lawson Wilkins Pediatric Endocrine Soc., Soc. Pediatric Rsch., Alpha Omega Alpha Med. Soc.

MACLAREN, ROY, Canadian government official, publisher; b. Vancouver, B.C., Can., Oct. 26, 1934; s. Wilbur and Anne (Graham) MacL.; m. Alethea Mitchell, June 25, 1959; children: Ian, Vanessa, Malcolm. BA, U. B.C., 1955; MA, U. Cambridge, Eng., 1957; postgrad., Harvard U., 1974; MDiv, U. Toronto, 1991; DSL honoris causa, U. toronto, 1996. Fgn. service officer Can. Diplomatic Service, Vietnam, Czechoslovakia, Switzerland, UN, 1957-69; dir. corporate pub. affairs Massey-Ferguson Ltd., Toronto, Ont., 1969-74; chmn., chief exec. officer Ogilvy & Mather, Can., Toronto, 1974-76; chmn. C.B. Media Ltd., 1976-93; mem. Toronto Planning Bd., 1974-76; mem. Parliament of Can., 1979-84, 88-96, parliamentary sec. to minister energy, mines and resources, 1980-82, minister of state (fin.), 1983-84, minister of nat. revenue, 1984—, minister of internat. trade, 1993-96; high commr. for Can. to U.K. of Gt. Britain and No. Ireland, 1996—; spl. lectr. U. Toronto, 1970-76; chmn. Can. Govt. Task Force on Rels. Between Govt. and Bus., 1976. Author: Canadians in Russia, 1918-19, 1976, Canadians on the Nile, 1882-1898, 1978, Canadians Behind Enemy Lines, 1939-1945, 1981, Honourable Mentions, 1986, African Exploits: The Diaries of William Stairs, 1997; contbr. articles to jours. Hon. col. 7th Toronto Regt., Royal Can. Arty. Fellow Royal Soc. Arts; mem. Royal Can. Yacht Club, Rideau Club (Ottawa), White's Club (London), Toronto Club. Address: High Commr for Canada, 1 Grosvenor Sq, London England W1X 0AB

MACLAUCHLIN, ROBERT KERWIN, communications artist, educator; b. Framingham, Mass., Oct. 8, 1931; s. Charles Lewis and Elinor Frances (Kerwin) MacL.; m. Elizabeth D'Ann Willson, June 13, 1964. BA in Sociology, U. Mass., Amherst, 1954; MEd, Bridgewater State Coll., 1958; MS in Radio and TV, Syracuse U., 1959; PhD in Speech, Radio, TV, Mich. State U., 1969. Personnel trainee Nat. Security Agy., Washington, 1954-55; elem. sch. tchr. Mattapoisett (Mass.) Pub. Schs., 1957-58; asst. prof., dir. programming Maine Ednl. TV Network, Orono, 1959-66; assoc. prof. speech communications, dir. TV-Radio instrn. Colo. State U., Ft. Collins, 1969-76, prof., dir. TV-Radio instrn., 1976—; cons. U. Maine, Orono, 1968, Ft. Collins Presbyn. Ch., 1976-78, Sta. KCOL-AM-FM, Ft. Collins, 1978, Pub. Health Assn., Ft. Collins, 1985; archives program guest Maine Pub. Broadcast, Orono, 1983. Served with inf. U.S. Army, 1955-57. Recipient Excellence in Teaching award Mich. State U., 1969, Friend of Broadcasting award Colo. Broadcasters Assn., 1985; named Disting. Vis. Prof. U. Vt., Burlington, 1983, A Teacher Who Makes A Difference Denver's Rocky Mountain News, KCNC-TV, 1987. Mem. NATA (panel Colo. chpt. 1989—), Broadcast Edn. Assn. (Industry State chmn. 1981-86, panel 1991—, chmn. faculty internship com. 1991—), Colo. Broadcasters Assn. (edn. com. 1972—, Hall of Fame com. 1980—, human resources com. 1991, Friends of Broadcast award 1985, panelist summer conv. 1994, panelist summer conv. 1995), Speech Comm. Assn., Broadcast Pioneers (charter Colo. chpt.), Kiwanis (Disting. past pres. 1979-80). Republican. Avocations: outdoor activities. Home: 1407 Country Club Rd Fort Collins CO 80524-1907 Office: Colo State U Dept Speech Communicat Fort Collins CO 80523 *Personal philosophy: Set high goals, enjoy people and laughter, and always seek to give back more to society than you take from it.*

MACLAUGHLIN, FRANCIS JOSEPH, lawyer; b. Davenport, Iowa, Oct. 5, 1933; s. Francis Joseph and Sylvia (Boone) MacL.; m. Joan Elizabeth Pfeiffer, Oct. 17, 1959; children: Lisa Ann, Christine Ann, Francis Joseph. B.A., Yale U., 1955; J.D., U. Mich., 1958. Bar: Ill. 1958, Calif. 1963. Assoc. Graham, Califf, Harper & Benson, Moline, Ill., 1958-59, Lillick, McHose & Charles, Los Angeles, 1963-70; ptnr. Lillick, McHose & Charles, L.A., 1970-90, White and Case, 1990—. Lt. USN, 1959-63. Mem. ABA, Calif. Bar Assn., Los Angeles County Bar Assn., Maritime Law Assn. U.S. Republican. Office: White & Case 633 W 5th St Ste 1900 Los Angeles CA 90071-2027

MACLAUGHLIN, HARRY HUNTER, federal judge; b. Breckenridge, Minn., Aug. 9, 1927; s. Harry Hunter and Grace (Swank) MacL.; m. Mary Jean Shaffer, June 25, 1958; children: David, Douglas. BBA with distinction, U. Minn., 1949, JD, 1956. Bar: Minn. 1956. Law clk. to justice Minn. Supreme Ct.; ptnr. MacLaughlin & Mondale, MacLaughlin & Harstad, Mpls., 1956-72; assoc. justice Minn. Supreme Ct., 1972-77; U.S. sr. dist. judge Dist. of Minn., Mpls., 1977—; part-time instr. William Mitchell Coll. Law, St. Paul, 1958-63; lectr. U. Minn. Law Sch., 1973-86; mem. 8th Cir. Jud. Council, 1981-83. Bd. editors: Minn. Law Rev, 1954-55. Mem. Mpls. Charter Commn., 1967-72, Minn. State Coll. Bd., 1971-72, Minn. Jud. Council, 1972; mem. nat. adv. council Small Bus. Adminstrn., 1967-69. Served with USNR, 1945-46. Recipient U. Minn. Outstanding Achievement award, 1995; named Best Fed. Dist. Ct. Judge in 8th Cir., Am. Lawyer mag., 1983. Mem. ABA, Minn. Bar Assn., Hennepin County Bar Assn., Beta Gamma Sigma, Phi Delta Phi. Congregational. Office: US Dist Ct 684 US Courthouse 110 S 4th St Minneapolis MN 55401-2244

MACLAURY, BRUCE KING, research institution executive; b. Mount Kisco, N.Y., May 7, 1931; s. Bruce King and Edith Mae (Wills) MacL.; m. Virginia Doris Naef, Jan. 8, 1955; children—John, David. B.A., Princeton, 1953; M.A., Harvard, 1958, Ph.D., 1961. Successively mgr., v.p. fgn. dept. Fed. Res. Bank N.Y., N.Y.C., 1958-69; dep. under sec. for monetary affairs U.S. Treasury Dept., Washington, 1969-71; pres. Fed. Res. Bank of Mpls., 1971-77, Brookings Instn., Washington, 1977-95; pres. emeritus Brookings Instn., Wahsington, 1995—; bd. dirs. Am. Express Bank Ltd., Nat. Steel Corp., St. Paul Cos., The Vanguard Group. Trustee Nat. Com. for Econ. Devel., 1978—; mem. Cou on Fgn. Rels., N.Y.C., 1962,; chair emergency trustees D.C. Pub. Schs. Recipient Exceptional Service award U.S. Treasury Dept., 1971. Mem. Phi Beta Kappa, Cosmos. Home: 5109 Yuma Pl NW Washington DC 20016-4309 Office: Brookings Instn 1775 Massachusetts Ave NW Washington DC 20036-2188

MACLAY, DONALD MERLE, lawyer; b. Belleville, Pa., Feb. 16, 1934; s. Robert Barr and Grace Virginia (Royer) M.; m. Nancy Margaret Hixenbaugh, Sept. 13, 1958; children: Susan Jo (dec.), Timothy Dean. A.B. magna cum laude, Grove City Coll., 1956; LL.B., U. Pa., 1961. Bar: D.C. 1968, Pa. 1970. Commd. fgn. svc. officer U.S. Dept. State, 1961; assigned Am. embassy, Cotonou, Dahomey (Benin), 1962-64, Am. Consulate Gen., Frankfurt, Fed. Republic Germany, 1964-66, U.S. Dept. State, Washington, 1966-69; dir. courses of study Am. Law Inst.-ABA Com. on Continuing Profl. Edn., Phila., 1969-87, dep. exec. dir., 1987—. Served with U.S. Army, 1956-58. Mem. ABA, Pa. Bar Assn., Am. Law Inst. Democrat. Presbyterian. Home: 936 Church Rd Springfield PA 19064-3935 Office: Am Law Inst-ABA 4025 Chestnut St Philadelphia PA 19104-3054

MACLAY, WILLIAM NEVIN, retired manufacturing and construction company executive; b. Belleville, Pa., Dec. 30, 1924; s. Robert Barr and Grace Virginia (Royer) M.; m. Betty Jane Boucher, June 4, 1949; children: Gary, Dennis, Rebekah, Bonnie, Beth. B.S. magna cum laude, Juniata Coll., 1947; Ph.D. in Phys. Chemistry, Yale U., 1950. Assoc. prof. chemistry Davis and Elkins Coll., Elkins, W.Va., 1950-51; research scientist B.F. Goodrich Co., Brecksville, Ohio, 1951-59; group mgr. Koppers Co., Inc., Monroeville, Pa., 1959-63, asst. sect. mgr., 1963-67; mgr. comml. devel. Koppers Co., Inc., Pitts., 1967-68; v.p. research Koppers Co., Inc., Monroeville, 1968-85; ret., 1985; dir. Indsl. Health Found., Pitts., 1974-77, Genex Corp., Rockville, Md., 1979-81, Kopvenco, Pitts., Ceramatec, Inc., Salt Lake City, 1981-85, Advanced Refractory Techs., Buffalo, 1984-85. Patentee in field. Deacon, ruling elder Presbyn. Ch., Pitts. Mem. Am. Chem. Soc. Republican. Presbyterian. Home: 539 Greenleaf Dr Monroeville PA 15146-1201

MACLEAN, CHARLES (BERNARD MACLEAN), public affairs and marketing consultant; b. Ann Arbor, Mich., Oct. 12, 1945. BS, Wis. State U., Oshkosh, 1967; MA, Mich. State U., 1969, PhD, 1973. Lic. profl. counselor, Tex. Dir. med. edn. Am. Coll. Emergency Physicians, Lansing, Mich. and Dallas, 1974-81; exec. dir. Soc. Tchrs. of Emergency Medicine, Lansing and Dallas, 1976-81; pres. Applied Foresight, Dallas, Tex., 1979—; ptnr. Inman, Maclean & Gaddy, Dallas, 1983-86; sr. v.p. Club Communities Retirement Ctrs., 1985-86; ptnr., exec. v.p. Metropolitan Retirement Ctrs., 1986-88; pres. Tri-East Ventures, Inc., 1988-90; Mem. Mazama Critical Incident Debriefing Team, Workforce Devel. Task Force. Author: (exec. briefing tapes) M.B.A.-Management by Acknowledgement, Acknowledgement-The Missing Piece in the Total Quality Puzzle, (video tng. package) Can't Happen...Here!, 1994, Workplace Violence, 1994; dir. (video documentary) Accelerated Career Transition for Ex-Military, 10 Virtual Commandments for Innovation; contbr. numerous articles to profl. jours. Chmn. community adv. bd. Youth at Risk, 1988-90; mem. Dallas Mayor's Adv. Com. on Crime, 1989-90, Trillgum Hollow Mktg. Team. Mem. ASTD (v.p. profl. devel. 1982), Assn. for Quality Participation, Nat. Eagle Scout Assn., Software Assn. Oreg., Oreg. Orgnl. Devel. Network, Spirituality in Workplace Grp., Oreg. Ethics Commons, Am. Electronics Assn. Innovation Now! Conf. Task Force, Mazama Critical Incident Stress Debriefing Team, Delta Kappa, Psi Chi, Delta Tau Kappa, Delta Sigma Phi. Office: 9601 NW Leahy Rd Portland OR 97229-6343

MACLEAN, DAVID BAILEY, chemistry educator, researcher; b. Summerside, P.E.I., Can., July 15, 1923; s. William and Lulu Adelaide (Stewart) McL.; m. Helen Shirley Canning, Dec. 28, 1945 (dec. 1950); 1 child, Susan; m. Regina Lane, Sept. 21, 1951; children—David, Richard, Robert, Gillian, stepchildren—Gary Hutton, Dariel Hutton. B.Sc., Acadia U., 1942; Ph.D., McGill U., 1946. Research chemist Dominion Rubber Co., Guelph, Ont., Can., 1946-49; assoc. prof. chemistry N.S. Tech. Coll., Halifax, Can., 1949-54; assoc. prof. chemistry McMaster U., Hamilton, Ont., 1954-60, prof., 1960-89, prof. emeritus, 1989—; mem. Council of Ont. Univs., Toronto, 1982-84. Fellow Royal Soc. Can., Chem. Inst. Can.; mem. Am. Chem. Soc., Am. Soc. Mass Spectroscopy. Home: 394 Queen St S, Hamilton, ON Canada L8P 3T9 Office: McMaster U Dept Chemistry, Main St W, Hamilton, ON Canada L8S 4M1

MACLEAN, DOUG, hockey coach; b. Summerside, P.E.I., Can., Apr. 12, 1954. Student, P.E.I.; M in Ednl. Psychology, We. Ont. Asst. coach London Knights of OHL, 1984-85, St. Louis Blues, 1986-87, 87-88, Washington Capitals, 1988-89, 89-90; asst. coach Detroit Red Wings, 1990-91, asst. gen. mgr., 1992-93, 93-94; gen. mgr. Adirondack, Red Wing orgn., 1992-93, 93-94; dir. player devel., scout Fla. Panthers, 1994-95, head coach, 1995—. Office: Florida Panthers 100 NE 3rd St Fl 10 Fort Lauderdale FL 33301-1047*

MACLEAN, JOHN, professional hockey player; b. Oshawa, Ont., Can., Nov. 20, 1964. Hockey player N.J. Devils, 1983—. Named to Meml. Cup All-Star team, 1982-83; played in NHL All-Star game, 1989, 91; mem. Stanley Cup championship team, 1995. Office: care NJ Devils PO Box 504 East Rutherford NJ 07073

MACLEAN, JOHN ANGUS, former premier of Prince Edward Island; b. Lewes, P.E.I., Can., May 15, 1914; s. George Allen and Sarah MacL.; m. Gwendolyn Esther Burwash, Oct. 29, 1952; children—Sarah Jean, Allan Duart, Mary Esther, Robert Angus. Student, U. B.C., Can.), Vancouver; B.Sc., Mt. Allison U., 1939, LL.D. (hon.), 1958. Farmer Lewes; mem. Can. House of Commons, Ottawa, Ont., 1951-76, Privy Council Can., 1957—; minister of fisheries Govt. Can., 1957-63; mem. P.E.I. Legislature, 1976-82; premier P.E.I., 1979-81. Leader Progressive Conservative Party of P.E.I., 1976-81; del. NATO Parliamentary Conf., Paris, 1956, Commonwealth Parliametary Conf., Wellington, N.Z., 1965, 18th Parliametary Course, Westminster, Eng., 1969; del. Inter-Parliamentary Conf. on European Cooperation and Security, Helsinki, 1973, Belgrade, 1975; leader Can. del. Colombo Plan Conf., Tokyo, 1960, FAO Conf., Rome, 1961; mem. Can.-Japanese Ministerial Del., Tokyo, 1963; Bd. regents Mt. Alison U.; bd. dirs. RCAF Meml. Fund. Served with RCAF, 1939-47; officer Most Venerable Order St. John of Jerusalem at Investiture Ceremony, Rideau Hall, Order of Can. Investiture, Rideau Hall, 1992; former mem. P.E.I. Energy Corp.; sr. adv. bd. Maritime Provinces Edn. Found.; P.E.I.'s Commr. to EXPO' 86; appointed officer of the Order of Can., 1992. Decorated D.F.C.; mentioned in Despatches. Mem. RAF Escaping Soc. (past pres. Can. br.), Commonwealth Parliamentary Assn. (past vice chmn. fed. br.), Mus. Nat. Scis., Nat. Mus. Can. Progressive Conservative. Presbyterian.

MACLEAN, JOHN RONALD, lawyer; b. Pueblo, Colo., Jan. 19, 1938; s. John Ronald and Mary Victoria (Curlin) MacL.; m. Carol Jean Turner, Aug. 18, 1962; children—Leslie Carol, John Ronald. Student, U. Okla., 1956; B.S., U.S. Mil. Acad., 1961; J.D., Vanderbilt U., 1967. Bar: Tex. 1967; cert. in personal injury trial law and criminal law Tex. Bd. Legal Splzn. Practicing atty. Turner & MacLean, Cleburne, Tex., 1967-68; county atty. Johnson County, Tex., 1968-76; dist. atty. 18th Jud. Dist. Tex., 1976-84; dist. judge 249th Jud. Dist. Tex., 1984-91; pvt. practice MacLean & Boulware, 1992—. Pres. Johnson County United Fund, 1976. Served with AUS, 1961-64. Fellow Tex. Bar Found.; mem. Tex. Bar Assn., Johnson County Bar Assn. (pres. 1969), Am. Bd. Trial Advocates (nat. dir.), Tex. Trial Lawyers Assn., Vanderbilt U. Law Sch. Bar Assn. (past pres.), Elks. Democrat. Methodist. Home: 1216 W Westhill Dr Cleburne TX 76031-6021 Office: 11 N Main St Cleburne TX 76031-5543

MAC LEAN, LLOYD DOUGLAS, surgeon; b. Calgary, Alta., Can., June 24, 1924; s. Fred Hugh and Azilda (Trudel) MacL.; m. Eleanor Colle, June 30, 1954; children—Hugh, Charles, Ian, James, Martha. B.Sc. (Viscount Bennett scholar), U. Alta., 1947, M.D. (Viscount Bennett scholar), 1949; Ph.D., U. Minn., 1957. Resident U. Minn. Hosp., Mpls., 1950-56; instr. dept. surgery U. Minn., Mpls., 1956-58, asst. prof. surgery, 1958-59, asso. prof., 1959-62; prof. McGill U., Montreal, Que., Can., 1962—, chmn. dept. surgery, 1968-73, 77-82, 87-88; surgeon-in-chief Ancker Hosp., St. Paul, 1957-62, Royal Victoria Hosp., Montreal, 1962-88; Edward Archibald prof. surgery McGill U., 1988-93, prof. surgery 1993—. Contbr. numerous articles on surgery, shock, host resistance and transplantation to profl. jours. Decorated officer Order Can. Fellow Royal Soc. Can.; mem. Am. Surg. Assn. (pres. 1992-93), A.C.S. (pres. 1993-94), Central Surg. Assn. (pres. 1985), Am. Physiol. Soc., Am. Assn. Thoracic and Cardiovascular Surgery, Soc. Surgery of Alimentary Tract. Home: # 1402-80 Berlioz, Montreal, PQ Canada H3E 1N9 Office: McGill Univ, 687 Pine Ave W, Montreal, PQ Canada H3A 1A1

MACLEAN, PAUL DONALD, government institute medical research official; b. Phelps, N.Y., May 1, 1913; s. Charles Chalmers and Elizabeth (Dreyfus) MacL.; m. Alison Stokes, July 16, 1942; children—Paul, David, Alexander, James, Alison. BA, Yale U., 1935; postgrad., U. Edinburgh, Scotland, 1935-36; MD cum laude, Yale U., 1940; DSci (hon.), SUNY, Binghamton, 1986. Intern in medicine Johns Hopkins U., 1940-41; asst. resident medicine New Haven Hosp., Yale Sch. Medicine, 1941-42, research asst. pathology, 1942, asst. prof. physiology, 1949-51, asst. prof. psychiatry, physiology and neurology, 1951-53, assoc. prof. physiology, 1956-57; clin. instr. medicine U. Wash. Med. Sch., Seattle, 1946-47; USPHS research fellow Harvard U. Med. Sch., also Mass. Gen. Hosp., 1947-49; dir. EEG lab. New Haven Hosp., 1951-52; assoc. prof. psychiatry, physiology and neurology, attending physician Grace-New Haven Hosp., 1953-56; sr. postdoctoral fellow NSF dept. physiology U. Zurich, 1956-57; chief sect. limbic integration and behavior Lab. Neurophysiology Intramural Research, NIMH, USPHS, Dept. Health and Human Services, Bethesda, Md., 1957-71; chief lab. brain evolution and behavior Intramural Research, Bethesda, Md., 1971-85; sr. research scientist Intramural Research Program, NIMH, 1985—. Author: The Triune Brain in Evolution, 1990; mem. editorial bd.: Jour. Nervous and Mental Disease. Emeritus trustee L.S.B. Leakey Found. Served to maj. M.C. AUS, 1942-46, PTO. Recipient award for disting. research Assn. for Research in Nervous and Mental Disease, 1964; Salmon medal and Lectureship award, 1966; Superior Service award HEW, 1967; Hincks Meml. lectr. Ont.; Spl. award Am. Psychopathol. Assn., 1971; G. Burroughs Mider NIH Lectureship award, 1972; Karl Spencer Lashley award Am. Philos. Soc., 1972; Adolph Meyer Lectureship award Am. Psychiat. Assn., 1982, Anokhin medal P.K. Anokhin Inst. Normal Physiology USSR Acad. Med. Scis., 1986; hon. Fulton fellow Yale U. Med. Sch., 1990. Mem. Am. Neurol. Assn., Am. Physiol. Soc., Am. Assn. Electroencephalographers, Am. Assn. Neurol. Surgeons, Soc. Neurosci., Am. Assn. Anatomists, Sigma Xi, Alpha Omega Alpha. Home: 10450 Lottsford Rd Apt 1218 Mitchellville MD 20721-2746 Office: NIMH Neuroscience Ctr 2700 Martin Luther King Jr Ave Washington DC 20032-2601

MACLEISH, ARCHIBALD BRUCE, museum director; b. White Plains, N.Y., May 6, 1947; s. Kenneth and Carolyn Elizabeth (de Chadenedes) MacL.; m. Patricia Ann McCue, Aug. 10, 1974; children: Kenneth Thomas, Padraic Andrew. BA, Johns Hopkins U., 1969; MA, SUNY, Oneonta, 1972. Asst. curator N.Y. State Hist. Assn., The Farmers' Mus., Cooperstown, 1972-73; assoc. curator N.Y. State Hist. Assn., Cooperstown, 1980-83, curator of collections, 1984-93, dir. collections, 1993—; curator of collections The Farmers' Mus., 1984-93, dir. collections, 1993—; curator The Ky. Mus., Bowling Green, 1973-80; mem. adj. tchg. faculty Cooperstown Grad. Program, 1980—. Author: Care of Antiques and Historical Collections, 1985; editor K.A.M. News, 1975-80. Sec. bd. dirs. Gallery 53, Cooperstown; mem. Ad Hoc Citizen's Com., Cooperstown, 1987—. Mem. Am. Assn. Mus., Am. Assn. for State and Local History, Mid-Atlantic Assn. Mus., Cooperstown Grad. Assn. Democrat. Methodist. Avocations: road running, gardening, guitar, fishing, cross-country skiing. Office: NY State Hist Assn PO Box 800 Lake Rd Cooperstown NY 13326

MACLENNAN, BERYCE WINIFRED, psychologist; b. Aberdeen, Scotland, Mar. 14, 1920; came to U.S., 1949, naturalized, 1965; d. William and Beatrice (MacRae) Mellis; m. John Duncan MacLennan, Nov. 29, 1944. BSc with honors, London Sch. Econs., 1947; PhD, London U., 1960. Diplomate Am. Bd. Clin. Psychology; cert. group therapist, trauma specialist. Group psychotherapist, youth specialist cons. N.Y.C. and Washington, 1949-63; dir. Ctr. for Prevention Juvenile Delinquency and New Careers, Washington, 1963-66; sect. chief NIMH, Mental Health Study Ctr., Adelphi, Md., 1967-70, chief, 1971-74; regional adminstr. Mass. Dept. Mental Health, Springfield, 1974-75; sr. mental health adv. GAO, Washington, 1976-90; pvt. practice, specialist psychotherapy Bethesda, Md., 1990—; clin. prof. George Washington U., 1970—; group therapy cons. D.C. Mental Health Svcs., 1993—, Washington Assessement and Therapy Svcs., 1992—; lectr. Montgomery C.C., 1988-91, Washington Sch. Psychiatry Geropsychiatric Program, 1997; mem. tech. adv. com. Prince George's County Mental Health Assn., 1968-84; cons. Washington Bus. Group on Health, 1990-91, KOBA, 1991. Mem. NIMH Prevention Intervention Rsch. Task Force, 1990-91, Montgomery County Victims Assistance Programs, 1990-95; v.p. Compliance, Federally Employed Women, 1979-81; pres. Glenecho chpt. Older Women's League, 1993-94. Fellow APA, Am. Orthopsychiat. Assn.; disting. fellow Am. Group Psychotherapy Assn.; mem. Bethesda Garden Club, Washington Mushroom Club. Democrat.

MACLENNAN, DAVID HERMAN, research scientist, educator; b. Swan River, Man., Can., July 3, 1937; s. Douglas Henry and Sigridur (Sigurdson) MacL.; m. Linda Carol Vass, Aug. 18, 1965; children: Jessica Lynn (dec.), Jeremy Douglas, Jonathan David. B.S.A., U. Man., 1959; M.S., Purdue U., 1961, Ph.D., 1963. Postdoctoral fellow Inst. Enzyme Research, U. Wis., Madison, 1963-64; asst. prof. U. Wis., Madison, 1964-68; assoc. prof. U. Toronto, 1969-74, prof., 1974-93, John W. Billes prof. med. rsch., 1987—, Univ. prof., 1993—, acting chmn., 1978-80, chmn., 1980-90; prin. investigator Can. Genetic Diseases Network of Ctrs. of Excellence, 1991—; mem. med. adv. bd. Muscular Dystrophy Assn. Can., 1976-87; mem. scientists' rev. panel Med. Rsch. Coun. Can., 1988-90; chmn. molecular biology and pathology grants com. Heart and Stroke Found. Can., 1995—; mem. rsch. rev. panel U. Ottawa Heart Inst., 1991—; cons. Merck, Sharp and Dohme, West Point, Pa., 1992—. Assoc. editor Can. Jour. Biochemistry, 1972-76; mem. editorial bd. Jour. Biol. Chemistry, 1975-80, 82-87; contbr. articles on muscle membrane biochemistry to profl. jours. Recipient Gairdner Found. Internat. award, 1991; Can. Med. Rsch. Coun. scholar, 1969-71, I.W. Killam Meml. scholar, 1977-78, I.W. Killam Meml. prize Health Scis., 1997. Fellow Royal Soc. Can., Royal Soc. London; mem. Can. Biochem. Soc. (Ayerst award 1974), Am. Soc. Biol. Chemists, Biophys. Soc. (Internat. Lectr. award 1990). Home: 293 Lytton Blvd, Toronto, ON Canada M5N 1R7 Office: U Toronto-Banting & Best Med Rsch, 112 College St, Toronto, ON Canada M5G 1L6

MACLEOD, DONALD, clergyman, educator; b. Broughton, N.S., Can., Dec. 31, 1914; s. Donald Archibald and Anne (MacKenzie) M.; m. Norma Eliner Harper, Jan. 5, 1948 (dec. Mar. 1972); children: John Fraser, David Ainslie, Anne, Leslie. A.B., Dalhousie U., Halifax, N.S., 1934, M.A., 1935, LL.D., 1978; B.D. (E.F. Grant scholar), Pine Hill Div. Hall, Halifax, 1938, D.D., 1970; Th.D., U. Toronto, 1947. Teaching fellow dept. English Dalhousie U., 1935-38; ordained to ministry Presbyn. Ch., 1938; minister First Ch., Louisburg, N.S., 1938-41; assoc. minister Bloor St. Ch., Toronto, 1941-45; sr. tutor Men's Residences Victoria Coll., Toronto, 1943-45; teaching fellow dept. homiletics Princeton Theol. Sem., 1946-47; asst. prof., 1947-53, assoc. prof., 1953-61, prof., 1961—, Francis L. Patton prof., 1982—; lectr. Princeton Summer Inst. Theology, 1948—; vis. lectr. Westminster Choir Coll., 1952, 55-58; lectr. Gettysburg Sem., 1952, Jr. Pastors Sch., Reading, Pa., 1954, Conf. on Evangelism, Whitby, Ont., 1957, Hampton (Va.) Inst., 1957, Union Sem., Richmond, Va., 1958, Crozier Sem., Chester, Pa., 1961, Ann. Pastors Conf. Am. Luth. Ch., Green Lake, Wis., 1966, Coll. Preachers, Nat. Cathedral Washington, 1967; lectr. continuing edn. Presbyn. Coll., Montreal, 1972-75; Mullins lectr. So. Baptist Theol. Sem., 1970; Kyes' lectr. Kirk in the Hills, Detroit, 1973; Oliver lectr. Nazarene Theol. Sem., 1985; Jameson Jones lectr. Duke U. Sch. Div., 1987; chmn. Synod Com. on Capital Ch., Trenton, N.J.; mem. coms. Christian edn., candidates and credentials, social edn. and action Presbytery New Brunswick; commr. Gen. Assembly United Presbyn. Ch., Oklahoma City, 1965; spl. preacher Princeton, Lehigh, Muhlenberg, Mt. Allison U., Duke U. and Rutgers U. Chapels, Chgo. Sunday Evening Club, Am. Preacher Series Eaton Meml. Ch., Toronto, Chatauqua Evangelist, Riverside Ch., N.Y.C., Fifth Ave. Presbyn Ch., N.Y.C., Nat. Presbyn. Ch., Washington, Preaching Mission McGuire AFB, Chaplains Seminars, USAF, 1967-68; adv. bd. Chapel of Princeton U. Author: Word and Sacrament, 1960, Presbyterian Worship, 1965, 2d edit., 1981, Higher Reaches, 1971, Proclamation, 1975; editor: Here Is My Method, 1952, Princeton Pulpit Prayers, 1987, Know the Way, Keep the Truth, Win the Life, 1987, The Problem of Preaching, 1987, Palms and Thorns, 1990; editor: Princeton Sem. Bull., 1956-82, Translator Dynamics of Worship, 1967; mem. editorial bd. Theology Today, 1948-61, Pulpit Preaching, 1970—, Pulpit Digest, 1980—; Am. corr.: The United Church Observer, 1947-56; N.J. corr.: The Christian Century, 1957-65; ecumenical editor Good News, Sunday Publs. Inc., 1983—; author bi-monthly book column. The Preachers Bookshelf, Monday Morning, 1985-96; contbr. Vols. I, IV and VI of Great Sermons and articles profl. publs. Established biennial series: Donald Macleod Lectureship on Preaching, Congl. Ch., Short Hills, N.J., 1989. Fellow Am. Assn. Theol. Schs.; mem. Am. Assn. Theol. Profs. in Practical Fields (exec. com.), Ch. Service Soc. (past v.p.), Clan Macleod Soc. Am. (chaplain), Am. Acad. Homiletics (founder, pres.). Address: Minister in Residence Charlestown Retirement Com 719 Maiden Choice Ln # 238 Baltimore MD 21228-6117 *Too often we interpret the Boy Scouts' slogan "Be Prepared" as a caution against danger or disaster, but its thrust is largely positive. It implies being prepared for every opportunity. Never did I have any particular position in mind, but every door which has opened to me found me ready and equipped for it.*

MACLEOD, GORDON ALBERT, retired lawyer; b. Buffalo, Mar. 29, 1926; s. Alexander D. and Loraine (Shea) MacL.; m. Lorraine King, July 7, 1951; children: Bruce King, Heather Lea. AB, Hamilton Coll., 1948; LLB, Harvard U., 1951. Bar: N.Y. 1951. Ptnr. Hodgson, Russ Andrews, Woods & Goodyear, Buffalo, 1960-93, of counsel, 1994—; lectr. N.Y. State Bankers Assn., Am. Soc. CLUs. Contbr. articles to profl. jours., other publs.; inventor several internationally marketed games. Trustee Creative Edn. Found., Buffalo. Fellow Am. Coll.. Trust and Estate Counsel; mem. ABA, N.Y. State Bar Assn. (lectr. trust and estates sect.), Phi Beta Kappa. Avocations: playing drums, backgammon, inventing toys and games, writing. Office: Hodgson Russ Andrews Woods 1800 One M & T Pla Buffalo NY 14203

MACLEOD, GORDON KENNETH, physician, educator; b. Boston, Jan. 30, 1929; s. Gordon Kenneth and Margaret J. MacL.; m. Janet B., Aug. 17, 1957; children—Gordon K. III, Alexander B. A.B., Blackburn Coll., 1954; M.D., U. Cin., 1960. Indsl. engr. Procter & Gamble Co., Cin., 1954-56; intern Boston City Hosp., 1960-61; resident, clin. fellow Mass. Gen. Hosp., Boston, 1961-64; research fellow Harvard U., 1962-64; sr. resident, sr. physician Boston VA hosp., 1964-66; asst. clin. prof. medicine Yale U., 1966-69, assoc. clin. prof. medicine and public health, 1969-71; dir. Health Maintenance Orgn. Service, HEW, 1971-73; prof. dept. health services adminstrn. Grad. Sch. Public Health, U. Pitts., 1974—, chmn. dept., 1974-83; assoc. clin. prof. medicine Pitts. (Sch. Medicine), 1976-86; clin. prof. medicine Grad. Sch. Public Health, U. Pitts. (Sch. Medicine), 1986—; pres. U. Pitts., 1997—; sec. health, State of Pa., 1979; mem. staff W. Penn Hosp.; mem. nat. adv. coun. divsn. rsch. resources NIH, 1983-87; cons. Shadyside Hosp.; cons. in field. Editor: (with Mark Perlman) Health Care Capital: Competition and Control, 1978; contbr. articles to profl. jours. Served with U.S. Army, 1948-49. Ford Found. travel grantee, 1973. Fellow ACP; mem. Allegheny County Med. Soc., AMA (editorial bd. jour. 1989-94), Am. Pub. Health Assn., Med. Adminstrs. Conf., Pa. Pub. Health Assn., Pa. State Med. Soc. (pres.), Pitts. Acad. Medicine. Office: 130 Desoto St Pittsburgh PA 15213-2535 *My first job as an industrial engineer with later training in internal medicine uniquely prepared me for an academic career in health management with intervals as a government executive at federal and state levels. My most challenging assignments were in initiating Health Maintenance Organizations nationally, in managing the health aspects of the nuclear accident at Three Mile Island, and in training young persons for careers in internal medicine and health management.*

MACLEOD, JOHN, college basketball coach; b. New Albany, Ind., Oct. 3, 1937; s. Dan J. and Ann Elizabeth (Welch) MacL.; m. Carol Ann McGroder, Jan. 18, 1974; children: Kathleen, Matthew. BA in History, Bellarmine Coll.; MA in History and Phys. Edn., Ind. State U., 1965. Coach high schs. Ky, Ind.; former coach U. Okla., Norman; head coach Phoenix Suns, NBA, 1973-87, Dallas Mavericks, NBA, 1987-89; former head coach New York Knicks, 1990; now head coach basketball program Notre Dame Univ., South Bend, Ind.; active hon. coach Ariz. Spl. Olympics. Active Soc. for Blind. Served with USAR, 1959-60. Named Coach of Yr. NBA, 1980. Mem. NBA Coaches Assn. (treas.). Office: care U Notre Dame Athletics Dept South Bend IN 46556

MACLEOD, JOHN AMEND, lawyer; b. Manila, June 5, 1942; s. Anthony Macaulay and Dorothy Lillian (Amend) M.; m. Ann Klee; children: Kerry, Jack. BBA, U. Notre Dame, 1963, JD, 1969. Bar: D.C. 1969, U.S. Supreme Ct. 1980. Assoc. Jones, Day, Reavis & Pogue, D.C., 1969-73; ptnr., 1974-79; ptnr. Crowell & Moring, Washington, 1979—, mem. mgmt. com., 1979-82, 83-86, 91-94, chmn., 1984-85, 93-94. Contbr. articles to profl. jours. Trustee, mem. exec. com. Eastern Mineral Law Found.; bd. dirs. St. Francis Ctr., 1982-91, C&M Internat. 1991-94. Served to lt. U.S. Army, 1963-65. Recipient Disting. Mining Lawyer award Nat. Mining Assn., 1995. Mem. ABA, D.C. Bar Assn., Notre Dame Law Assn. (dir., exec. bd.), Ptnrs. Leadership Forum, Metropolitan Club (Washington). Home: 4040 Swartz Rd Maurertown VA 22644-9759 Office: Crowell & Moring 1001 Pennsylvania Ave NW Washington DC 20004-2505

MACLEOD, JOHN DANIEL, JR., religious organization administrator; b. Robbins, N.C., Mar. 16, 1922; s. John Daniel Sr. and Sarah Cranor (McKay) MacL.; m. Helen Frances Boggs, Sept. 18, 1945 (dec. Aug. 1990); children: Sarah MacLeod Owens, Mary Marget MacLeod Silberstein, John Daniel III, William Boggs. AB, Davidson (N.C.) Coll., 1942; MDiv, Union Theol. Sem., Richmond, Va., 1945, ThM, 1949, PhD, 1952; DD (hon.), St. Andrews Presbyn. Coll., Laurinburg, N.C., 1992. Ordained to ministry Presbyn. Ch., 1945. Pastor Carolina Beach (N.C.) Presbyn. Ch., 1945-48, Brett-Reed Presbyn. Ch., Sweet Hall, Va., 1949-53, Keyser (W.Va.) Presbyn. Ch., 1953-63; exec. Appomattox Presbytery, Lynchburg, Va., 1963-67, Norfolk (Va.) Presbytery, 1967-76, Westminster Presbytery, St. Petersburg, Fla., 1976-81; exec. Synod of N.C., Raleigh, 1981-88, ret., 1988; interim exec. Coastal Carolina Presbytery, Fayetteville, 1991-93, Holston Presbytery, Kingsport, Tenn., 1993; interim parish assoc. White Meml. Presbyn. Ch., Raleigh, N.C., 1994; interim exec. Western N.C. Presbytery, Morganton, 1995, interim assoc. exec., 1996-97, interim pastor Trinity Presbyn. Ch., Starkville, Miss., 1997—; mem., chmn. various local and nat. Presbyn. Ch. Coms. Trustee Warren Wilson Coll., 1985-89, N.C. Presbyn. Hist. Soc., 1981—, Mary Baldwin Coll., 1960-68, Davis and Elkins Coll., 1955-61, Massanetta Springs Conf. Ctr., 1956-62, Barium Springs Children's Home, 1995-97, Black Mtn. Home for Children, 1995-97; active Mineral County Redevel. Commn., Keyser, 1960-63; mem. N.C. Gov's. Adv. com. on Citizen Affairs, Raleigh, 1983-84; bd. advisors Wake Forest U. Div. Sch., 1991-96. Nominee moderator Presbyn. Ch. USA Gen. Assembly, 1987, moderator Synod of Va., 1969, Synod of Mid-Atlantic, 1990. Fellow Soc. Antiquaries

(Scotland); mem. St. Andrews Soc. (Southern Pines, N.C. chpt., bd. dirs. Tampa, Fla. chpt. 1976-81), N.C. Scottish Heritage Soc. (pres. 1992—), Clan MacLeod Soc. (chaplain, bd. dirs. 1994). Democrat. Avocations: genealogy, history, travel. Office: 607 Hospital Rd PO Box 794 Starkville MS 39759

MACLEOD, JOHN MUNROE, radio astronomer; b. Vermilion, Alta., Can., Sept. 3, 1937; s. Munroe and Ruth Alberta (Williams) MacL.; m. Patricia Irene Nichols, Dec. 30, 1959; children: Carolyn, Audrey, Darryl. BSc, U. Alta., Edmonton, 1959; PhD, U. Ill., 1964. Radio astronomer NRC Can., Ottawa, 1964-86, head James Clerk Maxwell Telescope Group Herzberg Inst., 1986—. Union Carbide scholar, 1955-59, McKinley Found. scholar, 1963-64. Mem. Am. Astron. Soc., Can. Astron. Soc. (councillor 1977-80, v.p. 1980-84, pres. 1984-86). Mem. United Ch. of Can. Achievements include co-discovery of the radio variability of BL Lacertae, of long-chain interstellar molecules HC5N, HC7N, HC9N. Office: Nat Rsch Coun, 5071 W Saanich Rd, Victoria, BC Canada K1A 0R6

MACLEOD, RICHARD PATRICK, foundation administrator; b. Boston, Apr. 2, 1937; s. Thomas Everett and Margaret Gertrude (Fahey) MacL.; children: Kimberly Margaret Hamelin, Richard Alexander MacLeod. BA in Govt., U. Mass., 1960; MA in Internat. Rels., U. So. Calif., 1968. Instr. polit. sci. USAF Acad., 1968-71; Commd. 2d lt. USAF, 1960, advanced through grades to col., 1981; sr. rsch. fellow The Nat. Def. U., Washington, 1978-79; chief Space Policy Br., dep. chief Plans USAF Aerospace Def. Command, 1979-80; exec. officer to the comdr. in chief USAF Aerospace Def. Command, NORAD, 1980-81; chief of staff NORAD, 1981-84, USAF Space Command, 1982-84; ret. U.S. Space Found., 1985; exec. dir. U.S. Space Found., Colorado Springs, Colo., 1985-88; pres. U.S. Space Found., Colorado Springs, 1988-97, dir., 1997—; bd. dirs. Analytical Surveys, Inc., Colorado Springs, 1985—, U.S. Space Found., 1997—; space edn. advisor Coll. Engring. Adv. Coun., U. Colo., Colorado Springs. Author: Peoples War in Thailand, Insurgency in the Modern World, 1980. Mem. White House Space Policy Adv. Bd.; bd. dirs. Pike's Peak Coun. Boy Scouts Am., Colorado Springs; past pres. Colorado Springs Symphony Coun.; past dir. World Affairs Coun., Colorado Springs. Fellow Brit. Interplanetary Soc.; mem. AIA, Air Force Acad. Found. (bd. dirs., trustee), U.S. Space Found. (founding), Aviation Space Writers Assn., Air Force Space Ops. Assn., GPS Internat. Assn., Am. Legion, The Co. of Fifers and Drummers. Office: US Space Found 2860 S Circle Dr Ste 2301 Colorado Springs CO 80906-4107

MACLEOD, ROBERT ANGUS, microbiology educator, researcher; b. Athabasca, Alta., Can., July 13, 1921; s. Norman John and Eleonora Pauline Bertha (Westerhoff) MacL.; m. Patricia Rosemarie Robertson, Sept. 1, 1948; children—Douglas John, Alexander Robert, Kathleen Mary, David Gordon, Michael Norman, Susan Joan. B.A. with honors in Chemistry, U. B.C., Vancouver, Can., 1943, M.A. in Chemistry and Biology, 1945; Ph.D. in Biochemistry, U. Wis., Madison, 1949. Asst. prof. Queen's U., Kingston, Ont., Can., 1949-52; sr. biochemist Fisheries Research Bd. Can., Vancouver, B.C., 1952-60; assoc. prof. to prof., chmn. dept. microbiology Macdonald Coll., McGill U., Ste. Anne de Bellevue, Que., Can., 1960-86, prof. emeritus, 1986—; Cons. Def. Research Bd., Ottawa, Ont., 1965-75; assoc. editor Can. Jour. Microbiology, Ottawa, 1965-70. Author tech. papers. Recipient Harrison prize Royal Soc. Can., 1960; Can. Soc. Microbiologists award, 1973. Fellow Royal Soc. Can.; mem. Can. Soc. Microbiologists (pres. 1976-77, hon. mem. 1993), Am. Soc. Microbiology (hon. mem. 1992). Avocations: swimming, fishing. Home: 6 Grand Cedar Ct, Stittsville, ON Canada K25 1C8

MACLEOD, ROBERT FREDRIC, editor, publisher; b. Chgo., Oct. 15, 1917; s. Ernest F. and Martha W. (Ruzicka) MacL.; children—Merrill, Robert Fredric, E. Jay, Ian. B.A., Dartmouth Coll., 1939. Advt. mgr. Town & Country mag., N.Y.C., 1949; v.p., pub. Harper's Bazaar, N.Y.C., 1950-55, 55-60; v.p., advt. dir. Hearst Mags., N.Y.C., 1960-62; pub. Seventeen mag., N.Y.C., 1962-63; v.p., dir. mktg. Subscription TV Inc., Santa Monica, Calif., 1963-64; editor, pub. 'Teen Mag., Los Angeles, 1965—, now editorial dir., exec. pub.; sr. v.p. Petersen Pub. Co., L.A., 1976-95; ret., 1995, pub. cons., 1995—. Served to maj. USMC, 1941-46. Named to Football Hall of Fame, 1977. Club: Bel Air Country. Home: 110 Colony Dr Malibu CA 90265

MACLIN, ALAN HALL, lawyer; b. DuQuoin, Ill., Dec. 22, 1949; s. John E. and Nora (Hall) M.; m. Joan Davidson (div. Dec. 1981); children: Molly, Tess, Anne; m. Jeanne Sittlow, Nov. 17, 1984. B.A. magna cum laude, Vanderbilt U., 1971; J.D., U. Chgo., 1974. Bar: Minn. 1974, U.S. Dist. Ct. Minn. 1974, U.S. Ct. Appeals (8th cir.) 1974, U.S. Ct. Appeals (5th cir.) 1975, U.S. Supreme Ct. 1978. Asst. atty. gen. Minn. Atty. Gen., St. Paul, 1974-80; chief anti-trust div. Briggs & Morgan, St. Paul, 1980—, mem. bd. dirs. 1993—. Mem. Minn. State Bar Assn. (treas. anti-trust sect. 1978-80), Ramsey County Bar Assn. (sec. jud. com. 1980-82), Phi Beta Kappa. Unitarian. Office: Briggs & Morgan 2200 First National Bank Bldg Saint Paul MN 55101-1319

MACLIN, ERNEST, biomedical diagnostics company executive; b. N.Y.C., Jan. 25, 1931; s. Samuel and Dora (Sonsky) M.; m. Edith Samuel, Feb. 18, 1956; children—Alan David, Deborah Ellen, Julie Anne. B.M.E., CCNY, 1952, M.Engring., 1969. Registered profl. engr., N.Y., N.J. Engr. Reeves Instrument Corp., N.Y.C., 1952-54, Adrian Wilson Assocs., Nagoya, Japan, 1956-57; engr., unit head Kearfott div. Singer Corp., Little Falls, N.J., 1958-68; engr. Ford Instrument Co., L.I., N.Y., 1957-58, Technicon, Tarrytown, N.Y., 1968-69; v.p. research and devel. Electro-Nucleonics Inc., Fairfield, N.J., 1969-90; pres. The Product Devel. Group, 1990—; bd. dirs. Nat. Com. for Clin. Lab. Standards, Villanova, Pa., 1981-87. Contbr. articles to profl. jours.; patentee various instruments. Served to capt. USAF, 1954-57; mem. USAFR ret. Fellow ASME; mem. Am. Assn. Clin. Chemistry. Jewish. Home and Office: 659 Rutgers Pl Paramus NJ 07652-4207

MACMAHON, BRIAN, epidemiologist, educator; b. Sheffield, Eng., Aug. 12, 1923; came to U.S. 1952; s. Desmond and Gladys (Nelson) MacM.; m. Heidi Marie Graber, Aug. 28, 1948; children—Michael, Kevin, Kathleen Louise, Mary Anne. M.B., Ch.B., U. Birmingham, Eng., 1946, Ph.D., 1952, M.D., 1955; M.S., Harvard U., Boston, 1953; DMS (hon.), U. Athens, Greece, 1976; DSc (hon.), SUNY, Buffalo, 1986. Ship surgeon Alfred Holt & Co., Liverpool, Eng., 1946-48; assoc. prof. SUNY Downstate Med. Ctr., Bklyn., 1955-57, prof., 1957-58; prof., chmn. dept. epidemiology Harvard Sch. Pub. Health, Boston, 1958-89, emeritus prof. epidemiology, 1989—. Author: Epidemiologic Methods, 1960, Epidemiology: Principles and Methods, 1970, 2d edit., 1996; editor: Cancer Causes and Control, 1990; contbr. articles to profl. jours. Recipient Edwards Meml. medal U. Wales, 1974; Lucy Wortham James award Soc. Surg. Oncology, 1978; John Snow award Am. Pub. Health Assn., 1980; Lemuel Shattuck award Mass. Pub. Health Assn., 1982, Prix Antoinne Lacassagne Ligue National Francaise Contre le Cancer; Am. Cancer Soc. Medal of Honor, 1995, London Sch. Hygiene & Tropical Medicine Donald Reid medal, 1997. Fellow Am. Pub. Health Assn.; mem. Am. Epidemiol. Soc. Home: 89 Warren St Needham MA 02192-3115 Office: 89 Warren St Needham MA 02192-3115

MACMAHON, CHARLES HUTCHINS, JR., architect; b. Fort Seward, Alaska, June 6, 1918; s. Charles H. and Charlotte (Currie) MacM.; m. Ethel Hayward Pearce, Nov. 14, 1942; children—Charles H. III, Charlotte (Mrs. Douglas E. Neumann). Student, Bowdoin Coll., 1936-37, U. Pa., 1937-38; B.Arch., U. Mich., 1942. Dist. mgr. U.S. Gypsum Co., Chgo., 1947-52; gen. sales mgr. Spickelmeier Co., Indpls., 1952-55; with Smith, Tarapata, MacMahon, Inc., Birmingham, Mich., 1956-59; pres. Tarapata-MacMahon-Paulsen, Bloomfield Hills, Mich., 1959-73; cons. Tarapata-MacMahon-Paulsen, 1973—; pres. MacMahon-Cajacob Assos., DeLand, Fla., 1978-92; owner Charles MacMahon Architect, DeLand, Fla., 1992—; mem. Mich. Bd. Registration of Architects, Engrs. and Surveyors, 1964-68; mem. planning bd. City of DeLand, 1978-84. Works include Central Plaza, Canton, O., Gen. Motors Inst, Flint, Mich., Cloisters of DeLand, Fla., Washtenaw Community Coll, Ann Arbor, Mich. Chmn. bd. trustees Bloomfield Twp. Zoning Bd. Appeals, 1968-69; bd. dirs. Brookside Sch., Cranbrook, 1964-68; trustee Inst. for Advanced Pastoral Studies; mem. historic preservation bd. City of DeLand, 1993—. Lt. USNR, 1942-45. Fellow AIA; mem. Sch. Facilities Council (v.p., dir.), Mich. Soc. Architects (pres. 1962-64), Psi Upsilon. Episcopalian. Club: Lake Beresford Yacht. Address: 115 S Boundary Ave Deland FL 32720-5101

MACMAHON, PAUL, advertising executive; b. Orange, N.J., May 23, 1945; s. Paul J. and Joan (Schoenleber) MacM.; m. Mary Lee O'Neill, May 2, 1966 (div. May 1970); 1 child, Sandra; m. Barbara Jo Wernick, Mar. 8, 1972 (dec. Aug. 1988); children: Matthew, Timothy, Paul, Kathleen, Thomas, Julia; m. Ann Louise Dye, Aug. 7, 1993. A.A., Indian River Jr. Coll, 1966; B.S., Fla. State U., 1968; M.B.A., U. Mich., 1970. Acct. exec. Ted Bates & Co., N.Y.C., 1970-71; account dir. Ted Bates & Co., Ger. and Italy, 1972-74, v.p., 1975-79; sr. v.p. Ted Bates & Co., N.Y.C., 1979-80; sr. v.p. The Bloom Agy., Dallas, 1980-82, exec. v.p., 1982, gen. mgr., 1983-84, pres., 1984, chmn., 1985-88, chmn, ceo, 1988. Republican. Roman Catholic. Home: 126 Red Oak Ln Lewisville TX 75028-3501 Office: Publicis/Bloom 3500 Maple Ave Dallas TX 75219-3931

MACMANUS, SUSAN ANN, political science educator, researcher; b. Tampa, Fla., Aug. 22, 1947; d. Harold Cameron and Elizabeth (Riegler) MacM. BA cum laude, Fla. State U., 1968, PhD, 1975; MA, U. Mich., 1969. Instr. Valencia Community Coll., Orlando, Fla., 1969-73; rsch. asst. Fla. State U., 1973-75; asst. prof. U. Houston, 1975-79, assoc. prof., 1979-85, dir. M of Pub. Adminstrn. program, 1983-85, rsch. assoc. Ctr. Pub. Policy 1982-85; prof., dir. PhD program Cleve. State U., 1985-87; prof. pub. adminstrn. and polit. sci., U. South Fla., Tampa, 1987—, chairperson dept. govt. and internat. affairs, 1987-93; vis. prof. U. Okla., Norman, 1981—; field rsch. assoc. Brookings Instn., Washington, 1977-82, Columbia U., summer 1979, Princeton (N.J.) U., 1979—, Nat. Acad. Pub. Adminstrn., Washington, summer 1980, Cleve. State U., 1982-83, Westat, Inc., Washington, 1983—. Author: Revenue Patterns in U.S. Cities and Suburbs: A Comparative Analysis, 1978, Federal Aid to Houston, 1983, (with others) Governing A Changing America, 1984, (with Francis T. Borkowski) Visions for The Future: Creating New Institutional Relationships Among Academia, Business, Government, and Community, 1989, Reapportionment and Representation in Florida: A Historical Collection, 1991, Doing Business with Government: Federal, State, Local and Foreign Government Purchasing Practices for Every Business and Public Institution, 1992, Young v. Old: Generational Combat in the 21st Century, 1996; writer manuals in field; mem. editorial bds. various jours.; contbr. articles to jours. and chpts. to books. Bd. dirs. Houston Area Women's Ctr., 1977, past pres., v.p. fin., treas.; mem. LWV, Gov.'s Coun. Econ. Advisers, 1988-90, Harris County (Tex.) Women's Polit. Caucus, Houston; bd. dirs. USF Rsch. Found., Inc. Recipient U. Houston Coll. Social Scis. Teaching Excellence award, 1977, Herbert J. Simon Award for best article in 3d vol. Internat. Jour. Pub. Adminstrn., 1981, Theodore & Venette Askounes-Ashford Disting. Scholar award U. South Fla., 1991, Disting. Rsch. Scholar award, 1991; Ford Found. fellow, 1967-68; grantee Valencia Community Coll. Faculty, 1972, U. Houston, 1976-77, 79, 83; Fulbright Rsch. scholar, Korea, 1989. Mem. Am. Polit. Sci. Assn. (program com. 1983-84, chair sect. intergovtl. rels., award 1989, mem. exec. coun. 1994—, pres.-elect sect. urban politics 1994-95, pres. sect. urban politics 1995-96), So. Polit. Sci. Assn. (v.p. 1990-91, pres.-elect 1992-93, pres. 1993-94, V.O. key award com. 1983-84, best paper on women and politics 1988), Midwest Polit. Sci. Assn., Western Polit. Sci. Assn., Southwestern Polit. Sci. Assn. (local arrangements com. 1982-83, profession com. 1977-80), ASPA (nominating com. Houston chpt. 1983, bd. mem. Suncoast chpt., pres.-elect 1991, Lilly award 1992), Policy Studies Orgn. (mem. editorial bd. jour. 1981—, exec. coun. 1983-85), Women's Caucus Polit. Sci. (portfolio pre-decision rev. com. 1982-83, projects and programs com. 1981, fin.-budget com. 1980-81), Acad. Polit. Sci., Mcpl. Fin. Officers Assn., Phi Kappa Phi Artist/Scholar, U. South Fla., 1997, Phi Beta Kappa, Phi Kappa Phi, Pi Sigma Alpha (mem. exec. coun. 1994—), Pi Alpha Alpha. Republican. Methodist. Home: 2506 Collier Pky Land O'Lakes FL 34639-5228 Office: U South Fla Dept Govt & Internat Affairs Soc 107 Tampa FL 33620

MACMANUS, YVONNE CRISTINA, editor, videoscripter, writer, consultant; b. L.A., Mar. 18, 1931; d. Daniel S. and Josefina Lydia (Pina) MacM. Student, UCLA, NYU, U. So. Calif., U. London. Assoc. editor Bobbs-Merrill, N.Y.C., 1960-63; TV producer Leo Burnett Ltd., London, 1965-66; founding editor, editor-in-chief Leisure Books, L.A., 1970-72; tchr. pub. course UCLA Extension, 1972; sr. editor Major Books, 1974-77; co-pub., editor in chief Timely Books, Chattanooga, 1977; co-owner Write On...!, Chattanooga, 1977—; corp. videoscripting PR & video tng., 1983—; tchr. writing workshop Chattanooga State C.C., 1996. Author: Better Luck Elsewhere, 1966, With Fate Conspire, 1974, Bequeath Them No Tumbled House, 1977, Deadly Legacy, 1981, The Presence, 1982, You Can Write A Romance, 1983, (updated and expanded) 1996, (play) Hugo, 1990; contbr. articles to profl. publs. Home and Office: 4040 Mountain Creek Rd Ste 1304 Chattanooga TN 37415-6025

MACMASTER, DANIEL MILLER, retired museum official; b. Chgo., Feb. 11, 1913; s. Daniel Howard and Charlotte Louise (Miller) MacM.; m. Sylvia Jane Hill, Feb. 22, 1935; children—Daniel Miller, Jane Irene (Mrs. Robert W. Lightell). Student, Lakeside Press Tng. Sch., 1930-31, U. Chgo., 1931-34; L.H.D., Lincoln Coll., 1970; D.H.L., DePaul U., 1978. Mem. staff Mus. Sci. and Industry, Chgo., 1933—; acting dir. Mus. Sci. and Industry, 1950, dir., 1951-72, pres., 1968-78, pres. emeritus, 1978—, life trustee, 1968—; gen. mgr. Chgo. R.R. Fair, 1948-49. Author: (with others) Exploring the Mysteries of Physics and Chemistry, 1938; book reviewer; contbr. to newspapers, mags., encys. Mem. Homewood (Ill.) Bd. Edn., 1945-49, pres., 1948-49; mem. U. Ill. Citizen' Adv. Com., 1945—; sec. Higher Edn. Commn. Ill., 1955-59; dir. Hyde Park Bank and Trust Co., 1965-86; U.S. State Dept. Specialist to Ireland, Germany, Sweden, 1963; dir. Floating Seminar to Greece, 1960; guest mus. cons. Fed. Republic Germany, 1961, Iran, 1973, 74, 76, Hong Kong, 1978, 89, 90, 91, Singapore, Chili and Peru, 1978, Poland, Czechoslovakia and Hungary, 1979, Mexico, 1980, 81, Saudi Arabia, 1981, 82, 84, Columbia, Ecuador and Bolivia, 1983, Taiwan 1986-90, 92, 94, 96; mem. Nat. 4-H Svc. Com.; hon. dir. Chgo. Chamber Orch. Soc., pres., 1969-70; bd. dirs. Sears Roebuck Found., 1970-73, Internat. Coll. Surgeons Hall of Fame; mem. Lincoln Acad. Ill.; hon. trustee U. Chgo. Cancer Rsch. Found.; life trustee Adler Planetarium; dir. emeritus Monmouth Coll.; bd. govs. Chgo. Heart Assn., vice chmn., 1972-73. Decorated Golden Cross Royal Order Phoenix Greece; Officer's Cross Polonia Restituta Poland; Grand Badge of Honor Austria; Grand Badge of Honor of Burgenland Austria; Golden Badge of Honor Vienna; Officer's Cross 1st class Order of Merit Germany; Officer Order of Merit Luxembourg; Order Cultural Merit Poland; Royal Swedish Order North Star; recipient Patriotic Civilian Service award U.S. Army, St. Andrews Soc. Citizen of Yr. award, 1978. Fellow Assn. Sci. and Tech. Centers; mem. Kappa Sigma. Clubs: Tavern, Quadrangle, Commercial. Home: 2311 183rd St Apt 209 Homewood IL 60430-3146

MACMASTER, ROBERT ELLSWORTH, historian, educator; b. Winthrop, Mass., Oct. 10, 1919; s. Joseph Oscar and Ruby (Slocomb) MacM.; m. Ann Elizabeth Lynch, Apr. 28, 1942; children—Angus Michael, Martha Ann, David Joseph. A.B., Harvard, 1941, A.M., 1948, Ph.D., 1952. Mem. faculty MIT, 1952-90, prof. history and lit., 1967-90, prof. emeritus, 1990—, chmn. history sect., 1970-72. Author: Danilevsky: A Russian Totalitarian Philosopher, 1967. Served with AUS, 1941-46. Mem. Am. Assn. Advancement Slavic Studies. Home: 461 Main St Hingham MA 02043-4701 Office: MIT Dept History Cambridge MA 02139

MACMEEKEN, JOHN PEEBLES, foundation executive, educator; b. Glen Ridge, N.J., Aug. 15, 1924; s. John West and Esther (Strong) M.; m. Mary Swanberg, Nov. 26, 1949; children: Carol B. Macmeeken Luther, John W., Susan G. Student U. Calif., Berkeley, 1941-43, Ind. U., 1943-44; J.D., Harvard U., 1948. Bar: Calif. 1948. Assoc. Chickering & Gregory, San Francisco, 1948-60, ptnr., 1960-82; ptnr. Pettit & Martin, San Francisco, 1982-93; v.p. Zynk Indsl. Corp., 1995—; pres. Found. for Books to China, 1993; bd. dirs. Lanark West Corp.; pres. Clinton U., San Francisco, 1995-97; vice-chmn. The SOAR Found., 1996.; lectr. law Fudan U., Shanghai, China, East China Normal U., Shanghai, Nanking U., China. Sgt. U.S. Army, 1943-45. Mem. ABA, Calif. Bar Assn., San Francisco Bar Assn., Outlook Club Calif., World Trade Club, Commonwealth Club (Calif.). Republican. Congregationalist. Home: 5708 Glenbrook Dr Oakland CA 94618-1724

MACMILLAN, FRANCIS PHILIP, physician; b. Everett, Mass., June 19, 1937; s. Edward Joseph and Katherine H. (Hogan) M.; m. Nancy Marie Mirabello, May 18, 1963; children: Frank, Edward, Paul, John, Kerry. BS, Boston Coll., 1959; MD, N.Y. Med. Coll., 1964. Diplomate Am. Bd. Internal Medicine, Am. Bd. Gastroenterology. Intern Boston City Hosp., 1964-65, resident in internal med., 1965-66; resident Boston VA Hosp., Jamaica Plains, Mass., 1966-68; practice medicine specializing in gastroenterology Pentucket Med. Assn., Inc., Haverhill, Mass., 1968—; pres. med. staff Hale Hosp., Haverhill, 1975-78, chief of medicine, 1980-82; cons. in gastroenterology Lawrence (Mass.) Gen. Hosp., Holy Family Hosp., Methuen, Mass., Anna Jaques Hosp., Newburyport, Mass. Contbr. articles to profl. jours. Served to maj. USAR, 1968-71. Fellow Am. Coll. Physicians. Mem. Am. Med. Assn., Mass. Med. Assn., Am. Soc. Internal Med., Am. Gastroent. Assn., New England Endoscopy Soc. (pres. 1996—). Roman Catholic. Club: Haverhill Golf and Country (bd. dirs. 1983-86). Avocations: golf, tennis. Office: One Parkway Haverhill MA 01830 also: 203 Turnpike St North Andover MA 01845-5042

MACMILLAN, KENNETH, cinematographer. Cinematographer: (TV movies) Smiley's People, 1982, The Aerodrome, 1983, The Ghost Writer, 1984, Past Caring, 1985, Bleak House, 1985, Hotel du Lac, 1986, Pack of Lies, 1987, Day After the Fair, 1987, The Little Match Girl, 1987, (films) A Month in the Country, 1987, A Summer Story, 1988, The Tree of Hands, 1989, Henry V, 1989, King Ralph, 1991, Of Mice and Men, 1992, Rush, 1992, Lassie, 1994, Circle of Friends, 1995, Inventing the Abbotts, 1996. Office: Sandra Marsh Mgt 9150 Wilshire Blvd Ste 220 Beverly Hills CA 90212-3429*

MACMILLAN, KIP VAN METRE, foundation executive; b. Evanston, Ill., Dec. 18, 1937; s. Charles Daniel and Janet Marvia (Van Metre) M.; m. Linda Jean Griesbach, Dec. 22, 1962; children: Christopher, Julia. Sgt., lt., div. comdr. Evanston Police Dept., 1961-88; supr. Polio Plus campaign Rotary Found., Evanston, 1988-90, ret., 1990. Bd. dirs. Youth Orgn. Umbrella, Evanston, 1974, McGaw YMCA, Evanston, 1976-89, Shore Cmty. Svcs. for Retarded Citizens, Evanston, 1986-90, Teton County Crime Stoppers; pres. Teton Youth & Family Svcs.; chmn. Evanston March of Dimes, 1987, Teton County Congl. Awards Com., Browse and Buy Bd. St. John's Ch., Wildcat dist. com. Boy Scouts Am.; mem. adv. com. Cook County Dept. Children and Family Svcs., Chgo., 1987-90; mem. Ill. Coord. System Response Project-Mass Abuse of Children, Springfield, 1987-89; dir., treas. Evanston Sister City Found., 1989-90; vol. Grand Teton Music Festival; vestryman St. John's Episcopal Ch.; bd. dirs. Wyo. Spl. Olympics. Recipient Top Vol. of Yr. award North Shore mag., 1987, Jay Moore award Youth Orgn. Umbrella, 1988, William Harper award McGaw YMCA, 1975. Mem. Nat. Soc. Fundraising Execs., Rotary (bd. dirs. Evanston club 1986-89, bd. dirs. Jackson Hole club, pres. Jackson Hole club 1994-95, Outstanding Rotarian Evanston club 1988), Am. Soc. Indsl. Security, Teton County Peace Officers Assn., Rotary Dist. 5440 (asst. gov.). Republican. Episcopalian.

MACMILLAN, ROBERT FRANCIS, director university service; b. Easton, Pa., Oct. 3, 1925; s. William F. and Margaret (Woodruff) M.; m. Dolores G., June 7, 1952; 1 child, R. David. BS in Elec. Engring., Lafayette Coll., 1949; BD, Southern Bapt. Theol. Sem., 1952, ThM and MRE, 1954, 56; PhD, Am. U., 1969. Lic. psychologist, Pa. Assoc. pastor 1st Bapt. Ch., Washington, 1955-69; dir. psychol. svcs. U. Pa., East Stroudsburg, 1969—; pres., Assn. Pa. State Coll. U Faculty, 1980—. Chmn. Monroe County Planning Commn., Stroudsburg, 1974-85. Sgt. U.S. Army, 1943-46. Mem. Am. Psychol. Assn. Home: 32 Club Ct Stroudsburg PA 18360-1548 Office: East Stroudsburg U Dept of Psychol Stroudsburg PA 18301

MACMILLAN, ROBERT SMITH, electronics engineer; b. L.A., Aug. 28, 1924; s. Andrew James and Moneta (Smith) M.; BS in Physics, Calif. Inst. Tech., 1948, MS in Elec. Engring., 1949, PhD in Elec. Engring. and Physics cum laude, 1954; m. Barbara Macmillan, Aug. 18, 1962; 1 son, Robert G. Rsch. engr. Jet Propulsion lab. Calif. Inst. Tech., Pasadena, 1951-55, asst. prof. elec. engring., 1955-58; assoc. prof. elec. engring. U. So. Calif., L.A., 1958-70; mem. sr. tech. staff Litton Systems, Inc., Van Nuys, Calif., 1969-79; dir. systems engring. Litton Data Command Systems, Agoura Hills, Calif., 1979-89; pres. The Macmillan Group, Tarzana, Calif., 1989—; treas., v.p. Video Color Corp., Inglewood, 1965-66. Cons. fgn. tech. div. USAF, Wright-Patterson AFB, Ohio, 1957-74, Space Tech. Labs., Inglewood, Calif., 1956-60, Space Gen. Corp., El Monte, Calif., 1960-63. With USAAF, 1943-46. Mem. IEEE, Am. Inst. Physics, Am. Phys. Soc., Sigma Xi, Tau Beta Pi, Eta Kappa Nu. Research in ionospheric, radio-wave, propagation; very low frequency radio-transmitting antennas; optical coherence and statist. optics. Home: 350 Starlight Crest Dr La Canada Flintridge CA 91011-2839 Office: The Macmillan Group 5700 Etiwanda Ave Unit 260 Tarzana CA 91356-2546

MACMILLAN, WHITNEY, food products and import/export company executive. Chmn., CEO Cargill, Wayzata, Minn.; mem. bd. dirs. Deluxe Corp., Minn. Office: Cargill PO Box 9300 Minneapolis MN 55440-9300*

MACMILLAN, WILLIAM HOOPER, university dean, educator; b. Boston, Oct. 21, 1923; s. Alexander Stewart and Leslie (Hooper) M.; m. Anne Stearns, May 29, 1948; children: Leslie Jean, Robert Bruce, William Ian. BA, McGill U., 1948; PhD, Yale U., 1954. Instr. pharmacology U. Vt. Coll. Medicine, 1954-55, asst. prof., 1955-59, asso. prof., 1959-64, chmn. dept. pharmacology, 1962-63, prof. pharmacology, 1964-76, dean Grad. Coll., 1963-69, 71-76; rsch. fellow USPHS, U. Oxford, Eng., 1958-59; cons. New Eng. Assn. Schs. and Colls., 1967-76; Ford Found. project specialist, sci. adv. to Haile Sellassie I U., Addis Ababa., Ethiopia, 1969-71; prof. biology, dean Grad. Sch. U. Ala., 1976-91, prof. biology, dean emeritus, 1991—; cons. So. Assn. Colls. and Schs., 1976-91; exec. com. African grad. Fellowship Program, African-Am. Inst., N.Y.C., 1971-92; chmn. com. biomed. scis. Coun. of Grad. Schs., Washington, 1973-77, bd. dirs., 1985-88; exec. com. N.E. Assn. Grad. Schs., 1975-76; v.p. Conf. So. Grad. Schs., 1981, pres., 1982; pres. New Eng. Assn. Grad. Schs., 1971; bd. dirs. Oak Ridge Associated Univs., 1987-93. Officer USNR, 1943-46. Mem. Am. Soc. Pharmacology and Exptl. Therapeutics, AAAS, N.Y. Acad. Sci., AAUP, Sigma Xi.

MACMILLEN, RICHARD EDWARD, biological sciences educator, researcher; b. Upland, Calif., Apr. 19, 1932; s. Hesper Nichols and Ruth Henrietta (Golder) MacM.; m. Ann Gray, June 12, 1953 (div. 1975); children: Jennifer Kathleen, Douglas Michael; m. Barbara Jean Morgan, Oct. 23, 1980; 1 child, Ian Richard. BA, Pomona Coll., 1954; MS, U. Mich., 1956; PhD, UCLA, 1961. From instr. to assoc. prof. Pomona Coll., Claremont, Calif., 1960-68, Wig Disting. prof., 1965; assoc. prof., then prof. U. Calif., Irvine, 1968—, chair dept. population and environ. biology, 1972-74, chair dept. ecology and evolutionary biology, 1984-90; prof. emeritus, 1993—; adj. prof. biology So. Oreg. U., Ashland, 1996—; mem. award panel NSF, Washington, 1976-80; coord. U. Calif. Multi-Campus Supercourse in Environ. Biology, White Mountain Rsch. Sta., spring 1996, 97. Contbr. numerous articles to profl. jours. Chair sci. adv. bd. Endangered Habitats League, 1991-93. Recipient rsch. awards NSF, 1961-83; Fulbright-Hays advanced rsch. fellow Monash U., Australia, 1966-67. Fellow AAAS; mem. Am. Soc. Mammalogists (life), Ecol. Soc. Am. (cert. sr. ecologist), Am. Ornithologists Union, Cooper Ornithol. Soc. (life, bd. dirs. 1982-84). Democrat. Avocations: fly fishing, camping, hiking, nature photography. Home: 705 Foss Rd Talent OR 97540 Office: So Oreg State U Dept Biology Ashland OR 97520 *As world human populations continue to increase, our natural world continues to degrade. It is incumbent upon all of us to accept the responsibility of stewarding our land and its biota as precious and renewable resources.*

MACMILLIN, JAMES, religious organization administrator. Pres. John Milton Soc. for Blind Can., Toronto, Ont. Office: John Milton Soc For Blind, 60 St Clair Ave E Flr 9, Toronto, ON Canada M4T 1N5*

MACMINN, ALEENE MERLE B(ARNES), newspaper editor, columnist, educator; b. Salt Lake City, Sept. 19, 1930; d. Harold Sansom and Allie (Rasmussen) Barnes; m. Fraser K. MacMinn, July 28, 1961; children: Margaret A., Gregor Geordie. AA, Glendale Coll., 1950; BA, U. So. Calif., L.A., 1952. Women's page reporter Glendale (Calif.) News-Press, 1948-52; women's page reporter L.A. Times, 1953-57, asst. family editor, 1957-60, asst. TV editor, 1960-65, exec. TV editor, 1965-69, asst. entertainment editor, 1969-72, TV Times editor, 1972-91, asst. Calendar editor, entertainment columnist, 1989-93; sr. lectr. U. So. Calif. Sch. Journalism, 1979-92. Mem. Women in Communications, Alpha Gamma Delta. Mem. LDS Ch.

MACMULLEN, DOUGLAS BURGOYNE, writer, editor, retired army officer, publisher; b. Berkeley, Calif., Dec. 26, 1919; s. T. Douglas and Florence (Burgoyne) MacM.; ed. San Francisco State U., 1937-41, Stanford U., U. Calif., Fgn. Svc. Inst., Strategic Intelligence Sch., Indsl. Coll. of the Armed Forces, Air War Coll., Army Mgmt. Sch.; m. Sherry Bernice Auerbach, Mar. 11, 1942; 1 child, Douglas Burgoyne Jr. Commd. 2d lt. F.A. Res. U.S. Army, 1941; advanced through grades to col. M.I., 1967; Army gen. staff Psychol. Ops. Fgn. Svc., PTO; ret., 1972; exec. editor Am. Rsch. Assoc., Sherman Oaks, Calif.; cons. in communication; accredited corr. Def. Dept. Bd. govs. Monte Vista Grove Homes, Pasadena, Calif., Shriners Hosps. for Crippled Children, L.A.; pres. Clan MacMillan Soc. N.Am., 1973-77, trustee, 1975—; mem. L.A. Olympics Citizens Adv. Commn., 1982-84; mem. L.A. Philanthropic Found.; bd. dirs. Masonic Press Club, L.A., 1975, 84-88; mem. steering com. Mayor L.A. Coun. Internat. Visitors and Sister Cities, 1969; hon. dep. sheriff San Bernardino County, Calif., 1996—; chmn. Los Angeles-Glasgow Sister Cities Ad Hoc Com.; former mem. San Francisco Mayor's Mil. and Naval Affairs Com.; mem. wills and gifts com. Shriners Hosp. Crippled Children, Al Malaikah Temple, L.A., 1974-80; cons. com. on pub. info. Masons Grand Lodge of Calif., 1985-86. Decorated Legion of Merit, Army Commendation medal (U.S.), Knight Comdr. Order of Polonia Restituta (Free Poland), Red Cross of Constantine; Royal Order Scotland. Mem. Internat. Inst. Strategic Studies, Nat. Mil. Intelligence Assn., Assn. Former Intelligence Officers (pres. L.A. County chpt.), U.S. Naval Inst., Assn. U.S. Army, Company Mil. Historians, Am. Def. Preparedness Assn., St. Andrew's Soc. Los Angeles (past pres., trustee), Air Force Assn., Coun. Brit. Socs., Chinese Hist. Soc. Am., Ret. Officers Assn., Calif. State Sheriff's Assn., Friends Brit. Lib., Stanford U. Alumni Assn., Calif. Newspaper Pubs. Assn., Nat. Def. Exec. Res., Sigma Delta Chi. Republican. Presbyterian. Clubs: Press, Caledonian (London); Army & Navy Club (Washington), San Francisco Press. Lodges: Masons (32 deg.), K.T., Shriners (editor, pub. The Al Malaikahan, former imperial news editor Shrine of N.Am.), Quatuor Coronati C.C. Co-author: Psychological Profile of Cambodia, 1971; author-editor: A Sentimental Journey--The History of the First Hundred Years, 1988; numerous other publs. and articles; radio commentator and newspaper columnist on mil., polit. and internat. affairs. Address: PO Box 5201 Sherman Oaks CA 91413-5201

MACMULLEN, RAMSAY, retired history educator; b. N.Y.C., Mar. 3, 1928; s. Charles William and Margaret (Richmond) MacM.; m. Edith Merriman Nye, Aug. 7, 1954 (div. 1991); children: John A., Priscilla N., William R., Lucinda S.; m. Margaret McNeill, Aug. 1, 1992. A.B., Harvard, 1950, A.M., 1953, Ph.D., 1957. Instr., asst. prof. U. Oreg., 1956-61; asso. prof., prof. Brandeis U., 1961-67, chmn. dept. classics, 1965-66; prof. Yale U., 1967-93, Dunham prof. history and classics, 1979-93, chmn. dept. history, 1970-72, master Calhoun Coll., 1984-90. Author: Soldier and Civilian in the Later Roman Empire, 1963, Enemies of the Roman Order, 1966, Constantine, 1969, Roman Social Relations, 1974, Roman Government's Response to Crisis, 1976, Paganism in the Roman Empire, 1981, Christianizing the Roman Empire, 1984, Corruption and the Decline of Rome, 1988, Changes in the Roman Empire, 1990; (with E.N. Lane) Paganism and Christianity, 1992, Christianity and Paganism, 1997. Recipient Porter prize Coll. Art Assn., 1964; Fulbright fellow, 1960-61; Guggenheim fellow, 1964; Princeton Inst. for Advanced Study fellow, 1964-65; Nat. Endowment for Humanities sr. fellow, 1974-75. Mem. Soc. for Promotion Roman Studies, Assn. Ancient Historians (pres. 1978-81). Home: 25 Temple Ct New Haven CT 06511-6820 Office: Yale U Dept History New Haven CT 06520

MACMURREN, HAROLD HENRY, JR., psychologist, lawyer; b. Jersey City, Sept. 18, 1942; s. Harold Sr. and Evelyn (Almone) MacM.; m. Margaret Bartro, Nov. 21, 1970. BA, William Paterson Coll., Wayne, N.J., 1965; MA, Jersey City Coll., 1973; EdD, St. Johns U., N.Y.C., 1985; JD, Rutgers U., 1989. Cert. secondary tchr., N.J.; Bar: N.J. 1989. Instr. Wanaque (N.J.) Bd. Edn., 1965-66, cons. psychologist, 1983-84; instr. Elmwood Park (N.J.) Bd. Edn., 1967-70; coll. faculty mem., psychologist Assoc. Clinic, Jersey City, 1971-72; cons. psychologist Rockaway (N.J.) Bd. Edn., 1972-83; intern lawyer Environ. Law Clinic, Newark, N.J., 1988-89; cons. psychologist Pequannock (N.J.) Bd. Edn., 1984—; coord. of child study team Sandyston Walpack Sch. System; adj. prof. William Paterson Coll.; spkr. and writer in field. Mem. ABA, NEA, N.J. Edn. Assn., N.J. Psychologist Assn., N.J. Bar Assn., Sierra Club, Phi Delta Kappa. Avocations: reading, travel, skiing, hiking. Home: 4 Systema Pl Sussex NJ 07461-2833 Office: Pequannock Board of Ed Pequannock NJ 07440

MACMURREN, MARGARET PATRICIA, secondary education educator, consultant; b. Newark, Nov. 4, 1947; d. Kenneth F. and Doris E. (Lounsberry) Bartro; m. Harold MacMurren, Nov. 21, 1970. BA, Paterson State U., 1969; MA, William Paterson Coll., 1976; postgrad., Jersey City State Coll., 1976—. Tchr. Byram (N.J.) Twp. Schs., 1969-77; learning cons., child study team coord. Andover Regional Schs., Newton, N.J., 1977—. Mem. NEA, N.J. Edn. Assn., N.J. Assn. Learning Cons., Sussex Coutny Assn. Learning Cons. (pres. 1982-83, 93-94, sec.-treas. 1991-92, v.p. 1992-93), Andover Regional Edn. Assn. (pres. 1986-87). Avocations: skiing, dancing, weight training, travel, reading. Home: 4 Systema Pl Sussex NJ 07461-2833 Office: Andover Regional Schs 707 Limecrest Rd Newton NJ 07860-8801

MAC NAMARA, DONAL EOIN JOSEPH, criminologist; b. N.Y.C., Aug. 13, 1916; s. Daniel Patrick and Rita F.V. (Chambers) Mac N.; m. Margaret Elizabeth Scott, July 30, 1953 (dec. 1990); 1 child, Brian Scott. BS, Columbia U., 1939, M of Phil., 1948; M of Pub. Adminstrn., NYU, 1946; LLD (hon.), August Vollmer U., 1990. Instr. polit. sci. Rutgers U., New Brunswick, N.J., 1948-49; asst. dir. Delinquency Control Inst. L.A., 1949-50; dir. law enforcement program U. So. Calif., 1949-50; vis. prof. U. Louisville, 1950-71, Fla. State U., Tallahassee, 1958, St. Lawrence U., Canton, N.Y., 1954, 56; chmn. Law Enforcement Insts., NYU, 1950-57; coordinator police sci. programs Bklyn. Coll., 1954-57; with N.Y. Inst. Criminology, N.Y.C., 1950-63; assoc. dean N.Y. Inst. Criminology, 1955-56, dean, 1956-63; prof. criminology Center Corrections Tng., CUNY, 1966-67; in charge corrections programs John Jay Coll. Criminal Justice, 1965-85, emeritus disting. prof., 1985; dean doctoral programs August Vollmer U., Orange, Calif., 1987—; dir. summer session CUNY, Ireland, 1970; Disting. vis. prof. U. Melbourne, Australia, 1981; vis. prof. criminology Bar Ilan U., Ramat Gan, Israel, 1982-83; vis. prof. Calif. State U., Spring 1984, U. N.Mex., 1985, U. Tenn., 1986, Calif. State U., 1987-88, Bar Ilan U., Israel, Spring 1989; mng. ptnr. Flath-MacNamara Assocs., N.Y.C., 1958-64; dir. Crime Show Cons., N.Y.C., Traffic Mgmt. Survey Fund, Inc., N.Y.C.; Eastern regional dir. Character Underwriters, Inc., L.A.; vis. mem. faculty Hunter, Queens, Bklyn. colls., 1952-58; vis. lectr. criminology Brandeis U., Waltham, Mass., 1962; lectr. police adminstrn. SUNY, 1966-67; lectr. penology (CCNY), 1965-67; specialist police, correctional adminstrn. grad. program tng. pub. adminstrn., State of N.Y., Albany, 1951-56; criminol. cons. Am. Express Co., 1962-68; cons., Bergen County, N.J., 1967, N.J. Commn. Civil Disorders, 1967-68; vis. prof. criminology U. Utah, Salt Lake City, 1962; pres. League to Abolish Capital Punishment, 1958-70, chmn. bd., 1959-91; col. a.d.c. to commr. Ky. State Police, 1963; external assessor in police and pub. adminstrn. Republic of Ireland, 1975; vis. prof. Inst. Pub. Adminstrn., Dublin, 1974-75. Author: Problems of Sex Behavior, 1968, Perspectives on Correction, 1971, Corrections: Problems of Punishment and Rehabilitation, 1973, Police: Problems and Prospects, 1974, Criminal Justice, 1976, Sex, Crime and the Law, 1977, Incarceration: The Sociology of Imprisonment, 1978, Crime, Criminals and Corrections, 1981, Deviants: Victims or Victimizers, 1984, Deviance, Denigration and Dominance, 1990, also articles.; Am. editor: Excerpta Criminologica, 1965-85; editor-in-chief: Criminology: An Interdisciplinary Jour., 1975-78; asso. editor: Jour. Corrective Psychiatry; editor: UN Crime Conference: Keynote Document Edit., 1981. Exec. v.p. Real Estate Bd., Bronx, N.Y., 1964-65. Served to maj. AUS, 1942-48. Recipient award of honor Internat. Assn. Women Police, 1960, Herbert A. Bloch award Am. Soc. Criminology, 1967, Bruce Smith award Am. Acad. of Criminal Justice Scis., 1990, Lifetime Achievement in Criminal Justice award Am. Soc. for Pub. Adminstrn., 1991; named to Am. Police Hall Fame, 1996. Fellow AAAS (chmn. sci. criminology sect., mem. council 1957-82), Am. Acad. Criminalistics (presiding); mem. Internat. Police Officers Assn. (life), Am. Soc. Criminology (pres. 1960-64), Assn. Psychiat. Treatment Offenders (program coordinator 1954-58), M.P. Assn., Internat. Criminol. Soc., Am. Assn. Criminologists (hon. life), Edn. Research Assn. (exec. dir. 1965-69), Nat. Police Officers Assn. Am. (research dir. 1963-67), Pi Sigma Alpha. Home: 76 Four Corners Rd Warwick NY 10990-3020 Office: 899 10th Ave New York NY 10019-1029

MACNAMARA, THOMAS EDWARD, physician, educator; b. Airdrie, Scotland, May 23, 1929; came to U.S., 1956, naturalized, 1962; s. Edward Francis and Bridget Monica (Fawcett) M.; m. Julia B. Caulfield, Sept. 22, 1956; children: Edward, Brian, Mary, Bridget, Anne. Student, Paisley Tech. Coll., Glasgow U., 1947, MBChB, 1952. Diplomate: Am. Bd. Anesthesiology. Intern Victoria Infirmary, Glasgow, 1953, Leith Hosp., Edinburgh, Bellsdyke Hosp., Larbert, 1954, St. Martins Hosp., Bath, 1954, Birmingham (Eng.) Accident Hosp., 1955; resident in anesthesiology Mass. Gen. Hosp., Boston, 1956; practice medicine specializing in anesthesia Washington, 1957-59, 62—, Boston, 1960-62; mem. staff Mass. Gen. Hosp., Boston; instr. anesthesia Georgetown U., 1957-60, prof., chmn. dept. anesthesia Med. Center, 1962-90; prof. emeritus, 1995—; dir. anethesia and surg. svcs. Walter Grant Magnuson Clin. Ctr., NIH, Bethesda, Md., 1990-92; mem. faculty senate Georgetown U., 1967-75, v.p. senate, 1967-70, pres. senate, 1973-75; chief anesthesiology NIH Clin. Center, Bethesda, Md., 1975-83, 92-93; asst. in anesthesia Mass. Gen. Hosp., Harvard U. Med. Sch., 1960-62; cons. VA Hosp., Washington, 1962-92. Editor: Surgical Digest, 1966-70, Clinical Therapeutics, 1976-82. Bd. dirs. Georgetown U. Fed. Credit Union. Fellow Am. Coll. Anesthesiologists (chmn. bd. govs. 1986-87); mem. Md.-D.C. Soc. Anesthesiology (pres. sect. II 1966-67). Home: PO Box 7137 Arlington VA 22207-0137 Office: NIH Walter Grant Magnuson Clin Ctr Bldg 10 Bethesda MD 20892

MACNAUGHTON, ANGUS ATHOLE, finance company executive; b. Montreal, July 15, 1931; s. Athole Austin and Emily Kidder (MacLean) MacN.; children: Gillian Heather, Angus Andrew. Student, Lakefield Coll. Sch., 1941-47, McGill U., 1949-54. Auditor Coopers & Lybrand, Montreal, 1949-55; acct. Genstar Ltd., Montreal, 1955; asst. treas. Genstar Ltd., 1956-61, treas., 1961-64, v.p., 1964-70, exec. v.p., 1970-73, pres., 1973-76, vice chmn., chief exec. officer, 1976-81, chmn. or pres., chief exec. officer, 1981-86; pres. Genstar Investment Corp., 1987—; bd. dirs. Can. Pacific Ltd., Sun Life Assurance Co., Can., Ltd., Barrick Gold Corp., Diversified Collection Svcs., Inc., Varian Assocs., Inc.; past pres. Montreal chpt. Tax Execs. Inst. Bd. govs. Lakefield Coll. Sch.; past chmn. San Francisco Bay Area coun. Boy Scouts Am.; bd. dirs. San Francisco Opera; trustee World Affairs Coun. of No. Calif. Mem. Pacific Union Club, World Trade Club, Villa Taverna (San Francisco), Mt. Royal Club (Montreal), Toronto Club. Office: Genstar Investment Corp 950 Tower Ln Ste 1170 Foster City CA 94404-2127 also: Barrick Gold Corp, 200 Bay St Ste 2700, Toronto, ON Canada M5J 2J3

MACNAUGHTON, JOHN DAVID FRANCIS, aerospace company executive; b. Moose Jaw, Sask., Can., Apr. 10, 1932; s. Francis Maurice and Grace Elizabeth Ellen (Moore) MacN.; m. Joy Barbara Spencer; children: Paul, Neil, Jane. Diploma, deHavilland Aero. Tech. Sch., 1954; BSc, Hatfield Coll., U.K., 1954. Engrng. supr. deHavilland's Guided Missile Div., 1954-57; chief engr. Garrett Mfg. Ltd., 1958-61; chief mech. engr. deHavilland's Spl. Projects and Applied Research, 1962-68; dir. mech. products dept. Spar Aerospace Ltd., Toronto, Ont., Can., 1968-69, v.p. mktg. and planning, 1969-74, v.p., gen. mgr. remote manipulator systems div., 1974-80, v.p., group exec. space & electronics group, 1981-82, sr. v.p. systems sector, from 1982, exec. v.p., 1988-89, pres., CEO, 1989-96, bd. dirs., 1989—; chmn. Nat. Quality Inst.; invited spkr. various profl. confs. Contbr. papers to profl. publs. and profl. confs. Dir.-at-large Jr. Achievement Can. Recipient Engrng. medal Profl. Engrs. Ont., 1965, Pub. Service medal NASA, 1982, McGregor award Royal Can. Air Force Assn., 1983, Thomas W. Eadie medal Royal Soc. Can., 1984, 125th Can. Anniversary medal, 1993. Fellow Can. Aeronautics and Space Inst. (Casey Baldwin award 1963, McCurdy award 1983); mem. Assn. Profl. Engrs. of Province Ont., Info. Tech. Assn. Can. Rideau (Ottawa) Club, Mississauga Golf and Country Club, Bd. of Trade (Toronto), Founders Club (Toronto), Toronto Club.

MACNEAL, EDWARD ARTHUR, economic consultant; b. Winona Lake, Ind., Apr. 19, 1925; s. Kenneth Forsyth and Marguerite Josephine (Giroud) MacN.; m. Priscilla Creed Perry, Dec. 27, 1952; children: Catherine Wright, Madeleine Creed. Student Harvard, 1943; B.A., U. Chgo., 1948, M.A., 1951. Exec. sec. Internat. Soc. Gen. Semantics, Chgo., 1947-50; staff cons. James C. Buckley, Inc., N.Y.C., 1951-55; market researcher Socony Mobil Oil Co., N.Y.C., 1955-58; research dir. O.E. McIntyre, Inc., N.Y.C., 1958-61; econ. cons., N.Y., 1956-66, Wayne, Pa., 1966—; adv. local govt. agys. Served with AUS, 1943-46; ETO. Mem. ABA, Am. Statis. Assn., Am. Econ. Assn., Am. Mathematical Soc., Internat. Soc. Gen. Semantics (dir.), Inst. Gen. Semantics (dir.), Jean Piaget Soc., Am. Sociol. Assn., Am. Assn. Airport Execs., Travel and Tourism Rsch. Assn., Travel Rsch. Forum. Clubs: Nat. Aviation; Harvard (Phila.); Wings. Author: The Semantics of Air Passenger Transportation, 1981, MacNeal's Master Atlas of Decision Making, 1988, Mathsemantics: Making Numbers Talk Sense, 1994. Home: 348 Louella Ave Wayne PA 19087-4855 Office: PO Box 249 Wayne PA 19087-0249

MACNEE, ALAN BRECK, electrical engineer, educator; b. N.Y.C., Sept. 19, 1920; s. Forrest Frew and Ellen (Breck) M.; m. Lois Fuller Livermore, Feb. 16, 1946; children—Carol, Bruce Forrest, David Breck, Timothy Jay. S.B., S.M., M.I.T., 1943, Sc.D. (George Eastman fellow), 1948. Research asso. Chalmers Tech. U., Gothenburg, Sweden, 1949-50; vis. asso. prof. Chalmers Tech. U., 1961-62; mem. faculty U. Mich., Ann Arbor, 1950—; prof. elec. engring. U. Mich., 1959-89, prof. emeritus, 1989—; sr. research asso. Goddard Space Flight Center, NASA, 1971-72; mem. vis. tech. staff Sandia Labs., 1980-81. Co-author Modern Circuit Analysis, 1973; contbr. articles to profl. publs.; patentee in field. Recipient B.J. Thompson Meml. prize IRE, 1951, Western Electric Fund award Am. Soc. Engring. Edn., 1968-69. Fellow IEEE, AAAS; mem. Royal Soc. Sci. and Lit. (Gothenburg) (fgn. mem.), Sigma Xi, Eta Kappa Nu, Phi Kappa Phi. Congregationalist. Office: Univ Mich 1215 EECS Bldg Ann Arbor MI 48109

MACNEIL, IAN RODERICK, lawyer, educator; b. N.Y.C., June 20, 1929; s. Robert Lister and Kathleen Gertrude (Metcalf) Macneil; m. Nancy Carol Wilson, Mar. 29, 1952; children: Roderick, Jennifer, Duncan (dec.), Andrew. BA magna cum laude, U. Vt., 1950; LLB magna cum laude, Harvard U., 1955. Bar: N.H. 1956. Law clk. Hon. Peter Woodbury, 1955-56; asso. Sulloway Hollis Godfrey & Soden, Concord, N.H., 1956-59; mem. faculty Cornell U. Law Sch., Ithaca, N.Y., 1959-72, 74-80, Ingersoll prof. law, 1976-80; Wigmore prof. law Northwestern U. Sch. Law, Chgo., 1980—; vis. prof. U. East Africa, 1965-67, Duke U., 1971-72; prof. law, mem. Inst. Advanced Studies, U. Va., 1972-74; vis. fellow Centre for Socio-legal Studies and Wolfson Coll., Oxford U., 1979; hon. vis. fellow faculty law U. Edinburgh, 1979, 87; Rosenthal lectr. Northwestern U. Sch. Law, 1979; Braucher vis. prof. Harvard U., 1988-89. Author: Bankruptcy Law in East Africa, 1966, Contracts: Exchange Transactions and Relations, 2d edit., 1978, The New Social Contract, 1980, American Arbitration Law: Reformation Nationalization Internationalization, 1992; co-author: Federal Arbitration Law, 1994. Served with U.S. Army, 1951-53. Guggenheim fellow, 1978-79. Fellow Royal Soc. Antiquaries (Scotland); mem. ABA, Am. Law Inst., N.H. Bar Assn., Can. Assn. Law Tchrs., Soc. Pub. Tchrs. Law, Standing Coun. Scottish Chiefs. Home: 95/6 Grange Loan, Edinburgh EH9 2ED, Scotland

MAC NEIL, JOSEPH NEIL, archbishop; b. Sydney, N.S., Can., Apr. 15, 1924; s. John Martin and Kate (Mac Lean) Mac N. BA, St. Francis Xavier U., Antigonish, N.S., 1944; postgrad., Holy Heart Sem., Halifax, N.S., 1944-48, U. Perugia, 1956, U. Chgo., 1964; JCD, U. St. Thomas, Rome, 1958. Ordained priest Roman Cath. Ch., 1948. Pastor parishes in N.S., 1948-55; officialis Chancery Office, Antigonish, 1958-59; adminstrn. Diocese of Antigonish, 1959-60; rector Cathedral Antigonish, 1961; dir. extension dept. St. Francis Xavier U., Antigonish, 1961-69, v.p., 1962-69; bishop St. John, N.B., Can., 1969-73; chancellor U. St. Thomas, Fredericton, N.B., 1969-73; archbishop of Edmonton, Alta., 1973—; chmn. Alta Bishops' Conf., 1973—; chmn. bd. Newman Theol. Coll., Edmonton, 1973—, St. Joseph's Coll. U. Alta., Edmonton, 1973—. Vice chmn. N.S. Voluntary Econ. Planning Bd., 1965-69; bd. dirs. Program and Planning Agy., Govt. of N.S., 1969; exec. Atlantic Provinces Econ. Coun., 1968-73, Can. Coun. Rural Devel., 1965-75; bd. dirs. Futures Secretariat, 1981, Ctr. for Human Devel., Toronto, Ont., Can., 1985—; mem. bd. mgmt. Edmonton Gen. Hosp., 1983-92, Edmonton Caritas Health Group, 1992—; mem. Nat. Com. for Can. Participation in Habitat, 1976. Mem. Can. Assn. Adult Edn. (past pres. N.S.), Can. Assn. Dirs. Univ. Extension and Summer Schs. (past pres.), Inst. Rsch. on Pub. Policy (founding mem.), Can. Conf. Cath. Bishops (pres. 1979-81, mem. com. on ecumenism 1985-91, com. on missions 1991-96, mem. permanent coun. 1993-95). Address: Archbishop of Edmonton, 8421 101st Ave, Edmonton, AB Canada T6A 0L1

MACNEIL, ROBERT BRECKENRIDGE WARE, broadcast journalist; b. Montreal, Que., Can., Jan. 19, 1931; came to U.S., 1963; s. Robert A.S. and Margaret Virginia (Oxner) MacN.; m. Rosemarie Anne Copland, 1956 (div. 1964); children: Catherine Anne, Ian B.; m. Jane J. Doherty, May 29, 1965 (div. 1983); children: Alison N., William H.; m. Donna P. Richards, Oct. 20, 1984. Student, Dalhousie U., 1949-51; BA, Carleton U., 1955; LHD (hon.), William Patterson Coll., 1977, Beaver Coll., Bates Coll., 1979, Lawrence U., 1980, Bucknell U., 1982, George Washington U., Kings Coll., Trinity Coll., U. Maine, 1983, Brown U., 1984, Colby Coll., Carleton Coll., U. S.C., 1985, Franklin and Marshall Coll., 1987, Nazareth Coll., Washington Coll., 1988, Kenyon Coll., 1990, U. Western Ont., 1992, U. Miami, Clark U., 1994, Clark U., 1994, U. L.I., 1995, Columbia U., 1995, Princeton U., 1995, The Cooper Union, 1996. Radio actor CBC, Halifax, N.S., Can., 1950-52; radio/TV announcer CBC, 1954-55; announcer Sta.-CJCH, Halifax, 1951-52; announcer, news writer Sta. CFRA, Ottawa, Ont., Can., 1952-54; sub-editor to filing editor Reuters News Agy., London, 1955-60; news corr. NBC, London, 1960-63, Washington, 1963-65, N.Y.C., 1965-67; corr. Panorama program BBC, London, 1967-71, 73-75; sr. corr. Nat. Public Affairs Center for TV, Washington, 1971-73; exec. editor, co-anchor MacNeil/Lehrer Report, Sta. -WNET-TV, N.Y.C., 1975—; exec. editor, co-anchor MacNeil/Lehrer News Hour, PBS, 1983-95, ret., 1995. Author: The People Machine, The Influence of Television on American Politics, 1968, The Right Place at the Right Time, 1982, Wordstruck, 1989, Burden of Desire, 1992, The Voyage, 1995; co-author: The Story of English, 1986; editor The Way We Were 1963, 1988. Recipient Lifetime Achievement award Overseas Press Club, 1995, Broadcaster of Yr. Internat. Radio and TV Soc., 1991, Paul White award Radio TV News Dirs. Assn., 1990, Medal of Honor U. Mo. Sch. Journalism, 1980. Fellow AAAS, The MacDowell Colony (chmn. 1993); mem. AFTRA, Assn. Radio and TV News Analysts, Writers Guild Am., Century Club (N.Y.C.). Office: c/o MacNeil-Lehrer Prodns 2700 S Quincy St Ste 240 Arlington VA 22206-2226

MACNEILL, ARTHUR EDSON, physician, science consultant; b. Waltham, Mass., July 14, 1912; s. Charles Alfred and Florence (Wright) MacN.; m. Lydia Mae Rhoades, June 25, 1941; children: Marjorie Ann, Arthur Edson, Jr. AB, Harvard U., 1933, MD, 1937; grad., Army Sch. Aviation Medicine, 1942. Intern Mary Hitchcock Meml. Hosp., Hanover, N.H., 1937-38; physician Health Svc. Dartmouth Coll., 1938-41; acting med. dir. Dartmouth U., 1945-46, instr. anatomy, 1944-46, rsch. assoc. physiol. scis., 1946-50; univ. physician U. Fla., Gainesville, 1946-47; cons. med. and biol. rsch. Fgn. Svc. U.S. Dept. State, 1950; dir. lab. Chronic Disease Rsch. Inst. Buffalo Sch. of Medicine, 1950-56; lectr. medicine U. Buffalo, 1951-57, asst. prof. surgery, Buswell Rsch. fellow, 1957-61; assoc. rsch. prof. surgery SUNY, Buffalo, 1961-64; dir. Inst. Therapeutic Engring., Sunapee, N.H., 1964-65, Dialysis Rsch. Inst., Sunapee, 1964-84; mem. rsch. staff, med. bd. Buffalo Gen. Hosp., 1951-64, cons. surg. rsch. staff, 1957-64, dir. dept. therapeutic engring., 1958-64; rsch. advisor dept. surgery Buffalo Children's Hosp., 1957-66; chief clin. investigative cons. Respiratory Ctr., Buffalo, 1954-55; med. assoc. Crotched Mt. Rehab. Ctr., Greenfield, N.H., 1967-68; med. staff New London (N.H.) Hosp., 1980—, chmn. investigational review com., 1983—; pvt. cons. in field. Developer blood dialyzer, blood pumps, blood flowmeters, blood rheometer, other devices for profl. treatment vital organs; contbr. articles to profl. jours. Served from 1st lt. to maj. M.C. USAAF, 1941-44, surgeon 72d Fighter Wing, 1943-44, staff surgeon, 1944; maj. hon. res., USAF, 1951—. Recipient Maj. Louis Livingston Seaman award Assn. Mil. Surgeons U.S., 1949, 1st award sci. rsch. Med. Soc. State N.Y., 1953, Redway award, 1963. Mem. AAAS, AMA, Instrument Soc. Am. (dir. med. and biol. divsn. 1956-57), N.H. Med. Assn., Grafton County Med. Assn., Assn. Mil. Surgeons, N.Y. Acad. Scis., N.H. Orthopedic Assn., Nat. Kidney Found., Sigma Xi. Methodist. Home: 37 Fairway Dr Grantham NH 03753 Office: PO Box 577 Grantham NH 03753-0577

MACNEILL, JAMES WILLIAM, international environment consultant; b. Sask., Can., Apr. 22, 1928; s. Leslie William and Helga Ingeborg (Nohlgren) MacN.; m. Phyllis Beryl Ferguson, Nov. 30, 1953; children: Catherine Anne, Robin Lynne. BA, U. Sask., 1949, BE Mech., 1958, LLD (hon.), 1988; Diplome, U. Stockholm, 1951; DSc (hon.), McGill U., 1992; D of Environ. Studies (hon.), U. Waterloo, 1993; LHD (hon.), Lakehead U., 1994. Spl. adv. on constl. rev. Privy Council Office, Govt. Can., Ottawa, Ont., 1969-70; asst. sec. Can. Ministry of State for Urban Affairs, Ottawa, 1970-73; permanent sec. Can. Ministry of State for Urban Affairs, 1973-76; Can. AEP, Can. commr.-gen. UN Human Settlements Conf., Vancouver, B.C., 1975-78; dir. environ. directorate OECD, Paris, 1978-84; sec. gen. World Commn. Environment and Devel., Geneva, 1984-87; sr. fellow Inst. Research Pub. Policy, Ottawa, 1987-93; pres. J.W. MacNeill and Assocs., 1987—; chmn. Internat. Inst. for Sustainable Devel., 1994—; spl. advisor to adminstrn. UN Devel. Program, 1994—; apptd. officer Order of Can., 1995. Author: Environmental Management, 1971, Beyond Interdependence, 1991. Recipient Saskatchewan Achievement award, 1985, Silver medal City of Paris, 1984, Climate Inst. award, 1991, Swedish WASA award, 1991, Lifetime Achievement award Govt. of Can., 1993. Mem. Assn. Profl. Engrs. Ont., Assn. Profl. Engrs. Sask. Office: 13th Fl, 250 Albert St, Ottawa, ON Canada K2P 1L5

MAC NEISH, RICHARD STOCKTON, archaeologist, educator; b. N.Y.C., Apr. 29, 1918; s. Harris Franklin and Elizabeth (Stockton) MacN.; m. Phyllis Diana Walter, Sept. 26, 1963; children: Richard Roderick, Alexander Stockton. B.A., U. Chgo., 1940, M.A., 1944, Ph.D., 1949; LL.D. (hon.), Simon Frazer U., 1980; LL.D. Guggenheim fellow, Harvard U., 1956; LL.D. Aboriginal fellow, U. Mich., 1946. Supr., dir. U. Chgo. (W.P.A.), 1941-46; head dept. archaeology U. Calgary, 1964-68; anthropologist Nat. Mus. Can., 1949-62; dir. R.S. Peabody Found. for Archaeology, Andover, Mass., 1968-83; prof. dept. archeology Boston U., 1982-86; dir. Andover Found. for Archaeol. Research, 1986—. Contbr. numerous articles and revs. to profl. jours. Apptd. to U.S. Pres. Adv. Com. on Cultural Properties, 1992—. With AUS, 1942-43. Recipient Spinden medal for archaeology, 1964, Lucy Wharton Drexel medal for archaeol. research U. Pa. Mus., 1965, Addison Emery Verrill medal Peabody Mus., Yale U., 1966, hon. Disting. Prof. award Universidad Nacional de San Cristobal de Huamanga, Ayacucho, Peru, 1970, Cornplanter medal for Iroquois research Auburn, N.Y., 1977. Mem. Soc. Am. Archaeology (exec. council), Nat. Acad. Scis., Brit. Acad., Soc. Am. Archaeology (pres. 1971-72), Am. Anthrop. Assn. (Alfred Vincent Kidder award 1971), Sigma Psi, Alpha Tau Omega. Office: Andover Found Archaeol Research PO Box 83 Andover MA 01810-0002

MAC NELLY, JEFFREY KENNETH, cartoonist; b. N.Y.C., Sept. 17, 1947; s. Clarence Lamont and Ruth Ellen (Fox) Mac N.; m. Marguerite Dewey Daniels, July 19, 1969; children: Jeffrey Kenneth, Frank Daniels; m. Martha Scott Perry, July 13, 1985; 1 child, Matthew Perry; m. Susan Spekin, July 22, 1990. Grad., Phillips Acad., 1965; student, U. N.C., Chapel Hill, 1965-69. Cartoonist, staff artist Chapel Hill Weekly, 1969-70; cartoonist Richmond (Va.) News Leader, 1970-81, Chgo. Tribune, 1981—; creator syndicated comic strip Shoe. Recipient Pulitzer prize for editorial cartoons 1972, 78, 85. Office: Chicago Tribune 435 N Michigan Ave Chicago IL 60611*

MACNICHOL, EDWARD FORD, JR., biophysicist, educator; b. Toledo, Oct. 24, 1918; s. Edward Ford and Adelaide (Foster) MacN.; m. Anne Proctor Ayer, Sept. 7, 1940; children—Edward Ford III, Anne (Mrs. David A. Brownell). A.B., Princeton, 1941; student, U. Pa., 1946-48; Ph.D., Johns Hopkins, 1952. Staff mem. radiation lab. Mass. Inst. Tech., 1941-46; from instr. to prof. biophysics Johns Hopkins, 1952-68; research biophysicist, asst. dir. Marine Biol. Lab., Woods Hole, Mass., 1972-76; dir. Lab. Sensory Physiology, 1973-84; prof. physiology Boston U. Med. Sch., 1973—; dir. Nat. Inst. Neurol. Diseases and Stroke, 1968-72; acting dir. Nat. Eye Inst., NIH, 1968-69; Mem. visual scis. study sect. NIH, 1963-66; mem. bd. sci. counsellors Nat. Inst. Neurol. Disease, and Blindness, 1965-68, chmn., 1968—; mem. U.S. Nat. Com. Photobiology, 1966-68, U.S. Nat. Com. Pure and Applied Biophysics, 1966. Co-editor: Sensory Processes, 1978-82. Bd. dirs. Deafness Research Found., 1973-83, sec., 1976-78. Recipient certificate of appreciation War Dept.-Navy Dept., 1947. Fellow IEEE (Engrng. in Biology and Medicine prize award 1965, Centennial medal 1984, editor trans. biomed. engring. 1963-65); mem. AAAS, Am. Phys. Soc., Am. Physiol. Soc.,

Biophys. Soc., Soc. for Neurosci. Research in neurophysiology of vision; design instrumentation biol. research. Home: 120 Racing Beach Ave Falmouth MA 02540-1709 Office: Dept Physiology Boston Univ Sch Med 80 E Concord St Roxbury MA 02118-2307 *I have found a career, which has involved research, administration, engineering and teaching, to be both rewarding and challenging. I would regret not having had all these experiences; particularly the contact with different kinds of people having different ways of thinking. I would urge young people, above all, to understand thoroughly the basic principles involved in what they are doing, then work out the details, instead of just learning by rote the details of a narrow specialty.*

MACNIDER, JACK, retired cement company executive; b. Washington, Feb. 21, 1927; s. Hanford and Margaret Elizabeth (McAuley) MacN.; m. Margaret Hansen, Sept. 9, 1950; 1 son, Charles Hanford. Grad., Milton (Mass.) Acad., 1946; BA, Harvard U., 1950, MBA with distinction, 1952. With U.S. Steel Corp., 1952-54; with Northwestern States Portland Cement Co., Mason City, Iowa, 1954-90; v.p., asst. gen. mgr. Northwestern States Portland Cement Co., 1959-60, pres., gen. mgr., 1960-90, chmn. bd., 1979-90, ret., 1990; dir. Portland Cement Assn., 1962-9, chmn., 1974-76; sec.-treas., pres., dir. Mason City Hotel Corp.; pres., dir. Indian Farms, Inc., 1976—; trustee Equitable Life Ins. Co., Iowa, 1964-93. Chmn. North Iowa Med. Ctr., 1974-91; trustee Beloit Coll., Midwest Rsch. Inst., Kansas City, Mo., Iowa Natural Heritage Found., 1979-90, Herbert Hoover Presdl. Libr., 1985—; hon. trustee Upper Iowa U., Fayette; pres. Iowa Coll. Found., 1962. With USMCR, 1944-45. Mem. NAM (dir. 1978-85), Young Pres. Orgn., Portland Cement Assn. (chmn. bd. 1974-75, dir.), Iowa Mfrs. Assn. (chmn. 1971-72, dir.), Mason City C. of C. (pres. 1962), Am. Legion (past post comdr.), Masons, Euchre and Cycle Club (Mason City, Mason City Country Club, Mpls. Club, Univ. Club (Chgo.), Des Moines Club, Los Tree Club (Fla.). Republican. Congregationalist. Address: PO Box 623 Mason City IA 50402-0623

MACOMBER, JOHN D., construction executive; b. Boston, Oct. 8, 1955; s. George and Ann L. Macomber; m. Kristin Hodgkins, June 11, 1983; children: Ian D., Eric C. BA, Dartmouth Coll., 1978; MBA, Harvard U., 1983. Project mgr. George B.H. Macomber Co., Boston, 1987-90, v.p., 1983-87, pres., chief exec. officer, 1990—; lectr. MIT. Mem. exec. com. Appalachian Mountain Club, Boston, 1991—, Boys & Girls Clubs, Boston, 1989-93. Mem. U.S. Alpine Ski Team, 1974-76; NCAA All-America in skiing, 1974, 78. Mem. Harvard Bus. Sch. Assn., Young Pres. Orgn. Avocations: skiing, bicycling, tennis. Office: George BH Macomber Co 1 Design Center Pl Ste 600 Boston MA 02210-2313

MACOMBER, JOHN D., industrialist; b. Rochester, N.Y., Jan. 13, 1928; s. William Butts and Elizabeth Currie (Ranlet) M.; m. Caroline Morgan, Oct. 21, 1955; children: Janet Morgan, Elizabeth Currie, William Butts II. B.A., Yale U., 1950; M.B.A., Harvard U., 1952. Mng. dir. McKinsey & Co., N.Y.C., France and Switzerland, 1954-73; chmn., CEO Celanese Corp., N.Y.C., 1973-87; chmn. J.D. Macomber & Co., N.Y.C., 1987-89; pres., chmn. Export-Import Bank of U.S., Washington, 1989-92; prin. JDM Investment Group, Washington, 1992—. 1st lt. USAF, 1952-54. Mem. Links (N.Y.C.), River Club (N.Y.C.), Union Club (N.Y.C.), Metropolitan (Washington). Office: JDM Investment Group 2806 N St NW Washington DC 20007-3339

MACON, CAROL ANN GLOECKLER, micro-computer data base management company executive; b. Milw., Mar. 25, 1942; d. William Theodore and Gwendolyn Martha (Rice) Gloeckler; m. Jerry Lyn Macon, Aug. 28, 1981; children: Christian, Marie. BS in Edn. cum laude, U. Wis., Milw., 1969; postgrad., Midwestern State U., Wichita Falls, Tex., 1977, U. Tex., San Antonio, 1978, U. Colo., Colorado Springs. Tchr. Lubbock, Tex.; patient affairs coord. Cardiac Assocs., Colorado Springs; founder, CFO Macon Systems, Inc., Colorado Springs. Artist, Australia, Tex., Colo. Founding mem., bd. dirs. Pikes Peak Botanic Gardens. Mem. Software Pubs. Assn., Colorado Springs BBB, Colorado Springs Fine Arts Ctr., Pikes Peak Rose Soc. (v.p.), Glen Eyrie Garden Soc., Colo. Mountain Club, Phi Kappa Phi, Kappa Delta Pi, Sigma Tau Delta, Psi Chi.

MACON, JANE HAUN, lawyer; b. Corpus Christi, Tex., Sept. 26, 1946; d. E.H. and Johnnie Mae (De Mauri) Haun; m. R. Laurence Macon, Sept. 6, 1969. BA in Internat. Studies, U. Tex., 1967, JD, 1970. Bar: Tex. 1971, Ga. 1971, U.S. Dist. Ct. (we. dist.) Tex. 1973, U.S. Ct. Appeals (5th and 11th cirs.) 1973. Legal staff Office Econ. Opportunity, Atlanta, 1970-71; trial atty. City of San Antonio, 1972-77, city atty., 1977-83; ptnr. Fulbright & Jaworski, LLP, San Antonio, 1983—; pres. Internat. Women's Forum, Washington, 1987-89; mem. Com. of 200, 1988—; bd. dirs. Thousand Oaks Nat. Bank, San Antonio. Legal counsel Nat. Women's Polit. Caucus, 1981—; bd. dirs. Alamo council Boy Scouts Am., San Antonio, 1977—. Named to San Antonio Hall of Fame, 1984; named one of Rising Stars, 1984. Fellow Tex. Bar Found., Tex. Bar Assn. (chmn. women and the law 1984-85, client security fund com.), Southwest Research Found.; mem. San Antonio Bar Assn., San Antonio Young Lawyers Assn., Women Lawyers Tex. (pres. 1984-85), Tex. Banking Bd., Bexar County Women's Bar Assn. Democrat. Baptist. Home: 230 W Elsmere Pl San Antonio TX 78212-2349 Office: Fulbright & Jaworski LLP 300 Convent St Ste 2200 San Antonio TX 78205-3714

MACON, JERRY LYN, software company owner, software publisher; b. Okla., Jan. 10, 1941; s. James Westwood and Mary Isabelle (Hankins) M.; m. Carol Ann Gloeckler, Aug. 28, 1981; children: Heather, Scott, Karla. BS in Physics magna cum laude, Colo. Coll., 1963; MS in Physics, MIT, 1966; MBA in Fin., U. Colo., 1980. Physics instr. U.S. Naval Acad., Annapolis, Md., 1966-69; stockbroker Merrill Lynch, Colorado Springs, 1969-71; dir. systems analysis and programming Colorado Springs Pub. Schs., 1971-80; co-founder, pres. Alpine Software, Inc., Colorado Springs, 1980-82, Macon Systems Inc., Colorado Springs, 1981—. Author: (software) DB Master, 1980, Advanced DB Master, 1981, Advanced DB Master for Windows Version 6.0, 1995. Mem. Colorado Springs Fine Arts Ctr., 1982—, Colorado Springs Better Bus. Bur., 1990—. Cmdr. U&SN, 1966-69. Boettcher Found. scholar, 1959; Woodrow Wilson fellow, 1963; MIT rsch. assistantship, 1964. Mem. Nat. Fedn. Ind. Bus., Software Pubs. Assn., Pikes Peak Rose Soc., Colo. Mountain Club, Phi Beta Kappa. Avocations: mountain climbing, hiking, travel, reading history, growing roses. Office: Macon Systems Inc 724 S Tejon St Colorado Springs CO 80903-4042

MACON, MYRA FAYE, retired library director; b. Slate Springs, Miss., Sept. 29, 1937; d. Thomas Howard and Reba Elizabeth (Edwards) M. BS in Edn., Delta State U., 1959; MLS, La. State U., 1965; postgrad., U. Akron, Ohio; EdD, Miss. State U., 1977. Librarian Greenwood (Miss.) Jr. High Sch., 1959-62, Greenwood High Sch., 1962-63, Grenada (Miss.) High Sch., 1963-64; library supr. Cuyahoga Falls (Ohio) City Schs., 1964-71; assoc. prof. U. Miss., Oxford, 1971-83; dir. libraries Delta State U., Cleve., 1983-95. Editor: School Library Media Services for Handicapped; editor: ANRT Newsletter, Miss. Libraries; contbr. articles to profl. jours. Mem. ALA, Southeastern Library Assn., Miss. Library Assn., Exch. Club, Phi Delta Kappa, Beta Phi Mu, Delta Kappa Gamma, Omicron Delta Kappa. Home: RR 3 Box 215A Calhoun City MS 38916-9323

MACON, SETH CRAVEN, retired insurance company executive; b. Climax, N.C., Mar. 22, 1919; s. Oran T. and Kate (Craven) M.; m. Hazel Lee Monsees, June 27, 1942; children—Carol Susan, Randall Seth. A.B., Guilford Coll., 1940; grad., Am. Coll. Life Underwriters, 1949; postgrad., Inst. Ins. Marketing, So. Methodist U., 1947; exec. program, U. N.C., 1958. With Jefferson Standard Life Ins. Co., 1940-86, v.p., assoc. agy. mgr., 1964-67, v.p., agy. mgr., 1967-70, sr. v.p., dir., mem. finance com., 1970-84; v.p. Jefferson-Pilot Corp., 1974-86, also bd. dirs.; mem. adv. bd. Branch Bank & Trust Co. Author: Action in Recruiting, 1970, Recruiting—Today's Number One Priority in Agency Management, 1979. Trustee Guilford Coll., 1969—, chmn., 1980-88; trustee Life Underwriters Tng. Coun., 1974-76, So. Theol. Sem. Found., Louisville, 1983-93; bd. dirs. N.C. Bapt. Homes, 1983-92; mem. coordinating coun. Coop. Bapt. Fellowship, 1991-95. Recipient Disting. Alumnus award Guilford Coll., 1978. Mem. Life Ins. Marketing and Research Assn. (dir. 1974-78, chmn. 1976-77). Baptist (deacon 1960—, mem. fin. com. 1960-63). Lodge: Rotary. Home: 3803 Madison Ave Greensboro NC 27403-1035

MACOVSKI, ALBERT, electrical engineering educator; b. N.Y.C., May 2, 1929; s. Philip and Rose (Winogr) M.; m. Adele Paris, Aug. 5, 1950; children—Michael, Nancy. B.E.E., City Coll. N.Y., 1950; M.E.E., Poly. Inst. Bklyn., 1953; Ph.D., Stanford U., 1968. Mem. tech. staff RCA Labs., Princeton, N.J., 1950-57; asst. prof., then assoc. prof. Poly. Inst. Bklyn., 1957-60; staff scientist Stanford Research Inst., Menlo Park, Calif., 1960-71; fellow U. Calif. Med. Center San Francisco, 1971-72; prof. elec. engring. and radiology Stanford U., 1972—, endowed chair, Canon USA prof. engring., 1991—; dir. Magnetic Resonance Systems Research Lab.; cons. to industry. Author. Recipient Achievement award RCA Labs., 1952, 54; award for color TV circuits Inst. Radio Engrs., 1958; NIH spl. fellow, 1971. Fellow IEEE (Zworykin award 1973), Am. Inst. Med. Biol. Engring., Optical Soc. Am., Internat. Soc. Magnetic Resonance in Medicine (former trustee, gold medal); mem. NAE, Inst. Medicine, Am. Assn. Physicists in Medicine, Sigma Xi, Eta Kappa Nu. Jewish. Achievements include patents in field. Home: 2505 Alpine Rd Menlo Park CA 94025-6314 Office: Stanford U Dept Elec Engring Stanford CA 94305

MACPHAIL, JOY K., provincial agency administrator; b. Hamilton, Ont., Canada; one child, Jack. Degree in econs., U. Western Ont.; postgrad. degree, London Sch. Econs. With Svc. Employees Internat. Union, British Columbia Govt. Employees Union; economist, trade unionist British Columbia Fedn. Labour; apptd. Min. Social Svcs., 1993—, Govt. House Leader, 1996—, Min. Health, 1996—, Min. Responsible for Srs. and B.C. Transit, 1996—; chair standing com. on fin. and crown corps.; vice chair pub. accts. com.; co-chair legis. constitution com.; govt. caucus chair. Active Hastings Park, Vancouver Action Plan, Cmty. Svcs. Fund, VIEW Performing Arts Soc.; mem. Kidsafe Adv. Com. Office: Minister's Office, Rm 306 Parliament Bldgs, Victoria, BC Canada V8V 1X4

MACPHAIL, MORAY ST. JOHN, mathematics educator emeritus; b. Kingston, Ont., Can., May 27, 1912; s. James Alexander and Agnes Mary (Macmorine) M.; m. Frances Marian Patterson, Aug. 17, 1939; 1 child, James Alexander. B.A., Queen's U., 1933; M.A., McGill U., 1934; D.Phil., Oxford U., 1936; D.Sc. (hon.), Carleton U., 1978. Instr. Acadia U., Wolfville, N.S., Can., 1937-39, asst. prof., 1939-41, assoc. prof., 1942-44, prof., 1944-47; instr. Princeton U., N.J., 1941-42; vis. lectr. Queen's U., Kingston, Ont., Can., 1947-48; assoc. prof. Carleton U., Ottawa, Ont., Can., 1948-53, prof., 1953-67, 68-77, prof. emeritus, 1977—; vis. prof. U. Toronto, Ont., Can., 1967-68; assoc. dean Carleton U., Ottawa, Ont., Can., 1956-60, dir. grad. studies, 1960-63, dean grad. studies, 1963-69. Contbr. articles to profl. jours. Fellow Royal Soc. Can.; mem. Am. Math. Soc., Can. Math. Soc. Avocation: Music. Home: 165 Powell Ave, Ottawa, ON Canada K1S 2A2 Office: Carleton Univ, Dept Math and Stats, Ottawa, ON Canada K1S 5B6

MACPHEE, CRAIG ROBERT, economist, educator; b. Annapolis Royal, N.S., Can., July 10, 1944; came to U.S., 1950; s. Craig and Dorothy (Seney) MacP.; m. Kathleen Gray McCown, Feb. 6, 1966 (div. 1981); children: Paul, Heather, Rob; m. Andrea Joy Sime, June 26, 1983. BS, U. Idaho, 1966; MA, Mich. State U., 1968, PhD, 1970. Asst. prof., then assoc. prof. econs. U. Nebr., Lincoln, 1969-89, prof., 1989—, chmn. econs. dept., 1980-83, 89—; econ. affairs officer UN, Geneva, 1975-77; internat. economist U.S. Dept. Labor, Washington, 1983-84; cons. in field. Author: Economics of Medical Equipment and Supply, 1975, Restrictions on International Trade in Steel, 1974. Mem. Am. Econ. Assn., Midwest Econ. Assn., Nebr. Econ. and Bus. Assn., Delta Sigma Pi (faculty adviser 1982-95), Phi Eta Sigma, Omicron Delta Epsilon. Avocations: running, skiing, sailing, reading. Home: 631 Hazelwood Dr Lincoln NE 68510-4325 Office: U Nebr Coll Bus Dept Econs Lincoln NE 68588-0489

MACPHEE, DONALD ALBERT, academic administrator; b. Portland, Oreg., Jan. 3, 1928; s. Donald Lyman and Helen Adelaide (Randall) MacP.; m. Betty Jo Mincher, Sept. 9, 1950; children: Martha, William, Rebecca. BA, Seattle Pacific Coll., 1950; MA, U. Calif., Berkeley, 1952, PhD, 1959. Instr., asst., assoc. prof. history, acting dean ednl. svcs. and summer session San Francisco State Coll., 1956-64; assoc. prof. to prof. history Calif. State U., Dominquez Hills, 1964-85, mem. acad. planning staff, dean Sch. Social and Behavioral Scis., provost and v.p. acad. affairs, 1964-85; pres. SUNY Coll., Fredonia, 1985-96, pres. emeritus, 1996—. Contbr. scholarly articles on Am. politics, labor history, historiography, higher education to profl. jours.

MACPHERSON, COLIN R(OBERTSON), pathologist, educator; b. Aberdeen, Scotland, Sept. 2, 1924; came to U.S., 1956; s. Donald J.R. and Nora (Tait) M.; m. Margaret E. Mitchell, Dec. 21, 1949; children: Shelagh, Catherine, Janet, Mary. MBChB, U. Cape Town, Union South Africa, 1946, M.Med., MD in Pathology, 1954. Diplomate Anatomic and Clinical Pathology, Blood Banking. Resident, instr. U. Cape Town, 1948-54; fellow Postgrad. Med. Sch., London, 1955-56; asst., assoc. then prof. pathology Ohio State U., Columbus, 1956-75, vice chmn. lab. med., 1961-75; dir. lab. medicine U. Cin., 1975-87, dir. Hoxworth Blood Ctr., 1988-90, prof. dept. pathology and lab. medicine, 1991-95, prof. emeritus, 1995—. Contbr. articles to profl. jours. Chmn. bd. schs., rev. bd. Nat. Accrediting Agy. for Clin. Lab. Scis., 1968-74. Mem. Am. Assn. Blood Banks. Presbyterian. Avocations: music, color photography. Office: U Cin Med Ctr Goodman St Cincinnati OH 45267-0714

MACPHERSON, ELLE, model; b. Sydney, Australia, Mar. 29, 1964; m. Gilles Bensimon, May 24, 1986 (div.). Appeared on covers of Sports Illustrated swimsuit edit., 1986, 87, 88, 94, Elle, Cosmopolitan, Self; film appearences include Husbands and Wives, 1992, Sirens, 1994, If Lucy Fell, 1996. Office: Women Model Mgmt 107 Greene St Fl 2 New York NY 10012-3803*

MACPHERSON, ROBERT DUNCAN, mathematician, educator; b. Lakewood, Ohio, May 25, 1944; s. Herbert G. and Jeanette (Wolfenden) MacP. BA, Swarthmore Coll., 1966; MA, PhD, Harvard U., 1970; DSc (hon.), Brown U., 1994, U. Lille (France), 1993. Instr. Brown U., Providence, 1970-72, asst. prof., 1972-74, assoc. prof., 1974-77, prof., 1977-85, Florence Pirce Grant prof., 1985-87; prof. MIT, Cambridge, Mass., 1987-94, Inst. Advanced Study, 1994—; mem. Inst. des Hautes Etudes Sci., Paris, France, 1980-81, Steklov Math Inst., Moscow, USSR, 1980; vis. prof. U. Rome, 1985, U. Chgo., 1991, Max-Planck Inst. for Math, 1992. Co-author: Stratified Morse Theory, 1988, Nilpotent Orbits, 1989; contbr. numerous articles to profl. jours. Recipient Research Grant NSF, 1970—; named Herman Weyl Lectr. Inst. for Advanced Study, 1982. Mem. NAS (Math. award 1992), Am. Acad. Arts Scis., Am. Math. Soc., Soc. for Applied and Indsl. Math., Nat. Orgn. of Gay and Lesbian Sci. and Tech. Profs., Phi Beta Kappa. Home: 19 Haslet Ave Princeton NJ 08540-4913 Office: Inst for Advanced Study Princeton NJ 08540

MACQUEEN, CHER, newscaster, sportscaster; b. Kansas City, Mo., Mar. 20, 1952; . Ira Raymond and Peggy Estelle (Turner) Milks. AA in Liberal Arts, L.A. Valley Coll., 1982; BS in Broadcasting, U. New York, Albany, 1993; grad., Barbizon Sch. of Modeling, 1996. Lic. radio-TV operator. Personnel specialist U.S. Army, Honolulu, Hawaii, 1973-75; adminstrv. specialist U.S. Army, San Francisco, Calif., 1975-77; broadcast journalist U.S. Army, Vicenza, Italy, 1977-80; radio traffic specialist Armed Forces Radio & TV, L.A., 1980-84, radio prodn. specialist, 1984-86; supr. broadcast support specialist Armed Forces Radio & TV, Sun Valley, Calif., 1986-90; broadcast support mgr, Armed Forces Radio & TV, Sun Valley, 1990-91, internal info. mgr., 1991-94, news and sports specialist, 1994—. Mem. DAV (life), Armed Forces Broadcasters Assn. (v.p. L.A., 1991-93). Avocations: handcrafts especially crochet. Home: PO Box 276 Highland CA 92346-0276 Office: Armed Forces Radio & TV Svc 1363 Z St Bldg 2730 Riverside CA 92518-2073

MACQUEEN, ROBERT MOFFAT, solar physicist; b. Memphis, Mar. 28, 1938; s. Marion Leigh and Grace (Gilfillan) MacQ.; m. Caroline Gibbs, June 25, 1960; children: Andrew, Marjorie. BS, Rhodes Coll., 1960; PhD, Johns Hopkins U., 1968. Asst. prof. physics Rhodes Coll., 1961-63; instr. physics and astronomy Goucher Coll., Towson, Md., 1964-66; sr. research scientist Nat. Ctr. for Atmospheric Research, Boulder, Colo., 1967-90, dir. High Altitude Obs., 1979-86, asst. dir., 1986-87, assoc. dir., 1987-89; prof. physics Rhodes Coll., Memphis, 1990—; prin. investigator NASA Apollo program, 1971-75, NASA Skylab program, 1970-76, NASA Solar Maximum Mission, 1976-79, NASA/ESA Internat. Solar Polar Mission, 1978-83; lectr. U. Colo., 1968-79, adj. prof., 1979-90; mem. com. on space astronomy Nat. Acad. Scis., 1973-76, mem. com. on space physics, 1977-79; mem. Space Sci. Bd., 1983-86. Recipient Exceptional Sci. Achievement medal NASA, 1974. Fellow Optical Soc. Am.; mem. Am. Astron. Soc. (chmn. solar physics div. 1976-78), Assn. Univ. Research Astronomy (dir.-at-large 1984-93, chmn. bd. 1989-92), Am. Assn. Physics Tchrs., Sigma Xi.

MAC RAE, ALFRED URQUHART, physicist, electrical engineer; b. N.Y.C., Apr. 14, 1932; s. Farquhar and Eliza J. (Urquhart) Mac R.; m. Peggy M. Hazard, May 13, 1967; children: Susan, Pamela. B.S. in Physics, Syracuse U., 1954, Ph.D. in Physics, 1960. Dir. integrated circuit devel. Bell Labs., Murray Hill, N.J., 1979-83; dir. satellite communications systems Bell Labs., Homdel, N.J., 1983-95; pres. Mac Tech., Berkeley Heights, N.J., 1995—; adv. com. to bd. trustees N.J. Inst. Tech., 1981-85. Bd. editor: Vacuum Sci. and Tech, 1965-67, Rev. Sci. Instruments, 1969-71; contbr. articles to jours.; patentee in field. Bd. dirs. Summit Area ARC, 1996—. Fellow IEEE (chmn. field awards 1991-93), Am. Phys. Soc.; mem. Bohmische Phys. Soc., IEEE Electron Devices Soc. (pres. 1986-87, chmn. field awards 1989-93, Ebers award 1994). Office: 72 Sherbrook Dr Berkeley Heights NJ 07922-2346

MACRAE, CAMERON FARQUHAR, III, lawyer; b. N.Y.C., Mar. 21, 1942; s. Cameron F. and Jane B. (Miller) MacR.; m. Ann Wooster Bedell, Nov. 30, 1974; children: Catherine Fairfax, Ann Cameron. A.B., Princeton U., 1963; LL.B., Yale U., 1966. Bar: N.Y. 1966, D.C. 1967, U.S. Dist. Ct. (so. dist.) N.Y. 1975. Atty.-advisor Office of Gen. Counsel to Sec. Air Force, Washington, 1966-69; assoc. Davis, Polk & Wardwell, N.Y.C., 1970-72; dep. supt. and counsel N.Y. State Banking Dept., N.Y.C., 1972-74; sr. ptnr., vice chmn. LeBoeuf, Lamb, Greene & MacRae, N.Y.C., 1975—. Trustee, sec. St. Andrew's Dune Ch., 1982—; hon. chmn. Clear Pool Inc., 1990—. Capt. USAF, 1966-69. Mem. Assn. of Bar of City of N.Y. (past mem. securities regulation com., banking law com.), D.C. Bar Assn. Republican. Episcopalian. Clubs: Links, Racquet and Tennis, Union (N.Y.C.), Meadow (v.p., bd. govs.), Bathing Corp., Shinnecock Hills Golf (Southampton), Cottage (Princeton, N.J.). Note and comment editor Yale Law Jour., 1965-66. Office: LeBoeuf Lamb Greene & MacRae 125 W 55th St New York NY 10019-5369

MACRAE, DONALD ALEXANDER, astronomy educator; b. Halifax, Nova Scotia, Can., Feb. 19, 1916; s. Donald Alexander and Laura Geddes (Barnstead) M.; m. Margaret Elizabeth Malcolm, Aug. 25, 1939; children—David Malcolm, Charles Donald, Andrew Richard. B.A., U. Toronto, Ont., Can., 1937; A.M., Harvard U., Cambridge, Mass., 1940, Ph.D., 1943. Research asst. U. Pa., Phila., 1941-42; lectr. Cornell U., Ithaca, N.Y., 1942-44; scientist Carbide & Carbon Chem. Corp., Oak Ridge, Tenn., 1944-46; asst. prof. Case Inst. Tech., Cleve., 1946-53; assoc. prof. to prof. astronomy, dir. David Dunlap Observatory, U. Toronto, 1953-78, prof. and dir. emeritus, 1978—; trustee Univs. Space Research Assn., Lunar and Planetary Inst., Houston, 1969-76, Can.-France-Hawaii Telescope Corp., Kamuela, Hawaii, 1973-79, Cascatrust, 1991-94. Fellow Royal Soc. Can., Royal Astron. Soc. (London); mem. Can. Astron. Soc., Royal Astron. Soc. Can., Am. Astron. Soc. Home: 427 Glencairn Ave, Toronto, ON Canada M5N 1V4 Office: David Dunlap Observatory, Box 360, Richmond Hill, ON Canada L4C 4Y6

MACRAE, DUNCAN, JR., social scientist, educator; b. Glen Ridge, N.J., Sept. 30, 1921; s. Duncan and Rebecca Kyle (MacRae); m. Edith Judith Krugelis, June 24, 1950 (dec. Oct. 1995); 1 child, Amy Frances; m. Jane Stiles Sharp, May 1997. A.B., Johns Hopkins U., 1942; A.M., Harvard U., 1943, Ph.D., 1950. Mem. staff Radiation Lab., Mass. Inst. Tech., 1943-46; instr., then lectr. sociology Princeton, 1949-51; rsch. assoc. Lab. Social Rels., Harvard U., 1951-53; asst. prof. sociology U. Calif., Berkeley, 1953-57; mem. faculty U. Chgo., 1957-72, prof. polit. sci. and sociology, 1964-72; William Rand Kenan, Jr. prof. polit. sci. and sociology U. N.C., Chapel Hill, 1972—; chmn. curriculum in public policy analysis U. N.C., 1980-85; Pres. Policy Studies Assn., 1974-75. Author: Dimensions of Congressional Voting, 1958, Parliament, Parties and Society in France, 1946-58, 1967, Issues and Parties in Legislative Voting, 1970, The Social Function of Social Science, 1976, (with James A. Wilde) Policy Analysis for Public Decisions, 1979, Policy Indicators, 1985, (with Dale Whittington) Expert Advice for Policy Choice, 1997; editor: (with others) Electronic Instruments, 1948, Policies for America's Public Schools, 1988. Fulbright rsch. scholar France, 1956-57. Fellow AAAS, Am. Acad. Arts and Scis.; mem. Am. Polit. Sci. Assn., Am. Sociol. Assn., Am. Econ. Assn., Assn. Pub. Policy and Mgmt., Phi Beta Kappa. Home: 737 Gimghoul Rd Chapel Hill NC 27514-3815

MAC RAE, HERBERT FARQUHAR, retired college president; b. Middle River, N.S., Can., Mar. 30, 1926; s. Murdoch John and Jessie (Matheson) Mac R.; m. Mary Ruth Finlayson, Sept. 24, 1955; children—Roderick John, Elizabeth Anne, Christy Margaret, Mary Jean. Diploma NS, Agrl. Coll., 1952; BSc, McGill U., 1954, MSc, 1956, PhD, 1960, DSc (hon.), 1987. Chemist, food and drug directorate Dept. Nat. Health and Welfare, Ottawa, Ont., 1960-61; mem. faulty Macdonald Coll. McGill U., 1961-72, assoc. prof. animal sci. Macdonald Coll., 1967-70, prof., chmn. dept. Macdonald Coll., 1970-72; prin. N.S. Agrl. Coll., Truro, 1972-89, ret., 1989. Named to Can. Agrl. Hall of Fame, 1994. Fellow Agrl. Inst. Can.; mem. Can. Soc. Animal Sci., Mem. Order of Can., Rotary, Sigma Xi. Home: 7 Hickman Dr, Truro, NS Canada B2N 2Z2

MACRAKIS, KRISTIE IRENE, history of science educator; b. Boston, Mar. 11, 1958; d. Michael S. and Lily Macrakis. BA, Oberlin (Ohio) Coll., 1980; MA, Harvard U., 1983, PhD, 1989. Rsch. asst. Harvard U., Cambridge, Mass., 1980-82, lectr., 1989-90; postdoctoral fellow Humbolt Found., Bonn, Germany, 1990-91; asst. prof. Mich. State U., East Lansing, 1991-97, assoc. prof., 1997—. Author: Surviving the Swastika, 1993; contbr. articles to profl. jours. AAUW fellow, WAshington, 1987-88; Social Sci. Rsch. Coun. fellow, N.Y.C., 1984-86; Inst. for Advanced Study fellow, 1993-94. Mem. Am. Hist. Assn., German Studies Assn., N.Y. Acad. Sci., History of Sci. Soc., Sigma Xi. Avocations: music, sports. Office: Mich State U Dept History Morrill Hall # 301 East Lansing MI 48824-1036

MACRI, THEODORE WILLIAM, book publisher; b. N.Y.C.; s. Francis Carl and Emma Julia (Fantini) M.; m. Joan Michele Damato; children: Alicia, Theodore William. AB, Villanova U.; MA, NYU. With Doubleday & Co. Inc., N.Y.C., dir. domestic rights, 1978-82, editorial group dir., 1982-83, asst. to pres., 1983; v.p., pub. R.R. Bowker Co., 1983-85; v.p., dir. subs. rights Contemporary Books, Inc., 1985-90; v.p. Carol Pub. Group, Inc., N.Y.C., 1990-94; pres. Ted Macri Assocs., 1994—; Bd. dirs. CUNY Ctr. for Pub., 1983—, Nat. Book Awards. Mem. N.Y. County Republican Com., 1980-81; mem. men's com. Mus. Natural History, N.Y.C., 1978. Served to lt. (j.g.) USNR. Named Disting. Alumnus Villanova U., 1983. Mem. Assn. Am. Pubs. (edn. com.), Am. Bookseller's Assn. Republican. Roman Catholic. Club: N.Y. Athletic (N.Y.C.). Office: 10 E End Ave Apt 4E New York NY 10021-1110

MACRIS, MICHAEL, lawyer; b. Jackson Heights, N.Y., July 12, 1949. Student, Cornell U.; BA with distinction, Stanford U., 1971; JD, Columbia U., 1974. Bar: N.Y. 1975, Conn. 1976. Mem. Cahill Gordon & Reindel, N.Y.C. Bd. editors Columbia Law Rev., 1973-74. Harlan Fiske Stone scholar. Mem. ABA (chmn. com. on fiduciary responsibility, real property, probate and trust law sect. 1993—), Conn. Bar Assn. (exec. com. tax sect. 1979—, co-editor ERISA & Benefits Law Jour.), Phi Beta Kappa. Office: Cahill Gordon & Reindel 80 Pine St New York NY 10005-1702

MACRO, LUCIA ANN, editor; b. Rhinebeck, N.Y., May 15, 1959; d. Virgil Jordan and Jeannette Anastasia (Jakelski) M.; m. Richard Marchione, 1992. BA, Fordham U., Bronx, 1981. Asst. editor Silhouette Books, N.Y.C., 1985—, sr. editor, 1989—; sr. editor Avon Books, N.Y.C., 1997—; speaker in field nat. convs. Romance Writers Am., 1985—; interviewed Bus. Week, 1987, CNN, 1991, Sta. WNBC, various newspapers including N.Y. Daily News, Washington Post. Author articles Romantic Times, 1988-89, 93, Romance Writers Report, 1988-89. Recipient Rita award Romance Writers Am., 1990, 92, 94, 95, 96. Democrat. Office: Silhouette Books 300 E 42nd St New York NY 10017-5947

MACRURY, KING, management counselor; b. Manchester, N.H., Oct. 14, 1915; s. Colin H. and Lauretta C. (Shea) MacR.; 1 son, Colin C. A.B., Rollins Coll., 1938; postgrad., St. Anselms Coll., L.I. Coll. Medicine, Princeton. Asst. personnel dir. Lily-Tulip Cup Corp., 1939; asst. dir. market research Ward Baking Co., 1940-41; staff mem. Nat. Indsl. Conf. Bd., 1941-43; cons. indsl. relations and orgn. planning McKinsey & Co., 1946-48; internal cons. Oxford Paper Co., 1949-50; installer, dir. indsl. relations Champion Internat. Co., 1950-51; pvt. practice mgmt. counselor, 1951—; lectr. Indsl. Edn. Inst., 1962-68, Mgmt. Center, Cambridge, 1968-71, Dun & Bradstreet, 1979—; extension div. U. N.H., 1968—; extension program U. Maine, 1978—; also U. Bridgeport, extension program U. Conn.; coordinator mgmt. edn. extension div. U. Conn., 1964-68, Philippine Council Mgmt., 1969—, Econ. Devel. Found. Philippines, 1969—, Am. Metal Stamping Assn., 1969—; condr. mgmt. seminars for Asian Assn. Mgmt. Orgns. C.I.O.S., 1972; Mem. Indsl. Devel. Commn. Andover, 1957-58; manpower com. U.S. Dept. Labor Bus. Adv. Council, 1958-61. Author: Developing Your People Potential; Contbr. numerous articles in field to profl. jours. Served to lt. USNR, 1943-46. Mem. N.H. Dental Soc. (hon.), Smaller Bus. Assn. N.E., Res. Officers Assn. Office: PO Box 215 Rye NH 03870-0215 *As individuals or as corporations, we derive our vitality from the responsiveness of those to whom we are bound in interest or effort. So it becomes, necessarily, our primary goal to inspire and to nurture this elemental source of strength.*

MACSAI, JOHN, architect; b. Budapest, Hungary, May 20, 1926; came to U.S., 1947, naturalized, 1954; s. Ferenc and Margit (Rosenfeld) Lusztig; m. Geraldine Marcus, May 7, 1950; children: Pamela, Aaron, Marian, Gwen. Baccalaureate summa cum laude, Kolcsey Gimnasium, Budapest, 1944; student, Atelier Art Sch., Budapest, 1941-43, Poly. U., Budapest, 1945-47; BArch magna cum laude, Miami U., Oxford, Ohio, 1949. Archtl. designer Skidmore, Owings & Merrill, Chgo., Pace Assos., Chgo., Raymond Loewy Assos., Chgo., 1949-55; ptnr. Hausner & Macsai, Chgo., 1955-71, Campbell & Macsai, Chgo., 1971-74; prin. John Macsai & Assocs. Architects, Inc., Chgo., 1975-90, O'Donnell Wicklund Pigozzi & Peterson, Chgo., 1991—; prof. architecture U. Ill., Chgo., 1970-96. Author: High Rise Apartment Buildings: A Design Primer, 1972, Housing, 1976, 2d edit., 1982, Russian edit., 1980, Mexican edit., 1984; co-author: Designing Environments for the Aged, 1977, Housing for a Maturing Population, 1983, (ency.) Highrise Apartment Buildings, 1988, East European Modernism, 1996; prin. works include Nat. Opinion Rsch. Ctr., U. Chgo., 1967, High Energy Physics Bldg., 1968, Social Svcs. Ctr., 1970; apt. bldgs. Harbor House, 1965, Malibu East, 1972, Waterford apt. bldg., 1976, U. Chgo. faculty townhouses, 1986, Fairfield Ct. housing for the elderly, 1988, Evanston Pl. apt. bldg. and city garage, 1991, 2960 N. Lake Shore Dr. Housing for the Elderly, 1991. Fellow AIA (13 design award citations Chgo. chpt.). Jewish. Home: 1207 Judson Ave Evanston IL 60202-1316 Office: O Donnell Wicklund Pigozzi & Peterson 1 N Franklin St Chicago IL 60606-3421

MACTAGGART, BARRY, retired corporate executive; b. Kandos, Australia, Dec. 29, 1931; came to U.S., 1972; s. Malcolm Ian and Dorothy (Schroder) MacT.; m. Robin Margaret Wilson, Nov. 24, 1962; children: Susan, Ian, Cameron. Cert. acct., Inst. Chartered Accts., Australia, 1954. Audit mgr. Peat, Marwick, Mitchell, Sydney, Australia, 1950-58; auditor, controller eastern area Pfizer Internat., Hong Kong, 1959-64; controller Pfizer Asia, Tokyo, 1964-65, dir. adminstrn., 1966-67; mgr. country Pfizer Australia, 1967-68; pres. Pfizer Asia, Hong Kong, 1968-72; exec. v.p. Pfizer Internat., N.Y.C., 1972-80, pres., 1980-81, pres., chmn. bd. dirs., dir., 1981-91. Mem. Indian Harbor Yacht Club, Hong Kong Club, The Pilgrims Club, John's Island Club, Riomar Bay Yacht Club, Univ. and Schs. Club. Home: 180 N Shore Pt Vero Beach FL 32963-3726

MACTAVISH, CRAIG, hockey player; b. London, Ont., Can., Aug. 15, 1958. Hockey player Boston Bruins Nat. Hockey League, 1980-85, hockey player Edmonton Oilers, 1985-94, hockey player N.Y. Rangers, 1994, hockey player Phila. Flyers, 1994-96, hockey player St. Louis Blues, 1996—; mem. Stanley Cup championship team 1987, 88, 90, 94; capt. Edmonton Oilers, 1992-93, 93-94. Office: Saint Louis Blues 1401 Clark Ave Saint Louis MO 63103-2700

MACURDY, JOHN EDWARD, basso; b. Detroit, Mar. 18, 1929; s. Blanchard Archibald and Dorathea Rosalie (Radtke) Mc Curdy; m. Justine May Votypka, Apr. 12, 1958; children—Allison Anne, John Blanchard. Student, Wayne State U., 1947; student of Avery Crew, Detroit, 1946. Mem. N.Y.C. Opera, 1959-62, Met. Opera, 1962—. Appeared in U.S., Europe, including San Francisco Opera, La Scala; performances include world premieres Mourning Becomes Electra, Met. Opera, 1967, opening night Anthony and Cleopatra, Met. Opera, 1966, Wuthering Heights, Santa Fe Opera, 1958, Six Characters in Search of an Author, N.Y.C. Opera, 1959, Griffalkin, Tanglewood Festival, 1957; Am. premieres Capriccio, Santa Fe Opera, 1958, Murder in the Cathedral, Empire State Music Festival, Bear Mountain Park, N.Y., 1959, Inspector General, N.Y.C. Opera, 1960; appeared with numerous orchs.; film Don Giovanni, 1979; participant 40th Anniversary Sud-Deutsche Rundfunk, 100th Anniversary Gala Met. Opera, 1983. Served with USAF, 1950-54. Recipient medal for artistic merit during Mich. Week City of Detroit, 1969; inducted into Acad. Vocal Hall of Fame, 1985. Mem. Bohemians. Presbyterian. Clubs: Bohemian (San Francisco); Greenwich Country (Conn.). Office: Met Opera Lincoln Ctr New York NY 10023

MAC VICAR, ROBERT WILLIAM, retired university administrator; b. Princeton, Minn., Sept. 28, 1918; s. George William and Elizabeth (Brennan) MacV.; m. Clarice Chambers, Dec. 23, 1948; children—Miriam J., John R. BA, U. Wyo., 1939, LLD, 1977; MS, Okla. State U., 1940; PhD, U. Wis., 1946; DSc (hon.), Dankook U., Korea, 1980; HLD, Nat. U., 1995. Assoc. prof., prof. biochemistry Okla. State U., 1946-64, dean grad. sch., 1953-64, v.p. acad. affairs, 1957-64; v.p. acad. affairs So. Ill. U., Carbondale, 1964-68; chancellor So. Ill. U., 1968-70; pres. Oreg. State U., Corvallis, 1970-84; pres. emeritus Oreg. State U., 1984—; acting pres. Coll. of Ganado, Ariz., 1985; founding mem., bd. dirs. Central Ednl. Midwest Research Lab., chmn. exec. com., 1969-70. Exec. dir. regents task force Ariz. Bd. of Regents, 1987-88; chmn. N.W. Acad. Computing Consortium, 1987-90. Served with U.S. Army, 1939-45. Rhodes scholar, 1939. Mem. Am. Soc. Biol. Chemists, Am. Chem. Soc., Am. Inst. Nutrition, Okla. Acad. Sci., Phi Beta Kappa, Sigma Xi, Phi Kappa Phi. Presbyterian. Home: 1440 NW 14th St Corvallis OR 97330-4660 Office: Oreg State U Office of the Pres Corvallis OR 97331

MAC VITTIE, ROBERT WILLIAM, retired college administrator; b. Middletown, N.Y., Dec. 29, 1920; s. Mortimer, Jr. and Mary (Thompson) MacV.; m. Margaret L. Cooper, July 15, 1944; children—Robert William II, Beth Ann, Geralyn Amy. B.Ed., State U. N.Y., Oneonta, 1944; M.A., N.Y. U., 1946; Ed.D., 1954. Elementary tchr. Pine Plains (N.Y.) Central Sch., 1944; social sci. tchr. Meml. Jr. High Sch., Middletown, N.Y., 1944-48; supervising prin. Montowese Sch., North Haven, Conn., 1948-52, Ridge Rd. Sch., North Haven, 1952-53; prof. sch. adminstrn., prin. lab. sch. N.Y. State Coll. Tchrs., Buffalo, 1954-56; dir. div. elementary and secondary edn. State U. N.Y. Coll., Buffalo, 1956-58; dean coll. State U. N.Y. Coll., 1958-63; pres. State U. Coll., Geneseo, 1963-79; emeritus State U. Coll., 1979—; interim pres. SUNY-Fredonia, N.Y., 1985, SUNY-Geneseo, 1988-89. Mem. regional adv. bd. Key Bank, N.A., Oneonta, N.Y., 1978-86; mem. SUNY Commn. Univ. Purposes and Priorities; exec. com. Rochester Area Colls., Inc., 1972-79, SUNY Council Pres.'s, 1970-72, 76-78; bd. dirs. Adams Art Gallery. Author: Handbook for Substitute Teachers, 3d edit, 1959, also numerous articles. Mem. citizens salary adv. com. Kenmore, N.Y., 1957; cons. sch. program evaluation team Tchrs. Coll., Temple U., 1956-57; mem. Livingston County Planning Bd., 1967-73, chmn., 1972-73; bd. dirs. Chautauqua Co. Automobile Club, Inc., Am. Automobile Assn., 1986-93, No. Chautauqua Community Foundation, 1985—, Chautauqua Adult Day Care Ctrs., 1991-92, D.R. Barker Libr., 1992—; mem. adv. bd. Auto Club Western N.Y., 1993—. Paul Harris fellow Rotary Internat. Mem. Am. Assn. Higher Edn., Am. Assn. Sch. Adminstrs., Am. Assn. Univ. Adminstrs. (pres. 1971-73, dir. 1977-79, gen. sec. 1979-81, Disting. Svc. award 1994), Am. Assn. State Colls. and Univs. (bd. dirs. 1977-79), Am. Acad. Polit. and Social Scis., Livingston C. of C. (dir. 1970-79), Phi Delta Kappa, Kappa Delta Pi, Rotary Internat., SUNY of N.Y. and Conferations of SUNY Alumni Assns. (spl. citation Disting. Alumni Svc. award 1994). Lodge: Rotary Internat. Robert W. MacVittie Coll. Union named in his honor SUNY-Geneseo, 1989. Home and Office: 187 Chestnut St Fredonia NY 14063-1601

MAC WATTERS, VIRGINIA ELIZABETH, singer, music educator, actress; b. Phila.; d. Frederick-Kennedy and Idoleein (Hallowell) Mac W.; m. Paul Abée, June 10, 1960. Grad., Phila. Normal Sch. for Tchrs., 1933; student, Curtis Inst. Music, Phila., 1936. With New Opera Co., N.Y.C., 1941-42; artist-in-residence Ind. U. Sch. Music, 1957-58; assoc. prof. U. Ind. Sch. Music, 1958-68, prof. voice, 1968-82, prof. emeritus, 1982—. Singer: leading roles Broadway mus. Rosalinda, 1942-44, Mr. Strauss Goes to Boston, 1945, leading opera roles New Opera Co., N.Y.C., 1941-42, San Francisco, 1944, N.Y.C. Ctr., 1946-51; leading soprano for reopening of Royal Opera House, Covent Garden, London, 1947-48, Guatemala, El Salvador, Cen. Am., 1948-49; debut at Met. Opera, N.Y.C., 1952; TV spls. on NBC include Menotti's Old Maid and the Thief, 1949, Would-be Gentleman (R. Strauss), 1955; leading singer with Met. Opera Co. on coast to coast tour of Die Fledermaus, 1951-52,, Met. Opera debut, N.Y.C., 1952, leading soprano Cen. City Opera Festival, Colo., 1952-56; performed with symphony orchs. in U.S., Can., S.Am.; concert recitalist U.S., Can., 1950-62; opened N.Y. Empire State Music Festival in Ariadne auf Naxos (Strauss), 1959; soloist Mozart Festival, Ann Arbor, Mich. Recipient Mile award Album Familiar Music, 1949, Ind. U. Disting. Tchg. award, 1979; named One of 10 Outstanding Women of the Yr.; Zeckwer Hahn Phila. Mus. Acad. scholar, 1941-42; MacWatters chair donated by New Auer Grand Concert Hall, U. Ind. Sch. Music. Mem. Nat. Fedn. of Music Clubs, Nat. Soc. Arts and Letters, Nat. Soc. Lit. and Arts, Soc. Am. Musicians, Nat. Assn. Tchrs. of Singing, Internat. Platform Assn., Sigma Alpha Iota. Club: Matinee Musical (hon. mem. Phila., Indpls. chpts.). Only original recorded version of Zerbinetta aria from Ariadne auf Naxos (Strauss). Home: 3800 Arlington Rd Bloomington IN 47404-1347 Office: Ind U Sch Music Bloomington IN 47404

MACWHORTER, ROBERT BRUCE, retired lawyer; b. Phila., July 12, 1930; s. George Merritt and Marion (Ritchie) MacW.; m. Althea Lucille Davis, June 23, 1956; children: Susan Elizabeth (Mrs. Steven Young), Nancy Jeanne (Mrs. Matthew Oja), Marjorie Anne (Mrs. Carl Friedrichs). A.B., Oberlin Coll., 1953; LL.B., U. Va., 1956. Bar: Va. 1956, N.Y. 1957. Assoc. Shearman & Sterling, N.Y.C., 1956-65, ptnr., 1965-91. Mem. ABA, N.Y. Bar Assn., Order of Coif. Home: 85 Jefferson Ave Maplewood NJ 07040-1228

MACWILLIAMS, DEBRA LYNNE, secondary reading specialist, consultant; b. Buffalo, June 6, 1952; d. Charles Edward and Dorothy Elizabeth (Whitton) Fields; m. Thomas Michael MacWilliams, Aug. 18, 1979; children: Amy Claire, Matthew Brandon. BA in Liberal Arts, SUNY, Albany, 1977; cert. elem. teaching, SUNY, Geneseo, 1987, MS in Edn., 1988. Cert. elem. tchr., reading specialist, N.Y. Tchr. gifted and talented, reading specialist Letchworth Ctrl. Sch., Gainesville, N.Y., 1988—; reading cons., N.Y., 1988—. Sch. coord. Am. Cancer Soc. (Outstanding Svc. award 1992), Wyoming County Unit, 1988—; parent network coord. Assn. for Pediatric Patients, Buffalo, 1987; vol. Candlelighters Childhood Cancer Found., Washington, 1986—, Camp Good Days and Spl. Times, Rochester, N.Y., 1986—; exec. com. Cub Scouts Geneseo Region, Batavia, N.Y., 1991-92. Mem. Internat. Reading Assn., N.Y. State Reading Assn., N.Y. State Assn. Compensatory Educators, Advocacy for Gifted and Talented Edn., Mary Jemison Reading Coun., Inst. for Children's Lit., Phi Delta Kappa. Avocations: writing, boating, woodworking, traveling. Home: 180 Wyoming St Warsaw NY 14569-9580 Office: Letchworth Central Sch 5567 Jordon Rd Gainesville NY 14066-9700

MACWILLIAMS, KENNETH EDWARD, investment banker; b. Newburyport, Mass., Aug. 21, 1936; s. Harold Freeman and Helen (Melia) MacW.; m. Angelyn Wishnack, July 16, 1960 (div. 1975); children: Robert Hovey, James Stuart. BA, Harvard U., 1958, MBA, 1962. V.p. Morgan Guaranty Trust Co., N.Y.C., 1962-71; sr. assoc. Goldman Sachs & Co., N.Y.C., 1971-74; mng. dir., domestic merchant banking group Manfacturers Hanover Trust Co., N.Y.C., 1975-82; chmn., chief exec. officer Prudential Capital Corp. subs. Prudential Ins. Co. Am., Newark, 1982-90; pres. Prudential Equity Mgmt. Assn. subs. Prudential Ins. Co. Am., Newark, 1990-92, Woodrow Wilson Assocs., Princeton, N.J., 1993—. Office: 10 State St Newburyport MA 01950-6604

MACY, JOHN PATRICK, lawyer; b. Menomonee Falls, Wis., June 26, 1955; s. Leland Francis and Joan Marie (LaValle) M. BA, Carroll Coll., 1977; JD, Marquette U., 1980. Bar: Wis. 1980, U.S. Dist. Ct. (we. and ea. dists.) Wis. 1980, U. S. Ct. Appeals (7th cir.) 1980. Assoc. Hippenmeyer Reilly Arenz Molter Bode & Gross, Waukesha, Wis., 1980-83; ptnr. Arenz Molter Macy & Riffle, S.C., Waukesha, 1983--; lectr. in field. Mem. ABA, Waukesha County Bar Assn. (chair 1995-96), Silver Lake Environ. Assn. (officer 1988-89), Silver Lake Yacht Club (officer 1986-88). Republican. Roman Catholic. Home: 4839 Hewitts Point Rd Oconomowoc WI 53066-3320 Office: Arenz Molter Macy & Riffle SC 720 N East Ave Waukesha WI 53186-4800

MACY, RICHARD J., state judge; b. Saranac Lake, N.Y., June 2, 1930; m. Emily Ann Macy; children: Anne, Patty, Mark. BS in Bus., U. Wyo., 1955, JD, 1958. Pvt. practice Sundance, Wyo., 1958-85; justice Wyo. Supreme Ct., Cheyenne, 1985—; Crook County atty., 1970-85; mem. Nat. Conf. Commrs. on Uniform State Laws, 1982—. Mem. Sigma Chi (Nat. Outstanding Sig award 1986). Office: Wyo Supreme Ct Supreme Ct Bldg 2301 Capitol Ave Cheyenne WY 82001-3644*

MADAIO, MICHAEL P., medical educator, investigator, physician. BS in Biology cum laude, Fairfield U., 1970; MD, Albany Med. Coll., 1974. Diplomate Am. Bd. Internal Medicine, Am. Bd. Nephrology. Intern Med. Coll. Va., Richmond, 1974-75, resident, 1975-77, chief resident, 1977-78; clin. fellow in nephrology Boston U., 1978-79, rsch. fellow in nephrology, 1979-81; rsch. fellow in immunology Tufts U., Boston, 1981-82, instr. in medicine, 1981-82, asst. to assoc. prof., 1982-90; assoc. prof. medicine U. Pa., 1990-96, assoc. chief renal electrolye div., 1992—, prof. of medicine, 1996—; asst. physician New Eng. Med. Ctr., Boston, 1981-87, physician, 1988-90; reviewer manuscripts and grants in field; lectr. Pathology A Study Sect., NIH, 1992-96. Contbr. articles to profl. jours., publs. Vice-pres. Nat. Kidney Found. Mass., 1987-89, pres. 1989-90; active Lupus Found. Am., Phila., 1991—, chmn. med. adv. bd., 1995—. Mem. AAAS, Internat. Soc. Nephrology, Am. Soc. Nephrology, Am. Fedn. Clin. Rsch., Am. Heart Assn., Fedn. Am. Socs. for Exptl. Biology, Am. Assn. Immunologists, Nat. Kidney Found., Am. Soc. Clin. Investigation, Alpha Epsilon Delta. Office: Univ Pa 700 CRB 415 Curie Blvd Philadelphia PA 19104-4218

MADANSHETTY, SAMEER ISHWAR, mechanical engineer; b. Belgaum, Karnatak, India, Dec. 2, 1953; came to U.S., 1984; s. Ishwar Gurunath Mandanshetti; m. Isabel Morin Zambrano, Oct. 11, 1988. MS, Indian Inst. Tech., New Delhi, 1975; MA, Yale U., 1986, PhD, 1989. Engr. Telco Ltd., Poona, India, 1975-84; rsch. asst. Yale U., New Haven, 1984-89, tchg. fellow, 1987-88; lectr., rsch. assoc. engring. Harvard U., Cambridge, Mass., 1989-90; asst. prof. dept. mech. and aero. engring. Boston U., 1990—; with H.S. Outreach Program Boston U., North Andover H.S., 1991, 92; advisor Extracurricular Design Projects, Yale U., Harvard U., Boston U., 1988—; advisor Solar Car Club, Boston U., 1994. Contbr. articles to profl. jours. Recipient rsch. initiation award NSF, 1991; named Outstanding Engring. Prof. of Yr., Boston U., 1993. Mem. ASME, Acoustical Soc. Am., Am. Phys. Soc. Achievements include patents pending for apparatus for detection of particles in ultrapure liquids (acoustically), enhancing chemical reactions through acoustic cavitation, submicron particulate evictor. Home: 6923 Redbud Dr Manhattan KS 66503-9123 Office: Kans State U Mech and Nuclear Engring Dept Duriand Hall Manhattan KS 66506

MADANSKY, ALBERT, statistics educator; b. Chgo., May 16, 1934; s. Harry and Anna (Meidenberg) M.; m. Paula Barkan, June 10, 1990; children from previous marriage: Susan, Cynthia, Noreen, Michele. AB, U. Chgo., 1952, MS, 1955, PhD, 1958. Mathematician Rand Corp., Santa Monica, Calif., 1957-65; sr. v.p. Interpub. Group of Companies, N.Y.C., 1965-68; pres. Dataplan Inc, N.Y.C., 1968-70; prof. computer scis. CCNY, 1970-76; prof. bus. adminstrn. grad. sch. U. Chgo., 1976—, assoc. dean, 1985-90, dep. dean, 1990-93, H.G.B. Alexander prof. bus. adminstr., 1996—; bd. dirs. Analytic Services, Washington, 1975—. Author: Foundations of Econometrics, 1975, Prescriptions for Working Statisticians, 1988. Fellow: Ctr. for Advanced Study in Behavioral Scis., Am. Statis. Assn., Inst. Math. Stats., Econometric Soc. Home: 200 E Delaware Pl Apt 23F Chicago IL 60611-1736 Office: U of Chicago Grad Sch Business Chicago IL 60637

MADANSKY, LEON, particle physicist, educator; b. Bklyn., Jan. 11, 1923. B.S., U. Mich., 1942, M.S., 1944, Ph.D. in Physics, 1948. From asst. prof. to assoc. prof. Johns Hopkins U., Balt., 1948-58, chmn. dept., 1965-68, prof. physics, 1958-77, Decker prof., 1978—; research physicist Brookhaven Nat. Lab., 1952-53. Fellow NSF, 1961, 69, John S. Guggenheim Meml. Found., 1974-75. Fellow Am. Phys. Soc. Home: 6602 Edenvale Rd Baltimore MD 21209-2702 Office: Johns Hopkins U Dept Physics And Astro Baltimore MD 21218

MADARA, JAMES L., epitheliologist, pathologist, educator; b. Altoona, Pa., Sept. 16, 1950; s. Daniel Rodman and Margaret Jane (Hauser) M.; m. Victoria M. Madara, May 14, 1975; children: J. Maxwell, Alexis Lindsy. BA, Juniata Coll., 1971; MD, Hahnemann Med., 1975. Cert. anatomic and clin. pathology. Instr. pathology Harvard Med. Sch., Boston, 1980-81, asst. prof. pathology, 1981-85, assoc. prof. pathology, 1985-91; assoc. prof. of health scis. and tech. Harvard-M.I.T., Boston, 1986-91; prof. pathology Harvard U. Med. Sch., Boston, 1993-97; Timmie prof., chmn. dept. pathology & lab. medicine Emory U. Sch. Medicine, Atlanta, 1997—. Assoc. editor: Gastroenterology, 1986-91; editorial bd.: Jour. Clin. Investigation, 1987—; contbr. over 120 articles to profl. jours. Grantee NIH, 1980-91. Mem. Am. Soc. for Clin. Investigation (elected), Am. Soc. for Cell Biology, Am. Gastroenterological Assn. (rsch. coun. 1988-90, Ross Rsch. scholar award 1982), Am. Physiol. Soc., Am. Assn. Pathology (Parke/Davis award 1990), Assn. Am. Physicians. Achievements include description of functional sequellae of neutrophil-epithelial cell interactions; recognition that tight junctions between epithelial cells are regulated under physiological conditions. Office: Brigham and Womens Hosp 75 Francis St Boston MA 02115-6110

MADAY, CLIFFORD RONALD, insurance professional; b. Cin., Mar. 15, 1947; s. John J. and Betty (Kucha) M.; m. Ellen Doolittle, Aug. 31, 1968; children: Michael, Brian, Christina, Andrew. BS, Northeastern U., 1976. Cert. protection profl. With ITT Hartford Ins., 1977—; loss control mgr. ITT Hartford Ins., Manchester, N.H., 1981-83; loss control mgr. ITT Hartford Ins., Charlotte, N.C., 1983-93, loss control area coord., 1994—. Bd. dirs., soccer commr. and coach Matthews (N.C.) Athletic and Recreation Assn., 1983-91; select coach Charlotte United Soccer, 1991-95. 1st lt. U.S. Army, 1965-69, Vietnam. Decorated Bronze Star. Mem. Am. Soc. for Indsl. Security, Am. Soc. Safety Engrs. Avocations: soccer coach, gourmet cooking. Home: 1221 Seneca Pl Charlotte NC 28210-2424 Office: Hartford Ins 5525 Albemarle Rd Charlotte NC 28212-3610

MADDALA, GANGADHARRAO SOUNDARYARAO, economics educator; b. Hyderabad, Andhra, India, May 21, 1933; came to U.S., 1960; s. Soundarya Rao and Veera Lakshmi (Gollakota) M.; m. Kameswari Modali, May 21, 1967; children: Tara, Vivek. BA, Andhra U., Waltair, India, 1955; MA, Bombay U., 1957; PhD, U. Chgo., 1963. Asst. prof. Stanford (Calif.) U., 1963-67; assoc. prof. U. Rochester (N.Y.), 1967-70, prof. econs., 1970-75; grad. rsch. prof. U. Fla., Gainesville, 1975-93; univ. eminent scholar dept. econs. Ohio State U., Columbus, 1992—; dir. Ctr. for Econometrics and Decision Scis., Gainesville, 1979-93. Author: Econometrics, 1997, Spanish edit., 1989, Limdep Variables in Econometrics, 1983, Introduction to Econometrics, 1988, 2d edit., 1992, 3rd edit., 1997, Japanese edit., 1993, Microeconomics, 1989, Econometric Methods and Applications, 1994; editor Econometrica, 1971-79; co-editor Handbook of Statistics, vol. II, 1993, vol. 14, 1996, vol. 15, 1997, Advances in Econometrics, 1995; mem. editl. adv. bd. Econometric Theory. Fellow Econometric Soc.; mem. Am. Econ. Assn., Am. Statis. Assn. Office: Ohio State U Arps Hall 1945 N High St Columbus OH 43210-1120

MADDALENA, LUCILLE ANN, management executive; b. Plainfield, N.J., Nov. 8, 1948; d. Mario Anthony and Josephine Dorothy (Longo) M.; m. James Samonte Hohn, Sept. 7, 1975; children: Vincent, Nicholas, Mitchell. AA, Rider Coll., 1968; BS, Monmouth Coll., 1971; EdD, Rutgers U., 1978. Newscaster, dir. pub. relations Sta. WBRW, Bridgewater, N.J., 1971-73; editor-in-chief Commerce mag., New Brunswick, N.J., 1973-74; dir. pub. relations Raritan Valley Regional C. of C., New Brunswick, N.J., 1973-74; aide pub. relations to mayor City of New Brunswick, 1974; dir. communications United Way Cen. Jersey, New Brunswick, 1974-77; mgmt. cons. United Way Am., Alexandria, Va., 1977-78; pres., owner Maddalena Assocs., Chester, N.J., 1978—; sr. cons. United Research Co., Morristown, N.J., 1980-81; sr. ptnr., dir. OCD Group, Parsippany, N.J., 1984-87; chmn. bd. dirs. OCD Group (subs. Xicom Inc.), Morristown, N.J., 1988; pres. Morris Bus. Group, Chester, 1989—; adj. faculty Somerset County Coll., Bridgewater, N.J., 1970, Fairleigh Dickinson U., 1980; guest lectr. Rutgers U., New Brunswick, N.J., 1975-80; designer publicly offered seminars for Bell Atlantic, 1992—; cons. change Howmet, Alloy, Dover, N.J., 1993; consortium trainer Johnson & Johnson, 1988—. Author: A Communications Manual for Non-Profit Organizations, 1980; editor New Directions for Instl. Advancement, 1980-81. Chmn. pers. com., police com. Chester Borough Coun., 1984-87; pres. Chester Consolidation Study Commn., 1990. Recipient Mayor's Commendation City of New Brunswick, 1973, Chester Borough, N.J., 1988. Mem. AAUW, LWV, Nat. Assn. Press Women, N.J. Elected Women Officials, Kappa Delta Pi. Republican. Roman Catholic. Club: N.J. Sled Dog Assn. Avocation: sled dog racing. Home: 75 Melrose Dr Chester NJ 07930-2321 Office: Morris Bus Group 415 State Route 24 Chester NJ 07930-2920

MADDEN, ARTHUR ALLEN, nuclear pharmacist, educator; b. Atlanta, Sept. 19, 1960; s. Arthur Allen and Lillian Brandon (Vaughan) M.; m. Rebecca Kaye Teague, June 25, 1988; children: Kelley Vaughan, Arthur Allen, III. BA in English, U. of the South, Sewanee, Tenn., 1982; BS in Pharmacy, U. S.C., 1988, PharmD, 1990. Registered pharmacist, N.C., S.C.; bd. cert. nuclear pharmacist, 1994. Poison control specialist Palmetto Poison Ctr., Columbia, 1988-90; relief pharmacist Wal-Mart, Columbia, 1989-91; dir. S.C. Nuclear Pharmacy, Columbia, 1990-91; nuclear pharmacist Syncor Internat. Corp., Columbia, S.C., 1991-95; radiation safety cons. Syncor Internat. Corp., Columbia, 1990-95; dir. Cosource Nuclear Pharmacy Geodax Tech., Inc., Columbia, 1995—; mem. faculty U. S.C. Sch. Medicine, Columbia, 1990—, asst. prof. Coll. Pharmacy, 1990—; third party ins. expert, Columbia, 1983-93; mem. ad hoc com. for infectious disease policy. Mem. Am. Pharm. Assn., Am. Soc. Hosp. Pharmacists, S.C. Nuclear Medicine Soc., S.C. Sch. Medicine Hemotology/Oncology Jour. Club, Bd. Pharm. Specialties-Nuclear Pharmacy, Phi Lambda Sigma (sec. 1987-89), Order of the Thistle, Order of the Highlander. Home: 4626 Reamer Ave Columbia SC 29206-1541 Office: Cosource Nuclear Pharmacy 2501 Main St Columbia SC 29201

MADDEN, DAVID, author; b. Knoxville, Tenn., July 25, 1933; s. James Helvy and Emile (Merritt) M.; m. Roberta Margaret Young, Sept. 6, 1956; 1 son, Blake Dana. B.S., U. Tenn., 1957; M.A., San Francisco State Coll., 1958; postgrad., Yale Drama Sch., 1959-60. Faculty Appalachian State Tchrs. Coll., Boone, N.C., 1957-58, Centre Coll., Danville, Ky., 1960-62, U. Louisville, 1962-64, Kenyon Coll., Gambier, O., 1964-66, Ohio U., Athens, 1966-68; writer-in-residence La. State U., Baton Rouge, 1968-92, dir. creative writing program, 1992-94, dir. U.S. Civil War Ctr., 1992—; alumni prof. La. State U., 1994. Author: (novels) Cassandra Singing, 1969, Bijou, 1974, The Suicide's Wife, 1978, Pleasure Dome, 1979, On the Big Wind, 1980, Sharpshooter: A Novel of the Civil War, (stories) The Shadow Knows (Nat. Coun. on Arts selection), 1970, The New Orleans of Possibilities (lit. criticism) Wright Morris, 1964, Poetic Image in Six Genres, 1969, James M. Cain, 1970, A Primer of the Novel, 1980, Writers' Revisions, 1981, Cain's Craft, 1985, Revising Fiction, 1988, Rediscoveries II, 1988; asst. editor: The Kenyon Rev., 1964-66; editor: Remembering James Agee, 1974; co-editor: (with P. Bach) Classics of Civil War Fiction, 1991, Sharpshooter, 1996. Served with AUS, 1953-55. Recipient Rockefeller grant in fiction, 1969; John Golden fellow in playwriting, 1959. Mem. Authors League, Associated Writing Programs (bd). Democrat. Office: US Civil War Ctr La State U Raphael Semmes Dr Baton Rouge LA 70803

MADDEN, DONALD PAUL, lawyer; b. Winthrop, Mass., Dec. 26, 1933; s. Francis Patrick and Mary Josephine (Doherty) M.; m. Sarah Anne Donovan, Aug. 12, 1966; children—Matthew James, Andrew Peter, Peter Thomas. A.B., Princeton U., 1955; J.D., Harvard U., 1961. Bar: N.Y. 1962, U.S. Dist. Ct. (so. dist.) N.Y. 1962. Assoc. White & Case, N.Y.C., 1961-69, ptnr., 1969—; resident ptnr. Paris office, 1971-76. dir., sec. Am. Hosp. of Paris Found. Served to lt. USMC, 1955-58. Mem. ABA, Assn. Bar City N.Y. Club: Links (N.Y.C.). Office: White & Case 1155 Ave Of The Americas New York NY 10036-2711

MADDEN, EDWARD HARRY, philosopher, educator; b. Gary, Ind., May 18, 1925; s. Harry Albert and Amelia Dorothy (Schepper) M.; m. Marian Sue Canaday, Sept. 15, 1946; children: Kerry Arthur, Dennis William. A.B., Oberlin Coll., 1946, A.M., 1947; Ph.D., U. Iowa, 1950. Prof. philosophy U. Conn., 1950-59, San Jose State Coll., 1959-64, SUNY, Buffalo, 1964-82, U. Ky., 1982—; vis. prof. Brown U., 1954-55, Amherst Coll., 1962, U. Toronto, 1967, Am. U. Beirut, Lebanon, 1969-70; sr. research fellow Linacre Coll., Oxford U., 1978, Inst. Advanced Study, Princeton, 1980-81. Author: Philosophical Problems of Psychology, 1962, Chauncey Wright and the Foundations of Pragmatism, 1963, Evil and the Concept of God, 1968, Civil Disobedience and Moral Law, 1968, The Structure of Scientific Thought, 1960, Causal Powers, 1975, Causing, Perceiving and Believing, 1975, Freedom and Grace, 1982; co-author, editor: Theories of Scientific Method, 1960, Philosophical Perspectives on Punishment, 1968, The Idea of God, 1968; gen. editor: Harvard U. Press Source Books in History Sci.; mem. editl. bd.: The Works of William James, Thoreau Quar., History of Philosophy Quar., Philosophy of Sci., 1960-76; mem. adv. bd.: A Critical Edition of the Correspondence of William James (Am. Coun. Learned Socs.). Served with USNR, 1943-45. Recipient Am. Philos. Soc. research grant, 1961, Fulbright-Hays award, 1969-70, Herbert W. Schneider award Soc. for Advancement Am. Philosophy, 1991. Fellow Asa Mahan Soc.; mem. C.S. Peirce Soc. (pres. 1962-63, sec.-treas., editorial bd. Transactions of Soc.), Am. Council Learned Socs. (selection com.), Am. Philos. Assn. (co-chmn. com. publs. 1960-77), Phi Kappa Phi. Home: 106 Pickett Dr Wilmore KY 40390-1223 Office: Univ Ky Dept Philosophy Lexington KY 40506

MADDEN, HEATHER ANN, aluminum company executive; b. Sharon, Pa., Dec. 20, 1967; d. Edward Arthur and Mary Ann (McWilliams) M. BS in Bus., Salisbury (Md.) State U., 1991; MS in Bus., Johns Hopkins U., 1994. With Delmarva Aluminum Co., Inc., Delmar, Del., 1984-95, exec.'s asst., 1987-95, also dir., 1990—; instr. office sys. tech. Del. Tech. & C.C., Georgetown, 1995—. Vol. The Holly Ctr., Salisbury, 1992-94. Recipient Holly Svc. award The Holly Found., Salisbury, 1994. Avocations: women's softball, personal computers, dogs, swimming, gardening. Home: 8300 Robin Hood Dr Salisbury MD 21804

MADDEN, JAMES A., gifted and talented educator; b. Butler, Pa., Jan. 27, 1947; s. James Henry and Josephine Grace (Zagst) M.; m. Mary Ellen Adamcin, July 16, 1977; children: Joann Marie, Jamie Elyse. BS, U. Ariz., 1970, MEd, 1973. Cert. jr. coll. tchr. Tchr. Tucson Unified Sch. Dist., 1972—, tchr. of gifted, 1976—. Developer ednl. games and computer programs for math. and computer sci. Named Ariz. Tchr. of Yr., IBM, 1990. Home: 4442 E Cooper Cir Tucson AZ 85711-4260 Office: University High Sch 421 N Arcadia Ave Tucson AZ 85711-3032

MADDEN, JAMES COOPER, V, management consultant; b. Glen Cove, N.Y., June 18, 1961; s. James Cooper IV and Linda Marie (Lizza) M.; m. Jill Louise Howenstine, July 27, 1985; 1 child, Jennifer Louise. Student, Webb Inst. Naval Architecture, Glen Cove, 1979-80; BA cum laude, So. Meth. U., 1983, BBA magna cum laude, 1983. Cert. Soc. Naval Architects and Marine Engrs. Cons. Andersen Cons./Arthur Andersen, Houston, 1983-85, sr. cons., 1985-87; mgr. Andersen Cons./Arthur Andersen, L.A., 1987-90, sr. mgr., 1990-91; prin. Booz-Allen & Hamilton, L.A., 1991-93; v.p. mng. dir. MCI Systemhouse, L.A., 1993-95, pres. U.S. and Mexico ops., 1995-97, CFO, 1997—; mem. adv. bd. Claremont Grad. Sch., Mgmt. Info. Svcs. Program; mem. UCLA Anderson Sch., I.S. Assocs. Author industry papers. Scholar Webb Inst. Naval Architecture, 1979-80. Avocations: sailing, snow skiing, travel, reading. Office: MCI Systemhouse Corp 12750 Center Court Dr S Ste 700 Cerritos CA 90703-8580

MADDEN, JAMES DESMOND, forensic engineer; b. Jersey City; s. Louis A. and Ann Madden. BSChemE, U. S.C., 1963, ME, 1966. Lic. profl. engr., Ohio; cert. diplomate forensic engr. Process engr. Monsanto Co., Alvin, Tex., 1966-67; process and project engr. Union Carbide Corp., Houston, 1967-70; systems engr. M.W. Kellogg Co., Houston, 1970-73, prin. systems engr., 1974-77; sr. process engr. Litwin Co., Houston, 1973-74; sr. project engr. Davy Powergas, Houston, 1977-78, supervising project engr., 1978-79; mgr. equipment engring. DM Internat., Houston, 1979-80, project engring. mgr., 1980-83; owner, forensic engr. Madden Forensic Engring., Parma, Parma Heights and Brecksville, Ohio, 1983—. Pres. Houston Young Adult Rep. Club, 1970-73; chmn. Tex. Young Adult Rep. Clubs, 1973. NSF rsch. grantee, 1963; NASA fellow, 1963-65. Mem. ASTM, ASME, NSPE, Soc. Automotive Engrs., Nat. Fire Protection Assn., Am. Chem. Soc., Am. Inst. Chem. Engrs., Inst. Transp. Engrs., Transp. Rsch. Bd. (individual assoc.), Nat. Acad. Forensic Engrs., Sigma Xi, Sigma Pi Sigma, Tau Beta Pi, Omicron Delta Kappa. Office: 10175 Brecksville Rd Cleveland OH 44141-3205

MADDEN, JOHN, television sports commentator, former professional football coach; b. Austin, Minn., Apr. 10, 1936; s. Earl and Mary O'Flaherty M.; m. Virginia Madden; children: Mike, Joe. B.S., Calif. Poly. U., 1959, M.A., 1961. Player Phila. Eagles (NFL team), 1959; asst. coach Hancock Jr. Coll., Santa Maria, Calif., 1960-62; head coach Hancock Jr. Coll., 1962-64; defensive coordinator Calif. State U., San Diego, 1964-66; with Oakland Raiders, Am. Football League (now Am. Football Conf., Nat. Football League), 1967-79, linebacker coach, 1967-69, head coach, 1969-79; head coach NFL Pro Bowl team Am. Football Conf., 1971, 73, 74, 75; head coach 6 Western div. Am. Football Conf. championship teams, Super Bowl champions, 1976; sports commentator, football analyst CBS Sports, 1979-93; appears in TV and radio commls.; sports commentator, football analyst Fox Network, 1994—. Author: Hey, Wait a Minute, I Wrote a Book!, 1984; One Knee Equals Two Feet, 1986; developer (software) John Madden Football, 1988, John Madden Football II, 1993. Named Coach of Year Am. Football League, 1969, Sports Personality of the Yr., Am. Sportscasters Assn., 1985; recipient Emmy awards for sports broadcasting, 1982, 83, 85, 86, 87, 88. Office: care Fox Network PO Box 900 Beverly Hills CA 90213-0900*

MADDEN, JOHN PATRICK, lawyer; b. N.Y.C., Sept. 9, 1945; s. Eugene Patrick and Eileen Mary (Gaughan) M.; m. Sally Williams, Apr. 21, 1984; children: Samuel, Christopher. BCE, Manhattan Coll., 1967; MSCE, NYU, 1969; JD, St. John's U., 1978. Bar: U.S. Patent Office 1978, N.Y. 1979, N.J. 1982, U.S. Dist. Ct. (so. and ea. dists.) N.Y. 1982, U.S. Dist. Ct. N.J. 1982, U.S. Supreme Ct. 1985; cert. internat. arbitrator, constrn. panelist, comml. mediator, D.O.D. instr. Law clk., assoc. Buckley, Treacy, Shaffel Mackey & Abbate, N.Y.C., 1977-80; cons. Contractors Consulting Svcs. Inc., Greatneck, N.Y., 1980-81; ptnr. Madden, Sciarra & Muirhead, N.Y., N.J., 1981-82, Canfield, Venusti, Madden & Rossi, Manhattan, N.Y., 1983—; lectr. in field. Contbr. articles to profl. jours. V.p. N.Y.C. Jaycees, 1975-95. ROTC USAF, 1963-65. Mem. ABA (pub. contract law sect., forum com. on constrn. industry), London Ct. Internat. Arbitration, Swiss Arbitration Assn., Am. Trial Lawyers Assn., N.Y. State Bar Assn., N.Y. State Trial Lawyers Assn., Assn. of Bar of City of N.Y., Nat. Arts Club. Office: Canfield Venusti et al 230 Park Ave Rm 2525 New York NY 10169-2599

MADDEN, JOSEPH DANIEL, trade association executive; b. N.Y.C., Dec. 25, 1921; s. Thomas A. and Margaret (McFadden) M.; m. Eileen M. MacDonnell, Sept. 8, 1951; children: Joseph Daniel, Jr., Maureen A. BS, Fordham U., 1951; MBA, N.Y. U., 1956. Credit investigator Dun & Bradstreet, N.Y.C., 1947-48; credit mgr. Devoe & Raynolds Co., N.Y.C., 1948-50; accounts supr. credit dept. Admiral Corp., N.Y.C., 1950-51; asst. credit mgr. Standard Toch Chems., Inc., S.I., N.Y., 1951-52; with chems. and plastics div. Union Carbide Corp., Danbury, Conn., 1952-62; mgr. Detroit sales office, 1958-60; sr. staff adminstr. Soc. Plastics Industry, Washington, 1962-69; exec. v.p. Drug, Chem. and Allied Trades Assn., Syosset, N.Y., 1969-88, cons. assn. mgmt., 1988—. With U.S. Army, 1942-43. Mem. Am. Soc. Assn. Execs. (cert.), N.Y. Soc. Assn. Execs. (past bd. dirs., Exec. of Yr. award 1988), Soc. Friendly Sons of St. Patrick, Kiwanis (past pres. Bayside, sec.), Am. Assn. Ret. Persons (pres. local chpt.), Toastmasters Internat. (past pres. local club). Home: 201-26 38th Ave Flushing NY 11361-1849

MADDEN, JOSEPH MICHAEL, microbiologist; b. Yokohama, Japan, July 19, 1949; s. John Joseph and Anne Louise (Johnson) M.; m. Rennie K. Robb, Aug. 4, 1973; children: Loren, Mary Kate, Julie. BA, U. Calif., 1971; MS, Ariz. State U., 1974, PhD, 1976. Chief microbiologist Brook Army Med. Ctr., Ft. Sam Houston, Tex., 1976-78; rsch. microbiologist FDA Ctr. Food Safety and Applied Nutrition, Washington, 1978-88, dep. dir. microbiology divsn., 1988-91, dir., 1991-93, strategic mgr. microbiology, 1992—. Capt. U.S. Army, 1976-78, USPHS, 1978—. Fellow Am. Acad. Microbiology; mem. Am. Soc. Microbiology, Sigma Xi. Roman Catholic. Avocation: refereeing soccer. Office: FDA Ctr Food Safety and Applied Nutrition 200 C St SW Washington DC 20204-0001

MADDEN, LAURENCE VINCENT, plant pathology educator; b. Ashland, Pa., Oct. 10, 1953; s. Lawrence Vincent and Janet Elizabeth (Wewer) M.; m. Susan Elizabeth Heady, July 7, 1984. BS, Pa. State U., 1975, MS, 1977, PhD, 1980. Research scientist Ohio State U., Wooster, 1980-82, asst. prof., 1983-86, assoc. prof., 1986-91, prof., 1991—; invited univ. lectr. on plant disease epidemiology in more than 10 countries. Author: Introduction to Plant Disease Epidemiology; sr. editor Phytopathology, 1988-90, APS Press, 1988-90; editor-in-chief Phytopathology, 1991-93; contbr. 100 articles to profl. jours. U.S. Dept. Rsch. grantee, 1984, 85, 86, 87, 89, 90, 91, 95; Disting. scholar Ohio State U., 1991; recipient Outstanding Alumni award Pa. State U. Coll. Agrl. Scis. Fellow AAAS; mem. Am. Phytopathol. Soc. (chmn. com. 1983, 86, coun. 1991-93, Ciba Geigy Agrl. Achievement award 1990, v.p. 1994-95, pres.-elect 1995-96, pres. 1996-97), Biometric Soc., Brit. Soc. Plant Pathology, Sigma Xi (chpt. pres. 1985). Achievements include development of statistical models for understanding, predicting and comparing epidemics and assessing crop losses. Home: 677 Greenwood Blvd Wooster OH 44691-4923 Office: Ohio State U OARDC Dept Plant Pathology Wooster OH 44691

MADDEN, MARTIN GERARD, state legislator, insurance agent; b. Washington, May 24, 1949; s. Anthony M. and Catherine W. (Tracey) M.; m. Julia Gatewood Spangler, July 29, 1988; children: Donald Gerard, Thomas Martin, Christina Lynn, Marguerite Allen Spangler. BA in Econs., Iona Coll., 1971. Owner Marty Madden Ins. Ctr., Lanham, Md., 1971—; state del. State of Md. Gen. Assembly, Annapolis, 1991-95; state senator, 1995—; mem. fin. com., chmn. subcom. on welfare reform. Bd. dirs. St. Vincent Pallotti H.S. Mem. Sierra Club, K.C. Republican. Roman Catholic. Avocation: folk art collector. Office: James Senate Office Bldg 402-B Annapolis MD 21401-1991

MADDEN, MICHAEL DANIEL, finance company executive; b. Buffalo, Feb. 16, 1949; s. Daniel Francis and Miriam (Catron) M.; m. Mary Madden, May 1, 1976; children: Daniel, Kristina, Meagan, Michael. BA in Econs. magna cum laude, Le Moyne Coll., 1971; MBA with distinction, U. Pa., 1973. Assoc. Kidder, Peabody & Co., N.Y.C., 1973-77, v.p., 1977-80, mng. dir., 1980-85, dir. investment banking, 1985-88; head investment banking Lehman Bros., N.Y.C., 1989-93; exec. mng. dir. Global Capital Markets Kidder, Peabody Co., N.Y.C., 1993-94; vice chmn., chief origination officer Paine Webber Inc., N.Y.C., 1995-96; chmn., CEO Hannover Capital LLC, N.Y.C., 1996—. Bd. dirs. Freeport Properties, Inc., Cath. TV Ctr., N.Y.C., 1981-85, LeMoyne Coll., Syracuse, N.Y., 1987—, Canisius Preparatory Sch., Buffalo, N.Y., 1992—. Mem. Am. Petroleum Inst., MBA Assn., Univ. Club, The Creek, Longboat Key Club. Republican. Roman Catholic. Avocations: boxing, hunting, tennis, coin collecting. Office: Hannover Capital LLC 666 5th Ave New York NY 10103

MADDEN, MURDAUGH STUART, lawyer; b. Morgantown, W.Va., Feb. 26, 1922; s. Joseph Warren and Margaret (Liddell) M.; m. Eileen Dillon, June 17, 1978; children by previous marriage: Liddell Louise, Murdaugh Stuart Jr., Michael Mann. Student, Oberlin Coll., 1939-40; BA, George Washington U., 1942; JD, Harvard U., 1948. Bar: D.C. 1948, Va. 1948, U.S. Supreme Ct. 1953. Asst. counsel Bur. Aero., Washington, 1948-50; sole practice Washington, 1950-61, 71—; sr. ptnr. Shaw, Pittman, Potts, Trowbridge & Madden, Washington, 1961-71; gen. counsel Humane Soc. U.S., Atlantic Devel. Co. and related corps. Author: (with Sherman L. Cohn) The Legal Status and Problems of the American Abroad, 1966. Trustee Inst. for Study Nat. Behavior, Princeton, N.J., Friends of India Com., Washington; pres. World Fedn. for Protection Animals, Zurich; v.p. World Soc. forProtection Animals, London. With USAAF, 1942-45, ETO. Mem. ABA (past chmn. internat. and comparative law com. internat. transp., chmn. subcom. on charitable orgns. internat. law sect. 1985—), D.C. Bar Assn., (past dir., past chmn. com. bar ethics), Va. Bar Assn., The Barristers, Am. Soc. Internat. Law, Harvard Law Sch. Assn., Oberlin Alumni Assn., Metropolitan Club, Harvard Club N.Y., Internat. Lawn Tennis Club U.S., Chevy Chase Club, Phi Sigma Kappa. Episcopalian. Home: 2530 Queen Annes Ln NW Washington DC 20037-2148 Office: 2100 L St NW Washington DC 20037-1525

MADDEN, PALMER BROWN, lawyer; b. Milw., Sept. 19, 1945; m. Susan L. Paulus, Mar. 31, 1984. BA, Stanford U., 1968; JD, U. Calif., Berkeley, 1973. Bar: Calif. 1973, U.S. Dist. Ct. (no. dist.) Calif. 1973, U.S. Supreme Ct. 1982. Ptnr. McCutchen, Doyle Brown & Enersen, Walnut Creek, 1985—. Chair bd. govs. Continuing Edn. of the Bar, 1997; judge pro tem Contra Costa Superior Ct., 1991-96. Mem. Contra Costa County Bar Assn. (pres. 1996-97). Democrat. Episcopalian. Office: McCutchen Doyle Brown & Enersen 1331 N California Blvd Walnut Creek CA 94596-4537

MADDEN, PAUL ROBERT, lawyer; b. St. Paul, Nov. 13, 1926; s. Ray Joseph and Margaret (Meyer) M.; m. Rosemary R. Sorel, Aug. 7, 1974; children: Margaret Jane, William, James Patrick, Derek R. Sorel, Lisa T. Sorel. Student, St. Thomas Coll., 1944; AB, U. Minn., 1948; JD, Georgetown U., 1951. Bar: Ariz. 1957, Minn. 1951, D.C. 1951. Assoc. Hamilton & Hamilton, Washington, 1951-55; legal asst. to commr. SEC, Washington, 1955-56; assoc. Lewis and Roca, Phoenix, Ariz., 1957-59, ptnr., 1959-90; ptnr. Beus, Gilbert & Morrill, Phoenix, 1991-94; ptnr. Chapman and Cutler, Phoenix, 1994—. Sec. Minn. Fedn. Coll. Rep. Clubs, 1947-48; chmn. 4th dist. Minn. Young Rep. Club, 1948; nat. co-chmn. Youth for Eisenhower, 1951-52; mem. Ariz. Rep. Com., 1960-62; bd. dirs. Found. Jr. Achievement Ctrl. Ariz., Cath. Community Found., Phoenix, Heritage Hills Homeowners Assn., St. Joseph the Worker; past bd. dirs. Camelback Charitable Trust, The Samaritan Found., Phoenix; past bd. dirs., past. pres. Ariz. Club, Phoenix, 1990-93; past bd. dirs., past chmn. Found. for Sr. Living; past bd. dirs., vice chmn., Cen. Ariz. chpt. ARC; past bd. dirs., vice chmn., Cen. Ariz. chpt. ARC; past bd. dirs., past pres. Jr. Achievement Cen. Ariz., Inc.; mem. nat. bd. vis. U. Ariz. Law Sch. With USNR, 1946-48. Mem. ABA, Ariz. Bar Assn., Maricopa County Bar Assn., Fed. Bar Assn., Fedn. Ins. Counsel, Nat. Health Lawyers Assn., Am. Soc. Hosp. Attys., Phi Delta Phi. Clubs: The Barristers (Washington), Arizona. Home: 5847 N 46th St Phoenix AZ 85018-1234 Office: Chapman & Cutler Two N Central Ave Ste 1100 Phoenix AZ 85004

MADDEN, RICHARD BLAINE, forest products executive; b. Short Hills, N.J., Apr. 27, 1929; s. James L. and Irma (Twining) M.; m. Joan Fairbairn, May 24, 1958; children: John Richard, Lynne Marie, Kathryn Ann, Andrew Twining. B.S., Princeton U., 1951; J.D., U. Mich., 1956; M.B.A., NYU, 1959; PhD (hon.), St. Scholastica Coll., 1994. Bar: Mich. 1956, N.Y. 1958. Gen. asst. treas.'s dept. Socony Mobil Oil Corp., 1956-57; spl. asst. Socony Mobil Oil Corp., 1958-59, fin. rep., 1960; asst. to pres. Mobil Chem. Co.; also dir. Mobil Chems. Ltd. of Eng., 1960-63; exec. v.p., gen. mgr. Kordite Corp.; also v.p. Mobil Plastics, 1963-66; v.p. Mobil Chem. Co., N.Y.C., 1966-68; group v.p. Mobil Chem. Co., 1968-70; asst. treas. Mobil Oil Corp., 1970-71; chmn. Mobil Oil Estates Ltd., 1970-71; pres., chief exec. to chmn., chief exec. officer Potlatch Corp., San Francisco, 1971-94; ret., 1994; bd. dirs. Potlatch Corp., PG&E Corp., CNF Transp. Inc., URS Corp.; former bd. dirs. Del Monte Corp., AMFAC Inc., Bank Calif. N.A. and BankCal Tri-State Corp.; from lectr. to adj. assoc. prof. fin. NYU, 1960-63. Bd. dirs. Smith-Kettlewell Eye Rsch. Inst., Nat. Park Found., mem. fin. com., devel. com.; trustee emeritus, former chmn. Am. Enterprise Inst.; bd. govs., mem. adminstrv. compensation, audit & labor rels. com. San Francisco Symphony; hon. trustee Com. for Econ. Devel. Lt. (j.g.) USNR, 1951-54. Mem. N.Y. Bar Assn., Mich. Bar Assn. Roman Catholic. Clubs: Bohemian (San Francisco); Lagunitas (Ross, Calif.); Metropolitan (Washington).

MADDEN, ROBERT EDWARD, surgeon, educator; b. Oak Park, Ill., Sept. 16, 1925; s. Joseph Edward and Gertrude Celelia (McGowan) M.; m. Susan Ann Hale, May 24, 1958; children: Robert Joseph, Lisa Marie, Karen Louise, Kevin Francis. BS in Medicine, U. Ill., Chgo., 1950, MS in Biochemistry, 1952, MD, 1952. Diplomate Am. Bd. Surgery, Bd. Thoracic Surgery. Assoc. in surgery U. Ill. Coll. Medicine, Chgo., 1957-58; sr. surgeon Nat. Cancer Inst., Bethesda, Md., 1959-60; asst. prof. surgery N.Y. Med. Coll., N.Y.C., 1961-66, assoc. prof., 1966-71; prof. N.Y. Med. Coll., Valahlla, 1971—; mem. N.Y. State Health Rsch. Coun., Albany, 1976—. Author: (with Lippincott) Problems In General Surgery, 1988; editor: Gastrointestinal Bleeding, 1987; editor-in-chief N.Y. Med. Quarterly, 1979-90; contbr. articles to profl. jours. With U.S. Army, 1943-46. Recipient Borden Undergrad. Rsch. award Borden Corp., 1952; postdoctoral fellow Am. Cancer Soc., 1958-59. Fellow ACS; mem. Internat. Soc. Cardiovascular Surgery, Soc. Internat. Chirurgie, Am. Assn. Cancer Edn. (pres. 1979), N.Y. Cancer Soc. (pres. 1975-76), N.Y. State Cancer Progress Assn. (pres. 1975-76), Com. on Cancer, Knights of Holy Sepulchre, Knights of the Order of Malta, Pi Gamma Mu. Republican. Roman Catholic. Home: 6 Crows Nest Rd Bronxville NY 10708-4802 Office: NY Med Coll Munger Pavilion Valhalla NY 10595

MADDEN, TERESA DARLEEN, insurance agency owner; b. Dallas, Aug. 4, 1960; d. Tommy Joe Frederick Dodd and Mary Helen (Sterner) Smith; m. Kim Ashley Madden, June 2, 1989. Student, Tex. Tech U., 1978-81. Cert. ins. counselor. With personal lines svc. Charles R. Ervin Ins., Midland, Tex., 1981, Bryant Scalf Ins., Richardson, Tex., 1981-82; with comml. ins. svc. Street & Assocs. Inc., Dallas, 1982-84; with comml. ins. sales/svc. Hotchkiss Ins., Dallas, 1984-85; mgr. sales Abbott-Rose Ins. Agy., Dallas, 1985-89; owner Glenn-Madden & Assocs. Ins., Dallas, 1990—. Methodist. Office: Glenn Madden & Assocs Inc Ste 1470 9330 Lyndon B Johnson Fwy Dallas TX 75243-3448

MADDEN, THERESA MARIE, elementary education educator; b. Phila., Feb. 12, 1950; d. James Anthony and Marie Margaret (Clark) M. BA in Social Sci., Neumann Coll., 1977; postgrad., Beaver Coll.; Immaculata Coll. Cert. tchr., Pa. Tchr. elem. grades St. Anthony Sch., Balt., 1971-73, St. Mary-St. Patrick Sch., Wilmington, Del., 1973-74, Queen of Heaven Sch., Cherry Hill, N.J., 1974-77, St. Bonaventure Sch., Phila., 1977-78, 79-83, St. Stanislaus Sch., Lansdale, Pa., 1978-79; substitute tchr. various schs. Phila., 1983-84; tchr. 8th grade math. St. Cecilia Sch., Phila., 1984-94; tchr. math., vice prin. Corpus Christi Sch., Lansdale, Pa., 1994—; mem. visiting team Mid. States Assn., Phila., 1992; presenter workshops. Mem. Nat. Coun. Tchrs. Math., Pa. Coun. Tchrs. Math., Assn. Tchrs. Math. of Phila. and Vicinity. Roman Catholic. Avocations: crochet, cross-stitch, baking, walking. Office: Corpus Christi Sch 920 Sumneytown Pike Lansdale PA 19446-5414

MADDEN, WALES HENDRIX, JR., lawyer; b. Amarillo, Tex., Sept. 1, 1927; s. Wales Hendrix and Kathryn (Nash) M.; m. Alma Faye Cowden, Nov. 8, 1952; children: Wales Hendrix III, Straughn. B.A., U. Tex., 1950, LL.B., 1952. Bar: Tex. 1952. Practiced in Amarillo; mem. Tex. Constnl. Revision Commn., 1973. Bd. regents Amarillo Coll., 1958-59, U. Tex., 1959-65; mem. Tex. Coll. and Univ. System Coord. Bd., 1964-69, Amarillo Area Found., Cal Farley's Boys Ranch, Pres.'s Export Coun., 1981; trustee Trinity U., San Antonio; mem. Select Com. Higher Edn., 1985, 87; chmn. SWST Regional Panel, Pres.'s Commn. on White House Fellowships, 1989-90; chmn. bd. Internat. Food and Agrl. Devel., 1990-94; mem. Gov.'s Com. on Ad Valorem Taxes, 1996. Served with USNR. Named Outstanding Man of Amarillo, 1972; Disting. Alumnus U. Tex., 1979, U. Tex. Law Sch., 1986. Mem. ABA, Amarillo Bar Assn. (pres. 1956), Tex. Philos. Soc., Amarillo C. of C. (pres. 1968), State Bar Tex., State Jr. Bar Tex. (pres. 1956), Friar Soc., Phi Alpha Delta, Phi Delta Theta, Phi Eta Sigma, Pi Sigma Alpha. Presbyterian (elder). Home: PO Box 15288 Amarillo TX 79105-5288 Office: PO Box 15288 Amarillo TX 79105-5288

MADDEN, WANDA LOIS, nurse; b. Augusta, Kans., Apr. 26, 1929; d. George W. and Lillian B. (Dobyns) Provost; m. Laurence R. Madden, June 3, 1947 (div. 1961); children: Matthew, Mark, Luke, John, Michele. ADN, Pasadena City Coll., 1970; postgrad., Calif. State U. Consortium, 1986. RN, Calif.; ordained to ministry Am. Fellowship Ch., 1995. CCU nurse Huntington Meml. Hosp., Pasadena, Calif., 1970-71; ICU Community Hosp., Pico Rivera, Calif., 1971-72; CCU nurse Queen of the Valley Hosp., West Covina, Calif., 1973-74; ICU supr. Visalia (Calif.) Community Hosp., 1974-77, 89-90, ICU nurse, 1978; ICU nurse San Miguel Hosp. Assn., San Diego, 1978-79; supr. Casa Blanca Corp., San Diego, 1979-80; dir. nursing Visalia Convalescence Hosp., 1981-89, Westgate Gardens Convalescent Ctr., Visalia, 1990; psychiat. staff nurse Mill Creek Hosp., Visalia, 1990-91; AIDS case mgr. Tulare County Health Svcs., 1993-95; assoc. lay pastor Met. Cmty. Ch. of Sequoias, Visalia, 1994-95; ordained min. Tulare County Rainbow Cmty. Ch., 1995—; mem. Tulare County HIV Care Consortium, Tulare County HIV-AIDS Edn. and Prevention Planning Com.; gay and AIDS activist, Tulare County. Home: 2725 N Canary Dr Visalia CA 93291-1719 Office: 2725 N Canary Dr Visalia CA 93291-1719

MADDEX, MYRON BROWN (MIKE MADDEX), broadcasting executive; b. Champaign County, Ohio, May 20, 1924; s. Walter Omer and Eva Mae (Brown) M.; m. Wilma Jean Anderson, Mar. 29, 1943; children: James Michael, John Eugene, Martha Jean. Student, Coyne Elec. Sch., Chgo., Moody Bible Inst., Chgo., eves., 1956-58. With R.W. Schetter Jewelry & Radio, Mechanicsburg, Ohio, 1946-51; owner Maddex Radio & TV, Mechanicsburg, 1952-53; chief engr. sta. WJEL-AM&FM, Springfield, Ohio, 1953-54; engr. staf. WMBI-AM&FM, Chgo., 1954-55; traffic supr., asst. to mgr., then asst. mgr. staf. WMBI-AM&FM, 1956-65; gen. mgr., then exec. v.p. sta. WEEC, Springfield, 1965-72; pres. sta. WEEC, 1972—; dir. World Evangelistic Enterprise Corp., 1965—; past bd. dirs. Springfield Youth for Christ. Served with AUS, 1943-45. Mem. Nat. Religious Broadcasters (dir. 1968-89, 1st Midwest chpt. pres. 1969-71, nat. sec. 1982-85), Nat. Assn Evangelicals, Ohio Assn. Evangelicals (bd. dirs. 1984-92, sec. 1985-87, 1st v.p. 1987-89, pres. 1989-91), Springfield C. of C. Home: 1300 Shrine Rd Box 127 Springfield OH 45504-3966 Office: 2265 Troy Rd Springfield OH 45504-4229 *During high school, I felt radio was my field. That's about all that interested me. Pearl Harbor occurred 6 months prior to graduation, and the U.S. Army Signal Corps provided training and experience. Returning to civilian life in radio servicing came next. Then . . . I became a Christian. God directed me to Chicago and the pioneer Christian radio station, WMBI. From that day to this, radio, as a ministry, has been my calling.*

MADDIN, ROBERT, metallurgist educator; b. Hartford, Conn., Oct. 20, 1918; s. Isadore I. and Mae (Jacobs) Levine; married, July 8, 1945; children: Leslie, Jill. BS in Metall. Engring., Purdue U., 1942; DEng., Yale U., 1948. Registered profl. engr., Pa. Asst., assoc. prof. Johns Hopkins U., Balt., 1949-55; prof. U. Pa., phila., 1955-73, univ. prof., 1973-83; vis. prof. Harvard U., Cambridge, Mass., 1983-87, curator, 1987—; vis. prof. Oxford (Eng.) U., 1970, fellow Wolfson Coll., 1987; vis. prof. U. Birmingham, Eng., 1953-54; vis. scholar Hebrew U., Jerusalem, 1976; hon. prof. Beijing Sci. and Engring. U., 1986; hon. mem. Japan Metals. Contbr. more than 150 publs. to profl. jours. 1st Lt. USAF, 1942-45. Disting. Sr. Sci. fellow A. von Humboldt Found., Germany, 1989-90; recipient Pomerance award Archaeological Lust Am., 1994, medal of merit U. Pa. Fellow Am. Soc. Metallurgists, TMS. Avocations: history early metallurgy.

MADDOCK, JEROME TORRENCE, information services specialist; b. Darby, Pa., Feb. 7, 1940; s. Richard Cotton and Isobel Louise (Mezger) M.; m. Karen Rhueama Weygand, Oct. 2, 1965. BS in Biology, Muhlenberg Coll., 1961; MS in Info. Sci., Drexel U., 1968. Editorial assoc. Biol. Abstracts, Phila., 1962-63; mgr. rsch. info. Merck & Co., West Point, Pa., 1963-72; sr. cons. Auerbach Assocs., Inc., Phila., 1972-79; mgr. libr. and info. svcs. Solar Energy Rsch. Inst., Golden, Colo., 1979-88; mgr. info. svcs. Transp. Rsch. Bd., Washington, 1988—; del. Gov.;s Conf. on Libr. and Info. Svc., Pa., 1978; mem. blue ribbon panel to select archivist of U.S., Washington, 1979; U.S. del. to ops. com. on transp. rsch. info. Orgn. for Econ. Cooperation and Devel., 1988—. Bd. dirs. Paoli (Pa.) Pub. Libr., 1976-77. With USAFR, 1962-68. Mem. AAAS, Am. Soc. Info. Sci. (chmn. 1974-75),

Elks, Beta Phi Mu, Pi Delta Epsilon. Republican. Episcopalian. Achievements include projection of information science operations 10 years into the future. Home: 1162 E Riverbend St Superior CO 80027-8027 Office: Transp Rsch Bd 2101 Constitution Ave NW Washington DC 20418-0007

MADDOCK, LAWRENCE HILL, language educator, writer; b. Ogden, Utah, July 14, 1923; s. Lawrence J. and Nellie (Hill) M. Student, U. Fla., 1941-42; BA, George Peabody Coll., 1946, PhD, 1965; MA, U. So. Calif., 1949. Tchr. pub. schs. Jacksonville, Fla., 1949-52; instr. U. Fla., Gainesville, 1952-53; asst. prof. California (Pa.) State Coll., 1955-56, assoc. prof., 1956-64; assoc. prof. N.E. La. State Coll., Monroe, 1964-67, U. West Fla., Pensacola, 1967-90. Author: The Door of Memory, 1974, John Maddock: Mormon Pioneer, 1996; contbr. chpts. to books and articles to profl. jours. Mem. MLA (bibliographer 1978-93), Thomas Wolfe Soc., Mormon History Assn. Republican. Mormon. Home: 1012 Gerhardt Dr Pensacola FL 32503-3222

MADDOCKS, ROBERT ALLEN, lawyer, manufacturing company executive; b. Missouri Valley, Ia., Dec. 25, 1933; s. Clarence A. and Helen Louise (Unger) M.; m. JoAnn Skaggs, June 2, 1956; children—Todd Duncan, Susan Colette, Amy Annette. B.S., Drake U., 1956; J.D., 1958. Bar: Iowa 1958, U.S. Supreme Ct. 1969, Ohio 1970, Mo. 1972, Colo. 1992. Pvt. practice law Clarion, Ia., 1958-67; atty. Massey Ferguson, Inc., Des Moines, 1967-68; div. gen. counsel Akron, Ohio, 1968-69; asst. sec., gen. counsel, dir. corp. relations Kellwood Co., St. Louis, 1970-73, sec., gen. counsel, 1973-90, v.p., 1978-90, also bd. dirs. subs. cos.; dep. chmn., dir. Smart Shirts Ltd., Hong Kong, 1980-90; sec. Midwest Credit Corp.; Wright County atty., Clarion, 1961-65. Trustee Maryville Coll., St. Louis, 1975-78, Drake U., 1987-94; bd. dirs. Kellwood Found., 1975-90. Mem. Am. Bar Assn., Inter-Am., Ia., Ohio, Mo., Colo. bar assns., Am. Trial Lawyers Assn., Nat. Corporate Secs. Assn., Comml. Law League, Licensing Execs. Soc., Am. Apparel Mfrs. Assn. (legal com. 1972-90). Home: 266 Lookout Point Dr Osprey FL 34229-9738

MADDOX, ALVA HUGH, state supreme court justice; b. Andalusia, Ala., Apr. 17, 1930; s. Christopher Columbus and Audie Louella Maddox; m. Virginia Roberts, June 14, 1958; children: Robert Hugh, Jane Maddox. AB in Journalism, U. Ala., Tuscaloosa, 1952, JD, 1957. Bar: Ala. 1957. Law clk. to Judge Aubrey Cates, Ala. Ct. Appeals, Montgomery, 1957-58; field examiner Chief Atty.'s Office, VA, Montgomery, 1958-59; law clk. to Judge Frank M. Johnson, U.S. Dist. Ct., Montgomery, 1959-61; pvt. practice, Montgomery, 1961-65; cir. judge, spl. cir. judge Montgomery Cir. Ct., 1963, asst. dist. atty., 1964; legal advisor to govs. State of Ala., Montgomery, 1965-69; assoc. justice Supreme Ct. Ala., Montgomery, 1969—; mem. adv. bd. JUSTEC Rsch. Author: Alabama Rules of Criminal Procedure, 1991, supplements, 1992—. Founder youth jud. program YMCA, Montgomery, 1979, also mem. metro. bd. dirs. 2d lt. USAF, 1952-54, col. USAF Res. ret. Recipient Man of Yr. award YMCA, 1988, Disting. Program Svc. award, 1989. Mem. ABA, Ala. Bar Assn., Inst. Jud. Adminstrn., Christian Legal Soc., Federalist Soc. (bd. dirs.), Montgomery County Inns of Ct. (charter, founding), Ala. Law Inst., Am. Jud. Soc., Kiwanis (past bd. dirs. Montgomery). Democrat. Baptist. Office: Supreme Ct Ala 300 Dexter Ave Montgomery AL 36104-3741

MADDOX, HUGH, state supreme court justice. Justice Ala. Supreme Ct., Montgomery. Office: Ala Supreme Ct 300 Dexter Ave Montgomery AL 36104-3741

MADDOX, JESSE CORDELL, academic administrator; b. La Grange, Ga., Dec. 30, 1931; s. Jesse Garland and Esther Ann (Parmer) M.; m. Brona Faye Moorefield, Mar. 30, 1957; children: Cordell Jr., Michael, Brian, Gayle. BA, Furman U., 1954, LLD (hon.), 1976; M in Div., So. Bapt. Theol. Sem., 1957; DD (hon.), Bapt. Coll. at Charleston, S.C., 1972. Assoc. brotherhood dept. S.C. Bapt. Convention, Columbia, 1957-61; asst. to pres. Furman U., Greenville, S.C., 1961-71; pres. Anderson (S.C.) Coll., 1971-77, Carson Newman Coll., Jefferson City, Tenn., 1977—. Named Man. of Yr., Anderson Realtors, 1979; named to Athletic Hall of Fame Furman U., 1986. Mem. Nat. Jr. Coll. Council (pres. 1974-76), So. Assn. Colls. (commn. on colls. 1979-85), So. Assn., Ch. Related Colls. (pres. 1979), Assn. So. Bapt. Colls. and Schs. (pres. 1989-90). Lodge: Rotary (local pres. 1979). Avocations: tennis, jogging. Home: Laurel Hills RR 3 Jefferson Cy TN 37760-9803 Office: Carson-Newman Coll Office Pres Russell Ave Jefferson City TN 37760*

MADDOX, ROBERT LYTTON, lawyer; b. Middlesboro, Ky., May 18, 1924; s. Robert Lytton and Sybil (Sipher) M.; m. Inez Bentley Pryor, Nov. 23, 1955; children: William Granville, Julie Thornton, Robert Lytton III. AB, Harvard U., 1947, LLB, 1950. Bar: Ky. 1950, U.S. Dist. Ct. (ea. dist.) Ky. 1972, U.S. Dist. Ct. (we. dist.) 1979, U.S. Ct. Appeals (6th cir.) 1974. Assoc. Wyatt, Grafton & Sloss, Louisville, 1950-58; ptnr. Wyatt, Grafton & Sloss, 1958-80, Wyatt, Tarrant & Combs, 1980—; bd. dirs. Whip-Mix Corp., Louisville, Nugent Sand Corp., Louisville, Ky. Tax-Free Income Fund, Lexington, Orr Safety Corp., Louisville. Trustee/treas. Louisville Collegiate Sch., 1976-83, Lees Coll., Jackson, Ky., 1974-86; trustee/pres. Estate Planning Coun., Louisville, 1984-88. With U.S. Army, 1943-45. Decorated Bronze Star medal. Mem. Louisville Country Club, Harmony Landing Country Club, Jefferson Club, Wynn-Stay Club, Rotary. Democrat. Presbyterian. Avocations: golf, bicycling, investing. Home: 1412 Northwind Rd Louisville KY 40207-1665 Office: Wyatt Tarrant & Combs 2800 Citizens Plz Louisville KY 40202

MADDOX, ROBERT NOTT, chemical engineer, educator; b. Winslow, Ark., Sept. 29, 1925; s. R.L. and Mabel (Nott) M.; m. Paula Robinson, Oct. 6, 1951 (dec. Apr. 1984); children—Deirdre O'Neil, Robert Dozier; m. Pauline Razook, Nov. 30, 1987. Student, Iowa State Coll., 1944-45; B.S., U. Ark., 1948; M.S., U. Okla., 1950; Ph.D., Okla. State U., 1955; Sc.D. (hon.), U. Ark., 1991. Registered profl. engr., Okla. Mem. faculty Sch. Chem. Engring., Okla. State U., 1950-51, 52-58, prof., head dept., 1958-77, Leonard F. Sheerar prof., 1976-86, dir. phys. properties lab., 1976-86; design engr. process div. Black, Sivalls & Bryson, Inc., Oklahoma City, 1951-52; adminstrv. v.p., tech. dir. Fluid Properties Research, Inc., 1972-85; chem. engring. cons. Author: Gas and Liquid Sweetening, 1971, rev. ed. 1978, 83, (with J. Erbar) Gas Conditioning and Processing Vol. 3 - Computer Techniques and Applications, 1981, rev. ed. (with L. Lilly), 1988, (with A. Hines) Mass Transfer - Fundamentals and Applications, 1985; also numerous tech. papers. Served with USNR, 1944-45. Recipient award for personal achievement Chem. Engring. mag., 1988; Phillips lectr. in chem. engring. edn., Oklahoma State U., 1989; inducted into Engring. Hall of Fame, U. Ark., 1989, Okla. Higher Edn. Hall of Fame, 1996; Dr. Robert N. Maddox Professorship in Chem. Engring. established in his honor by Gas Processors Suppliers Assn. at Okla. State U., 1989, Founders award Am. Inst. of Chemical Engineers, 1994. Fellow AIChE (chpt. pres. 1956-57, André Wilkins Meml. award 1981, Founder's award 1994); mem. NSPE, Okla. Soc. Profl. Engrs. (chpt. pres. 1961-62, dir. 1966-68, Engr. of Yr. 1972), Am. Inst. Mining Engrs., Soc. Petroleum Engrs., Am. Chem. Soc. (treas. indsl. and engring. chemistry div. 1966-68, chmn. div. 1970, Stewart award 1971), Gas Processors Assn. (Hanlon award 1985, Svc. citation 1987), Gas Processors Suppliers Assn. (editorial adv. bd. Engring. Data Book 1972—), Sigma Xi, Omega Chi Epsilon (nat. pres. 1968-70), Tau Beta Pi, Alpha Chi Sigma, Omicron Deleta Kappa, Sigma Nu (high coun. 1966-70, regent 1972-74, Hall of Honor 1988). Episcopalian (lay reader, vestryman). Clubs: Elks, Masons. Home: 1710 Davinbrook Ln Stillwater OK 74074-2339

MADDOX, TIMOTHY DWAIN, natural gas company manager; b. Canton, Ohio, Aug. 17, 1960; s. Thomas and Marilyn May (Wharton) M. BS, Bowling Green State U., 1982; BS in Petroleum Engring., Marietta Coll., 1986. Lic. profl. geologist, Ky. Asst. prodn. engr. intern Mobil Oil Corp., Wichita Falls, Tex., 1985; monitoring & design engr. Columbia Gas Transmission Corp., Charleston, W.Va., 1986-90, mgr. storage engring.-east, 1990—; mem. gas storage workgroup State W.Va. Dept. Environ. Protection. Mem. NSPE, Soc. Petroleum Engrs. (publicity chmn. 1987-88, membership chmn. 1988-89, program chmn. 1989-90, chmn. 1990-91, exec officer 1991-93), Kappa Mu Epsilon. Avocation: jet-skiing. Office: Columbia Gas Transmission 1700 Maccorkle Ave SE Charleston WV 25314-1518

MADDREY, WILLIS CROCKER, medical educator, internist, academic administrator, consultant, researcher; b. Roanoke Rapids, N.C., Mar. 29, 1939; s. Milner Crocker and Sara Jean (Willis) M.; m. Ann Marie Matt; children: Jeffrey, Gregory, Thomas. BS, Wake Forest U., 1960; MD, Johns Hopkins U., 1964. Diplomate: Am. Bd. Internal Medicine. Intern Osler Med. Service Johns Hopkins Hosp., Balt., 1964-65, asst. resident, 1965-66, 68-69, chief resident, 1969-70; fellow in liver disease Yale U., 1970-71; asst. prof. medicine Johns Hopkins U., Balt., 1971-75, assoc. prof., 1975-79, prof., 1980-81, asst. dean Sch. Medicine, 1975-79; assoc. dir. dept. medicine Johns Hopkins U., Baltimore, 1979-82; prof., chmn. dept. medicine Jefferson Med. Coll., Phila., 1982-90; v.p. clin. affairs U. Tex. Southwestern Med. Ctr., Dallas, 1990-93, exec. v.p. clin. affairs, 1994—. Assoc. editor: Medicine, 1972-82, Hepatology, 1988-95, mem. editl. bd., 1981-84, 86-87, Gastroenterology, 1982-87, Am. Jour. Medicine, 1978-87; contbr. articles to profl. jours. Bd. dirs. Am. Liver Found., 1976-80, Dallas County Med. Soc., 1996—; trustee Magee Rehab. Hosp., Phila., 1982-87, St. Paul Med. Ctr., Dallas, 1996—. Served with USPHS, 1966-68. Mem. ACP (bd. regents 1984-94, pres. 92-93), Am. Soc. Clin. Investigation, Am. Gastroenterol. Assn., Am. Assn. Study Liver Disease (pres. 1982). Republican. Office: U Tex Southwestern Med Ctr 5323 Harry Hines Blvd Dallas TX 75235-7208

MADDUX, GREG(ORY ALAN), professional baseball player; b. San Angelo, Tex., Apr. 14, 1966. Grad. high sch., Las Vegas. Baseball player Chicago Cubs, 1984-92, Atlanta Braves, 1992—. Recipient Cy Young award Baseball Writers' Assn. Am., 1992, 93, 94, 95; named to All-Star team, 1988, 92, 94-5; recipient Gold Glove Award, 1990-96; Sporting News All-Star Team, 1992-94; named Nat. League Pitcher of Yr., Sporting News, 1993; Nat. League Innings Pitched Leader, 1991-92, earned run avg., 1995, fielding percentage, 1990-95. Mem. World Series championship team, 1995. Office: Atlanta Braves PO Box 4064 Atlanta GA 30302-4064*

MADDUX, PARKER AHRENS, lawyer; b. San Francisco, May 23, 1939; s. Jackson Walker and Jeanette Ahrens M.; m. Mathilde G.M. Landman, Mar. 20, 1966; 1 child, Jackson Wilhelmus Quentin. AB, U. Calif., 1961; JD, Harvard U., 1964. Bar: Calif. 1965, U.S. Dist. Ct. (no. so., ea., ctrl. dist.) Calif. 1965, U.S. Ct. Appeals (9th cir.) 1972, U.S. Ct. Claims, 1974, N.Y. 1981, U.S. Supreme Ct. 1982, Assoc., Pillsbury Madison & Sutro, San Francisco, 1965-72, ptnr., 1973-97; dir. litigation Tandem Computers Inc., Cupertino, Calif., 1997—; lectr. in field. Fulbright fellow, 1964-65. Mem. ABA, Calif. Bar Assn., San Francisco Bar Assn., Harvard Club (N.Y.C.), Pacific Union Club. Republican. Unitarian. Contbr. articles to profl. jours. Office: Tandem Computers Inc 10435 N Tantau Loc 200-16 Cupertino CA 95014

MADDY, JANET MARIE, retired educator, dean of students; b. Crestline, Ohio, Feb. 20, 1939; d. Hubert Franklin and Mabel May (Hotelling) M. AA, Pasadena City Coll, 1959; BA, Calif. State U., L.A., 1965, MA, 1972. Instr. Calif. State Coll., L.A., fall 1965; tchr. phys. edn. Irving Jr. High, L.A. Unified Sch. Dist., spring 1966, Bret Harte Jr. High Sch., L.A. Unified Sch. Dist., 1966-67; tchr., phys. edn. tchr., dept. chair Walton Jr. High Sch.-Compton (Calif.) Unified Sch. Dist., 1967-72; tchr. phys. edn./coach Dominguez H.S., Compton, 1972-78; prin. Westchester Luth. Schs., L.A., 1978-84; tchr. phys. edn., dept. chair Nimitz Middle Sch., L.A. Unified Sch. Dist., Huntington Park, Calif., 1985-94, dean of students-C Track, 1994-97; mem. shared decision making coun. Nimitz Middle Sch., Huntington Park, 1992-96; mentor tchr. selection com. L.A. Unified Sch. Dist., 1993-94; women in sports delegation to China, Citizen Amb. Program, Spokane, Wash., 1994, U.S. China Joint Conf. on Women's Issues, China, 1995, Internat. Conf. on Domestic Violence, Delhi, India, 1998. Synod womens orgn. bd. ELCA Women, L.A., 1990-93, 94-96, chair references and counsel com. triennial nat. conf., Washington, 1993, del. triennial conv., Mpls., 1996; chair cmty. com. Police Activity League, Ingelwood, Calif., 1990-93; co-chair Neighborhood Watch, Ingelwood, 1988-97. Comdr. USNR, ret., 1960-83. Mem. CAHPER, AAHPER, CTA, UTLA. Democrat. Lutheran. Avocations: reading, sports, travel. Home: 501 E Bucyrus St Crestline OH 44827

MADDY, PENELOPE JO, philosopher; b. Tulsa, July 4, 1950; d. Richard and Suzanne (Lorimer) Parsons. BA in Math., U. Calif., Berkeley, 1972; PhD in Philosophy, Princeton U., 1979. Asst. prof. U. Notre Dame (Ind.), 1978-83; assoc. prof. U. Ill., Chgo., 1983-87; assoc. prof. U. Calif., Irvine, 1987-89, prof., 1989—, dept. chair, 1991-95; mem. editorial bd. Jour. Philos. Logic, 1985—. Author: Realism in Mathematics, 1990; editor: Notre Dame Jour. Formal Logic, 1979-84, editl. bd., 1984—; editl. bd. Jour. Symbolic Logic, 1995—, Philosophia Mathematica, 1993—. Fellow AAUW, 1982-83, U. Calif., 1988-89; NSF grantee, 1986, 88-89, 90-91, 94-95, Marshall scholar, 1982-83, Westinghouse Sci. scholar, 1968-72. Mem. Assn. Symbolic Logic (mem. exec. com. 1993-96), Am. Philos. Assn. (mem. exec. com. 1993-95), Philosophy of Sci. Assn. (mem. governing bd. 1993-95). Office: U Calif Dept Philosophy Irvine CA 92697

MADEIRA, EDWARD W(ALTER), JR., lawyer; b. Phila., Feb. 10, 1928; s. Edward W. and Alice T. (Thompson) M.; m. Grace Lucer, Oct. 13, 1956; children: Martha L., Melissa P., Amanda T. A.B., U. Pa., 1949, LL.B., 1952. Bar: Pa. 1953. Law clk. Justice John C. Bell, Jr., Phila., 1952-53; ptnr. Pepper, Hamilton & Scheetz, 1961—, co-chmn., 1992-94, chmn. emeritus, 1994—; adj. prof. law Villanova Law Sch., 1992—. Pres. bd. dirs. Defender Assn. Phila. (pub. defender); assoc. trustee U. Pa. 1989—. Fellow Am. Coll. Trial Lawyers; mem. ABA (ho. of dels. 1989-92, chmn. com. on fed. jud. improvements 1991—), Jud. Conf. 3d Cir., Phila. Bar Assn., Pa. Bar Assn., Internat. Assn. Ins. Counsel. Republican. Episcopalian. Home: 227 Atlee Rd Wayne PA 19087-3835 Office: Pepper Hamilton & Scheetz 3000 Two Logan Sq 18th Arch St Philadelphia PA 19103

MADEIRA, FRANCIS KING CAREY, conductor, educator; b. Jenkintown, Pa., Feb. 21, 1917; s. Percy Childs and Margaret (Carey) M.; m. Jean E. Browning, June 17, 1947. Grad., Avon Old Farms, 1934; student, Julliard Grad. Sch., 1937-43; D.F.A. (hon.), Providence Coll., 1966; D.H.L., R.I. Coll., 1969; Mus.D. (hon.), Brown U., 1976. Instr. music Brown U., 1943-46, asst. prof. music, 1946-56, assoc. prof. music, 1956-66; founder, condr. R.I. Philharm. Orch., 1945-78; concert pianist recitals and condr. concerts, U.S. and Europe; also guest condr. U.S. and fgn. orchs. World premiere Trilogy (JFK-MLK-RFK) (by Ron Nelson), R.I. Philharmonic Orch., 1969. Mem. music panel Maine State Arts Commn., 1987-90; bd. trustees Saco River Festival Assn., 1988-94; mem. adv. bd., trustee Portland (Maine) Symphony Orch., 1996—. Recipient Gov.'s award for excellence in arts, 1972; John F. Kennedy award for service to community, 1978.

MADEIRA, ROBERT LEHMAN, professional society administrator; b. Elizabethtown, Pa., Aug. 30, 1915; s. Isaac Titus and Elsie Hernley (Lehman) M.; m. Mary Elizabeth Evans, Feb. 5, 1938; children: Terry Madeira Harsney, Chase Landre. Student, Juniata Coll., 1933-34; B.S. in Econs, Elizabethtown Coll., 1937; postgrad., Mpls. Honeywell Sch. Aero. Engring., U. Minn., 1945. Pianist, tchr. Elizabethtown, 1935-41; automobile salesman Packard Lancaster Co., Lancaster, Pa., 1937; owner, mgr. Conewago Foods, Elizabethtown, 1938-39; aircraft technician U.S. Air Force Middletown, Pa. and Columbia, S.C., 1941-42; project engr. Mpls. Honeywell, Chgo. and Mpls., 1942-45; mgr. Iceland, Inc., Elizabethtown, 1945-51; exec. sec. Nat. Frozen Food Locker Inst., Elizabethtown, 1951-55; exec. dir. Nat. Inst. Locker and Freezer Provisioners, Elizabethtown, 1955-73, Am. Assn. Meat Processors, Elizabethtown, 1973-80; exec. dir. emeritus Am. Assn. Meat Processors, 1980—; tchr. course in assn. mgmt. Yale U., Mich. State U., 1966-70; condr. internat. meat processing seminars, Europe, S.Am., Australia, New Zealand, The Orient, Africa, 1962-85. Chmn. Elizabethtown ARC, 1948-49, Elizabethtown Community Chest, 1952-53, Elizabethtown Park Dr., 1950; bd. dirs. Lancaster Com. of 100, 1953-57, Elizabethtown Music Found., 1951-57; bd. dirs. Norlanco Med. Center, Elizabethtown, 1972-75, chmn. fund dr., 1972-73. Recipient Man of Yr. award Nat. Inst. Locker and Freezer Provisioners, 1955; honor cert. Freedoms Found. at Valley Forge, 1976. Mem. Am. Soc. Assn. Execs. (Key award 1971, chartered assn. exec.), C. of C. U.S., Nat. Assn. Exhbn. Mgrs., Nat. Fedn. Ind. Bus., Gideons Internat., Nat. Right-to-Work Com. Republican. Presbyterian. Home: 660 Willow Valley Sq Apt M102 Lancaster PA 17602-4874 Office: Am Assn Meat Processors PO Box 269 Elizabethtown PA 17022-0269

MADER, BRYN JOHN, vertebrate paleontologist; b. N.Y.C., July 29, 1959; s. Walter Richard and Audrey Jeanne (Hargest) M. BS, SUNY, Stony Brook, 1982; MS, U. Mass., 1987, PhD, 1991. Curatorial asst. dept. vertebrate paleontology Am. Mus. Natural History, N.Y.C., 1982-83, asst. collection mgr., 1990-93, collections registrar dept. mammalogy, 1993—; trustee, founder, pres. L.I. Natural Hist. Mus., 1994—. Contbr. articles to profl. jours., chpts. to books. Mem. N.Y. Acad. Scis., Soc. Vertebrate Paleontology, Paleontol. Soc., Sigma Xi. Presbyterian. Achievements include publication of first and only significant review of brontotheres in almost 50 years (a major perissodactyl lineage known primarily from the Eocene and Oligocene epochs of North America and Central Asia). Office: Am Mus Natural History Cen Park West At 79th St W New York NY 10024

MADER, CHARLES LAVERN, chemist; b. Dewey, Okla., Aug. 8, 1930; s. George Edgar and Naomia Jane (Harer) M.; m. Emma Jean Sinclair, June 12, 1960; 1 child, Charles L. II. BS, Okla. State U., 1952, MS, 1954; PhD, Pacific Western U., 1980. Fellow Los Alamos (N.Mex.) Nat. Lab., 1955—; JIMAR sr. fellow U. Hawaii, Honolulu, 1985-94; pres. Mader Cons. Co., Honolulu, 1985—. Author: Numerical Modeling of Detonation, 1979, Numerical Modeling of Water Waves, 1988, Numerical Modeling of Explosives and Propellants, 1997; editor: Los Alamos Explosives Performance Data, 1982, LASL Phermex Data, vol. 1, 1980, vol. 2, 1980, vol. 3, 1981; contbr. numerous articles to profl. jours.; author 70 reports. Scoutmaster Boys Scouts Am., Los Alamos, 1971-85. Fellow Am. Inst. Chemists; mem. Am. Chem. Soc., Combustion Inst., Tsunami Soc. (editor 1985—), Marine Tech. Soc., Sigma Xi, Pi Mu Epsilon, Phi Lambda Upsilon. Methodist. Achievements include development and definition of field of numerical modeling of explosives and water waves. Home: 1049 Kamehame Dr Honolulu HI 96825-2860 Office: Mader Cons Co 1049 Kamehame Dr Honolulu HI 96825-2860

MADER, DOUGLAS PAUL, quality engineering manager; b. Brookings, S.D., May 16, 1963; s. Lawrence Harold Mader Jr. and Susan Margaret (Littleton) Burk; m. Darla Sue Hower, Dec. 30, 1991; children: Alyssa, Megan, Matthew. BS in Engring. Physics, S.D. State U., 1985; MS in Math., Colo. Sch. of Mines, 1990; PhD in Mech. Engring., Colo. State U., 1994. Cert. quality engr. Am. Soc. Quality Control, 1990-93. Quality control engr. Govt. Electronics Group, Motorola, Scottsdale, Ariz., 1985-87; integrated circuit test engr. Semiconductor Products sector, Motorola, Mesa, Ariz., 1987-88; sr. staff engr. Six Sigma Rsch. Inst., Motorola, Schaumburg, Ill., 1990-92, prin. staff scientist, 1992; cons. Rockwell Internat., Cedar Rapids, Iowa, 1992-93; quality engring. mgr. Advanced Energy Industries, Ft. Collins, Colo., 1993-95; instr. stats. and mech. engring. Colo. State U., 1993-94; statistician Hewlett-Packard Co., Greeley, Colo., 1995-96, sr. quality cons., 1996-97, quality engring. mgr., 1997—. Author: Process Control Methods, 1993 (videotapes) Concurrent Engineering - The Foundation of Six Sigma Quality, 1992; mem. editorial bd. Internat. Jour. of Ops. and Quantitative Mgmt., 1994—. Mem. Am. Statis. Assn., Inst. Indsl. Engrs., Am. Soc. Quality Control (mem. standing rev. and mix media rev. bd. 1992—, mem. editl. bd. for quality engring. 1994—), Inst. Ops. Rsch. and Mgmt. Sci., Decision Scis. Inc. Office: Hewlett-Packard Co 700 71st Ave Greeley CO 80634-9776

MADER, JON TERRY, physician; b. Madison, Wis., Mar. 21, 1944; s. John Henry and Louise E. (Hancock) M.; BA, Wabash Coll., 1966; MD, Ind. U., 1970; m. Donna Belinda Milner, May 7, 1994; children: Travis Jon, Amy Eileen, Bret Mark, Jason Darrel Samuel. Intern, U. Tex. Med. Br., Galveston, 1970-71, resident in internal medicine, 1971-73, fellow in infectious disease, 1973-74, 76-77, instr., 1977-78, asst. prof. dept. internal medicine, 1978-82, assoc. prof. internal medicine div. infectious diseases, 1982-89, prof., 1989—, acting chief div. infectious diseases, 1990-94; mem. med. staff, 1977—; prof. pathology, 1992—, adj. prof. orthopaedics, 1993—; chief hyperbaric medicine, div. marine medicine Marine Biomed. Inst., Galveston, 1979—; trainee in hyperbaric oxygenation therapy NASA Manned Spacecraft Center, Houston, 1973; bd. advisors Ocean Corp., Houston. Served with M.C., USN, 1974-76; capt. USNR, 1990. Diplomate Am. Bd. Internal Medicine; cert. Am. Bd. Infectious Diseases; recipient numerous fellowships and grants. Fellow Am. Bd. Internal Medicine; mem. Am. Soc. Microbiology, Undersea and Hyperbaric Med. Soc. (exec. com., past pres.), Am. Coll. Hyperbaric Medicine (pres.), Am. Fedn. Clin. Research, Can. Infectious Disease Soc., Infectious Disease Soc. Am., Musculoskeletal Infection Soc. (pres.), Am. Acad. Orthopedic Surgeons, ACP. Presbyterian. Contbr. articles to profl. jours. Home: 111 Lanai St Galveston TX 77554 Office: U Tex Med Br Dept Inernal Medicine 301 Univ Blvd Galveston TX 77555-1115

MADERA, JOSEPH J., bishop; b. San Francisco, Nov. 27, 1927. Ed., Domus Studiorum of the Missionaries of the Holy Spirit, Coyoacan, D.F., Mexico. Ordained priest Roman Cath. Ch., 1957. Coadjutor to bishop of Fresno, 1980; bishop of Fresno, 1980-91; aux. bishop Archdiocese for Mil. Svcs., Silver Springs, Md., 1991—. *

MADEWELL, JOHN EDWARD, radiologist. Student, Ctrl. State Coll., Oklahoma City, 1960-69; MD, U. Okla., 1969. Intern Madigen Gen. Hosp., Tacoma, 1969-70; resident in diagnostic radiology Walter Reed Med. Ctr., Washington, 1970-73; fellow in radiol. pathology Armed Forces Inst. Pathology, Washington, 1973-74; radiologist Milton S. Hershey Med. Ctr.; prof., chmn. dept. Milton S. Hershey Med. Ctr./Pa. State U., 1987—; exec. dir. Univ. Physicians/Pa. State U., Hershey, 1996—. Mem. Am. Coll. Radiology, Am. Roentgen Ray Soc., Assn. Univ. Radiologists, Internat. Skeletal Soc., Radiologic Soc. N.Am. Office: Pa State U Coll Medicine Hershey Med Ctr Dept Radiol PO Box 850 Hershey PA 17033-0850

MADEWELL, MARY ANN, nursing educator; b. Cin., Mar. 12, 1936; d. Joseph Anthony and Gertrude (Lietemeyer) Siegel; m. James Arthur Madewell, Sept. 12, 1959; children: Mary E., James J., Ann Marie, Larry J. BSN, U. Cin., 1958; MSN, Ind. U., 1982, D in Nursing Svc., 1994. RN, Ohio, Ind. Asst. head nurse The Christ Hosp., Cin., 1958; instr., tchr. trainer, evaluator Childbirth Edn. Assn., Cin., 1958-83; office, on-call nurse Drs. Graf and McCord, Cin., 1958-60; staff nurse Mt. Carmel Hosp., Columbus, Ohio, 1960-61; instr. U. Cin., 1977-78; tchr. asst. Ind. U., Indpls., 1981-82, 83-84; instr. adj. U. Cin., 1985-88; asst. vis. prof. Miami U., Hamilton, Ohio, 1992-94; asst. prof. U. Cin., 1994—; adv. bd. mem. Pregnancy Ctr. Cleremont, 1986—; cmty. educator abuse of children Women Helping Women, Cin., 1993—. Bd. dirs., 1st v.p. Great Rivers Girl Scout Coun., Cin., 1991—, presenter adolescent sexuality, 1987-91. Recipient Perinatal grant and nurse traineeship, 1978-79, 79-81, Rsch. award Sigma Theta Tau, 1985; prin. investigator March of Dimes, 1994, Ohio Dept. Health, 1994-97. Mem. Midwest Nursing Rsch. Soc. (presenter 1984), Assn. Women's Health, Obstetrical Neonatal Nurses (presenter, hospitality 1972—), Nat. Perinatal Assn., Health Mothers, Health Babies, Childbirth Edn. Assn. (con. 1983—), Southwestern Ohio Nurses Assn. Roman Catholic. Home: 5 Kris Cir Terrace Park OH 45174-1015

MADEY, THEODORE EUGENE, physics educator; b. Wilmington, Del., Oct. 24, 1937. BS, Loyola Coll., Balt., 1959; PhD in Physics, U. Notre Dame, 1963. Staff physicist Nat. Inst. Stds. & Tech., 1965-81, rsch. fellow, 1983-88, group leader surface structure & kinetics, 1981-88; dir. lab. surface modification, prof. dept. physics Rutgers U., Piscataway, N.J., 1988—; vis. scientist Inst. Phys. Chemistry Tech. U. Munich, 1973, Sandia Nat. Labs., Albuquerque, 1977, Fritz Haber Inst. of Max Planck, Gessellschaft, Berlin, 1982; Chevron vis. prof. chem. engring. Calif. Inst. Tech., 1981. Recipient Gold Medal award U.S. Dept. Commerce, 1981, E.W. Mueller award U. Wis., 1991. Fellow Am. Phys. Soc., Am. Chem. Soc., Am. Vacuum Soc. (pres. 1981, M.W. Welch award 1985); mem. Internat. Union Vacuum Sci. Tech. & Applications (sec. gen. 1986-89, pres.-elect 1989-92, pres. 1992-95), Am. Inst. Physics. Office: Rutgers U Lab Surface Modification PO Box 849 Serin Physics Lab Piscataway NJ 08855-0849

MADGETT, NAOMI LONG, poet, editor, educator; b. Norfolk, Va., July 5, 1923; d. Clarence Marcellus and Maude Selena (Hilton) Long; m. Julian F. Witherspoon, Mar. 31, 1946 (div. Apr. 1949); 1 child, Jill Witherspoon Boyer; m. William H. Madgett, July 29, 1954 (div. Dec. 1960); m. Leonard P. Andrews, Mar. 31, 1972 (dec. May 1996). BA, Va. State Coll., 1945; MEd, Wayne State U., 1956; PhD, Internat. Inst. for Advanced Studies, 1980; LHD (hon.), Siena Heights Coll., 1991, Loyola U., 1993; DFA (hon.), Mich. State U., 1994. Reporter, copyreader Mich. Chronicle, Detroit, 1946;

svc. rep. Mich. Bell Telephone Co., Detroit, 1948-54; tchr. English pub. high schs. Detroit, 1955-65, 66-68; rsch. assoc. Oakland U., Rochester, Mich., 1965-66; mem. staff Detroit Women Writers Conf. Ann. Writers Conf., 1968—; lectr. English U. Mich., 1970-71; assoc. prof. English Eastern Mich. U., Ypsilanti, 1968-73, prof., 1973-84, prof. emeritus, 1984—; editor-pub. Lotus Press, 1974—; editor Lotus Poetry Series, Mich. State U. Press, 1993—. Author: (poetry) Songs to a Phantom Nightingale (under name Naomi Cornelia Long), 1941, One and the Many, 1956, Star by Star, 1965, 70, Pink Ladies in the Afternoon, 1972, 90, Exits and Entrances, 1978, Phantom Nightingale: Juvenilia, 1981, Octavia and other Poems (Creative Achievement award Coll. Lang. Assn.), 1988, Remembrances of Spring: Collected Early Poems, 1993; (textbook) (with Ethel Tincher and Henry B. Maloney) Success in Language and Literature B, 1967, A Student's Guide to Creative Writing, 1980; editor: (anthology) A Milestone Sampler: 15th Anniversary Anthology, 1988, Adam of Ife: Black Women in Praise of Black Men, 1992; In Her Lifetime tribute Afrikan Poets Theatre, 1989. Participant Creative Writers in Schs. program. Recipient Esther R. Beer Poetry award Nat. Writers Club, 1957, Disting. English Tchr. of Yr. award, 1967; Josephine Nevins Keal award, 1979; Mott fellow in English, 1965, Robert Hayden Rungate award, 1985, Creative Artist award Mich. Coun. for the Arts, 1987, award Nat. Coalition 100 Black Women, 1984, award Nat. Coun. Tchrs. English Black Caucus, 1984, award Chesapeake/Virginia Beach chpt. Links, Inc., 1981, Arts Found. Mich. award, 1990, Creative Achievement award Coll. Lang. Assn., 1988; Arts Achievement award Wayne State U., 1985, The Black Scholar Award of Excellence, 1992; Am. Book award, 1993, Mich. Artist award, 1993; Creative Contbrs. award Gwendolyn Brooks Ctr. Black Lit. and Creative Writing Chgo. State U., 1993, George Kent award, 1995; Naomi Long Madgett Poetry award named for her, 1993—; inducted Summer H.S. Hall of Fame, St. Louis, 1997. Mem. NAACP, Coll. Lang. Assn., So. Poetry Law Ctr., Langston Hughes Soc., Nora Neale Hurston Soc., Am. Acad. Poets, Poetry Resource Ctr. Mich., Detroit Women Writers, Mus. African Am. History, Alpha Kappa Alpha. Congregationalist. Home: 18080 Santa Barbara Dr Detroit MI 48221-2531 Office: PO Box 21607 Detroit MI 48221-0607 *I have tried to set an example of excellence in the use of language, especially the language of poetry. If I can leave behind some enduring work—my own words and the words of others I have published—I will consider myself amply rewarded for my labors. The truly great people I have known have given a great deal of themselves in the service of others, have not been puffed up by their own importance, and have maintained integrity in their personal and professional lives. They have been my models.*

MADHUSOODANAN, SUBRAMONIAM, psychiatrist, educator; b. Trivandrum, India, Sept. 7, 1947; came to U.S., 1976; s. Subramoniam Pillai and Leelavathi K. Amma; m. Rama Sivathanu, Feb. 5, 1976 (div. Feb. 1991); children: Leena, Deepa; m. Gunjan Jain, Sept. 12, 1991; 1 child, Neha. MBBS, Trivandrum Med. Coll., 1971; Diploma in Otorhinolaryngology, Kurnool (India) Med. Coll., 1975; MD, SUNY, 1992. Diplomate in psychiatry and geriatric psychiatry Am. Bd. Psychiatry and Neurology, Am. Bd. Quality Assurance and Utilization Physicians. Instr. Mt. Sinai Sch. Medicine, CUNY, 1978-82; asst. attending psychiatrist Mt. Sinai Svcs., City Hosp. Ctr. at Elmhurst, N.Y., 1979-81; med. dir. outpatient alcohol program St. John's Episcopal Hosp., Far Rockaway, N.Y., 1983—, acting dir. psychiatry, 1984-86, assoc. chair psychiatry, 1986—, program dir. geriatric psychiatry fellowship program, 1993—; dir. psychiatry Peninsula Hosp., Far Rockaway, 1985-94; clin. asst. prof. dept. psychiatry SUNY Downstate Med. Ctr., Bklyn., 1989-95, 1995—; cons. psychiatrist St. John's Nursing Home, Peninsula Nurses Home, Far Rockaway Nursing Home, Lawrence Nursing Home, Rockaway Care Ctr., Brookhaven Nursing Home Haven Manor, 1981—. Mem. Am. Psychiat. Assn., Am. Geriatric Psychiatry Assn., World Fedn. Mental Health, Am. Geriatric Soc., Queens County Psychiat. Soc., Lawrence Assn. Democrat. Hindu. Avocations: gardening, photography, travel. Home: 249 Broadway Lawrence NY 11559-1511 Office: St John's Episcopal Hosp 327 B 19th St Far Rockaway NY 11691

MADIGAN, JOHN WILLIAM, publishing executive; b. Chgo., June 7, 1937; s. Edward P. and Olive D. Madigan; m. Holly Williams, Nov. 24, 1962; children: Mark W., Griffith E., Melanie L. BBA, U. Mich., 1958, MBA, 1959. Fin. analyst Duff & Phelps, Chgo., 1960-62; audit mgr. Arthur Andersen & Co., Chgo., 1962-67; v.p. investment banking Paine, Webber, Jackson & Curtis, Chgo., 1967-69; v.p. corp. fin. Salomon Bros., Chgo., 1969-74; v.p., CFO, dir. Tribune Co., Chgo., 1975-81, exec. v.p., 1981-91, pub., 1990-94, pres., CEO Tribune Pub. Co., 1991-94, pres., COO, 1994-5, pres., CEO, 1995—, chmn., pres., CEO, 1996—; bd. dirs. AP. Trustee Rush-Presbyn.-St. Luke's Med. Ctr., Mus. TV & Radio in N.Y., Northwestern U., Ill. Inst. Tech. Mem. Chicagoland C. of C. (bd. dirs.), Chgo. Coun. on Fgn. Rels. (bd. dirs.), Robert R. McCormick Tribune Found. (bd. dirs.), Newspaper Assn. Am. (bd. dirs.), Newspaper Mgmt. Ctr. at Northwestern U. (exec. com.), Econ. Club Chgo., Comml. Club Chgo. Office: Tribune Co 435 N Michigan Ave Chicago IL 60611

MADIGAN, JOSEPH EDWARD, financial executive, consultant, director; b. Bklyn., June 26, 1932; s. James Peter and Mary (Goldman) M.; m. Catherine Cashman, July 26, 1980; children: Kerri Ann, Kimberly Ann, Elizabeth Ann. BBA cum laude, Baruch Coll., CUNY, 1958; MBA, NYU, 1963. Adminstrv. asst. Assoc. Metals & Minerals Corp., 1961-63; fin. analyst, fgn. exch. trader, corp. portfolio trader AMAX, Inc., 1963-65; mgr. corp. portfolio, dir. cash mgmt., asst. treas. TWA, Inc., 1965-68; treas. Borden, Inc., 1968-76, v.p., treas., 1976-80; exec. v.p., chief fin. officer Wendy's Internat., Inc., Dublin, Ohio, 1980-87; bd. dirs. Skyline Chili, Inc., Voca Corp., Columbus Parts Supply, Inc., Columbus Paper & Supply Co., Frank Gates Svc. Co., RWS Enterprises, Cardinal Realty Svcs., Inc., chmn. bd. dirs.; bd. dirs. Columbus Show Case Co., Creative Control Designs, Inc. With USN, 1951-55. Mem. Fin. Execs. Inst., Nat. Investor Rels. Inst., Investor Rels. Assn., Exec. Forum NYU, Baruch Coll.-CUNY Alumni Assn., NYU Alumni Assn., Treas. Club N.Y., Country Club at Muirfield Village, Capital Club (Columbus), Imperial Golf Club (Naples, Fla.), Beta Gamma Sigma. Republican. Roman Catholic. Home: 5517 Carnoustie Ct Dublin OH 43017-8746

MADIGAN, MICHAEL JOSEPH, state legislator; b. Chgo., Apr. 19, 1942; m. Shirley Roumagoux; children: Lisa, Tiffany, Nicole, Andrew. Ed., U. Notre Dame, Loyola U., Chgo. Mem. Ill. Ho. of Reps., 1971—, majority leader, 1977-80, minority leader, 1981-82, house spkr., 1983-94, Dem. leader, 1995-96, ho. spkr., 1997—; lawyer. Sec. to Alderman David W. Healey; hearing officer Ill. Commerce Commn.; del. 6th Ill. Constnl. Conv.; trustee Holy Cross Hosp.; ex officio mem. adv. com. to pres. Richard J. Daley Coll.; adv. com. Fernley Harris Sch. for Handicapped; committeeman 13th Ward Democratic Orgn. Mem. Council Fgn. Relations, City Club Chgo. Office: House Reps State Capital Bldg Springfield IL 62706

MADIGAN, RICHARD ALLEN, museum director; b. Corning, N.Y., Oct. 29, 1937; s. Myles L. and Rebekah M. (Bacon) M.; AB, Drew U., 1959; m. Mary Jean Smith, June 11, 1960 (div. 1975); children: Richard Allen, Dana Smith, Reese Jennings; m. 2d, Alice Sturrock, Sept. 6, 1975 (div. May 1978); m. 3d, Cara Montgomery, Aug. 5, 1978 (div. July 1987); 1 son, James Myles. Pub. contact rep. Corning Glass Center, 1959, supr. visitor rels., 1959-60; dir. Andrew Dickson White Mus. Art, Cornell U., 1960-63; asst. dir., asst. sec. Corcoran Gallery Art, Washington, 1963-67; dir. N. Tex. Museums Resources Council, 1967-68, Bklyn. Children's Mus., 1968-69; exec. dir. Wave Hill Center Environ. Studies, 1969-74; instr. anthropology dept. Lehman Coll., 1968-74; dir. Norton Gallery and Sch. Art, West Palm Beach Fla., 1974-89; sec. Norton Gallery and Sch. of Art, Inc., 1974-80; pvt. art cons., 1989-91; columnist Palm Beach Daily News, 1990-91; contbr. Calif. mag.; exec. dir., CEO Atlantic Ctr. for Arts, New Smyrna Beach, Fla., 1990-91; dir. Decorative Arts Study Ctr., San Juan Capistrano, 1992-93, dep. dir., N.Y. Transit Mus. 1994—; past instr. art dept. George Washington U.; bd. dirs. Palm Beach Festival; lectr. Fgn. Svc. Inst., Dept. State. Mem. Am. Assn. Museums (chmn. coll. and univ. museums sect. 1962-63), Museums Council N.Y.C. (chmn. 1970-71), Fla. Art Mus. Dirs. Assn. (pres. 1978-79, 83-84), S.E. Museums Conf., Assn. Art Mus. Dirs., Palm Beach C. of C. (dir. 1979-91), West Palm Beach C. of C. (dir. 1981-82). Author: The Sculpture of Michael Schreck, 1983. Office: New York Transit Mus 130 Livingston St # E Brooklyn NY 11201-5106

MADISON, BERNARD L., academic dean, mathematics educator; b. Rocky Hill, Ky., Aug. 1, 1941; s. George G. and Neva (Crump) M.; m. Lyda Sue Madison Wood, June 1, 1969; children: Eva Camille, Blair Bernard. B.S., Western Ky. U., 1958-62; M.S., U. Ky., 1964, Ph.D., 1966. Asst. prof. La. State U., Baton Rouge, 1966-71, assoc. prof., 1971-79, dir. basic and applied math., 1976-79, prof. dept. math., 1979-80; prof., chmn. dept. math. U. Ark., Fayetteville, 1979-89, dean Fulbright Coll. Arts and Scis., 1989—; cons. NRC, 1986-87, project dir., 1987-88. Contbr. articles to profl. jours. Recipient Ogden medal Western Ky. U., 1962. Mem. Am. Math. Soc., Math. Assn. Am., AAUP, Sigma Xi, Sigma Pi Sigma, Pi Mu Epsilon, Lambda Chi Alpha. Democrat. Presbyterian. Home: 573 Rockcliff Rd Fayetteville AR 72701-3809 Office: U Ark Fulbright Coll Old Main # 525 Fayetteville AR 72701

MADISON, JAMES RAYMOND, lawyer; b. White Plains, N.Y., Apr. 27, 1931; s. Raymond S. and Katherine (Sherwin) M.; m. Mary Massey, Sept. 19, 1953; children: Michael, Matthew, Molly. BS, Stanford U., 1953, LLB, 1959. Bar: Calif. 1960, U.S. Dist. Ct. (no. dist.) Calif. 1960, U.S. Ct. Appeals (9th cir.) 1960, U.S. Dist. Ct. (ctrl. dist.) Calif. 1970, U.S. Supreme Ct. 1973, U.S. Dist. Ct. (ea. dist.) Calif. 1981, U.S. Dist. Ct. (so. dist.) Calif. 1988. Assoc. Orrick, Herrington & Sutcliffe, San Francisco, 1959-67, ptnr., 1968-95; pvt. practice Menlo Park, Calif., 1996—. Trustee Antioch U., Yellow Springs, Ohio, 1980-87; bd. dirs. Planned Parenthood Alameda/San Francisco, 1984-89. Lt. (j.g.) USN, 1953-56. Mem. ABA, ASCE, State Bar Calif., Bar Assn. San Francisco, San Mateo County Bar Assn., Am. Arbitration Assn. (large complex case panel arbitrators and mediators, No. Calif. regional adv. coun.). Democrat. Episcopalian. Avocation: soccer. Office: 750 Menlo Ave Ste 250 Menlo Park CA 94025-4735

MADISON, KENNETH EDWARD, career officer; b. Pensacola, Fla., Oct. 3, 1957; s. Willie James and Mary Francis (Tate) M.; m. Bonny Lou Ard, Apr. 10, 1984; children: Temeka S., Christopher M., Jazzlyn N. Assocs., C.C. of the Air Force, 1991; Bachelor's, Colo. Christian U., 1994; Master's, Webster U., 1997. Enlisted USAF, 1975, advanced through grades to Sr. Master Sgt., 1995; adminstrv. specialist U.S. Mil. Tng. Mission, Riyadh, Saudi Arabia, 1981-82; mgr. unsatisfactory reports Def. Nuclear Agy. Kirtland AFB, Albuquerque, 1982-85; info. mgr. USAF Spl. Activity Squadron, Naples, Italy, 1985-87, chief info. mgmt., 1987-88; air def. ops. info. mgr. Peterson AFB, Colorado Springs, Colo., 1988-89; chief info. mgmt., vice dir. Cheyenne Mountain AFB, Colorado Springs, 1991-92; supt. personnel info. mgmt. Peterson AFB, Colorado Springs, 1992-94; supt. complaints, inquiries and inspection support AFSPC/IG, 1994-97; supt. command sect. info. mgmt. HQ Airsouth, Naples, Italy, 1997—. Sec. King Solomon Bapt. Ch. Brotherhood, Colorado Springs, 1991-92, Peterson AFB Gospel Svc. Brotherhood, Peterson AFB, Colo., 1991-97. Mem. Protective Order of Elks (asst. sec. 1991), Prince Hall Free and Accepted Masons, Noncommd. Officers Assn., Air Force Sgts. Assn., Sr. Noncommd. Officers Orgn. (mem. chair 1992), Protestant Men of the Chapel. Democrat. Avocations: tennis, mountain biking, cars. Home and Office: HQ Airsouth PSC 813 Box 101 FPO AE 09620

MADISON, ROBERT PRINCE, architect; b. Cleve., July 28, 1923; s. Robert J. and Nettie (Brown) M.; m. Leatrice L. Branch, Apr. 16, 1949; children: Jeanne Marie, Juliette Branch. Student, Howard U., 1940-43, HHD, 1987; B.Arch., Western Res. U., 1946-48; M.Arch., Harvard, 1952. Mem. various archtl. firms, 1948-52; instr. Howard U., Washington, 1952-54; chmn., CEO Robert P. Madison Internat., architects, engrs. and planners, Cleve., 1954—; trustee Am. Automobile Assn.; vis. prof. Howard U., 1961-62; lectr. Western Res. U., 1964-65; mem. U.S. architects del. Peoples Repub. China, 1974. Prin. works include U.S. Embassy Dakar, Senegal, West Africa, 1966, State of Ohio Computer Ctr., 1988, Cuyahoga County Jail, 1990, Continental Airlines Hub Concourse, Cleve. Internat. Airport, 1991. Mem. tech. adv. com. Cleve. Bd. Edn., 1960—; mem. adv. com. Cleve. Urban Renewal, 1963—; mem. fine arts adv. com. to mayor, Cleve.; mem. archtl. adv. coun. Cornell U.; trustee Case Western Res. U., Cleve. Opera, 1990, NCCJ, 1990, Commn. on Higher Edn., 1990; bd. dirs. Jr. Achievement Greater Cleve.; trustee Cuyahoga County Hosp. Found., 1983—, Univ. Circle Inc., Midtown Corridor Inc.; mem. Ohio Bd. Bldg. Standards, 1986, Cleveland Heights City Planning Commn., 1987. 1st lt., inf. AUS, 1943-46. Decorated Purple Heart; Fulbright fellow, 1952-53; recipient Disting. Svc. award Case Western Res. U., 1989, Disting. Archtl. Firm award Howard U., 1989, Entrepreneur of Yt. award Ernst Young, Inc., Merrill Lynch, 1991, Arch. of Yr. Nat. Tech. Assn., 1996, Martin Luther King Jr. Corp. award African-Am. Archives Aux. Western Res. Hist. Soc., 1997; named to Corp. Hall of Fame, Ohio Assembly of Couns., 1991. Fellow AIA (chpt. pres., nat. task force for creative econs. 1976, mem. jury of fellows 1983-85, mem. nat. judicial coun. 1993, Gold Medal Firm award Ohio 1994); mem. Architects Soc. Ohio, Epsilon Delta Rho, Alpha Phi Alpha, Sigma Pi Phi. Home: 2339 N Park Blvd Cleveland OH 44106-3139 Office: Robert P Madison Internat Inc 2930 Euclid Ave Cleveland OH 44115-2416

MADISON, T. JEROME, business executive; b. N.Y.C., June 2, 1940; s. Theodore H. and Eleanor E. (Eveland) M.; m. Marsha A. Heeb, Sept. 26, 1964 (dec.); children: Jillian, Kimberly, Ryan. BS, U. Pa., 1962; MBA, Monmouth U., 1975. CPA, N.J. Mgr. KPMG Peat Marwick, Newark and Princeton, N.J., 1970-75; mgr. Abbott Labs., North Chicago, Ill., 1976; chief internal auditor Rhone-Poulenc Rorer Group, Inc., Fort Washington, Pa., 1977-78, corp. contr., 1979-82; v.p. fin. Cytogen Corp., Princeton, N.J., 1982-86; pres., chief exec. officer, dir. Outwater & Wells Ventures, Inc., 1981-85, Atlantic Capital Resources Group, Inc., 1985-87, Founders Court Investors Inc., Princeton, N.J., 1986-91, Montgomery Ptnrs. 1991—; chmn., chief exec. officer Pilling Co., 1986-91, AxCell Biosciences Corp., 1996—; chmn., dir. Bacus, Inc.; bd. dirs. Targon, Inc., Cytogen Corp., Serex, Inc. Naval flight officer USN, 1962-66. Mem. AICPA, Delaware Valley Venture Group, Fin. Execs. Inst.

MADIX, ROBERT JAMES, chemical engineer, educator; b. Beach Grove, Ind., June 22, 1938; s. James L. and Marjorie A. (Strohl) M.; children: Bradley Alan, David Eric, Micella Lynn, Evan Scott. BS, U. Ill., 1961; PhD, U. Calif., 1964. NSF postdoctoral fellow Max Planck Inst., Göttingen, Fed. Republic of Germany, 1964-65; asst. prof. chem. engr. Stanford (Calif.) U., 1965-72, assoc. prof., chem. engr., 1972-77; prof. chem. engring. Stanford U., 1977—, chmn., chem. engr., 1983-87, prof. chemistry, 1981—; cons. Monsanto Chem., St. Louis, 1975-84, Shell Oil Co., Houston, 1985-86; Peter Debye lectureship Cornell U., 1985; Eyring lectr. chemistry Ariz. State U., 1990; Barnett Dodge lectr. Yale U., 1996; disting. prof. lectr. U. Tex., Austin, 1980; chmn. Gordon Rsch. Conf. on Reactions on Surfaces, 1995. Assoc. editor Catalysis Rev., 1986—, Catalysis Letters, 1992—, Rsch. on Chem. Intermediates, 1994—; contbr. numerous articles to profl. jours. Recipient Alpha Chi Sigma award AIChemE, 1990, Paul Emmett award Catalysis Soc. N.Am., 1984, Humboldt U.S. Sr. Scientist prize, 1978; Ford Found. fellow, 1969-72. Mem. Am. Chem. Soc. (Irving Langmuir Disting. Lectr. award 1981, Arthur Adamson award 1997, Henry J. Albert award Precious Metals Inst., 1997), Am. Phys. Soc., Am. Vacuum Soc., AIChE, Calif. Catalysis Soc. Office: Stanford Univ Dept Chemical Engring Stanford CA 94305

MADNI, ASAD MOHAMED, engineering executive; b. Bombay, Sept. 8, 1947; came to U.S., 1966; s. Mohamed Taher and Sara Taher (Wadiwalla) M.; Gowhartaj Shahnawaz, Nov. 11, 1976; 1 child, Jamal Asad. Gen. cert. edn., U. Cambridge, Eng., 1964; AAS in Electronics, RCA Insts., Inc., 1968; BS in Engring., UCLA, 1969, MS in Engring., 1972; postgrad. exec. inst., Stanford U., 1984; cert. in engring. mgmt., Calif. Inst. Tech., 1987; PhD in Engring., Calif. Coast U., 1987; sr. exec. program, MIT, 1990. Sr. instr. Pacific States U., L.A., 1969-71; sr. electronics auditor Pertec Corp., Chatsworth, Calif., 1973-75; project engr., sr. engr., prog. mgr., dir. advanced programs Microwave div. Systron Donner, Van Nuys, Calif., 1975-82, dir. engring., 1982-92; gen. mgr. Microwave and Instrument div. Systron Donner, Van Nuys, Calif., 1985-90; chmn., pres., chief exec. officer Systron Donner Corp., 1990-92; pres., CEO Sensors and Controls Group BEI Electronics, Inc., 1992-93, BEI Motion Sys. Co., 1993-94, BEI Sensors & Sys. Co., 1994—; vice-chmn. IEEE-MTTS, San Fernando Valley chpt., 1991-92, chmn., 1992-94; tech. advisor Test and Measurement World, Boston, 1982-90; adv. Calif. State U. Northridge. Mem. editorial rev. bd., West coast chmn. Microwave Systems News and Communications Tech., 1982-90; contbr. more than 60 articles to numerous tech. publs.; patentee in field. Mem. AAAS, IEEE (sr.), NRA (life), Soc. Automotive Engrs., N.Y. Acad. Scis., Assn. Old Crows (life, gold cert. of merit 1992), Calif. Rifle and Pistol Assn. (life), MIT Soc. Sr. Execs. (life), UCLA Alumni Assn. (life), MIT Alumni Assn. (life). Home: 3281 Woodbine St Los Angeles CA 90064-4836 Office: BEI Sensors & Systems Co 13100 Telfair Ave Sylmar CA 91342-3573 *Personal philosophy: There is no substitute for talent and vision complemented by perseverance, dedication and integrity.*

MADONNA (MADONNA LOUISE VERONICA CICCONE), singer, actress; b. Bay City, Mich., Aug. 16, 1958; d. Sylvio and Madonna Ciccone; m. Sean Penn, Aug. 16, 1985 (div. 1989). Student, U. Mich., 1976-78. Dancer Alvin Ailey Dance Co., N.Y.C., 1979; CEO Maverick Records, L.A. Albums include Madonna, 1983, Like a Virgin, 1985, True Blue, 1986, (soundtrack)Who's That Girl, 1987, (with others) Vision Quest Soundtrack, 1983, You Can Dance, 1987, Like a Prayer, 1989, I'm Breathless: Music From and Inspired by the Film Dick Tracy, 1990, The Immaculate Collection, 1990, Erotica, 1992, Bedtime Stories, 1994, Something to Remember, 1995; film appearances include A Certain Sacrifice, 1980, Vision Quest, 1985, Desperately Seeking Susan, 1985, Shanghai Surprise, 1986, Who's That Girl, 1987, Bloodhounds of Broadway, 1989, Dick Tracy, 1990, Truth or Dare, 1991, Madonna, 1992, Body of Evidence, 1992, Dangerous Game, 1993, Blue in the Face, 1995, Four Rooms, 1996, Girl 6, 1996, Evita, 1996; Broadway theater debut in Speed-the-Plow, 1987; author: Sex, 1992. Roman Catholic. Office: Maverick Records 8000 Beverly Blvd Los Angeles CA 90048-4504 also: ICM 8942 Wilshire Blvd Beverly Hills CA 90211*

MADONNA, JON C., accounting firm executive. Chmn., CEO KPMG Peat Marwick, N.Y.C.; vice chmn. Travelers Group, N.Y.C., 1997—. Office: Travelers Group 388 Greenwich St New York NY 10013-0001*

MADORE, JOYCE LOUISE, gerontology nurse; b. Madison, Kans., Dec. 15, 1936; d. Lionel Wiedmer and Mary Elizabeth (Piley) Murphy; m. Robert Madore, Aug. 15, 1969; children: Carl, Clay. BS, Emporia State U., 1980; diploma, Newman Hosp., 1981. RN, Kans., Mo.; cert. gerontol. nurse, non profit adminstr.; cert. and lic. nursing home adminstr. Med. charge nurse St. Mary's Hosp., Emporia, Kans., 1971-72; dir. nursing Madison (Kans.) Manor, 1974-81, 82-83; staff nurse Newman Meml. Hosp., Emporia, 1981-82; dir. Daybreak Adult Day Svcs., dir. HELP program Springfield (Mo.) Area Coun. of Chs., 1983—; mem. Gov.'s Com. to Establish Rules and Regulations on Adult Day Care Patients State of Mo.; cons. U. Mo. Coop. Extension Svc. Program Guides on Adult Day Care. Contbr. video Understanding Aging Program; developer Home Guide for the Homebound, 1996. Named one of Outstanding Nurses in Mo. St. Louis U., 1989. Mem. NAFE, Adult Day Care Assn. (past sec., exec. past v.p. 1989-91), Mo. Nurses Assn., Mo. Adult Day Care Assn. (pres. 1991-95, Exec. award 1995), Mo. League Nursing. Home: 2003 S Link Sparta MO 65804

MADORY, JAMES RICHARD, hospital administrator, former air force officer; b. Staten Island, N.Y., June 11, 1940; s. Eugene and Agnes (Gerner) M.; m. Karen James Clifford, Sept. 26, 1964; children: James E., Lynn Anne, Scott J., Elizabeth Anne, Joseph M. BS, Syracuse U., 1964; MHA, Med. Coll. Va., 1971. Enlisted USAF, 1958; x-ray technician Keesler Area Med. Ctr., Biloxi, Miss., 1959-62; commd. 2d lt. USAF, 1964, advanced through grades to maj., 1979—; x-ray technician Keesler Area Med. Ctr., Biloxi, Miss., 1959-62; adminstr. Charleston (S.C.) Clinic, 1971-74, Beale Hosp., Calif., 1974-77; assoc. adminstr. Shaw Regional Hosp., S.C., 1977-79; ret. USAF, 1979; asst. adminstr. Raleigh Gen. Hosp., Beckley, W.Va., 1979-81; adminstr., dir., sec. bd. Chesterfield Gen. Hosp., Cheraw, S.C., 1981-87; pres., CEO Grand Strand Hosp., Myrtle Beach, S.C., 1987-95, trustee, 1987-95; elected vice chairman Horry County Planning Commn., 1996—; cons. Healthcare Adminstrn., 1995—; mem. adv. bd. Cheraw Nursing Home, 1984-85. Contbr. articles to profl. publs. Chmn. bd. W.Va. Kidney Found., Charleston, 1980-81; chmn. youth bd. S.C. TB and Respiratory Disease Assn., Charleston, 1972-73; county chmn. Easter Seal Soc., Chesterfield County, S.C., 1984-85; campaign crusade chmn. Am. Cancer Soc., Chesterfield County, 1985-86; chmn. dist. advancement com. Boy Scouts Am., 1987-90; bd. dirs. Horry County United Way, 1989-95, Horry County Access Care, 1989-91; trustee Cheraw Acad., 1982-85, Grand Strand Gen. Hosp., 1987-94, Coastal Acad., 1988-90; commr. Horry County Planning Commn., 1995—, vice chmn., 1996—. Decorated Bronze Star, Vietnamese Cross of Gallantry, Vietnamese Medal of Honor; named to S.C. Order of Palmetto Gov. David Beasley, 1995. Fellow Am. Coll. Hosp. Adminstrs., Am. Coll. Health Care Execs; mem. S.C. Hosp. Assn. (com on legislation 1984-86, trustee 1989-94), Am. Acad. Healthcare Adminstrs., Cheraw C. of C. (bd. dirs. 1982-83), Rotary (pres. 1984-85). Republican. Roman Catholic. Home and Office: 3710 Kinloch Dr Myrtle Beach SC 29577

MADOW, LEO, psychiatrist, educator; b. Cleve., Oct. 18, 1915; s. Solomon Martin and Anna (Meyers) M.; m. Jean Antoinette Weisman, Apr. 16, 1942; children: Michael, Robert. AB, Western Res. U., 1937, MD, 1942; MA, Ohio State U., 1938. Diplomate Am. Bd. Psychiatry and Neurology. Intern Phila. Gen. Hosp., 1942-43; resident Phila. Gen. Hosp., Jefferson Hosp., Inst. Pa. Hosp., 1943-46; practice medicine specializing in psychiatry Phila., 1948—; prof., chmn. dept. neurology Med. Coll. Pa., Phila., 1958-65; prof., chmn. dept. psychiatry and neurology Med. Coll. Pa., 1965-70, prof., chmn. dept. psychiatry, 1970-81, clin. prof. psychiatry Hershey Med. Ctr., 1982—; sr. cons. psychiatry Inst. Pa. Hosp., Phila., 1975—; tng. analyst, past pres. Phila. Psychoanalytic Inst.; past pres., mem. med. staff Inst. Pa. Hosp. Author: Anger, 1972, Love, 1983, Guilt, 1989; editor: Dreams, 1970, Sensory Deprivation, 1970, Psychomimetic Drugs, 1971, Integration of Child Psychiatry with Basic Resident Program, 1975. Served to capt. AUS, 1944-46. Named Outstanding Educator of Am. Med. Coll. Pa., 1972. Fellow ACP, Am. Psychiat. Assn. (life), Phila. Psychiat. Soc. (Lifetime Achievement award 1991) (past pres.), Am. Coll. Psychiatrists, Am. Coll. Psychoanalysts (pres. 1989-90, Laughlin award 1990); mem. Am. Psychoanalytic Assn., Am. Neurol. Assn., Phila. Psychoanalytic Soc. (past pres.), Alpha Omega Alpha, Phi Soc. Home: 135 Sibley Rd Narberth PA 19072-1318 Office: Inst of Pa Hosp 135 Sibley Ave Narberth PA 19072-1318

MADRID, OLGA HILDA GONZALEZ, retired elementary education educator, association executive; b. San Antonio, May 4, 1928; d. Victor A. and Elvira Ardilla Gonzalez; m. Sam Madrid, Jr., June 29, 1952; children: Ninette Marie, Samuel James. Student, U. Mex., San Antonio, St. Mary's U., San Antonio; BA, Our Lady of Lake U., 1956, MEd, 1963. Cert. bilingual tchr., adminstr., Tex. Sec. Lanier High Sch. San Antonio Ind. Sch. Dist., 1945-52, tchr. Collins Garden Elem. Sch., 1963-92; tutor Dayton, Ohio, 1952-54; bd. dirs., sch. rep. San Antonio Tchr.'s Coun., 1970-90; chair various coms. Collins Garden Elem., 1970-92. Elected dep. precinct, senatorial and state Dem. Convs., San Antonio, 1968—; apptd. commr. Keep San Antonio Beautiful, 1985; life mem., past pres. San Antonio YWCA; bd. dirs. Luth. Gen. Hosp., Nat. Conf. Christians and Jews, Cath. Family and Children's Svcs., St. Luke's Luth. Hosp.; nat. bd. dirs. YWCA, 1985-96, also mem. exec. com.; mem. edn. commn. Holy Rosary Parish, 1994—; mem. bus. assocs. com. Our Lady of the Lake U., 1995—. Recipient Outstanding Our Lady Lake Alumni award Our Lady Lake U., 1975, Guadalupana medal San Antonio Cath. Archdiocese, 1975, Yellow Rose Tex. citation Gov. Briscoe, 1977; Olga H. Madrid Ctr. named in her honor, YWCA San Antonio and San Antonio City Coun., 1983; Lo Mejor De Lo Nuestro honoree San Antonio Light, 1991, honoree San Antonio Women's History Month Coalition, 1996. Mem. San Antonio Bus. and Profl. Women, Inc. (mem. exec. com.), Salute Quality Edn. (honoree 1993), Delta Kappa Gamma (Theta Beta chpt., mem. exec. com.). Avocations: reading, gardening. Home: 2726 Benrus Blvd San Antonio TX 78228-2319

MADRY-TAYLOR, JACQUELYN YVONNE, educational administrator; b. Jacksonville, Fla., Sept. 27, 1945; d. Arthur Chester and Janie (Cowart) Madry; 1 child, Jana LeMadry. BA, Fisk U., 1966; MA, Ohio State U., 1969; EdD, U. Fla., 1975. Cert. Inst. for Ednl. Mgmt., Harvard U., 1981. Tchr. Spanish Terry Parker Sr. High Sch., Jacksonville, 1967-72; instr. U. Fla., Gainesville, 1972-75; asst. to v.p. for acad. affairs. Morris Brown Coll., Atlanta, 1975-76; dean for instructional svcs. No. Va. Community Coll., Annandale, Va., 1976-83; dean undergrad. studies Bridgewater (Mass.) State Coll., 1983-92, exec. asst. to acting pres., 1988, acting v.p. acad. affairs, 1988-90; dir. Acad. Leadership Acad. Am. Assn. State Coll. and Univs., Washington, 1992-94; dir. ednl. programs and svcs. United Negro Coll. Fund Hdqs., 1994—; cons. W.K. Kellog Found., 1993—; bd. dirs. Bridgewater

State Coll. Early Learning Ctr., 1984-88; evaluator U.S. Dept. State/Fgn. Svc., Washington, 1982—, U.S. Dept. Edn., 1989—; cons. in field. Vice chmn. No. Va. Manpower Planning Coun., Fairfax County, Va., 1981. Recipient Cert. Achievement Bridgewater State Coll. Black Alumni, 1988, Women Helping Women award Soroptimist Internat., 1983, Outstanding Young Women Am. award, 1976, 78; named Personalities of South, 1977; recipient Outstanding Tchr./Student Rels. Humanitarian award B'nai B'rith, 1972. Mem. Pub. Mem. Assn. U.S. Fgn. Svc., Soroptimist Internat., Boston Club (v.p. 1986-88), Jack and Jill of Am., Inc., Pi Lambda Theta, Phi Delta Kappa, Alpha Kappa Alpha, Links Inc. (Reston, Va. chpt.). Methodist. Avocations: playing piano, bike riding. Home: 12274 Angel Wing Ct Reston VA 22091 Office: United Negro College Fund PO Box 10444 8260 Willow Oaks Corp Dr Fairfax VA 22031-4511

MADSEN, BRIGHAM DWAINE, history educator; b. Magna, Utah, Oct. 21, 1914; s. Brigham and Lydia (Cushing) M.; m. Betty McAllister, Aug. 11, 1939; children—Karen Madsen Loos, David B., Linda Madsen Dunning, Steven M. B.A., U. Utah, 1938; M.A., U. Calif., Berkeley, 1940, Ph.D., 1948. Prin. Grade Sch. and Jr. High Sch., Pingree, Idaho, 1938-39; assoc. prof. history Brigham Young U., Provo, Utah, 1948-54; pres., mgr. Madsen Bros. Constrn. Co., Salt Lake City, 1954-61; prof. history Utah State U., Logan, 1961-64; asst. dir. tng. Peace Corps, Washington, 1964-65; first dir. tng. Vols. in Service to Am., Washington, 1965; dean div. continuing edn. U. Utah, Salt Lake City, 1965-66; dep. acad. v.p. U. Utah, 1966-67, adminstrv. v.p., 1967-71, dir. libraries, 1971-73, prof. history, 1973-84, chmn. dept. history, 1974-75. Author: Bannock of Idaho, 1958, The Lemhi: Sacajawea's People, 1980, Corinne: Gentile Capital of Utah, 1980, The Northern Shoshoni, 1980, (with Betty M. Madsen) North to Montana: Jehus, Bullwhackers and Muleskinners on the Montana Trail, 1980; Gold Rush Sojourners in Great Salt Lake City, 1849 and 1850, 1983, The Shoshoni Frontier and the Bear River Massacre, 1985, Chief Pocatello: The "White Plume", 1986, Glory Hunter: A Biography of Patrick Edward Connor, 1990; editor: The Now Generation, 1971, Letters of Long Ago, 1973, A Forty-niner in Utah: Letters and Journal of John Hudson, 1982, B.H. Roberts: Studies of the Book of Mormon, 1985, Exploring the Great Salt Lake: The Stansbury Expedition of 1849-50, 1989. Served to 1st lt., inf. AUS, 1943-46. Mem. Phi Beta Kappa, Phi Kappa Phi, Phi Alpha Theta. Mem. Ch. of Jesus Christ of Latter-day Saints. Home: 2181 Lincoln Ln Salt Lake City UT 84124-2759

MADSEN, DOROTHY LOUISE (MEG MADSEN), writer; b. Rochester, N.Y.; d. Charles Robert and Louise Anna Agnes Meyer; BA, Mundelein Coll., Chgo., 1978; m. Frederick George Madsen, Feb. 17, 1945 (dec.). Pub. rels. rep. Rochester Telephone Corp., 1941-42; feature writer Rochester Democrat & Chronicle, 1939-41; exec. dir. LaPorte (Ind.) chpt. ARC, 1964; dir. adminstrv. svcs. Bank Mktg. Assn., Chgo., 1971-74; exec. dir. The Eleanor Found., Chgo., 1974-84; founder Meg Madsen Assocs., Chgo., 1984-88; women's career counselor; founder, Clearinghouse Internat. Newsletter; founder Eleanor Women's Forum, Clearinghouse Internat., Eleanor Intern Program Coll. Students and Returning Women. Served to lt. col. WAC, 1942-47, 67-70. Decorated Legion of Merit, Meritorious Svc. award. Mem. Res. Officers Assn., Mundelein Alumnae Assn., Phi Sigma Tau (charter mem. Ill. Kappa chpt.). Home and Office: 3902 Joliet Rd La Porte IN 46350 also: 1030 N State St Chicago IL 60610-2844

MADSEN, GEORGE FRANK, lawyer; b. Sioux City, Iowa, Mar. 24, 1933; s. Frank O. and Agnes (Cuhel) M.; m. Magnhild Norstog, June 28, 1959; 1 child, Michelle Marie. BA, St. Olaf Coll., 1954; LLB, Harvard U., 1959. Bar: Ohio 1960, Iowa 196l, U.S. Dist. Ct. (no. and so. dists.) Iowa, U.S. Ct. Appeals (8th cir.), U.S. Supreme Ct. 1991. Trainee Cargill, Inc., Mpls., 1954; assoc. Durfey, Martin, Browne & Hull, Springfield, Ohio, 1959-6l; assoc., then ptnr. Shull, Marshall & Marks, Sioux City, 196l-85; ptnr. Marks & Madsen, Sioux City, 1985—. Author, editor: Iowa Title Opinions and Standards, 1978; contbg. author: The American Law of Real Property, 1991. Sec., bd.dirs. Sioux City Boys Club, 1969-76; mem. Sioux City Zoning Bd. Adjustment, 1963-65; past pres. Morningside Luth Ch., Sioux City; active Iowa Mo. River Preservation and Land Use Authority, 1992—. Lt. USAF, 1954-56. Fellow Iowa State Bar Found.; mem. ABA, Iowa Bar Assn., Woodbury County Bar Assn., St. Olaf Coll. Alumni Assn. (past pres. Sioux-land chpt.), Nat. Wildlife Assn., Mont. Wildlife Assn., Rocky Mountain Elk Found., Pheasants Forever, Phi Beta Kappa (past pres. Siouxland chpt.), Rotary Internat. Avocations: skiing, hunting, swimming, reading. Office: 700 4th St Ste 303 PO Box 3226 Sioux City IA 51102-3226

MADSEN, H(ENRY) STEPHEN, retired lawyer; b. Momence, Ill., Feb. 5, 1924; s. Frederick and Christine (Landgren) M.; m. Carol Ruth Olmstead, Dec. 30, 1967; children: Stephen Stewart, Christie Morgan, Kelly Ann. M.B.A., U. Chgo., 1948; LL.B., Yale U., 1951. Bar: Wash. 1951, Ohio 1953, U.S. Supreme Ct. 1975. Research asst. Wash. Water Power Co., Spokane, 1951; assoc. Baker, Hostetler & Paterson, Cleve., 1952-59, ptnr., 1960-88, sr. ptnr., 1989-92; ret., 1992; chmn. bd. trustees Blue Cross Northeastern, Ohio, 1972-81; Danish consul for Ohio, 1973—. Pres. Bus. Advisers Cleve.; trustee Breckenridge Ret. Cmty., Ohio Presbyn. Ret. Cmty. Served with AC U.S. Army, 1943-46. Decorated Knight Queen of Denmark, 1982. Fellow ABA (life); mem. Am. Coll. Trial Lawyers (life), Am. Law Inst., Am. Judicature Soc., Ohio Bar Assn., Cleve. Bar Assn., The Country Club of Cleve., The Club at Soc. Ctr. Office: Baker & Hostetler 3200 National City Ctr 1900 E 9th St Cleveland OH 44114-3401

MADSEN, LOREN WAKEFIELD, sculptor; b. Oakland, Calif., Mar. 29, 1943; s. Roy Sondergaard and Kathryn O. (Finerty) M.; m. Libbe Hurvitz, June 30, 1968; children: Anne Lea, Nora Karin. Student, Reed Coll., Portland, 1961-63; B.A., UCLA, 1966, M.A., 1970. One-man shows include Riko Mizuno Gallery, L.A., 1973, 74, McKee Gallery, N.Y.C., 1976, 77, 82, 84, 86, 90, 92, 96, L.A. Louver Gallery, Venice, Calif., 1976, 78, Hansen Fuller Goldeen Gallery, San Francisco, 1980, Wright State U., Dayton, 1980, U. mass., 1981, Cheryl Haines Gallery, San Francisco, 1991; group shows include Los Angeles County Mus. Art, 1974, 76, 83, Hayward Gallery, London, 1975, Walker Art Ctr., Mpls., 1976, Biennale of Sculpture, Sydney, Australia, 1976, Ft. Worth Mus. Art, 1977, Joslyn Art Mus., Omaha, 1979, Hirshhorn Mus., Washington, 1979, Newport Harbor Art Mus., 1982, Freedman Gallery, Albright Coll., 1987, others. Nat. Endowment for Arts grantee, 1975-76, 80-81. Office: 426 Broome St New York NY 10013-3251

MADSEN, MICHAEL, actor; b. Chicago, IL, Sept. 25; m. Jeannine Bisignano; 1 child, Christian. films include: Wargames, 1983, The Natural, 1984, Racing with the Moon, 1984, The Killing Time, 1987, Shadows in the Storm, 1988, Iguana, 1988, Blood Red, 1989, Kill Me Again, 1990, The Doors, 1991, The End of Innocence, 1991, Thelma and Louise, 1991, Fatal Instinct, 1992, Inside Edge, 1992, Reservoir Dogs, 1992, Straight Talk, 1992, Almost Blue, 1992, Free Willy, 1993, A House in the Hills, 1993, Money for Nothing, 1993, Trouble Bound, 1993, Wyatt Earp, 1993, The Getaway, 1994, Dead Connection, 1994, Species, 1995, Free Willy II: The Adventure Home, 1995, The Winner, 1996, Red Line, 1996, Mulholland Falls, 1996, Man With a Gun, 1996, The Last Days of Frankie the Fly, 1996, Rough Draft, 1997, The Maker, 1997, Donnie Brasco, 1997, Catherine's Grove, 1997; TV movies include: Special Bulletin, 1983, War and Remembrance, 1988, Montana, 1990, Baby Snatcher, 1992, Beyond the Law, 1994; TV series include: Our Family Honor, 1985-86. Office: c/o Grant and Tane 9100 Wilshire Blvd Beverly Hills CA 90212-3415 also: CAA Michael Manchal 9830 Wilshire Blvd Beverly Hills CA 90212*

MADSEN, STEPHEN STEWART, lawyer; b. Spokane, Wash., Oct. 13, 1951; s. H. Stephen Madsen and Sarah Pope (Stewart) Ruth; m. Rebecca Wetherill Howard, July 28, 1984; children: Stephen Stewart Jr., Lawrence Wetherill, Christina Wetherill, Benton Howard. BA, Harvard U., 1973; JD, Columbia U., 1980. Bar: N.Y. 1981, U.S. Dist. Ct. (so. dist.) N.Y. 1981, U.S. Ct. Appeals (6th cir.) 1983, U.S. Ct. Appeals (8th cir.) 1985, U.S. Ct. Appeals (2d, 7th and D.C. cirs.) 1994, U.S. Supreme Ct., 1996. Law clk. to presiding judge U.S. Ct. Appeals (2d cir.), N.Y.C., 1980-81; assoc. Cravath, Swaine & Moore, N.Y.C., 1981-88, ptnr., 1988—. Bd. visitors Columbia U. Sch. Law, 1991—; bd. govs. Hill-Stead Mus., 1995—; mem. vestry St. Bartholomew's Ch., 1995—. Mem. ABA, N.Y. State Bar Assn., New York County Lawyers Assn. Office: Cravath Swaine & Moore Worldwide Pla 825 8th Ave New York NY 10019-7416

MADSON, JOHN ANDREW, architect; b. Mankato, Minn., Nov. 12, 1920; m. Joyce Helen Madson, Sept. 4, 1949; children: Brian A., David G., Paul J., Thomas R., John E., Tracy Ann. BA, U. Minn., 1949, BArch, 1950. Archtl. draftsman, designer Perry E. Crosier & Son, Mpls., 1950-53; architect-in-tng. Magney Tusler & Setter, Mpls., 1953-55; ptnr., prin. Patch Erickson Madson Watten, Inc., Mpls., 1955-89; chief exec. officer Madson & Assocs., Mpls., 1989—. Capt. USAF, 1944-45, ETO. Corp. mem. AIA. Republican. Lutheran. Avocations: playing and collecting jazz, classical music, golf, directing church choir. Home: 17419 N 130th Ave Sun City West AZ 85375-5061

MADU, LEONARD EKWUGHA, lawyer, human rights officer, newspaper columnist; b. Ibadan, Nigeria, Mar. 17, 1953; came to U.S., 1977; s. Luke E. and Grace (Dureke) M.; m. Jaculine Stephanie Turner, June 4, 1980; children: Christine, Oscar. BA, Marshall U., 1980; JD, U. Tenn., 1988; MA, Sch. Internat. Svc., Am. U. Rsch. assoc. Lamberts Publs., Washington, 1980-82; data specialist Govt. Employees Ins. Co., Washington, 1982-85; law intern Knoxville (Tenn.) Urban League, 1986-88; cons. Morris Brown Coll., Atlanta, 1988; staff atty. East Carolina Legal Svc., Wilson, N.C., 1989-90; cons. youth devel. Nat. Crime Prevention Coun., Washington, 1990; contract compliance officer Walters State C.C., Morristown, Tenn., 1990; examiner Dept. of Human Svc., Nashville, 1990-93; human rights officer Human Rights Commn., Nashville, 1993—; pres. Panafrica, Nashville, 1994—; CEO Madu and Assoc. Internat. Bus. Cons., 1996—; polit. cons. Embassy of Nigeria, Washington, 1995; cons. Embassy of Swaziland, Washington, 1995, Embassy of Sierra Leone, Washington, 1995, Healthcare Internat. Mgmt. Co., 1996—; bd. dirs. Peace and Justice Ctr., Nashville. Editor: African Nations Handbook, 1994, Directory of African Universities and Colleges, 1994; editor-in-chief Panafrican Digest, 1994, Panafrican Jour. of World Affairs, 1994; columnist Met. Times, Nashville, 1991—, The African Herald, Dallas, 1995—, U.S./African Voice, Balt., 1995—, African Sun Times, 1995—, The Nigerian and African, 1995—. Co-chmn. Clergy and Laity Concerned, Nashville, 1992—; mem. curriculum and character com. Met. Sch. Bd., Nashville, 1994—; vice chmn. Nigerian Network Leadership awards N.Y., 1996; chmn. Internat. Women's Expo, Knoxville, Tenn., 1996; co-chairperson Miss Nigeria Internat. Beauty Pageant, Washington, 1995, Miss Africa Internat. Beauty Pageant, Nashville, 1996, Igbo Union Chieftaincy Coronation Ceremony, Nashville, 1995; chmn. Nigerian Patriotic Front, 1997—; active United Nigeria Congress Party, 1997—. Recipient World Hunger Devel. Program award Marshall U., 1978, 79, Hall of Nations scholar Am. U., 1980, 82, Mary Strohbel award United Way, 1994, 95, Non-profit Vol. award Nat. Conf. of Christians and Jews, 1994. Mem. NAACP, U.S. Com. on Fgn. Rels., Soc. Profl. Journalists, UN Assn., Orgn. African Natonals (pres. 1994). Avocations: reading, travelling, soccer, ping-pong, tennis. Office: Panafrica 1016 18th Ave S Nashville TN 37212-2105

MADURA, JAMES ANTHONY, surgical educator; b. Campbell, Ohio, June 10, 1938; s. Anthony Peter and Margaret Ethel (Sebest) M.; m. Loretta Jayne Sovak, Aug. 8, 1959; children: Debra Jean, James Anthony II, Vikki Sue. BA, Cogate U., 1959; MD, Western Res. U., 1963. Diplomate Am. Bd. Surgery. Intern in surgery Ohio State U., Columbus, 1963-64, resident in surgery, 1966-71; asst. prof. Surgery Ind. U., Indpls., 1971-76, assoc. prof. Surgery, 1976-80, prof. Surgery, 1980—; dir. gen. surgery Ind. U. Sch. Medicine, Indpls., 1985—. Contbr. articles to profl. jours. Capt. U.S. Army, 1964-66, Vietnam. Fellow Am. Coll. Surgeons; mem. Cen. Surg. Assn., Western Surg. Assn., Soc. Surgery Alimentary Tract, Midwest Surg. Assn., Internal Biliary Assn., Assn. Acad. Surgeons, The Columbia Club. Republican. Roman Catholic. Home: 9525 Copley Dr Indianapolis IN 46260-1422 Office: Indianapolis U Dept of Surgery 545 Barnhill Dr # 205 Indianapolis IN 46202-5112*

MADVA, STEPHEN ALAN, lawyer; b. Pitts., July 27, 1948; s. Joseph Edward and Mary (Zulick) M.; m. Bernadette A. McKeon; children: Alexander, Elizabeth. BA cum laude, Yale U., 1970; JD, U. Pa., 1973. Bar: Pa. 1973, U.S. Dist. Ct. (ea. dist.) Pa. 1975, U.S. Ct. Appeals (3d cir.) 1976, U.S. Ct. Appeals (11th cir.) 1987, U.S. Supreme Ct. 1985, N.Y. 1990. Asst. defender Defender Assn. Phila., 1973-75, fed. defender, 1975-77, also bd. dirs., 1985—; assoc. Montgomery, McCracken, Walker & Rhoads, Phila., 1977-81, ptnr., 1981—, mem. mgmt. com., 1993-96, chairman, litig. sect., 1996—; bd. dirs. Ctrl. Phila. Devel. Corp. Bd. dirs. Central Phila. Devel. Corp., 1995—. Mem. ABA, Am. Judicature Soc., Internat. Assn. Def. Counsel, Pa. Bar Assn., Phila. Bar Assn. (fed. cts. com.), Def. Rsch. Inst., Hist. Soc. Pa., Yale Alumni Assn. (schs. com.), Yale Rowing Assn. Democrat. Avocations: tennis, distance running. Home: 2055 Lombard St Philadelphia PA 19146-1314 Office: Montgomery McCracken Et Al 123 S Broad St Philadelphia PA 19109-1029

MAECHLING, CHARLES, JR., lawyer, diplomat, educator, writer; b. N.Y.C., Apr. 18, 1920; s. Charles and Eugenie H. M.; m. Janet Leighton, Sept. 2, 1944; children: Philip Leighton and Eugenie Elisabeth (Mrs. David Buchan). Attended, Birch Wathen Sch., N.Y.C., 1924-37; BA, Yale U., 1941; LLB, U. Va., 1949. Bar: N.Y. 1949, D.C. 1957. Assoc. Sullivan & Cromwell, N.Y.C., 1949-51; atty. Office Sec. Air Force, 1951-52; counsel Electronics Industries Assn., Washington, 1953-56; ptnr. Shaw, Pittman, Potts & Maechling, 1956-61; dir. for internal def. Dept. State, Washington, 1961-63; spl. asst. to undersec. for polit. affairs and amb.-at-large Averell Harriman, 1963-66; dep. gen. counsel NSF, 1966-71, spl. asst. to dir., 1972-74; prof. law U. Va., 1974-76; spl. counsel Kirlin, Campbell & Keating, Washington, 1976-81; sr. fellow Carnegie Endowment for Internat. Peace, 1981-85; vis. fellow, mem. law faculty Cambridge U. (Wolfson Coll.), Eng., 1985-88; guest scholar internat. law Brookings Inst., Washington, 1989-93; internat. cons., 1993—; legal adviser internat. matters NAS, 1970-73, mem. ocean policy com.; mem. law-of-sea and other adv. coms. Dept. State; gen. counsel Fairways Corp., 1959-61; adj. prof. Sch. Internat. Svc., Am. U.; mem. adv. bd. Internat. Peace Acad.; lectr. Acad. Internat. Law, Hague, Netherlands, Knight Ctr. U. Md.; arbitrator complex internat. cases Am. Arbitration Assn., Internat. C. of C.; chair U.S.-IIASA Plannig Group, 1981-83. Editor-in-chief Va. Law Rev., 1948-49; contbr. articles to N.Y. Times, Washington Post, L.A. Times, profl. and lit. jours.; occasional columnist Newsday, Miami Herald. Bd. dirs. Coun. for Ocean Law, Washington Inst. Fgn. Affairs, U.S. Com. for IIASA; mem. secretariat Joint Chiefs Staff, 1943-44, del., 1943, Cairo Conf.; outside counsel to CIA, 1957-60. Lt. comdr. USNR, 1941-46. Recipient Ross Essay award Am. Bar Assn., 1969. Mem. ABA (past com. chair), Am. Soc. Internat. Law, City Tavern Club (Washington), Cosmos Club (Washington), Yale Club (Washington). Avocation: languages. Home: 3403 Lowell St NW Washington DC 20016-5024 also (summer): Bar Rd, Saint Andrews, NB Canada E0G 2X0

MAEDA, J. A., data processing executive; b. Mansfield, Ohio, Aug. 24, 1940; d. James Shunso and Doris Lucille Maeda; m. Robert Lee Hayes; 1 child, Brian Sentaro Hayes. BS in Math., Purdue U., 1962, postgrad., 1962-63; postgrad., Calif. State U., Northridge, 1968-75; cert. profl. designation in tech. of computer operating systems and tech. of info. processing, UCLA, 1971. Cons., rsch. asst. computer ctr. Purdue U., West Lafayette, Ind., 1962-63; computer operator, sr. tab operator, mem. faculty Calif. State U., Northridge, 1969, programmer cons., tech. asst. II, 1969-70, supr. acad. applicatons, EDP supr. II, 1970-72, project tech. support coord. programmer II, office of the chancellor, 1972-73, tech. support coord. statewide timesharing tech. support, programmer II, 1973-74, acad. coord., tech. support coord. instrn., computer cons. III, 1974-83; coord. user svcs. info. ctr., mem. tech. staff IV CADAM INC subs. Lockheed Corp., Burbank, Calif., 1983-86, coord. user svcs., tech. specialist computing dept., 1986-87; v.p., bd. dirs. Rainbow Computing, Inc., Northridge, 1976-85; dir. Aki Tech/Design, Northridge, 1976—; mktg. mgr. thaumaturge Taro Quipu Cons., Northridge, 1987—; tech. cons. Digital Computer Cons., Chatsworth, Calif., 1988; computer tech., fin. and bus. mgmt., sys. integration, 1988-90; tech. customer software support Collection Data Sys., Westlake, Calif., 1991; sr. tech. writer Sterling Software Info. Mgmt. Divsn., 1992—. Author, editor more than 300 user publs., tutorials, reference manuals, user guides; contbr. articles and photos to profl. jours. Mem. IEEE, SHARE, DECUS (ednl. spl. interest group 1977-83, ednl. steering com. RSTS/E 1979-82), Soc. for Tech. Communicators. Avocations: photography, photojournalism, vintage automobiles. Office: Info Mgmt Divsn 5900 Canoga Ave Woodland Hills CA 91367-5009

MAEDA, KENJI, medical educator; b. Tsu-City, Japan, Apr. 1, 1939; s. Tamotsu and Sumi (Kubo) M.; m. Miyako Matsunaga, Mar. 30, 1975; children: Kayaho, Mayuho. MD, Nagoya U., 1965, PhD, 1978. Intern Nagoya U. Br. Hosp., 1965-66, asst., 1973-79, assoc. prof., 1979-91, prof., 1991—, dir., 1992-96. Editor: Contributions to Nephrology, 1993, 94; contbr. articles to profl. jours. Recipient Jinkenkyukai award Japan Kidney Found., Tokyo, 1993. Mem. N.Y. Acad. Sci., AAAS, Am. Soc. Nephrology. Home: c-1514 1-2 Sunadabashi, Higashi-ku, Nagoya/Aichi 461, Japan Office: Nagoya U Daiko Med Ctr, Higashi-Ku, 20-1-1 Daiko-Minami, Nagoya 461, Japan

MAEHL, WILLIAM HARVEY, historian, educator; b. Bklyn., May 28, 1915; s. William Henry and Antoinette Rose (Salamone) M.; m. Josephine Scholl McAllister, Dec. 29, 1941; children: Madeleine, Kathleen. BSc, Northwestern U., 1937, MA, 1939; PhD, U. Chgo., 1946. Asst. prof. history St. Louis U., 1941-42, Tex. A&M U., College Sta., 1943, De Paul U., Chgo., 1944-49; historian Dept. of Def., Karlsruhe, Stuttgart, Fed. Rep. Germany, 1950-52; chief briefing office U.S. hdqrs. U.S. Hdqs. European Command, Frankfurt, Germany, 1952-53; chief historian Arty. Sch., Okla., 1954; with War Plans Office, Hdqs. No. Air Materiel Area for Europe, Burtonwood, Eng., 1954-55; assoc. prof. European history Nebr. Wesleyan U., Lincoln, 1955-57, prof., 1958-62, 65-68; prof. German history Auburn (Ala.) U., 1968-81, prof. emeritus, 1981—; vis. prof. U. Nebr., 1962, U. Auckland, New Zealand, 1963-64, Midwestern U., Wichita Falls, Tex., 1965. Author: German Militarism and Socialism, 1968, History of Germany in Western Civilization, 1979, A World History Syllabus, 3 vols., 1980, August Bebel, Shadow Emperor of the German Workers, 1980, The German Socialist Party: Champion of the First Republic, 1918-33, 1986; author monographs for U.S. Army in Europe, chpts. in books, atomic, biol. and emergency war plans for No. Air Materiel Area for Europe; contbr. poetry to Question of Balance, Tears of Fire, Disting. Poets Am., Best Poems of 1995, Journey of Mind; contbr. articles to profl. jours. Grantee Nebr. Wesleyan U., 1959, Auburn U., 1969-73, 79-80, Am. Philosophical Soc., 1973-74, Deutscher Akademischer Austauschdienst, 1978. Mem. Am. Hist. Assn., Phi Kappa Phi, Phi Alpha Theta.

MAEHL, WILLIAM HENRY, historian, university administrator, educational consultant; b. Chicago Heights, Ill., June 13, 1930; s. William Henry and Marvel Lillian (Carlson) M.; m. Audrey Mae Ellsworth, Aug. 25, 1962; 1 child, Christine Amanda. B.A., U. Minn., 1950, M.A., 1951; postgrad (Fulbright fellow), King's Coll., U. Durham, Eng., 1955-56; Ph.D., U. Chgo., 1957; LHD (hon.), Fielding Inst., 1993. Asst. prof. Montclair (N.J.) State Coll., 1957-58; asst. prof. Washington Coll., Chestertown, Md., 1958-59, U. Okla., Norman, 1959-64; asso. prof. U. Okla., 1964-70, prof. English history, 1970-86; dean Coll. Liberal Studies, 1976-86, vice provost for continuing edn. and public service, 1979-86; pres. The Fielding Inst., Santa Barbara, Calif., 1987-93, pres. emeritus, 1993—; prin. investigator Project for a Nation of Lifelong Learners, Regents Coll., Albany, N.Y., 1994-97; vis. prof. U. Nebr., summer 1965; vis. fellow Wolfson Coll. Oxford (Eng.) U., spring 1975; fellow Salzburg Seminar in Am. Studies, 1976. Author: The Reform Bill of 1832, 1967; editor: R.G. Gammage, Chartist Reminiscences, 1981, Continuum: Jour. of the Nat. Continuing Edn. Assn., 1980-83, also articles. Bd. dirs. Alliance for Alternative Degree Programs, 1988-90; trustee Coun. for Adult and Exptl. Learning, 1990-94; mem. coun. Nat. Ctr. for Adult Learning, 1990—. Leverhulme Research fellow, 1961-62; grantee Am. Philos. Soc., 1961-62, 67-68, 71, 76. Fellow Royal Hist. Soc., Assn. of Grad. Liberal Studies Programs; mem. Am. Hist. Assn., Conf. on Brit. Studies, Soc. for Study Labour History. Office: PO Box 6580 Santa Fe NM 87502-6580

MAEHR, MARTIN LOUIS, psychology educator; b. Guthrie, Okla., June 25, 1932; s. Martin J. and Regina (Meier) M.; m. Jane M. Pfeil, Aug. 9, 1959; children—Martin, Michael, Katherine. B.A., Concordia Coll., 1953, M.A., 1959; Ph.D., U. Nebr., 1960. Counselor U. Nebr., Lincoln, 1959-60; asst. prof. to assoc. prof. Concordia Sr. Coll., Fort Wayne, Ind., 1960-67; assoc. prof. ednl. psychology U. Ill., Urbana, 1967-70, prof., 1970—, chmn. dept. ednl. psychology, 1970-75, assoc. dean grad. and internat. programs prof., 1975-77, research prof., dir. Inst. Research on Human Devel., prof. ednl. psychology, 1977-88, assoc. dir. Office Gerontology and Aging Studies, 1980-82; prof. edn. and psychology U. Mich., Ann Arbor, 1988—, chair combined program edn. and psychology, 1988-92; vis. prof. U. Queensland, Australia, 1981; vis. prof., cons. to dean Faculty Edn. U. Tehran, Iran, 1973-74. Author: Sociocultural Origins of Achievement, 1974, (with others) Being a Parent in Today's World, 1980, (with L.A. Braskamp) The Motivation Factor, 1986, (with Carol Midgley) Transforming School Cultures, 1996; editor: Advancement in Motivation and Achievement series; contbr. articles to profl. jours. Lutheran.

MAEROFF, GENE I., academic administrator, journalist; b. Cleve., Jan. 8, 1939; s. Harry B. and Charlotte (Szabo) M.; children: Janine Amanda, Adam Jonathan, Rachel Judith. B.S., Ohio U., 1961; M.S., Boston U., 1962. Teaching fellow Boston U., 1961-62; news bur. dir. R.I. Coll., 1962-64; religion editor Akron (Ohio) Beacon Jour., 1964-65; with Cleve. Plain Dealer, 1965-71, assoc. editor, 1969-71; edn. writer N.Y. Times, N.Y.C., 1971-86; sr. fellow Carnegie Found. for the Advancement of Teaching, Princeton, N.J., 1986-97; dir. Hechinger Inst. Tchr.'s Coll. Columbia U., N.Y.C., 1997—; contbr. mags. Author: Don't Blame the Kids, 1981, School and College, 1983, The Empowerment of Teachers, 1988, The School-Smart Parent, 1989, Sources of Inspiration, 1992, Team Building for School Change, 1993; (with others) The New York Times Guide to Suburban Public Schools, 1976, Scholarship Assessed, 1997; contbr. The Human Encounter: Readings in Education, 1976, Human Dynamics in Psychology and Education, 1977, Social Problems, 1978, Education Reform in the '90's, 1992, Teachers As Leaders, 1994. Trustee Guild-Times Scholarship Fund, Ed Bang Journalism Scholarship Found.; mem. adv. bd. Inst. Ednl. Mgmt., Harvard U., Ednl. Resources Info. Ctr., U.S. Dept. Edn., Nat. Ctr. for Postsecondary Governance. Recipient writing awards Press Club Cleve., A.P. Soc. Ohio, Edn. Writers Assn., AAUP, Internat. Reading Assn. Mem. Blue Key, Omicron Delta Kappa, Kappa Tau Alpha, Phi Sigma Delta. Office: 23 Carriage Pl Edison NJ 08820-4023

MAESTRONE, FRANK EUSEBIO, diplomat; b. Springfield, Mass., Dec. 20, 1922; s. John Battista and Margaret Carlotta (Villanova) M.; m. Jo Colwell, Jan. 20, 1951; children: Mark, Anne. BA, Yale U., 1943; grad. Naval War Coll., 1963. Assignments in Vienna and Salzburg, Austria, 1948, 54, Hamburg, Fed. Republic Germany, 1949, Khorramshahr, Iran, 1960; with NATO, Paris, 1963, Brussels, 1968; dep. asst. sec. gen. NATO, Brussels, 1968-71; counselor of embassy for polit. affairs, Manila, 1971-73; Dept. State adviser to pres. Naval War Coll., 1973; min.-counselor, Cairo, 1974; amb. State of Kuwait, 1976-79; diplomat-in-residence U. Calif., San Diego, 1979; spl. rep. of pres., dir. U.S. Sinai Support Mission, 1980; exec. dir. World Affairs Coun. San Diego, 1984-86; adj. prof. internat. rels., amb.-in-residence U.S. Internat. U., San Diego, 1986-90; bd. dirs. World Affairs Coun., San Diego; mem. adv. bd. Hansen Inst. for World Peace, San Diego State U. Found. With AUS, 1943-46, U.S. Fgn. Svc., 1948-84. Decorated chevalier du Merite Agricole (France). Mem. Internat. Inst. Strategic Studies.

MAFFEO, VINCENT ANTHONY, lawyer, executive; b. N.J., Jan. 22, 1951; s. Michael Anthony and Marie M.; BA summa cum laude, Bklyn. Coll., 1971; JD, Harvard U., 1974; m. Debra, Dec. 16, 1972. Admitted to N.Y. State bar, 1975, Calif. bar, 1982, Va. 1988, D.C. 1988, Mich. 1994; assoc. firm Simpson Thacher & Bartlett, N.Y.C., 1974-77; legal counsel Communications Systems div. ITT, Hartford, Conn., 1977-79, v.p., gen. counsel Bus. Communications div., Des Plaines, Ill., 1979-80, asst. counsel Western region, 1980-83, group counsel ITT Europe, Inc., 1983-86, v.p. gen. coun. ITT Defense Inc., 1987-91, v.p., gen. coun. ITT Automotive, Inc., 1992-95; sr. v.p., gen. counsel ITT Industries, Inc., 1995—. Served to lt. Judge Adv. Gen. Corps, USNR, 1975. Mem. Am. Bar Assn., Calif. State Bar, N.Y. State Bar Assn., Phi Beta Kappa. Office: ITT Industries Inc 4 W Red Oak Ln White Plains NY 10604-3603

MAFFIA, ROMA, actress. Appeared in films The Paper, 1994, Disclosure, 1994, Nick Of Time, 1995, Eraser, 1996. Office: Internat Creative Mgmt 8942 Wilshire Blvd Beverly Hills CA 90211*

MAFFITT, JAMES STRAWBRIDGE, lawyer; b. Raleigh, N.C., Oct. 29, 1942; s. James Strawbridge III and Lois (Handy) M.; children: Amy Maffitt

Barkley, Margaret Maffitt Kramer; m. Frances Holton, Aug. 15, 1981. BA, Washington and Lee U., 1964, LLB, 1966. Bar: Va. 1966, Md. 1969. Assoc. Apostolou, Place & Thomas, Roanoke, Va., 1966-67; trust officer Mercantile-Safe Deposit & Trust Co., Balt., 1967-71; from assoc. to ptnr. Cable, McDaniel, Bowie & Bond, Balt., 1971-82; ptnr. Maffit & Rothschild, Balt., 1982-85, Anderson, Coe & King, Balt., 1986-90, Miles, Stockbridge & Easton, Balt., 1990—. Chmn. Acad. of the Arts, 1994—; bd. dirs. United Fund of Talbot County, 1994—. Fellow Md. Bar Found.; mem. ABA (ho. dels. 1986-88), Md. Bar Assn. (bd. govs. 1989-91), Va. Bar. Assn., Balt. City Bar Assn. (pres. 1985-86), Wednesday Law Club, Talbot Country Club, Harbortown Country Club. Republican. Episcopal. Avocations: boating, waterfowl hunting, golf. Home: 9498 Martingham Cir Saint Michaels MD 21663-2238 Office: Miles & Stockbridge 101 Bay St Easton MD 21601-2748 also: Miles & Stockbridge 10 Light St Baltimore MD 21202-1435

MAFFLY, ROY HERRICK, medical educator; b. Berkeley, Calif., Nov. 26, 1927; s. Alfred Emil and Frances Elizabeth (Henderson) M.; m. Marilyn Miles, Feb. 2, 1952; children: Robert, Nancy, Laurie. A.B., U. Calif.-Berkeley, 1949; M.D., U. Calif.-San Francisco, 1952. Intern U. Calif.-San Francisco, 1952-53, resident in medicine, 1953-54, research fellow in medicine, 1959-61; resident in medicine Herrick Meml. Hosp., Berkeley, 1954-55; research fellow in medicine Mass. Gen. Hosp., Boston, 1957-59; asst. prof. medicine Stanford U., Palo Alto, Calif., 1961-65, assoc. prof., 1965-70, prof., 1970-92, assoc. dean students Sch. Medicine, 1983-92, chmn. dept. physiology, 1986-88; ret., 1992; chief renal service VA Med. Ctr., Palo Alto, Calif., 1968-83; mem. adv. com. on renal dialysis ctrs. State of Calif., 1966-70; mem. gen. med. B study sect. NIH, 1967-71; dir. Health Edn. Network, 1980-83; mem. medicine test com. Nat. Bd. Med. Examiners, 1981-88, chmn. medicine test com., 1983-88, mem. com. for comprehensive part II exam., 1987-89; established investigator Am. Heart Assn., 1961-66, mem. rsch. study com., 1972-82, rsch. com., 1976-82. Served to lt. USNR, 1955-57, PTO. Recipient Kaiser award for teaching Stanford U. Sch. Medicine, 1970, 72, 77, 79, 86, 87; recipient Bloomfield award for teaching Stanford U. Sch. Medicine, 1977, Gores award for teaching Stanford U., 1982; Disting. Achievement award Am. Heart Assn. Sci. Council, 1984; Gift of Life award Nat. Kidney Found. No. Calif., 1985. Mem. Am. Heart Assn., Am. Physiol. Soc., Am. Soc. Clin. Investigation (editorial com. 1970-75), Nat. Kidney Found. (sci. adv. bd. 1970-77). Home: 1401 Webster St Palo Alto CA 94301-3649 Office: Stanford Univ M-105 Sch Medicine Stanford CA 94305

MAFFRE, MURIEL, ballet dancer; b. Enghien, Val D'Oise, France, Mar. 19, 1966; came to U.S., 1990; d. Bernard and Monique (Berteaux) M. Diploma, Paris Opera Ballet Sch., 1981; Baccalauréat (hon.), France, 1984. Dancer Hamburg Ballet, Fed. Republic Germany, 1983-84; soloist Sarragoza Ballet, Spain; premiere danseuse Monte Carlo Ballet, Monaco, 1985-90; prin. dancer San Francisco Ballet, 1990—; guest artist with Berlinor Staatsoper and Lines Contemporary Ballet. Recipient 1st prize Nat. Conservatory, Paris, 1983, Grand prize and Gold medal Paris Internat. Ballet Competition, 1984, Isadora Duncan award, 1990. Office: San Francisco Ballet 455 Franklin St San Francisco CA 94102-4438

MAGA, JOSEPH ANDREW, food science educator; b. New Kensington, Pa., Dec. 25, 1940; s. John and Rose Maga; m. Andrea H. Vorperian, June 13, 1964; children: Elizabeth, John. BS, Pa. State U., 1962, MS, 1964; PhD, Kans. State U., 1970. Project leader Borden Foods Co., Syracuse, N.Y., 1964-66; group leader Cen. Soya Co., Chgo., 1966-68; asst. prof. Colo. State U., Ft. Collins, Colo., 1970-72, assoc. prof., 1972-74, prof. food sci., 1974—. Contbr. numerous articles to profl. jours. Mem. Inst. Food Technologists, Am. Chem. Soc., Am. Assn. Cereal Scientists. Office: Colo State U Dept Food Sci Nutrition Fort Collins CO 80523

MAGAD, SAMUEL, orchestra concertmaster, conductor; b. Chgo., May 14, 1932; s. Herman and Doris (Walder) M.; m. Miriam Seefor, Feb. 13, 1955; children: Debra, Carlen. Mus.B., De Paul U., 1955; student, Paul Stassevitch. Orch. violin soloist, beginning 1944; with Chgo. Symphony Orch., 1958—, asst. concertmaster, 1966-72, co-concertmaster, 1972—; concertmaster Grant Park Symphony Orch., 1970-71; dir., 1st violinist Chgo. Symphony Chamber Players; founder Chgo. Symphony Trio; music dir., condr. Kankakee Symphony Orch. (Ill.), from 1984; prof. violin Northwestern U., Evanston, Ill.; also 1st violinist Eckstein Quartet, Chgo. Symphony String Quartet; dir. music, condr. Northbrook Symphony Orch., 1980—; concertmaster Aspen Festival Orch., 1987—. Served with orch. AUS, 1955-58. Office: Northbrook Symphony Orch 801 Skokie Blvd Ste 213 Northbrook IL 60062-4027*

MAGAFAS, DIANIA LEE, geriatrics nurse consultant, administrator; b. Chgo., Oct. 17, 1963; d. Alec and Jacqueline Magafas; 1 child, Jason. BS, St. Xavier Coll., Chgo., 1986, MSN, 1991. Staff nurse Ingalls Meml. Hosp., Harvey, Ill., 1986-88; asst. DON Wedgewood Nursing Pavilion, Chgo., 1988-90; nursing cons. long term care Dynamics Healthcare Cons., Inc., Skokie, Ill., 1990—. Mem. Sigma Theta Tau.

MAGALNICK, ELLIOTT BEN, retail medical supply company executive; b. Cleve., Aug. 19, 1945; s. Joseph Hyman and Ann (Resnick) M.; m. Diane Kerner, May 26, 1968 (div. Feb. 1988); children: Joel A., David A.; m. Judy Banjavic, June 9, 1991; stepchildren: Daniel Banjavic, David Banjavic. BS in Bus. Mgmt., Temple U., 1968. Cert. orthopedic fitter Health Industries Dealer Assn. Retail mgr. Milner Surg. Supply Co., Phila., 1970-72, Colo. Surg. Supply Co., Denver, 1972-73; mgr. non wheelchair retail Wheelchairs, Inc., Englewood, Colo., 1973-77; asst. mgr. ops. Denver Surg. Supply Co., 1977-78; owner, founder The Get Well Shop, Inc., Aurora, Colo., 1978—. Mem. chorus Shir Ami Singers, Denver, 1978-95, Colo. Symphony Orch., Denver, 1986-96; vol. Allied Fedn. Denver, 1984-87; mem. Legion of Merit, Rep. Party, Denver, 1992; donor Belle Bonfils Blood Ctr., 1976—; cantor Temple Micah, Denver, 1991-95, Temple Shalom, Colorado Springs, Colo., 1996-97. Named Disting. Pres., Optimist Internat., 1987. Mem. Colo. Assn. Med. Equipment Suppliers (dealer mem., mem. state bd.), Health Industries Dealer Assn. (cert. orthopedic fitter, bd. dirs. 1986-87), Luncheon Optimist Club Windsor Gardens (pres. 1986), Masons (master mason Columbian lodge), Colo. Consistory, El Jebel Temple, Rocky Mtn. Cantors Assn. Jewish. Avocations: bicycling, cross-country skiing, singing, tennis, reading. Office: The Get Well Shop Inc 12028 E Mississippi Ave Aurora CO 80012-3294

MAGARGEE, W(ILLIAM) SCOTT, III, lawyer; b. Abington, Pa., Sept. 3, 1940; m. Annette Bruno, July 6, 1963; children: Scott, Todd, Ashley. AB, Princeton U., 1962; LLB, Yale U., 1966. Bar: Pa. 1966, U.S. Dist. Ct. (ea. dist.) Pa. 1966, U.S. Tax Ct. 1973. Admission officer Princeton (N.J.) U., 1962-63; assoc. Dechert Price & Rhoads, Phila., 1966-75, ptnr., 1975—. Supr. Tredyffrin Twp., Chester County, Berwyn, Pa., 1973-87; bd. trustees Paoli Meml. Hosp., 1988—; mem. citizens adv. com. Southeastern Pa. Transp. Authority, 1988—; bd. dirs. United Way Southeastern Pa., 1994—, chair human resources com., 1993—. Mem. ABA (sect. taxation, real estate, probate, trust law), Phila. Bar Assn.), Princeton Club Phila., Princeton Univ. Alumni Coun. (chmn. 1985-87). Office: Dechert Price & Rhoads 4000 Bell Atlantic Tower 1717 Arch St Philadelphia PA 19103-2713

MAGARIAN, ROBERT ARMEN, medicinal chemist, researcher, educator; b. East St. Louis, Ill., July 27, 1930; s. Leon and Pauline Mary (Struel) M.; m. Charmaine Virginia Kugler, June 24, 1950; children: Paula, Cindy, Leslie, Robert. Student, Washington U., St. Louis, 1951-52; B.A., U. Miss., 1956, B.S. in Pharmacy with highest honors, 1960, Ph.D., 1966. Registered pharmacist, Miss., Ill. Am. Found. for Pharm. Edn. fellow, 1961-66; NIH postdoctoral research fellow U. Kans., Lawrence, 1966-67; asst. prof. St. Louis Coll. Pharmacy, 1966-70; assoc. prof. U. Okla. Coll. Pharmacy, Norman, 1970-76; prof. U. Okla., Oklahoma City, 1978-96, prof. emeritus, 1996—; exec. dir. Kappa Psi, pharm. frat., 1980—. Assoc. editor Current Medicinal Chemistry. Served with U.S. Army, 1952-54, Korea. Recipient teaching awards Coll. Pharmacy, U. Okla., 1974, 786, 89, Excellence in Rsch. and Svc. award, 1985, Baldwin study-travel award, 1978, Assocs. Disting. Lectureship award, 1988; named Outstanding Prof. Okla. Soc. Hosp. Pharmacists, 1987, Alumni Teaching Excellence award, 1989, Outstanding Teaching award Gamma Omicron, 1990, 91, 92; Mead-Johnson grantee Am. Assn. Colls. Pharmacy, 1968, NSF grantee, 1968-70, Nat. Cancer Inst. grantee, 1987-93. Mem. Am. Assn. Colls. Pharmacy, Am. chem. soc., Sigma Xi, Phi Kappa Phi, Kappa Psi (exec. dir., assoc. editor Current Medicinal Chemistry, Tchr. Excellence award 1990, 92), Rho Chi (chpt. Rsch. award 1981). Episcopalian. Patentee in field. Office: U Okla Health Sci Ctr Coll of Pharmacy 1110 N Stonewall Ave Oklahoma City OK 73117-1200

MAGARITY, RUSSELL LYNN, banker; b. Corpus Christi, Tex., July 29, 1946; s. Roy Lee and Ira Oleuia (Patterson) M.; m. Susan Ann Byers, June 3, 1967; children: Jennifer Lynn, Jeffrey Alan, Allison Lee. BA in Internat. Rels., U. Okla., 1967; MBA in Fin., Thunderbird Sch. Internat. Mgmt., Ariz., 1973. Credit and mktg. officer Banco Lar Brasileiro, S.A., Rio de Janeiro, 1974-78; v.p., team leader Chase Manhattan Bank, N.A., N.Y.C., 1978; dir. adjutant, country corp. mgr. Banco Lar Brasileiro, S.A., Rio de Janeiro, 1979-80; country corp. mgr., country mgr. Chase Manhattan Bank, N.A., Mexico City, 1981-86; sr. v.p., credit supervising officer Asia Pacific Chase Manhattan Bank, N.A., Hong Kong, 1986-88; sr. v.p. Chase Manhattan Bank, N.A., N.Y.C., 1987-96; chief exec., bd. dirs. Chase Manhattan Asia Ltd., Hong Kong, 1989-96; mng. dir., area exec. Asia Bank of Boston, 1996—. Lt. USN, 1967-72, Vietnam. Mem. Young Reps., Am. C. of C. Avocations: sailing, flying, cycling, magic. Office: Bank of Boston, 8/F Jardine House, Hong Kong China

MAGAW, JOHN W., federal law enforcement official; b. Columbus, Ohio; m. Helen Mahley; 5 children. BA in Edn., Otterbein Coll., 1957. Patrolman State of Ohio, Columbus, 1958-66; joined U.S. Secret Svc., Columbus, 1967, spl. agt., 1967—; former head protection for U.S. President and First Lady U.S. Secret Svc., Washington, until 1992, 17th dir., 1992-93; dir. Bur. Alcohol, Tobacco & Firearms, Washington, 1993—. Bd. trustees Otterbein Coll., Westerville, Ohio. Recipient Presdl. Rank Meritorious award, 1991. Mem. Fed. Investigators Assn., Internat. Assn. Chiefs of Police (exec. com. adv. com. for internat. policy). Office: Dept Treasury Bur Alcohol Tobacco Firearm 650 Massachusetts Ave NW Washington DC 20001-3744*

MAGAW, ROGER WAYNE, construction company executive; b. Beaver, Ohio, Feb. 8, 1933; s. Cecil Elsworth and Thelma Mae (Howerton) M.; m. Virginia May Burdette, July 2, 1955; children: Wayne Robert, Rex Roger. BS, W.Va. State Coll., 1960. V.p. labor rels. Williams Power Corp., Nitro, W.Va., 1959—; bd. dirs. mgmt. chmn. Nat. Maintenance Agreements Policy Com., Washington, 1983—. Chmn. Putnam County Vocat. Adv. Com., W.Va., 1968-90. Served with U.S. Army, 1953-55. Mem. Am. Welding Soc., Nat. Assn. Constrn. Boilermaker Employers (pres., bd. dirs. 1983-87), Putnam County C. of C. (chmn., bd. dirs. 1985-87). Republican. Methodist. Lodges: Masons, Shriners. Avocations: motor home camping, farming. Home: RR 2 Box 112 Hurricane WV 25526-9683 Office: Williams Power Corp PO Box 425 Nitro WV 25143-0425

MAGAZINE, ALAN HARRISON, association executive, consultant; b. Cambridge, Mass., May 16, 1944; s. Arnold Lloyd and Ruth Magazine; m. June Ann O'Donohue, June 20, 1971 (div. Feb. 1984); children: Sarah Elizabeth, David Michael; m. Cynthia Louise Cordiner, Aug. 30, 1984. BA, Monmouth Coll., 1966; MPA, Kent State U., 1968; PhD, U.Md., 1976. Sr. cons. Real Estate Research Corp., Washington, 1969-72; exec. dir. Nat. Ctr. for Pub. Service Internships, Washington, 1972-75; nat. policy coordinator Internat. City Mgmt. Assn., Washington, 1973-76; dep. asst. dir. U.S. Commn. on Fed. Paperwork, Washington, 1976-78; dir. office of intergovernmental relations EPA, Washington, 1978-81; dir. Business-Higher Edn. Forum, Washington, 1981-86, pres. coun. on competitivenessadv. com. Congl. Tech. Policy Task Force, 1986-89; adv. bd. George Mason U. Ctr. Conflict Resolution, 1986-89; pres. Health Industry Mfgs. Assn., 1990—; adv. bd. George Mason U. Ctr. Conflict Resolution, 1986-89, Brookings Inst. Ctr. Econ. Progress and Employment, 1986-89; mem. U.S. China Joint Commn. on Commerce & Trade; bd. dirs. Congl. Econ. Leadership Inst., 1986-89—, Healthcare Tech. Inst. Bd. Advisors, 1992-95, Calif. Biomedical Found., 1994—. Author: Environmental Management in Local Government, 1977. Bd. dirs. Met. Washington Coun. of Govts., 1972-79; mem. Fairfax County Bd. Suprs., Va., 1972-79; chmn. No. Va. Transp. Commn., 1974-75; mem. No. Va. Planning Dist. Commn., Fairfax, 1976-79; mem. Dickinson Coll. Parents Coun., 1994—. Served with USAFR, 1968-71. Ford Found. fellow, 1970-71. Mem. Econ. Club of Washington D.C. Democrat. Jewish. Avocations: jogging, reading. Home: 1302 Chancel Pl Alexandria VA 22314-4707 Office: Health Industry Mfgs Assn 1200 G St NW Washington DC 20005-3814

MAGAZINER, ELLIOT ALBERT, musician, conductor, educator; b. Springfield, Mass., Dec. 25, 1921; m. Sari Fromkin; 2 children. Student, Nat. Orch. Assn., 1937-40, Princeton U., 1943, Juilliard School of Music, 1946-50. Music dir., prof. music Manhattanville Coll., Purchase, N.Y., 1970—; faculty Westchester Conservatory Music. Debut: Town Hall, N.Y.C., 1952; staff artist, concertmaster CBS-TV and Radio; Networks: condrs. Reiner, Ansermet, Beecham, Stokowski; condr. and sr. violin instr. Westchester Conservatory of Music; vis. condr. Dubuque Symphony; soloist N.Y. Philharm. Symphony, Symphony of the Air, Kol Visrael, symphonies in Chgo., Ft. Myers, Dubuque, York, St. Petersburg; recitals in N.Y.C., Washington, Detroit, Amsterdam, Paris, Jerusalem; star of CBS-TV, The Violin. Recs.: Charles Ives Sonata #2, Charles Ives Trio (with Frank Glazer and David Weber); Vivaldi Concerto in C and Concerto in B (with orchestre Symphonique de Paris); conductor Westchester All County Festival Orch. Mem. AAUP, N.Y. TV Musicians (pres.), CBS Musicians Fund (sec.). Avocations: collecting unique and ancient instruments. Home: 250 Garth Rd Apt 2b3 Scarsdale NY 10583-3922 Office: Westchester Conservatory Symphony Orch 20 Soundview Ave White Plains NY 10606-3302

MAGAZINER, FRED THOMAS, lawyer; b. Phila., July 4, 1947; s. Henry Jonas and Reba (Henken) M.; m. Phyllis Heller, June 28, 1970; children: Daniel, Andrew. BA, Columbia U., 1969, JD, 1976. Bar: Pa., U.S. Dist. Ct. (ea. dist.) Pa., U.S. Ct. Appeals (3rd cir.), U.S. Claims Ct. Law clk. to judge Max Rosenn U.S. Ct. Appeals (3rd cir.), Phila., 1976-77; assoc. Dechert, Price & Rhoads, Phila., 1977-84, ptnr., 1984—. Vice chair citizens adv. com. S.E. Pa. Transp. Authority, 1986—. Mem. ABA, Pa. Bar Assn., Phila. Bar Assn. Democrat. Jewish. Home: 1021 W Cliveden St Philadelphia PA 19119-3702 Office: Dechert Price & Rhoads 4000 Bell Atlantic Tower 1717 Arch St Philadelphia PA 19103-2713

MAGAZINER, HENRY JONAS, architect; b. Phila., Sept. 13, 1911; s. Louis and Selma (Jonas) M.; m. Reba Henken, June 19, 1938; children: Ellen Louise (Mrs. Alan I. Widiss), Fred Thomas. BArch, U. Pa., 1936. Cert. Nat. Coun. Arch. and Registration Bds.; registered arch. Pa., N.Y., N.J., Del., Md. Draftsman Phila. City Planning Project, 1936-37; draftsman Louis Magaziner (Architect), Phila., 1937-39, architect, 1946-48; chief Architects' Squad, Day & Zimmermann, Inc., Burlington, Iowa, 1940-41; architect Albert Kahn (Architect), Detroit, 1942; designer Wright Aero. Corp., Wood Ridge, N.J., 1943-45; ptnr. Louis & Henry Magaziner, Phila., 1948-56; architect, planner pvt. practice, 1956-72; regional hist. architect Mid-Atlantic region Nat. Pk. Svc., Phila., 1972-87; pvt. practice architecture, 1987—; archtl. adviser Phila. Hist. Commn., 1970-75, mem. archtl. com., 1979-85, chmn. archtl. com., 1972-75; mem. adv. bd. Preservation Alliance, Phila., 1994-96. Mem. Carpenters' Co. of City and County of Phila.; v.p. Phila. Health and Welfare Coun., 1957-61, Phila. chpt. Victorian Soc. Am., 1975; v.p. city planning Germantown Comty. Coun., 1957-62; bd. dirs. Downtown Children's (day care) Ctr., 1956-73, v.p., 1960-61; bd. dirs. Allens Ln. Art Ctr., 1945-67, Neighborhood Ctr. Phila., 1956-74, Hist. Soc. Pa., 1970-74, Chestnut Hill Hist. Soc., 1970-80, Phila. chpt. Assn. for Preservation Tech., 1991—, Clean Air Coun., 1980-92, Center City Residents Assn., 1995-96, Rittenhouse Plz., Inc., 1995-96; active Germantown Hist. Soc., bd. dirs., 1960-93; bd. dirs. Maxwell Mansion Mus., pres., 1964-67; trustee Stewardsom Meml. Fellowship in Arch., 1958-90. Recipient Presdl. award for Excellence in Design for the Govt., 1988; named to Germantown Hall of Fame, 1994. Fellow AIA (mem. com. on hist. resources); mem. ASTM (mem. com. on hist. preservation stds. 1981-90), Am. Inst. Conservation, Assn. for Preservation Tech., Ea. Nat. Pk. and Monument Assn., Fellows in Am. Studies (pres. 1983-84), Nat. Trust for Hist. Preservation (mem. preservation forum), Soc. Archtl. Historians (bd. dirs. 1977-80, mem. editl. bd. 58 vol. Buildings of the United States), Bldg. Conservation Internat., Am. Arbitration Assn. (arbitrator), Victorian Soc. Am., T-Square Atelier (pres. 1963-65), Pa. Soc. Architects, Pa. Acad. Fine Arts, Libr. Co. Phila., Sierra Club, Athenaeum of Phila., Preservation Action. Home: 2 Franklin Town Blvd (2404) Philadelphia PA 19103-1237 *I do hope that we can pass on to future generations a prejudice-free America having a natural environment without pollution and a man-made environment with its best elements both preserved and appreciated. Achieving these objectives is an unending struggle but one certainly worth winning. God willing, I expect to continue to fight for these ends.*

MAGAZINER, IRA, federal official; b. N.Y.C.; s. Louis and Sylvia M.; m. Suzanne Magaziner, 1981; children: Seth, Jonathan, Sarah. Grad., Brown U. With Boston Consulting Group; co-founder Telesis, 1979-88; issues advisor Clinton campaign, 1992; sr. advisor policy devel. The White House, 1993—. chief architect Health Security Act, 1993. Rhodes scholar Oxford U. Office: Domestic Policy Coun 1600 Pennsylvania Ave NW Washington DC 20500-0005

MAGDOL, MICHAEL ORIN, bank executive; b. N.Y.C., May 18, 1937; s. David Aaron and Ruth (Wein) M.; m. Alice Jane Gates, Aug. 29, 1940 (div. Sept. 1974); 1 child, David; m. Patricia Elizabeth Marshall, Feb. 1, 1943; 1 child, Jennifer. BSE, U. Pa., 1959. Internat. officer Mfrs. Hanover Trust Co., N.Y.C., 1959-65; exec. v.p. J. Henry Schroder Bank, N.Y.C., 1965-87; vice chmn., chief fin. officer, dir. Fiduciary Trust Co. Internat., N.Y.C., 1987—. Bd. dirs. Boy Scouts Am., N.Y.C., 1975—, Children Oncology Soc. N.Y., Lingnan Found. Mem. Am. Bankers Assn. (internat. bd. dirs. 1980-83), N.Y. State Bankers Assn. (chmn. internat. com. 1982—), Univ. Econs. Club, Onteora Club (Tannersville, N.Y.). Office: Fiduciary Trust Co Internat 2 World Trade Ctr New York NY 10048-0203

MAGEE, A. ALAN, artist; b. Newtown, Pa., May 26, 1947; s. Richard Forrest and Rena (Cook) M.; m. Monika Gabriele Ruth Siekmann, Jan. 4, 1969. Student, Tyler Sch. of Art, 1965-66, Phila. Coll. Art, 1967-69. Contbr. articles to profl. jours.; one-person shows include Allport Assocs. Gallery, Larkspur, Calif., 1978, 81, Clark Gallery, Lincoln, Mass., 1979, Staempfli Gallery, N.Y.C., 1980, 82, FIAC Grand Palais, Paris, 1983, Norton Gallery and Sch. of Art, West Palm Beach, Fla., 1983, San Jose Mus. of Art, 1983, Newport Art Mus., 1984, Farnsworth Art Mus., Rockland, Maine, 1984, U. Maine, 1985, Fresno Art Ctr., 1985, Los Angeles, 1986, Schmidt-Bingham Gallery, N.Y.C., 1986, 88, 89, Allport Assocs. Gallery, San Francisco, 1986, Joan Whitney Payson Gallery at Westbrook Coll., Portland, Maine, 1990, Farnsworth Art Mus., 1991, James A. Michener Art Mus., Doylestown, Pa., 1991, Ringling Sch. Art & Design, Sarasota, Fla., 1992, Fine Arts Ctr. at Cheekwood, Nashville, 1992, Edith Caldwell Gallery, San Francisco, 1992, 93, 95, 96, 97, Edity Lambert Gallery, Santa Fe, 1995; group shows include Farnsworth Art Mus., Rockland, Maine, 1985, Akron (Ohio) Mus. of Art, 1985, Maine Coast Artists, Rockport, 1985, Ark. Art Ctr, Little Rock, 1985, Smithsonian Instn., Nat. Air and Space Mus., Washington, 1985, Wunderlich & Co., N.Y.C., 1986, Light Gallery, N.Y.C., 1986, Schmidt-Bingham Gallery, N.Y.C., 1986, 88, Mus. Fine Arts, Springfield, 1986, Butler Inst. Am. Art, Youngstown, Ohio, 1987, Am. Acad. and Inst. of Arts and Letters, N.Y.C., 1987, Nat. Invitationnal Drawing Exhbn., 1989, Staempfli Gallery, N.Y.C., 1990, Albrecht Art Mus., St. Joseph, 1990, Nat. Acad. of Design, N.Y.C., 1990, Edith Caldwell Gallery, San Francisco, 1993, 94, 95, 96, Nora Eccles Harrison Mus. of Art, Logan Utah, 1992, Portland Mus. of Art, 1993, Creiger Dane Gallery, Boston, Mass., 1995, Phila. Pa., 1995, Forum Gallery, N.Y.C, 1996, Nat. Mus. Am. Art, Washington, 1997, and others; pub. collections include Farnsworth Art Mus., Rockland, Arco Collection, Los Angeles, Achenbach Collection, Palace of the Legion of Honour, San Francisco, Portland (Maine) Mus. of Art, Rutgers U. Art Mus., and others; author: Stones and Other Works, 1987, Alan Magee 1981-91; TV: Visions of Darkness and Light, 1988. Recipient Richard and Hinda Rosenthal Found. award N.Y.C., Am. Book award, Nevelson award, 1982; The Leo Meissner Prize, Nat. Acad. of Design, 1990. Home: Pleasant Point Rd RR 68 Box 132 Cushing ME 04563

MAGEE, BERNARD DALE, obstetrician, gynecologist; b. Niagara Falls, N.Y., June 8, 1950; s. Bernard Dale and Rose (Roffle) M.; m. Melanie Ann Ciszek, Aug. 31, 1974; 1 child, Ryan. Student, SUNY, Buffalo, 1968-71; MD, SUNY, Syracuse, 1975. Diplomate Am. Bd. Ob-Gyn, Am. Bd. Med. Examiners. Obstetrician-gynecologist Fallon Clinic, Worcester, Mass., 1979-83; pvt. practice Shrewsbury, Mass., 1983-96, U. Mass. Cmty. Physicians, Shrewsbury, 1996—; chmn. ob-gyn com. Ctrl. Mass. Health Care, Worcester, 1990—, trustee, 1993-95. Fellow Am. Coll. Ob-Gyn.; mem. AMA, Mass. Med. Soc., Worcester Dist. Med. Soc. (treas. 1988-94, pres. 1995-96), Maddox Soc. (pres. 1992-94). Avocations: medical history, antique medical books and instruments, skiing. Office: 604 Main St Shrewsbury MA 01545-5639

MAGEE, DENNIS, cultural organization administrator; b. Pala, Calif., Oct. 9, 1937; s. Raymond Milton and Prudence Theresa (Golsh) M. BSBA, San Diego State U., San Diego, 1961. Wholesaler Kroshel Industries, San Diego, 1962-69; adminstr. Indian Health Council Inc., Pauma Valley, Calif., 1970—; adv. bd. Masters in Pub. Health Program for Native Americans, U. Calif., Berkeley; bd. trustees Robert F. Kennedy Meml. Found., Washington; bd. dirs. Comprehensive Health Planning Assn. of San Diego, Riverside and Imperial Counties, Nat. Indian Health Bd., Denver; mem. San Diego State U. Athletic Found, San Diego State U. Alumni Assn., San Diego Council of Community Clinics; bd. chair Native Am. Tng. Assocs., Sacramento, D.Q. U., Davis, Calif., Calif. Rural Indian Health Bd., Sacramento. Bd. dirs. United Way of San Diego County, Nat. Neighborhood Ctrs. Am., N.Y.C., Citizens Equal Opportunity Commn., San Diego, Mental Health Assn., Sacramento, San Diego County Regional Criminal Justice Planning bd.; mem. tribal health coun., Sacramento; mem. San Diego County Human Relations Commn. Recipient Nat. Disting. Cmty. Svc. award Nat. Soc. Workers Techni-Culture Coalition, Cin., 1973, Indian Health Ctr. dedicated to Dennis Magee, 1976, Letter of Commendation Pres. Jimmy Carter, 1980; named One of Ten Outstanding Young Men of San Diego San Diego Jr. C. of C. Mem. Northern San Diego County Associated Cs. of C. (bd. dirs.). Democrat. Roman Catholic. Avocations: sports, bicycling, hunting, bullfighting. Home: Pala Mission Rd PO Box 86 Pala CA 92059-0086 Office: Indian Health Council Inc PO Box 406 Pauma Valley CA 92061-0406

MAGEE, DONALD EDWARD, retired national park service administrator; b. Trenton, N.J., Sept. 24, 1937; s. Donald A. and Anna C. (Bocskowics) M.; m. Linda Kimball, June 27, 1964; children: Kevin, Bonnie Magee Burch, Gale. BS in Forestry Mgmt., U. Mass., 1964. Pk. ranger Bryce Canyon (Utah) Nat. Pk., 1966-68; area mgr. Sunset Crater Nat. Monument, Flagstaff, Ariz., 1968-73; mgmt. analyst Nat. Capital Region, Washington, 1973-80; supt. Stones River Nat. Battlefield, Murfreesboro, Tenn., 1980-89, USS Ariz. Meml., Pearl Harbor, Hawaii, 1989-95; ret., 1995. With USN, 1956-58. Recipient Excellence of Svc. award Dept. of Interior, 1991. Home: 95-457 Kaukoe St Mililani HI 96789-1865

MAGEE, JOHN FRANCIS, research company executive; b. Bangor, Maine, Dec. 3, 1926; s. John Henry and Marie (Frawley) M.; m. Dorothy Elma Hundley, Nov. 19, 1949; children: Catherine Anne, John Hundley, Andrew Stephen. AB, Bowdoin Coll., 1947; MS, U. Maine, 1952; MBA, Harvard U., 1948; LLD, Bowdoin Coll., 1996. With Arthur D. Little, Inc., Cambridge, Mass., 1950—, v.p., 1961-72, pres., 1972-86, chief exec. officer, 1974-88, chmn., 1986—, also dir.; dir. John Hancock Mut. Life Ins. Co., Boston, Houghton-Mifflin Co., Boston. Author: Physical Distribution Systems, 1967, Industrial Logistics: Analysis and Management of Physical Supply and Distribution Systems, 1968, (with D. M. Boodman) Production Planning and Inventory Control, 1968; (with W. Capacino and W. Rosenfield) Modern Logistics Management, 1985. Trustee Boston U. Med. Ctr., New Eng. Aquarium, Woods Hole Oceanographic Instn., Bowdoin Coll. (emeritus), Emerson Hosp., Thompson Island Outward Bound Edn. Ctr. (chmn.). Mem. Ops. Research Soc. Am. (pres. 1966-67), Inst. Mgmt. Scis. (pres. 1971-72), Phi Beta Kappa, Phi Kappa Psi. Clubs: Concord (Mass.) Country (gov. 1971-74); The Country (Brookline, Mass.); Somerset (Boston). Office: Arthur D Little Inc 25 Acorn Park Cambridge MA 02140-2301

MAGEE, PAUL TERRY, geneticist and molecular biologist, college dean; b. Los Angeles, Oct. 26, 1937; s. John Paul and Lois Lorene (Cowgill) M.; m. Beatrice Buten, Aug. 6, 1964; children: Alexander John, Amos Hart. B.S., Yale U., 1959; Ph.D., U. Calif., Berkeley, 1964. Am. Cancer Soc. postdoctoral fellow Lab. Enzymologie, Gif-sur-Yvette, France, 1964-66; mem. faculty Yale U., 1966-77, asst. prof. microbiology, 1966-72, assoc. prof. microbiology and human genetics, 1972-75, assoc. prof. human genetics, 1975-77; dean Trumbull Coll., 1969-72; prof. microbiology, chmn. dept.

microbiology and pub. health Mich. State U., East Lansing, 1977-87, dir. Biotech. Research Ctr., 1985-87; dean Coll. Biol. Scis. U. Minn., 1987-95, prof. genetics and cell biology, 1987—; mem. genetics adv. panel NSF, 1978-83, mem. adv. com. biology directorate, 1992—, chair, 1995-96; chmn. BBS task force looking to 21st century, 1991; cons. Corning Glass Works, 1978-80, Pillsbury Rsch., 1990-96; mem. pers. com. Am. Cancer Soc., 1983-87; mem. microbial genetics and physiology study sect. NIH, 1984-88; co-chmn. com. grad. record exam. biochemistry cell and molecular biology Ednl. Testing Svc., 1988—; mem. microbiology infectious disease rsch. adv. group NIH, 1994—, chair, 1996-98; chair Burroughs Wellcome Fund Award Com. in Molecular Pathogenic Mycology, 1995—; traveling fellow Japanese Soc. for Promotion of Sci., 1995. Mem. editorial bd. Jour. Bacteriology, 1975-80, Molecular and Cell Biology, 1981-92, Fungal Genetics and Biology, 1996—. Named Mich. champion masters swimming, 1978-84, 86, Minn. champion masters swimming, 1988, 89, 91-97, nat. YMCA swimming champion, 1990. Mem. AAAS, Am. Soc. Microbiologists, Genetics Soc. Am. Jewish. Office: U Minn Coll Biol Scis Dept Genetics and Cell Biol Saint Paul MN 55108-1095

MAGEE, THOMAS ESTON, JR., minister; b. DeRidder, La., Aug. 9, 1947; s. Thomas Eston and Doris Maxine (Gallion) M.; m. Linda Ruth Lewis, Nov. 9, 1967. Student, McNeese State U., 1966-69; BTh, Tex. Bible Coll., 1972. Ordained to ministry United Pentecostal Ch., 1973. Asst. pastor United Pentecostal Ch., Pasadena, Tex., 1969-72; instr. Tex. Bible Coll., Houston, 1970-72, dean of women, 1970-71; evangelist United Pentecostal Ch., various locations, U.S., 1972-77; pastor 1st United Pentecostal Ch., Ragley, La., 1977—; sect. youth dir. La. Dist. United Pentecostal Ch., Ragley, 1979-83; sect. Sunday Sch. dir., 1984-86; sect. sec.-treas., 1989—. Named col., La. Gov., 1975. Democrat. Home: 319 N Frusha DeRidder LA 70634 Office: 1st United Pentecostal Ch PO Box 44 Ragley LA 70657-0044 *As a minister, I am looked upon as the one who has all the "right" answers to life's problems. I have discovered that life is not always fair but God is always just.*

MAGEE, THOMAS HUGH, lawyer; b. Rochester, N.Y., Aug. 15, 1943; s. Edward Charles and Jane Kathleen (Cranmer) M.; m. Judith Joy Stone, Oct. 2, 1982; 1 child, Michael Julian. BSME, U. Rochester, N.Y., 1965; JD, Syracuse U., 1973. Bar: N.J. 1974, U.S. Dist. Ct. N.J. 1974, U.S. Ct. Appeals (D.C. cir.) 1975, N.Y. 1981, U.S. Supreme Ct. 1978, U.S. Patent and Trademark Office. Sr. patent counsel RCA Corp., Princeton, N.J., 1973-86, GE/RCA Licensing Operation, Princeton, 1986-88; sr. counsel E.I. duPont de Nemours & Co., Wilmington, Del., 1988—. Lt. USN, 1965-70, Capt. USNR (ret.), 1991. Navy commendation medal with combat V, Vietnam, 1969. Mem. Am. Intellectual Property Law Assn. (com. chair 1974—), Phila. Intellectual Property Law Assn. (com. chmn. 1974—), N.J. Patent Law Assn., Justinian hon. law soc., Phi Alpha Delta. Republican. Presbyterian. Avocations: tennis, handball, coin-collecting. Home: 721 Severn Rd Wilmington DE 19803 Office: E I duPont de Nemours & Co Barley Mill Plz BMP 11-1126 Wilmington DE 19880

MAGEE, WAYNE EDWARD, biochemistry educator, researcher; b. Big Rapids, Mich., Apr. 11, 1929; s. William Fredrick and Elsie E. (Gifford) M.; m. Nannette A. Pierce, June 11, 1951; children: Lawrence, William, John. BA magna cum laude in Chemistry, Kalamazoo Coll., 1951; MS in Biochemistry, U. Wis., 1953, PhD in Biochemistry, 1955. Sci., then sr. sci. Upjohn Co., Kalamazoo, 1955-71; prof. life sci. Ind. State U., 1971-74; prof. biology, head divsn. allied health and life sci. U. Tex., San Antonio, 1975-80, prof., 1980-81; prof. biochemistry, head dept. bacteriology and biochemistry U. Idaho, 1981-85; dir. divsn. Life Scis., prof., head dept. biosci. and biotech. Drexel U., Phila., 1985-92, prof. biosci., 1985-95, W.R. Nes prof. bioscience, 1995—; adj. prof. biology Western Mich. U., 1970-71. Wis. Alumni Found. Grad. fellow, 1951-52; Predoctoral fellow NSF, 1952-55. Fellow AAAS, Am. Chem. Soc., Am. Inst. Biol. Sci., Am. Soc. Biochemistry and Molecular Biology, Am. Soc. Microbiology. Contbr. articles and abstracts to profl. jours., chpts. in books. Research on phospholipid membranes, liposomes as drug carriers, immune modulation, monoclonal antibodies. Home: 233 S 6th St Philadelphia PA 19106-3751 Office: Drexel U Dept Biosci Biotech Philadelphia PA 19104

MAGENHEIM, MARK JOSEPH, physician, epidemiologist, educator; b. Deland, Fla., Nov. 1, 1947; s. Milton David and Dolores Ella (Raithel) M. BA cum laude, Wash. U., 1969; MPH, Yale U., 1971; MD with honors, McMaster U., 1974. Diplomate Am. Bd. Preventive Medicine, Am. Bd. Pub. Health, Am. Bd. Family Medicine. Health officer, prof. Oreg. State U., Corvallis, 1976-78; prof. cmty. health U. Sierra Leone, Freetown, West Africa, 1978-81; asst. prof. McMaster U., Hamilton, Ont., Can., 1978-83; asst. state health officer State of Fla., Tallahassee, 1989-91; health officer Sarasota (Fla.) County Pub. Health Dept., 1984-95; med. dir. Hospice of S.W. Fla., Sarasota, 1994—; adj. prof. U. South Fla., Tampa, 1985—; mem. staff Doctor's Hosp. Sarasota; mem. CDC adv. com. for prevention of HIV and STD Infection, ACHSP chair, 1996—. Author, editor Clinics in Geriatric Medicine, 1986, (with others) Practice of Geriatrics, 1986; contbr. articles to profl. jours. Bd. dirs. Children & Youth Consortium, Sarasota, 1989—, Health Care Planning Coun., Sarasota, 1992—. Recipient Surgeon Gen.'s medallion of excellence USPHS, 1989, award of commendation, 1989, Leadership award Ctrs. for Disease Control, 1991-92; recipient numerous grants. Fellow Royal Soc. Tropical Medicine and Hygiene; mem. Pub. Health Leadership Soc. (chair 1993-95), Fla. Pub. Health Leadership Inst., Fla. Pub. Health Assn., Fla. Med. Assn., Fla. Soc. for Preventive Medicine, Sarasota County Med. Soc. (chair pub. health com. 1987—). Avocations: tennis, music, bicycling, international travel. Home: 3412 Clark Rd # 234 Sarasota FL 34231-8406 Office: Hospice of SW Fla 6055 Rand Blvd Sarasota FL 34238-5189

MAGER, ARTUR, retired aerospace company executive, consultant; b. Nieglowice, Poland, Sept. 21, 1919; came to U.S., 1939, naturalized, 1944; s. Herman and Ella (Kornbluh) M.; m. Phyllis R. Weisman, Aug. 19, 1942; 1 child, Ilana Gail. BS, U. Mich., 1943; MS, Case Inst. Tech., 1951; PhD in Aeros., Calif. Inst. Tech., 1953. Aero. rsch. scientist NASA Lewis Labs., Cleve., 1946-51; rsch. scientist Marquardt Corp., Van Nuys, Calif., 1954-60; dir. Nat. Engring. Sci. Co., Pasadena, Calif., 1960-61; dir. spacecraft scis. Aerospace Corp., El Segundo, Calif., 1961-64, gen. mgr. applied mechanics div., 1964-68, v.p., gen. mgr. engring. sci. ops., 1968-78, v.p. engring. group, 1978-82, cons., 1982—; mem. BSD Re-entry Panel, 1961-63, NASA com. missile and space vehicle aerodynamics, 1963-65; mem. adv. com. AFML, 1971-72; mem. NASA Adv. Council, 1982-86 ; chmn. NASA Space Applications Adv. Com., 1982-86 ; mem. Aeros. and Space Engring. Bd., NRC, 1982-87; mem. Space Sta. Task Force, NRC, 1983-87, Shuttle Criticality and Hazard Analysis Rev. Bd., 1986-88, DSB NASP Task Force, 1987-88, AFSB Hypersonic Task Force, 1987-88. Contbr. articles to profl. jours. Mem. alumni fund coun. Calif. Inst. Tech., 1972-74; trustee West Coast U., 1980-92; bd. councilors U. So. Calif. Sch. Engring., 1976-86; mem. devel. disabilities bd. Area X, 1976-80, chmn., 1976-78; 1st v.p. Calif. Assn. Retarded, 1983-85 ; pres. Exceptional Children's Found., 1970-72. Recipient Disting. Alumni award U. Mich., 1969, Golden Rule award Calif. Assn. Retarded, 1977, 89. Fellow Inst. Advanced Engring., AIAA (chmn. Los Angeles sect. 1967-68, bd. dirs. 1975-77, pres. 1980-81), AAAS; mem. Technion Soc., Nat. Acad. Engring., Sigma Xi. Home and Office: 1353 Woodruff Ave Los Angeles CA 90024-5129

MAGER, EZRA PASCAL, automobile dealership executive; b. N.Y.C., Nov. 1, 1941; s. Harold and Naomi (Levinson) M.; m. Sarah Johnson, Mar. 25, 1964 9div.); 1 child, Emma Rachel; m. Reeva Starkman, May 14, 1972; children: Camilla Elizabeth, Michael Johanon. BA, Cornell U., 1963; MBA, Harvard, 1966. Successively v.p., sr. v.p., exec. v.p. and dir. Seiden & DeCuevas, Inc., N.Y.C., 1966-73; exec. v.p., dir. Furman Selz Mager Dietz & Birney, Inc., N.Y.C., 1973-90; vice chmn. United Auto Group, Inc., N.Y.C., 1990-96, Cross Continent Auto Retailers, Inc., N.Y.C., 1996-97, First Team Auto Corp., N.Y.C., 1997—. Pres. Baron de Hirsch Fund. Mem. N.Y. Soc. Security Analysts, Alpha Delta Phi. Democrat. Club: Harvard (N.Y.C.). Home: 141 E 72nd St New York NY 10021-4367 Office: First Team Auto Corp 540 Madison Ave Ste 3000 New York NY 10022-3213

MAGGAY, ISIDORE, III, engineering executive, food processing engineer; b. San Diego, Calif., Sept. 12, 1952; s. Isidore Jr. and Dolores (Ambay) M.; m. Karen Elizabeth, Dec. 25, 1981; children: Adrienne Leigh, Brittany Elizabeth. BSME, Calif. Maritime Acad., 1973; MBA, Nat. U., 1980. Registered environ. assessor, Calif.; cert. hazardous material contractor, Calif. Project engr. Ralston Purina, San Diego, 1976-78; dist. engr. Carnation Co., L.A., 1978-81; dir. engring. Sara Lee Corp., San Francisco, 1981-85; v.p. engring. Alex Foods Inc., Anaheim, Calif., 1986-89; pres. Acad. Engring., Vista, Calif., 1989—; gen. engring. contractor, Contractors State Lic. Bd., Calif., 1989—. Commr. Environ. Quality Commn., Vista, 1991-92. Lt. Commdr. USNR, 1973—. Mem. Am. Inst. Plant Engrs., Environ. Assessment Assn., Nat. Soc. Profl. Engrs. Roman Catholic. Office: 1045 Linda Vista Dr Ste 107 San Marcos CA 92069-2622

MAGGIO, MICHAEL JOHN, artistic director; b. Chgo., July 3, 1951; s. Carlo and Genevieve (Sparacino) M.; m. Janice St. John, Sept. 7, 1974 (div. June 1977); m. Julie Carol Jackson, Mar. 29, 1980 (div. Dec. 1994); 1 child, Ben. BA, U. Ariz., 1973, MA, 1974. Artistic dir. Woodstock (Ill.) Music Theatre Festival, 1980-82, Northlight Theatre, Evanston, Ill., 1983-87; assoc. artistic dir. Goodman Theatre, Chgo., 1987—; artistic advisor Columbia Coll., Chgo., 1987—. Directed Another Midsummer Night, Brutality of Fact, Black Snow, Wings, Shakespeare's A Midsummer Night's Dream, Romeo and Juliet, Uncle Vanya, 1989-90, A Flea In Her Ear, A Christmas Carol, Sunday In The Park With George, Cyrano De Bergerac, The Front Page, The Dining Room; artistic dir. Northlight Theatre premieres of Dealing, City On The Make, Heart of A Dog, (Am. premiere) Ballerina, (world premiere) Sondheim Suite; dir. The Real Thing, West Memphis Mojo, Highest Standard of Living, Endgame, The Winter's Tale, Travesties, Tartuffe, Spokesong, Ladies In Waiting; dir. prodn. of Titus Andronicus for N.Y. Shakespeare Festival; prodns. include McCarter Theatre, Guthrie Theater in Mpls., The Cleve. Playhouse, Ariz. Theatre Co., Actors Theatre of Louisville, Seattle Repertory Co. chmn. Michael Merritt Award and Endowment Fund, Colubmia Coll, Chgo. Recipient Joseph Jefferson "Jeff" Citation 1975-76. 78, 93-94, Father of Yr. award, Chgo. Father's Day Com., 1986, Excellence in Arts award De Paul U. Theatre Sch., 1993, Obie award, 1993,. Office: Goodman Theatre 200 S Columbus Dr Chicago IL 60603-6402

MAGGIOLO, ALLISON JOSEPH, lawyer; b. New River, N.C., Aug. 29, 1943; s. Allison and Florence Celeste (Vago) M. Cert., U. Paris-Sorbonne, 1965; AB, Brown U., 1966; JD, U. Louisville, 1975. Bar: Ky. 1976, U.S. Dist. Ct. (we. dist.) Ky. 1981. Ops. mgr., stockbroker Bache & Co., Louisville, 1970-73; ptnr. Reisz, Blackburn, Manly & Treitz, Louisville, 1976-78, Greenebaum Boone Treitz Maggiolo & Brown, Louisville, 1978-91, Wyatt, Tarrant & Combs, Louisville, 1991—; workshop panelist Fin. Adv. Coun., 1994; panelist Seminar on Defaulted Bond Issues, 1987-89, Bond Counsel and the Corp. Trustee, 1990-92, Defaults and Workouts, 1993. Author: Indenture Trustee Liability and Defaulted Bond Issues, 1987, Minimizing Indenture Trustee Liability and Defaulted Bond Issues, 1991, Bond Default Resolution, 1993; co-author: The legal Aspects of Doing International Business in Kentucky, 1990. Exec. com. Louisville Com. Fgn. Rels., 1979—, chmn., 1991-96; bd. dirs. Ky. Opera, Louisville, 1978-91, mem. hon. coun., 1991—; bd. dirs. Ky. Show, Louisville, 1980-88. 1st lt. U.S. Army, 1966-69, Vietnam. Decorated Bronze Star. Mem. Internat. Bar Assn., Nat. Assn. Bond Lawyers, Bond Attys. Workshop (planning com. 1991-93), Pendennis Club, Wynn Stay Club, Jefferson Club. Office: Wyatt Tarrant & Combs Citizens Plz Louisville KY 40202

MAGGIORE, SUSAN, geophysical oceanographer; b. Newark, Mar. 14, 1957; d. John James and Marietta Nancy (Testa) M.; m. Stephen P. Garreffa, Oct. 21, 1989; children: Julianna Garreffa, Marietta Garreffa. BS in Geosci., Montclair State U., 1978; postgrad., U. So. Miss., 1981-84. Supr. rsch. and communications The Cousteau Soc., N.Y.C. and Norfolk, Va., 1979-81; geophysicist Naval Oceanographic Office, Bay St. Louis, Miss., 1981-85, NE Consortium Oceanographic Research, Narragansett, R.I., 1985-86; mem. tech. staff Lucent Technologies (formerly AT&T Bell Labs.), Whippany, N.J., 1986—; writer, creative cons. The Cousteau Soc., Los Angeles, 1981-89. Researcher book The Cousteau Almanac of the Environment, 1981; contbr. articles to profl. jours. Vol. Dover (N.J.) Gen. Hosp., 1987-88. Mem. Am. Geophys. Union, Marine Tech. Soc., Nat. Assn. Female Execs. Roman Catholic. Avocations: singing, playing musical instruments, reading, cooking, bridge. Office: Lucent Techs 67 Whippany Rd Whippany NJ 07981-1406

MAGGS, PETER BLOUNT, lawyer, educator; b. Durham, N.C., July 24, 1936; s. Douglas Blount and Dorothy (Mackay) M.; m. Barbara Ann Widenor, Feb. 27, 1960; children: Bruce MacDowell, Gregory Eaton, Stephanie Ann, Katherine Ellen. AB, Harvard U., 1957, JD, 1961; postgrad. (exchange student), Leningrad (USSR) State U., 1961-62. Bar: D.C. 1962. Research assoc. Law Sch. Harvard U., 1963-64; asst. prof. law U. Ill., 1964-67, assoc. prof., 1967-69, prof., 1969-88, William and Marie Corman prof., 1988—, acting dean, 1990; dir. rule of law program Washington, 1994; Fulbright lectr. Moscow State U., 1977; reporter Uniform Simplification of Land Transfers Act. Author: (with others) The Soviet Legal system, 1984, (with O.S. Ioffe) Soviet Law in Theory and Practice, 1983, (with others) Unfair Trade Practice and Consumer Protection, 1992; (with J. Sprowl) Computer Applications in the Law, 1987, (with others) Computer Law, 1992, The Mandelstam File, 1996; designer talking computers for the blind. Fulbright rsch. scholar, Yugoslavia, 1967; East-West Ctr. fellow, 1972, Guggenheim fellow, 1979. Mem. ABA (chmn. com. on Soviet law sect. internat. law 1976-80), Bar Assn. of the Dist. of Columbia, Am. Assn. Advancement Slavic Studies, Assn. Am. Law Schs. (chmn. sect. comparative law 1977), Am. Law Inst. (consultative group, UCC Article 2), Am. Acad. Fgn. Law, Internat. Acad. Comparative Law. Office: U Ill Coll Law 504 E Pennsylvania Ave Champaign IL 61820-6909

MAGID, GAIL AVRUM, neurosurgeon, neurosurgery educator; b. Chgo., Oct. 15, 1934; s. Harry M. and Henrietta (Busch) M.; m. Janet Louise Reinhardt, June 15, 1962 (div.); children: Allison Magid London, Jonathan Alward; m. Roseanne Cipra Muirhead, Sept. 4, 1982. BSc, U. Ill., 1954; MD, Chgo. Med. Sch., 1958. Diplomate Am. Bd. Neurol. Surgery. Intern Cook County Hosp., Chgo., 1958-59; resident, then fellow neurol. surgery Mayo Clinic, Rochester, Minn., 1959-61, 63-65; clin. instr. neurosurgery U. Calif., San Francisco, 1965-70, asst. clin. prof., 1970-79, assoc. prof., 1979—; chmn. Dominican Neurol. Inst., Santa Cruz, Calif., 1975—; bd. dirs. Dominican Found.; cons. neurosurgery U.S. Army, San Francisco Gen. Hosp. Assoc. editor: Clinical Neurosurgery, 1974. Bd. dirs. Santa Cruz Symphony Assn., 1983-85, U. Calif. Friends of Arts, Santa Cruz, 1985-86. Served to lt. comdr. USN, 1961-63. Fellow ACS, Internat. Coll. Surgeons; mem. AMA, Calif. Med. Assn., Internat. Soc. Pediatric Neurosurgeons, Am. Assn. Neurol. Surgeons, We. Neurosurg. Soc. (v.p. 1996—), Cong. Neurol. Surgeons, San Francisco Neurol. Soc. (pres.-elect 1991, pres. 1992), St. Francis Yacht Club (San Francisco). Republican. Home: 241 4th Ave Santa Cruz CA 95062-3815 Office: 1661 Soquel Dr Santa Cruz CA 95065-1709

MAGIELNICKI, ROBERT L., lawyer; b. Perth Amboy, N.J., Mar. 28, 1947; s. Leon C. and Dorothy M. (Hudanish) M.; m. Kathleen J. Urban, June 14, 1969; children: Robert Jr., Kimberly, Peter, Matthew. AB with honors, Rutgers U., 1967; JD with distinction, Cornell U., 1970. Bar: N.Y. 1971, U.S. Supreme Ct. 1974, D.C. 1990. Commd. lt. USN, 1968; assoc. Donovan Leisure Newton & Irvine, N.Y.C., 1970-71, 74-80; asst. staff judge advocate U.S. Naval Base Subic Bay, Republic of Philippines, 1971-73; asst. prof. law U.S. Naval Acad., Annapolis, Md., 1973-74; assoc. litigation and antitrust counsel Gen. Elec. Corp. Hdqs., Fairfield, Conn., 1980-83, counsel, 1989-90; divsn. gen. counsel Gen. Elec. Factory Automation Products, Charlottesville, Va., 1983-88; ptnr. Kutak Rock, Washington, 1990—. Avocations: tennis, golf, swimming, reading. Office: Kutak Rock 1101 Connecticut Ave NW Washington DC 20036-4303

MAGIERA, FRANK EDWARD, journalist, critic; b. Webster, Mass., Nov. 28, 1945; s. Charles Frank and Marion Margaret (Kralik) M.; m. Janice Lee Rayner, Aug. 20, 1977. BS, Worcester Poly. Inst., 1967. Reporter Worcester (Mass.) Telegram & Gazette, 1970—, drama critic, 1978-89, art critic, 1989—. Lt. (j.g.) USN, 1968-70. Democrat. Avocations: farming, painting, woodworking. Home: Lawrence Rd Dudley MA 01571 Office: Worcester Telegram & Gazette 20 Franklin St Worcester MA 01608-1904

MAGILL, DODIE BURNS, early childhood education educator; b. Greenwood, S.C., July 10, 1952; d. Byron Bernard and Dora Curry B.; m. Charles Towner Magill, May 4, 1974; children: Charles Towner II, Emily Curry. BA, Furman U., 1974; MEd, U. S.C., 1978. Cert. tchr., early childhood, elementary, elementary principal, supv., S.C. Kindergarten tchr. Sch. Dist. Greenville County, 1974-83; early childhood edn. instr. Valdosta (Ga.) State Univ., 1983-84; dir. lower sch. Valwood Sch., Valdosta, 1984-86; kindergarten tchr. Sch. Dist. Greenville County, 1986—; tchr.-in-residence S.C. Ctr. for Tchr. Recruitment, Rock Hill, 1993, mem. policy bd.; workshop presenter and lectr. in various schs. and sch. dists. throughout U.S., 1974—; chmn. S.C. Pub. Kindergarten Celebration, 1994; giv. S.C. State Readiness Policy Group; mem. Southeastern Region Vision for Edn. Adv. Bd., S.C. Coun. Ednl. Collaboration. Demonstration tchr. S.C. ETV (TV show) Sch. Begins with Kindergarten. Mem. Gov. of S.C.'s State Readiness Policy Group, Southeastern Regional Vision for Edn. Adv. Bd., South Carolina Ctr. Tchr. Recruitment Policy Bd. Recipient Ralph Witherspoon award S.C. Assn. for Children Under Six; named Tchr. of Yr., Greenville County, 1992, 93, State of S.C., 1993, S.C. Tchr. of Yr. Coun. of Chief State Sch. Officers, 1993, 94. Mem. Assn. for Childhood Edn. Internat., S.C. Tchr. Forum (chmn. 1993-94), S.C. Early Childhood Assn., Alpha Delta Kappa. Presbyterian. Office: Mountain Park Elem Sch 1500 Pounds Rd SW Lilburn GA 30047-6708

MAGILL, FRANK JOHN, federal judge; b. Verona, N.D., June 3, 1927; s. Thomas Charles and Viola Magill; m. Mary Louise Timlin, Nov. 22, 1955; children: Frank Jr., Marguerite Connolly, R. Daniel, Mary Elizabeth, Robert, John. BS in Fgn. Service, Georgetown U., 1951, LLB, 1955; MA, Columbia U., 1952. Ptnr. Nilles, Hansen, Magill & Davies, Ltd., Fargo, N.D., 1955-86; judge U.S. Ct. Appeals (8th cir.), Fargo, 1986—. Chmn. fin. disclosure com. U.S. Jud. Conf., 1993—. Fellow Am. Coll. Trial Lawyers; mem. N.D. Bar Assn. (chmn. legis. com. 1975), Cass County Bar Assn. (pres. 1970). Republican. Avocations: tennis, sailing, skiing. Home: 1711 7th St S Fargo ND 58103-4945 Office: US Ct Appeals 8th Circuit 248 US PO & Fed Bldg 657 2nd Ave N Fargo ND 58102-4727

MAGILL, SAMUEL HAYS, retired academic administrator, higher education consultant; b. Decatur, Ga., July 19, 1928; s. Orrin Rankin and Ellen Howe (Bell) M.; m. Martha H. Carmichael, 1988; children: Samuel Hays Jr., Katherine Magill Walters, Suzanne Magill Weintraub. A.B., U. N.C., 1950; B.D., Yale U., 1953; Ph.D., Duke U., 1962; LHD (hon.), Stockton State Coll., 1990. Ordained to ministry Congl. Christian Ch., 1953; gen. sec. Davidson Coll. YMCA, 1953-55; dir. student activities U. N.C., Chapel Hill, 1955-58, asst. dean student affairs, 1958-59; chaplain Dickinson Coll., 1962-63, asst. prof. religion, 1962-66, asso. prof. religion, 1966-68, dean coll., 1963-68; pres. Council Protestant Colls. and Univs., Washington, 1968-70; exec. asso., chief office acad. affairs Assn. Am. Colls., 1971-76; pres. Simon's Rock Early Coll., Great Barrington, Mass., 1976-79; pres. Monmouth U., West Long Branch, N.J., 1980-93, pres. emeritus, 1993—; higher edn. cons., 1993—; adj. prof. Duke U., 1996. Trustee Jersey Shore Med. Ctr., 1985-93; bd. overseers N.J. Gov.'s Schs., 1986-93. Guerney Harris Kearns fellow in religion, 1960-61; Danforth Found. spl. grad. fellow, 1959-61. Fellow Soc. Values in Higher Edn. (dir. 1969-81); mem. Am. Assembly Collegiate Sch. Bus. (accreditation task force 1989-90), NCAA (pres.'s commn. 1990-93), Am. Coun. Edn. (commn. leadership devel. 1982-85, commn. on minority affairs 1986-89), Harvard Inst. Ednl. Mgmt., Assn. Ind. Colls. and Univs. N.J. (dir. 1980-93, exec. com. 1983—, chair 1987-89), U.S. Assn. for Club of Rome, Order of Golden Fleece U. N.C., Delta Psi, Omicron Delta Kappa. Home: 1058 Fearrington Post Pittsboro NC 27312

MAGINN, STEPHEN ARTHUR, financial company executive; b. Orange, N.J., Mar. 5, 1952; s. Wallace Alton and La Verne (Chappell) M.; m. Linda Marie Stewart, Oct. 7, 1989; children: Brett Marshall, Todd Randall, Ryan Michael, Sean Christopher. BS in Commerce, U. Va., 1974. Cert. gen. securities prin. Nat. Assn. Securities Dealers. Securities broker Merrill Lynch, Newark, 1974-77, A.G. Becker, Inc., N.Y.C., 1977-79; regional v.p. Petro-Lewis Securities Corp., Denver, 1979-85; sr. v.p., co-founder Greystone Securities, Evergreen, Colo., 1985-86; regional v.p. NTS Securities, Louisville, 1986-87; sr. v.p., regional mgr. G.T. Global Fin. Svcs. (now GT Global, Inc.), San Francisco, 1987—. Mem. Internat. Assn. for Fin. Planning (nat. bd. dirs.). Avocations: golf, fine wine collecting, sailing. Home: 519 S Juanita Ave Redondo Beach CA 90277-3827 Office: GT Global Inc 50 California St Fl 27 San Francisco CA 94111

MAGLACAS, A. MANGAY, nursing researcher, educator. BSN, Vanderbilt U.; MPH, U. Minn.; DPH, Johns Hopkins U.; DSc (hon.), U. Ill. Chief sci. for nursing divsn. health manpower devel. WHO, Geneva, Switzerland; adj. prof. Coll. Nursing, U. Ill., Chgo.; various vis. prof. positions in several countries; cons. in field. Rockefeller fellow, 1964-67; Fulbright-Smith-Mundt scholar, 1952-54; recipient Alumni Internat. Leadership in Pub. Health award Vanderbilt U., 1986, Profl. Recognition award U. Philippines, 1989, Alumni award Johns Hopkins U., 1992. Mem. Internat. Coun. Nurses (bd. dirs.), NAS Inst. Medicine (fgn. assoc.). Office: 59 Chemin de Planta, CH-1223 Cologny Switzerland

MAGLICH, BOGDAN CASTLE, physicist; b. Yugoslavia, Aug. 5, 1938; came to U.S., 1956, naturalized, 1972; s. Cveta and Ivanka (Bingulac) M.; children: Marko Castle, Ivanka Taylor, Roberta Cveta, Angelica Dara, Aleksandra Mara Nadine. Diploma physics, U. Belgrade, 1951; MS, U. Liverpool, Eng., 1955; PhD, MIT, 1959. Staff mem. Lawrence Berkeley Lab., 1959-62; dep. group leader Brit. group, 1962-63; leader Swiss group CERN European Orgn. Nuclear Rsch., 1964-67; vis. prof., joint faculty mem. Princeton U.-U. Pa. accelerator U. Pa., 1967-69; prof. physics, prin. investigator high energy physics Rutgers U., 1969-74; pres., chmn. Fusion Energy Corp., Princeton, N.J., 1972-81, Aneutronix, Inc., 1982-83, Sci. Transfer Assocs., Inc., 1981-84, United Scis., Inc., 1984-87, AE Labs Aneutronic Energy Lab., Inc., 1986-88; pres. Advanced Physics Corp., 1988-94; chmn. Advanced Projects Group, Inc., 1994—, HiEnergy Microdevices, Ltd., 1995—; chmn. The Tesla Found., 1985—; resident scientist UN-ILO Seminar Econ. Devel. East Africa, Kenya, 1967; lectr. Postdoctoral Sch. Physics, Yerevan, USSR, 1965, Internat. Sch. Majorana, Italy, 1969; mem. U.S. delegation Internat. Conf. High Energy Physics, Vienna, 1968, Kiev, 1970; spl. rep. of U.S. Pres. to Yugoslavia, 1976; sci. project dir. Univ. Research Ctr., King Abdulaziz U., Saudi Arabia, 1981-82; prin. investigator for aneutronic energy USAF Weapons Lab., 1985-87, USAF Space Tech. Ctr., 1988-89. Editor: Adventures in Exptl. Physics, 1972-80, Living Physics Video Jour. Chmn. Yugoslav-Am. Bicentennial Com., 1975-76; co-chmn. Serbian-Am. Com. for a Dem. Yugoslavia, 1989—; pres. World Serbian Union, Geneva, 1990-92. Recipient White House citation, 1961; Bourgeois d'honneur de Lens Switzerland, 1973; UNESCO fellow, 1957-58. Fellow Am. Phys. Soc.; mem. Serbian Acad. Scis. and Arts (Yugoslavia), Ripon Soc. (bd. govs.), Nassau Club, MIT Club, Sigma Xi. Mem. Serbian Orthodox Ch. Discoverer omega-meson, sonic spark chamber, missing-mass spectrometer, delta-meson, g-meson, S, T and U-mesons, precetron, self collider migma, aneutronic energy process, minebuster, and bombuster; patentee in field.

MAGLIOCCA, LARRY ANTHONY, education educator; b. New Castle, Pa., Sept. 3, 1943; s. Anthony Norman Magliocca and Madeline Rose Ross; m. Judie Alene Kerr, Sept. 1, 1964 (div.); children: Jeannine Marie, Seth Bryan; m. Phyllis Marion Gentry, May 9, 1981 (div.); 1 child, Nicholas Rossi; m. Karen Elizabeth Sanders, Jan. 23, 1996. BSEd, Slippery Rock State Coll., 1967; MEd, U. Pitts., 1970; PhD, Ohio State U., 1978. Dir. Youth Devel. Ctr. of Pa., New Castle, 1967-70; state cons. S.D. Dept. Pub. Inst., Pierre, S.D., 1970-73; coord. Balt. City Pub. Schs., 1973-76; exec. dir. Ctr. for Spl. Needs Population, Columbus, Ohio, 1979—; assoc. prof. Ohio State U., Columbus, 1988—; vis. lectr. Melbourne (Australia) State Coll., 1978-79; adj. faculty Johns Hopkins U., Balt., 1974-76; blue ribbon task force, Chgo. City Pub. Schs., 1985. Author three books in spl. edn. field, 1978-92; contbr. articles to profl. jours.; editor: The Directive Teacher jour., 1976-84; author/designer instructional materials in math. problem solving, 1992. Founder Young Scientists Club, Westerville, Ohio, 1990-92; rsch. fellow Internat. Sys. Inst., 1994-96. Mem. Soc. for Gen. Systems Rsch., Am. Assn. for Artificial Intelligence, Coun. for Exceptional Children. Democrat. Unitarian-Universalist. Avocations: poetry, travel. Office: Ctr Spl Needs Populations 700 Ackerman Rd Ste 440 Columbus OH 43202-1559

MAGLIOCCO, JOHN, wholesale distribution executive; b. 1942. BS in Econs., U. Pa., 1963. With Peerless Importers Inc., 1963—, v.p., 1965-77, pres., 1978-85, chmn., 1986, CEO. Office: 16 Bridgewater St Brooklyn NY 11222-3804*

MAGLIONE, LILI, fine artist, art consultant; b. Manhasset, N.Y., Jan. 30, 1929; d. Angelo and Mary (Marciano) M.; m. Bernhert H. Rumphorst, June 1, 1957; children: Catherine, Douglas. AD, Traphagen Sch., N.Y.C., 1950; studetn, Art Students League, N.Y.C., 1950-52. Fashion artist Butterick Pattern Co., N.Y.C., 1952-53; fashion art cons. Miss. America Inc., N.Y.C., 1953-54; dept. head fashion art office Simplicity Pattern Co., N.Y.C., 1953-58, fashion art cons., 1958-62; art dept. cons. Nassau County Mus., Roslyn, N.Y., 1984-86; dir. decorative affairs Harbor Acres Assn., Port Washington, N.Y., 1987-89, Sands Point (N.Y.) Mus., 1989-91; art cons. Horst Design Assocs., Huntington, N.Y., 1992—. Exhibited paintings in one-woman shows at Palm Gallery, Southampton, N.Y., 1980, Art Internat., Chgo., 1985, Isis Gallery, Port Washington, 1987, Gallery 84, N.Y.C., 1989, 91, 93; one woman retrospective shows include Harkness Gallery, 1978, James Hunt Barker Gallery, 1984, Sands Point Mus., 1988, Fairfield U., 995. Mem. Nat. Assn. Women Artists, Nat. Mus. Women in the Arts. Roman Catholic. Avocations: horticulture, flower arrangement, nutrition, music, child care. Home: 7 Harmony Rd Huntington NY 11743

MAGNABOSCO, LOUIS MARIO, chemical engineer, researcher, consultant; b. Glarus, Switzerland, Nov. 29, 1938; s. Josef and Maria (Schlittler) M.; m. Vreni S. Zentner, Mar. 18, 1966 (div. Sept. 1985); 1 child, Henry Louis; m. D'Ella P. Phelon, Apr. 25, 1990; 1 child, Deon M. BSChemE, Swiss Fed. Inst. Tech., Zurich, 1961, MSChemE, 1963, ScD, 1967. Sr. scientist FMC Corp., Santa Clara, Calif., 1967-68; from engr. to project engr. Shell Devel. Co., Emeryville, Calif., 1968-72; sr. engr. Shell Devel. Co., Houston, 1972-74, staff engr., 1974-76; processing specialist ARCO, Harvey, Ill., 1976-79; mgr. process devel. ARCO, Harvey, 1979-85; cons. Magna Assocs., Olympia Fields, Ill., 1985-87; mgr. processes and catalysis Enimont, Zurich, 1987-90; pres. Chem. Engring. Ptnrs., Newport Beach, Calif., 1990-93; v.p. R&D Intercat, Sea Girt, N.J., 1993-94; cons. Magna Assocs., 1994—. Contbr. articles to internat. profl. jours.; conducted seminars and gave lectures on hydroprocessing internationally in petroleum field. Mem. AIChE, AAAS, Am. Chem. Soc. Catalysis Club. Achievements include: invention and development of Fluid Catalytic Cracking Sulfur Oxide Reduction Tech. (DESOX and NOSOX technologies); developer of math. models for: hydrotreating, hydrocracking, other petroleum processes, recycling tech. used motor oils, semi-synthetic lube oil process (H-H process). Avocations: reading, tennis, travels.

MAGNANO, SALVATORE PAUL, retired financial executive, treasurer; b. Portland, Conn., Jan. 10, 1934; s. Salvatore and Lucy (Dimodica) M.; m. Lois Jewel Johnson, July 16, 1955; children: Paul C., Mark J., Peter E. B.Metall. Engring., Rensselaer Poly. Inst., Troy, N.Y., 1955; MBA, Northwestern U., Chgo., 1959. Div. controller Sanders Assocs., Inc., Nashua, N.H., 1962-73; v.p., controller Teledyne Mec, Palo Alto, Calif., 1973-75; div. controller Sanders Assocs., Inc., Nashua, 1975-79; grp. controller Sanders Assocs., Inc., 1979-81, grp. v.p., controller, 1981-86, v.p. fin. and treas., 1986-96; ind. fin. & adminstrv. cons. Pres. Boys and Girls Club of Greater Nashua, 1988-89, bd. dirs., 1981—; bd. dirs. Boys and Girls Club of Greater Nashua Charitable Found., 1991—; trustee Daniel Webster Coll., Nashua, 1993—. Lt. USN, 1955-57. Mem. Fin. Execs. Inst., Beta Gamma Sigma (award for excellence 1959).

MAGNER, JEROME ALLEN, entertainment company executive; b. Bklyn., Mar. 14, 1929; s. Herman and Evelyn I. (Wolfe) M.; BBA cum laude, CCNY, 1951; m. Frances Ogens, Mar. 22, 1953; children: Merrill, Steven. Asst. to treas., chief acct. Grayson-Robinson Stores, Inc., S. Klein Dept. Stores, Inc., N.Y.C., 1951-59; controller Food Fair Properties, N.Y.C., 1959-61; v.p., controller Am. Leisure Products Corp., N.Y.C. and Providence, 1961-69; sr. v.p. fin., treas., CFO Nat. Amusements, Inc., NE Theatre Corp., Dedham, 1969—. Mem. Met. Controllers Congress, Nat. Assn. Accts., Am. Mgmt. Assn., Nat. Assn. Theatre Owners (bd. dirs.), CCNY Alumni Assn. Office: Nat Amusements Inc 200 Elm St Dedham MA 02026-4536

MAGNES, HARRY ALAN, physician; b. Orange, N.J., Dec. 3, 1948; s. Sam and Shirley (Daniels) M.; m. Patricia Bruce, Mar. 25, 1989; 1 child, Carlos Fontiveros. AB in Biology magna cum laude, Brown U., 1970; MD, Yale U., 1974. Diplomate Am. Bd. Internal Medicine, Am. Bd. Med. Mgmt. Intern, resident internal medicine U. Iowa Hosps. and Clinics, 1974-77; ptnr., med. dir., pres., CEO Gallatin Med. Clinic, Downey, Calif., 1977—; pres., CEO Gallatin Med. Corp., Downey, Calif., 1992-94; med. dir., bd. dirs. Gallatin Med. Found., Downey, Calif., 1993—; staff physician Downey Cmty. Hosp., 1977-96, Presbyn. Intercmty. Hosp., 1992—; clin. instr. Rancho Los Amigos Hosp., Downey, 1981-83; chairperson bd. dirs. Primehealth of So. Calif., 1997—; bd. dirs. California Health Network; project adv. bd. VA/UCLA/RAND Calif. MEd. Group, IPA Givernance Project, 1997—. Author: Rheumatic Fever in Connecticut, 1974. James Manning scholar Brown U., 1968. Mem. ACPE, Healthcare Assn. So. Calif., Am. Coll. Med. Practice Execs., Am. Med. Group Assn. (med. policy com. 1994—, legis. com. 1997—), Med. Group Mgmt. Assn., Sigma Xi, Phi Beta Kappa. Avocation: racquetball. Office: Gallatin Med Found 10720 Paramount Blvd Downey CA 90241-3306

MAGNESS, RHONDA ANN, microbiologist; b. Stockton, Calif., Jan. 30, 1946; d. John Pershing and Dorothy Waneta (Kelley) Wetter; m. Barney LeRoy Bender, Aug. 26, 1965 (div. 1977); m. Gary D. Magness, Mar. 5, 1977; children: Jay D. (dec.), Troy D. BS, Calif. State U., 1977. Lic. clin. lab. scientist Nat. Cert. Agy., Calif., med. technologist; cert. clin. lab. scientist. Med. asst. C. Fred Wilcox, MD, Stockton, 1965-66; clk. typist Dept. of U.S. Army, Ft. Eustis, Va., 1967, Def. Supply Agy., New Orleans, 1967-68; med. asst. James G. Cross, MD, Lodi, Calif., 1969, Arthur A. Kemalyan, MD, Lodi, 1969-71, 72-77; med. sec. Lodi Meml. Hosp., 1972; lab. aide Calif. State U., Sacramento, 1977; phlebotomist St. Joseph's Hosp., Stockton, 1978-79; supr. microbiology Dameron Hosp. Assn., Stockton, 1980—. Active Concerned Women Am., Washington, 1987—. Mem. AAUW, Calif. Assn. Clin. Lab. Technologists, San Joaquin County Med. Assts. Assn., Nat. Geog. Soc., Nat. Audubon Soc. Baptist. Lodge: Jobs Daus. (chaplain 1962-63). Avocations: boating, snow and water skiing, birding, sewing, reading. Home: 9627 Knight Ln Stockton CA 95209-1961 Office: Dameron Hosp Lab 525 W Acacia St Stockton CA 95203-2405

MAGNUS, FREDERICK SAMUEL, investment banker; b. Montclair, N.J., Aug. 26, 1932; s. Robert Frederick and Cora (Argue) M. BA, Rutgers U., 1954. Rep., T.L. Watson Co., 1956-57, Goodbody & Co., 1957-58; pres., dir. Godfrey Hamilton & Magnus Co., 1958-61; pres., dir. Magnus & Co., Inc., Clifton, 1961—. With U.S. Army, 1954-56. Office: Magnus & Co Inc 575 Grove St Clifton NJ 07013-3173

MAGNUS, KATHY JO, religious organization executive; b. Brainerd, Minn., Oct. 22, 1946; d. Fred L. and Doris K. (Anderson) Kunkel; m. Richard A. Magnus, Dec. 17, 1966; children: Erica Jo, Cory Allan. BS, U. Minn., 1968. Tchr. St. Paul Schs., 1968-69, Denver Pub. Schs., 1969-75; dir. comm. St. Paul Luth. Ch., Denver, 1979-81; adminstrv. asst. to bishop Rocky Mountain Synod Luth. Ch. Am., Denver, 1981-87; exec. staff Rocky Mountain Synod Evang. Luth. Ch. Am., Denver, 1988—; v.p. Evangel. Luth. Ch. in Am., 1991—. Named exemplar of univ. Calif. Luth. U., 1992. Avocations: writing, reading. Office: Evang Luthern Ch in Am 7000 Broadway Ste 401 Denver CO 80221-2926

MAGNUSON, HAROLD JOSEPH, physician; b. Halstead, Kans., Mar. 31, 1913; s. Joseph Simeon and Margaret Ethel (Matson) M.; m. Ruth Prusia, Feb. 16, 1935 (dec. 1941); children: Karen Margaret Magnuson Mauro), Ruth Ellen; m. Kathryne I. Bause, Dec. 20, 1941 (dec. 1993). AB, U. So. Calif., 1934, MD, 1938; MPH, Johns Hopkins U., 1942. Diplomate: Am. Bd. Preventive Medicine (mem. bd. 1964-75, vice chmn. occupational medicine 1968-75). Intern Los Angeles County Gen. Hosp., 1937-39; research fellow A.C.P., 1939-40; instr. medicine U. So. Calif., 1939-41; commd. asst. surgeon USPHS, 1941, med. dir., 1952; instr. medicine Johns Hopkins, 1943-46; research prof. exptl. medicine U. N.C., 1946-55; chief div. occupational health USPHS, 1956-62; ret., 1962; prof. internal medicine U. Mich. Sch. Medicine, prof. indsl. health, 1962-76, prof. emeritus, 1976—; chmn. dept. U. Mich. Sch. Pub. Health; also dir. U. Mich. Sch. Pub. Health (Inst. Indsl. Health), 1962-69; asso. dean U. Mich. Sch. Pub. Health (Sch. Pub. Health), 1969-76; Mem. U.S. delegation ILO Conf., 1958, 59; Chmn. U.S. indsl. toxicology delegation to, USSR, 1963. Fellow A.C.P., A.A.A.S., A.M.A. (chmn. sect. preventive medicine 1966, Hektoen bronze medal 1956), Am. Acad. Occupational Medicine, Am. Pub. Health Assn. (chmn. sect. occupational health 1966, Indsl. Med. Assn., Knudsen award 1970); mem. Soc. Clin. Investigation, Soc. Exptl. Biology and Medicine, Soc. Exptl. Pathology, Mich. Indsl. Med. Assn. (pres. 1965-66), Internat. Congress Indsl. Medicine (v.p. 1969), Rammazzini Soc., Phi Beta Kappa, Sigma Xi, Alpha Omega Alpha, Delta Omega. Home: 18755 W Bernardo Dr Apt 1125 San Diego CA 92127-3023

MAGNUSON, JOHN JOSEPH, zoology educator; b. Evanston, Ill., Mar. 8, 1934. BS, U. Minn., 1956, MS, 1958; PhD in Zoology, U. B.C., 1961. Chief tuna behavior program Biol. Lab. Bur. Comml. Fisheries U.S. Fish & Wildlife Svc., Honolulu, 1961-67; program dir. ecology NSF, Washington, 1975-76; asst. prof. to assoc. prof. U. Wis., Madison, 1968-74, chmn. oceanography & limnology grad. program, 1978-83, 86, prof. zoology, dir. Troup Lake Biol. Sta., 1974—, dir. Ctr. Limnology, 1982—; lead investigator North Temperate Lakes Long Term Ecol. Rsch. site, NSF, U. Wis., 1981—; chmn. Aquatic Ecol. sect. Ecol. Soc. Am., 1975-76; chair Com. Fisheries, Nat. Rsch. Coun., 1981-83, 93-94; chmn. Com. Sea Turtle Conservancy, 1989-90, chmn. Com. Protection & Mgmt. Pacific N.W. Anadromous Salmonids, 1992-94; chmn. com. Assessment Atlantic Bluefin, 1994; mem. Ocean Studies Bd., 1995—; working group on hydrology and aquatic ecology Intergovernmental Panel on Climate Change, 1993-95. NSF Midcareer fellow U. Wash., 1992. Fellow AAAS; mem. Am. Fisheries Soc. (pres. 1981, Disting. Svc. award 1980), Am. Soc. Limnology & Oceanography, Ecol. Soc. Am., Soc. Internat. Limnology. Office: Univ Wisconsin Madison Ctr Limnology 680 N Park St Madison WI 53706-1413

MAGNUSON, NANCY, librarian; b. Seattle, Aug. 15, 1944; d. James Leslie and Jeanette (Thomas) M.; 2 sons, Daniel Johnson, Erik Johnson. BA in History, 1977; MLS, U. Wash., 1978. With. King County Libr. System, Seattle, 1973-80; rsch. asst. Free Libr. Phila., 1980-81; asst. libr. Haverford (Pa.) Coll., 1981-87; libr. dir. Goucher Coll., Balt., Md., 1987—. Contbr. to profl. publs. Mem. ALA (com. on status of women in librarianship, various others), Online Computer Libr. Ctr. Users Coun., Md. Libr. Assn., Congress Acad. Libr. Dirs., NOW, Women's Internat. League for Peace and Freedom, Balt. Bibliophiles, Jane Austen Soc. N.Am. Democrat. Office: Goucher Coll Julia Rogers Libr 1021 Dulaney Valley Rd Baltimore MD 21204-2753

MAGNUSON, NORRIS ALDEN, librarian, history educator; b. Midale, Saskatchewan, Can., June 15, 1932; s. George August and Esther Lydia (Eliason) M.; m. Beverly Sue Carlson, Aug. 17, 1956; children: Douglas, Timothy, Kenneth, Daniel. BA, Bethel Coll., 1954; BD, Bethel Sem., 1958; MA, U. Minn., 1961, PhD, 1968. Instr., asst. libr. Bethel Theol. Sem., St. Paul, 1959-65, asst. prof., asst. libr., 1965-68, assoc. prof., assoc. libr., 1968-72, prof., head libr., 1972-97; archivist Bethel Bapt. Gen. Conf., 1993—; chair hist. com. Bapt. Gen. Conf., Arlington Heights, Ill., 1974—; mem. Conf. on Faith and History. Author: Salvation in the Slums, 1977, 2d edit., 1990, Missionsskolan: The History, 1982; editor: Proclaim the Good News, 1986; author: (with others) American Evangelicalism, 1990, 2d edit., 1996. Mem. Salem Bapt. Ch., chairperson, 1972-73. U. Minn. scholar, 1961-63; Inst. for Advanced Christian Studies fellow, 1968-69. Mem. Am. Theol. Libr. Assn., Minn. Theol. Libr. Assn. (pres. 1974-75, 79-80, 84-85, 88-89). Avocations: tennis, handball, racquetball, travelling. Office: Bethel Coll & Sem 3900 Bethel Dr Saint Paul MN 55112-6902

MAGNUSON, PAUL ARTHUR, federal judge; b. Carthage, S.D., Feb. 9, 1937; s. Arthur and Emma Elleda (Paulson) M.; m. Sharon Schultz, Dec. 21, 1959; children—Marlene, Margaret, Kevin, Kara. B.A., Gustavus Adolphus Coll, 1959; J.D., William Mitchell Coll., 1963. Bar: Minn. 1963, U.S. Dist. Ct. Minn. 1968. Claim adjuster Agrl. Ins. Co., 1960-62; clk. Bertie & Bettenberg Law Firm, 1962-63; ptnr. LeVander, Gillen, Miller & Magnuson, South St. Paul, Minn., 1963-81; judge U.S. Dist. Ct. Minn., St. Paul, 1981—, chief judge, 1995—; jurist-in-residence Hamline U. Law Sch., lectr., 1985; lectr. Augsberg Coll., 1986, Bethel Coll., 1986, Concordia Coll., St. Paul, 1987, U. Minn., Morris, 1987; instr. William Mitchell Coll. Law, 1984—. Mem. Met. Health Bd., St. Paul, 1970-72; legal counsel Ind. Republican Party Minn., St. Paul, 1979-81. Recipient Disting. Alumnus award Gustavus Adolphus Coll., 1982. Mem. ABA, 1st Dist. Bar Assn. (pres. 1974-75), Dakota County Bar Assn., Am. Judicature Soc. Presbyterian. Home: 3047 Klondike Ave N Lake Elmo MN 55042-9717 Office: US Dist Ct 730 Burger US Courthouse 316 Robert St N Saint Paul MN 55101-1423*

MAGNUSON, ROBERT MARTIN, retired hospital administrator; b. Chgo., June 28, 1927; s. Martin David and Adena Marie (Hallberg) M.; m. Patricia Ann McNaughton, Dec. 30, 1960; children: Thomas Martin, Dana Caroline. B.S. cum laude, Lake Forest (Ill.) Coll., 1951; M.B.A., Harvard U., 1955. Factory budget mgr., asst. budget dir. Zenith Radio Corp., Chgo., 1955-57; asst. adminstr., controller Elmhurst Meml. Hosp., (Ill.), 1957-64; asso. adminstr. Elmhurst Meml. Hosp., 1964-66, pres., 1966-92; officer, dir. Chgo. Hosp. Council, 1972-79, chmn. bd. dirs., 1983; mem. hosp. adv. council Ill. Dept. Pub. Health, 1972-76; faculty preceptor U. Chgo. Program in Hosp. Adminstrn., 1971-92, Northwestern U. Program in Hosp. and Health Sci. Adminstrn., 1972-92; dir. DuPage County Community Nursing Service, 1964-67, Health Chgo. HMO, 1984-92, Elmhurst Fed. Savs. & Loan Assn., 1971-92; pres. Meml. Health Services, Inc., 1980-92. Pres. Elmhurst Meml. Hosp. Found., 1980-92. Served with USN, 1945-48, 51-52. Mem. Am. Coll. Health Care Execs., Ill. Hosp. Assn. (dist. pres. 1967-69, bd. dirs. 1985-90), Inter-Hosp. Planning Assn. of Western Suburbs (pres., dir.). Republican. Club: Medinah (Ill.) Country.

MAGNUSON, ROGER JAMES, lawyer; b. St. Paul, Jan. 25, 1945; s. Roy Gustaf and Ruth Lily (Edlund) M.; m. Elizabeth Cunningham Shaw, Sept. 11, 1982; children: James Roger, Peter Cunningham, Mary Kerstin, Sarah Ruth, Elizabeth Camilla, Anna Clara, John Edlund. BA, Stanford U., 1967; JD, Harvard U., 1971; BCL, Oxford U., 1972. Bar: Minn. 1973, U.S. Dist. Ct. Minn. 1973, U.S. Ct. Appeals (8th, 9th, 10th cirs.) 1974, U.S. Supreme Ct. 1978. Chief pub. defender Hennepin County Pub. Defender's Office, Mpls., 1973; ptnr. Dorsey & Whitney, Mpls., 1972—; dean Oak Brook Coll. of Law and Govt. Policy, 1995—. Author: Shareholder Litigation, 1981, Are Gay Rights Right, The White-Collar Crime Explosion, 1992, Informed Answers To Gay Rights Questions, 1994; contbr. articles to profl. jours. Elder, Straitgate Ch., Mpls., 1980—. Mem. Christian Legal Soc., White Bear Yacht Club. Republican. Home: 625 Park Ave Saint Paul MN 55115-1663 Office: Dorsey & Whitney 220 S 6th St Minneapolis MN 55402-4502

MAGOR, LOUIS ROLAND, conductor; b. Auburn, Nebr., May 16, 1945; s. John William and Eleanor Lucille (Niemann) M. B.Mus. Edn., Northwestern U., 1967, Mus.M., 1974. Choral dir. Avoca Jr. High Sch., Wilmette, Ill., 1968-70; choral dir. Niles North High Sch., Skokie, Ill., 1970-73; dir. San Francisco Symphony Chorus, 1974-82, Schola Cantorum, 1982-85, San Francisco Boys Chorus, 1985-88; artistic dir. Seattle Bach Choir, 1990—; founder The Louis Magor Singers; mem. faculty San Francisco Conservatory of Music, 1976-78, San Francisco State U., 1979-80. Founder West Seattle Children's Chorus, 1990—; condr. Sing-It-Yourself Messiah, 1979-91, Calif. Symphony Chorus, 1990-92; exec. prodr. Sandy Bradley's Potluck, 1995-96. Mem. Pi Kappa Lambda.

MAGOWAN, PETER ALDEN, professional baseball team executive, grocery chain executive; b. N.Y.C., Apr. 5, 1942; s. Robert Anderson and Doris (Merrill) M.; m. Jill Tarlau (div. July 1982); children: Kimberley, Margot, Hilary; m. Deborah Johnston, Aug. 14, 1982. BA, Stanford U.; MA, Oxford U., Eng.; postgrad., Johns Hopkins U. Store mgr. Safeway Stores Inc., Washington, 1968-70; dist. mgr. Safeway Stores Inc., Houston, 1970-71; retail ops. mgr. Safeway Stores Inc., Phoenix, 1971-72; divsn. mgr. Safeway Stores Inc., Tulsa, 1973-76; mgr. internat. divsn. Safeway Stores Inc., Toronto, Ont., Can., 1976-78; mgr. western region Safeway Stores Inc., San Francisco, 1978-79; CEO Safeway Stores Inc., Oakland, Calif., 1980-93, chmn. bd. dirs., 1980—; pres., mng. gen. ptnr. San Francisco Giants, 1993—; bd. dirs. Chrysler Corp., Caterpillar. Office: San Francisco Giants 3 Com Park San Francisco CA 94124-3904

MAGRATH, C. PETER, educational association executive; b. N.Y.C., Apr. 23, 1933; s. Laurence Wilfrid and Giulia Maria (Dentice) M.; m. Deborah C. Howell, 1988; children: Valerie Ruth, Monette Fay. BA summa cum laude, U. N.H., 1955; PhD, Cornell U., 1962. Mem. faculty Brown U., Providence, 1961-68, prof. polit. sci., 1967-68, assoc. dean grad. sch., 1965-66; dean Coll. Arts and Scis. U. Nebr., Lincoln, 1968-69, dean faculties Coll. Arts and Scis., 1969-72, interim chancellor univ., 1971-72, prof. polit. sci., 1968-72, vice chancellor for acad. affairs, 1972; pres. SUNY, Binghamton, 1972-74, prof. polit. sci., 1972-74; pres. U. Minn., Mpls., 1974-84, U. Mo. System, 1985-91, Nat. Assn. State Univs. and Land Grant Colls., Washington, 1991—. Author: The Triumph of Character, 1963, Yazoo: Law and Politics in the New Republic, The Case of Fletcher v. Peck, 1966, Constitutionalism and Politics: Conflict and Consensus, 1968, Issues and Perspectives in American Government, 1971, (with others) The American Democracy, 2d edit., 1973, (with Robert L. Egbert) Strengthening Teacher Education, 1987; contbr. articles to profl. jours. Served with AUS, 1955-57. Mem. Assn. Am. Univs. (chmn. 1985-86), Phi Beta Kappa, Phi Kappa Phi, Pi Gamma Mu, Pi Sigma Alpha, Kappa Tau Alpha. Office: Nat Assn State U and Land Grant Colls 1 Dupont Cir NW Ste 710 Washington DC 20036-1133 *True personal success cannot be measured by public acclaim, recognition, or status. It grows out of an ability to recognize right from wrong, and to maintain principles of fairness and understanding in all human relationships - regardless of one's role in life. In my case I have tried to fulfill this ideal; I have been willing to exercise leadership by asserting my judgements and views openly and directly on the educational and human issues that came my way.*

MAGRILL, JOE RICHARD, JR., religious organization administrator, minister; b. Marshall, Tex., Aug. 7, 1946; s. Joe Richard and Mary Belle (Chadwick) M. BA summa cum laude, East Tex. State U., 1967; MDiv, Princeton Theol. Sem., 1970, MTh, 1972; MLS, Rutgers U., 1971. Ordained to ministry Cumberland Presbyn. Ch., 1970. Stated supply min. Newsome (Tex.) Cumberland Presbyn. Ch., 1966-67; Christian edn. asst. United Presbyn. Ch., Carlstadt, N.J., 1967-70; order libr. Princeton (N.J.) Theol. Sem., 1969-72; head libr., prof. Memphis Theol. Sem., 1972-79; pastor Brookhaven Cumberland Presbyn. Ch., Nashville, 1987-89; asst. to stated clk. Gen. Assembly Office, Cumberland Presbyn. Ch., Memphis, 1979-83, supr. ctrl. acctg. div., 1980-87, editor The Cumberland Presbyn., 1984-87, chief exec. bd. stewardship, 1989—, mem. Gen. Assembly Ctr., 1993—; mem. Trinity Presbytery of Cumberland Presbyn. Ch., 1970—; sec.-treas. Hist. Found. Cumberland Presbyn. Ch., Memphis, 1974—; bd. dirs. Hist. Found. Presbyn. Ch. U.S., Montreat, N.C., 1980-83. Editor: In the Valley of the Cauca, 1981, One Family Under God, 1982. Recipient achievement award Hist. Found. Cumberland Presbyn. Ch., 1980; scholar Phi Alpha Theta, 1967, Am. Theol. Libr. Assn., 1970. Democrat. Avocations: computers, historical research. Office: Cumberland Presbyn Ch 1978 Union Ave Memphis TN 38104-4134

MAGRILL, ROSE MARY, library director; b. Marshall, Tex., June 8, 1939; d. Joe Richard and Mary Belle (Chadwick) M. BS, E. Tex. State U., 1960, MA, 1961; MS, U. Ill., 1964, PhD, 1969. Asst. to dean women E. Tex. State U., Commerce, 1960-61, librarian II, 1961-63; teaching asst. U. Ill., Urbana, 1963-64; instr. to asst. prof. E. Tex. State U., Commerce, 1964-67; asst. prof. Ball State U., Muncie, 1969-70; asst. prof. to prof. U. Mich., Ann Arbor, 1970-81; prof. U. N. Tex., Denton, 1981—; dir. libr. E. Tex. Bapt. U., Marshall, 1987—; accreditation site visitor ALA, Chgo., 1975—; cons. in field. Co-author: Building Library Collections, 4th edit. 1974, Library Technical Services, 1977, Building Library Collections, 5th edit. 1979, Acquisition Management and Collection Development in Libraries, 2d edit. 1989. Trustee Memphis Theol. Sem., 1988—; treas. Mission Synod of Cumberland Presbyn. Ch., 1989—; bd. fin. Trinity Presbytery, 1989—; sec.-treas. Harrison County Hist. Commn., 1995—. Recipient award Cumberland Presbyn. History, 1995. Mem. ALA (RTSD Resources Sect. pub. award 1978), Tex. Libr. Assn. Home: 804 Caddo St Marshall TX 75670-2414 Office: E Tex Bapt Univ 1209 N Grove St Marshall TX 75670-1423

MAGRUDER, LAWSON WILLIAM, III, military officer; b. Bryan, Tex., Nov. 5, 1947; s. Lawson William Jr. and Maryanne (Windrow) M.; m. Gloria Ann Banton, July 26, 1969; children: Shannon, Loren, Matthew. BBA in Internat. Mktg., U. Tex., 1969; MA in Pers. Mgmt., Ctrl. Mich. U., 1979; student, U.S. Army Command Gen. Staff Coll., 1979, Army War Coll., 1986. Commd. 2d lt. U.S. Army, 1969, advanced through grades to maj. gen., 1995; rifle platoon leader 82d Airborne Divsn., Ft. Bragg, N.C., 1969-71, 23d Inf. Divsn., Vietnam; asst. brigade ops. officer, co. comdr. 82d Airborne Divsn., 1971-74; ranger co. comdr., bn. adj. 2d Ranger Bn., 1975-77; bn. ops. officer 9th Inf. Divsn., 1977-78; inf. assignment officer U.S. Total Army Pers. Command, 1979-82; brigade ops. officer 172d Light Inf. Brigade, Alaska; comdr. 5th bn. 327th Inf., Alaska, 1982-85; chief tactics, dep. dir. combined arms and tactics dept. U.S. Army Inf. Sch., Ft. Benning, Ga., 1986-88; comdr. 2d brigade 25th Inf. Divsn., Schofield Barracks, Hawaii, 1988-90; exec. asst. to dep. comdr.-in-chief, dep. dir. strategic policy and plans U.S. Pacific Command, 1990-92; asst. divsn. comdr. 10th Mountain Divsn.; comdr. Combined Task Force Kismayo, Somalia, 1992-93; comdg. gen. Joint Readiness Tng. Ctr. U.S. Army, Ft. Polk, La., 1993-95; comdg. gen. U.S. Army South, Ft. Clayton, Panama, 1995—. Pres. Ft. Benning Parish Coun., 1986-88; mem. Ft. Benning Sch. Bd., 1987-88. Decorated Bronze star medal with oak leaf cluster, Legion of Merit with two oak leaf clusters, Air medal, Army Commedation medal with one oak leaf cluster, Def. Superior Svc. medal, Meritorious Svc. medal with three oak leaf clusters. Roman Catholic. Avocations: golfing, running. Home: Quarters 1, West Corozal Panama Office: Hqs US Army S Ft Clayton Panama APO AA 34004

MAGRY, MARTHA J., elementary education educator; b. Paragould, Ark., Jan. 6, 1936; d. Burrell F. and Georgia M. (Watkins) Spence; m. James Magry, June 28, 1958; 1 child, David J. BS, Wheaton (Ill.) Coll., 1957; MS, Ind. U. Northwest, Gary, 1985; postgrad., Ark. State U., Jonesboro, 1964. Cert. elem., gen. sci. tchr. 4th grade tchr. Gary City Schs., sci. tchr.; 2d grade tchr. Merrillville (Ind.) Community Schs. Mem. NEA, Ind. State Tchrs. Assn., Merrillville Classroom Tchrs. Assn. Home: 5312 Pierce St Merrillville IN 46410-1364

MAGSIG, JUDITH ANNE, early childhood education educator; b. Saginaw, Mich., Nov. 9, 1939; d. Harold Howard and Catherine Louise (Barstow) Gay; m. George Arthur Magsig, June 22, 1963; children: Amy Catherine, Karl Joseph. BA, Alma Coll., 1961. Cert. tchr., early childhood tchr., Mich. 1st grade tchr. Gaylord (Mich.) Schs., 1961-64, spl. edn. tchr., 1965-67, kindergarten tchr., 1968—. instr. Suzuki violin method; second violinist Traverse (Mich.) Symphony Orch., 1985-92. Mem. ASCD, NEA, Mich. Edn. Assn., Gaylord Edn. Assn., Assn. for the Edn. of Young Children, Assn. for Childhood Edn. Internat., Suzuki Assn. Am., Am. String Tchrs. Assn., Order Eastern Star, Voyageurs, Alpha Delta Kappa (pres. Beta Rho chpt. 1980-82, 84-86). Methodist. Avocations: cross-stitch, camping, canoeing, sewing. Home: 2130 Evergreen Dr Gaylord MI 49735-9165 Office: S Maple Multi Age Program 590 E 5th St Gaylord MI 49735-1256

MAGUIRE, ALAN EDWARD, economist, public policy consultant; b. Paterson, N.J., Aug. 27, 1954; s. Edward Lawrence and Severna (Arens) M. BS in Econs., Ariz. State U., 1978. Legis. rsch. economist Ariz. State Senate, Phoenix, 1977-80, econ. advisor, 1980-83; chief dep. state treas. Ariz. State Treasury, Phoenix, 1983-87; 1st v.p. Rauscher Pierce Refsnes, Inc., Phoenix, 1987-91; pres. The Maguire Co., Phoenix, 1991—; forecaster Ariz. Blue Chip Econ. Forecast, Tempe, 1985—, Western Blue Chip Econ. Forecast, Tempe, 1988—. Bd. dirs. Ariz. Town Hall, 1994—, Ariz. Rep. Caucus, Phoenix, 1988-94, Ariz. State Bd. of Deposit, Phoenix, 1988—, Ariz. State Retirement System bd., 1987; active Ariz. Property Tax Oversight Commn., Phoenix, 1987—, Project SLIM Steering Com., 1991-92, Ariz. State Retirement Sys. Investment Adv. Coun., 1997—. Mem. Ariz. Econ. Forum (bd. dirs., v.p. 1983—), Ariz. Town Hall, Phoenix Econ. Club. Office: The Maguire Co PO Box 64382 Phoenix AZ 85082-4382

MAGUIRE, CHARLOTTE EDWARDS, retired physician; b. Richmond, Ind., Sept. 1, 1918; d. Joel Blaine and Lydia (Betscher) Edwards; m. Raymer Francis Maguire, Sept. 1, 1948 (dec.); children: Barbara, Thomas Clair II (dec.). Student, Stetson U., 1936-38, U. Wichita, 1938-39; BS, Memphis Tchrs. Coll., 1940; MD, U. Ark., 1944. Intern, resident Orange Meml. Hosp., Orlando, Fla., 1944-46; resident Bellevue Hosp. and Med. Ctr., NYU, N.Y.C., 1954, 55; instr. nurses Orange Meml. Hosp., 1947-57, staff mem., 1946-68; staff mem. Fla. Santarium and Hosp., Orlando, 1946-56, Holiday

House and Hosp., Orlando, 1950-62; mem. courtesy and cons. staff West Orange Meml. Hosp., Winter Garden, Fla., 1952-67; active staff, chief dept. pediatrics Mercy Hosp., Orlando, 1965-68; med. dir. med. svcs. and basic care Fla. Dept. Health and Rehab. Svcs., 1975-84; med. exec. dir., med. svcs. divsn. worker's compensation Fla. Dept. Labor, Tallahassee, 1984-87; chief of staff physicians and dentists Ctrl. Fla. divsn. Children's Home Soc. Fla., 1947-56; dir. Orlando Child Health Clinic 1949-58; pvt. practice medicine Orlando, 1946-68; asst. regional dir. HEW, 1970-72; pediat. cons. Fla. Crippled Children's Commn., 1952-70, dir., 1968-70; med. dir. Office Med. Svcs. and Basic Care, sr. physician Office of Asst. Sec. Ops., Fla. Dept. Health and Rehab. Svcs.; clin. prof. dept. pediat. U. Fla. Coll. Medicine, Gainesville, 1980-87; mem. Fla. Drug Utilization Rev., 1983-87; real estate salesperson Investors Realty, 1982—; bd. dirs. Stavros Econ. Ctr. Fla. State U., Tallahassee; mem. pres.'s coun. Fla. State U., U. Fla., Gainesville. Mem. profl. adv. com. Fla. Center for Clin. Services at U. Fla., 1952-60; del. to Mid-century White House Conf. on Children and Youth, 1950; U.S. del from Nat. Soc. for Crippled Children to World Congress for Welfare of Cripples, Inc., London, 1957; pres of corp. Eccleston-Callahan Hosp. for Colored Crippled Children, 1956-58; sec. Fla. chpt. Nat. Doctor's Com. for Improved Med. Services, 1951-52; med. adv. com. Gateway Sch. for Mentally Retarded, 1959-62; bd. dirs. Forest Park Sch. for Spl. Edn. Crippled Children, 1949-54, mem. med. adv. com., 1955-68, chmn., 1957-68; mem. Fla. Adv. Council for Mentally Retarded, 1965-70; dir. central Fla. poison control Orange Meml. Hosp.; mem. orgn. com., chmn. com. for admissions and selection policies Camp Challenge; participant 12th session Fed. Exec. Inst., 1971; del. White House Conf. on Aging, 1980; dir. Stavros Econ. Ctr. Fla. State U. Mem. AMA (life), Nat. Rehab. Assn., Am. Congress Phys. Medicine and Rehab., Fla. Soc. Crippled Children and Adults, Ctrl. Fla. Soc. Crippled Children and Adults (dir. 1949-58, pres. 1956-57), Am. Assn. Cleft Palate, Fla. Soc. Crippled Children (trustee 1951-57, v.p. 1956-57, profl. adv. com. 1957-68), Mental Health Assn. Orange County (charter mem.; pres. 1949-50, dir. 1947-52, chmn. exec. com. 1950-52, dir. 1963-65), Fla. Orange County Heart Assn., Am. Med. Women's Assn., Am. Acad. Med. Dirs., Fla. Med. Assn. (life, chmn. com. on mental retardation), Orange County Med. Assn., Orange Med. Soc. (life), Fla. Pediatric Soc. (pres. 1952-53), Fla. Cleft Palate Assn. (counselor-at-large, sec.), Nat. Inst. Geneal. Rsch., Nat. Geneal. Soc., Assn. Profl. Genealogists, Tallahassee Geneal. Soc., Fla. State U. Found. Inc. (bd. dirs. Stavoris Ctr. for Econ. Edn.), Capital City Tiger Bay Club, Fla. Econs. Club. Club: Governors. Home: 4158 Covenant Ln Tallahassee FL 32308-5765

MAGUIRE, DAVE, real estate manager; b. Macomb, Ill., Dec. 11, 1949; s. Davis and Martha Mae (Jennings) M. BA, So. Ill. U., 1973. Mgr. Chapman's Bookstore, Inc., Macomb, 1973-78; real estate mgr. Westbrook Village, Macomb, 1978-96; pres. University Park Apts. LLC, Macomb, 1996—. Pres. McDonough County Bd. Health, Macomb, 1985—; chmn. City/County Transit Commn., Macomb, 1982-89; alderman Macomb City Coun., 1979-89; precinct committeeman McDonough County Rep. Cen. Com., Macomb, 1977-94; trustee Spoon River Coll., Canton, Ill., 1993—, chmn. bd. dirs. 1995—. Mem. Ill. C.C. Trustees Assn. (bd. reps. 1993—, vice chmn. state rels. com. 1995-96, chmn. state rels. com. 1996—), Macomb Area Indsl. Devel. Corp. (exec. com. 1996—), Macomb Area C. of C. (bd. dirs. 1989—, pres.), Assn. Fraternity Advisors, Ill. DeMolay (Legion of Honor 1978, Cross of Honor 1980), Elks, Masons, Delta Upsilon (internat. sec. 1988-91, Meritorious Svc. award 1981). Methodist. Avocations: golf, bowling, travel. Home: 554 W Murray St Macomb IL 61455-1316 Office: University Park Apts 900 Linden Ln Macomb IL 61455-1074

MAGUIRE, D.E., electronics executive. CEO Kemet Electronic Corp., Greenville, S.C. Office: Kemet Electronic Corp PO Box 5928 Greenville SC 29606

MAGUIRE, JOHN DAVID, academic administrator, educator, writer; b. Montgomery, Ala., Aug. 7, 1932; s. John Henry and Clyde (Merrill) M.; m. Lillian Louise Parrish, Aug. 29, 1953; children: Catherine Merrill, Mary Elizabeth, Anne King. A.B. magna cum laude, Washington and Lee U., 1953, Litt.D. (hon.), 1979; Fulbright scholar, Edinburgh (Scotland) U., 1953-54; B.D. summa cum laude, Yale, 1956, Ph.D., 1960; postdoctoral research, Yale U. and U. Tübingen, Germany, 1964-65, U. Calif., Berkeley, 1968-69, Silliman U., Philippines, 1976-77; HLD (hon.), Transylvania U., 1990. Dir. Internat. Student Ctr., New Haven, 1956-58; mem. faculty Wesleyan U., Middletown, Conn., 1960-70; asso. provost Wesleyan U., 1967-68; vis. lectr. Pacific Sch. Religion and Grad. Theol. Union, Berkeley, 1968-69; pres. SUNY Coll. at Old Westbury, 1970-81, Claremont (Calif.) Grad. U., 1981—. Author: The Dance of the Pilgrim: A Christian Style of Life for Today, 1967; also numerous articles. Mem. Conn. adv. com. U.S. Commn. Civil Rights, 1961-70; participant White House Conf. on Civil Rights, 1966; advisor, permanent trustee and 1st chmn. bd. dirs. Martin Luther King Ctr. for Social Change, Atlanta, 1968—; bd. dirs. Nassau County Health and Welfare Coun., 1971-81, pres., 1974-76; trustee United Bd. Christian Higher Edn. in Asia, 1975-81, Inst. Internat. Edn., 1980-86; charter trustee Tomás Rivera Policy Inst., Claremont, Calif., 1984—, vice chmn., 1987-94, treas., 1995—, Assn. Ind. Calif. Colls. and Univs., 1985—, chmn. 1990-92, mem. exec. com., 1992—, The Calif. Achievement Coun., 1985-94, chmn. 1990-94, Transylvania U. Bingham Trust, 1987—, Lincoln Found. and Lincoln Inst. of Land Policy, Inc., 1987-94, The JL Found., 1988—, The Bus. Enterprise Trust, 1989—, Ednl. Found. for African Ams., 1991—; bd. dirs. Assn. Am. Colls. and Univs., 1981-86, chmn., 1984-85; bd. dirs. Legal Def. and Edn. Fund. NAACP, 1991—, west coast div., 1981—, Thacher Sch., Ojai, Calif., 1982-94, vice chmn., 1986-90, Salzburg Seminar, 1992-96; charter mem. Pacific Coun. Internat. Policy, 1995—; mem. Am. Com. on U.S.-Soviet Rels., 1981-92, Blue Ribbon Calif. Commn. on Teaching Profession, 1984-86; mem. governing coun. Aspen Inst. Wye Faculty Seminar, 1984-94; mem. Coun. on Fgn. Rels., 1983—; adv. bd. RAND Ctr. Rsch. Immigration Policy, 1994—; mem. Pres.'s Adv. Coun. to Commn. on Calif. Master Plan for Higher Edn., 1986-87, L.A. Ednl. Alliance for Restructuring Now, 1992—, Calif. Bus. Higher Edn. Forum, 1992—. Recipient Julia A. Archibald High Scholarship award Yale Div. Sch., 1956; Day fellow Yale Grad. Sch., 1956-57; Kent fellow, 1957-60; Howard Found. postdoctoral fellow Brown U. Grad. Sch., 1964-65; Fenn lectr., 7 Asian countries, 1976-77; recipient Conn. Prince Hall Masons' award outstanding contbns. human rights in Conn., 1965; E. Harris Harbison Gt. Tchr. prize Danforth Found., 1968. Fellow Soc. Values Higher Edn. (pres. 1974-81, bd. dirs. 1972-88); mem. Phi Beta Kappa, Omicron Delta Kappa. Democrat. Office: Claremont Grad U Office of Pres 160 E 10th St Claremont CA 91711-5909

MAGUIRE, JOHN PATRICK, investment company executive; b. New Britain, Conn., Apr. 1, 1917; s. John Patrick and Edna Frances (Cashen) M.; m. Mary-Emily Jones, Sept. 8, 1945; children: Peter Dunbar (dec.), Joan Guilford. Student, Holy Cross Coll., 1933-34; degree in bus. adminstrn. with distinction, Babson Inst., 1936; A.B. cum laude, Princeton U., 1941; BS (hon.), Babson Inst., 1995, Babson Coll., 1995; J.D., Yale U., 1943; PhD (hon.), St. Bonaventure U., 1965. Bar: Conn. 1943, N.Y. 1944. Asso. Cravath, Swaine & Moore (and predecessor), N.Y.C., 1943-50, 52-54; v.p., dir. Forbes, Inc.; also mng. editor Investors Adv. Inst., 1951-52; asst. counsel Gen. Dynamics Corp., 1954-60, sec., 1962-87, v.p., 1981-87; sec., gen. counsel Tex. Butadiene and Chem. Corp., 1960-62; with J.P. Maguire Investment Advisors, 1987-95; exec. v.p. Fiduciary Asset Mgmt. Co., 1995—. Mem. bd. govs. N.Y. Young Rep. Club, 1951-52; chmn. fin. and investment coms. St. Louis Art Mus., 1984-94; trustee St. Bonaventure U., 1965-71, Webster U., 1983-85, John Burroughs Sch. (chmn. investment com.) 1976-85. Mem. ABA. Clubs: Piping Rock (Locust Valley, L.I.); Yale (St. Louis); St. Louis Country; Princeton (St. Louis); Tiger Inn (Princeton). Home: 8 Chatfield Place Rd Saint Louis MO 63141-7850

MAGUIRE, ROBERT ALAN, Slavic languages and literatures educator; b. Canton, Mass., June 21, 1930; s. Frederick William and Ruth Spalding (Plunkett) M. A.B., Dartmouth Coll., 1951; M.A., cert., Russian Inst., Columbia U., 1953, Ph.D., 1961. Instr. Russian Duke U., 1958-60; asst. prof. Russian Dartmouth Coll., 1960-62, dir. NDEA Russian Lang. Inst., 1962; faculty Sch. Internat. Affairs and Harriman Inst. Columbia U., N.Y.C., 1962—, asst. prof. Russian lang. and lit., 1962-66; assoc. prof. Columbia U., 1966-70, prof., 1970—; Bakhmeteff prof. Russian studies Columbia U., N.Y.C., 1992—; chmn. dept. Slavic langs. Columbia U., 1977-83, 85-88; vis. lectr. Ind. U., 1961, 66, 69; vis. prof. U. Ill., 1976, Yale U., New Haven, 1984, Princeton (N.J.) U., 1991-92, Harvard U., 1995-96; vis. fellow St. Antony's Coll., Oxford (Eng.) U., 1971-72; mem. adv. bd. Sr. Fulbright-Hays program NEH, 1971-74; mem. selection bd. Internat. Rsch. and Exchs. Bd., 1971-74, 77, Coun. on Internat. Ednl. Exch., 1973, 78, 80; mem. planning and adv. bd. Am. Coun. Learned Socs.-USSR Acad. of Sci. Commn. on the Humanities and Social Scis., 1982; editor Soviet-Am. Lit. Project, Duke U./Leningrad U. Press; adv. com. on preservation of Russian periodicals N.Y. Pub. Libr.; mem. vis. com. dept. Slavic langs. Harvard U., 1988—, chmn., 1990—; selection com. Nat. Humanities Ctr. Author: Red Virgin Soil: Soviet Literature in the 1920's, 1968, 2d edit., 1987, Gogol from the Twentieth Century: Eleven Essays, 1974, 2d edit., 1976, Exploring Gogol, 1994, 2d edit., 1995, others; translator: Gogol (V.V. Gippius), 1981, 2d edit., 1989; co-translator Russian Short Stories, II, 1965, The Survivor and Other Poems (Tadeusz Rozewicz), 1976, Petersburg (Andrei Bely), 1978, 80, 83, Building the Barricade (Anna Swirszczynska), 1979, Sounds, Feelings, Thoughts: Seventy Poems (Wislawa Szymborska), 1981, 89, mem. editl. bd. Tchg. Lang. Through Lit., 1965-77, mng. editor, 1978-88; mem. editl. bd. Slavic Rev., 1966-69, 82-89, Polish Rev., 1980-88; mem. editl. adv. bd. Princeton Essays in Literature, 1972-77; contbr. articles to profl. jours. Sponsoring com. Leo Tolstoy Mus. and Rsch. Libr., 1979; bd. dirs. Chamber Music Conf. and Composers' Forum of the East, 1983-93. Served with U.S. Army, 1953-55. Mem. MLA (exec. com. divsn. on Slavic and E. European langs. 1986-92, Aldo and Jeanne Scaglione prize 1995), PEN, Am. Assn. Advancement of Slavic Studies (dir. 1977-79), Am. Assn. Tchrs. Slavic and E. European Langs., Nat. Assn. Scholars, Polish Inst. Arts and Scis., Kosciuszko Found., Irish-Am. Cultural Inst., Gogol Soc. Am. (pres. 1986). Roman Catholic (parish coun. 1979-89). Home: PO Box 69 Davenport Center NY 13751-0069 Office: Dept Slavic Langs Columbia U New York NY 10027

MAGUIRE, ROBERT EDWARD, retired public utility executive; b. Somerville, Mass., Jan. 25, 1928; s. Hugh Edward and Alice Theresa (Garrity) M.; m. Leona Rosemarie Beaulieu, June 21, 1952; children—Lynne Marie, Steven Francis, Judith Anne, David Robert. B.S. in Chem. Engring., Northeastern U., 1950, B.B.A. in Engring. and Mgmt., 1953. Vice pres., mgr. Lawrence Gas Co., Mass., 1960-68; vice pres., mgr. Mystic Valley Gas Co., Malden, Mass., 1968-70; v.p., regional exec. Mass. Electric Co., North Andover, 1970-71; v.p. New Eng. Power Service Co., Westboro, Mass., 1971-72, New Eng. Electric System, Westboro, Mass., 1972-75; exec. v.p., trustee Eastern Utilities Assocs., Boston, 1975-91. Contbr. to Gas mag., 1959. Vice chmn. Greater Lawrence United Fund Budget Com., 1967; treas., dir. ARC, Lawrence, 1966; trustee Essex-Broadway Savs. Bank, Lawrence, 1966-78; pres., dir. Greater Lawrence C. of C., 1962-64. Recipient Paul Revere Leadership medal Boston C. of C., 1963. Roman Catholic. Club: Lanam (Andover, Mass.). Home: 22 Ivy Ln Andover MA 01810-5018

MAGUIRE, ROBERT FRANCIS, III, real estate investor; b. Portland, Oreg., Apr. 18, 1935; s. Robert Francis Jr. and Jean (Shepard) M. B.A., UCLA, 1960. Vice pres. Security Pacific Nat. Bank, L.A., 1960-64; chmn. Maguire Thomas Ptnrs., L.A., 1964—; Exec. bd. med. scis. UCLA. Chmn. bd. dirs. Los Angeles County Mus. Art; trustee UCLA Found., Bard Coll.; bd. dirs. St. John's Hosp., Music Ctr. Bd. Govs., Calif. Clubs: California (Los Angeles); Valley (Montecito, Calif.), L.A. Country.

MAGURNO, RICHARD PETER, lawyer; b. Suffern, N.Y., June 29, 1943; s. Eugene and Rose (Foresta) M. BS, Georgetown U., 1964; MS, U. Wis., 1965; JD, Fordham U., 1968. Bar: N.Y. 1970, Fla. 1982, U.S. Supreme Ct. 1974, U.S. Ct. Appeals (2d, 5th, 11th cirs.) 1976, U.S. Dist. Ct. (so. and ea. dists.) N.Y. 1979. Atty. Eastern Air Lines, N.Y.C., 1970-73, sr. atty., 1973-76, gen. atty., 1976-79; dir. legal Eastern Air Lines, Miami, Fla., 1980, v.p. legal, asst. sec., 1980-84; gen. counsel, sr. v.p. legal, sec. Eastern Air Lines, 1984-88; ptnr. Lord Day & Lord, Barrett Smith, 1989-94; gen. counsel, sr. v.p. legal Trans World Airlines, St. Louis, 1994—. Author: Romantic Suffern, 1773-1973, 1973. Served in Peace Corps, 1968-69. Mem. ABA, Bar Assn. City of N.Y., Fla. Bar Assn. Democrat. Roman Catholic.

MAH, FENG-HWA, economics educator; b. Kaifeng, Honan, China, Mar. 25, 1922; s. Chiao-Hsiang and Wen-Chieh (Yang) M.; m. Judy Jiann Ting, Sept. 14, 1975. B.L. in Econs., Nat. Peking U., 1947; M.A. in Econs., U. Mich., 1956, Ph.D., 1959. Research asst. U. Mich., Ann Arbor, 1955-58; research fellow U. Calif.-Berkeley, 1959-60; asst. prof. Calif. State U.-Los Angeles, 1960-61; asst. prof. U. Wash., Seattle, 1961-64, assoc. prof., 1964-76, co-chmn. China Program, 1975-83, prof. econs., 1976-87, prof. emeritus, 1987—. Author: Communist China's Foreign Trade: Price Structure and Behavior 1955-1959, 1963, The Foreign Trade of Mainland China, 1971, Literary Essays of Mah Feng-hwa (in Chinese), 1993; contbr. numerous articles on Chinese economy to profl. jours. Orla B. Taylor fellow U. Mich., 1958-59; Fulbright faculty research fellow, 1967-68; Social Sci. Research Council grantee, 1962-65, 71. Mem. Am. Econs. Assn., Assn. Comparative Econ. Studies, Assn. Asian Studies, Phi Kappa Phi. Address: PO Box 15311 Seattle WA 98115-0311

MAH, RICHARD SZE HAO, chemical engineering educator; b. Shanghai, China, Dec. 16, 1934; came to U.S., 1961, naturalized, 1972; s. Fabian Soh Pai and E. Shang (Chang) M.; m. Shopin Stella Lee, Aug. 31, 1962; 1 child, Christopher. BSc, U. Birmingham, 1957; DIC, PhD; Leverhulme student, Imperial Coll. Sci. and Tech., U. London, 1961; DSc in Engring., U. London, 1992. Jr. chem. engr. A.P.V. Co., Ltd., Crawley, Sussex, Eng., 1957-58; research fellow U. Minn., 1961-63; research engr. Union Carbide Corp. Tech. Center, South Charleston, W.Va., 1963-67; group head/sr. project analyst Esso Maths. & Systems, Inc., Florham Park, N.J., 1967-72; assoc. prof. chem. engring. Northwestern U., Evanston, Ill., 1972-77; prof. Northwestern U., 1977-96, prof. emeritus, 1996—; trustee CACHE Corp., Cambridge, Mass., 1974—, sec., 1978-80, v.p., 1982-84, pres., 1984-86; cons. Argonne Nat. Lab., 1975-78, DuPont de Nemours & Co., 1981-89. Contbr. articles to profl. jours. Fellow Am. Inst. Chem. Engrs. (chmn. systems and process design com. 1978-80, chmn. cast div. programming bd. 1979-81, Computing in Chem. Engring. award 1981, E.W. Thiele award 1990); mem. Am. Chem. Soc., Am. Soc. Engring. Edn., Am. Soc. Quality Control (Youden prize 1986), Tau Beta Pi. Mem. United Ch. of Christ. Office: Northwestern U Dept Chem Engring Evanston IL 60208-3120 *Live every day as if it is our last. Each day of life is a marvelous gift of God. Let us count all our blessings and put to use every minute of our day and every resource of our life. Every morning let us marvel at the miraculous world which He has created for us. Every night let us thank God for giving us another day of fulfillment and go to sleep with the expectation of another great day of miracles for tomorrow.*

MAHA, GEORGE EDWARD, research facility administrator, consultant; b. Elgin, Ill., Feb. 15, 1924; s. George William and Agnes (Lux) M.; m. Mary Andrea Rasmussen, June 6, 1953; children: George, Richard, Mary, Andrea, Sarah. BS, U. Notre Dame, 1950; MD, St. Louis U., 1953. Diplomate Am. Bd. Internal Medicine. Intern Mt. Carmel Mercy Hosp., Detroit, 1953-54; resident in internal medicine VA Hosp., St. Louis, 1954-55; fellow St. Louis U. Hosp., 1955-56; NIH fellow in cardiology Duke U., Durham, N.C., 1956-58; chief outpatient svc. VA Hosp., Pitts., 1962-64; staff physician FDA, Washington, 1964-66; exec. dir. clin. rsch. Merck, Sharp & Dohme Rsch. Labs., West Point, Pa., 1966-88; asst. to pres. Clin. Rsch. Internat., Research Triangle Park, N.C., 1988-89; med. dir. Burroughs Wellcome, Research Triangle Park, 1989-91; cons., 1991—; chmn. med. sect. Pharm. Mfr.'s Assn., Washington, 1982-83, mem. steering com., 1975-84. Contbr. 17 articles to profl. jours. Tech. sgt. USAF, 1943-46, PTO. Recipient Mosby award St. Louis U., 1953. Mem. AMA, AAAS, Am. Coll. Cardiology, N.Y. Acad. Sci., Am. Heart Assn., Am. Soc. Clin. Pharmacology and Therapeutics, Alpha Omega Alpha. Roman Catholic. Avocations: reading, fishing, tennis. Home: 313 Marina Bay 2550 Harbourside Dr Longboat Key FL 34228-4170

MAHADEVAN, KUMAR, marine laboratory director, researcher; b. Madras, Tamilnadu, India, Sept. 29, 1948; came to U.S., 1971; s. Sockalingam Ponnusamy and Pankajam (Nadar) M.; m. Linda Claire Goggin, Sept. 27, 1980; children: Andrew, Alexander, Chad, Vijayan. BS, Madras U., 1967; MS, Annamalai U., Chidambaram, India, 1971; PhD, Fla. State U., 1977. Instr. Chingleput (India) Med. Coll., 1967-68, Lakshman's Coll., Madras, 1968-69; rsch. asst. Fla. State U., Tallahassee, 1971-75; staff scientist Conservation Cons., Inc., Palmetto, Fla., 1975-78; sr. scientist Mote Marine Lab., Sarasota, Fla., 1978-79, dir. div., 1979-86, interim co-dir., 1984, exec. dir., 1986—; mem. Coun. on Ocean Affairs, Washington, 1989-91, steering com. Gulf of Mex. Program, Atlanta, 1988—; mem. South Atlantic and Gulf States Coastal Protection Commn., 1990—; vice chmn. NOAA Marine Rsch. Bd., Gulf of Mex., 1992—. Contbr. articles to profl. publs. Mem. sch. adv. bd., Sarasota, 1988-89; mem. tech. adv. bd. Myakka River, Sarasota, 1987-90; legis. liason Parents Assn. of Sarasota Schs., 1988-89; bd. dirs. Jason Found. for Edn., 1991—. Nat. Merit scholar Univ. Grants Commn., India, 1969-71. Mem. N. Am. Benthological Soc., Oceanographic Soc., World Aquaculture Soc., Deep Sea Biol. Soc. (hon.), Fla. Acad. Scis. (councillor 1975), So. Assn. Marine Labs (pres. 1990, exec. bd. 1986-91, treas. 1995—), Assn. Marine Labs Caribbean (pres. 1987-88, exec. bd. 1984—), Nat. Assn. Marine Labs. (pres. 1994-95), Sigma Xi. Republican. Avocations: racquetball, fishing, gardening. Office: Mote Marine Lab 1600 Ken Thompson Pky Sarasota FL 34236-1004

MAHAFFEY, JAMES PERRY, education educator, consultant; b. Greenville, S.C., Sept. 29, 1935; s. Earl Perry and Flora Virginia (Painter) M.; m. Nora Dean Padgett, Dec. 22, 1961; 1 child, Janet E. BA cum laude, Furman U., 1957; MA, Vanderbilt U., 1958; PhD, U. S.C., 1974. Cert. edn. specialist-reading. Tchr. Greenville (S.C.) County Schs., 1958-61, reading supr., 1961-65; S.C. state reading supr. S.C. Dept. Edn., Columbia, 1965-69; asst. supt. for instrn. Anderson (S.C.) Pub. Schs., 1969-77; assoc. prof. edn. Furman U., Greenville, 1977-79; assoc. supt. for instrn. Horry County Schs., Conway/Myrtle Beach, S.C., 1979-91; prof. edn. Wofford Coll., Spartanburg, S.C., 1991—; adj. prof. Converse Coll., Spartanburg, 1961-65; instr. U. S.C., Columbia, 1973-74; mem. S.C. Basic Skills Comm., Columbia, 1981-89; bd. trustees So. Assn. Colls./Schs., Atlanta, 1990-93. Author, editor: Teaching Reading in South Carolina Secondary Schools, 1969; contbg. author: Elementary School Criteria: Focusing on Student Performance, 1994; contbr. articles to profl. jours. Named Outstanding Sch. Adminstr., S.C. Assn. Sch. Adminstrs., Columbia, 1989, Outstanding Educator, So. Assn. Colls./Schs., Atlanta, 1990; Carnegie fellow Peabody Coll. of Vanderbilt U., Nashville, 1958. Mem. Internat. Reading Assn. (S.C. pres. 1977). Baptist. Avocation: gardening. Home: 101 Heritage Dr Spartanburg SC 29307-3146 Office: Wofford Coll Edn Dept 429 N Church St Spartanburg SC 29303-3612

MAHAFFEY, JOHN CHRISTOPHER, association executive; b. Jefferson City, Mo., July 20, 1953; s. Fred Turner and Betty Cord (Woodfill) M.; m. Leslie Anne DenUyl Mahaffey, Oct. 24, 1987; children: Michael, Katherine. BA, Western Ill. U., Macomb, 1975; postgrad., DePaul U., 1997—. Legis. aide Congressman Harold R. Collier, Washington, 1972-73; legis. asst. Nat. Assn. Retail Druggists, Washington, 1975-76; dir. Commn. and Meetings Nat. Assn. Bds. of Pharmacy, Chgo., 1976-80; pres. Assn. Forum, Chgo., 1980—; mem. assn. com. of 100, U.S. C. of C., 1995—. Commr. City of Park Ridge Econ. Devel. Commn., Park Ridge, Ill., 1990-94, 96—; mem. exec. com. Chgo. Conv. and Tourism Bur., 1993—. Recipient Disting. Alumni award Western Ill. U., Macomb, 1993. Fellow Am. Soc. Assn. Execs. (mem. cert. commn. 1989-91, Key award 1994); mem. The Tower Club, Univ. Club Chgo. Presbyterian. Office: Assn Forum 20 N Wacker Dr Ste 3000 Chicago IL 60606-3101

MAHAFFEY, REDGE ALLAN, movie producer, director, writer, actor, scientist; b. Bethesda, Md., Dec. 15, 1949; s. George Newton and Lila Katherine (Drum) M.; m. Ellen Cecilia Cranston, May 30, 1973 (div. Dec. 1980); m. Patricia Jane Guy, Apr. 29, 1984 (div. Sept. 1994); children: Travis Guy, Morgan Nicole; m. Veronica Bird, Sept. 24, 1994; children: Ryan Alexander, Ramsey Blake. BS, U. Md., 1971, MS, 1973, PhD, 1976. NRC postdoctoral fellow Nat. Acad. of Scis., Washington, 1976-77; research physicist Naval Research Lab., Washington, 1977-78; sr. research physicist Sachs/Freeman Assocs., Bladensburg, Md., 1978-79; dir. research Sachs/Freeman Assocs., Bowie, Md., 1979-81; sr. v.p., sec., treas. Sachs/Freeman Assocs., Landover, Md., 1981-91, also bd. dirs., 1985—; mng. ptnr. Ramsway Pictures, 1991—; instr. George Washington U., Washington, 1979-80, Prince George's Coll., 1987; pres. Capitol Contracts, Bowie, 1981-83. Author: A Higher Education, 1989, Me, Myself and I, 1992, Deadly Rivals, 1992; exec. prodr., writer Deadly Rivals, 1992, Quest of the Delta Knight, 1993; prodr., actor, writer, dir. Life 101, 1995, Forst Encounter, 1997; prodr., actor, dir. She's Too Tall, 1997; contbr. articles on lasers and particle beams to sci. jours., also short stories, essays and poems to mags.; patentee laser, x-rays and particle beams. Recipient Research Publ. award Naval Research Lab., 1978, 1st Place Novel Internat. Lit. Awards, 1988. Mem. IEEE, Am. Phys. Soc., MENSA, Intertel, Nat. Writer's Club, Internat. Platform Assn., Internat. Soc. Phil. Enquiry, Writer's Assn. Anne Arundel County, Bethesda Writer's Ctr., Inst. Noetic Scis. Republican. Club: Sea Dragons Martial Arts(Washington) (treas. 1984-85, instr. 1987-91). Avocations: martial arts, softball. Office: Ramsway Pictures 738 Intrepid Way Davidsonville MD 21035-1307

MAHAJAN, SUBHASH, electronic materials educator; b. Gurdaspur, India; m. Sushma Sondhi, Sept. 3, 1965; children: Sanjoy, Sunit, Ashish. BS with highest honors, Panjab U., India, 1959; BE in Metallyrgy with highest honors, Indian Inst. Sci., 1961; PhD in Materials Sci. and Engring., U. Calif., 1965. Rsch. asst. U. Calif., Berkeley, 1961-65; rsch. metallurgist U. Denver, 1965-68; Harwell fellow Atomic Energy Rsch. Establishment, Harwell, Eng., 1968-71; mem. tech. staff AT&T Bell Labs., Murray Hill, N.J., 1971-83, rsch. mgr., 1981-83; prof. electronic materials dept. material sci. and engring. Carnegie Mellon U., Pitts., 1983-97; prof. electronic materials Ariz. State U., Tempe, 1997—; mem. site panel Materials Rsch. Lab., 1993; vis. prof. U. Antwerp, Belgium, 1991, École Ctrl. Lyon, Ecully, France, 1993; lectr., spkr., patentee, cons. in field. Editor: (with V.G. Keramidas) Electrochemical Society Symposium volume, 1983; (with L.C. Kimerling) The Concise Encyclopedia of Semiconducting Materials and Related Technologeis, 1992, Handbook on Semiconductors vol. 3, 1994; (with D. Bloor, R.J. Brook and M.C. Flemings) The Encyclopedia of Advanced Materials, 1994; contbr. over 170 articles to profl. jours. Mem. materials rsch. adv. com. divsn. materials rsch. NSF, 1989-92. DAAD fellow U. Göttingen, Germany, 1976. Fellow Am. Soc. Metals Internat.; mem. Materials Rsch. Soc. (editor symposium volume 1983, organizer symposium Am. Assn. Crystal Growers), Electrochem. Soc. (mem. electronics divsn. 1976-83, divisional editor 1976-86), Minerals, Metals and Materials Soc. (mem. phys. metallurgy com. 1976-83, vice chmn. mech. metallurgy com. 1978-79, mem. 1975-80, mem. electronic materials com. 1990-94, chmn. electronic, magnetic and photonic materials com. 1984-86, tech. dir. bd.), Sigma Xi. Home: 8824 S Poplar Tempe AZ 85284 Office: Ariz State U Dept Materials Sci and Engring Dept Chem Bio and Mats Engr Tempe AZ 85287

MAHAL, TAJ (HENRY ST. CLAIR FREDERICKS), composer, musician; b. Mass., May 17, 1942; s. Henry St. Clair and Mildred (Shields) Fredericks; m. Inshirah Geter, Jan. 23, 1976; children: Aya, Taj, Gahmelah, Ahmen, Deva, Nani. BA, U. Mass., Amherst, 1964. Ind. musician, composer, rec. artist, 1964—. Early appearances at Club 47, Boston; rec. artist with Columbia, Warner Brothers, Gramavision labels; tours throughout U.S., Europe, Australia, including State Dept.-sponsored tour of Africa; composer: (album) Taj Majal, 1968, The Natch'l Blues, 1968, Giant Steps, 1969, Brothers, 1971 (Ethnic Music award, Bay Area Musics award 1979), The Real Thing, 1971, Happy Just Like I am, 1971, Recycling the Blues, 1972, Oooh so Good 'n Blues, 1973, Mo' Roots, 1974, Music Keeps Me Together, 1975, Music Fuh Yuh, 1977, Evolution, 1977, Best of #1, 1981, Taj, 1986, Shake Sugaree, 1987, Live and Direct, 1987, Big Blues, 1988, Mulebone, 1991, Like Never Before, 1991, Rising Sun Collection, 1992, Taj's Blues, 1992, Rinsing Sons, 1992, Smilin' Island of Song, 1992, World Music, 1993, Dancin' the Blues-Private Music, 1993 (Grammy nomination traditional blues 1993), Mumtaz Mahal, 1995, An Evening of Acoustic Music, 1996, Phantom Blues, 1996; (film soundtracks) Sounder, Sounder II; (TV shows) Ewoks, The Man Who Broke a Thousand Chains, Brer Rabbit, 1990, The Hot Spot, 1990 (Grammy nomination as Best Contemporary Blues Album 1990); actor: (films) King of Ragtime, Sounder, Sounder II, (theater) Mule Bone: assoc. artist, Mark Taper Forum, L.A., 1992—. Office: Bill Graham Mgmt PO Box 429094 San Francisco CA 94142*

MAHAN, CHARLES SAMUEL, public health service officer; b. Pitts., Nov. 4, 1938. AB, W.Va. U., 1960; MD, Northwestern U., 1964. Diplomate Am. Bd. Ob-Gyn. Endocrine fellow Cook County Hosp., Chgo., 1964; intern Hennepin County Gen. Hosp., Mpls., 1964-65, assoc. and sr. assoc. physician, 1970-74; med. fellow in obstetrics and gynecology U. Minn. Hosp., Mpls., 1965-68; staff physician Shands Teaching Hosp., Coll. Medicine U. Fla., Gainesville, 1974-95, dir. divsn. ambulatory svcs. women,

1974-87, assoc. prof. dept. obstetrics and gynecology, 1974-80, prof., 1980—; mem. grad. faculty U. Fla., 1977-95, acting chmn. dept. obstetrics and gynecology, 1978-79; asst. and assoc. prof. dept. obstetrics and gynecology med. sch. U. Minn., Mpls., 1970-74; dir. maternal and child health State of Fla., 1982-86, acting asst. health officer pub. health and primary care, 1986-87; dep. sec. health, state health officer Fla. Dept. Health and Rehabilitative Svcs., 1988-95; prof. dept. cmty. and family health, maternal health program U. South Fla., Tampa, 1995—; sr. assoc. physician ob-gyn. Pilot City Health Ctr., Mpls., 1970-74; mem. Gov.'s Venereal Disease Awareness Com., Minn., 1971-74; med. dir. Red Door Venereal Disease Clinic, Mpls., 1972-74; mem. Minn. State Family Planning Adv. Bd., 1972-74; chmn. ambulatory care com. Hennepin County Gen. Hosp., 1973-74; dir. North Ctrl. Fla. Maternity and Infant Care, Family Planning, Teen-Age Pregnancy Team Projects, and WIC Program, 1974-87; assoc. dir. Tech. Assistance Health Rsch. Group, Gainesville, 1975-82; chmn. med. care evaluation com. Shands Teaching Hosp., 1976-80; mem. faculty senate U. Fla., 1976-78, 79-80, 87-88, mem. outpatient clinics com., 1978-86, mem. health policy task force, 1992—, mem. promotion and tenure com. coll. medicine, 1978-81, dir. undergrad. edn. dept. ob-gyn., 1980-85, pres. faculty, 1982-83, mem. faculty coun., 1982-85, dir. Fla. midwifery resource ctr., 1992—, mem. nurse-midwife tng. program adv. com. coll. nursing, 1982—, mem. adv. com. inst. HIV rsch. and edn., 1992—; mem. State of Fla. Family Planning Coun., 1976-79; chmn. 1st ann. med. alumni sci. seminar Hennepin County Med. Ctr., Minn., 1976; mem. Alachua County Child Advocacy Coun., 1977-79; mem. adv. bd. Rape Info. and Counseling Ctr., 1977-79; mem. nat. adv. coun. maternal, fetal and infant nutrition USDA, 1978-81; chmn. health com. Alachua County Human Svcs. Planning Coun., 1980-82, acting pres. coun., 1982; mem. adv. bd. Nat. Cesarean/Support, Edn. and Concern, 1984-89; gov.'s rep. Healthy Mothers/Healthy Babies Steering Com., 1985—; mem. children's med. svcs. Perinatal Adv. Coun. of State of Fla., 1985-88, chairperson, 1987-88; chmn. rsch. adv. com. nat. study freestanding birth ctrs. Nat. Assn. Childbearing Ctrs., 1986-88; chmn. Gov.'s Task Force AIDS, 1988-90; affiliate prof. inst. child health policy U. Fla., 1988—; mem. Fla. Task Force Govt. Financed Health Care, 1989-91; mem. bd. advisors Wellness Inst., Miami-Dade C.C., 1991—; mem. Statewide Health Coun., 1991—; mem. adv. com. to maternal and child health program at coll. pub. health U. South Fla., 1991—; mem. adv. bd. Healthy Kids Corp., 1992—; mem. child health initiative nat. adv. com. Robert Wood Johnson Found., 1992—, dir. healthy futures: a program to imporve maternal and infant care in the South, 1987-92; mem. bd. contbg. analysts Am. Health Line, 1992—; co-chair basic benefits com. Gov. Chiles' Health Care Reform Plan, 1993; mem. Commn. Minority Health, 1993—; mem. adv. com. to dir. Ctrs. Disease Control and Prevention, 1994—; vis. prof. various instns.; lectr. in field; bd. dirs. Corner Drug Store, Gainesville. Editor: Generally Funny: A Monograph of Medical Ancedotes and Cartoons, 1976; contbr. chpts. and revs. to books and articles to profl. jours. Active Nat. Found.-Mar. Dimes, 1978-88, chmn. edn. adv. com., 1978-82, 85-87; active Leadership Gainesville, 1978; mem. ob-gyn. alumni coun. med. sch. Northwestern U., 1986—; mem. Gov.'s Adv. Coun. Farmworkers Affairs, 1988—; mem. innovation coun. Ounce Prevention Fund Fla., 1994—. With USN, 1968-70, res. Recipient Cmty. Svc. award Gainesville Women's Health Ctr., 1976, Spl. MCH award Fla. Coun. Primary Care, 1984, Spl. Award for Mother-Infant Health, Coalition Fla. Childbirth Educators, 1984, Award for MCH Leadership, So. Health Assn., 1991, Mary E. Switzer award Assn. Schs. Applied Health Professions, 1992, State of Fla. Cabinet Disting. Svc. award, 1992; Rsch. fellow USN, Aviation Med. Acceleration Lab., 1961. Mem. AMA, APHA (mem. coun. maternal and child health 1985-88), Am. Coll. Ob-Gyn. (chmn. spl. interest group ambulatory reproductive health care 1978-80, chmn. dist. IV maternity mortality com. 1979-81, mem. com. health care underserved women 1988—, chmn. 1992, chmn. nat. fetal-infant mortality rev. steering com. 1990—), Nat. Assn. Childbearing Ctrs. (bd. dirs. 1983—), Nat. Perinatal Assn., Fla. Ctr. Children and Youth, Fla. Healthy Mothers/Healthy Babies Coalition (Spl. Award for MCH Leadership 1985), Fla. Med. Assn. (mem. com. pub. health 1988—, mem. com. AIDS 1988—), Fla. Obstet. and Gynecol. Soc., Fla. Perinatal Assn., Fla. Pub. Health Assn. (chmn. maternal and child health sect. 1987-88, mem. jour. editl. bd. 1987—), Fla. Soc. Childbirth Educators, Fla. Soc. Preventive Medicine, Childbirth Edn. Assn. Jacksonville (mem. adv. bd. 1989—), Assn. State and Territorial Health Ofcls. (mem. exec. com. 1991—, pres. 1993-94), Assn. Profs. Gynecology and Obstetrics, Capital Med. Soc., Internat. Childbirth Edn. Assn. (chairperson profl. cons. selection com. 1978-82, bd. dirs. 1978-82, profl. cons. 1982—), Internat. Physicians Prevention Nuclear War, Jacobs Inst. Women's Health (founding mem.), So. Med. Assn., W.Va. U. Alumni Assn. (life), Rotary Club Tallahassee (bd. dirs. 1989-90). Home: 1001 N Riverhills Dr Tampa FL 33617-4241 also: U Fla Dept Ob-Gyn Midwifery Resource Ctr 2705 Blairstone Ln Tallahassee FL 32301-6074

MAHAN, CLARENCE, retired govenment official, writer; b. Dayton, Ohio, Jan. 1, 1939; s. Clarence Mahan and Elsie (Crouch) Dlitz; m. Suky Mahan, May 27, 1962; children: Sean M., Christiane Elizabeth. BA, U. Md., 1963; MA, Am. U., 1968; MBA, Syracuse U., 1969. Dep. comtroller U.S. Army, Japan, 1974-76; dep. chief program and budget Defense Commn. Agy., Arlington, Va., 1976; aide Asst. Sec. Army, Washington, 1976-77; chief operating appropriations Dept. AF, Washington, 1979-80; dir. fin. and acctg. Dept. Energy, Washington, 1980-81, dep. comptroller, 1981-82; dir. fiscal and contracts mgmt. EPA, Washington, 1982-83, dep. comptroller, 1983-85, dir. Rsch. Program Mgmt. Office, 1985-95; instr., lectr. in field. Contbr. articles to profl. jours. and hort. mags. With U.S. Army, 1959-62, Korea. Mem. Am. Iris Soc. (bd. dirs., 2d v.p. 1991-95, 1st. v.p. 1995—), Hist. Iris Preservation Soc. (pres. 1991-93), Soc. Japanese Irises (pres. 1989-92), Reblooming Iris Soc. (bd. dirs. 1986-94). Democrat. Home and Office: 7311 Churchill Rd Mc Lean VA 22101-2001

MAHAN, DAVID JAMES, school superintendent; b. St. Louis, May 29, 1934; s. John William and Eleanor (Johnson) M.; m. Jane E. Pyle, Nov. 28, 1957; children: Elizabeth Mahan-Shaw, Kathryn Goodman. BA, Okla. Baptist Coll., 1956; MA, Washington U., St. Louis, 1962, EdD, 1968. Cert. elem., secondary English tchr., Mo., cert. elem. prin., Mo., cert. supt., Mo. Program devel. St. Louis Pub. Schs., 1968-69, dir. fed. programs, 1969-71, asst. to supt., 1971-72, asst. supt., instr., 1972-73, dist. supt., 1973-79, area II supt., 1979-84, asst. supt. mid. schs., 1984-90, interim supt. schs., 1990-91, supt. schs., 1991—. Co-author: The Faculty Team: School Organization for Results, 1971. Bd. dirs. Commerce and Growth Assn., St. Louis, 1990—, Asthma and Allergy Found. Am., St. Louis, 1990—, St. Louis Symphony Soc., 1992—, Boy Scouts Am., 1992—. Home: 5 Portland Ct Saint Louis MO 63108-1293 Office: U Mo St Louis 8001 Natural Bridge Rd Saint Louis MO 63121

MAHAN, GERALD DENNIS, physics educator, researcher; b. Portland, Oreg., Nov. 24, 1937; s. Thomas Finley and Julia Kay (Swails) M.; m. Sally Ann Spaugh, Feb. 20, 1965; children—Christopher Parker, Susan Thayer, Roy Finley. A.B., Harvard U., 1959; Ph.D. in Physics, U. Calif.-Berkeley, 1964. Research physicist Gen. Electric Co., Schenectady, 1963-67; part-time Gen. Electric Co., 1967-84; assoc. prof. physics U. Oreg., Eugene, 1967-73; prof. physics Ind. U., Bloomington, 1973-82; disting. prof. Ind. U., 1982-84; disting. prof. physics U. Tenn., Knoxville; disting. scientist Oak Ridge Nat. Lab.; guest prof. Niels Bohr Inst., Copenhagen, 1977-78. Author: Many-Particle Physics, 1981; contbr. numerous articles on physics to profl. jours. Alfred Sloan fellow, 1968-70. Fellow Am. Phys. Soc. Office: U Tenn Dept Physics Knoxville TN 37996

MAHAN, JAMES CAMERON, lawyer; b. El Paso, Tex., Dec. 16, 1943; m. Eileen Agnes Casale, Jan. 13, 1968; 1 child, James Cameron Jr. BA, U. Charleston, 1965; JD, Vanderbilt U., 1973. Bar: Nev. 1974, U.S. Dist. Ct. Nev. 1974, U.S. Ct. Appeals (9th cir.) 1975, U.S. Tax Ct. 1980, U.S. Supreme Ct. 1980. Assoc. Lee & Beasey, Las Vegas, Nev., 1974-75; mem. firm John Peter Lee Ltd., Las Vegas, 1975-82; sr. ptnr. Mahan & Ellis, Chartered, Las Vegas, 1982—. With USN, 1966-69. Office: Mahan & Ellis Chartered 510 S 9th St Las Vegas NV 89101-7011

MAHANES, DAVID JAMES, JR., retired distillery executive; b. Lexington, Ky., June 19, 1923; s. David James and Ethel (Brock) M.; m. Dorothy Jean Richardson, Oct. 28, 1950; 1 child, David James III. BS, U. Ky., 1947; MBA, Harvard U., 1950. Regional mgr. Jack Daniel Distillery, Nashville, 1960-65, v.p., 1965-70, sr. v.p., 1970-71, exec. v.p., 1971-85, pres., 1985-88, chmn. bd. dirs.; chmn. bd. dirs. Early Times Distillery Co., Can. Mist Distilling Co., Thoroughbred Plastics Co. Lt. inf. AUS, 1943-46, ETO; lt. col. AG ret. Recipient Bronze Star; Runnerup as outstanding sales exec. Gallagher Report, 1982. Mem. SAR (pres. Andrew Jackson chpt.), Soc. Colonial Wars in Tenn. (gov., dep. gov. gen.), English Speaking Union (pres.), Res. Officers Assn., The 200 Club, Belle Meade Country Club, Beaver Creek Club, Exch. Club, Tenn. Profl. Golfers Assn. (hon.), Kappa Alpha, Beta Gamma Sigma. Republican. Presbyterian. Home: 104 Adams Park Nashville TN 37205-4702

MAHANTHAPPA, KALYANA THIPPERUDRAIAH, physicist, educator; b. Hirehalli, Mysore, India, Oct. 29, 1934; s. Kalyana and Thippamma (Maddanappa) T.; m. Prameela Talkerappa, Oct. 30, 1961; children: Nagesh, Rudresh, Mahesh. BSc, Central Coll. Bangalore, India, 1954; MSc, Delhi U., 1956; PhD (Faculty Arts and Scis. fellow), Harvard, 1961. Research assoc. U. Cal. at Los Angeles, 1961-63; asst. prof. U. Pa., Phila., 1963-66; mem. Inst. Advanced Study, Princeton, N.J., 1964-65; assoc. prof. physics U. Colo., Boulder, 1966-69; prof. U. Colo., 1969—, faculty research fellow, 1970-71, 76-77, 83-84, 93-94; vis. prof./scientist U. Rome, 1970, Internat. Ctr. for Theoretical Physics, 1971, Cambridge U., 1976-77; cons. Aerojet-Gen., L.A., 1962-63; dir. Summer Inst. Theoretical Physics, Boulder, 1968-69, NATO Advanced Study Inst. in Elem. Particles, 1979, NATO Advanced Rsch. Workshop on Superstrings, 1987; gen. dir. Theoretical Advanced Study Inst. in Particle Physics, 1989—; sr. vis. rsch. fellow Imperial Coll., London, 1983-84. Contbr. articles to profl. jours. Fellow Am. Phys. Soc.; mem. AAAS, Sigma Xi. Research theoretical high energy and elementary particle physics. Home: 2865 Darley Ave Boulder CO 80303-6307

MAHAR, ELLEN PATRICIA, law librarian; b. Washington, Jan. 15, 1938; d. Richard A. and Lina C. (Chittick) M. BA, St. Joseph Coll., Emmitsburg, Md., 1959; MLS, U. Md., 1968. Asst. librarian Covington & Burling, Washington, 1971-73, libr. dir., 1978-92; librarian Shea & Gardner, Washington, 1974-78; mgr. info. ctr. Assn. Comml. Real Estate, Herndon, Va., 1992-94; head libr. Caplin & Drysdale Chtd., Washington, 1994—. Coeditor: Legislative History of the Securities Act of 1933 and the Securities Act of 1934, 11 vols., 1973. Mem. Am. Assn. Law Libraries, Spl. Libraries Assn., Law Librarians' Soc. Washington. Office: Caplin & Drysdale Chtd 1 Thomas Cir NW Washington DC 20005-5802

MAHARIDGE, DALE DIMITRO, journalist, educator; b. Cleve., Oct. 24, 1956; s. Steve and Joan (Kopfstein) M. Student, Cleve. State U., 1974-75. Free-lance reporter various publs., Cleve., 1976; reporter The Gazette, Medina, Ohio, 1977-78; free-lance reporter Cleve. Plain Dealer, 1978-80; reporter The Sacramento Bee, 1980-91; lectr. Stanford U., Palo Alto, Calif., 1992—. Author: Journey to Nowhere: The Saga of the New Underclass, 1985, repub. with introduction by Bruce Springsteen, 1996, And Their Children After Them, 1989 (Pulitzer Prize for gen. nonfiction 1990), The Last Great American Hobo, 1993, The Coming White Minority: California's Eruptions and the Nation's Future, 1996; contbr. articles to profl. jours. Nieman fellow Harvard U., 1988; grantee Pope Found., 1994, Freedom Forum, 1995. Democrat. Office: Stanford U Dept Comm Bldg 120 Stanford CA 94305

MAHER, BILL, talk show host, comedian, producer; b. N.Y.C., Jan. 20, 1956; s. Bill and Julie (Berman) M. BA, Cornell U., 1978. Creator, host Politically Incorrect, HBO, N.Y.C., 1993—. Performances include (theatre) Seymour Glick is Alive But Sick (Steve Allen); (stand-up) The Bob Monkhouse Show, Late Night with David Letterman, The Tonight Show Anniversary Show, The Tonight Show, HBO Spl., 1989, 92; (TV shows) Steve Allen's Music Room, Alice, Sara, Max Headroom, Hard Knocks, Newhart, Murder, She Wrote, The Midnight Hour, Say What?; (TV movies) Out of Time, Rags to Riches, Club Med; (films) D.C. Cab, Rat Boy, House II, Cannibal Women in the Avocado Jungle of Death, Pizza Man; author: (novel) True Story, 1994. Recipient Cableace award Nat. Acad. Cable Programming, 1990, Cableace award for best talk show series, 1995, Cableace award for best talk show host, 1995. Office: HBO Politically Incorrect 7800 Beverly Blvd Ste D Los Angeles CA 90036-2165*

MAHER, BRENDAN ARNOLD, psychology educator, editor; b. Widnes, Eng., Oct. 31, 1924; came to U.S., 1955; s. Thomas F. and Agnes (Power) M.; m. Winifred Barbara Brown, Aug. 27, 1952; children: Rebecca, Thomas, Nicholas, Liam, Niall. B.A. with honours, U. Manchester, Eng., 1950; M.A., Ohio State U., 1951, Ph.D., 1954; student, U. Ill. Med. Sch., 1952-53; A.M. (hon.), Harvard, 1972. Diplomate: Am. Bd. Examiners in Profl. Psychology. Psychologist Her Majesty's Prison, Wakefield, Eng., 1954-55; instr. Ohio State U., 1955-56; asst. prof. Northwestern U., 1956-58; asso. prof. La. State U., 1958-60; lectr. Harvard, 1960-64; chmn. Center Research Personality, 1962-64; prof. U. Wis., 1964-67, 71-72; vis. fellow U. Copenhagen, 1966-67, vis. fellow and research scientist, 1979; prof. psychology Brandeis U., 1967-72; dean Brandeis U. (Grad. Sch.), 1969-71, dean faculty, 1971-83; E. C. Henderson prof. psychology, 1983—; prof. Harvard U., 1972—, chmn. dept. psychology and social relations, 1973-78, chmn. dept. psychology, 1987-89, dean Grad. Sch. Arts and Scis., 1989-92; assoc. psychologist McLean Hosp., Belmont, Mass., 1968-77; psychologist McLean Hosp., 1977-84; cons. in medicine Peter Bent Brigham Hosp., Boston, 1977-85; cons. in psychology Mass. Gen. Hosp., 1977—. Author: Principles of Psychopathology, 1966, Introduction to Research in Psychopathology, 1970, A Passage to Sword Beach, 1996; co-editor: National Research Council: Research Doctorate Programs in the United States, 1995; editor Progress in Exptl. Personality Rsch., 1964-87, Jour. Cons. and Clin. Psychology, 1972-78; cons. editor Rev. Personality and Social Psychology, Clin. Psychology Rev. Served with Brit. Royal Navy, 1943-47. Fellow AAAS, Am. Psychol. Soc.; mem. Brit. Psychol. Assn. (chartered psychologist U.K.), Soc. Rsch. in Psychopathology (pres. 1985-87). Office: Harvard U William James Hall Cambridge MA 02138 also: Giffords Island, Mahone Bay, NS Canada

MAHER, DAVID L., drug store company executive; b. Iowa City, 1939. Grad., U. Iowa, 1964. Pres., COO Am. Stores Co., Salt Lake City. Office: American Stores Co 709 E South Temple Salt Lake City UT 84102-1205

MAHER, DAVID WILLARD, lawyer; b. Aug. 14, 1934, Chgo.; s. Chauncey Carter and Martha (Peppers) M.; BA Harvard, 1955, LLB, 1959; m. Jill Waid Armagnac, Dec. 20, 1954; children: Philip Armagnac, Julia Armagnac. Bar: N.Y. 1960, Ill. 1961; pvt. practice Boston, N.Y.C., 1958-60; assoc. Kirkland & Ellis, and predecessor firm, 1960-65, ptnr. 1966-78; ptnr. Reuben & Proctor, 1978-86, Isham, Lincoln and Beale, 1986-88, Sonnenschein, Nath & Rosenthal, 1988—; gen. counsel BBB Chgo. and No. Ill.; lectr. DePaul U. Sch. Law, 1973-79, Law Sch. of Loyola U., Chgo., 1980-84. Mem. vis. com. to the Div. Sch., U. Chgo., 1986—. Served to 2d lt. USAF, 1955-56. Fellow Am. Bar Found. (lifetime); mem. ABA, Am. Law Inst., Ill. Bar Assn., Chgo. Bar Assn. (chmn. internet interim policy oversight com.), Bull Valley Hunt Club, Chgo. Lit. Club, Union League Club, Tavern, Club. Roman Catholic. Home: 311 W Belden Ave Chicago IL 60614-3817 Office: Sonnenschein Nath & Rosenthal 233 S Wacker Dr Ste 8000 Chicago IL 60606-6342

MAHER, FRANCESCA MARCINIAK, air transportation executive, lawyer; b. 1957. BA, Loyola U., 1978, JD, 1981. Ptnr. Mayer, Brown & Platt, Chgo., 1981-93; v.p., sec. UAL Corp., Elk Grove Village, Ill., 1993—. Bd. dirs. United Ctr., YMCA Metro. Chgo. Mem. Ill. Humane Soc. (bd. dirs.). Office: UAL Corp PO Box 66100 Chicago IL 60666

MAHER, KIM LEVERTON, museum administrator; b. Washington, Feb. 25, 1946; d. Joseph Wilson and Helen Elizabeth (Bell) Leverton; m. William Fredrick Maher, June 12, 1965 (div. 1980); 1 child, Lauren Robinson. Student Duke U., 1963-65, George Washington U., 1966; B.A. in English, U. Fla., 1969. Social worker Fla. Health and Rehab. Service, Gainesville, 1969-71, Delray Beach, 1972-74, fraud unit supr., West Palm Beach, 1974-76, direct service supr., 1977-78; ctr. dir. Palm Beach County Employment and Tng. Adminstrn., West Palm Beach, 1979-81; exec. dir. Discovery Ctr., Inc., Ft. Lauderdale, Fla., 1981-92; exec. dir. Mus. Discovery & Sci., Ft. Lauderdale, 1992-94; CEO Va. Air and Space Ctr., Hampton, 1995—. Bd. dirs. Singing Pines Mus., Boca Raton, Fla., 1984-88, Broward Art Guild, Ft. Lauderdale, 1985-91, Va. space grant consortium Va. Aerospace Bus. Roundtable, Hampton, 1995—; mem. Leadersh ip Broward II, Ft. Lauderdale, 1983-84; mem. faculty Inst. New Sci. Ctrs., 1992. Recipient Cultural Arts award Broward Cultural Arts Found., 1985, Woman of Yr. award Women in Comm., 1990, Woman of Distinction award So. Fla. Mag., 1993, Outstanding Fundraiser Fla. Assn. Nonprofit Orgns., 1994. Mem. Am. Assn. Museums, A ssn. Sci. and Tech. Ctrs., Southeastern Museums Conf., Fla. Sci. Tchrs. Assn. (bd. dirs.), Fla. Assn. Mus. (bd. dirs. 1989—, pres. 1993-95), Leadership Broward Alumnae (curriculum com. 1984—), Fort Lauderdale Downtown Council (bd. dirs. 1992—),13), Women's Exec. Club, Phi Kappa Phi. Republican. Methodist. Avocations: scuba diving; piano; creative writing; collecting art and antiques; painting. Office: Va Air and Space Ctr 600 Settlers Landing Rd Hampton VA 23669-4033

MAHER, L. JAMES, III, molecular biologist; b. Mpls., Nov. 28, 1960; s. Louis James and Elizabeth Jane (Crawford) M.; m. Laura Lee Moseng, July 2, 1983; children: Elizabeth Lillian, Christina Ailene. BS in Molecular Biology, U. Wis., 1983, PhD in Molecular Biology, 1988. Fellow U. Wis., Madison, 1983-84, rsch. asst., 1984-88; postdoctoral fellow Calif. Inst. Tech., Pasadena, 1988-91; asst. prof. molecular biology Eppley Inst., U. Nebr. Med. Ctr., Omaha, 1991-95; assoc. prof. biochem. molecular biology Mayo Found., Rochester, Minn., 1995—. Editorial bd. Antisense Rsch. & Devel. Jour., 1991—; contbr. articles to profl. jours. Musician, Madison Symphony Orch., 1983-88, Calif. Inst. Tech. Symphony Orch., L.A., 1988-91. Gosney fellow, 1988; Am. Cancer Soc. postdoctoral fellow, 1988. Mem. AAAS, Phi Beta Kappa. Evangelical Christian Ch. Achievements include research in chemical and biochemical agents designed to artificially regulate the flow of genetic information in biological systems. Office: Mayo Found Dept Biochem and Molec Biol 200 1st St SW Rochester MN 55902-3008

MAHER, LOUIS JAMES, JR., geologist, educator; b. Iowa City, Iowa, Dec. 18, 1933; s. Louis James and Edith Marie (Ham) M.; m. Elizabeth Jane Crawford, June 7, 1956; children: Louis James, Robert Crawford, Barbara Ruth. BA, U. Iowa, 1955, MS, 1959; PhD, U. Minn., 1961. Mem. faculty dept. geology and geophysics U. Wis.-Madison, 1962—, prof., 1970—, chmn. dept., 1980-84. Contbr. articles to profl. jours. Served with U.S. Army, 1956-58. Danforth fellow, 1955-61; NSF fellow, 1959-61; NATO fellow, 1961-62. Fellow AAAS, Geol. Soc. Am.; mem. Am. Quaternary Assn., Ecol. Soc. Am., Wis. Acad. Sci., Arts and Letters, Sigma Xi. Episcopalian. Office: U Wis Dept Geology and Geoph 1215 W Dayton St Madison WI 53706-1600

MAHER, PATRICK JOSEPH, utility company executive; b. Dublin, Ireland, Apr. 20, 1936; came to U.S., 1946, naturalized, 1955; s. Pierce Albeus and Mary (Brady) M.; m. Catherine M. Sullivan, Oct. 13, 1962; children: Kathy, Kevin, Erin, Megan. BBA, Iona Coll., 1959; MBA, N.Y. U., 1965. With spl. devel. program Chase Manhattan Bank, N.Y.C., 1961-64, 2d v.p. fiduciary dept., 1964-68; asst. v.p. Nat. Comml. Bank, Albany, N.Y., 1968-70; chief sect. utility fin. N.Y. State Pub. Svc. Commn., Albany, 1970-74; v.p., chief fin. officer Washington Gas Light Co., 1974-80, exec. v.p. fin. and adminstrn., 1980-87, pres., 1987-92, 1992—, chmn. bd. dirs., CEO, 1993—. Served with USAR, 1960-61. Mem. Am. Gas Assn., Nat. Soc. Rate of Return Analysts, Natural Gas Men's Roundtable, Greater Washington Bd. Trade, Inst. Gas Tech., Associated Electric and Gas Ins. Svcs., U.S. C. of C., Rotary, N.Y. Athletic Club, Washington City Club. Roman Catholic. Home: 18781 Foggy Bottom Rd Bluemont VA 22012 Office: Washington Gas 1100 H St NW Washington DC 20080-0001

MAHER, PETER MICHAEL, university dean; b. North Battleford, Sask., Can., Mar. 4, 1940; s. Hugh James and Florence Andrea (Showell) M.; m. Illa Horning, Sept. 5, 1964; children: Andrea, Allison, Jennifer. BE, U. Sask., 1962; MBA, U. Western Ont., 1965; PhD, Northwestern U., 1970; D in Commerce, St. Mary's U., 1996. Registered prof. engr., Sask., Alta. Devel. engr. DuPont of Can., 1962-64, new venture analyst, 1965-67; teaching asst. Sir George Williams U., 1966-70; rsch. engr. dept. indsl. engring. and mgmt. sci. Northwestern U., 1968-76; prof., rsch. coord. Faculty of Bus. Adminstrn. and Commerce, U. Alta., 1970-76; dean, prof. adminstrn. Coll. of Commerce, U. Sask., 1976-81; dean, prof. faculty of mgmt. U. Calgary, Alta., 1981—, mem. univ. senate, 1989-92; bd.d irs. Calgary Airport Authority, Computalog Ltd., Can. Inst. for Petroleum Industry Devel., Pratt & Whitney Can., Inc., Theatre Calgary; witness House of Commons Spl. Commn. Employment Opportunities, 1981; mem. exec. com. Nu-West Ltd., 1982-88; audit com. Contbr. articles to profl. jours. Chmn. edn. div., mem. cabinet United Way, Calgary, 1989-90; creditor Northland Bank, 1985; trustee CNIB White Cane Found., 1989—; bd. dirs. Calgary Econ. Devel. Authority, 1983-90, Banff Mountain Acad., 1990—, Banff Sch. Advanced Mgmt., 1990—, chmn. acad. coun., 1992—, Theatre Calgary, 1992—; mem. corp. St. Thomas More Coll., Saskatoon, 1981—. Mem. Nat. Rsch. Coun. Can., Can. C. of C. (bd. dirs. 1984-86), Calgary C. of C. (bd. dirs. 1982-86), Am. Assembly Collegiate Schs. Bus. (faculty supply com. 1986—, initial/continuing accreditation com. 1989-94), Can. Fedn. Deans Mgmt. and Adminstrn. Studies (vice chmn. 1981-82, chmn. 1982-84, sec.-treas. 1990-96), Internat. Labour Orgn. (UN rep. 1985—), Can. Consortium Mgmt. Schs. (chmn. 1990-95, past chair 1995-97), Premier's Coun. on Sci. and Tech. (interman bd. dirs. 1984—). Home: 12 Varbrook Pl NW, Calgary, AB Canada T3A OA2 Office: U Calgary Faculty Mgmt. 2500 University Dr NW, Calgary, AB Canada T2N 1N4

MAHER, SHEILA, secondary school principal. Prin. R. L. Turner High Sch., Carrollton, Tex. Recipient Blue Ribbon Sch. award U.S. Dept. Edn., 1990-91. Office: RL Turner HS 1600 Josey Ln Carrollton TX 75006*

MAHER, TIMOTHY JOHN, pharmacologist, educator; b. Boston, Nov. 24, 1953; s. Robert Daniel and Veronica Irene (Cody) M.; m. Barbara Jean Walz, Aug. 20, 1977; children: Andrew Michael, Matthew Edward, Elizabeth Irene, Johnathan Daniel. BS, Boston State Coll., 1976; PhD, Mass. Coll. Pharmacy, 1980. Asst. prof. Mass. Coll. Pharmacy, Boston, 1980-83, assoc. prof., 1983-87, prof., 1987—, chmn., 1987-93, dir. pharm. scis., 1994—, Sawyer prof. pharm. scis., 1994—; postdoctoral fellow MIT, Cambridge, 1983-88, lectr., 1988—; bd. dirs. Mass. Soc. Med. Rsch., Chelmsford, 1985—; adv. bd. Mass. Poison Control System, Boston, 1990—. Contbr. 90 articles to profl. jours. Roman Catholic. Achievements include 4 patents, involving the use of L-Tyrosine to enhance/supplement the pharmacological activity of various sympathomimetic amine drugs. Office: Mass Coll Pharmacy 179 Longwood Ave Boston MA 02115-5804

MAHER, VINCENT F., academic administrator, educator, lawyer; b. Dublin, Ireland, Mar. 5, 1955; s. Denis V. and Bridget (Breen) M.; m. Ann M. Avitabile, May 26, 1979; 1 child, Elisabeth. BS, Coll. Mt. St. Vincent, 1979; MS, Columbia U., 1982; JD, Queens Coll., CUNY, 1986; MA, Fordham U., 1992; Profl. Diploma, U. Cambridge, Eng., 1993. Bar: N.J. 1987, N.Y. 1988, U.S. Dist. Ct. N.J. 1987, U.S. Dist. Ct. (ea. and so. dists.) N.Y. 1989; CRNA; RN, N.Y. Staff nurse anesthetist NYU/Bellevue, N.Y.C., 1983-84, St.Luke's/Roosevelt Hosp. Ctr., N.Y.C., 1980-86; cons. atty. Gair, Gair, Conason, Steigman and Mackauf, N.Y.C., 1989—; chmn. health svcs. adminstrn. Iona Coll., New Rochelle, N.Y., 1995—; nat., internat. lectr. Contbr. articles to profl. jours.; mem. editl. bd. Health Care Analysis, Jour. N.Y. State Nurses Assn., Jour. Nursing Law, Internat. Jour. Value Based Mgmt., others. Bd. dirs. Inst. Health Care Mgmt. Mem. ABA, ANA, AMWA, NHLA, N.Y. Bar Assn., Am. Pub. Health Assn., World Acad. on Med. Law, Am. Soc. Healthcare Execs., others. Office: Iona Coll 715 North Ave New Rochelle NY 10801-1830

MAHER, WILLIAM JAMES, investment executive; b. Chgo., Feb. 23, 1937; s. Alexander E. and Merle G. M.; B.B.A., Marquette U., 1961. Merchandising exec. Montgomery Ward & Co., Inc., Chgo., 1962-68; mgmt. cons. Cresap, McCormack & Paget, N.Y.C., 1968-69; v.p., treas. Solar Prodns., Inc., L.A., 1969-72; v.p., sec., treas. Creative Mgmt. Assocs., L.A., 1972-74; v.p., dir. Josephson Internat., Inc., L.A., 1975-83; pres. Tipperary Prodns., Inc., Beverly Hills, Calif., 1983-88; pres. Winter Park Capital Assets, Inc., 1989—. Office: Winter Park Capital Assets Inc 1031 W Morse Blvd Winter Park FL 32789-3715

MAHESH, VIRENDRA BHUSHAN, endocrinologist; b. India, Apr. 25, 1932; came to U.S., 1958, naturalized, 1968; s. Narinjan Prasad and Sobhagyawati; m. Sushila Kumari Aggarwal, June 29, 1955; children: Anita Rani, Vinit Kumar. BSc with honors, Patna U., India, 1951; MSc in Chemistry, Delhi U., India, 1953, PhD, 1955; DPhil in Biol. Sci, Oxford U., 1958. James Hudson Brown Meml. fellow Yale U., 1958-59; asst. rsch. prof. endocrinology Med. Coll. Ga., Augusta, 1959-63, assoc. rsch. prof., 1963-66, prof., 1966-70, Regents prof., 1970-86, Robert B. Greenblatt prof., 1979—, chmn. endocrinology, 1972-86, chmn., Regents prof. physiology and endocrinology, 1986—, chmn. physiology and endocrinology, 1986—; dir. Ctr. for Population Studies, 1971—; mem. reproductive biology study sect. NIH, 1977-81, mem. human embryology and devel. study sect. NIH, 1982-86, 90-93, chmn., 1991-93. Contbr. articles to profl. jours., chpts. to books; editor: The Pituitary, a Current Review, Functional Correlates of Hormone Receptors in Reproduction, Recent Advances in Fertility Research, Hirsuitism and Virilism, Regulation of Ovarian and Testicular Function, Excitatory Amino Acids: Their Role in Neuroendocrine Function; mem. editl. bd. Steroids, 1963—, Jour. of Clin. Endocrinology and Metabolism, 1976-81, Jour. Steroid Biochemistry and Molecular Biology, 1991—, Assisted Reproductive Tech./Andrology, 1993—; mem. adv. bd. Maturitas, 1977-81. Recipient Rubin award Am. Soc. Study Sterility, 1962, Billings Silver medal, 1965; Best Tchr. award freshman class Sch. Medicine, Med. Coll. Ga., 1969, Outstanding Faculty award Sch. Medicine, 1992, Outstanding Faculty award Sch. Grad. Studies, 1981, 94, Disting. Teaching award, 1988, Excellence in Rsch. award Grad. Faculty Assembly, 1987-91, 93-95; Disting. Scientist award Assn. Scientist Indian Origin in Am., 1989, rsch. grantee NIH, 1960—. Mem. Chem. Soc. (Eng.), Soc. Biochem. and Molecular Biol., Soc. Neurosci., Endocrine Soc., Soc. for Gynecologic Investigation, Internat. Soc. Neuroendocrinology, Soc. for Study Reproduction (Carl G. Hartman award 1996), Am. Physiol. Soc., Internat. Soc. Reproductive Medicine (pres. 1980-82), Soc. Exptl. Biology and Medicine, Am. Fertility Soc., Am. Assn. Lab. Animal Sci., N.Y. Acad. Scis., AAUP, Sigma Xi. Office: Med Coll of Ga Dept Physiology & Endocrinology Augusta GA 30912-3000

MAHEU, SHIRLEY, Canadian legislator; b. Montreal, Que., Can., Oct. 7, 1931; d. George William Johnson and Bertha Hunt; m. René Albert Maheu, Sept. 5, 1953; children: Ronald, Richard, Daniel, Marc. Ed., O'Sullivan Bus. Coll. Cert. ins. broker. Ins. broker; mcpl. councillor City of Saint-Laurent, Que., 1982-88; mem. from Saint-Laurent Ho. of Commons, 1988-96; mem. Can. Senate, Ottawa, Ont., 1996—. Pres. Saint-Laurent br. Red Cross Soc. Mem. Saint-Laurent C. of C. Roman Catholic. Office: Canadian Senate, Wellington St EB Rm 259, Ottawa, ON Canada K1A 0A4

MAHEY, JOHN ANDREW, museum director; b. DuBois, Pa., Mar. 30, 1932; s. Manasseh A. and Bernyce (Holdar) M. Student, Columbia U., 1950-52; B.A., Pa. State U., 1959, M.A., 1962. Asst. dir. Peale Mus., Balt., 1964-69; dir. E.B. Crocker Art Gallery, 1969-72, Cummer Gallery of Art, 1972-75, Meml. Art Gallery of U. Rochester, 1975-79; chief curator Philbrook Art Center, Tulsa, 1979-84; dir. San Antonio Mus. Art, 1984-89, Flint (Mich.) Inst. of Arts, 1989-96. Contbr. articles on artists to art his. jours.; author exhbn. catalogs. Served with USAF, 1952-57, 62-64. Fulbright scholar, 1962. Mem. Am. Assn. Museums, Assn. Art Mus. Dirs., Phi Beta Kappa, Phi Alpha Theta.

MAHFOOD, STEPHEN MICHAEL, governmental agency executive; b. Evansville, Ind., Feb. 12, 1949; s. George Mahfood and Bonnie Short Morse; m. Kathleen Kas; children: Nadia Joan, Leila Emma, Toni Henzler. BS, Rutgers U., 1971; grad. environ. leadership program, Yale U. Environ. dir. Project Hope, Tunisia, 1975-77; dir. prin. asst. Dept. of Health Mo. State Health Planning and Devel. Agy., Jefferson City, 1977-78, dir., 1978-81, 1982-84; gen. mgr. Chimney Rock (N.C.) Co., 1984—; dir. Mo. Environ. Improvement and Energy Resources Authority, Jefferson City; tchr. courses related to environ. and mgmt. Vol. YMCA, Beirut, Lebanon, 1974; past pres. Coun. of Pollution Control Fin. Agys., environ. fin. adv. bd. EPA Nat. Govs. Assn. Hazardous Minimization Assurance Adv. Group; appointed Congressman Anthony's Ho. Ways and Means Task Force on Pub. Fin.; past pres. Mo. Waste Control Coalition; mem. coun. Infrastructure Fin. Authorities. Recipient Achievement award Mo. Waste Control Coalition, 1986, 88, Presdl. Environ. Challenge award, 1992. Mem. Am. Mgmt. Assn., Am. Planning Assn., Nat. Assn. Environ. Profls., Coun. Infrastructure Fin. Authorities (co-founder). Avocations: canoeing, cross country skiing, hiking, motorcycling. Home: 7311 N Shore Dr Hartsburg MO 65039-9207 Office: Mo Environ Improvement & Energy Resources Authority Resources Authority PO Box 744 Jefferson City MO 65102-0744

MAHL, GEORGE FRANKLIN, psychoanalyst, psychologist, educator; b. Akron, Ohio, Nov. 27, 1917; s. Floyd Alexander and Margaret (Strecker) M.; m. Martha Jane Fenn, Jan. 10, 1944; 1 dau., Barbara Jessica. A. B., Oberlin Coll., 1939, M.A., 1941; PhD, Yale U., 1948; certificate, Western New Eng. Inst. Psychoanalysis, 1962. Asst. psychology Oberlin Coll., 1939-41; rsch. asst. in psychology Yale U., New Haven, 1941-42, mem. faculty, 1947—, prof. psychiatry and psychology, 1964-88, prof. emeritus, 1988—; tchr. Western New Eng. Inst. Psychoanalysis, 1961-85, pres., 1972-74. Served to 1st lt. AUS, 1942-46. Fellow AAAS, APA; mem. Ea. Psychol. Assn., Western New Eng. Inst. Psychoanalysis, Western New Eng. Psychoanalytic Soc., Internat. Psychoanalytical Assn., Inst. Psychoanalytic Tng. and Rsch. (N.Y.). Home: 106 Bayard Ave North Haven CT 06473-4303

MAHLE, CHRISTOPH ERHARD, electrical engineer; b. Stuttgart, Germany, Mar. 7, 1938; came to U.S., 1968; s. Ernst Johannes and Else (Wurth) M.; m. Mary Heavenrich, Mar. 23, 1975; children: Lisa, Charles. Diploma engring., Swiss Fed. Inst. Polytech., Zurich, 1961, D of Sci. Tech., 1966. Rsch. asst. Swiss Fed. Inst. Tech., Zurich, Switzerland, 1961-67; with tech. staff Comsat Labs., Clarksburg, Md., 1968-71, sect. head, 1971-73, dept. mgr., 1973-81, dir., 1981-83, exec. dir., 1983-94, v.p., 1995-96; ret., 1996. Patentee in field; contbr. articles to profl. jours. Fellow IEEE. Avocations: music, mountain climbing.

MAHLER, HALFDAN THEODOR, physician, health organization executive; b. Vivild, Denmark, Apr. 21, 1923; s. Magnus and Benedicte (Suadicani) M.; m. Ebba Fischer-Simonsen, Aug. 31, 1957; children: Per Bo, Finn. MD, U. Copenhagen, 1948, postgrad. degree in pub. health; LLD (hon.), U. Nottingham, Eng., 1975; MD (hon.), Karolinska Inst., Stockholm, 1977; Docteur, de l'Universite des Scis. Sociales de Toulouse, France, 1977; DPH (hon.), Seoul Nat. U., 1979; ScD (hon.), U. Lagos, Nigeria, 1979, Emory U., 1989; MD (hon.), Warsaw Med. Acad., 1980; LHD, U. Nacional Federico Villareal, Lima, Peru, 1980; LHD (hon.), U. Gand, Belgium, 1983, CUNY, 1989; MD (hon.), Charles U., Prague, 1982, Mahidol U., Bangkok, Thailand, 1982, Aarhus U., Denmark, 1988, U. Copenhagen, 1988, Aga Khan U., Pakistan, 1989; LHD (hon.), U. Nacional Autonoma de Nicaragua, 1983; Dr. honoris causa, The Semmelweis U. of Medicine, Budapest, Hungary, 1987; LLD (hon.), McMaster U., Can., 1989; DSc (hon.), SUNY, 1990; MD (hon.), U. Newcastle Upon Tyne, 1990; LLD (hon.), U. Exeter, 1990; LLD (honoris causa), U. Toronto, 1990. Specialized tng. in TB, active field of internat. pub. health work; planning officer mass Tb campaign Ecuador, 1950-51; sr. officer nat. Tb program WHO, India, 1951-61; chief Tb unit, Hdqrs., WHO, Geneva, 1962-69, sec. to expert adv. panel on Tb, 1962-69, dir. project systems analysis, 1969-70, asst. dir.-gen. div. health services and div. family health, 1970-73, dir.-gen., 1973-88, dir. gen. emeritus, 1988; sec. gen. Internat. Planned Parenthood Fedn., 1989-95. Contbr. articles on epidemiology and control of Tb, polit., social, econ, and technol. priorities in health sector, application of systems analysis to health care problems to profl. jours. Decorated Grand Officier de l'Ordre Nat. du Benin, 1975, Grand Officier de l'Ordre Nat. du Voltaique, Upper Volta, 1978, comdr. de l'Ordre Nat. du Mali, 1982, Grand Officer de l'Ordre du Merite de la Rep. du Senegal, 1982, comdr. 1st class Order White Rose (Finland), Grand Officier de l'Ordre nat. malgache, Madagascar, 1987, Grand Cross Icelandic Order of the Falcon, 1988, Grand Cordon of Order Sacred Treasure, Japan, 1988, Bourgeoisie d'Honneur, Geneva, Switzererland, Grand Croix De L'Ordre De Merite, Luxenbourg, 1990; recipient Jana Evangelisty Purkyne medal (Presdl. award) Prague, 1974, Comenius U. gold medal Bratislava, 1974, Carlo Forlanini gold medal Federazione Italiana contro la Tubercolosi et le Malattie Polmonari Sociali Rome, 1975, Ernest Carlsens Found. Prize Copenhagen, 1980, Georg Barfred-Pedersen prize Copenhagen, 1982, Hagedorn medal and prize Denmark, 1986, Freedom From Want medal Roosevelt Inst., 1988, Storkors Af Dannebrogsordenen, Denmark, 1988; hon. prof. U. Nacional Mayor de San Marcos, Lima, Peru, U. Chile Faculty of Medicine, Beijing Med. Coll., Rep. of China, Shanghai Med. U.; Bartel World Affairs fellow Cornell U., 1988; U.N. Population award, 1995, Andrija Stampar award, 1995. Fellow Royal Coll. Physicians (London), Faculty Community Medicine of Royal Colls. Physicians U.K. (hon.), Indian Soc. for Malaria and other Communicable Diseases (hon.), Royal Soc. Medicine (London) (hon., U.K.-U.S. Hewitt award 1992), London Sch. Hygiene and Tropical Medicine (hon.); mem. Med. Assn. Argentina (hon.), Latin Am. Med. Assn. (hon.), Italian Soc. Tropical Medicine (hon.), Belgium Soc. Tropical Medicine (assoc.), Societe medicale de Geneve (hon.), Union internationale contre la Tuberculose (hon.), Societe francaise d'Hygiene, de Medecine sociale et de Genie sanitaire (hon.), Uganda Med. Assn. (hon. life), Coll. Physicians and Surgeons, Bangladesh Royal Coll. Gen. Practitioners (ad eundem), List of Honour of the Internat. Dental Fedn., Am. Pub. Health Assn. (hon.), Nat. Acad. Medicine Mex. (hon.), Nat. Acad. Buenos Aires (hon.), Swedish Soc. Medicine (hon.), Brit. Medal Assn. (hon. fgn. corr. 1990), Inst. Medicine (NAS U.S.A.). Home and Office: 12 Chemin du Pont-Ceard, CH 1290 Versoix Switzerland

MAHLER, HARRY BEZ, architect, planner; b. Montclair, N.J., Aug. 8, 1928; s. Harry A. and Pauline Marie (Bez) M.; m. Elizabeth Willett, Oct. 2, 1954; children: Debra, Steven, Suzanne. B.Arch., Columbia U., 1954, William K. Fellows fellow, 1954-55. Successively draftsman, designer, chief designer, assoc., ptnr., sr. ptnr. for design, mem. mgmt. com. The Grad Partnership, Newark, 1949-90; chmn., chief exec. officer Grad. Assocs., P.A., Newark, 1990-94, chmn. emeritus, 1994—; prin. GLS Internat., 1994-96; pvt. practice Roseland, N.J., 1996-97; mgr. spl. products Edwards & Kelcey, Inc., Roseland, 19976; adj. prof. emeritus, curriculum coord. design and drawing Pratt Inst.; past mem. archtl. adv. bd. McGraw-Edison Corp.; chmn. adv. com., past chmn. fee com. N.J. Sch. Architecture; chmn. archtl. div. capital campaign, adv. com. Sch. Architecture N.J. Inst. Tech., mem. bd. overseers; design adv. com. State of N.J. Contbr. articles to profl. jours. Former commr., chmn. Montclair Redevel. Agy.; past chmn. barrier-free architecture com. Easter Seal Soc. N.J.; exec. v.p. Essex coun. Boy Scouts Am., chmn. camp study No. N.J. couns., mem. N.E. Regional Bd.; v.p. area 2 NE region Boy Scouts Am., past mem. Nat. Properties Com. Boy Scouts Am., mem. nat. coun.; past chmn., mem. real estate and corp. devel. luncheon, past mem. exec. bd., bd. govs. N.J. com. NCCJ; past trustee Montclair YMCA; mem. baseball boosters and kickoff classic coms. N.J. Sports Authority; mem., chmn., pres. Montclair State U. Found. Bd., others; pres., trustee Eagle Rock Condominium Assn.; pres., trustee, First United Meth. Ch. of Montclair. Recipient awards AIA, Illuminating Engrs. Soc., N.J. Soc. Architects, Bell System, Am. Concrete Inst., N.J. Bus. Mag., Am. Cons. Engrs. Coun., Archtl. Record Mag., Am. Planning Assn.; Humanitarian Brotherhood award NCCJ, 1987; Sch. of Architecture award N.J. Inst. Tech., 1987; Silver Beaver award Boy Scouts of Am., 1987, Silver Antelope award, 1991, Northeast Region award, 1987; named Bus. Leader of the Yr., N.J. Mag., 1991. Fellow AIA (past mem. nat. design com.); mem. N.J. Soc. Architects, Execs. Assn. N.J. (past chmn.), Regional Bus. Partnership (bd. dirs.), N.J. State C. of C. (bd. dirs.), N.J. Zool. Soc. (exec. v.p., past pres.), Beta Theta Pi. Methodist. Home: 72 Kent Dr Roseland NJ 07068-3706 Office: Grad Assocs PA 72 Kent Dr Roseland NJ 07068-3706

MAHLER, RICHARD T., finance executive; b. Galt, Ont., Can., May 15, 1943; s. Lawrence Herman and Therese (Trepanier) M.; m. Susan Jane Campbell, May 25, 1968; children: Stephen, Katherine. BSc, U. Waterloo, 1966; MBA, McMaster U., Hamilton, 1975. Asst. contr. Ford Motor Can., Oakville, Ont., 1967-81; v.p. fin., chief fin. officer Amdahl Can. Ltd., Toronto, Ont., 1981-90; exec. v.p., CFO Finning Internat. Inc., Vancouver, B.C., 1990—. Chmn. Oakville Galleries, Ont., 1971-79; pres. U. Waterloo Adv. Coun., 1984-90; bd. dirs. Nat. Ballet Sch., Toronto, 1989—; chmn. coop. coun. Simon Fraser U., 1993-95; mem. bus. coun. B.C. Econ. Policy Adv. Group, 1994—. Mem. Fin. Execs. Inst., Coun. Fin. Execs. Conf. Bd. Can., Hollyburn Country Club, Seymour Golf Club, Canadian Club Vancouver. Office: Finning Ltd, 555 Great Northern Way, Vancouver, BC Canada V5T 1E2

MAHLER, ROBERT LOUIS, soil scientist, educator; b. Huntington Park, Calif., Jan. 7, 1954; s. Robert Alfred and Emily Chonita (Ortega) M.; 1 child, Claudia. BS, Wash. State U., 1976, MS, 1978; PhD, N.C. State U., 1980. Asst. prof., assoc. prof., now prof. soil sci. U. Idaho, Moscow, 1980—, soil fertility researcher, 1980—, extension soil scientist, 1989—, water quality coord., 1990—. Contbr. more than 200 articles to profl. jours. Environ. sciences tchr. Knights of Columbus. Mem. Am. Soc. Agronomy, Soil Sci. Soc. Am., Western Soc. Soil Sci., Rotary, KC, Gamma Sigma Delta (pres. 1989-90). Roman Catholic. Avocations: hiking, camping, collecting baseball cards. Office: U Idaho Soil Sci Divsn Moscow ID 83843

MAHLMAN, JERRY DAVID, research meteorologist; b. Crawford, Nebr., Feb. 21, 1940; s. Earl Lewis and Ruth Margaret (Callendar) M.; m. Janet Kay Hilgenberg, June 10, 1962; children—Gary Martin, Julie Kay. A.B., Chadron State Coll., Nebr., 1962; M.S., Colo. State U., 1964, Ph.D., 1967. Instr. Colo. State U., Fort Collins, 1964-67; from asst. prof. to assoc. prof. Naval Postgrad. Sch., Monterey, Calif., 1967-70; rsch. meteorologist NOAA Geophys. Fluid Dynamics Lab., Princeton, N.J., 1970-84, lab. dir., 1984—; lectr. with rank of prof. Princeton U., 1980—; chmn. panel on mid-atmosphere program NAS-NRC, 1982-84, mem. climate rsch. com., 1986-89, mem. panel on dynamic extended range forecasting, 1987-90; mem. U.S.-USSR Commn. on Global Ecology, 1989-92; mem. Bd. on Global Change, 1991-95, Bd. on Sustainable Devel., 1995—; U.S. rep. world climate rsch. program Joint Sci. Commn., 1991-96. Contbr. over 80 articles to profl. jours. Elder Monterey Presbyterian Ch., 1968-70, Lawrence Road Presbyn. Ch., Lawrenceville, N.J., 1972-75; bd. dirs. Lawrence Non-Profit Housing Inc., 1978-88. Recipient Disting. Authorship award Dept. Commerce, 1980, 81, Gold medal, 1986, Disting. Svc. award Chadron State Coll., 1984, Presdl. Rank award disting. exec. 1994, Honor Alumnus award Colo. State U. 1995. Fellow Am. Geophys. Union (Jule Charney lectr. 1993), Am. Meterol. Soc. (awards com. 1984, 95, chmn. upper atmosphere com. 1979, assoc. editor Jour. Atmospheric Sci. 1979-86, councilor 1991-94, Editor's award 1978, Carl-Gustaf Rossby Rsch. medal 1994). Democrat. Home: 9 Camelia Ct Lawrenceville NJ 08648-3201 Office: Princeton U Geophys Fluid Dynamics Lab PO Box 308/NOAA Princeton NJ 08542-0308

MAHLMANN, JOHN JAMES, music education association administrator; b. Washington, Jan. 21, 1942; s. Charles Victor and Mary Elizabeth (Deye) M.; m. Ning Ning Chang, Feb. 5, 1972; 1 son, Justin Geng Ming. BFA, Boston U., 1962, MFA, 1963; postgrad., U. Notre Dame, summer 1962; EdD, Pa. State U., 1970. Grad. asst. Boston U., 1962-63, instr., supr. student tchrs., dir. masters degree candidates, 1964-66; grad. asst., research asst. Pa. State U., 1963-64, instr., 1966-67, dir. gallery, art edn. dept., 1966-67; asst. prof. Tex. Tech Coll., 1967-69; chmn. tenure and promotions com.; dir. publs., asst. exec. sec. Nat. Art Edn. Assn., Washington, 1969-71, exec. sec., 1971-82, also tour dir. to Japan and Orient; exec. dir. Music Educators Nat. Conf., 1983—; instr. drawing Lubbock Art Assn.; asst. debate coach, asst. coord. forensics Boston U.; vis. instr., mem. staff George Washington U., No. Va. C.C., Tchrs. Coll. N.Y. Exhibited at, Boston U., Pa. State U., Harvard U., Tex. Tech. U., Salem (Mass.) State Coll., Botolph Gallery, Boston, Inst. Contemporary Art, Boston, Barncellar Gallery, Orleans, Mass., State Gallery, State College, Pa., Halls Gallery, Lubbock, Lubbock Art Assn., Loft Gallery, San Antonio, Llano Estacado Art Assn., Hobbs, N.Mex., Purdue U., Cushing Gallery, Dallas, Religious Art Exhbn., Cranbrook Acad. Art, Bloomfield Hills, Mich., Upstairs Gallery, Arlington, Tex., S.W. Tex. State Coll., San Marcos.; Editor: Art Edn., 1970-81, Art Tchr., 1971-80; contbr. articles to mags. Mem. adv. bd. Hartt Sch., 1997—. Mem. Music Educators Nat. Conf., Nat. Art Edn. Assn., Am. Soc. Assn. Execs., Washington Soc. Assn. Execs., Phi Delta Kappa. Home: 10703 Cross School Rd Reston VA 20191 Office: Music Ed Nat Conf 1806 Robert Fulton Dr Reston VA 20191-4348

MAHMOOD, AAMER, computer system architect; b. Lahore, Pakistan, Jan. 27, 1956; came to U.S., 1979; s. Muhammad Iftikhar Quereshi and Farakh (Sultana) Iftikhar; m. Samira Aftab, June 28, 1985; children: Muhammad Bilal, Umer Ali. BSEE with honors, U. Engring. & Tech., Lahore, 1979; MSEE, Stanford U., 1980, PhD in Elec. Engring., 1986. Lectr. U. Engring. & Tech., 1979; teaching asst. Stanford (Calif.) U., 1980-82, rsch. asst., 1983-85; mem. tech. staff Rolm Milspec Computers, San Jose, Calif., 1986-88; sr. mgr., tech. leader CPU and memory systems Amdahl/Advanced Systems, Sunnyvale, Calif., 1988-93; sr. mgr. architect network hardware Cisco Systems, San Jose, 1994—. Contbr. articles to profl. jours. Bd. of Secondary Edn. merit scholar, Lahore, 1971, Bd. of Intermediate Edn. talent scholar, Lahore, 1973. Mem. IEEE (sr.), Assn. Computing Machinery, Stanford Alumni Assn. (life). Home: 1098 Cardinal Way Palo Alto CA 94303-3540

MAHMOUD, ADEL, infectious diseases, tropical medicine physician; b. Cairo, Egypt, Aug. 24, 1941; came to U.S., 1972; s. Abdel Fattah and Fathia (Osman) M.; m. Sally L. Hodder, Jan. 31, 1993. MD, Cairo U., 1963; MPH, Ain Shams U. Cairo, 1967; PhD, U. London, 1971. Lic. Ohio. Asst. lectr. Ain Shams Med. Sch., Cairo, 1965-68; fellow WHO U. London, 1969-72; postdoctoral fellow, instr., prof. Case We. Res. U., Cleve., 1973-80, chief divsn. geog. medicine, 1977-87, John H. Hord prof., chmn., 1987—; physician-in-chief Univ. Hosps., Cleve., 1987—; mem. adv. bd. Nat. Allergy and Infectious Diseases, Internat. Ctr., Bethesda, Md., Fogarty; program project NIH, Bethesda, 1994; program dir. Howard Hughes Med. Inst., 1996. Editor: The Eosinophil in Health and Disease, 1979, Tropical and Geographical Medicine, 1990. Mem. Natural History Mus., Cleve. Fellow Infectious Diseases Soc. Am.; mem. Am. Soc. Clin. Investigations, Assn. Am. Physicians, Inst. Medicine. Home: 18900 S Park Blvd Shaker Hts OH 44122-1851 Office: Case Western Reserve Univ Univ Hosps of Cleveland 11100 Euclid Ave Cleveland OH 44106-1736

MAHMOUD, ALY AHMED, electrical engineering educator; b. Cairo, Jan. 25, 1935; came to U.S., 1960, naturalized, 1970; s. Ahmed Aly and Amina Mohammed (Rashwan) M.; m. Lucinda Lou Keller, Dec. 20, 1962; children: Ramy, Samy. B.Sc. with distinction and honors (Nat. Honor student), Ain Shams U., Cairo, 1958; M.S., Purdue U., 1961, Ph.D., 1964. Diplomate: Registered profl. engr., Iowa, La. Instr. elec. engring. Ain Shams U., 1958-60; asst. prof. elec. engring. U. N.B., Fredericton, 1964; research engr. No. Electric Research and Devel. Lab., Ottawa, Ont., Can., summer 1964; asst. prof. elec. engring. U. Asyut, Egypt, 1964-66; sr. research elec. engr. Naval Civil Engring. Lab., Port Hueneme, Calif., 1968-69, summer 1970; asst. prof. elec. engring. U. Mo., Columbia, 1966-71; assoc. prof. U. Mo., 1971-73, prof., 1973-76; prof. elec. engring., dir. Iowa test and evaluation facility, program mgr. Power Affiliates Research Program; supr. Power System Computer Service, Iowa State U., Ames, 1976-85; dean Coll. Engring. U. New Orleans, 1985-88; dean Sch. Engring. and Tech. Ind. U.-Purdue U.-at Ft. Wayne, 1988—; with FPC, summer 1974; program mgr. NSF, 1975-76; cons. in field. Contbr. articles to profl. jours. Vice chmn. Water and Light Adv. Bd. City of Columbia, 1973-76. Am. Friends of Middle East fellow, 1960-68. Sr. mem. IEEE; Mem. Power Engring. Soc., Am. Phys. Soc., Egyptian Profl. Engring. Soc., Am. Soc. Engring. Edn., Sigma Xi, Tau Beta Pi, Eta Kappa Nu. Patentee in field. Home: 5640 Foxcross Ct Fort Wayne IN 46835-2802 Office: Ind U-Purdue U-Ft Wayne Dean Sch Engring and Tech 2101 E Coliseum Blvd Fort Wayne IN 46805-1445 *In this country there are outstanding opportunities for those who are willing to work hard to serve the society and their profession. I am thankful to be in the U.S. and to have found this type of opportunity.*

MAHMOUDI, HODA, academic administrator, sociology educator; b. Tehran, Iran, Oct. 24, 1948; came to U.S., 1959; s. Jalil and Badri (Behnam) M.; m. Richard W. DaBell, June 21, 1975; 1 child, Bijan Mahmoudi DaBell. BA, U. Utah, 1972, MA, 1973, PhD, 1979. Instr. U. Utah, Salt Lake City, 1976-78, acting dir. Middle East libr., 1978-79; adj. prof. Santa Monica (Calif.) Coll., 1984-86; asst. prof. Westminster Coll., Salt Lake City, 1979-84; assoc. dean for acad. affairs Calif. Luth. U., 1987-93, assoc. prof., 1986-96; assoc. prof. Olivet (Mich.) Coll., 1996—, assoc. v.p. for acad. affairs, 1997—; sec. Women for Internat. Peace and Arbitration, Santa Monica, 1975-96; adv. bd. mem. Nat. Conf. of Christians and Jews, Santa Monica, 1991—, Jour. of Baha'i Studies, Ottawa, Can., 1988—; statis. cons. in field. Author: (book chpt.) Altruism and Extensivity in the Baha'i Religion, 1992, Tahira: An Early Iranian Feminist, 1985; contbr. articles to profl. jours. Recipient Prof. of the Yr. award Westminster Coll., 1982, Award for Jour. Article, Assn. for Baha'i Studies, 1990. Mem. AAUW, Am. Sociol. Assn., Consortium on Peace Rsch., Edn. & Devel., World Future Soc., Western Social Sci. Assn. Baha'i. Avocations: photography, music. Office: Olivet Coll Olivet MI 49076

MAHNK, KAREN, law librarian, legal assistant; b. Bklyn., July 13, 1956; d. James V. and Mary M. (Jones) Mascari; 1 child, Adam Eugene. Student, Baruch Coll., 1974-75, Miami-Dade Community Coll., 1986-89, St. Thomas U., 1994; cert. in criminal justice, 1997. Asst. libr. Mershon, Sawyer et al, Miami, Fla., 1976-79; libr., legal asst. Steel Hecton & Davis, Miami, 1980-84; libr. Valdes-Fauli, et al, Miami, 1984-94, Pub. Defender's Office, 11th Jud. Cir., Miami, 1994—; asst. coord. Broward County Multi-Family Devel. Recycling Program, 1990-91. Chair ways and means com. Palm Cove Elem. PTO, 1993-94; active vol. Broward County Guardian Ad Litum Program, 1989-92. Mem. ABA (assoc. stat., family law sect., law libr. affiliate), Am. Assn. Law Librs., Southeastern Assn. Law Librs., South Fla. Assn. Law Librs. (bd. dirs. 1988-89, chair constn. and bylaws commn. 1988-91, sec. 1983-84, v.p.-elect 1986-88, nominating com. 1992, sec. 1993-95, chair union list com. 1995—), Spl. Librs. Assn., Internat. Platform Assn. Democrat. Baptist. Avocations: painting, sailing, chess. Office: 1320 NW 14th St Ste 313 Miami FL 33125-1609

MAHON, ARTHUR J., lawyer; b. N.Y.C., Jan. 13, 1934; s. Arthur Logan and Mary Agnes (Craine) M.; m. Myra E. Murphy, Aug. 10, 1957; children: Maura, Madonna, Arthur, Nancy. B.A., Manhattan Coll., 1955; JD, NYU, 1958. Bar: N.Y., Fla., D.C. Adj. prof. law NYU Sch. of Law, N.Y.C., 1964-78; ptnr. Mudge, Rose, Guthrie, Alexander & Ferdon, N.Y.C., 1970-94; counsel Donovan Leisure Newton & Irvine, N.Y.C., 1994—. Trustee Manhattan Coll., N.Y., 1988—, Adrian and Jesse Archbold Charitable Trust, N.Y.C., 1976—; mem. joint bd. N.Y. Hosp.-Cornell Med. Ctr., N.Y.C., 1990—; com. on trust and estate gift plans Rockefeller U., N.Y.C., 1984—; bd. dirs. United Way Internat., 1988-94, Alexandria, Va., chmn. planned giving and endowments com. Archdiocese, N.Y.C., 1985—; bd. overseers Cornell Med. Coll., N.Y.C., 1986-92, chmn., 1992-95; dir. Am. Skin Assn., N.Y.C., 1989—, Noel Found., San Francisco, 1990—; gov. N.Y. Hosp., N.Y.C., 1994—; counsel Ira W. De Camp Found., 1994—. Served to capt. USAF, 1958-60. Root-Tilden scholar NYU. Mem. N.Y. State Bar Assn., Bar Assn. City of N.Y., Fla. Bar Assn., D.C. Bar Assn. Home: 16 Cambridge Dr Madison CT 06443-3016 Office: Donovan Leisure 30 Rockefeller Plz New York NY 10112

MAHON, ELDON BROOKS, federal judge; b. Loraine, Tex., Apr. 9, 1918; s. John Bryan and Nola May (Muns) M.; m. Nova Lee Groom, June 1, 1941; children: Jana, Martha, Brad. B.A., McMurry Coll., 1939; LL.B., U. Tex., 1942. Bar: Tex. 1942. Law clk. Tex. Supreme Ct., 1945-46; county atty. Mitchell County, Tex., 1947; dist. atty. 32d Jud. Dist. Tex., 1948-60, dist. judge, 1960-63; v.p. Tex. Electric Service Co., Ft. Worth, 1963-64; mem. firm Mahon Pope & Gladden, Abilene, Tex., 1964-68; U.S. atty. U.S. Dist. Ct. (no. dist.) Tex., Ft. Worth, 1968-72, judge, 1972—, now sr. judge. Pres. W. Tex. council Girl Scouts U.S.A., 1966-68; Trustee McMurry Coll. Served with USAAF, 1942-45. Named an outstanding Tex. prosecutor Tex. Law Enforcement Found., 1957. Mem. ABA, Fed. Bar Assn., Ft.-Worth-Tarrant County Bar Assn., Am. Judicature Soc., State Bar Tex. Methodist (past del. confs.). Office: US Courthouse 501 W 10th St Ste 502 Fort Worth TX 76102-3643*

MAHON, MALACHY THOMAS, lawyer, educator; b. N.Y.C., Jan. 4, 1934; s. James and Alice (Rooney) M.; m. Margaret Phyllis Kirwan, Jan. 25, 1958; children: Veronica Mahon Grover, Laura Mahon Chandonnet, Malachy. B.A., Manhattan Coll., 1954; J.D., Fordham U., 1960. Bar: N.Y. 1960. Law clk. to chief magistrate John M. Murtagh N.Y.C., 1959-60; law clk. to justice Tom C. Clark U.S. Supreme Ct., 1960-61; assoc. Hale Russell & Stentzel, N.Y.C., 1961-62, Mudge Rose Guthrie & Alexander, N.Y.C., 1979-80; of counsel Farrell, Fritz, Caemmerer, Cleary, Barnosky & Armentano, Mineola, NY, 1982-83, Havens & Lombard, Flushing, N.Y., 1994-95; prof. Fordham U. Law Sch., 1962-68; prof. law Hofstra U. Law Sch., 1968—, founding dean, 1968-73, S.B. Wilzig disting. prof. banking, 1985—; vis. prof. U. Tex. Law Sch., 1973-74; exec. dir., spl. N.Y. State asst. atty. gen. Meyer Investigation of Coverup Charges Against the Spl. Attica Prosecutor's Office, 1975; Chief counsel N.Y. Gov.'s Spl. Com. on Criminal Offenders, 1966; mem. Nassau County Bd. Ethics, 1983-96, chmn., 1989-96. Staff author: Mental Illness, Due Process and the Criminal Defendant, 1968; monthly comml. law columnist: N.Y. Law Jour. 1976-78. Served with U.S. Army, 1954-56. Mem. ABA, N.Y. State Bar Assn., Assn. Bar City N.Y.,

Am. Law Inst. Home: 14 Duke of Gloucester Manhasset NY 11030-3210 Office: Hofstra U Law Sch Hempstead NY 11550

MAHON, ROBERT, photographer; b. Wilmington, Del., Dec. 28, 1949; s. Clifton and Mary Veronica (Figash) M.; m. Carol Joyce, Apr. 24, 1983. BA in Am. Studies, U. Del., 1971. One-man show Twining Gallery, N.Y.C., 1985, Mercer Coll., Trenton, N.J., 1993, Anne Reid Gallery, Princeton, 1996; exhibited in group shows Whitney Mus. Am. Art, 1982, Phila. Mus. Art, 1982, 95, Am. Ctr., Paris, 1982, Mus. Modern Art, N.Y.C., 1983, 84-85, 93, Kolnischer Kunstverein, 1983, Art Inst., Chgo., 1985, Twining Gallery, 1985-86, 88, 89, N.J. State Mus., 1990, Guggenheim Soho, 1994, Sandra Gering Gallery, N.Y.C., 1996, also others; represented in permanent collections Phila. Mus. Art, Mus. Modern Art, Met. Mus. Art, N.Y. Pub. Libr., Humanities Rsch. Ctr., U. Tex., Austin, Princeton U. Libr., Harvard U. Art Mus., N.J. State Mus., Newark Mus., Montclair Art Mus., Rutgers U. Zimmerli Mus., Noyes Mus., also pvt. collections. Guggenheim grantee, 1985; RCIP Printmaking fellow, 1996. Home and Studio: PO Box Q Stockton NJ 08559-0390

MAHONE, BARBARA JEAN, automotive company executive; b. Notasulga, Ala., Apr. 19, 1946; d. Freddie Douglas M. and Sarah Lou (Simpson). BS, Ohio State U., 1968; MBA, U. Mich., 1972; program for mgmt. devel., Harvard U., 1981. Sys. analyst GM, Detroit, 1968-71, sr. staff asst., 1972-74, mgr. career planning, 1975-78; dir. pers. adminstrn. GM, Rochester, N.Y., 1979-81; mgr. indsl. rels. GM, Warren, Ohio, 1982-83; dir. human resources mgmt. Chevrolet-Pontiac-Can. group GM, 1984-86; dir. gen. pers. and pub. affairs Inland divsn. GM, Dayton, Ohio, 1986-88; gen. dir. pers. Indland Fisher Guide divsn. GM, Detroit, 1989-91, gen. dir. employee benefits, 1991-93; dir. human resources truck group GM, Pontiac, Mich., 1994—; chmn. Fed. Labor Rels. Authority, Washington, 1983-84, Spl. Panel on Appeals; dir. Metro Youth; mem. bd. govs. U. Mich. Alumni. Bd. dirs. ARC, Rochester, 1979-82, Urban League Rochester, 1979-82, Rochester Aea Multiple Sclerosis; mem. human resources com. YMCA, Rochester, 1980-82; mem. exec. bd. Nat. Coun. Negro Women; mem. allocations com. United Way Greater Rochester. Recipient Pub. Rels. award Nat. Assn. Bus. and Profl. Women, 1976, Mary McLeod Bethune award Nat. Coun. Negro Women, 1977, Senate resolution Mich. State Legislature, 1980; named Outstanding Woman, Mich. Chronicle, 1975, Woman of Yr., Nat. Assn. Bus. and Profl. Women, 1978, Disting. Bus. Person, U. Mich., 1978, one of 11 Mich. Women, Redbook mag., 1978. Mem. Nat. Black MBA Assn. (bd. dirs., nat. pres. Disting. Svc. award, bd. dirs., nat. pres. Outstanding MBA), Women Econ. Club (bd. dirs.), Indsl. Rels. Rsch. Assn., Internat. Assn. for Pers. Women, Engring. Soc. Detroit. Republican. Home: 175 Kirkwood Ct Bloomfield Hills MI 48304-2927 Office: MC 483-550-221 1999 Centerpoint Pkwy Pontiac MI 48341-3150

MAHONEY, CATHERINE ANN, artist, educator; b. Macon, Mo., Nov. 18, 1948; d. Joe H. and Berniece Joyce (Garnett) Dickson; m. Michael W. Mahoney, July 19, 1969; children: Karin Lynn Mahoney Broeker, Ryan Michael. BS in Edn. with honors, Truman U., Kirksville, 1969. Mo. state life cert. for teaching art. Elem./secondary art instr. Bucklin (Mo.) R-I Schs., 1970-74; pvt. art instr. Groom (Tex.) Artist's Assn., 1974-75; substitute tchr. Gasconade R-I Schs., Hermann, Mo., 1977-89; pvt. art instr. Colorful Brushes Studio, Hermann, Mo., 1987-97; elem./secondary art instr. Crosspoint Christian Schs., Union, Mo., 1994—; pres. City of Hermann Arts Coun., 1983-87, membership chmn., 1980-82; dir. Summertime Childrn's Watercolor Workshops, Colorful Brushes, Hermann, 1987-97. One-woman shows at N.E. Mo. State U., Kirksville, 1969, Capitol City Art Guild, Jefferson City, Mo., 1983, Kolbe Gallery of Art, Hermann, 1984, Colorful Brushes Studio, Hermann, 1987-94; designer Sister Cities Emblem City of Hermann/Arolsen, Germany, 1989. Pres. Hermann Parent-Tchr. Orgn., 1985-87; organist, pianist, tchr. Hermann Cath. and Bapt. Chs., 1977-97; leader 4-H, Girl and Boy Scouts, Hermann, 1982-95. Named Outstanding Young Woman of Yr., Hermann Jaycees, 1984, 1st Pl. Mo. Artists Collection, Mo. Pub. Svc., Sedalia, Mo., 1992, 3d Pl. and Purchase prize Watercolor USA, Springfield (Mo.) Art Mus., 1995. Mem. Nat. Watercolor Soc. (assoc., included Nat. Art Show 1995), Okla. Watercolor Assn. (assoc., included Art Show 1989), St. Louis Artist Guild (mem. art sect., Honorable Mention 1993), Watercolor USA Honor Soc. (hon., Art Show award 1995), Oil Painters Am. Avocations: piano, reading, embroidery, sewing, knitting. Home: 1058 Old Stonehill Hermann MO 65041 Office: Colorful Brushes Studio 126 E 4th St Hermann MO 65041-1130

MAHONEY, DONALD SCOTT, financial industry marketing executive; b. Boston, May 18, 1953; s. Donald Richard and Gloria Joan (Lewis) M.; m. Cheryl Constance LeConche, Sept. 16, 1978; children: Brendon, Blake, Lawson, Gloria, Jacqueline. BS in Bus. Adminstrn., Fairleigh Dickinson U., 1977. Registered investment advisor. V.p. mktg. Fox & Carskadon Inc., San Mateo, Calif., 1984-87; 1st v.p. Met. Life Real Estate Investment Co., 1987-90; sr. v.p. The Colonial Group of Mut. Funds, Boston, 1990-95, cons. to adv. bd., 1993-94; v.p. Nicholas Applegate Money Mgmt. Co., San Diego, 1996—. Bd. dirs. Northridge Civic Assn., Atlanta, 1994, pres., 1995-96; mem. Ga. Republican Party, Atlanta, 1984-96. Mem. Internat. Assn. Fin. Planners, NRA. Roman Catholic. Avocations: jogging, Tai Kwan Do Karate (Brown Belt).

MAHONEY, GERALD FRANCIS, manufacturing company executive; b. Bklyn., July 31, 1943; s. Francis B. and Leona (Gray) M.; m. JoAnne A. Maselli, May 2, 1971; children: G. Scott, Ryan J. BA, Adelphi U., 1965; MBA, Northeastern U., 1966. CPA, N.Y. Mgr. Arthur Andersen & Co., N.Y.C., 1966-73; asst. contr. Bairnco Corp., N.Y.C., 1973-78, v.p. fin., 1980-81; gen. mgr. Bairnco Corp., Pensauken, N.J., 1979-80; v.p., div. pres. Bairnco Corp., Union, N.J., 1981-83; sr. v.p. fin. and adminstrn. Polychrome Corp., Yonkers, N.Y., 1984-87; pres. Transcrit Corp., Brewster, N.Y., 1987-90, Pavey Envelope & Tag Corp., Jersey City, 1991-94; chmn., CEO Mail-Well, Inc., Englewood, Colo., 1994—. Mem. AICPA, N.Y. State Soc. CPA's, Noyac Country Club (Sag Harbor, N.Y., bd. dirs. 1980-83), Glenmoor Country Club (Englewood, Colo.), Ridgewood Country Club (N.J.). Republican. Roman Catholic. Avocations: golf, tennis. Home: 21 Cherry Hills Farm Dr Englewood CO 80110-7170 Office: Mail-Well Inc 23 Inverness Way E Englewood CO 80112-5708

MAHONEY, JOHN JOSEPH, business executive, educator; b. Chattanooga, Nov. 9, 1921; s. John J. and Helen M. (Armstrong) M.; m. Elizabeth Dubose Porcher, June 25, 1949. BS in Commerce, The Citadel, 1946; MS in Indsl. Mgmt., Ga. Inst. Tech., 1967. Ordained deacon Roman Catholic Ch., 1979. Instr. dept. bus. adminstrn. The Citadel, Charleston, S.C., 1947-50, asst. prof., 1967—; founder, pres., gen. mgr. Carolinga Vending Inc., 1947-67, Shamrock System, Inc., 1960-67; dir. Charles F. Cates & Sons, Inc. Pickle Co., Faison, S.C., also mem. exec. com.; v.p., treas., dir. Cons. to Bus., Inc. (formerly Mahoney Cons., Inc.); dir., pres. Associated Distributors, Inc., Metro Stylists, Inc.; dir. Aunt Jane Foods, Inc. S.C. editor Diaconal Quarterly. Procurator/advocate diocesan tribunal Diocese of Charleston; mem. Bishop's Com. on Vocations; pres., Cath. Charities, 1958—; bd. dirs. Charleston Devel. Bd., 1957-60, United Fund, Charleston, 1955-56, Family Agy., Charleston, 1956-60; chmn. Pres.'s Export Expansion Council. Served to lt. AUS, 1943-46, capt. Res. Recipient Disting. Service award Jaycees, 1956. Fellow Found. Econ. Edn.; mem. So. Mgmt. Assn., Fellowship Cath. Scholars, Charleston C. of C., Hibernian Soc., Confederate Hist. Assn. Belgium (chargé d'affaires, S.C.), Sons Confederate Vets. (chaplain-in-the field S.C. div.), O'Mahoney Records Soc., Assn. Pvt. Enterprise Edn., Fund for Conservative Majority (bd. govs.). Republican. Club: Carolina Yacht. Home: 1602 Porchers Bluff Rd Mount Pleasant SC 29464-8942 Office: 276 E Bay St Charleston SC 29401-2600

MAHONEY, JOHN L., English literature educator; b. Somerville, Mass., Feb. 4, 1928. AB, Boston Coll., 1950, AM, 1952; PhD, Harvard U., 1957. Instr. of English Boston Coll., 1955-59, asst. prof. of English, 1959-62, assoc. prof., 1962-65, prof., 1965—, Rattigan prof. English, 1994—, chmn. dept., 1962-67, 69-70, dir. PhD program in English, 1970-75, 82-85, mem. ednl. licy com. Grad. Sch. Arts and Scis., 1985-87; vis. prof. of English Harvard . summer sch., 1963, 65, 67, 71, 80, 83, 86; cons. for self-study Weston oll. Schs. of Philosophy and Theology, Boston Coll., 1965; sem. leader programs for women, Boston Coll., Newton Coll., 1976, 78, 79; mem. numerous acad. coms. and couns.; cons., mem. English adv. com. Commonwealth of Mass., 1968-70; mem. acad. coun. Evening Coll. Arts and Scis. and Bus. Adminstrn., Boston Coll., 1969—, univ. core curriculum devel. com., 1991—; bd. trustees St. John's Sem., Brighton, Mass., com. on acad. affairs, 1980-86; sec. bd. trustees Katharine Gibbs Sch., Boston, 1982-90; mem. adv. bd. Jesuit Inst., Boston Coll., 1987—. Author: The Whole Internal Universe: Imitation and the New Defense of Literature in British Criticism, 1660-1830, 1985, The Persistence of Tragedy: Episodes in the History of Drama, 1985, The Logic of Passion: The Literary Criticism of William Hazlitt, rev. edit., 1978, 81, Wordsworth: A Poetic Life, 1997; editor, author intro. and notes: The Enlightenment and English Literature, 1980, The English Romantics: Major Poetry and Critical Theory, 1978, An Essay of Dramatic Poetry and Other Critical Writings by John Dryden, 1965, William Duff's Essay on Original Genius, 1964; contbr. Imagination and the Ways of Genius (in Approaches to Hazlitt), 1986, Teaching the Immortality Ode with Coleridge's Dejection: An Ode (in Approaches to Teaching Wordswòrth's Poetry), 1986, and others; editor: (with J. Robert Barth, S.J.) Coleridge, Keats, and the Imagination: Romanticism and Adam's Dream, 1990, Teaching Shelley's Skylark and the Defence of Poetry, (in Approaches to Teaching Shelley's Poetry) 1990; mem. editl. bd. Boston Coll. Mag., 1981-90; author articles, papers delivered at profl. confs.; reviewer for Studies in Romanticism, The Wordsworth Circle, Nineteenth Century Contexts, So. Humanities Rev. Active Sacred Heart Parish, Lexington, Mass., del. to Lexington Coun. Chs., 1968, chmn. parish coun., 1969-72, mem. parish coun., 1995—, vice chmn., 1996—, mem. religious edn. commn., 1974-79, 90—, sem. leader Christian Youth Edn., 1969-73, lector, 1972—; mem. Archdiocese of Boston Commn. for Promotion of Parish Couns., 1969-74, Patron Book Selection Com., Cary Meml. Libr., Lexington, Benjamin Mays Mentor Ahana program, 1993—. Boston Coll. Grad. Sch. fellow, 1950-52; Boston Coll. Faculty rsch. grantee, 1964, 68, 86, 92, Mellon Found. grantee for rsch. and faculty devel., 1981-82; grantee rsch. Am. Philos. Soc., 1987; recipient Boston Coll. Campus Coun. Tchr. of Yr. award, 1966, Boston Coll. alumni award for excellence in edn., 1978, Boston Coll. Faculty fellow, 1986, 94, Andrè Favat award Mass. Coun. Tchrs. English, 1988, Prof. of Yr. award Coun. for Advancement and Support of Edn. Mass., 1989. Mem. AAUP (pres. Boston Coll. chpt. 1962), MLA, N.E. MLA, Am. Soc. Eighteenth Century Studies, N.E. Soc. Eighteenth Century Studies, Wordsworth-Coleridge Assn. Am., Keats-Shelley Assn. Am., The Johnsonians, Alpha Sigma Nu, Phi Beta Kappa. Office: Boston Coll Dept English Chestnut Hill MA 02167

MAHONEY, LINDA KAY, mathematics educator; b. Bay Shore, N.Y., June 8, 1951; d. James Nathaniel and Katherine Pauline (Booth) Palmer Jr.; m. Peter Allan Mahoney, Jr., June 5, 1976; children: Matthew J., Michael J., Patrick A. BS, U. Md., 1972; MEd, 1979; postgrad., R.I. Coll., 1988-89, Providence Coll., 1989-90. Tchr. math. Prince George's County Pub. Schs., Benjamin Tasker Jr. High, Bowie, Md., 1973-76; tchr. substitute Warwick (R.I.) Pub. Schs., 1987-90, tchr. math., 1990-91; tchr. math. Ctrl. Tex. Coll., P.R., 1992-96; lectr. U. Tenn., Knoxville, 1996—. Vol. Sherman Elem. Sch., Warwick, 1989-90, Rohr Elem. Sch., Chula Vista, Calif., 1985-87. Mem. Nat. Coun. Tchrs. Math., Math. Assn. Am. Republican. Lutheran. Avocations: sewing, baking.

MAHONEY, LISA REEVES, dermatologist; b. N.Y.C., June 6, 1947; d. Jesse Waring and Mary Watkins (Reeves) M. BS, NYU at Washington Square, 1969; MD, NYU, 1974. Diplomate Am. Bd. Dermatology. Intern in medicine NYU Med. Ctr., N.Y.C., 1974-75; resident in dermatology U. Calif. Med. Ctr., San Francisco, 1975-78; attending dermatologist JT Mather Meml. Hosp., Port Jefferson, N.Y., 1979—, St. Charles Hosp., Port Jefferson, 1979—; pvt. practice Port Jefferson, 1979-90, Miller Place, N.Y., 1990—. Mem. Rotary Club of Port Jefferson. Mem. Am. Acad. Dermatology, N.Y. Dermatol. Soc., Suffolk Dermatol. Soc., Suffolk County Med. Soc., Long Island Dermatology Assn., Alpha Omega Alpha. Avocations: reading, gardening, travel, history, biography. Office: L Reeves Mahoney MD 565 Route 25 A Miller Place NY 11764

MAHONEY, MARGARET ELLERBE, foundation executive; b. Nashville, Oct. 24, 1924; d. Charles Hallam and Leslie Nelson (Savage) M.; BA magna cum laude, Vanderbilt U., 1946; LHD (hon.), Meharry Med. Coll., 1977, U. Fla., 1980, Med. Coll. Pa., 1982, Williams Coll., 1983, Smith Coll., 1985, Beaver Coll., 1985, Brandeis U., 1989, Marymount Coll., 1990, Rush U., 1993, SUNY, Bklyn., 1994, N.Y. Med. Coll., 1995. Fgn. affairs officer State Dept., Washington, 1946-53; exec. assoc., assoc. sec. Carnegie Corp., N.Y.C., 1953-72; v.p. Robert Wood Johnson Found., Princeton, N.J., 1972-80; pres. Commonwealth Fund, N.Y.C., 1980-94; pres. MEM Assocs., Inc., N.Y.C., 1995—. Contbr. articles to profl. jours. Trustee John D. and Catherine T. Mac Arthur Found., 1985—, Dole Found., 1984—, Smith Coll., 1988-93, Columbia U., 1991-96, Goucher Coll., 1995-96; vis. fellow Sch. Architecture and Urban Planning, Princeton U., 1973-80; bd. dirs. Council on Found., 1982-88; mem. N.Y.C. Commn. on the Yr. 2000, 1985-87, MIT Corp., 1984-89; bd. govs. Am. Stock Exchange, 1987-92; adv. bd. Office of the Chief Med. Examiner, N.Y.C., 1987—, Barnard Coll, Inst. Med. Research, 1986-92; vice chmn. N.Y.C. Mayor's Com. for Pub./Pvt. Partnerships, 1990-93; bd. dirs. Alliance for Aging Rsch., 1987—, Overseas Devel. Coun., 1988—, Nat. Found. Center for Disease Control and Prevention, Inc., 1994—; mem. vestry Parish of Trinity Ch., 1982-89, 91-95; active Atlantic Fellowships Selection Com., 1994—. Recipient Frank H. Lahey Meml. award, 1984, Women's Forum award, 1989, Walsh McDermott award, 1992, Disting. Grantmaker award Coun. Founds., 1993, Edward R. Loveland award Am. Coll. Physicians, 1994, Special Recognition award AAMC, 1994, Merit medal Lotos Club, 1994, Terrance Keenan Leadership award in Health Philanthrophy, Grantmakers in Health, 1995. Mem. AAAS, Inst. Medicine of NAS, Am. Acad. Arts and Scis., Am. Philos. Soc., Coun. Fgn. Rels., Fin. Women's Assn. N.Y., N.Y. Acad. Medicine (vice chmn. bd. govs.), N.Y. Acad. Scis., Alpha Omega Alpha. Office: MEM Assocs Inc 521 5th Ave Rm 2010 New York NY 10175-2099

MAHONEY, MICHAEL JAMES, investment executive; b. Spokane, Wash., July 18, 1960; s. James Lyle and Frances Edith (Castle) M.; m. Ann Dickinson, May 29, 1993; 1 child, James Junius Castle. BA in History cum laude, Whitman Coll., 1982; MBA, Stanford U., 1991. Analyst corp. fin. dept. E.F. Hutton & Co., Inc., N.Y.C., 1982-85; assoc. cons. Bain & Co., Inc., Boston, 1985-87, cons., 1987-89; summer assoc. Sachs & Co., N.Y.C., 1990; investment analyst Chancellor LGT Asset Mgmt., San Francisco, 1991-93; portfolio mgr., lead mgr. G.T. Global Telecomm. Fund, San Francisco, 1993—; founding ptnr. J&M Investments, Newport Beach, Calif., 1996—; guest lectr. in investments Stanford Grad. Sch. of Bus., 1994—. Pres. Spokane County Young Reps., 1976-78; campaign mgr. Malone for U.S. Senate, Boston, 1988. Recipient Pete Reid award Whitman Coll., 1997. Mem. Calif. Geneal. Soc., O'Mahony Records Soc., Ea. Wash. Geneal. Soc., Pacific Rsch. Inst. for Pub. Policy, No. Calif. Whitman Alumni Assn. (mem. steering com.), Stanford Alumni Assn. (life), Guardsmen (San Francisco), Spokane Club (Washington), Phi Beta Kappa, Sigma Chi (com. chmn. 1979-80). Avocations: skin diving, genealogy, swimming. Office: Chancellor LGT Asset Mgmt 27th Fl 50 California St San Francisco CA 94111-4624

MAHONEY, MICHAEL ROBERT TAYLOR, art historian, educator; b. Worcester, Mass., Jan. 24, 1935; s. Michael J. and Mary (Taylor) M. Grad., Phillips Acad., 1953; B.A., Yale U., 1959; Ph.D., Courtauld Inst., U. London, 1965. Finley fellow Nat. Gallery Art, 1962-64; fellow Harvard Center Italian Studies, Villa I Tatti, 1963; museum curator Nat. Gallery Art, 1964-69; prof. fine arts, chmn. dept. Trinity Coll., Hartford, Conn., 1969-86; Genevieve Harlow Goodwin prof. fine arts Trinity Coll., 1974—; Incorporator Hartford Pub. Library, 1970—; elector Wadsworth Atheneum, Hartford, 1974-85. Author: The Drawings of Salvator Rosa, 1977, (with Jean Cadogan) Wadsworth Atheneum Paintings II: Italy and Spain; editor: National Gallery of Art Report and Studies in the History of Art, 1968-69. Trustee Cesare Barbieri Found., Trinity Coll., 1977—, Watkinson Libr., Trinity Coll., 1985—, Somerset House Art History Found., N.Y.C., 1985—; bd. govs. Hill-Stead Mus., Farmington, Conn., 1992-95; mem. adv. coun. Am. Friends of Georgian Group, 1996—. Office: Trinity Coll Dept Fine Arts Hartford CT 06106

MAHONEY, MICHAEL SEAN, history educator; b. N.Y.C., June 30, 1939; s. Thomas Michael and Dorothy (Hopkins) M.; m. Jean Carmel Angelilli, Aug. 20, 1960; children: Colin Sean, Bridget Elizabeth. AB, Harvard U., 1960; postgrad., U. Munich., 1960-62; PhD, Princeton U., 1967. Instr. history Princeton (N.J.) U., 1965-67, asst. prof., 1967-72, assoc. prof., 1972-80, prof., 1980—. Author: The Mathematical Career of Pierre de Fermat, 1973, 94, (in Japanese) Mathematics in History, 1982. Bd. edn. regional schs., Princeton, 1983-86; trustee Nat. Faculty of Humanities, Arts and Sci., 1986—, chair, 1994—. Deutscher Akademischer Austauschdienst fellow, 1960, Dibner Inst. fellow, 1995-96, NSF fellow, 1964-69. Mem. History Sci. Soc. (council mem. 1980-82), Soc. for History of Tech. Home: 42 Hawthorne Ave Princeton NJ 08540-5355

MAHONEY, PATRICK MORGAN, retired judge; b. Winnipeg, Man., Can., Jan. 20, 1929; s. Paul Morgan and Joan Ethel Tracy (Patrick) M.; m. Mary Alma Sneath, June 28, 1958; children: Michael G., Patrick M., Sheila M., D'Arcy C. B.A., U. Alta., 1950, LL.B., 1951. Bar: Alta. 1952, apptd. Queen's counsel 1972, U.S. Ct. Mil. Appeals (hon.) 1983. Justice trial div. Fed. Ct. Can., Ottawa, Ont., 1973-83; judge Ct. Martial Appeal Ct. Can., Ottawa, 1973-82; chief justice Ct. Martial Appeal Ct. Can., 1982-94; ret.; judge Fed. Ct. Appeal, 1983-94; ret.; Mem. Parliament for Calgary South, 1968-72, sec. to minister of fin., 1970-71, minister of state, 1972. Mem. Can. Judges Conf. (dir. 1981), Calgary Golf and Country Club. Home: 3 Coltrin Pl, Ottawa, ON Canada K1M 0A5

MAHONEY, THOMAS HENRY DONALD, historian, educator, government official; b. Cambridge, Mass., Nov. 4, 1913; s. Thomas Henry, Jr. and Frances (Lucy) M.; m. Phyllis Norton, July 14, 1951; children: Thomas Henry IV, Linda, David, Peter, Philip. A.B., Boston Coll., 1936, A.M., 1937; Ph.D., George Washington U., 1944; M.P.A., Harvard U., 1967, D.P.A., 1989. Instr. Gonzaga Sch., Washington, 1937-39, Dunbarton Coll., Washington, 1938-39; instr., then asst. prof. history Boston Coll., 1939-44; asst. prof. history Holy Cross Coll., 1944-46; vis. lectr. history and govt. Smith Coll., 1944-45, Wellesley Coll., 1947-48; mem. faculty MIT, 1945-84, prof. history, 1961—, chmn. sect. history, 1963-65, 73-79; vis. prof. U. So. Calif., 1950; Lowell lectr. Boston, 1957; Carnegie fellow Harvard Law Sch., 1965-66; sec. elder affairs Commonwealth of Mass., 1979-83; head Mass. del. White House Conf. on Aging, 1981, mem. policy com., 1995; mem. ethnic com. U.S. Dept. Edn., 1979-83; mem. UNNGO Com. on Aging, N.Y.C., 1985—, chmn., 1987-91; corporator, trustee Cambridgeport Savs. Bank; adv. bd. Mildred & Claude Pepper Found., Washington, Tallahassee, 1989—; mem. Silver senate pres., bd. dirs. Nat. Silver Haired Congress, 1996—; panelist, cons. numerous internat. confs. on gerentology; keynote spkr., cons., panelist Interparliamentarian Union meetings on aging, Bangkok, Guatemala City, Sofia, Budapest, London, 1986-89, New Delhi, Canberra, 1993, Paris, Copenhagen, 1994, Madrid, Bucharest, 1995, Istanbul, 1996, Beijing 1996, Seoul 1997; prin. spkr. MIT Alumni Club Dinners Istanbul, 1988, Paris, 1988, Singapore, 1993, Madrid, 1995, Berlin, 1995, London, 1996, Beijing, 1996; rep. of Internat. Fedn. Aging, Montreal to UN, 1994—; acad. leader and lectr. MIT Alumni Tour, St. Petersburg, Russia, 1997; rev. essayist Futuribles Internat., Paris, 1996—; panelist UN conf. on aging populations in the context of urbanization, Sendai, Japan, 1991; guest spkr. Asia and Pacific conf. on scis. and tech. for Regional Sustainable Devel., Tokyo, 1994. Author: Edmund Burke and Ireland, 1960; co-author: Readings in International Order, 1951, China, Japan and the Powers, 3d edit., 1960, The U.S. in World History, 3d edit., 1963, Edmund Burke: The Enlightenment and the Modern World, 1977, 1776, 1977, Aging in Urbanization, 1990; editor: Burke's Reflections, 1955, Selected Writings and Speeches of Edmund Burke on America, 1964. Mem. Mass. Fulbright Com., 1953-74, chmn., 1966-74; observer Vatican City Consistories, 1956, 73, 85, World Assembly on Aging, Vienna, 1982; bd. dirs. Mass. Civic League, 1967—; state rep. Mass. Gen. Ct., 1971-78, chmn. energy and ethics coms., 1977-78; mem. community adv. coun. Jr. League Boston, 1982-86; UN rep. InterParliamentary Conf., Ottawa, 1985, Congress Latin Am. Socs. Gerontology and Geriatrics, Lima, 1984; N.Y. and Washington rep. Centre Internat. de Gérontologie, Paris, 1985-93; mem. Cambridge Sch. Com., 1948-54; chmn. trustees Cambridge Libr., 1948-54, Mass. State Libr., 1952-61; bd. dirs. Internat. Student Fedn.; mem. Cambridge City Coun., 1964-72; sr. advisor internat. issues and questions of aging Congressman Claude Pepper, 1985-88. Knight of Malta; Am. Coun. of Learned Socs. fellow, 1938, Guggenheim fellow, 1961-62, Carnegie fellow, 1954, Ford Internat. Rsch. fellow, 1975; recipient Humanitarian of Yr. award mass. Psychol. Soc., 1983. Fellow Royal Hist. Soc.; mem. Am. Hist. Assn., Am. Cath. Hist. Assn. (pres. 1957), Mass. Hist. Soc., cath. Commn. Cultural and Intellectual Affairs, Conf. Brit. Studies, Nat. Conf. State Legislators (sci. and tech. com., intergovtl. rels. com. 1973-78, mem. del. People's Republic of China 1976 and Republic of China, Taiwan 1978, keynote Singapore Internat. Conf. on Elders 1993), Japan-Am. Soc.s (keynote Honolulu 1995, keynote 1st internat. conf. on managed health care Seattle 1992). Home: 130 Mt Auburn St Apt 410 Cambridge MA 02138-5779

MAHONEY, WILLIAM FRANCIS, editor; b. Joliet, Ill., Jan. 24, 1935; s. Cletus George and Mildred Marie (Ochs) M.; m. Carroll Frances Johnson, June 28, 1958; children: Erin Michele Alderfer, Kevin William, Megan Ann, Sheila Marie, Nora Aileen. BS in Journalism, Marquette U., 1957. Reporter Ft. Wayne (Ind.) News Sentinel, 1958-59; pub. rels. mgr. Motorola, Inc., Franklin Park, Ill., 1959-66; sr. account exec. Young & Rubicam, Inc., Chgo., 1966-68; pub. info. dir. ABA, Chgo., 1969-71; investor rels. mgr. Chemetron Corp., Chgo., 1971-76; corp. comm. dir. Scott Paper Co., Phila., 1976-80; pub. rels. dir. Esmark Inc., Chgo., 1980-81; prin. Mahoney & Mitchell Incorp., Phila., 1981-89, Investor Rels. Ptnrs., Livingston, N.J., 1993—. Author: Investor Relations: The Professional's Guide to Financial and Marketing Communications, 1991, The Active Shareholder, 1993, The Strategy and Practice of Investor Relations, 1997; editor Investor Rels. Update, Valuation Issues. Mem. Nat. Investor Rels. Inst., Pub. Rels. Soc. Am., Vesper Club. Republican. Roman Catholic. Home and Office: 716 S Brandywine St West Chester PA 19382-3511

MAHONY, ROGER M. CARDINAL, archbishop; b. Hollywood, Calif., Feb. 27, 1936; s. Victor James and Loretta Marie (Baron) M. A.A., Our Lady Queen of Angels Sem., 1956; B.A., St. John's Sem. Coll., 1958, B.S.T., 1962; M.S.W., Catholic U. Am., 1964. Ordained priest Roman Cath. Ch., 1962, ordained bishop, 1975, created cardinal priest, 1991. Asst. pastor St. John's Cathedral, Fresno, Calif., 1962, 68-73, rector, 1973-80; residence St. Genevieve's Parish, Fresno, Calif., 1964—, adminstr., 1964-67, pastor, 1967-68; titular bishop of Tamascani, aux. bishop of Fresno, 1975-80; chancellor Diocese of Fresno, 1970-77, vicar gen., 1975-80; bishop Diocese of Stockton (Calif.), 1980-85; archbishop Archdiocese of L.A., 1985-91, cardinal priest, 1991—; diocesan dir. Cath. Charities and Social Svc. Fresno, 1964-70, exec. dir. Cath. Welfare Bur., 1964-70; exec. dir. Cath. Welfare Bur. Infant of Prague Adoption Service, 1964-70; chaplain St. Vincent de Paul Soc., Fresno, 1964-70; named chaplain to Pope Paul VI, 1967; mem. faculty extension div. Fresno State U., 1965-67; sec. U.S. Cath. bishops ad hoc com. on farm labor Nat. Conf. Bishops, 1970-75; chmn. com. on pub. welfare and income maintenance Nat. Conf. Cath. Charities, 1969-70; bd. dirs. West Coast Regional Office Bishops Com. for Spanish-Speaking, 1967-70; chmn. Calif. Assn. Cath. Charities Dirs., 1965-69; trustee St. Patrick's Sem., Archdiocese of San Francisco, 1974-75; mem. adminstrv. com. Nat. conf. Cath. Bishops, 1976-79, 82-85, 87-90, com. migration and refugees, 1976—, chmn. com. farm labor, 1981—, com. moral evaluation of deterrence, 1986-88; cons. com., chmn. for ProLife Activities, 1990—; mem. com. social devel. and world peace U.S. Cath. Conf., 1985, chmn. internat. policy sect., 1987-90; com. justice and peace, Pontifical Couns., 1984-89, 90—, pastoral care of migrants and itinerant people, 1986—, social communications, 1989—. Mem. Urban Coalition of Fresno, 1968-72, Fresno County Econ. Opportunities Commn., 1964-65, Fresno County Alcoholic Rehab. Com., 1966-67, Fresno City Charter Rev. Com., 1968-70, Mexican-Am. Council for Better Housing, 1968-72, Fresno Redevel. Agy., 1970-75, L.A. 2000 Com., 1985-88, Fed. Commn. Agrl. Workers, 1987—, Blue Ribbon Com. Affordable Housing City of L.A., 1988; mem. commn. to Draft an Ethics Code for L.A. City Govt., 1989-90; bd. dirs. Fresno Community Workshop, 1965-67; trustee St. Agnes Hosp., Fresno. Named Young Man of Yr. Fresno Jr. C. of C., 1967. Mem. Canon Law Soc. Am., Nat. Assn. Social Workers. Home: 114 E 2nd St Los Angeles CA 90012-3711 Office: Archdiocese of LA 3424 Wilshire Blvd Los Angeles CA 90010-2241*

MAHOWALD, ANTHONY PETER, geneticist, cell biologist, educator; b. Albany, Minn., Nov. 24, 1932; s. Aloys and Cecilia (Maus) Mahowald; m. Mary Lou Briody, Apr. 11, 1971; children: Maureen, Lisa, Michael. BS, Spring Hill Coll., 1958; PhD, Johns Hopkins U., 1962. Asst. prof. Marquette U., Milw., 1966-70; asst. staff mem. Inst. Cancer Rsch., Phila., 1970-72; assoc. prof. Ind. U., Bloomington, 1972-76, prof., 1976-82; Henry

Willson Payne prof. Case Western Res. U., Cleve., 1982-90, chmn. dept. anatomy, 1982-88, chmn. dept. genetics, 1988-90; Louis Block prof., chmn. dept molecular genetics and cell biology U. Chgo., 1990—; chmn. Com. Devel. Biology U. Chgo., 1991—. Woodrow Wilson Found. fellow, 1958, NSF fellow, 1958-62. Fellow AAAS, Am. Acad. Arts and Scis., Soc. Scholars Johns Hopkins U.; mem. Nat. Acad. Scis., Genetics Soc. Am. (sec. 1986-88), Soc. Devel. Biology (pres. 1989, editor-in-chief jour. 1980-85), Am. Soc. Cell Biology (coun. mem. 1995—). Office: U Chgo Dept Molecular Genetics/Cell Biology Chicago IL 60637

MAHR, GEORGE JOSEPH, financial service executive, real estate developer; b. Bklyn., Mar. 9, 1947; s. George Joseph and Mary Ann (Hanrahan) M.; m. Joan Valeroso, Mar. 21, 1970; children: Christopher, Courtney, Kelly. BS in Acctg., N.Y. Inst. Tech., 1970. Auditor Price Waterhouse & Co., Huntington Station, N.Y., 1973-77; mgr. internal audit United Techs. Corp., Hartford, Conn., 1977-83, contr., 1983-84, v.p. fin., chief fin. officer, 1985-86; v.p. fin., chief fin. officer Mostek Corp. div. United Techs. Corp., Carrollton, Tex., 1986, 1987; v.p. bus. devel. SGS-Thomson Microelectronics, Inc., Carrollton; CEO Mahr Leonard Mgmt. Co., Dallas, 1988—; chmn. Semicondr. Insights, Inc., Kanata, Ont., Can., Mahr Devel. Corp., Dallas, Lenmar Devel. Corp., Dallas, Mahr Devel. Corp. Fla., Dallas, Sailfish Enterprises, Inc., Dallas; ptnr. DJ Enterprises, Dallas. Home: 2616 Rothland Ln Plano TX 75023-1421 Office: Mahr Leonard Mgmt Co Ste 626 5420 Lyndon B Johnson Fwy Dallas TX 75240-2643

MAHRENHOLTZ, DAYLA DIANNE, elementary school principal; b. Glendale, Calif., Apr. 12, 1957; d. Preston Paul Buby and Evangeline Ruth (Sickler) B.; m. Laurence J. Mahrenholtz, Nov. 21, 1987 (div. Feb. 1993). AA, El Camino Jr. Coll., Torrance, Calif., 1975-77; BA, Calif. State U., Carson, 1979; MA, Calif. State U., L.A., 1990; EdD, U. LaVerne, Calif., 1996. Cert. edn. adminstr., Calif. Teller Ban of Am., Lawndale, Calif., 1977-79; tchr. Whittier (Calif.) City Sch. Dist., 1980-88, tchr., mentor, 1988-92; prin. Los Nietos Sch. Dist., Whittier, Calif., 1992—. Mem. AAUW, Calif. Assn. Bilingual Edn., Assn. Calif. Adminstrs., Computer Users in Edn., Whittier Area Sch. Adminstrs. (program chair 1993—). Democrat. Avocations: bird watching, running, bicycling, body building, reading. Office: Aeolian Sch 700 Esplanade Apt 21 Redondo Beach CA 90277-4629

MAHSMAN, DAVID LAWRENCE, religious publications editor; b. Quincy, Ill., Aug. 16, 1950; s. Alvin Henry and Dorothy Marie (Schnack) M.; m. Lois Jean Mohn, July 27, 1975. BS in Journalism, So. Ill. U., 1972; MDiv, Concordia Theol. Seminary, Fort Wayne, Ind., 1983; STM, Concordia Sem., St. Louis, 1995. Staff writer Paddock Publs., Arlington Heights, Ill., 1972-73, Decatur (Ill.) Herald & Rev., 1973-76; press asst. Hon. Tom Railsback U.S. Ho. Reps., Washington, 1976-79; campaign press sec. Hon. Dan Coats U.S. Ho. Reps., Ft. Wayne, Ind., 1979-80, 82; pastor Trinity Luth. Ch., Glen Cove, N.Y., 1983-85; dir. news and info. Luth. Ch.-Mo. Synod, St. Louis, 1985—; exec. editor, contbr. Luth. Witness, St. Louis, 1985—; exec. editor Reporter, St. Louis, 1985—; mem. Inter-Luth. task force on pornography Luth. Coun. U.S.A., 1986; mem. Washington adv. coun. Mo. Synod, Office of Govt. Info., Washington, 1987—. Editor: Augsburg Today: This We Believe, Teach and Confess, 1997. Recipient Jacob Scher Investigative Reporting award Women in Comm., 1974, Commendation award Concordia Hist. Inst., 1988. Mem. Concordia Hist. Inst. (life). Republican. Avocations: travel, photography, flying. Office: Luth Ch-Mo Synod 1333 S Kirkwood Rd Saint Louis MO 63122-7226

MAI, CHAO CHEN, engineer; b. Kwangchow, Canton, China, Feb. 26, 1936; came to U.S. 1962, naturalized 1973; m. Shao Shen Yam; children: Glenn, Kenneth. M.S.E.E., Oreg. State U., 1964; Ph.D. in E.E., Utah State U., 1967. Project engr. Sylvania Electric Co., Woburn, Mass., 1967-70; mgr. research and devel. Mostek Corp., Carrollton, Tex., 1970-76, v.p. research and devel., 1976-84; founder, sr. v.p. Dallas Semiconductor Corp., 1984—. Patentee Silicon gate combined with depletion load process, 1974; method for making a semicondr. device, 1985. MOSFET Fabrication Process, 1984. Mem. IEEE, Electrochem. Soc. Current work: Advanced processing technology in integrated circuits. Subspecialties: Integrated circuits; Microchip technology (engineering).

MAI, ELIZABETH HARDY, lawyer; b. Ithaca, N.Y., Nov. 7, 1948; d. William Frederick and Barbara Lee (Morrell) M.; m. Edward John Gobrecht III, May 19, 1990. BA in Am. Studies, Cornell U., 1970; JD, Dickinson Sch. Law, 1975. Bar: Pa. 1975, U.S. Dist. Ct. (mid. dist.) Pa. 1976. Atty. Keystone Legal Svcs., Inc., State Coll., Pa., 1975-76; asst. atty. gen. Pa. Dept. Commerce, Harrisburg, Pa., 1976-77; chief counsel Pa. Dept. Commerce, Harrisburg, 1978; assoc. Wolf, Block, Schorr and Solis-Cohen, Phila., 1979-83, ptnr., 1986—; v.p., gen. counsel EQK Ptnrs., Bala Cynwyd, Pa., 1983-86; chair environ. dept. Wolf, Block, Schorr and Solis-Cohen; chair Pa. state govt. affairs Internat. Coun. Shopping Ctrs., 1988-93; founding dir., mem. Comml. Real Estate Women, Phila.; bd. dels. Nat. Network Comml. Real Estate Women; adj. prof. Villanova (Pa.) U. Sch. Law, 1986—. Active Cornell U. Real Estate Coun., 1990—. Mem. ABA, Am. Coll. Real Estate Lawyers, Pa. Bar Assn., Phila. Bar Assn. Office: Wolf Block Schorr and Solis-Cohen 15th & Chestnut Sts 12th Fl Philadelphia PA 19102

MAI, HAROLD LEVERNE, retired judge; b. Casper, Wyo., Apr. 5, 1928. BA, U. Wyo., 1950, JD, 1952. Bar: Wyo. 1952, U.S. Supreme Ct. 1963. Sole practice, Cheyenne, Wyo., 1953-62, 67-71; judge Juvenile Ct., Cheyenne, 1962-67; U.S. bankruptcy judge, Cheyenne, 1971-93, ret., 1993. Mem. adv. bd. Salvation Army. Wyo. Mem. ABA, Wyo. Bar Assn., Laramie County Bar Assn., Nat. Conf. Bankruptcy Judges.

MAI, WILLIAM FREDERICK, plant nematologist, educator; b. Greenwood, Del., July 23, 1916; s. William Frederick and Laurana (Owens) M.; m. Barbara Lee Morrell, June 2, 1941; children: Virginia Mai Abrams, William Howard, Elizabeth Hardy. B.S., U. Del., 1939; Ph.D., Cornell U., 1945. Asst. prof. Cornell U., Ithaca, N.Y., 1946-49, assoc. prof., 1949-52, prof., 1952-81, Liberty Hyde prof. plant pathology, 1981-83, prof. emeritus, 1983—; cons. Nat. Acad. Scis., Internat. Potato Ctr., Brands Co., AID. Author (with H.H. Lyon), Pictoral Key to Genera of Plant Parasitic Nemtodes, 1960, 5th edit. 1993, Plant Parasitic Nematodes, 1971; editor: Control of Plant Parasitic Nematodes, 1968. Coach Little League Baseball and Football, Ithaca, 1955-60; chmn. Community Orgn., 1960-65. Recipient award of distinction Internat. Plant Protection Conf., 1979; Paul Harris fellow Rotary Found., 1997. Fellow Am. Phytopath. Soc. (pres. Northeastern div. 1968-69 award of merit Northeastern div); mem. AAAS, Soc. Nematologists (pres. 1969 hon. life), Helminthological Soc. Washington, Soc. European Nematologists, Potato Assn. Am. Lodge: Rotary. Home: 613 E Shore Dr Ithaca NY 14850-2135 Office: Cornell U Dept Plant Pathology Ithaca NY 14853

MAIALE, NICHOLAS F., healthcare communications executive. Grad., N.Y.C. C.C., Rutgers U. Account exec. Klemtner Advt., 1963-67; advt. planning mgr. E.R. squibb, 1967-69; advt. dir. Reed & Carnick, 1969-73; group product dir. USV Pharms., 1973-74; account dir. William Douglas McAdams, Inc., 1974-75; sr. v.p., account dir. Medicus Intercon, USA, 1975-83; rep. dir. Medicus Intercon K.K., Japan, 1983-85; regional dir. Far East Medicus Intercon Internat., Inc., 1985-88, exec. v.p., group dir. internat., 1988-92, pres. internat., 1992-95; pres. USA Medicus Group Internat., Inc., 1995-96, pres. N.Am., 1996—. Office: Medicus Group Internat Inc 1675 Broadway New York NY 10019-5820

MAIBACH, BEN C., JR., service executive; b. Bay City, Mich., 1920. With Barton-Malow Co., Detroit, 1938—, v.p., dir.-in-charge field ops., 1949-53, exec. v.p., 1953-60, pres., 1960-76, chmn. bd., 1976; chmn. and dir. Barton-Malow Ent.; chmn. bd. Cloverdale Equipment Co. Trustee Barton-Malow Found, Maibach Found., 1967—, Greater Del Safety Coun.; chmn. Apostolic Christian Woodhaven, Detroit; bishop Apostolic Christian Ch., Mich., Ont., Fla.; bd. dirs. S.E. Mich. chpt. ARC, United Found., Rural Gospel and Med. Missions of India. Home: 34050 Ramble Hills Dr Farmington MI 48331-4224 also: 5525 Azure Way Sarasota FL 34242-1857 Office: Barton-Malow Co 27777 Franklin Rd Ste 800 Southfield MI 48034-8258

MAIBACH, BEN C., III, construction company executive; b. 1946. BS, Mich. State U., 1969. With Barton-Malow Corp., Oak Park, Mich., 1964—, v.p. field ops., 1964-68, systems analyst, programmer, 1968-70, project adminstr., 1970-72, officer mgr., purchasing agt., 1972-73, v.p., 1973-76, exec. v.p., 1976-81, pres., 1981—. Office: Barton-Malow Co 27777 Franklin Rd Ste 800 Southfield MI 48034-8258*

MAIBACH, HOWARD I., dermatologist; b. N.Y.C., July 18, 1929; s. Jack Louis and Sidonia (Fink) M.; m. Siesel Wile, July 8, 1953; children—Lisa, Ed, Todd. A.B., Tulane U., 1950, M.D., 1955. Diplomate: Am. Bd. Dermatology. Intern William Beaumont Army Hosp., El Paso, Tex., 1955-56; resident, fellow in dermatology USPHS, Hosp. of U. Pa., 1959-61; asst. instr. U. Pa., 1958-61, lectr., 1960-61; practice medicine specializing in dermatology U. Calif. Hosps., San Francisco, 1961—; asst. prof. dermatology U. Calif. Sch. Medicine, San Francisco, 1961-63; asso. prof. U. Calif. Sch. Medicine, 1967-73; research asso. Cancer Research Inst., 1967—; mem. staff U. Calif.-H.C. Moffitt Hosps., 1961—; cons. Laguna Honda Hosp., 1962-66, chief dermatology service, 1963-67; cons. Letterman Gen. Hosp., Calif. Med. Facility, Vacaville, San Francisco Gen. Hosp., Sonoma State Hosp., Eldridge, Calif., Stanford Research Inst., Menlo Park, Calif., Calif. Dept. Public Health, Berkeley, VA Hosp., Research Inst. Fragrance Materials, Inc., David Grant USAF Hosp. of Travis AFB, Naval Hosp., San Diego, Wilford Hall AFB, Tex., Army Environ. Health Agy., Md.; mem. Internat. Contact Dermatitis Research Com. Editor: Animal Models in Dermatology, 1965; co-editor: Dermatotoxicology and Pharmacology, 1977, Skin Microbiology, 1981; bd. editors: Internat. Jour. Dermatology, 1974—; editorial bd.: Contact Dermatitis: Environ. Dermatology, 1974—, Clin. Toxicology, 1976—; internat. editorial bd.: Excerpta Media, 1976—; author, coauthor, editor of over 30 books and 750 publs. Served to capt. M.C. U.S. Army, 1955-58. Recipient awards Soc. Cosmetic Chemists, 1970, 71, 73. Fellow A.C.P.; mem. Am. Acad. Dermatology (award for essay 1961), San Francisco Dermatol. Soc. (pres. 1970-71), Pacific Dermatol. Assn., Soc. Investigative Dermatology, N.Y. Acad. Scis., Calif. Med. Assn., Am. Fedn. Clin. Research, AMA, San Francisco Med. Soc., Am. Dermatol. Assn., Internat. Soc. Tropical Dermatology, Am. Soc. Clin. Pharmacology and Therapeutics, Am. Coll. Toxicology; hon. mem. Swedish Dermatol. Soc., Am. Vet. Dermatol. Assn., Am. Acad. Vet. Dermatology, Danish Dermatol. Soc., German Dermatol. Soc. Office: U Calif Hosp San Francisco CA 94143

MAIBENCO, HELEN CRAIG, anatomist, educator; b. New Deer, Aberdeenshire, Scotland, June 9, 1917; came to U.S., 1917; d. Benjamin C. and Mary (Brown) Craig; children: Thomas Allen, Douglas Craig. BS, Wheaton (Ill.) Coll., 1948; MS, DePaul U., 1950; PhD, U. Ill., Chgo., 1956. Asst. prof., assoc. prof., then prof. U. Ill., Chgo., 1956-73; prof. Rush U., Chgo., 1973-86, prof. emerita, 1993—; anatomist dept. anatomy, dept. rehab. medicine Rush-Presbyn.-St. Luke's Med. Ctr., Chgo., 1986—, rsch. cons., 1973—; prof. emeritus Rush-U. Chgo., 1986—; cons. on grant application NIH, Bethesda, Md. Contbr. articles to profl. jours. Fellow ACS; mem. AAAS, Endocrine Soc., Am. Assn. Anatomists, Sigma Xi. Republican. Presbyterian. Home: 1324 S Main St Wheaton IL 60187-6480

MAICKEL, ROGER PHILIP, pharmacologist, educator; b. Floral Park, N.Y., Sept. 8, 1933; s. Philip Vincent and Margaret Mary (Rose) M.; m. Lois Louise Pivonka, Sept. 8, 1956; children: Nancy Ellen Maickel Ward, Carolyn Sue Maickel Anderson. B.S., Manhattan (N.Y.) Coll., 1954; postgrad., Poly. Inst. Bklyn., 1954-55; M.S., Georgetown U., 1957, Ph.D., 1960. Biochemist Nat. Heart Inst., Bethesda, Md., 1955-65; asso. prof. pharmacology Ind. U., 1965-69, prof., 1969—, head sect. pharmacology med. scis. program, 1971-77; prof. pharmacology and toxicology, head dept. Sch. Pharmacy and Pharmacal Scis. Purdue U., West Lafayette, Ind., 1977-83; dir. lab. animal program Purdue U., West Lafayette, 1988—; acting v.p. product acquisition and devel. BetaMED Pharms., Inc., Indpls., 1983-84. Adv. editor: Pergamon Press, 1970-88; adv. editorial bd.: Neuropharmacology, 1974-88. Bd. dirs. TEAMS, Inc., 1981-87, Am. Coun. on Sci. and Health, 1993—; trustee AAALAC, 1992-96. Recipient Alumni award in medicine Manhattan Coll., 1972. Fellow AAAS, Am. Coll. Neuropsychopharmacology, Am. Inst. Chemists (bd. dirs. 1989-92, pres.-elect 1992-94, pres. 1994-96, chmn. 1996—), Royal Soc. Chemistry, Collegium Internat. de Neuro-Psychopharmacologicum; mem. ASTM, Am. Chem. Soc., Am. Soc. Pharmacology and Exptl. Therapeutics, Am. Soc. Clin. Pharmacology and Therapeutics, Soc. Forensic Toxicologists, Internat. Assn. Chiefs Police, Internat. Soc. Psychoneuroendocrinology, N.Y. Acad. Scis., Soc. Neurosci., Soc. Toxicology, Sigma Xi, Rho Chi. Home: 3567 Canterbury Dr Lafayette IN 47905-3714 Office: R E Heine Pharmacy Bldg Purdue Univ West Lafayette IN 47907-1333 *As a human being, I hope to be able to do my best in the roles of scientist, teacher, and citizen by fulfilling the academic criteria of teaching, research, and service to the utmost degree humanly possible.*

MAICKI, G. CAROL, former state senator, consultant; b. Holden, Mass., July 16, 1936; d. John Arne and Mary Emily (Bumpus) Mannisto; m. Henry J. Maicki, May 4, 1957; children: Henry III, Matthew, Scott, Julia, Mary. BA, U. Mich., 1978. Exec. dir. Sweetwater County Task Force/Sexual Assault, Rocksprings, Wyo., 1978-81; program mgr. Family Violence/Sexual Assault, Cheyenne, Wyo., 1981-85; coord. S.D. Coalition Against Domestic Violence and Sexual Assault, Black Hawk, 1985-90; state senator S.D. Legislature, Pierre, 1990-92; cons. Black Hawk, 1990-94, Nat. Coalition Against Domestic Violence, 1987; spkr. Nat. Coalition Against Sexual Assault, Portland, Oreg., 1987, 96, Rutger Ctr. for Women in Politics, San Diego, 1991, Gov.'s Conf., Las Vegas, Nev., 1997; mem. planning com. Office for Victims of Crime, U.S. Justice, Phoenix, 1989; expert witness state and fed. cts., 1990-96, 97. Author: (manuals) Operating Standards, 1984, Rules and Regulations, 1986, Shelter Procedures, 1987, Administrative Procedures, 1995, Responders to Rope, 1996. Com. mem. Health and Human Svc. State Legislature, Pierre, 1990-92, local govt., 1990-92; commn. mem. local govt. study commn., Pierre, 1990-92; bd. dirs. Crisis Intervention Svcs., 1991—; apptd. def. adv. com. on women in svcs. Sec. of Def., 1995—; apptd. exec. com. def. adv. com. on women in the svcs., 1996—. Recipient award Gov. Wyo., 1985, Spirit of Peace award Women Against Violence, Rapid City, 1993, U.S. Dept. of Justice award, 1994, fellowship Share Our Strength, 1996—, Equity award S.D. chpt. AAUW, 1996. Mem. S.D. Alliance for Mentally Ill, Rapid City Womens Network, S.D. Advocacy Network for Women, Lions (Black Hawk), Women Against Violence. Democrat. Avocations: reading, crosswords, gardening. Home: PO Box 375 Black Hawk SD 57718-0375

MAIDA, ADAM JOSEPH CARDINAL, cardinal; b. East Vandergrift, Pa., Mar. 18, 1930. Student, St. Vincent Coll., Latrobe, Pa., St. Mary's U., Balt., Lateran U., Rome, Duquesne U. Ordained priest Roman Cath. Ch., 1956, consecrated bishop, 1984. Bishop Green Bay, Wis., 1984-89; archbishop Detroit, 1990-95; elevated to Cardinal, 1995—. Home: 75 E Boston Blvd Detroit MI 48202-1318 Office: Archdiocese of Detroit 1234 Washington Blvd Detroit MI 48226-1808*

MAIDEN, EVA WENKART, psychotherapist, school psychologist; b. Vienna, Austria, Apr. 8, 1935; d. Simon I. and Antonia (Taubes) Wenkart; m. Henry George Maiden, Aug. 26, 1956 (div. 1977); children: Peter David, Benjamin Paul; m. Martin Leonard Primack, Jan. 1, 1989. BA, Antioch U., 1957; MA, San Francisco State U., 1967. Cert. sch. psychologist, Calif.; lic. marriage, family and child counselor, Calif. Sch. psychologist Ravenswood Schs., East Palo Alto, Calif., 1967-69; tchr., sch. counselor Richmond (Ind.) Schs., 1969-70; sch. psychologist Yellow Springs (Ohio) Schs., 1970-72, Alum Rock Schs., San Jose, Calif., 1973-85; founder, psychotherapist Midpeninsula Mental Health Svcs., Palo Alto, 1976-91; psychotherapist Palo Alto, 1976—; instr. psychology Cen. State U., Wilberforce, Ohio, 1971; cons. psychologist Children's Hosp., Dayton, Ohio, 1972; counselor re-entry program DeAnza Coll., Cupertino, Calif., 1987. Chair for consciousness raising NOW, Palo Alto, 77-82; group leader women's support group Jewish Comty. Ctr., Palo Alto, 1983-89; v.p. bd. dirs. Tikvah network for Holocaust survivors, San Francisco, 1992—. Fellow Am. Orthopsychiat. Assn.; mem. Calif. Assn. Marriage and Family Therapists, Calif. Assn. Sch. Psychologists. Office: 550 S California Ave Palo Alto CA 94306-1401

MAIDIQUE, MODESTO ALEX, academic administrator; b. Havana, Cuba, Mar. 20, 1940; s. Modesto Maidique and Hilda Rodriguez; m. Ana Hernandez, July 18, 1981; children: Ana Teresa, Mark Alex. BS, MIT, 1962, MS, 1964, PhD, 1970. Instr. MIT, Boston, 1976-79; v.p., gen. mgr. Analog Devices Semiconductor, Boston, 1970-76; asst. prof. Harvard U., Boston, 1976-81; assoc. prof. Stanford U., Palo Alto, Calif., 1981-84; sr. ptnr. Hambrecht and Quist Venture Ptnrs., Palo Alto, Calif., 1981-86; co-founder, dir. U. Miami (Fla.) Innovation and Entepreneurship Inst., 1984-86; pres. Fla. Internat. U., Miami, 1986—. Mem. Pres.'s Edn. Policy Adv. Com.; chmn. Beacon Coun., 1992-93. Recipient Citizenship award HEW, 1973, Teaching award Stanford U., 1983. Mem. IEEE, Assn. Cuban Engrs. Republican. Roman Catholic. Home: 6821 SW 104th St Miami FL 33156-3253 Office: Fla Internat U Office of President Miami FL 33199

MAIDMAN, RICHARD HARVEY MORTIMER, lawyer; b. N.Y.C., Nov. 17, 1933; s. William and Ada (Seegle) M.; m. Lynne Rochelle Lateiner, Apr. 3, 1960 (div. Sept. 1987); children: Patrick, Mitchel, Dagny. BA, Williams Coll., 1955; JD, Yale U., 1959; postgrad. N.Y. U. Grad. Sch. Bus., 1957, Grad. Sch. Law, 1960, 77. Bar: N.Y. 1961, Fla., 1961, U.S. Dist. Ct. 1962, 79, U.S. Ct. Appeals 1966, U.S. Supreme Ct., 1978. Assoc. Saxe, Bacon & O'Shea, N.Y.C., 1962-64; ptnr. Weiner, Maidman & Goldman, N.Y.C., 1964-67; pvt. practice, N.Y.C., and Fla., 1968—; of counsel Maidman and Mittleman, 1996—; pres. MBS Equities, Inc., 1970-88, Fashion Wear Realty Co., Inc., N.Y.C., 1975—; mng. gen. ptnr. Richard and David Maidman, N.Y.C., 1972—, Barcelona Hotel Ltd., Miami Beach, Fla., 1975-84, New Haven Projects Co., 1987—; dir. The Farr Companies, Washington, 1990-92; legis. counsel Theodore R. Kupferman, 17th Congl. Dist. N.Y., 1966-68; of counsel Shwal, Thompson & Bloch, N.Y.C. and Geneva, 1976-87; receiver Halloran House Hotel, N.Y.C., 1981. Contbr. articles to profl. jours. Mem. ABA, N.Y. State Bar Assn., Fla. Bar Assn., Assn. Bar City N.Y., Bankruptcy Lawyers Assn. N.Y.C., Real Estate Bd. of N.Y. Home: Stamboat Landing 60-A Astor Ln Sands Point NY 11050 Office: 300 E 56th St Apt 4D New York NY 10022-4135

MAIDMAN, STEPHEN PAUL, lawyer; b. Hartford, Conn., Feb. 8, 1954; s. Harry and Roslyn (Mandell) M. AB summa cum laude, Bowdoin Coll., 1976; MBA, U. Pa., 1979, JD, 1980. Bar: Pa. 1980, U.S. Dist. Ct. (ea. dist.) Pa. 1980, U.S. Ct. Appeals (3d cir.) 1980, Mass. 1996, U.S. Dist. Ct. 1996, U.S. Ct. Appeals (1st cir.) 1996, U.S. Supreme Ct. 1997. Assoc. Drinker, Biddle & Reath, Phila., 1980-81; atty. IBM Corp., Boca Raton, Fla., 1981-84; atty. IBM Corp., N.Y.C., 1984-85, staff atty., 1985-87; staff atty. IBM Corp., Rye Brook, N.Y., 1987-88; lab. counsel IBM Corp., Poughkeepsie, N.Y., 1988-92; site counsel IBM Corp., Hopewell Junction, N.Y., 1992-95; pvt. practice Springfield, Mass., 1996—; vol. atty. Com. for Pub. Counsel Svcs., Pub. Defender Divsn., Springfield, Mass., 1996—. Co-class agt., fund dir. Bowdoin Coll. Alumni Fund; counselor Hugh O'Brian Youth Found., Western Mass. Leadership Seminar, 1996—; counselor Hugh O'Brian Youth Found., Conn. Leadership Seminar, 1989—. Mem. ABA, ATLA, Pa. Bar Assn., Phila. Bar Assn., Am. Corp. Counsel Assn., Corp. Bar Assn. Westchester and Fairfield, Mass. Bar Assn., Mass. Acad. Trial Attys., Hampden County Bar Assn., Springfield C. of CC., Western Mass. Software Assn. Avocations: reading, stamp collecting, running, biking, black Labradors. Home: 63 Fuller Dr West Hartford CT 06117-1315 Office: 1145 Main St Ste 417 Springfield MA 01103-2123

MAIDON, CAROLYN HOWSER, education director; b. Chgo., May 13, 1946; d. Lloyd Earl and Esther Lillian (Beck) Howser; m. Charles Randall Maidon, Nov. 21, 1970; children: Randall Scott, April Janel. BS in Edn., Okla. State U., 1968; MS in Edn., N.C. State U., 1984, postgrad., 1987—. Tchr. biology and English Cary (N.C.) High Sch., 1968-71; grad. instr. N.C. State U., Raleigh, 1984-85, asst. affirmative action officer, 1985-89, asst. dir. univ. undesignated program, 1989-95; dir. tchr. edn., 1995—. Home: 4204 Bellnap Dr Apex NC 27502 Office: NC State U Box 7801 Raleigh NC 27695-7801

MAIDON, GILLES, dancer; b. Paris. Studied with Raymond Franchetti, studied with Diane Carter. Soloist Ballet de Marseille, Paris, 1976-83; dancer Santiago (Chile) Ballet, 1983-90, Cin. Ballet, 1990-92; prin. artist Ballet West, Salt Lake City, 1992—; guest artist various ballet cos., galas and festivals. Dance performances include Notre Dame de Paris, Peer Gynt, Anna Karenina, Sergeant Early's Dream, Taming of the Shrew, The Great Gatsby, Swan Lake. Office: Ballet West 50 W 200 S Salt Lake City UT 84101-1642*

MAIENSCHEIN, FRED C., physicist; b. Belleville, Ill., Oct. 28, 1925; s. Fred and Ethel (Forsythe) M.; m. Joyce Kylander, Aug. 14, 1948; children: Jane, Jon. B.S. in Chem. Engring, Rose Hulman Inst. Tech., 1945; M.S. in Physics, Ind. U., 1948, Ph.D. in Physics, 1949. Physicist Oak Ridge Nat. Lab., 1951-60, assoc. dir. engring. physics div., 1960-66; co-dir. Oak Ridge Electron Linear Accelerator, 1965-74, dir. engring. physics div., 1966-90, ret., 1990; current neurosci. scholar; mem. com. reactor physics Nuclear Energy Agy., 1962-89; mem. adv. com. radiation aspects of SST, FAA, 1969-74; mem. subcoms. Nat. Com. Radiation Protection, 1959-71. Contbr. articles profl. jours., chpts. in books. Fellow Am. Nuclear Soc.; mem. Am. Phys. Soc., AAAS, Soc. Neurosci., Tau Beta Pi. Home: 838 W Outer Dr Oak Ridge TN 37830-8402

MAIER, ALFRED, neuroscientist; b. Bamberg, Bavaria, Fed. Republic of Germany, Sept. 16, 1929; came to U.S., 1958; s. Johan and Barbara (Rauh) M. BS in Zoology, Calif State U., Long Beach, 1967; PhD in Anatomy, UCLA, 1972. Postdoctoral fellow dept. kinesiology UCLA, 1972-74; instr. dept. cell biology UCLA, Birmingham, 1974-76, asst. prof, 1976-80; assoc. prof. U. Ala., Birmingham, 1980-89, prof., 1989-96, prof. emeritus, 1997—, sr. scientist cell adhesion and matrix rsch. ctr.; rsch. sabbatical Faculty Biology U. Konstanz, Fed. Republic of Germany, 1984, Dept. Physiology U. Otago, Dunedin, New Zealand, 1990; vis. prof. Faculty of Biology, U. Konstanz, 1985, '86. Contbr. articles and sci. papers to profl. jours and seminars. Recipient Pres.'s award for Excellence in Tchg., U. Ala., 1994, Didactic Instr. of Yr. Sch. Dentistry, 1993, 94, Best Basic Sci. Instr. Sch. Dentistry, 1978, 79, 83, 84. Mem. Soc. for Neurosci., Am. Assn. Anatomists. Avocations: photography, gardening, travel, camping.

MAIER, CHARLES STEVEN, history educator; b. N.Y.C., N.Y., Feb. 23, 1939; s. Louis and Muriel (Krailsheimer) M.; m. Pauline Alice Rubbelke, June 17, 1961; children—Andrea Nicole, Nicholas Winterer, Jessica Elizabeth Heine. A.B., Harvard U., 1960; postgrad., St. Anthony's Coll., Oxford, Eng., 1960-61; Ph.D., Harvard U., 1967. Instr. history Harvard U., Cambridge, Mass., 1967-69, asst. prof., 1969-73, lectr., 1973-75; vis. prof. U. Bielefeld, Fed. Republic Germany, 1976; assoc. prof. history Duke U., Durham, N.C., 1976-79, prof., 1979-81; prof. history Harvard U., Cambridge, Mass., 1981-91, Krupp Found. prof. European studies, 1991—; dir. Ctr. for European Studies, 1994—; rsch. fellow Lehrman Inst., N.Y.C., 1975-76; mem. assoc. staff Brookings Instn., Washington, 1978-84; mem. coun. Fondation Jean Monnet pour l'Europe, Lausanne, Switzerland; mem. joint comm. on W. Europe Social Sci. Rsch. Coun. and Am. Coun. Learned Socs., 1978-84, chmn., 1979-81. Author: Recasting Bourgeois Europe, 1975 (Am. Hist. Assn. George Louis Beer award 1976, Herbert Baxter Adams award 1977), In Search of Stability, 1987, The Unmasterable Past, 1988, Dissolution: The Crisis of Communism and the End of East Germany, 1997; editor: The Origins of the Cold War and Contemporary Europe, 1978, rev. edit., 1990, (with Dan S. White) The Thirteenth of May and the Advent of de Gaulle's Republic, 1967, (with Leon Lindberg) The Politics of Inflation and Economic Stagnation, 1985, Changing Boundaries of the Political, 1987, The Marshall Plan and Germany, 1991. Fellow NEH, 1977-78, German Marshall Fund, 1980-81, Guggenheim Found., 1984-85; rsch. grantee MacArthur Found., 1988-89. Fellow Woodrow Wilson Ctr. for Scholars (Washington); mem. Council on Fgn. Relations, Am. Hist. Assn., Soc. Italian Hist. Studies, Soc. Historians of Am. Fgn. Rels., Am. Acad. Arts and Scis., Phi Beta Kappa. Home: 60 Larchwood Dr Cambridge MA 02138-4639 Office: Harvard U Ctr for European Studies Cambridge MA 02138

MAIER, CRAIG FRISCH, restaurant executive; b. Cin., Sept. 20, 1949; s. Jack Craig and Blanche June (Frisch) M. BA, Trinity Coll., Hartford, Conn., 1971; MBA, Columbia U., 1975. With Frisch's Restaurant, Cin., 1975—, exec. v.p., 1987-89, pres., chief exec. officer, 1989—. Bd. dirs. Cin. Mus. Natural History, 1990—, Cin. Playhouse in the Pk., 1992—, Dan Beard coun. Boy Scouts Am., 1992—, Cin. Bus. Com., 1994—, Greater Cin. Cov. and Visitors Bur., 1995—. Mem. Greater Cin. Restaurant Assn. (bd. dirs. 1991—). Republican. Avocations: jogging, gardening, golf. Office: Frisch's Restaurants Inc 2800 Gilbert Ave Cincinnati OH 45206-1206

MAIER, DONNA JANE-ELLEN, history educator; b. St. Louis, Feb. 20, 1948; d. A. Russell and Mary Virginia Maier; m. Stephen J. Rapp, Jan. 3, 1981; children: Alexander John, Stephanie Jane-Ellen. BA, Coll. of Wooster, 1969; MA, Northwestern U., 1972, PhD, 1975. Asst. prof. U. Tex. at Dallas, Richardson, 1975-78; asst. prof. history U. No. Iowa, Cedar Falls, 1978-81, assoc. prof., 1981-86, prof., 1986—; cons. Scott, Foresman Pub., Glenview, Ill., 1975-94; editl. cons. Children's Press, 1975-76, Macmillan Pubs., 1989-90, Haper-Collins Pubs., 1994. Co-author: History and Life, 1976, 4th edit., 1990; author: Priests and Power, 1983; co-editor African Economic History, 1992—; contbr. articles to profl. jours., essays to books. Mem. Iowa Dem. Cen. Com., 1982-90, chmn. budget com., 1986-90; chmn. 3d Congl. Dist. Cen. Com., 1986-88. Fulbright-Hays fellow, Ghana, 1972, Arab Republic Egypt, 1987; fellow Am. Philos. Soc., London, 1978; recipient Iowa Bd. Regents Faculty Excellence award, 1996. Mem. Am. Hist. Assn., African Studies Assn., AAUW (fellow Ghana 1973), Quota Club. Home: 219 Highland Blvd Waterloo IA 50703-4229 Office: U No Iowa Dept History Cedar Falls IA 50614

MAIER, GERALD JAMES, natural gas transmission and marketing company executive; b. Regina, Sask., Can., Sept. 22, 1928; s. John Joseph and Mary (Passler) M. Student, Notre Dame Coll. (Wilcox), U. Man., U. Alta., U. Western Ont. With petroleum and mining industries Can., U.S., Australia, U.K.; responsible for petroleum ops. Africa, United Arab Emirates, S.E. Asia; chmn. TransCan. PipeLines, Calgary, 1985—, also bd. dirs.; chmn., bd. dirs. Epic Energy, Inc., 1996—; bd. dirs. BCE Inc., Bank of N.S., Petro-Can., XPronet Inc.; immediate past chmn. Can. Nat. Com. for World Petroleum Congresses; chmn. Van Horne Inst. for Internat. Transp.; dep. chmn. Coun. Can. Unity. Bd. dirs. Notre Dame Coll. Named Hon. Col. King's Own Calgary Rgt., Resource Man of Yr. Alta. Chamber of Resources, 1990; recipient Can. Engr.'s Gold medal Can. Coun. Profl. Engrs., 1990, Disting. Alumni award U. Alta., 1992, Mgmt. award McGill U., 1993, Centennial award Alta Assn. Engrs., Geologists and Geophysicists. Fellow Can. Acad. Engring.; mem. Assn. Profl. Engrs., Geologists and Geophysicists Alta. (past pres.), Can. Inst. Mining and Metallurgy (Past Pres.'s Meml. medal 1971). Avocations: golf, downhill skiing, shooting, fishing. Office: TransCan PipeLines Ltd, 2900 240-4 Ave SW, Calgary, AB Canada T2P 4L7

MAIER, HAROLD GEISTWEIT, law educator, lawyer; b. Cin., Mar. 25, 1937; s. Alfred F. and Alberta (Wilmes) M.; divorced; children: Marc L., Kurt S. BA in English Lit., U. Cin., 1959, JD, 1963; postgrad. Free U. Berlin, 1959-60; LLM, U. Mich., 1964; postgrad. U. Munich, 1964-65. Bar: Ohio 1963. Mem. faculty of law Vanderbilt U., Nashville, 1965—, prof., 1970—, dir. Transnat. Legal Studies Program, 1973—; David Daniels Allen prof. law, 1988—; faculty San Diego Internat. and Comparative Law Inst. King's Coll. U. London, 1986,87, Regent's Coll., 1989, 91, 96; vis. prof. law U. Pa., 1985, U. N.C., Chapel Hill, 1987; vis. Lyle T. Alverson prof. law George Washington U., Washington, 1987-88; vis. Woodruff prof. internat. law U. Ga., Atlanta, 1995; prof. law summer program LSU, Aix-en-Provence, France, 1995; cons. Office of Sec. Army, Panama Canal Treaty Negotiations, 1976; guest scholar Brookings Instn., Washington, 1976-77; dir. PDS Patrons, Inc. (Univ. Sch. of Nashville), 1975-87, pres., 1978-79; counselor on internat. law Office of Legal Adviser, U.S. Dept. State, 1983-84. Recipient Luftbrucke Dankstipendium, Free U. Berlin, 1959-60; Ford internat. studies fellow U. Mich., 1964-65; Vanderbilt U. faculty fellow, 1976-77. Mem. Am. Soc. Internat. Law (exec. coun. 1974-78, 84-87), Am. Soc. for Comparative Study of Law (bd. dirs. 1984—), Am. Law Inst., Order of Coif, Omicron Delta Kappa, Phi Alpha Delta, Tau Kappa Alpha, Pi Delta Epsilon. Bd. editors Am. Jour. Internat. Law, 1984-88; author: (with T. Buergenthal) Public International Law in A Nutshell, 1985, 2d edit., 1989, (with T. Buergenthal, K. Doehring, J. Kokott) Grundzüge des Völkerrechts, 1987, Manual de Derecho Internacional Publico, 1994; contbr. numerous articles in field to profl. jours. Office: Vanderbilt U Sch Law 21st Ave S Nashville TN 37240

MAIER, HENRY B., environmental engineer; b. Yonkers, N.Y., July 11, 1925; s. Henry and Adelaide (Boyce) M.; m. Elizabeth A. Maier, May 4, 1968. BA, Columbia U., 1947; postgrad., Adelphi U., Hofstra U. Prin. Maier Solar Developments, Hempstead, N.Y. Author: Techniques for Seascape Painting. Mem. AIAA, Am. Chem. Soc., N.Y. Acad. Scis. Achievements include patents for elapsed time indicator, multiple reflecting solar collecting system, electroresponsive coatings, fusion power pellets, and fusion power; design of initial stage of work for aerospace vehicle, comet flyby study; development of rapid method for perspective visualizations, for views of engineering and design concepts; definition of geometrics for placement of measuring points by approximation; research on inorganic sulfur and chlorine pollutants from combustion of fossil fuels and from incinerator processes, and their interactive roles in the progressive deterioration of the stratospheric ozone shield previously blocking frequencies in the infrared, far infrared and microwave frequencies, with particular regard to the prediction and pattern formation of major North Atlantic storm systems; study for a comet detecting telescope; design study for single span, steel beam highway bridge for enhanced safety from emerging situations of high-speed trucks, severe weather conditions and limited maintenance. Home: 6 Sealey Ave Apt 3K Hempstead NY 11550-1232

MAIER, PAUL LUTHER, history educator, author, chaplain; b. St. Louis, May 31, 1930; s. Walter A. and Hulda (Eickhoff) M.; m. Joan M. Ludtke, 1967; children: Laura Ann, Julie Joan, Krista Lynn, Katherine Marie. MA, Harvard U., 1954; BD, Concordia Sem., St. Louis, 1955; postgrad., U. Heidelberg, Fed. Republic Germany; PhD summa cum laude, U. Basel, Switzerland, 1957; LittD (hon.), Concordia Sem., St. Louis, 1995. Campus chaplain, 1958—; prof. ancient history Western Mich. U., Kalamazoo, 1961—; lectr. in field. Author: A Man Spoke, A World Listened, 1963, Pontius Pilate, 1968, First Christmas, 1971, First Easter, 1973, First Christians, 1976, The Flames of Rome, 1981, In the Fullness of Time, 1991, A Skeleton in God's Closet, 1994; editor: The Best of Walter A. Maier, 1980; editor: Josephus—The Jewish War, 1982; editor, transl.: Josephus—The Essential Writings, 1988, Josephus—The Essential Works, 1995; contbr. over 200 articles and revs. to profl. jours. Recipient Gold Medallion Book award ECPA, 1989, Disting. Faculty Scholar Western Mich. U., 1981, Alumni award tchg. excellence, 1974; named Outstanding Educator in Am., 1974-75, Prof. of Yr. Coun. for Advancement and Support of Edn., 1984, citation Mich. Acad. of Sci., Arts and Letters, 1985. Home: 8383 W Main St Kalamazoo MI 49009-8211 Office: Western Mich U Dept of History Kalamazoo MI 49008

MAIER, PAUL VICTOR, pharmaceutical executive; b. Seattle, Nov. 6, 1947; s. Norman Alvin and Rosalie (Godek) M.; m. Shirley Diehl, Aug. 11, 1979. BS, Pa. State U., 1969; MBA, Harvard U., 1975. Fin. analyst Greyhound Corp, Phoenix, 1975-76; asst. mgr. Wells Service Wells Fargo Bank, San Francisco, 1976-78; v.p. Fin. Cummins Service and Sales, Los Angeles, 1978-84; v.p., treas. ICN Pharms, Inc., Costa Mesa, Calif., 1984-90; v.p. fin. DFS West, 1990-92; sr. v.p., CFO Ligand Pharmaceuticals, Inc., San Diego, 1992—. Chmn. hosp. div. United Way Region V, L.A., 1983-84; bd. dirs. The Wellness Community, San Diego, 1993—. Served with USNR, 1969-95. Mem. Fin. Execs. Inst., The Athletic Congress, Pa. State Club of S.D., Harvard Bus. Sch. Assn. So. Calif., Ctr. for Non-Profit Mgmt., Vis. Nurse Assn. L.A. (bd. dirs. 1979-92, chmn.), Protection Mut. Inst. (West Coast adv. bd. 1985-90). Republican. Roman Catholic. Office: Ligand Pharmaceuticals 9393 Towne Centre Dr Ste 100 San Diego CA 92121-3093

MAIER, PAULINE, history educator; b. St. Paul, Apr. 27, 1938; d. Irvin Louis and Charlotte (Winterer) Rubbelke; AB, Radcliffe Coll., 1960; postgrad. London Sch. Econs., 1960-61; PhD in History, Harvard U., 1968, LLD (hon.), Regis Coll., 1987, DHL (hon.), Williams Coll., 1993; m. Charles Steven Maier, June 17, 1961; children: Andrea Nicole, Nicholas Winterer, Jessica Elizabeth Heine. Asst. prof., then assoc. prof. history U. Mass., Boston, 1968-77; Robinson-Edwards prof. history U. Wis., Madison, 1977-78; prof. history MIT, Cambridge, 1978—, William R. Kenan Jr. prof. history, 1990—, dept. head, 1979-88; mem. coun. Inst. Early Am. History, 1982-84; trustee Regis Coll., 1988-93; trustee Commonwealth Sch., 1991-96; bd. mgrs. Old South Meeting House, 1987-97. Recipient Douglass Adair award Claremont Grad. Sch.-Inst. Early Am. History, 1976, Kidger award New Eng. History Tchrs. Assn., 1981; fellow Nat. Endowment Humanities, 1974-75, 88-89; Charles Warren fellow, 1974-75; Guggenheim fellow, 1990. Mem. Orgn. Am. Historians (mem. exec. bd. 1978-82), Am. Hist. Assn. (mem. nominations com. 1983-85, chmn. 1985), Soc. Am. Historians, Am. Antiquarian Soc. (mem. exec. coun. 1984-89), Colonial Soc. Mass. (mem. exec. coun. 1990-93), Mass. Hist. Soc. Author: From Resistance to Revolution: Colonial Radicals and the Development of American Opposition to Britain, 1765-1766, 1972, The Old Revolutionaries: Political Lives in the Age of Samuel Adams, 1980, The American People: A History, 1986, American Scripture: Making the Declaration of Independence, 1997, Home: 60 Larchwood Dr Cambridge MA 02138-4639 Office: MIT E51-216 Dept History Cambridge MA 02139

MAIER, PETER KLAUS, law educator, investment adviser; b. Wurzburg, Germany, Nov. 20, 1929; came to U.S., 1939, naturalized, 1945; s. Bernard and Joan (Sonder) M.; m. Melanie L. Stoff, Dec. 15, 1963; children: Michele Margaret, Diana Lynn. BA cum laude, Claremont McKenna Coll., 1949; JD, U. Calif., Berkeley, 1952; LLM in Taxation, NYU, 1953. Bar: Calif. 1953, U.S. Supreme Ct. 1957; cert. specialist in taxation law, Calif. Atty. tax div. U.S. Dept Justice, Washington, 1956-59; mem. firm Bacigalupi, Elkus, Salinger & Rosenberg, San Francisco, 1959-69, Brookes & Maier, San Francisco, 1970-73, Winokur, Maier & Zang, San Francisco, 1974-81; chmn. Fromm Inst., U. San Francisco; prof. law Hastings Coll. Law, U. Calif., San Francisco, 1967-95; vis. prof. U. Calif. Boalt Sch. Law, Berkeley, 1988-89, Stanford U. Sch. Law, 1996—; pres. Maier & Siebel, Inc., Larkspur, Calif., 1981—; prin. Wood Island Investment Counsel, Inc., Larkspur, 1981—. Author books on taxation; contbr. articles to profl. jours. Chmn. Property Resources Inc., San Jose, Calif., 1968-77; pres. Calif. Property Devel. Corp., San Francisco, 1974-81. Capt. USAF, 1953-56. Mem. San Francisco Bar Assn. (chmn. sect. taxation 1970-71), Order of Coif. Home: PO Box 836 Belvedere CA 94920 Office: Maier & Siebel Inc 80 E Sir Francis Drake Blvd Larkspur CA 94939-1709

MAIER, ROBERT HAWTHORNE, biology educator; b. N.Y.C., Oct. 26, 1927; s. Ernest Henry and Clara Louise M.; m. Jane Hiob, Aug. 31, 1952; children: Pamela, David, Daniel. BS, U. Miami, 1951; MS, U. Ill., 1952, PhD, 1954. Asst. dean Grad. Coll., U. Ariz., 1966-67; asst. chancellor for instrn. and research U. Wis., Green Bay, 1967-69, vice chancellor and dep. chancellor, prof., 1969-75, prof. sci. and environ. change, public and environ. adminstrn., 1975-79; vice chancellor acad. affairs East Carolina U., Greenville, N.C., 1979-83; prof. exptl. surgery, biology, polit. sci. East Carolina U., 1983—, dir. Trace Element Ctr., Sch. Medicine, 1984—, adj. prof. physics, 1996—; pres., chmn. Nat. Investment Advisors, Inc., 1984—; mem. coun. biotech. U. N.C.; reviewer NC Tech. Devel. Authority, 1989—, NRC, 1990—. Contbr. articles to profl. jours. Bd. dirs. Lakeland chpt. ARC, 1978-79, Children's Svcs. Ea. N.C., 1987-94, fin. advisor, 1995—; mem. Edn. Task Force, City of Green Bay, 1977-78, N.C. State Panel Advancement of Women in Adminstrn., 1981-84, Gov.'s Commn. on Future of N.C., 1981-84; treas. Ronald McDonald House, 1987-94; mem. Vision Task Force, Global Transpark Devel. Commn., Kinston, N.C., 1996—. With U.S. Army, 1954-56. Fellow AAAS, Am. Inst. Chemists, Am. Soc. Agronomy, Soil Sci. Soc. Am.; mem. Am. Chem. Soc., Am. Inst. Biol. Scis. Presbyterian. Office: East Carolina U Sch Med Surgery Dept Greenville NC 27858-4354

MAIER, WILLIAM OTTO, martial arts school administrator, educator, consultant; b. Newark, July 15, 1949; s. Emil William Maier and Elizabeth Muriel Flader; children: William Wyatt, Kami Elizabeth. BA, Marietta (Ohio) Coll., 1971; MA, Coll. of Wooster (Ohio), 1973. Lic. sr. master instr. Internat. Bujinkan Dojo, Noda City, Japan. Tchr. Howard County (Md.) Pub. Schs., 1975-78; dean Martial Arts Am., Columbia, Md., 1975—; faculty mem. Martial Arts Am. Bus. Coll., Irvine, Calif. Featured on CNN, NBC and CBS; contbr. articles to profl. jours. Named Sch. of Month Black Belt Mag., Sept. 1992; recipient State Md. Govs. citation, 1992, Nat. Sch. of Yr. award U.S. Martial Arts Assn., 1992, 93, Cmty. Svc. award, 1993, Excellence award Martial Arts Bus. Info. Mag., 1996, recognition Md. Senate, 1995. Mem. Marishi Kai Instrs. Guild (charter mem.), U.S. Marital Arts Assn. (cons., bd. dirs. 1986-95, named Man of Yr. 1991, recipient award for best student retention 1988-93, Top Sch. award 1994), Martial Arts Am. (cons., bd. dirs. 1995—), Rotary. Office: Martial Arts Am 9042 Route 108 Columbia MD 21045-1952

MAIESE, KENNETH, neurologist; b. Audubon, N.J., Dec. 5, 1958; s. Charles and Margaret (Fioretti) M. BA summa cum laude, U. Pa., 1981; MD, Cornell U., 1985. Intern N.Y. Hosp., 1985-86, resident in neurology, 1986-89, asst. attending physician, 1989-94; asst. prof. Cornell U. Med. Coll., N.Y.C., 1989-94; assoc. prof. dept. neurology, dept. anatomy and cell biology Ctr. Molecular Medicine and Genetics, Sch. Medicine Wayne State U., Detroit, 1994—, dir. Lab. Molecular and Cellular Cerebral Ischemia, 1994—; with, 1995—; dir. neurol. diagnosis N.Y. Hosp., 1991-94. Author: Neurology and General Medicine, 1989, Neurological and Neurosurgical ICU Medicine, 1988; contbr. articles to Neurology, Jour. Cerebral Blood Flow and Metabolism, Jour. Intensive Care Medicine, Jour. Neurosci., Jour. Neurosci. Rsch., Neurosci. Lett., Jour. Brain Rsch., Jour. Neurochem. Joseph Collins scholar, 1981-85, Grupe Found. scholar, 1985; grantee NIH, 1990—, Nat. Stroke Assn., 1992-94, Alzheimer's Assn., 1994—, Am. Heart Assn., 1995—, United Cerebral Palsy Found., 1995—, Janssen Found., 1995—; recipient Young Scientist award Jours. Cerebral Blood Flow, 1991, Hoechst Investigaror award, 1993, Robert G. Siekert award in stroke, 1994, Johnson and Johnson Disting. Investigator award, 1996-99. Mem. Am. Acad. Neurology, N.Y. Acad. Scis., Assn. for Rsch. in Nervous and Mental Diseases, Am. Neurol. Assn. (elected), Soc. Neurosci. Roman Catholic. Achievements include rsch. in imidazole receptors, cerebral ischemia, nitric oxide toxicity, growth factor neuroprotection, signal cellular transduction mechanisms, metabotropic glutamate receptors, gene regulation, and gene therapy. Office: Wayne State U Sch Medicine 6E-19 Univ Health Ctr Dept Neurology 4201 Saint Antoine St Detroit MI 48201-2153

MAIHAFER, HARRY JAMES, retired banker, former army officer, writer; b. Watertown, N.Y., Aug. 8, 1924; s. George A. and Loretta Agnes (Daggett) M.; m. Jeanne Louise Mietzelfeld, June 9, 1949; children: Veronica Maihafer Barnes, Mary Maihafer Thompson, Margaret M., Douglas P. BS, U.S. Mil. Acad., 1949; MA, U. Mo., 1966. Commd. 2d lt. U.S. Army, 1949, col., 1968, ret., 1969; tng. dir. C&S Nat. Bank, Atlanta, 1970-73; sr. v.p., dir. pers. Union Planters Bank, Memphis, 1973-76; sr. v.p., dir. human resources Commerce Union Corp., Nashville, 1977-87, ret., 1987; pres. Middle Tenn. Human Resources Planners, Nashville, 1982-83. Author: From the Hudson to the Yalu--West Point '49 in the Korean War, 1993, Brave Decisions-Moral Courage from the American Revolution to Desert Storm, 1995, Oblivion: The Mystery of West Point Cadet Richard Cox, 1996; contbr. articles on mgmt. and mil. history to profl. jours. Pres. West Point Soc. Mid. Tenn., 1985-86; bd. dirs. St. Mary Villa, nashville, 1982-95, Cath. Charities Tenn., 1990-95. Mem. Assn. Grads. U.S. Mil. Acad., Ret. Officers Assn., Korean War Vets. Assn. Roman Catholic. Avocations: tennis, rose growing. Home: 6601 Fox Hollow Rd Nashville TN 37205-3956

MAILANDER, WILLIAM STEPHEN, lawyer; b. Dover, N.J., July 25, 1958; s. William Stephen and Doris Elizabeth (Post) M.; m. Judith Gay Burrows, May 20, 1989 (div. 1993). BA, NYU, 1984; JD, Temple U., 1988. Bar: Pa. 1988, N.J. 1991, D.C. 1996; U.S. Ct. Vets. Appeals 1991, U.S. Ct. Appeals (fed. cir.) 1993, U.S. Supreme Ct. 1994. Staff atty. Bd. Vets. Appeals, Washington, 1988-90, Coast Guard Chief Counsel, Washington, 1990-91, VA Gen. Counsel, Washington, 1991-93; asst. gen. counsel Paralyzed Vets. Am., Washington, 1993—; faculty continuing legal edn. seminars, various cities, 1993—. Contbr. articles to profl. jours. With USMC, 1976-79. Decorated Navy Achievement medal. Mem. Fed. Bar Assn. (chair membership vets. law sect. 1993-94). Avocations: reading, running. Office: Paralyzed Vets Am 801 18th St NW Washington DC 20006-3517

MAILER, NORMAN, author; b. Long Branch, N.J., Jan. 31, 1923; s. Issac Barnett and Fanny (Schneider) M.; m. Beatrice Silverman, 1944 (div. 1952); 1 dau., Susan; m. Adele Morales, 1954 (div. 1962); children: Danielle, Elizabeth; m. Jeanne Campbell, 1962 (div. 1963); 1 dau., Kate; m. Beverly Bentley, 1963 (div. 1980); children: Michael, Steven; m. Carol Stevens, 1980 (div. 1980); 1 dau., Maggie; m. Norris Church, 1980; 1 son, John Buffalo. SB cum laude, Harvard U., 1943; postgrad., Sorbonne, Paris, France, 1947-48. columnist Village Voice, 1946, Commentary, 1962-63, Esquire, 1962-63; contbg. editor Dissent, 1953-69; co-founding editor Village Voice, 1955. Author: No Percentage, 1941, The Naked and the Dead, 1948, Barbary Shore, 1951, The Deer Park, 1955, The White Negro: Superficial Reflections on the Hipster, 1957, Advertisements for Myself, 1959, Deaths for the Ladies and Other Disasters, 1962, The Presidential Papers, 1963, An American Dream, 1965, Cannibals and Christians, 1966, Why Are We in Vietnam?, 1967 (Nat. Book award nomination 1967), The Short Fiction of Norman Mailer, 1967, The Bullfight, 1967, The Armies of the Night, 1968 (Pulitzer prize for non-fiction 1969, George Polk award 1969), Miami and the Siege of Chicago, 1968 (Nat. Book award for non-fiction 1968), The Idol and the Octopus, 1968, Of a Fire On The Moon, 1970, King of the Hill, 1971, The Prisoner of Sex, 1971, The Long Patrol, 1971, Existential Errands, 1972, St. George and the Godfather, 1972, Marilyn, 1973, The Faith of Graffiti, 1974, The Fight, 1975, Some Honorable Men, 1975, Genius and Lust, 1976, A Transit to Narcissus, 1978, The Executioner's Song, 1979 (Pulitzer Prize for fiction 1980, Nat. Book Critics Circle award nomination 1979, Am. Book award nomination 1980), Of a Small and Modest Malignancy, Wicked and Bristling with Dots, 1980, Of Women and Their Elegance, 1980, Pieces and Pontifications, 1982, Ancient Evenings, 1983, Tough Guys Don't Dance, 1984, The Last Night, 1984, Harlot's Ghost, 1991, How the Wimp Won the War, 1991, Oswald's Tale, 1995, Portrait of Picasso as a Young Man, 1995, The Gospel According to the Song, 1997; (plays) The Deer Park: A Play, 1967, Strawhead, 1985; editor: Genius and Lust: A Journey Through the Major Writings of Henry Miller, 1976; screenwriter: (films) The Executioner's Song, 1982 (Emmy award nomination outstanding adapted screenplay 1983); screenwriter, prodr., dir., actor: (films) Wild 90, 1967, Maidstone: A Mystery, 1971; screenwriter, prodr.: (films) Beyond the Law, 1968; screenwriter, dir.: (films) Tough Guys Don't Dance, 1987; actor: (films) Ragtime, 1981. Served with AUS, 1944-46. Recipient Edward MacDowell medal MacDowell Colony, 1973, Nat. Arts Club Gold medal, 1976, Emerson-Thoreau Medal for lifetime of literary achievement, 1989; Nat. Inst. and Am. Acad. grantee, 1960; Pappas fellow U. Pa., 1983. Mem. PEN Am. Ctr. (pres. 1984-86), Nat. Inst. Arts and Letters. Office: care Random House Author's Mail 201 E 50th St New York NY 10022-7703

MAILER-HOWAT, PATRICK LINDSAY MACALPINE, investment banker; b. Edinburgh, Scotland, Feb. 4, 1955; came to U.S., 1985, naturalized 1993.; s. George Maxton Macalpine and Margaret Lorrain (Guild) M.; m. Rebecca Lynn Clifford, Mar. 30, 1985; children: Brodie Clifford, Lindsay Angevine. Grad. in Sovereign's Platoon, Royal Mil. Acad. Sandhurst, 1974. Lt. Scots Guards; trader J.H. Rayners Ltd., London, 1977-80; ptnr. investment mgr. Mailer Walker Internat. Ltd., London, 1980-85; mgr. trade svcs. Equator Bank Ltd., Hartford, Conn., 1985-88; v.p. Brazil sales First Nat. Bank Boston, N.Y.C., N.Y., 1989-93; dir. internat. banking First Nat. Bank Boston, 1993-95; sr. v.p. sales ING Baring Securities, N.Y.C., N.Y., 1995-96; dir. internat. equities Instinet Corp., N.Y.C., 1996—. Lt. Brit. Army, 1974-77. Mem. Pilgrims of the U.S.A., Union Club (N.Y.), Inst. CFP (cert.). Home: 41 Edgehill Rd Brookline MA 02146-7702 Office: Instinet Corp 875 3rd Ave New York NY 10022-6225

MAILES, KIM(BER DEAN), automotive executive; b. Abilene, Tex., Jan. 20, 1956; s. Harold Dean and Carmen Dale (Burr) M.; m. Carol Jean Carnes, May 19, 1979; 1 child, Colton Dean. Postgrad., Nova U., 1987-89; student, Mo. So. State Coll., 1977-79; BA, Ctrl. Bible Coll., 1983; MA, Assemblies God Theol. Sem., 1986. Announcer Radio Sta. KBTN, Neosho, Mo., 1972-74; sales rep. Burr Motor Co., Neosho, 1974-84, mgr., 1989—; founder, pastor Abundant Life Assembly God, Neosho, 1980-86; founder, gen. mgr. Radio Sta. KNEO (FM), Neosho, 1984-86; dist. youth dir. So. Mo. Dist. Assemblies God, Springfield, 1986-89; field dir. Gen. Coun. Assemblies God Internat., Springfield, 1988-89; founder, pres. Trinity Christian Fellowship, Neosho, 1990—; v.p. Joplin Metro 2000, 1983-86; baccalaureate speaker Neosho High Sch. Commencement, 1986, 93, East Newton (Mo.) High Sch., 1994, Assembly God Theol. Sem., Springfield, 1986; cons. Ch. God Apostolate Faith, Tulsa, 1989-91; speaker in field. Author: Destined for Hell, 1986; contbr. articles to mags. Precinct com. Newton County Rep. com., Neosho, 1974-86; commr. Mo.-Kans. coun. Boy Scouts Am., Joplin, Mo., 1982-86, leader, 1993—; bd. dirs. Crowder Coll. Found., Neosho, 1982-86; bd. dirs., v.p. Mid. Am. Concern Internat., Inc., Grand Haven, Mich., 1995—; v.p. MIA-Am.; v.p. Neosho Bd. Edn., 1983-86; mem. White River Band of No. Cherokee Nation; cub master Cub Scout Pack 100, Neosho, Mo. Recipient Cub Scouter award Boy Scouts Am., 1996. Mem. Trinity Christian Fellowship (pres. 1990—), Victory Fellowship Ministries, Mo. Master Gardeners, Kiwanis (bd. dirs. 1987-89), Neosho C. of C. (bd. dirs. 1995-96). Republican. Avocations: golf, reading, writing, spectator sports. Office: PO Box 15 Neosho MO 64850-0015

MAILHOT, LOUISE, judge; b. Montreal, Que., Can., July 23, 1940; d.Gerard and Jeanne (Bousquet) M.; m. Michael Oliver Lloyd, 1974; 2 children. BA, U. Montreal, LLL. Atty. pvt. practice, 1966-80, Justice Superior Ct., 1980-87, Justice Ct. Appeals, 1987—. Author: La Décision, guide pratique de Rédaction judiciaire, Ed. Y. Blais, Inc., 1996. Mem. Internat. Assn. Judges (v.p. 1996—). Office: Ct Appeals, 1 rue Notre Dame Est # 1786, Montreal, PQ Canada H2Y 1B6

MAILLET, ANTONINE, author, educator; b. Bouctouche, N.B., Can., May 10, 1929; d. Leonide Maillet and Virginie Cormier. BA, Coll. Notre-Dame D'Acadie, 1950; MA, Moncton U., N.B., 1959, D es L (hon.), 1972; LLD, Montreal U., Que., Can., 1962; PhD, Laval U., Que., 1970, DLitt (hon.), 1988; D es L (hon.), Acadia U., 1980, St. Mary's U., 1980, Laurentian U., 1981, McGill U., 1982; DLitt (hon.), Carleton U., 1978, Mount Allison U., 1979, St. Thomas U., 1986, Mt. St-Vincent U., 1987, U. Ste-Anne, 1987, Bowling Green U., 1988, Simon Fraser U., 1989. U. Maine, 1990, Concordia U., 1990; LLD (hon.), U. Alta., 1979, Dalhousie U., 1981, U. Toronto, 1982, Queen's U., 1982, St. Francis Xavier U., 1984, Lyon U., 1989, B.C. U., 1991, Royal Mil. Coll. Can., 1992; LittD (hon.), U. New Eng., 1994. Prof. Coll. Notre-Dame D'Acadie, Moncton, 1954-60, Moncton U., 1965-67, Coll. des Jesuites, Que., 1968-69, Laval U., Que., 1971-74, Montreal U., 1974-75, Nat. Drama Sch., Montreal, 1989-91; writer N.B. Hist. Resources Adminstrn., Central Registry, Fredericton, N.B.; assoc. prof. French studies Moncton U., chancelor, 1989; guest Michener Found., Queen's U., 1991. Author: (novels) Pointe-aux-coques, 1958 (Prix Champlain, 1960), On a mangé la dune, 1962, Don l'orignal, 1972 (Prix du Gouverneur General du Can. 1972), Par derrière chez mon père, 1972, Mariaagélas, 1973 (Prix des Volcans (France) 1975, Grand Prix Littéraire de la ville de Montréal, 1973, Prix France Can. 1975, Prix litteraire La Presse 1976), Emmanuel à Joseph à Dâvit, 1975, Les Cordes-de-Bois, 1977 (Prix des 4 jurys 1978), Pélagie-la-charrette, 1979 (Prix Goncourt 1979); Cent ans dans les bois, 1981, La Gribouille, 1982, Crache-à-Pic, 1984; Le Huitième Jour, 1986, L'Oursiade, 1990, Les Confessions de Jeanne de Valois, 1992; (texts) L'Ile-aux-Puces, 1996; (novel) Le Chemin St-Jacques, 1996; (plays): Poire-Acre, 1960 (Best Can. Play Vancouver Theatre Festival, 1960), Les Jeux d'Enfants sont faits, 1960 (Prix du Conseil des Arts 1960), Les Crasseux, 1968, Gapi et Sullivan, 1973, Evangéline Deusse, 1975, Gapi, 1976, La Veuve Enragée, 1977, Le Bourgeois Gentleman, 1978, La Contrebandière, 1981, Les drolatiques, horrifiques et épouvantables aventures de Panurge, ami de Pantagruel, 1983, Garrochés en Paradis, 1986, Margot la Folle, 1987, William S, 1991; (translations) Les Fantastiques (Tom Jones), 1988, Richard III (Shakespeare), 1989, (also adaptation) Valentine (Willy Russel), 1990, La Nuit des Rois (Shakespeare), 1993 (Prix de la traduction Association québécoise de critiques de théâtre saison 1992-93), (also adaptation) La Foire de la Saint-Barthélemy (Ben Jonson), 1994, La Fontaine ou la Comédie des Animaux, 1995, Le Chemin St. Jacques, 1996; (other) L'Acadie pour quasiment rien, 1973; author short stories, and children's literature. Mem. Conseil Littéraire Fondation Prince Pierre de Monaco, Haut Conseil Francophonie, 1987, Queen's Privy Coun. Can.; chancellor Moncton U., 1989; Conseil des gouverneurs associés de l'Université de Montréal. Decorated officer, comdr. Order of Can., officier des Palmes académiques françaises, knight l'Ordre de la Pléiade (Fredericton), officier l'Ordre Nat. du Québec, officier des Arts et des Lettres (France), comdr. l'Ordre du mérite culturel (Monaco); recipient Prix de la meilleure piece canadienne presented at Festival de Theatre, 1958, Prix Littéraire de la Presse, 1976. Mem. Assn. des Ecrivains de Langue Francaise, l'Ordre des francophones d'Amérique, l'Académie des Grands Montréalais, Soc. des Auteurs et Compositeurs Dramatiques de France (sec.), Soc. des Gens de Lettres de France, Soc. Royale du Canada, Academie Canadienne-Francaise, Tutular mem., European Acad. Arts, Scis. and Humanities (corr.), Pen Club of Quebec, 1988.

MAILLOUX, RAYMOND VICTOR, health services administrator; b. Haverhill, Mass., Feb. 8, 1959; s. Raymond Alfred and Elaine Irene (Tourville) M.; m. Donna Ann Murphy, Aug. 1, 1981; children: Matthew, Michael. BS, U. Lowell, 1980; MBA, N.H. Coll., 1984. Lic. nursing home adminstr., N.H., Mass. Comptroller Home Health Svcs., Haverhill, 1980-84; instr. Northern Essex C.C., Haverhill, 1984-86; adminstr. St. John's Nursing Home, Lowell, Mass., 1984-87; dir. health care svcs. N.H. Catholic Charities, Manchester, 1987—. Mem. Am. Coll. Health Care Adminstrs., Am. Health Care Assn. (region I non-proprietary com. rep. 1993—), N.H. Health Care Assn. (pres. 1993, 94), New Eng. Gerontol. Assn. (v.p. 1987—). Avocations: horses, traveling, reading. Home: 238 Jennifer Dr Chester NH 03036-4167 Office: NH Catholic Charities 215 Myrtle St Manchester NH 03104-4354

MAILLOUX, ROBERT JOSEPH, physicist; b. Lynn, Mass., June 20, 1938; s. Joseph H. and Nora S. M.; m. Marlene Schirf, Jan. 14, 1967; children: Patrice, Julie, Denise. BS, Northeastern U., 1961; SM, Harvard U., 1962, PhD, 1965. Physicist NASA Electronics Rsch. Ctr., Cambridge, Mass., 1965-70, Air Force Cambridge Rsch. Labs., Bedford, Mass., 1970-77, Rome Air Devel. Ctr., Bedford, 1977-80; chief antennas and components div., electromagnetic directorate Rome Air Devel. Ctr., 1980-91; sr. scientist Antennas Rome Lab., 1992—; lectr. Tufts U., Boston, 1985—. Author: Phased Array Antenna Handbook; contbr. chpts. to 8 textbooks, articles to sci. jours. Served with C.E. U.S. Army, 1966-68. Recipient Air Force Marcus O'Day paper award, 1971, Engineer of Yr. award RADC, 1988; RADC fellow, 1988. Fellow IEEE (spl. achievement award 1969, 76, nat. lectr., assoc. editor Transactions on Antennas and Propagation 1984-92, Harry Diamond award 1991); mem. Antenna and Propagation Soc. (chmn. Boston chpt. 1968, nat. meetings chmn. 1977-80, adcom mem. 1977-80, v.p. 1982, pres. 1983), Internat. Sci. Radio Union (Commn. B. tech. activities chmn. 1980—), Sigma Xi (pres. Hanscom chpt. 1980-81), Eta Kappa Nu, Tau Beta Pi. Achievements include 9 patents in field. Office: RL/ER 31 Grenier St Hanscom AFB MA 01731-3008

MAIN, A. DONALD, bishop. Bishop Upper Susquehanna region Evang. Luth. Ch. in Am., Lewisburg, Pa. Office: Evang Luth Ch in Am PO Box 36 192 Reitz Blvd Lewisburg PA 17837*

MAIN, BETTY JO, management analyst; b. Hatch, N.Mex., May 22, 1939; d. Truman Oliver and Madeline Kate (Bennett) Hickerson; m. Andrew Allan Burich, June 21, 1958 (div. Sept. 1977); children: Cari Lynn, Andrew Allan Jr.; m. Ralph Monroe Main, Apr. 21, 1979; stepchildren: Michael, Randall, Kelly. AA in Liberal Arts, Marymount Coll., 1988; BS in Bus. & Mgmt., U. Redlands, 1993, MBA, 1996. Escrow officer Palos Verdes Escrow, San Pedro, Calif., 1975-80; sec. City of L.A., San Pedro, 1980-85, wharfinger, 1985-87, mgmt. aide, 1987-89, mgmt. analyst II, 1989—. Mem. City of L.A. Tutoring Program, City of L.A. Spkrs. Bur. Mem. AAUW, Marymount Coll. Alumni, U. Redland Alumni, Alfred North Whitehead Leadership Soc., Emblem Club (L.A.). Episcopalian. Avocation: travel. Home: 2238 W Paseo Del Mar San Pedro CA 90732-4521 Office: City of LA 425 S Palos Verdes St San Pedro CA 90731-3309

MAIN, JACKSON TURNER, history educator; b. Chgo., Aug. 6, 1917; s. John Smith and Dorothy Kinsey (Turner) M.; m. Gloria Jean Lund, June 16, 1956; children: Jackson Turner, Eifiona Llewelyn, Judson Kempton. B.A., U. Wis., 1939, M.A., 1940, Ph.D., 1949; LL.D. (hon.), Washington and Jefferson Coll., 1980. Asst. prof. Washington and Jefferson Coll., Washington, Pa., 1948-50; prof. San Jose State U. (Calif.), 1953-65, U. Md., College Park, 1965-66; prof. history State U. N.Y. at Stony Brook, 1966-83. Author: The Antifederalists 1781-1788, 1961, The Social Structure of Revolutionary America, 1965, The Upper House in Revolutionary America, 1967, Political Parties Before the Constitution, 1973, The Sovereign States, 1775-1783, 1973, Connecticut Society in the Era of the American Revolution, 1977, Society and Economy in Colonial Connecticut, 1985. Served to sgt. USAF, 1941-45. Am. Council Learned Socs. fellow, 1962-63; Nat. Endowment Humanities fellow Center Advanced Studies in Behavioral Scis., Stanford, Calif., 1980-81. Mem. Am. Hist. Soc., Orgn. Am. Historians, Wis. Hist. Soc., others. Office: Univ of Colo Dept History Boulder CO 80309

MAIN, MARTHA LANE HUGHES, medical/surgical nurse; b. Waltham, Mass., Dec. 31, 1942; d. Francis Marion and Anna Jennie (Sanders) Hughes; m. Julian Harris Main; children: Mary-Martha, Michael, Patrick, Cynthia, Patricia. LPN, Assabet Valley Regional H.S., 1976; BSN, SUNY, Albany, 1986; MSN, Anna Maria U., 1992. RN, Mass., R.I., Calif.; cert. ACLS, Am. Heart Assn., pediat. advanced life support. Practical nurse Milford (Mass.) Whitinsville Regional Hosp., 1976-86, staff nurse, 1986-88, occupational health nurse, 1988-89; nurse mgr. Landmark Med. Ctr., Woonsocket, R.I., 1989-96; part-time clin. instr. R.I. Coll., Providence, 1993—; case mgr. Landmark Med Ctr, 1996-97, dir. nurses transitional living ctr, 1997—; poster presenter Nat. Symposium for Wound & Ostomy Care, Nashville, 1994, CHF Care Mgr., New Orleans, 1995. Mem. adv. bd. Assabet Valley Regional Vocat. Sch., Marlboro, Mass., 1984—; CPR instr. Am. Heart Assn., Providence, 1988—. Mem. R.I. Coun. Nurse Mgrs. (charter mem., steering com. 1992, sec. 1992-94), Greater Milford Profl. Cancer Educators, Am. Orgn. Nurse Execs. Episcopalian. Avocations: backpacking, photography, gardening. Home: 192 Hayden Rowe St PO Box 383 Hopkinton MA 01748

MAIN, MYRNA JOAN, mathematics educator; b. Kirksville, Mo., Oct. 31, 1947; d. Stanford H. and Jennie Vee (Nuhn) Morris; m. Carl Donet Main, Feb. 22, 1968; children: D. Christopher, Laura S. BSE, Northeast Mo. State U., 1968, MA, 1970. Instr. math. Callao (Mo.) Sch., 1968-73; tchr., chair dept. math. Macon (Mo.) R-I Schs., 1973—; regional dir. math. Mo. Middle Sch.; ext. staff Moberly (Mo.) Area C.C., 1983—, Cen. Meth. Coll., 1994; adj. faculty N.E. Mo. State U., Kirksville, 1987-93; mentor Mo. Math. Mentoring Project, Moberly, 1989—; trainer Mo. Show-Me Stds. and Frame Works, 1997. Organist, UBS tchr. Crossroads Christian Ch., Macon, 1981—; troop #503 leader Becky thatcher coun. Girl Scouts U.S.; team leader 4-H Series, 1993—; sponsor Macon R-I Gender Equity. Recipient Presdl. award for excellence in math., 1989; semi-finalist The Disney Co. Presents the Am. Tchr., 1991. Mem. AAUW (chpt. pres. 1980-81), Nat. Coun. Tchrs. Math., Mo. Coun. Tchrs. Math. (treas. 1978-79, v.p. 1976), Mo. Alliance for Sci., Math. and Tech. Edn. (bd. dirs., 1988—, mem. Mo. Framework writing team). Democrat.

MAINI, BALTEJ S., surgeon; b. Rawalpindi, India, Feb. 22, 1947; arrived in U.S., 1971; MD, All India Inst. of Med. Sci., 1969. Diplomate Am. Bd. Surgery. Dir. vascular lab. St. Vincent Hosp., Worcester, Mass., 1988—; acting chief, dept. surgery St. Vincent Hosp., 1990-91, dir. divsn. gen. and vascular surgery, 1991—, chief dept. surgery, 1991—; chmn. surg. svcs. The Fallon Clinic, Worcester, 1988—; clin. instr. health sci. Northeastern U., Boston, 1991—; assoc. prof. surgery U. Mass., Worcester, 1991—; bd. dirs. The Fallon Clinic, 1995—. Mem. Internat. Soc. for Endovascular Surgery, Am. Coll. Physician Execs., New Eng. Surgical Soc., New Eng. Soc. Vascular Surgery. Office: St Vincent Hosp 25 Winthrop St Worcester MA 01604-4543

MAINORD, WILLIAM RONALD, pilot; b. Emory, Tex., Feb. 6, 1941; s. William T. and Faye (Cochran) M.; m. Jackquelin Jean Budny, Nov. 25, 1969. BS, U. Nebr., 1965; MA, Webster Coll., 1976. Cert. flight instr., airline transport pilot FAA. Enlisted USAF, 1961, commd. 2d lt., 1962; chief C-130 pilot Mil. Airlift Command USAF, Scott AFB, Ill., 1976-79; cmdr. Det 2 1400 Mil. Airlift Squadron USAF, Randolph AFB, Tex., 1979-81; cmdr. 1402 Mil. Airlift Squadron USAF, Andrews AFB, Md., 1981-82; br. chief Joint Chiefs Staff USAF, Pentagon, 1982-85; cmdr. 2d air divsn. USAF, Hurlburt AFB, Fla., 1986-87; def. & air attache U.S. Embassy, Caracas, Venezuela, 1988-91; ret. USAF, 1991; owner, chief pilot Lake Granbury Aviation Inc., Granbury, Tex., 1994-97. Mem. Granbury Lions (pres. 1994-95). Methodist. Home and Office: 1720 Old Cleburne Rd Granbury TX 76048

MAINOUS, BRUCE HALE, foreign language educator; b. Appalachia, Va., Aug. 2, 1914; s. William Lazarus and Sibyl (Hale) M.; m. Ruth Marie Daugherty, June 7, 1941; children: Mary Michele (Mrs. Robert F. Chinn), Martha Hale (Mrs. Gary Dougherty). A.B., Coll. William and Mary, 1935; M.A., U. Ill., 1939, Ph.D., 1948; certificates, Sorbonne, Paris, 1958, U. Besançon, France, 1975. Asst. d'anglais Lycée de Nimes, France, 1935-36; prin. Derby Grade Sch., Va., 1936-37; mem. faculty U. Ill., Urbana, 1937—; prof. French U. Ill., 1964-84, prof. emeritus, 1984—, head dept., 1965-73; dir. Unit for Fgn. Lang. Study and Research, 1972-76, Lang. Learning Lab., 1976-84. Author: (with H.C. Woodbridge) A Sainte-Beuve Bibliography, 1954, Basic French, 2d edit, 1968, (with Donald J. Nolan) Basic French, Workbook and laboratory Manual, 1968; co-author: Spanish for Agricultural Purposes, 1984, (with Maria T. Rund) A Glossary of Spanish-American Agricultural Terms, 1987. Served to lt. USNR, 1942-46; comdr. Res. ret. Decorated officier Ordre des Palmes Académiques; Camargo Found. fellow, 1975. Mem. MLA, Am. Assn. Tchrs. French, Ill. Fgn. Lang. Tchrs. Assn. (pres. 1966-68), Am. Council Teaching Fgn. Langs., Inst. d'Etudes Occitanes, N.Am. Catalan Soc., Corda Fratres Assn. Cosmopolitan Clubs, Phi Kappa Phi, Sigma Delta Pi, Pi Delta Phi. Methodist. Clubs: Dial, Exchange. Home: 502 W Washington St Urbana IL 61801-4052

MAINWARING, THOMAS LLOYD, motor freight company executive; b. Cleve., Aug. 25, 1928; s. Hugh Trevor and Mary Beatrice (Ottman) M.; m. Gladys Fraser Mehr, June 10, 1983; children by previous marriage—Kevin, James, Eileen, Scott, Bruce. B.A., Albion Coll., 1950; M.B.A., Western Res. U., 1958. C.P.A., Ohio. Controller Cleve. Cartage Co., 1959-61, v.p., treas., 1961-64; controller Associated Truck Lines, Inc., Vandenberg Ctr., Grand Rapids, Mich., 1964-69; v.p. fin. Associated Transport, Inc., N.Y.C., 1969-70, exec. v.p. fin. and adminstrn., 1970-72; pres. Ryder Truck Lines Inc., Jacksonville, Fla., 1972-78, exec. v.p., chief operating officer, 1978-81, chief exec. officer, 1981-84; pres. Freight System div. Ryder System Inc., Miami, Fla., 1984-86; cons. trucking industry affairs Arlington, Va., 1986-88; pres., chief oper. officer H & M Internat. Transp., Inc., 1989-91, vice chmn., 1991-92; transp. cons., 1992-93; pres., gen. mgr. E.I. Kane Intermodal Transport, Inc., Balt., 1993-95, vice chmn., 1995, transp. cons., 1996—; bd. dirs. Trucking Mgmt., Inc. Mem. exec. com. United Way Jacksonville, 1981-84; trustee Albion Coll., 1977; bd. dirs. Goodwill Industries North Fla. Served with AUS, 1950-53. Mem. Am. Trucking Assn. (nat. acctg. and fin. council 1964, pres. 1971, chmn. ATA Found. 1986-88, exec. com. 1985-88), Fla. Trucking Assn. (bd. dirs. 1973, pres. 1979), Am. Mgmt. Assn. (lectr. seminars), Jacksonville Area C. of C. (bd. govs., com. of 100, v.p. internat. 1984), Cen. and So. Motor Freight Tariff Assn. (bd. dirs. 1981-84, pres. 1983, exec. com. transp. rsch. bd. 1987-89), Sigma Nu. Home: PO Box 2665 Purcellville VA 20134

MAINWARING, WILLIAM LEWIS, publishing company executive, author; b. Portland, Oreg., Jan. 17, 1935; s. Bernard and Jennie (Lewis) M.; m. Mary E. Bell, Aug. 18, 1962; children: Anne Marie, Julia Kathleen, Douglas Bernard. B.S., U. Oreg., 1957; postgrad., Stanford U., 1957-58. With Salem (Oreg.) Capital Jour., 1958-76, editor, pub., 1962-76; pub. Oreg. Statesman, 1974-76; pres. Statesman-Jour. Co., Inc., Salem, 1974-76, Westridge Press, Ltd., 1977—; pres. MediAmerica, Inc., Portland, 1981-96, CEO, 1988-96; bd. dirs. MediAmerica, Inc. Author: Exploring the Oregon Coast, 1977, Exploring Oregon's Central and Southern Cascades, 1979, Exploring the Mount Hood Loop, 1992, Government, Oregon-Style, 1996. Pres. Salem Beautification Coun., 1968, Marion-Polk County United Good Neighbors, 1970, Salem Social Svcs. Commn., 1978-79, Salem Hosp. Found., 1978-81. 2d lt. AUS, 1958; capt. Res. Ret. Mem. Salem Area C. of C. (pres. 1972-73), Oreg. Symphony Soc. Salem (pres. 1973-75), Salem City Club (pres. 1977-78), Sigma Chi. Republican. Presbyterian (ruling elder). Home and Office: 1090 Southridge Pl S Salem OR 97302-5947

MAIO, F. ANTHONY, lawyer; b. Passaic, N.J., Mar. 30, 1937; s. Anthony J. and Santina (Sciarra) M.; m. Maureen Margaret McKeown, Dec. 30, 1960; children: Christopher, Duncan, Todd. BS in Mech. Engring., Stevens Inst. Tech., 1959; LLB cum laude, Boston Coll., 1968. Bar: Wis. 1968, D.C. 1971. Engr., project mgr. Hazeltine Corp., Greenlawn, N.Y. and Avon, Mass., 1959-64; project mgr. Raytheon Corp., Portsmouth, R.I., 1964-65; atty. Foley & Lardner, Milw., 1968-70; ptnr. Foley & Lardner, Washington, 1971-86, Milw., 1986-97. Editor Boston Coll. Law Rev., 1967-68. Dir. Arthritis Found., Milw., 1986-88, ARC, Milw., 1986-94. Mem. Order of Coif, Milw. Yacht Club (dir. 1989-95), Naples Sailing & Yacht Club. Avocations: boating, fishing.

MAIOCCHI, CHRISTINE, lawyer; b. N.Y.C., Dec. 24, 1949; d. George and Andreina (Toneatto) M.; m. John Charles Kerecz, Aug. 16, 1980; children: Charles George, Joan Christine. BA in Polit. Sci., Fordham U., 1971, MA in Polit. Sci., 1971, JD, 1974; postgrad., NYU, 1977—. Bar: N.Y. 1975, U.S. Dist. Ct. (so. and ea. dists.), N.Y. 1975, U.S. Ct. Appeals (2nd cir) 1975. Law clk. to magistrate U.S. Dist. Ct. (so. dist.) N.Y., N.Y.C., 1973-74; atty. corp. legal dept. The Home Ins. Co., N.Y.C., 1974-76; asst. house counsel corp. legal dept. Allied Maintenance Corp., N.Y.C., 1976; atty. corp. legal dept. Getty Oil Co., N.Y.C., 1976-77; v.p., mgr. real estate Paine, Webber, Jackson & Curtis, Inc., N.Y.C., 1977-81; real estate mgr. GK Techs., Inc., Greenwich, Conn., 1981-85; real estate mgr., sr. atty. MCI Telecom. Corp., Rye Brook, N.Y., 1985-93; real estate and legal cons. Wallace Law Registry, 1994-96; sr. assoc. counsel Met. Transp. Authority, 1996—. Bd. dirs. League Women Voters, Dobbs Ferry, N.Y., 1988; co-pres. The Home/Sch. Assn., Immaculate Conception Sch., Irvington, N.Y. Mem. ABA, Nat. Assn. Corp. Real Estate Execs. (pres. 1983-84, treas. 1985-86, bd. dirs. 1986), Indsl. Devel. Rsch. Coun. (program v.p. 1985, Profl. award 1987), N.Y. Bar Assn., Women's Bar Assn. Manhattan, The Corp. Bar (sec. real estate divsn. 1987-89, chmn. 1990-92), Jr. League Club, Dobbs Ferry Women's Club (program dir. 1981-92, 94-96, publicity dir. 1992-94). Avocations: sports, theatre, gardening. Home: 84 Clinton Ave Dobbs Ferry NY 10522-3004

MAIORIELLO, RICHARD PATRICK, otolaryngologist; b. Phila., Mar. 17, 1936; s. Gesumino Theodore and Angelina (Del Rossi) M.; A.B., U. Pa., 1960; M.D., Jefferson Med. Coll., 1964; M.S., Thomas Jefferson U., 1972; m. Susan Hemenway, Mar. 6, 1979; children—Gabriel, Angela, Richard. Commd. 2d lt., U.S. Air Force, 1963, advanced through grades to col., 1977; ret., 1979; intern Keesler Hosp., 1965-67; chief flight medicine USAF Base, Bitburg, W. Ger., 1965-68; resident in otolaryngology Thomas Jefferson Hosp., Phila., 1968-71, 72-73; fellow in physiology Thomas Jefferson U., 1971-72; dir. med. edn. Andrews AFB, 1974-78; assoc. prof. uniformed services Univ. Health Scis., 1978-79; assoc. prof. Northeastern Ohio U. of Medicine, 1983—; mem. staff Aultman Hosp., 1979—; assoc. staff Timken Mercy Med. Ctr., 1981—, Union Hosp., 1988—; cons. otolaryngology to Surgeon Gen., 1977—; pres. Mid-Ohio Dressage Assn. Served with USNR, 1954-58. Decorated Air Force Commendation medal; diplomate Nat. Bd. Med. Examiners, Am. Bd. Otolaryngology. Fellow ACS, Am. Soc. Head and Neck Surgery; mem. Am. Acad. Otolaryngology, Am. Acad. Facial Plastic and Reconstructive Surgery, Am. Assn. Cosmetic Surgery, Vail Cosmetic Surg. Soc., Hanoverian Soc. (exec. v.p.), U.S. Dressage Fedn. (chmn. all-breeds coun.), Centurion Club. Republican. Roman Catholic. Office: 1445 Harrison Ave NW Canton OH 44708-2620

MAIR, BRUCE LOGAN, interior designer, company executive; b. Chgo., June 5, 1951; s. William Logan and Josephine (Lee) M. BFA, Drake U., 1973; postgrad., Ind. Wesleyan U., 1990—. Mgr., head designer Reifers of Indpls., 1973-79; pres. Interiors Internat., Indpls., 1979-87; sr. designer Kasler Group, Indpls., 1987-89; dir. devel. Tillery Interiors and Imports, Greenwood, Ind., 1990; v.p. Tillery Interiors and Imports, Indpls., 1990-92; owner Mair Interior Design Group, Indpls., 1992—; pres. Tokens Inc., Indpls., 1982-88, Meg-A-Wat Enterprises Inc., Indpls., 1985-87, Luxury Ice Creams Inc., Indpls., 1986-87. Cover designer Indpls. Home and Garden mag., 1978, feature designer 1980; feature designer Builder mag., 1979; co-designer feature Indpls. At Home mag., 1979. Campaigner Anderson for Pres., 1980. Mem. Am. Soc. Interior Designers (treas. Ind. chpt. 1982-83, Pres. awards 1981-82), U.S. Rowing Assn. (master 1987—), St. Joseph Hist. Neighborhood Assn., Columbia Club (rowing crew coxswain 1986—), Highland Model A Club, Tower Harbor Yacht Club (Douglas, Mich.), Alpha Epsilon Pi. Avocations: sculling, historic preservation, model A Ford restoration, fishing, farming. Home: 219 E 10th St Indianapolis IN 46202-3303 Office: Mair Interior Design Group 2047 SE 29th Ln Cape Coral FL 33904-3011

MAIR, DOUGLAS DEAN, medical educator, consultant; b. Mpls., May 29, 1937; s. Lester Alexander and Irene Clare (Fisher) M.; m. Joanne Mary Elliott, Aug. 18, 1963; children: Scott, Michele, Todd. BA, U. Minn., 1959, MD, 1962. Bd. cert. pediats. and pediat. cardiology. Cons. Mayo Clinic, Rochester, Minn., 1971—; from asst. prof. pediats. to assoc. prof. pediats. Mayo Med. Sch., Rochester, 1972-80, prof. pediats., 1980—, assoc. prof. internal medicine, 1978—. Contbr. numerous articles and book chpts. to profl. pubis. Capt. USAF, 1966-67.

MAIRS, DAVID, symphony conductor; b. Morristown, N.J., Jan. 30, 1943; s. G. Donald and Frances P. (Johnson) M.; children from previous marriage: Stephen, Gregory: m. Elizabeth Ann Powell, May 24, 1975; children: Ellen, Sarah. BM, U. Mich., 1965, MM, 1966; MDiv, Pitts. Theol. Sem., 1983. Cert. tchr. K-12, Mich. 3d horn San Antonio Symphony, 1969-70; assoc. prin. horn Pitts. Symphony, 1970-80; condr. wind ensemble Duquesne U., Pitts., 1981-83; asst. pastor 1st Presbyn. Ch., Flint, Mich., 1983-86, 87-88; asst. condr., music adminstr. Flint Symphony, 1984-88; artistic advisor Adrian (Mich.) Symphony, 1987-88; resident condr. San Antonio Symphony, 1988—; pops condr. Charlotte (N.C.) Symphony, 1993-95; music dir. Mid-Tex. Symphony, 1996—; music dir. Flint Youth Symphony, 1986-88; chmn. vision 2000 com. N.E. Ind. Sch. Dist., San Antonio, 1990-92. Hon. life mem. Tex. PTA. With U.S. Army, 1966-69. Mem. Am. Symphony Orch. League, Condr.'s Guild. Office: San Antonio Symphony 222 E Houston St Ste 200 San Antonio TX 78205-1836

MAISEL, HERBERT, computer science educator; b. N.Y.C., Sept. 22, 1930; s. Hyman and Dora (Goldstein) M.; m. Millicent Sherry Kushner, Apr. 13, 1957; children—Scott Alan, Raymond Bruce. B.S., CCNY, 1951; M.S., NYU, 1952; Ph.D., Catholic U. Am., 1964. Mathematician, statistician Dept. Army, Aberdeen, Md., Washington, 1954-63; dir. acad. computer ctr. Georgetown U., Washington, 1963-76, prof. computer sci., 1963—; systems advisor Social Security Adminstrn., Balt., 1976-84; cons. Nat. Bur. Standards, Gaithersburg, Md., 1968-72, Balt. Housing Authority, 1972-73, Social Security Adminstrn., Balt., 1966-73; mem. study group HHS, Washington, 1975-76. Author: An Introduction to Electronic Digital Computers, 1969; Simulation of Discrete Stochastic Systems, 1972; Computers for Social and Economic Development, 1974; Computers: Programming and Applications, 1975; also others. Contbr. articles to profl. jours. Mem. Community Housing Resources Bd., Montgomery County, Md., 1975. Recipient spl. service award Internat. Assn. Parents of Deaf, 1982. Fellow Assn. Computing Machinery (chmn. external activities bd. 1981-86, chmn. mems. and chpts. bd. 1978-80, chmn. nominating com. 1983-84, mem. council, chmn. Washington chpt. 1971-73, Outstanding Contribution award 1986); mem. Phi Beta Kappa (chmn. Georgetown chpt. 1974-76), Sigma Xi. Jewish. Office: Georgetown Univ Computer Sci Dept 37th & O Sts NW Washington DC 20057

MAISEL, SHERMAN JOSEPH, economist, educator; b. Buffalo, July 8, 1918; s. Louis and Sophia (Beck) M.; m. Lucy Cowdin, Sept. 26, 1942; children: Lawrence C., Margaret L. A.B., Harvard U., 1939, M.P.A., 1947, Ph.D., 1949. Mem. bd. govs. FRS, 1965-72; economist, fgn. service res. officer Dept. State, 1945-46; teaching fellow Harvard U., 1947-48; asst. prof., assoc. prof., prof. bus. adminstrn. U. Calif. at Berkeley, 1948-65, 72-86; sr. economist Nat. Bur. Econ. Research-West, 1973-78; chmn., bd. dirs. Farmers Savings & Loan, 1986-88; pres. Sherman J. Maisel & Assocs. Inc., 1986—; fellow Fund For Advancement Edn., 1952-53, Inst. Basic Math. with Application to Bus., 1959-60, Center for Advanced Study in Behavioral Scis., 1972; mem. adv. coms. to Bur. Census, FHA, State of Calif., Ford Found., Social Sci. Research Council; mem. bldg. research adv. bd. NRC. Author: Housebuilding in Transition, 1953, Fluctuations, Growth, and Forecasting, 1957, Managing the Dollar, 1973, Real Estate Investment and Finance, 1976, Risk and Capital Adequacy in Commercial Banks, 1981, Macroeconomics: Theories and Policies, 1982, Real Estate Finance, 1987, 2d edit., 1992. Bd. dirs. Berkeley Unified Sch. Dist., 1962-65. Served to capt. AUS, 1941-45. Mem. Am. Fin. Assn. (pres. 1973), Am. Econ. Assn., Am. Statis. Assn. Home: 2164 Hyde St San Francisco CA 94109-1701 Office: U Calif Haas Bus Sch Berkeley CA 94720

MAISLIN, ISIDORE, hospital administrator; b. N.Y.C., Aug. 4, 1919; s. Solomon and Rose (Baruch) M.; m. Frances Mussman, Jan. 18, 1948; children—Wendy Sue (Mrs. Neil Robbins), Steven William. B.S., Columbia, 1950, M.S., 1951. Asso. dir. Albert Einstein Med. Center, Phila., 1950-59; asso. dir. Mt. Sinai Hosp. Greater Miami, Mimai Beach, Fla., 1959-63; adminstr. Scranton (Pa.) Gen. Hosp., 1963-64; exec. dir. Jewish Home of Eastern Pa., Scranton, 1964-67; adminstr. South Mountain (Pa.) Restoration Center, 1967—. Served with AUS, 1943-46. Fellow Am. Coll. Hosp. Adminstrs., Am. Pub. Health Assn., Royal Soc. Health. Home and Office: 535 Colfax Ave Scranton PA 18510-2364

MAISSEL, LEON ISRAEL, physicist, engineer; b. Cape Town, South Africa, May 31, 1930; came to U.S., 1956; s. Charles and Emily (Cohen) M.; m. Raina Eve Corren, Jan. 26, 1956; children: Simon, Gerda, Joseph. B.Sc., U. Cape Town, 1949, M.Sc., 1951; Ph.D., U. London, 1955. Staff scientist Philco Corp., Phila., 1956-60; adv. physicist IBM Corp., Poughkeepsie, N.Y., 1960-63, sr. engr., 1963-81, sr. tech. staff mem., 1981-93; patent writer, 1994—. Author, editor: Handbook of Thin Film Technology, 1969, An Introduction to Thin Films, 1970; contbr. articles profl. jours.; patentee in field. Recipient Outstanding Invention award IBM Corp., 1968; recipient Outstanding Contbn. award IBM Corp., 1969. Fellow IEEE; mem. Am. Vacuum Soc. (Dir. 1966-68). Democrat. Jewish. Lodge: B'nai B'rith. Home: 16 Smoke Rise Ln Wappingers Falls NY 12590-1220 *Most people, properly trained, can solve well-defined problems. The ability to deal with poorly-defined problems is much rarer and is the key to success in science.*

MAISTO, JOHN F., ambassador; b. Braddock, Pa., Aug. 28, 1938; married; 3 children. BSFS, Georgetown U., 1961; MA, San Carlos Coll., Guatemala, 1962. With BiNational Ctr., Cordoba, Argentina, 1963-66; asst. cultural affairs officer USIA, Cochabamba, Bolivia, 1966-68; with Fgn. Svc., 1968—; adminstrv. asst. Fgn. Svc. Inst. Dept. State, 1968-69; econ. and comml. officer U.S. Embassy, La Paz, Bolivia, 1969-71; internat. rels. officer Ops. Ctr., 1971-72; spl. asst. Office of Counselor, 1972-73; internat. rels. officer office Andean affairs, bur. inter-Am. affairs Dept. State, 1973-75; polit. officer U.S. Embassy, San Jose, Costa Rica, 1975-78, Manila, 1978-82; dep. dir. office Philippine affairs, bur. East Asian and Pacific affairs Dept. State, 1982-84, dir., 1984-86; dep. chief of mission and charge d'affaires Am. Embassy, Panama, 1986-89; dep. permanent U.S. rep. to OAS, 1989-92; dep. asst. sec. state for Ctrl. Am. and Panama Dept. State, 1992-93; U.S. amb. to Nicaragua, 1993-96, U.S. amb. to Venezuela, 1997—. Office: USEmb Unit 4910 APO AA 34037-4910 also: Am Embassy, PO Box 62291, 1060-A Caracas Venezuela

MAITIN, SAM(UEL CALMAN) (SAM MAITIN), artist; b. Phila., Oct. 26, 1928; s. Isaac Boris and Ruth (Pollack) M.; m. Lilyan Miller, Aug. 29, 1964; children—Izak Joshua, Ana Raquel. Grad., Phila. Coll. Art, 1949; B.A., U. Pa., 1951. instr. art Phila. Coll. Art, 1949-59, Moore Coll. Art, 1950-52, Phila. Mus. Art, 1961-73, 80-81, Annenberg Sch. Comm. U. Pa., 1964-70; vis. lectr. Kent (Eng.) Inst. Art & Design, Canterbury, 1990, Camberwell Coll. Art, London, 1990. Creator 50 posters for YM/YWHA Arts Council.; one-man shows include: Yoseido Gallery, Tokyo, 1967, 69, 70, Curwen Gallery, London, 1969, Fleisher Gallery, Phila. Mus. Art, 1971, Associated Am. Artists Gallery, Phila., 1979, Joanne Lyon Gallery, Aspen, Colo., 1981, 82, 84, Dolan/Maxwell Gallery, Phila., 1985, 87, Noyes Mus., N.J., 1985, Woodmere Art Mus., Phila., 1994, Art Inst. Phila., 1994; group shows include Phila. Mus. Art Bicentennial Exhbns., 1976, Tate Gallery, 1977, Phila. Artists, Tel Aviv, 1978; represented in permanent collections Library of Congress, Mus. Modern Art, N.Y.C., Nat. Gallery Art, Oakland Mus., Calif., Phila. Mus. Art, Currier Gallery Art, Manchester, N.H., Tate Gallery, London, Pa. Acad Fine Arts, Smithsonian Instn., U. Pa., Picker Mus., Colgate U.; commissions include: (tapestry) Ark Covering, Adath Jeshurun Synagogue, Elkins Park, Pa., 1976, (mural painting) Phila. Dept. Recreation swimming pool, 1978, (mural) Academy House, Phila., 1984, (mural) Christian Assn., U. Pa., 1985, (tapestry) Abington Hosp., Pa., 1985, (dimensional mural) Annenberg Sch. Communications lobby, U. Pa., 1975, expanded, 1985, (3 story dimensional mural) law offices of Morgan, Lewis & Bockius, Miami, Fla., 1987, (ceiling and wall mural banners) Wharton Sch., U. Pa., 1988, (dimensional mural) Children's Hosp., Phila., 1992, (dimensional diptych) Kaiserman YM/YWHA, Haverford, Pa., 1992, (50 dimensional paintings) Brady Cancer Treatment Ctr., Voorhees, N.J., 1993, (mural) Settlement Music Sch., West Phila., (66 foot mural-banner) Tai Cang Tape

Factory, Shanghai, China, 1996. Guggenheim fellow, 1968; recipient award of excellence Art Matters, 1988, Percy M. Owens Meml. award Fellowship of Pa. Acad. Fine Arts, 1997. Home and Studio: 704 Pine St Philadelphia PA 19106-4005

MAITRA, SUBIR RANJAN, medical educator; b. Calcutta, India, Oct. 2, 1943; came to U.S., 1983; s. Sudhir R. and Nilima (Sanyal) M.; m. Sakti Sanyal, July 6, 1975; 1 child, Soma. BS, Calcutta U., 1964, MS, 1966, PhD, 1971, DSc, 1990. Lectr. in Physiology Banaras U., Varanasi, India, 1973-78, 81-83; sr. Fulbright rsch. scholar Henry Ford Hosp., Detroit, 1979-80, rsch. assoc. in hypertension, 1983-85; rsch. assoc. in physiology Loyola U., Chgo., 1985-86, asst. prof. physiology, 1987-88; dir. trauma rsch. surgery SUNY, Stony Brook, 1988-90, asst. prof., dir. trauma rsch. emergency medicine, surgery, 1990-93, assoc. prof., dir. rsch. emergency medicine, 1993—. Recipient Gold medal Calcutta U., 1966; prin. investigator Indian Coun. Med. Rsch., 1981, Univ. Grants Commn., 1983; grantee NIH, 1993-96, 96-99. Mem. AAAS, Am. Physiol. Soc., Shock Soc. Avocations: travel, community activities, sports.

MAIWURM, JAMES JOHN, lawyer; b. Wooster, Ohio, Dec. 5, 1948; s. James Frederick and Virginia Anne (Jones) M.; m. Wendy S. Leeper, July 31, 1971; children: James G., Michelle K. BA, Coll. Wooster, 1971; JD, U. Mich., 1974. Bar: Ohio 1974, D.C. 1986, Md. 1987, N.Y., 1987. Ptnr. Squire, Sanders & Dempsey, Cleve. and Washington, 1974-90; ptnr., group head Crowell & Moring, Washington, 1990—. Contbr. articles to profl. jours. Bd. trustees Davis Meml. Goodwill Industries, 1996—. Mem. ABA, D.C. Bar Assn., Leadership Washington, Fed. City Coun., Econ. Club Washington, George Mason U. Century Club (bd. dirs. 1994-95, chair tech. resource alliance 1995—). Home: 9419 Brian Jac Ln Great Falls VA 22066-2002 Office: Crowell & Moring 1001 Pennsylvania Ave NW Washington DC 20004-2505

MAJD, MASSOUD, radiology and nuclear medicine educator; b. Yazd, Iran, July 23, 1935; came to U.S., 1961; s. Jalil and Khadijeh Majd; m. Fereshteh H.S. Javadi, June 23, 1968; children: Kurosh, Katayoon. MD, Tehran U., 1960. Diplomate Am. Bd. Radiology, Am. Bd. Nuclear Medicine. Intern Deaconess Hosp., Buffalo, 1961-62; resident Georgetown U., Washington, 1962-66, instr. radiology, 1965-66, 68-70; asst. prof. Pahlavi U., Shiraz, Iran, 1966-68; asst. prof. George Washington U., 1970-72, assoc. prof., 1972-79, prof. radiology and pediatrics, 1979—; radiologist, dir. pediatric nuclear medicine Children's Nat. Med. Ctr., Washington, 1968—; adj. prof. radiology Georgetown U., 1981—; staff radiologist Georgetown U. Hosp., 1965-66; radiologist Pahlavi U. Hosps, Shiraz, 1966-68; assoc. staff radiology Children's Med. Ctr., 1968-72, sr. attending staff radiology, 1972—, founder dir. sect. nuclear medicine, 1969—; presenter in field. Contbr. chpts. to books and articles to profl. jours. Fellow Soc. Uroradiology, Am. Coll. Radiology, Am. Coll. Nuclear Physicians, Am. Acad. Pediatrics; mem. Am. Roetgen Ray Soc., Radiologic Soc. N.Am., European Soc. Pediatric Radiology (affiliate), Soc. Pediatric Radiology, Soc. Nuclear Medicine, Pediatric Imaging Coun., John Caffey Soc. Home: 8605 Stirrup Ct Potomac MD 20854-4843 Office: Childrens Nat Med Ctr 111 Michigan Ave NW Washington DC 20010-2916

MAJDA, ANDREW J., mathematician, educator; b. East Chicago, Ind., Jan. 30, 1949; m. Gerta Keller. BS, Purdue U., 1970; MS, Stanford U., 1971, PhD, 1973. Instr. Courant Inst. NYU, 1973-76; from asst. prof. to assoc. prof. U. Calif., L.A., 1976-78, prof., 1978; prof. U. Calif., Berkeley, 1979-84; vis. prof. Princeton (N.J.) U., 1984-85, prof., 1985-95; Morse prof. arts and sci. Courant Inst./NYU, N.Y.C., 1995—. Alfred P. Sloan Found. fellow, 1977-79; recipient medal of college de France, 1982, John von Neumann award Soc. for Indsl. and Applied Math., 1990. Mem. NAS (Applied Math. and Numerical Analysis award 1992). Office: Courant Institute 251 Mercer St New York NY 10012-1110

MAJERUS, PHILIP WARREN, physician; b. Chgo., July 10, 1936; s. Clarence Nicholas and Helen Louise (Mathis) M.; m. Janet Sue Brakensiek, Dec. 28, 1957; children: Suzanne, David, Juliet, Karen. BS, Notre Dame U., 1958; MD, Washington U., 1961. Resident in Medicine Mass. Gen. Hosp., Boston, 1961-63; research assoc. NIH, Bethesda, Md., 1963-66; asst. prof. biochemistry Washington U., St. Louis, 1966-75, asst. prof. medicine, 1966-69, assoc. prof. medicine, 1969-71, prof. medicine, 1971—, dir. div. hematology, 1973—, prof. biochemistry, 1976—. Mem. editorial bd. numerous jours. and profl. mags.; contbr. numerous articles to profl. jours. Recipient numerous awards including Am. Cancer Soc. Faculty Rsch. Assoc. award, 1966-75, Disting. Career award for Contbns. to Hemostasis Internat. Soc. for Thrombosis and Hemostasis, 1985, Alumni/Faculty award Washington U. Sch. Medicine, 1986, The Robert J. and Claire Pasarow Found. award, 1994. Fellow ACP; mem. NAS, Inst. Medicine of NAS, Am. Acad. Arts and Scis., Assn. Am. Physicians, Am. Soc. Hematology (pres. 1991), Am. Fedn. Clin. Rsch., Am. Soc. Biol. Chemists, Am. Soc. Clin. Investigation (pres. 1981-82), Sigma Xi, Alpha Omega Alpha. Home: 7220 Pershing Ave Saint Louis MO 63130-4248 Office: Wash Univ Sch of Med Dept Int Med Saint Louis MO 63110*

MAJERUS, RICK, collegiate basketball team coach; b. Sheboygan, Wis.. BS, Marquette U., 1970, MS, 1979. Asst. coach Marquette U., 1971-83, head coach, 1983-86; asst. coach Milw. Bucks, 1986-87; head coach Ball State U., 1987-89, U. Utah, Salt Lake City, 1989—; asst. coach U.S.A. Dream Team 2, summer 1994. Named Coach of Yr. Hoop Scoop, 1989, UPI Coach of Yr., 1991, Coach of Yr. Basketball Times, 1991, Utah Sports Person of Yr. 1992, Playboy Coach of Yr., 1992, Kodak Dist. Coach of Yr., 1991, 93, 95, Western Athletic Conf. Coach of Yr., 1994, 95. Office: U Utah Jon M Huntsman Ctr Salt Lake City UT 84112*

MAJESTY, MELVIN SIDNEY, psychologist, consultant; b. New Orleans, June 6, 1928; s. Sidney Joseph and Marcella Cecilia (Kieffer) M.; m. Bettye Newanda Gordon, Dec. 18, 1955; 1 child, Diana Sue. BA, La. State U., 1949; MS, Western Res. U., 1951; PhD (USAF Inst. Tech. fellow), Case-Western Res. U., 1967. Commd. 2d lt. USAF, 1951, advanced through grades to lt. col., 1968; program mgr., ast. dir. tng. rsch. Air Force Human Resources Lab., 1967-69; dir. faculty and profl. edn. rsch. USAF Acad., 1969-72; dir. plot tng. candidate selection program Officer Tng. Sch., Air Tng.Command, 1972-76; ret. USAF, 1976; personnel selection cons. to Calif. State Pers. Bd., Sacramento, 1976-92. Patentee listening center; founded pers. testing for ballistic missile and space systems; directed largest study of fighter pilot selection since World War II; pioneered use of phys. testing as replacement for the maximum age requirement in law enforcement jobs; developed phys. fitness tests and established psychol. screening standards for state highway patrol officer and police officers; contbr. numerous articles to profl. publs. Decorated Commendation medal (2), Meritorious Svc. medal (2). Mem. Am. Psychol. Assn., Internat. Pers. Mgmt. Assn., Calif. Psychol. Assn., Western Psychol. Assn., Soc. Indsl. and Orgnl. Psychology, Personnel Testing Coun., VFW, DAV, Am. Legion, Amvets, Vietnam Vets. Am. Office: 801 Capitol Mall Sacramento CA 95814-4806

MAJEV, HOWARD RUDOLPH, lawyer; b. N.Y.C., Dec. 10, 1952; s. Benny and Hela (Wolnowicz) M.; m. Janet Brandt; children: Brendan Joshua, Collin Campbell. BA, Johns Hopkins U., 1973; JD, U. Md., 1976. Bar: Md. 1978, D.C. 1995. Exec. asst. to city coun. pres. City of Balt., Balt., 1976-79; assoc. Weinberg and Green, Balt., 1979-84; ptnr. Weinberg & Green, Balt., 1985-94, Rudnick & Wolfe, Balt., Washington, 1994-96, Rudnick, Wolfe, Epstein, Washington, 1996—. Author: (with K.S. Koenig) How to be a Legal Eagle: A Checklist for Remodelers, 1988; dir. Lex Mundi, 1992-94. Dir. Citizens Planning and Housing Assn., Balt., 1985-95, pres., 1990-92; bd. dirs. Md. Food Bank, Inc., 1988-92, Florence Crittenton Svcs. Balt., 1986-87, Sinai Hosp. Balt., 1990-92, Levindale Hebrew Geriat. Home and Hosp., 1991; devel. coun. The Kennedy Krieger Inst., 1988-92; participant Leadership-Greater Balt. Com., 1986. Mem. ABA, D.C. Bar Assn., Md. State Bar Assn., Balt. City Bar Assn. Avocations: running, rotisserie league baseball, reading, stamp collecting. Office: Rudnick Wolfe Epstein & Zeidman 1201 New York Ave NW Ph Washington DC 20005-3917

MAJOR, ANDRÉ, radio producer, writer, educator; b. Montréal, Que., Can., Apr. 22, 1942; s. Arthur and Anna (Sharp) M.; m. Ginette Lepage, June 30, 1970; children—Eric, Julie. Student, Coll. de Montréal, 1955-60. Lit. critic La Presse, Montreal, 1965-79, Le Devoir, Montreal, 1967-70; lecteur Editions du Jour, Montreal, 1964-67, Lemeac, Montreal, 1972-75; radio producer CBC, Radio Canada, Montreal, 1973—; prof. lit. and creative writing Ottawa U., 1977-78, U. Que., 1977, McGill U., 1990. Works include Le Chair de poule, 1965, L'Epouvantail, 1974, L'Epideie, 1975, Les Rescapés, 1978 (Gov. Gen. Can. award), Histoires de Deserteurs, 1991, La Vie Provisoire, 1995; poetry collections include Poèmes pour durer, 1969; dramas include Un Soirée en octobre, 1975; short stories include La Folle d'Elvis, 1981, L'Hiver au coeur, 1987 (Can.-Belgium award 1991, prix Athanase-David, 1992). Mem. Union des Ecrivains québécois (sec. 1976-79).

MAJOR, CLARENCE LEE, novelist, poet, educator; b. Atlanta, Dec. 31, 1936; s. Clarence and Inez (Huff) M.; m. Pamela Ritter, May 8, 1980. BS, SUNY, Albany; PhD, Union Inst. Prof. U. Colo., Boulder, 1977-89, U. Calif., Davis, 1989—. Author: All-Night Visitors, 1969, Dictionary of Afro-American Slang, 1970, No, 1973, Reflex and Bone Structure, 1975, rev. edit., 1996, Emergency Exit, 1979, My Amputations, 1986, Such Was the Season, 1987, Painted Turtle: Woman with Guitar, 1987, Fun and Games, 1990, Calling the Wind, 1993, Juba to Jive: A Dictionary of African American Slang, 1994, Dirty Bird Blues, 1996; poetry: Swallow the Lake, 1970, Symptoms & Madness, 1971, Private Line, 1971, The Cotton Club, 1972, Inside Diameter: The France Poems, 1985, Painted Turtle, 1988, Surfaces and Masks, 1988, Some Observations of a Stranger at Zuni in the Latter Part of the Century, 1989, Parking Lots, 1992, The Garden Thrives, 1996; contbr. articles to Washington Post Book World, L.A. Times Book Rev., N.Y. Times Book Rev. Recipient Nat. Council on Arts award, Washington, 1970; Western States Book award, Western States Found., Santa Fe, 1986; Fulbright grantee, 1981-83. Office: U Calif Dept of English 211 Sproul Hall Davis CA 95616

MAJOR, COLEMAN JOSEPH, chemical engineer; b. Detroit, Sept. 7, 1915; s. Coleman I. and Anna (Galik) M.; m. Marjorie Lois Shenk, Nov. 21, 1941; children: Roy Coleman, Marilyn M. Phillips Bever. B.S., U. Ill., 1937; Ph.D., Cornell U., 1941. Chief prodn. engr., supt. services Sharples Chems., Inc., Wyandotte, Mich., 1941-50; asso. prof. chem. engring. U. Iowa, 1950-56; head high energy chems. Am. Potash & Chem. Corp., Whittier, Calif. and Henderson, Nev., 1956-59; prof. chem. engring. U. Iowa, 1959-64; prof., head dept. chem. engring. U. Akron, 1964-70; dean Coll. Engring., also dir. Inst. Technol. Assistance, 1970-80; dir. Inst. Biomed. Engring. Rsch., 1979-80; cons. computers. Contbr. articles to tech. jours. Named Chem. Engr. of Yr., 1979; C.J. Major Scholarship award established in his honor, 1990; recipient Disting. Svc. award U. Akron, 1993. Fellow Am. Inst. Chem. Engrs.; mem. Am. Chem. Soc., Sigma Xi, Tau Beta Pi. Patentee in field. Home: 7838 Jaymes St Dublin OH 43017-8812 *A few guidelines that I have used: 1. Work very hard but find time to relax. 2. Push yourself ahead, but don't hold anyone else back. 3. When gathering facts, be rigorous and unrelenting but when making decisions involving people, use the art of compromise.*

MAJOR, JAMES RUSSELL RICHARDS, historian, educator; b. Riverton, Va., Jan. 7, 1921; s. Julian Neville and Jean (Richards) M.; m. Blair Louise Rogers, June 9, 1945; children: Blair Louise, Randon Leigh, Clara Jean, James Russell Richards. AB, Va. Mil. Inst., 1942; MA, Princeton U., 1948, PhD, 1949. Mem. faculty Emory U., 1949-90, Charles Howard Candler prof. history, 1980-90, chmn. dept., 1966-70, 76-79, 87-89; vis. prof. Harvard, 1965-66; mem. Inst. Advanced Study Princeton, 1967-68, 79-80; Vice pres. H.W. Dick Co., 1975—. Author: The Estates General of 1560, 1951, Representative Instns. in Renaissance France, 1421-1559, 1960, The Deputies to the Estates General of Renaissance France, 1960, The Western World: Renaissance to the Present, 2d edit, 1971, The Age of the Renaissance and Reformation, 1970, Bellièvre, Sully and The Assembly of Notables of 1596, 1974, Representative Government in Early Modern France, 1980, The Monarchy, The Estates and The Aristocracy in Renaissance France, 1988, From Renaissance Monarchy to Absolute Monarchy: French Kings, Nobles, and Estates, 1994; also articles; bd. editors: Jour. Modern History, 1966-69, French History, 1986-90. Served to capt. AUS, 1942-46. Decorated Silver Star, Bronze Star, Purple Heart with 2 clusters; Fulbright fellow France, 1952-53; Guggenheim fellow, 1953-54, 67-68; Faculty Research fellow Soc. Sci. Research Council, 1955-58; fellow, 1961-62; sr. fellow Nat. Endowment for Humanities, 1973-74. Mem. AAUP (pres. S.E. regional conf. 1965-67, mem. nat. coun. 1966-69), Am. Hist. Assn. (com. on PhD programs in history 1969-71, program com. 1976, mem. rsch. divsn. 1978-81, Leo Gershoy prize com. 1990-92, Leo Gershoy award 1996), Internat. Commn. History Rep. and Parliamentary Instn. (pres. N.Am. sect. 1975-81), Renaissance Soc. Am. (mem. coun. 1971-73), Sixteenth Century Studies Conf. (Nancy Syman Roelker prize 1987), Soc. French Hist. Studies (William C. Koren prize 1966, co-winner 1987), So. Hist. Assn. (vice chmn. program com. 1967, chmn. European sect. 1970-71), Sodiété de l'Histoire de France, Européenne d'Histoire, Phi Beta Kappa (senator United chpts. 1970-76). Home: 2223 Hill Park Ct Decatur GA 30033-2716

MAJOR, JEAN-LOUIS, author, French literature educator; b. Cornwall, Ont., Can., July 16, 1937; s. Joseph and Noella (Daoust) M.; m. Bibiane Landry, June 4, 1960; 1 dau., Marie-France. B.A. with honors, U. Ottawa, Ont., 1959, B.Phil., 1959, Licenciate of Philosophy, 1960, M.A., 1961, Ph.D., 1965; research fellow, Ecole Pratique des Hautes Etudes, Paris, 1968-69. Lectr. philosophy College Bruyere, Ottawa, 1960-61; lectr. dept. philosophy U. Ottawa, 1961-65, asst. prof. departement lettres Francaises, 1965-67, assoc. prof. lettres Francaises, 1967-71, prof. lettres Francaises, 1971—, assoc. dean rsch., Faculty of Arts, 1991—; lit. critic, dir. lit. sect. Le Droit (newspaper), 1963-65; vis. prof. U. Toronoto, Ont., 1970-71; editor Corpus d'editions critiques, 1981—, Bibliothèque du Nouveau Monde; chmn. acad. adv. com. Ont. Coun. on Univ. Affairs, 1991-93. Author books including Saint-Exupéry, l'écriture et la pensée, 1968, Léone de Jean Cocteau, 1975, Anne Hébert et le miracle de la parole, 1976, Radiquet, Cocteau "Les joues en feu," 1977, Le jeu en étoile, 1978, Paul-Marie Lapointe: la nuit incendiée, 1978, Entre l'ecriture et la parole, 1984, Journal d'Henriette Dessaulles, 1989, Ringuet, Trente arpents, 1991; also numerous articles. Fellow Can. Coun., 1968, 69, 71; grantee Humanities Rsch. Coun. Can., 1975, 85, 90, 95. Fellow Royal Soc. Can., Academie des Lettres et des Sciences humaines. Home: PO Box 357, St-Isidore, ON Canada K0C 2B0 Office: Faculty Arts, U Ottawa, Ottawa, ON Canada K1N 6N5

MAJOR, JOHN CHARLES, judge; b. Mattawa, Ont., Can., Feb. 20, 1931; s. William and Elsie (Thompson) M.; m. Hélène Provencher, 1959; children: Suzan, Peter, Paul, Steven. BComm, Loyola Coll., Montreal, 1953; LLB, U. Toronto, 1957. Bar: Alberta 1958, Queen's Counsel, 1972, Alberta Ct. of Appeal, 1991. With Bennett, Jones & Verchere, Calgary, 1957-91, sr. ptnr., 1967; sr. counsel City of Calgary Police Svc., 1975-85; counsel McDonald Commn., 1978-82; sr. counsel Province of Alta., 1987; mem. Supreme Ct. of Can., 1992—. Fellow Am. Coll. Trial Lawyers; mem. Can. Bar Assn., Can. Inst. of the Adminstrn. of Justice, Can. Judges Conf., The Glencoe Club (Calgary), Calgary Golf and Country Club, Ottawa Hunt and Golf Club. Avocation: golf. Office: Supreme Court of Can, Wellington St, Ottawa, ON Canada K1A 0J1

MAJOR, JOHN KEENE, radio broadcasting executive; b. Kansas City, Mo., Aug. 3, 1924; s. Ralph Hermon and Margaret Norman (Jackson) M.; m. Gracemary Somers Westing, Apr. 9, 1950 (div.); children: John Westing, Ann Somers, Richard Jackson; m. Lee Adair Jordan, June 25, 1970. Student, U. Kansas City, 1940-41; BS, Yale U., 1943; MS, 1947; DSc, U. Paris, 1951. Lab. asst. physics Yale U., 1943-44, instr., research asst. physics, 1952-55; sci. staff spl. studies group, div. war research Columbia U., 1944; instr. physics and chemistry Am. Community Sch., Paris, 1948-49; research fellow Centre National de la Recherche Scientifique, Laboratoire de Chimie Nucleaire, Coll. de France, Paris, 1951; Carnegie Found. fellow Laboratoire Curie, Institut du Radium, Paris, 1951; assoc. prof. physics Western Res. U., 1955-57, chmn. dept., 1955-60, 61-64, Perkins prof. physics, 1957-66; staff assoc. univ. sci. devel. sect. div. instl. programs NSF, 1964-68; prof. physics, dean Grad. Sch. Arts and Scis., U. Cin., 1968-71; prof. physics NYU, 1971-74, dean Grad. Sch. Arts and Scis., 1971-73; vis. scholar Alfred P. Sloan Sch. Mgmt., MIT, 1973-74; prof. physics Northeastern Ill. U., Chgo., 1974-77; v.p. acad. affairs Northeastern Ill. U., 1974-75; cons. NSF, 1968-69; sci. cons. Sonar Analysis Group, 1946-47; gen. mgr. Sta. WONO, Syracuse, N.Y., 1977; dir. research and mktg. Sta. WFMT, Chgo., 1978-81; chmn. bd., pres. KCMA, Inc., 1980—; gen. mgr. Sta. KCMA, 1981-88; mem. exec. com. radio project Ctr. for Pub. Resources, 1980-81. Contbr. articles to profl. jours. Bd. dirs. Concertime, 1985—, prs. 1993-95; bd. dirs. Tulsa Opera, 1984-95, Tulsa Philharm. Soc., 1988-95. Lt. (j.g.) USNR, 1944-46. Fellow at Lab. für Technische Physik, Technische Hochschule Munich, 1960-61; Fulbright fellow U. Paris, 1949-50. Mem. Classical Music Broadcasters Assn. (exec. v.p., 1979-80, bd. dir. 1979-82, 85-87, 89-93, pres. 1980-81, 90-91), Cosmos Club (Washington), Sigma Xi. Home: 126 E 26th Pl Tulsa OK 74114-2422

MAJOR, MARY JO, dance school artistic director; b. Joliet, Ill., Dec. 5, 1955; d. George Francis and Lucille Mae (Ballun) Schmidberger; m. Perry Rex Major, June 9, 1979. AA, Joliet Jr. Coll., 1976; BA, Lewis U., 1978; MS, Ill. State U., 1983; postgrad., No. Ill. U., Nat. Louis U., Gov.'s State U. Cert. tchr., Ill. Tchr., softball coach St. Rose Grade Sch., Wilmington, Ill., 1977-78; tchr., coach volleyball, basketball, softball Reed Custer High Sch., Braidwood, Ill., 1978-79; pvt. tutor, 1979; tchr. Coal City (Ill.) Middle Sch., 1980—, basketball coach, 1980-84; owner, dir., choreographer Major Sch. Dance, Inc., Coal City, 1984—; owner Technique Boutique, 1991—; aerobics instr. Wilmington Park Dist., 1977-82, Coal City Shape Shoppe, 1980-82; cheerleading sponsor Joliet Jr. Coll., 1976-77, aerobics instr., 1980-81; pvt. dance instr., Coal City, 1981; dancer, choreographer Coal City Bi-Centennial Celebration, 1981, Coal City Community Celebration, 1982; founder Major Motion Dancers, 1984—; tchr., Russia, 1990; dancer, choreographer various performances for ch. and civic orgns.; televised half-time performance and tour Citrus Bowl. Commd. to choreograph and appear in video prodn.: Jacinta, Not an Ordinary Love, The Patty Waszak Show A Bit of Branson, 1995—; performer on televised Easter Seals Telethon from the Empress Casino, Joliet. Mem. Arts Coun. Co-op. Recipient Proclamation of Achievement award Dance Olympus, Chgo., 1986-97, Best Choreographer award 1990, Merit award Tremaine Dance Conv., 1991-92; named Best Actress, Joliet Kiwanis, 1989, Best Musician, 1990. Mem. NEA, Ill. Edn. Assn., Coal City Cmty. Unit Edn. Assn. Office: Major Sch Dance Inc 545 E 1st St Coal City IL 60416

MAJOR, PATRICK WEBB, III, principal; b. Wai, Maharastra, India, Mar. 12, 1947; s. Patrick W. Jr. and Alice (Seeland) M.; m. Daphnelynn Jantz, June 26, 1971; children: Mindy Joy, Matthew Patrick Webb. BA, Biola U., 1972; MA, Point Loma Coll., 1979; postgrad., U. Calif., Irvine. Cert. secondary tchr., adminstr., Calif. Prin. Omega High Sch., Bakersfield, Calif., 1980-84; headmaster Bakersfield (Calif.) Christian Life Schs., 1984-86; prin. North Kern Christian Sch., Wasco, Calif., 1986-88; prin., adminstr. Yucaipa (Calif.) Christian Schs., 1988—. Mem. ASCD, Assn. Christian Schs. Internat. (former dist. rep., exec. bd. mem.), Ctrl. Redwood League (pres. 1985-86), CIF Ctrl Sect., Internat. Fellowship Christian Sch. Adminstrs., Nat. Assn. Elem. Sch. Prins.

MAJORS, JOHNNY (JOHN TERRILL MAJORS), university athletic coach; b. Lynchburg, Tenn., May 21, 1935; m. Mary Lynn Barnwell, June 27, 1959; children—John Ireland, Mary Elizabeth. B.S., U. Tenn., 1957. Head football coach Iowa State U., 1968-72, U. Pitts., 1973-76, U. Tenn., 1977-92; head football coach U. Pitts., 1993-96, spl. asst. to chancellor, dir. athletics, 1996—. Chmn. E. Tenn. Easter Seals Com., 1977, March of Dimes, 1977. Named Nat. Coll. Coach of Yr., 1973, 76; won nat. championship NCAA Divsn. 1A, 1976; inducted into Nat. Football Hall of Fame, 1987, Tenn. Hall of Fame (charter). Mem. Am. Football Coaches Assn. (bd. dirs., past pres.), Pitts. Athletic Assn., Univ. Club, Pitts. Field Club, Honors Club in Ooltewah (Tenn.), Sigma Chi, Omicron Delta Kappa. Home: 4215 Bigelow Blvd Pittsburgh PA 15213-2649 Office: U Pitts PO Box 7436 Pittsburgh PA 15213-0436

MAJORS, NELDA FAYE, physical therapist; b. Houston, Aug. 3, 1938; d. Columbus Edward and Mary (Mills) M. Cert. in Phys. Therapy, Hermann Sch. Phys. Therapy, Houston, 1960; BS, U. Houston, 1963. Lic. phys. therapist, Tex. Staff therapist Tex. Med. Ctr. Hermann Hosp., Houston, 1960-61; phys. therapist Chelsea Orthopedic Clinic, Houston, 1961-63; dir. phys. therapy Meml. Hosp. Southwest, Houston, 1963-75; owner, pres. Nelda Majors, Inc., Houston, 1975—; mem. profl. adv. bd. Logos Home Health Agy., Houston, 1985-86; adv. dir. 1st Northwestern Bank, Houston. Active Meml. Dr. Meth. Ch., Houston, 1983—; ptnr. Houston Proud Ptnr., 1986—; founder, pres. Instnl. Safety Advs. Inc., 1994—; bd. dirs. Texans for the Improvement of Long Term Care Facilities, 1995—. Named All Am. Softball Pitcher, Amateur Softball Assn., 1964, All-Regional and All-State Pitcher, Tex. Amateur Softball Assn., 1954-70; named to Houston Amateur Softball Assn. Softball Hall of Fame, 1994. Mem. Am. Phys. Therapy Assn. (pvt. practice sect.), Tex. Phys. Therapy Assn., U. Houston Alumni Assn., E. Cullen Soc. (U. Houston), N.W. Crossing Optimist Club (Houston, charter mem., bd. dirs.), River Oaks Rotary (Houston), Phi Kappa Phi. Republican. Club: U. Houston Cougar. Avocations: softball, bicycling, traveling, golf, reading.

MAJORS, RICHARD GEORGE, psychology educator; b. Ithaca, N.Y.; s. Richard G. II and Fannie Sue Majors; legal guardian: Lillian A. McGill. AA, Auburn (N.Y.) Community Coll., 1974; BA in History, Plattsburgh State Coll., 1977; PhD in Ednl. Psychology, U. Ill., 1987. Various social svc. positions, 1976-79; probation officer, ct. investigator Plattsburgh, 1979; clin. intern McKinley Health Ctr., Urbana, Ill., 1981; rsch. asst. U. Minn., Mpls., 1981, U. Ill., Urbana, 1981-84; instr. Parkland C.C., Champaign, Ill., 1985; rsch. asst. U. Ill., Champaign, 1985-86; postdoctoral fellow U. Kans., Lawrence, 1987-89; postdoctoral fellow, clin. fellow Harvard Med. Sch., Boston, 1989-90; asst. prof. psychology U. Wis. Sys., 1990-93; sr. rsch. assoc. The Urban Inst., Washington, 1993-95; vis. fellow, scholar David Walker Rsch. Inst., Mich. State U., East Lansing, 1995—; vis. scholar Georgetown U., 1996-97; hon. Leverhulme vis. fellow for rsch. in Eng., 1996-97. Co-author: Coolpose: The Dilemmas of Black Manhood in America, 1992, The American Black Male: His Present Status and Future, 1994; founder Jour. of African Am. Men. Named one of Outstanding Young Men of Am., 1987. Fellow APA (predoctoral minority fellow 1984, Minority Achievement award for Rsch. in Psychology 1995); mem. Nat. Coun. African Am. Men (chmn., co-founder), Soc. for Psychol. Study of Ethnic Minority Issues, Am. Orthopsychiat. Assn., Greenpeace, Kappa Delta Pi, Phi Delta Kappa. Avocations: reading, traveling, cycling. Office: David Walker Rsch Inst Mich State U B421 West Fee Hall East Lansing MI 48824

MAJUMDAR, SHARMILA, research scientist, educator; b. Calcutta, W. Bengal, India, Nov. 23, 1961; d. Anil Kumar and Sipra (Roy) M. BSc., U. Delhi, India, 1979-82; MS, Yale U., 1984, MPhil, 1985, PhD, 1987. Assoc. rsch. scientist Yale U., New Haven, Conn., 1987-88, prof., 1988-89; asst. prof. U. Calif., San Francisco, 1989-95, assoc. prof., 1995—; mem. alumni sch. com. Yale U., 1988—. Contbg. author; contbr. papers in field. Recipient Engring. award Whittaker Found., 1990—, NIH Career Devel. award, 1993; NIH-RO1 rsch. grantee, 1992, 96. Mem. AAPM, Am. Phys. Soc., Soc. Magnetic Resonance in Medicine, Sigma Xi. Avocations: cooking, reading. Home: 244 Diapian Bay Alameda CA 94502-7911 Office: U Calif Dept Radiology MRSC 1 Irving St San Francisco CA 94143-1250

MAJUMDER, SABIR AHMED, physical and analytical chemist; b. Chandpur, Bangladesh, July 15, 1957; came to U.S., 1986; s. Quashem Majumder and Momtaz Begum; m. Hamida Khanam, Dec. 15, 1985; children:Faryha, Nabilah. BS in Chemistry with honors, U. Dhaka, Bangladesh, 1981, MS, 1983; MS, Duquesne U., 1988; PhD, U. N.Mex., 1994. Corr. The Daily Janapad, Dhaka, Bangladesh, 1973-74; rsch. fellow U. Dhaka, 1983-84, lectr. in Chemistry, 1984-86; teaching asst. Duquesne U., Pitts., 1986-88, U. N.Mex., Albuquerque, 1988-90; Assoc. Western Univs. grad. lab. fellow Sandia Nat. Labs., Albuquerque, 1991-93, postdoctoral fellow, 1994-96; postdoctoral fellow U. Minn., Mpls., 1997—. Contbr. articles to profl. jours. Gen. Sec. Bangladesh Youth Coun., Dhaka, 1982; mem. Nat. Student League Ctrl., Dhaka, 1983. Trainee Youth Leadership Tng. Inst., Singapore, 1981; recipient Link Energy Fellowship Link Found., Rochester, N.Y., 1987. Mem. AAAS, Am. Chem. Soc., Bangladesh Chem. and Biol. Soc. N.Am. (elected gen. sec. 1993-94, pres. 1997—). Democrat. Muslim. Achievements include patent disclosure: photocatalytic degradation of aromatic compounds by metalloporhyrins adsorbed into alumina using visible light. Office: U Minn Dept Chemistry Minneapolis MN 55455

MAJZOUB, MONA KATHRYNE, lawyer; b. Memphis, June 19, 1949; d. A. Joseph and Mary Majzoub. BA, U. Mich., 1970, MA, 1972; JD, U. Detroit, 1976. Bar: Mich. 1977, U.S. Dist. Ct. (ea. dist.) Mich. 1977, U.S.

Supreme Ct. 1988. Sr. prin. Kitch, Drutchas, Wagner & Kenney, P.C., Detroit, 1977—. Bd. dirs. Saratoga Community Hosp., Detroit, 1986—, Family Svcs. Detroit and Wayne County, 1988—. Mem. ABA, State Bar Mich. (tort law review com.), Detroit Bar Assn., Women Lawyers Assn. of Mich., Am. Arab Bar Assn. (treas. 1982-86, pres. 1986-94), Am. Hosp. Assn., Mich. Soc. of Hosp. Attys., Nat. Assn. of Women Lawyers, Assn. of Def. Trial Counsel, Inc., Assn. Trial Lawyers of Am., Mich. Def. Trial Counsel, Leadership Detroit XVI. Office: Kitch Drutchas Wagner et al 1 Woodward Ave Fl 10 Detroit MI 48226-3422

MAK, BEN BOHDAN, engineer; b. Chortkiw, Ukraine, June 11, 1926; s. Iwan and Antonya (Smerechynska) M.; children: Loretta, Audrey, Donald. Student, U. Cracow (Poland) Poly., 1948, Frieburg U., 1949, Ukrainian Tech. Husbandry Inst, 1951, U. Miami, 1959, War Coll., 1965; MSME, N.J. Inst. Tech., 1968, MBA, 1968, MS in Mgmt. Engring., 1968, MS in Ordnance Engring., 1968. Registered profl. engr.; cert. plant engr. Design engr., engring. mgr. Bernard & Burk-Huston Corp., Miami, Fla., 1956-60; instr. value engring. U. Miami, Fla., 1959-60; prof. ordnance engring., logistic armament Air Force Inst. Tech.; gen. engr., mgr. Wiz Kids; project mgr. Sec. Def. Office Dept. Def., 1961-69; v.p. engring. Metal Improvement Co. and Valiant Metal Products Co., 1969-78; engring. mgr. Coll. Medicine and Dentistry N.J., 1979-82; dean facilities Dutchess C.C., 1982-89; pvt. practice cons. mgmt., engring., mktg. North Port, Fla., 1970—. Author: Value Engineering, 1963, Bomb Fragmentation, 1964, Value Analysis for Industry, 1965, Sydor-Shelest, 1966; author rsch. papers. Recipient awards and merit citations U.S. Army, USN, USAF, Sec. of Def., Pres.'s office, univs. Mem. NSPE, ASME, Assn. Phys. Plant Adminstrs. of Univs., Soc. Cert. Plant Engrs., Ukrainian Engrs. Soc. Am., Assn. Energy Engrs., Ordnance Assn., others. Achievements include fluency in English, German, Polish, Russian, Ukrainian, Yiddish and understands Spanish. Avocations: architecture, history.

MAKADOK, STANLEY, management consultant; b. N.Y.C., Mar. 30, 1941; s. Jack and Pauline (Speciner) M.; BME, CCNY, 1962; MS in Mgmt. Sci., Rutgers U., 1964; m. Neilia A. David, Nov. 12, 1989; 1 child from previous marriage, Richard. Bus. systems analyst Westinghouse Electric Corp., Balt., 1964-65; project engr., corp. cons. Am. Cyanamid Corp., Pearl River, N.Y., Wayne, N.J., 1965-68; v.p., bus. devel. and planning Pepsico Inc. and affiliates, Purchase, N.Y., Miami, Fla., 1968-75; mgr. fin. and planning cons. Coopers & Lybrand, N.Y.C., 1975-77; pres. Century Mgmt. Cons., Inc., Ridgewood, N.J., 1977—. Contbr. articles to profl. jours. Office: Century Mgmt Cons Inc 4 Wilsey Sq Ste 9 Ridgewood NJ 07450-3728

MAKAR, BOSHRA HALIM, mathematics educator; b. Sohag, Egypt, Sept. 23, 1928; came to U.S., 1966, naturalized, 1971; s. Halim and Hakima (Khair Mikhail) M.; m. Nadia E. Eissa, Jan. 1, 1960; children—Ralph, Roger. B.Sc., Cairo U., 1943-47, M.Sc., 1952, Ph.D., 1955. Mem. faculty Cairo U., 1948-65; vis. assoc. prof. Am. U., Beirut, Lebanon, 1966, Mich. Tech. U., Houghton, 1967; prof. math. St. Peter's Coll., Jersey City, 1967-95, prof. emeritus, 1996—. Mem. Math. Assn. Am., AAUP, U.S. Naval Inst. Republican. Roman Catholic. Clubs: Poetry Soc. London; United Poets Internat. (Philippines) (v.p.). Home: 410 Fairmount Ave Jersey City NJ 07306-5910

MAKAR, NADIA EISSA, secondary education educator, educational administrator; b. Cairo, Oct. 7, 1938; came to U.S., 1966.; d. Michel and Yvonne (Bitar) Issa; m. Boshra Halim Makar, Jan. 1, 1960; children: Ralph, Roger. Cert., Moscow U., 1964; BA, St. Peter's Coll., 1969, MA, 1981; postgrad., Hope Coll. and Brown U., 1972, 1973. Cert. tchr., supr., prin., N.J. Tchr. Hudson Cath. H.S., Jersey City, 1970-72, sci. dept. chairperson, 1972-79; coord. Convocation Model Project Union City N.J. Bd. Edn., 1979-81, tchr., coord. industry and coll. rels., 1989-96, sci. supr., 1996—; mem. Bd. Edn., Jersey City; cons. Stevens Inst. Tech. Hughes Grant, Hoboken, N.J., 1989-94; cons./advisor Project RISE. Author: Health; Space; Environment, 1980; co-editor NSSA mag., 1974-76; contbr. articles to profl. jours. Co-founder N.J. Bus./Industry/Sci. Edn. Consortium, 1981; pres. Bus./Profl. Women, Jersey City, 1984-86, sec. N.J., 1985, dir. dist. III, 1995—; treas. Mental Health Assn., Hudson County, 1977-80; bd. dirs. N.J. Math. Coalition; U.S. del. 1st U.S./Russian Meeting for Math. Educators. Recipient Outstanding Secondary Educator Am. award U.S. Sec. Edn., 1973, award Mfg. Chemists Assn., 1975, recognition award Gov. State of N.J., 1988, Presdl. award for excellence in math. and sci. teaching, 1989, Sigma Xi award of encouraging rsch. at pre-coll. level. Mem. Am. Chem. Soc. (chmn. Hudson-Bergen sect. 1980-82, sec. N.Y. sect. 1994—, reviewer for Chem. Edn. Jour., bd. dirs. Home PC Mag., Nicol award 1975, Outstanding Achievement award New Eng. region 1976), St. Peter's Coll. Alumni Assn. (v.p. 1982-88, treas.), Nat. Coun. Tchrs. Math (reviewer). Office: Union Hill High Sch 3808 Hudson Ave Union City NJ 07087-6020

MAKARA, CAROL PATTIE, education educator, consultant; b. Norwich, Conn., Feb. 27, 1943; d. Howard G. and Ruth R. Robinson; m. Benjamin Makara, Feb. 19, 1966; children: Cheryl A., John J. AS, Three Rivers Community-Tech. Coll., 1988; BS, Cen. Conn. State U., 1965; MA, U. Conn., 1967. Cert. tchr., Conn. Tchr. Ledyard (Conn.) Bd. of Edn., 1965-66, Preston (Conn.) Bd. of Edn., 1974—; continuing edn. unit mgr. Preston (Conn.) Pub. Schs., 1993—; computer analyst Clinton (Conn.) plant Stanley Bostitch, summers 1987-92; evening instr. Three Rivers Cmty. Tech. Coll., 1989—; evening mgr. AutoCad Tng. Ctr., 1990-95; coop. mentor tchr. Dept. Edn., Conn., 1988—; advisor Conn. Educators' Computer Assn., 1992—; tchr. assessor The Begining Educator Support and Tng. Program, Conn. State Dept. Edn., 1995—. Author: (with others) Pedagogical Guide: Strategies for Improving Instruction, 1992. Active Fellowship Program for Disting. Tchrs., 1987-94. Fellow Conn. Bus. and Industry Assn.; mem. NEA, Conn. Edn. Assn. Home: 89 Mathewson Mill Rd Ledyard CT 06339-1114 Office: Preston Plains Sch 1 Route 164 Preston CT 06365-8818

MAKE, ISABEL ROSE, multicultural studies educator, small business owner; b. Phila., Oct. 6, 1947; d. Aaron M. and Lillian (Simon) Rose; m. Barry Jay Make, June 13, 1970; children: Jonathan David, Jeremy Simon. BA, George Wash. U., 1969; EdM, Temple U., 1970; cert. advanced grad. studies, W.Va. U., 1975. Cert. tchr., Pa., Mich., W.Va., Mass. Dir. learning ctr. Kirkbride Elem. Sch., Phila., 1970-71, Huron High Sch., Ann Arbor, 1971-73; learning disabilities tutor Brookline (Mass.) Pub. Schs., 1976-82; ednl. cons. Newton, Mass., 1982-84; child care cons. Isabel Make Assocs., Newton, 1984-88; adj. prof. reading and multicultural studies Metro State Coll., Denver, 1989—; pres. Top Hat Gourmet, 1992—; bus. lectr. on The Art of Corp. Giving, 1993—; ednl. counselor Phila. Home for Emotionally Disturbed Girls, 1970; cons. Ann Arbor Pub. Schs., 1971; child care cons. Newton Community Schs., 1985; founding mem. Denver Parenting Ctr., 1989—; chairperson legis. and regulations subcom. Commonwealth of Mass., Boston, 1984-88. ednl. counselor Phila. Home for Emotionally Disturbed Girls, 1970; cons. Ann Arbor Pub. Schs., 1971; child care cons. Newton Cmty. Schs., 1985; founding mem. Denver Parenting Ctr., 1989—; chairperson legis. and regulations subcom. Commonwealth of Mass., Boston, 1984-88; adj. prof. Metro. State Coll., 1984-88, 94—, Cmty. Coll. Denver, 1992—. Founder Temple Shalom Nursery Sch., Newton, 1975; chmn. childcare task force The U. Hosp., Boston U. Med. Ctr., 1985-88; bd. dirs. Greenwood Village Arts and Humanites Coun., 1991—; mem. at large Colo. Consortium Community Arts Couns., 1992—, Greenwood Village Arts and Humanities Coun. (chair A Space of my Own, Parent-Child Art Day), 1991—; mem. steering com. Colo. Alliance for Arts in Edn., 1993. Democrat. Jewish. Avocations: gourmet cooking, swimming. Home and Office: 2600 E Belleview Ave Littleton CO 80121-1627

MAKELA, BENJAMIN R., editor, research director; b. Hancock, Mich., Mar. 23, 1922; s. Charles Robert and Engel (Kruka) M.; m. Betty Virginia Shade, June 26, 1954; 1 son, Gregory Strickler. B.A., George Washington U., 1943; M.A., Stanford, 1954. Statistician Dept. Commerce, 1946, Nat. Fertilizer Assn., 1947-48; research economist U.S. C. of C., 1948-53; asso. dir. Financial Execs. Inst., N.Y.C., 1953-63; editor Financial Exec., 1963-72; research dir. Financial Execs. Research Found., 1966-83; cons., 1983—. Editor: (with Richard F. Vancil) The CFO's Handbook, 1970, How to Use and Invest in Letter Stock, 1970, (with William Chatlos) Strategy of Corporate Tender Offers, 1971, (with D.R. Carmichael) Corporate Financial Reporting: The Benefits and Problems of Disclosure, 1986, (with Mark E. Haskins) The CFO Handbook, 1997: mem. editorial adv. bd. also author chpt. Financial Exec.'s Handbook. Served with AUS, 1943-46, 51-53. Mem. Am. Acctg. Assn., Stanford Alumni Club, Squadron A Club, Halifax Club, Smyrna Yacht Club, Men's Garden Club of New Smyrna Beach, Phi Beta Kappa, Pi Gamma Mu, Omicron Delta Gamma, Sigma Nu. Republican. Baptist. Home: 686 Rochester Ct New Smyrna Beach FL 32168-2105

MAKEPEACE, DARRYL LEE, consulting company executive; b. Pitts., Oct. 24, 1941; s. Thomas Henry Makepeace and Nevada Ruth (Wagener) Desin. BS in Indsl. Engring., Pa. State U., 1969; MBA, Pepperdine U., 1982. Dept. mgr. Procter & Gamble, Cin., 1969-72; plant mgr. CBS Mus. Instruments, Fullerton, Calif., 1972-76; dir. mfg. Frigid Coil/Wolf Range, Whittier, Calif., 1977-79; mgr. materials mgmt. Nat. Supply, Los Nietos, Calif., 1979-85; assoc. prof. mgmt. Calif. State U., Fullerton, 1982-86; mgr. mfg. Nat. Supply, Los Nietos, Calif., 1985-86; program mgr. Armco Cumberland Group, Middletown, Ohio, 1986; ptnr., cons. Armco Cumberland Group, Mason, Ohio, 1986-87; prin., owner Cumberland Group, Cin., 1988—; owner Phoenix Cons., Inc., Cin., 1991-96; owner, pres. D.L. Makepeace & Assocs., West Chester, Ohio, 1991—; assoc. prof. mgmt. Wright State U., Dayton, Ohio, 1987-88, Miami U., Oxford, Ohio, 1988-89. Author: The System, American Iron and Steel Institute, Steel Body Panel Performance Characteristics, 1991; contbr. articles to profl. jours. Served with U.S. Army, 1960-61. Named to Honorable Order of Ky. Cols. Mem. Am. Prodn. and Inventory Control Soc., Inst. Indsl. Engrs., Alpha Pi Mu, Tau Beta Pi, Sigma Tau. Avocations: reading, chess, traveling.

MAKER, CAROL JUNE, gifted and talented educator; b. Caneyville, Ky., Aug. 7, 1948; d. Arnold David and Bernice (Smith) Shartzer. BS, Western Ky. U., 1970; MS, So. Ill. U., 1971; PhD, U. Va., 1978. Cert. elem. edn. tchr. Tchr. Caneyville (Ky.) Pub. Schs., 1970; tchr. of gifted Edwardsville (Ill.) Pub. Sch., 1971; regional supr. Ill. Office Edn., Springfield, 1971-74; adminstrv. intern U.S. Office Edn., Washington, 1974-75; grad. instr. U. Va., Charlottesville, 1976-77, off-campus instr., 1977-78; asst. prof. U. N.Mex., Albuquerque, 1978-81; asst. prof. U. Ariz., Tucson, 1981-83, assoc. prof., 1983-96, prof., 1996—; keynote spkr. World Coun. for Gifted, Oporto, Portugal, 1986, Sydney, Australia, 1989, Victorian Assn for the Gifted, Melbourne, 1996. Author: Teaching Models in Education of Gifted, 1982, 2d edit., 1995, Curriculum Development for the Gifted, 1982, Curriculum Development and Teaching Strategies for Gifted Learners, 2d edit., 1996; coauthor: Intellectual Giftedness in Disabled Persons, 1985, Nurturing Giftedness in Young Children, 1996; editor: (book series) Critical Issues in Education of Gifted, Vol. I, 1986, Vol. II, 1989, Vol. III, 1994; mem. editl. bd. Jour. for Edn. of Gifted, 1977—, Gifted Edn. Internat., 1985—. Mem. H.S. task force Tucson (Ariz.) Unified Sch. Dist., 1983, 85; mem. task force gifted concerns Ariz. State Bd. Edn., Phoenix, 1985-87; steering com. China-U.S. Conf. Edn., 1996—; bd. dirs. Arts Genesis, Inc., Tucson, 1994—. Fulbright scholar U. de las Ams., Mexico City, 1987; Rsch. grantee U.S. Dept. Edn., Office of Bilingual Edn., 1987-89, 93-96, U.S. Dept. Edn., Javits Gifted Edn. Program, 1993—. Mem. Nat. Assn. for Gifted (bd. dirs., sec. 1972-89), Ariz. Assn. for Gifted and Talented (bd. dirs., sec. 1981-87), World Coun. for Gifted and Talented (com. chair 1986-93), Coun. for Exceptional Children (com. chair 1975-94). Democrat. Avocations: photography, yoga, hiking, gardening. Home: 503 E 2nd St Tucson AZ 85705 Office: Univ Ariz Dept Special Edn & Rehab Tucson AZ 85721

MAKHIJA, MOHAN, nuclear medicine physician; b. Bombay, Oct. 1, 1941; came to U.S., 1969; m. Arlene Zambito, Nov. 11, 1978. MD, Bombay U., 1965. Diplomate Am. Bd. Nuclear Medicine, Am. Bd. Radiology; cert. spl. competence in nuclear radiology. Resident in radiology Morristown (N.J.) Meml. Hosp., 1972-75; resident in nuclear medicine Yale-New Haven Hosp., 1975-76; post-doctoral fellow Yale U. Sch. Medicine, New Haven, 1976-77; jr. attending physician Helene Fuld Med. Ctr., Trenton, N.J., 1977-78; acting dir. dept. nuclear medicine Monmouth Med. Ctr., Long Branch, N.J., 1978, dir. nuclear medicine sect., 1979—, asst. attending radiology, 1978-80, assoc. attending radiology, 1980-83, attending radiologist, 1983—; sr. instr. Hahneman U., Phila., 1978-80, clin. asst. prof., 1980-83, clin. assoc. prof., 1983-91, clin. prof., 1991-94, clin. prof. of Radiologic Scis., Med. Coll. of Pa. and Hahnemann U., 1994—; radiol. cons. to N.J. State Bd. Med. Examiners., 1994. Contbr. articles to profl. jours. Fellow ACP, Am. coll. Nuclear Physicians (spkr. ho. of dels. 1992-93), Am. Coll. Radiology; mem. Monmouth County Med. Soc. (pres. 1991-92), Radio Soc. N.J. (chmn. nuclear medicine 1988-94, treas. 1994-95, sec. 1995-96, v.p. 1996-97, pres.-elect 1997-98), Indo-Am. Soc. Nuclear Medicine (pres. 1992-93), Soc. Nuclear Medicine (bd. govs. greater N.Y. chpt. 1992—). Home: 5 High Ridge Rd Ocean NJ 07712-3460 Office: Monmouth Med Ctr 300 2nd Ave Long Branch NJ 07740-6300

MAKHOLM, MARK HENRY, lawyer, former insurance company executive; b. Maple Valley, Wis., Jan. 10, 1915; s. Henry and Emma Dorothy Agnet (Johnson) M.; m. Phylis Shoger, Nov. 11, 1950; children: Linda Marie, Mark Henry, Martha Marie. B.A. magna cum laude, Northland Coll., Ashland, Wis., 1937; JD, U. Wis., 1950. Bar: Wis. 1950, U.S. Supreme Ct 1950. Asst. prof. Northland Coll., 1937-38; high sch. tchr. Washburn, Wis., 1939-41; operational supr. E.I. duPont de Neumours & Co. Inc., also U.S. Rubber Co., Kankakee, Ill., 1941-45; high sch. tchr. West Bend, Wis., 1945-47; engaged in retail clothing bus. West Bend, 1947-48; practice in Ashland, 1950-52; mem. firm Anderson, Fisher, Shannon, O'Brien and Rice, Stevens Point, Wis., 1980-86; with Sentry Ins. a Mut. Co.-Sentry Life Ins. Co., Stevens Point, Wis., 1952-80; v.p., gen. counsel Sentry Ins. a Mut. Co.-Sentry Life Ins. Co., 1962-78, exec. v.p., 1978-80, also dir., until 1980; former dir. Middlesex Ins. Co., Gt. S.W. Fire Ins. Co., The Sentry Corp., Dairyland Ins. Co., Sentry Indemnity Co. Dir. Delta Dental Plan Wis., 1980—. Mem. Am., Wis. bar assns., Internat. Assn. Ins. Counsel, Order of Coif, Phi Delta Phi. Home: 3717 Combs Creek Ln Stevens Point WI 54481-7621

MAKHOUL, JOHN IBRAHIM, electrical engineer, researcher; b. Deirmimas, Lebanon, Sept. 19, 1942; came to U.S., 1964; s. Ibrahim Hanna and Badia (Masoud) M. BEE, Am. U. Beirut, 1964; MEE, Ohio State U., 1965; PhDEE, MIT, 1970. Successively scientist, sr. scientist, supervisory scientist, prin. scientist to chief scientist BBN Corp., Cambridge, Mass., 1970—; rsch. affiliate MIT, Cambridge, 1970—; adj. prof. Northeastern U., Boston, 1982—. Contbr. over 100 articles on speech processing and character recognition by computer and spectral estimation to profl. jours. Recipient Citation Classic award for paper on linear prediction Inst. Scientific Info., 1982. Fellow IEEE, Acoustical Soc. Am.; mem. Signal Processingoc. of IEEE (Sr. award 1978, Tech. Achievement award 1982, Soc. award 1988), Computer Soc. of IEEE, Communications Soc. of IEEE, Info. Theory Soc. of IEEE, Pattern Recognition Soc. Avocation: music. Home: 18 Amberwood Dr Winchester MA 01890-2202 Office: BBN Corp 70 Fawcett St Cambridge MA 02138-1110

MAKI, DENNIS G., medical educator, researcher, clinician; b. River Falls, Wis., May 8, 1940; m. Gail Dawson, 1962; children: Kimberly, Sarah, Daniel. BS in Physics with honors, U. Wis., 1962, MS in Physics, 1964, MD, 1967. Diplomate Am. Bd. Internal Medicine, Am. Bd. Infectious Diseases, Am. Bd. Critical Care Medicine. Physicist, computer programmer Lawrence Radiation Lab., AEC, Livermore, Calif., 1962; intern, asst. resident Harvard Med. unit Boston City Hosp., 1967-69, chief resident, 1972-73; with Hosp. Infections sect. Ctrs. for Disease Control, USPHS, Atlanta, 1969-71; acting chief nat. nosocomial infections study Ctr. for Disease Control, USPHS, Atlanta, 1970-71; sr. resident dept. medicine Mass. Gen. Hosp., 1971-72, clin. and research fellow infectious disease unit, 1973-74; asst. prof. medicine U. Wis., Madison, 1974-78, assoc. prof., 1978-82, prof., 1982—; hosp. epidemiologist, U. Wis. Hosp. and Clinic, Madison, 1974—; Ovid O. Meyer chair in medicine U. Wis., Madison, 1975—, head sec. infectious diseases, 1979—; attending physician Ctr. for Trauma and Life Support U. Wis., 1976—; clinician, rschr., educator in field; mem. program com. Intersci. Conf. on Antimicrobial Agts. and Chemotherapy, 1987-94; mem. Am. Bd. Critical Care Medicine, 1989-95. Sr. assoc. editor Infection Control and Hosp. Epidemiology, 1979-93; mem. editl. bd. Jour. Lab. and Clin. Investigation, 1980-86, Jour. Critical Care, 1985-96, Jour. Infectious Diseases, 1988-90, Critical Care Medicine, 1989-94; contbr. articles to med. jours. Recipient 1st award for disting. rsch. in Antibiotic Rev., 1980, Internat. CIPI award, 1994, numerous teaching awards and hon. lectrs. Fellow ACP, Am. Coll. Chest Physicians, Infectious Diseases Soc. Am. (coun. 1993-96), Soc. for Critical Care Medicine, Surg. Infection Soc.; mem. Soc. Hosp. Epidemiologists Am. (pres. 1990), Ctrl. Soc. for Clin. Rsch., Am. Soc. Microbiology, Am. Fedn. Clin. Rsch., Alpha Omega Alpha (nat. bd. dirs. 1983-89). Office: U Wis Hosp and Clinics H4/574 Madison WI 53792

MAKI, JERROLD ALAN, health system executive; b. Duluth, Minn., Sept. 4, 1947; s. Willio John and Eleanor Edla (Savela) M.; m. Carolyn Helen Dack, Aug. 2, 1969; children: Eric Edward, Emily Miriam, David Dack. BA cum laude, U. Min., Duluth, 1969; MHA, U. Min., Mpls., 1973. Lic. nursing home adminstr., Ohio. Asst. to supr. Investors Diversified Svcs., Inc., Mpls., 1969-71; assoc. adminstr. North Ottawa Community Hosp., Grand Haven, Mich., 1973-77; v.p. St. Mary's Hosp., Grand Rapids, Mich., 1977-80, Bapt. Med. Ctr., Oklahoma City, 1980-85; exec. v.p., COO Svc. Frontiers, Inc., Lafayette, Ind., 1985-86; exec. v.p., COO Mercy Med. Ctr., Springfield, Ohio, 1986-90, pres., CEO, 1990-95, bd. dirs., 1987-95; sr. v.p. Mercy Health System-We. Ohio, Springfield, 1995-96; pres., CEO Mercy Health Sys.-Western Ohio, Springfield, 1996—, also bd. dirs.; sr. v.p. Mercy Health System, Cin., 1996—; chairperson accreditation and quality com. Ohio Hosp. Assn., 1993-96; pres. Mercy Health Ventures, 1996—; chmn. bd. dirs. Mercy Primary Care, 1996—; bd. dirs. Mercy Managed Care, Ltd. Bd. dirs. Mental Health Svcs. Clark County, Springfield, 1987—, Friends of Mercy, Springfield, 1988-95, Springfield Physician-Hosp. Orgn., 1991—; v.p. Springfield Acad. for Cmty. Leadership, 1988-89; bd. deacons for ch., 1990-92, bd. trustees, 1993—, Mercy Found., 1996—. Fellow Am. Coll. Healthcare Execs.; mem. Ohio Hosp. Assn. (bd. dirs., pres.-elect S.W. dist. 1997—), Springfield C. of C., Springfield CountryClub, Rotary. Presbyterian. Avocations: stamp and coin collecting, sailing, golf. Home: 2006 W Mile Rd Springfield OH 45503-2732 Office: Mercy Health Sys-Western Ohio 1 S Limestone St Ste 600 Springfield OH 45502-1243

MAKI, KAZUMI, physicist, educator; b. Takamatsu, Japan, Jan. 27, 1936; s. Toshio and Hideko M.; m. Masako Tanaka, Sept. 21, 1969. B.S., Kyoto U., 1959, Ph.D., 1964. Research asso. Inst. for Math. Scis., Kyoto U., 1964; research asso. Fermi Inst., U. Chgo., 1964-65; asst. prof. physics U. Calif., San Diego, 1965-67; prof. Tohoku U., Sendai, Japan, 1967-74; vis. prof. Universite Paris-Sud, Orsay, France, 1969-70; prof. physics U. So. Calif., Los Angeles, 1974—; vis. prof. Inst. Laue-Langevin, U. Paris-Sud, France, 1979-80, Max Planck Inst. fur Festkorper Forschung, Stuttgart, Germany, 1986-87, U. Paris-7, 1990, Hokkaido U., Sapporo, Japan, 1993, Centre de Recherche sur Tres Basses Temperatures, Grenoble, France, 1993-94, Instituto de Ciencia de Materiales, Madrid, Spain, 1994. Assoc. editor Jour. Low Temperature Physics, 1969-91; contbr. articles to profl. jours. Guggenheim fellow, 1979-80, Japan Soc. Promotion of Sci. fellow, 1993; Fulbright scholar, 1964-65; recipient Nishina prize, 1972, Alexander von Humboldt award, 1986-87. Fellow Japan Soc. Promotion of Sci., Am. Phys. Soc.; mem. AAAS, Phys. Soc. Japan. Office: U So Calif Dept Physics Los Angeles CA 90089-0484

MAKINEN, MARVIN WILLIAM, biophysicist, educator; b. Chassell, Mich., Aug. 19, 1939; s. William John and Milga Katarina (Myllyla) M.; m. Michele de Groot, July 30, 1966; children: Eric William, Stephen Matthew. AB, U. Pa., 1961; postgrad., Free U. Berlin, 1960-61; MD, U. Pa., 1968; DPhil, U. Oxford, Eng., 1976. Diplomate Am. Bd. Med. Examiners. Intern Columbia-Presbyn. Med. Ctr., N.Y.C., 1968-69; rsch. assoc. NIH, Bethesda, Md., 1969-71; vis. fellow U. Oxford, Eng., 1971-74; asst. prof. biophysics U. Chgo., 1974-80, assoc. prof., 1980-86, prof. biochemistry and molecular biology, 1986—, chmn. dept., 1988-93; established investigator Am. Heart Assn., 1975-80; lectr. in field. Contbr. numerous articles to profl. jours. Mem., advisor The Raoul Wallenberg Com. of U.S., 1991—. Sr. surgeon USPHS, 1969-71. John E. Fogarty Sr. Internat. fellow, 1984-85, European Molecular Biology Orgn. sr. fellow, 1984-85, NIH spl. fellow, 1971-74, Berquist fellow Am. Scandinavian Found., 1970, John Simon Guggenheim fellow, 1997-98. Fellow Am. Inst. Chemists; mem. Am. Chem. Soc., Biophys. Soc., Am. Soc. Biochemistry and Molecular Biology, The Protein Soc., AAAS. Office: U Chgo Dept Biochemistry/Mol Biol 920 E 58th St Chicago IL 60637-1432

MAKINO, SHOJIRO (MIKE MAKINO), chemicals executive; b. Roppongi, Tokyo, Japan, June 5, 1929; s. Taro and Tomiko M.; m. Sachi Hirose, Apr. 24, 1965; 1 child, Genta. BA, Keio U., Tokyo, 1951; MBA, U. Oreg., 1961. Salesman Getz Bros. Shokai, Tokyo, 1951-55; mgr. indsl. sales Getz Bros. and Co., Okinawa, Japan, 1955-59; mgmt. trainee Getz Bros. and Co., San Francisco, 1959-61; sales rep., mgr. Far East Omark Industries, Inc., Portland, Oreg., 1962-67; v.p., gen. mgr. Omark Japan, Inc., Tokyo, 1967-69; v.p. W.R. Grace K.K., Tokyo, 1969-70; pres. W.R. Grace K.K. changed to Grace Japan K.K. (1985), Tokyo, 1970—; corp. v.p. W.R. Grace and Co., N.Y.C., 1988—; v.p. W.R. Grace & Co., Asia Pacific, 1992—, also sr. advisor, bd. dirs., 1995; vice chmn. Polyfibron Techs., Inc., 1995. Past mem. Prime Min.'s Deregulation Com., 1994; mem. Govt. Adminstrn. Com. Mem. Am. C. of C. (bd. govs. Tokyo chpt. 1988—), Tokyo Golf Club, Hakone Country Club, Hodogaya Country Club, Tokyo East Rotary Club. Office: Polyfibron Techs Inc. 2-4-1 Nishi ShinjukuNS Bldg 6F, Tokyo 163-08, Japan

MAKIOS, VASILIOS, electronics educator; b. Kavala, Greece, Dec. 31, 1938; s. Thrassivoulos and Sophia M. Dipl.Ing., Tech. U. Munich, 1962; Dr. Ing., Max Planck Inst. for Plasmaphysics and Tech. U. Munich, 1966. Profl. engr., Ger., Ont., Greece. Research assoc. Max Planck Inst., Munich, 1962-67; asst. prof. dept. electronics Carleton U., Ottawa, Ont., 1967-70, assoc. prof., 1970-73, prof., 1973-77; prof. and head electromagnetics lab. U. Patras, Greece, 1975—; cons. in field; dean engring. U. Patras, 1980-82; hon. rsch. prof. Carleton U., 1977—. Contbr. over 120 articles to profl. jours. Patentee in field. Recipient Silver medal German Elec. Engring. Soc., 1984; numerous grants for research in Can., Greece and European community. Mem. IEEE, German Phys. Soc., German Inst. Elec. Engrs., Can. Assn. Physicists & Engrs., Greek Tech. Chamber. Greek Orthodox. Avocations: classical music; swimming; skiing. Home: 2 Lefkosias St, 26441 Patras 41, Greece Office: U Patras, Lab Electromagnetics, Patras Greece

MAKISE, YOSHIHIRO, lawyer; b. Osaka, Japan, Dec. 16, 1930; s. Yoshihiko and Keiko (Matsumoto) M. BL, U. Tokyo, 1955; D Pvt. Internat. Law, U. Paris, 1975. With Dai-Tokyo Fire & Marine Ins. Co., Tokyo, 1955-59; legal apprentice Legal Rsch. and Tng. Inst., Supreme Ct. Japan, Tokyo, 1960-62; staff lawyer Dai-ichi Tokyo Bar Assn., 1962-67; legal cons. in collaboration with French lawyers Paris, 1968-75; prin. Makise Law Office, Tokyo, 1975—. Author: The Legal Theory of Money, 1991, New Civil Law, 1992, Money and the Future of Japan, 1993. Scholar of Boursier technique Dept. Fgn. Affairs, Govt. of France, 1967-68. Mem. Japan Assn. Internat. Econ. Law, French-Japanese Soc. Legal Sci., The Acad. Experts (London). Avocations: reading, classical music, photography, travel, museums. Home: 1-6-15-408 Kichijoji-Minami, Musashino Tokyo 180, Japan Office: Makise Law Office, 1-6-15-408 Kichijoji-Minami, Musashino Tokyo 180, Japan

MAKKAY, MAUREEN ANN, broadcast executive; b. Chgo.; d. John Paul and Bernice Ann (Williams) Monaghan; m. Albert Makkay, Oct. 20, 1962; children: Allison, Albert Jr., Colleen. BA, U. R.I., 1974. Cert. secondary sch. tchr., Mass. Adminstr. Ednl. Records Bur., Wellesley, Mass., 1979-81; local sales mgr. Sta. WKZE, Orleans, Mass., 1981-83; nat. sales mgr. Sta. WKFM, Syracuse, N.Y., 1983-85; pres. Sta. WPXC-FM, Hyannis, Mass., 1987—; v.p. Sta. WRZE, Nantucket, Mass., Sta. WCIB-FM, Falmouth, Mass. Pres. Cape and Islands unit Am. Cancer Soc., 1988-91, bd. dirs., 1989-95; mem. pers. bd. Town of Barnstable, Mass., 1989-94, chmn., 1990-91; bd. dirs. Cape Cod Alcoholism Intervention and Rehab., Inc., 1995—. Mem. Bus. and Profl. Women Cape Cod (bd. dirs. 1989—), Am. Women in Radio and TV, Nat. Assn. Broadcasters. Office: Sta WPXC-FM Radio 154 Barnstable Rd Hyannis MA 02601-2930

MAKOUS, WALTER LEON, visual scientist, educator; s. Lawrence and Ruth Lorraine (Luehring) M.; m. Marilyn Ann Carlson, Feb. 2, 1958 (div. 1974); children: Ann, James, Matthew; m. Joyce Brown Menconi, 1974 (div. 1981); m. Barbara Anne Duggins, Apr. 29, 1982. B.S., U. Wis., 1958; M.Sc., Brown U., 1961, Ph.D., 1964. Mem. staff IBM, Yorktown Heights, N.Y., 1963-66; asst. prof. psychology U. Wash., 1966-69, lectr. in physiology and biophysics, 1966-69, assoc. prof. psychology, 1969-74, prof. psychology, 1974-79; prof. psychology, ophthalmology and visual sci. U. Rochester, 1979-95; prof. brain and cognitive sci., ophthalmology & visual sci., 1995—; dir. Ctr. for Visual Sci. U. Rochester, 1979-90; northwest rep., charter mem.

steering com. West Coast Regional Consortium Univs. in Neuroscis., 1976-79; mem. coun. on energy saving through more efficient lighting, NAS-NRC, 1978-79, night vision coun., 1985-86; chmn. ctr. symposium U. Rochester, 1981-82; sensory processes panelist NSF, Washington, 1977-82, mem. adv. com, applied sci. and rsch. applications policy, 1978-81, rev. com. Presdl. Young Investigator award program, 1984; vis. scientist IBM Rsch., 1970-71. Cons. editor Sensory Processes, 1977-79, Jour. of the Optical Soc. Am., 1982-86; contbr. over 100 articles to profl. jours. Served with USNR, 1953-55. Grantee Nat. Eye Inst., 1969—; NSF grantee, 1959-62, 81-82. Fellow AAAS, Am. Psychol. Soc., Optical Soc. Am. (mem. coord. vision and physiol. optics com. 1983-89, coord. vision and med. optics com. 1983-89, publs. com. 1985-89, chmn. fellows and hon. mems. com. 1986, editor vision and color 1982-86, feature editor applied vision 1989-90); mem. Assn. Rsch. in Vision and Ophthalmology (chmn. sect. pshcyo-physics 1977), Soc. Neurosci., Psychonomic Soc., Human Factors and Ergonomics, Am. Nat. Standards Inst./Human Factor & Ergonomics Sic-100 (rev. com. 1992—). Office: U Rochester Ctr for Visual Sci Rochester NY 14627

MAKOVSKY, KENNETH DALE, public relations executive; b. St. Louis, Oct. 3, 1940; s. Jack and Minnie (Freedman) M.; m. Phyllis Ann Peck, Oct. 15, 1972; children: Evan, Matthew. BA, Washington U., St. Louis, 1962, JD, 1965. Asst. account exec. Curtis Hoxter Inc., N.Y.C., 1965-66; account exec. Ruder & Finn Inc., N.Y.C., 1966-69; account exec. Harshe-Rotman & Druck, N.Y.C., 1970-72, v.p., 1973-75, sr. v.p., 1975-79, sr. v.p., dep. gen. mgr. N.Y. office, 1978-79; founder, pres. Makovsky & Co., Inc., N.Y.C., 1979—; founder, past pres. Internat. Pub. Rels. Exchange; chmn. Makovsky & Co., Inc., N.Y.C. Contbr. articles to profl. pubs. Speechwriter 17th Dist. Congl. Campaign, N.Y.C., 1972; v.p. Am. Jewish Com. N.Y., N.Y.C., 1985—, N.Y. bd. dirs., 1978—, nat. bd. govs., 1993—, chmn. Diplomatic Outreach, 1987—; bd. dirs. Postgrad. Ctr. for Mental Health, N.Y.C., 1981—. Recipient Gold Quill IABC, 1990, Cipra award Inside Pub. Rels., 1994; named Pub. Rels. All Star, Inside Pub. Rels., 1992; co. named one of ten fastest growing pub. rels. firms in U.S., O'Dwyer Rankings, 1985, 86, 87, 89, 90, 91, one of four top pub. rels. firms in N.Y.C., Small Agy. Yr. Inside Pub. Rels., 1990, among 12 Best Managed Firms in U.S., 1993. Mem. Pub. Rels. Soc. Am. (Silver Anvil award for Chem. Spltys. Mfrs. Assn. 1978, for Am. Superconductor, 1994), Nat. Investor Rels. Inst., Washington U. Alumni Club N.Y.C. (pres. 1970), India House, 200 East Club (N.Y.C.), Arthur Page Soc. Avocations: theatre, movies, travel. Office: Makovsky & Co Inc 575 Lexington Ave New York NY 10022*

MAKOWKA, LEONARD, medical educator, surgeon; b. Toronto, Ont., Can., Nov. 25, 1953. MD, U. Toronto, Can., 1977, MS in Pathology, 1979, PhD in Pathology, 1982. Intern in surgery The Mount Sinai Hosp., Toronto, Ont., Can., 1977-78; with gen. surgery course U. Toronto, Can., 1978; Can. fellow med. rsch. coun., dept. surgery and pathology Toronto Gen. Hosp., U. Toronto, Can., 1978-82; rsch. assoc., dept. surgery and pathology U. Toronto, Can., 1982; asst. resident gen. surgery Toronto Gen. Hosp., Can., 1982; sr. resident gen. surgery Women's Coll. Hosp., 1983; chief resident surgery Toronto Western Hosp., Can., 1983-84; fellow in hepatobiliary surgery Toronto Gen. Hosp., Can., 1984-85; rsch. assoc. dept. surgery and pathology U. Toronto, Can., 1984-85, asst. prof. dept. surgery and pathology, 1985; asst. prof. surgery, dept. surgery U. Pitts., Pa., 1986-87, assoc. prof. surgery, dept. surgery, 1987-89; dir. surgery and transplantation svcs., dept. surgery Cedars Sinai Med. Ctr., 1989-92; prof. surgery UCLA Med. Sch., 1989—; chmn. dept. surgery, dir. transplantation svcs. Cedars Sinai Med Ctr., 1992—; exec. dir. comprehensive liver disease & treatment ctr. St. Vincent Med. Ctr., L.A., 1995—; vis. asst. prof. U. Pitts., Pa., 1985; lectr. in the field. Contbr. to over 345 jours. Recipient Charles E. Frost Bronze medal, 1979, Royal Coll. Physicians and Surgeons of Can. Surgery medal, 1980, 85, First Place award Second Annual Assembly of Gen. Surgeons, 1979, Gallie Bateman Essay award, 1980, Davis and Geck Surgical Essay award, 1981-82, Can. Found. of Ileitis and Colitis Rsch. award, 1981, U. Toronto Rsch. Papers award, 1981; Charles E. Frost scholar, 1979, Schering scholar Am. Coll. Surgeons, 1981; Graham Campbell fellow Faculty of Medicine U. Toronto, 1982, Centennial fellow Med. Rsch. Coun. of Can., 1985-87; named Humanitarian of the Yr. World Children's Transplant Fund, 1992. Mem. Alpha Omega Alpha. Office: St Vincent Med Ctr Institute Plz 2200 W 3rd St Los Angeles CA 90057-1932*

MAKOWSKI, EDGAR LEONARD, obstetrician and gynecologist; b. Milw., Oct. 27, 1927; s. Adam and Ernestine (Horn) M.; m. Patricia M. Nock, Nov. 1, 1952; children: Peter, James, Ann, Mary, Thomas, Paul. B.S., Marquette U., 1951, M.D., 1954. Intern Deaconess Hosp., Milw., 1954-55; resident in Ob/Gyn U. Minn., Mpls., 1955-59; asst. prof. U. Minn., 1959-66, asso. prof., 1966; asso. prof. Ob/Gyn U. Colo., Denver, 1966-69; prof. U. Colo., 1969-93, chmn. dept., 1976-88, prof. emeritus, 1993—. Contbr. articles to sci. jours., chpts. to books. Served with AUS, 1946-47. NIH spl. fellow in physiology Yale U., 1963. Mem. Am. Gynecol. and Obstet. Soc. (pres.), Am. Coll. Obstetricians and Gynecologists, Soc. Gynecol. Investigators, Central Assn. Obstetricians and Gynecologists, Colo. Soc. Ob/Gyn., Perinatal Research Soc. (pres.). Roman Catholic. Achievements include radioactive microsphere technique for determination of organ blood flow.

MAKOWSKI, M. PAUL, electronics research executive; b. Warsaw, Poland, Jan. 15, 1922; Arrived in U.S. July 1949.; s. Antoni and Stanislawa (Leszowska) M.; m. Eugenia Sawczyn, Dec. 1, 1945; children: Paul, Teresa. BA in Chem., Case Western Reserve U., 1957, MS in Physical Chem., 1961, PhD in Electrochem., 1964. Mgr. Smith Phoenix Co., Cleve., 1950-55; chemist Clevite Research Ctr., Clevite Corp., Cleve., 1955-64; mgr. chemistry Materials Research Lab., Gould Inc., Cleve., 1964-73; assoc. dir. Materials Research Gould Inc., Cleve.; dir. Materials Research Lab., Gould Inc., Cleve., 1976-80; v.p. tech. adminstrn. Gould Inc., Rolling Meadows, Ill., 1980-81, v.p. scientific affairs, 1981-87; pres. TECTRA Cons. Inc., Rolling Meadows, Ill., 1988-93; cons. Rolling Meadows, 1994—; mem. Frontiers in Chem. Com. Cleve. 1976-80; bd. dirs. Microelectronics and Computer Corp. Austin, Tex. 1986-87. Inventor several patents in electrodeposition and catalysis. Mem. Ill. Gov.'s Commn. on Sci. and Tech. Chgo., 1986-87, Tech. Commercialization Coun. Ill. Dept. Commerce and Community Affairs. Mem. Am. Chem. Soc., Electrochem. Soc. Chgo., Materials Rsch. Avocation: stamp collecting. Home: 305 Shady Dr Palatine IL 60067-7551

MAKRI, NANCY, chemistry educator; b. Athens, Greece, Sept. 5, 1962; came to the U.S., 1985; d. John and Vallie (Tsakona) M.; m. Martin Gruebele, July 9, 1992; children: Alexander Makris Gruebele, Valerie Gruebele. BS, U. Athens, 1985; PhD, U. Calif., Berkeley, 1989. Teaching asst. U. Calif., Berkeley, 1985-87; rsch. asst. U. Calif., 1986-89; jr. fellow Harvard U., Cambridge, Mass., 1989-91; asst. prof. U. Ill., Urbana, 1991-96, assoc. prof., 1996—. Recipient Beckman Young Investigator award Arnold & Mabel Beckman Found., 1993, Ann. medal Internat. Acad. Quantum Molecular Sci., 1995; named NSF Young Investigator, 1993; Packard fellow for sci. and engring. David and Lucille Packard Found., 1993, Sloan Rsch. fellow Alfred Sloan Found., 1994, Cottrell scholar Rsch. Corp., 1994. Home: 2208 Wyld Dr Urbana IL 61801-6753 Office: U Ill at Urbana Dept Chem 601 S Goodwin Ave Urbana IL 61801-3617

MAKRIANES, JAMES KONSTANTIN, JR., management consultant; b. Springfield, Mass., Jan. 15, 1925; s. James K. and Clara (Allen) M.; m. Judith Alden Erdmann, Sept. 30, 1960; children—Mary, James, Susan, Jane, Mahady. B.A., Amherst Coll., 1949. V.p., gen. mgr. Nat. Paper Box Co. and Nat. Games, Inc., Springfield, 1949-59; merchandising and acct. exec. Young & Rubicam, Inc., N.Y.C., 1959-63; v.p., acct. supr. Young & Rubicam, Inc., 1963-67, sr. v.p., mgmt. supr., 1963-73, exec. v.p., dir., 1973-78; sr. v.p., dir. Haley Assocs., Inc., N.Y.C., 1978-80, pres., 1980—, chief exec. officer, 1985-89; ptnr., dir. Ward & Howell Internat., Inc., N.Y.C., 1989-95; dir. Webb Johnson Assocs., N.Y.C., 1995—. Trustee Boys' Club N.Y., 1976—. With USNR, 1943-46. Mem. Maidstone Club, Racquet and Tennis Club, Links. Home: 415 E 52nd St New York NY 10022-6424 Office: Webb Johnson Assocs 280 Park Ave New York NY 10017-1216

MAKRIS, ANDREAS, composer; b. Salonica, Greece, Mar. 7, 1930; came to U.S., 1950, naturalized, 1962; s. Christos and Kallitza (Andreou) M.; m. Margaret Lubbe, June 12, 1959; children: Christos, Myron. Grad. with highest honors, Nat. Conservatory, Salonica, 1950; postgrad., Kansas City (Mo.) Conservatory, 1953, Mannes Coll. Music, 1956, Aspen Music Festival, 1956-57, Fontainbleau (France) Sch., 1958; pupil of Nadia Boulanger. adv. to Maestro Rostropovich for new music, 1979-90. Compositions premiered and performed in U.S., Can., S.Am., Europe, Japan, USSR; composer-in-residence Nat. Symphony Orch., 1979-90; prin. works include Scherzo for Violins, 1966, Concerto for Strings, 1966, Aegean Festival, 1967, Anamnesis, 1970, Viola Concerto, 1970, Concertino for Trombone, 1970, Efthymia, 1972, Five Miniatures, 1972, Mediterranean Holiday, 1974, Fantasy and Dance for Saxaphone, 1974, Chromatokinesis, 1978, In Memory, 1979, Variations and Song for Orchestra, 1979, Fanfare Alexander 1980, Fourth of July March, 1982, Violin Concerto, 1983, Nature-Life Symphonic Poem, 1983, Caprice "Tonatonal", 1986, Intrigues for Solo Clarinet and Wind Ensemble, 1987, Concertante for Violin, Cello, Clarinet, French Horn, Percussion and Orchestra, 1988, Sonata for Cello and Piano, 1989, Symphony to Youth for Full Orchestra, 1989, Trilogy for Orchestra, 1990, Polychornion Chorus and Orchestra, 1990, Procession Chorus and Brass Quintet, 1990, Intrigues for Solo Clarinet, Strings, Brass and Percussion, 1991, Concertino for Organ, Flute and Strings, 1992, A Symphony for Soprano and Strings, 1992, Woodwind Quintet, 1993, Decalog (ten songs for young students), 1995, Antithesis for Orch., 1995, J.F.K. Commemorative Fanfare for Strings and Snare Drum, 1995, Concerto for Violin and Strings, 1996, Introduction and Kalamatianos for solo trumpet, strings, snare and bass drums, 1997; also works for violin, string quartets, voice quintets, duets and arrangements of Paganini, Bach, Corelli and Fiorillo. Recipient citation Greek Govt., 1980; Student Program grantee Phillips U., Enid, Okla., 1950, grantee Nat. Endowment Arts, 1967, grantee Martha Baird Rockefeller Fund, 1970, grantee Damrosh Found., 1958. Mem. ASCAP (ann. awards 1980-97), Internat. Platform Assn. Greek Orthodox. Home: 11204 Oak Leaf Dr Silver Spring MD 20901-1313 Office: Nat Symphony Orch Kennedy Ctr Washington DC 20566 *Two important elements have contributed tremendously to my composing: As a child I was in the midst of war in Greece, and, while all wars are terrible, it taught me both self-discipline and an appreciation for simplicity. Just being alive and able to compose makes me very happy. As a student I was not able to have a piano, the most valuable instrument for a composer. I learned to write with only a pencil and paper for full orchestra, and this liberated me both musically and practically.*

MAKSYMOWICZ, JOHN, electrical engineer; b. Bklyn., Feb. 3, 1956; s. Theodore John and Helen Mary (Kisinski) M. BEE with highest honors, Pratt Inst., Bklyn., 1983. Elec. engr. RF and digital automated test equipment IBM, Poughkeepsie, N.Y., 1983; elec. engr. AWACS airborne early warning radar Grumman Aerospace Corp., Bethpage, N.Y., 1983-87; elec. engr. radar and spread spectrum comm. Plessey Electronics, Totowa, N.J., 1987-88; sr. mem. tech. staff, radar design and systems engring. The Aerospace Corp., L.A., 1989—; sr. mem. tech. staff, radar design and engring. The Aerospace Corp., Herndon, Va., 1995—. Cook-Marsh scholar Pratt Inst., 1979-83, Samuel Brown scholar, 1979-83, Fred G. Flickinger scholar, 1980-83. Mem. IEEE, SPIE, U.S. Space Found., Old Crows Assn., Tau Beta Pi (pres. coll. chpt. 1981-82), Eta Kappa Nu (pres. coll. chpt. 1981-82). Roman Catholic. Avocations: photography, reading, music, running, astronomy.

MAKUPSON, AMYRE PORTER, television station executive; b. River Rouge, Mich., Sept. 30, 1947; d. Rudolph Hannibal and Amyre Ann (Porche) Porter; m. Walter H. Makupson, Nov. 1, 1975; children: Rudolph Porter, Amyre Nisi. BA, Fisk U., 1970; MA, Am. U., Washington, 1972. Asst. dir. news Sta. WGPR-TV, Detroit, 1975-76; dir. pub. rels. Mich. Health Maintenance Orgn., Detroit, 1974-76, Kirwood Gen. Hosp., Detroit, 1976-77; mgr. pub. affairs, news anchor Sta. WKBD-TV, Southfield, Mich., 1977—, Children's Miracle Network Telethon, 1989—. Mem. Co-Ette Club, Inc., Met. Detroit Teen Conf. Coalition; mem. adv. com., bd. dirs. Alzheimers Assn.; mem. exec. com. March of Dimes; pres. bd. dirs. Detroit Wheelchair Athletic Assn.; bd. dirs. Providence Hosp. Found., Sickle Cell Assn., Kids In Need of Direction, Drop-out Prevention Collaborative, Merrill Palmer Inst. Recipient Emmy award for best commentary NATAS, 1993, 12 Emmy nominations NATAS, Editorial Best Feature award AP, Media award UPI, Oakland County Bar Assn., TV Documentary award, Detroit Press Club, numerous svc. awards including Arthritis Found. Mich., Mich. Mchts. Assn., DAV, Jr. Achievement, City of Detroit, Salvation Army, Spirit award City of Detroit, Spirit award City of Pontiac, Golden Heritage award Little Rock Bapt. Ch., 1993; named Media Person of the Yr. So. Christian Leadership Conf., 1994, Humanitarian of the Yr. March of Dimes, 1995. Mem. Pub. Rels. Soc. Am., Am. Women in Radio and TV (Outstanding Achievement award 1981, Outstanding Woman in TV Top Mgmt. 1993, Mentor award 1993), Women in Communications, Nat. Acad. TV Arts and Scis., Detroit Press Club, Ad-Craft. Roman Catholic. Office: 26955 W 11 Mile Rd Southfield MI 48034-2292

MALA, THEODORE ANTHONY, physician, consultant; b. Santa Monica, Calif., Feb. 3, 1946; s. Ray and Galina (Liss) M.; children: Theodore S., Galina T.; m. Cynthia A. Mala, 1996; 1 stepchild, Rebecca Smith. BA in Philosophy, DePaul U., 1972; MD, Autonomous U., Guadalajara, Mex., 1976; MPH, Harvard U., 1980. Spl. asst. for health affairs Alaska Fedn. Natives, Anchorage, 1977-78; chief health svcs. Alaska State Div. of Corrections, Anchorage, 1978-79; assoc. prof., founder, dir. Inst. for Circumpolar Health Studies, U. Alaska, Anchorage, 1982-90; founder Siberian med. rsch. program U. Alaska, Anchorage, 1982, founder Magadan (USSR) med. rsch. program, 1988; commr. Health and Social Svcs. State of Alaska, Juneau, 1990-93; pres. chief exec. officer Ted Mala, Inc., Anchorage, 1993—; pres., ptnr. Mexican-Siberian Trading Co., Monterrey, Mex., 1994—; mem. Alaska rsch. and publs. com. Indian Health Svc., USPHS, 1987-90; advisor Nordic Coun. Meeting, WHO, Greenland, 1985; mem. Internat. Organizing Com., Circumpolar Health Congress, Iceland, 1992-93; chmn. bd. govs. Alaska Psychiat. Inst., Anchorage, 1990-93; cabinet mem. Gov. Walter J. Hickel, Juneau, 1990-93; advisor humanitarian aid to Russian Far East U.S. Dept. State, 1992—; cons. USAID on U.S.-Russian Health Programs, 1994. Former columnist Tundra Times; contbr. articles to profl. jours. Trustee United Way Anchorage, 1978-79; chmn. bd. trustees Alaska Native Coll., 1993—. Recipient Gov.'s award, 1988, Outstanding Svc. award Alaska Commr. Health, 1979, Ministry of Health citation USSR Govt., 1989, Citation award Alaska State Legislature, 1989, 90, 94, Commendation award State of Alaska, 1990, Alaska State Legislature, 1994, Honor Kempton Svc. to Humanity award, 1989, citation Med. Comty. of Magadan region, USSR, 1989; Nat. Indian fellow U.S. Dept. Edn., 1979. Mem. Assn. Am. Indian Physicians, N.Y. Acad. Scis., Internat. Union for Circumpolar Health (permanent sec.-gen. 1987-90, organizing com. 8th Internat. Congress on Circumpolar Health 1987-90). Avocations: cross-country skiing, hiking, photography, travel. Office: 205 E Dimond Blvd Ste 544 Anchorage AK 99515-1909 *Personal philosophy: Progress in the North will come only when circumpolar countries put aside their geopolitical thinking and work together as one northern family.*

MALABRE, ALFRED LEOPOLD, JR., journalist, author; b. N.Y.C., Apr. 23, 1931; s. Alfred Leopold and Marie (Leonard) M.; m. Mary Patricia Wardropper, July 28, 1956; children: Richard C., E. Ann, John A. B.A., Yale U., 1952. Copy editor Hartford (Conn.) Courant, 1957-58; successively reporter, Bonn bur. chief, econs. editor, news editor and Outlook columnist Wall St. Jour., 1958-94, news editor, 1969-94; contbg. editor Harvard Bus. Review, 1995—. Author: Understanding the Economy: For People Who Can't Stand Economics, 1976, America's Dilemma: Jobs vs. Prices, 1978, Investing for Profit in the Eighties, 1982, Beyond Our Means, 1987, Understanding the New Economy, 1988, Within Our Means, 1991, Lost Prophets, 1993. Served with USNR, 1953-56, Korea. Poynter fellow, 1976; Hoover Instn. fellow, 1991; recipient Eccles prize Columbia U., 1988. Mem. Authors Guild, Pilgrim Soc. U.S., Union Club, Nat. Golf Links Am. Address: PO Box 208 Quogue NY 11959

MALACARNE, C. JOHN, insurance company executive, lawyer; b. St. Louis, Dec. 26, 1941; s. Claude John and Virginia E. (Miller) M.; m. Kathleen M. Morris, Aug. 27, 1966; children: Tracy, Kristen, Lisa. AA, Harris-Stowe State Coll., 1962; BS in Pub. Adminstrn., U. Mo., 1964, JD, 1967. Bar: Mo. 1967. Asst. counsel Kansas City (Mo.) Life, 1967-71, assoc. counsel, 1971-74, asst. gen. counsel, 1974-76, assoc. gen. counsel, 1976-80, gen. counsel, 1980-81, v.p., gen. counsel, sec., 1981—; bd. dirs. Kansas City Life Ins. Co., Sunset Life Ins. Co. Am., Calif. Life Ins. Guaranty Assn.; sec., bd. dirs. Old Am. Ins. Co. Sec., bd. dirs. Mid-Continent coun. Girl Scouts U.S.A., Kansas City, 1986-88; v.p., bd. dirs. Kansas City Eye Bank, 1986-91; pres., bd. dirs. Shepherd's Ctr., Kansas City, 1982-84; bd. dirs. Shepherd's Ctr. Internat., 1986-92, Community Mental Health Svcs. Found., sec. rsch., 1992-94, v.p., 1995—; mem. Bd. Edn. Consolidated Sch. Dist. #4, Jackson County, Mo., 1989-91. Mem. ABA, Kansas City Met. Bar Assn. (vice chmn. corp. counsel com. 1986-87, vice chmn. corp. law 1993-94, chmn. corp. law com. 1994-95), Lawyers Assn. Kansas City (bd. dirs. 1976), Internat. Assn. Def. Counsel (chmn. accident health and life sect. 1982-84, ins. exec. com. 1986, v.p., mem. exec. com. 1988-90), Jr. C. of C. (bd. dirs. 1972), Kiwanis (pres. Kansas City 1975-76). Home: 604 Tam O Shanter Dr Kansas City MO 64145-1240 Office: Kansas City Life Ins Co PO Box 419139 Kansas City MO 64141-6139

MALACH, MONTE, physician; b. Jersey City, Aug. 15, 1926; s. Charles and Yetta (Pascher) M.; m. Ann Elaine Glazer, June 15, 1952 (dec. June 1989); children: Barbara Sandra, Cathie Tara, Matthew David; m. Barbara Meryl Lipstein, Dec. 24, 1994; stepchildren: Heather Ilene, Jennifer Beth, Matthew Howard. BA, U. Mich., 1949, MD, 1949. Diplomate Am. Bd. Internal Medicine, Nat. Bd. Med. Examiners. Intern Beth Israel Hosp., Boston, 1949-50; resident Beth Israel Hosp., 1950-51, chief resident, 1951-52; chief resident Kings County Hosp., Bklyn., 1954-55; practice medicine specializing in internal medicine and cardiology Bklyn., 1955—; dir. CCU Bklyn. Hosp., 1965-91, dir. emeritus CCU, 1991—; med. dir., annual coord. Medicare IPRO Downstate N.Y., 1990—; pres. profl. staff Bklyn. Hosp., 1966-69, chmn. med. bd., 1971-72; attending staff Caledonian Hosp., pres. profl. staff, 1984-85; pres. profl. staff Bklyn. Hosp.-Caledonian Hosp., 1987-89, chmn. med. bd., 1988-89; cons. Kings County Hosp.; tchg. fellow Tufts U. Med. Sch., 1951-52; instr. medicine Downstate Med. Ctr., Bklyn., 1955-59, clin. asst. prof. medicine, 1959-68, clin. assoc. prof., 1969-76, clin. prof., 1976—; clin. prof. medicine NYU Med. Ctr., 1994—; bd. dirs. Bay St. Landing One Owners Corp., 1985-87; v.p. Ocean View Condos, 1989-90, pres., 1990-95; med. dir. IPRO Medicare Rev., N.Y. State, 1990—. Kings County committeeman Democratic Party, 1964, 65. Served with USNR, 1944-46, to 1st lt. M.C. U.S. Army, 1952-54. Recipient 1st Prize for Crisis Mgmt. Habitat Mag., 1987. Fellow Am. Coll. Chest Physicians, ACP, Am. Coll. Cardiology (task force Health Care Quality Improvement Initiative 1996—); mem. AMA (chmn. sect. coun. ofr internal medicine 1980), N.Y. Heart Assn., Am. Soc. Internal Medicine (trustee 1975-79, sec.-treas. 1979—, pres. elect 1981, pres. 1982-83, chmn. investment com. 1985-93), N.Y. State Soc. Internal Medicine (pres. 1973-74, dir. 1966-84, chmn. Bklyn. chpt., v.p. 1971, award of merit 1978), Bklyn. Soc. Internal Medicine (mem. council 1965, pres. 1969-72), Med. Soc. State of N.Y. (chmn. sect. internal medicine 1976, chmn. med. care ins. com. 1988-93), Federated Council for Internal Medicine (chmn. 1979-80), Med. Soc. County Kings (censor 1985-91). Office: 55 Rugby Rd Brooklyn NY 11226-2607 *There is a place for hard work, scrupulous ethics and pride of accomplishment. A great marriage and a fine close family are buffers against adversity.*

MALAFRONTE, DONALD, health executive; b. Bklyn., Dec. 16, 1931; s. Pasquale and Amalia (Castaldo) M.; m. Diane Freedenberg, Jan. 7, 1960 (dec. Nov. 14, 1970); children: Philip, Victor.; m. Hillary Demby, Oct. 30, 1982. B.S., NYU, 1954. Reporter L.I. Daily Press, 1956-58; reporter, editor Newark Star-Ledger, 1958-65, art columnist, 1963-70; adminstrv. asst. to mayor of Newark, 1965-70; dir. Newark Model Cities Program, 1967-70, Newark Community Devel. Adminstrn., 1968-70; chief urban field operations N.J. Regional Med. Program, 1970-73; pres. Urban Health Inst., Roseland, N.J., 1973—; cons. to hosps., local govts., 1970—. Author articles in field. Served with AUS, 1954-56. Recipient Joyce Kilmer fiction prize NYU, 1953. Home: 78 Crestview Rd Mountain Lakes NJ 07046-1223 Office: Urban Health Inst 101 Eisenhower Pky Roseland NJ 07068-1028

MALAGA, STANLEY, accounting educator; b. Bronx, N.Y., Dec. 16, 1942; s. Benjamin and Rita Malaga; m. Leda Malaga, June 7, 1964; children: Ross, Meredith, Mitchell. BS, L.I. U., 1964; MBA, Bernard Baruch Coll., 1971. CPA, N.Y.; cert. valuation analyst. Acct. Stanley Katz & Co., N.Y.C., 1964-68, Hurdman and Cranston, N.Y.C., 1968-71; prof. acctg. and taxation L.I. U., Brookville, N.Y., 1971—; ptnr. Bertucelli & Malaga LLP, Hauppauge, N.Y., 1994—, Malaga & Malaga PC, Hauppauge, 1984-94; lectr. in field. Author: Automatic Tax Planner, 1984. Active Hauppauge Indsl. Assn., 1989; bd. dirs. Suffolk County Girl Scouts, Hauppauge, 1989. Mem. AICPA, Am. Acctg. Assn., N.Y. State Soc. CPAs, C.W. Post Tax Inst. (dir.), Acad. Mktg. Sci., Nassau/Suffolk Soc. CPAs (chmn. fed. tax com.). Avocations: golf, swimming, bridge. Office: Bertucelli & Malaga LLP 3033 Expressway Dr N Hauppauge NY 11788-5309

MALAKHOV, VLADIMIR, dancer; b. Krivoy Rog, Ukraine, USSR, Jan. 7, 1968; arrived in Can., 1994; s. Anatoly and Elena Malakhov. Grad., Bolshoi Ballet Acad., Moscow, 1986. Prin. dancer Vienna State Opera, 1992—, Nat. Ballet Can., 1994—, Am. Ballet Theatre, N.Y.C., 1995—; guest artist Am. Ballet Theatre, 1994. Appeared in Giselle, Swan Lake, Nutcracker, Manon, Romeo and Juliette, others; performed in major opera houses worldwide. Recipient Gold medal Varna Ballet Competition, 1986, Gold medal Moscow Ballet Competition, 1986, Serge Lifar prize, 1991.

MALAKOFF, JAMES LEONARD, management information executive; b. Phila., June 20, 1933; s. John and Ida Vera (Partman) M.; m. Anne Bronstein Frisch, June 26, 1955; children: Randi Ellen, John Seymour. B in Aerospace Engring., Rensselaer Poly. Inst., 1954, MS, 1955. Structural methods specialist Grumman Aircraft, Bethpage, N.Y., 1955-62; mem. tech. staff Northrop Corp., Hawthorne, Calif., 1962-65; chief, math. analyst Beckman Instruments, Inc., Fullerton, Calif., 1965-68; dir. data processing Beckman Instruments, Inc., Fullerton, 1968-82, v.p. data processing, 1982-85, v.p., mgmt. info., 1985-93, cons. to mgmt., 1993—; bd. dirs. Little Co. Mary Health Svcs., Little Co. Mary Hosp., San Pedro (Calif.) Peninsula Hosp.; vis. prof. computer sci. Calif. State U., Fullerton, 1981-82, mem. indsl. adv. coun. Sch. Engring. and Computer Sci. Fellow AIAA (assoc.); mem. IEEE (computer group), U.S. Council Internat. Bus. (bus. and industry adv. com., West Coast com. Internat. Info. and Telecommunications Policy), Assn. Computing Machinery, Data Processing Mgmt. Assn.

MALAMED, SEYMOUR H., motion picture company executive; b. N.Y.C., June 17, 1921; s. Abraham and Bess (Kaisin) M.; m. Doris Raphael, May 19, 1946; children—Margery, Susan, Nancy. B.B.A., City Coll. N.Y., 1942. Engaged in entertainment field, 1954—; asst. to v.p., treas. Screen Gems Co., 1956-62; treas. parent co. Columbia Pictures Corp., 1962—, v.p., 1963-73, exec. v.p., 1973—. Served with AUS, World War II. Mem. Motion Picture Acad. Arts and Scis. Clubs: Friars (N.Y.C.); Metropolis Country (Westchester County); High Ridge Country (Palm Beach, Fla.), Metropolis Country Club. Home: 135 Central Park W Apt 9nc New York NY 10023-2465 Office: 301 W 57th St Ste 336 New York NY 10019-3114

MALAMUD, DANIEL, biochemistry educator; b. Detroit, June 5, 1939; s. Jack and Jennie (Ashe) M.; m. Judith Disner, Mar. 7, 1961; children: Randy, Lisa. BS, U. Mich., 1961; MA, Western Mich. U., 1962; PhD, U. Cin., 1965; MA, U. Pa., 1983. Post-doctoral fellow Temple U., Phila., 1966-68, asst. prof. pathology, 1968-69; asst. biologist Mass. Gen. Hosp., Boston, 1969-72, assoc. biologist, 1972-77; assoc. prof. biochemistry Sch. Dental Medicine, U. Pa., Phila., 1977-84, prof. biochemistry, 1984—, chmn. biochemistry, 1985—; asst. prof. pathology Harvard U., Boston, 1970-77; vis. assoc. prof., Fulbright lectr. U. Philippines, Manila, 1975; vis. scientist Wistar Inst., Phila., 1985; affiliated scientist Monell Chem. Senses Ctr., Phila., 1985—; exchange scientist Hebrew U., Jerusalem, 1982. Author: Autoradiography, 1969; contbr. over 80 articles to profl. jours. and chpts. to books. Recipient Career Devel. award NIH, 1972-77. Mem. Am. Soc. Biol. Chemists, N.Y. Acad. Scis., Am. Soc. Cell Biologists, Am. Soc. Microbiologists. Office: Univ of Pa Sch of Dental Medicine 4001 Spruce St Philadelphia PA 19104-4118

MALAMY, MICHAEL H(OWARD), molecular biology and microbiology educator; b. Bklyn., Apr. 20, 1938; s. Henry R. and Rhoda A. (Resnick) M.; m. Frances E. Siegel, June 15, 1958; children: Adam C., Jocelyn E. B.A., NYU, 1958, Ph.D., 1963. Postdoctoral fellow Pasteur Inst., Paris, 1963-65, Princeton U., N.J., 1965-66; asst. prof. microbiology Tufts U., Boston, 1966-71, assoc. prof. molecular biology, microbiology, 1971-76, prof., 1976—. Mem. editorial bd.: Jour. Bacteriology, Washington, 1971-80. Mem. Am. Soc. Biochemistry and Molecular Biology, Am. Soc. Microbiology. Home: 39 Wildwood St Winchester MA 01890-1748 Office: Tufts U/Molecular Biology 136 Harrison Ave Boston MA 02111-1817

MALARKEY, MARTIN FRANCIS, JR., cable television executive; b. Pottsville, Pa., May 1, 1918; s. Martin Francis and Gertrude (Cress) M.; m. Catherine Clare McCarthy, May 30, 1935; 1 child, Clare Ann (Mrs. John E. Hampford); m. Elizabeth Koehn Onesto, May 29, 1961. BS in Acctg., LaSalle U., Phila., 1939. V.p. Malarkey's, Inc., Pottsville, 1939-42, pres., 1946-50; pres., dir. Trans Video Corps., Washington, 1950-59; pres., dir. radio Sta. WRTA, Altoona, Pa., 1956-84; owner Eastern Shore Microwave Relay Co., Washington, 1961-75; chmn. Malarkey, Taylor Assocs., Inc., Washington, 1959-92, MTA/EMCI, Washington, 1992-97; chmn. emeritus The Strategis Group, Washington, 1997—; pres. radio sta. WMBT, Shenandoah, Pa., 1970-86. Pres. Washington Internat. Horse Show Assn., 1976-77; trustee emeritus Am. U., Washington; trustee Washington Hosp. Ctr.; chmn. emeritus Washington Hosp. Ctr. Found. Served with USNR, World War II. Mem. Nat. Cable TV Assn. (founder, 1st pres.), Washington Club, City Tavern Assn., F St. Club, Univ. Club, Army and Navy Club. Pioneer in devel. cable television. Home: 1817 Kalorama Sq NW Washington DC 20008-4021

MALASANOS, LOIS JULANNE FOSSE, nursing educator; b. LaPorte City, Iowa, Sept. 1, 1928; d. Lewis Reginald and Hennetta Marie Fosse; widowed; children: John, Toree. BSN, U. Tex., 1948; BA in Gen. Sci., U. Iowa, 1952; MA in Nursing Edn., U. Chgo., 1959; PhD in Physiology, U. Ill., 1973. Assoc. dir. nursing U. Iowa Hosps., Iowa City, 1950-51, staff charge nurse, 1951; instr. operating room Sch. Nursing, Michael Reese Hosp., Chgo., 1951-58; charge nurse, med.-surg. U. Chgo., Billings Hosp., 1952-59; pvt. duty nurse Ill., 1959-60; charge nurse, maternal-infant nursing Weiss Meml. Hosp., Chgo., 1963-66; asst. prof. Loyola U., Chgo., 1966-69; teaching asst. in physiology U. Ill., Chgo., 1969-73, assoc. prof., assoc. head gen. nursing dept. Coll. Nursing, 1973-76, prof., assoc. head gen. nursing dept., 1976-80; prof., dean Coll. Nursing U. Fla., Gainesville, 1980-95, Disting. Svc. prof., 1995—; instr. anatomy and physiology Cook County Hosp., Chgo., 1973; lectr. endocrinology Chgo. Coll. Osteopathic Medicine, 1973-80; active Pres. Clinton's Task Force on Health Care, 1993; cons. Am. Assn. Med. Colls., 1977-78, Am. Heart Assn., 1977-94, Am. Jour. Nursing, 1978-79, Gainesville (Fla.) Vets. Ctr., 1980-95, Lake Butler Receiving Ctr., 1980—; presenter papers in field; cons. to numerous colls. and univs. regarding curriculum, nursing care and endocrinology; chair Deans and Dirs. of Fla. Colls. Nursing, 1981-89; chair edn. com. State Bd. Nursing, 1983, 87, chair probable course com.; vis. prof. Dokuz English U., Izmir, Turkey, 1995-96. Co-author, editor: Manual of Medical Surgical Nursing, 1983, Translating Comitment to Reality, 1986, Health Assessment, 1977 (Am. Jour. Nursing Book of Yr. award 1977), 4th edit., 1989; editor: Vital Signs, 1981-90, Fla. Cancer Nursing News, 1983-84; co-editor: Fla. Nursing Rev., 1986-90; mem. editl. rev. bd. Image, 1980—; editl. cons. Nursing, 1982—; manuscript referee Rsch. in Nursing and Health, 1980—, Jour. Profl. Nursing, 1985—; chairperson adv. com. Nursing Outlook, 1986-91, Peer Rev., 1986—; contbr. more than 100 articles, revs. to profl. jours. Mem. nursing com., scholarship com. and rsch. rev. com. Am. Cancer Soc., Tampa, Fla., 1980—. Recipient Bronze medal Fla. Heart Assn., 1986, Silver medal Fla. Heart Assn., 1989, 93; named Disting. Alumnus U. Tex. Med. Br., 1985; named to Disting. Faculty, Albany State U., 1988, Hall of Fame, U. Tex. Med. Br., 1992; NEH fellow, 1981; Fulbright awardee to Turkey, 1995-96. Mem. ANA (mem. coun. nurse rschrs.), AACN, AASN, AAUP, Am. Acad. Nursing (mem. pub. com. 1986-89) Am. Assn. Higher Edn., Am. Assn. Colls. Nursing, Fla. Nurses Assn. (mem. dist. 10), Fla. League Nursing, Nat. League Nursing (mem. coun. baccalaureate and higher degree programs, Dirs. award 1995), So. Regional Edn. Bd., Sigma Xi, Sigma Theta Tau, Phi Kappa Phi (pres. 1987-88). Office: U Fla Coll Nursing PO Box 100187 Gainesville FL 32610-0197

MALASHEVICH, BRUCE PETER, consulting economist; b. Ridgewood, N.J., Feb. 21, 1952; s. Peter Gabriel and Olga Julia (Pelenko) M.; m. Linda Christine Kauskay, May 11, 1985; children: Jason Kauskay, Jessica Alexandra Kauskay. B.A. cum laude, Woodrow Wilson Sch. Pub. and Internat. Affairs, Princeton U., 1974; M.A., Johns Hopkins U., 1976. Internat. economist U.S. Treasury Dept., Washington, 1975-76; asst. to dir. Econ. Cons. Services div. Wolf and Co., C.P.A.s, Washington, 1976-78; v.p. Econ. Cons. Services Inc., Washington, 1978-88, pres., chief exec. officer, 1988—, also dir. Contbr. articles to internat. studies jours. and nat. bus. newspapers. Crown-Zellerbach scholar Johns-Hopkins U., 1975. Clubs: Princeton of N.Y.; Princeton of Washington; Kenwood Golf and Country. Avocations: tennis; squash; travel; reading history. Office: Econ Cons Svcs Inc 1225 19th St NW Ste 210 Washington DC 20036-2485

MALAYERY, NASRIN, educator, consultant; b. Tehran, Iran, Jan. 27, 1943; U.S. citizen, 1990; d. Mahmoud Malayery and Ghamar Narjis Kia. BA with spl. honors in history, George Washington U., 1964; EdM in Edn. and Social Studies, Boston U., 1967, EdM in Media and Tech., 1977, EdD in Media Tech., 1986. Editor in-house mgmt. jour. Oil Consortium, Employee Comm., Tehran, 1970-74; mgr. documents and publs. Iran-UNESCO Adult Literacy Program, Tehran, 1974-76; instr., instrnl. designer Shiraz (Iran) U. Med. Sch., 1977-81; ednl. cons. WHO Eastern Mediterranean Regional Orgn., Alexandria, Egypt, 1981-87; sr. ednl. cons. Digital Equipment Corp., Littleton, Mass., 1987—. Mem. Internat. Soc. for Performance Improvement, Nat. Mus. of Women in the Arts (assoc.), Phi Beta Kappa. Avocations: writing, reading, gardening, ballet, yoga. Home: 88 Tower Hill Rd Osterville MA 02655-1618

MALCOLM, ANDREW HOGARTH, journalist, writer; b. Cleve., June 22, 1943; s. Ralph Monteith and Beatrice Florence (Bowles) M.; m. Connie D'Amelio, Nov. 28, 1981; children: Christopher, Spencer, Emily, Keddy. BJ, Northwestern U., 1966, MJ, 1967. Clk. The N.Y. Times, N.Y.C., 1967-68, met. reporter, 1969-70; nat. corr. The N.Y. Times, Chgo., 1971-73, San Francisco, 1974-75; fgn. corr. The N.Y. Times, Vietnam, Thailand, Guam, 1975, Tokyo, 1975-78, Republic of Korea, 1975-78; bur. chief The N.Y. Times, Toronto, Ont., Can., 1978-82, Chgo., 1982-87; asst. nat. editor The N.Y. Times, N.Y.C., 1987-88, nat. affairs corr., columnist, 1988-93; exec. asst., dir. comm. Govs. Office, Helena, Mont., 1993—. Author: Unknown America, 1975, The Canadians, 1985, Final Harvest, 1986, This Far and No More, 1987, Someday, 1991, U.S. 1: America's Original Main Street, 1991, The Land and People of Canada, 1991, Huddle: Fathers, Sons, and Football, 1992, Mississippi Currents: A Journey Through Time and A Valley, 1996, Fury, 1997. Recipient George Polk award L.I. U., 1975, Page One award N.Y. Newspaper Guild, 1975, 83. Office: Governor's Office State Capitol Helena MT 59620-0801

MALCOLM, DAWN GRACE, family physician; b. L.A., Nov. 3, 1936; d. Thomas N. and Grace S. (Salisian) M. BA, UCLA, 1959; MD, Med. Coll. Pa., 1973. Diplomate Am. Bd. Family Practice. Tchr. elem. music Fullerton (Calif.) Sch. Dist., 1960-61; tchr. Ahlman Acad., Kabul, Afghanistan, 1961-65; intern and resident in family practice Kaiser Found. Hosp., L.A., 1973-76; family physician So. Calif. Permanente Med. Group, L.A., 1976—; mem. faculty family practice residency program Kaiser Found. Hosp., L.A., 1976—. Fellow Am. Acad. Family Physicians. Office: So Calif Permanente Med Grp 4747 Sunset Blvd Los Angeles CA 90027-6021

MALCOLM, DOUGLAS RAYMOND, insurance agent, real estate developer; b. Connellsville, Pa., Oct. 4, 1958. BS, Ohio State U., 1980, MBA, 1981. Investment broker L.F. Rothschild, Unterberg, Towbin, N.Y.C., 1981-82, McDonald and Co., Columbus, Ohio, 1982-83; pres. Malcolm Ins. Group, Canton, Ohio, 1983—. Mem. Congress Lake Club, Glenmoor Country Club. Office: Malcolm Ins Group 4819 Munson St NW Canton OH 44718-3614

MALCOLM, GAROLD DEAN, architect; b. Belle Fouche, S.D., Apr. 25, 1940; s. Gifford Garold Malcolm and Ellen Eve Liming; m. Breta Lois Bailey, 1966 (div. 1982); children; Heather Marie, Allison Clare; m. Lucia Eagon Stenson, 1991. BArch, U. Oreg., 1966. Ptnr. McAdoo, Malcolm & Youel, Architects, 1981—. Prin. works include Creston-Nelson Elec. Substation, Seattle (Honor award Wash. Aggregates and Concrete Assn.), Arboretum Visitor's Ctr., Seattle (Honor award Builders Community Awards Program, People's Choice award Seattle chpt. AIA), Des Moines (Wash.) Libr., Queen Anne Swimming Pool, Seattle. Mem. AIA, Matsumura Kenpo Karate Assn. (black belt). Office: McAdoo Malcolm & Youel Architects 1718 E Olive Way Seattle WA 98102-5615

MALCOM, JOSEPH ADAMS, retired military officer, project manager; b. Social Circle, Ga., Oct. 29, 1944; s. Archie Preston Malcom and Sarah Rebecca (Adams) Malcom-Anderson; m. Mary Carol Anderson, May 7, 1967; children: Mary Elizabeth, Susan Rebecca. BBA, North Ga. Coll., 1966; MS in Econs., Clemson U., 1968; grad., Command and Gen. Staff Coll., 1984. Commd. 2d lt. U.S. Army, 1966, advanced through grades to lt. col., 1985; chief, fin. mgr. U.S. Army Inventory Control Ctr., Long Binh, Vietnam, 1971; instr., inventory mgt. U.S. Army Quartermaster Sch., Ft. Lee, Va., 1972-73; co. commdr. XVIII Airborne Corps, Ft. Bragg, N.C., 1974-77; asst. prof. U. Tenn., Martin, 1977-80; finance officer 3d Infantry Divsn., Wuerzburg, Germany, 1980-83; chief exercise divsn. U.S. Army Logistics Ctr., Ft. Lee, 1984-88; chief logistics assistance officer 82nd Airborne Divsn., Ft. Bragg, 1989-93; ret. U.S. Army, 1997; project mgr. Logistics Mgmt. Resources, Inc., 1997—; adj. prof. U. Richmond, Ft. Lee, 1970, Chapman Coll., Ft. Lee, 1972-74, U. Md., Wuerzburg, 1980-82. Author: Civil War Organization, 1979; editor: Civil War Press Corps newsletter, 1980-87. Decorated Bronze Star (2), Meritorious Svc. medal (4), Army Commendation medal (3). Mem. SAR, SCV, Assn. U.S. Army, Soc. Civil War Necrologists, Assn. Quartermaster Officers, Assn. for Gravestone Studies, 3d Inf. Divsn. Marne Assn. Republican. Baptist. Avocation: necrology, genealogy. Home: PO Box 722 Social Circle GA 30279-0722 Office: LMR Inc Box 722 Social Circle GA 30279

MALDE, HAROLD EDWIN, retired federal government geologist; b. Reedsport, Oreg., July 9, 1923; s. Emil and Bessie May (Alspaugh) M.; m. Caroline Elizabeth Rose, Dec. 21, 1954; children: Margaret Jean, Melissa Ruth. AB, Willamette U., 1947; postgrad. Harvard U., 1947-48, U. Colo., 1948-51. Geologist, U.S. Geol. Survey, Denver, 1951-87, emeritus, 1987—; mem. Colo. com. for Nat. Register Hist. Places, 1972-80; vol. photographer Nature Conservancy, 1987—; mem. paleoanthropology del. to Peoples Republic China, Nat. Acad. Scis., 1975, mem. various coms. for study surface mining; mem. oil shale environ. adv. panel U.S. Dept. Interior, 1976-80. Contbr. numerous sci. papers to profl. lit. Served to ensign USNR, 1942-44. Recipient Meritorious Service award U.S. Dept. Interior, 1979, Oak Leaf award Nature Conservancy, 1993. Fellow Geol. Soc. Am. (Kirk Bryan award 1970, assoc. editor 1982-88), AAAS, Ariz.-Nev. Acad. Sci.; mem. Am. Quaternary Assn., Explorers Club. Democrat. Unitarian. Home: 842 Grant Pl Boulder CO 80302-7415

MALDEN, KARL (MALDEN SEKULOVICH), actor; b. Chgo., Mar. 22, 1914; s. Peter and Minnie (Sebera) Sekulovich; m. Mona Graham, Dec. 18, 1938; children—Mila, Carla. Student, Goodman Theatre, Chgo., 1935-38. pres. Acad. of Motion Arts and Scis.; mem. Citizens Stamp Com., U.S. Govt., Washington. Actor, 1935—; stage plays include Golden Boy, 1938, Gentle People, 1939, Key Largo, 1940, Flight to the West, 1942, Uncle Harry, 1940, All My Sons, 1949, A Streetcar Named Desire, 1950, Desire Under the Elms, 1952, Desperate Hours, 1954; in motion pictures, 1940—, films include: Boomerang, Gunfighter, 1945, Halls of Montezuma, 1950, A Streetcar Named Desire (Acad. award for best supporting actor), 1951, Ruby Gentry, 1952, I Confess, 1953, On the Waterfront, 1954, Baby Doll, 1956, Desperate Hours, 1957, Fear Strikes Out, 1957, The Hanging Tree, 1959, Pollyanna, 1960, One Eyed Jacks, 1961, Parrish, The Adventures of Bullwhip Griffin, 1967, Patton, 1970, Beyond the Poseidon Affair, 1978, Meteor, 1979, Sting II, 1982, Twilight Time, 1982, Billy Galvin, 1987, Nuts, 1987; TV films include: Word of Honor, 1981, Miracle on Ice, 1981, Intent to Kill, 1983, Fatal Vision, 1984 (Emmy award), My Father My Son, 1988, The Hijacking of the Achille Lauro, 1989, Call Me Anna, 1990, Absolute Strangers, 1991, Back to the Streets of San Francisco, 1992; dir.: Time Limit, 1957, Billion Dollar Brain, 1967, Hot Millions, 1968, Hotel, Cat O'Nine Tails, 1971, Wild Rovers, 1971, Summertime Killer, 1973, Nuts, 1987; star TV series Streets of San Francisco, 1972-77, Skag, 1980. Recipient Donaldson award, 1950, Critic's award, 1950. Mem. Acad. Motion Picture Arts and Scis. (pres. 1989-92). Address: 1845 Mandeville Canyon Rd Los Angeles CA 90049-2222

MALDON, ALPHONSO, JR., federal official, retired military officer; b. Bonifey, Fla., Oct. 6, 1950; m. Carolyn Maldon; 1 child, Kiamesha Racha'el. BS, Fla. A&M U., 1972; M in Human Rels., U. Okla., 1975; grad., Armed Forces Staff Coll., 1985. Commd. U.S. Army, 1972, advanced through grades to lt. col.; chief orgnl. effectiveness mgmt. U.S. Army, Stuttgart, Germany, 1981-83; pers. officer, comdr. 259th Pers. Svc. Co. U.S. Army, Bamberg, Ger., 1983-84; exec. officer Armed Forces Staff U. U.S. Army, Norfolk, Va., 1985-89; congl. liaison officer U.S. Army Legis. Liaison, U.S. Ho. of Reps. U.S. Army, 1989-93, ret., 1993; spl. asst. to Pres., legis. affairs The White House, Washington, 1993-94, dep. asst. to Pres., milit. affairs, 1994—, dep. asst. to Pres., legis. affairs, 1994—; admissions, pub. affairs officer West Point. Contbr. features Army pubs. Decorated Def. Meritorious Svc. medal with 2 oak leaf clusters, Army Meritorious Svc. medal with 2 oak leaf clusters, Army Commendation medal with 2 oak leaf clusters, Legion of Merit; Congl. scholar. Office: Legis Affairs 1600 Pennsylvania Ave NW Washington DC 20500-0005

MALDONADO-BEAR, RITA MARINITA, economist, educator; b. Vega Alta, P.R., June 14, 1938; d. Victor and Marina (Davila) Maldonado; m. Larry Alan Bear, Mar. 29, 1975. BA, Auburn U., 1960; PhD, NYU, 1969. With Min. Wage Bd. & Econ. Devel. Adminstrn., Govt. of P.R., 1960-64; assoc. prof. fin. U. P.R., 1969-70; asst. prof. econs. Manhattan Coll., 1970-72; assoc. prof. econs. Bklyn. Coll., 1972-75; vis. assoc. prof. fin. Stanford (Calif.) Grad. Bus. Sch., 1973-74; assoc. prof. fin. and econs. Grad. div. Stern Sch. Bus. NYU, 1975-81, prof., 1981—, acting dir. markets, ethics and law, 1993-94; cons. Morgan Guaranty Trust Co., N.Y.C., 1972-77, Bank of Am., N.Y.C., 1982-84, Res. City Bankers, N.Y.C., 1978-87, Swedish Inst. Mgmt., Stockholm, 1982-91, Empresas Master of P.R., 1985-90; bd. dirs. Medallion Funding Corp., 1985-87; mem. N.Y.U. Senate and Faculty Coun., 1995—; chairperson Fin. Com., 1996—; apptd. adv. bd. dirs. equity and diversity in ednl. environs. Mid. States Commn. on Higher Edn., 1991—; trustee Securities Industry Assn., N.Y. Dist. Econ. Edn. Found., 1994—; chairperson NSF, Nat. Vis. Com. Curriculum Devel. Project Networked Fin. Simulation, 1995—. Author: Role of the Financial Sector in the Economic Development of Puerto Rico, 1970; co-Author: Free Markets, Finance, Ethics, And Law, 1994; contbr. articles to profl. jours. Trustee Bd. Edn., Twp. of Mahwah, N.J., 1991-92. P.R. Econ. Devel. Adminstrn. fellow, 1960-65; Marcus Nadler fellow, NYU, 1966-67, Phillip Lods Dissertation fellow, 1967-68. Mem. Am. Econs. Assn., Am. Fin. Assn., Metro. Econ. Assn. N.Y., Assn. for Social Econs. (trustee exec. coun. 1994-96). Home: 95 Tam O Shanter Dr Mahwah NJ 07430-1526 Office: Mgmt Edn Ctr 44 W 4th St Ste 9-190 New York NY 10012-1106

MALE, ROY RAYMOND, English language educator; b. Bklyn., Mar. 15, 1919; s. Roy Raymond and Mary Edwards (Brooks) M.; m. Carolyn Kate Conlisk, Aug. 19, 1944; children: Marilyn, Frank. B.S., Hamilton Coll., 1939; M.A., Columbia U., 1940; Ph.D., U. Tex., 1950. Instr. English U. Tex., 1946-50; asst. prof. Tex. Tech. Coll., 1950-55; mem. faculty U. Okla., 1955-84, Boyd prof. English emeritus; vis. prof. Bowling Green U., 1962, U. Wash., 1968, U. Tex. at Arlington, 1971. Author: Hawthorne's Tragic Vision, 1957, Enter, Mysterious Stranger, 1979; editor: Types of Short Fiction, 2d edit, 1970, Money Talks, 1981; co-editor: Am. Literary Masters, 1974. Served with AUS, 1940-45. Ford Found. fellow, 1954-55; Recipient Regents award excellence teaching U. Okla., 1968. Mem. Modern Lang. Assn., South Central Modern Lang. Assn. (pres. 1968). Home: Hilton Head Plantation 40 Field Sparrow Rd Hilton Head Island SC 29926-1813

MALEC, WILLIAM FRANK, utilities company executive; b. Broadalbin, N.Y., June 22, 1940; s. Henry and Anna Frances M.; m. Sarah Powell, Sept. 11, 1965; children: Charles A., Mariah E. BS cum laude, Niagara U., 1962; MBA, Ind. U., 1967; AMP, Harvard U., 1987. Mgmt. trainee Marine Midland Bank, Buffalo, 1962-63; project budget analyst Cleve. Electric Illuminating Co., 1967-68; asst. treas. Mid-Continent Telephone Co., Hudson, Ohio, 1968-75; v.p., treas. Gulf States Utilities, Beaumont, Tex., 1975-78; treas. Cen. and S.W. Corp., C&W Leasing Inc., CSW Energy Inc., CSW Fin., Inc., Dallas; v.p., treas. Cen. and S.W. Services, Inc., Dallas, 1978-89; pres. C&W Credit, Inc., 1985-89; exec. v.p., CFO TVA, Knoxville, 1989-95. Served with U.S. Army, 1963-65. Mem. Nat. Mgmt. Assn., Leading Chief Fin. Officers. Republican. Roman Catholic. Office: TVA 110 N Nilam St No 123 Fredericksburg TX 78624

MALECHA, MARVIN JOHN, architect, academic administrator; b. Lonsdale, Minn., June 26, 1949; s. George and Barbara Malecha; m. Cynthia Marie Miller, Aug. 8, 1970; children: Peter, Michelle. Student, St. Thomas Coll.; BArch, U. Minn.; MArch, Harvard U. Registered architect, Calif. Designer Wallace and Mundt Architects, Edina, Minn., 1969-73, Hugh Stubbins and Assocs., Cambridge, Mass., 1973-76; instr. Cambridge Urban Awareness Program, 1973-76, Boston Archtl. Ctr., 1974-76; asst. chmn., asst. prof. dept. arch. Coll. Environ. Design Calif. State Poly. U., Pomona, 1976-77, chmn., assoc. prof., 1979-82, prof., dean Coll. Environ. Design, 1982-94; dean sch. design N.C. State U., 1994—; chmn. Univ. Fall Conf. com. Calif. State Poly. U., 1984; mem. steering com. Architects for Social Responsibility; mem. bd. advisors Tchrs. cert. program City Bldg. Edn. Program, planning com. So. Calif. Assn. Govts.; vis. critic UCLA, 1985, U., Minn., 1981-83, 87, U. So. Calif., 1980-87, Calif. Poly. State U., San Luis Obispo, 1979-87, Clemson U., 1988, Columbia U., 1993, U. Tenn., 1994, U. Md., 1995, Miss. State U., 1995, U. Wis., Milw., 1996, Roger Williams U., 1997; lectr. to schs. and archtl. assns.; cons. in architecture and research, Claremont, Calif., 1976—; master juror Nat. Council Archtl. Registration Bds.; mem. edn. equity com. Calif. State U. System, 1985-86; pres. Calif. Coun. Archtl. Edn., 1986-88; mem. accreditation vis. team for collegiate programs in landscape architecture, 1988—; bd. dirs. Nat. Archtl. Accreditation Bd.; campus architect cons. U. Calif., Riverside, 1990-94. Author: Form of Performance, The Fabric of Architecture, The Pomona Method; co-sgner, author internat. protocol for internat. exch. in arch. edn.; contbr. articles to profl. jours. Mem. Art and Liturgy com. Our Lady Assumption Ch., Claremont, Calif., 1982-94; mem. bldg. and real estate com. Archdiocese of Raleigh; bd. dirs. United Arts Raleigh, City Gallery Raleigh, 1995—. Recipient Ellerbe Archtl. award, 1972, Hon. Mention Mass. Housing Dept., 1976; Rotch scholar, 1980. Fellow AIA (bd. dirs. L.A. chpt. 1982-83, chmn. state and nat. awards coms. 1983-85, chmn. Monterey design conf. com., Henry Adams award 1973, mem. steering com. archs. in edn. com. 1991, chair archs. in edn. com. 1994-95, presdl. citation L.A. chpt. 1987, mem. Calif. coun. 1994, Excellence in Arch. Edn. award), Soc. Am. Registered Archs., Assn. Collegiate Schs. Arch. (v.p. 1988-89, chair ann. meeting, pres. 1988-89, adminstrs. conf. Washington 1985), Calif. Coun. Archtl. Edn. (pres. 1988-89). Office: NC State U Sch Design Raleigh NC 27695

MALECKI, EDWARD STANLEY, JR., political science educator; b. Chgo., Nov. 16, 1938; s. Edward Stanley and Lucille Clara (May) M.; m. Judith Evelyn Sobczak, Aug. 24, 1962; children: Stephen, Robert. B.A., U. Ill., 1961, LL.B., 1963, M.A., 1965, Ph.D. (Charles Merriam fellow), 1969. Bar: Ill. 1963. Asst. prof. polit. sci. Calif. State U., Los Angeles, 1967-71; assoc. prof. Calif. State U., 1971-76, prof., 1976—, chair dept. Polit. Sci., 1993—. Author: (with H.R. Mahood) Group Politics: A New Emphasis, 1972; contbr. articles to profl. jours. Chmn. Caucus for a New Polit. Sci., 1970-71; ednl. cons. Foothill Urban League, 1969-70; bd. dirs. Pasadena Area Democratic Council, 1974. Calif. State U. Los Angeles Found. grantee, 1971-72, 84-85; HEW-Urban League grantee, 1969-70; NEH fellow, 1987. Mem. Ill. Bar Assn., Am. Polit. Sci. Assn., Am. Sociol. Assn., United Profs. Calif. (chpt. sec. 1974), ACLU (chpt. pres. 1974, 85-86, bd. dirs. So. Calif. 1981), Phi Kappa Phi. Home: 2225 Midwick Dr Altadena CA 91001-2828 Office: 5151 State University Dr Los Angeles CA 90032-4226

MALEFAKIS, EDWARD E., history educator; b. Springfield, Mass., Jan. 2, 1932; s. Emmanuel A. and Despina (Sophoulakis) M.; m. Cali Doxiadis, 1988; children from previous marriage: Michael, Laura. A.B., Bates Coll., 1953; M.A., Johns Hopkins U., 1955; Ph.D., Columbia U., 1965. Instr. Northwestern U., 1962-63, assoc. prof., 1968-71; asst. prof. Wayne State U., Detroit, 1963-64; asst. prof. modern European history Columbia U., 1964-67, prof., 1975—; prof. U. Mich., Ann Arbor, 1971-74. Author: Agrarian Reform and Peasant Revolution in Spain, 1970, Southern Europe in the 19th and 20th Centuries, 1992; editor: Indalecio Prieto, 1975, La guerra de España, 1936-39, 1996. Recipient Herbert Baxter Adams award Am. Hist. Assn., 1971, Faculty Teaching award Northwestern U., 1971, medal of honor U. Internacional Menendez Pelayo, 1982, Orden de Mérito Civico (Spain), 1988; Social Scis. Rsch. Coun. grantee, 1967, NEH grantee, 1977; Guggenheim fellow, 1974, Inst. Juan March fellow, 1991. Mem. Modern Greek Studies Assn. (exec. com. 1981-87), Soc. for Spanish and Portuguese Hist. Studies (exec. council 1969-72), Spanish Inst. N.Y.C. (bd. dirs. 1982—). Democrat. Greek Orthodox. Home: 380 Riverside Dr New York NY 10025-1858 Office: Columbia Univ 524 Fayerweather Hall New York NY 10027

MALEK, FREDERIC VINCENT, finance company executive; b. Oak Park, Ill., Dec. 22, 1936; s. Fred W. and Martha (Smickilas) M.; m. Marlene A. McArthur, Aug. 5, 1961; children: Fred W., Michelle A. BS, U.S. Mil. Acad., 1959; MBA, Harvard U., 1964; D of Humanities (hon.), St. Leo Coll., St. Petersburg, Fla., 1970. Assoc. McKinsey & Co., Inc., L.A., 1964-67; chmn. exec. com. Triangle Corp., Columbia, S.C., 1967-69; dep. under sec. HEW, Washington, 1969-70; spl. asst. to Pres. U.S., Washington, 1970-73; dep. dir. U.S. Office of Mgmt. and Budget, Washington, 1973-75; with Marriott Corp., Washington, 1975-88, sr. v.p., 1975-77, exec. v.p., 1978-88; pres. Marriott Hotels and Resorts, 1981-88; pres. Northwest Airlines, Mpls., 1989-90, vice chmn., 1990-91, also bd. dirs.; campaign mgr. Bush-Quayle '92, 1991-92; co-chmn. CB Comml. Real Estate Group, 1989-96; chmn. Lodging Opportunities Fund, 1991—, Thayer Capital Ptnrs., 1992—, Thayer Hotel Investors, 1994—; chmn. 1996 Rep. Presdl. Trust, 1995-96; bd. dirs. Automated Data Processing Corp., Am. Mgmt. Sys. Inc., Choice Hotels, Inc., N.W. Airlines, FPL Group Inc., Paine Webber Funds, Manor Care Inc.; dir. with rank of amb., 1990 Econ. Summit, 1989—; adj. prof. U.S.C., 1986-89; lectr. Kennedy Sch. Govt., Harvard U., 1976. Mem. Pres.'s Commn. on White House Fellows, 1971-75, White House Domestic Coun., 1974-75, Pres.'s Commn. on Pers. Interchange, 1974-76; dep. dir. com. for Re-election of Pres., 1972; Pres.'s Commn. on Pvt. Sector Initiatives, 1982-85, dir. conv. Bush for Pres., 1988; mem. Nat. Coun. on Surface Transp. Rsch., 1993-95; nat. adv. bd. Nat. Ctr. Econ. Edn. of Children, 1980-82; mem. Pres.'s Coun. on Phys. Fitness and Sports, 1986-91. Mem. Am.-Israel Friendship League (bd. trustees 1991—), Aspen Inst. (bd. trustees 1996—). Episcopalian. Avocations: biking, skiing. Office: 1455 Pennsylvania Ave NW Washington DC 20004-1008

MALENKA, BERTRAM JULIAN, physicist, educator; b. N.Y.C., June 8, 1923; s. Morris and Mollie (Wichtel) M.; m. Ruth D. Stolper, Mar. 28, 1948; children—David Jonathan, Robert Charles. AB, Columbia, 1947; MA, Harvard, 1949, PhD, 1951. Research fellow Harvard, 1951-54; asst. prof. physics Washington U., St. Louis, 1954-56; assoc. prof. Tufts U., Medford, Mass., 1956-60; faculty Northeastern U., Boston, 1960—; prof. physics Northeastern U., 1962-93, prof. emeritus, 1993—; Mem. sci. adv. group Harvard-Mass. Inst. Tech. Cambridge Electron Accelerator, 1956—. Mem. vis. com. dept. conservation Mus. Fine Arts, Boston, 1997—. Mem. Am., Italian phys. socs., N.Y. Acad. Scis., Phi Beta Kappa, Sigma Xi. Research and publs. on theory of nuclear forces and structure of nucleus, explanation polarization phenomena in high-energy scattering, gamma radiation, electric polarization deuteron, accelerator design. Home: 16 Rutledge Rd Belmont MA 02178-3323 Office: Northeastern Univ Dept Of Physics Boston MA 02115

MALES, WILLIAM JAMES, film producer, make-up artist; b. Mesa, Ariz.; s. James W. and Oveta (Bradshaw) M. Student, Pepperdine U., 1982-86; studies with Vincent J. R. Kehoe, 1980-82, studies with Dick Smith, 1981-83. Make-up artist William J. Males and Assocs., Hollywood, Calif., 1976—; exec. v.p. Bonaire Films, 1984-88; producer AZRAK Films, Inc., Hollywood, Calif., 1986—; co-producer with Bruce Boxleitner Diplomatic Immunity Distbr. Fries Entertainment, Hollywood, Calif., 1991; mgr. market rsch. Universal Pictures, Universal City, Calif., 1993—; CFO Calif. Pension Adminstrs., 1993-95. Studio make-up artist for numerous projects including (films) Aftershock, Family Reunion, Winds of War, Necromancer, Conan the Barbarian, Return of the Living Dead, Scanners, Ragedy Anne, (TV shows) The Blue and the Gray, Crisis at Central High, Skyward, Printer to the Territory, Golden Girls, Hollywood Squares, 21 Jump Street, 9 to 5, (theatrical prodns.) Mama Bear Papa Bear, I'm Not Rappaport, Man of La Mancha, The Gospel Truth, Camelot, Chorus Line (nat. tour), Grease, Godspell, Crucible; line producer (films) Aftershock, (distbr. Paramount Pictures) Dead Time, Lock Down, Necromancer, Ms. Frankenstein, Family Reunion, Rocky I; assoc. producer (films) Castle of Revenge, Alien Warrior, Californio, (TV comml.) Coppertone, Pepsi, Beechcraft, Levi Strauss, Chanel; prodn. dir. Danza/Floricanto USA; prodr. Lord Chamberlain's

Players. Mem. NATAS, Acad. TV Arts and Scis. (Emmy nomination 1982), Brit. Acad. Film and TV Arts, Am. Soc. Makeup Artists, Soc. Motion Picture and TV Engrs., Assn. Film Craftsmen (local 531), Nat. Assn. Broadcast Employees and Technicians, Prodrs. Guild Am. Republican. Office: Universal Pictures 8721 Santa Monica Blvd Ste 26 West Hollywood CA 90069-4511

MALESKA, MARTIN EDMUND, publishing executive; b. Yonkers, N.Y., Apr. 3, 1944; s. Edmund Joseph and Marian (Kolton) M.; m. Elissa Mary Delfini, Apr. 27, 1968; children: Christine, Matthew, Danielle. BS in Chemistry, Fordham U., 1966; MBA in Fin., NYU, 1968. Dir. fin. Celanese do Brasil, São Paulo, Brazil, 1972-77; mng. dir. internat. ops. Pfizer Med. Systems, N.Y.C., 1977-80; dir. planning Macmillan Inc., N.Y.C., 1980-82, now bd. dirs., bd. dirs., v.p., group exec., 1984-88; pres. Nat. Register Pub. Co., N.Y.C., 1982-83; sr. v.p. corp. devel. Maxwell Communication Corp., N.Y.C., 1989-91; bd. dirs. Macmillan Inc., N.Y.C.; mng. dir. Verons, Suhler & Assocs., N.Y.C., 1991-95; pres. Internat. and Profl. Publishing Grps., Simon and Schuster Inc., 1995—. Capt. USAF, 1968-72. Republican. Roman Catholic. Avocation: racquet sports. Home: 3 Deborah Ln Chappaqua NY 10514-3003 Office: Simon & Schuster 1230 Avenue Of The Americas New York NY 10020-1513

MALETTA, DIANE STANLEY, gifted and talented educator, education educator; b. Fairmont, W.Va., July 1, 1960; d. Dan Jarrell and LaModa June (Forth) Stanley; m. Robert Thomas Maletta, May 22, 1993; children: Adam Robert, Derek Nathaniel, Jasmine Elizabeth, Robert Thomas II. BS in Edn. with honors and distinction, Valparaiso U., 1982; MS in Edn. summa cum laude, Butler U., 1986; PhD in Lang. Edn., Ind. U., 1996; gifted/talented endorsement, Purdue U., 1992. State of Ind. life license: gen. elem., reading minor, gifted/talented endorsement. Tchr. grade 1, Spanish tchr. grades 7-8, coach St. John's Luth. Sch., Indpls., 1983-86; tchr. grade 1 River Grove (Ill.) Sch., 1986-87; tchr. grades 2 and 4, intramural dir. Washington Twp. Sch., Valparaiso, Ind., 1987-89; asst. prof. edn. Valparaiso (Ind.) U., 1989-92; tchr. gifted and talented Valparaiso (Ind.) Cmty. Schs., 1992—; mem., rec. sec. Ind. Dist. Luth. Tchrs., Indpls., 1983-85; mem. Luth. Edn. Assn., Indpls., 1983-86, Nat. Orgn. Tchr. Educators in Reading, 1989-92, Ind. Reading Profs., Indpls., 1989-92; adv. bd. mem. The Learning Pl., Valparaiso, 1990-92; asst. planner Nat. Assessment Symposium, 1990; adj. prof. edn. Ind. U. N.W., Gary, spring 1995, Valparaiso U., 1996—; tutor, spkr. and conf. presenter in field. Choir mem. St. John's Luth. Ch., Indpls., 1983-86, Immanuel Luth. Ch., Valparaiso, 1987-89; road race runner Lakeshore Striders, Chgo., N.W. Ind., 1989-94; mem. Augsburg Luth. Ch., Porter, Ind., 1992-94; runner, phone vol. Dem. Election Com., Porter, 1994. Mem. ASCD, Internat. Reading Assn. (past sec.), Porter County Reading Assn. (past sec., bd. mem., com. chairperson), Kappa Delta Pi, Pi Lambda Theta, Phi Delta Kappa, Mortar Bd. Avocations: running, biking, swimming, traveling, reading. Home: 1140 Dune Meadows Dr Porter IN 46304-1286 Office: Valparaiso Cmty Schs 405 Campbell St Valparaiso IN 46385-4625

MALETZ, HERBERT NAAMAN, federal judge; b. Boston, Oct. 30, 1913; s. Reuben and Frances (Sawyer) M.; m. Catherine B. Loebach, May 8, 1947; 1 son, David M. A.B., Harvard, 1935, LL.B., 1939. Bar: Mass. bar 1939, D.C. bar 1952. Mem. staff Truman com. U.S. Senate, 1941-42; atty. anti-trust div. Dept. Justice, 1946-50; with OPS, 1950-53, chief counsel, 1952-53; chief counsel anti-trust subcom. U.S. Ho. of Reps., 1955-61; commr. U.S. Ct. Claims, 1961-67; judge U.S. Ct. Internat. Trade, N.Y.C., 1967-87; vis. judge with various fed. cts., including U.S. Ct. Customs and Patent Appeals, U.S. Cts. of Appeals for the 1st and 2nd Cirs., U.S. Dist. Cts. for Mass., N.H., Maine, R.I., Ea. Dist. N.Y., Ea. Dist. N.C., Cen. Dist. Calif., So. Dist. Calif., 1972-87; vis. judge U.S. Dist. Md., 1987—. Served with AUS, 1942-46; lt. col. Res. Office: US Dist Ct Md 101 W Lombard St Baltimore MD 21201-2626

MALEY, PATRICIA ANN, preservation planner; b. Wilmington, Del., Dec. 25, 1955; d. James Alfred and Frances Louise (Fenimore) M.; m. Scott A. Stone, Dec. 7, 1991. AA, Cecil C.C., 1973; BA, U. Del., 1975, MA, 1981. Cert. planner: cert. secondary tchr., Del. Analyst econ. devel. City of Wilmington, 1977-78, evaluation specialist, 1978-80, planner II mayor's office, 1980-86, cons. preservation, 1986-87; dir. Belle Meade Mansion, Nashville, 1987-88; dir. planning, devel. Children's Bur. of Del., Wilmington, 1988; prin. preservation planner Environ. Mgmt. Ctr., Brandywine Conservancy, Chadds Ford, Pa., 1988-92; planning cons., 1992-95; design review and preservation commn. coord. Wilmington Dept. Planning, 1995—; cons. cultural resources M.A.A.R. Inc., Newark, Del., 1987, ITC Cons., Wilmington, 1985-86. Contbg. photographer America's City Halls, 1984; author numerous Nat. Register nominations, 1980-86; 88—. Pres., founder Haynes Park Civic Assn., Wilmington, 1977-80; photographer Biden U.S. Senate Campaign, New Castle County, Del., 1984; sec. parish coun. Our Lady Fatima Roman Cath. Ch., 1985-86, choir dir., 1983-87; mem. com. on design & renovation of worship spaces Diocese of Wilmington, also mem. com. on music; bd. dirs. Del. Children's Theatre; music dir. St. Elizabeth Ann Seton parish, Bear, Del., 1988—. U. Del. fellow, 1976-77. Mem. Nat. Trust Hist. Preservation, Am. Inst. Cert. Planners, Am. Planning Assn. (exec. com. Del. chpt. 1997), Nat. Pastoral Musicians Assn., Del. Soc. Architects, Del. Archeol. Soc., Del. Hist. Soc., Pi Sigma Alpha. Democrat. Avocations: photography; choral, piano, organ music. Office: City of Wilmington Dept Planning 800 N French St Fl 7 Wilmington DE 19801-3590

MALEY, SAMUEL WAYNE, electrical engineering educator; b. Sidney, Neb., Mar. 1, 1928; s. Samuel Raymond and Inez (Moore) M.; m. Elizabeth Anne Green, June 11, 1963; children—Karen Margaret, Laura Elaine. B.S., U. Colo., 1952, M.S., 1957, Ph.D., 1959; student, U. N.M., 1957-58. Geophysicist Stanolind Oil Co., Lubbock, Tex., 1952; design engr. Beach Aircraft Corp., Wichita, Kan., 1952-53, Dynalectron Corp., Cheyenne, Wyo., 1953-56; research scientist U. Colo., Boulder, 1959-60, vis. lectr., 1960-61, asst. prof., 1961-62, assoc. prof. elec. engring., 1962-67, prof., 1967-91, prof. emeritus, 1991—; mem. Nat. Ctr. Computer Aided Design, Millimeter and Microwave Systems U. Colo., 1988—; cons. Nat. Center Atmospheric Research, 1964, Automation Industries Research Div., Boulder, Colo., 1960-71, Midwec Corp., Ogallala, Neb., 1969-70, IBM, Boulder, 1969—. Author: Combinational Logic Circuits, 1969; contbg. author to 5 survey books on sci. and engring. Served with AUS, 1946-47; Served with USAF, 1947-48. Mem. I.E.E.E., A.A.A.S., Soc. Indsl. and Applied Math. Research electromagnetic theory; communication theory; computer design. Home: PO Box 1172 Boulder CO 80306

MALEY, WAYNE ALLEN, engineering consultant; b. Stanley, Iowa, Mar. 9, 1927; s. Neil Gordon and Flossie Amelia (Wharram) M.; m. Marianne Nelson, Aug. 2, 1959; children: James G., Mary G., Mark A. BS in Agrl. Engring., Iowa State U., 1949; postgrad., Purdue U., Ga. Tech., IIT. Power use advisor Southwestern Electric, Greenville, Ill., 1949-53; field agt. Am. Zinc Inst., Lafayette, Ind., 1953-59; mktg. devel. specialist U.S. Steel, Des Moines, Iowa, 1959-65; mktg. rep. U.S. Steel, Pitts., 1965-71, bar products rep., 1972-76; assoc. Taylor Equipment, Pitts., 1977-81; mgr. pub. rels. Am. Soc. Agrl. Engrs., St. Joseph, Mich., 1981-84, dir. mem. svcs., 1984-92; cons. Tech. Tours, St. Joseph, 1992—. Author: Iowa Really Isn't Boring, 1992, (textbook) Farm Structures, 1957, (computer program/workbook) Rim Lift Material Handling, 1970 (Blue Ribbon award 1971); editor: Agriculture's Contract with Society, 1991. Pres. Ednl. Concerns for Hunger Orgn., Ft. Myers, Fla., 1979-81; dist. activity dir. Boy Scouts Am., Moon Twp., 1969-70. With USN, 1945-46. Named Hon. Star Farmer, FFA Ill., 1958. Fellow Am. Soc. Agrl. Engrs. (bd. dirs. 1979-81 hon. for forum leadership 1991); mem. Agrl. Editors Assn., Coun. Engring. Soc. Execs. (bd. dirs. 1984-85), Sigma Xi (pres./del. Whirlpool chpt. 1993-94). Presbyterian. Achievements include patent for fence building machine, for material handling system; design of cable fences; design and installation of steel beverage can recycling center. Home and Office: Tech Tours 2592 Stratford Dr Saint Joseph MI 49085-2714

MALGIERI, NICK, chef, author, educator; b. Newark, Sept. 30, 1947; s. Nufre and Antoinette (LoConte) M. BA in French, Seton Hall U., 1970; AOS in Culinary Arts, Culinary Inst., Hyde Park, N.Y., 1973. Pastrycook Seehotel Meierhof, Zurich, 1973-74, Hotel de Paris, Monte Carlo, 1974, Sporting Club, Monte Carlo, 1974-76, Hotel la Reserve, Beaulieu, France, 1974; pastry chef Windows on the World, N.Y.C., 1976-79; asst. pastry chef Hotel Waldorf Astoria, N.Y.C., 1979; chmn. baking dept. N.Y. Restaurant Sch., N.Y.C., 1979-83; v.p., dir. baking program Peter Kump Cooking Sch., N.Y.C., 1984—; founder, owner Total Heaven Baking Co.; exec. chef Paine Webber; pastry chef Board Room; cons. Inhilco, Inc.; guest lectr. Smithsonian Instn. Author: Nick Malgieri's Perfect Pastry, 1989, Great Italian Desserts, 1990, How to Bake, 1995 (James Beard Found. Cookbook award/ Best Book on Baking/Deserts of 1995); contbr. articles, recipes to newspapers, profl. jours. Mem. Internat. Assn. Culinary Profls. (cert. culinary profl., chmn. certification 1989-91), Amicale Culinaire de Monaco, Societe Culinaire Philanthropique N.Y., Federazione Italiana dei Cuochi, James Beard Found. (coord. competitions 1991—), N.Y. Assn. Cooking Tchrs. (former bd. dirs.), Cooking Advancement, Rsch. and Edn. Found. (former trustee). Home: 277 W 10th St New York NY 10014-2562 Office: Peter Kump Cooking Sch 307 E 92nd St New York NY 10128-5401

MALHERBE, ABRAHAM JOHANNES, VI, religion educator, writer; b. Pretoria, South Africa, May 15, 1930; came to U.S., 1951; s. Abraham Johannes V and Cornelia Aletta (Meyer) M.; m. Phyllis Melton, May 28, 1953; children: Selina, Cornelia, Abraham Johannes VII. BA, Abilene Christian U., 1954; STB, Harvard U., 1957; student, U. Utrecht, The Netherlands, 1960-61; ThD, Harvard U., 1963; LLD (hon.), Pepperdine U., 1981; LHD (hon.), Centre Coll., 1990; STD (hon.), Providence Coll., 1994. Minister Ch. of Christ, Lexington, Mass., 1956-63; asst. and assoc. prof. Abilene (Tex.) Christian U., 1963-67; vis. scholar Harvard Divinity Sch., Cambridge, Mass., 1967-68; assoc. prof. Abilene Christian U., 1968-69, Dartmouth Coll., Hanover, N.H., 1969-70; assoc. prof. Yale Divinity Sch., New Haven, Conn., 1970-77, prof., 1977-81, Buckingham prof., 1981-94, assoc. dean acad. affairs, 1987-89; prof. eremitus, 1994—; guest prof. U. Pretoria, South Africa, 1989. Author: Social Aspects of Early Christianity, 1983, Moral Exhortation, 1986, Paul and the Thessalonians, 1987, Ancient Epistolary Theorists, 1988, Paul and the Popular Philosophers, 1989; mem. editl. bd. Bible Rev., 1986—; contbr. articles to profl. jours.; inspiration for book: Greeks, Romans and Christians: Essays in Honor of Abraham J. Malherbe, 1990. Recipient tchg. award Abilene Christian U., 1965, 67, Outstanding Alumni citation, 1993; NEH fellow 1973. Mem. Soc. Bibl. Lit., N.Am. Patristic Soc., Studiorum Novi Testamenti Societas, South African New Testament Soc. (hon.), Religious Studies Rev. (editl. bd. 1980—), Novum Testamentun (editl. bd. 1991—). Mem. Ch. of Christ. Home: 71 Spring Garden St Hamden CT 06517-1913 Office: Yale Divinity Sch 409 Prospect St New Haven CT 06511-2167

MALHOTRA, ASHOK KUMAR, philosophy educator; b. Ferozepur, India, Apr. 1, 1940; came to U.S., 1963, naturalized, 1977; s. Nihal Chand and Vidya (Wanti) M.; m. Nina Judith Finestone, Oct. 24, 1966; children: Raj Kumar, Ravi Kumar. B.A., U. Rajasthan, 1961, M.A., 1963; Ph.D., U. Hawaii, 1969. Asst. prof. SUNY-Oneonta, 1967-70, assoc. prof., 1970-80, prof., 1980—, chmn. philosophy dept., 1975—; vis. prof. SUNY-Buffalo, summer 1970, Kurukshetra U. and Birla Inst., Pilani, India, spring 1980; grants reviewer NEH, 1978—. bd. dirs. SUNY Press editorial, 1989—, dir. SUNY study abroad, program to India, 1980—; cons. TV series Kung Fu: The Legend Continues. East-West Ctr. fellow, 1963-65, 66-67; N.Y. State Dept. Edn. grantee, 1967-68, 68-69, summer 1969; NEH grantee, summer 1979; recipient Excellence in Teaching award United Univ. Profession. Mem. Am. Philos. Assn., Soc. Asian and Comparative Philosophy, Assn. Asian Studies, N.Y. State Asian Studies Soc., Internat. Phenomenol. Soc. Author: Sartre's Existentialism in Nausea and Being and Nothingness, 1978, Pathways to Philosophy: A Multidisciplinary Approach, 1996; articles, revs. Home: 17 Center St Oneonta NY 13820-1445

MALHOTRA, DAVINDER KUMAR, finance educator, consultant, researcher; b. New Delhi, Delhi, India, May 25, 1961; came to U.S., 1988; s. Jagat Ram and Sushila (Vohra) M.; m. Rashmi Nagpal, July 1, 1990; 1 child, Kunal. B in Commerce, U. Delhi, India, 1980, M in Commerce, 1982; MA in Fin., U. Ala., 1991, PhD in Fin., 1993. Sr. lectr. in commerce U. Delhi, Delhi, India, 1982-88; asst. prof. fin. Phila Coll. Textiles and Sci., 1993—; advisor MBA program Phila. Coll., 1993—; cons. Ctr. for Internat. Bus. Excellence, 1995—. Contbr. articles to profl jours. including Jour. Fin. Rsch., Advance in Futures and Options, Jour. of Retail Banking, Jour. of Comml. Lending, Jour. of Global Bus., Banker's Mag. Recipient various rsch. and best paper awards at fin. confs. Mem. Fin. Mgmt. Assn., Ea. Fin. Assn., Midwest Fin. Assn., So. Fin. Assn., Acad. Fin. Svcs., Acad. Internat. Bus. Home: 2991 School House Ln B 24E Philadelphia PA 19144 Office: Phila Coll Sch of Bus School House Ln & Henry Ave Philadelphia PA 19144

MALHOTRA, NARESH KUMAR, management educator; b. Ambala, Punjab, India, Nov. 23, 1949; came to U.S., 1975; s. Har Narian and Satya (Kakkar) M.; m. Veena Bahl, Aug. 13, 1980; children: Ruth Veena, Paul Naresh. BTech with honors, I.I.T., Bombay, India, 1971; MBA, I.I.M., Ahmedabad, India, 1973; MS, SUNY, Buffalo, 1978, PhD, 1979. Mgmt. cons. ASCI, Hyderabad, India, 1971-73; asst. prof. Ga. Tech. Inst., Atlanta, 1979—, assoc. prof. mgmt., coord. mktg., 1982-87, 89—, prof., 1988, regents' prof. 1992—; organizer several nat., internat. mktg. mgmt. confs. Contbr. articles to profl. jours. Lay preacher of the Gospel. Ranked the Top Researcher in U.S.A. based on publs. in Jour. Mktg. Rsch., 1980-85, Top Researcher Jour. Health Care Mktg., 1980-94. Fellow Acad. Mktg. Sci. (disting., program chmn. 1984-85, 85-86, v.p. programs 1988-90, chmn. bd. 1990-92, pres.-elect 1992-94, pres. 94-96, chmn. found. 1996—, Top Rschr. Jour.), Decision Scis. Inst.(track chmn. 1984-86); mem. Am. Mktg. Assn. (track chmn. 1983-84), Am. Statis. Assn. Republican. Baptist. Avocations: reading, writing, church activities, outdoor activities. Home: 1956 Lenox Rd NE Atlanta GA 30306-3035 Office: Ga Tech Inst Sch Mgmt Atlanta GA 30332

MALHOTRA, SURIN M., aerospace manufacturing executive; b. New Delhi, Dec. 27, 1948; came to U.S., 1970; s. Shiv D. and Gur D. (Kaushalya) M.; m. Rita Kashyap, Mar. 11, 1977; children: Tina, Amie. BSME, Delhi U., 1970; MSME, Wichita State U., 1971, MS in Adminstrn., 1973; JD cum laude, U. Bridgeport, 1992. Grad. asst. Wichita State U., Wichita, Kans., 1971-73; proj. engr. Norco Inc., Ridgefield, Conn., 1973-75, data processing mgr., 1975-78, program mgr., 1978-81, dir. materials, 1981-84, dir. contracts, 1984-86, v.p. sales, 1986-88, v.p. mfg. and sales, 1988-89; v.p. ops. Ridgefield, Conn., 1989-95; exec. v.p., COO Norco Inc., Ridgefield, Conn., 1995—; advisor BHS Mock Trial Team; notary pub. Inventor, patentee reversing mechanism. Vice chmn. Bethel (Conn.) Ethics Commn. Bridgeport scholar, 1989. Mem. ABA, Conn. Bar Assn., Phi Delta Phi. Republican. Hindu. Home: 104 Rockwell Rd Bethel CT 06801-3006 Office: Norco Inc 139 Ethan Allen Hwy Ridgefield CT 06877-6207

MALICKI, GREGG HILLARD, engineer; b. Chgo., Feb. 13, 1947; s. Hillard Lawrence and Virginia Valerie (Vosen) M.; 1 child, James Michael. BSBA, U. Ill., Champaign, 1975; MBA, U. Iowa, 1985; student, Coll. DuPage, Glen Ellyn, Ill., 1972-73, Ill. Inst. Technol., 1965-68. First lt. U.S. Army, 1969-72; sr. engring. analyst Deere & Co., Moline, Ill., 1975-87; sr. cons. engr. Deere & Co., Ill., 1987-94; regional mgr. Internat. Supply Mgmt. Svcs., Moline, 1994-97, mgr., 1997—; pres. Inst. Indsl. Engrs., Moline Ill., 1987—. Lt. col. Army NG, 1975—. Recipient Letter of Commendation Nat. Merit 1965. Sr. mem. Inst. Indsl. Engrs. (pres. 1987—); mem. Am. Prodn. & Inventory Control Soc., Phi Theta Kappa, Chi Gamma Iota. Roman Catholic. Avocation: fluent in German. Home: 3418 49th St Moline IL 61265-6614 Office: Deere & Co John Deere Rd Moline IL 61265-8098

MALICKY, NEAL, college president; b. Sour Lake, Tex., Sept. 14, 1934; s. George and Ethel L. (Reed) M.; m. Margaret A. Wilson, Sept. 2, 1956; children: Michael Neal, Eric Scott, David Matthew. A.B., Baker U., 1956; B.D., So. Meth. U., 1959; Ph.D., Columbia U., 1968; postgrad., Harvard U., 1978. Ordained to ministry Meth. Ch., 1959; pastor Meth. Ch., Moran, Kans., 1959-62, Van Cortlandtville, N.Y., 1962-66; asst. prof., dir. semester on UN Drew U., 1966-69; prof. polit. sci., dean Coll., Baker U., Baldwin City, Kans., 1969-75; acting pres. Coll., Baker U., 1973-75; v.p. acad. affairs, also dean Baldwin-Wallace Coll., Berea, Ohio, 1975-81; pres. Baldwin-Wallace Coll., 1981—. Author: To Keep the Peace, 1965, Non-Governmental Organizations at the United Nations, 1968; contbr. articles to profl. jours. Mem. Leadership Cleve., Nat. Conf. Christian and Jews, Cleve. Commn. Higher Edn., Cleve. Coun. World Affairs, Greater Cleve. Roundtable (chmn. edn. com.), Cleve. Initiative Edn. (vice chmn.), Summit on Edn. (co-convenor), Assn. Independent Colls. Ohio (chmn.). Mem. UN Assn. Clubs: Union of Cleve., Fifty of Cleve. Office: Baldwin-Wallace Coll Office of Pres 275 Eastland Rd Berea OH 44017-2005*

MALIGAS, MANUEL NICK, metallurgical engineer; b. Thimena, Greece, May 9, 1943; came to U.S., 1950; s. Nick and Jane M.; children: James Paul, John Michael. BE, Youngstown U., 1966; MS, Youngstown State U., 1974. Sr. material engr. Goodyear Aerospace, Akron, Ohio, 1966-76; plant metallurgist Tex. Bolt, Houston, 1976-81; sr. material engr. N.L. Shaffer, Houston, 1981-83; ind. cons. M&M Metall., Houston, 1983; materials engring. specialist FMC Corp., Houston, 1983—; engring. material specialist, instr. materials U. Houston; presenter symposia. Contbr. articles to profl. publs. Mem. Am. Soc. Metals (past officer), Am. Petroleum Inst. (chmn. material and welding coms.), Nat. Assn. Corrosion Engrs. (chmn.). Achievements include early design of carbon composite brake for commercial aircraft, use of laser and HVOF process for hard facing. Home: 5907 Winged Foot Dr Houston TX 77069-1322 Office: FMC Corp PO Box 3091 Houston TX 77253-3091

MALIK, HAFEEZ, political scientist, educator; b. Lahore, Pakistan, Mar. 17, 1930; m. Lynda P. Malik; children: Cyrus, Dean. BA, Government Coll., Lahore, Pakistan, 1949; grad. diploma in Journalism, U. Punjab, Lahore, 1952; MS in Journalism, Syracuse U., 1955, MA in Polit. Sci., 1957, PhD in Polit. Sci., 1961. Asst. prof. polit. sci. Villanova (Pa.) U., 1961-63, assoc. prof., 1963-67, prof., 1967—; pub. rels. officer City of Lahore, 1950-53; White House corr. The Nawa-i-Waqt, 1958-61, The Shabaz, 1958-61; mem. grad. com. dept. Polit. Sci. Villanova U., 1961-67, chmn., 1967-78; vis. prof. Fgn. Svc. Inst., Washington, 1961-63, 66-68, 70-85, Syracuse U. 1964, 65, Drexel U., Phila., 1968-69; mem. grad. coun. com. rsch. and publs., 1969-70, mem. grad. adv. com. liberal arts and social studies, 1964-67, mem. faculty libr. com., 1964-67, mem. undergrad. com. polit. sci., 1980—, mem. rank and tenure com., 1991-92; pres. Am. Inst. Pakistan Studies, 1972-88, Pakistan Am. Found., 1972—; exec. dir. Am. Coun. Study of Islamic Socs., 1983—; cons. Soviet Acad. Scis., 1979, Dept. Def., 1980, Pakistan-U.S. subcommn. edn. and culture, 1985, 88, USIA, 1986; presenter in field. News editor The Daily Magharabi Pakistan, 1948-50; tech. editor: Meteorological and Geoastrophysical Abstracts, Am. Meteorological Soc. 1960-63; author: Muslim Nationalism in India and Pakistan, 1963, rev. edit. 1980, Sir Sayyid Ahmed Khan's History of the Bijnore Rebellion, 1972, rev. edit. 1980, Political Profile of Sir Sayyid Ahmed Khan: A Documentary Record, 1982, Domestic Determinants of Soviet Foreign Policy Towards South Asia and the Middle East, 1990, Dilemmas of National Security and Cooperation in India and Pakistan, 1993, Soviet-Pakistan Relations and Post-Soviet Dynamics, 1994, Central Asia: Its Strategic Importance and Future Prospects, 1994, U.S., Russia, China in the New World Order, 1996; editor: Iqbal: Poet-Philosopher of Pakistan, 1971, rev. edit., 1982, Soviet-American Relations with Pakistan, Iran, and Afghanistan, 1986; mem. editorial adv. bd. Islam and the Modern Age, Islam Awr Aser-i Jadid, 1969-79; editor Jour. South Asian and Middle Eastern Studies, 1977—; contbr. articles to profl. jours., encyclopedias, chpts. to books. Grantee Office Health, Edn. Welfare, 1974, 1978, Assn. Pakistan and Indic-Islamic Studies/Pakistan Am. Found, 1982. Office: Villanova U 416-421 SAC 800 E Lancaster Ave Villanova PA 19085-1603

MALIK, OM PARKASH, electrical engineering educator, researcher; b. Sargodha, Punjab, India, Apr. 20, 1932; arrived in Can., 1966; s. Arjan Dass and Kesar Bai (Ahuja) M.; m. Margareta Fagerstrom, Dec. 22, 1968; children: Ola Parkash, Mira, Maya. Nat. Diploma in Elec. Engring., Delhi (India) Poly., 1952; M in Engring., Roorkee (India) U., 1962; PhD, London U., 1965; D.I.C., Imperial Coll., London, 1966. Registered profl. engr., Ont., Alta. Asst. engr. Punjab State Elec. Bd., 1953-61, asst. to chief engr., 1957-59; rsch. engr. English Elec. Co., Eng., 1965-66; asst. prof. U. Windsor, Ont., Can., 1966-68; assoc. prof. U. Calgary, Alta., Can., 1968-74, prof., 1974—; assoc. dean student affairs, faculty engring. U. Calgary, Alta., Can., 1995—; assoc. acad. dean faculty engring. U. Calgary, Alta., Can., 1979-90, acting dean, 1981; cons. prof. Huazhong U. Sci. and Tech., Wuhan, People's Republic China, 1986—. Assoc. editor Can. Elec. and Computer Engring. Jour., 1988—; contbr. 400 articles to profl. jours. Indsl. tng. scholar Govt. India, 1952-53, sr. indsl. tng. scholar Confedn. Brit. Industries, 1959-60; recipient Can. Pacific Rwy. engring. medal Engring. Inst. Can., 1997. Fellow IEEE (Centennial medal 1984, chmn. Western Can. coun. 1983-84, Merit award 1986, chmn. student activities Can. region 1979-82), Inst. Elec. Engrs.; mem. IEEE Power Engring. Soc. (machine theory subcom. 1979—, excitation sys. subcom. 1988—, sys. dynamic performance com. 1988—, energy devel. and power generation com. 1990—), Assn. Profl. Engrs., Geologists and Geophysicists Alta. (Vol. Svc. award 1990), Assn. Profl. Engrs. Ont., Am. Soc. Engring. Edn., Can. Elec. Assn. (assoc., controls com.1977-92, chmn. digital control com. 1977-85, chmn. edn. com. 1983-85, mem. expert sys. com. 1989-94), Confederacion Panamericana de Ingenieria Mecanica, Electica y Ramas Afines (v.p. 1987—, bd. dirs. region I, 1991-93). Hindu. Home: 1917-10A Street SW, Calgary, AB Canada T2T 3K2 Office: U Calgary Dept Elec & Computer Engring, 2500 University Dr NW, Calgary, AB Canada T2N 1N4

MALIK, RAYMOND HOWARD, economist, scientist, corporate executive, inventor, educator; b. Lebanon, Feb. 4, 1933; came to U.S., 1948, naturalized, 1963; s. John Z. and Clarice R. (Malik) M. BA, Valparaiso U., 1950; BSBA and Econs., Simpson Coll., 1951; MSBA, So. Ill. U., 1956, PhD in Electronics and Econs., 1959. Supr. Arabian Am. Oil Co., Beirut, 1952-54; mem. grad. faculty, advisor Ill. State U., 1954-59; prof., head world trade programs Central YMCA Community Coll., Chgo., 1966-74; pres. Malik Internat. Enterprises Ltd., Chgo., 1959—; advisor U.S. Congl. Adv. Bd. Author: The Guide to Youth, Health and Longevity, 1980, Do You Really Need Glasses, 1988; inventor selectric typing elements and mechanism, 1959, heater-humidifier-dehumidifier, 1963, ednl. math toys, 1965, 85, circle of sound concept of sound propogation, 1967; designed, introduced Computer and Others, 1962; introduced modular concept in color TV (system-three and others), 1973, gamma ray breast cancer detector, 1976, auto-ignition instant hot water heater, 1981, water filter, purifier and softener, 1984, no doze warner, 1985, indoor-outdoor barbeque grill, 1985, infra-red heat massager, 1986; designed and introduced telephone shoulder rest with adjustable mechanism, 1962, electronic telephone (Trimline, others), 1964, modular telephone, 1975, video phone, 1991; pioneer developer interplanetary communications system, 1961. Deacon, mem. pastor-congl. com., youth and young adult ednl. com. St. George Orthodox Ch., Cicero, Ill.; fundraiser March of Dimes, St. Jude Hosp., Am. Cancer Soc., Am. Heart Fund, numerous others; mem. Am. Task Force for Lebanon, 1992—. Fulbright scholar, 1948-50, Meth. Ch. scholar, 1950-51; So. Ill. U. fellow, 1954-59. Mem. IEEE, AAAS, Am. Mgmt. Assn., Am. Econ. Assn., Am. Mktg. Assn., Import Clubs U.S., Internat. Bus. Coun., Internat. Platform Assn., Pres.'s Assn., Nat. Assn. Self-Employed, Imperial Austrian Legion of Honor, Internat. Students Assn., Soc. Mfg. Engrs., Am. Legion, Highlander Club, Phi Beta Kappa, Sigma Xi, Delta Rho, Beta Gamma Sigma, Alpha Phi Omega. Avocation: multi-linguist. Address: PO Box 3194 Chicago IL 60654-0194 *My duties and responsibilities are: to be of service to my community, working and aiding my countrymen and women in the development of leaders, for the betterment of America's future and the world.*

MALIK, SOHAIL, chemistry educator, researcher, consultant; b. Karachi, Pakistan, Nov. 7, 1958; came to U.S., 1986; s. Bakhtiar Malik and Amna Begum; m. Rubina Sial, Jan. 1, 1990; 1 child, Shahbaz. BSc with honors, U. Karachi, 1980, MS, 1982, PhD, 1986; postgrad., Stanford U., 1986-88. Instr. div. chemistry and nephrology, depts. lab. medicine and medicine U. Wash., Seattle, 1988-89, asst. prof. depts. lab. medicine and medicine, 1989-96; head natural products lab. dept. lab. medicine, 1990-96; co-dir. div. chemistry, dept. lab. medicine U. Wash., Seattle, 1991-96; pres., dir. R&D BioFrontiers, Inc., Redmond, Wash., 1996—; postdoctoral rsch. assoc. dept. chemistry Stanford (Calif.) U., 1986-88; peer rev. cons. NIH/Alcohol Drug Abuse and Mental Health Adminstrn. Mem. editorial bd. Current Medicinal Chemistry; contbr. articles to profl. jours.; patentee in field. Fellow Am. Inst. Chemists, Stanford U. scholar, 1986-88. Mem. Am. Assn. Advancement Sci., Am. Chem. Soc., Am. Soc. Pharmacognosy, Internat. Isotope Soc., Acad. Clin. and Lab. Physicians and Scientists. Avocations: reading, travel, music, poetry, photography. Office: BioFrontiers Inc 14712 NE 87th St Redmond WA 98052-3400

MALIN, HOWARD GERALD, podiatrist; b. Providence, Dec. 2, 1941; s. Leon Nathan and Rena Rose (Shapiro) M. AB, U. R.I., 1964; MA, Brigham Young U., 1969; BSc, Calif. Coll. Podiatric Medicine, 1969, DPM, 1972; MSC, Pepperdine U., 1978; postgrad. in classic, U. So. Calif., 1983—. Diplomate Am. Bd. Podiatric Pub. Health, Am. Bd. Podiatric Orthopedics. Extern in podiatry VA Med. Ctr., Wadsworth, Kans., 1971-72, Marine Corps Res. Dept., San Diego, 1972; resident in podiatric medicine and surgery N.Y. Coll. Podiatric-Medicine, N.Y.C., 1972-73; resident in podiatric surgery, instr. in podiatric surgery N.Y. Coll. Podiatric Medicine, N.Y.C., 1973-74; pvt. practitioner in podiatric medicine and surgery Bklyn., 1974-77; mem. staff Prospect Hosp., Bronx, N.Y., 1974-77; chief podiatry service, mem. staff, cons. sports medicine David Grant U.S. Air Force Med. Ctr., Travis AFB, Calif., 1977-80; chief podiatric sect., mem. staff VA Med. Ctr., Martinsburg, W.Va., 1980—; instr. ednl. devel. program VA Med. Ctr., Martinsburg, W.Va., 1980—; clin. prof. med. sci. Alderson-Broaddus Coll., U. Osteopathic Medicine and Health Scis.; adj. prof. Barry U. Sch. Podiatric Medicine; dir. extern program Pa. Coll. Podiatric Medicine. Editorial rev. bd. Jour. Contemporary Podiatric Physician, 1991—. Lt. col. USAF, 1977-80, with Res. Fellow Am. Coll. Foot Orthopedics, Am. Coll. Podiatric Physicians, Am. SOc. Podiatric Medicine (past pres., archivist), Am. Soc. Podiatric Radiologists (v.p., archivist, pres. elect), Royal Soc. Health; mem. Am. Acad. Podiatric Sports Medicine (assoc.), Assn. Mil. Surgeons U.S. (life), Am. Coll. Podiatric Surgery (assoc.), Am. Assn. Podiatric Med. Writers (archivist), Phi Kappa Theta, Phi Kappa Psi. Home: 210 Shenandoah Rd Apt 2D Martinsburg WV 25401-3723 Office: VA Med Ctr Dept Podiatry Martinsburg WV 25401

MALIN, IRVING, English literature educator, literary critic; b. N.Y.C., Mar. 18, 1934; s. Morris and Bertha (Silverman) M.; m. Ruth Lief, Dec. 18, 1955; 1 child, Mark. BA, Queens Coll., 1955; PhD, Stanford U., 1958. Acting instr. English Stanford U., 1955-58; instr. Ind. U., 1958-60; from instr. to prof. CCNY, 1960-72, prof., 1972—; cons. Jewish Publ. Soc., 1964, Am. Quar., 1964, NEH, 1972, 79, 80, 81, 82, B'nai B'rith, 1974-75, Yaddo, 1975-77, Jewish Book Coun., 1976, 79, PEN, 1978-82, Princeton U. Press, 1979, Fairleigh Dickinson Press, 1980, Wayne State U. Press, 1980, INternat. Coun. Exch. of Scholars, 1980-81, Duke U. Press, 1981, Jewish Daily Forward, 1981, U. Pitts. Press, 1981, Papers on Lang. and Lit., 1981, U. Ga. Press, 1983, UMI Rsch., 1989, Gordian Press, 1990, Ctr. for Study of Higher Edn., 1990, Mosiac, 1991, MacArthur Found., 1996. Author: William Faulkner: An Interpretation, 1957, New American Gothic, 1962, Jews and Americans, 1965, Saul Bellow's Fiction, 1969, Nathanael West's Novels, 1972, Isaac Bashevis Singer, 1972; co-editor: Breakthrough: A Treasury of Contemporary American Jewish Literature, 1964, William Styron's The Confessions of Nat Turner: A Critical Handbook, 1970, The Achievement of William Styron, 1975, William Goyen, 1997; editor: Psychoanalysis and American Fiction, 1965, Saul Bellow and the Critics, 1967, Truman Capote's in Cold Blood: A Critical Handbook, 1968, Critical Views of Isaac Bashevis Singer, 1969, Contemporary American-Jewish Literature: Critical Essays, 1973, Conrad Alken's Prose, 1982; adv. editor: Studies in American Jewish Literature, Jour. Modern Literature, Review of Contemporary Fiction, Saul Bellow Jour., 20th Century Literature; reviewer: Hollins Critic, So. Quarterly; co-editor Paul Bowles, 1986, Spl. Issue of 20th Century Lit., James Dickey spl. Issue of S.C. Rev., 1994, So. Quarterly, 1995, James Dickey's Fiction Spl. Tex. Rev., 1996. Fellow Yaddo, 1963, Nat. Found. for Jewish Culture, 1963-64, Huntington Libr., 1978. Mem. MLA, AAUP, Am. Studies Assn., Am. Jewish Hist. Soc., Melville Soc., Authors League Am., Soc. Study of So. Lit., Poe Studies Assn., English Inst., Nathaniel Hawthorne Soc., N.Y. Acad. Scis., Poetry Soc. Am., Popular Culture Assn., Nat. Book Critics Circle, Sherwood Anderson Soc., Internat. Assn. Univ. Prof. English, Kafka Soc., English-Speaking Union, Multi-Ethnic Lit. U.S. Soc., Hastings Ctr., Am. Jewish Congress, Assoc. Writing Programs, Nat. Coun. Tchrs. of English, Vladimir Nabokov Soc., Phi Beta Kappa. Jewish. Home: 96-13 68th Ave Forest Hills NY 11375-5039 Office: CCNY Dept English New York NY 10031

MALIN, ROBERT ABERNETHY, investment management executive; b. Mt. Vernon, N.Y., Dec. 13, 1931; s. Patrick Murphy and Caroline Cooper (Biddle) M.; m. Gail Lassiter, Nov. 5, 1960; children: Alison Campbell, Robert Lassiter. A.B., Dartmouth Coll., 1953, M.B.A., 1954. Asst. to comptroller Biddle Purchasing Co., N.Y.C., 1958-59; with Blyth & Co., Inc., N.Y.C., 1960-71; v.p. Blyth & Co., Inc., 1965-71, dir., 1968-71, sr. v.p., mem. exec. com., 1971-72; sr. v.p. corp. fin. Reynolds Securities Inc., N.Y.C., 1972-74; dir. Reynolds Securities Inc., 1973-74; mng. dir. First Boston Corp., N.Y.C., 1974-90; gen. ptnr. Tiedemann Investment Group, N.Y.C., 1991-96; mng. dir. SeaBridge Investment Advisors, Summit, N.J., 1997—. Mem. adv. council Fin. Acctg. Standards Bd., 1973-78. Served as lt. (j.g.) USNR, 1954-57. Mem. Investment Bankers Assn. Am. (v.p. exec. com. 1970-71), Securities Industry Assn. (acctg. com.), Links Club, Bond Club, Beacon Hill Club (Summit, N.J.), Morris County (N.J.) Club, Harbour Ridge Club (Stuart, Fla.). Republican. Home: 105 Whittredge Rd Summit NJ 07901-3709 Office: SeaBridge Investment Advisors 450 Springfield Ave Summit NJ 07901-2611

MALINA, MICHAEL, lawyer; b. Bklyn., Mar. 20, 1936; s. William and Jean (Kutlowitz) M.; m. Anita May Oppenheim, June 22, 1958; children: Rachel Lynn, Stuart Charles, Joel Martin. AB, Harvard U., 1957, LLB, 1960. Bar: N.Y. 1961, U.S. Dist. Ct. (so. and ea. dists.) N.Y. 1962, U.S. Ct. Appeals (2d, 3d, 4th, 9th, and D.C. cirs.) 1965, U.S. Supreme Ct. 1965, U.S. Tax Ct. 1991. Assoc. Kaye, Scholer, Fierman, Hays & Handler, N.Y.C., 1960-69, ptnr., 1969—. Contbr. articles to profl. jours. Mem. ABA (antitrust sect.), N.Y. State Bar Assn. (vice chmn. antitrust sect. 1996-97, sec. 1995-96), Assn. of Bar of City of N.Y. (profl. ethics com. 1985-88), Phi Beta Kappa. Democrat. Jewish. Home: 12 Innes Rd Scarsdale NY 10583-7110 Office: Kaye Scholer Fierman Hays & Handler 425 Park Ave New York NY 10022-3506

MALINA, ROGER F., astronomer; b. Paris, July 6, 1950; married; children: Xavier, Juri, Giselle. BS in Physics, MIT, 1972; PhD in Astronomy, U. Calif., Berkeley, 1979. Rsch. aide MIT Ctr. for Space Rsch., Cambridge, 1969-72; summer rsch. aide Cambridge (Mass.) Electron Accelerator, 1971; teaching asst. U. Calif., Berkeley, 1972-73, rsch. asst. space scis. lab., 1973-79, assoc. rsch. astronomer space scis. lab., 1980—; project mgr. for NASA sounding rockets, 1974; organizer Sierra Astrophysics Conf., 1974-76; project scientist for NASA sounding rockets, 1976-78, Berkeley-London-Utrecht extreme ultraviolet spectrometer, 1979-82, FAUST Spacelab 1 Instrument, 1977-84, Extreme Ultraviolet Explorer, 1978-86; co-investigator IUE observations of HZ43, 1981, NGC4242, 1983; co-dir. grant from the Nat. Endowment for the Arts to the Jour. Leonardo, 1984; dir. grant from the Nat. Endowment for the Arts to the Jour. Leonardo, 1985-87; prin. investigator Extreme Ultraviolet Explorer Sci. Instruments, 1985-92; exec. dir. EON Astrophysics; dir. Lab. Astronomy Spatiale, 1995—, NASA EUVE Obs., 1997—. Exec. editor Jour. Leonardo, 1982-95; co-author and contbr. various articles to profl. jours., 1974—; author numerous papers delivered to sci. meetings, 1974—; speaker on profl. confs., 1977—. Bd. dirs. Bay Area Energy Action, San Francisco, 1977-80, Sun Found. Fellow Brit. Interplanetary Soc. (assoc. 1976), Royal Astron. Soc.; mem. Am. Astron. Soc., Optical Soc. of Am., Internat. Soc. for the Arts, Scis. and Tech. (chmn. bd.), Internat. Acad. of Astronautics (corr. mem. 1987), Sigma-Xi. Office: U Calif Ctr for EUV Astrophysics 2150 Kittredge St Berkeley CA 94704-1426

MALINDZAK, GEORGE STEVE, JR., cardiovascular physiology, biomedical engineer; b. Cleve., Jan. 3, 1933; s. George Steve Sr. and Mary (Zemancik) M.; m. Marianne Beamer, June 27, 1959; children: Katherine, Scott, Edward, Eric. AB cum laude in Chemistry and Biology, Western Res. U., 1956; MSc in Physiology and Biophysics, Ohio State U., 1959, PhD in Physiology and Biophysics, 1961; postgrad., MIT, 1963-65, Stanford U., 1969. Metallurgist Thompson & Co., Cleve., 1956-57; from instr. to asst. prof. dept. physiology Bowman Gray Sch. Medicine, Winston-Salem, N.C., 1962-68, assoc. prof., 1968-73; rsch. physiologist U. N.C.-EPA, Chapel Hill, 1973-76; prof., chmn. dept. physiology N.E. Ohio U. Coll. Medicine, Rootstown, 1976-85; prof., chmn. dept. biomed. engring. La. Tech. U., Ruston, 1985-88; health sci. adminstr. NIH, Nat. Inst. Environ. Health Scis., Rsch. Triangle Park, N.C., 1988-96, branch chief, 1996—; cons. Internat. Chelation Rsch. Found., 1982—, Tech. Adv. Svc. for Attys., 1979—. Contbr. more than 140 articles and abstracts to profl. pubs. Mem. U.S. Power Squadron (boating), 1967—. With U.S. Army, 1950-53. Grantee NIH, 1961-73, N.C. Heart Assn., 1962-73, EPA, 1973-76, Am. Heart Assn., 1977-85. Mem. AAAS, Am. Soc. Engring. Edn., Am. Physiol. Soc., Am. Soc. Pharmacology and Exptl. Therapeutics, Assn. Chmn. Depts. Physiology, IEEE Engring. in Medicine and Biology Group, Biomed. Engring. Soc., Am. Heart Assn. (basic sci. coun.), Assn. Computing Machinery, AAUP, Biophys. Soc., La. Engring. Soc., Sigma Xi, Beta, Beta, Beta, Alpha Eta Mu. Achievements include research in cardiopulmonary toxicology, coronary and cerebral vascular reactivity and spasm, coronary and cerebral ischemia and hypoxia and vascular control, carbon monoxide toxicity, autonomic and receptor physiology and pharmacology, control of blood flow in health and disease, microcirculation of the heart, cardiopulmonary function and environmental toxicology, hypoxia, ischemia and circulatory function, pathophysiology of coronary and peripheral vascular atherosclerosis, echocardiography and ventricular function, spinal cord trauma, cardiac function and rehabilitation of alcoholics, peripheral vascular disease, medical electronics and medical engineering, cardiovascular modeling, indicator-dilution techniques and analyses, mathematical and computer analyses of biological systems. Home: 10009 Bushveld Ln Raleigh NC 27613-6145 Office: Nat Inst Environ Health Sci PO Box 12233 Durham NC 27709-2233

MALING, GEORGE CROSWELL, JR., physicist; b. Boston, Mass., Feb. 24, 1931; s. George Croswell and Marjory (Bell) M.; m. Norah J. Horsfield, Dec. 29, 1960; children: Ellen P., Barbara J., Jeffrey C. A.B., Bowdoin Coll., 1954; S.B., S.M., MIT, 1954, Elec. Engr., 1958, Ph.D., 1963. Rsch. asst., postdoctoral fellow MIT, 1957-65; adv. physicist IBM Corp., 1965-71; sr. physicist IBM Corp., Poughkeepsie, N.Y., 1971-92; pres. Empire State Software Systems, Ltd., 1992-93; dir. Noise Control Found., Inc., Poughkeepsie, 1975—; chmn. com. Sl-acoustics Am. Nat. Standards Com., 1976-79; dir. Inst. Noise Control Engring. Found., Inc., 1993—; mng. dir. Inst. of Noise Control Engring., 1994—. Editor: Noise/News, 1972-92; mng. editor: Noise/News, 1972-92; mng. editor: Noise/News Internat., 1993—; assoc. editor Jour. Acoustical Soc. Am., 1976-83; editor tech. proc.; contbr. numerous articles to profl. jours. Served with U.S. Army, 1955-57. Fellow IEEE, AAAS, Acoustical Soc. Am. (exec. coun. 1980-83, Silver medal in noise 1992), Audio Engring. Soc.; mem. Inst. Noise Control Engring. (bd. dirs. 1972-77, pres. 1975), Internat. Inst. Noise Control Engring. (bd. dirs. 1980-86, 90—). Office: Noise Control Foundation PO Box 2469 Arlington Br Poughkeepsie NY 12603-8880

MALINO, JEROME R., rabbi; b. N.Y.C., June 7, 1911; s. Wolf and Henrietta (Rosenbaum) M.; m. Rhoda Simon, June 9, 1936; children: Frances, Jonathan. B.A., CCNY, 1931; M.H.L., Jewish Inst. Religion, 1935; L.H.D. (hon.), Alfred (N.Y.) U., 1958; D.D. (hon.), Hebrew Union Coll., 1960. Rabbi Baldwin (N.Y.) Jewish Center, 1934-35, United Jewish Center, Danbury, Conn., 1935-81; rabbi emeritus United Jewish Center, 1981—; chaplain Fed. Correctional Inst., Danbury, 1940-83; lectr. Western Conn. State U., 1983-84; adj. lectr. Hebrew Union Coll.-Jewish Inst. Religion, 1983—; a founder Jewish Fedn. Danbury, pres., 1947-50. Mem. Danbury Bd. Edn., 1949-69, pres. alternate yrs., 1951-69; bd. dirs. Danbury Cmty. Action Com.; mem. Danbury Charter Revision Com., 1976, Mayor of Danbury Ad Hoc Com. Racism, 1976. Mem. Central Conf. Am. Rabbis (pres. 1979-81), Assn. Religious Communities (pres. 1982-84), Jewish Peace Fellowship, Inst. Religion in Age of Sci., Danbury Music Center, Danbury Concert Assn. Home: 77 Garfield Ave Danbury CT 06810-7906 Office: 141 Deer Hill Ave Danbury CT 06810-7726 *The best way to enhance the meaning of one's own life is to place human values everywhere before all other considerations.*

MALINO, JOHN GRAY, real estate executive; b. N.Y.C., Oct. 15, 1939; s. Joseph and Dorothy (Gray) M.; m. Geraldine Seibel, Mar. 24, 1963 (div.); m. Phyllis Susan Alter, Mar. 29, 1987; children: Joanne, Linda. BA, NYU, 1961. Lic. real estate broker, N.Y. Real estate broker Robert Joseph, N.Y.C., 1961-64; asst. v.p. Loews Corp., N.Y.C., 1964-83, v.p., 1983—. Chmn. Young Men's and Women's Real Estate Assn., N.Y., 1974, N.Y.C. Real Estate Bd., 1982. Lodge: B'nai B'rith (pres. real estate div.). Home: 553 Barnard Ave Woodmere NY 11598-2707 Office: Loews Corp 667 Madison Ave New York NY 10021-8029

MALINOWSKI, PATRICIA A., community college educator; b. Buffalo, N.Y., Jan. 19, 1950; d. Raymond J. and Emily M. (Ferek) Cybulski; m. Leonard T. Malinowski, July 12, 1975; children: Adam, Christopher. BA, SUNY, Fredonia, 1971; MEd, Bowling Green State U., 1972. Prof. devel. studies Finger Lakes C.C., Canandaigua, N.Y., 1987-92, assoc. prof., 1992-96, prof. devel. studies, 1996—, chairperson devel. studies dept., 1991—. Editor: Rsch. and Teaching in Devel. Edn., 1990—, (monographs) Perspectives on Teaching in Development Edn., 1992, 93, Issues in Assessment, 1993, 94, 95; contbr. articles to profl. jours. Mem. sch. bd. St. Mary's Sch., Canandaigua, 1993—, sec. parent's adv. com., 1994-95; mem. program com. Literacy Vols., Canandaigua, 1994—. Mem. N.Y. Coll. Learning Skills (v.p., sec., conf. chair 1987—), NADE (Outstanding Publ. award 1995), N.Y. State Reading Assn., Nat. C.C. Chair Acad. (editl. bd. 1992—), Internat. Reading Assn. (editl. bd. 1994—), Nat. Coun. Tchrs. English. Avocations: family, reading, travel, walking. Office: Finger Lakes CC 4355 Lakeshore Dr Canandaigua NY 14424-8347

MALIS, LEONARD IRVING, neurosurgeon; b. Phila., Nov. 23, 1919; s. Morris Melvin and Dorothy (Brodsky) M.; m. Ruth Gornstein, June 24, 1942; children: Larry Alan, Lynne Paula. MD, U. Va., 1943. Intern Phila. Gen. Hosp., 1943-44; resident in neurology Mt. Sinai Hosp., N.Y.C., 1947, resident in neurosurgery, 1948-50, neurosurgeon in chief, dir. dept. neurol. surgery, 1970-92; prof., chmn. dept. neurosurgery Mt. Sinai Sch. Medicine, CUNY, 1970-92, prof. emeritus dept. neurosurgery, 1993—; fellow in neurophysiology Med. Sch., Yale U., 1951; practice medicine specializing in neurosurgery N.Y.C., 1951—; cons. in field. Contbr. numerous articles to profl. jours.; developer various surg. and electronic instruments. Capt. M.C., U.S. Army, World War II. Mem. ACS, Am. Assn. Neurol. Surgery, Congress Neurol. Surgeons, Am. Physiol. Soc., Soc. Neuroscis., Am. Acad. Neurol. Surgery, Soc. Neurol. Surgeons, Alpha Omega Alpha. Office: 219-44 Peck Ave Hollis NY 11427

MALISH, DAVID MARC, physician; b. Phila., Dec. 29, 1947; s. Irvin and Esther (Divor) M.; (div. 1990); children: Jennifer, Scott; m. Shari Boxer, Sept. 26, 1992; 1 child, Jack. BS, Knox Coll., 1969; MD, Hahnemann U., 1973. Diplomate Am. Bd. Internal Medicine, Am. Bd. Allergy and Immunology. Intern Hahnemann Hosp., Phila., 1973-74; internal medicine resident Monmouth Med. Ctr., Long Branch, N.J., 1974-76; fellow in allergy and immunology Kaiser Found. Hosp.-Sunset facility, UCLA Immunodeficiency Clinic, Children's Hosp., L.A., 1976-78; locum tenems Drs. Cenci and Krall, West Hartford and Hartford, Conn., 1978-79; pvt. practice San Jose, Calif., 1979—; staff internist Monte Villa Hosp., Morgan Hill, Calif., 1979-81; med. dir., staff internist Good Samaritan Recovery Ctr., Good Samaritan Hosp., San Jose, 1991-94, med. cons. Samaritan Pain Ctr., San Jose. Bd. dirs. Am. Lung Soc., Santa Clara, 1980—; med. dir. Camp Superstuff-Asthmatic Camp for Children, 1985—; head pediat. asthma sect. Am. Lung Assn., Santa Clara County, 1994—; mem. fin. bd. for physicians Com. to Reelect Congressman Norm Mineta. Fellow Am. Acad. Allergy and Immunology, Am. Coll. Allergy; mem. Am. Acad. Physicians, Calif. Soc. Addiction Medicine (cert.), Santa Clara Med. Assn. Avocations: photography, art, weight lifting, computers. Office: 2505 Samaritan Dr Ste 606 San Jose CA 95124-4016

MALITZ, SIDNEY, psychiatrist, educator, researcher; b. N.Y.C., Apr. 20, 1923; s. Benjamin and Etta (Cohen) M. Student, NYU, 1940-42, Tulane U., 1942-43; BM, Chgo. Med. Coll., 1946, MD, 1947. Diplomate Am. Bd. Psychiatry and Neurology. Intern St. Mary's Hosp., Huntington, W.Va., 1946-47; sr. intern Bethesda, Hosp., Cin., 1947-48; resident N.Y. State Psychiat. Inst., N.Y.C., 1948-51; sr. research psychiatrist N.Y. State Psychiat. Inst., 1954-56, acting prin. research psychiatrist, 1956-58, acting chief psychiat. research, chief dept. exptl. psychiatry, 1958-64, chief psychiat. research dept. exptl. psychiatry, 1964-72, dep. dir., 1972-75, acting dir., 1975-76, 81-84, dep. dir., 1976-78, dir. dept. biol. psychiatry, 1984-91; in charge psychiat. drug clinic Vanderbilt Clinic, Presbyn. Hosp., N.Y.C., 1956-75, asst. attending psychiatrist, 1960-66, assoc. attending psychiatrist, 1966-71, attending psychiatrist, 1971-93, acting dir. psychiatry service, 1975-76, 81-84, 93—, consulting psychiatrist; asst. dept. psychiatry Coll. Physicians and Surgeons, Columbia U., N.Y.C., 1955-57, assoc., 1957-59, asst. clin. prof., 1959-65, assoc. prof., 1965-69, prof., 1969-93, vice chmn. dept. psychiatry, 1972-75, acting chmn., 1975-76, 81-84, vice chmn., 1976-78, prof. emeritus, 1993—; mem. panel impartial psychiat. experts N.Y. State Supreme Ct., 1960—; mem. adv. com. subcom.; cons. U.S. Pharmacopeia; mem. adv. com. subcom. health N.Y. State Constl. Conv.; cons. div. med. scis. NRC, Washington, 1967-70; cons. Rush Found., Los Angeles, 1968-75; mem. ad hoc rev. com. to select Nat. Drug Abuse Research Ctrs., Ctr. Studies Narcotic and Drug Abuse, NIMH, 1972-73. Contbr. numerous articles to profl. jours. Recipient Leonard Caemmer award N.Y. State Psychiatric Inst., 1984. Fellow Royal Soc. Medicine (life), Am. Psychiat. Assn. (life, chmn. com. biol. psychiatry 1961-62, program com. 1961-62, sec-treas. chpt. 1962-63, com. rsch. 1966-68, pres. chpt. 1969-70, chmn. Coun. Rsch. and Devel. 1971-73, History and Libr. com. 1989-91), Am. Coll. Neuropsychopharmacology (life); mem. AAAS (coun. 1969-72), N.Y. Acad. Medicine (life), Collegium Internationale Neuropsychopharmacologicum (life), Am. Coll. Psychiatrists (archivist-historian 1978—, liaison to Royal Coll. Psychiatrists 1985—, Bowis award 1989), Royal Coll. Psychiatrists, Am. Coll. Psychoanalysts, N.Y. Soc. Clin. Psychiatry, Assn. Research Nervous and Mental Disease, N.Y. State, N.Y. County med. socs., AMA (cons. coun.l drugs 1960-70), Group Advancement of Psychiatry (rsch. com. 1986-91), N.Y. Acad. Scis, N.Y. Psychiat. Soc. (v.p. 1989-91, pres. 1991-92), Am. Psychopath. Assn., Soc. Biol. Psychiatry, Benjamin Rush Soc. (pres.-elect 1989, pres. 1990-91), Vidonian Soc. (pres. 1989-93), Alpha Omega Alpha. Office: Columbia U Dept Psychiatry 161 Fort Washington Ave New York NY 10032-3713

MALKASIAN, GEORGE DURAND, JR., physician, educator; b. Springfield, Mass., Oct. 26, 1927; s. George Dur and Gladys Mildred (Trombley) M.; m. Mary Ellen Koch, Oct. 16, 1954; children: Linda Jeanne, Karen Diane, Martha Ellen. AB, Yale U., 1950; MD, Boston U., 1954; MS, U. Minn., 1963. Diplomate Am. Bd. Ob-Gyn. Intern Worcester (Mass.) City Hosp., 1954-55; resident in ob-gyn Mayo Grad. Sch. Hosp., Rochester, Minn., 1955-58, 60-61; mem. faculty Mayo Med. Sch., 1962—, prof. ob-gyn, 1976—, chmn. dept. ob-gyn, 1976-86. Author articles in field. Served to lt. comdr. M.C., USNR, 1958-60. Named Tchr. of Yr., Mayo Grad. Sch. Medicine, 1973, 77, Alumnus of Yr., Boston U. Sch. Med., 1990. Mem. ACS, Am. Coll. Obstetricians and Gynecologists, Am. Gynecol. and Obstet. Soc., Am. Radium Soc., Soc. Gynecologic Oncologists, Assn. Profs. Ob-gyn., N.Am. Ob-gyn. Soc., Ctrl. Assn. Obstetricians and Gynecologists, Minn. Soc. Obstetricians and Gynecologists, Am. Coll. Obstetricians and Gynecologists (pres. 1989-90), Zumbro Valley Med. Soc. (exec. dir. 1996—). Home: 1750 11th Ave NE Rochester MN 55906-4215 Office: Mayo Clinic 200 1st St SW Rochester MN 55902-3008

MALKAWI, ALI MAHMOUD, architecture educator, researcher; b. Irbid, Jordan, Feb. 12, 1967; came to U.S., 1989; s. Mahmoud Ahmed and Safia (Khatib) M.; m. Jenae Joy Huey, Dec. 21, 1991. BS in Archtl. Engring. with honors, Jordan U. Sci. and Tech., Irbid, 1989; MArch, U. Colo., Denver, 1990; PhD with honors, Ga. Inst. Tech., 1994. Project designer Malkawi Cons. Engrs., Amman, Jordan, 1989; instr. Ga. Inst. Tech., Atlanta, 1992-94, doctoral fellow, 1991-94, project coord., 1994; asst. prof. architecture U. Mich., Ann Arbor, 1994—; coord., asst. prof., 1994—; postdoctoral/Oberdick fellow U. Mich., Ann Arbor, 1994-95; pres. Intelligenet Energy Optimization Cons., Ann Arbor, 1995—. Mem. ASHRAE, Acoustical Soc. Am., Illumination Engring. Soc., Am. Solar Energy Soc. Achievements include copyrighted theory development and implementation of intelligent CAD software. Office: U Mich Coll Architecture 2000 Bonisteel Dr Ann Arbor MI 48109-2021

MALKEMES, WILLIAM CHARLES, career military officer; b. Phila., Oct. 29, 1948. Enlisted U.S. Army, 1970; advanced through ranks to col.; with Camber Corp, Huntsville, Ala.; sr. mem. Space Exec. Group, Washington, 1992—, Distributed Interactive Simulation, Huntsville, Ala., 1992—; adv. bd. Directed Energy Coun., Huntsville, 1994—, Theater Missile Def., Washington, 1994—. Avocations: tennis, coaching youth basketball, squash. Home: 131 Winfield Chase Dr Madison AL 35758 Office: Camber Corp 635 Discovery Dr NW Huntsville AL 35806-2801

MALKIEL, BURTON GORDON, economics educator; b. Boston, Aug. 28, 1932; s. Sol and Celia (Gordon) M.; m. Judith Ann Atherton, July 16, 1954 (dec. 1987); 1 child, Jonathan; m. Nancy Weiss, July 31, 1988. BA, Harvard, 1953, MBA, 1955; PhD, Princeton, 1964. Assoc. Smith Barney & Co., N.Y.C., 1958-60; asst. prof. dept. econs. Princeton U., 1964-66, assoc. prof., 1966-68, prof., 1968-81, Rentschler prof. econs., 1969-81, chmn. dept. econs., 1974-75, 77-81; dean Sch. Orgn. and Mgmt., Yale U., 1981-87; Chem. Bank chmn.'s prof. econs. Princeton U., 1988—; mem. Pres.'s Council Econ. Advisors, 1975-77; dir. Amdahl Corp., Jeffrey Co., So. New Eng. Telephone Co., Prudential Life Ins. Co. Am., Baker, Fentress & Co., Vanguard Group. Author: The Term Structure of Interest Rates, 1966, (with others) Strategies and Rational Decisions in the Securities Options Market, 1969, A Random Walk Down Wall Street, 1973, 6th edit., 1996, The Inflation-Beater's Investment Guide, 1980. Served to 1st lt. AUS, 1955-58. Mem. Am. Fin. Assn. (dir., pres. 1978). Home: 76 North Rd Princeton NJ 08540-2430 Office: Princeton U Dept Econs Princeton NJ 08544

MALKIEL, NANCY WEISS, college dean, history educator; b. Newark, Feb. 14, 1944; d. William and Ruth Sylvia (Puder) W.; m. Burton G. Malkiel, July 31, 1988. BA summa cum laude, Smith Coll., 1965; MA, Harvard U., 1966, PhD, 1970. Asst. prof. history Princeton (N.J.) U., 1969-75, assoc. prof., 1975-82, prof., 1982—, master Dean Mathey Coll., 1982-86, dean of coll., 1987—. Author (as Nancy J. Weiss): Charles Francis Murphy, 1858-1924: Respectability and Responsibility in Tammany Politics, 1968, (with others) Blacks in America: Bibliographical Essays, 1971, The National Urban League, 1910-1940, 1974, Farewell to the Party of Lincoln: Black Politics in the Age of FDR, 1983 (Berkshire Conf. of Women Historians prize 1984), Whitney M. Young Jr., and the Struggle for Civil Rights, 1989. Trustee Smith Coll., Northampton, Mass., 1984-94, Woodrow Wilson Nat. Fellowship Found., 1975—. Fellow Woodrow Wilson Found., 1965, Charles Warren Ctr. for Studies in Am. History, 1976-77, Radcliffe Inst., 1976-77, Ctr. for Advanced Study in Behavioral Scis., 1986-87. Mem. Am. Hist. Assn., Orgn. Am. Historians (chmn. status women hist. profession 1972-75), So. Hist. Assn., Phi Beta Kappa. Democrat. Jewish. Office: Princeton U Office Dean Of College Princeton NJ 08544

MALKIEL, YAKOV, linguistics educator; b. Kiev, Russia, July 22, 1914; came to U.S., 1940, naturalized, 1946; s. Léon and Claire (Saitzew) M.; m. María Rosa Lida, Mar. 2, 1948 (dec. Sept. 1962). Matura, Werner-Siemens Realgymnasium, Berlin-Schöneberg, 1933; PhD magna cum laude, Friedrich-Wilhelms Universität, Berlin, 1938; LHD (hon.), U. Chgo., 1969; LLD (hon.), U. Ill., 1976; Dr honoris causa, U. Paris, 1983, Free U., W. Berlin, 1983, Georgetown U., 1987, Oxford U., 1989, Salamanca U., 1992. Instr. U. Wyo., 1942; lectr. U. Calif.-Berkeley, 1942-45, instr., 1945-46, asst. prof., 1946-48, assoc. prof., 1948-52, prof. Romance philology, 1952-66, mem. grad. council, 1953-57, assoc. dean grad. div., 1963-66, prof. linguistics and Romance philology, 1966-85, 86, 88, research fellow in the humanities, 1968-69, research prof. humanities, 1981; research assoc. Mills Coll., summers 1942-43; vis. assoc. prof. U. So. Calif., summer 1949; vis. lectr. Ind. U., summer 1953; vis. prof. U. Colo., summer 1958, U. Tex. Linguistic Inst., summer 1960, Linguistic Inst., Ind. U., summer 1964, Linguistic Inst., UCLA, 1966; Collitz prof. Linguistics Inst., 1980; vis. lectr. cursos superiores Melsaga U., 1989-92; lectr. Jennifer summer inst., Soria, Spain; cons. various panels NEH, 1978—; participant symposium Inst. Italian Ency., Rome. Editor in chief Romance Philology Quar., 1947-82, cons. editor, 1982—; assoc. editor Hispanic Rev., Jour. Hispanic Rsch. (London), Romance Quar. (Ky.), Revista de Filologia Española, Voz y Letra (Málaga); author: Essays on Linguistic Themes, 1968, Etymological Dictionaries: A Typological Survey, 1976, Theory and Practice of Romance Etymology, 1989, Etymology; also monographs, articles U.S. and fgn. countries; contbr. to Dictionary of the Middle Ages, Ency. of Romance Linguistics, Ency. of Lexicography. Recipient Guggenheim Meml. Found. 3d award, 1967; Berkeley citation U. Calif., 1985; Faculty Rsch. lectr. U. Calif. Berkeley, 1988-89; Guggenheim fellow, 1948-49, 59; NSF sr. postdoctoral fellow, 1966; Princeton U. fellow, 1977. Mem. Am. Acad. Arts and Scis., Linguistic Soc. Am. (pres. 1965), MLA (founder Romance linguistics group 1946), Linguistic Soc. Paris, Am. Oriental Soc., Philol. Assn. Pacific Coast (v.p. 1963, pres. 1965), Société de Linguistique Romane (exec. com. 1977, 79, 89), Royal Spanish Acad. (corr. mem. 1987—), Società di linguistica italiana (hon.), Ctr. Romance Studies, U. London. Home: 1 Arlington Ln Kensington CA 94707-1108

MALKIN, BARRY, film editor, consultant; b. N.Y.C., Oct. 26, 1938; s. Richard and Helen (Kandix) M.; m. Stephanie Byer, Apr. 5, 1971; 1 child, Sacha Janine. BA, Adelphi U., 1960. Freelance film editor Sacha Prodns., Inc., N.Y.C., 1964—. Editor: (films) The Rain People, 1969, They Might Be Giants, 1971, Who is Harry Kellerman and Why Is He Saying All Those Terrible Things About Me?, 1971, Cops and Robbers, 1973, One Summer Love, 1976, Somebody Killed Her Husband, 1978, Last Embrace, 1979, (with Edward Beyer and David Ray) One Trick Pony, 1980, Windows, 1980, (with Mark Laub) Four Friends, 1981, (with Laub, Robert Q. Lovett and Randy Roberts) Hammett, 1982, Rumble Fish, 1983, (with Lovett) The Cotton Club, 1984 (Acad. award nominee for best film editing 1984), Peggy Sue Got Married, 1986, Gardens of Stone, 1987, Big, 1988, New York Stories ("Life Without Zoe"), 1989, The Freshman, 1990, (with Lisa Fruchtman and Walter Murch) The Godfather Part III, 1990 (Acad. award nominee for best film editing 1990), Honeymoon in Vegas, 1992, It Could Happen to You, 1994, Jack, 1996, The Rainmaker, 1997. Mem. Acad. Motion Picture Arts and Scis., Motion Picture Editors. Home and Office: 275 Central Park W New York NY 10024

MALKIN, CARY JAY, lawyer; b. Chgo., Oct. 6, 1949; s. Arthur D. and Perle (Slavin) M.; m. Lisa Klimley, Oct. 27, 1976; children: Dorothy R., Victoria S., Lydia R. BA, George Washington U., 1971; JD, Northwestern U., 1974. Bar: Ill. 1974, U.S. Dist. Ct. (no. dist.) Ill. 1974. Assoc., Mayer, Brown & Platt, Chgo., 1974-80, ptnr., 1981—. Chmn. spl. events com. Mental Health Assn., 1984-85; mem. steering com. Endowment Campaign of the Latin Sch. Chgo, 1988-92; chmn. annual fund The Latin Sch. of Chgo., 1990-91, trustee, 1991—, v.p., 1992—, chmn. capital campaign, 1995—; mem. exec. com. Friends of Prentice Women's Hosp., 1991-92; bd. dirs. SOS Children's Village Ill., 1992-96; mem. M.S. Weiss fund bd. Children's Meml. Hosp., 1989-93; mem. Graziano Fund bd. Children's Meml. Hosp., 1993-96; mem. steering com. Founder's Cup, Field Mus., 1995—. Mem. Order of the Coif, Chgo. Club, Saddle and Cycle Club, Standard Club, Phi Beta Kappa. Home: 233 E Walton St Chicago IL 60611-1526 Office: Mayer Brown & Platt 190 S La Salle St Chicago IL 60603-3410

MALKIN, MOSES MONTEFIORE, employee benefits administration company executive; b. Revere, Mass., Sept. 18, 1919; s. Irving and Annie (Helfant) M.; m. Hannah Lacob, Oct. 11, 1941. AB, U. N.C., 1941; BSME, Columbia U., 1948. Enrolled actuary and chartered life underwriter. Engr. GE, Schenectady, N.Y., 1948-50; engr. Gen. Bronze, Inc., Jersey City, 1950-51; v.p. Malkin Warehouse, Inc., New Haven, 1951-57; pvt. practice actuary New Haven, 1957-72; chmn., actuary Profl. Pensions, Inc., East Haven, Conn., 1972—; presenter pension issues at numerous confs., 1970-80. Pres., founder Milford, Conn., 1962, Milford Child Guidance Clinic, 1966; pres. Clifford Beers Child Guidance, New Haven, 1971, Jewish Family Svc., New Haven, 1973. With U.S. Army, 1941-46, ETO. Mem. Am. Acad. Actuaries, Am. Soc. Pension Actuaries (instr. 1984), Am. Soc. Chartered Life Underwriters, Grads. Club (New Haven), Phi Beta Kappa, Tau Beta Pi. Jewish. Home: 1514 Heron Dr Sun City Center FL 33573 Office: Profl Pensions Inc 444 Foxon Rd New Haven CT 06513-2019

MALKIN, PETER LAURENCE, lawyer; b. N.Y.C., Jan. 14, 1934; s. Samuel and Gertrude (Greenberger) M.; m. Isabel L. Wien, July 10, 1955; children: Scott David, Cynthia Allison, Anthony Edward. Grad. cum laude, Poly. Prep. Country Day Sch., 1951; AB summa cum laude, Harvard Coll., 1955; LLB magna cum laude, Harvard U., 1958. Bar: N.Y. 1958, Conn. 1976, Fla. 1977. Sr. ptnr., chmn. Wien & Malkin LLP, N.Y.C., Fla., 1960—; gen. ptnr. Empire State Bldg. Assocs., 1961—, 1185 Ave. of Ams. Assocs., N.Y.C., 1978—; bd. dirs. U.S. Trust Corp., N.Y.C. Partnership and C. of C., 1992—; chmn. W&M Properties, Inc., Grand Ctrl. Partnership Inc., 34th St. Partnership, Inc.; dir. Fashion Ctr. Bus. Improvement Dist.; dir. Realty Found. N.Y., 1981—, v.p., 1995—; mem. adv. com. Greenwich (Conn.) Japanese Sch., 1992—; gov. Real Estate Bd., N.Y., 1993—. Nat. vice-chmn. Harvard Law Sch. Fund, 1967-71, chmn. nat. scholarship com., 1975-76, chmn. N.Y.C. com., 1981-83; founder, bd. dirs. Urban League Southwestern Fairfield County, 1969-73, treas., 1969-71; bd. dirs., mem. exec. com. Lincoln Ctr. for Performing Arts, 1979—; bd. dirs. Inst. Internat. Edn., 1983-89, hon. 1994—; mem. devel. com. N.Y. Pub. Libr., 1979—; trustee Nat. Trust for Hist. Preservation, 1988-91; founding chmn. Greenwich (Conn.) Green & Clean, Inc., 1986—; v.p., mem. exec. com. Greenwich chpt. NAACP, 1967-69; trustee Citizens Budget Commn., N.Y.C., 1971-91, Jewish Communal Fund, N.Y., 1976-81; hon. trustee Assoc. YM and YWHA Greater N.Y.; dean's coun., Harvard U., 1987—; chmn. capital campaign and mem. overseers com. to visit Kennedy Sch. Govt., 1976-82, 83-89, 90—, to visit Harvard Law Sch. 1977-83; exec. com. Program for Ctr. for Jewish Studies, 1974-80; bd. overseers Harvard Coll., 1989-95, overseers com. univ resources, 1972—, exec. com., 1985—; dean's adv. com., Harvard Law Sch., 1988-90; mem. steering com. N.Y. Major Gifts, Harvard Coll. Fund, 1989-93, chmn., 1989-93; elected dir. Harvard Alumni Assn., 1981-83; chmn. schs. and scholarship com. Harvard U., Greenwich, 1973-79; exec. com. Assn. Better N.Y., 1972—; founding chmn. Greenwich Adopt-A-Read, 1996—. Recipient Nat. Preservation Honor award Nat. Trust Hist. Preservation, 1987, President's award Grad. Sch. and Univ. Ctr. CCNY, 1989, Crain's All-Star award, 1994, Nacore Disting. Man of Yr. award, 1995; named Outstanding Young Man, N.Y.C. Jaycees, 1969, fellow Brandeis U., 1970—, Man of Yr., Hist. Soc. Greenwich, Conn., 1993. Mem. Harvard Law Sch. Assn. N.Y.C. (trustee 1968-70, v.p. 1973-74, mem. coun.), Assn. Bar City N.Y. (mem. com. admissions 1965-68, com. assn. bldgs. 1968-72, chmn. com. ins. assn. bldgs. 1967-68), Am. Arbitration Assn. (nat. panel arbitrators), Century Assn., The Links N.Y., The Hasty Pudding Inst. 1770, AD Hon., Harvard Varsity Club (Cambridge), Harvard Club N.Y.C. (bd. mgrs. 1979-81), Harvard Club (Fairfield County, Conn., v.p. 1974-75, bd. dirs. 1976-80), Bailwick Club (founding pres.), Blind Brook Club, Sky Club, Phi Beta Kappa. Office: 60 E 42nd St New York NY 10165

MALKIN, STANLEY LEE, neurologist; b. Pitts., Nov. 11, 1942; s. Maurice and Bessie Beatrice (Serbin) M.; children: Justin Ross, Keith Richard. BA with honors, U. Pa., 1964; MD, U. Pitts., 1968; Intern, Montefiore Hosp., Pitts., 1968-69; resident in neurology Columbia-Presbyn. Med. Center, N.Y.C., 1969-72; chief neurology service Wright-Patterson AFB, Dayton, Ohio, 1972-74; practice medicine specializing in neurology, N.Y.C.; attending staff Mt. Sinai Hosp.; former dir. Neuro-Diagnostic Lab, Englewood; asst. clin. prof. neurology Mt. Sinai Sch. of Medicine; founder Bergen-Passaic Tomography Center, Fairlawn, N.J.; neurology cons. Regent Hosp.; med. dir. Pain Suppression Labs., Inc.; med. dir. Efficient Health Systems, Inc.-N.Y.C. Healthline; founder, med. dir., exec. v.p. Hosp. Diagnostic Equipment Corp., 1987—; pres. Cancer Treatment Holdings, Inc, 1993-95, dir. 1993-94, sr. med. dir. 1995—; founder Montvale Med. Imaging Assocs. (N.J.), N.Y. Med. Imaging, N.Y.C., Hosp. Diagnostic Equipment Corp. Co-mcpl. coord. Ft. Lee Citizens for McGovern, 1972; ptnr. Sall/Myers Med. Assocs., prin. 1995—; mem. Edgewater Rent Control Bd., 1978, Nat. Headache Found. Maj. M.C., USAF, 1972-74. Diplomate Am. Bd. Psychiatry and Neurology, Nat. Bd. Med. Examiners. Mem. Am. Acad. Neurology, Am. Assn. Electrodiognostic Medicine, Am. Soc. Neuro-Imaging (charter), Am. Med. EEG Soc., Am. Assn. for Study of Headache, Nat. Headache Found., Internat. Headache Soc., N.Y. Acad. Scis., N.Y.U. Bellevue Psychiat. Soc., European Fedn. Neurol. Socs. Office: 120 W 44th St Ste 701 New York NY 10036-4011 also: 136 E 57th St Ste 600 New York NY 10022

MALKINSON, FREDERICK DAVID, dermatologist; b. Hartford, Conn., Feb. 26, 1924; s. John Walter and Rose (Volkenheim) M.; m. Una Zwick, June 15, 1979; children by previous marriage: Philip, Carol, John. Student, Loomis Inst., 1937-41; 3 yr. cert. cum laude, Harvard U., 1943, D.M.D., 1947, M.D., 1949. Intern Harvard-Beth Israel Hosp., Boston, 1949-50; resident in dermatology U. Chgo., 1950-54, from instr. to assoc. prof. dept. dermatology, 1954-68; prof. medicine and dermatology U. Ill., Chgo., 1968-71; chmn. dept. dermatology Rush Med. Coll. and Rush-Presbyn.-St. Luke's Med. Ctr., Chgo., 1971-92, Clark W. Finnerud, M.D. prof. dept. dermatology, 1981-95, 95—; trustee Sulzberger Inst. Dermatol. Comm. and Edn., 1976-96; pres. Sulzberger Inst. Dermatol. Communication and Edn., 1983-88, 93-96. Editor: Year Book of Dermatology, 1971-78; chief editor: AMA Archives of Dermatology, 1979-83; bd. editors, 1976-84, Jour. AMA, 1979-83; editorial cons. World Book Medical Encyclopedia, 1991—; contbr. articles and abstracts to profl. jours., chpts. to books. Active Evanston (Ill.) Libr. Bd., 1988-94, pres., 1993-94. With M.C. USN, 1950-52. Grantee U.S. Army, 1955-61, USPHS, 1962-73. Mem. AAAS, Am. Acad. Dermatology (v.p. 1987-89, dir. 1964-67), Am. Dermatol. Assn., Soc. Investigative Dermatology (v.p. 1978-79, dir. 1963-68), Am. Fedn. Clin. Rsch., Cen. Soc. Clin. Rsch., Radiation Rsch. Soc., Assn. Profs. of Dermatology (dir. 1982-85), Dermatology Found. (trustee 1980-93, pres. 1983-85), Nat. Coun. on Radiation Protection and Measurements (mem. com. on cutaneous radiobiology 1986-92), Chgo. Dermatol. Soc. (pres. 1964-65, Gold Medal award 1992), Chgo. Lit. Club.

MALKOVICH, MARK PAUL, III, musician, artistic director, scientist, sports agent; b. Eveleth, Minn., July 10, 1930. s. Mark II and Mary Frances (Greben) M.; m. Joan Shewring, Feb. 7, 1959; children: Mark IV, Erik, Kent, Kara. BS in Chemistry, Columbia U., 1952, MS, 1953; studied piano with Dorothy Crost Bourgin, Chgo. Mus. Coll., 1947-50, William Beller, ch. Piano Dept. Columbia U. 1951-1954; Adele Marcus, Juilliard Sch., 1959-62; MusD (hon.) Salve Regina, 1993; DFA, U. R.I., 1994. Pres. Chem. Gum Industries, Ltd., N.Y.C., 1964-69. Artistic and gen. dir. Newport Music Festival, 1975—; exec. dir. Palm Beach Festival, Fla., 1984-86; guest lectr. TV and radio appearances and adjudicator at music competitions; pres. Chopin Found. of U.S., Miami, Fla., 1985; presented N. Am. debuts of Bella Davidovich, Jean-Philippe Collard, Dmitry Sitkoveksky, Andrei Gavrilov, others; founder Sports US*A*SR; negotiator/agt. for USSR leading hockey players-Fetisov, Krutov, Larionov, and Makarov, 1989—. Mem. Harvard Mus. Assn. Office: care Newport Music Festival PO Box 3300 Newport RI 02840-0992

MALKUS, DAVID STARR, mechanics educator, applied mathematician; b. Chgo., June 30, 1945; s. Willem V.R. Malkus and Joanne (Gerould) Simpson; m. Evelyn R. (div.); children: Christopher, Annelise, Byron, Renata. AB, Yale U., 1968; PhD, Boston U., 1976. Mathematician U.S. Nat. Bur. Standards, Gaithersburg, Md., 1975-77; asst. prof. math. Ill. Inst. Tech., Chgo., 1977-83, assoc. prof., 1983-84; assoc. prof. mechanics U. Wis., Madison, 1984-87, prof., 1987—, chmn. Rheology Rsch. Ctr., 1991-94; chair prof. Nanjing (People's Republic China) Aero. Inst., 1986. Co-author: Concepts and Applications of Finite Element Analysis, 1989; contbr. articles to Computer Methods Applied Mech. Engring., Jour. Computational Physics. Mem. Soc. Rheology. Achievements include research on finite element methods--reduced and selective integration techniques, a unification of concepts. Home: 5595 Mary Lake Rd Waunakee WI 53597-9124 Office: U Wis Dept NEEP 1500 Engineering Dr Madison WI 53706-1609

MALL, WILLIAM JOHN, JR., aerospace executive, retired air force officer; b. Pitts., Jan. 13, 1933; s. William John and Margaret (Henry) M.; m. Vivian Lea Fenton; children—Michele, William, Catherine. B.B.A., U. Pitts., 1954; M.B.A., George Washington U., 1966; sr. mgrs. in govt. program, Harvard U., 1980. Commd. officer USAF, 1954, advanced through grades to maj. gen., 1981; insp. gen. Mil. Airlift Command., Scott AFB, Ill., 1978; comdr. 436 wing Mil. Airlift Command., Dover AFB, Del., 1979; DCS personnel Mil. Airlift Command, Scott AFB, Ill., 1979-81; comdr. Air Rescue Service, Scott AFB, Ill., 1981-83, 23d AF/MAC, Scott AFB, Ill., 1983-85; assigned to Hdqrs USAF, Bolling AFB, D.C., 1985-86; ret.; dir. integrated logistics support div. Douglas Aircraft Co., Long Beach, Calif., 1987-89, gen. mgr. human resources, 1989-91; exec. dir. LAX Two Corp., L.A., 1991—. Decorated Legion of Merit, Bronze Star, Air medal. Mem. Airlift Assn., Daedalians, Jolly Green Pilots Assn. Avocations: tennis, sailing. Office: LAX Two Corp 200 World Way Los Angeles CA 90045-5859

MALLARD, STEPHEN ANTHONY, retired utility company executive; b. Jersey City, Sept. 15, 1924; s. Stephen F. and Gertrude V. (Donahue) M.; m. Winifred Anne Carey, June 7, 1947; children: Stephen Kevin, Catherine Anne, Eileen Rosemary Mallard McClenehan. M.E., Stevens Inst. Tech, Hoboken, N.J., 1948, M.S.E.E., 1951. With elec. distbn., system planning and devel. Pub. Service Electric and Gas Co., Newark, 1951-77, v.p. system planning, 1977-80, sr. v.p. planning and research, 1980-88, sr. v.p. transmission systems, 1989; pvt. practice engring. Nutley, N.J., 1990—; advisor Brookhave Nat. Lab.; cons. Manhattan Coll. Bd. dirs. Essex chpt. ARC, East Orange, N.J., 1985—, bd. dirs. No. N.J. chpt., 1988—; bd. dirs. Essex County Grand Jury Assn., 1978-87. With USN, 1944-46, PTO. Fellow IEEE; mem. Nat. Soc. Profl. Engrs., , Conf. Internationale des Grands Reseaux Electriques a Haute Tension, Eta Kappa Nu, Tau Beta Pi. Roman Catholic. Home and Office: 68 High St Nutley NJ 07110-1134

MALLARDI, VINCENT, organization executive; b. N.Y.C., Sept. 5, 1942; s. Dominic and Wanda Ruth (Ballard) M.; m. Susan Snyder; m. Avril Y. Stone, Dec. 27, 1986; children: Douglas M., Karen R., Kevan Stone. BBA in Mgmt., St. John's U., N.Y.C., 1971; MBA in Fin., Lehigh U., 1979. Cert. mgmt. cons. Announcer Sta. WLIR-FM, N.Y.C., 1960-61; sound-recording prodr. Audio Rec. & Mfg. Co., N.Y.C., 1961-67; pub. G. Riccordi, music, N.Y.C. and Milan, Italy, 1965-67, Synectics Network Inc., news weekly, Bethlehem, Pa., 1967-72, SNI/Re:Print, Phila., 1973-84; cons. SNI/Caribbean, Miami, Fla., 1985—; chmn. Printing Brokerage/Buyers Assn., Inc., Palm Beach, Fla., 1992—; bd. dirs., chmn. exec. com. IFH Capital Mgmt. Corp., Ft. Lauderdale, Fla., 1990—, Mapasa/Sistemas Unidas de Mex., Toluca, sec. Author over 12 books; contbg. editor Am. Printer mag., 1979—; editor-in-chief Who's Printing What Monthly, 1989—; pub. Exitos mag. (Latin Am.); pub. Miss Universe Mag. (worldwide). Recipient Disting. Salesman award Sales and Mktg. Execs. Internat. Fellow Soderstrom Soc. of Nat. Assn. Printers and Lithographers; mem. Chaine des Rotisseurs (chevalier). Republican. Episcopalian. Office: Printing Brokerage/Buyers Assn 277 Royal Poinciana Way Palm Beach FL 33480-4047

MALLARY, GERTRUDE ROBINSON, civic worker; b. Springfield, Mass., Aug. 19, 1902; d. George Edward and Jennie (Slater) Robinson; m. R. DeWitt Mallary, Sept. 15, 1923; children: R. DeWitt, Richard Walker; student, Bennett Coll., 1921-22, U. Conn., 1941-42; LLD (hon.), U. Vt., 1996. Co-owner, ptnr. Mallary Farm, Bradford, Vt., 1936-93; mem. Vt. Ho. of Reps., 1953-56. Pres., Jr. League, Springfield, 1931-33; trustee Wesson Meml. Hosp., Springfield, 1937-42, chmn. nursing services, 1939-42; chmn. Springfield Council Social Agys., 1938-40; mem. Mass. Commn. Pub. Safety, 1941-42; mem. Vt. Bd. Recreation, 1959-65; trustee Fairlee (Vt.) Public Library, 1953-84, Justin Smith Morrill Found., 1964-71, pres., 1968-71; chmn. Fairlee Bicentennial Com., 1974-77. Recipient Theresa R. Brungardt award, 1979, co-recipient with husband Master Breeders award New Eng. Holstein Assn., 1969, Disting. Svc. award, 1989. Mem. Vt. Hist. Soc. (hon.). Editor New Eng. Holstein Bull., 1947-50. Address: Mallary Farm RR1 Box 620 Bradford VT 05033

MALLARY, ROBERT, sculptor; b. Toledo, Dec. 2, 1917; s. Benjamin E. and Laura (Grossman) M.; m. Margot Handrahan, Oct. 29, 1942; children: Michelle, Michael, Martine, Dion. Certificate, La Escuela de las Artes del Libro, Mexico D.F., 1939. mem. faculty U. N.M., 1955-59, Pratt Inst., 1959-67; prof. art U. Mass., Amherst, 1967—. Exhbt. One-man shows, San Francisco Mus. Art., 1944, one-man shows, Crocker Art Gallery, Sacramento, 1944; Calif. Exhibitors Gallery, Los Angeles, 1951, Santa Barbara Mus. Art, 1952, Gumps, San Francisco, 1953, Fine Arts Gallery San Diego, 1953, Urban Gallery, N.Y.C., 1954, Coll. Fine Arts, U. N.M., 1956, Jonson Gallery, Albuquerque, 1957-59, Santa Fe, 1958, Allan Stone Gallery, N.Y.C., 1961, 62, 66, Los Angeles Mus. Art, 1951, 53, 54, Colorado Springs Fine Art Center, 1953, Denver Art Mus., 1955, exhibited in group shows, Denver Art Mus., Sao Paulo, Brazil, 1955, 63, Mus. Modern Art, 1959, 61, 65, Gt. Jones Gallery, N.Y.C., 1959, Guggenheim Mus., 1960, Whitney Mus. Am. Art, 1960, 62, 64, 66, 68, Pace Gallery, Boston, 1960, Stable Gallery, N.Y.C., 1960, Martha Jackson Gallery, N.Y.C., 1961, Inst. Contemporary Art, Houston, 1961, 62, Am. Fedn. Art, Riverside Mus., N.Y.C., 1961, Paris, 1962, Exhbt., Seattle Worlds Fair, 1962, Carnegie Inst., 1962, Denver Mus. Fine Arts, 1962, Art Inst. Chgo., 1962, Allan Stone Gallery, 1961, 62, 66, N.Y. State Coll., Potsdam, 1969; represented in permanent collections, Mus. Modern Art, rep., Whitney Mus. Am. Art, Maremont Found., Smith Coll., Brandeis U., Womens Coll. of U. N.C., U. Tex., Kalamazoo Art Center, U. Cal. at Berkeley, Roswell (N.M.) Mus., Los Angeles Mus. Art, U. N.M., Santa Fe, Denver Coll., N.J.; commd. by, N.Y. Worlds Fair, 1963-64, collaborator (with Dale Owne), mural, Beverly Hilton Hotel, Beverly Hills, Cal., 1955; Dir.: Arstecnica: Interdisciplinary Center for Art and Tech. Guggenheim grantee, 1964-65; fellow Tamarind Workshop, 1962. Mem. Computer Arts Soc., Siggraph/ACM. Research in computer art and computer-supported studies in aesthetics; projects in art and tech.; aesthetics of surface mine reclamation; application of computer-aided design techniques to large-scale environ. sculpture and landscape design; devel. of library of art-oriented computer-graphic programs, subroutines and tutorial exercises for dedicated and time-sharing systems; creative work with computer-graphic paint and image-processing systems and research-and-development projects in computer and video stereographic projection; assemblage relief sculpture; and in stereoscopic projection, in assemblage relief sculpture, and in self-referential and self-documenting installations. Home: PO Box 605 Conway MA 01341-0605

MALLENBAUM, ALLAN ELIYAHU, marketing executive; b. Bklyn., Nov. 26, 1931; s. Arthur I. and Sophie Mallenbaum; m. Irene Bright, Nov. 16, 1953; children: Stephan J., David N., Sandra L., Cheryl D., Lisa G. B in Psychology, NYU, 1952; postgrad., Università Di Padova, Padua, Italy, 1956-60; MBA in Mktg./Internat. Commerce, Baruch Grad. Sch., 1968. Mktg. rsch. Lennon & Newell Advt., N.Y.C.; mktg. dir. Steifel Labs., Oak Hill, N.Y., Belvac Internat., L.I. City, N.Y.; pres. Copeless Concepts, Ltd., N.Y.C.; adminstrv. v.p. Alliance Communication Group, N.Y.C., 1984-86; exec. v.p. Resource Network Internat., N.Y.C., 1986-88; mng. dir./founder Kensington High St. Assocs., Plainview, N.Y., 1988—; arbitrator Better Bus. Bur., N.Y.C. Founder United Zionists of the Americas, N.Y.C., Rosa Robota Found., Plainview, N.Y., Family Rsch. Found., Plainview, L.I. Genealogy Fedn., Plainview, Ukrainian Genealogy Soc. of Ams.; co-founder Jewish Survival Legion, N.Y.C.; pres. L.I. Genealogy Computer Soc.; v.p. L.I. Jewish Genealogy Soc. With U.S. Army, 1954-56. Mem. Jewish War Vets., Mensa. Avocations: computer science, new technologies, photography, genealogy.

MALLENBAUM, SIDNEY, neurologist; b. Milford, Conn., July 14, 1960; s. Victor Mallenbaum; m. Rita Hixson, June 15, 1986; children: Joshua John, Isaac Chaim. BSc, McGill U., Montreal, Que., Can., 1982; MD, U. N.C., 1986. Diplomate Am. Bd. Psychiatry and Neurology, Am. Bd. Electrodiagnostic Medicine. Intern in internal medicine Royal Victoria Hosp., Montreal, 1986-87; resident in neurology Montreal Neurol. Inst. and Montreal Neurol. Hosp., 1987-90, chief resident, 1989; active staff and cons. neurologist Virginia Beach (Va.) Gen. Hosp., 1990—; pvt. practice, Virginia Beach, 1990—; cons. neurologist Sentara Bayside Hosp., Virginia Beach, 1990—; prin. investigator Stroke Treatment with Ancrod Trial, 1995-96, Lubeluzole in Acute Ischemic Stroke Study, Cervena in Acute Ischemic Strike Trial, 1996, Thrombolytic Therapy in Acute Ischemic Stroke Trial; electrodiagnostic cons. Dynamic Engring. Corp., Madison, Wis., 1992—; lectr. Va. Pediat. Soc., Virginia Beach, 1993. Univ. scholar McGill U., 1978-79, faculty scholar, 1979-80. Fellow Am. Assn. Electrodiagnostic Medicine; mem. Am. Acad. Neurology, Virginia Beach Med. Soc. Avocations: tennis, swimming, cooking, travel. Office: Neurol Cons Va Beach Inc 1008 First Colonial Rd Ste 101 Virginia Beach VA 23454-3002

MALLERY, ANNE LOUISE, elementary education educator, consultant; b. Myersdale, Pa., June 14, 1934; d. Samuel Addison and Ruth Elizabeth (Meehan) M.; m. Richard Gwen Jones, Mar. 9, 1953 (div. 1974); children: Valerie Anne, Joseph Samuel, Richard Alan (dec.). BS in Edn., Calif. U., Pa., 1970, MEd, 1972; EdD, Pa. State U., 1980. From proficiency coord. to prof. elem. edn. Millersville (Pa.) U., 1980—; asst. to pres. for planning MobileVision Tech., Inc., Coral Gables, Fla., 1990—; editor Innovative Learning Strategy, Nat. Publ., 1989—; cons. East Brunswick Pub. Schs., 1995; cons. Pequea Valley H.S., Lancaster, Pa., 1985, Cambridge Adult Edn. Co., 1987, Conawago Elem. Sch., York, Pa., 1991; co-dir. NEH grant, 1993-94. Co-author The Secret Cave Multimodal Reading Program; contbr. numerous articles to profl. jours. Judge Intelligencer Reg. Spelling Bee, Lancaster, 1990,91. Mem. Assn. Pa. State Coll. and U. Faculty, Internat. Reading Assn., Lancaster Lebanon Reading Assn., Assn. Tchr. Educators, Am. Assn. Colls. Tchr. Edn., Am. Reading Forum. Republican. Presbyterian. Avocations: swimming, walking, reading, films. Home: 24 Strawberry Ln Lancaster PA 17602-1639 Office: Millersville Univ Stayer Education Ctr Millersville PA 17551

MALLETT, CONRAD LEROY, JR., state chief supreme court justice; b. Detroit, Oct. 12, 1953; s. Conrad LeRoy and Claudia Gwendolyn (Jones) M.; m. Barbara Straughn, Dec. 22, 1984; children: Alex Conrad, Mio Thomas, Kristan Claudia. BA, UCLA, 1975; MPA, U. So. Calif., 1979, JD, 1979. Bar: Mich. 1979. Legal asst. to congressman Detroit, 1979-80; dep. pol. div. Dem. Nat. Com., Washington, 1980-81; assoc. Miller, Canfield, Paddock & Stone, Detroit, 1981-82; legal counsel, dir. to gov. State of Mich., Lansing, 1983-84; sr. exec. asst. to Mayor City of Detroit, 1985-86; ptnr. Jaffe, Raitt, Heuer & Weiss, Detroit, 1987-90; justice Mich. Supreme Ct., Lansing, 1990—. Mem. NAACP, Kappa Alpha Psi. Democrat. Roman Catholic. Avocations: writing, fiction. Office: Supreme Ct Office 500 Woodward Ave Fl 20 Detroit MI 48226-3423

MALLETT, HELENE GETTLER, elementary education educator; b. Goshen, N.Y., Aug. 20, 1937; d. John and Anna Gettler; m. Richard David Mallett, July 29, 1967; 1 child, Anna Alma. BS in Fgn. Svc., Georgetown U., 1959; MA, SUNY, Stonybrook, 1989. Supr. Fulbright Program/Europe Inst. Internat. Edn., N.Y.C., 1961-65; editor Am. Assn. Fund Raising Coun., N.Y.C., 1965-67; coord. adult GED/ESL programs BOCES 3, Deer Park, N.Y., 1973-85; tchr. UFSD #3 and UFSD #4, Huntington, N.Y., 1967—; trustee Eastwood Sch., Oyster Bay, N.Y., 1977-83; alumni interviewer, Georgetown U., Washington, 1989—. Mem. ASCD, Nat. Coun. for the Social Studies, N.Y. State United Tchrs. (com. 100), Chemist Club. Avocations: travel, Angora rabbits, diplomatic history, robots, geography. Home: 79 Little Neck Rd Centerport NY 11721-1615

MALLETTE, MALCOLM FRANCIS, newspaper editor, educator; b. Syracuse, N.Y., Jan. 30, 1922; s. Ralph Joseph and Hermia Ruth (Barry) M.; m. Eleanor Christine Ingram, Sept. 21, 1946; children: Gary, Bruce, David. BS magna cum laude, Syracuse U., 1947. Profl. baseball pitcher Norfolk, Va., Newark, Kansas City, Memphis, Sacramento, Bklyn., Montreal, 1946-52; sports reporter Asheville (N.C.) Times, 1951-54; sports editor Asheville Citizen, 1954-56; sports dir. Winston-Salem (N.C.) Jour. & Sentinel, 1956-59; mng. editor Winston-Salem Jour., 1959-66; assoc. dir. Am. Press Inst., Reston, Va., 1966-69; mng. dir. Am. Press Inst., 1969-75, sec., dir., 1975-79, dir. devel., 1979-87; dir. projects World Press Freedom Com., 1987—; guest lectr. Grad. Sch. Journalism, Columbia, 1969-71, Am. Press Inst., Columbia, 1961-66, U. N.C. Sch. Journalism, 1964; Def. Info. Sch. Ft. Benjamin Harrison, Ind., 1987. Author (with others), editor: Handbook for Journalists of Central and Eastern Europe, 1990, transl. to Polish, Czechoslovakian, Hungarian, Romanian, Bulgarian, Albanian, Russian; author (Seminar) The Story of the American Press Institute, 1992; contbr. articles to various mags. Served to capt. Signal Corps, AC AUS, 1943-46. Mem. AP Mng. Editors Assn. (dir. 1961-66, regent 1976—), AP News Coun. (pres. N.C. 1964), Assn. Profl. Baseball Players (life). Baptist. Club: Rotarian. Home: 2419 Silver Fox Ln Reston VA 20191-2628

MALLETTE, PHYLLIS SPENCER COOPER, medical/surgical nurse; b. Chestertown, Md., Nov. 18, 1944; d. Charles P. and Elma (Brown) Spencer; children: Winsor A. Cooper, III and Elma Cooper Henderson; m. Arthur E. Mallette, June 5, 1982. ASN, Rutgers U., 1965; BSN cum laude, Trenton State Coll., 1978. Cert. critical care, IV therapy, acute respiratory care, OSHA regulations, advanced coronary care, med. office mgmt., case mgmt., utilization rev.; RN, Md., N.J., Pa. Nurse delivery room St. Francis Med. Ctr., Trenton, N.J., 1971-73; nurse ICU Delaware Valley Med. Ctr., Langhorne, Pa., 1973-74; coord. nights Robert Wood Johnson U. Hosp., New Brunswick, N.J., 1974-75; occupational health RN Warner-Lambert/Parke-Davis Co., Morris Plains, N.J., 1977-79; sr. profl. rep. hosp., coord. sales tng. Merck Human Health Svcs. Divsn., Phila., 1979-89; co-coord. 400 trainee field force expansion Merck Sharp & Dohme, Denver, 1989; clin. nurse Johns Hopkins Hosp., Balt., 1989-90; office mgr. Arthur E. Mallette, M.D., Pikesville, Md., 1990-94; quality mgmt. specialist United Health Care, Inc., Balt., 1994-96; quality improvement coord. United Health Care of Fla., 1996—; med. cons. N.J. Pub. TV, Trenton, 1974. Mem. Sigma Theta Tau. Democrat. Methodist. Avocations: computer, career coaching youth, mystery and adventure novels. Home: 28229 CR 33 # 18C Leesburg FL 34748

Office: United Health Care of Fla 800 N Magnolia Ave Ste 600 Orlando FL 32803-3263

MALLEY, JAMES HENRY MICHAEL, industrial engineer; b. Providence, Oct. 15, 1940; s. Leo Henry and Gladys Elizabeth (Canning) M.; children: James Michael, Julie Michele; m. Joyce Sue Marie Greenwell, Aug. 28, 1993. BS in Engring., U.S. Mil. Acad., 1962; MS in Indsl. Engring., U. R.I., 1977. Commd. U.S. Army, 1962-84, advanced through grades to lt. col., ret., 1984; milt. advisor U.S. Army, Rep. of Vietnam, 1964-65; co. comdr. Army Tng. Ctr., Ft. Benning, Ga., 1965-67; ops. and exec. officer First Air Cavalry Divsn., Vietnam, 1968-69; asst. prof. U. R.I., Kingston, 1969-73; asst. inspector gen. U.S. Army Criminal Investigation Command, Washington, 1973-76; ops. rsch. analyst and study dir. U.S. Army Concepts Analysis Agy., Bethesda, Md., 1977-80; dir. tng. U.S. 7th Army Combined Arms Tng. Ctr., Vilseck, Germany, 1980-81; chief of ops. rsch. and sys. analysis U.S. Army Europe, Heidelberg, Germany, 1981-84; mgr. engring. svcs. Orion Internat. Tech., Inc., Albuquerque, 1985-90; temp. recall, Ops. Desert Shield/Desert Storm U.S. Army, 1991; army after action report integrator ODCSOPS-HQDA, Washington, 1991; prin. analyst Gen. Rsch. Corp., Washington, 1992; ops. rsch. and analysis exec. Lockheed-Sanders, Merrimack, N.H., 1992—; mgmt. advisor to pres. PC Support, Inc., Albuquerque, 1986—; presenter numerous symposia, U.S. and Europe. Decorated Silver Stars (2), Legion of Merit, Bronze Stars (3), Air medals (4), Purple Heart, Vietnamese Cross of Gallantry with Gold Star (1) with Palm (2). Mem. Ops. Rsch. Soc. Am., Assn. of U.S. Army, U.S. Naval Inst., Internat. Test & Evaluation Assn. Avocations: volksmarching, kayaking, skiing, rafting, mathematics. Home: PO Box 746 Merrimack NH 03054-0746

MALLEY, KENNETH CORNELIUS, retired military officer, corporation executive; b. Newark, Dec. 12, 1934; s. Raymond Cornelius and Catherine Mary (Pisarcik) M.; m. Catherine Margaret Potter, June 8, 1958; children: William B., Paul K. BS in Naval Sci., U.S. Naval Acad., 1957; MSEE, Naval Postgrad. Sch., 1963. Commd. ensign USN, 1957, advanced through grades to vice adm., 1991; gunnery officer USS Borden USN, Norfolk, Va., 1957-59, staff ops. officer Destroyer Divsn. 322, 1959-60; weapons officer USS Farragut USN, Mayport, Fla., 1963-64; proj. officer Bur. Naval Ordnance USN, Washington, 1964-67, head engring. sect., 1970-75, head missile br., 1975-80, tech. dir., 1980-85, 1985-91, dir. strategic programs, comdr. naval sea sys. command, 1991-94; pres. Malley Assocs., 1994-95; support dir. naval ordnance sta. USN, Indian Head, Md., 1975-76; head missile br. naval plan rep. office USN, Sunnyvale, Calif., head. engring div., 1969-70; mem. Charles Stark Draper Lab., Inc., Cambridge, Mass.; v.p. ARINC Inc., 1995—. Bd. dirs. Constellation Found., Balt.; vol. spkr. Chesapeake Bay Found., Annapolis, 1987, 89, 90, 91; mem. maritime tech. adv. com. South Eastern Univs. Rsch. Assn. Decorated DSM, Legion of Merit with oak leaf cluster, Meritorious Svc. medal, Navy Achievement medal. Mem. Am. Soc. Naval Engrs. (Gold medal 1986), U.S. Naval Inst., Naval Submarine League. Republican. Roman Catholic. Avocations: duck carving, boating. Home: 136 Riverside Rd Edgewater MD 21037-1405

MALLEY, RAYMOND CHARLES, retired foreign service officer, industrial executive; b. Cambridge, Mass., Dec. 22, 1930; s. William and Evangeline (Vautour) M.; m. Rita Ann Masse, May 26, 1951 (dec. June 1989); children: Keith, Bruce, Gregory; m. Josette Lucile Vidril Murphy, Aug. 11, 1995. AA, Boston U., 1950, BS, 1952; MA Equivalent, U. Geneva, Switzerland, 1955; MA and PhD A.B.D., Fletcher Sch. Law & Diplomacy (Tufts U. and Harvard U.), Medford, Mass., 1956. Economist, fin. analyst Texaco, Inc., N.Y.C., 1957-61; fgn. svc. officer U.S. Dept. State/A.I.D., Washington & fgn. posts, 1961-82; dir. U.S. Trade and Devel. Program, Washington, 1980; v.p. Silopress, Inc., Sioux City, Iowa, 1982-87; cons., advisor Labat-Anderson Internat., Arlington, Va., 1988-93; sr. group advisor, N. Am. rep. Halla Bus. Group, Seoul (Korea), N.Y.C., Washington, 1991—; chmn. Halla Am. Inc., 1996—. Mem. exec. bd. Coll. of Mgmt., Long Island U., Brookville, N.Y., 1994. Major U.S. Air Force, 1952-54, active reserve 1954-70. Mem. Acadian Cultural Soc., Am. Fgn. Svc. Assn., U.S. Profl. Tennis Registry, Ft. Myer Officers Club, Arlington, Va., Harvard Club, Boston. Roman Catholic. Avocation: tennis (ranked sr. player, cert. tennis instr.). Home: 6224 Loch Raven Dr McLean VA 22101 Office: Halla Bus Group 60 Oxford Dr Moonachie NJ 07074-1022

MALLEY, WILLIAM, production designer. Prodn. designer: (films) Prime Cut, 1972, The Exorcist, 1973 (Academy award nomination best art direction 1973), Huckleberry Finn, 1973, Alex & Gypsy, 1976, Citizen's Band, Handle with Care, 1977, The Fury, 1978, (with Dennis Washington) The Ninth Configuration, 1980, Defiance, 1980, Mommie Dearest, 1981, The Star Chamber, 1983, Deal of the Century, 1983, The House of God, 1984, Protocol, 1984, Uforia, 1985, Vision Quest, 1985, Walk Like a Man, 1987, Big Shots, 1987, (with Alan Locke) Dr. Giggles, 1992, (TV movies) The Great Ice Rip-Off, 1974, Pray for the Wildcats, 1974, The Red Badge of Courage, 1974, Griffin and Phoenix, 1976, World War III, 1982, Something About Amelia, 1984, Margaret Bourke-White, 1989, Common Ground, 1990, Dark Avenger, 1990, The Whereabouts of Jenny, 1991, (TV episodes) Alfred Hitchcock Presents, 1986. Office: Smith Gosnell Nicholson & Assoc PO Box 1166 1515 Palisades Dr Pacific Palisades CA 90272*

MALLIK, MUHAMMAD ABDUL-BARI, soil microbiologist; b. Pabna, Bangladesh, Mar. 15, 1927; s. Monsur Ali and Ataharun-Nisa Mallik; m. Rowshan Jahan Hamida, Sept. 24, 1966; 1 child, Abds-Sami. BSc, Rajshahi (Bangladesh) Coll., 1949; MSc, Dhaka (Bangladesh) U., 1952; MS, Minn. U., 1961; PhD, Okla. U., 1964. Lectr. botany U. Karachi, Pakistan, 1956-59, asst. prof., 1964-68, 69-72; vis. scholar dept. botany Baghdad (Iraq) U., 1968-69; asst. prof. Dhaka (Bangladesh) U., 1973-74; rsch. assoc. dept. botany and microbiology u. Okla., Norman, 1974-75; assoc. rsch. prof. agrl. rsch. program Langston (Okla.) U., 1975-82, rsch. prof. agrl. rsch. program, 1982—. Author: Introduction to Fungi, 1973; contbr. articles to profl. and popular publs. Fulbright scholar Minn. U., St. Paul, 1961; rsch. grantee Pakistan Agrl. Rsch. Coun., Karachi, 1968-69, USDA, Langston, 1982—. Mem. Am. Soc. Agronomy, Internat. Allelopathy Soc., Okla. Acad. Sci., Bangladesh Bot. Soc. Democrat. Muslim. Avocation: gardening. Home: 2611 S Oxford Dr Stillwater OK 74074 Office: Langston Univ Agrl Rsch Program PO Box 730 Langston OK 73050

MALLINCKRODT, GEORGE W., bank executive; b. Eichholz, Germany, Aug. 19, 1930; s. Arnold Wilhelm and Valentine (von Joest) von M.; m. Charmaine Brenda Schroder, July 31, 1958; children: Claire, Philip, Edward, Sophie. Student, various bus. schs.; DCL (hon.), Bishops U., Lennoxville, Can., 1994. With AGFA A.G., Munich, 1948-51, Munchmeyer and Co., Hamburg, 1951-53, Kleinwort Sons and Co., London, 1953-54, J. Henry Schroder Banking Corp., N.Y.C., 1954-55, 57-60, Union Bank Switzerland, 1956; with J. Henry Schroder & Co. Ltd., London, 1960—, also bd. dirs.; chmn. Schroders PLC, London, 1984-95, pres., 1995—; chmn. bd. dirs. J. Henry Schroder Bank A.G., Zurich, 1967; chmn., pres. Schroders Inc., N.Y.C., 1985; bd. dirs. Schroders Australia Ltd., Sydney, 1984—, Schroder Wertheim and Co. Inc., N.Y.C., 1986—, Schroders Ltd., Bermuda, 1991, British Invisibles, 1995—; bd. dirs. Euris S.A., Paris, Siemens plc., London, Schroder Internat. Mcht. Bankers Ltd., Singapore, Fgn. and Colonial German Investment Trust plc.; mem. Brit. N.Am. com., 1988—; trustee Kurt Hahn Trust, 1991—. V.p. German Brit. C. of C., London, 1992-95; chmn. Coun. World Econ. Forum, Davos, 1992—; mem. CBI City Adv. Group, London; mem. Brit. Mus. Devel. Trust, 1995—, Nat. Art Collection Devel. Coun., 1995—. Recipient Verdienstkreuz Am. Bande Des Verdienstordens Der Bundesrepublik Deutschland, 1986, Verdienstkeuz 1 Klasse Verdienstordens, 1990; apptd. Hon. Knight Comdr. of the Most Excellent Order of Brit. Empire, 1997. Fellow Royal Soc. Arts; mem. Inst. Mgmt. (companion 1986—). Office: Schroders PLC, 120 Cheapside, London EC2V 6DS, England also: Schroders Inc 787 7th Ave New York NY 10019-6018

MALLISON, N DANIELE, elementary school educator; b. Portsmouth, Va., Aug. 16, 1962; d. Howard Danford and Norma Mae (Gibbs) M. BFA in Art Edn., Va. Commonwealth U., 1984. Cert. tchr. K-12, Va.; cert. therapeutic recreation asst. Activity dir. Eldercare Gardens Nursing Home, Charlottesville, Va., 1985-86; itinerant art tchr. Henry County Pub. Schs., Collinsville, Va., 1986-87; contract substitute Louisa County (Va.) Pub. Schs., 1988; middle/h.s. art tchr. Grayson County Pub. Schs., Independence, Va., 1988-90; elem. art resource tchr. Orange County (Va.) Pub. Schs., 1990—; Upward Bound art tchr. Wytheville (Va.) C.C., summer 1990; tchr./cons. Henry County Pub. Schs. in conjunction with Va. Dept. Edn., Collinsville, 1987. Lifetime mem. Va. 4-H All Stars; chmn. young adults Gordonsville United Meth. Ch., 1994—. Folk Artist grantee Va. Commn. for the Arts, 1992-93, 93-94. Mem. NEA, Va. Edn. Assn., Nat. Art Edn. Assn., Va. Art Edn. Assn., Nat. Therapeutic Recreation Assn., Gordonsville Jaycees (sec. 1992, 94, state dir. 1993). Avocations: arts and crafts, reading, travel, horses, researching native American heritage. Office: Orange County Pub Schs PO Box 349 Orange VA 22960-0204

MALLO-GARRIDO, JOSEPHINE ANN, advertising agency owner; b. Agana, Guam, Mar. 20, 1955; d. Benjamin Corneja and Salvacion (Lacuesta) Mallo; m. John Marco Haniu Garrido, Feb. 16, 1980; children: Josiah Michael, Jordan Thaddeus. Student, U. Guam, Agana, 1972-74; BA in Journalism, Seattle U., 1976; MBA, Pepperdine U., 1982. Reporter Pacific Daily News, Agana, 1976, features editor, 1977-78, asst. city editor, 1978-79; copy editor features Honolulu Star-Bull., 1979-81; advt. copywriter Advt. Factors, Honolulu, 1981-83; communications specialist Liberty House, Honolulu, 1983-84; editor, advt. copywriter Safeway Stores Inc., Oakland, Calif., 1984-88; features writer Tracy (Calif.) Press, 1988-91; mktg. mgr. ComputerLand of Guam, Maite, 1992-93; mktg. officer Citibank, Agana, 1993-94; owner JMG Advt., 1994—; newspaper graphics cons. Pacific Daily News, 1984. Editor/writer Foods Unltd., 1984-88, Tracy Community Hosp. Health Beat and Update, 1988-91; editor Pacific Voice, 1977-78; contbr. articles to profl. jours. Vol. Engaged Encounter, Honolulu, 1989, Trans-Pacific Yacht Race, Honolulu, 1983, United Way, Oakland, 1986; organist St. Patrick's Ch., Honolulu, 1980-84, Immaculate Heart of Mary Ch., Toto, Guam, 1994—; advt. coord. Easter Seals, Oakland, 1987; mem. adv. bd. Cath. Social Svcs., Agana, Guam, 1993-97, bd. dirs. Recipient Cert. Achievement award Advt. Age Mag., 1985, Cert Appreciation award Am. Heart Food Festival, 1985, Best in the West award Am. Advt. Fedn., 1986, Retail Nutrition award Nat. Potato Promotion Bd., 1986, Spl. Achievement award Newspaper Spl. Sect. Mother's Day/Father's Day Coun., 1989, 90, Best Feature Story 2d place Calif. Newspaper Pubs. Assn., 1989, 1st place Classified Advt. Assn., 1989, 1st place appetizer Spam Food Festival, 1991. Mem. Guam C. of C. (media coord. 1993-95), Citiclub (exec. sec. 1994-95). Roman Catholic. Avocations: piano, travel.

MALLON, MEG, professional golfer. Winner Women's U.S. Open, 1991; 4th ranked woman LPGA Tour, 1992; winner Cup Noodles Hawaiian Ladies Open, 1996, Sara Lee Classic, 1996; 2nd major LPGA championship, 1991; winner 6 LPGA titles. Office: care LPGA 2570 Volusia Ave Ste B Daytona Beach FL 32114-7103*

MALLON, PETER, archbishop; b. Prince Rupert, Can., Dec. 5, 1929; s. Joseph P. and Sheila M. (Keenan) D. Grad., Seminary Christ the King, Burnaby and Mission, B.C. ordained to ministry Roman Cath. Ch., 1956;. Asst. Holy Rosary Cath., Vancouver, B.C., 1956-64, rector, 1966-82; chancellor Archdiocese Vancouver, 1964-65, dir. religious edn., 1971-73; adminstr. Guardian Angels Parish, Vancouver, 1964-65; pastor St. Anthony's, West Vancouver, 1982-89; bishop Nelson, B.C., 1989-95; archbishop of Regina Sask., Can., 1995—. Address: 445 Broad St N, Regina, SK Canada S4R 2X8

MALLORY, ARTHUR LEE, university dean, retired state official; b. Springfield, Mo., Dec. 26, 1932; s. Dillard A. and Ferrell (Claxton) M.; m. Joann Peters, June 6, 1954; children: Dennis Arthur (dec.), Christopher Lee, Stephanie Ann, Jennifer Lyn. B.S., S.W. Mo. State Coll., 1954; M.Ed., U. Mo., 1957, Ed.D., 1959; H.H.D., S.W. Bapt. Coll., Mo., 1972. History supr. U. Mo. Lab. Sch., Columbia, 1956-57; asst. to supt. schs. Columbia, 1957-59; asst. supt. schs. Parkway Sch. Dist., St. Louis County, Mo., 1959-64; dean evening div. U. Mo., St. Louis, 1964; pres. S.W. Mo. State U., Springfield, 1964-70, dean Coll. Edn., 1991-94; commr. edn. Mo. Dept. Edn., Jefferson City, 1971-87; dir. Internat. House, U. Mo., Columbia, 1956-59. V.p. Ozarks coun. Boy Scouts Am., 1967, pres. Gt. Rivers coun., 1972-73, Greene County Assn. for Retarded Citizens, 1989—, pres., 1991-96, mem. north ctrl. region exec. bd., 1984—; bd. dirs. Meml. Cmty. Hosp., Mid-Continent Regional Ednl. Lab., Ozark Pub. Telecoms. Inc., 1989—; chmn. bd. Mo. Coun. on Econ. Edn.; bd. regents Mo. State Univs.; trustee Pub. Sch. Retirement, William Jewell Coll., 1972-74; chmn. com. bds. So. Bapt. Conv., 1972-73, mem. com. or bds., 1981—; mem .exec. bd. Mo. Bapt. Conv., 1972-75, 77-80, 2d v.p., 1995-96, pres., 1996-97; trustee Southwestern Bapt. Theol. Sem., Fort Worth, 1995—; mem. adv. com. Young Audiences, Inc., 1986, ARC Bd., Greene County, 1986, Children's Svcs. Commn., chmn., 1986—, Edn. Commn. U.S.; bd. dirs. Ozark Pub. TV; chmn. bd. advisors Windemere Bapt. Assembly, 1992—. With U.S. Army, 1954-56. Recipient Disting. Service award Mo. Jr. C. of C., 1966; Distinguished Service award U. Mo., 1976; Faculty/Alumni award U. Mo., 1976; Silver Beaver award Boy Scouts Am., 1983, Good Shepherd and Cross, 1986, Disting. Citizen award, 1986; hon. life mem. Mo. Congress Parents and Tchrs.; named Springfield's Outstanding Young Man of Yr., 1965; Champion of Excellence PUSH, 1978. Mem. Am. Assn. State Colls. and Univs., N. Central Assn. Colls. and Secondary Schs., Council Chief State Sch. Officers, Mo. Assn. Sch. Adminstrs., NEA, Mo. Tchrs. Assn. So. Baptist (deacon). Clubs: Masons (33 deg.), Rotary.

MALLORY, FRANK BRYANT, chemistry educator; b. Omaha, Mar. 17, 1933; s. Deane Havercroft and Helen (Bryant) M.; m. Patricia Ann Livingston, June 30, 1951; children—Mary Susan, Paul Deane, Philip Howard (dec.), Michele; m. Clelia Sara Wood, Nov. 26, 1965. B.S., Yale U., 1954; Ph.D., Calif. Inst. Tech., 1958. Asst. prof. Bryn Mawr (Pa.) Coll., 1957-63, assoc. prof., 1963-69; prof. chemistry Bryn Mawr Coll. (Pa.), 1969—, W. Alton Jones prof. chemistry, 1985—, chmn. dept., 1982-92; acad. dep. to pres. Bryn Mawr (Pa.) Coll., 1978-81; vis. assoc. Calif. Inst. Tech., 1963-64; vis. prof. Yale U., 1968, 78-79, lectr., 1977-78; vis. prof. SUNY-Albany, summer 1967; vis. fellow Cornell U., 1970-71; vis. prof. U. Pa., 1988-89. Mem. adv. bd. Jour. Organic Chemistry, 1988-93; contbr. articles to profl. jours. Mem. sci. and arts com. Franklin Inst., Phila. Recipient Bond award Am. Oil Chemists Soc., 1970, Lindback award for disting. tchg., 1992; John Simon Guggenheim fellow, 1963-64, Alfred P. Sloan rsch. fellow, 1964-68, NSF sr. postdoctoral fellow, 1970-71. Mem. Am. Chem. Soc. (exec. com. of organic divsn. 1986-95, symposium officer 1989-95, award Phila. sect. 1989), Phila. Organic Chemists Club (past sec., chmn.). Home: 321 Caversham Rd Bryn Mawr PA 19010-2927 Office: Bryn Mawr Coll Dept Chemistry Bryn Mawr PA 19010

MALLORY, FRANK LINUS, lawyer; b. Calgary, Alta., Can., May 5, 1920; s. Frank Louis and Anna Amy (Allstrum) M.; m. Jean Ellen Lindsey, Jan. 29, 1944; children: Susan Mallory Remund, Ann, Bruce R. AB with distinction, Stanford U., 1941, LLB, 1947. Bar: Calif. 1948. Assoc. Gibson, Dunn & Crutcher, L.A., 1947-54; ptnr. L.A. and Orange County, Calif., 1955-88; cert. specialist taxation law Calif. Bd. Legal Specialization, 1973-89. Pres. Town Hall of Calif., L.A., 1970, Boys Republic, Chino, Calif., 1962-64; pres. Braille Inst. Am., L.A., 1988-92. Lt. (j.g.) USNR, 1942-46. Mem. ABA, Calif. Bar Assn., Los Angeles County Bar Assn., Orange County Bar Assn., Newport Harbor Yacht Club, Big Canyon Country Club, Transpacific Yacht Club (staff commodore). Republican. Home: 633 Bayside Dr Newport Beach CA 92660-7213

MALLORY, ROBERT MARK, controller, finance executive; b. Mattoon, Ill., Apr. 15, 1950; s. Robert Monroe and Betty Ann (Mudd) M.; m. Diana Marie Burde, Aug. 19, 1972; 1 child, Laura Elizabeth. BS in Accountancy, U. Ill., 1972; M Mgmt., Northwestern U., 1986. CPA, Ill. Staff acct. Price Waterhouse, Chgo., 1972-74, sr. acct., 1974-77, mgr., 1977-79; dir. internal audit Mark Controls Corp., Skokie, Ill., 1979-81; corp. contr. Mark Controls Corp., Skokie, 1981-86, v.p., contr., 1986-88; contr., dir. planning Tribune Co., Chgo., 1988-91, v.p., contr., 1991—. Mem. Am. Inst. CPA's (Elijah Watts Sells award 1972), Ill. CPA Soc., Fin. Execs. Inst., Beta Gamma Sigma. Methodist. Home: 3312 Lakewood Ct Glenview IL 60025-2505 Office: Tribune Co 435 N Michigan Ave Chicago IL 60611

MALLORY, V(IRGIL) STANDISH, geologist, educator; b. Englewood, N.J., July 14, 1919; s. Virgil Sampson and Sarah Lauris (Baum) M.; m. Miriam Elizabeth Rowan, Feb. 3, 1946; children—Charles Standish, Stefan Douglas, Peter Sommers, Ingrid Lauris. A.B., Oberlin Coll., 1943; M.A., U. Calif. at Berkeley, 1948, Ph.D. (Standard Oil of Calif. fellow in paleontology), 1952. Preparator U. Calif. Museum Paleontology, Berkeley, 1946-48; curator foraminifera U. Calif. Museum Paleontology, 1948-50, cons., 1951; lectr. paleontology U. Calif. at Berkeley, 1951; asst. prof. geology U. Wash., 1952-59, asso. prof., 1959-62; prof., chmn. div. geology and paleontology, curator of paleontology Burke Meml. Wash. State Mus., 1962-84, prof. emeritus, mus. curator, 1984—; cons. in petroleum geology and mus. curation, in wines to restaurants; lectr. geology of wine; mem. Gov. of Wash. Commn. on Petroleum Regulations, 1956-57; mem. NSF Paris Basin Field Inst., Paris, Belgium and Luxembourg, 1964; co-dir. NSF Inst. Secondary Sch. Tchrs., Western Wash. State Coll., summers 1963, 65. Author: Lower Tertiary Biostratigraphy of California Coast Ranges, 1959, Lower Tertiary Foraminifera From Media Agua Creek Drainage Area, Kern County, California, 1970, Biostratigraphy—A Major Basis of Paleontologic Correlation, 1970; contbg. author: Lincoln Library Essential Knowledge, 1965, Ency. Brit., 15th edit, 1974; Editor paleontology: Quaternary Research Jour, 1970-77; Contbr. articles to profl. jours. Served with AUS, 1944-46, PTO. Am. Assn. Petroleum Geologists Revolving Fund grantee, 1957; U. Wash. Agnes Anderson Fund grantee, 1963. Fellow AAAS (coun. 1964—), Geologic Soc. Am.; mem. Am. Assn. Petroleum Geologists (sect. coun. 1964-84, com. on stratigrahic correlations 1979-85), Paleontologic Soc. (chmn. sect. 1956-58), Geol. Soc. Am., Soc. Econ. Paleontology and Mineralogy, Paleontol. Rsch. Soc., Paleontologische Gesellschaft, Geologische Gesellschaft, Internat. Paleontological Union, N.W. Sci. Soc., Am. Assn. Mus., Mineral Mus. (adv. coun. 1974-87), N.W. Fedn. Mineralogical Socs. (hon. award 1995, 96), N.W. Paleontol. Assn. (hon. mem.), Sigma Xi, Theta Tau. Home: 5209 Pullman Ave NE Seattle WA 98105-2139 Office: U Wash Burke Meml Wash State Mus DB10 Seattle WA 98195

MALLORY, WILLIAM BARTON, III, lawyer; b. New River, N.C., June 8, 1944; s. William B. and Marion (Lucas) M.; m. Margaret Mary Milnor; children: Barton, Bennett, Brian, Allison. BA, U. Va., 1966; JD, U. Tenn., 1969. Bar: Tenn. 1969. Assoc. Heiskell, Donelson, Adams, Williams & Wall, Memphis, 1969; gen. counsel Guardsmark Inc., N.Y.C., 1969-73; v.p., gen. counsel The Crump Cos. Inc., Memphis, 1973-86; vice chmn., gen. counsel Guardsmark Inc., Memphis, 1986-93; v.p., gen. counsel Terminix Internat., Memphis, 1994—. Mem. ABA. Club: Memphis Country.

MALLOT, MICHAEL E., gastroenterologist; b. N.Y.C., Mar. 11, 1943; s. Sam and Ruth (Bernstein) M.; m. Anita Claire Sopian, Dec. 15, 1963 (div. Dec. 1990); children: Scot, Darren; m. Kathleen A. Rizzo, Apr. 22, 1995. BA, UCLA, 1964; MD, U. Calif., Irvine, 1968. Diplomate Am. Bd. Internal Medicine. Resident in internal medicine U. Calif., Orange, 1968-71, 73-75; pvt. practice L.A., 1975-92, Nacogdoches, Tex., 1993—. Maj. U.S. Army, 1971-73. Fellow Am. Coll. Gastroenterology; mem. AMA, ACP, Am. Soc. Gastrointestinal Endoscopy, Tex. Med. Assn., Alpha Omega Alpha. Office: Nacogdoches Gastroent PA 1225 N Mound St Nacogdoches TX 75961-4028

MALLOY, CRAIG RIGGS, physician, educator; b. Pasadena, Calif., Feb. 8, 1952; s. John Atherton and Frances Dwight (Riggs) M.; m. Deborah Finger, May 24, 1980; children: William Atherton, Mary Margaret, George Joseph. BS, Stanford U., 1973; MD, U. Calif., San Francisco, 1977. From asst. to prof. U. Tex., Dallas, 1984—; dir. Southwestern Biomedical Magnetic Resonance Ctr., Dallas, 1993. Contbr. articles to profl. jours.

MALLOY, DANNEL PATRICK, mayor; m. Cathy Malloy; children: Dan, Ben, Sam. Grad., Boston Coll. Bar: Conn., Mass., N.Y., U.S. Dist. Ct. Conn., U.S. Dist. Ct. (ea. and so. dists.) N.Y. Asst. dist. atty. Bklyn., N.Y. Dist. Atty.'s Office, 1980-84; ptnr. Abate & Fox, Stamford, Conn., 1984-95; mayor City of Stamford, 1995—; mem. bd. fin. City of Stamford, 1983-94, Stamford Bd. Edn., 1994-95; spl. master Conn. Superior Ct.; lectr. Family Law Tng. Seminar. Past bd. dirs. Teen Life Ctr., Liberation Programs, Inc., CTE. Mem. ABA, ATLA, Nat. Trial Lawyers Assn., Conn. Bar Assn., Conn. Trial Lawyers Assn. Office: Office of Mayor PO Box 10152 Stamford CT 06904-2152

MALLOY, EDWARD ALOYSIUS, priest, university administrator, educator; b. Washington, May 3, 1941; s. Edward Aloysius and Elizabeth (Clark) M. BA, U. Notre Dame, 1963, MA, 1967, ThM, 1969; PhD, Vanderbilt U., 1975. Joine Congregation Holy Cross, 1963, ordained priest Roman Cath. Ch., 1970. Instr. U. Notre Dame, Ind., 1974-75, asst. prof., 1975-81, assoc. prof., 1981-88, prof. theology, 1988—, assoc. provost, 1982-86, pres. elect, 1986, pres., 1987—; bd. regents U. Portland, Oreg., 1985—. Author: Homosexuality and the Christian Way of Life, 1981, The Ethics of Law Enforcement and Criminal Punishment, 1982, Culture and Commitment: The Challenge of Today's University, 1992; contbr. articles to profl. jours. Chmn. Am. Coun. on Edn.; bd. dirs. NCAA Found., 1989—; mem. Bishops and Pres.' com. Assn. Cath. Colls. and Univs., 1988—; bd. dirs. Internat. Fedn. Cath. Univs., 1988—; mem. Pres.'s Adv. Coun. on Drugs, 1989—; mem. adv. bd. AmeriCorps and Nat. Civilian Community Corps, 1994-97; interim chmn. Ind. Commn. on Community Svc., 1994-97; mem. Boys and Girls Clubs Am., 1997—; trustee St. Thomas U., 1997—; bd. advisors Bernardin Ctr., 1997—; bd. dirs. Points of Light; chmn. Campus Compact. Mem. Cath. Theol. Soc., Am. Soc. Christian Ethics, Bus.-Higher Edn. Forum, Assn. Governing Bds. of Univs. and Colls. (vice chair 1996—), The Conf. Bd. Office: U Notre Dame Office Pres Notre Dame IN 46556

MALLOY, EILEEN ANNE, ambassador; b. Teaneck, N.J., July 9, 1954; d. John Joseph and Mary Kathryn (Langan) M.; m. Ilmar Paegle, Jan. 13, 1975 (div. Aug. 1982); 1 child, Mary Kathryn; m. James George McLachlan, July 6, 1985; 1 child, Christina Alana. BS, Georgetown U., 1975. Analyst, divsn. mgr. Dunn & Bradstreet, Staten Island, N.Y., 1975-78; consular officer, spl. asst. to amb. U.S. Embassy, London, 1978-79; counselor, sci. officer U.S. Embassy, Moscow, 1980-82, chief arms control unit, 1988-90; consul U.S. Consulate, Calgary, A.B., Can., 1982-85; chief consular sect. U.S. Consulate, Dublin, Ireland, 1987-88; sr. U.K. desk officer Dept. of State, Washington, 1990-92, asst. to under sec. political affairs, 1992-93, dir. sec. staff, 1993-94, U.S. ambassador to Kyrgyz Republic, 1994—. Mem. Am. Fgn. Svc. Assn., Georgetown Alumni Assn. Office: US Ambassador Bishkek Kyrgzstan Dept of State Washington DC 20521-7040

MALLOY, JAMES MATTHEW, managed care executive, health care consultant; b. N.Y.C., Aug. 26, 1939; s. Peter Joseph and Catherine (Cunningham) M.; m. Joan Elizabeth Wagner, Sept. 9, 1967; children—Stephen, Christopher. B.S., Manhattan Coll., 1961; M.P.H., Yale U., 1967. Asst. to dir. Yale New Haven Hosp., New Haven, Conn., 1967; assoc. adminstr. Waterbury Hosp., Conn., 1969-75; exec. dir., CEO Jersey City Med. Ctr., N.J., 1975-77; dir., CEO U. Conn. Hosp., Farmington, 1977-82, U. Ill. Hosp. and Clinics, Chgo., 1982-87; exec. v.p. Our Lady of the Resurrection Med. Ctr., Chgo., 1988-89; pres., CEO, St. Dominic Jackson Meml. Hosp., Jackson, Miss., 1989-91; sr. v.p. health affairs Miss. and La. Blue Cross/Blue Shield, Jackson, Miss., 1991-92; health care cons., pres. Malloy Assocs., Jackson, 1992—; pres., CEO S.E. Managed Care Orgn., Jackson, 1993-95; cons. NIH, Bethesda, Md., 1976-84; dir. Univ. Health Consortium; chmn. Compass Health Plan, Chgo., 1983-87; dir. Hosp. Fund, Inc., New Haven, Comprends Inc., Chgo.; lectr. Yale U. Sch. Medicine; adj. prof. U. Ill. Coll. Medicine, Chgo.; assoc. prof. U. Ill. Sch. Pub. Health. Contbr. articles to profl. jours. Past chmn. Miss. chpt. Nat. Multiple Sclerosis Assn. Dr. Stuart Hamilton fellow Capital Area Health Consortium, 1982. Fellow Inst. Medicine Chgo., Am. Coll. Healthcare Execs.; mem. Ill. Hosp. Assn. (bd. dirs. 1984-86), Met. Chgo. Healthcare Coun., Yale Alumni Fund, Yale Club (pres. Miss. chpt.), Miss. Bus. Coalition on Health Care (bd. dirs.). Avocations: golf, jogging. Home and Office: 177 St Andrews Dr Jackson MS 39211-2532

MALLOY, JOHN RICHARD, lawyer, chemical company executive; b. Boston, Nov. 26, 1932; s. Thomas Francis and Mary (Field) M.; m. Maraleta Ellerson, May 24, 1960; children: Maureen, John, Megan, Elizabeth. BA, St. John's Sem., Brighton, Mass., 1954; LLB, Boston Coll., 1957. Bar: Mass. 1957. V.p., dir. fin. Remington Arms Co., Inc., Bridgeport, Conn., 1975-78; chief counsel, energy and raw materials E. I. du Pont de Nemours and Co., Wilmington, Del., 1978-79, asst. gen. counsel legal, 1979-83, dir. pub. affairs, 1983-85, v.p. pub. affairs, 1983-85, sr. v.p. external affairs, 1985-92, v.p., spl. counsel to chmn. bd., 1992-93; ret. Chmn. Jobs for Del. Grads, Wilmington, 1985-97, Del. Compensation Commn., 1988-96; trustee Med. Ctr. of Del., Christiana, 1985—, Del. Pension Fund, 1993—; bd. dirs. Del. Cmty. Found.,

1996—, Children's Beach House; mem. Minner Commn. (Del.), 1993-96; chmn. Del. Coun. on Transp., 1994—. Mem. ABA, Fed. Bar Assn. Democrat. Roman Catholic. Avocations: tennis, golf, skiing.

MALLOY, MICHAEL TERRENCE, journalist, newspaper editor; b. Chgo., Feb. 26, 1936; s. Medard Valentine and Lucille (Zehrol)M.; m. Ruth Gwendolyn Lor, June 5, 1965; children: Linda Jo, Terrence. Student, Reed Coll., 1953-54, Columbia U., 1966-67. Police reporter City News Bur. Chgo., 1956-58; reporter, then bur. chief and chief corr. S.E. Asia UPI, Japan, Laos, India, Vietnam and Thailand, 1960-66; reporter Nat. Observer, Washington, 1968-76, mng. editor, 1976-77; reporter Asian Wall St. Jour., Manila, 1977-80, mng. editor, Hong Kong, 1980-84; mng. editor Dow Jones Can., Toronto, Ont., 1984-94; chief corr. Dow Jones India Report, 1995-97. Author: Racing Today, 1967, The Art of Retirement, 1967. With U.S. Army, 1958-60.

MALLOY, WILLIAM MICHAEL, book editor, reviewer, writer; b. Cleve., Oct. 29, 1960; s. Leroy Joseph Francis and Betty Jayne (Kubicek) M.; m. Claire Zion, Feb. 14, 1989; children: Rose Zion, Quinn Zion. BA in Lit., Yale U., 1982. Copyright mgr. G. Schirmer, Inc., N.Y.C., 1982-84; creative dir. Cloverdale Press, N.Y.C., 1985; mng. editor The Mysterious Press, N.Y.C., 1985-88; editor-in-chief The Mysterious Press/Warner Books, N.Y.C., 1988—; cons. 20th Century Crime and Mystery Writers, London, 1989—. Author: The Mystery Book of Days, 1990; contbg. editor The Armchair Detective, 1989—; contbr. critical essays to reference work. Democrat. Avocations: saxophone, flute, reading, cooking. Office: The Mysterious Press/Warner 1271 Avenue Of The Americas New York NY 10020-1300

MALLOZZI, COS M., public relations executive; b. Utica, N.Y., Aug. 16, 1951. BA, Syracuse U., 1973. Pub. rels. coun. and legis. intern Congressman D. Mitchell, Washington, 1973-74; assr. pub. rels. dir., sports info. dir. Siena Coll., 1974-75; pub. rels. dir. SUNY, 1975-76; acct. supv. group mgr. Gibbs & Soell, Inc., N.Y.C., 1978-80, gen. mgr., 1980-81, exec. v.p., gen. mgr., 1981-88, pres., 1988—, CEO, 1993—. Office: Gibbs & Soell Inc 600 3rd Ave New York NY 10016-1901*

MALLUCHE, HARTMUT HORST, nephrologist, medical educator; b. Breslau, Fed. Republic Germany, Jan. 1, 1943; came to U.S., 1975, naturalized, 1985; s. Harald E. and Renate (Muenzberg) M.; m. Gisela Gleich, Dec. 19, 1975; children: Nadine, Danielle, Tiffany. Abitur, Albertus Magnus Coll., Koenigstein, Germany, 1963; postgrad. Phillips U., Marburg/Lahn, Fed. Republic of Germany, 1963-65, U. Innsbruck, Austria, 1965-66, U. Vienna, Austria, 1966; MD, J. W. Goethe U., Frankfurt, Fed. Republic of Germany, 1969. Diplomate German Bd. Internal Medicine. Intern, County Hosp., Aichach, Fed. Republic of Germany, 1969-70; resident in internal medicine and fellow in nephrology Ctr. Internal Medicine, Univ. Hosp., Frankfurt am. Main, 1970-75, asst. prof. medicine U. So. Calif., Los Angeles, 1975-78, assoc. prof., 1978-81; prof., dir. Div. Nephrology, Bone and Mineral Metabolism U. Ky. Med. Ctr., Lexington, 1981—; cons. NIH, FDA; Va. merit Rev. bd. nephrology. Author (monograph) Atlas of Mineralized Bone Histology, 1986; contbr. articles to profl. jours. and books. Grantee NIH, 1982—, Shriner's Hosp. for Crippled Children, Lexington, 1982—. Fellow ACP; mem. Am. Soc. Nephrology, Am. Soc. Clin. Investigation, Am. Soc. Bone and Mineral Research, Am. Soc. Physiol. Endocrinology, European Dialysis and Transplantation Assn., Am. Fedn. Clin. Research, Internat. Soc. Nephrology, AAAS.

MALME, CHARLES IRVING, acoustical engineer; b. Crookston, Minn., Aug. 13, 1931; s. Charles Martin and Idella Hilma (Efteland) M.; m. Jane Elton Hamlett, June 17, 1961; children: Robert, Karen. BS, BEE, U. Minn., 1954; MS, MIT, 1958, Elec. Engr., 1959. Ensign, lt.(j.g.) USNR, 1954-56; rsch. asst. Acoustics Lab. MIT, Cambridge, Mass., 1956-59; scientist Bolt Beranek and Newman Inc., Cambridge, Mass., 1960-65, mgr. instrumentation lab., 1965-67, sr. scientist, 1968-93; cons., owner C. Malme Engrng. and Scientific Svcs., Hingham, Mass., 1993—; mem. sci. rev. bd. Minerals Mgmt. Svc., Anchorage, 1994-95. Contbr. chpts. to books, articles to profl. jours. Chmn. bldg. com. First Parish Ch., Hingham, Mass., 1994—. Mem. Acoustical Soc. Am. Democrat. Unitarian. Achievements include patent in Wide Range Electrostatic Loudspeaker, Method for Reducing the Bubble Pulse From Underwater Explosions; development of methods for determining the sensitivity of marine species to high level underwater sound. Home: 25 Rockwood Rd Hingham MA 02043-1937 Office: Engring & Scientific Svcs 25 Rockwood Rd Hingham MA 02043-1937

MALME, JANE HAMLETT, lawyer, educator, researcher; b. N.Y.C., Dec. 2, 1934; d. Robert T. and Minnie (Means) Hamlett; m. Charles I. Malme, June 17, 1961; children: Robert H., Karen I. AB, Brown U., 1956; cert., U. Kobenhavn, Copenhagen, Denmark, 1959; JD, Northeastern U., 1977. Bar: Mass., 1977. Counsel Mass. Tax Commn., Boston, 1978-79; chief bur. local assessment Mass. Dept. Revenue, Boston, 1978-90; owner Mcpl. Mgmt. and Taxation Cons. Svcs., Hingham, Mass., 1990—; fellow Lincoln Inst. Land Policy, Inc., Cambridge, Mass., 1993—; faculty Lincoln Inst. Land Policy, Inc., Cambridge, 1989—; cons. state, provincial coun. Internat. Assn. Assessing Officers chgo., 1990—; adv. property tax OECD, Paris, 1993—; legal adv. property tax USAID, Russia, 1995-97, Korea Tax Inst., 1995-96. Co-author: (with Joan Youngman) Internat. Survey of Taxes on Land and Buildings, 1994; contbr. articles to tax jours., papers for Lincoln Inst. of Land Policy, Inc., 1991—. Mem. Dem. Town Com., Hingham, 1990-96; trustee Old Ship Ch., Hingham, 1992—; treas. Betty Taymor Scholarship Fund, Boston, 1992—; pres. Network for Women in Politics and Govt., McCormick Inst., Boston, 1992-94. Mem. Internat Assn. Assessing Officers (founder, state and prov. adminstrv. sec., Presidential citation 1983), Mass. Assn. Assessing Officers (hon. lifetime), Mass. Bar Assn., Womens Bar Assn., Nat. Assn. Tax Adminstrs. (chair property tax sect. 1988). Unitarian Universalist. Avocations: community service, women in politics, travel. Office: Lincoln Inst Land Policy 113 Brattle St Cambridge MA 02138-3407

MALMGREN, HARALD BERNARD, economist; b. Boston, July 13, 1935; s. Berndt Birger and Magda Helena (Nilsson) M.; m. Patricia A. Malmgren, 1959 (div. 1975); children: Karen Philippa, Britt Patricia, Erika Nina; m. Linda V. Einberg, Oct. 3, 1987; children: Markus Harald, Liivia Linda, Viivianne Vaike. BA summa cum laude, Yale U., 1957; postgrad., Harvard U., 1959; PhD, Oxford U., 1961. Asst. prof. dept. engring. and econs. Cornell U., Ithaca, N.Y., 1961-62; head, econ. group Inst. for Def. Analyses, Washington, 1962-64; asst. U.S. trade rep. Exec. Office Pres. The White House, Washington, 1964-69; sr. fellow Overseas Devel. Coun., 1969-71; ambassador, dep. U.S. trade rep., 1972-75; sr. fellow Woodrow Wilson Internat. Ctr. for Scholars, Washington, 1975-76; prof. George Washington U., Washington, 1976-77; pres. Malmgren, Inc., Washington, 1977—; mng. dir. Malmgren, Golt, Kingston, Ltd., London, 1979—; mem. adv. coun. Ctr. Strategic and Internat. Studies, Washington, 1987—; adv. Senate Fin. Com., Washington, 1970-71, 75-76, Interaction Coun., 1985—. Author: International Economic Peace Keeping, 1972; co-author: Assisting Developing Countries, 1972; editor: Pacific Basin Development, 1972; bd. editors: The International Economy, 1987—, The Washington Quarterly, 1987-95, The World Economy, 1980-90; contbr. articles to profl. jours. Mem. Am. Econ. Assn. Met. Club, Reform Club. Home: Summerfield Farm 7620 Cannonball Gate Rd Warrenton VA 20186 Office: Malmgren Group 1001 22nd St NW Ste 320 Washington DC 20037-1803

MALMSTAD, JOHN EARL, Slavic languages and literatures, educator; b. Bismarck, N.D., June 25, 1941; s. Manley Ellsworth and Joyce Evelyn (David) M. BA summa cum laude with distinction and departmental honors in Russian Lang. and Lit., Northwestern U., 1963; MA in Slavic Langs. and Lits., Princeton U., 1965, PhD in Slavic Langs. and Lits., 1969; AM (hon.), Harvard U., 1985. Instr. Columbia U., N.Y.C., 1968-69, asst. prof. Russian Lit., 1969-73, assoc. prof., 1973-79, prof. dept. slavic langs. and lits., 1979-85; Samuel Hazzard Cross prof. Slavic langs. and lits. Harvard U., Cambridge, Mass., 1985—, assoc. dean, 1993-94; vis. assoc. prof. Stanford U., 1971-72, U. Calif. Berkeley, 1977-78; vis. prof. Harvard U., fall 1982; cons., referee NEH translation awards; lectr. in field; attendee internat. symposia. Editor: (with others) The Poetry of Mikhail Kuzmin (3 vols.), 1977, The Poetry of Andrei Bely (3 vols.), 1982-85, Gibel Senatora, 1986, Vladislav Khodasevich Sobranie sochinenii, 1983, Andrei Bely, Spirit of Symbolism, 1987, Readings in Russian Modernism to Honor Vladimir Markov, 1993, Mikhail Kuzmin: Zhizn' Tvorchestvo, Epokha, 1996; Russian book rev. editor Slavic Rev., 1975-86; assoc. editor Russian Rev., 1986-88; mem. editl. bd. Minuvshee, Feniks, Opyty, Novoe Literaturnoe obozrenie, Experiment, Philologica; manuscript rev. profl. jours., univ. presses; contbr. articles to profl. jours. Woodrow Wilson fellow, 1963, NDFL fellow Columbia U., 1963-66, Princeton U., 1967-68, Fulbright-Hays fellow, 1966-67, spring 1981, spring 1987, Woodrow Wilson Dissertation fellow, 1966, ACLS rsch. fellow, 1972, Rsch. fellow Russian Inst. Columbia U., summer 1977, 79, 83, 84, IREX fellow, 1975, John Simon Guggenheim fellow, 1980-81; ACLS grant-in-aid, summer, 1980, IREX/ACLS grantee exch. Acad. Scis. USSR, fall 1981, spring 1987, 91, IREX travel grantee Moscow, 1992. Mem. Am. Assn. Advancement of Slavic Studies, Modern Lang. Assn., Assn. Tchrs. of Slavic and East European Langs., Institut d'Etudes Slaves (Paris), Phi Beta Kappa. Avocations: fine arts, ballet, reading. Home: 8A Cogswell Ave Cambridge MA 02140-2001 Office: Harvard U Dept Slavic Langs/Lit 301 Bolyston Hall Cambridge MA 02138

MALMUTH, NORMAN DAVID, scientist, program manager; b. Brooklyn, N.Y., Jan. 22, 1931; s. Jacob and Selma Malmuth; m. Constance Nelson, 1970; children: Kenneth, Jill. AE, U. Cin., 1953; MA in Aero. Engring., Polytech. Inst. of N.Y., 1956; PhD in Aeronautics, Calif. Inst. Tech., 1962. Rsch. engr. Grumman Aircraft Engring. Corp., 1953-56; preliminary design engr. N.A. Aviation Div., L.A., 1956-68; teaching asst. Calif. Inst. Tech., L.A., 1961; mem. maths. sci. group Rockwell Internat. Sci. Ctr., 1968-75, project mgr. fluid dynamics rsch., 1975-80, mgr. fluid dynamics group, 1980-82, sr. scientist, project mgr., 1982—; cons. Aerojet Gen., 1986-89; lectr. UCLA, 1971-72; mem. adv. group for aerospace R&D Fluid Dynamics Panel, 1995; vis. scientist Rensselaer Poly. Inst. Referee AIAA Jour.; bd. editors Jour. Aircraft; contbr. articles to Jour. of Heat Transfer, Internat. Jour. Heat Mass Transfer, and others. Named Calif. Inst. Tech. fellow; recipient Outstanding Alumnus award Univ. Cin., 1990. Fellow AIAA (Aerodynamics award 1991); mem. Am. Acad. Mechanics, Am. Inst. Physics (fluid dynamics divsn.), Soc. Indsl. and Applied Math. Achievements include patent in Methods and Apparatus for Controlling Laser Welding; pioneering development of high aerodynamic efficiency of hypersonic delta wing body combinations, hypersonic boundary layer stability, transonic wind tunnel interference web dynamics, combined asymptotic and numerical methods in fluid dynamics and aerodynamics. Home: 182 Maple Rd Newbury Park CA 91320-4718 Office: Rockwell Sci Ctr PO Box 1085 1049 Camino Dos Rios Thousand Oaks CA 91358

MALONE, DAN F., journalist; b. Dallas, Jan. 22, 1955; s. Charles Ted and Ela Grace (Darden) M.; m. Kathryn Jones, June 27, 1981. BJ, U. Tex., 1978. Editor-in-chief The Daily Texan, Austin, Tex., 1977-78; intern Harte-Hanks Austin Bur., 1978-79; staff writer Corpus Christi (Tex.) Caller-Times, 1979-81, Ft. Worth Star-Telegram, 1981-85; staff writer Dallas Morning News, 1985—, Ft. Worth bureau chief, 1992—; Fox fellow Nat. News Coun., N.Y.C., summer 1978. Recipient Pulitzer prize for investigative reporting, 1992, 1st Place Freedom of Info. Category award Tex. AP Mng. Editor's Assn., 1992, 1st Place Investigative Reporting Inst. Southern Studies, 1992. Office: Dallas Morning News 500 Main St Ste 800 Fort Worth TX 76102-3945

MALONE, DANIEL PATRICK, lawyer; b. Albany, N.Y., Jan. 25, 1953; s. Paul Timothy and Miriam Rose (Connolly) M.; m. Claudia Ann Hebel, June 3, 1978; children: Danny Jr., Emily, Molly. AB, Cornell U., 1975; JD, U. Detroit, 1978. Bar: Mich. 1978. Law clk. to judge U.S. Dist. Ct. (ea. dist.) Mich., Detroit, 1978-79; ptnr. Butzel Long (formerly Butzel, Long, Gust, Klein & Van Zile), Detroit, 1979—; faculty midwest region Nat. Inst. Trial Advocacy; instr. rsch., writing Detroit Coll. Law, 1979—, adj. prof. trial advocacy, 1984—; adj. prof. evidence Wayne State Sch. Law; speaker Mich. Inst. Continuing Edn., 1986—; pres. Fed. Bar Assn. (ea. dist. Mich.). Pres., bd. dirs. Boysville Mich.; founder Generation of Promise Program; bd. dirs. U. Detroit Jesuit High Sch., 1991—. Mem. ABA, Mich. Bar Assn. (negligence sect., entertainment sect.), Detroit Bar Assn. Avocations: music, athletics. Home: 372 Westwood Dr Bloomfield Hills MI 48301-2649 Office: Butzel Long 150 W Jefferson Ave Ste 900 Detroit MI 48226-4430

MALONE, DAVID ROY, state senator, university administrator; b. Beebe, Ark., Nov. 4, 1943; s. James Roy and Ila Mae (Griffin) M.; m. Judith Kaye Huff, June 20, 1965 (div. Feb. 1990); 1 child, Michael David. BSBA, U. Ark., 1965, JD, 1969, MBA, 1982. Bar: Ark. 1969, U.S. Dist. Ct. (we. dist.) Ark. 1969, U.S. Tax Ct. 1972, U.S. Ct. Appeals (8th cir.) 1972, U.S. Supreme Ct. 1972. Pvt. practice Fayetteville, Ark., 1969-72; atty. City of Fayetteville, 1969-72; asst. prof. bus. U. Ark., Fayetteville, 1972-76, asst. dean law, 1976-91; mem. Ark. Ho. of Reps., 1980-84, Ark. Senate, 1984—; exec. dir. U. Ark. Found., 1991—; chair senate edn. com.; bd. dirs. Bank of Elkins, S.W. Edn. Devel. Lab., Austin, Tex., 1988-94; legal adv. coun. So. Regional Edn. Bd., Atlanta, 1991—. Contbr. articles to profl. jours.; bd. dirs. Ark. Law Rev., 1978-92; contbg. author U. Ark. Press, 1989. Mayor City of Fayetteville, 1979-80; mem. Jud. Article Task Force, Little Rock, 1989-91; chair Motor Voter task force, 1994-95; bd. dirs. Music Festival Ark., 1989-91, Washington County Hist. Soc., 1993—; chmn. bd. Walton Arts Ctr. Found., 1994—; chmn. bd. dirs. Washington County Law Libr., 1970-84. Recipient Svc. award Ark. Mcpl. League, 1980, Disting. Service award U. Ark., 1988. Mem. Ark. Bar Assn. (ho. of dels. 1977-81, award of merit 1980, exec. 1981-82, Outstanding Lawyer-Citizen award 1990), Washington County Bar Assn., Ark. Inst. Continuing Legal Edn. (bd. dirs. 1979-88), Fayetteville C. of C. (bd. dirs. 1984—), Ark. Genealogy Soc. (bd. dirs. 1990—). Democrat. Methodist. Avocations: genealogy, stamp collecting. Home: 2848 Club Oak Dr Fayetteville AR 72701-9168 Office: PO Box 1048 Fayetteville AR 72702-1048

MALONE, EDWARD H., financial executive; b. Forest Hills, N.Y., Nov. 11, 1924; s. Edward H. and Gertrude (Gibson) M.; m. Margaret A. Rakers, Sept. 8, 1951; children: Mary Malone Tilney, Edward, Patricia J. Malone Palmer, Jo-Ann Malone Huber. B.S., Columbia U., 1949; M.B.A., N.Y. U., 1950. Bank examiner Fed. Res. Bank of N.Y., N.Y.C., 1949-52; trust officer Lincoln Rochester (N.Y.) Trust Co., 1952-55; with Gen. Electric Co., 1955-86; mgr. private placement investments Gen. Electric Co., N.Y.C., 1959-61, mgr. trust portfolios, 1961-67, mgr. trust investment ops., 1967-70; v.p. Gen. Electric Co., Stamford, Conn., 1970-86; trustee Prudential Savs. Bank, 1966-77; bd. dirs. Allegheny Power Sys. Inc., Butler Capital Corp., GenRe Corp., Mattel Inc., Warburg Pincus Capital, Fidelity Mutual Funds; chmn. CT Ret. Sys. Investment Adv., 1985-87; mem. Pres.'s Commn. for Fin. Structure and Regulation, 1970-71; dir. Darien chpt. ARC, 1982-88. Trustee Rensselaer Poly. Inst.; bd. dirs. Naples Philharm. Ctr. for Arts. Served with USAAF, 1943-45.

MALONE, EDWIN SCOTT, III, radio and television producer, public relations consultant; b. Vernon, Tex., Mar. 25, 1938; s. Edwin Scott and Pauline (King) M.; m. Sandra Sue Ballard, Aug. 19, 1960; children: Melissa, Michael Scott, Paula Sue. BA, So. Meth. U., 1960; MA, Burton Coll.; PhD, Burton Coll. Seminary; HumD (hon.), Golden State U. Pres. Ed Malone Enterprises, Arlington, Tex., 1960—; account exec. David Wade & Assocs., Dallas, 1963-66; ptnr. COMAL Pub. Rels. Cons., Arlington, 1970-75; v.p. radio So. Bapt. Radio-TV Commn., Ft. Worth, 1965-87; cons. Tyndale House Pubs., Inc., Wheaton, Ill. Performer Gourmet TV series, Dallas and Ft. Worth, 1955-60; author: Religious Landmarks of America, 1973; prodr. (series) Accent on Youth, Assignment Travel. Tex. del. White House Conf. on Children and Youth, 1960, 70. Mem. SAR, NATAS, Am. Soc. Travel Writers, Religious Heritage Am., Nat. Press Club, Pacific Pioneer Broadcasters, Am. Broadcast Pioneers, Broadcasters Found., Nat. Press Club, Soc. War of 1812, Sertoma (past pres.), Acacia, Order of Pythagorus (hon.), Order of St. Dennis of Zante (grand cross, charge d'affair Tex.), Order of Crown of Thorns (grand master), Masons, Shriners (past presiding officer York Rite), DeMolay, Legion of Honor. Home: 1608 Hawthorne Dr Arlington TX 76012-2229

MALONE, JAMES WILLIAM, retired bishop; b. Youngstown, Ohio, Mar. 8, 1920; s. James Patrick and Katherine V. (McGuire) M. AB, St. Mary Sem., Cleve., 1945; MA, Cath. U. Am., 1952, PhD, 1957. Ordained priest Roman Catholic Ch., 1945; asst. pastor Youngstown, 1945-50; supt. schs. Diocese of Youngstown, 1952-65; instr. ednl. adminstrn. St. John's Coll., Cleve., 1953; aux. bishop of Youngstown, 1960-68; bishop, 1968-96; ret. Diocese Youngstown, 1996; v.p. Nat. Conf. cath. Bishops, 1980-83; pres. Nat. Conf. Cath. Bishops, 1983-86. consultor Com. on Social Devel. and World Peace; mem. ad. hoc com. on health care, ex corde ecclesiae com. Nat. Conf. Cath. Bishops; mem. Nat. Interfaith Commn. for Worker Justice. Trustee Cath. U. Am.

MALONE, JOHN C., telecommunications executive; b. 1941; m. Leslie. Attended Yale U., Johns Hopkins U. Formerly pres. Jerrold Electronics Corp.; pres., chief exec. officer Tele-Communications, Inc., Denver, chmn. and CEO, 1996—. Office: Tele-Comm Inc 5619 DTC Pkwy Englewood CO 80111-3017*

MALONE, JOSEPH D., state treasurer; b. Waltham, Mass., Nov. 18, 1954; m. Linda Ploen; children: Joe Jr., Sam, Carolyn Adele. Educated at Harvard Univ., 1978. Treas. state of Mass., 1991—. Office: State House Rm 227 Office Of Treasurer Boston MA 02133

MALONE, JOSEPH JAMES, mathematics educator, researcher; b. St. Louis, Sept. 9, 1932; s. Joseph James and Aurelia Theresa (Schomaker) M.; m. Dorothy Sue Cleary, Nov. 24, 1960; children: Michael, Barbara, Philip, Patrick. BS, St. Louis U., 1954, MS, 1958, PhD, 1962. Instr. math. Rockhurst Coll., Kansas City, Mo., 1960-62; asst. prof. U. Houston, 1962-67; assoc. prof. Tex. A&M U., College Station, 1967-70, prof., 1970-71; prof. Worcester (Mass.) Poly. Inst., 1971—, chmn. dept. math., 1971-78. Contbr. articles to profl. jours. Mem. Town of Westborough (Mass.) Pub. Schs. Bd., 1974-83, 84-87, Fin. Com., 1992—. With U.S. Army, 1954-56. Mem. AAUP, Am. Math. Soc., Math. Assn. Am. Democrat. Roman Catholic. Achievements include research in near-ring theory and group theory. Home: 45 Adams St Westborough MA 01581-3610 Office: Worcester Poly Inst 100 Institute Rd Worcester MA 01609-2247

MALONE, JOSEPH LAWRENCE, linguistics educator; b. N.Y.C., July 2, 1937; s. Joseph Timothy and Katherine Veronica (O'Connor) M.; m. Pamela Joan Altfeld, Jan. 31, 1964; children—Joseph Timothy II, Otis Taig. B.A., U. Calif.-Berkeley, 1963, Ph.D., 1967. Mem. faculty Barnard Coll., N.Y.C., 1967—, prof. linguistics, 1975—, chmn. dept., 1967—; vis. lectr. U. Pa., 1970; linguistics advisor Grolier Pub. Co. Author: The Science of Linguistics in the Art of Translation, 1988, Tiberian Hebrew Phonology, 1992; editor, contbr. Acad. Am. Ency.; mem. editorial bd. Hellas; contbr. articles to profl. jours. Served with U.S. Army, 1957-60. Grad. fellow U. Calif.-Berkeley, 1965-66, Am. Council Learned Socs., 1966-67. Mem. Linguistics Soc. Am., Am. Oriental Soc., AAUP, N.Am. Conf. Afro-Asiatic Linguistics, Phi Beta Kappa. Democrat. Home: 169 Prospect St Leonia NJ 07605-1929 Office: Barnard Coll New York NY 10027-6598

MALONE, JULIA LOUISE, news reporter, White House correspondent; b. Memphis, Sept. 16, 1947; d. William Battle and Alice Avery (Allen) M. BA, Vanderbilt U., 1969. Copy aide Christian Sci. Monitor, Boston, 1969-71, editorial asst., 1971-72, local reporter, 1972-73, editor Living Page, 1978-80, Congl. reporter, 1980-86; TV corr. Christian Sci. Monitor, Washington, 1987-88; bull. editor Harvard Div. Sch., Cambridge, Mass., 1971; reporter The Fauquier Democrat, Warrenton, Va., 1975-77; nat. reporter Cox Newspapers, Washington, 1986-87, 89—; elected mem. standing com. corrs. House and Senate press galleries, Washington, 1983-85. Recipient award for excellence in bus. and econ. reporting John Hancock Fin. Services, Boston, 1986. Gridiron Club. Home: 3101 New Mexico Ave Washington DC 20016 Office: Cox Newspapers 2000 Pennsylvania Ave NW Washington DC 20006-1812

MALONE, KARL, professional basketball player; b. Summerfield, La., July 24, 1963. Student, La. Tech. U., 1981-85. Basketball player Utah Jazz, 1985—; mem. U.S. Olympic Basketball Team (received Gold medal), 1992. Mem. NBA All-Star team, 1988-94; recipient NBA All-Star Game MVP award, 1989, co-recipient, 1993; mem. All-NBA first team, 1989-94; mem. All-NBA second team, 1988; mem. NBA All-Defensive second team, 1988; mem. NBA All-Rookie Team, 1986; co-leader most seasons (8) with 2000 points, 1987-95; NBA Most Valuable Player, 1997. Office: Utah Jazz Delta Ctr 301 W South Temple Salt Lake City UT 84101-1216*

MALONE, MARK, sports reporter. Football player Pitts. Steelers, San Diego Chargers, N.Y. Jets, 1970-90; starting quarterback Pitts. Steelers, 1984; host Pitts. Steelers pre-game show, sports reporter/anchor Sta. WPXI-TV, Pitts., 1990-93; color commentator preseason games Sta. WPXI-TV, 1990—; NFL reporter, SportsCenter anchor ESPN, 1993—, Sunday Night NFL sideline reporter, host Edge NFL Match-up, 1994—. Active various charities including Multiple Sclerosis, Children's Hosp., Ronald McDonald House, West Penn Burn Unit, Literacy Found., Epilepsy Found., Phila. Recipient AFC Championship as Pitts. Steeler, 1984; holds records for most touchdown passes in one game (1985), highest completion percentage in one game (1984). Office: c/o ESPN ESPN Pla Bristol CT 06010

MALONE, MICHAEL PETER, academic administrator, historian; b. Pomeroy, Wash., Apr. 18, 1940; s. John Albert and Dolores Frances (Cheyne) M.; m. Kathleen Malone, Apr. 17, 1983; children: John Thomas, Molly Christine. BA in History, Gonzaga U., 1962; PhD in Am. Studies, Wash. State U., Pullman, 1966. Asst. prof. history Tex. A&M U., College Station, 1966-67; asst. prof., prof. history Mont. State U., Bozeman, 1967—, dean grad. studies, 1979-89, v.p. acad. affairs, 1989-90; pres. Mont. State U., 1991—; bd. dirs. Buttrey Food and Drug, Commn. on Colls. of N.W. Assn. of Schs. and Colls. Author: The Battle for Butte, 1981 (Sick award 1981), Historians and The American West, 1983, (with others) Montana: A History of Two Centuries, 1976, 2d edit., 1991, The American West: A 20th Century History, 1989, James J. Hill, Empire Builder of the Northwest, 1995. Mem. Western History Assn., Nat. Assn. State Univs. and Land-Grant Colls. (exec. bd. dirs.). Home: 2310 Springcreek Dr Bozeman MT 59715-6035 Office: Montana State U Bozeman MT 59717

MALONE, MICHAEL WILLIAM, electronics executive, software engineer; b. Belmore L.I., N.Y., Mar. 31, 1956; s. Daniel Joseph Malone and Frances Ann (Reilly) Coppersmith; m. Jane Pauline Raese, Aug. 20, 1988. BS in Elec. Engring. and Computer Sci., U. Colo., 1986. Test engr. Catalina Controls, Longmont, Colo., 1984-86; design engr. Inlab, Inc., Broomfield, Colo., 1986-87, mgr. engring., 1987-89; software engr. UMG, Inc., Golden, Colo., 1989-90, sr. software engr., 1990-91, v.p., 1991-94; sr. software engr. RELA, Boulder, Colo., 1994—. Developer software. With USN, 1975-79. Avocations: rock climbing, sailing, aikido, skiing. Office: Rela Inc 6175 Longbow Dr Boulder CO 80301-3205

MALONE, NANCY, actor, director, producer; b. Queens Village, N.Y.; d. James and Bridget (Sheilds) M. Freelance actress, dir., producer, writer. Performer (TV series) The First Hundred Years, Naked City, The Long, Hot Summer (Best Performance by an Actress award); Broadway debut in Time Out For Ginger, other stage performances include Major Barbara, The Makropoulis Secret, A Touch of the Poet, The Trial of the Catonsville Nine; touring performances include The Chalk Garden, The Seven Yr. Itch, A Place For Dolly; actress (films) The Violators, I Cast No Shadow, An Affair of the Skin, Intimacy, The Trial of the Cantonsville Nine, The Man Who Loved Cat Dancing, Capricorn One; producer (TV series) including Bionic Woman, 1978, Husbands, Wives and Lovers, 1978, The Great Pretender, 1984, (special) Bob Hope: The First 90 Years, 1993 (Emmy award, Outstanding Variety, Musical or Comedy Special, 1993), Womanspeak, 1983; dir. (TV series) Dynasty, 1984-87, Hotel, 1984-87, Colbys, 1985, Cagney and Lacey, 1987, Rosie O'Niel (Emmy nomination), Sisters (Emmy nomination), Melrose Place, Beverly Hills, Picket Fences; producer, dir. (film) There Were Times Dear, 1986 (John Muir Trustees award, Cine Golden Eagle, Blue Ribbon); founder Nancy Malone Prodns., 1975, Lilac Prodns., 1979. Fellow Leaky Found.; mem. Am. Film Inst. (mem. founder), Women in Film (trustee, Chrystal award, Founders award 1996). Home: 11624 Sunshine Terr Studio City CA 91604

MALONE, PERRILLAH ATKINSON (PAT MALONE), retired state official; b. Montgomery, Ala., Mar. 17, 1922; d. Odolph Edgar and Myrtle (Fondren) Atkinson. BS, Oglethorpe U., 1956; MAT, Emory U., 1962. Asst. editor, then acting editor Emory U., 1958-64; asst. project officer Ga. Dept. Pub. Health, Atlanta, 1965-68; asst. project dir. Ga. Ednl. Improvement Coun., 1968-69, assoc. dir., 1970-71; dir. career svcs. State Scholarship

Commn., Atlanta, 1971-74; rev. coord. Div. Phys. Health, Ga. Dept. Human Resources, Atlanta, 1974-79; project dir. So. Regional Edn. Bd., 1979-81; specialist Div. Family and Children Svcs., Atlanta, 1982-91, ret., 1991; mem. Gov.'s Commn. on Nursing Edn. and Nursing Practice, 1972-75, Aging Svcs. Task Force, Atlanta Regional Commn., 1985-95; book reviewer Atlanta Jour.-Constn., 1962-79. Recipient Recognition award Ga. Nursing Assn., 1976, Korsell award Ga. Ga. League for Nursing, 1974, Alumni Honor award Emory U., 1964. Mem. APHA, Ga. Gerontology Soc. (editor GGS Newsletter 1988-92, Lewis Newman award 1991). Methodist. Home: 1146 Oxford Rd NE Atlanta GA 30306-2608

MALONE, ROBERT JOSEPH, bank executive; b. Sept. 3, 1944. With Bank of Am., 1969-81; chmn., pres., CEO First Interstate Bank Boise, Idaho, 1981-84; pres., CEO First Interstate Bank Denver, 1984-90; chmn., pres., CEO Western Capital Investment Corp. (now First Bank System, Inc.), Denver, 1990-92; chmn., CEO Bank Western/Central Banks (now First Bank System, Inc.), Denver, 1992-93; CEO Colo. Nat. Bank, Denver, 1993—, chmn., 1996—. Office: Colorado Nat Bank 950 17th St Denver CO 80202-2828

MALONE, ROBERT ROY, artist, art educator; b. McColl, S.C., Aug. 8, 1933; s. Robert Roy and Anne (Matthews) M.; m. Cynthia Enid Taylor, Feb. 26, 1956; 1 child, Brendan Trevor. B.A., U. N.C., 1955; M.F.A., U. Chgo., 1958; postgrad., U. Iowa, 1959. Instr. art Union U., Jackson, Tenn., 1959-60, Lambuth Coll., 1959-61; asst. prof. art Wesleyan Coll., Macon, Ga., 1961-67; assoc. prof. Wesleyan Coll., 1967-68, W.Va. U., 1968-70, So. Ill. U., Edwardsville, 1970-75; prof. So. Ill. U., 1975—. One-man shows at Gallery Illien, Atlanta, 1969, De Cinque Gallery, Miami, 1968, 71, Ill. State Mus., Springfield, 1974, U. Del., Newark, 1978, Elliot Smith Gallery, St. Louis, 1985, Merida Galleries, Louisville, 1985, Yvonne Rapp Gallery, Louisville, 1990, 92, 93, 96, St. John's Coll., Santa Fe, 1991, Yzelac Gallery, Pontiac, Mich., 1997, others; group shows include Bklyn. Mus., 1966, Assoc. Am. Artists Gallery, N.Y.C., 1968, Musée d'Art Modern, Paris, 1970, DeCordova Mus., 1973, 74, St. Louis Art Mus., 1985, Wake Forest U., 1985, New Orleans Mus. Art, 1990, Dakota Internat., Vermillion, 1994; represented in numerous permanent collections including Smithsonian Instn., Washington, USIA, Washington, Library of Congress, Calif. Palace of Legion of Honor, San Francisco, N.Y. Pub. Library, N.Y.C., Victoria and Albert Mus., London, Chgo. Art Inst., Indpls. Mus. Art, Humana Inc., Louisville, State of Ill. Ctr., Chgo., Speed Mus., Louisville, N. Ill. Univ., Capital Devel. Bd., Ill. Recipient numerous regional, nat. awards in competitive exhbns.; Ford fellow, 1977; So. Ill. U. at Edwardsville sr. research scholar, 1976, 84. Home: 600 Chapman St Edwardsville IL 62025-1260 Office: Dept Art and Design So Ill U Edwardsville IL 62025

MALONE, THOMAS FRANCIS, academic administrator, meteorologist; b. Sioux City, Iowa, May 3, 1917; s. John and Mary (Hourigan) M.; m. Rosalie Doran, Dec. 30, 1942; children—John H., Thomas Francis, Mary E., James K., Richard K., Dennis P. B.S., S.D. Sch. Mines, 1940, D.Eng., 1962; Sc.D., MIT, 1946; L.H.D., St. Joseph Coll., West Hartford, Conn., 1965; Sc.D. (hon.), Bates Coll., 1988. Instr. MIT, 1942-43, asst. prof., 1943-51, assoc. prof., 1951-56; dir. Travelers Research Ctr., Travelers Ins. Co., Hartford, Conn., 1955-56; dir. research Travelers Research Ctr., Travelers Ins. Co., 1956-69, sr. v.p., 1968-70; chmn. bd. Travelers Research Ctr., Inc., 1961-70; dean Grad. Sch., U. Conn., Storrs, 1970-73; chmn. bd. Center for Environment and Men, 1970-71; dir. emeritus Holcomb Research Inst., Butler U., Indpls., 1983—; scholar in residence St. Joseph Coll., 1983-91; Nat. Scis. fellow Resources for Future, 1983-84; chmn. bd. Univ. Corp. for Atmospheric Research.; mem. Conn. Weather Control Bd., 1959-73; mem. panel on sci. and tech., com. on sci. and astronautics U.S. Ho. of Reps., 1960-1970; nat. adv. com. community air pollution HEW, 1962-66; mem. sci. info. council NSF, 1962-66; rep. Am. Geophys. Union to U.S. Nat. Commn. for UNESCO, 1963-73 chmn. U.S. Nat. Commn., 1965-67; mem. nat. adv. com. on oceans and atmosphere, 1972-75, mem. Conn. Research Commn., 1965-71; mem. com. application sci. and tech. New Eng. Council; chmn. Nat. Motor Vehicle Safety Adv. Council, 1967-70; mem. sci. adv. com. climate impact assessment and response program UN Environ. Program, 1992—. Editor: Compendium of Meteorology, 1951; contbg. editor: Environment, 1992—; bd. editors: Jour. of the Marine Tech. Soc., 1995—. Bd. dirs. Engrs. Joint Coun., 1968-70; bd. govs. Ins. Inst. Hwy. Safety, 1968-70; mem. oversight rev. bd. Nat. Acid Precipitation Assessment Program, 1990—. Recipient Robert M. Losey award Inst. Aero. Sci., 1960, Charter Oak Leadership medal Greater Hartford C. of C., 1962, Charles Franklin Brooks award, 1964, Cleveland Abbe award Am. Meteorol. Soc., 1968, Conn. Conservationist of Yr. award, 1966, Guy E. March Silver medal S.D. Sch. Mines, 1976, Internat. Meteorol. Orgn. prize, 1984, Internat. St. Francis Assissi prize for environment, 1991, AAAS Internat. prize, 1994; N.C. State U. disting. scholar, 1990—. Fellow AAAS (internat. sci. coop., 1994), N.Y. Acad. Scis., Am. Meteorol. Soc. (pres. 1960-62), Am. Geophys. Union (past pres., sec. internat. participation 1964, Waldo E. Smith award 1986); mem. NAS (chmn. geophysics research bd. 1969-76, chmn. bd. on internat. orgns. and programs, dep. fgn. sec. 1969-73, fgn. sec. 1978-82), NRC (space application bd. 1973-77), Am. Acad. Arts and Scis., Internat. Council Sci. Unions (v.p., sec.-gen. sci. com. problems environ. 1970-76, treas. 1978-82) Am. Geog. Soc. (council 1971-77), Royal Irish Acad. (hon.), Conn. Acad. Sci. and Engring. (exec. scientist 1987-91), Acad. Polit. Scis., Sigma Xi (bd. dirs. 1983—, pres. 1988-89, dir. Sigma Xi Ctr. 1992-95, chief scientist 1996—). Home: 5 Bishop Rd Apt 203 West Hartford CT 06119-1536 Office: NC State U Dept Marine and Atmospheric Scis Box 8208 Raleigh NC 27695

MALONE, WILLIAM GRADY, lawyer; b. Minden, La., Feb. 19, 1915; s. William Gordon and Minnie Lucie (Hortman) M.; m. Marion Rowe Whitfield, Sept. 26, 1943; children: William Grady, Gordon Whitfield, Marion Elizabeth, Helen Ann, Margaret Catherine. BS, La. State U., 1941; JD, George Washington U., 1952. Bar: Va. 1952, U.S. Supreme Ct 1971. Statis. analyst Dept. Agr., Baton Rouge, 1941; investigator VA, Washington, 1946-59; legal officer, dep., gen. counsel, asst. gen. counsel VA, 1959-79; pvt. practice law Arlington, Va., 1979—. Editor: Fed. Bar News, 1972-73. Pres. Aurora Hills Civic Assn., 1948-49; spl. asst. to treas. Com. of 100, 1979-81, chmn., 1982-83; pres. Children's Theater, 1968-69; trustee St. George's Episc. Ch., 1979—; chmn. Arlington County Fair Assn., 1979-83. Lt. col. AUS, 1941-46, ETO. Decorated Legion of Merit; recipient Disting. Svc. award, 1979, 3 Superior Performance awards, 1952-72, Outstanding Alumni award George Washington Law Sch., 1978. Mem. Fed. Bar Assn. (pres. D.C. chpt. 1970-71, nat. pres. 1978-79), Va. Bar Assn., Arlington County Bar Assn., Nat. Lawyers Club (dir.), Arlington Host Lions, Ft. Myer Officers Club. Home: 224 N Jackson St Arlington VA 22201-1253 Office: 2060 14th St N Ste 310 Arlington VA 22201-2519 *Success is not measured by dollars accumulated but by service to others.*

MALONE, WINFRED FRANCIS, health scientist; b. Revere, Mass., Feb. 10, 1935; s. Winfred and Marguerite (Meehan) M.; m. Eleanor Malone, Aug. 1974. BS, U. Mass., 1957, MS, 1961; MS, Rutgers U., 1963; PhD, U. Mich., 1970. Health scientist Nat. Cancer Inst., Bethesda, Md., 1970-81, chief chemoprevention br., 1981-95, acting assoc. dir., 1991-93; chief ACRES Nat. Cancer Inst., 1995—. Contbr. articles on drug devel. scis. to profl. jours. Mem. AAAS, Am. Coll. Toxicology, N.Y. Acad. Scis., Drug Info. Assn. Home: 3209 Wake Dr Kensington MD 20895-3216 Office: Nat Cancer Inst EPN # 201 Bethesda MD 20892

MALONEY, CAROLYN BOSHER, congresswoman; b. Feb. 19, 1948; d. R.G. and Christine (Clegg) Bosher; m. C.H.W. Maloney, 1976; children: Christina, Virginia. Student, Greensboro Coll. Former mem. N.Y. State Assembly Housing Com., N.Y.C Council dist. 8; mem. 103rd Congress from 14th N.Y. dist., Washington, 1993—, mem. banking and fin. svcs. com., subcom. monetary policy, mem. fin. instns. and consumer credit com., mem. govt. reform and oversight com. govt. mgmt., info. and tech., mem. joint economic com. Past chmn. Common Cause; active Assn. for a Better N.Y., Manahattan Women's Polit. Caucus. Mem. NAACP, Nat. Orgn. Women, Hadassah. Home: 49 E 92nd St Apt 1A New York NY 10128-1326 Office: US Ho of Reps 1330 Longworth Bldg Washington DC 20515-3214

MALONEY, DIANE MARIE, legal nurse consultant; b. Aug. 15, 1951; d. John J. and Ruthe E. (Fournier) Perron; m. Patrick J. Maloney, Apr. 26, 1975; children: Melissa, Shawnas. Grad., Miller Hosp. Sch. Nursing, St. Paul, 1970; degree, Inver Hills Community Coll., Inver Grove Heights, Minn., 1988, cert. in paralegal/medical studies, 1989. Orthopedic specialist St. Luke's Hosp., St. Paul; head nurse Otolaryngology Profl. Assocs., St. Paul; charge nurse Southview Health Ctr., West St. Paul, Minn.; legal nurse cons. Milavetz and Assocs., Bloomington, Minn.; with Milavetz, Gallop & Milavetz, Edina, Minn. Mem. NAACOG, Am. Assn. Legal Nurse Cons., Minn. Assn. Legal Nurse Cons. (steering com.), Interstitial Cystitis Assn.

MALONEY, FRANCIS PATRICK, physiatrist, educator; b. Pitts., Mar. 4, 1936; s. Francis Barrington and Esther Elizabeth (Kuhn) M.; m. Kathryn Brassell Anderson, June 25, 1960 (dec. June 6, 1987); children: Timothy J., Kevin P., J. Christopher; m. Billie Barbara Galloway, Feb. 14, 1990. BA, St. Vincent Coll., 1958; MD, U. Pitts., 1962; MPH, Johns Hopkins U., 1966. Diplomate Am. Bd. Phys. Medicine and Rehab., Am. Bd. Preventive Medicine, Am. Bd. Med. Mgmt. Intern St. Francis Hosp., Pitts., 1962-63; resident gen. preventive medicine Johns Hopkins U. Sch. of Hygiene & Pub. Health, Balt., 1965-67; fellow medicine, med. genetics Johns Hopkins U. Sch. of Medicine, Balt., 1966-68; resident phys. medicine and rehab. U. Minn., Mpls., 1968-70; staff physician Sister Kenny Inst., Mpls., 1970-72; asst. clin. prof. U. Minn., Mpls., 1970-72; asst. prof. phys. medicine and rehab., assoc. prof. U. Colo., Denver, 1972-78, 78-84; prof. head div. of rehab. medicine U. Ark., Little Rock, 1984-91, prof., chmn. dept. phys. medicine and rehab., 1991—; med. dir. Bapt. Rehab. Inst., Little Rock, 1985—; chief rehab. medicine svc. VA Med. Ctr., Little Rock, 1984—. Editor: Interdisciplinary Rehabilitation of Multiple Sclerosis and Neuromuscular Disease, 1984; editor, author: Physical Medicine & Rehabilitation State of the Art Reviews, 1987, Primer on Management, 1987, Rehabilitation of Aging, 1989, Management for Rehabilitation Medicine II, 1993; alt. editor: Archives of Physical Medicine and Rehabilitation, 1989-93. Mem. exec. bd. Greater No. Colo. Chpt. of Muscular Dystrophy Assn. of Am., 1972-82; spl. edn. adv. com. Cherry Creek Sch. Dist., Denver, 1975, vice chmn., 1976, chmn., 1977; med. advisor Denver Commn. on Disabled and Coun. on Aging, Denver, 1980-82, Denver Commn. on Human Svcs., 1982-84; external examiner King Saud U. Med. Sch., Saudi Arabia, 1983; med. adv. bd. Ark. Multiple Sclerosis Soc., Little Rock, 1985-88; chmn. chmn's. coun. Assn. Acad. Physiatrists, Indpls., 1992-94. Fellow Am. Acad. Phys. and Rehab.; mem. AMA, Am. Congress of Rehab. Medicine, Am. Acad. Cerebral Palsy, Am. Pub. Health Assn., Am. Bd. Physical Medicine and Rehbilitation (dir. 1988—), Soc. for Exptl. Biology and Medicine, Assn. Acad. Physiatrists, Ark. Med. Soc., Pulaski County Med. Soc., Soc. for Neuroscis. Office: U Ark Med Scis 4301 W Markham Slot #602 Little Rock AR 72205

MALONEY, FRANK, judge, lawyer; b. Worcester, Mass., Nov. 20, 1927; s. Francis James and Dora Marie (Berthiaume) M.; children: Catharine Frances, Edward James. BA, U. Tex., Austin, 1953, LLB, 1956. Bar: Tex. 1956, U.S. Supreme Ct. 1962, Mass. 1969. Asst. dist. atty. Travis Co., Austin, Tex., 1956-60; chief Law Enforcement div. Atty. Gen. State of Tex., Austin, 1960-61; ptnr. Stayton, Maloney, Hearne & Babb, Austin, 1961-79; owner Frank Maloney & Assocs., P.C., Austin, 1979-90; judge Tex. Ct. Criminal Appeals, Austin, 1991-96; vis. judge Trial and Appelate Tex. Cts., 1996—; of counsel Sheinfeld, Maley & Kay, 1996—; adj. prof. law U. Tex. Sch. of Law, 1962-85, 97—. Co-author: (with Stumberg) Criminal Law and Administration, 1964. Capt. U.S. Army, 1946-51. Fellow Tex. Bar Found.; mem. ABA, Nat. Assn. Criminal Def. Lawyers (pres. 1987-88), Mass. Bar Assn., Tex. Bar Assn., Tex. Criminal Def. Lawyers Assn. (pres. 1971-72), Am. Bd. Trial Advocates, Am. Bd. Criminal Lawyers, Travis County Bar Assn. Home: 1414 Wathen Ave Austin TX 78703-2528 Office: 300 Congress Ave Ste 1400 Austin TX 78701-4024

MALONEY, GERALD P., utility executive; b. Lawrence, Mass., Mar. 9, 1933; s. Thomas P. and Concetta M.; m. Dorothea Ames. BSEE, MIT, 1955, BSBA, 1955; MBA, Rutgers U., 1962. With Am. Electric Power Co., Inc., Columbus, Ohio, 1955—; controller Am. Electric Power Co., Inc., 1965-70, v.p. fin., 1970-75, sr. v.p. fin., 1975-90, exec. v.p., CFO, 1990—; dir., v.p. fin. Appalachian Power Co., Ind., Mich. Power Co., Ohio Power Co., Ky. Power Co., Wheeling Power Co., Kingsport Power Co., Columbus So. Power Co.; bd. dirs. Energy Ins. Mut., Ltd., chmn., 1990-92; bd. dirs. Nuclear Electric Ins., Ltd. Mem. Edison Electric Inst. (fin. com.), Beta Gamma Sigma. Home: 275 S Parkview Ave Bexley OH 43209-1649 Office: Am Electric Power Co 1 Riverside Plz Columbus OH 43215-2355

MALONEY, JAMES EDWARD, lawyer; b. Hackensack, N.J., Apr. 28, 1951; s. Edward James Maloney and Kathleen Elizabeth (Lamont) Leaf. BA, Yale U., 1972; JD, Harvard U., 1975. Bar: Tex. 1975, U.S. Dist. Ct. (no., so., ea. and we. dists.) Tex., U.S. Ct. Appeals (2d, 3d, 5th, 9th and D.C. cirs.), U.S. Supreme Ct. Assoc. Baker & Botts, Houston, 1975-82, ptnr., 1982—; chmn. bd. dirs. Fotofest, Inc.; bd. dirs. Houston Ctr. for Photography. Trustee Woodberry Forest (Va.) Sch., 1991—. Mem. ABA, Tex. Bar Assn., Tex. Bar Found., Houston Bar Assn., Houston Bar Found., Yale Club (Houston, Assn. Yale Alumni rep. 1984-86). Republican. Episcopalian. Home: 2129 Tangley St Houston TX 77005-1640 Office: Baker & Botts 3000 One Shell Plz 910 Louisiana St Houston TX 77002-4916

MALONEY, JAMES HENRY, congressman; b. Quincy, Mass., Sept. 17, 1948; s. James Henry Jr. and Katherine Smith (Murphy) M.; m. Mary Angela Draper, Aug. 16, 1980; children: Adele, Anna, Ellen. BA cum laude, Harvard U., 1972; JD, Boston U., 1980. Vol. VISTA, Gary, Ind., 1969-70; exec. dir. Community Action Com. Danbury, Conn., 1974-78; atty. Pinney, Payne, VanLenten, Burrell, Wolfe & Dillman, P.C., Danbury, 1980-86; ptnr. Dice, Maloney & Lenz, P.C., Danbury, 1986-93, Maloney, Leaphart & Associates, PC, Danbury, 1995—; mem. Conn. Senate, Hartford, 1987-95; mem 105th Congress from 5th Conn. dist., 1997—; asst. majority leader and senate chair fin., revenue and bonding com., 1993-95. Chmn. Danbury Cmty. Endowment, 1984-94, dem. candidate for U.S. Congress, 1994, 96. Recipient Disting. Svc. award Jaycees North Fairfield County, 1984, Community Svc. award Midwestern Conn. Coun. on Alcoholism, 1990, Spl. Recognition award Jewish Home for the Elderly, Fairfield County, 1993; named Legislator of Yr., Caucus Conn. Dems., 1990, Conn. Assn. Ind. Ins. Agts., 1992. Roman Catholic. Avocation: sailing. Office: 1213 Longworth Washington DC 20515-0705

MALONEY, JOHN JOSEPH, writer; b. N.Y.C., Jan. 15, 1929; s. John J. and Breda T. (O'Leary) M.; m. Helen Martin; children: Peter, Elizabeth, Mary Ellen. BA, Fordham Coll., 1951. City editor Patent Trader, Mt. Kisco, N.Y., 1953-59; news bureau mgr. N.Y. Stock Exchange, N.Y.C., 1959-63; dir. pub. rels. Lehman Bros., N.Y.C., 1963-71, Warnaco, Inc., Bridgeport, Conn., 1971-77; v.p. charge of media rels. Citicorp/Citibank, N.Y.C., 1977-91; writer Easton, Conn., 1991—. With U.S. Army, 1951-53. Avocation: sailing. Home: 65 Sport Hill Pkwy Easton CT 06612-2239

MALONEY, JOHN WILLIAM, lawyer, retired; b. Santa Barbara, Calif., Dec. 6, 1930; s. John Joseph and Mildred (Brunenmeyer); m. Jean Anderson, Nov. 18, 1966; children: Patrick Maloney, Cynthia Maloney. BA in Econs., U. Calif., Santa Barbara, 1953; JD, UCLA, 1958. Bar: Calif. 1959, U.S. Dist. Ct. (no., ctrl., ea., so. dists.) Calif. 1959. Assoc. Fogel McInery, Santa Monica, Calif., 1959-62; ptnr. Rhodes Barnard & Maloney, Santa Monica, 1963-82, Rhodes, Maloney et al., Santa Monica, 1983-88; prin. Maloney & Mullen, Santa Monica, 1989-96, ret., 1997; ptnr. Real Estate Investors, 1970—. Pres. Santa Monica Legal Aid Soc., 1960-63. Capt. U.S. Army, 1953-55. Mem. Bel Air Bay Club, Riviera Tennis Club, Bear River Club. Republican. Roman Catholic. Avocations: fly fishing, duck hunting, tennis.

MALONEY, MARYNELL, lawyer; b. Hutchinson, Kans., Jan. 14, 1955; d. Robert Edgar and Marian Ellen (Benson) Baker; m. Michael D. Maloney, Nov. 30, 1977; children: Michelle M., Erica O., Dennis Jr. BA, Oberlin Coll., 1975; MA, Trinity U., San Antonio, 1978; JD, St. Mary's U., San Antonio, 1980. Cert. by Tex. bd. of legal specialization. Assoc. Law Offices Pat Maloney, P.C., San Antonio, 1981-82; ptnr., owner Maloney & Maloney, San Antonio, 1982—. Bd. dirs. San Antonio Internat. Keyboard Competition, 1988-90; bd. govs. St. Peters/St. Joseph's Children's Home, San Antonio, 1989-92. Mem. ACLU (bd. dirs. 1990—, v.p. 1995-96, Tex. chpt. 1992—, SACLU 1990—), Am. Trial Lawyers Assn., State Bar Tex., Tex. Trial Lawyers Assn. (assoc. bd. dirs. 1989-90, bd. dirs. 1991—, chair coun. local leadership 1990-92, cert. personal injury trial law), San Antonio Bar Assn., San Antonio Trial Lawyers Assn. (pres. 1991-92). Democrat. Avocations: reading, writing. Office: Maloney & Maloney PC 2000 Milam 115 E Travis San Antonio TX 78205

MALONEY, MAUREEN, government official; b. Burnley, England, Nov. 23, 1955; arrived in Canada, 1980; d. Michael and Mary (O'Dea) M.; m. Jamie Lloyd Cassels, June 23, 1989 (div. Dec. 1995). LLB, U. Warwick, 1977; LLM, U. Toronto, 1981. Bar: Supreme Ct. England & Wales 1980; barrister, solicitor Br. Columbia, 1992. Assoc. Pinsent & Co., Birmingham, England, 1978-80; from asst. prof. to assoc. prof. U. Victoria, B.C., Canada, 1981-93; dep. min. justice Govt. British Columbia, 1993—; dean faculty of law U. Victoria, 1990-93; adv. bd. Canadian Lawyer. Office: Min Atty Gen, 910 Govt St Ste 910, Victoria, BC Canada V8V 1X4

MALONEY, MICHAEL JAMES, research scientist; b. Madison, Wis., Aug. 29, 1942; s. James Edward and Wanda Marie (Berry) M; m. Diane Lois Best, Apr. 20, 1962; children—Lance, Robin Maloney Judd, Tracy, Scott. Staff scientist Bjorksten Research Labs., Inc., Madison, Wis., 1962-79, v.p., 1979-84, pres., 1984—. Inventor in field. Contbr. articles to profl. jours. Chmn., Fitchburg Parks Commn., Wis., 1972—; mem. Fitchburg Planning Commn., 1972—. Mem. ASTM, ASM, Soc. Plastics Engrs. Roman Catholic. Office: Bjorksten Rsch Labs Inc 2998 Syene Rd PO Box 259444 Madison WI 53725-9444

MALONEY, MICHAEL PATRICK, lawyer, corporate executive; b. Syracuse, N.Y., June 1, 1944; s. Randolph Bartholomew and Alice Mary (Loban) M.; m. Jane McBurney, May 21, 1977; children: Christopher, Kara. A.B., Georgetown U., 1966; M.B.A., Cornell U., 1968, J.D., 1971. Bar: N.Y. 1972. Assoc. Donovan Leisure Newton and Irvine, N.Y.C., 1971-78; asst. dir. div. market regulation SEC, Washington, 1978-79; sr. v.p., gen. counsel, sec. Orion Capital Corp., N.Y.C., 1979—; bd. dirs. Am. Arbitration Assn.; mem. Corp. Governance Com. Mem. N.Y. Bar Assn., Am. Soc. Corp. Secs. (pres. N.Y. chpt.), Am. Corp. Counsel Assn. (bd. dirs. N.Y. chpt.), Scarsdale Golf Club (Hartsdale, N.Y.), Rockefeller Ctr. Club. Home: 7 Kings Grant Way Briarcliff Manor NY 10510-2521 Office: Orion Capital Corp 600 5th Ave New York NY 10020-2302

MALONEY, MILFORD CHARLES, retired internal medicine educator; b. Buffalo, Mar. 15, 1927; s. John Angelus Maloney and Winifred Hill; m. Dione Ethyl Sheppard. BS, Canisius Coll., 1947, postgrad., 1947-49; MD, U. Buffalo, 1953. Diplomate Am. Bd. Internal Medicine. Rsch. chemist Buffalo Electrochem. Co., 1947-49; intership Mercy Hosp./Georgetown U., 1953-54; med. residency Buffalo VA Hosp., 1954-56; cardiology fellow Buffalo Gen. Hosp., 1956-57; chmn. dept. medicine Mercy Hosp., 1969-94; program dir., internal medicine residency Mercy Hosp., Buffalo, 1972-89; with steering com. Assn. Program Dirs. in Internal Medicine, 1976, coun. mem., 1977-80; clin. prof. medicine SUNY, Buffalo, 1981-94; trustee Am. Soc. Internal Medicine, 1984-90; edn. leader med. seminar Am. Soc. Internal Medicine, Austria, Switzerland, France, 1987, Argentina, Brazil, Paraguay, 1988; bd. dirs. Internal Medicine Ctr. for Advancement and Rsch. Edn.; pres. Heart Assn. Western N.Y., Buffalo, 1969; sr. cancer rsch. physician Roswell Park Meml. Cancer Inst., 1959-62; mem. internal medicine liaison com. N.Y. State, 1980-90. Editor (newsletter) N.Y. State Soc. Internal Medicine, 1972-78. Bd. dirs. Health Sys. Agy. Western N.Y., Buffalo, 1981; mem. exec. com., bd. dirs. Blue Cross Western N.Y., Buffalo, 1987; mem. bd. regents Canisius Coll., Buffalo, 1987—; mem. pres. assocs. SUNY, Buffalo. Capt. M.C., U.S. Army, 1957-59. Recipient merit award N.Y. State Soc. Internal Medicine, 1980, Man of Yr. award Heart Assn. Western N.Y., 1982, ann. honoree award Trocaire Coll., 1986, Disting. Alumni award Canisius Coll., 1991, Berkson Excellence award in tchg. and art of medicine, SUNY at Buffalo, 1992, Outstanding Med. Tchg. Attending award Mercy Hosp./SUNY Med. Residents, 1994; named to Sports Hall of Fame, Canisius Coll., 1978. Fellow ACP (Upstate Physician Recognition award 1989), Am. Coll. Cardiology; mem. AMA (SUNY rep. 1986-94, rep. to sect. med. schs. at ann. meetings 1984-94, chmn. sect. on internal medicine 1990-91), Am. Soc. Internal Medicine (bd. dirs. Internal Medicine Ctr. for Advancement of Rsch. Edn. 1988-91, trustee 1984-90, pres. 1990-91, chmn. long range planning com., rep. to Federated Coun. on Internal Medicine 1990-91, rep. to AMA nat. practice parameters and guidelines com. 1989-91), N.Y. State Soc. Internal Medicine (pres. 1974-75), Alumni Assn. SUNY (pres. 1975), Med. Soc. County Erie (pres. 1969), Va. Soc. Internal Medicine (hon.). Home: 116 Cove Point Ln Williamsburg VA 23185-8613

MALONEY, PATSY LORETTA, university official, nursing educator; b. Murfreesboro, Tenn., Feb. 19, 1952; d. Buford Leon Browning and Ina (Bush) Dubose; m. Richard J. Maloney, July 26, 1975; children: Katherine Nalani, Nathaniel Allen, Elizabeth Maureen. BS in Nursing, U. Md., 1974; MA, Cath. U., 1984, MS in Nursing, 1984; EdD, U. So. Calif., 1994. Commd. 1st lt. U.S. Army, 1974, advanced through grades to lt. col., 1989; asst. chief nurse evenings and nights DeWitt Army Hosp., Ft. Belvoir, Va.; chief nurse, tng. officer 85th EVAC Hosp., Ft. Lee, Va.; clin. head nurse emergency rm./PCU Tripler Army Med. Ctr., Honolulu, chief nursing edn.; chief surg. nursing sect. and acute care nursing sect. Madigan Army Med. Ctr., Tacoma, 1991-94; ret., 1994; dir. Ctr. for Continued Nursing Learning Pacific Luth. U., Tacoma, Wash., 1994—; asst. prof., dir. ctr. for continued nursing learning Pacific Luth. U., Tacoma, 1994—. Mem. Emergency Nurses Assn., Nat. Nursing Staff Devel. Orgn., Assn. Mil. Surgeons, Acad. Med. Surg. Nurses, Sigma Theta Tau, Phi Kappa Phi. Home: 7002 53rd St W University Place WA 98467-2214 Office: Pacific Luth U Ctr Cont Nursing Learning Tacoma WA 98467

MALONEY, ROBERT B., federal judge; b. 1933. BBA, So. Meth. U., 1956, postgrad., 1960. Asst. dist. atty. County of Dallas, 1961-62; ptnr. Watts, Stallings & Maloney, 1962-65, Maloney, Miller & McDowell, 1966-75, Maloney & McDowell, 1976-78, Maloney & Hardcastle, 1979-80, Maloney & Maloney, 1981-84; assoc. judge Tex. Ct. Appeals (5th cir.), Tex., 1983-85; judge U.S. Dist. Ct. (no. dist.) Tex., Dallas, 1985—. State rep., Austin, Tex., 1973-82. Mem. Tex. Bar Assn. Office: US Dist Ct Rm 15 E 26 1100 Commerce St Dallas TX 75242-1027

MALONEY, ROBERT E., JR., lawyer; b. San Francisco, Sept. 17, 1942; s. Robert E. and Mara A. (Murphy) M.; children: Michael, Sarah. BA magna cum laude, U. Portland, 1964; JD summa cum laude, Willamette U., Salem, Oreg., 1967. Bar: Oreg., Wash., U.S. Dist. Ct. Oreg., U.S. Dist. Ct. (we. dist.) Wash., U.S. Dist. Ct. (ea. dist.) Wash., U.S. Ct. Appeals (9th cir.). Ptnr. Lane Powell Spears Lubersky, Portland, 1967—; bd. dirs., sec. Norm Thompson Outfitters, Inc., Portland, 1981—, Capital Credit Inc., 1996—; chmn. bd. visitors Willamette U. Law Sch., 1993-95; chair, mem. exec. com. Portland Trial Dept.; lawyers del. 9th Cir. Jud. Conf., 1995—. Bd. dirs. Oreg. chpt. Multiple Sclerosis Soc.; judge pro tem Multnomah County Cir. Ct., 1994—. Mem. ABA (co-chair products liability com., trial practice com. 1990-94), Nat. Assn. R.R. Trial Counsel, Fedn. Ins. Corp. Counsel, Oreg. Assn. Def. Counsel (bd. dirs. 1987-94, sec. 1991-92, v.p. 1993-94, pres. 1994), Fed. Bar Assn. (exec. com. Oreg. divsn. 1988—, pres. 1994-95), Multnomah Athletic Club. Republican. Roman Catholic. Office: Lane Powell Spears Lubersky 520 SW Yamhill St Portland OR 97204-1335

MALONEY, ROBERT KELLER, ophthalmologist, medical educator. AB in Mathematics summa cum laude, Harvard U., 1979; MA in Philosophy, Politics and Econs., Oxford (Eng.) U., 1981; MD, U. Calif., San Francisco, 1985. Diplomate Am. Bd. Ophthalmology. Rsch fellow dept. physiology Cambridge (Eng.) U., 1985; intern U. Calif., L.A., 1985-86; resident Wilmer Ophthalmol. Inst. Johns Hopkins Hosp., Balt., 1986-89; head fellow cornea and refractive surgery Emory U., Dept. Ophthalmology, Atlanta, 1989-91; assoc. prof. ophthalmology UCLA Sch. Medicine, Jules Stein Eye Inst., 1991—; cons. Premier Laser Systems, for devel. of Erbium-YAG sys. for corneal refractive surgery. Contbr. numerous articles to profl. jours.; presenter and spkr. in field; assoc. editor (N.Am.) Jour. Refractive and Corneal Surgery, 1991-95; internat. editl. bd. European Jour. Implant and Refractive Surgery, 1995; reviewer Am. Jour. Ophthalmology, Ophthalmology, Archives of Ophthalmology, Jour. Cataract and Refractive Surgery, Ophthalmic Surgery and Lasers. Rhodes scholar, 1979, Heed Found. fellow, 1989-90, Heed/Knapp fellow, 1990-91, John Harvard scholar, 1978; recipient Detur and Edward Whitaker prizes, Harvard U., Rsch. to Prevent Blindness Career Devel. award, 1992, Mericus Whittier award, 1997.

Mem. Am. Acad. Ophthalmology (long-range planning com. 1989-92, quality of care com. 1987-91, retina preferred practice pattern subcom., refractive errors preferred practice pattern subcom.; chmn. ann. meeting program com. for young ophthalmologists, 1990-92; adv. group to ad hoc com. on orgnl. design 1991, young ophthalmologists' com. 1992-94; Honor award 1993), Assn. Rsch. in Vision and Ophthalmology, Internat. Soc. Refractive Surgery, Calif. Assn. Ophthalmology, Max Fine Corneal Soc., Phi Beta Kappa. Office: UCLA Sch Medicine 100 Stein Plz Los Angeles CA 90095-7065

MALONEY, THERESE ADELE, insurance company executive; b. Quincy, Mass., Sept. 15, 1929; d. James Henry and F. Adele (Powers) M. BA in Econs., Coll. St. Elizabeth, Convent Station, N.J., 1951; AMP, Harvard U. Bus. Sch., 1981. CPCU. With Liberty Mut. Ins. Co., Boston, 1951-94, asst. v.p., asst. mgr. nat. risks, 1974-77, v.p., asst. mgr. nat. risks, 1977-79, v.p., mgr. nat. risks, 1979-86, sr. v.p. underwriting mktg. and adminstrn. 1986-87, exec. v.p. underwriting, policy decision, 1987-94, also bd. dirs.; pres. and bd. dirs. subs. Liberty Mut. (Bermuda) Ltd., 1981-94, LEXCO Ltd.; bd. dirs., dep. chmn. Liberty Mut. (U.K.) Ltd., London; bd. dirs. Liberty Mut. Ins. Co., Liberty Mut. Fire Ins. Co., Liberty Mut. Life Assurance Co., Liberty Fin. Cos.; mem. faculty Inst. Inst., Northeastern U., Boston, 1969-74; mem. adv. bd., risk mgmt. studies Ins. Inst. Am., 1977-83; mem. adv. coun. Suffolk U. Sch. Mgmt., 1984-96; mem. adv. coun. to program in internat. bus. rels. Fletcher Sch. Law and Diplomacy, 1985-94; cons. Exec. Svd. Corp., 1994—. Mem. Soc. CPCUs (past pres. Boston chpt.), Univ. Club, Boston Club.

MALOOF, GILES WILSON, academic administrator, educator, author; b. San Bernardino, Calif., Jan. 4, 1932; s. Joseph Peters and Georgia (Wilson) M.; m. Mary Anne Zimker, Sept. 5, 1958 (dec. Oct. 1976); children: Mary Jane, Margery Jo. BA, U. Calif. at Berkeley, 1953; MA, U. Oreg., 1958; PhD, Oreg. State U., 1962. Petroleum reservoir engr. Creole Petroleum Corp., Venezuela, 1953-54; mathematician electronics div. research dept. U.S. Naval Ordnance Rsch. Lab., Corona, Calif., 1958-59; asst. prof. math. Oreg. State U., Corvallis, 1962-68, rsch. assoc. dept. oceanography, 1963-68, vis. prof. math., 1977-78; prof. math. Boise (Idaho) State U., 1968—, head dept., 1968-75, dean grad. sch., 1970-75; project dir. Dept. Energy Citizens' Workshop Energy Environment Simulator for Eastern Oreg., No. Nev. and Idaho, 1976—. Served with Ordnance Corps, AUS, 1950, 54-56. Author, reviewer of coll. textbooks; contbr. to profl. jours. Recipient Carter award, 1963, Mosser prize, 1966, Oreg. State U. Mem. Math. Assn. Am., Am. Math. Soc., Soc. Indsl. and Applied Math., Northwest Coll. and Univ. Assn. for Sci. (dir. 1973—, pres. 1990-92), Northwest Sci. Assn. (trustee 1977-80), Assoc. Western Univs. (mem. edn. and rsch. com. 1993—), Sigma Xi, Pi Mu Epsilon, Phi Kappa Phi. Home: 1400 Longmont Ave Boise ID 83706-3730

MALOOF, JAMES A., mayor, real estate company executive; b. Peoria, Ill., Oct. 18, 1919; s. Nimer and Sarah (Hamady) M.; m. Gertrude Mae Burson, June 28, 1941; children—James Michael, Mark (dec.), Nicholas, Janice. Grad. high sch., Peoria. Pres., owner Jim Maloof Realtor, Peoria, 1969—; mayor City of Peoria, 1985—. Mem. adv. bd. Peoria Civic Ctr. Commn., Jr. League Peoria, Boy's Club Peoria, Lebanon Task Force, local Peoria County Emergency Planning Com., Bradley Community Action Advisory Council; mem. exec. mgmt. bd. St. Jude Children's Research Hosp., Memphis, chmn. bd. dirs. and co-founder midwest affiliate at Meth. Med. Ctr., chmn. first telethon, 1978, past nat. exec. v.p.; chmn. Christian edn. fund drive St. Philomena Parish, Bradley U. Athletic Fund Dr.; chmn. adv. com. Peoria Big Bros. and Big Sisters; mem. Gov.'s Build Ill. Com., Ill. Job Tng. Coordinating Council, Gov.'s Statewide Taskforce on the Homeless; mem. fundraising com. Lakeview Ctr.; bd. dirs. Econ. Devel. Council Peoria Area, Peoria Conv. and Visitors Bur., Peoria Symphony, Peoria YMCA, Meth. Med. Ctr. Found. Served with USAAF, 1943-45. Recipient Pope John award, Jefferson award, Midwest Fedn. Am-Syrian Lebanese Clubs award, Gov.'s Citation award, Cited Congl. Record, Silver Good Citizenship medal SAR, Internat. Communication and Leadership award Toastmasters Internat., County Old Settler's Assn. award, Appreciation award Zeller Clinic, Patriotism award U.S. Marine Corps, Boss of Yr. award Am. Bus. Womens Assn., Achievement award Phoenician Club, Enterprise award Observer newspaper; named Man of Yr. B'nai Brith, Tri-County Kiwanis. Mem. Peoria Area C. of C. (bd. dirs., exec. com.), Orpheus Club, Italian Am. Soc. (hon.), Peoria Fedn. Musicians (hon.), Epsilon Sigma Alpha (hon.). Republican. Roman Catholic. Club: Creve Coeur (bd. dirs.). Lodge: Kiwanis (past pres. Southwest Peoria chpt.). Established Jim Maloof Realtor scholarship, Bradley Univ. Office: City of Peoria City Hall Bldg 419 Fulton St Ste 207 Peoria IL 61602-1217

MALOON, JERRY L., lawyer, physician, medicolegal consultant; b. Union City, Ind., June 23, 1938; s. Charles Elias and Bertha Lucille (Creviston) M.; children: Jeffrey Lee, Jerry Lee II. BS, Ohio State U., 1960, MD, 1964; JD, Capital U. Law Sch., 1974. Intern Santa Monica (Calif.) Hosp., 1964-65; tng. psychiatry Cen. Ohio Psychiat. Hosp., 1969, Menninger Clinic, Topeka, 1970; clin. dir. Orient (Ohio) Devel. Ctr., 1967-69, med. dir., 1971-83; assoc. med. dir. Western Electric, Inc., Columbus, 1969-71; cons. State Med. Bd. Ohio, 1974-80; pvt. practice law, Columbus, 1978—; pres. Jerry L. Maloon Co., L.P.A., 1981—; medicolegal cons., 1972—; pres. Maloon, Maloon & Barclay Co., L.P.A., 1990-95; guest lectr. law and medicine Orient Devel. Ctr. and Columbus Devel. Ctr., 1969-71; dep. coroner Franklin County (Ohio), 1978-84. Served to capt. M.C., AUS, 1965-67. Fellow Am. Coll. Legal Medicine; mem. AMA, ABA, Ohio Bar Assn., Columbus Bar Assn., Am. Trial Lawyers Assn., Ohio Trial Lawyers Assn., Columbus Trial Lawyers Assn., Ohio State U. Alumni Assn., U.S. Trotting Assn., Am. Profl. Practice Assn. Clubs: Ohio State U. Pres.'s, Buckeye. Home: 2140 Cambridge Blvd Upper Arlington OH 43221 Office: 1335 Dublin Rd Columbus OH 43215-1000

MALORZO, THOMAS VINCENT, lawyer; b. Rome, N.Y., Jan. 10, 1947; s. Helen Adeline (Grande) M.; m. CAtherine Marie Healy, Dec. 28, 1968; children: Amy, Craig, Mary, Thomas Jr. BA, Walsh U., Canton, Ohio, 1969; JD, Cleve. State U., 1979. Bar: Ohio 1979, Tex. 1981, U.S. Dist. Ct. (no. dist.) Ohio 1980, U.S. Dist. Ct. (no. dist.) Tex. 1981, U.S. Patent Office 1980, U.S. Ct. Appeals (7th cir.) 1994. Environ. regulations analyst Diamond Shamrock Corp., Dallas, 1979-81; ind. adv. counsel Southwestern Corp., Dallas, 1981-83; staff atty. NCH Corp., Irving, Tex., 1983-89; gen. counsel Wormald US, Inc., Dallas, 1989-90; patent atty. Otis Engring. Corp., Carrollton, Tex., 1990-93; pvt. practice Addison, Tex., 1993-95; ptnr. Falk, Vestal & Fish LLP, 1995-96; pvt. practice Addison, Tex., 1996—; asst. prof. law Dallas/Ft. Worth Sch. Law, Irving, Tex., 1990-92. Dist. com. Circle 10 Boy Scouts Am., Dallas, 1985—; first aid team ARC, Cleve., 1972-80. Recipient Silver Beaver award Boy Scouts of Am., 1997. Mem. State Bar Tex. (chmn. trademark com. intellectual property sect. 1989). Office: 15800 Addison Rd Ste 112 Dallas TX 75248-3213

MALOTT, ADELE RENEE, editor; b. St. Paul, July 19, 1935; d. Clarence R. and Julia Anne (Christensen) Lindgren; m. Gene E. Malott, Oct. 24, 1957. B.S., Northwestern U., 1957. Coordinator news KGB Radio, San Diego, 1958-60; asst. pub. relations dir. St. Paul C. of C., 1961-63; night editor Daily Local News, West Chester, Pa., 1963-65; editor, co-pub. Boutique and Villager, Burlingame, Calif., 1966-76; sr. editor mag. The Webb Co., St. Paul, 1978-84; editor GEM Pub. Group, Reno, 1985—; co-pub. The Mature Traveler, 1987—; mem. faculty Reader's Digest Writers' Workshops. Co-author: Get Up and Go: A Guide for the Mature Traveler, 1989, The Mature Traveler's Book of Deals, 1997. Recipient numerous awards Nat. Fedn. Press Women, Calif. Newspaper Pubs. Assn., San Francisco Press Club, Calif. Taxpayers Assn., White House Citations. Mem. Internat. Assn. Bus. Communicators (Merit award 1984), Press Women Minn. (numerous awards), Press Women Nev., Soc. Am. Travel Writers (chair Western chpt. 1996—). Avocations: historical research; golf; travel; photography; reading.

MALOTT, JOHN RAYMOND, foreign service officer; b. Kankakee, Ill., Nov. 5, 1946; s. Raymond Roderick and Ruth Pearl (Jacobs) M.; m. Hiroko Iwami, Nov. 23, 1971; children: David Iwami, Rumi Justine. BA, Northwestern U., 1967; grad., Nat. War Coll., 1983. Civilian advisor U.S. Dept. State, Vietnam, 1969-70; China desk officer U.S. Dept. State, Washington, 1970-71; Am. consul U.S. Dept. State, Kobe, Japan, 1971-73; 1st sec. Am. Embassy U.S. Dept. State, Tokyo, Japan, 1974-77; Sri Lanka desk officer U.S. Dept. State, Washington, 1977-78, India desk officer, 1978-80; Am. consul &, Bombay, India, 1980-82; with Nat. War Coll. &, Washington, 1982-83, dep. dir. Japan Affairs, 1983-85, spl. asst. to Under Sec. State Econ. Affairs, 1985-86; Am. consul gen. &, Osaka, Japan, 1986-89; dir. Japan Affairs &, Washington, 1989-91, sr. seminar, 1991-92, dep. asst. sec. state South Asian Affairs, 1992-93; sr. advisor to Undersec. State for Econ. Affairs, Washington, 1993-95; U.S. amb. to Malaysia Dept. State, 1995—. Author: Partners, 1992. Recipient Vietnam Svc. award, 1970, Meritorious Honor award Dept. State, 1982, Superior honor award, 1991. Mem. Am. Fgn. Svc. Assn. Presbyterian. Office: US Embassy, PO Box No. 10035, 50700 Kuala Lumpur Malaysia

MALOUFF, FRANK JOSEPH, health care association executive; b. La Junta, Colo., Aug. 21, 1947; s. Phillip Francis and Lillian Aileen (Sayklay) M.; m. Virginia Lynn Frye, Aug. 24, 1968; children: Lynnea, Joseph, J. Daniel, David. BS in Journalism, U. Colo., Boulder, 1969; MS in Health Adminstrn., U. Colo., Denver, 1974; LLD (hon.), Ohio Coll. Podiatric Medicine, 1988. Program adminstr. U. Colo. Health Scis. Ctr., Denver, 1974-83; exec. dir. Ohio Podiatric Med. Assn., Columbus, 1983-89, Am. Podiatric Med. Assn., Bethesda, Md., 1989—; dir. Fund for Podiatric Med. Edn., Bethesda, 1986—, Foothealth Found. Am., Bethesda, 1991—. Contbg. author: Handbook of Healthcare Human Resources Management, 1981; co-author: Pursuing Mastery: Professional Development Tools and Techniques, 1991; columnist in field. Leader Boy Scouts Am., various locations. 1st lt. U.S. Army, 1969-72, Korea. Mem. Am. Soc. Healthcare Edn. and Tng. (officer 1977-81, Disting. Svc. award 1982, past dir.), Am. Soc. Assn. Execs., Am. Inst. Parliamentarians. Roman Catholic. Avocation: lay church ministry. Office: Am Podiatric Med Assn 9312 Old Georgetown Rd Bethesda MD 20814-1646

MALOUIN, JEAN-LOUIS, university dean, educator; b. Three-Rivers, Que., Can., Oct. 5, 1943; m. Hélène Pépin; children: Pascale, Philippe. B in Commerce, Université Laval, Que., 1965, MSc, 1966; PhD, UCLA, 1970. Prof. Bus. Sch., U. Laval, 1966-89, dir. OSD dept., 1971-75, 78-79, assoc. dean acad. affairs, 1979-84, dean, 1984-89; dean faculty of bus. U. Alta., Edmonton, Alta., Can., 1989-92; dean faculty of adminstrn. U. Ottawa, Ottawa, Ont., Can., 1992—; coord. Can. Consortium for the Suuport of the Sea. Editor: The Generation of Scientific Administrative Knowledge, 1986; co-author: L'Innovation Technologique dans les PME Manufacturières: études de cas enquête, 1992. Bd. dirs. Centre québécois de Productivité, du Vêtement, Montréal, 1983-86, Nat. Rsch. Ctr., London, 1986-87, Banff Sch. Advancement Mgmt., 1989-92. Mem. Can. Fedn. Deans (v.p. 1987), Edmonton C. of C. (bd. dirs. 1989-92). Home: 1410 Clay Ct, Gloucester, ON Canada K1C 4T2 Office: U Ottawa Fac Adminstrn, 136 Jean-Jacques Lussier St, Ottawa, ON Canada K1N 6N5

MALOZEMOFF, PLATO, mining executive; b. Russia, 1909. BS, U. Calif., Berkeley, 1931; MS, Mont. Sch. Mines, 1932. Metall. engr. Pan-Am. Engring., Berkeley, 1933-39; mgr. of mines of pvt. co.'s Argentina and Costa Rica, 1939-42; mining analyst OPA, Washington, 1942-45; with Newmont Mining Corp., N.Y.C., 1945-87, chief exec. officer, 1954-85, chmn. emeritus, 1985—. Bd. dirs. Boys' and Girls' Clubs Am., Tolstoy Found., Inc., South Am. Gold and Copper Co., Inc.; dir., trustee Am. Mus. Natural History; mem. James Madison coun. Libr. of Congress. Office: 230 Park Ave Rm 1154 New York NY 10169-1199

MALPASS, LESLIE FREDERICK, retired university president; b. Hartford, Conn., May 16, 1922; s. Fred J. and Lilly (Elmslie) M.; m. Winona Helen Cassin, May 17, 1946; children: Susan Heather (Mrs. J. Poulton), Peter Gordon, Jennifer Joy (Mrs. T. Droege), Michael Andrew. BA, Syracuse U., 1947, MA, 1949, PhD, 1952. Diplomate Am. Bd. Profl. Psychology. Psychologist Onondaga County (N.Y.) Child Guidance Center Syracuse, 1948-52; lectr. Syracuse U., also U. Buffalo, 1949-52; asst. prof. then assoc. prof. So. Ill. U., 1952-60; vis. prof. U. Fla., 1959-60; prof. psychology, chmn. div. behavioral scis. U. So. Fla., 1960-65; dean Coll. Arts and Scis., Va. Poly Inst., Blacksburg, 1965-68; v.p. acad. affairs Va. Poly Inst., 1968-74; pres. Western Ill. U., Macomb, 1974-87, pres. emeritus, 1987—; cons. in field; lectr. Duke U., 1988-93. Author books and articles in field. Mem. Mayor's Adv. Coun., Durham, N.C., 1989-93; bd. dirs. N.C. Poverty Program, 1989-95; mem. N.C. Human Rels. Commn., 1994—; adv. bd. Durham Salvation Army, 1992—. Fellow APA; mem. AAAS, AAUP, Assn. for Higher Edn., Sigma Xi, Psi Chi, Theta Chi Beta, Omicron Delta Kappa, Beta Gamma Sigma, Phi Mu Alpha. Home: 3927 Swarthmore Dr Durham NC 27707-5313

MALPHURS, ROGER EDWARD, biomedical marketing executive; b. Lake Worth, Fla., Dec. 15, 1933; s. Cecil Edward and Muriel Thelma (Ward) M.; m. Carolyn Sue Calapp, Feb. 2, 1963(div. 1993); children: Steven, Brian, Darren, Regina, Victoria. *The generations preceding the name Malphurs, had their origins in Switzerland (Malpas), Italy (Malpaso), France (Malphrus), England (Malpass), and maybe even as far back as 711 AD when a Malpass led a military contingent against the Moors during the invasion of Spain in that year*. BS, U. Utah, 1961; D of Chiropractic, Palmer Coll. Chiropractic West, 1990. Cert. med. technologist; lic. chiropractor, Calif., Ariz. Supr. spl. chemistry Cen. Pathology Lab., Santa Rosa, Calif., 1968-73; mgr. lab. Cmty. Hosp., Santa Rosa, 1973-76; supr. chem., staff asst. Meml. Hosp., Santa Rosa, 1976-85; pres., CEO R.E. Malphurs Co., Sunnyvale, Calif., 1972—; owner, developer REMCO Mktg. Assocs., Santa Rosa, 1970-71; pvt. commodity trader, 1974—; owner Better Bus. Forms and Typeset, Santa Rosa, 1977-81, commodity pool operator, 1979-80; dept. mgr. immunochemistry Spectra Labs., Fremont, Calif., 1990-95; clin. trials cons. hematology Abbott Diagnostics, Santa Clara, Calif., 1995-97. Author: A New, Simple Way to Win at Blackjack, 1972. Served as squadron commdr. CAP USAF Aux., 1982-84. Mem. APHA, Am. Chiropractic Assn., Calif. Chiropractic Assn., Optimists Internat. (youth awards chmn. 1969-74), Toastmasters (sec./treas. 1988-89), Rep. Senatorial Inner Circle. Republican. Avocations: flying, computers, pistol shooting, oil painting, writing.

MALSACK, JAMES THOMAS, retired manufacturing company executive; b. Milw., Apr. 4, 1921; s. Leonard Henry and Florence Alice (Webb) M.; m. Joyce Irene Niemi, Aug. 1, 1963; children: Thomas James, Claudia Irene, Robert Richard, Thomas John, Pamela Joyce. BSBA, Marquette U., 1946; D Pub. Svc. (hon.), No. Mich. U., 1990. Acct. Price Waterhouse & Co., Milw., 1946-51; with Lake Shore, Inc., Iron Mountain, Mich., 1951-88; exec. v.p. Lake Shore, Inc., 1959-72, pres., chief exec. officer, 1972-84, chmn., 1984-88. Bd. control No. Mich. U., trustee emeritus. With USN, 1942-45. Mem. Masons, Shriners. Republican. Episcopalian. Home (winter): 8326 E LaSenda Scottsdale AZ 85255

MALSON, REX RICHARD, drug and health care corporation executive; b. Stanberry, Mo., Nov. 26, 1931; s. Albert J. Curtis and Nellie E. Coburn (Bussey) M.; m. Jimmie S., May 25, 1956 (dec. 1980); children: Richard Gary, Gregory Neil; m. Vicki L., Feb. 10, 1983 (div. Aug. 1984). B.B.A., Ga. State U., 1961; postgrad. grad. exec. program, U. Chgo., 1967; postgrad. exec. program hon., Stanford U., 1983; LHD (hon.), L.I. U., 1989. Gen. transp. mgr. John Sexton & Co., Chgo., 1964-68; dir. distbn. system Keebler Co., Chgo., 1968-73; with drug and health care group McKesson Corp., San Francisco, 1973-92, vice pres., 1984-86, exec. v.p. ops., 1986-89, pres. & chief operating officer, 1989-92, also vice chmn.,bd. dirs.; ret., 1992; bd. dirs. Sunbelt Beverage Co., Balt., Stationers Distbg. Co., Ft. Worth; chmn. bd. dirs. Armor All Products Corp. Served with U.S. Navy, 1951-55, Korea. Mem. Am. Soc. Traffic and Transp. Republican.

MALSON, VERNA LEE, special education educator; b. Buffalo, Wyo., Mar. 29, 1937; d. Guy James and Vera Pearl (Curtis) Mayer; m. Jack Lee Malson, Apr. 20, 1955; children: Daniel Lee, Thomas James, Mark David, Scott Allen. BA in Elem. Edn. and Spl. Edn. magna cum laude, Met. State Coll., Denver, 1975; MA in Learning Disabilities, U. No. Colo., 1977. Cert. tchr., Colo. Tchr.-aide Wyo. State Tng. Sch., Lander, 1967-69; spl. edn. tchr. Bennett Sch. 29J, Colo., 1975-79, chmn. health, sci., social studies, 1977-79; spl. edn. tchr. Deer Trail Sch., Colo., 1979—, chmn. careers, gifted and talented, 1979-87, spl. edn./preschool tchr. 1992—; course cons. Regis Coll., Denver, 1990; mem. spl. edn. parent adv. com. East Central Bd. Coop. Edn. Services, Limon, Colo. Colo. scholar Met. State Coll., 1974; Colo. Dept. Edn. grantee, 1979, 81; recipient Cert. of Achievement, Met. State Coll., 1993. Mem. Council Exceptional Children, Bennett Tchrs. Club (treas. 1977-79), Kappa Delta Pi. Republican. Presbyterian. Avocations: coin collecting; reading; sports. Home: PO Box 403 Deer Trail CO 80105-0403 Office: Deer Trail Pub Schs PO Box 26J Deer Trail CO 80105-0026

MALT, RONALD A., surgeon, educator; b. Pitts., 1931; married, 3 children. A.B., Washington U., 1951; M.D., Harvard U., 1955. Diplomate Am. Bd. Surgery, Am. Bd. Thoracic Surgery, Am. Bd. Vascular Surgery. Resident Mass. Gen. Hosp., Boston, 1955-56, 58-62, chief gastrointestinal surg. sect., 1972—; from asst. in surgery to assoc. prof. surgery Harvard U. Med. Sch., Boston, 1962-74, prof., 1975—. Co-author: Regeneration of Liver and Kidney, 1972. Editor: Colonic Carcinogenesis, 1983, Complex Operations, 1984, Surgical Techniques Illustrated, 1985, The Practice of Surgery, 1993, Oxford Textbook of Surgery, 1994 co-editor: Micromolecular Synthesis and Growth, 1967; assoc. editor New Eng. Jour. Medicine, Boston, 1966-93. Contbr. articles to profl. jours. Served to lt. comdr. USNR, 1956-62. Mem. Am. Surg. Assn., Am. Soc. Clin. Investigation, Am. Physiol. Soc., Internat. Cardiovascular Surgery Soc., Soc. Surg. Oncology, Societe Internat. Chirurgie, Somerset Club, St. Botolph Club, Thursday Evening Club, Clug of Odd Vols. Republican. Episcopalian. Achievements include first replantation of a severed limb, 1962; development of replantation surgery. Office: Mass Gen Hosp Boston MA 02114-2620

MALTBY, RICHARD ELDRIDGE, JR., theater director, lyricist; b. Ripon, Wis., Oct. 6, 1937; s. Richard Eldridge and Virginia (Hosegood) D.; m. Janet Brenner, 1987; children: Nicholas Avery, David Stevenson, Jordan Brenner, Emily Celia, Charlotte Perry. BA, Yale U., 1959. Lyricist: Starting Here, Starting Now, 1977 (Grammy nomination); dir.: Ain't Misbehavin', 1978 (N.Y. Drama Critics Circle award, Drama Desk award, Obie award Best Musical, Tony award Best Dir.); dir., lyricist: Baby, 1983 (3 Tony award nominations); dir., co-lyricist: Song and Dance, 1985 (Tony award nomination); co-lyricist: Miss Saigon, 1989 (London Evening Standard Best Musical, London Drama Critics award, 3 Tony awards); dir., lyricist: Closer Than Ever, 1989 (2 Outer Critics' Circle awards, Best Off-Broadway Musical, Best Score), Nick and Nora, 1993 (Tony award nomination), Big, 1996 (Tony award nomination). Mem. ASCAP, Dramatists Guild, Soc. Stage Dirs. and Choreographers. Office: care Flora Roberts Inc 157 W 57th St New York NY 10019-2210

MALTBY, SUE ELLEN, special education educator; b. Waterford, Ohio, Apr. 30, 1950; d. James Lawrence and Agatha Macel (Crosby) Starcher; m. Marshall Martin Maltby, Nov. 25, 1978; stepchildren: Laura Leigh Maltby Karanthasis, Lisa Michelle Maltby Atkinson. BA, Marietta Coll., 1972; MA, Ga. Coll., 1976. Cert. tchr., adminstr., W.Va. Psychology technician Cen. State Hosp., Milledgeville, Ga., 1972-74, psychologist, 1976-77; psychologist Ga. War Vets. Home, Milledgeville, 1974-76; mental retardation specialist Albany (Ga.) Mental Health/Mental Retardation Ctr., 1977-81; dir. residential program Colin Anderson Ctr., St. Marys, W.Va., 1981-84; tchr. spl. edn. W.Va. Dept. Edn., St. Marys, 1984-91; lead tchr. W.Va. Dept. Edn., Waverly, 1991—; tech. asst. cons. County Bds. Edn., W.Va., 1985—, insvc. presenter, 1985—. Recipient Outstanding Svc. award Ga. Assn. Retarded Citizens, 1978. Mem. Assn. Retarded Citizens, Assn. Severely Handicapped, Coun. Exceptional Children/Persons, Nat. Down Syndrome Assn. Republican. Methodist. Avocations: crafts, travel, volunteer work. Home: RR 1 Box 21C Waterford OH 45786-9705

MALTER, JAMES SAMUEL, pathologist, educator; b. Tooele, Utah, May 18, 1956; s. Robert Henry Malter and Evvajean (Harris) Mintz; m. Elaine Gadzicki, May 26, 1988. AB, Dartmouth Coll., 1979; MD, Washington U., 1983. Diplomate Am. Bd. Clin. Pathology. Resident in pathology U. Pa., Phila., 1983-88, chief resident, 1987-88; asst. prof. pathology Tulane U., New Orleans, 1988-91; dir. exptl. pathology Tulane Med. Ctr., New Orleans, 1988-91, dir. Blood Ctr., 1989-91; asst. prof. pathology Sch. Medicine U. Wis., Madison, 1991—; med. dir. Blood Bank U. Wis. Hosp. & Clinic, Madison, 1991—. Mem. editorial bd. Hepatology jour., 1991—. Recipient Nat. Rsch. Svc. award NIH, 1986-88, Clin. Investigator award NCI-NIH, 1988-91, Ind. Investigator award NIH, 1991—. Mem. Am. Assn. Blood Banks, Am. Assn. Pathologists, Am. Coll. Pathologists (diplomate). Office: U Wis Hosp & Clinic Dept of Pathology 600 Highland Ave # B4 263 Madison WI 53792-0001*

MALTESE, GEORGE JOHN, mathematics educator; b. Middletown, Conn., June 24, 1931; s. Giorgio and Sebastiana (Morello) M.; m. Marlene Erika Kunz, Apr. 14, 1956; children: Christopher, Michelle. BA, Wesleyan U., Middletown, Conn., 1953; postgrad., U. Frankfurt, Germany, 1953-54; PhD, Yale U., 1960. Instr. MIT, 1961-63; asst. prof. U. Md., College Park, 1963-66, assoc. prof., 1966-69; prof. U. Md., 1969-73, U. Münster, Fed. Republic Germany, 1973—; vis. prof. U. Frankfurt, 1966-67, 70-71, U. Palermo, Italy, 1967, 71, 76. U. Pisa, Italy, 1972, U. Kuwait, 1977, U. Bahrain, 1988, U. Oman, 1991. Contbr. articles to profl. jours. Served with AUS, 1954-56. Fulbright fellow, 1953-54; NATO postdoctoral fellow, 1960-61. Mem. Am. Math. Soc., Math. Assn. Am., Unione Matematica Italiana, Deutsche Mathematiker Verein. Home: 35 Orange Rd Govenors Grove Middletown CT 06457 Office: Dept Math Wesleyan U Middletown CT 06457

MALTESE, SERPHIN RALPH, state senator, lawyer; b. N.Y.C., Dec. 7, 1932; s. Paul and Frances (Scafidi) M.; m. Constance Mary Del Vecchio, Aug. 27, 1955; children—Andrea Constance, Leslie Serphine, Serphin Ralph (dec.). B.A., Manhattan Coll., 1958; LL.B., J.D. (War Service scholar 1958-62), Fordham U., 1962. Bar: N.Y. bar 1963. Trial atty. for ins. cos., 1963-66; asst. dist. atty., dep. chief homicide bur. Queens County, N.Y., 1966-69; asso. counsel N.Y. State Com. Campus Disorders, 1969-70; counsel N.Y. State Com. Deaf and Multiple Impaired, 1970; chmn. law com. Buckley for U.S. Senator, 1970; counsel N.Y. State Assembly, 1972-76; counsel N.Y. State Senate, Albany, 1976-88, state senator, 1988—, chmn. senate standing com. on elections, mem. com. on aging, cities, civil svc. and pensions, mem. codes higher edn., investigations and govt. ops. com.; pres. N.Y. Conf. of Italian Am. Legislators; exec. dir. N.Y. State Conservative Party, 1971-86, exec. vice chmn., 1978-86, state chmn., 1986-88. Chmn. trustees Christ the King Regional H.S., 1976—; pres. We Care Civic Assn., 1968-76, chmn. exec. bd., 1978-88; past cmty. chmn. local Boy Scouts Am.; N.Y. State chmn. Conservatives for Ronald Reagan, 1980. With AUS, 1952-54, Korea. Recipient Charles Edison Meml. award N.Y. State Conservative Party, 1977, St. John's U. Pres.'s medal, 1994. Mem. N.Y. State Bar Assn., Queens Asst. Dist. Attys. Assn., Christopher Columbus Assn. (chmn. 1970—), Young Ams. for Freedom (nat. sr. adv. bd.), Am. Conservative Union (nat. bd. dirs.), Internat. Assn. Space Philatelists, Queens C. of C., Alexander Hamilton Conservative Club (chmn. exec. com. 1971-88), Harold Gray Collectors Soc. (pres.), Met. Post Card Collectors Club, Am. Legion, VFW, Alpha Phi Delta. Roman Catholic. Home: 60-16 74th St Flushing NY 11373-5218 Office: 71-04 Myrtle Ave Glendale NY 11385-7254 Office: 803 Legislative Office Bldg Albany NY 12247

MALTIN, LEONARD, television commentator, writer; b. N.Y.C., Dec. 18, 1950; s. Aaron Isaac and Jacqueline (Gould) M.; m. Alice Tlusty, Mar. 15, 1975; 1 child, Jessica Bennett. BA, NYU, 1972. Mem. faculty New Sch. for Social Rsch., N.Y.C., 1973-81; curator Am. Acad. Humor, N.Y.C., 1975-76; guest curator dept. film Mus. Modern Art, N.Y.C., 1976; film critic and corr. Entertainment Tonight, Hollywood, Calif., 1982—; columnist Microsoft Cinemania Online, 1996—, Modern Maturity, 1996—, Satellite Direct, 1997. Author: Movie Comedy Teams, 1970, rev. edit., 1985, Behind the Camera (reprinted as The Art of the Cinematographer), 1971, The Great Movie Shorts (reprinted as Selected Short Subjects), 1971, The Disney Films, 1973, rev. edit., 1995, The Great Movie Comedians, 1978, Of Mice and Magic: A History of American Animated Cartoons, 1980, rev. edit., 1987, The Great American Broadcast, 1997; co-author: Our Gang: The Life and Times of the Little Rascals, 1977, reprinted as The Little Rascals: The Life and Times of Our Gang, 1992; editor: Leonard Maltin's Movie & Video Guide, 1969, rev. annually, Leonard Maltin's Movie Encyclopedia, 1994; producer, writer, host (video) Cartoons for Big Kids, 1989; writer (TV spl.) Fantasia: The Making of a Disney Classic, 1990; writer, host (video) The Making of The Quiet Man, 1992, The Making of High Noon, 1992, Cartoon Madness: The Fantastic Max Fleischer Cartoons, 1993, Cliffhanger!, 1993. Mem. steering com. Hollywood Entertainment Mus., 1989—. Mem. Authors Guild, Soc. for Cinephiles (pres. 1990-91, Man of Yr. 1973), L.A. Film Critics Assn. (pres. 1995-96). Office: care Entertainment Tonight Paramount TV 5555 Melrose Ave Los Angeles CA 90038-3112

MALTZAN, MICHAEL THOMAS, architect; b. Roslyn Heights, N.Y., Oct. 10, 1959; s. William George and Jacqualine (Cain) M.; m. Amy Louise Murphy, Sept. 25, 1988. Student, Wentworth Inst. Tech., 1977-79; BFA, RISD, 1984, BArch, 1985; MArch with letter of distinction, Harvard U., 1988. Lic. architect, Calif. Architect The Architects, Glastonbury, Conn.,

1978-80, Williamd D. Warner Assocs., Exeter, R.I., 1980-83, Steven Lerner Assocs., Providence, 1983-84, Schwartz/Silver Assocs., Boston, 1984-86, Machado-Silvetti Assocs., Boston, 1986-88, Frank O. Gehry Assocs., L.A., 1988-95; pvt. practice architecture L.A., 1995—; instr. RISD, Providence, 1987, Harvard U., Cambridge, Mass., 1988; co-instr. UCLA, 1989; invited jury critic Harvard U., RISD, So. Calif. Inst. Architecture, L.A., Ariz. State U., tempe, Calif. Coll. Arts and Crafts, San Francisco, U. SO. Calif., L.A., UCLA, Iowa State U., Ames, Miami (Ohio) U. Prin. works include Unitarian-Universalist Ch., Vernon, Conn., 1979, Providence Riverfront Study, 1982, Harvard Law Sch. Alumni Bldg. Addition, Cambridge, 1984, 330 Congress St. Renovation, Boston, 1985, 280 Summer St. Renovation, Boston, 1986, City of Leonforte, Italy Master Plan, 1987 (Progressive Arch. award), North Park Apt. Complex Renovation, Chevy Chase, Md., 1988, Walt Disney Concert Hall, 1988— (Progressive Arch. award), Culver City (Calif.) Retail Complex Master Plan, 1990, Villa Olympica Retail and Entertainment Complex, Barcelona, Spain, 1992, U. Toledo Art Sch., 1992 (AIA award), Inner-City Arts Sch., L.A., 1994, Harvard West Lake Art Ctr., 1997, Getty Culture Lab., 1997. Recipient Coll. Gold medal AIA. Office: 2801 Hyperion Ave Apt 107 Los Angeles CA 90027-2571

MALTZMAN, IRVING MYRON, psychology educator; b. Bklyn., May 9, 1924; s. Israel and Lillian (Mass) M.; m. Diane Seiden, Aug. 21, 1949; children—Sara, Kenneth, Ilaine. B.A., N.Y. U., 1946; Ph.D., State U. Iowa, 1949. Mem. faculty UCLA, 1949—, assoc. prof., 1957-60, prof. psychology, 1961—, chmn. dept., 1970-77. Co-author: Handbook of Contemporary Soviet Psychology, 1969. Fellow APA, AAAS; mem. Phi Beta Kappa, Sigma Xi. Home: 11260-22B Overland Ave Culver City CA 90230-5559

MALVEAUX, FLOYD JOSEPH, academic dean. BS, Creighton U., 1961; MS, Loyola U.; PhD in Microbiology and Pub. Health, Mich. State U., 1968; MD, Howard U., 1974; postgrad., Washington Hosp. Ctr., 1974-76, Johns Hopkins U., 1976-78. Asst. prof. microbiology Howard U. Med. Sch., Washington, 1968-70, chmn. microbiology, assoc. prof. microbiology and medicine, 1989-96, current dean, interim v.p. health affairs; mem. faculty Johns Hopkins U., Balt., 1984-89; founder, pres. Urban Asthma and Allergy Ctr., Balt., 1986-89; mem. numerous med. panels; lectr. in field. Contbr. articles to profl. jours. Recipient Nat. Rsch. Svc. award NIH, Clemens von Pirquet Rsch. award Georgetown U. Sch. Medicine, 1991; Vivian B. Allen Found. fellow; Grantee Nat. Inst. Allergy and Infectious Diseases, Nat. Heart, Lung and Blood Inst. of NIH, Hasbro Children's Found., Robert Wood Johnson Found. Mem. NAACP (life), Alpha Omega Alpha, Sigma Xi, Sigma Pi Phi, Kappa Alpha Psi. Office: Howard U Med Sch 520 W St NW Washington DC 20001-2337

MALVERN, DONALD, retired aircraft manufacturing company executive; b. Sterling, Okla., Apr. 22, 1921; s. George Michael and Anna Francesca (Elsass) M.; m. Ruth Marie Vogler, June 4, 1949; 1 son, Michael John. BSME, U. Okla., 1946. Engr. Victory Architects and Engrs., Clinton, Okla., 1943, Douglas Aircraft Co., Santa Monica, Calif., 1943; with McDonnell Aircraft Co., St. Louis, 1946-88; exec. v.p. McDonnell Aircraft Co., 1973-82, pres., 1982-86; v.p. McDonnell Douglas Corp., 1973-88; aerospace cons. St. Louis, 1988—; pres. McDonnell Douglas Services, Inc., 1978-82. Trustee Falcon Found., 1983—; bd. visitors Def. Sys. Mgmt. Coll., 1983-86, U. Okla. Coll. Engring., 1988-91; pres. Wings of Hope, 1989-92, chmn., 1992—. 1st lt. USAAF, 1943-46; capt. Mo. Air NG, 1946-51. Inducted into Okla. Aviation and Space Mus.'s Hall of Fame, 1987. Fellow AIAA (Tech. Mgmt. award 1968, Reed Aeros. medal 1980); mem. Am. Def. Preparedness Assn. (pres. St. Louis chpt. 1979-80), Navy League U.S. (life), Nat. Aeros. Assn., Air Force Assn., Armed Forces Mgmt. Assn., Pi Tau Sigma, Tau Beta Pi, Tau Omega, Sigma Tau Beta. Clubs: Bellerive Country, St. Louis. Home: 213 Grand Banks Ct Chesterfield MO 63017-9507

MALVERN, LAWRENCE EARL, engineering educator, researcher; b. Sterling, Okla., Sept. 14, 1916; s. George Michael and Anna Francesca (Elsass) M.; m. Marjorie Malene McCarther, Aug. 8, 1939 (dec. Jan. 1985); 1 dau., Maureen; m. Myra Louise Engelhardt, Sept. 18, 1987. Sc.B., Southwestern Okla. State Coll., 1937; M.A., U. Okla., 1939; Ph.D., Brown U., 1949. High sch. tchr. Marlow, Clinton, El Reno, Okla., 1937-38, 39-40, 40-42; asst. prof. math and mechanics Carnegie-Mellon U., Pitts., 1949-53; assoc. prof. applied mechanics Mich. State U., East Lansing, 1953-58, prof., 1958-69; prof. engring. scis. U. Fla., Gainesville, 1969-93; prof. emeritus. Assoc. editor: Jour. Applied Mechanics, 1978-85; author: Introduction to the Mechanics of a Continuous Medium, 1969, Engineering Mechanics-Statics and Dynamics, 2 vols., 1976. Served to lt. (j.g.) USNR, 1944-46. Guggenheim fellow, 1959. Fellow ASME (Worcester Reed Warner medal 1989), Am. Acad. Mechanics; mem. Soc. Engring. Sci. (dir. 1967-70), Sigma Xi. Home: 3901 NW 21st Ln Gainesville FL 32605-3566 Office: U Fla 231 Aerospace Bldg Gainesville FL 32611

MALY, KURT JOHN, computer science educator; b. Modling, Austria, Aug. 20, 1944; came to U.S., 1969; s. Anton and Editha (Gneist) M.; m. Christiana Peterlik, Mar. 18, 1972; 1 child, Angela Claudia. Diplom Ingenieur summa cum laude, U. Tech., Austria, 1968; MS, Courant Inst. NYU, 1970, PhD, 1973. Asst. prof. U. Minn., Mpls., 1972-78, assoc. prof., 1978-85, acting head, 1980-82, head, 1982-85; eminent prof., chmn. computer sci. Old Dominion U., Norfolk, Va., 1985—, Kaufman prof., 1991—; hon. prof. Chengdu U. of Sci. and Tech., People's Republic of China, 1986—, Hefei U., People's Republic of China, 1991—, Guangxi Computer Inst., People's Republic of China, 1993—; bd. dirs. Inst. of Info. Tech., Ctr. for Innovative Tech., Blacksburg, Va., 1988-92; bd. dirs., exec. co-dir. Microelectronic and Info. Scis. Ctr., Mpls., 1980-85. Author: Fundamentals of the Computing Sciences, 1978; assoc. editor: Jour. for Microcomputer Application Tech., PRC; contbr. articles to profl. jours. Served with Austrian Air Force, 1963-64. Fellow Sorbonne U., Paris, 1966, Courant Inst., N.Y.C., 1968-72. Mem. Assn. Computing Machinery, IEEE, Sigma Xi. Roman Catholic. Office: Old Dominion U Norfolk VA 23508

MALZAHN, RAY ANDREW, chemistry educator, university dean; b. Fort Madison, Iowa, July 8, 1929; s. Arnold Frederick and Inez (Russell) M.; m. Elizabeth Mae Barrett, Aug. 23, 1953; children—Karen Louise, Janet Elizabeth. B.A., Gustavus Adolphus Coll., 1951; M.S., U. N.D., 1953; Ph.D., U. Md., 1962. Research assoc. U. Ariz., Tucson, 1961-63; asst. prof. chemistry West Tex. State U., Canyon, 1963-65, assoc. prof., 1965-67, prof. chemistry, 1967-80, dean Coll. Arts and Scis., 1967-71, v.p. acad. affairs, 1971-77; prof., dean Sch. Arts and Scis. Mo. So. State Coll., Joplin, 1980-95, interim v.p. for acad. affairs, 1993-94. Served with AUS, 1954-56. Mem. Am. Chem. Soc. Home: 1215 Goetz Blvd Joplin MO 64801-1433

MAMANA, JOSEPH, editor; b. Easton, Pa., Sept. 3, 1909; s. Domenico Louis and Maria Filippe (Sacchetti) M.; m. Julia Cericola, Sept. 20, 1935; children: Joseph Jr., James, John, Julianne, June. BS, U. Notre Dame, MA, 1932; postgrad., Muhlenberg Coll., 1932. Cert. tchr., guidance counselor, prin., supt. Tchr. Pocono Sch. for Girls, Pocono Manor, Pa., 1929-30; tchr. U. Notre Dame, Notre Dame, Ind., 1931-32, Easton Sch. Dist., Easton, Pa., 1933-46; guidance counselor Easton Sch. Dist., 1947-50, prin., 1951-72; editor PASSP Schoolmaster Publs., Harrisburg, Pa., 1970-92, editor emeritus, 1992—; investment mgr. Boyd Investment Svcs., Easton, 1974—; pres. Easton Edn. Assn., 1957-59; dist. XI commr. Pa. Interscholastic Athletic Assn., Easton High Sch. Assn., 1955-72; pres. Investment Svcs. Cons., 1974—. Contbr. edn. articles to PASSP Jour., 1970— . Edn. chmn. N.C. Am. Cancer Soc., Bethlehem, Pa., 1947-57, N.C. Am. Heart Assn., Bethlehem, 1957-67; mem. bd. 112U.S. SSS, Easton, 1967-73; police commn. mem. to study police brutality, Easton. Recipient Medal of Honor (educator) Freedoms Found., Valley Forge, Pa., 1965, Notre Dame U. Alumni award, 1992; named Nat. Prin. of Yr., A.C. Croft Publs., Vision Inc., N.J., 1963; named to Dist. XI Wrestling Hall of Fame, Pa. Interscholastic Athletic Assn., 1981; established Joseph Mamana Award of Merit, Pa. Prins. Assn., 1990. Mem. NEA (life, del. 1957-59), Pa. Assn. Secondary Sch. Prins. (life, chmn. real estate com. 1980-90), Easton Area Schoolmen's Assn. (life, pres. 1948-72, Schoolman of Yr. 1955, 89), Prins. Assn., Notre Dame Univ. Club (Alumni Svc. award 1992), Investments Club (mgr. 1974-96). Avocations: stone masonry, swimming, track, wrestling, collecting rare books. Home: 200 Burke St Easton PA 18042

MAMAT, FRANK TRUSTICK, lawyer; b. Syracuse, N.Y., Sept. 4, 1949; s. Harvey Sanford and Annette (Trustick) M.; m. Kathy Lou Winters, June 23, 1975; children: Jonathan Adam, Steven Kenneth. BA, U. Rochester, 1971; JD, Syracuse U., 1974. Bar: D.C. 1976, U.S. Ct. Appeals (D.C. cir.) 1976, Fla. 1977, U.S. Supreme Ct. 1979, US. Dist. Ct. (ea. dist.) 1983, U.S. Ct. Appeals (6th cir.) 1983, Mich. 1984, U.S. Dist. Ct. (no. dist.) Ind. 1984. Atty. NLRB, Washington, 1975-79; assoc. Proskauer, Rose, Goetz & Mendelsohn, Washington, N.Y.C. and L.A., 1979-83; assoc. Fishman Group, Bloomfield Hills, Mich., 1983-85, ptnr., 1985-87; sr. ptnr. Honigman, Miller, Schwartz and Cohn, 1987-94; pres. Morgan Daniels Co., Inc., West Bloomfield, Mich., 1994—; ptnr. Clark Klein & Beaumont, P.L.C., Detroit, 1995-96, Clark Hill, P.L.C., Detroit, 1996—; bd. dirs. Mich. Food and Beverage Assn., Air Conditioning Contractors of Am., Air Conditioning Contractors of Mich., Associated Builders and Contractors, Am. Subcontractors Assn., Mich. Mfrs. Assn. Labor Counsel. Gen. counsel Rep. Com. of Oakland County, 1986—, Constrn. Code commn. Mich., 1993—; bd. dirs. 300 Club, Mich., 1984-90; pres. 400 Club, 1990-93, chmn., 1993—; mem. Associated Gen. Contractors Labor Lawyers Coun.; mem. Rep. Nat. Com. Nat. Rep. Senatorial Com., Presdl. Task Force, Rep. Labor Coun., Washington; city dir. West Bloomfield, 1985-87; pres. West Bloomfield Rep. CLub, 1985-87; fin. com. Rep. Com. of Oakland County, 1984-93; pres. Oakland County Lincoln Rep. Club, 1989-90; bd. dirs. camping svcs. and human resources com. YMCA, 1989-93, Anti-Defamation League, 1989—; vice chmn. Lawyers for Reagan-Bush, 1984; v.p. Fruehauf Farms, West Bloomfield, Mich., 1985-88; mem. staff Exec. Office of Pres. of U.S. Inquiries/Comments, Washington, 1981-83. Mem. ABA, Fed. Bar Assn., Mich. Bar Assn., Fla. Bar Assn. (labor com. 1977—), Mich. Bus. and Profl. Assn., Am. Subcontractors Assn. (Southeastern Mich., bd. dirs.), Founders Soc. (Detroit Bar Assn., Oakland County Bar Assn., B'nai B'rith (v.p. 1982-83, trustee Detroit coun. 1987-88, bd. dirs. Detroit Barristers unit 1983-91, pres. 1985-87), Oakpointe Country Club, Detroit Soc. Clubs, Skyline Club, Fairlane Club, Renaissance Club. Office: Clark Hill PLC 500 Woodward Ave Ste 3500 Detroit MI 48226-3435 also: Morgan Daniels Co Inc 5484 Crispin Way Rd West Bloomfield MI 48323-3402

MAMATEY, VICTOR SAMUEL, history educator; b. North Braddock, Pa., Feb. 19, 1917; s. Albert Paul and Olga (Darmek) M.; m. Denise M. Perrone, Nov. 20, 1945; children: Albert R., Peter V. Student, Wittenberg Coll., 1938-39, U. Chgo., 1939-40; AM, Harvard U., 1941; PhD, U. Paris, 1949. Asst. prof. history Fla. State U., Tallahassee, 1949-55, assoc. prof., 1955-58, prof., 1958-67, chmn. dept. history, 1964-67; rsch. prof. hist. U. Ga., Athens, 1967-82, acting dean Coll. Arts and Scis., 1972-73; vis. prof. Columbia U., 1961, Tulane U., 1963. Author: The United States and East Central Europe, 1914-18, 1957, Soviet RussianImperialism, 1964, (with Geoffrey Brunn) The World in the Twentieth Century, 1967, The Rise of the Hapsburg Empire, 1526-1815, 1971, (with Radomir Luza) History of the Czechoslovak Republic, 1918-1948, 1973. With U.S. Army, 1942-46. Guggenheim fellow, 1959. Mem. Am. Hist. Assn. (George Louis Beer prize for best book on internat. history 1958), Am. Assn. For Advancement Slavic Studies. Home: 142 Spruce Valley Rd Athens GA 30605-3332

MAMER, STUART MIES, lawyer; b. East Hardin, Ill., Feb. 23, 1921; s. Louis H. and Anna (Mies) M.; m. Donna E. Jordan, Sept. 10, 1944; children: Richard A., John S., Bruce J. A.B., U. Ill., 1942, J.D., 1947. Bar: Ill. bar 1947. Assoc. Thomas & Mulliken, Champaign, 1947-55; partner firm Thomas, Mamer & Haughey, Champaign, 1955—; lectr. U. Ill. Coll. Law, Urbana, 1965-85; Mem. Atty. Registration and Disciplinary Commn. Ill., 1976-82. Chmn. fund drive Champaign County Community Chest, 1955; 1st pres. Champaign County United Fund, 1957; Pres., dir. U. Ill. McKinley Found., Champaign, 1957-69; trustee Children's Home and Aid Soc. of Ill., v.p., 1977-96. Served as pilot USAAF, 1943-45. Mem. Am. Coll. Trust and Estate Counsel (bd. regents 1984-90), Phi Beta Kappa, Phi Gamma Delta. Republican. Presbyterian. Home: 6 Montclair Rd Urbana IL 61801-5824 Office: Thomas Mamer & Haughey 30 E Main St Fl 5 Champaign IL 61820-3629

MAMET, DAVID ALAN, playwright, director, essayist; b. Chgo., Nov. 30, 1947; s. Bernard Morris and Lenore June (Silver) M.; m. Lindsay Crouse, Dec. 1977 (div.), m. Rebecca Pidgeon, Sept. 22, 1991. B.A., Goddard Coll., Plainfield, Vt., 1969; DLitt (hon.), Dartmouth Coll., 1996. Artist-in-residence Goddard Coll., 1971-73; artistic dir. St. Nicholas Theatre Co., Chgo., 1973-75; guest lectr. U. Chgo., 1975, 79, NYU, 1981; assoc. artistic dir. Goodman Theater, Chgo., 1978; assoc. prof. film Columbia U., 1988; chmn. bd. Atlantic Theater Co. Author: (plays) The Duck Variations, 1971, Sexual Perversity in Chicago, 1973 (Village Voice Obie award 1976), Reunion, 1973, Squirrels, 1974, American Buffalo, 1976 (Village Voice Obie award, N.Y. Drama Critics Circle award), A Life in the Theatre, 1976, The Water Engine, 1976, The Woods, 1977, Lone Canoe, 1978, Prairie du Chien, 1978, Lakeboat, 1980, Donny March, 1981, Edmond, 1982 (Village Voice Obie award 1983), The Disappearance of the Jews, 1983, The Shawl, 1985, Glengarry Glen Ross, 1984 (Pulitzer prize for drama, N.Y. Drama Critics Circle award), Speed-The-Plow, 1987, Bobby Gould in Hell, 1989, The Old Neighborhood, 1991, Oleanna, 1992, The Cryptogram, 1994 (Obie award 1995), (dir. only) Ricky Jay and His 52 Assistants, 1994, (one act) Death Defying Acts, 1995; screenplays: The Postman Always Rings Twice, 1979, The Verdict, 1980, The Untouchables, 1986, House of Games, 1986, (with Shel Silverstein) Things Change, 1987, We're No Angels, 1987, Homicide, 1991 (also dir.), Hoffa, 1991, Oleanna, 1994, The Edge, 1996, The Spanish Prisoner, 1996, Wag The Dog, 1997; (children's books) Warm and Cold with drawings by Donald Sultan, 1985, The Duck and the Goat; (essays) Writing In Restaurants, 1986, SomeFreaks, 1989, on Directing Film, 1990, The Cabin, 1992; (novels) The Village, 1994, The Old Religion, 1996, True and False, 1996, (books) Passover, The Duck and the Goat, 1996, Make-Believe-Town, 1996, (poetry) The Hero Pony, 1990; dir. (films) House of Games, 1986, Things Change, 1987, Homicide, 1991, Oleanna, 1994, (play) Dangerous Corner (J.B. Priestly), 1995. Recipient Outer Critics Circle award for contbn. to Am. theater, 1978; Acad. award nominee for best screen play adaptation, 1983; Rockefeller grantee, 1977; CBS Creative Writing fellow Yale U. Drama Sch., 1976-77.

MAMLOK, URSULA, composer, educator; b. Berlin, Feb. 1, 1928; d. John and Dorothy Lewis; m. Dwight G. Mamlok, Nov. 27, 1947. Student, Mannes Coll. Music, 1942-45; MusB, Manhattan Sch. Music, 1955, MusM, 1958. Mem. faculty dept. music NYU, 1967-74, CUNY, 1971-74; prof. composition Manhattan Sch. Music, N.Y.C., 1974—. Composer numerous works including Variations and Interludes for 4 percussionists, 1973, Sextet, 1977, Festive Sounds, 1978, When Summer Sang, 1980, piano trio Panta rhei, 1981, 5 recital pieces for young pianists, 1983, From My Garden for solo viola or solo violin, 1983, Concertino for wind quintet, strings and percussion, 1984, Der Andreas Garten for voice, flute and harp, 1986, Alariana for recorder, clarient, bassoon, violin and cello, 1986, 3 Bagatelles for harpsichord, 1987, 5 Bagatelles for clarinet, violin, cello, 1988, Rhapsody for clarinet, viola, piano Inward Journey for Piano, 1989, Sonata for violin and piano, 1989, Music for flute, violin, cello, 1990, Girasol, a sextet for flute, violin, viola, cello and piano, 1991, Constellations for orch., 1993, Polarities for flute, violin, cello, piano, 1995, Festive Sounds for Organ, String Quartet II, 1996-97. Recipient Serge Koussevitzky Found. commn., 1988, Walter Hinrichsen award Acad. Inst. Arts and Letters, 1989, commn. San Francisco Symphony, 1990; Nat. Endowment Arts grantee, 1974, Am. Inst. Acad. Arts and Letters grantee, 1981, 89, Martha Baird Rockefeller grantee, 1982; John Simon Gugenheim fellow, 1995. Mem. Am. Composers Alliance (dir., Opus One Rec. award 1987), Am. Soc. Univ. Composers, Am. Women Composers, N.Y. Women Composers, Internat. League Women Composers, Music Theory Soc. N.Y., Am. Music Ctr., Internat. Soc Contemporary Music (bd. dirs.), Fromm Found. Commn., Am. Guild Organists Com. Address: 315 E 86th St New York NY 10028-4714 *In my music, I have never striven for novelty nor originality for its own sake. Rather, my primary concern as a composer has been the consolidation of older and newer techniques, as they best serve the work at hand.*

MAMMEL, RUSSELL NORMAN, retired food distribution company executive; b. Hutchinson, Kans., Apr. 28, 1926; s. Vyvian E. and Mabel Edwina (Hursh) M.; m. Betty Crawford, Oct. 29, 1949 (dec. Oct. 1994); children: Mark, Christopher, Elizabeth, Nancy. BS, U. Kans., 1949. With Mammel's Inc., Hutchinson, 1949-57, pres., 1957-59; retail gen. mgr. Kans. divsn. Nash Finch Co., Hutchinson, 1959-61; retail gen. mgr. Iowa divsn. Nash Finch Co., Cedar Rapids, 1961-66; dir. store devel. Nash Finch Co., Mpls., 1966-75, v.p., 1975-83, exec. v.p., 1983-85, pres., COO, 1985-91; also bd. dirs. Nash Finch Co., Mpls., Mpls., 1991; pvt. investments, 1991—. With AUS, 1944-46. Home: 6808 Cornelia Dr Minneapolis MN 55435-1608 Office: Nash Finch Co 7600 France Ave S Minneapolis MN 55435-5924

MAMMEN, SAM, publishing executive, entrepreneur; b. Kerala, India, June 22, 1949; came to U.S., 1972; s. K.O. and Mariamma M.; m. Lori J. Hummel, Dec. 20, 1973; children: Sarah Nalini, Suzanne Kamala, Christopher Ashok. BS in Biology and Chemistry, U. Kerala, 1969; MA in English Lit., Kanpur (India) U., 1971; MA in Edn., U. Tex., San Antonio, 1979. Cert. profl. supr., Tex. Edn. Agy. Tchr. St. James Sch., San Antonio, 1973-76, St. Gerard Sch., San Antonio, 1976-77, Comal Ind. Sch. Dist., Bulverde, Tex., 1978-83; owner Ednl. Cons. Svc., San Antonio, 1982-86; pres. ECS Learning Systems, Inc., San Antonio, 1986—; coach Tex. Future Problem Solving Program State Finals, 1981-83. Founding pres. Assn. Educators Gifted Students, San Antonio, 1980-81; pres. San Antonio Assn. for Gifted and Talented Children, San Antonio, 1987-88. Teaching grantee Tex. Assn. for the Improvement Reading, 1978, Tchr. Tng. grantee Tex. Dept. Human Resources, 1986; Grad. Student scholar Nat. Assn. for Gifted Children, 1983. Mem. Ednl. Press Assn. Am. (regional rep. 1993-94), Am. Creativity Assn., Ednl. Dealers and Suppliers Assn., Nat. Sch. Supply and Equipment Assn., India/Asia Entrepreneur's Assn., Tex. Assn. for the Gifted and Talented (charter mem., 2d v.p. 1981-82, exec. bd. dirs. 1979-82). Avocations: travel, reading, gardening, tennis, San Antonio Spurs fan. Office: ECS Learning Systems Inc PO Box 791437 San Antonio TX 78279-1437

MAMPRE, VIRGINIA ELIZABETH, communications executive; b. Chgo., Sept. 12, 1949; d. Albert Leon and Virginia S. (Joboul) M. BA with honors, U. Iowa, 1971; Masters degree, Ind. U., 1972; spl. cert., Harvard U., 1981. Cert. tchr. Harris Intern WTTW-TV Sta., Chgo., 1972, asst. dir., 1972-73; prod. and dir. WSIU/WUSI-TV Sta., Carbondale, Ill., 1973-74; instr. So. Ill. U., Carbondale, 1972-77; prog. and prod. mgr. WSIU/WUSI-TV, Carbondale, 1974-77; prog. dir. KUHT-TV Sta., Houston, 1977-83; pres. Victory Media, Inc., Houston, 1984-89, Mampre Media Internat., Houston, 1984—; pres. A.I.C.B.; cons. Corp. for Pub. Broadcasting, Washington, 1981-83; chmn. AWRT/YCOC Houston Metro Area, 1983-85, pres., 1983—, nat. v.p., 1985-90; adv. coun. PBS, Washington, 1981-83; bd. and programming chmn. So. Edn. Comms., Columbia, S.C., 1978-83; bd. dirs. TVPC; program bd. EEN; bd. dirs. IFEA, 1994—; mem. IFEA Found. Bd., 1996—; spkr., presenter in field, Europe, Asia, Australia, S.Am. Contbg. author/editor to mags. including Focus, 1989, News & Views, 1987-88, In the Black, 1984-93, Festivals; creator: (report card campaign) Multi-media, U.S., 1985—; exec. prodr. TV spls., pub. affairs and info., 1977-83 (awards 1978-91). Pres. bd. dirs. Houston Fin. Coun., 1983—; pres. Child Abuse Prevention Coun., Houston, 1984—; bd. dirs. Child Abuse Prevention Network, 1990—; officer bd. dirs. Crime Stoppers Houston, 1984—; chmn. exhbns. Mayor's 1st Hearing, Children and Youth, Houston, 1985-88; founder, bd. dirs. Friends of WSIU-TV, 1974-77; chmn. Evening Guild St. John the Divine, St. Kevork/ACYO Nat. sports fair, 1990; rep. for Houston 2d World Conf. on Mayors, Japan, 1989; exec. bd. nat. com. to prevent child abuse, 1990—; bd. dirs. Houston Read Com., 1995—; mem. nat. faculty Ctr. for Children's Issues, 1995—. Fellow W.K. Kellogg Found., Battle Creek, Mich., 1987-90; recipient award for Excellence Pres. Pvt. Sector, White House, Washington, 1987, Ohio State U., Columbus, 1983, Feddersen award for excellence in Pub. TV Ind. U., Bloomington, 1981, Heritage award Child Abuse Prevention Coun., 1990, Dona J. Stone Founders award Nat. Assn. for Prevention of Child Abuse, 1990; named among Outstanding Women Vols. for community, civic and profl. contbns., Fedn. Houston Profl. Women, 1989; finalist Woman on the Move, 1987, Rising Star, 1987. Mem. Am. Women in Radio and TV (nat. v.p. 1986-90, award 1987, pres. Houston chpt. 1990, bd. dirs. 1985—), Houston Fed. Profl. Women (pres., del. 1986-93, chmn. 1994), Nat. Assn. Ednl. Broadcasters (presenter nat. conv. 1975-76), Tex. Lyceum (v.p., bd. dirs. 1990—), Dephians, Nat. Assn. for Programming TV Execs., Fedn. Houston Profl. Women Ednl. Found. (bd. dirs. 1994—), Ctr. for Bus. Women's Devel. (bd. dirs. 1993-94). Republican. Episcopalian. Avocations: photography, swimming, sailing, languages, travel. Office: Mampre Media Internat 5123 Del Monte Dr Houston TX 77056-4316

MAN, EUGENE HERBERT, chemist, educator, business executive; b. Scranton, Pa., Dec. 14, 1923; s. E. Lester and Celia (Cohen) M.; m. Priscilla R. Perry, Sept. 15, 1976; children—Elizabeth Sue Man Eichenberger, Barbara Ruth, Linda Jeanne Man Manley, Bruce Jonathan, Pamela Irene Perry, Aaron Benjamin Perry. A.B., Oberlin Coll., 1948; Ph.D. (Office Naval Research fellow, E.I. duPont fellow), Duke, 1952. Rsch. chemist E.I. duPont de Nemours & Co., Inc., Wilmington, Del., 1952-60; supr. tech. sect. E.I. duPont de Nemours & Co., Inc., Chattanooga, 1960-61; sr. supr. E.I. duPont de Nemours & Co., Inc., 1961-62; coordinator research U. Miami, Coral Gables, Fla., 1962-66; dean rsch. coordination U. Miami, 1966-77, dean research and sponsored programs, 1977-79, prof. chemistry, 1967-93, prof. marine and atmospheric chemistry, 1971-93, prof. emeritus, 1994—; pres., chief exec. officer Ctr. for Health Techs. Inc., Miami, 1990—; vis. investigator Scripps Instn. Oceanography, 1971-72; Lady Davis faculty fellow Technion, Israel, 1990; bd. dirs. Health Planning Coun., Dade County, Fla., 1970-71; dir. Gulf Univs. Rsch. Consortium, Galveston, Tex., chmn., 1969-71, cons., 1979-81. Contbr. articles profl. jours. Trustee, v.p. Cmty. Mental Health Svc., Dade County, 1967-71; trustee United Fund Dade County, 1967-69; mem., chmn. exec. com. Mental Health Consortium, Dade County, 1966-71; mem. Met. Dade County Cultural Affairs Coun., 1984-89, chmn. sci. com., 1986-90, 1st vice chmn., 1988-89; mem. exec. com. Nat. Coun. Univ. Rsch. Adminstrs., 1967-72; trustee, vice chmn. Hospice Found. of Am., 1992—; mem. coun. Oak Ridge Assoc. Univs., 1973-79; trustee Miami Mus. Sci., 1990-94, adv. bd., 1995—; trustee Greater Miami C. of C. 1st lt. AUS, 1943-46. Recipient Harry N. Holmes award in chemistry Oberlin Coll., 1948; NIH grantee, 1983-91. Fellow Am. Inst. Chemists; mem. Am. Chem. Soc., AAAS, Phi Beta Kappa, Sigma Xi (pres. U. Miami chpt. 1981-82), Phi Lambda Upsilon. Patentee in field. Home: 1627 Brickell Ave Apt 1107 Miami FL 33129-1249

MAN, LAWRENCE KONG, architect; b. Kowloon, Hong Kong, July 4, 1953; s. Hon-Kwong Man and Sau-Ching Luk. Student, U. Redlands, 1971-72; BArch, U. Oreg., 1977; MArch, Harvard U., 1978. Registered architect, Mass. Designer, project architect Shepley Bulfinch Richardson & Abbott, Boston, 1978-86; project designer, project architect E. Verner Johnson & Assoc., Boston, 1987-91; owner Lawrence Man Architect, Cambridge, Mass., 1992-95, L.A., 1994-95. Prin. works include LCP Studio, Somerville, Mass., New Asia Restaurants, Danvers and Arlington, Mass., Tai Pan Restaurant, Cambridge, Mass. (Honor award AIA 1993, New Eng. award Excellence in Architecture 1993, Design Excellence award Nat. Orgn. Minority Architects 1993), Ti-Sales Office, Sudbury, Mass. (Design Excellence award Nat. Orgn. Minority Architects 1993), Dental Clinic, Reading, Mass. (AIA Interior Architecture award 1992, Interior Design Project award Am. Soc. Interior Designers 1991, Boston Exports citation AIA 1990, Boston Soc. of Architects/New Eng. Healthcare Assembly honor award, 1994), Mus. Ctr. Union Terminal, Cin. (Reconstrn. award 1991), Ramesses Pavilion Boston Mus. Sci. (Double Vision award/Double Silver Soc. Environ. Graphics 1990), Smithsonian South Quadrangle Mus., Washington (Boston Exports award/citation AIA 1990, Honor award AIA 1989), Pub. Mus. Grand Rapids (Mich.) River Front Devel., U. Vt. Student Ctr., Burlington, Campus Ctr. Study and Libr. addition Franklin & Marshall Coll., Andover (Mass.) Co. Corp. Hdqs., Emerson Hosp., Concord, Mass., pvt. residences, others. Mem. AIA, Am. Assn. Mus., Boston Soc. Architects, Nat. Orgn. Minority Architects. Avocations: dancing, traveling, music. Home: 2158 Valentine Pl San Marino CA 91108-2343 *There are ups and downs in life. It is more rewarding to experience them all, nomatter how hard it may get sometimes. It allows you to become a more complete person. That is, in my view, a ture achievement.*

MANABE, SYUKURO, climatologist; b. Shingu-Mura, Uma-Gun, Ehime-ken, Japan, Sept. 21, 1931; came to U.S., 1958; s. Seiichi and Sueko (Akashi) M.; m. Nobuko Nakamura, Jan. 21, 1962; children: Nagisa M. Bianchini, Yukari C. BS, Tokyo U., 1953, MS, 1955, DS, 1958. Rsch. meteorologist U.S. Weather Bur., Washington, 1958-63; sr. rsch. meteorologist Geophys. Fluid Dynamics Lab. NOAA, Washington, 1963-68; sr. rsch. meterologist geophys. fluid dynamics lab. NOAA, Princeton, N.J., 1968-95, mem. sr. exec. svc. of U.S., 1979-95, sr. scientist, 1995—; lectr. with rank of prof. Princeton U., 1968—; mem. joint sci. com. World Climate Rsch. Program, 1981-87; mem. bd. on atmospheric sci. and climate NRC, 1988-91; mem. Commn. on Geoscis., Environ. and Resources, NRC, 1990-93; mem. panel on climate and global change NOAA, 1988—. Recipient Fujiwara award Japan Meterol. Soc., 1967, gold medal U.S. Dept. Commerce, 1970, Presdl. Rank Meritorious Exec. award Pres. of U.S., 1989, Acad. award of Blue Planet prize Asahi Glass Found., 1992, Asahi prize Asahi Shinbun newspaper, 1996. Fellow Am. Geophys. Union (Revelle medal 1993), Am. Meteorol. Soc. (Meisinger award 1967, 2d half century award 1977, Rossby medal 1992); mem. NAS, Acad. Europaea (fgn.), Royal Soc. Can. (fgn.). Achievements include the first modeling study of global warming. Home: 6 Governors Ln Princeton NJ 08540-3666 Office: NOAA Geophys Fluid Dynamics Lab Princeton U PO Box 308 Princeton NJ 08542

MANAHAN, KENT, newscaster; b. Long Beach, Calif.; s. Edward Henry and Mary Ann (Denning) Kohlschreiber; m. Peter D. Manahan, July 2, 1966; children: Marc, Matthew, Eric, Sean, Bryan, Erin. BA in English, Dunbarton Coll. of Holy Cross; LLD (hon.), Stockton State Coll., Kean Coll., 1993. Host, writer, prodr. WMTR radio sta., Cedar Knolls, N.J., 1974-76; sr. anchor, corr. N.J. Network, Trenton, 1975—. Prodr., reporter (TV program) Broken Lives, Broken Hearts, New Jersey Personalities, (documentary) Battered Wived, Shatter Lives (award Internat. Film and TV Festival N.Y.); host 1st live satellite transmission of high definition TV from Princeton, N.J. to Washington. Mem. bd. regents Seton Hall U.; bd. dirs. Tri-County Scholarship Fund for Disadvantaged Youngsters; spokesperson Literacy Vols. Am., N.J.; debate moderator Lincoln-Douglas H.S., 1992; host EAster Seal Telethon. Recipient Virginia Apgar Arts and Lit. award, Woman of Achievement award Kean Coll., Broadcaster of Yr. award Montclair State Coll. DuMont TV Ctr., Woman of Yr. award Ironbound Mfrs. Assoc., Belitta Bentz award for Women's Achievements, Presdl. award Caldwell Coll., 3 Emmy awards, 16 Emmy nominations, Scripps-Howard Nat. Journalism award, Cath. Women of Achievement award Coll. of St. Elizabeth, citations Phila. Press Assn., N.J. AP Broadcasters Assn., Am. Women in Radio and TV. Office: NJ Network 25 Stockton St Trenton NJ 08619-1950

MAÑAS, RITA, educational administrator; b. Newark, N.J., Dec. 6, 1951; d. John and Sofia Mañas. BA, Kean Coll., 1974; MA, Seton Hall U., 1977; PhD, Rutgers U., 1990. Cert. tchr. K-12, N.J. Ednl. counselor Aspira Inc. of N.J., Newark, 1974-75; student devel. specialist ednl. opportunity program Seton Hall U., South Orange, N.J., 1975-88; asst. dir. ednl. opportunity fund program Fairleigh Dickinson U., Madison, N.J., 1988-89; dir. office of minority edn. William Paterson Coll., Wayne, N.J., 1990-95; asst. prof. dept. modern langs. Coll. N.J., 1995-96; dir. ednl. opportunity fund program Centenary Coll., Hackettstown, N.J., 1996—; adj. instr. Ctr. for African Am. Studies, English dept. Seton Hall U., South Orange, 1978-79, modern langs. dept., 1981-82, 85-91, 91-93; adj. instr. fgn. langs. dept. Bergen C.C., Paramus, N.J., 1990; adj. instr. langs. and cultures dept. William Paterson Coll., Wayne, N.J., 1991, 95. Bd. dirs. North End Nursery, Newark, 1993-94; mem. adv. bd. Sch. and Comty. Organized to Promote Edn. Program (S.C.O.P.E.), Paterson, N.J., 1993-95. Recipient Achievement award P.R. Inst. of Seton Hall U., 1977, Svc. award Black Student Assn. of William Paterson Coll., 1991, 92, Orgn. of Latin Am. Students of William Paterson Coll., 1991, 93, Tri State Disting. Alumni award Tri-State Consortium of Opportunity Programs in Higher Edn., 1993. Mem. MLA (del. 1993-95, P.R. Lit. and Culture com. 1995—), Am. Assn. Tchrs. of Spanish and Portuguese, N.E. MLA, Mid. Atlantic Coun. Latin Am. Studies, N.J. Ednl. Opportunity Fund Profl. Assn. (20th anniv. conf. planning com. 1989, Svc. award 1989, 93), Hispanic Women's Task Force (Svc. award 1991), Hispanic Assn. Higher Edn. Avocations: crocheting, reading, traveling.

MANASSON, VLADIMIR ALEXANDROVICH, physicist; b. Chernovtsy, Ukraine, Mar. 4, 1952; came to U.S., 1991; s. Alexander and Chaya (Finkelsteyn) M.; m. Katrine Kokhanovskaya, Aug. 2, 1975; children: Alexander, Julia. BSEE, Moscow Inst. Electronic Mfg., 1973, MSEE, 1974; PhD in Physics, Chernovtsy U., 1984. Entr. Acad. of Scis. of the Ukraine Material Sci. Inst., 1975-78, sr. engr., 1978-80, jr. rsch. assoc., 1980-85, sr. rsch. assoc., 1985-90; rsch. scientist Phys. Optics Corp., Torrance, Calif., 1991-94, sr. scientist, 1994-95; leader antenna devel. WaveBand Corp., Torrance, Calif., 1996—. Patentee several photosensitive devices and antennae. Grantee NSF, 1993-94, 97, Dept. Def., 1994-97, Dept. Transp., 1994, 95. Mem. IEEE, Optical Soc. Am., Assn. of Old Crows. Avocations: playing piano, reading, children. Office: 375 Van Ness Ave Torrance CA 90501-1420

MANATOS, ANDREW EMANUEL, policy consultant, former government official; b. Washington, July 7, 1944; s. Mike N. and Dorothy V. (Varanakis) M.; m. Tina G. Weber, June 25, 1967; children: Mike A., Nick A., Tom A., George A. B.A., Am. U., 1968, M.A., 1969. Staff post office and civil service com. U.S. Senate, Washington, 1969-73; assoc. staff dir. post office com., legis. asst. Senator Thomas Eagleton, 1973-77; asst. sec. congl. affairs Dept. Commerce, Washington, 1977-81; owner Manatos & Manatos Inc., Washington, 1981—; creator White House Conf. on Productivity, U.S. Senate Productivity Award, Greek Independence Day Resolution, (videotapes) U.S. Congress and You, Your Court System and You; bd. dirs. Washington Coord. Coun. Productivity, 1981-88, Com. for Citizen Awareness, 1985—. Contbr. articles to N.Y. Times, Washington Post, Indianapolis Star. Dem. precinct chmn., 1974-81; chmn. Montgomery County Dollars for Dems., 1975; bd. dirs., mem. nat. fin. com., co-chmn. Washington fin. com. Dukakis for Pres., 1987-88, Inst. Confidence in Cong.; mng. trustee Dem. Nat. Com. Victory Fund, 1988; mem. Archdiocesan Coun. & Leadership 100 Greek Orthodox Ch. Recipient Cross of Holy Sepulcher, Medal of St. Andrew; named Archon, Greek Orthodox Ch. Office: Manatos & Manatos 601 13th St NW Ste 1150 S Washington DC 20005-3807

MANATT, CHARLES TAYLOR, lawyer; b. Chgo., June 9, 1936. BS, Iowa State U., 1958; JD, George Washington U., 1962. Bar: Calif. 1962, U.S. Supreme Ct. 1967, D.C. 1985. Ptnr. Manatt, Phelps & Phillips, Washington. Bd. editors George WAshington Law Rev., 1960-62. Pres. Calif. Bankers Assn.; chmn. Nat. Democratic Inst., Calif. Democratic Com., Nat. Democratic Com., Internat. Found. for Election Sys. Mem. ABA, Calif. State Bar, L.A. County Bar Assn., San Fernando Valley Bar Assn. (pres. 1971-72), Century City Bar Assn., Phi Delta Phi, Delta Sigma Rho. also: Manatt Phelps & Phillips Trident Ctr E Tower 11355 W Olympic Blvd Los Angeles CA 90064-1614

MANATT, RICHARD, education educator; b. Odebolt, Iowa, Dec. 13, 1931; s. William Price and Lucille (Taylor) M.; m. Sally Jo Johnson, Aug. 20, 1952; children—Tamra Jo, Ann Lea, Joel Price; m. Jacquelyn M. Nesset, Feb. 25, 1970; 1 child, Megan Sue. B.Sc., Iowa State U., 1953, M.S., 1956; Ph.D., U. Iowa, 1964. Prin. Oskloosa (Iowa) Schs., 1959-62; research asso. U. Iowa, Iowa City, 1962-64; mem. faculty Iowa State U., Ames, 1964—; prof. Iowa State U., 1972—, chmn. dept. ednl. adminstrn., 1970-80, 93—, dir. Sch. Improvement Model Projects, 1980—; cons. performance evaluation for public and independent schs.; disting. vis. prof. Calif. State U., L.A. Author: Educator's Guide to the New Design, When Right is Wrong, The Fundamentalists and the Public Schools, The Clinical Manual for Teacher Performance Evaluation Compendias of Professional Growth Plans, (computer software program) Computer Assisted Teach Evaluation/Supervision; editor Coll. Scene, Internat. Jour. Ednl. Reform. Served with AUS, 1953-55. Named Disting. Prof., Nat. Acad. Sch. Execs., 1979, Regents' Prof. Edn., 1994. Mem. NEA, Nat. Assn. Secondary Sch. Prins., Am. Assn. Sch. Adminstrs., Assn. Supervision and Curriculum Devel. (named Outstanding Cons. 1981), Phi Kappa Phi, Phi Delta Kappa, Delta Chi. Democrat. Methodist. Home: 2926 Monroe Dr Ames IA 50010-4362

MANBECK, HARVEY B., agricultural and biological engineer, wood engineer, educator; b. Reading, Pa., Jan. 11, 1942; m. Glenda Manbeck; children: Eric, Christina. BS, Pa. State U., 1963, MS in Agrl. Engring., 1965; PhD in Engring., Okla. State U., 1970. Rsch. assoc. agrl. engring. dept. Pa. State U., 1965, instr. agrl. engring. dept., 1966, prof. agrl. engring., 1980-96; asst. prof. agrl engring. dept. U. Ga., 1970-75, assoc. prof. agrl. engring. dept., 1977-80; assoc. prof., extension agrl. engr. Ohio State U., 1975-77; adminstrv. intern rsch. office Pa. Agrl. Experiment Sta., 1991-92; Disting. prof. agrl. and biol. engring. Pa. State U., 1996—; vis. prof. agrl. engring. U. Manitoba, 1986-87, Shenyang Agrl. U., 1988; interim dir. Housing Rsch. Ctr., Pa. State U., 1995. Contbr. chpts. to books and articles to profl. jours. Coach Little League Baseball, 1981-84, leader YMCA Indian Princess Longhouse, 1983-85, Webelo's Cub Scouts 1984, com. mem. Troop 31 Boy Scouts of Am. 1985—. Recipient Outstanding and Premier Teaching award, Outstanding Rsch. award Coll. of Engring., Pa. State U., Atherton Excellence in Teaching award Pa. State U. Mem. ASCE, Am. Soc. Agrl. Engrs. (mem. structures group, vice chair 1978-79, chair, 1979-81, Pa. State sect. sec.-treas. 1983-84, chair 1985-86, tech. dir. S.E. divsn. 1993-95, Henry Giese S & E award 1990), Nat. Frame Builders Assn. (mem. editl. rev. com. for the post-frame profl., chair 1988—), Ga. Soc. Profl. Engrs (state dir. at large 1974-75, named Outstanding Young Engr. of the Year, 1972, recipient Outstanding Chpt. Pres. award, 1974, various other coms.), Ohio Soc. Profl. Engrs., Am. Soc. for Engring. Edn., Forest Products Rsch. Soc., Gamma Sigma Delta, Alpha Epsilon, Sigma Xi, numerous others. Achievements include development of standard designs and specs for hardwood glulam highway bridges, authorship of national engineering practice for post-frame structural diaphragm design, development of FEM for predicting thermal pressures in grain bins, development of FEM for predicting structural performance of wood-framed, metal-clad diaphagm and development of quality control schemes for poultry housing systems. Home: 912 Anna St Boalsburg PA 16827-1214 Office: Penn State U 210 Agr Engring Bldg University Park PA 16802

MANCALL, ELLIOTT LEE, neurologist, educator; b. Hartford, Conn., July 31, 1927; s. Nicholas and Bess Tuch M.; m. Jacqueline Sue Cooper, Dec. 27, 1953; children: Andrew Cooper, Peter Cooper. BS, Trinity Coll., Hartford, 1948; MD, U. Pa., 1952. Diplomate Am. Bd. Psychiatry and Neurology (dir. 1983-91, dir. emeritus, 1991—). Intern Hartford Hosp., 1952-54; clk. in neurology Nat. Hosp. Nervous Disease, London, 1954-55; asst. resident neurology Neurol. Inst. N.Y., 1955-56; resident neuropathology Mass. Gen. Hosp., 1956-57, also clin. and research fellow, 1957-58; teaching fellow neuropathology Harvard Med. Sch., 1956-57; asst. prof. neurology Jefferson Med. Coll., 1958-64, asso. prof., 1964-65; prof. medicine Hahnemann Med. Coll. and Hosp., 1965-76, prof. neurology, chmn. dept., 1976-93; prof. neurology Jefferson Med. Coll., Phila., 1995—, Med. Coll. Pa.-Hahnemann U., 1993-95; dir. Hahnemann U. ALS Clinic; chmn. bd. dirs. Phila. Profl. Standards Rev. Orgn., 1981-84; del. Am. Bd. Med. Specialties, 1984—. Author: (with others) The Human Cerebellum: A Topographical Atlas, 1961, (with B.J. Alpers) Clinical Neurology, 1971, Essentials of the Neurological Examination, 1971, 81; contbr. numerous articles to profl. jours. Served with USN, 1945-47. Recipient Christian R. and Mary F. Lindback award, 1969; Oliver Meml. prize ophthalmology U. Pa., 1952. Fellow Am. Acad. Neurology (alt. del. to AMA 1982-86, gen. editor CONTINUUM 1991—, A.B. Baker award for excellence in neurol. edn. 1997); mem. Am. Neurol. Assn., Am. Assn. Neuropathology, Assn. Rsch. in Nervous and Mental Diseases, Soc. Neurosci., AAUP, Pa. Med. Peer Rev. Orgn. (dir. 1979-84), Phila. Neurol. Soc., Alpers Soc. Clin. Neurology, Coll. Physicians Phila., Sydenham Coterie, Phila. County Med. Soc., Pa. State Med. Soc., AMA (sec.-treas. sect. coun. neurology 1983-86), Am. Med. Soc. on Alcoholism, Neurology Intersoc. Liaison Group, Intersoc. Com. Neurol. Resources, Assn. Univ. Prof. Neurology (pres. 1988-90), Soc. for Exptl. Neuropathology, Am. Bd. Med. Specialities (exec. bd., chair COSEP, 1992—), Am. Bd. Psychiatry and Neurology (v.p. 1990, del. to Am. Bd. Med. Specialities, emeritus dir. 1991—), Pa. Blue Shield (profl. adv. coun. 1991—). Home: PO Box 498 Lafayette Hill PA 19444 Office: 1025 Walnut St Philadelphia PA 19107-5001

MANCEL, CLAUDE PAUL, household product company executive; b. Paris, Oct. 27, 1942; s. Pierre Mancel and Marcelle E. (Grimaud) Mirowicz; m. Annie Simon, Sept., 1967; children: Pacome, Elodie, Sebastien. Diploma in engring., E.N.S.C., Bordeaux, France, 1966, ENSIC, Nancy, France, 1967; MS in Chem. Engring., Worcester (Mass.) Poly. Inst., 1971, PhD in Chem. Engring., 1974; hon. doctorate, Worcester Poly Inst., 1990. Mem. R & D staff Procter & Gamble European Tech. Ctr., Brussels, 1973-80; dir. R & D Procter & Gamble European Tech. Ctr., 1981-85, Procter & Gamble U.S., Cin., 1986-87; mgr. R & D Procter & Gamble European Tech. Ctr., Brussels, 1987-88; v.p. R & D Procter & Gamble Europe and Middle East, 1989-92, v.p. R & D Europe and Middle East and worldwide (dish, hard surface cleaner and bleach products), 1993—; chmn. adv. com. dept. chem. engring. Worcester Poly. Inst., 1988—, bd. trustees, 1992—; bd. trustees ENSIC, 1996—; vice chmn., treas., bd. dirs. Assn. Internat. Savonnerie, 1990; bd. dirs., vice chmn., treas. European Ctr. Ecotoxicology and Toxicology of Chems. Fulbright Found. grantee, 1969. Mem. Sigma Xi. Home: 115 Ave Bellevue, 1410 Waterloo Belgium Office: Procter & Gamble, Temselaan 100, 1853 Strombeek Bever Belgium

MANCHER, RHODA ROSS, federal agency administrator, strategic planner; b. N.Y.C., Sept. 28, 1935; d. Joseph and Hannah (Karpf) Ross; m. Melvin Mancher, May 27, 1962 (dec.); children: Amy Backus, James Marc. B.S. in Physics, Columbia U., 1960; M.S. in Ops. Research, George Washington U., 1978. Cons. pvt. practice, Bethesda, Md., 1994—; staff FEA, Washington, 1974-77; dir. info. systems devel. div. The White House, Washington, 1977-79; dir. office systems devel. Social Security Adminstrn., Balt., 1979-80; dep. asst. atty. gen. Office Info. Tech., Dept. Justice, Washington, 1980-84; assoc. dir. info. resources mgmt. Dept. Navy, Washington, 1985-87; dir. Office Info. Tech. VA, Washington, 1987-94; pres. H.W.& W., Inc., 1994—; mem. ad hoc com. on recommendations to merge chem. and biol. info. systems Nat. Cancer Inst., Washington; chmn. permanent com. on info. tech. Iternat. Criminal Police Orgn. (INTERPOL); mem. curriculum com. USDA, adv. bd. computer system security and privacy U.S. Govt.; internat. tech. com. AFCEA. Contbr. articles to profl. publs. Recipient Assoc. Commr.'s citation Social Security Adminstrn., 1980, managerial excellence award Interagy. Com. on ADP, 1983; Meritorious award Sr. Exec. Svc., 1982, 83, 85, 87, 88, 91-93, Presdl. Rank of Meritorious Exec., 1990. Mem. Am. Fedn. Info. Processing Socs. (nat. info. issues panel).

MANCHESTER, KENNETH EDWARD, electronics executive, consultant; b. Winona, Minn., Mar. 22, 1925; s. Laurence Edwin and Daisy Idel (Finley) M.; m. Bonnie Lee Hardgrave, June 24, 1946; children: Cynthia Lee, David Scott. AB, San Jose State Coll., 1949; MS, Stanford U., 1950, PhD, 1955. Sr. chemist Shell Devel. Co., Emeryville, Calif., 1955-62; head chemistry sect. Sprague Electric Co., North Adams, Mass., 1962-63, head chemistry dept., 1963-69, dir. semiconductor rsch., devel. and engring., 1969-79; dir. quality assurance and reliability Sprague Electric Co., Worcester, Mass., 1979-85; v.p. corp. R & D Sprague Electric Co., North Adams, 1985-89, Sprague fellow, 1985; cons. semiconductor industry, 1989—; lectr. Rensselaer Poly. Inst., Troy, N.Y., 1967. Contbr. articles to profl. jours.; patentee in field. Chmn. com. Troop 70 Boy Scouts Am. Sgt. U.S. Army Ground Forces, 1943-46, ETO. Mem. Am. Chem. Soc., AIME, Optimist Club, Sigma Xi. Republican. Avocations: woodworking, golf.

MANCHESTER, ROBERT D., venture capitalist; b. Windsor, Ont., Can., Dec. 16, 1942; came to U.S., 1956; s. Lewis R. and Mary I. (Suave) M.; m. Shirley A. Manchester, Sept. 24, 1971; children: Sara A., Robert D., Geoffrey A. B.S., Boston U., 1974; M.B.A., Amos Tuck Sch., Dartmouth U., 1976. Shipping mgr. N. Am. Pharmacal, Dearborn, Mich., 1961-64, plant mgr., 1968-72; investment analyst Narragansett Capital Corp., Providence, 1976-78, v.p., 1978-80, pres., chief operating officer, 1980-86; mng. dir. Narragansett Capital, Inc., Providence, 1986-88; pres., chief exec. officer Manchester & Co., Inc., 1989-91; pres. Manchester Humphreys Inc., 1992—, also bd. dirs.; bd. dirs. Data Indsl. Corp. Served to capt. U.S. Army, 1964-68. Home: 2 Harbour Rd Barrington RI 02806-4411 Office: Manchester Humphreys Inc 101 Dyer St Providence RI 02903-3908

MANCHESTER, WILLIAM, writer; b. Attleboro, Mass., Apr. 1, 1922; s. William Raymond and Sallie Elizabeth (Thompson) M.; m. Julia Brown Marshall, Mar. 27, 1948; children: John Kennerly, Julie Thompson, Laurie. BA, U. Mass., 1946; AM, U. Mo., 1947; LHD (hon.), U. Mass., 1965, U. New Haven, 1979, Russell Sage Coll., 1990; LittD (hon.), Skidmore Coll., 1987, U. Richmond, 1988. Reporter Daily Oklahoman, 1945-46; reporter, fgn. corr., war corr. Balt. Sun, 1947-55; mng. editor Wesleyan U. Publs., 1955-64; fellow Ctr. for Advanced Studies Wesleyan U., Middletown, Conn., 1959-60; writer-in-residence Wesleyan U., Middletown, 1975—, adj. prof. history, 1979-92; fellow Pierson Coll. Yale U., 1991—; prof. of history emeritus Wesleyan U., 1992—. Author: Disturber of the Peace, 1951, The City of Anger, 1953, Shadow of the Monsoon, 1956, Beard the Lion, 1958, A Rockefeller Family Portrait, 1959, The Long Gainer, 1961, Portrait of a President, 1962, The Death of a President, 1967 (Book-of-the-Month Club selection), The Arms of Krupp, 1968 (Lit. Guild selection), The Glory and the Dream, 1974 (Lit. Guild selection), Controversy and Other Essays in Journalism, 1976, American Caesar: Douglas MacArthur, 1880-1964, 1978 (Book-of-Month Club selection), Goodbye, Darkness, 1980 (Book-of-the-Month Club selection), The Last Lion: Winston Spencer Churchill Visions of Glory 1874-1932, 1983 (Book-of-the-Month Club selection), One Brief Shining Moment: Remembering Kennedy, 1983 (Book-of-the-Month Club selection), The Last Lion: Winston Spencer Churchill Alone 1932-1940, 1988 (Book-of-the-Month Club selection), In Our Time, 1989, A World Lit Only by Fire: The Medieval Mind and the Renaissance, Portrait of an Age, 1992; contbr. to Ency. Brit., various publs. Pres. bd. trustees Friends of U. Mass. Libr., 1970-71, trustee, 1970-74; bd. dirs. Winston Churchill Travelling Fellowships, 1990—. Sgt. USMC, 1942-45, PTO. Decorated Purple Heart; recipient Dag Hammarskjöld prize Assn. Internatonale Correspondents Diplomatiques, Rome, 1967, citation for best book on fgn. affairs Overseas Press Club, 1968, U. Mo. Honor award for disting. svc. in journalism, 1969, Conn. Book award, 1975, Pres.'s Cabinet award U. Detroit, 1981, Frederick S. Troy medal U. Mass., 1981, McConnaughy award Wesleyan U., 1981, N.Y. Pub. Libr. Lit. Lion award, 1983, Disting. Pub. Svc. award Conn. Bar Assn., 1985, Lincoln Lit. award Union League Club N.Y., 1983, Blenheim award Internat. Churchill Soc., 1986, Washington Irving award, 1988, Sarah Josepha Hale award, 1993; Guggenheim fellow, 1959-60. Mem. PEN, Soc. Am. Historians, Am. Hist. Assn., Authors Guild, Century Club. Democrat. Avocation: photography. Office: Wesleyan U History Dept Middletown CT 06459

MANCINI, ERNEST ANTHONY, geologist, educator, researcher; b. Reading, Pa., Feb. 27, 1947; s. Ernest and Marian K. (Filbert) M.; m. Marilyn E. Lee, Dec. 27, 1969; children—Lisa L., Lauren N. B.S., Albright Coll., 1969; M.S., So. Ill. U., 1972; Ph.D., Tex. A&M U., 1974. Petroleum exploration geologist Cities Service Oil Co., Denver, 1974-76; asst. prof. geology U. Ala., Tuscaloosa, 1976-79, assoc. prof., 1979-84, prof., 1984—; state geologist, oil and gas supr. State Ala., Tuscaloosa, 1982-96. Cushman Found. fellow; recipient Nat. Coun. citation Albright Coll., 1983, Pratt-Haas Disting. Lectr. award, 1987-88. Fellow Geol. Soc. Am.; mem. Am. Assn. Petroleum Geologists (A.I. Levorsen petroleum geology Meml. award Gulf Coast assn., geol. socs. sect. 1980), Assn. Am. State Geologists (hon., past pres.), Soc. Econ. Paleontologists and Mineralogists Gulf Coast sect. (hon., past pres.), Paleontol. Soc. (past pres. southeast sect.), N.Am. Micropaleontology Soc., Internat. Micropaleontology Soc., Geol. Soc. Am., (Chair, southeast sect.), Ala. Geol. Soc. (past pres.), Sigma Xi (past chpt. pres.), Phi Kappa Phi (past chpt. pres.), Phi Sigma. Presbyterian. Contbr. articles to profl. jours. Home: 15271 Four Winds Loop Northport AL 35475-3325 Office: U Ala Dept Geology Box 870338 Tuscaloosa AL 35487

MANCINI, MARY CATHERINE, cardiothoracic surgeon, researcher; b. Scranton, Pa., Dec. 15, 1953; d. Peter Louis and Ferminia Teresa (Massi) M. BS in Chemistry, U. Pitts., 1974, MD, 1978; postgrad. in Anatomy and Cellular Biolog, La. State U. Med. Ctr., 1994—. Diplomate Am. Bd. Surgery (speciality cert. critical care medicine), Am. Bd. Thoracic Surgery. Intern in surgery U. Pitts., 1978-79, resident in surgery, 1979-87; fellow pediatric cardiac surgery Mayo Clinic, 1987-88; asst. prof. surgery, dir. cardiothoracic transplantation Med. Coll. Ohio, Toledo, 1988-91; assoc. prof. surgery, dir. cardiothoracic transplantation La. State U. Med. Ctr., Shreveport, 1991—. Author: Operative Techniques for Medical Students, 1983; contbr. articles to profl. jours. Rsch. grantee Am. Heart Assn., 1988; recipient Pres. award Internat. Soc. Heart Transplantation, 1983, Charles C. Moore Tchg. award U. Pitts., 1985, Internat. Woman of Yr. award Internat. Biog. Inst., Eng., 1992-93, Internat. Order of Merit award, 1995, Nina S. Braunwald Career Devel. award Thoracic Surgery Found., 1996-98. Fellow ACS, Am. Coll. Chest Physicians, Internat. Coll. Surgeons (councillor 1991—); mem. Assn. Women Surgeons, Rotary (gift of life program 1991). Roman Catholic. Achievements include first multiple organ transplant in La., first pediatric heart transplant in La., 1993. Office: La State U Med Ctr 1501 Kings Hwy Shreveport LA 71103-4228

MANCINO, DOUGLAS MICHAEL, lawyer; b. Cleve., May 8, 1949; s. Paul and Adele (Brazaitis) M.; m. Carol Keith, June 16, 1973. BA, Kent State U., 1971; JD, Ohio State U., 1974. Bar: Ohio 1974, U.S. Tax Ct. 1977, Calif. 1981, D.C. 1981. Assoc. Baker & Hostetler, Cleve., 1974-1980; ptnr. Memel & Ellsworth, Los Angeles, 1980-87, McDermott, Will & Emery, Los Angeles, 1987—; bd. dirs. Physician Partners, Inc., Health Net. Author: Taxation of Hospitals and Health Care Organizations, 1995, (with others) Hospital Survival Guide, 1984, Navigating the Federal Physician Self-Referral Law, 1995; co-author quar. tax column Am. Hosp. Assn. publ. Health Law Vigil, (with L. Burns) Joint Ventures Between Hosps. and Physicians, 1987; contbr. articles to profl. jours. Chmn. bd. dirs. The Children's Burn Found. Mem. ABA (tax, bus., real property, probate and trust sects., chair exempt orgns. com. 1995-97), Calif. State Bar Assn. (tax, bus. law sects.), Ohio Bar Assn., Calif. State Bar, D.C. Bar Assn., Nat. Health Lawyers Assn., Am. Acad. Healthcare Attys. (bd. dirs. 1986-95, pres. 1993-94), Calif. Soc. for Healthcare Attys., Bel Air Country Club, The Regency Club. Office: McDermott Will & Emery 2049 Century Park E Fl 34 Los Angeles CA 90067-3101

MANCKE, RICHARD BELL, economics writer and investor; b. Bethlehem, Pa., Jan. 11, 1943; s. Donald Bell and Elizabeth (Schlottman) M.; m. Barbara Hobbie, Sept. 4, 1970; 1 child, Max. BA, Colgate U., 1965; PhD, MIT, 1969. Instr. MIT, Cambridge, Mass., 1968-69; staff economist U.S. President's Oil Imports Task Force, Washington, 1969-70; asst. prof. Grad. Sch. Bus., U. Chgo., 1969-71; asst. prof. econs. and law U. Mich. Law Sch., Ann Arbor, 1971-74; assoc. prof. Fletcher Sch. Tufts U., Medford, Mass., 1974-81, prof., 1981-86; mng. ptnr. Wolfeboro (N.H.) Ventures, 1985-92, 96—; vis. prof. Fgn. Affairs Coll., Beijing, 1987, Colgate U., Hamilton, N.Y., 1990; prof. Fletcher Sch. Tufts U., 1990-96; acad. dean Fletcher Sch., Tufts U., 1991-94; interim dean Fletcher Sch. Tufts U., Medford, Mass., 1994-95; expert witness Cravath, Swaine & Moore, N.Y.C., 1974-82; dir. Intellitech Corp., Key Largo, Fla., 1985-90; rsch. dir. Twentieth Century Fund Energy Policy Task Force, N.Y.C., 1976-77. Author: The Failure of U.S. Energy Policy, 1974, Squeaking By, 1976, Mexican Oil and Natural Gas, 1979; co-author: IBM and the U.S. Data Processing Industry, 1983 (outstanding acad. book award Choice) 1984. Testified before various coms. U.S. Senate, 1972-76; mem. various town bds., Wolfeboro, N.H., 1981-94. Fellow NSF, 1967, Earhart Found., 1981, Goethe Inst., 1995. Mem. Am. Econs. Assn., Appalachian Mountain Club. Avocations: reading, cycling, hiking. Home: PO Box 432 Wolfeboro NH 03894-0432

MANCOFF, NEAL ALAN, lawyer; b. Chgo., May 7, 1939; s. Isadore and Sarah (Leviton) M.; m. Alys Belofsky, June 26, 1966; children: Wesley, Frederick, Daniel. BBA, U. Wis., 1961; JD, Northwestern U., 1965. Bar: Ill. 1965, U.S. Dist. Ct. (no. dist.) Ill. 1965. Assoc. Aaron Aaron Schimberg & Hess, Chgo., 1965-72, ptnr., 1972-80; ptnr. Schiff Hardin & Waite, Chgo., 1980—. Author: Qualified Deferred Compensation Plans, 1983, Nonqualified Deferred Compensation Agreements, 1987. 1st lt. U.S. Army, 1961-62. Mem. Chgo. Bar Assn. (chmn. employee benefits com. 1984). Office: Schiff Hardin & Waite 7500 Sears Tower Chicago IL 60606-6327

MANCUSO, FRANK G., entertainment company executive; b. Buffalo, July 25, 1933; married. Ed., SUNY. Film buyer, ops. supr. Basil Enterprises, 1959-63; joined Paramount Pictures Corp., 1963, booker Buffalo br., 1963-64, sales rep. Buffalo br., 1964-67, br. mgr., 1967-70; v.p., gen. sales mgr. Paramount Pictures Can. Ltd., 1970-72, pres., 1972-76; U.S. we. divsn. mgr. Paramount Pictures Corp., L.A., 1976-77; gen. sales mgr. Paramount Pictures Corp., N.Y.C., 1977; v.p. domestic distbn. Paramount Pictures Corp., 1977-79, exec. v.p. distbn. and mktg., 1979-83, pres. motion picture divsn., 1983-84; chmn., CEO Paramount Pictures Corp., N.Y.C., 1984-91; chmn, CEO Metro-Goldwyn-Mayer, 1993—. Bd. dirs. Will Rogers Meml. Fund, N.Y.-Cornell Med. Ctr., Burke Rehab. Ctr., UCLA Med. Ctr., Mus. of Broadcasting. Mem. Acad. Motion Picture Arts and Scis. (bd. dirs.), Motion Picture Assn. (bd. dirs.), Am. Film Inst. (bd. dirs.), Motion Picture Pioneers (bd. dirs.), Variety Clubs Internat. (bd. dirs.). also: Metro-Goldwyn-Mayer Inc 2500 Broadway Santa Monica CA 90404-3065 also: Metro-Goldwyn-Mayer Inc 1350 Avenue Of The Americas New York NY 10019-4702

MAND, MARTIN G., financial executive; b. Norfolk, Va., Sept. 26, 1936; s. Meyer J. and Lena (Sutton) M.; m. Shelly Cohen, Aug. 29, 1965; children: Gregory S., Michael E., Brian C. BS in Commerce, U. Va., 1958; MBA, U. Del., 1964. Various fin. staff and mgmt. positions E.I. du Pont de Nemours

& Co., Wilmington, Del., 1961-83, v.p. taxes and fin. services, 1983-84; v.p., comptroller, 1984-88, v.p., treas. 1989-90 ; sr. v.p., CFO No. Telecon Ltd., Mississauga, Ont., Can., 1990-93, exec. v.p., CFO, 1993-94; chmn. pres., CEO Mand Assocs., Ltd., 1995—; dir. First Fed. Savs. and Loan, Wilmington, 1977-83, Bimcor, Inc., Toronto, Can., 1990-94, Fuji Bank & Trust Co, N.Y.C., 1995—, Sun Healthcare Group, Inc., Albuquerque, 1996—; pres. Fin. Execs. Research Found., 1988-90. Lt. USN, 1958-61. Mem. Fin. Execs. Inst., Am. Mgmt. Assn (chmn. fin. coun.).

MANDA, JOSEPH ALEXANDER, III, veterinary consulting executive; b. Orange, N.J., Jan. 17, 1952; s. Joseph Alexander and Caroline (Barnes) M. BS in Edn., Okla. State U., 1973, BS, 1978; MS, Rutgers U., 1979; DVM, Universidad Nacional de Pedro Henriquez Urena, Santo Domingo, Dominican Republic, 1981; MBA, Hood Coll., Frederick, Md., 1989; cert. in veterinary practice adminstrn., Purdue U., Am. Animal Hosp. Veterinarian Cameron Animal Hosp., Montclair, N.J., 1981-82; veterinarian, mgr. Whitesburg (Ky.) Animal Clinic, 1982-83; rsch. assoc. Coll. Vet. Medicine, U. Wis., Madison, 1983-84; vet. researcher W.Va. U. Sch. Medicine, Morgantown, 1984-86; sr. veterinarian/prin. investigator Hazelton Labs./Am., Rockville, Md., 1986-90; pres., CEO Vet. Consulting Corp., Gainesville, Fla., 1984—; asst. dir. U. Fla. Biotech. Inst., Gainesville, 1990-93; adj. prof. Coll. Vet. Medicine, U. Fla., Gainesville, 1990—; lectr. various profl. orgns., 1986—; radio talk show host WPAZ Radio. Author: Problems in Management, 1992; contbr. articles to profl. jours. Grantee Bionetics Corp., Rockville, Md., 1986-90, NIH, Rockville, 1986-90, USDA/State Fla., Alachua, 1990-93. Mem. Am. Vet. Medicine Assn., Am. Assn. Lab. Animal Sci. (nat. steering com., editorial rev. bd. jours. 1991—), Am. Assn. Lab. Animal Practitioners, Am. Heartworm Soc., Am. Animal Hosp. Assn. (nat. mgmt. com. 1992), Gainesville Area Innovation Network. Avocations: sailing, golf, swimming. Office: care 28 Battle Hill Rd Basking Ridge NJ 07920

MANDAL, ANIL KUMAR, nephrologist, medical educator; b. West Bengal, India, Nov. 12, 1935; came to U.S., 1967; s. Nirmal Chandra and Kamala Bala (Sarkar) M.; m. Pranati Ganguly, June 18, 1964 (dec.); children: Aditi, Atashi. MB, BS, Calcutta Nat. Med. Coll., 1959. Diplomate Am. Bd. Internal Medicine, Am. Bd. Nephrology. Instr. U. Ill., Chgo., 1971-72; asst. prof. U. Okla., Oklahoma City, 1972-75, assoc. prof., 1975-82; VA career investigator VA Med. Ctr., Oklahoma City, 1975-77; prof. medicine Med. Coll. Ga., 1982-87, Wright State U., Dayton, Ohio, 1987—; chief nephrology VA Med. Ctr., Dayton, 1987—; cons. Vets. Affairs Med. Ctr., Chillicothe, Ohio, 1995—; chmn. med. adv. bd. Nat. Kidney Found., 1996—. Author: Nephrology Asian Pacific Physicians, 1995, Diagnosis and Management Renal Disease and Hypertension, 1994; editl. bd. Jour. Clin. Pharmacology, 1994-96, Kidney, 1994—. Fulbright scholar, 1992, 96. Avocation: rose gardening. Home: 571 Pine Needles Dr Centerville OH 45458 Office: VA Med Ctr 4100 E 3rd St # 111W Dayton OH 45403-2244

MANDEL, BABALOO, scriptwriter; b. N.Y.C.. Screenwriter: (with Lowell Ganz) Night Shift, 1982, (and with Bruce Jay Friedman) Splash, 1984 (Academy award nomination best original screenplay 1984), (and with Dan Aykroyd) Spies Like Us, 1985, Gung Ho, 1986, Vibes, 1988, Parenthood, 1989, City Slickers, 1991, A League of Their Own, 1992, (and with Billy Crystal) Mr. Saturday Night, 1992, Greedy, 1994, City Slickers II: The Legend of Curley's Gold, 1994, (and with Crystal) Forget Paris, 1995, Multiplicity, 1996; writer: (TV series) Laverne and Shirley, 1976-83, Busting Loose, 1977, (TV pilots) Herndon and Me, 1983; writer, exec. prodr.: (TV pilots) Gung Ho, 1986, Channel 99, 1988, Knight and Daye, 1989, Parenthood, 1990, A League of their Own, 1993; creator, writer, creative cons.: (with Ganz) Take Five, 1987; appearances include (film) Splash, 1984, (TV) Naked Hollywood, 1991. Office: CAA 9830 Wilshire Blvd Beverly Hills CA 90212-1804*

MANDEL, CAROLA PANERAI (MRS. LEON MANDEL), foundation trustee; b. Havana, Cuba; d. Camilo and Elvira (Bertini) Panerai; ed. pvt. schs., Havana and Europe; m. Leon Mandel, Apr. 9, 1938. Mem. women's bd. Northwestern Meml. Hosp., Chgo. Trustee Carola and Leon Mandel Fund Loyola U., Chgo. Life mem. Chgo. Hist. Soc., Guild of Chgo. Hist. Soc., Smithsonian Assos., Nat. Skeet Shooting Assn. Frequently named among Ten Best Dressed Women in U.S.; chevalier Confrerie des Chevaliers du Tastevin. Capt. All-Am. Women's Skeet Team, 1952, 53, 54, 55, 56; only woman to win a men's nat. championship, 20 gauge, 1954, also high average in world over men, 1956, in 12 gauge with 99.4 per cent; European women's live bird shooting championship, Venice, Italy, 1957, Porto, Portugal, 1961; European woman's target championship, Torino, Italy, 1958; woman's world champion live-bird shooting, Sevilla, Spain, 1959, Am. Contract Bridge League Life Master, 1987. Named to Nat. Skeet Shooting Assn. Hall of Fame, 1970; inducted in U.S. Pigeon shooting Fedn. Hall of Fame, 1992. Mem. Soc. Four Arts. Club: Everglades (Palm Beach, Fla.), The Beach. Home: 324 Barton Ave Palm Beach FL 33480-6116

MANDEL, DAVID MICHAEL, lawyer; b. N.Y.C., Dec. 20, 1951; s. Seymour and Henrietta (Gersoni) M.; m. Alice Elizabeth Stanley, June 10, 1973; 1 child, Michael Stanley. BA, Yale U., 1973; JD, Harvard U., 1976. Bar: Mass. 1977, U.S. Dist. Ct. Mass. 1978, U.S. Ct. Appeals (1st cir.) 1979, U.S. Supreme Ct. 1982. Clk. Judge Murray I. Gurfein, N.Y.C., 1976-77; assoc. Ropes & Gray, Boston, 1977-1985, ptnr., 1985—. Mem. ABA (Labor and Employment sect.), Mass. Bar Assn. (Labor and Employment sect.), Sudbury (Mass.) Pers. Bd. (chair 1988-94). Office: Ropes & Gray One International Pl Boston MA 02110

MANDEL, HERBERT MAURICE, civil engineer; b. Port Chester, N.Y., May 11, 1924; s. Arthur William and Rose (Schmeiser) M.; m. Charlotte Feldman, Aug. 22, 1954; children: Rosanne Mandel Levine, Elliott D., Arthur M. BSCE, Va. Poly. Inst., 1948, M Engring., Yale U., 1949. Registered profl. engr., N.Y., Conn., Fla., Md., Mich., Minn., Ohio, Pa., Va., W.Va. Structural engr. Madigan Hyland Co., Long Island City, N.Y., 1949-50; with firm Parsons, Brinckerhoff, Quade & Douglas, Inc., 1950-86; v.p. GAI Cons. Inc., 1986—, prin. staff cons., 1993—, project mgr., Atlanta, 1962, N.Y.C., 1963-70, Honolulu, 1970-74, v.p., 1974, sr. v.p., Pitts., 1977-86; faculty Yale U., 1948-49; adj. faculty Bklyn. Poly. Inst., 1956-64, U. Pitts., 1986; gen. chmn. 6th Internat. Bridge Conf., Pitts., 1989. Author tech. papers; prin. works include (prin.-in-charge) Williamstown-Marietta Bridge, W.Va.-Ohio, Dunbar Bridge, W.Va., I-64 Bridge over Big Sandy River, W.Va.-Kentucky, Davis Creek Bridge, Charleston, W.Va., Tygart R. Bridge, W.Va., Easley Bridge, Bluefield, W.Va., Fayette Sta. Bridge, Fayetteville, W.Va., Mon Valley Expwy., W.Va., (project mgr.) Newport Bridge, Narragansett Bay, R.I., (designer/project engr.) Hackensack River Bridge, N.J., Housatonic River Bridge, Conn., Arthur Kill Vertical Lift R.R. Bridge, S.I., N.Y., 62nd St. Bridge, Pitts., Savannah River Cantilever Bridge, Ga., I-84 Bridges, Danbury, Conn., (structural rehab designer) Avondale Bridge, N.J., Lincoln Bridge, N.J., B&O R.R. Bridge, Vincennes, Ind., Hawk St. Viaduct, Albany, N.Y., Congress Ave. Bridge, Austin, Tex., Ohio St. Bridge, Buffalo, Panhandle Bridge, Pitts.; project mgr. Interstate Rt. H-3, Honolulu, 1970-74; project dir. design and constrn. Pitts. Light Rail Transit System, 1977-84; designer Elizabeth R. Tunnel, Norfolk, Va., 1950. Served to 1st lt. U.S. Army, 1943-46, 50-52; ETO. Fellow ASCE, Soc. Am. Mil. Engrs. (pres. Pitts. post 1987-88); mem. Am. Ry. Engring. Assn. (steel structures specifications com., 1974—), Nat. Soc. Profl. Engrs., Profl. Engrs. in Pvt. Practice (bd. govs. 1994-96, profl. devel. coun. 1995—), Pa. Profl. Engrs. in Pvt. Practice (state vice-chmn. 1992-94, chmn. 1994-96), Pa. Soc. Profl. Engrs. (dir. Pitts. chpt. 1995—), Internat. Assn. Bridge and Structural Engring., Assn. for Bridge Constrn. and Design, Tau Beta Pi, Chi Epsilon, Omicron Delta Kappa, Phi Kappa Phi, Pi Delta Epsilon, Scabbard and Blade. Jewish. Club: Engineers (Pitts.). Home: 920 Parkview Dr Pittsburgh PA 15243-1116 Office: GAI Cons Inc 570 Beatty Rd Monroeville PA 15146-1334

MANDEL, IRWIN DANIEL, dentist; b. Bklyn., Apr. 9, 1922; s. Samuel A. and Shirley (Blankstein) M.; m. Charlotte Lifschutz, Apr. 1, 1944; children: Carol, Nora, Richard. BS, CCNY, 1942; DDS, Columbia U., 1945; DSc (hon.), U. Medicine and Dentistry of N.J., 1981; DOdont (hon.), U. Göteborg, 1984; DSc (hon.), Columbia U., 1996. Rsch. asst. Dental Sch. Columbia U., 1946-48, mem. faculty Dental Sch., 1946—, prof. dentistry, dir. div. preventive dentistry Dental Sch., 1969-84, dir. Ctr. Clin. Rsch. in Dentistry Dental Sch., 1984-91, assoc. dean rsch., 1991-92; prof. emeritus Dental Sch., 1992—; pvt. practice dentistry, 1946-68; vis. prof. various dental schs.; chmn. oral biology and medicine study sect. Nat. Inst. Dental Rsch., 1974-76. Co-author: The Plaque Diseases, 1972; contbr. over 250 articles to profl. publs., chpts. to books. Active local chpt. ACLU, Peace Action, Physicians for Social Responsibility. Lt. Dental Corps USNR, 1945-46, 52-54. Recipient Career Scientist award N.Y.C. Health Rsch. Council, 1969-72, Leadership award in periodontology Tufts U. Dental Sch., 1971, Internat. award U. Conn. Sch. Dental Medicine, 1979, ann. Seymour J. Kreshover NIDR lecture award, 1986. Fellow AAAS, Am. Coll. Dentists; mem. ADA (chmn. coun. dental rsch. 1978-80, Gold medal for excellence in rsch. 1985), Dental Soc. (Henry Spenadel award 1973, Jarvie-Burkhart Internat. award 1990), Am. Assn. Dental Rsch. (pres. 1980), Am. Assn. Pub. Health Dentists (Disting. Svc. award 1991), Fed. Dentair Internat. (W. D. Miller prize 1992), Internat. Assn. Dental Rsch. (Salivary Rsch. award 1994), N.Y. Acad. Scis., Sigma Xi, Omicron Kappa Upsilon. Home: 60 Pine Dr Cedar Grove NJ 07009-1036 Office: 630 W 168th St New York NY 10032-3702

MANDEL, JACK N., manufacturing company executive; b. Austria, July 16, 1911; s. Sam and Rose M.; m. Lilyan, Aug. 14, 1938. Student, Fenn Coll., 1930-33. Founder, now chmn. fin. com. Premier Indsl. Corp., Cleve. Mem. exec. com. NCCJ; trustee Wood Hosp., 1969—, Fla. Soc. for Blind; life trustee South Broward Jewish Fedn., Cleve. Jewish Welfare Fedn.; pres. Montefiore Home for Aged; pres. adv. bd. Barry U.; hon. trustee Hebrew U.; trustee Tel Aviv U. Mus. of the Diaspora; life trustee The Temple, Woodruff Found.; trustee Cleve. Play House. Mem. Emerald Hills Country Club, Beachmont Country Club, Commede Club. Office: Premier Indsl Corp 4500 Euclid Ave Cleveland OH 44103-3736

MANDEL, JOSEPH DAVID, university official, lawyer; b. N.Y.C., Mar. 26, 1940; s. Max and Charlotte Lee (Goodman) M.; m. Jean Carol Westerman, Aug. 18, 1963; children: Jonathan Scott, Eric David. AB, Dartmouth Coll., 1960, MBA, 1961; JD, Yale U., 1964. Bar: Calif. 1965. Law clk. U.S. Ct. Appeals, 9th crct., L.A., 1964-65; lectr. law U. So. Calif. Law Ctr., L.A., 1965-68; assoc. atty. Tuttle & Taylor, L.A., 1965-69, mem., 1970-82, 90-91, of counsel, 1984-90; vice chancellor UCLA, 1991—; lectr. UCLA Law Sch., 1993; v.p., gen. counsel, sec. Natomas Co., San Francisco, 1983; mem. Calif. Legal Corps, 1993—; bd. dirs. Legal Rsch. Network, Inc., 1993—. Pres. Legal Aid Found., L.A., 1978-79; trustee Southwestern U. Sch. Law, 1982, UCLA Pub. Interest Law Found., 1981-82, L.A. County Bar Found., 1974-79, 82, Coro Found., 1989-92, Armand Hammer Mus. Art and Cultural Ctr., 1995—, Geffen Playhouse, Inc., 1995—; trustee Coro Soc. Calif. Ctr., 1985-92, bd. dirs. pub. coun., 1989-94, cmty. v.p., 1992-94; mem. L.A. Bd. Zoning Appeals, 1984-90, vice chmn., 1985-86, 89-90, chmn., 1986-87; mem. L.A. City Charter Reform Commn., 1996—; bd. dirs. Western Justice Ctr. Found., 1989—, v.p., 1992-95, 1st v.p., 1995—; bd. dirs. Harvard Water Polo Found., 1990-96; bd. advisors Pub. Svc. Challenge Nat. Assn. for Pub. Interest Law, 1990—; bd. govs. Inner City Law Ctr., 1991—; mem. alumni coun. Dartmouth Coll., 1992-95. Recipient Maynard Toll award Legal Aid Found. of L.A., 1991, Shattuck-Price award L.A. County Bar Assn., 1993, West Coast Liberty award Lambda Legal Def. and Edn. Fund, 1994, Cmty. Achievement award Pub. Coun., 1996. Mem. State Bar Calif. (legal svcs. trust fund commn. 1985-87, chmn. 1985-86), Yale U. Law Sch. Assn. (exec. com. 1983-88, 90-96, v.p. 1986-88, chmn. planning com. 1990-92, pres. 1992-94, chmn. exec. com. 1994-96). Democrat. Jewish. Home: 15478 Longbow Dr Sherman Oaks CA 91403-4910 Office: UCLA Office of the Chancellor 2135 Murphy Hall Los Angeles CA 90095

MANDEL, LEONARD, physics and optics educator; m. Jeanne Elizabeth Kear, Aug. 20, 1953; children: Karen Rose, Barry Paul. B.Sc., U. London, Eng., 1947, U. London, Eng., 1948; Ph.D., U. London, Eng., 1951. Tech. officer Imperial Chem. Industries, 1951-54; lectr., sr. lectr. Imperial Coll., U. London, 1954-64; prof. physics U. Rochester, N.Y., 1964—, prof. optics, 1977-80, Lee Du Bridge prof. physics and optics, 1994—; joint sec. Rochester Confs. on Coherence and Quantum Optics, 1966, 72, 77, 83, 89,, 1995; vis. prof. U. Tex., Austin, 1984; vis. scientist Am. Inst. Physics; Internat. Commn. Optics traveling lectr., 1992. Editor books; co-author: (with E. Wolf) Optical Coherence and Quantum Optics; contbr. more than 290 articles to profl. jours.. Recipient Marconi medal Italian Nat. Rsch. Coun., 1987, Thomas Young medal Inst. Physics Gt. Britain, 1989, 1st recipient Max Born medal, 1982, Ives medal, 1993. Fellow AAAS, Am. Phys. Soc., Am. Acad. Arts and Scis., Optical Soc. Am. (bd. dirs. 1985-87, assoc. editor jour. 1970-76, 82-84, Optics Letters 1977-79, bd. editors Phys Rev. 1987-89, Jour. Quantum Optics 1989-93, chmn. com. for society objectives and policy 1977, Wood prize com. 1988, Max Bon medal com. 1994). Office: U Rochester Dept Physics Astronomy Rochester NY 14627

MANDEL, LEWIS RICHARD, pharmaceutical company executive; b. Bklyn., Nov. 13, 1936; s. Murray and Belle (Teller) M.; m. Rochelle Holtzman, Mar. 27, 1960; children: Beth, Susan, Stefanie. BS, Columbia U., 1958, PhD, 1962. Registered pharmacist, N.Y., N.J., Pa. Lectr. in biochemistry, then asst. prof. pharmacology Columbia U., N.Y.C., 1961-64; rsch. biochemist Merck & Co., Inc., Rahway, N.J., 1964-76, dir. biochemistry, 1976-79, sr. dir. univ. and indsl. rels., 1979-89, exec. dir. indsl. and acad. rels., 1989—, exec. dir. external sci. affairs worldwide, 1993. Patentee in field; contbr. articles to profl. publs. Grantee NIH, 1963-64; recipient Wellcome travel award Burroughs Wellcome, 1963. Mem. Am. Soc. Pharmacology and Exptl. Therapeutics, Am. Soc. Biochemistry and Molecular Biology. Office: Merck and Co Inc PO Box 2000 Rahway NJ 07065-0900

MANDEL, MORTON, molecular biologist; b. Bklyn., July 6, 1924; s. Barnet and Rose (Kliner) M.; m. Florence H. Goodman, Apr. 1, 1952; children: Robert, Leslie. BCE, CUNY, 1944; MS, Columbia U., 1949, PhD in Physics, 1957. Scientist Bell Telephone Labs., Murray Hill, N.J., 1956-57; asst. prof. physics dept. Stanford (Calif.) U., 1957-61; scientist Gen. Telephone & Telegraph, Mountain View, Calif., 1961-63; rsch. assoc. dept. genetics Stanford U., 1963-64; rsch. fellow Karolinska Inst., Stockholm, Sweden, 1964-66; assoc. prof. sch. of medicine U. Hawaii, Honolulu, 1966-68, prof., 1968—; founder, dir. Hawaii Biotechnology Group, Inc., 1982-95; cons. Fairchild Semiconductor, Hewlett Packard, Lockheed, Rheem, Palo Alto, Calif., 1957-61. Contbr. articles to profl. jours. Lt. (j.g.) USN, 1944-46. Recipient Am. Cancer Soc. Scholar award Am. Cancer Soc., 1979-80, Eleanor Roosevelt Internat. Cancer fellowship, 1979; named NIH Spl. fellow Karolinska Inst., 1964-66. Fellow Am. Phys. Soc.; mem. Sigma Xi. Achievements include citation classics; optimal conditions for mutagenesis by N-methyl-N-nitro-N-nitrosoguanidine in E. coli K12; calcium dependent bacteriophage DNA infection. Office: Dept of Biochemistry 1960 E West Rd Honolulu HI 96822-2319

MANDEL, OSCAR, literature educator, writer; b. Antwerp, Belgium, Aug. 24, 1926; came to U.S., 1940; m. adrienne Schizzano. BA, NYU, 1947; MA, Columbia U., 1948; PhD, Ohio State U., 1951. Asst. prof. English U. Nebr., 1955-60; Fulbright lectr. U. Amsterdam, 1960-61; vis. assoc. prof. English Calif. Inst. Tech., 1961-62, assoc. prof. English, 1962-68, prof. Lit., 1968—. Author: A Definition of Tragedy, 1961, The Theater of Don Juan, 1963, Seven Comedies by Marivaux, 1968, The Collected Plays, 1970-72, Ariadne, 1982, Collected Lyrics and Epigrams, 1981, Three Classic Don Juan Plays, 1981, Philoctetes and the Fall of Troy, 1981, Annotations to Vanity Fair, 1981, The Book of Elaborations, 1985, The Kukkurrik Fables, 1987, Sigismund, Prince of Poland, 1989, August von Kotzebue: The Comedy, The Man, 1990, The Virgin and the Unicorn: Four Plays, 1993, The Art of Alessandro Magnasco: An Essay on the Recovery of Meaning, 1994, The Cheerfulness of Dutch Art: A Rescue Operation, 1996, Two Romantic Plays: The Spaniards in Denmark and The Rebels of Nantucket, 1996, Fundamentals of the Art of Poetry, 1997; contbr. articles to profl. jours. Office: Calif Inst Tech Humanities Divsn Pasadena CA 91125

MANDELBAUM, HOWARD ARNOLD, marketing and management consultant; b. Newark, May 17, 1941; s. Morris and Minna (Eisenberg) M.; m. Susan Ganz, June 9, 1963; children: Joel Barry, Sari Beth, Matthew Gary. BS in Indsl. Engring., Lafayette Coll., 1963; MS in Mgmt., MIT, 1965. Advt. rsch. mgr. Hoffmann-La Roche Inc., Nutley, N.J., 1965-68; mgr. mktg. rsch. USV Pharms., N.Y.C., 1968-69; product mgr. Warner-Chilcott, Morris Plains, N.J., 1969-71; v.p. Mabico Automotive Warehouse, Maplewood, N.J., 1972; exec. v.p. William Douglas McAdams Inc., N.Y.C., 1973-93; pres. Mng. Dynamics, Inc., Livingston, N.J., 1994—. Trustee Temple Beth Shalom, Livingston, N.J., 1984-91. Mem. Healthcare Mktg. and Comms. Coun. Office: Mng Dynamics Inc 50 Tremont Ter Livingston NJ 07039-3340

MANDELBAUM, SAMUEL ROBERT, lawyer; b. N.Y.C., June 9, 1951; s. Alvin J. and Florence (Geller) M.; m. Erica Gottfried Mandelbaum, Sept. 27, 1980; children: Lia, Ben. BA, SUNY, 1973; student, Columbia U., 1974-75; JD, Vermont Law Sch., 1977; LLM, Georgetown U., 1995. Bar: Fla. 1979, N.Y. 1985, U.S. Dist. Ct. (mid. dist.) 1979, U.S. Dist. Ct. (so. dist.) 1983, U.S. Ct. Appeals (11th cir.) 1981, U.S. Ct. Appeals (4th cir.) 1984, U.S. Supreme Ct. 1982. Sr. asst. atty. gen. Atty. Gen's. Office, Tampa, Fla., 1981-82; ptnr. Anderson & Orcutt, P.A., Tampa, Fla., 1996—; adj. prof. law Stetson U. Coll. of Law, De Land, Fla., 1995—; editor, trial section Fla. Bar Jour., Tallahassee, 1988—. Fund distbr. com. mem. United Way, Tampa, Fla., 1991—. Recipient Outstanding Svc. to Ct. Arbitration Program award U.S. Dist. Ct. Fla., Tampa, 1991. Mem. Fla. Bar Assn. (exec. coun. internat. sect.), Hillsborough County Bar Assn. (chmn. internat. sect.), Davis Island Yacht Club, Rotary Club. Avocations: sailing, golf, jogging, photography. Office: Anderson & Orcutt PA 401 E Jackson St Fl 24 Tampa FL 33602

MANDELBROT, BENOIT B., mathematician, scientist, educator; b. Warsaw, Poland, Nov. 20, 1924; came to U.S., 1958; s. Charles and Belle (Lurie) M.; m. Aliette Kagan, Nov. 5, 1955; children: Laurent, Didier. Diploma, Ecole Polytechnique, Paris, 1947; MS in Aeronautics, Calif. Inst. Tech., 1948; PhD in Math., U. Paris, 1952; DSc (hon.), Syracuse U., 1986, Syracuse U., 1985, Laurentian U., 1986, Boston U., 1987, SUNY, 1988, U. Bremen, 1988, U. Guelph, Ont., Can., 1989, U. Dallas, 1992, Union Coll., 1993, U. Buenos Aires, 1993, U. Tel Aviv, 1995; DHL (hon.), Pace U., 1989. Jr. mem. and Rockefeller scholar Inst. for Advanced Study, Princeton, N.J., 1953-54; jr. prof. math. U. Geneva, 1955-57, U. Lille and Ecole Polytechnique, Paris, 1957-58; rsch. staff mem. IBM Watson Rsch. Ctr., Yorktown Heights, N.Y., 1958-74, IBM fellow, 1974-93, IBM fellow emeritus, 1993—; prof. math. scis. Yale U., New Haven, 1987—; prof. Acad. des Scis., Paris, 1995; vis. prof. econs. Harvard U., 1962-63, vis. prof. applied math., 1963-64, vis. prof. math., 1979-80, prof. practice math., 1984-87; vis. prof. engring. Yale U., 1970; vis. prof. physiology Einstein Coll. Medicine, 1970; Hitchcock prof. U. Calif., Berkeley, 1992; visitor MIT, 1953, also Inst. lectr.; visitor U. Paris, 1966, Coll. de France, Paris, 1973, Inst. des Hautes Etudes Scientifiques, Bures, 1980, Mittag-Leffler Inst., Sweden, 1984, Max Planck Inst. Math., Bonn, Germany, 1988; lectr. Yale U., 1970, Cambridge U., 1990, Oxford U., 1990, Imperial Coll., London, 1991, Accademia di Lincei, Rome, Math. Centrum, Amsterdam, The Netherlands, U. Barcelona, Spain, U. Uppsala, Sweden; spkr. and organizer profl. confs. Author: Logique, Langage et Théorie de l'Information, 1957, Les Objets Fractals: Forme, Hasard et Dimension, 1975, 4th edit., 1995, Fractals: Form, Chance and Dimension, 1977, The Fractal Geometry of Nature, 1982, La Geometria della Natura, 1987, Fractals and Scaling in Finance: Discontinuity and Concentration, Risk, 1997; contbr. articles to profl. jours. Recipient Franklin medal Franklin Inst., 1986, Alexander von Humboldt Preis, 1987, Caltech disting. svc. award, 1988, Moet-Hennessy prize, 1988, Harvey prize, 1989, Nev. prize U. Nev. Sys., 1991, Wolf prize for physics, 1993, Honda prize, 1994, Medal of City of Paris, 1996; nat. lectr. Sigma Xi, 1980-82; Guggenheim fellow, 1968. Fellow AAAS, IEEE (Charles Proteus Steinmetz medal 1988), Am. Acad. Arts and Scis., European Acad. Arts, Scis. and Humanities, Am. Phys. Soc., Inst. Math. Stats., Econometric Soc., Am. Geophys. Union, Am. Statistic Assn.; mem. NAS U.S.A. (fgn. assoc., Barnard medal 1985), Internat. Statis. Inst. (elected), Am. Math. Soc., French Math. Soc. Achievements include orgination of theory of fractals, an interdisciplinary enterprise concerned with financial data, mountains, clouds, attroctors, and all other shapes and phenomena that are equally rough, irregular or broken-up at all scales. Office: IBM PO Box 218 Yorktown Heights NY 10598-0218 also: Yale Univ Math Dept New Haven CT 06520-8283 *Science would be ruined if (like the Olympics) it were to put competition above everything else, and if it were to clarify the rules of competition by withdrawing entirely into narrowly defined specialties. The rare scholars who are wanderers-by-choice are essential to the intellectual welfare of the settled disciplines.*

MANDELKER, DANIEL ROBERT, law educator; b. Milw., July 18, 1926; s. Adolph Irwin and Marie (Manner) M.; divorced; children: Amy Jo, John David. BA, U. Wis., 1947, LLB, 1949; JD, Yale U., 1956. Bar: Wis. 1949. Asst. prof. law Drake U., 1949-51; atty. HHFA, Washington, 1952-53; asst. prof., then assoc. prof. law Ind. U., 1953-62; mem. faculty Washington U., St. Louis, 1962—; prof. law Washington U., 1963-74, Howard A. Stamper prof. law, 1974—; Walter E. Meyer rsch. prof. law Columbia U., 1971-72; Ford Found. law faculty fellow, London, 1959-60; cons. State of Hawaii Dept. Planning and Econ. Devel., 1972-78, State of Hawaii Office of State Planning, 1993-94; legal resources adv. group Transp. Rsch. Bd., 1991-94; mem. local govt. adv. bd. intergovtl. rels. U.S. Adv. Commn., 1985-88; mem. devel. regulations coun. Urban Land Inst., 1980-96; cons. housing subcom., banking and currency com. U.S. Ho. of Reps., 1970-71, cons. policy studies, ins. subcom., banking, fin., urban affairs coms., 1989-91; cons. state and local govts. on land use regulation; Nat. Disting. lectr. Fla. State Jour. Land Use and Environ. Law, 1992; 15th Denman lectr. U. Cambridge, Eng., 1992, Inaugural Robert E. Boden lectr. Marquette U. Sch. Law, 1997. Author: Green Belts and Urban Growth: English Town and Country Planning in Action, 1962, Controlling Planned Residential Developments, 1966, Managing Our Urban Environment-Cases, Text and Problems, 1966, 2d edit., 1971, Case Studies in Land Planning and Development, 1968, The Zoning Dilemma, 1971, (with W.R. Ewald) Street Graphics and the Law, 1971, 2d edit., 1988, (with R. Montgomery) Housing in America: Problems and Perspectives, 1973, 2d edit., 1979, Housing Subsidies in the United States and England, 1973, New Developments in Land and Environmental Controls, 1974, Environmental and Land Controls Legislation, 1976, supplement, 1982, (with D. Netsch) State and Local Government in a Federal System, 1977, supplement, 1981, (with D. Netsch and P. Salsich) 2d edit., 1983, supplement, 1987, (with Netsch, Salsich and Wegner) 3rd edit., 1990, supplement, 1992, (with R. Cunningham) Planning and Control of Land Development, 1979, 3d edit., 1990, (with R. Cunningham and J. Payne) 4th edit., 1995, Environment and Equity, 1981, (with others) Cases and Materials on Housing and Urban Development, 1981, 2d edit., 1989, Land Use Law, 1982, 3d edit., 1993, supplement, 1996, (with F. Anderson and D. Tarlock) Environmental Protection Law and Policy, 2d edit., 1990, NEPA Law and Litigation, 2d edit., 1992, supplement, 1997, (with J. Gerard and T. Sullivan) Federal Land Use Law, 1986, supplement, 1997; mem. editl. adv. bd. various land use jours. Mem. nat. adv. com. on outdoor advt. and motorist info. Dept. Transp., 1980-81; mem. adv. com. on housing Dem. Caucus, U.S. Ho. of Reps., 1981-82; pres. Nat. Coalition for Scenic Beauty, 1987-88; sr. fellow Urban Land Inst., 1989-95; mem. law sch. editl. bd. Michie Co., 1989—. Mem. NAS (com. social and behavioral urban rsch. 1967-68), Am. Planning Assn. (bd. dirs. 1981-84, Housing Policy Task Force 1990-93, property rights task force 1994-95, amicus curiae com. 1995—), Order of Coif, Phi Beta Kappa, Phi Kappa Phi. Office: Washington U Sch Law Campus Box 1120 Saint Louis MO 63130

MANDELKER, LESTER, veterinarian; b. Memphis, July 31, 1945; s. Maurice and Alice (Herman) M.; m. Brenda Conger, Oct. 21, 1989; children: Zev and Blakelee (twins). BS, Mich. State U., 1968, DVM, 1969. Diplomate Am. Bd. Vet. Practitioners. Assoc. veterinarian Yarbrough Animal Hosp., Miami, Fla., 1969-71, Gulf Bay Animal Hosp., Clearwater, Fla., 1971-72; owner, dir. Cmty. Vet. Hosp., Largo, Fla., 1972—; mem. Am. Bd. Vet. Practitioners; mem. adv. bd. Vet. Forum, N.Y.C., 1980—, Vetoquinol USA, Inc., Tampa, Fla., 1996—; computer specialist, pharmacology moderator Network of Animal Health, Chgo., 1995—; pharmacology cons. Vet. Info. Network. Author: Veterinary Practice Tips I, 1980, II, 1985, Pharmaceutical Index, 1994. Founder, past pres. Class Inc., Clearwater, 1973-80. Mem. AVMA, Am. Animal Hosp. Assn., Pinellas County Vet. Med. Soc. (past pres.). Jewish. Avocations: tennis, cooking, dancing, computers. Office: Cmty Vet Hosp 1631 W Bay Dr Largo FL 33770-3001

MANDELKERN, LEO, biophysics and chemistry educator; b. N.Y.C., Feb. 23, 1922; s. Israel and Gussie (Krostich) M.; m. Berdie Medvedoff, May, 1946; children: I. Paul, Marshal, David. BA, Cornell U., 1942, PhD, 1949. Postdoctoral rsch. assoc. Cornell U., Ithaca, N.Y., 1949-52; phys. chemist Nat. Bur. Standards, Washington, 1952-62; prof. chemistry and biophysics Fla. State U., Tallahassee, 1962—, R.O. Lawton Disting. prof., 1984—; vis. prof. U. Miami (Fla.) Med. Sch., 1963, U. Calif. Med. Sch., San Francisco,

1964, Cornell U., 1967; mem. biophysics fellowship com. NIH, 1967-70; mem. study panel crystal growth and morphology NRC, 1960; cons. in field. Author: Crystallization of Polymers, 1964, An Introduction to Macromolecules, 1972, 1983; contbr. numerous articles to profl. jours. 1st lt. USAAF, 1942-46, PTO. Recipient Meritorious Svc. award U.S. Dept. Commerce, 1957, Arthur S. Fleming award Washington Jaycees, 1958, Mettler award N.Am. Thermal Analysis Soc., Phila., 1984, Disting. Svc. in Advancement of Polymer Sci. award Soc. Polymer Sci., Japan, 1993. Mem. AAAS, N.Y. Acad. Scis., Am. Inst. Chemists, Am. Chem. Soc. (Polymer Chemistry award 1975, Fla. award 1984, Rubber divsn. Whitby award 1988, Charles Goodyear medal 1993, Applied Polymer Sci. award 1989, Disting. Svc. in Advancement of Polymer Sci. 1993, Polymer Divsn. P.J. Flory award 1994, Polymer Materials Sci. & Engring. Divsn. Coop. Rsch. award 1995), Polymer Soc. Japan, Biophys. Soc., Am. Phys. Soc. (Outstanding Educator of Am. 1973, 75), Cosmos Club Washington, Alpha Epsilon Pi. Home: 1503 Old Ft Dr Tallahassee FL 32301-5637 Office: Fla State U Dept Chemistry Tallahassee FL 32306

MANDELL, ARLENE LINDA, writing and communications educator; b. Bklyn., Feb. 19, 1941; d. George and Esther Kostick; m. Lawrence W. Mandell, May 23, 1982; children by previous marriage: Bruce R. Rosenblum, Tracey B. Grimaldi. BA magna cum laude, William Paterson Coll., 1973; MA Columbia U., 1989. Newspaper reporter Suburban Trends, Riverdale, N.J., 1972-73; writer Good Housekeeping mag., N.Y.C., 1976-78; account exec. Carl Byoir & Assocs., N.Y.C., 1978-86; v.p. Porter/Novelli, N.Y.C., 1986-88; adj. prof. composition, lit., poetry, women's studies William Paterson Coll., Wayne, N.J., 1989—. Contbr. articles to profl. jours. and newspapers, poetry to N.Y. Times and poetry jours. Recipient 1st place women's interest writing N.J. Press Assn., 1973; named John W. Stahr Writer of Yr., Carl Byoir & Assocs., N.Y.C., 1981. Mem. N.J. Coll. English Assn.

MANDELL, GERALD LEE, physician, medicine educator; b. N.Y.C., Aug. 20, 1936; s. Herman and Sylvia (Keller) M.; m. Judith Rensin Mandell, Dec. 22, 1960; children: James, Pamela, Scott. BA, Cornell U., 1958; MD, Cornell U., N.Y.C., 1962. Diplomate Am. Bd. Internal Medicine. Intern, resident N.Y. Hosp. Cornell Med. Ctr., N.Y.C., 1965-67; instr. Med. Coll., Cornell U., N.Y.C., 1968-69; asst. prof. U. Va., Charlottesville, 1969-71, assoc. prof., 1972-75, prof., 1976—, Owen R. Cheatham prof. sci., 1981—, head infectious diseases, 1970—. Editor: Principles and Practice of Infectious Diseases, 1979, 4th edit., 1995. Lt. comdr. USPHS, 1963-65. Recipient MERIT award NIH, 1986. Master ACP; mem. Assn. Am. Physicians, Am. Soc. Clin. Investigation, Phi Beta Kappa, Alpha Omega Alpha. Jewish. Avocations: photography, tropical fish, sculling. Office: U Va Med Ctr Box 385 Charlottesville VA 22908-0385

MANDELL, MARSHALL, physician, allergist, consultant; b. N.Y.C., Feb. 4, 1922; s. Albert and Beatrice (Roth) M.; m. Thelma Sylvia Cantor, Aug. 1, 1944 (div. 1974); children: Joan Arlene, Steven Marshall, Nori Lyn; m. Sandra Jane Bodnar, Dec. 6, 1988. BA in Zoology, U. Conn., 1943; MD, L.I. Coll. Medicine, 1946. Diplomate Am. Bd. Pediats., Am. Bd. Allergy, Am. Bd. Allergy and Immunology. Intern in pediats. Yale U. Med. Sch./New Haven Hosp., 1946; jr. resident in pediats. St. Louis Children's Hosp./Washington U., 1946-49; resident in pediats. Gen. Hosps. #1 and #2, Kansas City, Mo., 1950; instr., clin. asst. N.Y. Med. Coll., 1955-58, asst. prof. allergy, 1958-80; adj. prof. nutrition and allergy U. Bridgeport, Conn., 1976-90; cons. in allergy and clin. ecology in mental illness Fuller Meml. Sanitarium, South Attleboro, Mass., 1972-76. Author: 5-Day Allergy Relief, 1979, Lifetime Arthritis Relief, It's Not Your Fault You're Fat Diet; editor: Let's Have Healthy Children; contbr. more than 30 articles to profl. jours. Capt. U.S. Army, 1942-49. Recipient Huxley Soc. Founders medal. Fellow Am. Coll. Allergy, Asthma, and Immunology, Am. Acad. Environ. Medicine (Jonathan Formam gold medal), Acad. Orthomolecular Medicine (Spl. Commendation for Contbns. to Mental Illness), Internat. Acad. Nutrition and Preventive Medicine; mem. Lions (pres. Norwalk club 1956-58), Phi Sigma Delta (pres. 1941-43). Avocations: writing, computers, wood carving, gardening, swimming. Home and Office: 6721 Oakmont Way Bradenton FL 34202-1702

MANDELSTAM, CHARLES LAWRENCE, lawyer; b. Brookline, Mass., July 6, 1927; s. Felix and Sarah (Odence) M.; m. Gloria Messinger, June 2, 1957; children: Emily F., Peter D. BA, Harvard Coll., 1949; LLB, Yale U., 1952. Bar: Conn. 1952, N.Y. 1953, D.C. 1953. Mem. staff office of gen. counsel Internat. Ladies' Garment Workers Union, N.Y.C., 1952-56; assoc. Kaye, Scholer, Fierman, Hays & Handler, N.Y.C., 1956-60; ptnr. Dornbush Mensch Mandelstam & Schaeffer, LLP, N.Y.C., 1968—; bd. dirs. Société d' Exploitation Agricole Rhodanienne, Ampuis, France; counsel North Salem (N.Y.) Open Land Found., 1975—. Comment editor Yale Law Jour., 1951-52; contbr. articles to Yale Law Jour., 1951, 52;. Bd. dirs. Samuel Rubin Found., 1975—, N.Y.C. Sch. Vol. Program, 1991—. With U.S. Army, 1945-46. Mem. Assn. of the Bar City of N.Y., Phi Beta Kappa. Home: 27 W 86th St New York NY 10024-3615 Office: 747 3rd Ave New York NY 10017-2803

MANDELSTAM, STANLEY, physicist; b. Johannesburg, South Africa, Dec. 12, 1928; came to U.S., 1963; s. Boris and Beatrice (Liknaitzky) M. BSc, U. Witwatersrand, Johannesburg, 1952; BA, Cambridge U., Eng., 1954; PhD, Birmingham U., Eng., 1956. Boese postdoctoral fellow Columbia U., N.Y.C., 1957-58; prof. math. physics U. Birmingham, 1960-63; asst. rsch. physicist U. Calif., Berkeley, 1958-60, prof. physics, 1963-94; prof. emertitus U. Calif., 1994—; vis. prof. physics Harvard U., Cambridge, Mass., 1965-66, Univ. de Paris, Paris Sud, 1979-80, 84-85. Editorial bd. The Phys. Rev. jour., 1978-81, 85-88; contbr. articles to profl. jours. Recipient Dirac medal and prize Internat. Ctr. for Theoretical Physics, 1991. Fellow AAAS, Royal Soc. London, Am. Phys. Soc. (Dannie N. Heineman Math. Physics prize 1992). Jewish. Office: Univ of Calif Dept Of Physics Berkeley CA 94720

MANDELSTAMM, JEROME ROBERT, lawyer; b. St. Louis, Apr. 3, 1932; s. Henry and Estelle (London) M.; stepchildren: Amy E., John M. Gagliardi, Maria A. Amundson. A.B., U. Pa., 1954; LL.B., Harvard U., 1957. Bar: Mo. 1957. Since practiced in St. Louis; partner Greenfield, Davidson, Mandelstamm & Voorhees, 1969-81, Schmitz, Mandelstamm, Hawker & Fischer, 1981-82; sole practice, 1982—; bd. dirs. Legal Aid Soc. City and County St. Louis, 1967-75, pres., 1969-70; bd. dirs. Lawyers Reference Service Met. St. Louis, 1976-83, chmn., 1978-83; bd. dirs. Mo. Legal Aid Soc., 1977-82; mem. 22d Jud. Cir. Bar Com., 1983-85, gen. chmn., 1984-85. Mem. St. Louis County Bd. Election Commrs., 1973-77. Served with AUS, 1957. Mem. ABA, Mo. Bar Assn., Am. Arbitration Assn. (panel of arbitrators 1984—), Bar Assn. Met. St. Louis (v.p. 1974-75, treas. 1975-76). Home: 4525 Laclede Ave # 3 Saint Louis MO 63108-2117 Office: 1010 Market St Ste 1600 Saint Louis MO 63101-2000

MANDELSTEIN, PAUL STANLEY, book publishing executive; b. Bklyn., May 18, 1946; s. Max and Esther (Friedman) M.; m. Cornelia S. Pratt, Feb. 21, 1973 (div. June 1993); children: Zachary, Naomi, Nicolas. Student, Bklyn. Coll., 1965. Pres. Quantum Pub., Mill Valley, Calif., 1984—, The Book Pub. Co., Summertown, Tenn.; mktg. cons. Farm Foods, Summertown, Tenn., 1975—, Solar Electronics, Summertown, 1976—, Shambhala Pubs., 1994—; bus. cons. Audio Scholar, Mendocino, Calif., 1991. Author: The Nightingale and the Wind, 1993, The Lute Player, 1994, The Divorced Father's Survival Guide, 1996. Avocations: tennis, mythology, mythopoetics, basketball, music. Home: 1204 El Cide Ct Mill Valley CA 94941-3401 Office: 65 Main St Saint Johnsbury VT 05819-2204

MANDERS, KARL LEE, neurosurgeon; b. Rochester, N.Y., Jan. 21, 1927; s. David Bert and Frances Edna (Cohan) Mendelson; m. Ann Laprell, July 28, 1969; children: Karlanna, Maidena; children by previous marriage; Karl, Kerry, Kristine. Student, Cornell U., 1946; MD, U. Buffalo, 1950. Diplomate Am. Bd. Neurol. Surgery, Am. Bd. Clin. Biofeedback, Am. Bd. Hyperbaric Medicine, Am. Bd. Pain Medicine, Nat. Bd. Med. Examiners. Intern U. Va. Hosp., Charlottesville, 1950-51, resident in neurol. surgery, 1951-52; resident in neurol. surgery Henry Ford Hosp., Detroit, 1954-56; pvt. practice Indpls., 1956—; med. dir. Cmty. Hosp. Rehab. Ctr. for Pain, 1973—; chief hosp. med. and surg. neurology Cmty. Hosp., 1983, 93; coroner Marion County, Ind., 1977-85, 92-96. Served with USN, 1952-54, Korea. Recipient cert. achievement Dept. Army, 1969. Fellow ACS, Internat. Coll Surgeons, Am. Acad. Neurology; mem. Am. Assn. Neurol. Surgery, Congress Neurol. Surgery, Internat. Assn. Study of Pain, Am. Assn. Study of Headache, N.Y. Acad. Sci., Am. Coll. Angiology, Am. Soc. Contemporary Medicine and Surgery, Am. Holistic Med. Assn. (co-founder), Undersea Med. Soc., Am. Acad. Forensic Sci., Am. Assn. Biofeedback Clinicians, Soc. Cryosurgery, Pan Pacific Surg. Assn., Biofeedback Soc. Am., Acad. Psychosomatic Medicine, Pan Am. Med. Assn., Internat. Back Pain Soc., North Am. Spine Soc., Am. Soc. Stereotaxic and Functional Neurosurgery, Soc. for Computerized Tomography and Neuroimaging, Ind. Coroners Assn. (pres. 1979), Royal Soc. Medicine, Nat. Assn. Med. Examiners, Am. Pain Soc., Midwest Pain Soc. (pres. 1988), Am. Acad. Pain Medicine, Cen. Neurol. Soc., Interurban Neurosurg. Soc., Internat. Soc. Aquatic Medicine, James A. Gibson Anat. Soc., Am. Bd. Med. Psychotherapists (mem. profl. adv. council), James McClure Surg. Soc., Brendonwood Country Club, Highland Country Club. Home: 5845 High Fall Rd Indianapolis IN 46226-1017 Office: 7209 N Shadeland Ave Indianapolis IN 46250-2021

MANDERS, SUSAN KAY, artist; b. Burbank, Calif., Dec. 29, 1948; d. Gus H. and Erika (Stadelbauer) M.; m. Allan D. Yasnyi, Dec. 18, 1992; children: Brian Mallut. Attended, U. Guadalajara, 1969; BA, Calif. State U., 1971; postgrad., Otis Parsons, L.A., 1985, Royal Coll. of the Arts, London, 1987; grad., Silicon Digital Arts. Owner, dir., tchr. The Art Experience Sch. and Gallery, Studio City, Calif., 1978—; cons. in field. One-woman shows include La Logia, Studio City, Calif., 1991, Il Mito, Studio City, 1991, Bamboo, Sherman Oaks, Calif., 1991—, L.A. Art Installations, 1990, 92, Fed. Bldg., L.A., 1993, Art Experience, Studio City, 1993, Emerson's Gallery, Sherman Oaks, 1994, Raphael's, Beverly Hills, Calif., 1994; group shows include Beverly Hills Affair in the Gardens, 1984, 94, Otis Parsons, L.A., 1987, Hilderbrand Galleries, New Orleans, 1993, Studio City Art Festival, 1994, Parents Found., New Haven, Conn., 1994, Project Studio 8, San Francisco, 1994, Bistango Studio-Gallery, Irvine, Calif., 1994—, Montserrat Gallery, N.Y.C., 1995, Annenberg Ctr., U. So. Calif., 1997—; creator, publ. prints Iron Jane Collections, 1994, Children's Hosp. Docent UCLA; active Tuesday's Child, Pillars of Hope Project San Fernando Valley County Fair, 1995. Mem. L.A. Art Assn., Beverley Hills Art Assn., Nat. Mus. Women in the Arts, L.A. County Mus. of Art, Dada, L.A., Mus. Contemporary Art Coun., Women in Animation. Office: The Art Experience 11830 Ventura Blvd Studio City CA 91604-2617

MANDERSCHEID, LESTER VINCENT, agricultural economics educator; b. Andrew, Iowa, Oct. 9, 1930; s. Vincent John and Alma (Sprank) M.; m. Dorothy Helen Varnum, Aug. 29, 1953; children: David, Paul, Laura, Jane. BS, Iowa State U., 1951, MS, 1952; PhD, Stanford U., 1961. Grad. asst. Iowa State U., Ames, 1951-52, Stanford (Calif.) U., 1952-56; asst. prof. Mich. State U., East Lansing, 1956-65, assoc. prof., 1965-70, prof., 1970-73, prof., assoc. chmn., 1973-87, prof., chmn., 1987-92, prof., 1992-95, prof. emeritus, 1996—, coord. Grad. Sch., 1993; reviewer Tex. A&M Agrl. Econ. Program, College Station, 1989; con. Consortium Internat. Earth Sci. Info. Network, Ann Arbor, 1990. Co-author: Improving Undergraduate Education, 1967; contbr. articles to jours. in field. Pres. parish coun. St. Thomas, East Lansing, 1984-87; coll. coord. United Way, East Lansing, 1983-84. Recipient Disting. Faculty award Mich. State U., 1977. Mem. Am. Agrl. Econ. Assn. (pres. 1988-89, bd. dirs. 1982-85, excellence in teaching award 1974), Am. Statis. Assn., Am. Evaluation Assn., Am. Econ. Assn., University Club, Sigma Xi (pres. 1986-87), Phi Kappa Phi (pres. 1979-80). Roman Catholic. Home: 2372 Burcham Dr East Lansing MI 48823-3885 Office: Mich State U Dept of Agrl Econs Circle Dr East Lansing MI 48824-1039

MANDERY, MATHEW M., principal. BS, Bklyn. Coll., 1965, MA, 1971; EdD, Fordham U., 1990; LHD (hon.), Adelphi U., 1997. Asst. prin. supr. math. Midwood H.S., Bklyn.; prin. Newtown H.S., Bklyn. Tech. H.S., Jericho (N.Y.) High Sch., 1987—. Author: Achieving Competence in Mathematics, 1987, Achieving Proficiency in Mathematics, 1994. Recipient Blue Ribbon Sch. award U. S. Dept. Edn., 1990-91; named N.Y. State Prin. of Yr., 1992-93, Educator of Yr. Assn. Tchrs. N.Y.C., 1985; Danforth fellow; recipient Disting. Svc. award for Contbns. to Math. Edn., 1984, Cert. of Honor Westinghouse Sci. Talent Search, Disting. Alumnus award Bklyn. Tech. H.S. Alumni Assn., 1993; Alumni Achievement award Fordham U., 1997. Mem. Nassau County Secondary Sch. Adminstrs. Assn. (pres.), Headmasters Assn., Phi Delta Kappa (past pres. St. John's U. chpt., Educator of Yr., 1995). Office: Jericho High Sch Cedar Swamp Rd Jericho NY 11753

MANDEVILLE, CRAIG H., aircraft company executive, retired military officer; b. Chickasha, Okla., Sept. 22, 1940. BA, Okla. State U., 1963. Commd. 2d lt. U.S. Army, 1963, advanced through grades to lt. col., 1979; battery comdr. Battery A 2d Battalion 320th Field Artillery, 101st AIrborne Divsn. U.S. Army, Vietnam, 1967-68, dep. regimental advisor 15th Inf. Regiment, 9th ARVN Divsn., 1971-72; staff officer, dep. chief of staff ops. and plans, requirements directorate Hdqrs. DA U.S. Army, Washington, 1978-82; battalion comdr. 1st Battalion (LANCE) 12th Field Artillery U.S. Army, Ft. Sill, Okla., 1982-83; ret. U.S. Army, 1983; mgr. C-17 program devel. Douglas Aircraft Co.-McDonnell Douglas Corp., Long Beach, Calif., 1983-89, bus. unit mgr. C-17 program devel., 1989-91, acting gen. mgr. C-17 program exts., 1991, now exec. asst. to C-17 sr. v.p., program mgr. Founder, dir. L.A. Rams Pro-Am Celebrity Tennis Tournament; assisted clubs with tennis clinics, tournaments; instr. tennis. Decorated Silver Star (2), Bronze Star (3), Legion of Merit, Purple Heart (3), Combat Infantryman's Badge, Parachute Badge, others. Mem. U.S. Tennis Assn. Avocations: running, aerobics, cert. profl. U.S. profl. tennis registry. Home: 16521 Grunion #200 Huntington Beach CA 92649-3484 Office: McDonnell Douglas Aerospace 54-44 2401 E Wardlow Rd Long Beach CA 90807-5309

MANDEVILLE, ROBERT CLARK, JR., former naval officer, business executive; b. Princeton, W.Va., July 18, 1927; s. Robert Clark and Grace (Oney) M.; m. Elizabeth Anne Perry, Oct. 10, 1953; children: Cathy, Karen, Christy, Scott. B.S., U.S. Naval Acad., 1950; M.S., Princeton U., 1959. Commd. ensign U.S. Navy, 1950, advanced through grades to rear adm., 1976; assigned carrier-based fighter and attack squadrons; project mgr. A-6/EA-6 Weapons Systems, Washington, 1970-73; comdg. officer Naval Air Sta. Oceana, Virginia Beach, Va., 1973-74; dir. aviation plans and requirements Navy Dept., Washington, 1974-78; comdr. Light Attack Wing, Pacific, Lemoore, Calif., 1978-80; dep. chief Naval Material for Logistics, Washington, 1980-81; ret., 1981; v.p. Science Applications, Inc., 1981-83; sr. v.p. ManTech Internat., Fairfax, Va., 1983-94; ind. cons., 1994—. Decorated D.F.C. (6), Air medal (13), Bronze Star, Meritorious Service medal, Legion of Merit (2). Mem. Assn. Naval Aviation, Tailhook Assn., Soc. Old Crows, Sigma Xi. Home: 5016 Althea Dr Annandale VA 22003-4144

MANDIA, STEPHEN ERNEST, urologist; b. Engelwood, N.J., Dec. 30, 1958; s. Ernest James and Anita Joan (Turrisi) M. BS, Georgetown U., Washington, 1980; MSA in Health Svcs. Adminstrn., Cen. Mich. U., Mt. Pleasant, 1996; MD, Georgetown U., 1984. Diplomate Am. Bd. Urology, Am. Coll. Healthcare Execs. Resident in surgery St. Vincent's Med. Ctr., Bridgeport, Conn., 1984-85; commd. ensign USN, 1980, advanced through grades to comdr., 1995; flight surgeon USN, San Diego, 1985-88, resident in urology, 1988-92; head urology dept. USN, Rota, Spain, 1992-94, chief surg. svcs., 1994; head urology dept. USN, Jacksonville, Fla., 1994—; assoc. clin. prof. Uniformed Svcs. U. of Health Scis., Bethesda, Md., 1994—. Fellow ACS; mem. AMA, Am. Urol. Assn., Fla. Med. Assn. (bd. govs. 1995—). Republican. Roman Catholic. Avocations: private pilot, motorcycling, golf. Office: US Naval Hosp 2080 Child St Jacksonville FL 32214-5005

MANDIL, I. HARRY, nuclear engineer; b. Istanbul, Turkey, Dec. 11, 1919; s. Harry Robert and Bertha (Presente) M. (parents Am. citizens); m. Beverly Ericson, June 22, 1946; children: Jean Dale, Eric Robert. B.S., U. London, Eng., 1939; M.S., MIT, 1941; grad., Oak Ridge Sch. Reactor Tech., 1950; D.Sc. (hon.), Thiel Coll., Greenville, Pa., 1960. Devel., design process controls for textile mills and chem. plants Norcross Corp., 1941-42, asst. to pres. charge field engring., 1946-49; asst. to tech. dir. naval reactors br. reactor devel. div. AEC, 1950-54, dir. reactor engring. div., 1954-64; prin. officer, dir. MPR Assos., Inc. (engrs.), Washington, 1964-85; cons., dir. MPR Assos., Inc. (engrs.), Alexandria, Va., 1985—; developer nuclear power for propulsion naval vessels, also for Shippingport Atomic Power Ctrl. Sta.; mem., sec. Energy Adv. Bd., Washington, 1990-93; mem. corp. vis. com. for nuclear engring. dept. MIT, 1984-93; mem. sr. tech. rev. group for plutonium, Amarillo, Tex., 1995—. Author numerous papers in field. Served with USNR, 1942-46. Recipient Naval Letter of Commendation, 1946, Meritorious Civilian Svc. award Navy Dept., 1952, ASME Prime Movers award, 1956, Disting. Civilian Svc. award, 1959. Home: 701 Heathery Ln Pelican Bay Naples FL 34108 Office: 320 King St Alexandria VA 22314-3230

MANDLE, EARL ROGER, academic administrator, former museum administrator; b. Hackensack, N.J., May 13, 1941; s. Earl and Phyllis (Key) M.; m. Gayle Wells Jenkins, July 11, 1964; children: Luke Harrison, Julia Barnes. BA cum laude, Williams Coll., 1963; MA, NYU, 1967, cert. in Museum Training, 1967, postgrad.; DFA (hon.), U. Toledo, 1983, Kenyon Coll., 1986. Intern in drawings Met. Mus. Art, N.Y.C.; intern in sculpture and architecture Victoria and Albert Mus., London, 1966-67; assoc. dir. Mpls. Inst. Arts, 1967-74; assoc. dir. Toledo Mus. Art, 1974-76, dir., 1977-88; dep. dir. Nat. Gallery of Art, Washington, 1988-93; pres. Rhode Island Sch. Design, Providence, R.I., 1993—; chmn. exec. com. Am. Fedn. of Arts, 1987-93; mem. adv. panel New Zealand-U.S. Arts Found.; trustee Internat. Exhbns. Found., Sterling & Francine Clark Art Inst.; adv. panel Mus. Mgmt. Inst.; mem. NEA, Nat. Coun. on Arts; mem. adv. council Nat. Mus. Act, Smithsonian Instn.; mem. adv. com. on mus. mgmt. J. Paul Getty Trust; adv. bd. Charles Hosmer Morse Found., Inc.; trustee Spanish Found. for Restoration of Toledo (Spain); chmn. U.S. Com. on Restoration of Toledo; cons. Nat. Mus. Western Art, Tokyo, Kerr Found., Oklahoma City; chair cultural adv. council Netherlands-Am. Amity Trust, Inc., mem., exec. Ohio Arts Council; mem. exec. com. Williams Coll. Mus. Art; mem. arts adv. com. Barnes Found., 1991—; com. for the preservation of the Treasury Bldg., hist. advisor, 1989-93; vis. prof. Robert Sterling Clark Prof. of Art Williams Coll., Williamstown, Mass., 1993. Contbr. to profl. mags. and jours. Chmn., bd. dirs. Health and Edn. Leadership for Providence; trustee Providence Found.; mem. City Film Commn.; bd. dirs. Cranston Print Works; mem. adv. bd. Corp. Design Found., Alliance of ARtists' Cmtys. Decorated by the His Majesty Juan Carlos Knight of the Order of Isabel the Cath., Spain, 1985; Andover teaching fellow, 1963-64; Ford Found. fellow, 1966; Nat. Endowment Arts fellow, 1974; recipient Am. Hellenic Educational Progressive award, 1983, Distinguished Citizen for Art award Ohio Art Edn. Assn., 1983, Resolution for Leadership award Ohio Senate, 1983, Governor's award State of Ohio, 1983, Marketer of the Year award Am. Marketing Assn., 1983. Mem. Am. Assn. Mus. (trustee, v.p.), Art Mus. Assn. (pres.), Assn. Art Mus. Dirs., Am. Arts Alliance (trustee, policy com.), Coll. Art Assn. (mem. pres.' adv. bd.), Internat. Council Mus., Intermus. Conservation Assn. (exec. com.), Ohio Found. for Arts, Ohio Art Council, Am. Assn. 18th Century Studies (treas.), Young Pres. Orgn., R.I. Ind. Higher Edn. Assn., Providence C. of C., R.I. Commodores, Confrerie des Chevaliers du Tastevin, Phi Kappa Phi. (hon. mem.), Providence Art Club, Univ. Club, Brown Faculty Club, Tile Club, Century Club (N.Y.C.), The Answer Club, Williams Club (N.Y.C.). Office: Rhode Island Sch Design Office of the President 2 College St Providence RI 02903-2717

MANDLER, GEORGE, psychologist; b. Vienna, Austria, June 11, 1924; came to U.S., 1940, naturalized, 1943; s. Richard and Hede (Goldschmied) M.; m. Jean Matter, Jan. 19, 1957; children: Peter Clark, Michael Allen. B.A., NYU, 1949; M.S., Yale U., 1950, Ph.D., 1953; postgrad., U. Basel, Switzerland, 1947-48. Asst. prof. Harvard U., 1953-57, lectr., 1957-60; prof. U. Toronto, Ont., Can., 1960-65; prof. psychology U. Calif., San Diego, 1965-94, chmn. dept. psychology, 1965-70, prof. emeritus, 1994—; dir. Ctr. Human Info. Processing, U. Calif., San Diego, 1965-90; hon. rsch. fellow Univ. Coll. London., 1977-78, 82-90, vis. prof., 1990—. Author: Mind and Emotion, 1975, (German edit.), 1980, Mind and Body, 1984, (Japanese edit.), 1987, Cognitive Psychology, 1985, Japanese edit., 1991; contbr. articles and revs. to profl. jours.; editor: Psychol. Rev., 1970-76. Served with U.S. Army, 1943-46. Fellow Ctr. for Advanced Study in Behavioral Scis., 1959-60; vis. fellow Oxford U., Eng., 1971-72, 78; Guggenheim fellow, 1971-72. Fellow AAAS, Am. Acad. Arts and Scis.; mem. AAUP, Am. Assn. Advancement Psychology (1974-82); Psychonomic Soc. (governing bd., chmn. 1983), Am. Psychol. Soc., Am. Psychol. Assn. (pres. div. exptl. psychology 1978-79, pres. div. gen psychology 1982-83, mem. coun. reps. 1978-82, William James prize 1986), Internat. Union Psychol. Scis. (U.S. com. 1985-90), Soc. Exptl. Psychologists, Fedn. Behavioral Psychol. and Cognitive Scis. (pres. 1981). Home: 1406 La Jolla Knoll La Jolla CA 92037-5236 Office: U Calif San Diego Dept Psychology La Jolla CA 92093-0109 also: 3 Perrins Lane, London NW3 1QY, England

MANDLER, JEAN MATTER, psychologist, educator; b. Oak Park, Ill., Nov. 6, 1929; d. Joseph Allen and May Roberts (Finch) Matter; m. George Mandler, Jan. 19, 1957; children: Peter Clark, Michael Allen. Student, Carleton Coll., 1947-49; BA with highest honors, Swarthmore Coll., 1951; PhD, Harvard U., 1956. Rsch. assoc. lab. social rels. Harvard U., 1957-60; rsch. assoc. dept. psychology U. Toronto, Ont., Can., 1961-65; assoc. rsch. psychologist, lectr. U. Calif. at San Diego, La Jolla, 1965-73, assoc. prof., 1973-77, prof. psychology, 1977-88, prof. cognitive sci., 1988—; mem. adv. com. on memory and cognitive processes NSF, 1978-81; hon. rsch. fellow U. Coll., London, 1978-89, vis. prof., 1990—; hon. mem. Med. Rsch. Coun. Cognitive Devel. Unit, 1982—. Author: (G. Mandler) Thinking: From Association to Gestalt, 1964, Stories, Scripts and Scenes, 1984; assoc. editor Psychol. rev., 1970-76; mem. editl. bd. Child Devel., 1976-89, Discourse Processes, 1977-94, Jour. Exptl. Psychology, 1977-85, Text, 1979—, Jour. Verbal Learning and Verbal Behavior, 1980-88, Lang. and Cognitive Processes, 1985—, Cognitive Devel., 1990—; contbr. articles to profl. jours. Pres. San Diego Assn. Gifted Children, 1968-71; v.p. Calif. Parents for Gifted, 1970-71; mem. alumni council Swarthmore Coll., 1975-78. NIMH research grantee, 1968-81; NSF research grantee, 1981—. Fellow APA (mem. exec. com. divsn. 3 1983-85), Am. Acad. Arts and Scis.; mem. Psychonomic Soc. (mem. governing bd. 1982-87, chmn. 1985-86), Soc. Rsch. in Child Devel., Cognitive Sci. Soc., Soc. Exptl. Psychologists, Phi Beta Kappa. Office: Dept Cognitive Sci U Calif San Diego La Jolla CA 92093-0515

MANDLER, SUSAN RUTH, dance company administrator; b. Kew Gardens, N.Y., Feb. 11, 1949; d. Ernest and Clea (Reisner) M.; m. Robert Morgan Barnett, July 30, 1982. B.S., Boston U., 1971. Mgr. Pilobolus, Inc., Washington, Conn., mgr., 1977—. Office: PO Box 166 Washington Depot CT 06794-0166

MANDRA, YORK T., geology educator; b. N.Y.C., Nov. 24, 1922; s. Raymond and Irene (Farruggio) M.; m. Highoohi Kechijian, Jan. 26, 1946. BA, U. Calif., Berkeley, 1947, MA in Paleontology, 1949; PhD in Geology, Stanford U., 1958. From instr. to assoc. prof. geology San Francisco State U., 1950-63, prof., 1964—, head geology sect., chmn. dept., 1960-67; vis. prof. U. Aix-Marseille, France, 1959, Syracuse U., summer 1963, U. Maine, summer 1969, U. Calif., Santa Barbara, summers 1972—; research assoc. U. Glasgow, 1959, Calif. Acad. Scis., 1966-88; vis. scientist New Zealand Geol. Survey, fall 1970. Contbr. numerous articles to profl. jours. Pres. David S. Sohigian Found., 1975—. Served with USAAF, 1942-46. Recipient Neil A. Miner Disting. Coll. Teaching award, 1984; Danforth Found. teaching fellow, 1958, NSF fellow, 1959; NSF rsch. grantee, 1967-77. Fellow Geol. Soc. Am. (Sr.), Calif. Acad. Scis., AAAS; mem. Nat. Assn. Geology Tchrs. (pres. Far Western sect. 1953-54, 73-74, Robert Wallace Webb award 1977), Paleontol. Soc., Soc. Econ. Mineralogists and Paleontologists, Soc. for Environ. Geochemistry and Health. Avocations: walking, reading, music. Office: San Francisco State U Dept Geoscis 1600 Holloway Ave San Francisco CA 94132-1722

MANDRACCHIA, VIOLET ANN PALERMO, psychotherapist, educator; b. N.Y.C.; d. Anthony and Anna (Yetto) Palermo; m. John J. Mandracchia (dec. 1979); children: Dona Williams, Anne Marino, Marisa, John, Matthew, Lisa. Student, Coll. Mt. St. Vincent, 1946-48; BA, St. John's U., 1950; MA, Bklyn. Coll., 1953; cert. in ednl. adminstrn. & supervision, Hofstra U., 1978; MSW, SUNY, Stony Brook, 1990; advanced study in psychotherapy, L.I. Gestalt Ctr., 1988-92. Cert. social worker, secondary sch. adminstr., supr., English and social studies. Tchr. English Bay Ridge H.S., Bklyn,, 1951-55, Ctrl. Islip (N.Y.) H.S., 1967-68, Smithtown (N.Y.) H.S., 1968-77; asst. prin. Shoreham-Wading River (N.Y.) H.S., 1977-81; prin. West Islip (N.Y.) H.S., 1981-83; pvt. practice as psychotherapist Stony Brook and Manhattan,

1990—; satellite psychotherapist Health House, Islandia, N.Y., 1988—, supr., 1990—. Active Suffolk County (N.Y.) Human Rights Commn., 1979-84, 88-92; chair adv. bd. Office for Women, Suffolk County, 1986-89; treas. bd. dirs. Women's Ctr., SUNY, Farmingdale, N.Y., 1985-87; chair Women's Equal Rights Coalition, Suffolk County, 1979-84, 88-92; chair North Fork Task Force in Arts, Suffolk County, 1977-79. Recipient Woman of Yr. award Suffolk County Exec. Office for Women, 1989; named Citizen of Yr., Smithtown LWV, 1984, Educator of Yr., Suffolk County Exec. & Women's Equal Rights Coalition, 1982; practitioner writing grantee Harvard U. Grad. Sch. Edn., 1981. Mem. NASW, NOW, Nat. Assn. Secondary Sch. Prins. Avocations: writing, film, theater, travel, painting. Home: 15 Shore Oaks Dr Stony Brook NY 11790 Office: 211 Thompson St New York NY 10012-1365

MANDRELL, BARBARA ANN, singer, entertainer; b. Houston, Dec. 25, 1948; d. Irby Matthew and Mary Ellen (McGill) M.; m. Kenneth Lee Dudney, May 28, 1967; children: Kenneth Matthew, Jaime Nicole, Nathaniel. Grad. high sch. Country music singer and entertainer, 1959—, performed throughout U.S. and in various fgn. countries; mem., Grand Ole Opry, Nashville, 1972—; star TV series Barbara Mandrell and the Mandrell Sisters, 1980-82, Barbara Mandrell: Get to the Heart, 1987; albums include Midnight Oil, Treat Him Right, He Set My Life To Music (Grammy award, Dove award 1983), This Time I Almost Made It, This is Barbara Mandrell, Midnight Angel, Barbara Mandrell's Greatest Hits, Christmas at Our House, 1987, Morning Sun, 1990, Greatest Country Hits, 1990, Standing Room Only, 1993; star TV series Barbara Mandrell and the Mandrell Sisters, 1980-82, TV movie Burning Rage, 1984, TV specials Barbara Mandrell, Something Special, 1985, The Lady is A Champ; guest star TV series The Commish, Touched By an Angel, Dr. Quinn, Medicine Woman, Baywatch, Diagnosis Murder, others. Author (with George Vecsey): Get To the Heart: My Story, 1990. Named Miss Oceanside, Calif., 1965; Named Most Promising Female Singer, Acad. Country and Western Music, 1971; Female Vocalist of Yr., 1978; Female Vocalist of Yr., Music City News Cover Awards, 1979; Female Vocalist of Yr., Country Music Assn., 1979, 81, Entertainer of Yr., 1980, 81; People's Choice awards (9), 1983-87. Mem. Musicians Union, Screen Actors Guild, AFTRA, Country Music Assn. (v.p.). Mem. Order Eastern Star. Home: PO Box 620 Hendersonville TN 37077-0620 Office: Creative Artists Agy 3310 W End Ave Fl 5 Nashville TN 37203*

MANDULA, JEFFREY ELLIS, physicist; b. N.Y.C., July 23, 1941; s. Andrew and Gertrude Phyllis (Entenberg) M.; m. Barbara Blumenstein, June 2, 1963. BA, Columbia U., 1962; MA, Harvard U., 1964, PhD, 1966. Postdoctoral fellow Harvard U., Cambridge, Mass., 1966-67; research fellow Calif. Inst. Tech., Pasadena, 1967-69, asst. prof. theoretical physics, 1970-73; mem. Inst. for Advanced Study, Princeton, N.J., 1969-70; assoc. prof. applied math. MIT, Cambridge, 1973-79; prof. physics Washington U., St. Louis, 1979-87; sr. scientist theoretical physics Dept. Energy, Washington, 1987—; program dir. for theoretical physics NSF, Washington, 1980-81; sec. Signition Corp., Los Alamos, N.Mex., 1986—; vis. prof. U. Minn., Mpls., 1979, U. Southampton, Eng., 1979; invited prof. U. Louvain, Belgium, 1980; adj. prof. physics Washington U., St. Louis, 1987—. Contbr. over 80 articles to profl. jours. NSF fellow, 1966, Alfred P. Sloan Found. fellow 1973; recipient Cottrel Research award Research Corp., 1984. Mem. AAAS, Am. Phys. Soc., Fedn. Am. Scientists. Home: 500 23rd St NW Washington DC 20037-2828 Office: US Dept Energy Divsn High Energy Physics Washington DC 20585

MANEA, NORMAN, writer, educator; b. Suceava, Bukovina, Romania, July 19, 1936; came to U.S., 1988; s. Marcu and Janeta (Braunstein) M.; m. Josette-Cella Boiangiu, June 28, 1969. MS in Engring., Inst. Constrn., Bucharest, Romania, 1954. Engr. Romania, 1959-74, writer, 1969-86; fellow Deutscher Akademischer Austauschdienst, West Berlin, Germany, 1987; fellow Internat. Acad. Scholarship and the Arts Bard Coll., Annandale On Hudson, N.Y., 1989-92, writer in residence, 1992-96, Francis Flournoy prof. in European studies and culture, 1997—. Author: October, eight o'clock, 1992, On Clowns: The Dictator & the Artist, 1992, Compulsory Happiness, 1993, The Black Envelope, 1995; contbr. articles, stories to profl. jours. Recipient MacArthur Found. award, 1992, Nat. Jewish Book award Jewish Book Coun., 1993, Literary Lion award Nat. Pub. Libr., 1993; Guggenheim grantee, 1992; Fulbright fellow, 1988. Mem. Am. Pen. Home: 201 W 70th St Apt 10-I New York NY 10023-4301 Office: Bard Coll Dept Lang and Lit Annandale On Hudson NY 12504

MANEATIS, GEORGE A., retired utility company executive; b. 1926. BSEE, Stanford U., 1949, MSEE, 1950. With GE, 1950-53; with Pacific Gas & Elec. Co., San Francisco, 1953-91, v.p., 1979-81, sr. v.p., 1981-82, exec. v.p., 1982-86, pres., 1986-91, also bd. dirs. Office: Pacific Gas & Electric Co PO Box 770000 123 Mission St H17F San Francisco CA 94177

MANEKER, DEANNA MARIE, advertising executive; b. Albany, N.Y., Dec. 13, 1938; d. Marion K. and Florence R. (Krell) Colle; m. Morton Maneker, Sept. 15, 1957 (div. Feb. 1981); children: Meryl C., Amy J., Marion Kenneth. AB, Barnard Coll., 1960. Dir. circulation Westchester Mag., Mamaroneck, N.Y., 1971-73; pub. Change Mag., New Rochelle, N.Y., 1973-78; gen. mgr. Ctr. for Direct Mktg., Westport, Conn., 1978-81; sr. v.p. The Stenrich Group, Glen Allen, Va., 1981-88, exec. v.p., 1988-94; COO Martin Direct (formerly The Stenrich Group), Glen Allen, Va., 1994-96, exec. v.p. database, fulfillment, call ctr. svcs., 1995—. Home: 206 Tamarack Rd Richmond VA 23229-7039 Office: The Martin Agency One Shockoe Plz Richmond VA 23219-4132

MANEKER, MORTON M., lawyer; b. N.Y.C., Nov. 14, 1932; s. Arthur and Estelle (Hochberg) M.; m. Roberta S. Wexler, 1985; children: Meryl Colle, Amy Jill, Marion Kenneth. A.B., Harvard U., 1954, LL.B., 1957. Bar: N.Y. State 1957. Assoc. Shearman & Sterling, N.Y.C., 1957-62; trial atty. antitrust div. Dept. Justice, 1962-63; ptnr. Proskauer, Rose, Goetz & Mendelsohn, N.Y.C., 1963-94; arbitrator, 1995—. Trustee Beth Israel Hosp., N.Y.C., 1977—. Mem. Am. Law Inst., N.Y. State Bar Assn., Harvard Club N.Y.C. Jewish. Home: 30 E 65th St New York NY 10021-7005

MANELLI, DONALD DEAN, screenwriter, film producer; b. Burlington, Iowa, Oct. 20, 1936; s. Daniel Anthony and Mignon Marie (Dean) M.; m. Susan Linda Allen, June 16, 1964 (div. Aug. 1973); children: Daniel, Lisa. BA, U. Notre Dame, 1959. Communications specialist Jewel Cos., Melrose Park, Ill., 1959; script writer Coronet Films, Chgo., 1960-62; freelance writer Chgo., 1962-63; creative dir. Fred A. Niles Communications Ctrs., Chgo., 1963-67; sr. writer Wild Kingdom NBC-TV, Chgo., 1967-70; freelance film writer, producer Chgo., 1970-76; pres. Donald Manelli & Assocs., Inc., Chgo. and Paris, 1976—. Screenwriter, prodr. over 200 documentary films, 1970—, numerous episodes Wild Kingdom, 1967-82 (Emmy award 1969, 70). Recipient numerous awards various orgns. including N.Y. Internat. Film Festival, Houston Internat. Film Festival, Berlin, Paris, Venice Internat. Film Festivals, CINE, 1976—. Mem. Writers Guild Am. Roman Catholic. Avocations: photography, traveling, tennis. Office: 1 E Delaware Pl Chicago IL 60611-1459 also: 1 Rue Goethe, 75116 Paris France *A simple truth is played out in most lives: what we believe ourselves to be, we are. We may be tested with adversity, our own failed efforts, and plain bad luck, but our personal vision gives us strength and persistence. Success brings the satisfaction of fulfilled dreams, and the responsibility to help others form and follow their own visions.*

MANERI, REMO R., management consultant; b. Cleve., Aug. 16, 1928; s. Quinto Peter and Lucia (Massenzi) M.; m. Camille Ann Caranna, Aug. 26, 1950; children: Peter, Alisa, Leonard, Celia. B.S. in Chem. Engring., Case Inst. Tech., 1950; grad., Advanced Mgmt. Program, Harvard U., 1969. Devel. engr. Dow Corning, 1950-53, market researcher, 1956, comml. devel. mgr., 1957-63, chief engr., 1964-66, unit mfg. mgr., 1967-69, dir. tech. service and devel., 1970-72, bus. mgr., v.p., 1973-74, mgr. bus., group v.p., 1975-76; pres. Dow Corning U.S.A., 1977-80; exec. v.p. Dow Corning Corp., 1981-82, also bd. dirs.; chmn. bd. Quantum Composites, 1982-85, pres., chmn. bd., 1985-87, chmn. bd., 1987-89, also bd. dirs.; mgmt. cons., 1989—; bd. dirs. Comerica Bank-Midland, Duro-Last Roofing, Inc., Quantum Composites, Inc.; cons. in field. Contbr. articles to profl. jours. Bd. dirs. Midland Hosp. Assn. Served with Signal Corps, U.S. Army, 1954-56. Named Man of Year Adhesives and Sealants Coun., 1988. Mem. Chem. Spltys. Mfg. Assn. (dir.), Am. Chem. Soc., AAAS, Sigma Xi, Tau Beta Pi, Alpha Chi Sigma. Roman Catholic. Club: Midland Country. Patentee in field. Home and Office: 5808 Siebert St Midland MI 48640-2753

MANES, STEPHEN GABRIEL, concert pianist, educator; b. Bennington, Vt., Apr. 11, 1940; s. Julius H. and Edna E. (Silberstein) M.; m. Frieda Green, July 7, 1963; children: Sonya Ruth, Daniel Ira. B.S., Juilliard Sch. Music, 1961, M.S., 1963; postgrad. (Fulbright fellow), Acad. Music, Vienna, 1963-64. Vis. instr. music Oberlin Coll. Conservatory, Ohio, 1966-67; asst. prof. Ball State U., Muncie, Ind., 1967-68; prof. music SUNY-Buffalo, 1968—, chair, 1989-93; co-music dir. Sebago-Long Lake Region Chamber Music Festival, North Bridgton, Maine, 1982-85. Concert piano soloist maj. orchs. U.S. and abroad; debuts in Washington, 1962, N.Y.C., 1963, Vienna, Austria, 1964, Berlin, 1975, Amsterdam, 1975, London, 1975, chamber music concerts, radio, TV appearances, four-hand piano recitals with Frieda Manes in U.S., Australia, Can. and P.R.; rec. artist Orion Master Records, 1974—, Spectrum Records, 1986—; mem. Baird Piano Trio, 1986-90. Recipient Kosciuszko Chopin prize, 1960, Town Hall award Concert Artists Guild, 1962; finalist Leventritt Internat. Competition, 1962; Harriet Cohen Internat. Beethoven prize, 1964. Mem. Music Tchrs. Nat. Assn., Coll. Music Soc., Am. Fedn. Musicians. Home: 89 High Park Blvd Amherst NY 14226-4210 Office: SUNY-Buffalo Dept of Music 414 Baird Hall Buffalo NY 14260

MANESS, STEPHEN RAY, manufacturing engineer, retired army officer; b. Greensboro, N.C., Dec. 21, 1946; s. Roy Stevenson and Mary Etta (Gunter) M; m. Sandra Leigh Liles, Aug. 29, 1966 (div. Jan. 1970); 1 child, Michael; m. Mailyn Ruth Chandler, Mar. 15, 1974; children: Melanie, Gregory. BBA, Campbell U., Buies Creek, N.C., 1975; MA, Webster U., St. Louis, 1976; postgrad., Nat. Def. U., Washington, 1988, Duke U., 1992. Cert. acquisition mgr. and profl. logistician. Commd. U.S. Army, advanced through grades to col., 1990; procurement officer Army Tank - Auto Command, Warren, Mich., 1975-79, dir. nat. maintenance point, 1988-90; comdr. Mainz (Germany) Army Depot, 1990-92; comdr. Europe Army Materiel Command, Heidelberg, Germany, 1992-94; dir. mfg. tech. Army Materiel Command, Alexandria, Va., 1994—; ret. U.S. Army, 1996; sr. dir. mfg. engring. biomed. svcs. Am. Red Cross, Arlington, Va., 1996—; Pres. PTA, Dodds Sch., Karlsruhe, Germany, 1981-82, sch. adv. coun., The Netherlands, 1984-86. Decorated Silver Star. Recipient Legion of Merit with 2 oak leaf clusters, Bronze Star, Vietnamese Cross of Gallentry. Avocations: running, biking, skiing, reading. Home: 9730 S Park Circle Fairfax Station VA 22039 Office: Am Red Cross 1616 Ft Meyer Dr Arlington VA 22209

MANEVAL, DAVID RICHARD, mineral engineering consultant; b. Williamsport, Pa., Dec. 18, 1928; s. Paul David and Julia May (Heisler) M.; m. Lyne Page Heisley, Feb. 25, 1951; children: David R. Jr., Michael W., Holly M. McDonough, Laurie M. Zellers. BS, Pa. State U., 1950, MS, 1957, PhD, 1961. Asst. prof. Pa. State U., State College, 1961-63, dir. rsch. Pa. dept. of mines, 1963-69, dep. sec. Pa. dept. environment, 1969-70; sci. advisor Appalachian Regional Com., Washington, 1971-78; asst. dir. Office of Surface Mining, Washington, 1979-81; prof. U. Alaska, Fairbanks, 1981-89; mineral engring. cons. State College, 1989—; cons. in field, 1961—; extramural reviewer Alaska Sci. and Engring. Found., Anchorage, Alaska, 1989—; lectr. Pa. State U., 1992—. Author: (book chpts.) Mining Engineering Handbook, 1973, Coal Preparation, 1979; contbr. articles to profl. jours. Mem. College Area Sch. Bd., State College, 1957-63; mem. adv. com. Bur. Land Mgmt., Fairbanks, 1983-89; exec. bd. dirs. Juniata Valley Boy Scout Coun., 1993—. With U.S. Army, 1950-52. Recipient Superior Svc. award U.S. Dept. of Interior, 1979, Silver Beaver award Juniata Valley Boy Scout Coun., 1962. Mem. Am. Inst. Mining, Metallurg. and Petroleum Engrs. (disting. mem. 1990, Distin. Svc. award for environ. conservation 1980), Rotary Club State College (sr. active mem., bd. dirs. 1995-97, Paul Harris fellow 1988), Pa. State Ret. Faculty Club (treas. 1995—). Republican. Presbyterian. Avocations: gardening, travel, photography. Home: 126 W Lytle Ave State College PA 16801

MANEY, MICHAEL MASON, lawyer; b. Taihoku, Japan, Aug. 13, 1936; s. Edward Strait and Helen M. M.; m. Suzanne Cochran, Oct. 22, 1960; 1 child, Michele. B.A., Yale U., 1956; M.A., Fletcher Sch. Law and Diplomacy, Tufts U., 1957; LL.B., U. Pa., 1964. Bar: N.Y. 1966, D.C. 1977. Case officer CIA, 1957-61; law clk. Justice John Harlan, Supreme Ct. U.S., Washington, 1964-65; asso. Sullivan & Cromwell, N.Y.C., 1965-70, ptnr., 1971-77, 81—; mng. ptnr. Sullivan & Cromwell, Washington, 1977-81; law fellow Salzburg Seminar in Am. Studies, 1967; bd. overseers Fletcher Sch. Law and Diplomacy. Trustee, chmn. bd. Am. Found. for the Blind, Inc. Lt. USAF, 1958-60. Mem. ABA, Am. Law Inst., Am. Coll. Trial Lawyers, N.Y. State Bar Assn., Union Club, Harvard Club of Boston, Down Town Assn., Madison Beach Club, Madison Country Club, Met. Opera Club. Home: 1220 Park Ave New York NY 10128-1733 also: 48 Neptune Ave Madison CT 06443-3210 Office: Sullivan & Cromwell 125 Broad St New York NY 10004-2400

MANFREDI, DAVID PETER, architect; b. Hartford, Conn., Aug. 9, 1951; s. Domenic George and Elizabeth Frances (Ferrando) M. BA, U. Notre Dame, 1973; MA, U. Chgo., 1976; BArch, U. Notre Dame, 1979. Registered architect. V.p. The Architects Collaborative, San Francisco & Cambridge, Mass., 1979-88, Elkus/Manfredi Architects, Boston, 1988—. Prin. works include SONY Gallery, 1992 (Chgo. Interiors Grand Prize 1993), West Roxbury Dist. Courthouse, 1992, Franklin Pierce Law Ctr., 1992. Mem. AIA, Boston Soc. Architects, Phi Beta Kappa. Office: Elkus/Manfredi Architects 530 Atlantic Ave Boston MA 02210-2218

MANFREDI, JOHN FREDERICK, food products executive; b. N.Y.C., Dec. 1, 1940; s. John Frederick and Angela (Morano) M.; m. Doreen Honore Molloy, July 19, 19180; children: Nicole, Kendre, Hadley. Student, Yale U., 1958-61; BA, Columbia U., 1967. Asst. trader Singer & Mackie, N.Y.C., 1964; editor New Haven Jour. Carrier, Fairchild Publs., 1965-68; dir. pub. rels. Gen. Foods, White Plains, N.Y., 1968-74, dir. corp. communications, 1975-80, dir. internat. pub. affairs, 1981-86, dir. pub. affairs worldwide, 1986-87; v.p. pub. affairs Nabisco, Inc., Parsippany, N.J., 1988, sr. v.p. external and govt. affairs, 1988—, exec. v.p. corp. affairs, 1995—; chmn. Internat. Food Info. Coun., Washington, 1990—; chmn. Commn. on Mktg. and Advt., U.S. Coun. for Internat. Bus., N.Y.C., 1990—, Internat. C. of C., Paris, 1990—; mem. govt. affairs coun. GMA, 1995. Mem. Internat. Advt. Assn. (bd. dirs. 1990—), U.S. Olympic Com. N.J. (chmn.), Internat. Pub. Rels. Assn., Pub. Rels. Soc. Am., Arthur Page Soc., The Wisemen, Nat. Press Club. Office: Nabisco Foods Group 7 Campus Dr Parsippany NJ 07054-4404

MANGAN, JOHN LEO, retired electrical manufacturing company executive, international trade and trade policy specialist; b. Lakewood, Ohio, May 24, 1920; s. Mark A. and Celia M. (Motley) M.; m. Mildred J. Livingston, June 21, 1946; children: John, Scott. BSME, Carnegie Inst. Tech., 1942. Registered profl. engr., Mass., N.Y. Turbine design engr. Gen. Electric Co., Lynn, Mass., 1946-48; turbine application and sales engr. Gen. Electric Co., Fitchburg and Lynn,, Mass., Schenectady, St. Louis,, 1948-55; mgr. gas turbine indsl. sales Gen. Electric Co., Schenectady, 1955-60, mgr. gas turbine product planning, 1960-64, mgr. turbine bus. strategy devel., 1966-86; mgr. turbine indsl. customer requirements Boeing Co., Seattle, 1964-66. Contbr. articles profl. jours., chpts. in books; inventor in field. Mem. com. Boy Scouts Am., 1955-59, 64-66; bd. dirs. United Way Schenectady County, Inc., 1991-96, chmn., 1992-93. 1st lt. U.S. Army, 1942-46. Recipient Profl. and Social Activities award Gen. Electric Co., 1977. Fellow ASME (v.p. 1975-79, bd. govs. 1983-87, Gas Turbine citation, Centennial medal 1980, Dedicated Svc. award 1988); mem. Internat. Combustion Engine Coun. (CIMAC, permanent com. 1974-81, v.p. 1977-81), Mohawk Golf Club (Schenectady). Home: 1345 Ruffner Rd Niskayuna NY 12309-2505

MANGAN, MONA, association executive, lawyer; b. Pittston, Pa., Dec. 29, 1945; d. Joseph H. and Mona C. Mangan; m. Roy N. Watanabe, Oct. 24, 1987; 1 child, Julia. BA, Lock Haven U., 1966; AM, Duke U., 1969; JD, Columbia U., 1975. Bar: N.Y. 1976, U.S. Dist. Ct. (ea. and so. dists.) N.Y. 1979. Congl. staff Senator Wayne Morse of Oreg., 1967-68; staff atty. U.S. Dept. Labor, N.Y.C., 1975-79; trial atty. EEOC, N.Y.C., 1979; asst. exec. dir. Writers Guild Am. East, Inc., N.Y.C., 1979-84, assoc. exec. dir., 1984, exec. dir., 1984—. Recipient Gross award for contbn. to journalism Lock Haven U., 1984. Mem. Assn. Bar City N.Y., ABA, Dept. for Profl. Employees, AFL-CIO (v.p.), Coalition Motion Picture and TV Unions (v.p.), Pan Am. Fedn. Arts, Mass Media and Entertainment Unions (regional v.p. 1993—), Unions for Performing Arts (treas.), Internat. Affiliation Writers Guilds (treas.), Columbia U. Law Sch. Alumni Assn. Office: Writers Guild Am East Inc 555 W 57th St New York NY 10019-2925

MANGANARO, FRANCIS FERDINAND, naval officer; b. Providence, Feb. 27, 1925; s. Ralph and Ada Susanna (Hobden) M.; m. Carol Anne Slater, Sept. 8, 1948; children: Carol Sue, William Francis, John Thomas, Linda Anne, Mary Kathryn. Student, U. R.I., 1943-44; B.S. in Elec. Engring, U.S. Naval Acad., 1944-47; Naval Engr., MIT, 1956; cert., Advanced Mgmt. Program, Harvard U. Sch. Bus., 1971; cert. pub. utilities exec. program, U. Mich., 1984. Registered profl. engr., Conn. Commd. ensign U.S. Navy, 1947, advanced through grades to rear adm., 1975; served in destroyers Atlantic Fleet, 1947-49, served in submarines Pacific Fleet, 1949-53, repair officer, submarines Pearl Harbor Naval Shipyard, 1956-59, design project officer, submarines Bur Ships, 1959-63; inspection and planning officer Office Supr. of Shipbldg. Groton, Conn., 1963-68; prodn. officer Portsmouth Naval Shipyard, 1968-72, comdg. officer Puget Sound Naval Shipyard, 1972-76, chmn. navy claims settlement bd. Naval Material Command, 1976-78; vice comdr. Naval Sea Systems Command Washington, 1978-80; ret. (Naval Sea Systems Command), 1980; v.p., dir. GPU Nuclear Corp., 1980-90; cons. Burns & Roe Utility Mgmt. Cons., 1990-94; cons. Raytheon Engrs. & Constructors, Inc., 1994-96. Decorated Legion of Merit, DSM. Mem. Soc. Naval Architects and Marine Engrs., Am. Soc. Naval Engrs., Sigma Xi, Tau Beta Pi, Beta Psi Alpha.

MANGANELLO, JAMES ANGELO, psychologist; b. Cambridge, Mass., Nov. 30, 1944; s. Almando and Carmella (Spera) M.; m. Rosemarie Bombara, Dec. 26, 1965; children: Jason, Jennifer. BA, Eastern Nazarene Coll., 1966; MA, Boston U., 1970; EdM, Suffolk U., 1969; EdD, Boston U., 1977; M in Pub. Health, Harvard U., 1980. Instr. biology N.Y. Christian Acad., Bklyn., 1966-67; minister youth, edn. St. Paul Ch., Somerville, Mass., 1967-69; dir., founder Community Nursery Sch., Somerville, 1967-69; resident dir., instr. Malone Coll., Canton, Ohio, 1969-70; clin., research fellow dept. psychiatry Mass. Gen. Hosp., Boston, 1973-75; psychologist North Shore Counseling Ctr., Beverly, Mass., 1975-79; instr. North Shore Community Coll., Beverly, 1975-78; pres. Health Integration Services, Peabody, Mass., 1978-83; clin. fellow dept. psychiatry Harvard U. Med. Sch., Boston, 1983-84; pres. Dr. Manganello & Assocs., Danvers, Mass., 1983—; cons. psychologist Erich Lindemann Mental Health Ctr., Boston, 1971-75, Westwood Lodge, 1973-74. Contbr. articles to profl. jours. Chpt. mem. Rep. Presdl. Task Force, Washington, 1983—; mem. guidance adv. bd. Lexington Christian Acad., Mass., 1977—; mem. pres.'s council Gordon-Conwell Theol. Sem., Hamilton, Mass., 1983—. Mem. AAAS, Am. Orthopsychiat. Assn., Am. Pub. Health Assn., Am. Coll. Health Care Execs., Am. Sci. Affiliation, Soc. for Sci. Study of Religion, MIT Enterprise Forum, Pi Lambda Theta. Avocations: tennis, basketball, music. Home: 2920 NW 26th Ct Boca Raton FL 33434-3656 Office: Liberty Tree Med Ctr Danvers MA 01923

MANGANIELLO, JANICE MARIE, peri-operative nurse; b. Pittston, Pa., July 29, 1966; d. Ludwig Sr. and Dorothy Manganiello. AAS, Luzerne County Community Coll., Nanticoke, Pa., 1989; student, Coll. Misericordia, Dallas, Pa., 1989—; cert., Luzerne County Community Coll., 1992. Cert. RN first asst. CNOR, perioperative nurse Nat. Certification. Bd Perioperative Nursing, Inc. Emergency svcs. nurse Pittston Med. Emergency Ctr., 1989; obstetrics nurse Wilkes Barre (Pa.) Gen. Hosp., 1989, surg. svcs. nurse, 1989-91; RN first asst. Office of Sam C. DePasquale, 1992-93; perioperative nurse, charge nurse urology/renal transplant Temple U. Hosp., Phila., 1993—; clin. specialist Laser Surgery, 1993—, clin. coord. for students, 1993—; instr. continuing edn. planning, Luzerne County C.C., 1993. Vol. Big Bros./Big Sisters, Am. Cancer Soc., Valley Santa; religious edn. tchr. St. Rocco's Ch., Pittston; mem. Long Range Planning Comm. Pittston Area Sch. District, 1992. Recipient St. John Neumann award, St. Pius X award religious edn. Mem. ANA, NAFE, Am. Heart Assn., Assn. Operating Rm. Nurses (chairperson project Alpha 1990-91, chair rsch. 1993—, RN first asst. interest group), Soc. for Urology Nurses Assn., Orgn. for Advancement Assoc. Degree Nurses, Nat. League for Nursing, Soc. Peripheral Vascular Nursing, Nat. Assn. Orthopaedic Nurses, Couns. Cardiovascular Nursing and Circulation. Home: 1134 Fitzgerald St Philadelphia PA 19148-3612

MANGANO, LOUIS, lawyer; b. Passaic, N.J., Sept. 19, 1939; s. Salvatore and Mary Mangano; m. Arlene M. Triolo, Sept. 20, 1964; children: Kenneth L., Eileen M., Louis M., Michael S. BS in Bus. Adminstrn., Seton Hall U., 1970; MA in Criminal Justice, John Jay Coll., 1973; JD, Seton Hall U., 1979. Bar: N.J. 1981, U.S. Dist. Ct. N.J. 1981, U.S. Supreme Ct. 1985. With Elmwood Park (N.J.) Police Dept., 1966-83; pvt. practice atty. Elmwood Park, 1981—; adj. prof. Fairleigh Dickinson U., Rutherford, N.J., 1973-75, Jersey City (N.J.) State Coll., 1973-75; asst. prof. William Paterson Coll., Wayne, N.J., 1983-84; adv. bd. mem. Berkeley Coll., West Paterson, N.J., 1983—. Trustee, pres. Elmwood Park (N.J.) Bd. Edn., 1980-83, 89-93. With U.S. Army, 1959-61. Mem. Bergen County Bar Assn. Office: PO Box 305 395 River Dr Elmwood Park NJ 07407

MANGELSDORF, THOMAS KELLY, psychiatrist, consultant; b. St. Louis; s. Albert Henry and Hazel (Kelly) M.; m. Helen Louise Kareth, Apr. 12, 1958 (div. Jan. 1986); children: Ellen S., Steven T., Thomas K. Jr., Laura E. BS, U. Notre Dame, 1952; MD, St. Louis U., 1956. Diplomate Am. Bd. Psychiatry and Neurology (examiner 1968, 95), Am. Bd. Forensic Examiners; cert. Am. Bd. Profl. Disability Cons. Cons. in mental health various municipalities and pvt. practice, 1972—. Author and editor computerized system to interpret Minn. Multiphasic Personality Inventory profiles of patients to predict optimal psychiat. and pharmacologic interventions. Served to capt. U.S. Army, 1960-62. Fellow Am. Psychiat. Assn.; mem. Eastern Mo. Psychiat. Assn. (sec. 1983-85). Avocation: sailing. Office: 621 S New Ballas Rd Saint Louis MO 63141-8232

MANGER, WILLIAM MUIR, internist; b. Greenwich, Conn., Aug. 13, 1920; s. Julius and Lilian (Weissinger) M.; m. Lynn Seymour Sheppard, May 30, 1964; children: William Muir, Jr., Lilian Wade (Mrs. Porter Fleming), Stewart Sheppard, Charles Seymour. BS, Yale U., 1944; MD, Columbia U., 1946; PhD, Mayo Found., U. Minn., 1958. Intern, Presbyn. Hosp., N.Y.C., 1946-47, resident, 1949-50; fellow internal medicine Mayo Found., 1950-55; asst. physician Presbyn. Hosp., 1957—; dir. Manger Rsch. Found., 1961-77; clin. asst. vis. physician Columbia div. Bellevue Hosp., 1964-68; asst. attending physician NYU Bellevue Hosp. 1969-77; assoc. attending physician, 1977-83, attending physician, 1983—; instr. medicine Columbia U. Coll. Phys. and Surg., 1957-66, assoc. medicine, 1966-70, lectr., 1981—; asst. attending physician Presbyn. Hosp., 1966-68; asst. clin. prof. medicine N.Y.U. Med. Ctr., 1968-75, assoc. clin. prof. medicine, 1975-83, prof. clin. medicine, 1983—; mem. devel. com. Mayo Clinic, 1981-87; vice chmn. bd. Manger Hotels, Inc., 1957-73. Mem. bd. govs. St. Albans Sch., Washington, 1958-64, 67-73, 83-89, chmn., 1967-69; trustee Found. Rsch. in Medicine and Biology, 1971-77, Buckley Sch., 1975-85, Lycee Francais, N.Y., 1996—, Found. for Advancement Internat. Rsch. in Microbiology, 1977-82, Thyroid Found., 1980-85; mem. bd. visitors Boston U. Med. Sch., 1992—; trustee Found. for Depression and Manic Depression, 1978-89, pres., 1980-89; elder Presbyn. Ch., 1968-70, 92-93, trustee, 1962-67, 80-84, deacon, 1959-61. Lt. (j.g.) M.C., USNR, 1947-49. Recipient Mayo Found. Alumni award for Meritorious Rsch., 1955, Disting. Alumnus award, 1992. Diplomate Nat. Bd. Med. Examiners, Am. Bd. Internal Medicine. Fellow ACP, Acad. Psychosomatic Medicine, Am. Geriatric Soc., Coun. on Geriatric Cardiology, N.Y. Acad. Medicine (admission com. 1976-78, edn. com. 1979-92), Am. Coll. Cardiology, Am. Coll. Clin. Pharmacology, Royal Soc. Health, Am. Inst. Chemists; trustee Nat. Hypertension Assn. (chmn. 1977—), AMA, Am. Soc. Internal Medicine, N.Y. State Med. Soc., N.Y. County Med. Soc., Am. Heart Assn. (fellow council on circulation and council for high blood pressure rsch.), Nat. High Blood Pressure Edn. Program (mem. Coord. Com.), Inter-Am. Soc. Hypertension, Internat. Soc. Hypertension, Am. Soc. Hypertension, Am. Thoracic Soc., N.Y. Acad. Sci., AAAS, Am. Physiol. Soc., Am. Chem. Soc., Am. Soc. Pharmacology and Exptl. Therapeutics, Am. Soc. for Clin. Pharmacology and Therapeutics, Clin. Autonomic Rsch. Soc., Am. Autonomic Soc., Med. Strollers, N.Y.C., Endocrine Soc., Pan Am. Med. Assn., Harvey Soc., Soc. Exptl. Biology and Medicine, Rsch. Discussion Group (founding mem., sec.-treas. 1958-80), Am. Fedn. Clin. Rsch., Am. Soc. Nephrology, Royal Soc. Medicine (affiliate), Fellows Assn. Mayo

Found. (v.p., pres. 1953), Mayo Alumni Assn. (v.p. 1981-82, exec. com. 1981-89, pres. elect 1982-85, pres. 1985-87), Catecholamine Club (founder, sec.-treas. 1967-80, pres. 1981-82), Doctors Mayo Soc., Albert Gallatin Assos., New Eng. Soc., S.R. (chmn. admissions com. 1959-67, bd. mgrs. 1959-67, 69-70), Soc. Colonial Wars, Sigma Xi, Nu Sigma Nu, Phi Delta Theta, Explorers, Meadow (L.I., N.Y.); Univ.; Yale; N.Y. Athletic (N.Y.C.); Southampton Bathing Corp.; Jupiter Island. Co-author: Chemical Quantitation of Epinephrine and Norepinephrine in Plasma, 1959, Pheochromocytoma, 1977, Clinical and Experimental Pheochromocytoma, 1996; author: Catecholamines in Normal and Abnormal Cardiac Function, 1982; editor, contbr. Hormones and Hypertension, 1966; editor: Am. Lecture Series in Endocrinology, 1962-75; guest editor First Irvine H. Page Internat. Hypertension Rsch. Symposium, 1990; contbr. articles to profl. and lay jours. Achievements include research on the mechanism of salt-induced hypertension, and on pheochromocytoma. Home: 8 E 81st St New York NY 10028-0201

MANGES, JAMES HORACE, investment banker; b. N.Y.C., Oct. 8, 1927; s. Horace S. and Natalie (Bloch) M.; m. Joan Brownell, Oct., 1969 (div.); m. Mary Seymour, Mar. 28, 1974; children: Alison, James H. Jr. Grad., Phillips Exeter Acad., 1945; BA, Yale U., 1950; MBA, Harvard U., 1953. With Kuhn, Loeb & Co., N.Y.C., 1954-77, ptnr., 1967-77; mng. dir. Lehman Bros., Kuhn Loeb Inc., N.Y.C., 1977-84, Shearson Lehman Hutton, Inc., N.Y.C., 1984-90; adv. dir. Lehman Bros., N.Y.C., 1990-96; dir. Baker Industries, Inc., 1967-77, Proudfoot PLC 1996—; dir., exec. com. Metromedia, Inc. 1970-86. Trustee The Episcopal Sch., 1978-92, St. Bernard's Sch., 1985—, Phillips Exeter Acad., 1985-89, mem. trustee coun., 1989-95. Mem. Bond Club, Yale Club (N.Y.C.), City Midday, Century Country Club (Purchase, N.Y.). Home: 875 Park Ave New York NY 10021-0341 Office: 20th Fl 45 Rockefeller Plz Fl 20 New York NY 10111-0100

MANGHAM, R. HAROLD, church administrator. V.p. for ch. ministries The Christian and Missionary Alliance, 1997. Office: Christian & Missionary Alliance PO Box 35000 Colorado Springs CO 80935-3500

MANGHIRMALANI, RAMESH, international trade corporation executive; b. Bombay, Dec. 31, 1953; came to U.S., 1968; s. Chatur Thakurdas and Maya Mansukhani; m. Mona Gour, 1988. BA in History, Oxford U., 1975; MBA, London Sch. Econs., 1977; cert. internat. law and trade, U. Paris, 1979; diploma Exec. Devel. Program, Harvard U., 1984. Chief planner UN, Geneva, 1977-81; cons. Fin. Corp. Am., L.A., 1981-85; mgr. mktg. Calif. Fed. Savs. and Loan, L.A., 1985-86; pres. Marco Polo Assocs., San Francisco, 1986—; dir. Wall St. Cons. Assn., 1986—; pres. Indian Tourism Devel. Corp., 1988—; spl. advisor Hoover Inst., Stanford U., Palo Alto, Calif. Author: Thirld World Debt Solution, 1987, Marketing of Financial Instruments, 1988, India's Role in International Economy, 1988. Dir. Indian Children's Assn., New Delhi; pres. Children's World. Mem. Am. Mgmt. Assn., World Affairs Coun., Commonwealth Club. Office: Global Markets Ltd 230 Powhattan Ct Danville CA 94526-5500

MANGIAPANE, JOSEPH ARTHUR, consulting company executive, applied mechanics consultant; b. N.Y.C., Aug. 1, 1926; s. Michael and Rose D'Amico M.; m. Marcia Balut, Oct. 30, 1954 (div. Apr. 1974); children: Rosemarie, Michael, Diana, Joseph J., Susan. BS, Fordham U., 1950. Stress analyst Republic Aviation, Farmingdale, N.Y., 1951-55; pvt. practice tech. cons., 1955-58; sect. mgr. Aerojet-Gen., Sacramento, 1958-61; project engr. Pratt & Whitney Aircraft, East Hartford, Conn., 1961-71; pvt. practice tech. cons., 1971-79; pres. Joseph A. Mangiapane & Assocs., Inc., Tampa, Fla., 1979-92. Author numerous tech. reports. Served as cpl. USAAF, 1945-47, ETO. Assoc. fellow AIAA; mem. Pine Acres Club (Wethersfield, Conn.) (pres. 1968-69). Republican. Roman Catholic. Avocations: reading, photography, golf. Home: 4713 W San Rafael St Tampa FL 33629-5507

MANGIN, CHARLES-HENRI, electronics company executive; b. Riom, France, Apr. 16, 1942; s. Louis Eugene and Monique (Mathivon) M.; m. Marguerite Stern, Nov. 27, 1974; children: Charlotte, Louis-David, Maxence. MBA, Ecole Superieure de Commerce, Reims, France, 1965. Computer salesman IBM, Paris, 1967-68; asst. to pres. EDC, Rome, 1969-71; gen. mgr. CEGI, Paris, 1971-77; pres. CEERIS, Paris, 1977-81, CEERIS Internat., Inc., Old Lyme, Conn., 1982—; cons. The Mitre Corp., Washington, 1973-78, Coyne & Bellier, Paris, 1973-76, IITRI, Chgo., 1979-81, PRC, London, 1980-81. Author: Lebanon, 1965, The Atlantic Facade, 1973, Flights Over Europe, 1974, Surface Mount Technology, 1986, Managing the SMT Challenge, 1990; contbg. editor Electronic Packaging and Prodn., 1988-97; contbr. articles to profl. jours. Mem. IEEE, Surface Mount Tech. Assn., Soc. Mfg. Engrs., Internat. Microelectronics and Packaging Soc., Am. Soc. Test Engrs., Internat. Soc. Hybrid Microelectronics, N.Y. Yacht Club, Ocean Cruising Club, Ski Club (Les Arcs, France). Roman Catholic. Avocations: sailing, skiing, opera. Office: Ceeris Internat Inc PO Box 939 Old Lyme CT 06371-0939

MANGINO, KRISTIN MIKALSON, secondary education educator; b. Spokane, Wash., July 7, 1939; d. Norman Lillard and Mabel Mae Mikalson; m. Paul Angelo Mangino, Aug. 15, 1965; children: Kyle Aaron, Lisan Kristin. Student, Cottey Coll., 1957-58, Ea. Wash. Coll. Edn. (now Ea. Wash. U.), 1958-61; BS in Psychology, Wash. State U., 1961; student, Calif. State U., Fullerton, 1961-66; postgrad., U. Calif., Irvine, 1966; MS in Spl. Edn., Portland State U., 1983. Cert. elem. and secondary tchr., Calif., Wash., Oreg. Tchr. English and reading Jr. High Sch., Anaheim and Monterey, Calif., 1961-68; substitute tchr. Elma (Wash.) Sch. Dist., 1970-71, Evergreen Sch. Dist., Vancouver, Wash., 1974-75; tutor Evergreen Sch. Dist., Vancouver, 1975-84; tutor, substitute tchr. Vancouver and Evergreen Sch. Dists., 1984-88, tutor, 1988—; bd. dirs. Arden Tree Farms; hostess with svc. sales City Welcome Svc., 1986-87; co-pres. Spl. Edn. Adv. Coun., Vancouver, 1986-87; mem. direction svc. bd. Ednl. Svc. Dists. 112, 1980. Sec. Spl. Olympics, Evergreen Sch. Dist., 1989-90; mem. D.D. Parent Coalition of Clark County, 1993—. Mem. Philanthropic Ednl. Orgn. (G.X. chpt. officer), The Arc (bd. dirs. 1992-93), Internat. Rett Syndrome Found., Berg Freunde Ski Club. Presbyterian. Avocations: travel, reading, gardening, vol. work. Home and Office: PO Box 5542 Vancouver WA 98668-5542

MANGINO, MATTHEW THOMAS, lawyer; b. New Castle, Pa., Oct. 3, 1962; s. Thomas Michael and Connie (Frigone) M.; m. Juliann Galmarini, Aug. 6, 1988. BA, Westminster Coll., 1985; JD, Duquesne U., 1988. Bar: Pa. U.S. Dist. Ct. (we. dist.) Pa., U.S. Ct. Appeals (3d cir.), U.S. Supreme Ct. Jud. clk. Hon. Francis X. Caiazza, New Castle, 1988-89; asst. pub. defender County of Lawrence, New Castle, 1989; pvt. practice New Castle, 1990—; chmn. New Castle Airport Authority, 1990-92; solicitor County of Lawrence, New Castle, 1992-96; instr. Pa. State U., 1992—; legal cons. O.J. Simpson Trial, Sta. WBZY-AM, New Castle, 1995; bd. dirs. Allied Human Svcs.; seminar plan mem. on gang violence Pa. Bar Inst., 1996. Prodr. (TV program) Gang Violence Curbing the Epidemic, 1996; columnist, New Castle News, 1989-90; contbr. chpt. to book, article to profl. jours. Mem. campaign staff Dukakis for Pres., Pitts., 1988; del. Dem. Nat. Conv., Atlanta, 1988; com. mem. Lawrence County Econ. Devel. Corp.; sec. Lawrence County Bd. Assistance, New Castle; bd. dirs. Family Ctr. of Lawrence County. Mem. ABA (vice chmn. law and media com.), Pa. Bar Assn. (state exec. bd. young lawyers divsn., jud. selection and reform com., co-chair spl. project on gang violence), Pa. Trial Lawyers Assn., Lawrence County Bar Assn., Lawrence County C. of C. (bd. dirs. 1990), Wolves (bd. dirs. pres. 1996-97). Roman Catholic. Avocations: golf, writing, reading. Office: 312 N Jefferson St New Castle PA 16101-2222

MANGION, RICHARD MICHAEL, health care executive; b. Haverhill, Mass., Apr. 26, 1941; s. Michael Anthony and Evelyn (Cote) M.; m. Gail Elizabeth Donne, Apr. 27, 1968; children: Catherine Jean, James Richard, Ian Kyle. BBA, Suffolk U., 1963; MBA, Syracuse U., 1965; MPH, U. Calif., Berkeley, 1972. Asst. adminstr. Nashua (N.H.) Meml. Hosp., 1972-75, assoc. adminstr., 1975-77; pres. and chief exec. officer Harrington Meml. Hosp., Southbridge, Mass., 1977—; lectr. U. N.H., Durham, 1972-74. Pres. Tri-Community Devel. Corp., Southbridge, 1983-88. Capt. USAF, 1966-70. Fellow Am. Coll. Health Care Execs. (regent Mass. area B 1995—); mem. Am. Hosp. Assn., Mass. Hosp. Assn., Ctrl. Mass. Hosp. Coun. (pres. 1982-84), Ctrl. Mass. Health Care Found., Tri-Cmty. C. of C. (pres. 1983-84). Democrat. Roman Catholic. Club: Hosp. Supts. Lodge: Rotary. Avocations: tennis, swimming, hiking. Home: 50 Old Village Rd Sturbridge MA 01566-1069 Office: Harrington Meml Hosp 100 South St Southbridge MA 01550-4051

MANGIONE, CHUCK (CHARLES FRANK MANGIONE), jazz musician, composer; b. Rochester, N.Y., Nov. 29, 1940; children: Nancy, Diana. MusB in Music Edn., Eastman Sch. Music, U. Rochester, 1963, MusD (hon.), 1985. Formed quintet with brother Gap, Jazz Bros., 1958-64; tchr. elem. sch. music Rochester, 1963-64; dir. Eastman Jazz Ensemble; mem. faculty Eastman Sch. Music, 1968-72. Freelance musician with bands of Maynard Ferguson and Kai Winding, 1965, trumpet player with, Art Blakey's Jazz Messengers, 1965-67; formed Chuck Mangione Quartet, 1968; guest condr. Rochester Philharm. Orch., 1970, appeared at Montreux Internat. Jazz Festival, 1972; starred on PBS-TV spl. Live from Wolftrap; performed on PBS-TV spl. Grammy Awards show, 1981; ann. tours to Europe, Japan, Australia and S. Am.; performed benefit concerts for Spl. Olympics; also 8-hour marathon to aid Italy's earthquake victims; compositions include Hill Where the Lord Hides (Grammy nomination 1971), Land of Make Believe, 1973 (Grammy nomination for Best Big Band Performance and Best Instrumental Arrangement Accompanying a Vocalist), Bellavia, 1976 (Grammy award), Give It All You Got, Chase the Clouds Away, 1995; theme for 1980 Winter Olympics (Emmy award Music Composition/Direction), 1980 (Grammy nomination for Best Instrumental Composition); albums include Chuck Mangione Quartet, 1972, Chase the Clouds Away, 1975 (gold album, 2 Grammy nominations), Main Squeeze, 1976, Feels So Good, 1977 (gold, platinum and double-platinum album), Children of Sanchez, Save Tonight For Me, 1986 Eyes of the Veiled Temptress, 1988; movie soundtrack, 1978 (Grammy award Best Pop Instrumental Performance), Live at the Hollywood Bowl, 1979, Fun and Games, 1980 (Grammy nomination), Tarentella, 1981. Commd. by Sesquicentennial Com. of City of Rochester to compose and premier spl. work in honor of city's 150th birthday. Made acting debut in film Paradise Blues, 1984; guest star Magnum PI; 1st music video Diana D, completed 1984 (directed by Zbigniew Rybczynski). Named Most Promising Male Jazz Artist, Record World 1975, Jazz Artist of Yr., Instrumentalist of Yr., Most Promising Instrumentalist, Top Fusion Artist, Top Producer, Top Instrumentalist, Outstanding Jazz Artist, Internat. Jazz award winner 1978-79, Georgie award for Instrumental Act of Yr., AGVA 1980, winner Playboy mag. ann. music poll, several times, also 1980 winner for Best Brass, Best Composer and Best Group.; recipient Entertainment award Big Bros. 4th Ann. Sidewalks of N.Y. Awards Dinner, 1983, Regents medal of excellence N.Y. State Bd. Regents, 1984, Jazz Music Campus Entertainment award Nat. Assn. Campus Activities, 1987. His performance at Montreal Internat. Jazz Festival, July 1986, drew largest crowd in history of the event. *

MANGIONE, JERRE GERLANDO, author, educator; b. Rochester, N.Y., Mar. 20, 1909; s. Gaspare and Giuseppina (Polizzi) M.; m. Patricia Anthony, Feb. 18, 1957. BA, Syracuse U., 1931; MA (hon.), U. Pa., 1971, LittD (hon.), 1980; LHD (hon.), SUNY, Brockport, 1987. Writer, Time mag., 1931; book editor Robert M. McBride & Co., N.Y.C., 1934-37; nat. coordinating editor Fed. Writers' Project, 1937-39; spl. asst. to U.S. commr. immigration and naturalization, 1942-48; advt. writer, pub. relations dir., 1948-61; mem. faculty U. Pa., 1961—, dir. writing program, 1965-77, prof. English, 1968-77, emeritus, 1977—, founding dir. Italian Studies Center, 1978-80, coord. cultural events, 1980-82; vis. lectr. Bryn Mawr Coll., 1966-67; vis. prof. Trinity Coll., Rome, summer 1973, Queens Coll., 1980; chmn. Leon lectr. com. U. Pa., 1964-85; acting dir. Yaddo, 1977-78; editor WFLM Phila. Guide, 1960-61; book reviewer, 1931—; adv. editor Italian Americana, 1974-84, 90—; mem. lit. panel NEA, 1980-81; spkr. main address Symposium on Italian and Italian-Am. Women in '90s, SUNY, Stony Brook, 1993. Author: Mount Allegro: A Memoir of Italian Life, 1943, 6th edit., 1989 (hist. marker commemorating area erected in Rochester, 1986, stage adaptation premiere, Rochester), 1992, Spanish edit., 1944, Italian edit., 1947, rev., 1983, (novel) Ship and the Flame, 1948, Swedish edit., 1949, Reunion in Sicily, 1950, 2d edit., 1984, Italian edit., 1992, Night Search, 1965, To Walk the Night, Brit. edit., 1966, Italian edit., 1987, Life Sentences for Everybody, 1966, (fables) A Passion for Sicilians: The World Around Danilo Dolci, 1968, 3d edit., 1985, America is Also Italian, 1969, The Dream and the Deal: Federal Writers Project (1935-43), 1972, 3d edit., 1983 (nominated for Nat. Book award 1972), Mussolini's March on Rome, 1975, An Ethnic At Large: A Memoir of America in the Thirties and Forties, 1978, 2d edit., 1983, (with Ben Morreale) La Storia: Five Centuries of the Italian American Experience, 1992; (pamphlet on Phila. lit. history) By Reason of Birth or Residence, 1988; contbr. to newspapers and mags. Chmn. lit. arts com. Phila. Art Alliance, 1958-61; mem. adv. bd. U. Pa. Press, 1983-84; founding mem. exec. bd. Am.-Italy Soc., 1959-94, Inst. Contemporary Art U. Pa., 1964-77, Am. Italian Hist. Assn., 1969—, Am. Inst. Italian Studies, 1975-82, Amici, 1981—; pres. Friends Danilo Dolci, Inc., 1969-71. Guggenheim fellow,1945; Fulbright Rsch. fellow, 1965; MacDowell Colony fellow, Yaddo fellow; Va. Ctr. Arts fellow; Rockefeller grantee, 1968; Am. Philos. Soc. grantee, 1971; Earhart Found. grantee, 1975; NEH grantee, 1980-83; decorated Knight Comdr. Order Star Solidarity, Italy, 1971; recipient Key to City Rochester, 1963, 10th Ann. Lit. award Friends Rochester Pub. Libr., 1966, Justinian Soc. award, 1966, Phila. Athenaeum Lit. award, 1973, Presdl. award Am. Inst. for Italian Culture, 1979, Outstanding Achievement award Am.-Italian Hist. Assn., 1985, Key to City New Orleans, 1988, Pa. Gov.'s award for Excellence in Humanities, 1989, Leonardo da Vinci award Italian Heritage and Culture Month Com., 1989; named Person of Yr. Italian Ams. Delaware County, 197, 86, Premio Nazionale Empedocie, 1984, Legion of Honor medal Chapel Four Chaplains, 1984; Mangione papers housed at U. Rochester Libr. Dept. of Rare Books and Spl. Collections; recipient Internat. Arts award Columbus Countdown, 1990, 92; honored by Libr. of Congress for lit. career with an exhibit titled: Jerre Mangione, An Ethnic at Large, 1992, Fed. Writer's Project, Christopher Columbus Quincentenary award, 1992, Mariano DiVito Human Achievement award Amici Friends of Italian Studies U. Pa., 1993, Distinction in Lit. Achievement award Columbus Citizens Found., 1993. Fellow Soc. Am. Historians; mem. Author's Guild, Franklin Inn, Assn. Writers of Agrigento in Sicily (nominated hon. pres. 1994), Sons of Italy. Home: 3300 Darby Rd Apt 7315 Haverford PA 19041-1075 Office: U Pa Dept English Philadelphia PA 19104

MANGLER, ROBERT JAMES, lawyer; b. Chgo., Aug. 15, 1930; s. Robert H. and Agnes E. (Sugrue) M.; m. Geraldine M. Delich, May 2, 1959; children: Robert Jr., Paul, John, Barbara. BS, Loyola U., Chgo., 1952, MA, 1983; JD, Northwestern U., 1955. Bar: Ill. 1958, U.S. Dist. Ct. (no. dist.) Ill. 1959, U.S. Supreme Ct. 1976, U.S. Ct. Appeals (7th cir.) 1980. Author: (with others) Illinois Land Use Law, Illinois Municipal Law. Village atty., prosecutor Village of Wilmette, 1965-93; mcpl. prosecutor City of Evanston, 1963-65; chmn. Ill. Traffic Ct. Conf., 1977—; pres. Ill. Inst. Local Govt. Law; mem. home rule attys. com. Ill. Mcpl. League. Mem. ABA (chmn. adv. com. traffic ct. program), Nat. Inst. Mcpl. Law Officers (past pres.), Ill. Bar Assn. (former chmn. traffic laws and ct. com.), Chgo. Bar Assn. (former chmn. traffic ct. seminar, former chmn. traffic laws com.), Caxton Club, Phi Alpha Delta.

MANGO, WILFRED GILBERT, JR., construction company executive; b. Weehawkin, N.J., July 11, 1940; s. Wilfred Gilbert and Mildred B.M.; children from previous marriage; Christian P., Peter H.; m. Charlene Holt, Feb. 14, 1985; children: Alison L., David H. BS., Lehigh U., 1963; M.B.A., NYU, 1969. Auditor Hurdman & Cranstown, N.Y.C., 1963-69; dir. fin. Thomas Crimmins Contracting Co., N.Y.C., 1969-77; v.p. fin., mgr. fin. controls ITT Teleplant, Inc., N.Y.C., 1977-78; v.p. fin. George A. Fuller Co. div. Northrop Corp., N.Y.C., 1978-81, now pres., chief exec. officer, dir., 1981—. Past chmn. bd. trustees Marymount Manhattan Coll.; adv. bd. N.Y. Real Estate Inst.; bus. adv. coun. Lehigh U.; bus. coun. Lighthouse for the Blind; mem. Urban Land Inst. Mem. AICPA, N.Y. State Soc. CPA's. Clubs: Lehigh U. of N.Y., Univ. (N.Y.C.). Home: 12 Dwight Ln Greenwich CT 06831 Office: Fuller Group Inc 451 Park Ave S New York NY 10016-7390

MANGO-HURDMAN, CHRISTINA ROSE, psychiatric art therapist; b. Garden City, N.Y., May 13, 1962; d. Camillo Andrew and Dorothy Mae (Harrison) Mango; Keith Hurdman, Sept. 11, 1993; 1 child, Clarissa Rose Hurdman. BFA summa cum laude, Coll. of New Rochelle, 1984; MA, NYU, 1987. Registered art therapist; bd. cert. structural family therapy tng.; cert. psycho-edn. multi family therapy tng. Art therapist Bronx Mcpl. Hosp. Ctr., 1984-88; art therapist, clin. supr. Fordham-Tremont Cmty. Mental Health Ctr., Bronx, 1988—; art therapy fieldworker Bronx State Hosp., 1984, art therapy intern Bronx Children's Hosp., 1985, Saint Lukes Hosp., N.Y.C., 1986. Contbr. articles to profl. jours. Mem. N.Y. Art Therapy Assn., No. N.J. Art Therapists Assn., Am. Art Therapy Assn. Home: 11 Turnure St Bergenfield NJ 07621-2035

MANGOLD, JOHN FREDERIC, manufacturing company executive, former naval officer; b. La Grange, Ill., Jan. 24, 1927; s. John Frederic and Helvig Victoria (Anderson) M.; m. Margaret Ellen Gore, Oct. 25, 1947; children: John, Andrew, Jennifer. BS, U.S. Naval Acad., 1947; MSEE, U.S. Naval Postgrad. Sch., Monterey, Calif., 1958. Registered profl. engr., Conn. Commd. ensign USN, 1947, advanced through grades to comdr., 1962, comdg. officer nuclear submarine U.S.S. Halibut, 1962-63, comdg. officer nuclear tng. unit, 1963-67, ret., 1967; v.p. mfg. Combustion Engring., Inc., Windsor, Conn., 1972-78, group pres., 1982-86, v.p. utility boilers, 1990-91; pres. Vetco, Inc., Ventura, Calif., 1978-82; cons., 1992; pres. Detrex Corp., Southfield, Mich., 1992-93, bd. dirs., 1993—; bd. dirs. Detrex Corp. Mem. IEEE, U.S. C. of C. (energy com. 1984-87). Republican. Office: 1000 Prospect Hill Rd Windsor CT 06095-1521

MANGOLD, SYLVIA PLIMACK, artist; b. N.Y.C., Sept. 18, 1938; d. Maurice and Ethel (Rein) Plimack; m. Robert Mangold. Student, Cooper Union, 1956-59; BFA, Yale U., 1961. Exhibited one-person shows Daniel Weinberg Gallery, San Francisco, 1974, Fischbach Gallery, N.Y.C., 1974, 75, Annemarie Verna Gallery, Zurich, 1978, 91, Droll-Kolbert Gallery, N.Y.C., 1978, 80, Young Hoffman Gallery, Chgo., 1980, Ohio State U., Columbus, 1980, Pa. Acad., 1981, Contemporary Arts Mus., Houston, 1981, Madison Art Ctr., (Wis.), 1982, Brooke Alexander, Inc., 1982, 83, 84, 85, 86, 89, 92, 95, Duke Art Mus., N.C., 1982, Rhona Hoffman Gallery, Chgo., 1985, Tex. Gallery, 1986, Fuller Goldeen Gallery, San Francisco, 1987, U. Mich, Ann Arbor, 1992, Minn. Inst. Arts, 1992, Grunwald Ctr. for Graphic Arts, UCLA, 1992, Neuberger Mus. Art, SUNY, Purchase, 1993, Davison Art Ctr., Wesleyan U., Middletown, Conn., 1993, Albright-Knox Art Gallery, Buffalo, 1994, Wadsworth Atheneum, Hartford, Conn., 1994, Blaffer Gallery U. Houston, 1994, Mus. Fine Arts, Boston; group shows at Young Hoffman Gallery, Chgo., 1979, Walker Art Ctr., Mpls., 1979, Droll-Kolbert Gallery, 1979, Denver Art Mus., 1979, U. So. Calif., 1979, Honolulu Acad. Art, 1979, Oakland Mus., (Calif.), 1979, Univ. Art Mus. of U. Tex.-Austin, 1979, Internat. Biennial Ljibljana, Yugoslavia, Phoenix Art Mus., 1979, Art Latitute Gallery, N.Y.C., 1980, Thorpe Intermedia Gallery, Sparkhill, N.Y., 1980, U. Colo. Art Galleries, Boulder, 1980, Nina Freudenheim Gallery, Buffalo, 1980, U.S. Pavillion of Venice Biennial, 1980-81, Inst. Contemporary Art of U. Pa., Phila, 1980-81, Yale U. Art Gallery, 1981, San Antonio Mus. Art, 1981, Indpls. Mus. Art, 1981, Tucson Mus. Art, 1981, Pa. Acad., 1981, Mus. Art of Carnegie Inst., Pitts., 1981, Brooke Alexander, Inc., N.Y.C., 1982, Ben Shahn Ctr. Visual Arts, 1982, Castle Gallery, Coll. of New Rochelle, N.Y., 1983, Thomas Segal Gallery, Boston, 1982-83, Siegel Contemporary Art, N.Y., 1983, Freedman Gallery, Albright Coll., Reading, Pa., 1983, Fuller Goldeen, San Francisco, 1983, Yale U. Art Gallery, New Haven, 1983-84, 86, Wilcox Gallery, Swarthmore, Pa., 1984, The Hudson River Mus., Yonkers, N.Y., 1984, Sardonia Art Gallery, Wilkes Coll., Wilkes-Barre, Pa., 1985, Kent State U. Gallery, Ohio, 1985, Brooke Alexander, N.Y., 1985, John C. Stoller Co., Minn., 1985, Knight Gallery, Spirit Sq. Arts Ctr., Charlotte, N.C., 1986, Mus. Art, R.I. Sch. Design, Providence, 1986, Yale U. Gallery, 1986, CUNY, 1986-87, Lorence Monk Gallery, N.Y.C., Vanquard Gallery, Phila., 1986-087, Aldrich Mus., Ridgefield, 1986-87. Flander's Contemporary Art, Mpls., 1987, Annemarie Verna Galerie, Zurich, 1988, U. N.C., 1988, R.I. Sch. Design, 1988, Grace Borgenicht Gallery, N.Y.C., 1988, Fay Gold Gallery, Atlanta, 1988, U. N.C., Greensboro, Three Rivers Arts Festival, Pitts., 1989, Cin. Art Mus., New Orleans Mus. Art, Denver Art Mus., Pa. Acad. Fine Arts, 1989, U. Mich., 1992, Mpls. Inst. Arts, 1992, Grunwald Ctr. Graphic Arts, UCLA, L.A., Neuberger Mus. Art, SUNY Purchase, 1993, Davison Art Ctr., 1993; exhibited in permanent collections, Albright-Knox Art Gallery, Buffalo, Allen Meml. Art Mus., Oberlin, Ohio, Bklyn. Mus., Dallas Mus. Fine Arts, Detroit Inst. Art, Mus. Fine Arts, Houston, Indpls. Mus. Art, Madison (Wis.) Art Ctr., Milw. Art Mus., Yale U. Art Gallery, Mus. Modern Art, N.Y.C., Mus. Fine Arts, U. Utah, Tampa (Fla.) Mus., Walker Art Mus., Mpls., Whitney Mus. Am. Art, N.Y., Weatherspoon Art Gallery, Greensboro, N.C., Wadsworth Athenaeum, Hartford, U. Mich., Utah Mus. Fine Art. Work reviewed in newspapers and mags.

MANGONE, GERARD J., international and maritime law educator; b. N.Y.C., Oct. 10, 1918; s. Gerard Francis and Viola (Schumm) M.; m. Emma Haddad, Apr. 13, 1958; children—Cleopatra, Regina, Flaminia. A.B., CCNY, 1938; M.A., Harvard, 1947, Ph.D. (Charles Summer prize), 1949. Asst. prof. polit. sci. Wesleyan U., Middletown, Conn., 1948-51; assoc. prof. Swarthmore Coll., 1951-56; prof. polit. sci. and internat. relations Syracuse U., 1956-67; dir. grad. overseas tng. program, exec. officer Maxwell Center Study Overseas Operations, 1958-60; exec. asst. to dean Maxwell Grad. Sch., 1961-64, asso. dean dir. internat. relations program, 1961-67; dean Coll. Liberal Arts, v.p., provost Temple U., Phila., 1967-69; sr. fellow Woodrow Wilson Internat. Ctr., 1970-72; prof. internat. law U. Del., Newark, 1972-74, dir. Ctr. for Study of Marine Policy, 1973-89, H. Rodney Sharp prof. internat. law and orgn., 1975-89, univ. rsch. prof. internat. and maritime law, 1989—, coord. grad. studies, 1976-79; adj. prof. Maine Maritime Acad., 1992—; vis. prof. Trinity Coll., Mt. Holyoke Coll., Yale, Princeton, Johns Hopkins; Tagore law prof. U. Calcutta, 1979; disting. lectr. U. Ind., 1980; vis. scholar U. Western Australia, 1983, 87, Peking U., 1984, Capetown U., 1986, 89, U. Natal, 1989; mem. Presdl. Commn. Trust Territory Pacific, 1963; cons. AID, 1965-67, Nat. Commn. Marine Resources and Engring. and State Dept., 1967-73, UN, 1965, U.S. Corps Engrs., 1975; vice chmn. exec. com. Commn. Study Orgn. Peace; exec. dir. Pres.' Commn. on UN, 1970-71. Author: The Idea and Practice of World Government, 1951, A Short History of International Organization, 1954, The Elements of International Law, 2d edit, 1967, Marine Policy for America, 1977, 2d edit., 1989, Law for the World Ocean, 1981, Mangone's Concise Marine Almanac, 2d edit., 1991, United States Admiralty Law, 1997; co-author, editor: The Art of Overseasmanship, 1958, The Overseas Americans, 1960, European Political Systems, 1960, UN Administration of Economic and Social Programs, 1966, Energy Policies of the World, 3 vols, 1976-79, Internat. Straits of the World, 11 vols., 1978-89; editor: Future of Gas and Oil from Sea, American Strategic Minerals, 1984; editor in chief: Marine Policy Reports, 1981-91, Internat. Jour. Marine and Coastal Law, 1991— . Capt. AUS, 1942-46. Mem. Am. Soc. Internat. Law, Internat. Law Assn., Maritime Law Assn., Port of Wilmington Maritime Soc. (bd. dirs. 1980—, chmn. 1989), Francis Alison Soc. (sec. 1990—, award 1983), Del. Acad. Sci. (pres. 1993), Cosmos Club (Washington), Harvard Club (N.Y.C.). Home: 201 Unami Trl Newark DE 19711-7508 Office: Univ Del Grad Coll Marine Studi Newark DE 19716

MANGOUNI, NORMAN, publisher; b. Detroit, Oct. 19, 1932; s. Nazareth Lazarus and Isabelle (Garabedian) M.; m. Anahid Apelian, May 10, 1964; 1 child, Marie-Isabelle. A.B., U. Mich., 1954; M.S., Columbia U., 1955; postgrad., U. Mich. Law Sch., 1957-58. Reporter Ann Arbor (Mich.) News, 1957-59; editor Mich. Alumnus, U. Mich., Ann Arbor, 1959-62; sr. editor Coll. Entrance Exam. Bd., N.Y.C., 1962-64; dir. fin. aid U. Miami, Coral Gables, Fla., 1965-66; dir. State U. N.Y. Press, Albany, 1966-78; pres., gen. editor Scholars' Facsimiles & Reprints, Delmar, N.Y., 1972—; pres. Caravan Books, Delmar, 1972—, Acad. Resources Corp., Las Vegas, Nev., 1988—; corr. DuPont-Columbia Survey and Awards, 1976-78; rep. to com. on standards in field of library work, documentation and related pub. practices Am. Nat. Standards Inst., 1974-78; Exec. asst. to majority caucus Mich. State Senate, 1964. Co-translator: The Gaucho Martin Fierro, 1974; contbr. articles to profl. jours.; mem. editorial bd.: Ararat mag, 1962-66, 77-78. Served to lt. USAF, 1955-57. Mem. Modern Lang. Assn. Am., Middle East Studies Assn. N.Am., Mensa, Phi Sigma Kappa, Sigma Delta Chi, Phi Alpha Delta. Club: Rotary Internat. Home: 410 Lenawee Dr Ann Arbor MI 48104-1866

MANGRU, BASDEO, secondary school educator; came to U.S., 1987; m. Doreen Nadia Permaul, Aug. 4, 1965; children: Rajendra, Tricia Nadini (Mangru) Dhanraj. Tchr. cert., Tchrs. Coll., Guyana, 1964; BA, U. Guyana, 1970, MA in Guyanese, West Indian History, 1976; PhD in S. Asian Studies, U. London, Eng., 1981. Cert. social studies tchr., NYC bd. edn.; grade I, class I, trained tchrs. cert., Guyana. Tchr. Guyana High Sch., 1959-74; lectr. U. Guyana, 1974-76, asst. prof., 1976-80, assoc. prof., 1980-84; tchr., rscher. London, Eng., 1984-87; social studies tchr. N.Y.C. Bd.

Edn., 1987—; Coord. Caribbean Studies Course for non-history majors, U. Guyana, student evaluator, interviewer freshmen history majors; participant in seminars, symposiums, lectr. on East Indian Diaspora to ednl. and cultural groups; adj. prof. York Coll., CUNY. Author: Benevolent Neutrality, Indian Government Policy and Labour Migration to British Guiana, 1854-1884, 1987, Indenture and Abolition, Sacrifice and Survival on the Guyanese Sugar Plantations, 1993; editor: (with others) The East Indian Diaspora: 150 Years of Survival, Contributions and Achievements, 1993, A History of East Indian Resistance on the Guyana Sugar Estates, 1996; asst. editor The East Indian Diaspora Newsletter; resident historian The East Indian Diaspora Com.; contbr. articles to profl. jours. vol. civilian asst. to Richmond Hill police dept. working with youth and teenage problems; organizer remedial reading and citizenship classes for local residents. Recipient Bookers' Sugar Estates scholarship, Guyana, 1966-70, Commonwealth Acad. Staff fellowship, Commonwealth Scholarship Commn., UK, 1978-81, Ednl. Achievement award, Corentyne Comprehensive High Sch. Student-Tchr. Reunion Orgn., 1989, Rockefeller Residency fellowship in Humanities, Queens Coll. Asian-Am. Ctr., CUNY, 1990-91. Mem. Am. Hist. Assn. (Albert J. Beveridge Rsch. award 1990), Assn. Caribbean Historians, Assn. Caribbean Studies, Assn. Third World Studies, E. Indian Diaspora Com. (asst. sec., history cons., conf. coord.). Avocations: reading, writing, music, cricket, lawn tennis. Home: 10941 115th St Jamaica NY 11420-1112

MANGUM, GARTH LEROY, economist, educator; b. Delta, Utah, July 23, 1926; s. James L. and Golda (Elder) M.; m. Marion Poll, Nov. 20, 1953; children: Stephen, David, Mary, Elizabeth. BS, Brigham Young U., 1956; MPA, Harvard U., 1958, PhD, 1960; JD, U. Utah, 1989. Instr. econs. Harvard U., 1960; asso. prof. econs. Brigham Young U., 1960-63; sr. staff analyst Presdl. R.R. Commn., 1961; research dir., subcom. employment and manpower U.S. Senate, 1963-64; exec. dir. President's Com. Manpower, 1964-65; exec. sec. Nat. Com. Tech., Automation and Econ. Progress, 1965-66; research prof. econs. George Washington U., 1967-71; co-dir. George Washington U. (Center Manpower Policy Studies), 1967-69; Max McGraw prof. econs. and mgmt. U. Utah, Salt Lake City, 1969-97, prof. emeritus, 1997—, dir. Inst. Human Resource Mgmt., 1969-90; lectr. U. Tel Aviv, Israel, 1969, 84, Am. Seminar at Salzburg, 1975, U. South Africa, 1977, Monash U., Australia, 1984; Spl. mediator Fed. Mediation and Conciliation Service, 1962-63; mem. Adv. Council Vocational Edn., 1966-67; vice chmn. Nat. Manpower Policy Task Force, 1966-69, chmn., 1969-71, mem., 1966-76; mem. Nat. Council on Employment Policy, 1976—, chmn., 1979-81, sec.-treas., 1990—; chmn. Nat. Inst. Career Edn., 1976-81; cons. fed., state and local govts., bus. firms, govts. of, Saudi Arabia, Kuwait, Jordan, Yemen, Bahrain, United Arab Emirates, Indonesia, Yugoslavia, Romania, Uganda, Nigeria, Israel, South Africa, Russia, Korea, China, other countries; cons. AID, ILO, World Bank; also arbitrator. Author: The Operating Engineers: Economic History of a Trade Union, 1964, MDTA, Foundation of Federal Manpower Policy, 1968, The Emergence of Manpower Policy, 1969, Federal Work and Training Program in the 1960's, 1969, Economic Opportunity in the Ghetto, 1970, Human Resources and Labor Markets, 1971, Career Education: What It Is and How To Do It, 1972, A Decade of Manpower Development and Training, 1973, Career Education and the Elementary School Teacher, 1973, Career Education in the Middle/Junior High School, 1973, Manpower Planning for Local Labor Markets, 1974, Career Education for the Academic Classroom, 1975, Employability, Employment and Income, 1976, Career Education in the High School, 1976, Your Child's Career, 1977, The Lingering Crisis of Youth Unemployment, 1978, Coming of Age in the Ghetto, 1978, Job Market Futurity, 1979, The Coal Industry and its Industrial Relations, 1985, Capital and Labor in American Copper, 1992, Labor Struggle in The Post Office, 1992, The Mormons War on Poverty, 1993, Union Resilience in Troubled Times, 1994, Portable Pension Plans for Casual Labor Markets, 1995, Transnational Industrial Marriages, 1996, The Rise, Fall and Replacement of Industry-Wide Bargaining in the Basic Steel Industry, 1996, Programs in Aid of the Poor, 1997, On Being Poor in Utah, 1997; also articles, monographs.; editor: The Manpower Revolution: Its Policy Consequences, 1965, Automation and Economic Progress, 1966, Metropolitan Impact of Manpower Programs, 1973, The T in CETA, 1981, Of Heart and Mind: Social Policy Essays in Honor of Sar A. Levitan, 1996. With USAAF, 1944-45. Mem. Ch. of Jesus Christ of Latter-day Saints (missionary 1950-53, bishop 1971-78). Home: 1539 Preston St Salt Lake City UT 84108

MANGUM, JOHN K., lawyer; b. Phoenix, Mar. 7, 1942; s. Otto K. and Catherine F. Mangum; m. Deidre Jansen, Jan. 10, 1969; children: John Jansen, Jeffery Jansen. Student, Phoenix Coll. 1960-62; BS, U. Ariz., 1965, JD, 1969. Bar: Ariz. 1969. Sr. trial atty. criminal div. Maricopa County Atty.'s Office, Phoenix, 1969-71; ptnr. Carmichael, McClue and Stephens, P.C., Phoenix, 1972-74; sr. ptnr. O'Connor, Cavanagh, 1992-94, Phoenix; pvt. practice, Phoenix, 1994—; ct. commr., judge pro tem Maricopa County super. ct., Phoenix, 1974-78, spl. commr., 1979-82; legal csl. to speaker of Ariz. Ho. of Reps., Phoenix, 1975-86; mem. John K. Mangum and Assocs., P.C., Phoenix, 1974-92; sr. mem. O'Connor & Cavanaugh, 1992-94; pvt. practice, 1994—. Mem. Maricopa County Bd. Health, 1974-79, Ariz. State Commn. on Elected Ofcls. Salaries, 1987-93; chmn. curriculum com., mem. legal asst. adv. com. Phoenix Coll., 1973-75; legal counsel Maricopa County Rep. Com., 1986-90; mem. task force com. on career edn. Phoenix Mayor's Youth Commn., 1972-73; v.p. The Samaritans, 1984-87. Mem. State Bar Ariz. (exec. bd. young lawyers sect. 1974-76), Maricopa County Bar Assn. (pres. young lawyers sect. 1974-75, dir. 1973-75), Ariz. C. of C. (dir. 1974-79), Phoenix Country Club, Ariz. Club, Rotary. Republican. Office: 340 E Palm Ln Ste 100 Phoenix AZ 85004-4529

MANGUN, CLARKE WILSON, JR., public health physician, consultant; b. Iowa Falls, Iowa, Feb. 12, 1919; s. Clarke Wilson and Vallie Hazel (Hoffman) M.; m. Edith Lauretta DuBois, May 13, 1945; children: Edith Ann, Nancy June, Laura Jane. BS, U. Iowa, 1940, MD, 1943; MPH, Columbia U., 1947. Diplomate Am. Bd. Preventive Medicine. Commd. officer USPHS, 1945-66; med. adminstr. Am. Hosp. Assn., Chgo., 1966-67, Chgo. Heart Assn., 1967-68, AMA, Chgo., 1969-80; long-term cons. Abbott Labs., North Chicago, Ill., 1980—. Recipient award Nat. Bd. Med. Examiners, 1944. Fellow APHA, Am. Coll. Preventive Medicine; mem. AMA (Physician's Recognition award, 1970-96), Ill. State Med. Soc., Chgo. Med. Soc. Avocations: photography, travel, gardening. Home: 733 S Greenwood Ave Park Ridge IL 60068-4539

MANHART, MARCIA Y(OCKEY), art museum director; b. Wichita, Kans., Jan. 14, 1943; d. Everett W. and Ruth C. (Correll) Yockey; children: Caroline Manhart Sanderson, Emily Alexandrea Morrison. BA in Art, U. Tulsa, 1965, MA in Ceramics, 1971. Dir. edn. Philbrook Art Ctr., Tulsa, 1972-77, exec. v.p., asst. dir., 1977-83, acting dir., 1983-84; exec. dir. Philbrook Mus. Art (formerly Philbrook Art Ctr.), Tulsa, 1984—; instr. Philbrook Art Ctr. Mus. Sch., Tulsa, 1963-72; gallery dir. Alexandre Hogue Gallery, Tulsa U., 1967-69; NEH Challenge Grant panelist, 1991, presenter to AAM Conv., 1991; MAAA Craft Fellowship panelist, 1988, 93, NEA Craft Fellowship panelist, 1990; NEA spl. exhbn. panelist, 1996; curator nat. touring exhibit Nature's Forms/Nature's Forces: The Art of Alexandre Hogue, 1984-85; co-curator internat. exhbn.: The Eloquent Object, 1987-90; curator Sanford and Diane Besser Collection exhbn., 1992. Vis. com. Smithsonian Instn./Renwick Gallery, Washington, 1986; cultural negotiator Gov. George Nigh's World Trade Mission (Okla.), China., 1985; com. mem. State Art Coll. of Okla., 1985—; mem. Assocs. of Hillcrest Med. Ctr., 1983-88, exec. com., 1985-88; com. mem. Neighborhood Housing Services, 1985-87; mem. Mapleridge Hist. Dist. Assn., 1982—; steering com. Harwelden Isnt. for Aesthetic Edn., 1983; com. mem. River Parks Authority, 1976; mem. Jr. League of Tulsa Inc., 1974-78; adv. panel mem. Nat. Craft Planning Project, NEA, Washington, 1978-81; craft adv. panel mem. Okla. Arts and Humanities Council, 1974-76; juror numerous art festivals, competitions, programs; reviewer Inst. Mus. Services, Washington, 1985, 88, 92; auditor Symposium on Language & Scholarship of Modern Crafts, NEA and NEH, Washington, 1981; nominator MacArthur Fellows Program, 1988. Recipient Harwelden award for Individual Contbrn. in the Arts, 1989, Gov.'s award State of Okla., 1992. Mem. Assn. Am. Mus., Assn. Art Mus. Dirs., Art Mus. Assn. Am., Mountain Plains Assn. Mus., Am. Craft Coun., Okla. Mus. Assn., Rotary. Office: Philbrook Mus Art PO Box 52510 Tulsa OK 74152-0510

MANHEIMER, BERNARD HENRY, federal agency administrator, consultant; b. N.Y.C., Nov. 24, 1926; s. Joseph Henry and Frieda (Lichtman) M.; m. Sheila Schectman, June 4, 1953; children: Susan, Kenneth, Lisa. BS, CCNY, 1949; MS, Case Western Res. U., 1955. Exec. engr. ITT Fed. Electric Corp., Paramus, N.J., 1959-61; city councilman N.Y.C. Coun., 1961-65; mem. profl. staff Ctr. for Naval Analyses U. Rochester, Arlington, 1966-69; various positions HUD, Washington, 1970-81, energy mgmt. specialist, 1981—; v.p. Publ. Engring. Consul, N.Y.C., 1958-59; chmn. workshop UN Conf. on Sci. and Tech. for Devel., Vienna, 1979; panel session chmn., organizer Fourth Joint Conf. on Sensing Environ. Pollutants, New Orleans, 1977, Internat. Conf. on Environ. Sensing and Assessment, 1975, among others; speaker at numerous confs. Co-author: (guidebook) Making Rental Housing Energy Efficient, 1990; assoc. editor IEEE Transactions on Man Machine Systems, 1960-68; contbr. articles to profl. jours. Co-founder FDR Ind. Dem. Club of the N.W. Bronx, N.Y.C., 1959. With USN, 1945-46, PTO. Mem. IEEE (Profl. Achievement award 1989, chmn. profl. group on man/machine systems 1968, chmn. environ. quality com. 1971-74, 83-85, del. to UN confs. on human environment Stockholm 1972, human settlements in Vancouver 1976, sci. and tech. for devel. in Vienna 1979), Intersoc. Liaison Com. on the Environment (founder, mem., vice chmn. 1971-77, chmn. 1977-81, 1982-83), Am. Assn. Engring. Socs. (del., chmn. coord. com. on the environment 1982-83. Avocations: tennis, stamp collecting. Home and Office: 2204 Richland St Silver Spring MD 20910

MANIERI-HARVEY, MICHELE DAWN, musician, educator; b. Melbourne, Fla., Apr. 25, 1955; d. Ettore Don and June Laclaire (Spaur) Manieri; m. Joseph Howard Harvey, May 27, 1989. AA, U. Fla., 1976, B in Music Edn., 1978; M in Early Childhood and Elem. Edn., Nova U., 1983; M in Guidance and Counseling, U. South Fla., 1993. Cert. tchr., Fla. Profl. vocalist Fla., 1973—; vocal tchr. in pvt. practice Gainesville, Fla., 1978-80; substitute tchr. Alachua Sch. Bd., Gainesville, 1978-79; music specialist Levy County Sch. Bd., Williston, Fla., 1979-82, kindergarten tchr., 1982-83; tchr. 2d grade Hernando County/Moton Elem., Brooksville, Fla., 1983-84, tchr. 1st grade, 1984-86, music specialist with integrated counseling concepts and basic skills, 1986—; chair calendar plus com. Moton, 1994—; adj. prof. St. Leo Coll., 1984—; Fla. cert. observer and peer tchr., 1986—; mem. Hernando County Fine Arts Curriculum Writing Team, 1994-96. Featured vocalist Hernando Symphony Orch., Spring Hill, Fla., 1992, 95, 96, Nature Coast Festival Singers, 1994, 96, Brooksville Music Club Christmas Ho., 1985, 87, 94, 95; dir., prodr. 15 sacred cantata-dramas, 42 children's musicals. Music dir. 1st Bapt. Ch., Brooksville, 1989—. Named 1994 Hernando County Tchr. of Yr., 1994, Best Musical Actress, Stage West, 1995, Best Musical Supporting Actress, Outstanding Young Woman of Am., 1981. Mem. FTP-NEA, Nat. Music Educators Assn., Fla. Music Educators Assn., Fla. League Tchrs., Fla. Counseling Assn., Hernando Counseling Assn. (Counseling Advocate of Yr. 1994), Hernando County Bd. Fine Arts Coun., Hernando Edn. Found. (sec. 1995-96), Hernando Classroom Tchrs. Assn. (exec. bd. 1985-86), Hernando Acad. Tchrs. (vice chair 1994-95, chair 95-96), Alpha Delta Kappa Internat. Educators Hon. Fraternity (1985-96). Office: Moton Elem Sch 7175 Emerson Rd Brooksville FL 34601-5752

MANIGAULT, PETER, media executive; b. Charleston, S.C., Jan. 13, 1927; s. Edward and Mary (Hamilton) M.; m. Landine Sanford Legendre, Aug. 8, 1959 (div.); children: Gabrielle, Pierre; m. Patricia Lucas Bennett, Dec. 14, 1986. A.B., Princeton U., 1950. With Eve. Post Pub. Co. and subs., Charleston, 1959—; pres., pub. Eve. Post Pub. Co. and subs., 1960-85, chmn., 1985—. Trustee Nat. Trust Historic Preservation, 1963, vice chmn., 1965-74. Served with USNR, 1945-46, 52-53; capt. Res. Decorated Legion of Merit with combat V; Order Mil. Merit (Republic of Korea). Mem. Nat. Audubon Soc. (dir. 1968-74). Office: 134 Columbus St Charleston SC 29403-4809

MANILOFF, JACK, biophysicist, educator; b. Balt., Nov. 6, 1938; s. Boris and Edith (Cohen) M.; m. Sandra Sue Steele, Dec. 22, 1960; children: Beth Susan, Eric Steele. BA in Biology, Johns Hopkins U., 1960; MS in Biophysics, Yale U., 1964, PhD in Biophysics, 1965. Research assoc. in chemistry Brown U., Providence, 1964-66; asst. prof. microbiology Sch. Medicine and Dentistry, U. Rochester, N.Y., 1966-71; assoc. prof. Sch. Medicine and Dentistry, U. Rochester, 1971-79, prof., 1979—; dir. core nucleic acid lab. U. Rochester; lectr. Am. Soc. Microbiology Found., 1989-90; mem. Internat. Com. on Taxonomy of Viruses, 1975—, mem. exec. com., 1990—, chair bacterial virus subcom., 1993—; cons. subcom. on taxonomy of mycoplasmatales Internat. Com. Systematic Bacteriology, 1978—. Adv. bd. Archives of Virology, 1995—; contbr. articles to profl. jours. Recipient Research Career Devel. award USPHS, 1970-75; Fogarty Sr. Internat. fellow, 1987-88; Disting. vis. fellow Christ's Coll., Cambridge, Eng., 1987-88; Lady Margaret lectr. Christ's Coll., 1988. Mem. Am. Soc. Microbiology (chmn. mycoplasma divsn. 1993-94), Am. Soc. Virology, Sigma Xi. Office: Univ Rochester Med Ctr Dept Microbiology & Immunology Box 672 Rochester NY 14642-0001

MANILOW, BARRY, singer, composer, arranger; b. N.Y.C., June 17, 1946; s. Harold Pincus and Edna M. Student, N.Y. Coll. Music. Former positions include mailroom CBS; film editor WCBS-TV. Dir. music Callback series, Ed. Sullivan's Pilots; dir. music, condr., arranger, producer for Bette Midler, singer and composer; recorded hit songs: Can't Smile Without You, I Write the Songs, At the Copa (Grammy award, best male pop performance, 1979), Mandy, Looks Like We Made It; albums include Even Now, 1977, Manilow, 1985, 2 A.M. Paradise Cafe, 1985, Swing Street, 1987, Barry Manilow, 1989, Because It's Christmas, 1990, Showstoppers, 1991, The Complete Collection, Then Some, 1992, Manilow Box Set, 1992; star TV movie Copacabana, 1985; appeared TV specials The Barry Manilow Special (Emmy award, 1977), The Second Barry Manilow Special, also Big Fun on Swing Street, 1988, Barry Manilow: SRO on Broadway, 1989; TV appearances Murphy Brown, 1992; Broadway prodn.: Barry Manilow at the Gershwin, 1989; author Sweet Life: Adventures on the Way to Paradise; recipient Spl. Tony award, 1977, Ruby award After Dark mag. 1976, Photoplay Gold medal award 1976. Office: Arista Records 6 W 57 th St New York NY 10019*

MANINGER, R(ALPH) CARROLL, engineering executive, consultant; b. Harper, Kans., Dec. 24, 1918; s. Earl Dotterer and Mabel Velma (Haskin) M.; m. Jean Graves Kidder, July 1, 1942; children: Margaret Elisabeth, Mary Carroll, Emily Catherine. BS, Calif. Inst. Tech., 1941. Br. mgr. Gen. Precision Inc., Sunnyvale, Calif., 1953-62; head electronic engring. rsch. Lawrence Livermore Nat. Lab., Livermore, Calif., 1962-72, sr. scientist, 1972-85; owner Holidyne, Danville, Calif., 1985—. Contbr. articles to profl. jours.; patentee in field. Pres. Contra Costa (Calif.) Concert Guild, 1972-76. Fellow IEEE (life); mem. Nuclear and Plasma Scis. Soc. of IEEE (pres. 1980-82). Home and Office: Holidyne 146 Roan Dr Danville CA 94526-1915

MANION, DANIEL ANTHONY, federal judge; b. South Bend, Ind., Feb. 1, 1942; s. Clarence E. and Virginia (O'Brien) M.; m. Ann Murphy, June 29, 1984. BA, U. Notre Dame, 1964; JD, Ind. U., 1973. Bar: Ind., U.S. Dist. Ct. (no. dist.) Ind., U.S. Dist. Ct. (so. dist.) Ind. Dep. atty. gen. State of Ind., 1973-74; from assoc. to ptnr. Doran, Manion, Boynton, Kamm & Esmont, South Bend, 1974-86; judge U.S. Ct. Appeals (7th cir.), South Bend, 1986—. Mem. Ind. State Senate, Indpls., 1978-82. Home: 20725 Riverlan Rd South Bend IN 46637-1029 Office: US Ct Appeals 301 Federal Bldg 204 S Main St South Bend IN 46601-2122*

MANION, THOMAS A., college president; b. Aug. 10, 1934; m. Maureen O'Mara; children: Gregory, Marcy, Andrew, Margaret, Vicki, Tina, Thomas. B.B.A., St. Bonaventure U., 1959; M.B.A., Boston Coll., 1962; Ph.D., Clark U., 1968; D.Pedagogy, Bryant Coll., 1973. Chmn. econs. dept., dean grad. sch., acad. provost v.p. Bryant Coll., Smithfield, R.I.; pres. Coll. Saint Rose, Albany, N.Y., 1973-83, St. Nobert Coll., De Pere, Wis., 1983—; bd. dirs. Associated Kellogg Bank, Green Bay, Wis. Bd. dirs. Higher Edn. Aids Coun., State of Wis. Mem. NCAA, Nat. Assn. Ind. Colls. and Univs. (mem. commn. on campus concerns), Am. Assn. Higher Edn., Am. Coun. Edn., Nat. Cath. Edn. Assn., Assn. Cath. Colls. and Univs., Coun. Ind. Colls. (bd. dirs.), Wis. Assn. Ind. Colls. and Univs. (pres.), Wis. Found. Ind. Colls., Delta Epsilon, Delta Mu Delta. Office: St Norbert Coll De Pere WI 54115

MANIRE, GEORGE PHILIP, bacteriologist, educator; b. Roanoke, Tex., Mar. 25, 1919; s. Ernest L. and Zera (Ballew) M.; m. Ruth Jacobs, Apr. 10, 1943; children—Sarah, Philip. B.S., N. Tex. State Coll., 1940, M.S., 1941; Ph.D., U. Calif. at Berkeley, 1949. Instr. Southwestern Med. Sch., U. Tex., Dallas, 1949-50; mem. faculty U. N.C. Med. Sch., Chapel Hill, 1950—; prof. bacteriology and immunology U. N.C. Med. Sch., 1959-89, asst. vice chancellor health affairs, 1965-66, chmn. dept., 1966-79, Kenan prof., 1971—, vice chancellor, dean grad. sch., 1979-87; vis. scientist Lister Inst., London, Eng., 1971-72; Fulbright Research scholar Statens Seruminstut, Copenhagen, Denmark, 1956; Alan Gregg Travel Fellow in med. edn. China Med. Bd., 1963-64; vis. prof. Inst. for Virus Research, Kyoto (Japan) U., 1963-64, Inst. for Virus Research, Kyoto (Japan) U. (Japan Soc. Promotion Sci.), 1979. Club: Cosmos (Washington), Carolina Club (Chapel Hill). Research, publs. on chem. biol. and structural characteristics of chlamydiae, microbial pathogenesis. Home: 708 Coker Ln Chapel Hill NC 27514-4945

MANIRE, JAMES MCDONNELL, lawyer; b. Memphis, Feb. 22, 1918; s. Clarence Herbert and Elizabeth (McDonnell) M.; m. Nathalie Davant Latham, Nov. 21, 1951 (div. 1979); children: James McDonnell, Michael Latham, Nathalie Manire Willard; m. Nancy Whitman Colbert, Dec. 30, 1995. LL.B., U. Va., 1948. Bar: Tenn. 1948, U.S. Supreme Ct. 1957. Pvt. practice Memphis, 1948—, city atty., 1968-71; of counsel Waring Cox, Memphis, 1986—. Editor in chief Va. Law Rev., 1947-48. Served to lt. comdr. USNR, 1941-46. Fellow Am. Coll. Trial Lawyers, Am. Bar Found. (life); mem. ABA, Tenn. Bar Assn. (pres. 1966-67), Memphis and Shelby County Bar Assn. (pres. 1963-64), Tenn. Bar Found. (charter), 6th Circuit Jud. Conf. (life), Raven Soc. Clubs: Memphis Country, Memphis Hunt and Polo. Home: 2927 Frances Pl Memphis TN 38111-2401 Office: Waring Cox PLC 1300 Morgan Keegan Twr 50 N Front St Memphis TN 38103-2126

MANIS, MELVIN, psychologist, educator; b. N.Y.C., Feb. 18, 1931; s. Alex and Hanna (Oyle) M.; m. Jean Denby, May 28, 1954; children: Peter Eugene, David Denby. AB in Psychology, Franklin and Marshall Coll., 1951; PhD, U. Ill., 1954. Instr. psychology U. Pitts., 1956-58; rsch. psychologist Ann Arbor VA Med. Ctr., Mich., 1958-89; prof. psychology U. Mich., Ann Arbor, 1966—, assoc. chair dept. psychology, 1990-91. Author: Cognitive Processes, 1966, An Introduction to Cognitive Psychology, 1971; editor Jour. Personality and Social Psychology, 1980-84. Served with USPHS, 1954-56. Mem. APA, Am. Psychol. Soc., Midwestern Psychol. Assn., Soc. Exptl. Social Psychology, AAUP, Phi Beta Kappa, Sigma Xi. Democrat. Jewish. Club: Racquet (Ann Arbor). Home: 20 Harvard Pl Ann Arbor MI 48104-1726 Office: U Mich Dept Psychology Ann Arbor MI 48109

MANK, EDWARD WARREN, marketing professional; b. Boothbay Harbor, Maine, Oct. 2, 1962; s. Edward Raymond Jr. and Sandra Gail (Strahan) M. Assoc. in Liberal Arts, C.C. Vt., 1985; cert. ophthalmic technician, Nat. Edn. Ctr., San Francisco, 1992; cert. real estate broker, Am. Sch. Mortgage Banking, Walnut Creek, Calif., 1994. Lic. real estate salesman, Calif.; cert. Am. Bd. Optometry Dispensing. Tng. coord. Burger King Corp., South Burlington, Vt., 1985-87, San Francisco, 1988-89; asst. mgr. Bonanza Family Restaurant, South Burlington, 1987-88; supr. U.S. Census Bur., San Francisco, 1990; sales rep. Viacom Cablevision, San Francisco, 1991; programming researcher NBC, San Francisco, 1992; mktg. cons. Calyx & Corolla, San Francisco, 1993; mktg. rep. Alliance Bancorp, Millbrae, Calif., 1993—. Sustaining mem. Rep. Nat. Com., Washington, 1989—; sponsor Heritage Found., Washington, Cato Inst., Washington. Mem. Acad. Polit. Sci., Coun. Fgn. Rels., World Affairs Coun., Nat. Rifle Assn. (life), Reason Found. Republican. Episcopalian. Home: 3401 E 18th St Apt 3 Oakland CA 94601-3003 Office: Alliance Bancorp 800 El Camino Real Millbrae CA 94030-2010

MANKA, RONALD EUGENE, lawyer; b. Wichita, Kans., Dec. 12, 1944; s. James Ashford and Jane Bunn (Meeks) M.; m. Frances Ann Patterson, Aug. 7, 19665 (dec. Dec. 1985); children: Kimberly Ann, Lora Christine; m. Linda I. Bailey, Mar. 11, 1995. BBA cum laude, U. Kans., 1967; JD cum laude, U. Mich., 1970. Bar: Conn. 1970, Mo. 1974, Kans. 1985. Assoc. Day, Barry & Howard, Hartford, Conn., 1970-73; assoc. Lathrop & Gage L.C., Kansas City, Mo., 1973-78, mem., 1979-82, 85—; group counsel Butler Mfg. Co., Kansas City, 1982-83, div. gen. mgr., 1983-84. Trustee, clk., elder Village Presbyn. Ch., Prairie Village, Kans.; dir., treas. Lyric Opera of Kansas City, 1995—; pres. Genesis Sch., Kansas City, 1987-89; devel. chmn. Kansas City Friends of Alvin Ailey, 1987-89; chmn. Kansas City Mus., 1988-92, gen. counsel, 1994—; gen. counsel Spirit Festival, Kansas City, 1985-87, Kansas City C. of C., 1989—; pres. Ctr. for Mgmt. Assistance, Kansas City, 1991-93. Mem. ABA, Mo. Bar Assn. (alt. dispute resolution com. 1986—), Lawyers Assn. Kansas City, Silicon Prairie Tech. Assn. (bd. dirs. 1990-92), Homestead Country Club (pres. 1984-85). Republican. Avocations: bicycling, swimming. Office: Lathrop & Norquist PC 2345 Grand Blvd Ste 2600 Kansas City MO 64108-2625

MANKEL, FRANCIS XAVIER, former principal, priest; b. Knoxville, Tenn., Nov. 8, 1935; s. George Whitehead Sr. and Willia Frances (Duncan) M. BA, St. Ambrose U., 1957; STB, St. Mary's Coll., Balt., 1959, STL, 1961; MEd, Loyola Coll., Balt., 1965. Ordained priest, Roman Cath. Ch., 1961. Assoc. pastor Holy Ghost Ch., Knoxville, 1962-67; prin. Knoxville Cath. High Sch., 1967-79; pastor Sacred Heart Ch., Lawrenceburg, Tenn., 1979-84, St. John Neumann Ch., Knoxville, 1984-87, Sacred Heart Cathedral, Knoxville, 1987—; vicar gen., chancellor Cath. Diocese Knoxville, 1988—; supt. Cath. Schs., Diocese of Knoxville, 1989-92. Bd. dirs. Knoxville area chpt. ARC, 1986—. Mem. Am. Guild Organists, Knoxville Ministerial Assn. Home: 711 Northshore Dr SW Knoxville TN 37919-7549 Office: 805 Northshore Dr Knoxville TN 37919

MANKILLER, WILMA PEARL, tribal leader; b. Stilwell, Okla., Nov. 18, 1945; d. Charley and Clara Irene (Sitton) M.; m. Hector N. Olaya, Nov. 13, 1963 (div. 1975); children: Felicia Marie Olaya, Gina Irene Olaya; m. Charlie Soap, Oct. 13, 1986. Student, Skyline Coll., San Bruno Coll., 1973, San Francisco State Coll., 1973-75; BA in Social Sci., Union Coll., 1977; postgrad., U. Ark., 1979; DHL (hon.), U. New Eng., 1986; PhD in Pub. Svc. (hon.), R.I. Coll., 1989; DHL (hon.), Yale U., 1990; PhD (hon.), Dartmouth Coll., 1991; LLD (hon.), Mills Coll., 1992. Cmty. devel. dir. Cherokee Nation, Tahlequah, Okla., 1977-83, dep. chief, 1983-85, prin. chief, 1985-95; Montgomery fellow Darmouth Coll., 1996; mem. exec. bd. Coun. Energy Resource Tribes; bd. dirs. Okla. Indsl. Devel. Commn. Author: Mankiller: A Chief and Her People, 1993. Bd. dirs. Okla. Acad. for State Goals, 1985—. Recipient Donna Nigh First Lady award Okla. Commn. for Status of Women, 1985, Am. Leadership award Harvard U., 1986; inducted Okla. Women's Hall of Fame, 1986. Mem. Nat. Tribal Chmn. Assn., Nat. Congress Am. Indians, Cherokee County Dem. Women's Club. Avocations: reading, writing. Home: PO Box 308 Park Hill OK 74451

MANKIN, CHARLES JOHN, geology educator; b. Dallas, Jan. 15, 1932; s. Green and Myla Carolyn (Bohmert) M.; m. Mildred Helen Hahn, Sept. 6, 1953 (dec. Oct. 26, 1995); children: Sally Carol, Helen Francis, Laura Kay. Student, U. N.Mex., 1949-50; B.S., U. Tex. at Austin, 1954, M.A., 1955, Ph.D., 1958. Asst. prof. geology Calif. Inst. Tech., 1958-59; asst. prof. geology U. Okla., 1959-63, asso. prof., 1963-64, prof., 1964—; dir. Sch. Geology and Geophysics, 1963-77, Energy Resources Inst., 1978-87; mem. U.S. Nat. Commn. on Geology, 1977-80; dir. Okla. Geol. Survey, 1967—; former chmn. bd. mineral and energy resources, former mem. commn. on phys. sci., math. and resources Nat. Acad. Scis.; former commr. Commn. Fiscal Accountability of Nation's Energy Resources; former chmn. Royalty Mgmt. Adv. Com. Dept. Interior; bd. dirs. Environ. Inst. for Waste Mgmt. Studies, U. Ala.; bd. trustees Nat. Inst. Global Environ. Change. Contbr. articles profl. jours. Recipient Conservation Service award Dept. Interior, 1983. Fellow Geol. Soc. Am. (co-project leader Decade N.Am. Geology, former councillor, chmn. found.), Mineral. Soc. Am.; mem. Am. Assn. Petroleum Geologists (pub. svc. award 1988), Am. Inst. Profl. Geologists (v.p., past pres., Martin Van Couvering Meml. award 1988, mem. found., hon. life), Clay Minerals Soc., Geochem. Soc., AAAS, Assn. Am. State Geologists (past pres.), Am. Geol. Inst. (past pres., Ian Campbell medal 1987), Soc. Econ. Paleontologists and Mineralogists (past pres. Mid-Continent sect.), Oklahoma City Geol. Soc. (hon., life), Sigma Gamma Epsilon (nat. sec.-treas.). Home: 2220 Forister Ct Norman OK 73069-5120 Office: Okla Geol Survey Energy Ctr 100 E Boyd St Rm 131N Norman OK 73019-1001

MANKIN, HENRY JAY, physician, educator; b. Pitts., Oct. 9, 1928; s. Hyman Isaac and Mary (Simons) M.; m. Carole Jane Pinkney, Aug. 20, 1952; children: Allison Joan, David Philip, Keith Pinkney. B.S. magna cum laude, U. Pitts., 1952, M.D., 1953; M.A. (hon.), Harvard U., 1973. Diplomate Am. Bd. Orthopaedic Surgery (mem. bd. 1976-82, pres. bd. 1980-81). Intern U. Chgo. Clinics, 1953-54; resident orthopaedics Hosp. for Joint Diseases, N.Y.C., 1957-60; instr. orthopaedics U. Pitts. Sch. Medicine, 1960-62, asst. prof., 1962-64, assoc. prof., 1964-66; dir., prof. orthopaedics Hosp. for Joint Diseases and Mt. Sinai Sch. Medicine, 1966-72; chief orthopaedics Mass. Gen. Hosp., Boston, 1972-96; Edith M. Ashley prof. orthopaedics Harvard Med. Sch., 1972—; mem. surgery B study sect. NIH, 1969-73; mem. adv. com. on surg. treatment FDA, 1973-75; corporator Boston Five Cent Savs. Bank, 1982-83; mem. exec. com. Am. Bd. Med. Spltys., 1982-85; adv. council on grad. med. edn., 1986-96; mem. Nat. Arthritis Avd. Bd., 1986-89; mem. human resources and research rev. group A Nat. Inst. Arthritis, Metabolism and Digestive Diseases, 1981-85, chmn., 1983-85. Assoc. editor Arthritis and Rheumatism, 1967-77, Jour. Bone and Joint Surgery, 1967-82; mem. editorial bd. Jour. Orthopedic Research, 1982-85; trustee Jour. Bone and Joint Surgery, 1985-91, chmn. bd., 1988-91; contbr. numerous articles to profl., med. jours. Served to lt. comdr. USNR, 1955-57. Fellow ACS, Royal Coll. Surgeons (hon.); mem. Am. Acad. Orthopaedic Surgeons, Acad. Orthopaedic Soc. (pres. 1991-92), Am. Orthopaedic Assn. (pres. 1982-83), Orthopaedic Research Soc. (pres. 1969-70), Musculoskeletal Tumor Soc. (pres. 1991-92), Brit. Orthopaedic Research Soc., Argentine Orthopedic Assn. (hon.), N.Y. Acad. Medicine (chmn. orthopaedic sect. 1971-72), Am. Rheumatism Assn., Soc. Internat. Chirurgerie Orthopaedice et Traumatologia, Hip Soc., Interurban, Forum Orthopaedic clubs, Brit. Orthopaedic Assn. (hon.), Can. Orthopaedic Assn. (hon.), Australian Orthopaedic Assn. (hon.), N.Z. Orthopaedic Assn. (hon.), Japanese Orthopaedic Assn. (hon.), Israel Orthopaedic Assn. (hon.), Thai Orthopaedic Assn (hon.). Home: 185 Dean Rd Brookline MA 02146-4201 Office: Mass Gen Hosp 32 Fruit St Boston MA 02114-2620

MANKIN, ROBERT STEPHEN, financial executive; b. N.Y.C., Mar. 26, 1939; s. Samuel Harry Mankin and Dorothy (Rosenblum) Goldstein; m. Joyce Marie Cabel, June 13, 1971; children: Seth Howard, Laura Nicole, Gina Danielle. BA cum laude, Bklyn. Coll., 1961; MBA, Bernard Baruch Coll., 1970; Dr. Profl. Studies with distinction, Pace U., 1982. Mgr. ABC, N.Y.C., 1969-71, Babcock and Wilcox, N.Y.C., 1971-74; v.p. Chase Manhattan Bank, N.Y.C., 1974-84; sr. v.p. 1st Interstate Bank, N.Y.C., 1984-87; mng. dir., sr. v.p., co-head fixed income, mem. mgmt. com. Nomura Securities Internat., N.Y.C., 1987-94; mng. dir. Paine Webber, N.Y.C., 1994-95; pres., CEO Lakeside Fin. Svcs., Hoboken, N.J., 1995—; bd. dirs., sec. Nomura Mortgage Capital Corp., N.Y.C.; bd. dirs., pres., CEO Nomura Asset Capital Corp., N.Y.C., 1988-94; bd. dirs. PaineWebber Real Estate, 1994-95. Contbr. articles to profl. jours. Mem. Planning Forum, Assn. for Computing Machinery, Assn. Computer Programmers and Analysts (chmn. bd. 1971). Home: 21 Shield Dr Woodcliff Lake NJ 07675-8127 Office: Lakeside Fin Svcs LLC 209 Garden St Hoboken NJ 07030-3705

MANKO, JOSEPH MARTIN, SR., lawyer; b. Phila., Oct. 7, 1939; s. Horace David and Vivian (Greenberg) M.; m. Lynn Kimmelman, June 17, 1962; children: Joseph Jr., Glenn, Wendy. BA magna cum laude, Yale U., 1961; JD cum laude, Harvard U., 1964. Bar: Pa. 1964. Regional counsel EPA, Phila., 1973-75; assoc. Wolf, Block, Schorr & Solis-Cohen, Phila., 1964-72, ptnr., 1972-73, 75-89, chmn. environ. law, 1978-89; founding ptnr. Manko, Gold & Katcher, Bala Cynwyd, Pa., 1989—; adj. prof. U. Pa. Law Sch., 1988—, Grant Irey lectr., 1989-90; dir. Pa. Environ. Council, Phila., 1978-85, treas., 1986-87, pres., 1987-89, chmn. 1989—; chair or co-chair numerous environ. bar assn. coms. Commr. Lower Merion Twp., Ardmore, Pa., 1979-91, 94—, v.p., 1992, pres. 1993; mem. Com. of 70, Phila., 1978-88; pres. Beth David Reform Congregation, Gladwyne, Pa., 1983-86, trustee, 1978-83, 86—; trustee Fedn. Jewish Agys., Phila., 1982-86; bd. dirs. Golden Slipper Camp, 1981-84, 88—, Jewish Cmty. Rels. Coun., 1983-88, Lower Merion Conservancy, 1976—, Phila. Geriatric Ctr., 1990—, Delaware River Basin Water Resources Assn., 1993-96; mem. Dem. State Com., 1986-90; bd. dirs. 21st Century Environ. Commn., 1997—. Mem. ABA, Pa. Bar Assn., Pa. Bar Inst. (bd. dirs. 1997—), Phila. Bar Assn., Phi Beta Kappa. Clubs: Germantown Cricket, Bala Golf (Phila.), Hamilton Bridge, Vesper. Avocations: tennis, golf, walking, classical music. Home: 96 E Levering Mill Rd Bala Cynwyd PA 19004-2611 Office: Manko Gold & Katcher 401 E City Ave Ste 500 Bala Cynwyd PA 19004-1122

MANKO, WESLEY DANIEL, financial advisor; b. Kenosha, Wis., Oct. 14, 1957; s. Antoni Stanley and Sophie (Jerzowski) M.; m. Theresa Lee Mulrooney (div.); m. Sandra Lynn Hansen, May 22, 1992. AS, Gateway Tech. Coll., Kenosha, Wis., 1978; BS in Criminal Justice, Edgewood Coll., 1981; MPA, U. Wis., Kenosha, 1987. Job placement specialist Kenosha Schievement Ctr., 1986-88, State of Wis. Job Svc., 1986; vocat. cons. Kaiser Group Inc., 1988; membership rep. U.S. C. of C., Washington, 1989-90; case mgr. Goodwill Industries, Kenosha, 1990-91; account mgr. Lakeshore Employment Specialists, Kenosha, 1991-92; pres. Competitive Edge Employment Mktg. Svcs., Kenosha, 1991—; mktg. cons. Bus. Connections Mag., Kenosha, 1992—; fin. adv. Cigna Fin. Advisors, 1993. lAuthor: Women's Guide to Practical Self Defense, 1979. Chmn. Kenosha County Dem. Party, 1991-92. Recipient Rookie of Yr. award Prin. Fin. Group, 1994. Mem. Kenosha Jaycees (chpt. pres. 1985, Past Pres. award 1986), Toastmasters (area gov. 1989, pres. 1989, Best Speaker 1985, Best Table Topics Speech 1985, 86, 87, 90, 92), Masons, Shriner, Order DeMolay. Avocations: biking, tennis, travel, martial arts. Home: 4947 N Wildwood Ave Milwaukee WI 53217-6015

MANKOFF, ALBERT WILLIAM, cultural organization administrator, consultant; b. Newark, Aug. 24, 1926; s. Albert and Dorothy M.; m. Audrey Emery, Mar. 18, 1972; 1 child, Robert Morgan. BLS, U. Okla., 1967. With Am. Airlines, Inc., 1947-69; mgr. mgmt. tng. and devel. Am. Airlines Inc., 1957-67; mgr. orgn. devel. Am. Airlines, Inc., Tulsa, 1968-69; dir. personnel Peat, Marwick, Mitchell & Co., Chgo., 1969-72; ptnr. Lexicon, Inc. Cons., Raleigh, N.C., 1972-77; Pacific area mgr. safety and tng. Trailways, Inc., L.A., 1978-80; tng. cons. State of Sacramento, Sacramento, 1980-91; pres. Inst. Am. Hist. Tech., Weaverville, N.C., 1987—. Author: Trolley Treasures, 4 vols., 1986-87, The Glory Days, 1989, Tracks of Triumph, 1993, Tarnished Triumph, The Edison Paradigm, 1994, Sacramento's Shining Rails, 1995, Trolleys in America: The Long Road Back, 1995; contbr. articles to profl. jours. Bd. dirs., v.p. OASIS; Midwest Centre for Human Potential, Chgo., 1970-72, Tulsa Urban League, 1962-69; v.p., bd. dirs. Meditation Groups Inc., Ojai, Calif., Psychosynthesis Internat., Ojai Internat. Assn. Managerial and Orgnl. Psychosynthesis, Thousand Oaks, Calif. Avocations: street car and light rail technology, historical trolley photographs, cat humor. Home and Office: 36 Cedar Hill Ln Weaverville NC 28787 *Personal philosophy: I believe that the love principle is the most powerful force in the universe, and fear is the most destructive; that we create our own heaven or hell as a consequence of our thought; that we die and are reborn countless times until we master life in the human framework.*

MANKOFF, DAVID A., nuclear medicine physician; b. July 10, 1959. BS in Physics summa cum laude, Yale U., 1981; MD, PhD in Bioengring., U. Pa., 1988. Diplomate Am. Bd. Internal Medicine, Am. Bd. Nuclear Medicine. Rsch. scientist UGM Med. Systems, Phila., 1988-89, dir. engring., 1989-90; rsch. assoc. nuclear medicine sect. U. Pa., Phila., 1988-90; resident in internal medicine U. Wash., Seattle, 1990-92, resident in nuclear medicine, 1992-96, asst. prof. radiology, 1996—. Office: Divsn Nuclear Medicine U Wash Med Ctr Box 356113 1959 NE Pacific St Seattle WA 98195-0004

MANKOFF, RONALD MORTON, lawyer; b. Gettysburg, S.D., Oct. 13, 1931; s. Harry B. and Sarah (Frank) M.; m. Joy Faith Shechtman, Nov. 3, 1959; children: Jeffrey Walker, Douglas Frank. BSL, U. Minn., JD, 1954; LLM in Taxation, NYU, 1959. Bar: Minn. 1954, Tex. 1959. With Leonard, Street & Deinard, Mpls., 1957-58; research analyst Inst. Jud. Adminstrn., N.Y.C., 1958-59; assoc. Lyne, Blanchette, Smith & Shelton, Dallas, 1959-60; ptnr. Durant and Mankoff, Dallas, 1960-85; pres. Brice & Mankoff P.C., Dallas, 1985-89, Mankoff, Hill, Held & Metzger, L.L.P., Dallas, 1989-95; chmn./gen. counsel RAC Fin. Group, Inc., 1994-96; lectr. law So. Meth. U., 1974-77; speaker in field. Contbr. articles to profl. jours. Chmn. bd. Dallas chpt. Am. Cancer Soc., 1976-77, bd. dirs. Tex. divsn., 1981-94; chmn. Dallas Crusade, 1974-75, bd. dirs., mem. exec. com., 1963-88; mem. Dallas Mcpl. Libr., 1973-75; exec. com. Dallas Citizens Charter Assn., 1971-75; pres. Dallas Arts Found., Inc., 1973-75; mem. exec. com. Nat. Pooled Income Fund, Coun. Jewish Welfare Fedns. and Funds, 1975-77; adv. dir. Dallas Cmty. Chest Trust Fund, 1976-78; chmn. Found. Dallas Jewish Fedn., 1976-77; pres. Temple Emanu-el, Dallas, 1977-79; bd. dirs. Jewish Fedn. Greater Dallas, 1977-79, Dallas Civic Opera, 1981-83, World Union Progressive Judaism, 1981-90; mem. S.W. regional liaison com. IRS, 1980-83; exec. com. Union Am. Hebrew Congregations, 1979-89, trustee, 1979—, chmn. nat. coll. com., 1983-87, vice chmn. bd. dirs., 1984-88; sec. Dallas Assembly, 1979-84; exec. com. Jewish Cmty. Rels. Coun., 1982-83, Com. for Qualified Judiciary, 1982—; sec. Child Care Partnership, 1984-86, bd. dirs., 1986-88; bd. dirs. Dallas Women's Found., 1985-89, adv. coun., 1989—; bd. dirs. Am. Jewish Com., 1982-88, pres. Dallas chpt. 1986-90; bd. dirs. Tex. coun. Girl Scouts U.S., 1982-85, Goodwill Industries of Greater Dallas, 1979-83, Title One Home Improvement Lender's Assn., 1994-96; mem. Mayor's Task Force on Child Care, 1984; bd. govs. Dallas Symphony Assn., 1988-96; chmn. Temple Emanu El Found., 1988-95. Lt. (j.g.) USN, 1954-57. Mem. ABA, State Bar Tex., Dalls Bar Assn., North Dallas C. of C. (adv. bd. 1986-88), Columbian Country Club (bd. dirs. 1967-73), Zeta Beta Tau, Delta Sigma Rho. Democrat. Jewish. Home: 22 Lakeside Park Dallas TX 75225-8110 Office: 5950 Berkshire Ln Ste 500 Dallas TX 75225-5833

MANLEY, AUDREY FORBES, medical administrator, physician; b. Jackson, Miss., Mar. 25, 1934; d. Jesse Lee and Ora Lee (Buckhalter) Forbes; m. Albert Edward Manley, Apr. 3, 1970. A.B. with honors (tuition scholar), Spelman Coll., Atlanta, 1955; M.D. (Jesse Smith Noyes Found. scholar), Meharry Med. Coll., 1959; MPH, Johns Hopkins U.-USPHS traineeship, 1987; LHD (hon.), Tougaloo (Miss.) Coll., 1990, Meharry Med. Coll., Nashville, 1991; LLD (hon.), Spelman Coll., 1991. Diplomate: Am. Bd. Pediatrics. Intern St. Mary Mercy Hosp., Gary, Ind., 1960; from jr. to chief resident in pediatrics Cook County Children's Hosp., Chgo., 1960-62; NIH fellow neonatology U. Ill. Rsch. and Ednl. Hosp., Chgo., 1963-65; staff pediatrician Chgo. Bd. Health, 1963-66; practice medicine specializing in pediatrics Chgo., 1963-66; assoc. Lawndale Neighborhood Health Ctr. North, 1966-67; asst. med. dir., 1967-69; asst. prof. Chgo. Med. Coll., 1966-67; instr. Pritzker Sch. Medicine, U. Chgo., 1967-69; asst. dir. ambulatory pediatrics, asst. dir. pediatrics Mt. Zion Hosp. and Med. Center, San Francisco, 1969-70; med. cons. Spelman Coll., 1970-71, med. dir. family planning program, chmn. health careers adv. com., 1972-76; med. dir. Grady Meml. Hosp. Family Planning Clinic, 1972-76; with Health Services Adminstrs., Dept. Health and Human Services, 1976—; commd. officer USPHS, 1976—; chief genetic diseases services br. Office Maternal and Child Health, Bur. Community Health Services, Rockville, Md., 1976-81; acting assoc. adminstr. clin. affairs Office of Adminstr. Health Resources and Services Adminstrn., 1981-83, chief med. officer, dep. assoc. adminstr. planning, evaluation and legis., 1983-85; sabbatical leave USPHS Johns Hopkins Sch. Hygiene and Pub. Health, 1986-87; dir. Nat. Health Service Corps.; asst. surgeon gen., 1988; dep. asst. Sec. for Health USPHS/HHS, 1989-93, acting asst. Sec. Health, 1993, dep. asst. Sec. Health/intergovtl. affairs, 1993-94; dep. surgeon gen., acting dep. asst. sec. for minority health USPHS, 1994-95; acting surgeon gen., 1995—; mem. U.S. del. UNICEF, 1990-94. Author numerous articles, reports in field. Trustee Spelman Coll., 1966-70. Recipient Meritorious Svc. award USPHS, 1981, Mary McLeod Bethune award Nat Coun. Negro Women, 1979, Dr. John P. McGovern Ann. Lectureship award Am. Sch. Health Assn., Disting. Alumni award Meharry Med. Coll., 1989, Spelman Coll. 108 Founder's Day Convocation, 1989, Disting. Svc. medal USPHS, 1992, Hildrus A. Poindexter award OSG/PHS, 1993, numerous other svc. and achievement awards. Fellow Am. Acad. Pediatrics; mem. Nat. Inst. Medicine of Nat. Acad. Sci., Nat. Med. Assn., APHA, AAUW, AAAS, Spelman Coll. Alumnae Assn., Meharry Alumni Assn., Operation Crossroads Africa Alumni Assn., Delta Sigma Theta (hon.). Home: 2807 18th St NW Washington DC 20009-2205 Office: 5600 Fishers Ln Rockville MD 20852-1750

MANLEY, FRANK, English language educator; b. Scranton, Pa., Nov. 13, 1930; s. Aloysius F. and Kathryn L. (Needham) M.; m. Carolyn Mary Holliday, Mar. 14, 1952; children: Evelyn, Mary. B.A., Emory U., 1952, M.A., 1953; Ph.D., Johns Hopkins U., 1959. Instr., then asst. prof. Yale U., New Haven, 1959-64; assoc. prof., then prof. dept. English Emory U., Atlanta, 1964—; chmn. dept. Emory U., 1968-70, Candler prof. English, 1982—, dir. creative writing program, 1990—. Editor: The Anniversaries (John Donne), 1963, A Dialogue of Comfort (St. Thomas More), vol. 12, 1977 and Epistola ad Pomeranum, vol. 7, 1990, Yale edit. More's complete works; author: Resultances, 1980 (Devins award for poetry 1980), Two Masters (co-winner Gt. Am. New Play Contest 9th Ann. Humana Festival New Am. Plays 1985), (with F. Watkins) Some Poems and Some Talk About Poetry, 1985, Within the Ribbons: 9 Stories, 1989, (play) The Trap, 1993. With U.S. Army, 1952-55. Guggenheim Found. fellow, 1966-67, 78-79; recipient NEH transl. program fellowship, 1981-83, Nat. Endowment Arts Creative Writing Fellowship in Fiction, 1995-97, Disting. Teaching award, 1984, Univ. scholar/Tchr. of yr. award, 1989, Disting. Alumnus award The Marist Sch., 1993. Mem. MLA, AAUP. Roman Catholic. Home: 401 Adams St Decatur GA 30030-5207 also: RR5 Box 228 Ellijay GA 30540 Office: Emory U Dept English Atlanta GA 30322

MANLEY, GERTRUDE ELLA, librarian, media specialist; b. Phila., Dec. 29, 1930; d. William Eugene and Anna G. (Price) Lomas; m. Harley E. Manley, Jr., July 20, 1957; children: Marc Alan, Karen Sue Manley Thornton, Gail Ann Manley Rivera. BRE, Shelton Coll., 1955; MSEd, Queens Coll., 1958, MS in Libr. Edn., 1958; postgrad., various. Libr. tchr. Plainedge (N.Y.) Sch. Dist., 1955-60; libr. dir. Huntington (N.Y.) Christian Sch., 1968-70; libr./media specialist Connetquot Ctrl. Sch. Dist. of Islip, Bohemia, N.Y., 1970—. Editor: Manley Family Newsletter, 1983—; contbr. articles to profl. jours. Mem. nursery sch. bd. New Life Community Ch. Nursery Sch., Sayville, N.Y., 1985-89; adminstr. pre-sch. story time program, E.J. Bosti Sch., Bohemia, 1972—, sign lang. instr., 1988—, Huffine award chairperson, 1985—, spell bee judge, 1984—, arranger speakers program, 1988—, kindergarten screening participant, 1988—, numerous in-house site-base planning and mgmt. coms., 1990-93. Mem. N.Y. State Ret. Tchrs. Assn. (life), N.Y. State United Tchrs., Western Suffolk Ret. Tchrs. Assn. (life), Connetquot Tchrs. Assn. (chmn. scholarship com.1978-93), Connetquot Ret. Tchrs. Assn. (rec. and corr. sec. 1993—). Baptist/Reformed Ch. of Am. Avocations: family history rsch., genealogy, authoring history articles, reading. Home: 171 Nathan Dr Bohemia NY 11716-1319 Office: Connetquot Ctrl Sch Dist Islip 780 Ocean Ave Bohemia NY 11716-3631

MANLEY, JOAN A(DELE) DANIELS, retired publisher; b. San Luis Obispo, Calif., Sept. 23, 1932; d. Carl and Della (Weinmann) Daniels; m. Jeremy C. Lanning, Mar. 17, 1956 (div. Sept. 1963); m. Donald H. Manley, Sept. 12, 1964 (div. 1985); m. William G. Houlton, May 31, 1991. BA, U. Calif., Berkeley, 1954; DBA (hon.), U. New Haven, 1974; LLD (hon.), Babson Coll., 1978. Sec. Doubleday & Co., Inc., N.Y.C., 1954-60; sales exec. Time Inc., 1960-66, v.p., 1971-75, group v.p., 1975-84, also bd. dir.; circulation dir. Time-Life Books, 1966-68, dir. sales, 1968-70, pub., 1970-76; chmn. bd. Time-Life Books Inc., 1976-80; vice chmn. bd. Book-of-the-Month Club, Inc., N.Y.C., until 1984; supervising dir. Time-Life Internat. (Nederland) B.V., Amsterdam, until 1984; bd. dirs. Viking Office Products Inc., AON Corp., Sara Lee Corp., BFP Holdings, Inc. Past trustee Mayo Found., Rochester, Minn., Nat. Repertory Orch., William Benton Found.; former mem. adv. coun. Stanford U. Bus. Sch., Haas Sch. Bus. U. Calif.; trustee Vail Valley Inst., Keystone Ctr. Named to Direct Mktg. Hall of Fame, 1993; U. Calif.-Berkeley fellow, 1989. Mem. Assn. Am. Pubs. (past chmn.).

MANLEY, JOHN, Canadian government official; b. Ottawa, Ontario, Canada, Jan. 5, 1950; s. John Joseph Manley and Mildred Charlotte (Scharf) M.; m. Judith Mary Rae, April 21, 1973; children: Rebecca Jane, David John, Sarah Kathleen. Attended, Carleton U., U. Ottawa. Law clerk for Rt. Hon. Bora Laskin Chief Justice Can., 1976-77; chair Ottawa-Carleton Bd. Trade, 1985-86; min. industry Canada, 1993—, min. western economic diversificatio & min. of industry, min. for the atlantic Canada oppurtunities agency & min. responsible for the off. of reg. dev, 1996. elected to H. of C. g.e., 1988. Office: Industry, 235 Queen St 11th Fl East, Ottawa, ON Canada K1A 0H5 also: 200 1885 Bank St, Ottawa, ON Canada K1V 0W3*

MANLEY, JOHN FREDERICK, political scientist, educator; b. Utica, N.Y., Feb. 20, 1939; s. John A. and Gertrude Manley; children from previous marriage: John, Laura; m. Kathy Lynn Sharp, 1991; 1 child, Cole Sharp Manley. B.S., Le Moyne Coll., 1961; Ph.D., Syracuse U., 1966. Asst. prof. polit. sci. U. Wis., 1966, assoc. prof., 1969-71; prof., chmn. dept. polit. sci. Stanford U., 1977-80; fellow Center for Advanced Study in Behavioral Scis., 1976-77; vis. prof. Stanford in Oxford, 1996. Author: The Politics of Finance, 1970, American Government and Public Policy, 1976; author, co-editor: The Case Against the Constitution, 1987. Congressional fellow, 1963-64; Brookings Instn. fellow, 1965-66; Guggenheim fellow, 1974-75; Fulbright fellow U. Bologna, 1992. Office: Stanford U Dept Polit Sci Stanford CA 94305

MANLEY, JOHN HUGO, computing technology executive, educator; b. Highland Park, Mich., July 9, 1932; s. Hugo Edward and Linda Amelia (Kuure) M.; m. Josephine Theresa Catanzaro, Sept. 3, 1958; children: Lisa Linn, Michele Ann, John David, Marc Darrin. B. Metall. Engring., Cornell U., 1955; MS Indsl. Engring., U. Pitts., 1965, PhD, 1971. Metall. engr. GE, Schenectady, N.Y., 1955-56; commd. 2d lt. USAF, 1956, advanced through grades to lt. col., 1973, ret., 1976; asst. to dir. Johns Hopkins Applied Physics Lab., Laurel, Md., 1976-80; exec. ITT Corp., Stratford, Conn., 1980-83; v.p. Nastec Corp., Southfield, Mich., 1983-85; dir. Software Engring. Inst. Software Engring. Inst. Carnegie Mellon U., Pitts., 1985-87; pres., chmn. Computing Tech. Transition, Inc., Wilmington, Del., 1983—; prof. manufacturing and info. tech. systems engring., dir. mfg. sys. engring. prog. U. Pitts., 1987—; mem. tech. adv. bd. Tartan Inc., Pitts.; dir. Concurrent Techs. Corp., Johnstown, Pa.; mem. com. on nat. weather svc. modernization NRC, 1991-94. Editor-in-chief Jour. Systems and Software, 1978-82; contbr. articles to profl. jours. Pres. Point Field Community Assn., Millersville, Md., 1979-80; v.p. Greater Severna Park Coun., Severna Park, Md., 1980. Lt. col. USAF, 1955-76, Vietnam. Decorated Legion of Merit, Bronze Star. Mem. IEEE Computer Soc. (TC exec. bd.), Soc. Mfg. Engrs., Assn. Computing Machinery, Am. Soc. Engring. Edn., Pitts. Athletic Assn. Republican. Episcopalian.

MANLEY, NORLEE K., nurse, chemical dependence program administrator; b. Middleport, Ohio; d. James Norwood Van Cooney and Esther Marie Searles; m. Virgil James Manley; children: Michael James, Sandra René. ADN, Cuyahoga Community Coll., 1975; BSN, Kent State U., 1986; MSN in Adminstrn., U. Akron, 1991. Cert. in nursing adminstrn.; cert. chem. dependence counselor. Head nurse Vets. Addiction Recovery Ctr. VA Med. Ctr., Cleve., coord. Drug Depencence Treatment prog., dep. dir. Vets. Addiction Recovery Ctr., dir. Vets. Addiction Recovery Ctr. Contbr. to profl. jours. Chairperson 24th Ann. Nurses Conf. Recipient award for outstanding supr. Fed. Exec. Bd., 1991. Mem. ANA, Ohio Nurses Assn., Greater Cleve. Nurses Assn., Nat. Consortium of Chem. Dependence Nurses, Nurses Orgn. of VA (bd. dirs., Excellence in Nursing award 1986, Regional Adminstrs. award for Excellence in Nursing 1990), Sigma Theta Tau. Home: 4820 Sentinel Dr Cleveland OH 44141-3149

MANLEY, RICHARD WALTER, insurance executive; b. Malone, N.Y., Dec. 26, 1934; s. Walter E. and Ruth (St. Mary) M.; m. Linda Kimberlin, Dec. 18, 1965; children: Stephanie, Christopher. BS in Bus., U. So. Miss., 1960. Cert. real estate broker. Account exec. Colonial Life and Accident, Hattiesburg, Miss., 1960-63; dist. mgr. Colonial Life and Accident, Oklahoma City, 1963-66; regional dir. Colonial Life and Accident, Denver, 1966-76, zone dir., 1976-82; pres. Commonwealth Gen. Group, Denver, 1982-96, Manley Properties Inc., Denver, 1982-90, Richard W. Manley Commonwealth Gen. Grps., Inc., Denver, 1982—; cons. Capitol Am. Life Ins. Co., Cleve., 1987-96; bd. dirs. (merco) Mercy Hosp., Denver, 1982-87. With USAF, 1956-59. Mem. Cherry Hills C. of C., Rotary, Alpha Tau Omega. Roman Catholic. Avocations: golfing, racquetball, running. Home: 6510 E Lake Pl Englewood CO 80111-4411

MANLEY, ROBERT EDWARD, lawyer, economist; b. Cin., Nov. 24, 1935; s. John M. and Helen Catherine (McCarthy) M.; m. Roberta L. Anzinger, Oct. 21, 1971 (div. 1980); 1 child, Robert Edward. ScB in Econs, Xavier U., 1956; AM in Econ. Theory, U. Cin., 1957; JD, Harvard U., 1960; postgrad., London Sch. Econs. and Polit. Sci., 1960, MIT, 1972. Bar: Ohio 1960, U.S. Supreme Ct. 1970. Pvt. practice law Cin., 1960—; pres. Manley, Burke, Lipton & Cook, 1977; Taft teaching fellow econs. U. Cin., 1956-57, vis. lectr. community planning law Coll. Design, Architecture and Art, 1967-73, adj. assoc. prof. urban planning Coll. Design, Architecture, Art and Planning, 1972-81, adj. prof., 1981—, adj. prof. law, 1980—. Author: Metropolitan School Desegregation, 1978, (with Robert N. Cook) Management of Land and Environment, 1981, others; chmn. editl. adv. bd. Urban Lawyer, 1986-95. Mem. Hamilton County Pub. Defender Commn., 1976-79; trustee HOPE, Cin., Albert J. Ryan Found.; counsel, co-founder Action Housing for Greater Cin.; mem. Spl. Commn. on Formation U. Cin. Health Maintenance Orgn., Mayor Cin. Spl. Com. on Housing; chmn. Cin. Environ. Adv. Coun., 1975-76; trustee The Americas Fund for Ind. Univs., 1987—; trustee Ohio Planning Conf., 1982-91, pres., 1987-89, trustee, 1987-90; sec. Cin. Mounted Patrol Com., 1993—; active Bd. Cin. Downtown Coun., 1991—. Mem. ABA (coun. sect. local govt. law 1976-80, 81-85, 88-92), Ohio Bar Assn., Cin. Bar Assn., Am. Judicature Soc., Law and Soc. Assn., Nat. Coun. Crime and Delinquency, Harvard U. Law Sch. Assn. Cin. (pres. 1970-71), Am. Econ. Assn., Am. Acad. Polit. and Social Sci., Queen City Club, Explorers Club (N.Y.C.) (trustee, sec. Clark chpt. 1992—), Athenaeum Club (Phila.), S.Am. Explorers Club (Lima, Peru). Republican. Roman Catholic. Office: Manley Burke Lipton & Cook 225 W Court St Cincinnati OH 45202-1012

MANLEY, WALTER WILSON, II, lawyer; b. Gainesville, Fla., Mar. 16, 1947; s. Walter Wilson and Marjorie Iley (Watkins) M.; children: Marjorie, Benjamin. BA, Fla. So. Coll., 1969; JD, Duke U., 1972; MBA, Harvard U., 1975. Atty. Blackwell, Walker & Gray, Miami, Fla., 1972-75; pvt. practice law Lakeland, Fla., 1975-84; prof. bus. adminstrn. Fla. State U., Tallahassee, 1985—; ptnr. MacFarlane, Ferguson, Allison & Kelly, Tallahassee, 1991-94; vis. prof. bus. adminstrn. Ridley Hall Coll. and Cambridge Fedn. Theol. Colls., Eng., 1988-90, Cambridge U. Faculties of Mgmt. Studies, Philosophy, Law, Social and Polit. Scis. and Divinity, 1989-90; pres. Exeter Leadership Cos. Inst., Inc., Tallahassee, 1989-94, Fla. North Shore Tech. Ctrs., Inc., 1995—. Author: Critical Issues in Business Conduct, 1990, Executive's Handbook of Model Business Conduct Codes, 1991, Handbook of Good Business Practice, 1992, What Florida Thinks, 1996, The History of the Supreme Court of Florida and Its Predecessor Courts, 1821-1917, 1997. Pres. Fla. Endowment Found. for Vocat. Rehab., 1991-93; bd. dirs. Fla. Real Property and Casualty Joint Underwriters Assn., 1987-91, Consumer Coun. Fla., 1992—; bd. visitors Duke U. Sch. Law, 1991—; trustee The Webb Sch., BellBuckle, Tenn., 1983-92, nat. fund chmn., 1982; pres. Polk County Legal Aid Soc. Mem. ABA, Fla. Bar Assn. (Pres.' Pro Bono Svc. award 1985), Lakeland Bar Assn. (pres.), Capital Duke Club (pres.), Tallahassee Quarterback Club Found. (chmn., Biletnikoff award), Psi Chi, Omicron Delta Kappa, Sigma Alpha Epsilon, Phi Delta Phi. Episcopalian. Avocations: hot air balloons, gliders, fly fishing, wing shooting. Home: 2804 Rabbit Hill Rd Tallahassee FL 32312-3137

MANLY, SARAH LETITIA, state legislator, ophthalmic photographer, angiographer; b. Greenville, S.C., Feb. 1, 1927; d. Victor Harris and Elsie Clippard (Burnett) Gillespie; m. Basil Manly IV, Sept. 11, 1947; children: Sarah Manly Cornish, Basil V, Jean Manly McDowell, Mary Manly Grant. BS cum laude, Furman U., 1947; postgrad., MIT, 1972; MEd, Clemson U., 1974; postgrad., Cambridge (Eng.) U., 1981. Cert. physics tchr., Pa., S.C.; cert. retinal angiographer. Ward sec. Roper Hosp., Charleston, S.C., 1947; analytical chemist Parker Labs., Charleston, 1948; tchr. sci. Upper Darby (Pa.) Sch. Dist., 1961-63; tchr. physics Sch. Dist. Greenville (S.C.) County, 1963-64, 70-76; ophthalmic photographer Basil Manly IV, MD, Greenville, 1976-96; lectr. physics Clemson (S.C.) U., 1979-81; state rep. S.C. Ho. of Reps., Columbia, 1989-93; cons. MIT, Cambridge, 1972-75, Georgetown U., Washington, 1974-76, NASA, Houston, 1974-76. Editor, cons. physics study guides MIT, 1972-75; editor lab. materials NASA, 1974-76; contbr. articles to profl. jours. Trustee Sch. Dist. Greenville County, 1976-88. Named S.C. Legislator of Yr., S.C. Sch. Bds. Assn., 1991. Mem. Greenville County Med. Aux. (sec. 1953-54), Delta Kappa Gamma. Democrat. Baptist. Avocations: travel, reading, gardening. Home: 2 Chanticleer Dr Greenville SC 29605-3106

MANLY, WILLIAM DONALD, metallurgist; b. Malta, Ohio, Jan. 13, 1923; s. Edward James and Thelma (Campbell) M.; m. Jane Wilden, Feb. 9, 1949; children—Hugh, Ann, Marc, David. Student, Antioch Coll., 1941-42; B.S., U. Notre Dame, 1947, M.S., 1949; postgrad., U. Tenn., 1950-55. Metallurgist Oak Ridge Nat. Lab., 1949-60, mgr. gas cooled reactor program, 1960-64; mgr. materials research Union Carbide Corp., N.Y.C., 1964-65; gen. mgr. Union Carbide Corp. (Stellite div.), N.Y.C., 1967-69; v.p. Union Carbide Corp. (Stellite div.), Kokomo, Ind., 1969-70; sr. v.p. Cabot Corp., Boston, 1970-83; exec. v.p. Cabot Corp., 1983-86; ret., 1986; also dir. chmn. adv. com. for reactor safety AEC, 1964-65. Served with USMC, 1943-46. Recipient Honor award U. Notre Dame, 1974, Nat. Medal of Tech., Nat. Sci. Found., 1993. Fellow Am. Soc. Metals (hon. mem., pres. 1972-73, medal for advanced rsch. 1987), AIME, Am. Nuclear Soc. (Merit award 1966); mem. Nat. Acad. Engring., Nat. Assn. Corrosion Engrs., Metall. Soc., Cosmos Club, Masons. Presbyterian. Home: 300 Chamberlain Cove Rd Kingston TN 37763-6030

MANN, ALFRED, musicology educator, choral conductor; b. Hamburg, Germany, Apr. 28, 1917; came to U.S. May 2, 1939, naturalized, 1943; s. Wilhelm and Edith (Weiss) M.; m. Carolyn Owens, Aug. 23, 1948; children: Adrian, John, Timothy. Cert., State Acad. Music, Berlin, Germany, 1937, Royal Conservatory, Milan, Italy, 1938; diploma, Curtis Inst. Music, Phila., 1942; M.A., Columbia U., 1950, Ph.D., 1955; MusD (hon.), Whitworth Coll., 1947, Baldwin-Wallace Coll., 1984, Muhlenberg Coll., Allentown, Pa., 1985. Instr. State Acad. Music, Berlin, 1937-38; instr. Scuola Musicale, Milan, Italy, 1938-39; research asst. Curtis Inst. Music, Phila., 1939-42; chmn. to prof. emeritus Rutgers U., New Brunswick, N.J., 1947—; prof. emeritus musicology Eastman Sch. Music/U. Rochester, N.Y., 1980—; condr. Cantata Singers, N.Y., 1952-59, Bach Choir, Bethlehem, Pa., 1970-80, recs. G.F. Handel, Chandos Anthems, 3 vols., 1964, 65, 66; dir. publs. Am. Choral Found., Phila., 1962—. Author: Study of Fugue, 1958, Theory and Practice, 1987, Bach and Handel: Choral Performance Practice, 1992; editor vols. for Complete Works of Handel, Mozart, Schubert, 1965—, J.J. Fux, Gradus ad Parnassum, 1938, 43, 85, Messiah critical edit. of Handel's conducting score, 1959, 65, 89, Am. Choral Rev., 1962—, Handel, The Orchestral Music, 1996. Bd. dirs. G.F. Handel Gesellschaft, Halle, Germany. Served with CIC, U.S. Army, 1943-45. Guggenheim fellow, 1958. Fellow Am. Coun. Learned Soc., Am. Philos. Soc., Nat. Found. Humanities; mem. Am. Musicological Soc., Internat. Musicological Soc., Am. Bach Soc. (sec. 1972-92), Am. Handel Soc. (hon., bd. dirs. 1965—), Internat. Bach Soc. (hon.), Internat. Schuetz Soc. (bd. dirs. Am. chpt. 1983—), Bach Riemenschneider Inst. (hon.). Home: 1536 Scribner Rd Penfield NY 14526-9723 Office: Eastman Sch Music 26 Gibbs St Rochester NY 14604-2505

MANN, BERNARD (BERNIE MANN), professional basketball team executive. Former pres. N.J. Nets, East Rutherford, now bd. dirs. Office: NJ Nets 405 Murray Hill Pkwy East Rutherford NJ 07073-2136*

MANN, BRUCE ALAN, lawyer; b. Chgo., Nov. 28, 1934; s. David I. and Lillian (Segal) M.; m. Naomi Cooks, Aug. 31, 1980; children: Sally Mann Stull, Jonathan Hugh, Andrew Ross. BBA, U. Wis., 1955, SJD, 1957. Bar: Wis. 1957, N.Y. 1958, Calif. 1961. Assoc. Davis, Polk & Wardwell, N.Y.C., 1957-60; assoc. Pillsbury, Madison & Sutro, San Francisco, 1960-66, ptnr., 1967-83; adminstrv. mng. dir. L.F. Rothschild Unterberg Towbin, San Francisco, 1983-87; ptnr. Morrison & Foerster, San Francisco, 1987—; cons. SEC, 1978; vis. prof. law Georgetown U., 1978; lectr. in field; mem. adv. bd. San Diego Securities Regulation Inst., 1973—. Contbr. articles to profl. jours. Served with USAR, 1957. Mem. Am. Law Inst., Am. Bar Assn. (chmn. fed. regulation of securities com. 1981-83, mem. bus. law sect. coun. 1996—), State Bar Calif., Bar Assn. San Francisco (bd. dirs. 1974-75), Nat. Assn. Securities Dealers (gov. at large 1981-83). Club: The Family. Office: Morrison & Foerster 425 Market St San Francisco CA 94105

MANN, CEDRIC ROBERT, retired institute administrator, oceanographer; b. Auckland, N.Z., Feb. 14, 1926; came to Can., 1949; s. Duncan and Winifred Mary (Hood) M.; m. Muriel Frances May, Dec. 19, 1950; 1 child, Robin Carl. B.Sc., U. N.Z., Auckland, 1948, M.Sc., 1950; Ph.D., U. B.C., Vancouver, Can., 1953; D.Eng., N.S. Tech. Coll., Halifax, Can., 1972. Physicist Naval Research Establishment, Halifax, N.S., Can., 1953-61; oceanographer Atlantic Oceanographic Lab., Halifax, N.S., Can., 1961-75, dir., 1975-78; dir. gen. Bedford Inst. Oceanography, Halifax, N.S., Can., 1978-79, Inst. Ocean Scis., Sidney, B.C., Can., 1979-87; Assoc. prof. Dalhousie U., Halifax, 1961-75; chmn. sci. adv. bd. Intergovtl. Oceanographic Commn., Paris, 1978-81; mem. Can. Climate Planning Bd., Ottawa, 1983-86; chmn. Sea Use Council, Seattle, 1981-86. Contbr. articles to profl. jours. Fellow Royal Soc. Can.; mem. Can. Meteorol. and Oceanographic Soc. (life, recipient J.P. Tully medal in Oceanography, 1994). Anglican. Avocations: golf; gardening. Home: 9751 Ardmore Dr, Sidney, BC Canada V8L 5H5

MANN, CLARENCE CHARLES, real estate company official; b. Oradell, N.J., Oct. 15, 1929; s. Clarence Theodore and Martha Barbara (Koster) M.; m. Joan Elizabeth Schnoor, Nov. 25, 1951 (div. Jan. 1985); 1 child, Gary John. BA, NYU, 1951; MA, U. Pa., 1958, Am. U., Beirut, Lebanon, 1963. Grad. Realtors Inst.; accredited buyers rep. grad. Commd. 2d. lt. U.S. Army, 1951, advanced through grades to col., ret., 1977; def. attache to Jordan, 1973-77; mktg. mgr. Litton Industries, Jordan, Saudi Arabia, 1977-81; mktg. mgr. Mid-East Hughes Aircraft Co., Fullerton, Calif., 1981-91; dir. relocation ERA Gem Realty, Tucson, 1992—. Author: Abu Dhabi: Birth of an Oil Shaikhdom, 1964. Decorated Legion of Merit. Mem. Met. Tucson Conv. and Visitors Bureau, Chamber Mil. Affairs Com., Tucson C. of C. Avocations: music, gardening.

MANN, DAVID SCOTT, lawyer; b. Cin., Ohio, Sept. 25, 1939; s. Henry M. and Helen Faye M.; m. Elizabeth Taliaferro, Oct. 5, 1963; children: Michael, Deborah, Marshall. AB cum laude, Harvard Coll., 1961, LLB magna cum laude, 1968. Bar: Ohio 1968. Assoc. Dinsmore & Shohl, Cin., 1968-74, ptnr., 1974-83; ptnr. Taliaferro and Mann, Cin., 1983-92; councilman City of Cin., 1974-92, mayor, 1980-82, 91; mem. 103d Congress 1st Ohio dist., Washington, 1993-94; mem. armed svcs. com., mem. jud. com. Washington; of counsel Thompson, Hine and Flory, Cin., 1995-96; pvt. practice Cin., 1997—; adj. prof. Coll. of Law, U. Cin., 1995—. Editor Harvard Law Rev., 1966-68, notes editor, 1967-68; contbr. articles to profl. jours. Mem., chmn. Cin. Bd. Health, 1972-74. With USN, 1961-65. Mem. Cin. Bar Assn. Democrat. Methodist. Home: 568 Evanswood Pl Cincinnati OH 45220-1527

MANN, DAVID WILLIAM, minister; b. Elkhart, Ind., Apr. 17, 1947; s. Herbert Richard and Kathryn (Bontrager) M.; m. Brenda Marie Frantz, June 7, 1969; children: Troy, Todd, Erika. BA, Bethel Coll., 1969; MS, Nat. Louis U., 1986. Ordained to ministry Missionary Ch., 1978. Campus life dir. Youth for Christ, Elkhart, 1969-77; denominational youth dir. Missionary Ch., Ft. Wayne, Ind., 1977-81, Christian edn. dir., 1981-88, U.S. dir. missions, 1990—; assoc. dir. World Ptnrs., Ft. Wayne, 1988-90; dir. Missionary Ch. Vol. Svc., Ft. Wayne, 1983—. Author: (with others) Youth Leaders Source Book, 1985; contbr. articles to profl. jour. Mgr. Little League, Ft. Wayne, 1981-89, bd. dirs. 1986. Mem. Nat. Assn. Evangelicals, Evangelical Fgn. Mission Assn., Denominational Execs. in Christian Edn. (chmn. 1988), Aldersgate Pub. Assn. (bd. dirs. 1985, 87), Nat. Christian Edn. Assn. (exec. com. 1987-89). Avocations: baseball, skiing, fishing, woodworking. Home: 10025 Crown Point Dr Fort Wayne IN 46804-4391 Office: Missionary Ch 3811 Vanguard Dr Fort Wayne IN 46809-3304*

MANN, DELBERT, film, theater, television director and producer; b. Lawrence, Kans., Jan. 30, 1920; s. Delbert Martin and Ora (Patton) M.; m. Ann Caroline Gillespie, Jan. 13, 1942; children: David Martin, Frederick G., Barbara Susan, Steven P. B.A., Vanderbilt U., 1941; M.F.A., Yale U.; LL.D. (hon.), Northland Coll. Dir. Town Theatre, Columbia, S.C., 1947-49; stage mgr. Wellesley Summer Theater, 1947-48; floor mgr., asst. dir. NBC-TV, N.Y.C., 1949, dir., 1949-55; freelance film and TV dir., 1954—; former bd. govs. Acad. TV Arts and Scis.; former co-chmn. Tenn. Film, Tape and Music Commn.; former pres. Dirs. Guild, Ednl. and Benevolent Found., Cinema Circulus; former lectr. Claremont (Calif.) McKenna Coll. Dir., Philco-Goodyear TV Playhouse, 1949-55, also Omnibus, Ford Star Jubilee, Playwrights 56, Producers Showcase, DuPont Show of the Month, Playhouse 90; films Marty, 1954 (Palme d'Or, Cannes Internat. Film Festival, Acad. Award), The Bachelor Party, 1956, Desire Under the Elms, 1957, Separate Tables, 1958, Middle of the Night, 1959, The Dark at the Top of the Stairs, 1960, The Outsider, 1960, Lover Come Back, 1961, That Touch of Mink, 1962, A Gathering of Eagles, 1962, Dear Heart, 1963, Mister Buddwing, 1965, Fitzwilly, 1967, Kidnapped, 1972, Birch Interval, 1976, Night Crossing, 1982; TV spl. Heidi, 1968, David Copperfield, 1970, Jane Eyre, 1971, The Man Without a Country, 1973, A Girl Named Sooner, 1975, Breaking Up, 1977, Tell Me My Name, 1977, Home To Stay, 1978, All Quiet on the Western Front, 1979, To Find My Son, 1980, All the Way Home, 1981, Bronte, 1982, The Member of the Wedding, 1982, The Gift of Love, 1983, Love Leads the Way, 1984, A Death in California, 1985, The Last Days of Patton, 1986, The Ted Kennedy Jr. Story, 1986, April Morning, 1987, Ironclads, 1991, Against Her Will: An Incident in Baltimore, 1992, Incident in a Small Town, 1993, Lily in Winter, 1994, The Memoirs of Abraham Lincoln, 1996; plays include A Quiet Place, 1956, Speaking of Murder, 1957, Zelda, 1969, The Memoirs of Abraham Lincoln, 1996,; opera Wuthering Heights, N.Y.C. Ctr., 1959. Bd. trustees Vanderbilt U., 1962—. 1st lt. USAAF, WWII; B-24 pilot and squadron intelligence officer, 1944-45. Recipient Acad. Award for dir. Marty, 1955. Mem. Dirs. Guild Am. (past pres. 1967-71) (Dirs. Guild award, 1955), Kappa Alpha. Democrat. Presbyterian. Avocation: reading history. Home and Office: Caroline Prodns Inc 401 S Burnside Ave Apt 11D Los Angeles CA 90036-5305

MANN, DONEGAN, lawyer; b. Birmingham, Ala., Mar. 6, 1922; s. Ephriam DeValse and Edna Atkins (Donegan) M.; m. Frances Virginia Hindman, Apr. 6, 1957 (dec. May 1993); m. Frances M. Jenkins, Jan. 7, 1995. Student, Birmingham-So., 1940-41; AB, George Washington U., 1947, JD, 1950. Bar: U.S. Dist. Ct. D.C. 1950, U.S. Ct. Appeals (D.C. cir.) 1950, U.S. Ct. Claims 1957, U.S. Supreme Ct. 1961, U.S. Ct. Appeals (fed. cir.) 1982. Acting bur. counsel Civil Aeronautics Bd., Washington, 1953-55; gen. rates atty. GAO, Washington, 1955-57; spl. rate counsel Gen. Svcs. Administrn., Washington, 1957-60; assoc. Wolf & Case, Washington, 1960-66; sr. atty., office gen. counsel. U.S. Dept. Treasury, Washington, 1966-79; of counsel Shands & Stupar, Washington, 1979-82; pvt. practice Washington, 1984—. Pres. Friends of Great Falls Tavern, Inc., Potomac, Md., 1977-80, bd. dirs., 1981-82. With USN, 1943-46, PTO. Mem. ABA (treas. pub. contracts sect. 1965-66, chair awards com. 1975-76, Svc. award sr. lawyers' divsn. 1991, counsel sr. lawyers divsn., 1995—, chair guardianship and conservatorship com. 1989-95, sr. lawyers' divsn. task force to reform guardianship laws 1992-94, vice chair, wills probate and trust com., 1995—, chair citizenship com. 1996—), Bar Assn. D.C., Fed. Energy Bar Assn., Fed. Bar Assn., D.C. Bar Assn., Montgomery County Hist. Soc. (exec. v.p. 1980-83, bd. dirs. 1984-86). Democrat. Episcopalian. Avocations: fishing, hunting, golf, tennis, gardening. Office: 1000 Connecticut Ave NW Ste 204 Washington DC 20036-5337

MANN, EMILY BETSY, writer, artistic director, theater and film director; b. Boston, Apr. 12, 1952; d. Arthur and Sylvia (Blut) M.; 1 child, Nicholas Isaac Bamman. BA, Harvard U., 1974; MFA, U. Minn., 1976. Resident dir. Guthrie Theater, Mpls., 1976-79; dir. BAM Theater Co., Bklyn., 1980-81; freelance writer, dir. N.Y.C., 1981-90; artistic dir. McCarter Theater Ctr. for the Performing Arts, Princeton, N.J., 1990—; cons. N.Y. Theatre Workshop, 1987. Author: (plays) Annulla, An Autobiography, Still Life (6 Obie awards 1981, Fringe First award 1985), Execution of Justice (Helen Hayes award, Bay Area Theatre Critics Circle award, HBO/USA award, Playwriting award Women's Com. Dramtists Guild for Dramatizing Issues of Conscience 1986), Greensboro: A Requiem, Having Our Say; co-author: (with Ntozake Shange) (musical) Betsey Brown; (screenplays) Fanny Kelly, The Winnie Mandela Story, Having Our Say; dir. Hedda Gabbler, A Doll House, Annulla, Still Life (Obie award), Execution of Justice (Guthrie and Broadway), Betsey Brown, The Glass Menagerie, Three Sisters, Cat on a Hot Tin Roof, Twilight: L.A., 1992 (L.A. NAACP award for best dir.), The Perfectionist, The Matchmaker: adaptor, dir. Miss Julie, Having Our Say (Tony nomination-direction of a play 1995, Dramatist Guild's Hull Warriner award), Greensboro, A Requiem, The Mai, Betrayal; translator: Nights and Days (Pierre Laville), 1985; pub. in New Plays U.S.A. 1, New Plays 3, American Plays and the Vietnam War, The Ten Best Plays of 1986, Out Front, Testimony: 4 Plays by Emily Mann, 1997. Recipient BUSH fellowship, 1975-76, Rosamond Gilder award New Drama Forum Assn., 1983, NEA Assocs. grant, 1984, Guggenheim fellowship, 1985, McKnight fellowship, 1985, CAPS award, 1985, NEA Playwrights fellowship, 1986. Mem. Soc. Stage Dirs. and Choreographers, Theatre Comms. Group (v.p.), New Dramatists, PEN, Writers' Guild, Dramatists' Guild (exec. bd. mem.), Phi Beta Kappa.

MANN, GEORGE STANLEY, real estate and financial services corporation executive; b. Toronto, Ont., Can., Dec. 23, 1932; s. David Philip and Elizabeth (Green) M.; m. Saundra Sair, Jan. 2, 1955; children: Michael, Tracy. Attended, North Toronto Collegiate Sch.; LLD (hon.), U. Windsor. Ptnr. Mann & Martel Co. Ltd., 1959-68, chief exec. officer, 1968-70; chief exec. officer United Trust Co., 1970-76; pres. Unicorp Canada Corp., Toronto, 1972-76, chmn. bd., 1976-90; dir. Nat. Bank Canada, 1978-91; chmn. bd. Union Gas Ltd., 1986-93; pres. chmn. bd. Lincorp Holdings, Inc., N.Y.C. Bd. govs. Mt. Sinai Hosp., Toronto. Clubs: Oakdale Golf & Country (Toronto); High Ridge Country (Palm Beach, Fla.). Avocation: golf. Office: Ste 1004, 2 St Clair Ave W, Toronto, ON Canada M4V 1L5 Home: 18 Old Forest Hill Rd, Toronto, ON Canada M5P 2P7 also: 930 S Ocean Blvd Palm Beach FL 33480-4909

MANN, HERBIE, flutist; b. N.Y.C., Apr. 16, 1930; s. Harry C. and Ruth (Brecher) Solomon; m. Ruth Shore, Sept. 8, 1956 (div. 1971); children: Paul J., Claudia; m. Jan Clonts, July 11, 1971 (div. 1990); 2 children: Laura, Geoffrey; m. Susan Janeal Arison, 1991. Student, Manhattan Sch. Music, 1952-54. Founder, pres. Herbie Mann Music Corp., N.Y.C., 1959—; founder Kokopelli Music, Santa Fe, 1992—; toured Africa for Dept. State, 1960, Brazil, 1961-62, Japan, 1964, Scandanavia, Cyprus and Turkey, 1971; pres. Herbie Mann Orch., Inc., 5 Face of Music Prodns., Inc., Rupadia Music, Inc. Recorded over 100 albums under own name, 1954—; Memphis Underground, 1969, Push, Push, 1971, Missippi Gambler, 1974, Bird in a Silver Cage, 1977, Caminho De Casa, 1990. Deep Pocket, 1992, The Evolution of Mann: The Herbie Mann Anthology, 1994. Served with AUS, 1948-52. Recipient Downbeat award for flute, 1958-70. Mem. ASCAP, Nat. Acad. Rec. Arts and Scis.

MANN, J. KEITH, arbitrator, law educator, lawyer; b. May 28, 1924; s. William Young and Lillian Myrle (Bailey) M.; m. Virginia McKinnon, July 7, 1950; children: William Christopher, Marilyn Keith, John Kevin, Susan Bailey, Andrew Curry. BS, Ind. U., 1948, LLB, 1949; LLD, Monmouth Coll., 1989. Bar: Ind. 1949, D.C. 1951. Law clk. Justice Wiley Rutledge and Justice Sherman Minton, 1949-50; practice, Washington, 1950; with Wage Stblzn. Bd., 1951; asst. prof. U. Wis., 1952; asst. prof. Stanford U. Law Sch., 1952-54, assoc. prof., 1954-58, prof., 1958-88, prof. emeritus 1988—, assoc. dean, 1961-85, acting dean, 1976, 81-82, cons. to provost, 1986-87; vis. prof. U. Chgo., 1953; mem. Sec. of Labor's Adv. Com., 1955-57; mem. Pres.'s Commn. Airlines Controversy, 1961; mem. COLC Aerospace Spl. Panel, 1973-74; chmn., mem. Presdl. Emergency Bds. or Bds. of Inquiry, 1962-63, 67, 71-72; spl. master U.S. vs. Alaska, U.S. Supreme Ct., 1980—. Ensign USNR, 1944-46. Sunderland fellow U. Mich., 1959-60; scholar in residence Duke U., 1972. Mem. ABA, AAUP, Nat. Acad. Arbitrators, Indsl. Rels. Rsch. Assn., Acad. Law Alumni Fellows Ind. U., Order of Coif, Tau Kappa Epsilon, Phi Delta Phi. Editor: book rev. and articles Ind. U. Law Jour. Democrat. Presbyterian. Home: 872 Lathrop Dr Stanford CA 94305-1053 Office: Stanford U Law Sch Stanford CA 94305-8610

MANN, JACK MATTHEWSON, bottling company executive; b. Marshall, Tex., Apr. 14, 1932; s. Jack Slater and Mary (Matthewson) M.; m. True Sandlin, Sept. 4, 1954 (div. 1989); children: Jack, Robert, Daniel, Nathaniel. Student, N.Mex. Mil. Inst., 1952; BBA, U. Tex., 1954; MBA, Harvard U., 1960. Credit analyst Republic Nat. Bank, Dallas, 1959; chem. coord. Humble Oil and Refining Co., Baytown, Tex., 1960-61; asst. sales mgr. The Made-Rite Co., Marshall, Tex., 1957-58; asst. gen. mgr. The Made Rite Co., Marshall, Tex., 1961-63; gen. mgr. The Made Rite Co., Longview, Tex., 1963—, pres., 1972—, owner, chmn., 1982—; v.p. Longview Econ. Devel. Corp., 1994—, treas., 1995-96, pres., 1996—; bd. dirs. Longview Nat. Bank; mem. pres.'s adv. coun. Le Tourneau U., 1994-97. Exec. com. Rep. Party Tex., 1962-65; mem. exec. bd. Episcopal Diocese Tex., Houston, 1974-76; mem. small bus. adv. com. Tex. Dept. Commerce, 1988-91. Mem. Tex. Soft Drink Assn. (pres. 1972), Nat. Dr. Pepper Bottlers Assn. (pres. 1983-85), Longview C. of C. (dir. 1965-68, 84-86). Club: Summit (Longview) (gov. 1982-94). Avocation: hunting. Home: 45 Stonegate Dr Longview TX 75601-3600 Office: The Made Rite Co PO Box 3283 Longview TX 75606-3283

MANN, JAMES ROBERT, congressman; b. Greenville, S.C., Apr. 27, 1920; s. Alfred Cleo and Nina (Griffin) M.; m. Virginia Thomason Brunson, Jan. 15, 1945; children—James Robert, David Brunson, William Walker, Virginia Brunson. B.A., The Citadel, 1941, LL.D. (hon.), 1978; JD, U. S.C., 1947. Bar: S.C. 1947, U.S. Ct. Appeals (4th cir.) 1948, U.S. Supreme Ct. 1970. Practice in Greenville, 1947—; del. S.C. Ho. of Reps. from Greenville County, 1949-52; solicitor 13th Jud. Circuit, 1953-63; mem. 91st-95th Congresses 4th Dist., S.C. Sec. Greenville County Planning Commn., 1963-67; Trustee Greenville Hosp. System, 1965-68; bd. govs. Greenville Shriners Hosp., 1983-90. Served to lt. col. AUS, 1941-46; col. USAR ret. Mem. Am., S.C., Greenville County bar assns., Am. Judicature Soc., Greater Greenville C. of C. (pres. 1965), V.F.W. (dep. comdr. 1951-52), Am. Legion. Democrat. Baptist. Lodges: Mason; Shriners; Kiwanis; Elks; Woodmen of World. Office: 102 W Stone Ave Greenville SC 29609-5524

MANN, JIM (JAMES WILLIAM MANOUSOS), editor, publisher; b. Cambridge, Mass., Dec. 9, 1919; s. Demetrios Peter and Germaine (Lambertz) Manousos; m. Mary Dimitrakis, July 21, 1962. MFA, Fordham U., 1954. Assoc. editor View mag., Yonkers, N.Y., 1951-58; various editorial jobs N.Y.C., 1959-71; pres., editor The Gallagher Report, N.Y.C., 1971-74; pres., treas. Jim Mann & Assocs., Gales Ferry, Conn., 1974—; editor, pub. Media Mgmt. Monographs, 1978-90; editor in chief Pub. Trends & Trendsetters, 1991-95; adj. prof. mktg. U. New Haven, Orange, Conn., 1976-82. Author: Solving Publishing's Toughest Problems, 1982, Magazine Editing, 1985, Ad Sales, 1987. Pres. Cmty. Action Network, 1990-95. *Success is realizing one's potential; happiness is exercising it.*

MANN, JONATHAN MAX, international agency administrator, public health director; b. Boston, July 30, 1947; s. James and Ida (Laskow) M.; m. Marie-Paule Bondat, Jan. 30, 1970; children: Naomi, Lydia, Aaron. BA, Harvard U., 1969, MPH, 1980; MD, Washington U., St. Louis, 1974. Epidemic intelligence service officer USPHS, Ctrs. Disease Control, Atlanta and Santa Fe, 1975-77; med. epidemiologist, dir. AIDS research program, Kinshasa, Zaire, 1984-86; dir. global program AIDS, WHO, Geneva, 1986-90; state epidemiologist, chief med. officer N.Mex. Health Dept., Santa Fe, 1977-84. Mem. editorial bd. Control of Communicable Diseases in Man, Western Jour. Medicine, 1984—. Contbr. articles to profl. jours. Recipient Spl. Commendation N.Mex. Med. Soc., 1980, Friend of N.Mex. Journalism award Sigma Delta Chi, 1979, Disting. Service award School Nursing Com., 1979. Fellow Am. Coll. Preventive Medicine (Recognition award 1982), Am. Coll. Epidemiology; mem. Santa Fe County Med. Soc. (treas. 1981-82, pres. 1983-84), U.S.-Mex. Border Health Assn., Am. Pub. Health Assn.*

MANN, KENNETH HENRY, marine ecologist; b. Dovercourt, Essex, Eng., Aug. 15, 1923; emigrated to arrived Canada, 1967, naturalized, 1973; s. Harry and Mabel (Ashby) M.; m. Isabella Gilmour Ness, Apr. 18, 1946; children: Ian Malcolm, Sheila Helen, Colin Gilmour. B.Sc., U. London, 1949, Ph.D., U. Reading, 1953; D.Sc., U. London, 1965. Lectr. zoology, then reader U. Reading, Eng., 1949-64; 64-67; sr. biologist marine ecology lab. Bedford Inst. Oceanography, Dartmouth, Can., 1967-72, dir. marine ecology lab., 1980-86, sr. rsch. scientist, 1986-93, emeritus rsch. scientist, 1993—; prof., chmn. biology Dalhousie U., Halifax, N.S., Can., 1972-80, adj. prof. biology, 1980—. Author: Leeches: Their Structure, Phyiology, Ecology and Embryology, 1961, Ecology of Coastal Waters: A Systems Approach, 1982; co-author: (with J. Lazier) Dynamics of Marine Ecosystems: Biological-Physical Interactions in the Sea, 1991; 2d edit., 1996; (with R.S. Barnes) Fundamentals of Aquatic Ecology, 1991; editor, contbr.: Network Analysis in Marine Ecology, 1989; editor Jour. Animal Ecology, 1966-67. Served with Royal Air Force, 1942-46. Fellow Royal Soc. Can.; mem. Brit. Ecol. Soc., Am. Assn. Limnology and Oceanography. Home: 23 Woodward Cres, Halifax, NS Canada B3M 1J6 Office: Bedford Inst Oceanography, Box 1006, Dartmouth, NS Canada B2Y 4A2

MANN, KENNETH WALKER, retired minister, psychologist; b. Nyack, N.Y., Aug. 22, 1914; s. Arthur Hungerford and Ethel Livingston (Walker) M. AB, Princeton U., 1937; STB, Gen. Theol. Sem., N.Y.C., 1942; MS, U. Mich., 1950, PhD, 1956. Ordained priest Episcopal Ch., 1942; diplomate Am. Assn. Pastoral Counselors; lic. clin. psychologist, Calif., Conn.; lic. marriage, family and child counselor, Calif. Vicar in Valley Cottage, Pearl River, N.Y., 1941-43; priest in charge Yonkers, N.Y., 1943-45; dir. youth work and Christian edn. Diocese L.A., 1945-47; curate in Beverly Hills, Calif., 1947-49; counselor Bur. Psychol. Svcs., U. Mich., 1951-52; chaplain, clin. psychologist dept. psychiatry St. Luke's Hosp., N.Y.C., also priest-psychotherapist Cathedral St. John Divine, N.Y.C., psychol. examiner ministerial candidates Diocese N.Y., 1952-58; assoc. chaplain Hosp. Good Samaritan, L.A., 1958-65; exec. pastoral svcs., exec. coun. Episc. Ch. N.Y.C., 1965-70; program officer Acad. Religion and Mental Health, N.Y.C., 1970-72; sr. adviser profl. affairs Inst. Religion and Health, 1972-74; sr. psychol. staff Silver Hill Found., New Canaan, Conn., 1974-84; pres. Rockland County (N.Y.) Mins. Assn., 1942-43; exec. sec. social svc. commn. Diocese N.Y., 1943-45; chmn. div. pastoral svcs. Diocese L.A., 1958-65; field dir. Western region Acad. Religion and Mental Health, 1958-61; assoc. nat. chaplain U.S. Power Squadrons, 1956-57. Author: On Pills and Needles, 1969, Deadline for Survival—A Survey of Moral Issues in Science and Medicine, 1970; contbr. articles to profl. jours. Pres. Adoption Inst. L.A., 1964; mem. edn. com. Calif. Heart Assn., 1962-64; trustee, treas. Acad. Religion and Mental Health, 1954-59, mem. profl. bd., 1960-70; trustee Vis. Nurse Assn. L.A., 1963-65, Children's Home Soc. Calif. in L.A., 1964-65, North Conway Inst., 1966-80. USPHS grantee, 1950-51. Fellow AAAS; mem. APA (chmn. com. rels. between psychology and religion 1956-58), Western Psychol. Assn., Calif. Psychol. Assn., L.A. County Psychol. Assn., N.Y. Acad. Scis., Planetary Soc., Assembly Episc. Hosps. and Chaplains, Upper Nyack Tennis Club, Princeton Club N.Y. Republican. Home: 32 Tallman Ave Nyack NY 10960-1606 *I have strongly held to the principle that the total "health" of mankind cannot be considered apart from the values and aspirations by which people live, and by which they may even be prepared to die. Amidst the confusions that exist today over loyalties, traditions, and ideals, many are asking: What is the right way to behave? How should I think? What kind of person am I supposed to be? To help such people in quandary to live responsibly, and still be true to their individuality, is a large task, but it is one that is central to a religious ministry. It has always been my chief concern.*

MANN, LESTER PERRY, mathematics educator; b. Milford, Mass., May 30, 1921; s. Lester P. and Viola E. (Tracy) M.; m. Dorothy M. Davis, Oct. 11, 1947; children: Kelly P., Leslie P. BS with high honors, U. Md., 1964; MEd, U. Alaska, Anchorage, 1974; EdD, Boston U., 1983. Cert. elem. tchr., reading specialist and supr., Mass.; cert. elem. tchr., reading specialist, Alaska. Commd. 2nd lt. USAAF, 1941; advanced through grades to maj. USAF, 1954, navigator, weather officer, 1941-64; ret., 1964; resident counselor OEO-Job Corps, 1965-66; flight navigator Südflug, Braniff, Capitol and Japan Air Lines, 1966-73; instr. math., adminstr., curriculum developer U. Alaska, 1974-86, adj. instr., 1987—; instrnl. assoc. Mann Assocs., Applied Lifelong Learning, Anchorage, 1983—; instr. Anchorage Community Coll., 1974-86; asst. prof. Embry-Riddle Aero. U., Anchorage, 1987—, acad. advisor, 1987-90; mem. for remedial reading Alaska Talent Bank; vis. adult educator German Adult Edn. Assn., 1984. Mem. Math. Assn. Am., Nat. Coun. Tchrs. Math., Internat. Reading Assn., Am. Assn. Adult and Continuing Edn. (profl., past mem. nomination and election com.), Am. Meteorol. Soc., Phi Alpha Theta, Phi Kappa Phi. Avocations: fishing, sport flying, classical guitar. Home and Office: 2304 Turnagain Pky Anchorage AK 99517-1124

MANN, LINDA MARIE, elementary school educator; b. Pitts., July 11, 1949; d. Howard Robert and Matilda Elizabeth Mann. BA in Edn., Syracuse U., 1972; MS in Instructional Systems Tech., Ind.U., 1975; post-grad. studies Edn.-related, SUNY, Oswego, Plattsburgh, Albany, 1991-92. Cert. tchr. lifetime (N-6), libr. media specialist (K-12), English (7-12) permanent, N.Y. Secondary English tchr. Liverpool (N.Y.) Ctrl. Schs., 1972-74, media specialist, 1975-91, elem. tchr. vertical team grades 3-4-5, 1992, elem. tchr., 1992—; edn. cons., mem. educators' adv. bd. Ste Marie Mus., Liverpool, 1976-92; tour guide, guest speaker Hist. Assn. Greater Liverpool, 1989-92. Tchr., tchr. trainer, supt. Sunday sch., chairperson curriculum com., coord. ref. libr. Greater Love in Christ Ch., Syracuse, N.Y., 1985-92. Mem. ASCD, Internat. Reading Assn., Tchrs. Applying Whole Lang., Ctrl. N.Y. Coun. Social Studies, Delta Kappa Gamma. Avocations:

journal writing, literature, singing, speedwlking, bicycling, hiking. Office: Liverpool Ctrl Sch 800 4th St Liverpool NY 13088-4455

MANN, LOUIS EUGENE, financial planner; b. Balt., Jan. 24, 1947; s. Manfred and Ruth Eleanor (Kates) M.; m. Marjorie Ruth Friedman, Mar. 23, 1971; children: Lisa Renee, Brian Michael. Student, Balt. Poly. Inst., 1964, Towson State Coll., 1964-67; postgrad., U. Pa., 1969-70; CFP, Coll. for Fin. Planning, 1993. CFP; securities licenses; lic. ins. broker, N.J., Pa. Clk. Food Fair Stores, Inc., Balt., 1964-68; v.p. Friendly Grocer, Inc., Cherry Hill, N.J., 1968-79; sales mgr. Frito-Lay Inc., Cinnaminson, N.J., 1979-82; salesman N.Y. Life Ins. Co., Cherry Hill, 1982-89; ptnr. Custom Fin. Svcs., Marlton, N.J., 1988-93; pres. Louis E. Mann Fin. Svcs., Inc., Phila., 1993—; v.p. Orion Fin. Svcs., Inc., Phila., 1994-96; comptroller Shusterman & Davis, LLC, Marlton, N.J., 1996—; cons. fin. Congregation Beth Tikvah, Marlton. Developer: (math. formula) Law of Squares of Consecutive Numbers, 1963. Mgr., coach Greentree Athletic Assn., Mount Laurel, N.J., 1985-94; pres. Congregation Beth Tikvah Men's Club, Marlton, 1988-89, 90-91, 94-95, bd. dirs., exec. bd. mem., 1994-95. Recipient Coll. scholarship State of Md.-Senatorial, 1964. Mem. Inst. CFPs, Million Dollar Round Table (membership com. 1984), Rotary Club of Moorestown (com. chmn., bd. dirs. 1984-94, 1st v.p. 1996-97, pres. 1997—), Rotary Internat. (dist. planned giving chmn. Dist. 7500, 1994-95), Fedn. Jewish Men's Clubs (bd. trustees mid. Atlantic region). Democrat. Jewish. Avocations: sports, hist. readings, fin. readings, music, gardening. Home: 121 Colony Pl Mount Laurel NJ 08054-2404 Office: LEMFS Inc 110 Pavilions at Greentree Marlton NJ 08053-4808

MANN, LOWELL D., religious organization executive. Chmn. Bd. for World Missions. *

MANN, LOWELL KIMSEY, retired manufacturing executive; b. LaGrange, Ga., June 28, 1917; s. Otis A. and Georgia B. (Mundy) M.; m. Helen Margaret Dukes, Feb. 11, 1944; children: Margaret Ellen, Lowell Kimsey. Grad., Advanced Mgmt. Program, Harvard, 1962. Foreman Callaway Mills, LaGrange, 1935-39, indsl. engr., 1939-42; indsl. engr. Blue Bell, Inc., Greenboro, N.C., 1946-52, chief engr., 1952-61, v.p. engring., 1961-62, v.p. mfg., 1962-68, exec. v.p., 1968-73, pres., 1973-82, chief exec. officer, 1974-83, chmn. bd., 1982-84, ret., 1984; dir. Shadowline Inc., Morganton, N.C., Wachovia Bank & Trust Co., Greensboro, Quality Mills, Mt. Airy, N.C.; mem. So. adv. bd. Arkwright-Boston Ins. Co., 1975-84. Bd. dirs. Learning Inst., N.C., 1969-76; trustee Southeastern Legal Found., 1977-84; deacon Bapt. Ch., 1984-88, chmn., 1986-87. Served to capt. AUS, 1942-46. Recipient Disting. Citizen award Greensboro C. of C., 1983; named Clothing Mfg. Industry CEO of Yr. Fin. World, 1978. Mem. Piedmont Assoc. Industries (bd. dirs., pres. 1966-68), Am. Apparel Mfrs. Assn. (bd. dirs. 1972-78), Nat. MS Soc., NAM (bd. dirs. 1977-84), Beta Gamma Sigma (hon.). Democrat. Club: Sedgefield Country (bd. dirs. 1970-73, 85-88, pres. 1986-88) (Greensboro). Home: Sedgefield 5503 Currituck Pl Greensboro NC 27407-7217 *I believe that honesty, integrity, and fairness are essential in our relationships with others. These shared values will encourage understanding, and, in turn, will create pride in us, opportunities for us, and accomplishments by us.*

MANN, MARION, physician, educator; b. Atlanta, Mar. 29, 1920; s. Levi James and Cora (Casey) M.; m. Ruth Maurine Reagin, Jan. 16, 1943; children: Marion Jr., Judith (Mrs. Kenneth Walk). B.S. in Edn, Tuskegee Inst., Ala., 1940; M.D., Howard U., 1954; Ph.D., Georgetown U., 1961, D.Sc. (hon.), 1979; D.Sc. (hon.), U. Mass., 1984; grad., U.S. Army Command and Gen. Staff Coll., 1965, U.S. Army War Coll., 1970. Diplomate: Nat. Bd. Med. Examiners, Am. Bd. Pathology. Intern USPHS Hosp., Staten Island, N.Y., 1954-55; resident Georgetown U. Hosp., 1956-60; practice medicine, specializing in pathology Washington, 1961—; instr. pathology Georgetown U., 1960-61; professorial lectr. Georgetown U. (Sch. Medicine), 1970-73; asst. prof. pathology Howard U. Coll. Medicine, 1961-67, assoc. prof., 1967-70, prof., 1970, dean, 1970-79; v.p. rsch. Howard U., 1988-91. Capt. AUS, 1942-50; brig. gen. Res. Mem. Inst. Medicine, Nat. Acad. Scis., Alpha Omega Alpha. Mem. United Ch. of Christ. Home: 1453 Whittier Pl NW Washington DC 20012-2845 Office: 520 W St NW Washington DC 20001-2337

MANN, MARVIN L., electronics executive; b. Birmingham, Ala., Apr. 22, 1933; s. Jesse Marvin and Nannie Leola (Thomason) M.; m. Frances Nell Marlin, Dec. 24, 1953; children: Tara Jane, Jeffery Loy. BS, Samford U., 1954; MBA, U. Ala., 1958. Chmn., pres., chief exec. officer Lexmark Internat., Inc., Lexington, Ky.; bd. dirs. M.A. Hanna, Inc., Imation, Inc., Fidelity Investments. Office: Lexmark Internat Inc 740 New Circle Rd NW Lexington KY 40511-1806

MANN, MICHAEL K., producer, director, writer; b. Chgo.. Ed., U. Wis., London Film Sch. Dir. (documentary) 17 Days Down the Line, 1972; dir, scriptwriter (TV movie) The Jericho Mile, 1979 (Best Dir. award Dir. Guild Am., Emmy award); dir, exec. prodr., scriptwriter (film) Thief, 1981; dir, scriptwriter (films) The Keep, 1983, Manhunter, 1986; dir., co-prodr., scriptwriter (films) Last of the Mohicans, 1992, Heat, 1995, (TV movie) LA Takedown, 1989; exec. prodr. (TV show) Miami Vice, Crime Story, (TV miniseries) Drug Wars: Camarena Story (Emmy award), Drug Wars: Cocaine Cartel; scriptwriter (TV episodes) Police Story, Starsky and Hutch. Mem. Writers Guild., Dirs. Guild. Office: care CAA 9830 Wilshire Blvd Beverly Hills CA 90212-1804

MANN, MICHAEL MARTIN, electronics company executive; b. N.Y.C., Nov. 28, 1939; s. Herbert and Rosalind (Kaplan) M.; m. Mariel Joy Steinberg, Apr. 25, 1965. BSEE, Calif. Inst. Tech., 1960, MSEE, 1961; PhD in Elec. Engring. and Physics, U. So. Calif., 1969; MBA, UCLA, 1984. Cert. bus. appraiser, profl. cons., mgmt. cons., lic. real estate broker, Calif. Mgr. high power laser programs office Northrop Corp., Hawthorne, Calif., 1969-76; mgr. high energy laser systems lab. Hughes Aircraft Co., El Segundo, Calif., 1976-78; mgr. E-0 control systems labs. Hughes Aircraft Co., El Segundo, 1978-83, asst. to v.p., space & strategic, 1983-84; exec. v.p. Helionetics Inc., Irvine, Calif., 1984-85, pres., chief exec. officer, 1985-86, also bd. dirs.; ptnr. Mann Kavanaugh Chernove, 1986-87; sr. cons. Arthur D. Little, Inc., 1987-88; chmn. bd., pres., CEO, Blue Marble Devel. Group, Inc., 1988—; exec. assoc. Ctr. Internat. Cooperation and Trade, 1989—; sr. assoc. Corp. Fin. Assocs., 1990—; exec. assoc. Reece and Assocs., 1990—; dir. Reece & Assocs., 1991—; mng. dir. Blue Marble Ptnrs. Ltd, 1991—; chmn. bd. dirs., CEO Blue Marble Ptnrs., 1992—; chmn., CEO, En Compass Techs., Inc., Torrance, Calif., 1994—; mem. Army Sci. Bd., Dept. Army, Washington, 1986-91; chmn. Ballistic Missile Def. Panel, Directed Energy Weapon Panel, Rsch. and New Initiatives Panel; cons. Office of Sec. of Army, Washington, 1986—, Inst. of Def. Analysis, Washington, 1978—, Dept. Energy, 1988—, Nat. Riverside Rsch. Inst., 1990—; bd. dirs. Datum, Inc.,1988—, Fail-Safe Tech., Corp., 1989-90, Safeguard Health Enterprises, Inc., 1988—, Am. Video Communications, Inc., Meck Industries, Inc., 1987-88, Decade Optical Systems, Inc., 1990—, Forum Mil. Application Directed Energy, 1992—, Am. Bus. Consultants, Inc., 1993—; chmn. bd. Mgmt. Tech., Inc. 1991—, Encompass Tech., Inc., 1994—; bd. dirs., mem. adv. bd. Micro-Frame, Inc., 1988-91; chmn. bd. HLX Laser, Inc., 1984-86; bd. dirs. Cons's. Roundtable, 1992—, Am. Bus. Cons., Inc., 1993—; rsch. assoc., mem. extension teaching staff U. So. Calif., L.A., 1964-70; chmn. Ballistic Missile Def. Subgroup, 1989-90, Tactical Directed Energy Weapons Subgroup, 1988-90; chmn., chief exec. officer Mgmt. Tech., Inc., 1991—; dir. Am. Bus. Cons., Inc., 1993—. Contbg. editor, mem. adv. bd. Calif. High-Tech Funding Jour., 1989-90; contbr. over 50 tech. articles to profl. jours.; patentee in field. Mem. adv. com. to Engring. Sch., Calif. State U., Long Beach, 1985—; chmn. polit. affairs Am. Electronics Assn., Orange County Coun., 1986-87, mem. exec. com., 1986-88; adv. com. several Calif. congressmen, 1985—; mem. dean's coun. UCLA Grad. Sch. Mgmt., 1984-85; bd. dirs. Archimedes Circle U. Soc. Calif., 1983-85, Ctr. for Innovation and Entrepreneurship, 1986-90, Caltech/MIT Venture Forum, 1987-91; chmn. adv. coun. and adj. prof., indsl. and sys. engring. U. So. Calif., 1996—. Hicks fellow in Indsl. Rels. Calif. Inst. Tech., 1961, Hewlett Packard fellow. Mem. IEEE (sr.), So. Calif. Tech. Execs. Network, Orange County CEO's Network, Orange County CEO's Roundtable, Pres. Roundtable, Nat. Assn. Corp. Dirs., Aerospace-Def. CEO's Roundtable, Am. Def. Preparedness Assn., Security Affairs Support Assn., Acad. Profl. Cons. and Advisors, Internat. Platform Assn., Inst. Mgmt. Cons. (bd. dirs. So. Calif. chpt.), Pres. Assn., Cons. Roundtable, King Harbor Yacht Club. Republican. Avocations: sailing, photography, writing. Home: 4248 Via Alondra Palos Verdes Peninsula CA 90274-1545 Office: Blue Marble Partners 406 Amapola Ave Ste 200 Torrance CA 90501-6229

MANN, NANCY LOUISE (NANCY LOUISE ROBBINS), entrepreneur; b. Chillicothe, Ohio, May 6, 1925; d. Everett Chaney and Pauline Elizabeth R.; m. Kenneth Douglas Mann, June 19, 1949 (div. June 1979); children: Bryan Wilkinson, Laura Elizabeth. BA in Math., UCLA, 1948, MA in Math., 1949, PhD in Biostatistics, 1965. Sr. scientist Rocketdyne Div. of Rockwell Internat., Canoga Park, Calif., 1962-75; mem. tech. staff Rockwell Sci. Ctr., Thousand Oaks, Calif., 1975-78; rsch. prof. UCLA Biomath., L.A., 1978-87; pres., CEO, owner Quality Enhancement Seminars, Inc., L.A., 1982—; pres., CEO Quality and Productivity, Inc., L.A., 1987—; curriculum adv. UCLA Ext. Dept. of Bus. and Mgmt., L.A., 1991—; mem. com. on Nat. Statistics, Nat. Acad. Scis., Washington, 1978-82; mem adv. bd. to supt. U.S. Naval Posgrad. Sch., Monterey, Calif., 1979-82. Co-author: Methods for Analysis of Reliability and Life Data, 1974; author: Keys to Excellence, 1985, The Story of the Deming Philosophy, 2d edit., 1987, 3d edit., 1989; contbr. articles to profl. jours. Recipient award IEEE Reliability Soc., 1982, ASQC Reliability Divsn., 1986. Fellow Am. Statis. Assn. (v.p. 1982-84); mem. Internat. Statis. Inst. Office: Quality and Productivity Inc 1081 Westwood Blvd # 213 Los Angeles CA 90024-2911

MANN, OSCAR, physician, internist, educator; b. Paris, Oct. 13, 1934; came to U.S., 1953; s. Aron and Helen (Biegun) M.; m. Amy S. Mann, July 19, 1964; children: Adriana, Karen. AA with distinction, George Washington U., 1958; MD cum laude, Georgetown U., 1962. Diplomate Am. Bd. Med. Examiners, Am. Bd. Internal Medicine, Am. Bd. Internal Medicine subspecialty Cardiovascular Disease; cert. advanced achievement in internal medicine; re-cert. in internal medicine. Intern Georgetown U. Med. Ctr., Washington, 1962-63, jr. asst. med. resident, 1963-64, clin. fellow in cardiology with Proctor Harvey program, 1965-66; sr. asst. resident in medicine Georgetown svc. D.C. Gen. Hosp., Washington, 1964-65; clin. prof. medicine Georgetown U. Sch. Medicine, 1985—; nat. chmn. med. alumi fund Georgetown U. Med. Sch., Washington, 1993-95; pvt. practice internal medicine and cardiology, Washington, 1966—; mem. Med.-Nursing Audit Com., CME adv. com., teaching. adv. com., Opthamology dept. rev. com., surgery dept. rev. com., faculty com., search com. for a new dean for acad. affairs Georgetown U. Med. Ctr.; appointed coun. to the dean Georgetown U. Sch. Medicine, 1977—; mem. Instnl. Self Study Task Force. Contbr. articles to profl. jours. Served with the U.S. Army, 1953-55. Recipient Mead Johnson Postgrad. Scholar ACP, 1964-65, Physicians Recognition award AMA, 1987-96, Advanced Achievement in Internal Medicine, 1987. Fellow ACP, Am. Coll. Cardiology, Am. Coll. Chest Physicians; mem. AMA, Am. Soc. Internal Medicine, Am. Heart Assn. (coun. clin. cardiology), Med. Soc. D.C., Cosmos Club, Georgetown U. Alumni Assn. (bd. govs. 1993—, chair med. alumni bd. 1995—), Alpha Omega Alpha, Phi Delta Epsilon. Home: 4925 Weaver Ter NW Washington DC 20016-2660 Office: Foxhall Internists PC 3301 New Mexico Ave NW Washington DC 20016-3622

MANN, PHILIP ROY, lawyer; b. N.Y.C., Jan. 31, 1948; s. Elias and Gertrude Esther (Levbarg) M. AB, Cornell U., 1968; JD, NYU, 1971, LLM, 1975. Bar: N.Y. 1972, U.S. Dist. Ct. (so. and ea. dists.) N.Y. 1983, U.S. Ct. Appeals (2nd cir.) 1973, U.S. Dist. Ct. (no. dist.) N.Y. 1974, U.S. Ct. Mil. Appeals 1974, U.S. Supreme Ct. 1975, D.C. 1976, U.S. Dist. Ct. (we. dist.) N.Y. 1976, U.S. Tax Ct. 1976, U.S. Ct. Appeals (D.C. cir.) 1978, Conn. 1983, U.S. Dist. Ct. D.C. 1983, U.S. Ct. Claims 1983, U.S. Ct. Appeals (3rd and fed. cirs.) 1983. Assoc. Levin & Weintraub, N.Y.C., 1971-74; assoc. Shea & Gould, N.Y.C., 1974-79, ptnr., 1979-84; sole practice N.Y.C., 1984—. Lt. col. J.A., USAR, 1969—. Mem. ABA, Fed. Bar Assn. Democrat. Jewish. Home and Office: 250 E 87th St Apt 26H New York NY 10128-3117

MANN, PREM SINGH, economics educator; b. Punjab, India, Nov. 20, 1947; came to U.S., 1980; s. Malkiat Singh and Darshan Kaur (Gill) M.; m. Sarabjeet K. Bains, May 9, 1975; children: Harpreet K., Kulwinder S., Sukhwinder S. BA, Panjab U., Chandigarh, India, 1968, MA in Econs., 1970; MA in Econs., U. Manchester (Eng.), 1977; PhD in Econs., UCLA, 1988. Tchr. D.S.N. High Sch., Nawanshahr, India, 1970-71; lectr. Panjab U., 1971-75, Calif. State U., L.A., 1981-82; asst. prof. Calif. State U., Fullerton, 1982-86; asst. prof. Ea. Conn. State U., Willimantic, 1986-89, assoc. prof., 1989-94, prof., 1994—, chair dept. econs., 1994—. Author: Introductory Statistics, 1992, 2d edit., 1995, Statistics for Business and Economics, 1995; contbr. articles to profl. publs. Mem. Am. Econ. Assn. Sikh. Avocations: sports, reading. Office: Ea Conn State U Willimantic CT 06226

MANN, ROBERT WELLESLEY, biomedical engineer, educator; b. Bklyn., Oct. 6, 1924; s. Arthur Wellesley and Helen (Rieger) M.; m. Margaret Ida Florencourt, Sept. 4, 1950; children: Robert Wellesley, Catherine Louise. SB, MIT, 1950, SM, 1951, ScD, 1957. With Bell Telephone Labs., N.Y.C., 1942-43, 46-47; with U.S. Army Signal Corps, 1943-46; research engr. MIT, 1951-52, rsch. supr., 1952, mem. faculty, 1953—, prof. mech. engring., 1963-70, Germeshausen prof., 1970-72, prof. engring., 1972-74, Whitaker prof. biomed. engring., 1974-92, Whitaker prof. emeritus, sr. lectr., 1992—, head systems and design div., mech. engring. dept., 1957-68, 82-83, founder, dir. engring. projects lab., 1959-62; founder, chmn. steering com. Center Sensory Aids Evaluation and Devel., 1964-86, chmn. div. health scis., tech., planning and mgmt., 1972-74, founder, dir. Newman biomechanics and human rehab. lab., 1975-92; dir. bioengring. programs Whitaker Coll. MIT, 1986-89; dir. Harvard-MIT Rehab. Engring. Ctr., 1988-93; mem. exec. com. Divsn. Health Scis. and Tech. Harvard U. MIT, 1972-85; prof., 1979—, mem. Com. on Use of Humans as Exptl. Subjects MIT, 1984-93, co-chair Pub. Svc. Ctr., 1988-92; lectr. engring. Faculty of Medicine, Harvard U., 1973-79; rsch. assoc. in orthopedic surgery Children's Hosp. Med. Ctr., 1973—; cons. in engring. sci. Mass. Gen. Hosp., 1969—; cons. in field, 1953—; mem. Nat. Commn. Engring. Edn., 1962-69; com. prosthetics rsch. and devel. NRC, 1963-69; chmn. sensory aids subcom., 1965-68, com. skeletal sys., 1969; mem. com. interplay engring. with biology and medicine Nat. Acad. Engring., 1969-73; mem. nat. bd. health scis. policy Inst. Medicine, 1973-74, 82-86; mem. com. on nat. needs for rehab. physically handicapped Nat. Acad. Scis., 1975-76; mem.-at-large confs. com. Engring. Found., 1975-81; chair sensory aids panel scis. merit rev. bd. Rehab., R & D, Dept. Vets. Affairs, 1983-95; mem. Commn. on Life Scis. NRC, 1984-88, Com. on Strategic Tech. for U.S. Army, NRC, 1989-93; NRC Com. on Space Biology and Medicine, 1992-95. Consulting editor: Ency. Sci. and Tech., 1962-67; assoc. editor: IEEE Trans. in Biomed. Engring., 1969-78, ASME Jour. Biomech. Engring., 1976-82; mem. editl. bd. Jour. Visual Impairment and Blindness, 1976-80, SOMA, 1986-92; mem. editl. adv. bd. new liberal arts program Alfred P. Sloan Found., 1986-92; contbr. over 350 articles to profl. jours. Pres., trustee Amanda Caroline Payson Scholarship Fund, 1965-86; bd. dirs. Carroll Ctr. for Blind, 1967-74, pres., 1968-74; mem. corp. Perkins Sch. for Blind, 1970—, Mt. Auburn Hosp., 1972—; trustee Nat. Braille Press, 1982—, pres., 1990-94; mem. Cardinal's adv. com. on social justice Archdiocese of Boston, 1993—; bd. overseers St. Marguerite D'Youville Found., Youville Lifecare Inc., 1994—. With U.S. Army Signal Corps, 1943-46. Recipient Sloan award for Outstanding Performance, 1957, Talbert Abrams Photogrammetry award, 1962, Assn. Blind of Mass. award, 1969, IR-100 award for Braillemboss, 1972, Bronze Beaver award MIT, 1975, UCP Goldenson Rsch. for Handicapped award, 1976, New Eng. award, 1979, J.R. Killian Faculty Achievement award MIT, 1983, Martin Luther King Leadership award MIT, 1995, Distng. Alumnus lectr. dept. mech. engring. MIT, 1997. Fellow Am. Acad. Arts and Scis., Am. Inst. Med. and Biol. Engring., IEEE (mem. editl. bd. Spectrum 1984-86), AAAS, ASME (gold medal 1977, H.R. Lissner award for biomed. engring. 1977); mem. NAS, Inst. Medicine NAS, NAE, Biomed. Engring. Soc. (bd. dirs. 1981-84), Orthopedic Rsch. Soc., Rehab. Soc. N.Am., MIT Alumni Assn. (pres. 1983-84, Alumni Fund Bd. 1978-80, bd. dirs. 1980-86, 93-95, corp. joint adv. com. 1983-84, chair nat. selector com. 1985-88, awards com. 1992-94, chmn. 1994, bd. Tech. Rev. 1986-95, chmn. 1993-95), Sigma Xi (nat. lectr. 1979-81), Tau Beta Pi, Pi Tau Sigma, Sigma Xi. Roman Catholic. Achievements include patents on missile power units, founding of computer aided design in 1963, earliest braille translation software and hardware in 1962, cybernetic amputation prosthesis, 1966, in vivo measurements of cartilage pressures, 1984. Home: 5 Pelham Rd Lexington MA 02173-5707 Office: MIT 77 Massachusetts Ave Rm 3-137 Cambridge MA 02139-4301

MANN, SALLY, photographer; b. Lexington, Va., 1951. Student, Putney Sch., 1966-69, Bennington Coll., 1969-71, Praestegaard Film Sch., Denmark, 1971-72, Aegean Sch. Fine Arts, Greece, 1971-72; BA summa cum laude, Hollins Coll., 1974, MA, 1975. guest lectr. Honolulu Acad. Arts, 1989, Women Photog. Conf., 1989, Md. Inst. Art, 1989, Bard Coll., 1989, San Francisco Cameraworks, 1990, Photog.-Retrospect/Prospect Conf., 1990, others; instr. Maine Photog. Workshops, 1985-89, Palm Beach Photog. Workshops, 1987-89, Ctr. Photog. Woodstock, 1988, 90, Internat. Ctr. Photog., N.Y., 1989, Image Found., Honolulu, 1989, Okla. Arts Found., 1989, Friends Photog. Workshops, 1990. One-woman shows include Cleve. Ctr. Contemporary Art, 1990, Edwynn Houk Gallery, Chgo., 1990, 92, Tartt Gallery, Washington, 1990, Md. Art Pl., Balt., 1991, Houk Friedman, N.Y., 1992-94, Mus. Contemporary Photog., Chgo., 1993-94, Mus. Modern Art, N.Y., 1991, Milw. Mus. Art, 1991, Whitney Mus. Am. Art, N.Y., 1991, Met. Mus. Art, N.Y., 1991, Frumpkin Adams Gallery, N.Y., 1994, Elizabeth Leach Gallery, Portland, Oreg., 1994, Bard Coll., Mass., 1994, Wellesley Coll., Mass., 1995; exhibited in group shows Corcoran Gallery Art, Washington, 1977, Va. Mus. Fine Arts, Richmond, 1988, New Orleans Mus. Art, 1990; represented in permanent collections Addison Gallery Am. Art, Andover, Mass., Balt. Mus. Art, Birmingham (Ala.) Mus. Art, Boston Mus. Fine Art, Corcoran Gallery Art, Hirshhorn Mus. and Sculpture Garden, Nat. Mus. Am. Art, Smithsonian Inst., Washington, Met. Mus. Art, N.Y., Mus. Modern Art, N.Y., Whitney Mus. Am. Art, N.Y., San Francisco Mus. Art, Va. Mus. Fine Arts, Richmond, others. Fellow Nat. Endowment Arts, 1982, 88, 92, Guggenheim Found., 1987, Southeastern Ctr. Contemporary Arts, 1989, Artists Visual Arts, 1989. Office: c/o Houk Friedman Gallery 851 Madison Ave New York NY 10021-4908*

MANN, SAM HENRY, JR., lawyer; b. St. Petersburg, Fla., Aug. 2, 1925; s. Sam Henry and Vivian (Moore) M.; m. Mary Joan Bishop, Sept. 7, 1948; children: Vivian Louise, Sam Henry III, Wallace Bishop. BA, Yale U., 1948; LLB, Fla. U., 1951, JD, 1967. Bar: Fla. 1951, U.S. Dist. Ct. (mid. and so. dists.) Fla. 1951, U.S. Ct. Appeals (5th cir.) 1955, U.S. Ct. Appeals (11th cir.) 1996, U.S. Supreme Ct. 1971. Ptnr. Greene, Mann, Rowe, Stanton, Mastry & Burton, St. Petersburg, 1951-84, Harris, Barrett, Mann & Dew, St. Petersburg, 1984—. Trustee, v.p. Mus. Fine Arts, St. Petersburg, 1980-94, Eckerd Coll., St. Petersburg, 1976-79, Webb Sch., Bell Buckle, Tenn., 1966-75; bd. dirs. Regional Community Blood Ctr., St. Petersburg, 1966—, Fla. Blood Svcs., 1993-94, mem. emeritus 1996—; mem. Disting. Alumni Soc. Webb Sch.; mem., chmn. H. Milton Rogers Heart Found.; bd. dirs., pres. Family and Children's Svc., Inc., 1956-61. Served to lt. (j.g.) USNR, 1943-48. Fellow Am. Coll. Trial Lawyers, Am. Bar Found., Fla. Bar Found.; mem. ABA, Fla. Bar Assn., Fla. Supreme Ct. Hist. Soc., Am. Counsel Assn., Def. Rsch. Inst., Internat. Assn. Def. Counsel, Pinellas County Trial Lawyers Assn., Nat. Assn. Railroad Trial Counsel, Fla. Def. Lawyers Assn., Assn. Hostp. Attys., Bay Area Vanderbilt, Yale and U. Fla. Assns., Phi Alpha Delta. Republican. Presbyterian. Avocations: RV travel, boating, gardening, workshop. Home: 531 Brightwaters Blvd NE Saint Petersburg FL 33704-3713 Office: Harris Barrett Mann & Dew Ste 1500 Southtrust Bank Bldg Saint Petersburg FL 33731-1441

MANN, SEYMOUR ZALMON, political science and public administration educator emeritus, union official; b. Chgo., Mar. 29, 1921; s. Morris and Sarah (Julius) M.; m. Irene Eincig, Aug. 30, 1942; children: Martin R., Sheldon H., Jeanette P. Student, Wright Coll., 1938-40; BE, No. Ill. U. (formerly No., Ill. State Tchr.'s Coll.), 1942; MA, U. Chgo., 1948, PhD, 1951. Instr. polit. sci. Triple Cities Coll., Syracuse U., 1948-51; asst. prof. Harpur Coll., State U. N.Y., 1951-55, asso. prof. polit. sci., 1955-60, chmn. dept., 1953-58; dir. pub. adminstrn. and met. affairs program, prof. govt. So. Ill. U., Edwardsville, 1960-67; chmn., prof. urban affairs dept. urban affairs Hunter Coll./CUNY, 1967-77; dir. Urban Research Center, 1967-68, chmn. dept. urban affairs, 1968-73; dep. to execs. dist. council 37, Am. Fedn. State, County and Mcpl. Employees, AFL-CIO, 1977-79; prof. govt. and public adminstrn., asso. dir. Nat. Center Public Productivity, John Jay Coll. Criminal Justice, CUNY, 1980-86; mem. profl. staff Congress; vis. expert rsch. staff Office Pub. Affairs, High Commr.'s Office, Germany, 1954; cons. Southwestern Ill. Govtl. Study Comm., 1961-62; vis. prof. U. So. Calif. Sch. Pub. Adminstrn., 1967; co-chmn. Ill. U.-State Agy. Coun., 1965-67; chmn. nat. commn. on urban affairs Am. Jewish Congress, 1977-81, mem. nat. governing coun., 1991—; cons., coord. spl. projects dist. coun. 37 Am. Fedn. State, County and Mcpl. Employees, N.Y.C., 1972-77. Author: (with others) From the Wagner Act to the Taft-Hartley Act, 1950, (with Charlotte B. Smart) Land Use and Planning in the Cleveland Metropolitan Area, 1959, (with R.R. Boyce) Urbanism in Illinois: Its Nature Importance and Problems, 1965, Chicago's War on poverty, 1966; contbr. to: Cases in State and Local Government, 1961, Cases in American National Government and Politics, 1978, The Politics of Productivity: State and Local Focus, 1980, Labor Management Cooperation and Worker Participation: A Public Sector Focus, 1989, play Summing Up in Public Voices, 1993; mem. editl. bd. Public Productivity and Management Rev., Pub. Voices. Served with AUS, 1943-45, ETO. Fellow Social Sci. Research Council, 1949-50; Fulbright prof. W. Germany, 1953-54; Fulbright prof. Tel Aviv (Israel) U., 1974-75. Mem. Am. Polit. Sci. Assn., Am. Soc. for Pub. Adminstrn. (pres. St. Louis met. chpt. 1964-65), Am. Arbitration Assn. (nat. labor panel), Soc. of Children's Book Writers and Illustrators, Poetry Soc. Va. Home and Office: 203 S Yoakum Pky Apt 1111 Alexandria VA 22304-3731 *It will have to be left to others to judge what success I may have obtained. There have, however, been some guiding principles which seemed to have given direction to my life's course and undoubtedly impacted on whatever professional recognition has come my way. These include: a profound respect for democratic ideology—particularly the notion that each person should have the opportunity to achieve his/her fullest potential; a clear recognition that wisdom and knowledge are not the same; and that listening is harder than talking, though it is the most important element in human communication.*

MANN, SUSAN, history educator; b. Ottawa, Ont., Can., Feb. 10, 1941; d. Walter and Marjorie Mann; m. Nicholas Trofimenkoff; 1 child, Britt. BA in Modern History, U. Toronto, 1963; MA in History, U. Western Ont., 1965; PhD, U. Laval, Que., Can., 1970; LLD (hon.), Concordia U., Montreal, Que, Can., 1989, U. Ottawa, 1994, U. Montréal, 1997. Lectr. English Toyo Eiwa Jogakuin, Tokyo, 1963-64; lectr. in history U. Montreal, 1966-70; asst. prof. history U. Calgary, Alta., Can., 1970-72; from asst. to assoc. prof. U. Ottawa, Ont., Can., 1972-83, prof. history, 1983—, chmn. dept. history, 1977-80, vice rector acad., 1984-90; pres. York U., Toronto, Ont., 1992-97; mem. stamp adv. com. Can. Post Corp., Ottawa, 1988-92; chmn. adv. bd. Nat. Archives Can., 1989-91. Author: (as Susan Mann Trofimenkoff) Action Française: French Canadian Nationalism in the 1920s, 1975, Stanley Knowles: The Man From Winnipeg North Centre, 1982, Dream of Nation: A Social and Intellectual History of Quebec, 1983 (Sec. of State Canadian Studies prize 1984), Visions nationales: Une histoire du Québec, 1986; editor: The Twenties in Western Canada, 1972, Abbé Groulx: Variations on a Nationalist Theme, 1973, (with Alison Prentice) The Neglected Majority: Essays in Canadian Women's History, vol. I, 1977, vol II, 1985; acad. editor Social Scis. in Can., 1974-76; assoc. editor Social History, 1982-84; contbr. articles to profl. jours. Assessor of projects SSHRCC, 1972—; chmn., aid to scholarly publs. com. Social Sci. Fedn. Can., 1976-79; mem. appraisals com. Ont. Coun. Grad. Studies, 1983-84; pres. Can. Hist. Assn., 1984-85; chair status of women com. Coun. Ont. Univs., 1985-88; mem. Summer Inst. Women in Higher Edn. Adminstrn. Bryn Mawr (Pa.) Coll., 1986; co-founder Sr. Women Acad. Adminstrs. Can. Publ. grantee SSHRCC, 1975, Leave fellow, 1980-81, Doctoral fellow Can. Coun., 1968-70; U. Toronto scholar, 1959-61, U. Western Ont. scholar, 1964. Fellow Royal Soc. Can., Canadian Rsch. Inst. Advancement Women (hon., life, founder, bd. dirs. 1976-78). Office: York Univ Office of Pres, 4700 Keele St, North York, ON Canada M3J 1P3

MANN, TED, screenwriter. Screenwriter VT series Bionic Showdown: The Six-Million Dollar Man and the Bionic Woman, 1989, Miami Vice, 1989, Civil Wars, 1991-92; prodr. N.Y.P.D. Blue (Emmy award for outstanding drama series 1995). Office: Hansen & Jacobson Teller Hoberman 450 N Roxbury Dr Fl 8 Beverly Hills CA 90210-4222*

MANN, THEODORE, theatrical producer and artistic director; b. N.Y.C., May 13, 1924; s. Martin M. and Gwen (Artson) Goldman; m. Patricia A. Brooks, Oct. 5, 1953; children: Andrew, Jonathan. Asso. B.A., Salinas (Calif.) Jr. Coll., 1945; LL.B., Bklyn. Law Sch., 1949. Co-founder, co-prodr., co-artistic dir. Circle in the Square Theatre, N.Y.C., 1951—; co-founder

Circle in the Sq. Theatre Sch., 1961. Co-prodr.: Long Day's Journey into Night, 1956 (Tony award best prodn. of yr. 1956-57, Pulitzer prize, N.Y. Drama Critics award); prodr.: Carnegie Hall Concert Series, 1955-69; co-founder: Washington Sq. Park Concert Series, 1955; dir.: A Moon for the Misbegotten, Ah Wilderness!, Mourning Becomes Electra, Trumpets of the Lord, Morning, Noon and Night, Arsenic and Old Lace, John and Abigail, The Iceman Cometh, Where's Charley?, The Glass Menagerie, Pal Joey, Romeo and Juliet, Awake and Sing, Seven Days of Mourning, The Last Analysis, F. Jasmine Addams, An American Millionaire, Past Tense, The Boys in Autumn, The Night of the Iguana, Anna Karenina, (mus. and opera) The Small Jewel Box; prodr.-dir.: Ford's Theatre, Washington, 1968—; host: radio show Conversations with Circle in the Square Sta., WNYC, 1978; author: Producers on Producing, 1975. Served with USAAF, 1943-45. Recipient Vernon Rice award, 1956, Page One award Newspaper Guild, 1960, Tony spl. award, 1976, Tony award nomination for best revival, 1995. Office: Circle in the Sq Theatre 1633 Broadway New York NY 10019-6708*

MANN, THEODORE R., lawyer; b. Kosica, Czechoslovakia, Jan. 31, 1928; came to U.S., 1929, naturalized, 1930; s. Aaron and Bertha (Schreiber) M.; m. Rowena Joan Weiss, 1954; children: Julie Ellen, Rachel Beth, Marcus Eliyahu. Pvt. practice Phila., 1953—; ptnr. Mann, Ungar, Spector & Labovitz; advocate in civil liberties, anti-trust and securities fraud cases.; advocate in civil liberties, anti-trust and securities fraud cases. Chmn., pres. Nat. Jewish Community Rels. Adv. Coun., 1976-80; Conf. Pres. Major Am. Jewish Orgns., 1978-80; Nat. Conf. Soviet Jewry, 1981-83; Am. Jewish Congress, 1984-88; Mazon-A Jewish Response to Hunger, 1985-90; co-chair Project Nishma, 1988—; trustee New Israel Fund, Jewish Fund for Christian Rescuers. Fellow Temple U. Alumni. Office: 1709 Spruce St Philadelphia PA 19103-6103

MANN, THOMAS EDWARD, political scientist; b. Milw., Sept. 10, 1944; s. Edward Emil and Eleanor (Hoffman) M.; m. Sheilah Rosenhack, June 4, 1976; children: Edward Matthew, Stephanie Rachael. B.A., U. Fla., 1966; M.A., U. Mich., 1968, Ph.D., 1977. Staff assoc. Am. Polit. Sci. Assn., Washington, 1970-76, asst. dir., 1977-81, exec. dir., 1981-87; co-dir. congress project Am. Enterprise Inst., Washington, 1979-81; dir. govtl. studies Brookings Instn., 1987—, W. Averell Harrimann sr. fellow in Am. governance, 1991—; mem. bd. overseers Nat. Election Study, 1987-94, chmn., 1990-94. Author: Unsafe At Any Margin, 1978; co-author: Vital Statistics on Congress, 1980, 82, 84-85, 87-88, 89-90, 91-92, 93-94, 95-96; Renewing Congress, 1992, 93; co-editor: The New Congress, 1981, The American Elections of 1982, 1983, Media Polls in American Politics, 1992, Values and Public Policy, 1994, Elections at Home and Abroad, 1994, Congress, the Press, and the Public, 1994, Intensive Care: How Congress Shapes Health Policy, 1995; editor: A Question of Balance: The President, The Congress and Foreign Policy, 1990. Mem. Democratic Nat. Com.'s Commn. on Presdl. Nomination and Party Structure, 1975-78; mem. tech. com. Dem. Nat. Com. Commn. on Presdl. Nominations, 1981-82, The Fairness Commn., 1985. U. Mich. NDEA grad. fellow, 1966-69; Am. Polit. Sci. Assn. Congl. fellow, 1969-70. Fellow Am. Acad. Arts and Scis., Nat. Acad. Pub. Adminstrn.; mem. Coun. on Fgn. Rels., Phi Beta Kappa. Home: 6508 Goldleaf Dr Bethesda MD 20817-5837 Office: Brookings Instn 1775 Massachusetts Ave NW Washington DC 20036-2188

MANN, TIMOTHY, corporate executive; b. Hackensack, N.J., July 24, 1942; s. Conklin and Hermione (Hatch) M.; m. Rosemary Teresa Connell, Feb. 26, 1965 (div. July 1993); children: Timothy, Sean Douglas, Patrick Devlin; m. Margaret Ann Tyrie, Nov. 20, 1993. Student U. Colo., 1960-61, Monmouth Coll., 1961-65, BS, 1965; postgrad. U. North Fla., 1980. Product mgr. Am. Brands, Inc., N.Y.C., 1965-70; account supr. Cargill Wilson & Acree, Inc., Richmond, Va., 1970-74; sr. mktg. mgr. Liggett & Myers Tobacco Co., Durham, N.C., 1974-78; sr. v.p. mktg. and sales Swisher Internat., Inc., Jacksonville, Fla., 1978-86, pres., 1986—, mem. mgmt. com., 1978—; pres., CEO export divsn. Swisher Internat., Inc., 1990—. Bd. dirs. Jr. Achievement of Jacksonville, Jacksonville Pvt. Industry Coun.; active Jacksonville Community Coun., Inc., 1980-87, N.E. Fla. Coun. Boy Scouts Am. Recipient N.J. Mortgage Bankers award, 1965. Mem. Cigar Assn. Am. (dir., v.p.), Am. Wholesale Marketers Assn., Tobacco Mchts. Assn. (bd. dirs.), Am. Mgmt. Assn., River Club. Office: Swisher Internat Inc PO Box 2230 Jacksonville FL 32203-2230

MANN, WESLEY F., newspaper editor. Editor Investor's Business Daily, L.A. Office: Investor's Business Daily 12655 Beatrice St Los Angeles CA 90066-7300*

MANNE, HENRY GIRARD, lawyer, educator; b. New Orleans, May 10, 1928; s. Geoffrey and Eva (Shainberg) M.; m. Bobbette Lee Taxer, Aug. 19, 1968; children: Emily Kay, Geoffrey Adam. B.A., Vanderbilt U., 1950; J.D., U. Chgo., 1952; LL.M., Yale U., 1953, J.S.D., 1966; LLD, U. Puget Sound, 1987, U. Francisco Marroquin, Guatemala, 1987. Bar: Ill. 1952, N.Y. 1969. Practice in Chgo., 1953-54; asso. prof. Law Sch., St. Louis U., 1956-57, 59-62; prof. Law Sch., George Washington U., 1962-68; Kenan prof. law and polit. sci. U. Rochester, 1968-74; Disting. prof. law, dir. Law and Econs. Center, U. Miami Law Sch., 1974-80; prof. law Law and Econs. Center, Emory U., Atlanta, 1980-86; dean Law Sch., univ. prof., hon. chmn. Law and Econs. Ctr. George Mason U., 1986-96, dir. planning and devel., chmn. bd. advisors Law Econs. Ctr., 1996—; vis. prof. law U. Wis., Madison, 1957-59, Stanford (Calif.) Law Sch., 1971-72; dir. Econs. Insts. Fed. Judges, 1976-89. Author: Insider Trading and the Stock Market, 1966, (with H. Wallich) The Modern Corporation and Social Responsibility, 1973, (with E. Solomon) Wall Street in Transition, 1974, Med. Malpractice Guidebook: Law and Economics, 1985; editor: (with Roger LeRoy Miller) Gold, Money and the Law, 1975; editor: (with Roger LeRoy Miller) Auto Safety Regulation: The Cure or the Problem, 1976, Economic Policy and the Regulation of Corporate Securities, 1968, The Economics of Legal Relationships, 1975; editor: (with James Dorn) Econ. Liberties and the Judiciary, 1987. Served to 1st lt. USAF, 1954-56. Recipient Salvatori award Excellence in Acad. Leadership, 1994; named Cultural Laureate of Va., 1992. Fellow Am. Bar Found.; mem. Am. Law Inst., Am. Econs. Assn., Am. Law and Econs. Assn. (hon. life, Salvatori award for excellence in acad. leadership 1994), Mont Pelerin Soc., Order of Coif, Phi Beta Kappa.

MANNERING, JERRY VINCENT, agronomist, educator; b. Custer, Okla., June 14, 1929; s. James Bryan and Verta (Bates) M.; m. Marjorye McVicker, June 20, 1953; children: Debra Lynn Mannering Zerman, Stephen Scott, Lisa Gaye Mannering Schwingendorf. B.S., Okla. State U., 1951; M.S., Purdue U., 1956, Ph.D., 1967. Cert. profl. soil scientist, profl. soil erosion and sediment control specialist. Grad. asst. Purdue U., West Lafayette, Ind., 1954-56, extension agronomist, prof. agronomy, 1967-89; prof. emeritus, 1990—; research agronomist U. Idaho, Aberdeen, 1956-58; research soil scientist Agrl. Research Sta., USDA, West Lafayette, 1958-67; cons. FAO, Bulgaria, 1972, Govt. of Brazil, 1975. Contbr. numerous articles on agronomy to profl. jours. Served to 1st lt. U.S. Army, 1951-54. Decorated Purple Heart; recipient Hovde award Purdue U. and Ind. Farm Bur., 1982. Fellow Soil Conservation Soc. Am., Soil Sci. Soc. Am., Am. Soc. Agronomy; mem. Internat. Soil Sci. Soc., Internat. Soil Tillage Research Orgn., Lions Club.

MANNERS, GEORGE EMANUEL, business educator, emeritus dean; b. N.Y.C., Nov. 26, 1910; s. John Emanuel and Demetra (Kremida) M.; m. Claire Gibson, Oct. 14, 1939; children—George Emanuel, Susan Demetra. B.S. in Commerce, Ga. State U., 1935; M.B.A. in Econs, U. Ga., 1946; Ph.D. in History, Emory U., 1959. Bookkeeper and acct. Ga., 1927-37; pub. acct., 1937; high sch. tchr. Atlanta, 1937-39, 41-42, 46-47; test technician merit system Ga. Labor Dept., 1939-41; mem. faculty Ga. State U. (and predecessor), 1947—; dean Sch. Bus. Adminstrn. Ga. State U., 1950-69, asst. v.p., 1969-70, assoc. v.p., 1970—, Regents' prof., 1971—, dean emeritus, 1977—; dean Sch. Mgmt., Rensselaer Poly. Inst., Troy, N.Y., 1979-80; dir. Univ. Ctr. in Ga., Inc., 1980-83; dean protem, Sch. Bus. and Econs. Mercer U. Atlanta, 1986-87; Mem. Met. Planning Commn., Atlanta, 1949-59, Atlanta Regional Export Expansion Council. Author: History of Life Insurance Company in Georgia, 1891-1955, 1959, also articles. Served to maj. AUS, 1942-46. Mem. So. Econ. Assn., So. Hist. Assn., Atlanta C. of C., Hellenic Study Group, Delta Sigma Pi, Beta Gamma Sigma. Methodist (Sunday sch. tchr.). Club: Kiwanian. Home: 338 Nelson Ferry Rd Decatur GA 30030-2320 Office: 33 Gilmer St SE Atlanta GA 30303-3044 *I have noted that a life devoted to a sound ideal, pursued steadily with character and tolerance, brings the keenest and most lasting happiness. Others feel the fire and assist on the way; impediments become adventures. Challenge and zest accompany one each day; horizons widen. This spirit can be applied by all, in every walk of life, in every field of endeavor, in every land, at all times in history.*

MANNERS, PAMELA JEANNE, middle school educator; b. Holyoke, Mass., Mar. 20, 1951; d. Francis Edward and Helen Mary (Kurtyka) Herbert; div. 1985; children: Tracy, Kristen. BA, U. So. Miss., 1986, MEd, 1993. Cert. elem. edn. K-3, 4-8, secondary Eng., Social Studies; cert. elem. prin., secondary prin., elem. and secondary adminstrn. Registrar Michel Mid. Sch., Biloxi, Miss., 1987-88, tchr. Eng. and Social Studies, 1988-90, tchr. reading/law related edn., 1990-95; curriculum coord. Biloxi Pub. Schs., 1995—; dir. ABA Reading Cirriculum Program; law-related edn. trainer Miss. Law-Related Edn. Ctr., Jackson, 1990—; law-related trainer Ctr. Civic Edn., Calabasas, Calif., 1993; law-related trainer Constitutional Right Found., 1994—. Participant program Lawyer in Every Class Miss. Bar Assn., Jackson, 1990-93. On-site target grantee Miss. Bar/Dept. Justice, 1992; A+ Site recognition U.S. Dept. Edn. Mem. NEA, Miss. Edn. Assn., Leadership Gulf Coast C. of C. Roman Catholic. Office: Curriculum Office Biloxi Pub Schs 1424 Father Ryan Ave Biloxi MS 39530-3523

MANNES, ELENA SABIN, film and television producer, director; b. N.Y.C., Dec. 3, 1943; d. Leopold Damrosch and Evelyn (Sabin) M. BA, Smith Coll., 1965; MA, Johns Hopkins U., 1967. Researcher Pub. Broadcast Lab. Nat. Ednl. TV, N.Y.C., 1968-70; writer Sta. WPIX-TV, N.Y.C., 1970-73; assignment editor Sta. ABC-TV, N.Y.C., 1973-76; producer, writer Sta. WCBS-TV, N.Y.C., 1976-80; producer CBS News, N.Y.C., 1980-87, Pub. Affairs TV/Bill Moyers PBS Documentaries, N.Y.C., 1987-90; ind. documentary dir. and producer, 1987—. Recipient Emmy award NATAS, 1984, 85, 87, 90, 94, 96, Peabody award, 1985, Cine Golden Eagle award, 1988, 90, 93, 94, 95, Robert F. Kennedy journalism award, 1989, DGA awards, 1987, 90. Mem. Writers Guild Am., Dirs. Guild Am., Am. Film Inst. (dir. Workshop for Women). Avocations: tennis, still photography.

MANNES, PAUL, judge; b. Washington, Dec. 25, 1933; A.B., Dartmouth Coll., 1955; LL.B., Georgetown U., 1958, LL.M., 1962. Bar: D.C. 1958, Md. 1965. Judge U.S. Bankruptcy Ct. Dist. Md., 1981—; mem. Jud. Conf. adv. com. on Bankruptcy Rules, 1987-96, chmn., 1993-96; pres. Nat. Conf. Bankruptcy Judges, 1991-92; bd. dirs. Am. Bankruptcy Inst., 1992-97. Mem. Am. Coll. Bankruptcy, Bar Assn. Montgomery County (pres. 1979-80), Md. Bar Found. Office: US Courthouse 6500 Cherrywood Ln Greenbelt MD 20770-1249

MANNICK, JOHN ANTHONY, surgeon; b. Deadwood, S.D., Mar. 24, 1928; s. Alfred and Catherine Elizabeth (Schuster) M.; m. Alice Virginia Gossard, June 9, 1952; children—Catherine Virginia, Elizabeth Eleanor, Joan Barbara. BA, Harvard U., 1949, MD, 1953. Diplomate: Am. Bd. Surgery (dir. 1971-77). Intern Mass. Gen. Hosp., 1953-54, resident in surgery, 1956-60; instr. in surgery to asst. prof. Med. Coll. Va., 1960-64; asso. prof. to prof. surgery Boston U., 1964-76, chmn. div. surgery, 1973-76; Moseley prof. surgery Harvard U., 1976-94, Moseley Disting. prof. surgery, 1994—; dir. ednl. programs Harvard Med. Internat., 1994-96; chmn. dept. surgery Peter Bent Brigham Hosp. and Brigham and Women's Hosp., Boston, 1976-94; mem. surgery, anesthesiology and trauma study sect. NIH, 1978-82, mem. medicine study sect., 1967-70; rsch. com. Med. Found., Inc., 1970-76. Author: (with others) Modern Surgery, 1970, Core Textbook of Surgery, 1972, Surgery of Ischemic Limbs, 1972, The Cause and Management of Aneurysms, 1990; mem. editorial bd. AMA Archives of Surgery, 1973-84, Clin. Immunology and Immunopathology, 1972-84, Surgery, 1982—, Brit. Jour. Surgery, 1982-92, European Jour. Vascular Surgery, 1988—; mem. editorial bd. Advances in Surgery, 1979—, editor, 1984-86; mem. editorial bd. Jour. Vascular Surgery, 1984—, assoc. editor, 1990—; also articles. Served to capt. M.C. USAF, 1954-56. Markle scholar in acad. medicine, 1961-66. Fellow ACS (gov.), Royal Coll. Surgeons (hon., Eng.), Royal Coll. Surgeons (hon., Edinburgh); mem. Am. Fedn. Clin. Rsch., Am. Assn. Immunologists, Am. Soc. Exptl. Pathology, Soc. Clin. Investigation, Soc. Clin. Surgery, Soc. Univ. Surgeons, Soc. Surg. Chmn. (sec. 1985-87, pres. 1987-88), Am. Surg. Assn. (pres. 1989-90), Internat. Cardiovascular Soc. (recorder N.Am. chpt., 1973-76, pres. N.Am. chpt. 1991-92, internat. v.p. 1993), Soc. Vascular Surgery (pres. 1981), N.E. Surg. Soc., New Eng. Soc. Vascular Surgery (pres. 1994-95), So. Surg. Assn., So. Soc. Vascular Surgery, Surg. Infection Soc., Halstead Soc., Phi Beta Kappa. Home: 81 Bogle St Weston MA 02193-1056 Office: 75 Francis St Boston MA 02115-6110

MANNIELLO, JOHN BAPTISTE LOUIS, research scientist; b. N.Y.C., Oct. 31, 1923; s. George and Susan Manniello; m. Rosa Ann Gulotta; children: George, John, Stephen. B of Mech. Engring., Poly. Inst. N.Y., 1953; cert. with honors, Indsl. Coll. Armed Forces, 1962; DSc (hon.), N.Y. Inst. Tech., 1989, DMS, 1991. Engring. exec. Fairchild Camera, N.Y.C., 1946-60; dir. labs. div. CBS, Stamford, Conn., 1960-73, v.p. govt. ops. labs. div., 1973-77; diplomat State Dept., Rome, 1977-78; chief Am. scientist NATO Labs., 1978-79; with Office of Chmn. Western Union, Mahwah, N.J., 1978-79; v.p. N.Y. Inst. Tech., N.Y.C., 1979-91; exec. v.p. Artificial Intelligence Techs., Inc., N.Y.C., 1991-94; mem. adv. bd. CUNY, 1968-70; advisor to pres. Staten Island (N.Y.) C.C., 1970-72; permanent chair Inst. Mech. Studies, Trieste, Italy, 1975—; vis. prof. Med. Coll., U. Rome, 1977—, Hahnemann Med. Ctr., 1967—, U. Naples; pres., chief exec. officer San Marino (Italy) Telecom., 1958-59; instr. physics and engring. Hofstra U.; mem. governing bd. Clinica Moscati, Rome; apptd. mem. Commn. on Application Am. Sci. and Tech. to improvement of Italian med. care delivery, sci. advisor Nat. Rsch. Coun., Pres. of Italy; chmn. various confs., symposiums and workshops; active Office Navy Intelligence Adv. Com., 1991—, Def. Intelligence Agy. Adv. Com., 1990-91; sci. advisor Vatican, 1994; with info. sci. divsn. Argonne Nat. Labs. Author: Marketing Research and Developmentt for the Government, vols. 1 and 2, 1972, The NATO Market, 1978, (autobiography) A Life, 1993; mem. adv. panel Electronics Mag., contbr. to books, papers and publs. Chmn. N.Y. Civic Assn., 1962-63; co-chmn. Cerebral Palsy Assn., N.Y., 1965-66; counselor Eagle Scouts; mem. VITA; founder Arnaldo Marie Àngelini Scholarship Fund, John Manniello Scholarship Fund; sponsor Lennard Perroots Intelligence Rsch. fellowship, William Doyle Internat. Rels. award; bd. dirs. Office Teleport. With USAAF, 1942-46, ETO, prisoner of war. Decorated Purple Heart with three oak leaf clusters, Air medal with three oak leaf clusters, DFC, Ordine Merito, Republic of Italy, 1977, comdr. and knight Cavaliere di Gran Croce-Etoile de la Paix, Order of St. John; recipient Presdl. Service award, ECO Gold Medal award. Mem. Am. Astron. Soc. (sr.), Soc. Photo-Optical Instrumentation Engrs., Soc. Photographic Scientists and Engrs., Am. Soc. Photogrammetry, Soc. for Info. Display, Am. Mgmt. Soc., Mus. Holography (bd. dirs.), N.Y. Acad. Scis., Internat. Innovation Group, Exec. Service Corps, Pan Am. Med. Assn., Acad. Incammenatti, Acad. Gentium Pro Pace, Marconi Inst. (mem. telecommunications commn.), Tau Beta Pi, Pi Tau Sigma, Sigma Alpha. Republican. Roman Catholic. Clubs: Army and Navy (Washington), Caterpillar (N.J.), Pres.'s (N.Y.), Goldfish. Achievements include implementation of ultrasound for medical diagnosis, compass link system for transmission and reception of hi-resolution photography between Vietnam and the U.S., color TV on the moon, pioneer wireless TV, videoconferencing. Home: 9 Island Ave Unit 801 Miami FL 33139

MANNING, BLANCHE M., federal judge; b. 1934. BEd, Chgo. Tchrs. Coll., 1961; JD, John Marshall Law Sch., 1967; MA, Roosevelt Univ., 1972; LLM, Univ. of Va. Law Sch., 1992. Asst. states atty. State's Atty.'s Office (no. dist.), Ill., 1968-73; supervisory trial atty. U.S. EEOC, Chgo., 1973-77; gen. atty. United Airlines, Chgo., 1977-78; asst. U.S. atty. U.S. Dist. Ct. (no. dist.) Ill., 1978-79; assoc. judge Cir. Ct. of Cook County, 1979-86, circuit judge, 1986-87; appellate court judge Ct. of Review Ill. Appellate Ct., 1987-94; district judge U.S. Dist. Ct. (no. dist.) Ill., Chgo., 1994—; tchr. A. O. Sexton Elem. Sch. James Wadsworth Elem. Sch., Wendell Phillips H.S. Adult Program, Morgan Park H.S. Summer Sch. Program, South Shore H.S. Summer Sch. Program, Carver H.S. Adult Edn. Program; lectr. Malcolm X C.C., 1970-71; adj. prof. NCBL C.C. of Law, 1978-79, DePaul Univ. Law Sch., 1992-94; tchg. team mem. Trial Advocacy Workshop, Harvard Law Sch., U. Chgo. Law Sch., 1991-94; chmn. Com. on Recent Devels. in Evidence, Ill. Judicial Conf., 1991; faculty mem. New Judges Seminar, Ill. Judicial Conf.; past faculty mem. Profl. Devel. Seminar for New Assoc. Judges, Cook County Cir. Ct.; mem. bd. dirs., trained intervenor Lawyers' Assistance Program, Inc.; mem. adv. coun. Lawyer's Asst. Program, Roosevelt U. Trustee Sherwood Music Conservatory Bd. Mem. Cook County Bar Assn. (second v-p 1974), Nat. Bar Assn., Nat. Judicial Coun., Ill. Judicial Coun. (treas. 1982-85, chmn. 1988, chmn. judiciary com. 1992), Ill. Judges Assn., Women's Bar Assn. of Ill., Nat. Assn. of Women Lawyers, Ill. State Bar Assn. (bd. dirs. Lawyers Assistance Program Inc.), Am. Bar Assn. (fellow 1991), Chgo. Bar Assn. (bd. dirs. Lawyers Assistance Program Inc.), Nat. Assn. of Women Judges, Appellate Lawyers Assn. (hon.); John Marshall Law Sch. Alumni Assn. (bd. dirs.), Chgo. State Univ. Alumni Assn. (bd. dirs.). Office: US Dist Ct 2156 US Courthouse 219 S Dearborn St Chicago IL 60604*

MANNING, BRENT V., lawyer; b. Preston, Idaho, Jan. 18, 1950; s. Leon W. and Gwen (Briscoe) M.; m. J. Christine Coffin, Oct. 25, 1969; children: Justin, Britten, John. BA, Idaho State U., 1972; JD, Harvard U., 1975. Bar: Colo. 1975, Utah 1981, U.S. Ct. Appeals (10th cir.) 1978. Assoc. Holme Roberts & Owen, Denver, 1975-80, ptnr., 1980—; ptnr. Holme Roberts & Owen, Salt Lake City, 1981-97; founding ptnr. Manning Curtis Bradshaw & Bednar, LLC, Salt Lake City, 1997—; cooperating atty. ACLU, Denver, 1979-81, Salt Lake City, 1987-91; mem. panel mediators and arbitrators U.S. Dist. Ct. Utah, 1993—; mediation & settlement judge pro tempore 3rd Jud. Dist. State of Utah, 1996—. Trustee Bountiful (Utah) Davis Art Found., 1985-91, Utah Tibetan Resettlement Project. Mem. ABA, Utah Bar Assn. (chmn. continuing legal edn. com. 1988, mem. disciplinary com. 1991-93, cts. and judges com. 1993—, chmn. 1996-97), Am. Inns of Ct. (pres.-elect 1996-97, master of bench 1988—), Sierra Club, Am. Alpine Club (N.Y.C.). Democrat. Avocations: climbing, bicycling, running. Home: 2079 Maple Grove Way Bountiful UT 84010-1005 Office: Holme Roberts & Owen 111 E Broadway Ste 1100 Salt Lake City UT 84111-5233

MANNING, BURT, advertising executive; b. 1931. Chmn., chief exec. officer J. Walter Thompson Co., Worldwide, N.Y.C., 1987—. Bd. dirs. nat. Assn. for Depressive Illness, Nat. Players Co., Advt. Edn. Found.; trustee Neuroscis. Inst., New Sch. for Social Rsch. Mem. Lotus Club. Office: J Walter Thompson Co 466 Lexington Ave New York NY 10017-3140*

MANNING, CHARLES TERRILL, retired lawyer; b. Empress, Alta., Can., Mar. 27, 1925; s. N. Folsom and Mary E. (Terrill) M.; m. H. Joyce Johnson, 1946; children—A. Terrill, Timothy F., Heather J., Annabelle H. B.A., Bishop's U., 1946; B.C.L., McGill U., 1949. Bar: Que. Ptnr. Hackett-Mulvena-Hackett, Montreal, Que., Can., 1946-56; gen. counsel, v.p. Brit. Nfld., Churchill Falls, Montreal, 1956-69; v.p., sec., chief legal officer Royal Trust, Montreal and Toronto, Ont., Can., 1970-85; counsel McMaster Meighen, Montreal, 1985-90; assoc. Meighen Demers, Toronto, 1991-94; ret., 1994. Served with Royal Can. Navy, 1944-45. Named to Queen's Counsel, Minister of Justice, Que., Can., 1968. Mem. Can. Bar Assn., Que. Bar Assn. Anglican. Home: 1000 King Sr W 703, Kingston, ON Canada K7M 8H3

MANNING, CHARLES W., academic administrator; b. Mar. 18, 1943; s. Charles Manning; m. Sharon Fischer; children: Shannon, Charles, Kelly. BS in Chemistry, Western Md. Coll., 1965; PhD in Analytical Chemistry, U. Md., 1969; postgrad., Inst. Anorganische und Kernchemie, Johannes Gutenberg U., Mainz, Germany, 1969-70. Sr. staff assoc. Nat. Ctr. Higher Edn. Mgmt. Systems, Boulder, Colo., 1971-74; asst. provost, asst. prof. chemistry U. Mo., Kansas City, 1974-79; assoc. exec. dir. acad. affairs Colo. Commn. Higher Edn., Denver, 1979-81, dep. exec. dir., 1982-88; v.p. acad. affairs U. No. Colo., Greeley, 1981-82; exec. vice chancellor Okla. State Regents for Higher Edn., Oklahoma City, 1988-90; chancellor U. System W.Va., Charleston, 1991—; cons. as v.p. for planning and fin. Fed. U., Ceara, Brazil, 1976-77; presenter in field. Contbr. articles to profl. jours. Capt. U.S. Army, 1970-71. Mem. Rotary. Office: U System WVa 1018 Kanawha Blvd E Ste 700 Charleston WV 25301-2827

MANNING, DANIEL RICARDO, professional basketball player; b. Hattiesburg, Miss., May 17, 1966; s. Ed Manning. Student, U. Kans. Basketball player L.A. Clippers, 1988-94, Atlanta Hawks, 1994, Phoenix Suns, 1994—. Recipient Bronze medal U.S. Olympic Basketball Team, 1988; named Most Outstanding Player NCAA Divsn. I Tournament, 1988, Naismith award, 1988, Wooden award, 1988; named to Sporting News NCAA All-Am. first team, 1987, 88, NBA All-Star Team, 1993-94. First pick overall NCAA draft, 1988; mem. NCAA Divsn. I Championship team, 1988. Office: Phoenix Suns 201 E Jefferson St Phoenix AZ 85004-2412*

MANNING, DARRELL V., national guard officer; b. Preston, Idaho, July 17, 1932; s. Virgil and Olive Ann (Jenks) M.; m. Rochelle Cole, June 4, 1954; children: David Scott, Michael Alan. BS, Utah State U., 1955; postgrad., Idaho State U., 1969. Enlisted USAF, 1955, pilot, 1955-60, advanced through grades to maj. gen., 1987; v.p. Manning Inc., Pocatello, Idaho, 1960-71; dir. Idaho Dept. Aeronautics, Boise, 1971-74, Idaho Dept. Transp., Boise, 1974-85; adjutant-gen., chief Idaho N.G., Boise, 1985-95; chmn. Trans Research Bd. Nat. Acad. Scis., 1982. State rep., Boise, 1960-63; Idaho sen., 1970-71. Mem. Am. Assn. State Hwy. and Transp. Officials (nat. pres. 1978, Disting. Service award 1985, MacDonald Meml. award 1985), Western Assn. State Hwy. and Transp. Officials, Adjutant-Gens. Assn. U.S., N.G. Assn. U.S., Air Force Assn., Assn. U.S. Army, VFW, Rotary. Home: 8260 Golse Cir Boise ID 83704-4455

MANNING, DAVID LEE, health care executive; b. Birmingham, Ala., Jan. 30, 1950; s. William L. and Lula L. (Lively) M.; m. Donna H. Holley, Dec. 29, 1972; children: Emily Anne, Laura Elizabeth. BA, U. Ala., Tuscaloosa, 1973, MPA, 1974. Budget analyst State of Tenn., Nashville, 1974-79, asst. state treas., 1979-87, commr. fin. and adminstrn., 1987-95; v.p. Columbia/HCA Healthcare Corp., 1995-97, sr. v.p., 1997—. So. Regional Tng. Program in Pub. Adminstrn. fellow, 1973. Democrat. Baptist. Office: Columbia/HCA Healthcare Corp One Park Plz PO Box 550 Nashville TN 37202-0550

MANNING, DEBORAH A., physician; b. Clinton, N.C., Dec. 21, 1952; d. George A. and Virginia M. (McLaurin) M. BS, George Washington U., 1974; MD, Howard U., 1977. Diplomate Am. Bd. Internal Medicine. Intern Harbor Gen. Hosp., Torrance, Calif., 1977-78; resident Martinez (Calif.) VA Hosp., 1978-79, Providence Hosp., Washington, 1979-80; physician United Neighborhood Health Svcs., Nashville, 1980-82; pvt. practice Nashville, 1982-93; physician State of Tenn. Corrections, Nashville, 1993-94; med. dir. Matthew Walker Comp. Health Ctr., Nashville, 1994-95; physician Johns Hopkins Med. Svcs. Corp., 1996—. Mem. task force Meharry-Gen. merger Nashville C. of C., 1991; chair nat. trends Music City Links, Nashville, 1992-94; mem. Harbor City Links, 1996—. Mem. ACP, Tenn. Women Medicine (mem. exec. com. 1992-94).

MANNING, ERIC, computer science and engineering educator, university dean, researcher; b. Windsor, Ont., Can., Aug. 4, 1940; g. George Gorman and Eleanor Katherine (Koehler) M.; m. Betty Goldring, Sept. 16, 1961; children: David, Paula. BSc, U. Waterloo, Ont., 1961, MSc, 1962; PhD, U. Ill., 1965. Registered profl. engr., B.C. With MIT and Bell Telephone Labs., 1965-68; prof. computer sci. U. Waterloo, 1968-86, founding dir. computer comms. networks group, 1973-82; founding dir. Inst. for Computer Rsch., 1982-86; prof., dean engring. U. Victoria, B.C., Can., 1986-92, prof. computer sci., elec. engring., 1993—; dir. Natural Sci. and Engring. Rsch. Coun. Can., mem. exec. com., chair strategic grants com., 1982-87; dir. Comms. Rsch. Centre, Govt. of Can., 1995—, Consortium for Software Engring. Rsch., Ottawa, 1997—; trustee B.C. Advanced Sys. Found., 1986-93; dir. Sci. Coun. B.C., 1988-91; bd. dirs. Can. Microelectric Corp.; adv. com. on artificial intelligence NRC, 1987-91; IBM chair computer sci. Keio U., Yokohama, 1992-93; hon. prof. South East U., Nanjing, People's Republic of China. Author: Fault Diagnosis of Digital Systems, 1970; also numerous articles. V.p. Greater Victoria Concert Band, 1995-96. Fellow IEEE, Engring. Inst. Can.; mem. Assn. Profl. Engrs. B.C., Soc. for Computer Simulation, Can. Inst. for Advanced Rsch. (adv. com. on artificial intelligence and robotics 1986-90), Can. Assn. for Computer Sci. (pres. 1994—), Can. Soc. for Fifth Generation Rsch. (trustee 1987-88), B.C. Microelectronics Soc. (bd. dirs. 1986-87). Avocations: squash, scuba diving, sailing, flying, music. Home: 2909 Phyllis St, Victoria, BC Canada V8N 1Y8 Office: U Victoria Faculty Engring, PO Box 3055, Victoria, BC Canada V8W 3P6

MANNING, FARLEY, retired public relations executive; b. Shelburne, Mass., Oct. 30, 1909; s. John Farley and Bessie (Learmont) M.; m. Ruth Fulton Koegel, 1932 (div. 1968); 1 child, Toni Ruth; m. Jean Yeager, Nov. 17, 1982. Student Northeastern U., 1927-29, Boston U., 1929-31. Reporter, editor various newspapers, New Eng., 1931-42; acct. exec. Dudley Anderson Yutzy, N.Y.C., 1946-54; pres., chmn. Manning Selvage & Lee, N.Y.C., 1954-79; chmn. G. & M. Creative Svcs., 1958-81; treas. Cascade Olympic Corp., Olympia, Wash., 1982—; dir. Cascade Olympic Corp., Capital Cascade Inc., Capitol Ctr. Inc. Contbr. articles on dog care and tng. to nat. mags. Maj. USAF, 1943-46. Mem. Pub. Rels. Soc. Am., Olympia Yacht Club, N.Y. Yacht Club, Beaverkill Fly Fishers Club, Overseas Press Club, Thunderbird Country Club, Comm. 25 Club, Rotary. Home: 5510 Cooper Point Rd NW Olympia WA 98502-3646

MANNING, FREDERICK JAMES, insurance company executive; b. Chgo., Oct. 20, 1947; s. Herbert and June Betty (Cohen) M.; m. Gail Hilary Phillips, Feb. 9, 1980; children: Elizabeth Sarah, David Charles. BS, U. Pa., 1969; JD, Harvard U., 1972. Treas. The Marmon Group, Inc., Chgo., 1973-77; chmn. bd. dirs., chief exec. officer Celtic Life Ins. Co., Chgo., 1978—; also chmn. bd. dirs., pres., chief exec. officer Celtic Group, Inc., Chgo.; bd. dirs. Engineered ControlsInternat., Inc. Trustee, chmn. bd. trustees Michael Reese Health Trust; trustee, v.p., asst. sec. Pritzker Family Philanthropic Fund; mem., pres. coun. U. Pa.; mem. adv. com. Dispute Resolution Rsch. Ctr., Kellogg Grad. Sch. Mgmt., Northwestern U., Evanston, Ill.; trustee, mem. planning and mktg. com., mem. budget com. Children's Meml. Med. Ctr. Mem. Young President's Orgn., Std. Club, East Bank Club, Met. Club, Northmoor Country Club (Highland Park, Ill.). Home: 442 W Wellington Ave Chicago IL 60657-5804 Office: Celtic Life Ins Co 233 S Wacker Dr Ste 700 Chicago IL 60606-6300

MANNING, FREDERICK WILLIAM, retired retail executive; b. Youngstown, Ohio, Aug. 15, 1924; s. John Carroll and Mary Matilda Manning; m. Martha Ann Gross, May 9, 1953 (dec. Feb. 1992); children: William, Patricia, Joan, Donna, David. BS, Youngstown U., 1948; LLB, Case Western Res. U., 1951. With F.W. Woolworth Co., N.Y.C., 1951-88, dir. real estate N.Y. office, 1960-79, v.p., 1980-88, ret., 1988. 2nd lt. USAAF, 1943-45. Mem. Ohio State Bar. Roman Catholic. Home: 77 Huron Dr Chatham NJ 07928-1205

MANNING, J. FRANCIS, school administrator; b. Syracuse, N.Y., May 11, 1963; s. Thomas Michael and Elena Ann (Corbacio) M. BS, SUNY, Buffalo, 1986; MS, Syracuse U., 1987; CAS, SUNY, Cortland, 1991; postgrad., Century U., 1991—. Math. tchr. Huntington Elem. Sch., Syracuse, N.Y., 1987-91; adminstrv. intern Henniger High Sch., Syracuse, 1991; vice prin. Levy Middle Sch., Syracuse, 1991-92; asst. prin. West Genesee Mid. Sch., Camillus, N.Y., 1992—; grade level adminstr. Pine Grove Jr. H.S., East Syracuse, N.Y.; la crosse coach Syracuse High Sch. Dist., 1987-90; cooperating tchr. SUNY at Cortland, 1987-91; resident mentor Syracuse Tchr. Ctr., 1990-93; supt.'s issue team, Syracuse City Sch. Dist., 1990-92; prin. Henniger High Sch. Summer Sch., 1991, '92; facilitator Syracuse City Sch. Dist., 1992-3. Recipient scholaship Syracuse U., 1986. Mem. N.Y. State Assn. for Supervision, Curriculum Devel., Sch. Adminstrs. Assn. N.Y., Nat. Assn. Secondary Prins., N.Y. State Middle Sch. Assn., N.Y. State Devel. Coun., Commn. on Adult Basic Learning. Avocations: Tae Kwon Do Karate Black Belt. Home: 209 Seward St Syracuse NY 13203-1542 also: Pine Grove Jr HS Fremont Rd East Syracuse NY 13057

MANNING, JACK, photographer, columnist, author; b. N.Y.C., Nov. 21, 1920; s. Mathew and Sally (Markowitz) Mendelsohn; m. Marie Louise Koch, Oct. 9, 1970; 1 child, Sarah-Jeanne. Student, CCNY. Free-lance photographer for nat. mags., 1941-63; staff photographer N.Y. Times, N.Y.C., 1964—, photographic columnist, 1976—. Author: Venezuela, 1958, Young Puerto Rico, 1966; Young Spain, 1967, Young Ireland, 1968, Young Brazil, 1969, Portrait of Spain, 1970, The Fine 35mm Portrait, 1979, 82; photographs represented in permanent collections Mus. Modern Art, Met. Mus. Art, Nat. Gallery Arts, Toronto. Recipient numerous photog. awards. Mem. Nat. Press Photographers, N.Y. Press Photographers. Home: 75 Pearce Pky Pearl River NY 10965-1923 Office: NY Times 229 W 43rd St New York NY 10036-3913

MANNING, JAMES FORREST, computer executive; b. Washington, July 31, 1929; s. James Forrest and Marguerite (Wise) M.; m. Joan Morris, Nov. 5, 1955; children: Katherine W., James Forest IV, Robert M. Student in Math., Dayton U., 1951-53; B.A. in Econs., Williams Coll., 1954. With IBM Corp., 1954—, sales rep. data processing div., Pittsfield, Mass., 1954-57, branch mgr., Erie, Pa., from 1957, custom systems mgr., systems devel. div., 1965-66, systems mgr., intermediate systems, 1966-68, dir. intermediate/medium systems, systems devel. div., 1968-69, v.p. mktg., data products div., 1969-71, group dir. operational programs, data processing group, 1971-72, v.p. plans and controls, gen. products div., 1972-78, v.p. plans and controls, systems products div., 1978-81, asst. group exec., from 1981, corp. v.p., asst. group exec. business info. systems group, 1985-87; pvt. practice cons., 1987-95; pres., vice chmn. Staff Leasing, Bradenton, Fla., 1995—. Served to tech. sgt. USAF, 1950-53. Avocations: reading; sports. Home: Hilltop Rd Wilson Pt Norwalk CT 06854

MANNING, JEROME ALAN, lawyer; b. Bklyn., Dec. 31, 1929; s. Emanuel J. and Dorothy (Levine) M.; m. Naomi Jacobs, Oct. 31, 1954; children: Joy, Stephen, Susan. BA, NYU, 1950, LLB, 1952; LLM, Yale U., 1953. Bar: N.Y. 1953, Fla. 1977. Assoc. Joseph Trachtman, N.Y.C., 1956-61; ptnr. Stroock & Stroock & Lavan, N.Y.C., 1961-96; prof. NYU Sch. Law, 1956-96. Editor: NYU Law Review; author: Estate Planning, 1980, rev. edit. 1995, Estate Planning for Laymen, 1992. Trustee Jewish Communal Fund, N.Y. Capt. USAF, 1953-56. Mem. ABA. Home: 1835 Franklin St San Francisco CA 94109

MANNING, JOHN WARREN, III, retired surgeon, medical educator; b. Phila., Nov. 24, 1919; s. John Warren Jr. and Edith Margaret (Reagan) M.; m. Muriel Elizabeth Johnson, Oct. 11, 1944; children: John, Melissa, Susan. BS in Chemistry with honors, Ursinus Coll., 1940; MD, U. Pa., 1943; postgrad., 1978. Diplomate Am. Bd. Surgery. Naval intern Pa. Naval Hosp., 1946; resident Saginaw (Mich.) Gen. Hosp., 1947-50; preceptor Dr. H.M. Bishop, 1950-52; pvt. practice Saginaw, 1950—; sr. staff mem. Saginaw Gen. Hosp., St. Luke's Hosp., Saginaw; past chief of surgery, chmn. tissue com. St. Mary's Hosp., Saginaw; cons. VA Hosp., Saginaw; assoc. clin. prof. surgery Mich. State U., assoc. prof. surgery, 1976-92, prof. emeritus, 1992—; mem. search com. Saginaw Coop. Hosp. Contbr. articles to profl. publs. Lt. USN, 1942-46, PTO. Fellow ACS; mem. AMA, Mich. State Med. Soc., Saginaw Surg. Soc., Soc. Abdominal Surgeons, Am. Coll. Angiology, Soc. Am. Gastrointestinal Endoscopic Surgeons. Home: PO Box 3236 Key Largo FL 33037 Office: PO Box 3236 Key Largo FL 33037-8236

MANNING, KENNETH ALAN, lawyer; b. Buffalo, July 22, 1951; Jack Edwin and Dorothea Ann (Ruhland) M.; m. Diane Louise Garrold, Aug. 11, 1973; children: Michael John, Kathryn Ann. BS in Engring. Sci., SUNY, Buffalo, 1974, JD, 1977. Bar: N.Y. 1978, U.S. Dist. Ct. (we. dist.) N.Y. 1978, U.S. Dist. Ct. (no. dist.) N.Y. 1980, U.S. Ct. Appeals (2d cir.) 1983, U.S. Ct. Appeals (3d cir.) 1988. Confidential law asst. to assoc. justice Appellate Div. 4th Dept., Buffalo, 1977-79; assoc. Phillips, Lytle, Hitchcock, Blaine & Huber, Buffalo, 1979-84, ptnr., 1985—. Vol. Lawyers Project, Erie County, 1985—, Criminal Appeals Program, Erie County, 1988-89; mem. coun. Western N.Y. region NCCJ. Woodburn fellow SUNY, Buffalo, 1973-76. Mem. ABA (TIP sect.), N.Y. State Bar Assn. (ins. negligence sect.), Erie County Bar Assn., Gyro Club (pres. 1988), Park Club. Avocations: sports, hunting. Office: Phillips Lytle Hitchcock Blaine & Huber 3400 Marine Midland Ctr Buffalo NY 14203-2887

MANNING, KENNETH PAUL, food company executive; b. N.Y.C., Jan. 18, 1942; s. John Joseph and Edith Helen (Hoffmann) M.; m. Maureen Lambert, Sept. 12, 1964; children: Kenneth J., John J., Elise, Paul, Carolyn, Jacqueline. BMechEngring., Rensselaer Poly. Inst., 1963; postgrad. in Statistics George Washington U., 1965-66; M.B.A. in Ops. Research, Am. U., 1968. With W.R. Grace & Co., N.Y.C., 1973-87, v.p. European consumer div., 1975-76, pres. edn!. products div., 1976-79, pres. real estate div., 1979-81, v.p. corp. tech. group, 1981-83, pres., chief exec. officer Ambrosia Chocolate Co. div., Milw., 1983-87; with Universal Foods Corp., Milw., 1987—, group v.p., 1987-89, exec. v.p., dir., 1989-92, pres., COO, dir., 1992-96, pres., CEO, dir., 1996—, chmn., CEO, 1997—; bd. dirs. Firstar Trust Co., Milw., Badger Meter, Inc., Milw.; trustees Cardinal Stritch Coll. Bd. dirs. United Performing Art Found. Milw. Served as lt. USN, 1963-67; rear adm., USNR, (ret.). Decorated Legion of Merit, Nat. Def. medal, Armed Forces Res. medal. Mem. Greater Milw. Com., Navy League, US. Naval Inst., Naval Res. Assn. Republican. Roman Catholic. Clubs: Union League (N.Y.C.), Milw. Club. Home: 2914 E Newberry Blvd Milwaukee WI 53211-3429 Office: Universal Foods Corp 433 E Michigan St Milwaukee WI 53202-5104

MANNING, KEVIN JAMES, academic administrator; b. N.Y.C., Nov. 8, 1944; s. James and Helen (Gurry) M.; m. Sara Garrity; children: Elizabeth Ann, Meagan Garrity, Kevin James. BA in Theatre, Webster U., St. Louis, 1967; MS in Pers., Shippensburg (Pa.) U., 1976; PhD in Ednl. Adminstrn., Ohio State U., 1982; attended, Inst. Ednl. Mgmt., Harvard U., 1989. Adminstr., intr. Webster U., St. Louis, 1967-68; mgmt recruiter L.S. Brady, Inc., St. Louis, 1969; adminstr. Washington U., St. Louis, 1969-71; admissions counselor Elizabethtown (Pa.) Coll., 1972-76, dir. admissions, 1976-80, spl. asst. to pres., 1982-83; rsch. asst. Ohio State U., Columbus, 1980-82; chief staff Gov.'s Commn. Higher Edn., Harrisburg, Pa., 1983-84; v.p. devel. Immaculata (Pa.) Coll., 1984—; workforce adv. panel Commonwealth of Pa. Mem. workforce adv. panel Commonwealth of Pa.; bd. dirs. Chester County Export Ctr., Exton, Pa., 1990; mem. attractions com. Phila. Econ. Devel. Coalition, 1988—. Mem. Coun. Advancements and Support Edn., Am. Assn. Higher Edn. (chmn. 1994-95), Sr. Devel. Officers Phila. (chmn. 1995-96), Great Valley C. of C. (bd. dirs.). Avocations: reading, arts, film. Home: 17 Pine Rd Malvern PA 19355-1623 Office: Immaculata Coll Villa Maria Hall Immaculata PA 19345

MANNING, NOEL THOMAS, publishing company executive; b. Ayden, N.C., Oct. 10, 1939; s. James Samuel and Tinie (McGlohon) M.; m. Edith Joyce Reagan, Jan. 1, 1964 (div. Jan. 1973); 1 son, Noel Thomas. BS in Intermediate Edn., East Carolina U.; student, Free Will Bapt. Coll., 1960. Cert. tchr. reading diagnosis, Eng., lang. arts, social studies and art. Staff illustrator Free Will Bapt. Press, Ayden, 1959-61, 1963-68; editor Free Will Bapt. Press Found., 1968-80; tchr. creative writing Pitt Community Coll., Greenville, N.C., 1972-80; instr. piano, 1974-80; tchr. composition and creative writing Greenville Recreational Dept., 1974—; mng. editor The Christian Jew Found., San Antonio, Tex., 1980—. Writer/dir. plays and musicals (with wife), 1968-70; dancer, drama, entertainer civic groups; singer, dancer, dramatic and humorous monologues, 1959-63. Youth dir. Cragmont Assembly Religious Camp, Black Mountain, N.C., 1968-80; musician Reedy Br. Free-Will Bapt. Ch., organist, 1968-80; choir dir. Good Shepherd Presbyn. Ch., San Antonio, 1983—; mem. Kinston Little Theatre Group. East Carolina U. honor scholar, Columbus (Ohio) Sch. Art scholar, 1959; recipient nat. awards for poetry. Democrat. Baptist. Composer church music. Home: 2503 Jackson Keller Rd Apt 619 San Antonio TX 78230-5249 Office: Christian Jewish Found 611 Broadway St San Antonio TX 78215-1823 *How be it so? I have the choice to live or die—and in my hands I hold the tools to make life good—or to make it bad...One abbreviates his life when he dissociates himself from others and their concerns. In order to relate meaningfully, one must share both the sorrows and the joys of his fellowman. Identifying thus has certainly made life for me more beneficial. Accordingly, each day I live, I try to make life more livable for at least one person—be it a needed pat on the back or an extended word of greeting. I am convinced that the manner in which one approaches all situations will determine the outcome. I further believe that a smile communicates all messages best and receives in like measure.*

MANNING, PETER KIRBY, sociology educator; b. Salem, Oreg., Sept. 27, 1940; s. Kenneth Gilbert and Esther Amelia (Gibbard) M.; m. Victoria Francis Shaughnessy, Sept. 1, 1961 (div. 1981); children—Kerry Patricia, Sean Peter, Merry Kathleen; m. Betsy Cullum-Swan, Aug. 4, 1991. B.A., Willamette U., 1961; M.A., Duke U., 1963, Ph.D., 1966; M.A. (hon.), Oxford U., Eng., 1983. Instr. sociology Duke U., 1964-65; asst. prof. sociology U. Mo., 1965-66, Mich. State U., East Lansing, 1966-70; assoc. prof. sociology and psychiatry Mich. State U., 1970-74, prof., 1974—; prof. criminal justice, 1993—; Beto chair lectr. Sam Houston State U., 1990; Ameritech lectr. E. Ky. U., 1993; cons. Nat. Inst. Law Enforcement and Criminal Justice (now Nat. Inst. Justice), U.S. Dept. Justice, Rsch. Triangle Inst., NSF, Nat. Health and Med. Rsch. Coun., Australia, 1980—, Social Sci. Rsch. Coun. Eng., AID (Jamaica), 1991, Sheehy com. Police Pay and Performance, Eng., 1993. Author: Sociology of Mental Health and Illness, 1975, Police Work, 1977, 2d edit., 1997, The Narcs' Game, 1980, Semiotics and Fieldwork, 1987, Symbolic Communication, 1988, Organizational Communication, 1992, other books; also book chpts., articles in profl. jours.; editor Security Annual, 1996—; cons. editor series: Principal Themes in Sociology; co-editor Sage Series in Qualitative Methods; mem. editorial bd. numerous jours. in social scis. Recipient Bruce Smith Sr. award Acad. Criminal Justice Scis., 1993, O.W. Wilson award, 1997, Charles H. Cooley award Mich. Sociol. Assn., 1994; NDEA fellow, 1962-64, NSF fellow, 1965, fellow Balliol Coll., Oxford U., 1982-83, vis. fellow Wolfson Coll., Oxford U., 1981, 82-83, fellow, 1984-86. Mem. Am. Soc. Criminology, Am. Sociol. Assn., Brit. Soc. Criminology, Internat. Sociol. Assn., Midwest Sociol. Soc., Soc. Study of Social Problems, Soc. for the Study of Symbolic Interaction (spl. recognition award 1990, v.p. 1992-93, program chair 1993), Internat. Soc. for Semiotics and Law. Office: Mich State U 516 Baker Hall East Lansing MI 48824-1118

MANNING, RICHARD DALE, writer; b. Flint, Mich., Feb. 7, 1951; s. Harold J. Manning and Juanita Mayo; m. Margaret B. Saretsky, June 5, 1971 (div.); 1 child, Joshua; m. Tracy M. Stone, Sept. 8, 1990. AB in Polit. Sci., U. Mich., 1973. News dir. Sta. WATZ, Alpena, Mich., 1975-79; reporter Alpena News, 1977-79; city editor Post-Register, Idaho Falls, Idaho, 1979-81; editor, columnist Wood River Jour., Hailey, Idaho, 1981-82; city editor, columnist Times-News, Twin Falls, Idaho, 1982-85; reporter, columnist Missoulian, Missoula, Mont., 1985-89; John S. Knight fellow in journalism Stanford (Calif.) U., 1994-95. Author: Last Stand: Timber, Journalism and the Case for Humility, 1991, A Good House, 1993, Grassland, 1995. Recipient Blethen award for investigative reporting Allied Newspapers, 1986-87.

MANNING, ROBERT HENDRICK, media consultant; b. Soerabaja, Java, Indonesia, Aug. 23, 1941; s. William and Gertrude (Unk) M. BS, No. Mich. U., 1974. Instr. sailing USCG Acad., New London, Conn., 1959-63; dir. audio visual svcs. No. Mich. U., Marquette, 1965-93; dir. devel. Bresnan Comm. Co., Marquette, 1993-97; ind. media cons., Marquette, 1969—, comm. cons., 1996—. Pub. TV host PBS Sta. WNMU-TV, 1977—. Mem. Marquette-Alger County Med. Soc. (hon., assoc. exec. dir. 1970—, capt. univ rsch. vessel 1977-79), U.S. Distance Learning Assn., Assn. Ednl. Comm. and Tech. Avocations: astronomy, navigation, med. history, sailing, amateur radio. Home and Office: PO Box 309 Marquette MI 49855-0309

MANNING, ROBERT JOSEPH, editor; b. Binghamton, N.Y., Dec. 25, 1919; s. Joseph James and Agnes Pauline (Brown) M.; m. Margaret Marinda Raymond, Dec. 28, 1944 (dec. 1984); children: Richard Raymond, Brian Gould, Robert Brown; m. Theresa M. Slomkowski, July 11, 1987. Nieman fellow, Harvard, 1945-46; LittD (hon.), Tufts U., 1966; LHD, St. Lawrence U., 1971. Reporter Binghamton (N.Y.) Press, 1936-41, AP, 1942; State Dept. and White House corr. UPI, 1944-46; chief UN corr. United Press, 1946-49; writer Time mag., 1949-55, sr. editor, 1955-58; chief London bur. Time, Life, Fortune, Sports Illus. mags., 1958-61; Sunday editor N.Y. Herald Tribune, 1961-62; asst. sec. state for pub. affairs Washington, 1962-64; exec. editor Atlantic Monthly, 1964-66, editor-in-chief, 1966-80; v.p. Atlantic Monthly Co., 1966-80; editor-in-chief Boston Pub. Co., 1981-87; pres., editor-in-chief Bobcat Books Inc., Boston, 1987—. Served with AUS, 1942-43. Fellow Kennedy Inst. Politics, Harvard U., 1980. Mem. AAAS, Century Assn. (N.Y.C.), Tavern Club, St. Botolph Club. Home and Office: 191 Commonwealth Ave Boston MA 02116-2210

MANNING, ROBERT THOMAS, physician, educator; b. Wichita, Kans., Oct. 16, 1927; s. Thomas Earl and Mary Francis (Schlegel) M.; m. Jane Bell, July 29, 1949; children: Mary Kay Travers, Phillip Trenton, Susan Ann Shiba. A.B., Wichita U., 1950; M.D., Kans. U., 1954; DHL, Med. Coll. Hampton Rds., 1991. Diplomate Am. Bd. Internal Medicine. Intern Kansas City (Mo.) Gen. Hosp., 1954-55; resident Kans. U., Kansas City, 1955-58; from assoc. prof. to prof. Kans. U. Med. Ctr. Sch. of Medicine, Kansas City, 1958-71; assoc. dean students Kans. U. Med. Ctr. Sch. of Medicine, 1969-71; dean Eastern Va. Med. Sch., Norfolk, Va., 1971-74; chmn., prof. internal medicine Eastern Va. Med. Sch., 1974-77; prof. internal medicine U. Kans. Sch. of Medicine, Wichita, 1977-93; prof. emeritus U. Kans. Sch. Medicine, Wichita, 1993—; assoc. dean, clin. affairs U. Kans. Sch. of Medicine, Wichita, 1985-89; chmn. internal medicine U. Kans. Sch. Medicine, Wichita, 1991-93; pres. Wesley Med. Rsch. Inst., 1986-88; nat. cons. surgeon gen. USAF, 1973-78. Author: Major's Physical Diagnosis, 9th edit., 1982; contbr. articles to profl. jours. Served with USAF, 1945-47. Recipient Advanced Achievement award Am. Bd. Internal Medicine, 1987. Fellow ACP (laureate Kans. chpt., bd. govs. Kans. 1984-88); mem. Am. Fedn. Clin. Rsch., Cen. Soc. Clin. Rsch., Am. Assn. Study Liver Disease, Sigma Xi, Alpha Omega Alpha. Presbyterian. Avocations: hunting, fishing. Home: 156 N Maize Rd # 31 Wichita KS 67212-4649 Office: U Kans Sch Medicine 1010 N Kansas St Wichita KS 67214-3124

MANNING, SYLVIA, English studies educator; b. Montreal, Que., Can., Dec. 2, 1943; came to U.S., 1967; d. Bruno and Lea Bank; m. Peter J. Manning, Aug. 20, 1967; children—Bruce David, Jason Maurice. B.A., McGill U., 1963; M.A., Yale U., 1964, Ph.D. in English, 1967. Asst. prof. English Calif. State U.-Hayward, 1967-71, assoc. prof., 1971-75, assoc. dean, 1972-75; assoc. prof. U. So. Calif., 1975-94, prof., assoc. dir. Ctr. for Humanities, 1975-77, assoc. dir. Ctr. for Humanities, 1975-77, chmn. freshman writing, 1977-80, chmn. dept. English, 1980-83, vice provost, exec. v.p., 1984-94; prof. English U. Ill., 1994—, v.p. for acad. affairs, prof. English, 1994—. Author: Dickens as Satirist, 1971; Hard Times: An Annotated Bibliography, 1984. Contbr. essays to mags. Woodrow Wilson fellow, 1963-64, 66-67. Mem. MLA, Dickens Soc. Office: U of Ill 377 Henry Adm Bldg 506 S Wright St Urbana IL 61801-3620

MANNING, THOMAS EDWIN, II, aeronautical engineer; b. Randolph, Vt., Feb. 2, 1969; s. Thomas Edwin Manning and Jane Kate (Sadd) Fletcher. BS, Pa. State U., 1991, MS, 1993. Commd. USAF, 1991, advanced through grades to capt., 1996; aircraft test project mgr. USAF, Arnold AFB; chief joint STARS aircraft engring. USAF, Hanscom AFB, Mass., 1996—. With USAF, 1993-96. Mem. AIAA, Pa. State U. Alumni Assn., U.S. Hang Gliding Assn. (pilot), Company Grade Officers Assn. Avocations: physical fitness, hang gliding, computers. Home: 45 Georgetown Dr Apt 12 Framingham MA 01702-7531 Office: ESC/JS1P 75 Vandenberg Dr Hanscom AFB MA 01731-2103

MANNING, WALTER SCOTT, accountant, former educator, consultant; b. nr. Yoakum, Tex., Oct. 4, 1912; BBA, Tex. Coll. Arts and Industries, 1932; MBA, U. Tex., 1940; m. Eleanor Mary Jones, Aug. 27, 1937; children: Sharon Frances, Walter Scott, Robert Kenneth. Asst. to bus. mgr. Tex. Coll. Arts and Industries, Kingsville, 1932; tchr. Sinton (Tex.) High Sch., 1933-37, Robstown (Tex.) High Sch., 1937-41; prof. Tex. A&M U., College Station, 1941-77; cons. C.P.A., Tex. Walter Manning Outstanding Jr. and Outstanding Sr. awards at Coll. Bus. Adminstrn., Tex. A&M U. named in his honor. Mem. AICPA, AAUP, Am. Acctg. Assn., Tex. Soc. CPAs, College Station C. of C. (past pres.), Tex. Assn. Univ. Instrs. Acctg. (pres. 1963-64), SAR (independence chpt. past pres.), Knights York Cross of Honor, Alpha Chi, Beta Gamma Sigma, Beta Alpha Psi. Democrat. Presbyterian (elder). Clubs: Masons, (32 degree), Shriners, K.T., Kiwanis (past pres., past lt. gov. div. IX Tex. Okla. dist., Kiwanis Internat. Legion of Honor). Home: 405 Walton Dr College Station TX 77840-2224

MANNING, WILLIAM DUDLEY, JR., retired specialty chemical company executive; b. Tampa, Fla., Mar. 7, 1934; s. William Dudley and Rebecca (Reid) M.; m. Carol Randolph Gillis, June 30, 1962; children: Carol Randolph, Rebecca Barrett, Anne Gillis. BA in Chemistry, Fla. State U., 1957. Sales rep. Amoco Chem. Co., St. Louis and Cleve., 1959-63; sales engr. The Lubrizol Corp., Tulsa, 1963-64, southwestern regional sales mgr., 1964-66; mgr. chem. product sales The Lubrizol Corp., Wickliffe, Ohio, 1966-72, sales mgr., western U.S., 1972, gen. sales mgr., asst. div. head-sales, 1972-79, mktg. mgr., asst. div. head-sales, 1979-80, v.p. mktg., 1980-81, v.p., bus. devel. div., 1981-85, sr. v.p. sales and mktg., 1985-87; pres. Lubrizol Petroleum Chems. Co., Wickliffe, 1987-94; sr. v.p., asst. to pres. The Lubrizol Corp., 1994; cons., investor, 1994—; bd. dirs. Fletcher Paper Co., Alpena, Mich., Robbins and Myers, Dayton, Ohio, UNIFRAX Corp., Niagara Falls, N.Y., Park Ave. Marble Co., Brooksville, Fla. Chmn. bd. trustees Vocat. Guidance Svcs., Cleve., 1991—. With USAR, 1957-63. Mem. Soc. Automotive Engrs. (assoc.), Am. Petroleum Inst., Nat. Petroleum Refiners Assn., Soc. of Chem. Industry, Kirtland Country Club (v.p. 1986-88, pres. 1988-89), Tavern Club (trustee 1986-91), Chagrin Valley Hunt Club. Republican. Roman Catholic. Office: 2550 SOM Center Rd Ste 105 Willoughby OH 44094

MANNING, WILLIAM FREDERICK, wire service photographer; b. Gardner, Mass., Aug. 18, 1920; s. Seth Newton and Jennie May (Bennett) M.; m. Yvonne J.C. Winslow, Feb. 29, 1964; children: Pamela Ann, Jeffrey Newton. A.A., Boston U., 1950, B.S. in Communications, 1952. With AP, Boston, 1951-53; photographer UPI, Boston, 1953-88, ret. Contbr. photos to books, mags., newspapers throughout the world. Served with USN, 1940-46, PTO. Recipient Look 1st Prize All Sports award, 1958; Pictures of the Yr. award U. Mo., 1964, 74; Nat. Headliners Club award for outstanding syndicate photography, 1974. Mem. Boston Press Photographers Assn., Delta Kappa Alpha. Congregationalist. Club: Nat. Headliners. Home: 23 Sunset Dr Beverly MA 01915-2319 Office: One Herald Sq 300 Harrison Ave Boston MA 02118-2237

MANNING, WILLIAM HENRY, lawyer; b. Dallas, Feb. 5, 1951. BA, Creighton U., 1973; JD, Hamline U., 1978. Bar: Minn. 1978, U.S. Dist. Ct. Minn. 1978, U.S. Ct. Appeals (8th cir.) 1979; cert. civil trial specialist. Spl. asst. atty. gen. Minn. Atty. Gen.'s Office, St. Paul, 1980-83, dir. tort litigation div., 1984-86; ptnr. Robins, Kaplan, Miller & Ciresi, Mpls., 1986—. Office: Robins Kaplan Miller & Ciresi 800 Lasalle Ave Minneapolis MN 55402-2006

MANNING, WILLIAM JOSEPH, lawyer; b. N.Y.C., Aug. 11, 1926; s. Joseph Michael and Eileen Johanna (Walsh) M.; m. Maryanne Cullen, June 23, 1956; children—William Joseph, Michael P., Maura G., Marian T., John A., Mary E. B.B.A. magna cum laude, St. John's U., N.Y.C., 1949, LL.B. magna cum laude, 1952. Bar: N.Y. 1952. Assoc. firm Simpson Thacher & Bartlett, N.Y.C., 1952-62; ptnr. Simpson Thacher & Bartlett, 1962—, sr. ptnr., 1968-88, of counsel, 1989—; dir. Brascan Ltd., Toronto, Ont., Can., 1970-79; bd. dirs. N.Y. Lawyers for Public Interest, 1977-88. Notes editor: St. John's Law Rev, 1951-52. Trustee Inst. for Muscle Disease, N.Y.C., 1963-70; bd. dirs. Mercy Hosp., Rockville Centre, N.Y., 1975-87. Served with inf. U.S. Army, 1944-46. Fellow Am. Coll. Trial Lawyers, Am. Law Inst., Am. Bar Found.; mem. ABA (chmn. sect. litigation 1977-78, founding mem. coun. 1973), Assn. Bar City N.Y., N.Y. State Bar Assn., N.Y. County Lawyers Assn., Am. Judicature Soc., Downtown Assn., Garden City Golf Club, Westhampton Country Club (pres. 1989—), Cherry Valley Club. Roman Catholic. Home: 64 1st St Garden City NY 11530-4321 also: 156 Dune Rd Westhampton Beach NY 11978-3003 also: 15865 Westerly Ter Jupiter FL 33477-1337 Office: Simpson Thacher & Bartlett 425 Lexington Ave New York NY 10017-3903

MANNING, WINTON HOWARD, psychologist, educational administrator; b. St. Louis, Feb. 9, 1930; s. Winton Harry and Jane (Swanson) M.; m. Nancy Mercedes Groves, Aug. 1, 1959; children: Cecelia Groves Tazelaar, Winton H. III. AB with honors, William Jewell Coll., 1947; PhD in Psychology, Washington U., St. Louis, 1959. Instr. psychology William Jewell Coll., Liberty, Mo., 1954-55, asst. prof., acting head dept. psychology, 1955-56; rsch. psychologist Washington U., St. Louis, 1956-58, rsch. assoc., 1958-59; vis. lectr. Washington U., summer, 1961, 62; asst. prof. psychology Tex. Christian U., Fort Worth, 1959-61, assoc. prof., 1961-64, prof., 1964-65, assoc. dir. univ. honors program, 1962-65; assoc. dir. rsch. Coll. Entrance Examination Bd., N.Y.C., 1965-66, dir. program devel., 1966-68, exec. dir. rsch.and devel., 1968-69; dir. devel. rsch. div. Ednl. Testing Svc., Princeton, N.J., 1969-70, v.p., 1970-77, sr. v.p. devel. and rsch., 1977-83, sr. scholar, 1983-93; pres. Ednl. Devel. Svc., Princeton, 1993—; vis. fellow Princeton U., 1982-83; cons. Gallup Internat. Inst., 1990—, Applied Ednl. Rsch., 1993-95;

cons. Grad. Mgmt. Admissions Coun., 1992-95, Carnegie Found. for the Advancement of Tchg. 1993-95. Author: The Pursuit of Fairness in Admissions to Higher Education, 1977; Student Manual for Essentials of Psychology, 1960. Contbr. articles on ednl. measurement and psychology of learning to profl. publs. Patentee in field U.S. and Europe. Trustee Assn. for Advancement of Handicapped People, 1975-78, Nat. Chicano Coun. on Higher Edn., 1977-85, N.J. Arts Festival, 1980-85; vice-chair Found. for Books to China, 1980—; chair bd. trustees Princeton Day Sch., 1981-93; trustee Princeton Area Found., 1991-94, Our House Found., 1991-92; bd. mem. The Princeton Singers, 1992—, Christian Renewal Effort in Emerging Democracies, 1992-94, George H. Gallup Internat. Inst., 1992—; chair, trustee Trinity-All Saints' Cemetery, 1993—; chair Affordable Housing Bd. of Princeton Borough, 1987-89; chair and commr. Princeton Pub. Housing Authority, 1995—; sr. warden All Saints Episc. Ch., 1987-89; chair ins. com. Diocese N.J., 1993-95; mem. Diocese Coun., Diocese of N.J., 1996—; adv. coun. U. Okla. Ctr. for Rsch. on Minority Edn., 1987-92, Ind. Sch. Chmn. Assn., 1987-92; trustee Friends of Princeton Open Space, 1995—; trustee Russian Ministry Network, 1995—; cons. Carnegie Found. for Advancement of Teaching, 1987-95; cons. The Coll. Bd., 1988-91; spl. cons. Commn. on Admission to Grad. Mgmt. Edn., 1987-89. Recipient Alumni Achievement citation William Jewell Coll., 1970; named Gallup Scholar in Edn., 1995. Fellow Am. Psychol. Soc. (charter), Eastern Psychol. Assn., Psychometric Soc., Am. Ednl. Rsch. Assn., Nat. Coun. on Measurement in Edn. (mem. com. on legal issues in measurement 1977-79), N.Y. Acad. Scis., Nassau Club, Pendragon Club, Oratory of Good Shepherd, Phi Beta Kappa, Sigma Xi, Order of St. John of Jerusalem. Home: 12 Morven Pl Princeton NJ 08540-3024 Office: Ednl Devel Svc PO Box 441 Princeton NJ 08542-0441

MANNING-WEBER, CLAUDIA JOY, medical radiography administrator, consultant; b. Oak Park, Ill., Mar. 17, 1950; d. Charles Lawrence and Carrie Joy (Lund) Manning. AAS, Coll. of DuPage, 1980; BA with honors, Nat. Coll. of Edn., 1986, MS, 1989. Registered med. radiography technologist, Am. Registry of Radiologic Technologists; cert. med. radiography technologist, Ariz.; cert. adult and continuing edn. tchr., Ariz. State Cmty. Coll. Bd. Faculty Coll. of DuPage, Glen Ellyn, Ill., 1987-90, South Suburban Coll., South Holland, Ill., 1989-91; mentor tchr. Prescott (Ariz.) Coll., 1992—; dir. Ariz. Continuing Edn. Svcs., Avondale, 1992—; clin. instr. Phoenix Bapt. Hosp., 1992-93; program dir. PTR Bryman Sch., 1993-95; program dir. med. radiography Apollo Coll., 1995—; contbr., cons. EDUMED Co., Lakeville, Minn., 1995—; treas. ASSRT, Mesa, Ariz., 1993-94; cons. Coll. of DuPage, 1988-91. Author: Distance Delivered Education in Nuclear Medicine Technology, 1989. Mem. ASCD, AAUW, Internat. Soc. Radiographers and Radiologic Technicians, Assn. for Educators in Radiologic Sci., Am. Soc. Radiologic Technologists, Ariz. State Soc. Radiologic Technologists (ednl. dir. 1992-93, treas. 1993-94, seminar presenter 1991, 92), Delta Kappa Gamma. Avocations: reading, writing, hiking, horseback riding. Home: 10938 W Bermuda Dr Avondale AZ 85323 Office: Apollo Coll 2701 W Bethany Home Rd Phoenix AZ 85017-1705

MANNINO, EDWARD FRANCIS, lawyer; b. Abington, Pa., Dec. 5, 1941; s. Sante Francis and Martha Anne (Hines) M.; m. Mary Ann Vigilante, July 17, 1965 (div. 1990); m. Antoinette K. O'Connell, June 25, 1993; children: Robert John, Jennifer Elaine. B.A. with distinction, U. Pa., 1963, LL.B. magna cum laude, 1966. Bar: Pa. 1967. Law clk. 3d cir. U.S. Ct. Appeals, 1966-67; assoc. firm Dilworth, Paxson, Kalish & Kauffman, Phila., 1967-71; ptnr. Dilworth, Paxson, Kalish & Kauffman, 1972-86, co-chmn. litigation dept., 1980-86, sr. ptnr., 1982-86; sr. prin. Elliott, Mannino & Flaherty, P.C., Phila., 1986-90; chmn. Mannino Griffith P.C., Phila., 1990-95; sr. ptnr. Wolf, Block, Schorr & Solis-Cohen, Phila., 1995—; hearing examiner disciplinary bd. Supreme Ct. Pa., 1986-89; lectr. Temple U. Law Sch., 1968-69, 71-72; mem. Phila. Mayor's Sci. and Tech. Adv. Com., 1976-79; mem. adv. com. on appellate ct. rules Supreme Ct. Pa., 1989-95; project mgr. Pa. Environ. Master Plan, 1973; chmn. Pa. Land Use Policy Study Adv. Com., 1973-75; chmn. adv. com., hon. mem. faculty history dept. U. Pa., 1980-85. Author: Lender Liability and Banking Litigation, 1989, Business and Commercial Litigation: A Trial Lawyer's Handbook, 1995, The Civil RICO Primer, 1996; mem. editl. bd. Litigation mag., 1985-87, Lender Liability News, 1988—, Bank Bailout Litigation News, 1989-93, Bus. Torts Reporter, 1988—, Practical Litigator, 1989—, Civil RICO Report, 1991—; contbr. articles to profl. jours. Pres. parish coun. Our Mother of Consolation Ch., 1977-79; bd. overseers U. Pa. Sch. Arts and Scis., 1985-89, chmn. recruitment and retention of faculty com.; commonwealth trustee Temple U., 1987-90, mem. audit, bus. and fin. coms. Named one of Nation's Top Litigators Nat. Law Jour., 1990. Fellow Am. Bar Found., ABA (chmn. various coms.), Am. Law Inst., Hist. Soc. U.S. Dist. Ct. Ea. Dist. Pa. (bd. dirs.), Pa. Bar Assn., Phila. Bar Assn. (gov. 1975), Pyramid Club, Sharswood Law Club, Order of Coif, Phi Beta Kappa, Phi Beta Kappa Assocs. Democrat. Office: Wolf Block Schorr et al 12th Fl Packard Bldg 15th & Chestnut Sts Philadelphia PA 19102

MANNION, KEVIN, publishing executive. Pub. Computer Reseller News CMP Media, Inc., Jericho, N.Y. Office: CMP Media Inc 1 Jericho Plaza Jericho NY 11753*

MANNIX, CHARLES RAYMOND, law educator; b. Elizabeth, N.J., Aug. 2, 1950; s. Charles Raymond and Helen Joan (French) M. BA, Duquesne U., 1972, MA, 1976, JD, 1976. Bar: Iowa 1976, N.Y. 1996, U.S. Ct. Claims 1976, U.S. Tax Ct. 1976, U.S. Ct. Mil. Appeals 1976, U.S. Ct. Internat. Trade 1976, U.S. Ct. Appeals (4th and 5th cirs.) 1977, U.S. Ct. Appeals (D.C. cir.) 1977, U.S. Dist. Ct. Va. 1980, U.S. Supreme Ct. 1980, Va. 1980, D.C. 1980, U.S. Ct. Appeals (D.C. cir.) 1980, U.S. Ct. Appeals (fed. cir.) 1982, N.Y. 1996. Commd. 2d lt. U.S. Air Force, 1973, advanced through grades to lt. col., 1982; intern UN Office of Legal Affairs, N.Y.C., 1975; various legal assignments; lectr. USAF Med. Law Cons. Program, 1981-83; adj. faculty Georgetown U., Washington, 1984—; assoc. prof. and chmn. dept. med. jurisprudence, asst. prof. mil. medicine, gen. counsel Uniformed Svcs. U. Health Scis. Decorated Meritorious Service medal with Oak Leaf Cluster, Air Force Commendation medal with Oak Leaf clusters. Mem. ABA, FBA, ATLA, D.C. Bar Assn., Va. State Bar Assn., Am. Soc. Internat. Law, Inter-Am. Bar Assn., Internat. Bar Assn., Am. Soc. Law and Medicine, Am. Arbitration Assn. (arbitrator), Am. Acad. Hosp. Attys., Nat. Assn. Coll. l. and U. Attys., N.Y. State Bar Assn., Bar City N.Y. Home: 10205 Walker Lake Dr Great Falls VA 22066-3501 Office: Unif Svcs U Health Scis Gen Coun Jones Bridge Rd Bethesda MD 20815-5737

MANNIX, KEVIN LEESE, lawyer; b. Queens, N.Y., Nov. 26, 1949; s. John Warren Sr. and Editta Gorrell M.; m. Susanna Bernadette Chiocca, June 1, 1974; children: Nicholas Chiocca, Gabriel Leese, Emily Kemper. BA, U. Va., 1971, JD, 1974. Bar: Oreg. 1974, U.S. Ct. Appeals (9th cir.) 1976, U.S. Supreme Ct. 1978, Guam 1979. Law clk. to judge Oreg. Ct. Appeals, Salem, 1974-75; asst. atty. gen. Oreg. Dept. Justice, Salem, 1975-77, Govt. of Guam, Agana, 1977-79; judge adminstrv. law Oreg. Workers' Compensation Bd., Salem, 1980-83; assoc. Lindsay, Hart, Neil & Weigler, Portland, Oreg., 1983-86; pres. Mannix, Nielsen & Crawford Profl. Corp., Salem, 1986—. Chmn. St. Joseph Sch. Bd., Salem, 1981-86; pres. Salem Cath. Schs. Corp., 1985; v.p. Salem Cath. Schs. Found., 1985-88, pres., 1988-90, 91-94, state rep., 1989-97; pres. bd. dirs. Blanchet Sch. Mem. Marion Bar Assn., Rotary (bd. dirs. East Salem 1985-89, pres. 1987-88), KC. Republican. Avocations: photography, scuba diving, travel. Home: 375 18th St NE Salem OR 97301-4307 Office: 2003 State St Salem OR 97301-4349

MANNO, VINCENT PAUL, engineering educator; b. N.Y.C., Dec. 4, 1954; s. Paul Thomas and Jennie (Toia) M.; m. Mariann Margaret Montine, Feb. 16, 1980; children: Elizabeth Ellen, Michael Vincent, Christopher Lawrence. BS, Columbia U., 1976; MS, MIT, 1978, ScD, 1983. Engr. Am. Electric Power Co., N.Y.C., 1978-81; engr. Stone & Webster Corp., Boston, 1981-82; postdoctoral assoc. MIT, Cambridge, 1983-84; assoc. prof. Tufts U., Medford, Mass., 1984—; chmn. mech. engring. dept., 1993—; cons. high tech. and power industry, 1983—. Contbr. articles to engring. sci. and energy jours.; reviewer for tech. jours. and pub. cos.; guest editor tech. jours. Recipient Student award Am. Nuclear Soc., Ralph R. Teetor award, 1986; U.S. Dept. Energy fellow, 1983, sr. faculty fellow USN, 1988. Mem. AAAS, Am. Soc. Engring. Edn., AAUP, ASME (tech. conf. session chmn.), IEEE (chair conf. and program com.), Sigma Xi. Roman Catholic. Avocation: coaching youth sports. Office: Tufts U Dept Mech Engring Medford MA 02155

MANNY, CARTER HUGH, JR., architect, foundation administrator; b. Michigan City, Ind., Nov. 16, 1918; s. Carter Hugh and Ada Gage (Barnes) M.; m. Mary Alice Kellett, Dec. 6, 1942 (dec. Jan. 1994); children: Elizabeth, Carter Hugh III; m. Maya Moran, Dec. 27, 1995. A.B. magna cum laude, Harvard U., 1941, Indsl. Adminstr., 1942; Taliesin fellow, Scottsdale, Ariz., 1946; B.S. in Architecture, Ill. Inst. Tech., 1948. With Murphy/Jahn (name formerly Naess & Murphy and C.F. Murphy Assocs.), Chgo., 1948-83; partner Murphy/Jahn (name formerly Naess & Murphy and C.F. Murphy Assocs.), 1957-61; dir. 1st Citizens Bank, Michigan City, Ind., 1970-86; sr. v.p. Murphy/Jahn (name formerly Naess & Murphy and C.F. Murphy Assocs.), 1978-83; mem. adv. com. on architecture Art Inst. of Chgo., 1982—, oversight com. Ill. Inst. Tech. Sch. of Architecture, Chgo., 1989-94; trustee Graham Found. Advanced Studies in Fine Arts 1956-74, exec. dir., 1972-93, hon. trustee, 1994—. Projects include O'Hare Internat. Airport, Chgo., FBI Hdqrs, Washington, First Nat. Bank Chgo, Chgo. Civic Center, Chgo. Bd. Trade. Fellow AIA (pres. Chgo. chpt. 1973, dir. Ill. council 1972-73), Soc. Archtl. Historians (dir. 1982-85), Chgo. Bldg. Congress (dir. 1978-83); mem. Phi Beta Kappa, Pottawattomie Country Club, Mich. City Yacht Club, Tavern Club, Arts Club, Cliff Dwellers Club (Chgo., hon.). Home: 200 Lake Ave Michigan City IN 46360 also: 1448 N Lake Shore Dr Chicago IL 60610-1625 Office: Graham Found 4 W Burton Pl Chicago IL 60610-1416

MANOFF, DINAH BETH, actress; b. N.Y.C., Jan. 25, 1958; d. Arnold and Lyova (Rosenthal) (Lee Grant) M. Student public schs., N.Y. and Calif. Appeared in: TV series Soap, 1977-78, Empty Nest, 1989-95; TV movie appearances include Raid on Entebbe, 1977, High Terror, 1977, The Possessed, 1977, For Ladies Only, 1981, A Matter of Sex, 1984, The Seduction of Gina, 1984, Celebrity, 1984, Flight #90, 1984, Classified Love, 1986, The Cover Girl and The Cop, 1989, Babies, 1990, (also co-exec. prodr.) Maid for Each Other, 1992; stage performances include I Ought To Be In Pictures, 1980 (Tony award, Theatre World award), Leader of the Pack, 1985, Alfred and Victoria: A Life, Los Angeles Theatre Ctr., 1986-87; films include Grease, 1977, Ordinary People, 1979, I Ought To Be in Pictures, 1981, Gifted Children, 1983, Child's Play, 1988, Staying Together, 1989, Bloodhounds of Broadway, 1989, Welcome Home Roxy Carmichael, 1990. Mem. Screen Actors Guild, Actors Equity, AFTRA. Jewish. Office: The Gersh Agy 232 N Canon Dr Beverly Hills CA 90210-5302 *So far, so good.**

MANOFF, RICHARD KALMAN, advertising executive, public health consultant, author; b. Bklyn., June 24, 1916; s. Kalman and Sarah (Glatman) M.; m. Lucy B. Deutscher, Nov. 27, 1942; children: Robert K., Gregory P. B.S., CCNY, 1937, M.S., 1940. Asst. regional dir. War Manpower Commn., 1942-45; marketing dir. Welch Grape Juice Co., 1949-53; v.p. Kenyon & Eckhardt Advt., N.Y.C., 1953-56; pres., chmn. bd. Richard K. Manoff Inc. Advt., N.Y.C., from 1956; now pres. Manoff Internat. Inc.; spl. adv. mktg. and communications to exec. dir. UNICEF, 1980—; dir. Thomas J. Lipton, Inc.; adj. prof. dept. health scis. Sargent Coll. Allied Health Professions, Boston U., 1978—; lectr. pub. health Columbia U. Sch. Medicine, 1982-83; Mem. U.S. del. FAO World Conf., Rome, Italy, 1966; spl. advisor UNICEF and WHO, 1968-78; cons. spl. mission to Food and Agr. Ministry, Govt. India, AID, 1969; Ford Found. offices Pub. Edn. Pub. Broadcasting for children's TV; participant 1st World Conf. on Social Communication for Devel. Mass Communications, Mexico, 1970, 7th Asian Advt. Congress, Delhi, 1970, 3d Western Hemisphere Nutrition Congress, Fla., 1971, Internat. Conf. Nutrition, Nat. Devel. and Planning, Mass. Inst. Tech., 1971, Symposium Eating Patterns and Their Influence on Purchasing Behavior and Nutrition, Nev., 1971, Nutrition Workshop, AID, 1971, 9th Annual Summer Workshop Family Planning, 1971, 4th & 5th Seminar Workshop on Mgmt. and Planning of Population Family Planning Programs, 1971, New Products Symposium, 1971, Communication Seminar series Cornell U., 1971, Exploration The Frontiers of Nutritional Edn. Seminar, 1972, 9th Internat. Congress of Nutrition, Mexico, 1972, East-West Center Comml. Resources Conf. on Family Planning, Hawaii, 1972; Protein adv. group UN Systems Annual Mtg., 1973; mem. panel White House Conf. Food, Nutrition and Health, 1969; mem. Sec.'s Adv. Com. on Population Affairs, Dept. HEW, 1971-76; mem. adv. com. Population Reference Bur., Washington, 1977—, Population Inst., 1980—; mem. Nelson A. Rockefeller's Commn. on Critical Choices for Ams.; cons. HRSA Healthy Start Campaign to reduce infant mortality, 1991; bd. dirs. Population Comm. Internat.; Martin J. Forman Meml. lectr., Washington, 1993. Author: Social Marketing: New Imperative for Public Health, 1985. Bd. dirs. Planned Parenthood World Population, Pathfinder Fund, Boston, 1977-80, United Nutrition Edn. Found., Alexandria, Va., 1978—; mem. com. on internat. nutrition programs NAS-NRC, 1973; founder, mem. Com. for Shakespeare Festival, N.Y.C.; bd. visitors Grad. Sch. and Univ. Ctr., CUNY; mem. adv. bd., cons. to the pres. Henry J. Kaiser Family Found., 1987-91; dir. City Coll. Fund, 1990—. Recipient 5th Ann. Global award for media excellence Population Inst., China, 1985, Townsend Harris medal Alumni Assn. CCNY, 1986. Mem. Am. Assn. Advt. Agys. (gov. 1967—, sec.-treas. 1975—), Population Comms. Internat. (dir. 1992—), Friars Club, Harmonie Club (N.Y.C.), Century Assn. Home: 14 Donahue Rd Litchfield CT 06759 also: 322 E 57th St New York NY 10022-2949

MANOLAKAS, STANTON PETER, watercolor artist; b. Detroit, July 25, 1946; s. Constantine Stamatios and Angela (Kaloyeropolous) M.; m. Barbara Soldathos, July 25, 1971. Student, Eastman Sch. of Music, 1964-65; BA in Psychology, U. So. Calif., L.A., 1969; postgrad., Calif. State U., Long Beach, 1969-70. Represented by Art Angle's Gallery, Orange, Calif., 1985-94, Gallery Tatewari, Sedona, Ariz., 1995—, Wild Wings, Lake City, Minn., 1995—. Exhibited in group show at Zantman Galleries, Carmel, Calif., 1989, Dossin Great Lakes Mus., 1994; demonstration artist City Art exhibit Millard Sheets Gallery, L.A. County Fair, Pomona, Calif., 1994, L.A. Heritage Sq. Mus., 1994; represented in permanent collections Bechtel Industries, San Francisco, Marriott Hotel Corp., Newton, Mass., Gallagher & Heffernan Inc., San Francisco, The Borovay Group, L.A., Datum Inc., Anaheim, Calif., Tarbell Realty Inc., Costa Mesa, Calif. Active AFL-CIO County Fedn. of Labor, L.A., 1982-92; mem. Saint Sophia Cathedral Choir, L.A., 1970-82, Burbank Symphony Orch., 1973-76, Glendale (Calif.) Symphony Orch., 1975-77. Mem. Am. Fedn. of Musicians (local 47). Republican. Eastern Orthodox. Avocations: distance running, music, photographic collector of historic photos. Home: 2500 Las Flores Dr Los Angeles CA 90041-1021

MANOLIU, MARIA, linguist; b. Galatz, Romania, Mar. 12, 1934; came to U.S., 1978, naturalized, 1987; d. Ion T. and Ana S. (Codescu) Manoliu. BA, French Coll., Galatz, 1951; MA, U. Bucharest, Romania, 1955, PhD, 1966. Asst. prof. Romance linguistics U. Bucharest, 1957-61, assoc. prof., 1961-68, prof., 1968-77; prof. linguistics U. Calif., Davis, 1978—; vis. prof. U. Chgo., 1972-74, H. Heine Universitat, Dusseldorf, 1994; cons. NEH, 1980—; mem. adv. bd. Revue Romane, Copenhagen, 1972—, Romance Philology, Berkeley, Calif., 1984—, Philologica Canariensia, Spain, 1992—. Author: Sistematica Substitutelor, 1968 (Ministry of Edn. award 1968), Gramatica Comparata a limbilor romanice, 1971, El Estructuralismo Lingüístico, 1979, Tipologia e Historia, 1985, Gramatica, Pragmasemantica si Discurs, 1993, Discourse and Pragmatic Constraints on Grammatical Choices. A Grammar of Surprises, 1994; editor-in-chief Bull. de la S.R.L.R., Bucharest, 1975-78; contbr. articles to profl. jours. Recipient Evenimentul award for Outstanding Contbn. to Romanian Culture, 1991; grantee Internat. Com. Linguists, 1972, Fulbright Found., 1972-74, 91, 92, IREX, 1993, U. Calif., 1970—. Mem. MLA, Am. Romanian Acad. (pres. 1982-95, hon. pres. 1995—), Academia Română (hon.), Soc. de Linguistique Romane, Soc. Roumaine de Linguistique Romane (v.p. 1974—), Internat. Assn. Hist. Linguistics, Linguistics Soc. Am., Internat. Assn. Pragmatics, Romanian Studies Assn. Am. (pres. 1986-88). Avocations: tourism, classical music, cinema. Office: U Calif Dept French and Italian 509 Sproul Hall Davis CA 95616

MANOOGIAN, RICHARD ALEXANDER, manufacturing company executive; b. Long Branch, N.J., July 30, 1936; s. Alex and Marie (Tatian) M.; children: James, Richard, Bridget. B.A. in Econs, Yale U., 1958. Asst. to pres. Masco Corp., Taylor, Mich., 1958-62, exec. v.p., 1962-68, pres., 1968-85, chmn. bd., CEO, 1985—; chmn., dir. Mascotech, Inc., Trimas Corp.; dir. First Chgo. NBD Corp., Detroit Renaissance, Am. Bus. Conf. Trustee U. Liggett Sch., State Dept. Fine Arts Commn., Founder's Soc., Detroit Inst. Arts, Center for Creative Studies; trustee coun. Nat. Gallery Art. Mem. Yale Alumni Assn. Clubs: Grosse Pointe Yacht, Grosse Pointe Hunt, Country Club Detroit, Detroit Athletic. Office: Masco Corp 21001 Van Born Rd Taylor MI 48180-1340

MANOS, JOHN, editor-in-chief. Editor-in-chief Consumer's Digest, Chgo. Office: Consumer Digest 8001 N Lincoln Ave Skokie IL 60077-3657

MANOSEVITZ, MARTIN, psychologist; b. Mpls., June 22, 1938; s. Julius and Ethel (Cohen) M.; m. Carolyn Heather Margulius, Sept. 17, 1959; children—Bradley, Jason. B.A., U. Minn., Mpls., 1960, Ph.D., 1964. Diplomate in clin. psychology Am. Bd. Profl. Psychology. Asst. prof. psychology Rutgers U., 1964-67; asst. prof. psychology U. Tex., Austin, 1967-69; assoc. prof. U. Tex., 1969-75, prof., 1975-87; pvt. practice clin. psychology Austin, 1975—; adj. prof. psychology U. Tex., 1987-93; dir. psychol. svcs. CPC Capital Hosp., Austin, 1987-93, Shoal Creek Hosp., Austin, 1994-95. Trustee Austin-Travis County Mental Health-Mental Retardation Center, 1978-80. Fellow APA, Am. Orthopsychiat. Assn.; mem. Soc. Rsch. and Child Devel., Tex. Psychol. ASsn., Capital Area Psychol. Assn., Austin Soc. for Psychoanalytic Psychology (pres. 1994-95). Home: 3703 Kennelwood Rd Austin TX 78703-2008 Office: Ste 245 8140 N Mo Pac Expy Bldg 1 Austin TX 78759-8837

MANOUKIAN, RITA CHAKE, sales executive; b. Manhasset, N.Y., Feb. 14, 1964; d. Aram Manoukian and Astrid Tchalekian Torosian. BS, St. John's U., 1985. Sales system analyst Bristol-Myers Products, N.Y.C., 1987-88, sales devel. asst., 1988-89; sales and promotion devel. mgr. Bristol-Myers Products, Bridgewater, N.J., 1989-90; div. sales devel. mgr. Bristol-Myers Products, Irvine, Calif., 1990, mgr. category devel., 1990-93; dir. key account sales Intactix Internat., Manhattan Beach, Calif., 1993-94; regional v.p. Intactix Internat., Laguna Niguel, Calif., 1994-96; gen. mgr. U.S. Intactix Internat., Atlanta, 1996. Office: 3100 Medlock Bridge Rd Norcross GA 30071-1432

MANOUSOS, JAMES WILLIAM See **MANN, JIM**

MANOWITZ, PAUL, biochemist, researcher, educator; b. Monticello, N.Y., Dec. 13, 1940; s. Jacob M. and Rose (Levine) M.; m. Joyce L. Swartz, June 16, 1968; children: Neal J., Lauren H. BA in Chemistry with honors, Cornell U., 1962; PhD in Biochemistry, Brandeis U., 1967. Postdoctoral fellow NYU Sch. Medicine, 1967-70, instr., 1970-72; asst. prof. psychiatry U. Medicine and Dentistry N.J. Robert Wood Johnson Med. Sch., Piscataway, 1972-78, assoc. prof. psychiatry, 1978-96, assoc. prof. psychiatry and neurology, 1991-96, prof. psychiaty, 1996—; rsch. cons. VA Med. Ctr., Lyons, N.J., 1987—. Editorial bd. Jour. of Studies on Alcohol, 1993—; contbr. articles to profl. jours. Grantee Nat. Inst. on Alcohol Abuse and Alcoholism, UNICO Found. Mem. AAAS, Am. Soc. for Neurochemistry, Internat. Soc. for Biomed. Rsch. on Alcoholism, Soc. Biol. Psychiatry, Rsch. Soc. on Alcoholism, Soc. for Neurosci., World Fedn. of Socs. Biol. Psychiatry. Home: 7 Guernsey Ln East Brunswick NJ 08816-3506 Office: U Medicine and Dentistry NJ Robert Wood Johnson Med Sch 675 Hoes Ln Piscataway NJ 08854-5627

MANSBERGER, ARLIE ROLAND, JR., surgeon; b. Pitts., Oct. 13, 1922; s. Arlie Rol and Mayme (Smith) M.; m. Anna Ellen Piel, July 27, 1946; children—Ellen Lynn, John Arlie, Leigh Ann. B.A., Western Md. Coll., 1943, D.Sc. (hon.), 1974; M.D., U. Md., 1947, D.Sc. (hon.), 1978. Diplomate: Am. Bd. Surgery (dir., vice chmn.). Intern U. Md. Hosp., 1947-49, resident in surgery, 1947-54; chief wound shock br. biophysics div. Army Chem. Center, 1954-56; instr. surgery U. Md., 1956-59, asst. prof., 1959-61, asso. prof., 1961-69, prof. surgery, 1969-73; clin. dir. shock-trauma unit, 1962-73; prof. surgery, chmn. dept. Med. Coll. Ga., Augusta, 1973-91; prof. surgery emeritus, chmn., 1991—; cons. surgeon Dwight David Eisenhower Army Med. Center, VA Hosp. Editor: Essence of General Surgery, 1975; chmn. editorial bd.: Bull. U. Md, 1971-73; editor-in-chief: The Am. Surgeon, 1973-89; surg. editor: Resident and Staff Physician, 1979-91; contbr. articles to profl. jours., chpts. to books. Trustee Western Md. Coll., 1971—, Med. Research Found. Ga., 1973-91; bd. dirs. Nicholas J. Pisican Found., 1993—. Served to col. U.S. Army, 1943-46, 54-56. Recipient Man of Yr. award U. Md., 1970, 72, Golden Apple teaching award U. Md., 1968, 72, Disting. Faculty award Med. Coll. Ga., 1979, Gold Medal Alumni award U. Md., 1989, Disting. Svc. award (medal) Southeastern Surg. Congress, 1990. Fellow A.C.S. (gov.); mem. Am. Surg. Assn., Soc. Univ. Surgeons, So. Surg. Assn., Soc. Internationale de Chirurgie, Am. Assn. Surgery of Trauma, Southeastern Surg. Congress, Soc. Surgery of Alimentary Tract, AMA, Soc. Consultants to Armed Forces, Med. Assn. Ga. (editorial bd. 1987-92), Am. Bd. Family Practice (bd. dirs. 1987-92), 29th Div. Assn., Alpha Omega Alpha. Episcopalian. Home: One 7th St Unit 1502 Augusta GA 30901-1343 Office: Dept Surgery Med Coll Ga Augusta GA 30912

MANSBRIDGE, JANE JEBB, political scientist, educator; b. N.Y.C., Nov. 19, 1939; d. Ronald and Georgia St. Claire (Mullen) M.; m. Christopher Jencks; 1 child, Nathaniel Mansbridge Jencks. BA, Wellesley Coll., 1961; MA, Harvard U., 1966, PhD, 1971. Asst. prof. polit. sci. U. Chgo., 1973-80; assoc. prof. Northwestern U., Evanston, Ill., 1980-86, prof. polit. sci., 1986-91, Jane W. Long prof. arts and scis., 1991-96; prof. J.F. Kennedy Sch. Govt. Harvard U., 1996—; fellow Ctr. for Advanced Study in Behavioral Scis., 1997—. Author: Beyond Adversary Democracy, 1980, Why We Lost the ERA, 1986; editor : Beyond Self-Interest, 1990, (with Susan M. Okin) Feminism 2 vols., 1994; mem. editorial bd.: Signs, Jour. Polit. Philosophy. Scholar Russell Sage Found., 1991-92; fellow Inst. for Advanced Study, 1985-86, Rockefeller Humanities, 1982-83, NSF, 1971-72. Mem. Am. Polit. Sci. Assn. (v.p. 1992-93, exec. com. 1987-89, coun. 1987-89, program chair 1990), Am. Acad. Arts and Scis. Office: JF Kennedy Sch Govt 79 Jfk St Cambridge MA 02138-5801

MANSBRIDGE, JOHN B., art director, production designer. Prodn. designer: (films) The Love Bug, 1969, Bedknobs and Broomsticks, 1971 (Academy award nomination best art direction 1971), Deliverance, 1972, (with Mark Mansbridge) Amy, 1981, (with Leon Harris) The Devil and Max Devlin, 1981, Baby: Secret of the Lost Legend, 1985, Stone Cold, 1991; art dir.: (films) The Island at the Top of the World, 1974 (Academy award nomination best art direction 1974), No Deposit, No Return, 1976, The Shaggy D.A., 1976, Treasure of Matecumbe, 1976, Freaky Friday, 1976, Herbie Goes to Monte Carlo, 1977, Pete's Dragon, 1977, Hot Lead and Cold Feet, 1978, Return from Witch Mountain, 1978, The North Avenue Irregulars, 1979, The Last Flight of Noah's Ark, 1980, Midnight Madness, 1980, Herbie Goes Bananas, 1980, Tex, 1982, Tron, 1982, Something Wicked This Way Comes, 1983, Trenchcoat, 1983, Splash, 1984, Country, 1984, The River Wild, 1994, (TV movies) The Man Who Fell to Earth, 1987, (TV series) Beauty and the Beast, 1988 (Emmy award outstanding art direction 1989). Office: care Art Directors Guild 11365 Ventura Blvd Ste 315 Studio City CA 91604-3148*

MANSBRIDGE, MARK, art director, production designer. Art dir.: (films) Smokey and the Bandit, 1977, Amy, 1981, The Man with Two Brains, 1983, 8 Million Ways to Die, 1986, The Witches of Eastwick, 1987, The War of the Roses, 1989, Ghost, 1990, Chaplin, 1992 (Academy award nomination best art direction 1992), Fire in the Sky, 1993; prodn. designer: (films) Say Anything, 1989, (TV movies) Dream Breakers, 1989. Office: care Art Directors Guild PO Box 3182 Lake Isabella CA 93240*

MANSELL, DARREL LEE, JR., English educator; b. Canton, Ohio, Apr. 9, 1934; s. Darrel Lee and Virginia (Shepherd) M.; m. Elizabeth Meihack, Jan. 1957 (div. July 1970); 1 child, Benjamin Lloyd; m. Adriana Saviane, July 16, 1983. BA, Oberlin Coll., 1956; student, Oxford U., 1961-62; PhD, Yale U., 1963; MA (hon.), Dartmouth Coll., 1975. Instr. Dartmouth Coll., Hanover, N.H., 1962-64, asst. prof., 1964-68, assoc. prof., 1968-74, prof., 1974—. Author: The Novels of Jane Austen, 1973; contbr. articles to scholarly jours. Mem. Victorian Lit. Assn., Internat. Assn. for Phenomenology and Lit., Soc. for Literature and Sci., Jane Austen Soc. N.Am. (founding patron), Phi Beta Kappa. Home: 2 Dana Rd Hanover NH 03755-2227 Office: Dartmouth Coll Dept English Hanover NH 03755

MANSELL, HENRY J., bishop; b. N.Y.C., Oct. 10, 1937. Student, Cathedral Coll., St. Joseph's Sem. and Coll., N.Am. Coll., Gregorian U. Ordained priest Roman Catholic Ch., 1962. Ordained priest N.Y., 1962; titular bishop Marzane and aux. bishop N.Y.C., 1993—. Office: Chancery Office 795 Main St Buffalo NY 14203

MANSELL, JOYCE MARILYN, special education educator; b. Minot, N.D., Dec. 17, 1934; d. Einar Axel and Gladys Ellen (Wall) Alm; m. Dudley J. Mansell, Oct. 31, 1954; children: Michael, Debra Mansell Richards. BS, U. Houston, 1968; MEd, Sam Houston State U., 1980. Cert. provisional elem. tchr. 1-8, provisional mentally retarded tchr., provisional lang. and/or learning disabilities tchr., profl. elem. tchr. gen. 1-8, profl. reading specialist. From 1st grade tchr. to 3rd grade tchr. Johnson Elem. Sch., 1968-77; spl. edn. tchr. mentally retarded/learning disabled Meml. Parkway Jr. H.S., 1982-86, Waller Mid. Sch., 1986-90; spl. edn. tchr. mentally retarded Royal Mid. Sch., Tex., 1990-95, Royal H.S., 1995-96; ret., 1996; tchr. Am. sign lang. for retarded students Holy Three and One Luth. Ch. of Deaf. Lutheran. Avocations: reading, fishing, grandchildren and family, signing choir. Home: 2155 Paso Rello Dr Houston TX 77077-5622

MANSFIELD, CARL MAJOR, radiation oncology educator; b. Phila., Dec. 24, 1928; m. Sarah Lynn Flower; children: Joel, Kara. AB in Chemistry, Lincoln U., 1951; postgrad., Temple U., 1952; MD, Howard U., 1956; ScD (hon.), Lincoln U., 1991. Diplomate Am. Bd. Radiology, Am. Bd. Nuclear Medicine. Rotating intern Episcopal Hosp., Phila., 1956-57, resident in radiology, 1957-58, 60, 61-62; resident in radiation therapy and nuclear medicine Thomas Jefferson Med. Coll. Hosp., Phila., 1960-61, NIH fellow in radiation therapy and nuclear medicine, 1962-63, instr. radiology, chief div. nuclear medicine, 1964-65, Chernicoff fellow in pediatric radiation therapy, 1964-66, assoc. in radiology, chief div. nuclear medicine, 1966-67, asst. prof. radiology, chief div. nuclear medicine, 1967-69, assoc. prof. dept. radiation therapy and nuclear medicine, chief sect. of ultrasound, 1970-74, prof., chief div. nuclear medicine and sect. of ultrasound, 1974-76, prof., chmn. dept. radiation therapy and nuclear medicine, 1983-95; assoc. dir. divsn. cancer treatment Nat. Cancer Inst. NIH, Bethesda, Md., 1995—; NIH postdoctoral fellow in radiation therapy Middlesex Hosp. and Med. Sch., London, 1963-64; lectr. in radiology U. Pa. Sch. Medicine, Phila., 1967-73; vis. prof. radiation therapy and nuclear medicine Hahnemann Med. Coll. Hosp., 1971; sabbatical leave Myerestein Inst. Radiotherapy, Middlesex Hosp. and Med. Sch., London, 1972-73; mem. grad. faculty in radiation biophysics U. Kans. Med. Ctr., Kansas City, 1977-83, prof., chmn. dept. radiation therapy, 1976-83; chmn. dept. radiation therapy Menorah Med. Ctr., Kansas City, Mo., 1977-83. Author 2 books, also author or co-author over 129 articles in med. jours. Served with USAF, 1958-60. Fellow Am. Coll. Radiology, Coll. Physicians of Phila., Am. Coll. Nuclear Medicine; mem. AMA, Am. Coll. Radiology, Am. Cancer Soc. (dir.-at-large, nat. bd. dirs. 1981-85, med. and sci. com. 1981-88, profl. edn. com. 1981-88, pres. Phila. divsn. 1989), Am. Radium Soc. (pres. 1988), Radiation Rsch. Program Nat. Cancer Inst. (dir.), Sigma Xi. Office: NCI DCTDC RRP Bldg EPN Rm 800 6130 Exec Blvd MSC 7440 Bethesda MD 20892-7440

MANSFIELD, CHRISTOPHER CHARLES, insurance company legal executive; b. 1950; married. BA, Boston Coll., 1972, JD, 1975. With Liberty Mut. Ins. Co., Boston, 1975—, v.p., 1983, sr. v.p., gen. counsel, 1983—; underwriter Liberty Lloyds of Tex. Ins. Co., 1984-94; v.p., dir. Liberty Ins. Corp., 1985—; v.p. Liberty Mut. Fire Ins. Co., 1985—, Stein Roe Svcs. Co., 1986-95; v.p., gen. counsel LEXCO Ltd., 1986—, Liberty Mut. Capital Corp., 1986—; bd. dirs. Liberty Fin. Cos., Liberty Mut. Bermuda, Liberty Internat. Office: Liberty Mut Ins Co PO Box 140 175 Berkeley St Boston MA 02117

MANSFIELD, EDWARD PATRICK, JR., advertising executive; b. Warren, Pa., Oct. 29, 1947; s. Edward Patrick and Frieda (Dahler) M.; m. Norma L. Johnson, Apr. 17, 1971. AS in Acctg., Jamestown Bus. Coll., 1967; BS in Mktg. Advt., David N. Myers Coll., 1970. Promotion mgr., ad dir. The News-Herald, Lake County, Ohio, 1973-77; dir. advt. The Eagle, Butler, Pa., 1977-78; dir. mktg. Baltimore Mag., 1978-79; dir. advt. The Washingtonian, Washington, 1979—. Founder, chmn. Warm-A-Heart Fund, 1988—; bd. dirs. Columbia Lighthouse for the Blind, 1988—, chmn., 1988-93; bd. dirs. The Lighthouse; mem. adv. bd. Ann Arundel County Mental Health. Avocations: amateur radio operator gen. class, sailing. Home: 347 Cottswold Pl Riva MD 21140-1528 Office: Washingtonian Mag 1828 L St NW Ste 200 Washington DC 20036-5104

MANSFIELD, EDWIN, economist, educator; b. Kingston, N.Y., June 8, 1930; s. Raymond and Sarah M.; m. Lucile Howe, Feb. 21, 1955; children: Edward, Elizabeth. AB, Dartmouth Coll., 1951; MA, Duke U., 1953, PhD, 1955; cert. diploma, Royal Statis. Soc., 1955; MA (hon.), U. Pa., 1971. Asst. prof., assoc. prof. econs. Carnegie-Mellon U., 1955-60, 62-63; vis. assoc. prof. econs. Yale U., New Haven, 1961-62; vis. prof. econs. Harvard U., Cambridge, Mass., 1963-64, Calif. Inst. Tech., Pasadena, 1967-68; prof. econs. U. Pa., Phila., 1964—; dir. Ctr. Econs. and Tech. U. Pa., 1985—; guest prof. Chalmers U. Tech. Gothenburg, Sweden, 1983, Nat. Technol. U., 1989-95; cons. Exec. Office Pres. of U.S., U.S. Dept. Commerce, U.S. Gen. Acctg. Office, U.S. Dept. Labor, HHS, NSF, Nat. Inst. Edn., Fed. Power Commn., Inst. for Def. Analysis, SBA, FTC, U.S. Army, Ford Found., RAND Corp., Can. Royal Commn., New Zealand Rsch. Inst., Nat. Inst. Standards and Tech., Internat. Fin. Corp., World Bank, others; mem. Gov.'s Sci. Adv. Com., 1965-66; chmn. U.S.-USSR Working Party on Sci. and Tech., 1974-75; panelist Nat. Bur. Standards/NAS, 1974-76; bd. examiners Grad. Record Exam, 1975-76; econ. adv. com. U.S. Bur. Census, 1982-85; Nat. Tech. Medal Com., 1984-87; chmn. vis. com. Rensselaer Poly. Inst., 1986-91; mem. adv. com. Ctr. for Drug Devel., U. Rochester, 1976-83. Author: The Economics of Technological Change, 1968, Industrial Research and Technological Innovation, 1968, Defense, Science and Public Policy, 1968, Research and Innovation in the Modern Corporation, 1971, The Production and Application of New Industrial Technology, 1977, Monopoly Power and Economic Performance, 4th edit., 1978, Technology Transfer, Productivity and Economic Policy, 1982, Managerial Economics and Operations Research, 5th edit., 1987, Economics, 7th edit., 1992, Economics USA, 4th edit., 1995, Managerial Economics, 1990, 3d edit., 1996, Microeconomics, 9th edit., 1997, Statistics, 5th edit., 1994, (with Elizabeth Mansfield) The Economics of Technical Change, 1993, Applied Microeconomics, 2d edit., 1997, Leading Economic Controversies, 3d edit., 1997, Innovation, Technology, and the Economy, 1995, others; editor Jour. of the Am. Statistical Assn., 1964-67, Am. Economist, 1969-90, Jour. of Econ. Edn., 1982-90, Review of Industrial Organization, 1984—, IEEE Transactions on Engring. Mgmt., 1985—, Managerial and Decision Econs., 1988-92, Univ. Wis. series on tech. change, 1984-88, Pub. Rsch. Quar., 1993—, and others. Fulbright fellow, 1954-55, Ford Found. rsch. fellow, 1960-61, Ctr. for Advanced Study Behavioral Scis. fellow, 1971-72; NSF grantee, 1962—; recipient Cert. Appreciation U.S. Sec. Commerce, 1979, Publ. award Patent Law Assn., 1984, Honor award Nat. Tech. U., 1992, Citation Classic award Inst. for Sci. Info., 1992, Spl. Creativity award NSF, 1994, Hall of Fame award Prentice Hall, 1995, Enterprise award Kenan Charitable Trust, 1996. Fellow Econometric Soc., Am. Acad. Arts and Scis.; mem. AAAS (sci., engring. and pub. policy com. 1981-84), Am. Econ. Assn., Royal Statis. Soc. (cert.), Phi Beta Kappa. Home: 202 Plush Mill Rd Wallingford PA 19086-6021 Office: U Pa Dept Econs Philadelphia PA 19104

MANSFIELD, ELAINE SCHULTZ, molecular geneticist, automation specialist; b. Boulder, Colo., Apr. 20, 1954; d. William Varley and Juanita M. (Zingg) M.; m. Gary G. Schultz, Nov. 24, 1983; children: Matthew, Greggory Mark. BA in Molecular Biology, San Jose State U., 1975; MS in Genetics, U. Calif., Berkeley, 1978, PhD in Genetics, 1983. Diplomate Am. Bd. Med. Genetics (fellow), Am. Bd. Clin. Molecular Genetics. Customer cons. IntelliGenetics, Mountain View, Calif., 1980-81; staff scientist Applied Biosys., Foster City, Calif., 1978-80; sr. staff scientist Molecular Dynamics, Sunnyvale, Calif., 1993—; lectr. in the field. Author (with others) Mutations in the Human Genome, 1993; contb. to profl. jours.; patentee in field. U. Calif. grant, Chancellors Patent Fund grant U. Calif. Mem. AAAS, Am. Soc. Human Genetics, Am. Soc. Histocompatibility and Immunogenetics, Women in Sci., Black Masque (pres. 1975). Avocations: skiing, quilting. Office: Molecular Dynamics 928 E Arques Ave Sunnyvale CA 94086-4520

MANSFIELD, JOHN H., legal educator; b. 1928. AB, Harvard U., 1952, LLB, 1956. Bar: Calif., Mass. John H. Watson, Jr. prof. law Harvard U., Cambridge, Mass. Mem. Assn. for Asian Studies. Editor: (with Weinstein, Abrams and Berger) Cases and Materials on Evidence, 1988. Office: Sch Law Harvard U Cambridge MA 02138

MANSFIELD, KAREN LEE, lawyer; b. Chgo., Mar. 17, 1942; d. Ralph and Hilda (Blum) Mansfield; children: Nicole Rafaela, Lori Michele. BA in Polit. Sci., Roosevelt U., 1963; JD, DePaul U., 1971; student U. Chgo., 1959-60. Bar: Ill. 1972, U.S. Dist. Ct. (no. dist.) Ill. 1972. Legis. intern Ill. State Senate, Springfield, 1966-67; tchr. Chgo. Pub. Schs., 1967-70; atty. CNA Ins., Chgo., 1971-73; law clk. Ill. Apellate Ct., Chgo., 1973-75; sr. trial atty. U.S. Dept. Labor, Chgo., 1975—, mentor Adopt-a-Sch. Program, 1992-95. Contbr. articles to profl. jours. Vol. Big Sister, 1975-81; bd. dirs. Altgeld Nursery Sch., 1963-66, Ill. div. UN Assn., 1966-72, Hull House Jane Addams Ctr., 1977-82, Broadway Children's Ctr., 1986-90, Acorn Family Entertainment, 1993-95; mem. Oak Park Farmers' Market Commn., 1996—; rsch. asst. Citizens for Gov. Otto Kerner, Chgo., 1964; com. mem. Ill. Commn. on Status of Women, Chgo., 1964-70; del. Nat. Conf. on Status of Women, 1968; candidate for del. Ill. Constl. Conv., 1969. Mem. Chgo. Council Lawyers, Women's Bar Assn. Ill., Lawyer Pilots Bar Assn., Fed. Bar Assn. Unitarian. Clubs: Friends of Gamelan (performer), 99's Internat. Orgn. Women Pilots (legis. chmn. Chgo. area chpt. 1983-86, legis. chmn. North Cen. sect. 1986-88, legis. award 1983, 85). Home: 204 S Taylor Ave Oak Park IL 60302-3307 Office: US Dept Labor Office Solicitor 230 S Dearborn St Fl 8 Chicago IL 60604-1505

MANSFIELD, NORMAN CONNIE, bookkeeper; b. Rayle, Ga., Apr. 27, 1916; s. Boykin Carswell and Cleo (Norman) M.; m. Ila Ruth Poss, Jan. 3, 1943; children: Jonathan Norman, Jerry Carswell. Cert., U. Ga. Notary Pub., Ga. Mgr. Railway Express Agy., Washington, Ga., 1943-78; semi-retired bookkeeper Russell Transfer Co. Inc., Washington, 1979—; mgr. Rwy. Express. Exec. bd. mem. Ga. Carolina Coun.; deacon First Baptist Ch., Washington; cubscout master, Washington, Ga., 1962. With USNG. Recipient Baseball and Little League award Coca Cola Co., Washington, Ga., 1951, 68, Woodmen of World award Life Ins. Soc., Augusta, Ga., 1978; named Boy Scout of Yr., Ga. Carolina Coun., Thomson, 1956. Mem. Masons (Shriner, worship master 1984), Order of Eastern Star (worthy patron), Woodman of the World (pres.), Lions (pres.), Washington (Ga.) Country Club, Ida Cason Callaway Found., Ga. Sheriffs Assn. Home: 209 Hudson Dr Washington GA 30673-1527 Office: The News-Reporter 116 W Robert Toombs Ave Washington GA 30673-1664

MANSFIELD, STEPHEN W., judge; b. Brookline, Mass., Aug. 21, 1952; s. Clarence E. and Mary Ann (Zeyer) M.; divorced; children: Eric, Mark, Greg. BA cum laude, Tufts U., 1974; JD, Boston U., 1977. Bar: Tex., Mass. Assoc. gen. counsel Corbel & Co., Jacksonville, Fla., 1984-86; sr. counsel VALIC, Houston, 1986-94; pvt. practice Houston, 1994; judge Tex. Ct. of Criminal Appeals, Austin, 1995—. Republican. Avocations: numismatics, rugby, running. Office: Ct Criminal Appeals Box 12308 Austin TX 78711*

MANSHIP, DOUGLAS, broadcast and newspaper executive; b. Baton Rouge, Nov. 3, 1918; s. Charles P. and Leora (Douthit) M.; m. Jane French, Jan. 31, 1942 (div. 1981); children—Douglas Lewis, Richard French, David Charles, Dina. Student, La. State U., 1936-41, U. Heidelberg, 1937, U. Colo., 1938-39. Reporter State Times and Morning Advocate, 1945-47, pub., 1970—; with Baton Rouge Broadcasting Co., 1947—, pres., 1948—; pres., chmn. bd. La IV Broadcasting Corp., 1953—; vice chmn. bd. Radio Free Europe/Radio Liberty, 1978—; chmn. Mobile Video Tapes, Inc., 1960; pres. Capital City Press, 1970; bd. dirs. City Nat. Bank, TV Stas. Inc. Campaign chmn. Community Chest, 1950, bd. dirs., 1950-52, pres., 1951. With USAAF, World War II. Mem. Baton Rouge C. of C. (pres. 1963), La. C. of C. (v.p.), Assn. for Profl. Broadcasting Edn., Council for A Better La., Assn. La. Chambers Commerce, So. Newspaper Pubs. Assn. (pres. 1977-78), Kappa Alpha, Sigma Delta Chi. Episcopalian. Office: Capital City Press 525 Lafayette St Baton Rouge LA 70802-5410

MANSI, JOSEPH ANNEILLO, public relations company executive; b. Oct. 8, 1935; s. Joseph C. and Vinnie (Chirico) M.; m. Mary P. Fusco, Aug. 1, 1959; children: Karen M. D'Attore, Jeanine V. Dimenna. B.S., NYU, 1957. Newsman Internat. News Service, UPI, 1953-58; mem. pub. relations staff Lawrence Orgn., N.Y.C., 1960-63; acct. supr. Philip Lesly Co., N.Y.C., 1963-67; dir. corp. communications Ward Foods, Inc., N.Y.C., 1967-72; dir. pub. relations Metromedia Inc., N.Y.C., 1973-75; pres. Corp. Relations Network, Inc., N.Y.C., 1975-80; mng. ptnr. KCSA Pub. Rels., N.Y.C., 1980—. Served with AUS, 1958-60. Mem. Pub. Rels. Soc. Am. (accredited). Home: 10 Beatrice Ln Glen Cove NY 11542-1202 Office: KCSA Pub Rels 820 2nd Ave New York NY 10017-4504

MANSKE, PAUL ROBERT, orthopedic hand surgeon, educator; b. Ft. Wayne, Ind., Apr. 29, 1938; s. Alfred R. and Elsa E. (Streufert) M.; m. Sandra H. Henricks, Nov. 29, 1975; children: Ethan Paul, Claire Bruch, Louisa Hendricks. BA, Valparaiso U., 1960, DSc (hon.), 1985; MD, Washington U., St. Louis, 1964. Diplomate Am. Bd. Surgery. Surg. intern U. Wash., Seattle, 1964-65, surg. resident, 1965-66; orthopedic surg. resident Washington U., St. Louis, 1969-72; hand surgery fellow U. Louisville, 1971; instr. orthopedic surgery Washington U. Med. Sch., St. Louis, 1972-76, asst. prof. orthopedic surgery, 1976-83, prof., 1983—, chmn. dept., 1983-95. Editor-in-chief Jour. Hand Surgery, 1996—; contbr. more than 215 articles and abstracts to profl. jours. Lt. comdr. USN, 1966-69, Vietnam. Lt. comdr. USN, 1966-69, Vietnam. Fellow AMA, Am. Acad. Orthopaedic Surgery, Am. Orthopaedic Assn.; mem. Am. Soc. Surgery of the Hand, Alpha Omega Alpha. Lutheran. Office: Washington Univ Dept Orthop Surgery 1 Barnes Hosp Plz Saint Louis MO 63110

MANSKI, WLADYSLAW JULIAN, microbiology educator, medical scientist; b. Lwow, Poland, May 15, 1915; came to U.S., 1958, naturalized, 1964; s. Julian and Helena (Lewicka) M.; m. Anna Z. Artymowicz, June 20, 1941; children: Chris, Louis. M.Phil., U. Warsaw, Poland, 1939, D.Sc., 1951. Instr. U. Warsaw, 1936-39; rsch. asst. Inst. Lwow, 1940-41, Inst. Lwow (Inst. Agr.), Pulawy, Poland, 1942-44; instr. Inst. U. Lublin, Poland, 1944-45; instr. dept. microbiology Med. Sch., Wroclaw, Poland, 1945-49; Rockefeller fellow Columbia U., N.Y.C., 1949-50; head immunochemistry lab. Inst. Immunology and Exptl. Therapy, Polish Acad. Sci., Wroclaw, 1951-55; head Macromolecular Biochemistry Lab. Inst. Immunology and Exptl. Therapy, Polish Acad. Sci., Warsaw, 1955-57; head dept. virology Biochemistry Lab., State Inst. Hygiene, Warsaw, 1955-57; research worker Coll. Physicians and Surgeons, Columbia U., 1958-62, rsch. assoc., 1962-64, asst. prof., 1964-67, assoc. prof. microbiology, 1967-74, prof. microbiology, 1974-85, prof. emeritus, 1986; dir. rsch. Harkness Eye Inst., Columbia U., N.Y.C., 1985-90. Contbr. articles to profl. jours. NIH grantee, 1960-86. Mem. AAAS, Am. Assn. Immunologists, AAUP, Research in Vision and Ophthalmology Assn., Am. Chem. Soc., Brit. Biochemical Soc., N.Y. Acad. Scis., Soc. Exptl. Biology and Medicine, Soc. Study of Evolution, Internat. Soc. Eye Research, Harvey Soc., Transplantation Soc. Home: 10 Downing St New York NY 10014 Office: 630 W 168th St New York NY 10032-3702

MANSMANN, CAROL LOS, federal judge, law educator; b. Pittsburgh, Pa., Aug. 7, 1942; d. Walter Joseph and Regina Mary (Pilarski) Los; m. J. Jerome Mansmann, June 27, 1970; children: Casey, Megan, Patrick. B.A., J.D., Duquesne U., 1964, 67; LL.D., Seton Hill Coll., Greensburg, Pa., 1985; PhD (hon.), La Roche Coll., 1990; LLD (hon.), Widener U., 1994. Asst. dist. atty. Allegheny County, Pitts., 1968-72; assoc. McVerry Baxter & Mansmann, Pitts., 1973-79; assoc. prof. law Duquesne U., Pitts., 1973-82; judge west dist. U.S. Dist. Ct. Pa., Pitts., 1982-85; judge U.S. Ct. Appeals (3rd cir.), Phila., 1985—; mem. Pa. Criminal Procedural Rules Com., Pitts., 1972-77; spl. asst. atty. gen. Commonwealth of Pa., 1974-79; co-adminstr. Local Criminal Rules Reorg. Project, 1978-79; chair 2 Bar Assn. CLE programs, 1982; bd. govs. Pa. Bar Inst., Harrisburg, 1984-90; mem. 3d Cir. jud. coun., 1985—; adj. prof. law U. Pitts., 1987-96; mem. U.S. Jud. Conf. on adminstrn. of magistrate-judge sys., 1990-96. Mem. bd. consultors Villanova U. Law Sch., 1985-91; trustee Duquesne U., 1987—, Sewickley Acad., 1988-91. Recipient St. Thomas More award, Pitts., 1983, Phila., 1984, Ann. Dinner award Duquesne U. Law Alumni Assn., 1986, Faculty Alumni award Duquesne U., 1987. Mem. ABA, Nat. Assn. Women Judges, Pa. Bar Assn., Fed. Judges Assn., Am. Judicature Soc., Allegheny County Bar Assn. (gov., bd. govs. 1982-85), Phi Alpha Delta. Republican. Roman Catholic. Office: US Ct Appeals 712 US Courthouse Pittsburgh PA 15219

MANSMANN, J. JEROME, lawyer; b. Pitts., Aug. 14, 1942; s. C. Rex and Margaret G. (McArdle) M.; m. Carol M. Los, June 27, 1970; children: Kathleen, Megan, Patrick. BA, U. Dayton, 1963; JD, Duquesne U., 1967. Bar: Pa., U.S. Dist. Ct. (we. dist.) Pa., U.S. Ct. Appeals (3d cir.), U.S. Supreme Ct. Assoc. Law Offices of P.J. MCArdle, Pitts., 1969-70; ptnr. Mansmann & Mansmann, Pitts., 1970-72, Gondelman, Baxter, Mansmann McVerry & Cindrich, Pitts., 1972-81, Mansmann Cindrich & Titus, Pitts., 1981-91; shareholder Buchanan Ingersoll, P.C., Pitts., 1991—; spl. asst. Atty. Gen. Commonwealth of Pa., Pitts., 1974-80. Past legal svcs. com. Cath. Health Assn., St. Louis. With USAF, 1967-68. Mem. Pa. Bar Assn., Allegheny County Bar Assn. Home: Backbone Rd Sewickley PA 15143 Office: Buchanan Ingersoll PC One Oxford Ctr 301 Grant St Ste 20 Pittsburgh PA 15219-1408

MANSMANN, PARIS TAYLOR, medical educator; b. Pitts., Feb. 19, 1957; s. Herbert Charles Jr. and Margaret Marshal (Miller) M.; m. Leslie Ann Windstein, July 8, 1978; children: Erin Hart, Paris Corey, Maureen Ellyse. Student, Lafayette Coll., 1975-76; BS in Math., St. Joseph's U., Phila., 1980; MD, Jefferson Med. Coll., 1984. Diplomate Am. Bd. Medicine, Am. Bd. Internal Medicine, Am. Bd. Pediatrics, Am. Bd. Allergy and Immunology. Resident in medicine, pediatrics Geisinger Med. Ctr., Danville, Pa., 1984-88, chief resident, 1987-88; fellow in allergy, immunology Duke U. Med. Ctr., Durham, N.C., 1988-90; asst. prof. medicine and pediat. W.Va. U., Morgantown, 1990-93, asst. prof. medicine, 1990-95, assoc. prof. medicine, 1995—; program coord. medicine, pediat., W.Va. U., Morgantown, 1990-93. Author: (with others) Current Pediatric Therapy, 1994; contbr. articles to profl. jours. Recipient Outstanding Commitment award Vis. Clinicians, 1990. Fellow Am. Acad. Pediatrics, Am. Coll. Allergy and Immunology, ACP, Am. Acad. Allergy and Immunology, European Acad. Allergy and Clin. Immunology, W.Va. Allergy Soc. (pres. 1992—). Republican. Roman Catholic. Avocations: fishing, farming, cross country skiing, soccer. Office: WVa U Sch Medicine Box 9167 Health Scis Ctr Morgantown WV 26506-9167

MANSON, JOSEPH LLOYD, III, lawyer; b. Richmond, Va., May 5, 1949; s. Joseph Lloyd Jr. and Nan Smith (Copley) M.; m. Martha Forman Foltz, Sept. 8, 1973; children: Martha Stuart, Joseph Scott, Rachel Smith. BS, U. Va., 1970; JD, Emory U., 1974. Assoc. Verner, Liipfert, Bernhard & McPherson, Washington, 1974-80; ptnr. Verner, Liipfert, Bernhard, McPherson & Hand, Washington, 1981—; bd. dirs. Barrow Grocery Co. Founder Alexandria Youth Sports Found., 1993, co-chmn. Exec. Com. bd. dirs., 2d lt. U.S. Army, 1973. Mem. ABA (ry. and airline labor law com., co-chmn. mgmt. 1993-94), D.C. Bar Assn. Republican. Episcopalian. Avocations: music, tennis, theatre, movies. Office: Verner Liipfert Bernhard McPherson & Hand 901 15th St NW Ste 700 Washington DC 20005-2327

MANSON, KEITH ALAN MICHAEL, lawyer; b. Warwick, RI, Oct. 26, 1962; s. Ronald Frederick and Joan Patricia (Reardon) M.; m. Jennifer Annette Stearns; children: Kristin Elizabeth, Michelle Nicole. BA, R.I. Coll., 1985; cert. computer info. systems, Bryant Coll., 1988; cert. law, U. Notre Dame, London, 1990; JD, Thomas M. Cooley Law Sch., 1991. Bar: Ind. 1991, U.S. Dist. Ct. (no. dist.) Ind. 1991, U.S. Dist. Ct. (so. dist.) Ind. 1991, U.S. Dist. Ct. (so. dist.) Ga. 1992, U.S. Dist. Ct. Mil. Appeals 1991. Spl. asst. U.S. atty. U.S. Dist. Ct. Ga., Brunswick, 1992-93; pvt. practice Fernandina Beach, Fla., 1994—; cons. The Law Store Ltd. Paralegal Svcs., Fernandina Beach, 1994—. Contbr. articles to profl. jours. Commnr. Fla. coun. Boy Scouts Am., Jacksonville, 1993—; com. mem. sea scout ship 660 St. Peter's Ch., Fernandina Beach, 1994—; chmn. Scouting for Food Dr., Nassau County, Fla., 1994. Lt. USN, 1985-86, 90-94. F.C. Tanner Trust, Fed. Products Inc. scholar, Providence, 1981-85, Esterline Corp. scholar, Providence, 1986. Mem. ABA, Judge Advocate Assn., Jacksonville Bar Assn., Navy League U.S., Rotary (project mgr. Webster-Dudley Mass. chpt. 1986-88), Phi Alpha Delta. Avocations: gardening, rugby, sports history, military history, collecting historical items. Home and Office: 1908 Reatta Ln Fernandina Beach FL 32034-8936

MANSON, LEWIS AUMAN, energy research executive; b. Cleve., July 12, 1918; s. Lewis Frederick and Ina Josephine (Auman) M.; m. Alva Anne London, Sept. 3, 1960 (div. 1982); children: Anita, Howard; m. Shirley Anne Traeger, Jan. 27, 1982; children: Lewis, Jean, Phillip, Edward. Student, Gen. Motors Tech. U., 1943-44, Purdue U., 1942-43, Rice U., 1950-54. Cons. numerous oil, gas, and mining cos., 1951-57; cons. The Space Agy., Washington, 1958-59, Douglas Aircraft, El Segundo, Calif., 1964; dir. Copper Range Mines, Wyo., 1965; dir. explorations, cons. Nico Internat., S.A. de C.V., Mex., 1968-71; builder Spring, Tex., 1971-74; dir., conductor explorations Minerals of the Sun, S.A. de C.V., Honduras, 1975; dir. Asheville Petroleum Corp., Ill., 1976; conductor explorations Neozoic Minerals & Petroleum, Ltd., Colo., N.Mex., Tex., 1976-77; conductor explorations, dir. Primal Energy Rsch. Found., Houston, 1982—; pres. Transzoic Orebody Locators, Ltd., Vancouver, B.C., Pleiades Petroleum Corp., Lexington, Tenn. and Houston; lectr. grade schs., high schs., Kiwanis, and Rotary, 1962—. Author: The Primal Energy Transverter, 1966, Birth of the Moon, 1978, Origins of Solar Flares and Keys to Predicting Them, 1978, Automatic Recording of Deep Space (interplanetary) Gravity, 1978, Arriving Ionospheric High Energy (Solar Generated), 1978, Out of the Grey Mist, 1994, Life's Continuum, 1992, The Real Origin of Stellar Energy, 1993, The Great Mystery, 1994; patentee in field; inventor Quakaster, Affinity Sys., The Cradle System equipment to prevent and/or cure decubitis ulcers by Ocean Motion (tm). Scoutmaster Boy Scouts Am., Houston, 1956-63; cubmaster Cub Scouts, Pasadena, Calif., 1962. With Ind. NG, 1942-43. Republican. Avocations: mineral and fossil collecting, mountaineering, boating, archeology, metal and wood working. Office: Primal Energy Rsch Found 11250 Taylor Draper Ln Apt 113 Austin TX 78759-3976

MANSON, MALCOLM HOOD, educational administrator; b. Melton Mowbray, Leicester, Eng., May 31, 1938; s. James Milne and Williamina (Hood) M.; m. Snowden Sandra Johnston. BA, Oxford U., Eng., 1961, MA, 1964. Tchr. The Choate Sch., Wallingford, Conn., 1961-63, adminstr., 1963-69; headmaster Marin Country Day Sch., Corte Madera, Calif., 1969-82, Ore. Episcopal Sch., Portland, Oreg., 1982-90; canon headmaster Cathedral Sch. for Boys, San Francisco, 1990—. Mem. Calif. Assn. Ind. Schs. (bd. dirs., v.p. 1976-80), Pacific N.W. Assn. Ind. Schs. (pres. 1985-86). Episcopal. Office: Cathedral Sch for Boys 1275 Sacramento St San Francisco CA 94108-1910

MANSON, PAUL DAVID, retired military officer, electronics executive; b. Trail, B.C., Can., Aug. 20, 1934; s. Robert Edwin and Mary Leonora (McLeod) M.; m. Margaret Nickel, May 11, 1957; children: Robert, Catherine, Peter, Karen. Diploma, Royal Roads Mil. Coll., Victoria, B.C., Can., 1954, Royal Mil. Coll., Kingston, Ont., Can., 1956; BS, Queen's U., 1957; D Mil. Sci. honoris causa, Royal Roads, 1990. Joined RCAF, 1957; advanced through grades to gen. Can. Armed Forces, 1989; various squadron duties Can. Armed Forces, France and Federal Republic of Germany, 1957-62, 67-72; ops. research, Hqrs. Can. Armed Forces, Ottawa, 1963-66; exec. asst. to chief of def. staff Nat. Def. Hdqrs., Can. Armed Forces, Ottawa, 1972-73, chief of air doctrine and ops., 1982-83, asst. dep. minister personnel, 1985-86, chief of def. staff, 1986-89; student Nat. Def. Coll., Kingston, 1973-74; base comdr. Can. Forces Base, Chatham, 1974-76; program mgr. New Fighter Aircraft Program, Ottawa, 1977-80; comdr. 1 Can. Air Group, Fed. Republic of Germany, 1980-81, Air Command, Winnipeg, Man., Can., 1983-85; chmn. Lockheed Martin Can., Inc., Montreal, 1985—. Recipient Order of Mil: Merit Govt. of Can., 1981, Comdr. Legion of Merit U.S., 1989, C.D. Howe award for achievements in aeronautics and space, 1992. Mem. Aerospace Industries Assn. Can. (past chmn.). Anglican. Avocations: astronomy, music, golfing, home computing. Office: Lockheed Martin Can Inc, 6111 Royalmount Ave, Montreal, PQ Canada H4P 1K6

MANSON, PAUL NELLIS, plastic surgeon; b. Kansas City, Mo., Dec. 28, 1943; s. Nellis Emanuel and Alice Winifred (Olson) M.; m. Kathryn Garland, 1968; children: Ted, Jenner. BA in Chemistry, Northwestern U., 1965, MD, 1968. Prof., chmn. plastic surgery Johns Hopkins Sch. Medicine, Balt., 1990—. Maj. U.S. Army, 1970-73. Republican. Presbyterian. Office: 8152 F McElderry Wins 601 N Caroline St Baltimore MD 21205-1809

MANSON-HING, LINCOLN ROY, dental educator; b. Georgetown, Guyana, May 20, 1927; m. Joyce Louise Chin, Aug. 21, 1949; children: Collin James, Jennifer Lynn, Jeffrey Paul. D.M.D. cum laude, Tufts U.,

1948; M.S., U. Ala., 1961. Practice dentistry Kingston, Jamaica; also dir. Schs.' Dental Clinic, St. Mary Parish, Jamaica, 1948-56; asst. prof. dentistry U. Ala., 1956-59, asso. prof., 1959-68, prof. dentistry, 1968-88, chmn. dept. dental radiology, 1962-88, prof. emeritus dentistry, 1988—; Cons. Am. Dental Assn., Am. Standards Assn., VA Hosp., Birmingham, Ala., Tuskegee, Ala.; cons. USAF, Ala. State Crippled Children Cleft Palate Clinic, 1957-69; Fulbright-Hays lectr., Egypt., 1964-65. Author: (with A.H. Wuehrmann) Dental Radiology, 1965, Panoramic Dental Radiology, 1975, Fundamentals of Dental Radiology, 1979; also articles, textbook chpts.; sect. editor: Jour. Oral Surgery, Oral Medicine and Pathology, 1967-80. Mem. ADA, Am. Acad. Dental Radiology (pres. 1967, editor 1967-80), Internat. Assn. Dento-maxillofacial Radiology (v.p. 41977—), Internat. Assn. Dental Research, AAAS, Sigma Xi, Omicron Kappa Upsilon. Home: 205 Mecca Ave Birmingham AL 35209-3459 Office: 1919 7th Ave S Birmingham AL 35233-2005

MANSOUR, GEORGE P., Spanish language and literature educator; b. Huntington, W.Va., Sept. 4, 1939; s. Elia and Marie (Yazbek) M.; m. Mary Ann Rogers, Dec. 27, 1961; children: Alicia, Philip. AB, Marshall U., 1961; MA, Mich. State U., 1963, PhD, 1965. Assoc. prof. Mich. State U., East Lansing, 1968-77, prof., 1977—, chmn. dept. Romance and Classical langs., 1982—; cons. Mich. Dept. Edn., Lansing, 1984-85. Contbr. articles to profl. jours. Mem. Am. Assn. Tchrs. Spanish and Portuguese (v.p. 1969-71), Mich. Fgn. Lang. Assn. (pres. 1982-84). Democrat. Mem. Eastern Orthodox Ch. Avocations: Pysanky, golf. Home: 1303 Lucerne Dr Dewitt MI 48820-9528 Office: Mich State U Dept Romance & Classical Langs East Lansing MI 48824

MANSOUR, TAG ELDIN, pharmacologist, educator; b. Belkas, Egypt, Nov. 6, 1924; came to U.S., 1951, naturalized, 1956; s. Elsayed and Rokaya (Elzayat) M.; m. Joan Adela MacKinnon, Aug. 6, 1955; children—Suzanne, Jeanne, Dean. DVM, Cairo U., 1946; PhD, U. Birmingham, Eng., 1949, DSc, 1974. Lectr. U. Cairo, 1950-51; Fulbright instr. physiology Howard U., Washington, 1951-52; sr. instr. pharmacology Case Western Res. U., 1952-54; asst. prof., assoc. prof. pharmacology La. State U. Med. Sch., New Orleans, 1954-61; assoc. prof., prof. molecular pharmacology Stanford U. Sch. Medicine, 1961—, chmn. dept. pharmacology, 1977-91, Donald E. Baxter prof., 1977—; cons. USPHS, WHO, Nat. Acad. Scis.; Mem. adv. bd. Med. Sch., Kuwait U.; Heath Clarke lectr. London Sch. Hygiene and Tropical Medicine, 1981. Contrbr. sci. articles to profl. jours. Commonwealth Fund fellow, 1965; Macy Found. scholar NIMR, London, 1982. Fellow AAAS; mem. Am. Soc. Pharmacology and Exptl. Therapeutics, Am. Soc. Biol. Chemists, Am. Heart Assn., Sierra Club, Stanford Faculty Club. Office: 300 Pasteur Dr Palo Alto CA 94304-2203

MANSOURI, LOTFOLLAH (LOTFI MANSOURI), opera stage director, administrator; b. Tehran, June 15, 1929; arrived in Can., 1976; s. Hassan and Mehri (Jalili) M.; m. Marjorie Anne Thompson, Sept. 18, 1954; 1 child, Shireen Melinda. AB, UCLA, 1953. Asst. prof. UCLA, 1957-60; resident stage dir. Zurich Opera, 1960-65; chief stage dir. Geneva Opera, 1965-75; gen. dir. Can. Opera Co., Toronto, Ont., 1976-88, San Francisco Opera, 1988—; dramatic coach Music Acad. West, Santa Barbara, Calif., 1959; dir. dramatics Zurich Internat. Opera Studio, 1961-65, Centre Lyrique, Geneva, 1967-72; artistic adviser Tehran Opera, 1973-75; opera adviser Nat. Arts Centre, Ottawa, Ont., 1977; v.p. Opera America, 1979—; operatic cons. dir. Yes, Giorgio, MGM, 1981; dir. opera sequence for film Moonstruck (Norman Jewison), 1987. Guest dir. opera cos. including Met. Opera, San Francisco Opera (60 prodns.), N.Y.C. Opera, Lyric Opera of Chgo., Canadian Opera Co. (30 new prodns.), Houston Grand Opera, La Scala, Covent Garden, Verona Opera, Kirov Opera, Australian Opera, Vienna Staatsoper, Vienna Volksoper, Salzburg Festival, Amsterdam Opera, Holland Festival, Nice (France) Opera, Festival D'Orange, France, Verona Arena Festival; co-author: An Operatic Life, 1982. Decorated chevalier Order Arts and Letters (France), 1992. Mem. Am. Guild Mus. Artists, Can. Actors Equity Assn. Initiated above-stage projection of subtitles as a simultaneous translation of opera, 1983.

MANTEL, SAMUEL JOSEPH, JR., management educator, consultant; b. Indpls., Nov. 17, 1921; s. Samuel Joseph and Beatrice Smith (Talmas) M.; m. Dorothy Jean Friedland, June 28, 1950; children—Michael Lee, Samuel Joseph, III, Margaret Irene, Elizabeth Baer. A.B., Harvard U., 1948, M.P.A., 1950, Ph.D., 1952. Asst. prof. social sci. Ga. Inst. Tech., 1953-56; asst. prof., then assoc. prof. econs., dir. Econs.-in-Action program, Case Western Res. U., 1956-69; prof. mgmt. and quantitative analysis U. Cin., 1969-89, prof. emeritus quantitative analysis and ops. mgmt., 1989—, Joseph S. Stern prof. mgmt., 1973-89, emeritus, 1989, exec. dir. Grad. Ctr. for Mgmt. of Advanced Tech. and Innovation, 1987-89, emeritus, 1989; mgmt. cons., condr. mgmt. seminars. Author: Cases in Managerial Decisions, 1964, Project Management: A Managerial Perspective, 1985, 2d edit. 1989, 3d edit. 1995, Operations Management for Pharmacists: Strategy and Tactics, 1992; co-author several books; mem. editl. bd. Technovation; contbr. articles to profl. jours. Vice pres. Jewish Fedn. Cin., 1978-80; past pres., life mem. Cin. Hillel Found., Cleve. Hillel Found.; historian Rockdale Temple, 1969-77; mem. mgmt. and adminstrn. com. Anti-Defamation League, B'nai B'rith, 1976; trustee Jewish Hosp., Cin., 1975-84, Sarah Marvin Found. for Performing Arts, 1990—; mem. mgmt. adv. com. Cin. Police Dept., 1991-92. Maj. USMCR, 1942-46, 51-53. Decorated D.F.C. with 3 oak leaf clusters, Air medal with 11 oak leaf clusters; Econs.-in-Action fellow, 1955; fellow Inst. Policy Research, 1980; named Prof. of Year, Delta Sigma Pi, 1974. Mem. IEEE, Project Mgmt. Inst., Iota Epsilon, Beta Gamma Sigma. Home: 608 Flagstaff Dr Cincinnati OH 45215-2525

MANTELL, SUZANNE RUTH, editor; b. West Orange, N.J., Nov. 26, 1944; d. Milton A. and Florence B. M.; m. Peter Gray Friedman, 1985; 1 child, Erica Mantell Friedman. Student, U. Chgo., 1962; B.F.A., Pratt Inst., 1967. Formerly assoc. editor Harper's mag., N.Y.C., exec. editor, 1977-80; editor Harper's Bookletter, 1974-77, Learning Mag., 1980-81, Family Learning Mag., 1983-84; reader Book of the Month Club, 1985-87, 91—; editor Travel Bookstore Catalogue, Banana Republic, 1985-87; assoc. editor The N.Y. Observer, N.Y.C., 1987-91; acting Book News editor Pubs. Weekly, 1992-93, contbg. editor, 1993—; also lectr. mag. writing Stanford U., U. Calif. at Santa Cruz. Consulting editor Spelman Coll. Messenger, 1994—. Mem. PEN, Nat. Book Critics Circle. Home: 101 Warwick Pl South Pasadena CA 91030

MANTHEI, RICHARD DALE, lawyer, health care company executive; b. Olivia, Minn., Dec. 23, 1935; s. Alvin R. and Sidonia (Klatt) M.; m. Karen J. Peterson, Sept. 6, 1959 (dec. Mar. 1985); children: Steven, Jana, Kari, John, Rebecca; m. Lynn E. Graham, Aug. 9, 1986. B.S. in Pharmacy (Rexall award 1960), S.D. State U., 1960; J.D., U. Minn., 1967. Bar: Ind. 1967, Ill. 1970, D.C. 1987, U.S. Supreme Ct. 1987. Sales rep. Eli Lilly & Co., Indpls., 1962-64, atty., 1967-70; atty., then asst. corp. sec., dir. regulatory affairs Am. Hosp. Supply Corp., Evanston, Ill., 1970-79, corp. sec., dep. gen. counsel, 1979-85; assoc. gen. counsel Baxter Travenol Labs., Deerfield, Ill., 1986-87; ptnr. Burditt, Bowles & Radzius, Washington, 1987-90, McKenna & Cuneo, Washington, 1990-96; v.p. sci. affairs C.R. Bard, Inc., Murray Hill, N.J., 1996—. Author articles in field.; Editorial adv. staff: Med. Devices and Diagnostic Industry, 1979. Mem. bd. edn. Libertyville High Sch., 1984-87; mem. governing bd. Spl. Edn. Dist. of Lake County, Ill., 1985-87. Served with AUS, 1954-56. Mem. ABA, Health Industry Mfrs. Assn. (chmn. law sect. 1976), Health Industry Assn. (chmn. legal com. 1973), Am. Soc. Corp. Secs. (com. practices com. 1983-88, group pres. 1985-86, Chgo. regional group 1986-87), Ill. Bar Assn., Ind. Bar Assn., D.C. Bar Assn., Univ. Club (Evanston, Ill., bd. dirs. 1984-86), Hidden Creek Country Club (Reston, Va.), Fiddler's Elbow Country Club (Far Hills, N.J.). Home: 33 Sandalwood Dr Warren NJ 07059 Office: CR Bard Inc 730 Central Ave New Providence NJ 07974-1139

MANTHEY, FRANK ANTHONY, physician, director; b. N.Y.C., Dec. 2, 1933; s. Frank A.J. and Josephine (Roth) M.; m. Douglas Susan Falvey, Sept. 14 1958 (div. 1979, dec. 1989); children: Michael P., Susan M., Peter J.; m. Doris Jean Pulley, Oct. 11, 1979. BS, Fordham U., 1954; MD, SUNY, Syracuse, 1958. Diplomate Am. Bd. Anesthesiology, Am. Bd. Med. Examiners. Intern Upstate Med. Ctr., Syracuse, 1958-59; resident in anesthesiology Yale-New Haven Med. Ctr., 1962-64; physician Yale-New Haven Hosp., 1964-75; pvt. practice medicine Illmo, Mo., 1975-79; dir. Manthey Med. Clinic, Elkton, Ky., 1979—; clin. instr. anesthesiology Yale U. Med. Sch., New Haven, 1964-69, asst. clin. prof. anesthesiology, 1969-75; cons. Conn. Dept. Aeros., Hartford, 1969-70; sr. med. examiner Fed. Aviation Adminstrn., Illmo, 1975-79. Contbr. articles to profl. jours. Chmn. gen. works Little Folks Fair, Guilford, Conn., 1967-71; mem. Rep. Town Com., Guilford, 1969-75; chmn. Guilford Sch. Bldg. Com., 1973-75. Capt. USAF (M.C.), 1956-62. Mem. Ky. Med. Assn., Aerospace Med. Assn. (assoc. fellow 1973-75), Flying Physicians Assn. (v.p. NE chpt. 1973-75, v.p. nat. 1974-75, 79-80, bd. dirs. 1970-73, 75-78, bd. dirs. nat. 1975-78), Aircraft Owners and Pilots Assn., Mercedes Benz Club Am., Alpha Kappa Kappa. Avocations: philately, aviation, skiing, automobile mechanics and restoration, photography. Home: 105 Sunset Dr Elkton KY 42220-9257 Office: Manthey Family Practice Clinic 203 Allensville St PO Box 368 Elkton KY 42220

MANTHEY, THOMAS RICHARD, lawyer; b. St. Cloud, Minn., May 5, 1942; s. Richard Jesse and Dolores Theresa (Terhaar) M.; m. Janet S. Barth, Dec. 18, 1965; children: Molly, Andrew, Luke. BA cum laude, St. John's U., Collegeville, Minn., 1964; JD cum laude, Harvard U., 1967. Bar: Minn. 1967. Assoc. Dorsey & Whitney, Mpls., 1967-73, ptnr. real estate dept., 1974—, also mem. Indian and gaming law practice group, chmn. real estate workout practice group. Contbr. articles to profl. jours. Capt. U.S. Army, 1968-70. Mem. Minn. State Bar Assn. (real estate sect.), Hennepin County Bar Assn. (real estate sect.). Roman Catholic. Avocations: volleyball, golf, fishing. Home: 1834 Summit Ave Saint Paul MN 55105-1427 Office: Dorsey & Whitney 220 S 6th St Minneapolis MN 55402-4502

MANTIL, JOSEPH CHACKO, nuclear medicine physician, researcher; b. Kottayam, Kerala, India, Apr. 22, 1937; came to U.S., 1958; s. Chacko C. and Mary C. Manthuruthil; m. Joan J. Cunningham, June 18, 1966; children: Ann Marie, Lisa Susan. BS in Physics, Chemistry and Math. with distinction, Poona U., India, 1956; MS, U. Detroit, 1960; PhD, Ind. U., 1965; MS in Biological Scis., Wright State U., 1975; MD, U. Autonoma de Ciudad Juarez, Mex., 1977. Diplomate Am. Bd. Internal Medicine, Am. Bd. Nuclear Medicine; lic. physician, Ohio, Ind., Ky. Rsch. physicist Aerospace Rsch. Lab, Wright Patterson AFB, Ohio, 1964-75; chief resident, resident in internal medicine Good Samaritan Hosp., Dayton, Ohio, 1977-80; chief resident, resident in nuclear medicine Cin. Med. Ctr., 1980-82; assoc. dir., divsn. nuclear med. Kettering (Ohio) Med. Ctr., 1982-86, dir. dept. nuclear medicine/PET, 1986—; dir. Kettering-Scott Magnetic Resonance Lab., Kettering Med. Ctr. Wright State U. Sch. Medicine, Kettering, 1985—, clin. prof. medicine, chief divsn. nuclear medicine, dept. medicine, 1988—; served as session chmn., speaker, amd co-organizer for five internat. confs. Author: Radioactivity in Nuclear Spectroscopy Vol. I and II, 1972; contbr. 38 articles to profl. jours. Mem. ACP, Am. Physical Soc., Soc. Nuclear Medicine, Soc. Magnetic Resonance in Medicine, Soc. Magnetic Resonance Imaging. Achievements include research in proton and phosphorous NMR spectroscopy and glucose metabolism (using PET) in various types of dementia; use of carbon-13 NMR spectroscopy in the study of a saturated and unsaturated fatty acid composition of body fat in patients with heart disease, diabetes and other diseases; normal pressure hydrocephalus with NMR spectroscopy and radionuclide cisternography; general muscle metabolism study with phosphorous NMR spectroscopy and PET and in atrophy, steroid myopathy, and various muscle disorders; use of NMR spectroscopy (both proton and phosphorous) and positron emission tomography (measurement of glucose and protein metabolism) in the study of tumors and assessment of thier reponse to chemotherapy and radiation therapy; positron emission tomography in the study of myocardial viabilty; PET in the diagnosis of coronary artery disease; PET in seizure disorders; use of monoclonal antibody in the diagnosis of maglignant tumors. Home: 6040 Mad River Rd Dayton OH 45459-1508 Office: Kettering Med Ctr 3535 Southern Blvd Kettering OH 45429-1221

MANTLE, RAYMOND ALLAN, lawyer; b. Painesville, Ohio, Oct. 15, 1937; s. Junius Dow and Ada Louise (Stinchcomb) M.; m. Judith Ann LaGrange, Nov. 26, 1967; children: Amanda Lee, Rachel Ann, Leah Amy. BSBA summa cum laude, BA summa cum laude Kent State U., 1961; LLB cum laude, NYU, 1964. Bar: N.Y. 1964, N.J. 1976, U.S. Supreme Ct. Asst. counsel Gov. Nelson A. Rockefeller, N.Y., 1964-65; assoc. Paul Weiss Rifkind Wharton & Garrison, 1967-69; mem. firm Varet & Fink P.C. (formerly Milgrim Thomajan & Lee, P.C.), N.Y.C., 1969-95; ptnr. Piper & Marbury L.L.P., N.Y.C., 1995—; lectr. in computer law field. Contbg. author Doing Business in China. Served to capt. U.S. Army, 1965-67. Mem. N.Y. State Bar Assn., N.J. Bar Assn. Republican. Methodist. Office: Piper & Marbury LLP 1251 Avenue Of The Americas New York NY 10020-1104

MANTON, EDWIN ALFRED GRENVILLE, insurance company executive; b. Earls Colne, Essex, Eng., Jan. 22, 1909; came to U.S., 1933; s. John Horace and Emily Clara (Denton) M.; m. Florence V. Brewer, Feb. 1, 1936; 1 child, Diana H. Manton Morton. Student, London (Eng.) U., 1925-27, N.Y. Ins. Soc., 1933-35; DHL (hon.), Coll. of Ins., 1994. With B.W. Noble Ltd., Paris, 1927-33; casualty underwriter Am. Internat. Underwriters Corp., N.Y.C., 1933-37, sec., 1937-38, v.p., 1938-42, pres., 1942-69, chmn., 1969-75; sr. advisor Am. Internat. Group, Inc.; hon. dir. C.V. Starr & Co., Inc. Trustee St. Luke's-Roosevelt Hosp., N.Y.C. Mem. Salmagundi Club, City Midday Drug and Chem. Club, Mendelssohn Glee Club, Williams Club, St. George's Soc. Episcopalian. Office: Am Internat Group Inc 70 Pine St New York NY 10270-0002

MANTON, THOMAS JOSEPH, congressman; b. N.Y.C., Nov. 3, 1932; m. Diane Schley; children: Cathy, Tom, John, Jeanne. BBA, St. John's U., 1958, LLB, 1962. Mem. N.Y.C. Police Dept., 1955-60; mktg. rep. IBM, 1960-64; practice law, 1964-84; mem. 99th-105th Congresses from 9th (now 7th) N.Y. Dist., Washington, 1984—; mem. commerce com.; ranking mem. subcom. fin. and hazardous materials, mem. subcom. telecomms., trade and consumer protection. Mem. N.Y.C. Council, 1970-84. Served with USMC, 1951-53. Democrat. Office: US Ho of Reps 2235 Rayburn HOB Washington DC 20515

MANTONYA, JOHN BUTCHER, lawyer; b. Columbus, Ohio, May 26, 1922; s. Elroy Letts and Blanche (Butcher) M.; m. Mary E. Reynolds, June 14, 1947 (dec. 1987); children: Elizabeth Claire, Mary Kay, Lee Ann; m. Carole L. Lugar, Sept. 28, 1989. A.B. cum laude, Washington and Jefferson Coll., 1943; postgrad., U. Mich. Law Sch., 1946-47; J.D., Ohio State U., 1949. Bar: Ohio 1949. Assoc. A.S. Mitchell (Atty.), Newark, Ohio, 1949-50, C.D. Lindrooth, Newark, 1950-57; partner firm Lindrooth & Mantonya, Newark, 1957-74; firm John B. Mantonya, 1974-81, John B. Mantonya, L.P.A., 1981—. Mem. North Fork Local Bd. Edn., 1962-69; adv. com. Salvation Army, Licking County, 1965—, Mayor of, Utica, Ohio, 1953-59. Served with AUS, 1943-45. Mem. Am. Bar Assn., Ohio Bar Assn., Licking County Bar Assn. (pres. 1967), Phi Delta Phi, Beta Theta Pi. Home: 11055 Reynolds Rd Utica OH 43080-9549 Office: 3 N 3rd St Newark OH 43055-5506

MANTOVANI, JOHN FRANCIS, neurologist, educator; b. St. Louis, Jan. 17, 1949; s. John F. and Marinelle (Pouyer) M.; m. Janis M. Barnes, July 8, 1972; children: John R. and Ann Marie. BA cum laude, U. Evansville, 1971; MD, U. Mo., 1974. Diplomate Am. Bd. Pediatrics, Am. Bd. Psychiatry and Neurology. Resident pediatrics, neurology, fellow child neurology Washington U. & St. Louis Childrens Hosp., 1974-79; practitioner adult & child neurology Dean Clinic, Madison, Wis., 1979-84; dir. child neurology, vice chmn. dept. pediatrics St. John's Mercy Med. Ctr., St. Louis, 1984—; clin. asst. prof. neurology U. Wis., Madison, 1980-84; instr. clin. pediatrics and neurology Washington U., St. Louis, 1985-95, asst. prof. clin. pediatrics. and neurology, 1995—. Contbr. articles to profl. jours. Mem. AMA, Alpha Omega Alpha; fellow Am. Acad. Pediatrics, Am. Acad. Cerebral Palsy and Developmental Medicine (com. mem. 1985-87, 1989-91, bd. dirs. 1994-96, v.p. 1997—), Am. Acad. Neurology, Child Neurology Soc. Office: Ste 5009 621 S New Ballas Rd Saint Louis MO 63141-8200

MANTSCH, HENRY HORST, chemistry educator; b. Mediasch, Transylvania, Romania, July 30, 1935; emigrated to Can., 1968; s. Heinrich Johann and Olga Augusta (Gondosch) M.; m. Amy Emilia Kory, Nov. 2, 1959; children: Monica, Marietta. B.Sc., U. Cluj, Transylvania, 1958, Ph.D., 1964. Rsch. scientist Romanian Acad. Sci., Cluj, 1958-65, Tech. U. Munich, Germany, 1966-68; with NRC, Ottawa, Can., 1968-72; prof. biochemistry U. Cluj, 1973-74, Liebig U., Giessen, Germany, 1975-76; head molecular spectroscopy NRC, Ottawa, 1977—; mem. Can. Rsch. Coun., Ottawa, 1977-91, Winnipeg, Can., 1992—; adj. prof. Carleton U., Ottawa, 1978-90, U. Ottawa, 1990-92, U. Manitoba, Winnipeg, 1992—. Contbr. articles to profl. jours.; patentee in field. Recipient medal Ministry of Edn., Bucharest, 1972; recipient Humboldt Found. award and medal Bonn, 1980; Chem. Inst. Can. fellow, 1979; Royal Soc. Can. fellow, 1982; recipient Herzberg award, 1984. Mem. Am. Biophys. Soc., Soc. Applied Spectroscopy, Chem. Inst. Can. (chmn. biol. chem. div. 1980-81), Can. Spectroscopy Soc. (mem. nat. exec. com. 1981-90). Home: 222 W Taylor Blvd, Winnipeg, MB Canada R3P 2J5 Office: NRC Can, 435 Ellice Ave, Winnipeg, MB Canada R3B 1Y6

MANTY, BRIAN ALAN, high technology company executive; b. Quincy, Mass., Aug. 2, 1944; s. Allan E. and Ellen Manty; m. Barbara Adamson, Mar. 13, 1965; children: George, Mark. BS in Chemistry, Fla. State U., 1966; MS in Electrochemistry, Fla. Atlantic U., 1969; MBA, Nova U., 1989. Chemist Pratt & Whitney Aircraft Co., West Palm Beach, Fla., 1966-71; group leader, surface finishing Pratt & Whitney Aircraft Co., West Palm Beach, 1971-77, supr. chemistry and machining, 1976-93, program mgr. govt. contracts, 1975-93; tech. dir. Concurrent Techs., Johnstown, Pa., 1993—; adj. instr. Palm Beach C.C., 1989-93; cons. in field. Patentee in field. Mem. Am. Chem. Soc., Am. Electroplaters and Surface Finishers Soc. (dir. 1991-95, pres. 1995-96), Soc. Mfg. Engrs., Robotics Internat. (cert. mfg. engr.), Nat. Assn. Corrosion Engrs. (cert. corrosion specialist), Am. Metals Soc., Air Force Assn. Home: 119 Luna Ln Johnstown PA 15904-3070 Office: 1450 Scalp Ave Johnstown PA 15904-3374

MANTYLA, KAREN, sales executive; b. Bronx, N.Y., Dec. 31, 1944; d. Milton and Sylvia (Diamond) Fischer; m. John A Mantyla, May 30, 1970 (div. 1980); 1 child, Michael Alan. Student, Rockland Community Coll., Suffern, N.Y., 1962, NYU, 1967, Mercer U., 1981. Mktg. coordinator Credit Bur., Inc., Miami, Fla., 1973-79; dist. mgr. The Research Inst. Am., N.Y.C., 1979-80, regional dir., 1980-85, field sales mgr., 1985-86, nat. sales mgr., 1986-87; dir. mktg. TempsAmerica, N.Y.C., 1987-88; nat. accounts mgr. The Rsch. Inst. Am., N.Y.C., 1989; v.p. sales Bur. Bus. Practice/Paramount Comm., Inc., Waterford, Conn., 1989-93; pres. Quiet Power, Inc., Washington, 1993—. Author: Consultative Sales Power, 1995; co-author: Distance Learning: A Step-By-Step Guide for Trainers, 1997. Mem. ASTD, Sales and Mktg. Execs. (past bd. dirs. N.Y. chpt., v.p. Ft. Lauderdale chpt. 1979), U.S. Distance Learning Assn., Nat. Assn. Women Bus. Owners, U.S. C. of C., Women Entrepreneurs. Avocations: antiques, tennis, writing, swimming. Home: 5449 Grove Ridge Way Rockville MD 20852-4648 Office: Quiet Power Inc 655 15th St NW Ste 300 Washington DC 20005-5701

MANTZ, ARLAN W., physics educator; b. Slatington, Pa., July 25, 1940; s. Harold H. and Irene A. (Herber) M.; m. Barbara Dae Mantz, Dec. 28, 1963; 1 child, Yves Andre. BA, Catawba Coll., 1962; MSc, Ohio State U., 1966, PhD, 1969. Sr. scientist Air Force Avionics Lab., Ohio, 1966-73; postdoctoral fellow Labo Aime Cotton, Orsay, France, 1973-74; sr. scientist Digilab, Inc., Cambridge, Mass., 1974-76; engrng. mgr. Laser Analytics Inc., Bedford, Mass., 1976-79, pres., gen. mgr., 1979-89; assoc. prof. Franklin and Marshall Coll., Lancaster, Pa., 1990-95; Oakes Ames prof. physics Conn. Coll., New London, 1995—. Editl. adv. bd. Spectrochemica Acta, 1990, revs. editor, 1995. Mem. AAAS, Optical Soc. of Am., Am. Chem. Soc., Am. Phys. Soc., N.Y. Acad. Sci. Avocation: sailing. Home: 145 Wamphassuc Pt Rd Stonington CT 06378

MANUEL, RALPH NIXON, private school executive; b. Frederick, Md., Apr. 21, 1936; s. Ralph Walter and Frances Rebecca (Nixon) M.; m. Sarah Jane Warner, July 22, 1960; children: Mark, David, Stephen, Bradley. A.B., Dartmouth Coll., 1958; M.Ed., Boston U., 1967; Ph.D., U. Ill., 1971. Assoc. dean Dartmouth Coll., Hanover, N.H., 1971-72, dean of freshmen, 1972-75, dean, 1975-82; pres. Culver (Ind.) Acad. and Culver Edn. Found., 1982—. Bd. dirs. Ind. Sch. Cen. States, 1986—, chair, 1993-95. NDEA fellow, 1968-69. Mem. Assn. Mil. Colls. and Schs. of U.S. (pres., bd. dirs.), Nat. Assn. Ind. Schs. (bd. dirs. 1995—). Office: Culver Acads 1300 Academy Rd Culver IN 46511-1234

MANUEL, VIVIAN, public relations company executive; b. Queens County, N.Y., May 6, 1941; d. George Thomas and Vivian (Anderson) M. BA, Wells Coll., Aurora, N.Y., 1963; MA, U. Wyo.-Laramie, 1965. Mgmt. analyst Dept. Navy, 1966-68; account supr. Gen. Electric Co., N.Y.C., 1968-72, corp. rep. bus. and fin., 1972-76; dir. corp. comm. Standard Brands Co., N.Y.C., 1976-78; pvt. cons., N.Y.C., 1978-80; pres. V M Comm. Inc., N.Y.C., 1980—. Mem. com. Girls Club N.Y., 1983-84; trustee Wells Coll., 1983-90; mem. adv. bd. Glenholme Sch., 1991-92. Mem. AAUW, N.Y. Women in Comm. (bd. v.p. 1983-85, chair Matrix awards 1985), Women Execs. in Pub. Rels. (bd. dirs. 1985-88), Women's Econ. Roundtable, Friend N.Y.C. Commn. on Status of Women. Office: 400 Hayes Ave Helena MT 59601-6149

MANULIS, MARTIN, film producer; b. N.Y.C., May 30, 1915; s. Abraham and Anne (Silverstein) M.; m. Katharine Bard, June 14, 1939; children: Laurie, Karen, John Bard. BA, Columbia, 1935. Mng. dir. Bahamas Playhouse, 1951-52; exec. head TV prodn. Twentieth Century Fox, 1958-60, ind. motion picture producer, 1960—; artistic dir. Ahmanson Theatre, Music Ctr., Los Angeles, 1987-89; dir. Am. Film Inst. West, 1974-76. Producer, dir. (with John C. Wilson) Broadway; dir. Private Lives, Laura, Made in Heaven, The Show Off, Westport Country Playhouse, 1946-50; (TV) Suspense, Studio One, Best of Broadway, Climax, Playhouse 90, 1952-58, Requiem for a Heavyweight (Emmy award Best Show 1956-57), The Commedian (Emmy Best Show 1957-58); producer: (films) Dear Heart, Days of Wine and Roses, Luv and Duffy; producer TV miniseries Chiefs, James Michener's Space, Grass Roots. Served as lt. USNR, 1942-45. Recipient spl. Svc. award Crusade for Freedom, 1954, Look TV award for Best Dramatic Series, 1955, 56, 57, eleven TV Emmy awards Nat. Acad. TV Arts and Scis., 1956, 57; named to Producers Guild of Am. Hall of Fame for Studio One and Playhouse 90, 1992. Office: Martin Manulis Prodns Ltd PO Box 818 Beverly Hills CA 90213-0818

MANUTA, DAVID MARK, research chemist; b. Bklyn., June 10, 1957; s. Gerald and Vivian Bernice (Chartoff) M.; m. Ruth Pauline Krog, Mar. 27, 1988 (dec. Dec. 1993). BS in Chemistry, SUNY, Oneonta, 1979; PhD in Chemistry, SUNY, Binghamton, 1985. Lab. tech. Scientific Process & Rsch., Somerset, N.J., 1980-81; from tchg. asst. to postdoctoral fellow SUNY, Binghamton, 1981-86; asst. prof. Upper Iowa U., Fayette, 1986-88; asst. prof. II Shawnee State U., Portsmouth, Ohio, 1989-90; rsch. staff Lockheed Martin Utility Svcs., Piketon, Ohio, 1990—; tchr. Christ the King Regional H.S., N.Y.C., 1986; instr. Stanley Kaplan Exam. Prep. Svcs., Garden City, N.Y., 1986; cons. City of Portsmouth, 1989; mem. strategic planning com. Ohio Acad. Sci., 1996. Bd. dirs. Big Bros./Big Sisters of South Ctrl. Ohio, 1996; pres. Waverly Heights Crime Watch, 1995; treas. Pike County Humane Soc., Ohio, 1997; bd. mem. Portsmouth employees chpt. Nat. Mgmt. Assn., 1997. Served in U.S. Navy, 1978-79. IBM Corp. grad. fellow, 1984-85. Fellow Am. Inst. of Chemistry; mem. AAAS, ASTM, Am. Chem. Soc. Avocations: chess, reading, running, bicycling, traveling. Home: 431 Gordon Ave Waverly OH 45690-1208 Office: Lockheed Martin Utility Svc 3930 US Rte 23 S PO Box 628 M/S 2220 Piketon OH 45661-0628

MANVEL, ALLEN DAILEY, fiscal economist; b. Spokane, Wash., June 29, 1912; s. Arthur Orlando and Agnes Louise (Johnson) M.; m. Helen Louise de Werthern, Oct. 9, 1937; children: Sarah Katherine, Bennet. AB in Econs., Occidental Coll., 1934; postgrad., U. Chgo., 1935-36, Harvard U., 1939-40; DSc (hon.), Ohio State U., 1976. Rsch. assoc. Ill. Dept. Fin., Springfield, 1936-41; rsch. dir. Ill. Agrl. Assn., Chgo., 1941-42; state budget supr. Ill. Dept. Fin., Springfield, 1942-43; adminstrv. analyst U.S. Bur. Budget, Washington, 1943-46; chief govts. div. U.S. Bur. Census, Washington, 1946-67; assoc. dir. Nat. Com. on Urban Problems, Washington, 1967-68; asst. dir. Adv. Com. on Intergovt. Rels., Washington, 1968-71; rsch. asst., sr. fellow The Brookings Instn., Washington, 1972-75; econ. cons. Tax Analysts, Inc., Arlington, Va., from 1976; now ret.; lectr. in pub. adminstrn. George Washington U., Washington, 1946-48; cons. Fiscal Div. UN, N.Y.C., 1953, N.Y.C. Commn. on Statis. Programs, 1954-55. Author: (book) Paying for Civilized Society, 1986; co-author: (books) Measuring Fiscal Capacity and Effort, 1971, Monitoring Revenue Sharing, 1975; contbr. numerous articles to profl. jours. Recipient Louis Brownlow award, Nat. Mcpl. League, 1966.

Mem. Nat. Tax Assn. (past. bd. dirs.), Nat. Acad. Pub. Administrn., Cosmos Club, Washington. Democrat. Unitarian. Avocations: reading, travel. Home and Office: 10450 Lottsford Rd Unit 3009 Mitchellville MD 20721

MANVILLE, STEWART ROEBLING, archivist; b. White Plains, N.Y., Jan. 15, 1927; s. Leo and Margaret (Roebling) M.; m. Ella V. Grainger, Jan. 19, 1972 (dec.). Student U. Wyo., 1944-46; BS, Columbia U., 1962. Various office positions, N.Y.C., 1947-51, 56-58; asst. stage dir. several European opera houses, 1951-55; editor Jas. T. White & Co., N.Y.C., 1959-63; archivist, curator Percy Grainger Library, White Plains, N.Y., 1963—. Mem. SAR, Hist. House Assn. Am., Nat. Trust Hist. Preservation, Victorian Soc. in Am. (past dir. N.Y. chpt.), Société des Antiquaires de Picardie, Soc. Archtl. Historians, Brit. Music Soc., Westchester County Hist. Soc., Titanic Hist. Soc., White Plains Battle Monument Com., Appalachian Trail Conf., Westchester Trails Assn. (past dir.), St. Nicholas Soc. N.Y., Quaker. Author: The Manville/Manvel Families in America; contbr. articles and revs. on music to mags. and newspapers. Office: 7 Cromwell Pl White Plains NY 10601-5005

MANWILL, DIANE RACHEL, counselor; b. Palo Alto, Calif., Sept. 14, 1959; d. Harry and Geraldine Ann (Caliri) Copelan; m. Walter Blair Manwill, Aug. 4, 1979; 1 child, Rachel Anna. BS summa cum laude, U. Md., 1987; MEd, Boston U., 1989. Lic. ind. adoption svcs. investigator; lic. profl. clin. counselor, S.C., N.Mex.; cert. mediator; diplomate Acad. Forensic Counseling. Mental health counselor U. Cambridge (Eng.) Counseling Clinic, 1988-89; program dir. IV Jud Dist Casa Program, Boise, Idaho, 1990-92; substance abuse instr. Boise Sch. Dist., 1990-91; coll. lectr. Chapman U., Cannon AFB, N.Mex., 1992-94; exec. dir. IX Jud. Dist. Family & Children's Ct. Svcs., Clovis, N.Mex., 1992—, counselor, play therapist, 1994—; pvt. divorce mediator Columbia, S.C., 1994—; cons., clin. supr. Oasis-Child's Safe House, Clovis, 1992-93; clin. supr. Youth Opportunities Unltd., Clovis, 1994-95; chief mental health counselor, clinic dir. Lexington County Cmty. Mental Health Ctr., West Columbia, S.C., 1996—. Co-author: Idaho State Gal Standards, 1992; compiler: (workbook) Custody Education Workshop Manual, 1994; author: A Practical Guide to Family Mediation, (video tng.) Introduction to Mediation, How to Mediate, Using Mediation to Deal With Difficult Former Spouses, Using Mediation to Develop Equitable Plans in Special Cases. Mem. Families in Need Svcs. Team, Clovis, 1994-96; pres. bd. Idaho Case Assn., Boise, 1990-91; legis. liaison for children's issues Gali Casa, Boise, 1992; treas. bd. Cmty. Ptnrs., Inc., 1994—. Recipient Cambridge internship Boston U., 1988, Liberty Bell awards 4th Dist. Bar Assn., Boise, 1992, 9th Dist. Bar Assn., Clovis, N.Mex., 1994. Mem. ACA, Assn. Family and Conciliation Cts., Am. Mental Health Counselors Assn., Acad. Family Mediators, Phi Kappa Phi. Democrat. Avocations: skiing, hiking, gardening. Home: 2801 Bratton St Columbia SC 29205

MANWORREN, DONALD B., church administrator; b. Galesburg, Ill., Jan. 25, 1937; m. Elaine K. Jensen, June 15, 1957; children: Julia, Susan, John. BA, Drake U., 1957, BD, 1961, DD (hon.), 1981; STM, Yale U., 1962; postgrad., Sch. Theology, Claremont, Calif., 1977, Assumption Coll., 1980. Pastor 1st Christian Ch., Keota, Iowa, 1962-64, Convenant Christian Ch., Urbandale, Iowa, 1965-71, Ctrl. Christian Ch., Waterloo, Iowa, 1971-77; exec. coord. Iowa Inter-Ch. Forum, Des Moines, 1977-85; dep. gen. min., pres. Christian Ch. (Disciples of Christ) U.S. and Can., 1986—; mem. gen. bd. Christian Ch. (Disciples of Christ) U.S. and Can., 1975-83, mem. adminstrv. com., 1975-81, mem. regional commn. witness and Soc., 1979-81, mem. Upper Midwest regional bd., parliamentarian, 1981-85; mem. Disciples Ecumenical Consultative Coun., Jamaica, 1979; bd. dirs. Coun. Christian Unity, 1979-85. Commr. Iowa Comm. Aging, 1976-80; bd. dirs. Ramsey Meml. Home, Des Moines, 1975-85; trustee Christian Theol. Sem., Indpls., 1976-87, 89—. Rsch. fellow Yale U., 1983. Mem. NCCC-USA (chmn. commn. regional and local ecumenism 1985-87), Nat. Coun. Chs. (mem. governing bd. 1979-87, mem. study panel ecumenical commitment and purposes 1979-87), Phi Beta Kappa. Home: 12571 Spring Violet Pl Carmel IN 46033 Office: PO Box 1986 Indianapolis IN 46206-1986

MANY, ROBERT TODD, telecommunications executive; b. Oneonta, N.Y., Dec. 3, 1958; s. Wesley Allen and Margaret Louise (Ames) M.; m. Marina Ann Teglia, June 20, 1982; children: Michael Wesley, Julie Ann, Kristine Marie. BS, No. Ill. U., 1980, MBA, 1990. Tchr. Riverside-Brookfield High Sch., Riverside, Ill., 1980-84; sr. account mgr. sales NCR Corp., Dayton, Ohio, 1984-86; sales mgmt. staff MCI, Chgo., 1986-90; dir. sales Teradyne, Chgo., 1990-93, nat. sales mgr., 1994-95, dir. N.Am. sales, 1995-96; bus. devel. dir. Andersen Cons., Chgo., 1996—. Mem. Am. Mgmt. Assn., Beta Gamma Sigma. Avocations: sports, books, travel, wine, cooking. Home: 483 Quail Dr Naperville IL 60565-4159

MANZ, BETTY ANN, nurse administrator; b. Paterson, N.J., Nov. 30, 1935; d. James Albert and Elsie (Basse) Brown; diploma Newark Beth Israel Hosp. Sch. Nursing, 1955; BSN, Seton Hall U., 1964; m. Roger A. Johnson, Feb. 1988; children: Laura, Richard, Garry. Staff nurse oper. room Newark Beth Israel Hosp., 1955-56, recovery room head nurse, 1956-57, oper. room head nurse, 1957-58, supr. oper. room, 1958-60; substitute tchr. pub. schs. Harding Twp., 1966-70; charge nurse St. Barnabas Med. Ctr., Livingston, N.J., 1965-70, head nurse emergency room, 1970-72; oper. room supr. St. Clares Hosp., Denville, N.J., 1972-77; asst. dir. for oper. rooms and post anesthesia rooms Newark Beth Israel Med. Ctr., 1977-82; asst. dir. nursing oper. room care program Thomas Jefferson U. Hosp., Phila., 1982-84; asst. dir./assoc. nursing dir. oper. room, anesthesia ICU, ambulatory surgery Univ. Hosp., SUNY-Stony Brook, 1984-87 dir. oper. room/post anestesia care ambulatory surgery Med. Ctr. Del., Wilmington and Christiana, Del., 1987-88; practice mgr. Del. Orthopaedic Ctr., Wilmington, 1989-96; sr. cons. and lectr. AIME, New Haven, 1996—; faculty mem. postgrad. course in microsurgy for Am. Coll. Obstetricians and Gynecologists, Newark, 1982; profl. cons. oper. room products, also health cons. Henry E. Wessel Assocs., Moraga, Calif.; profl. tech. cons., lectr. Surgicot, Inc., Smithtown, N.Y. Dep. dir. Harding Twp. CD, 1967-75. Recipient Service award Essex County Med. Soc., 1979. Mem. AAMI, MGMA, Nat. Assn. Orthopaedic Nurses, Assn. Oper. Room Nurses, Am. Soc. Post Anesthesia Nurses, Del. Med. Group Mgmt. Assn. (sec.), Bones Soc. Orthopedic Mgrs., Newark Beth Israel Hosp. Nursing Alumnae Assn., Seton Hall U. Alumnae Assn., Harding Twp. Civic Assn., Am. Field Svc., Colonial States Knitters Guild (pres.). Republican. Club: Mt. Kemble Lake Community. Editor operating room sect. SCORE mag. Home & Office: 2620 Lamper Ln Wilmington DE 19808-3808

MANZ, CHARLES C., management educator. Prof. mgmt. Ariz. State U., Tempe; Nirenberg prof. bus. leadership U. Mass., 1997—. Author: The Art of Self Leadership: Achieving Personal Effectiveness in Your Life and Work, 1983, Mastering Self-Leadership: Empowering Yourself for Personal Excellence, 1992; co-author: Superleadership, 1990, Business Without Bosses: How Self-Managing Teams are Building High-Performance Companies, 1993, Company of Heroes: Unleashing the Power of Self-Leadership, 1996, For Team Members Only, 1997. Office: Ariz State U Dept Mgmt Tempe AZ 85287

MANZ, JOHANNES JAKOB, Swiss diplomat; b. Zurich, Switzerland, Dec. 15, 1938; s. Jakob J. and Margaret (Ruegg) M.; m. Marie-Antoinette Kunz, May 26, 1966; children: Alexander Cyril, Isabel Carmela. Student, Oreg. State U., 1958-59; LLD, U. Zurich, 1969. Sec. Mission of Switzerland, N.Y.C., 1971-75; counselor Swiss Embassy, Vienna, Austria, 1975-81; min., dep. head mission Mission of Switzerland, Geneva, 1981-84; amb., chief protocol Swiss Confedn., Bern, 1984-88; amb., dir. adminstrn. and pers. Swiss Dept. for Fgn. Affairs, Bern, 1988-91; under sec. gen., spl. rep. to sec. gen. for Western Sahara, UN, N.Y.C., 1990-91; amb., head of mission, permanent observer to UN, Mission of Switzerland, N.Y.C., 1992—. Contbg. author: Manual of Swiss Foreign Policy, 1991. Pres. Platform for Young Citizens, Zollikon, Switzerland, 1967-68. Mem. Delta Upsilon (hon. Oreg. State U. chpt.). Avocations: cross-country skiing, golf, swimming, classical music. Office: Mission of Switzerland 757 3rd Ave Fl 21 New York NY 10017-2013

MANZO, DAVID WILLIAM, human services administrator; b. Waterbury, Conn., Apr. 16, 1954; s. Louis G. and Elaine (Harlamon) M.; m. Noreen S. MacEvoy, Dec. 13, 1980; 1 child, Louis. BA summa cum laude, Boston Coll., 1977; MEd, Harvard U., 1980. Co-dir. Haley House Inc., Boston, 1977-80; cons. Boston Basics, Boston, 1980-81, program coord., 1981-82; lectr. Boston Coll., 1980—; asst. exec. dir. COMPASS, Boston, 1982-84, exec. dir., 1984—; bd. dirs. Pine St. Inn, Boston, 1988—, Mass. Assn. Approved Pvt. Schs., 1985—; bd. dirs., pres. Haley House, Inc., 1980-91. Bd. dirs. Victory House, 1981-87, Greater Boston Assn. Approved Pvt. Schs., 1985-88. Recipient William J. Kenneally award Boston Coll., 1990, Order of Cross and Crown, 1977, Award of Excellence in Pub. Svc., 1993; named Boston Neighborhood Superstar, 1997. Avocations: coaching Little League baseball. Office: COMPASS 26 Sunnyside St Jamaica Plain MA 02130-1215

MANZO, SALVATORE EDWARD, retired business developer; b. Bklyn., Oct. 23, 1917; s. Salvatore and Mary (Sireci) M.; B.S., U.S. Mil. Acad., 1939; m. Flournoy Davis, Mar. 11, 1960; children: Janeen, John, Joanne, Molly. Commd. 2d lt. USAF, 1939, advanced through grades to col., 1944, ret., 1962; v.p. C.H. Leavell & Co., El Paso, 1962-65; exec. dir. Met. Airlines Com., N.Y.C., 1965-67; dir. aviation City of Houston, 1967-69; pres. Trans-East Air Inc., Bangor, Maine, 1969-70; aviation mgmt. cons., Bangor, 1970-72, Sao Paulo, Brazil, 1972-74; exec. asst. to pres. Hidroservice, Sao Paulo, 1974-77; assoc. Charter Fin. Group, Inc., Houston, 1977-79; dir. exec. devel. Jesse H. Jones Grad. Sch. Adminstrn., Rice U., Houston, 1979-85, asst. dean for exec. devel., 1985-89; pres., bd. dirs. Manzo Devel. Co., 1969-90; 1st Tex. Venture Capital Corp., 1983-89; dir. Headlines U.S.A., Houston, 1987-91; ind. gen. partner Equus Capital Ptnrs., Ltd. 1989—; pres. El Paso Indsl. Devel. Corp., 1965; dir. Bus. Devel. and Financing Greater Houston Partnership's Econ. Devel. Div., 1989-93; ret., 1993. Vestryman Christ Ch. Cathedral, Houston, 1979-81. Decorated Silver Star, Legion of Merit, D.F.C. (2), Soldier's medal, Air medal (5), Commendation medal (2); Croix de Guerre with palm (France); recipient Entrepreneur of Yr. award Arthur Young and Venture Mag., 1988. Mem. Houston C. of C., El Paso C. of C. (pres. 1965). Republican. Episcopalian. Author: (with Edward E. Williams) Business Planning for the Entrepreneur: How to Write and Execute a Business Plan, 1983. Home: 610 Keswick Ct Granite Bay CA 95746-7156

MANZULLO, DONALD A, congressman, lawyer; b. Rockford, Ill., 1944; s. Frank A. Sr. and Kathryn M.; m. Freda Teslik; children: Neil, Noel, Katie. BA in Polit. Sci./Internat. Rels., American U., 1967; JD, Marquette U. Law Sch. Atty., 1970—; mem. 103th Congress from 16th Ill. Dist., 1993—; mem. House Com. on Internat. Rels., subcom. internat. econ. policy and trade, subcom. on Asia and the Pacific, House Com. on small bus., chmn. on subcom. on tax, fin. and exports, Banking Com. and its domestic andinternat. monetary policy subcom. Mem. No. Ill. Alliance for Arts, Friends of Severson Dells, Citizens Against Govt. Waste, Rep. Nat. Com. Recipient George Washington honor medal for excellence in pub. comm. Freedoms Found., Valley Forge, Pa., 1991. Mem. ABA, Ill. Bar Assn., Ogle County Bar Assn. (pres. 1971, 73), Nat. Legal Found., Acad. Polit. Sci., Ill. Press Assn., Ill. C. of C., Oregon City C. of C., Nat. Land Inst., Nat. Fedn. Ind. Bus., Ogle County Hist. Soc., Aircraft Owners and Pilots Assn., Ogle County Pilots Assn., Ill. Farm Bur., Ogle County Farm Bur. Office: US Ho of Reps 409 Cannon Bldg Ofc Bld Washington DC 20515-1316

MAPEL, WILLIAM MARLEN RAINES, retired banking executive; b. Maryville, Mo., Sept. 17, 1931; s. William and Evelyn (Raines) M.; m. Gail Manchee, June 21, 1958; children: Daniel B., Susan L., Stephen W. B.A., Yale U., 1953. Indsl. relations asst. Union Carbide Corp., N.Y.C., 1953-57; with Citibank (N.A.), N.Y.C., 1957-88; asst. cashier Citibank (N.A.), 1959-62, asst. v.p., 1962-64, v.p., 1964-69, sr. v.p., 1969-88; chmn. Merc. and Gen. Reins. Co. Am.; bd. dirs. Merc. & Gen. Life Reassurance Co. Am., Brundage, Story & Rose Investment Trust, Churchill Ptnrs., Galey & Lord, NSC Corp., U.S. Life Income Fund, Inc., Atlantic Salmon Fedn., Que.-Labrador Found. Mem. U.S. Srs. Golf Assn., Woodway Country Club, Anglers Club, Pine Valley Golf Club, Links, Wolf's Head, Delta Kappa Epsilon. Home: 18 Stephanie Ln Darien CT 06820-2723

MAPES, GLYNN DEMPSEY, newspaper editor; b. N.Y.C., July 15, 1939; s. John George and Dorothy (Glynn) M.; m. Elizabeth Adlum, Apr. 13, 1963; children—Timothy Glynn, Susannah Glynn. B.A., Williams Coll., 1961. Reporter Wall St. Jour., San Francisco, 1965-67; bur. chief Wall St. Jour., Phila., 1967-70; fgn. editor Wall St. Jour., N.Y.C., 1970-71, bur. chief, 1971-75, Page One editor, 1975-88, Reports editor, 1988-89; bur. chief Wall St. Jour., London, 1989-93; money and investing editor Wall St. Jour., N.Y.C., 1993—. Served to lt. (j.g.) USN, 1961-65. Democrat. Club: Collegiate Chorale, London Concert Choir. Home: 570 1st St Brooklyn NY 11215-2353 Office: Wall St Jour 200 Liberty St New York NY 10281-1003

MAPES, JEFFREY ROBERT, journalist; b. San Francisco, Nov. 21, 1954; s. James Robert and Phyllis June (Bloemker) M.; m. Karen Jane Minkel, Aug. 20, 1978; children: Katharine, James. BA, San Jose State U., 1976. Reporter Napa (Calif.) Register, 1976-79; Washington corr. Scripps League Newspapers, 1979-83; reporter The Oregonian, Portland, 1984-87, chief polit. reporter, 1987—. Office: The Oregonian 1320 SW Broadway Portland OR 97201-3411

MAPLES, WILLIAM ROSS, anthropology educator, consultant; b. Dallas, Aug. 7, 1937; s. William Hunter and Agnes Ross (Bliss) M.; m. Margaret Jane Kelley, Dec. 20, 1958; children: Lisa Linda, Cynthia Lynn. BA, U. Tex., 1959, MA, 1962, PhD, 1967. Diplomate Am. Bd. Forensic Anthropology. With Darajani (Kenya East Africa) Primate Rsch. Sta., 1962-63; teaching asst. U. Tex., Austin, 1963-64; mgr. S.W. Primate Rsch. Ctr., Nairobi, Kenya, East Africa, 1964-66; asst. prof. Western Mich. U., Kalamazoo, 1966-68; from asst. prof. to prof. anthropology U. Fla., Gainesville, 1968—; with Fla. Mus. Natural History, Gainesville, 1972-78, chmn. dept. social scis., 1973-87, curator in charge human indentificaion lab., 1986—; Disting. Svc. prof. Fla. Mus. Natural History, 1994-96; disting. svc. prof. anthropology U. Fla., Gainesville, 1996—; cons. Armed Forces Graves Registration Office, Honolulu, 1986—, Armed Forces Inst. Pathology, 1989, N.Y. State Police Forensic Unit, Albany, 1987—; cons. in residence U.S. Army Ctrl. Identification Lab., Honolulu, 1986-87; post mortem examination in hist. cases include: Don Francisco Pizarro, Lima, Peru, The Elephant Man, Joseph Merrick, London, Pres. Zachary Taylor, Louisville, Czar Nicholas II and family, Ekaterinburg, Russia. Author: (with Michael Browning) Dead Men Do Tell Tales, 1994; contbr. articles to profl. jours. Recipient Disting. Tchr. Cert., U. Fla., 1973, Cert. of Honor, City of Lima, Peru, 1985., Disting. Faculty award Fla. Blue Key, 1996, award Fla. Assn. Med. Examiners, 1996. Fellow Am. Anthropol. Assn., Am. Assn. Physics Anthropologists; mem. Am. Acad. Forensic Scis (v.p. 1986-87, bd. dirs. 1989-93, Phys. Anthropology Sect. award 1996T. Dale Steward award 1996), Forensic Scis. Found. (trustee, treas. 1988-95), Am. Bd. Forensic Anthropology (treas. 1984-87, pres. 1987-89). Avocations: photography, sailing. Office: U Florida PO Box 112545 Gainesville FL 32611

MAPOTHER, DILLON EDWARD, physicist, university official; b. Louisville, Aug. 22, 1921; s. Dillon Edward and Edith (Rubel) M.; m. Elizabeth Beck, June 29, 1946; children: Ellen, Susan, Anne. B.S. in Mech. Engring, U. Louisville, 1943; D.Sc. in Physics, Carnegie-Mellon U., 1949. Engr. Westinghouse Research Labs., East Pittsburgh, Pa., 1943-46; instr. Carnegie Inst. Tech., Pitts., 1946; mem. faculty U. Ill., Urbana, 1949-94; prof. physics U. Ill., 1959-94, dir. acad. computing services, 1971-76, assoc. vice chancellor for research, 1976-94, acting dean grad. coll., vice chancellor research, 1977-78, assoc. dean grad. coll., 1979-94; assoc. vice chancellor rsch. emeritus U. Ill., Urbana, 1995—, assoc. dean emeritus grad. coll., prof. emeritus physics, 1995—; cons. in field. DuPont fellow, 1947-49; Alfred P. Sloan fellow, 1958-61; Guggenheim fellow, 1960-61. Fellow Am. Phys. Soc.; mem. AAAS, Assn. Univ. Tech. Mgrs., Am. Assn. Physics Tchrs., Sigma Xi. Research on ionic mobility in alkali halides, thermodynamic properties of superconductors, calorimetric study of critical points, administration of university research, commercialization of academic research technology. Home: 1013 Ross Dr Champaign IL 61821-6631 Office: U Ill Physics Dept Loomis Lab 1110 W Green St Urbana IL 61801-3003

MAPOTHER, TOM CRUISE, IV *See* **CRUISE, TOM**

MAPP, ALF JOHNSON, JR., writer, historian; b. Portsmouth, Va., Feb. 17; s. Alf Johnson and Lorraine (Carney) M.; m. Hartley Lockhart, Mar. 28, 1953; 1 son, Alf Johnson III; m. Ramona Hartley Hamby, Aug. 1, 1971. A.A., Coll. William and Mary, 1945, A.B. summa cum laude, 1961. Editorial writer Portsmouth Star, 1945-46, assoc. editor, 1946-48, editorial chief, 1948-54; news editor, editorial writer Virginian-Pilot, Norfolk, 1954-58; free-lance writer, 1958—; lectr. Old Dominion U., 1961-62, instr., 1962-67, asst. prof. English and history, 1967-73, asso prof. English, journalism, creative writing, history, 1973-79, prof., 1979-82, eminent prof., 1982-89, eminent scholar, 1989-92, eminent scholar emeritus, 1992—, Louis I. Jaffe prof. English, 1990-92; Louis I. Jaffe prof. emeritus, 1992—; radio commentator WSAP, Portsmouth, Va., 1947-48; profl. lectr., 1984—; frequent analyst or guest on radio and TV including individual stas. and Universal Studio and BBC radio networks, CBS-TV, 1985—. Host TV series Jamestown to Yorktown, 1975-77; author: The Virginia Experiment, 1975, 3d edit., 1987, Frock Coats and Epaulets, 1963, 5th edit., 1996, America Creates Its Own Literature, 1965, Just One Man, 1968, The Golden Dragon: Alfred the Great and His Times, 1974, 4th edit., 1990, Thomas Jefferson: A Strange Case of Mistaken Identity, 1987, 3d edit., 1989 (Book-of-Month Club feature selection 1987), Thomas Jefferson: Passionate Pilgrim, 1991, 3d edit., 1993 (Book-of-Month Club feature selection 1991), (novel) Bed of Honor, 1995; co-author: Chesapeake Bay in the Revolution, 1981, Portsmouth: A Pictorial History, 1989, Constitutionalism: Founding and Future, 1989, Constitutionalism and Human Rights, 1991, Great American Presidents, 1995; mem. editl. bd. Jamestown Found., 1967—. Mem. Portsmouth-Norfolk County Savs. Bond Com, 1948-51, Va. Com. on Libr. Devel., 1949-50; mem. publs. com. 350th Anniversary of Rep. Govt. in the Western World, 1966-69, War of Independence Commn., 1967-83; chmn. Portsmouth Revolutionary Bicentennial Com., 1968-81; chmn. awards jury Baruch award United Daus. Confederacy-Columbia U., 1976, mem., 1980; chmn. Portsmouth Mus. and Fine Arts Commn., 1983-85, Southeastern Va. Anglo-Am. Friendship Day, 1976, Bicentennial Commemoration of Cornwallis' Embarkation for Yorktown, 1981, World Premiere of Mary Rose Marine Archeol. Exhibit, 1985; mem. grant rev. com. Va. Commn. for the Arts, 1986-87; bd. dirs. Portsmouth Pub. Libr., 1948-58, v.p., 1954-56; bd. dirs. Va. Symphony, 1986-87, trustee, 1987—; mem. taxes and mandates com. City of Portsmouth, 1982-86; mem. adv. com. City Mgr. of Norfolk, 1988-94; bd. dirs. Portsmouth Area Cmty Chest, 1948-52, Va. YMCA Youth and Govt. Found., 1950-52; mem. All-Am. cities com. for award-winning city Nat. League Municipalities, 1976; bd. advisors Ctr. Study Interactive Learning, Pasadena, Calif., 1993—; mem. steering com. Old Dominion U. Friends of the Libr., 1994-95, dir., 1995—; trustee Coun. for Am.'s First Freedom, 1994—. Named Portsmouth Young Man of Year, 1951; recipient honor medal Freedoms Found., 1951, Disting. Rsch. award Old Dominion U., 1987, Great Citizen award Hampton Roads 8 Cities, 1987, Notable Citizen award Portsmouth, Va., 1987; English award Old Dominion Coll., 1961; Troubadour, Great Tchrs. award, 1969; Outstanding Am. Educator award, 1972, 74; Nat. Bicentennial medal Am. Revolution Bicentennial Adminstrsn., 1976; medal Comité Francais du Bicentenaire de l'Independence des Etats-Unis, France, 1976; (with Ramona Mapp) Nat. Family Svc. award Family Found. Am., 1980; Laureate award Commonwealth of Va., 1981; Disting. Alumnus award Old Dominion U., 1982; Liberty Bell award Portsmouth Bar Assn., 1985; Old Dominion U. Triennial Phi Kappa Phi Scholar award, 1986, 91; History medal Nat. Soc. Daus. Am. Revolution; Portsmouth Downtown Merchants award, 1984, 85, Nat. Founders and Patriots award, 1995; Old Dominion U. Outstanding Achievement award, 1995; Gladstone Hill Friend of the Arts award (with Ramona H. Mapp), 1995, Richard Hakluyt award for Am. history, 1996; named to Order of the Crown of Charlemagne, 1993. Mem. Am. Hist. Assn., Va. Hist. Soc., Portsmouth Hist. Soc. (historiographer 1975-82, v.p. 1982-84, pres. 1985), Norfolk Hist. Soc. (dir. 1965-72), No. Neck Hist. Soc., Hist. Socs. Eastern Va. (dir. 1971—), SAR, Am. Assn. U. Profs., Authors Guild, Va. Library Assn. (legislative com. 1950-51), Poetry Soc. Va. (pres. 1974-75, adv. com. 1976—), Va. Writers Club, Assn. Preservation of Va. Antiquities, Order of Cape Henry (dir. 1970—, nat. pres. 1975-76), Jamestowne Soc. (chief historian 1975-77, internat. sec. state 1978-79), English Speaking Union (dir. 1976-77), Modern Lang. Assn., Order of First Families Va. 1607-1624 (councillor 1996—), Nat. Historians Circle, Phi Theta Kappa, Delta Phi Omega (chpt. pres. 1961), Phi Kappa Phi. Baptist. Home: Willow Oaks 2901 Tanbark Ln Portsmouth VA 23703-4828 *Reared in an intellectual family with high ethical standards, enthusiasm for the arts, and firm belief in hard work, I also had impressed on me that advantages conferred obligations. In an historic environment, I became aware of my generation's responsibility to those that had preceded it (to preserve the good they had created) and to those that would follow (to create things that would enrich their lives). This concept, with personal ambition, imbues my professional life.*

MAPP, KENNETH E., lieutenant governor of Virgin Islands. Lt. gov. V.I., Charlotte Amalie. Office: Office of Lt Gov 18 Kongens Gade Charlotte Amalie VI 00802

MAQUET, JACQUES JEROME PIERRE, anthropologist, writer; b. Brussels, Belgium, Aug. 4, 1919; came to U.S., 1967, naturalized, 1974; s. Jerome and Jeanne (Lemoine) M.; m. Emma de Longrée, June 17, 1946; children: Bernard, Denis; m. Gisèle Cambresier, Nov. 13, 1970. JD, U. Louvain, Belgium, 1946, D.Phil., 1948; student, Harvard, 1946-48; PhD, U. London, Eng., 1952; Dr. ès-lettres, Sorbonne, France, 1973. Field anthropologist Inst. Sci. Research in Central Africa, 1949-51; head Inst. Sci. Research in Central Africa (Social Scis. Center), 1951-57; prof. State U. of Congo, Elisabethville, 1957-60; research dir. Ecole pratique des Hautes Etudes, U. Paris, 1961-68; prof. anthropology Case Western Res. U., 1968-71; prof. UCLA, 1971-91, chmn. dept. anthropology, 1978-83, prof. emeritus anthropology, 1991—; vis. prof. Northwestern U., 1956, Harvard, 1964, U. Montreal, 1965, U. Pitts., 1967; extraordinary prof. U. Brussels, 1963-68. Author: The Sociology of Knowledge, 1951, Aide-mémoire d'ethnologie africaine, 1954, Ruanda, 1957, (with others) Elections en Société féodale, 1957, The Premise of Inequality in Ruanda, 1961, Power and Society in Africa, 1971, Civilizations of Black Africa, 1972, Africanity, The Cultural Unity of Black Africa, 1972, Introduction to Aesthetic Anthropology, 1979, The Aesthetic Experience, 1986; co-editor: (with others) Dictionary of Black African Civilization, 1974. Recipient Waxweiler award Royal Acad. Belgium, 1961; First World Festival of Negro Arts award Dakar, 1966. Mem. Am. Anthrop. Assn., Internat. Assn. Buddhist Studies, Pali Text Soc., AAUP, Fedn. Am. Scientists. Office: UCLA Dept Anthropology Los Angeles CA 90095-1553

MAR, EUGENE, lawyer, financial consultant; b. Hong Kong, July 5, 1940; s. Timothy T. and Shuh Yin L. (Lu) M.; came to U.S., 1946, naturalized, 1963; m. Sara C., Aug. 5, 1965; children: Christopher E., Jonathan. M. B.S. in Metall. Engring., U. Md., 1964; J.D., Cath. U. Am., 1969. Bar: Va. 1970, U.S. Ct. Mil. Appeals, U.S. Supreme Ct., U.S. Tax Ct., U.S. Ct. Appeals D.C. Assoc. Philpitt, Steininger & Priddy, 1964-65; examiner U.S. Patent Office 1965-68; assoc. Arthur Schwartz, Arlington, Va., 1968-72; ptnr. Bacon & Thomas, Arlington, 1978—, mng. ptnr., 1981—; bus./fin. cons., 1978—. Mem. ABA, Am. Intellectual Property Law Assn., Licensing Execs. Soc., Phi Alpha Delta, Phi Kappa Sigma. Home: 4304 Victoria Ln Alexandria VA 22304-7400 Office: 625 Slaters Ln 4th Fl Alexandria VA 22314

MARA, JOHN LAWRENCE, veterinarian, consultant; b. Whitesboro, N.Y., May 17, 1924; s. William Edward and Olive Pearl (Brakefield) M.; m. Kathleen Keefe, 1946 (div. 1958); children: William, Michael, Daniel, Patrick; m. Patricia Louise Paulk, 1970 (div. 1994); children: Jennifer Lee, Kennon. DVM, Cornell U., 1951. Diplomate Am. Coll. Vet. Nutrition. Intern N.Y. State Coll. Vet. Medicine, Cornell U., Ithaca, 1951-52; assoc. veterinarian L.W. Goodman Animal Hosp., Manhasset, N.Y., 1952-55; owner, pres. Mara Animal Hosp., Huntington, N.Y., 1955-79; profl. rep. Hills Pet Products, Topeka, Kans., 1979-80, mgr. profl. rels., 1980-81, dir. profl. affairs, 1981-88, dir. vet. affairs, 1988-94, sr. fellow profl. and acad. affairs, 1994—. V.p. Huntington United Fund; chmn. Huntington Taxpayers Party, 1968-78, Ch. in the Garden, Garden City, N.Y., 1975-77, trustee, 1975-77; trustee, v.p. vet. divsn. Morris Animal Found. Sgt. U.S. Army, 1943-45, ETO. Recipient Disting. Svc. award We. Vet. Conf., 1988; named hon. alumnus Coll. Vet. Medicine, Wash. State U. Mem. AVMA (Pres.'s award), L.I. Vet. Medicine Assn., N.Y. State Vet. Medicine Assn., Am. Animal Hosp. Assn. (Outstanding Svc. award Western Region 1996, Outstanding Svc. award 1997), Kans. Vet. Medicine Assn., Am. Coll. Vet. Nutrition (hon. diplomate). Republican. Baptist. Avocations: gardening, swimming, reading. Home: 6439 SW Castle Ln Topeka KS 66614-4392

MARA, VINCENT JOSEPH, college president; b. Worcester, Mass., Sept. 19, 1930; s. Edward Stephan and Mary Stephanie (Kavanaugh) M.; m. Clare Owens, Feb. 15, 1958; children: John, Kevin, Maryellen, Thomas, Clare. BS in Edn., Worcester State Coll.; EdM, U. Conn.; PhD; LLD (hon.), Framingham State Coll., 1995; LHD, Fitchburg State Coll., 1995. Asst. prof., then assoc. prof. Framingham (Mass.) State Coll., 1960-63, dir. admissions, 1963-69, acad. dean, 1969-76; acting pres. Salem (Mass.) State Coll., 1974-75; pres. Fitchburg (Mass.) State Coll., 1976-95, prof. emeritus, 1995—, pres. emeritus, 1955—; corporator Fitchburg Savs. Bank, 1976-85; mem. Montachusett Region Pvt. Industry Coun., 1983—; dir. Safety Fund Nat. Bank. Contbr. articles to profl. jours. Trustee Notre Dame Prep. Sch., Fitchburg, 1985-86; trustee Worcester Pub. Libr., 1967-70, pres. bd. trustees, 1970; bd. dirs Fitchburg Civic Ctr., 1977-80, Cushing Acad., 1978-80, North Ctrl. Mass. Mental Health Assn., 1979-81, United Way, 1981-87, Montachusett Region Pvt. Industry Coun., 1983-93; bd. dirs. Thayer Symphony Orch., 1987-90, pres., 1994-95; mem. Mass. Commn. Edn. Telecomm., 1983-90, Fitchburg Bd. Health, 1982-93. With U.S. Army, 1952-53. Named Outstanding Young Man of Yr. Worcester C. of C., 1960; recipient Disting. Citizen award City of Fitchburg, 1989. Mem. NEA, Am. Conf. Acad. Deans, Am. Assn. State Colls. and Univs., N.Am. C. of C. (bd. dirs. 1984-91), Fitchburg C. of C. (bd. dirs. 1977-83), Fay Club, Phi Delta Kappa, Kappa Delta Pi. Democrat. Roman Catholic. Home: 242 Pearl Hill Rd Fitchburg MA 01420-2019 Office: Fitchburg State Coll 160 Pearl St Fitchburg MA 01420-2631

MARA, WELLINGTON T., professional football team executive; b. Aug. 8, 1916. Pres. N.Y. Giants, East Rutherford, N.J., also co-chief exec. officer. elected to Pro Football Hall of Fame, 1997. Office: NY Giants Giants Stadium East Rutherford NJ 07073 also: Nat Football League 410 Park Ave New York NY 10022-4407*

MARABLE, SIMEON-DAVID, artist; b. Phila., May 10, 1948; s. Daniel Berry and Marsima (Maddela); B.A. in Art and English, Lea Coll., Minn., 1970; postgrad. Tyler Sch. Art, Phila.; m. Pamela Joyce Sorenson, June 1, 1969; children: Simeon-David dePaul, Daniel-Dale Christopher, Jason-Andrew Bartley, Jo Anna Lee, Benjamin Arthur Kurtis. Tchr. 7th and 8th grade art Pennsbury (Pa.) Sch. System, 1970-88; tchr. 9th and 10th grade art Charles H. Boehm High Sch., Pennsbury, 1988—, Medill Bair High Sch., Pennsbury, 1990—; tchr. Neshaminy Adult Edn., 1972-82; resident artist Middletown Hist. Assn., 1976, Three Arches Corp., 1975, also treas.; sculptures represented in Albert Lea (Minn.) Library; painting in chapel Ft. Dix, N.J.; portraits of Mr. Mike Schmidt, 1986, Mr. Lee Elia, 1986; creator Phila. City of Champs logo. Mgr. Boys Soccer League, Boys Little League, Middletown Twp.; sr. Babe Ruth coach, mgr. Langhorne Athletic Assn., 1988-89; sr. coach Babe Ruth League, 1989; J.V. Baseball coach, 1989; mem. Presdl. Task Force; elected to Nat. Trust for Historic Preservation, 1995. Served with USAR, 1970. Creator children's ednl. programs Falls Twp. 300th, Pa. statehood; artwork represented in Middletown twp. 300th ann. calandar, 1992, Falls Twp. 300th ann. calandar, 1992. Named Artist of Year, Albert Lea Lions Club, 1970. Mem. Buck County Art Educators (pres. 1973-74), Levittown Artists Assn., Nat. Soc. Arts and Lit., Internat. Platform Assn. Roman Catholic. Home: 18 Spindletree Rd Levittown PA 19056-2215 Office: 600 S Olds Blvd Fairless Hills PA 19030-2441

MARADONA, REMIGIO MARTIN, international diplomat; b. Buenos Aires, Dec. 6, 1963; came to U.S., 1981, naturalized, 1986; BA in Polit. Sci., History, CUNY, 1988; MPA, Audrey Cohen Coll., N.Y.C., 1992. Freelance writer Hispanic publs.; co-founder, exec. v.p., sec. Internat. Cons. for Latin Am. Inc., N.Y.C., 1993—; prin. coord. events UN, 1986, 88, 89, 91, alt. rep. to UN Dept. Info., 1993—; city of N.Y. ofcl. Author: (poem) My Inner Self, 1997. Recipient Mayoral Letter of Appreciation, N.Y.C., 1989, Golden Poet award U.S. Acad. Poetry Instituto Cultural Ruben Dario. Mem. World Assn. Former UN Interns and Fellows. Avocations: poet, soccer coach UN internat. sch.

MARADUDIN, ALEXEI A., physics educator; b. San Francisco, Dec. 14, 1931. BS, Stanford U., 1953, MS, 1954; PhD in Physics, Bristol U., 1957. Rsch. assoc. physics U. Md., College Park, 1956-57, rsch. asst. prof., 1957-58; asst. rsch. prof. Inst. Fluid Dynamics & Applied Math., 1958-60; physicist Westinghouse Rsch. Labs., Churchill Borough, Pa., 1960-65; cons. semicondr. br. U.S. Naval Rsch. Lab., Washington, 1958-60, Los Alamos Sci. Lab., 1965-67, 83-89; cons. semiconductor br. Gen. Atomic Divsn. Gen. Dynamics Corp., 1965-71; chmn. dept. U. Calif., Irvine, 1968-71, prof. physics, 1965—. Recipient Alexander von Humboldt U.S. sr. scientist award, 1980-81. Fellow Am. Phys. Soc.; mem. Optical Soc. Am., Sigma Xi. Office: U Calif Irvine Dept Physics and Astronomy Phys Scis Bldg 2 Rm 2180 Irvine CA 92697

MARAMAN, KATHERINE ANN, judge; b. Los Alamos, N.Mex., Aug. 13, 1951; d. William Joseph and Katherine Ann (Thorpe) M. BA, Colorado Coll., 1973; JD, U. N.Mex., 1976. Bar: N.Mex. 1976, Guam 1978, Trust Territory Pacific Islands, Commonwealth of No. Mariana Islands, U.S. Ct. Appeals (9th cir.), U.S. Supreme Ct. Draftsperson N.Mex. Legis. Coun. Svc., Santa Fe, 1976-77; atty. Brooks & Klitzkie, P.C., Agana, Guam, 1977-84; pvt. practice Agana, 1985-88; counsel Office of Gov., Agana, 1988-94; judge Superior Ct., Agana, 1994—; mem. asst. legis. counsel Guam Legis., Agana, 1977-80, mem. minority counsel, 1981-87; bd. dirs. Pub. Defender Svc. Corp., Agana, 1988-94. Trustee Guam Terr. Law Libr., 1994—. Mem. Guam Bar Assn. Counsel Rep. Party, Agana, 1981-94; bd. dirs. Guam Rehab. and Workshop, Inc., Tumon, Guam, 1983-95; deacon First Presbyn. Reformed Ch., Agana. Office: Superior Ct Guam 120 W Obrien Dr Agana GU 96910-5174

MARAMOROSCH, KARL, virologist, educator; b. Vienna, Austria, Jan. 16, 1915; came to U.S., 1947, naturalized, 1952; s. Jacob and Stefanie Olga (Schlesinger) M.; m. Irene Ludwinowska, Nov. 15, 1938; 1 dau., Lydia Ann. M.S. magna cum laude in Entomology, Agrl. U., Warsaw, Poland, 1938; student, Poly. U. Bucharest, Rumania, 1944-46; fellow, Bklyn. Bot. Garden, 1947-48; Ph.D. (predoctoral fellow Am. Cancer Soc. 1948-49), Columbia, 1949. Civilian internee in Rumania, 1939-46; asst., then assoc. Rockefeller Inst., N.Y.C., 1949-61; sr. entomologist Boyce Thompson Inst., Yonkers, N.Y., 1961-74, program dir. virology and insect physiology, 1962-74; prof. microbiology Waksman Inst., Rutgers U., New Brunswick, N.J., 1974-85; prof. entomology Cook Coll., Rutgers U., New Brunswick, 1985—, Robert L. Starkey prof., 1983—; vis. prof. agr. U. Wageningen, Netherlands, 1953, Cornell U., 1957, Rutgers U., 1967-68, Fordham U., 1973, Sapporo U., Japan, 1980, Justus Liebig U., Giessen, Ger., 1983; Mendel lectr. St. Peters Coll., Jersey City, 1963; virologist FAO to Philippines, 1960; Disting. Vis. prof. Fudan U., Shanghai, 1982; cons. FAO-UN, World-wide survey, 1963; chmn. U.S.-Japan Coop. Seminar, 1965, 74, 85; mem. panel food and fiber Nat. Acad. Scis., 1966; cons. rice virus diseases AID-IRRI, Hyderabad, India, 1971; cons. UNDP, Bangalore, India, 1978-79; virologist FAO/UNDP, Sri Lanka, 1981, 82, 83, Mauritius, 1985; AIBS lectr., 1970-72, Found. Microbiology Nat. lectr., 1972-73, Fulbright Disting. prof., Yugoslavia, 1972, 78; mem. tropical medicine and parasitology study sect. NIH, 1972-76; chmn. 1st-3d Internat. Confs. Comparative Virology, 1969, 73, 76. Author: Comparative Symptomatology of Coconut Diseases of Unknown Etiology, 1964; editor: Biological Transmission of Disease Agents, 1962, Insect Viruses, 1968, Viruses, Vectors and Vegetation, 1969, Comparative Virology, 1971, Mycoplasma Diseases, 1973, Viruses, Evolution and Cancer, 1974, Invertebrate Immunity, 1975, Legume Diseases in the Tropics, 1975, Invertebrate Tissue Culture: Research Applications, 1976, Invertebrate Tissue Culture: Applications in Medicine, Biology and Agriculture, 1976, Aphids as Virus Vectors, 1977, Insect and Plant Viruses: An Atlas, 1977, Viruses and Environment, 1978, Practical Tissue Culture Applications, 1979, Leafhopper Vectors and Plant Disease Agents, 1979, Vectors of Plant Pathogens, 1980, Invertebrate Systems in Vitro, 1980, Vectors of Disease Agents, 1981, Mycoplasma Diseases of Trees and Shrubs, 1981, Mycoplasma and Allied Pathogens of Plants, Animals and Human Beings, 1981, Plant Diseases and Vectors: Ecology and Epidemiology, 1981, Invertebrate Cell Culture Applications, 1982, Pathogens, Vectors and Plant Diseases: Approaches to Control, 1982, Subviral Pathogens of Plants and Animals, 1985, Viral Insecticides for Biological Control, 1985, Biotechnology Advances in Insect Pathology and Cell Culture, 1987, Mycoplasma Diseases of Crops, 1988, Invertebrate and Fish Tissues Culture, 1988, Biotechnology for Biological Controls of Pests and Vectors, 1991, Viroids and Satellites: Molecular Parasites at the Frontier of Life, 1991, Plant Diseases of Uncertain Etiology, 1992, Insect Cell Biotechnology, 1994, Arthropod Cell Culture Systems, 1994, Forest Trees and Palms: Diseases and Control, 1996, Invertebrate Cell Culture: Novel Directions and Biotechnology Applications, 1997, Invertebrate Cell Culture: Looking Toward the XXI Century, 1997; Methods in Virology, 1964—, Advances in Virus Research, 1972—, Archives of Virology, 1973-78, Intervirology, 1973-77, Advances in Cell Culture, 1979—; editor in chief Jour. N.Y. Entomol. Soc, 1972-84; assoc. editor: Virology, 1964-68, 75-79. Recipient Sr. Research award Lalor Found., 1957; Nat. Ciba-Geigy award in agr., 1976; Wolf prize in agr., 1980; Jurzykowski prize in biology, 1980; Disting. Service award Am. Inst. Biol. Scis., 1983. Fellow AAAS (Campbell award 1958), Entomol. Soc. Am., N.Y. Acad. Scis. (A. Cressy Morrison prize natural sci. 1951, chmn. div. microbiology 1956-60, rec. sec. 1960-61, v.p. 1962-63), Nat. Acad. Scis. India (hon.); mem. Harvey Soc., Growth Soc., Phytopath. Soc., Indian, Japan, Can. phytopath. socs., Leopoldina Acad., Internat. Com. Virus Nomenclature, Electron Microscope Soc., Am. Soc. Microbiology (Waksman award 1978), Tissue Culture Assn. (pres. N.E. br. 1978-81, pres. history br. 1988-90), Soc. Invertebrate Pathology (founder's lectr., Adelaide 1990), Internat. Assn. Medicinal Forest Plants (pres. 1989—), Sigma Xi (pres. Rugers chpt. 1978). Home: 17 Black Birch Ln Scarsdale NY 10583-7456 Office: Rutgers U Dept Entomology New Brunswick NJ 08903

MARAN, STEPHEN PAUL, astronomer; b. Bklyn., Dec. 25, 1938; s. Alexander P. and Clara F. (Schoenfeld) M.; m. Sally Ann Scott, Feb. 14, 1971; children: Michael Scott, Enid Rebecca, Elissa Jean. B.S., Bklyn. Coll., 1959; M.A., U. Mich., 1961, Ph.D., 1964. Astronomer Kitt Peak Nat. Obs., Tucson, 1964-69; project scientist for orbiting solar observatories NASA-Goddard Space Flight Center, Greenbelt, Md., 1969-75; head advanced systems and ground observations br. NASA-Goddard Space Flight Ctr., 1970-77, mgr. Operation Kohoutek, 1973-74, sr. staff scientist Lab. for Astronomy and Solar Physics, 1977-95; asst. dir. Space Scis. for Info. and Outreach, 1995—; Cons. Westinghouse Rsch. Labs., 1966; vis. lectr. U. Md., College Park, 1969-70; sr. lectr. UCLA, 1976; press officer Am. Astron. Soc., 1985—; A. Dixon Johnson lectr. in sci. comm., Pa. State U., 1990; vis. scholar Univ. Ctr. Ga., 1997; lectr. on astronomy cruises and eclipse tours. Author: (with John C. Brandt) New Horizons in Astronomy, 1972, 2d edit., 1979, Arabic edit., 1979, (with Jacqueline Mitton) Gems of Hubble-Superb Images fm the Hubble Telescope, 1996; editor: Physics of Nonthermal Radio Sources, 1964, The Gum Nebula and Related Problems, 1971, Possible Relations Between Solar Activity and Meteorological Phenomena, 1975, New Astronomy and Space Science Reader, 1977, A Meeting with the Universe, 1981, Astrophysics of Brown Dwarfs, 1986, The Astronomy and Astrophysics Encyclopedia, 1991; assoc. editor: Earth, Extraterrestrial Scis, 1969-79; editor: Astrophys. Letters, 1974-77, assoc. editor, 1977-85; contbg. editor Air & Space/Smithsonian, 1990—; mem. editl. adv. bd. Astronomy Mag., 1997—, Astronomy and Graphics, 1997—; contbr. articles on astronomy, space to popular mags. Named Disting. Visitor Boston U., 1970; recipient Group Achievement awards NASA, 1969, 74, Exceptional Achievement medal, 1991. Fellow AAAS; mem. Internat. Astron. Union (editor daily newspaper 1988), Am. Astron. Soc. (Harlow Shapley vis. lectr. 1981—), press. officer 1985—), Royal Astron. Soc., Am. Phys. Soc., Am. Geophys. Union. Office: Code 600 NASA Goddard Space Flight Ctr Greenbelt MD 20771

MARANDA, GUY, oral maxillofacial surgeon, Canadian health facility executive, educator; b. Paris, May 9, 1936; arrived in Canada, 1937; s. Emilien and Lucille (Fortin) M.; married; children: Lucille, Jean, Isabelle. BA, U. Ottawa, Ont., Can., 1957; DDs, U. Montreal, Can., 1962; cert. oral surgeon, U. Pa., 1965. Pvt. practice Quebec, 1965-70; mem. faculty U. Laval, Ste. Foy, Que., Can., 1970—, asst. prof., 1987-94, prof., 1995—; bd. dirs. Ordre Dentistes du Québec; pres. Quebec Assn. Oral Surgeons, 1985; cons. Quebec Health Bd., Assurance Auto Quebec, various law firms. Mem. Royal coll. Dentists Can. (diplomate, pres. 1991), Internat. Assn. Oral Surgeons, Can. Assn. Oral Surgeons, Am. Assn. Oral Surgeons, Can. Dental Assn. Ordre Dentistes Que. Roman Catholic. Home: 822 Bellevue, Sainte Foy, PQ Canada G1V 2R5 Office: U Laval, Faculty Dental Medicine, Sainte Foy, PQ Canada G1V 7P4

MARANDA, PIERRE JEAN, anthropologist, writer; b. Quebec, Que., Can., Mar. 27, 1930; s. Lucien and Marie Alma (Rochette) M.; m. Elli Köngäs, Mar. 12, 1963 (dec.); children: Erik Pierre, Nicolas Martin. BA, U. Laval, Quebec, 1949; MA, U. Montreal, Que., 1953; PhD, Harvard U., 1966; Dr honoris causa, Meml. U. Nfld., 1984. Asst. prof. anthropology U. Laval, 1955-58, research prof., 1975—, prof., 1976—, dept. head, 1989—; tutor Harvard U., 1964-65, research fellow, 1966-70; dir. studies Ecole Pratique des Hautes Etudes, 6th Sect., Paris, 1968-69; assoc. prof. U. B.C. (Can.), Vancouver, 1969-73; prof. U. B.C. (Can.), 1973-75; prof. étranger College de France, Paris, 1975; bd. dirs. several internat. rsch. insts.; vis. prof. Universidade Federal, Rio de Janeiro, 1983, U. Toronto, 1987, 89, U. B.C., 1988, U. Libreville, Gabon, 1990, 91. Author: (with Köngäs Maranda) books, including Structural Models in Folklore and Transformational Essays, 1962, 2d rev. edit., 1970, Introduction to Anthropology: A Self-Guide, 1972, French Kinship: Structure and History, 1974, Soviet Structural Folkloristics, 1974, Dialogue Conjugal, 1985; DiscAn: A Computer System for Contents and Discourse Analysis, 1989, (with Fidèle Nze-Guema) L'Unité culturelle dans la diversité: Une Geste bantu, 1994; contbr. numerous articles to profl. jours. Pres. Comité des Citoyens de Belvedere, Que., 1976-83. Recipient Medaille du College de France, 1975, Molson prize in social scis. and humanities, 1996. Fellow Royal Soc. Can., Am. Anthrop. Assn.; mem. Internat. Semiotics Assn., Internat. Center Linguistics and Semiotics, Can. Inst. Advanced Research (council), Can. Ethnol. Soc. (former pres.), Can. Anthropology and Sociology Assn. (former pres.), Can. Semiotics Research Assn. (bd. dirs.), Can. Folklore Studies Assn.

MARANGI, VITO ANTHONY, SR., claim administrator; b. Utica, N.Y., Jan. 1, 1932; s. Mary Margaret Lokey, Apr. 10, 1960 (div. July 1973); children: Vito Anthony Jr., Vanetta Gayle, Gregory Alan; m. Diann Louise Bunch, Apr. 11, 1987. BS, SUNY, Potsdam, 1958. Asst. regional claims mgr. Hartford Ins. Group, Fresno, Calif., 1958-67; supervising adjuster Underwriters Adjusting Co., Fresno, 1967-70; home office claim supr. Meritplan Ins. Co., Newport Beach, Calif., 1970-71; appeals referee State of Nev., Reno and Carson City, 1971-73, 76-79; br. mgr. Brown Bros. Adjusters, Reno, 1974-87; ind. ins. adjuster Tony Marangi, Adjuster, Carson City, 1987—; vice chmn., bd. trustees Carson-Tahoe Hosp., 1991-96. Scout master Boy Scouts Am., Utica, N.Y., Fresno, Calif., Carson City, 1953-85. With USN, 1949-53. Mem. Nev. State Claims Assn. (pres., v.p., treas., sec.), No. Nev. Claims Assn. (pres., v.p., treas., sec.), Nat. Assn. of Adminstrv. Law Judges, Internat. Assn. of Arson Investigators (Nev. chpt.), Carson City Elks Lodge, VFW, Carson City C. of C. (bus. edn. com. 1987—, transp. com. 1987—). Avocations: photographer, bowling, dancing, classic car owner, musician. Home: PO Box 843 Carson City NV 89702-0843 Office: Carson Tahoe Hosp PO Box 2168 Carson City NV 89702-2168

MARANISS, DAVID, reporter; b. 1949. Reporter, now staff writer The Washington Post. Author: First in His Class: A Biography of Bill Clinton, 1995. Recipient Pulitzer Prize for nat. reporting, 1993. Office: Washington Post 1150 15th St NW Washington DC 20071-0001*

MARANO, ANTHONY JOSEPH, cardiologist; b. White Plains, N.Y., Apr. 14, 1934; s. Anthony Joseph and Mary Antoinette (Perrotta) M.; m. Mary Regina Marbach, Aug. 23, 1958; children—Thomas, Kathryn, Michele. B.A., Williams Coll., 1956; M.D., Cornell Med. Coll., 1960. Diplomate Am. Bd. Internal Medicine, Am. Bd. Cardiovascular Disease. Intern Bellevue Hosp., N.Y.C., 1960-61; resident St. Luke's Hosp., N.Y.C., 1961-63; NIH fellow in cardiology Mt. Sinai Hosp., N.Y.C., 1963-64, research assoc., 1964-75; clin. assoc. in medicine Coll. Physicians and Surgeons, N.Y.C., 1970-86; pres. med. staff White Plains Hosp., 1984-86, chief cardiology, 1985-91, chief cardiology emeritus, 1991—, bd. dirs., 1983-88; cons. in cardiology Burke Rehab. Ctr.; med. dir., founder Paramedic Ambulance, White Plains, 1976-82. Contbr. articles to med. jours. Trustee Pace U., N.Y.C., 1975—, Home Savs. Bank, White Plains, 1973-90; bd. dirs. YMCA, White Plains, 1978-82; team physician White Plains High Sch., 1967—; cons. physician Dept. Pub. Safety, White Plains, 1968—; cons. physician City of White Plains Sch. System, 1994—; bd. dirs. Westchester County Sports Hall of Fame, 1993—; alumni trustee Tyng Found., Williams Coll., 1994—. Tyng scholar Williams Coll., 1952-59; recipient Outstanding Achievement award Emergency Med. Services Council, 1982. Fellow ACP, Am. Coll. Cardiology; mem. AMA, Am. Coll. Sports Medicine, Am. Heart Assn., N.Y. State Heart Assn. (bd. dirs. 1982-85), Westchester Heart Assn. (v.p. 1983-86, pres. 1987-90), Phi Beta Kappa. Clubs: University (White Plains) (pres. 1970-71); Westchester Country (Harrison, N.Y.). Avocations: tennis, skiing, gardening. Home: 9 Fairway Dr White Plains NY 10605-4107 Office: 20 Old Mamaroneck Rd White Plains NY 10605-2060

MARANO, RICHARD MICHAEL, lawyer; b. Waterbury, Conn., June 22, 1960; s. Albert Nicholas and Angeline Domenica (Viotti) M.; m. Eileen N. Barry. BA, Fairfield U., 1982; JD, Seton Hall U., 1985. Bar: Conn. 1985, U.S. Dist. Ct. Conn. 1985, U.S. Tax Ct. 1986, U.S. Supreme Ct. 1990, U.S. Ct. Appeals (2d cir.) 1991. Assoc. Moynahan, Ruskin, Mascolo & Mariani, Waterbury, 1985-87; ptnr. Marano & Diamond, Waterbury, 1987—; alderman City of Waterbury 1988-90. Author: History of the Order Sons of Italy of Waterbury, Connecticut, 1995; co-editor: Counsel for the Defense, 1991-93, editor, 1993—; contbr. law articles to Conn. Bar Jour. Bd. dirs. Italian-Am. Dem. Club, Waterbury, 1988—, Ctrl. Naugatuck Valley HELP, 1992—, Anderson Boys Club, 1989— (pres. 1996—), Waterbury Housing Police Fund, 1992-94, Waterbury Crime Stoppers Inc., 1994-97; pres. Conn. Young Dems., 1981-82; state coord. McGovern for U.S. Presdl. campaign, 1983-84; campaign mgr. Orman for Congress, 1984; commr. Waterbury Pub. Assistance, 1986-88; justice of the peace, Waterbury, 1989—; gen. counsel Waterbury Dem. Town Com., 1990-96; commr. Waterbury Fire Bd., 1996—; trustee Our Lady of Lourdes Ch., 1993—. Mem. ABA, ATLA, KC, Conn. Bar Assn., Nat. Assn. Criminal Def. Lawyers, Conn. Criminal Def. Lawyers Assn. (sec. 1994-96, v.p. 1996—), Conn. Italian-Am. Bar Assn. (pres. 1993-95), Conn. Trial Lawyers Assn., Waterbury Bar Assn. (bd. dirs. 1993-96, pres. 1996—), New Haven County Bar Assn., Nat. Italian-Am. Bar Assn., Sons of Italy (pres. lodge # 66 1994-96), Unico Club, Elks, Alpha Mu Gamma, Pi Sigma Alpha. Roman Catholic. Home: 22 Stephana Ln Waterbury CT 06710-1126 Office: Marano & Diamond 61 Field St Waterbury CT 06702-1907 *Notable cases include: State vs. Rafael Molina Jud. dist. Waterbury, CR4-145496, acquittal on a first degree sexual assault charge; Davis vs. Alaska 415 U.S. 308, 1974; State vs. Dawn Marotta, Jud. Dist. Waterbury Crs-18353, State's evidence of cocaine was suppressed; Petruzzi vs. Sterling, Jud. dist. Waterbury, 87-792347, violation of Conn. statutes pertaining to prescription and dispensing of drugs.*

MARANS, J. EUGENE, lawyer; b. Butte, Mont., May 26, 1940; s. Edward and Florence M.; m. Anne Marie Borger, Sept. 3, 1978; children: Julia C., John E. A.B., Harvard U., 1962, LL.B., 1965. Bar: N.Y. 1966, D.C. 1971. Law clk. to Judge John M. Wisdom U.S. Ct. Appeals (5th cir.), New Orleans, 1965-66; assoc. Cleary, Gottlieb, Steen & Hamilton, N.Y.C., 1966-70, Paris, 1970-71; assoc. Cleary, Gottlieb, Steen & Hamilton, Washington, 1971-74, ptnr., 1975-90, 93—; ptnr. Cleary, Gottlieb, Steen & Hamilton, Hong Kong, 1990-93; mem. N.Y. State adv. com. U.S. Commn. Civil Rights, 1969-70; mem. nat. eval. com. on simplified method of determining eligibility in pub. assistance HEW, 1969-70; sec., counsel Bipartisan Com. on Absentee Voting, 1973—. Contbr. articles to legal jours. Bd. dirs. New Leadership Fund, chmn. 1977-79; mem. Sabre Found., pres. 1990. Mem. Assn. Ams. Resident Overseas, Ripon Soc. (nat. governing bd. 1962—, chmn. 1969-70), Council on Fgn. Relations, ABA, D.C. Bar (chmn. internat. sect. 1978-79), Assn. of Bar of City of N.Y., Am. Soc. Internat. Law, Union Internat. des Avocats, Washington Fgn. Law Soc. (pres. 1985-86), Am. Law Inst. Office: 1752 N St NW Washington DC 20036-2907 also: 2000 Pennsylvania Ave NW Washington DC 20006-1801

MARANS, ROBERT WARREN, architect, planner; b. Detroit, Aug. 3, 1934; s. Albert and Anne Rose (Siegel) M.; m. Judith Ann Bloomfield, Jan. 24, 1956; children: Gayl Elizabeth, Pamela Jo. BArch, U. Mich., 1957; M in Urban Planning, Wayne State U., 1961; PhD, U. Mich., 1971. Reg. architect, Mich. Archtl. engr., planner Detroit City Planning Commn., 1957-61; planning cons. Blair & Stein Assocs., Providence, 1961-64; architect-urban designer Artur Glikson, Architect, Tel Aviv, Israel, 1964-65; regional planner Detroit Area Transp. Land Use Study, 1965-67; asst. prof. Fla. State U., Talahassee, 1967; rsch. assoc., sr. study dir. Inst. Social Rsch., Ann Arbor, Mich., 1968-74, program dir., 1974—; from lectr. to assoc. prof. Coll. Architecture Urban Planning, Ann Arbor, 1971-78; prof. architecture and urban planning U. Mich., Ann Arbor, 1978—; cons. TVA, 1972, UN, 1974; chmn. urban and regional planning program, 1987—. Co-author: Planned Residential Environments, 1970, Quality of NonMetropolitan Living, 1978, Evaluating Built Environments, 1981, Retirement Communities: An American Original, 1984; co-editor: Methods of Environmental and Behavioral Research, 1987, Environmental Stimulation: Research and Policy Perspectives, 1993, Advances in Environment, Behavior and Design, vol. IV, 1997; contbr. articles to profl. jours. and tech. reports. Sec. Washtenaw County Parks Recreation Commn., Ann Arbor, 1972—; chmn. Huron-Clinton Met. Parks Authority, Brighton, Mich., 1986—. Recipient fellow Social Sci. Rsch. Coun., 1969-70; Fulbright Rsch. award Coun. Internat. Exchange Scholars, Israel, 1977; Progressive Architecture Applied Rsch. award Progressive Architecture Mag., 1982; Design Rsch. Recognition award Nat. Endowment for Arts, 1983. Mem. Am. Planning Assn., Nat. Recreation Pk. Assn., Environ. Design Rsch. Assn. Avocations: swimming, stamp collecting. Office: U Mich Coll Arch and Urban Planning Ann Arbor MI 48109

MARASCO, JOSEPH A., JR., radiologist. Physician dept. radiology Forbes Regional Hosp., Monroeville, Pa. Recipient Gold award Am. Coll. Radiology, 1995. Office: Forbes Regional Hosp Dept Radiology 2570 Haymaker Rd Monroeville PA 15146-3513

MARASH, STANLEY ALBERT, consulting company executive; b. Bklyn., Dec. 18, 1938; s. Albert Samuel and Esther (Cunio) M.; m. Muriel Sylvia Sutchin, June 24, 1961; children: Judith Ilene, Alan Scott. Student, Bklyn. Coll., 1956-58; BBA, CCNY, 1961; student, U. Idaho, 1962-63, Boston U., 1964-66; MBA, Baruch Coll., 1970, PhD, 1995. Registered profl. engr., Calif.; cert. quality engr., reliability engr. Statistician Electric Boat Gen. Dynamics, Groton, Conn., 1961-62; statistician Idaho Nat. Energy Lab. Electric Boat Gen. Dynamics, Idaho Falls, 1962-63; mgr. quality assurance memory product ops. RCA, Needham, Mass., 1963-65; cons. engr. astroelectronics div. RCA, Princeton, N.J., 1965-66; corp. mgr. quality assurance Ideal Corp., Bklyn., 1966-68; mgr. quality assurance Gen. Instrument, Signalite, Neptune, N.J., 1968; pres. STAT-A-MATRIX, Inc., Edison, N.J., 1968-90; chmn. bd. STAT-A-MATRIX Inst., Edison, N.J., 1975—; chmn., CEO STAT-A-MATRIX Group, Edison, N.J., 1990-94, The SAM Group - STAT-A-MATRIX, Edison, N.J., 1994—; trustee Ellis R. Ott Found., Edison, 1982-95; chmn. Quality N.J., 1989-94, chmn. emeritus, 1994—; advisor quality tech. Middlesex County Coll., Edison, 1970-94; vis. prof. U. Sao Paulo, Brazil, 1974, 75, 77, Madrid Poly. U., 1976; expert cons. Internat. Atomic Energy Agy., Vienna, 1974-77; cons. various govt. agys. and pub. and pvt. cos., 1972—; mem. indsl. adv. com. dept. stats. Rutgers U., 1977-78; mem. exec. stds. coun. Am. Nat. Stds. Inst., N.Y.C., 1979-80; chmn. World Quality Coun., 1996—. Author: (tng. manual) Statistically Aided Management: What Every Executive Needs to Know, 1987; contbr. numerous articles, manuals and tng. texts. Examiner Malcolm Baldridge Nat. Quality Award, 1990, 91. Fellow Am. Soc. Quality Control (chmn. met. sect. 1966-68, Ellis R. Ott award 1981, chmn. internat. cooperation com. 1989—); mem. IEEE (sr.), ASTM, ASME, Am. Statis. Assn., Am. Soc. Tng. Devel., Am. Nuclear Soc. Office: The SAM Group/STAT-A-MATRIX One Quality Pl Edison NJ 08820-1073

MARATEA, JAMES MICHAEL, healthcare administrator, editor, consultant; b. Riverside, N.J., Nov. 26, 1946; s. Domenic J. and Martha C. (Moloney) M.; m. Linda Jean Morgan, Sept. 6, 1970; children: Jennifer A., Jill M., Patrick J. BS in Bus. Adminstrn., Trenton (N.J.) State Coll., 1973; MA in Mgmt., Cen. Mich. U., 1977. Staff technologist Del. Valley Hosp., Bristol, Pa., 1966-68; supr. Zurbrugg Meml. Hosp., Riverside, 1968-74; v.p. Maratea Med. Lab., Riverside, 1966-84; rep. Thomas Jefferson U., Phila., 1974-75, lab. mgr., 1975-85, adminstr. dept. clin. and anatomic pathology, 1985-93, adminstr. clin. lab. and emergency svcs., 1992—; adminstr. Dept. of Pathology and Emergency Svcs., Thomas Jefferson U., Phila., 1993—; cons. to maj. league baseball, N.Y.C., 1990—; instr. Thomas Jefferson U., 1985—; mem. Univ. Hosp. Cons. Tech. Adv. Com., Chgo., 1989—. Contbg. author: Sharpening Management Skills, A Laboratorian's Guide, 1978; contbr. articles to profl. jours. Mem. Camden County (N.J.) Com., 1991—; v.p.

Merchantville (N.J.) Rep. Club, 1991, pres., 1992; mem. Bd. Health, Merchantville, 1986—. Recipient MLO Writing award Med. Econs., 1977, 80, 81, 82. Mem. Am. Med. Technologists, Clin. Lab. Mgmt. Assn. (v.p. Delaware Valley 1981-82, pres. 1982-84), Am. Soc. Med. Technologists, Am. Bd. Bionalysts. Roman Catholic. Avocations: gardening, home remodeling. Home: 118 Westminster Ave Merchantville NJ 08109-2640 Office: Thomas Jefferson U 11th and Walnut Sts Philadelphia PA 19107

MARAYNES, ALLAN LAWRENCE, filmmaker, television producer; b. N.Y.C., Apr. 26, 1950; s. Harry and Dorothy (Kaufman) M.; m. Bitsy Healy, Oct. 14, 1978; children: Sean, Megan, Matthew. BA, Queens Coll., 1972; MA, Loyola U., L.A., 1974. Assoc. prodr. CBS News, N.Y.C., 1976-77, prodr. 60 Minutes, 1974-88, writer, dir. 60 Minutes, 1976-88; pres. No. Films, N.Y.C., 1988-90; exec. prodr. "SST" program ABC, 1989; prodr. 20/20 ABC News, N.Y.C., 1990-93, sr. investigative prodr. 20/20, 1994-96; sr. investigative prodr. Dateline NBC, N.Y.C., 1996—; lectr. New Sch., N.Y.C., 1979, Columbia U., N.Y.C. Author: (play) A Straight Line to the Market Place, 1975, (screenplay) The Scrambler, 1996. Recipient Emmy award NATAS, 1981, 85, 89, 91, 93, 95, George Foster Peabody award, 1989. Mem. NATAS, Writers Guild Am. Avocations: N.Y. Yankees. Office: NBC 30 Rockefeller Plz New York NY 10112

MARBLE, DUANE FRANCIS, geography educator, researcher; b. Seattle, Dec. 10, 1931; s. Francis Augustus and Beulah Belle (Simmons) M.; m. Jacquelynne Hardester, Aug. 18, 1957; children: Kimberley Eileen, Douglas Craig. BA, U. Wash., 1953, MA, 1956, PhD, 1959. Asst. prof. real estate U. Oreg., Eugene, 1959; asst. prof. regional sci. U. Pa., Phila., 1960-63; from assoc. prof. geography to prof. geography Northwestern U., Evanston, Ill., 1963-73, assoc. dir. Transp. Ctr., 1966-73; prof. geography and computer sci. SUNY at Buffalo, Amherst, N.Y., 1973-87; prof. geography and natural resources Ohio State U., Columbus, 1987—; chmn. com. on geog. data sensing and processing Internat. Geog. Union, 1980-88; bd. dirs. Castlereagh Enterprises, Phoenix; founder Internat. Symposium Spatial Data Handling; cons. on geog. info. systems to U.S. Bur. Census, UN, also pvt. orgns. Editor: Intro Readings in GIS, 1990, Taylor & Francis, 1990-95; author computer program (best software award Assn. Am. Geogs. 1990). Mem. AAAS, Assn. Am. Geographers (honors 1993), IEEE Computer Soc. Home: 1310 Langston Dr Columbus OH 43220 Office: Ohio State U Dept Geography Columbus OH 43210-1361

MARBLE, MELINDA SMITH, writer, editor; b. Ponca City, Okla., June 17, 1960; d. Monte Gene and Dorothy Worthington Smith; m. Sanford Marble. BA with high hons., spl. hons. English, U. Tex., 1984. Mktg. Data Base Publs., Austin, Tex., 1986-87; assoc. editor Austin Area Bus. Women Directory, 1987-88; asst. pub. Travelers' Times, Austin, 1988-89; assoc. editor Tex. Bar Jour., Austin, 1989-95; freelance editor, Austin, 1989-95, novelist, freelance journalist, Morristown, N.J., 1995—. Contbr. articles to newspapers and profl. jours. Recipient Gold Quill award of merit Internat. Assn. Bus. Communicators, 1993, Gold Quill Excellence award for First Person Articles, 1995; Best of Austin 4 Color Mag. award, 1993, 2 awards of merit, 1995, Presdl. Citation, State Bar of Tex., 1993, Nat. Assn. Govt. Communicators award of Honor 4 Color Mag., 1994, Best of Austin Feature Writing award, 1995, Best of Austin Advocacy Writing award, 1995. Avocations: reading, writing, traveling, skiing.

MARBURGER, JOHN ALLEN, food manufacturing company executive; b. Wabash, Ind., Jan. 17, 1956; s. John Marburger and L. Betty (Hall) McFarling; m. Rosemary J. Walker, June 12, 1976; children: Billy, Melissa, Joseph. BS in Gen. Mgmt., Purdue U., 1977. Mgr. Rolling Greens Golf & Supper Club, Peru, Ind., 1977-80; mgr., owner M.M.S., Inc., Peru, 1977-92; plant mgr. Marburger Packing Inc., Peru, 1980-84, v.p. mfg., 1984-89; pres., CEO Marburger Foods, Peru, 1989—. Campaign mgr. Ind. State Rep. Dist. #23, Ind., 1992; trustee Dukes Meml. Hosp., Peru, 1992—. Named Hon. Commr. of Agr., Lt. Gov. Ind., Indpls., 1986; recipient Cert. of Appreciation, Nat. Com. for Support Nat. Guard, Grissom AFB, 1991. Mem. Am. Orgn. Analytical Chemists, Pres. Coun. Purdue U., Peru Rotary Club (Paul Harris fellow). Republican. Roman Catholic. Avocation: golf, sportfishing. Office: Marburger Foods PO Box 387 Peru IN 46970-0387

MARBURY, RITCHEY MCGUIRE, III, engineering executive, surveyor; b. Albany, Ga., May 18, 1938; s. Ritchey McGuire and Shirley Kathryn (VanHouten) M.; m. Fonda Gayle Starnes, June 16, 1962; children: Mary Kathryn, Ritchey McGuire IV. BCE, Ga. Tech. Inst., 1960, M in City Planning, 1966. Registered profl. engr., Ga., Fla., Idaho, Ala.; land surveyor, Ga. V.p. Marbury Engring. Co., Albany, Ga., 1965-78, pres., chmn. bd., 1981—; pres. Marbury, Ritter, Scott & Turner, Inc., Albany, 1970-78, 81-92, Marbury Assocs., Inc., 1991—, Idaho Boise Mission of Latter-day Saints Ch., 1978-81; presenter seminars on total quality mgmt. to nat. convs. of Am. Cons. Engrs. Coun., Design Constrn. Quality Inst., Sml. Firm Coalition of Cons. Engrs., Assn. for Project Mgrs. Exec. bd. Boy Scouts Am., Southwest Ga., 1982—. Served to 1st lt. U.S. Army, 1963-65. Mem. NSPE (South Ga. chpt. pres. 1993-95), Am. Cons. Engrs. Coun., Surveying and Mapping Soc. of Ga. (bd. dirs. 1966-78), Ga. Planning Assn., Home Builders Assn. (bd. dirs. 1985-86), Rotary. Mem. LDS Ch. Avocations: fishing, writing, music, computer, golf. Home: 1824 Green Valley Dr Albany GA 31707-3116 Office: 2334 Lake Park Dr Albany GA 31707-3132 *Always be a role model of Christlike behavior and do those things that make a significant differenc for good. Do what's right simply because it's the right thing to do. The greatest results come through kindness.*

MARBUT, ROBERT GORDON, communications and broadcast executive; b. Athens, Ga., Apr. 11, 1935; s. Robert Smith and Laura Gordon (Powers) M.; m. Margo Susan Spitz, Sept. 24, 1989; children: Robert Gordon, Laura Dodd, Michael Powers, Marcy Lizbeth. B Indsl. Engring., Ga. Inst. Tech., 1957; MBA with distinction, Harvard U., 1963. Registered profl. engr., Calif. Engr. Esso Standard Oil Co., Baton Rouge, 1957; corp. dir. engring. and plans Copley Press, La Jolla, Calif., 1963-70; v.p. named changed to Harte-Hanks Newspapers, Inc., San Antonio, 1970-71; pres., CEO named changed to Harte-Hanks Comm., Inc., San Antonio, 1971-91, also dir., 1971-91, vice chmn. bd. dirs., 1991; founder, chmn., CEO Argyle Comm., Inc, San Antonio, 1992—; founder, CEO, dir. Argyle TV Holding, Inc., San Antonio, 1993-95; co-founder, chmn., CEO Argyle TV, Inc., San Antonio, 1994—; dir. AP, 1979-88, vice chmn. 1987-88; chmn. Newspaper Advt. Bur., 1988-90, exec. com. dir. 1974-80, 82-90; bd. dirs Tupperware, Inc., Diamond Shamrock, Inc., Tracor, Inc., Katz Media Group; pres. adv. bd. U Ga. Henry W. Grady Sch. Journalism, 1975—, mem. adv. Found. for Comm. Sch. U. Tex., 1975—; bd. dirs. Tex. Rsch. League, 1975—, Salzburg Inst. Am. Studies, 1978-81; mem. adv. bd. Ga. Tech., 1978-81; founding mem. Am. Bus. Conf., 1981-89; mem. U. Tex. Centennial comm., 1981-83; pres. adv. coun. U. Tex. Coll. Comm., 1982-83; bd. dirs. Up With People, 1983—, exec. com., 1984—; instr. Armstrong Coll., 1951, Calif. State, Los Angeles, 1964, Woodbury Coll., 1964. Author: (with Healy, Henderson and others) Creative Collective Bargaining, 1965; also articles in mags., jours.; frequent spkr. Coordinating chmn. San Antonio Target 90 commn., 1983-84; campaign chmn. United Way, San Antonio, 1985, chmn. bd. dirs., 1988-89; vice chmn. Tex. select com. on Tax Equity, 1987-89; mem select com. Tex. Revenues, 1991-92; mem. Tex. World Trade Coun., 1986-87. Served with USAF, 1958-61. Recipient Isaiah Thomas award Rochester Inst. Tech., 1980, EXCEL award in comm., 1987, People of Vision award, 1991; selected to Acad. Disting. Engring. Alumni Ga. Tech., 1995. Mem. Am. Newspaper Pubs. Assn. Rsch. Inst. (exec. com. 1973—), Am. Newspaper Publs. Assn. (chmn. task group on future, chmn. telecomm. com. 1974—, bd. dirs. 1976—, chmn. future task group), So. Newspaper Pubs. Assn. (pres. 1979-80, dir. 1975-81, treas. 1977, chmn. bus. and adminstrn. com. 1976), Am. Newspaper Pubs. Assn. Found. (trustee 1976—), Tex. Daily Newspaper Assn. (pres. 1979, Tex. Newspaper Leader of Yr., 1981), Greater San Antonio C. of C. (chmn. long range planning task force, dir. 1979—, exec. com. 1981—, chmn., 1984), Delta Tau Delta, Omicron Delta Kappa, Phi Eta Sigma. Protestant. Club: San Antonio Country, Argyle. Office: Argyle Communications 200 Concord Plaza Dr Ste 700 San Antonio TX 78216-6943*

MARCEAU, MARCEL, pantomimist, actor, director, painter, poet; b. Strasbourg, France, Mar. 22, 1923; s. Charles and Anne (Werzberg) Mangel. Student, Sch. Dramatic Art, Sarah Bernhardt Theatre, Paris, 1946; D (hon.), Linfield Coll., Princeton U., U. Mich. Dir. artistique Ecole De Mimodrame de Paris Marcel Marceau. Performer role of Arlequin, pantomime Baptiste; Praxitele and the Golden Fish, Sarah Bernhardt Theatre; creator character Bip, 1947; performer Maggio Musicale in Florence and Edinburgh festivals; organizer, Pantomime Co., Paris; producer: The Overcoat, The Three Wigs, 14th of July, The Pawn Shop, Pierrot de Montmartre,Paris qui rit Paris qui pleure, Don Juan; performer extensive tours U.S., S.Am., Africa, Australia, China, Japan, South East Asia, Russia, Europe, 1950—; performer worldwide TV shows; appeared in motion pictures: Barbarella, 1967, Shanks, 1974, Silent Movie, 1976; appeared as Scrooge in TV film A Christmas Carol, 1973; author, illustrator: The Story of Bip, Pimporello; lithographer The 7 Deadly Sins, The Third Eye. Decorated Officier Legion d'Honneur; comdr. Order Arts and Letters; Commandeur of Merit (France); recipient Emmy awards, 1956, 68, Medaille Vermeil de la ville de Paris, 1978. Mem. Acad. Fine Arts Berlin, Acad. Fine Arts Munich, Academie Des Beaux Arts France. Office: 32 Rue de Londres, 75009 Paris France Office: Ecole Internat Mimodrame Paris, 17 Rue Rene Boulanger, 75010 Paris France

MARCEAU, YVONNE, ballroom dancer. Ballet dancer Ballet West; ptnr. with Pierre Dulaine, 1976; founder, artistic dir. Am. Ballroom Theatre, N.Y.C., 1984—; guest tchr. Sch. Am. Ballet, N.Y.C.; tchr. ballroom dancing Juilliard Sch. Appearances include The Smithsonian Inst., JFK Ctr. for Performing Arts, N.Y. State Theater, N.Y.C., Sadlers Wells, London, (Broadway and London show) Grand Hotel, 1989-92; toured with Pierre Dulaine and Am. Ballroom Theatre worldwide. Recipient Brit. Theatrical Arts Championships 4 times, Spl. Astaire award, Dance Educator awards, Outstanding Achievement in Dance award Nat. Coun. Dance Am., 1992, Dance Mag. award, 1993. Office: Am Ballroom Theatre 129 W 27th St Ste 705 New York NY 10001-6206*

MARCELLUS, JOHN ROBERT, III, trombonist, educator; b. Overton, Tex., Sept. 17, 1939; s. John Robert and Grace (Stockman) M.; children: Robert Gray, John Frederick. BS., U. Md., 1964; Mus.M., Catholic U. Am., 1970, D.Mus. Arts, 1972. Adj. prof. trombone Cath. U. Am., dir. trombone choir and brass ensembles, 1966-78; prof. N.C. Sch. Arts, 1965-68; mem. rotating faculty Inst. Advanced Mus. Studies, Montreux, Switzerland, 1974, Am. U., 1970-78; prof. trombone Eastman Sch. Music, Rochester, N.Y., 1978—, acting chmn. woodwind, brass and percussion, 1981, dir. internat. trombone workshop, 1991; co-dir. Ea. Trombone Workshop, Towson, Md., 1974-80, Internat. Trombone Workshop, 1991; guest condr. Chautauqua Symphony Orch., Penfield Symphony Orch., Chautauqua Wind Ensemble, U.S. Naval Acad. Band, Nat. Music Camp, Interlochen. Trombonist USN Band, Washington, 1960-64, Balt. Symphony, 1964-65; trombonist Nat. Symphony, Washington, 1965-78, prin. trombone, 1970-78; prin. trombone Chautauqua Symphony Orch., 1978; mem. Eastman Brass Quintet; clinician, soloist King Benge Mus. Instruments; solo tours to Scandinavia, Japan, Germany, Greece, Austria, Poland, Australia, England, France; performer with Art Mooney, Ray Eberle, Charlie Spivak, Vaughn Monroe, Henry Mancini Orchs.; music dir. Brighton Symphony Orch., 1980—; contbr. articles to Music Educators Jour., Instrumentalist, Accent, Internat. Trombone Assn. Jour. Mem. Internat. Trombone Assn. (founder, bd. dirs., pres. 1988-90), Am. Fedn. Musicians, Nat. Assn. Wind and Percussion Instruments, Music Educators Nat. Conf., Phi Mu Alpha. Office: Eastman Sch Music 26 Gibbs St Rochester NY 14604-2505 *Dedication, drive and determination to the art of music has been center front on my career in music.*

MARCH, BERYL ELIZABETH, animal scientist, educator; b. Port Hammond, B.C., Can., Aug. 30, 1920; d. James Roy and Sarah Catherine (Wilson) Warrack; m. John Algot March, Aug. 31, 1946; 1 dau., Laurel Allison. B.A., U. B.C., Vancouver, 1942, M.S.A., 1962; D.Sc., U. B.C., 1988. Mem. indsl. research staff Can. Fishing Co. Ltd., 1942-47; mem. research staff, faculty U. B.C., 1947—, prof. animal sci., 1970—. Recipient Poultry Sci. Assn.-Am. Feed Mfrs. award, 1969, Queen's Jubilee medal, 1977, Earle Willard McHenry award Can. Soc. Nutritional Sci., 1986, 125th Can. Confederation Annv. medal, 1993. Fellow Agrl. Inst. Can., Royal Soc. Can., Poultry Sci. Assn.; mem. Profl. Agrologists, Agr. Inst. Can., Can. Soc. Nutritional Sci., Poultry Sci. Assn., Am. Soc. Exptl. Biology and Medicine, Am. Inst. Nutrition, Can. Soc. Animal Sci., Aquaculture Assn. Can. Avocation: researching poultry and fish nutrition and physiology. Office: U BC Dept Animal Sci, Vancouver, BC Canada V6T 2A2

MARCH, JACQUELINE FRONT, retired chemist; b. Wheeling, W.Va.; m. A.W. March (dec.); children: Wayne Front, Gail March Cohen. BS, Case Western Res. U., 1937, MA, 1939; postgrad. U. Chgo., U. Pitts. (1942-45), Ohio State U. Clin. chemist, Mt. Sinai Hosp., Cleve.; med. rsch. chemist U. Chgo.; rsch. analyst Koppers Co., also info. scientist Union Carbide Corp., Carnegie-Mellon U., Pitts.; propr. March Med. Rsch. Lab., etiology of diabetes, Dayton, Ohio; guest scientist Kettering Found., Yellow Springs, Ohio; Dayton Found. fellow Miami Valley Hosp. Rsch. Inst.; chemistry faculty U. Dayton, computer/chem. info. scientist Rsch. Inst. U. Dayton; on-base prin. investigator Air Force Info. Ctr. Wright-Patterson AFB, 1969-79; chem. info. specialist Nat. Inst. Occupl. Safety and Health, Cin., 1979-90; propr. JFM Cons., Ft. Myers, Fla., 1990-93; ret., 1993; designer info. sys., spkr. in field. Contbr. articles to profl. pubis. Active Retired & Sr. Vol. Program Lee County Sch. Dist., 1992-93, Lee County Hosp. Med. Libr., Rutenberg County Libr., Wyeth Gastrointestinal fellow med. rsch. U. Chgo., 1940-42. Mem. AAUP (exec. bd. 1978-79), Am. Soc. Info. Sci. (treas. South Ohio chpt. 1973-75), Am. Chem. Soc. (emeritus, Fla. chpt., pres. Dayton 1977), Dayton Engring. Soc. (hon.), Soc. Advancement Materials & Process Engring. (Fla. chpt., pres. Midwest chpt. 1977-78), Dayton Affiliated Tech. Socs. (Outstanding Scientist and Engr. award 1978), Sigma Xi (emeritus, Fla. chpt., pres. Cin. fed. environ. chpt. 1986-87).

MARCH, JAMES GARDNER, social scientist, educator; b. Cleve., Jan. 15, 1928; s. James Herbert and Mildred (MacCorkle) M.; m. Jayne Mary Dohr, Sept. 23, 1947; children: Kathryn Sue, Gary Clifton, James Christopher, Roderic Gunn. BA, U. Wis., 1949; MA, Yale U., 1950, PhD, 1953; hon. doctorate, Copenhagen Sch. Econs., 1978, Swedish Sch. Econs., 1979, U. Wis., Milw., 1980, U. Bergen, 1980, Uppsala U., 1987, Helsinki Sch. Econs., 1991, Dublin City U., 1994. From asst. prof. to prof. Carnegie Inst. Tech., 1953-64; prof., dean Sch. Social Scis. U. Calif., Irvine, 1964-70; prof. mgmt., higher edn., polit. sci. and sociology Stanford (Calif.) U., 1970-95, prof. emeritus, 1995—; cons. in field, 1954—; Mem. Nat. Council Ednl. Research, 1975-78; mem. Nat. Sci. Bd., 1968-74; mem. sociol.-social psychology panel NSF, 1964-66; social sci. tng. com. NIMH, 1967-68; mem. math. social sci. com. Social Sci. Research Council, 1958-60; mem. Assembly Behavioral and Social Sci., NRC, 1973-79, chmn. com. on aging, 1977-82, chmn. com. on math., sci., tech. edn., 1984-86. Author: (with H.A. Simon) Organizations, 1958, 2nd edit., 1993, (with R.M. Cyert) A Behavioral Theory of the Firm, 1963, 2nd edit., 1992, Handbook of Organizations, 1965, (with B.R. Gelbaum) Mathematics for the Social and Behavioral Sciences, 1969, (with M.D. Cohen) Leadership and Ambiguity, 1974, 2nd edit., 1986, Academic Notes, 1974, (with C.E. Lave) An Introduction to Models in the Social Sciences, 1975, (with J.P. Olsen) Ambiguity and Choice in Organizations, 1976, Aged Wisconsin, 1977, Autonomy as a Factor in Group Organization, 1980, Pleasures of the Process, 1980, Slow Learner, 1985, (with R. Weissinger-Baylon) Ambiguity and Command, 1986, Decisions and Organizations, 1988, (with J.P. Olsen) Rediscovering Institutions, 1989, Minor Memos, 1990, A Primer on Decision Making, 1994, Fornuft og Forandring, 1995, (with J.P. Olsen) Democratic Governance, 1995; contbr. articles to profl. jour. Fellow Ctr. Advanced Study in Behavioral Scis., 1955-56, 73-74; recipient Wilbur Lucius Cross medal Yale U., 1968; named knight 1st class Royal Norwegian Order of Merit, 1995. Mem. NAS, Nat. Acad. Edn., Accademia Italiana di Economia Aziendale, Royal Swedish Acad. Scis., Norwegian Acad. of Sci. and Letters, Am. Acad. Arts and Scis., Am. Econ. Assn., Am. Polit. Sci. Assn. (v.p. 1983-84, John Gaus award 1997), Am. Psychol. Assn., Am. Sociol. Assn., Acad. Mgmt., Russell Sage Found. (trustee 1985-94, chmn. 1990-93), Finnish Soc. Scis. and Letters, Phi Beta Kappa, Sigma Xi. Home: 837 Tolman Dr Stanford CA 94305-1025 Office: Stanford U Scancor 509 Ceras Stanford CA 94305-3084

MARCH, MARION D., writer, astrologer, consultant; b. Nürnberg, Germany, Feb. 10, 1923; came to the U.S., 1941; d. Franz and Grete Dispeker; m. Nico D. March, Sept. 1, 1948; children: Michele, Nico F. Diploma, Ecole de Commerce, Lausanne; attended, Columbia U. Cons. astrologer L.A., 1970—; founder, pres., tchr. Aquarius Workshops, L.A., 1975—; internat. lectr. in field, 1976—; chmn. bd. dirs., convention dir. United Astrology Congress, 1986, 89, 92; co-founder, mem. bd. dirs. Assn. for Astrological Networking; cons. in astrology to psychology profls. Author: (books) (with Joan McEvers) The Only Way To... Learn Astrology, 1981-94 (6 vol. series), Astrology: Old Theme, New Thoughts, 1984; editor (mag.) ASPECTS, 1976-93; contbr. numerous articles to jours. in field. Recipient Regulus award for edn. United Astology Congress, 1989, for community svc., 1992, PAI Annual award Profl. Astrologers, Inc., 1990, Syotisha Ratna award Syotish Samsthan of Bombay, India, 1986, Robert Carl Jansky Astrology Leadership award, 1994. Mem. Nat. Coun. for Geocosmic Rsch. (mem. adv. bd.), Internat. Soc. Astrological Rsch., Profl. Astrologers Inc., Astrological Assn. Great Britain. Avocations: reading, gardening, music, skiing, travelling. Office: care Publisher ACS PO Box 34487 San Diego CA 92163-4487

MARCH, RALPH BURTON, retired entomology educator; b. Oshkosh, Wis., Aug. 5, 1919; s. Albert Harold and Vanita Ida Cora (Siewert) M.; m. Robinetta Tompkin, Dec. 26, 1942; children: John S., Janice A., Susan E. Student, Oshkosh State Tchrs. Coll., 1937-38; B.A., U. Ill., 1941, M.A. (Grad. scholar 1941-42), 1946, Ph.D. (Grad. fellow 1947-48), 1948. Faculty U. Calif. at Riverside, 1948—, entomologist, 1957—, prof. entomology, 1961-83, prof. entomology emeritus, 1983—, dean grad. div., 1961-68, head div. toxicology and physiology dept. entomology, 1968-72, chmn. dept. entomology, 1978-83. Served with USAAF, 1942-46. Mem. Entomol. Soc. Am., Am. Chem. Soc., AAAS, Phi Beta Kappa, Sigma Xi, Phi Kappa Phi, Phi Sigma. Home: 300 Deer Valley Rd # 4A San Rafael CA 94903-5514

MARCHAK, MAUREEN PATRICIA, anthropology and sociology educator; b. Lethbridge, Alta., Can., June 22, 1936; d. Adrian Ebenezer and Wilhelmina Rankin (Hamilton) Russell; m. William Marchak, Dec. 31, 1956; children: Geordon Eric, Lauren Craig. BA, U. B.C., Vancouver, Can., 1958, PhD, 1970. Asst. prof. U. B.C., Vancouver, 1972-75, assoc. prof., 1975-80, prof., 1980—, head dept. anthropology and sociology, 1987-90, dean faculty arts, 1990-96. Author: Ideological Perspectives on Canada, 1975, 2d edit., 1981, 3d edit., 1988, In Whose Interests, 1979, Green Gold, 1983 (John Porter award 1985), The Integrated Circus, The New Right and The Restructuring of Global Markets, 1991, Logging The Globe, 1995, Racism, Sexism and the University, the Political Science Affair of UBC, 1996; author, co-editor: Uncommon Property, 1987; mem. editorial bd. Can. Rev. Sociology and Anthropology, Montreal, Que., 1971-74, Studies in Polit. Economy, Ottawa, Ont., Can., 1980-87, Current Sociology, 1980-86, Can. Jour. Sociology, 1986-90, B.C. Studies, 1988-90. Bd. dirs., chairperson ethics com. U. B.C. Hosp., 1992-93, Cedar Lodge Trust Soc., 1989-92; mem. adv. coun. Ecotrust, 1991-93, bd. dirs., 1993—; chmn. bd. dirs. B.C. Bldgs. Corp., 1992-95; mem. B.C. Forest Appeals Commn., 1996—. Fellow Royal Soc. Can. (v.p. Acad. II 1994-96); mem. Can. Sociology and Anthropology Assn. (pres. 1979-80, other offices), Internat. Sociol. Assn., Can. Polit. Sci. Assn., Assn. for Can. Studies, Forest History Soc. (mem. exec. com. 1991-92). Mem. New Dem. Party (Can.). Avocations: hiking, swimming, traveling. Home: 4455 W 1st Ave, Vancouver, BC Canada V6R 4H9 Office: U BC, Dept Anthropol & Sociology, 6303 NW Marine Dr, Vancouver, BC Canada V6T 121

MARCHALONIS, JOHN JACOB, immunologist, educator; b. Scranton, Pa., July 22, 1940; s. John Louis and Anna Irene (Stadner) M.; m. Sally Ann Sevy, May 5, 1978; children: Lee, Elizabeth, Emily. A.B. summa cum Laude, Lafayette Coll., 1962; Ph.D., Rockefeller U., 1967. Grad. fellow Rockefeller U., 1962-67; fellow Am. Cancer Soc. Walter and Eliza Hall Inst. Med. Research, 1967-68; asst. prof. biomed. scis. Brown U., 1969-70; head molecular immunology lab. Walter and Eliza Hall Inst. Med. Research, Melbourne, Australia, 1970-76; head cell biology and biochemistry sect. Frederick Cancer Research Ctr., 1977-80; prof. adj. faculty dept. pathology U. Pa., 1977-83; prof., chmn. dept. biochemistry and molecular biology Med. U. S.C., Charleston, 1980-88; prof., chmn. dept. microbiology and immunology U. Ariz., Tucson, 1988—, prof. pathology, 1991—, prof. medicine, 1992—; bd. dirs. Am. Type Tissue Culture Collection. Author: Immunity in Evolution, 1977; editor: Comparative Immunology, 1976, The Lymphocyte: Structure and Function, 1977, (with N. Cohen) Self/Non-Self Discrimination, 1980, (with G.W. Warr) Antibody as a Tool, 1982, The Immunobiology and Molecular Biology of Parasitic Infections, 1983, Antigen-Specific T Cell Receptors and Factors, 1987, The Lymphocyte: Structure and Function, 2d edit., 1987, (with Carol Reinisch) Defense Molecules, 1989, (with Gregory Beck, Edwin L. Cooper and Gail S. Habicht) Primordial Immunity, 1994; edtl. bd. jours. in field. Active Nat. Commn. Damon Runyon-Walter Winchel Cancer Fund. Named among 1,000 most highly cited sci. authors Inst. for Sci. Info.; Frank R. Lillie fellow, 1974; grantee in field. Fellow Am. Inst. Chemists, Am. Acad. Microbiology; mem. AAAS, Am. Assn. Immunology, Am. Soc. Biol. Chemists, Sigma Xi, Phi Beta Kappa. Episcopalian. Achievements include development of microchemical (radioimmunochemical) approaches for proteins and surface receptors of living cells; characterization of immunoglobulin-like antigen receptors of thymus-derived lymphocytes; application of synthetic peptide technology to antibodies, T cell receptors and autoimmunity; pioneered investigation of the molecular evolution of immunity. Home: 5661 N Camino Arturo Tucson AZ 85718-3933 Office: U Ariz Health Sci Ctr Tucson AZ 85724

MARCHAND, LESLIE ALEXIS, language educator, writer; b. Bridgeport, Wash., Feb. 13, 1900; s. Alexis and Clara Adele (Buckingham) M.; m. Marion Knill Hendrix, July 8, 1950. B.A., U. Wash., 1922, M.A., 1923; Ph.D., Columbia U., 1940; postgrad., Sorbonne, Paris, 1927-28, U. Munich, Germany, summer 1932; L.H.D. hon., U. Alaska, 1976; Litt.D. (hon.), Rutgers U., 1981. Asst. in English U. Wash., Seattle, 1920-23; instr., summer U. Wash., 1924, vis. prof., 1925, 58; prof. English and French Alaska Agrl. Coll. and Sch. Mines (now U. Alaska), 1923-27, 34-35; extension tchr. English Columbia U., 1928-34, instr., summers 1929-31, vis. prof., summers 1945-46, 65; lectr. Columbia U. (Coll. Pharmacy), 1936-37; instr. Rutgers U., 1937-42, asst. prof., 1942-46, asso. prof., 1946-53, prof., 1953-66, emeritus, 1966—; Fulbright prof. U. Athens, Greece, 1958-59; lectr. English Hunter Coll., 1960-62; Berg vis. prof. N.Y. U., 1962-63; vis. prof. Ariz. State U., 1966-67; Adams chair English Hofstra U., 1967-68; vis. prof. U. Calif. at Los Angeles, summer 1949, U. Ill., summer 1954, Harvard U., summer 1969. Author: The Athenaeum: A Mirror of Victorian Culture, 1941, Byron: A Biography, 1957, Byron's Poetry: A Critical Introduction, 1965, Byron: A Portrait, 1970; editor: Letters of Thomas Hood, 1945, Selected Poetry of Lord Byron, 1951, Lord Byron: Don Juan, 1958, Byrons's Letters and Jours., Vols. 1-12, 1973-82, supplementary vol., 1994, Lord Byron: Selected Letters and Jours., 1982; editl. bd.: Keats-Shelley Jour.; contbr. articles to profl. jours. Recipient Ivan Sandrof award Nat. Book Critics Circle, 1982; Guggenheim fellow, 1968-69, 79-80; Nat. Endowment for Humanities grantee, 1972-73, 74-75, 76-79. Fellow Royal Soc. Lit. (Eng.); mem. PEN, MLA (James Russell Lowell prize), Keats-Shelley Assn. Am. (dir.), Byron Soc., Phi Beta Kappa. Home: 570 Foxwood Blvd Englewood FL 34223-6100

MARCHAND, NANCY, actress; b. Buffalo, June 19, 1928; d. Raymond L. and Marjorie F. M.; m. Paul Sparer, July 7, 1951; children: David, Kathryn, Rachel. BFA, Carnegie Inst. Tech., 1949. Vol. actress Actors studio, N.Y.C.; TV appearances include A Touch of the Poet, Marty, Of Famous Memory, Cheers, Coach, Night Court; series regular on TV show Lou Grant, 1977-82 (Emmy award 1978, 1980, 1981, 1982); theater: performed at Circle in the Sq., N.Y.C., L.A. Music Center, Lincoln Center, N.Y.C., Am. Shakespeare Festival, Goodman Theater, Chgo., Ahmanson Theater, Los Angeles; appeared on Broadway in And Miss Reardon Drinks a Little, After the Rain, Miss Isobel, Three Bags Full, Mornings at Seven, 40 Carats, Octette Bridge Club; off-Broadway plays: Children, Sister Mary Ignatius, The Balcony (Obie award 1959), Cocktail Hour (Obie Award 1989), The End of the Day, 1992, White Liars and Black Comedy, 1993, The Importance of Being Earnest, 1996; films include Bachelor Party, 1957, Ladybug, Ladybug, 1963, Me, Natalie, 1969, Tell Me That You Love Me Junie Moon, 1969, The Hospital, 1971, The Bostonians, 1984, From the Hip, 1987, Naked Gun, 1988, Brain Doners, 1991, Jefferson in Paris, 1994, Sabrina, 1995; TV films include Some Kind of Miracle, North and South Book II. Recipient Drama Desk award, Outstanding Ensemble Performances, 1979.

MARCHAND, RUSSELL DAVID, II, fire chief; b. Lafayette, Ind., May 14, 1950; s. Russell David and Mable May (Gean) M.; m. Sandra Green, June 12, 1951 (div. Nov. 1986); 1 child, Russell David III; m. Carol Bella Flashenburg, May 31, 1987 (div. Feb., 1996). AA in Fire Sci., Clark County Community Coll., Las Vegas, Nev., 1979. Cert. fire service instr., supr. instr. Firefighter North Las Vegas Fire Dept., 1973-78, engr., 1978-82, capt., 1982-95, divsn. chief, officer-in-charge bldg. and constrn., 1990—; pres. Local 1607 Internat. Assn. Fire Fighters, Las Vegas, 1980— (v.p. 1976-80); instr. N. Las Vegas Fire Dept., 1986. Chmn. N. Las Vegas Firefighters Polit. Action Com., 1980—, Muscular Dystrophy Assn., 1980-83, 85. Sgt. USMC, 1966-72, South Vietnam. Named Fireman of Yr., Optimist Club, 1981, Lions Club Nev., 1989, Profl. Ins. Agts. of Am.; received citation of merit Muscular Dystrophy Assn., 1982, commendation City of N. Las Vegas, 1980, 83, 85. Mem. Fed. Firefighters Nev. (received commendation 1982), Internat. Assn. Fire Fighters (local 1607 pres. emeritus 1990). Avocations: sailing, computers. Office: 2626 E Carey Ave North Las Vegas NV 89030-6215

MARCHANT, DAVID JUDSON, lawyer; b. Oakland, Calif., Jan. 12, 1939; s. Luther Brusie and Marian Hand (Fisher) M.; m. Susan Robbins (div. 1980); children: Michael Hilton, Robbins Fisher, Lauren Payton. BA, U. Calif., Berkeley, 1961; JD, U. Calif., San Francisco, 1967. Bar: Calif. 1967. Atty. Calif. Pub. Utilities Commn., San Francisco, 1967-68; ptnr. Graham & James, San Francisco, 1968—; sr. counsel MCI Telecom. Corp., San Francisco. Mem. ABA (pub. utility law sect.). Office: MCI Telecom Corp 201 Spear St Fl 9 San Francisco CA 94105-1630

MARCHANT, MAURICE PETERSON, librarian, educator; b. Peoa, Utah, Apr. 20, 1927; s. Stephen C. and Beatrice (Peterson) M.; m. Gerda VaLoy Hansen, June 3, 1949; children: Catherine, Barrie, Alan, Roxanne, Claudia, David, Theresa. BA, U. Utah, 1949, MS, 1953; AM in Libr. Sci., U. Mich., 1966, MA, 1968, Ph.D., 1970. Tchr. area h.s. Altamont, Utah, 1949-50; libr. area h.s. Salt Lake City and Preston, Idaho, 1950-53; chief tech. libr. Dugway (Utah) Proving Ground, 1953-58; libr. Carnegie Free Libr., Ogden, Utah, 1958-66; mem. faculty Brigham Young U., Provo, Utah, 1969-92, prof. libr. and info. scis., 1976-92, dir. Sch. Libr. and Info. Scis., 1975-82; prof. emeritus libr. and info. scis. Brigham Young U. (Sch. Library and Info. Scis.), Provo, Utah, 1992—; exec. dir. Nat. Libr. Week, Utah, 1961-62. Author: Participative Management in Academic Libraries, 1976, SPSS as a Library Research Tool, 1977, Books That Made a Difference in Provo, 1989, Why Adults Use the Public Library, 1994, also articles. Served with USN, 1945-46. Mid-career fellow Coun. Libr. Resources, 1972. Mem. AAUP, ALA (rsch. paper award Libr. Rsch. Round Table 1975), Utah Libr. Assn. (pres. 1964-65, Disting. Svc. award 1986). Address: 2877 N 220 E Provo UT 84604-3906 *Man has the potential of learning to love or exploit, to become wise or remain ignorant. God intends us to become charitable and wise, preparing us to contribute to human progress. My measure of success as a librarian and educator must reflect my commitment to lifelong learning and to honest respect of others.*

MARCHANT, TRELAWNEY ESTON, retired national guard officer, lawyer; b. Columbia, S.C., Dec. 9, 1921; s. Trelawney Eston and Lila (Cave) M.; m. Caroline Melton Bristow, Nov. 10, 1951; children—Trelawney Eston, III, Walter Bristow, Caroline M., Nancy Lila. B.S., U. S.C., 1942, LL.B., 1947; grad. various USMC and U.S. Army schs. Bar: S.C. 1947. Pvt. practice Columbia, 1948-78; mem. S.C. N.G., 1947-95, maj. gen., 1979; comdr. Palmetto Mil. Acad., 1968-71; adj. gen. State of S.C., 1978-95. Mem. bd. visitors The Citadel, Charleston, S.C., 1979-95; trustee U. S.C., 1965-70, chmn., 1970-78, mem. devel. adv. coun., 1963-77; chmn. Nat. Found., 1953-60; v.p. U. S.C. Ednl. Found., 1957-77; chmn. Richland County Dem. Party, 1964-68. Served as officer USMCR, 1942-46. Mem. ABA, Am. Judicature Soc., 4th Cir. Jud. Conf., Adjs. Gen. Assn. U.S. (pres. 1989-91), Acad. Polit. Sci., S.C. Bar Assn., Richland County Bar Assn. (pres. 1970-71), Mil. Order World Wars (past chpt. pres.), Am. Legion, N.G. Assn. S.C. (past pres.), U. S.C. Alumni Assn. (past pres.), Order of Palmetto (S. Carolinian of Yr. 1990), Sigma Nu, Omicron Delta Kappa. Episcopalian. Clubs: Columbia Cotillion (pres. 1991-92), Columbia Ball, Tarantella, Summit, Forest Lake. Home: 5046 Courtney Rd Columbia SC 29206-2909

MARCHELLO, JOSEPH MAURICE, mathematics and physical science educator; b. East Moline, Ill., Oct. 6, 1933; s. Anton Joseph and Katherine Margaret (Scavarda) M.; m. Mary Louise Coulson, Jan. 27, 1960; children—Sara Leigh, Katherine C. B.S. in Chem. Engring, U. Ill., 1955; Ph.D., Carnegie-Mellon U., 1959. Asst. prof. chem. engring. Okla. State U., 1959-61; asst. prof. U. Md., 1961-62, assoc. prof., 1962-66, prof., 1966-78, chmn. dept. chem. engring., 1967-73, provost div. math. and phys. scis. and engring., 1973-78; chancellor U. Mo.-, Rolla, 1978-85; pres. Old Dominion U., Norfolk, Va., 1985-88; prof., 1985—; Pres. Mo. Council Pub. Higher Edn., 1981-82. Author: Control of Air Pollution Sources, 1976; editor: (with John J. Kelly) Gas Cleaning for Air Pollution Control, 1975, (with Albert Gomezplata) Gas-Solids Handling in the Process Industry, 1976; contbr. numerous articles to profl. jours. Mem. Md. Air Quality Control Adv. Council, 1966-78, chmn., 1971-78; mem. Md. Adv. Commn. on Atomic Energy, 1973-78; chmn. Md. Power Plant Siting Com., 1978. Mem. AAAS, NSPE, Air Pollution Control Assn., Am. Inst. Chem. Engrs., Am. Chem. Soc., Mo. Soc. Profl. Engrs., N.Y. Acad. Sci., Mo. Acad. Sci., Cosmos Club. Presbyterian. Home: 6 Rhoda Ct Hampton VA 23664-1769 Office: Coll Engring Old Dominion Norfolk VA 23508

MARCHESANO, JOHN EDWARD, electro-optical engineer; b. N.Y.C., Aug. 20, 1927; s. John R. and Maria J. (Mollino) M.; divorced; children: Pamela, Debra, Scott, Neal. BEE, CCNY, 1951; postgrad., U. Pa., 1954-56. Project engr. Philco Rsch., Pa., 1951-56; sr. engr. Am. Bosch Arma, Garden City, N.Y., 1956-60; pres. Automation Labs. Inc., Mineola, N.Y., 1960-66; pres., CEO Decilog, Inc., Melville, N.Y., 1966—. Achievements include development and design of wide angle lens for aircraft collision avoidance, modulation transfer system for low light level TV evaluation, long wavelength infared missile research, laser eye protection devices. Office: Decilog Inc 555 Broadhollow Rd Melville NY 11747-5001

MARCHESE, MICHAEL JAMES, JR., radiation oncologist; b. N.Y.C., Mar. 9, 1955; s. Michael James Sr. and Mabel Gladys (Rosero) M.; m. Kathryn Allen, Aug. 7, 1982 (div. May 1993); 1 child, Michael James III. BA magna cum laude, NYU, 1976; MD, Baylor Coll. Medicine, 1979. Diplomate Am. Bd. Radiology. Intern Monmouth Med. Ctr., Hahnemann Med. Coll., Long Branch, N.J., Phila., 1979-80; resident and chief resident radiation therapy Presbyn. Hosp., Columbia U. Coll. Physicians and Surgeons, N.Y.C., 1980-83, asst. attending physician radiation oncology, 1983-87; resident brachytherapy svc. Meml. Hosp. Cancer & Allied Diseases, Cornell U. Med. Coll., N.Y.C., 1982; asst. clin. prof. radiation oncology Columbia U. Coll. Physicians & Surgeons, N.Y.C., 1983-84, asst. prof. radiation oncology, 1984-87; attending staff radiology/radiation oncology Cmty. Med. Ctr., Toms River, N.J., 1987-96, Kimball Med. Ctr., Lakewood, N.J., 1994—, Med. Ctr. Ocean County, Brick, N.J., 1996—; investigator Nat. Cancer Inst., 1983-87, investigator radiation therapy oncology group, 1983-87, 95—, physician surveyor, 1983-85, investigator cancer and leukemia group B, 1986-87, investigator Ea. Coop. Oncology Group, 1995—; physician surveyor practice accreditation program Am. Coll. Radiology, 1986-87. Author: (with others) Radiation Therapy of Gynecological Cancers, 1987, Frontiers of Radiation Therapy and Oncology, vol. 22, 1988; contbr. articles to profl. jours. Bd. dirs. Am. Cancer Soc., Ocean County, N.J., 1993—, v.p., 1993-94, pres., 1994—. Recipient Resident/Fellow award Am. Radium Soc., Travel award European Soc. Therapeutic Radiology and Oncology, Clin. Oncology Career Devel. award Am. Cancer Soc. Mem. Am. Coll. Radiology, Am. Soc. Therapeutic Radiology and Oncology, Am. Soc. Clin. Oncology, Acad. Medicine N.J., Radiation Rsch. Soc., N.Y. Acad. Sci., Ocean County Med. Soc., Med. Soc. N.J. Roman Catholic. Home: 44 Lake Shore Dr Red Bank NJ 07701-5840 Office: Ocean Radiation Therapy Ctr 19 Mule Rd Toms River NJ 08755-5029

MARCHESE, RONALD THOMAS, ancient history and archaeology educator; b. Fresno, Calif., Mar. 17, 1947; s. John Anthony and Julie Rita (Ferrarese) M.; m. Marcia Lynn Schneider, Apr. 6, 1974 (div. Apr. 1980); children: Stephanie Jo, Kayla Marie. BA summa cum laude, Calif. State U., Fresno, 1970; MA, N.Y.U., 1972, PhD with distinction, 1976; postgrad., Columbia U., 1972-73. Asst. prof. Va. Poly. Inst., Blacksburg, 1976-77; asst. to assoc. prof. ancient history and archaeology U. Minn., Duluth, 1977-87, prof., 1987—; rsch. assoc. dept. classics NYU, 1972-74; evaluator grant proposals NEH, HSF; excavator numerous sites in Israel and Turkey; lectr. in field. Author 4 books; contbr. articles to profl. jours. Recipient Fulbright-Hays Sr. Research fellowship, Turkey, 1984-85, 91-92, The Am. Council Learned Socs. fellowship, 1977-78, NDEA Title VI Fgn. Languages fellowship, 1972-75, Spl. Commendation for Excellence award Phi Alpha Theta, 1979; grantee NEH, 1978, 80, nat. Geographic Soc., 1974, Andrew Mellon Found., NSF, Ford Found., 1971-72, U. Minn., others. Mem. NEH, Nat. Assn. Scholars, Coun. for Internat. Exchange, Am. Coun. Learned Socs., Fulbright Alumni Assn., Phi Alpha Theta, Sigma Xi. Roman Catholic. Avocations: tennis, golf, dressage. Home: 5789 220th St N Forest Lake MN 55025-9677

MARCHESI, VINCENT T., biochemist, educator; b. N.Y.C., Sept. 4, 1935; married, 1959; three children. BA, Yale U., 1957, MD, 1963; PhD in Pathology, Oxford (Eng.) U., Eng., 1961. Intern, resident in pathology Wash. U., Bethesda, Md., 1963-65; rsch. assoc. cell biology Rockefeller U., New Haven, 1965-66; staff assoc. Nat. Cancer Inst., 1966-68; chief sect. chem. pathology Nat. Inst. Arthritis, Metabolism & Digestive Disorders, 1968-77; Anthony N. Brady prof. pathology Sch. Medicine Yale U., 1977—; dir. Boyer Ctr. Molecular Medicine Yale U., New Haven, 1987—; cons. Miles Pharm., West Haven, Conn., 1982—. Bd. dirs. Am. Cyanamid, N.J., 1992-94. Lt. comdr. USPHS, 1966-72. Mem. Inst. Medicine-NAS, Histochem. Soc., N.Y. Acad. Sci., Am. Soc. Cell Biology. Avocations: tennis, history. Office: Yale U Sch Medicine Dept Pathology Brady Meml Lab New Haven CT 06520 also: Boyer Ctr Molecular Medicine 295 Congress Ave New Haven CT 06519-1417*

MARCHI, JON, cattle rancher, exporter, former investment brokerage executive; b. Ann Arbor, Mich., Aug. 6, 1946; s. John Robert and Joan Trimble (Toole) M.; m. Mary Stewart Sale, Aug. 12, 1972; children: Aphia Jessica, Jon Jacob. Student Claremont Men's Coll., 1964-65; BS, U. Mont., 1968, MS, 1972. Sec., treas. Marchi, Marchi & Marchi, Inc., Morris, Ill., 1968-69; account exec. D. A. Davidson & Co., Billings, Mont., 1972-75, asst. v.p., office mgr., 1976-77, v.p. mktg. and adminstrn., Great Falls, Mont., 1977—; sec., dir., v.p. fin. svcs. and exec. devel., D. A. Davidson Realty Corp., Great Falls, 1978-85, chmn. rsch. com., 1980; cattle rancher, Polson, Mont., 1985—; bd. dirs. Big Sky Airlines, Billings, Mont., chmn. bd. dirs., 1995; bd. dirs. Energy Overthrust Found., Mansfield Found., Mont. Beverages, Mont. Venture Capital Network, Direct Advantage, Inc., Hamilton, Mont., Mont. Naturals Internat., Inc., Eclipse Techs., Inc., Mont. Small Bus. Investment Corp.; chmn., dir. Devel. Corp. Mont., Helena, 1995. Chmn. Mont. Gov.'s Subcom. for Venture Capital Devel., Mont. Cmty. Fin. Corp., Helena; chmn. investment com., State of Mont. Sci. and Tech. Alliance, 1985—; chmn. seed capital com. State of Mont., bd. dirs. job svc. com. Mem. Mont. Peoples Action; sec.-treas. Valley View Assn., 1987—; trustee sch. dist. # 35, Polson, Mont., 1990—, chmn., 1991—; bd. dirs. Mont. Entrepreneurship Ctr., Missoula, Mont., 1990—; pres., dir., sec./treas. Mont. Pvt. Capital Network, Bozeman, Mont., 1990—, pres., 1992—; chmn., dir. Mont. Naturals Internat., Inc., 1991; dir. Mont. State Rural Devel. Coun., 1992, Mont. SBA Adv. Coun., 1992; dir. Ctr. Econ. Renewal and Tech. Transfer Mont. State U., Bozeman, 1994—; del. to White House Conf. on Small Bus., Washington, 1994-95; chmn. Glacier Venture Fund, Helena, Mont., 1996—. With U.S. Army, 1969-71. Mem. Nat. Cattlemen's Assn. (fgn. trade com.), Am. Wagyu Assn., Can. Wagyu Assn., Polson C. of C. (bd. dirs.), Valley View Assn. (bd. dirs.), Mont. Cattle Feeders Assn., Montana Angus Assn., Am. Angus Assn., Western Mont. Stockgrowers Assn., Securities Industry Assn., Mont. Stock Growers Assn., Mont. Ambassadors (dir. 1995), Polson C. of C. (dir.), Leadership Great Falls Club, Ski Club, Mont. Club, Helena Wilderness Riders Club, Rotary. Episcopalian. Home: 7783 Valley View Rd Polson MT 59860-9302 Office: Marchi Angus Ranches 7783 Valley View Rd Polson MT 59860-9302

MARCHI, LORRAINE JUNE, association executive; b. San Francisco, June 5, 1923; d. Leopold Pulverman and Josephine Lillian (Trieber) Heiman; m. Gene Marchi, Apr. 10, 1943 (div. 1973); children: Gene, Jeffrey, Debra, Beth; m. Robert L. Fastie, Oct. 21, 1973. Student Stanford U., 1941-42, U. Calif.-Berkeley, 1942-43. Founder Com. To Aid Visually Handicapped Children, San Francisco, 1954-57; pres. Aid to Visually Handicapped, San Francisco, 1957-59; founder, exec. dir. Nat. Assn. for Visually Handicapped, San Francisco, 1972—; sec. Calif. Conf. for Exceptional and Rehab. Needs, San Francisco, 1955-66; chmn. bd. Langley Porter Neuropsychiat. Inst., San Francisco, 1966-73. Recipient spl. svc. award Los Angeles County Soc. Ophthalmology, 1971; honor award Am. Acad. Ophthalmology and Otolaryngology, 1971, Lifetime Achievement award Nat. Assn. for Visually Handicapped, 1989; cert. of appreciation Am. Acad. Ophthalmology, 1978; named Woman of Yr. San Francisco sect. Nat. Council Jewish Women, 1957, one of Ten Disting. Women San Francisco Examiner Bay Area, 1959. Home: 305 E 24th St New York NY 10010-4011

MARCHI, SERGIO SISTO, Canadian government official; b. Buenos Aires, May 12, 1956; s. Ottavio and Luisa (D'Agostinis) M.; m. Laureen Storozuk, Oct. 1, 1983. BA with honors, York U., Toronto, 1979. Exec. asst. to Ron Irwin and Hon. Jim Flemming, 1980-82; alderman City of North York, 1982-84; M.P. for York West dist. Ho. of Commons, Ottawa, 1984—, min. citizenship and immigration, 1993-96; min. of environment, 1996—; mem. cabinet coms. on treasury bd., social policy and program review. Mem. Cabinet Com. on Treas. bd., Social Policy and Program Review; vice chmn. North York Planning Bd., Toronto, 1982-84, Standing Com. on Transport, Ottawa, 1990-93; chmn. Nat. Liberal Caucus, Ottawa, 1990-93. Mem. Liberal Party. Roman Catholic. Avocations: reading, walking, fishing, skiing. Office: Environment, 10 Wellington St 28th Fl, Hull, PQ Canada K1A 0H3

MARCHIBRODA, TED (THEODORE JOSEPH MARCHIBRODA), professional football coach; b. Mar. 15, 1931; m. Henrietta Marchibroda; children: Jodi, Teddy, Lonni, Robert. Student, St. Bonaventure Coll., 1950-51, U. Detroit, 1952. Football player Pitts. Steelers, 1953-54, 55-56, Chgo. Cardinals, 1957-58; asst. coach Washington Redskins, 1961-65, offensive coord., 1971-74; asst. coach L.A. Rams, 1966-70; head coach Balt. Colts, 1975-79; offensive coord., quarterbacks coach Chgo. Bears, 1981; offensive coord. Detroit Lions, 1982-83; offensive coord., quarterbacks coach Phila. Eagles, 1984-85; quarterbacks coach Buffalo Bills, 1987-88, offensive coord., 1989-92; head coach Indpls. Colts, 1992-95, Balt. Ravens, 1996—. Served with U.S. Army, 1954-55. Office: Baltimore Ravens 11001 Owings Mills Blvd Owings Mills MD 21117-2857*

MARCHINI, CLAUDIA CILLONIZ, artist; b. Lima, Peru, Feb. 3, 1959; came to U.S., 1983; d. Alberto Peschiera and Matilde Spiers (Toledo) Cilloniz; m. Carlos Edwards, Nov. 14, 1983; 1 child, Renzo. BFA in Painting, Memphis Coll. Art, 1987; MFA in Painting, U. Tex., San Antonio, 1989. Part-time mgr. Lung Clinic, Grants Pass, Oreg. Executed mural Oreg. State Capitol bldg., Salem, 1994, One woman shows at Foyer Auditorium and Gallery, U. Tex., San Antonio, 1990, GPHS Libr. Gallery, Oreg., 1991, Instituto Cultural Peruano Norteamericano, Lima, 1992, 93, Rogue Gallery, Medford, Oreg., 1992, Portland (Oreg.) State U., 1994, Firehouse Gallery, Grants Pass, Oreg., 1995, D.O.T. N.W., Portland, 1995, Galeria Cecilia Gonzalez, Lima, 1996, Gallery at Stevenson Union, So. Oreg. State Coll., Ashland, 1996, Lisa Harris Gallery, Seattle, 1997; group exhbns. include Instituto Cultural Peruano Norteamericano, 1988, 110 Broadway, San Antonio, 1988, Mexic-Arte, Austin, Tex., 1988, Bank One, San Antonio, 1989, Rolling Oaks Mall, San Antonio, 1989, Art League Gallery, Beaumont, Tex., 1990, U. Toronto, Can., 1990, Art Gallery at Lower Columbia Coll., 1991, Newport (Oreg.) Visual Arts Ctr., 1991, 92, Grants Pass Mus., 1991, 92, 93, Rogue Gallery, 1991, 92, 95, Stonington Gallery, Seattle, 1992, 93, Wiseman Gallery, Grants Pass, 1993, Paris Gibson Sq. Mus. of Art, Great Falls, Mont., 1993, Ctr. Contemporary Art, Seattle, 1993, Pulliam Deffengaugh Gallery, Portland, 1994, Ctr. for Visual Arts, Oakland, Calif., 1994, Washington State Convention and Trade Ctr., 1995, D.O.T. Northwest, 1995, Graven Images Gallery, Ashland, Oreg., 1995, Portland Mus. of Art, 1995, So. Oreg. Art Exhbn., Grants Pass, 1996, Coleman Gallery, Albuquerque, 1996; represented in various pvt. collections. Mem. Nat. Mus. Women in the Arts, Grants Pass Mus. of Art, Ctr. on Contemporary Art, Greenpeace, Wofld Wildlife Fund, Arts Coun. So. Oreg., U.S. Squash Racquet Assn. Avocations: squash, hiking, travel, animals. Office: Lung Clinic 874 NE 7th St Grants Pass OR 97526-1635

MARCHIONE, SHARYN LEE, computer scientist; b. Schenectady, Oct. 1, 1947; d. Albert Jr. and Estelle Mabelle (Christiansen) O'Brien; m. Joseph Michael Marchione, May 4, 1972; 1 child, Heather E. AS in Engring., Hudson Valley Community Coll., Troy, N.Y., 1967; BS in Computer Sci., Skidmore Coll., 1987; MBA, Coll. of St. Rose, Albany, N.Y., 1993. Computer programmer info. systems GE, Schenectady, 1967-72, 78-81, shift leader CAD-CAM systems, 1981-84, advanced techniques specialist, 1984-88, mgr. end user computing decision support ops., 1988-95; mgr. info. systems Westinghouse, 1995—; chmn. windows spl. interest group Westinghouse, Schenectady, 1990-95; mem. adv. coun. Software Pub. Co., 1991. Vol. Rep. Town Supr. Campaign, Halfmoon, N.Y., 1987-91, Concerned for Hungry, Schenectady, 1988—; cons. Schenectady Econ. Devel. Coun., 1991—, Cobleskill Coll., SUNY, 1991—. Avocations: mountain hiking, camping, bicycling, reading, tennis.

MARCHIONI, ALLEN, publishing company executive. Pres., CEO Wililam Morrow & Co. Inc., N.Y.C. Office: William Morrow & Co Inc 1350 Avenue Of The Americas New York NY 10019-4702

MARCHISHIN, DANIEL, construction executive; b. Paterson, N.J., May 16, 1934; s. William and Mary (Hepak) Marchisen; m. Marie Gruber, Oct. 31, 1965; children: Rita, Geoffrey, Rachel, Michael. BSCE, Newark Coll. Engring. Hwy. engr. U.S. Forest Svc., Placerville, Calif., 1961-67; environ. engr. U.S. EPA, N.Y.C. and Edison, N.J., 1967-72; gen. engr. U.S. Dept. HUD, Newark, 1972-80; modernization coord., constrn. mgr. Newark Housing Authority, 1980-89; self-employed constrn. mgr. cons. Bound Brook, N.J., 1990—. Commr. U.S. Commn. on Ukrainian Famine, Washington, 1985-90, N.J. Commn. on Eastern European History, 1985—, chmn., 1991—; fin. officer N.J. Divsn. Ukrainian Am. Vets., 1991—; pres. Plainfield Area Coalition for Environment, 1970, St. Andrew's Fed. Credit Union, 192-94, Masthope Property Owners Assn., 1995; chmn. Captive Nations Com., N.J., 1967-72; treas. Ascension of Our Lord Serbian Orthodox Ch., 1974-75, N.J. Coalition for Dem. Majority, 1975; coord. Henry Jackson for Pres., N.J. Citizens, 1976, Com. for Def. Valentin Moroz, 1978-80; shop steward, NFFE profl. staff, HUD Newark office, 1975-81; v.p. Ams. for Human Rights in Ukraine, 1980-87; chmn. N.J. Ethnic Cmtys. Congress, 1974-81; active Orgn. for Def. Lemkivshchina; pres. U.S. EPA Employees Sunshine Club, 1969-72; coord. Pan-Orthodox Youth Group, 1963-67; chmn. Captive Nations Com., San Francisco, 1963-67; treas. St. John Serbian Orthodox Ch. Choir, 1963-67. With U.S. Army, 1954-55. Mem. NAACP, League of Ukranian Voters (bd. dirs., coord. 1985-96), Serbian Am. Voters Alliance (bd. dirs.), Ukrainian Congress Com. Am., Serb Nat. Def. Coun. Democrat. Ukrainian Orthodox. Avocations: reading, chess, football, golf, singing. Home and Office: 518 Church St Bound Brook NJ 08805-1729

MARCHUK, DOUGLAS ALAN, medical educator; b. Cleve., July 17, 1956. BS in Biology cum laude, U. Dayton, 1978; MS in Microbiology, U. Conn., 1980; PhD in Molecualr Genetics and Cell Biol., U. Chgo., 1985. Postdoctoral U. Mich. Med. Sch., Ann Arbor, 1987-91, asst. rsch. scientist, 1991-93; asst. prof. genetics Duke U. Med. Ctr., Durham, N.C., 1993—; vis. asst. prof. biology Hope Coll., Holland, Mich., 1985-87; lectr. in field. Mem. editorial bd. jour. Genome Rsch., 1993—; ad hoc reviewer jours.; contbr. chpts. to books and numerous articles to profl. jours. Mem. med. adv. bd. Hereditary Hemorrhagic Telengietasis Found., 1992—. Baxter Found. scholar, 1983—; grantee NIH, 1992—, Share Found., 1992-93, Am. Heart Assn., 1995—, Sandoz Pharms. Corp., 1995, Baxter Found., 1993—. Mem. Alpha Sigma Tau. Office: Duke U Med Ctr Rm 277 CARL Bldg Box 3175 Research Dr Durham NC 27710*

MARCIALIS, ROBERT LOUIS, planetary astronomer; b. N.Y.C., Sept. 14, 1956; s. Louis Angelo and Joan Regina (Dippolito) M. SB in Aero. and Astronautical Engring., MIT, 1978, SB in Earth and Planetary Scis., 1980; MS in Physics and Astronomy, Vanderbilt U., 1983; PhD in Planetary Scis., U. Ariz., 1990. Teaching asst. dept. earth and planetary scis. MIT, Cambridge, 1976-80; lab. instr. dept. physics and astronomy Vanderbilt U., Nashville, 1981, 82-83, rsch. asst. Arthur J. Dyer Obs., 1981-82; rsch. asst. Lunar and Planetary Lab. U. Ariz., Tucson, 1983-86, rsch. assoc., 1986-90; JPL postdoctoral fellow Jet Propulsion Lab., Pasadena, Calif., 1990-92; adj. faculty Pima C.C., Tucson, 1992—; sr. rsch. specialist U. Ariz., 1996—; founding mem. Pluto/Charon Mut. Eclipse Season Campaign. Contbr. articles to Nature, Bull. Am. Astron. Soc., Astron. Jour., Minor Planet Circular, Lunar and Planetary Sci., Sci., Jour. Brit. Astron. Assn., Astrophys. Jour., Icarus, also others. Instr. water safety ARC, 1981-82; ednl. counselor MIT, 1983—; fastpitch softball umpire, 1975—. Rsch. fellow NASA, 1986-89. Mem. AAAS, Am. Astron. Soc., Am. Geophys. Union, Astron. Soc. Pacific, Internat. Occultation Timing Assn., Sigma Pi Sigma. Roman Catholic. Achievements include discovery of water ice on surface of Pluto's moon Charon; construction of an albedo map for surface of Pluto; research on Pluto, Charon and Triton, icy satellites, outer solar system formation and evolution, solar system photometry, occultation astronomy, RS Canum Venaticorum binary stars. Office: U Ariz Lunar and Planetary Lab Tucson AZ 85716

MARCIANO, MAURICE, apparel executive. CEO Guess?, L.A. Office: Guess Inc 1444 S Alameda St Los Angeles CA 90021-2448*

MARCIANO, RICHARD ALFRED, research executive; b. Providence, Apr. 9, 1934; s. Eugene and Venera (Stramondo) M.; children: Melissa, Cristina. Student Brown U., 1951-52; BA, Syracuse U., 1970. Computer programmer RAND Corp., Santa Monica, Calif., 1956-58; computer scientist, mgr. System Devel. Corp., Santa Monica, 1958-65; sr. staff SRI Internat., Menlo Park, Calif., 1965-76, dir. edn. rsch., 1976-81, asst. to pres., 1981-93, v.p. technology commercialization, 1983-87, v.p. commercialization and ventures, 1987-93; founder, pres. The Agrari Group, San Francisco, 1993—; dir. TGV Software Inc. Santa Cruz, Calif.; mem., chmn. bd. dirs., Confirma Tech. Corp., Menlo Park. Mem. Assn. Computing Machinery, Ops. Rsch. Soc. Am., Inst. Mgmt. Scis., Assn. Univ. Tech. Mgrs., Licensing Execs. Soc. Office: The Agrari Group 1221 Jones St Apt D4 San Francisco CA 94109-4215

MARCINEK, MARGARET ANN, nursing educator; b. Uniontown, Pa., Sept. 29, 1948; d. Joseph Hugh and Evelyn (Bailey) Boyle; m. Bernard Francis Marcinek, Aug. 11, 1973; 1 dau., Cara Ann. R.N., Uniontown Hosp., 1969; B.S. in Nursing, Pa. State U., 1970; M.S.N., U. Md., 1973; Ed.D., W.Va. U., 1983. Staff nurse Presbyn. U., Pitts., 1970-71; instr. nursing W.Va. U., Morgantown, 1973-77, asst. prof., 1977-80, assoc. prof., 1980-83; assoc. prof. California U. of Pa., 1983-87, prof., 1987—, dept. chmn., 1985—. Contbg. author: Critical Care Nursing. Contbr. articles to profl. jours. Mem. adv. coun. In Home Health, Inc.; mem. adv. coun. Albert Gallatin VNA. Mem. Am. Nurses Assn., Am. Assn. Critical Care Nurses, Nat. League for Nurses, Sigma Theta Tau, Phi Kappa Phi.

MARCO, GUY ANTHONY, librarian, educator; b. N.Y.C., Oct. 4, 1927; s. Gaetano Mongelluzzo and Evelyn Capobianco; m. Karen Csontos, July 23, 1949; 1 son, Howard William. Student, DePaul U., 1947-50; B.Mus., Am. Conservatory Music, Chgo., 1951; M.A. in Music, U. Chgo., 1952, M.L.S., 1955, Ph.D. in Musicology, 1956. Librarian, instr. musicology Chgo. Mus. Coll., 1953-54; asst. classics library U. Chgo., 1954; asst. librarian, instr. music Wright Jr. Coll., Chgo., 1954-56; librarian, instr. music Amundsen Jr. Coll., Chgo., 1957-60; asso. prof. library sci., chmn. dept. Kent State U., 1960-66; prof., dean Kent State U. (Sch. Library Sci.), 1966-77; chief gen. reference and bibliography div. Library of Congress, Washington, 1977-78; dir. for N.Am., Library Devel. Cons.'s, London, 1979-81; prof., dir. div. library sci. San Jose State U., 1981-83; exec. dir. Global Research Services, Washington, 1984-85; chief libr. activities U.S. Army, Ft. Dix, N.J., 1985-89; sr. fellow, adj. prof. libr. sci., editor Third World Librs. Rosary Coll., River Forest, Ill., 1989-96; pres. Global Rsch. Svcs., Chgo., 1996—; vis. lectr. library sci. U. Wis., summer 1955; reference librarian Chgo. Tchrs. Coll., summer 1957; vis. prof. library sci. N.Y. State Coll. Tchrs., Albany, summer 1956, 58; guest lectr. library sci. U. Denver, summer 1959; vis. prof. U. Okla., summer 1960, Coll. Librarianship, Wales, summer 1974, 76, 77, U. Md., summer 1978. Author: The Earliest Music Printers of Continental Europe, 1962, An Appraisal of Favorability in Current Book Reviewing,

1959, (with Claude Palisca) The Art of Counterpoint, 1968, Information on Music, vol. I, 1975, vol. II, 1977, vol. III, 1984, Opera: A Research and Information Guide, 1984, Ency. of Recorded Sound in the United States, 1993, Literature of American Music, 1997; contbr. 150 articles to profl. jours., also book revs. Served with AUS, 1946-47. Mem. ALA, Am. Musicological Soc. Home: 3450 N Lake Shore Dr Apt 3508 Chicago IL 60657-2864

MARCOCCIA, LOUIS GARY, accountant, university administrator; b. Syracuse, N.Y., Nov. 6, 1946; s. George A. and Rose J. (Misita) M.; m. Susan Evelyn Miller, June 21, 1974; 1 child: Rachel Kathryn. BS, Syracuse U., 1968, MS, 1969. CPA, N.Y. Acct. Price Waterhouse & Co., Syracuse, N.Y., 1969-75; dir. internal audit Syracuse U., 1975-76, comptroller, 1976-82, v.p., controller, 1985-95, sr. v.p. bus., fin. and adminstrv. svcs., 1985-95, 1995—; bd. dirs. Syracuse Bd. Chase Lincoln First Bank N.A., Lincoln Life and Annuity Co. N.Y., Univ. Hill Corp.; spkr. Harvard U. Inst. Ednl. Mgmt., 1984-88, 90-91. Pres. parish coun. St. Michael's Ch., Syracuse, 1985-88, Syracuse U. Theatre Corp., 1987—; bd. dirs. Friends of Burnet Park Zoo, 1987-93, Syracuse U. Press., 1982—, Syracuse Sports Corp., 1990-91. Mem. AICPA, N.Y. Soc. CPAs, Nat. Assn. Accts., Fin. Execs. Inst., Inst. Internal Auditors. Republican. Roman Catholic. Clubs: Drumlins (pres. 1976—); Century. Avocations: swimming, golf. Home: Hedge Ln Cazenovia NY 13035 Office: Syracuse U Off of VP Bus Fin Adminstrv Svc Skytop Rd Syracuse NY 13244

MARCOPOULOS, GEORGE JOHN, history educator; b. Salem, Mass., June 30, 1931; s. John George and Urania Christou (Moustakis) M. BA, Bowdoin Coll., 1953; MA, Harvard U., 1955, PhD, 1966. Instr. Tufts U., Medford, Mass., 1961-66, asst. prof., 1966-71, assoc. prof., 1971-92, prof., 1992—. Contbr. articles to profl. jours. and Am. Ann. yearbooks. Bd. dirs., treas. Gerondelis Found., Inc., Lynn, Mass., 1987—. Recipient Mellon Faculty Devel. grant Tufts U., 1983. Mem. AAUP, Am. Assn. Advancement Slavic Studies, Am. Hist. Assn., New Eng. Hist. Assn., Danforth Assocs. New Eng., Modern Greek Studies Assn., Phi Beta Kappa. Greek Orthodox. Avocations: music, films, reading, performing arts, excursions. Office: Tufts U Dept History East Hall Medford MA 02155

MARCOSSON, THOMAS I., service company executive; b. N.Y.C., Jan. 31, 1936; s. Mark and Mollie (Schreiber) M.; m. Carla F. Hunt, May 15, 1988; children: Mark, Susan, Samuel, Jill. Student, Union Coll., Schenectady, 1953-55; B.S., NYU, 1959. CPA, N.Y. Mgr. Touche Ross & Co., N.Y.C., 1959-63; v.p. fin., dir. Superior Surg. Mfg. Co., Inc., Huntington, N.Y., 1964-66; div. pres., gen. mgr. OEI div., Vernitron Corp., Great Neck, N.Y., 1967-71; controller Allied Maintenance Corp., N.Y.C., 1972-75; v.p. fin. Allied Maintenance Corp., 1975-82; chief fin. officer Remco Maintenance Corp., N.Y.C., 1982-84; exec. v.p., chief operating officer Remco Maintenance Corp., 1984-88; pres. MBW Advt. Network Inc., N.Y.C., 1988-89; founder, pres. Dunmarc Assocs., Inc., N.Y.C., 1989—; exec. v.p. Greater Talent Network, Inc., 1991—. Office: 150 5th Ave Ste 900 New York NY 10011-4311

MARCOTTE, BRIAN, transportation executive. BAS in Civil Engring., U. Toronto, Ont., 1971; Diploma in Local Govt. Adminstrn., U. Alta., 1985; Cert., U. Va., 1994. With Ont. Ministry of Transp., North Bay, Toronto, 1971-74, Regional Municipality of York, Newmarket, Ont., 1974-81; exec. dir. planning and programming br. Alta. Transp. & Utilities, Edmonton, 1981—. Office: Dept Transp & Utilities, Twin Atria Bldg 4999 98th Ave NW, Edmonton, AB Canada T6B 2X3

MARCOUX, CARL HENRY, former insurance executive, writer, historian; b. San Francisco, Jan. 6, 1927; s. Henry Roderick and Margaret (Carlin) M.; m. Ana Virginia Penate-Melara, Nov. 11, 1967; children: Eric Henry, Grant Reynold. B.A., Stanford U., 1950; M.B.A., Golden Gate U., San Francisco, 1958; M.A. in Latin Am. History, U. Calif., Irvine, 1988; PhD in Latin Am. History, U. Calif., Riverside, 1994. Gen. mgr. Nat. Union Ins. Co., Pitts., 1953-68; exec. v.p. Transam. Ins. Co., 1968-85. Served with U.S. Mcht. Marine, 1944-46; USAF, 1951-53. Mem. Stanford Alumni Assn. Republican. Home: 1967 Port Cardigan Pl Newport Beach CA 92660-5347

MARCOUX, JULES EDOUARD, physicist, educator, writer; b. Charny, Que., Can., Jan. 26, 1924; s. Romeo Joseph and Atala (Fontaine); m. Hermina Manz, July 2, 1955; children: Daniel, Edouard, Elise, Vincent, Pierre, Paul. B.A., Laval U., 1946, B.S., 1952; M.A., Toronto U., 1952, Ph.D. (Burton fellow), 1956. Research assoc. U. Montreal, Que., 1957; assoc. prof. physics U. Laval, Quebec, Que., 1962-64; prof. physics Royal Mil. Coll., St.-Jean, Que., 1958-62, 64-90, ret., 1990. Author in French: (with A. Ares) Physics Textbook, 6 vols, 1970-76, Astronauts and Astronautics, 1975, Energy: Its Sources, Its Future, 1982, Mechanics for Engineers, 1983; contbr. articles to profl. publs. Exec. com. bd. dirs. College de St.-Jean-sur-Richelieu, Que., 1981—. Postdoctoral fellow NRC Can., 1957. Mem. Am. Assn. Physics Tchrs., Can. Assn. Univ. Tchrs., Can. Mil. Colls. Faculty Assn. (pres. 1980-82). Home: 29 rue de Tilleuls, Saint Luc, PQ Canada J2W 1B4

MARCOUX, JULIA A., midwife; b. St. Helens, England, Aug. 7, 1928; d. Robert Patrick and Margaret Mary Theresa (White) Ashall; m. Albert Marcoux, Apr. 23, 1955; children: Stephen, Ann Marie, Richard, Michael, Maureen, Patrick, Margaret, Julie. Diploma, Withington Hosp., Manchester, England, 1950; grad., Cowley Hill Hosp., St. Helens, England, 1952; BS in Pub. Adminstrn., St. Joseph's Coll. RN, Conn.; lic. midwife, Conn. Nurse, labor, delivery rm. and nursery Day Kimbal Hosp., Putnam, Conn.; sch. nurse Marianapolis Prep. Sch., Thompson, Conn.; occupational nurse U.S. Post Office, Hartford, Conn.; pvt. duty and gerontology nurse Conn.; day care nurse cons. Contbr. articles to profl. jours. Named Internat. Cath. Family of Yr., 1982.

MARCOUX, WILLIAM JOSEPH, lawyer; b. Detroit, Jan. 20, 1927; s. Lona J. and Anna (Ransom) C.; m. Kae Marie Sanborn, Aug. 23, 1952; children: Ann K., William C. B.A., U. Mich., 1949, LL.B., 1952. Bar: Mich. 1953. Pvt. practice Pontiac, Mich., 1953; assoc. McKone, Badgley, Domke and Kline, Jackson, Mich., 1953-65, ptnr., 1965-75; dir. Marcoux, Allen, Abbott, Schomer & Bower, P.C., Jackson, Mich., 1975-93. Mem. exec. bd. Great Sauk Trail council Boy Scouts Am., pres., 1965-66; bd. dirs. Jackson County United Way, pres., 1983-84. Served with USNR, 1945-46. Recipient Silver Beaver award Boy Scouts Am., 1969, Disting. Citizen award Land O'Lakes coun. Boy Scouts Am., 1991. Fellow Am. Coll. Trial Lawyers; mem. Mich. Bar Assn., Jackson County Bar Assn. (pres. 1979-80). Methodist (chmn. adminstrv. bd., chmn. bd. trustees 1976-78, chmn. fin. com. 1986-89). Clubs: Rotarian (pres. 1963-64), Country, Clark Lake Yacht (hon. mem.; commodore 1959). Home: 1745 Malvern Dr Jackson MI 49203-5378 Office: Marcoux Allen Abbott Schomer & Bower PC 145 S Jackson St Jackson MI 49201-2211

MARCOUX, YVON, financial executive, lawyer; b. St. Lambert, Que., Can., Mar. 26, 1941; s. Henry Marcoux and Irène Simard; m. Odette Marcoux, Sept. 5, 1964; children: Stéphane, Sylvain, Sébastien, Valérie. BA, Université Laval, Que., Can., 1960, LL.L., 1963, postgrad., 1966; LL.M., U. Toronto, Can., 1965. Prof. Université Laval, Faculty Law, 1966-70; asst. sec. treasury bd., asst. dep. min. mcpl. affairs Govt. Que., 1970-78; v.p., sec. Nat. Bank Can., Montréal, 1978-81; sr. v.p. adminstrn. Laurentian Bank, Montréal, 1981-86; pres., chief exec. officer Trust La Laurentienne, Montréal, 1985-86; chmn., chief exec. officer Groupe SGF, Montréal, 1986-88; exec. v.p. adminstrn. Provigo, Montreal, 1988—; bd. dirs. Groupe LGS, Montreal, Corp. d'assurance de personnes La Laurentienne. Pres. Inst. for Pub. Adminstrn. Can., 1977-78, Found. U. Laval, 1992-93, 93-94, Que. C. of C., 1992-93, Montreal C. of C., 1985-86; bd. dirs. La Fondation Jean Duceppe, Inst. de Design de Montréal, Found. Paul Gérin-Lajoie, Can. Coun. of Grocery Distbrs. Mem. Can. Bar Assn., Bar Que., Club St. Denis. Office: Provigo, 1611 Crémazie Blvd E, Montreal, PQ Canada H2M 2R9

MARCOVICH, MIROSLAV, classics educator; b. Belgrade, Yugoslavia, Mar. 18, 1919; came to U.S., 1969; s. Svetozar and Mila (Sakich) M.; m. Verica Tosich, May 30, 1948; 1 son, Dragoslav. B.A., U. Belgrade, 1942; DLitt (hon.), U. Ill., 1994. Lectr. in classics U. Belgrade, 1946-55; prof. Los Andes U., Merida, Venezuela, 1955-69; prof. classics U. Ill., Urbana, 1969-89, chmn. dept., 1973-77, lectr. humanities, 1987. Author: M. Maruli Davidias, 1957, Fr. Natalis Carmina, 1958, Bhagavadgita, 1958, Heraclitus, 1967, Eraclito: Frammenti, 1978, Three-Word Trimeter in Greek Tragedy, 1984, Hippolytus Elenchos, 1986, Studies in Gnosticism, 1988, Alcestis Barcinonensis, 1988, Prosper of Aquitaine, De Providentia Dei, 1989. Athenagoras, Legatio pro Christianis, 1990, Ps.-Justin, Cohortatio, 1990, Studies in Greek Poetry, 1991, Theodorus Prodromus, Rhodanthe and Dosicles, 1992, Justin Martyr, Apologies, 1994, Patristic Textual Criticism I, 1994, Tatian, Oratio, 1994, Theophilus, Ad Autolycum, 1995, Clementis Alexandrini Protrepticus, 1995, Justin Martyr, Dialogus cum Tryphone, 1997, others; founder, editor Illinois Classical Studies, 1976—; contbr. numerous articles to profl. jours. Guggenheim fellow, 1980, 83, NEH, 1990; U. Ill. scholar, 1973, sr. scholar, 1986, Sackler scholar Tel Aviv U., 1990-91; recipient Premio Sesquicentenario Gold medal Venezuela, 1962, 64, Silver Cross Mt. Athos, Greece, 1963, Beckman award, 1991, 93, 94. Mem. Am. Philol. Assn. (mem. adv. com. Thesaurus Linguae Graecae 1973-80). Home: 2114 S Vine St Urbana IL 61801-6616

MARCOVITZ, LEONARD EDWARD, retail executive; b. Bismarck, N.D., Sept. 6, 1934; s. Jacob and Frieda M. Asst. mgr. Greengard's Clothing, Mandan, N.D., 1955-58; mgr. K-G Men's Stores, Inc., Bismarck, 1958-61, Billings, Mont., 1961-69; v.p. store ops. K-G Men's Stores, Inc., 1969-73; pres. Leonard's Men's Stores, Yakima, Wash. and Billings, Mont., 1973-77; chief exec. officer K-G Retail div. Chromalloy Am. Corp., Englewood, Colo., 1977-81; pres. DeMarcos Men's Clothing, Casper, Wyo., 1982—, Idaho Falls, Idaho, 1984—, Billings, Mont., 1986-96, Twin Falls, Idaho, 1996—. Mem. Menswear Retailers Am. (past dir.), Billings Petroleum Club, Order of Demolay (Degree of Chevalier 1952, Internat. Master Councilor 1953, Demolay Dad 1959), Elks. Home: PO Box 23344 Billings MT 59104-3344

MARCUCCIO, PHYLLIS ROSE, association executive, editor; b. Hackensack, N.J., Aug. 25, 1933; d. Filippo and Rose (Henry) M. AB, Bucknell U., 1955; MA, George Washington U., 1976. Trainee Time, Inc., 1956-57; art prodn. for mags. of Med. Econs., Inc., 1958-60; mem. staff Nat. Sci. Tchrs. Assn., Washington, 1961—; assoc. editor Sci. and Children, 1963-65, editor, 1965-95, dir. divsn. elem. edn., 1974-78, dir. div. program devel. and continuing edn., 1978-83, pub., 1993—; dir. publs. Nat. Sci. Tchrs. Assn., 1983—, assoc. exec. dir., 1990—; pub. Dragonfly, 1996—; lectr., cons. in field. Author, photographer, illustrator numerous articles; co-author: Investigation in Ecology, 1972; editor: Science Fun, 1977, 2d edit., 94; illustrator: Selected Readings for Students of English as a Second Language, 1966; compiler: Opportunities for Summer Studies in Elementary Science, 1968, 2d edit., 1969. Apptd. commr. Rockville (Md.) Housing Authority, 1981-91, chairperson, 1984-86; bd. dirs. Nat. Sci Resource Ctr., Nat. Acad. Sci., 1986—, Hands on Sci. Outreach, Inc., 1988—. Recipient Citizenship medal DAR, 1951; hon. life mem. Ohio Council Elem. Sch. Sci., 1974. Life mem. Nat. Sci. Tchrs. Assn.; mem. Council Elem. Sci. Internat. (Internat. award outstanding contbns. sci. edn. 1971, 72, 86, 94), Am. Nature Study Soc., Soil Conservation Soc. Am., Nat. Free Lance Photographers Assn., Photog. Soc. Am., Nat. Wildlife Fedn., Nat. Audubon Soc., Nat. Geog. Soc., Wilderness Soc., AAAS, Washington Edn. Press Assn. (treas. 1966-67, pres. 1975-76), Ednl. Press Assn. Am. (regional dir. 1969-71, sec. 1979—, Disting. Achievement award 1969, 71-74, 76, 77, 80, 88, 93, 95, Eleanor Fishburn award 1978), Sci. Teaching Assn. N.Y. (Outstanding Service to Sci. Edn. award 1987), Nat. Assn. Industry Edn. Coop. (bd. dirs. 1980-86), Pocono Environ. Edn. Ctr. (bd. dirs. 1989—), Nat. Press Club, Theta Alpha Phi, Phi Delta Gamma, Phi Delta Kappa., Sigma Delta Chi. Home: 406 S Horners Ln Rockville MD 20850-1556 Office: Nat Sci Tchrs Assn 1840 Wilson Blvd Arlington VA 22201-3000

MARCUM, DEANNA BOWLING, library administrator; b. Salem, Ind., Aug. 5, 1946; d. Anderson and Ruby (Mobley) Bowling; m. Thomas P. Marcum, June 13, 1974; 1 child, Ursula. BA, U. Ill., 1967; MA, So. Ill. U., 1969; MLS, U. Ky., 1971; PhD, U. Md., 1991. Tchr. Deland-Weldon (Ill.) High Sch., 1967-68; instr. English U. Ky., Lexington, 1969-70, cataloging librarian, 1970-73, asst. to dir., 1973-74; asst. dir. pub. svcs. Joint U. Librs., Nashville, 1974-77; mgmt. tng. specialist Assn. Rsch. Librs., Washington, 1977-80; sr. cons. Info. Systems Cons., Inc., Washington, 1980-81; v.p. Coun. on Libr. Resources, Washington, 1981-89; dean Sch. Libr. and Info. Sch. Cath. U., Washington, 1989-92; dir. pub. svcs. and collections mgmt. Libr. of Congress, Washington, 1993-95; pres. Coun. on Libr. Resources, Washington, 1995—; adv. bd. So. Edn. Found., Atlanta, 1986-91; chmn. grants com. Coun. on Libr. resources, Washington, 1990-94. Author: Good Books in a Country Home, 1993; co-author: (with Richard Boss) The Library Catalog, 1980, On-Line Acquisitions Systems, 1981; contbr. articles to profl. jours. Pres., Commn. on Preservation and Access, 1995—. Mem. ALA, Am. Studies Assn., Orgn. Am. Historians, Am. Antiquarian Soc. (adv. bd. 1989—), Beta Phi Mu, Phi Kappa Phi. Home: 3315 Wake Dr Kensington MD 20895 Office: Coun on Libr Resources 1400 16th St NW Ste 715 Washington DC 20036-2224

MARCUM, JOSEPH LARUE, insurance company executive; b. Hamilton, Ohio, July 2, 1923; s. Glen F. and Helen A. (Stout) M.; m. Sarah Jane Sloneker, Mar. 7, 1944; children: Catharine Ann Marcum Lowe, Joseph Timothy (dec.), Mary Christina Marcum Manchester, Sarah Jennifer Marcum Shuffield, Stephen Sloneker. B.A., Antioch Coll., 1947; M.B.A. in Fin, Miami U., 1965. With Ohio Casualty Ins. Co. and affiliates, 1947—, now chmn. bd., also bd. dirs. Trustee Miami U., Oxford, Ohio. Capt., inf. U.S. Army. Mem. Soc. CPCU, Queen City Club, Bankers Club, Princeton Club N.Y., Little Harbor club, Walloon Lake Country Club, Mill Reef Club. Presbyterian. Home: 475 Oakwood Dr Hamilton OH 45013-3466 Office: Ohio Casualty Corp 136 N 3rd St Hamilton OH 45011-2726

MARCUM, WALTER PHILLIP, manufacturing company executive; b. Bemidji, Minn., Mar. 1, 1944; s. John Phillip and Johnnye Evelyn (Edmiston) M.; m. Barbara Lynn Maloof, Apr. 17, 1976. BBA, Tex. Tech U., 1967. Researcher Collins Securities, Denver, 1968-70, Hanifin Imhoff, Denver, 1970-71; cons. Marcum-Spillane, Denver, 1971-76; with MGF Oil Corp., Midland, Tex., 1976-87, sr. v.p., 1978, exec. v.p., 1979-83, pres., chief exec. officer, 1983-87; sr. v.p. corp. fin. Boettcher & Co., Denver, 1987-90; pres., chief exec. officer Marcum Natural Gas Svcs., Inc., Denver, 1991—; dir. Hydrologic Inc., Asheville, N.C., Key Energy Group, East Brunswick, N.J. Republican. Presbyterian. Home: 676 Monroe St Denver CO 80206-4451 Office: 1675 Broadway Ste 2150 Denver CO 80202-4621

MARCUS, ALAN C., public relations consultant; b. N.Y.C., Feb. 26, 1947; s. Percy and Rose (Fox) M.; m. Judith Lamel, June 21, 1979; 1 child, Allison. Student Hun Sch., Princeton, 1966. Dir. pub. relations Bergen County Rep. Com., Hackensack, N.J., 1968; clk. N.J. Gen. Assembly, Trenton, 1969, sec. to majority party of assembly, 1970; pres. The Marcus Group, Inc., Secaucus, 1971—; adj. prof. Rutgers U. Grad. Sch., 1986-88. Trustee Nat. Leukemia Assn., 1976-82, Hun Sch. of Princeton, 1977-88, Passaic River Coalition, 1980-82. Recipient Youth Enterprise award Jim Walter Corp., 1972. Mem. Pub. Relations Soc. Am. (N.J. chpt. pres.'s award 1975, past pres. and bd. dirs. N.J. chpt. 1976-77), N.J. C. of C., N.J. Bus. and Industry Assn., N.J. Press Assn., Apple Ridge Country Club, Capitol Hill Club, Fed. City Club (Washington). Office: 300 Lighting Way Secaucus NJ 07094 also: 50 W State St Trenton NJ 08608-1220

MARCUS, BERNARD, lawyer; b. Wilkes-Barre, Pa., Mar. 10, 1924; m. Frances Frank; children: Kate, Aaron, Charles, Mary. Student, U. Pa., 1941-43, Carnegie-Mellon U., 1943-44; LL.B., Harvard U., 1948; postgrad., Loyola U. of South, New Orleans, 1958. Bar: D.C. 1949, La. 1958. Atty. legis. reference service Library of Congress, 1949-50; acting counsel small bus. com. Ho. of Reps., 1950; atty. NLRB, Washington, Cin., Buffalo and New Orleans, 1950-57; assoc. Deutsch, Kerrigan & Stiles, New Orleans, 1957-58; ptnr. Deutsch, Kerrigan & Stiles, 1958-95, mng. ptnr., 1985-89, emeritus ptnr., 1995—; cons. Dept. State, 1965-69; labor arbitrator Am. Arbitration Assn., Fed. Mediation and Conciliation Svc., USDA, U.S. Dept. Def., U.S. Dept. Transp., City of Houston, Fla. Power and Light, Internat. Paper Co., Celotex, Mead Paper, Inland Paper, Gaylord Container, ADM Corp., GTE, SW Bell, Ingalls Shipbldg., Gulf States Utilities, PPG Industries, Ga. Pacific Corp., Westvaco, Hertz, Memphis Comml. Appeal, Schering Plough, Chevron, Bryan Foods, Savannah Elec. & Power, Citgo, also others. Author: Congress and the Monopoly Problem, 1950; contbr. to casebooks. Pres. New Orleans Jewish Community Center, 1973-75; mem. Nat. Jewish Welfare Bd., 1974-83; bd. dirs. New Orleans Jewish Welfare Bd., Jewish Family and Children's Service, New Orleans, Communal Hebrew Sch.; v.p. New Orleans Home for Jewish Aged, 1978-80, Florence Heller Rsch. Found. Served U.S Army, 1943-46. Mem. ABA, Fed. Bar Assn., La. Bar Assn., New Orleans Bar Assn. (exec. com. 1971-74), D.C. Bar Assn. Home: 630 Burdette St New Orleans LA 70118-3937 Office: 755 Magazine St New Orleans LA 70130-3698

MARCUS, BERNARD, retail executive; b. 1929; married. BS, Rutgers U., 1954. V.p. Vornado Inc., 1952-68; pres. Odell Inc., 1968-70; v.p. Daylin Inc., 1970-73; with Handy Dan Home Improvement, Los Angeles, 1972-78; with Home Depot Inc., Atlanta, 1978—, now chmn., chief exec. officer, sec., also bd. dirs. Office: Home Depot Inc 2727 Paces Ferry Rd NW Atlanta GA 30339-4053*

MARCUS, CLAUDE, advertising executive; b. Paris, Aug. 28, 1924; s. Jacques and Louise (Bleustein) M.; m. Claudine Pohl, May 27, 1948; children: Michele, Pierre, Anne-Marie, Isabelle. Diploma in Econs., U. Paris, 1947; Lic., Paris Law Sch., 1947. Sec. gen. Publicis, Paris, 1948-55, dir. comml. to dir. gen. adjoint, 1961, dir. gen., 1962-68; mng. dir. Publicis Conseil, Paris, 1968-83; pres. Publicis Internat., Paris, 1984-88; vice-chmn. Publicis Communication, Paris, 1988—; vice chmn. Metrobus Publicities, Paris, 1994; vice chmn. supr. bd. Publicis SA, 1996. Decorated Chevalier de la Legion d'Honneur, 1970. Mem. Bur. de Verification de la Publicite (vice chmn.), Racing Club (France). Home: 12 Rue Felicien David, 75016 Paris France Office: Publicis, 133 Champs Elysees, 75008 Paris France also: 304 E 45th St New York NY 10017-3425

MARCUS, CRAIG BRIAN, lawyer; b. Boise, Idaho, May 30, 1939; s. Claude Virgil and Marie Louise M.; m. Lynne Merryweather, Sept. 3, 1960; children: Shawn, Brian, Trent. Student, Boise Jr. Coll., 1958, U. Pa., 1958-59, Mexico City Coll., 1959-60; JD, U. Idaho, 1963. Bar: Idaho 1963, U.S. Dist. Ct. Idaho 1963. Ptnr. Marcus, Merrick & Montgomery, predecessors, Boise, 1963—. Ada County dir. Rep. Congl. Campaigns, Boise, 1964-66; Ada County coord. Rep. Senatorial Campaigns, 1969; chmn. jud. campaign Idaho Ct. of Appeals, 1984, 90. Mem. ABA, Idaho Bar Assn. (peer rev. com. 1971-73), 4th Dist. Bar Assn. (treas. 1967-68, ct. trial porcedural rules com. 1973-74), Lincoln Day Banquet Assn. (pres. 1975), Elks. Avocations: fishing, hunting, golf, skiing, trap shooting. Home: 7711 Apache Way Boise ID 83703-1903 Office: Marcus Merrick & Montgomery 737 N 7th St Boise ID 83702-5504

MARCUS, DEVRA JOY COHEN, internist; b. Bronx, N.Y., Sept. 5, 1940; d. Benjamin and Gertrude (Siegel) Cohen; m. Robert A. Marcus, Apr. 1963 (div. 1974); children: Rachel, Adam; m. Michael J. Horowitz, Mar. 2, 1975; 1 child, Naomi. BA, Brandeis U., 1961; MD, Stanford U., 1966. Diplomate Am. Bd. Internal Medicine. Intern in internal medicine Stanford U., 1966-67, resident, 1967-68; gen. internist D.C. Dept. Pub. Health, 1968-69, Cardozo Neighborhood Health Ctr., Washington, 1969-73; med. dir. East of the River Health Assn., Washington, 1973-75; fellow in infectious disease Washington Hosp. Ctr., 1975-77; gen. internist Police and Fire Clinic, Washington, 1977-78; gen. internist, pvt. practice Washington, 1977—; assoc. clin. prof. medicine George Washington U. Med Ctr., Washington, 1978—; gen. internist World Bank, Washington, 1978-81; ptnr. Traveller's Med. Svc. D.C., 1980-82; gen. internist Community of Good Hope Med. Clinic, Washington, 1984-85; assoc. clin. prof. medicine Georgetown U. Med. Ctr., Washington, 1987—; preceptor Georgetown U. Hosp., 1986—. Contbr. articles to profl. jours. Exec. com. Woodley Park Citizen's Assn., 1979-80; chair mayor's adv. com. on prevention, 1982-83; bd. dirs. Exodus Youth Svcs., 1987-89. Fellow ACP; mem. AMA (Physicians Recognition award, 1981, 84, 87, 90, 93), Med. Soc. D.C. (credentials com., communicable disease com., founder com. on women 1983, pres. 1985-87, med. ethics and judiciary com. 1987-91, judiciary coun. 1992-96). Home: 1205 Crest Ln Mc Lean VA 22101-1837 Office: 2021 K St NW Washington DC 20006-1003

MARCUS, DONALD HOWARD, advertising agency executive; b. Cleve., May 16, 1916; s. Joseph and Sarah (Schmitman) M.; m. Helen Olen Weiss, Feb. 12, 1959; children: Laurel Kathy Heifetz, Carol Susan Greene, James Randall (dec.), Jonathan Anthony. BA, Cleve. State U., 1996. Mem. publicity dept. Warner Bros. Pictures, Cleve., 1935-37; mem. advt. dept. RKO Pictures, Cleve., 1937-40; mem. sales dept. Monogram Pictures, Cleve., 1940-42; pres. Marcus Advt. Inc., Cleve., 1946-85, chmn., 1986—. Mem. Ohio Democratic exec. com., 1969-70, del. nat. conv., 1968; vice-chmn. communication div. Jewish Welfare Fund Appeal Cleve., 1964-70, chmn., 1971-72; trustee Jewish Community Fedn., 1973-74; trustee Cleve. Jewish News, 1974-96, v.p., 1983-85; trustee No. Ohio regional office Anti Defamation League of B'nai B'rith, 1986—, Jewish Community Ctr., 1988-90; bd. dirs. Cuyahoga County unit Am. Cancer Soc., 1979—, Cleve. State U. Devel. Found., 1987—, Achievement Ctr. for Children, 1991-96. Served to 1st lt. USAAF, 1942-46. Mem. Nat. Acad. TV Arts and Scis. (Silver Circle award 1994), Ohio Commodores, Cleve. Advt. Club (elected to Hall of Fame), Cleve. Growth Assn., Mensa, Union Club of Cleve., Beechmont Country Club (past pres.). Jewish (temple trustee). Home: 22449 Shelburne Rd Cleveland OH 44122-2053 Office: Marcus Advt Inc 25700 Science Park Dr Cleveland OH 44122-7312

MARCUS, EDWARD, economist, educator; b. Bklyn., Apr. 29, 1918; s. Herman and Rose (Marayna) M.; m. Mildred Rendl, Aug. 10, 1956. B.S., Harvard, 1939, M.B.A., 1941; student, King's Coll., Cambridge (Eng.) U., 1946-47; Ph.D., Princeton, 1950. Economist Fed. Res. Bd., 1950-52; prof. econs. Bklyn. Coll., 1952-81, chmn. dept., 1966-79; cons. Nat. Acad. Scis., 1959, UN Conf. Trade and Devel., 1966; dir. Syracuse U. Maxwell Sch. Nigerian Project, 1961; participant Internat. Econometrics Assn., Amsterdam, Holland, 1968. Author: Canada and the International Business Cycle, 1927-1938, 1954, (with Mildred Rendl Marcus) Investment and Development Possibilities in Tropical Africa, 1960, International Trade and Finance, 1965, Monetary and Banking Theory, 1965, Economic Progress and the Developing World, 1971, Economics, 1978. Served with AUS, 1941-42; Served with USCGR, 1942-46. Grantee Merrill Found., 1953. Mem. Am. Econ. Assn., Canadian Econ. Assn., N.Y. Met. Econ. Assn. (pres. 1966-67), Am. Finance Assn., Royal Econ. Soc., Econ. Soc. S. Africa, Am. Assn. U. Profs., New Canaan Hist. Soc. Treas. 1983—), Phi Beta Kappa. Home: PO Box 814 New Canaan CT 06840-0814

MARCUS, EILEEN, public relations and advertising executive; b. Naples, Italy, June 11, 1946; came to U.S., 1947; d. Isaac and Mina (Cyplowicz) Einik; m. Zvi Marcus, May 24, 1974; children: Neely, Kerren. BS in Journalism, U. Fla., 1967. Acct. exec. EV Clay Assocs., Miami, Fla., 1972-74; account exec., pub. relations dir. Hume Smith Mickleberry Advt. Co., Miami, 1974-77; dir. publs. Fla. Internat. U., Miami, 1977-81; dir. mktg. Northshore Hosp., Miami, 1981-85; ptnr. Mktg. Mix, Inc., Miami, 1985-88; sr. v.p., gen. mgr. Burson-Marsteller, Miami, 1988-96; exec. v.p. Zynyx Mktg. Comms. Inc., Miami, 1996—. Mem. South Fla, Hosp. Assn. (pres. 1985-86), South Fla. Advt. Fedn. (Gold, Silver and Bronze Addy awards 1988). Office: Zynyx Mktg Comms Inc 407 Lincoln Rd Fl 3 Miami Beach FL 33139-3008

MARCUS, ERIC PETER, lawyer; b. Newark, Aug. 31, 1950; s. John J. and Alice M. (Zeldin) M.; m. Terry R. Toll, Oct. 9, 1983. BA, Brown U., 1972; JD, Stanford U., 1976. Bar: N.Y. 1977, N.J. 1977. Assoc. Kaye, Scholer, Fierman, Hays & Handler, N.Y.C., 1976-84, ptnr., 1985—. Contbr. articles to profl. jours. Mem. Phi Beta Kappa. Office: Kaye Scholer Fierman Hays & Handler 425 Park Ave New York NY 10022-3506

MARCUS, ERIC ROBERT, psychiatrist; b. N.Y.C., Feb. 16, 1944; s. Victor and Pearl (Maddow) M.; m. Eslee Samberg, Nov. 24, 1985; children: Max, Pia. AB, Columbia U., 1965; MD, U. Wis., 1969. Diplomate Am. Bd. Psychiatry and Neurology. Intern NYU Med. Ctr. Bellevue Hosp., 1969-70; resident Columbia Presbyn. Med. Ctr.-N.Y. State Psychiatric Inst., 1972-75; dir. St. Marks Free Clinic, N.Y.C., 1971-75; from co-dir. to dir. neuropsychiatric/diagnostic treatment unit Columbia-Presbyn. Med. Ctr., N.Y.C., 1975-84; dir. med. student edn. in psychiatry Columbia U. Coll. Physicians and Surgeons, N.Y.C., 1981—; supervising-tng. analyst Columbia U. Ctr. for Psychoanalytic Tng.-Rsch., N.Y.C., 1994—; clin. prof. psychiatry and social medicine Columbia U. Coll. Physicians and Surgeons, N.Y.C., 1995—; bd. govs. student health Columbia U., 1986—. Author: Psychosis and Near

Psychosis, 1992; mem. editorial bd. The Psychoanalytic Study of Society, 1989-94; contbr. articles to profl. jours. Recipient Weber rsch. award Columbia U. Psychoanalytic Ctr., 1991, O'Connor Teaching award, 1995. Fellow Am. Psychiat. Assn. (Roeske award 1991), Am. Psychoanalytic Assn., Am. Coll. Psychoanalysts, N.Y. Acad. Medicine. Avocations: classical music, photography, swimming, reading. Office: Columbia U Dept Psychiatry 722 W 168th St New York NY 10032-2603

MARCUS, FRANK ISADORE, physician, educator; b. Haverstraw, N.Y., Mar. 23, 1928; s. Samuel and Edith (Sattler) M.; m. Janet Geller, June 30, 1957; children: Ann, Steve, Lynn. BA, Columbia U., 1948; MS, Tufts U., 1951; MD cum laude, Boston U., 1953. Diplomate Am. Bd. Internal Medicine, subspecialty cardiovascular diseases. Intern Peter Bent Brigham Hosp., Boston, 1953-54; asst. resident Peter Bent Brigham Hosp., 1956-57, research fellow in cardiology, 1957-58; clin. fellow in cardiology Georgetown U. Hosp., 1958-59, chief med. resident, 1959-60; chief of cardiology Georgetown U. Med. Service, D.C. Gen. Hosp., Washington, 1960-68; instr. medicine Georgetown U. Sch. Medicine, 1960-63, asst. prof., 1963-68, assoc. prof., 1968; prof. medicine, chief cardiology sect. U. Ariz. Coll. Medicine, Tucson, 1969-82, disting. prof. internal medicine (cardiology), 1982—, dir. electrophysiology, 1982—; cons. cardiology VA Hosp., Tucson, 1969, USAF Regional Hosp., Davis-Monthan AFB, Tucson, 1969; mem. panel drug efficacy study, panel on cardiovascular drugs Nat. Acad. Scis.-NRC, 1967-68; chmn. undergrad. cardiovascular tng. grant com. HEW-NIH, 1970. Editor: Modern Concepts of Cardiovascular Disease, 1982-84; mem. editl. bd.: Circulation, 1976-81, Current Problems in Cardiology, 1976-80, Cardiovascular Drugs and Therapy, 1986—, New Trends in Arrythmias, 1984—, Jour. Am. Coll. Cardiology, 1984-87, 96—, Am. Jour. Cardiology, 1984—, Jour. Cardiovasc. Drugs and Therapy, 1994—, Jour. Cardiovasc. Pharmacology and Therapeutics, 1994—, Pacing and Clin. Electrophysiology, 1995—; contbr. numerous articles to med. jours. Chmn. Washington Heart Assn. High Sch. Heart Program, 1966-68. Served to capt. USAF, 1954-56. Recipient Career Devel. award NIH, 1965, Student AMA Golden Apple award Georgetown U. Sch. Medicine, 1968; Mass. Heart Assn. fellow, 1957-58; John and Mary Markle scholar, 1960-65. Fellow Coun. on Clin. Cardiology Am. Heart Assn., ACP (Ariz. laureate award 1987), Am. Coll. Cardiology (bd. govs. Ariz. 1984-87, asst. sec. 1987-89, trustee); mem. Assn. Univ. Cardiologists, Inc. (v.p. 1989-90, pres. 1990-91), Ariz. Heart Assn. (dir. 1970, v.p. 1972-73, chmn. rsch. com. 1970-72), So. Ariz. Heart Assn. (dir. 1969), N.Am. Soc. for Pacing and Electrophysiology, Alpha Omega Alpha. Home: 4949 E Glenn St Tucson AZ 85712-1212 Office: U Ariz Univ Med Ctr 1501 N Campbell Ave Tucson AZ 85724-0001

MARCUS, GREIL GERSTLEY, critic; b. San Francisco, June 19, 1945; s. Gerald Dodd and Eleanore (Hyman) M.; m. Jenelle Bernstein, June 26, 1966; children: Emily Rose, Cecily Helen. BA, U. Calif., Berkeley, 1967, MA, 1968. Record editor Rolling Stone mag., San Francisco and N.Y.C., 1969-70; book columnist Rolling Stone mag., 1975-80, Calif. Mag., L.A., 1982-83, 88-90; pop music columnist Music Mag., Tokyo, 1978-94, New West mag., L.A., 1978-82, Artforum mag., N.Y.C., 1983-87, 90—, Village Voice newspaper, N.Y.C., 1986-90, Interview Mag., N.Y.C., 1992—; dir. Pagnol et Cie, operators Chez Panisse restaurant, Berkeley, Falter newspaper, Vienna, 1997—. Author: Mystery Train: Images of America in Rock 'n Roll Music, 1975, U.S. rev. , 1982, 90, 97 (Brit., German, Greek, Dutch and Japanese edits.), Real Life Rock (Japanese), 1984, Lipstick Traces: A Secret History of the 20th Century, 1989 (Brit., Italian, Spanish and German edits.), Dead Elvis: A Chronicle of a Cultural Obsession, 1991 (Brit., Japanese and German edits.), Ranters and Crowd Pleasers: Punk in Pop Music, 1977-92, 93, In The Fascist Bathroom: Writings on Punk (Brit. and German edits.), The Dustbin of History (Brit. and German edits.), 1995, Invisible Republic: Bob Dylan's Basement Tapes, 1997 (Brit., German and Dutch edits.); editor: Stranded, 1979, rev. 1996, Psychotic Reactions and Carburetor Dung (Lester Bangs), 1987; contbr. criticism to publs. including N.Y. Times, N.Y. Times Book Rev., Creem, Express-Times, Boston Phoenix, New Mus. Express, Another Room, L.A. Times, Newsday, IT, RAW, Rock and Roll Confidential, Threepenny Rev., Representations, Common Knowledge.

MARCUS, HAROLD, physician, health facility administrator; b. N.Y.C., May 28, 1915; s. Abraham and Yetta (Salb) M.; m. Beatrice Falk, Apr. 27, 1943; children: Robert Michael, Alan David. BS, Columbia U., 1935; BS in Medicine, W.Va. U., 1936; MD cum laude, Boston U., 1939. Diplomate Nat. Bd. Med. Examiners, Am. Bd. Internal Medicine. Intern Maimonides Med. Ctr., Bklyn., N.Y., 1939-41; resident in pathology Nassau County Med. Ctr., Hempstead, N.Y., 1941, 46, resident in internal medicine, 1947-48; resident in neurology Kingsbrook Med. Ctr., Bklyn., 1948-49; pvt. practice Bklyn., 1949-88; chief medicine Internat. Ladies Garment Workers Union Health Ctr., N.Y.C., 1953-96. Contbr. articles to profl. jours. Lt. col. U.S. Army, 1941-46. Decorated Bronze Star; recipient Merit Citation Gen. Chiang Kai Shek, China, 1945. Mem. ACP, Phi Delta Epsilon. Avocations: golf, tennis, leather work. Home: 180 Marlborough Rd Brooklyn NY 11226-4510

MARCUS, HARRIS LEON, mechanical engineering and materials science educator; b. Ellenville, N.Y., July 5, 1931; s. David and Bertha (Messite) M.; m. Leona Gorker, Aug. 29, 1962; children: Leland, M'Risa. BS, Purdue U., 1963; PhD, Northwestern U., 1966. Registered profl. engr., Tex. Tech. staff Tex. Instruments, Dallas, 1966-68; tech. staff Rockwell Sci. Ctr., 1968-70, group leader, 1971-75; prof. mech. engring. U. Tex., Austin, 1975-79, Harry L. Kent Jr. prof. mech. engring., 1979-90, Cullen Found. prof., 1990-95, dir. ctr. for Materials Sci. and Engring., dir. program, 1979-95; prof. metallurgy and materials engring., dir. Inst. for Material Sci., U. Conn., 1995—; cons. numerous orgns. Contbr. numerous articles to profl. publs. Recipient U. Tex. faculty U. Tex. Engring. Found., 1983; Krengel lectr. Technion, Israel, 1983; Alumni Merit medal Northwestern U., 1988, Disting. Purdue Univ. Engring. Alumnus award, 1994. Fellow Am. Soc. Metals; mem. ASTM, ACS, AIME (bd. dirs. Metall. Soc. 1976-78, 84-86), Materials Rsch. Soc. Achievements include 17 patents. Home: 48 Dog Ln Storrs Mansfield CT 06268-2220 Office: Univ Conn Inst Materials Scis 97 Eagleville Rd U-136 Storrs Mansfield CT 06269

MARCUS, HYMAN, business executive; b. Roumania, May 3, 1914; s. Morris and Fannie M.; m. Sydelle Allen, June 29, 1935; children: Beverly Faith, Carole Ann. BA, Columbia U., 1932; MA, CCNY, 1993. Math instr., 1932-39; pres. Empire Designing Corp., 1939-46, Manhattan Capital Co., 1946-54; pres., chmn. U.S. Hoffman Machinery Corp., 1954-58; ptnr. Van Alstyne Noel & Co., 1956-59; chmn. bd. Artloom Industries, 1958—, pres., 1959—; chmn. bd. Hoffman Internat., 1957-59; pres., chmn. bd. Trans-United Industries, 1958; chmn. First Capital Corp., 1968—, Maralco Enterprises Inc., 1969—. Chmn. planning commn. Village of Atlantic Beach; trustee Riverside Sch., Jewish Meml. Hosp. Home: 159 W 53rd St New York NY 10019-6005 Office: 200 W 51st St New York NY 10019-6208

MARCUS, JANET CAROL, cytotechnologist; b. N.Y.C., Mar. 15, 1941; d. David and Adele (Rosenberg) M. BS, Fairleigh Dickinson U., 1963; student, N.Y. Hosp./Cornell Med. Ctr., 1965-66. Cert. cytotechnologist. Cytotechnology trainee N.Y. Hosp.-Cornell Med. Ctr., 1965-66; cytotechnologist Good Samaritan Hosp., Suffern, N.Y., 1966-70; cytotechnology supr. Newark (N.J.) Beth Israel Med. Ctr., 1970-76; chief cytotechnologist Gyn Cytology and Pathology Assocs. merged Bio Reference Lab., Englewood, N.J., 1976-94; rsch. cytotechnologist Neurmed. Systems, Inc., Suffern, 1994—; guest lectr. U. of Medicine and Dentistry of N.J., Newark, 1980-85. Mem. N.J. Assn. Cytology (pres. 1983-85), N.J. Assn. of Cytology, Greater N.Y. Assn. of Cytotechnologists, Delaware Valley Soc. of Cytology, Am. Soc. of Clin. Pathologists (assoc. mem., cert. cytotechnology, specialist in cytotechnology), Am. Soc. of Cytopathology (assoc.), Am. Soc. for Cytotech. Avocations: opera and concert goer, photography, making beaded flowers, attending museum exhibits. Home: 162 Jefferson Ave River Edge NJ 07661-2107 Office: Neuromedical Systems Inc Ste 102 2 Executive Blvd Ofc 102 Suffern NY 10901-4164

MARCUS, JERRY, broadcasting executive; b. N.Y.C.; m. Mary Jane Marcus; children: Stuart, Lee, Nancy. Student, L.A. State Coll., UCLA. Account exec., local sales mgr., nat. sales mgr. KTLA, L.A., Ea. sales mgr., asst. gen. sales mgr.; ptnr. Hunter, Whillhite, Marcus Advt., Inc., L.A.; account exec., local sales mgr. KTTV, L.A.; v.p., gen. sales mgr. WTTG, Washington; v.p., gen. mgr. KRIV, Fox 26, Houston, 1978—. Mem. bd. Nat. Leukemia Soc., March of Dimes; past mem. Arbitron Adv. Bd.; life mem. Houston Livestock Show and Rodeo Com.; mem. Keep Houston Clean Com., End Hunger Network. Recipient Torch of Liberty award Nat. Leukemia Soc., 1986. Mem. Advt. Fedn. Houston, Tex. Area Broadcasters (mem. bd.). Office: Fox 26 3935 Westheimer Rd Houston TX 77027-5011

MARCUS, JOEL DAVID, pediatrician; b. Bklyn., June 16, 1932. BA, Columbia Coll., 1954; MD, George Washington U., 1958. Diplomate Am. Bd. Pediats. Rotating intern/pediat. resident The Jewish Hosp. of Bklyn., 1958-61; pvt. practice Rye, N.Y., 1963—; attending pediatrician United Hosp., Port Chester, N.Y., 1963—. Sch. pediatrician Rye Sch. Sys., 1963—. Capt. USAF, 1961-63. Fellow Am. Acad. Pediats. Avocations: sculpture, barbershop quartet. Office: 33 Cedar St Rye NY 10580-2031

MARCUS, JOHN, wholesale distribution executive; b. N.Y.C., Oct. 18, 1941; s. Sam and Margaret (McCoy) M.; m. Helen S. Bondurant, Aug. 14, 1965; children: Lisa Marie, Lynn Michelle. AA, Wentworth Mil. Acad., Lexington, Mo., 1961. Buyer Foley Bros. Dept. Stores, Houston, 1963-65; owner JOMARC, Houston, 1965-66; sales mgr. Firestone Tire & Rubber Co., Houston, 1966-67; distbn. mgr. Matthews Book Co., St. Louis, 1967-69, office mgr., 1969, gen. mgr., 1970, v.p. ops., 1971, pres., 1972—; pres. McCoy Collegiate Svcs., St. Louis, 1969—, NACSCORP Inc., Oberlin, Ohio, 1983, Coll. Stores Rsch. and Edn. Found., 1984-85; chmn. Coll. Stores Am., St. Louis, 1986—; bd. dirs. Quality Med. Pubs. Contbr. articles to publs. Mem. Nat. Assn. Coll. Stores (pres. 1981-82), The ESOP Assn. Office: Matthews Book Co 11559 Rock Island Ct Maryland Heights MO 63043

MARCUS, JOSEPH, child psychiatrist; b. Cleve., Feb. 27, 1928; s. William and Sarah (Marcus) Schwartz; m. Cilla Furmanovitz, Oct. 3, 1951; children: Oren, Alon. B.Sc., Western Res. U., 1963; M.D., Hebrew U., 1958. Intern Tel Hashomer Govt. Hosp., Israel, 1956-57; resident in psychiatry and child psychiatry Ministry of Health, Govt. of Israel, 1958-61; acting head dept. child psychiatry Ness Ziona Rehab. Ctr., 1961-62; sr. psychiatrist Lasker dept. child psychiatry Hadassah U. Hosp., 1962-64; research asso. Israel Inst. Applied Social Research, 1966-69; practice medicine specializing in psychiatry Jerusalem, 1966-72; assoc. dir. devel. neuropsychiatry Jerusalem Infant and Child Devel. Ctr., 1969-70; dept. head Eytanim Hosp., 1970-72; cons. child psychiatrist for Jerusalem Ministry of Health, 1970-72; dir. dept. child psychiatry and devel. Jerusalem Mental Health Ctr., 1972-75; prof. child psychiatry, dir. unit for research in child psychiatry and devel. U. Chgo., 1975-85, prof. emeritus, co-dir. unit for research in child psychiatry and devel., 1986—; vis. research psychiatrist UCLA Dept. Psychiatry, 1987—. Chief editor: Early Child Devel. and Care, 1972-76; mem. editorial bd.: Israel Annals of Psychiatry and Related Disciplines, 1965-70, Internat. Yearbook of Child Psychiatry and Allied Professions, 1968-74; contbr. articles to med. jours. Mem. Am. Acad. Child Psychiatry (com. on research, com. on psychiat. aspects of infancy), Soc. Research in Child Devel., Internat. Assn. Child Psychiatry and Allied Professions (asst. gen. sec. 1966-74), European Union Paedopsychiatry (hon.), World, Israel psychiatry assns., Internat. Coll. Psychosomatic Medicine, Israel Center Psychobiology. Home: 910 Chelham Way Santa Barbara CA 93108-1049 Office: # MC 3077 5841 S Maryland Ave Chicago IL 60637-1463

MARCUS, KAREN MELISSA, foreign language educator; b. Vancouver, B.C., Can., Feb. 28, 1956; came to the U.S., 1962; d. Marvin Marcus and Arlen Ingrid (Sahlman) Bishop; m. Jorge Esteban Mezei, Jan. 7, 1984 (div. Mar. 1987). BA in French, BA in Polit. Sci., U. Calif., Santa Barbara, 1978, MA in Polit. Sci., 1981; MA in French, Stanford U., 1984, PhD in French, 1990. Lectr. in French Stanford (Calif.) U., 1989-90; asst. prof. French No. Ariz. U., Flagstaff, 1990-96, assoc. prof. French, 1996—; cons. Houghton Mifflin, 1993, Grand Canyon (Ariz.) Natural History Soc., 1994. Vol., letter writer Amnesty Internat. Urgent Action Network, 1991-95; vol. No. Ariz. Aids Outreach Orgn., Flagstaff, 1994-95. Recipient medal for outstanding achievement in French, Alliance Francaise, Santa Barbara, 1978; named Scholarship Exch. Student, U. Geneva, Switzerland, 1979-80; doctoral fellow Stanford (Calif.) U., 1981-85. Mem. MLA, Am. Assn. Tchrs. French, Am. Coun. on the Tchg. Fgn. Langs., Am. Literary Translators Assn., Women in French, Coordination Internat. des Chercheurs Sur Les Litteratures Maghrebines, Phi Beta Kappa, Pi Delta Phi, Alpha Lambda Delta. Democrat. Jewish. Avocations: walking, yoga, reading, writing short stories, photography. Office: No Ariz Univ Modern Lang Dept Box 6004 Flagstaff AZ 86011

MARCUS, LARRY DAVID, broadcasting executive; b. N.Y.C., Jan. 27, 1949; s. Oscar Moses and Sylvia (Ackerman) M.; m. Noreen Mary Marcus, Dec. 24, 1975; children: Julia Ilene, Barbara Maureen. BBA, CUNY, 1970, postgrad. studies Bus. Admistrn., 1970-72. Acctg. mgr. Sta. WPLG-TV, Miami, Fla., 1974-75; v.p., bus. mgr. Sta. KPLR-TV-Koplar Communications, Inc., St. Louis, 1976-82; chief fin. officer Koplar Communications, Inc., St. Louis, 1982-88, River City Broadcasting Co., St. Louis, 1988-96; gen. ptnr. Marcus Investments, L.P., 1996—; bd. dirs. Citation Computer Sys. Inc., Kupper-Parker Advt., St. Louis. Mem. exec. com., treas. St. Louis Art Fair. Mem. Broadcast Cable Fin. Mgmt. Assn. (bd. dirs. 1976-89, treas. 1989-90, sec. 1990-91, v.p. 1991-92, pres. 1992-93). Jewish. Avocations: sports, skiing, golf. Office: Marcus Investments LP 34 Brentmoor Park Clayton MO 63105-3071

MARCUS, LAURENCE RICHARD, education policy and planning educator; b. Brookline, Mass., July 23, 1947; s. Herbert M. and Joyce (Chaban) M.; m. Maureen Flanagan; children: Yvette, Christina Ann. BA in Polit. Sci. and Am. Govt., U. Mass., Amherst, 1969; MEd, 1972, EdD, 1976. Staff asst. U. Mass., Amherst, 1970-76; asst. to v.p. acad. affairs Stockton State Coll., Pomona, N.J., 1976-79, interim dean gen. studies, 1977; asst. to chancellor N.J. Dept. Higher Edn., Trenton, 1979-81, dir. state colls., 1981-87; dir. N.J. Fund for Improvement of Collegiate Edn., 1984-87, Div. Faculty Devel. and Ednl. Policy, 1987-89, dep. asst. chancellor, 1989-91, asst. chancellor for academic and fiscal affairs, 1991-94; prof. ednl. leadership and policy Rowan Coll. of N.J., Glassboro, 1994—. tchr. U. Mass., Stockton State Coll.; cons. race relations, ednl. administrn. and leadership; trustee Glassboro State Coll., 1986-87, Trenton State Coll, 1986-87, 89-94, Montclair State Coll., 1989-91, Kean Coll. of N.J., 1990-94; trustee, N.J. Marine Scis. Consortium, 1990-94, exec. com., 1990-94. Mem. Amherst Town Meeting, 1971-73, Franklin-Hampshire Concil for Children, 1974-76, N.J. Commn. Future of State Colls., 1982-84; adv. Commn. on Investing in State Colls., 1993-94. Mem. Assn. Study of Higher Edn., Am. Ednl. Research Assn. (chair div. J govt. relations com., 1986-88, chair div. J comm. on publs. 1988-89, chair spl. interst group futures rsch. and strategic planning 1995—), Am. Polit. Sci. Assn., Policy Studies Orgn., Adelphia (past pres.). Co-author: (with Benjamin D. Stickney) Race and Education: The Unending Controversy, 1981; (with A. Leone, E. Goldberg) The Path to Excellence, 1983; (with Benjamin D. Stickney) The Great Education Debate-Washington and the Schools, 1984, (Choice's award as Outstanding Academic Book, 1985-86), (with Janet Johnson) Blue Ribbon Commissions and Higher Education: Changing Academe from the Outside, 1986, (with Benjamin D. Stickney) Politics and Policy in the Age of Education, 1990. Fighting Words: The Politics of Hateful Speech, 1996; mem. editorial bd. Review of Higher Edn., 1991-95, On the Horizon, 1994—; consulting editor: ASHE/ERIC Higher Edn. Report Series, 1994—; contbr. numerous articles to profl. jours. Home: 33 Forest Ave Medford NJ 08055-3447 Office: Rowan U NJ Dept Ednl Leadership Glassboro NJ 08028-1701

MARCUS, LINDA SUSAN, dermatologist; b. Brooklyn; d. Nathaniel and Eugenia (Portnay) Marcus; m. Ronald Carlin, July 5, 1976; children: Robert Adam, Neal Marc. BS, Adelphi U., Garden City, N.J., 1970; MD, Downstate Med. Sch., Brooklyn, 1975. Diplomate Am. Bd. Dermatology. Intern Long Island (N.Y.) Jewish Med. Ctr., 1975-76; resident in dermatology Columbia-St. Luke's, N.Y.C., 1976-77, Boston U.-Tuft's, 1977-79; pvt. practice Wyckoff, N.J., 1980—. Contbr. articles to profl. jours. Mem. Am. Acad. Dermatology, Am. Soc. Dermatology Surgeons, Internat. Soc. Dermatology Surgeons. Avocations: swimming, ice skating. Office: 271 Godwin Ave Wyckoff NJ 07481-2057

MARCUS, MARIA LENHOFF, lawyer, law educator; b. Vienna, Austria, June 23, 1933; came to U.S., 1938, naturalized, 1944; d. Arthur and Clara (Gruber) Lenhoff; m. Norman Marcus, Dec. 23, 1956; children: Valerie, Nicole, Eric. BA, Oberlin Coll., 1954; JD, Yale Law Sch., 1957. Bar: N.Y. 1961, U.S. Dist. Ct. (so. and ea. dists.) N.Y. 1962, U.S. Ct. Appeals (2d cir.) 1962, U.S. Supreme Ct. 1964. Assoc. counsel NAACP, N.Y.C., 1961-67; asst. atty. gen. N.Y. State, N.Y.C., 1967-78; chief litigation bur. Atty. Gen. N.Y. State, 1976-78; adj. assoc. prof., Law Sch. NYU, 1976-78; assoc. prof. law Fordham Law Sch., N.Y.C., 1978-86, prof. law, 1986—; arbitrator Nat. Assn. Securities Dealers; chair subcom. interrogatories U.S. Dist. Ct. (so. dist.) N.Y., 1983-85. Contbr. articles to profl. jours. Fellow N.Y. Bar Found.; mem. Assn. Bar City of N.Y. (v.p. 1995-96, long range planning com. 1996—, exec. com. 1976-80, com. audit 1988-91, labor com. 1981-84, judiciary com. 1975-76, chmn. civil rights com. 1972-75), N.Y. State Bar Assn. (exec. com. 1979-81, ho. dels. 1978-81, com. constitution and by-laws 1984-93). Office: Fordham Law Sch 140 W 62nd St New York NY 10023-7407

MARCUS, MARIANO NAKAMURA, secondary school principal; b. Weno Chuuk, Federated States Micronesia, Sept. 5, 1961; s. Teruo Ignacio and Machko Ursula (Nakamura) M.; m. Marcelly Kantito, Feb. 28, 1987; children: Antinina, Antinisi, Anter, Anterina, Ancher, Mariano, Mark Metek. BSW, U. Guam, Mangilao, 1986; MA, U. San Francisco, 1997. Registrar Xavier H.S., Weno Chuuk, 1979-80, dean students, 1981-83; rschr. Micronesian Seminar, Weno Chuuk, 1986-87; health educator Dept. Health, Weno Chuuk, 1987-89, mental health counselor, 1989-90; prin. Saramen Chuuk Acad., Weno Chuuk, 1990-96; mem. rsch./devel. cadre Pacific Regional Ednl. Lab., Honolulu, 1992—. Sec.-treas. Mechitiw Village, Weno Chuuk, 1990—; chmn. Youth Commn., Weno Chuuk, 1992-94; bd. consultors Xavier H.S., Weno, 1992—; chmn. non-pub. schs., Weno, 1993—; mem. Close Up Washington Program, 1992-94. Mem. ASCD, Nat. Cath. Edn. Assn., Cath. Sch. Adminstrs. Roman Catholic. Home: 1400 Floyd Ave #9 Modesto CA 95355 Office: Saramen Chuuk Academy PO Box 662 Chuuk FM 96942

MARCUS, MARVIN, mathematician, educator; b. Albuquerque, July 31, 1927; s. David Clarence and Esther (Rosenthal) M.; m. Arlen Ingrid Sahlman, Sept. 14, 1951; children: Jeffrey Thomas, Karen Melissa; m. Rebecca Elizabeth Michael, Oct. 12, 1965. B.A., U. Calif. at Berkeley, 1950, Ph.D., 1953. Instr., then asst. prof. U. B.C., 1954-56, asso. prof., 1957-62; postdoctoral research fellow Nat. Bur. Standards, Washington, 1956-57; prof. U. Calif. at Santa Barbara, 1962—; dir. Inst. for Interdisciplinary Applications of Algebra and Combinatorics, 1973-79, chmn. dept. math., 1963-68, dean research devel., 1978, assoc. vice-chancellor research and acad. devel., 1979-86; vis. distinguished prof. U. Islamabad, West Pakistan, 1970; Cons. Bur. Naval Ordnance, Pasadena, Calif. Author books and articles in field.; Editor: Linear and Multilinear Algebra. Served with USN, 1945-46. Mem. Am. Math. Soc., Math. Assn. Am., Soc. Indsl. and Applied Math., Assn. for Computing Machinery, Sigma Xi, Pi Mu Epsilon. Home: 2937 Kenmore Pl Santa Barbara CA 93105-2223

MARCUS, NORMAN, lawyer; b. N.Y.C., Aug. 31, 1932; s. David and Evelyn (Freed) M.; m. Maria Eleanor Lenhoff, Dec. 23, 1956; children: Valerie, Nicole, Eric. BA, Columbia U., 1953; LLB, Yale U., 1957. Bar: N.Y. 1958, U.S. Dist. Ct. (so. dist.) 1960, U.S. Supreme Ct. 1964. Assoc. LaPorte & Meyers, N.Y.C., 1957-61; assoc. counsel Stanley Warner Corp., N.Y.C., 1961-63; gen. counsel N.Y.C. Planning Commn. and Dept. of City Planning, 1963-85; ptnr. Finley, Kumble, Wagner, Heine, Underberg, Manley, Myerson & Casey, N.Y.C., 1985-87; counsel Bachner, Tally, Polevoy & Misher, N.Y.C., 1987—; adj. prof. Pratt Inst., Bklyn., 1965-85, NYU Law Sch., 1977—, Benjamin N. Cardozo Sch. Law, N.Y.C., 1983-85, NYU Wagner Sch. Pub. Svc., 1986—, Princeton (N.J.) U. Sch. Architecture, 1990-91. Contbr. articles to profl. jours. Recipient Meritorious Achievement award Am. Planning Assn., 1986. Mem. N.Y. State Bar Assn., Assn. of Bar of City of N.Y. (com. on land use planning and zoning), N.Y. County Lawyers Assn. (bd. dirs., chmn. com. on urban devel. and land use), Am. Coll. Real Estate Lawyers, The Fine Arts Fedn. N.Y. (v.p.), Century Club. Avocations: antique books, swimming, drama criticism. Home: 91 Central Park W New York NY 10023-4600 Office: Bachner Tally Polevoy & Misher 380 Madison Ave New York NY 10017-2513 *Solve problems and you leave the world a better place.*

MARCUS, NORMAN, tax and financial consultant; b. Aleppo, Syria, Feb. 16, 1919; (parents Am. citizens); s. Ezra and Jamille (Dweck) M.; m. Harriet Spero, Jan. 23, 1943; children: Eric G., Amy L., Beth I. Marcus Haughney. B Mech. Engring., CCNY, 1950; MA, Hofstra U., 1957; EdD, U. Sarasota, 1970. Enrolled agt., IRS; registered profl. engr., Conn. Test engr. Sperry Corp., Lake Success, N.Y., 1950-53; engr. Servo Corp. Am., New Hyde Park, N.Y., 1953-56; devel. engr. Perkin-Elmer Corp., Norwalk, Conn., 1956-59; rsch. engr. Sperry Semicondr., Norwalk, 1959-62; supervisory engr. Nat. Semicondr., Danbury, Conn., 1962-67; prof. Norwalk State Tech. Coll., 1967-85, prof. emeritus, 1985—; pres. The Profl. Men, Inc., Bridgeport, Conn., 1985—. Author: Technical Mathematics, 1972. Judge sci. fair Norwalk Bd. Edn., 1980-84; former moderator Norwalk Bd. Elections. With U.S. Army, 1943-45. Named Fin. Planner of Month, Main Street Mgmt., 1983. Mem. Nat. Assn. Tax Practitioners, Sigma Pi Sigma, Pi Tau Sigma, Sigma Pi Sigma. Jewish. Avocation: sstill and video photography. Home: 13 Mohawk Dr Norwalk CT 06851-1825 Office: The Profl Men Inc 900 Madison Ave Bridgeport CT 06606-5534

MARCUS, PAUL, lawyer, educator; b. N.Y.C., Dec. 8, 1946; s. Edward and Lillian (Rubin) M.; m. Rebecca Nimmer, Dec. 22, 1968; children: Emily, Beth, Daniel. AB, UCLA, 1968, JD, 1971. Bar: Calif. 1971, U.S. Dist. Ct. (cen. dist.) Calif. 1972, U.S. Ct. Appeals (D.C. cir.) 1972, U.S. Ct. Appeals (7th cir.) 1976. Law clk. U.S. Ct. Appeals (D.C. cir.), 1971-72; assoc. Loeb & Loeb, L.A., 1972-74; prof. law U. Ill., Urbana, 1974-83; dean Coll. Law U. Ariz., Tucson, 1983-88, prof., 1988-92; Haynes prof. law Coll. William and Mary, Williamsburg, Va., 1992—; reporter, cons. Fed. Jud. Ctr. Commn. Author: The Entrapment Defense, 1989, 2d edit., 1995, The Prosecution and Defense of Criminal Conspiracy, 1978, 4th edit., 1997, Gilbert Law Summary, 1982, 5th edit., 1995, Criminal Law: Cases and Materials, 1982, 3d edit., 1995; nat. reporter on criminal law Internat. of Comparative Law, 1978—. Nat. reporter on criminal law Internat. of Comparative Law, 1978—. Office: Coll of William and Mary Williamsburg VA 85721

MARCUS, PHILIP IRVING, virology educator, researcher; b. Springfield, Mass., June 3, 1927; s. Julius and Marley Amelia (Speir) M.; m. Angela Joan Francis, Dec. 4, 1953; children: Craig F., Wendy L., Valerie L. B.S., U. So. Calif., 1950; M.S., U. Chgo., 1953; Ph.D., U. Colo., 1957. Asst. prof. biophysics U. Colo. Sch. Medicine, Denver, 1957-60; asso. prof. microbiology Albert Einstein Coll. Medicine, Bronx, N.Y., 1961-66; prof. Albert Einstein Coll. Medicine, 1967-69; prof. microbiology U. Conn., Storrs, 1969-75, head dept., 1969-75, prof. virology, 1969—, dir. Biotech. Ctr., 1990-95; dir. Nat. Cancer Inst. Program Project, 1973-83; cons. NIH, NSF; mem. sci. adv. coun. Damon Runyon-Walter Winchell Cancer Fund, 1970-74, Am. Cancer Soc., 1986-88, Am. Found. for AIDS Rsch., 1990—. Editor Jour. Cellular Physiology, 1969-96; editor in chief Jour. Interferon Rsch., 1984-95, Jour. Interferon & Cytokine Rsch., 1995—; contbr. numerous articles to profl. jours. Served with USAAC, 1945-47. Recipient USPHS rsch. career devel. award, 1960-70, excellence in rsch. award U. Conn. Alumni Assn., 1987; NIH grantee, 1960-94, NSF, USDA grantee. Mem. AAAS, Am. Soc. Microbiology, Am. Soc. Cell Biology, Am. Soc. Virology, Brit. Soc. Microbiology, Internat. Soc. Interferon and Cytokine Research, Tissue Culture Assn., Conn. Acad. Sci. and Engring. Home: 24 Thompson Rd Storrs Mansfield CT 06268-1806 Office: U Conn Dept Molec & Cell Biol U44 Storrs CT 06269-3044

MARCUS, RICHARD LEON, lawyer, educator; b. San Francisco, Jan. 28, 1948; s. Irving Harry and Elizabeth (McEvoy) M.; m. Andrea June Saltzman, Apr. 26, 1981; 1 child, Ruth. BA, Pomona Coll., 1969; JD, U. Calif., Berkeley, 1972. Bar: Calif. 1973, U.S. Dist. Ct. (no. dist.) Calif. 1976, U.S. Dist. Ct. (cen. dist.) Calif. 1978, U.S. Ct. Appeals (9th cir.) 1981. Law clk. to judge Calif. Supreme Ct., San Francisco, 1972; assoc. Boalt Hall U. Calif., 1973-74; law clk. to judge U.S. Dist. Ct. Calif., San Francisco, 1974-75; from assoc. to ptnr. Dinkelspiel, Pelavin, Steefel & Levitt, San Francisco, 1976-81; assoc. prof. law U. Ill., Champaign, 1981-84, prof. law, 1984-89; prof. law U. Calif., Hastings, 1989-97, disting. prof. law, 1997—; vis. prof. law U. Mich., 1986-87, U. Calif., Hastings, 1988; assoc. reporter Fed. Cts. Study Com., 1989-90; reporter com. civil motions Ill. Jud. Conf., Chgo.,

1984, com. on evidence, 1985; cons. Nat. Commn. on Judicial Discipline and Removal Act Adv. Group No. Dist. of Calif., 1992—, chair local rules adv. com. No. Dist. Calif., 1994—; spl. reporter advisory commn. on the civil rules, jud. conf. of the U.S., 1996—; mem. 9th Cir. local rules and internat. operating procedures com., 1996—. Author: Complex Litigation, 1985, 2d edit., 1992, Civil Procedure: A Modern Approach, 1989, 2d edit., 1995, Federal Practice and Procedure, vols. 8, 8A, and 12, 2d edit., 1994, 1997; rsch. editor U. Calif. Law Rev., 1971-72; contbr. articles to profl. jorus. Named Order of Coif. Mem. ABA, Am. Law Inst., Am. Assn. Law Schs. (chmn. sect. civil procedure 1988,chmn. complex litigation com. 1991). Democrat. Home: 70 Domingo Ave Berkeley CA 94705-2436 Office: U Calif Coll Law 200 Mcallister St San Francisco CA 94102-4707

MARCUS, RICHARD STEVEN, lawyer; b. Cin., May 26, 1950; s. Bernard Benjamin and Norma (Ginsberg) M.; m. Jane Iris Schreiber, Sept. 12, 1971; children: Rebecca, Sarah. BA in English, U. Wis., 1972; JD, Harvard U., 1975. Bar: Wis. 1975, U.S. Tax Ct. 1976, U.S. Ct. Appeals (7th cir.) 1977, U.S. Dist. Ct. (ea. dist.) Wis. 1979, U.S. Ct. Claims 1979. Assoc. Godfrey & Kahn, S.C., Milw., 1975—. Pres., Milw. Assn. for Jewish Edn., 1992; bd. dirs. Milw. Jewish Fedn., 1992, Milw. chpt. Jewish Nat. Fund, 1992. Office: Godfrey & Kahn SC 780 N Water St Milwaukee WI 53202-3512

MARCUS, ROBERT, aluminum company executive; b. Arlington, Mass., Feb. 24, 1925; s. Hymen David and Etta (Arbetter) M.; m. Emily Patricia Ulrich, 1988; children: Lawrence Brian, Janie Sue, Clifford Scott, Emily. AB, Harvard U., 1947; MBA, U. Mich., 1949; MEd, Tufts U., 1950. Market analyst Govt. Commodity Exch., N.Y.C., 1952-54; market rsch. analyst Gen. Electric Co., 1954-55; corp. market analyst Amax Inc., N.Y.C., 1955-62, staff market mgr. aluminum group, 1962-65, pres. internat. aluminum div., 1965-70, v.p., 1970-71; exec. v.p. Amax Pacific Corp., San Mateo, Calif., 1971-72; exec. v.p., dir. Alumax Inc., San Mateo, 1973-82, pres., chief exec. officer, dir., 1982-86; ptnr. Am. Indsl. Ptnrs., San Francisco, 1987-92; dir. Saybrook Inst., 1992—; dir. Domtar, Montreal, 1984-90, Kaiser Aluminum Corp., 1990—. Trustee Mex. Mus., 1988-93, World Affairs Coun., 1975-90. With USN, 1943-46. Mem. Japan Soc. (bd. dirs.), Harvard (N.Y.C.). Clubs: Harvard (N.Y.C.); University, Commonwealth, (San Francisco). Home: 2700 Scott St San Francisco CA 94123-4637

MARCUS, ROBERT D., historian, educator; b. Bklyn., Jan. 14, 1936; s. Leonard Roger and Dorothy (Zimmerman) M.; m. Deborah Irene Weisstein, Aug. 13, 1961 (div. 1970); children: Anthony Allen, Elizabeth Sarah; m. Grania Bolton, Mar. 14, 1971 (div. 1989); children: Abigail Whitney, Benjamin Luke; m. Jill Gussow, Dec. 3, 1989; 1 child, Zora Marcus Gussow. B.A., Columbia U., 1957, M.A., 1963; postgrad., Oriel Coll., Oxford U., 1957-58; Ph.D., Northwestern U., 1967. Lectr. in history Ind. U., Bloomington, 1964-67; asst. prof. history SUNY-Stony Brook, 1967-71, assoc. prof., 1971-80, dean undergrad. studies, 1974-80; v.p. acad. affairs Rollins Coll., Winter Park, Fla., 1980-83; v.p. acad. affairs SUNY-Brockport, 1983-92, prof. history, 1992—. Author: Grand Old Party, 1971, A Giant's Strength, 1971, A Brief History of the United States Since 1945, 1975, (with others) America: A Portrait in History, 1978, American Voices, 1992, American Firsthand, 4th edit., 1997; editor: Brandywine Monograph Series in American History. Mem. Am. Hist. Assn., Orgn. Am. Historians, Phi Beta Kappa. Democrat. Office: State Coll Dept History Brockport NY 14420

MARCUS, RUDOLPH ARTHUR, chemist, educator; b. Montreal, Que., Can., July 21, 1923; came to U.S., 1949, naturalized, 1958; s. Myer and Esther (Cohen) M.; m. Laura Hearne, Aug. 27, 1949; children: Alan Rudolph, Kenneth Hearne, Raymond Arthur. BS in Chemistry, McGill U., 1943, PhD in Chemistry, 1946, DSc (hon.), 1988; DSc (hon.), U. Chgo., 1983, Poly. U., 1986, U. Göteborg, Sweden, 1987, U. N.B., Can., 1993, Queens U., Can., 1993, U. Oxford, Eng., 1995, Yokohama Nat. U., 1996, U. N.C., 1996, U. Ill., 1997. Rsch. staff mem. RDX Project, Montreal, 1944-46; postdoctoral rsch. assoc. NRC of Can., Ottawa, Ont., 1946-49, U. N.C., 1949-51; asst. prof. Poly. Inst. Bklyn., 1951-54, assoc. prof., 1954-58, prof., 1958-64; prof. U. Ill., Urbana, 1964-78; Arthur Amos Noyes prof. chemistry Calif. Inst. Tech., Pasadena, 1978—; vis. prof. theoretical chemistry U. Oxford, 1975-76; Baker lectr. Cornell U., Ithaca, N.Y., 1991; Linnett vis. prof. chemistry Cambridge (Eng.) U., 1996; hon. prof. Fudan U., Shanghai, 1994—; hon prof. Inst. Chemistry Chinese Acad. Scis., Beijing, 1995—; professorial fellow Univ. Coll., Oxford, hon. fellow, 1995—; vis. prof. theoretical chemistry U. Oxford, Eng., IBM, 1975-76; also professorial fellow Univ. Coll.; Linnett vis. prof. chemistry Cambridge (Eng.) U., 1996; mem. Courant Inst. Math. Scis., NYU, 1960-61; trustee Gordon Rsch. Confs., 1966-69, chmn. bd. dirs., 1968-69, mem. coun., 1965-68; mem. rev. panel Argonne Nat. Lab., 1966-72, chmn., 1967-68; mem. rev. panel Brookhaven Nat. Lab., 1971-74; mem. rev. com. Radiation Lab., U. Notre Dame, 1975-80; mem. panel on atmospheric chemistry climatic impact com. NAS-NRC, 1975-78, mem. com. kinetics of chem. reactions, 1973-77, chmn., 1975-77, mem. com. chem. scis., 1977-79, mem. com. to survey opportunities in chem. scis., 1982-86; mem. math. panel Internat. Benchmarking of U.S. Rsch. Fields, 1996—; adv. com. for chemistry NSF, 1977-80, external adv. bd. NSF ctr. Photoinduced Charge Transfer, 1990—, mem. presdl. chairs com., Chile, 1994-96; advisor Ctr. for Molecular Scis., Chinese Acad. Scis. and State Key Lab. for Structural Chemistry of Unstable and Stable Species, Beijing, 1995—. Former mem. editl. bd. Jour. Chem. Physics, Ann. Rev. Phys. Chemistry, Jour. Phys. Chemistry, Accounts Chem. Rsch., Internat. Jour. Chem. Kinetics Molecular Physics, Theoretica Chimica Acta, Chem. Physics Letters, Faraday Trans., Jour. Chem. Soc.; mem. editl. bd. Laser Chemistry, 1982—, Advances in Chem. Physics, 1984—, World Sci. Pub., 1987—, Internat. Revs. in Phys. Chemistry, 1988—, Progress in Physics, Chemistry and Mechanics (China), 1989—, Perkins Transactions 2, Jour. Chem. Soc., 1992—, Chem. Physics Rsch. (India), 1992—, Trends in Chem. Physics Rsch. (India), 1992—; hon. editor Internat. Jour. Quantum Chemistry, 1996—. Treas. L.A. Cen. City Assn., 1995. Alfred P. Sloan fellow, 1960-61, sr. postdoctoral fellow NSF, 1960-61; sr. Fulbright-Hays scholar, 1972; recipient Sr. U.S. Scientist award Alexander von Humboldt-Stiftung, 1976, Electrochem. Soc. Lecture award Electrochem. Soc., 1979, 96, Robinson medal Faraday divsn. Royal Soc. Chemistry, 1982, Centenary medal Faraday divsn., 1988, Chandler medal, Columbia U., 1983, Wolf prize in Chemistry, 1985, Nat. Medal of Sci., 1989, Evans award Ohio State U., 1990, Nobel prize in Chemistry, 1992, Hirshfelder prize in Theoretical Chemistry, U. Wis., 1993, Golden Plate award Am. Acad. Achievement, 1993, Lavoisier medal French Chem. Soc., 1994; named Hon. Citizen, City of Winnipeg, 1994, Treasure of L.A., Ctrl. City Assn., 1995. Fellow AAAS, Am. Acad. Arts and Scis. (hon., exec. com. western sect., co-chmn. 1981-84, rsch. and planning com. 1989-91), Am. Phys. Soc., Internat. Soc. Electrochemistry (hon.), Royal Soc. Chemistry (hon.), Royal Soc. London (hon.), Internat. Acad. Quantum Molecular Sci. (hon.), Royal Soc. Can. (hon.); mem. NAS (hon.), Am. Philos. Soc. (hon.), Korean Chem. Soc. (hon.), Am. Chem. Soc. (past divsn. chmn., mem. exec. com., mem. adv. bd. petroleum rsch. fund, Irving Langmuir award in chem. physics 1978, Pter Debye award in phys. chemistry 1988, Willard Gibbs medal Chgo. sect. 1988, S.C. Lind Lecture, East Tenn. sect. 1988, Theodore William Richards medal Northwestern sect. 1990, Edgar Fahs Smith award Phila. sect. 1991, Ira Remsen Meml. award Md. sect. 1991, Pauling medal Portland, Oreg., and Puget Sound sect. 1991, Auburn-Kosolapoff award 1996, Theoretical Chemistry award 1997), Internat. Acad. Quantum Molecular Sci. (hon.), Korean Chem. Soc. (hon.). Achievements include responsibility for the Marcus Theory of electron transfer reactions in chemical systems and RRKM theory of unimolecular reactions. Home: 331 S Hill Ave Pasadena CA 91106-3405

MARCUS, RUTH BARCAN, philosopher, educator, writer, lecturer; b. N.Y.C.; d. Samuel and Rose (Post) Barcan; divorced; children: James Spencer, Peter Webb, Katherine Hollister, Elizabeth Post. BA, NYU, 1941; MA, Yale U., 1942, PhD, 1946; LHD (hon.), U. Ill., 1995. Rsch. assoc. in anthropology Inst. for Human Relations, Yale U., New Haven, Conn., 1945-47; AAUW fellow, 1947-48; vis. prof. (intermittently) Northwestern U., 1950-57, Guggenheim fellow, 1953-54; asst. prof., assoc. prof. Roosevelt U., Chgo., 1957-63; NSF fellow, 1963-64; prof. philosophy U. Ill. at Chgo., 1964-70, head philosophy dept., 1963-69; fellow U. Ill. Center for Advanced Study, 1968-69; prof. philosophy Northwestern U., 1970-73; Reuben Post Halleck prof. philosophy Yale U., 1973-93; sr. rsch. scholar, 1994—; fellow Ctr. Advanced Study in Behavioral Sci., Stanford, Calif., 1979; vis. fellow Inst. Advanced Study, U. Edinburgh, 1983, Wolfson Coll., Oxford U., 1985, 86; vis. fellow Clare Hall, Cambridge U., 1988, lifetime mem. common room, 1989—; past or present mem. adv. coms. Princeton U., MIT, Calif. Inst. Tech., Cornell U. Humanities Ctr., Columbia U., UCLA, others. Author: Modalities, 1993; editor: The Logical Enterprise, 1975, Logic Methodology and Philosophy of Science VII, 1986; mem. editorial bd. Past or Present Metaphilosophy, Monist, Philos. Studies, Signs, Jour. Symbolic Logic, The Philosophers Annual; editor, contbr. to profl. jours. and books. Recipient Machette prize for contbn. to profession; Medal, College de France, 1986; Mellon sr. fellow Nat. Humanities Ctr., 1992-93; vis. disting. prof. U. Calif., Irvine, 1994, 96, 97; fellow Conn. Acad. Arts & Scis. Fellow Am. Acad. Arts and Scis.; mem. Coun. on Philos. Studies (pres. 1988-90), Assn. for Symbolic Logic (past exec. coun., exec. com. 1973-83, v.p. 1980-82, coun. 1980-85, pres. 1982-84), Am. Philos. Assn. (past sec., treas., nat. bd. dirs. 1967-83, pres. ctrl. divsn. 1975-78, chmn. nat. bd. officers 1977-85), Philosophy of Sci. Assn., Inst. Internat. Philosophie (past exec. com., v.p. 1983-86, pres. 1990-93, hon. pres. 1994—), Fedn. Internat. Philosophy (exec. com., steering com. 1985—), Elizabethan Club (v.p. 1989, pres. 1989-90), Phi Beta Kappa (professorial lectr. 1993).

MARCUS, SHELDON, social sciences educator; b. N.Y.C., Aug. 4, 1937; s. Manny and Sarah (Lande) M.; m. Phyllis Knight; children: Beth, Jonathan, Evan. B.A., CCNY, 1959, M.S., 1960; Ed.D., Yeshiva U., 1970. Tchr. N.Y.C. Pub. Schs., 1959-68; lectr. social sci. CUNY, 1965-68; mem. faculty Fordham U., N.Y.C., 1968-70, chmn. div. urban edn., 1970-76, assoc. dean grad. edn. Tarrytown campus, 1976-93, prof., 1993—; mem. exec. bd. tchr. corps program U.S. Office Edn., 1974-82; trustee Doctoral Assn. N.Y., 1973-82; co-dir. Fordham Inst. for Rsch. on Supervision and Tchg., 1992-94, Fordham U./N.Y.C. Supts. Network, 1995—. Author or co-author: Conflicts in Urban Education, 1970; Urban Education: Crisis or Opportunity?, 1972; Father Coughlin: The Tumultuous Life of the Priest of the Little Flower, 1973, (nominated for Pulitzer Prize); The Urban In-Service Education Experience, 1977; Administrative Decision Making in Schools: A Case Study Approach to Strategic Planning, 1986, Strategic Planning: A Case Study Approach to Administrative Decision Making. Case Teaching Notes, 1987; contbr. articles to profl. jours. Recipient Scanlon award for contbns. to edn., 1992, Adminstr. of Yr. award Phi Delta Kappa, 1993. Mem. Am. Ednl. Rsch. Assn. (proposal reviewer 1992—). Home: 36 Pocantico River Rd Pleasantville NY 10570-3510 Office: Fordham U Sch Educ Tarrytown NY 10591

MARCUS, STANLEY, federal judge; b. 1946. BA, CUNY, 1967; JD, Harvard U., 1971. Assoc. Botein, Hays, Sklar & Herzberg, N.Y.C., 1974-75; asst. atty. U.S. Dist. Ct. (ea. dist.) N.Y., 1975-78; spl. atty., dep. chief U.S. organized crime sect. Detroit Strike Force, 1978-79, chief U.S. organized crime sect., 1980-82; U.S. atty. So. Dist. of Fla., Miami, 1982-85; judge U.S. Dist. Ct. (so. dist.) Fla., Miami, 1985—. Office: US Dist Ct 301 N Miami Ave Fl 5 Miami FL 33128-7702*

MARCUS, STEPHEN HOWARD, lawyer; b. N.Y.C., June 30, 1945; s. Jacob and Mildren (Cohen) M.; m. Carol Sylvia Beatrice, June 11, 1967; children: Joshua David, Rebecca Lynn, Daniel Benjamin. BME, MIT, 1967; JD, Harvard U., 1970. Bar: Calif. 1971, U.S. Dist. Ct. (cen. dist.) Calif. 1971, U.S. Dist. Ct. (so. dist.) Calif. 1974, U.S. Dist. Ct. (so. dist.) Calif. 1975, U.S. Ct. Appeals (9th cir.) 1980. Assoc. Mitchell, Silberberg & Knupp, L.A., 1971-72, Greenberg, Bernhard, Weiss & Karma, L.A., 1972-76; ptnr. Greenberg, Bernhard, Weiss & Rosin, L.A., 1976-85; assoc. Frandzel & Share, L.A., 1985-87, ptnr., 1987—; judge pro tem L.A. Mcpl. Ct., 1976-83. Editor Harvard Law Rev., 1970. Mem. Los Angeles County Bar Assn. (client rels. com. arbitrator 1982—, vice chair, 1996—), Century City Bar Assn. (bd. govs. 1984-90), MIT Club So. Calif. (pres. 1978-79, bd. govs. 1979—), Sigma Xi, Tau Beta Pi. Democrat. Jewish. Avocations: senior soccer, skiing, square dancing. Office: Frandzel & Share 6500 Wilshire Blvd Los Angeles CA 90048-4920

MARCUS, STEVEN, dean, English educator; b. N.Y.C., Dec. 13, 1928; s. Nathan and Adeline Muriel (Gordon) M.; m. Gertrud Lenzer, Jan. 20, 1966; 1 son, John Nathaniel. Ph.D., Columbia U., 1961; D.H.L. (hon.), Clark U., 1985. Prof. English Columbia U., 1966—, George Delacorte prof. humanities, 1976—, chmn. dept. English and comparative lit., 1977-80, 85-89, v.p. Arts and Scis., 1993-95; dean Columbia Coll., 1993-95; dir. planning Nat. Humanities Center, 1974-76; chmn. exec. com. bd. dirs. Nat. Humanities Ctr., 1976-80, 96—, also bd. dirs.; chmn. Lionel Trilling Seminars, 1976-80. Author: Dickens: From Pickwick to Dombey, 1965, The Other Victorians, 1966, Engels, Manchester and the Working Class, 1974, Representations, 1976, Doing Good, 1978, Freud and The Culture of Psychoanalysis, 1984; Assoc. editor: Partisan Rev. Co-dir. Heyman Ctr. for the Humanities. With AUS, 1954-56. Guggenheim Found. fellow, 1967-68; Nat. Humanities Ctr. fellow, 1980-82; Rockefeller Found. fellow in humanities, 1980-81; fellow Ctr. Advanced Studies in the Behavioral Scis., 1972-73. Fellow Am. Acad. Arts and Scis., Acad. Lit. Studies; mem. Columbia Soc. Fellows in Humanities (co-chmn.), Am. Psychoanalytic Assn. (hon.), Inst. for Psychoanalytic Tng. and Rsch. (hon.), Am. Acad. Psychoanalysis (sci. assoc.). Home: 39 Claremont Ave New York NY 10027-6824

MARCUS, STEVEN IRL, electrical engineering educator; b. St. Louis, Apr. 2, 1949; s. Herbert A. and Peggy L. (Polishuk) M.; m. Jeanne M. Wilde, June 4, 1978; children: Jeremy A., Tobin L. BA, Rice U., 1971; SM, MIT, 1972, PhD, 1975. Research engr. The Analytic Scis. Corp., Reading, Mass., 1973; asst. prof. U. Tex., Austin, 1975-80, assoc. prof., 1980-84, prof., 1984-91, assoc. chmn., dept. elec. and computer engring., 1984-89, L.B. Meaders prof. engring., 1987-91; prof. elec. engring. U. Md., College Park, 1991—, dir. Inst. for Sys. Rsch., 1991-96; cons. Tracor Inc., Austin, 1977, 90. Assoc. editor Math. of Control Signals and Systems, 1987—, Jour. on Discrete Event Dynamic Systems, 1990, Acta Applicandae Mathematicae, 1983—. NSF fellow, 1971-74; Werner W. Dornberger Centennial Teaching fellowship in engring., U. Tex., Austin, 1982-84. Fellow IEEE (prize paper awards com. 1985-88, field awards com. 1989-90, assoc. editor Transactions Info. Theory 1990-92), IEEE Control Systems Soc. (bd. govs. 1985-90, chmn. conf. on decision and control program com. 1983, chmn. working group on stochastic control and estimation 1984-87, assoc. editor Transactions Automatic Control 1980-81); mem. Am. Math. Soc., Soc. Indsl. and Applied Math. (editor Jour. Control and Optimization 1990—), Acta Applicandae Math., 1983—, Eta Kappa Nu, Tau Beta Pi. Home: 9516 Thornhill Rd Silver Spring MD 20901-4836 Office: U Md Inst for Systems Rsch 2167 Ave Williams Bldg 115 College Park MD 20742

MARCUS, WILLIAM MICHAEL, rubber and vinyl products manufacturing company executive; b. Boston, Jan. 31, 1938; s. Richard and Diana (Litch) M.; m. Cynthia Steinman, Dec. 9, 1962; children: Melanie, Daniel, Richard. B.S. in Bus. Adminstrn., Babson Inst., 1959. With Am. Biltrite Inc., Wellesley Hills, Mass., 1960—; exec. v.p., treas. Am. Biltrite Inc., 1983—, also dir.; bd. dirs. Reebok Internat. Inc., Congoleum Corp. Served with U.S. Army, 1960-61. Office: Am Biltrite Inc 57 River St Wellesley MA 02181-2006

MARCUSA, FRED HAYE, lawyer; b. Paterson, N.J., Jan. 31, 1946; s. Harry and Alice Marcusa; m. Andrea Disario, Jun. 28, 1986; children: Michael, Daniel. A.B., Dartmouth Coll., 1967; J.D., U. Pa., 1970. Bar: N.Y. 1971. Assoc. Davis, Polk & Wardwell, N.Y.C., 1970-79; v.p., gen. counsel The Coca-Cola Bottling Co. of N.Y., Inc., N.Y.C., 1979-81; ptnr. Kaye, Scholer, Fierman, Hays & Handler, N.Y.C., 1981—. Office: Kaye Scholer Fierman Hays & Handler 425 Park Ave New York NY 10022-3506

MARCUSE, ADRIAN GREGORY, academic administrator; b. N.Y.C., Mar. 25, 1922; s. Maxwell Frederick and Mildred Ann (Hitter) M.; m. Janet Constance Radlo, Oct. 28, 1945 (dec. Mar. 22, 1980); children: Nancy Ruth Marcuse Marshall, Sally Ann Marcuse Crawford, Elizabeth Susan Marcuse Peterman; m. Betty Jane Lieberman Rossman, Jan. 11, 1985; 1 stepchild, Amy Beth Rossman Schurtz. BS, MIT, 1942, MS, 1946; LLD (hon.), Lab Inst. Merchandising, 1992. Registered profl. engr. N.Y., Fla. Rsch. assoc. MIT, Cambridge, Mass., 1945-46; rsch. scientist United Aircraft Co., E. Hartford, Conn., 1946-47; application engr. Westinghouse Electric Corp., Boston, N.Y.C., 1947-60; consulting engr. pvt. practice, N.Y.C., 1955-62; v.p. mktg. and sales Corrosion Control Corp., N.Y.C., 1960-62; sales & merchandising mgr. B. Altman & Co., N.Y.C., 1962; v.p., chief operating officer Lab. Inst. of Merchandising, N.Y.C., 1962-72, pres., chief exec. officer, 1972—; pres. LIM Fashion Edn. Found., N.Y.C., 1978—; chmn. Assn. Regionally Accredited Prvt. Colls. and Univs., Washington, 1990-93. Charter commr. City of Glen Cove, N.Y., 1964, chmn. bd. engrs., 1964-68, mem. planning bd., 1980-87; past treas. Community Concert Assn., Glen Cove; past trustee and budget chmn. North Country Reform Temple, Glen Cove; past mem. YMCA Fund-Raising Coun., Glen Cove. 1st lt. USAAF, 1942-45, PTO. Mem. Am. Assn. Higher Edn., Nat. Assn. Coll. Admissions Counselors, Assn. Proprietary Colls. (former pres., chmn.), N.Y. State Assn. Two-Yr. Colls., N.Y. State Counselors Assn., Soc. Sigma Xi. Republican. Avocations: sailing, bicycling, travel, theater. Office: Lab Inst of Merchandising 12 E 53rd St New York NY 10022-5208

MARCUSE, DIETRICH, retired physicist; b. Koenigsberg, East Prussia, Germany, Feb. 27, 1929; came to U.S., 1957; s. Richard and Gertrud (Solty) M.; m. Haide Schwarz, Jan. 13, 1959; children: Christina, Mikel. Diplom Physiker, Freie Universität, Berlin, 1954; Doktor Ingenieur, Karlsruhe Universität, 1962. Mem. tech. staff Siemens and Halske, Berlin, 1954-57; mem. tech. staff AT&T Bell Labs., Holmdel, N.J., 1957-94, dist. mem. tech. staff, 1982-94; ret., 1994; vis. rsch. prof. U. Md., Balt. County, 1995—. Author: Principles of Quantum-Electronics, 2d edit., 1980, Light Transmission Optics, 2d edit., 1982, Theory of Dielectric Optical Wave-guides, 1972, 2nd edit.,1991, Principles of Optical Fiber Measurements, 1981; also over 200 articles. Fellow IEEE (Quantum Electronics award 1981), Optical Soc. Am. (Max Born award 1989).

MARCUSE, MANFRED JOACHIM, paper products executive; b. Berlin, Apr. 17, 1927; came to U.S., 1947, naturalized, 1951; s. Bruno and Hedwig Elisabeth (Ettling) M.; m. Charlotte Kraemer, Sept. 23, 1950. Grad. high sch., Berlin. Export clk. ERICO Corp., N.Y.C., 1947-49; sales rep. Roseda Mills, Buffalo, 1950, various companies, 1953-58; systems engr. Nebr. Salesbook Co., Lincoln, 1958-64; prin., owner, chmn. Marc Bus. Forms Inc., Chgo., 1964—. Contbr. articles to profl. jours. Supporting mem. Selfhelp Home for the Aged, Chgo., 1988—, Chgo. Symphony, Lyric Opera, Chgo. United Jewish Appeal. With U.S. Army, 1951-52. Jewish. Office: Marc Business Forms Inc 2722 W Peterson Ave Chicago IL 60659-3920

MARCUSS, ROSEMARY DALY, economist; b. Stamford, Conn., Aug. 27, 1945; d. Eugene Lawrence and Margaret Mary (Murphy) Daly; B.A. in Econs. cum laude, Newton (Mass.) Coll., 1967; M.S., U. Md., 1973, Ph.D., 1979; m. Stanley J. Marcuss, July 6, 1968; children—Elena Daly, Aidan Stanley. Jr. staff economist President's Council of Econ. Advisers, 1968-70; economist, asst. to pres. Am. Fedn. State, County and Mcpl. Employees, Washington, 1973; economist, mgmt. cons. Data Resources, Inc., Washington, 1974-78; dep. asst. dir. tax analysis Congressional Budget Office, Washington, 1980-83, asst. dir. tax analysis, 1983—. NSF fellow, 1970-73. Mem. Am. Econ. Assn., Nat. Tax Assn., Tax Inst. Am., So. Econ. Assn., Soc. Govt. Economists, Nat. Economists Club, Washington Women Economists. Home: 4616 29th Pl NW Washington DC 20008-2105 Office: Congressional Budget Office House Office Bldg # 2 Washington DC 20515-0001

MARCUSS, STANLEY JOSEPH, lawyer; b. Hartford, Conn., Jan. 24, 1942; s. Stanley Joseph and Anne Sutton (Leone) M.; m. Rosemary Daly, July 6, 1968; children: Elena Daly, Aidan Stanley. BA, Trinity Coll., 1963, Cambridge U., 1965; MA, Cambridge U., 1968; JD, Harvard U., 1968. Bar: D.C., N.Y., Conn., U.S. Supreme Ct. Staff atty. office of gen. counsel HUD, Washington, 1968; atty. firm Hogan and Hartson, Washington, 1968-73; counsel to internat. fin. subcom. U.S. Senate Com. on Banking, Housing and Urban Affairs, 1973-77; dep. asst. sec. for trade regulation Dept. Commerce, Washington, 1977-78; sr. dep. asst. sec. for industry and trade Dept. Commerce, 1978-79, acting asst. sec. for industry and trade, 1979-80, acting asst. sec. for trade regulation, 1980; mem. firm Milbank, Tweed, Hadley & McCloy, Washington, 1980-93, Bryan Cave, 1993—; former adj. prof. Am. U. Law Sch. Author: Effective Washington Representation, 1983; mem. bd. overseers U. Calif. Berkeley Law Jour.; contbr. articles to profl. jours. Former trustee Trinity Coll., Hartford. Marshall scholar. Mem. ABA, D.C. Bar (former chmn., steering com. internat. law div.), Phi Beta Kappa. Home: 4616 29th Pl NW Washington DC 20008-2105

MARCUVITZ, NATHAN, electrophysics educator; b. Bklyn., Dec. 29, 1913; s. Samuel and Rebecca (Feiner) M.; m. Muriel Spanier, June 30, 1946; children—Andrew, Karen. B.E.E., Poly. Inst. Bklyn., 1935, M.E.E., 1941, D.E.E., 1947; Laurea Honoris Causa, Politecnico Di Torino, 1993. Engr. RCA Labs., 1936-40; research asso. Radiation Lab., Mass. Inst. Tech., 1941-46; asst. prof. elec. engring. Poly. Inst. Bklyn., 1946-49, asso. prof., 1949-51, prof., 1951-65; dir. Poly. Inst. Bklyn. (Microwave Research Inst.), 1957-61; v.p. research, acting dean Poly. Inst. Bklyn. (Grad. Center), 1961-63, prof. electrophysics, 1961-66, dean research, dean, 1964-65; asst. dir. def. research and engring. Dept. Def., Washington, 1963-64; prof. applied physics N.Y.U., 1966-73; prof. electrophysics Poly. Inst. N.Y., 1973—, prof. emeritus, 1978—; vis. prof. Harvard U., spring 1971. Author: Waveguide Handbook, Vol. 10, 1951, (with L. Felsen) Radiation and Scattering of Waves, 1973; also numerous articles. Recipient Microwave Career award IEEE Microwave Theory and Techniques Soc., 1985. Fellow IEEE (Heinrich Hertz medal 1989); mem. Nat. Acad. Engring., Am. Phys. Soc., Sigma Xi, Tau Beta Pi, Eta Kappa Nu. Home: 7 Ridge Dr E Great Neck NY 11021-2806 Office: Polytech U Rt 110 Farmingdale NY 11735

MARCY, CHARLES FREDERICK, food packaging company executive; b. Buffalo, Aug. 25, 1950; s. Charles and Mary Jane (Frederick) M.; m. Helen Jean Shank, May 6, 1972 (div. Dec. 1986); children: Michelle Catherine, Adam Charles; m. Cynthia Louise Shockey, June 17, 1989; 1 child, Brooke Allison. BA, Washington and Jefferson Coll., Washington, Pa., 1972; MBA, Harvard U., 1974. Various mktg. and strategic planning positions Gen. Foods Corp., White Plains, N.Y., 1974-84; v.p. mktg. Sara Lee Bakery, Deerfield, Ill., 1984-86; v.p., gen. mgr. Wolferman's Inc. divsn. of Sara Lee Corp., Lenexa, Kans., 1987-89; v.p. strategy and mktg. Kraft Gen. Foods Frozen Products, Glenview, Ill., 1989-90; pres. Kraft Gen. Foods Nat. Dairy Products Corp., Phila., 1991-92, Golden Grain Co., Pleasanton, Calif., 1993-95; pres., CEO Sealright Packaging Co., Inc., DeSoto, Kans., 1995—. Bd. dirs. Phila. Police Athletic League, 1991-92, Boys and Girls Club of Kansas City, Mo., 1987-90, Lake Forest (Ill.) Symphony, 1984-87. Office: Sealright Co Inc 9201 Packaging Dr DeSoto KS 66018-2708

MARDEN, ANNE ELLIOTT ROBERTS, paralegal, estates and trust specialist; b. N.Y.C., Dec. 17, 1935; d. James Ragan and Jane Ziegler (Elliott) Roberts; m. George Linn Davis, May 29, 1955 (div. Aug. 1967); children: James Roberts, Elliott Britton, George Linn Jr., William Vaughn (dec.); m. Robert Gray Peck III, Oct. 24, 1969 (div. April 1993); children: Andrew Adams, Matthew Canfield Roberts; m. John Newcomb Marden, June 26, 1993 (dec. 1996). BA in English with honors, Wellesley Coll., 1957; MA in English and Comparative Lit. with honors, Columbia U., 1966; postgrad. in law Villanova U., 1978-80, U. Bridgeport, 1988; Bus. Law and Corp. Fin. diploma, The Phila. Inst., 1988. Contbg. editor Newsfront mag., 1960-63; English tchr. The Masters Sch., Dobbs Ferry, N.Y., 1963-65; sports feature writer Westchester-Rockland newspapers, Reporter Dispatch, Gannett chain, White Plains, N.Y., 1969-70; corr., weekly column Knickerbocker News-Union Star, Schenectady Gazette, Capital Newspapers, Hearst chain, Albany and Schenectady, N.Y., 1971-73; on-screen TV pub. affairs panel moderator "Access", Channel 17, Albany, 1971-73; pub. and exec. tax preparer H & R Block, Inc., Wayne, Pa., 1976-79; sr. estate planning trust officer Provident Nat. Bank-Trust div. PNC Bank, Phila., 1981-86; asst. v.p., trust officer estate planning dept., trusts and investments div. Mellon Bank (East) N.A., 1986-87; asst v.p., trust officer People's Bank, Stamford, Conn., 1987-88; estates and trusts paralegal estates dept. Pepper, Hamilton and Scheetz, Berwyn, Pa., 1988-89; estate and trusts paralegal adminstr. Blank, Rome, Comisky and McCauley, Phila., 1989-90. Mem. Mus. Art and Sci. acquisitions com., Schenectady, N.Y., 1970-73; asst. prodr. "Poetry", Channel 25-TV, N.Y.C.; bd. dirs., legis. chmn. Greenacres Sch. PTA, 1967-69; pub. rels. chmn. Planned Parenthood League, Schenectady; sec., parliamentarian N.Y. State Legis. Forum, 1971-73; pres., founder The Career Group, Phila., 1983-85; editor congregation directory St. David's Episcopal Ch., 1976, mem. exec. com. every-member canvass, 1977; ann. fair gateskeeper, Episcopal Diocese Phila., 1974-80, rep. Merion Deanery; lector St. James the Less Ch., Scarsdale, N.Y., 1995-97; maj. gift solicitor Planned Parenthood Southeastern Pa., 1975-76; mem. plant sale exec. com. and Merry Mart com. Haverford Sch., 1976, 77; Rep. pollchecker Tredyffrin Twp., 1978-79; majority insp. of elections Tredyffrin Twp. E-2, 1980—;

mem. ARC; vol. Armed Svcs. to Mil. Families and Vets. and Emergency Svcs., Phila., Major Gifts Campaign, White Plains, N.Y., 1994-95, Hospice of Westchester, Inc. (diploma), 1994. Recipient prize Coll. Bd. Contest Mademoiselle mag., 1954, Prix de Paris, Vogue mag., 1957. Mem. DAR (bd. mgrs.-pub. rels. Phila. chpt., treas. 1983) Phila. Bicentennial Celebration com. 1976), AAUW (bd. dir. Schenectady 1971-73, legis. chmn. Valley Forge br., Albany-Schenectady br.), Schenectady County Mus. of Arts and Sci., N.Y. State Women's Press Club (Capital dist. br.), Jr. League Phila. (sustainer, pub. affairs com., art com., edn. com., child abuse ctr. com., Bicentennial Cookbook com., Waterworks Restoration com., 1984, bd. dirs. 1960-61), Schenectady Curling Club, Valley Forge Coun. Rep. Women, Mohawk Golf Club (Schenectady), Shenorock Shore Club (Rye, N.Y.), The Merion Cricket Club (Haverford, Pa.), Acorn Club (Phila.), Little Acorns Investment Club, Career Group W. in P. (founder, chair 1983-85), Nat. Soc. Daus. Am. Revolution, Jeptha Abbott Chap (Bryn Mawr), Wellesley Alumnae (Phila.), Phila. Assn. Paralegals, Phila. Bar Assn. (probate and trust law sect., non-lawyer assoc.), Phila. Estate Planning Coun., Chester County Estate Planning Coun., Little Egg Harbor Yacht Club (Beach Haven, N.J.), Jr. League of Phila. (sustainer, waterworks restoration com., pub. affairs com.). Republican. Episcopalian.

MARDEN, KENNETH ALLEN, advertising executive; b. Englewood, N.J., Dec. 12, 1928; s. Allen H. and Doris (Littlefield) M.; m. Julia Lee Black, June 11, 1949; children—Priscilla Anne, Emily Gage. B.A., U. Maine, 1950. Hosp. salesman Johnson & Johnson, New Brunswick, N.J., 1959-61, product dir. hosp. div., 1962-68, advt., pub. relations mgr. hosp. div., 1969-71, group product dir., patient care div., 1972-74, advt. dir. patient care div., 1974-78; v.p. E.J. Axelrod, Inc., N.Y.C., 1978-80; v.p. account mgmt. Vicom/FCB, Phila., 1980-87; pres. Am. Kennel Club, N.Y., 1987-90, cons. on dog legislation, 1990—, also bd. dirs.; pres. Crossing Creek Comm., 1991—; bd. dirs. The Dog Mus., 1995—. 1st lt. U.S. Army, 1951-53. Mem. DogWriters Assn. Am. Republican. Episcopalian. Clubs: German Shorthaired Pointer of Am. (del. 1976—, v.p. 1985-86), Eastern German Shorthaired Pointer (pres. 1972-74, 95-96), Jersey Rag Racers (pres. 1994-96), Kennel Club Phila. (bd. dirs.), Hunterdon Hills Kennel, Nat. Animal Interest Alliance (bd. dirs. 1994—), Nat. Breed Clubs Alliance (v.p. 1996—). Home: Crossing Creek Farm 53 Nedsland Ave Titusville NJ 08560-1715 Office: Crossing Creek Communications 53 Nedsland Ave Titusville NJ 08560-1715

MARDEN, PHILIP AYER, physician, educator; b. Newport, N.H., Oct. 31, 1911; s. Albion Sullivan and Laura Isobel (McEchern) M.; m. Magdalen Rekus, Aug. 5, 1950. A.B., Dartmouth, 1933; student, Med. Sch., 1933-34; M.D., U. Pa., 1936. Intern Presbyn. Hosp., Phila., 1936-38; chief resident Delaware County Hosp., Drexel Hill, Pa., 1938-39; fellow otolaryngology U. Pa. Hosp., 1939-40, chief otolaryngology, 1959-72; mem. faculty U. Pa. Med. Sch., 1940—, prof. dept. otolaryngology, 1959—; chief otolaryngology, div. A Phila. Gen. Hosp., 1959-94; emeritus prof. dept. otolaryngology U. Pa. Med. Sch., 1994—; cons. Presbyn. Hosp., Phila., VA Hosp., Phila., Phila. Gen. Hosp. Served to maj., M.C. AUS, 1942-46, CBI. Mem. AMA, Am. Acad. Ophthalmology and Otolaryngology, A.C.S., Coll. Physicians Phila., Phi Beta Kappa, Sigma Xi. Home: 163 Vassar Rd Bala Cynwyd PA 19004-2135

MARDER, JOHN G., real estate investor, marketing consultant, corporate director; b. N.Y.C., Dec. 27, 1926; s. Joseph T. and Rhea (Greenspun) M.; m. Barbara Sand, 1956 (div. 1971); children; Jonathan Allen, Susan Zelouf, Jane Alison; m. Joan Kron, 1971. Student, Cornell U., 1944-45; BS, Columbia U., 1950. Merchandising exec. Macy's, N.Y.C., 1951-56; exec. v.p. Grey Advt. Inc., N.Y.C., 1956-86; real estate investor-developer Miami Beach, Anguilla B.W.I., 1986—; bd. dirs. several profit, not-for-profit and ednl. corps. Served as radio officer U.S. Maritime Service, U.S. Army Transport Service, 1945-46; 2d Lt. Q.M.C. U.S. Army, 1951-53. Home: 205 E 63rd St New York NY 10021-7425 also: 18 Hedges Banks Dr East Hampton NY 11937-3505

MARDER, MICHAEL ZACHARY, dentist, researcher, educator; b. N.Y.C., Aug. 30, 1938; s. Jospeh Theodore and Rhea (Greenspun) M.; (widowed); children: Sherri Ellen, Robert Whitney. Student, Tufts U., 1959; D.D.S., Columbia U., 1963. Diplomate: Am. Bd. Oral Medicine. Practice dentistry N.Y.C., 1963-66, 68—; asst. Sch. Dental and Oral Surgery, Columbia U., N.Y.C., 1963-66, instr., 1968, asst. clin. prof., 1968-72, assoc. clin. prof., 1972-76, clin. prof. dentistry, 1976—, researcher, 1963—; dir. oral medicine, 1972-84, dir. clin. cancer tng., 1993—; asst. attending dental surgeon Presbyn. Hosp., 1972-76; assoc. attending dentist, 1976-82, attending dentist, 1982—; cons. Good Samaritan Hosp., Suffern, N.Y.; lectr. in field. Author 2 textbooks in dental medicine; contbr. chpts. to med. and dental textbooks, articles to profl. jours. Served to capt. U.S. Army, 1966-68. Recipient Cert. of Achievement U.S. Army, 1968. Fellow N.Y. Acad. Dentistry; mem. ADA, Internat. Assn. Dental Rsch., Am. Acad. Oral Medicine, Frist Dist. Dental Soc. N.Y., Omicron Kappa Upsilon, Sigma Xi. Office: 119 W 57th St New York NY 10019

MARDIAN, DANIEL, construction company director; b. Pasadena, Calif., Apr. 10, 1917; s. Samuel and Akabe (Lekerian) M.; m. Katherine Evkhanian, Jan. 30, 1942; children: Daniel Jr., Tom, John, Paul, Scott. Student, Pasadena City Coll., 1937; diploma, U.S. Army Engring. Sch., Ft. Belvoir, Va., 1944, U.S. Army Command and Gen. Staff Coll., 1961. Commd. U.S. Army, 1942, advances through grades to lt. col., 1962, ret., 1970; ptnr. Mardian Constrn. Co., Phoenix, 1945-47, exec. v.p., 1947-66, pres., 1966-78, also bd. dirs.; past chmn., mem. Nat. Joint Apprenticeship/Tng. commn. Oper. Engrs., Washington, 1975-78; mem. adv. bd. constrn. programs Ariz. State U., Tempe, 1957—, mem. adv. bd. Coll. Engring., 1957—; mem. adv. bd. constrn. program No. Ariz. U., Flagstaff; bd. dirs. Citibank, Phoenix, 1962-87. Pres. Am. Coun. Constrn. Edn., Monroe, La., 1991-93; past pres., bd. dirs. Fiesta Bowl, Tempe, 1986-92; gen. campaign chmn. United Way, Phoenix, 1967; pres. Met. Phoenix C. of C., 1967-68. Capt. C.E., U.S. Army, 1942-46, PTO, 1970—. Recipient Hall of Fame award Ariz. State U., 1990, medallion of merit, 1984, Excellence in Constrn. award Am. Subcontractors Assn., 1988, Hall of Fame award Nat. Football Found., 1987, Brotherhood award Ariz. chpt. NCCJ, 1981, Fellow award Am. Inst. Constructors, 1996. Mem. Associated Gen. Contractors Am. (life bd. dirs., chmn. yr. award 1970, mem. workforce devel. com., trustee, chmn. laborers tng. com., 1969—), Sun Angel Found. (chmn. 1989-91), Ariz. Acad., Phoenix Country Club (bd. dirs., pres. 1985-86), Phoenix Kiwanis Club (past dir.). Republican. Mem. United Ch. Christ. Avocations: golfing, fishing. Home: 7215 N 3rd St Phoenix AZ 85020-4904 Office: Perini Building Co 360 E Coronado Rd Phoenix AZ 85004-1524

MARDIN, ARIF, musician; b. Istanbul, Turkey, 1932. Grad., Istanbul U.; postgrad., London Sch. Econs., Berklee Coll. Music; D (hon.), Berklee Coll. Music. V.p. Atlantic Records, 1969, sr. v.p. Prodr. The Young Rascals, Dusty Springfield, Aretha Franklin, Roberta Flack, Donny Hathaway, Hall & Oates, John Prine, Willie Nelson, The Average White Band, , the Bee Gees, Phil Collins, Bette Midler, Judy Collins, Carly Simon, Laura Nyro, Dionne Warwick, Culture Club, Howard Jones, George Benson, Melissa Manchester, CHaka Kahn. Recipient Man of Yr. award Assembly Turkish Am. Assns., 1990, Shofar of Peace award Sephardic Hebrew Acad., 1992, Best Musical Show Album Grammy award, 1996, inducted into Nat. Acad. Record Arts & Scis. Hall of Fame, 1990; Quincy Jones scholar, 1958. Office: Atlantic Records 75 Rockefeller Plz New York NY 10019-6908

MARDIS, HAL KENNEDY, urological surgeon, educator, researcher; b. Lincoln, Nebr., Apr. 4, 1934; s. Harold Corson and Marie (Swaim) M.; m. Janet Reimers Schenken, June 22, 1956; children: Michael Corson, Anne Lucille, Jeanne Marie. BS, U. Nebr., Lincoln, 1955; MD, U. Nebr., Omaha, 1958. Diplomate Am. Bd. Urology. Intern Nebr. Meth. Hosp., Omaha, 1958-59, med. dir. The Stone Ctr.,, 1966—; resident in urology Charity Hosp. La., New Orleans, 1959-62, chief resident in urology, 1962-63; pvt. practice Omaha, 1965—; instr., asst. prof. La. State U. Sch. Medicine, New Orleans, 1963-65; asst. prof., assoc. prof. surgery U. Nebr. Med. Ctr., 1965-85, prof., 1985—; investigator North Cen. Cancer Treatment Group, Rochester, Minn., 1988—, Technomed Internat., Inc., Danvers, Mass., 1988—; cons. Boston Sci. Corp., Watertown, Mass., 1988—. Assoc. editor Jour. Stone Disease; contbr. articles to Jour. AMA, So. Med. Jour., Jour. Urology, Urology, Urol. Clinics N.Am., Seminars in Interventional Radiology. Sec., pres. Omaha Symphony Assn., 1973-76; advisor United Arts Omaha, 1983-88. Recipient Outstanding Contbn. award dept. surgery U. Nebr. Med. Ctr., 1990. Fellow ACS; mem. AMa (del. med. staff sect. 1983-86), Am. Urol. Assn. (pres. South Cen. chpt. 1990-91, 1st prize 1976, best clin. exhibit award 1977), Am. Lithotripsy Soc. (pres. 1989-90), Alpha Omega Alpha (pres. 1991-92). Republican. Achievements include development of guidewire techniques for angiography and endourology, thermoplastic internal ureteral stent; description of benefits of hydrophilic polymers for endourologic devices. Office: The Urology Ctr 111 S 90th St Omaha NE 68114-3907

MAREADY, WILLIAM FRANK, lawyer; b. Mullins, S.C., Sept. 13, 1932; s. Jesse Frank and Vera (Sellers) M.; m. Brenda McCanless, Nov. 3, 1979. AB, U. N.C., 1955, JD with honors, 1958. Bar: N.C. 1958, U.S. Dist. Ct. N.C. 1960, U.S. Ct. Appeals (4th cir.) 1962, U.S. Supreme Ct. 1968. Assoc. Mudge, Stern, Baldwin & Todd, N.Y.C., 1958-60, Hudson, Ferrell, Carter, Petree & Stockton, Winston-Salem, N.C., 1960-65; ptnr. Petree, Stockton & Robinson, Winston-Salem, 1965-92, Robinson, Maready, Lawing & Comerford, 1992—; N.C. chmn. Winston-Salem/Forsyth County Bd. Edn., 1968-70, chmn., bd. dirs. and mem. exec. com. N.C. State Port Authority, 1984—. Served with Green Berets, U.S. Army, 1952-54. Recipient Disting. Svc. award N.C. Sch. Bds. Assn. Fellow Am. Coll. Trial Lawyers, Am. Bar Found.; mem. ABA (chmn. standing com. on aero. law 1979-82, chmn. forum com. on air and space law 1982-86), N.C. Bar Assn. (chmn. litigation sect. 1981-82, adminstrn. of justice com. 1981-82), Nat. Parent Tchr. Assn. (life), Order of Coif, Phi Delta Phi, Phi Beta Kappa. Republican. Methodist. Clubs: Forsyth County. Lodge: Rotary of Winston Salem. Office: Maready Comerford & Britt LLP 250 W 1st St Ste 300 Winston Salem NC 27101-4010

MAREE, WENDY, painter, sculptor; b. Windsor, Eng., Feb. 10, 1938. Student, Windsor & Maidenhead Coll., 1959; studied with Vasco Lazzlo, London, 1959-62. Exhibited in group shows at Windsor Arts Festival, San Bernardino (Calif.) Mus.; one-woman shows include Lake Arrowhead (Calif.) Libr., 1989, Amnesty Internat., Washington, 1990, Phyllis Morris Gallery, Many Horses Gallery, L.A., 1990, Nelson Rockefeller, Palm Springs, Calif., 1992, 94, Stewart Gallery, Rancho Palos Verdes, Calif., Petropavlovsk (Russia) Cultural Mus., Kamchatka, Russia, 1993, Coyle-Coyle Gallery, Blue Jay, Calif., 1995, La Quinta Sculpture Park, Calif., 1995, Avante-Garde Gallery, Palm Springs, 1996, Avante-Garden Gallery, La Jolla, Calif., 1996, Avante Garde Gallery, La Jolla, 1996, Carmichael Gallery, Rancho Mirage, Calif., 1997, Art in the Courtyard, Palm Springs, Calif., 1997, others; represented in pvt. collections His Royal Highness Prince Faisal, Saudi Arabia, Gena Rowlands, L.A., John Cassavetes, L.A., Nicky Blairs, L.A., Guilford Glazer, Beverly Hills, Calif., June Allyson, Ojai, Calif., Amnesty Internat., Washington; commd. Ingleside Inn, Palm Springs. Recipient award San Bernardino County Mus., 1988, Gov. Kamchatka of Russia, 1993. Mem. Artist Guild of Lake Arrowhead.

MAREK, VLADIMIR, ballet director, educator; b. Uzhorod, Czechoslovakia, Sept. 26, 1928; came to U.S., 1969; s. Jaroslav and Julia (Valkova) Sourek. Student Bus. Acad., Czechoslovakia, ballet schs., Czechoslovakia, 1945-47. Soloist Nat. Theater Ballet, Prague, Czechoslovakia, 1947-50, prin. dancer, Bratislava, Czechoslovakia, 1950-69, ballet master, 1958-68; ballet tchr. Our Lady of Lake U., San Antonio, 1970-78; owner, tchr. V. Marek Ballet Acad., San Antonio, 1970—; founder, artistic dir. San Antonio Ballet, 1970—. Home and Office: San Antonio Ballet 212 E Mulberry Ave San Antonio TX 78212-3041

MARELLA, PHILIP DANIEL, broadcasting company executive; b. Italy, Sept. 9, 1929; came to U.S., 1930; s. T. Joseph and Julia (Santolina) M.; m. Lucinda Minor, Dec. 30, 1955; children: Philip Daniel, Laura Ann, William Scott. BS, Calif. State U., 1955; MS, Syracuse U., 1956. Account exec. WGR-TV, Buffalo, 1956-57; account exec., sales mgr. WIIC-TV, Pitts., 1957-66; gen. mgr. WCHS-TV, Charleston, W.Va., 1966-68; v.p. radio and television Rollins, Inc., Atlanta, 1968-70; pres. WAVY-TV, Inc., Tidewater, Va., 1970—; v.p. ops. Lin Broadcasting, Inc., N.Y.C.; also dir.; pres., owner WMGC-TV, Binghamton, N.Y., 1978-86; CEO, pres. Pinnacle Comm., Inc., 1987—; CEO Pinnacle Broadcasting Co., 1987; owner radio stas. WFXC-FM, WDUR, WFXK, Raleigh, N.C., WRNS-AM-FM, WANG-FM, WMSQ-AM, WERO-FM, WDLX-AM, Coastal, N.C., WKOO-FM, WKJA-FM, Jacksonville, N.C., WYAV-FM, WRNN-FM, WMYB-FM, WYAK-FM, Myrtle Beach, S.C., KLLL-AM-FM, KONE-FM, KMMX-FM, Lubbock, Tex., WYNG-FM, Evansville, Ind., WSOY-AM-FM, WDZQ-FM, WDZ-AM, WCZQ-FM, Decatur, Ill., WPXX-FM, Danville, Va. Bd. dirs. Salvation Army, 1966-68; bd. dirs., v.p. United Fund; bd. dirs. Portsmouth chpt. ARC, Tidewater Regional Health and Planning Commn.; bd. dirs., v.p. Binghamton Symphony. Served with USMC, 1948-49, 50-52. Mem. Nat. Assn. Broadcasters (v.p.), Va. Assn. Broadcasters, N.C. Broadcasters Assn., Variety Club Pitts., Radio and TV Club, Portsmouth C. of C. (pres.-elect), Norfolk C. of C., Newport News C. of C., Cavalier Golf and Yacht Club (Virginia Beach, Va.), N.Y. Athletic Club, Binghamton Country Club. Home: 2073 Cheshire Rd Binghamton NY 13903-3199 also: Central Pk Pl 301 W 57th St Apt 43C New York NY 10019-3180 Office: 331 W 57th St Ste 288 New York NY 10019-3101

MARELLI, SISTER M. ANTHONY, secondary school principal. Prin. Boylan Ctrl. Cath. High Sch., Rockford, Ill. Recipient Blue Ribbon Sch. award U.S. Dept. Edn., 1986-87, 90-91. Office: Boylan Ctrl Cath High Sch 4000 Saint Francis Dr Rockford IL 61103-1661

MARES, MICHAEL ALLEN, ecologist, educator; b. Albuquerque, Mar. 11, 1945; s. Ernesto Gustavo and Rebecca Gabriela (Devine) M.; m. Lynn Ann Brusin, Aug. 27, 1966; children: Gabriel Andres, Daniel Alejandro. BS in Biology, U. N.Mex., 1967; MS, Ft. Hays Kans. State U., 1969; PhD, U. Tex.-Austin, 1973. Adj. prof. U. Nacional de Cordoba, Argentina, 1971-72; adj. prof. U. Nacional de Tucuman, Argentina, 1972, vis. prof., 1974; from asst. to assoc. prof. U. Pitts., 1973-81; vis. scientist U. Ariz., Tucson, 1980-81; assoc. prof., curator mammals U. Okla., Norman, 1981-83, dir. Okla. Mus. Nat. Hist., 1983—, assoc. prof. zoology, 1983-85, prof., 1985—; NUS cons., Venezuela, 1980-81; cons. Argentine Nat. Sci. Found., Inst. Arid Zone Research, Mendoza, 1983; World Wildlife Fund cons., Brazil, 1986; mem. Council Internat. Exchange of Scholars, Am. Republics Bd., Fulbright Commn., 1983-86, 88-91; bd. dirs. Coun. Internat. Exchange of Scholars, 1988-91; Okla. rep. to U.S. Fish and Wildlife Service Endangered Mammal Species Commn., 1987-95; co-chair Internat. Programs Com. Systematics 2000, 1991-94; sci. cons. interim working group White House Biodiversity, Ecology, and Ecosystems, 1992-94; apptd. adv. bd. Ctr. Biol. Diversity, Dept. Interior; mem. Commn. on Future of Smithsonian Instns., 1993-96. NSF grantee, 1974-79, 82-93; Nat. Fulbright research fellow, 1976; Nat. Geog. Soc. grantee, 1992-95. Active Chicano Council on Higher Edn. rsch. fellow, 1978; Ford Found. Minority Rsch. fellow, 1980-81; Brazilian Nat. Acad. Sci. rsch. award, 1975-78. Mem. AAAS (Western Hemispheric coop. com. 1989-93), Am. Soc. Mammalogists (1st v.p. 1990-94), Am. Ecol. Soc., Interam. Assn. Advancement Sci., Am. Inst. Biol. Sci., Am. Soc. Naturalists, Soc. Study of Evolution, Southwestern Assn. Naturalists (Donald W. Tinkle rsch. excellence award), Paleontol. Soc., Sigma Xi, Phi Kappa Phi, Beta Beta Beta. Contbr. articles to profl. jours. Home: 3930 Charing Cross Ct Norman OK 73072-3201 Office: U Okla Okla Mus Natural History 1335 Asp Ave Norman OK 73019-6070

MARESH, ALICE MARCELLA, retired educational administrator; b. Chgo., Sept. 17, 1922; d. Joseph Anton and Barbara Magdalene (Slad) M. BEd, Chgo. Tchrs. Coll., 1944; MEd, Loyola U., Chgo., 1962. Chemist Best Foods, Inc., Chgo., 1944-54; tchr. Chgo. Bd. Edn., 1954-65, counselor, 1965-67, asst. prin., 1967-69, prin., 1969-93; retired, 1993. Recipient Outstanding and Dedicated Svc. award Puerto Rican Congress, 1975, Those Who Excel award Ill. Bd. Edn., 1978, Whitman award for excellence in ednl. mgmt. Whitman Acad., Chgo., 1990, Outstanding Svc. to Edn. in Chgo. award Nat. Coun. Negro Women, 1992. Mem. Chgo. Prins. Assn., Chgo. Area Reading Assn., Aquin Guild (Dedicated Svc. award 1976), Delta Kappa Gamma (pres. 1976-78), Phi Delta Kappa, Pi Lambda Theta (sec. 1995—). Democrat. Roman Catholic. Avocations: music, travel, calligraphy, theater. Home: 3850 W Bryn Mawr Ave #308 Chicago IL 60659-3135

MARETH, PAUL, communications consultant; b. N.Y.C., Nov. 16, 1945; s. Josef Gleicher and Elisabeth Gay; m. Evelyn Heineman, Dec. 26, 1968 (div. 1980); children: Leda J., Joanna R. BA, Brandeis U., 1967; MFA, UCLA, 1969. Lectr. U. Pitts., 1976-77; asst. prof. communications Temple U., Phila., 1977-81; vis. faculty fellow in history of sci. Princeton (N.J.) U., 1981-82; founder, owner Projections Co., White Plains, N.Y., 1982—; cons. IBM, RCA, Bell Labs., Ednl. Testing Svc., Children's TV Workshop, Prodigy. Contbr. to Acad. Am. Ency., 1985—, Channels of Communications, 1983-85; editorial advisor IEEE Jour., IEEE Spectrum, 1983-84; contbr. numerous articles to profl. jours. Bd. dirs. Westchester Choral Soc., 1991—, v.p. Grantee WGBH Pub. TV, Boston, 1974, Swedish Film Inst./Swedish Broadcasting Corp., 1973, Pa. Coun. on the Arts, 1976, 79. Mem. Soc. Motion Picture and TV Engrs., Internat. Interactive Communications Soc. (chmn. program com. 1987-90), Univ. Film/Video Assn. Avocation: choral singing. Office: Projections Co 14 Nosband Ave Apt 6D White Plains NY 10605-2074

MARG, ELWIN, physiological optics, optometry educator; b. San Francisco, Mar. 23, 1918; s. Sigmund and Fannie (Sockolov) M.; m. Helen Eugenia Kelly, Apr. 1, 1942; 1 child, Tamia. AB, U. Calif., Berkeley, 1940, PhD, 1950. Asst. prof. vision sci. U. Calif., Berkeley, 1950-56, assoc. prof., 1956-62, prof., 1962—; bd. dirs., v.p., Minerva Found., Berkeley. Author: Computer Assisted Eye Examination, 1980; also articles. Served to lt. col. USAF, 1941-46, 50-52, ETO. NSF fellow, Nobel Inst. Stockholm, 1957, Guggenheim, Madrid, 1964; recipient Miller Research Professorship U. Calif.-Berkeley, 1967. Fellow AAAS, Optical Soc. Am., Am. Acad. Optometry; mem. Soc. Neurosci., Assn. Rsch. Vision and Ophthalmology, Internat. Soc. Magnetic Resonance in Medicine. Office: U Calif Sch Optometry Berkeley CA 94720-2020

MARGARITIS, JOHN PAUL, public relations executive; b. N.Y.C., June 8, 1949; s. George H. and Mary (Liakos) M.; m. Charlene Corenman, Feb. 21, 1982. BA in English, Washington and Jefferson Coll., 1971; MA in Media Studies, New Sch. Social Rsch., 1977. Account exec. Hank Boerner & Assocs., Uniondale, N.Y., 1974-76; account exec. Manning, Selvage & Lee, N.Y.C., 1976-77; account supr. Gen. Electric Co., N.Y.C., 1977-79, Burson-Marsteller, Inc., Chgo., 1979-80; v.p., dir. client services Burson-Marsteller, Inc., Los Angeles, 1980-82; exec. v.p., gen. mgr., sr. ptnr. Fleishman-Hillard, Inc., Los Angeles, 1982-88; chmn., chief exec. officer Ogilvy & Mather Pub. Relations, N.Y.C., 1988-92; pres., COO Ogilvy Adams and Rinehart, N.Y.C., 1992-94, pres., CEO, 1994-97; also bd. dirs. Ogilvy Adams and Rinehart; bd. dirs. Rsch. Am., Young Pres. Orgn., Arthur Ashe Found. 2nd lt. U.S. Army, 1972-74. Mem. Pub. Rels. Soc. Am. (hons. and awards com. 1986-89, counselors acad. 1985—), Alpine Country Club. Republican. Greek Orthodox. Home: 38 Hidden Ledge Rd Englewood NJ 07631-5125 Office: Ogilvy Adams and Rinehart 708 3rd Ave New York NY 10017-4201

MARGEN, SHELDON, public health educator, nutritionist emeritus; b. Chgo., May 19, 1919; s. Paul and Sarah M.; m. Jeanne Carmel Sholtz, Mar. 16, 1943; children: Claude, Paul, Peter, David. BA, UCLA, 1938, MA, 1939; MD, U. Calif., San Francisco, 1943. Diplomate Am. Bd. Internal Medicine. Assoc prof. U. Calif. , Berkeley, 1963-68, prof. pub. health and nutrition, 1968-89, prof. emeritus, 1989—; cons., mem. adv. coms. NIH, WHO,; bd. dirs. Omnicare. Cin., 1980—. Editor-in-chief U. Calif. Wellness Letter; author and editor 10 books on Nutrition and/or Pub. Health. Bd. dirs. Calif. Wellness Found., Woodland Hills, 1991-96. Capt. M.C., U.S. Army, 1943-48, ETO. Grantee NIH, State of Calif., Ford Found., numerous others. Fellow Am. Inst. Nutrition and many other profl. orgns. in fields of ntutrition and pub. health. Office: Univ Calif Sch of Pub Health Berkeley CA 94720

MARGERISON, RICHARD WAYNE, diversified industrial company executive; b. Phila., Nov. 5, 1948; s. Kenneth Hilton and Edythe (Helmuth) M.; m. Leah Blythe Creed, July 18, 1970; children: Andrew Kenneth, Ashley Creed. BA in Econs., U. N.C., 1970; MBA with distinction, Harvard U., 1977. Mgr. So. Bell Telephone Co., Greensboro, N.C., 1972-75; mgr. sub. liaison Atlas Powder Co. subs. Tyler Corp., Dallas, 1978-79, dir. mktg. svcs., 1979-80; exec. v.p. Micro-Term, Inc., St. Louis, 1980-83, pres., chief exec. officer, 1983-85; mgr. acquisitions Tyler Corp., Dallas, 1977-78, v.p., 1985-88, sr. v.p., 1988-89, exec. v.p., 1989-94, pres., COO, 1994—, also bd. dirs. Mem. Northway Christian Ch., Dallas, 1985—; coach Youth Soccer, Dallas, 1987—; advisor YMCA Indian Princess and Indian Guides, 1987-89; adult leader Boy Scouts Am., 1988-93; mem. Dallas Citizens Coun.; active Dallas United Way, 1990. Love fellow Harvard Grad. Sch. Bus., 1975-77. Mem. Harvard Bus. Sch. Club of Dallas, Lakewood Country Club, Order of Old Well, Phi Beta Kappa. Avocations: golf, youth soccer, running. Office: Tyler Corp 2121 San Jacinto St Ste 3200 Dallas TX 75201-6704

MARGERUM, DALE WILLIAM, chemistry educator; b. St. Louis, Oct. 20, 1929; s. Donald C. and Ida Lee (Nunley) M.; m. Sonya Lora Pedersen, May 16, 1953; children: Lawrence Donald, Eric William, Richard Dale. BA, S.E. Mo. State U., 1950; PhD, Iowa State U., 1955. Research chemist Ames Lab., AEC, Iowa, 1952-53; instr. Purdue U., West Lafayette, Ind., 1954-57; asst. prof. Purdue U., 1957-61, asso. prof., 1961-65, prof., 1965—, head dept. chemistry, 1978-83; inorganic-analytical chemist, vis. scientist Max Planck Inst., 1963, 70; vis. prof. U. Kent, Canterbury, Eng., 1970; mem. med. chem. study sect. NIH, 1965-69; mem. adv. com. Research Corp., 1973-78; mem. chemistry evaluation panel Air Force Office Sci. Research, 1978-82. Cons. editor McGraw Hill, 1962-72; mem. editorial bd. Jour. Coordination Chemistry, 1971-81, Analytical Chemistry, 1967-69, Inorganic Chemistry, 1985-88. Recipient Grad. Rsch. award Phi Lambda Upsilon, 1954, Alumni Merit award S.E. Mo. State U., 1991, Sagamore of the Wabash, State of Ind., 1994; NSF sr. postdoctoral fellow, 1963-64. Fellow AAAS; mem. AAUP, Am. Chem. Soc. (chmn. Purdue sect. 1965-66, com. on profl. tng. 1993—, Disting. Svc. award in advancement of inorganic chemistry 1996), Sigma Xi, Phi Lambda Upsilon. Office: Dept Chemistry Purdue U West Lafayette IN 47907

MARGERUM, J(OHN) DAVID, chemist; b. St. Louis, Oct. 20, 1929; s. Donald Cameron and Ida Lee (Nunley) M.; m. Virginia Bolen, June 5, 1954; children: John Steven, Kris Alan, Julie Ellen. A.B., S.E. Mo. State Coll., 1950; Ph.D., Northwestern U., 1956. Rsch. chemist Shell Oil Co., Wood River, Ill., 1954-55; chief spectroscopy sect. U.S. Army QMR&E Center, Natick, Mass., 1957-59; research specialist Sundstrand Corp., Pacoima, Calif., 1959-62; with Hughes Research Labs., Malibu, Calif., 1962—, sr. scientist, head chemistry sect., 1967—, head material scis. sect., 1988—, asst. dept. mgr. exploratory studies dept., 1989—, mgr. dept. materials sci., lab. chief scientist, 1991—; prin. rsch. scientist, 1993—. Contbr. articles to profl. jours.; patentee in field. Served with U.S. Army, 1955-57. Recipient Holley medal ASME, 1977. Fellow AAAS; mem. Am. Chem. Soc., Electrochem. Soc., Soc. Info. Display, Inter-Am. Photochem. Soc., Internat. Liquid Crystal Soc., Sigma Xi. Democrat. Unitarian. Home: 5433 Rozie Ave Woodland Hills CA 91367-5760 Office: 3011 Malibu Canyon Rd Malibu CA 90265-4737

MARGESON, THEODORE EARL, judge; b. New Glasgow, N.S., Can., Aug. 15, 1938; children: Theodore Jason, Mark Andrew Earl. BA, Mt. Allison U., Sackville, N.B., Can., 1959, BEd, 1960; LLB, Dalhousie U., Halifax, N.S., 1965. Barrister, solicitor, notary pub. Tchr. Shelburne (N.S.) H.S., 1960-61, New Glasgow H.S., 1961-62; barrister, solicitor New Glasgow and Toronto, Ont., 1965-90; judge Tax Ct. of Can., Ottawa, 1990—; bd. dirs. N.S. Legal Aid. Recipient Confedn. medal Govt. of Can., 1992. Mem. Can. Judges Conf., N.S. Barrister's Soc. (mem. of coun.), Continuing Legal Edn. Soc. (dir.). Avocations: golf, hockey, squash. Office: Tax Ct of Can, 200 Kent St 3d Fl, Ottawa, ON Canada K1A OM1

MARGESSON, MAXINE EDGE, professor; b. Cordele, Ga., Aug. 29, 1933; d. Bryant Peak and Maxie (Grantham) Edge; m. Burland Drake Margesson, June 24, 1956; children: Anda Margesson Foxwell, Risa Margesson Carpenter. BS, Bob Jones U., 1958; MEd, SUNY, Buffalo, 1971; EdD, Western Mich. U., 1983. Elem. tchr. Cheektowaga (N.Y.) Cen. Sch. Dist., 1965-72; elem. prin. Grand Rapids (Mich.) Bapt. Acad., 1972-85; reading rsch. Wake Forest U., Winston-Salem, N.C., 1987-90; prof. Piedmont Bible Coll., Winston-Salem, 1985-90; reading specialist Randolph (N.Y.) Ctrl. Sch. Dist., 1990—; bd. dirs. Salem Day Sch., Winston-Salem. Mem. Forsyth County Coalition for Literacy Com. Mem. Assn. for

Supervision and Curriculum Devel., Assn. Christian Schs. Internat. Republican. Baptist. Avocations: travel, reading, sewing. Office: Randolph Ctrl Sch Randolph NY 14772

MARGETON, STEPHEN GEORGE, law librarian; b. Elizabeth, N.J., Mar. 22, 1945; s. Louis George and Josephine A. (Bednarik) M.; m. Margaret Mary Salter, May 14, 1977; children: Catherine Ann, Elizabeth Ann. AB, Mt. St. Mary's Coll., 1967; JD, George Washington U., 1970; MLS, Cath. U., 1973. Reference librarian Am.-Brit. law div. Library of Congress, Washington, 1968-72; law libr. Steptoe & Johnson, Washington, 1972-85; librarian Supreme Ct. of U.S., Washington, 1985-88; dir. Judge Kathryn J. DuFour Law Libr. The Cath. Univ. Am., 1988—; instr. George Mason Law Sch., Arlington, Va., 1977-80. Mem. Am. Assn. Law Libraries, Internat. Assn. Law Libraries. Office: Cath U Am Kathryn J DuFour Law Libr 3600 John McCormack Rd NE Washington DC 20064-8206

MARGILETH, ANDREW MENGES, physician, former naval officer; b. Cin., July 17, 1920; s. Elmer C. and Bertha (Menges) M.; m. Catherine Lanier, Oct. 31, 1994; children: R. Lynn, Andrew C., Elle C., David Lanier. B.A., Washington and Jefferson Coll., 1943; B.S., Mass. Inst. Tech., 1944; M.D., U. Cin., 1947. Diplomate Am. Bd. Pediatrics. Commd. ensign USN, 1943, advanced through grades to capt., 1963; intern, resident pediatrics Nat. Naval Med. Center, 1947-49; resident pediatrics Johns Hopkins Hosp., 1949-50; chief pediatrics U.S. Naval Hosps., Corona, Calif., 1953-57, Chelsea, Mass., 1957-63, Bethesda, Md., 1963-67; prof. pediatrics Uniformed Svcs. U. Health Scis., 1979-90; clin. prof. pediatrics U. Va. Health Scis. Ctr., 1990-95, Mercer Univ. Sch. Medicine, 1995—; council mem. Nat. Inst. Child Health and Human Devel., 1963-67; sr. attending physician Childrens Hosp., Washington; assoc. clin. prof. pediatrics Med. Sch., Howard U.; adj. prof. pediatrics Med. Sch., George Washington U. Contbr. chpt. to Current Pediatric Therapy, 1970, 72, 74, 76, 80, 83, 85, 90, 93, 95; contbr.: (textbooks) Neonatology, 1975, 81, 86, 94, Pediatrics, 1977, 81, 86, 91, 95, 96, Medicine, 1978, 82, 86, 88, 91, Current Therapy Medicine, 1996, Pediatric Dermatology, 1978, 86, 88, also 150 articles to profl. jours.; co-editor Clin. Procs. of Children's Hosp. Nat. Med. Ctr., 1970-79. Fellow Am. Acad. Pediatrics, ACP; mem. Assn. Mil. Surgeons, Am. Pediatric Soc., Soc. Pediatric Dermatologists, Soc. Pediatric Infectious Diseases, Alpha Omega Alpha. Address: 20 Kingston Rd Hilton Head Island SC 29928

MARGO, KATHERINE LANE, physician; b. Buffalo, June 3, 1952; d. Warren Wilson and Virginia (Penney) Lane; m. Geoffrey Myles Margo, Apr. 20, 1980; 1 child, Benjamin; stepchildren: Jenny, Judy. BA, Swarthmore Coll., 1974; MD, SUNY Health Sci. Ctr., Syracuse, 1978. Resident physician St. Joseph's Hosp., Syracuse, 1979-82; attending physician Health Svcs. Assn., Syracuse, 1982-90, asst. med. dir. for quality assurance, 1985-90; asst. prof. family medicine SUNY-HSC at Syracuse, 1990-94; residency faculty Harrisburg (Pa.) Hosp., 1994—; med. dir. Harrisburg Family Practice Ctr., 1996—. Contbr. articles to profl. jours. Bd. of trustees Pt. Choice, Syracuse, 1993-94, Harrisburg, 1996—; chair med. com. Planned Parenthood, Syracuse, 1984-94; bd. dirs. Planned Parenthood Susquehanna Valley, 1996—; active Friends of Chamber Music, Syracuse, 1985-94; keyboard player Old World Folk Band. Mem. Soc. Tchrs. of Family Medicine, Am. Acad. of Family Practitioners (v.p. Syracuse chpt.), Pa. Med. Soc. Home: 4705 Maple Shade Dr Harrisburg PA 17110-3217

MARGOL, IRVING, personnel consultant; b. St. Louis, May 28, 1930; s. William and Dora (Karsh) M.; m. Myrna Levy, Dec., 1959; children—Bradley, Lisa, Cynthia. B.A., Washington U., St. Louis, 1951, M.A., 1952. Employment mgr. Am. Car & Foundry div. ACF, St. Louis, 1955-59; asst. personnel dir. Vickers Inc. div. Sperry-Rand, St. Louis, 1959-60; instr. personnel mgmt. Washington U. (St. Louis), 1960-62; personnel dir. Energy Controls div. Bendix Corp., South Bend, Ind., 1962-69; exec. v.p. community/employee affairs group, community rels. dept., employee assistance program Security Pacific Nat. Bank, L.A., 1969-92; mng. dir. Southern Calif. Jannotta, Bray & Assocs., Inc., 1992—; pres. Security Pacific Found., L.A., 1989-94; mng. dir. Jannotta Bray & Assocs., L.A., 19092-94, Right and Assocs., L.A., 1995—; instr. UCLA Extension Div., Los Angeles; Grad. Sch. Banking, Rutgers U., Notre Dame U. Bd. dirs. L.A. chpt. ARC, Am. Heart Assn., Am. Cancer Soc., Nat. Conf. Christians & Jews, Braille Inst.; bd. overseers Southwestern U. Law. Mem. Am. Bankers Assn. (exec. com. 1979—), Am. Soc. Tng. and Devel., Am. Soc. Personnel Adminstrs., Am. Inst. Banking, Washington U. Alumni Assn. Democrat. Jewish. Office: Right and Assocs 5320 Pacific Councourse Dr Los Angeles CA 90045

MARGOLIASH, EMANUEL, biochemist, educator; b. Cairo, Feb. 10, 1920; s. Wolf and Bertha (Kotler) M.; m. Sima Beshkin, Aug. 22, 1944; children: Reuben, Daniel. BA, Am. U., Beirut, 1940, MA, 1942, MD, 1945. Rsch. fellow, lectr., acting head cancer rsch. labs. Hebrew U., Jerusalem, 1945-58; rsch. fellow Molteno Inst. Cambridge (Eng.) U., 1951-53; Dazian fellow Nobel Inst., 1958; rsch. assoc. U. Utah, Salt Lake City, 1958-60, McGill U., Montreal, Que., Can., 1960-62; rsch. fellow Abbott Labs., North Chicago, Ill., 1962-69; sr. rsch. fellow Abbott Labs., 1969-71, head protein sect., 1962-71; prof. biochemistry and molecular biology Northwestern U., Evanston, Ill., 1971-90, prof. chemistry, 1985-90, Owen L. Coon prof. molecular biology, 1988-90, Owen L. Coon prof. molecular biology emeritus, 1990—; prof. biol. scis. U. Ill., Chgo., 1989—, coord. lab. for molecular biology, 1990-93; mem. com. on cytochrome nomenclature Internat. Union Biochemistry, 1962—; mem. adv. com. Plant Research Lab., Mich. State U./AEC, 1967-72; co-chmn. Gordon Research Conf. on Proteins, 1967. Editl. bd. Jour. Biol. Chemistry, 1966-72, Biochem. Genetics, 1966-80, Jour. Molecular Evolution, 1971-82, Biochemistry and Molecular Biology Internat., 1981—, Jour. Protein Chemistry, 1982-86, Chemtracts, Biochem. Molecular Biology, 1990—; contbr. over 275 articles and revs. to sci. jours. Rudi Lemberg fellow Australian Acad. Sci., 1981; Guggenheim fellow, 1983. Fellow Am. Acad. Arts and Scis., Am. Acad. Microbiology; mem. Nat. Acad. Scis., Biochem. Soc. (Keilin Meml. lectr. 1970), Harvey Soc. (lectr. 1970-71), Am. Soc. Biochem. Molecular Biology (publs. com. 1973-76), Am. Chem. Soc., Can. Biochem. Soc., Soc. Devel. Biology, Biophys. Soc. (exec. com. U.S. bioenergetics group 1980-83), N.Y. Acad. Sci., Ill. Acad. Sci., Am. Soc. Naturalists, Sigma Xi (nat. lectr. 1972-73, 74-77). Home: 353 Madison Ave Glencoe IL 60022-1809 Office: Univ Ill Chgo Dept Bio-Scis 845 W Taylor St Chicago IL 60607

MARGOLIN, ARTHUR STANLEY, distillery company executive; b. N.Y.C., Aug. 7, 1936; s. Samuel and Belle (Gelb) M.; m. Barbara Jane Lester, June 27, 1965; children: Sarah Jennifer, Julie Ellen, Carolyn Leigh. BA in Econs., NYU, 1957, postgrad. in bus., 1961. Analyst, sr. analyst Asch Market Research (div. JES), N.Y.C., 1961-63; field asst. to eastern div. mgr. Calvert Distillers, N.Y.C., 1963-64, asst. to asst. and met. N.Y. mgr., 1964-72, asst. to exec. v.p. sales, asst. to pres., 1972-78; exec. asst. to pres. House of Seagram, N.Y.C., 1978-80; dir. U.S. ops. Seagram Europe, London, 1980-82; asst. to pres. Seagram Internat. Joseph E. Seagram & Sons Inc., N.Y.C., 1982, asst. to office of chmn. and pres., 1982-85, v.p. spl. asst. to office of chmn. and pres., 1985—; bd. dirs. Forhan Forwarding and Handling Co., N.V., Antwerp, Belgium. Mng. editor Heights Daily News, 1956-57. Bd. dirs. Fifth Ave. Assn., N.Y.C., 1987—, USO of Metro N.Y., 1994—. Republican. Jewish. Avocations: collecting stamps and coins, baseball. Office: Joseph E Seagram & Sons Inc 375 Park Ave New York NY 10152-0002

MARGOLIN, HAROLD, metallurgical educator; b. Hartford, Conn., July 12, 1922; s. Aaron David and Sonia (Krupnikoff) M.; m. Elaine Marjorie Rose, July 4, 1946; children: Shelley, Deborah, Amy. B in Engring., Yale U., 1943; M in Engring., Yale Univ., 1947, DEng, 1950. Rsch. assoc./scientist divsn. rsch. NYU, N.Y.C., 1949-56, assoc. prof. metall. engring., 1956-62, prof., 1962-73; prof. phys. metallurgy Poly. U. N.Y., Bklyn., 1973-93, disting. rsch. prof., 1993—; ret. U. N.Y., Bklyn., 1995; cons. in field. Contbg. author books; contbr. articles to profl. publs. With USNR, 1944-46. Named Theodore W. Krengel vis. prof. Technion, Haifa, Israel, 1983; appt. Disting. Rsch. prof. Polytechnic U., 1993, 96. Fellow Am. Soc. Metals (edn. award N.Y. chpt. 1967); mem. Metall. Soc. (honoree symposium in his name San Francisco 1994), Am. Soc. Materials, TMS. Democrat. Jewish. Patentee in field. Home: 19 Crescent Rd Larchmont NY 10538-1733
Achievement, work, and refusal to accept defeat are intimately intertwined.

MARGOLIN, SOLOMON BEGELFOR, pharmacologist; b. Phila., May 16, 1920; s. Nathan and Fannie (Begelfor) M.; m. Gerda Levy, Jan. 17, 1947 (div. Feb. 1985); children: David, Bernard, Daniel; m. Nancy A. Cox, Apr. 30, 1987. BSc, Rutgers U., 1941, MSc, 1943, PhD, 1945. Asst. Rutgers U., New Brunswick, N.J., 1943-45; rsch. biologist Silmo Chem. Co., Vineland, N.J., 1947-48; rsch. pharmacologist Schering Corp., Bloomfield, N.J., 1948-52, dir. pharmacology dept., 1952-54; chief pharmacologist Maltbie Labs., Belleville, N.J., 1954-56; chief pharmacologist Wallace Labs, Carter-Wallace, Inc., Cranbury, N.J., 1956-60, dir. pharmacology dept., 1960-64, v.p. biol. rsch., 1964-68; pres. AMR Biol. Rsch., Inc., Princeton, N.J., 1968-78; from prof., chmn. pharmacology dept. to emeritus prof. St. George's (Grenada) U. Sch. Medicine, 1978—; pres. MARNAC, Inc., Dallas, 1990—. Author: Harper's Handbook Therapeutic Pharmacology, 1981; author: (with others) Physiological Pharmacology, 1963, World Review, Nutrition & Dietetics, 1980; contbr. more than 60 articles to profl. jours. including Annals of Allergy, Proc. Soc. Exptl. Biol. & Med., Nature. Mem. AAAS, Endocrino Soc., Am. Chem. Soc., Soc. Exptl. Biology and Medicine, Am. Soc. Pharmacology and Exptl. Therapeutics, N.Y. Acad. Scis., Drug Information Assn. Achievements include U.S., European, and Japanese patents for Prevention and Treatment of Fibrotic Lesions; research in anti-histamines anti-cholinergics, endorphins, sedative-hypnotics, tranquilizers, muscle relaxants, glucocorticoids, cardiovascular agents, anti-inflammatory drugs, anti-fibrotic agents. Home: 6723 Desco Dr Dallas TX 75225-2704

MARGOLIS, BERNARD ALLEN, library administrator; b. Greenwich, Conn., Oct. 2, 1948; s. Sidney S. and Rose (Birkenfeld) M.; m. Amanda Batey, Nov. 2, 1973. BA in Polit. Sci., U. Denver, 1970, MLS, 1973. Cert. libr., Mich. Libr. asst. Denver Pub. Libr., 1970-72; br. head Virginia Village Libr., Denver Pub. Libr., 1972-73; dep. dir. Monroe County Libr. Sys., Mich., 1973-75; dir. Raisin Valley Libr. Sys., Monroe, 1976-78, S.E. Mich. Regional Film Libr., Monroe, 1976-88, Monroe County Libr. Sys., 1976-88, Pikes Peak Libr. Dist., Colorado Springs, Colo., 1988-97; pres. Colo. Ctr. for Books, 1989-92, Colo. Ctr. for the Book, 1993-97; pres. Boston Pub. Libr., 1997—; cons. in libr. pub. rels., 1976—; founding trustee United Colo. Investment Trust, 1993-95; chmn. Colo. Gov.'s Conf. on Libr. and Info. Svcs., 1990; lectr. Western Mich. U., Kalamazoo, 1978-81; appraiser rare books, Monroe, Colorado Springs, 1970—. Contbr. articles to profl. jours; mem. editl. bd. Bottom Line Mag. Fin. Mgmt. for Librs., 1986—. Bd. dirs. Monroe Sen. Citizens Ctr., 1976-80, Monroe Fine Arts Coun., 1978-81, Am. the Beautiful Centennial Celebration, Inc., 1993, The Libr. Consortium, 1993-97, Downtown Colo. Springs, Inc., 1994-97, Care & Share, Inc., sec., 1994—, vice chmn., 1995, chmn., 1995-97; chmn. Blue Cross-Blue Shield Consumer Coun., Detroit, 1984-88; mem. adv. bd. Access Colo. Libr. and Info. Network (ACLIN), 1991—, Mercy Meml. Hosp., Monroe, 1984-86, 5th Congl. Art Competition Com., 1992-97; Dem. candidate for Mich. Senate, 1986; mem. allocations com. Pikes Peak United Way, 1988-91, chmn., 1990-91, bd. dirs., 1990-91, 94—; chmn. Great Pikes Peak Cowboy Poetry Gathering, 1990, 91, 92, 94, 95, 96; del. White House Conf. on Libr. and Info. Scis.; mem. El Paso County, Colo. Retirement Bd., 1995—, sec. 1996-97. Recipient Mayoral Cert. Commendation award Denver, 1972, 73; named Mich. Libr. of Yr., 1985, Colo. Libr. of Yr., 1990; commendation John F. Kennedy Ctr. for Performing Arts, 1993, Frank Waters award Pikes Peak Writer's Conf., 1996; Mem. ALA (governing coun. 1986—, endowment trustee 1989-93, sr. endowment trustee 1993—, chmn. resolutions com. 1991-92, cons. ann. swap and shop 1979-84, John Cotton Dana award 1977, 91, Libr. Awareness Idea Search award Washington 1982), Colo. Libr. Assn. (mem. legis. com., Intellectual Freedom award 1993), Libr. Adminstrv. Mgmt. Assn., Pub. Libr. Assn. Democrat. Jewish. Home: 99 Grayfield Ave Boston MA 02132 Office: Boston Pub Libr Copley Sq Boston MA 02116

MARGOLIS, DANIEL HERBERT, lawyer; b. Montgomery, W.Va., Feb. 11, 1926; s. Morris Abraham and Miriam M.; m. Anabel Tendler, Dec. 23, 1951 (dec.); children—Peter, Beth, Lura, James; m. Sidney Millman Moore, Feb. 5, 1983. B.A., Johns Hopkins U., 1948; LL.B., Harvard U., 1951. Bar: D.C. 1951, U.S. Supreme Ct. 1959. Atty adv. Office Price Stblzn., Washington, 1951-52; trial atty. Antitrust div. Dept. Justice, Washington, 1952-56; sr. ptnr. Bergson, Borkland, Margolis & Adler, Washington, 1956-86; ptnr. McGuire, Woods, Battle & Boothe, 1986-89, Patton, Boggs L.L.P., 1989—. Contbr. articles to profl. jours. Mem. adv. bd. Internat. Human Rights Law Group, 1989—. Served with USN, 1945-46, PTO. Fellow ABA (chmn. spl. com. on jury comprehension, litigation sect. 1983-90), Washington Lawyers for Civil Rights. Democrat. Avocations: sailing, skiing, cooking. Office: Patton Boggs LLP 2550 M St NW Washington DC 20037-1301

MARGOLIS, DAVID I(SRAEL), corporate executive; b. N.Y.C., Jan. 24, 1930; s. Benjamin and Celia (Kosofsky) M.; m. Barbara Schneider, Sept. 7, 1958; children: Brian, Robert, Peter, Nancy. BA, CCNY, 1950, MBA, 1952; postgrad., NYU, 1952-55. Asst. treas. Raytheon Co., 1956-59; treas. IT&T, N.Y.C., 1959-62; with Coltec Industries Inc., N.Y.C., 1962-95, pres., 1968-91, CEO, 1984-95, chmn. bd. dirs., 1985-95; chmn. exec. com., 1995—; bd. dirs. Burlington Industries, Ft. Howard Corp., Offitbank. Mem. bd. trustees Presbyn. Hosp. City N.Y.; bd. overseers NYU Stern Sch. Bus. Mem. Coun. Fgn. Rels. Office: 147 E 48th St New York NY 10017-1223

MARGOLIS, EMANUEL, lawyer, educator; b. Bklyn., Mar. 18, 1926; s. Abraham and Esther (Levin) M.; m. Edith Cushing; m. Estelle Thompson, Mar. 1, 1959; children: Elizabeth Margolis-Pineo, Catherine, Abby Margolis Newman, Joshua, Sarah. BA, U. N.C., 1947; MA, Harvard U., 1948, PhD, 1951; JD, Yale U., 1956. Bar: Conn. 1957, U.S. Dist. Ct. Conn. 1958, U.S. Sup. Ct. 1969. Instr. dept. govt. U. Conn. 1951-53; assoc. Silberberg & Silverstein, Ansonia, Conn. 1956-60; assoc. Wofsey Rosen Kweskin & Kuriansky Stamford, Conn. 1960-66, ptnr. 1966—; arbitrator State of Conn., 1984-85; trial referee, 1985—; adj. prof. Quinnipiac Coll. Sch. Law, 1986—. Sr. editor Conn. Bar Jour., 1971-80, 83—, editor-in-chief, 1980-83; contbr. to legal jours. Mem. nat. bd. ACLU, 1975-79; mem. Westport (Conn.) Planning & Zoning Commn., 1971-75; chmn. Conn. CLU, 1988-95, legal advisor, 1995—. Served with U.S. Army, 1944-46. Decorated Purple Heart; recipient First Award for Disting. Service to Conn. Bar, Conn. Law Tribune, 1987. Fellow Conn. Bar Found. (James W. Cooper fellow 1996—); mem. ABA, Conn. Bar Assn. (chmn. human rights sect. 1970-73), Nat. Assn. Criminal Def. Lawyers. Home: 72 Myrtle Ave Westport CT 06880-3512 Office: 600 Summer St Stamford CT 06901-1403

MARGOLIS, EUGENE, lawyer, government official; b. Bronx, N.Y., Dec. 19, 1935; s. Louis and Minnie (Kaplan) M.; m. Sally Fay Gellman, Sept. 22, 1962; children—Judith Miriam, Linda Aileen, Aaron Keith, Pamela June. BME, Rensselaer Poly. Inst., 1957; JD, Georgetown U., 1960, M in Patent Law, 1962. Bar: N.Y. 1961, U.S. Supreme Ct. 1969; cert. exec. U.S. Office Personnel Mgmt., 1983. Patent examiner U.S. Patent Office, Washington, 1957-60; trial atty. antitrust div. U.S. Dept. Justice, Washington, 1960-66, N.Y.C., 1966-67; chief consumer protection div. N.Y.C. Dept. Law, 1967-71; gen. counsel Mayor's Interdeptl. Com. on Pub. Utilities, N.Y.C., 1972-73; spl. counsel to commr. N.Y.C. Dept. Gen. Services, 1974-79; dir. N.Y.C. Office of Energy Conservation, 1975-79; sr. legal adviser U.S. Dept. Energy, Washington, 1979-95, dep. asst. gen. counsel, 1995—; adj. prof. Cooper Union, 1978-79; adj. assoc. prof. Grad. Sch., CUNY, 1974-80. Mem. editorial bd. Georgetown Law Jour., 1958-60. Chmn. govtl. relations and grants com. Village of Larchmont, N.Y., 1977-79, mem. cable TV com., 1977-79, mem. tax base com., 1974-79; chmn. Larchmont Democratic Com., 1976-77; vice chmn. Mamaroneck Dem. Com., 1979; mem. Westchester County Dem. Com., 1975-77, 79; bd. dirs. Jewish Community Coun. Greater Washington, 1986-94; mem. adv. bd. Dept. Volunteerism, Commonwealth Va., 1987-91; mem. pub. social policy com. United Jewish Appeal-Fedn. Greater Washington, 1988—,mem. No. Va. leadership coun. 1990—; sr. v.p. B'nai Brith Internat., 1996—, bd. govs., 1992-94, 95—, internat. coun., 1992-94, Hillel com., 1991-94, mem. nat. fund raising cabinet, 1987-90, com. on community vol. svcs., 1985-89, pres. dist. 5, 1993-94, pres. Va. State Assn., 1986-87, pres. Va. Hillel Found., 1985-86. Recipient Cert. of Appreciation U.S. Dept. Energy, 1984, Sec. of Energy's Award, Outstanding Community Svc. Vol., 1990, Gov. Va.'s Cmty. Svc. and Volunteerism award, 1995. Mem. N.Y. State Bar Assn., ASME, Phi Delta Phi, Pi Delta Epsilon, Tau Epsilon Phi. Jewish. Clubs: Rensselaer Alumni (sec. chpt. 1976-77), U. Va. Fund Parents, Town and Village Synagogue Men's (pres. 1970-71). Lodge: B'nai Brith (pres. Mcpl. lodge 1976-78, Larchmont-Mamaroneck lodge 1978-80, Masada lodge 1984-85, Internat. Lodge Col. Elliot A. Niles Community Svc. award 1984, Dist. 5 Outstanding Ben Brith award 1988, Outstanding State Pres. award 1987, Hillel award 1986, Community Vol. Svc. award 1984, Va. State Assn. Herman G. Koplen Meml. award 1987, Sherry B. Rose Leadership award 1984). Home: 6504 Sparrow Point Ct Mc Lean VA 22101-1638 Office: US Dept Energy Forrestal Bldg 1000 Independence Ave SE Washington DC 20585-0001

MARGOLIS, GERALD JOSEPH, psychiatrist, psychoanalyst; b. Bronx, N.Y., May 7, 1935; s. Max and Sophie (Siegel) M.; A.B., U. Rochester, 1957; M.D., U. Chgo., 1960; postgrad. Inst. Phila. Assn. Psychoanalysis, 1972; m. June Edelman Greenspan, July 13, 1976; children: David J., Peter S., Steven J. Intern, psychiat. resident, Upstate Med. Center, SUNY, Syracuse, 1960-64, instr. psychiatry, 1966-67; from instr. to clin. prof. psychiatry Med. Sch., U. Pa., Phila., 1967—; practice medicine specializing in psychiatry and psychoanalysis, Cherry Hill, N.J.; tng. and supervising analyst Inst. of Phila. Assn. for Psychoanalysis. Served with M.C., USAF, 1964-66. Diplomate Am. Bd. Psychiatry and Neurology. Mem. Am. Psychoanalytic Assn. (cert.), Am. Psychiat. Assn., AMA, Phila. Assn. for Psychoanalysis (tng. and supervising analyst), Phi Beta Kappa. Club: B'nai B'rith. Contbr. articles to profl. publs. Home: 408 Park Ln Moorestown NJ 08057-2000

MARGOLIS, HAROLD STEPHEN, epidemiologist; b. Tucson, Ariz., Feb. 22, 1946; s. Maurice H. and Helen (Letz) M.; m. Susan Helen Quinn, July 3, 1971; children: Ellis, Leah, Amber. BS, U. Ariz., 1968, MD, 1972. Diplomate Am. Bd. Med. Examiners. Resident in pediatrics U. Colo. Health Scis. Ctr., Denver, 1972-75; med. epidemiologist Ctrs. for Disease Control, Anchorage, 1975-79, Phoenix, Ariz., 1981-83; dep. chief hepatitis br. Ctrs. for Disease Control, Atlanta, 1983-87; chief hepatitis br., 1995—; chief Ctrs. for Disease Control, Atlanta, 1987—; rsch. fellow Nat. Jewish Hosp., Denver, 1979-81; dir. WHO Collaborative Ctr. for Rsch. and Reference in Viral Hepatitis, Atlanta, 1987—; cons. WHO, 1988, 89, Agy. for Internat. Devel.; guest advisor Inst. Medicine, 1989, 92. Editor: Viral Hepatitis and Liver Disease, 1991; contbr. articles to profl. jours. Capt. USPHS, 1975—. Fellow Am. Acad. Pediats., Infectious Disease Soc. Am.; mem. Alpha Omega Alpha, Sigma Xi. Achievements include development of strategies to prevent viral hepatitis through immunization; research in characterization of hepatitis A viruses and molecular pathogenesis of viral hepatitis. Office: Nat Ctr for Infectious Diseases Hepatitis Branch 1600 Clifton Rd NE Atlanta GA 30329-4018

MARGOLIS, JULIUS, economist, educator; b. N.Y.C., Sept. 26, 1920; s. Sam and Fannie (Weiner) M.; m. Doris Lubetsky, Oct. 30, 1942; children—Jane S., Carl W. B.S.S., City Coll. N.Y., 1941; Ph.M. in Econs, U. Wis., 1943; M.P.A. in Econs, Harvard, 1947, Ph.D., 1949. Instr. econs. Tufts Coll., 1947-48; asst. prof. econs. and planning U. Chgo., 1948-51; asst. prof. econs. Stanford, 1951-54; prof. bus adminstrn. U. Calif. at Berkeley, 1954-64; prof. econs. and engring. econ. systems Stanford, 1964-69; prof., dir. Fels Center of Govt., U. Pa., 1969-76; prof. econs. U. Calif. at Irvine, 1976—; dir. Ctr. on Global Peace and Conflict Studies, 1985—; cons. to govt. and industry, 1958—. Author: (with others) The Public Economy of Urban Communities, 1965, The Northern California's Water Industry, 1966, Public Economics, 1969, Public Expenditure and Policy Analysis, 1984; also articles. Served with AUS, 1943-46. Mem. Am. Econ. Assn., Royal Econ. Soc. Home: 45 Whitman Ct Irvine CA 92612-4059 Office: U Calif Dept Econ Irvine CA 92697

MARGOLIS, LAWRENCE STANLEY, federal judge; b. Phila., Mar. 13, 1935; s. Reuben and Mollie (Manus) M.; m. Doris May Rosenberg, Jan. 30, 1960; children: Mary Aleta, Paul Oliver. BSME, Drexel U., 1957; JD, George Washington U., 1961. Bar: D.C. 1963. Patent examiner U. S. Patent Office, Washington, 1957-62; patent counsel Naval Ordnance Lab., White Oak, Md., 1962-63; asst. corp. counsel D.C., 1963-66; atty. criminal div., spl. asst. U.S. atty. Dept. of Justice, Washington, 1966-68; asst. U.S. atty. for D.C., 1968-71; U.S. magistrate judge U.S. Dist. Ct., Washington, 1971-82; judge U.S. Ct. Fed. Claims, Washington, 1982—; chmn. task force on discovery reform U.S. Claims Ct., Washington, chmn. alt. dispute resolution; mem. faculty Fed. Jud. Ctr. Editor-in-chief The Young Lawyer, 1965-66, D.C. Bar Jour., 1967-73; bd. editors The Dist. Lawyer, 1978-82. Trustee Drexel U., 1983-89; bd. govs. George Washington U. Alumni Assn., 1978-85, 93-96. Recipient Contbn. award D.C. Jaycees, 1966, Svc. award Boy Scouts Am., 1970, Alumni Svc. award George Washington U., 1976, Disting. Alumni Achievement award George Washington U., 1985, Disting. Alumni Achievement award Drexel U., 1988, Drexel 100 award, 1992, Alt. Dispute Resolution award Ctr. for Pub. Resources, 1988, Alumni Recognition award George Washington U., 1996. Fellow Inst. Jud. Adminstrn., Am. Bar Found.; mem. ABA (chmn. jud. adminstrn. divsn., Disting. Svc. award 1981), ABA Nat. Conf. Spl. Ct. Judges (chmn., Disting. Svc. award 1978), D.C. Jud. Conf., Bar Assn. D.C. (bd. dirs. 1970-72, jour. editor-in-chief, Contbn. award young lawyers sect. 1983), Fed. Bar Assn., George Washington U. Nat. Law Assn. (pres. D.C. chpt. 1974-76, pres. 1983-84), Univ. Club., Rotary (bd. dirs. Washington 1984-90, pres. 1988-89, dist. gov. 1991-92, Rotarian of Yr. 1984), Charles Fahy Am. Inn of Ct. Office: US Ct Fed Claims 717 Madison Pl NW Ste 703 Washington DC 20005-1011

MARGOLIS, PHILIP MARCUS, psychiatrist, educator; b. Lima, Ohio, July 7, 1925; s. Harry Sterling and Clara (Brunner) M.; m. Nancy Nupuf, July 26, 1959; children: Cynthia, Marc, David, Laurence. B.A. magna cum laude, U. Minn., 1945, M.D., 1948. Diplomate Am. Bd. Psychiatry and Neurology (examiner 1973—). Intern Milw. County Hosp., 1948-49; resident VA Hosp. and U. Minn., 1949-52, Mass. Gen. Hosp. and Harvard U., Boston, 1952-54; instr. U. Minn., Milw., 1953-55; asst. prof. dept. psychiatry Med. Sch., U. Chgo., 1955-60, assoc. prof., 1960-66; prof. psychiatry Med. Sch. U. Mich., 1966—, prof. cmty. mental health, 1968—, mem. civil liberties bd., 1995—, chair civil liberties bd., 1996—; chief psychiat. inpatient service U. Chgo. Hosps. and Clinics, 1956-66; cons. Forensic Psychiat. Ctr., State of Mich., 1972—, coord. med. student edn. program, 1975-78, dir., 1978-82; cons. Turner Geriatric Clin., 1978-86, cons. Breast Cancer Clinic, 1988, Powertrain subs. Gen. Motors, 1984—, Dept. Mental Health, U.S. Dept. Justice; assoc. chief clin. affairs U. Mich. Hosps., 1981-85, chair legis. govt. com., 1996—, chmn. ethics com.; bd. dirs., mem. profl. rev. com. PSRO Area VII, 1982-86; mem. Mich. State Bd. Medicine, 1986-94, chmn. 1992-94, senate adv. com. Univ. Affairs., 1986-89; bd. dirs. Fedn. of State Med. Bds., 1994—, Mich. del., 1988—, FLEX Com. Nat. Bd. Med. Examiners. Author: Guide for Mental Health Workers, 1970, Patient Power: The Development of a Therapeutic Community in a General Hospital, 1974; also articles.; cons. editor: Community Mental Health jour, 1967—. Recipient Commonwealth Fund fellow award, 1964, Career Svc. award, 1992, Resident Appreciation award, 1991. Fellow Am. Coll. Psychiatrists, Am. Psychiat. Assn. (life, chmn. membership com. 1979-83, cons. ethics com. 1983-86, trustee 1985-88, sec. 1989-91, cons. steering com. on practical guidelines, 1991—, mem. assembly 1992—, coun. med. edn. and career devel. 1993—, budget com. 1991—, chmn. ethics appeals bd. 1989—, pres. Lifers 1994—); mem. Washtenaw County Med. Soc. (exec. coun. 1982—, chmn. ethics com. 1983-87, pres. 1987-88, editl. bd. 1995—), Mich. Psychiat. Soc. (pres. 1980-81, chmn. ethics com. 1983-86, resolutions officer student rights responsibilities 1996—), Mich. State Med. Soc. (bioethics com., 1989—, com. on med. licensure and discipline, 1995—, legis. and regulations com., 1995—, mental health liaison com., 1995—, Internat. Assn. Social Psychiatry, World Fedn. Mental Health, Am. Acad. Psychoanalysis, Am. Acad. Psychiatry and Law (com. on psychoanalytic edn. 1995—). Home: 228 Riverview Dr Ann Arbor MI 48104-1846 Office: 900 Wall St Ann Arbor MI 48105-1910

MARGOLIS, RICHARD MARTIN, photographer, educator; b. Lorain, Ohio, June 10, 1943; s. Harold and Claudine (Martin) M.; m. Sherry Lynn Phillips. BS, Kent State U., 1969; MFA, Rochester Inst. Tech, 1978. Asst. prof. SUNY-Brockport, 1981-88; presenter Bridge Project, Stories about Bridges, Soc. for Indsl. Archeology Nat. Conf., 1995; delivered 1995 Barbara L. Bush Meml. Lectr., Longwood Coll., Farmville, Va. Exhibitor over 70 one-person shows, including Foto, N.Y.C., 1976, 79, 81, 83, Carpenter Ctr., Harvard U., 1978, George Eastman House, Rochester, N.Y., 1978, Camden Arts Ctr., London, 1981, NAS, Washington, 1990, Magic Powers, Rochester, 1991, Bridges: Symbols of Progress, catalog and exhbn. on nat. tour, 1991-94, Rochester's Landmarks Airport Art Project Permanent Insallation; group shows 130 Yrs. of Ohio Photography, Columbus, 1978, Contemporary Expression, Catskill Ctr. for Photography, Woodstock, N.Y., 1979, Wells Coll., Aurora, N.Y., 1996; curator (exhbns.), 1980, 82; curator: Photography Art of State, 1983, Computers and Photography, 1989; contbr.

Contemporary Photographers, 3rd edit., 1995, Photographers Encyclopedia International, 1939 to the Present, 1985, Photographic Artists and Innovators, 1983. Creative Artists Pub. Svc. Found. grantee N.Y. State Coun. on Arts, 1977-78; N.Y. State Coun. on Arts grantee to photograph N.Y. bridges, 1985, 90; SUNY Rsch. Found. incentive grantee, 1983; Lift grantee, 1989; recipient Individual Artist award Rochester N.Y. Arts and Cultural Alliance, 1994. Mem. Soc. for Photog. Edn. (chmn. 1982-83), Photog. Heritage Assn. (founder, steering com.), Soc. for Indsl. Archaeology. Studio: Studio #4-9 250 North Goodman St Rochester NY 14607

MARGOLIS, VIVIENNE O., psychotherapist; b. Dayton, Ohio, Jan. 11, 1922; d. Sol and Cecelia (Salowitz) M.; m. Leonard Eisner (div. 1976); children: Charna, Andrew, Jonathan. BS, George Washington U., 1944; MS with honors, So. Conn. U., 1966; PhD with honors, Calif. Coast, 1980. Tchr. Fairfield (Conn.) U., 1970-72, Norwalk (Conn.) Community Coll., 1970-75, Bicultural Day Sch., Stamford, Conn., 1960-70; therapist Hackensack (N.J.) Hosp., 1976-81; tchr. Towson (Md.) State U., 1987-89, Towson State U., Columbia, 1988-90; pvt. practice Washington, 1985-87, Columbia, 1989—. Author: Newspaper Everything Book, 1975, 77, Boat, Bat and Beanie, 1977, Quick and Easy Holiday Costumes, 1977, Fanfare for a Feather, 1991. Avocations: collage, small-box constructions, clay sculpture. Home and Office: 6037 Majors Ln Columbia MD 21045-4133

MARGOLIUS, HARRY STEPHEN, pharmacologist, physician; b. Albany, N.Y., Jan. 29, 1938; s. Irving Robert and Betty (Zweig) M.; m. Francine Rockwood, May 22, 1964; children: Elizabeth Anne, Craig Matthew. BS, Union U., 1959, PhD, 1963; MD, U. Cin., 1968. Diplomate Nat. Bd. Med. Examiners, 1969, chmn. pharmacology test com., 1990-94. Intern, resident Harvard Med. Svc. Boston City Hosp., 1968-70, pharmcology rsch. assoc., 1970-72; sr. clin. investigator NHLBI NIH, Bethesda, 1972-74; assoc. prof. pharmacology, asst. prof. medicine Med. U. S.C., Charleston, 1974-77, prof. pharmacology, assoc. prof. medicine, 1977-80, prof. pharmacology, prof. medicine, 1980—, chmn. pharmacology, 1989—; cons. NIH, FDA, VA, NSF, Washington, Bethesda, 1975—; mem. editorial bd. Am. Heart Assn., Dallas, 1980—. Editor: Kinins IV, 1986, Renal Function, Hypertension and Kallikrein-Kinin System, 1988; contbr. numerous articles to profl. jours. Commdr. USPHS, 1967-74. Recipient S.C. Gov.'s award for sci. S.C. Acad. Scis., 1988, Frey-Werle Commemorative medal for biomed. rsch., 1997; Burroughs-Wellcome scholar, 1976; vis. scholar U. Cambridge, Eng., 1980-81; sr. fellow Fitzwilliam Coll., 1996; NIH grantee, 1975—; named Theodore Cooper Meml. Lectr., 1995. Fellow Coun. for High Blood Pressure Rsch., Am. Heart Assn.; mem. Am. Soc. for Pharmacology and Exptl. Therapeutics, Am. Soc. for Clin. Investigation and 10 additional med., sci. socs. Jewish. Achievements include studies of the role of kallikreins and kinins in human and animal forms of hypertension; discovery of abnormalities which signify roles in causing high blood pressure. Office: Medical Univ of SC College of Medicine 171 Ashley Ave Charleston SC 29425-0001

MARGON, BRUCE HENRY, astrophysicist, educator; b. N.Y.C., Jan. 7, 1948; s. Leon and Maxine E. (Margon) Siegelbaum; m. Carolyn J. Bloom, May 8, 1976; 1 dau., Pamela. A.B., Columbia U., 1968; M.A., U. Calif.-Berkeley, 1971, Ph.d., 1973. Asst. rsch. astronomer U. Calif.-Berkeley, 1973-76; assoc. prof. astronomy UCLA, 1976-80; prof. astronomy U. Wash., Seattle, 1980—, chmn., 1981-87, 90-95; bd. govs. Astrophys. Rsch. Consortium, Inc., Seattle; chmn. bd. dirs. AURA, Inc., Washington; co-investigator Hubble space telescope NASA, Washington, 1977—. NATO postdoctoral fellow, 1973-74; Sloan Found. research fellow, 1979-83. Fellow AAAS, Am. Phys. Soc.; mem. Internat. Astron. Union, Am. Astron. Soc. (Pierce Prize 1981), Royal Astron. Soc. Office: Univ Wash Box 351580 Astronomy Dept Seattle WA 98195-1580

MARGRAVE, JOHN LEE, chemist, educator, university administrator; b. Kansas City, Kans., Apr. 13, 1924; s. Orville Frank and Bernice J. (Hamilton) M.; m. Mary Lou Davis, June 11, 1950; children: David Russell, Karen Sue. B.S. in Engring. Physics, U. Kans., 1948, Ph.D. in Chemistry, 1950. AEC postdoctoral fellow U. Calif. at Berkeley, 1951-52; from instr. to prof. chemistry U. Wis., Madison, 1952-63; prof. chemistry Rice U., 1963—, E.D. Butcher chair, 1986—, chmn. dept., 1967-72, dean advanced studies and research, 1972-80, v.p., 1980-86; v.p. for research Houston Advanced Research Ctr., 1986-89, chief sci. officer, 1989—; dir. Materials Sci. Ctr., 1986-93; vis. prof. chem. Tex. So. U., 1993—; dir. Council for Chem. Research, 1985-88; Reilly lectr. Notre Dame, 1968, Phi Lambda Upsilon lectr. Kans. State U., 1995; vis. distinguished prof. U. Wis., 1968, U. Iowa, 1969, U. Colo., 1975, Ga. Inst. Tech., 1978, U. Tex. at Austin, 1978, U. Utah, 1982; Seydel-Wooley lectr. Ga. Inst. Tech., 1970; Dupont lectr. U. S.C., 1971; Abbott lectr. U. N.D., 1972; Cyanamid lectr. U. Conn., 1973; Sandia lectr. U. N.Mex., 1981; R.A. Welch lectr., 1985; NSF-Japan Joint Thermophys. Properties Symposium, 1983; chmn. com. on chem. processes in severe nuclear accidents NRC, 1987-88, chmn. molten salt reactor remediation com., 1996—, mem. armor and armarments panel, 1996—; mem. Wilhelm und Else Heraeus Stiffung Found. Symposium on Alkali Metal Reactions, Fed. Republic Germany, 1988; various nat. and internat. confs. on chem. vapor deposition of thin diamond films, 1989-96; orgnl. com. First, Second Third and Fourth World Superconductivity Congresses, 1989, 90, 92, 94, NATO Conf. on Supercooled Metals, Il Ciocio, Italy, 1993; mem. adv. coms. chem., materials sci., rsch. U. Tenn. Knoxville, Ohio State U., Tex. So. U., La. Bd. Regents, sci. adv. bd. SI Diamond Tech., 1992—, BioNumerik, 1993—, Intrepid Tech., 1994—; cons. to govt. and industry, 1954—; pres. Mar Chem., Inc., 1970—, High Temperature Sci., Inc., 1976—; dir. Rice Design Center, Houston Area Research Ctr.; U. Kans. Research Found., Gulf Univs. Research Consortium, Energy Research and Edn. Found., Spectroscopic Assocs., World Congress on Superconductivity; advisor NROTC Assn., 1984—. Editor: Modern High Temperature Sci., 1984; contbg. editor Characterization of High Temperature Vapors, 1967, Mass. Spectrometry in Inorganic Chemistry, 1968; editor High Temperature Sci., 1969—, Procs. XXIII and XXIV Confs. on Mass Spectrometry, 1975, 76; author: (with others) Bibliography of Matrix Isolation Spectroscopy, 1950-85, 87; contbr. articles to profl. jours. Served with AUS, 1943-46; capt. Res. ret. Sloan research fellow, 1957-58; Guggenheim fellow, 1960; recipient Kiekhofer Teaching award U. Wis., 1957; IR-100 award for CFX lubricant powder, 1970, IR-100 award for Cryolink, 1986; Tex. Honor Scroll award, 1978; Disting. Alumni citation U. Kans., 1981, Sci. and Tech. award North Harris Montgomery Cmty. Coll., 1994. Fellow AAAS, Am. Inst. Chemists, Am. Phys. Soc., Tex. Acad. Sci.; mem. AAUP, NAS, Am. Chem. Soc. (Inorganic Chemistry award 1967, S.W. Regional award 1978, Fluorine Chemistry award 1980, S.E. Tex. Sect. award 1993, chem. edn. com. 1968-70, publs. com. 1973-74, patents and related matters com. 1994—), Am. Ceramic Soc., Am. Soc. Mass Spectrometry (dir.), Am. Soc. Metals, Electrochem. Soc., Chem. Soc. London, Tex. Philos. Soc., Materials Rsch. Soc., Sigma Xi (Disting. Svc. award 1994), Omicron Delta Kappa, Sigma Tau, Tau Beta Pi, Alpha Chi Sigma. Methodist. Patentee in field. Home: 5012 Tangle Ln Houston TX 77056-2114 Office: Rice University Dept of Chemistry MS-60 6100 Main St Houston TX 77005-1827

MARGULIES, ANDREW MICHAEL, chiropractor; b. Bklyn.; s. Irving R. and Marion (Steiner) M.; m. Lorraine Raffa, Dec. 23, 1990; children: Samantha Cara, Maxwell Scott. D. Chiropractic, Palmer Coll. Chiropractic, Davenport, Iowa, 1981; MSc in Spinal Biomechanics, Intercontinental U., 1995. Diplomate Nat. Bd. Chiropractic, Am. Acad. Pain Mgmt., Am. Bd. Disability Analyst (sr. disability analyst), Am. Bd. Disability Analysts; cert. chiropractic sports physician. Dir., chiropractic physician Margulies Chiropractic and Sports Injuries Ctr., Massapequa, N.Y., 1981—; chiropractor, mem. med. team N.Y. Long Island Marathon, 1986—, USA/Mobil Track and Field Nat. Championships, 1991—; cons. Massapequa Rd. Runners, Long Island, 1985—. Recipient Silver Star award Markson/Svc. to Community, Flushing, N.Y., 1984, Markson Mgmt. Annual award, 1984, Community Svc. and Profl. award Success Systems, 1993. Fellow Am. Acad. Applied Spinal Biochem. Engring.; mem. APHA, AAAS, N.Y. Acad. Scis., Am. Chiropractic Assn. (coun. on sports injuries and phys. fitness, coun. on diagnostic imaging), Found. for Chiropractic Edn. and Rsch., N.Y. Chiropractice Coun. Office: Margulies Chiropractic and Sports Injury Ctr 1148 Hicksville Rd Massapequa NY 11758-1222

MARGULIES, JAMES HOWARD, editorial cartoonist; b. Bklyn., Oct. 8, 1951; s. Henry Norman and Miriam Margulies; m. Martha Anne Golub, May 21, 1978; children: Elana, David. BFA, Carnegie-Mellon U., 1973. Editorial cartoonist Jour. Newspapers, Springfield, Va., 1980-84, Houston Post, 1984-90, The Record, Hackensack, N.J., 1990—; syndicated cartoonist various newspapers, 1985—. Author: My Husband is Not a Wimp, 1988; contbr. columns to profl. jours.; cartoons featured on TV programs. Mem. leadership com. Jewish Community Ctr., Houston, 1987, 88. Recipient Best Cartoon award Population Inst., 1985, Global Media award, 1985, 2d Place Editl. award Pavillion of Humor, 1985, Judges award World Hunger Media awards, 1986, Katie award Press Club of Dallas, 1989, Best Black and White Illustration in Advt. and Graphic Arts Addy award Houston Advt. Fedn., 1990, John Peter Zenger award N.Y. State Bar Assn., 1992, Nat. Headliner award for editl. cartoons Press Club of Atlantic City, 1996, 1st prize Fischetti Editl. Cartoon Competition, Columbia Coll., Chgo., 1996; named One of Texans Who Made the Eighties Winter, Ultra mag., 1990. Mem. Assn. Am. Editl. Cartoonists. Avocation: running. Office: The Record 150 River St Hackensack NJ 07601-7110

MARGULIES, LAURA JACOBS, lawyer; b. Bklyn., Feb. 5, 1956; d. David and Marcia (Reichman) Jacobs; children: Moshe, Yaakov, Miriam, Yehuda, Shira. BS in Edn., HTD, Yeshiva U., 1977; JD, U. Balt., 1988. Bar: Md. 1988, D.C. 1990. Jud. intern to Hon. James F. Schneider U.S. Bankruptcy Ct., Balt., 1986; law clk. Shawe & Rosenthal, Balt., 1987-88; law clk. to Hon. Paul E. Alpert Md. Ct. Spl. Appeals, Towson, 1988-89; assoc. Semmes, Bowen & Semmes, Balt., 1989-92, Shaw, Pittman, Potts & Trowbridge, Washington, 1992-93; pvt. practice Rockville, Md., 1993—; adj. prof. U. Md. U. Coll., College Park, 1993—; civil mediator Cir. Ct. of Balt. City, 1991-93. Editor U. Balt. Law Review, 1986-88. Recipient David Gann scholarship U. Balt. Sch. Law, 1987. Mem. Bankruptcy Bar Assn. for Dist. of Md. (so. div. co-chmn. 1994-95, chmn. 1995-96), Md. State Bar Assn., D.C. Bar Assn. Avocations; walking, reading, swimming. Office: 5870 Hubbard Dr Rockville MD 29852

MARGULIES, LEE, newspaper editor. Television editor Los Angeles Times, Calif. Office: Los Angeles Times Times Mirror Sq Los Angeles CA 90053

MARGULIES, MARTIN B., lawyer, educator; b. N.Y.C., Oct. 6, 1940; s. Max N. and Mae (Cohen) M.; m. Beth Ellen Zeldes, July 26, 1981; children: Max Zeldes, Adam Zeldes. AB, Columbia Coll., 1961; LLB, Harvard U., 1964; LLM, NYU, 1966. Bar: N.D. 1968, N.Y. 1974, Mass. 1977, U.S. Dist. Ct. Mass. 1977, U.S. Ct. Appeals (2d cir.) 1984, Conn. 1988. Asst. prof. law U. N.D., Grand Forks, 1966-69; editor-in-chief Columbia Coll. Today, Columbia U., N.Y.C., 1969-71; assoc. editor Parade Mag., N.Y.C., 1971-72; assoc. prof. law Western New Eng. Law Sch., Springfield, Mass., 1973-76; Bernard Hersher prof. law U. Bridgeport, Conn., 1977-92; prof. law Quinnipiac Coll., 1992—. Author: The Early Life of Sean O'Casey, 1970. Contbr. articles to profl. jours. Cooperating atty. Conn. Civil Liberties Union, Hartford, 1979—, bd. dirs., 1982-94; bd. dirs. Conn. Attys. for Progressive Legislature, New Haven, 1982—; bd. dirs. ACLU, 1987-94, mem. free speech-assn. and poverty constitutional rights com. 1988-94; chmn. bd. dirs. Fairfield County Civil Liberties Union, 1982-87, Hampden County Civil Liberties Union, 1976-78; bd. dirs. Civil Liberties Union Mass., Boston, 1975-78, Greater Springfield Urban League, 1976-78, Conn. Civil Liberties Union, 1982-94, ACLU, 1987-94. Ctr. for First Amendment Rights, Inc., 1993—. Recipient Media award N.Y. State Bar Assn., 1972, Gavel award ABA, 1973, Outstanding Tchr. award U. Bridgeport Law Sch., 1986, 87. Mem. Mass. Bar Assn., N.Y. State Bar Assn. Jewish. Home: 79 High Rock Rd Sandy Hook CT 06482-1623 Office: Quinnipiac Coll Sch Law 275 Mt Carmel Ave Hamden CT 06518-1961

MARGULIS, ALEXANDER RAFAILO, physician, educator; b. Belgrade, Yugoslavia, Mar. 21, 1921; came to U.S., 1946; s. Rafailo and Olga (Weiss-Belic) M.; m. Hedvig Hricak, Feb. 26, 1983; 1 son, Peter Hricak-Margulis. Student, U. Belgrade, 1939-41, 45-46; MD, Harvard U., 1950; hon. doctorates, Aix-Marseille U. Sch. Medicine, 1980, Med. Coll. Wis., 1986, Cath. U. Louvain, 1986, Karolinska Inst., Stockholm, 1986, U. Munich, 1987, U. Toulouse, 1987, U. Montpellier, 1993. Diplomate Am. Bd. Radiology. Intern Henry Ford Hosp., Detroit, 1950-51; resident in radiology U. Mich. Hosps., 1951-53; jr. clin. instr. U. Mich., 1953-54; instr., then asst. prof. U. Minn., 1954-59; asst. prof. sch. medicine Washington U., St. Louis, 1959-60, assoc. prof. to prof., 1960-63; prof. radiology, chmn. dept. U. Calif., San Francisco, 1963-89, dir. magnetic resonance Sci. Ctr., assoc. chancellor spl. projects, 1989-93; spl. cons. to vice chancellor U. Calif.; radiologist in chief U. Calif. Hosps., 1963-89; cons. VA Hosp., Letterman Gen. Hosp., San Francisco, U.S. Naval Hosp., Oakland, Calif.; cons. in radiology Office Surgeon Gen., 1967-71. Author (with others) Roentgen Diagnosis of Abdominal Tumors in Childhood, 1957; co-editor Alimentary Tract Roentgenology; editorial bd. Calif. Medicine, 1964-74, Radiology, 1975-93; assoc. editor Investigative Radiology, 1980-89; editor Opinion in Radiiology, 1988-91. Served to capt. AUS, 1957-59. Recipient J.P. Allyn medal P. Roberts Rsch. Inst., 1989. Fellow Faculty Radiologists (hon.); sr. mem. Nat. Acad. Scis.-Inst. Medicine; mem. AMA (cons. drugs 1961—), Royal Coll. Radiologists, Roentgen Ray Soc., Assn. Univ. Radiologists (pres. 1966-67, chmn. adv. com. acad. radiology 1971), Am. Gastroenterology Assn., Soc. Chmn. Acad. Radiology Depts. (pres. 1968-69), Radiol. Soc. N.Am., San Francisco Radiol. Soc. (pres. 1973-74), Rocky Mountain Radiol. Soc. (hon.)., Calif. Acad. Medicine (pres. 1978), Soc. Magnetic Resonance in Medicine (pres. 1983), Serbian Acad. Scis. (fgn.), Russian Acad. Med. Scis. (fgn.). Home: 8 Tara Hill Rd Belvedere Tiburon CA 94920-1554 Office: Univ Calif 3333 California St Ste 16 San Francisco CA 94118-1944

MARHIC, MICHEL EDMOND, engineering educator, entrepreneur, consultant; b. Ivry, Seine, France, June 25, 1945; came to U.S., 1968; s. Jean-Marie and Yvonne Marie (Nenez) M. Ingenieur, Ecole Sup. D'Electricite, Paris, 1968; MS, Case Western Res. U., 1970; PhD, UCLA, 1974. Asst. prof. Northwestern U., Evanston, Ill., 1974-79, assoc. prof., 1980-84, prof., 1985—; vis. asst. prof. U. So. Calif., L.A., 1979-80; vis. prof. Stanford U., 1984-85, 93-94; bd. dirs. Holographic Industries, Lincolnshire, Ill. Contbr. and co-contbr. over 140 jour. articles and conf. publs.; holograhic portrait Ronald Reagan, 1991. Mem. IEEE (sr.), Optical Soc. Am., Tau Beta Pi. Achievements include 8 patents in field. Office: Northwestern U Dept Elec Engring 2145 Sheridan Rd Evanston IL 60208-0834

MARICHAL, JUAN ANTONIO SANCHEZ, retired baseball player, agency administrator. Baseball player San Francisco Giants, 1960-73, Boston Red Sox, 1974, L.A. Dodgers, 1975; sec. state Sports, Phys. Edn. & Recreation, Dominican Republic, 1996—. Named to Baseball Hall of Fame, 1983. Office: Apdo 497, Calle Pedro Henriquez Uren, Santo Domingo Dominican Republic

MARIE, LINDA, artist, photographer; b. Cheverly, Md., Nov. 8, 1960; d. Thomas Grason Jr. and Rosalinda (Wepf) McWilliams; 1 child, Ann Marie. AA with honors, Cecil C.C., North East, Md., 1991. One-woman shows include Franklin Hall Arts Ctr., Chesapeake City, Md., 1993, Humanities and Arts Gallery-Essex (Md.) C.C., 1993, Widner Art Mus., Chester, Pa., 1996, Gallery B.A.I., N.Y.C., 1997; group exhbns. include Del. Ctr. Contemporary Art, Wilmington, 1991, Md. Fedn. Art, Annapolis, 1991-93, Acad. of Arts, Easton, Md., 1992, Elkton (Md.) Arts Ctr., 1990-92, Md. Gallery East, Havre de Grace, 1992, Chautaqua (N.Y.) Inst., 1992, Washington Project for Arts, 1992, Ward-Nasse Gallery, N.Y.C., 1994, Sinclair C.C., Dayton, Ohio, 1994, AAAS, Washington, 1994-95, ACP, College Park, Md., 1994, Gallery B.A.I., Barcelona, Spain, 1996, Sullivan County Mus., N.Y., 1997; represented in permanent collections at AAAS, Cecil C.C. Mem. Del. Ctr. Contemporary Arts, Md. Fedn. Art, Cecil County Arts Coun., Alpha Alpha Theta. Home and Studio: 6 Walnut St North East MD 21901

MARIELLA, RAYMOND P., chemistry educator, consultant; b. Phila., Sept. 5, 1919; s. Angelo Raphael and Sophia (Peel) M.; m. Miriam Margaret McMahon, Nov. 26, 1943; children: Miriam Margaret, Raymond P., Anne Marie, Patricia Sue. B.S., U. Pa., 1941; M.S., Carnegie Inst. Tech., 1942, D.Sc., 1945; postdoctoral fellow, U. Wis., 1946. Instr., then asst. prof. chemistry Northwestern U., 1946-51; mem. faculty Loyola U., Chgo., 1951-77; prof. chem. Loyola U., 1955-77, chmn. dept., 1951-70; asso. dean Loyola U. (Grad. Sch.), dir. grad. sci. programs, 1968-69, dean, 1969-77, sci. cons. indsl. orgns., 1951-77; assoc. exec. dir. Am. Chem. Soc., 1977, exec. dir., 1978-82; Sec.-treas. Midwestern Assn. Grad. Schs., 1972-77; exec. com. Council of Grad. Schs., 1972-74; Scientific adviser to gov. Ill. Producer, performer sci. TV shows Chgo. networks, 1956-65; Author: Laboratory Manual of Organic Chemistry and Biochemistry, 1953, Inorganic Qualitative Analysis, (with J. L. Huston), 1958, Chemistry of Life Processes, (with Rose Blau), 1968, Selected Laboratory Experiments for Chemistry of Life Processes, 1968, also articles. Recipient McCormack Freud Hon. lectr. award chemistry and chem. engring. Omicron chpt. Phi Lambda Upsilon, 1961; Merit award Chgo. Tech. Socs. Council, 1962. Mem. Am. Chem. Soc. (chmn. Chgo. 1960-61, nat. councilor 1956-82, chmn. bd. com. on profl. relations 1974-75, cons. to chmn. bd.), AAAS, N.Y. Acad. Scis., Sigma Xi (pres. Loyola chpt. 1956-57), Phi Kappa Phi, Alpha Chi Sigma, Phi Lambda Upsilon, Lambda Chi Sigma, Sigma Delta. Home and Office: 21215 N 123rd Dr Sun City West AZ 85375-1944

MARIENTHAL, GEORGE, telecommunications company executive; b. Kansas City, Mo., Nov. 15, 1938; s. George and Sadie (James) M.; children: Shawn Ann Capon, Patrick James, Shannon Lee Van Winter. B.S., U.S. Naval Acad., 1962; M.S., Stanford U., 1963; M.B.A., Am. U., 1974. Sr. rsch. assoc. Logistics Mgmt. Inst., Washington, 1967-71; dir. regional ops. EPA, 1971-75, dir. water policy, 1984-85; dep. asst. sec. def. Dept. Def., Washington, 1975-81; v.p. Survival Tech., Inc., Bethesda, Md., 1981-84; dep. asst. sec. agr. Dept. Agr., Washington, 1985-86; dep. adv. programs Titan Systems, Inc., 1986-87; mgr. mktg. Computer Scis. Corp., Falls Church, Va., 1987-89; dir. MCI Communications Corp., McLean, Va., 1989—; bd. dirs. Home Security Title Ins. Co. Served with USAF, 1962-67. Mem. Inst. Indsl. Engrs., Am. Def. Preparedness Assn., Armed Forces Communications and Electronics Assn., Internat. Telephone Pioneers Assn. Republican. Episcopalian. Club: Masons. Home: 10202 Parkwood Dr Kensington MD 20895-4130

MARIMOW, WILLIAM KALMON, journalist; b. Phila., Aug. 4, 1947; s. Jay and Helen Alma (Gitnig) M.; m. Diane K. Macomb, Oct. 18, 1969; children: Ann Esther, Scott Macomb. BA, Trinity Coll., Conn., 1969. Asst. editor Comml. Car Jour., Chilton Co., Bala Cynwyd, Pa., 1969-70; asst. to econ. columnist Phila. Bull., 1970-72; staff writer Phila. Inquirer, 1972—, city hall bur. chief, 1979-81, editor Main Line Neighbors, 1986-87, N.J. editor, 1987-89, city editor, 1989-91; city editor, asst. to pub. Phila. Inquirer and Daily News, 1991-93; met. editor Balt. Sun, 1993, assoc. mng. editor, 1993-95, mng. editor, 1995—; instr. urban studies U. Pa., 1979; instr. English Rutgers U., Camden, N.J., 1981; mem. nominating jury Pulitzer Prize, 1991-92, 96-97. Recipient 1st pl. award for team reporting Phila. Press Assn., 1977, 1st pl. award for deadline reporting AP Mng. Editors of Pa., 1977, Pub. Svc. awards, 1978, 85, Nat. Pub. Svc. award Sigma Delta Chi, 1978, 1st pl. award for best news story Sigma Delta Chi Phila., 1977, 2nd pl. award for deadline reporting, 1980, Pub. Svc. awards, 1978, 85, Pub. Svc. awards Sigma Delta Chi N.J., 1978, Pulitzer prize for disting. pub. svc., 1978, Pulitzer prize for investigative reporting, 1985, Silver Gavel award ABA, 1978, 82, Roy W. Howard Pub. Svc. award Scripps-Howard Found., 1978, Robert F. Kennedy Journalism award, 1978, 2nd pl. award for investigative reporting Keystone Press Assn., 1978, 85, 1st pl. award for best news story, 1982, Media Achievement award Phila. Bar Assn., 1982, William Schnader award Pa. Bar Assn., 1982, Nat. Headliners award, 1985, Trinity Coll. Alumni Achievement award, 1984; Nieman fellow Harvard U., 1982-83. Mem. Pen and Pencil Club, Investigative Reporters and Editors, Inc. Home: 1025 Winding Way Baltimore MD 21210-1232 Office: The Baltimore Sun PO Box 1377 501 N Calvert St Baltimore MD 21202-3604

MARINACCIO, CHARLES LINDBERGH, lawyer; b. Stratford, Conn., Dec. 10, 1933. BA, U. Conn., 1957; JD with honors, George Washington U., 1962. Bar: Conn. 1962, D.C. 1982. Trial lawyer U.S. Dept. Justice, Washington, 1963-69; advisor supervisory and regulation div. Fed. Res. Bd., Washington, 1969-73; dir., exec. sec. law enforcement asstistance adminstrn. U.S. Dept. Justice, Washington, 1973-75; gen. counsel banking housing and urban affairs com. U.S. Senate, Washington, 1975-84; commr. SEC, Washington, 1984-85; ptnr. Kelley, Drye & Warren, Washington, 1985-94; ind. cons. Washington, 1995—; apptd. by Pres. Clinton to bd. dirs. Securities Investor Protection Corp. Home and Office: 4911 Massachusetts Ave NW Washington DC 20016-4310

MARINACCIO, PAUL JOHN, JR., marketing professional; b. Oceanside, N.J., Sept. 1, 1957; s. Paul J. and Jeanette (Romanescu) M. AB, Rutgers U., 1979. Polit. writer The N.J. Herald, Newton, 1979-82; reporter, bur. chief The Star Ledger, Newark, 1982-85; staff writer Newsday, Melville, N.Y., 1985-87; nat. econs. writer, bus. writer Newsday, N.Y. Newsday, N.Y.C., 1987-91; exec. dir. Econ. Policy Mktg. Group City of N.Y., 1991-94; mktg. exec. Deloitte and Touche, Wilton, Conn., 1994-95, nat. dir. bus. devel., 1995—; contbg. editor N.J. Monthly, Princeton, N.J., 1979-82; cons. Ctr. for Capital Studies CUNY, N.Y.C., 1994. Editor: New York City 1991: the World's Capital in Transition, 1991, Strong Economy, Strong City: Jobs for New Yorkers, 1993. Recipient 1st place award for deadline reporting Press Club L.I., 1986, for bus. writing N.Y. State AP, 1988, for labor reporting Newspaper Guild N.Y., 1989, Golden Quill award Garden State Scholastic Press Assn., 1991; Davenport fellow U. Mo. Sch. Journalism, 1990.

MARINACE, KENNETH ANTHONY, financial advisor; b. N.Y.C., May 2, 1944; s. Anthony and Hilda Marinace; children: Steven Joseph, Douglas Anthony. Student, Am. Inst. Fin., 1962-63, Am. Coll., 1975; CLU, Coll. Fin. Planning, 1981. CFP, CFP Bd. Owner, CEO Comprehensive Fin. Svcs., Burbank, Calif., 1967—; bd. dirs. Life Underwriters Assn. L.A., 1980-82. Host radio series You and Your Money, 1988-90, TV series You and Your Money, 1990—. Bd. dirs. San Gabriel coun. Girl Scouts U.S., Arcadia, Calfi., 1987, Burbank Family YMCA, 1989, Econ. Coun., Mus. Sci. and Industry, L.A., 1990-93, St. Joseph Med. Ctr. Found., 1997—, Burbank corps Salvation Army, 1996—; mem. adv. panel Royal Alliance Assocs., Inc., N.Y.C., 1989-91; pres. Burbank Cmty. Healthcare Found., 1989. Recipient Bus. Person of Yr. award Profl. Econs. Svcs., 1974, Outstanding Citizen Commendations, City of Burbank, 1988, City of L.A., 1988, County of L.A., 1993. Mem. Internat. Assn. Fin. Planning, Inst. CFP, Am. Soc. CLU and ChFC, Kiwanis (bd. dirs. Burbank Found. 1989—), Oakmont Country Club, Jonathan Club. Avocations: golf, music, travel. Office: Comprehensive Fin Svcs 3811 W Burbank Blvd Burbank CA 91505-2116

MARINE, CLYDE LOCKWOOD, agricultural business consultant; b. Knoxville, Tenn., Dec. 25, 1936; s. Harry H. and Idelle (Larue) M.; m. Eleanor Harb, Aug. 9, 1958; children: Cathleen, Sharon. B.S. in Agr., U. Tenn., 1958; M.S. in Agrl. Econs., U. Ill., 1959; Ph.D. in Agrl. Econs., Mich. State U., 1963. Sr. market analyst Pet Milk Co., St. Louis, 1963-64; mgr. market planning agr. chems. div. Mobile Chem. Co., Richmond, Va., 1964-67; mgr. ingredient purchasing Central Soya Co., Ft. Wayne, Ind., 1970-73, corp. economist, 1967-70, v.p. ingredient purchasing, 1973-75, sr. v.p., 1975-90; pres. Marine Assocs., Ft. Wayne, 1991—; bd. dirs. SCAN, 1992—; mem. agrl. policy adv. com. U.S.D.A. Bd. dirs. Ft. Wayne Fine Arts Found., 1976-79; bd. dirs. Ft. Wayne Pub. Transp. Corp., 1975-83; v.p. Ft. Wayne Philharm., 1974-76. Served with U.S. Army, 1959-60. Mem. Nat. Soybean Processors Assn. (chmn.), U.S. C. of C., Am. Agrl. Econs. Assn., Am. Feed Mfrs. Assn. (chmn. purchasing coun.). Episcopalian. Club: Ft. Wayne Country. Office: Marine Assocs 4646 W Jefferson Blvd Fort Wayne IN 46804-6832

MARINE, SUSAN SONCHIK, analytical chemist; b. Maple Heights, Ohio, Mar. 10, 1954; d. Stephen Robert and Gloria Ann (Hach) Sonchik; m. Michael D. Marine; 1 child, Matthew Robert Marine. BS in Chemistry magna cum laude, John Carroll U., 1975; MS in Analytical Chemistry, Case Western Res. U., 1978, PhD in Phys. Chemistry, 1980. Asst. chemist Horizons Research Inc., Beachwood, Ohio, 1974-75; chemist specialist Standard Oil of Ohio, Warrensville Heights, Ohio, 1975-79; organic chemistry br. mgr. Versar, Inc., Springfield, Va., 1980-83; mgr. gas chromatography program IBM Instruments Inc., Danbury, Conn., 1983-87, radiation safety officer, 1985-87; expert witness, cons. Martin, Craig, Chester & Sonnenschein, Chgo., 1981-83; adv. engr. in advanced lithography IBM Corp., Essex Junction, Vt., 1987-95; vis. assoc. prof. chemistry Centre Coll., Danville, Ky., 1995—; tchr. chemistry and math. Heritage Coll., 1991-92; speaker in field. Author: African Walking Safari, 1985; editorial adv. bd. Jour. Chromatographic Sci., 1977-93, guest editor, 1987. Mem. Danbury Conservation Commn., 1986-87, tchr. and tutor chemistry, 1985-89, 91-92, 94; troop leader Lake Erie coun. Girl Scouts U.S.A., 1971-80, Southwestern

Conn., 1983-87; leader explorer post Cleve. coun. Boy Scouts Am., 1977-78; managerial advisor Jr. Achievement, Warrensville Heights, Ohio, 1977-78; judge State Sci. Fair, 1977, 80, 89-91, Odyssey of the Mind, 1994; asst. leader Internat. Folk Dancers, Newtown, Conn., 1985-87; tchr. religion, 1981-84, 87-90, 93-94. Recipient Overall Best Paper award Eastern Analytical Symposium, 1984, First Gas Chromatograph award IBM Instruments Inc., 1985, contbn. award (tech. paper) 10th Internat. Congress of Essential Oils, Flavors, Fragrances, Washington, 1986. Mem. ASTM (exec. com. E-19 1985—, chmn. subcom. 1986—, vice chmn. arrangements 1994—), Am. Chem. Soc. (chmn. membership com. Green Mountain sect. 1988-89, chair elect 1989-90, chmn. 1990-91, local coord. Nat. Chemistry Week 1991, 93—, Phoenix award 1994), Iota Sigma Pi (pres. N.E. Ohio chpt. 1978-79, mem.-at-large fin. mgr. 1993-97, nat. v.p. 1996—), No. Vt. Canoe Cruisers (treas. 1990-92), Green Mountain Steppers (sec. 1993-95), Centre Coll. Outdoors Club (faculty liaison 1996—). Roman Catholic. Avocations: camping, dancing, travel. Home: 1116 Bluegrass Pike Danville KY 40422-9207 Office: Centre Coll Dept Chem 600 W Walnut St Danville KY 40422-1309

MARINELLI, LYNN M., county official; b. Akron, Ohio, Aug. 4, 1962; d. Michael and Christine (Golonka) Madden; divorced; 1 child, Jessica. BA in English, Daemen Coll., 1985. Pub. rels. coord. Bison Baseball Inc., Buffalo, 1985-86; exec. asst. to Assemblyman William B. Hoyt N.Y. State Assembly, Buffalo, 1986-92; exec. dir. Erie County Commn. on Status of Women, Buffalo, 1992-96; chair Erie County Coalition Against Family Violence, 1992-95; co-chair domestic violence com. Multidisciplinary Coordinating Coun., 1992—; mem. adv. bd. Dept. Social Svcs., Erie County, 1992-96. Sec. dem. com. Town of Tonawanda, 1991—; active Dem. Jud. Adv. Com. Erie County, 1990—, Reapportionment Com., Erie County, 1991, Ct. Care Project, 1992, Compass House, Erie County, 1993—, Women for Downtown, 1993-96, Citizens Com. on Rape and Sex Assault, 1993-96, Leadership Buffalo, 1994, United Way Family Support and Safety, 1994—. Recipient Disting. Svc. award Coalition Against Family Violence, 1992; named Young Careerist, Bus. and Profl. Women, 1991; named to 40 Under Forty list, Bus. First, 1993. Roman Catholic. Avocations: skiing, reading. Office: Erie County Legis 11th Dist 25 Delaware Ave Rm 7 Buffalo NY 14202-3903

MARINETTI, GUIDO V., biochemistry educator; b. Rochester, N.Y., June 26, 1918; s. Michael and Nancy (Lippa) M.; m. Antoinette F. Francione, Sept. 19, 1942; children: Timothy D., Hope L. B.S., U. Rochester, 1950, Ph.D., 1953. Research biochemist Western Regional Lab., Albany, Calif., 1953-54; instr. U. Rochester, N.Y., 1954-57; asst. prof. U. Rochester, 1957-60, assoc. prof., 1960-66, prof. sch. medicine and dentistry, 1966-79; prof. emeritus dept biochemistry and biophysics, 1997—; cons. Eastman Kodak, 1978, Rochester Gas & Electric, 1979. Author: Disorders of Lipid Metabolism, 1990; editor: Lipid Chromatographic Analysis, 3 vols., 1969, 2nd edit., 1976; contbr. 160 pub. articles in sci. jours. Served with USAAF, 1942-46. Recipient Nat. Infantile Paralysis award, 1952; recipient Glycerine Research award, 1957; NSF grantee, 1953; recipient Lederle Med. Faculty award, 1955, 56. Mem. Am. Soc. Biol. Chemists, Am. Chem. Soc., AAAS, Sigma Xi, Phi Beta Kappa. Rsch. area: membrane structure and function, biochemistry of phospholipids, phosphatidylinositiol metabolism in isolated synaptomsomes. Office: Univ Rochester Med Ctr 601 Elmwood Ave Rochester NY 14642-0001

MARINI, ELIZABETH ANN, civilian military executive; b. Dubuque, Iowa, Feb. 8, 1940; d. Cletus Nicholas and Catherine Margaret (Blasen) Freiburger; m. John J. Marini, Jan. 12, 1980. BA, Cardinal Stritch Coll., 1962; MPA, George Washington U., 1982. Claims examiner Social Security Adminstrn., Chgo., 1962-64; supply systems analyst Navy Electronic Supply Office, Great Lakes, Ill., 1964-67; investment rep. Investors Planning Corp. Am., N.Y.C., 1967; supply systems analyst Naval Electronic Systems Command, Washington, 1968-76, head Saudi naval expansion program, 1976-80, head def. security assistance office internat. program, 1979-80; chief East Asia/Latin Am. divsn. Office of Sec. of Def. Def. Security Assistance Agy., Washington, 1980-84; chief East Asia Pacific divsn. Office of the Sec. of Def., DSAA, Washington, 1984-90; chief arms coop. and policy analysis divsn. Office of the Sec. of Def., Def. Tech. Security Adminstrn., Washington, 1990—. Tchr. religion classes Blessed Sacrament Ch., Alexandria, Va., 1972-73. Mem. Kappa Gamma Pi, Pi Alpha Alpha. Roman Catholic. Avocations: reading, walking. Office: Def Tech Security Adminstrn 400 Army Navy Dr Arlington VA 22202-2885

MARINI, FRANK NICHOLAS, political science and public administration educator; b. Melrose Park, Ill., June 18, 1935; s. Joseph and Lillian Lee (Stuart) M.; m. Elsie B. Adams; children: Lisa M., Katherine D. B.A., Ariz. State U., 1960, M.A., 1961; Ph.D., U. Calif., Berkeley, 1966. Instr. U. Mo., Columbia, 1963-64; asst. prof. polit. sci. U. Ky., 1966-67; asst. prof. Syracuse U., 1967-70; assoc. prof., asso. dean Syracuse U. (Maxwell Sch.), dir. public adminstrn. programs, 1970-73; dean Coll. Arts and Letters, San Diego State U., 1973-80; provost, v.p. acad. affairs Calif. State U., Fullerton, 1980-84; sr. adviser chancellor's office Calif. State U., 1984-85; sr. v.p., provost U. Akron, Ohio, 1985-90, prof. pub. adminstrn., urban studies, polit. sci., 1990-96, prof. emeritus, 1996—. Author pamphlets; contbr. numerous articles to profl. jours.; editor: Toward a New Public Administration, 1971; mng. editor: Public Administrn. Rev, 1967-77; editor-in-chief Jour. Pub. Adminstrn. Edn., 1994—. Served with USAF, 1954-58. Mem. Am. Soc. Pub. Adminstrn.

MARINI, ROBERT CHARLES, environmental engineering executive; b. Quincy, Mass., Sept. 29, 1931; s. Larry and Millie (Cirillo) M.; m. Myrna Lydia Pellegrini, June 26, 1955 (dec. June 1994); children: Debra, Robert Charles, Larry; m. B. Anne Jones, May 27, 1995. B.S.C.E. with honors, Northeastern U., 1954; S.M.S.E., Harvard U., 1955, postgrad. Advanced Mgmt. Program, 1985. Registered profl. engr., Mass., N.Y., Maine, R.I., N.H., Conn., Vt., Calif., N.C., Wash., Colo., Mich., Fla., Wis., Tenn., La., Ariz., Ohio, Ill., Va. Jr. engr. Camp Dresser & McKee Inc., Boston, 1955-56, project engr., 1958-64, assoc., 1964-67, ptnr., sr. v.p., 1967-77, pres. environ. engring. div., 1977-82, exec. v.p., 1982-84, pres., 1984-90, chief exec. officer, 1989—, also chmn. bd. dirs.; mem. civil engring. adv. com. Worcester (Mass.) Poly. Inst., 1985-90, U. Mass., 1986-90, U. Tex., Austin, 1989-91, chmn., 1991-92, mem. engring. found. adv. coun., 1991—. Contbr. articles to profl. jours. Dir. nat. coun. Northeastern U., Boston, 1983—, mem. corp. bd., 1983—, bd. overseers, 1985-89, trustee, 1989—; chmn. Leadership Phase Century II Fund, 1989-91, chmn. devel. com., 1991—; corporator Weymouth Savs. Bank, 1988—, trustee, 1991—; bd. dirs. Mass. Bus. Round Table, 1991—, vice chmn., 1995-97, chmn., 1997—. Recipient Disting. Eagle Scout award Boy Scouts Am., 1986, W. Erwin Story award, 1991, Outstanding Civil Engring. Alumni award Northeastern U., 1992, Outstanding Alumni award, 1993. Fellow ASCE, NAE, Instn. Engrs. Australia; mem. Am. Pub. Works Assn. (Man of the Yr. award New Eng. chpt. 1981), Am. Water Works Assn., Mass. Soc. Profl. Engrs. (Young Engr. of Yr. award 1966), Am. Acad. Environ. Engrs. (diplomate, trustee at large 1989-92, v.p. 1992-93, pres.-elect 1993-94, pres. 1994-95, Stanley E. Kappe award 1992), Water Environment Fedn. (hon.), Internat. Assn. Water Pollution Rsch. and Control, Engring. Soc. New Eng. (New Eng. award 1994), Tau Beta Pi, Phi Kappa Phi. Roman Catholic. Home: 1 Nevin Rd Weymouth MA 02190-1610 Office: Camp Dresser & McKee Inc 1 Cambridge Ctr Cambridge MA 02142-1605

MARINIS, THOMAS PAUL, JR., lawyer; b. Jacksonville, Tex., May 31, 1943; s. Thomas Paul and Betty Sue (Garner) M.; m. Lucinda Cruse, June 25, 1969; children—Courtney, Kathryn, Megan. B.A., Yale U., 1965; LL.B., U. Tex., 1968. Bar: Tex. Assoc. Vinson & Elkins, Houston, 1969-76, ptnr., 1977—. Served with USAR, 1968-74. Fellow Tex. Bar Found; mem. ABA (sec. taxation sect. 1984-85), Tex. Bar Assn. (chmn. taxation sect. 1986-87). Clubs: Houston Country, Houston Ctr., Coronado.

MARINO, ANN DOZIER, real estate broker; b. Durham, N.C., Apr. 22, 1944; d. Walter Joseph and Ellen G. (Cheek) Dozier; m. John Harrison Marino, Oct. 15, 1966 (div. Jan. 1981); children: John Harrison Jr., Ann Southerlyn. BA, Salem Coll., 1966. Sales assoc. Rector Assocs. Realtors, Alexandria, Va., 1984—. Vol. Jr. League, Chgo., 1970-74; bd. dirs. Jr. League, Washington, 1979-95, Vol. Clearing House, Washington, Project Open Rd., Chgo., Fire and Burn Inst., Washington; mem. parents coun. Burgundy Farm Sch., 1983; mem. parish coun. St. Mary's, Oldtown, 1977-80. Recipient Rookie of Yr. award No. Va. Bd. Realtors, 1985, Lifetime Top Producer award, Million Dollar Club, No. Va. Bd. Realtors, 1985-94. Mem. Salem Coll. Alumnae Club (pres. Chgo. chpt. 1970-73), Million Dollar Club (life). Republican. Roman Catholic. Office: Pardoe and Graham 310 King St Alexandria VA 22314-3212

MARINO, DANIEL CONSTANTINE, JR., professional football player; b. Pittsburgh, Sept. 15, 1961. BA, communications, U. Pitts., 1983. Profl. football player Miami Dolphins, NFL, 1983—. Film appearance Ace Ventura: Pet Detective, 1994. Named All-America team quarterback, The Sporting News, 1981; Rookie of the Year, The Sporting News, 1983, NFL All-Pro team, The Sporting News, 1984-86, MVP, Nat. Football League, 1984-85; named to Pro Bowl Team, 1983-87, 91-92. NFL career record for most games (12) with 400 or more yards passing; NFL records for most seasons (6) with 4,000 or more yards passing, most seasons (9) with 3,000 or more yards passing, 1984-1992, most consecutive games (4) with four or more touchdown passes, 1984; NFL record for lowest percentage (2.03) of passes intercepted by a rookie, 1983; NFL record for most games (17) with four or more touchdown passes, 1984. Office: care Miami Dolphins Joe Robbie Stadium 2269 NW 199th St Opa Locka FL 33056-2600*

MARINO, EUGENE LOUIS, publishing company executive; b. N.Y.C., Jan. 7, 1929; s. Salvatore A. and Florence M. (Casabona) M.; student Columbia U., 1945-48; m. Patricia Ryan, Mar. 11, 1948; children—Jeanette, Anthony, John, Eugene III. Credit mgr. Sears, Roebuck Inc., L.I., N.Y., 1951-60; gen. credit mgr. Davison-Paxon div. R.H. Macy, Inc., Atlanta, 1960-63, Grand-Way div. Grand Union Co., N.Y.C., 1963-66; v.p., gen. credit mgr. Consumer Products div. Singer Co., N.Y.C., 1966-75, Grolier, Inc., Danbury, Conn., 1975-90, ret.; officer, v.p., gen. credit mgr., dir. numerous subsidiaries. Recipient Quarter Century cert. Internat. Consumer Credit Assn., 1981. Mem. Mchts. Research Council, Internat. Consumer Credit Assn., Nat. Assn. Credit Mgmt., Alpha Sigma Phi. Home: 4858 Tivoli Ct Sarasota FL 34235-3653

MARINO, IGNAZIO ROBERTO, transplant surgeon, researcher; b. Genova, Italy, Mar. 10, 1955; s. Pietro Rosario and Valeria (Mazzanti) M.; m. Rossana Parisen-Toldin, Sept. 15, 1990; 1 child, Stefania Valeria. Maturità-Classica, Coll. of Merode, Rome, 1973; MD, Cath. U., Rome, 1979. Diplomate Nat. Bd. Gen. Surgery, Nat. Bd. Vascular Surgery. Intern, then resident Gemelli U. Hosp., Rome, 1979-84; temp. asst. dept. surgery Cath. U., Rome, 1981, asst. prof. surgery, 1983-92; asst. prof. surgery Transplantation Inst., U. Pitts., 1991-95; assoc. prof. surgery Transplantation Inst./U. Pitts., 1995—; prof. surgery postgrad. Sch. Microsurgery, Exptl. Surgery U. Milan, 1994—; prof.surgery Sch. Medicine U. Perugia, 1994—; attending surgeon U. Pitts. Med. Ctr., Pitts., 1991—; assoc. dir. transplant divsn. VA Med. Ctr., Pitts., 1992—; attending surgeon Children's Hosp. Pitts., 1993—; mem. surg. team 1st and 2d baboon to human liver transplants U. Pitts. Med. Ctr., 1992, 93, dir. European med. divsn., 1995—; sci. journalist Agenzia Nazionale Stampa Associata, 1992—; mem. nat. ad hoc donations com. United Network for Organ Sharing, 1995—. Author: New Technique to Avoid the Revascularization Syndrome in Liver Transplantation, 1985 (Ann. prize Italian Soc. Surgery 1986), New Technique in Liver Transplantation, 1986 (De Angelis award 1986); mem. editl. bd. Clin. Transplantation, Leadership Medica; contbr. more than 350 articles to profl. jours. Mem. Italian Ordine Giornalisti, 1994—. Grantee Italian Nat. Coun. Rsch., 1979, 86, 87, 88, 89-93, Gastroenterology Soc., 1988; recipient award Instituto Nazionale Previdemza Dirigenti Aziende Industriali, 1982. Mem. ACS, Am. Soc. Transplantation Surgeons, Am. Soc. Transplant Physicians, Italian Soc. Surgery, Transplantation Soc. (grant 1988), European Soc. for Organ Transplantation, Soc. Surgeons Under 40 (Ann. prize 1986), Cell Transplant Soc. (founding mem.), Acad. Surg. Rsch., Soc. Critical Care Medicine, Internat. Liver Transplantation Soc., Assn. Italian Correspondents in N.Am. (assoc.), Xenotransplantation Club (founding mem.), Internat. Coll. Surgeons (U.S. sect.), Assn. for Acad. Surgery, Nat. Assn. VA Physicians. Avocations: reading (history books), sailing, Annibale (pet cat). Home: Corso Italia 29, Rome 00198, Italy Office: Univ Pitts Transplant Inst 4W Falk Clinic 3601 5th Ave Pittsburgh PA 15213-3403

MARINO, JOSEPH ANTHONY, retired publishing executive; b. Geneva, N.Y., Apr. 1, 1932; s. Anthony Rocco and Antoinette (DePalma) M.; m. Catherine Colville, Dec. 18, 1953; children: Joseph, Michael, Paul. B.S., Tri-State U., 1959; M.B.A., Mich. State U., 1960. Mgr. Gillette Co., Boston, 1960-82; pres., chief exec. officer Liquid Paper Corp. div. Gillette, Dallas, 1979-82, Western Pub. Co., Inc., Racine, Wis, 1982-89; mem. adv. bd. Heritage Bank, Racine, 1983—; bd. dirs. Wickes Furniture Co., Aerosol Svcs. Co., Inc., Prairie Sch., Youth Leadership Acad. Mem. bus. alumni adv. bd. Mich. State U., 1987. Served with USAF, 1951-54. Recipient award of Honor Fedn. Jewish Philanthropies, 1973. Mem. Racine Country Club (Wis.).

MARINO, MICHAEL FRANK, III, lawyer; b. Little Falls, N.Y., Feb. 19, 1948; s. Michael Frank and Betty (Roberts) M.; m. Catherine Viladesau, Aug. 31, 1970 (div. Nov. 1996); m. Ann Buttfield Feb. 15, 1997; children: Michael John, Lisa Kathryn, Matthew Christopher. BS, Cornell U., 1971; JD, Syracuse U., 1974; LLM, Georgetown U., 1982. Bar: D.C. 1975, U.S. Dist. Ct. D.C. 1975, U.S. Ct. Mil. Appeals 1975, N.Y. 1976, U.S. Dist. Ct. (ea. and we. dists.) Va. 1977, U.S. Dist. Ct. Md. 1980, U.S. Ct. Appeals (4th cir.) 1982, Va. 1982, U.S. Ct. Appeals (9th cir.) 1994. Civilian employee head rels. br. Office of the Judge Adv. of the Navy, Washington, 1975-76; spl. asst. to the gen. counsel Office of Sec. of Navy, Washington, 1977; asst. gen. counsel labor and employment Office of the Gen. Counsel of the Navy, Washington, 1978; assoc. Pierson, Ball & Dowd, Washington, 1978-81; ptnr. Boothe, Prichard & Dudley, Fairfax and Mc Lean, Va., 1981-87, McGuire, Woods, Battle & Boothe, Mc Lean, 1987-89, Reed, Smith, Shaw & McClay, Mc Lean, 1989—; labor group head, Washington, Va.; mng. ptnr. McLean Office. Author: Virginia Employer's Guide to Labor Law, 1982; co-author: New York Employer's Guide, 1989, 92-94, Fla. Labor and Employment Law, 1994, Labor Employment Law in Pa., 1994. Mem. planning com. SMU Multi State labor Law Conf., Dallas; chmn. Arlington (Va.) Chamber Employee Rels. Com.; bd. dirs. Arlington Chamber Bd. of Dirs.; mem. Va. Chamber Mgmt. Rels. Com. Richmond, 1980—. Capt. USMC, 1971-78. Named Best Lawyer in Am., 1986-97. Mem. ABA (labor law com. 1974—), D.C. Bar Assn. (labor law com. 1974—), Va. Bar Assn. (labor law com. 1974—, sec.-treas. labor law sect. 1995, vice chair 1996-97), N.Y. Bar Assn. (labor law com. 1974—), Riverbead Country Club. Roman Catholic. Avocations: jogging, fitness, hunting, fishing. Office: Reed Smith Shaw & McClay 8251 Greensboro Dr Ste 1100 Mc Lean VA 22102-3809

MARINO, PAMELA ANNE, health sciences administrator; b. Milford, Conn., Feb. 28, 1951; d. Angelo and Christine M. BA in Biology with honors, U. Conn., 1973; PhD in Biomed. Scis., U. Conn., Farmington, 1986. Rsch. assoc. to lab. supr. Yale Med. Sch., New Haven, 1973-80; from postdoctoral fellow to sr. staff fellow Nat. Cancer Inst., Bethesda, Md., 1986-93; sr. staff fellow FDA, Bethesda, Md., 1993-94; program dir. Nat. Inst. Gen. Med. Scis., Bethesda, Md., 1994—. Contbr. articles to profl. jours. Tchr. NIH Sci. Alliance with Pub. Schs., Rockville, Md., 1994-96. Conn. State scholar, 1969-73; U. Conn. fellow, 1980-86, Nat. Cancer Soc. fellow, 1986-90; recipient Performance award NIGMS, 1994. Mem. Am. Soc. Biol. Chemists and Molecular Biologists (assoc.), Women in Cancer Rsch. (co-chair mentoring com. 1995-96, chair database com., chair commns. com. 1995-97), Am. Assn. for Cancer Rsch. Home: Apt 201 17128 King James Way Gaithersburg MD 20877-2219 Office: Nat Inst Gen Med Scis 45 Center Dr Bethesda MD 20892

MARINO, PAUL LAWRENCE, physician, researcher; b. Everett, Mass., Feb. 10, 1946; s. Charles Joseph and Jean Marie (Casale) M.; 1 child, Daniel Joseph. BA, Merrimack Coll., 1967; MD, PhD, U. Va., 1974. Diplomate Am. Bd. Internal Med. Resident physician U. Mich., Ann Arbor, 1974-77; fellow in pulmonary medicine U. Pa., Phila., 1977-80; med. faculty U. Pa. Sch. Medicine, Phila., 1980-90; assoc. prof. Mt. Sinai Sch. Medicine, N.Y.C., 1990-92; dir. critical care Presbyn. Med. Ctr., Phila., 1992—. Author: The ICU Book, 1991; editorial bd. Jour. Internal Medicine; adv. bd. Medical Tribune; software designer The Expert Series. Mem. coun. on critical care Am. Heart Assn., 1995; exec. bd. Nemir Surg. Found., 1995. Recipient Nat. Rsch. Svc. award NIH, 1969-74. Fellow Am. Coll. Critical Care Medicine, Phila. Coll. Physicians (hon. 1990); mem. Found. Med. Edn. (founder, chmn.), Pa. Thoracic Soc. (critical care chmn. 1989-91). Home: 1830 Spruce St Philadelphia PA 19103-6603 Office: Presbyn Med Hosp 39th and Market Sts Philadelphia PA 19104

MARINO, RAUL, JR., neurosurgeon; b. São Paulo, Brazil, Mar. 22, 1936; s. Raul and Brigida Quartim (de Albuquerque) M.; m. Angela Zacarelli; children: Ricardo, Rodolfo. MD, U. São Paulo Med. Sch., 1961. Medical Diplomate. Resident Lahey Clinic, Boston, 1964-65; rsch. fellow Harvard Med. Sch., Boston, 1965-66; resident McGill U., Can., 1966-67; vis. scientist NIH, Bethesda, 1967-68; neurosurgeon, founder functional neurosurgery divsn. U. São Paulo, 1970-90; prof., chmn. divsn. neurosurgery Hosp. das Clínicas/U. São Paulo Med. Sch., 1990—. Author: The Japanese Brain, 1990; editor: Functional Neurosurgery, 1979. Med. lt. Brazilian Army, 1961. Mem. São Paulo Acad. Medicine (pres. 1993-95). Avocations: philosophy, theology, history of medicine. Office: S Paulo Neurol Inst, Rua Maestro Cardim 808, 01323001 São Paulo Brazil

MARINO, RICHARD J., publishing executive. With Harcourt/Brace/Jovanovich; sr. v.p. advtg. and mktg. ABC Cap Cities Pub. Corp.; assoc. pub. PC World Communications, 1990-92, pub.; pres., COO, 1994—. Office: PC World 501 2nd St Ste 600 San Francisco CA 94107-1431*

MARINO, SHEILA BURRIS, education educator; b. Knoxville, Nov. 24, 1947; d. David Paul and Lucille Cora (Maupin) Burris; m. Louis John Marino, Dec. 19, 1969; children: Sheila Noelle, Heather Michelle. BS, U. Tenn., 1969, MS, 1971, EdD, 1976; postgrad., W.Va. U., Europe. Elem./early childhood tchr. Knoxville City Schs., 1969-71; cooperating tchr. U. Tenn., Knoxville, 1969-71; dir. early childhood edn./tchr. Glenville (W.Va.) State Coll., 1971-72, Colo. Women's Coll., Denver, 1972-73; asst. prof. edn. Lander U., Greenwood, S.C., 1973-75; instr., spl. asst. coordinator of elem./early childhood edn. U. Tenn., 1975-76; prof. edn., dir. clin. experiences, asst. dean Sch. Edn. Lander U., 1976-95, dean sch. edn., 1993-94; cons. in field; dir. Creative Activities Prog. for Children, Lander U., 1979—; mem. W.Va. Gov.'s Early Childhood Adv. Bd., 1971-72, Gov.'s Team of Higher Edn. Profls. on Comprehensive Plan for S.C. Early Childhood Edn., 1982. Contbr. articles to profl. jours.; author: International Children's Literature, 1989. Bd. dirs. Greenwood Lit. Coun., v.p., 1990, pres., 1991; bd. dirs. St. Nicholas Speech and Hearing Ctr., Greenwood, pres., 1992; bd. dirs. Old Ninety-Six coun. Girl Scouts U.S.A., 1987-92; vol. March of Dimes Program, Greenwood, 1987. Mem. AAUW (pres. 1990—), AAUP, SNEA (state advisor 1981-88), S.C. Student Edn. Assn., Piedmont Assn. Children and Adults with Learning Disabilities (pres. 1986—, exec. bd.), Learning Disabilities Assn. S.C. (pres. 1990-94), S.C. Edn. Assn., S.C. Assn. for Children Under Six, So. Assn. for Children under Six, S.C. Assn. Tchr. Educators, Piedmont Reading Coun. (v.p. 1985-86, 90-91, pres. 1986-88, 91-92, 96—), S.C. Coun. Internat. Reading Assn. (exec. bd. 1986-88, 91—), Delta Kappa Gamma (pres. Epsilon chpt. 1984-88, 92-94, mem. exec. bd.), Pi Lambda Theta, Kappa Delta Pi (pres. U. Tenn. chpt. 1974-75), Phi Delta Kappa (v.p. 1988-90, pres. Lander U. chpt. 1990-91, 94-96). Democrat. Presbyterian. Avocations: reading, gardening, swimming, music, arts and crafts. Home: 103 Essex Ct Greenwood SC 29649-9561 Office: Lander U Stanley Avenue Greenwood SC 29649

MARINO, WILLIAM FRANCIS, telecommunications industry executive, consultant; b. Phila., Dec. 28, 1948; s. William F. and Edith Ellen (Dougherty) M.; m. Mary Ellen Klems, Sept. 29, 1979; children: Kiersten Leigh, Meghan Lyn. Student, Ohio State U., 1967; BS in Fin. and Acctg., Widener U., 1970. Sr. acctg., fin. positions U.S. Steel Corp., Pitts., 1970-83; v.p. U.S. Steel Credit Corp., Pitts., 1983-85; dir. fin. programs CIS Corp., Syracuse, N.Y., 1985, v.p. instl. sales, 1986; pres. CIS Credit Corp., Syracuse, N.Y., 1987, v.p. fin., 1988; v.p., chmn. reorganization com. Continental Info. Systems Corp., Syracuse, N.Y., 1989; v.p. fin., CFO ITEC Corp., Lake Bluff, Ill., 1990-91; pres., CEO ITEC Corp., Lake Bluff, 1991—; chmn. The Telecare Group, Inc.; advisor, cons. Chong & Assocs., N.Y.C., 1989. Advisor Hiawatha coun. Boy Scouts Am., Syracuse, 1987; dir. Cystic Fibrosis Found., Syracuse, 1987-88. Recipient Century award Boy Scouts Am., Syracuse, 1988. Mem. Am. Assn. Equipment Lessors, Am. Mgmt. Assn., Fin. Execs. Inst., Aircraft, Owners & Pilots Assn. Republican. Avocations: pvt. pilot, cross country skiing. Home: 1280 Thornbury Ln Libertyville IL 60048-2361 Office: ITEC Corp 999 Sherwood Dr Lake Bluff IL 60044-2203

MARIO, ERNEST, pharmaceutical company executive; b. Clifton, N.J., June 12, 1938; s. Jerry and Edith (Meijer) M.; m. Mildred Martha Daume, Dec. 10, 1961; children: Christopher Bradley, Gregory Gerald, Jeremy Konrad. B.S. in Pharmacy, Rutgers U., 1961; M.S. in Phys. Scis., U. R.I., 1963, Ph.D. in Phys. Scis., 1965. Registered pharmacist, R.I., N.Y. Vice pres. mfg. Smith Kline Corp., Phila., 1975-77; v.p. mfg. ops. U.S. Pharm. Co. (divsn. E. R. Squibb), New Brunswick, N.J., 1977-79; v.p., gen. mgr. chem. div. E. R. Squibb, Princeton, N.J., 1979-81; pres. chem. and engring. div., sr. v.p. Squibb Corp., Princeton, 1981-84; v.p. Squibb Corp., 1984-86; pres., COO Glaxo Inc., 1986-88, chmn., CEO, 1988, chmn., 1989-91; CEO Glaxo Holdings plc, 1989-93, dep. chmn., 1991-93; co-chmn., CEO, Alza Corp., Palo Alto, Calif., 1993—; grad. asst., instr. U. R.I., Kingston, 1961-66; research fellow Inst. Neurol. Diseases, Bethesda, Md., 1963-65. Contbr. articles to profl. jours. Trustee Duke U., Rockefeller U., U. R.I. Found.; mem. pres.'s coun. U. R.I.; chmn. Am. Found. for Pharm. Edn.; bd. dirs. Nat. Found. Infectious Diseases, Antigenics, Pharm. Product Devel., Stanford Health Svcs., Tech. Mus. Innovation; mem. Calif. gov.'s coun. on biotech. Office: Alza Corp 950 Page Mill Rd Palo Alto CA 94304-1012

MARION, GAIL ELAINE, reference librarian; b. Bloomington, Ill., May 31, 1952; d. Ralph Herbert and Norma Mae (Crump) Nyberg; m. David Louis Marion, May 13, 1972 (div. Apr. 1983). AA in Liberal Arts, Fla. Jr. Coll., 1976; BA in U.S. History, U. North Fla., 1978; MS in Libr. and Info. Sci., Fla. State U., 1985. Law libr., legal rschr. Mathews Osborne et al, Jacksonville, Fla., 1979-82; reference libr. City of Jacksonville-Pub. Librs., 1982—. With U.S. Army, 1970-72, maj. U.S. Army Res., 1978—, with Fla. Army N.G., 1974-78. Named to Outstanding Young Women of Am., 1985; N.G. Officers Assn. scholar, 1980. Mem. ALA, WAC Vets. Assn., Adj. Gen. Regimental Corps, Res. Officers Assn., Fla. Libr. Assn., Fla. Paleontol. Soc., Jacksonville Gem and Mineral Soc. Republican. Methodist. Avocations: art, history, photography, reading, rock hounding. Home: 3200 Hartley Rd Apt 70 Jacksonville FL 32257-6719 Office: Jacksonville Pub Librs 122 N Ocean St Jacksonville FL 32202-3314

MARION, JOHN LOUIS, fine arts auctioneer and appraiser; b. N.Y.C., Nov. 27, 1933; s. Louis John and Florence Adelaide (Winters) M.; children: John L., Deborah Mary, Therese Marie, Michelle Marie; m. Anne Burnett Windfohr, May 26, 1988. BS, Fordham U., 1956; postgrad., Columbia U., 1960-61. With Sotheby Parke Bernet Inc., N.Y.C., 1960—, dir., 1965—, v.p., 1966-70, exec. v.p., 1970-72, pres., 1972-87; chmn. bd. Sotheby's Inc., N.Y.C., 1975—, now hon. chmn.; bd. dirs. Sotheby Holdings Inc., London. Chmn. fine arts N.Y.C. div. Am. Cancer Soc., 1983—; vice chmn. bldg. steering com. Dobbs Ferry (N.Y.) Hosp., 1975; bd. dirs. Internat. Found. Art Research, Ctr. for Hope. Served as lt. (j.g.) USN, 1956-60. Mem. Appraisers Assn. Am., Lotos Club, Eldorado Club, Shady Oaks, Vintage Club. Home: 1400 Shady Oaks Ln Fort Worth TX 76107-3538 Office: Sotheby's Inc 1334 York Ave New York NY 10021-4806*

MARION, JOHN MARTIN, academic administrator; b. Fitchburg, Mass., Jan. 11, 1947; s. Don Louis and Violet Pearl Marion; m. Joann Elizabeth Trzcinski, Aug. 8, 1970; children: Benjamin Andrew, Jessica Noelle. BS in Edn., Fitchburg State Coll., 1969, M in Edn., 1971; postgrad., Pepperdine U. Tchr. Groton (Mass.) Dunstable Regional Schs., 1969-84; computer tchr. Littleton (Mass.) Pub. Schs., 1985-86; computer coord. K-12th grades Newburyport (Mass.) Pub. Schs., 1986-90; chair Acad. Computing Endicott Coll., Beverly, Mass., 1990—; instr. Merrimack Edn. Ctr., Chelmsford, Mass., 1980-90; trainer, cons. Logo Computer Sys., Inc., N.Y.C., 1984-90; tchr. trainer Lego-Decta, Lego Sys., Inc., Enfield, Conn., 1987-90; mem. adv. bd. Claris Software Co.; bd. dirs. Mass. Computer Using Educator, 1989-90. Fulbright scholar tchr. exch., Southampton, Eng., 1973-74. Mem. Internat. Soc. Tech. in Edn. Home: 123 Chestnut St Pepperell MA 01463-1019 Office: Endicott Coll 376 Hale St Beverly MA 01915-2096

MARION, MARJORIE ANNE, English educator; b. Winterset, Iowa, May 6, 1935; d. Virgil Arthur and Marilyn Ruth (Sandy) Hammon; m. Robert H.

Marion, Dec. 20, 1964; 1 dau., Kathryn Ruth. BA, Colo. Coll., 1958; MA, Purdue U., 1969; postgrad., Inst. Mgmt. Lifelong Edn. Harvard U., 1981. Chairperson English dept. Lincoln-Way High Sch., New Lenox, Ill., 1964-68; dir. pub. rels. Coll. St. Francis, Joliet, Ill., 1968-70, chairperson English dept., 1971-75, chairperson div. humanities and fine arts, 1975-79, coord. instructional devel., 1979-80, dir. continuing edn., 1980-84, acting v.p. for acad. affairs, 1984-85, dean of faculty, 1985-89, assoc. prof. English, 1989—; dir. Freshman Core Program, 1993-95; dir. Writing Ctr., 1996; mem. vis. team North Cen. Assn., Joliet & Lockport, Ill, 1975-79; lectr. at ednl. workshops and insts.; TV and radio appearances regarding lifelong edn., Chgo., St. Louis, Albuquerque, Phoenix, 1982-85. Drama critic Joliet Herald News, 1970-82. Recipient Pres.'s award Coll. St. Francis, 1975. Mem. Am. Assn. Higher Edn., Nat. Coun. Tchrs. of English, Nat. Acad. Advising Assn. Roman Catholic.

MARION, MILDRED RUTH, honor society executive; b. St. Louis, Nov. 3, 1904; d. Charles G. and Cora B. (Sutton) Bryan; m. Leroy B. Bale, Mary 29, 1930 (div. May 1, 1940); m. Eugene H. Marion, Dec. 24, 1941 (dec.). PhB, U. Chgo., 1928; MBA, Northwestern U., 1953, postgrad., 1976-90. CPCU. Underwriter Liberty Mut. Ins. Co., Chgo., 1929-69; ret., 1969; exec. sec., editor newsletter, del. Delta Mu Delta Honor Soc., Chgo., 1970—; counsellor Chgo. Campus, Northwestern U., 1958-69. Mem. Northwestern U. Guild (chmn. bylaws 1983-85), Fedn. Bus. Honor Socs. (bd. govs. 1991), Assn. Coll. Honor Socs. (chmn. ins. com.), Woman's Club Evanston (membership com. 1974-76, corr. sec. 1991-92, chmn. printing, chmn. elections), Order Ea. Star (worth matron 1974-76), Phi Chi theta (nat. pres. 1964-66, chmn. bylaws alumni chpt. 1984-90, Cert. 1989, Gold Key award 1991), Delta Mu Delta (nat. pres. 1962-64, rep., spl. plaque Beta chpt. 1969, nat. spl. plaque 1986, 91). Republican. Avocations: sewing, reading, music, art.

MARIONI, TOM, artist; b. Cin., May 21, 1937; s. John D. and Jennie (Geiss) M.; m. Kathan Brown, June 14, 1983; children by previous marriage: Marino, Anthony, Miles. MFA, Cin. Art Acad., 1959. Curator, Richmond Art Ctr. (Calif.), 1968-71; founding dir. Mus. Conceptual Art, San Francisco, 1970-84. Exhibited one-man shows: Galeria Foksal, Warsaw, Poland, 1975, DeYoung Mus., San Francisco, 1977, Modern Art Gallery, Vienna, Austria, 1979, Crown Point Press, San Francisco, 1993, Margarete Roeder Gallery, N.Y.C., 1994; group shows include: Tate Gallery, London, 1982, Belca House, Kyoto, Japan, 1982, Mus. Contemporary Art, L.A., 1995; editor, designer Vision, 1975-81. Mem. tech. assistance com. San Francisco Redevel. Agy., 1982—. Served with U.S. Army, 1960-63. W.Ger. Nat. Endowment Arts grantee, 1980; Guggenheim Found. fellow, 1981; Awards in Visual Arts grantee, 1984. Address: 657 Howard St San Francisco CA 94105-3915

MARIOTTI, JAY ANTHONY, journalist; b. Ellwood City, Pa., June 22, 1959; s. Geno Anthony and Dolores Virginia (Lordi) M.; m. Dana Lynne Barnard, Apr. 19, 1985; children: Karina, Allison. Student, Ohio U., 1976-80. Sports writer The Detroit News, 1980-85; sports columnist The Cin. Post, 1985-87, The Rocky Mountain News, Denver, 1987-89, The Denver Post, 1989-90, The Nat. Sports Daily, N.Y.C., 1990-91, The Chgo. Sun-Times, 1991—. Recipient AP Sports Editors award, 1987, 1993, Crain's Forty under 40 award Crain's Chgo. Bus., 1992, Peter Lisagor award Chgo. Headline Club, 1992. Avocations: reading, tennis, golf, travel. Office: Chicago Sun-Times 401 N Wabash Ave Chicago IL 60611-5642*

MARIS, STEPHEN S., lawyer, educator; b. Dallas, Dec. 19, 1949; m. Bronwyn Holmes; children: Shane, Kara. BS, Stephen F. Austin State, 1971; JD, So. Meth. U., 1975. Bar: U.S. Dist. Ct. (no. dist.) Tex. 1975, U.S. Dist. Ct. (ea. dist.) Tex. 1986, U.S. Dist. Ct. (so. dist.) Tex. 1992, U.S. Ct. Appeals (5th cir.) 1980, U.S. Ct. Appeals (11th cir.) 1981, U.S. Supreme Ct. Tex. 1975. Assoc. Passman & Jones, Dallas, 1975-80, ptnr., 1980-87; ptnr. Fulbright & Jaworski, Dallas, 1987—; prof. So. Ill. U., 1979-80, So. Meth. U., Dallas, 1980—; mem. faculty Nat. Inst. Trial Advocacy, 1980—. Editor: Southwest Law Journal, 1973-75. Mem. ABA, State Bar Tex., Dallas Bar Assn., Barristers, Order Coif, Phi Delta Phi. Office: Fulbright & Jaworski 2200 Ross Ave Ste 2800 Dallas TX 75201-2750

MARISOL (MARISOL ESCOBAR), sculptor; b. Paris. Ed., Ecole des Beaux-Arts, Paris, 1949, Art Students League, N.Y.C., 1950, New Sch. for Social Research, 1951-54, Hans Hofmann Sch., N.Y.C., 1951-54; DFA (hon.), Moore Coll. Arts, Phila., 1969, R.I. Sch. Design, 1986, SUNY, Buffalo, 1992. One-woman shows include Leo Castelli Gallery, 1958, Stable Gallery, 1962, 64, Sidney Janis Gallery, N.Y.C., 1966, 67, 73, 75, 81, 84, 89, Hanover Gallery, London, 1967, Moore Coll. Art, Phila., 1970, Worcester (Mass.) Art Mus., 1971, N.Y. Cultural Center, 1973, Columbus (Ohio) Gallery of Fine Arts, 1974, Makler Gallery, Phila., 1982, Boca Raton Mus. Art, Fla., 1988, Galerie Tokoro, Tokyo, 1989, Hasagawa Gallery, Tokyo, 1989, Nat. Portrait Gallery, Washington, 1991, Marlborough Gallery, 1995, Hakone Open Air Mus., Kanagawa, Japan, 1995, Mus. Modern Art, Shiga, Japan, 1995, Iwai City Art Mus., Fukushima, Japan, 1995, Kagoshima City (Japan) Mus. Art, 1995, Museo de Arte Contempo Ranio, Caracas, Venezuela, 1996, numerous others; exhibited in group shows including Painting of a Decade, Tate Gallery, London, 1964, New Realism, Municipal Mus., The Hague, 1964, Carnegie Internat., Pitts., 1964, Art of the U.S.A. 1670-1966, Whitney Mus. Am. Art, N.Y.C., 1966, American Sculpture of the Sixties, Mus. of Art, Los Angeles, 1967, Biennale, Venice, 1968, Art Inst. Chgo., 1968, Boymans-van Beuningen Mus., Rotterdam, The Netherlands, 1968, Inst. Contemporary Art, London, 1968, Fondation Maeght, Paris, 1970, Hirshhorn Mus. and Sculpture Garden, 1984, Nat. Portrait Gallery, Washington, 1987, Heckscher Mus., Huntington, N.Y., 1987, Whitney Mus. at Philip Morris, N.Y.C., 1988, Rose Art Mus., Waltham, Mass., 1990, Nat. Portrait Gallery, London, 1993; represented in permanent collections at Mus. Modern Art, N.Y.C., Whitney Mus. Am. Art, Albright-Knox Gallery, Buffalo, Hakone Open Air Mus., Tokyo, Nat. Portrait Gallery, Washington, Harry N. Abrams Collection, N.Y.C., Yale U. Art Gallery, Art Inst. Chgo., Met. Mus., N.Y.C., numerous others; pub. installation Am. Mcht. Mariner's Meml., Promenade Battery Pk. Pier A., Port of N.Y., N.Y.C. Mem. Am. Acad. and Inst. Arts and Letters (v.p. art 1984-87). Address: 427 Washington St 7th Fl New York NY 10013

MARITZ, WILLIAM E., communications company executive; b. St. Louis; m. Phyllis Mesker; 4 children. Grad., Princeton U., 1950. With Maritz Inc., St. Louis, now pres., chmn. bd. Bd. dirs. Community Sch., John Burroughs Sch., Princeton U., Sta. KETC, Mo. Bot. Garden, St. Luke's Hosp., Washington U., Brown Group, Am. Youth Found., Camping and Edn. Found., Cystic Fibrosis, others; founder, chmn. bd. Laclede's Landing Devel. Corp., St. Louis; chmn. bd. VP Fair Found. Recipient Levee Stone award Downtown St. Louis; Right Arm of St. Louis award, Regional Commerce and Growth Assn. Served with USN. Home: 10 Upper Ladue Rd Saint Louis MO 63124-1630 Office: Maritz Inc 1375 N Highway Dr Fenton MO 63026-1929*

MARK, ALAN SAMUEL, lawyer; b. N.Y.C., Mar. 13, 1947; s. Stanley M. and Miriam (Gordon) M.; m. Paula Calimafde, Oct. 14, 1978; children: Ilana, Clifford, Clayton. Student, Johns Hopkins U., 1965-66; BA, NYU, 1969; JD cum laude, Am. U., 1973; LLM in Taxation, George Washington U., 1977. Bar: D.C. 1973, Maryland 1979. Ptnr. Verner, Liipfert, Bernhard, McPherson, Washington, 1982-85, Finley, Kumble, Wagner et al, Washington, 1986-88, Perito & Dubuc, Washington, 1988-91; sr. counsel Paley, Rothman Goldstein, Rosenberg & Cooper Chtd., Bethesda, Md., 1991—; adj. prof. law Georgetown Law Sch., Am. U. Washington Coll. Law. With U.S. Army. 1969-75. Mem. ABA. Avocation: tennis.

MARK, HANS MICHAEL, aerospace engineering educator, physicist; b. Mannheim, Germany, June 17, 1929; came to U.S., 1940, naturalized, 1945; s. Herman Francis and Maria (Schramek) M.; m. Marion G. Thorpe, Jan. 28, 1951; children: Jane H., James P. A.B. in Physics, U. Calif. at Berkeley, 1951; Ph.D., MIT, 1954; Sc.D. (hon.), Fla. Inst. Tech., 1978; D. Eng. (hon.), Poly. U. N.Y., 1982; DEng (hon.), Milw. Sch. Engring., 1991; LHD (hon.), St. Edward's U., 1993. Research assoc. MIT, 1954-55, asst. prof., 1958-60; research physicist Lawrence Radiation Lab., U. Calif. at Livermore, 1955-58, 60-69, exptl. physics div. leader, 1960-64; assoc. prof. nuclear engring. U. Calif. at Berkeley, 1960-66, prof., 1966-69, chmn. dept. nuclear engring., 1964-69; lectr. dept. applied sci. U. Calif. at Davis, 1969-73; cons. prof. engring. Stanford, 1973-84; dir. NASA-Ames Research Center, 1969-77; undersec. Air Force, Washington, 1977-79; sec. Air Force, 1979-81; dep. adminstr. NASA, Washington, 1981-84; chancellor U. Tex. System, Austin, 1984-92; prof. aerospace engring. and engring. mechanics U. Tex., Austin, 1988—; mem. Pres.'s Adv. Group Sci. and Tech., 1975-76; bd. dirs. BDM Internat. Corp., Astronautics Corp. Am., MAC Equipment Co., Arrowsmith Techs., Inc.; trustee Poly. U., 1984—. Author: (with N.T. Olson) Experiments in Modern Physics, 1966 (with E. Teller and J.S. Foster, Jr.) Power and Security, 1976, (with A. Levine) The Management of Research Institutions, 1983, The Space Station-A Personal Journey, 1987; also numerous articles.; Editor: (with S. Fernbach) Properties of Matter Under Unusual Conditions, 1969, (with Lowell Wood) Energy in Physics, War and Peace, 1988. Recipient Disting. Svc. medal NASA, 1972, 77, medal for exceptional engrng. achievement, 1984, Exceptional Civilian Svc. award USAF, 1979, Disting. Pub. Svc, medal, Dept. Def., 1981. Fellow AIAA (Von Karman lectr. astronautics 1992), Am. Phys. Soc.; mem. Nat. Acad. Engring., Am. Nuclear Soc., Am. Geophys. Union, Coun. Fgn. Rels., Cosmos Club. Achievements include research on nuclear energy levels, nuclear reactions, applications, nuclear energy for practical purposes, atomic flourescence yields, measurement X-rays above atmosphere, spacecraft and experimental aircraft design. Office: U Tex Dept Aerospace Engring & Engring Mechs Austin TX 78712-1085

MARK, HARRY HORST, ophthalmologist, researcher; b. Breslau, Germany, Jan. 21, 1931; came to U.S., 1957; s. Lothar and Ruth Mark. MD, U. Vienna, Austria, 1957. Diplomate Am. Bd. Ophthalmology. Intern George Washington U., Washington, 1957; resident Boston U., 1958-60, SUNY, Bklyn., 1960-62; pvt. practice New Haven, 1963—; attending ophthalmologist Yale-New Haven Hosp., 1963—, St. Raphael Hosp., New Haven, 1963—. Author: Optokinetics, 1982; contbr. articles to profl. jours. Avocations: optics, history, sailing. Home: 16 Broadway North Haven CT 06473-2301 Office: 2 Church St S New Haven CT 06519-1717

MARK, HENRY ALLEN, lawyer; b. Bklyn., May 16, 1909; s. Henry Adam and Mary Clyde (McCarroll) M.; m. Isobel Ross Arnold, June 26, 1940; BA, Williams Coll., 1932; JD, Cornell U., 1935. Bars: N.Y. 1936, Conn. 1981, U.S. Dist. Ct. (so. dist.) N.Y. 1943. Assoc. firm Allin & Tucker, N.Y.C., 1935-40; mng. atty. Indemnity Ins. Co. of N.Am., N.Y.C., 1940-43; assoc. firm Mudge, Stern, Williams & Tucker, N.Y.C., 1943-50, Cadwalder, Wickersham & Taft, N.Y.C., 1950-53; ptnr. Cadwalader, Wickersham & Taft, 1953-74; lectr. Practicing Law Inst., N.Y.C., 1955-68. Mem. adv. com. zoning Village of Garden City (N.Y.), 1952-54, planning commn., 1957-59, zoning bd. appeals, 1959-61, trustee, 1961-65, mayor, 1965-67; chmn. planning commn. Town of Washington (Conn.), 1980-84; trustee The Gunnery Sch., Washington, Conn., 1980-86; mem. adv. com. on continuing care State of Conn., 1996—. Recipient Disting. Alumnus award Cornell U., 1983. Mem. ABA, N.Y. Bar Assn., Assn. Bar City of N.Y., Conn. Bar Assn., Hartford County Bar Assn., Cornell Law Assn. (pres. 1971-73), Bar Assn. Nassau County (grievance com. 1974-77), St. Andrew's Soc., Phi Beta Kappa, Sigma Phi, Phi Delta Phi. Republican. Congregationalist. Lodge: Masons. Address: 80 Loeffler Rd # G405 Bloomfield CT 06002-2274

MARK, JAMES B. D., surgeon; b. Nashville, June 26, 1929; s. Julius and Margaret (Baer) M.; m. Jean Rambar, Feb. 5, 1957; children: Jonathan, Michael, Margaret, Elizabeth, Katherine. B.A., Vanderbilt U., 1950, M.D., 1953. Intern, resident in gen. and thoracic surgery Yale-New Haven Hosp., 1953-60; instr. to asst. prof. surgery Yale U., 1960-65; assoc. prof. surgery Stanford U., 1965-69, prof., 1969-97, Johnson and Johnson prof. surgery, 1972-97, head div. thoracic surgery, 1972-97, assoc. dean clin. affairs, 1988-92; chief staff Stanford U. Hosp., 1988-92; governing bd. Health Systems Agy., Santa Clara County, 1978-80; sr. Fulbright-Hays fellow, vis. prof. surgery U. Dar es Salaam, Tanzania, 1972-73. Mem. editl. bd.: Jour. Thoracic and Cardiovasc. Surgery, 1986-94, World Jour. Surgery, 1995—; contbr. numerous articles to sci. jours. Bd. dirs. Stanford U. Hosp., 1992-94. With USPHS, 1955-57. Fellow ACS (pres. No. Calif. chpt. 1980-81), Am. Coll. Chest Physicians (pres. 1994-95); mem. Am. Assn. Thoracic Surgery, Am. Surg. Assn., Western Surg. Assn., Pacific Coast Surg. Assn., Halsted Soc. (pres. 1984), Western Thoracic Surg. Assn. (pres. 1992-93), Calif. Acad. Medicine (pres. 1978), Santa Clara County Med. Soc. (pres. 1976-77). Home: 921 Casanueva Pl Stanford CA 94305-1001 Office: Stanford U CVRB Surgery Med Ctr Stanford CA 94305

MARK, JOHN, film company executive. With John Mark Film Co., L.A., 1971—; chmn., ceo John Mark Film Co., Beverly Hills, Calif., 1992—. Office: John Mark Film Corp 421 N Rodeo Dr # 15283 Beverly Hills CA 90210-4500*

MARK, LAURENCE MAURICE, film producer; b. N.Y.C., Nov. 22; s. James Mark and Marion Lorraine (Huebner) Green. BA, Wesleyan U., 1971; MA, NYU, 1973. Exec. dir., publicity Paramount Pictures, N.Y.C., 1978-80; v.p., West Coast mktg. Paramount Pictures, L.A., 1980-82, v.p., prodn., 1982-84; exec. v.p., prodn. Twentieth Century Fox, L.A., 1984-86; pres. Laurence Mark Prodns., L.A., 1986—. Exec. prodr.: (films) Black Widow, 1987, My Stepmother is an Alien, 1988, Working Girl, 1988, Mr. Destiny, 1990, Sister Act 2: Back in the Habit, 1993, Old Friends, 1997, (TV) Sweet Bird of Youth, 1989, Oliver Twist, 1997; prodr.: (films) Cookie, 1989, True Colors, 1991, One Good Cop, 1991, The Adventures of Huck Finn, 1993, Cutthroat Island, 1995, Tom and Huck, 1995, Jerry Maguire, 1996, Romy and Michele's High School Reunion, 1997, Deep Rising, 1997; prodr. (theatre) Brooklyn Laundry, 1991, (Broadway) Big, 1996. Mem. Acad. Motion Pictures Arts and Scis. Home: 7888 Woodrow Wilson Dr West Hollywood CA 90046-1256 Office: Hollywood Pictures Walt Disney Studios 500 S Buena Vista St Burbank CA 91521-0001

MARK, MELVIN, consulting mechanical engineer, educator; b. St. Paul, Nov. 15, 1922; s. Isadore William and Fannye (Abrahamson) M.; m. Elizabeth J. Wyner, Sept. 9, 1951; children: Jonathan S., David W., Peter B. B.M.E., U. Minn., 1943, M.S., 1946; Sc.D. (Teaching, Research fellow), Harvard, 1950. Registered profl. engr., Mass., Minn. Instr. N.D. State U., 1943-44, U. Minn., 1945-47; project mgr. Gen. Electric Co., Lynn., Mass., 1950-52; mgr. Raytheon Co., Wayland, Mass., 1952-56; cons. engr., 1956—; prof. Lowell Technol. Inst., 1957-59, dean faculty, 1959-62; prof. mech. engring. Northeastern U., Boston, 1963-84; dean engring. Northeastern U., 1968-79, provost, sr. v.p. for acad. affairs, 1979-84; vis. lectr. Mass. Inst. Tech., 1955, Brandeis U., 1958; vis. prof. U. Mass., 1984-86; mem. Mass. Bd. Registration of Profl. Engrs. and Land Surveyors, 1990—. Author: Thermodynamics: An Auto-Instructional Text, 1967, Concepts of Thermodynamics, 1975, Thermodynamics: Principles and Applications, 1979, Engineering Thermodynamics, 1985. Contbr. articles to profl. jours. Served with USAAF, 1944-45. Recipient prize Lincoln Arc Welding Found., 1947. Hon. fellow ASME (fellow 1948-50); mem. Am. Soc. Engring. Edn., Sigma Xi, Tau Beta Pi, Pi Tau Sigma, Phi Kappa Phi. Patentee in field. Home: 17 Larch Rd Newton MA 02168-1413 Office: 93 Union St Suite 400 Newton Center MA 02159

MARK, MICHAEL LAURENCE, music educator; b. Schenectady, N.Y., Dec. 1, 1936; s. David and Ruth (Garbowitz) M.; m. Lois Nitekman, Jan. 28, 1942; children: Michelle, Diana. BM, The Cath. U. of Am., 1958, DMA, 1969; MA, George Washington U., 1960; M in Music Edn., U. Mich., 1962. Tchr. Prince George's County, Md. Pub. Schs., 1958-60, 61-66; assoc. prof. music Morgan State U., Balt., 1966-70; supr. music Auburn (N.Y.) Enlarged Sch. Dist., 1970-72; dir. music Elmira (N.Y.) Enlarged Sch. Dist., 1972-73; assoc. prof., sch. music Cath. U. Am., Washington, 1973-81; dean grad. sch., prof. music Towson (Md.) State U., 1981-95, prof. music, 1995—; Edtl. com. five jours. in field. Author: Contemporary Music Education, 1978, 3rd rev. edit., 1996, Source Readings in Music Education Histor, 1982; co-author: A History of American Music Education, 1992. Mem. Music Educators Nat. Conf. (numerous coms.), Coll. Music Soc., Md. Music Educators Assn. (pres.-elect 1997—). Avocations: travel, woodworking. Office: Music Dept Towson State U Towson MD 21204

MARK, PETER, director, conductor; b. N.Y.C., Oct. 31, 1940; s. Irving and Edna M.; m. Thea Musgrave, Oct. 2, 1971. BA (Woodrow Wilson fellow), Columbia U., 1961; MS, Juilliard Sch. Music, 1963. Prof. music and dramatic art U. Calif., Santa Barbara, 1965-94; fellow Creative Arts Inst., U. Calif., 1968-69, 71-72; guest condr. Wolf Trap Orch., 1979, N.Y.C. Opera, 1981, L.A. Opera Theater, 1981, Royal Opera House, London, 1982, Hong Kong Philharm. Orch., 1984, Jerusalem Symphony Orch., 1988, Tulsa Opera, 1988, Compania Nacional de Opera, Mexico City, 1989, 92, N.Y. Pops, Carnegie Hall, 1991. Concert violist U.S., S.Am., Europe, 1961-67; artistic dir., condr. Va. Opera, Norfolk, 1975—, gen. dir., 1978—; condr.: Am. premier of Mary, Queen of Scots (Musgrave), 1978; World premier of A Christmas Carol (Musgrave), 1979, of Harriet, the Woman Called Moses (Musgrave), 1985, of Simon Bolivar (Musgrave), 1984, Porgy and Bess, Buenos Aires, Mexico City and São Paulo, 1992, Orlando Opera co., 1993, Richmond Symphony, 1993, Krakow Opera, 1995, Pacific Opera Victoria (Can.), 1996, Cleve. Opera, 1996, Festival Pucciniano-Torre del Lago, Italy, 1996. Recipient Elias Lifchey viola award Juilliard Sch. Music, 1963; named hon. citizen of Norfolk (Va.). Mem. Musicians Union, Phi Beta Kappa. Office: Va Opera PO Box 2580 Norfolk VA 23501-2580

MARK, REUBEN, consumer products company executive; b. Jersey City, N.J., Jan. 21, 1939; s. Edward and Libbie (Berman) M.; m. Arlene Slobzian, Jan. 10, 1964; children: Lisa, Peter, Stephen. AB, Middlebury Coll., 1960; MBA, Harvard U., 1963. With Colgate-Palmolive Co., N.Y.C., 1963—; pres., gen. mgr. Colgate-Palmolive Co., Venezuela, 1972-73, Can., 1973-74; v.p., gen. mgr. Far East div. Colgate-Palmolive Co., 1974-75, v.p., gen. mgr. household products div., 1975-79, group v.p. domestic ops., 1979-81, exec. v.p., 1981-83, chief operating officer, 1983-84, pres., 1983-86, chief exec. officer, 1984—, chmn. bd., 1986—; lectr. Sch. Bus. Adminstrn., U. Conn., 1977. Served with U.S. Army, 1961. Mem. Soap and Detergent Assn. (bd. dirs.), Grocery Mfrs. Am. (dir.), Nat. Exec. Service Corp. Office: Colgate-Palmolive Co 300 Park Ave New York NY 10022-7402*

MARK, RICHARD KUSHAKOW, internist; b. N.Y.C., Feb. 11, 1951; s. Eugene and Gertrude (Kushakow) M.; m. Harriet Bass, Sept. 17, 1989; children: Sabrina, Ari Etan. BS, Hofstra U., 1972; MD, U. Autonomous Guadalajara, 1976, SUNY, Bklyn., 1977. Diplomate Am. Bd. Internal Medicine. Resident in medicine Maimonides Med. Ctr., Bklyn., 1977-82; clin. instr. medicine Downstate Med. Ctr., Bklyn., 1982-90, asst. prof. medicine, 1990-93; prof. clin. medicine CUNY, 1993—; pvt. practice internal medicine Bklyn., 1982—; dept. attending emergency Cabrini Med. Ctr., N.Y.C., 1982-84; med. cons. The Lighthouse. Author: Consumer's Guide to Preventive Medicine, 1996. Mem. N.Y.C. Coalition for the Homeless, 1986—, The Children's Fund., N.Y.C., 1990—. Recipient Cmty. Svc. award Borough of Bklyn., 1986, Physicians Recognition award AMA, 1993-97, Preceptorship award ACP, 1996, Tchr. of Yr. Maimonides Clin. Tchg. award CUNY, 1995, 96; recipient Tchr. of the Yr. 1982, 83. Mem. Acad. Medicine, Inter-Am. Coll. Medicine, King's County Med. Soc. Democrat. Jewish. Avocations: sailing, photography, skiing. Office: 8023 19th Ave Brooklyn NY 11214-1753

MARK, SHELLEY MUIN, economist, educator, government official; b. China, Sept. 9, 1922; came to U.S., 1923, naturalized, 1944; s. Hing D. and S. (Wong) M.; m. Janet Chong, Sept. 14, 1946 (dec. Mar. 1977); children—Philip, Diane, Paul, Peter, Steven; m. Tung Chow, July 8, 1978. B.A., U. Wash., 1943, Ph.D., 1956; M.S., Columbia, 1944; postgrad. (Ford Found. fellow), Harvard, 1959-60. Fgn. news reporter CBS, N.Y., 1945-46; instr. U. Wash., 1946-48; asst. prof. Ariz. State Coll., 1948-51; territorial economist OPS, Honolulu, 1951-53; prof. econs. U. Hawaii, 1953-62, dir. econ. rsch. ctr., 1959-62; dir. planning and econ. devel. State of Hawaii, 1962-74, state land use commr., 1962-74, state energy coord., 1973-74; dir. Office Land Use Coordination EPA, Washington, 1975-77; prof. econs. U. Hawaii, 1978—; rsch. fellow East-West Ctr., Inst. Econ. Devel. and Policy, 1984-94; Asian advisor Internat. Ctr. Econ. Growth, 1992—; sr. advisor Dept. Bus., Econ. Devel. and Tourism, Hawaii, 1995—; vis. scholar Harvard U., 1986; vis. faculty Grad. Sch. People's Bank of China, 1988; also econ. cons. Philippines Inst. Devel. Studies, Devel. Rsch. Ctr. State Coun., China, also other orgns.; mem. Gov.'s Adv. Com. Sci. and Tech., 1963-74, Oahu Transp. Policy Com., 1964-74, Regional Export Expansion Coun., 1964-74;. Author: Economics in Action, 4th edit., 1969, Macroeconomic Performance of Asia-Pacific Region, 1985, Development Economics and Developing Economies, 1990, Aspects of Chinese Economic Development, 1991; editor: Economic Interdependence and Cooperation in Asia-Pacific, 1993, Asian Transitional Economies, 1996; contbr. articles to profl. jours. Bd. dirs. U. Hawaii Rsch. Corp.; bd. dirs. Coun. State Planning Agys., pres., 1973-74, hon. mem., 1975—; governing bd. Coun. State Govts., 1972-74. Recipient Sackett Meml. award Columbia, 1944. Mem. Hawaii Govt. Employees Assn. (pres. univ. chpt., dir. 1958-59), Am. Econ. Assn., Royal Econ. Soc., Western Regional Sci. Assn. (pres. 1974-75, dir.), Phi Beta Kappa, Sigma Delta Chi. Mem. United Ch. of Christ. Home: 2036 Keeaumoku St Honolulu HI 96822-2526

MARK, SHEW-KUEY TOMMY, physics educator; b. Canton, China, Aug. 8, 1936; emigrated to Can., 1952, naturalized, 1952; s. Yook Sue and Nuey (Fong) M.; m. Yan Chu Woo, Sept. 9, 1961; children: Bethany Mark, Terence Mark. BSc, McGill U., 1960, MSc, 1962, PhD, 1965. Postdoctoral fellow NRC of Can., U. Man., 1965-66; asst. prof. McGill U., Montreal, 1966-70; assoc. prof. McGill U., 1970-75, prof. physics, 1975—; dir. McGill U. (Foster Radiation Lab.), 1971-79; chmn. dept. physics McGill U., 1982-90. Contbr. articles to profl. jours. Grantee Natural Scis. and Engring. Rsch. Coun. of Can., 1965—, DOE of U.S., 1990—. Mem. Canadian Assn. Physicists, Am. Phys. Soc., Canadian Assn. Univ. Tchrs. Home: 660 Victoria Ave, Westmount, PQ Canada H3Y 2R9 Office: 3600 University St, Montreal, PQ Canada H3A 2T8

MARKE, JULIUS JAY, law librarian, educator; b. N.Y.C., Jan. 12, 1913; s. Isidore and Anna (Taylor) M.; m. Sylvia Bolotin, Dec. 15, 1946; 1 child, Elisa Hope. BS, CCNY, 1934; LLB, NYU, 1937; BS in Lib. Sci., Columbia U., 1942. Bar: N.Y. 1938. Reference asst. N.Y. Pub. Libr., 1937-42; pvt. practice law N.Y.C., 1939-41; prof. law, law libr. NYU, 1949-83, prof. law emeritus, 1983—, interim dean of librs., 1975-77; Disting. Prof., dir. Law Libr. St. John's U. Sch. Law, 1983-95; disting. rsch. prof. law St. John's U. Sch. Law, Jamaica, N.Y., 1995—; lectr. Columbia Sch. Library Service, 1962-78, adj. prof., 1978-85; cons. Orientation Program Am. Law, 1965-68, Found. Overseas Law Libraries Am. Law, 1968-79, copyright Ford Found., law libraries, Coun. Fgn. Rels., 1990—, Shubert Archives, 1991, others. Author: Vignettes of Legal History, 1965, 2d series, 1977, Copyright and Intellectual Property, 1967 (with R. Sloane) Legal Research and Law Library Management, rev. edit., 1990, 96, 97; editor: Modern Legal Forms, 1953, The Holmes Reader, 1955, The Docket Series, 1955—, Bender's Legal Business Forms, 4 vols., 1962; compiler, editor: A Catalogue of the Law Collection at NYU with Selected Annotations, 1953, Dean's List of Recommended Reading for Pre-Law and Law Students, 1958, 84, and others; chmn. editl. bd. Oceana Group, 1977—, Index to Legal Periodicals, 1978—; columnist N.Y. Law Jour., 1970—; contbr. articles to profl. jours. Mem. publs. coun. N.Y.U., 1964-80. Sgt. AUS, 1943-45. Decorated Bronze Star. Mem. ABA, Am. Assn. Law Librs. (pres. 1962-63, Disting. Svc. award 1986), Assn. Am. Law Schs., Coun. of Nat. Libr. Assns. (exec. bd., v.p. 1959, 60), Law Libr. Assn. Greater N.Y. (pres. 1949, 50, chmn. joint com. on libr. edn. 1950-52, 60-61), NYU Law Alumni Assn. (Judge Edward Weinfeld award 1987, mem. exec. bd. 1988—), Columbia Sch. Libr. Svc. Alumni Assn. (pres. 1973-75), Order of Coif (pres. NYU Law Sch. br. 1970-83), NYU Faculty Club (pres. 1966-68), Field Inn, Phi Delta Phi. Home: 4 Peter Cooper Rd Apt 8F New York NY 10010-6746

MARKEE, KATHERINE MADIGAN, librarian, educator; b. Cleve., Feb. 24, 1931; d. Arthur Alexis and Margaret Elizabeth (Madigan) M. AB, Trinity Coll., Washington, 1953; MA, Columbia U., 1962; MLS, Case Western Res. U., 1968. Employment mgr., br. store tng. supr. The May Co., Cleve., 1965-67; assoc. prof. libr. sci., data bases libr. Purdue U. Libr., West Lafayette, Ind., 1968—. Contbr. articles to profl. jours. Mem. ALA, AAUP, Spl. Librs. Assn., Ind. Online Users Group, Sigma Xi (Rsch. Support award 1986). Avocations: photography, sailing, gardening. Office: Purdue U Libr West Lafayette IN 47907-1530

MARKEL, ROBERT THOMAS, mayor; b. Wilmington, Del., Apr. 4, 1943; s. Robert H. and Margaret T. (Dillon) M.; m. Mary C. Alby, Aug. 5, 1967; children: Robert J., Katharine C. BA, Notre Dame U., 1965, PhD, 1975. Assoc. prof. Am. Internat. Coll., Springfield, Mass., 1969-92; city councillor City of Springfield, 1978-92, mayor, 1992-96; exec. dir. Boston Mgmt. Consortium, 1996—; mem. Springfield Conservation Commn., 1976-78, Springfield Preservation Trust, 1982—, local govt. adv. commn. Commonwealth of Mass., Boston, 1982-90; bd. dirs. World Affairs Coun. Western Mass., 1979—, Mass. Mcpl. Assn., Boston, 1981-88; pres. Springfield City Coun., 1986. Bd. dirs. Stage West Resident Theatre, 1987—. Mem. Am. Polit. Sci. Assn. Democrat. Roman Catholic. Avocations: skiing, fishing, running. Home: 53 Florentine Gdns Springfield MA 01108-2507 Office: Boston Mgmt Consortium Adminstrn Bldg 43 Hawkins St Boston MA 02114-2907

MARKELL, ALAN WILLIAM, linguistic company executive; b. Boston, June 6, 1933; s. Edward and Frances B. Markell; m. Carol Markell (div. Apr. 1978); children: Jennifer, Adam. AB, Bowdoin Coll., 1954; MBA, Columbia U., 1956. Fin. analyst RCA Corp., Camden, N.J. and N.Y.C., 1956-58; controller Jenkins Spirits Corp., Somerville, Mass., 1958-60, Marum Knitting Mills, Lawrence, Mass., 1960-63; pres. Norfolk Fluoridation Corp., Dedham, Mass., 1963-65, Car Mark Inc., Brookline, Mass., 1965-78; v.p. Linguistic Systems Inc., Cambridge, Mass., 1978-90, also bd. dirs.; pres. Cambridge Inst. Inc., Boston, 1979-86, instr. in mgmt.; ptnr. Moss Roberts and Co., Cambridge, 1978-90, bd. dirs. Bd. dirs. Miami Chamber Symphony, 1991—. Home: 200 Ocean Lane Dr Key Biscayne FL 33149-1461 Summer Address: Box 596 Basin Point Rd Harpswell ME 04079

MARKEN, GIDEON ANDREW, III, advertising and public relations executive; b. Hampton, Iowa, June 24, 1940; s. Gideon Andrew Jr. and Cleone (Marie Riss) M.; m. Jeannine Gay Hill, Dec. 28, 1963; children: Tracy Lynn, Gideon Andrew. BS, Iowa State U., 1962; MBA, Hamilton Inst., 1967. Pub. relations mgr. Fairchild Instrumentation, Mountain View, Calif., 1967-68; pub. relations dir. Barnes-Hind Pharms., Sunnyvale, Calif., 1968-69; v.p. acct. supr. Hal Lawrence, Inc., Palo Alto, Calif., 1969-74, Bozell-Jacobs, Palo Alto, 1974-77; pres. Marken Communications, Sunnyvale, Calif., 1977—. Contbr. articles to profl. jours. Served as sgt. USAF, 1963-67. Mem. Pub. Relations Soc. of Am., Peninsula Mktg. Assn., Bus. Publishing Advt. Assn., Am. Mgmt. Assn., Am. Electronics Assn., Am. Med. Writers Assn. (pres. 1968-70, 72-74). Republican. Methodist. Club: San Rafael Yacht. Home: 1428 Bellingham Ave Sunnyvale CA 94087-3811 Office: Marken Comm 3375 Scott Blvd Ste 108 Santa Clara CA 95054-3111

MARKEN, WILLIAM RILEY, magazine editor; b. San Jose, Calif., Sept. 2, 1942; s. Harry L. and Emma Catherine (Kraus) M.; m. Marilyn Tonascia, Aug. 30, 1964; children—Catherine, Elizabeth, Michael, Paul. Student, Occidental Coll., 1960-62; BA, U. Calif., Berkeley, 1964. From writer to editor-in-chief Sunset Mag., Menlo Park, Calif., 1964-96; editor-at-large Sunset Publ. Corp., Menlo Park, Calif., 1996—. Bd. dirs. Calif. Tomorrow, 1979-83; pres. League to Save Lake Tahoe, 1994-97. Avocations: tennis; skiing; basketball. Office: Sunset Mag 80 Willow Rd Menlo Park CA 94025-3661

MARKER, DAVID GEORGE, university president; b. Atlantic, Iowa, Mar. 20, 1937; s. Calburt D. and Vera (Smith) M.; children—Paul C., Elizabeth A. A.B., Grinnell Coll., 1959; M.S., Pa. State U., 1962, Ph.D., 1966; L.H.D. (hon.), Hope Coll., 1984; ScD (hon.), Grinnell Coll., 1993. Instr., asst. prof., assoc. prof., prof. physics Hope Coll., Holland, Mich., 1965-84, adminstrv. dir. Computer Ctr., 1969-74, chmn. dept. computer sci., 1973-79, assoc. dean acad. affairs, 1973-74, provost, 1974-84; pres. Cornell Coll., Mount Vernon, Iowa, 1984-94, U. of Osteo. Medicine and Health Scis., Des Moines, 1994-96; exec. dir. Svc. Ctr. of Iowa, Des Moines, 1996—; bd. dirs. Firstar, Des Moines, Sci. Ctr. Iowa, Mercy Coll. of Health Scis.; cons. in field. Contbr. articles to profl. jours. Bd. dirs. St. Luke's Hosp., 1987-90; mem. adv. com. NSF Project Kaleidoscope, 1990-94. Recipient Bishop's Service Cross. Mem. NCAA (pres. commn. 1989-93), Nat. Assn. Colls. and Univs. (chmn. commn. on policy analysis 1991), Iowa Assn. Ind. Colls. and Univs. (exec. com. 1986-93, chmn. 1991-92), Iowa Coll. Found. (exec. com. 1987-92, chmn. 1990-91), Rotary, Phi Beta Kappa, Sigma Xi. Episcopalian. Avocations: cycling; music; photography. Home: 3131 Fleur Dr Apt 601 Des Moines IA 50321-1741 Office: Sci Ctr of Iowa 4500 Grand Ave Des Moines IA 50312-2402

MARKER, LORETTA IRENE, medical/surgical cardiac nurse; b. Memphis, Tenn., June 10, 1956; d. John Wesley and Kathleen Ann (Robbins) M.; divorced; 1 child, Timothy John. AS, Lorain County Community Coll., 1980; student, Cuyahoga Community Coll., 1989, Cleve. State U., 1991-92. RN, Ariz.; cert. med.-surg. nurse, ACLS, PALS. Staff nurse Cleve. Clinic Found., 1980-81, surg. nurse, 1981-86, head nurse cardiac surgery, 1986-89, surg. nurse clinician, 1989-90, nurse clinician, 1990-94; C.V.O.R. nurse Cigna Healthcare of Ariz., 1994-96; cardiology nurse mgr. Cigna Healthcare of Ariz., Phoenix, 1996—. Me. Am. Assn. Oper. Rm. Nurses, Airplane Owners and Pilots Assn. Roman Catholic. Avocations: private pilot, 4-wheel drive truck owner, classic cars. Home: 5121 N 40th St Apt B121 Phoenix AZ 85018-2128

MARKER, MARC LINTHACUM, lawyer, investor; b. Los Angeles, July 19, 1941; s. Clifford Harry and Voris (Linthacum) M.; m. Sandra Yocom, Aug. 29, 1965; children: Victor, Gwendolyn. BA in Econs. and Geography, U. Calif.-Riverside, 1964; JD, U. So. Calif., 1967. Asst. v.p., asst. sec. Security Pacific Nat. Bank, L.A., 1970-73; sr. v.p., chief counsel, sec. Security Pacific Leasing Corp., San Francisco, 1973-92; pres. Security Pacific Leasing Svcs. Corp., San Francisco, 1977-85, dir., 1977-92; bd. dirs., sec. Voris, Inc., 1973-86; bd. dirs. Refiners Petroleum Corp., 1977-81, Security Pacific Leasing Singapore Ltd., 1983-85, Security Pacific Leasing Can. Ltd., 1989-92; lectr. in field. Served to comdr. USCGR. Mem. ABA, Calif. Bar Assn., D.C. Bar Assn., Am. Assn. Equipment Lessors. Republican. Lutheran. Club: Univ. (L.A.). Office: 471 Magnolia Ave # B Larkspur CA 94939-2034

MARKERT, CLEMENT LAWRENCE, biology educator; b. Las Animas, Colo., Apr. 11, 1917; s. Edwin John and Sarah (Norman) M.; m. Margaret Rempfer, July 29, 1940; children—Alan Ray, Robert Edwin, Betsy Jean. B.A. summa cum laude, U. Colo., 1940; M.A., UCLA, 1942; Ph.D., Johns Hopkins U., 1948. Merck-NRC fellow Calif. Inst. Tech., 1948-50; asst. prof. zoology U. Mich., 1950-56, assoc. prof., 1956-57; prof. biology Johns Hopkins, 1957-65; chmn. dept. biology Yale U., 1965-71, prof. biology, 1965-86, dir. Center for Reproductive Biology, 1974-86; Disting. Univ. Research prof. N.C. State U., 1986-93, disting. univ. prof. emeritus, 1993-96; vis. prof. Kyoto U., Japan, 1996-97; panelist NSF, 1959-63; panelist subcom. on marine biology President's Sci. Adv. Com., 1965-66; mem. council Am. Cancer So., 1976-78; co-chmn. devel. biology interdisciplinary cluster Pres.' Biomed. Research Panel, 1975; mem. com. on animal models and genetic stocks NRC, 1979-85; trustee Bermuda Biol. Sta. for Research, 1959-83, life trustee, 1983—; bd. sci. advisers La Jolla Cancer Research Found.; mem. bd. sci. advs. Jane Coffin Childs Meml. Fund for Med. Research, 1979-86; chmn. bd. trustees BIOSIS, 1981, mem., 1976-81. Editor Prentice-Hall Series in Developmental Biology, Procs. 3d, 5th, 6th, 7th Internat. Congress Isozymes, 1974, 86, 89, 92; assoc. editor The Physiology of Reproduction; mng. editor Jour. Exptl. Zoology, 1963-85; mem. editl. bd. Archives of Biochemistry and Biophysics, 1963-81, Sci. mag., 1979-83, Differentiation, 1973—, Developmental Genetics, 1979-92, Cancer Rsch., 1982-85, Tansgenics, 1993—; mem. spl. adv. bd. Jour. Reprodn. and Devel., 1992—. Served with Internat. Brigades, 1938, Spain; with Mcht. Marine, 1944-45. Mem. Am. Inst. Biol. Scis. (pres. 1965), NAS (governing council 1970-71, 77-80), Inst. Medicine, Am. Soc. Biochemistry and Molecular Biology, Internat. Soc. Developmental Biologists, Am. Soc. Developmental Biology (pres. 1963-64), Soc. Study of Reprodn., Am. Acad. Arts and Scis. (governing council 1980-84), Am. Genetic Assn. (pres. 1980), Am. Soc. Naturalists (v.p. 1967), Am. Soc. Zoologists (pres. 1967), Genetics Soc. Am., Am. Soc. Animal Sci., Phi Beta Kappa, Sigma Xi. Home: 4005 Wakefield Dr Colorado Springs CO 80906-4324

MARKEY, EDWARD JOHN, congressman; b. Malden, Mass., July 11, 1946; s. John E. and Christine M. (Courtney) M. B.A., Boston Coll., 1968, J.D., 1972. Bar: Mass. Mem. Mass. Ho. of Reps., 1973-76, 94th-104th Congresses from 7th Mass. Dist., 1975—, New Eng. Congl. Caucus, N.E.-Midwest Econ. Advancement Coalition, Dem. Study Group, Environ. Study Conf. Freshman Caucus, now chmn. subcom. telecomm. and fin.; ranking minority mem., mem. commerce subcom. on telecomm. and fin. Mem. editorial staff: Boston Coll. Law Rev. Served with USAR, 1968-73. Mem. Mass. Bar Assn. (Mass. Legislator of Year 1975). Club: K.C. Home: 7 Townsend St Malden MA 02148-6322 Office: US Ho of Reps 2133 Rayburn HOB Washington DC 20515-2107*

MARKEY, ROBERT GUY, lawyer; b. Cleve., Feb. 25, 1939; s. Nate and Rhoda (Gross) M.; children: Robert Jr., Randolph; m. Nanci Louise Brooks, Aug. 25, 1990. AB, Brown U., 1961; JD, Case Western Res., 1964. Bar: Ohio 1964. Assoc., ptnr. Kahn and Kleinman, Cleve., 1964-75; ptnr. Arter & Hadden, Cleve., 1975-83, Baker & Hostetler, Cleve., 1983—; dir., sec. Blue Coral, Inc., Cleve.; bd. dirs. Matrix Essentials, Inc., Cleve., McKay Chem. Co., L.A. Chmn. attys. div. United Way Svcs., Cleve., 1978; trustee Fedn. Community Planning, Cleve., 1980-87, Cleve. Ctr. Contemporary Art, 1993—, pres. 1995—. Mem. ABA, Cleve. Bar Assn. (chmn. securities law com. 1974-75), Ohio State Bar Assn., Union Club, Chagrin Valley Hunt Club. Republican. Jewish. Office: Baker & Hostetler 3200 National City Ctr 1900 E 9th St Cleveland OH 44114-3401

MARKEY, THOMAS ADAM, financial officer; b. Dayton, Ohio, June 12, 1956; s. Paul Robert Markey and Cathleen Wilgus. BA, Ariz. State U., 1980, MBA, 1992. CPA. Fin. analyst Maricopa County Sch. Supt., Phoenix, 1982-84; EDP acct. Maricopa County Fin. Dept., Phoenix, 1984-88, sr. fin. acct., 1988-90, sr. budget analyst, 1990-92; dir. bus. and human resources East Valley Inst. Tech., Mesa, Ariz., 1992—. Sustaining mem. SW Assn. Indian Affairs, Santa Fe, N.Mex., 1990—; active mem. Intertribal Indian Ceremonial Assn., Gallup, N.Mex., 1990—. Mem. AICPA, Ariz. Soc. CPAs, Ariz. Assn. Sch. Bus. Ofcls., Western Govtl. Rsch. Assn., Gov. Fin. Officers Assn., Beta Gamma Sigma. Democrat. Avocations: piano, reading, classical music, hiking. Office: East Valley Inst Tech 200 S Center St Mesa AZ 85210-1502

MARKEY, WILLIAM ALAN, health care administrator; b. Cleve., Dec. 29, 1927; s. Oscar Bennett and Claire (Feldman) M.; m. Irene Nelson, Oct. 31, 1954; children—Janet Ellen Markey-Hisakawa, Suzanne Katherine Markey-Johnson. Student, Case Inst. Tech., 1945-48; BA, U. Mich., 1950; MS, Yale U., 1954. Resident hosp. adminstrn. Beth Israel Hosp., Boston, 1953-54; asst. dir. Montefiore Hosp., Pitts., 1954-56; asst. adminstr. City of Hope Med. Ctr., Duarte, Calif., 1956-57; adminstrv. dir. City of Hope Med. Ctr., 1957-66; assoc. dir. cancer hosp. project, instr. pub. health U. So. Calif. Sch. Medicine, 1966-67, asst. clin. prof. pub. health and community medicine, 1968-70, asst. prof., 1970-75, dep. dir. regional med. programs, 1967-71; adminstr. Health Care Agy., County of San Diego, 1971-74; health services cons. Health Care Agy., 1974-75; dir. Maricopa County Dept. Health Services, Phoenix, 1975-79; cons. Maricopa County Dept. Health Services, 1979-80; adminstr. Sonoma Valley Hosp., Calif., 1980-83;; lectr. pub. health Sch. Pub. Health, UCLA, 1969-74; lectr. comty. medicine Sch. Medicine, U. Calif.-San Diego, 1973-75; cons. L.A. County Dept. Hosps., 1966-71, cons. Hosp./Health Svcs., 1983—; CEO Chinese Hosp., San Francisco, 1985-86, 90-91; adj. instr. Golden Gate U., 1992-96. Mem. bd. edn. Duarte Unified Sch. Dist., 1967-72, pres., 1970-72; bd. dirs. Hosp. Coun. So. Calif., 1963-67, sec., 1966-67, Duarte Pub. Libr. Assn., 1965-72, Duarte-Bradbury chpt. Am. Field Svc., 1965-72, Duarte-Bradbury Comty. Chest, 1961-68, Cen. Ariz. Health Svcs. Agy., 1975-80, Vis. Nurse Assn. The Redwoods, Santa Rosa, Calif., 1985-86, Sonoma Greens Homeowners Assn., 1990-95, Sonoma City Opera, 1987, 93, United Way, Sonoma, 1996—; com. chmn. Sonoma County Bd. Realtors, 1990-92; active Sonoma County Multiple Listing Svc., 1987—. With AUS, 1950-52. Fellow Am. Coll. Health Care Execs. (life); mem. Am. Hosp. Assn. (life), Am. Pub. Health Assn., Royal Soc. Health, Calif. Hosp. Assn. (trustee 1966-69, dir. 1966-69), Internat. Fedn. Hosps., Hosp. Coun. No. Calif. (dir. 1981-83), Kiwanis, Rotary (past pres. Duarte). Home: 866 Princeton Dr Sonoma CA 95476-4186 Office: PO Box F Sonoma CA 95476-0370

MARKEY, WINSTON ROSCOE, aeronautical engineering educator; b. Buffalo, Sept. 20, 1929; s. Roscoe Irvin and Catherine L. (Higgins) M.; m. Phoebe Anne Sproule, Sept. 10, 1955; children: Karl Richard, Katherine Ilse, Kristina Anne. BS, MIT, 1951, Sc.D., 1956. Engr. MIT, 1951-57, asst. prof., 1957-62, assoc. prof., 1962-66, prof., 1966—, chmn. undergrad. com., 1988—, dir. Measurement Systems Lab., 1961-89; chief scientist USAF, 1964-65, mem. sci. adv. bd., 1966-69. Author: (with J. Hovorka) The Mechanics of Inertial Position and Heading Indication, 1961; Assoc. editor: AIAA Jour, 1963-66. Recipient Exceptional Civilian Service award USAF, 1965. Mem. Sigma Xi, Tau Beta Pi, Gamma Alpha Rho. Home: 11 Edgewood Rd Lexington MA 02173-3501 Office: MIT Bldg 33-208 Cambridge MA 02139

MARKGRAF, J(OHN) HODGE, chemist, educator; b. Cin., Mar. 16, 1930; s. Carl A. and Elizabeth (Hodge) M.; m. Nancy Hart, Apr. 4, 1957; children: Carrie G., Sarah T. A.B., Williams Coll., 1952; M.Sc., Yale U., 1954, Ph.D., 1957; postgrad., U. Munich, W. Ger., 1956-57. Research chemist Procter & Gamble Co., Cin., 1958-59; asst. prof. chemistry Williams Coll., Williamstown, Mass., 1959-65; assoc. prof. Williams Coll., Williamstown, 1965-69, prof., 1969—, Ebenezer Fitch prof. chemistry, 1977-85, 94—, provost, 1980-83, v.p. for alumni relations and devel., 1985-94, coll. marshal, 1995—; vis. prof. U. Calif., Berkeley, 1964-65, 68-69, 76-77, Duke U., 1983-84. Contbr. articles to profl. jours. NSF sci. faculty fellow, 1964-65; NSF grantee, 1961-63, Am. Chem. Soc.-Petroleum Rsch. Fund grantee, 1965-68, 70-72, 93-95, Merck & Co. grantee, 1967, Rsch. Corp. grantee, 1963, 75, 90-92, Pfizer Inc. grantee, 1996, 97. Mem. Am. Chem. Soc., Phi Beta Kappa, Sigma Xi. Patentee in field. Home: 104 Forest Rd Williamstown MA 01267-2029 Office: Williams College Dept Chemistry Williamstown MA 02167-2692

MARKHAM, CHARLES BUCHANAN, lawyer; b. Durham, N.C., Sept. 15, 1926; s. Charles Blackwell and Sadie Helen (Hackney) M. A.B., Duke U., Durham, N.C., 1945; postgrad., U. N.C. Law Sch., Chapel Hill, 1945-46; LL.B., George Washington U., Washington, 1951. Bar: D.C. 1951, N.Y. 1961, N.C. 1980, U.S. Ct. Appeals (2d cir.) 1962, U.S. Ct. Appeals (D.C. cir.) 1955, U.S. Supreme Ct. 1964. Reporter Durham Sun, N.C., 1945; asst. state editor, editorial writer Charlotte News, N.C., 1947-48; dir. publicity and research Young Democratic Clubs Am., Washington, 1948-49, exec. sec., 1949-50; polit. analyst Dem. Senatorial Campaign Com., Washington, 1950-51; spl. atty. IRS, Washington and N.Y.C., 1952-60; assoc. Battle, Fowler, Stokes and Kheel, N.Y.C., 1960-65; dir. research U.S. Equal Employment Opportunity Commn., Washington, 1965-68; dep. asst. sec. U.S. Dept. Housing and Urban Devel., Washington, 1969-72; asst. dean Rutgers U. Law Sch., Newark, 1974-76; assoc. prof. law N.C. Central U., Durham, 1976-81, prof. law, 1981-83; mayor City of Durham, N.C., 1981-85; ptnr. Markham and Wickham, Durham, 1984-86; Trustee Hist. Preservation Soc. Durham, 1982-86; bd. dirs. Stagville Ctr., 1984-86; mem. Gov.'s Crime Commn., Raleigh, 1985; dep. commr. N.C. Indsl. Commn., Raleigh, 1986-93. Editor: Jobs, Men and Machines: The Problems of Automation, 1964. Mem. Carolina Club, Phi Beta Kappa, Omicron Delta Kappa, Phi Delta Phi, Phi Delta Theta. Republican. Episcopalian. Home: 204 N Dillard St Durham NC 27701-3404

MARKHAM, JESSE WILLIAM, economist; b. Richmond, Va., Apr. 21, 1916; s. John James and Edith (Luttrell) M.; AB, U. Richmond, 1941; postgrad. Johns Hopkins U., 1941-42, U.S. Fgn. Service Sch., 1945; MA, Harvard U., 1947, PhD, 1949; m. Penelope Jane Anton, Oct. 15, 1944; children: Elizabeth Anton Markham McLean, John James, Jesse William. Accountant, E.I. duPont de Nemours Co., Richmond, 1935-38; teaching fellow Harvard U., 1946-48; asst. prof. Vanderbilt U., 1948-52, asso. prof., 1952-53; chief economist FTC, Washington, 1953-55; asso. prof. Princeton U., 1955-57, prof. econs., 1957-68; prof. Harvard Grad. Sch. Bus. Adminstrn., 1968-72, Charles Edward Wilson prof., 1972-82, prof. emeritus, 1982—; prof. Harvard U. Extension Svcs., 1984—; vis. prof. Columbia U., 1958; Ford Found. vis. prof. Harvard Grad. Sch. Bus. Adminstrn., 1965-66; rsch. prof. Law and Econs. Ctr., Emory U., 1982-84; rsch. staff, mem. bd. editors Patent Trademark Copyright Rsch. Inst., George Washington U., 1955-70; econs. editor Houghton Mifflin Co., 1961-71; U.S. del. commn. experts on bus. practices European Productivity Agy., OEEC, 1956, 57, 58, 59, 61; vis. prof. Harvard U., 1961-62; dir. Ford Found. Seminar Region II, 1961; adv. com. mktg. to sec. commerce, 1967-71; mem. Am. Bar Assn. Commn. to study FTC, 1969. Del. People to People Diplomacy Mission to USSR, 1989; active Boy Scouts Am.; chmn. Harvard Parents Com., 1969-72. Served as lt. USNR, World War II. Ford Found. research prof., 1958-59. Mem. Am. Econ. Assn., U.S. C. of C. (econ. policy com.), Harvard Club (N.Y.C., Sarasota, Fla.), The Cedars Club. Episcopalian. Author: Competition in the Rayon Industry, 1952; The Fertilizer Industry: Study of an Imperfect Market, 1958; The American Economy, 1963; (with Charles Fiero and Howard Piquet) The European Common Market: Friend or Competitor, 1964; (with Gustav Papanek) Industrial Organization and Economic Development, 1970; Conglomerate Enterprise and Public Policy, 1973 (with Paul Teplitz) Baseball Economics and Public Policy, 1982; sect. on oligopoly Internat. Ency. Social Scis.; contbr. articles to econ. jours. Mem. Phi Beta Kappa. Home: 663 Martin Rd Friendship ME 04547 Office: Harvard U Grad Sch Bus Adminstrn 300 Cumnock Boston MA 02163

MARKHAM, JORDAN J., physicist, retired educator; b. Samokov, Bulgaria, Dec. 25, 1916; s. Reuben Henry and Mary (Gall) M.; m. Lillian Cagnon, Feb. 6, 1943; children—Linda C., Roger H. B.S., Beloit (Wis.) Coll., 1938; M.S., Syracuse U., 1940; Ph.D., Brown U., 1946. With div. war research Columbia U., 1942-45; trainee Clinton Lab., Oak Ridge, 1946-47; instr. physics U. Pa., 1947-48; asst. prof. Brown U., 1948-50; physicist Applied Physics Lab., Johns Hopkins U., 1950-53; research lab. Zenith Radio Corp., 1953-60; sci. adv. Armour Research Found., 1960-62; prof. physics Ill. Inst. Tech., 1962-81, ret., 1981; vis. prof. Phys. Inst., U. Frankfurt, Germany, summer 1965; sabbatical leave U. Reading, Eng., 1977. Author: F-centers in Alkali Halides, 1966, also articles. Home and Office: Villa 128 Carolina Meadows Chapel Hill NC 27514

MARKHAM, REED B., education educator, consultant; b. Alhambra, Calif., Feb. 14, 1957; s. John F. and Reeda (Bjarason) M. BA, Brigham Young U., 1982, MA, 1982; BS, Regents Coll., 1981, MA, 1982; MPA, U. So. Calif., 1983; MA, UCLA, 1989; PhD, Columbia Pacific U., 1991. Mem. faculty Brigham Young U., Provo, Utah, 1984; mem. faculty Calif. State U., Fullerton and Long Beach, 1984, Northridge, 1985; mem. faculty El Camino Coll., Torrance, Calif., 1986, Orange Coast Coll., Costa Mesa, Calif., 1986, Pasadena (Calif.) Coll., 1986, Fullerton (Calif.) Community Coll., 1986; instr., mem. pub. rels. com. Chaffey (Calif.) Coll., 1986-87; prof., CARES dir. Calif. State Poly. U., Pomona, 1987—; adj. prof. Calif. State U., L.A., 1992-93, dir. Ctr. for Student Retention, 1995—; rsch. asst. to pres. Ctr. for the Study of Cmty. Coll., 1985; mem. faculty Riverside (Calif.) Coll., 1989-90, Rio Hondo (Calif.) Coll., 1989-90, English Lang. Inst., 1994, Calif. Poly Summer Bridge, 1989-95, East L.A. Coll.; speechwriter U.S. Supreme Ct., Washington, 1980; cons. gifted children program Johns Hopkins U./Scripps Coll., Claremont, Calif., 1987-88; mem. faculty PACE Program East L.A., 1995-96; faculty East L.A. Coll., 1996-97. Author: Power Speechwriting, 1983, Power Speaking, 1990, Public Opinion, 1990, Advances in Public Speaking, 1991, Leadership 2000: Success Skills for University Students, 1995; co-author: Student Retention: Success Models in Higher Education, 1996, Upward Bound Program Grant Proposal, 1996, editor Trojan in Govt., U. So. Calif., 1983; editl. bd. mem. Edn. Digest, Speaker and Gavel, Innovative Higher End., Pub. Rels. Rev., Nat. Forensic Jour., The Forensic Educator, Clearinghouse for the Contemporary Educator, Hispanic Am. Family Mag.; writer N.Y. times, Christian Sci. Monitor; ednl. columnist San Bernardino (Calif.) Sun., 1992-97. Pres. bd. trustees Regents Coll., 1986. Mem. Doctorate Assn. N.Y. Scholars, Nat. Assn. Pvt. Nontraditional Colls. (accrediting com. 1989—), Pub. Rels. Soc. Am. (dir.-at-large inland empire 1992-93, faculty advisor). LDS. Home: 801 E Alosta Ave # T-307 Azusa CA 91702-2744 Office: Calif Polytech U Communications Dept 3801 W Temple Ave Pomona CA 91768-2557

MARKHAM, RICHARD LAWRENCE, chemist; b. Texarkana, Ark., July 31, 1940; s. Andre Lawrence and Elizabeth Ella (Beck) M.; m. Judith Lynn Roberts, Aug. 5, 1972. BS, Okla. State U., 1962; MS, U. Ariz., 1969. Rsch. scientist Celanese Plastics Co., Summit, N.J., 1969-72; narcotics analyst U.S. Army Crime Lab., Frankfurt, Germany, 1973-74; from plant chemist to mfg. mgr. Amerace Corp., Kehlen, Luxembourg, Butler, NJ, Johnson City, Tenn., 1974-79; from project mgr. to product mgr. Battelle Meml. Inst., Columbus, Ohio, 1979-90, bus. devel. mgr., 1991—; adv. bd. Plastics Cons. Dir., Tucson, 1990—. Author, editor: Identification of Major Developments in Polymer Blends, 1987, Reactive Processing of Polymeric Materials, 1988, Compatibilization of Polymer Blends, 1994; contbr. articles to profl. jours. Founder, pres. East. Tenn. chpt. St. Jude Rsch. Hosp., Johnson City, 1977, 78, 79; pres., trustee Lakeside Forest Homeowners Assn., Westerville, Ohio, 1993-94. Mem. Am. Chem. Soc. (polymer chem. div., polymeric materials sci. & engring. div.), Sigma Xi. Patentee in field. Avocations: fastpitch softball, racquetball, photography. Home: 425 S Spring Rd Westerville OH 43081 Office: Battelle Meml Inst 505 King Ave Columbus OH 43201-2696

MARKIN, ALLAN P., professional sports team executive. BSChE, U. Alberta. Chmn. Canadian Natural Resources Ltd.; co-owner Calgary (Canada) Flames; mem. steering com. Markin-Flanagan Disting. Writers Progam U. Calgary. Recipient Pinnacle award for bus. excellence in Alberta, 1993, Prodr. of Yr. award Oilweek, 1993, Gold award Wall St. Jour. Office: Calgary Flames, PO Box 1540 Sta M, Calgary, AB Canada T2P 3B9

MARKIN, DAVID ROBERT, motor company executive; b. N.Y.C., Feb. 16, 1931; s. Morris and Bessie (Markham) M.; children: Sara, John, Christopher, Meredith. B.S., Bradley U., 1953. Foreman Checker Motors Corp., Kalamazoo, 1955-57, factory mgr., 1957-62, v.p. sales, 1962-70, pres., 1970—, dir.; bd. dirs. Jackpot Inc. Trustee Kalamazoo Coll. Served to 1st lt. USAF, 1953-55. Mem. Alpha Epsilon Pi. Clubs: Standard (Chgo.); Park (Kalamazoo). Home: 2121 Winchell Ave Kalamazoo MI 49008-2205 Office: Internat Controls Corp 2016 N Pitcher St Kalamazoo MI 49007-1869*

MARKINSON, MARTIN, theatre owner, producer; b. Bklyn., Dec. 23, 1931; s. Abraham and Dora (Rosenthal) M.; m. Arlene Francis Gelfand, Apr. 15, 1962; children: Brett, Keith, Sydney. Owner, operator Helen Hayes Theatre, N.Y.C.; bd. govs. Am. League of Theatre and Producers, N.Y.C. Producer Broadway plays including: Poor Murderer, Some of My Best Friends, Cheaters, Whoopee, Ned and Jack, Snoopy, Torch Song Trilogy (Tony award 1983), Passion, And a Nightingale Sang, Corpse, Dusky Sally, Last Minstral Show and Daddy Goodness. Sgt. USAF, 1951-53, Korea. *

MARKLAND, FRANCIS SWABY, JR., biochemist, educator; b. Phila., Jan. 15, 1936; s. Francis Swaby Sr. and Willie Lawrence (Averritt) M.; m. Barbara Blake, June 27, 1959; children: Cathleen Blake, Francis Swaby IV. B.S., Pa. State U., 1957; Ph.D., Johns Hopkins U., 1964. Postdoctoral fellow UCLA, 1964-66, asst. prof. biochemistry, 1966-73; vis. asst. prof. U. So. Calif., Los Angeles, 1973-74, assoc. prof., 1974-83, prof., 1983—, acting chmn. dept. biochemistry, 1986-88, vice-chmn., 1988-92; cons. Clin. Lab. Med. Group, L.A., 1977-88, Cortech, Inc., Denver, 1983-88.; mem. biochem., endocrinology study sect. NIH, 1986-90. Editorial bd. Toxicon., Internat. Jour. of Toxinology; contbr. articles, chpts. and abstracts to profl. publs.; patentee in field. Mem. Angeles Choral, Northridge, Calif. Served to capt. USNR. Recipeint NIH rsch. career devel. award USPHS, NIH, 1968-73; rsch. grantee Nat. Cancer Inst., 1979-86, 91-93, Nat. Heart Lung and Blood Inst., 1984-88, 95—. State of Calif. Breast Cancer Rsch. Program, 1995—. Mem. Am. Soc. Biochem. and Molecular Biology, Am. Chem. Soc., Internat. Soc. on Toxinology, Internat. Soc. on Thrombosis and Haemostasis (subcom. exogenous hemostatic factors, chair 1994-96), Am. Assn. Cancer Rsch., Am. Soc. Hematology, Protein Soc., Sigma Xi, Alpha Zeta. Avocations: singing, skiing, aerobics. Office: U So Calif Sch Medicine Cancer Rsch Lab Rm 106 1303 N Mission Rd Los Angeles CA 90033-1020

MARKLE, CHERI VIRGINIA CUMMINS, nurse; b. N.Y.C., Nov. 22, 1936; d. Brainard Lyle and Mildred (Schwab) Cummins; m. John Markle, Aug. 26, 1961 (dec. 1962); 1 child, Kellianne. RN, Ind. State U. and Union Hosp., 1959; BS in Rehab. Edn., Wright State U., 1975; BSN, Capital U., 1987; postgrad. in nursing adminstrn., Wright State U., 1987-89; MS, Calif. Coll. Health Sci. Administration, 1994; postgrad., Columbia Pacific U., 1996—. Cert. clin. hypnotherapist Nat. Guild Hypnotherapists. Coordinator Dayton (Ohio) Children's Psychiat. Hosp., 1962-75; dir. nursing Stillwater Health Ctr., Dayton, 1975-76; rehab. cons. Fairborn, Ohio, 1976-91; sr. supr. VA, Dayton, 1977-85, nurse coord. alcohol rehab., 1985-86; DON Odd Fellows, Springfield, Ohio, 1987-88, Miami Christel Manor, Miamisburg, Ohio, 1988—; DON, rehab. cons. NMS Tng. Sys., Dayton, 1989-91; psychiat. unit nurse VA Med. Ctr., N.Y. Rehab., 1991, mem. com. women vets., 1991-93; advisor Calif. Coll. Health Sci. Newspaper columnist Golden Times, Clark County. Bd. dirs. Temple Universal Judaism; active Women of Reform Judaism Sisterhood, Village Temple. 1st lt. USAF, 1959-61; advisor Calif. Coll. Health Sci. Mem. ANA (cert. adminstrn. 1983, cert. gerontology 1984), NAFE, AAUW, Nat. Rehab. Nursing Soc., Nurse Mgrs. Assembly, Gerontol. Nurse Assembly, Rehab. Soc., Nat. Guild Hypnotherapists, Internat. Assn. Counselors and Therapists, Wright State U. Alumni

Assn., Am. Legion, Women's City Club N.Y., Gilbert & Sullivan Soc., Internat. Consortium Parse Scholars, Alpha Sigma Alpha, Sigma Theta Tau. Democrat. Jewish. Avocations: cats, reading, music, needlework, swimming. Office: VA Med Ctr 423 E 23rd St New York NY 10010-5050

MARKLE, GEORGE BUSHAR, IV, surgeon; b. Hazleton, Pa., Oct. 29, 1921; s. Alvan and Gladys (Jones) M.; m. Mildred Donna Umstead, July 3, 1944; children: Donna Markle Partee, Melanie Jones Markle, George Bushar, Christian; m. Teresa Damm, Mar. 31, 1996. B.S., Yale U., 1943; M.D., U. Pa., 1946. Diplomate Am. Bd. Surgery. Intern Geisinger Med. Ctr., Danville, Pa., 1946-47, resident, 1947-49; surg. fellow Mayo Clinic, Rochester, Minn., 1949-52; chief surgery U.S. Army Hosp., Ft. Monroe, Va., 1952-54; practice gen. surgery Carlsbad, N.Mex., 1954-94; surg. staff Carlsbad Regional Med. Ctr., 1954-77, Guadalupe Med. Ctr., 1977-94; ret., 1994; panelist Voice of Am. Author: Ill Health and Other Foolishness, 1966, How to Stay Healthy All Your Life, 1968, The Teka Stone, 1983, How to Be Healthy, Wealthy and Wise, 1991, Donna's Story, 1991; contbr. articles to profl. jours.; radio health series. Mem. Eddy County Ctrl. Rep. Com.; candidate N.Mex. Ho. of Reps., 1996. With M.C., U.S. Army, 1952-54. Recipient Distinguished Service award Jr. C. of C., 1956. Fellow Internat. Coll. Surgeons (regent, Regent of Yr. 1991), Southwestern Surg. Congress, Priestley surg. Soc., Western Surg. Assn.; mem. Eddy County Med. Soc., Kiwanis. Presbyterian. Home: 1003 N Shore Dr Carlsbad NM 88220-4635 *Those blest in family and fortune, things not of their own making, ought, I believe, to strive to deserve those blessings through service to God and Man. Even the least of us has some power to influence others through our examples and attitudes, and through each we influence, for good or bad, we may affect sequentially many others, like ever widening ripples on the water.*

MARKLE, JOHN, JR., lawyer; b. Allentown, Pa., July 20, 1931; s. John Markle II and Pauline (Powers) Mulligan; m. Mary B. McLean, Apr. 19, 1952 (div. Apr. 1990); children: Ellen, John III, Patricia, Stephen, Mary; m. Kathryn E. Wheeler, July 14, 1990. Grad., The Hill Sch., Pottstown, Pa., 1949; BA, Yale U., 1953; LLB, Harvard Law Sch., 1958. Assoc. Drinker Biddle & Reath, Phila., 1958-64, ptnr., 1964—; chmn. Pa. Labor Rels. Bd., 1996—. Contbg. editor: The Developing Labor Law, 1976—. Chmn., bd. dirs. Paoli (Pa.) Meml. Hosp. Found., 1982—. Lt. col. USMCR, 1951-73. Named Most Outstanding Young Rep. (Pa.), 1966. Mem. ABA, Pa. Bar Assn., Am. Arbitration Assn. Republican. Clubs: Union League of Phila., Yale of Phila., Merion Golf. Avocations: golf, photography. Home: 205 Cambridge Chase Exton PA 19341-3137 Office: Drinker Biddle & Reath 1000 Westlakes Dr Ste 300 Berwyn PA 19312-2409

MARKLE, ROGER A(LLAN), retired oil company executive; b. Sidney, Mont., Dec. 12, 1933; s. Forrest William and Mary Elizabeth (Hartley) M.; m. Mary Elizabeth Thompson, Jan. 13, 1967. B.S. in Mining Engring, U. Alaska, 1959; M.S., Stanford U., 1965; M.B.A., U. Chgo., 1972. Mgr. mine devel. Amoco Minerals, Inc., Chgo., 1973-74; pres. western div. Valley Camp Coal Co., Salt Lake City, 1974-78; pres., chief exec. officer Valley Camp Coal Co., Cleve., 1979-82; pres. Quaker State Corp., Oil City, Pa., 1982-86, chief operating officer, 1986-88, also bd. dirs.; vice chmn. Quaker State Corp., Oil City, 1988-89; pres. Nerco Oil & Gas, Vancouver, Wash., 1990-92; dir. U.S. Bur. Mines, Washington, 1978-79. Served with USN, 1951-54. Mem. AIME.

MARKMAN, HOWARD J., psychology educator; b. Oct. 27, 1950; s. Arnold J. and Claire (Fox) M.; m. Fran Dickson, June 29, 1980; children: Mathew Lee, Leah Deborah. BA, Rutgers U., 1972; MA in Clin. Psychology, Ind. U., 1976, PhD in Clin. Psychology, 1977. Lic. clin. psychologist, Colo. Assoc. instr. psychology Ind. U., 1973-75; psychology trainee, consultation team Monroe County Community Mental Health Ctr., Bloomington, Ind., 1975-76; clin./community psychology intern U. Colo. Sch. Medicine, Denver, 1976-77; asst. prof. psychology Bowling Green (Ohio) U., 1977-80, U. Denver, 1980-83; dir. Denver Ctr. for Marital and Family Studies, U. Denver, 1980—; dir. clin. tng. U. Denver, 1983-86, assoc. prof. psychology, 1983-89, prof. psychology, 1989—; presenter in field. Author: Couples' Guide to Communication, 1976, Prevention and Relationship Enhancement Program, 1980, We Can Work it Out, Fighting for your Marriage; mem. editorial bd. Jour. Consulting and Clin. Psychology, 1988-90, Behavioral Assessment, Jour. Family Psychology, Contemporary Psychology, Am. Assn. for Marriage and Family Therapy, Am. Jour. Family Therapy; guest assoc. editor Behavioral Assessment, 1989, Human Communication Rsch.; contbr. articles and reviews to profl. jours. Bd. dirs. Assn. Children and Youth, Boulder, Colo., 1985-86. NIMH grantee, 1980-82. Fellow APA; mem. NIMH (adhoc reviewer 1980—), NSF (adhoc reviewer 1980—), APA, Internat. Soc. Social and Personal Relationships (world conf. planning com. 1990—), Colo. Psychol. Assn. (co-chmn. 1990—), Nat. Coun. on Family Rels., Am. Assn. Marriage and Family Therapy (clin. mem.), Rocky Mountain Conf. Family Rels. (bd. dirs.). Democrat. Jewish. Avocations: softball, photography, tennis, hockey, skiing. Office: Univ of Denver Ctr Marital & Family Studies Dept of Psychology Denver CO 80208

MARKMAN, RAYMOND JEROME, marketing executive; b. Bklyn., Dec. 26, 1927; s. Julius and Celia (Schroeder) M.; m. Frances Pauline Heyman, June 4, 1949; children: Leslie Jane Stern, Janet Beth Meyer, Thomas Irion. BJ in Advt., U. Mo., 1949; postgrad., U. Chgo., 1955-58. Creative dir. Chicago Tribune, 1949-53; pres., founder Salespower Inc., Chgo., 1953-55; brand dir. Helene Curtis Industries, Chgo., 1955-58; account supr. Leo Burnett Co., Chgo., 1958-63; v.p., mgmt. supr. McCann-Erickson, Chgo., 1964-71; v.p. mktg. GRI Corp., Chgo., 1971-74; exec. v.p. mktg. Ency. Britannica, Chgo., 1974-83; pres., founder Heritage Home Video, Chgo., 1983-86, Magic Video Pub. Co., Chgo., 1986—, Life Planning Co., Chgo., 1988—; bd. dirs., founder Seago Realty Co., Chgo., 1970-86; bd. dirs. Chgo. City Bank; pres. Raymond J. Markman Assocs., Chgo., 1983—. Author: Handbook of Direct Marketing, 1983. Mem. Chgo. Crime Commn., 1951, Park Board Sports Coun., Highland Park, Ill., 1971-77, Mayor's Com., Highland Park, 1980-82; organizer Little League, Highland Park, 1965-70. Mem. Direct Mail Mktg. Assn., Chgo. Direct Mktg. Assn. (lectr. 1977-85, chmn. echos com.), Execs. Club. Home and Office: Life Planning Co 424 Lakeside Manor Rd Highland Park IL 60035-5040

MARKMAN, RONALD, artist, educator; b. Bronx, N.Y., May 29, 1931; s. Julius and Mildred (Berkowitz) M.; m. Barbara Miller, Sept. 12, 1959; 1 dau., Ericka Elizabeth. B.F.A., Yale U., 1957, M.F.A., 1959. Instr. Art Inst. Chgo., 1960-64; prof. fine arts Ind. U., 1964—; color cons. Hallmark Card Co., 1959-60. One-man shows Kanegis Gallery, 1959, Reed Coll., 1966, Terry Dintenfass Gallery, 1965, 66, 68, 70, 76, 79, 82, 85, The Gallery, Bloomington, Ind., 1972, 79, Indpls. Mus., 1974, Tyler Sch. Art, Phila., 1976, Franklin Coll., 1980, Dart Gallery, Chgo., 1981, Patrick King Gallery, Indpls., 1983, 86, John Heron Gallery, Indpls., 1985, New Harmony Gallery, 1985; two-man show Dintenfass Gallery, 1984; group shows include Kanegis Gallery, Boston, 1958, 60, 61, Boston Arts Festival, 1959, 60, Mus. Modern Art, 1959, 66, Whitney Mus., N.Y.C., 1960, Art Inst. Chgo., 1964, Gallery 99, Miami, Fla., 1966, Ball State Coll., 1966, Butler Inst., 1967, Indpls. Mus., 1968, 69, 72, 74, Phoenix Gallery, N.Y.C., 1970, Harvard U., 1974, Skidmore Coll., 1975, Am. Acad. Arts and Letters, 1977, 89, Tuthill-Gimprich Gallery, N.Y.C., 1980, Patrick King Gallery, 1988, numerous others; represented in permanent collections Met. Mus. Art, Mus. Modern Art, Art Inst. Chgo., Library of Congress, Cin. Art Mus., Bklyn. Mus., Ark. Art Center, others; commns. include 5 murals Riley Children's Hosp., Indpls., 1986; installation Evanston (Ill.) Art Ctr., 1989, 2-part installation Ortho Child Care Ctr., Raritan, N.J., 1991; illustrator Acid and Basics-A Guide to Acid-Base Physiology, 1992. Served with U.S. Army, 1952-54. Recipient Ind. Arts Commn. award, 1990, 93; Fulbright grantee, Italy, 1962, grantee Ctr. for New TV, Chgo., 1992; Lilly Endowment fellow, 1989, honorable mention, Ohio Film Festival, 1995. Home: 719 S Jordan Ave Bloomington IN 47401-5123 Office: Ind U Dept Fine Arts Bloomington IN 47401

MARKMAN, SHERMAN, investment banker, venture capital investor, corporate financier; b. Denver, Aug. 21, 1920; s. Abe and Julia (Rosen) M.; m. Paula Elaine Henderson. Student So. Meth. U., 1962-64; children: S. Michael, Joan, Lori. V.p. Lester's, Inc., Oklahoma City, 1940-59; exec. v.p. Besco Enterprises, San Francisco, 1960-61; sr. v.p. Zale Corp., Dallas, 1962-69; pres., chief exec. officer Leased Jewelry div., 1965-69, pres. Designcraft Industries, N.Y.C., 1969-75, chief exec. officer, 1969-75; pres. Tex. Internat. Export Co., Dallas, 1975—, CAC Fin. Group (Tex.), Dallas, 1975—; fin. advisor Vocational Video, Huntington, N.Y., Consolidated Transplant Network, Metairie, La., Thera-Test Diagnostic Labs., Chgo., Kemper Mil. Acad., Boonville, Mo., Soft-Trac Info. Systems, Jasper, Ala., client referal arrangement The Dai-Ichi Kangyo Bank, Ltd.; former bd. dir. Pipelife Svc. Corp., Chem. Applicators, Lafayette, La., Coverage Cons., N.Y.C., Transworld Ins. Intermediaries, Ltd.; former cons. Homecare Mgmt., Ronkonkoma, N.Y., Credicorp, Chgo., The Windy City Group, Chgo.; charter mem. N.Y. Ins. Exch.; guest lectr. fin. risk confs., 1982—, speaker Am. Real Estate Investment Conf., London, 1986; pres., chief exec. officer The Markman Fin. Orgn., Dallas, 1975—. Contbr. articles to profl. jours. Vol. social worker Presbyn. Hosp., Dallas; mem. Dallas Coun. World Affairs, 1962—; active NCCJ. With USMCR, 1942-45; PTO. Clubs: Press, City (Dallas); India Temple (Oklahoma City); L.A. Athletic, Columbian Golf and Country Club, Young Men's Philanthropic League N.Y.C. Office: RR 1 Box 1236 Keswick VA 22947-9747

MARKO, ANDREW PAUL, school system administrator; b. Kingston, Pa., Aug. 16, 1936; s. Andrew Paul and Anna (Stragis) M.; m. Janet Thimm, Aug. 10, 1988; 1 child, Danielle. BA, Kings Coll., Wilkes-Barre, Pa., 1962; MA, Scranton U., 1968, prin.'s cert., 1971; postgrad., Oxford (Eng.) U., 1988, Lehigh U., 1991, Widener U., 1991—. Cert. tchr., secondary prin., supt.'s letter of eligibility, Pa. Elem. tchr. Dundalk Elem. Sch., Balt., 1963-64; English tchr. Kingston (Pa.) High Sch., 1964-66; English tchr. Wyoming Valley West High Sch., Plymouth, Pa., 1966-90, vice prin., 1980, 89; secondary curriculum adminstr. Wyoming Valley West Sch. Dist., Kingston, 1990, dir. instrnl. svcs. and pupil svcs., 1991-95, asst. supt., 1995—; wrestling coach Kingston High Sch., 1964-69; jr.-sr. class advisor Wyoming Valley West High Sch., Plymouth, 1968-88, newspaper advisor, 1970-90, literary mag. advisor, 1970-90, publs. bus. mgr., 1988-90. Councilman Kingston Borough Coun., 1969-77; pres. Holy Name Soc.; ward capt. Heart Fund and March of Dimes. With USN, 1954-57. Mem. ASCD, Pa. Assn. Student Assistance Profls., Pa. Assn. for Supervision and Curriculum Devel., Pa. Assn. Pupil Svcs. Adminstrs., Nat. Assn. Pupil Svcs. Adminstrs., Pa. Staff Devel. Coun., Nat. Mid. Sch. Assn., Ptnrs. for Quality Learning, VFW, Am. Legion, KC. Democrat. Roman Catholic. Avocations: sports, gardening, building, reading. Home: 6 Halowich Rd Harveys Lake PA 18618-0108 Office: Wyoming Valley West Sch Dist 450 N Maple Ave Kingston PA 18704-3630

MARKO, HAROLD MEYRON, diversified industry executive; b. Detroit, Oct. 29, 1925; s. Louis Meyron and Mae (Goldberg) M.; m. Barbara Soss, July 2, 1951; children—Clifford S., Neil L., Matthew P. B.A., U. Mich., 1948. Salesman Core Industries Inc (formerly SOS Consol. Inc.), Bloomfield Hills, Mich., 1951-57; v.p. sales Core Industries Inc (formerly SOS Consol. Inc.), 1957-60, pres., 1960-91; chmn. emeritus, chmn. exec. com. Core Industries Inc. (formerly SOS Consol. Inc.), 1991—; also dir. Core Industries Inc (formerly SOS Consol. Inc.), chmn. bd. dirs., chief exec. officer, 1986. Editorial adv. bd. Fin. World mag.; contbr. chpt. to book. Mem. Founders' Soc., Detroit Inst. Arts; trustee Nat. Jewish Hosp., Denver, Mich. Opera Theatre; bd. dirs. Detroit Symphony Orch.; mem. adv. bd. Greater Detroit Round Table; bd. govs. Cranbrook Acad. Art. Served with AUS, 1943-45. Club: Bloomfield Open Hunt. Home: 1132 Woburn Grn Bloomfield Hills MI 48302-2300 Office: Core Industries Inc 500 N Woodward Ave Bloomfield Hills MI 48304-2961

MARKOE, FRANK, JR., lawyer, business and hospital executive; b. Balt., Sept. 5, 1923; s. Frank and Margaret (Smith) M.; m. Margaret McCormack (div.); children: Andrée Markoe Caldwell, Ritchie Harrison Markoe Scribner. AB, Washington and Lee U., 1947; LLB, U. Md., 1950. Bar: Md. 1950. Pntr. Karl F. Steinmann, Balt., 1948-50, 50-53, Cable & McDaniel, Balt., 1954-55; gen. counsel, dir. Emerson Drug Co., Balt., 1955-56; adminstrv. v.p. Emerson Drug Co., 1957-58; v.p., sec., dir., gen. counsel Warner-Lambert Pharm. Co., 1958-67, exec. com., sr. v.p., dir., gen. counsel, sec., 1967-69, exec. asst. chmn. bd., 1970-71, sr. v.p., 1971-73; exec. v.p. Warner-Lambert Co., Morris Plains, N.J., 1973-77; vice chmn. bd. Warner-Lambert Co., 1977-81; vice chmn. adv. bd. N.Y. Hosp.-Cornell Med. Ctr., 1987—, also chmn. major gifts com. Capital Campaign; hon. holder Alfred E. Driscoll chair Fairleigh Dickinson U. Trustee Morristown Meml. Hosp., Morris County Soc. for Crippled Children and Adults; bd. dirs. N.J. Coll. Medicine and Dentistry, Bd. Internat. Broadcasting, Radio Free Europe/Radio Liberty, Kips Bay Boys; bd. dirs., exec. com., pres. N.J. Ballet. With USAAF, 1942-45, PTO. Mem. U.S. C. of C., Proprietary Assn. (chmn., bd. dirs., exec. com.), Pharm. Mfrs. Assn. (bd. dir., exec. com.), N.J. State C. of C. (bd. dir.), Phi Beta Kappa. Home and Office: 201 Grenville Rd Hobe Sound FL 33455-2414 also: Peacock Point Locust Valley NY 00001

MARKOFF, BRAD STEVEN, lawyer; b. N.Y.C., July 29, 1957; s. Daniel and Geri (Skitol) M.; m. Danna Kay Schmidt, May 17, 1980; children: Andrew David, Paul Steven. AB, Duke U., 1979; JD, Washington U., St. Louis, 1982. Bar: Mo. 1982, U.S. Tax Ct. 1984, N.C. 1985. Assoc. Stolar Partnership, St. Louis, 1982-84; assoc., ptnr. Moore & Van Allen, Raleigh, N.C., 1984-92; ptnr. Smith Helms Mulliss & Moore, Raleigh, 1992—; bd. dirs. Coun. for Entrepreneurial Devel., Research Triangle Park, N.C.; spl. coun. apptd. by N.C. Gov. N.C. R.R. Study Group, 1992-93. Contbr. articles to profl. jours. Mem. ABA, Nat. Assn. Bond Lawyers, Mo. Bar Assn., N.C. Bar Assn. Avocations: golf, astronomy. Office: Smith Helms Mulliss & Moore LLP 2800 Two Hannover Sq Raleigh NC 27601

MARKOFF, STEVEN C., finance company executive. CEO A. Mark Fin. Office: A-Mark Financial 100 Wilshire Blvd Fl 3 Santa Monica CA 90401-1121*

MARKOS, CHRIS, real estate company executive; b. Cleve., Nov. 25, 1926; s. George and Bessie (Papathatou) M.; m. Alice Zaharopoulos, Dec. 11, 1949; children: Marilyn, Irene, Betsy. BA, Case Western Reserve, Cleve., 1960; LLB, LaSalle U., Chgo., 1964. Cert. gen. real estate appraiser, Ohio. Vice-pres. Herbert Laronge Inc., Cleve., 1963-76; v.p. Calabrese, Racek and Markos Inc., Cleve., 1976-83; v.p. Herbert Laronge Inc., Cleve., 1983-87, pres., 1987-88; v.p. Cragin Lang, Inc., Cleve., 1989-91; sr. cons. Grubb & Ellis, Cleve., 1991-93; sr. v.p. Realty One Appraisal Divsn., Independence, Ohio, 1993—; pres. Alcrimar Inc., 1989—. Co-author: Ohio Supplement to Modern Real Estate Practice, 5th-7th edits.; cons. editor, co-author: Modern Real Estate Praactice in Ohio, 1st-3rd edits. Bd. dirs. David N. Meyers Coll., Cleve., 1984—. With U.S. Army, 1945-46. Named Realtor of the Year, Cleve. Bd Realtors, 1976. Mem. Am. Soc. Appraisers (sr., pres. 1973, state dir. 1976), Cleve. Bd. Realtors (pres. 1974, Realtor of Yr. 1976). Republican. Greek Orthodox. Home: 6731 Hidden Lake Trail Brecksville OH 44141-3189 Office: Realty One 6000 Rockside Woods Blvd Cleveland OH 44131-7304 *Everyone's life has a beginning and an ending. It is what happens between these two points that makes up the essence of a person.*

MARKOSKI, JOSEPH PETER, lawyer; b. Floral Park, N.Y., Nov. 7, 1948; s. Stephen Nicholas and Josephine Veronica (Lapkofsky) M.; m. Julie Ann Angus, June 30, 1979; children: Katherine, Caroline, Peter. BSFS, Georgetown U., 1970, JD, 1973. Bar: D.C. 1973. Law clk. Hon. Thomas A. Flannery U.S. Dist. Ct., Washington, 1973-74; assoc. Wilkinson, Cragun & Barker, Washington, 1975-80, ptnr., 1980-82; ptnr. Squire, Sanders & Dempsey, Washington, 1982-96, mng. ptnr., 1991-96; mng. ptnr. Squire, Sanders & Dempsey, London, 1996—; mng. ptnr. Europe, Sanders & Dempsey, London, 1996—; co-chmn. task force on open network initiatives Strategic Planning Group of .S. CCITT Nat. Com., 1988-92; bd. dirs. Cmty. Lodgings, Inc. Author: (with others) Internat. Telecommunications Handbook, 1986; contbr. articles to profl. jours. Capt., USAR, 1970-78. Mem. ABA (vice-chmn. common carrier com. sci. and tech. sect. 1986-88, internat. common carrier project 1980-86), Fed. Commn. Bar Assn. (com. common carrier practice and procedure 1980—), Computer Law Assn. (bd. dirs., chmn. telecomm. bar liaison com. 1994-96), Internat. Bar Assn. (mem. comm. and internat. computer and tech. law coms.), Am. C. of C. (Eng.). Democrat. Roman Catholic. Office: Squire Sanders & Dempsey, Royex Ho Aldermanbury Sq, London EC2V 7HR, England

MARKOU, PETER JOHN, economic developer; b. Keene, N.H., Apr. 11, 1940; s. Peter John and Zoe Nicholas (Kussku) M.; m. Ann Corcoran Gibbons, June 25, 1983; 1 child, Justin Peter. BSBA cum laude, Suffolk U., 1964, MSBA, 1965; cert. in taxation, U. Hartford, 1977; PhD in Econ. Devel., Am. U. London, 1993. Purchasing agt. Fed. Prison Industries, Danbury, Conn., 1965; instr. Becker Jr. Coll., Worcester, Mass., 1967-70; assoc. prof. Post Coll., Waterbury, Conn., 1976-77; asst. prof. bus. North Adams (Mass.) State Coll., 1970-76, assoc. prof., 1977-84, prof., 1984-94; dir. dept. econ. devel. Greene County, Catskill, N.Y., 1996—; exec. dir. Green Mountain Econ. Devel. Corp., White River Junction, Vt., 1994-96. Contbr. articles to small bus. and econ. devel. proc. Pres. North Adams Community Devel. Corp., 1985-91, Hardman Indsl. Pk. Corp., North Adams, 1989-91; mem. North Adams Mgmt. Improvement Com., 1987-88; mem., sec. Mass. Mus. Contemporary Art Cultural Commn., North Adams, 1988—; bd. dirs. No. Berkshire Community Action, North Adams, 1989-91; mem. adv. bd. Salvation Army, North Adams, 1988-90. Recipient Mass. Pride in Performance award Commonwealth of Mass., 1989. Mem. Nat. Coun. Urban Econ. Devel., Nat. Soc. Pub. Accts. (educator mem.), Am. Econ. Devel. Coun. (mem. bd. dirs.), N.E. Indsl. Developers Assn., N.E. Econ. Developers Assn., Capital Region Econ. Devel. Corp., N.Y. State Econ. Devel. Coun., Waterfront Ctr., Pvt. Industry Coun. Home: PO Box 861 Catskill NY 12414-0861 Office: Greene County Dept Econ Devel Catskill NY 12414

MARKOVICH, PATRICIA, economist; b. Oakland, Calif.; d. Patrick Joseph and Helen Emily (Prydz) Markovich; BA in Econs., MS in Econs., U. Calif.-Berkeley; postgrad. (Lilly Found. grantee) Stanford U., (NSF grantee) Oreg. Grad. Rsch. Ctr.; children: Michael Sean Treece, Bryan Jeffry Treece, Tiffany Helene Treece. Cert. Emergency Mgmt. Planner. Pub. rels. Pettler Advt., Inc.; pvt. practice polit. and econs. cons.; aide to majority whip Oreg. Ho. of Reps.; lectr., instr., various Calif. instns., Chemeketa (Oreg.) Coll., Portland (Oreg.) State U.; commr. City of Oakland (Calif.), 1970-74; chairperson, bd. dirs. Cable Sta. KCOM; mem. gen. plan commn. City of Piedmont, Calif.; with Oakland Mus. Archives of Calif. Artists. Mem. Internat. Assn. Feminist Economists, Mensa (officer San Francisco region), Bay Area Artists Assn. (coord., founding mem.), Berkeley Art Ctr. Assn., San Francisco Arts Commn. File, Calif. Index for Contemporary Arts, Pro Arts, YLEM: Artists Using Sci. and Tech., NAFE, No. Calif. Pub. Ednl. and Govt. Access Cable TV Com. (founding), Triple Nine Soc., Nat. Coord. Coun. Emergency Mgmt., Am. Econ. Assn., Allied Social Scis. Assn., N.Y. Acad. Scis., Internat. Assn. for Feminist Economists.

MARKOVITZ, ALVIN, molecular biologist, geneticist, educator; b. Chgo., May 30, 1929; s. Raymond and Fannie (Rudich) M.; m. Harriet June Porter, Aug. 24, 1952; children—Diane (dec.), Paula, Ellen, Nancy. B.S., U. Ill., 1950, M.S., 1952; Ph.D., U. Wash., 1955. Instr., U. Chgo., 1957-59; asst. prof., 1959-64, assoc. prof. microbiology, 1964-74, prof. microbiology, 1974-84, prof. biochemistry and molecular biology, 1984—. Contbr. articles to sci. publs. Grantee NIH, 1964-88. Mem. Am. Soc. for Microbiology, Am. Soc. for Biochemistry and Molecular Biology, AAAS. Jewish. Avocations: piano, sports.

MARKOWICZ, VICTOR, video company executive; b. Tynda, USSR, July 6, 1944; s. Szymon and Gustawa (Goldstain) M.; m. Monica A. Minkiewicz, July 10, 1971; children: Clara, Daniela. Student, U. Warsaw, Poland, 1962-64; BS in Maths., Technion U., Haifa, Israel, 1966. Software mgr. Elbit Computers, Ltd., Haifa, 1966-69; tech. dir., co-founder System Ops., Inc., Princeton, N.J., 1970-76; pres., co-founder Gaming Dimensions, Providence, 1976-78; v.p. Datatrol Inc., Hudson, Mass., 1978-80; chmn., dir., co-founder GTech Corp., Providence, 1981—; bd. dirs. Intervoice, Dallas, Nat. TV Network Mgmt., Pasadena. Designer of state lottery games, 1970—; exec. producer (movie) South of Reno, 1987. Jewish. Avocations: bridge, skiing, tennis. Office: Gtech Corp 55 Technology Way West Greenwich RI 02817-1711*

MARKOWITZ, HARRY M., finance and economics educator; b. Chicago, Ill., Aug. 24, 1927; s. Morris and Mildred (Gruber) M.; m. Barbara Gay. PhB, U. Chgo., 1947, MA, 1950, PhD, 1954. With research staff Rand Corp., Santa Monica, Calif., 1952-60, 61-63; tech. dir. Consol. Analysis Ctrs., Inc., Santa Monica, 1963-68; prof. UCLA, Westwood, 1968-69; pres. Arbitrage Mgmt. Co., N.Y.C., 1969-72; pvt. practice cons. N.Y.C., 1972-74; with research staff T.J. Watson Research Ctr. IBM, Yorktown Hills, N.Y., 1974-83; Speiser prof. fin. Baruch Coll. CUNY, N.Y.C., 1982-93; dir. rsch. Daiwa Securities Trust Co, Jersey City, N.J., 1990—; v.p. Inst. Mgmt. Sci., 1960-62. Author: Portfolio Selection: Efficient Diversification of Investments, 1959, Mean-Variance Analysis in Portfolio Choice, 1987; co-author: SIMSCRIPT Simulation Programming Language, 1963; co-editor: Process Analysis of Economic Capabilities, 1963. Recipient John von Neumann Theory prize Ops. Rsch. Soc. Am. and Inst. Mgmt. Sci., 1989, Nobel Prize in Econs., 1990. Fellow Econometric Soc., Am. Acad. Arts and Scis.; mem. Am. Fin. Assn. (pres. 1982—). Office: 1010 Turquoise St Ste 245 San Diego CA 92109-1266 also: Daiwa Securities 1 Evertrust Plz Jersey City NJ 07302-3051

MARKOWITZ, SAMUEL SOLOMON, chemistry educator; b. Bklyn., Oct. 31, 1931; s. Max and Florence Ethel (Goldman) M.; children: Michael, Daniel, Jonah; m. 2d Lydia de Antonis, Oct. 31, 1993. BS in Chemistry, Rensselaer Poly. Inst., 1953; MA, Princeton U., 1955, PhD, 1957; postgrad. Brookhaven Nat. Lab., 1955-57. Asst. prof. chemistry U. Calif.-Berkeley, 1958-64, assoc. prof., 1964-72, prof., 1972—; faculty sr. scientist Lawrence Berkeley Lab., 1958—; vis. prof. nuclear physics Weizmann Inst. Sci., Rehovot, Israel, 1973-74. Mem. Bd. Edn. of Berkeley Unified Sch. Dist., 1969-73, pres. bd., 1971-72. Recipient Elizabeth McFeely D'Urso Meml. Pub. Ofcl. award Alameda County Edn. Assn., 1973; LeRoy McKay fellow Princeton U., 1955; Charlotte Elizabeth Proctor fellow Princeton U., 1956; NSF postdoctoral fellow U. Birmingham, Eng., 1957-58; NSF sr. postdoctoral fellow Faculte des Scis. de L'Universite de Paris a Orsay, Laboratoire Joliot-Curie de Physique Nucleaire, 1964-65. Fellow AAAS; mem. Am. Chem. Soc. (bd. dirs. Calif. sect., chmn. 1991, 93-94), Am. Phys. Soc., Am. Inst. Chemists, N.Y. Acad. Scis., Calif. Inst. Chemists, Sigma Xi. Home: 317 Tideway Dr Alameda CA 94501-3540 Office: U Calif Dept Chemistry Berkeley CA 94720

MARKOWSKA, ALICJA LIDIA, neuroscientist, researcher; b. Warsaw, Poland, Aug. 22, 1948; came to U.S., 1986; d. Marian Boleslaw and Eugenia Krystyna (Wodzynska) Pawlak; m. Janusz Jozef Markowski, Oct. 23, 1971; children: Marta Agnieszka, Michal Jacek. BA, MSc, Warsaw U., 1971; PhD, Nencki Inst., Warsaw, 1979. Postdoctoral fellow Nencki Inst., 1979-81, asst. prof., 1981-86; assoc. rschr. Johns Hopkins U., Balt., 1987-91, rsch. scientist, 1991-92, prin. rsch. sci., prof., 1992-94, head of neuromnemonic lab., 1994—; vis. fellow Czechoslovak Acad. Sci., Prague, 1981; rschr., lectr. U. Bergen, Norway, 1983; vis. faculty Johns Hopkins U., 1986-87; cons. Sigma Tau & Otsuka Co., Italy, Japan, 1990-92. Reviewer Neurobiology of Aging, 1992—, Behavioral Brain Rsch., 1992—' contbr. chpts. to Preoperative Events, 1989, Prospective on Cognitive Neuroscience, 1990, Encyclopedia of Memory, 1992, Neuropsychology of Memory, 1992, Methods in Behavioral Pharmacology, 1993. Grantee Nat. Inst. Age, 1993—, NSF, 1990-93, NIH, 1992—. Mem. AAAS, Soc. for Neuroscience, Internat. Brain Rsch., N.Y. Acad. Sci. Achievements include first evidence that pharmacological interventions with cholinergic against, oxotremorine, through intracranial stimulation of the septohippocampal system can alleviate age-related mnemonic impairments, research has focused on an importance of the septohippocampal cholinergic system in memory function, brain mechanisms involved in different kinds of memory and sensorimotor skills and their relations to aging, amnesia, and dementia, animal models to examine the effect of nerve growth factor treatment. Office: Johns Hopkins U 34th Charles St Baltimore MD 21218 Office: Dept Psychology Neuromnemonic Lab Johns Hopkins U Baltimore MD 21218

MARKOWSKI, JOHN JOSEPH, human resources executive; b. N.Y.C., Jan. 12, 1947; s. Stanley J. and Helen (Krawiecki) M.; m. Christine Cipriano, Sept. 15, 1974; children: Alexis Marie, Laura Jane. BSEE, Poly. U., Bklyn., 1968, MS in Mgmt., 1973. Engr. Gen. Dynamics Corp., Pomona, Calif., 1968-69; mgr. employee rels. Unisys Corp., Great Neck, N.Y., 1969-82; dir. compensation Merck & Co. Inc., Rahway, N.J., 1982-91; dir. human resources Astra Merck, Wayne, Pa., 1991-95; asst. v.p. human resources Am. Home Products Corp., Madison, N.J., 1995—. Mem. coun. on compensation The Conf. Bd., N.Y.C., 1988-91; sponsor Ctr. for Advanced Human Resources Studies, Ithaca, N.Y., 1991-95. Named Exec. Human Resources Champion, Cornell U., 1993. Mem. Am. Compensation Assn., Soc. for Human Resources Mgmt., Human Resources Planning Soc. Avocation:

Dept. 56 Dickens village collecting. Office: Am Home Products Corp 5 Giralda Farms Madison NJ 07940-1027

MARKS, ARNOLD, journalist; b. Phila., Aug. 4, 1912; s. Morris M. and Esther (Joel) M.; m. Isabelle Ruppert, Oct. 3, 1942 (dec.); 1 son, Rupert William Joel (dec.); m. Emi Seligman Simon. B.A., U. Wash., 1935; M.S., Columbia U., 1939. Editor Pasco (Wash.) Herald, 1946; with Oreg. Jour., Portland, 1946-78; drama, TV, entertainment editor Oreg. Jour., 1948-58, entertainment editor, 1958-78, ret., 1978, freelance writer. Served with AUS, 1942-46. Mem. Sigma Delta Chi, Sigma Alpha Mu. Club: University (Portland). Home: PO Box 590 Gleneden Beach OR 97388-0590 also: 2393 SW Park Pl Portland OR 97205-1056 *In retrospect, there is great satisfaction in the thought that the years seem more loaded with heartwarming memories than with disappointments.*

MARKS, BARBARA HANZEL, publishing executive; b. Providence, Sept. 8, 1955; d. Albert and Pearl (Garfinkel) Hanzel; m. Alan D. Marks, Apr. 3, 1982; children: Harrison Douglas, Eleanor Kate. B.A. in English and Am. Lit., Harvard U., 1977, M.B.A., 1980. Circulation mgr. New Age Mag., Brookline, Mass., 1977-78; dir. planning Leisure Mags., N.Y.C., 1980-81; dir. planning ABC Pub., N.Y.C., 1981-82, v.p. strategic planning, 1982-83, v.p. ops., fin., 1984-88, v.p. ops. and fin., 1988-89. Class fund agt. Harvard U. Sch. Bus., 1987—; chmn. learning to look com. Fox Meadow Sch., 1996—. Honoree, ABC Pub., N.Y.C., 1985; named to City YWCA Acad. Women Achievers. Mem. Mag. Pubs. Assn., Am. Bus. Press. Club: Harvard (N.Y.C.). Home: 20 Kensington Rd Scarsdale NY 10583-2217

MARKS, BERNARD BAILIN, lawyer; b. Sioux City, Iowa, Sept. 6, 1917; s. Meyer A. and Beulah (Bailin) M.;m. Betty L. Marks; 1 child, Susan E. BA, Harvard U., 1939, JD, 1942. Bar: Iowa 1942. With firm Shull, Marshall & Marks, Sioux City, 1946-85, ptnr., 1949-85; ptnr. Marks & Madsen, Sioux City, 1985—; sec., asst. treas., dir. Flavorland Industries, Inc. (formerly Needham Packing Co., Inc.), Sioux City, 1962-81; sec., dir. KTIV-TV Co., Sioux City, 1965-74; bd. dirs. First Nat. Bank, Firstar Bank, Sioux City, 1963-91. Bd. dirs. Iowa Heart Assn., 1960, Woodbury County chpt., 1958-64, pres., 1962-64; bd. dirs. Sioux City Art Center, 1952-54, Sioux City United Fund, 1965-71, Sioux City Community Appeals Bd., 1965-68; trustee Briar Cliff Coll., Sioux City, 1968-74. Served with USAAF, 1942-46. Fellow Iowa Bar Assn. Found.; mem. ABA, Iowa Bar Assn., Woodbury County Bar Assn. (prews. 1958), Am. Coll. Trust and Estate Counsel, Sioux City C. of C. (bd. dirs. 1964-67, treas. 1965-66), Sioux City Lawyers Club (pres. 1951), Sioux City Country Club (bd. dirs. 1963-64). Clubs: Sioux City Lawyers (pres. 1951), Sioux City Country (bd. dirs. 1963-64). Office: Marks & Madsen 303 Piper Jaffray Bldg PO Box 3226 Sioux City IA 51102

MARKS, BRUCE, artistic director, choreographer; b. N.Y.C., Jan. 23, 1937; s. Albert and Helen (Kosersky) M.; m. Toni Pihl Petersen, Jan. 27, 1966 (dec. May 1985); children: Erik Antony, Adam Christopher, Kenneth Rikard. Student, Brandeis U., 1954-55, Juilliard Sch., 1955-56; DFA (hon.), Wheaton Coll., 1986, Franklin Pierce Coll., 1990, U. Mass., 1995, Juilliard Sch., 1996, Northeastern U., 1997. Prof. U. Utah, 1981, 84-86; artistic dir. Boston Ballet Co., 1985—; mem. dance adv. panel Nat. Endowment for Arts, 1979, chmn. internat. selection com., 1979, chmn. dance adv. panel, 1981, mem. nat. adv. bd. on arts and edn., 1989; bd. dirs., mem. exec. com., Dance/USA 1989, 92—, chmn., 1990-92, chmn. govt. affairs, 1992—; mem. U.S.-USSR Commn. on Dance and Theatre Studies, Am. Coun. Learned Socs./IREX; mem. jury Internat. Moscow Internat. Ballet Competition, 1989. Prin. dancer Met. Opera, 1956-61, Am. Ballet Theatre, 1961-72, Royal Swedish Ballet, 1963, Festival Ballet, London, 1965, Royal Danish Ballet, 1971-76; artistic dir. Ballet West, Salt Lake City, 1976-85; choreographer Eliot Feld Ballet Co., 1970, Royal Danish Ballet, 1972-73, Netherlands Dance Theatre, 1974, Ballet West, 1976-85; artistic fellow Aspen Inst. for Humanistic Studies, 1979—. Bd. dirs. Am. Arts Alliance, 1983-85, Am. Coun. for Arts, 1985—; bd. dirs. Dance U.S.A., 1988-94, chmn., 1990-92; chmn. U.S.A. Internat. Ballet Competition, Jackson, Micc., 1990—, vice chair jury Helsinki, Finland, 1991, judge Helsinki Ballet Competition 1995; mem. nat. adv. bd. on arts and edn. NEA, 1989-91; mem. internat. jury 1st Japan Internat. Ballet Competition, Nagoya, Japan, 1993, 96, Am. jury for Prix de Lausanne, 1994; mem. Brandeis Creative Arts Awards Commn., 1993, chmn. Brandeis Creative Arts Awards Dance, 1994; chair Grants to Dance Cos. panel NEA, 1993, overview panel, 1994. Recipient Disting. Svc. award for artistic prodn. Nat. Govs. Assn., 1994, Capezio award Balletmakers, Inc., 1995, Hon. Doctorate Fine Arts, Julliard, 1996, Dance Mag. award, 1997. Office: Boston Ballet 19 Clarendon St Boston MA 02116-6107

MARKS, CHARLES CALDWELL, retired investment banker, retired industrial distribution company executive; b. Birmingham, Ala., June 1, 1921; s. Charles Pollard and Isabel (Caldwell) M.; m. Jeanne Vigeant, Jan. 12, 1945; children: Randolph C., Margaret Marks Porter, Charles P. Student, Birmingham U., 1930-38; BS in Physics, U. of South, 1942; grad. mgmt. seminar, Harvard U., 1957; DCL (hon.), U. of the South, 1989; LLD (hon.), U. Ala., Birmingham, 1990. With Owen-Richards Co. (name changed to Motion Industries, Inc. 1970), Birmingham, 1946—; chmn. bd. Owen-Richards Co. (name changed to Motion Industries, Inc. 1970), 1952-73, pres., 1973-83; vice chmn. bd. Porter White & Yardley Cos., Inc., 1984-92, ret., 1992; bd. dirs. emeritus Genuine Parts Co., BE & K Inc., emeritus; bd. dirs., chmn. Birmingham br. Fed. Res. Bank of Atlanta. Bd. dirs. So. Rsch. Inst., exec. com., 1987-95, dir. emeritus, 1995—; bd. govs. Indian Springs Sch., dir. emeritus, 1995—; pres., bd. dirs. Workshop for Blind, Birmingham, 1958-61, Children's Aid Soc. Birmingham, 1962; chmn. Com. of 100, Birmingham, 1963; co-chmn. United Appeals of Jefferson County, 1963; trustee, regent U. of South; pres. St. Vincent's Found., 1987; bd. dirs. U. Ala.-Birmingham Rsch. Found., Exec. Svcs. Corps. of Birmingham, 1984-96. Lt. USNR, WWII, ATO, MTO. Mem. Navy League, The Club, Redstone Club, John's Island Club, Mountain Brook Club, Willow Point Club, Ala. Newcomen Soc., Blue Key, Phi Beta Kappa, Sigma Alpha Epsilon. Episcopalian. Home: 2828 Cherokee Rd Birmingham AL 35223-2607 Office: 2160 Highland Ave Suite 301 Birmingham AL 35205

MARKS, CHARLES DENNERY, insurance salesman; b. New Orleans, Nov. 22, 1935; s. Sidney Leroy Marks and Melanie Dennery; m. Gillian E. Otter, Sept. 1, 1963; children: Elizabeth Dennery, Richard Dennery. BA, Yale U., 1957. CLU; ChFC; accredited estate planner. With Charles Dennery, Inc., 1959-63; sales rep. Prudential Ins. Co., New Orleans, 1964—. Past bd. dirs. Boys Club Greater New Orleans, Big Bros. Greater New Orleans, United Way; past pres. Goodwill Rehab. Ctr.; vice chmn. Jr. Achievement; active Temple Sinai Synagogue. 1st lt. U.S. Army, 1957-59. Recipient award Volunteer Activist, 1983. Mem. Am. Soc. CLU and ChFC (pres. New Orleans chpt. 1984-85), Assn. Advanced Life Underwriting, Life Underwriters Pol. Action Com. (diplomat, sec./treas. 1982-87), La. Assn. Life Underwriters (Life Underwriter of Yr. 1985, 87, pres. 1986-87), New Orleans Estate Planning Coun. (pres. 1986-87), New Orleans Life Underwriters Assn. (Life Underwriter of Yr. 1981, pres. 1982-83), Million Dollar Round Table (Top of the Table 1986-89, exec. com. 1990-94, pres. 1993) Nat. Assn. Life Underwriters (vice chmn. fin. com. 1993—), Life and Health Found. for Edn. (life. chmn. 1996—). Republican. Home: 1525 Eleonore St New Orleans LA 70115-4242 Office: 1250 Poydras St Ste 325 New Orleans LA 70113-1826

MARKS, CRAIG, management educator, consultant, engineer; b. Salt Lake City, Oct. 9, 1929; s. Elmer Lester and Louie Thelma (Marks) M.; m. Lois Marie Brinkman, June 11, 1950 (div. 1972); children—Gary C., Diane Marks White, Marian Marks Deming; m. Anne Mary Crowe, Oct. 28, 1972. B.S.M.E., Calif. Inst. Tech., 1950, M.S.M.E., 1951, Ph.D. in Mech. Engring., 1955. Instr. Calif. Inst. Tech., Pasadena, 1953-55; supr. Ford Motor Co., Detroit, 1955-56, Gen. Motors Research Labs., Warren, Mich., 1956-57; asst. engr.-in-charge engring. staff Gen. Motors Corp., Warren, 1957-67; engr.-in-charge Gen. Motors Corp., 1967-72, exec. asst. to v.p., 1972-79, exec. dir. environ. activity staff, 1979-83; v.p. engring. and tech. TRW Inc., Cleve., Ohio, 1983-88; v.p. tech. and productivity Allied Signal Inc., Southfield, Mich., 1988-91; prof. U. Mich., 1991—; pres. CMS-Creative Mgmt. Solutions, Bloomfield Hills, Mich., 1991—; co-dir. Tauber Mfg. Inst. U. Mich., 1995—. Contbr. articles to profl. jours.; patentee in field. Speaker civic leaders meetings Gen. Motors Corp., 1977-82. Fellow Soc. Automotive Engrs. (bd. dirs.); mem. NAE, ASME, Engring. Soc. Detroit (bd. dirs.), Sigma Xi, Tau Beta Pi. Christian Scientist. Avocations: flying; tennis; golf. Home and Office: 174 Kirkwood Ct Bloomfield Hills MI 48304-2926

MARKS, EDWARD B., international social service administrator; b. N.Y.C., Apr. 22, 1911; s. Edward B. and Miriam (Chuck) M.; m. Margaret Levi (dec. 1980); 2 children; m. Vera J. Barad, 1987. BA cum laude, Dartmouth Coll., 1932; MA in Sociology, Columbia U., 1938. Assoc. editor Am. Wine and Liquor Jour., N.Y.C., 1933-36; mng. editor Better Times mag. Welfare Coun. N.Y.C., 1937-38; dir. div. for social and cultural adjustment Nat. Refugee Svc., N.Y.C., 1938-42; refugee program officer War Relocation Authority, Dept. Interior, Washington, 1942-46; chief of mission for Greece UN Internat. Refugee Orgn., Geneva and Athens, 1947-50; chief of mission successively for Greece, N.Y., and Yugoslavia Internat. Migration Orgn., 1951-58; exec. dir. U.S. Com. for Refugees, N.Y.C., 1958-62; dep. chief office cen. African affairs AID, Washington, 1962-65; asst. dir. for relief and rehab., Vietnam AID, 1965-66, aid coordination officer, Am. Embassy, U.K., 1966-68, asst. dir. for relief and rehab., Nigeria, 1969-71, voluntary agy. liaison officer for Asia, 1973-75; various emergency and liaison assignments UNICEF, N.Y.C., Paris, Geneva, 1971-73; dep. dir. secretariat Internat. Yr. of Child UNICEF, N.Y.C., 1976-80, liaison rep. for UN Yr. for Disabled, 1981-82, internat. cons., 1983-85; interim pres. U.S. Com. for UNICEF, N.Y.C., 1985, bd. dirs., mem. exec. com., chmn. nominating com., 1986-92; pres. then chmn. Immigration and Refugee Svcs. Am., 1985—; instr. Boston U. Sch. Social Work, 1988, 89. Author: A World of Art--The United Nations Collection, 1996; contbr. articles to The New Yorker, N.Y. Times Mag., other jours. Recipient 1st Disting. Career award AID, 1976; Nat. Endowment for Arts grantee, 1994. Address: 333 E 46th St New York NY 10017-7401 also: 4 Channing St Cambridge MA 02138-4714

MARKS, EDWIN S., investment company executive; b. N.Y.C., June 3, 1926; s. Carl and Edith R. (Smith) M.; m. Nancy Lucille Abeles, June 21, 1949; children: Carolyn Gail, Linda Beth, Constance Ann. Student, Princeton U., 1944-45; BS, U.S. Mil. Acad., 1949. V.p. Carl Marks & Co., Inc., N.Y.C., 1958-61, pres., 1961—, also bd. dirs.; dir., exec. v.p. CMNY Capital Co. Inc., 1962—. Author: What I Know about Foreign Securities, 1958. Trustee Lincoln Ctr. Fund, 1966-77, Hofstra U., 1974-79, Sarah Lawrence Coll., 1979-81, North Shore Univ. Hosp., Manhasset, N.Y.; chmn. bd. overseers Rsch. Lab., North Shore Univ. Hosp.; bd. dirs. Chief Execs. Orgn. Cold Spring Harbor Labs., 1992, Smith New Court PLC, London, 1988-94; bd. dirs., exec. com. Lincoln Ctr. for the Performing Arts. Mem. West Point Soc., N.Y. Bd. Trade, Harmonie Club. Office: Carl Marks & Co Inc 135 E 57th St New York NY 10022-2050

MARKS, ELAINE, French language educator; b. N.Y.C., Nov. 13, 1930; d. Harry and Ruth (Elin) M. BA, Bryn Mawr Coll., 1952; MA, U. Pa., 1953; PhD, NYU, 1958. Asst. prof. French NYU, N.Y.C., 1958-60; assoc. prof. U. Wis., Milw., 1963-65; prof. U. Wis., Madison, 1967-68, prof. French, Italian and women's studies, 1980—; prof. French U. Mass., Amherst, 1965-66; dir. Women's Studies Rsch. Ctr., 1977-85. Author: Colette, 1960, 2d edit., 1981, Simone de Beauvoir: Encounters with Death, 1973, Marrano as Metaphor: the Jewish Presence in French Writing, 1996; co-editor: Homosexualities and French Literature, 1979, 2d edit., 1990, New French Feminisms, 1980, 81; editor: Critical Essays on Simone de Beauvoir, 1987. Decorated officier Ordre Palmes Académiques (France), 1994; recipient Disting. Alumni award NYU Grad. Sch. Arts and Sci. Alumni Assn., 1994; Wis. Alumni Rsch. Found. U. House Professorship, 1988; Fulbright fellow, France, 1956-57, Guggenheim fellow, 1992. Mem. MLA (pres. 1993), Midwest MLA, Am. Assn. Tchrs. French, Nat. Women's Studies Assn. Home: 2040 Field St Madison WI 53713-1159

MARKS, ESTHER L., metals company executive; b. Canton, Ohio, Oct. 3, 1927; d. Jacob and Ella (Wisman) Rosky; m. Irwin Alfred Marks, June 29, 1947; children: Jules, Howard, Marilyn. Student, Ohio State U., 1945-46, Youngstown State U., 1946-47. V.p. Steel City Iron & Metal, Inc., Youngstown, Ohio. Pres. Jr. Hadassah, Youngstown, 1943-45, Pioneer Women, Youngstown, 1951, Anshe Emeth Sisterhood, Youngstown, Broadway Theatre League, Youngstown, 1958, B'nai B'rith Women, Youngstown, 1962, Dist. 2 B'nai B'rith Women, Cleve., 1969-70, Jewish Cmty. Ctr., Youngstown, Youngstown Area Jewish Fedn., 1988-90; v.p. United Way, Youngstown, 1991, chmn., 1996; grad. Leadership Youngstown, 1991; bd. Akiva Acad. Commn. for Jewish Edn., Temple El Emeth, Stambaugh Auditorium. Named Guardian of the Menorah B'nai B'rith, Youngstown, 1978; recipient B'nai B'rith Girls Alumda award, Washington, 1989, Woman of Valor award Jewish Fedn., 1996. Mem. LMV, YWCA, Ohio Hist. Soc. Democrat. Jewish. Avocations: knitting, organizational work. Home: 3511 5th Ave Youngstown OH 44505-1907 Office: 703 Wilson Ave Youngstown OH 44506-1445

MARKS, FLORENCE CARLIN ELLIOTT, retired nursing informaticist; b. Louisville, Ky., Oct. 15, 1928; d. David Carlin and Anna Marie (Lance) Elliott; m. George Edward Marks, Mar. 18, 1961; children: Mary Ellen Marks Fox, Ruth Ann, Charles Douglas. BS in Chemistry and Zoology, U. Cin., 1949; BSN, U. Minn., 1953, M in Nursing Adminstrn., 1956. RN, Minn. From staff nurse to asst. head nurse U. Minn. Hosps., Mpls., 1953-54; staff nurse Marseilisbog Hosp., Aarhaus, Denmark, 1954-55; nursing supr. U. Minn. Hosps., Mpls., 1956-61, spl. asst. to dir. of nursing svc., 1962; rsch. asst. Hill Family Found. Nursing Rsch. Project, Mpls., 1966-69; writer Sch. Nursing U. Minn., Mpls., 1976, cons., 1976, 78, mem. adj. faculty, 1991-96; nursing program specialist Hennepin County Med. Ctr., Mpls., 1978-84, nursing info. sys. dir., cons., 1987-96, ret., 1996; nursing utilization system coord. U. Minn. Hosps., Mpls., 1984-87; cons. Creative Nursing Mgmt., 1992-96; spkr., lectr. various nursing confs. in U.S. Contbr. articles to profl. publs., chpts. to profl. books, posters, abstracts; co-author: (with Joan Williams) (TV series) TLC, 1953 (McCall's award 1954); editor: Tomorrow's Nurse, 1960-62; Minn. Nursing Accent (commemorative issue 60th anniversary) May, 1965. Prin. flutist St. Anthony Civic Orch., 1975—, bd. dirs., 1988-92, adminstrv. bd. Hennepin Ave. United Meth. Ch., 1974-77, tchr., 1966-83 intermittently, cmty. outreach ministry, chair adv. com., 1992-95; mem. U. Minn. Sch. Nursing Densford Recognition Com., 1992-96; troop leader Mpls. coun. Girl Scouts USA, 1971-85, bd. dirs., 1977-79, svc. unit mgr., 1973-77; den leader Cub Scouts Webelo den, Viking coun. Boy Scouts Am., 1977-79; v.p. Wilshire Park PTSA, 1975-76, pres., 1976-77. Recipient Thanks Badge Greater Mpls. Girl Scout Coun. Mem. Minn. Nurses Assn. (various coms., bd. dirs. 1959-61), Minn. League for Nursing, Minn. Heart Assn. (profl. edn. com. 1959-61), Nursing Info. Discussion Group (chmn. Twin City program com. 1985-91, 95—), U. Minn. Sch. Nursing Alumni Assn. (bd. dirs. 1963-67, pres. 1965-66), Mortar Bd., Zeta Tau Alpha, Tau Beta Sigma, Sigma Theta Tau (bd. dirs. Zeta chpt. 1969-73, 89-91, pres. 1972-73, heritage com. 1990). Home: 3424 Silver Lake Rd NE Minneapolis MN 55418-1605

MARKS, HERBERT EDWARD, lawyer; b. Dayton, Ohio, Nov. 3, 1935; s. I.M. and Sarah S. M.; m. Marcia Frager; children: Jennifer L., Susan E. A.B. with high distinction, U. Mich., 1957; J.D., Yale U., 1960; post-grad., George Washington U. Law Sch., 1965-67. Bar: Ohio 1960, D.C. 1964, U.S. Supreme Ct. 1965. Law clk. to chief judge U.S. Ct. Claims, 1964-65; assoc. Wilkinson, Cragun & Barker, Washington, 1965-69, ptnr., 1969-82; ptnr. Squire, Sanders & Dempsey, Washington, 1982—; assoc. gen. counsel Presdl. Inaugural Coms., 1969, 73, 81; chmn. U.S. State Dept. Adv. Panel on Internat. Telecomm. Law, 1987-91; mem. adv. com. on internat. comm. and info. policy U.S. State Dept., 1988-91; mem. U.S. del. ITU European Telecomm. Devel. Conf., 1991. Contbr. articles to legal jours. Served to capt. JAG USAF, 1960-64. Mem. ABA (chair sci. and tech. sect. 1990-91, chmn. communications div. 1986-88), D.C. Bar Assn., Computer Law Assn. (pres. 1975-77, bd. dirs. 1972-85, adv. bd. 1985—), Fed. Communications Bar Assn., Cosmos Club, Kenwood Golf & Country Club, Phi Beta Kappa. Office: Squire Sanders & Dempsey 1201 Pennsylvania Ave NW PO Box 407 Washington DC 20004 also: 5317 Cardinal Ct Bethesda MD 20816-2908

MARKS, JAMES FREDERIC, pediatric endocrinologist, educator; b. Pitts., Dec. 18, 1928; s. Alfred Mozelle and Cecil (Cuff) M.; m. Mary Fay Clement, Jan. 29, 1959; 1 child, Roland Phillip. BA, Princeton U., 1950; MD, Harvard U., 1954; MPH, U. Pitts., 1984. Intern Montefiore Hosp., Pitts., 1954-55; resident in pediatrics Children's Hosp. of Pitts., 1955-57; rsch. fellow in pediatric endocrinology U. Pitts., 1959-61; asst. prof. dept. pediatrics U. Tex. Southwestern Med., Dallas, 1961-68, assoc. prof. pediatrics, 1968—; bd. dirs. State Newborn Screening Program, Tex., 1980—. Contbr. articles to profl. publs., chpts. to med. textbooks. Capt. U.S. Army, 1957-59. Sr. rsch. fellow USPHS, 1983-84. Mem. Am. Diabetes Assn. (bd. dirs. Tex. affiliate 1992-97), Am. Acad. Pediatrics, Endocrine Soc., Soc. for Pediatric Rsch. Achievements include research in thyroid function in infancy, delineation of early clinical course in Lesch-Nyhan disease, observations on the possible genetic factors in diabetic microvascular disease. Office: U Tex Southwestern Med 5323 Harry Hines Blvd Dallas TX 75235-7208

MARKS, JAMES GARFIELD, JR., dermatologist; b. Trenton, N.J., May 19, 1945; s. James Garfield and Lavinia May (Ellis) M.; m. Joyce Lynne Turner, Aug. 9, 1969; 1 child, Shannon. BA, Wilkes Coll., 1967; MD, Temple U., 1971. Intern Geisinger Med. Ctr., Danville, Pa., 1971-72; resident Wilford Hall USAF Med. Ctr., San Antonio, 1975-78; staff dermatologist Pa. State U. Coll. Medicine, Hershey, 1980—, asst. prof., 1980-85, assoc. prof., 1985-91, prof. medicine, 1991—; clin. instr. dermatology U. Tex. Health Sci. Ctr., San Antonio, 1978-80. Author: Contact and Occupational Dermatology, 1997, Principles of Dermatology, 1993, (with others) Principles of CLinical Diagnosis, 1992, Principles and Practice of Dermatology, 1990, Occupational Skin Diseases, 1990, Conn's Current Therapy, 1988, 89; contbr. articles to profl. jours. Bd. dirs. Braun Sta. East Cmty., 1976. Lt. col. USAF, 1972-80. Decorated Meritorious Svc. Commendation meadl; Am. Acad. Dermatology Exch. fellow, 1984; recipient Roerig Pharms. Challenges in Dermatology Ednl. award, 1982. Mem. Am. Acad. Dermatology, Am. Contact Dermatitis Soc., N.Am. Contact Dermatitis Group, Pa. Acad. Dermatology, Phila. Dermatology Soc., European Soc. Contact Dermatitis, World Fragrance Rsch. Team, Soc. Investigative Dermatology, Assn. Mil. Dermatologists, Dermatology Found., Agromedicine Consortium, Lions (v.p. 1982, pres. 1983). Office: Hershey Med Ctr 500 University Dr # 850 Hershey PA 17033-2360

MARKS, JAMES S., public health service administrator; b. May 13, 1948. AB cum laude, Williams Coll., 1969; MD, SUNY, Buffalo, 1973; MPH, Yale U., 1980. Diplomate Am. Bd. Pediatrics. Intern in pediat. U. Calif., San Francisco, 1973-74, resident in pediat., 1974-75, chief resident pediatric outpatient dept., 1975-76; resident in preventive medicine Ctrs. for Disease Control, Atlanta, 1977-78; fellow Robert Wood Johnson Clin. Scholars Program Yale U., New Haven, Conn., 1978-80; resident in preventive medicine Ctrs. for Disease Control, Atlanta, 1981-82, chief epidemiology and rsch. br., nutrition divsn., 1982-84, asst. dir. preventive medicine residency program, 1985-87, dir. divsn. reproductive health, 1987, coord. for chronic disease control activities, 1987-88, acting dir. divsn. diabetes transl., 1988-89, acting dir. divsn. chronic disease control, 1990-91, dir. divsn. reproductive health, 1992-95, dir. Nat. Ctr. Chronic Disease Prevention/Health Promotion, 1995—; adj. assoc. prof. Emory U. Sch. Pub. Health, Atlanta, 1990—; asst. surgeon general, 1996—; editor Chronic Disease Notes and Reports, 1989-92; clinic physician Planned Parenthood of San Francisco Teen Clinic, San Francisco, 1975-76; cons. physician Ohio Dept. Health Bur. Preventive Medicine, 1978-79; cons. PAHO Consultative Group on Perinatal Care, Washington, 1982, WHO Malaysia Ministry of Health, 1982, 83, WHO Maternal and Child Health Unit Geneva, 1983, World Bank China Program Third Health Project, 1988, 1991, World Bank Poland, Health Promotion/Chronic Disease Prevention, 1992, World Bank China, Seventh Health Project, 1993. Contbr. articles to profl. jours, chpts. to books. Exec. sec. Diabetes Tech. Adv. com., 1989-92; liaison mem. Nat. Diabetes Adv. Bd., 1988-89; mem. Diabetes Mellitus Interagy. Coording. com., 1988-89; mem. subcom. adult edn., Am. Cancer Soc., 1987-92; staff White House Task Force on Infant Mortality, 1989; presenter in field. Epidemic Intelligence Svc. Officer USPHS Field Svcs. Divsn., 1976-78. Recipient Alexander D. Langmuir award, 1978, CDC Group award, 1984, Commendation Medal USPHS, 1984, and many other awards and citations. Fellow Am. Coll. Epidemiology; mem. APHA (active in com. work), Am. Epidemiol. Soc., Soc. Epidemiol. Rsch., Am. Acad. Pediat. (com. pediatric rsch. 1994-95), Internat. Epidemiol. Assn., Physicians for Social Responsibility, Soc. on Med. Decision Making, Epidemic Intelligence Svc. Alumni Assn., Sigma Xi. Home: 3158 Kings Arms Court Atlanta GA 30345 Office: Ctrs for Disease Control Health Promotion Chronic Disease Prevention Atlanta GA 30333

MARKS, JEROME, lawyer; b. N.Y.C., June 24, 1931; m. Margarita A. Shuhukin; children: Susan Marks Schmetterer, David J., Ilyse Marks Kelly, Laurence K. BA, Northwestern U., 1952, JD summa cum laude, 1955. Bar: Ill. 1955. Assoc. Friedman & Koven, Chgo., 1956-63, ptnr., 1963-86; ptnr. Rudnick & Wolfe, Chgo., 1986—. Asst. editor-in-chief Northwestern U. Law Rev., 1954-55. Co-chmn. No. Suburbs div. Operation Breadbasket, Chgo. and Highland Park (Ill.), 1968-72. Mem. Chgo. Bar Assn., Chgo. Coun. Lawyers, Order of Coif. Democrat. Avocations: walking, swimming, horse racing. Office: Rudnick & Wolfe 203 N La Salle St Ste 1800 Chicago IL 60601-1225

MARKS, JOHN HENRY, Near Eastern studies educator; b. Denver, Aug. 6, 1923; s. Ira and Clara E. (Dralle) M.; m. E. Aminta Willis, July 21, 1951; children: Peter A., Fleur A., John B. B.A., U. Denver, 1946; B.D. (O.T. fellow), Princeton Theol. Sem., 1949; Th.D., U. Basel, (Switzerland), 1953. Instr. Princeton Theol. Sem., 1953-54; instr. Princeton U., 1954-55, asst. prof. to assoc. prof. Near Eastern studies, 1955-61, prof., 1979-93; dir. Am. Schs. Oriental Research, Jerusalem, 1966-67; pres. Am. Ctr. Oriental Research, Amman, Jordan, 1969-79; trustee Am. Schs. Oriental Research, Phila, 1971-86 ; Acting dean Princeton U. Chapel, 1980. Author: Der Textkritische Wert des Psalterium Hieronymi iuxta Hebraeos, 1956, Visions of One World, Legacy of Alexander, 1985; also translator. Pres. Sch. Bd. Princeton, 1969-71; mem. Planning-Zoning Bds. Princeton, 1964-66. Served with U.S. Army, 1943-45. Mem. Soc. Bibl. Lit. Democrat. Presbyterian. Home: 107 Moore St Princeton NJ 08540-3308 Office: Princeton U 110 Jones Dr Princeton NJ 08540

MARKS, JONATHAN BOWLES, lawyer, consultant, educator; b. Washington, Dec. 17, 1943; s. Herbert Simon Marks and Rebecca (Bowles) Marks Hawkins; m. Nandita Wagle, Dec. 18, 1971; children—Joshua Benegal, Natasha Bowles. B.A. cum laude, Harvard U., 1966, J.D. cum laude, 1972. Bar: Fla. 1972, D.C. 1973, Calif. 1976. Asst. U.S. Atty., Washington, 1973-76; assoc. Munger, Tolles & Rickershauser, Los Angeles, 1976-78, ptnr., 1979; counsel, assoc. dir. planning and evaluation Peace Corps, Washington, 1979-80; gen. counsel Internat. Devel. Coop. Agy., Washington, 1980-81; dispute resolution cons., Washington, 1981-82; pres. EnDispute, Inc., Washington, 1982-94; vice chmn. Jams-EnDispute, 1994—. Author: Dispute Resolution in America: Processes in Evolution, 1984. Campaign staff Sargent Shriver for Vice Pres., 1972; campaign dir. Calif. for Ct., Los Angeles, 1978. Democrat. Home: 3600 Macomb St NW Washington DC 20016-3164 Office: 700 11th St NW Ste 450 Washington DC 20001-4507

MARKS, LAWRENCE EDWARD, psychologist; b. N.Y.C., Dec. 28, 1941; s. Milton and Anne (Parnes) M.; m. Joya Ellen Cazes, Dec. 24, 1963; children: Liza, Laura. AB, Hunter Coll., N.Y.C., 1962; PhD, Harvard U., Cambridge, Mass., 1965; PhD honoris causa, Stockholm U., 1994. Rsch.-assoc. prof. Yale U., New Haven, 1966-84; asst.-assoc. fellow John B. Pierce Lab., New Haven, 1966-84; prof. psychology Yale U., New Haven, 1984—; fellow John B. Pierce Lab., New Haven, 1984—. Author: Sensory Processes: The New Psychophysics, 1974, The Unity of the Senses, 1978. Named to Hall of Fame, Hunter Coll., N.Y.C., 1985; recipient Jacob Javits award NIH, Washington, 1987. Fellow AAAS, Am. Psychol. Assn., Am. Psychol. Soc., N.Y. Acad. Sci. Democrat. Jewish. Achievements include elucidation of common principles underlying sensory processes in various sense modalities; development of validational scheme for quantifying magnitudes of sensory experience; indication of role of cross-modal (synesthetic) perception in relation to language and literature. Home: 48 Maplevale Dr Woodbridge CT 06525-1118 Office: John B Pierce Lab 290 Congress Ave New Haven CT 06519-1403

MARKS, LEONARD, JR., retired corporate executive; b. N.Y.C., May 22, 1921; s. Leonard M. and Laura (Colegrove) Rose; m. Antonia Saldaña Riley, July 19, 1986; children from previous marriage: Linda, Patricia Anne, Peter K. A.B. in Econs., Drew U., 1942; M.B.A., Harvard U., 1948, D.B.A., 1961. Asst. prof. bus. adminstrn. Harvard U., 1949-55; prof. fin. Stanford U., 1955-64; asst. sec. USAF, Washington, 1964-68; v.p. corp. devel. Times Mirror Co., Los Angeles, 1968-69; sr. v.p. Wells Fargo Bank, San Francisco,

1969-72; exec. v.p. Castle & Cooke Inc., San Francisco, 1972-85; gen. ptnr. Marks-Hoffman Assocs., Venture Capital, 1985-92; ind. corp. dir., 1992—; bd. dirs. Airlease Mgmt. Svcs., Alexion Pharm. Inc., No. Trust Bank of Ariz. Co-author: Case Problems in Commercial Bank Management, 1962; contbg.: Credit Management Handbook, 1958. Capt. AUS, 1942-46, ret. brig. gen. USAFR.

MARKS, LEONARD HAROLD, lawyer; b. Pitts., Mar. 5, 1916; s. Samuel and Ida (Levine) M.; m. Dorothy Ames, June 3, 1948; children: Stephen Ames, Robert Evan. B.A., U. Pitts., 1935, LL.B., 1938. Bar: Pa. 1938, D.C. 1946. Asst. prof. law U. Pitts. Law Sch., 1938-42; prof. law Nat. U., 1943-55; asst. to gen. counsel FCC, 1942-46, ops. counsel, 1986—; ptnr. Cohn & Marks, Washington, 1946-65, 69-86; chmn. exec. com. Nat. Savs. and Trust Co., 1977-85; chmn. Internat. Conf. on Comm. Satellites, 1968-69; Am. del. Internat. Broadcasting Confs., 1948-69; pres. Internat. Rescue Com., 1973-79, Honor Am. Com., 1977-86; chmn. U.S. Adv. Commn. on Internat. Ednl. and Cultural Affairs, 1973-78; chmn. Fgn. Policy Assn., 1981-87, exec. com., 1987-96; head U.S. del. Internat. Telecom. Union, 1983, 87; chmn. U.S. del. to London Info. Forum, Commn. on Security and Cooperation in Europe, 1989. Mem. ABA (ho. of dels. 1962-64), Fed. Communications Bar Assn. (pres. 1959-60), Bar Assn. D.C., World Affairs Council Washington (chmn.), Phi Beta Kappa, Order of Coif, Omicron Delta Kappa, Sigma Delta Chi. Clubs: Cosmos, Metropolitan, Federal City, Broadcasters, (pres. 1957-59), Alfalfa (Washington). Home: Shoreham West Apt 714 2700 Calvert St NW Washington DC 20008 Office: 1333 New Hampshire Ave NW Washington DC 20036-1511

MARKS, MARTHA ALFORD, author; b. Oxford, Miss., July 27, 1946; d. Truman and Margaret Alford; m. Bernard L. Marks, Jan. 27, 1968. BA, Centenary Coll., 1968; MA, Northwestern U., 1972, PhD, 1978. Tchr. Notre Dame High Sch. for Boys, Niles, Ill., 1969-74; teaching asst. Northwestern U., Evanston, Ill., 1974-78, lectr., lang. coord., 1978-83; asst. prof. Kalamazoo (Mich.) Coll., 1983-85; writer Riverwoods, Ill., 1985—; cons. WGBH Edn. Found., Boston, 1988-91, Am. Coun. on the Tchg. of Fgn. Langs., 1981-92, Ednl. Testing Svcs., 1988-90, Peace Corps., 1993. Co-author: Destinos: An Introduction to Spanish, 1991, 96, Al corriente, 1989, 93, 97, Que tal?, 1986, 90, author: (workbook) Al corriente, 1989, 93; contbr. articles to profl. jours. Mem. Lake County (Ill.) Bd., Forest Preserve Commn., 1992—, Lake County Conservation Alliance; vice chmn. Friends of Ryerson Conservation Area Bd.; co-founder, pres. Rep Am., Reps. for Environ. Protection. Home: 2940 Cherokee Ln Riverwoods IL 60015-1609 Office: County Bd Office County Bldg Rm 1001 18 N County St Waukegan IL 60085-4304

MARKS, MERTON ELEAZER, lawyer; b. Chgo., Oct. 16, 1932; s. Alfred Tobias and Helene Fannie (Rosner) M.; m. Radee Maiden Feiler, May 20, 1966; children: Sheldon, Elise Marks Vazelakis, Alan, Elaine Marks Ianchiou. BS, Northwestern U., 1954, JD, 1956. Bar: Ill. 1956, U.S. Ct. Mil. Appeals 1957, Ariz. 1958, U.S. Dist. Ct. Ariz. 1960, U.S. Ct. Appeals (9th cir.) 1962, U.S. Supreme Ct. 1970. Assoc. Moser, Compere & Emerson, Chgo., 1956-57; ptnr. Morgan, Marks & Rogers, Tucson, 1960-62; asst. atty. gen. State of Ariz., Phoenix, 1962-64, counsel indsl. commn., 1964-65; assoc., then ptnr. Shimmel, Hill, Bishop & Greunder, Phoenix, 1965-74; ptnr. Lewis & Roca, Phoenix, 1974—; lectr. on pharm., health care, product liability, ins. and employers' liability subjects; Judge Pro Tempore Ariz. Ct. Appeals, 1994. Contbr. more than 35 articles to profl. jours. Capt. JAGC, USAR, 1957-64. Mem. ABA (tort and ins. practice sect., chmn. spl. com. on fed. asbestos legis. 1987-89, chmn. workers compensation and employers liability law com. 1983-84), Am. Bd. Trial Advocates, Am. Coll. Legal Medicine, Internat. Bar Assn., Drug Info. Assn., Am. Soc. Pharmacy Law, State Bar Ariz. (chmn. workers compensation sect. 1969-73), Nat. Coun. Self Insurers, Ariz. Self Insurers Assn., Fedn. Ins. and Corp. Counsel (chmn. pharm. litig. sect. 1989-91, chmn. workers compensation sect. 1977-79, v.p. 1978-79, 81, bd. dirs. 1981-89), Internat. Assn. Def. Counsel, Ariz. Assn. Def. Counsel (pres. 1976-77), Maricopa County Bar Assn., Def. Rsch. Inst. (drug and device com., chmn. workers compensation com. 1977-78), Assn. Internat. Droit Assurances, Union Internat. des Avocats. Office: Lewis & Roca 40 N Central Ave Phoenix AZ 85004-4424

MARKS, MICHAEL J., lawyer, corporate executive; b. 1938. AB, Cornell U., 1960; JD, U. Chgo., 1963. Assoc. Stroock & Stroock & Lavan, 1964-70, Chun, Kerr & Dodd, 1970-72; counsel Kelso, Spencer, Snyder & Stirling, 1972-75; asst. gen. counsel Alexander & Baldwin Inc., Honolulu, 1975-80, v.p., gen. counsel, 1980-84, v.p., gen. counsel, sec., 1984-85, sr. v.p., gen. counsel, sec., 1985—. Office: Alexander & Baldwin Inc 822 Bishop St Honolulu HI 96813-3924

MARKS, PAUL ALAN, oncologist, cell biologist, educator; b. N.Y.C., Aug. 16, 1926; s. Robert R. and Sarah (Bohorad) M.; m. Joan Harriet Rosen, Nov. 28, 1953; children: Andrew Robert, Elizabeth Susan Marks Ostrer, Matthew Stuart. AB with gen. honors, Columbia U., 1945, MD, 1949; D in Biol. Sci. (hon.), U. Urbino, Italy, 1982; PhD (hon.), Hebrew U., Jerusalem, Israel, 1987, U. Tel Aviv, 1992. Fellow Columbia U. Coll. Physicians and Surgeons, 1952-53, assoc., 1955-56, mem. faculty, 1956-82, dir. hematology tng., 1961-74, prof. medicine, 1967-82, prof. human genetics and devel., 1969-82, dean faculty of medicine, v.p. med. affairs, 1970-73, dir. Comprehensive Cancer Ctr., 1972-80, v.p. health scis., 1973-80, Frode Jensen prof. medicine, 1974-80; prof. medicine and genetics Cornell U. Coll. Medicine, N.Y.C., 1982—, prof. medicine Grad. Sch. Med. Scis., 1983—; instr. Sch. Medicine, George Washington U., 1954-55; cons. VA Hosp., N.Y.C., 1962-66; attending physician Presbyn. Hosp., N.Y.C., 1967-82; pres., CEO Meml. Sloan-Kettering Cancer Ctr., 1980—; attending physician Meml. Hosp. for Cancer and Allied Diseases, 1980—; mem. Sloan-Kettering Inst. for Cancer Rsch., 1980—; adj. prof. Rockefeller U., 1980—; vis. physician Rockefeller U. Hosp., 1980—; hon. staff N.Y. Hosp., 1981—; bd. sci. counselors divsn. cancer treatment Nat. Cancer Inst., 1980-83; mem. steering com. Nat. Cancer Inst. Frederick Cancer Rsch. Facility, 1982-86; chmn. program adv. com. Robert Wood Johnson Found., 1983-89; mem. Gov.'s Commn. on Shoreham Nuclear Plant, 1983; mem. Mayor's Commn. Sci. and Tech. City of N.Y., 1984-87; mem. adv. com. on NIH to Sec. HHS, 1989-90, 93—, external adv. com. Intramural Rsch. Program Rev. NIH; mem. gov. com. NYPRHA, 1996; mem. coun. biol. scis. Pritzker Sch. Medicine U. Chgo., 1977-88; first lectr. Nakasone Program for Cancer Control U. Tokyo, 1984; Ayrey fellow, vis. prof. Royal Postgrad. Med. Sch. U. London, 1985; William Dameshek vis. prof. hematology Mt. Sinai Med. Ctr., 1985; nat. vis. com. CUNY Med. Sch., 1986-89; trustee Feinberg Grad. Sch. Weizmann Inst. Sci., Rehovot, Israel, 1986—; William H. Resnick lectr. in medicine Stamford Hosp., 1986; disting. faculty lectr. M.D. Anderson Hosp. U. Tex., 1986; Maurice C. Pincoffs lectr. U. Md., Balt., 1987; Japan Soc. Hematology Disting. lectr., 1989; vis. prof. Coll. de France, 1988; Alpha Omega Alpha vis. prof. N.Y. Med. Coll., 1990; Mario A. Baldini vis. prof. Harvard Med. Sch., 1991; mem. sci. adv. bd. City of Hope Nat. Med. Ctr., Duarte, Calif., 1987-92, Raymond and Beverly Sackler Found., Inc., 1989, Jefferson Cancer Inst., Phila., 1989; mem. Found. Biomed. Rsch., 1989—; advisor Third World Acad. Sci.; mem. sci. adv. com. Imperial Cancer Rsch. Fund, 1994; mem. bd. govs. Friends of Sheba Med. Ctr., Tel Hashomer; bd. trustees Hadassah Med. Ctr., Jerusalem, 1996. Editor: Monographs in Human Biology, 1963; author 11 books; contbr. over 375 articles to profl. jours.; mem. editl. bd. Blood, 1964-71, assoc. editor, 1976-77, editor-in-chief, 1978-82; assoc. editor Jour. Clin. Investigation, 1967-71; mem. editl. bd. Cancer Treatment Revs., 1981—, Cancer Preventions, 1989, Sci., 1990; guest editl. bd. Japanese Jour. Cancer Rsch., 1985—; assoc. editor Molecular Reprodn. and Devel., 1988—; expert analyst Chemistry and Molecular Biology edit. of Chemtracts, 1990-92; mem. adv. bd. Internat. Jour. Hematology, 1992, Stem Cells; bd. contbg. editors Blood Cells, Molecules and Diseases, 1994, Comité des Sages, 1994. Trustee St. Luke's Hosp., 1970-80, Roosevelt Hosp., 1970-80, Presbyn. Hosp., 1972-80, Metpath Inst. Med. Edn., 1977-79, Hadassah Med. Ctr., Jerusalem, 1996; mem. jury Albert Lasker awards, 1974-82; bd. govs. Weizmann Inst., 1976—; bd. dirs. Revson Found., 1976-91, Am. Found. for Basic Res. Israel, Israel Acd. Scis., 1991; mem. tech. bd. Milbank Meml. Fund, 1978-85; bd. govs. Friends of Sheba Med. Ctr., Tel Hashomer. Recipient Charles Janeway prize Columbia U., 1949, Joseph Mather Smith prize, 1959, Stevens Triennial prize, 1960, Swiss-Am. Found. award in med. rsch., 1965, Columbia U. Coll. Physicians and Surgeons Disting. Achievement medal, 1980, Centenary medal Inst. Pasteur, 1987, Disting. Oncologist award Hipple Cancer Ctr. and Kettering Ctr., 1987, Found. for Promotion of Cancer Rsch. medal, 1984 (Japan), Disting. Svc. medal Robert Wood Johnson Found., 1989, Outstanding Achievement award in hematopoiesis U. Innsbruck, 1991, Pres.'s Nat. Medal Sci., 1991, Gold medal for Disting. Acad. Accomplishments, Coll. Physicians and Surgeons, 1994, Joseph Mather Smith prize Columbia U., 1995, Japan Found. for Cancer Rsch. award, 1995, John Jay award for disting. profl. achievement, Columbia Coll., N.Y., 1996, Lifetime Achievement award Greater N.Y. Hosp. Assn., 1997; Commonwealth Fund fellow Pasteur Inst., 1961-62. Master ACP, Coll. Phys. Surgeons; fellow AAAS, Royal Soc. Medicine, Am. Acad. Arts and Scis., Pasteur Inst. Paris; mem. NAS (chmn. sect. med. genetics, hematology and oncology 1980-83, chmn. Acad. Forum Adv. Com. 1980-81, mem. coun. 1984-87, del. biol. warfare com. Internat. Security and Arms Control 1986-89), Royal Soc. Medicine (London), Inst. Medicine (mem. coun. 1973-76, chmn. com. study resources clin. investigation with NAS 1988), Red Cell Club (past chmn.), Am. Fedn. Clin. Rsch. (past councillor Ea. dist.), Am. Soc. Clin. Investigation (pres. 1972-73), Am. Soc. Biol. Chemists, Am. Soc. Human Genetics (past mem. program com.), Am. Assn. Cancer Rsch., Assn. Am. Cancer Insts. (bd. dirs. 1983-88), Soc. Cell Biology, Am. Soc. Hematology (pres.-elect 1983, pres. 1984, chmn. adv. bd. 1985), Assn. Am. Physicians, Harvey Soc. (pres. 1973-74), Internat. Soc. Devel. Biologists, Italian Assn. Cell Biology and Differentiation (hon.), Chinese Anti-Cancer Assn. (hon.), Soc. for Devel. Biology, Japanese Cancer Assn. (hon.), Japan Soc. Hematology (Disting. lectr. 1989), Internat. Leadership Ctr. on Longevity and Soc. Interurban Clin. Club, Soc. for Study Devel. and Growth, Third World Acad. Scis., Sci. Adv. Bd. Hong Kong Cancer Inst., Chinese U. Hong Kong, Weizmann Inst. Sci. (gov. emeritus, Israel), Health Scis. Adv. Coun. Columbia U., Century Assn., Econ. Club (N.Y.C.), Univ. Club (N.Y.C.), Alpha Omega Alpha. Office: Meml Sloan-Kettering Cancer Ctr 1275 York Ave New York NY 10021-6007

MARKS, RICHARD DANIEL, lawyer; b. N.Y.C., June 21, 1944; s. Morris Andrew and Dorothy (Schill) M.; m. Cheryl L. Hoffman, Nov. 13, 1971. BA, U. Va., 1966; JD, Yale U., 1969. Bar: D.C., U.S. Ct. Appeals (3rd, 4th, 8th, 11th and D.C. cir.), U.S. Supreme Ct. Assoc. Dow, Lohnes & Albertson, Washington, 1972-78, ptnr., 1978-97; ptnr. Vinson & Elkins, Washington, 1997—. Co-author: Legal Problems in Broadcasting, 1974. Capt. U.S. Army, 1970-72. Mem. ABA (chmn. contracting for computer com., sect. for sci. and tech., computer law div., chmn. computer law div. 1994—), Fed. Comms. Bar Assn., Capital Area Assn. Flight Instrs. (pres. 1989-90), UVA Club of Washington (pres. 1991-92). Avocations: aviation, skiing. Office: Vinson & Elkins 1455 Pennsylvania Ave NW Washington DC 20004-1008

MARKS, ROBERT HUTCHINSON, publishing executive; b. Bklyn., May 2, 1926; s. Robert John and Martha Jean (Hutchinson) M.; m. Dorothy Beatrice Alexander, Feb. 3, 1951 (dec. Feb. 1974); m. 2d, Joyce Marie Goodwin, July 23, 1983. BS in Civil Engring., MIT, 1947. Application engr. Permutit Co., N.Y.C., 1948-56, dist. mgr., 1960-62; assoc. editor Power Mag., McGraw-Hill, Inc., N.Y.C., 1956-60, mng. editor 1962-69; mgr. pub. relations Michel-Cather, Inc., N.Y.C., 1969-70; assoc. dir. pub. Am. Inst. Physics, N.Y.C., 1970-84, dir. pub., 1985-88. dir. pub. div. Am. Chem. Soc., 1988-96. Cons., Carnegie Found., N.Y.C., 1979—, Sci-tech Pub., 1997—; treas., dir. Nat. Fedn. of Abstracting and Info. Svcs., Phila., 1980-83, pres. 1984-85; pres. Masonic Assn. for Charity, Bklyn., 1981; trustee Hanson Pl. Cen. United Meth. Ch., Bklyn., 1970-87, Engring. Info., Inc., 1976-82. Served to lt. USNR, 1944-46. Mem. Coun. Engring. and Sci. Soc. Execs., Soc. Scholarly Pub., AAAS, Am. Chem. Soc., Am. Inst. Chem. Engrs., ASME, ASCE, Am. Waterworks Assn., Nat. Assn. Corrosion Engrs. Republican. Methodist. Lodge: Masons. Home and Office: 1200 N Nash St Apt 214 Arlington VA 22209-3613

MARKS, SHELDON HARRIS FEILER, urologist; b. L.A., Apr. 15, 1956. Student, U. Ariz., 1974-76; AB, Occidental Coll., L.A., 1978; MD, U. Ariz., 1982. Bd. cert. Am. Bd. Urology. Intern in gen. surgery Mayo Clinic, Rochester, Minn., 1982-84; resident in urology Tufts U./New Eng. Med. Ctr., Boston, 1984-87; specialist in adult and pediat. urology Thomas-Davis Med. Ctr., 1987-89; specialist in adult urology and urologic oncology So. Ariz. Surg. Oncology, 1989-90; pvt. practice Tucson, 1990—; affiliated with hosps. Tucson Med. Ctr., El Dorado Hosp., Tucson, St. Joseph's Hosp., Tucson, U. Med. Ctr., Tucson, HealthSouth Rehab. Hosp., Tucson; mem. Medicare Preservation Task Force, 1995; mem. adv. panel Prostate Cancer Infolink web site, 1995—; mem. quality assurance com. Sutter Tucson Surgery Ctr., 1990—; quality advisor dept. surgery med. exec. quality assurance com. Tucson Med. Ctr., 1994-95, mem. laser safety com., 1995; comty. mem. S.W. Oncology Group, 1992—; lectr. on prostate cancer, urinary incontinence, vasectomy reversals and other topics to local and regional hosps., srs. groups, bus. groups, and physicians. Author: Prostate and Cancer: A Family Guide to Diagnosis, Treatment and Survival, 1995, 96; appeared on radio and TV programs; contbr. numerous articles to profl. jours. Co-chair health care divsn. United Way Greater Tucson, 1995. Recipient 40 Under 40 award Inside Tucson Bus., 1996. Fellow Am. Urol. Assn. (western sect. 1995—); mem. Am. Cancer Soc. (pres. 1993-95), Ariz. Urol. Soc. (pres. 1992-94), Pima County Med. Soc. (pres. 1995). Office: 6369 E Tanque Verde Rd Ste 160 Tucson AZ 85715-3833

MARKS, STANLEY JACOB, lawyer, historian, lecturer, author; b. Chgo., Apr. 26, 1914; s. Samuel and Sarah Marks; m. Ethel Milgrom, Aug. 1, 1936; 1 child, Roberta E. AB, U. Ill., 1934; LLB, JD, John Marshall Law Sch., Chgo., 1937. Bar: Ill. 1939. Pres., chmn. bd. Beauti-Dor, Inc., Chgo., 1939—, Glamour Glass Door, Inc., Chgo., 1939—; pvt. practice Calif., 1964—; internat. and nat. legal and bus. cons. L.A., 1964—; lectr. on polit. and social/econ. events worldwide. Author: (with Ethel Marks) The Bear That Walks Like a Man, 1943, Murder Most Foul, 1967, Two Days of Infamy, 1969, Coup d'Etat!, 1970, Through Distorted Mirrors, 1974, Juadism Looks at Christianity, 1986, A Year in the Lives of the Damned, Reagn, Reaganism, 1986, The 1991 U.S. Consumer Market, 1991, Yes, Americans, A Conspiracy Murdered JFK!, 1992, Jews, Judaism and the U.S., 1992, Justice For Whom?, 1996, others; playwright: Judgement Day, 1997, Judaism - Civilization's Las Hope, 1997; pub. weekly polit. newsletter Diogenes, 1984, 88. Writer Dem. Nat. Com., 1936, 40, 48, 52, 60, 91, 96. With AUS, 1944-46. Recipient various Army decorations. Mem. Am. Acad. Polit. and Social Scis., Soc. Am. Mil. Engrs., Authors League Am., Libr. of Congress Assn., Anti-Defamation League, Dramatists Guild (life), Masons, Shriners, Anti Discrimination League, World Jewish Congress, Dramatist Guild.

MARKS, WILLIAM H., organ transplant program director, pharmacologist, pharmacognosist, and director for laboratory transplantation biology; b. Chgo., Aug. 16, 1948; s. Louis M. and Bertha M. (Michaelson) M.; m. Christine M. Marks, Nov. 1971; children: Annika, Daniel, Susie, Julia. BS, Loyola U., Chgo., 1970; MS, U. Ill., Chgo., 1973; MD, Loyola U., 1977; PhD, Lund U., 1983. Instr. U. Mich., Ann Arbor, 1973-85; asst. prof. surgery and biochemistry Loyola U., Maywood, Ill., 1985-87; assoc. prof. surgery Yale U., New Haven, Conn., 1987-93; adj. assoc. prof. pharmacology Nat. Products Chemistry U. Ill., Chgo., 1987—; dir. organ transplantation Swedish Med. Ctr., Seattle, 1994—; dir. lab. for transplant biology; surg. adv. bd. Smith Kline Beecham, Phila., 1992—; USMLE surg. step II Nat. Bd. Med. Examiners, Phila., 1992-95. Editor Resident Surgery, 1992—, Phytomedicine, 1994; editl. bd. Resident Surgery, 1992—; contbr. articles to profl. jours.; patentee in field. Mem. exec. com. N.W. Kidney Ctrs., Seattle, 1993; sec. bd. dirs. Life Ctr. NW, 1996—; bd. dirs. CenterSpan, Inc., 1996—. Fellow ACS (SK&F fellowship 1985, 86); mem. Am. Soc. Transplant Surgeons, Am. Soc. Transplant Physicians, Soc. Univ. Surgeons, The Transplant Soc., Soc. Surgery of the Alimentary Tract. Avocations: writing, skiing, mountaineering. Office: Organ Transplant Program 1120 Cherry St Ste 400 Seattle WA 98104-2023

MARKSON, DANIEL BEN, real estate developer, consultant, syndicator; b. Boston, Dec. 19, 1959; s. Morris Eliot and Gertrude (Hurvitt) M. BA, Clark U., 1981; MBA, Babson Coll., 1983. Projects mgr. Hist. Mill Properties, Milton Village, Mass., 1983-84; freelancer Markson Devel., Boston, 1984-85; asst. v.p. New England Communities Inc., Wellesley, Mass., 1985-88; sr. v.p. Boston Capital Ptnrs. Inc., 1988-96; exec. v.p. Nat. Housing Corp., Virginia Beach, Va., 1996—; exec. v.p. Affordable Landmarks Inc., Miami Beach, Fla., 1989—; pres. Charlesview Inc., Allston, Mass., 1988-91, dir., 1981—; dir. North Harvard, Allston, 1981-91. Participant Boston City Housing Task Force, 1990—; v.p. Miami Supportive Housing Corp., 1994—. Mem. Nat. Home Builders (trustee, multi-family coun.). Republican. Avocations: hist. property restoration, antique Cadillacs, swimming, weight tng. Home: 2421 Lake Pancoast Dr Miami FL 33140 Office: Nat Housing Corp 208 Golden Oak Ct Ste 450 Virginia Beach VA 23452-6767

MARKULIS, HENRYK JOHN, career military officer; b. Columbia, S.C., July 10, 1945; s. Henryk F. Markulis and Judith E. (Taylor) Kassman; children: Mark C., Melinda L. BA, U. Buffalo, 1968; MA, Ctrl. Mich. U., 1977. Commd. USAF, 1969; advanced through ranks to col.; aircraft cmdr. 53d Weather Recon Squadron Ramey AFB, P.R., 1970-74; gunship aircraft cmdr. 16th Spl. Ops. Squadron Korat RTAB, Thailand, 1974-75; cmdr. 437th Field Maintenance Squadron Sect. Charleston AFB, S.C., 1975-78; exercise and contingency support 1701st Mobility Support Shaw AFB, S.C., 1978-82; air staff action officer Joint Chiefs of Staff Pentagon, 1982-84, chief internat. programs Singapre, Malaysia & Brunei, 1984-93; dep. cmdr., chief staff Iceland Def. Force NATO, 1993-95, ret.; pres., CEO Internat. Security and Mktg. Cons., 1996—. Mem. Am. Legion, VFW, Ret. Officers Assn., Aircraft Owners & Pilots Assn., Army Navy Country Club, Order of Daedalians, Kiwanis. Avocation: golf. Home: PO Box 310 Orchard Park NY 14127 Office: 52 Union St Hamburg NY 14075-4910

MARKUS, KENT RICHARD, lawyer; b. Cleve., Feb. 1, 1959; s. Richard and Carol (Slater) M.; m. Susan Mary Gilles, Apr. 15, 1987. BS, Northwestern U., 1981; JD with honors, Harvard U., 1984. Bar: Ohio 1984, U.S. Dist. Ct. (no. dist.) Ohio 1984, U.S. Ct. Appeals (6th cir.) 1986. Jud. clk. to Hon. Alvin I. Krenzler U.S. Dist. Ct. (no. dist.) Ohio, Cleve., 1984-86; litigation assoc. Gold, Rotatori, Schwartz & Gibbons, Cleve., 1986-89; transition dir. Ohio Atty. Gen. Office, Columbus, Ohio, 1990-91; first asst. atty. gen., chief of staff Ohio Atty. Gen. Office, Colombus, Ohio, 1991-93; counsel to dep. atty. gen. U.S. Dept. Justice, Washington, 1994, dep. assoc. atty. gen., 1994-95, acting asst. atty. gen. legis affairs, 1995, counselor to atty. gen, 1996—; adj. prof. law Cleveland-Marshall Coll. Law, 1987-88. Co-editor: Trial Handbook for Ohio Lawyers, 2nd edit., 1988; contbn. editor for law Webster's New World Dictionary, 3d edit., 1988. Bd. dirs., former legis. chair Handgun Control Fedn. of Ohio, 1984—; mem. adv. coun. Northwestern U. Sch. Speech, 1985—; spl. projects dir. Celeste for Gov. Com., Cleve., 1986; campaign mgr. Lee Fisher for Atty. Gen., Cleve. and Columbus, 1989-90; bd. dirs., trustee, life mem. Cleve. NAACP, 1986-87; chief of staff Dem. Nat. Com., Washington, 1993-94. Named Rising Star of Dem. Party, Campaigns and Elections mag., 1991. Mem. ATLA, Cleve. Bar Assn., Ohio State Bar Assn. (former chair young lawyers divsn.), Ohio Legal Needs Implementation Com. (former chair fin. resources subcom.), Cuyahoga County Bar Assn. (mem. grievance com.). Home: 7215 MacArthur Blvd Bethesda MD 20816 Office: Office Atty Gen 950 Pennsylvania Ave NW Rm 5131 Washington DC 20530-0001

MARKUS, LAWRENCE, retired mathematics educator; b. Hibbing, Minn., Oct. 13, 1922; s. Benjamin and Ruby (Friedman) M.; m. Lois Shoemaker, Dec. 9, 1950; children: Sylvia, Andrew. BS, U. Chgo., 1942, MS, 1946; PhD, Harvard U., 1951. Instr. meteorology U. Chgo., 1942-44; rsch. meteorologist Atomic Project, Hanford, 1944; instr. math. Harvard U., 1951-52; instr. Yale U., 1952-55; lectr. Princeton U., 1955-57; asst. prof. U. Minn., Mpls., 1957-58, assoc. prof., 1958-60, prof. math., 1960-93, assoc. chmn. dept. math., 1961-63, dir. control scis., 1964-73, Regents' prof. math., 1980-93, Regents' prof. emeritus, 1993—; dir. Control Sci. and Dynamical Systems Ctr. U. Minn., 1980-89; Leverhulme prof. control theory, dir. control theory centre U. Warwick, Eng., 1970-73, Nuffield prof. math., 1970-85, hon. prof., 1985—; regional conf. lectr. NSF, 1969; vis. prof. Yale U., Columbia U., U. Calif., U. Warsaw, 1980, Tech. Inst. Zurich, 1983, Peking U. (China), 1983; dir. conf. Internat. Centre Math., Trieste, 1974; lectr. Internat. Math. Congress, 1974, Iranian Math. Soc., 1975, Brit. Math. Soc., 1976, Japan Soc. for Promotion Sci., 1976, Royal Instn., London, 1982, U. Beer Sheva, Israel, 1983; vis. prof. U. Tokyo, 1976, Tech. U., Denmark, 1979; mem. panel Internat. Congress Mathematicians, Helsinki, 1978; sr. vis. fellow Sci. Rsch. Coun., Imperial Coll., London, 1978; mem. UNESCO sci. adv. com. Control Symposium, U. Strasbourg, France, 1980; IEEE Plenary lectr., Orlando, Fla., 1982; Sci. and Engring. Rsch. Coun. vis. prof. U. Warwick, Eng., 1982-90; Neustadt Meml. lectr. U. So. Calif., 1985, prin. lectr. symposium U. Minn., 1988, dir. NSF workshop, 1989; mem. adv. bd. Office Naval Rsch., Air Force Office Sci. Rsch. Author: Flat Lorentz Manifolds, 1959, Flows on Homogeneous Spaces, 1963, Foundations of Optimal Control Theory, 1967, rev. edit., 1985, Lectures on Differentiable Dynamics, 1971, rev. edit., 1980, Generic Hamiltonian Dynamical Systems, 1974, Distributed Parameter Control System, 1991; editor Internat. Jour. Nonlinear Mechanics, 1965-73, Jour. Control, 1963-67; mem. editorial bd. Proc. Georgian Acad. Sci. Math., 1993—; contbr. articles to profl. jours. Lt. (j.g.) USNR, 1944-46. Recipient Rsch. prize Internat. Conf. Nonlinear Oscillations, Ukrainian Acad. Sci., Kiev, 1969, Festschrift volume, 1993; Fulbright fellow Paris, 1950; Guggenheim fellow Lausanne, Switzerland, 1963. Mem. Am. Math. Soc. (past mem. nat. coun.), Am. Geophys. Soc., Soc. Indsl. and Applied Math. (past nat. lectr.), Phi Beta Kappa, Sigma Xi. Office: U Minn Math Dept 127 Vincent Hall Minneapolis MN 55455

MARKUS, RICHARD M., lawyer; b. Evanston, Ill., Apr. 16, 1930; s. Benjamin and Ruby M.; m. Carol Joanne Slater, July 26, 1952; children: Linda, Scott, Kent. BS magna cum laude, Northwestern U., 1951; JD cum laude, Harvard U., 1954. Bar: D.C. 1954, Ohio 1956, Fla. 1994. Appellate atty., civil div. Dept. Justice, Washington, 1954-56; ptnr. civil litigation law firms Cleve., 1956-76, 89—; judge Cuyahoga County (Ohio) Common Pleas Ct., 1976-80, Ohio Ct. Appeals, 1981-88; instr. M.I.T., 1952-54; adj. prof. Case Western Res. U. Law Sch., 1972-78, 84-87, Cleve. State U. Law Sch., 1960-80; prof. Harvard Law Sch., 1980-81; mem. Nat. Commn. on Med. Malpractice, 1971-73; chmn. Nat. Inst. Trial Advocacy, 1978-81, trustee 1971—. Author: Trial Handbook for Ohio Lawyers, 1973, 3d edit., 1991; contbr. articles to profl. jours.; editor Harvard U. Law Rev. 1952-54. Republican nominee Justice of Ohio Supreme Ct., 1978; co-founder Nat. Advocacy Coll., 1970; bd. dirs. Lutheran Coun. Greater Cleve., 1979-81, Fairview Luth., Hosp., 1985—. Mem. Ohio State Bar Assn. (pres. 1991-92), Cuyahoga County Bar Assn., Greater Cleve. Bar Assn. (trustee 1967-70, 85-90), Assn. Trial Lawyers Am. (nat. pres. 1970-71), Ohio Acad. Trial Lawyers (pres. 1965-66), Phi Beta Kappa, Pi Mu Epsilon, Delta Sigma Rho, Phi Alpha Delta. Home: 3903 N Valley Dr Cleveland OH 44126-1716 Office: Porter Wright Morris & Arthur 925 Euclid Ave Cleveland OH 44115

MARKUS, ROBERT MICHAEL, journalist, retired; b. Chgo., Jan. 30, 1934; s. David White and Anna (Tonkonogy) M.; m. Leslie Winnifred Ator, Aug. 25, 1962; children—Catherine Mary, Patricia Anne, Michael Hughes. B.J., U. Mo., 1955. Gen. assignment reporter Moline (Ill.) Dispatch, 1955-59; successively copy editor, sports columnist, feature writer, baseball writer, coll. sports writer, hockey writer Chgo. Tribune, 1959-96, ret., 1996. Mem. Northbrook (Ill.) Caucus, 1967. Served with U.S. Army, 1956-58. Recipient Nat. Headliner award as best columnist, 1973; named Ill. Sports Writer of Year, 1970, 71, 72. Mem. Football Writers Assn. Am., Baseball Writers Assn. Am., Am. Auto Racing Writers and Broadcasters Assn., Hockey Writers Assn. Home: 402 Willow Rd Winnetka IL 60093-4132 Office: Chgo Tribune PO Box 25340 Chicago IL 60625-0340

MARKWARDT, KENNETH MARVIN, former chemical company executive; b. St. Paul, Mar. 6, 1928; s. Rudy A. and Kathryn M. (Thell) M.; m. Bernice M. Kimmel, Aug. 5, 1950; children: Ronald, Mary Ellen, Gary, Thomas, Jean. BBA, Coll. St. Thomas, 1950. With Ecolab, Inc., St. Paul, 1951-83, contr., 1961-69, v.p., contr., 1968-73, v.p., treas., sr. v.p. fin., 1973-83, also bd. dirs. Treas. St. Patrick's Guild, bd. dirs., 1951—; bd. dirs., sec. Health East, St. Paul. Served with AUS, 1946-47. Mem. Cath. Athletic Assn. (pres. 1956-57, dir. 1953-80, trustee 1980—), Tax Execs. (pres. Minn. chpt. 1962-63), K.C. Home: 100 Imperial Dr W Apt 304 West Saint Paul MN 55118-2244

MARKWOOD, SANDRA REINSEL, human services administrator; b. Washington, Aug. 27, 1955; d. Francis Eugene and Delores Jean (Horning) Reinsel-Kahn; m. James Scott Markwood, Aug. 4, 1984; children: Christopher Scott, Anne Meredith. BA with distinction, U. Va., 1977, M in Urban and Environ. Planning, 1979. Sr. rsch. asst. Nat. League of Cities, Washington, 1979-80; rsch. assoc./ project dir. Nat. Assn. Counties, Washington, 1980-84; asst. to county exec. Albemarle County, Charlottesville, Va., 1984-86; sr. rsch. assoc./ project dir. Nat. Assn. Counties, Washington,

1986—; exec. sec. Nat. Assn. County Aging Programs, Washington, 1986—; co-staff dir. Local Collaboration for Children and Youth; com. co-chair Generations United, Washington, 1988-90; intergovtl. liaison Nat. Hwy. Traffic Safety Adminstrn., Washington, 1989-91; chair Aging Needs Assessment Com., Charlottesville, 1985-86. Author: (handbook) Local Officials Guide to Urban Recreation, 1980, (guide) Building Support for Traffic Safety Programs, 1991; co-author: (guide) Graying of Suburbia, 1988; editor: Counties and Volunteers, Partners in Service, 1992-95; co-author: Counties Care for Kids: Programs That Work, Bridging the Generations. Vol. tchr. St. Louis Cath. Sch., Alexandria, Va., 1980-83, St. Rita's Cath. Sch., Alexandria, 1987-89; vol. Jr. Friends of Campaign Ctr., Alexandria; coord. Sister Cities Exch. Program, Charlottesville, 1985. Recipient Cert. of Appreciation, Nat. Hwy. Traffic Safety Adminstrn., 1991. Mem. Women's Transp. Seminar, Smithsonian Assocs., Generations United. Roman. Catholic. Avocations: reading, jogging, walking, sailing. Home: 5018 W Dauber Dr Toledo OH 43615

MARLAND, ALKIS JOSEPH, leasing company executive, computer science educator, financial planner; b. Athens, Greece, Mar. 8, 1943; came to U.S., 1961, naturalized, 1974; s. Basil and Maria (Pervanides) Mouradoglou; m. Anita Louise Malone, Dec. 19, 1970; children: Andrea, Alyssa. BS, Southwestern U., 1963; MA, U. Tex., Austin, 1967; MS in Engring. Adminstrn., So. Meth. U., 1971. Cert. in data processing, enrolled agt., fund specialist, ChFC, CLU, CFP, RFC, CTP, ATA, ATP. With Sun Co., Richardson, Tex., 1968-71, Phila., 1971-76; mgr. planning and acquisitions Sun Info. Svcs. subs. Sun Co., Dallas, 1976-78; v.p. Helios Capital Corp. subs. Sun Co., Radnor, Pa., 1978-83; pres. ALKAN Leasing Corp., Wayne, Pa., 1983—, bd. dirs., 1983—; prof. dept. computer scis. and bus. adminstrn. Eastern Coll., St. David's, Pa., 1985-87; prof. math. Villanova (Pa.) U., 1987-89. Bd. dirs. Radnor Twp. Sch. Dist., 1987-91, Delaware County Intermediate Unit, 1988-91, Phila. Fin. Assn., 1989-92, Delaware Valley Soc. ICFP, 1993—. Mem. IEEE, Assn. Computing Machinery, Data Processing Mgmt. Assn., Internat. Assn. Fin. Planners, Am. Soc. CLUs and ChFC, Am. Assn. Equipment Lessors, Inst. Cert. Fin. Planners (bd. dirs. Del. Valley Soc. 1993—, v.p. mem. 1994-95, treas. 1995—), Nat. Assn. Enrolled Agts., Nat. Assn. Tax Practitioners, Nat. Assn. Pub. Accts., Fin. Analysts Phila., Phila. Fin. Assn. (sec. 1989-92, mem. award 1988, bd. dirs. 1989-92), Fgn. Policy Rsch. Inst., World Affairs Coun. Phila., Phila. Union League, Main Line C. of C., Assn. Investment Mgmt. and Rsch., Rotary (pres. Wayne club 1989-90, gov.'s rep. dist. 7450, 1990-91, 93-94), Masons (32 degree). Republican. Home: 736 Brooke Rd Wayne PA 19087-4709 Office: PO Box 8301 Radnor PA 19087-8301

MARLAS, JAMES CONSTANTINE, holding company executive; b. Chgo., Aug. 22, 1937; s. Constantine J. and Helen (Cotsirilos) M.; m. Kendra S. Graham, 1968 (div. 1971); m. Glenn Close, 1984 (div. 1987); m. Marie Nugent-Head, 1993. A.B. cum laude, Harvard U., 1959; M.A. in Jurisprudence, Oxford (Eng.) U., 1961; J.D., U. Chgo., 1963. Bar: Ill. 1963, N.Y. 1966. Assoc. firm Baker & McKenzie, London and N.Y.C., 1963-66; exec. v.p. South East Commodity Corp., N.Y.C., 1967-68; chmn. bd. Union Capital Corp., N.Y.C., 1968—; vice chmn. bd. Mickelberry's Food Products Co., N.Y.C., 1970-71; pres., dir. Mickelberry Comm. Corp., N.Y.C., 1972—; chief exec. officer Mickelberry Comm. Corp., 1973—; chmn. bd. Mickleberry Commn. Corp., 1984—; chmn. bd., CEO Newcourt Industries, Inc., 1976—; chmn. bd. dirs. Bowmar Instrument Corp., chmn. exec. com., 1983-92. Co-editor: Univ. Chgo. Law Rev, 1962-63; Contbr. articles to profl. jours. Bd. dirs. N.Y.C. Opera, Commanderie de Bordeaux, Brasenose Coll. Charitable Found. Mem. Am. Fgn. Law Assn., Young Pres.'s Orgn. Clubs: Boodle's (London); Racquet and Tennis (N.Y.C.). Office: Mickelberry Comm Corp 405 Park Ave New York NY 10022-4405

MARLEAU, DIANE, Canadian government official; b. Kirkland Lake, Ont., Can., June 21, 1943; d. Jean-Paul and Yvonne (Desjardins) LeBel; m. Paul C. Marleau, Aug. 3, 1963; children: Brigitte, Donald, Stéphane. Student, U. Ottawa, Ont., 1960-63; BA in Econs., Laurentian U., Sudbury, Ont., 1976. With Donald Jean Acctg. Svcs., Sudbury, 1971-75; receiver mgr. Thorne Riddell, Sudbury, 1975-76; treas. No. Regional Residential Treatment Program for Women, Sudbury, 1976-80, Com. for the Industry and Labour Adjustment Program, Sudbury, 1983; mem. transition team Ont. Premier's Office, Toronto, 1985; firm adminstr. Collins Barrow-Maheu Noiseux, Sudbury, 1985-88; M.P. from Sudbury House of Commons, Ottawa, 1988—; minister of health for Can., 1993-96; min. of public works Canada, 1996; councilor Regional Municipality of Sudbury, 1980-85, chair fin. com., 1981; alderman City of Sudbury, 1980-85; mem. No. Devel. Coun., Sudbury, 1986-88; vice chair Nat. Liberal Standing Com. on Policy, 1989; chair Ont. Liberal Caucus, 1990; apptd. nat. exec. Liberal Party Can., 1990, assoc. critic Govt. Ops., 1990, Dep. Opposition Whip, 1991, assoc. critic Fin., 1992; vice chair standing com. fin., 1992. Chmn. fund-raising Canadian Cancer Soc., Sudbury, 1987-88; co-chmn. Laurentian Hosp. Cancer Care Svcs. fund-raising campaign, Sudbury, 1988; chair bd. govs. Cambrian Coll., 1987-88, bd. govs., 1983-88; mem. Sudbury and Dist. Health Unit Bd., 1981-82; mem. fin. com., bd. dirs. Laurentian Hosp., 1981-85; chair Can. Games for the Physically Disabled, 1983; apptd. Ont. Adv. Coun. Women's Issues, 1984. Recipient Paul Harris award, 1996. Mem. Sudbury Bus. and Profl. Women Club. Avocations: playing piano, gardening, cooking. Office: Public Works & Gov't Svc 11 Laurier, 18A1 Place du Portage Phs III, Hull, PQ Canada K1A 0S5 also: 36 Elgin St, Sudbury, ON Canada P3C 5B4

MARLEAU, ROBERT, parliamentary clerk; b. Cornwall, Ont., Can., Apr. 27, 1948; m. Ann Spilsbury; children: Stéphane, Kristian. Grad., Cornwall Classic Coll., 1967, U. Ottawa, 1969. French high sch. tchr., 1969-70; com. clk. Coms. and Pvt. Legis. Br., 1970-74; dep. sec. gen., Parliamentary Relations Secretariat Can. Ho. Commons, Ottawa, 1974-81, prin. clks., 1981-83, asst. clk., 1983-87, clk., 1987—; adv. bd. faculty of adminstrn. U. Ottawa. Decorated comdr. Ordre de la Pléiade. Mem. Can. Study Parliament Group, Can. Soc. Clks. at the Table, Assemblée Sec. Gén. Parlements Membres l'Assemblée Internationale des Parlementaires de Langue Française, Ordre de la Pléiade (comdr.), Mil. and Sovereign Order Malta (knight magistral grace), Forum for Young Canadians (dir., 125th medal 1992). Office: Ho of Commons, Ottawa, ON Canada K1A 0A6

MARLEN, JAMES S., chemical-plastics-building materials manufacturing company executive; b. Santiago, Chile, Mar. 14, 1941; came to U.S., 1961; grad. U. Ala., 1965; MBA, U. Akron, 1971; m. Carolyn S. Shields, Jan. 23, 1965; children: James, Andrew, John. With GenCorp., Akron, Ohio, 1965-93, engring., marketing and gen. mgmt. positions domestic and internat. ops., 1965-76; divsn. pres. GTR Coated Fabrics Co., 1977-80, group pres. 1980-87; pres., GenCorp Polymer Products, Akron, Ohio, 1988—, v.p., GenCorp, Akron, 1988-93; pres., CEO Ameron Internat., Inc., Pasadena, Calif., 1993—, bd. dirs., Ameron, Inc., chmn. bd. dirs., pres. and CEO, 1995—; dir. A. Schulman, Inc., Tamco Steel, Gifford-Hill, gen., hon. chmn. Nat. Inventors Hall of Fame Induction, 1993. Bd. dirs. YMCA Met. L.A., The Employers Group of Calif., Town Hall of L.A., gov.; mem. The Beavers; dir. L.A. Sports Coun. Mem. Am. Mgmt. Assn. (mem. pres. assn.), Chem. Mfrs. Assn. (past pres.), Assocs. Caltech, Calif. C. of C., L.A. C. of C. (dir.), Portage Country Club (Akron, Ohio), Calif. Club. (L.A.), Annandale Golf Club (Pasadena), Valley Hunt Club (Pasadena), Soc. Fellows of Huntington Libr. Office: Ameron Inc 245 S Los Robles Ave Pasadena CA 91101-2820

MARLER, LARRY JOHN, private investor; b. Chgo., Sept. 22, 1940; s. Walter William and Lena Inez (Killen) M.; m. Katy Jo Hibbits, Oct. 17, 1962 (div. Apr. 1971); 1 child, Preston Scott; m. Linda Lee Sorg, Sept. 2, 1982. BA, Christian Coll. Am., 1987; MA, Houston Grad. Sch. Theology, 1988; PhD, U.S. Internat. U., San Diego, 1992. Acct. Shell Oil Co., New Orleans and Houston, 1964-73; acctg. supr. We. Geophys. Co. Am., Houston, 1974; payroll supr. Olsen Inc., Houston, 1975-77; corp. credit mgr. Grant Corps., Houston, 1977-82; rschr., student contractor Navy Pers. R&D Ctr., San Diego, 1990-92; entrepreneur Denver, 1992—. Served with USCG, 1959-62. Mem. Am. Psychol. Soc., Am. Soc. Quality Control, Toastmasters Internat. Republican. Protestant. Avocations: reading, jogging, swimming, hiking, downhill skiing.

MARLETT, DE OTIS LORING, retired management consultant; b. Indpls., Apr. 19, 1911; s. Peter Loring and Edna Grace (Lombard) M.; m. Ruth Irene Pillar, Apr. 10, 1932 (dec. Feb., 1969); children: De Otis Neal, Marilynn Ruth; m. Marie Manning Ostrander, May 1, 1970 (dec. Apr. 1982); m. Peggie P. Whittlesey, Jan. 15, 1983 (dec. Oct., 1993); m. Estelle B. Brewer, Sept. 23, 1994. B.A., M.A., U. Wis., 1934; postgrad., Northwestern U., (part time), 1934-39, Harvard U.; postgrad. (Littauer fellow in econs. and govt.), 1946-47. CPA, Wis., 1935. Staff mem. Ill. Commerce Commn., 1934-39; lectr. in econs. and pub. utilities Northwestern U., (part time), 1936-39; staff mem. Bonneville Power Adminstrn., U.S. Dept. Interior, 1939-45, asst. adminstr., 1945-52; acting adminstr. Def. Electric Power Adminstrn., 1950-51; asst. to v.p., gen. mgr. Dicalite and Perlite divs. Great Lakes Carbon Corp., 1952-53; v.p., also gen. mgr. Dicalite, Perlite, Mining and Minerals divs. Gt. Lakes Carbon Corp., 1953-62, v.p. property investment dept., 1962-81; pres., chief exec. officer Great Lakes Properties, Inc., 1981-83, ret., 1983; past pres., dir. Rancho Palos Verdes Corp., G.L.C. Bldg. Corp., Del Amo Energy Co., Torrance Energy Co.; former mem. L.A. arbitration panel N.Y. Stock Exch. Contbr. articles and reports on public utility regulation, operation and mgmt. to profl. jours. Past bd. dirs. United Cerebral Palsy Assn. Los Angeles County; bd. dirs., past co-chmn. So. Calif. region NCCJ, mem. nat. trustee, mem. nat. exec. bd., nat. protestant co-chmn., 1987-90; past mem. Orthopaedic Hosp. Adv. Coun.; past trustee City of Hope; past pres., dir. Los Angeles area coun., past chmn. relationships com., past pres. Sunshine area, pres. Western region Boy Scouts Am., 1978-81, nat. exec. bd., 1978-88, past mem. nat. exec. com., past chmn. properties com., chmn. logistics for world jamboree delegation to Australia, 1987-88; past trustee Nat. Scouting Mus.; mem. internat. com. Baden Powell fellow World Scouting Found., 1984; past mem. Western Govs. Mining Adv. Coun., Calif. State Mining Bd.; bd. govs. Western div. Am. Mining Congress, chmn., 1962-63; incorporator, past pres., bd. dirs. Torrance Meml. Med. Center Health Care Found.; region III dir., past mem. corp. adminstrn. and fin. com., Los Angeles United Way. Recipient Disting. Service medal U.S. Dept. Interior, 1952; named knight Order of Crown Belgium; commd. Ky. Col.; recipient Silver Beaver, Silver Antelope, Silver Buffalo awards Boy Scouts Am., 1984. Mem. AIME, AICPA, Fin. Execs. Inst., L.A. World Affairs Coun., Wis. Alumni Assn., Perlit Inst. (past pres., dir.), L.A. C. of C. (past dir., chmn. mining com.), Mining Assn. So. Calif. (past pres., dir.), Calif. Mine Operators Assn. (past dir.), Bldg. Industry Assn. So. Calif., Calif. Club, Portuguese Bend Club (past pres.), Palos Verdes Bay Club (past v.p.), Phi Kappa Phi, Beta Gamma Sigma, Phi Beta Kappa, Beta Alpha Psi, Lambda Alpha Internat. Democrat. Home: 32759 Seagate Dr Unit 204 Palos Verdes Peninsula CA 90275

MARLETT, JUDITH ANN, nutritional sciences educator, researcher; b. Toledo. BS, Miami U., Oxford, Ohio, 1965; PhD, U. Minn., 1972; post-grad., Harvard U., 1973-74. Registered dietitian. Therapeutic and metabolic unit dietitian VA Hosp., Mpls., 1966-67; spl. instr. in nutrition Simmons Coll., Boston, 1973-74; asst. prof. U. Wis., Madison, 1975-80, assoc. prof. dept. nutritional scis., 1981-84, prof. dept. nutritional scis., 1984—; cons. U.S. AID, Leyte, Philippines, 1983; acting dir. dietetic program dept. Nutritional Scis. U. Wis., 1977-78, dir., 1985-89; cons. grain, drug and food cos., 1985—, adv. bd. U. Ariz. Clin. Cancer Ctr., 1987-95; sci. bd. advisors Am. Health Found., 1988—; reviewer NIH, 1982—. Mem. editl. bd. Jour. Sci. of Food and Agrl., 1989—, Jour. Food Composition and Analysis, 1994—; contbr. articles to profl. jours. Mem. AAAS, NIH (Diabetes amd Digestive and Kidney Disease spl. grant rev. com. 1992-96), Am. Inst. Nutrition, Am. Dietetic Assn., Am. Soc. Clin. Nutrition, Inst. Food Technologists, Am. Assn. Cereal Chemists. Achievements include research and international speaker on human nutrition and disease, dietary fiber and gastrointestinal function. Office: U Wis Dept Nutritional Sci 1415 Linden Dr Madison WI 53706-1527

MARLETTA, MICHAEL, biochemistry educator, researcher, pharmacologist; b. Rochester, N.Y., Feb. 12, 1951; m. Margaret Gutowski, 1991. BA, SUNY, 1973; PhD in Pharm. Chemistry, U. Calif., 1978. Fellow MIT, Cambridge, 1978-80, from asst. prof. to assoc. prof. toxicology, 1980-87; assoc. prof. med. chemistry U. Mich., Ann Arbor, 1987-91, assoc. prof. biol. chemistry, 1989-91, John G. Searle prof. med. chemistry, prof. biol. chemistry, 1991—. John D. and Catherine T. MacArthur fellow, 1995. Mem. AAAS, Am. Soc. Biochem. and Molecular Biology, Am. Chem. Soc. Achievements include research in protein/structure function with a particular interest in enzyme reaction mechanisms and molecular mechanisms of signal transduction, study of nitric oxide syntase, guanylate cyclase and related enzymes in this signaling system. Office: U Michigan 428 Church St Ann Arbor MI 48109-1065

MARLETTE, DOUGLAS NIGEL, editorial cartoonist, comic strip creator; b. Greensboro, N.C., Dec. 6, 1949; m. Melinda Hartley; 1 child, Jackson Douglas. Student, Fla. State U. Editorial cartoonist The Charlotte (N.C.) Observer, 1972-87, The Atlanta Constn., 1987-89, N.Y. Newsday, N.Y.C., 1989—; syndicated to over 200 newspapers through Creators Syndicate, Inc., L.A., 1988—. Creator syndicated comic strip Kudzu; works reproduced in Time, Newsweek, Christian Century, Rolling Stone, Der Spiegel, Esquire mags., also textbooks and encys.; author: The Emperor Has No Clothes, If You Can't Say Something Nice, Drawing Blood, Kudzu, 1982, Preacher, The Wit and Wisdom of Will B. Dunn, 1984, Just A Simple Country Preacher, 1985, It's a Dirty Job But Somebody Has To Do It, There's No Business Like Soul Business, 1987, Chocolate is My Life, Shred This Book, I Am Not a Televangelist, Doublewide with a View, 1989, In Your Face, A Cartoonist At Work, 1991, (children's book) The Before and After Book, Even White Boys Get the Blues, 1992, Gone With the Kudzu, 1995; co-wrote screenplay "EX"; TV appearances include ABC's Nightline, Good Morning Am., Today Show, CBS Morning News, Nat. Pub. Radio's Morning Edition; syndicated animated editorial cartoons NBC Today Show. Nieman fellow, 1st for editorial cartoonist, Harvard U.; recipient Nat. Headliners award 1983, 88, Robert F. Kennedy Meml. award 1984, Sigma Delta Chi Disting. Service award 1986, First Amendment award, 1986, 1st Pl. award John Fischetti Editorial Cartoon Competition, 1986, The Golden Plate Acad. of Achievement award, 1991; named to Register of Men and Women Who Are Changing Am., Esquire Mag., 1984; recipient Pulitzer Prize for editorial cartooning Newsday, 1988; 1st Prize, John Fischetti Editorial Cartoon Competition, 1992. Office: NY Newsday 2 Park Ave New York NY 10016-5675 also: care Creators Syndicate Inc 5777 W Century Blvd Ste 700 Los Angeles CA 90045-5677*

MARLEY, EVERETT ARMISTEAD, JR., lawyer; b. Memphis, June 15, 1933; s. Everett Armistead and Elizabeth (Alexander) M.; m. Carolyn Marie McKay, June 21, 1958; children: Elizabeth Ann, Jill Marie. B.A. in Econs., Rice Inst., 1955; LL.B., U. Tex.-Austin, 1959. Bar: Tex.; cert. specialist in estate planning State Bar of Tex., 1977. C.P.A., Tex. Assoc. Butler & Binion L.L.P., Houston, 1959-68; ptnr. Butler & Binion, L.L.P., 1968—. Trustee Schreiner Coll., Kerrville, Tex., 1980-88, San Francisco Theol. Sem., San Anselmo, Calif., 1991—; elder St. Philip Presbyn. Ch., Houston. Fellow Am. Coll. Trust and Estate Counsel; mem. ABA. Presbyterian. Avocation: bass fishing. Office: Butler & Binion LLP 1000 Louisiana St Ste 1600 Houston TX 77002-5009

MARLIN, ALICE TEPPER, research organization administrator; b. Long Branch, N.J., Aug. 10, 1944; d. Walter L. and Grace A. (Comins) Tepper; m. John Tepper Marlin, Sept. 25, 1971; children—John Joseph, Caroline. Ed. The Baldwin Sch., 1962; B.A., in Econs., Wellesley Coll., 1966; postgrad. in Bus. Adminstrn., N.Y.U. Securities analyst Burnham & Co. (now Drexel Burnham), N.Y.C., 1966-68; scheduler, advance planner McCarthy for Pres. Campaign, 1968; fin. analyst T. O'Connell Mgmt. and Research, Boston, 1968-69; pres., founder Council on Econ. Priorities, N.Y.C., 1969—; bd. dirs. Fund for Constl. Govt., Washington, 1983—, Winston Found. for World Peace, N.Y.C., 1985—, Green Seal, D.C., 1991. Author: Shopping for a Better World, 1986, 7th edit., 1994, Rating America's Corporate Conscience, 1986, Corporate Report Card, 1987. Editor: (monthly) Council Econ. Rsch. Report; editor more than 30 books. Contbr. articles to profl. jours. Mem. Bus. for Social Responsibility, Social Venture Network, Social Investment Forum, Women's Forum, Harvard (N.Y.C.) Club, Devon (Amagansett) Yacht Club. Recipient Inventory of Hope award Saturday Review, disting. alumnae award The Baldwin Sch., Right Livelihood award, Investor's Cir. Pioneer award; named woman of Yr., Mademoiselle mag.; Point fellow, 1972; Japan Soc. Leadership fellow, 1985-86. Democrat. Unitarian. Avocations: tennis, gardening. Address: Council on Econ Priorities 30 Irving Pl New York NY 10003-2303

MARLIN, JOHN TEPPER, economist, writer, consultant; b. Washington, Mar. 1, 1942; s. Ervin Ross and Hilda (van Stockum) M.; AB cum laude, Harvard U., 1962; BA, Oxford (Eng.) U., 1965, MA, 1969; PhD in Econs., George Washington U., 1968; m. Alice Rose Tepper, Sept. 25, 1971; children: John Joseph Tepper (Jay), Caroline Alice Tepper. Fin. economist Fed. Res. Bd., FDIC and SBA, Washington, 1964-69; asst. prof. Baruch Coll., City U. N.Y., 1969-73; founder, pres. Council Mcpl. Performance, N.Y.C., 1973-88; pres. JTM Reports, Inc., 1989-92; social auditor Ben and Jerry's Homemade, 1989; dir. Conversion Info. Ctr., Coun. on Econ. Priorities, 1991-92; chmn., bd. advisers CIC, CEP, 1992-95, adviser internat. security program, 1995—; cons. J.M. Kaplan Fund, 1991-92; chief economist for Office of Comptr., City of N.Y., 1992-94, 97—, sr. policy adviser, 1994-97. Donor-adviser E.R. Marlin Fund, N.Y. Cmty. Trust. Mem. Am. Econ. Assn. (life), Fin. Mgmt. Assn. (life), Nat. Assn. Bus. Economists, Economists Allied for Arms Reduction (treas., mem. exec. com.), City Club (N.Y.C.), Harvard Club (N.Y.C.), Devon Yacht Club, Trinity (Oxford) Soc. U.S.A. (pres. 1969-94), Oxford U. Alumni Assn. N.Y. (sec., mem. exec. com.), Oxford-Cambridge dinner Com. (N.Y.C., pres.), Oxford Soc. (mem. exec. com.), Money Marketeers NYU. Author: The Wealth of Cities, 1974, Cities of Opportunity, 1988, Catalogue of Healthy Food, 1990, The Livable Cities Almanac, 1992, (with others) Book of American City Rankings, 1983, Contracting Municipal Services, 1984, Book of World City Rankings, 1986, Soviet Conversion, 1991, Building a Peace Economy, 1992 ; founding editor Jour. Fin. Edn., 1972-73; editor Nat. Civic Rev., 1987-88, Privatization Report, 1986-88, Econ. Notes, 1992-94, 97—. Home: 360 W 22nd St New York NY 10011-2600 Office: City of New York Office Comptr 1 Centre St Rm 510 New York NY 10007-1602

MARLIN, KENNETH BRIAN, information and software company executive; b. N.Y.C., Feb. 2, 1955; s. Elmer David and Edith Barbara (Stern) M.; m. Marcia A. Levis, Dec. 15, 1988; 1 child, Victoria Rae. BA, U. Calif., Irvine, 1977; MBA, UCLA, 1979; advanced profl. cert., NYU, 1981. Mgr. Dun & Bradstreet Corp., N.Y.C., 1981-85; v.p. Dun & Bradstreet Internat., N.Y.C., 1985-88; sr. v.p. fin. info. group Dun & Bradstreet Corp., N.Y.C., 1988-92; pres. Telekurs (N.Am.), Inc., Stamford, Conn., 1992-95; pres., CEO Telesphere Corp., N.Y.C., 1995—. Trustee Hurricane Island Outward Bound Sch., Rockland, Maine, 1990—; bd. mem., vice chmn. N.Y. chpt. Red Cross of Greater N.Y., N.Y.C., 1991—. Office: Telesphere Corp One State St Plz 22nd Fl New York NY 10004

MARLIN, RICHARD, lawyer; b. N.Y.C., June 1, 1933; s. Edward and Lillian (Milstein) M.; m. Merrel Pincus, June 12, 1955 (div. 1972); children: John F., Elizabeth; m. Jenesta Rutherford, July 29, 1974 (div. 1981); m. Caroline Mary Hirsch Magnus, Nov. 1, 1981. BA magna cum laude, Yale U., 1955, LLB, 1958; LLM, NYU, 1964. Bar: N.Y. 1959, Fla. 1978. Law clk. to presiding justice U.S. Dist. Ct. Conn., New Haven, 1958-59; assoc. Cleary, Gottlieb, Steen & Hamilton, N.Y.C., 1959-62, Wien Lane & Klein, N.Y.C., 1962-64; ptnr. Mnuchin Moss & Marlin, N.Y.C., 1964-66, Marshall, Bratter, Greene, Allison & Tucker, N.Y.C., 1966-79; sr. ptnr. Kramer, Levin, Naftalis & Frankel, N.Y.C., 1979—; bd. dirs. FAB Industies, N.Y.C. Bd. editors Yale Law Jour. Mem. ABA, N.Y. State Bar Assn., Assn. Bar City N.Y., N.Y. County Lawyers' Assn. (corp. law com., chmn. subcom.), Glen Oaks Club (Old Westbury, N.Y.) (bd. govs. 1979-85, 92-94), Phi Beta Kappa. Office: Kramer Levin Naftalis & Frankel 919 3rd Ave New York NY 10022

MARLIN, STERLING, professional race car driver. Winner Daytona 500, 1994, 1995. Office: NASCAR PO Box 2875 Daytona Beach FL 32120-2875

MARLING, KARAL ANN, art history and social sciences educator; b. Rochester, N.Y., Nov. 5, 1943; d. Raymond J. and Marjorie (Karal) M. PhD, Bryn Mawr Coll., 1971. Prof. art history and Am. studies U. Minn., Mpls., 1977—. Author: Federal Art in Cleveland, 1933-1943: An Exhibition, 1974, Wall-to-Wall America: A Cultural History of Post-Office Murals in the Great Depression, 1982, The Colossus of the Roads: Myth and Symbol along the American Highway, 1984, Tom Benton and His Drawings: A Biographical Essay and a Collection of His Sketches, Studies, and Mural Cartoons, 1985, Frederick C. Knight (1898-1979), 1987, George Washington Slept Here: Colonial Revivals and American Culture, 1876-1986, 1988, Looking Back: A Perspective on the 1913 Inaugural Exhibition, 1988, Blue Ribbon: A Social and Pictorial History of the Minnesota State Fair, 1990, (with John Wetenhall) Iwo Jima: Monuments, Memories, and the American Hero, 1991, Edward Hopper, 1992, As Seen on T.V.: The Visual Culture of Everyday Life in the 1950's, 1994, Graceland: Going Home with Elvis, 1995; editor (with Jessica H. Foy) The Arts and the American Home, 1890-1930, 1994, Norman Rockwell, 1997, Designing the Disney Theme Parks: The Architecture of Reassurance, 1997; contbr. essays to exhbn. catalogs. Recipient Minn. Humanities Commn. award 1986, Minn. Book award History, 1994, Robert C. Smith award Decorative Arts Soc., 1994. Office: 1920 S 1st St Apt 1301 Minneapolis MN 55454-1048

MARLING, LYNWOOD BRADLEY, lawyer; b. Cin., Apr. 17, 1944; s. John Bertron Marling and Florence Mary (Kelly) Lyman;m. Patricia Lynne Coté, June 13, 1981; children: Burke, Brady, Dustin. B Ceramic Engring., Ga. Inst. Tech., 1967; MBA, Stanford U., 1969; JD, Tex. Tech U., 1976. Bar: Tex. 1976, U.S. Dist. Ct. (no. dist.) Tex. 1977; cert. in family law Tex. Bd. Legal Specialization. Distbn. cons. Jos. Schlitz Brewing Co., Milw., 1969-71; pres., owner Marling Industries, Lubbock, Tex., 1971-74; pvt. practice, Hurst, 1981-88; ptnr. Caston and Marling, Hurst, Tex., 1976-81, 88—; legal cons. St. John the Apostle Sch., Ft. Worth, 1982-91. Contbr. articles to legal jours. Mem. St. John the Apostle Sch. Bd., 1982-84; campaign mgr. Robert Caston for State Rep., Tarrant County, Tex., 1980, Rick Barton for Mayor, Bedford, Tex., 1992. Recipient svc. award St. John the Apostle Sch., 1988. Mem. ABA, State Bar Tex. (coll. 1987—), Tarrant County Bar Assn., N.E. Tarrant County Bar Assn. (pres. 1990-92), Soto Grande Tennis Club (Outstanding Mem. award 1980). Avocations: snow skiing, tennis, officiating high school football, public speaking. Office: 1848 Norwood Plaza Ct Ste 214 Hurst TX 76054-3752

MARLOW, AUDREY SWANSON, artist, designer; b. N.Y.C.; d. Sven and Rita (Porter) Swanson; student (scholarships) Art Students League, 1950-55; spl. courses SUNY (Stony Brook), L'Alliance Française m. Roy Marlow, Nov. 30, 1968. With Cohn-Hall-Marx Textile Studio, 1961-65, R.S. Assocs. Textile Studio, 1965-73; freelance designer, illustrator Prince Matchabelli, Lester Harrison Agy., J. Walter Thompson Agy., 1957-78; portrait and fine artist, Wading River, N.Y., 1973—; instr. Phoenix Sch. Design (N.Y.C.); illustrator children's books: Breads of Many Lands and 4H Club Bakes Bread, 1966, Anna Smith Strong and the Setauket Spy Ring, 1991, Timothy and the Acrobat, 1992; exhibits include: Nat. Arts Club, NAD, Parish Art Mus., South Hampton, N.Y., Guild Hall, East Hampton, N.Y., Portraits Inc., Lincoln Ctr., Chung-Cheng Art Gallery, St. John's U., Mystic (Conn.) Art Assn., Harbour Gallery, St. Thomas, V.I., Palais Rameau, Lisle, France, 1988, Sumner Mus., Washington, 1992, East End Arts & Humanities Coun., L.I., N.Y., 1996; one-person shows: Salmagundi Club, 1982, Rockefeller Gallery, N.Y.C., 1992; portrait commns. include: Millicent Fenwick, Harrison J. Goldin, Thomas R. Bayles, Mons. John Fagan, others. Trustee, Middle Island Public Library, 1972-76. Recipient John W. Alexander medal, 1976, award Council on Arts, 1978, award of excellence Cork Gallery, Lincoln Center, 1982; Grumbacher Bronze medal, 1983; Grumbacher Silver medal 1986; Best in Show award N.Y. Arts Council, 1986, Suburban Art League, 1993, Excellence award Town of Oyster Bay, 1995. Mem. Pastel Soc. Am. (award 1977, 80, 90), Am. Artists Profl. League (2 1st prize awards), Hudson Valley Art Assn. (award), Knickerbocker Artists (2 awards), Catharine Lorillard Wolfe Art Club (award 1982), Salmagundi Club (5 awards), Nat. League Am. Pen Women (Gold award, Gold medal of Honor, Best in Show 1990). Works represented at NYU, Longwood Pub. Libr., Sr. Citizen's Complex, Newark, St. Theresa of the Child Jesus Convent, Wading River Congl. Ch., L.I., pvt. collections. Home: 147 Northside Rd Wading River NY 11792-1112

MARLOW, JAMES ALLEN, lawyer; b. Crossville, Tenn., May 23, 1955; s. Dewey Harold and Anna Marie (Hinch) M.; m. Sabine Klein, June 9, 1987; children: Lucas Allen, Eric Justin. BA, U. Tenn., 1976, JD, 1979; postgrad., Air War Coll., Maxwell AFB, Ala., 1990-91, Internat. Studienzentrum, Heidelberg, Fed. Republic Germany, 1985-86. Bar: Ga. 1979, D.C. 1980, Tenn. 1980, U.S. Dist. Ct. (mid. dist.) Tenn. 1984, U.S. Ct. Fed. Claims

1987, U.S. Ct. Internat. Trade 1988, U.S. Tax Ct. 1987, U.S. Ct. Mil. Appeals 1980, U.S. Ct. Appeals (fed. cir.) 1987, U.S. Supreme Ct. 1987. Assoc. Carter & Assocs., Frankfurt, Fed. Republic Germany, 1984-85; chief internat. law USAF, Sembach AFB, Fed. Republic Germany, 1986-96; adj. prof. Embry-Riddle Aero. U., Kaiserslauten, Fed. Republic Germany, 1985—, Ctrl. Tex. Coll., Kaiserslauten, 1997—. Capt. USAF, 1980-84. Mem. Phi Beta Kappa. Avocations: genealogy, basketball, chess, German and Spanish languages. Home and Office: 5746 Hwy 127 South Crossville TN 38555

MARLOWE, EDWARD, research company executive; b. N.Y.C., May 5, 1935; children: Shari Marlowe Kasten, Steven Richard. B.S., Columbia U., 1956, M.S., 1958; Ph.D., U. Md.-Balt., 1962. Research assoc. Merck, Sharp & Dohme Research Lab., West Point, Pa., 1962-64; sr. scientist Ortho Pharm. Corp. div. Johnson & Johnson, Raritan, N.J., 1964-67; dir. research and devel. Whitehall Labs. div. Am. Home Products Corp., Hammonton, N.J., 1967-72; v.p. research and devel. Plough Products div. Schering-Plough Corp., Memphis, 1972-81; v.p. research and devel., consumer products group Warner-Lambert Co., Morris Plains, N.J., 1981-83, pres. consumer products div. rsch. and devel., 1983-91, v.p., 1984-91, v.p. parent Co.; v.p. R&D Clairol Inc., Stamford, Conn., 1992-97; sr. v.p. Bristol-Myers Squibb World Wide Beauty Care, 1997—. Contbr. articles to profl. publs. Bd. dirs. Lowenstein Found., Overlook Hosp., 1985-94. Recipient award Skin Cancer Found., 1979; Pfizer fellow, 1958; Robert Lincoln McNeil fellow, 1961. Mem. Am. Pharm. Assn., Acad. Pharm. Scis., Soc. Cosmetic Chemists, Indsl. Rsch. Inst., Cosmetic, Fragrance and Toiletry Assn. (sci. affairs com. 1976-79), Non-Prescription Drug Mfrs. Assn. (sci. affairs com. 1976-91, policy planning subcom. 1977-91, bd. dirs. 1981-83), N.Y. Acad. Sci., Sigma Xi, Rho Chi. Home: 56 Kean Rd Short Hills NJ 07078-1430 Office: Clairol Inc 2 Blachley Rd Stamford CT 06902-4149

MARMARELIS, VASILIS ZISSIS, engineering educator, author, consultant; b. Mytilini, Greece, Nov. 16, 1949; came to U.S., 1972; s. Zissis P. and Elpis V. (Galinos) M.; m. Melissa Emily Orme, Mar. 12, 1989; children: Zissis Eugene and Myrl Galinos. Diploma in elec. and mech. engring., Nat. Tech. U. of Athens, Greece, 1972; MS in Info. Sci., Calif. Inst. Tech., 1973, PhD in Engring. Sci., 1976. Rsch. fellow Calif. Inst. Tech., Pasadena, 1976-78; asst. prof. U. So. Calif., L.A., 1978-83, assoc. prof., 1983-88, prof., 1988—, also dir. biomed. simulations resource, 1985—, chmn. dept. biomed. engring., 1990-96; pres. Multispec Corp., L.A., 1986—. Author: Analysis of Physiological Systems, 1978, translated in Russian 1981, translated in Chinese 1990; Advanced Methods of Physiological Systems Modeling, vol. I, 1987, vol. II, 1989, vol. III, 1994; contbr. numerous articles to profl. jours. Fellow IEEE; mem. AAAS, Internat. Fedn. Automatic Control, N.Y. Acad. Scis., Biomed. Engring. Soc., Neural Networks Soc. Office: U So Calif OHE 500 Los Angeles CA 90089-1451

MARMAS, JAMES GUST, retired businees educator, retired college dean; b. Virginia, Minn., July 11, 1929; s. Gust George and Angela (Fatili) M.; m. Ruth Phyllis Leinonen, May 23, 1952; children—James Matthew, Lynn Marie, Brenda Kay. B.S., St. Cloud (Minn.) State Coll., 1951; M.A., U. Minn., 1956; Ed.D., Stanford, 1961. Tchr. bus. Littlefork (Minn.) High Sch., 1951-53, Lake City (Minn.) High Sch., 1953-55, Austin (Minn.) High Sch., 1955-59; asst. prof. bus. edn. Los Angeles State Coll., 1961-62; chmn. dept. bus. edn., dir. Center Econ. Edn., St. Cloud State Coll., 1962-66; dean Coll. of Bus. St. Cloud State Coll. (Sch. Bus.), 1966-87; bd. dirs. Ins. and Savs. and Loan. Author articles in field. Bd. dirs., mem. exec. com. Minn. Council Econ. Edn.; bd. dirs. St. Cloud (Minn.) Econ. Devel. Ptnrship., chmn. research and planning com. (sec., bd. dirs.). Mem. Nat. Bus. Edn. Assn., Minn. Bus. Edn. Assn., N. Central Bus. Edn. Assn. (2d v.p.), Midwest Bus. Adminstrn. Assn., St. Cloud C. of C., Phi Delta Kappa, Delta Pi Epsilon (nat. research com.), Beta Gamma Sigma. Club: Rotary (pres. St. Cloud). Home: 13215 County Road 4 N Nisswa MN 56468-8514

MARMER, ELLEN LUCILLE, pediatrician; b. Bronx, N.Y., June 29, 1939; d. Benjamin and Diane (Goldstein) M.; m. Harold O. Shapiro, June 5, 1960; children: Cheri, Brenda. BS in Chemistry, U. Ala., 1960; MD, U. Ala., Birmingham, 1964. Cert. Nat. Bd. Med. Examiners; diplomate Am. Bd. Sports Medicine, Bd. Pediatrics, Bd. Qualified and Eligible Pediatric Cardiology, Bd. cert. sports medicine. Intern Upstate Med. Ctr., Syracuse, N.Y., 1964-65, resident, 1965-66; fellow in pediatric cardiology Columbia Presbyn. Med. Ctr.-Babies Hosp., N.Y.C., 1967-69; pvt. practice Hartford, Vernon, Conn., 1969—; examining pediatrician child devel. program Columbia Presbyn. Med. Ctr.-Babies Hosp., N.Y.C., 1967, instr. pediatrics, 1967-69; dir. pediatric cardiology clinic St. Francis Hosp., Hartford, 1970-80; asst. state med. examiner, Tolland County, Conn., 1974-79; sports physician Rockville (Conn.) High Sch., 1976—; advisor Cardiac Rehab. com., Rockville, 1984-90; mem. bd. examiners Am. Bd. Sports Medicine, 1991—, chmn. credentials com., 1991—. Mem. Vernon Town Coun., 1985-89; bd. dirs. Child Guidance Clinic, Manchester, Conn., 1970—; life mem. Tolland County chpt. Hadassah, v.p., 1969-70, pres., 1970-72, bd. dirs., 1973-74; mem. B'nai Israel Congregation and Sisterhood, Vernon, 1969—, chmn. youth commn., 1970-72. Recipient Outstanding Svc. award Indian Valley YMCA, 1985. Fellow Am. Acad. Pediatrics, Am. Coll. Cardiology, Am. Coll. Sports Medicine (bd. examiners 1991—, chmn. credentials com. 1991—); mem. Conn. Med. Soc., Am. Heart Assn. (mem. coun. cardiovascular disease in young 1969—, chmn. elect New Eng. regional heart com. 1990-91), Conn. Heart Assn. (bd. dirs. 1974-75, 83-84, pres. 1986-88), Heart Assn. Greater Hartford (bd. dirs. 1970-89, mem. exec. com. 1972-73, 79-84, pres. 1982-84), Tolland County Med. Assn. (sec. 1971-72), Vis. Nurse and Community Care Tolland County, LWV (state program chairperson Vernon chpt. 1971-73). Democrat. Jewish. Avocation: sports. Office: 520 Hartford Tpke Vernon Rockville CT 06066-5037

MARMER, NANCY, editor; b. N.Y.C., Nov. 19, 1932; d. Carl and Frances Marmer; m. Gerald Jay Goldberg, Jan. 23, 1954; 1 child, Robert. BA magna cum laude, Queens Coll., 1954; postgrad., U. Minn., 1954-57, UCLA, 1968-71. L.A. corr. Art Internat., 1965-67; West Coast editor Artforum, 1976-77; sr. editor Art in America, N.Y.C., 1979-81, exec. editor, 1981-83, book rev. editor, 1983—, mng. editor, 1983—; lectr. Mellon seminar R.I. Sch. Design, 1983; lectr. art criticism Visual Arts dept. U. Calif., San Diego, 1978; faculty expository writing Dept. English, U. Minn., 1954-57. Author: The Modern Critical Spectrum, 1962; contbr. numerous articles to profl. jours.; art critic/reviewer for Art in America, Art Internat., Artforum, L.A. Times. Recipient Samuel Kress Found. Award in Art History; Nat. endowment for the Arts fellow in art criticism. Mem. Phi Beta Kappa. Office: Art in America 575 Broadway New York NY 10012-3230

MARMET, PAUL, physicist; b. Levis, Que., Can., May 20, 1932; s. Albert and Corinne (Filteau) M.; m. Jacqueline Cote, June 6, 1959; children—Louis, Marie, Nicolas, Frederic. B.Sc., Laval U., Quebec, Que., 1956, D.Sc., 1960. Research asst. Commonwealth Sci. and Inds. Research Orgn., Melbourne, Australia, 1960-61; asst. prof. physics Laval U., 1961-66, asso. prof., 1966-70, prof., 1970-84; sr. research officer Herzberg Inst. Astrophysics, 1984-91; prof. physics dept. U. Ottawa, 1991—; vis. prof. U. Liège, Belgium, 1967; com. mem. NRC Can.; bd. dirs. Atomic Energy Control Bd. of Can., 1979-84. Author: (with others) Case Studies in Atomic Physics I, 1969, A New Non-Doppler Redshift, 1981, Absurdities in Modern Physics: A Solution, 1993; contbr. (with others) numerous articles to internat. sci. jours. Recipient Sci. prize Province Que., 1962; Royal Soc. Can. Rutherford Meml. fellow Melbourne, 1960; decorated officer Order of Can. Fellow Royal Soc. Can.; mem. AAAS, Can. Assn. Physicists (pres. 1981-82, Herzberg medal 1971), Am. Phys. Soc., Royal Astron. Soc. Can. (Svc. award 1977), Assn. canadienne-francaise pour l'avancement des scis. (Parizeau medal 1976). Patentee energy analyser of charged particules. Office: Univ Ottawa, Physics Dept, Ottawa, ON Canada K1N 6N5

MARMION, WILLIAM HENRY, retired bishop; b. Houston, Oct. 8, 1907; s. Charles Gresham and Katherine (Rankin) M.; m. Mabel Dougherty Nall, Dec. 28, 1935; children: William Henry, Roger Mills Nall. B.A., Rice U., 1929; M.Div., Va. Theol. Sem., 1932, D.D. (hon.), 1954. Ordained to ministry Episc. Ch., 1932. Priest-in-charge St. James, Taylor, Tex., and Grace Ch., Georgetown, Tex., 1932-35; asso. rector St. Mark's Ch., San Antonio, 1935-38; rector St. Mary's-on-the-Highlands, Birmingham, Ala., 1938-50, St. Andrew's Ch., Wilmington, Del., 1950-54; bishop Episcopal Diocese of Southwestern Va., Roanoke, 1954-79, ret., 1979; Former dir. diocesan camps for young people in, Tex. and Ala., headed diocesan youth work, several yrs; dep. to Gen. Conv. Episcopal Ch., 1943, 46, alternate dep., 1949, 52; del. to Provincial Synod; mem. exec. council Episcopal Ch., 1963-69; chmn. Ala. Com. on Interracial Cooperation, 4 yrs. Trustee Va. Theol. Sem., Va. Episc. Sch., St. Paul's Coll.; pres. Appalachian Peoples Svc. Orgn.; interim warden Coll. of Preachers, 1981-82, diocesan coord. of pastoral ministry to retired clergy and families, 1990—. Home: 2730 Avenham Ave SW Roanoke VA 24014-1527

MARMOR, JUDD, psychiatrist, educator; b. London, May 1, 1910; came to U.S., 1911, naturalized, 1916; s. Clement K. and Sarah (Levene) M.; m. Katherine Stern, May 1, 1938; 1 son, Michael Franklin. AB, Columbia U., 1930, MD, 1933; DHL, Hebrew Union Coll., 1972. Diplomate: Am. Bd. Psychiatry and Neurology, Nat. Bd. Med. Examiners. Intern St. Elizabeth Hosp., Washington, 1933-35; resident neurologist Montefiore Hosp., N.Y.C., 1935-37; psychiatrist Bklyn. State Hosp., 1937; psychoanalytic tng. N.Y. Psychoanalytic Inst., N.Y.C., 1937-41; pvt. practice psychiatry, psychoanalysis and neurology N.Y.C., 1937-46, L.A., 1946—; instr. assoc. in neurology Columbia Coll. Physicians and Surgeons, 1938-40; adj. neurologist, neurologist-in-charge clinic Mt. Sinai Hosp., N.Y.C., 1939-46; lectr. New Sch. Social Rsch., N.Y.C., 1942-43; vis. prof. social welfare UCLA, 1949-64, clin. prof. psychiatry sch. medicine, 1953-80, adj. prof. psychiatry, 1980—; vis. prof. psychology U. So. Calif., 1946-49; tng. analyst, also pres. So. Calif. Psychoanalytic Inst., 1955-57; sr. attending psychiatrist L.A. County Gen. Hosp., 1954—; dir. divs. psychiatry Cedars-Sinai Med. Ctr., L.A., 1965-72; Franz Alexander prof. psychiatry U. So. Calif. Sch. Medicine, 1972-80, emeritus, 1980—; sr. cons. regional office social svc. VA, L.A., 1946-50; cons. psychiatry Brentwood VA Hosp., Calif., 1955-65; mem. Coun. Mental Health of Western Interstate Commn. Higher Edn., 1966-72. Editor: Sexual Inversion-The Multiple Roots of Homosexuality, Modern Psychoanalysis: New Directions and Perspectives, Psychiatry in Transition: Selected Papers of Judd Marmor, Homosexual Behavior: A Modern Reappraisal; (with S. Woods) The Interface Between the Psychodynamic and Behavioral Therapies, Psychiatrists & Their Patients: A National Study of Private Office Practice; (with S. Elsenstein and N.A. Levy) The Dyadic Transaction: An Investigation into the Nature of the Psychotherapeutic Process; (with P. Nardi and D. Sanders) Growing Up Before Stonewall; mem. editl. bd. Am. Jour. Psychoanalysis, Contemporary Psychoanalysis, Archives Sexual Behavior; contbr. articles in field to profl. jours. Served as sr. attending surgeon USPHS USNR, 1944-45. Fellow Am. Psychiat. Assn. (life mem., pres. 1975-76), N.Y. Acad. Medicine (life mem.), Am. Acad. Psychoanalysis (pres. 1965-66), Am. Orthopsychiat. Assn. (dir. 1968-71), AAAS, Am. Coll. Psychiatrists; mem. AMA, Calif. Med. Assn., Group for Advancement Psychiatry (dir. 1968-70, pres. 1973-75), Am. Fund for Psychiatry (dir. 1955-57), So. Calif. Psychiat. Soc., So. Calif. Psychoanalytic Soc. (pres. 1960-61), Am. Psychoanalytic Assn., Los Angeles County Med. Soc., Phi Beta Kappa, Alpha Omega Alpha. Home: 655 Sarbonne Rd Los Angeles CA 90077-3214 Office: 1100 Glendon Ave Ste 921 Los Angeles CA 90024-3513

MARMOR, MICHAEL FRANKLIN, ophthalmologist, educator; b. N.Y.C., Aug. 10, 1941; s. Judd and Katherine (Stern) M.; m. C. Jane Breeden, Dec. 20, 1968; children: Andrea K., David J. AB, Harvard U., 1962, MD, 1966. Diplomate Am. Bd. Ophthalmology. Med. intern UCLA Med. Ctr., 1967; resident in ophthalmology Mass. Eye and Ear Infirmary, Boston, 1970-73; asst. prof. ophthalmology U. Calif. Sch. Medicine, San Francisco, 1973-74; asst. prof. surgery (ophthalmology) Stanford (Calif.) U. Sch. Medicine, 1974-80, assoc. prof., 1980-86, prof., 1986—, head. div. ophthalmalogy, 1984-88, chmn. dept., 1988-92, dir. Basic Sci. Course Ophthalmology, 1993—; mem. assoc. faculty program in human biology Stanford U., 1982—; chief ophthalmology sect. VA Med. Ctr., Palo Alto, Calif., 1974-84; mem. sci. adv. bd. No. Calif. Soc. to Prevent Blindness, 1984-92, Calif. Med. Assn., 1984-92, Nat. Retinitis Pigmentosa Found., 1985-95. Author: (with J.G. Ravin) The Eye of the Artist, 1996; editor: The Retinal Pigment Epithelium, 1975, The Effects of Aging and Environment on Vision, 1991; editor-in-chief Doc. Ophthalmologica, 1995—; editl. bd. Healthline, Lasers and Light in Ophthalmology; contbr. more than 175 articles to sci. jours., 25 chpts. to books. Mem. affirmative action com. Stanford U. Sch. Medicine, 1984—. Sr. asst. surgeon USPHS, 1967-70. Recipient Svc. award Nat. Retinitis Pigmentosa Found., Balt., 1981, Rsch. award Alcon Rsch. Found., Houston, 1989; rsch. grantee Nat. Eye. Inst., Bethesda, Md., 1974-94. Fellow Am. Acad. Ophthalmology (bd. councillors 1982-85, pub. health com. 1990-93, rep. to NAS com. on vision 1991-93, Honor award 1984, Sr. Honor award 1996); mem. Internat. Soc. Clin. Electrophysiology of Vision (v.p. 1990—), Assn. Rsch. in Vision and Ophthalmology, Internat. Soc. for Eye Rsch., Macula Soc. (rsch. com.), Retina Soc. Democrat. Avocations: tennis, race-walking, chamber music (clarinet), art, medical history. Office: Stanford U Sch Medcine Dept Ophthalmology Stanford CA 94305

MARNEY, SAMUEL ROWE, physician, educator; b. Bristol, Va., Feb. 15, 1934; m. Elizabeth Ann Bingham, Oct. 1, 1966; children: Samuel Rowe III, Annis Morison. BA in Chemistry, U. Va., 1955, MD, 1960. Diplomate Am. Bd. Internal Medicine, Am. Bd. Allergy and Immunology; cert. in Diagnostic Lab. Immunology, 1988. Staff physician VA Hosp., Nashville, 1968-69, clin. assoc., 1969-71, clin. investigator, 1971-74, staff physician, infectious disease and allergy cons., 1974—; asst. prof. medicine Med. Ctr. Vanderbilt U., Nashville, 1971-76, assoc. prof., 1976—, dir. allergy and immunology, 1974—; vis. investigator Scripps Clinic and Rsch. Found., La Jolla, Calif., 1973-74. Capt. USAF, 1962-64, Korea. Fellow ACP, Am. Acad. Allergy and Immunology, Am. Coll. Allergy and Immunology; mem. Southeastern Allergy Assn. (pres. 1986-87, Hal M. Davison Meml. award, 1981), Tenn. Soc. Allergy and Immunology. Home: 4340 Sneed Rd Nashville TN 37215-3242 Office: Vanderbilt U Med Ctr Allergy & Immunology 1500 21st Ave S Ste 3500 Nashville TN 37212-3157

MAROCKIE, HENRY R., state school system administrator. Instr., rsch. assoc., asst. to dean W.V. Univ., Morgantown, 1968; asst. supt. Fin., Secondary Schs., Parkersburg, W.V., 1971; supt. Ohio County Schs., Wheeling, W.V., 1972-89; state supt. schs. Charleston, W.V., 1989—; chair Nat. gov. bd. Project Use It, W.V. Literacy Coun.; co-chair Learning Techs. com. Coun. Chief State Sch. Officers; pres. W.V. Sch/ Bldg. Authority; exec. com. mem. W.V. Edn. Fund; past officer W.V. Bd. Edn.; dir. reorgn. W.V. Dept. Edn., new evaluation systems tchrs., adminstrs.; launched Tobacco Control Policy W.V. schs.; est. Student, Tchr. Code Conduct, policies to modernize curriculum to State Bd., Gov's, Am. 2000 goals. Contbr. articles to profl. jours. Officer W.Va. Bd. Dirs., W.Va. Bd. Trustees, W.Va. Gov.'s Honors Acad., W.Va. Profl. Devel. Ctr., W.Va. Joint Commn. Vocat., Tech., Occupational Edn. Recipient W.Va. Supt. Yr. award, W.Va. Leader Learning award Dept. Edn., 1984, Supt. Yr. award W.Va. Assn. Music Educators, 1986, Leadership award Coll. Human Resources and Edn., W.Va. U., 1988, Alumni Achievement award West Liberty State Coll., 1985, citation edn. excellence W.Va. Ho. of Dels., 1982, Disting. Svc. award Nat. Alliance Health/Phys. Edn. Mem. W.V. Bd. Pub. Works, Ednl. Broadcasting Authority, Labor Mgmt. Coun., Tchrs. Retirement Bd., Drug Control Policy Bd., State Job Tng. Coord. Coun., Private Ind. Coun. W.V. Inc. Office: State Dept Edn 1900 Kanawha Blvd E Rm 358 Charleston WV 25305-0330*

MAROHN, ANN ELIZABETH, health information professional; b. Grand Rapids, Mich., Feb. 26, 1946; d. Luther Alfonse and Mary Inez (Pinkstaff) M. BS, Ind. U., 1968; MS, SUNY, Buffalo, 1978. Asst. med. record dir. Highland Park (Mich.) Gen. Hosp., 1968-70; asst. dir. med. record svcs. Meml. Hosp., Elmhurst, Ill., 1970-73; dir. med. record tech. program Alfred (N.Y.) State Coll., 1974-76; mem. faculty med. record adminstrn. dept. Lincoln Coll., Melbourne, Australia, 1977-78, Kean Coll., Union, N.J., 1984-85, Med. U. S.C., Charleston, 1985-87; mem. faculty health record dept. Ferris State Coll., Big Rapids, Mich., 1979-80; dir. health info. mgmt. Armstrong State Coll., Savannah, Ga., 1980-84; dir. med. record dept. Tucson Gen. Hosp., 1988-89, N.D. State Hosp., Jamestown, 1990-92; cons. Prospective Payment Specialists, Tucson, 1992-93; health info. mgr. Sierra Med. Ctr., El Paso, Tex., 1993-94; dir. health info. mgmt. program Southern U., Shreveport, La., 1994-97; dir. health info. mgmt. N. VA Mental Health Inst., Falls Church, Va., 1997—; cons. Oglethorpe Ctr., Savannah, 1983-84. Columnist Australian Med. Record Jour., 1981-87, Communique, 1981-84, Palmetto Breeze, 1985-87, Progress Notes, 1984-85. Recipient disting. mem. award Ga. Med. Record Assn., 1984. Mem. NAFE, Am. Health Info. Mgmt. Assn., Ariz. Health Info. Mgmt. Assn. (program chmn. 1988-89, sec. 1989—), Tex. Health Info. Mgmt. Assn. (dist. III v.p.), Va. Health Info. Mgmt. Assn. (behavioral health sect.). Episcopalian. Avocations: swimming, reading, travel, photography, cooking. Home: 3307 Cannongate Rd Apt 40 Fairfax VA 22031

MAROLDA, ANTHONY JOSEPH, management consulting company executive; b. Winthrop, Mass., Sept. 7, 1939; s. Daniel Arthur and Rose Marie (Pagliarulo) M.; m. Maria Theresa Rizzo, Oct. 10, 1970; children: Matthew, Ria. BS in Physics, Northeastern U., 1962; MS in Physics, Northeaster U., 1968; MBA, Harvard U., 1970. Rsch. physicist High Voltage Engring. Corp., Burlington, Mass., 1962-65; sr. scientist E.G. & G. Inc., Wellsley, Mass., 1965-68; v.p. Arthur D. Little, Inc., Cambridge, Mass., 1970-85; pres. The Winbridge Group, Inc., Cambridge, Mass., 1985—; bd. advs. Daetwyler N.Am., Burlington, N.J., Altdorf, Switzerland, 1995-96. Inventor Apparatus High Density Plasma, 1965; co-author: Business Problem Solving, 1980, Modern Marketing, 1986, Regional Resiliance and Defense Conversion, 1997. Adv. Waterbury-Leningrad. Intersport, Waterbury, Conn., 1988-92. Recipient Hayden Meml. Scholarship, Northeastern U., 1957. Mem. Harvard Club, Harvard Bus. Sch. Alumni Assn. Republican. Roman Catholic. Avocations: hiking, sailing, tennis. Office: The Winbridge Group Inc University Place 124 Mount Auburn St Ste 200 Cambridge MA 02138-5758

MARON, ARTHUR, pediatrician, medical administrator; b. Asbury Park, N.J., Apr. 15, 1933; s. Isidore Chaim and Sadie (Raskin) M.; m. Lynn Sunshine Maron, Aug. 5, 1956 (dec. Aug. 1994); children: Stuart Glenn, Andrea Kim, Scott Michael; m. Ruth Fuerth, Dec. 17, 1995. BS in Biology, Rutgers U., 1954; MD, Union U., 1958; MPA in Health Care, Seton Hall U., 1994. Diplomate Am. Bd. Pediats. Rotating intern USPHS Hosp., Norfolk, Va., 1958-59; pediat. resident Babies Hosp., Newark, 1961-63; pvt. practice specializing in pediats. West Orange, N.J., 1963-94; dir. med. edn. St. Barnabas Med. Ctr., Livingston, N.J., 1988—; assoc. dean for acad. affairs Mount Sinai Sch. of Medicine; pres. Med. Practice Assocs., Roseland, N.J., 1990-93; pres. med. staff St. Barnabas Med. Ctr., Livingston, 1991-93; med. dir. Found. Health Plan, Short Hills, N.J., 1989-91; bd. dirs. Alliance Ind. Acad. Med. Ctrs. Mem. bd. health West Orange Twp., 1970-90, Roseland Bd., 1996—; chmn. physicians divsn. United Jewish Appeal, 1994—. Recipient Maimonides award State of Israel Bonds, 1992. Fellow Am. Acad. Pediats. (bd. dirs., chmn. 1982-88, Presdl. award 1989); mem. AMA, (residency rev. com. for pediats. 1989-96, chmn. 1994-96, nat. residency matching program, bd. dirs. 1996—), Am. Hosp. Assn. (com. on med. edn. 1996—), Assn. for Hosp. Med. Edn. of N.J. (pres.). Jewish. Avocation: travel. Office: St Barnabas Med Ctr 94 Old Short Hills Rd Livingston NJ 07039-5672

MARON, MELVIN EARL, engineer, philosopher, educator; b. Bloomfield, N.J., Jan. 23, 1924; s. Hyman and Florence (Goldman) M.; m. Dorothy Elizabeth Mastin, Aug. 16, 1948; children—Nadia, John. B.S. in Mech. Engring, U. Nebr., 1945, B.A. in Physics, 1947; Ph.D. in Philosophy, U. Calif. at Los Angeles, 1951. Lectr. philosophy UCLA, 1951-52; tech. engr. IBM Corp., San Jose, Calif., 1952-55; mem. tech. staff Ramo-Wooldridge Corp., 1955-59; mem. sr. staff, computer scis. dept. RAND Corp., 1959-66; prof. Sch. Libr. and Info. Studies U. Calif., Berkeley. Served with AUS, 1943-46. Fellow AAAS; mem. Assn. Computing Machinery, Am. Soc. Info. Sci. Home: 63 Ardilla Rd Orinda CA 94563-2201 Office: U Calif Sch Libr & Info Studies Berkeley CA 94720

MARONDE, ROBERT FRANCIS, internist, clinical pharmacologist, educator; b. Monterey Park, Calif., Jan. 13, 1920; s. John August and Emma Florence (Palmer) M.; m. Yolanda Cerda, Apr. 15, 1970; children—Robert George, Donna F. Maronde Varnau, James Augustus, Craig DeWald. B.A., U. So. Calif., 1941, M.D., 1944. Diplomate: Am. Bd. Internal Medicine. Intern L.A. County-U. So. Calif. Med. Ctr., 1943-44, resident, 1944-45, 47-48; asst. prof. physiology U. So. Calif., L.A., 1948-49, asst. clin. prof. medicine, 1949-60, assoc. clin. prof. medicine, 1960-65, assoc. prof. medicine and pharmacology, 1965-67, prof. medicine and pharmacology, 1968-90, emeritus, 1990—, prof. emeritus, 1990—; spl. asst. v.p. for health affairs, 1990—; cons. FDA, 1973, Medco Containment Co. Inc., 1991-97, State of Calif. Dept. Health Svcs., 1993; mem. adv. panel State of Calif., 1997—. Served to lt. (j.g.) USNR, 1945-47. Fellow ACP; mem. Am. Soc. Clin. Pharmacology and Therapeutics, Alpha Omega Alpha. Home: 785 Ridgecrest St Monterey Park CA 91754-3759 Office: U So Calif 2025 Zonal Ave Los Angeles CA 90033-4526 *Scientific integrity, objectivity, concern for the quality of life and adherence to the ethics of Nuremberg are ingredients for the evaluation of therapy for human illness. This is the ultimate objective of the practice of medicine.*

MARONI, DONNA FAROLINO, biologist, researcher; b. Buffalo, Feb. 27, 1938; d. Enrico Victor and Eleanor (Redlinska) Farolino; m. Gustavo Primo Maroni, Dec. 16, 1974. BS, U. Wis., 1960, PhD, 1969. Project assoc. U. Wis., Madison, 1960-63, 68-74; Alexander von Humboldt fellow Inst. Genetics U. Cologne, Fed. Republic Germany, 1974-75; Hargitt fellow Duke U., Durham, N.C., 1975-76, rsch. assoc., 1976-83, rsch. assoc. prof., 1983-87; sr. program specialist N.C. Biotech. Ctr., Research Triangle Park, 1987-88, dir. sci. programs div., 1988-92, v.p. for sci. programs, 1992-94, ret., 1995; mem. adv. com. MICROMED at Bowman Gray Sch. Medicine, Winston-Salem, N.C., 1988—, Minority Sci. Improvement Alliance for Instrn. and Rsch. in Biotech. Ala. A & M U., Normal, 1990-91. Contbr. over 20 articles and revs. to profl. jours. Grantee NSF, 1977-79, NIH, 1979-82, 79-83, 82-87. Mem. Am. Soc. Cell Biology, Genetics Soc. Am., N.C. Acad. Sci., Inc. (bd. dirs. 1983-86), Sigma Xi (mem. exec. com. Duke U. chpt. 1989-90). Achievements include research in electron microscopy, evolution of chromosomes, chromosome structure, evolution of mitosis, and mitosis and fungal phylogeny.

MARONI, PAUL L., finance executive; b. Scranton, Pa., June 20, 1947; s. L. Paul and Mary M. (Manzo) M.; m. Margaret Garretson Bronner, Apr. 27, 1985; 1 child, Emily Garretson. BA, U. Scranton, 1969; MLS, Rutgers U., 1972; MBA, Cornell U., 1980. Reference libr. SUNY Coll., Oneonta, 1972-78; fin. analyst Continental Grain Co., N.Y.C., 1980-82; asst. treas. Newmont Mining Corp., N.Y.C., 1982-88; treas. Newmont Mining/Newmont Gold, N.Y.C., Denver (Colo.), 1988-93; v.p. Newmont Mining/Newmont Gold, Denver, 1990-91, sr. v.p., chief fin. officer, 1991-93; sr. v.p. fin. Consolidated Hydro, Inc., Greenwich, Conn., 1994—. Mem. Fin. Execs. Inst., Nat. Assn. Corp. Treas. Office: Consolidated Hydro Inc 1 Greenwich Plz Greenwich CT 06830-6352

MAROTTA, JOSEPH THOMAS, medical educator; b. Niagara Falls, N.Y., May 28, 1926; emigrated to Can., 1930; s. Alfred and Mary (Montemuro) M.; m. Margaret Hughes, Aug. 31, 1953; children: Maureen, Patricia, Margaret, Fred, Thomas, Jo Anne, Michael, Martha, John, Virginia. M.D., U. Toronto, 1949. Trainee in internal medicine U. Toronto, 1949-52; trainee in neurology Presbyn. Hosp., N.Y.C., 1952-55, U. London, Eng., 1955-56; mem. faculty U. Toronto, 1956—, prof. medicine, 1969—; former assoc. dean clin. affairs U. Toronto (Faculty of Medicine), 1981-89; hon. prof. of neurology U. Western Ontario, 1990—; consulting staff Dept. of Neurol. Scis. Victoria Hosp., U. Hosp., London. Fellow Royal Coll. Physicians (Can.); mem. Alpha Omega Alpha, Phi Chi. Home and Office: 46 Carnforth Rd, London, ON Canada M6G 4P6

MAROVICH, GEORGE M., federal judge; b. 1931. AA, Thornton Community Coll., 1950; BS, U. Ill., 1952, JD, 1954. Atty. Chgo. Title & Trust Co., 1954-59; mem. firm Jacobs & Marovich, South Holland, Ill., 1959-66; v.p., trust officer South Holland Trust & Savs. Bank, 1966-76; judge Cir. Ct. Cook County, Ill., 1976-88; dist. judge U.S. Dist. Ct. (no. dist.) Ill., Chgo., 1988—; adj. instr. Thornton Community Coll., 1977-88. Mem. Ill. Judges Assn., Ill. Jud. Conf., Chgo. Bar Assn., South Suburban Bar Assn. Office: US Dist Ct Chambers 1956 219 S Dearborn St Chicago IL 60604*

MAROVITZ, ABRAHAM LINCOLN, judge; b. Oshkosh, Wis., Aug. 10, 1905; s. Joseph and Rachel (Glowitz) M. JD, Chgo.-Kent Coll. Law, 1925; LHD, Lincoln (Ill.) Coll., 1956; LLD, Winston Churchill Coll., 1968; HHD, Chgo. Med. Sch., 1984; LLD (hon.), Ill. Inst. Tech., 1988, Roosevelt U., 1989, Nat.-Louis U., 1991. Bar: Ill. bar 1927. Asst. state's atty. Cook County, Ill., 1927-33; practiced in Chgo., 1933-50; judge Superior Ct. Cook County, 1950-63; chief justice Cook County Criminal Ct., 1958-59; U.S. judge No. dist. Ill., 1963-75, sr. judge, 1975-89; ret., 1989; chmn. bd. Lincoln

Nat. Bank, 1946-63; Past nat. chmn. Nat. Conf. State Ct. Trial Judges; past mem. lawyer's adv. council U. Ill. Law Forum. Mem. Ill. Senate, 1938-50; Bd. dirs. Hebrew Theol. Coll.; mem. adv. bd. YMCA Met. Chgo.; trustee Chgo.-Kent Coll. Law, Chgo. Med. Sch.; former trustee Ill. Hist. Library; past mem. Jewish Bd. Edn. Served to sgt. maj. USMCR, 1943-46. Named Outstanding Legislator, Ind. Voters Ill., 1949; named to Wisdom Hall of Fame, 1979; recipient Founders' Day award Loyola U. in Chgo., 1967, awards Chgo. Press Club, Chgo. Press Photographers Assn., 1968, Man of Yr. award Jewish Nat. Fund, Israel Bond Orgn., 1973, Horatio Alger award, 1979, Na. Americanism medal DAR, 1980, Citizens' award Chgo. Police Dept., 1982, Lincoln The Lawyer award, 1985, Chgo. Park Dist. Sr. Citizen of Yr. award, 1985, Spirit of Lincoln award Anti-Defamation League, 1985, Celtic Man of Yr. award Celtic Legal Soc. Chgo., 1989, Disting. Pub. Svc. award Union League Club, 1990, Jack Robbins award Boys Brotherhood Republic Alumni Assn., 1990, Excellence in Pub. Svc. award North Shore Retirement award, 1990, Recognition award B'nai B:rith Sports Lodge, 1990, award Immigration and Naturalization Svc., 1993, Sr. medal of honor Cook County Sheriff, 1994, plaque Intellectual Property Law Assn., 1994, Profl. Achievement award Chgo. Kent Law Sch., 1995, Making History award Chgo. Hist. Soc., 1995, Commitment to a Dream award United Neighborhood Orgn. Chgo., 1995, Humanitarian award Jesse Owens Found., 1995, Benjamin Cardozo award B'nai B'rith Anti-Discrimination League, 1996, Raoul Wallenberg Humanitarian awrd, 1990, Order of Lincoln award, 1987, others; named to Chgo. Jewish Sports Hall of Fame, 1994; Judge Abraham Lincoln Marovitz Ct. in Chgo. named in his honor, 1992, Judge Abraham Lincoln Marovitz Courtroom at Chgo. Kent Law Sch. named in his honor, 1992, Chgo. chpt. Am. Inns. of Ct. named in his honor, 1994. Mem. ABA, Ill. State Bar Assn., Chgo. Bar Assn. (past mgr., Exemplary Svc. award 1987), Internat. Assn. Jewish Lawyers & Jurists, Decalogue Soc. of Lawyers (ann. merit award 1968), Jewish War Vets. U.S. (past dept. comdr., Man of Yr. 1994), Am. Legion (past comdr. Marine post Chgo.). Jewish (bd. dirs. synagogue). Home: 3260 N Lake Shore Dr Apt 8A Chicago IL 60657-3955 Office: U S Dist Ct 219 S Dearborn St Rm 1900 Chicago IL 60604-1801

MAROVITZ, JAMES LEE, lawyer; b. Chgo., Feb. 21, 1939; s. Harold and Gertrude (Luster) M.; m. Gail Helene Florsheim, June 17, 1962; children: Andrew, Scott. BS, Northwestern U., 1960, JD, 1963. Bar: Ill. 1963, U.S. Dist. Ct. (no. dist.) Ill. 1963, U.S. Ct. Appeals (7th cir.) 1990. Assoc. Leibman, Williams, Bennett, Baird & Minow, Chgo., 1963-70, ptnr., 1970-72; ptnr. Sidley & Austin, Chgo., 1972—; bd. dirs. Cobra Elec. Corp., Chgo. Plan commr. Village of Deerfield, Ill., 1972-79, trustee, 1983-93. Mem. ABA, Ill. Bar Assn., Chgo. Bar Assn. Club: Univ. (Chgo.). Office: Sidley & Austin 1 First Natl Plz Chicago IL 60603-2003

MARPLE, DOROTHY JANE, retired church executive; b. Abington, Pa., Nov. 24, 1926; d. John Stanley and Jennie (Stetler) M. A.B., Ursinus Coll., 1948; M.A., Syracuse U., 1950; Ed.D., Columbia U. Tchrs. Coll., 1969; L.H.D., Thiel Coll., 1965, Gettysburg Coll., 1979, Ursinus Coll., 1981; D. Humanitarian Services, Newberry Coll., 1977; DD, Trinity Luth. Sem., 1987. Counselor, asst., office dean undergrad. women Women's Coll., Duke, 1950-53; dean women, fgn. student adv. Thiel Coll., 1953-61; asst. social dir. Whittier Hall, Columbia Tchrs. Coll., 1961-62; exec. dir. Luth. Ch. Women, Luth. Ch. Am., Phila., 1962-75; asst. to bishop Luth. Ch. Am., 1975-85; coord. Transition Office Evang. Luth. Ch. Am., 1986-87; asst. gen. sec. ops. Nat. Coun. Chs. of Christ in U.S., N.Y.C., 1987-89; coordinator Luth. Ch. in Am. commn. on function and structure, 1970-72. Home: 8018 Anderson St Philadelphia PA 19118-2936

MARPLE, GARY ANDRE, management consultant; b. Mt. Pleasant, Iowa, Feb. 22, 1937; s. Kenneth Lowry and Truma Janice (Cook) M.; m. Ellen I. Metcalf, May 29, 1971 (div. 1981); m. Meredith Ann Rutter, July 23, 1988; children: Brian Edward, Stephen Lowry. BS, Drake U., 1959; MBA, Mich. State U., 1962, DBA, 1963. Postdoctoral fellow mgmt. MIT, 1963; cons. Arthur D. Little Inc., Cambridge, Mass., 1963-82; pres. Commonwealth Strategies, Inc., Acton, Mass., 1982—, Oceanus Holding, Ltd., S.W., Harbor, Maine, 1985—; treas. Bramar, Inc., Stow, Mass., 1988—; exec.-in-residence Ctr. for Entrepreneurial Leadership, Ewing Marion Kauffman Found., Kansas City, Mo. Editor, author: Grocery Manufacturing in the U.S., 1968; contbr. to Conquering Government Regulation, 1982. Mem. Arthur D. Little Alumni Assn. (bd. dirs., past pres. Lexington, Mass. 1992—).

MARPLE, STANLEY LAWRENCE, JR., electrical engineer, signal processing researcher; b. Tulsa, Sept. 7, 1947; s. Stanley Lawrence and Geraldine Doris M.; m. Suzanne Eileen Stevens, Aug. 31, 1974; children: Darci Leah, Rebecca Anne, Matthew Lawrence. BA, Rice U., 1969, MEE, 1970; DEng, Stanford U., 1976. Staff engr. Argo Systems, Inc., Sunnyvale, Calif., 1972-78; sr. staff engr. Advent Systems, Inc., Mountain View, Calif., 1978-79, The Analytic Scis. Corp., Mc Lean, Va., 1980-82; sr. devel. engr. Schlumberger Well Svcs., Houston, 1983-85; mgr., devel. engr. Martin Marietta Aero & Naval Systems, Balt., 1986-88; chief scientist Orincon Corp., San Diego, 1989-93, 96—, Acuson Corp., Mountain View, Calif., 1993-96. Author: Digital Spectral Analysis, 1987, Digital Time, Frequency, and Space Analysis, 1997. Capt. Signal Corps, U.S. Army, 1972-80. Fellow IEEE; mem. IEEE Signal Processing Soc. (editor Trans. on Signal Processing 1982-86, Sr. Paper award 1984, adminstrv. com. 1985-88, chmn. spectral estimation and array processing com. 1989-91). Avocations: stamp collecting, hiking, writing. Office: Orincon 9363 Towne Centre Dr San Diego CA 92121-3016

MARQUARDT, ANN MARIE, small business administrator; b. Plainview, N.Y., Oct. 28, 1964; d. Steven Peter Paul and Virginia Ann (Gallo) M.; m. Paul W. Minerva, Dec. 24, 1996. Grad., Harry B. Ward Occupational Ctr, Riverhead, N.Y., 1982; student, Dowling Coll., 1982-84; Assoc. Acctg., Suffolk Community Coll., 1990; BS in Bus. Mgmt., St. John's U., 1993. Sec. Dowling Coll., Oakdale, N.Y., 1982-84; sec., office mgr. Pudge, Peteco & Peanuts Corp., Southold, N.Y., 1984-86, Era Albo Agy., Mattituck, N.Y., 1986-87; legal asst. manage estate dept. Wickham, Wickham & Bressler, P.C., Mattituck, 1987-89, 93—; bus., gen. mgr. Mattituck Laundromat, 1987-89, Gaslight Cafe, Ltd., Mattituck, 1989; office/bus. mgr., bookkeeper accounts payable/receivable Minerva's Tree Svcs. Ltd., Cutchogue, N.Y., 1990-96; office/bookkeeping cons. Dickerson's Marine, Mattituck, 1990, Hobby's Plus, Southold. Author poetry and short stories. Mem. NOW, NAFE, AAUW, Am. Mgmt. Assn., Nat. Arborist Assn., Nat. Assn. for Self-Employed, Legal Secs. Ea. L.I., Am. Soc. Notaries. Avocations: modeling, dance, creative writing, boating, fishing. Office: Wickham Wickham & Bressler 10315 Main Rd Mattituck NY 11952-1529 Address: PO Box 527 Cutchogue NY 11935-0527

MARQUARDT, CHRISTEL ELISABETH, lawyer; b. Chgo., Aug. 26, 1935; d. Herman Albert and Christine Marie (Geringer) Trolenberg; children: Eric, Philip, Andrew, Joel. BS in Edn., Mo. Western Coll., 1970; JD with honors, Washburn U., 1974. Bar: Kans. 1974, Mo. 1992, U.S. Dist. Ct. Kans. 1974, U.S. Dist. Ct. (we. dist.) Mo. 1992. Tchr. St. John's Ch., Tigerton, Wis., 1955-56; pers. asst. Columbia Records, L.A., 1958-59; ptnr. Cosgrove, Webb & Oman, Topeka, 1974-86, Palmer & Marquardt, Topeka, 1986-91, Levy and Craig P.C., Overland Park, Kans., 1991-94; sr. ptnr. Marquardt and Assocs., L.L.C., Fairway, Kans., 1994—; judge Kans. Ct. Appeals, 1995—; mem. atty. bd. discipline Kans. Supreme Ct., 1984-86. Mem. editorial adv. bd. Kans. Lawyers Weekly, 1992—; contbr. articles to legal jours. Bd. dirs. Topeka Symphony, 1983-92, Arts and Humanities Assn. Johnson County, 1992—, Brown Found., 1988-90; hearing examiner Human Rels. Com., Topeka, 1974-76; local advisor Boy Scouts Am., 1973-74; bd. dirs., mem. nominating com. YWCA, Topeka, 1979-81; bd. govs. Washburn U. Law Sch., 1987—, v.p., 1994-95; mem. dist. bd. adjudication Mo. Synod Luth. Ch., Kans., 1982-88. Names Woman of Yr., Mayor, City of Topeka, 1982; Obee scholar Washburn U., 1972-74. Fellow Am. Bar Found., Kans. Bar Found. (trustee 1987-89); mem. ABA (labor law, family and litigation sects., mem. ho. dels. 1988—, state del. 1995—, specilization com. 1987-93, chmn. 1989-93, lawyer referral com. 1993—, bar svcs. and activities, 1995—. standing com. on comms. 1996—), Kans. Bar Assn. (sec., treas. 1981-82, 83-85, v.p. 1985-86, pres. 1987-88, bd. dirs.), Kans. Trial Lawyers Assn. (bd. govs. 1982-86, lectr.), Topeka Bar Assn., Am. Bus. Women's Assn. (lectr., corr. sec. 1983-84, pres. career chpt. 1986-87, named one of Top 10 Bus. Women of Yr., 1985). Home: 3408 Alameda Dr Topeka KS 66614 Office: 4330 Shawnee Mission Pkwy Fairway KS 66205-2507

MARQUARDT, KATHLEEN PATRICIA, professional society administrator; b. Kalispell, Mont., June 6, 1944; d. Dean King and Lorraine Camille (Buckmaster) Marquardt; m. William Wewer, Dec. 6, 1987; children: Shane Elizabeth, Montana Quinn. Purser, Pan Am. World Airways, Washington, 1968-75; info. specialist Capital Systems Group, Kensington, Md., 1979-81; dir. pub. affairs Subscription TV Assn., Washington, 1981-83, exec. dir., 1983-86; pres. Internat. Policy Studies Orgn., 1983-90; pres., designer Elizabeth Quinn Couture; lectr. in field. Chmn. bd. Friends of Freedom, 1982-90, Putting People First, 1990—, Mont. Matters, 1996—; v.p. Am. Policy Ctr., 1996—; treas. Mont. Tax Reduction Movement. Author: Animal Scam-The Beastly Abuse of Human Rights, 1993, (national newpaper column) From the Trenches; contbr. articles to syndicated newspapers and mags.; host Grass Roots radio. Recipient Citizen Achievement award Ctr. fo Def. Free Enterprise, 1992, Gold Medal award Pa. State Fish and Game Protective Assn., 1993. Mem. Outdoor Writers Assn. Am. Home: 533 5th Ave Helena MT 59601-4359 Office: Putting People First 21 N Last Chance Gulch St Helena MT 59601-4137

MARQUARDT, SANDRA MARY, activist, lobbyist, researcher; b. Dhahran, Saudi Arabia, Mar. 5, 1959; parents Am. citizens; d. Donald Edward and Mary Eleanor (Lindsay-Rea) M.; m. Hans Kristensen. BA, U. Wis., 1982. Editor, organizer Nat. Coalition Against the Misuse of Pesticides, Washington, 1983-87; rschr., author Environ. Policy Inst., Washington, 1987-88; rschr., lobbyist Greenpeace, Washington, 1988-95; rschr. Consumer's Union., 1995-96; program dir. Mothers and Others for a Livable Planet, San Francisco, 1996—; mem. steering com., former chmn. Pesticide Action Network, San Francisco, 1984-89, 92—; consumer rep. Calif. Organic Food Adv. Bd., 1997—. Authored reports on pesticide exports, bottled water, organic cotton, golf courses, sanitary products, diapers. Avocation: bicycling, running, photography. Office: Mothers and Others for a Livable Planet 870 Market St Ste 654 San Francisco CA 94102-3014

MARQUARDT, STEPHEN ALAN, ironworks company executive; b. St. Paul, Ark., Feb. 1, 1950; s. Kurt Walter and Violet (Klein) M.; m. Gloria Fern Evans, May 19, 1984; children: Sol, Mok. Grad., H.S., Mason City, Iowa, 1968; student, Bethel Coll., St. Paul, 1968-69, U. Ark., Fayetteville, Ark., 1978-79. Plant foreman Wash. Fish & Oyster Co., Seattle, 1976-79; shop foreman White River Ironworks, Fayetteville, Ark., 1979-82; pres., CEO Great Southern Metals Co., Fayetteville, 1982—; cons. various midwest metal mfrs., 1984—. Poet: Individual poems published in London, 1988-89; artist: architectural metalwork, 1984—; inventor: machine and building design, 1992—. Mem. Artists and Blacksmith's Assn. of N.Am., Nat. Ornamental and Miscellaneous Metals Assn. Avocations: reading, writing, gardening, art metalwork, meditation. Office: Great So Metals Co 600 W Meadow St Ste A Fayetteville AR 72701-5011

MARQUARDT, STEVE ROBERT, library director; b. St. Paul, Sept. 7, 1943; s. Robert Thomas and Dorothy Jean (Kane) M.; m. Judy G. Brown, Aug. 4, 1968; 1 child, Sarah. BA in History, Macalester Coll., 1966; MA in History, U. Minn., 1970, MLS, 1973, PhD in History, 1978. History instr. Macalester Coll., St. Paul, 1968-69; cataloger N.Mex. State U. Libr., Las Cruces, 1973-75; acting univ. archivist, acting dir. Rio Grande Hist. Collections N. Mex. State U. Libr., Las Cruces, 1973-74; acquisitions librarian Western Ill. U. Libr., Macomb, 1976-77, head cataloger, Online Computer Libr. Ctr. coord., 1977-79; asst. dir. resources & tech. svcs. Ohio U. Libr., Athens, 1979-81; dir. librs. U. Wis., Eau Claire, 1981-89; dir. univ. librs. No. Ill. U., DeKalb, 1989-90; dir. librs. U. Wis., Eau Claire, 1990-96; dean of librs. S.D. State U., Brookings, 1996—. Editor Jour. Rio Grande History, 1974; contbr. articles to profl. jours. Coord. Amnesty Internat. Adoption Group 275, Eau Claire, 1985-88; pres. Chippewa Valley Free-net, 1994-96. Mem. ALA, Assn. Coll. and Rsch. Librs. (chmn. performance measures in acad. librs. com. 1985-89). Lutheran. Avocations: tennis, bicycling. Office: SD State U Briggs Libr Box 2115 Brookings SD 57007-1098

MARQUART, CHRISTOPHER LOUIS, neurosurgeon; b. Wheeling, W.Va., Aug. 2, 1955; s. Louis August and Beatrice Anne (Pagenparm) M.; m. Marisa Dee Boggs, Apr. 16, 983; children: Matthew Christopher, Andrew Stuart. AB in Biology magna cum laude, W.Va. U., 1977, MD, 1981. Diplomate Am. Bd. Neurol. Surgery. Gen. surgery intern Ind. U., Indpls., 1981-82, neurosurgery resident, 1982-87; attending neurosurgeon Wheeling (W.Va.) and OVMC Hosp., 1987—; clin. asst., prof. W.Va. U. Hosp., 1989; chmn. intensive care unit OVMC, Wheeling, 1989—; chmn. dept. neuroscis. OVMC/Wheeling Hosp., 1994. Mem. AMA, Ohio County Med. Soc., Congress of Neurol. Surgeons, Neurosurg. Soc. of the Virginias, W.Va. Med. Soc., W.Va. Neurosurg. Soc. (v.p.), Am. Trauma Soc., Am. Assn. of Neurol. Surgeons, Jacob Schwinn Study Club, Alpha Omega Alpha, Alpha Epsilon Delta, Phi Kappa Phi. Republican. Roman Catholic. Office: 40 Medical Park Ste 406 Wheeling WV 26003-6392

MARQUEZ, ALFREDO C., federal judge; b. 1922; m. Linda Nowobilsky. B.S., U. Ariz., 1948, J.D., 1950. Bar: Ariz. Practice law Mesch Marquez & Rothschild, 1957-80; asst. atty. gen. State of Ariz., 1951-52; asst. county atty. Pima County, Ariz., 1953-54; adminstrv. asst. to Congressman Stewart Udall, 1955; judge U.S. Dist. Ct. Ariz., Tucson, 1980—. Served with USN, 1942-45. Office: US Dist Ct US Courthouse Rm 327 55 E Broadway Blvd Tucson AZ 85701-1719

MARQUEZ, JOAQUIN ALFREDO, lawyer; b. Humacao, P.R., Aug. 1, 1942; s. Joaquin and Emelina (Tudela) M.; m. Jocelyn Christiansen, Mar. 27, 1967; children: Joaquin A. Jr., Julian A. BS in Econs., U. Pa., 1964; LLB, U. P.R., 1967; LLM in Taxation, Georgetown U., 1974. Bar: P.R. 1967, U.S. Dist. Ct. P.R. 1968, U.S. Ct. Appeals (lst cir.) 1968, D.C. 1972, U.S. Dist. Ct. D.C. 1972. Assoc. Goldman, Antonetti & Subira, San Juan, P.R., 1967-68; adminstrv. asst. to resident commr. from P.R. Washington, 1971-72, 77-78; sr. atty.-advisor AID U.S. Dept. State, Washington, 1973-76; dir. P.R. Fed. Affairs Adminstrn., Washington, 1978-81; ptnr. Hopkins & Sutter, Washington, 1981-94, Drinker, Biddle & Reath, Washington, 1994—; mem. P.R. Export Promotions Coun., San Juan, 1979-81; staff dir. So. Govs.' Assn., Washington, 1980-81. Capt. U.S. Army, 1968-70, Vietnam. Decorated Bronze Star. Mem. ABA, P.R. Bar Assn., D.C. Bar Assn. Republican. Roman Catholic. Avocations: sailing, reading. Office: Drinker Biddle & Reath 901 15th St NW Washington DC 20005-2327

MARQUIS, HARRIET HILL, social worker; b. Rocky Mount, N.C., Sept. 4, 1938; d. Robert Foster and Anne Ruth (Daughtry) Hill; m. James Ralph Marquis, Apr. 23, 1967; children: Margaret Anne, Karen Lee. BA in English, Meredith Coll., 1960; MA in English, Seton Hall U., 1971; PhD in English, Drew U., 1984; MSW, NYU, 1987. Cert. diplomate in social work; cert. in psychoanalyst psychotherapy, N.Y. Tchr. English S.C. Pub. Schs., 1960-62, Peace Corps, Sierra Leone, West Africa, 1963-65; psychotherapist Child Guidance & Family Svc. Ctr., Orange, N.J., 1987; staff clinician Esther Dutton Counseling Ctr., Morristown, N.J., 1987-90; psychotherapist Ctr. Evaluation & Psychotherapy, Morristown, N.J., 1990-93; clin. social worker pvt. practice, Madison, N.J., 1990—; adj. prof. English Fairleigh Dickenson U., Madison, 1983-85; speaker in field. Fellow N.J. Assn. Clin. Social Workers; mem. NASW, Nat. Fedn. of Socs. for Clin. Social Work (nat. membership com. psychoanalysis in clin. social work), N.J. Soc. Study of Multiple Personality and Dissociative Disorders, Internat. Conf. Advancement of Pvt. Practice Clin. Social Work, Coun. Psychoanalytic Psychotherapists. Democrat. Methodist. Avocations: reading, walking, writing, travel. Office: Clin Psychotherapy Assocs Madison NJ 07940

MARQUIS, ROLLIN PARK, retired librarian; b. Badin, N.C., Nov. 29, 1925; s. Rollin Howard and Carmen (Park) M.; m. Marian Horton Bonstein, Aug. 21, 1954 (dec. Aug. 1995); children: Rollin Hilary, Jeffrey Perrin, Anne-Louise. B.A., Columbia, 1948; postgrad. linguistics, St. Catherines Soc. U. Oxford, 1948-50; painting, Art Students League N.Y., 1950-52; M.L.S., Carnegie Inst. Tech., 1958. Catalog asst. Columbia Med. Library, 1952-53; adminstrv. asst. Nat. Council Chs. Christ in U.S.A., N.Y.C., 1953-56, Friends Com. on Nat. Legislation, Washington, 1956-57; reference asst. Carnegie Library, Pitts., 1957-58; dir. Citizens Library, Washington, Pa., 1958-59, River Edge (N.J.) Free Pub. Library, 1959-63, Allegany County Library, Cumberland, Md., 1963-64; city librarian Dearborn (Mich.) Dept. Libraries, 1964-89, ret., 1989. Active Fine Arts Assocs., U. Mich., Dearborn. With AUS, 1944-46. Mem. ALA, Better Edn. thru Simplified Spelling, Dearborn Orchestral Soc., Fair Lane Music Guild, Schoolcraft Coll. Cmty. Choir, Torch Club (Detroit), Rotary. Democrat. Mem. Soc. of Friends. Home: 16351 Rotunda Dr Ste 369 Dearborn MI 48120-1159 *The things obtained through cooperation, sharing and mutual goodwill are the achievements which satisfy—as significantly for public and business life, as for private life.*

MARR, CARMEL CARRINGTON, retired lawyer, retired state official; b. Bklyn.; d. William Preston and Gertrude Clementine (Lewis) Carrington; BA, Hunter Coll., 1945; JD, Columbia U., 1948; m. Warren Marr, II, Apr. 11, 1948; children: Charles Carrington, Warren Quincy III. Bar: N.Y. 1948, U.S. Dist. Ct. (ea. dist.) N.Y. 1950, U.S. Dist. Ct. (so. dist.) N.Y. 1951; clk. Dyer & Stevens, N.Y.C., 1948-49; pvt. practice, N.Y.C., 1949-53; adviser legal affairs U.S. mission to UN, N.Y.C., 1953-67, sr. legal officer Office Legal Affairs, UN Secretariat, 1967-68; mem. N.Y. State Human Rights Appeal Bd., 1968-71; mem. N.Y. State Pub. Svc. Commn., 1971-86; cons. Gas Rsch. Inst., 1987-91; lectr. N.Y. Police Acad., 1963-67. Contbr. articles to profl. jours. Mem. N.Y. Gov.'s Com. Edn. and Employment of Women, 1963-64; mem. Nat. Gen. Svcs. Pub. Adv. Council, 1969-71; mem., former chmn. adv. coun. Gas Rsch. Inst.; mem., chmn. tech. pipeline safety standards com. Dept. Transp., 1979-85; former mem. task force Fed. Energy Regulatory Commn. and EPA to examine PCBs in gas supply system; past chmn. gas com. Nat. Assn. Regulatory Utility Commrs.; past pres. Great Lakes Conf. Pub. Utilities Commrs., mem. exec. com.; mem. UN Devel. Corp., 1969-72; bd. dirs. Amistad Rsch. Ctr., New Orleans, 1970—, chmn. bd. dirs., 1981-94; bd. dirs. Bklyn. Soc. Prevention Cruelty to Children, Nat. Arts Stblzn. Fund, 1984-93, Prospect Park Alliance, 1987—; bd. visitors N.Y. State Sch. Girls, Hudson, 1964-71; mem. exec. bd. Plays for Living, N.Y.C., 1968-75; pres. bd. dirs. Billie Holiday Theatre, 1972-80; mem. nat. adv. coun. Hampshire Coll.; pres.'s. coun. Tulane U., 1988-95. Mem. Phi Beta Kappa, Alpha Chi Alpha, Alpha Kappa Alpha. Republican. Episcopalian.

MARR, DAVID FRANCIS, television announcer, former professional golfer, journalist; b. Houston, Dec. 27, 1933; s. David Francis and Grace Anne (Darnell) M.; m. Caroline Elizabeth Dawson, Sept. 25, 1972; children by previous marriage: Elizabeth S., David Francis III, Anthony J. Student, Rice U., 1950-51, U. Houston, 1951-52. Profl. golfer, 1953—, tour player, 1960-72, part-time tour player, 1973—; golf announcer ABC Sports, 1970-91, BBC Sports, 1992—, NBC Sports, 1995—; dir. Nabisco-Dinah Shore Tournament, 1981-86. Elected to Coll. Golf Hall of Fame, 1977, Tex. Golf Hall of Fame, 1981; named to Ryder Cup Team, 1965. Mem. Profl. Golfers Assn. (nat. champion 1965, Player of Year 1965), AFTRA. Roman Catholic. Clubs: Lochinvar Golf (Houston); Houston City; Champions Golf (Houston); Brae-Burn Country; Loch Lomond (Scotland). Capt. Ryder Cup Team, 1981. Office: care Hans Kramer IMG 1 Erieview Plz Ste 1300 Cleveland OH 44114-1715

MARR, JACK WAYNE, lawyer; b. Ft. Worth, Aug. 19, 1949; s. Norman L. and Florence (Mohn) M.; m. Sharon Lee Hutto, Jan. 2, 1971; children: Justin, Dallas. BBA, Tex. Tech. U., 1971, JD, 1974. Bar: Tex. 1994. Briefing counsel 13th Ct. Civil Appeals, Corpus Christi, Tex., 1974-75; assoc. Guittard & Henderson, Victoria, Tex., 1975-79; ptnr. Lewis & Kelly, Victoria, 1979-81, Kelly, Stephenson & Marr, Victoria, 1981-91, Kelly, Marr, Meier & Hartman, Victoria, 1991-93, Marr, Meier & Hartman, Victoria, 1993—. Contbr. articles to profl. jours. Pres. Southwest Little League, Victoria, 1991-92. Mem. State Bar Tex. (family law coun., legis. com., practice manual com.), Tex. Acad. Family Law Specialists (pres. 1994-95).

MARR, LUTHER REESE, communications executive, lawyer; b. Kansas City, June 23, 1925; s. Luther Dow and Aileen (Shimfessel) M.; m. Christelle Lois Taylor, July 12, 1956; children—Michelle Lois, Stephen Luther, Christelle Elizabeth. A.B., U. Calif. at Los Angeles, 1946; J.D., U. So. Calif., 1950. Bar: Calif. 1951. With firm Hasbrouck & Melby, Glendale, 1952-54; atty. The Walt Disney Co., Burbank, Calif., 1954-92; corp. sec. The Walt Disney Co., 1957-78, v.p. corp. and shareholder affairs, 1978-87, v.p. shareholder svc., 1987-92. Trustee Le Lycée Français de Los Angeles. Served with USNR, 1946-47. Mem. Am. Soc. Corp. Secs., Calif., Los Angeles Bar Assns., Phi Beta Kappa, Phi Alpha Delta. Republican. Methodist. Home: 1785 Cielito Dr Glendale CA 91207-1023

MARR, PHEBE ANN, historian, educator; b. Mt. Vernon, N.Y., Sept. 21, 1931; d. John Joseph and Lillian Victoria (Henningsen) Marr. B.A., Barnard Coll., 1953; Ph.D., Harvard U., 1967. Research assoc. ARAMCO, Dhahran, Saudi Arabia, 1960-62; dir. middle east program Fgn. Service Inst., 1963-66; research fellow Middle East Ctr., Harvard U., Cambridge, Mass., 1968-70; asst. prof. Stanislaus State Coll., Turlock, Calif., 1970-71, assoc. prof., 1971-74; assoc. prof. history U. Tenn., Knoxville, 1974-85, chmn. Asian Studies Program, 1977-79; sr. fellow Nat. Def. U., Washington, 1985—; cons. ARAMCO, 1979-83. Harvard U. traveling fellow, 1956; mem. Coun. Fgn. Rels. Author: The Modern History of Iraq, 1985; co-editor: Riding the Tiger: Middle East Challenge After the Cold War, 1993; contbr. articles to profl. jours. Mem. Middle East Inst. (bd. govs.), Middle East Studies Assn. Home: 2902 18th St NW Washington DC 20009-2954 Office: Nat Def U 4th & P Sts SW Fort Mcnair DC 20319

MARR, ROBERT BRUCE, physicist, educator; b. Quincy, Mass., Mar. 25, 1932; s. Ralph George and Ethel (Beals) M.; m. Nancy Rosa Parkes, June 12, 1954; children: Richard, Jonathan, Rebecca. B.S., MIT, 1953; M.A., Harvard U., 1955, Ph.D., 1959. Research assoc. Brookhaven Nat. Lab., Upton, N.Y., 1959-61; assoc. physicist Brookhaven Nat. Lab., 1961-64, physicist, 1964-68, sr. physicist, 1968-95, assoc. chmn. applied math. dept., 1974-75, 83-88, chmn., 1975-78; ret., 1995; adj. assoc. prof. Columbia U., 1969; lectr. SUNY at Stony Brook, 1969-70, vis. prof. dept. computer sci., 1979; guest mathematician U. Colo., 1970; vis. mathematician Lawrence Berkeley Lab., 1978; cons. NSF, NIH, 1969—. Contbr. articles to profl. jours. Served with U.S. Army, 1958-59. NSF grantee, 1974. Mem. Soc. for Magnetic Resonance in Medicine (trustee 1982-87, sec.-treas. 1984-86, treas. 1986-87). Home: 368 Private Rd Patchogue NY 11772-5827 Office: Brookhaven Nat Lab Applied Sci Dept Upton NY 11973

MARRA, ANTHONY TULLIO, audio visual specialist; b. Newark, N.J., June 26, 1947; s. John and Christine (Sapparito) M.; m. Erica Jane Curci, Nov. 25, 1987; children: Becky Michelle George, Antonio Tullio, Becky Lynn George, Crystal Marra, Heather Leigh Marra. Advisor Govt. Liason for Ednl. Insts., Washington, 1978-91; media specialist, advisor Washington & Lee U., Lexington, Va., 1978-91; media specialist Longwood Coll., Farmville, Va., 1978-91, Hollins Coll., Salem, Va., 1978-91, Lynchburg (Va.) Coll., 1978-91, Randolph Macon Women's Coll., Lynchburg, Va., 1978-91; dir. audio-visual Sweet Briar (Va.) Coll., 1978-91; media cons. Africa Global Perspectives, 1994—; pres., owner Audio/Visual Advisors, 1997—; agt. bus. comms. sys. divsn. Lucent Techs./Bell Labs, 1997—; acoustic expert rsch. and devel. NASA Langley Field, Hampton, Va., 1971-78. Author: (books) Poetry in LIfe To Be in Death I Am, 1972, The Holy Quran-The Hereafter, 1989; inventor: overhead copy stand for ch.-sch. system, 1991, marking device for NASA Test Flights, 1972; designer TV studio and control room, 1994. Bd. dirs. S.W. Va. Free Clinic. With USMC, 1964-68, Vietnam. Recipient cert. appreciation NASA fors rsch. 1976, 78. Avocations: photgraphy, videography, working with bldg. computers, cmty. work. Home: PO Box 3104 Lynchburg VA 25603 Office: 2822 Rivermont Ave Lynchburg VA 24503-1402

MARRETT, CORA B., university educator, science educator; b. Richmond, Va., June 15, 1942; d. Horace Sterling and Clora Ann (Boswell) Bagley; m. Louis Everard Marrett, Dec. 24, 1968. BA, Va. Union U., 1963; MS, U. Wis., 1965, PhD, 1968. Asst. prof. U. N.C., Chapel Hill, 1968-69; from asst. to assoc. prof. Western Mich. U., Kalamazoo, Mich., 1969-73; from assoc. prof. to full prof. U. Wis., Madison, 1973—; asst. dir. NSF, Arlington, Va., 1992-96; mem. sci. adv. panel U.S. Army, Washington, 1976-77; mem. Naval Rsch. Adv. Com., Washington, 1978-81, Pres. Commn. on the Accident at Three Mile Island, 1979; bd. govs. Argonne (Ill.) Nat. Lab., 1983-90, 96-99. Editor: Research in Race and Ethnic Relations, 1988, Gender and Classroom Interaction, 1990. Resident fellow NAS, 1973-74; fellow Ctr. for Advanced Study in Behavioral Scis., 1976-77. Mem. AAAS, ASA, Phi Kappa Phi.

Avocations: reading, travel, film appreciation. Home: 1745 Norman Way Madison WI 53705 Office: U Wis Dept Sociology 4201 Wilson Blvd Madison WI 53706

MARRINER, SIR NEVILLE, orchestra conductor; b. Lincoln, Eng., Apr. 15, 1924; s. Herbert Henry and Ethel May (Roberts) M.; m. Elizabeth Sims, Dec. 20, 1957; children: Susan Frances, Andrew Stephen. Ed., Royal Coll. Music, Paris Conservatory. Violinist Martin String Quartet, 1946-53, Virtuoso String Trio, 1950, Jacobean Ensemble, 1952, London Symphony Orch., from 1956; condr. L.A. Chamber Orch., 1969-77; music dir. Minn. Orch., 1979-86, Stuttgart (Germany) Symphony Orch., 1986-89; dir. South Bank Festival Music, 1975-78, Meadow Brook Festival, Detroit, 1979-84. Condr. Béatrice et Bénédict, Festival Hall, 1989; recs. include CDs of Dvořák Serenades, Haydn Violin Concerto in C, Mozart Serenade K361, Il Barbiere di Siviglia, Schubert 4th and 5th Symphonies, The English Connection (Vaughan Williams The Lark Ascending, Elgar Serenade and Tippett Corelli Fantasia), Trumpet Concertos, with Håkan Hardenberger, Mendelssohn Piano Works with Murray Perahia, Mozart Haffner Serenade, 200 other recordings include Bach Concertos, Suites and Die Kunst der Fuge, Vivaldi, The Four Seasons and other concertos, Concerti Grossi by Corelli, Geminiani, Torelli, Locatelli and Manfredini, Mozart Symphonies, Concertos, Serenades and Divertimenti, Handel Messiah, Opera overtures and Water and Fireworks music, Die Zauberflöte, Handel Arias with Kathleen Battle, Il Turco in Italia and Don Giovanni, complete cycles of symphonies of Beethoven, Schubert, Schumann, Tchaikowsky, complete Mozart Piano Concertos with Alfred Brendel. Bd. dirs., founder Acad. of St. Martin-in-the Fields, 1959—. Decorated Comdr. of Brit. Empire, KBE; recipient Grand Prix du Disque, Edison award, Mozart Gemeinde prize, Tagore prize, Grammy award, Shakespeare prize, KT of Polar Star, others. Fellow Royal Coll. Music, Royal Acad. Music. Office: Acad St Martin Fields Raine House, Raine St, London E1 9RG, England

MARRINGA, JACQUES LOUIS, manufacturing company executive; b. Rotterdam, The Netherlands, Aug. 8, 1928; came to U.S., 1965; s. Jakob and Christine Antoinette (Vandervalk) M.; m. Joan Kathryn Potter, Oct. 23, 1965; children—Jack, Bob, Katy. student, Erasmus U., Rotterdam, 1946-49, Doctors in Econs., 1954, Advanced Mgmt. Program Harvard U., 1984. Rsch. asst. Chem. Projects, N.Y.C., 1955; product mgr. Philips,N.V., Eindhoven, Netherlands, 1956-61; product line mgr. ITT, Brussels and N.Y.C., 1961-70; v.p. Elco Corp., Willow Grove, Pa., 1970-72, v.p. Crouse-Hinds, Syracuse, N.Y., 1972-77; group v.p. Sta-Rite Industries, Milw., 1977-94; pres. Marringa Internat. Corp, 1994—; bd. dirs. Marlo Inc., Racine, Wis. Mem. Milw. Country Club, Rotary (Milw.). Home: 2520 W Dean Rd Milwaukee WI 53217-2019

MARRINGTON, BERNARD HARVEY, retired automotive company executive; b. Vancouver, B.C., Can., Nov. 9, 1928; s. Fredrick George and Constance Marie (hall) M.; m. Patricia Grace Hall, Sept. 3, 1953 (div. 1993); children: Jodie Lynn, Stacey Lee. Student, U. Pitts., 1982, Bethany Coll., W.Va., 1983; BS in Mktg. Mgmt., Pacific Western U., 1985. V.p., sales mgr. W & L of La Mesa, Calif., 1960-66; pres., gen. mgr. W & L of La Mesa, 1966-68; regional mgr. PPG Industries, Inc., L.A., 1977-88, regional mgr. profit ctr., 1988-91; cons. L.A. Unified Sch. Dist., 1972, South Coast Air Quality Mgmt. Dist., El Monte, Calif., 1987-91; adv. com. So. Calif. Regional Occupational Ctr., Torrance, 1978-91; mem. Ford Arbitration bd. U. Wis., 1997. Contbr. articles to profl. jours. Sustaining sponsor Ronald Reagan Presdl. Found., Simi, 1987—; sustaining mem. Rep. Nat. Com., L.A., 1985-92, Rep. Presdl. Legion of Merit, 1986-94; del. Rep. Platform Planning com., L.A., 1992; charter mem. Nat. Tax Limitation Com., Washington, 1988, Jarvis Gann Taxpayers Assn., L.A., 1979-94; sponsor Reagan Presdl. Libr., 1986; mem. Fotd Arbitration Bd., U. Wis., 1997. Recipient Award for Outstanding Community Support, So. Calif. Regional Occupational Ctr., 1986. Episcopalian. Avocations: rose gardening, circus culture, golf, sailing, classical music.

MARRIOT, SALIMA SILER, state legislator, social work educator; b. Batl., Dec. 5, 1940; d. Jesse James and Cordie Susie (Ayers) Silver; m. David Small Mariott, Sept. 24, 1964 (div. 1972); children: Terrez Siler, Patrice Kenyatta. BS, Morgan State Coll., 1964; M in Social Work, U. Md., 1972; D in Social Work, Howard U., 1988. Tchr. Balt. City Pub. Sch., 1964-65; social worker N.Y.C. Social Svcs., 1965-67, Balt. City Social Svcs., 1968-72; instr., asst. prof. Morgan State U., Balt., 1972-96; mem. Md. Ho. of Dels., 1990—; chair Park Heights Devel. Corp., Balt., 1976-92, Nat. Black Women's Health Project, 1993-94. Co-editor: U.S. Policy Toward Southern Africa, 1984. Cons. Balt. City Head Start, 1985-94; del. Dem. Conv., Atlanta, 1988; active Md. Dem. Ctrl. Com., 1988-90; sec. Nat. Rainbow Coalition; exec. bd. Nat. Black Caucus of State Legislators; vice chmn. Md. Legis. Black Caucus, 1995-96. Flemming fellow, 1995. Mem. Delta Sigma Theta. Office: Md House of Dels 2901 Druid Park Dr Ste A 11 Baltimore MD 21215-8104

MARRIOTT, DAVID M., public relations executive; b. Port Townsend, Wash., Oct. 1, 1943. BA in Radio and TV Comm., U. Wash., 1966. Reporter Sta. KVI, Seattle, 1966-68; gen. assignment and city hall reporter Sta. KIRO-TV, Seattle, 1968-72; press sec. Mayor of Seattle, 1972-77; dir. corp. comm. Alaska Airlines, 1977-82; area dir. Sheraton Corp. N.Am., 1982-84; v.p. Corp. Comm., Inc., 1984-86; ptnr. Bean/Marriott Pub. Rels., 1986; eec. v.p., gen. mgr. Evans/Kraft/Bean Pub. Rels., 1986-90; sr. v.p., mng. dir. pub. rels. Elgin Syferd, 1990-95; pres. Elgin Syferd Pub. Rels., Seattle, 1995—. Office: Elgin Syferd Pub Rels 1008 Western Ave Ste 601 Seattle WA 98104-1058

MARRIOTT, JOHN WILLARD, JR., hotel and food service chain executive; b. Washington, Mar. 25, 1932; s. John Willard and Alice (Sheets) M.; m. Donna Garff, June 29, 1955; children: Deborah, Stephen Garff, John Willard, David Sheets. B.S. in Banking and Fin, U. Utah, 1954. V.p. Marriott Hot Shoppes Inc., 1959-64, exec. v.p., bd. dirs., 1964; pres. Marriott Corp., 1964—, chief exec. officer, 1972—, chmn. bd., 1985—; bd. dirs. Outboard Marine Corp., Waukegan, Ill., GM, U.S.-Russia Bus. Coun., Host Marriott Corp. (formerly Marriott Corp.). Trustee Mayo Found., Nat. Geog. Soc., Eisenhower Med. Ctr., Exec. Coun. on Fgn. Diplomats; mem. nat. adv. bd. Boy Scouts Am.; mem. conf. bd. Bus. Coun., Bus. Roundtable. Lt. USNR, 1954-56. Recipient Bus. Leader of Yr. award, Georgetown U. Sch. Bus. Adminstrn., 1984, Svc. Above Self award, Rotary Club at JFK Internat. Airport, 1985, Am. Mgr. of Yr. award, Nat. Mgmt. Assn., 1985, Golden Chain award, Nation's Restaurant News, 1985, Hall of Fame award, Consumer Digest Mag., 1985, Citizen of Yr. award, Boy Scouts of Am., 1986, Restaurant Bus. Leadership award, Restaurant Bus. Mag., 1986, Gold Plate award, Am. Acad. Achievement, 1986, Hall of Fame, Am. Hotel and Motel Assn., 1986, Hall of Fame award, Culinary Inst. of Am., 1987, Hospitality Exec. of Yr. award, Pa. State U., 1987, Bronze winner in Fin. World's Chief Exec. Officers award, 1988, Silver Plate award Lodging Hospitality Mag., 1988, Chief Exec. Officer of Yr. Chief Exec. Officer Mag., 1988, Signature award CA chpt. Nat. Multiple Scelerosis, 1988; named Outstanding Mktg. Exec. Gallagher Report, 1988. Mem. Conf. Bd., U.S. C. of C., Sigma Chi. Mem. LDS Ch. Clubs: Burning Tree (Washington), Met. (Washington). Office: Marriott Int'l Inc 1 Marriott Dr Washington DC 20058-0001*

MARRIOTT, MARCIA ANN, human resources administrator, educator, consultant; b. Rochester, N.Y., Mar. 21, 1947; d. Coyne and Alice (Schepler) M.; children: Brian, Jonathan. AA, Monroe C.C., Rochester, 1967; BS, SUNY, Brockport, 1970, MA, 1975; PhD, S.W. U. La., 1985. Program adminstr. N.Y. Dept. of Labor, N.Y.C., 1970-75; employment mgr. Rochester Gen. Hosp., 1975-77, salary adminstr., 1982—; dir. wage and salary dept. Gannett Newspapers, Rochester, 1977-80; compensation and benefits adminstr. Sybron Corp., Rochester, 1980-82; compensation mgr. Rochester Gen. Hosp., 1996—; dir. compensation Via Health, Rochester, 1996—; pres. Compensation Link, 1996—; instr. N.Y. State Sch. Indsl. Rels., Cornell U., N.Y.C., 1976-79; assoc. prof. Rochester Inst. Tech., 1978—, Monroe C.C., 1981—, dir. career adv. coun., 1989—; cons. in field; dir. Rochester Presbyn. Home, 1987-91, 96—, v.p. bd. dirs., 1997—; dir. area hosp. coun. Kidney Svc. Ctrs., Rochester, 1988-91. Author: (pamphlets) Guideline for Writing Job Descriptions, 1983, (manual) Career Planning Manual, 1985, (booklet) Guideline for Writing Criteria-Based Job Descriptions, 1988, Skill-based Job Descriptions: A Quality Approach, 1994, Redesigning the Performance Appraisal Process, 1996. Campaign mgr. Carter Campaign Commn., Rochester, 1975; mem. coun. Messiah Luth. Ch., Rochester, 1991-94. Davenport-Hatch Found. grantee, 1973, Wegman Found. grantee, 1975. Mem. Am. Compensation Assn., Single Adopted Parents Group (pres. 1988-93). Avocations: tennis, hiking, reading, swimming, skiing. Office: Rochester Gen Hosp 1425 Portland Ave Rochester NY 14621-3001

MARRO, ANTHONY JAMES, newspaper editor; b. Middlebury, Vt., Feb. 10, 1942; s. Francis James and Esther Martha (Butterfield) M.; m. Jacqueline Helen Cleary, June 5, 1965; 1 child, Alexandria. B.A. in History, U. Vt., 1965; M.S. in Journalism, Columbia U., 1968. Reporter Rutland (Vt.) Herald, 1964-67; Reporter Newsday, L.I., N.Y., 1968-74, chief Washington bur., 1979-81, mng. editor, 1981-86, exec. editor, 1986-87, editor, 1987—; reporter Newsweek, Washington, 1974-76, N.Y. Times, Washington, 1976-79. Co-recipient Pulitzer prizes for Pub. Service Reporting, 1970, 74. Office: Newsday 235 Pinelawn Rd Melville NY 11747-4226

MARRON, DONALD BAIRD, investment banker; b. Goshen, N.Y., July 21, 1934; m. Catherine D. Calligar. Student, Baruch Sch. Bus., 1949-51, 55-57. Investment analyst N.Y. Trust Co., N.Y.C., 1951-56, Lionel D. Edie Co., N.Y.C., 1956-58; mgr. research dept. George O'Neill & Co., 1958-59; pres. D.B. Marron & Co. Inc., N.Y.C., 1959-65; pres. Mitchell Hutchins & Co. Inc. (merger with D.B. Marron & Co. Inc. 1965), N.Y.C., 1965-69, pres., chief exec. officer, 1969-77; pres. PaineWebber Inc. (merger with Mitchell Hutchins & Co. Inc. 1977), N.Y.C., 1977-88, chief exec. officer, 1980—, chmn. bd., 1981—, also bd. dirs.; co-founder, former chmn. Data Resources, Inc.; former dir. N.Y. Stock Exchange. Vice chmn. bd. trustees Mus. of Modern Art; bd. overseers and mgrs. Meml. Sloan-Kettering; trustee for cultural resources N.Y.C., trustee Dana Found.; bd. dirs. N.Y.C. Partnership; bd. dirs. Bus. Com. for the Arts, Inc.; mem. Govs.'s Sch. and Bus. Alliance Task Force, N.Y.; mem. Coun. on Fgn. Rels., Inc.; mem. pres.'s com. on The Arts and The Humanities, Inc. Office: Paine Webber Group Inc 1285 Avenue Of The Americas New York NY 10019-6028 also: Mus Modern Art 11 W 53rd St New York NY 10019-5401*

MARRON-CORWIN, MARY-JOAN, neonatologist; b. Flushing, N.Y., July 21, 1955; d. James Joseph and Joan Marie (Quinn) Marron; m. Andrew David Corwin, Oct. 2, 1988; children: Matthew Thomas, Timothy James. RN, St. Vincent's Hosp., 1973-76; BS in Biology cum laude, Molloy Coll., 1978-80; MD, Far Eastern U., 1981-85. Diplomate Am. Bd. Pediatrics, Neonatal Perinatal Medicine; lic. N.Y., N.J. Intern in pediatrics St. Vincent's Hosp., Manhattan, N.Y., 1985-86, resident in pediatrics, 1986-87, chief resident, 1987-88; fellow neonatal intensive care medicine, asst. clin. ped. Babies Hosp. Coll. Physician & Surgeons, Columbia U., N.Y., 1988-90; asst. prof. clin. pediatrics Columbia U., 1990-97, assoc. prof. clin. pediatrics, 1997—; asst. attending pediatrician Presbyn. Hosp., N.Y.C., 1988-97, dir. neonatology Allen pavilion, 1990—, assoc. attending pediatrician, 1997—; med. bd. Allen Pavilion, 1990—, quality assurance com., 1990—. Reviewer Pediatrics, 1993; contbr. articles to profl. jours.; lectr. and presenter in field. Fellow Am. Acad. Pediatrics; mem. AMA, N.Y. Perinatal Soc., Irish-Am. Pediatric Soc. Roman Catholic. Office: Columbia Presbyn Med Ctr 5141 Broadway Ste 1095 New York NY 10034-1159

MARRONE, DANIEL SCOTT, business, production and quality management educator; b. Bklyn., July 23, 1950; s. Daniel and Esther (Goodman) M.; m. Portia Terrone, Sept. 1, 1979; children: Jamie Ann. BA, Queens Coll., 1972, MLS, 1973; MBA, N.Y. Inst. Tech., 1975; PhD, NYU, 1988; diploma in Quality Engring., Quality Inst. L.I., 1992, diploma in Mfg. Engring., 1993; cert. in reliability engring., 1995; cert. in quality tech., Total Bus. Svc. Ctr., 1997, Total Bus. Svc. Ctr., 1997. Cert. prodn. and inventory mgmt., integrated resource mgmt. Am. Prodn. & Inventory Mgmt.; cert. quality auditor, quality engr., quality mgr., quality technician Am. Soc. Quality Control; cert. sr. indsl. technologist Nat. Assn. Indsl. Tech.; cert. purchasing mgr. Nat. Assn. Purchasing Mgmt. Auditor/investigator N.Y. State Spl. Pros., N.Y.C., 1977-78; asst. prof. Delehanty Inst., N.Y.C., 1978-79, Ladycliff Coll., Highland Falls, N.Y., 1979-80, Am. Bus. Inst., Bklyn., 1980-82; asst. dir. Adelphi Inst., Bklyn., 1982-85; asst. prof. Coll. St. Elizabeth, Convent Station, N.J., 1986-88; prof., co-dir. computer integrated mfg. ctr./dir. mgmt. tech SUNY Coll. of Tech., Farmingdale, 1987—. Editor: Research Techniques in Business Education, NYU Business Education Doctoral Abstracts, 1981—, Agnew lecture by P.M. Sapre, 1989, NYU Symposium, 1989. Recipient Paul S. Lomax award, NYU, 1989, Bus. Edn. Leadership award, 1993. Mem. Nat. Assn. Indsl. Tech., Inst. Mgmt. Accts., Am. Prodn. and Inventory Control Soc., Production and Ops. Mgmt. Soc., Nat. Assn. Purchasing Mgmt., Am. Soc. for Quality Control, Delta Pi Epsilon (Cert. of Merit 1988). Republican. Home: 493 Lariat Ln Bethpage NY 11714-4017

MARROU, CHRIS RENÉ, television newscaster; b. San Antonio, Nov. 12, 1947; s. André Noel and Annette (Deason) M.; m. Kathleen Mary O'Connor, Aug. 17, 1974; children: Mirage Marie and Molly O'Connor (twins). Student, Princeton U., 1964-67. News editor, anchor KRLD Radio, Dallas, 197-73; news anchor KENS-TV, San Antonio, 1973-80, news anchor, mng. editor, 1981—; news anchor WBZ-TV, Boston, 1980-81; pres., owner Alamo.com. Internet Directory of San Antonio, 1997. Contbr. weekly column San Antonio Light, 1986-93. Recipient award Tex. AP Broadcasters, 1976, 77, 87, Most Respected Local TV News Anchor award TV-Radio Age Mag., 1985, My Turn, Newsweek mag., 1996. Office: KENS-TV 5400 Fredericksburg Rd San Antonio TX 78229-3504

MARRS, SHARON CARTER, librarian; b. Andover, Va., May 7, 1943; d. Wallace Ralph and Dorothy (Stout) Carter; m. Glenn Robert Marrs, July 3, 1965. BS, East Tenn. State U., 1965; MLS, U. Pitts., 1974, postgrad., 1983—. Cert. libr. sci. and English, Pa. Tchr. English grades 8 and 10 Powell Valley H.S., Big Stone Gap, Va., 1964-65; libr. Coeburn (Va.) Elem., 1967-68, tchr. grade 2, 1968; libr. Wise (Va.) Elem., 1968-69; tchr. English grade 7 Christiansburg (Va.) Elem. Sch., 1969-70, libr., 1970-71; libr. Myrtle, Vernridge and Kelton Schs., Pitts., 1972—; apptd. to serve on Microcomputer in the Media Ctr. Award com., Am. Assn. Sch. Librs.; presenter workshops in field. Inventor games for children on use of card catalog, the Dewey Decimal System, various ref. books. Mem. ALA, Pa. State Libr. Assn. (mem. tech. com.), Internat. Assn. Sch. Librarianship, Beta Phi Mu. Home: 620 Broughton Rd Bethel Park PA 15102-3775

MARS, FORREST E., JR., candy company executive; s. Forrest Mars Sr.; married. Grad., Yale U., 1953. Co-pres., CEO Mars Inc. Office: Mars Inc 6885 Elm St Mc Lean VA 22101-3810*

MARS, JOHN F., candy company executive; b. 1935; married. Student, Yale U., 1957. Chmn. Kal Kan Foods Inc.; co-pres., CEO Mars Inc., 1973—. Office: Mars Inc 6885 Elm St Mc Lean VA 22101-3810*

MARSALA-CERVASIO, KATHLEEN ANN, medical/surgical nurse; b. Mar. 22, 1955; d. James Patrick and Kathleen (McLoughlin) Waters. AAS with honors, S.I. Coll., 1974, BS in Nursing with honors, 1984; MS in Nursing with honors, CUNY, 1986; postgrad., Kensington U. RN, N.Y.; cert. CS, CCRN, CNAA. Staff nurse USPHS Hosp., S.I., 1974-80; head nurse MICU-critical care unit-surg. ICU Bayley Seton Hosp., N.Y., 1980-82; staff nurse surg. ICU, MICU, critical care unit East Orange (N.J.) VA Med. Ctr., 1982-86, critical care nurse specialist; clin. specialist, cons. Med. Ctr. Bklyn. VA Med. Ctr., 1989-95; dep. dir. nursing svcs. U. Hosp./SUNY Health Sci. Ctr., Bklyn., 1990—; asst. clin. prof. SUNY Health Sci. Ctr. Mem. ANA (coun. clin. nurse specialists), AACN (no. N.J. chpt., N.J. chpt.), Am. Coll. Healthcare Execs. (assoc.), N.Y. Orgn. Nurse Execs., Nat. League for Nursing, Sigma Theta Tau. Home: 8898 16th Ave Brooklyn NY 11214-5804

MARSALIS, BRANFORD, musician; b. New Orleans, Aug. 26, 1960; s. Ellis Marsalis. Student, So. U., 1978, Berklee Coll. Music, 1979-81. Mem. Art Blakey Group, 1981, Wynton Marsalis Quintet, 1982; ind. saxophonist, 1983—; bandleader The Tonight Show, L.A., 1992-95. Rec. Artist: (with Wynton Marsalis) Wynton Marsalis, Think of One, Hot House Flowers, Black Codes (From the Underground), (with Art Blakey) Keystone 3, (with Kevin Eubanks) Opening Nights, (with Dizzy Gillespie) New Faces, Closer to the Source, (with Andy Jaffe) Manhattan Projects, (with Sting) Dream of the Blue Turtles, Bring on the Night; (solo albums) Romances for Saxophone, 1986, Royal Garden Blues, 1986, Renaissance, 1987, Random Abstract, 1988, Tio Jeepy, 1989, Crazy People Music, 1990, The Beautiful Ones Are Not Yet Born, 1991, Bloomington, 1993, Scenes in the City, I Heard You Twice the First Time, (Guru) Jazzmatazz, 1993; composer various pieces including No Backstage Pass, Solstice, Waiting for Rain, (video) David and Goliath, 1993, (film) Bring on the Night, 1985, Throw Momma From The Train, 1987, School Daze, 1988, Mo' Better Blues, 1990, The Music Tells You, 1992, Mr. and Mrs. Loving, 1996, Eve's Bayou, 1997, (TV movie) To My Daughter with Love, 1994. Winner Down Beat magazine's readers' poll, best soprano sax player, 1991-92; Grammy award, Best Pop Instrumental 1994 for "Barcelona Mona" with Bruce Hornsby. Office: Columbia Records 550 Madison Ave Los Angeles CA 10019*

MARSALIS, WYNTON, musician; b. New Orleans, Oct. 18, 1961; s. Ellis and Dolores Marsalis. Studied with John Longo; student, New Orleans Ctr. for Performing Arts, Berkshire Music Ctr., Juilliard Sch. Music, 1979-81. Trumpet soloist with New Orleans Philharm. Orch., 1975; recitalist with New Orleans Ctr. for Creative Arts, 1979; played with various New Orleans and N.Y.C. orchs.; with Art Blakey's Jazz Messengers, 1980-81, Herbie Hancock's V.S.O.P. quartet; formed own group, 1981; albums include Fathers and Sons, 1982, Hummel/Haydn/L. Mozart Trumpet Concertos, 1983 (Grammy award), Wynton Marsalis (Best Jazz Record, Downbeat readers' poll 1982), Think of One, 1983 (Grammy award), Handel, purcell, Torelli, Fasch, Moler (Grammy award), Trumpet Concertos, 1983, Hot House Flowers, 1984, Black Codes from the Underground, 1985 (2 Grammy awards), J Mood, 1986, Carnaval, 1987, Marsalis Standard Time, Vol. 1, 1987 (Grammy award), Majesty of the Blues, 1989, Standard Time, Vol. 3, 1990, Intimacy Calling Standard Time, Soul Gestures in Southern Blue, Vols. 1, 2, 3, 1991, Blue Interlude, 1992, Citi Movement, 1993, In This House, On This Morning, 1994, Wynton Marsalis, 1995, (with others) The All-American Hero, 1996, Live at Bubba's, 1996. Named Jazz Musician of Yr., Downbeat readers' poll, 1982, 84-86, 89, Best Trumpet Player, Downbeat critics' poll, 1984, Acoustic Jazz Group of Yr., 1984, Best Trumpet Player, Downbeat readers' poll, 1985 ; recipient Grammy award for best solo jazz instrumental, 1983-85, Grammy award for best solo classical performance with orch., 1984-85, Grammy award for best jazz instrumental performance with group, 1985, 87; musician of the Year, Down Beat Readers' poll, 1992, Pulitzer prize for music, 1997, Algur H. Meadows award, Southern Methodist University, 1997. Office: care Agy for Performing Arts Jim Gozmel 9000 W Sunset Blvd Ste 1200 West Hollywood CA 90069-5801*

MARSALISI, FRANK BERNARD, obstetrician-gynecologist; b. N.Y.C., Feb. 11, 1955; s. Bernard J. and Margaret (Sievers) M.; m. Elinor Miranda, June 21, 1978; children: Elinor Clarissa, Frank Phillip, Christina Danielle, Priscilla Alexis. BS in Biology, Fordham U., 1977; MD, Mich. State U., 1983; postgrad., U. South Fla., 1987. Diplomate Am. Bd. Ob-Gyn., Nat. Bd. Med. Examiners. Rsch. asst. USV Pharm., Tuckahoe, N.Y., 1977-78; rsch. assoc. Upjohn Co., Kalamazoo, Mich., 1978-79; resident dept. ob-gyn U. South Fla/Tampa Gen. Hosp., 1983-87; adminstrv. chief resident dept. ob-gyn U. South Fla., Tampa, 1986-87, clin. asst. prof., 1988—; dir. ob-gyn. Ruskin Migrant and Cmty. Health Ctr., Ruskin, Fla., 1987-91; dir. gynecology, ob-gyn. residency program Bayfront Med. Ctr., St. Petersburg, Fla., 1991—; sec.-treas. ob-gyn. sect. Tampa Gen. Hosp., 1990-91. Contbr. articles to profl. jours. Recipient Regional Health Adminstr.'s award USPHS, 1991, Nat. Faculty award Coun. on Resident Edn. in Ob-Gyn., 1994; named Tchr. of Yr. Bayfront Med. Ctr., 1992, 93. Fellow ACOG; mem. AMA (Physician's Recognition award), Am. Uro-Gynecologic Soc., Fla. Ob-Gyn. Soc., Phi Beta Kappa. Avocations: organist, boating, skiing, hiking. Office: 603 7th St S Ste 560 Saint Petersburg FL 33701-4734

MARSAN, JEAN-CLAUDE, architect, urban planner, educator; b. St-Eustache, Que., Can., Oct. 7, 1938; s. Aimé and Gertrude (Bolduc) M.; children: Jean-Sébastien, Marc-Aurèle. BA, U. Montreal, 1960, BArch, 1965; MSc in Urban Planning, U. Edinburgh, Scotland, 1968, PhD in Urban Planning, 1975. Assoc. prof. Sch. Architecture U. Montreal, 1975-84, prof., 1984—, dean Faculté de L'Aménagement, 1984-93, dir. Sch. Architecture, 1975-79; rsch. prof. Inst. québécois de recherche sur la culture, 1980-82; pres. Com. to Study the Future of Olympic Installations, Montreal, 1977. Author: Montréal en évolution, 1974, Montréal une esquisse du futur, 1983, Sauver Montréal, 1990; contbr. articles to profl. jours. and newspapers, chpts. to books. Founding mem. Save Montreal, 1973-78, Mcpl. Action Group, 1978; pres. Heritage Montreal, 1983-88; bd. dirs. Mus. Fine Arts Montreal, 1975-87, v.p., 1978-87, Hôtel Dieu Hospital Montréal, 1996-97, Commn. de la Capitale Nationale Du Quebec, 1995—. Decorated officer Order of Can. Mem. Ordre des Architectes du Que. (Priz Paul-Henri Lapointe 1984, 85, 87, Prix Gérard Morisset 1992, govt. of Que.), Royal Soc. Can., Ordre des Urbanistes du Què. Office: U Montreal Box 6128 Sta A, Faculté de l'Aménagement, Montreal, PQ Canada H3C 3J7

MARSCHING, RONALD LIONEL, lawyer, former precision instrument company executive; b. N.Y.C., Mar. 30, 1927; m. Marjory Fleming Duncan, Dec. 31, 1964; children: Christine, Jane. BA cum laude, Princeton U., 1950; JD, Harvard U., 1953. Bar: N.Y. 1954. Assoc. White & Case, N.Y.C.; vice chmn., gen. counsel Timex Corp., Waterbury, Conn., 1967-86, also bd. dirs. Served with U.S. Army, 1953-55. Mem. ABA, Nat. Assn. Dirs., University Club (N.Y.C. chpt.). Home: 41 E Hill Rd Woodbury CT 06798-3017

MARSDEN, BRIAN GEOFFREY, astronomer; b. Cambridge, Eng., Aug. 5, 1937; came to U.S., 1959; s. Thomas and Eileen (West) M.; m. Nancy Lou Zissell, Dec. 26, 1964; children: Cynthia Louise, Jonathan Brian. BA, Oxford U., U.K., 1959, MA, 1963; PhD, Yale U., 1965. Rsch. asst. Yale U., New Haven, 1959-65; lectr. astronomy Harvard U., Cambridge, Mass., 1966-83; astronomer Smithsonian Astrophys. Obs., Cambridge, 1965-86; assoc. dir. planetary scis. Harvard-Smithsonian Ctr. for Astrophysics, Cambridge, 1987—; dir. Cen. Bur. Astron. Telegrams, 1968—, Minor Planet Ctr. Internat. Astron. Union, 1978—. Editor: The Earth-Moon System, 1966, The Motion, Evolution of Orbits and Origin of Comets, 1972, Catalogue of Cometary Orbits, 1996, Catalogue of Orbits of Unnumbered Minor Planets, 1996. Recipient Merlin medal Brit. Astron. Assn., 1965, Goodacre medal, 1979; Van Biesbroeck award U. Ariz., 1989, Camus-Waitz prize Societé astronomique de France, 1993. Dirk Brouwer award Am. Astron. Soc., 1995. Fellow Royal Astron. Soc.; mem. Am. Astron. Soc. (chmn. div. on dynamical astronomy 1976-78), Internat. Astron. Union (pres. commn. 1976-79), Astron. Soc. Pacific, Sigma Xi. Office: Harvard-Smithsonian Ctr Astrophysics 60 Garden St Cambridge MA 02138-1516

MARSDEN, CHARLES JOSEPH, financial executive; b. N.Y.C., Dec. 18, 1940; s. David Joseph and Louise (Noell) M.; m. Marilyn Weber, Nov. 12, 1988 ; children from previous marriage: Anne Brewer, George David. A.B. cum laude, Amherst Coll., 1962; M.B.A. with distinction, Harvard U., 1965. Credit analyst Irving Trust Co., N.Y.C., 1962-63; with W.R. Grace & Co., 1965-81; treas. Polyfibron Div. W.R. Grace & Co., Cambridge, Mass., 1969-72; v.p. fin. adminstrn. Cryovac Div. W.R. Grace & Co., Duncan, S.C., 1972-78; v.p. fin. Indsl. Chems. Group W.R. Grace & Co., N.Y.C., 1978-81; exec. v.p., chief fin. officer The Grand Union Co., Elmwood Park, N.J., 1981-83; also dir. The Grand Union Co.; v.p. fin. Pan Am. World Airways, Inc., 1984-85; v.p. fin., CFO, dir. Crompton & Knowles Corp., 1985-96, sr. v.p., CFO, dir., 1996—. Mem. Harvard Club. Office: Crompton & Knowles Corp 1 Station Pl Stamford CT 06902-6800

MARSDEN, HERCI IVANA, classical ballet artistic director; b. Omis-Split, Croatia, Dec. 2, 1937; came to U.S., 1958; d. Ante and Magda (Smith) Munitic; m. Myles Marsden, Aug. 10, 1957 (div. 1976); children—Ana, Richard, Mark; m. Dujko Radovnikovic, Aug. 27, 1977; 1 child, Dujko. Student, Internat. Ballet Sch., 1955. Mem. corps de ballet Nat. Theatre, Split, 1954-58; founder Braecrest Sch. Ballet, Lincoln, R.I., 1958—; founder State Ballet of R.I., Lincoln, 1960—, artistic dir., 1976—; artistic dir. U. R.I. Classical Ballet, Kingston, 1966—, lectr., 1966—. Office: Brae Crest School of Ballet 52 Sherman Ave Lincoln RI 02865-3809

MARSDEN, JERROLD ELDON, mathematician, educator, engineer; b. Ocean Falls, British Columbia, Aug. 17, 1942; married 1965; 1 child. BSc, U. Toronto, Canada, 1965; PhD in Math., Princeton U., 1968. Instr. math. Princeton U., N.J., 1968; lectr. U. Calif., Berkeley, 1968-69, asst. prof., 1969-

72, assoc. prof., 1972-77, prof. math., 1977—; asst. prof. U. Toronto, Canada, 1970-71. Recipient Norbert Weiner Applied Math. prize Am. Math. Soc., 1990. Mem. Am. Phys. Soc. Achievements include research in mathematical physics, global analysis, hydrodynamics, quantum mechanics, nonlinear Hamiltonian systems. Office: Control and Dynamical Sys Caltech 116-81 Pasadena CA 91125

MARSDEN, LAWRENCE ALBERT, retired textile company executive; b. Mpls., May 28, 1919; s. Lawrence N. and Carrie Elizabeth (Ross) M.; m. Millicent Irene Snyder, Mar. 24, 1941; children: Millicent Carrie, Andrea Leigh, Lawrence Stewart, John Daniel. B.S. in Law, U. Minn., 1941; LL.B., George Washington U., 1946. Bar: D.C. 1946. Ptnr. Onion, Marsden & New, Washington, 1947-48; pres. Marsden-Slate, Inc., High Point, N.C., 1949-68; v.p. Guilford Mills, Inc., Greensboro, N.C., 1968-72, sr. v.p., 1973-84; chmn. Marcor, Inc., High Point, 1980—; ptnr. SPM Investments; pres. Fabrilux Products, Inc., High Point, 1995-96. Served to lt. comdr. USN, 1941-46, PTO. Mem. Am. Assn. Textile Chemists and Colorists, Sportsman Pilots Assn. (past pres.), Aircraft Owners and Pilots Assn., Rolls Royce Owner's Club, Quiet Birdmen, High Point Country Club, Willow Creek Golf Club (High Point), Isla Del Sol Yacht and Country Club (St. Petersburg, Fla.), Phi Delta Phi, Phi Delta Theta. Republican. Home: 1706 Maryfield Ct High Point NC 27260-2684

MARSDEN, WILLIAM, government official; b. Cambridge, Eng., Sept. 15, 1940; s. Christopher Alexander Marsden and Ruth Kershaw; m. Kaia Collingham, Sept. 9, 1964; children: Inge, Thomas. BSc in Econs., London U., 1973; MA, Cambridge U., 1962. 3d sec. U.K. Del. to NATO, Paris, 1964-66; 2d sec. Brit. Embassy, Rome, 1966-70; 1st sec. Brit. Embassy, Moscow, 1976-78; min. trade Brit. Embassy, Washington, 1992-94; 1st sec. sci. and tech. Fgn. Office, London, 1971-75, asst. head European community dept., 1978-81, head African dept., commr. Brit. Indian Ocean Ter., 1985-89, amb. to Costa Rica and Nicaragua, 1989-92, asst. under sec. of state For the Americas, 1994—; counsellor U.K. Representation to EEC, Brussels, 1981-85. Named Companion of Order St. Michael and St. George by Her Majesty the Queen. Mem. Brit. Inst. Mgmt., The City London (freeman), The Grocers' Co. London (freeman), The Univ. Club, The Lansdowne Club. Office: Under Sec For the Americas, Fgn Office, London SW1A 2AH, England

MARSEE, STUART (EARL), educational consultant, retired; b. Gardener, Oreg., Sept. 30, 1917; s. William and Clare (Grimes) M.; m. Audrey Belfield, June 1, 1940; children: Frederic, Jeffrey, Wayne. BS, U. Oreg., 1939, MS, 1942; EdD, U. So. Calif., 1947; LLD, Pepperdine U., 1977. Asst. supt. for bus. Pasadena City Schs., Calif., 1949-57, acting supt., 1957-58, asst. supt., 1949-58; pres. El Camino Coll., 1958-82, cons., 1982—; lectr. UCLA, 1965, U. So. Calif., 1956-57; adj. prof. Pepperdine U., 1978-79. Author: History of the Rotary Club of Torrance, 1962-74, 1974; contbr. articles to profl. jours. Recipient Disting. Service award Los Angeles County Bd. Suprs., 1958, Disting. Service Leadership award Kiwanis Internat., 1970; named Citizen of Yr., Torrance, Calif., 1981, Redondo Beach, Calif., 1986. Mem. Am. Assn. Cmty. and Jr. Colls. (pres. 1968), Nat. Commn. Accrediting (dir. 1970-74), Coun. Postsecondary Accreditation (dir. 1974-78), Western Coll. Assn. (mem. exec. com. 1978-81). Office: 358 Camino De Las Colinas Redondo Beach CA 90277-6435

MARSEE, SUSANNE IRENE, lyric mezzo-soprano; b. San Diego, Nov. 26, 1941; d. Warren Jefferson and Irene Rose (Wills) Dowell; m. Mark J. Weinstein, May, 1987; 1 child, Zachary. Student, Santa Monica City Coll., 1961; BA in History, UCLA, 1964. Mem. voice faculty Am. Mus. and Dramatic Acad., N.Y.C., 1994-97; assoc. prof. La State U. Appeared with numerous U.S. opera cos., 1970—, including N.Y.C. Opera, San Francisco Opera, Boston Opera, Houston Grand Opera; appeared with fgn. cos., festivals, Mexico City Bellas Artes, 1973, 78, Canary Islands Co., 1976, Opera Metropolitana, Caracas, Venezuela, 1977, Spoleto (Italy) Festival, 1977, Aix en Provence Festival, France, 1977, Calgary, Alta., Can., 1986; recorded Tales of Hoffmann, ABC/Dunhill Records; TV appearances include Live from Lincoln Center, Turk in Italy, Cenerentola, 1989, Live from Wolftrap Roberto Devereux, 1975, Rigoletto, 1988, A Little Night Music, 1990, Marriage of Figaro, 1991, (PBS TV) Rachel, La Cubana; recs. and CDs Anna Bolena with Ramey, Scotto, Roberto Devereux with Beverly Sills, Roberto Devereux with Monserat Caballé, Tales of Hoffmann with Beverly Sills, Rigoletto with Quilico and Carreras; videotape Roberto Devereux with Beverly Sills. Recipient 2d place award Met. Opera Regional Auditions, 1968, San Francisco Opera Regional Auditions 1968; named winner Liederkranz Club Contest, 1970; Gladys Turk Found. grantee, 1968-69; Corbett Found. grantee, 1969-73; Martha Baird Rockefeller grantee, 1969-70, 71-72. Mem. AFTRA, Am. Guild Mus. Artists (past bd. dirs.), Nat. Assn. Tchrs. of Singing (bd. dirs. for N.Y.). Democrat.

MARSELLA, ANTHONY JOSEPH, psychologist, educator; b. Cleve., Sept. 12, 1940; m. Joy Anne Marsella, June 22, 1963; children: Laura Joy, Gianna Malia. BA in Psychology with honors, Baldwin-Wallace Coll., 1962; PhD in Clin. Psychology, Pa. State U., 1968. Lic. psychologist, Hawaii. Intern Worcester (Mass.) State Hosp., 1966-67; Fulbright rsch. scholar Alteneo de Manila U., Quezon City, The Philippines, 1967-68; postdoctoral rsch. scholar NIMH Culture-Mental Health Program, East-West Ctr., Honolulu, 1968-69; prof. psychology, dir. clin. studies program U. Hawaii, Honolulu, 1969—; dir. WHO Psychiat. Rsch. Ctr., Honolulu; cons. Inst. Stress Rsch. of Karolinska Inst., Stockholm, Divsn. Mental Health, WHO, Geneva; v.p. acad. affairs U. Hawaii, 1985-89; vis. prof. Melbourne U., Monash U., Korea U., King George Med. Coll., India, Shanghai Psychiat. Inst., Ateneo de Manila U., Johns Hopkins U., Balt.; lectr. in field. Author 10 books and over 100 articles to profl. jours.; assoc. editor: Encyclopedia of Psychology; jour. reviewer. Recipient Medal of Highest Honor, Soka U., Tokyo, 1995. Fellow APA (Internat. Advancement of Psychology award 1997); mem. Hawaii Psychol. Assn., Internat. Assn. for Cross-Cultural Psychology, Soc. for Study of Culture and Psychiatry, World Fedn. Mental Health, Amnesty Internat., Psi Chi, Omicron Delta Kappa, Sigma Xi. Home: 1429 Laamia St Honolulu HI 96821

MARSH, BENJAMIN FRANKLIN, lawyer; b. Toledo, Apr. 30, 1927; s. Lester Randall and Alice (Smith) M.; m. Martha Kirkpatrick, July 12, 1952; children: Samuel, Elizabeth. BA, Ohio Wesleyan U., 1950; JD, George Washington U., 1954. Bar: Ohio 1955. Pvt. practice law Toledo, 1955-88, Maumee, Ohio, 1988—; assoc., ptnr. Doyle, Lewis & Warner, Toledo, 1955-71; ptnr. Ritter, Boesel, Robinson & Marsh, Toledo, 1971-88, Marsh & McAdams, Maumee, 1988—; personnel officer AEC, 1950-54; asst. atty. gen. State of Ohio, 1969-71; asst. solicitor City of Maumee, 1959-63, solicitor, 1963-92; mem. U.S. Fgn. Claims Settlement Commn., Washington, 1990-94; counsel N.W. Ohio Mayors and Mgrs. Assn., 1993—; mem. regional bd. rev. Indsl. Commn. Ohio, Toledo, 1993-94; mem. Ohio Dental Bd. U.S. rep. with rank spl. amb. to 10th Anniversary Independence of Botswana, 1976; past pres. Toledo and Lucas County Tb Soc., citizens for metro pks.; past mem. Judges Com. Notaries Pub.; formerly mem. Lucas County Bd. Elections; former chmn. bldg. commn. Riverside Hosp., Toledo; past trustee Com. on Rels. with Toledo, Spain; past chmn. bd. trustee Med. Coll., Ohio; past treas. Coglin Meml. Inst.; chmn. Lucas County Rep. Exec. Com., 1973-74; precinct commiteeman, Maumee, 1959-73; legal counsel, bd. dirs. Nat. Coun. Rep. Workshops, 1960-65; pres. Rep. Workshops, Ohio, 1960-64; alt. del. Rep. Nat. Conv., 1964; candidate 9th dist. U.S. Ho. of Reps., 1968; adminstrv. asst. to Rep. state chmn. Ray C. Bliss, 1954; chmn. Lucas County Bush for Pres., 1980; co-chmn. Reagan-Bush Com. for Northwestern Ohio, 1980, vice chmn. fin. com. Bush-Quayle, 1992; co-chmn. Ohio steering com. Bush for Pres., mem. nat. steering com., 1988; del. Rep. Nat. Conv., 1988; past bd. dirs. Ohio Tb and Respiratory Disease Assn.; apptd. Ohio chmn. UN Day, 1980, 81, 82; adminstrv. asst. Legis. Svc. Commn., Columbus, 1954-55; mem. Lucas County Charter Commn., Toledo, 1959-60; vice-chmn. U.S. Nat. Commn. for UNESCO, mem. legal com., del. 17th gen. conf., Paris, 1972, U.S. observer meeting of nat. commns., Africa, 1974, Addis Ababa, Ethiopia; past mem. industry functional adv. com. on standards trade policy matters; mem. nat. def. exec. res. Dept. Commerce; active Am. Bicentennial Presdl. Inauguration, Diplomatic Adv. Com. With USNR, 1945-46. Named Outstanding Young Man of Toledo, 1962. Mem. ABA, Maumee C. of C. (trustee), Ohio Bar Assn., Toledo Bar Assn., Nat. Inst. Mcpl. Law Officers, Ohio Mcpl. League (past pres.), Am. Legion, Maumee Valley Hist. Soc. (trustee), George Washington Law Assn., Internat. Inst. Toledo, Ohio Mcpl. Attys. Assn. (past pres.), Ohio Hist. Soc., Ohio State Dental Bd., Am. Canal Soc., Canal Soc. Ohio, Toledo Mus. Art, Ohio Wesleyan U. Alumni Assn. (past pres.), Toledo C. of C., Ohio State Bar Found., Rotary, Laurel Hill Swim and Tennis Club, Faculty Club Med. Coll., Toledo Country Club, Press Club, Omicron Delta Kappa, Delta Sigma Rho, Theta Alpha Phi, Phi Delta Phi. Presbyterian. Home: 124 W Harrison St Maumee OH 43537-2119 Office: 312 Conant St Maumee OH 43537-3358

MARSH, BRUCE DAVID, geology educator; b. Munising, Mich., Jan. 4, 1947; s. William Roland and Audrey Jane (Steinhoff) M.; m. Judith Anne Congdon, Jan. 24, 1970; children: Hannah Eyre, William Noah. BS, Mich. State U., 1969; MS, U. Ariz., 1971; PhD, U. Calif.-Berkeley, 1974. Geologist, geophysicist Anaconda Co., Tucson, 1969-71; asst. prof. dept. earth/planet sci. Johns Hopkins U., Balt., 1974-78, assoc. prof., 1978-81, prof., 1981—; chmn., 1989-93; vis. prof. Calif. Inst. Tech., Pasadena, 1985, U. Maine, 1992-93; co-chmn. Gordon Rsch. Conf. on Inorganic Geochemistry, Holderness, N.H., 1983-84; advisor NASA, Washington, 1975-84, NSF, Washington, 1978-90, NRC, 1985-91; Hallimond lectr. Mineral. Soc. Great Britain and Ireland, 1995. Assoc. editor Geology, 1981-83, Jour. Volcanology and Geothermal Rsch., 1978—, Jour. Petrology, 1986—. Fellow Geol. Soc. Am. (assoc. editor Bulletin 1986-92), Royal Astron. Soc.; Fellow Am. Geophys. Union (sec. sect. on volcanology, geochemistry and petrology 1984-86, pres. elect 1988-90, pres. 1990-92, Bowen award 1993); mem. Model A Ford Club Am. Office: Johns Hopkins U Dept Earth & Planetary Scis 322 Olin Hall Baltimore MD 21218

MARSH, CARYL AMSTERDAM, museum exhibitions curator, psychologist; b. N.Y.C., Mar. 9, 1923; d. Louis and Kitty (Weitz) Amsterdam; m. Michael Marsh, Sept. 3, 1942; children: Susan E., Anna L. B.A., Bklyn. Coll., 1942; M.A., Columbia U., 1946; Ph.D., George Washington U., 1978. Lic. psychologist, D.C. Asst. cultural attache Am. Embassy, Paris, 1946-48; psychologist D.C. Recreation Dept., 1957-69; spl. asst. Smithsonian Instn., Washington, 1966-73; curator exhbns. Nat. Archives, Washington, 1978-85, sr. exhbns. specialist, 1985-86; dir. traveling psychology exhbn. Am. Psychol. Assn., 1986-93, sr. advisor, 1993-95; chair humanities seminars in sci. mus. Assn. Sci. Tech. Ctrs., 1994—; rsch. fellow exptl. gallery Smithsonian Instn., 1992; rsch. cons. Nat. Zoo, 1981-92, Smithsonian Folk Life Festival, Nat. Mus. Am. History, 1977-78; organizer Discovery Room Nat. Mus. Natural History, 1969-73; cons. Meyer Found., 1964-66. Editor: Exhibition: The American Image, 1979. Organizer Anacostia Neighborhood Mus., Washington, 1967, bd. dirs., 1974—, v.p. 1993; sec. D.C. Commn. on Arts and Humanities, 1969-72; pres. Pre-Sch. Parents Coun., Washington, 1956-57. Fellow Nat. Mus. Am. Art, 1975-77; vis. scholar Nat. Mus. Am. Art, 1978—; grad. fellow CUNY, 1945-46; scholar George Washington U.; noted for Disting. Contbn. to Pub. Understanding of Psychology, APA, 1993. Mem. AAAS, APA (Outstanding Svc. award 1992, Disting. Contbn. to Pub. Understanding of Psychology award 1993), D.C. Psychol. Assn., Am. Assn. Mus., Mus. Edn. Roundtable (bd. dirs. 1983-87). Home and Office: 3701 Grant Rd NW Washington DC 20016-1819

MARSH, CHERYL LEPPERT, marketing professional; b. Upper Darby, Pa., July 24, 1946; d. Edward Franklin and Jeanne Isabelle (Stults) Leppert; m. John Nicholas Marsh III, July 24, 1972; children: Barnaby, Jessica, Wellesley, Brooks, Forbes. Student, Art Inst./Carnegie Tech., 1968, Barnes Found., 1972. Advt. and sales promotion mgr. Binney and Smith Inc., N.Y.C., 1974-75; advt. and sales promotion dir. consumer and indsl. products Carborundum Corp., N.Y.C., 1972-74, Union Carbide Corp., N.Y.C., 1968-72; sr. planner IV State of Alaska, Anchorage, 1982-83; mktg. and art svcs. staff Mkt. Rsch. and Design Assocs., N.Y.C., 1975-78; pres. Epicurean Delights, Cambridge, Mass. Recipient Senatorial scholarship Art Inst/Carnegie Tech., 1968. Mem. NAFE, Am. Mgmt. Assn., Art Dirs. Club. Home: 462 Apple Dr Exton PA 19341-3148 Office: Market Rsch & Design 200 Park Ave New York NY 10166-0005 also: Box 1215 Harvard Sq Cambridge MA 02238

MARSH, DAVE, writer, publisher, editor; b. Pontiac, Mich., Mar. 1, 1950; s. Oliver Kenneth and Mary A. (Evon) M.; m. Barbara E. Carr, July 21, 1979; stepchildren: Sasha J. Carr, Kristen A. Carr (dec.). Student, Wayne State U., 1968-69. Editor Creem Mag., Detroit and Birmingham, Mich., 1969-73; music critic Newsday, Garden City, N.Y., 1973, 74-75; assoc. editor Rolling Stone Mag., N.Y.C., 1975-78, contbg. editor, 1978-85; contbg. editor The Record, N.Y.C., 1982-84; editor, pub. Rock & Rap Confidential, L.A., 1983—; music critic Playboy, 1985—, Rock Today (syndicated radio), 1987-92; contbg. editor Entertainment Weekly, 1991-93. Author: Born to Run: The Bruce Springsteen Story, 1979, The Book of Rock Lists, 1981, Elvis, 1982, Before I Get Old, 1983, Fortunate Son, 1985, Michael Jackson and the Crossover Dream, 1985, Glory Days: Bruce Springsteen in the 1980s, 1987; The Heart of Rock and Soul, 1989, 50 Ways to Fight Censorship, 1991, Louie, Louie, 1993, Merry Christmas Baby, 1993, The New Book of Rock Lists, 1994, (with Kathi Goldmark) The Great Rock & Roll Joke Book, 1997; editor: Rolling Stone Record Guide, 1979, The First Rock and Roll Confidential Report, 1985, Pastures of Plenty (Woody Guthrie, Harper and Row), 1990, (with Don Henley) Heaven Is Under Our Feet: Essays for Walden Woods, 1991, Mid-Life Confidential: The Rock Bottom Remainders Tour America, 1994, (book series) Liner Notes, 1996, On The Record, 1997—; host Radio Mafia, Finland, 1990-96. Trustee Kristen Ann Carr Fund; active The Critics Chorus, Rock Bottom Remainders, 1992-95. Office: Rock & Rap Confidential PO Box 341305 Los Angeles CA 90034-9305

MARSH, DONALD JAY, college dean, medical educator; b. N.Y.C., Aug. 5, 1934; m. Wendy G. Clough; 2 children. AB, U. Calif., Berkeley, 1955; MD, U. Calif., San Francisco, 1958. Intern in medicine UCLA Hosp., 1958-59; postdoctoral fellow dept. physiology NYU, 1959-60, instr. dept. physiology, 1960-61, asst. prof. physiology and biophysics, 1963-67, assoc. prof. physiology and biophysics, 1967-71; prof. biomed. engring. U. So. Calif., 1971-92, prof., chmn. dept. physiology and biophysics, 1978-92, prof. medicine, 1982-92, rsch. prof. physiology and biophysics, 1992—; prof. physiology Brown U., Providence, 1992—, dean medicine and biol. scis., 1992—, Frank L. Day prof. biology, 1995—; mem. engring. in medicine and biology tng. com. NIH, 1973, cardiovascular renal study sect., 1983-86, ad hoc mem. med. lab. scis. rev. com., 1976, inst. gen. med. scis. adv. com., 1982; ad hoc reviewer NSF; mem. rsch. com. Am. Heart Assn., 1979-82, rev. coms. for grants-in-aid, pub. affairs com., 1986-88; cons. com. interdisciplinary rsch. Nat. Rsch. Coun.- Inst. of Medicine, 1989; mem. med. schs. sect. task force AMA, 1994—; lectr. in field. Mem. editorial bd. Annals of Biomed. Engring., 1972-74, mng. editor, 1974-78; mem. editorial bd. Am. Jour. Physiology and Jour. of Applied Physiology, 1972-76, Am. Jour. Physiology: Regulatory, Integrative and Comparative Physiology, 1977-79, Am. Jour. Physiology: Renal, Fluid and Electrolyte Physiology, 1977-82, 88-94, Am. Jour. Physiology: Modelling Methodology Forum, 1984-91; guest reviewer Biophys. Jour., Circulation Rsch., Jour. Clin. Investigation, Jour Theoretical Biology, Kidney Internat., Sci., Pfluegers Archiv European Jour. Physiology; contbr. articles to profl. jours., chpts. to books. Named Career Scientist, Health Rsch. Coun. N.Y., 1964-71; Spl. fellow NIH, 1970-71; NIH grantee, 1963—. Fellow AAAS; mem. Assn. Am. Med. Colls. (coun. of deans), Am. Soc. Nephrology, Am. Physiol. Soc. (com. on coms. 1980-83, chmn. renal sect. 1982-83, long range planning com. 1990-93), Biophys. Soc., Microvascular Soc., Soc. Gen. Physiologists, Soc. Math. Biology (nominating com. 1983, publs. com. 1984-85, bd. dirs. 1986-88), Alpha Omega Alpha. Home: 148 Pratt St Providence RI 02906-1411 Office: Brown U Sch of Medicine Box G-A1 Providence RI 02912*

MARSH, FRANK (IRVING), former state official; b. Norfolk, Nebr., Apr. 27, 1924; s. Frank and Delia (Andrews) M.; m. Shirley Mac McVicker, Mar. 5, 1943; children: Sherry Anne Marsh Tupper, Corwin Frank, Stephen Alan (dec.), Mitchell Edward, Dory Michael, Melissa Lou. BS, U. Nebr., 1950; hon. degree in commerce and bus., Lincoln Sch. Commerce, 1975. Builder, businessman, part-time instr. Lincoln Sch. System, 1946-52; sec. of state State of Nebr., Lincoln, 1953-71, lt. gov., 1971-75, state treas., 1975-81, 87-91; state dir. Farmers Home Adminstrn., Lincoln, 1981-85; with Tabitha, Inc., Lincoln, 1986; ptnr. Lincoln Landscaping and Landscape Interiors Inc., 1983—; organizer, CEO Lincoln FoodNet, Inc. Ops., 1985—; U.S. State Dept. escort, interpreter, cons. Ctr. Continuing Edn., U. Nebr., 1986-87; mem. Foodchain Assn. (prepared perishable food rescue programs); bd. dirs. Ultras Pharmaceuticals; founder/CEO Agates Etc. Bd. dirs., treas. Lincoln Mayor's Com. Internat. Friendship, 1967—; affiliate mem., past pres. Nat. Coun. Internat. Visitors, Washington, 1967; bd. dirs. Nebraskaland Found., Inc., Lincoln, 1970—, Lincoln-Lancaster Food and Hunger Coalition, Good Neighbor Ctr.; hunger coord. Lincoln Dist. United Meth. Ch.; port insp., past fleet adm. Soc. Nebr. Adms. With AUS, 1943-46, ETO. Recipient Gov.'s Citation, State of Nebr., 1984, Outstanding Svc. award U.S. Info. Agy., 1990, Lincoln Parks and Recreation award, 1991, Mayor's Waste and Recycling award, 1993, Lincoln Dist. Outstanding Laity award United Meth. Ch., 1993, Citation of Achievement Nebr. Game and Parks Commn., 1993, Unsung Hero award United Way, 1996. Mem. VFW (life), Internat. Livestock Identification Assn. (life), Am. Legion (life), Disabled Am. Vets. (life), Nebr. Alumni Assn. (Outstanding Alumni award 1975, life), Nebr. Nut Growers Assn., Nebr. Hist. Soc. (life), Alpha Phi Omega (life), Sertoma (past pres. Gateway Club). Republican. Methodist. Home: 2701 S 34th St Lincoln NE 68506-3211 Office: 1911 R St Lincoln NE 68503-2931

MARSH, FREDERICK WILLIAM, accountant; b. Newark, Aug. 11, 1946; s. Fred Charles and Rita Elizabeth (Foerst) M.; children: William, Harold, Aimee. BS, Monmouth Coll., 1976, MBA, 1981. Registered pub. acct. Mgr. Acctg. office Teledyne Still-Mah Mfg., Lakewood, N.J., 1976-77; asst. to contr. Freehold (N.J.) Area Hosp., 1977-78; sr. auditor N.J. Office Legis. Svcs., Trenton, N.J., 1978—; pvt. practice acctg. Morrisville, Pa., 1975—. Publicity chmn. Belmar (N.J.) Bicentennial Com., 1976; treas. Belmar C. of C., 1986-87. With U.S. Army, 1966-69. Mem. VFW (comdr. 1976-91), N.J. Assn. Pub. Accts. (editor 1986-88, state sec. 1989-90, pres. 1989-91), Am. Legion (sr. vice comdr. 1988-90), Richard Skoluda DAV (truste 1989-90), Elks (lecturing knight 1977-78). Avocations: photography, travel. Home: 105 Annamarie Dr Morrisville PA 19067-0264

MARSH, JAMES C., JR., secondary school principal. Headmaster Westminster Christian Acad., St. Louis. Recipient Blue Ribbon Sch. award U.S. Dept. of Edn., 1990-91. Office: Westminster Christian Acad 10900 Ladue Rd Saint Louis MO 63141-8425

MARSH, JEAN LYNDSEY TORREN, actress, writer; b. London, July 1, 1934; d. Henry Charles John and Emmeline Susannah Nightingale Poppy (Bexley) M.; m. Jon Devon Roland Pertwee, Apr. 2, 1955 (div. 1960). Student in dance, voice and mime; DHL (hon.), Marymount Coll. Photographers' model; with repertory cos.; Broadway debut in Much Ado About Nothing, 1959; other theatrical appearances include Travesties, The Importance of Being Earnest, 1977, Too True to Be Good, 1977, My Fat Friend, Whose Life Is It Anyway?, 1979, Hamlet, Blithe Spirit, Habeas Corpus, Uncle Vanya, Pygmalion, The Chalk Garden; movie appearances include Cleopatra, 1963, Frenzy, 1972, Dark Places, The Eagle Has Landed, 1977, The Limbo Line, 1969, The Changeling, 1980, Return to Oz, Willow, 1988; artistic dir. Adelphi U. Theatre, 1981; co-creator, story cons., starred in I.T.V. series Upstairs, Downstairs, 1974-77, The House of Elliott, 1992, also starred The Grover Monster/Jean Marsh Cartoon Special, 1975, A State Dinner for Queen Elizabeth II, 1976, Mad About the Boy: Noel Coward--A Celebration, 1976; other TV appearances include The Ring, The Rory Bremner Show, The Alexei Sayle Show, (series) Nine to Five, (film) Jane Eyre, Master of the Game, Act of Will, A Connecticut Yankee at the Court of King Arthur, Dr. Who, Tomorrow People, Adam Bede, Carlton Lives, Fatherland (HBO); author: (novel) House of Elliott, Fiennders Keepersk 1997. Named Most Outstanding New Actress of 1972; Recipient Emmy award, 1975, Cable-Ace Best Supporting Actress award for Fatherland. Office: Fifi Oscard Agy Inc 24 W 40th St New York NY 10018-3904

MARSH, JEANNE CAY, social welfare educator, researcher; b. Madison, Wis., July 9, 1948; d. Herbert Louis and Helen Irene (Moeckly) M.; m. Steven King Shevell, Oct. 3, 1976; children: Lee Catherine Marsh, Lauren Elisabeth Marsh. BA, Mich. State U., 1969; MSW, U. Mich., 1972, PhD, 1975. Postdoctoral fellow Inst. for Social Rsch., U. Mich., Ann Arbor, 1975-77; asst. prof. Sch. Social Svc. Adminstrn., U. Chgo., 1978-83, assoc. prof., 1983-88, prof., dean, 1988—; acad. vis. London (Eng.) Sch. Econ.; vis. fellow Clare Hall U. Cambridge, Eng., 1987-88. Author: (with N. Caplan and A. Geist) Rape and the Limits of Law Reform, 1982, (with S. Berlin) Informing Practice Decisions, 1993; editor (with others) spl. issues of Jour. Social Issues, 1982, Evaluation and Program Planning, 1991; chair editorial bd. Social Svc. Rev., 1988—; mem. editorial bd. Social Work Rsch. and Abstracts, 1982-92, Internat. Applied Social Svc. Index, 1988—. Trustee Chgo. Theol. Sem., 1988—. Recipient Disting. Alumna award Sch. Social Work, U. Mich., 1987; Leadership Greater Chgo. fellow, 1985-86. Mem. NASW, Am. Psychol. Assn., Am. Evaluation Assn., Leadership Fellows Assn., Phi Beta Kappa. Office: U Chgo Sch Social Svc Adminstrn 969 E 60th St Chicago IL 60637-2640

MARSH, JOHN HARRISON, environmental planner, lawyer; b. Auburn, Wash., June 25, 1954; s. F. A. Buzz and Margery Ann (Greene) M.; m. Debra Rose Raniere, June 18, 1977; children: Jenna Rose, Christian John. BS in Fisheries Scis., Oreg. State U., 1977; JD, Lewis & Clark Coll., 1985, cert. natural resources and environ. law, 1985. Bar: Oreg. 1986. Rsch. asst. EPA, Corvallis, Oreg., 1975-77; fisheries biologist Nat. Marine Fisheries Svc., Portland, Oreg., 1977-78, Oreg. Dept. Fish and Wildlife, Astoria, 1978; pub. info. officer Columbia River Inter-Tribal Fish Commn., Portland, 1978-79, fisheries ecologist, 1979-85; system planning coord. N.W. Power Planning Coun., Portland, 1985-96, mgr. habitat and prodn., 1996—; speaker, expert witness in field; guest lectr. Lewis and Clark Coll., 1984, 95. Contbr. articles to profl. publs. Organizer food drive Friends of Seasonal Workers, 1987; chair ann. NPPC food drive Sunshine Divsn., 1987-96; bd. dirs. Panavista Park Homeowners Assn., 1991-93, mem. archtl. rev. com., 1990—, chair, 1991—; Riverwest Ch. lead Sunday sch. instr. grades 5-6, 1992-96, adult Bible study instr., 1995—, Kinship leader, 1994—, Mex. Youth Mission team, 1994, 95, libr. coord., 1995—; asst. scoutmaster Boy Scouts Am., 1972-73. Mem. Am. Fisheries Soc. (cert. profl. fisheries scientist, exec. com. Portland chpt. 1981-84, v.p. 1981-82, pres. 1982-83, chair legis. com. Oreg. chpt. 1988-89, program com. 1980-81, riparian com. Western div. 1982-83, convenor various sessions, mem. native peoples fisheries com. 1982-88, chair 1984-86, resolutions com. 1985-86, strategic plan devel com., 1993-95, other coms.), Oreg. State Bar Assn., Native Am. Fish and Wildlife Assn., Oreg. Wine Brotherhood (chair Benefit Auction and Barrel Tasting 1995), Great Lovers of Wine Soc. Oreg. (pres. 1988). Avocations: fishing, hunting, wine, cooking. Office: NW Power Planning Coun 851 SW 6th Ave Ste 1100 Portland OR 97204-1348

MARSH, JOHN S., JR., newspaper editor; b. Niagara Falls, N.Y., Apr. 23, 1949; s. John S. and Muriel (MacLaren) M.; m. Elizabeth Poreda, July 10, 1971; children: Beth, Colleen. BA in Govt., Baldwin-Wallace Coll., 1971. Reporter, then various editing positions Times-Union, Rochester, N.Y., 1971-82; mng. editor Daily Press, Utica, N.Y., 1982-84; exec. editor Observer-Dispatch, Utica, 1984-91; pub., pres. Daily Jour., Vineland, N.J., 1991-92; exec. editor Argus Leader, Sioux Falls, S.D., 1992—. Bd. dirs. Forward Sioux Falls, Univ. Sioux Falls. Mem. Am. Soc. Newspaper Editors, AP Mng. Editors, S.D. Associated Press Mng. Editors Assn. (pres. 1994-95), Rotary Club Downtown Sioux Falls (bd. dirs.). Office: Argus Leader PO Box 5034 Sioux Falls SD 57117-5034

MARSH, JOSEPH FRANKLIN, JR., emeritus college president, educational consultant; b. Charleston, W.Va., Feb. 24, 1925; s. Joseph Franklin and Florence (Keller) M. Student, Concord Coll., 1941-42; W.Va. U., 1942-43; A.B., Dartmouth Coll., 1947; student, Nat. Inst. Pub. Affairs, Washington, 1947-48; M.P.A., Harvard U., 1949; LL.D., Davis and Elkins Coll., 1968; L.H.D., Alderson-Broaddus Coll., 1982. Cons. Hoover Commn., Washington, 1948; instr. in gt. issues Dartmouth, 1952-54, instr. econs., 1953-55, asst. prof., 1955-59; pres. Concord Coll., Athens, W.Va., 1959-73, pres. emeritus, 1985—; ednl. cons., 1973-74; pres. Waynesburg (Pa.) Coll., 1974-83, pres. emeritus, 1983—; v.p. The Armand Hammer United World Coll. of the Am. West, Montezuma, N. Mex., 1984-85; pres. Marsh Edn Cons., Athens, W.Va., 1985—; Dir. One Valley Bank of Mercer County. Author articles. Mem. State Dept. Ednl. Mission to U.A.R., 1964, Mercer County (W.Va.) Planning Commn., 1964-74, 83-94, hon., 1994—; vice chmn. W.Va. Com. for Constnl. Amendments, 1966; mem. regional coun. Internat. Edn. Study Mission to Europe, 1970; bd. dirs. Am. Assn. State Colls. and Univs., 1972-73, Regional Coun. for Internat. Edn., 1973, Hospice Care Mercer County, W.Va., 1987-91, Faculty Merit Found. W.Va., 1990—; bd. dirs. Pa. Assn. Colls. and Univs., 1974-83, exec. com., 1980-82; bd. dirs. Pa. Commn. for Ind. Colls. and Univs., 1974-83, sec.-treas., 1976-77, vice chmn.,

1977-80, chmn., 1980-82; trustee Found. Ind. Colls. Pa., 1974-83, mem. exec. com., 1979-82; bd. visitors Midway Coll., Ky., 1979-93; adv. com. Pa. State Coun. Higher Edn., 1980-82; trustee Concord Coll. Found., 1986, bd. dirs., 1987—; active Town of Athens Planning Commn., 1986-94, pres. commn. 1987-94; vice chmn. bd. trustees, Princeton (W.Va.) Cmty. Hosp. Found., 1989—; Gov's. appointee to bd. dirs. State Coll. System W.Va., 1989-96, chmn. adminstrv. com., 1990-91, vice chmn. of bd., 1991-95, chmn., 1995-96. Served as gunnery officer USNR, 1943-46. Named Outstanding Young Man, W.Va. Jr. C. of C., 1960; recipient Alumnus of Yr. award Concord Coll., 1973, Golden Alumnus award, 1992, Outstanding Alumnus award for Career Achievement, 1996; Outstanding Citizen award Athens Woman's Club, 1992; Rotary fellow Oxford (Eng.) U., 1950-52. Mem. AAUP, Am. Assn. Univ. Adminstrs., Am. Econ. Assn., Royal Inst. Pub. Adminstrn., Oxford Union Debating Soc. (life), Oxford Soc. (life), Pa. Soc., Duquesne Club (Pitts.), Univ. Club (Bluefield), Masons, Rotary (dist. gov. 1992-93), Phi Beta Kappa, Phi Tau, Phi Delta Pi, Phi Sigma Kappa, Alpha Kappa Psi (hon.). Methodist. Home: 106 First Ave Athens WV 24712 Office: PO Box 734 Athens WV 24712-0734

MARSH, MALCOLM F., federal judge; b. 1928. BS, U. Oreg., 1952, LLB, 1954, JD, 1971. Ptnr. Clark & Marsh, Lindauer & McClinton (and predecessors), Salem, Oreg., 1958-87; judge U.S. Dist. Ct. Oreg., Portland, 1987—. With U.S. Army, 1946-47. Fellow Am. Coll. Trial Lawyers; mem. ABA. Office: US Dist Ct 114 US Courthouse 620 SW Main St Portland OR 97205-3037

MARSH, MICHAEL, track and field athlete. Olympic runner Barcelona, Spain, 1992. Recipient 200m Track and Field Gold medal Olympics, Barcelona, 1992. Office: US Olympic Com 1750 E Boulder St Colorado Springs CO 80909-5724*

MARSH, MILES L., textile company executive; b. 1947. With various divsns. Dart & Kraft Inc., Gen. Foods USA; chmn., CEO, Pet Inc., St. Louis, until 1995; pres., CEO, James River Corp. Va., Richmond, 1995—, chmn. bd., 1996—. Office: James River Corp Va 120 Tredegar St Richmond VA 23219-4306

MARSH, OWEN ROBERT, education educator; b. Springfield, Ill., Oct. 4, 1935; s. Owen Rainey and Dorothea Nell (Frutiger) M.; m. Evelyn Joyce Mathews, Aug. 19, 1958; children: Jeffrey, John, Thomas. BS in Edn., Ill. State Normal U., 1957, MS in Edn., 1958; EdD, Ill. State U., Normal, 1967. Tchr. Galesburg (Ill.) Pub. Schs., 1958-61; instr. edn. Western Ill. U., Macomb, 1962-64, Ill. State U., Normal, 1967; rsch. assoc. Ill. Bd. Higher Edn., Springfield, 1967-69; registrar U. Ill., Springfield, 1969-72; dean of admissions and records Tex. Ea. U., Tyler, 1972-80; registrar U. Tex., Tyler, 1980-89, assoc. prof., 1989—. Author: Illinois Board of Higher Education, 1969; contbr. articles to mags. Pres. Springfield Lions Club, 1967-72, Tyler Evening Lions, 1979-80, 86-87; treas. Assn. of Retarded Citizens, Springfield, 1971-72; mem. Human Rights Com., Tyler, 1992—. Served with USAF, 1961-62. Recipient Roy A. Clark scholarship Ill. State U., 1967. Mem. St. Louis Performance Coun., Kappa Delta Pi (counselor 1992-95, area rep. 1994—). Methodist. Avocation: camping. Home: 3613 Glendale Dr Tyler TX 75701-8642 Office: Univ Tex Tyler 3900 University Blvd Tyler TX 75701-6622

MARSH, QUINTON NEELY, banker; b. Omaha, July 1, 1915; s. Arthur J. and Rose L. (Baysel) M.; m. Thelma May Beck, Nov. 24, 1944. B.C.S., Benjamin Franklin U., Washington, 1949, M.C.S., 1950; student, Am. U., 1950-51; diploma, Sch. Bank Adminstrn., U. Wis., 1959. Chartered bank auditor; cert. internal auditor; cert. protection profl. V.p., gen. auditor Am. Security & Trust Co., Washington, 1972, sr. officer auditing and security, 1972-77; sr. v.p., cashier Bank of Columbia N.A., Washington, 1977-79; sr. v.p. United Nat. Bank of Washington, 1979-80. Mem. Bank Adminstrn. Inst. (pres. D.C. 1966-67, auditing commn. 1968-70), Inst. Internal Auditors (pres. D.C. 1962-63), Am. Soc. Indsl. Security. Lodges: Masons, Shriners. Home: # 312 4801 Connecticut Ave Washington DC 20008-2203

MARSH, ROBERT BUFORD, chemical engineer, consultant; b. Chgo., Nov. 16, 1946; s. Ivar Buford and Blanche Julien (Morrisette) M.; m. Claudia Ann Werner, Feb. 14, 1970; children: Julie Ann, Kristy Louise. BS in chem. engr., Mich. Tech. U., 1968. Registered profl. engr., Mass. Engr. 1 design engr. Chevron Rsch., Richmond, Calif., 1968-70, tech. svc. engr., 1970-73; lustrex supr. Monsanto, Long Beach, Calif., 1973-78; mfg. supr. Monsanto, Everett, Mass., 1978-83, environ. engr., 1984-85, mfg. tech. specialist, 1986-91; worldwide plasticizer tech. expert engring. specialist Monsanto, Everett, Indian Orchard, Mass., 1992-93; pres. Marsh Engr., Inc., Andover, Mass., 1992—; environ. instr., U. Mass., 1994; cons. Mass. Dept. Environ. Protection, Lowell, 1993-94; cons. EPA Rsch. grant, 1994; speaker in field. Adv., co. leady Jr. Achievement, Long Beach, 1975-77; vol. Andover Sch. System, 1983-84, Chicopee River Watershed Assn., Springfield, Mass., 1993, Shawsheen River Watershed Assn., Tewksbury, Mass., 1994; election com. State Senator O'Brien com., 1994-95. Mem. Nat. Soc. Profl. Engrs., AIChE. Democrat. Methodist. Achievements include orginal research and published a Chevron Report on Ammonia-Hydrogen Sulfide Equilibrium in the 10-50% range. Avocations: reading, camping, tennis, swimming, stock market. Home: 8 Mulberry Cir Andover MA 01810 Office: Marsh Engring Inc PO Box 3232 Andover MA 01810

MARSH, ROBERT CHARLES, writer, music critic; b. Columbus, Ohio, Aug. 5, 1924; s. Charles L. and Jane A. (Beckett) M.; m. Kathleen C. Moscrop, July 4, 1956 (div. 1985); m. Ann Noren, Feb. 25, 1987; 1 child, James MacArtain. BS, Northwestern U., 1945, AM, 1946; postgrad., U. Chgo., 1948; EdD, Harvard U., 1951; postgrad., Oxford U., 1952-53, Cambridge U., 1953-56. Instr. social sci. U. Ill., 1947-49; lectr. humanities Chgo. City Jr. Coll., 1950-51; asst. prof. edn. U. Kansas City, 1951-52; vis. prof. edn. SUNY, 1953-54; humanities staff U. Chgo., 1956-58, lectr. in social thought, 1976; music critic Chgo. Sun-Times, 1956-91; dir. Chgo. Opera Project, Newberry Libr., 1983—; pres. Zerbinetta Corp., 1996. Author: Toscanini and the Art of Orchestral Performance, 1956, rev. edit., 1962, The Cleveland Orchestra, 1967, Ravinia, 1985, James Levine at Ravinia, 1993; editor: Logic and Knowledge, 1956. Co-recipient Peabody award for ednl. broadcasting, 1976; Ford Found. fellow, 1965-66. Mem. Harvard U. Faculty Club. Roman Catholic. Home and Office: 1001 7th St New Glarus WI 53574-0790

MARSH, ROBERT HARRY, chemical company executive; b. Camden, N.J., Sept. 6, 1946; s. Harry Louis and Margaret Charlotte (Starke) M.; BA, BS in Mech. Engring., Rutgers U., 1969; MBA in Mgmt. and Fin., Temple U., 1980; m. Margaret Sammartino, Mar. 21, 1970. From mech. engr. to mech. specialist and project engr. Rohm & Haas Engring., Bristol, Pa., 1969-76; from staff engr. to sr. engring. specialist Hercules, Inc., Wilmington, Del., 1976-80, sr. fin. analyst for corp. strategic planning, 1980-81, sr. bus. analyst bus. group, 1982-83; mgr. bus. analysis Himont, Inc., 1983-86, dir. strategy and planning, 1988, dir., bus. mgmt., 1988-91, mng. dir. China, 1991-95, dir. strategy 1991-95, prin. Marsh & Assoc., 1995. Founder, owner, bd. dirs. Motionweave, Inc. Active Moorestown civic affairs. Mem. ASME (nat. power com. 1977-84, vice chmn. awards com. 1980, membership chmn. 1982), NSPE, Pyramid Club Phila., Engrs. Club Phila., Beta Gamma Sigma. Contbr. articles to profl. jours. Home: 355 Tavistock Cherry Hill NJ 08034-4025

MARSH, ROBERT MORTIMER, sociologist, educator; b. Everett, Mass., Jan. 22, 1931; s. Henry Warren and Ruth (Dunbar) M.; children: Eleanor L., Christopher S.H., Diana E. Student, Boston U., 1948-50; A.B., U. Chgo., 1952; M.A., Columbia, 1953, Ph.D., 1959. Fellow Ford Found., Japan, Taiwan, Hong Kong, 1956-58; instr. sociology U. Mich., 1958-61; asst. prof. sociology Cornell U., 1961-65; asso. prof. Duke, 1965-67; mem. faculty Brown U., 1967—, prof. sociology, 1968—, chmn. dept., 1971-75; manpower personnel and tng. rsch. prof. U.S. Naval Acad., Annapolis, 1987-88; vis. prof. Nat. Tsing Hua U., Taiwan, 1991. Author: The Mandarins: The Circulation of Elites in China, 1961, Comparative Sociology: A Codification of Cross-Societal Analysis, 1967; (with H. Mannari) Modernization and the Japanese Factory, 1976, Organizational Change in Japanese Factories, 1988, The Great Transformation: Social Change in Taipei, Taiwan Since the 1960s, 1996; also articles; assoc. editor Adminstrv. Sci. Quar., 1963-67, Jour. Comparative Family Studies, 1970-74; co-editor: (with J. Michael Armer) Comparative Sociological Research in the 1960s and 1970s. East Asian Inst. summer fellow Chinese Columbia, 1955; Ford Found. and Guggenheim Found. fellow Japan, 1969-70; Japan Soc. Promotion Sci. fellow, 1976, 83; Chiang Ching Kuo Found. and Nat. Sci. Coun. fellow (Taiwan, Republic of China). 1991-93. Mem. Am. Sociol. Assn., Ea. Sociol. Assn., Assn. Asian Studies, Internat. Studies Assn. (exec. com. comparative interdisciplinary studies sect. 1971-76), Japan Human Rels. Assn. (councilor 1970—). Office: Dept Sociology Brown Univ Providence RI 02912

MARSH, ROBERTA REYNOLDS, elementary education educator, consultant; b. Kokomo, Ind., June 2, 1939; d. Elwood Bert and Mildred Bell Reynolds; m. Ronald Dean Marsh Sr., Apr. 5, 1958; children: Ronald Jr., Bryan William, Joel Allen. BEd, Ind. U., Kokomo, 1970; MEd, Ind. U., Bloomington, 1971. Cert. tchr., spl. edn. tchr., Ind., Ariz. Tchr. spl. edn. Kokomo Ctr. Schs., 1970-77; tchr. spl. edn. Tempe (Ariz.) Elem. Dist. #3, 1978-86, tchr. civics, geography, English/lit., 1986—. Local dir. Spl. Olympics, Kokomo, 1974-77, Tempe Assn. Retarded Citizens, 1978-88; den mother Boy Scouts Am., Kokomo, 1967-73; leader 4-H Club, Kokomo, 1974-77. Recipient Excellence in Edn. award Tempe Diablo, 1991. Mem. Coun. for Exceptional Children (state pres. 1986-87, Tempe chpt. pres. 1994-95, outstanding leader award 1985, outstanding regular tchr., 1996, Tempe coun. 1995-96), Internat. Reading Assn., Assn. for Children with Learning Disabilities, Ind. U. Alumni Assn., Alpha Delta Kappa (corr. sec. 1986-88, Theta pres. 1990-92). Democrat. Avocations: bridge, traveling, reading, collecting apples and bells. Home: 4113 E Emelita Cir Mesa AZ 85206-5109 Office: Hudson Sch 1325 E Malibu Dr Tempe AZ 85282-5742

MARSH, SCOTT CLYDE, financial consultant, writer, lecturer; b. Salt Lake City, Aug. 2, 1953; s. Mearle C. and Virginia (Welch) M.; m. Mary Louise Bunker, June 9, 1983; children: Landon David, Christopher Scott, Clayton Bunker, Jordan William, Spencer Robert. BS in Econs. magna cum laude, U. Utah, 1977, BS in Acctg. magna cum laude, 1978, MBA, 1979; MS in Fin. Svcs., Am. Coll., 1989. ChFC; CLU; registered investment advisor. Prin. Profl. Edn. Inst., Salt Lake City, 1980—, Scott C. Marsh Fin., Salt Lake City, 1982—; lic. rep. Intermountain Fin. Svcs., Salt Lake City, 1982—; owner, mgr. Wasatch Yamaha Sch. Music, Salt Lake City, 1987-92; lic. agt. Marsh Realtors, Salt Lake City, 1974—; ind. ins. agt., Salt Lake City, 1983—; cert. course monitor Life Underwriters Tng. Coun., Salt Lake City, 1992—; cert. ins. instr. Utah State Ins. Dept., Salt Lake City, 1987—, Nev. State Ins. Dept., Carson City, 1986—, Calif. State Ins. Dept., Sacramento, 1993; mem. faculty Brigham Young U. Edn. Week, Provo, Utah, 1992, 93, 94, 95, 96. Author: Investments and Securities Markets, 1983, Risk Management and Insurance Planning, 1985, 1986 Tax Reform Act and Tax Law Since Then, 1986, Financial Prosperity, The Wisdom and Order of Acquisition, 1991, Making the Moneymakers Make You Money, 1992. Exec. cabinet Associated Students U. Utah, 1977; active Nat. Com. Planned Giving, bd. dirs. Greater Salt Lake coun. Boy Scouts Am., 1981, chmn., coord., 1992; bd. dirs., chmn. planned giving Granite Edn. Found., 1991—. Mem. Utah Planned Giving Roundtable, Beehive Honor Soc. (pres.), Sigma Gamma Chi, Phi Kappa Phi, Beta Gamma Sigma. Mem. LDS Ch. Avocations: memory training and research, gardening, graphic art. Home and Office: 1313 E 4170 S Salt Lake City UT 84124-1456

MARSH, TERENCE, production designer. Prodn. designer: (films) (with John Box) Doctor Zhivago, 1965 (Academy award best art direction 1965), (with Box) A Man for All Seasons, 1966, (with Wallis Smith) The Wild Affair, 1966, (with Box) Oliver!, 1968 (Academy award best art direction 1968), (with Robert Laing) Perfect Friday, 1970, The Looking Glass War, 1970, (with Robert Cartwright) Scrooge, 1970, (with Cartwright) Mary, Queen of Scots, 1971 (Academy award nomination best art direction 1971), (with Cartwright) The Public Eye, 1972, Follow Me!, 1972, (with Alan Tomkins) The Mackintosh Man, 1973, (with Tomkins) A Touch of Class, 1973, (with Tomkins) Juggernaut, 1974, The Abdication, 1974, The Adventures of Sherlock Holmes' Smarter Brother, 1975, (with Tomkins) Royal Flash, 1975, A Bridge Too Far, 1977, (with Richard Lawrence) Magic, 1978, (with Marvin March) The Frisco Kid, 1979, (with others) Sunday Lovers, 1980, Absence of Malice, 1981, (with Peter Lamont and Gil Parrondo) Sphinx, 1981, (with J. Dennis Washington) To Be or Not to Be, 1983, (with Tomkins) Haunted Honeymoon, 1986, (with Fernando Ramirez, El Polo, George Richardson, and Craig Edgar) Miracles, 1987, (with Harold Michelson) Spaceballs, 1987, (with Dianne Wager) Bert Rigby, You're a Fool, 1989, (with Richardson) Havana, 1990, (with Wager, Donald Woodruff, and William Cruse) The Hunt for Red October, 1990, Basic Instinct, 1992, The Shawshank Redemption, 1994, Forget Paris, 1995, (TV movies) Great Expectations, 1974; prodn. designer, prodr.: (films) (with Steve Sardanis) The World's Greatest Lover, 1977; prodn. designer, co-prodr. (with Washington), co-screenwriter (with Ronny Graham and Charles Dennis): (films) Finders Keepers, 1984. Office: Sandra Marsh Mgt 9150 Wilshire Blvd Ste 220 Beverly Hills CA 90212-3429*

MARSH, WILLIAM DOUGLAS, lawyer; b. Sikeston, Mo., Feb. 22, 1947; s. Ray Carl and Mary Louis (Buchanan) M.; m. Georgia Kay Trigg, June 3, 1967; children: Kristin Elizabeth, Kelly Anne. BSBA, S.E. Mo. State U., 1971; JD, U. Mo., Kansas City, 1973. Bar: Fla. 1974, U.S. Dist. Ct. (no., mid. and so. dists.) Fla., U.S. Ct. Appeals (5th and 11th cir.). Shareholder Emmanuel, Sheppard & Condon, Pensacola, Fla., 1973—. Contbr. articles to profl. jours.; reviewer Fla. Torts, 1990. Active numerous polit. campaigns/polit. action groups. 1st lt. U.S. N.G., 1967-73. Mem. ABA (litigation sect., torts and ins. practice sect., com. on auto. law), Assn. Trial Lawyers Am. (diplomate), Acad. Fla. Trial Lawyers (sustaining), Am. Bd. Trial Advocacy (cert. trial lawyer), Fla. Bar Assn. (rules of civil procedure com. 1991—, trial lawyers sect. exec. coun. 1979-88, sec. 1984-85, editor trial sect. newsletter 1982-83, chmn. 1986-87). Democrat. Methodist. Avocation: sailing. Office: Emmanuel Sheppard & Condon 30 S Spring St Pensacola FL 32501-5612

MARSH, WILLIAM LAURENCE, retired research pathology executive; b. Cardiff, Wales, Great Britain, Apr. 21, 1926; came to U.S., 1969; s. William and Violet (Hill) M.; m. Jean Beryl Margaret Hill, June 6, 1952; children: Christine Margaret, Nicholas John. Fellow, Inst. Med. Lab. Sci., London, 1954, Inst. Biology, London, 1969; PhD, Columbia Pacific U., 1968; fellow, Royal Coll. Pathologists, London, 1985. Lab. chief Regional Blood Transfusion Ctr., Brentwood, Eng., 1955-69; assoc. investigator N.Y. Blood Ctr., N.Y.C., 1969-79, investigator, 1980-83, sr. investigator, 1984-87; sr. v.p. rsch. Lindsley Kimball Rsch. Inst. of N.Y. Blood Ctr., N.Y.C., 1987-94; ret.; editorial bd. Transfusion jour., 1979-91, Blood Transfusion and Immunohematology jour., 1980-86; sci. reviewer various jours. Author chpts. on human blood groups in textbooks, 1965-91; contbr. over 250 articles to profl. jours. Recipient Blood Donors award of merit Blood Donor Assn., Eng., 1961. Fellow Inst. Med. Lab. Sci. (Race prize 1976), Inst. Biology, Royal Coll. Pathologists; mem. Internat. Soc. Blood Tranfusion, Am. Assn. Blood Banks (Dunsford Meml. award 1975, Emily Cooley award 1988, Grove-Rasmussen award 1990, Karl Landsteiner award 1995), Am. Soc. Clin. Pathologists (Philip Levine Outstanding Rsch. award 1993), Brit. Soc. Hematology, Brit. Soc. Blood Transfusion. Avocations: sailing, flying, photography. Home: 101 Hillcrest Dr Moneta VA 24121-3003 Office: NY Blood Ctr S310 E 67th St New York NY 10021-6204

MARSHAK, ALAN HOWARD, electrical engineer, educator; b. Miami Beach, Fla., Mar. 21, 1938; s. Jerome and Yetta (Feiner) M.; children: Jerry Brian. B.Sc.E.E., U. Miami, 1960; M.S., La. State U., 1962; Ph.D., U. Ariz., 1969. Asst. prof. elec. engring. La. State U., Baton Rouge, 1969-73; assoc. prof. La. State U., 1973-78, prof., 1978—, chmn. dept. elec. and computer engring., 1983—; vis. prof. Electron Device Rsch. Ctr., U. Fla., Gainesville, 1979-80; tech. reviewer NSF, 1976—, panelist, 1993-96; panelist NRC, 1993; mem. Southeastern Ctr. Elec. Engring. Edn., 1984—, chmn., CEO, 1992—; spkr. profl. confs. Tech. referee various jours. including Solid-State Electronics, Jour. Applied Physics; editor: Device and Process Modeling, IEEE Trans. Electron Devices, 1991—; author: (with D. J. Hamilton and F. A. Lindholm) Principles and Applications of Semiconductor Device Modeling, 1971, Basic Experiments in Electronics: A Laboratory Manual, 1978, also tech. papers. NSF grad. trainee, 1967-69; grantee, 1970, 73, 75, 78; named F.H. Coughlin/CLECO prof. of elec. engring., 1993. Fellow IEEE; mem. Electron Devices Soc., Sigma Xi, Eta Kappa Nu. Home: 320 Misty Creek Dr Baton Rouge LA 70808-8174 Office: La State U Elec And Computer Dept Baton Rouge LA 70803

MARSHAK, HILARY WALLACH, psychotherapist, owner; b. N.Y.C., May 27, 1950; d. Irving Isaac and Suni (Fox) Wallach; m. Harvey Marshak, Jan. 1, 1981; children: Emily Fox, Jacob Randall. BA, U. Conn., Storrs, 1973; MSW, N.Y.U., 1992; cert., Inst. for Study of Culture, and Ethnicity, N.Y.C., 1994. Cert. social worker, N.Y. Tchr. English Glastonbury (Conn.) High Sch., 1973, U. Autonoma de Guerrero, Acapulco, Mexico, 1974; administrv. asst. 4M Pub. Svcs. Corp., N.Y.C., 1975, bus. mgr.; exec. v.p. Vitalmedia Enterprises Inc., N.Y.C., 1977-87, pres., chief exec. officer, 1987—; psychotherapist Fifth Ave. Ctr. Counseling and Psychotherapy, N.Y.C., 1992-95; pvt. practice N.Y.C., 1992—; mktg. cons. Frana Ltd., London, 1988-89. Editor: Before the Bar, 1978-80, Guide to Higher Edn., 1980; reviewer vol 32, The Jour. of Sex Rsch. Founder Women's Radical Caucus, U. Conn., 1970; broadcaster Sta. WHUS; bd. dirs. N.Y. Theater Ballet, 1990—, Am. AIDS Assn., 1992-97; mem. writers coun. Writers in Performance series Manhattan Theater Club. Recipient 2nd Place Flowers Ulster County Agrl. Fair, New Paltz, N.Y., 1987, 1st Place Herbs, 1988. Mem. NASW, Soc. for Sci. Study of Sex, Sex Edn. and Info. Coun. of U.S., Nat. Coun. Family Rels. Jewish. Avocations: gardening, birdwatching, cooking, reading. Home and Office: 95 Horatio St New York NY 10014-1543

MARSHAK, MARVIN LLOYD, physicist, educator; b. Buffalo, Mar. 11, 1946; s. Kalman and Goldie (Hait) M.; m. Anita Sue Kolman, Sept. 24, 1972; children: Rachel Kolman, Adam Kolman. AB in Physics, Cornell U., 1967; MS in Physics, U. Mich., PhD in Physics, 1970. Rsch. assoc. U. Minn., Mpls., 1970-74, asst. prof., 1974-78, assoc. prof., 1978-83, prof. physics, 1983—, dir. grad. studies in physics, 1983-86, prin. investigator high energy physics, 1982-86, head sch. of physics and astronomy, 1986-96, sr. v.p. for acad. affairs, 1996—. Contbr. articles to profl. jours. Trustee Children's Theater Co., 1989-94. Mem. Am. Phys. Soc. Home: 2855 Ottawa Ave S Minneapolis MN 55416-1946 Office: U Minn Acad Affairs 100 Church St SE Minneapolis MN 55455-0110

MARSHAK, ROBERT REUBEN, former university dean, medical educator, veterinarian; b. N.Y.C., Feb. 23, 1923; s. David and Edith (Youselovsky) M.; m. Ruth Emilie Lyons, Dec. 4, 1948; children: William Lyons, John Ball, Richard Best.; m. Margo Post Marshall, June 25, 1983. Student, U. Wis., 1940-41; D.V.M., Cornell U., 1945; D.V.M. (hon.), U. Bern, 1968; M.A. (hon.), U. Pa., 1971. Diplomate: Am. Coll. Vet. Internal Medicine (charter). Practice vet. medicine Springfield, Vt., 1945-56; prof., chmn. dept. medicine Sch. Vet. Medicine, U. Pa., Phila., 1956-58; prof. medicine Grad. Sch. Medicine, 1957-64; chmn. dept. clin. studies Sch. Vet. Medicine, 1958-73; dir. Bovine Leukemia Research Center, 1965-73; dean Sch. Vet. Medicine, 1973-87; co-dir. Center on Interactions Animals and Soc., 1975-79, also mem. grad. group com. in comparative med. scis.; prof. medicine, chief sect. epidemiology and pub. health Sch. Vet. Medicine U. Pa., 1990-93, prof. medicine emeritus, 1993—; mem. adv. bd. Pa. Dept. Agr., 1973-87; chmn. Gov.'s Study Group on Horse Racing Industry in Pa., 1979; mem. del. to evaluate vet. med. and rsch. Chinese Ministry Agr.; mem. adv. com. Stroud Water Rsch. Ctr., 1992—; mem. adv. coun. Coll. Vet. Medicine, Cornell U., 1993—. Sr. co-editor Advances in Veterinary Science and Comparative Medicine; contbr. numerous articles to sci. jours. Bd. dirs. Humane Soc. U.S., 1978-82, Bide-a-wee Home Assn., 1980-85; sci. adv. bd. mem. Sch. Vet. Medicine The Hebrew U., Jerusalem, 1984—; chmn. external com. Sch. Vet. Medicine Tuskegee U.; trustee Upland Country Day Sch., 1988-91; mem. animal adv. com. City of Phila., 1989-93. Served with AUS, 1943-44. Recipient Disting. Veterinarian award Pa. Vet. Med. Assn., 1984, Barnraiser award Pa. Farmers Assn., 1987. Fellow Phila. Coll. Physicians; mem. AAAS, John Morgan Soc. (pres. 1967-68), Am. Assn. Cancer Rsch., Am. Vet. Med. Assn., Pa. Vet. Med. Assn, NAS Inst. Medicine (sr.), Pa. Livestock Assn. (dir.), Westminster Kennel Club, James A. Baker Inst. for Animal Health (mem. adv. coun. 1977—), Phila. Soc. for Promoting Agr., Pa. Friends of Agr. Found., Phila. Zool. Soc. (bd. dirs. 1986-87), Sigma Xi, Phi Zeta.

MARSHALEK, EUGENE RICHARD, physics educator; b. N.Y.C., Jan. 17, 1936; s. Frank M. and Sophie (Weg) M.; m. Sonja E. M. Lennhart, Dec. 8, 1962; children: Thomas, Frank. BS, Queens Coll., 1957; PhD, U. Calif., Berkeley, 1962. NSF postdoctoral fellow Niels Bohr Inst., Copenhagen, Denmark, 1962-63; rsch. assoc. Brookhaven Nat. Lab., Upton, N.Y., 1963-65; asst. prof. U. Notre Dame, Ind., 1965-69, assoc. prof., 1969-78, prof., 1978—. Contbr. articles to profl. jours. Recipient Alexander von Humboldt sr. scientist award, 1985. Mem. AAAS, Am. Phys. Soc., Sigma Xi. Office: U Notre Dame Dept Physics Notre Dame IN 46556

MARSHALL, ALAN GEORGE, chemistry and biochemistry educator; b. Bluffton, Ohio, May 26, 1944; s. Herbert Boyer Marshall Jr. and Cecile (Mogil) Rosser; m. Marilyn Gard, June 13, 1965; children: Gwendolyn Scott, Brian George. BA in Chemistry with honors, Northwestern U., 1965; PhD in Phys. Chemistry, Stanford U., 1970. Instr. II U. B.C., Vancouver, Can., 1969-71, asst. prof., 1971-76, assoc. prof., 1976-80; prof. chemistry and biochemistry Ohio State U., Columbus, 1980-93; prof. chemistry Fla. State U., Tallahassee, 1993—; cons. Extrel FTMS, Madison, Wis., 1989-92, Oak Ridge (Tenn.) Nat. Lab., 1990—; dir. Ion Cyclotron Resonance Program Nat. High Magnetic Field Lab., 1993—. Author: Biophysical Chemistry, 1978, Fourier Transforms in Spectroscopy, 1990; editor ICR/ION Trap newsletter, 1986—; N.Am. editor Rapid Comm. on Mass Spectrometry, 1988—; mem. editorial bd. Analytical Chemistry, 1990-92, Internat. Jour. Mass Ion Procs., 1987—, Jour. Am. Soc. Mass Spectrometry, 1989—, Mass Spectrometry Rev., 1994—, Jour. Magnetic Resonance, 1995—; contbr. more than 240 articles to profl. jours. Recipient Disting. Scholar award Ohio State U., 1988, Maurice F. Hasler award Spectroscopy Soc. Pittsb., 1997. Fellow AAAS, Am. Phys. Soc.; mem. Am. Chem. Soc. (award in chem. instrumentation, Akron sect. award, award in analytical chemistry Ea. Analytical Symposium 1991, Frank H. Field and Joe L. Franklin award 1995), Soc. Applied Spectroscopy (chmn. local sect. 1990-91), Am. Soc. Mass Spectroscopy (bd. dirs. 1991-92). Office: Fla State Univ Nat High Magnetic Field Lab 1800 East Paul Dirac Dr Tallahassee FL 32310

MARSHALL, ALTON GARWOOD, real estate counselor; b. Flint, Mich., Sept. 19, 1921; s. William Robert and Lela Christine (Brabon) M.; m. Mary Lee Golden, June 22, 1945 (div. July 1971); children: William A., Stephen B., Bruce S., Mary Ann Marshall Trebian, John L.; m. Sarah Elizabeth DeLand, Sept. 4, 1971; 1 child, Sarah Graham. BA, Hillsdale Coll., 1942; MS, Syracuse U., 1948, LLD (hon.), 1974; D Pub. Service & Bus. Adminstrn. (hon.), Hillsdale Coll., 1980. Sec. utility regulations pub. svc. commn. N.Y. State, Albany, 1953-61, dep. dir. div. budget, 1961-65, exec. officer, then sec. to gov., Office of Gov., 1965-70; pres., bd. dirs. Rockefeller Ctr., N.Y.C., 1971-81; pres. A.G. Marshall Assocs., N.Y.C., 1981—; chmn., pres., chief exec. officer Lincoln Savs. Bank, N.Y.C., 1984-88, chmn., chief exec. officer, 1988-91, also bd. dirs.; mem. exec. com. Nat. Realty Com., Washington, 1970—; bd. dirs. N.Y. State Electric & Gas Corp., 1971—; ind. gen. ptnr. Equitable Capital Ptnrs. and Equitable Capital Ptnrs. Retirement Fund, 1989—; trustee Hudson River Trust, 1991—. Mem. exec. com., steering com. Assn. for a Better N.Y., 1971—; mem. exec., landmarks and polit. action coms. Real Estate Bd. N.Y.; chmn. Nat. Assn. on Drug Abuse Problems, 1990-92. Sr. fellow The Nelson A. Rockefeller Inst. Govt., 1991-94. Mem. Am. Soc. Real Estate Counselors. Office: Alton G Marshall Assocs Inc 136 E 79th St New York NY 10021-0328

MARSHALL, ARTHUR K., lawyer, judge, arbitrator, educator, writer; b. N.Y.C., Oct. 7, 1911. BS, CUNY, 1933; LLB, St. John's U., N.Y.C., 1936; LL.M., U. So. Calif., 1952. Bar: N.Y. State 1937, Calif. 1947. Practice law N.Y.C., 1937-43, Los Angeles, 1947-50; atty. VA, Los Angeles, 1947-50; tax counsel Calif. Bd. Equalization, Sacramento, 1950-51; inheritance tax atty. State Controller, Los Angeles, 1951-53; commr. Superior Ct. Los Angeles County, 1953-62; judge Municipal Ct., Los Angeles jud. dist., 1962-63, Superior Ct., Los Angeles, 1963-81; supervising judge probate dept. Superior Ct., 1968-69, appellate dept., 1973-77; presiding judge Appellate Dept., 1976-77; pvt. practice arbitrator, mediator, judge pro tem, 1981—; acting asst. prof. law UCLA, 1954-59; grad. faculty U. So. Calif., 1955-75; lectr. Continuing Edn. of the Bar; mem. Calif. Law Revision Commn., 1984—, chmn., 1986-87, 92-93; chmn. com. on efficiency and econs. Conf. Calif. Judges, past chmn. spl. action com. on ct. improvement; past chmn. probate law cons. group Calif. Bd. Legal Specialization. Author: Joint Tenancy Taxwise and Otherwise, 1953, Branch Courts, 1959, California State and

Local Taxation Text, 2 vols., 1962, rev. edit., 1969, supplement, 1979, 2d edito., 1981, Triple Choice Method, 1964, California State and Local Taxation Forms, 2 vols., 1961-75, rev. edit., 1979, California Probate Procedure, 1961, 5th rev. edit., 1994, Guide to Procedure Before Trial, 1975; contbr. articles to profl. jours. Mem. Town Hall. With AUS, 1943-46; lt. col. JAGC, USAR ret. Named Judge of Yr. Lawyers Club L.A. County, 1975; first recipient Arthur K. Marshall award established by estate planning, trust and probate sect. L.A. Bar Assn., 1981, Disting. Jud. Career award L.A. Lawyers Club, award L.A. County Bd. Suprs., 1981. Fellow Am. Bar Found.; mem. ABA (probate litigation com. real property, probate and trust sect.), Am. Arbitration Assn. (mem. nat. panel of arbitrators), Internat. Acad. Estate and Trust Law (academician, founder, 1st pres., now chancellor), Calif. State Bar (advisor to exec. com. real property, probate and trust sect. 1970-83), Santa Monica Bar Assn. (pres. 1960), Westwood Bar Assn. (pres. 1959), L.A. Bar Assn., Am. Legion (comdr. 1971-72), U. So. Calif. Law Alumni Assn. (pres. 1969-70), Phi Alpha Delta (1st justice alumni chpt.). Office: 300 S Grand Ave Ste 28 Los Angeles CA 90071-3110

MARSHALL, BARRY JAMES, gastroenterologist; b. Kalgoorlie, Western Australia, Australia, Sept. 30, 1951; came to U.S., 1986; s. Robert William and Marjory Jean (Donald) M.; m. Adrienne Joyce Feldman, Dec. 27, 1972; children: Luke, Bronwyn, Caroline, Jessica. MBBS, U. Western Australia, Perth, 1974, postgrad., 1986. Intern Sir Charles Gairdner Hosp., Western Australia, 1975-76, resident, 1976-77, med. registrar, 1977-78; med. registrar Royal Perth Hosp., Western Australia, 1979-82; med. registrar Fremantle Hosp., Western Australia, 1983-84, microbiology register, 1984; research scientist Royal Perth Hosp., Western Australia, 1985-86; research fellow U. Va. Sch. Med., Charlottesville, 1986-87, asst. prof. medicine, 1988—; cons. Procter and Gamble Co., Cin., 1984—, Delta West Perth, 1985—; bd. dirs. JARM Pty. Ltd., Perth, 1987—. Inventor Clotest (rapid urease test), 1985, Carbon-14 Urea Breath Test, 1985; co-discoverer Helicobacter Pylori bacilli in stomach of patients with gastritis and peptic ulcers, 1984; first person to culture Helicobacter Pylori bacilli. Named one of Outstanding West Australians, Perth Jaycees, 1985; research grantee Australian Nat. Health and Med. Research Council, 1985-86; recipient Albert Lasker Clinical Medical Rsch. award Albert and Mary Lasker Foundation, 1995. Fellow Royal Australian Coll. Physicians, Am. Coll. Gastroenterology; mem. Australian Med. Assn., Australian Gastroent. Soc. Avocations: computer hardware and software, photography, skin diving, American cuisine. Office: care Helicobacter Foundation PO Box 7965 Charlottesville VA 22906-7965

MARSHALL, BRIAN LAURENCE, trade association executive; b. Kingston-on-Thames, England, Apr. 6, 1941; came to U.S., 1949; s. John and Marguerite Elizabeth (Sandele) M. BA in European History, U. N.C., 1963; MS in Internat. Mgmt., Am. Grad. Sch. Internat. Mgmt., Glendale, Ariz., 1973. Commd. 2d lt. USAF, 1964, advanced through grades to capt., 1972; instr. Armed Forces Air Intelligence Tng. Ctr., Denver, 1965-68; intelligence analyst Task Force Alpha, Nakhon Phanom, Thailand, 1968-69; intelligence systems analyst Headquarters Tactical Air Command, Langley AFB, Va., 1969-72, resigned, 1972; cons. Gen. Research Corp., McLean, Va., 1974; systems analyst Computer Scis. Corp., Falls Ch., Va., 1974-87; dir. U.S. membership and pubs. U.S.-Mexico C. of C., Washington, 1987-91; v.p. pub. affairs, bd. dirs. N.Am. Free Trade Assn., Washington, 1991—; v.p. internat. N.Am. Trade and Investment Group, Washington, 1991—, also bd. dirs.; contract team leader, strategic planning studies and analyses U.S. Dept. Defense, Joint Chiefs of Staff, Washington, 1976-82. Contbr. articles to booklets and newsletters. Vol. Pres. Ford Com., Washington, 1976; bd. dirs. Columbia Plaza Tenants Assn., Washington, 1981-84. Mem. VFW, Assn. Former Intelligence Officers, World Affairs Coun., Fgn. Policy Assn. (group leader discussion program), Thunderbird Alumni Assn. (pres. Washington chpt. 1980-87), Washington Mgmt. and Bus. Assn. (vice chmn. 1981-83, treas. 1987-91). Republican. Lodge: Hash House Harriers. Avocations: jogging, tennis, travel, discussion groups, reading. Home: 5304 Albemarle St Bethesda MD 20816-1827 Office: N Am Free Trade Assn 1130 Connecticut Ave NW Ste 500 Washington DC 20036-3919

MARSHALL, BRYAN EDWARD, anesthesiologist, educator; b. London, Oct. 24, 1935; came to U.S., 1965, naturalized, 1979; m. Carol Davies, Sept. 1957; children—Leisa, David. M.D., Leeds U., 1959. Diplomate: Am. Bd. Anesthesiology. Rotating intern Hereford (Eng.) Gen. Hosps., 1959-60; sr. house officer anesthesia Taunton Gen. Hosps., Cambridge, Eng., 1960-61; registrar anesthesia United Cambridge Hosps., 1961-63; research scholar Cambridge U., 1963-65; research fellow U. Pa. Med. Sch., 1965-66, mem. faculty, 1966—, prof. anesthesia, 1972—; prof. comparative anesthesia U. Pa. Vet. Sch., 1973—, Horatio C. Wood prof. research in anesthesia, dir. anesthesia research, 1982; vis. prof., U.S., Can., Europe, Asia, Australia; lectr. throughout, U.S.; mem. merit rev. bd. VA; study sect. NIH. Author textbooks and numerous articles in field.; editor: Anesthesiology, 1975—, Circulatory Shock; mem. editorial bds. profl. jours. Recipient Career Devel. award NIH, 1971-76. Fellow Am. Coll. Anesthesiologists, Royal Coll. Physicians; mem. AAUP, AAAS, Assn. Univ. Anesthesiologists (Rsch. Excellence award 1995), Am. Physiol. Soc. Am., Soc. Exptl. Biology and Medicine, Assn. Anesthesiologists Gt. Britain and Ireland (Rsch. prize 1964), Anesthesia Rsch. Group Gt. Britain, Shock Soc., Phila. Med. Sco., Pa. Soc. Anesthesiologists, Phila. Physiol. Soc., Pa. Thoracic Soc., Laennec Soc. Phila., Circanes Soc., John Morgan Soc., Sigma Chi. Home: 119 Adrienne Ln Wynnewood PA 19096-1205 Office: Hosp U Pa 773 Dudley St Bldg Philadelphia PA 19148-2423

MARSHALL, BURKE, law educator; b. Plainfield, N.J., Oct. 1, 1922. A.B., Yale U., 1944, LL.B., 1951, M.A., 1970. Bar: D.C. bar 1952. Assoc., then partner firm Covington and Burlington, Washington, 1951-61; asst. atty. gen. U.S., 1961-65; gen. counsel IBM Corp., Armonk, N.Y., 1965-69; sr. v.p. IBM Corp., 1969-70; prof. law Yale U. Law Sch., 1970—, Nicholas deB. Katzenbach prof. emeritus; chmn. Nat. Adv. Commn. SSS, 1967. Author: Federalism and Civil Rights, 1965; co-author: The Mylai Massacre and Its Cover-up, 1975; editor: The Supreme Court and Human Rights, 1982, A Workable Government?, 1989; contbr. articles, revs. to legal publs. Bd. dirs. Ctr. Community Change, Washington, 1968—, Robert F. Kennedy Meml., 1969—, Vera Inst. Justice, N.Y.C., 1965—. Home: Castle Meadow Rd Newtown CT 06470 Office: Yale U Sch Law 127 Wall St New Haven CT 06511-6636

MARSHALL, C. TRAVIS, manufacturing executive, government relations specialist; b. Apalachicola, Fla., Jan. 31, 1926; s. John and Estelle (Marks) M.; m. Katherine Rose Lepine; children: Melanie, Monica, Katharine. BS, U. Notre Dame, 1948. Chief clk. Firestone Tire & Rubber Co., Detroit, 1948-51; gen. sales mgr. The Hallicrafters, Chgo., 1952-65; v.p. mktg. E. F. Johnson, Waseca, Minn., 1965-70; v.p. mktg. ops. Motorola, Inc., Schaumburg, Ill., 1970-72, dir., govt. relations, communications div., 1972-74; v.p., dir. govt. relations Motorola, Inc., Washington, 1974-85, sr. v.p., dir., gov. relations, 1985-92; telecomm. cons., 1992—; bd. dirs. Iridium, Inc. Appointed amb. by Pres. Bush to Internat. Telecomm. Union Conf.; trustee Md. Youth Symphony Orch. Recipient Disting. Service award Electronics Industries Assn., Washington, 1987. Mem. Electronics Industries Assn. (treas. 1982-92, treas. emeritus 1992—, v.p. 1975-88), Burning Tree Country Club (Bethesda), Columbia Country Club (Chevy Chase), Met. Club (Washington), Crystal Downs Country Club (Frankfort, Mich.). Republican. Roman Catholic. Avocations: sailing, golf. Office: Motorola Inc 1350 I St NW Washington DC 20005-3305

MARSHALL, CAROL SYDNEY, labor market analyst, employment counselor; b. N.Y.C., Nov. 21, 1930; d. Charles Herbert and Tillie (Muriel) Helman; m. Bogdan Branislav Denitch, 1952 (div. 1954); m. Charles Marshall, Oct. 9, 1954 (div. Aug. 1973); children: Katrina, Peter Morgan Helman, Bonnie Sophia Brija, Athena. Student, Antioch Coll., 1948-50, Hunter Coll., 1953-61, U. Mo., 1967-68; AB in Geography & Urban Planning with honors & distinction, San Diego State U., 1971, postgrad., 1972-73. Copy person, cub reporter Chgo. Sun-Times, 1949-50; adminstrv. asst. Hudson Guild Child Care Ctr., N.Y.C., 1951-54; rsch. asst. City of Antioch Planning Dept., Calif., 1971-72; planning aide San Diego County Planning Dept., 1972-73; labor market analyst Labor Market Info. Divsn. Calif. Employment Devel. Dept., San Francisco, 1973-94; employment rep. Job Svc. Calif. Employment Devel. Dept., San Francisco, 1994—; speaker, panelist on labor mkt. issues, 1985-94; labor mkt. rsch. cons. San Francisco Pvt. Industry Coun., 1986-94, San Mateo Pvt. Industry Coun., 1986-91, Alameda County Econ. Devel. Adv. Bd., 1991-94; mem. profl. working group Health Occupations Study Nat. Ctr. for Rsch. in Vocat. Edn., Berkeley, Calif., 1989-91; mem. adv. bd. Dept. Health Info. Tech. City Coll. San Francisco, 1992-94. Contbr. articles to profl. jours. Mem. Young Peoples Socialist League, N.Y.C., 1947-54, nat. sec., 1952-53; mem. Young Socialist League, N.Y.C., 1954-62; organizer, co-founder San Diego State U.Child Care Ctr., 1971. Mem. Dem. Socialists of Am., Ctr. for Sci. in the Pub. Interest, Pub. Citizens Health Rsch. Group, East Bay Bicycle Coalition, San Francisco Bicycle Coalition, League of Am. Bicyclists. Jewish. Avocations: bicycling, classic rock & roll, photography, theatre. Office: Calif Employment Devel Dept Job Svc 363 Civic Dr Pleasant Hill CA 94523-1920

MARSHALL, CAROLYN ANN M., church official, consultant; b. Springfield, Ill., July 18, 1935; d. Hayward Thomas and Isabelle Bernice (Hayer) McMurray; m. John Alan Marshall, July 14, 1956 (dec. Sept. 1990); children: Margaret Marshall Bushman, Cynthia Marshall Kyrouac, Clinton, Carol. Student, De Pauw U., 1952-54; BSBA, Drake U., 1956; D of Pub. Svc. (hon.), De Pauw U., 1983; LHD (hon.), U. Indpls., 1990. Corp. sec. Marshall Studios, Inc., Veedersburg, Ind., 1956-89, exec. cons., 1989-93; sec. Gen. Conf., lay leader South Ind. conf. United Meth. Ch., 1988—; Carolyn M. Marshall chair in women studies Bennett Coll., Greensboro, N.C., 1988; fin. cons. Lucille Raines Residence, Inpls., 1977—. Pres. Fountain Ctrl. Band Boosters, Veedersburg, 1975-77; del. Gen. Conf., United Meth. Ch., 1980, 84, 88, 92, 96, pres. women's divsn. gen. bd. global ministries, 1984-88; bd. dirs. Franklin (Ind.) United Meth. Ch. Home: 204 N Newlin St Veedersburg IN 47987-1358*

MARSHALL, CHARLES, communications company executive; b. Vandalia, Ill., Apr. 21, 1929; s. William Forman and Ruth (Corson) M.; m. Millicent Bruner, Jan. 2, 1953; children: Ruth Ann, Marcia Marshall Rinek, William Forman, Charles Tedrick. B.S. in Agr. U. Ill., 1951. With Ill. Bell Telephone Co., 1953-59, 61-64, 65-70, 71-72, 77-81; pres., chief exec. officer Ill. Bell Telephone Co., Chgo., 1977-81; with AT&T, 1959-61, 64-65, 70-71, 76-77, 81-89; chmn., chief exec. officer Am. Bell, Morristown, N.J., 1983-84, AT&T Info. Systems, 1984-85; vice chmn. AT&T, N.Y.C., 1985-89; bd. dirs. Ceridian, GATX, Sundstrand, Sonat, Hartmarx; trustee U. Ill. Found. Served to 1st lt. USAF, 1951-53. Mem. Econ. Club Chgo., Comml. Club Chgo., Club of Pelican Bay, Tavern Club, Chgo. Club. Avocations: fishing, golfing, reading. Home: Ph-B 6001 Pelican Bay Blvd Naples FL 34108-8166

MARSHALL, CHARLES BURTON, political science consultant; b. Catskill, N.Y., Mar. 25, 1908; s. Caleb Carey and Alice (Beeman) M.; m. Betty Louise O'Brien, Aug. 1, 1958 (dec. July, 1991); children (by previous marriage) Charles Richard, Jean Marshall Vickery. BA, U. Tex., 1931, MA, 1932; PhD, Harvard U., 1939; LHD, Johns Hopkins U., 1987. With newspapers in El Paso and Austin, Tex., 1925-31; With newspapers in Detroit, 1934-38; instr., tutor govt. Harvard U. and Radcliffe Coll., 1938-42; vis. lectr. Harvard U., summer 1963; cons. Intergovtl. Com. Refugees, 1946-47; staff cons. com. fgn. affairs U.S. Ho. of Reps., 1947-50; mem. policy planning staff State Dept., 1950-53; adviser to prime minister Pakistan, 1955-57; research assoc. Washington Center Fgn. Policy Research, 1957-74, acting dir., 1969-70; vis. prof. Sch. Advanced Internat. Studies, Johns Hopkins, 1965-66, prof., 1966-67, Paul H. Nitze prof. internat. politics, 1967-75; Alumni prof. internat. studies U. N.C., 1960-61; Centennial vis. prof. Tex. A&M U., 1976; cons. in field, 1961—; U.S. govt. rep. XIV Conf. Internat. Red Cross, Toronto, Can., 1952; mem. Gen. Adv. Com. Arms Control and Disarmament, 1982-92. Author: The Limits of Foreign Policy, 1954, The Exercise of Sovereignty, 1965, The Cold War: A Concise History, 1965, Crisis Over Rhodesia: A Skeptical View, 1967; Cons. editor: New Republic, 1959-64; contbg. editor: Nat. Rev, 1979-83. Served to lt. col. AUS, 1942-46. Fellow Carnegie Endowment Internat. Peace, 1934-35; vis. scholar, 1958-59. Mem. Washington Inst. Fgn. Affairs, Cosmos Club. Home: 4106 N Randolph St Arlington VA 22207-4808

MARSHALL, CHARLES NOBLE, railroad consultant; b. Phila., Feb. 18, 1942; s. Donnell and Cornelia Lansdale (Brooke) M.; m. Ann Shaw Donovan, Jan. 12, 1971; children—Elizabeth, Caroline, Cornelia, Edward. B.S. in Engring., Princeton U., 1963; J.D., U. Mich., 1967. Bar: Md. 1967, D.C. 1975, Pa. 1978. Atty. Balt. & Ohio R.R., Balt. and Cleve., 1967-73; gen. atty. So. Ry., Washington, 1973-78; gen. counsel commerce Conrail, Phila., 1978-83, v.p. mktg., 1983-85, sr. v.p. mktg. and sales, 1985-89, sr. v.p. devel., 1989-95; bd. dirs. Phila. Reg. Port Authority, Pa. Chamber, Inc. Republican. Episcopalian.

MARSHALL, CODY, bishop. Bishop No. Ill. Ch. of God in Christ, Chgo. Office: Ch of God in Christ 8836 Blackstone Chicago IL 60637*

MARSHALL, CONRAD JOSEPH, entrepreneur; b. Detroit, Dec. 23, 1934; s. Edward Louis Fedak and Maria Magdalena Berzsenyi; m. Dorothy Genieve Karnafil, Dec. 1, 1956 (div. 1963); children: Conrad Joseph Jr., Kevin Conrad, Lisa Marie; m. Beryle Elizabeth Callahan, June 15, 1965 (div. 1972); children: Brent Jasmer, Farah Elizabeth. Diploma, Naval Air Tech. Tng. Ctr., Norman, Okla., 1952; student, Wayne State U., 1956-59; Diploma, L.A. Police Acad., 1961. Dir. mktg. Gulf Devel., Torrance, Calif., 1980-83; sales mgr. Baldwin Piano Co., Santa Monica, Calif., 1977-80; dir. mktg., v.p. Western Hose, Inc., L.A., 1971-76; city letter carrier U.S. Post Office, L.A., 1969-71; writer freelance L.A., 1966—; police officer L.A. Police Dept., 1961-66; asst. sales mgr. Wesson Oil Co., Detroit, 1958-60; agt. Life Ins. Co. of Va., Wayne, Mich., 1956-58; pres. Am. Vision Mktg., L.A., 1990—, Con-Mar Prodns., L.A., 1983—; sr. v.p. Pacific Acquisition Group, 1992—, Invest. Admin. HealthCom., Int., 1993—; pres. Midway TV Co., 1994—; tech. advisor Lion's Gate Films, Westwood, Calif., 1970-74, Medicine Wheel Prodns., Hollywood, Calif., 1965-75; mng. gen. ptnr. Encino Wireless #1, 1994—; CEO Midway TV Inc., 1995; v.p. nat. bus. affairs MMA Internat., 1997. Author: (series) "Dial Hot Line", 1967, (screenplay) "Heads Across the Border", 1968, "The Fool Card", 1970, "Probable Cause", 1972; co-author: The Fedak File, 1995; albums include Song Shark, 1992, Conrad Marshall Quintet, 1991. Campaign vol. Dem. Ctrl. Com., L.A., 1976, Rep. Ctrl. Com., 1994. Mem. Screen Actors Guild, Internat. Platform Assn. Avocations: poetry, song writing, club singing, philosophy, theology. Home: 11853 Kling St Apt 17 Valley Village CA 91607-4048 Office: Con-Mar Prodns 2026 Holly Hill Ter Hollywood CA 90068-3812

MARSHALL, CONSUELO BLAND, federal judge; b. Knoxville, Tenn., Sept. 28, 1936; d. Clyde Theodore and Annie (Brown) Arnold; m. George Edward Marshall, Aug. 30, 1959; children: Michael Edward, Laurie Ann. A.A., Los Angeles City Coll., 1956; B.A., Howard U., 1958, LL.B., 1961. Bar: Calif. 1962. Dep. atty. City of L.A., 1962-67; assoc. Cochran & Atkins, L.A., 1968-70; commr. L.A. Superior Ct., 1971-76; judge Inglewood Mcpl. Ct., 1976-77, L.A. Superior Ct., 1977-80, U.S. Dist. Ct. Central Dist. Calif., L.A., 1980—; lectr. U.S. Information Agy. in Yugoslavia, Greece and Italy, 1984, in Nigera and Ghana, 1991, in Ghana, 1992. Contbr. articles to profl. jours.; notes editor Law Jour. Howard U. Mem. adv. bd. Richstone Child Abuse Center. Recipient Judicial Excellence award Criminal Cts. Bar Assn., 1992; research fellow Howard U. Law Sch., 1959-60;. Mem. State Bar Calif., Calif. Women Lawyers Assn., Calif. Assn. Black Lawyers, Calif. Judges Assn., Black Women Lawyers Assn., Los Angeles County Bar Assn., Nat. Assn. Women Judges, NAACP, Urban League, Beta Phi Sigma. Office: US Dist Ct 312 N Spring St Ste 155 Los Angeles CA 90012-4703*

MARSHALL, DALE ROGERS, college president, political scientist, educator; b. Mar. 22, 1937; m. Donald J. Marshall; children: Jessica, Cynthia, Clayton. BA in Govt., Cornell U., 1959; MA in Polit. Sci., U. Calif., Berkeley, 1960; PhD in Polit. Sci. with distinction, UCLA, 1969. Lectr. in polit. sci. UCLA, 1969-70, U. Calif., Berkeley, 1970-72; from asst. prof. to prof. U. Calif., Davis, 1972-86, faculty asst. to vice chancellor acad. affairs, 1980-82, assoc. dean Coll. Letters and Scis., 1983-86; acting pres. Wellesley (Mass.) Coll., 1987-88, dean of coll., prof. polit. sci., 1986-92; pres. Wheaton (Mass.) Coll., 1992—; mem. exec. bd. Calif. Assembly Fellowship Program, 1980-86; bd. trustees, bd. overseers Newton-Wellesley Hosp., 1989-93; bd. trustees Cornell U., Ithaca, N.Y., 1983-93, chair Cornell Fund, co-chair Coll. Arts and Scis. Capital Campaign, 1990-93; bd. trustees New Eng. Zenith Fund, New Eng. Mut. Life Ins. Co., 1995—; bd. dirs. Am. Student Assistance Guarantor, Am. Student Assistance Corp., 1994—. Author: (with John C. Bollens) Guide to Participation: Field Work, Role Playing Cases and Other Forms, 1973, (with Roger Montgomery) Housing Policy for the 80's, 1980, (with Rufus P. Browning and David H. Tabb) Protest is Not Enough: The Struggle of Blacks and Hispanics for Eqauality in Urban Politics, 1984 (APSA Ralph J. Bunche award for best book on ethnic rels. 1985, Gladys Kammerer award for best book in Am. policy 1985); editor: Urban Policy Making, 1979, (with David K. Leonard) Institutions of Rural Development for the Poor: Decentralization and Organizatonal Linkages, 1982, (with Rufus P. Browning and David H. Tabb, co-editor), Racial Politics in American Cities, 1990, 2d edit., 1997; mem. editl. bd. Am. Polit. Sci. Rev., 1972-76, Pub. Adminstrn. Rev., 1985-86; contbr. articles to profl. jours. Woodrow Wilson fellow, 1959-60, Calif. Regents fellow, 1966-67, 67-68; NSF grantee, 1976-78, 79-80; recipient Disting. Teaching award Significant Contbn. to Status of Women citation Chancellor's Com. on Status of Women at U. Calif. at Davis, 1978. Mem. Am. Polit. Sci. Assn. (mem. exec. coun. 1974-76, v.p. 1985-86, mem. nominating com. 1988-90), Western Polit. Sci. Assn. (mem. exec. coun. 1973-75, pres. 1984-85), Nat. Acad. Pub. Adminstrn., Nat. Assn. Ind. Colls. and Univs. (bd. dirs.), Assn. Ind. Colls. and Univs. Mass. (exec. com.), Mortar Bd., Phi Beta Kappa, Phi Kappa Phi. Office: Wheaton Coll Office of Pres Norton MA 02766

MARSHALL, DANIEL STUART, advertising executive; b. London, Eng., Nov. 14, 1930; came to U.S., 1964; s. Leslie Stuart and Jessie (Morrison) M.; m. Solange Goohier, Sept. 2, 1985. Student, St. Johns Coll., Hassocks, Eng., 1944. Dir. art J. Walter Thompson, Santiago, Chile, 1958-61, San Paulo, Brazil, 1961-64, N.Y.C., 1964-96; exec. v.p., creative dir. Marshall Jacomma & Mitchell, N.Y.C., 1978-96; creative dir., ptnr. Poppe-Tyson, N.Y.C., 1996—. Artist, designer (book) The Dream Theatre, 1975, In a Monastery Kitchen, 1975. Office: Marshall Jacomma & Mitchell 41 Madison Ave New York NY 10010-2202

MARSHALL, DONALD GLENN, English language and literature educator; b. Long Beach, Calif., Sept. 9, 1943; s. Albert Louis and Margaret Corinne (Morrison) M.; m. Kathleen Bonann, June 21, 1975; children: Stephanie Deborah, Zachary Louis. AB summa cum laude, Harvard U., 1965; MPhil, Yale U., 1969, PhD, 1971. Asst. prof. English UCLA, 1969-75; from assoc. prof. to prof. English U. Iowa, Iowa City, 1975-90; honors dir. U. Iowa Coll Liberal Arts, 1981-85; prof., head English dept. U. Ill., Chgo., 1990—. Editor: Philosophy as Literature/Literature as Philosophy, 1986; compiler: Contemporary Critical Theory: A Selective Bibliography, 1993; translator: (with Joel Weinsheimer) Truth and Method by Hans-Georg Gadamer, 1989; contbr. articles and revs. to profl. jours. Recipient Bell prize Harvard U., 1965, Webster prize Yale U., 1967; NEH Younger Humanist fellow, 1973-74; grantee UCLA, U. Iowa. Mem. MLA, Internat. Assn. Philosophy and Lit. (bd. dirs. conf. Christianity and lit. 1995—), Ill. Humanities Coun. (bd. dirs. 1994—, Chgo. humanities festival 1997—). Democrat. Roman Catholic. Office: U Ill Dept English Univ Hall 601 S Morgan St Chicago IL 60607-3401

MARSHALL, DONALD STEWART, computer systems company executive; b. Saskatoon, Sask., Can., Nov. 18, 1938; s. Arthur Stewart and Helen Margaret (Pederson) M.; children: Douglas Stewart, Andrew Christopher. B Applied Sci. in Civil Engring., Queen's U., Kingston, Ont., Can., 1962. Registered profl. engr., Ont. Progressed from computer systems analyst to branch mgr. Honeywell, IBM and AGT Data Systems, 1962-71; pres. Ventek Ltd., London, 1971-80; v.p. CDC Data Systems Ltd., Toronto, Ont., 1980-83; exec. v.p. Meridian Techs. Inc., Toronto, 1983-93; pres. Nextest Ltd (formerly Atelco Ltd.), Markham, Ont., 1993—; bd. dirs. Incontext Sys. Inc., Halozone Tech. Inc., Nextest Ltd. Mem. Assn. Profl. Engrs. Ont. Avocations: golf, squash, tennis. Home: 54 Anderson Ave, Toronto, ON Canada M5P 1H7 Office: Nextest Ltd, Ste 241, 50 McIntosh Dr, Markham, ON Canada L4B 3H6

MARSHALL, DONALD THOMAS, medical technologist; b. Omaha, June 9, 1955; s. William A. and Alma J. (Jorgensen) M.; m. Beverly Ann Everett, Sept. 22, 1990. Med. tech., Pikes Peak Inst. Med. Tech., 1977; EMT, Pikes Peak C.C., Colorado Springs, 1979; PhD of Religion, Universal Life Ch., 1995, D of Metaphysics (hon.), 1995. Registered med. technologist; cert. clin. lab. technologist. Technician x-ray/med. St. Joseph Hosp. of Plains, Cheyenne Wells, Colo., 1977-79; technician med. lab. Conejos County Hosp., La Jara, Colo., 1979-84; med. technologist Nat. Health Lab., Englewood, Colo., 1984-91; lab. tech. cons. neighborhood health program Denver Dept. Health and Hosps., 1996—. EMT, fireman La Jara Vol. Fire Dept., 1979-84, Meritorious Svc. Citation, 1983. Mem. Internat. Soc. Clin. Lab. Tech., Am. Med. Technologists, East Denver Masonic Lodge Ancient, Free and Accepted Masons (Master 1994). Republican.

MARSHALL, ELAINE F., state official; b. Lineboro, Md., Nov. 18, 1945; d. Donald and Pauline Folk; m. Sol Marshall; 3 stepchildren. BS in Textiles and Clothing, U. Md., 1968; JD, Campbell U., 1981. Bar: N.C., U.S. Dist. Ct. (ea. and mid. dists.), U.S. Ct. Appeals (4th cir.), U.S. Supreme Ct. Owner retail bus., 1986-79; ptnr. Marshall & Marshall, Lillington, N.C., 1981-96; sec. state State of N.C., 1997—; legal advisor bus. and prol. women, N.C., 1982—; mem. 15th dist. N.C. Senate, 1993-94, N.C. Planning Commn., 1993-94, N.C. Cts. Commn., 1993-94. Bd. dirs. Harnett County United Way, 1987-97, N.C. 4-H Devel. Fund, Inc., 1990—, N.C. Rural Econ. Devel. Fund, 1993-95, N.C. Bd. Econ. Devel., 1993-94, N.C. Ctr. Pub. Policy Rsch., 1994—, N.C. Justice Acad. Fund, 1994—; mem. Divine St. United Meth. Ch.; founding chmn., hon. chmn. Harnett HelpNet Children, 1992—. Recipient N.C. Friends Ext. award, 1992. Fellow N.C. Inst. Polit. Leadership; mem. Women's Forum N.C. Office: Office Sec State 300 N Salisbury St Raleigh NC 27603-5909*

MARSHALL, ELLEN RUTH, lawyer; b. N.Y.C., Apr. 23, 1949; d. Louis and Faith (Gladstone) M. AB, Yale U., 1971; JD, Harvard U., 1974. Bar: Calif. 1975, D.C. 1981, N.Y. 1989. Assoc. McKenna & Fitting, Los Angeles, 1975-80; ptnr. McKenna, Conner & Cuneo, Los Angeles and Orange County, Calif., 1980-88, Morrison & Foerster, LLP, Orange County, Calif., 1988—. Mem. ABA (bus. law sect., savs. inst. com., asset securitization com., tax sect., employee benefits com.), Orange County Bar Assn. Club: Center (Costa Mesa, Calif.). Office: Morrison & Foerster 19900 Macarthur Blvd Irvine CA 92612-2445

MARSHALL, FRANCIS JOSEPH, aerospace engineer; b. N.Y.C., Sept. 5, 1923; s. Francis Joseph and Mary Gertrude (Leary) M.; m. Joan Eager, June 14, 1952; children—Peter, Colin, Stephen, Dana. B.S. in Mech. Engring, CCNY, 1948; M.S., Rensselaer Poly. Inst., 1950; Dr. Eng. Sci., N.Y. U., 1955. Engr. Western Union Co., N.Y.C., 1948, Gen. Electric Co., Schenectady, 1948-50; engr. Wright-Aero Corp., Woodridge, N.J., 1950-52; group leader Lab. for Applied Scis., U. Chgo., 1955-60; instr. Ill. Inst. Tech., 1957-59; prof. Sch. Aeros. and Astronautics, Purdue U., West Lafayette, Ind., 1960—; engr. U.S. Naval Underseas Warfare Center, Pasadena, Calif., 1966-68; faculty fellow NASA-Langley, 1969-70; vis. prof. Inst. Tech. Mara-Midwest Univs. Consortium for Internat. Activities, Malayasia, 1989. Contbr. articles to profl. jours. Served with U.S. Army, 1943-46. Decorated Combat Inf. badge.; NASA research grantee, 1970-76; Fulbright scholar, Turkey, 1988-89. Assoc. fellow AIAA; mem. Am. Soc. Engring. Edn., AAUP. Home: 120 Leslie Ave West Lafayette IN 47906-2410 Office: Sch Aeros and Astronautics Purdue U West Lafayette IN 47907

MARSHALL, FRANK W., film producer, director. Student, UCLA. Location mgr.: The Last Picture Show, 1971, What's Up Doc?, 1972; assoc. prodr.: Paper Moon, 1973, Daisy Miller, 1974, At Long Last Love, 1975. Nickelodeon, 1976, The Driver, 1978; line prodr.: Orson Welles' The Other Side of the Wind (unreleased), Marin Scorsese's The Last Waltz, 1977; prodr.: (films) Raiders of the Lost Ark, 1981 (Academy award nomination for best picture 1981), Noises Off, 1992; (with Steven Spielberg) Poltergeist, 1982; (with Spielberg, Quincy Jones, and Kathleen Kennedy) The Color Purple, 1985 (Academy award nomination for best picture 1985), (with Kathleen Kennedy and Kane Startz) Indian in a Cupboard; (with Spielberg and Kennedy) Empire of the Sun, 1987, Always, 1989; (with Robert Watts) Who Framed Roger Rabbit, 1988; (with Kennedy and Gerald R. Molen) Hook, 1991; (with Kennedy) Milk Money, 1994; exec. prodr.: (films) The Warriors, 1979, Twilight Zone-The Movie, 1983; (with George Lucas) Indiana Jones and the Temple of Doom, 1984; (with Kennedy and Spielberg) Gremlins, 1984, The Goonies, 1985, Back to the Future, 1985, Young Sherlock Holmes, 1985, *batteries not included, 1987, Dad, 1989, Back to the Future Part II, 1989, Gremlins 2: The New Batch, 1990, Back to the

Future Part III, 1990, Joe Versus the Volcano, 1990, Cape Fear, 1991, We're Back! A Dinosaur's Story, 1993; (with Kennedy) Fandango, 1985; (with Kennedy, Spielberg, and David Kirschner) An American Tail, 1986; (with Kennedy and Art Levinson) The Money Pit, 1986; (with Kennedy, Spielberg, Peter Guber, and Jon Peters) Innerspace, 1987; (with Kennedy, Lucas, and Spielberg) The Land Before Time, 1988; (with Kennedy and Lucas) Indiana Jones and the Last Crusade, 1989; (with Kennedy and Kirschner) An American Tail: Fievel Goes West, 1991; (with Chris Meledandri) Swing Kids, 1993; (with Kennedy and Molen) A Far Off Place, 1993; exec. prodr. (with Spielberg, Robert W. Cort, and Ted Field), dir.: Arachnophobia, 1990; dir.: Alive, 1993, Congo, 1995; exec. producer: TV Roger Rabbit and the Secret of Toontown; prodr., dir. TV Johnny Bago. Office: Kennedy/Marshall Co 1620 26th St Ste 1030 N Santa Monica CA 90404-4013*

MARSHALL, GAILEN DAUGHERTY, JR., physician, scientist, educator; b. Houston, Sept. 9, 1950; s. Gailen D. and Evelyn C. (Gresham) M.; m. Elizabeth M. Marek, Nov. 5, 1978; children: Sarah Elizabeth, Jonathan David, Rebecca Marie. BS, U. Houston, 1972; MS, Tex. A&M U., 1975; PhD, U. Tex., 1979, MD, 1984. Rsch. sci. U. Tex., Galveston, 1981-84; rsch. fellow U. Iowa, Iowa City, 1985-86; lab. dir. Biotherapeutics Inc., Memphis, 1986-88; chief med. resident Bapt. Meml. Hosp., Memphis, 1988-89; assoc. dir. Rsch. for Health Inc., Houston, 1989-90; clin. asst. prof. medicine U. Tex., Houston, 1990-91, asst. prof. medicine, 1991-94, assoc. prof. medicine and pathology, 1994—, dir. divsn. allergy and immunology, 1990—; mem. sci. adv. com. Carrington Labs., Dallas, 1992-94. Mem. editl. bd. Molecular Biotherapy, 1992-93, Cancer Biotherapy, 1994-96, Allergy Proceedings, 1994—, Annals Allergy, Asthma and Immunology, 1995-99; contbr. articles to profl. jours. Judge Greater Houston Sci. Fair, 1992—. Fellow ACP, Am. Coll. Allergy and Immunology, Am. Acad. Allergy-Immunology (chair com.); mem. Tex. Allergy-Immunology Soc. (chair com.), Greater Houston Allergy Soc. Republican. Baptists. Avocations: amateur radio, classical music, fishing. Office: U Tex Houston Med Sch 6431 Fannin St Ste 4044 MSB Houston TX 77030-1501

MARSHALL, GARLAND ROSS, biochemist, biophysicist, medical educator; b. San Angelo, Tex., Apr. 16, 1940; s. Garland Ross and Jewel Wayne (Gray) M.; m. Suzanne Russell, Dec. 26, 1959; children: Chris, Keith, Melissa, Lee. BS, Calif. Inst. Tech., 1962; PhD, Rockefeller U., 1966; DSc (hon.), Politechnika, Lodz, Poland, 1993. Instr. Washington U., St. Louis, 1966-67, asst. prof., 1967-72, assoc. prof., 1972-76, prof. biochemistry, 1976—, prof. pharmacology, 1985—, dir. Ctr. for Molecular Design, 1988—; vis. prof. Massey U., Palmerston North, New Zealand, 1975; vis. prof. chemistry U. Florence, Italy, 1991; pres. Tripos Assocs., Inc., St. Louis, 1979-87; chmn. 10th Am. Peptide Symposium, St. Louis, 1986-88; councilor Am. Peptide Soc., 1990-93; established investigator Am. Heart Assn., Washington, 1970-75. Editor: Peptides: Chemistry and Biology, 1988, Peptides: Chemistry, Structure and Biology, 1990; editor-in-chief Jour. Computer-Aided Molecular Design, 1986—. Recipient medal XL-Lecia Tech. U., Lodz, Poland, 1987, Vincent de Vigneaud award Am. Peptide Soc., 1994, Sci. and Tech. award St. Louis Regl. Commerce and Growth Assn., 1996. Mem. Am. Chem. Soc. (Medicinal Chemistry award 1988, Midwest award 1996), Am. Soc. for Biochemistry and Molecular Biology, Am. Soc. for Pharmacology and Exptl. Therapeutics, Biophys. Soc., Am. Peptide Soc. (Vincent du Vigneaud award 1994). Office: Washington U Ctr for Molecular Design 700 S Euclid Ave Saint Louis MO 63110-1012

MARSHALL, GARRY, film producer, director, writer; b. N.Y.C., Nov. 13, 1934. B.S., Northwestern U. Writer I Spy, Jack Paar Show, Joey Bishop Show, Danny Thomas Show, Lucy Show, Dick Van Dyke Show; writer, creator Hey Landlord; exec. prodr. The Odd Couple, 1968; creator, exec. prodr. Evil Roy Slade, 1972, Happy Days, Laverne and Shirley, Mork and Mindy, Angie, Joanie Loves Chachi; writer, prodr. films, How Sweet It Is, 1968, The Grasshopper, 1970: dir. Young Doctors in Love, 1982; screenwriter, dir. Flamingo Kid, 1984; dir. films Nothing in Common, 1987, Overboard, 1987, Beaches, 1988, Pretty Woman, 1990, Frankie & Johnny, 1991, Exit to Eden, 1994; film appearance includes Psych-out, 1968, Lost in America, 1985, Soapdish, 1991, A League of Their Own, 1992, Hocus Pocus, 1993, (TV movie) Frank Capra's American Dream, 1997; prodr., actor (film) Twilight of the Golds, 1997; actor, dir. Dear God, 1996. also: Pkwy Prodns 10202 W Washington Blvd Culver City CA 90232*

MARSHALL, GEOFFREY, university official; b. Lancaster, Pa., Feb. 6, 1938; s. Ray Ardell and Mary (Elsen) M.; m. Mary Gale Beckwith, June 17, 1961; children: Eden Elizabeth, Erin Elizabeth. BA, Franklin and Marshall Coll., 1959; MA, Rice U., 1961, PhD, 1965; LHD (hon.), Mansfield State Coll., 1980, Ursinus Coll., 1990. Assoc. prof. English U. Okla., Norman, 1964-74; asst. provost U.Okla., Norman, 1973-74; dir. div. state programs Nat. Endowment for Humanities, Washington, 1974-78, dir. div. edn. programs, 1978-80, dep. chmn., 1981-85; assoc. provost and dean for acad. affairs Grad. Sch. CUNY, 1985-92, acting provost and v.p. for acad. affairs, 1992-94, provost, sr. v.p., 1994—; bd. dirs. Ursinus Coll., 1986—. Author: Restoration Serious Drama, 1975; contbr. articles to profl. jours. Trustee Norman Pub. Library, 1970-74; chmn. Okla. Humanities Com., 1971-74; mem. Norman Human Rights Commn., 1972-73. Assoc. Danforth Found., 1968-74; recipient Couch Scholars award for excellence in undergrad. edn. U. Okla., 1967. Mem. MLA, Nat. Council Tchrs. English, Am. Soc. 18th Century Studies, Nat. Collegiate Honors Council (exec. com. 1972-74). Home: 125 Cypress Dr Hightstown NJ 08520-2315 Office: CUNY Grad Sch and Univ Ctr 33 W 42nd St New York NY 10036-8003

MARSHALL, GEORGE DWIRE, retired supermarket chain executive; b. Washington, Feb. 7, 1940; s. Joseph Paull and Jane Schouler (Dwire) M.; m. Sharon Ruth Carter, Nov. 17, 1968; children: Sarah Dwire, Benjamin Carter. BA, Amherst Coll., 1962; JD, U. Calif., Berkeley, 1965. Bar: Calif. 1966. Atty., then sr. atty. legal div. Safeway Inc., Pleasanton, Calif., 1970-79, v.p., mgr. labor rels. divsn., 1979-97; employer trustee UFCW Internat. Union-Industry Pension Fund, 1980—. Served to lt. USNR, 1966-70, Korea, Vietnam. Mem. State Bar Calif., Bar Assn. San Francisco, Psi Upsilon, Phi Delta Phi. Republican. Presbyterian.

MARSHALL, GERALD FRANCIS, optical engineer, consultant, physicist; b. Seven Kings, Eng., Feb. 26, 1929. BSc in Physics, London U., 1952. Physicist Morganite Internat., London, 1954-59; sr. research devel. engr. Ferranti Ltd., Edinburgh, Scotland, 1959-67; project mgr. Diffraction Limited Inc., Bedford, Mass., 1967-69; dir. engring. Medical Lasers, Inc., Burlington, Mass., 1969-71; staff cons. Speedring Systems, Troy, Mich., 1971-76; dir. optical engring. Energy Conversion Devices, Inc., Troy, Mich., 1976-87; sr. tech. staff specialist Kaiser Electronics, San Jose, Calif., 1987-89; cons. in optics design and engring., 1989—. Editor, contbg. author: Laser Beam Scanning, 1985, Optical Scanning, 1991; patentee in field. Fellow Inst. Physics, Internat. Soc. Optical Engring. (syymposia chair 1990), bd. dirs. 1991-93, exec. chair Internat. Symposium on Electronic Imaging Device Engring., Munich 1993); mem. Optical Soc. Am. (program chair 1979-80, pres. Detroit sect. 1980-81, bd. dirs. No. Calif. sect. 1990-92).

MARSHALL, HERBERT A., lawyer; b. Clinton, Ill., Aug. 20, 1917; s. Harry A. and Andrea (Pederson) M.; m. Helen Christman, May 3, 1941; children—James A., Thomas O., Mary (Mrs. William Nichols). A.B., Washburn U., 1940, LL.B., J.D., 1943. Bar: Kans. bar 1943. Law clk. U.S. Ct. Appeals, 1943-44; asst. county atty. Shawnee County, Kans., 1944-50; practiced in Topeka, 1944—; instr. practice ct. Washburn U. Law Sch., 1963—; mem. Kans. Supreme Ct. Nominating Commn., 1968-79. Trustee, elder Presbyn. Ch. Fellow Am. Bar Found. (life), Kans. Bar Found. (life), Am. Coll. Trial Lawyers; mem. ABA, Kans. Bar Assn. (exec. council 1968—, v.p. 1977, pres. 1979), Am. Judicature Soc., Topeka Bar Assn. (pres. 1968), Topeka C. of C., Optimist Club, Masons, Elks. Home: 4722 SW Brentwood Rd Topeka KS 66606-2204

MARSHALL, HOWARD LOWEN, music educator, musicologist; b. Nokesville, Va., July 21, 1931; s. Howard Hampton and Florence Annie (Nash) M.; m. Doris Mae Rosencranz, July 14, 1962. B of Music Edn., Shenandoah U., 1952; MusM, U. Cin., 1958; PhD, U. Rochester, 1968. Asst. prof. music Lake Forest (Ill.) Coll., 1966-73; Charles B. Thompson prof. music, chmn. music dept. Mercer U., Macon, Ga., 1974—. Author: The Four-Voice Motets of Thomas Crecquillon, Symbolism in Schubert's Winterreise in Studies in Romanticism, The Motets of Georg Prenner. Lt. comdr. USNR, ret. Mem. Am. Musicological Soc., AAUP, Phi Mu Alpha, Phi Kappa Lambda. Avocation: photography. Home: 1324 Maplewood Dr Macon GA 31210-3106 Office: Mercer U Music Dept 1400 Coleman Ave Macon GA 31207-0001

MARSHALL, IRL HOUSTON, JR., residential and commercial cleaning company executive; b. Evanston, Ill., Feb. 28, 1929; s. Irl H. and Marjorie (Greenleaf) M.; m. Barbara Favill, Nov. 5, 1949; children: Alice Marshall Vogler, Irl Houston III, Carol Marshall Allen. AB, Dartmouth Coll., 1949; MBA, U. Chgo., 1968; cert. franchise exec., La. State U., 1991. Gen. mgr. Duraclean Internat., Deerfield, Ill., 1949-61; mgr. Montgomery Ward, Chgo., 1961-77; pres., chief exec. officer Duraclean Internat., 1977—. Inventor/patentee in field. Pres. Cliff Dwellers, Chgo., 1977; exec. com., treas., dir. Highland Park Hosp., 1971-80; dir. Continential Ill. Bank Deerfield, 1982-90; bd. dirs. Better Bus. Bur. Chgo. & No. Ill., Chgo., 1988—. Mem. Internat. Franchise Assn. (bd. dirs. 1981-90, pres. 1985, chmn. 1985-86), Econ. Club Chgo., Exmoor Country Club, Univ. Club Chgo. Presbyterian. Home: 1248 Ridgewood Dr Northbrook IL 60062-3725

MARSHALL, JAMES JOHN, publishing executive; b. Fall River, Mass., Apr. 15, 1930; s. John and Florence (Carr) M.; m. Kathleen Seibert, Apr. 14, 1967 (dec. Jan. 1988); children: Kathleen C., Mary E. BS, Providence Coll., 1953; MS, Columbia U., 1954. Reporter Providence Jour., 1954-55, 57-60; seminarian Maryknoll, Ossining, N.Y., 1960-62; press sec. Office of R.I. Gov. John H. Chafee, Providence, 1962-67; pub. affairs dir. Rep. Govs. Assn., Washington, 1967-69, Citizens Com. for Postal Reform, Washington, 1969-70; pres. Govt. Info. Svcs., Arlington, Va., 1971—, Edn. Fund Rsch. Coun., Arlington, 1971—; pres. Newsletter Press of New Eng., East Providence, R.I., 1976—, Internat. Law Libr., Arlington, 1994—; bbd. dirs. Manisses Comms., Providence. With USN, 1955-57. Mem. Newsletter Pubs. Assn. (founding mem., bd. dirs. 1977-87, pres. 1984), Newsletter Pubs. Found., Ind. Newsletter Assn. (pres. 1976), Nat. Press Club. Roman Catholic. Home: 10906 Quimby Point Ln Reston VA 22091 Office: Govt Info Svcs 4301 Fairfax Dr Ste 875 Arlington VA 22203-1627

MARSHALL, JANE PRETZER, newspaper editor; b. Chase County, Kans.; married; 2 children. BS in Home Econs. and Journalism, Kans. State U., 1967; student, Tex. A&M, U. Mo., Tex. Christian U., Brite Divinity Sch. Asst. editor dept. agr. info. Tex. Agrl. Ext. Sta. Tex. A&M U., College Station, 1967-70; staff writer Gazette-Telegraph, Colorado Springs, Colo., 1970-72; editor corporate publ. Colorado Interstate, Colorado Springs, 1972-75; co-editor The Pampa (Tex.) News, 1975-78; exec. features editor Ft. Worth Star-Telegram, 1978-84; features editor Denver Post, 1984-88, Houston Chronicle, 1988—. Author: (children's book) Going for the Gold: Hakeem Olajuwon, 1996. Recipient 1st place for feature writing Tex. AP Mng. Editors Assn., 1978. Mem. Am. Assn. Sunday and Features Editors (bd. dirs., founding chairperson Features First), Women's Fund Health Edn. and Rsch. (bd. dirs.), Journalism and Women Symposium (1st pres.). Office: Houston Chronicle 801 Texas St Houston TX 77002-2906

MARSHALL, JEAN MCELROY, physiologist; b. Chambersburg, Pa., Dec. 31, 1922; d. Frank Lester and Florence (McElroy) M. A.B., Wilson Coll., 1944; M.A., Mt. Holyoke Coll., 1946; Ph.D., U. Rochester, 1951. Instr. Johns Hopkins U. Med. Sch., Balt., 1951-56; asst. prof. Johns Hopkins U. Med. Sch., 1956-60; research postdoctoral fellow Oxford (Eng.) U., 1954-55; asst. prof. Harvard U. Med. Sch., Boston, 1960-66; assoc. prof. physiology Brown U., Providence, 1966-69; prof. Brown U., 1969-88, prof. emerita, 1988, E. Brintzenhof Prof. Med. Sci., 1987—; mem. physiology study sect. NIH, 1967-71, mem. tng. com. engring. in biology and medicine, 1971-74, mem. tng. com. lab. medicine, 1976-77; physiol. test com. Nat. Bd. Med. Examiners, 1972-76, neurobiology adv. com., 1977-80. Editor: The Initiation of Labor, 1964; mem. editorial bd. Jour. Pharmacology and Exptl. Therapeutics, 1963-69, Am. Jour. Physiology, 1969-73, Circulation Research, 1973-81; contbr. articles to profl. jours. Mem. Am. Physiol. Soc., Am. Pharmacol. Soc., N.Y. Acad. Scis., Soc. Reproductive Biology, Soc. Gen. Physiologists, Phi Beta Kappa, Sigma Xi. Home: 14 Aberdeen Rd Weston MA 02193-1733 Office: R I Hosp/Brown Univ Dept Medicine Providence RI 02903

MARSHALL, JEFFREY SCOTT, mechanical engineer, educator; b. Cin., Feb. 10, 1961; s. James C. and Norma E. (Everett) M.; m. Marilyn Jane Patterson, July 16, 1983; children: Judith K., Eric G., Emily J. BS summa cum laude, UCLA, 1983, MS, 1984; PhD, U. Calif., Berkeley, 1987. Asst. rsch. engr. U. Calif., Berkeley, 1988; engr. Creare, Inc., Hanover, N.H., 1988-89; from asst. to assoc. prof. dept. ocean engring. Fla. Atlantic U., 1989-93; assoc. prof. dept. mech. engring., rsch. scientist Iowa Inst. Hydraulic Rsch. U. Iowa, Iowa City, 1993—. Contbr. articles to profl. jours. Rsch. grantee Am. Soc. Engring. Edn./USN Summer Faculty Rsch. Programs, 1991-94. ARO Young Investigator Program, 1992-95. Mem. ASME (assoc., Henry Hess award 1992), Am. Phys. Soc. , Tau Beta Pi. Achievements include research in fluid mechanics, three-dimensional vortex dynamics and geophysical flows. Office: U Iowa Iowa Inst Hydraulic Rsch Dept Mech Engring Iowa City IA 52242

MARSHALL, JOHN CROOK, internal medicine educator, researcher; b. Blackburn, Lancashire, Eng., Feb. 28, 1941; came to U.S., 1976; s. Albert Acey and Marion Miller (Crook) M.; m. Marilyn Dallas Parry, Sept. 20, 1969; children—Samantha Jane, Susannah Crook. B.S., Victoria U., Manchester, Eng., 1962, M.B., Ch.B., 1965, M.D., 1973. Diplomate Am. Bd. Internal Medicine, Am. Bd. Endocrinology and Metabolism. Intern Manchester Royal Infirmary, 1965-66; resident Brompton Hosp., Nat. Heart Hosp., London, 1966-69; resident Hammersmith Hosp., 1966-69, research fellow, London, 1969-72; lectr. U. Birmingham, Eng. 1972-76; assoc. prof. internal medicine U. Mich., Ann Arbor, 1976-79, prof., 1979-90; chief endocrinology and metabolism, 1987-91; prof. U. Va., Charlottesville, 1991—; sci. counselor NIH, Bethesda, Md., 1983-84; dir. Ctr. for Rsch. in Reproduction U. Va., 1996—. Editor Endocrinology Jour., 1979-97; editor: Endocrinology Text, 1990; contbr. articles to profl. jours. NIH grantee 1977-97. Fellow Royal Coll. Physicians, Royal Soc. Medicine, ACP; mem. Central Soc. for Clin. Research (council 1983—), Assn.. Am. Physicians, Am. Soc. for Clin. Investigation, Am. Clin. and Climatological Soc. Anglican. Avocations: vintage racing cars; golf; tennis.

MARSHALL, JOHN DAVID, lawyer; b. Chgo., May 19, 1940; s. John Howard and Sophie (Brezenk) M.; m. Marcia A. Podlasinski, Aug. 26, 1961; children: Jacquelyn, David, Jason, Patricia, Brian, Denise, Michael, Catherine. BS in Acctg., U. Ill., 1961; JD, Ill. Inst. Tech., 1965. Bar: Ill. 1965, U.S. Tax Ct. 1968, U.S. Dist. Ct. (no. dist.) Ill. 1971; CPA, Ill. Ptnr. Mayer, Brown & Platt, Chgo., 1961—. Bd. dirs. Levinson Ctr. for Handicapped Children, Chgo., 1970-75. Fellow Am. Coll. Probate Counsel; mem. Ill. Bar Assn., Chgo. Bar Assn. (agribus. com. 1978—, trust law com. 1969—, probate practice com. 1969—, com. on coms. 1983—, vice chmn. 1988-89, chmn. 1989-90, legis. com. of probate practice com. 1983—, chmn. and vice chmn. legis. com. of probate practice com. 1983-84, chmn. exec. com. probate practice com. 1982-83, vice chmn. exec. com. 1981-82, sec. exec. com. 1980-81, div. chmn. 78-79, div. vice chmn. 1977-78, div. sec. 1976-77, Appreciation award 1982-83), Chgo. Estate Planning Council. Roman Catholic. Club: Union League (Chgo.). Home: 429 Willow Wood Dr Palatine IL 60067-3831 Office: Mayer Brown & Platt 190 S La Salle St Chicago IL 60603-3410

MARSHALL, JOHN ELBERT, III, foundation executive; b. Providence, July 2, 1942; s. John Elbert Jr. and Millicent Edna (Paige) M.; m. Diana M. Healy, Aug. 16, 1968; children: Nelson John, Priscilla Anne. B.A., Brown U., 1964. Advt. mgr. U.N. Alloy Steel Corp., Boston, 1968-70; assoc. dir. devel. Brown U., 1970-74; exec. dir. R.I. Found., Providence, 1974-79; v.p. Kresge Found., Troy, Mich., 1979-82, exec. v.p., 1982-87, pres., 1987—, trustee, 1991—; CEO, 1993—; bd. dirs., former chmn. Coun. Mich. Founds.; bd. dirs. Ind. Sector; former chmn. Mich. Cmty. Found. Youth Project. Bd. dirs. United Way Cmty. Svcs., Detroit Symphony Orch. Hall, Mich. Campus Compact, Greater Downtown Partnership, Schs. for 21st Century; former bd. dirs., vice chmn. Family Svc. Detroit and Wayne County; past pres. Bloomfield Village Assn.; former trustee Coun. on Founds., Washington. Office: Kresge Found PO Box 3151 Troy MI 48007-3151

MARSHALL, JOHN HARRIS, JR., geologist, oil company executive; b. Dallas, Mar. 12, 1924; s. John Harris and Jessie Elizabeth (Mosley) M.; BA in Geology, U. Mo., 1949, MA in Geology, 1950, LHD, Garrett Evangelical Theological Seminary, 1996; m. Betty Eugenia Zarecor, Aug. 9, 1947; children: John Harris III, George Z., Jacqueline Anne Marshall Leibach. Geologist, Magnolia Oil Co., Jackson, Miss., 1950-59, assoc. geologist Magnolia/Mobil Oil, Oklahoma City, 1959-63, dist. and divsn. geologist Mobil Oil Corp., L.A. and Santa Fe Springs, Calif., 1963-69, divsn. geologist, L.A. and Anchorage, 1969-71, exploration supt., Anchorage, 1971-72, western region geologist, Denver, 1972-76, internat. and offshore geol. mgr., Dallas, 1976-78, chief geologist Mobil Oil Corp., N.Y.C., 1978-81, gen. mgr. exploration for Western Hemisphere, 1981-82; chmn. Marshall Energetics, Inc., Dallas, 1982—; dir. exploration Anschutz, 1985-91; pres. Madera Prodn. Co., 1992—, Summit Oil and Gas Worldwide, 1993-96; CEO Marshall Energetics Ltd., 1994—; active Geology Devel. Bd. U. Mo., 1982—; past pres. Coll. Arts and Sci. Devel. Coun., U. Mo. Councilman, City of Warr Acres (Okla.), 1962-63; various positions United Meth. Ch., 1951—, Boy Scouts Am., 1960-68; Manhattan adv. bd. Salvation Army, 1980-82; trustee The Sci. Place., Dallas, 1995—. Served with U.S. Army, 1943-46. Decorated with 3 Battle Stars U.S. Army; recipient U. Mo. Bd. Curators medal, ROTC Most Outstanding Student, 1949, Disting. Alumni Svc. award U. Mo., 1996; registered geologist, Calif., Wyo., Ky. Mem. Am. Assn. Petroleum Geologists (Pacific sect.), Am. Geol. Inst., Petroleum Exploration Soc. N.Y., Dallas Geol. Soc., Rocky Mountain Assn. Geologists, Alaska Geol. Soc., Oklahoma City Geol. Soc., N.Y. Acad. Sci., L.A. Basin Geol. Soc. (pres. 1969-70)., Am. Sci. Affiliation, Assn. Christian Geologists, Meth. Men Club, Denver Petroleum Club, Sigma Xi. Democrat. Office: Marshall Energetics Inc 12720 Hillcrest Rd Ste 105 Dallas TX 75230-2010

MARSHALL, JOHN PATRICK, lawyer; b. Bklyn., July 3, 1950; s. Harry W. and Mary Margaret (Kelly) M.; m. Cheryl J. Garvey, Aug. 10, 1975; children: Kelly Blake, Logan Brooke. BA, Rutgers U., 1972; JD cum laude, N.Y. Law Sch., 1976. Bar: N.Y. 1977, N.J. 1977, U.S. Dist. Ct. N.J. 1977, U.S. Dist. Ct. (so. and ea. dists.) N.Y. 1978, U.S. Ct. Appeals (3rd cir.) 1982, U.S. Dist Ct. (no. dist.) N.Y. 1991. Assoc. Kelley Drye & Warren, N.Y.C., 1976-84; ptnr. Kelley Drye & Warren, N.Y.C. and Parsippany, 1985—; bd. dirs. Am. Foreign Shipping Co., Inc., Westfield, N.J. Editorial bd. N.Y. Law Sch. Law Rev., 1975-76, staff mem., 1974-75; contbr. articles to profl. jours. Mem. jud. screening com. N.Y. Dem. Com., N.Y. New Dem. Coalition, 1988; exec. v.p. Humanitarian Found. for Nicaragua, 1991; mem., sec. Respect for Law Found., 1996; mem. Southern Dist. N.Y. Mediation Panel, 1994—; mem. Coun. on Jud. Adminstrn., 1996—. Fellow Am. Bar Found.; mem. ABA, N.Y. State Bar Assn. (sec. com. on cts. and the cmty. 1993-95), N.Y. County Lawyers' Assn. (sec. 1984-87, mem. com. on Supreme Ct. 1984-94, mem. legal edn., admission to bar and lawyer placement com. 1983-93), Am. Arbitration Assn. (mem. nat. panel arbitrators N.Y. and N.J. regions 1991—, mem. corp. counsel com. 1993—), Assn. of Bar of City of N.Y. (sec. judiciary com. 1989-92, mem. com. on arbitration 1994-96, sec. coun. on judical adminstrn. 1996—). Office: Kelley Drye & Warren 101 Park Ave New York NY 10178 also: 5 Sylvan Way Parsippany NJ 07054-3805

MARSHALL, JOHN PAUL, broadcast engineer; came to U.S., 1967; Degree, U. Grenoble, France, 1963; student, U. Munich, 1964-65, San Francisco State, 1969-71, John O'Connell Tech. Inst., 1973-74. Mem. faculty law and econ. scis. U. Grenoble, 1963-64; mem. Expo '67 staff City of Montreal, Que., Can., 1967; filmmaker Cinemalab, San Francisco, 1970; engr. film and TV Able Studios, San Francisco, 1971-73; radio and TV engr. Sta. KALW-FM (Nat. Pub. Radio), San Francisco, 1973-74; broadcast engr. Sta. KRON-TV (NBC), San Francisco, 1974-91; intern Centre d'Informatique et de Maintenance Automatisme, Tunisia, 1993; founder Marshall U.S.A., San Francisco, 1994; freelance broadcast engr. KPIX-TV (CBS), KGO-Radio (ABC), KSFO-Radio (ABC), KPST-TV, San Francisco, 1995—, also Sta. KPST-TV (Home Shopping Network), San Francisco; freelance audio visual tech. advisor, San Francisco area, 1975—, lectr. radio, TV, motion pictures, 1975—, cons. customized electronic effects; tech. advisor, assoc. Broadkast Skills Bank. Translator tech. pubs. and manuals, 1975—. Mus. dir., participant in theater prodns., 1950-59; active Boy Scouts Am. Govt. of France scholar, 1960-63. Mem. Rolls Royce Owners Club Found. (life), Internet Soc., Soc. Broadcast Engrs. (cert. broadcast technologist). Avocations: classical pianist, polyglot, world traveler. Office: 298 4th Ave Ste 419 San Francisco CA 94118-2468 *Personal philosophy: (French proverb) Aide toi, le ciel t'aidera--Use your own resources and you will always receive a helping hand from heaven.*

MARSHALL, JOHN STEVEN, artist, educator, museum administrator; b. Oct. 20, 1957. Spl. studies, U. of the South, 1979-80; AA, Motlow State Community Coll., Tullahoma, Tenn., 1981; BFA, Middle Tenn. State U., 1983; MFA, U. N.C., 1985. Registrar, curatorial asst. Weatherspoon Art Gallery, U. N.C., Greensboro, 1983-85, asst. curator, lectr., 1985, acting curator, 1986; instr./curator Meridian C.C., 1986—; dir. Meridian Mus. Art, 1986-89; represented by Artworks Gallery Laurel, Miss.; Artworks Gallery, Laurel, Miss.; co-owner Horne-Marshall Gallery, Meridian; lectr. art various Tenn. and Miss. orgns.; curator, jury mem. various exhbns. One-man shows include Meridian Mus. Art, 1989, Miss. State U., 1990, 92, Miss. U. for Women, 1990, Tusculum Coll., 1992, Gen. Art Gallery, Miss., 1993, Coleman Art Ctr., Ala., 1995, Meridian C.C., 1995, Lauderdale Cmty. Gallery, 1995, Meridian Underground Gallery, 1996, Arts in the Park, 1996, Eula Bass Lewis Gallery, Miss., 1996, Dauphin Way Gallery, Mobile, Ala., 1997, Horne-Marshall Gallery, Meridian, 1997; 2-person show Winfield Gallery, 1991; exhibited in group shows Elliot U. Ctr. Gallery, Brentwood and Nashville, 1984, Weatherspoon Art Gallery, Greensboro, 1985, 86, Waterworks Gallery, Winston-Salem, N.C., 1985, Meridian Mus. Art, 1987, 89, Casteel Art Gallery, Meridian, 1987, U. So. Miss., 1988, Greenville Art Gallery, 1988, Space-One-Eleven Gallery, 1990, Birmingham-So. Coll., 1990, Winfield Gallery, 1991; represented in pvt. collections. Named Arts Educator of the Yr., Meridian, Miss., 1996; recipient Lamplighter Ednl. Excellence award, 1996. Office: Meridian Community Coll 910 Highway 19 N Meridian MS 39307-5801

MARSHALL, JOHN TREUTLEN, lawyer; b. Macon, Ga., Nov. 1, 1934; s. Hubert and Gladys (Lucas) M.; m. Katrine White, May 1, 1959; children: Allison, Rebecca, Paul, Mary Anne. BA, Vanderbilt U., 1956; LLB, Yale U., 1962. Bar: Ga. 1962, U.S. Dist. Ct. (no., mid. and so. dists.) Ga. 1962, U.S. Ct. Appeals (5th cir.) 1962, U.S. Supreme Ct. 1978, U.S. Ct. Appeals (11th cir.) 1982. Ptnr. Powell, Goldstein, Frazer & Murphy, Atlanta, 1962—; adj. prof. law Emory U. Sch. Law, 1968-86, mem. coun.; chmn. No. Dist. Ga. Bar Coun., 1989; chmn. Ga. State Commn. on Continuing Lawyer Competency, 1991-93. Bd. editors: Yale Law Jour. Bd dirs. Atlanta Legal Aid, 1972-73; trustee Ga. Inst. Continuing Legal Edn., 1983-90; chmn. adv. bd. Atlanta Vol. Lawyers Found. Recipient S. Phillip Heiner award Atlanta Vol. Lawyers Assn., 1992, A. Gus cleveland award Ga. Commn. on Continuing Edn., Tradition of Excellence award State Bar Ga., 1995. Fellow Am. Coll. Trial Lawyers (state chmn. 1985-86), Am. Acad. Appellate Lawyers, Am. Bar Found., Ga. Bar Found.; mem. ABA (ho. of dels. 1976-86, Harrison Tweed award 1986), State Bar Ga. (chair stds. pf profession), Atlanta Bar Assn. (pres. 197475, Charles E. Watkins Jr. award 1988, Leadership award 1996), Ga. Inst. Trial Advocacy (chmn. 1982-830, Cherokee Town and Country Club, 191 Club, Lawyers Club. Office: Powell Goldstein Frazer & Murphy 191 Peachtree St NE Fl 16 Atlanta GA 30303-1740

MARSHALL, JOSEPH FRANK, electronic engineer; b. Wyoming, Pa., Mar. 2, 1917; s. Anthony Marchel and Mary (Moosic) M.; m. Margaret Mary Kennedy, June 17, 1961. BSEE, Pa. State Coll., 1941; MSEE, Harvard U., 1951. Registered profl. engr., Mass., N.J. Devel. engr., project mgr. Stromberg Carlson Co., Rochester, N.Y., 1941-49; design engr., staff engr. Bell Aircraft Corp., Buffalo, 1952-60; fellow engr. Electronics div. Westinghouse, Balt., 1961-62; sr. staff engr. Avco Corp., Wilmington, Mass., 1962-64; rsch. electrical engr. Cornell Lab., Buffalo, 1964-65; systems engr. Radio div. Bendix, Balt., 1966-67, Raytheon Corp., Sudbury, Mass., 1967-69, Astro Electronics div. RCA, Princeton, N.J., 1969-72; broadcast engr. N.J. Pub. TV, Princeton, 1972-74; sr. staff engr. Office of Engring. Tech. FCC, Washington, 1974-92; with Luther Acoustic Rsch., Pittsford, N.Y.; IRE subcom. mem. Industry Audio Amplifier Standards, 1944-46; served on EIA TR-8 ad hoc com. Nationwide Cellular Mobile Radio Standards, 1979-80. Violinist Pa. State Coll. Symphony Orch., 1937-40. Fellow Radio Club of

Am., Inc.; mem. Inst. Elec./Electronics Inc. (life), Radio Club of Washington, Violin Soc. Am., Catgut Acoustical Soc. Inc., Harvard Club of Rochester, Eta Kappa Nu, Sigma Tau, Tau Beta Pi, Pi Mu Epsilon. Democrat. Roman Catholic. Achievements include patents for selective tuning and damping of partials of rods and method of clamping tunable rods for electronic carillons, for critical components employed in a Navy secure missile command guidance system. Home: 9 Kimberly Rd Pittsford NY 14534-1505

MARSHALL, JULIE W. GREGOVICH, engineering executive; b. Pasadena, Calif., Mar. 3, 1953; d. Gibson Marr and Anna Grace (Peterson) Wolfe; m. Michael Roy Gregovich Dec. 18, 1976 (div. June 1994); children: Christianna, Kerry Leigh; m. Robert Brandon Marshall, Aug. 6, 1994. BA magna cum laude, Randolph-Macon Woman's Coll., 1975; MBA, Pepperdine U., 1983. cert. tchr. K-12, Calif. Test engr. Westinghouse Hanford, Richland, Wash., 1975-76; startup engr. Bechtel Power Corp., Norwalk, Calif., 1976-77; test engr. Wash. Pub. Power, Richland, 1978-80; from mgr. to v.p. Sun Tech. Svcs., Mission Viejo, Calif., 1983-93; cons. Mission Energy Co., Irvine, Calif., 1993-94; owner, CEO, pres. Key Employee Svcs., Inc., Key Largo, Fla., 1994—; assoc. Hawk Assocs., Inc. Investor Rels., Tavernier, Fla., 1996—. contbr. article to jour. Named Young Career Woman of the Yr. Wash. Pub. Power Supply System, 1979. Mem. Am. Nuc. Soc. (mem. bd. trustees pub. edn. program 1992—), Phi Beta Kappa.

MARSHALL, KATHRYN SUE, lawyer; b. Decatur, Ill., Sept. 12, 1942; d. Edward Elda and Frances M. (Minor) Lahniers; m. Robert S. Marshall, Sept. 5, 1964 (div. Apr. 1984); m. Robert J. Arndt, June 25, 1988; children: Stephen Edward, Christine Elizabeth. BA, Lake Forest Coll., 1964; JD, John Marshall Law Sch., Chgo., 1976. Intern U.S. Atty.'s Office, Chgo., 1974-76; mng. ptnr. Marshall and Marshall Ltd., Waukegan, Ill., 1976-84; pvt. practice Waukegan, 1984-93. Contbr. articles to profl. jours. Cert. jud. candidate Dem. party, Lake County, Ill.; bd. mem. Camerata Soc., Lake Forest; bd. mem., v.p. Lake Forest (Ill.) Fine Arts Ensemble. Fellow ABA (gov. 1993-96, Ill. Bar Assn., Coll. Law Practice Mgmt.; mem. Navy League (life). Avocations: boating, reading, travel.

MARSHALL, KEITH, pharmaceutical consultant; b. Leeds, Yorkshire, Eng., June 17, 1929; came to U.S., 1976; s. Thomas George and Dorothy (Bickerdike) M.; widowed; children: Neil Anthony, Carol Louise, Christopher Ian. BSC, London U., 1963; PhD, U. Bradford, 1970. Cert. pharm. chemist. Dir. Risdales Chemists, Leeds, Eng., 1954-56; lectr. Bradford Inst. Tech., Eng., 1956-60; head indsl. pharmacy unit U. Bradford, Eng., 1960-76; research dir. Colorcon Inc., Westpoint, Pa., 1976-78; dir. Inst. Applied Pharm.Scis., East Brunswick, N.J., 1978-83; assoc. dir. Smith Kline & French Labs., Phila., 1983-92; pres. Keith Marshall Assocs. Cons. Firm, 1992—; adj. prof. U. R.I., Kingston, 1985—, Phila. Coll. Pharmacy and Sci., 1996—, U. Md., 1994—. Author: Modern Pharmaceutics, 1987, Industrial Pharmacy: Theory and Practice, 1987. Served with M.C., Brit. Army, 1948-50. Fellow Assn. Am. Pharm. Scientists; mem. Royal Pharm. Soc. Gt. Britain, Fedn. Internat. Pharmacy. Avocation: boats. Home: 10 Royal Dr Brick NJ 08723-6731 Office: 144 Tices Ln East Brunswick NJ 08816-2014

MARSHALL, KERRY JAMES, artist; b. Birmingham, Ala., Oct. 17, 1955. BFA, Otis Art Inst., L.A., 1978. Prodn. designer Praise House & Sankofa, 1991; assoc. prof. U. Ill., Chgo.; art instr. L.A. City Coll., 1980-83; art faculty L.A. S.W. Coll., 1981-85; adj. asst. prof. Sch. Art and Design, U. Ill., Chgo., 1993-94. One man exhibits include James Turcotte Gallery, L.A., 1983, Pepperdine U., Malibu, 1984, Koplin Gallery, 1985, 91, Studio Mus. Harlem, 1986, Terra Incognito, Chgo. Cultural Ctr., 1992, Jack Shainmen Gallery, N.Y.C., 1993, 95, Koplin Gallery, Santa Monica, Calif., 1993, Cleveland Ctr. Contemporary ARts, 1994, Drawings III, Koplin Gallery, Santa Monica, 1993, Markts of Resistance, White Columns Gallery, N.Y.C. 1993, 43rd Biennial of Contemporary Am. Painting, Corcoran Gallery Art, Washington, 1993, Document X, Kassel, Germany, 1997, Whitney Biennial Whitney Mus. Am. Art, N.Y.C., 1997, Saddlebrook Coll. Art Gallery, Mission Viejo, Calif., 1994, Addison Gallery Am. Art, 1997; contbr. articles to profl. jours. Recipient Herb Alpert award Cal Arts, 1997; fellow Nat. Endowment Arts Visual Art, 1991, Mac Arthur Found., 1997; visual arts grantee Ill. Arts Coun., 1992; grantee Tiffany Found., 1993. Mem. Ill. Arts Coun. Office: 4122 S Calumet Ave Chicago IL 60653-2649

MARSHALL, L. B., clinical lab scientist; b. Chgo., Feb. 10; s. Gillman and Ethel (Robinson) M.; m. Esther Wood, Sept. 28, 1961; children: Lester B. III, Kiti B., Lelani. AA City Coll. San Francisco, 1957; BS in Podiatric Medicine, U. Puget Sound, 1961; ScD, London Inst., Eng., 1972. Pres., Med. Offices Health Svcs. Group Inc., San Francisco, 1964—. Mem. NAACP. With U.S. Army, 1947-53. Decorated Bronze Star, Med. Combat Badge; recipient Cert. Appreciation Pres. Nixon, 1973, Urban League, 1973, Calif. Dept. Human Resources, 1973. Mem. Am. Calif. Assns. Med. Technologists, Oyster Point Yacht Club, Press Club, Commonwealth Club (San Francisco).

MARSHALL, LEE DOUGLAS, entertainment company executive; b. Pitts., Sept. 23, 1956; s. Joseph Samuel and Lois Jean (Mickey) M.; m. Karen Lynne Drumm, Mar. 17, 1984; children: Jessica Lee, Lauren Lee. B in Communication, Ohio U., 1978. Account exec. Energy Talent Agy., Beachwood, Ohio, 1978-81; v.p. Magic Promotions & Theatricals, Inc., Aurora, Ohio, 1984—; pres. S. and S. Mgmt., Inc., Beachwood, 1981-84; The Touring Artists Group, 1992—; pres., COO Magicworks Entertainment, Inc., 1996—; mgr. Boxcar Willie and Tonia Kwiatkowski; prodr. 1996 Worldwide Gymnastics Tour., Deathtrap. Prodr.: The Magic of David Copperfield, South Pacific, Elvis, An American Musical, Jesus Christ Superstar, Man of La Mancha, Hello Dolly (starring Carol Channing), The Phantom of the Opera (with Ken Hill), Aint Misbehavin' (starring the Pointer Sisters), A Chorus Line, Nutcracker on Ice (starring Oksana Baiul, Brian Boitano and Viktor Petrenko), Deathtrap (starring Elliot Gould and Mariette Hartley), Gershwin on Ice, World Gold Gymnastics Tour (starring Kerri Strug). Mem. League of Am. Theatres and Producers. Mem. League of Am. Theatres and Prodrs. Avocations: boating, golfing, snow skiing. Office: Magic Promotions Inc 199 E Garfield Rd Aurora OH 44202-8886

MARSHALL, LINDA LANTOW, pediatrics nurse; b. Tulsa, Dec. 13, 1949; d. Lawrence Lee and Lena Mae (Ross) Lantow; m. David Panke Hartson, Aug. 25, 1970 (div. 1982); children: Michael David, Jonathan Lee; m. Roger Nathan Marshall, Dec. 11, 1985; 1 child, Sarabeth Megan. A, U. Okla., 1970; BSN, U. Tulsa, 1983. Cert. pediatric nurse, 1995. Pediats. nurse Youthcare, Claremore, Okla., 1983-85, 87—; staff nurse ICU Doctors Hosp., Tulsa, 1985-87. Bd. dirs. PTA Barnard, Tulsa, 1993-95; leader Brownie troop Girl Scouts U.S., Tulsa, 1994-95, leader jr. scouts, 1995—. Mem. Sigma Theta Tau. Avocation: gardening. Home: 2628 E 22nd St Tulsa OK 74114-3123 Office: Youth Care of Rogers County 525 E Blue Starr Dr Claremore OK 74017-4401

MARSHALL, MARGARET ELIZABETH, psychologist-therapist; b. Phoenix, Feb. 13, 1935; d. Glenn and Blanche (Chambers) Blankenship; m. John Raymond Hickman, May 26, 1956 (div. Mar. 1968); children: Diane Marie Hickman, John Noel Hickman; m. Charles Edward Marshall, 1971, (div. Oct. 1982). BA, Ariz. State U., 1956, MA, 1959, PhD, 1970. Lic. psychologist, Ariz. Lifeguard Salt River Recreation, Phoenix, 1956; tchr. Madison Elem. Dist., Phoenix, 1956-67; counselor Neighborhood Youth Corps, Phoenix, 1967-68, Maricopa County Conciliation Ct., Phoenix, 1969-80; pvt. practice psychology Anchor Counseling Centre, Phoenix, 1980—; pub. speaker; forensic expert witness to cts. Contbr. articles to profl. jours. Mem. Am. Psychol. Assn., Ariz. Chpt. Family and Conciliation Cts., Ariz. State Psychol. Assn., Assn. Family Conciliation Ct., Nat. Edn. Assn. (life). Avocations: swimming, bridge, continuing education classes, art. Home: 6316 N 30th Pl Phoenix AZ 85016-2224 Office: Anchor Counseling Centre 5150 N 16th St #A112 Phoenix AZ 85016

MARSHALL, MARGO, artistic director; b. Louisville, Nov. 3, 1934; d. Irving Robert and Elizabeth (Greenleaf) Lisbony; m. Jay C. Marshall, 1952 (div. 1971); 1 child, Dennis. BA, U. Houston, 1953. Pvt. tchr. dance Houston, 1950-58, owner, operator pvt. dance sch., 1958—; guest tchr. Joffrey Sch., N.Y., Internat. Acad. Dance, Portugal, Louisville Ballet, Boston Ballet's Summer Workshops, 1981-85, The Place, London, and others; part-time faculty mem. High Sch. for the Performing and Visual Arts, Houston; tchr. dance U. Houston, Sam Houston State U. Artistic dir. City Ballet Houston, 1967—; mem. dance panel Cultural Arts Coun. Houston; advisor Tex. Commn. on the Arts. Recipient Adjudicator for Mid-States Regional Ballet Assn., 1986. Mem. Southwestern Regional Ballet Assn. (officer 1965—), Houston Grand Opera (trustee). Office: City Ballet of Houston 9902 Long Point Rd Houston TX 77055-4116

MARSHALL, MARILYN JEAN, social services director, consultant; b. Phila., Oct. 11, 1930; d. Emery W. and Katherine (Rothermel) Sparrow; m. Samuel C. Marshall, June 14, 1952 (dec. July 1958); children: Catherin, James Scott, Jennifer Louise. Diploma in nursing, Thomas Jefferson U., 1951; BSN, Millersville U., 1970. RN, Pa. Staff nurse, head nurse Lancaster (Pa.) Gen. Hosp., 1952-54, 56-57; staff nurse emergency and recovery rm. Lancaster Gen. Hosp., 1956-60; supr. Homemaker Svc. Family and Children's Svc., Lebanon, Pa., 1966-74; staff nurse Good Samaritan Hosp., Lebanon, Pa., 1962-66, dir. social svcs., 1974-95; cmty. health needs assessment coord., 1995—. Bd. dirs. Helping Our People in Emergency, Lebanon; chmn. adv. bd. Victim/Witness. Mem. Am. Hosp. Assn., Soc. for Social Work Dirs. (Ea. Pa. chpt.), Hosp. Assn. Pa., Mental Health Interagy. Coun. Republican. Avocations: walking, fixing things around house. Office: Good Samaritan Hosp 4th and Walnut Sts PO Box 1281 Lebanon PA 17042-1281

MARSHALL, MARTIN VIVAN, business administration educator, business consultant; b. Kansas City, July 22, 1922; s. Vivan Dean and Marie (Church) M.; m. Rosanne Borden, Sept. 5, 1951 (dec. Feb. 8, 1986); children: Martin Dean, Michael Borden, Neil McNair; m. Hildegard Meyer, June 24, 1988. A.B., U. Mo., 1943; M.B.A., Harvard U., 1947, D.C.S., 1953. Instr. mktg. and advt. U. Kans., 1947-48; mem. faculty Harvard U., 1948—, Henry R. Byers prof. bus. adminstrn., 1960—, chmn. mktg. area faculty, 1962-66, chmn. Smaller Co. Mgmt. Program, 1981-84; chmn. Owner/Pres. Mgmt. Program, 1985-94; mem. faculty Inst. Ednl. Mgmt. Harvard U., 1981-90; cons. U.S. and internat. bus., 1950—; dir. ann. seminar mktg. and advt. Am. Advt. Fedn., 1958-78; vis. prof. mktg. IMEDE Mgmt. Inst., Lausanne, 1965-66; sr. prof., ednl. dir. Internat. Mktg. Inst., 1967-71; vis. prof. Indian Inst. Mgmt., Agra, 1968, IPADE, Mexico City, 1969, U. Melbourne, Australia, 1977, 79; bd. dirs. Western Stone & Metal. Author: Automatic Merchandising, 1954, (with N.H. Borden) Advertising Management, 1960, Notes on Marketing, 1983, 88, 90, 92, 93. Bd. dirs. Youth Svcs. Internat., Inc., 1994—. Served to lt. (s.g.) USNR, 1943-46. Home: 130 Mount Auburn St Apt 309 Cambridge MA 02138-5779 Office: Harvard U Cumnock Hall Boston MA 02163

MARSHALL, MARY JONES, civic worker; b. Billings, Mont.; d. Leroy Nathaniel and Janet (Currie) Dailey; m. Harvey Bradley Jones, Nov. 15, 1952 (dec. 1989); children: Dailey, Janet Currie, Ellis Bradley; m. Boyd T. Marshall, June 27, 1990. Student, Carleton Coll., 1943-44, U. Mont., 1944-46, UCLA, 1959. Owner Mary Jones Interiors. Founder, treas. Jr. Art Council, L.A. County Mus., 1953-55, v.p., 1955-56; mem. costume council Pasadena (Calif.) Philharm.; co-founder Art Rental Gallery, 1953, chmn. art and architecture tour, 1955; founding mem., sec. Art Alliance, Pasadena Art Mus., 1955-56; benefit chmn. Pasadena Girls Club, 1959, bd. dirs., 1958-60; chmn. L.A. Tennis Patron's Assn. Benefit, 1965; sustaining Jr. League Pasadena; mem. docent council L.A. County Mus.; mem. costume council L.A. County Mus. Art., program chmn. 20th Century Greatest Designers; mem. blue ribbon com. L.A. Music Ctr.; benefit chmn. Venice com. Internat. Fund for Monuments, 1971; bd. dirs. Art Ctr. 100, Pasadena, 1988—; pres. The Pres.'s L.A. Children's Bur., 1989; co-chmn. benefit Harvard Coll. Scholarship Fund, 1974, steering com. benefit, 1987, Otis Art Inst., 1975, 90th Anniversary of Children's Bureau of L.A., 1994; mem. Harvard-Radcliffe scholarship dinner com., 1985; mem. adv. bd. Estelle Doheny Eye Found., 1976, chmn. benefit, 1980; adv. bd. Loyola U. Sch. Fine Arts, L.A., Art Ctr. Sch. Design, Pasadena, Calif., 1987—; patron chmn. Benefit Achievement Rewards for Coll. Scientists, 1988; chmn. com. Sch. Am. Ballet Benefit, 1988, N.Y.C.; bd. dirs. Founders Music Ctr., L.A., 1977-81; mem. nat. adv. council Sch. Am. Ballet, N.Y.C., nat. co-chmn. gala, 1980; adv. council on fine arts Loyola-Marymount U.; mem. L.A. Olympic Com., 1984, The Colleagues; founding mem. Mus. Contemporary Art, 1986; chmn. The Pres.'s Benefit L.A. Children's Bur., 1990; exec. com. L.A. Alive for L.A. Music Ctr., 1992; mem. exec. com. Children's Bur. of L.A. Found., 1992; chmn. award dinner Phoenix House, 1994, 96; bd. dirs. Andrews Sch. Gerontology, U. So. Calif., 1996—, Leakey Found., 1996—; bd. regents Children's Hosp. L.A., 1996—. Mem. Am. Parkinson Disease Assn. (steering com. 1991), Valley Hunt Club (Pasadena), Calif. Club (L.A.), Kappa Alpha Theta. Home: 10375 Wilshire Blvd Apt 8B Los Angeles CA 90024-4728

MARSHALL, NANCY HAIG, library administrator; b. Stamford, Conn., Nov. 3, 1932; d. Harry Percival and Dorothy Charlotte (Price) Haig; m. William Hubert Marshall, Dec. 28, 1953; children—Bruce Davis, Gregg Price, Lisa Reynolds, Jeanine Haig. B.A., Ohio Wesleyan U., 1953; M.A.L.S., U. Wis., 1972. Dir. Wis. Inter Libr. Svcs., Madison, 1972-79; Reference librarian U. Wis., Madison, 1972, assoc. dir. univ. libraries, 1979-86; dean univ. librs. Coll. William and Mary, Williamsburg, Va., 1986—; mem. adv. com. Copyright Office, Washington, 1978-82; dir. USBE, Inc., Washington, 1983-86; trustee OCLC, Inc., Dublin, Ohio, 1982-88. Contbr. articles to profl. jours. Mem. ALA (coun. 1980-88, 90-93), Wis. Libr. Assn. (Libr. of the Yr. award 1982), Va. Libr. Assn., Beta Phi Mu. Office: Coll William and Mary E G Swem Libr Williamsburg VA 23185

MARSHALL, NATALIE JUNEMANN, economics educator; b. Milw., June 13, 1929; d. Harold E. and Myrtle (Findlay) Junemann; m. Howard D. Marshall, Aug. 7, 1954 (dec. 1972); children: Frederick S., Alison B.; m. Phillip Shatz, May 27, 1988. AB, Vassar Coll., 1951; MA, Columbia U., 1952, PhD, 1963, JD, 1994. Instr. Vassar Coll., Poughkeepsie, N.Y., 1952-54, 59, 59-60, 63, dean studies, prof. econs., 1973-75, v.p. for student affairs, 1975-80, v.p. for adminstrn. and student services and prof. econs., 1980-91, prof. econs., 1991-94; teaching fellow Wesleyan U., Middletown, Conn., 1955-56; from asst. prof. to prof. SUNY, New Paltz, 1964-73; prof. econs. Vassar Coll., Poughkeepsie, N.Y., 1973-94; of counsel Anderson, Banks, Curran and Donoghue, Mt. Kisco, N.Y., 1994—. Editor: (with Howard Marshall) The History of Economic Thought, 1968; Keynes, Updated or Outdated, 1970; author: (with Howard Marshall) Collective Bargaining, 1971. Trustee St. Francis Hosp., 1979-88, Area Fund Dutchess County, 1981-87, Coll. New Rochelle, 1994—, Hudson Valley Philharm., 1985-92, pres., 1989-91. Mem. AAUP, Am. Assn. Higher Edn., Am. Econ. Assn., AAUW (v.p. N.Y. State div. 1964-66), Poughkeepsie Vassar Club (pres. 1965-67). Home: PO Box 2470 Poughkeepsie NY 12603-8470

MARSHALL, NATHALIE, artist, writer, educator; b. Pitts., Nov. 10, 1932; d. Clifford Benjamin and Clarice (Stille) Marshall; m. Robert Alfred Van Buren, May 1, 1952 (div. June 1965); children: Christine Van Buren Popovic, Clifford Marshall Van Buren, Jennifer Van Buren Lake; m. David Arthur Nadel, Dec. 30, 1976 (div. Oct. 1995). AFA, Silvermine Coll. Art, New Canaan, Conn., 1967; BFA, U. Miami, Coral Gables, 1977, MA, 1982, PhD in English and Fine Art, 1982. Instr. humanities Miami Ednl. Consortium, Miami Shores, Fla., 1977-79, Barry U., Miami Shores, 1979-81, U. Miami, Coral Gables, 1977-81; sr. lectr. Nova U., Ft. Lauderdale, Fla., 1981-84, assoc. prof. humanities, 1985-86; prof. art, chair dept. art. Old Coll., Reno, Nev., 1986-88; chief artist Rockefeller U., N.Y.C., 1973-75; asst. registrar Lowe Art Mus., Coral Gables, 1976-78; co-founder, dir. The Bakehouse Art Complex, Miami, 1984-86; advisor, bd. mem. NAH YAH EE (Indian children's art exhibits), Weimar, Calif., 1984—; mem. adv. bd. New World Sch. Arts, Miami, 1985-86. One-woman shows include Silvermine Coll. Art, New Canaan, Conn., 1968, Ingber Gallery, Greenwich, 1969, Capricorn Gallery, N.Y.C., 1969, Pierson Coll. at Yale U., New Haven, 1970, The Art Barn, Greenwich, 1972, Art Unltd., N.Y.C., 1973, Benevy Gallery, N.Y.C., 1974, Richter Libr., U. Miami, 1985, Nova U., Ft. Lauderdale, 1985, Ward Nasse Gallery, N.Y.C., 1985, Old Coll., Reno, 1986, Washoe County Libr., Reno, 1987, Sabal Palms Gallery, Gulfport, Fla., 1992, Ambiance Gallery, St. Petersburg, 1995, 96, Gulfport Libr., 1996, Richter Lib. U. Miami, 1997; group shows include: Capricorn Gallery, N.Y.C., 1968, Ingber Gallery, Greenwich, 1968, Compass Gallery, N.Y.C., 1970, Optimums Gallery, Westport, Conn., 1970, Finch Coll. Mus., N.Y.C., 1971, Town Hall Art Gallery, Stamford, Conn., 1973, 74, Jewish Community Ctr., Miami Beach, 1981, Continuum Gallery, Miami Beach, 1982, South Fla. Art Inst., Hollywood, Fla., 1984, Met. Mus., Coral Gables, Fla., 1985, Ward Nasse Gallery, N.Y.C., 1985, Brunnier Mus., Iowa State U., Ames, 1986, Nat. Mus. of Women in The Arts Libr., Washington, 1987, 89, U.S. Art in Embassies Program, 1987-88, UN World Conf. Women, Nairobi, 1987, Raymond James Invitational, St. Petersburg, Fla., 1989-92, Arts Ctr., St. Petersburg, 1990, 91, 92, Global Gallery, Tampa, Fla., 1990, 91, Sabal Palms Gallery, Gulfport, Fla., 1992, No. Nat. Nicolet Coll., Rhineland, Wis., 1992, Internat. Biennale, Bordeaux, France, 1993, Salon de Vieux Colombier, Paris, 1993, Synchronicity Space, N.Y.C., 1993, Women's 1st Internat. Biennal of Women Artists, Stockholm, 1994-95 (gold medal), Tampa Arts Forum, Fla., 1995, 96, Salon Internat. des Seigneurs de l'Art, Aix-en-Provence, France, 1995 (silver medal), World's Women Online Internet Installation Ariz. State U. 1995-96, UN 4th Conf. on Women, Beijing, 1995-96, Artemisa Gallery, Chgo., 1995-96; author, artist: Vibrations on Revelations, 1973, The Firebird, 1982, Homage to John Donne's Holy Sonnets 10 & 13, 1987, Tidepool, 1995, What is a Book?, 1997; numerous artist books, 1968—; author: Be Organized for College, 1980; artist: (children's book) The Desert: What Lives There?, 1972; editor, designer: Court Theaters of Europe, 1982; writer, dir. T.V. programs Moutain Mandala: Autumn, Mountain Mandala: Winter, The Unexpected, 1992; contbr. poems to poetry mags., articles to profl. jours. Recipient Sponsor's award for Painting Greenwich Art Soc., 1967; Steven Buffton Meml. award Am. Bus. Women's Assn., 1980; grantee Poets & Writers, 1993; one of 300 global artists in Internat. Hope and Optimism Portfolio, Oxford. Mem. MLA, Coll. Art Assn., Nat. Women's Studies Assn., Women's Caucus for Art (nat. adv. bd. 1983-88, pres. Miami chpt. 1984-86, southeast regional v.p. 1986). Address: 3209 58th St S # 238 Gulfport FL 33707-6050

MARSHALL, NINA COLLEEN CLUBB, elementary school educator; b. Beaumont, Tex., Apr. 11, 1960; d. Thomas Joseph and Ella Lucille (Garvin) Clubb; m. David Louis Marshall, June 21, 1986; children: Sarah Lynn, Aaron Thomas. BS, Lamar U., 1981, M in Elem. Edn., 1988. Cert. elem., kindergarten, early childhood and math. tchr. Elem. tchr. East Chambers Ind. Sch. Dist., Winnie, Tex., 1982-85; middle sch. tchr. Conroe (Tex.) Ind. Sch. Dist., 1985-86, Nederland (Tex.) Ind. Sch. Dist., 1986-87, Port Arthur (Tex.) Ind. Sch. Dist., 1987-93, Hamshire-Fannett Ind. Sch. Dist., 1994—. Mem. ASCD, Nat. Coun. Tchrs. Math., Tex. Math. & Sci. Coaches Assn., Tex. State Tchrs. Assn., Tex. Classroom Tchrs. Home: RR 2 Box 2548 Beaumont TX 77705-9755

MARSHALL, (C.) PENNY, actress, director; b. N.Y.C., Oct. 15, 1943; d. Anthony W. and Marjorie Irene (Ward) M.; m. Michael Henry (div.); 1 child, Tracy Lee; m. Robert Reiner, Apr. 10, 1971 (div. 1979). Student, U. N.Mex., 1961-64. Appeared on numerous television shows, including The Odd Couple, 1972-74, Friends and Lovers (co-star), 1974, Let's Switch, 1974, Wives (pilot), 1975, Chico and the Man, 1975, Mary Tyler Moore, 1975, Heaven Help Us, 1975, Saturday Night Live, 1975-77, Happy Days, 1975, Battle of Network Stars (ABC special), 1976, Barry Manilow special, 1976, The Tonight Show, 1976-77, Dinah, 1976-77, Mike Douglas Show, 1975-77, Merv Griffin Show, 1976-77, Blansky's Beauties, 1977, Network Battle of the Sexes, 1977, Laverne and Shirley (co-star), 1976-83; TV films More Than Friends, 1978, Love Thy Neighbor, 1984, Challenge of a Lifetime, 1985, The Odd Couple: Together Again, 1993; appeared in motion pictures How Sweet It Is, 1967, The Savage Seven, 1968, The Grasshopper, 1970, 1941, 1979, Movers and Shakers, 1985, She's Having a Baby, 1988, The Hard Way, 1991, Hocus Pocus, 1993, Get Shorty, 1995; dir. films: Jumpin' Jack Flash, 1986, Big, 1988, Awakenings, 1990, A League of Their Own, 1992, Renaissance Man, 1994, The Preacher's Wife, 1996; co-exec. prodr. TV series A League of Their Own, 1993 (also dir. pilot); prodr. Getting Away With Murder, 1995.

MARSHALL, PHILIPS WILLIAMSON, insurance agency executive; b. Orange, N.J., Aug. 28, 1935; s. Herbert Jr. and Evelyn Lenore (Philips) M.; m. Sandra Richards Vose, Mar. 29, 1958; children: Tracy Anne Marshall Santa Florentina, Laurie Williamson Marshall Holbrook. BS in Econs., U. Pa., 1957. Enlisted U.S. Army, 1958, advanced through grades to capt., 1964, resigned, 1970; underwriter Continental Ins. Co., N.Y.C., 1957-60; salesman A.W. Marshall & Co., Newark, 1960-65; spl. agt. Aetna Ins. Co., Millburn, N.J., 1965-66; v.p. Woodward & Williamson, Jersey City, 1966-88; pres. Woodward & Williamson, 1988—; pres. Ind. Ins. Agts. Hudson County, Jersey City, 1979-80. Chmn. ARC-Millburn (N.J.)-Short Hills, 1971-74, Harriman Div. coun. ARC, N.Y.C., 1976-77; chief Millburn Aux. Police, Millburn, 1976-81. Mem. Ind. Ins. Agts. N.J. (exec. com. 1982-86, Presdl. Citation 1986), Ducks Unltd. (chmn. State of N.J. 1990-92), Short Hills Club. Republican. Episcopalian. Avocations: tennis, fishing, hunting. Home: 24 Meadowview Ln Berkeley Heights NJ 07922-1370 Office: Woodward & Williamson 25A Hanover Rd Florham Park NJ 07932-0165

MARSHALL, RICHARD, art historian, curator; b. L.A., 1947. B.A., Calif. State U., Long Beach, 1969; postgrad. U. Calif., Irvine, 1969-70. Advisor Mus. Modern Art, N.Y., 1974-77, Whitney Mus. Am. Art, curator, 1974-93. Art editor Paris Rev. mag., 1977-94; ind. curator, 1995—.

MARSHALL, RICHARD TREEGER, lawyer; b. N.Y.C., May 17, 1925; s. Edward and Sydney (Treeger) M.; m. Dorothy M. Goodman, June 4, 1950; children—Abigail Ruth Marshall Bergerson, Daniel Brooks; m. 2d, Sylvia J. Kelley, June 10, 1979. B.S., Cornell U., 1948; J.D., Yale U., 1951. Bar: Tex. 1952, U.S. Ct. Appeals (5th cir.) 1966, U.S. Ct. Appeals (10th cir.) 1980, U.S. Supreme Ct., 1959; lic. Tex. Dept. Ins. Sole practice, El Paso, Tex., 1952-59, 61-79; assoc. Fryer & Milstead, El Paso, 1952; sr. ptnr. Marshall & Wendorf, El Paso, 1959-61; sr. ptnr. Marshall & Volk, El Paso, 1979-81; sr. atty. Richard T. Marshall & Assocs., P.C., El Paso, 1981-85; sr. ptnr. Marshall, Thomas & Winters, El Paso, 1985-87, sr. atty. Marshall & Winters, 1987-88; sr. atty. Marshall, Sherrod & Winters, 1988-90, pvt. practice law, 1990—; instr. polit. sci. U. Tex., El Paso, 1961-62; instr. ins. law C.L.U. tng. course Am. Coll.; officer, dir. Advance Funding, Inc., El Paso. Mem. ABA, Coll. State Bar Tex., El Paso Bar Assn., El Paso Trial Lawyers Assn. (pres. 1965-66), Tex. Trial Lawyers Assn., Assn. Trial Lawyers Am. (sec. personal injury law sect. 1967-68, nat. sec. 1969-70, sec.-treas. environ. law sect. 1970-71, vice chmn. family law litigation sect. 1971-72); Roscoe Pound-Am. Trial Lawyers Found. (Commn. on Profl. Responsibility 1979-82). Editor: El Paso Trial Lawyers Rev., 1973-80; contbr. articles to legal jours. Office: 5959 Gateway Blvd W El Paso TX 79925-3331

MARSHALL, ROBERT CHARLES, computer company executive; b. Berwyn, Ill., June 19, 1931; s. Joseph H. and Rose M.; m. Sarane Virruso, Aug. 1, 1954; children—Joseph, Lisa, Jim. B.S.E.E., Heald Engring. Coll., 1956; M.B.A., Pepperdine U., 1976. Engr. Lawrence Radiation Lab., Livermore, Calif., 1956-64; systems engr. Electronics Assos., Palo Alto, Calif., 1964-69; v.p. mfg. Diablo Systems, Hayward, Calif., 1969-75; with Tandem Computers, Inc., Cupertino, Calif., 1975—; sr. v.p., chief operating officer, dir. Tandem Computers, Inc., 1979-96; pres., CEO Info Gear, 1996—. Served with U.S. Army, 1952-54.

MARSHALL, ROBERT GERALD, language educator; b. Houston, Feb. 19, 1919; s. Luther Pierce and Nancy (May) M.; m. Kathryn Keller, Aug. 27, 1949; children—Christoph Patton, Ann Patterson, Philip Sanburn. B.A., Rice U., 1941, M.A., 1946; Ph.D., Yale, 1950; diploma, U. Siena, Italy, 1954. Asst., then instr. French Yale, 1947-49; asst. prof. fgn. langs. Tex. Women's U., 1949-51; mem. faculty Wells Coll., Aurora, N.Y., 1951—; prof. Romance langs. Wells Coll., 1958—, chmn. dept., 1956-72, coordinator summer programs, 1963-67; dir. NDEA Inst. Advanced Study French, 1963-67; prof.-in-charge Sweet Briar Coll. Jr. Year In Paris, France, 1967-68; dir. Jr. Year in France, 1972-84. Contbr. to profl. jours.; editor-in-chief: Catalogue of 16th Century Italian Books in American Libraries, 1970; editor: (with F. C. St. Aubyn) Les Mouches (Sartre), 1963, Trois Pièces Surréalistes, 1969, Abraham de Vermeil in Textes et Contexts, 1986, American, French, Italian Relationships in Mélanges André Bordeaux, 1988, Historic St. Michaels, An Architectural History; contbr. to Columbia Dictionary of Modern European Lit., 18th Century Bibliography. Commr., Historic Area Commn., St. Michaels, Historic Preservation Commn., Talbot County, Md. Served to capt. AUS, 1942-46. Decorated chevalier dans L'Ordre des Palmes Academiques France); R.G. Marshall scholarship named in his honor Sweet Briar Coll.; grantee Am. Council Learned Socs., 1953; Fulbright research grantee Rome, Italy, 1959-60. Mem. Am. Assn. Tchrs. French (v.p. Central N.Y. chpt. 1965-67, pres. Va. chpt. 1979-84), South Atlantic Modern Lang. Assn., Soc. Profs. français à l'Etranger. Episcopalian. Home: PO Box 1059 Saint Michaels MD 21663-1059

MARSHALL, ROBERT HERMAN, economics educator; b. Harrisburg, Pa., Dec. 6, 1929; s. Mathias and Mary (Bubich) M.; m. Billie Marie Sullivan, May 31, 1958; children: Mellisa Frances, Howard Hylton, Robert Charles. A.B. magna cum laude, Franklin and Marshall Coll., 1951; M.A., Ohio State U., 1952, Ph.D., 1957. Teaching asst. Ohio State U., 1952-57; mem. faculty, then prof. econs. U. Ariz., Tucson, 1957-95, prof. emeritus, 1995; dir. Internat. Bus. Studies Project, 1969-71; research observer Sci.-Industry Program, Hughes Aircraft Co., Tucson, summer 1959. Author: Commercial Banking in Arizona: Structure and Performance Since World War II, 1966, (with others) The Monetary Process, 2d edit. 1980. Bd. dirs. Com. for Econ. Opportunity, Tucson, 1968-69. Faculty fellow Pacific Coast Banking Sch., summer 1974. Mem. Am. Econ. Assn., Phi Beta Kappa, Beta Gamma Sigma, Pi Gamma Mu, Phi Kappa Phi, Delta Sigma Pi. Democrat. Roman Catholic. Home: 6700 N Abington Rd Tucson AZ 85743-9795

MARSHALL, ROBERT LEWIS, musicologist, educator; b. N.Y.C., Oct. 12, 1939; s. Saul and Pearl (Shapiro) M.; m. Traute Maass, Sept. 9, 1966; children—Eric, Brenda. A.B., Columbia U., 1960; M.F.A., Princeton U., 1962, Ph.D., 1968; postgrad., U. Hamburg, W. Ger., 1965. Instr. dept. music U. Chgo., 1966-68, asst. prof., 1968-71, assoc. prof., chmn. dept., 1972-78, prof., 1978-83; prof. Brandeis U., 1983—, chmn. dept., 1985-93, incumbent endowed chair Louis, Frances and Jeffrey Sachar prof. music, 1986—; vis. assoc. prof. Princeton U., 1971-72; endowed prof. Univ. Ala., 1994; mem. rev. bd. rsch. materials program NEH, 1982, rev. bd. edits., 1991. Author: The Compositional Process of J.S. Bach, 2 vols., 1972, The Music of Johan Sebastian Bach: The Sources; The Style; The Significance, 1989, Mozart Speaks: Views on Music, Musicians and the World, 1991, Dennis Brain on Record: A Comprehensive Discography of His Solo, Chamber, and Orchestral Recordings, 1996; editor New Bach Edit., Eighteenth Century Keyboard Music, 1994; contbr. articles to musical jours. in U.S., Gt. Brit., Germany. Mem. music adv. bd. Ill. Arts Council, 1977-79. Recipient Deems Taylor award ASCAP, 1990; NEH fellow, 1978-79; Hon. Harold Spivacke consultantship Library of Congress. Mem. Am. Musicol. Soc. (bd. dirs. 1974-75, v.p. 1985-86, editl. bd. jour. 1975-80, rev. editor 1986-89, chmn. publs. com. 1991-94, Otto Kinkeldey prize 1974), New Bach Soc. (chmn. Am. chpt. 1977-80), Phi Beta Kappa. Home: 100 Chestnut St Newton MA 02165-2538 Office: Music Dept Brandeis U Waltham MA 02254

MARSHALL, ROBERT WILLIAM, lawyer, rancher; b. L.A., Apr. 12, 1933; s. Kenneth I. and Helen (Putnam) M.; m. Nanette Hollenbeck, June 10, 1965; children: Thomas, Victoria, Rebecca, Kathleen. AB in Pre Law, Stanford U., 1955, JD, 1957. Bar: Calif. 1958, Nev. 1958, U.S. Dist. Ct. (so. dist.) Calif. 1958, U.S. Dist. Ct. Nev. 1958. Assoc. Vargas & Bartlett, Reno, Nev., 1958-64; ptnr. Vargas & Bartlett, Reno, 1964-85, sr. ptnr., 1985-94; chmn. of bd. Marshall, Hill, Cassas & de Lipkau, 1994—. Advisor Explorer Boy Scouts Am., Reno, 1971-76, 87-89, scoutmaster Troop 444 Boy Scouts Am., Reno, 1981-85; state chmn. Nev. Young Reps., 1962-64. Mem. ABA, Nat. Cattlemen's Assn., Calif. Bar Assn., Nev. Bar Assn., Washoe County Bar Assn., Rocky Mountain Mineral Law Inst., No. Nev. Indsl. Gas Users (organizer), No. Nev. Large Power Users (organizer), So. Nev. Large Power Users (organizer), Nev. Cattlemen's Assn., Reno Stanford Club (pres. Reno chpt. 1974). Republican. Mormon. Office: Marshall Hill Cassas et al 333 Holcomb Ave Ste 300 Reno NV 89502-1664

MARSHALL, ROBERTA NAVARRE, middle school educator; b. Martinez, Calif., Sept. 26, 1949; d. Robert Frank and Navarre (Baggett) M. BS, Calif. Polytech. State U., 1971; MS in voc. edn., Calif. State U., 1981. Cert. secondary educator, Calif. Consumer-homemaking tchr. Hanford (Calif.) H.S., 1972-73, Eagle Mountain (Calif.) H.S., 1974-79, Solano Jr. H.S., Vallejo, Calif., 1980—; co-chairperson applied acads. dept. Solano Jr. H.S., Vallejo; competitive recognition events coord. FHA-HERO Region 3, 1991-95; workshop presenter. Middle grades curriculum task force Calif. Dept. Edn., Sacramento, 1987-88. Recipient home econs. curriculum grants, 1985-86, 89-90; named Tchr. of Yr. Elks Lodge, 1988-89. Mem. Calif. Tchrs. Assn., Home Econs. Tchrs. Assn. Calif. (v.p. 1991-93), Am. Assn. Univ. Women, Am. Voc. Assn., Am. Assn. Family & Consumer Scis., Future Homemakers of Am. (adv. 1972), Home Econs. Related Occupations, Delat Kappa Gamma (Theta Iota chpt.). Avocations: reading, needlework, walking, traveling. Home: 5038 Brittany Dr Suisun City CA 94585-6855 Office: Solano Jr H S 1025 Corcoran Ave Vallejo CA 94589-1844

MARSHALL, RUSSELL FRANK, consulting company executive; b. Fort Madison, Iowa, Sept. 10, 1941; s. William Frank and Dorothy Eleanor (Mikels) M.; m. Mary Jean Bailey, June 19, 1966; children: William Russell, Robert Scott, Gregory Howard. AB, Monmouth Coll., 1963; MS, U. Ill., 1965, PhD, 1971. Rsch. engr. Materials Rsch. Lab, Urbana, Ill., 1970-75; mgr. acad. computing Drake U., Des Moines, 1975-80; v.p. GMI Ltd., Des Moines, 1980-83; sr. v.p., treas. Communication Devel. Co., West Des Moines, 1983-96; pres. Marshall Assocs., West Des Moines, Iowa, 1996—; dir. info. svcs. Grand View Coll., Des Moines, 1996—. Contbr. articles to profl. jours. Active Boy Scouts Am., 1982—; mem. Des Moines Cmty. Theatre. Grantee AEC, 1964-71. Mem. Assn. Computing Machinery, Am. Phys. Soc., Assn. for Systems Mgmt., Sigma Xi. Presbyterian. Avocations: music, reading. Home: 1625 19th St West Des Moines IA 50265-1622

MARSHALL, SCOTT, advertising agency executive. V.p. Ogilvy & Mather, N.Y.C., sr. v.p., 1986-88; pres. Cole & Weber, Inc., Seattle, 1988—; pres Hal Riney & Ptnrs., Inc., San Francisco. Office: Hal Riney & Ptnrs 735 Battery St San Francisco CA 94111-1501

MARSHALL, SHARON BOWERS, nursing educator, director clinical trials; b. Alameda, Calif.; d. Stanley Jay and Rosalie Kathryn (Soldati) Bowers; m. Lawrence F. Marshall; children: Derek, Kathryn, Samantha. BS in Nursing, San Francisco State U., 1970. Charge nurse med./surg. unit Mt. Zion Hosp., San Francisco, 1970-73, charge nurse med./surg. ICU, 1973-75; clin. nurse U. Calif. San Diego Med. Ctr., 1975-78, coordinator neurotrauma study, 1978-79, project coordinator Nat. Traumatic Coma Data Bank, 1979-88, project mgr. Comprehensive Cen. Nervous System Injury Ctr., 1979-86, mgr. neurotrauma research, 1984-91, asst. clin. prof. neurol. surg. U. Calif. San Diego Sch. Medicine, 1992—; study dir. Internat. Tirilazad Study, 1991-95; prin. investigator Internat. Selfotel Trial, 1994-96. Author: Head Injury, 1981; Neuroscience Critical Care: Pathophysiology and Patient Management, 1990; contbr. articles to profl. jours. Mem. Internat. Soc. Study of Traumatic Brain Injury, Am. Assn. Neurosci. Nursing. Avocations: skiing, traveling. Office: 4130 La Jolla Village Dr La Jolla CA 92037-1480

MARSHALL, SHEILA HERMES, lawyer; b. N.Y.C., Jan. 17, 1934; d. Paul Milton and Julia Angela (Meagher) Hermes; m. James Josiah Marshall, Sept. 30, 1967; 1 child, James J.H. BA, St. John's U., N.Y.C., 1959; JD, NYU, 1963. Bar: N.Y. 1964, U.S. Ct. Appeals (2d, 3d, 5th and D.C. cirs.), U.S. Supreme Ct. 1970. Assoc. LeBoeuf, Lamb, Greene & MacRae, N.Y.C., 1963-72, ptnr., 1973—; specialist in field. Mem. ABA, N.Y. State Bar Assn., Assn. of Bar of City of N.Y. Republican. Home: 1035 Park Ave New York NY 10028-0912 Office: LeBoeuf Lamb Greene & MacRae 125 W 55th St New York NY 10019-5369

MARSHALL, SHERRIE, newspaper editor. Metro editor Star Tribune, Mpls. Office: Star Tribune 425 Portland Ave Minneapolis MN 55415-1511*

MARSHALL, SIRI SWENSON, corporate lawyer. BA, Harvard U., 1970; JD, Yale U., 1974. Bar: N.Y. 1975. Assoc. Debevoise & Plimpton, 1974-79; atty., sr. atty., asst. gen. counsel Avon Products, Inc., N.Y.C., 1979-85, v.p. legal affairs, 1985-89, sr. v.p., gen. counsel, 1990-94; sr. v.p., gen. counsel Gen. Mills, Inc., Mpls., 1994—. Office: Gen Mills Inc Number One Gen Mills Blvd Minneapolis MN 55426

MARSHALL, STANLEY, former educator, business executive; b. Cheswick, Pa., Jan. 27, 1923; s. Walter W. and Mildred (Crawford) M.; m. Ruth Cratty, June 10, 1944 (div. 1966); children: David, Sue, John; m. Shirley Ann Slade, Sept. 10, 1966; children: Kimberly, James Andrew. B.S., Slippery Rock (Pa.) State Tchrs. Coll., 1947; M.S., Syracuse U., 1950, Ph.D., 1956. Tchr. sci. Mynderse Acad., Seneca Falls, N.Y., 1947-52; asst. prof. sci. State U. N.Y. Coll. Edn., Cortland, 1953-55; asso. prof. State U. N.Y. Coll. Edn., 1956-57, prof., 1957-58; instr. Syracuse U., 1955-56; prof., head dept. sci. edn. Fla. State U., Tallahassee, 1958; asso. dean Fla. State U. (Sch. Edn.), 1965-67; dean Fla. State U. (Coll. Edn.), 1967-69, pres., 1969-76; pres. Sonitrol of Tallahassee, Inc., 1978-87, COMSAFE Inc., 1981-84; pres. James Madison Inst. for Pub. Policy Studies, 1987-90, chmn. bd. dirs., 1990—; pres. Marshall Land Co., 1989—; pres. So. Scholarship and Research Found., 1968-69. Author: (with E. Burkman) Current Trends in Science Education, 1966, (with I. Podendorf and C. Swartz) The Basic Science Program, 1965; Editor: Jour. of Research in Sci. Teaching, 1962-66; Mem. editorial bd.: Science World, 1962-65; Contbr. articles to profl. jours. Mem. U.S. Navy Sec.'s adv. bd. edn. and tng. U.S. Army adv. panel ROTC, 1975-79; bd. regents Nat. Libr. Medicine, 1970-75; bd. dirs. Tallahassee Meml. Regional Med. Ctr., 1980-86; mem. Citizens Commn. on the Fla. Cabinet, 1995-96; trustee Bethune Cookman Coll., 1993—. Fellow AAAS; mem. Am. Inst. Physics, Nat. Sci. Tchrs. Assn., Fla. Acad. Scis., Fla. Assn. Sci. Tchrs., So. Assn. State Univs. and Land-Grant Colls (pres. 1971-72), Nat. Assn. Research Sci. Teaching, NEA, Fla. Edn. Assn., Sigma Xi, Phi Delta Kappa, Kappa Delta Pi. Home: 5000 Brill Pt Tallahassee FL 32312-5600

MARSHALL, SUSAN, choreographer; b. Hershey, Pa.. Student, Julliard Sch. Founder, artistic dir. Susan Marshall & Co., N.Y.C., 1982—. Recipient Dance Mag. award, 1995. Office: Dance Continuum Inc Box 707 Cooper Sta New York NY 10276-0707

MARSHALL, THOM, columnist. Columnist The Houston Chronicle, Tex. Office: Houston Chronicle 801 Texas St Houston TX 77002-2906*

MARSHALL, THOMAS CARLISLE, applied physics educator; b. Cleveland, Ohio, Jan. 29, 1935; s. Stephen Irby and Bertha Marie (Bieger) M.; children—Julian, John. B.Sc., Case Inst. Tech., 1957; M.Sc., U. Ill., 1958, Ph.D., 1960. Asst. prof. elec. engring. U. Ill., 1961-62; mem. faculty Columbia U., 1962—, asst. prof. elec. engring., 1962-65, assoc. prof., 1965-70, prof. engring. sci., 1970-78, prof. applied physics, 1978—. Author: Free Electron Lasers, 1985, Book of the Toade, 1992; contbr. over 100 articles to profl. jours. Research grantee Dept. Energy, Office Naval Research, NSF. Fellow Am. Phys. Soc. (study group on directed energy weapons 1985-87), Free Election Lasers and Accelerator Physics. Office: Columbia U 213 Mudd Bldg New York NY 10027

MARSHALL, THOMAS OLIVER, JR., lawyer; b. Americus, Ga., June 24, 1920; s. Thomas Oliver and Mattie Louise (Hunter) M.; m. Angie Ellen Fitts, Dec. 20, 1946; children: Ellen Irwin Marshall Beard, Anne Hunter Marshall Peagler, Mary Olivia Marshall Hodges. BS in Engring., U.S. Naval Acad., 1941; JD, U. Ga., 1948. Bar: Ga. 1947. Pvt. practice law Americus, Ga., 1948-60; judge S.W. Judicial Circuit, Americus, 1960-74, Ga. Ct. Appeals, Atlanta, 1974-77; justice Ga. Supreme Ct., Atlanta, 1977-86, chief justice, 1986-89; pvt. practice Atlanta, 1989—; chmn. bd. visitors U. Ga. Law Sch., 1970. Trustee Andrew Coll., So. Ga. Meth. Home for Aged; active ARC, 1948-60, United Givers Fund, 1948-54. Served with USN, World War II, Korean War. Decorated Bronze Star; named Young Man of Yr. Americus, 1953. Mem. ABA, Ga. Bar Assn. (bd. govs. 1958-60), Atlanta Bar Assn., State Bar Ga., Am. Judicature Soc., Nat. Jud. Coll., Jud. Coll. Ga., VFW, Am. Legion. Methodist. Lodges: Kiwanis, Masons, Shriners. Home: 238 15th St NE Apt 3 Atlanta GA 30309-3594 Office: 230 Peachtree St NW Ste 1100 Atlanta GA 30303-1513

MARSHALL, TREVOR GORDON, computer company executive, editor; b. Adelaide, Australia, Nov. 16, 1948; came to U.S., 1982; s. Jeffrey Gordon Marshall and Cynthia Olive (Overall) Paton; m. Frances Elizabeth Schuman, June 1, 1970; 1 child, Karen Nicole. BE, U. Adelaide, 1974, ME, 1978; PhD, U. Western Australia, 1985. Sr. tutor Papua New Guinea U. of Tech., 1974; lectr. Curtin U., Perth, Australia, 1975-80; COO Definicon Sys. Inc., Newbury Park, Calif., 1984-87; chmn., CEO YARC Sys. Corp., Newbury Park, 1988—. Cons. editor: Byte Mag., Peterborough, N.H., 1989—. 1st lt. Australian Army, 1966-82. Recipient Region 10 Student Paper prize IEEE, 1974. Office: YARC Sys Corp 975 Business Center Cir Newbury Park CA 91320-1126

MARSHALL, TREVOR JOHN, engineering professional; b. Faversham, Kent, U.K., Jan. 5, 1954; came to U.S., 1992; s. John Rodney and Margaret (Hutchinson) M.; m. Kathleen Patricia Keenan, May 22, 1994. B of Chemistry, Leicester U., 1975. Rsch. chemist Ever Ready Batteries, London, 1975-80; tech. devel. coord. Ever Ready Batteries, Oxford, U.K., 1981-83; project mgr. Renata Batteries, Sissach, Switzerland, 1983-84; tech. coord. Alupower, Inc., Bernardsville, N.J., 1985-86; battery devel. cons. UKAEA (Lithium Batteries), Harwell, U.K., 1987-88; industry mgr. Freudenberg, Halifax, U.K., 1988-92; product engr. mgr. Seatronics, Inc., Hatboro, Pa., 1992—; cons. Piles Wonder, Paris, 1984, Gold Peak Industries, Hong Kong, 1984. Mem. Internat. Battery Data Registry. Avocation: indsl. archaeology. Office: Seatronics Co Inc 3235 Sunset Ln Hatboro PA 19040-4528

MARSHALL, VICTOR FRAY, physician, educator; b. Culpeper, Va., Sept. 1, 1913; s. Otis and Marie Josephine (Riton) M.; m. Barbara Walsh, Dec. 11, 1943; children—Fray F., Victor R., Philip S. M.D., U. Va., 1937; D.Sc., Washington and Lee U., 1975. Diplomate: Am. Bd. Urology (past pres.). Intern N.Y. Hosp., 1937-38; tng. in gen. surgery and urology Cornell U. Med. Coll.-N.Y. Hosp., 1938-43, staff mem., 1943-88; attending-in-charge urology James Buchanan Brady Found., 1949-78; faculty Med. Coll., Cornell U., 1938-81, asso. prof. clin. surgery urology, 1947-57, prof. clin. surgery (urology), 1957-78, James J. Colt prof. urology in surgery, 1970-78, head service urology, 1946-78, emeritus, 1978-88; prof. urology U. Va., Charlottesville, 1979-83; cons., 1983-88, ret., 1988; asst. attending surgeon Meml. Center for Cancer and Allied Diseases, 1943-52, assoc. attending, 1952-67, attending surgeon, 1967-83, emeritus, 1983—. Contbr. articles to med. jours. Fellow ACS, N.Y. Acad. Medicine (Valentine medal 1974); mem. AAAS, N.Y. Urol. Soc. (past pres.), Am. Urol. Assn. (Guiteras award 1975), N.Y. Cancer Soc. (past pres.), Soc. Pelvic Surgeons (past pres.), Mexican Acad. Surgery, Am. Surg. Assn., Am. Acad. Pediatrics, Soc. Pediatric Urology, Clin. Soc. Genito-Urinary Surgeons (pres. 1976), Surg. Soc. Venezuela, Mexican Urol. Soc., Brit. Assn. Urol. Surgeons, Venezuelan Soc. Urology, Am. Assn. Genito-Urinary Surgeons (Barringer medal 1970, Keyes medal 1994), Canadian Urol. Assn. (hon.), Royal Coll. Surgeons Ireland (hon.), Alpha Omega Alpha, Pi Kappa Alpha, Nu Sigma Nu. Home: The Colonades C8 2600 Barracks Rd Charlottesville VA 22901-2100

MARSHALL, VINCENT DE PAUL, industrial microbiologist, researcher; b. Washington, Apr. 5, 1943; s. Vincent de Paul Sr. and Mary Frances (Bach) M.; m. Sylvia Ann Kieffer, Nov. 15, 1986; children from previous marriage: Vincent de Paul III, Amy. BS, Northeastern State Coll., Tahlequah, Okla., 1965; MS, U. Okla. Health Sci. Ctr., Oklahoma City, 1967, PhD, 1970. Rsch. assoc. U. Ill., Urbana, 1970, postdoctoral fellow, 1971-73; rsch. scientist The Upjohn Co., Kalamazoo, Mich., 1973-74, rsch. head, 1975, sr. rsch. scientist, 1976-91, sr. scientist, 1991—. Mem. editorial bd. Jour. of Antibiotics, 1990—, Jour. Indsl. Microbiology, 1989—, Devels. in Indsl. Microbiology, 1990; contbr. numerous articles to profl. jours., chpts. to books; patentee in field. Served with U.S. Army Nat. Guard, 1960-65. NIH predoctoral fellow, 1967-70; NIH postdoctoral fellow, 1971-73. Fellow Am. Acad. Microbiology; mem. Soc. for Indsl. Microbiology (membership com. 1988-90, co-chair edn. com. 1989-93, local sects. com. 1991—, chair nominating com. 1993-94, co-chair program com. 1993-94, dir. 1994-96, pres. Ind. sect. 1992-95), Am. Soc. Microbiology, Am. Soc. Biochemistry and Molecular Biology, Internat. Soc. for Antimicrobial Activity of Non-Antibiotics (sci. adv. bd.), Sigma Xi. Republican. Episcopalian. Home: 203 Paisley Ct Kalamazoo MI 49006-4359 Office: Pharmacia and Upjohn Inc Chem & Biol Screening 7000 Portage Rd Kalamazoo MI 49001-0102

MARSHALL, VIRGINIA MARY, technology educator; b. Medford, Mass., Nov. 2, 1940; d. Frederick Edward and Louise Angela (Lombardi) Gordinier; m. Dana Philip Marshall, Apr. 17, 1970; children: Jennifer Susanne, Kristin Terese Justyne Marshall. BS in Secondary Edn. cum laude, Salem (Mass.) State Coll., 1962; MS in Secondary Edn., Boston State Coll., 1967; MS in Edn. Libr. Media, Bridgewater State Coll., 1992. Cert. secondary tchr. and libr. media specialsit, Mass. Tchr. English Somerville (Mass.) Sch. System, 1962-73; tchr. jr. high Blessed Sarament Sch., Walpole, Mass., 1983—, sch. libr. media sepcialist, 1991—; literary cons. Koller Enterprises, 1971; pres. Glass Castle, 1974-83, Ginny's Pincushion, 1983-87. Named Outstanding Young Educator, Somerville Jaycees, 1970, Am. Yearbook Outstanding Advisor, 1970, 71. Mem. NEA, Mass. Sch. Libr. Media Assn., Nat. Coun. English Tchrs. Avocations: reading, mountain climbing, sewing, bee keeping. Home: 17 Country Club Dr Walpole MA 02081-3417

MARSHALL, WAYNE KEITH, anesthesiology educator; b. Richmond, Va., Feb. 9, 1948; s. Chester Truman and Lois Ann (Tiller) M.; m. Dale Claire Reynolds, June 18, 1977; children: Meredith Reynolds, Catherine Truman, Whitney Wood. BS in Biology, Va. Poly. Inst. and State U., 1970; MD, Va. Commonwealth U., 1974. Diplomate Am. Bd. Anesthesiology, Nat. Bd. Med. Examiners; bd. cert. in pain mgmt. Surg. intern U. Cin., 1974-75, resident in surgery, 1975-77; resident in anesthesiology U. Va. Coll. Medicine, Charlottesville, 1977-79, rsch. fellow, 1979-80; asst. prof. anesthesia Pa. State U. Coll. Medicine, Hershey, 1980-86, assoc. prof., 1986-95, assoc. clin. dir. oper. rm., 1982-95, dir. pain mgmt. svc., 1984-95, chief divsn. pain mgmt., 1992-95; prof., chmn. dept. anesthesiology Med. Coll. Va., Richmond, 1995—; med. dir. operating rms. MCV Hosp., 1995—; moderator nat. meetings. Mem. editorial bd. Am. Jour. Anesthesiology, 1987—, Jour. Neurosurg. Anesthesiology, 1988—; contbr. articles and abstracts to med. jours. Recipient Antarctic Svc. medal NSF, 1980. Mem. AMA, Soc. Neurosurg. Anesthesia and Critical Care (sec.-treas. 1985-87, v.p. 1987-88, pres. 1989-90, bd. dirs. 1985-91), Assn. Univ. Anesthetists, Am. Soc. Anesthesiologists (del. ASA ho. of dels. 1990-92), Internat. Anesthesia Rsch. Soc., Pa. Soc. Anesthesiology. Republican. Baptist. Office: VCU Med Coll Va Dept Anesthesiology PO Box 980695 Richmond VA 23298-0695

MARSHALL, WILLIAM, III, think tank executive; b. Norfolk, Va., 1952; m. Katryn S. Nicolai; children: Olivia, William. BA in English and History, U. Va., 1975. Reporter Richmond Times-Dispatch; various positions on Capitol Hill and electoral politics; policy dir. Dem. Leadership Coun., 1985—; pres. Progressive Found.; pres., founder Progressive Policy Inst., Washington, 1989—; Sr. editor 1984 House Dem. Caucus policy, Renewing America's Promise; participant in drafting nat. legis., including a demonstration project for vol. nat. svc. Nat. Cmty. Svc. Act of 1990; press sec., spokesman, speechwriter for 1984 U.S. Senate campaign of current N.C. Gov. Jim Hunt; speechwriter, policy analyst for late U.S. Rep. Gillis Long of La., chmn. of House Dem. Caucus; spokesman, speechwriter 1982 U.S. Senate campaign of former Va. Lt. Gov. Dick Davis. Co-editor: Mandate for Change, 1992; contbr. articles to profl. jours. Office: Progressive Policy Inst 518 C St NE Washington DC 20002-5810*

MARSHALL, WILLIAM EDWARD, historical association executive; b. St. Paul, Apr. 19, 1925; s. William Edward and Louise (White) M.; m. Ruth Marie Winner, Sept. 3, 1947 (div.); children: Michael Scott, Terry Lee, Sharon; m. Loretta E. Slota, Nov. 6, 1976; children: Marc William, Matthew Ryan. B.A., Mont. State U., 1950; B.F.A., Wittenberg U., 1951; postgrad., Ohio State U., 1951-52. Owner, operator Public Library Public Relations Service, 1952-55, Specialized Press, 1952-60; graphic and exhibits designer Ohio Hist. Soc., 1952-60, State Historic Soc. Colo., Denver, 1960-61; dep. exec. dir. State Historic Soc. Colo., 1961-63, exec. dir., 1963-79; cons. to hist. agys., author, 1979—; founding mem. Little Kingdom Hist. Found.; condr. historic interpretation seminars and workshops. Author historic TV and film prodns., books, fiction and non-fiction in nat. publs.; editor: Humboldt Historian, 1990-91, CEO MediFacts, 1992—; illustrator, photographer books and periodicals; contbr. articles to profl. jours. Bd. dirs. Rocky Mountain Center on Environment, 1967-72, Trinidad Mus. Soc., 1986-89; chmn. Colo. Humanities Program Com., 1971, 75. With USMCR, 1943-45. Mem. Am. Assn. Museums (exec. com. 1973-74, mus. accreditation evaluator), Am. Assn. State and Local History (mem. council 1966-72, awards com. 1966-80, com. on fed. programs in history), Orgn. Am. Historians (hist. sites com. 1974-75). Presbyterian. Home: Moonstone Heights 719 Driver Rd Trinidad CA 95570-9722

MARSICANO, HAZEL ELLIOTT, education educator; b. Wilkes-Barre, Pa., Sept. 1, 1932; d. Paul Good and Helen Grace (Buckalew) Elliott; m. Joseph R. Marsicano, Sept. 29, 1951; children: Joselle A., Elizabeth A. BS in Nursery-Elem. Edn., SUNY, Buffalo, 1966, MS in Elem. Sch. Prin. and Supr. Elem. S, 1970, EdD in Early Childhood Edn., 1977. Cert. kindergarten, elem. tchr., elem. prin. Tchr., presch. dir. Niagara Falls (N.Y.) Pub. Schs., 1966-77; asst. prof. Ea. Mont. Coll., Billings, 1977-78, W.Va. U., Morgantown, 1978-83; prof. early childhood edn. Troy (Ala.) State U., dir. devel. reading program, 1983—; dir. Trojan Learning Ctr., Troy, Ala. Author numerous short stories and interactive video programs. Mem. Nat. Assn. Edn. Young Children, Ala. Assn. Tchr. Educators (Outstanding Tchr. Educator award 1990), Ea. Edn. Rsch. Assn., Ala. Assn. Young Children, So. Assn. for Children Under Six, Ala. Assn. Early Childhood Tchr. Educators (Outstanding Leadership award 1990), Post Secondary Reading Coun. Ala., Phi Delta Kappa, Delta Kappa Gamma (past pres.), Kappa Delta Pi. Avocations: leading workshops, cons. Home: 218 W Walnut St Troy AL 36081-2038

MARSIK, FREDERIC JOHN, microbiologist; b. Camden, N.J., June 22, 1943; s. Ferdinand Vincent and Helen (Reidl) M.; children: Terri Jean, Kristi Ann Marsik McCann. BA, Lebanon Valley Coll., 1965; MS, U. Mo., 1970, PhD, 1973. Diplomate Am. Bd. Med. Microbiology. Clin. microbiology staff Hartford (Conn.) Hosp., 1973-76; asst. prof. U. Va. Sch. Medicine, Charlottesville, 1976-80; tech. dir. microbiology and serology Children's Hosp. Wis., Milw., 1980-84; assoc. prof. microbiology and internal medicine Oral Roberts U. Sch. Medicine, Tulsa, 1984-87; dir. microbiology Crozer-Chester Med. Ctr., Upland, Pa., 1987-88; dir. R&D Becton Dickinson Microbiology Sys., Cockeysville, Md., 1988-96; microbiologist FDA, Rockville, Md., 1996—; mem. adv. com. Milw. Area Tech. Coll., Milw., 1983-84, Tulsa Jr. Coll., 1985-87; mem. rev. bd. Clin. Lab. Sci. Publ., Washington, 1990—. Contbr. chpts. to textbooks. Treas. Rose Fire Co. and Ambulance Svc., New Freedom, Pa., 1989—; alumni amb. Lebanon Valley Coll., 1991—; adult edn. com. So. York County Sch. Dist., Glen Rock, Pa., 1989—. Lt. col. USAR. Recipient Best Rsch. Project award S.W. Assn. for Clin. Microbiology, 1984. Mem. Am. Soc. Microbiology (mem. lab. practices com. 1990—), Am. Soc. Med. Tech., N.Y. Acad. Scis. Congregationalist. Avocations: fishing, camping, basketball. Home: 244 E Main St New Freedom PA 17349 Office: FDA 5600 Fishers Ln # 520 Rockville MD 20857-0001

MARSOLAIS, HAROLD RAYMOND, trade association administrator; b. Troy, N.Y., Mar. 10, 1942; s. Harold George and Viola Marie (Chamberlain) M.; m. Susan Lemieux, Jul. 5, 1964; children: Michelle, Harold R. BS, U. So. Miss., 1974; MS, Webster Coll., 1979. Officer US Army, 1961-82; CEO Minn. Dak. Hardware Assn., Mpls., 1982-84, Penn. ATL. Sbd. Hardware Assn., Harrisburg, Pa., 1984-87; v.p. sales Natl. Retail Hardware Assn., Indpls., Ind., 1987-89; CEO Nat. Retail Hardware Assn., Indpls., 1989-94; pres. Marsolais & Assoc., 1995—; exec. dir. Russell Mueller Found. 1989-94, Home Center Inst. 1987-94; exec. v.p. Profl. Ins. Agts. Fla., Tallahassee, 1996. Author: Guide to FAA Reg., 1971, In Store Merchandising, 1987, Doing the Right Thing: An Environmental Guide, 1994. Dir. Jr. Chamber, Hattiesburg, Pa., Rotary Intl., Harrisburg, Pa. Recipient W.B. Harlan Business award U. So. Miss., 1974, Outstanding Young Man Jaycees, Hattiesburg, 1974. Decorated Distinguished Flying Cross. Mem. Am. Soc. Assn. Exec. Avocations: golf, boating, flying. Office: Marsolais and Assocs 115 S Lake Cir Saint Augustine FL 32095-1750

MARSTERS, GERALD FREDERICK, retired aerospace science and technology executive; b. Summerville, N.S., Can., Dec. 18, 1932; s. Ralpha Roland and Madge Thelma (Harvey) M.; m. Lorena May Gunter, Oct. 23, 1954; children: Mariko Collette, Cynthia Denise. BS, Queens U., Kingston, Ont., Can., 1962; PhD, Cornell U., 1967. Registered profl. engr., Ont., Can. Prof. mech. engring. Queen's U., 1967-82; dir. airworthiness Dept. of Transport, Ottawa, 1982-87; dir. gen. Inst. for Aerospace Rsch., Nat. Rsch. Coun., Ottawa, 1987-94; ret., 1994; proprietor, cons. AeroVations Aerospace Tech. Specialists; nat. del. adv. group Aerospace Rsch. (NATO), Paris, 1987-94. Flying officer Royal Can. Airforce, 1953-58. Recipient Gold medal for Extraordinary Svc. FAA, 1986. Fellow AIAA, Can. Aero. and Space Inst. (past pres. 1992-93), Can. Acad. Engring., Can. Soc. for Mech. Engring.; mem. SAE (aerospace coun. 1985). Avocations: recreational flying, model railroads. Home: 39 Westpark Dr, Gloucester, ON Canada K1B 3G6

MARSTON, EDGAR JEAN, III, lawyer; b. Houston, July 5, 1939; s. Edgar Jr. and Jean (White) M.; m. Graeme Meyers, June 21, 1961; children: Christopher Graham, Jonathan Andrew. BA, Brown U., 1961; JD, U. Tex., 1964. Bar: Tex. 1964. Law clk. to presiding justice Supreme Ct. Tex., Austin, 1964-65; assoc. Baker & Botts, Houston, 1965-71; ptnr. Bracewell & Patterson, Houston, 1971-89, 96—, of counsel, 1990-96; exec. v.p., gen. counsel Southdown, Inc., Houston, 1987-95, also bd. dirs. Mem. ABA, Tex. Bar Assn., Tex. Bar Found., Houston Bar Assn., Houston Country Club, Coronado Club. Episcopalian. Avocations: hunting, fishing, philately, reading. Office: Bracewell & Patterson 711 Louisiana St Ste 2900 Houston TX 77002-2721

MARSTON, MICHAEL, urban economist, asset management executive; b. Oakland, Calif., Dec. 4, 1936; s. Lester Woodbury and Josephine (Janovic) M.; m. Alexandra Lynn Geyer, Apr. 30, 1966; children: John, Elizabeth. BA, U. Calif., Berkeley, 1959; postgrad. London Sch. Econs., 1961-63. V.p. Larry Smith & Co., San Francisco, 1969-72, exec. v.p. urban econ. divsn., 1969-72; chmn. bd. Keyser Marston Assocs., Inc., San Francisco, 1973-87; gen. ptnr. The Sequoia Partnership, 1979-91; pres. Marston Vineyard and Winery, 1982—, Marston Assocs., Inc., 1982—, The Ctr. for Individual and Instnl. Renewal, 1996—. Cert. rev. appraiser Nat. Assn. Rev. Appraisers and Mortgage Underwriters, 1984—. Chmn., San Francisco Waterfront Com., 1969-86; chmn. fin. com., bd. dirs., mem. exec. com., treas. San Francisco Planning and Urban Rsch. Assn., 1976-87, Napa Valley Vintners, 1986—, mem. gov. affairs com.; trustee Cathedral Sch. for Boys, 1981-82, Marin Country Day Sch., 1984-90; v.p. St. Luke's Sch., 1986-91; pres. Presidio Heights Assn. of Neighbors, 1983-84; chmn. Presidio Com. 1991—; v.p., bd. dirs., mem. exec. com. People for Open Space, 1972-87; mem. Gov.'s Issue Analysis Com. and Speakers Bur., 1966; mem. speakers bur. Am. Embassy, London, 1961-63; v.p., bd. dirs. Dem. Forum, 1968-72; v.p., trustee Youth for Service. Served to lt. USNR. Mem. Napa Valley Vintners, Urban Land Inst., World Congress Land Policy (paper in field), Order of Golden Bear, Chevalier du Tastevin, Bohemian Club, Pacific Union Club, Lambda Alpha. Contbr. articles to profl. jours. Home: 3375 Jackson St San Francisco CA 94118-2018 *Personal philosophy: Success is what you do with what you have not what others think or what is in vogue.*

MARSTON, ROBERT ANDREW, public relations executive; b. Astoria, N.Y., Aug. 6, 1937; s. Frank and Lena (DiDomenico) M.; m. Maryann Doherty, Sept. 23, 1990; children: Robert Brendan, Bradford Scott. BA, Hofstra U., 1959. Sr. v.p. Rowland Co., N.Y.C., 1959-68, Rogers & Cowen, Inc., N.Y.C., 1968-70; founder, chmn., CEO Robert Marston And Assocs., Inc., N.Y.C., 1970—. Contbr. articles and photographs to profl. jours. and popular mags. Mem. Pub. Rels. Soc. Am. (counselors sect.), Marco Polo Club, Doubles Club, Southampton Bath & Tennis Club. Roman Catholic. Home: 570 Park Ave New York NY 10021-7370 also: 130 Captains Neck Ln Southampton NY 11968-4561 Office: 485 Madison Ave New York NY 10022-5803

MARSTON, ROBERT QUARLES, university president; b. Toano, Va., Feb. 12, 1923; s. Warren and Helen (Smith) M.; m. Ann Carter Garnett, Dec. 21, 1946; children: Ann, Robert, Wesley. B.S., Va. Mil. Inst., 1943; M.D., Med. Coll. Va., 1947; B.Sc. (Rhodes scholar 1947-49), Oxford (Eng.) U., 1949; B.Sc. 6 hon. degrees. Intern Johns Hopkins Hosp., 1949-50; resident Vanderbilt U. Hosp., 1950-51; resident Med. Coll. Va., 1953-54, asst. prof. medicine, 1954; asst. prof. bacteriology and immunology U. Minn., 1958-59; asso. prof. medicine, asst. dean charge student affairs Med. Coll. Va., 1959-61; dean U. Miss. Sch. Medicine, 1961-66; dir. U. Miss. Sch. Medicine (Med. Center), 1961-65, vice chancellor, 1965-66; asso. dir. div. regional med. programs NIH, 1966-68; adminstr. Fed. Health Services and Mental Health Adminstrn., 1968; dir. NIH, Bethesda, Md., 1968-73; scholar in residence U. Va., Charlottesville, 1973-74; Disting. fellow Inst. of Medicine, Nat. Acad. Scis., 1973-74; pres. U. Fla., 1974-84, pres. emeritus, emeritus prof. medicine, emeritus prof. fish and aquaculture; bd. dirs. Johnson and Johnson, Nat. Bank Alachua, Wackenhut Corp.; chmn. bd. dirs. Cordis Corp.; chmn., mem. Fla. Marine Fisheries Commn. Author articles in field. Chmn. Commn. on Med. Edn. for Robert Wood Found.; chmn. Safety Adv. Bd. Three Mile Island; chmn. adv. com. med. implications of nuclear war NAS; exec. coun. Assn. Am. Med. Coll., 1964-67; past chmn. exec. com. Nat. Assn. State Univs. and Land Grant Colls., chmn., 1982. 1st lt. AUS, 1951-53. Decorated Knight of North Star (Sweden); Markle scholar, 1954-59; hon. fellow Lincoln Coll. Oxford U. Fellow Am. Pub. Health Assn.; mem. Inst. Medicine of NAS, AAAS, Am. Hosp. Assn. (hon.), Nat. Med. Assn. (hon.), Assn. Am. Rhodes Scholars, Assn. Am. Physicians, Assn. Am. Med. Colls. (disting. mem.), Am. Clin. and Climatol. Assn., Soc. Scholars Johns Hopkins, Alpha Omega Alpha. Episcopalian. Home: 19810 Old Bellamy Rd Alachua FL 32615

MARSTON-SCOTT, MARY VESTA, nurse, educator; b. St. Stephen, N.B., Can., Apr. 5, 1924; d. George Frank and Betsey Mildred (Babb) M.; m. John Paul Scott, June 30, 1979. B.A., U. Maine, 1946; M.N., Yale U., 1951; M.P.H., Harvard U., 1957; M.A., Boston U., 1964, Ph.D., 1969. Research asst. Roscoe B. Jackson Meml. Lab., Bar Harbor, Maine, 1946-48; nurse, 1952-54; instr. Yale U. Sch. Nursing, 1955-56; nurse cons. Div. Nursing, Washington, 1957-62; asso. prof. Frances Payne Bolton Sch. Nursing, Case-Western Res. U., Cleve., 1969-74; prof. grad. program community health nursing Boston U., 1974-86; assoc. prof. Coll. Nursing U. Ill., Chgo., 1986-94, assoc. prof. emerita, 1994—; cons. in field. Contbr. articles to profl. jours. Served with USPHS, 1957-62. Fellow Am. Acad. Nursing; mem. Am. Psychol. Assn., Am. Public Health Assn., Am. Nurses Assn., Sigma Theta Tau. Home: 1052 Pinewood Ct Bowling Green OH 43402-2173 Office: U Ill Coll Nursing 845 S Damen Ave Chicago IL 60612-7350

MARTEL, JACQUES G., engineer, adminstrator. BA, Coll. Jean-de-Bréboeuf, Montreal, 1964; BScA in Engring. Physics, U. Montreal, 1968; PhD in Nuclear Engring., MIT, 1971. Dir. Gen. Indsl. Materials Inst. Nat. Rsch. Coun. Can., Boucherville, PQ, Canada. Office: Indsl Materials Rsch Inst, 75 De Mortagne Blvd, Boucherville, PQ Canada J4B 6Y4

MARTEL, PETRA JEAN HEGSTAD, elementary school educator; b. Oakland, Calif., May 27, 1944; d. Lorentz Reginald and Hazel Dorothy (Danielson) Hegstad; m. Curtis Wayne Martel, Apr. 30, 1966 (div. 1989); children: Christopher W., Peter L., Loren R. BS in Elem. Edn. and German, Concordia Coll., Moorhead, Minn., 1966; MS in Elem. Edn., Bemidji (Minn.) State U., 1989. Cert. German, elem. edn., reading cons., remedial and devel. reading tchr. K-12, Minn. 2d grade tchr. Rice Creek and Hayes Elem. Schs., Fridley, Minn., 1966-72; chpt. 1 reading tchr. Chief Bug-O-Nay-Ge-Shig Sch., Cass Lake, Minn., 1986-92; tchr. English/reading Rochester (Minn.) Pub. Schs., 1992-93; Chpt. I lead reading tchr. English/reading Moorhead (Minn.) Jr. H.S., 1993—, student newspaper advisor, 1993—. Vol. den mother Cub Scouts, Bismarck, N.D., 1976-77; vol. com. to establish kindergarten Bismarck Pub. Schs., 1974-75; vol. com. to help refugees relocate Bismarck, 1976; vol. Bemidji Sch. System, 1985. Mem. NEA, Northland Reading Coun. (pres. 1985-86, honor coun. 1986), Minn. Reading Assn. (sec. 1993—), Internat. Reading Assn., Minn. Edn. Assn., Kappa Delta Pi. Avocations: skiing, golf, music, art, travel. Home: 2333 Calihan Ave NE Bemidji MN 56601-2333

MARTEL, WILLIAM, radiologist, educator; b. N.Y.C., Oct. 1, 1927; s. Hyman and Fanny M.; m. Rhoda Kaplan, Oct. 9, 1956; children: Lisa, Pamela, Caryn, Jonathan, David. M.D., NYU, 1953. Intern, Kings County Hosp., N.Y., 1953-54; resident in radiology Mt. Sinai Hosp., N.Y.C., 1954-57; instr. radiology U. Mich., 1957-60, asst. prof., 1960-63, asso. prof., 1963-67, prof., 1967—, Fred Jenner Hodges prof., 1984—, chmn. dept. radiology, 1981-92, dir. skeletal radiology, 1970-81. Contbr. articles to Radiol. Diagnoses of Arthritic Diseases. Served with USAAF, 1945-46. Recipient Amoco U. Mich. Outstanding Teaching award, 1980. Mem. Radiol. Soc. N.Am., Am. Roentgen Ray Soc., Assn. Univ. Radiologists. Home: 2972 Parkridge Dr Ann Arbor MI 48103-1737 Office: Univ Mich Hosps Dept Radiology 1500 E Med Ctr Dr Ann Arbor MI 48109

MARTELL, ARTHUR EARL, chemistry educator; b. Natick, Mass., Oct. 18, 1916; s. Ambrose and Dorina (Lamoureaux) M.; m. Norma June Saunders, Sept. 2, 1944; children: Stuart A., Edward S., Janet E., Judith S., Jon V., Elaine C.; m. Mary Austin, 1965; children: Helen E., Kathryn A. B.S., Worcester Poly. Inst., 1938, D.Sc. (hon.), 1962; Ph.D., NYU 1941. Instr. Worcester Poly. Inst., 1941-42; mem. faculty Clark U., 1942-61, prof. chemistry, 1951-61, chmn. dept., 1959-61; prof. chemistry, chmn. dept. Ill. Inst. Tech., 1960-66; prof. chemistry Tex. A&M U., College Station, 1966—; Disting. prof. Tex. A&M U., 1973—, dept. head, 1966-80, adv. to pres., 1980-82; rsch. on chem equilibria, kinetics, catalysis, metal chelate compounds in solution. Author: (with M. Calvin) Chemistry of the Metal Chelate Compounds, 1952, (with S. Chaberek, Jr.) Organic Sequestering Agents, 1959, (with L.G. Sillen) Stability Constants, 1964; supplement, 1971, (with M.M. Taqui Khan) Homogeneous Catalysis by Metal Complexez, 2 vols., 1973, (with R.M. Smith) Critical Stability Constants, Vol. 1, 1974, Vol. 2, 1975, Vol. 3, 1977, Vol. 4, 1976, Vol. 5, 1982, Vol. 6, 1989, (with R.J. Motekaitis) Determination and Use of Stability Constants, 1989, 2nd edit., 1992, (with R.D. Hancock) Metal Complexes in Aqueous Solutions, 1996; editor: ACS Monograph on Coordination Chemistry, Vol. 1, 1973, Vol. 2, 1978, ACS Symposium Series 140, inorganic Chemistry in Biology and Medicine, 1980, Jour. Coordination Chemistry, 1970-80; mem. editl. bd. Bioinorganic Chemistry, Jour. Inorganic and Nuclear Chemistry, Inorganic Chemsty; contbr. articles to profl. jours. Mem. sch. bd. Northborough, Mass., 1958-61, chmn., 1959-61. Research fellow U. Calif. at Berkeley, 1949-50; Guggenheim fellow U. Zurich, Switzerland, 1954-55; NSF sr. postdoctoral fellow, also fellow Sch. Advanced Studies Mass. Inst. Tech., 1959-60; NIH Spl. fellow U. Calif. at Berkeley, 1964-65. Fellow N.Y. Acad. Scis. (hon. life); mem. AAAS, Am. Chem. Soc. (chmn. ctrl. Mass. sect. 1957-58, chmn. Tex. A&M sect. 1990-91, S.W. Regional award 1976, Nat. award for Disting. Svc. 1980, Patterson-Crane award 1995), Am. Acad. Arts and Scis., Japan Soc. for Analytical Chemistry (hon.), Sigma Xi, Phi Lambda Upsilon (hon.). Home: 9742 Myrtle Dr College Station TX 77845-6786

MARTELL, DENISE MILLS, lay worker; b. Newberry, S.C., Apr. 8, 1965; d. Wyman Harman and Evangeline (Berry) Mills; m. Marty Martell, Feb. 29, 1992; 1 child, Thomas Peter. Grad., Newberry High Sch., 1983. Tchr. Vacation Bible Sch., Newberry, 1984-95, Sun. Sch., Newberry, 1989-92; dir. Bapt. Young Women, Newberry, 1989-92; sec. Sunday Sch. Bapt. Ch., Newberry, S.C., 1993-95, Sun. Sch. tchr. 1-3 grades, 1995-96; tchr. mission trips, various locations, 1987-89; tchr. Mission Friends, Newberry, 1987-96, mem. choir, 1986—, mem. Newberry Cmty. choir, 1992-95, tchr. children's choir, 1993-95; leader Weekday Bible Club, 1990-92, missionary to Bolivia, South Am., 1996. Active March of Dimes Walk Am., Am. Diabetes Assn. Bike-a-thon. Home: 8769 Monticello Rd Columbia SC 29203-9708 *We are to be an encourager to share Christ love with all we meet. There is no task we can not handle. What ever God calls us to do, He has already equipped us to handle—standing faithful and firm in Christ to be a light in this world.*

MARTEN, GORDON CORNELIUS, research agronomist, educator, federal agency administrator; b. Wittenberg, Wis., Sept. 14, 1935; s. Clarence George and Cora Levina (Verpoorten) M.; m. Lynette Joy Hanson, Sept. 9, 1961; 1 dau., Kimberly Joy. BS, U. Wis., 1957; MS, U. Minn., 1959, PhD, 1961; postgrad., Purdue U., 1962. Rsch. agronomist U.S. Dept. Agr., U. Minn., St. Paul, 1961-72, supervisory rsch. agronomist, rsch. leader, 1972-89; adj. prof. agronomy U. Minn., St. Paul, 1971-96; assoc. dir. USDA-Agr. Rsch. Svc., Beltsville, Md., 1989-96; prof. emeritus U. Minn., St. Paul, 1996—; mem. governing body and U.S. rep. to OECD Biol. Resource Mgmt. Program, Paris, 1990-96; adminstrv. coun. USDA Sustainable Agrl. Rsch. and Edn. Program, 1993-95. Assoc. editor: Crop Sci., 1972-74; sr. editor USDA Handbook Near Infrared Reflectance Spectroscopy: Analysis of Forage Quality, 1985, rev. edit., 1989; mem. edit. bd. Sci. of Food and Agriculture, 1985-90; contbr. numerous articles to profl. jours. Recipient Merit award Am. Forage and Grassland Coun., 1976, Outstanding Svc. award, 1981, Civil Servant of Yr. award Twin Cities, Minn., 1976; NSF grad. fellow, 1959-61; numerous cert. merit USDA Agrl. Rsch. Svc., Northrup King Faculty Outstanding Performance award U. Minn., 1986, Superior Svc. award USDA, 1987. Fellow Am. Soc. Agronomy, Crop Sci. Soc. Am. (bd. dirs. 1975-77); mem. Am. Forage and Grassland Coun. (bd. dirs. 1977-80), Coun. Agr. Sci. and Tecch. (bd. dirs. 1985-90), Agronomic Sci. Found. (trustee 1984-89), Biol. Club, Sigma Xi, Gamma Sigma Delta (Adminstrn. award of merit/Nat. Capital Area 1994), Alpha Zeta, Delta Theta Sigma. Lutheran. Home: 1312 Willow Cir Roseville MN 55113-3235

MARTENS, ERNESTO, air, aerospace transportation executive. CEO AeroMexico, Mexico City. Office: AeroMexico, Paseo de la Reforma 444-501, Mexico City 06500, Mexico

MARTENS, LYLE CHARLES, state education administrator; b. Wausau, Wis., June 22, 1935; s. Norman Theodore and Eloise Loretta (Kreger) M.; m. Darlene Carrol Pyatt, Dec. 22, 1956; children: William Lyle, Robert Michael. BS in Indsl. Edn., Stout State U., 1957, MS in Indsl. Tech., 1962. Tchr. indsl. arts Mercer (Wis.) Pub. Schs., 1957-62; high sch. prin. Seymour (Wis.) Community Schs., 1962-65, supt. schs., 1965-87; supt. schs. Green Bay (Wis.) Area Pub. Schs., 1987-89; asst. state supt. State Dept. Edn., Madison, Wis., 1989-90, dep. state supt., 1990-93; coord. sch.-to-work Cesa 7, Green Bay, Wis., 1993—; dir. Ctr. for Edn. and Workforce Competitiveness U. Wis., Green Bay, 1996—. Chair United Way Edn. Fund Dr., Brown County, Wis., 1989; mem. bd.dirs. Green Bay C. of C., Good Shepherd Nursing Home, Seymour, Wis., 1975-87; mem. Econ. Devel. Corp., Outagamie County, Wis., 1985-86; founder Fallen Timber's Environment Ctr., 1972. Recipient Martens Praire Honor, 1995. Mem. Am. Assn. Sch. Dist. Adminstrs., Wis. Assn. Sch. Dist. Adminstrs. (pres. 1978-79), Assn. Svc./Curriculum Devel., North Cen. Regional Ednl. Lab., Fox Valley Tech. Inst., Masons, Phi Delta Kappa. Lutheran. Avocations: fishing, hunting, flying, woodworking, raising and showing dogs. Home: 6504 County Road R Denmark WI 54208-9729 Office: Cesa 7 595 Baeten Rd Green Bay WI 54304-5763

MARTENS, ROY MICHAEL, commercial loan broker; b. Des Moines, Feb. 7, 1950; s. Roy Edwin and Maxine Hayworth M. BA, Luther Coll., 1972; MBA, U. Minn., 1978. Auditor Honeywell, Mpls., 1972-75; supr. Norwest, Mpls., 1989-91; fin. analyst Amhoist, St. Paul, 1979-81; sr. fin. analyst AgriBank, St. Paul, 1981-88; lease finance rep. Dataserv, Eden Prairie, Minn., 1988-89; contract employment and tax cons., 1989-91; pres. Comml. Financing Resources, inc., Mpls., 1991—. Mem. Nat. Assn. Indsl. and Office Parks, Assn. Corp. Growth, Minn. Multi Housing Assn., Minnetonka Yacht Club, New Warrior Minn. Avocations: skiing, sailing, running, photography. Home: 2511 Chestnut Ave Minneapolis MN 55405-1736 Office: Comml Fin Resources Inc 2511 Chestnut Ave Minneapolis MN 55405-1736

MARTH, ELMER HERMAN, bacteriologist, educator; b. Jackson, Wis., Sept. 11, 1927; s. William F. and Irma A. (Bublitz) M.; m. Phyllis E. Menge, Aug. 10, 1957. BS, U. Wis., 1950, MS, 1952, PhD, 1954. Registered sanitarian, Wis. Teaching asst. bacteriology U. Wis., Madison, 1949-51; research asst. U. Wis., 1951-54, project asso., 1954-55, instr. bacteriology, 1955-57, assoc. prof.food sci., bacteriology and food microbiology and toxicology, 1966-71, prof., 1971-90, prof. emeritus, 1990—; vis. prof. Swiss Fed. Inst. Tech., Zurich, 1981; with Kraft Foods, Inc., Glenview, Ill., 1957-66, bacteriologist, 1957-59, rsch. bacteriologist, 1959-61, sr. rsch. bacteriologist, 1961-63; group leader microbiology, 1963-66; assoc. mgr. microbiology, 1966; mem. Intersoc. Coun. on Std. Methods for Exam. Dairy Products, 1968-84, chmn., 1972-78. Contbg. author books; editor: Jour. Milk and Food Tech, 1967-76, Jour. Food Protection, 1977-87; contbr. articles to profl. publs. Sec. Luth. Acad. Scholarship, 1961-71; WHO travel fellow, 1975. Recipient Nordica award for rsch. Am. Cultured Dairy Products Inst., 1979, Meritorious Svc. award APHA, 1977, 83, Sanitarian of Yr. award Wis. Assn. Milk and Food Sanitarians, 1983, Meritorious Svc. award Nat. Confectioners Assn., 1987, Joseph Mityas Meml. Laboratorian of Yr. award Wis. Lab. Assn., 1989, Quality of Comm. award Am. Agrl. Econs. Assn., 1992. Fellow Inst. Food Technologists (Nicholas Appert award 1987, Babcock-Hart award 1989); mem. Am. Soc. Microbiology, Am. Dairy Sci. Assn. (Pfizer rsch. award 1975, Dairy Rsch. Found. award 1980, Borden award 1986, Kraft Inc. teaching award 1988), Internat. Assn. Milk, Food, and Environ. Sanitarians (hon. life, Educator award for rsch. and teaching food hygiene 1977, citation award 1984), Coun. Biology Editors, Inst. Food Technologists, Sigma Xi, Alpha Zeta, Kappa Eta Kappa, Phi Sigma, Phi Tau Sigma, Delta Theta Sigma, Gamma Sigma Delta, Gamma Alpha. Patentee in field. Office: U Wis Dept Food Sci 1605 Linden Dr Madison WI 53706-1519

MARTH, FRITZ LUDWIG, sports association executive; b. Essen, Germany, Feb. 23, 1935; s. Fritz and Elizabeth (Dietrich) M.; came to U.S., 1952, naturalized, 1959; student pub. schs. Essen; m. Sonja Wiehl, June 17, 1964; children: Fritz Thomas, William Robert. Stock clk. Hamilton Art Metal Co., N.Y.C., 1952-55; with Keystone Metal Finishers, Inc., Secaucus, N.J., 1955—, asst. plant mgr., 1962-66, plant mgr., 1966-83; adminstr. amateur div. U.S. Soccer Fedn., N.J. 1983—. Pres. N.J. State Soccer Assn., 1965-70; sec. So. N.Y. State Soccer Assn., 1972-83; gen. sec. Cosmopolitan Soccer League, 1961—; mem. div. soccer U.S. Olympic Com. With U.S. Army, 1958-59, Korea. Lutheran. Mem. Hoboken (N.J.) Soccer Football. Home: 121 W Passaic Ave Bloomfield NJ 07003-4528 Office: 7800 River Rd North Bergen NJ 07047-6221

MARTI, ERWIN ERNST, physicochemist, researcher; b. Basel, Switzerland, Dec. 27, 1932; s. Ernst and Martha (Kistler) M.; m. Alice Magrit Stieger, Jan. 18, 1936; children: Dominik, Barbara Siegrist-Marti, Florian. PhD, U. Basel, 1963. Postdoctoral fellow U. Calif., Berkeley, 1966-68; with mgmt. Ciba-Geigy Ltd., Basel, 1968-96, sci. expert, 1978—, rsch. group leader, 1984—; with Novartis Svcs. AG, Basel, 1997; head sci. project team Swiss Fed. Office of Oecology, Incineration of Dioxin containing waste from Seveso, 1983-87; chmn. organizing com. European Symposium Thermal Analysis and Calorimetry 3, Interlaken, Switzerland, 1984; sci. chmn. Symposium Pharmacy and Thermal Analysis, Freiburg, Germany, 1993, Geneva, 1995, Monte Verita, Switzerland, 1997. Mem. editl. bd. Thermochimica Acta, 1994; regional editor Jour. Thermal Analysis, 1995; patentee in field. Bd. dirs. Free Dem. Party of Canton Basel-Stadt, 1986—; active Guild of Heaven, Basel, 1968—. Mem. Swiss Soc. Thermal Analysis and Calorimetry (pres.), European Soc. Thermal Analysis, Calorimetry, Thermodynamics and Chem. Reactivity (pres.). Avocations: hiking, downhill skiing. Home: Im Langen Loh 181, CH-4054 Basel Switzerland Office: Novartis Svcs AG, Klybeckstrasse, CH-4002 Basel Switzerland

MARTIG, JOHN FREDERICK, anesthesiologist; b. Salem, Oreg., Mar. 19, 1947; s. Kenneth W. and Virginia P. (Young) M.; m. Susan J. Chinworth; children: Daniel R., Thomas. A of Tech. Arts, Olympic Coll., 1968, AS, 1972; BSEE, U. Wash., 1974; DO, COMP, 1987. Registered profl. engr., Wash. Cons. Rockwell Internat., Anaheim, Calif., 1984, Honeywell, Silverdale, Wash., 1985; resident Ball Meml. Hosp., Muncie, Ind., 1987-89; physician Drs. Imediate Med. Ctr., Muncie, Ind., 1988—; resident Met. Hosp., Grand Rapids, Mich., 1990-93; chief anesthesia Jay County Hosp., Portland, Ind., 1993—. With USN, 1969-83. Mem. AMA, Am. Osteo. Assn., Am. Soc. Anesthesiologists, Am. Osteo. Coll. Anesthesiologists, Am. Coll. Osteo. Family Physicians, Am. Soc. Regional Anesthesia, Ind. State Med. Assn. Avocations: flying, tennis, hiking, photography, gardening. Home: 703 W 7th St Portland IN 47371-2314 Office: Jay County Hosp 500 W Votaw St Portland IN 47371-1322

MARTIN, AGNES, artist; b. Maklin, Sask., Can., 1912; came to U.S., 1932, naturalized, 1950; Student, Western Wash. State Coll., 1935-38; BS, Columbia U., 1942, MFA, 1952. One-woman shows include Betty Parsons Gallery, N.Y.C., 1958, 59, 61, Robert Elkon Gallery, N.Y.C., 1961, 63, 72, 76, Nicolas Wilder Gallery, Los Angeles, 1963-66, 67, Visual Arts Ctr., N.Y.C., 1971, Kunstraum, Munich, 1973, Inst. Contemporary Art U. Pa., Phila., 1973, Pace Gallery, N.Y.C., 1975, 76, 77, 78, 79, 80-81, 81, 83, 84, 85, 86, 89, 91, 92, 94, 95, Mayor Gallery, London, 1978, 84, Galerie Rudolf Zwirner, Cologne, Fed. Republic Germany, 1978, Harcus/Krakow Gallery, Boston, 1978, Margo Leavin Gallery, Los Angeles, 1979, 85, Mus. N.Mex., Santa Fe, 1979, Richard Gray Gallery, Chgo., 1981, Garry Anderson Gallery, Sydney, Australia, 1986, Waddington Galleries Ltd., London, 1986, Stedelijk Mus., Amsterdam, 1991, Whitney Mus. Am. Art, N.Y.C., 1992; exhibited in group shows at Carnegie Inst., Pitts., 1961, Whitney Mus. Am. Art, N.Y.C., 1962, 66, 67, 74, 77, 92, Tooth Gallery, London, 1962, Gallery Modern Art, Washington, 1963, Wadsworth Atheneum, Hartford, Conn., 1963, Solomon R. Guggenheim Mus., N.Y.C., 1965, 66, 76, Mead Corp., 1965-67, Mus. Modern Art, N.Y.C., 1967, 76, 85, Inst. Contemporary Art, Phila., 1967, Detroit Inst. Art, 1967, Corcoran Gallery Art, Washington, 1967, 81, Finch Mus., N.Y., 1968, Phila. Mus., 1968, Zurich Art Mus., Switzerland, 1969, Ill. Bell Telephone Co., Chgo., 1970, Mus. Contemporary Art, Chgo., 1971, Inst. Contemporary Art U. Pa., Phila., 1972, Randolph-Macon Coll., N.C., 1972, Kassel, Fed. Republic Germany, 1972, Stedelijk Mus., Amsterdam, 1975, U. Mass., Amherst, 1976, Venice Biennale, Italy, 1976, 80, Cleve. Mus. Art, 1978, Albright-Knox Gallery, Buffalo, 1978, Inst. Contemporary Art, Boston, 1979, Art Inst. Chgo., 1979, San Francisco Mus. Modern Art, 1980, ROSC Internat. Art Exhbn., Dublin, Ireland, 1980, Marilyn Pearl Gallery, N.Y.C., 1983, Kemper Gallery, Kansas City Art Inst., 1985, Am. Acad. and Inst. Arts and Letters, N.Y.C., 1985, Charles Cowles Gallery, N.Y.C., 1986, Moody Gallery Art U. Ala., Birmingham, 1986, Butler Inst. Am. Art, 1986, Art Gallery Western Australia, Perth, 1986, Mus. Contemporary Art, Los Angeles, 1986, Boston Fine Arts Mus., 1989; represented in permanent collections Mus. of Modern Art, N.Y.C., Albright-Knox Gallery, Aldrich Mus., Ridgefield, Conn., Art Gallery Ont., Can., Australian Nat. Gallery, Canberra, Grey Art Gallery and Study Ctr., N.Y.C., Solomon R. Guggenheim Mus., High Mus. Art, Atlanta, Hirshhorn Mus. and Sculpture Garden, Washington, Israel Mus., Jerusalem, La Jolla (Calif.) Mus. Contemporary Art, Los Angeles County Mus. Art, Mus. Art R.I. Sch. Design, Providence, Mus. Modern Art, Neuegalerie der Stadt, Aachen, Fed. Republic Germany, Norton Simon Mus. Art at Pasadena, Calif., Stedelijk Mus., Amsterdam, The Netherlands, 1992, Mus. Modern Art, paris, 1992, Tate Gallery, London, Wadsworth Atheneum, Walker Art Ctr., Mpls., Whitney Mus. Am. Art, 1993, Sofia, Madrid, 1993, Huosten, 1993, Worcester (Mass.) Art Mus., Yale U. Art Gallery, New Haven; subject of various articles. Office: 414 Placitas Rd # 37 Taos NM 97571-2513

MARTIN, ALAN EDWARD, gasket company executive; b. Pasadena, Tex., Feb. 6, 1965; s. Alvin and Marjorie (Ballard) M.; m. Miriam Deane Sellers, June 7, 1984; 1 child, Alan E. Jr. Grad., high sch., Deer Park, Tex. Inventory control supr. Furon Metallic Gasket, Houston, 1986-90, inventory control and purchasing mgr., 1990-94; tech. customer svc. Seal-Pac Profl. Svcs., Baytown, Tex., 1994—. Capt. Pasadena (Tex.) Fire Dept.; EMT-I, Rural Metro Corp., Pasadena. Mem. Nat. Assn. of Purchasing Mgrs., Purchasing Mgmt. Assn. Houston, Am. Prodn. and Inventory Control Soc., Tex. State Fireman's & Fire Marshall's Assn., Harris County Firefighters Assn. Avocations: hunting, shooting.

MARTIN, ALBERT CAREY, architect; b. Los Angeles, Aug. 3, 1913; s. Albert Carey and Carolyn Elizabeth (Borchard) M.; m. Dorothy Virginia Dolde, Nov. 15, 1937; children—Albert Carey III, David Charles, Mary Martin Marquardt, Claire, Charles Dolde. B.Arch. cum laude, U. So. Calif., 1936. Registered architect, Calif. Architect Albert C. Martin and Assocs., Los Angeles, 1937-42; ptnr. Albert C. Martin and Assocs., 1942—; dir. Rancho Los Alamitos Found. Prin. works include Los Angeles Dept. Water and Power, ARCO Twin Towers, St. Basil's Ch., Union Bank Sq. Trustee Los Angeles Orthopaedic Hosp.; bd. dirs. Long Beach Mus. Art Found. Recipient Annual Spirit of Los Angeles award Los Angeles Hdqrs. City Assn., 1980, Brotherhood award NCCJ, 1980, Asa V. Call Achievement award U. So. Calif. Alumni Assn., 1984, Boy Scouts Am. Good Scout award L.A. Area Coun., 1989; named Constrn. Man of Yr. Los Angeles C. of C., 1971. Fellow AIA (past dir., pres. So. Calif. chpt., past v.p. Calif. Coun.); mem. U. So. Calif. Archtl. Guild (advisor, disting. alumnus 1990), L.A. C. of C. (past pres.), Calif. C. of C. (past dir.), Lambda Alpha, Automobile Club of So. Calif. Republican. Roman Catholic. Clubs: California, Jonathan (Los Angeles). Avocation: sailing. Office: Albert C Martin and Assocs 811 W 7th St Los Angeles CA 90017-3408

MARTIN, ALBERT CHARLES, manufacturing executive, lawyer; b. San Lucido, Italy, Sept. 20, 1928; s. Joseph and Carmela M.; m. Jean Perrin, Aug. 22, 1953 (dec.); children: Lynne, Ken; m. Frances Doughty, June, 1996. B.S., Mich. State U., 1952; M.S., U. Mich., 1953; J.D., Detroit Coll. Law, 1962. Bar: Mich. 1962. Corp. counsel, sec. Udylite Corp., Detroit, 1963-68; corp. counsel Hooker Chem. Corp., N.Y.C., 1968-70, Grow Chem. Co., N.Y.C., 1970-71; group v.p. Leeds & Northrup Internat., North Wales, Pa., 1971-79, pres., 1979—. Served with U.S. Army, 1946-48. Mem. Mich. Bar Assn.

MARTIN, ALLEN, lawyer; b. Manchester, Conn., Aug. 12, 1937; s. Richard and Ruth Palmer (Smith) M.; m. Bonnie Reid, Sept. 8, 1979; children: Elizabeth Palmer, Samuel Bates. B.A., Williams Coll., 1960, Oxford U., 1962; LL.B., Harvard U., 1965. Ptnr. firm Downs, Rachlin and Martin, Burlington, Brattleboro and St. Johnsbury, Vt., 1971—; chmn. bd. dirs. Elcon Inc., 1991—; bd. dirs., chmn. fin. com. Union Mut. Ins. Co., New Eng. Guaranty Ins. Co.; mem. Vt. Jud. Responsibility Bd., vice-chmn., 1978-80. Chmn. Vt. Bd. Edn., 1978-83; chmn. Vt. Rep. Party, 1991-95; mem. Rep. Nat. Com., 1991-95. Mem. Am. Law Inst., Am., Vt. bar assns. Republican. Home: 283 S Union St Burlington VT 05401-5507 also: Six Chimneys Orford NH 03777 Office: PO Box 190 199 Main St Burlington VT 05402-0190

MARTIN, ALVIN CHARLES, lawyer; b. Bklyn., Oct. 25, 1933; s. George and Dora (Gitlin) M.; m. Susan Goldman, Sept. 3, 1959 (div. Jan. 1980); children: Robert, Peter; m. Gail Leichtman, Oct. 25, 1985; stepchildren: Hilary Macht, Timothy Macht. BBA, CCNY, 1954; JD, Harvard U., 1957; LLM in Taxation, NYU, 1963. Bar: N.Y. 1958, N.J. 1977, Fla. 1991. Pvt. practice N.Y.C., 1958-76, Newark and Morristown, N.J., 1977—; with Office of Regional Counsel, IRS, 1959-64; assoc. Curtis Mallet-Prevost Colt & Mosle, 1964-66; ptnr. Zissu, Halper & Martin, 1966-76; ptnr. Shanley & Fisher, 1977-88, counsel, 1988—; of counsel Ruden, McClosky, Smith, Schuster & Russell P.A., Ft. Lauderdale, Fla., 1990-97; sec. Vornado, Inc., 1966-79, exec. v.p., asst. to chmn. bd., 1971-76, also bd. dirs.; adj. prof. taxation NYU, 1972-86; mem. taxation faculty Pace Coll. Grad. Sch. Bus. Adminstrn., 1964-70, Baruch Sch. Bus. and Pub. Adminstrn., 1959-62. Author: New Jersey Estate Planning, Will Drafting and Estate Administration Forms, 1988, 95. Bd. dirs. Met. Jewish Geriatric Ctr., 1980-84. With U.S. Army, 1957. Fellow Am. Coll. Trust and Estate Counsel. Clubs: Boca West (Fla.). Home: 20179 Fairfax Dr Boca Raton FL 33434-3235 Office: 2000 Glades Rd Boca Raton FL 33431-8504 also: 200 E Broward Blvd Fort Lauderdale FL 33301-1963

MARTIN, ANDREW AYERS, lawyer, physician, educator; b. Toccoa, Ga., Aug. 18, 1958; s. Wallace Ford and Dorothy LaTranquil (Ayers) M. BA, Emory U., Atlanta, 1980, MD, 1984; JD, Duke U., 1988. Bar: Calif. 1989, La. 1990, D.C. 1991; diplomate Am. Bd. Pathology, Nat. Bd. Med. Examiners; lic. physician, La., Miss. Intern in pediatrics Emory U./Grady Meml. Hosp., Atlanta, 1984; intern Tulane U./Charity Hosp., New Orleans, 1989-90, resident in anatomic and clin. pathology, 1990-94; surg. pathology fellow Baylor Coll. Medicine, Houston, 1994-95; law clk. Ogletree, Deakins, Smoak, Stewart, Greenville, S.C., summer 1986, Thelen Marrin Johnson Bridges, L.A., summer 1987, Duke Hosp. Risk Mgmt., 1987-88; assoc. Haight Brown Bonesteel, Santa Monica, Calif., 1988; pvt. practice L.A., 1989; physician/atty. Tulane Med. Ctr./Charity Hosp., New Orleans, 1989-94, Baylor Coll. Medicine/Tex. Med. Ctr., Houston, 1994-95; lab. dir., sr. ptnr. King's Daus. Hosp., Greenville, Miss., 1995—; bd. dirs. Martin Bldrs., Inc., Toccoa; mem. AIDS Legis. Task Force for La.; case cons. Office of Tech. Assessment, Washington; tech. cons. and autopsy extra Oliver Stone's "JFK"; adj. clin. faculty Moorhead Coll. Contbr. articles to profl. jours.; author: Reflections on Rusted Chrome (book of poetry). Fellow Coll. Am. Pathologists, Coll. Legal Medicine, La. State Med. Soc. (del. meeting 1992-93). Home: 935 Lake Hall Rd Lake Village AR 71653 also: 4104 Alabama Kenner LA 70065 Office: Kings Daughters Hosp PO Box 5880 Greenville MS 38704-5880

MARTIN, ARTHUR MEAD, lawyer; b. Cleveland Heights, Ohio, Mar. 29, 1942; s. Bernard P. and Winifred (Mead) M. AB, Princeton U., 1963; LLB, Harvard U., 1966. Bar: Ill. 1966, U.S. Dist. Ct. (no. dist.) Ill. 1969, U.S. Ct. Appeals (7th cir.) 1970, U.S. Supreme Ct. 1980. Instr. law U. Wis., Madison, 1966-68; assoc. Jenner & Block, Chgo., 1968-74, ptnr., 1975—; co-trustee Dille Family Trust, 1982—; bd. dirs. Sleepeck Printing Co. Author: Historical and Practice Notes to the Illinois Civil Practice Act and Illinois Supreme Court Rules, 1968-88. Trustee 4th Presbyn. Ch., Chgo., sec. 1997—, exec. com. 1997—. Mem. ABA, Am. Law Inst., Ill. Bar Assn., Chgo. Bar Assn. (bd. editors 1972-86), Am. Arbitration Assn. (panel), Lake Mich. Fedn. (bd. dirs. 1993—, exec. com. 1994—), Law CLub Chgo., Legal Club Chgo. Office: Jenner & Block 1 IBM Plz Chicago IL 60611-3586

MARTIN, BARBARA ANN, secondary education educator; b. Lexington, Ky., Apr. 11, 1946; d. Robert Newton and Juanita June (Karrick) M. AA, Beckley Coll., 1966; BS in Edn., Concord Coll., 1969; MA, Western Ky. U., 1974, rank I, 1982. Standard teaching cert., adminstrn., secondary edn., Ky. Tchr. Daviess County Mid. Sch., Owensboro, Ky., 1969—; inservice speaker Daviess County Schs., Owensboro, 1969—; acad. writer Ky. Acad. Assn., Frankfort, 1992—. Author: Social Studies for Gifted Student, 1977; contbr.: (game) National Geographic Global Pursuit, 1988. Ky. rep. tchr. adv. coun. Nat. Rep. Party, Washington, 1993—; exec. com. Daviess County Rep. Party, 1987—. Named Outstanding Young Woman, 1978, Outstanding Social Studies Tchr., Ky. Coun. for Social Studies, 1978; recipient Outstanding Comty. Svc. award Owensboro (Ky.) City Commn. and Mayor, 1982. Mem. NEA (del., mid-atlantic coord. women's caucus 1969—), Ky. Edn. Assn. (del., legis. com. 1969—), 2d Dist. Assn. (del., pres. 1969—), Daviess County Edn. Assn. (del., pres. 1969—). Presbyterian. Avocations: writing, photography, gardening, family history, Ky. Wildcat basketball. Home: 4325 Fischer Rd Owensboro KY 42301-8109 Office: Daviess County Mid Sch 1415 E 4th St Owensboro KY 42303-0134

MARTIN, BARBARA JEAN, elementary education educator; b. St. Louis, May 20, 1949; d. Robert Clarke and Ruth Eloise (Baseler) M. BS in Elem. Edn., N.E. Mo. State U., 1971; MA in Elem. Edn., Maryville U., 1991. Classroom instr. Hazelwood (Mo.) Sch. Dist., 1971—; mem. curriculum revision com., Hazelwood Sch. Dist., 1974-97, profl. devel. Com., 1992-94, 96, 97, steering com. 1993-94; advisor/cons. Hazelwood Sch. Dist. Early Childhood Parents and Staff, 1985—. Mem. chmn. PTA, Russell Sch., 1989—; tchr., musician Bermuda Bible Chapel, St. Louis, 1965—; asst. dir., sec., musician, tchr. Hickory Cove Bible Camp, Hickory, N.C., 1975—. Recipient Disting. Vol. award Christian Camping Internat., 1986; recipient Robert D. Elsea scholarship St. Louis Cooperating Sch. Dist., St. Louis County, 1989. Mem. Assn. for Edn. of Young Children (pres. seminar 1994), Christian Educators Assn., Sigma Alpha Iota (pres. 1978-81, v.p. 1976-78, scholarship chmn. 1981—), Sword of Honor 1981, Rose of Honor 1996). Avocations: music, sewing, ch. youth activities. Home: 18 Buckeye Dr Ferguson MO 63135-1515 Office: Russell Sch 7350 Howdershell Rd Hazelwood MO 63042-1306

MARTIN, BECCA BACON, editor, journalist; b. Ontario, Oreg., Nov. 26, 1957; d. Raymond A. and Ruth (Wilson) Bacon; m. Daniel P. Martin, Sept. 1, 1984; adopted daughter, Amanda Kathryn. AA, Allen County Coll., Iola, Kans., 1978; student, U. Ark., 1990. Wire and page 1 editor Iola Register, 1979-84; asst. mng. editor Benton County Daily Record, Bentonville, Ark., 1985-87, news editor, 1987-88; editor living, entertainment and weekend mag. Morning News of N.W. Ark., Springdale, 1988-96; free-lance writer, photographer, cons. Fayetteville, Ark., 1996—; bus. editor Morning News N.W. Ark., 1997—. Editorial asst. Arkansas County Judges Mag., 1989; founding editor (monthly mag.) Bella Vista Village Voice, 1985; contbr. investigative reports to Ark. Bus. mag., 1988; author spl. arts sect. U. Ark. Alumni Mag., 1990; play producer Ozark Stage Works, 1990; mem. editl. adv. bd. Inside Arts Mag., 1997. Former mem. adv. bd. Fayetteville West Campus Child Care/Parenting Ctr.; troop leader Girl Scouts U.S.A., Farmington, Ark., 1988-89; mem. adv. bd. Ark. Better Chance, Fayetteville, 1991-92; chmn. publicity Miss N.W. Ark. Pageant, Springdale, 1990—; charter mem. Altrusa Internat., Springdale, 1994. Recipient Excellence in Journalism award Am. Cancer Soc., 1990-95, award AP Mng. Editors, 1991, 94, WISE award Northwest Ark. Women's Festival and Conf., 1995; named Best Humorous Column Ark. Press Assn., 1992-94, Best Family Pages in Ark., APA, 1995, 2d place in both humorous and serious col. categories, 1995; Writing grant Nat. League Am. Pen Women, 1995. Mem. Internat. Thespian Soc. (hon.), Nat. League Jr. Cotillions Washington County (adv. bd.), Alpha Psi Omega (hon.). Avocations: animal rights support, pageant judging, cycling, book collecting, public speaking on adoption and special-needs children. Home: 173 S Hill Ave Fayetteville AR 72701-5768 Office: Morning News PO Box 7 Springdale AR 72765-0007

MARTIN, BENJAMIN GAUFMAN, ophthalmologist; b. Louisville, Aug. 18, 1937; s. Benjamin and Catherine L. Martin; m. Caroline Sue Martin, May 25, 1975; children: Benjamin, Lori, Tamara, Farrell, Steven, David. BME, U. Louisville, 1954, M. Engring., 1973; MD, U. So. Calif., 1964. Design engr. Philco/Ford, Palo Alto, Calif., 1957-60; rsch. engr. N.Am./Rockwell, Inglewood, Calif., 1961-63; intern Wright-Patterson Med. Ctr., Dayton, Ohio, 1964-65; ophthalmology resident Wilford Hall Med. Ctr., San Antonio, 1968-71; commd. USAF, 1963, advanced through grades to col., ret., 1980; CEO Cape Coral (Fla.) Eye Ctr., 1980—. With USN, 1954-57. Decorated Legion of Merit, DFC, Bronze Star, Air medal. Mem. Daedalions, Masons, Shriner. Republican. Lutheran. Office: Cape Coral Eye Ctr 4120 Del Prado Blvd S Cape Coral FL 33904-7165

MARTIN, BERNARD LEE, former college dean; b. Dayton, Ohio, May 29, 1923; s. Harley L. and Clare (Murphy) M.; m. Mary Patricia McDonald, Nov. 23, 1950; children: Joseph, Mary, David, Patrick, Paul, Timothy, Michael, Christopher. B.A., Athenaeum of Ohio, 1941-45; M.A. in History, Xavier U., 1950, M.B.A., 1955; Ph.D. in Econs, U. Cin., 1963; Ph.D. honoris causa, Canisius Coll., 1978. Mem. faculty Xavier U., Cin., 1948-65; asst. prof. bus. adminstrn. Xavier U., 1955-62, assoc. prof. mktg., 1962-65, chmn. mktg. dept., 1961; chmn., prof. mktg. Eastern Mich. U., Ypsilanti, 1965-66; dean Sch. Bus. Adminstrn. Canisius Coll., Buffalo, 1966-71, 1973-78, acting acad. v.p. of coll., 1971-73; dean McLaren Coll. Bus. Adminstrn., U. San Francisco, 1978-86, prof. mktg., 1986-91; prof. emeritus U. San Francisco, 1992. Author: (with others) Contemporary Economic Problems and Issues, 3d edit, 1973. Ford Found. grantee Harvard, 1964. Mem. Am. Mktg. Assn., Am. Econ. Assn. Home: 1062 Cherry Ave San Jose CA 95125-4311

MARTIN, BERNARD MURRAY, painter, educator; b. Ferrum, Va., June 21, 1935. Student, Wake Forest Coll.; BFA, Richmond Profl. Inst.; MA, Hunter Coll. Prof. emeritus Va. Commonwealth U., 1961—; represented by Reynolds Gallery, Richmond, Va. One-man shows include Gallery K, Washington, 1978, 80, Gallery Contemporary Art, Winston-Salem, Mass., 1972, Va. Mus. Fine Art, Richmond, 1996, Longwood Coll., 1997, Reynolds Gallery, 1996; exhibited in Am. Fedn. Arts Traveling Exhibit, 1968, Va. Mus. Fine Art, 1970, Corcoran Gallery, Washington, 1971; represented in permanent collections Va. Mus. Fine Arts, Walter Rawls Mus., Chrysler Mus., Nat. Collection, First & Merchants Nat. Bank. Recipient Certificate of Distinction, Va. Mus. Fine Arts, 1964, 66, 68, 70; first prize Gallery Contemporary Art, 1970, 71, award Nat. Endowment for Visual Arts, 1995. Address: 1015 Francisco Rd Richmond VA 23229

MARTIN, BETTY J., speech, language pathologist; b. East St. Louis, Ill., Nov. 2, 1950; d. Nathaniel and Minnie Mae (Long) Gause; m. Leander Martin, Jr.; children: Leander III, Lavell, Kenneth. BS, So. Ill. Univ., 1978, MS, 1980. Cert. speech-lang. pathologist, Ill., Mo.; lic. in Ill. Bd. sec. State C.C., East St. Louis, 1970-75; speech-lang. pathologist East. St. Louis Sch. Dist. 189, 1980—. site coord. Educom, St. Peter's, Mo., 1993. Tutor Project Love, East St. Louis, 1990; tchr. Vacation Bible Sch., East St. Louis, 1994, 95; sec. Steward BBd. #2, East St. Louis, 1994-96. Mem. Am. Speech Hearing Lang. Assn. (cert.), Ill. Speech Hearing Assn., So. Ill. Speech Hearing Assn. Methodist. Home: 520 Green Haven Dr Swansea IL 62226-1801 Office: Mandela Elem Sch East Saint Louis IL 62201

MARTIN, BILL, artist, art educator; b. South San Francisco, Calif., Jan. 22, 1943; s. Gordon and Zelia (Sonderman) M.; m. Shelley Persistence Balaban, Feb. 22, 1975. BFA, San Francisco Art Inst., 1968, MFA, 1970. instr. Acad. Art, San Francisco, 1970-71, U. Calif., Berkeley, 1972, San Francisco Art Inst., 1972, Calif. State U., San Jose, 1973, Coll. Marin, Kentfield, Calif., 1975-78, Coll. of the Redwoods, Mendocino, Calif., 1983—. One-man shows, San Francisco Mus. Art, 1973, Nancy Hoffman Gallery, N.Y.C., 1977, 79, 82, Zara Gallery, San Francisco, 1978, 80, Joseph Chowning Gallery, 1983, 85, 87, 89, 92, 94, U. Nev., 1988, Clatsop Coll., Oreg., 1989, Joseph Chwoning Gallery, San Francisco, 1989, Joseph Chowning Gallery, 1996, 97, Monterey Mus. Art, 1996, Chabot Coll., Hayward, Calif., 1990, Kabutoya Gallery, Tokyo, 1991; Joseph Chowning Gallery, San Francisco, 1992, Atrium Galley, San Francisco, 1992; group shows include, San Francisco Art Inst., 1966, 68, 70, 71, Unicorn Gallery, San Francisco, 1969, Sun Gallery, San Francisco, 1969, Richmond (Calif.) Art Center, 1970, Pioneer Mus., Stockton, Calif., 1970, U. So. Calif., Los Angeles, 1971, Whitney Mus. Am. Art, N.Y.C., 1972-73, U. Pa., 1972, Calif. State U., San Jose, 1973, Nancy Hoffman Gallery, N.Y.C., 1974, State U. Albany, 1974, Milw. Arts Center, 1974, Chgo. Art Inst., 1974, Mus. Modern Art, Paris, 1975, Tri-Ann. Invitational of India, 1978, European traveling exhbn. organized by New Mus., N.Y.C., 1979-81, Zara Gallery, 1979, 80, Western Assn. Arts Mus., 1980-81, Joseph Chowning Gallery, 1983, 85, 87, Mendocino (Calif.) Art Gallery, 1987, Cheney Cowles Mus., Spokane, Wash., 1988, Humbolt State Univ., 1988, Muscarelle Mus. Art Coll. William & Mary Coll., 1988, Salt Lake City, 1988, Mus. of Rockies, Bozeman, Mont., 1988, Lancaster (Calif.) Mus., 1988, Humboldt State U., Arcata, Calif. 1988, City Coll. San Francisco, 1988, Medocino (Calif.) Art Ctr., 1989, So. Utah State U., 1989, Springfield (Mo.) Art Mus., 1989, From the Studio: Recent Painting and Sculpture by 20 California Artists, Oakland (Calif.) Mus., 1992; painting and sculptures represented in permanent collections, Neue Gallerie der Stadt Acchen, Germany, AT&T, San Francisco Internat. Airport, Oakland Mus., Calif., Owens Corning, Vesti Corp., Boston, Varney Collection, San Francisco, Ohio, Capital Group Inc., Los Angeles, McDermott, Will & Emery, N.Y.C., Clayton E. Michael CPA., San Fancisco, Police Data Systems, Dublin, Calif., John F. Kennedy U., Orinda, Calif., Madison (Wis.) Art Ctr.; author: Visions, Bill Martin Paintings 1969-1979, Composition In Painting Drawing, Joy of Drawing, Lost Legends, 1995, (videotape series) Principles of Painting. Home: PO Box 511 Albion CA 95410-0511

MARTIN, BOE WILLIS, lawyer; b. Texarkana, Ark., Oct. 6, 1940; s. E. H. and Dorothy Annette (Willis) M.; m. Carol J. Edwards, June 12, 1965; children—Stephanie Diane, Scott Andrew. B.A., Tex. A&M U., 1962; LL.B., U. Tex., 1964; LL.M., George Washington U., 1970. Bar: Tex. 1964. Law clk. Tex. Supreme Ct. 1966-67; assoc. Snakard, Brown & Gambill, Fort Worth, 1967-69; legis. asst. counsel U.S. Senate Labor and Pub. Welfare Com., 1969; legis. asst. U.S. Senator Ralph W. Yarborough, 1969-71; assoc., ptnr. Snakard, Brown & Gambill, Fort Worth, 1971-72; assoc., ptnr. Stalcup & Johnson, Dallas, 1972-77; assoc., ptnr. Coke & Coke, Dallas, 1977-80; ptnr., shareholder Johnson & Gibbs, Dallas, 1981-95, Hutcheson & Grundy, LLP, 1995-96, Bell & Nunnally, 1996—; vis. prof. law So. Meth. U. Sch. Law, 1972, 73, 75, 88, 89, U. Tex. Sch. Law, 1977, 79. Mem. Carter-Mondale Campaign staff, 1976, 1980; cons. to Vice-Pres. of U.S., 1977-80; cons. Mondale for Pres. Campaign, 1983-84, Dukakis for Pres. campaign, 1988, State of Minn., for visit of Pres. Mikhail Gorbachev, 1990. Served to capt. U.S. Army, 1964-69. Mem. ABA, Tex. Bar Assn., Dallas Bar Assn. Democrat. Methodist. Contbr. articles to legal jours. Home: 4435 Arcady Ave Dallas TX 75205-3604 Office: Bell & Nunnally 3232 Mckinney Ave Ste 1400 Dallas TX 75204-7422

MARTIN, BOYCE FICKLEN, JR., federal judge; b. Boston, Oct. 23, 1935; s. Boyce Ficklen and Helen Artt M.; m. Mavin Hamilton Brown, July 8, 1961; children: Mary V. H., Julia H.C., Boyce Ficklen III, Robert C. G. II. AB, Davidson Coll., 1957; JD, U. Va., 1963. Bar: Ky. 1963. Law clk. to Shackelford Miller, Jr., chief judge U.S. Ct. Appeals for 6th Circuit, Cin., 1963-64; asst. U.S. atty. Western Dist. Ky., Louisville, 1964; U.S. atty. Western Dist. Ky., 1965; pvt. practice law Louisville, 1966-74; judge Jefferson Circuit Ct., Louisville, 1974-76; chief judge Ct. Appeals Ky., Louisville, 1976-79; judge U.S. Ct. Appeals (6th cir.), Cin. and Louisville, 1979-96, chief judge, 1996—; mem. judicial coun. U.S. Ct. Appeals (6th cir.), 1979-96, chmn., 1996—, judicial conf. of U.S., 1996—. Mem. vestry St. Francis in the Fields Episcopal Ch., Harrods Creek, Ky., 1979-83; bd. visitors Davidson (N.C.) Coll., 1980-86, trustee, 1994—; trustee Isaac W. Bernheim Found., Louisville, 1981—, chmn., 1982-95; trustee Blackacre Found., Inc., Louisville, 1983-94, chmn., 1986-94; trustee Hanover (Ind.) Coll., 1983—, vice chmn., 1992—; mem. exec. bd. Old Ky. Home coun. Boy Scouts of Am., 1968-72; pres. Louisville Zool. Commn., 1971-74. Capt. JAGC U.S. Army, 1958-66. Fellow Am. Bar Found.; mem. Inst. Jud. Adminstrn., Am. Judicature Soc., Fed Bar Assn., ABA (com. effective appellate advocacy Conf. Appellate Judges), Ky. Bar Assn., Louisville Bar Assn. Office: US Ct Appeals 209 US Courthouse 601 W Broadway Louisville KY 40202-2238

MARTIN, BOYD ARCHER, political science educator emeritus; b. Cottonwood, Idaho, Mar. 3, 1911; s. Archer Olmstead and Norah Claudine (Imbler) M.; m. Grace Charlotte Swingler, Dec. 29, 1933; children: Michael Archer, William Archer. Student, U. Idaho, 1929-30, 35-36, B.S., 1936; student, Pasadena Jr. Coll., 1931-32, U. Calif. at Los Angeles, summer 1934; A.M., Stanford, 1937, Ph.D., 1943. Rsch. asst. Stanford U., 1936-37, teaching asst., 1937-38; instr. polit. sci. U. Idaho, 1938-39; acting instr. polit. sci. Stanford U., 1939-40; John M. Switzer fellow, summer 1939-40; chief personnel officer Walter Butler Constrn. Co., Farragut Naval Tng. Center, summer 1942; instr. polit. sci. U. Idaho, 1940-43, asst. prof. polit. sci., 1943-44, asso. prof. polit. sci., 1944-47; prof., head dept. social sci., asst. dean coll. letters and sci. U. Idaho, 1947-55, dean, 1955-70, Borah Distinguished prof. polit. sci., 1970-73, prof., dean emeritus, 1973—; vis. prof. Stanford U., summer 1946, spring 1952, U. Calif., 1962-63; affiliate Center for Study Higher Edn., Berkeley, 1962-63; mem. steering com. N.W. Conf. on Higher Edn., 1960-67, pres. conf., 1966-67; mem. bd. Am. Assn. of Partners of Alliance for Progress; chmn. Idaho Adv. Coun. on Higher Edn.; del. Gt. Plains UNESCO Conf., Denver, 1947; chmn. bd. William E. Borah Found. on Causes of War and Conditions of Peace, 1947-55; mem. Commn. to Study Orgn. Peace; dir. Bur. Pub. Affair Rsch., 1959-73, dir. emeritus, 1973—; dir. Martin Peace Inst., 1970—. Author: The Direct Primary in Idaho, 1947, (with others) Introduction to Political Science, 1950, (with other) Western Politics, 1968, Politics in the American West, 1969, (with Sydney Duncombe) Recent Elections in Idaho (1964-70), 1972, Idaho Voting Trends: Party Realignment and Percentage of Voters for Candidates, Parties and Elections, 1890-1974, 1975, In Search of Peace: Starting From October 19, 1980, 1980, Why the Democrats Lost in 1980, 1980, On Understanding the Soviet Union, 1987; editor: The Responsibilities of Colleges and Universities, 1967; contbr. to: Ency. Britannica, 1990, 91; also articles. Mem. Am. Polit. Sci. Assn. (exec. council 1952-53), Nat. Municipal League, Am. Soc. Pub. Adminstrn., Fgn. Policy Assn., UN Assn., AAUP, Western Polit. Sci. Assn. (pres. 1950), Phi Beta Kappa, Pi Gamma Mu, Kappa Delta Pi, Pi Sigma Alpha. Home: 516 N Eisenhower St Moscow ID 83843-9596 *Attempt to contribute to society to the maximum of your ability. Assume responsibility in positions commensurate with the obligations and accountability of the position. In making decisions, first gather all factual data, interpret it fairly, make the decision, and assume responsibility for the decision. In dealing with people, whether family, friends, professionals, or adversaries, try to remember the sensitivity of personal feelings and personal pride. Commend people who achieve and contribute. Be completely honest; when you don't know, admit it.*

MARTIN, BRUCE JAMES, newspaper editor; b. Pontiac, Mich., Sept. 2, 1956; s. James Patrick and Patricia Ann (Taylor) M.; m. Elizabeth Hartley Nutting, July 30, 1988. BJ, U. Mo., 1982. Reporter Spinal Col. Newsweekly, Union Lake, Mich., 1982; sports editor Northville (Mich.) Record/Novi News, 1982-85; news editor Novi News, Northville, 1984-85; copy editor Kalamazoo Gazette, 1985-89; copy editor Ann Arbor (Mich.) News, 1989-91, homes editor, 1991, arts and entertainment editor, 1991—. Recipient 1st Place in Sports Writing in Circulation Category, Mich. Press Assn., 1993. Avocations: songwriting, playing piano and guitar. Office: Ann Arbor News 340 E Huron St Ann Arbor MI 48104-1909*

MARTIN, BRYAN LESLIE, allergist, immunologist; b. Macomb, Ill., June 25, 1954; s. George Albert and Vernal Louise (Stutsman) M.; m. Deborah Ann Schettig, June 22, 1979; children: Emily, Stephanie, Scott. BA, St. Vincent Coll., 1976; postgrad., Ohio U., 1976-79; DO, U. Osteo. Medicine/Hlth. Scis., 1984; M of Mil. Art and Sci., Command & Staff Officer Coll., 1994. Diplomate Am. Bd. Internal Medicine, Am. Bd. Allergy and Immunology, Nat. Bd. Osteo. Med. Examiners. Commd. 2d lt. U.S. Army, 1980, advanced through grades to lt. col., 1996, comdr. med. troop 3d armored cavalry regiment, 1990-91; resident in internal medicine William Beaumont Army Med. Ctr., 1987-90, chief med. resident, 1990-91; with U.S. Army Command and Gen. Staff Coll., 1993-94. Student body pres. U. Osteopathic Medicine and Health Scis., Des Moines, 1981-82. Allergy/immunology fellow Fitzsimons Army Med. Ctr., Aurora, Colo., 1991-93; Health Professions scholar U.S. Army, 1980-84; decorated Bronze star. Fellow Am. Coll. Allergy, Asthma and Immunology (fellow-in-tng. rep. to bd. regents 1991-93, chmn. fellow-in-tng. sect. 1992-93, chmn. VIT Bowl planning com. 1995—), Am. Acad. Allergy, Asthma and Immunology; mem. ACP, AMA (del. resident physicians sect. 1991-93, young physicians sect. 1993—), Am. Osteo. Assn. (del. 1981-83), Dustoff Assn., Nat. Med. Vets. Soc., Sigma Sigma Phi. Avocations: mountain biking, karate, photography, model railroading, computers. Office: SW Allergy and Asthma Ctr 7711 Louis Pasteur Dr Ste 901 San Antonio TX 78229-3424

MARTIN, CAROL JACQUELYN, educator, artist; b. Ft. Worth, Tex., Oct. 6, 1943; d. John Warren and Dorothy Lorene (Coffman) Edwards; m. Boe Willis Martin, Oct. 6, 1940; children: Stephanie Diane, Scott Andrew. BA summa cum laude, U. N. Tex., 1965; MA, U. Tex., El Paso, 1967. Tchr. Edgemere Elem. Sch., El Paso, Tex., 1965-66, Fulmore Jr. H.S., Austin, 1966-67, Monnig Jr. H.S., Ft. Worth, 1967-68, Paschal H.S., Ft. Worth, 1968-69; instr. Tarrant County Jr. Coll., Ft. Worth, 1968-69, 71-72; press sec. U.S. Sen. Gaylord Nelson, Washington, 1969-71; instr. Eastfield C.C., Dallas, 1981, Richland C.C. Dist., 1982. Editor The Avesta Mag., 1964-65; exhibited in group shows at City of Richardson's Cottonwood Park, 1970-86, Students of Ann Cushing Gantz, 1973-85, Art About Town, 1979, 80, shows by Tarrant County and Dallas County art assns. Active Dallas Symphony Orch. League, Easter Seal Soc., Women's Auxiliary of Nexus, Dallas Hist. Soc., Women's Bd. of the Dallas Opera, Dallas Arboretum and Garden Club, Dallas County Heritage Soc. Mem. Internat. Platform Assn., Mortar Bd., Alpha Chi, Sigma Tau Delta, Kappa Delta Pi, Delta Gamma. Democrat. Methodist. Avocations: travel, photography, snow skiing, oil painting. Address: 4435 Arcady Ave Dallas TX 75205-3604

MARTIN, CATHERINE ELIZABETH, anthropology educator; b. N.Y.C., Feb. 14, 1943; d. Walter Charles and Ruth (Crucet) Strodt; children: Kai Stuart, Armin Wade. BA, Reed Coll., 1965; MA, UCLA, 1967, PhD, 1971. Cert. C.C. tchr., Ariz., Calif. From asst. to full prof. anthropology Calif. State U., L.A., 1970-96; prof. emeritus —, —, 1996; coord. women's studies Calif. State U., L.A., 1979-88, acting dir. acad. advisement, 1992-93, dir. Can. studies, 1991, advisement coord., 1996, prof. emeritus, 1996; assoc. faculty Mohave C.C., Kingman, Ariz., 1996—; adj. prof. No. Ariz. U., 1997—. Contbr. chpts. to books and poetry to profl. publs. Cubmaster, den mother Boy Scouts Am., L.A. and Pasadena, 1982-85; leader Tiger Cubs, Boy Scouts Am., 1983. Recipient Outstanding Tiger Cub Leader award Boy Scouts Am., L.A., 1983, Cub Scout Growth award Boy Scouts Am., L.A., 1984. Fellow Soc. Applied Anthropology; mem. Am. Anthropol. Assn., Southwestern Anthropol. Assn. Avocations: reading, traveling, new experiences.

MARTIN, CHARLES WALLACE, travel executive, retired university administrator; b. Columbia, S.C., Feb. 1, 1916; s. Earle Purkerson and Caroline Louise (Keenan) M.; m. Nancy Miles Chisolm, Sept. 30, 1944; children: Nancy Miles, Charles Wallace, Louise Elizabeth. B.A., U. S.C., 1936. Br. office employee N.Y. Life Ins. Co., Columbia, 1936-38; mgr. Palmetto Theatre Co., Columbia, 1938-42, Reamer Appliance Co., Columbia, 1946-47; local sales mgr. WIS Radio, Columbia, 1947-50; pres., gen. mgr. WMSC Radio, Columbia, 1950-60; dir. devel. U. S.C., Columbia, 1960-66; exec. dir. ednl. found. U. S.C., 1960-77, v.p. for devel., 1966-77, instr. English, 1948-52; chmn. Carolina V.I.P. Tours, 1977—; adv. bd. Bankers Trust S.C., Columbia, 1960-78. Chmn. United Way Columbia, 1954; pres. Columbia Philharm. Orch., 1967-68; commr. Columbia Housing Authority, 1971-76, chmn., 1974-76; bd. dirs. Bus. Ptnrs. Found., 1969-77, Providence Hosp. Found., 1977-82; trustee Columbia Mus. Arts and Sci., 1977-80, 88-94, life mem.; co-chmn. S.C. Gov.'s Mansion Found., 1979-83; vestryman Trinity Cathedral, Columbia; chmn. Trinity Found. Lt. USNR, 1942-45. Named Young Man of Year Columbia, 1951. Mem. Columbia Stage Soc. (dir. 1947-59, 66-69), Greater Columbia C. of C. (pres. 1959), S.C. Broadcasters Assn. (pres. 1954), Am. Coll. Pub. Relations Assn. (dir., treas. Mason-Dixon dist. 1967-72), English-Speaking Union U.S. (pres. Columbia br. 1973-75, nat. dir. 1972-75), Sigma Nu, Omicron Delta Kappa, Pi Gamma Mu. Episcopalian. Clubs: Kiwanian (pres. 1957), Forest Lake, Pine Tree Hunt (pres. 1985-86) Centurion Soc., Columbia Ball (pres. 1959), Forum (pres. 1989-90), Palmetto. Home: 1718 Madison Rd Columbia SC 29204

MARTIN, CHESTER Y., sculptor, painter; b. Chattanooga, Nov. 2, 1934; s. Woodfin Ballenger and Mabel Willett (Young) M.; m. Patricia Ann Parnell, Aug. 15, 1963; 1 child, Sharon Elizabeth (Mrs. Christopher Pruitt). Student, U. Chattanooga, 1952-55, 60-61, Internat. Medallic Workshop-Pa. State U., 1984. Freelance artist Chattanooga, 1967-86; sculptor, engraver U.S. Mint, Phila., 1986-92. One-man shows include Hunter Mus. Art, Chattanooga, 1979; group shows: Kottler Galleries, N.Y.C., 1966; Internat. Exposition Contemporary Medals, Italy, 1983, Sweden, 1985, Finland, 1990; U.S. Dept. State, 1984, Nat. Sculpture Soc., N.Y.C., 1984, 85, Cast Iron Gallery, N.Y.C., 1992, Internat. Exhbn. of Contemporary Medals, Brit. Mus., London, 1992, Hungarian Nat. Gallery, Budapest, 1994, Neuchatel, 1996, numerous others; permanent collections: British Mus., London; Smithsonian Instn.; Food and Agrl. Orgn., Rome; Am. Numismatic Soc., N.Y.C.; Julius Wile Sons and Co., N.Y.C.; Brookgreen Gardens, S.C., U.S. Mint, Phila.; major comms.: World Food Day Medal, UN, 1984, others; other major works: History of Chattanooga Mural, 1974; Centennial Mural for Chattem Inc., Chattanooga, 1980; sculptured Congl. Bicentennial Silver Dollar, 1989, Eisenhower Centennial Dollar reverse, Mt. Rushmore Dollar obverse, 1991; designer Andrew Wyeth Congl. medal, 1989, George Bush Presdl. medal reverse; designer Yosemite Nat. Park Centennial Congressional Medal, 1991, Gen. Colin L. Powell Congressional Medal, 1992, White House Bicentennial Dollar reverse, 1992. Served with USAF, 1956-60. Recipient numerous art awards, most recent being Purchase award Benedictine Art Competition, 1975, Medallic Sculpture award Am. Numismatic Assn., 1993. Mem. Fedn. Internationale de la Medaille (Am. del.), Am. Medallic Sculpture Assn. (v.p. 1987). Methodist. Avocations: modern languages. Mailing Address: 4110 Sunbury Ave Chattanooga TN 37411-5232

MARTIN, CHRISTY, professional boxer; b. Orlando, Fla., June 12, 1968. Named Women's Lightweight Champion. Achievements include a record of 36 wins, two losses, and two ties, including 26 knock-outs. Office: c/o Consejo Mundial de Boxeo, Genova 33 Oespacho # 503, 06600 Mexico City Mexico

MARTIN, CLARA RITA, elementary education educator; b. Steubenville, Ohio, Oct. 14, 1953; d. Robert Emmett and Mary Agnes (Flynn) Joyce; m. Gary Dean Martin, July 8, 1978; children: Bradley A., Douglas A. BS in Elem. Edn., Coll. Steubenville, 1975; MS in Interdisciplinary Skills, U. Dayton, 1984. Cert. tchr., Ohio. Reading specialist Steubenville City Sch. Dist., 1975; tchr. elem. schs. Harrison Hills City Sch. Dist., Jewett and Hopedale, Ohio, 1975—; coord. spelling bee Harrison News Herald Spelling Bee, Cadiz, Ohio, 1984—. Jump Rope for Heart coord., asst. coord. Meml. Day Program, 1992. Mem. Harrison Hills Tchrs.' Assn. (grievance chair, chief negotiator 1980—, bldg. rep. 1985—, del. Ohio Edn. Assn. Conv., 1981—), Ladies Ancient Order Hibernians (sec. 1991-92). Roman Catholic. Avocations: reading, travel. Home: 4059 State Hwy 43 Richmond OH 43944-7912

MARTIN, CLAUDE RAYMOND, JR., marketing consultant, educator; b. Harrisburg, Pa., May 11, 1932; s. Claude R. and Marie Teresa (Stapf) M.; m. Marie Frances Culkin, Nov. 16, 1957; children: Elizabeth Ann, David Jude, Nancy Marie, William Jude, Patrick Jude, Cecelia Marie. B.S., U. Scranton, 1954, M.B.A, 1963; Ph.D., Columbia U., 1969. Newsman Sta. WILK-TV, Wilkes-Barre, Pa., 1953-55; news dir. Sta. WNEP-TV, Scranton, Pa., 1955-60; dir. systems Blue Cross & Blue Shield Ins., Wilkes-Barre, 1960-63; lectr. mktg. St. Francis Coll., Bklyn., 1964, U. Mich., Ann Arbor, 1965-68; asst. prof. U. Mich., 1968-73, asso. prof., 1973-77, prof., 1977-80, Isadore and Leon Winkelman prof. retail mktg., 1980—, chmn. mktg. dept., 1986-90; bd. dirs. Perry Drug Stores, cons. mktg., 1983-89; spl. cons. on rsch. changes in U.S. currency Fed. Res. Sys., 1978—; pub. mem. Nat. Advt. Rev. Bd., 1989-94. Contbr. articles on mktg. analysis, consumer research to profl. publs. Trustee U. Scranton, 1996—. Served with USNR, 1955-57. Mem. Acad. Mktg. Sci., Am. Mktg. Assn., S.W. Mktg. Assn., Bank Mktg. Assn., Assn. Consumer Research, Am. Collegiate Retailing Assn., Am. Acad. Advt. Roman Catholic. Home: 1116 Aberdeen Dr Ann Arbor MI 48104-2812

MARTIN, CLYDE VERNE, psychiatrist; b. Coffeyville, Kans., Apr. 7, 1933; s. Howard Verne and Elfrieda Louise (Moehn) M.; m. Barbara Jean McNeilly, June 24, 1956; children: Kent Clyde, Kristin Claire, Kerry Constance, Kyle Curtis. Student Coffeyville Coll., 1951-52; AB, U. Kans., 1955; MD, 1958; MA, Webster Coll., St. Louis, 1977; JD, Thomas Jefferson Coll. Law, Los Angeles, 1985. Diplomate Am. Bd. Psychiatry and Neurology. Intern, Lewis Gale Hosp., Roanoke, Va., 1958-59; resident in psychiatry U. Kans. Med. Ctr., Kansas City, 1959-62, Fresno br. U. Calif.-San Francisco, 1978; staff psychiatrist Neurol. Hosp., Kansas City, 1962; practice medicine specializing in psychiatry, Kansas City, Mo., 1964-84; founder, med. dir., pres. bd. dirs. Mid-Continent Psychiat. Hosp., Olathe, Kans., 1972-84; adj. prof. psychology Baker U., Baldwin City, Kans., 1969-84; staff psychiatrist Atascadero State Hosp., Calif., 1984-85; clin. prof. psychiatry U. Calif., San Francisco, 1985—; chief psychiatrist Calif. Med. Facility, Vacaville, 1985-87; pres., editor Corrective and Social Psychiatry, Olathe, 1970-84, Atascadero, 1984-85, Fairfield, 1985—. Contbr. articles to profl. jours. Bd. dirs. Meth. Youthville, Newton, Kans. 1965-75, Spofford Home, Kansas City, 1974-78. Served to capt. USAF, 1962-64, ret. col. USAFR. Oxford Law & Soc. scholar, 1993. Fellow Am. Psychiat. Assn., Royal Soc. Health, Am. Assn. Mental Health Profls. in Corrections, World Assn. Social Psychiatry, Am. Orthopsychiat. Assn.; mem. AMA, Assn. for Advancement Psychotherapy, Am. Assn. Sex Educators, Counselors and Therapists (cert.), Assn. Mental Health Adminstrs. (cert.), Kansas City Club, Masons, Phi Beta Pi, Pi Kappa Alpha. Methodist (del. Kans. East Conf. 1972-80, bd. global ministries 1974-80). Office: PO Box 3365 Fairfield CA 94533-0587

MARTIN, CRAIG LEE, engineering company executive; b. Dodge City, Kans., Nov. 23, 1949; s. Ray N. and Nadia C. Martin; m. Diane E. Hensley, Mar. 19, 1977. BS in Civil Engring., U. Kans., 1971; MBA, U. Denver, 1982. Project mgr. Martin K. Eby Constrn. Co., Wichita, Kans., 1972-83; exec. v.p., COO CRSS Constructors, Inc., Denver, 1983-89; exec. v.p. CRSS Comml. Group, Houston, 1989-90; sr. v.p. CRSS Capital, Houston, 1990-92, CRSS Inc., Houston, 1992-94; pres. CRSS Architects, Inc., Houston, 1992-94; sr. v.p. ops. Jacobs Engring. Group Inc., 1994-95; pres. Jacobs Constructors, Inc., 1994-95; sr. v.p. gen. sales and mktg. Jacobs Engring. Group, Inc., 1995—; mem. adv. bd. Constrn. Bus. Rev., 1993—; bd. dirs. Meridian Engrs. Mem. ASCE, Am. Mgmt. Assn. Avocations: golf, clay shooting, fishing. Home: 930 S El Molino Ave Pasadena CA 91106-4414 Office: Jacobs Engring Group Inc 251 S Lake Ave Pasadena CA 91101-3003

MARTIN, CURTIS, professional football player; b. Pitts., May 1, 1973. Student, U. Pitts. Running back New Eng. Patriots, Foxboro, Mass., 1995—. Selected to Pro Bowl, 1995, 96. Office: care New England Patriots 60 Washington St Foxboro MA 02035*

MARTIN, DALE, vocational rehabilitation executive; b. N.Y.C., May 10, 1935; d. Byron Pink Molter and Ruth (Nobel) Gestram; m. Robert A. Wishart, Dec. 13, 1985; children by previous marriage: Elizabeth, Devon. BS, U. Conn., 1957. RN, cert. case mgr., ins. rehab. specialist, lic. rehab. counsellor, Mass. Dental asst. Hempstead, N.Y., 1951; with Weston Maternity Hosp., Springfield, Mass., 1957-58, Huntington Hartford Meml. Hosp., Pasadena, Calif., 1958-59; office mgr. Indsl. By Products Inc., Kalamazoo, Mich., 1969-72; controller Indsl. By Products Inc., Chgo., 1970-74; cons. Mgmt. Resources Inc., Broomall, Pa., 1978-81; cons., owner Martin-Collard Assocs., Inc., Monmouth Beach, N.J., 1980-84; cons., owner, chmn. bd. dirs. MCA, Inc., Boston, 1984—; bd. dirs. Consortium Advantage, Inc., Boston; ind. rep. JewelWay Internat., Inc., Platinum Exec.; cons. Viewfinder, Old Chatham, N.Y., 1987—, Phoenix Inc., Global Explorations, Inc. Contbr. articles to profl. jours.; painter, sculptor. Bd. govs. Rumson-Fair Haven H.S., N.J., 1976-78; benefit tennis co-chair Jordan Hosp.-White Cliffs Country Club. Mem. Nat. Assn. Rehab. Profls. in Pvt. Sector (forensic sect., past rep. region I to bd. dirs.), Nat. Rehab. Assn. (pvt. sector group), Internat. Assn. Psychosocial Rehab. Specialists, New Eng. Claims Assn., Individual Case Mgmt. Assn., Mass. Nurses Assn. (chmn. image com. 1984-85), Town Club (v.p.), Mountain Lakes Ski Club (founder), Jr. Women's Club, Jr. League, Sigma Theta Tau, Alpha Delta Pi. Avocations: painting, tennis, N.J. state girls gymnastic judge. Office: MCA Inc PO Box 1617 Sagamore Beach MA 02562 also: MCA Inc PO Box 789 Port Salerno FL 34992-0789

MARTIN, DANIEL C., surgeon, educator; b. St. Louis, Apr. 7, 1946; s. Dan Allen and Ruth Keel (Fields) M.; m. Glenn Ann Blakemore, July 7, 1970; children: Josh, Adam. BS in Physics, Emory U., 1968, MD, 1972. Diplomate Am. Bd. Ob-Gyn. Rsch. asst. physics and radiology Emory U., Atlanta, 1968-69; intern, resident, fellow, instr. The Johns Hopkins Med. Instns., Balt., 1972-77; from asst. prof. to clin. asst. prof. U. Tenn., Memphis, 1977-90, clin. assoc. prof., 1990—; surgeon Reproductive Surgery, P.C., Memphis, 1977—; reproductive surgeon Bapt. Meml. Hosp., 1977—; Axel Munthe presenter, Naples, Italy, 1992; guest spkr. 15th Annual Japanese Endometriosis Symposium, Osaka, 1994; dir. gynecologic laser and endoscopy workshops, 1982-93. Editor: (textbooks) Lasers in Endoscopy, 1990, Laparoscopic Appearance of Endometriosis, 1990, Manual of Endoscopy, 1990, Atlas of Endometriosis, 1993, Endoscopic Management of Gynecologic Disease, 1996. Basketball coach Grace St. Luke's Ch., Memphis, 1992-95. Picker Found. fellow Emory U., 1969; Tex. Assn. Ob-Gyn. hon. fellow, 1989; recipient Bridges trophy for athletics Emory U., 1968, Codman surg. award, 1982, 83, Video award Am. Fertility Soc., 1992, Physician Recognition awrd Endometriosis Assn., 1995; named one of Best Drs. Am. Woodward and White Inc., 1992, 94, Hon. mem. Australian Gynecol. Endoscopy Soc., 1993. Mem. ACOG (sect. chair jr. fellows Md.), Tenn. Med. Assn., Memphis and Shelby County Med. Soc. (comm. com.), Am. Nat. Std. Inst. (subcom. on laser safety in med. facility), Am. Assn. Gynecol. Laparoscopists (pres. 1990-91, Videoendoscopy award 1993), Gynecologic Surgery Soc. (pres. 1994-96, chmn. bd. 1996—), Australian Gynecol. Endoscopy Soc. (hon.). Office: Reproductive Surgery PC 1717 Kirby Pkwy Ste 100 Memphis TN 38120-4331

MARTIN, DANIEL RICHARD, pharmaceutical company executive; b. Lima, Peru, June 9, 1937; s. James Marion and Clemmy Caroline (Valencia) M.; m. Barbara Artemis Cyrus, June 23, 1962; children: Daniel Richard Jr., John Alexander, Christopher Andrew. BA, Cornell U., 1958; MS, Columbia U., N.Y.C., 1959. Area sales supr. Schering Corp., Bloomfield, N.J., 1960-64; assoc. McKinsey & Co., N.Y.C., 1964-69; treas. Harper & Row, Pubs., N.Y.C., 1969-72; mng. dir. Merck & Co., Rahway, N.J., 1972-77; group v.p. Bell & Howell Co., Chgo., 1977-80; pres. Howland Martin Corp., N.Y.C., 1980-85; pres. Sterling Europe, Middle East, Africa Sterling Drug, Inc., N.Y.C., 1986-89; pres., CEO E-Z-EM, Inc., Westbury, N.Y., 1990—; adj. prof. mgmt. Pace U., N.Y.C., 1996—. Co-chmn. Accion Internat., Cambridge, Mass., 1988—; trustee Bangor (Maine) Theol. Sem., 1991—; dir. Americas Found.; bd. dirs., fin. com. White Plains (N.Y.) Hosp. Decorated Order of Merit (Ecuador). Mem. Coun. on Fgn. Rels., Americas Soc., Univ. Club (N.Y.C., Chgo.), Cornell Club (N.Y.C.). Republican. Congregationalist. Home: 2 Dolma Rd Scarsdale NY 10583-4506 Office: E-Z-EM Inc 717 Main St Westbury NY 11590-5021

MARTIN, DANIEL WILLIAM, acoustical physicist; b. Georgetown, Ky., Nov. 18, 1918; s. Dean William and Ethel (Weigle) M.; m. Martha Elizabeth Parker, June 9, 1941; children: Mary Elizabeth, David William, Nancy Jane, Donald Warren. A.B., Georgetown Coll., 1937, Sc.D., 1981; M.S., U. Ill., 1939, Ph.D., 1941. Asst. physics U. Ill. at Urbana, 1937-41; with RCA, 1941-49, tech. coordinator, 1946-49; acoustical research supr. Baldwin Piano Co., Cin., 1949-57; research dir. D.H. Baldwin Co., Cin., 1957-70, 74-83; chief engr. D.H. Baldwin Co., 1970-74; acoustical cons., 1983—; extension instr. math. Purdue U., 1941-46; asst. prof. mus. acoustics U. Cin., 1964-73, assoc. prof., 1973-75. Author; Editor: I.R.E. Trans. on Audio, 1953-55; assoc. editor: Sound, 1961-63; patent reviewer Jour. Acoustical Soc. Am, 1950—, assoc. editor, 1977-85, editor-in-chief, 1985—. Trustee Pikeville Coll., 1976-82; mem. theology and worship ministry unit Presbyn. Ch. (U.S.A.), 1987-93, vice-chair, 1987-89, 91-92, vice-chmn. Presbyn. Assn. for Sci., Tech. and Christian Faith, 1992-97. Recipient Ohio Engr. of Yr. award Nat. Soc. Profl. Engrs., 1972. Fellow Acoustical Soc. Am. (exec. council 1957-60, pres.-elect 1983-84, pres. 1984-85), Audio Engring. Soc. (pres. 1964-65), IEEE (nat. chmn. audio group 1956-57); mem. Engring. Soc. Cin. (dir. 1964-67, pres. 1969-70), Tech. and Sci. Socs. Council Cin. (pres. 1967-68, Cin. Engr. Year 1972), Nat. Council Presbyn. Men (pres. 1977). Republican. Patentee in field. Home and Office: 7349 Clough Pike Cincinnati OH 45244-3745 *A Christian home, economic need, and early choice of profession gave me momentum. Generous personal assistance and teaching, professional opportunity and family stability sustained my efforts. The byproducts of striving for goals are just as valuable as the realization of goals. Building bridges between disciplines is difficult but intellectually stimulating. Great are the rewards of service to profession, people and the church.*

MARTIN, DARRIS LEE, quality assurance executive; b. Greenville, Miss., June 2, 1950; s. Robert Talis and L'Vee (Preston) M. BS in Bus. and Fin., Ind. U., 1971; diploma in theology, Gospel Crusade Inc., Bradenton, Fla., 1977. Fin. cons., traveling bible tchr. Gospel Crusade, Inc., 1977-78; estimator Sign Mart Neon Co., Daytona Beach, Fla., 1978-79; with GE, 1971-77, 79—; supr. plant, taxes and expense acctg. GE, Daytona Beach, Fla., 1982-83; specialist reliability & quality assurance program planning GE, Binghamton, N.Y., 1983-84, project leader quality control engring., 1984-85, mgr. quality systems, 1985-87, mgr. ops. planning, 1987-88, mgr. ops. compliance aerospace control systems, 1988-90; mgr. AOD quality programs GEO Aerospace Ops. Divsn. (now Lockheed Martin Elec. Sector), Valley Forge, Pa., 1990-95; mgr. material quality Acquisition Ctr. GEO Aerospace Ops. Divsn. (now Lockheed Martin Elec. Sector), Utica, N.Y., 1995; mgr. site SQA inte. MAC-MAR Lockheed Martin, Syracuse, N.Y., 1996-97; acting dir. SQA MAC-MAR Lockheed Martin, Moorestown, N.J., 1997—. Formerly vol. supr. Agape Crisis Ctr., active numerous programs including Park Outreach activities for youth, big. brother Halifax Area Youth in Action, counselor, religious instr. Fla. Dept. Corrections. Named MM2 Outstanding Tchr. of Yr., Fla. Dept. Corrections, 1976. Mem. Am. Soc. Quality Control (membership chmn. 1988-89), Zeta Epsilon chpt. Omega Psi Phi (keepr of fin. 1969-71, Man of Yr. 1971). Pentacostal. Avocation: oil portrait artist. Home: 2 C Gardenia Dr Maple Shade NJ 08052

MARTIN, DAVID ALAN, law educator, government official; b. Indpls., July 23, 1948; s. C. Wendell and Elizabeth Bowman (Meeker) M.; m. Cynthia Jo Lorman, June 13, 1970; children: Amy Lynn, Jeffrey David. BA, DePauw U., 1970; JD, Yale U., 1975. Bar: D.C. Law clk. Hon. J. Skelly Wright U.S. Ct. Appeals (D.C. cir.), 1975-76; law clk. Hon. Lewis F. Powell U.S. Supreme Ct., Washington, 1976-77; assoc. Rogovin, Stern & Huge, Washington, 1977-78; spl. asst. bur. human rights and humanitarian affairs U.S. State Dept., Washington, 1978-80; from asst. prof. to assoc. prof. U. Va. Sch. Law, Charlottesville, 1980-86, prof., 1986-91, Henry L. & Grace Doherty prof. law, 1991—, F. Palmer Weber Rsch. prof. civil liberties and human rights, 1992-95; on leave U.S. Immigration and Naturalization Svc., Washington, 1995—; cons. Adminstrv. Conf. U.S., Washington, 1988-89, 91-92, U.S. Dept. Justice, 1993-95; gen. counsel U.S. Immigration and Naturalization Svc., 1995—. Author: Immigration: Process and Policy, 1985, 2d edit., 1991, 3d edit., 1995, Asylum Case Law Sourcebook, 1994, The Endless Quest: Helping America's Farm Workers, 1994; editor: The New Asylum Seekers, 1988; contbr. numerous articles to profl. jours. Mem. nat. governing bd. Common Cause, Washington, 1972-75; elder Westminster Presbyn. Ch., Charlottesville, 1982-84, 89-92. German Marshall Fund Rsch. Fellow, Geneva, 1984-85. Mem. Am. Soc. Internat. Law (ann. book award 1986), Internat. Law Assn. Democrat. Office: Immign & Naturaliz Svc 425 I St NW Rm 6100 Washington DC 20536-0001

MARTIN, DAVID BRITON HADDEN, JR., lawyer; b. Beverly, Mass., Dec. 9, 1946; s. David Briton Hadden and Mary Louise (Ward) M.; m. Martha Bacon, June 21, 1969; children: Charlotte, Jessica, Benjamin Ward. BA, Yale U., 1969; JD, U. Va., 1976. Bar: Va. 1976, D.C. 1977. Assoc. Dunnells, Duvall, Bennett & Porter, Washington, 1976-79, Dickstein, Shapiro & Morin, Washington, 1979-80; spl. counsel SEC, Washington, 1980-84, spl. counsel to chmn., 1984-85; assoc. Hogan & Hartson, Washington, 1985-87, ptnr., 1987—. Mng. editor U. Va. Law Review, 1975-76. Chair The Washington Revels, 1993-96; mem. adv. bd. Jubilee Jobs, 1993—; bd. dirs. First Night Alexandria, Va., 1995—, Alexandria Indsl. Devel., 1980-82. Mem. Metro. Club. Office: Hogan & Hartson 555 13th St NW Washington DC 20004-1109

MARTIN, DAVID EDWARD, health sciences educator; b. Green Bay, Wis., Oct. 1, 1939; s. Edward Henry and Lillie (Luckman) M. B.S., U. Wis., 1961, M.S., 1963, Ph.D., 1970. Ford Found. research trainee Wis. Regional Primate Ctr., Madison, 1967-70; asst. prof. health scis. Ga. State U., Atlanta, 1970-74, assoc. prof., 1974-80, prof., 1980-91, regents prof., 1992—; affiliate scientist Yerkes Primate Rsch. Ctr., Emory U., Atlanta, 1970—; U.S. rep. to Internat. Olympic Acad., 1978; sports medicine rsch. assoc. U.S. Olympic Com., 1981-84; chmn. sports scis. U.S.A. Track and Field; mem. coaching staff U.S. teams to world championships in distance running, Rome, 1982, Gateshead, Eng., 1983, Budapest, Hungary, 1994, head coach, Paris, 1980, Madrid, 1984, Hiroshima, Japan, 1985, Warsaw, Poland, 1987, Antwerp, Belgium, 1991; mem. Olympic med. support group Atlanta Olympic Games. Author: Laboratory Experiments in Human Physiology, 4th edit., 1980, The Marathon Footrace, 1979, La Corsa Di Maratona, 1982, The High Jump Book, 1982, 2d edit., 1987, Respiratory Anatomy and Physiology, 1987, Training Distance Runners, 1991, 2d edit., 1997, German edit., 1992, Spanish edit., 1995; contbr. articles to profl. jours. Trustee Ga. Found. for Athletic Excellence. Recipient fed. and univ. grants for physiol. research; named Disting. prof. Ga. State U., 1975, 81, 85. Fellow Am. Coll. Sports Medicine; mem. Internat. Soc. Olympic Historians, Am. Physiol. Soc., Atlanta Track Club. Home: 510 Coventry Rd Apt 13A Decatur GA 30030-5038 Office: Ga State U Dept Cardiopul Surg Atlanta GA 30303

MARTIN, DAVID GEORGE, lawyer; b. George, Iowa, Nov. 7, 1945; s. William David and Frances R. (Harms) M.; m. Karen Cox, Aug. 7, 1966 (div. 1970); 1 child, Stephanie; m. Elizabeth Hoene, May 1, 1987. BS, Sterlin (Kans.) Coll., 1967; JD, U. Minn., 1971. Tchr. Maple Lake (Minn.) Sr. High Sch., 1967-68; assoc. Salland & Faricy, St. Paul, 1971-74; from assoc. to ptnr. Doherty, Rumble & Butler, P.A., St. Paul, 1974—; spl. mcpl. judge White Bear Lake (Minn.) 1973-74. Author: Federal Trial Court Practice, Civil Litigation Environmental Practice, 1990. Mem. Minn. Bar Assn., Assn. Trial Lawyers Am., Minn. Trial Lawyers Assn., Gamma Eta Gamma. Republican. Presbyterian. Office: Doherty Rumble & Butler 2800 Minn World Trade Ctr 30 7th St E Saint Paul MN 55101-4901

MARTIN, DAVID HUBERT, physician, educator; b. Detroit, Mar. 24, 1943; s. Hubert Cillis and Mable Anita (Stewart) M.; m. Jane Ellen Schlichtemeier, Nov. 22, 1970; children: Jennifer, Jason. BA with distinction, U. Kans., 1965; MD cum laude, Harvard Coll., 1969. Diplomate Nat. Bd. Med. Examiners, Am. Bd. Internal Medicine, Infectious Disease Subspecialty Bd. Am. Bd. Internal Medicine. Intern Bronx (N.Y.) Mcpl. Hosp. Ctr., 1969-70; staff assoc. Nat. Inst. Allergy and Infectious Diseases, Mid. Am. Rsch. Unit, NIH, Panama Canal Zone, 1970-73; med. resident U. Wash. Affiliated Hosps., 1973-75; sr. fellow in infectious diseases U. Wash., 1976-78; chief resident in medicine USPHS Hosp., Seattle, 1975-76, staff internal medicine clinic, 1975, attending physician internal medicine, 1976-78; staff dept. internal medicine USPHS Hosp., New Orleans, 1979-81; staff Hotel Dieu Hosp., New Orleans, 1982-94; clin. asst. prof. medicine La. State U. Med. Sch., New Orleans, 1979-81, asst. prof. medicine divsn. infectious diseases, 1981-82, assoc. prof. medicine divsn. infectious diseases, 1982-88, assoc. prof. microbiology, 1986-88, prof. internal medicine and microbiology, 1988, asst. chief sect. infectious diseases, 1988-89, chief sect. infectious diseases, 1990—, Harry E. Dascomb M.D. prof. of medicine, 1990—; instr. dept. medicine U. Wash. Sch. Medicine, Seattle, 1975-78, acting asst. prof. medicine, 1978-79; chmn. infection control com., chmn. instnl. rev. bd. human rsch. com., chmn. antibiotic utilization com., sec. rsch. and editl. com., sec. animal welfare com. USPHS Hosp., New Orleans, 1979-81, dep. chief clin. rsch. dept., 1979-81, chmn. credentials com., 1980-81; mem. infection control com. Hotel Dieu Hosp., New Orleans, 1983-84, chmn. pharmacy and therapeutics com., 1988-94, mem. infection control com., 1990-94; vis. physician Charity Hosp. (now Med. Ctr. of La. at New Orleans), New Orleans, 1982—, chmn. antiobiotics com., 1982—, dir. infection control program, 1993—, chmn. infection control com., 1993—, vice chmn. pharmacy and therapeutics com., 1995—; cons. sexually transmitted diseases control program Dept. Health and Human Resources, State of La., 1985—; staff physician Jefferson Parish Venereal Disease Clinic, 1986-90, New Orleans (La.) Sexually Transmitted Disease Clinic, 1992—; cons. pharmacy and therapeutics com. Mercy Hosp., New Orleans, 1989-91; cons. La. AIDS Cmty. Rsch. Project, 1989-92; chmn. comprehensive medicine head search com. La. State U. Med. Sch., 1989-90, dept. medicine faculty promotion com., 1988—, AIDS policy com., 1992; mem. La. State Labs. Adv. Bd., 1993—, State La. Pub. Health Lab. Adv. Com., 1994—, U.S. Pub. Health Region 6 Infertility Prevention Adv. Com., 1995—; cons. Ctr. Disease Control; lectr., workshop presenter and rschr. in field; others. Peer reviewer various jours. including Sexually Transmitted Diseases, The Jour. of Infectious Diseases, The Am. Jour. of the Med. Scis., Archives of Internal Medicine, Clin. Infectious Diseases, New Eng. Jour. Medicine, Annals Internal Medicine, Jour. AMA; contbr. chpts. to books and articles to profl. jours. With USPHS, 1970-82. Achievements include established the first chlamydia laboratory in the Gulf South. Fellow ACP (La. chpt. program chmn. 1994-95), Infectious Diseases Soc. Am.; mem. Internat. Soc. for Sexually Transmitted Disease Rsch. (bd. dirs. 1991—, chmn. 1995 meeting organizing com. 1993-95), Am. Fedn. for Clin. Rsch., Am. Sexually Transmitted Diseases Assn. (v.p. 1992-94, pres. 1994—), Am. Soc. for Microbiology, European Soc. for Clin. Microbiology and Infectious Diseases, So. Soc. for Clin. Investigation, La./Miss. Infectious Diseases Soc. (bd. dirs., sci. program chmn. 1993, pres. 1997—), Southeastern Clin. Club, Phi Beta Kappa. Achievements include research in the effect of sexually transmitted microorganisms on pregnancy outcome; antibiotic treatment of sexually transmitted diseases and in particular C. trachomatis; the epidemiology of C. trachomatis in normal populations; Chancroid and other genital ulcer diseases. Office: La State U Med Sch 1542 Tulane Ave New Orleans LA 70112-2825

MARTIN, DAVID HUGH, private investigator, business executive, writer; b. Ft. Worth, Mar. 24, 1952; s. Joesph Morgan Jr. and Jane Maurine (Harriss) M.; children: David Christian, Thomas Joshua, Michael Morgan. Ordained to ministry Meth. Ch., 1979; lic. pvt. investigator, Tex. CEO Woodland West Corp., Houston, 1977-84; owner D. H. Martin & Assocs. Investigations, Austin, Tex., 1980—; fin. mgr. The Williams Trust, Austin, 1982—; chmn. Biologic, Inc., Austin, 1983—; pres. Terminal Recovery, Inc., 1995—; exec. dir. Grace Ministries, Austin, 1980—. Author: Rain Music, 1990; albums include Voice of a Child, 1987. Recipient Prism award Nat. Homebuilders Assn., 1979, 80, 82. Mem. MENSA, SAG, Tex. Assn. Lic. Investigators, Tex. Assn. Nurserymen, Rep. Nat. Com. Avocations: deep sea fishing, coin and relic hunting. Office: DH Martin & Assocs PO Box 5581 Austin TX 78763-5581

MARTIN, DAVID S., educator, administrator; b. N.Y.C., May 14, 1941; s. Perry Johnson and Polly Edith (Shedlov) M.; m. Florence E. Martin, Jan. 14, 1989; children: Drew Michael, Amy Davida. BA, Adelphi Coll., 1962, MA, 1966; profl. cert., Hofstra U., 1969. Cert. secondary tchr., sch. dist. adminstr., N.Y. Adj. assoc. prof. Pace U., White Plains, N.Y., 1978—; tchr., computer coord. Jericho (N.Y.) Pub. Schs., 1962—. Author: Teachers Manual for Introduction to Pascal; co-author: How To Prepare for SAT II: Physics, 6th edit.; also author other books; contbr. articles to profl. jours. Fulbright-Hays grantee, 1967-68; recipient Grand award L.I. Sci. Congress, 1958, Disting Achievement award Electronic Learning, 1983, Outstanding Accomplishment award RITEC, 1984. Mem. IEEE (sr.), Internat. Soc. for Technology in Edn., Am. Assn. Physics Tchrs., Assn. Computing Machinery, Authors Guild, Jericho Tchrs. Assn., N.Y. State United Tchrs., Flambeau, Phi Delta Kappa, Sigma Pi Sigma. Home: 16 Elm Pl Sea Cliff NY 11579-1634 Office: Jericho Pub Schs Cedar Swamp Rd Jericho NY 11753

MARTIN, DAVID STANDISH, education educator; b. New Bedford, Mass., Aug. 24, 1937; s. Theodore Tripp and Elinor Louise (Raymond) M.; m. Susan Katherine Orowan, June 30, 1962. BA, Yale U., 1959; MEd, Harvard U., 1961, CAS, 1968; PhD, Boston Coll., 1971. Cert. tchr., prin. Tchr. Newton (Mass.) Pub. Schs., 1961-68, asst. prin., 1969-70; teaching asst. Boston Coll., Chestnut Hill, Mass., 1968-69; curriculum dir. Beverly (Mass.) Pub. Schs., 1970-73; prin. Mill Valley (Calif.) Pub. Schs., 1973-75, curriculum dir., 1975-80; chmn. dept. edn. Dominican Coll., San Rafael, Calif., 1978-80; coordinator undergrad. tchr. edn. Gallaudet U., Washington, 1980-85, dean sch. edn. and human svcs., 1985-95, prof. edn., 1995—; cons. Curriculum Devel. Assocs., Washington, 1975—; mem. bd. examiners Nat. Coun. Accreditation Tchr. Education; bd. dirs. USA-SINO Tchr. Education Consortium, Western Pa. Sch. for the Deaf. Author: Case Studies in Curriculum, 1989; editor: Cognition, Education and Deafness, 1985, Advances in Cognition Education and Deafness, 1991; contbr. articles to profl. jours. U.S. Dept. Edn. grantee, 1970, 85. Mem. D.C. Assn. Colls. Tchr. Edn. (pres. 1989-92), Assn. for Supervision and Curriculum Devel., Nat. Coun. for Social Studies, Am. Ednl. Rsch. Assn., Am. Assn. Colls. for Tchr. Edn. (bd. dirs.), Coun. for Exceptional Children, Phi Delta Kappa, Kappa Delta Pi (chair publ.). Democrat. Unitarian. Avocations: genealogy, sailing, classical organ, astronomy. Home: 4709 Blagden Ter NW Washington DC 20011-3719 Office: Gallaudet U 800 Florida Ave NE Washington DC 20002-3660

MARTIN, DEANNA COLEMAN, university director; b. Kansas City, Mo., Feb. 6, 1939; d. Olaf Arthur and Dolores Augustine (Judd) Coleman; m. Robert Allan Blanc, Apr. 28, 1982; children: Chris Robert Martin, Coleman O'Brian Martin. BA in English, U. Kansas City, 1960; MA in Reading Edn., U. Mo., Kansas City, 1974, PhD in Reading Edn., 1976. Cert. tchr., Mo. Tchr. Raytown (Mo.) H.S., 1964-74, Lee's Summit (Mo.) H.S., 1964-74; coord. learning resources U. Mo., Kansas City, 1974, dir. student learning ctr., 1975, dir. ctr. for acad. devel., 1980—, assoc. prof. sch. edn., 1987—; cons., presenter in field. Cons. editor Unit. for Rsch. into Higher Edn.--Ctr. for Sci. Devel. of the South African Human Scis. Rsch. Coun.; co-author: Supplemental Instruction: A Guide to Student Retention, 1983, Study Guide and Readings for Abnormal Psychology: Current Perspectives, 1984, Supplemental Instruction: Improving First-Year Student Success in High Risk Courses, 1992, Supplemental Instruction: Increasing Student Achievement and Persistence, 1994, also book chpts., monographs; contbr. articles to profl. publs. Trustee Multi-Media Network Trust, Johannesburg, South Africa. Grantee HEW, 1976, 81, Kansas City Assn. Trusts and Founds., 1977, 84, 85, U. Mo.-Kansas City, 1978, 79, 80, Nat. Basic Skills Improvement Schs. Program, 1980, Nat. Assn. State Univs. and Land-Grant Colls., 1984-85, Ctr. Sch. Dist., 1994, Sch. Dist. of City of Independence, Mo., Ft. Osage Sch. Dist., 1984, Consol. Sch. Dist. Raytown, 1984, Kansas City Pub. Sch. Dist., 1984, Coalition of 100 Black Women, 1985, U.S. Dept. Edn., 1989—, Nat. Diffusion Network, Office Edn., 1984—; recipient Retention Excellence award Noel/Levitz Nat. Ctr. for Student Retention, 1990, Cert. of REcognition, Nat. Assn. of Student Pers. Adminstrs., 1981. Mem. Nat. Assn. for Developmental Edn., Am. Assn. for Higher Edn. Avocations: hiking, biking. Office: U Mo Kansas City Ctr Acad Devel 5100 Rockhill Rd Kansas City MO 64110-2446

MARTIN, DEBRA MICHELE, nurse; b. Hagerstown, Md., Sept. 19, 1950; d. James Kingsley and Mary Madalan (Bultman) Noel; m. David Richard Rawls, June 9, 1973 (div. June 1981); children: Derek Joseph, Dayna Noel; m. Sydney Lee Martin, June 25, 1982 (div. Oct. 1988). RN, Sinai Hosp., Balt., 1971. RN, Pa., Md.; cert. ACLS, CPR, CEN, BTLS, PALS, emergency vehicle operators course, hazardous materials tng. Asst. head RN Sinai Hosp., Balt., 1971-73, postpartum charge RN, 1975-77; ob-gyn. office RN Scher, Muher & Lowen, PA, Balt., 1973-74; emergency dept. RN Meml. Hosp., York, Pa., 1978-80, advance life charge RN, 1980—; teaching EMT's and paramedics Harrisburg (Pa.) Area C.C., 1984—, St. Joseph's Hosp., Lancaster, Pa., 1984—. Health profl. Pa. Dept. of Health, Harrisburg, 1988—. Named ALS Provider of Yr., Emergency Med. Svcs. Assn. of York County, 1990. Mem. Emergency Health Sys. Fedn. (RN adv. bd. 1986—, automated early defibrillator instr.), Emergency Nurses Assn. Democrat. Roman Catholic. Avocations: biking, skiing, self-improvement, golf, hiking. Home: 123 S Main St Shrewsbury PA 17361-1528

MARTIN, DIANE CARAWAY, school librarian; b. Dallas, Nov. 2, 1956; d. Stone Walker and Eleanor Lynn (DeBray) C.; m. C.A. Martin III, July 30, 1977; children: C.Allan IV, Wesley Walker. BS magna cum laude, La. Tech. U., 1977; MLS, La. State U., 1978. Cert. English tchr., libr., La. Libr. Northwood Elem. Sch., Baton Rouge, 1978-80; reference libr. Ouachita Valley Pub. Libr., West Monroe, La., 1980-82; libr. River Oaks Elem. Sch., Monroe, La., 1988-90, River Oaks High Sch., Monroe, 1990-93; substitute tchr. Bd. dirs. Monroe YWCA, 1982-85, La. Tech. Alumni, Ruston, 1991-95, Teen Ct. Northeast La., Monroe, 1990-93, Children's Mus. N.E. La.; coord. Parents in Edn. Project Self Esteem, Monroe, 1992-94; coord. elem. dept. St. Paul's United Meth. Ch., Monroe, 1992—; rep. Ouachita Valley coun. Boy Scouts Am., 1991—, wolf den leader, 1993-94; mem., room mother PTO; exec. com. Parents' Adv. Com. for Gifted and Talented, Monroe City Schs.; youth coord. St. Paul's United Meth. Youth, 1995-97. Mem. ALA, Northeast La. Libr. Network, Monroe Jr. League (recording sec. 1992-93, chmn. social svcs. 1993—, corresponding sec. 1994), Monroe Racquet Club Tennis League, United Meth. Women (past pres.). Republican. Avocations: tennis, reading, singing, piano, cooking. Home: 3509 Lake Desiard Dr Monroe LA 71201-2078

MARTIN, DONALD WALTER, author, publisher; b. Grants Pass, Oreg., Apr. 22, 1934; s. George E. and Irma Ann (Dallas) M.; m. Kathleen Elizabeth Murphy, July, 1970 (div. May 1979); children: Daniel Clayton, Kimberly Ann; m. Betty Woo, Mar. 18, 1985. Enlisted USMC, 1952; advanced through grades to staff sgt. USMC, Japan, Republic of Korea, Republic of China, 1956-61; reporter Blade-Tribune, Oceanside, Calif., 1961-65; entertainment editor Press-Courier, Oxnard, Calif., 1965-69; mng. editor Argus-Courier, Petaluma, Calif., 1969-70; assoc. editor Motorland mag., San Francisco, 1970-88; founder, prin., CEO Pine Cone Press, Inc., Columbia, Calif., 1988—. Author: Best of San Francisco, 1986, 90, 94, Best of the Gold Country, 1987, 92, San Francisco's Ultimate Dining Guide, 1988, Inside Francisco, 1991, Best of the Wine Country, 1991, 95, Oregon Discovery Guide, 1993, 95, 96, Northern California Discovery Guide, 1993, The Ultimate Wine Book, 1993, Washington Discovery Guide, 1994, Utah Discovery Guide, 1995, Adventure Cruising, 1996, Arizona Discovery Guide, 1996, Arizona in Your Future, 1991, 93, 97, The Toll-Free Traveler, 1997, Las Vegas: The Best of Glitter City, 1997. Recipient Diane Seely award Ventura County Theatre Council, 1968. Mem. Soc. Am. Travel Writers. Republican. Avocations: traveling, hiking, white water rafting, biking. Home: 1649 Justin Cir Henderson NV 89015 Office: Ste 138 631 N Stephanie St Henderson NV 89014

MARTIN, DONALD WILLIAM, psychiatrist; b. Columbus, Ohio, Aug. 13, 1921; s. Olin R. and Clara (Jahraus) M.; m. Clara Jane Jones, June 23, 1951; children: Jennifer Christine, David Lawrence. B.A., Ohio State U., 1942, M.D., 1944. Diplomate: Am. Bd. Psychiatry and Neurology. Intern Met. Hosp., N.Y.C., 1944-45; resident psychiatrist Kings Park (N.Y.) State Hosp., 1945-46, sr. psychiatrist, 1948-49; supervising psychiatrist Central Islip (N.Y.) State Hosp., 1950-56; staff psychiatrist Summit County Receiving Hosp. (name now Fallsview Psy. Hosp.), Cuyahoga Falls, Ohio, 1956-59; supt. Summit County Receiving Hosp. (name now Fallsview Psy. Hosp.), 1959-63; dir. Pontiac (Mich.) State Hosp. (name now Clinton Valley Center), 1963-79; pvt. practice cons. psychiatry, 1979-90, ret., 1990. Served from 1st lt. to capt. M.C., U.S. Army, 1946-48. Fellow Am. Psychiat. Assn. (life). Home: 608 Millwright Ct # 21 Millersville MD 21108 *My experiences over the years have only strengthened my belief that our happiness and growth as human beings derives above all else from our relationships with others. The life's theme I have evolved is: becoming and being a loving person.*

MARTIN, DONNA LEE, publishing company executive; b. Detroit, Aug. 7, 1935; d. David M. Paul and Lillian (Paul); m. Rex Martin, June 5, 1956; children: Justin, Andrew. B.A., Rice U., 1957. Mng. editor trade dept. Appleton-Century-Crofts Co., N.Y.C., 1961-62; dir. publs. Lycoming Coll., Williamsport, Pa., 1966-68; editor Univ. Press of Kans., Lawrence, 1971-74; mng. editor Andrews & McMeel, Kansas City, Mo., 1974-80, v.p., editorial dir., 1980-95, v.p., editor-at-large, 1995; v.p. Universal Press Syndicate, Kansas City, 1980—; lectr. U. Mo., Kansas City. Author: (adaptation) Charles Dickens' A Christmas Carol: Adapted for Theatre; contbr. articles to profl. jours. Named Disting. Alumna Rice U., 1990. Mem. Women in Comms., The Groucho Club (London), Phi Beta Kappa. Office: Universal Press Syndicate 4520 Main St Fl 7 Kansas City MO 64111-1816

MARTIN, DONNIS LYNN, adult education educator; b. Knox City, Tex., Sept. 7, 1948; s. Derrell Lee Martin and Audie Lee (Qualls) Kempe; m. Karen Marie Hanzevack, Dec. 24, 1988; children: Christina, Dustin, Shara. BA/BS, Met. State Coll. Denver, 1979; MA in Mgmt., U. Phoenix, 1990; EdD, N.C. State U., 1991. Cert. tchr. lang. arts. Program supr. wind energy sys. Rockwell Internat., Golden, Colo., 1980-83, mgr. plant tng., 1983-84, prin. orgn. devel. specialist, 1984-87; mgr. computer-based tng. courseware devel. No. Telecom, Inc., Raleigh, N.C., 1987-88, program mgr. documentation, 1988-89; edn. program specialist N.C. Dept. Community Colls., 1991-92; pres. ERC Assocs., Cary, N.C., 1992-96; asst. prof. N.C. State U. Dept. Adult and C.C. Edn., Raleigh, 1996—. Contbr. articles to profl. jours. With USAF, 1973-80. Fellow Acad. Human Resource Devel.; mem. Am. Soc. for Tng. and Devel., Am. Ednl. Rsch. Assn., Am. Vocat. Edn. Rsch. Assn., Internat. Soc. Performance Improvement, Soc. Applied Learning Technologies, Soc. for Tech. Comm. (sr.), Omicron Tau Theta. Avocations: photography, boating. Home: 110 Talon Dr Cary NC 27511-8604 Office: N C State U PO Box 7801 Raleigh NC 27695-7801

MARTIN, EARL DEAN, physical therapist; b. Mammoth Springs, Ark., July 30, 1959; s. Earl Eudell and Ruth (Standley) M.; m. Mary Ellen Eckstein, June 10, 1989; children: Tyler Joseph, Jenny Catherine, Kelsey Elizabeth, McKenzie Mae. BS in Biology, U. Ill., 1982; MS in Phys. Therapy, Boston U., 1987. Lic. phys. therapist, Ill.; bd. cert. pediatric clin. specialist. Phys. therapist Carle Hosp., Urbana, Ill., 1987-88; prin. phys. therapist Phys. Therapy Svcs. for Children, Philo, Ill., 1988—; phys. therapist Champaign Children's Home, 1988-90, Devel. Svc. Ctr., Champaign, 1988-90, 1996—; sch. phys. therapist Urbana Schs., 1988-97, Ford-Iroquois Assn. for Spl. Edn., Gilman, Ill., 1988-89, Vermilion County Assn. for Spl. Edn., Danville, Ill., 1992-97, Champaign Cmty. Schs., 1994-95, Champaign County Rural Coop., Rantoul, Ill., 1994-96; clin. instr. phys. therapist. asst. program Lakeland Coll., Effingham, Ill., 1993—; clin. instr. phys. therapy program Midwestern U., Downers Grove, Ill., 1996—; ind. evaluator State of Ill. Registry Ind. Sch. Evaluators, Springfield, Ill., 1993—; pediat. phys. therapist Cerebral Palsy Clinic, Vermilion County, Danville, 1994-97; mem. adv. bd. Champaign County Arthritis Found., Urbana, Ill. 1995—. Vol. Champaign Park Dist., 1984, Spl. Olympics, Boston, 1986, Grand Prairie Olympics, Watseka, Ill., 1989. Mem. Am. Phys. Therapy Assn, Ill. Phys. Therapy Assn. (mem. pediats. sect.). Roman Catholic. Avocations: marble collecting, gardening, canoeing, competitive walking, 3 on 3 basketball. Home: 808 S Garfield St Philo IL 61864-9784 Office: Phys Therapy Svc for Children 808 S Garfield St Philo IL 61864-9784

MARTIN, EDWARD BRIAN, electrical engineer; b. Lawrence, Kans., Feb. 9, 1936; s. Edward Brian and Dorothy Irene (Dowers) M.; m. Sharon Anne Zimmerman, Dec. 21, 1955; children: Terry Brian, Ricky Lynn, Mindy Anne, Timothy Alan. BSEE, U. Kans., 1958; MSEE, St. Louis U., 1969. Registered profl. engr., Mo. Program mgr. McDonnell Douglas, St. Louis, 1980-85, mgr. avionics, 1985-86, dir. engring., 1986-88, dir. electronics, 1988-89, sr. dir. tech. processes, 1989-91, sr. dir. avionics tech., 1991-92, dir. advanced missile systems, 1992-95, dir. advanced weapon systems, 1995—; chmn. bd. dirs. Martin Internat., Ltd. Contbr. numerous articles to profl. jours. Pres. PTA, St. Louis, 1972; founder Martin Family Found. Mem. AIAA. Avocations: running, mountain climbing, writing. Home: 5 Baron Ct Florissant MO 63034-1203

MARTIN, EDWARD CURTIS, JR., landscape architect, educator; b. Albany, Ga., Aug. 21, 1928; s. Edward Curtis and Mildred Lee (Tyler) M.; m. Roberta Inman Parker, Mar. 18, 1967; children: Edward Curtis III, Andrew Parker. BFA, U. Ga., 1950, M of Landscape Architecture, 1969. Registered landscape architect, Miss. Landscape architect Norman C. Butts Landscape Contractor, Atlanta, 1950; M.T. Brooks Office of Landscape Architecture, Birmingham, Ala., 1950-56; univ. landscape architect, horticulturalist Miss. State U., Mississippi State, 1956-70, prof. landscape architecture, 1970-92, Disting. prof., 1988, prof. emeritus, 1992—, part-time prof., 1992—; originator, chmn. Miss. Landscape Design Sch., Mississippi State, 1957—; guest lectr. U. San Luis Potosi, Mex., 1990, U. Mexico, Mex. City, 1991, La. State U., 1990, 91, 92, 94, 96, Biendenharn Found., Monroe, La., 1991, Longue Vue Found., New Orleans, 1991, So. Garden Symposium, 1993, St. Francisville, La., 1993, Southern Regional Meeting Garden Writers Assn. Am., Memphis, 1993, Rotary Internat. Dist. Conf., Memphis, 1993, Deep S. Regional Conf. Nat. Coun. State Garden Clubs, Lafayette, La., 1993, NAt. Capital Area Garden Coun., U. Md., 1996; guest instr. Nat. Landscape Design Study Courses Nat. Coun. State Garden Clubs, Inc., U.S., Mex., 1960—, Guatemala first study course, 1995, 96; originator, lectr. Garden Design Workshops, Miss. State U., 1988—; host Flower and Garden Tour of British Isles, Southland Travel Svcs., 1985, Flower and Garden Tour of Europe, 1981, 82; photographic landscape architecture rsch. study: Europe, 1958, 66, 74, 85, S.Am., 1960, Israel, 1993, 95; vis. prof. La. State U., 1990-93, vis. landscape architecture prof., 1994; instr. landscape design Botanical Gardens, Huntsville, Ala., 1996; host, lectr. historic southern gardens on Miss. River, New Orleans to Vicksburg, Delta Queen Steamboat; host Chelsea Flower Show and English Gardens Tour, 1994, Nat. Coun. State Garden Clubs, 1994, Fla. Wild Flower Conf. Fla. Fedn. Garden Clubs, Inc., 1994; instr. ecology tour Copper Canyon, Mex., 1994; spkr. in field. Author: Landscape Plants in Design, A Photographic Guide, 1983; co-author: Home Landscapes, Planting Design and Management, 1994; invited to participate in Attingham Summer Program in Historic Preservation (English country houses and gardens) Eng., 1985; author/photographer of 80-captioned slide series, one on Home Landscapes, another on Urban Landscape Design for use by Nat. Coun. State Garden Clubs, Inc., 1994. Mem. Miss. State Bd. Landscape Architects for Profl. Registration, 1973-74; mem. Starkville (Miss.) Park and Recreation Bd., 1973-79. Recipient Silver Seal award Nat. Coun. State Garden Clubs 1969, honoree 1995; recipient Landscape Heritage award Fraser Found. Calif. 1986, Helent S. Hull Lit. award, 1996. Fellow Am. Soc. Landscape Architects (chmn. edn. com. 1960-61, pres. Miss. sect. S.W. chpt. 1975, chmn. S.W. chpt. ann. awards com. 1976, trustee Miss. chpt. 1977-81); mem. Nat. Trust for Historic Preservation, So. Garden History Soc., Coun. of Educators in Landscape Architecture, Nat. Coun. State Garden Clubs (chmn. landscape design 1993—), Garden Clubs Miss. (bd. dirs. 1958—, Silver Trophy 1961, Spl. Silver award 1980, Gold trophy 1993). Presbyterian. Home: 1335 Ridgewood Rd Starkville MS 39759-9177 Office: Dept Landscape Architecture Box 9725 Mississippi State MS 39762

MARTIN, EDYTHE LOUVIERE, business educator; b. Breaux Bridge, La., Dec. 30, 1940; d. James Ivy and Volna Mary (Landry) L.; m. James Henry Martin, Aug. 23, 1969; 1 child, Lois Elizabeth. BS in Bus. Edn., U. Southwestern La., 1972; MEd in Supervision, La. State U., 1977, Specialist Degree in Ednl. Adminstrn., 1988, postgrad studies in Ednl. Adminstrn., 1989—. Geol. sec. Sohio Petroleum Co., Lafayette, La., 1960-67, Bintliff Oil & Gas Co., Lafayette, 1967-69; bus. tchr. Cottonport (La.) H.S., 1972-74; bus. instr. Acadian Tech. Coll., Crowley, La., 1975—; team leader, mem. accrediting teams So. Assn. Colls. and Schs., 1978—, chmn. of steering com. for Acadian Tech. evaluation, 1991; speaker, presenter at meetings and seminars of educators. Publicity chairperson Miss Eunice (La.) Pageant, 1981-88; chairperson Eunice Lady of Yr. award, 1982; organizer chairperson, St. Jude Children's Hosp., Fund Raiser, Memphis, Eunice, 1985-91; PTC sec. St. Edmund Sch., Eunice, 1982-84; vol. March of Dimes, 1995—. Mem. Office Occupations Assn., La. Vocat. Assn. Inc., La. Vocat. Assn. (trade and indsl. divsn.). Democrat Roman Catholic. Avocations: collecting, travel. Home: 750 Viola St Eunice LA 70535-4340 Office: Acadian Tech Coll 1933 W Hutchinson Ave Crowley LA 70526-3215

MARTIN, ELLIOT EDWARDS, theatrical producer; b. Denver, Feb. 25, 1924; m. Marjorie Cuesta, Oct. 7, 1949; children: Richard, Linda Lisa. Student, U. Denver, 1943-46. Actor, singer, stage mgr., assoc. producer Theatre Guild, N.Y.C. and London, 1947-53; prodn. stage mgr. 20 Broadway plays and musicals, 1953-61; theatrical producer Never Too Late, Nobody Loves an Albatross, N.Y.C., 1962-66; theatre producer London, 1963; mng. dir. Center Theatre Group, Music Ctr., Los Angeles, 1966-71; producer Elliot Martin Prodns., N.Y.C., 1972—; mem. exec. bd. Nat. Theatre of the Deaf, Chester, Conn., 1981—, Westport-Weston Arts Council, 1976—. Prodns. on Broadway include: Dinner at Eight, 1966, More Stately Mansions, 1967, Abelard and Heloise, 1971, Emperor Henry IV, 1973, A Moon for the Misbegotten, 1973 (spl. Tony award), When You Comin' Back, Red Rider, 1974 (Outer Critics award), Of Mice and Men, 1975, Touch of the Poet, 1976, Dirty Linen and New Found Land, 1977, Caesar and Cleopatra, 1977, Kingfisher, 1979, Clothes for a Summer Hotel, 1980, Kingdoms, 1981, American Buffalo, 1981, Angels Fall, 1983, Glengarry Glen Ross, 1984 (Pulitzer prize), Woza Albert, 1984, American Buffalo, 1984, Harrigan 'n' Hart, 1985, Arsenic and Old Lace (Broadway and nat. tour), 1986-87, Joe Turner's Come and Gone (7 Tony nominations, N.Y. Drama Critic's award best play), 1988, Steel Magnolias (nat. tour), 1989, The Circle, 1989-90, Shadowlands, 1990-91, Breaking Legs, 1991-92, She Loves Me (9 Tony noms.), 1993-94, Death of a Salesman, 1995-96. Mem. bd. assocs. U. Bridgeport, 1978-83. Recipient Tony award for most innovative revival, 1977-78, Larry Tajiri award for outstanding contbn. to arts Denver Post, 1970, Congl. commendation, 1970, Profl. Achievement award U. Denver, 1987. Mem. Platform Speakers Am., League N.Y. Theatres and Producers. Republican. Club: N.Y. Athletic (N.Y.C.). Office: Elliot Martin Prodns 152 W 58th St New York NY 10019-2139

MARTIN, ERNEST LEE, academic administrator, historian, theologian, writer; b. Meeker, Okla., Apr. 20, 1932; s. Joel Chester and Lula Mae (Quinn) M.; m. Helen Rose Smith, Aug. 26, 1957 (div. 1980); children: Kathryn, Phyllis, Samuel; m. Ramona Jean Kinsey, June 27, 1987. BA, Ambassador U., 1958, MA, 1960, PhD, 1966. Dean faculty Ambassador U., St. Albans, Eng., 1965-72; chmn. dept. theology Ambassador U., Pasadena, Calif., 1972-74; dir. Found. for Bibl. Rsch., Pasadena, 1974-84, Acad. for Scriptural Knowledge, Portland, 1985—; dir. 450 coll. students with Prof. Benjamin Mazar Herodian Temple archaeol. excavations, Jerusalem, 1969-74. Author: Birth of Christ Recalculated, 1978, 2d edit., 1980, The Original Bible Restored, 1984, Secrets of Golgotha, 1987, 2d edit., 1996, The Star That Astonished the World, 1996, 101 Bible Secrets That Christians Do Not Know, 1993, The People That History Forgot, 1993, The Place of the New Third Temple, 1994, Restoring the Original Bible, 1994, The Biblical Manual, 1995, The Temples that Jerusalem Forgot, 1997, Angels-The Facts and the Fictions, 1997, Essential Theology of the New Testament, 1997, ABC's of the Gospel, 1997. Tech. sgt. USAF, 1950-54. Mem. SBL (advisor to original Bible project), Planetarium Soc. Home: PO Box 25000 Portland OR 97298-0990 Office: Acad for Scriptural Knowledge 4804 SW Scholls Ferry Rd Portland OR 97225-1668 *Christianity is the teaching that all humanity is destined to be reconciled to God, and that is my prime philosophical belief.*

MARTIN, FRANK BURKE, statistics consultant; b. Cleve., Mar. 21, 1937. BA, St. Mary's Coll., Minn., 1958; MS, Iowa State U., 1966, PhD in Stats., 1968. Instr. math. St. Mary's Coll., Minn., 1960-63; teaching asst. stats. Iowa State U., Ames, 1963-65, rsch. assoc., 1965-67; asst. prof. to assoc. prof. U. Minn., St. Paul, 1967-78, statistician Exptl. Sta., 1967—; dir. Statis. Ctr. U. Minn., Mpls., 1980—. Mem. Biometric Soc., Am. Statis. Assn. Home: 726 Lincoln Ave St Paul MN 55105 Office: U Minn Statis Ctr/1994 Buford Ave 352 Classroom Office Bldg Saint Paul MN 55108

MARTIN, FRED, artist, college administrator; b. San Francisco, June 13, 1927; s. Ernest Thomas and Leona (Richey) M.; m. Genevieve Catherine Fisette, Jan. 29, 1950 (dec.); children: T. Demian, Fredericka C., Anthony J.; m. Stephanie Zuperko Dudek, 1992. BA, U. Calif., Berkeley, 1949, MA, 1954; postgrad., Calif. Sch. Fine Arts, 1949-50. Registrar Oakland (Calif.) Art Mus., 1955-58; dir. exhbns. San Francisco Art Inst., 1958-65, dir. coll., 1965-75, dean acad. affairs, 1983-92; dean acad. affairs emeritus; represented by Frederick Spratt Gallery, San Jose, Calif., Ebert Gallery, San Francisco. Exhibited one man shows, Zoe Dusanne Gallery, Seattle, 1952, M.H. deYoung Meml. Mus., San Francisco, 1954, 64, Oakland Art Mus., 1958, San Francisco Mus. Modern Art, 1958, 73, Dilexi Gallery, San Francisco, 1961, Minami Gallery, Tokyo, 1963, Royal Marks Gallery, N.Y.C., 1965-70, Hansen Fuller Gallery, San Francisco, 1974, 75, 76, Quay Gallery, San Francisco, 1979, 81, 84, Natsoulas Gallery, Davis, Calif., 1991, Belcher Studios Gallery, San Francisco, 1994, Frederick Spratt Gallery, San Jose, 1996, Ebert Gallery, San Francisco, 1997, Art and Consciousness Gallery/John F. Kennedy U., Berkeley, 1997; represented in permanent collections, Mus. Modern Art, N.Y.C., San Francisco Mus. Modern Art, Oakland Art Mus., Whitney Mus., Fogg Mus.; author: Beulah Land, 1966, Log of the Sun Ship, 1969, Liber Studiorum, 1973, A Travel Book, 1976, From an Antique Land, 1979; Bay area corr.: Art Internat., 1967-69, 75-76; contbg. editor Art Week, 1976-93. Recipient prizes Oakland Art Mus., 1951, 58, prizes San Francisco Mus. Art, 1957, 58, prizes Richmond (Calif.) Art Center, 1962, prizes Nat. Found. for Arts, 1970. Home: 232 Monte Vista Ave Oakland CA 94611-4922 Office: San Francisco Art Inst 800 Chestnut St San Francisco CA 94133-2206

MARTIN, FRED, retired municipal official; b. Detroit, Oct. 21, 1925; s. Fred McKinley and Eva Irene (Agnew) M.; m. Ernestine Robinson, Sept. 20, 1947 (div. 1980); children: Robin K. Turner, Keith R. BA, Wayne State U., 1953, MEd, 1954, postgrad., 1970-74. Tchr. Detroit Schs., 1953-61, asst. prin., 1961-63, personnel adminstr., 1963-67, asst. to supt., 1967-74, exec. dir. pers., 1974-78, pers. dir., dep. supt., 1978-81; pers. dir. City of Detroit, 1981-82, chief exec. asst. to mayor, 1981-92, personnel dir., 1992-94; instr. Wayne State U., 1968-75, U. Mich., Detroit, 1972; cons. U. Detroit, 1968. Author: Corrective Discipline - Management Grade, 1978. Bd. dirs. Greater Detrout Resource Recovery Authority, 1985, Detroit Sci. Ctr., 1987; pres. Northwest Activities Ctr., Detroit, 1987-94; mem. libr. commn. Detroit Pub. Libr., 1987; trustee Detroit Med. Ctr. With U.S. Army, 1944-46, ETO, PTO. Mem. Forum Black Pub. Adminstrs. (bd. dirs. 1984-92), Your Heritage House, Detroit Inst. Arts. (Founders Soc.), Kappa Alpha Psi. Democrat. Baptist. Avocations: reading, music, sports. Home: 1300 E Lafayette St Apt 1401 Detroit MI 48207-2921

MARTIN, FREDDIE ANTHONY, agronomist, educator; b. Raceland, La., Nov. 17, 1945; s. of Abraham and Flossie Margarette (Foret) M.; m. Rose Ann Hill, Aug. 23, 1969; children: Samson, Jonathan, Robert. BS, Francis T. Nicholls State Coll, Thibodaux, La., 1966; MS, Cornell U., 1968, PhD, 1970. Asst. prof. Plant Pathology Dept. La. State U., Baton Rouge, 1971-76; assoc. prof. Plant Pathology Dept. La. State U., 1976-80, prof. Plant Pathology Dept., 1980, prof. Agronomy Dept., 1980—, head Sugar Sta./Audubon Sugar, 1988—. Editor Am. Soc. Sugar Cane Technologists jour., 1980-94; author profl. manuscripts, jours. Recipient Rsch. Excellence Award, La. Agricultural Experimental Sta., 1984, Svc. Award, St. James Sugar Growers, 1989. Mem. Internat. Soc. Sugarcane Technologists (biology commr. 1995—), Am. Soc. Agronomy, Crop Sci. Soc. Am., Am. Soc. Sugarcane Tech., Gamma Sigma Delta. Office: Louisiana State Univ Sugar Station Audobon Sugar Inst Baton Rouge LA 70803

MARTIN, FREDERICK NOEL, audiology educator; b. N.Y.C., July 24, 1931; s. Philip and Mildred Ruth (Austin) M.; m. Mary Catherine Robinson, Apr. 4, 1954; children: David C., Leslie Anne. B.A., Bklyn. Coll., 1957, M.A., 1958; Ph.D., CUNY, 1968. Audiologist, Lenox Hill Hosp., N.Y.C., 1957-58; Audiologist Ark. Sch. for the Deaf, Little Rock, 1958-60; dir. audiology Bailey Ear Clinic, Little Rock, 1960-66; mem. faculty Bklyn. Coll., 1966-68; mem. faculty U. Tex., Austin, 1968—, endowed prof. audiology, 1982—. Author: Introduction to Audiology, 1975, 6th edit., 1997, Pediatric Audiology, 1978, Medical Audiology, 1981, Basic Audiometry, 1986; editor: Remediation of Communication Disorders, Vol. 10, 1978, Hearing Disorders in Children, 1986, Effective Counseling in Audiology, 1994, Hearing Care for Children, 1996; contbr. over 100 articles to profl. jours. Served with USAF, 1951-55. Fellow Am. Speech-Language Hearing Assn., Am. Acad. Audiology; mem. Tex. Speech-Lang.-Hearing Assn., Am. Auditory Soc. Home: 8613 Silver Ridge Dr Austin TX 78759-8144 Office: U Tex Austin TX 78712

MARTIN, GARY J., retired business executive, mayor; b. Des Moines, Feb. 8, 1937; s. William Carl Martin and Mary Louise (Festner) Sweeney; m. Carolyn J. Karau, July 28, 1956; children: Victoria, Cheryl, Dennis. BBA, Marquette U., 1972. CPA Wis., 1973. Mfr. GM, Milw., 1957-68, engring. mgr., 1968-73; CFO Miller Brewing Co., Milw., 1974-76, dir. corp. planning, 1977-78; pres. Better Brands of N.Y., N.Y.C., 1978-79; exec. v.p. Seven Up Co., St. Louis, 1979-85; v.p. mktg. Schenley Industries, Dallas, 1985-86; cons. Martin & Assocs., Dallas, 1986-89; mayor Osage Beach, Mo., 1992-95. Bd. dirs. Family Hosp., Milw., 1976-78; mem. lay bd. St. Mary Health Ctr., St. Louis, 1980-85. With USN, 1954-57. Avocations: computers, boating, golfing, travel. Home: 2166 Springmeadow Dr Spring Hill FL 34606

MARTIN, GARY JOSEPH, medical educator; b. Chgo., Mar. 12, 1952; m. Helen Gartner; children: Daniel T., David G. BA in Psychology, U. Ill., 1974, MD, 1978. Diplomate Am. Bd. Internal Medicine, Am. Bd. Cardiovascular Disease, Nat. Bd. Med. Examiners; lic. physician, Ill. Intern, resident internal medicine Northwestern U. Med. Sch., Chgo., 1978-81, instr. medicine, 1981-82, asst. prof. medicine, 1984-90, assoc. prof., 1990-96, prof., 1996—, divsn. chief, divsn. gen. internal medicine, 1988—; cardiology fellow Loyola U. Med. Ctr., 1982-84; attending physician Northwestern Meml. Hosp./Northwestern Med. Faculty Found., Chgo., 1984—; chief med. resident, attending physician Northwestern Meml. Hosp., Chgo., 1981-82; faculty and course dir. Nat. Ctr. for Advanced Med. Edn., 1984—; chmn. outpatient utilization rev. and quality assurance com., 1985-93; chmn. Northwestern Meml. Hosp./Lakeside VA Rsch. Com., 1988-91; dir. tng. gen. internal medicine residency program, 1985—; bd. dirs. com. Northwestern Med. Faculty Found., 1993—; cons. health care divsn. Ernst & Young, 1991—; peer reviewer Faculty Devel. Rev. Com. Panel 1, 1994. Contbr. articles to profl. jours. Fellow Buehler Ctr. on Aging. Fellow Am. Coll.

Cardiology; mem. ACP, Am. Fedn. Clin. Rsch., Soc. Gen. Internal Medicine, Am. Heart Assn., Soc. Med. Decision Making. Home: 215 N Home Ave Park Ridge IL 60068-3029 Office: Northwestern U Med Sch Divsn Gen Internal Medicine 303 E Ohio St Ste 300 Chicago IL 60611

MARTIN, GARY O., film company executive; b. Santa Monica, Calif., Aug. 14, 1944; s. Ivan C. and Helen M. (Werner) M.; m. Susan Alden Seaton, Sept. 2, 1967; 1 child, Sean Robert. Student, Calif. State U., Northridge, 1962-65. V.p. prodn. Columbia Pictures, Burbank, Calif., 1984-86, exec. v.p. prodn., exec. prodn. mgr., 1986-88; pres. prodn. adminstrn. Columbia Pictures and Tri Star Pictures, Culver City, Calif., 1988-95, Columbia Tri Star Motion Picture Cos., Culver City, 1995—. Mem. Motion Picture Acad. Arts and Scis., Dirs. Guild. Republican. Home: 8605 Amestoy Ave Northridge CA 91325-3405 Office: Columbia Pictures 10202 Washington Blvd Culver City CA 90232-3119

MARTIN, GARY WAYNE, lawyer; b. Cin., Feb. 14, 1946; s. Elmer DeForrest and Nellie May (Hughes) M.; m. Debra Lynn Goldsmith, June 25, 1982; children: Christopher, Jeremy, Joie, Casey. BA, Wilmington Coll., 1967; JD, U. Cin., 1974. Bar: Fla. 1974. Head casualty dept. Fowler White Gillen Boggs Villareal & Banker, Tampa, Fla., 1974—, also bd. dirs. Lt. USNR, 1967-71. Mem. Harbour Island Athletic Club. Republican. Presbyterian. Avocation: tennis. Office: Fowler White Gillen Boggs Villareal & Banker 501 E Kennedy Blvd Ste 1600 Tampa FL 33602-5200

MARTIN, GEORGE, psychologist, educator; b. L.A., May 8, 1940; s. George Leonard and Margaret (Padigamus) M.; m. Penny Harrell, June 22, 1963 (div. 1986); children: Jeni, Kimberle. BA, UCLA, 1965; MA, Calif. State U., L.A., 1967; MS, Calif. State U., Fullerton, 1994. Systems analyst L.A. Dept. Water & Power, 1965-67; project coord. L.A. Police Dept., 1967-70, edn. cons., 1980-83; alcohol researcher Pomona (Calif.) Coll., 1970-73; tng. systems researcher Lanterman State Hosp., Pomona, 1973-77; prof. psychology Mt. San Antonio Coll., Walnut, Calif., 1970—, dir. rsch., 1986-94. Contbr. articles to profl. jours. Rsch. dir. Orange County Dem. Party, 1985-86. With U.S. Army, 1959-61. Grantee Nat. Inst. Law Enforcement, 1967-70, Nat. Inst. Alcohol, 1970-74. Mem. APA, NSA. Avocations: photography, computers. Home: 1313 N Grand Ave Ste 326 Walnut CA 91789-1317 Office: Mt San Antonio Coll 1100 N Grand Ave Walnut CA 91789-1341

MARTIN, GEORGE COLEMAN, aeronautical engineer; b. Everett, Wash., May 16, 1910; s. Walter Franklin and Minnie (Coleman) M.; m. Mary Sturart Patrick, June 29, 1935; children: Marian Coleman, Edith Patrick. B.S. cum laude, U. Wash., 1931. With Boeing Airplane Co., Seattle, 1931—; successively chief of stress, staff engr. stress and power plant, XB-47 project engr., preliminary design chief, B-47 project engr., chief project eng Boeing Airplane Co., 1951-53; chief engr. Boeing Airplane Co. (Seattle div.), 1953-58, v.p., 1958-64, v.p. engring., 1964-72, cons., 1972—. Recipient Disting. Alumnus award Dept. Aeros. and Astronautics, Coll. of Engring. of U Wash., 1983, Pathfinders award Mus. of Flight, 1987. Fellow Am. Inst. Aeros. and Astronautics; mem. Aerospace Industries Assn. (chmn. aerospace tech. council 1969), Phi Beta Kappa, Tau Beta Pi. Club: Seattle Yacht. Home: 900 University St Apt 5P Seattle WA 98101-2728

MARTIN, GEORGE CONNER, pomology educator; b. San Francisco, Sept. 15, 1933; s. Henry B. and Doris E. (Brockman) M.; m. C. Patricia Thayer, June 28, 1953; children: Steven P., Pamela J. MS, Purdue U., 1960, PhD, 1962. Plant physiologist USDA, Wenatchee, Wash., 1962-67; assoc. prof. dept. pomology U. Calif., Davis, 1967-73, prof. dept. pomology, 1973-94; ret., 1994. Contbr. over 245 articles to scholarly and profl. jours. 1st lt. USMC, 1955-58. Fellow Am. Soc. Hort. Sci. (pres. 1989-90, chmn. bd. 1990-91, Gourley award 1971, Membership award 1976, 81, 83, 85, Stark award 1980, Miller award 1981, Popenoe award 1982, Rschr. of Yr. award 1987, Fruit Publ. award 1992).

MARTIN, GEORGE FRANCIS, lawyer; b. Yuba City, Calif., July 7, 1944; s. John Severd and Albina Marie M.; m. Linda Louise D'Aoust, Mar. 17, 1968; children: Brandon, Bry. BA in Govt., Calif. State U., Sacramento, 1968; JD, U. Calif., Davis, 1971. Bar: Calif. Adminstr. asst. Assemblyman E. Richard Barnes, Sacramento, 1967-68; with Borton, Petrini & Conron, Bakersfield, Calif., 1971—; mng. gen. ptnr. Borton, Petrini & Conron, Bakersfield, 1977—; dean Calif. Pacific Sch. Law, Bakersfield, 1993-95; holdings numerous ventures, partnerships; lectr. in field; founder, owner theatrical bus. Mgmt. by Martin, Inc., Shower of Stars, Frantic Records, 1962-67. Editor-in-chief Verdict Jour. of Law, 1984-85, Calif. Def. Mag.; newspaper reporter Appeal Democrat, Marysville, Calif., 1959-62. Former vice chmn. Kern County Rep. Ctrl. Com.; past pres. So. Calif. Def. Counsel; past chmn. Ctrl. Calif. Heart Inst.; bd. dirs. Calif. State U. at Bakersfield Found., Kern County Food Bank, Calif. Coun. Partnerships, Kern Hospice, Kern Econ. Devel. Corp. Mem. Greater Bakersfield C. of C. (bd. dirs., past pres.). Office: Borton Petrini & Conron 1600 Truxtun Ave Bakersfield CA 93301-5104

MARTIN, GEORGE J., JR., lawyer; b. Port Chester, N.Y., June 7, 1942; s. George J. and Eileen Ann (Buckley) M.; m. Joanne L. Frost, Aug. 21, 1965 (div. May 1986); children: Amy Anne, Ryan Frost; m. Anna Marie Cipriati, June 21, 1986; children: Marissa McCreay, Jill McCreay. BA, Georgetown U., 1964, JD, 1967. Bar: N.Y. 1969; conseil juridique, France, 1977. From assoc. to ptnr. Mudge Rose Guthrie Alexander & Ferdon, N.Y.C., 1967-95; ptnr. Coudert Bros., N.Y.C., 1995—. Mem. Friends Vieilles Maisons Francaises Inc. (dir.-sec.). Roman Catholic. Home: 232 Clinton St Brooklyn NY 11201-6208 Office: Coudert Bros 1114 Avenue Of The Americas New York NY 10036-7703

MARTIN, GEORGE M., pathologist, gerontologist, educator; b. N.Y.C., June 30, 1927; s. Barnett J. and Estelle (Weiss) M.; m. Julaine Ruth Miller, Dec. 2, 1952; children: Peter C., Kelsey C., Thomas M., Andrew C. BS, U. Wash., 1949, MD, 1953. Diplomate Am. Bd. Pathology, Am. Bd. Med. Genetics. Intern Montreal Gen. Hosp., Quebec, Can., 1953-54; resident-instr. U. Chgo., 1954-57; instr.-prof. U. Wash., Seattle, 1957—; vis. scientist Dept. Genetics Albert Einstein Coll., N.Y.C., 1964; chmn. Gordon Confs. Molecular Pathology, Biology of Aging, 1974-79; chmn., nat. res. Plan on Aging Nat. Inst. on Aging, Bethesda, Md., 1985-89; dir. Alzheimer's Disease Rsch. Ctr. U. Wash., 1985—. Editor Werner's Syndrome and Human Aging, 1985, Molecular Aspects of Aging, 1995; contbr. articles in field to profl jours. Active Fedn. Am. Scientists. With USN, 1945-46. Recipient Allied Signal award in Aging, 1991, Rsch. medal Am. Agy. Assn., 1992, Kleemeier award, 1994; named Disting. Alumnus, U. Wash. Sch. Medicine, 1987; USPHS rsch. fellow dept. genetics, Glasgow U., 1961-62; Eleanor Roosevelt Inst. Cancer Rsch. fellow Inst. de Biologie, PHysiologie, Chimie, Paris, 1968-69; Josiah Macy faculty scholar Sir William Din Sch. Pathology, Oxford (Eng.) U., 1978-79, Humboldt Disting. scientist dept. genetics U. Wurzburg, Germany, 1991. Fellow AAAS, Gerontol. Soc. Am. (chmn. Biol. Sci. 1979, Brookdale award 1981), Tissue Culture Assn. (pres. 1986-88); mem. Inst. Medicine, Am. Assn. Univ. Pathologists (emeritus), Am. Soc. Human Genetics, Am. Soc. Investigative Pathology. Democrat. Avocations: internat. travel, jazz music, biography. Home: 2223 E Howe St Seattle WA 98112-2931 Office: U Wash Sch Medicine Dept Pathology Sm # 30 Seattle WA 98195

MARTIN, GEORGE (WHITNEY), writer; b. N.Y.C., Jan. 25, 1926; s. George Whitney and Agnes Wharton (Hutchinson) M. B.A., Harvard U., 1948; student, Trinity Coll., Cambridge (Eng.) U., 1950; LL.B., U. Va., 1953. Bar: N.Y. 1955. With firm Emmet, Marvin & Martin, N.Y.C., 1955-59; engaged in writing, 1959—. Author: The Opera Companion, A Guide for the Casual Operagoer, 1961, 5th edit., 1997, The Battle of the Frogs and Mice, An Homeric Fable, 1962, 2d edit., 1987, Verdi, His Music, Life and Times, 1963, 4th edit., 1992, The Red Shirt and The Cross of Savoy, The Story of Italy's Risorgimento, 1748-1871, 1969, Causes and Conflicts, The Centennial History of the Association of the Bar of the City of New York, 1870-1970, 1970, 2d edit., 1997, Madam Secretary: Frances Perkins, 1976, The Companion to Twentieth Century Opera, 1979, 3d edit., 1989, The Damrosch Dynasty, America's First Family of Music, 1983, Aspects of Verdi, 1988, 2nd edit., 1993, Verdi at the Golden Gate, San Francisco in the Golden Years, 1993; contbr. articles to profl. jours., mags. Home: 21 Ingleton Cir Kennett Square PA 19348-2000

MARTIN, GEORGE WILBUR, trade association administrator; b. Oklahoma City, Aug. 24, 1930; s. Jeff Frank and George Mullineaux (Bullard) M.; m. Maryellen Brokaw, June 20, 1953; 1 son, Michael Blake. Student, Okla. A&M Coll., 1951. Real estate salesman Washington, 1955-59; jr. analyst CIA, Washington, 1953-55; advt. mgr. Guns and Ammo Mag., Petersen Pub. Co., Los Angeles, 1959-66; editor Guns and Ammo Mag., Petersen Pub. Co., 1967-73; pub. Petersen's Hunting, Guns and Ammo and shooting splty. books, 1974-78; exec. dir. publs. NRA, Washington, 1978-93, exec. dir. industry rels., 1993-95; publishing cons., 1995—; cons. White House Com. Firearms Legis., 1971—. Served with USAF, 1951-52. Named hon. lt. gov. State of Okla.; recipient Anschutz-Precision Sales Internat. Outstanding Writer award, 1988. Mem. NRA (endowment mem.), Internat. Profl. Hunters Assn., Alaska Profl. Hunters Assn., Hunting Hall of Fame Found. (charter, life), Am. Handgunner Awards Orgn. (endowment). Home: 1593 Paiute Rd Saint George UT 84790

MARTIN, GERALD WAYNE, professional football player; b. Forest City, Ark., Oct. 26, 1965. Degree in Criminal Justice, U. Ark., 1990. Defensive end New Orleans Saints, 1989—. Named to The Sporting News coll. All-Am. 1st team, 1988; selected to Pro Bowl, 1994. Office: New Orleans Saints 7800 Airline Hwy Metairie LA 70003-6480*

MARTIN, GUY, lawyer; b. Los Angeles, Jan. 22, 1911; s. I.G. and Mary Pearl (Howe) M.; m. Edith Kingdon Gould, Oct. 12, 1946; children—Guy III, Jason Gould, Christopher Kingdon, Edith Maria Theodosia Burr. A.B., Occidental Coll., 1931; B.A. (1st class hons.), Oxford U., 1934, M.A., 1944; LL.B., Yale, 1937. Bar: N.Y. 1938, D.C. 1947. Practiced with Donovan, Leisure, Newton & Lumbard, N.Y.C., 1938-41; gen. counsel All Am. Aviation, Inc., 1942, Am. Mexican Claims Commn., U.S. Dept. State, 1945-47; ptnr. Martin, Whitfield, Smith & Bebchick (and predecessors), Washington, 1952-80; counsel Martin and Smith (and predecessors), 1981-86; pres., vice chmn. bd., dep. chief exec. officer Internat. Bank, 1981-86; with Law Office of Saltzstein & Martin, 1988—. Served with USN; sea duty 1942-45. Mem. ABA, Assn. of Bar of City of N.Y., Bar Assn. D.C, Phi Beta Kappa, Sigma Alpha Epsilon. Episcopalian. Clubs: Yale, Brook, Knickerbocker (N.Y.C.); Metropolitan, City Tavern (Washington). Home: 3300 O St NW Washington DC 20007-2813

MARTIN, HAROLD CLARK, humanities educator; b. Raymond, Pa., Jan. 12, 1917; s. Henry Floyd and Anna May (Clark) M.; m. Elma Hicks, Dec. 21, 1939; children—Thomas, Joel, Ann, Rebecca. A.B., Hartwick Coll., Oneonta, N.Y., 1937, LL.D. (hon.), 1965; A.M., U. Mich., 1941; Ph.D., Harvard, 1954; student, U. Wis., 1936, Columbia, 1941; L.H.D. (hon.), Elmira Coll., 1967, Siena Coll., 1968, Concord Coll., 1968; D.H.L. (hon.), Trinity Coll., Conn., 1970; Litt.D. (hon.), Skidmore Coll., 1974; L.H.D. (hon.), Coll. St. Rose, 1974, Union Coll., 1975. High sch. tchr. English and French langs. Adams, N.Y., 1937-39; high sch. tchr. English Goshen, N.Y., 1939-44; prin. high sch., 1944-49; mem. faculty Harvard U., 1951-65, dir. gen. edn., 1951-63, lectr. comparative lit., 1954-65; chancellor Union U.; also pres. Union Coll., Schenectady, 1965-74; pres. Am. Acad., Rome, Italy, 1974-76; Margaret Bundy Scott prof. Williams Coll., 1977; Charles A. Dana prof. humanities Trinity Coll., Conn., 1977-82, prof. emeritus, 1982—, sr. lectr. humanities, 1982—. Author: Logic and Rhetoric of Exposition, 1958, Spanning Three Centuries, 1984, Outlasting Marble and Brass, 1986. Editor: Inquiry and Expression (with Richard Ohmann), 1958, Style in Prose Fiction, 1959. Chmn. Mass. Com. Fulbright Awards, 1955-65, Coll. Bd. Com. English, 1959-64; Trustee Hartwick Coll., Siena Coll., Franklin Coll., Switzerland, Wenner-Gren Found. Served with USNR, 1945-46. Home: 87 Spurwink Rd Scarborough ME 04074

MARTIN, HAROLD EUGENE, publishing executive, consultant; b. Cullman, Ala., Oct. 4, 1923; s. Rufus John and Emma (Meadows) M.; m. Jean Elizabeth Wilson, Nov. 25, 1945; children: Brian, Anita. B.A. in History with honors, Howard Coll., Birmingham, Ala., 1954; M.A. in Journalism, Syracuse U., 1956. Asst. gen. mgr. Birmingham News Newhouse Newspapers, 1960-63, asst. prodn. mgr. St. Louis Globe-Democrat, 1958-60, asst. bus. mgr. Syracuse Herald Jour., 1957-58; pub. Montgomery Advertiser and Ala. Jour., Ala., 1963-70; pres. Multimedia Newspapers, editor and pub. Montgomery Advertiser and Ala. Jour. Multimedia, Inc., 1970-78, v.p., mem. mgmt. bd., 1973-78, also corp. dir.; exec. v.p., chief exec. officer So. Baptist Radio and TV Commn., Ft. Worth, 1979; pres. Jefferson Pilot Publs., Inc., Beaumont, Tex., 1980-85; pres., pub. Beaumont Enterprise, 1981-85; owner, pub. Herald Citizen daily newspaper, Cookeville, Tenn., 1970-78, News-Observer, Crossett, Ark., 1970-78; co-owner, pub Baxter Bull., Mountain Home, Ark., 1970-78; disting. vis. prof. Sch. Journalism, U. Fla., 1979-80; adj. prof. Samford U., 1961; juror Pulitzer Prize, 1971-72; dir. exec. Svc. Corp. of Ft. Worth. Contbr. articles to newspapers. Bd. dirs. Billy Graham Evangelistic Assn., Mpls.; coun. Samford U. Study Ctr., London. Recipient awards for articles; recipient citation Howard Coll, 1965, award of Outstanding Merit Ala. Dental Assn., 1966, Community Service award AP Assn., 1969, 72, 73, Pulitzer prize, 1970, First Place Newswriting award AP, 1971, Newswriting award for Best Stories of Yr. by Ala. Reporters AP, 1974, 75, Canon award, 1972, Ann. award for outstanding contbn. to health care Ala. State Nurses's Assn., 1973, News award Ala. State Nurses' Assn., 1976, Ala. Bapt. Communications award Ala. Bapt. State Conv., 1975; named Alumnus of Yr. Samford U., 1970. Mem. Alumni Assn. Samford U. (pres. 1967, 92, 93, adv. bd. Samford London Centre), Sigma Delta Chi (Green Eye Shade citation for Reporting 1969). Baptist. Home: 4958 Overton Woods Ct Fort Worth TX 76109-2433

MARTIN, HARRY CORPENING, lawyer, retired state supreme court justice; b. Lenoir, N.C., Jan. 13, 1920; s. Hal C. and Johnsie Harshaw (Nelson) M.; m. Nancy Robiou Dallam, Apr. 16, 1955; children: John, Matthew, Mary. A.B., U. N.C., 1942; LL.B., Harvard U., 1948; LL.M., U. Va., 1982. Bar: N.C. 1948. Sole practice Asheville, N.C., 1948-62; judge N.C. Superior Ct., Asheville, 1962-78, N.C. Ct. Appeals, Raleigh, 1978-82; justice N.C. Supreme Ct., 1982-92; ptnr. Martin & Martin, Attys., Hillsborough, N.C., 1992—; adj. prof. U. N.C. Law Sch., 1983-92, Dan K. Moore disting. vis. prof., 1992—; sr. conf. atty. U.S. Ct. Appeals for 4th Cir., 1994—; adj. prof. Duke U., 1990-91. Served with U.S. Army, 1942-45, South Pacific. Mem. U.S. Supreme Ct. Hist. Soc., N.C. Supreme Ct. Hist. Soc. (pres.). Democrat. Episcopalian. Home: 702 E Franklin St Chapel Hill NC 27514-3823 Office: U NC Law Sch Van Hecke-Wettach Hall Chapel Hill NC 27599

MARTIN, HENRY ALAN, lawyer; b. Nashville, Sept. 5, 1949; s. James Alvin and Mary Elizabeth (Long) M.; m. Gloria B. Ballard, May 9, 1975; children: Nathan Daniel, Anna Elizabeth. BA, Vanderbilt U., 1971, JD, 1974. Bar: Tenn. 1975, U.S. Dist. Ct. (mid. dist.) Tenn. 1975, U.S. Ct. Appeals (6th cir.) 1976, U.S. Supreme Ct. 1979. Pvt. practice Nashville, 1975-76; ptnr. Haile & Martin, P.A., Nashville, 1976-82; assoc. firm Barrett & Ray, P.C., Nashville, 1982-85; fed. pub. defender U.S. Dist. Ct. (mid. dist.) Tenn., Nashville, 1985—; mem. adv. com. on rules criminal procedure U.S. Judicial Conf., 1994—. CO-author, co-editor trial manual, Tools for the Ultimate Trial, 1985, 2d edit., 1988; contbr. articles to profl. jours. Del., Witness for Peace, Managua, Nicaragua, 1987. Mem. ABA (coun. criminal justice sect. 1993-96), NACDL, Nat. Lawyers Guild, Assn. Fed. Defenders (pres. 1995—), Nashville Bar Assn., Napier Looby Bar Assn., Nat. Legal Aid and Def. Assn., Tenn. Assn. Criminal Def. Lawyers (bd. dirs. 1978-94, pres. 1984-85, Pres.'s award 1984). Democrat. Avocations: jogging, swimming. Home: 3802 Whitland Ave Nashville TN 37205-2432 Office: Fed Pub Defender 810 Broadway Ste 200 Nashville TN 37203-3810

MARTIN, J. LANDIS, manufacturing company executive, lawyer; b. Grand Island, Nebr., Nov. 5, 1945; s. John Charles and Lucile (Cooley) M.; m. Sharon Penn Smith, Sept. 23, 1978; children: Mary Frances, Sarah Landis, Emily Penn. BS in Bus. Adminstrn., Northwestern U., 1968, JD cum laude, 1973. Bar: Ill. 1974, D.C. 1978, Colo. 1982. Assoc. Kirkland & Ellis, Chgo., 1973-77; ptnr. Kirkland & Ellis, Washington, 1978-81; mng. ptnr. Kirkland & Ellis, Denver, 1981-87, firm com. mem., Chgo., 1983-87; chmn., bd. dirs. Titanium Metals Corp., 1987—, CEO, 1995—; pres., CEO NL Industries Inc., Houston, 1987—; also bd. dirs. NL Industries Inc.; chmn., CEO Baroid Corp., Houston, 1987-94; chmn. bd., pres., CEO Tremont Corp., 1990—, also bd. dirs.; dir. Dresser Industries, Dallas, Aimco. Editor-in-chief: Exchange Act Guide to SEC Rule 144, 1973; articles editor Northwestern U. Law Rev., 1972-73. Pres Ctrl. City Opera House Assn., Denver, 1986-88, chmn. 1987; pres. Ctrl. City Opera House Endowment Fund, 1992—; vis. com. Northwestern U. Sch. Law, 1987—; mem. exec. com. Houston Grand Opera, 1991—, sr. v.p. devel. 1992—, pres. 1993-95, chmn. 1995—; bd. trustees Denver Art Mus., 1994—, Graland Country Day Sch., 1992—. With U.S. Army, 1969-71. Mem. ABA, Ill. Bar Assn., Colo. Bar Assn., D.C. Bar Assn. Clubs: Chevy Chase (Md.), John Evans (Evanston, Ill.), Denver, Denver Country, Castle Pines Golf. Office: NL Industries Inc 16825 Northchase Dr Ste 1200 Houston TX 77060-6004

MARTIN, J. PATRICK, lawyer; b. Detroit, Apr. 19, 1938; s. Joseph A. and Kathleen G. (Rich) M.; m. Denise Taylor, June 27, 1964; children: Timothy J., Julie D. Martin Digiovanni. AB magna cum laude, U. Notre Dame, 1960; JD with distinction, U. Mich., 1963; postgrad., London Sch. Econs., 1964. Bar: Mich. 1963, U.S. Dist. Ct. (ea. dist.) Mich. 1963, U.S. Ct. Appeals (6th cir.) 1967, U.S. Supreme Ct. 1979, U.S. Dist. Ct. (we. dist.) Mich. 1981. Spl. asst. to gen. counsel Ford Motor Co., Dearborn, Mich., 1962; assoc. Dykema, Wheat, Spencer et al, Detroit, 1963-66; assoc., then ptnr. Poole Littell Sutherland, Detroit, 1966-76; sr. atty., ptnr., shareholder Butzel Long, Detroit and Birmingham, Mich., 1976-94; sr. atty., shareholder Vlcko, Lane, Payne & Broder PC, Bingham Farms, Mich., 1994-96; settlement moderator Mich. Ct. Appeals, 1995—; sr. atty. Gourwitz and Barr PC, Southfield, Mich., 1996—; adj. prof. law U. Detroit Law Sch., 1989—, Wayne State U. Law Sch., 1996—; arbitrator Am. Arbitration Assn., Southfield, Mich., 1986—, Nat. Assn. Security Dealers, 1988—, N.Y. Stock Exch., 1991—; mediator, facilitator Oak County Cir. Ct., Pontiac, Mich., 1985—, Lex Mundi. author, editor: Laches-Oak County Bar Assn. Legal Jour., 1984, 92, 96, Real Property Rev., 1989-90, Mich. Law Weekly, 1990. Scholar Cook Found., Ford Found., London, 1963-64. Mem. ABA, Mich. Bar Assn., Detroit Met. Bar Assn., Oakland County Bar Assn. Roman Catholic. Avocations: gardening, golf, walking, bridge. Home: 200 Town Center Ste 1400 Southfield MI 48075-1147 Office: Gourwitz and Barr PC 2000 Town Ctr Ste 1400 Southfield MI 48075-1147

MARTIN, JACK, physician; b. Northport, Ala., Aug. 11, 1927; s. Marvin Oscar and Glenavis (Rice) M.; m. Ann Inman, Apr. 7, 1957; children: Sarah, Richard, Charles Randall, Robert. BS, U. Ala., 1949; MD, Valderbilt U., 1953. Intern Charity Hosp., New Orleans, 1953-54; resident in adult and child psychiatry Cin. Gen. Hosp., Richardson, Tex., 1954-58; dir. child psychiatry U. Tex. Health Scis. Ctr., Dallas, 1958-67; med. dir. Shady Brook Res. Ctr., Richardson, 1963-81; physician pvt. practice, Dallas, 1981—. With USNR, 1945-47. Independent. Episcopalian. Avocations: bridge, golf. Office: 3636 Dickason Ave Dallas TX 75219-4911

MARTIN, JAMES ALFRED, JR., religious studies educator; b. Lumberton, N.C., Mar. 18, 1917; s. James Alfred and Mary (Jones) M.; m. Ann Bradsher, June 1, 1936 (dec. 1982); m. Nell Gifford, Jan. 6, 1984. AB, Wake Forest Coll., 1937, LittD, 1965; MA, Duke U., 1938; PhD, Columbia U., 1944; student, Union Theol. Sem., 1940-43; M.A. (hon.), Amherst Coll., 1950. Ordained to ministry Bapt. Ch., 1944; asst. pastor Roxboro (N.C.) Ch., 1937-38; instr. philosophy and psychology Wake Forest Coll., 1938-40; asst. philosophy religion Union Theol. Sem., N.Y.C., 1941-44; Danforth prof. religion in higher edn. Union Theol. Sem., 1960-67, adj. prof. philosophy religion, 1967-82; prof. religion Columbia U., 1967-82, prof. emeritus, 1982—, chmn. dept., 1968-77; asst. prof. religion Amherst Coll., 1946-47, asso. prof., 1947-50, prof., 1950-54, Marquand and Stone prof., 1954-57, Crosby prof. religion, 1957-60; ordained deacon P.E. Ch., 1953; vis. prof. Cornell U., summer 1948, Mt. Holyoke Coll., 1949-50, 52-53, 59-60, State U. Iowa, summer 1959, U. N.C., summer 1964; Univ. prof. Wake Forest U., 1984—; vis. prof. religious studies U. Va., 1984; asso. mem. East-West Philosophers Conf., U. Hawaii, 1949. Author: Empirical Philosophies of Religion, 1944, (with J.A. Hutchison) Ways of Faith, 1953, rev., 1960, Fact, Fiction, and Faith, 1960, The New Dialogue between Philosophy and Theology, 1966, Beauty and Holiness, 1990; contbr. articles to profl. jours. and encys., chpts. to books. Chmn. bd. visitors Wake Forest Coll., 1981-83. Served as lt. chaplain USNR, 1944-46, PTO. Recipient Disting. Alumnus award Wake Forest U., 1971, Nat. Faculty award Assn. of Grad. Liberal Studies Programs, 1995. Mem. Soc. Values in Higher Edn. (Kent fellow, pres. 1964-69), Am. Theol. Soc. (v.p. 1981-82, pres. 1982), Soc. Theol. Discussion, Soc. Philosophy of Religion, Phi Beta Kappa, Omicron Delta Kappa, Pi Kappa Alpha. Home: PO Box 6746 Winston Salem NC 27109-6746 *My experience of life has increasingly underscored the central importance of honesty-in understanding of oneself, and in perceptions of and relations to others. The quest for honesty entails a relentless and often painful search for truth. Acceptance of truth, and of others as they truly are, requires grace. The goal is to speak the truth in love.*

MARTIN, JAMES DOUGLAS, neurologist; b. Cullman, Ala., Dec. 10, 1926; s. Charles L. and Sylvia J. (Johnson) M.; m. Elizabeth Mason, June 22, 1956; children: James, Julia, Ann. BA, Vanderbilt U., 1949, MD, 1959. Diplomate Am. Bd. Psychiatry and Neurology. Med. intern U. Va., Charlottesville, Va., 1959-60; neurology resident U. Va., Charlottesville, 1960-63; fellow in neuropathology Harvard Med. Sch., Boston, 1963-65; asst. prof. neurology W. Va. U., Morgantown, 1965-70, assoc. prof., 1970-72, prof., 1972—. Fellow Am. Acad. Neurology. Office: W Va Univ Dept Neurology PO Box 9180 Morgantown WV 26506-9180

MARTIN, JAMES FRANCIS, state legislator, lawyer; b. Atlanta, Aug. 22, 1945; s. Joseph Grant and Helen (Hester) M.; m. Joan Vohryzek, Jan. 30, 1970; children: Morgan, Rebecca, James, Frank. AB, U. Ga., 1967, JD, 1969, LLM, 1972; MBA, Ga. State U., 1980. Bar: Ga. 1972. Asst. legis. counsel Ga. Gen. Assembly, Atlanta, 1972-77; staff atty. Atlanta Legal Aid and Ga. Legal Svc. Programs, 1977-80; ptnr. Martin and McDuffie, 1980-86; of counsel Martin and Wilkes, 1986—, Martin Bros. P.C., 1986—; mem. Ga. Ho. of Reps., 1983—. Chmn. Judiciary Com., 1997—. 1st lt. U.S. Army, 1969-71, Vietnam. Democrat. Presbyterian. Office: State Capitol Rm 132 Atlanta GA 30334

MARTIN, JAMES FRANKLIN, physician, lawyer; b. Chattanooga, Feb. 22, 1929; s. Delbert Chester and Doshia (Locke) M.; m. Mary Edna Connelly, June 5, 1950; children: Samuel Franklin, Mary Karen, John Delbert, Molly Frances. MD, U. Tenn., Memphis, 1960; LLB, U. Tenn., Knoxville, 1952. Bar: Tenn. 1952, U.S. Ct. Mil. Appeals 1953. Engring. draftsman Combusion Engring. Co., Chattanooga, 1947-48; engr. mech. Combustion Engring. Co., Chattanooga, 1952; lawyer Harold Stone Law Firm, Knoxville, 1955-60; atty. Tenn. Valley Authority, Knoxville, 1955-56; intern James Walker Meml. Hosp., Wilmington, N.C., 1960-61, attending staff mem., 1962-66; pvt. practice in family practice Wilmington, N.C., 1961-66, Yuma, Ariz., 1968—; med. dir. Provident Life Accident Ins. Co., Chattanooga, 1966-68; instr. medicine James Walker Meml. Hosp., 1962-64; bd. dirs. Yuma Regional Med. Ctr., Mutual Ins. Co. of Ariz., Phoenix. Editor Tenn. Law Rev., 1951-52; author: Principal Security Devices in Tennessee, 1952. Capt. U.S. Army, 1952-55. Fellow Am. Acad. Family Practice, Am. Coll. Legal Medicine; mem. AMA, Ariz. Med. Assn., Am. Coll. Legal Medicine. Democrat. Avocations: reading, Southwest border history, Spanish language, quail hunting, tennis. Home: 1733 W Arcadia Ln Yuma AZ 85364-5064 Office: 2503 South Ave A Yuma AZ 85364

MARTIN, JAMES GILBERT, university provost emeritus; b. Paris, Ill., Dec. 10, 1926; s. James and Ruth Ann (Gilbert) M.; m. Doris E. Edmonson, Aug. 23, 1969; children—Bradley Keith, Philip Roger. B.A., Ind. State Coll., 1952, M.A., 1953; Ph.D., Ind. U., 1957. Instr. Ind. State Coll., Terre Haute, 1952-53; lectr. Ind. U., Bloomington, 1953-56; instr. sociology Okla. U., Norman, 1956-57; asst. prof. sociology No. Ill. U., DeKalb, 1957-65; asso. prof. No. Ill. U., 1959-64; asst. dean Coll. Arts and Scis., Ohio State U., Columbus, 1965-68; asso. dean Coll. Arts and Scis., Ohio State U. (Coll. Social and Behavioral Scis.), 1968-70, acting dean, 1970-71; v.p., provost U. No. Iowa, Cedar Falls, 1971-89, provost emeritus, 1989—; intern academic adminstrn. E.L. Phillips Found., 1963-64. Author: The Tolerant Personality, 1964, Minority Group Relations, 1973. Mem. Iowa Peace Inst. Bd., 1989-92. With AUS, 1945-48. Home: 749 Hidden Cir Dayton OH 45458-3317

MARTIN, JAMES GRUBBS, medical research executive, former governor; b. Savannah, Ga., Dec. 11, 1935; s. Arthur Morrison and Mary Julia (Grubbs) M.; m. Dorothy Ann McAulay, June 1, 1957; children: James Grubbs, Emily Wood, Arthur Benson. BS, Davidson Coll., 1957; PhD, Princeton U., 1960. Assoc. prof. chemistry Davidson (N.C.) Coll., 1960-72;

mem. 93d to 98th Congresses from N.C., 1973-85; gov. State of N.C., 1985-92; v.p. rsch. Carolinas HealthCare System, Charlotte, N.C., 1993—; mem. Mecklenburg (N.C.) Bd. County Commrs., 1966-72, chmn., 1967-68, 70-71; v.p. Nat. Assn. Regional Couns., 1971-72; pres. N.C. Assn. County Commrs., 1970-71; mem., tuba player Charlotte Symphony, 1961-66; dir. J.A. Jones Constrn., 1993—, Duke Power Co., 1994—; chmn. Global Transport Found., 1993—; trustee Wake Forest U. Danforth fellow, 1957-60. Mem. Beta Theta Pi (v.p., trustee 1966-69, pres. 1975-78), Masons (33 deg.), Shriners. Presbyterian. Office: Carolinas Med Ctr PO Box 32861 Charlotte NC 28232-2861

MARTIN, JAMES HANLEY, deputy state attorney general; b. N.Y.C., Dec. 22, 1960; s. James Patrick and Josephine Anne (Hanley) M. AB, Georgetown U., 1983; JD, Fordham U., 1986. Bar: N.J. 1986, U.S. Dist. Ct. N.J. 1986, N.Y. 1987, D.C. 1988, U.S. Dist. Ct. (so. and ea. dists.) N.Y. 1991, U.S. Ct. Appeals (D.C. and 3d cirs.) 1991, U.S. Supreme Ct. 1991. Dep. atty. gen. State of N.J., Newark, 1987—. Mem. ABA, Am. Judicature Soc., Essex County Bar Assn., N.J. State Bar Assn., D.C. Bar, Assn. Bar of City of N.Y. Roman Catholic. Office: State of NJ Divsn Law PO Box 45029 124 Halsey St Newark NJ 07101

MARTIN, JAMES JOHN, JR., retired consulting research firm executive, systems analyst; b. Paterson, N.J., Feb. 3, 1936; s. James John and Lillian (Lea) M.; m. Lydia Elizabeth Bent, June 11, 1954; children: David, Peter, Laura, Daniel, Lucas. B.A., U. Wis.-Madison, 1955; postgrad., Div. Sch., Harvard U., 1955-57; M.S., Navy Postgrad. Sch., 1963; Ph.D., MIT, 1965. Commd. ensign USN, 1957, advanced through grades to comdr., 1971, ret., 1977; sector v.p. Sci. Applications Internat. Corp., La Jolla, Calif., 1977-95. Author: Bayesian Decision Problems and Markov Chains, 1967; editor: On Not Confusing Ourselves, 1991; author articles on nat. security. Bd. dirs. Mil. Conflict Inst., 1986-92. Decorated Legion of Merit; recipient Superior Svc. medal Dept. Def. Mem. Internat. Inst. Strategic Studies, Ops. Research Soc. Am., Mil. Ops. Research Soc. (bd. dirs. 1974-77). Republican. Avocation: cooking. Home: 6603 Aranda Ave La Jolla CA 92037-6216

MARTIN, JAMES KAY, government official; b. Montreal, Que., Sept. 20, 1948; s. Douglas Kay and Margaret (Sherren) M.; m. Guillerma Lim Abrenica, Sept. 12, 1986. B.Math., U. Waterloo, Ont., 1970; PhD, U. Toronto, 1974. Sr. analyst Health & Welfare, Ottawa, 1974-79; asst. dir. transfer payments Social Devel. Ministry, Ottawa, 1980-84; exec. dir. planning Dept. Agr., Ottawa, 1984-90; exec dir. regulatory affairs Treasury bd. Can., Ottawa, 1990—; chmn. regulatory mgmt. group OECD, Paris, 1995—. Contbr. articles to profl. jours. Chmn. grad. students union U. Toronto, 1973, mem. bd. govs., 1974. Fellow Nat. Rsch. Coun., 1970, Ont. Inst. for Edn., 1971, Can. Coun., 1972, 73. Mem. Ottawa Humane Soc. Roman Catholic. Avocations: squash, skiing, swimming. Office: Treasury Board of Canada, 140 O'Connor St, Ottawa, ON Canada K1A 0R5

MARTIN, JAMES KIRBY, historian, educator; b. Akron, Ohio, May 26, 1943; s. Paul Elmo and Dorothy Marie (Garrett) M.; m. Karen Wierwille, Aug. 7, 1965; children: Darcy Elizabeth, Sarah Marie, Joelle Kathryn Garrett. B.A. summa cum laude, Hiram Coll., 1965; M.A., U. Wis., 1967, Ph.D., 1969. Asst. prof. history Rutgers U., New Brunswick, N.J., 1969-73, assoc. prof., 1973-79, prof., 1979-80, asst. provost, 1972-74, v.p. acad. affairs, 1977-79; vis. prof. Rutgers Ctr. of Alcohol Studies, 1978-88; prof. history U. Houston, 1980—, chmn. dept., 1980-83; vis. prof. history Rice U, 1992; chmn. bd. sponsors Papers of Thomas Edison Project, 1977-80; mem. editorial adv. bd. Papers of William Livingston Project, 1973-80. Author: Men in Rebellion, 1973, In the Course of Human Events, 1979, (with M.E. Lender) A Respectable Army: The Military Origins of the Republic, 1982 (contemporary mil. reading list), Drinking in America: A History, 1982, rev. edit. 1987, (with others) America and Its Peoples, 1989, 2d edit., 1993, 3d edit., 1997, concise edit. 1995, Benedict Arnold: Revolutionary Hero, 1997; editor: Interpreting Colonial America, 1973, 2d edit. 1978, The Human Dimensions of Nation Making, 1976, (with K. Stubaus) The America Revolution, Whose Revolution?, 1977, 81, (with M.E. Lender) Citizen-Soldier: The Revolutionary War Journal of Joseph Bloomfield, 1982 (R.P. McCormick prize), Ordinary Courage: The Revolutionary War Adventures of Joseph Plumb Martin, 1993; mem. bd. editors Houston Rev., 1981—, N.J. History, 1986—, Conversations with the Past Series, 1993-95; gen. editor Am. Social Experience Series, 1983—. Recipient N.J. Soc. of the Cin. prize for Disting. Achievement in Am. History, 1995, Hiram Coll. Alumni Achievement award, 1996. Mem. Tex. Assn. for Advancement History (bd. dirs. 1981-93, v.p. 1986-90), Inst. for Internat. Bus. Analysis (adv. coun. 1982-86), Am. Hist. Assn. (Beveridge-Dunning prize com. 1990-93), Orgn. Am. Historians, So. Hist. Assn., Soc. Historians Early Am. Republic (adv. coun. 1985-88), Phi Beta Kappa, Phi Kappa Phi, Pi Gamma Mu, Omicron Delta Kappa, Phi Alpha Theta. Office: U Houston Dept History 4800 Calhoun Rd Houston TX 77004-2610

MARTIN, JAMES ROBERT, identification company executive; b. Indpls., Mar. 31, 1943; s. Walter and Helen (Snider) M.; m. Jan. 24, 1970 (div. Dec. 1990); children: Julia, Justin; m. Tamara Hicks, Dec. 21, 1991; stepchildren: Hunter Hoskins, Laura Hoskins. BA, DePauw U., 1965; MBA, Ind. U., 1967. Bus. analyst TRW, Inc., Redondo Beach, Calif., 1967-70; fin. analyst Internat. Industries, Beverly Hills, Calif., 1970; v.p. fin., treas. A & E Plastik Pak Co., Inc., Industry, Calif., 1970-75; pres. Plasti-Line, Inc., Knoxville, Tenn., 1975-92, chmn., CEO, 1992—; bd. dirs. 1st Am. Corp., Nashville, Signal Thread Co., Chattanooga, Tenn. Bd. dirs. Knoxville Symphony Soc., 1976, Knoxville United Way, Webb Sch., Knoxville, 1986, Knoxville Mus. Art; bd. dirs., chmn. fin. com. Thompson Cancer Survival Ctr., Knoxville, 1985. Mem. Chief Execs. Orgn., Club LeConte (bd. dirs.), East Tenn. Automobile Club (bd. dirs.), St. Francis Yacht Club, Cherokee Country Club. Republican. Episcopalian. Home: 1029 Scenic Dr Knoxville TN 37919-7641 Office: Plasti-Line Inc PO Box 59043 Knoxville TN 37950-9043

MARTIN, JAY HERBERT, psychoanalysis and English educator; b. Newark, Oct. 30, 1935; s. Sylvester K. and Ada M. (Smith) M.; m. Helen Bernadette Saldini, June 9, 1956; children: Helen E., Laura A., Jay Herbert. AB with honors, Columbia U., 1956; MA, Ohio State U., 1957, PhD, 1960; PhD in Psychoanalysis, So. Calif. Psychoanalytic Inst., 1983. Instr. English Pa. State U., 1957-58; instr., then asst. to assoc. prof. English and Am. Studies Yale U., New Haven, Conn., 1960-68; prof. English and comparative culture U. Calif., Irvine, 1968-79; asst. prof. psychiatry and human behavior, clin. supr. residency program Calif. Coll. Medicine Calif. Coll. Medicine U. Calif., Irvine, 1978-96; Leo S. Bing prof. English and Am. lit. U. So. Calif., Irvine, 1979-96, dir. undergrad. program in Am. studies, 1968-69, dir. program in comparative culture, 1969-71, dir. edn. abroad program, 1971-75, dir. grad. studies dept. English, 1980-83; dir. civilization program Claremont (Calif.) McKenna Coll., 1996—; instr. psychoanalysis So. Calif. Psychoanalytic Inst., 1984-96; Bicentennial prof. Am. lit. and culture Moscow State U., USSR, 1976; vis. Parmenter lectr. Children's Hosp., San Francisco, 1989, Ann. William Faulkner Lecture, 1991, Herman Serota Found. lecture, 1992; cons. to pub. houses; lectr. USSR, Poland, Norway, France, Costa Rica, Fed. Republic Germany, Brazil, Can., U. London, Hebrew U., Jerusalem, Seoul, Rep. Korea, Bergen, Norway, China; dir. NEH summer sems., 1976, 77; mem. evaluation com. dept. pvt. post-secondary edn. State of Calif., 1986; cons. numerous univs., pubs., NEA, NEA, J.S. Guggenheim Found., Calif. Coun. for Humanities and Pub. Policy, U.S. Congress Com. on Edn. and Labor; faculty assoc. Coun. Internat. Exch. of Scholars; frequent speaker profl. orgns. and sems., univs., confs., hosps. Author: (criticism and biography) Conrad Aiken: A Life of His Art, 1962, Harvests of Change: American Literature 1865-1914, 1967, Nathanael West: The Art of His Life, 1970 (U. Calif. Friends Libr. award), Robert Lowell, 1970, Always Merry and Bright. The Life of Henry Miller, 1978, (U. Calif. Friends of Libr. award, Phi Kappa Phi Best Faculty Publ. prize U. So. Calif., transl. in French, Japanese and German), (fiction) Winter Dreams: An American in Moscow, 1979, Who Am I This Time, Uncovering the Fictive Personality, 1988 (trans. Portuguese, Burlington No. Found. award 1989); Swallowing Tigers Whole, 1996, A Corresponding Leap of Love: Henry Miller, 1996, Henry Miller's Dream Song, 1996; author one hour radio drama, William Faulkner. Sound Portraits of Twentieth-Century Humanists, starring Tennessee Williams, Glenn Close, Colleen Dewhurst, Nat. Pub. Radio, 1980; author sects. 24 books including most recently American Writing Today, vol. I, 1982, The Haunted Dusk: American Supernatural Fiction, 1820-1902, 1983, Frontiers of Infant Psychiatry, vol.II, 1986, Centenary Essays on Huckleberry Finn, 1985, Robert Lowell: Essays on the Poetry, 1987, William Faulkner: The Best from American Literature, 1989, The Homosexualities: Reality, Fantasy and the Arts, 1991, Life Guidance Through Literature, 1992, Biography and Source Studies, 1995, William Faulkner and Psychology, 1995, Psychotherapy East and West, 1996; contbr. numerous articles and revs. to profl. jours., bulls., L.A. Times Book Rev., Partisan Rev., N.Y. Times Book Rev., Internat. Rev. Psycho-Analysis, Am. Lit., London Times Lit. Supplement, Psychoanalytic Quarterly; editor: Winfield Townley Scott (Yale series recorded poets), 1962, Twentieth Century Interpretations of the Waste Land: A Collection of Critical Essays, 1968, Twentieth Century Views of Nathanael West, 1972, A Singer in the Dawn: Reinterpretations of Paul Laurence Dunbar (with intro.), 1975, Economic Depression and American Humor (with intro.), 1986; mem. editl. bd. Am. Lit., 1978-81, Humanities in Society, 1979-1983; editor-in-chief Psychoanalytic Edn., 1984-89; appearances on TV and radio including Connie Martinson Talks Books, Barbara Brunner Nightline, Sonya Live in L.A., Oprah Winfrey Show, 1988-89. Pres. Friends of Irvine Pub. Libr., 1974-75; mem. Com. for Freud Mus. Recipient Fritz Schmidl Meml. prize for rsch. applied psychoanalysis Seattle Assn. Psychoanalysis, 1982, Marie H. Briehl prize for child psychoanalysis, 1982, Franz Alexander prize in psychoanalysis, 1984; Morse rsch. fellow, 1963-64, Am. Philos. Soc. fellow, 1966, J.S. Guggenheim fellow, 1966-67, Rockefeller Found.humanities sr. fellow, 1975-76, Rsch. Clin. fellow So. Calif. Psychoanalytic Soc. 1977-81, Rockefeller fellow, Bellagio, Italy, 1983, NEH sr. fellow, 1983-84. Mem. So. Calif. Am. Studies Assn. (pres. 1969-71), Am. Studies Assn. (exec. bd. 1969-71, del. to MLA Assembly 1974, chmn. Ralph Gabriel prize com. 1975-77), MLA (chmn. prize com. Jay B. Hubbell Silver medal in Am. lit. 1978-84), Nat. Assn. Arts and Letters (prize com. 1987-88), Nat. Humanities Faculty (advisor to Valhalla High Sch., El Cajon, Calif. 1979-81), Nat. Am. Studies Faculty, Internat. Psychoanalytic Assn., Internat. Assn. Empirical Aesthetics, Internat. Assn. U. Profs. English, Internat. Karen Horney Soc., Phi Beta Kappa. Home: 748 Via Santo Tomas Claremont CA 91711

MARTIN, JEFFREY ALLEN, anesthesiologist; b. Sacramento, Dec. 3, 1956; s. Edward and Doris Ester (Marsch) M.; m. Sherry Lee Kroll, Oct. 16, 1993. BA in Psychology cum laude, Washington and Jefferson Coll., 1978; M of Med. Sci., Emory U., 1983; MD, Med. Coll. Ga., 1991. Diplomate Nat. Bd. Med. Examiners, Am. Bd. Anesthesiology; lic. physician asst., Ga., lic. physician, Pa. Physician asst. dept. anesthesiology divsn. cardiothoracic anesthesia Emory U. Hosp., Atlanta, 1983-91, mem. sci. staff, 1983-91, chief anesthetist cardiac transplant team, 1985-87; intern in medicine Nat. Naval Med. Ctr., Bethesda, Md., 1991-92, resident in anesthesiology, 1992-95, chief resident in anesthesiology, 1995; clin. scholar in anesthesiology Yale U., 1995-96; asst. dept. head, clin. dir. anesthesiology Naval Hosp. Submarine Base, Groton, Conn., 1995-96, attending anesthesiologist, 1995—; dir. ambulatory surgery Pain Consultation Svc.; clin. instr. cardiothoracic anesthesia, Emory U. Sch. Medicine, Atlanta, 1983-91; tng. cardiothoracic anesthesia Yale New Haven Hosp.; mem. med. staff Yale-New Haven Hosp., Nat. Naval Med. Ctr. Contbr. articles to profl. jours. Lt. Cmdr. 1991-95. Mem. AMA, Am. Soc. Anesthesiologists, Am. Acad. Anesthesia Assocs. (v.p. 1985, pres. 1986), Undersea and Hyperbaric Med. Soc., Pa. Med. Soc., Wayne Pike Med. Soc., Navy Anesthesia Soc., Soc. Air Force Physicians, Ducks Unltd., Delta Tau Delta (Outstanding Young Am. award 1977). Republican. Avocations: skiing, scuba, hunting, fishing, martial arts. Home: 33 Mott Ave New London CT 06320-2841 Office: Naval Hosp Submarine Base Groton CT 06322

MARTIN, JERRY C., oil company executive; b. Indpls., May 10, 1932; s. Joel C. and Blanche J. (Traubel) M.; m. Marilyn L. Brock, Sept. 7, 1952 (div. 1976); children: Cathy J., Kiefer, Douglas E.; m. Connie B. Young, May 8, 1979 (div. 1988); m. Rachel M. Fulgieri, Aug. 22, 1990. BS in Acctg., Butler U., 1953. Acct. Allison div. Gen. Motors, Indpls., 1953-57; acctng. and budget mgr. Standard Oil, Indpls., 1957-60; budget dir. Inland Container Corp., Indpls., 1960-71; corp. controller Storm Drilling and Marine Co., Chgo., 1971-75; v.p. Scottsman Norwood, Houston, 1975-76; corp. controller Internat Systems and Controls, Houston, 1976-79; v.p., controller Global Marine Drilling Co., Houston, 1979-85; sr. v.p., chief fin. officer Global Marine, Inc., Houston, 1985—. Bd. dirs. Global Marine Inc., 1993—. Mem. Fin. Execs. Inst., Mensa, Westlake Club, Westside Tennis Club, Houstonian Club. Republican. Avocation: tennis. Office: Global Marine Inc 777 N Eldridge Pky Houston TX 77079-4425

MARTIN, JERRY LEE, organization executive, philosophy educator; b. Turkey, Tex., Oct. 16, 1941. Student, San Diego State Coll., 1961; BA in Polit. Sci., U. Calif., Riverside, 1963; MA in Philosophy and Polit. Sci., U. Chgo., 1966; PhD in Philosophy, Northwestern U., 1970. Asst. prof. U. Colo., Boulder, 1967-74, chmn. dept. philosophy, 1979-81, assoc. prof., 1974-84, adjunct prof., 1984—; rsch. analyst House Rep. Rsch. Com., 1982-87; legis. asst. Congressman Hank Brown, 1982-87; dir. divsn. edn. programs NEH, Washington, 1987-88, asst. chmn. studies and evaluation, 1988-89, asst. chmn. programs and policy, 1989-95, acting chmn., 1993; adj. prof. Georgetown U., 1993—; adj. scholar Am. Enterprise Inst., 1993—; dir. Ctr. Study Values and Social Policy, U. Colo., Boulder, 1981-82; founding mem. organized rsch. program State of Colo., 1981-82; mem. exec. com. faculty adv. coun. Colo. Commn. Higher Edn., 1980-82; pres. Nat. Alumni Forum, 1995—; spkr. in field, frequent guest on radio and TV. Contbr. articles to profl. jours. Andrew W. Mellon Found. Congl. fellow, 1992-93. Mem. AAUP (state pres. 1977-79), Am. Philos. Assn., Soc. Historians Early Am. Republic, Am. Polit. Sci. Assn., Soc. Social, Polit. and Legal Philosophy. Avocations: tennis, baseball, hist. tours. Home: 5902 Mount Eagle Dr Apt 108 Alexandria VA 22303-2514 Office: Nat Alumni Forum 1625 K St NW Ste 310 Washington DC 20006-1612

MARTIN, JIM, publishing executive. Pub., CEO Infoworld, San Mateo, Calif. Office: Infoworld 755 Boret Rd Ste 800 San Mateo CA 94402*

MARTIN, JIM G., church renewal consultant; b. Mannington, W.Va., Nov. 16, 1933; s. Jacob Calvin and Dona Marie (Edgel) M.; m. R. Carolyn Holdman, Dec. 28, 1957; children: Susan Diane Martin Fenker, Stephen Glen. Pastor Bloom Ctr. Ch. of God, Bloomdale, Ohio, 1955-57, Esther (Mo.) Ch. of God, 1957-61, Silver Creek Ch. of God, Silver Lake, Ind., 1961-69, Oak Grove Ch. of God, Columbia City, Ind., 1969-77, Enola (Pa.) Ch. of God, 1977-81; sr. pastor Chambersburg (Pa.) Ch. of God, 1985-92; renewal assoc. Chs. of God Gen. Conf., Findlay, Ohio, 1992—. Office: Churches of God PO Box 926 700 E Melrose Ave Findlay OH 45840-4417

MARTIN, JOANNE, business educator; b. Salem, Mass., Sept. 25, 1946; d. Richard Drake and Nathalie (Ashton) M.; m. Beaumont A. Sheil, July 9, 1977; 1 child, Beaumont Martin Sheil. BA, Smith Coll., 1968; PhD in Social Psychology, Harvard U., 1977. Assoc. cons. McBer & Co. (formerly Behavior Sci. Ctr. of Sterling Inst.), 1968-70, dir. govt. mktg., 1970-72; asst. prof. orgnl. behavior and sociology Grad. Sch. Bus., Stanford (Calif.) U., 1977-80; assoc. prof. grad. sch. bus. Stanford (Calif.) U., 1980-91, prof. grad. sch. bus., 1991—, dir. doctoral programs, grad. sch. bus., 1991-95, Fred H. Merrill prof. orgn. behavior and sociology, 1996—, mem./vice-chair univ. adv. bd., 1995—; vis. scholar Australian Grad. Sch. of Mgmt., U. N.S.W., Dept. Psychology, Sydney (Australia) U., 1989-90; Ruffin fellow bus. ethics Darden Grad. Sch. of Bus. Adminstrn., U. Va., 1990. Author/co-author four books; contbr. over four dozen articles to profl. jours. Lena Lake Forrest Rsch. fellowship Bus. and Profl. Women's Found., 1978, James and Doris McNamara Faculty fellowship Grad. Sch. of Bus., Stanford U., 1990-91. Fellow APA (dissertation award), Acad. of Mgmt. (western divsn. promising young scholar award 1982, rep.-at-large 1983-85, divsn. program chair 1985-87, divsn. chair 1987-89, nat. bd. govs. 1992-95), Am. Psychol. Soc.; mem. Cons. Psychologists Press (bd. dirs.). Office: Stanford U Grad Sch Bus Stanford CA 94305

MARTIN, JOHN, airport executive. Dir. San Francisco Airport Commn. Office: San Francisco Airport Commn PO Box 8097 San Francisco CA 94128

MARTIN, JOHN BRUCE, chemical engineer; b. Auburn, Ala., Feb. 2, 1922; s. Herbert Marshall and Lannie (Steadham) M.; m. Mildred Jane Foster, Aug. 7, 1943 (dec. Nov. 1960); children—Shirlie Martin Briggs, John Bruce; m. 2d, Phyllis Barbara Rodgers, June 25, 1963; 1 child, Richard Kipp. B.S., Ala. Poly. Inst., 1943; M.Sc., Ohio State U., 1947, Ph.D., 1949. Registered profl. engr., Ohio. With Procter & Gamble Co., Cin., 1949-82, coordinator orgn. devel., research and devel., 1967-77, mgr. indsl. chem. market research, 1977-82; sr. assoc. Indumar Inc., Cin., 1982-86, sr. v.p., 1986-87; lectr. U. Cin., 1982-88; adj. assoc. prof. Auburn U., 1983-88. Contbr. articles to profl. jours.; patentee in field. Served with AUS, 1943-46. Decorated Air Medal, Bronze Star with oak leaf cluster; recipient Disting. Alumnus award Coll. Engring., Ohio State U., 1970, Disting. Engr. award Tech. Socs. Council Cin., 1982. Fellow AIChE (bd. dirs. 1968-70, chmn. mktg. divsn. 1985, Mktg. Hall of Fame 1988, Chem. Engr. of Yr. award Ohio Valley 1971); mem. Am. Chem. Soc., Am. Soc. Engring. Edn., Engring. Soc. Cin. (pres. 1972-73), Tech. and Sci. Socs. Cin. (pres. 1972-73), Chem. Mgmt. and Resources Assn., Sigma Xi, Tau Beta Pi, Phi Kappa Phi, Phi Lambda Upsilon. Republican. Mem. Disciples of Christ Ch. Home: 644 Doepke Ln Cincinnati OH 45231-5045

MARTIN, J(OHN) EDWARD, architectural engineer; b. L.A., Oct. 23, 1916; s. Albert C. and Carolyn Elizabeth (Borchard) M.; m. Elizabeth Jane Hines, May 27, 1944; children: Nicolas Edward, Peter Hines, Sara Jane McKinley Reed, Christopher Carey, Elizabeth Margaret Ferguson. Student, U. So. Calif., 1934-36; BS in Archtl. Engring., U. Ill., 1939. Registered profl. engr., Calif., Ill. Structural engr. Albert C. Martin & Assocs., L.A., 1939-42, ptnr., 1945-75, mng. ptnr., 1975-86. Founding mem. bd. trustees Thomas Aquinas Coll., Santa Paula, Calif., 1971—. Lt. USNR, 1942-45. Fellow ASCE; mem. Structural Engrs. Assn. Calif., Cons. Engrs. Assn. Calif., Jonathan Club (bd. dirs. 1978-81), Calif. Club (Ranchero Visitadores), Valley Hunt Club, Flintridge Riding Club, West Hills Hunt Club (Master of Fox Hounds 1975-88), Saddle & Sirloin Club, Rep. Assn. L.A., Heritage Found., Traditional Mass Soc. (founder). Republican. Roman Catholic. Avocation: horsemanship. Office: Albert C Martin & Assocs 811 W 7th St Los Angeles CA 90017-3408

MARTIN, JOHN HUGH, lawyer, retired; b. Los Angeles, Apr. 19, 1918; s. John Hume and Carrie Suzanne (Hatcher) M.; m. Jean Morrison Park, Sept. 17, 1945; 1 dau., Suzanne L. B.S., Monmouth Coll., 1939; J.D., U. Chgo., 1942. Bar: Ill. 1943, Calif. 1962. Practice law Chgo., 1943-52; sec., gen. counsel Am. Community Builders, Park Forest, Ill., 1952-54; dep. counsel Bur. Aero., Dept. Navy, Washington, 1954-57; with Lockheed Aircraft Corp., Burbank, Calif., 1957-79; European counsel Lockheed Aircraft Corp., 1960-61, div. counsel, 1961-71, asst. sec., chief counsel, 1971-77, corp. adv., 1977-79; pvt. practice law, 1980-94, retired, 1994. Mem. Am., Fed., Internat., Los Angeles County bar assns., Phi Alpha Delta. Democrat. Episcopalian. Club: Legal (Chgo.);. Home: 1611 Arboles Dr Glendale CA 91207-1127

MARTIN, JOHN JOSEPH, journalist; b. N.Y.C., Dec. 3, 1938; s. John and Marie Agnes (Jacobsen) M.; children from previous marriage: Sophie Suzanne, Claire Catherine; m. Katherine Fitzhugh, Feb. 14, 1987. BA in Journalism, San Diego State U., 1995. Copy editor, reporter San Diego Union, 1958-62; copy editor Augusta (Ga.) Chronicle, 1963, N.Y. Times Internat. Edit., Paris, 1964-65; editorial asst. Temple Fielding Publs., Mallorca, Spain, 1965-66; reporter, producer Sta. KCRA-TV News, Sacramento, 1966-75; corr. ABC-TV News, 1975—. Served with U.S. Army, 1962-64. Recipient Nat. Headliner awards, 1980, 89, NSPE award, 1982, Nat. Assn. Home Care award, 1992, Emmy award, 1993, George Polk award, 1994, DuPont-Columbia U. Gold baton. Mem. AFTRA, U.S. Tennis Assn., Coffee House Club N.Y.C., Nat. Press Club, Overseas Press Club. Office: 1717 Desales St NW Washington DC 20036-4401

MARTIN, JOHN L., state legislator; b. Eagle Lake, Maine, June 5, 1941; s. Frank and Edwidge (Raymond) M. BA in History and Govt., U. Maine, 1963, postgrad., 1963-64. Tchr. Am. govt. and history Ft. Kent (Maine) Community High Sch., 1966-72; instr. U. Maine, Ft. Kent, 1972—; asst. prof. U. Maine, 1989—; mem. from Eagle Lake and St. Francis dist. Maine Ho. of Reps., 1964-94, minority fl. leader, 1970-74, speaker of ho., 1975-94, chmn. com. on energy & natural resources, 1994-95; adj. lectr.; mem. intergovtl. rels. com. Nat. Legis. Conf., 1970—; chmn. Maine Land Use Regulation Commn., 1972-73, Maine Bur. Human Rels., 1972, State Legis. Leaders Found., 1979—; mem. exec. bd. Nat. Conf. State Legislatures, chmn. state-fed. assembly, 1985-86, chair task force on reapportionment, 1987-88, vice chmn. budget, fiscal and rules com., 1986-87, v.p., 1988-89, pres.-elect, 1989-90, pres., 1990-91, immediate past pres., 1991-92; mem. exec. com. New Eng. Caucus of State Legislatures, 1978-95, chmn., 1982; mem. regional exec. com. Nat. Dem. State Legis. Leaders Assn., 1991-95, chmn., 1987—; bd. dirs. Found. for State Legislatures, 1988-94; mem. exec. com. Dem. Nat. Com., 1991-94. Trustee Eagle Lake Water and Sewer Dist., 1966—, No. Maine Gen. Hosp., Ft. Kent, Ea. Maine Health Care, 1991-92; mem. rural health steering com. Nat. Acad. for State Health Policy; advisor White House Task Force on Health Care Reform; dir. intergovtl. affairs Nat. Health Care Campaign, 1994. Mem. New Eng. Polit. Sci. Assn. Home: PO Box 250 Eagle Lake ME 04739-0250 Office: Maine Ho of Reps State House Augusta ME 04333

MARTIN, JOHN S., JR., federal judge; b. Bklyn., May 31, 1935. BA, Manhattan Coll., 1957; LLB, Columbia U., 1961. Law clk. to Hon. Leonard P. Moore U.S. Ct. Appeals (2d cir.), 1961-62; asst. U.S. atty. U.S. Dist. Ct. (so. dist.) N.Y., 1962-66; ptnr. Johnson, Hekker & Martin, Nyack, N.Y., 1966-67; asst. to solicitor gen., 1967-69, sole practitioner, 1969-72; ptnr. Martin, Obermaier & Morvillo, 1972-79, Schulte, Roth & Zabel, 1979-80; U.S. atty. U.S. Dist. Ct. for So. Dist. N.Y., N.Y.C., 1980-83; ptnr. Schulte, Roth & Zabel, 1983-90; judge U.S. Dist. Ct. for So. Dist. N.Y., N.Y.C., 1990—. Fellow Am. Coll. Trial Lawyers; mem. Assn. Bar City N.Y. Office: US Dist Ct So Dist NY 500 Pearl St New York NY 10007-1316

MARTIN, JOHN THOMAS, physician, author, educator; b. Cleve., June 8, 1924; s. Clarence Henry and Clara May (Feeney) M.; m. Marion Elizabeth George, Feb. 18, 1946; children: Thomas R., David B., Richard G., Janet E., Patricia L., Robert W. MD, U. Cin., 1948. Commd. 1st lt. USAF, 1949, advance through grades to maj., 1953; resident in anesthesiology Lackland AFB Hosp., San Antonio, 1953-55; asst. chief USAF Sch. Anesthesiology, Lackland AFB, 1955-57; attending anesthesiologist Baylor U. Hosp., Dallas, 1957-58; cons. dept. anesthesiology Mayo Clinic, Rochester, Minn., 1958-72; head Meth sect. anesthesiology Mayo Clinic, 1966-72; chmn. dept. anesthesiology Ochsner Med. Ctr., New Orleans, 1972-74; clin. assoc. prof. anesthesiology Tulane U. Sch. Medicine, New Orleans, 1972-74; prof. anesthesiology Med. Coll. Ohio, Toledo, 1974-90; chmn. dept. anesthesiology Med. Coll. Ohio, 1980-89, emeritus prof. anesthesiology, 1990—. Editor, author: Positioning Patients Anesthesia/Surgery, 1978, 2d edit., 1987, 3d edit., 1997; editor ASA Handbook of Hosp. Facilities for Anesthesia, 1972, 2d edit., 1974; contbr. articles to profl. jours. Chmn. conductor selection com. Rochester Symphony Orch., 1963-66; pres. Rochester Civic Music, 1965. Mem. Internat. Anesthesia Rsch. Soc. (chmn. 1979-81, trustee 1965-90), Minn. Soc. Anesthesiologists (pres. 1966-67), Ohio Soc. Anesthesiologists (pres. 1988-89), Am. Med. Writers Assn. (pres. Minn. chpt. 1970-71), Assoc. Physicians Med. Coll. Ohio (bd. dirs. 1974-89), Am. Soc. Anesthesiology, Sigma Xi, Alpha Omega Alpha, Sigma Chi, Phi Chi. Republican. Avocations: medical writing, computers, music, fishing. Home: 4605 Woodland Ln Sylvania OH 43560-3221 Office: Med Coll of Ohio Toledo PO Box 10008 Toledo OH 43699

MARTIN, JOHN WILLIAM, JR., lawyer, automotive industry executive; b. Evergreen Park, Ill., Sept. 1, 1936; s. John William and Frances (Hayes) M.; m. Joanne Cross, July 2, 1966; children: Amanda Hayes, Bartholomew McGuire. AB in History, DePaul U., 1958, JD, 1961. Bar: Ill. 1961, D.C. 1962, N.Y. 1964, Mich. 1970. Antitrust trial atty. Dept. Justice, Washington, 1961-62; assoc. Donovan, Leisure, Newton & Irvine, N.Y.C., 1962-70; sr. atty. Ford Motor Co., Dearborn, Mich., 1970-72, assoc. counsel, 1972-74, counsel, 1974-76, asst. gen. counsel, 1976-77, assoc. gen. counsel, 1977-89, v.p., gen. counsel, 1989—; trustee Ford Motor Co. Fund, 1989—; bd. dirs. Ctr. Social Gerontology, Inc., Nat. Women's Law Ctr. Contbr. articles to profl. jours. Mem. Assn. Gen. Counsel, Am. Law Inst. Coun., Nat. Legal Aid and Defender Assn. (bd. dirs.), Little Traverse Yacht Club. Republican. Roman Catholic. Office: Ford Motor Co The American Rd Dearborn MI 48121

MARTIN, JOSEPH, JR., retired lawyer, former ambassador; b. San Francisco, May 21, 1915; m. Ellen Chamberlain Martin, July 5, 1946; children: Luther Greene, Ellen Myers. AB, Yale U., 1936, LLB, 1939. Assoc. Cadwalader, Wickersham & Taft, N.Y.C., 1939-41; ptnr. Wallace, Garrison, Norton & Ray, San Francisco, 1946-55, Pettit & Martin, San Francisco, 1955-70, 73-95; gen. counsel FTC, Washington, 1970-71; ambassador, U.S. rep. Disarmament Conf., Geneva, 1971-76; ret.; mem. Pres.'s Adv. Com. for Arms Control and Disarmament, 1974-78; bd. dirs. Astec Industries, Inc. Pres. Pub. Utilities Commn., San Francisco, 1956-60; Rep. nat. committeeman for Calif., 1960-64; treas. Rep. Party Calif., 1956-58; bd. dirs. Patrons of Art and Music, Calif. Palace of Legion of Honor, 1958-70, pres., 1963-68; bd. dirs. Arms Control Assn., 1977-84; pres. Friends of Legal Assistance to Elderly, 1983-87. Lt. comdr. USNR, 1941-46. Recipient Ofcl. commendation for Outstanding Service as Gen. Counsel FTC, 1973, Distinguished Honor award U.S. ACDA, 1973, Lifetime Achievement award Legal Assistance to the Elderly, 1981. Fellow Am. Bar Found. Clubs: Burlingame Country, Pacific Union. Home: 2879 Woodside Rd Woodside CA 94062-2441

MARTIN, JOSEPH BOYD, neurologist, educator; b. Bassano, Alta., Can., Oct. 20, 1938; s. Joseph Bruce and Ruth Elizabeth (Ramer) M.; m. Rachel Ann Wenger, June 18, 1960; children: Bradley, Melanie, Douglas, Neil. BSc, Eastern Mennonite Coll., Harrisonburg, Va., 1959; MD, U. Alta., 1962; PhD, U. Rochester, N.Y., 1971; MA (hon.), Harvard U., 1978; ScD (hon.), McGill U., 1994, U. Rochester, 1996. Resident in internal medicine Univ. Hosp., Edmonton, Alta., 1962-64; resident in neurology Case-Western Res. U. Hosps., 1964-67; rsch. fellow U. Rochester, N.Y., 1967-70; mem. faculty McGill U. Faculty Medicine, Montreal, Que., Can., 1970-78; prof. medicine and neurology, neurologist-in-chief Montreal Neurol. Inst., 1976-78; chmn. dept. neurology Mass. Gen. Hosp., Boston, also Dorn prof. neurology Harvard U. Med. Sch., 1978-89; dean Sch. Medicine U. Calif., San Francisco, 1989-93; chancellor U. Calif., San Francisco, 1993-97; dean faculty medicine Harvard U., Boston, 1997—; mem. med. adv. bd. Gairdner Found., Toronto, 1978-83; adv. council neurol. disorders program Nat. Inst. Neurol., Communicative Disorders and Stroke, 1979-82. Co-author: Clinical Neuroendocrinology, 1977, The Hypothalmamus, 1978, Clinical Neuroendocrinology: A Pathophysiological Approach, 1979, Neurosecretion and Brain Peptides: Implications for Brain Functions and Neurological Disease, 1981, Brain Peptides, 1983; editor Harrison's Principles of Internal Medicine, 1980—, Clin. Neuroendocrinology 2d edit., 1987. Recipient Moshier Meml. gold medal U. Alta. Faculty Medicine, 1962, John W. Scott gold med. award, 1962; Med. Research Council Can. scholar, 1970-75. Mem. NAS, Am. Neurol. Assn. (pres. 1990), Am. Physiol. Soc. (Bowditch lectr. 1978), Royal Coll. Phys. and Surg. Can., Endocrine Soc., Soc. Neurosci., Am. Soc. Clin. Investigation, Assn. Am. Physicians, Am. Acad. Arts and Scis., Inst. of Medicine, Nat. Adv. Coun., Nat. Inst. Aging. Office: U Calif 513 Parnassus Ave Ste 126 San Francisco CA 94122-2722

MARTIN, JOSEPH PAUL, university department director; b. Liverpool, Eng., June 28, 1936; m. Joseph and Winifred (Austin) M.; m. Roberta Martin, Aug. 7, 1971; children: Christopher, Elizabeth. PhL, Angelicum, Rome, 1960, STL, 1964; PhD, Columbia U., 1973. Cert. comparative and internat. edn. Missionary Oblate Fathers, Lesotho, 1964-67; dir. Earl Hall Ctr. Columbia U., N.Y.C., 1972-86, exec. dir. ctr. study of human rights, 1977—. Lt. Brit. Artillery, 1954-56. Mem.ACLU (ch.-state com. 1987—), African Studies Assn., Amnesty Internat. Office: Columbia U Ctr Human Rights 1108 International Affairs Bldg New York NY 10027

MARTIN, JOSEPH ROBERT, financial executive; b. Phila., Dec. 9, 1947; s. Robert and Elva Ruth (Griffen) M.; m. Catherine Marie Kelly, Sept. 5, 1970; children: Joseph Robert Jr., Jennifer H., Patrick F., Kathleen K., Mariah E. BS, Embry Riddle U., 1974; MBA, U. Maine, 1976. Sr. corp. fin. analyst Keyes Fibre Co., Waterville, Maine, 1976-80; mgr. fin. analysis and planning Schlumberger, Fairchild, South Portland, Maine, 1980-83; div. contr. Schlumberger, Factron, Clifton Park, N.Y., 1983-84; corp. contr. VTC, Inc., Bloomington, Minn., 1984-87; v.p. fin., chief fin. officer VTC, Inc., Bloomington, 1987-88, sr. v.p., chief fin. officer, 1989-90; dir. fin. Nat. Semiconductor, South Portland, Maine, 1990-91; v.p. fin. std. products group Nat. Semicondr., Santa Clara, Calif., 1991-95; v.p. fin. worldwide ops. Nat. Semiconductor, Santa Clara, Calif., 1995-96; exec. v.p., CFO, bd. dirs. Fairchild Semiconductor, South Portland, Maine, 1996—. Served to capt. U.S. Army, 1967-72, Vietnam. Decorated D.F.C., Purple Heart, Bronze Star medal, Air medal. Home: 21 Beechtree Ln Yarmouth ME 04096-1062 Office: Nat Semiconductor 1090 Kifer Rd Santa Clara CA 95051

MARTIN, JUDITH SYLVIA, journalist, author; b. Washington, Sept. 13, 1938; d. Jacob and Helen (Aronson) Perlman; m. Robert Martin, Jan. 30, 1960; children: Nicholas Ivor, Jacobina Helen. BA, Wellesley Coll., 1959; DHL (hon.), York Coll., 1985, Adelphi U., 1991. Reporter-critic, columnist Washington Post, 1960-83; syndicated columnist United Feature Syndicate, N.Y.C., 1978—; critic-at-large Vanity Fair, 1983-84. Author: The Name on the White House Floor, 1972, Miss Manners' Guide to Excruciatingly Correct Behavior, 1982, Gilbert, 1982, Miss Manners' Guide to Rearing Perfect Children, 1984, Common Courtesy, 1985, Style and Substance, 1986, Miss Manners' Guide for the Turn-of-the-Millennium, 1989, Miss Manners on (Painfully Proper) Weddings, 1996, Miss Manners Rescues Civilization, 1996, Miss Manners' Basic Training: Communications, 1997, Miss Manners' Basic Training: Eating, 1997; mem. editl. bd. The American Scholar. Bd. dirs. Washington Concert Opera; mem. nat. adv. coun. Inst. Govtl. Studies, U. Calif., Berkeley. Mem. Cosmos Club (bd. mgmt.). Office: United Feature Syndicate 200 Madison Ave New York NY 10016-3903

MARTIN, JUDSON PHILLIPS, retired education educator; b. Butler, Wis., Feb. 4, 1921; s. Darwin H. and Emma (Phillips) M.; m. June Ruth Elletson, June 19, 1948 (div.); children: Christopher Alan, Karen Marie; m. Mary Belle Jepson, Sept. 23, 1971 (dec. Apr. 1995); stepchildren: Stephen, Susan, Sandra, Christopher; m. Kathryn L. Tompkins, Feb. 17, 1996; stepchildren: David, Dale. BS, U. Wis., 1942, MA, 1946, PhD, 1955. Registrar, acad. dean Bemidji (Minn.) State U., 1946-68; dean grad. study, prof. edn. N.E. Mo. State U., 1968-71, prof. edn., 1971-80, 82-85, head div. edn. and head tchr. edn., 1980-82; substitute tchr. Seminole County, Fla., 1990-96. Dist. officer Minn. Boy Scouts Am.; mem. Bemidji City Coun., 1951; pres. Red Barn Cmty. Arts Coun.; sch. vol. Seminole County, Fla., 1994-96; newspaper reader for the blind Sta. WMFE, Orlando, Fla. With AUS, 1942-45. Decorated Bronze Star; Croix de Guerre (France) avec etoille. Mem. NEA, Am. Legion, Minn. Edn. Assn. (past pres. higher edn. sect.), Mo. Edn. Assn., Am. Assn. Higher Edn., Mo. Fiber Artists Assn., Weavers of Orlando, Handweavers of Am. Tropical Weavers of Fla., Masons, K.T., Elks, Kiwanis (dist. lt. gov. 1974-75), Phi Delta Kappa. Presbyn. Home: 35 Granada Ave Merritt Island FL 32592-5035

MARTIN, JUDY BRACKIN HEREFORD, higher education administrator; b. York, Ala., May 25, 1943; d. Julian Byron and Willie Lee (Aiken) B.; m. Roy Nichols Hereford, Jr., Apr. 1, 1962 (dec. Mar. 1988); children: Leanne, Roy Nichols III, Rachel, Samantha; m. John Lawrence Martin Sr., Nov. 23, 1988. BA, Judson Coll., 1964. Co-owner, ptnr. Hereford Haven Farms, Faunsdale, Ala., 1962-93; ptnr. The Mustard Seed, Demopolis, Ala., 1974-76; ptnr., sales mgr. Hereford & Assocs. Auction Co., Faunsdale, Ala., 1967-91; alumnae dir., dir. admissions Judson Coll., Marion, Ala., 1988-90, asst. to pres., 1990-94, interim v.p. for instnl. advancement, 1996—; exec. sec.-treas. Ala. Women's Hall of Fame, Judson Coll., Marion, 1991-97; exec. dir. Ala. Rural Heritage Found., Thomaston, 1991-95. Officer Marengo County Red. Cross, 1987-88; mem. Marengo County Hist. Soc., Econ. Devel. Assn. Ala., 1991—; com. mem. Marengo Dem. Exec. Com.; bd. dirs. Dept. Human Resources, Marengo County, 1987-95, Marengo County Farmers Fedn. Bd., 1985-95; reporting sec. Ala. Women's Comm., 1993-97; mem. Ala. Women's Leadership Data Base, 1995—; bd. dirs. Perry County C. of C., 1995—; mem. So. Arts Fedn. Adv. Coun., 1994-95; mem. steering com. Leadership Marengo, 1994; chmn. bd. Faunsdale United Meth. Ch., 1989-91. Mem. Blackbelt Tourism Coun. (bd. dirs. 1991), Judson Coll. Alumnae Assn. (treas. 1992-96). Methodist. Avocations: cattle farming, sewing, painting.

MARTIN, JUNE JOHNSON CALDWELL, journalist; b. Toledo, Oct. 6; d. John Franklin and Eunice Imogene (Fish) Johnson; m. Erskine Caldwell, Dec. 21, 1942 (div. Dec. 1955); 1 child, Jay Erskine; m. Keith Martin, May 5, 1966. AA, Phoenix Jr. Coll., 1939-41; BA, U. Ariz., 1941-43, 53-59; student Ariz. State U., 1939, 40. Free-lance writer, 1944—; columnist Ariz. Daily Star, 1956-59; editor Ariz. Alumnus mag., Tucson, 1959-70; book reviewer, columnist Ariz. Daily Star, Tucson, 1970-94; ind. book reviewer and audio tape columnist, Tucson, 1994—; panelist, co-producer TV news show Tucson Press Club, 1954-55, pres., 1958; co-founder Ariz. Daily Star Ann. Book & Author Event. Contbg. author: Rocky Mountain Cities, 1949; contbr. articles to World Book Ency., and various mags. Mem. Tucson CD Com., 1961; vol. campaigns of Samuel Goddard, U.S. Rep. Morris Udall, U.S. ambassador and Ariz. gov. Raul Castro. Recipient award Nat. Headliners Club, 1959, Ariz. Press Club award, 1957-59, 96, Am. Alumni Council, 1966, 70. Mem. Nat. Book Critics Circle, Jr. League of Tucson, Tucson Urban League, PEN U.S.A. West, Planned Parenthood of So. Ariz., Pi Beta Phi. Democrat. Methodist. Club: Tucson Press. Home: Desert Foothills Sta PO Box 65388 Tucson AZ 85728

MARTIN, KEITH, lawyer; b. Mpls., May 5, 1953; s. L. John and Lois Ann (Henze) M.; m. Linda Harvill, 1977 (div. 1985). BA, Wesleyan, 1974; JD, George Washington U., 1977; MSc, London Sch. Econs., 1978. Bar: D.C. 1978, N.Y. 1985. Legis. asst. Sen. Henry M. Jackson Washington, 1974-77, legis. counsel Sen. Daniel Patrick Moynihan, 1979-82; ptnr. Chadbourne & Parke, Washington, 1983—, mng. ptnr., 1989-93. Democrat. Office: Chadbourne & Parke LLP 1200 New Hampshire Ave NW Washington DC 20036-6802

MARTIN, KEVIN JOHN, nephrologist, educator; b. Dublin, Ireland, Jan. 18, 1948; came to U.S., 1973; s. John Martin and Maura Martin; m. Grania E. O'Connor, Nov. 16, 1972; children: Alan, John, Ciara, Audrey. MB BCh, Univ. Coll. Dublin, 1971. Diplomate Am. Bd. Internal Medicine, Am. Bd. Nephrology. Intern St. Vincent's Hosp., Dublin, 1971-72, resident, 1972-73; resident Barnes Hosp., St. Louis, 1973-74, fellow, 1974-77; asst. prof. Washington U., St. Louis, 1977-84, assoc. prof., 1984-89; prof., dir. div. nephrology St. Louis U., 1989—. Contbr. numerous articles to med. jours. Office: Saint Louis Univ Med Ctr 3635 Vista Ave Saint Louis MO 63110-2539

MARTIN, LEE, mechanical engineer; b. Elkhart, Ind., Feb. 7, 1920; s. Ross and Esther Lee (Schweitzer) M.; m. Geraldine Faith Fitzgarrald, July 20, 1945; children: Jennifer L., Casper, Rex, Elizabeth L. SBME, SMME, MIT, 1943; LLD (hon.), Ind. U., 1997. Seaman Brit. Merchant Marine, St. John's, Newfoundland, 1939; with GE, 1940-42; with NIBCO Inc., Elkhart, 1943—, pres., 1957-76, chmn., 1975-95, vice chmn., 1995—. Chmn. Samaritan Inst., Denver, 1980-86; dir. Interlochen (Mich.) Ctr. for Arts, 1983-94; trustee Tri-State U., Angola, Ind., 1973-88. Mem. Union League Club (Chgo.), The Club at Pelican Bay (Naples, Fla.).

MARTIN, LELAND MORRIS (PAPPY MARTIN), history educator; b. Patrick Springs, Va., Aug. 8, 1930; s. Rufus Wesley and Mary Hilda (Biggs) M.; m. Mildred Greer, May 12, 1956; children: Lee Ann Martin Powell, Mitzi Jo. AB, Berea Coll., 1953; MS, U. Tenn., 1954; grad., Air War Coll., Maxwelll AFB, Ala., 1978; MA in History, U Tex. Pan-Am., 1993; cert. machinist, Tex. State Tech. Coll., 1997. Cert. machinist, Tex. Enlisted USAF, 1954, advanced through grades to col., 1977; comdr. RAF, Greenham Common, Welford, 1974-76; comdt., comdr. Mil. Airlift Command Noncommissioned Officers Acad., McGuire AFB, N.J., 1976-79; vice comdr., comdr. RAF Mildenhall and RAF Chicksands, Eng., 1979-83; chief of staff 21st Air Force, McGuire AFB, 1983-84; pres. Air Force Phys. Evaluation Bd., Randolph AFB, N.J., 1984-86; ret., 1986; dep. exec. dir. Confederate Air Force, Harlingen, Tex., 1986-88; exec. dir. Am. Airpower Heritage Found., Harlingen, 1986-88; tchg. asst., lectr. in history Pan Am. dept. U. Tex., Edinburg, 1989-93; adj. prof. history Tex. State Tech. Coll., Harlingen, 1994—; co-chair (with Sir Douglas Bader) 1976 Internat. Air Tatoo at RAF Greenham Common; chair Air Fete 80 and 81, RAF Mildenhall, Eng. Co-editor: History of Military Assistance Command, Vietnam, 1970. Decorated Legion of Merit with two oak leaf clusters, Bronze Star; Cross of Gallantry (Vietnam); recipient Amb.'s award Ct. St. James, London, 1974, 83. Mem. Air Force Assn., Am. Watchmakers Inst., Nat. Assn. Watch and Clock Collectors, Brit. Officers Club Phila. (hon.), Rotary (gov. internat. dist. 5930 1995-96), Order of Daedalians, Phi Alpha Theta, Phi Kappa Phi. Republican. Presbyterian. Avocations: clock repairs, photography, golf, fishing. Home: 3001 Emerald Lake Dr Harlingen TX 78550-8621 Office: Tex State Tech Coll Dept History Harlingen TX 78550-3697

MARTIN, LEROY E., finance company executive; b. Mpls., Apr. 9, 1941; m. Gayle Martin; children: Lisa, Michelle, Bradley. BSBA in Acctg., U. Minn., 1963. CPA, Minn. Mem. client svc. staff, ptnr. McGladrey & Pullen, Mpls., 1962-74, dir. audit, acctg. and SEC practice, 1974-76, ptnr. in charge St. Paul office, 1976-79, coord. audit and acctg., 1979-83, regional mng. ptnr., 1983-89, mng. ptnr., 1989—; mem. SEC Practice Sect. Exec. Com., chmn. Group B adv. com.; past mem. Auditing Standards Exec. Com. Fin. Acctg. Standards Adv. Coun.; chmn. RSM Internat. Mem. AICPA, Minn. Soc. CPAs, Accts. Liability Assurance Co. Ltd. (bd. dirs.). *

MARTIN, LINDA GAYE, demographer, economist; b. Paris, Ark., Dec. 17, 1947; d. Leslie Paul and Margie LaVerne (Thomas) M. BA in Math., Harvard U., 1970; MPA, Princeton U., 1972, PhD in Econs., 1978. Dir. mgmt. info. sr. ctrs. bur. purchased social svcs. for adults City of N.Y., 1972-74; rsch. assoc., rsch. dir. U.S. Ho. of Reps. Select Com. on Population, Washington, 1977-79; rsch. assoc. East-West Population Inst., Honolulu, 1979-89, asst. dir., 1982-84; asst. prof. econs. U. Hawaii, Honolulu, 1979-81, assoc. prof., 1981-89, prof., 1989; dir. com. on population Nat. Acad. Scis., Washington, 1989-93; dir. domestic rsch. divsn., v.p. RAND, Santa Monica, Calif., 1993-95, v.p. for rsch. devel., 1995—; mem. neurosci. behavior and sociology of aging rev. com. Nat. Inst. on Aging, Bethesda, 1991-95; chair panel on aging in developing countries NAS, Washington, 1987, mem. com. on population , 1993—. Editor: The ASEAN Success Story, 1987; co-editor: Demographic Change in Sub-Saharan Africa, 1993, Demographic Effects of Economic Reversals in Sub-Saharan Africa, 1993, The Demography of Aging, 1994; author: (monograph) The Graying of Japan, 1989; contbr. articles to profl. jours. Recipient Fulbright Faculty Rsch. award Coun. for Internat. Exch. of Scholars, 1988. Mem. Gerontol. Soc. Am., Internat. Union for Scientific Study Population, Population Assn. Am. (bd. dirs. 1991-93), Japan Am. Soc. So. Calif. (bd. dirs. 1994—). Democrat. Office: Rand PO Box 2138 Santa Monica CA 90407-2138

MARTIN, LORRAINE B., humanities educator; b. Utica, N.Y., Aug. 18, 1940; d. Walter G. and Laura (Bochenek) Bolanowski; m. Charles A. Martin; children: Denise M. Stringer, Tracy M. Weinrich. Student, SUNY, Albany, 1958-60, postgrad.; BA in English and Edn. magna cum laude, Utica Coll. of Syracuse U., 1977; MS in Edn. and Reading, SUNY, Cortland, 1979, CAS in Edn. Adminstrn., 1984; postgrad., Syracuse U., 1990—, SUNY, Albany, 1992—. Cert. elem. tchr., secondary tchr., sch. adminstr. and supr., sch. dist. adminstr., reading specialist, N.Y. Tchr. Poland (N.Y.) Cen. Sch., 1972-80, reading specialist, 1980-84; instr. reading Utica Coll. of Syracuse U., summer 1982-84; adminstr. spl. edn. and chpt. 1 remedial program Little Falls (N.Y.) City Sch. Dist., 1984-85; adminstr. adult and continuing edn. Madison-Oneida Bd. Coop. Ednl. Svcs., Verona, N.Y., 1985-86; dir. gen. programs Herkimer (N.Y.) Bd. Coop. Ednl. Svcs., 1986-88; assoc. prof. English, children's lit., reading, freshman seminar, and honors program Herkimer County Community Coll., Herkimer, 1988—; ednl. cons., 1979—; pvt. cons. for reading and writing, 1980—; participant SUNY brainstorming session on underprepared students, 1993; trainer tchr. performance evaluation program N.Y. State Dept. Edn., Herkimer, 1984, facilitator effective schs. program, 1986-88; cons. Two-Yr. Coll. Devel. Ctr. SUNY, 1985-89, tchr. trainer for the Writing Process; developer summer reading, writing and study skills course for Bridge program. Author: The Bridge Program—Easing the Transition from High School to College, 1990; editorial bd. Research and Teaching in Developmental Education; contbr. to Teaching Writing to Adults Tips for Teachers: An Idea Swap, 1989; textbook reviewer for pubs., 1993—. Vol. arts and crafts fair HCCC Found.; active Myasthenia Gravis Found., 1988—, Muscular Dystrophy Assn., 1989—, Thyroid Found. of Am., 1988—; advisor Network for Coll. Re-Entry Adults; mem. Profl. Devel. Com., Acad. Computer Com. Recipient Leader Silver award for volunteerism 4-H Coop. Extension, Utica, 1980; HCCC Found. grantee, Writing grantee Reader's Digest. Mem. Internat. Reading Assn., N.Y. State Reading Assn., Assn. Supervision and Curriculum Devel., Nat. Coun. Tchrs. English, Conf. on Coll. Composition and Communication, N.Y. Coll. Learning Skills Assn., N.Y. State Assn. Two-Yr. Colls., Inc., Phi Kappa Phi, Alpha Lambda Sigma. Avocations: English, current events, travel, public and satellite television, computers. Home: 7099 Crooked Brook Rd Utica NY 13502-7203 Office: Herkimer County Comm Coll SUNY Reservoir Rd Herkimer NY 13350-1545

MARTIN, LUCY Z., public relations executive; b. Alton, Ill., July 8, 1941; d. Fred and Lucille J. M. BA, Northwestern U., 1963. Adminstrv. asst., copywriter Batz-Hodgson-Neuwoehner, Inc., St. Louis, 1963-64; news reporter, Midwest fashion editor Fairchild Publs., St. Louis, 1964-66; account exec. Milici Advt. Agy., Honolulu, 1967; publs. dir. Barnes Med. Ctr., St. Louis, 1968-69; comms. cons. Fleishman-Hillard, St. Louis, 1970-74; comms. cons., CEO, pres. Lucy Z. Martin & Assocs., Portland, Oreg., 1974—; spkr. Marylhurst Coll., 1991, 92, 93, Concordia Coll., 1992, Women Entrepreneurs of Oreg., 1992, Oreg. Assn. Hosps. and Health Sys. Trustees, 1992, Healthcare Assn. Hawaii, Honolulu, 1993, USBancorp for Not-for-Profits, 1993, Multnomah County Ret. Srs. Vol. Program, 1993, Healthcare Fin. Mgmt. Assn., N.W., 1993, Healthcare Comms. Oreg., 1994, Area Health Edn. Ctrs., OHSU/statewide, 1994, Columbia River chpt. Pub. Rels. Soc. Am., 1994, 96; spkr., workshop conducter Healthcare Assn. Hawaii, 1993, USBancorp Not-for-Profit, 1993, Healthcare Communicators Oreg., 1994, Pathways to Career Transition, 1995, among others; bd. dirs. Ctrs. Airway Sci. Featured in Entrepreneurial Woman mag.; contbr. articles to profl. jours. Chmn. women's adv. com. Reed Coll., Portland, 1977-79; mem. Oreg. Commn. for Women, 1984-87; bd. dirs. Ronald McDonald House Oreg., 1986, Oreg. Sch. Arts and Crafts, 1989—, Northwestern U. Alumni Coun., 1992—; bd. dirs. Good Samaritan Hosp. Assocs., 1991-94, chair 1993-94; mem. pub. policy com. YMCA, 1993-95; mem. adv. bd. Jr. League, 1994-97. Recipient MacEachern Citation Acad. Hosp. Pub. Relations, 1978, Rosey awards Portland Advt. Fedn., 1979, Achievement award Soc. Tech. Comms., 1982, Disting. Tech. Comm. award, 1982, Exceptional Achievement award Coun. for Advancement and Support Edn., 1983, Monsoon award Internat. Graphics, Inc., 1984; named Woman of Achievement Daily Jour. Commerce, 1980. Mem. Pub. Rels. Soc. Am. (pres. Columbia River chpt. 1984, chmn. bd. 1980-84, Oreg. del. 1984-86, jud. panel N. Pacific dist 1985-86, exec. bd. health care sect. 1986-87, mem. Counselors Acad., Spotlight awards 1985, 86, 87, 88, nat. exec. com. 1987-91), Portland Pub. Rels. Roundtable (chmn. 1985, bd. dirs. 1983-85), Assn. Western Hosps. (editl. adv. bd. 1984-85), Best of West awards 1978, 80, 83, 87), Oreg. Hosp. Pub. Rels. Orgn. (pres. 1981, chmn. bd. 1982, bd. dirs. 1992-93), Acad. Health Service Mktg., Am. Hosp. Assn., Am. Mktg. Assn. (Oreg. chpt. bd. dirs. 1992-93), Am. Soc. Hosp. Mktg. & Pub. Rels., Healthcare Communicators Oreg. (conf. keynote speaker 1994), Internat. Assn. Bus. Communicators (18 awards 1981-87), Oreg. Assn. Hosps. (keynote speaker for trustee, 1991, speaker, 1993, bd. dirs. 1992-93), Oreg. Press Women, Nat. and Oreg. Soc. Healthcare Planning and Mktg., Women in Comms. (Matrix award 1977), Bus. Social Responsibility, Inst. for Managerial and Profl. Women (bd. dirs. 1992-94). Office: 1881 SW Edgewood Rd Portland OR 97201-2235

MARTIN, MALCOLM ELLIOT, lawyer; b. Buffalo, Dec. 11, 1935; s. Carl Edward and Pearl Maude (Elliot) M.; m. Judith Hill Harley, June 27, 1964; children: Jennifer, Elizabeth, Christina, Katherine. AB, U. Mich., Ann Arbor, 1958, JD, 1962. Bar: N.Y. 1963, U.S. Ct. Appeals (2d cir.) 1966, U.S. Supreme Ct. 1967. Assoc., Chadbourne, Parke, Whiteside & Wolff, N.Y.C., 1962-73, ptnr., 1974—, now Chadbourne & Parke LLP, 1986; dir., sec. Carl and Dorothy Bennett Found., Inc.; sec., counsel Copper Devel. Assn., Inc.; sec., treas. Jute Carpet Backing Council, Inc., Burlap and Jute Assn. Served with U.S. Army, 1958-60. Mem. ABA, N.Y. State Bar Assn., Assn. Bar City N.Y., St. Andrew's Soc. of State of N.Y., Met. Opera Guild. Clubs: Oratamin (Blauvelt, N.Y.), Nyack Boat, Rockefeller Center, Copper (N.Y.C.). Home: 74 S Highland Ave Nyack NY 10960-3602 Office: Chadbourne & Parke LLP 30 Rockefeller Plz New York NY 10112

MARTIN, MARGARET ANNE See STEELE, ANITA MARTIN

MARTIN, MARILYN JOAN, library director; b. Golden Meadow, La., Jan. 17, 1940; d. Marion Francis Mobley and Audrey Virna (Goza) Sapaugh; m. James Reginald Martin, Dec. 16, 1958; children: James Michael, Linda Jill Michaels. BA in History, U. Wash., 1975, MLS, 1976; MA in Pub. History, U. Ark., 1992; PhD in Libr. Sci., Tex. Woman's U., 1993. Cataloger, reference libr. St. Martin's Coll., Lacey, Wash., 1976-78; asst. reference libr. Pacific Luth. U., Tacoma, 1978-85; serials libr. Henderson State U., Arkadelphia, Ark., 1985-86, collection devel. libr., 1987-88, dir. learning resources, 1989-95; dean libr. svcs. Rowan Coll. of N.J., Glassboro, 1995—. Contbr. articles to profl. jours. Bd. dirs. N.J. Acad. Libr. Network; mem. exec. com. Tri-state Coll. Libr. Mem. ALA (rsch. com. 1993—, stds. com. 1994—), Assn. Coll. and Rsch. Librs. Republican. Avocations: walking, reading, collecting names. Office: Library Rowan Coll of NJ Glassboro NJ 08028-1701

MARTIN, MARK, professional race car driver; b. Batesville, Ark., Jan. 9, 1959; m. Arlene Martin; children: Heather, Rachel, Stacy, Matthew Clyde. profl. race car driver 1978—, winner ASA Championship 1978, 79, 80, 86, IROC Championship, 1994; raced in NASCAR Winston Cup, 1981—; winner Budweiser at the Glen, Watkins Glen, N.Y., 1994; winner Tyson Holly Farms 400, North Wilkesboro, N.C., 1995, UAW-GM 500, Charlotte, N.C., 1995, Budweiser at the Glen, 1995, Winston-Select 500, Talladega, Ala., 1995. Office: c/o NASCAR PO Box 2875 Daytona Beach FL 32120-2875

MARTIN, MARSHA PYLE, federal agency administrator; married; 2 children. BA, Tex. Woman's U.; MS, Tex. A&M U. Sr. officer Fed. Intermediate Credit Bank Tex., 1970-94; apptd. chmn. Farm Credit Adminstrn. Bd., 1994—; bd. dirs. Farm Credit Sys. Ins. Corp. Office: Farm Credit Adminstrn 1501 Farm Credit Dr Mc Lean VA 22102-5004

MARTIN, MARY COATES, genealogist, writer, volunteer; b. Gloucester County, N.J.; d. Raymond and Emily (Johnson) Coates; m. Lawrence O. Kupillas (dec.); m. Clyde Davis Martin (dec.); 1 child, William Raymond. Contbg. editor Md. & Del. Genealogist, St. Michaels, Md., 1985—. Author: The House of John Johnson (1731-1802) Salem County, N.J. and His Descendants, 1979, Fifty Year History of Daughters of Colonial Wars in the State of New York, 1980, 350 Years of American Ancestors: 38 Families: 1630-1989, 1989, Colonial Families: Martin and Bell Families and Their Kin: 1657-1992, Clifton--Coates Kinfolk and 316 Allied Families, 1995. Pres. Washington Hdqrs. Assn., 1970-73, bd. dirs., 1962—; Centennial pres. Sorosis, Inc., 1966-68; bd. dirs. Soldiers Sailors Airmen's Club, N.Y.C., 1976-81, Yorkville Youth Coun., N.Y.C., 1954-60; co-chmn. Colonial Ball, N.Y.C., 1965-67; rec. sec. Parents League of N.Y., Inc., 1954-57; mem. com. Internat. Debutante Ball, N.Y.C., 1977-81; mem. Am. Flag Inst., N.Y.C., 1963-72. Mem. Hereditary Order of Descendants of Colonial Govs. (gov. gen. 1981-83), Nat. Soc. Colonial Dames of Seventeenth Century (N.Y. State pres. 1977-79, parlimentarian 1979-81), Nat. Soc. Daus. of Colonial Wars (N.Y. State pres. 1977-80), Nat. Soc. DAR (regent 1962-65, pres. roundtable 1964-65, N.Y. State chaplain 1968-71, parliamentarian 1980-83, nat. platform com. 1970-76, certificate of award 1971, nat. vice chmn. lineage rsch. com. 1977-80, geneal. com. 1980-83), Nat. Soc. New Eng. Women (dir. gen. 1972-77, nat. vice chmn. helping hand disbursing fund 1968-71), Order of Crown of Charlemagne U.S.A. (corr. sec. gen. 1985-88, 3rd v.p. 1988-89, 2nd v.p. 1989-91), Nat. Soc. Children Am. Revolution, Nicasius de Sille Soc. (pres. 1960-62), Order Ams. of Armorial Ancestry (1st v.p. gen. 1985-88, councillor gen. 1988—), Nat. Gavel Soc., Nat. Soc. Magna Carta Dames, Descendants of Soc. of Colonial Clergy, Huguenot Soc. Am., Descendants of a Knight of Most Noble Order Garter, Nat. Soc. Daus. Am. Colonists, Nat. Soc. U.S. Daus. 1812, Order of Descendants of Colonial Physicians and Chirurgiens, Plantagenet Soc., Vt. Soc. Colonial Dames, Del. Geneal. Soc., Huguenot Hist. Soc., DuBois Family Assn. (1st v.p.), Cumberland County N.J. Hist. Soc., Gloucester County N.J. Hist. Soc., Md. Hist. Soc., Hist. Soc. Del., Salem County N.J. Hist. Soc., Woodstown-Pilesgrove N.J. Hist. Soc., Hereditary Order First Families of Mass., Inc. Avocation: travel. Home: Hague Towers # 1815 330 W Brambleton Ave Norfolk VA 23510-1307

MARTIN, MARY-ANNE, art gallery owner; b. Hoboken, N.J., Apr. 26, 1943; d. Thomas Philipp and Ruth (Kelley) M.; m. Henry S. Berman, June 9, 1963 (div. 1976); 1 child, Julia Berman. Student, Smith Coll., 1961-63; BA, Barnard Coll., 1965. Head dept. painting Sotheby Parke Bernet, N.Y.C.,

1971-78; sr. v.p. Sotheby's, N.Y.C., 1978-82; pres. Mary-Anne Martin, Fine Art, N.Y.C., 1982—; founder Latin Am. dept. Sotheby's, 1977. Mem. Art Dealers Assn. Am. (v.p., bd. dirs.). Avocations: art collecting, scuba diving. Office: 23 E 73rd St New York NY 10021-3522

MARTIN, MAURICE JOHN, psychiatrist; b. Tuscola, Ill., July 6, 1929; s. Daniel Ambrose and Mary Alta (Payne) M.; m. Ada Himma, Aug. 15, 1953; children: Daniel, Mark, Matthew, Tina, Lisa. BS, U. Ill., 1951, MD, 1954; MS, U. Minn., 1960. Diplomate Am. Bd. Internal Medicine, Am. Bd. Psychiatry and Neurology (bd. dirs. 1984-92, treas. 1988-90, v.p. 1991), Am. Bd. Emergency Medicine (bd. dirs. 1990-94, 96—), Am. Bd. Med. Spltys. (v.p. 1992, pres. elect 1993, pres. 1994-96), Am. Bd. Med. Spltys. Edn. Rsch. Found. (pres. 1992-94). Intern Presbyn. Hosp., Chgo., 1954-55; resident Mayo Grad. Sch. Medicine, Rochester, Minn., 1955-57, 59-62; cons. in adult psychiatry Mayo Clinic, Rochester, 1962—; head adult psychiatry Mayo Clinic, 1968-74, sr. cons. adult psychiatry, 1985—; chmn. dept. psychiatry and psychology Mayo Clinic and Mayo Med. Sch., 1974-85, asst. prof. psychiatry and psychology, 1965-70, assoc. prof., 1970-75, prof., 1975—; pres. staff Mayo Clinic, 1981-82; mem. Minn. Bd. Med. Practice, 1989-97, v.p., 1995, pres., 1996; pres., pres. exec. com. Am. Bd. of Med. Specialists, U.S. Med. Lic. Exam Step 3 Com., 1995—. Contbr. articles on psychiatry and psychosomatic medicine to profl. jours. Served to col., M.C. USAR, 1955-95. Decorated Order Mil. Med. Merit; recipient H.V. Jones award Mayo Found., 1960, Burlingame award Inst. of Living, 1994. Fellow Am. Psychiat. Assn. (life), Am. Coll. Psychiatrists (regent 1980-83, v.p. 1986-89, pres.-elect 1988, pres. 1989-90, sec. gen. 1993—, Bowls award 1992), Acad. Psychosomatic Medicine (pres. 1974-75, Prestigious Achievement award 1986), Fedn. State Med. Bds. (exam com. 1992-95); mem. Minn. Psychiat. Soc. (pres. 1977-79), Benjamin Rush Soc. (sec.-treas. 1993-96, v. pres. 1996—), Minn. Med. Assn. (Pres. award 1994), Edn. Commn. Fgn. Med. Grads. (trustee 1996—), Sigma Xi (chpt. pres. 1981-82), Alpha Omega Alpha. Home: 914 Sierra Ln NE Rochester MN 55906-4227 Office: 200 1st St SW Rochester MN 55902-3008 *Diligence, perseverance, and hard work —all virtues learned on the farm in Illinois, along with a strong desire for excellence in the altruistic service of sick patients have led to accomplishment. The jump from horse-drawn farm equipment to professor and chairman of a large department of psychiatry in 25 years required the above factors in addition to being in the right place at the right time.*

MARTIN, MELISSA CAROL, radiological physicist; b. Muskogee, Okla., Feb. 7, 1951; d. Carl Leroy and Helen Shirley (Hicks) Paden; m. Donald Ray Martin, Feb. 14, 1970; 1 child, Christina Gail. BS, Okla. State U., 1971; MS, UCLA, 1975. Cert. radiol. physicist, Am. Bd. Radiology, radiation oncology, Am. Bd. Med. Physics. Asst. radiation physicist Hosp. of the Good Samaritan, L.A., 1975-80; radiol. physicist Meml. Med. Ctr., Long Beach, Calif., 1980-83, St. Joseph Hosp., Orange, Calif., 1983-92, Therapy Physics, Inc., Bellflower, Calif., 1993—; cons. in field. Editor: (book) Current Regulatory Issues in Medical Physics, 1992. Fund raising campaign div. mgr. YMCA, Torrance, Calif., 1988-92; dir. AWANA Youth Club-Guards Group, Manhattan Beach, Calif., 1984—. Named Dir. of Symposium, Am. Coll. Med. Physics, 1992. Fellow Am. Coll. Med. Physics (chancellor western region 1992-95); mem. Am. Assn. Physicists in Medicine (profl. coun. 1990-95), Am. Coll. Radiology (econs. com. 1992-95), Calif. Med. Physics Soc. (treas. 1991-95), Am. Soc. for Therapeutic Radiology and Oncology, Health Physics Soc. (pres. So. Calif. chpt. 1992-93), Am. Brachytherapy Soc. Baptist. Avocations: Christian youth group dir. Home: 507 Susana Ave Redondo Beach CA 90277-3953 Office: Therapy Physics Inc 9156 Rose St Bellflower CA 90706-6420

MARTIN, MICHAEL LEE, orthodontist; b. Long Beach, Calif., May 30, 1947; s. Troy Lee and Ruth Elizabeth (Hummer) M.; m. Sharon Lee Johnson, Aug. 23, 1969; 1 child, Tanya Lee. Student, Northwestern U., 1973; AA, Cerritos (Calif.) Coll., 1976; student, UCLA, 1976. Diplomate Am. Bd. Orthotists and Prosthetist. Cable splicer Gen. Telephone, Dairy Valley, Calif., 1965-66; orthotic technician Johnson's Orthopedic, Santa Ana, Calif., 1969-73, orthotist, 1974—; pres. Johnson's Orthopedic, Orange, Calif., 1989—; rsch. orthotist Rancho Los Amigos Hosp., Downey, 1973; mem. rsch. adv. bd. Rancho Los Amigos Hosp. Mem. rsch. adv. com. on tech. for children Rancho Los Amigos Hosp., Downey. With U.S. Army, 1966-68, Vietnam. Mem. Am. Acad. Orthotists and Prosthetists (sec., pres. So. Calif. chpt. 1976-79, sec., pres. Region IX 1979-87, bd. dirs. 1994—, Practitioner of Yr. award 1992), Orthotic and Prosthetic Provider Network (pres. Calif. chpt. 1988—), Internat. Soc. for Prosthetics and Orthotics. Democrat. Avocations: fishing, golf, surfing. Home: 19 Fontaire Coto De Caza CA 92679-4904 Office: Johnson's Orthopedic 1920 E Katella Ave Ste G Orange CA 92867-5146

MARTIN, MICHAEL TOWNSEND, racing horse stable executive, sports marketing executive; b. N.Y.C., Nov. 21, 1941; s. Townsend Bradley and Irene (Redmond) M.; m. Jennifer Johnston, Nov. 7, 1964 (div. Jan. 1977); children: Ryan Bradley, Christopher Townsend; m. Jean Kathleen Meyer, Mar. 1, 1980. Grad., The Choate Sch., 1960; student, Rutgers U., 1961-62. Asst. gen. mgr. N.Y. Jets Football Club, N.Y.C., 1968-74; v.p. NAMANCO Prodns., N.Y.C., 1975-76; v.p., gen. mgr. Cosmos Soccer Club, N.Y.C., 1976-77; exec. asst. Warner Communications, N.Y.C., 1978-84; owner, operator Martin Racing Stable, N.Y.C., 1983—; pres. Sports Mark, Inc., N.Y.C., 1990—; ptnr. Halstead Property Co., N.Y.C., 1987—; bd. dirs. Night Kitchen, N.Y. Bd. dirs. Very Spl. Arts, Mote Marine Lab., Sarasota, Fla., Phipps Houses, V2V Rsch. Found., Inc., Julliard Sch. Mem. Athletics Congress (life, cert. official 1984—), U.S. Tennis Assn. (life), Internat. Oceanographic Found. (Miami life mem.), Thoroughbred Horsemens Assn. (pres. 1995), Fla. Thoroughbred Breeders Assn., Quogue Field Club, The Union Club. Republican. Episcopalian. Avocation: collecting Inuit (Eskimo) art. Home: 131 E 69th St Apt 11A New York NY 10021-5158 Office: 575 Madison Ave Ste 1006 New York NY 10022-2511

MARTIN, MURRAY SIMPSON, librarian, writer, consultant; b. Lower Hutt, N.Z., July 21, 1928; came to U.S., 1966, naturalized, 1974; s. Francis Roy and Sarah Isabel (Mitchell) M.; m. Noelene Phyllis Ax, Aug. 28, 1954. B.A., U. New Zealand, Auckland, 1948; M.A., U. New Zealand, 1949; B.Comm., U. New Zealand, Auckland and Wellington, 1958; Diploma, New Zealand Library Sch., Wellington, 1950. Cert. pub. acct., N.Z. With New Zealand Nat. Library Service, Wellington, 1951-63; br. serials librarian U. Sask., Saskatoon, Can., 1963-66; acquisitions-collections devel. librarian Pa. State U., University Park, 1967-73; assoc. dean librs. Pa. State U., 1973-81; univ. librarian, prof. library sci. Tufts U., Medford, Mass., 1981-89, prof. libr. sci. emeritus, univ. libr. emeritus, 1990—, spl. asst. to provost for libr. planning and devel., 1989-90; sr. acad. library planner Aaron Cohen Assocs., 1990-91; interim exec. sec. Coll. and Univ. Librs. Assn., 1990-92; treas. Universal Serials and Book Exchange Washington, 1979-80, 82-84, v.p., 1985, pres., 1986; pres. Pitts. Regional Library Ctr., 1980-81, Boston Library Consortium, 1984-85; mem. adj. faculty Simmons Coll., 1989—. Author: Budgetary Control in Academic Libraries, 1979, Issues in Personnel Management in Academic Libraries, 1981, Academic Library Budgets, 1993, Collection Development and Finance, 1995; editor: Financial Planning in Libraries, 1983, Library Finance: New Needs, New Models, 1994, Issues in Collection Management, 1995, Genre and Ethnic Collections: Collected Essays; assoc. editor: Bottom Line, 1990—, Guide to Reference Books, 1993-94; column editor: Technicalities, 1995—; mng. editor: Advances in Library and Information Science, JAI Press, Inc., 1990—; contbr. articles and revs. to profl. and lib. publs. Mem. ALA, MLA, Can. Libr. Assn., New Zealand Libr. Assn. (chmn. fiction com. 1960-63, assoc.), Am. Comparative Lit. Assn., Am. Assn. Australian Lit. Studies, N.E. MLA, soc. for Scholarly Pub. Democrat. Avocations: bird-watching; stamp-collecting; conservation; travel.

MARTIN, NATHANIEL FRIZZEL GRAFTON, mathematician, educator; b. Wichita Falls, Tex., Oct. 10, 1928; s. James Thelbert and Ethel Elizabeth (Nycum) M.; m. Joan Bowman, Apr. 10, 1954; children: Nathaniel Grafton, Jonathan Bowman. BS, North Tex. State U., 1948, MS, 1950; PhD, Iowa State U., 1958. Instr. Midwestern U., Wichita Falls, 1950-52; teaching asst. Iowa State U., Ames, 1955-59; from instr. to prof. math. U. Va., Charlottesville, 1959-96, prof. emeritus math., 1996, assoc. dean Grad. Sch. Arts and Scis., 1976-82; rsch. assoc. U. Calif., Berkeley, 1965-66; guest lectr. U. Copenhagen, 1969-70; rsch. assoc. U. Warwick, Coventry, Eng., 1982; vis. mem. MSRI, Berkeley, 1992; vis. faculty Univ. Coll., London, 1992. Author: Mathematical Theory of Entropy, 1981; editor: McGraw-Hill Dictionary of Physics & Math, 1978, Sci. & Tech. Terms, 1974. Lt. USNR, 1952-55. Mem. Am. Math. Soc., Math. Assn. Am., Sigma Xi, Pi Mu Epsilon. Office: U Va Dept Math Kerchof Hall Charlottesville VA 22903

MARTIN, NED HAROLD, chemistry educator; b. New Brunswick, N.J., May 18, 1945; s. Harold and Gertrude (Link) M.; m. Lynda Susan Blackadar, June 14, 1980; 1 child, Tara Elizabeth. BA, Denison U., 1967; PhD, Duke U., 1972. NDEA trainee Duke U., Durham, N.C., 1967-69; rsch. chemist Research Triangle Inst., Research Triangle Park, N.C., 1969-70; rsch. asst. Duke U., Durham, 1970-72, lectr., 1971-72; asst. prof. U. N.C., Wilmington, 1972-77, assoc. prof., 1977-82, prof., 1982—, chair chemistry dept., 1992—, Will S. DeLoach prof. chemistry, 1996—; cons. Corning Glass, Wilmington, 1979-80, LaQue Ctr. for Corrosion Tech., Wrightsville Beach, N.C., 1983-87, Condux, Inc., Newark, Del., 1989-90, Trinity Mfg., Inc., 1991; postdoctorate researcher U. Geneva, 1980-81. Co-author: Organic Chemistry Lab Manual with Waste Management and Molecular Modeling, 1993, Chemistry 211/212 Lab Manual, 1987. Mem. N.C. Acad. Sci. (v.p. 1988-90, pres.-elect 1989-90, pres. 1990-91, past pres. 1991-92), Am. Chem. Soc., Sigma Xi (assoc.), Phi Beta Kappa, Omicron Delta Kappa, Phi Soc., Phi Eta Sigma, Phi Lambda Upsilon. Office: UNCW 601 S College Rd Wilmington NC 28403-3201

MARTIN, NOEL, graphic design consultant, educator; b. Syracuse, Ohio, Apr. 19, 1922; s. Harry Ross and Lula (Van Meter) M.; m. Coletta Ruchty, Aug. 29, 1942; children—Dana, Reid. Cert. in Fine Arts, Art Acad. Cin., Doctorate (hon.), 1994. Designer Cin. Art Mus., 1947-93, asst. to dir., 1947-55; freelance designer for various ednl., cultural and indsl. orgns., 1947—; instr. Art Acad. Cin., 1951-57, artist-in-residence, 1993—; design cons. Champion Internat., 1959-82, Xomox Corp., 1961—, Federated Dept. Stores, 1962-83, Hebrew Union Coll., 1969—; designer-in-residence U. Cin., 1968-71, adj. prof., 1968-73; mem. adv. bd. Carnegie-Mellon U., R.I. Sch. Design, Cin. Symphony Orch., Am. Inst. Graphic Arts; lectr. Smithsonian Instn., Libr. of Congress, Am. Inst. Graphic Arts, Aspen Design Conf., various additional schs. and orgns. nationally. One man shows include Contemporary Arts Ctr., Cin., 1954, 71, Addison Gallery Am. Art, 1955, R.I. Sch. Design, 1955, Soc. Typographic Arts, Chgo., 1956, White Mus. of Cornell U., 1956, Cooper & Beatty, Toronto, Ont., Can., 1958, Am. Inst. Graphic Arts, 1958, Ind. U., 1958, Ohio State U., 1971; exhibited in group shows at Mus. Modern Art, N.Y.C., Library of Congress, Musee d'Art Moderne, Paris, Grafiska Inst., Stockholm, Carpenter Ctr., Cambridge, Gutenberg Mus., Mainz, U.S. info. exhbns. In Europe, South America and USSR; represented in permanent collections Mus. Modern Art, Stedelijk Mus., Amsterdam, Cin. Art Mus., Boston Mus. Fine Arts, Cin. Hist. Soc., Library of Congress; contbr. to various publs. Served to sgt. U.S. Air Force, 1942-45. Recipient Art Directors medal, Phila., 1957, Sachs award, Cin., 1973, Lifetime Achievement award Cin. Art Dirs., 1989.

MARTIN, PATRICIA ANN, music educator; b. Salinas, Calif., Mar. 11, 1939; d. Kenneth Duane and Hazel Gertrude (Setser) Lowe; m. Raymond Dalton Martin, Aug. 22, 1959; children: William Dalton, Brian David. BA, Calif. State U., 1965. Choir accompanist Salinas Christian Ch., 1954-57; choir accompanist North Fresno Christian Ch., Fresno, Calif., 1957-93, organist, 1965-96, choir dir., 1968-70; tchr. music pvt. lessons Fresno, 1962—; tchr. music Mountain View Christian Sch., Fresno, 1992-93; organist for weddings, various chs., Fresno, 1962-96; dir. bell choir North Fresno Christian Ch., 1985-86, dir. ministry, 1989-90. Composer songs, piano teaching pieces, 1974—; contbr. poetry to anthologies, 1981—. Mem. AAUW, Am. Guild Organists (sec. 1978-79), Calif. Fedn. Music Clubs (pres. 1988-91), Music Tchrs. Assn. Calif. (state chmn. Cal-Plan 1981-83, pres. 1983-85, condr. workshops 1978—, dir. pianorama 1976-88), Jr. Music Festival (pres. 1987-91, performer in New Wrinkles Sr. Theatre 1993—). Republican.

MARTIN, PATRICK, business equipment company executive; b. N.Y.C., Mar. 16, 1941; s. Michael and Theresa (Devaney) M.; children: Julia, Margaret, Brendan, Patrick, Sean Patrick; m. Donna Knutson, 1995. BS in Math., Iona Coll., 1962; MS in Math., George Washington U., 1965, PhD in Elec. Engring. and Computer Sci., 1971. Sr. scientist Research Analysis Corp., 1962-64; sr. mgr. Informatics Inc., 1964-66; pres. NCS Computing Corp., 1966-72; assoc. prof. George Washington U., 1966-77; dep. asst. sec. USDA, 1972-77; v.p., gen. mgr. China bus. devel. Xerox Corp., Rochester, N.Y., 1977-91; pres., gen. mgr. Am. Customer Ops., Stamford, Conn., 1991—. Contbr. numerous articles and research papers in computer sci. and mgmt. jours. Avocations: squash, skiing, reading, ethnic dances. Home: 14 Creekside Ln Rochester NY 14618 Office: Xerox Corp 800 Long Ridge Rd Stamford CT 06902-1227

MARTIN, PAUL, Canadian government official; b. Windsor, Ont., Can., Aug. 28, 1938; s. Paul Joseph and Eleanor (Adams) M.; m. Sheila Ann Cowan, Sept. 11, 1965; children—Paul William James, Robert James Edward, David Patrick Anthony. BA in Philosophy and History, U. Toronto, Can., 1962, LLB, 1965; LLB, U. Toronto, Can., 1965. Bar: Ont. 1966. Exec. asst. to pres. Power Corp. Can. Ltd., 1966-69, v.p., 1969-71; v.p. spl. projects Consol.-Bathurst Ltd., 1971-73; v.p. planning and devel. Power Corp., Can., 1973-74; pres. Can. S.S. Lines Ltd., Montreal, 1974-80, chief exec. officer, 1976-80; pres., chief exec. officer CSL Group Inc., 1980-88; M.P. Ho. of Commons, 1988-93; min. of finance Dept. of Finance Canada, 1993—; former min. for fed. office of regional devel. Can. Govt., 1993-95. Former mem. C.D. Howe Inst. Policy Analysis Com., Birt, N.Am. Com., Ctr. Rsch. Action on Race Rels.; former bd. dirs. Can. Coun. Christians and Jews; founding dir. emeritus North-South Inst., Can., Coun. Native Bus.; bd. govs. Concordia U., coun., v.p., past mem. bd. advisors. Liberal. Avocations: sports, reading. Office: Dept of Finance Canada, 140 O'Connor St, Ottawa, ON Canada K1A 0G5

MARTIN, PAUL CECIL, physicist, educator; b. Bklyn., Jan. 31, 1931; s. Harry and Helen (Salzberger) M.; m. Ann Wallace Bradley, Aug. 7, 1957; children: Peter, Stephanie Glennon, Daniel. A.B., Harvard U., 1952, Ph.D., 1954. Mem. faculty Harvard U., Cambridge, Mass., 1957—, prof. physics, 1964-82, J. H. VanVleck prof. pure and applied physics, 1982—, chmn. dept. physics, 1972-75, dean div. applied scis., 1977-97, assoc. dean Faculty Arts and Scis., 1981—; vis. prof. Ecole Normale Superieure, Paris, 1963, 66, U. Paris, Orsay, 1971; mem. materials rsch. adv. coun. NSF, 1986-89; bd. dirs. Mass. Tech. Pk. Corp., 1990—, exec. com., 1992—. Bd. editors: Jour. Math Physics, 1965-68, Annals of Physics, 1968-82, Jour. Statis. Physics, 1975-80. Bd. dirs. Assoc. Univs. for Rsch. in Astronomy, 1979-85; bd. dirs. Assoc. Univs ., Inc., 1981—, exec. com., 1986-90, 92-94, chmn. bd. dirs., 1987-98. NSF postdoctoral fellow, 1955; Sloan Found. fellow, 1959-62; Guggenheim fellow, 1966, 71. Fellow AAAS (chair physics sect. 1986), NAS, Am. Acad. Arts and Scis., Am. Phys. Soc. (councillor-at-large 1982-84, panel on pub. affairs 1983-86, chmn. nominating com. 1994), N.Y. Acad. Scis. Office: Harvard U Dept Physics Cambridge MA 02138

MARTIN, PAUL EDWARD, retired insurance company executive; b. Santa Claus, Ind., Sept. 10, 1914; s. James F. and Anna (Singer) M.; m. Pauline Peva, Dec. 22, 1939 (dec. Feb. 1982); 1 child, Peter McDowell; m. Ann Parker, Oct. 14, 1983. B.A., Hanover Coll., 1936. With actuarial dept. State Life Ins. Co., Indpls., 1936-42; asst. actuary Ohio Nat. Life Ins. Co., Cin., 1946-48; asso. actuary Ohio Nat. Life Ins. Co., 1948-49, actuary, 1949-55, actuarial v.p., 1955-56, adminstrv. v.p., 1956-67, sr. v.p. ins. adminstrn., 1967-71, pres., 1971-72, chmn. bd., chief exec. officer, 1972-79, also dir. Trustee Hanover (Ind.) Coll. Served to maj. F.A. AUS, 1942-46, PTO. Fellow Soc. Actuaries, Acad. Actuaries; mem. Comml. Club, Skyline Club, Masons, Shriners, Gamma Sigma Pi, Beta Theta Pi. Presbyterian. Home: 7146 N Finger Rock Pl Tucson AZ 85718-1406

MARTIN, PAUL ROSS, editor; b. Lancaster, Pa., May 14, 1932; s. Paul Rupp and Amanda (Minnich) M.; m. Julia Ibbotson, June 5, 1954 (div. Apr. 1979); children: Monica Martin Goble, Julia, Paul Jr., Barbara, Drew, Eric. BA, Dartmouth Coll., 1954. Reporter, wire editor Lancaster New Era, Lancaster Newspapers Inc., 1954-60; copyreader, makeup man Wall St. Jour. divsn. Dow Jones & Co., N.Y.C., 1960-63, copy editor nat. news, 1963-69, editor bus. and fin. column, 1969-72, nat. copydesk chief, 1972-75, page one sr. spl. writer, 1975-90, asst. to mng. editor, 1990-93, asst. mng. editor, 1993—. Editor: The Possible Dream, 1978, Retirement Without Fear, 1981, Wall Street Journal Style Book, 1981, 2d edit., 1987, 3d edit., 1992, 4th edit., 1995; co-author, editor: American Dynasties Today, 1983. Bd. dirs. Community Bd. 1, S.I., N.Y., 1976-84. Mem. N.Y. Fin. Writers Assn. (past officer). Avocations: basketball, tennis, travel. Office: Wall St Jour 200 Liberty St New York NY 10281-1003

MARTIN, PETER GERARD, infosystems specialist, consultant, teacher; b. Weymouth, Mass., May 2, 1952; s. John Augustine and Jean Anita (Murphy) M.; m. Elizabeth Anne Collins, Aug. 24, 1974; children: Derek Grant, Erin Jean. BA, Nasson Coll., 1974; MS, U. R.I., 1979; postgrad., Boston Coll., U. So. Maine, 1977, 79; MA, Columbia Pacific U., 1991. Computer programmer Baybank Data Services, Waltham, Mass., 1975-76; mathematician Factory Mut. Engring., Norwood, Mass., 1976-78; tchr. Kennebunk (Maine) High Sch., 1978-79; v.p. strategic planning The Foxboro (Mass.) Co., 1979-84, systems cons., 1984-85, mgr. system product planning, 1986-88, v.p. market strategies and comm., 1996—; v.p. mktg. Intec Controls Corp., 1993-94; v.p. Automation Rsch. Corp., 1996; instr. Dean Jr. Coll., Franklin, Mass. 1980-96; tech. cons. Balance Inc., Wiscassett, Maine, 1985-89. Author: Dynamic Performance Management: A Path to World Class Manufacturing, 1992; contbr. articles to profl. jours. Pres. East Woonsocket Sch. Parent Council, R.I., 1983-85; mem. Parents Involvement Com., Woonsocket, 1985; Cub Scout den leader, Woonsocket, 1985-86; instr. religious edn. Our Lady of Lourdes Ch. Mem. Soc. Mfg. Engrs., Mfrs. Automation Protocol Users Group, Inst. Soc. of Am. Roman Catholic. Avocations: camping, tennis, boating. Office: The Foxboro Co Bristol Park Foxboro MA 02035

MARTIN, PETER ROBERT, psychiatrist, pharmacologist; b. Budapest, Hungary, Sept. 6, 1949; came to U.S.,1980; s. Nicholas M. and Eva (Horvat) M.; m. Barbara Bradford, Dec. 23, 1985; 1 child, Alexander Bradford. BSc with honors, McGill U., Montreal, Que., Can., 1971, MD, CM, 1975; MSc, U. Toronto (Ont., Can.), 1978. Diplomate Am. Bd. Psychiatry and Neurology, Psychiatry, Addiction Psychiatry. Resident Dept. Medicine U. Toronto, Can., 1975-76, Psychiatry, U. Toronto, 1978-80; fellow Clin. Pharmacology Addiction Rsch. Found., Toronto, 1976-78; chief Sect. Clin. Sci., Nat. Inst. on Alcohol Abuse & Alcoholism, Bethesda, 1983-86; assoc. prof. Vanderbilt U. Sch. Medicine, Nashville, 1986-92, prof., 1992—; dir. Addiction Rsch. Ctr. Vanderbilt U., Nashville, 1994—, chief psychiatrist Vanderbilt Addiction Care Ctr., 1995—; vis. scientist Lab. of Clin. Sci., NIMH, Bethesda, Md., 1980-83; investigator John F. Kennedy Ctr. for Rsch. on Human Devel., Nashville, 1993—. Fellow Royal Coll. Physicians (Can.), Am. Psychiatric Assn.; mem. AAAS, Am. Soc. Clin. Pharmacology and Therapeutics, Am. Acad. Addiction Psychiatry, Am. Coll. Psychiatrists, Rsch. Soc. on Alcoholism, Internat. Soc. Biomed. Rsch. in Alcoholism. Office: Vanderbilt U Sch Medicine Dept Psychiatry MCN A2205 Nashville TN 37232

MARTIN, PETER WILLIAM, lawyer, educator; b. Cin., Apr. 11, 1939; s. Wilfred Samuel and Elizabeth (Myers) M.; m. Ann Wadsworth, Nov. 28, 1964; children: Leah, Elliot, Isaac. B.A., Cornell U., 1961; J.D., Harvard U., 1964. Bar: Ohio 1964. Atty. AF Gen. Counsel's Office, 1964-67; asso. prof. law U. Minn., 1967-71; vis. asso. prof. law Cornell U., 1971-72, prof. law, 1972—, dean, 1980-88, Edward Cornell prof. law, 1989-92, Jane Foster prof. law, 1992—; co-dir. Legal Info. Inst., 1992—; pres. Ctr. for Computer Assisted Legal Instrn., 1986-88; cons. Adminstrv. Conf. U.S., 1977-79; reporter Am. Bar Assn. Task Force on Lawyer Competency and the Role of the Law Schs. Author: The Ill-Housed, 1971, (with others) Social Welfare and the Individual, 1971, Cases and Materials on Property, 1974, 3d edit., 1992, Social Security Law, 1990, Basic Legal Citation, 1992, Social Security Plus, 1994; editor Jour. Legal Edn., 1985. Chmn. Ithaca Bd. Zoning Appeals, 1974-79. Served to capt. USAF, 1964-67. Mem. ABA (task force on law schs. and legal profession 1990-92), Am. Bar Found. (vis. com.), Am. Assn. Law Schs. (chmn. law and computers sect. 1987-88, 93-94). Office: Cornell U Law Sch Myron Taylor Hall Ithaca NY 14853

MARTIN, PHILLIP DWIGHT, bank consulting company executive, mayor; b. Nevada, Mo., Jan. 4, 1943; s. E. Dwight and Berniece E. (Leedy) M. BS, U. Mo., 1964, MBA, 1965, cert. math. and bus. edn., 1966. Tchr. Warson (Mo.) Pub. Schs., 1966-68; investment analyst Bus. Men's Assurance Co. Am., Kansas City, Mo., 1968-70; exec. v.p. Farmer's Bank Walker, Mo., 1970-71; banking cons. Howard J. Blender Co., Dallas, 1971-84; chmn. Profit Motivators Internat., Inc., Boulder, Colo., 1984—; mayor City of Walker, 1986—. Mem. Walker R-4 Alumni Assn. (pres. 1994-96). Home: 214 E Marvin Ave Walker MO 64790-9106 Office: Profit Motivators Internat 2146 Linden Dr Boulder CO 80304-0477

MARTIN, PHILLIP HAMMOND, lawyer; b. Tucson, Jan. 4, 1940; s. William P. and Harriet (Hammond) M.; m. Sandra S. Chandler, June 17, 1961 (div. Mar. 1989); children: Lisa, Craig, Wade, Ryan; m. Erika Zetty, May 9, 1990. BA, U. Minn., 1961, JD, 1964. Bar: Minn. 1964, U.S. Tax Ct. 1967, U.S. Dist. Ct. Minn. 1968, U.S. Ct. Appeals (8th cir.) 1973, U.S. Supreme Ct. 1981, U.S. Claims Ct. 1983, U.S. Ct. Appeals (fed. cir.) 1988, U.S. Ct. Appeals (7th cir.) 1989. Assoc. Dorsey & Whitney, Mpls., 1964-69, ptnr., 1970—. Home: 487 Portland Ave Saint Paul MN 55102-2216 Office: Dorsey & Whitney 220 S 6th St Minneapolis MN 55402-4502

MARTIN, PRESTON, financial services executive; b. L.A., Dec. 5, 1923; s. Oscar and Gaynell (Horne) M.; 1 child, Pier Preston. BS in Fin., U. So. Calif., 1947, MBA, 1948; PhD in Monetary Econs., U. Ind., 1952. Prof. fin. Grad. Sch. Bus. Adminstrn. U. So. Calif., 1950-60; prin. in housebldg. firm, 1952-56; with mortgage fin. and consumer fin. instns., 1954-57; commr. savs. and loan State of Calif., 1967-69; chmn. Fed. Home Loan Bank Bd., Washington, 1969-72; founder, CEO PMI Mortgage Ins. Co., 1972-80; chmn., CEO Seraco Group subs. Sears, Roebuck & Co., 1980-81, also bd. dirs. parent co.; chmn., CEO WestFed Holdings Inc., L.A., 1986-92, SoCal Holdings, Inc., L.A., 1987-93, H.F. Holdings, Inc., San Francisco, 1986-92; vice-chmn. Fed. Res. Bd., Washington, 1982-86; founder Fed. Home Loan Mortgage Corp.; prof. bus. econ. and fin. Inst. per lo Studio Organizitzatione Aziendale, Italy. Author: Principles and Practices of Real Estate, 1959. Mem. President's Commn. on Housing, 1980-81; prin. Coun. Excellence in Govt., Washington. Recipient House and Home award, 1969, award Engring. News Record, 1971, Turntable award Nat. Assn. Home Builders, 1973. Mem. Lambda Chi Alpha. Presbyterian.

MARTIN, QUINN WILLIAM, lawyer; b. Fond du Lac, Wis., Mar. 12, 1948; s. Quinn W. and Marcia E. (Petrie) M.; m. Jane E. Nehmer; children: Quinn W., William J. BSME, Purdue U., 1969; postgrad., U. Santa Clara, 1969-70; JD, U. Mich., 1973. Bar: Wis. 1973, U.S. Dist. Ct. (ea. dist.) Wis. 1973, U.S. Ct. Appeals (7th cir.) 1973. Sales support mgr. Hewlett-Packard, Palo Alto, Calif., 1969-70; assoc. Quarles & Brady, Milw., 1973-80, ptnr., 1980—; bd. dirs. Associated Bank Milw., U-Line Corp., Martin Comms., Inc., Kaukauna, Gen. Timber and Land, Inc., Fond du Lac. Active McCallum for Lt. Gov., Wis., U. Mich. Law Sch. Fund; bd. dirs. Milw. Zool. Soc., Found. for Wildlife Conservation. Mem. ABA, Wis. Bar Assn., Milw. Bar Assn., Milw. Club, Ozaukee Country Club, Chaine des Rottiseurs, Delta Upsilon (sec.), Milw. Alumni Club. Office: Quarles & Brady 411 E Wisconsin Ave Milwaukee WI 53202-4409

MARTIN, R. KEITH, business and information systems educator, consultant; b. Seattle, Sept. 5, 1933; s. Jerome Milton and Winifred (Gifford) M.; m. Carolyn Joanne Carosella, June 15, 1957; children: Jefferson, Sean, Jennifer, Katherine. AB, Whitman Coll., 1955; MBA with high honors, CCNY, 1965; PhD, U. Wash., 1973. Registered, lic. profl. engr.; cert. data processing, cert. systems profl., cert. computer profl. Div. mgr. Campus Merchandising Bur., Inc., N.Y.C., 1955-56; sales rep IBM, Seattle, 1956, Service Bur. Corp. subs. IBM, N.Y.C., 1957-58; specialist mgmt. adv. services Price Waterhouse & Co., N.Y.C., 1959-65; specialist mgmt. adv. services Price Waterhouse & Co., Seattle, 1965-66, mgr., 1966-67; dir. mgmt. systems dept. U. Wash., 1967-71, lectr. dept. acctg. Sch. Bus. Adminstrn, 1971-73; asst. prof. dept. accountancy Baruch Coll., CUNY, 1973-76, assoc. prof., 1977-79; prof. acctg. and info. systems Fairfield U., 1979-94, assoc. dean Sch. Bus., 1980-82, dean, 1982-93, acting dean grad. Sch. of Communications, 1988-90, prof. info. systems, 1994—; v.p. Eastalco Systems, 1971-72; faculty fin. div. Am. Mgmt. Assn., 1963-64; part-time lectr. Bellevue Community Coll., 1967-69, Shoreline Community Coll., 1968-72, Seattle U., 1971-72. Co-author: Management Control of Electronic Data Processing, 1965; author: Management Information Systems in Higher Education: Case Studies at

Three Universities, 1973, Effective Business Communications, 1976, 79, 91, Systems Development and Computer Concepts, 1977; assoc. editor: Industry Guides for Accountants and Auditors, 2 vols., 1980; mem. editorial rev. bd. Dickenson Pub. Co., 1974-75, Prentice-Hall, Inc., 1977-78, 87-88, 90-91, Reston Pub. Co., 1977-78, Jour. Acctg. Edn., 1981-83; author numerous monographs; contbr. numerous articles to profl. jours. Mem. Mendelssohn Choir of Conn., Amateur Comedy Club. Recipient cert. of appreciation Am. Mgmt. Assn., 1966, cert. of merit for disting. service to Mgmt. Scis., 1969, for disting. service to info. systems profession, 1973; Merit award Assn. Systems Mgmt., 1971, Achievement award, 1972, Internat. award World Assn. for Case Method Rsch. and Application; cert. for service City of Seattle, 1973; named Outstanding Young Man Am., 1970, One of 300 Outstanding Alumni, Whitman Coll., 1979; Kellogg fellow, 1971-72, Price Waterhouse faculty fellow, 1976. Mem. Am. Inst. Indsl. Engrs. (dir. Seattle chpt. 1967-70, chmn. regional conf. 1969), Inst. Mgmt. Accts. (assoc. dir. N.Y. chpt. 1963-64, 75-85 Seattle chpt. 1967-70), Assn. Systems Mgmt. (sec. 1968-69, v.p. 1969-70, pres. Pacific N.W. chpt. 1970-71), Data Processing Mgmt. Assn., Assn. Computing Machinery, Soc. Cert. Data Processors, NSPE, N.Y. Soc. Profl. Engrs., Soc. Mgmt. Info. Systems, AAUP, Am. Acctg. Assn., Phi Delta Theta (province pres. 1986-87), Mu Gamma Tau, Phi Delta Kappa, Beta Alpha Psi. Clubs: Bronxville Field, Amateur Comedy. Home: 2 Normandy Rd Bronxville NY 10708-4808

MARTIN, RALPH DRURY, lawyer, educator; b. Pitts., Mar. 4, 1947; s. Kent Wills and Kathleen (Drury) M.; m. Ruchirawan Meemeskul, Oct. 28, 1982; 1 child, Chanida Kathleen. BA, Tulane U., 1969; JD, Washington U., 1972. Bar: La. 1972, D.C. 1981, Calif. 1992, U.S. Dist. Ct. (mid. dist.) La. 1985, U.S. Dist. Ct. D.C. 1991, U.S. Ct. Appeals (9th cir.) 1979, U.S. Ct. Appeals (D.C. cir.) 1991, U.S. Supreme Ct. 1976. Law clk. to Hon. Frederick J.R. Heebe U.S. Dist. Ct., Ea. Dist. La., New Orleans, 1972-74; spl. asst. to U.S. atty. U.S. Dept. Justice, Washington, 1974-75, trial atty. civil rights div., 1975-80; dep. asst. legal advisor U.S. Dept. State, Washington, 1980-82; sr. prosecutor pub. integrity sect. U.S. Dept. Justice, Washington, 1982-90; spl. counsel U.S. Dept. State, Washington, 1990-91; ptnr. Storch & Brenner, Washington, 1991—; adj. prof. Washington Coll. Law, The Am. Univ., 1991-92. Comments editor Washington U. Law Quarterly, 1971-72 (honors scholar award 1971). Network mem. Dem. Leadership Conf., Washington, 1991; dir. Thomas and Bertie T. Smith Found., 1996—. Mem. ABA, ATLA, Am. Soc. Internat. Law, Nat. Assn. Criminal Def. Lawyers, Univ. Club, Order of Coif. Democrat. Avocations: jogging, Spanish literature, Thai-American relations. Home: 3511 30th St NW Washington DC 20008-3251 Office: Storch & Brenner 1001 Connecticut Ave NW Washington DC 20036-5504

MARTIN, RALPH GUY, writer; b. Chgo., Mar. 4, 1920; s. Herman and Tillie (Charno) M.; m. Marjorie Jean Pastel, June 17, 1944; children: Maurice Joseph, Elizabeth, Tina. B.J., U. Mo., 1941. Reporter, mng. editor Box Elder News Jour., Brigham, Utah, 1940-41; contbr. mags. including Sunday N.Y. Times, Look, Harpers mag., 1945-53; assoc. editor New Republic mag., 1945-48; assoc. editor charge spl. reports Newsweek mag., 1953-55; exec. editor House Beautiful mag., 1955-57; pub., pres. Bandwagon, Inc. Author: Boy From Nebraska, 1946, The Best is None Too Good, 1948, Ballots and Bandwagons: Five Key Conventions since 1900, 1964, Skin Deep, 1964, The Bosses, 1964, President from Missouri, 1964, Wizard of Wall Street, 1965, World War II, Pearl Harbor to V-J Day, 1966, The GI War, 1967, A Man for All People, 1968, Jennie: The Life of Lady Randolph Churchill, The Romantic Years, 1969, vol. II, The Dramatic Years, 1971, Lincoln Center for the Performing Arts, 1971, The Woman He Loved: The Story of the Duke and Duchess of Windsor, 1974, Cissy, The Extraordinary Life of Eleanor Medill Patterson, 1979; A Hero For Our Time, An Intimate Study of the Kennedy Years, 1983, Charles and Diana, 1985, Golda, Golda Meir: The Romantic Years, 1988, Henry and Clare: An Intimate Portrait of the Luces, 1991, Seeds of Destruction: Joe Kennedy and His Sons; co-author: Stevenson Speeches, 1952, Eleanor Roosevelt: Her Life in Pictures, 1958, The Human Side of FDR, 1960, Front Runner, Dark Horse, 1960, Money, Money, Money, 1960, Man of Destiny: Charles DeGaulle, 1961, Man of the Century: Winston Churchill, 1961, The Three Lives of Helen Keller, 1962, World War II: From D-Day to VE-Day, 1962; Contbr. to: Yank The GI History of The War, Social Problems in America, 1955, Democracy in Action, 1962, others. Dep. dir. pub. relations Nat. Vols. for Stevenson-Kefauver, 1956; mem. Dem. Nat. Campaign Com. Combat corr. Stars and Stripes, Yank mag., 1941-45. Recipient Lifetime Achievement in Lit. award Westport Art Ctr., 1996. Mem. Author's League Am., Author's Guild, English-Speaking Union, Tenn. Squires, Dramatist's Guild, Author's League. Clubs: Century, Overseas Press. Home: 135 Harbor Rd Westport CT 06880-6918

MARTIN, RANDI CHRISTINE, psychology educator; b. Salem, Oreg., May 24, 1949; d. Harold Raymond and Maxine Constance (Torgeson) M.; m. Lawrence P. Chan, Aug. 30, 1974. BA, U. Oreg., 1971; MA, Johns Hopkins U., 1977, PhD, 1979. Lectr. U. Calif., Santa Cruz, 1979-80; assoc. rsch. scientist Johns Hopkins U., Balt., 1980-82; asst. prof. Rice U., Houston, 1982-87, assoc. prof., 1987-93, prof., 1993—. Assoc. editor Psychonomic Bulletin & Rev., Austin, Tex., 1995—; editl. bd. mem. Cognitive Neuropsychology, London, 1994—, Jour. Neurolinguistics, Cambridge, Eng., 1994—; contbr. articles to profl. jours. Recipient Claude Pepper award NIH Deafness and Comm. Disorders Inst., 1995—. Fellow APA; mem. Psychonomic Soc. (sec./treas. 1993-95, bd. dirs. 1997—), Acad. Aphasia (program com. 1990-93). Achievements include research in short term memory deficits in brain damaged patients. Office: Rice U Psychology Dept 6100 Main St Houston TX 77005-1827

MARTIN, RAYMOND BRUCE, plumbing equipment manufacturing company executive; b. N.Y.C., Oct. 23, 1934; s. Raymond M. and Margaret (Lennon) M.; m. Suzanne Ruth Longpre, Sept. 3, 1960; 1 son, Christopher Haines. A.B., Villanova U., 1956. With Corning Glass Works (N.Y.), 1956-68, nat. plumbing sales mgr., 1966-68; v.p. mktg. Briggs Mfg. Co., Warren, Mich., 1968-69, v.p., gen. mgr. plumbing fixture div., 1969-72; pres., chief exec. officer Water Control Internat. Inc., Troy, Mich., 1972-91; dir. Internat. Tech. Corp., Cash Control Products Inc.; pres., chief exec. officer W/C Technology Corp., 1991; mem. plumbing harmonization Fed. North Am. Free Trade Delegation, 1992. Served with AUS, 1957-58. Mem. Am. Soc. Plumbing Engrs., Plumbing Mfrs. Inst. (chmn. HUD Task Group 1981-82, chmn. communications com. 1983-86, chmn. fed. water conservation com. 1988-90), Am. Soc. Sanitary Engrs., ASME (panel 19, chmn. definitions task group 1993-94, chmn. water closet hyraulic performance task group 1993-94), Republican. Roman Catholic (trustee 1982-86). Clubs: Orchard Lake Country, L'Arbre Croche Club (chmn. archtl. com. 1989-96, bd. dirs., v.p. 1996—). Patentee in field. Office: 2820 W Maple Rd Troy MI 48084-7011

MARTIN, REBECCA REIST, librarian; b. Princeton, N.J., Mar. 2, 1952; d. Benjamin A. and Harriet (Nold) Reist; 1 child, Benjamin R. BA, U. Calif., Santa Cruz, 1973; MA, San Jose State U., 1975; DPA, U. So. Calif., 1992. Med. libr. VA Med. Ctr., San Francisco, 1975-77, chief libr. svc., 1977-81; head biology libr. U. Calif., Berkeley, 1981-85; assoc. libr. dir. San Jose (Calif.) State U., 1985-90; dean of librs. U. Vt., Burlington, 1990—. Author: Libraries and the Changing Face of Academia, 1994; contbr. articles to profl. jours., chpts. in books. Mem. Libr. Commn. San Jose, 1989-90. Mem. ALA (coun. 1996—), New England Libr. Assn., Am. Soc. Pub. Adminstrn., Am. Assn. Coll. and Rsch. Librs., Libr. Adminstrn. and Mgmt. Assn. (bd. dirs. 1987-89), NELINET (bd. dirs. 1995—). Office: U Vt Bailey/Howe Libr Burlington VT 05405

MARTIN, REX, manufacturing executive. CEO Nibco, Elkhart, Ind. Office: Nibco Inc 1516 Middleberry St PO Box 1167 Elkhart IN 46516*

MARTIN, RICHARD HARRISON, curator, art historian; b. Bryn Mawr, Pa., Dec. 4, 1946; s. Frank Harrison and Margaret Dever M. BA, Swarthmore Coll., 1967; MA, Columbia U., 1969, M.Phil., 1971. Instr. William Paterson Coll. of N.J., Wayne, 1972-73; editor Arts Mag., N.Y.C., '74-88; prof. Fashion Inst. Tech., SUNY, N.Y.C., 1973-93, Ednl. Found. ; the Fashion Industries, 1991-93; exec. dir. Shirley Goodman Resource enter, 1980-93; critic-in-residence Md. Inst. Coll. Art, 1985-87; editor, pub. Textile & Text, 1989-93; curator The Costume Inst., Met. Mus. Art, N.Y.C., 1993—; adj. faculty Sch. Visual Arts, N.Y.C., 1975-80, 93—; adj. prof. NYU, 1977—, Columbia U., 1987-89, 95—, Vt. Coll., 1991-93. Author: Fashion and Surrealism, 1987, Jocks and Nerds, 1989, The Historical Mode, 1989, The New Urban Landscape, 1990, Giorgio Armani: Images of Man, 1990, Flair: Fashion Collected by Tina Chow, 1992, Infra-Apparel, 1993, Diana Vreeland: Immoderate Style, 1993, Waist Not, 1994, Madame Grès, 1994, Orientalism: Visions of the East in Western Dress, 1994, Bloom, 1995, Contemporary Fashion, 1995, Haute Couture, 1995, Christian Dior, 1996. Mem. Coll. Art Assn. Am., Victorian Soc. Am. (dir. 1980-84, chpt. dir. 1981-83), Soc. Archtl. Historians, Am. Soc. for Aesthetics, Art Libraries Soc. N.Am., N.Y. Hist. Soc., Soc. for History of Tech., Costume Soc. Am. (dir. 1983-89, Region II pres. 1984-87). Home: 225 E 79th St New York NY 10021-0855 Office: Met Mus Art The Costume Inst 1000 5th Ave New York NY 10028-0113

MARTIN, RICHARD JAY, medical educator; b. Detroit, May 16, 1946; s. Peter Aaron and Tillie Jean (Munch) M.; m. Helene Iris Horowitz, Dec. 23, 1967; children: Elizabeth Hope, David Evan. BS, U. Mich., 1967, MD, 1971. Diplomate Am. Bd. Internal Medicine and Pulmonary Disease. Intern Ariz., 1971-72; resident Tulane U., New Orleans, 1974-76; asst. prof. medicine U. Okla., Okla. City, 1978-80; asst. prof. medicine U. Colo., Denver, 1980-85, assoc. prof., 1985-92, prof., 1992—; dir. Cardiorespiratory Sleep Rsch., Nat. Jewish Ctr. for Immunology and Respiratory Medicine, Denver, 1980-89, staff physician, 1980—, head divsn. pulmonary medicine, 1993—. Author: Cardiorespiratory Disorders During Sleep, 1984, 2d edit., 1990, (with others) Current Therapy in Internal Medicine, 1984, Clinical Pharmacology and Therapeutics in Nursing, 1985, Interdisciplinary Rehabilitation of Multiple Sclerosis and Neuromuscular Disorders, 1984, Drugs for the Respiratory System, 1985, Current Therapy in Pulmonary Medicine, 1985, Abnormalities of Respiration During Sleep, 1986, Mitchell's Synopsis of Pulmonary Medicine, 1987, Pulmonary Grand Rounds, 1990, Asthma and Rhinitis, 1994, The High Risk Patient: Management of the Critically Ill, 1995, Manual of Asthma Management, 1995, Severe Asthma: Pathogenesis and Clinical Management, 1995, Curret Pulmonology, 1995, Pulmonary and Respiratory Therapy Secrets, 1996; editor: Nocturnal Asthma: Mechanisms and Interventions, 1993; author, editor: Nocturnal Asthma: Mechanisms and Treatment, 1993; mem. editl. bd.: (jour.) Am. Jour. of Respiratory and Critical Care Medicine, 1994—, Bronchial Asthma: Index and Review, 1996—; assoc. editor: Clinical Care for Asthma, 1995—; contbr. articles, reviews, reports on respiratory and neuromuscular diseases to profl. jours. Pres. Congregation Rodef Shalom, Denver, 1984-85; regional v.p. United Synagogues of Am., Denver, 1988-89. Pulmonary fellow Am. Lung Assn., 1977-79; James F. Hammarsten Outstanding fellow U. Okla. Health Scis. Ctr., 1978; grantee Am. Lung Assn., VA, U. Okla. Lung Assn., NIH, Parker B. Francis Found.; recipient Best Paper in Internal Medicine award Okla. Soc. Interna. Medicine, 1977, 78, U. Okla. Gastroenterology sect, 1977. Mem. Am. Thoracic Soc., Am. Fedn. for Clin. Rsch., Am. Coll. Chest Physicians (rep. to Young Pulmonary Physician Conf., St. Charles, Ill. 1979), ACP, Colo. Trudeau Soc., Western Soc. Clin. Investigation. Avocations: biking, golf, karate. Office: Nat Jewish Ctr Immun & Resp Med 1400 Jackson St Denver CO 80206-2761

MARTIN, RICHARD KELLEY, lawyer; b. Tulsa, June 30, 1952; s. Richard Loye and Maxine (Kelley) M.; m. Reba Lawson, June 12, 1993; children from previous marriage: R. Kyle, Andrew J. BA, Westminster Coll., 1974; JD, So. Meth. U., 1977. Bar: Tex. 1977, U.S. Tax Ct. 1979. Ptnr. Akin, Gump, Strauss, Hauer & Feld, LLP, Dallas, 1977-95; prnt. Haynes and Boone LLP, Dallas, 1995—. Bd. dirs. Goodwill Industries, Dallas, 1986—, v.p., 1986-91; bd. dirs. Greater Dallas Youth Orchs., 1987-90; bd. dirs., v.p., pres. Big Bros. and Sisters Met. Dallas, 1988-91; bd. dirs. Tejas coun. Girl Scouts U.S. Mem. Tex. Bar Assn., Salesmanship Club Dallas. Republican. Methodist. Office: Haynes and Boone LLP 3100 NationsBank Plz 901 Main St Dallas TX 75202-3714

MARTIN, RICHARD L., insurance executive; b. Franklin, N.J., Feb. 2, 1932; s. Richard Lewis and Elizabeth (Roe) M.; m. Susan Mazuy, June 20, 1970; children: David Cory, Scott Mazuy. BEd, U. Miami, 1958; MA, Columbia U., 1963. Chartered Property Casualty Underwriter. Educator Franklin (N.J.) Sch. Dist., 1958-60; mng. dir. Sparta (N.J.) Sch. Dist., 1960-66; adminstr. Orange (N.J.) Sch. System, 1966-71; chief exec. officer Montague (N.J.) Sch. Dist., 1971-72, Stanhope (N.J.) Sch. System, 1972-73; v.p. Selective Ins. Group, Branchville, N.J., 1973-87; pres., chief exec. officer Med. Malpractice Ins. Assn., N.Y.C., 1987—; chmn. N.J. Anti-Car Theft Com., Trenton, 1980-87; treas. N.J. Ins. News Svc., Newark, 1982-87; chmn. AIA-N.J. State Conf., Trenton, 1983-87. Contbr. several articles to mags. With USMC, 1952-54. Mem. CPCU, Am. Mgmt. Assn., Soc. Ins. Research, Soc. for Corp. Planning, City Midday, Newton Country, Branchville Rotary, Sons of Am. Revolution, Mayflower Soc. Presbyterian. Avocations: golf, hunting. Home: Two Plains Rd Augusta NJ 07822 Office: Med Malpractice Ins Assn 110 William St New York NY 10038-3901

MARTIN, ROBERT BRUCE, chemistry educator; b. Chgo., Apr. 29, 1929; s. Robert Frank and Helen (Woelffer) M.; m. Frances May Young, June 7, 1953. B.S., Northwestern U., 1950; Ph.D., U. Rochester, 1953. Asst. prof. chemistry Am. U., Beirut, Lebanon, 1953-56; research fellow Calif. Inst. Tech., 1956-57, Harvard U., 1957-59; asst. prof. chemistry U. Va., Charlottesville, 1959-61, assoc. prof., 1961-65, prof., 1965—, chmn. dept., 1968-71; spl. fellow Oxford U., 1961-62; Program dir. Molecular Biology Sect., NSF, 1965-66. Author: Introduction to Biophysical Chemistry, 1964. Fellow AAAS; mem. Am. Chem. Soc. Office: Univ Va Dept Chemistry Charlottesville VA 22901

MARTIN, ROBERT DAVID, judge, educator; b. Iowa City, Oct. 7, 1944; s. Murray and G'Ann (Holmgren) M.; m. Ruth A. Haberman, Aug. 21, 1966; children: Jacob, Matthew, David. A.B., Cornell Coll., Mt. Vernon, Iowa, 1966; J.D., U. Chgo., 1969. Bar: Wis. 1969, U.S. Dist. Ct. (we. dist.) Wis. 1969, U.S. Dist. Ct. (ea. dist.) Wis. 1974, U.S. Supreme Ct. 1973. Assoc. Ross & Stevens, S.C., Madison, Wis., 1969-72, ptnr., 1973-78; chief judge U.S. Bankruptcy Ct. We. Dist. Wis., 1978—; instr. gen. practice course U. Wis. Law Sch., 1974, 76, 77, 80, lectr. debtor/creditor course, 1981-82, 83, 85, 87, farm credit seminar, 1985, advanced bankruptcy problems, 1989; co-chmn. faculty Am. Law Inst.-ABA Fin. and Bus. Planning for Agr., Stanford U., 1979; faculty mem. Fed. Jud. Ctr. Schs. for New Bankruptcy Judges, 1985-93; chmn. Ann. Continuing Legal Edn. Wis. Debtor Creditor Conf., 1981—. Author: Bankruptcy: Annotated Forms, 1989; co-author: Secured Transactions Handbook for Wisconsin Lawyers and Lenders, Bankruptcy-Text Statutes Rules and Forms, 1992, Ginsberg and Martin on Bankruptcy, 4th edit., 1996. Bd. dirs., exec. com. Luth. Social Svcs. for Wis. and Upper Mich. Mem. Wis. State Bar, Am. Coll. Bankruptcy, Am. Judicature Soc., Nat. Conf. Bankruptcy Judges (bd. govs. 1989-91, sec. 1993-94, v.p. 1994-95, pres. 1995-96), Nat. Bankruptcy Conf. Office: 120 N Henry Rm 340 PO Box 548 Madison WI 53701-0548

MARTIN, ROBERT EDWARD, architect; b. Dodge City, Kans., Mar. 17, 1928; s. Emry and Alice Jane (Boyce) M.; m. Billie Jo Lange, Aug. 16, 1952 (div. Feb. 1970); m. Kathryn M. Arvanitis, June 26, 1971; children: Lynn, Amy, Blaine. Student, McPherson Coll., 1946-48; BArch, U. Cin., 1954. Registered architect, Ohio. Architect Samborn, Steketee, Otis & Evans, Inc., Toledo, 1956-58; prin. Schauder & Martin, Toledo, 1958-72, The Collaborative, Inc., Toledo, 1972-93; mem. Bd. Examiners Archs., Ohio, 1985-95, pres., 1989-94; bd. examiners Nat. Coun. Archtl. Registration Bds., 1986—, edn. com., 1992; chmn. site design divsn. Archtl. Registration Exam., 1989, 90, 91; mem. Nat. Coun. Archtl. Registration Bds. Grading, 1987-94; chmn. study of Toledo Fire & Rescue Dept., Corp. for Effective Govt., 1994. Artist numerous paintings. Mem. Toledo Planning Commn., 1971-74, Toledo Zoning Appeals Bd., 1973, Toledo Bd. Bldg. Stds., 1967-84, Citizens Fire Adv. Commn., 1974-80, Citizens Urban Area Adv. Commn., 1962, Toledo Area Coun. Govts., 1977-80, Com. of 100, Toledo, 1987-89, Spectrum Friends Fine Arts, Inc., Toledo; chmn. bd. Toledo Area Govtl. Rsch. Assn., 1981-90; chmn. Corp. for Effective Govt., Study of Toledo Fire and Rescue Dept., 1994; chmn. Cystic Fibrosis, Toledo. 1985. Served to capt. USAF, 1954-56. Recipient numerous watercolor awards. Fellow AIA (pres. Toledo chpt. 1966, Arch. of Yr. 1993), Archs. Soc. Ohio (pres. 1975), Ohio Watercolor Soc., N.W. Ohio Watercolor Soc., Toledo Fedn. Art Socs. (pres. 1989, 90), Spectrum, Tile Club (v.p.), Toledo Artists Club, Toledo Artists Club, Sylvania Country Club, Rotary, Masons, Shriners, Jesters. Mem. Ch. of Brethren. Avocation: painting. Home: 5119 Regency Dr Toledo OH 43615-2946 Office: 1700 N Reynolds Rd Toledo OH 43615-3628

MARTIN, ROBERT FINLAY, JR., retired judge; b. Akron, O., May 4, 1925; s. Robert Finlay and Olive (Dexter) M.; m. Eleanor A. Gunn, Sept. 3, 1948; children—Roberta C. (Mrs. Bobby P. Grimes), Craig J., Scott D. B.A., Kent State U., 1949; J.D., U. Akron, 1954. Bar: Ohio bar 1955, Okla. bar 1963, U.S. Supreme Ct. bar 1974, Supreme Ct. Okla. bar 1963, Supreme Ct. Ohio bar 1955, U.S. Dist. Ct. Northeastern Dist. Okla. bar 1971. Claims atty. Ohio Farmers Ins. Cos., LeRoy, 1951-59; claims supr. Selman & Co., Tulsa, 1959-63; practiced in Tulsa, 1963-66; judge Common Pleas Ct., Tulsa, 1967-69, Dist. Ct., Tulsa, 1969-88. City solicitor City of Seville, Ohio, 1958-59; Trustee Bd. Pub. Affairs, LeRoy, 1957-59, Ct. Fund Trustees Tulsa County, 1971-74. Served with USNR, 1943-46. Lodge: Masons. Home: 2315 S Fulton Pl Tulsa OK 74114-3746

MARTIN, ROBERT FRANCIS, roof maintenance systems executive; b. Bronx, N.Y., Sept. 16, 1942; s. James Edward and Loretta Rita (Martin); children: Craig, Keith, Dana. Student, St. Mary's Coll., Ky., 1960-64; BS in Mktg. Econs., Fordham U., 1967. Registered roof cons. Mgr. Owens Corning Fiberglass, N.Y.C., 1965-70; gen. sales mgr. Bradco Supply, Avenel, N.J., 1970-73; pres. Roof Maintenance Systems, Farmingdale, N.J., 1973—; mem. teaching staff Ctr. for Profl. Advancement, 1989-93. Coach referee Jackson Vics Soccer Club, N.J., 1973-91; coach Holbrook Little League, N.J., 1976-86, Pop Warner Football, N.J., 1979-85; founder Drug Prevention Program for Children, N.Y.C., 1965-69. Fellow Am. Inst. Plant Engrs. (pres. 1987-89, Engr. of Yr. 1981), Roof Cons. Inst. (past officer, region I bd. dirs., registered roof cons., post officer); mem. Constrn. Specification Inst., Bldg. Owners and Mgrs., Nat. Roofing Contractors, N.E. Roofing Contractors Assn., Bldg. Trades Assn., Single Ply Roofing Inst. Republican. Office: Roof Maintenance Systems PO Box 67 Farmingdale NJ 07727-0067

MARTIN, ROBERT LESLIE, physician; b. Abilene, Tex., Oct. 28, 1934; s. Leslie Resa and Garnet Iva (Brown) M.; m. Henrietta Montgomery, 1956; children: Randal, Christopher. BA, U. Kans., 1956, MD, 1960. Diplomate in clin. pathology Am. Bd. Pathology; diplomate Nat. Bd. Med. Examiners; lic. physician, Calif., Fla. Intern U. Kans., 1960-61, resident and fellow in pathology, 1964-67; asst. prof. pathology Case We. Res. U., Cleve., 1967-78; dir. clin. labs. Univ. Hosps. of Cleve., 1972-76; assoc. prof. pathology U. South Fla., Tampa, 1978-82; chief clin. pathology James A. Haley Vets. Hosp., Tampa, 1978-82; project mgr. Scott Sci. & Tech., Albequerque, N.Mex., 1982-83; physician advisor Profl. Found. for Health Care Inc., Tampa, 1984-89; primary care physician Tampa, Fla., 1986—. Contbr. articles to profl. jours. Fellow Coll. Am. Pathologists; Alpha Omega Alpha, Phi Gamma Delta. Republican. Episcopalian. Home: 15840 Sanctuary Dr Tampa FL 33647-1075

MARTIN, ROBERT WILLIAM, corporate director; b. Toronto, Ont., Can., June 7, 1936; s. William George and Evelyn Irene (Phillips) M.; m. Patricia Lorraine Norris, June 27, 1959; children: Stephen Gregory, Robert Scott, Adrienne Christine Teron. B.A.Sc., U. Toronto, 1958. V.p. ops. Consumers Gas, Toronto, 1973-80, pres., dir., 1981-92, CEO, ret., 1992; chmn. Silcorp. Ltd.; bd. dirs. IPL Energy Inc., Cara Ops. Ltd., Peoples Jewellers Ltd., Peadaries Petroleums Ltd., Reed Stenhouse Cos., Goldfarb Corp. Bd. dirs. York U.; campaign chmn. United Way Toronto, 1988; chmn. Toronto Symphony Orch.; pres. West Park Hosp. Found. Recipient Meritorious Svc. award U. Toronto, 1983, Arbor award. Mem. Assn. Profl. Engrs. Ont., Can. Gas Assn. (past chmn.), Ont. Natural Gas Assn. (past pres.), Mad River Golf Club, Mississauga Golf and Country Club, Toronto Club. Home: 118 Farnham Ave, Toronto, ON Canada M4W 1H4

MARTIN, ROBLEE BOETTCHER, retired cement manufacturing executive; b. St. Louis, Apr. 21, 1922; s. Henry W. and Esther (Boettcher) M.; m. Lillian Seegraves, July 15, 1940; children: Mary Katherine, Bruce Daniel, Amy Lee. B.S. in Chem. Engring., Columbia U., 1943, M.S. in Chem. Engring., 1947; D.Sc. in Bus. Adminstrn. (hon.), Cleary Coll., 1962. Prodn. supr. Monsanto Chem. Co., St. Louis, 1946-49; dir. research and devel. Miss. Lime Co., Ste. Genevieve, Mo., 1949-59; pres. Dundee Cement Co., Mich., 1959-69; v.p. Fruehauf Corp.; gen. mgr. (Fruehauf Bldgs. div.), Detroit, 1969-72; pres. Presidents Assn. div. Am. Mgmt. Assn., N.Y.C., 1972-74; pres. insulation div. Keene Corp., Princeton, N.J., 1974-76; chmn., chief exec. officer Keystone Cement Co., Bath, Pa., 1976-89, Giant Cement Co., Harleyville, S.C., 1985-89; sr. v.p., dir. Giant Group Ltd., Beverly Hills, Calif., 1985-89. Served to lt. (j.g.) USNR, 1944-46, PTO. Mem. Sigma Xi, Tau Beta Pi, Phi Lambda Upsilon. Baptist. Home: 2151 Palermo Pl Charleston SC 29406-9231

MARTIN, ROGER BOND, landscape architect, educator; b. Virginia, Minn., Nov. 23, 1936; s. Thomas George and Audrey (Bond) M.; m. Janis Ann Kloss, Aug. 11, 1962; children: Thomas, Stephen, Jonathan. BS with high distinction, U. Minn., 1958; M. Landscape Arch., Harvard U., 1961. Asst. prof. U. Calif.-Berkeley, 1964-66; assoc. prof. U. Minn., Mpls., 1966, prof., 1968—, chmn. dept. landscape architecture, 1966-77, 83-87, dir. grad. studies in landscape architecture, 1983-84, dir. undergrad. studies, 1987-94, dir. profl. studies, 1994—; owner Roger Martin & Assoc., site planners and landscape architects, Mpls., 1966-68; prin. InterDesign, Inc., Mpls., 1968-84, Martin & Pitz Assocs., Inc., 1984—; vis. prof. U. Melbourne, 1979-80. Prin. works include Minn. Zool. Gardens, 1978 (merit award Am. Soc. Landscape Archs. 1978), Mpls. Pky. Restorations, 1972-87 (merit award 1978, Minn. Classic award Am. Soc. Landscape Archs. 1994), South St. Paul Ctrl. Sq., 1978 (merit award 1978), Festival Park, Chisholm, Minn., 1986, Miss. Wildlife Refuge (visual image assessment merit award 1985), Nicollet Island Park (merit award 1989), Hennepin Avenue Master Plan, 1995 (merit award 1995). Recipient Fredrick Mann award for svc. to edn. U. Minn., 1990, Disting. Educator award Sigma Lambda Alpha, 1990; fellow Am. Acad. in Rome, 1962-64. Fellow Am. Soc. Landscape Archs. (pres. Minn. chpt. 1970-72, trustee 1980-84, nat. pres. 1987, chmn.-elect coun. fellows 1991, chmn. 1992-94, past chmn. 1994-96, Pub. Svc. award 1985); mem. Nat. Coun. Instrs. Landscape Architecture (pres. 1973-74), Can. Soc. Landscape Archs. (hon.). Home: 2912 45th Ave S Minneapolis MN 55406-1829 Office: Martin & Pitz Assocs Inc 1409 Willow St Minneapolis MN 55403-2249

MARTIN, ROGER HARRY, college president; b. N.Y.C., June 26, 1943; s. Edwin Diller and Emma (Neuenburg) M.; m. Susan Bradford, Aug. 29, 1970; children: Katherine R., Emily G. BA, Drew U., 1965; BD, Yale U., 1968, STM, 1969; DPhil, Oxford (Eng.) U., 1974. Program officer Edn. Incentive Program, N.Y.C., 1969-70; devel. officer NYU, 1970-71, 75-76; asst. dir. devel. Rensselaer Polytech Inst., Troy, N.Y., 1974-75; asst. prof. history, exec. asst. to pres. Middlebury (Vt.) Coll., 1976-80; assoc. dean Harvard Div. Sch., Cambridge, Mass., 1980-86; prof. history, pres. Moravian Coll., Bethlehem, Pa., 1986-97; pres. Randolph-Macon Coll., 1997—. Author: Evangelicals United: Ecumenical Stirrings in Pre-Victorian Britain, 1795-1830, 1983. Mem. Harvard Club (N.Y.C.). Mem. Soc. of Friends. Avocations: skiing, running. Home: 305 Caroline St Ashland VA 23005 Office: Randolph-Macon Coll Office of the President Ashland VA 23005

MARTIN, ROGER JOHN, computer scientist, computer systems analyst; b. Ft. Atkinson, Iowa, Sept. 11, 1947; s. Raymond Charles and Linda R. (Kuennen) M.; m. Jane Degnan, Nov. 21, 1970; children: John, Kathryn, Susan, Jacquelyn. BS in Computer Sci., Iowa State U., 1969, MS in Computer Sci., 1971. Computer specialist Naval Ship R & D Ctr., Bethesda, Md., 1971-76; supervisory systems analyst Exec. Office of Pres., Washington, 1976-82; computer scientist, mgr. software engring. group Inst. for Computer Scis. and Tech., Nat. Inst. Standards and Tech., Washington, 1982-92, chief System and Software Technology Divsn., 1993-95, mgr. Software Methods, 1995-96, standards strategy mngr., Sun Microsystems, 1996—, program co-chmn. Conf. on Software Maintenance, 1985, gen. chair, 1987; gen. chair Computer Standards Conf. 1988. Coach soccer Montgomery County Recreation Dept., Rockville, Md., 1979-83; treas., del. Mill Creek Towne Elem. Sch. PTA, Rockville, 1981-84, pres. 1986-87; Magruder cluster PTA coordinator, 1984-86; leader Cub Scouts, Rockville, 1983-84, asst. scoutmaster troop, 1984-92. Recipient Outstanding Performance award Naval Ship R & D Ctr., 1976; Outstanding Performance award Exec. Office of Pres., 1979, Spl. Achievement award, 1981, Interagency Com. on Info. Resources Mgmt. award for Tech. Excellence, 1989, Fed. Computer Week award, 1992; cert. of recognition Nat. Bur. Standards, 1983; Dept. Commerce Bronze medal award, 1984, Silver Medal award, 1989, . Mem. Assn. for Computing Machinery, IEEE Computer Soc. (chmn. working group on test methods for POSIX 1986-93, chmn. tech. com. on operating system steering com. on conformance testing 1989-94, cert. recognition 1987, tech. com. on operating system project mgmt. com. 1991-93, Meritorious Svc. award 1991, Standards Medallion, 1992), IEEE Hans Karslsson award, 1995 Home: 7413 Cliffbourne Ct Rockville MD 20855-1101 Office: Sun Microsystems 2250 Garcia Ave MPK17-307 Mountain View CA 94041

MARTIN, ROGER LLOYD, management consultant; b. Kitchener, Ont., Can., Aug. 4, 1956; s. Lloyd Milton and Delphine Elvera (Horst) M.; m. Nancy Lorraine Lang, Sept. 24, 1983; children: Robert Lloyd, Jennifer Frances, Daniel Roger. BA in Econs., Harvard U., 1979, MBA, 1981. Prin. Can. Cons. Group, Toronto, Ont., Can., 1981-85; chmn. Monitor Co. Can. Ltd., Toronto, 1986—; dir. Monitor Co. Inc., Boston, 1988—, co-head, 1994—; chmn., CEO Monitor U., 1993—; mem. editorial bd. Can. Competition Policy Record, Ottawa, Ont., 1986—; bd. dirs. Hamilton Group Ltd., Mississauga, Ont., 1986-93. Contbr. antitrust and internat. trade articles to profl. jours. Mem. Osler Bluffs Ski Club Collingwood. Home: 27 Chestnut St Wellesley MA 02181-3005 Office: Monitor Co 25 1st St Cambridge MA 02141-1802

MARTIN, RON, editor, superintendent of schools, consultant, minister; b. Rock Island, Tenn., Aug. 5, 1942; s. Houston and Bernie (Gribble) M.; m. Carolyn J. Odineal, Oct. 5, 1969. AA, Freed-Hardeman Coll., Henderson, Tenn., 1963; BA with honor, David Lipscomb Coll., 1973; MEd with highest honors, Mid. Tenn. State U., 1983; student, Leadership Inst., Harvard U. Grad. Sch. Edn., Oxford (England) U. Entered ministry Ch. of Christ, 1963. Cons. Tenn. Dept. Edn., Nashville, 1977-82; tchr. remedial reading Warren County Schs., McMinnville, Tenn., 1972-74, elem. prin., 1974-77; tchr. Warren County Schs., Viola, Tenn., 1981-82; asst. prin. sr. high sch. Warren County Schs., McMinnville, 1982-85, supt. schs., 1987-92, editor newsletter, 1987—; min., Bible tchr. Warren County Chs. of Christ, McMinnville, 1963—; announcer, news reporter Cumberland Valley Broadcasting, McMinnville, 1963-90. Vice chmn. Warren County Dem. Com., 1984-86; mem. bd. rev. Eagle Scouts, Boy Scouts Am., McMinnville, 1986—; pres. Warren County Drug Task Force, 1987, 92; chmn. Leadership McMinnville, 1997. Named Young Educator of Yr., Warren County Jaycees, 1976, Leader of Yr., 4-H Club, Warren County, 1974-76, Leadership award Tenn. Acad. Sch. Leaders, 1983. Mem. NEA, ASCD, Am. Adult Edn. Coun., Nat. Assn. Secondary Sch. Prins., Nat. Staff Devel. Coun., Am. Assn. Sch. Adminstrs., Coun. Adult Basic Edn., Tenn. Edn. Assn., Tenn. Adult Edn. Coun., Tenn. Literary Coun., Warren County Edn. Assn. (rep. assembly 1976, 83, Leadership award), Warren County Aviators and navigators (sec.), Commn. on Adult Basic Edn. (southeast regional rep. 1003-95), Commn. on Adult Basic Edn. (nat. sec. 1995), Kiwanis (Warren County pres., disting. pres. 1995, lt. gov. 1997—). Avocations: reading, working on community projects, visiting outstanding school systems, teaching young people, developing educational ideas. Home: 4200 Crisp Springs Rd Mc Minnville TN 37110-5239 Office: Warren County Schs 109 Lyon St Mc Minnville TN 37110-2545

MARTIN, ROY BUTLER, JR., museum director, retired broker; b. Norfolk, Va., May 13, 1921; s. Roy Butler and Anne (Holman) M.; m. Louise Eggleston, Apr. 17, 1948; children: Roy Butler III, Anne Beverly Martin Sessoms. Student, William and Mary Coll., Norfolk, 1939-40; BS in Commerce, U. Va., 1943. Chmn. bd. Commonwealth Brokers Inc., 1955-88; mayor City of Norfolk, 1962-74; pres. Chrysler Mus., Norfolk, 1989-961989—; pres. U.S. Conf. Mayors, Washington, 1973-74; trustee Sentara Health System, 1985-96. Chmn. Douglas MacArthur Found., 1963—, Civic Facilities Commn., Norfolk, 1986—; bd. dirs. Norfolk Forum; exec. com., pres. Va. Mcpl . League, 1968-69; past mem. Va. State Water Control Bd.; past mem. exec. com., adv. bd. Nat. League of Cities, com. on community devel., U.S. Conf. Mayors, Southeastern Va. Planning Dist. Commn; chmn. Southeastern Tidewater Area Manpower Planning System, Mayor's Youth Commn.; Gov.'s Com. on Youth; past bd. dirs. Norfolk Urban Coalition; past mem. VALC Zoning Procedures Com.; past bd. dirs. Norfolk Symphony Orch., Boys Club Norfolk, Old Dominion U. Edns. Found.; past mem. Norfolk Cerebral Palsy Tng. Ctr., vestry Ch. of Good Shepherd, Norfolk. Lt. USNR, 1943-46, USNR, 1948-52. Decorated officer in Order of the Crown (Belgium); recipient Outstanding Alumni award Old Dominion U., 1964, Sales of Yr. award Sales and Mktg. Club Tidewater, 1971, Meritorious Pub. Svc. Citation Dept. Navy, 1974, Cmty. Svc. award Jewish Cmty. Ctr., 1974, Cert. Appreciation Va. Food Dealers Assn., 1974, Fall Guy award Saints and Sinners, 1974, Brotherhood award NCCJ, 1976, First Citizen award City of Norfolk, 1974. Mem. Norfolk Yacht and Country Club (pres. 1990-92), Va. Club (bd. dirs. 1991-93), Chi Phi, Alpha Kappa Psi. Episcopalian. Home: 1519 Commonwealth Ave Norfolk VA 23505-1719

MARTIN, SAM See MOSKOWITZ, SAM

MARTIN, SLATER NELSON, JR., retired basketball player; b. Houston, Oct. 22, 1925. Grad., U. Tex., 1949. Basketball player Mpls. Lakers, 1949-56, N.Y. Knicks, 1956-57; basketball player St. Louis Hawks, 1957-60, coach, 1956-57; coach Houston Rockets, 1967-69. Named to Basketball Hall of Fame, 1981; selected All-NBA 2d Team, 1954, 56, 57, 58, 59; mem. NBA Championship Team, 1950, 52, 53, 54, 58. Office: c/o Basketball Hall Fame PO Box 179 Springfield MA 01101-0179

MARTIN, STANLEY A., lawyer; b. Logansport, Ind., Apr. 9, 1955; s. Richard James and Helen Elizabeth (Newburn) M.; m. Kellie Lea McCabe, Aug. 14, 1988. BS, MIT, 1977; JD, Boston Coll., 1984. Bar: Mass. 1985, U.S. Dist. Ct. Mass. 1985, U.S. Ct. Appeals (1st cir.) 1985, N.H. 1986, U.S. Dist. Ct. N.H. 1987. Prin. Stan Martin, Designer/Builder, Andover, Mass., 1977-84; assoc. Gadsby & Hannah LLP, Boston, 1984-91, ptnr., 1992—; lectr. Northeastern Univ., Boston, 1989—. Author: Mechanic's Liens, Performance and Payment Bonds under Massachusetts Law, 1989, 7th rev. edit., 1996; co-author: Architect-Engineer Liability Under Massachusetts Law, 1985, 5th rev. edit., 1990, Wiley Construction Law Update Annual; contbr. articles to profl. jours. Bd. dirs. Andover Com./A Better Chance-ABC, 1981-84. Mem. ABA (pub. contract sect., chair region I 1990—), Am. Arbitration Assn. Constrn. Industry Panel, Mass. Bar Assn. (chair pub. law sect. 1993-94), Internat. Bar Assn., N.H. Bar Assn. Home: 13 Brown St Andover MA 01810-5302 Office: Gadsby & Hannah LLP 225 Franklin St Boston MA 02110-2804

MARTIN, STEVE, comedian, actor; b. Waco, Tex., 1945; s. Glenn and Mary Lee Martin; m. Victoria Tennant, Nov. 20, 1986 (div. 1994). Student, Long Beach State Coll., UCLA. Exec. prodr. TV show Domestic Life, 1984. TV writer for Smothers Bros. (co-winner Emmy award 1969), Sonny and Cher, Pat Paulsen, Ray Stevens, Dick Van Dyke, John Denver, Glen Campbell; nightclub comedian; guest and host appearances NBC's Saturday Night Live, Tonight Show; appeared on Carol Burnett Show; starred in TV spls. Steve Martin: A Wild and Crazy Guy, 1978, Comedy is Not Pretty, 1980, Steve Martin's Best Show Ever, 1981; rec. comedy albums Let's Get Small, 1977 (Grammy award 1977), A Wild and Crazy Guy, 1978 (Grammy award 1978), Comedy is Not Pretty, 1979, The Steve Martin Brothers, 1982; actor, screenwriter (films) The Absent Minded Waiter, 1977 (Academy award nomination best short film 1977), The Jerk, 1979, Pennies From Heaven, 1981, Dead Men Don't Wear Plaid, 1982, The Man With Two Brains, 1983, All of Me, 1984 (Nat. Soc. Film Critics award best actor 1984, New York Film Critics' Circle award best actor 1984), Three Amigos, 1986, Roxanne, 1987, (Nat. Soc. Film Critics award best actor 1988, Los Angeles Film Critics' award best actor 1988), L.A. Story, 1991; actor (films) Sergeant Pepper's Lonely Hearts Club Band, 1978, The Muppet Movie, 1979, The Kids Are Alright, 1979, The Lonely Guy, 1984, Little Shop of Horrors, 1986, Planes, Trains and Automobiles, 1987, Dirty Rotten Scoundrels, 1988, Parenthood, 1989, My Blue Heaven, 1990, Father of the Bride, 1991, Grand Canyon, 1991, Housesitter, 1992, Leap of Faith, 1993, Mixed Nuts, 1994, Twist of Fate, 1994, Sgt. Bilko, 1995; (theatre) Waiting For Godot, 1988; (television) And the Band Played On, 1993; screenwriter (films) Easy Money, 1983; author Cruel Shoes, 1977; playwright Picasso at the Lapin Agile, 1993. Recipient Georgie award Am. Guild Variety Artists 1977, 78; Grammy award 1978. Office: care ICM 8942 Wilshire Blvd Beverly Hills CA 90211-1934 also: Rogers & Cowan c/o Michelle Bega 1888 Century Park E Ste 500 Los Angeles CA 90067-1709

MARTIN, SUSAN KATHERINE, librarian; b. Cambridge, Eng., Nov. 14, 1942; came to U.S., 1950, naturalized, 1961; d. Egon and Jolan (Schonfeld) Orowan; m. David S. Martin, June 30, 1962. BA with honors, Tufts U., 1963; MS, Simmons Coll., 1965; PhD, U. Calif., Berkeley, 1983. Intern libr. Harvard U., Cambridge, Mass., 1963-65, systems libr., 1965-73; head systems office gen. libr. U. Calif., Berkeley, 1973-79; dir. Milton S. Eisenhower Libr. Johns Hopkins U., Balt., 1979-88, exec. dir. Nat. Commn. on Libraries and Info. Sci., 1988-90; univ. libr. Georgetown U., Washington, 1990—; mem. libr. adv. com. Princeton (N.J.) U., 1987-95; mem. vis. com. Harvard U. Libr., 1987-93, 94—; bd. overseers for univ. libr. Tufts U., 1986—; mem. libr. adv. com. Hong Kong U. Sci. Tech., 1988-95; mem. acad. libr. adv. group U. Md. Sch. Librs. and Info. Sci., 1994-96; cons. to various librs. and info. cos., 1975—; mem. adv. bd. ERIC, 1990-92, History Assocs., Inc., 1990-92; mem. Chadwyck-Healey North Am. Adv. Com. on Lit. Online, 1997—; vice chair, chair Chesapeake Info. and Rsch. Libr. Alliance, 1996-98. Author: Library Networks; Libraries in Partnership, 1986-87; editor; Jour. Libr. Automation, 1972-77; mem. editl. bd. Advanced Tech./Librs., 1973-93, Jour. Libr. Adminstrn., 1986—, Libr. Hi-Tech., 1989-93, Jour. Acad. Librarianship, 1994—; contbr. articles to profl. jours. Trustee Phila. Area Libr. Network, 1980-81; bd. dirs. Universal Serials and Book Exch., 1981-82, v.p., 1983, pres., 1984; trustee Capital Consortium, 1992-95; mem. bd. Potomac Internet, 1995-96. Recipient Simmons Coll. Disting. Alumni award, 1977; Council on Library Resources fellow, 1973. Mem. ALA (coun. 1988-92, structure revision TF, 1995-97), Internat. Fedn. Libr. Assns. Commn. on Access to Info. and Freedom of Expression, Rsch. Librs. Group (gov., exec. com. 1985-87), Libr. and Info. Tech. Assn. (pres. 1978-79), Assn. Rsch. Librs., Libr. of Congress (optical disk pilot project adv. com. 1985-89), Coalition for Networked Info. (leader working group 1990-92), Assn. Coll. and Rsch. Librs. (pres. 1994-95), Cosmos Club (libr. com. 1989-96), Phi Beta Kappa. Home: 4709 Blagden Ter NW Washington DC 20011-3719 Office: Georgetown U Lauinger Libr Washington DC 20057

MARTIN, SUSAN TAYLOR, newspaper editor; b. N.Y.C., Aug. 3, 1949; d. Lewis Randolph and Carolyn Emmons (Douthat) Taylor; m. James Addison Martin Jr., Nov. 15, 1975; 1 child, Steven Randolph. BA in Polit. Sci., Duke U., 1971. Reporter Ft. Myers (Fla.) News Press, 1972-75, Tampa (Fla.) Tribune, 1975-77, Associated Press, Detroit, 1977-78; bur. chief Detroit News, 1978-81; asst. city editor Orlando (Fla.) Sentinel, 1981-82; exec. bus. editor St. Petersburg (Fla.) Times, 1982-86, city editor, 1986-87, nat. corr., 1987-91, asst. mng. editor, 1991-93, dep. mng. editor, 1993-97, chief fgn. corr., 1997—. Trustee Poynter Fund, St. Petersburg, 1992—. Recipient Non-Deadline Reporting award Soc. Profl. Journalists, 1990, Investigative Reporting award, 1991, Feature, Depth Reporting award Fla. Soc. Newspaper Editors, 1990, Depth Reporting award, 1991. Mem. Suncoast Figure Skating Club. Democrat. Episcopalian. Avocations: figure skating, travel, antiques, reading. Home: 1312 51st Ave NE Saint Petersburg FL 33703-3209 Office: St Petersburg Times 490 1st Ave S Saint Petersburg FL 33701-4204

MARTIN, SUZANNE CAROLE, health facility administrator; b. Columbus, Ohio, Aug. 29, 1945; d. John Fredrick and Clairmae (Kelley) Belknap; m. Daniel C. Martin, Mar. 16, 1968 (div. Apr. 1974); m. Richard Wayne Shadburn, Sept. 10, 1986. Diploma in nursing, Mount Carmel Sch. Nursing, Columbus, Ohio, 1977; BA in Sociology, Ohio Dominican Coll., 1976; JD cum laude, Capital U., 1983. Bar: Ohio 1983. From staff nurse to unit dir., med. dir. medicine Mount Carmel Med. Ctr., Columbus, 1966-77; dir. nursing McNamara-Mercy Hosp., Fairplay, Colo., 1977-78; staff nurse Nurse Pro Nurses Registry, San Diego, 1978-80; from dir. ambulatory care to asst. v.p., quality assurance to v.p. quality, utilization and risk mgmt. to v.p. patient care svcs. Mount Carmel Med. Ctr., Columbus, 1981-92; sr. cons. Deloitte & Touche, 1992-93; v.p. patient care svcs. Santa Rosa Health Care, San Antonio, 1993-95; exec. dir. Health Info. Measurement Systems Inc., San Antonio, 1995—; bd. dirs. United Ostomy Assn. Ctrl. Ohio, Columbus; com. mem. Franklinton Health Ctr., Columbus, 1985-92; mem. ethics com. Cath. Conf., Columbus, 1989-92; lectr. various group and orgns. on nursing and legal aspects. Mem. Columbus Zoo, 1990-93, Friends of Sta. WOSU, Columbus, 1990-93. Mem. Am. Acad. Hosp. Attys., Am. Soc. Hosp. Risk Mgrs., Am. Orgn. Nurse Execs., Ohio Soc. Nurse Execs., Ohio Soc. Risk Mgrs., Wilderness Soc., Mount Carmel Alumni Assn., Capital U. Alumni Assn. Roman Catholic. Home: 20210 Bat Cave Rd Garden Ridge TX 78266-2300 Office: Health Info Measurement Systesm 4402 Vance Jackson Rd Ste 201 San Antonio TX 78230-5334

MARTIN, TERESA ANN HILBERT, special education educator; b. Kingsport, Tenn., May 16, 1959; d. Bryan Hagan and Patsy Ruth (Owens) Hilbert; m. Harold Tony Martin, June 10, 1989. BS in Spl. Edn., Tenn. Tech. U., 1982, MA in Spl. Edn., 1983. Spl. edn. tchr. Gunnings Sch., Blountville, Tenn., 1984-85, S.E. H.S., Dalton, Ga., 1985-89, Murray County H.S., Chatsworth, Ga., 1989-94, N.W. H.S., Tunnel Hill, Ga., 1994—. Mem. Coun. for Exceptional Children, Delta Kappa Gamma (pres. 1994-96). Baptist. Avocations: reading, collecting Norman Rockwell memorabilia, needle work. Home: 100 Sims Dr Ringgold GA 30736 Office: Northwest Whitfield HS 1651 Tunnel Hill Varnell Rd Tunnel Hill GA 30755-9247

MARTIN, THEODORE KRINN, former university administrator (deceased); b. Blue Mountain, Miss., Jan. 2, 1915; s. Thomas Theodore and Ivy (Manning) M.; m. Lorene Garrison, Sept. 6, 1947; children: Glenn Krinn, Mary Ann, Janet Kay. A.B., Georgetown (Ky.) Coll., 1935; M.A., La. State U., 1941; Ph.D., George Peabody Coll., 1949. Tchr. Consol. Sch., Dumas, Miss., 1935-36; prin. Mississippi Heights Acad., 1936-39; tchr. Murphy High Sch., Mobile, Ala., 1940-41; registrar Miss. State U., 1949-53, registrar, adminstrv. asst. to pres., 1953-56, dean Sch. Edn., 1956-61, exec. asst. to pres., 1961-66, v.p., 1966-85, dir. Summer Sch., 1956-70, ret., 1985. Served as capt. AUS, 1941-46. Mem. Masons, Kappa Alpha, Phi Kappa Phi, Omicron Delta Kappa, Kappa Delta Pi, Phi Delta Kappa. Home: 1151 East Dr Starkville MS 39759-9216

MARTIN, THOMAS HOWARD, pastor; b. Clovis, N.Mex., Aug. 22, 1952; s. Howard Venson and Gertrude Ernestine (Winkler); children: Tara Catherine, Aubrey Lynn, Andrew Thomas, Benjamin Luke; m. Kathryn Ann Brinson, May 19, 1984. BBA, Eastern N.Mex. U., 1974; MDiv, Southwestern Bapt. Theol. Sem., 1978; D.Min., New Orleans Bapt. Theol. Sem., 1986. Lic. to Preach, 1975; ordained to Min., 1977. Pastor Hilltop Bapt. Ch., Fort Worth, 1976-77, Pioneer Drive Bapt. Ch., Irving, Tex., 1977-80, Buckner Terr. Bapt. Ch., Dallas, 1980-83; v.p. DBC Found. Dallas Bapt. Coll., 1983-84; stewardship cons. Resource Svcs., Inc., Dallas, 1984-85; minister with single adults Pioneer Drive Bapt. Ch., Abilene, Tex., 1985-87; v.p. advancement Howard Payne U., Brownwood, Tex., 1987-88; dir. client rels. Community Svc. Bur., Inc., Dallas, 1988-89; pastor Sandia Bapt. Ch., Clovis, N.Mex., 1989-93, First Bapt. Ch., Hobbs, N.Mex., 1993—; mem. exec. bd. The Bapt. Convention N.Mex., 1990-94, vice-chmn. exec. bd., 1991-92, chmn. exec. bd., 1992-93, 93-94, pres., 1994-95, 95-96. Contbr. articles to profl. jours. Named Outstanding Young Men Am., 1981, 86, 88. Baptist. Avocations: golf, reading. Home: 100 W Wolfcamp Dr Hobbs NM 88240-1911 Office: First Bapt Ch 301 E Snyder St Hobbs NM 88240-8338

MARTIN, THOMAS LYLE, JR., university president; b. Memphis, Sept. 26, 1921; s. Thomas Lyle and Malvina (Rucks) M.; m. Helene Hartley, June 12, 1943 (dec. Sept. 1983); children: Michele Marie, Thomas Lyle; m. Mildred L. Moore, June 5, 1984. B.E.E., Rensselaer Poly. Inst., 1942, M.E.E., 1948, D.Eng., 1967; Ph.D., Stanford U., 1951. Prof. elec. engring. U. N.Mex., 1948-53; prof. engring. U. Ariz., 1953-63, dean engring., 1958-63; dean engring. U. Fla., Gainesville, 1963-66, So. Meth. U., Dallas, 1966-74; pres. Ill. Inst. Tech., Chgo., 1974-87, pres. emeritus, 1987—; bd. dirs. Cherry Corp. Capt. Signal Corps AUS, 1943-46. Fellow IEEE; mem. Nat. Acad. Engring. Home and Office: PO Box 167845 Irving TX 75016-7845

MARTIN, TODD, professional tennis player; b. Hinsdale, Ill., July 8, 1970. Student, Northwestern U. Profl. tennis player, 1990—. Moved into world's top ten in tennis 1994; 3 pro singles titles 1993, 94 (2); winner Rolex Nat. Indoor Collegiate Championship award, 1990. Office: US Tennis Assn 70 W Red Oak Ln White Plains NY 10604-3602*

MARTIN, TONY, football player; b. Miami, Fla., Sept. 5, 1965. Student, Bishop Coll., Mesa State U. Wide receiver Miami Dolphins, 1990-93, San Diego Chargers, 1994—. Named to Pro Bowl, 1996. *

MARTIN, ULRIKE BALK, laboratory analyst; b. Kelheim, Germany, Oct. 28, 1965; d. Gunther Anton and Elfriede Babette (Eiser) Balk; m. Kent Daniel Martin, May 1, 1988. BS summa cum laude, Stephen F. Austin State U., Nacogdoches, Tex., 1992; MS, 1994. Lab. analyst Eastman Chem. Co., Longview, Tex., 1994—. Author: An Analysis of Heavy Metals on Forest Stream Ecosystems Receiving Run Off from an Oil Field, 1992. Mem. Tex. Acad. Sci., Sigma Xi. Home: 3019 B Tryon Rd Longview TX 75605

MARTIN, VERNON EMIL, librarian; b. Guthrie, Okla., Dec. 15, 1929; s. Vernon E. Sr. and Marian (Brandon) M.; m. Arlan Stone, June 30, 1956 (div. 1977); children: Vernon Martin III, Jeffrey Martin; m. Elizabeth Jean Chapin, June 16, 1979; 1 child, Amy Chapin Hathaway. MA in Music, Columbia U., 1959, MS in Libr., 1965. Libr. Lincoln Ctr. Libr. Mus., N.Y.C., 1964-66; music libr. North Tex. State U., Denton, 1966-70; libr. dir. Morningside Coll., Sioux City, Iowa, 1970-74; head art dept. Hartford (Conn.) Pub. Libr., 1974-93, ret., 1993. Composer operas including Ladies Voices, 1956, Waiting For The Barbarians, 1956, Fables By Thurber, 1986, (ballet) Dancing Back The Buffalo, 1996. CHmn. Cultural Affairs Commn., Hartford, 1984-86. Mem. ASCAP (Standard award 1969-97). Home: 110 Arch St Keene NH 03431

MARTIN, VINCENT GEORGE, management consultant; b. N.Y.C., Feb. 9, 1922; s. Joseph R. and Mae B. (Mulligan) M.; m. Alice Ann McGovern, June 8, 1946; children—Kathleen (Mrs. Michael Greiner), Joseph F. Student, Pace Coll., 1948-49, Am. Internat. Coll., 1950. Salesman Lavigna Jewels, N.Y.C., 1945-47; indsl. engr. Barton Watchcase Mfg., N.Y.C., 1948-49; office procedures Local Loan Co., N.Y.C., 1950-51; sr. time study engr. Perkins Machine & Gear Co., West Springfield, Mass., 1951-52; with Milton Bradley Co., East Longmeadow, Mass., 1952-79; mgr. mfg. Milton Bradley Co., 1962-64, v.p. mfg., 1964-69, exec. v.p., 1969—, dir., 1971—, gen. mgr., 1972-79; with Vincent G. Martin Assos. (Mgmt. Consultants), 1979—; trustee Springfield Inst. for Savs., 1978-81; dir. Armoury Corp., Stockbridge Corp., 1978-80. Past pres. Springfield Speech and Hearing Center; mem. East Longmeadow Indsl. Park Steering Com.; gen. campaign chmn. United Fund Pioneer Valley, 1976; bd. dirs. Springfield Symphony Orch.; corporate Springfield Coll., 1976-79, Wesson Meml. Hosp., 1976-80. Served with AUS, 1942-45. Decorated Bronze Star. Mem. Soc. Advancement Mgmt. (pres. Western Mass. chpt. 1954-56), Am. Mgmt. Assn., Toy Mfrs. Am. (dir. 1973-75), Springfield C. of C. (dir. 1974-78), Newcomen Soc. N.Am., East Longmeadow C. of C. (pres., dir. 1965-68). Club: Rotarian (dir. 1970-72). Home: 3555 John Anderson Dr Ormond Beach FL 32176-2176 Office: 8 Flume Ave PO Box 505 Marstons Mills MA 02648

MARTIN, VINCENT LIONEL, manufacturing company executive; b. Los Angeles, June 29, 1939; s. Arthur Seymon and Alice Maria (Miller) M.; m. Janet Ann Dowler, Mar. 25, 1961; children: Jennifer Lynn, Karen Arlene, Timothy Paul. B.S., Stanford U., 1960; M.B.A., Harvard U., 1963. Various staff positions FMC Corp, Chgo, 1966-74; gen. mgr. Crane and Excavator div. FMC Corp, Cedar Rapids, Iowa, 1974-79; pres. Equipment Systems div. AMCA Internat. Corp., Houston, 1979-81; group v.p. AMCA Internat. Corp., Brookfield, Wis., 1981-85; pres. Jason Inc., Milw., 1986-96, chmn. CEO, 1996—. Mem. Phi Beta Kappa, Tau Beta Pi. Republican. Presbyterian. Home: 2601 W Cedar Ln Milwaukee WI 53217-1138 Office: Jason Inc 411 E Wisconsin Ave Milwaukee WI 53202-4409

MARTIN, VIRVE PAUL, licensed professional counselor; b. Tallinn, Estonia, Nov. 19, 1928; came to U.S., 1949; d. Walter Gerhard and Alice (Haas) Paul; m. Albert Lynn Martin Jr., May 31, 1952; children: Lynda Lee, Elaine Lynne, Monique Louise. Student, U. Heidelberg, Germany, 1948-49; BA, Wesleyan Coll., Macon, Ga., 1952; MA, U. Minn., 1970. Cert. profl. counselor, Ga. Interpreter Internat. Refugee Orgn., Nuremberg, Frankfurt, Heidelberg, Fed. Republic of Germany, 1947-49; rsch. asst. Kenny Inst., Mpls., 1966-67; vocat. evaluator Dept. Human Resources, Atlanta, 1970-73, rehab. counselor, 1973-96; interpreter Mpls. C. of C., 1963-65, Dem. Nat. Conv., Atlanta, 1988; attaché Estonian Olympic Com. 1996 Olympics, Atlanta. Writer, editor World Pen Pals, 1964-66. V.p., bd. dirs. Ms. JCs, Minn., 1959-62; pres. Valley View Mothers' Club, Bloomington, Minn., 1961-62. Mem. AAUW, Nat. Rehab. Assn., Ga. Rehab. Assn. (membership chair 1988), Ga. Mental Health Counselors Assn. Avocations: travel, reading, metaphysics, dancing, knitting. Home: 1106 Norwich Cir NE Atlanta GA 30324-2908

MARTIN, WALTER EDWIN, biology educator; b. DeKalb, Ill., Jan. 14, 1908; s. Walter Sylvester and Tillie Lula (Secora) M.; m. Ruth Virginia Butler, June 16, 1934; children: Carol Ann, John Walter, Judith Kathryn, David Butler. B.E., No. Ill. State Tchrs. Coll., 1930; M.S., Purdue U., 1932, Ph.D., 1937. Asst. Purdue U., 1930-34, instr., 1934-37; instr. No. Ill. State Tchrs. Coll., summers 1930-31; mem. sci. expdn. Honduras, summer 1934; mem. staff Marine Biol. Lab., summers 1935-42; asst. prof. DePauw U., 1937-41, assoc. prof., 1941-46, prof., 1946-47; assoc. prof. U. So. Calif., 1947-48, prof., 1948—, head zoology dept., 1948-54, head biology dept., 1954-58; naval technician to, Egypt, summer 1953, 55, Japan, Taiwan and Philippines, 1957; sabbatical leave Marine Lab., U. Hawaii, 1956-57; sabbatical year Neuchatel, Switzerland, 1963-64, U. Queensland, Brisbane, Australia, 1970-71. Fellow Ind. Acad. Sci., AAAS, So. Calif. Acad. Sci.; mem. Am. Soc. Zoologists, Am. Soc. Parasitologists, Am. Micros. Soc., Western Soc. Naturalists, Phi Sigma, Alpha Epsilon Delta. Home: 2185 Warmouth St San Pedro CA 90732-4530 Office: U of Southern California Dept Bio Los Angeles CA 90007

MARTIN, WILFRED WESLEY FINNY, psychologist, property owner and manager; b. Rock Lake, N.D., Dec. 3, 1917; s. William Isaac and Anna Liisa (Hendrickson-Juntunen) M.; m. Stella Helland, Sept. 25, 1943; children: Sydney Wayne, William Allan. BA, Jamestown Coll., 1940; army specialized tng. program, Hamilton Coll., 1944; MS, EdD, U. So. Calif., 1956. Highsch. prin., coach pub. sch., Nekoma, N.D., 1940-42; contact rep., psychologist VA, L.A., 1946-49, psychologist, chief rehab., 1972-77; guidance dir. Moorehead (Minn.) Pub. Schs., 1951-53; instr. Concordia Coll., Moorhead, 1951-53; from intern to resident Fargo (N.D.) VA Hosp., Moorhead, Minn., 1953-58; psychologist VA, Fargo, N.D., 1953-57; assoc. Sci. Rsch. Assoc./IBM, Boulder, Colo., 1957-65; regional dir. Sci. Rsch. Assoc./IBM, L.A., 1966-72; owner, mgr. Martin Investments, Huntington Beach, Calif., 1977—; adjutant U. Miss., Oxford, 1942; trustee Wilfred W. and Stella Martin Trust, Huntington Beach, 1991. Author: Veterans Administration Work Simplification, 1948, 57. Charter mem. Rep. Presdl. Task Force, 1980; adv. sr. ptnrs. bd. dirs. U. Calif. Med. Sch., Irvine, 1990; donor Dr. and Mrs. W.W. Martin Endowment, Jamestown Coll., N.D., 1985; mem. Assocs. of James Ford Bell Libr., U. Minn. With U.S. Army, 1942-45. Mem. Am. Psychol. Assn., Cardinal & Gold U. So. Calif., Jamestown Coll. Heritage Circle (charter), Suomi Coll. Second Century Soc., Elks. Republican. Lutheran. Avocations: reading, Finnish heritage, swimming, sports, card playing. Home: PO Box 5445 Huntington Beach CA 92615-5445 *The dominant force in my life is described by the Finnish word SISU, which means perseverence, determination, competitiveness, and tenacity toward goal-oriented achievements. Due to SISU, faith, and hard work I enjoy an active successful life.*

MARTIN, WILLIAM BRYAN, chancellor, lawyer; b. Lexington, Ky., Apr. 11, 1938; s. William Stone and Alice Bryan (Spiers) Martin; m. Mary Ellen Matson, Aug. 11, 1973; children: Chanley Morgan, Matson Bryan, Evan Andrew. AB, Transylvania U., 1960; JD, U. Ky., 1964; LLM, Georgetown U., Washington, 1965; MDiv summa cum laude, Emory U., 1979. Bar: Ky. 1964, D.C. 1964; ordained to ministry Christian Ch. (Disciples of Christ), 1981. Legal intern Pub. Defender, Washingotn, 1964-65; asst. U.S. atty. Western Dist. Ky., 1965-67; assoc. McElwain, Denning, Clarke and Winstead, Louisville, 1967-69; asst. atty. gen. Commonwealth of Ky., 1969-70; prof. U. Louisville Sch. Law, 1970-81; dean Oklahoma City U. Sch. Law, 1982-83; pres. Franklin Coll. Ind., 1983-97; bd. dirs. Coun. Ind. Colls. and Univs., 1992—; bd. dirs. Ind. Colls. Ind. Found., 1983—, 1st vice chmn., 1992—, chmn., 1993—, mem. spl. study com. and strategic planning com., mem. transition task force, 1991—; mem. Ind. Colls., Ind. Conf. Higher Edn., 1983—; sec. Am. Bapt. Assn. Colls. and Univs., 1989—; cons.-evaluator North Ctrl. Assn., Commn. on Instns. Higher Edn., 1985. Columnist Scripps Howard News Svc., 1991—; contbr. articles to profl.

jours. Mem. adv. bd. Heartland Film Festival, 1995—; bd. regents Ind. Acad., 1988—, chair nominating com.; bd. trustees Christian Theol. Sem., 1986—, past mem. investment com., chair ednl. policies com.; bd. dirs., exec. com. Historic Landmarks Found. Ind., 1987-91, adv. coun., 1991—; first chmn. coun. pres. Ind. Collegiate Athletic Conf., 1987-90; elder Tabernacle Christian Ch., Franklin, 1983-91, North Christian Ch., Columbus, 1994—; mem. Progress Forum Johnson County, 1987-92; mem. adv. bd. Greater Johnson County Cmty. Found., inc., 1992—; mem. Historic Preservation Task Force, Divsn. Historic Preservation and Archaeology, Ind. Dept. Natural Resources; mem. Nat. Environ. Task Force.ship com., tchr. family life class Douglass Blvd. Christian Ch.; deacon Crown Heights Christian Ch., Okla. Recipient Svc. award Franklin Heritage, 1986, Man of Yr. award Franklin C. of C., 1986, Disting. Svc. cert. Transylvania U., 1987. Mem. Ben Franklin Soc., Ind. Soc. Chgo., Econ. Club Indpls., Junto Club Indpls., Columbia Club Indpls., Rotary of Franklin, Hillview Country Club, Alpha Soc. Home: Pres Residence & Reception 253 S Forsythe Franklin IN 46131 Office: Franklin Coll Ind 501 E Monroe St Franklin IN 46131-2512

MARTIN, WILLIAM C., sociology educator, writer; b. San Antonio, Dec. 31, 1937; s. Lowell Curtis and Joe Bailey (Brite) M.; m. Patricia Dale Summerlin, Dec. 31, 1957; children: Rex Martin, Jeff Martin, Elisabeth Dale Martin Thomas. BA, Abilene Christian U., 1958, MA, 1960; BD, Harvard Divinity Sch., 1963; PhD, Harvard U., 1969. Instr. history Dana Hall Sch., Wellesley, Mass., 1965-68; instr. sociology Rice U., Houston, 1968-69, asst. prof. sociology, 1969-73, assoc. prof. sociology, 1973-79, prof. sociology, 1979—, Chavanne prof. religion and pub. policy, 1996—, master Sid W. Richardson Coll., 1976-81, chair dept. sociology, 1983-86, 89-94; cons. films and TV documentaries; speaker in field. Author: These Were God's People, 1966, Christians in Conflict, 1972, A Prophet With Honor: Billy Graham Story, 1991 (Christianity Today's Critic's Choice award 1992), My Prostate and Me: Dealing With Prostate Cancer, 1994, With God on our Side: The Rise of the Religious Right in America, 1996; contbg. editor Tex. Monthly (Nat. Headliner award 1982); contbr. numerous articles to profl. jours. and pop mags.; numerous radio and TV appearances. Dir. House of the Carpenter, Inc., inner-city youth program, Boston, 1963-66, pres. and bd. dirs. non-profit housing corp.; bd. dirs. Fellowship Racial and Econ. Equality, 1970-71; mem. exec. com. Houston Coun. Human Rels. Recipient Nicholas Salgo Outstanding Tchr. award Rice U., 1971, 93, Brown Coll. award for Teaching in the Humanities Rice U., 1974, 76, George R. Brown Award for Superior Teaching, alumni Rice U., 1974, 76, 77, 84, for Excellence in Teaching, 1975, 82, Life Honor award, 1985, Sr. scholar James A. Baker Inst. Pub. Policy; grantee Am. Coun. Learned Socs. and Am. Philos. Soc., 1974. Mem. Am. Sociol. Assn., Soc. Scientific Study Religion, Religious Rsch. Assn., Tex. Inst. Letters (J. Frank Dobie/Paisano fellowship 1980). Democrat. Protestant. Avocation: bicycling. Home: 2148 Addison Rd Houston TX 77030-1222 Office: Rice U Dept Sociology 6100 Main St Houston TX 77005-1827

MARTIN, WILLIAM EDWIN, government official; b. Bowling Green, Ky., Oct. 16, 1943; s. John Edwin and Bess Carolyn (Matherly) M.; children: Anne Whitson, William Whitson; m. Jean Clinton Nelson, Aug. 1, 1981. BA, Vanderbilt U., 1965, JD, 1968. Bar: Tenn. 1968. Ptnr. Waller Lansden Dortch & Davis, Nashville, 1968-75; sr. ptnr. Harwell Martin & Stegall, Nashville, 1975-93; dep. asst. sec. for internat. affairs U.S. Dept. Commerce-NOAA, Washington, 1993—. Contbr. articles to newspapers and law revs. Dir. polar programs Wilderness Soc., Washington, 1990-92; pres. Environ. Action Fund, Nashville, 1982; bd. dirs. Tenn. Environ. Coun., Nashville, 1992, So. Appalachian Highland Conservancy, Johnson City, Tenn., 1988-90. Mem. Nashville Bar Assn. (bd. dirs. 1979-80). Democrat. Episcopalian. Avocations: mountain climbing, photography, running, tennis. Office: Nat Oceanic and Atmospheric Admn 14th & Constitution Ave NW Washington DC 20230

MARTIN, WILLIAM GIESE, lawyer; b. Canton, Ohio, Nov. 4, 1934; s. George Denman and Emily (Giese) M.; m. Martha Justice, June 14, 1958; children: William E.J., Peter J.D., George F.D. BA, Yale U., 1956; LLB, Harvard U., 1959. Bar: Ohio 1959, U.S. Dist. Ct. (so. dist.) Ohio 1963. Assoc. Porter, Stanley, Treffinger & Platt, Columbus, Ohio, 1963-68; ptnr. Porter, Wright, Morris & Arthur, Columbus, 1967, of counsel, 1967—. Lt. USNR, 1959-63. Mem. ABA, Ohio State Bar Assn., Columbus Bar Assn., Capital Club, Rocky Fork Hunt and Country Club, Yale Club of N.Y. Home: 6169 Havens Corners Rd Blacklick OH 43004-9676 Office: Porter Wright Morris & Arthur 41 S High St Columbus OH 43215-6101

MARTIN, WILLIAM ROBERT, accountant; b. Cocoa, Fla., Nov. 26, 1927; s. Roy Nmi and Ella (Barton) M.; m. Lurline Lillian Powell, Apr. 30, 1954; children: Lurline Lillian, Nancy Louise, William Robert, Jr. BA in Acctg., Stetson U., 1949. CPA, Fla. Staff acct. Potter, Loucks & Bower, CPAs, Orlando, 1949-51; in-svc. auditor Army Audit Agy., Atlanta, 1951-53; sr. acct. Potter, Bower & Co., CPAs, Orlando, 1954-55; ptnr. Kurtz and Martin, CPAs, Orlando, 1956-68, Osburn, Henning & Co., CPA, Orlando, 1968-92; mem. Bd. of Accountancy Dept. Profl. Regulation, 1987-92, vice chmn. 1989, chmn. 1990; adj. faculty Valencia Community Coll. Acctg. Founding treas., past bd. dirs. Orlando Opera Co., Inc.; bd. dirs., fin. advisor Open Door Mission, Inc.; treas. Bill McCollum for Congress, 1982—; v.p., bd. dirs. Cen. Fla. Crew Boosters Assn., Inc., 1979-81; charter dir. Cen. Fla. Crime Watch Program, Inc., 1977-79; mem. Fla. Symphony Orch., Inc., Assoc. Bd., 1959-72; active Indsl. Devel. Commn. Mid-Fla., 1977-89; past treas., bd. dirs. United Cerebral Palsy Orange County, 1960-64, We Care, Inc., 1971. Mem. AICPA (mem. legis. key contact program), Fla. Inst. CPAs (founding chmn., local practitioners com., chmn. pub. rels. com., 1984-85), Nat. Assn. Bds. Accountancy administrv. and fin. com. 1991—), Greater Orlando C. of C. (bd. dirs. 1985, asst. v.p. fin. 1986, v.p. fin. 1987). Republican. Presbyterian. Avocations: fishing, water sports. Office: Osburn Henning & Co CPAs 617 E Colonial Dr Orlando FL 32803-4602

MARTIN, WILLIAM ROYALL, JR., association executive; b. Raleigh, N.C., Sept. 3, 1926; s. William Royall and Edith Ruth (Crocker) M.; m. Betty Anne Rader, June 14, 1952; children: Sallie Rader Martin Busby, Amy Kemp Martin Lewis. AB, U. N.C., 1948, MBA, 1964; BS, N.C. State U., 1952. Chemist Stamford (Conn.) rsch. labs. Am. Cyanamid Co., 1952-54; chemist Dan River Mills, Danville, Va., 1954-56, Union Carbide Corp., South Charleston, W.Va., 1956-59; rsch. assoc. Sch. Textiles N.C. State U., 1959-63; tech. dir. Am. Assn. Textile Chemists and Colorists, Research Triangle Park, N.C., 1963-73, exec. dir., 1974-96; adj. asst. prof. Coll. Textiles, N.C. State U., 1966-88, adj. assoc. prof., 1989—; del. Internat. Orgn. Standardization, Pan Am. Standards Commn. With USNR, 1944-46. Fellow Am. Inst. Chemists, Soc. Dyers and Colourists, Textile Inst.; mem. Am. Chem. Soc., Coun. Engring. and Sci. Soc. Execs. (past pres. 1992-93), Fiber Soc., Am. Assn. Textile Chemists and Colorists, Masons, Rotary, Phi Kappa Phi, Phi Gamma Delta. Methodist. Home and Office: 224 Briarcliff Ln Cary NC 27511-3901

MARTIN, WILLIAM RUSSELL, nuclear engineering educator; b. Flint, Mich., June 2, 1945; s. Carl Marcus and Audrey Winifred (Rosene) M.; m. Patricia Ann Williams, Aug. 13, 1967; children: Amy Leigh, Jonathn William. B.S.E. in Engring. Physics, U. Mich., 1967; MS in Physics, U. Wis., 1968; M.S.E. in Nuclear Engring., U. Mich., 1975, PhD in Nuclear Engring., 1976. Prin. physicist Combustion Engring., Inc., Windsor, Conn., 1976-77; asst. prof. nuclear engring. U. Mich., Ann Arbor, 1977-81, assoc. prof. nuclear engring., 1981-88, prof. nuclear engring., 1988—, dir. lab. for sci. computation, 1986—, chmn. nuclear engring., 1990-94, assoc. dean for acad. affairs Coll. Engring., 1994—; cons. Lawrence Livermore Nat. Lab., Livermore, Calif., 1982—, Los Alamos (N.Mex.) Nat. Lab., 1980-89, IBM, Inc., Kingston, N.Y., 1984, Rockwell Internat., Pitts., 1985. Author: Transport Theory, 1979; author tech. and conf. papers. Recipient Glenn Murphy award Am. Soc. for Engring. Edn., 1993; Disting. scholar U. Mich. Coll. Engring., 1967; vis. fellow Royal Soc., London, 1989. Fellow Am. Nuclear Soc.; mem. Am. Phys. Soc., Soc. for Indsl. and Applied Math., IEEE. Avocations: running, reading, skiing, sailing. Home: 1701 Crestland St Ann Arbor MI 48104-6329 Office: U Mich Dept Nuclear Engring Ann Arbor MI 48109

MARTIN, WILLIE PAULINE, elementary school educator, illustrator; b. Pendleton, Tex., May 27, 1920; d. Lester B. and Stella (Smith) M.; m. Charles M., June 23, 1946; 1 child, Charles Jr. BS, Middle Tenn. State U., Murfreesboro, 1944; MS, U. Tenn., 1965; postgrad., U. Ga., 1980. Cert. tchr., Tenn., Tex., Ga. Elem. tchr. Bd. Edn., Sparta, Tenn., 1940-44; home econs. tchr. Bd. Edn., Salado, Tex., 1944-46; rsch. technician Oak Ridge (Tenn.) Nat. Lab., 1946-50; art, gen. sci. tchr. Bd. Edn., State of Tenn., 1965-69; art, reading, elem. tchr. Bd. Edn., State of Ga., 1970-83; elem. tchr. Bd. Edn., Augusta, Ga., 1984-86; tchr. aerospace edn. workshop Middle Tenn. State U., 1969; spkr. in field. Contbr. articles in field to profl. jours. Exhibitor Oak Ridge (Tenn.) Festival. Mem. Nat. Art Edn. Assn. (del. conv. Washington 1989, Balt. 1994), Ga. Art Edn. Assn. (del. state conv., dist. pres. 1974, del. conv. Savannah 1986, Augusta 1993, del. state conv. Athens 1994), Tenn. Edn. Assn. Methodist. Avocations: art, crafts, music, singing, reading. Home: 1406 Flowing Wells Rd Augusta GA 30909-9767

MARTIN-BOWEN, (CAROLE) LINDSEY, freelance writer; b. Kansas City, Kans., Aug. 4, 1949; d. Lawrence Richard and V. Marie (Schaffer) Pickett; m. Frederick E. Nicholson, July 3, 1971 (div. 1977); 1 child, Aaron Frederick; m. Edwin L. Martin, June 18, 1980 (div. 1987); 1 child, Ki Elise; m. Michael L. Bowen, Dec. 23, 1988. BA in English Lit., U. Mo., Kansas City, 1972, MA in English and Creative Writing, 1988, postgrad., 1991-94; postgrad., U. Mo. Kansas City Sch. Law, Kansas City, 1995—. Tech. editor Office Hearings and Appeals, U.S. Dept. Interior, Washington, 1976-77; reporter, photographer Louisville Times, 1982-83; reporter, features editor Sun Newspapers, Overland Park, Kans., 1983-84; assoc. editor Modern Jeweler, Overland Park and N.Y.C., 1984-85; writer Coll. Blvd. News, Overland Park, 1985-89, KC View, Kansas City, Mo., 1988-89; editor Number One, Kansas City, Mo., 1986-88, cons., 1988-89; copywriter Sta KXEO/KWWR Radio, Mexico, Mo., 1989; editorial asst. New Letters, 1985—; features writer, columnist The Squire, Prairie Village, Kans., 1990-95; instr. English U. Mo., Kansas City, 1986-88, Johnson County C.C., 1988-95; tchr. English and fiction Longview C.C., 1988-95; instr. writing and mass comm. Webster U., 1990—; instr. world lit., Am. lit., women in lit., creative writing Penn Valley C.C., 1993—, faculty sponsor The Penn; owner, writer Paladin Freelance Writing Svc., Kansas City, 1988—; prodn. editor Nat. Paralegal Reporter, 1992-95, editor 1994—; staff writer, editor Nat. Fedn. Paralegal Assns., Inc. books and pubs.; writing contest judge New Letters, 1987—. Author: (novel) The Dark Horse Waits in Boulder, 1985, (poetry) Waiting for the Wake-Up Call, 1990, Second Touch, 1990, (fiction) Cicada Grove and Other Stories, 1992; contbr. poems, book revs., features, cartoon artwork, and photographs to numerous publs. including New Letters, Lip Service and Contemporary Lit. Criticism; lead actress prodns. Coach House Players, 1969-70; extra HBO film Truman, 1995. Campaigner McGovern for Pres. Campaign, Kansas City, 1971-72. Regents scholar, 1967; GAF fellow, 1986. Mem. U. Mo.-Kansas City Alumni Assn. (media com. 1983-84), Phi Kappa Phi. Roman Catholic. Avocations: acrylic and oil painting, downhill skiing, music, Greek cooking, paralegal work. Home: 7109 Pennsylvania Ave Kansas City MO 64114-1316 Office: Nat Paralegal Reporter Hdqs 32 W Bridlespur Ter Kansas City MO 64114

MARTINDALE, CARLA JOY, librarian; b. Ladysmith, Wis., Sept. 9, 1947; d. Howard Walter and Audrey Elizabeth (Stanton) M. BA, Mt. Senario Coll., 1970; MLIS, U. South Fla., 1990. Sch. librarian Blackhawk Schs., South Wayne, Ind., 1975-79; librarian Osceola County Libr., Kissimee, Fla., 1989-90, Fla. Tech. Coll., Orlando, 1991-92, Orlando Coll. South, 1993—; chair for libr. 21st curriculum Phillips Coll., Orlando, 1995, acad. com., 1993—, accreditation steering com., 1996. Library named in her honor Orlando Coll. South, 1995. Mem. Fla. Libr. Assn. Avocations: reading, pets, stock investing. Home: 705 Bear Way Kissimmee FL 34759-4213 Office: Orlando Coll South 2411 Sand Lake Rd Orlando FL 32809-7641

MARTINEAU, JULIE PEPERONE, social worker; b. Kilgore, Tex., Oct. 31, 1956; d. Angelo Gerad and Jane Margaret (Reppel) Peperone; m. Russell Joseph Martineau, Dec. 30, 1950; children: Adria Helen, Brittany Jane. AA, Marymount Palos Verdes Coll., Calif., 1976; BA, Calif. State U., Long Beach, 1979. Staff cons. United Way of L.A., 1979-83; group mgr. United Way of the Tex. Gulf Coast, Houston, 1983; dir. cmty. devel. Tri-County Mental Health and Mental Retardation Svcs., Conroe, Tex., 1984-87; exec. dir. Montgomery County Com. on Aging, Conroe, 1987-97; chmn. South Montgomery County Healthier Cmty. Forum, Conroe, 1996—; pres. Montgomery County United Way, The Woodlands, 1997—; chmn. Project CARE Monitoring Coun., Conroe, 1989—; mem. long term care task force Tex. Health and Human Svcs. Commn., Austin, 1993-95; mem. aging programs adv. coun. Houston-Galveston Area Coun., 1987—; mem. aging and disabled adv. coun. Dept. Human Svcs., Houston, 1993—. Bd. dirs. Conroe Regional Med. Ctr., 1993—, United Way of Montgomery County, Conroe, 1984-87; congl. del. 1995 White House Conf. on Aging; chmn. Leadership Montgomery County, 1995-96; v.p. Bluebonnet chpt. Nat. Charity League. Named Oustanding Woman of Yr., YWCA of Montgomery County, 1990, recipient awards. Mem. John Ben Sheperd Leadership Forum, Leadership Conroe, Area Agy. on Aging Execs. Network, South Montgomery C. of C. (chmn. bd. 1992-93), LWV of Montgomery County (pres. 1990-92, v.p. 1995—). Roman Catholic. Avocations: singing, cooking, volleyball, riding. Office: Montgomery County United Way 1600 Lake Front Cir The Woodlands TX 77380-3633

MARTINEN, JOHN A., travel company executive; b. Sault St. Marie, Mich., June 26, 1938; s. John Albert and Ina Helia (Jarvi) M.; BS with highest honors, Mich. State U., 1960; LLB, NYU, 1963. With Grace Line, N.Y.C., 1963-69; cons. Empresa Turistica Internat., Galapagos Cruises, Quito, Ecuador, 1969-70; regional mgr. Globus & Cosmos (Group Voyagers Inc.), N.Y.C., 1971-73, v.p., 1974-76, exec. v.p., 1977-78, pres., CEO, 1979-92, Littleton, Colo., 1993—. Pres., bd. dirs. Edbrooke Condominium Assn. Mem. U.S. Tour Operators Assn. (bd. dirs., sec.), Am. Soc. Travel Agts., Tour Operator Plan (chmn.), Denver Acad. Travel & Tourism (bd. dirs.), Lotos, Sky and Wings Clubs (N.Y.), Columbine Country Club, Denver Athletic Club. Democrat. Home: 1450 Wynkoop St Denver CO 80202-1116 Office: 5301 S Federal Cir Littleton CO 80123-2980

MARTINES, LAURO, historian, writer; b. Chgo., Nov. 22, 1927; m. Julia O'Faolain, Nov. 20, 1957; 1 child, Lucien. A.B., Drake U., 1950; Ph.D., Harvard, 1960. Asst. prof. history Reed Coll., 1958-62; fellow Villa I Tatti, Harvard Center for Italian Renaissance Studies, Florence, Italy, 1962-65; prof. history UCLA, 1966-92; vis. prof. Warburg Inst., U. London, 1985; vis. dir. studies Ecole des Hautes Etudes en Sces Sociales, Paris, spring 1992, 94. Author: The Social World of the Florentine Humanists, 1963, Lawyers and Statecraft in Renaissance Florence, 1968, Power and Imagination: City-States in Renaissance Italy, 1979, Society and History in English Renaissance Verse, 1985, An Italian Renaissance Sextet: Six Tales in Historical Context, 1994; co-author: Not in God's Image: Women in Western Civilization, 1973; Editor: Violence and Civil Disorder in Italian Cities 1200-1500, 1972, Riti e rituali nelle societa medievali, 1994. Served with AUS, 1945-47. Fellowships include Am. Council Learned Socs., 1962-63, Harvard U. Ctr. Italian Renaissance Studies, Villa i Tatti, Florence, Italy, 1962-65, Guggenheim Meml. Found., 1964-65;, sr. fellow Nat. Endowment for Humanities, 1971, 78-79; resident fellow Rockefeller Found. Bellagio Ctr., Italy, 1990. Fellow Mediaeval Acad. Am., Italian Deputation for History Tuscany (fgn.); mem. Am. Hist. Assn., Renaissance Soc. Am. Home: 8 Gloucester Crescent, London NW1 7DS, England

MARTINETTI, RONALD ANTHONY, lawyer; b. N.Y.C., Aug. 13, 1945; s. Alfred Joseph and Frances Ann (Battipaglia) M. Student, U. Chgo., 1981-82; JD, U. So. Calif., 1982. Bar: Calif. 1982; U.S. Dist. Ct. (cen. and no. dists.) Calif. 1982, U.S. Dist. Ct. Ariz., 1992; U.S. Ct. Appeals (9th cir.) 1982. Ptnr. Kazanjian & Martinetti, Glendale, Calif., 1986—; co-founder Am. Legends Website, 1996, Am. Legends Pub., 1996. Author: James Dean Story, 1995. Vol. trial lawyer Bet Tzedek Legal Svcs., 1987—; judge pro tem L.A. Superior Ct., 1994—. Mem. Calif. Bar Assn. Roman Catholic. Office: Kazanjian & Martinetti 520 E Wilson Ave Glendale CA 91206-4374

MARTINEZ, AL, journalist, screenwriter; b. Oakland, Calif., July 21, 1929; s. Alfredo Martinez and Mary (Larragoite) Lehmann; m. Joanne Cinelli, July 30, 1949; children: Cinthia, Linda, Allen. Student, San Francisco State U., 1949-50, U. Calif., Berkeley, 1952-53, Contra Costa Jr. Coll., Walnut Creek, Calif., 1953-54; LHD (hon.), Whittier U., 1996. Reporter, feature writer Richmond (Calif.) Ind ., 1952-55; reporter, feature writer Oakland Tribune, 1955-71, columnist, 1963-71; profilist, feature writer L.A. Times, 1972-84, columnist, 1984—; screenwriter CBS, ABC, NBC, L.A., 1975—; tech. advisor Lou Grant TV Series, CBS, Los Angeles, 1979-80. Author: Rising Voices, 1974, Jigsaw John, 1976, Ashes in the Rain, 1989, Dancing Under the Moon, 1992, Rising Voices: A New Generation, 1993, City of Angles, 1995; screenwriter TV movie That Secret Sunday, 1988, Out on the Edge, 1990 (nominated for Emmy Best Screenplay 1990), other TV movies, pilots, 1975—. Recipient Nat. Headliner award Atlantic City Press Club, 1987, 88, Best Columnist award Nat. Soc. News Columnist, St. Louis, 1986, Pulitzer prize (shared Gold medal to L.A. Times) Columbia U., 1984, Nat. Ernie Pyle award, 1991; named Best Print Journalist of 1996 Soc. Profl. Journalists, L.A., 1997. Mem. PEN, Writers Guild Am. Office: Los Angeles Times Editorial Dept Times Mirror Sq Los Angeles CA 90053

MARTINEZ, ARTHUR C., retail company executive; b. N.Y.C., Sept. 25, 1939; s. Arthur F. and Agnes (Caulfield) M.; m. Elizabeth Rusch, July 30, 1966; children: Lauren, Gregory. BSME, Polytech. U., 1960; MBA, Harvard U., 1965; JD (hon.), U. Notre Dame, 1997. Dir. planning Internat. Paper Co., N.Y.C., 1967-69; asst. to pres. Talley Industries, Mesa, Ariz., 1969-70; dir. fin. RCA Corp., N.Y.C., 1970-73, v.p., 1973-80; sr. v.p., CFO Saks Fifth Ave., N.Y.C., 1980-84, exec. v.p., 1984-87, vice chmn., 1990-92; sr. v.p. and group chief exec. Batus Inc., Louisville, 1987-90; chmn., CEO Sears Merchandise Group, Chgo., 1992-95; chmn., ceo Sears, Roebuck and Co., 1995—; bd. dirs. Sears, Roebuck and Co., Sprout Venture Capital Group, N.Y.C., Ameritech, Defenders of Wildlife; dep. chmn. Fed. Res. Bank, Chgo.; trustee Polytechnic U., Northwestern U., chmn. Nat. Minority Supplier Devel. Coun., Inc. Bd. dirs. Defenders of Wildlife, 1992—; chmn. bd. trustees Polytech. U., 1990—, chmn. devel. com.; trustee Art Inst., Orch. Assn. Chgo. Symphony Orch.; adv. bd. Northwestern U. J.L. Kellog Grad. Sch. Mgmt. 1st lt. U.S. Army, 1961-63. Named CEO of Yr., Fin. World Mag., 1996. Mem. Nat. Retail Fedn. (bd. dirs.). Avocations: tennis, golf, gardening. Office: Sears Roebuck and Co 3333 Beverly Rd Hoffman Est IL 60192-3322

MARTINEZ, ARTURO, newspaper editor. Entertainment editor The Star-Ledger, Newark. Office: The Star-Ledger One Star Ledger Plz Newark NJ 07102-1200*

MARTINEZ, BUCK, baseball analyst; b. Nov. 7, 1948; married; 1 child. Student, Sacramento City Coll., Sacramento State U., Southwestern Mo. State U. Baseball player Kansas City, 1969-77, Milw., 1978-81, Toronto Blue Jays, 1981-86; color commentator World Series, Am. League Championship Telemedia Radio Network, 1982-88, color commentator All-Star Game, 1982-88, post-game analyst Major League Baseball coverage, 1982-88; analyst The Sports Network Toronto Blue Jays, 1986—; reporter The Manager's Show and Sports Desk TSN, 1986—, host The Boys of Winter and Knockout, 1986—; analyst Wednesday night nat. telecasts Major League Baseball ESPN, 1992—. Author: (seasons with Toronto Blue Jays) From Worst to First, 1985, The Last Out, 1986.

MARTINEZ, CONSTANTINO, professional baseball player; b. Tampa, Fla., Dec. 7, 1967. Baseball player Seattle Mariners, 1988-95, N.Y. Yankees, 1996—; mem. U.S. Olympic baseball team, 1988. Named 1st baseman Sporting News Coll. All-Am. team, 1988, Pacific Coast MVP, 1991. Achievements include member 1996 World Series Champions. Office: New York Yankees East 161 St and River Ave Bronx NY 10451

MARTINEZ, EDGAR, professional baseball player; b. N.Y.C., Jan. 2, 1963. Student, American Coll., Puerto Rico. Baseball player Seattle Mariners, 1982—. Named. to Am. League All-Star Team, 1992, 95, 96, Am. League Silver Slugger Team, 1992, 95. Am. League Batting Champion, 1992, 95. Office: Seattle Mariners PO Box 4100 Seattle WA 98104*

MARTINEZ, ELIZABETH, professional association administrator; b. Upland, Calif.. B in Latin Am. Studies, UCLA; MLS, U. So. Calif.; cert. in mgmt. and exec. mgmt., U. Calif., Irvine. County libr. Orange County Pub. Libr.; chief pub. svcs., regional adminstr. west and ctrl. regions L.A. County Libr.; lectr. Calif. State U. Sch. Libr. Sci., Fullerton; city libr. L.A. Pub. Libr.; exec. dir. ALA, Chgo., 1994—; del. to White House Conf. Libr. and Info. Svcs., 1979, 91. Named one of Women of Achievement, County of Orange, 1988, Hispanic Libr. of Yr., Hispanic Book Distbrs., 1990; recipient Women's Alert award Orange County, 1990, Freedom to Write award Pen West USA, 1993. Office: ALA 50 Huron St Chicago IL 60611

MARTINEZ, ELUID, government official. Degree, N.Mex. State U. Lic. profl. engr., land surveyor. With N.Mex. Engrs. Office, 1973-96, state engr., sec. N.Mex. Interstate Coun. on Water Policy; commr. Bur. Reclamation, Washington, 1996—. Office: Bur of Reclamation 1849 C St NW Washington DC 20240-0001

MARTINEZ, GAYLE FRANCES, protective services official; b. Joplin, Mo., June 25, 1954; d. Jackie Ray Jackson and Shirley Joann (Williams) Jackson Hulett; m. Randy Louis Brown (div. Sept. 1974); 1 child, Randy Louis Brown II; m. Alan John Dwinells, July 15, 1975 (div. Sept. 1977); children: Christopher Ray Dwinells. AA, Longview Coll., 1979; indsl. drafting cert., Marin County Adult Sch., 1984; BA, Sacramento State Coll., 1989. Cert. peace officer. Computer operator JC Penney, Kans., 1977-81; air cargo specialist USAF, 1980-92; ins. agent Prudential, Richmond, Calif., 1983-85; peace officer Calif. State Prison, Vacaville, 1985—; trainer Calif. Dept. Corrections, Vacaville, 1989—. Author: Whispers in the Wind. Mem. Calif. Correctional Peace Officers Assn. Democrat. Assembly of God. Avocations: sewing, interior decorating, bowling, camping, piano. Home: 599 Greenwood Dr Vacaville CA 95687-6215

MARTINEZ, GUSTAVE See **SOLOMONS, GUS, JR.**

MARTINEZ, HERMINIA S., economist, banker; b. Havana, Cuba; came to U.S., 1960, naturalized, 1972; d. Carlos and Amelia (Santana) Martinez Sanchez; m. Mario Aguilar, 1982; children: Mario Aguilar, Carlos Aguilar; BA in Econs. cum laude, Am. U., 1965; MS in Fgn. Svc. (Univ. fellow), MS in Econs., Georgetown U., 1967, PhD in Econs., 1969; postgrad. Nat. U. Mex. Instr. econs. George Mason Coll., U. Va., Fairfax, 1967-68; researcher World Bank, 1967-69, indsl. economist, industrialization div., 1969-71, loan officer, Central Am., 1971-79, loan officer, economist, Mex., 1973-74, Venezuela and Ecuador, 1973-77, sr. loan officer in charge of Panama and Dominican Republic, Washington, 1977-81, sr. loan officer for Middle East and North Africa, 1981-84, sr. loan officer for Western Africa region, 1985-87, sr. economist Africa Region, 1988-91, prin. ops. officer Africa region, 1991—. Mid-Career fellow Princeton U., 1988-89. Mem. Am. Econ. Assn., Soc. Internat. Devel., Brookings Inst. Latin Am. Study Group. Roman Catholic. Contbg. author: The Economic Growth of Colombia: Problems and Prospects, 1973, Central American Financial Integration, 1975. Home: 5145 Yuma St NW Washington DC 20016-4336 Office: World Bank 1818 H St NW Washington DC 20433-0001

MARTINEZ, MARIA DOLORES, pediatrician; b. Cifuentes, Cuba, Mar. 16, 1959; d. Demetrio and Alba Silvia (Perez) M.; m. James David Marple, Apr. 25, 1992. MD, U. Navarra, Pamplona, Spain, 1984. Med. diplomate. Resident in pediatrics Moses Cone Hosp., Greensboro, N.C., 1986-89; pvt. practice Charlotte, N.C., 1989-93, Mooresville, N.C., 1993-96; pediat. pulmonary fellow Univ. Med. Hosp., Tucson. Mem. AMA, Am. Acad. Pediatrics, N.C. Med. Soc., Mecklenburg County Med. Soc. Republican. Roman Catholic. Avocations: horseback riding, travel. Office: Univ Med Hosp 1501 Campbell Ave Tucson AZ 85741

MARTINEZ, MATTHEW GILBERT, congressman; b. Walsenburg, Colo., Feb. 14, 1929; children: Matthew, Diane, Susan, Michael, Carol Ann. Cert of competence, Los Angeles Trade Tech. Sch., 1959. Small businessman and bldg. contractor; mem. 97th-105th Congresses from 30th (now 31st) Calif. dist., 1982—; mem. edn. and labor com., fgn. affairs com. Mem. Monterey Park Planning Commn., 1971-74; mayor City of Monterey Park, 1974-75; mem. Monterey Park City Council, 1974-80, Calif. State Assembly, 1980-82; bd. dirs. San Gabriel Valley YMCA. Served with USMC, 1947-50. Mem. Congl. Hispanic Caucus, Hispanic Am. Democrats, Nat. Assn. Latino Elected and Apptd. Ofcls., Communications Workers Am., VFW, Am. Legion, Latin Bus. Assn., Monterey Park C. of C., Navy League (dir.).

Democrat. Lodge: Rotary. Office: US Ho of Reps 2234 Rayburn Bldg Ofc Washington DC 20515-3306*

MARTINEZ, PATRICIA ANN, middle school educator, administrator; b. Phoenix, Oct. 12, 1963; d. Jack Leon and Eleanor Jean (Gripman) McMullen; m. Gerald Marc Martinez, Aug. 11, 1984. BA, Calif. State U., 1986, MA magna cum laude, 1994. Cert. tchr. Calif. Tchr. St. Athanasius Elem. Sch., Long Beach, Calif., 1987-93; vice prin. St. Athanasius Elem. Sch., Long Beach, 1990-93; lang. arts specialist Washington Mid. Schs., Long Beach, 1993-96, spl. edn. tchr., 1996-97, U.S. history tchr., 1997—; mentor tchr. St. Athanasius Elem. Sch., Long Beach, 1988-90, mem. restructuring team, family leader Site-Based Decision Making Com. Mem. ACLU, Greenpeace, 1988—. Mem. ASCD, NEA, AAUW, Nat. Cath. Edn. Assn., Internat. Reading Assn., Internat. Platform Assn., Tchrs. Assn. Long Beach, Calif. Tchrs. Assn., Kappa Delta Pi, Phi Kappa Phi. Democrat. Lutheran. Avocations: volleyball, weight-lifting, Stephen King books, church choir, skiing. Home: 3601 Gardenia Ave Long Beach CA 90807-4303 Office: Washington Mid Sch 1450 Cedar Ave Long Beach CA 90813-1705

MARTINEZ, PEDRO JAIME, professional baseball player; b. Manoquayabo, Dominican Republic, July 25, 1971. With L.A. Dodgers, 1992-93; pitcher Montreal Expos, 1994—. Named Minor League Player Sporting News, 1991. Office: Montreal Expos, 4549 Pierre de Coubertin, Montreal, PQ Canada H1V 3N7*

MARTINEZ, RAMON JAIME, professional baseball player; b. Santo Domingo, Dominican Rep., Mar. 22, 1968. Grad. high sch., Dominican Rep. Pitcher L.A. Dodgers, 1988—. Achievements include mem. Dominican Rep. Olympic Baseball Team, 1988. Office: LA Dodgers 1000 Elysian Park Ave Los Angeles CA 90012-1112*

MARTINEZ, RAUL L., mayor, publisher; b. Santiago, Oriente, Cuba, Mar. 6, 1949; came to U.S., 1960; s. Chin and Aida Martinez; m. Angela Callava, Jan. 10, 1970; children—Aida, Raul. AA, Miami Dade Coll.; BS in Criminal Justice, Fla. Internat. U., Miami. Pub., founder El Sol de Hialeah, Fla., 1969—; pres. Martex Realty, Fla., 1975—; mem. city council City of Hialeah, 1977-81, mayor, 1981—; Mem. Dem. Policy Commn.'s Roundtable on Defense and Fgn. Policy, State Comprehensive Plan Com., Dade Clean Inc.; past vice chmn. Beacon Council; chmn. Dade County Council Mayors, So. Fla. Employment and Tng. Consortium, Hialeah Dade Devel. Inc.; bd. dirs. Hialeah Pk. racecourse; mem. franchise and environ. rev. com. High Speed Rail, 1987; mem. Gov.'s Commn. on Statewide Prosecution Function, 1984-85, Fla. State Commn. on Hispanic Affairs, 1979-82;pres. Fla. League of Cities. Mem. Dade County Assn. Chiefs Police, Little Havana Nutrition and Activities Ctr., State Fla. Planning Commn., United Way of Dade County (community devel. com.), Little Havana Activity Ctrs. Commn., St. John Home Health Care Inc.; adv. bd. Barry U.; hon. adviser Miami Dade Community Coll., North Campus-Hialeah Ctr. Fedn. Hispanic Students; chmn. So. Mcpl. Conf.; bd. dirs. Nat. League of Cities; former pres. Fla. League of Cities. Recipient Legion of Honor award, 1977, Citizen Involvement award Crime Commn. of Greater Miami, 1977, Over the Top award Hialeah-Miami Springs YMCA, 1979, Pub. Adminstr. of Yr. award South Fla. chpt. Am. Soc. Pub. Adminstrn., 1984. Mem. U.S. Conf. of Mayors, Hialeah-Miami Springs-N.W. Dade Area C. of C., Nat. League Cities, Fla. League Cities (pres.), Dade County League (past. pres.), Hialeah Latin C. of C., Kiwanis. Lodge: Kiwanis. Office: City of Hialeah 501 Palm Ave Hialeah FL 33010-4719*

MARTINEZ, RICARDO, federal agency administrator; m. Robin Rosser. MD, La. State U. Sch. Medicine, 1980. Intern Lafayette (La.) Charity Hosp., 1980-81; resident Charity Hosp., New Orleans, 1983-85; vis. fellow accident rsch. unit Ctr. Automotive Engring./U. Birmingham, U.K., 1989; adminstr. Nat. Hwy. Traffic Safety Adminstrn, Washington; assoc. prof. emergency medicine Emory U. Sch. Medicine, Atlanta, assoc. dir. Ctr. for Injury Control. Home: 1218 Dartmouth Rd Alexandria VA 22314

MARTINEZ, ROMAN, IV, financial executive; b. Santiago, Cuba, Dec. 29, 1947; came to U.S., 1960, naturalized, 1971; s. Roman and Virginia G. (Gomez) M.; B.S., Boston Coll., 1969; MBA, U. Pa., 1971; m. Helena Hackley, Dec. 20, 1974; children—Roman, Helena Catalina. Asso., Kuhn Loeb & Co., N.Y.C., 1971-73, v.p., 1974-77; corp. v.p. Lehman Bros. Kuhn Loeb Inc., N.Y.C., 1977, mng. dir., 1978-84; mng. dir. Lehman Bros. (formerly Shearson Lehman Bros. Inc.), N.Y.C., 1984—; mem. bd. trustees Presbyn. Hosp. city of N.Y.; bd. dir. Internat. Rescue com.; chmn. Internat. Adv. Coun., Am. Soc. Republican. Roman Catholic. Clubs: Racquet and Tennis, Links, River, Piping Rock. Home: 555 Park Ave New York NY 10021-8166 Office: Lehman Bros 3 World Fin Ctr New York NY 10285

MARTINEZ, WALTER BALDOMERO, architect; b. Havana, Cuba, Sept. 21, 1937; came to U.S., 1961; s. Baldomerò and Maria J. Amparo (Rodriguez) M.; m. Olga Justa Sardina, July 23, 1961; children: Teresita Maria, Gabriel Jose. Cert. in civil constrn., Arts and Craft Vocat. Sch., Havana, 1957; student, U. Havana, 1958-60; student Sch. Architecture, U. Miami, 1963-64, cert. fallout shelter analyst, 1970. Registered architect, Fla.; cert. gen. contractor, Fla. Job capt. Tony Sherman Architect, Miami, Fla., 1961-63; project mgr. Ken Miller Architect, Miami, 1968-69; designer, project mgr. Russell-Melton & Assocs., Miami, 1969-70; head archtl. dept. Sanders & Thomas, Miami, 1971-72; assoc. Russell-Wooster & Assoc., Miami, 1973-77; prin. Russell-Martinez & Holt, Miami, 1977-84; prin., pres. The Russell Partnership, Miami, 1985—; uniform bldg. code insp., 1991—; insp. So. Bldg. Code Cong. Internat. Inc., 1997. Contbr. articles to Constrn. mag. Bd. dirs. Biscayne Nature Ctr., Miami, 1982—; vice chmn. Latin Quarters Rev. Bd., Miami, 1989, 95. Fellow AIA (nat. chmn. minority resources com. 1985, pres. Miami chpt. 1982, Silver medal 1981); mem. Nat. Assn. Cuban Archs. (bd. dirs. Miami chpt. 1986-87, Gold medal 1984), Latin Builders Assn., Fla. Bd. Archs. (chmn. 1991), NCARB, Greater Miami C. of C. (Hispanic affairs com. 1988-90, chmn. affordable housing com. 1989), Nat. Arch. Accrediting Bd., Inc. (accreditation team mem. 1992-95). Republican. Roman Catholic. Avocations: boating, photography. Home: 4130 Malaga Ave Coconut Grove FL 33133 Office: Russell Partnership Inc 2733 SW 3rd Ave Miami FL 33129-2335

MARTINEZ-CARRION, MARINO, biochemist, educator; b. Felix, Almeria, Spain, Dec. 2, 1936; came to U.S., 1957; naturalized, 1961.; s. Juan Martinez and Maria Carrion; m. Ana J. Iriarte, Apr. 20, 1987; children: Victoria, Marino Juan. BA, U. Calif, Berkeley, 1959, MA, 1961, PhD, 1964. NIH postdoctoral fellow U. Rome, 1964-65; asst. prof. U. Notre Dame, Ind., 1965-68, 1968-74, prof., 1974-77; chmn. Va. Commonwealth U., Richmond, 1977-86; dean Sch. Biol. Sci. U. Mo., Kansas City, 1986—; dir. Ctr. for Innovative Tech. Inst. Biotech., Richmond, 1984-86; chmn. biophys. chemistry study sect. NIH, Washington, 1977-82; mem. cell neurobiol. panel NSF, Washington, 1985-89; panelist Howard Hughes Med. Inst. postdoctoral fellowships, 1995—. Contbr. numerous articles on biochem. subjects to profl. jours.; mem. Jour. Protein Chemistry; mem. editorial bd. Archives Biochemistry and Biophysics, Jour. Biol. Chemistry. Rsch. grantee NIH, 1965—, NSF, 1974—, Am. Heart Assn., 1974-77, career devel. grantee NIH, 1972-77. Fellow N.Y. Acad. Scis.; mem. Am. Chem. Soc., Am. Soc. Biochemistry and Molecular Biology, Pan Am. Assn. Biochem. and Molecular Biology (treas. 1987-90, vice chmn. 1990-93, chmn. 1993—), Internat. Soc. Neurochemistry, Biophys. Soc. Democrat. Roman Catholic. Office: U Mo Sch Biol Scis Kansas City MO 64110

MARTINEZ DE LA ESCALERA, GONZALO, neuroendocrinologist; b. Montevideo, Uruguay, Jan. 1, 1956; arrived in Mex., 1969; s. Fernando and Raquel (Lorenzo) M.; m. Carmen Clapp, June 19, 1980; children: Daniela, Lucia. BS, Met. U. Mex., 1978; PhD, Nat. U. Mex., 1984. Rsch. asst. Biomed. Rsch. Inst., Mex., 1977-81, asst. prof., 1982-85, assoc. prof., 1988-90, prof., 1991-94; prof. Neurobiology Ctr., Mex., 1994—; vis. scientist U. Calif., San Francisco, 1989, 90, 91-92, 93. Editor: Neuroendocrine Communication: Molecular and Cellular Bases, 1993; editl. bd. Neuroendocrinology, 1994—; contbr. articles to profl. jours. Recipient Syntex Found. award, 1995, Sci. Rsch. Acad. award, 1995, Young Scientist award Nat. U. Mex., 1995; fellow U. Calif., San Francisco, 1985-88, Andrew William Mellon Found. fellow, N.Y., 1985, Rockefeller Found. fellow, N.Y., 1988, 92, John Simon Guggenheim Meml. Found. fellow, N.Y., 1993. Mem. The Endocrine Soc., Soc. Neurosci., Internat. Soc. Neuroendocrinology. Home: Ingenio de Zacatepec 68, 14330 Mexico City Mexico Office: Ciudad U Neurobiology Ctr, PO Box 70228, 04510 Mexico City Mexico

MARTINEZ-LÓPEZ, ENRIQUE, Spanish educator; b. Granada, Spain, Aug. 18, 1928; came to the U.S., 1959, naturalized 1967; s. Francisco and Amparo (Lopez Mesa) M.; m. Maria Teresa Leal, Feb. 10, 1954 (div. 1965); children: Maria Teresa, Maria Isabel, Enrique; m. Natalie Louise Campbell, Nov. 10, 1966. BA, U. Granada, 1947; MA in Romance Philology, U. Madrid, 1952, PhD, 1964. Instr. SPanish and Hispanic Lit. U. da Paraiba, João Pessoa, Brazil, 1954-56, U. do Recife, Brazil, 1956-59; asst. prof. Spanish U. Houston, 1959-63; asst. prof. Spanish U. Calif., Santa Barbara, 1963-66, assoc. prof., 1966-72, chmn. dept. Spanish and Portuguese, 1970-74, prof., 1972—; vis. lectr. U. Wis., Madison, 1966, 67; fellow, rschr. Cervantes INst. Consejo Superior de Investigaciones Cientificas, Madrid, 1952-54; conf. organizer III Ann. So. Calif. Cervantes Symposium, Santa Barbara, 1992. Author: Sor Juana Ines de la Cruz en Portugal, 1968, Granada, Paraiso Cerrado, 1971, 89, La Variacion en el Corrido Mexicano, 1979, El Rival de Garcilaso, 1981, Mezclar Berzas con Capachos, 1992, Tablero de Ajedrez: Imagenes del Negro Heroico, 1995, 97; editor: Camoniana Californiana, 1985; editor: Ency. Britannica Editores, 1962-64. Chair intercultural com. YWCA, Houston, 1960-62; chair com. on culture Alianza Cultural Mexicana, Santa Barbara, 1973-75. 2d lt. Spanish Army, 1953-54. Recipient award Cruz de Caballero, Orden del Merito Civil Govt. of Spain, 1955; grantee Am. Philos. Soc. Inst. Humanities, 1966, 71, 74. Mem. MLA, Am. Assn. Tchrs. Spanish and Portuguese, Internat. Assn. Hispanists, Internat. Inst. Iberoam. Lit., Am. Soc. Sephardic Studies, Internat. Assn. Golden Age Studies, Inst. Brasileiro de Cultura Hispanica (pres. 1956-58). Democrat. Roman Catholic. Home: 503 Miramonte Dr Santa Barbara CA 93109-1400 Office: U Calif Dept Spanish and Portuguese Santa Barbara CA 93106-4150

MARTINEZ-MALDONADO, MANUEL, medical service administrator, physician; b. Yauco, P.R., Aug. 25, 1937; s. Manuel Martinez and Josefa Maldonado; m. Nivia Elena Rivera, Dec. 18, 1959; children: Manuel, David, Ricardo, Pablo. BS, U. P.R., 1957; MD, Temple U., 1961. Diplomate Am. Bd. Internal Medicine (assoc. mem. nephrology com. 1982-86), Am. Bd. Nephrology. Intern St. Charles Hosp., Toledo, 1961-62; resident VA Hosp., San Juan, 1962-65, chief resident, 1964-65; instr. U. Tex. Southwestern Med. Sch., Dallas, 1967-68; asst. prof. medicine Baylor Coll. Medicine, Houston, 1968-71, assoc. prof. medicine, 1971-73, prof. medicine, dir. renal sect., 1973; prof. medicine U. P.R. Sch. Medicine, 1973-90, prof. physiology, 1974-90; prof. medicine U. Caribbean, Bayamon, P.R., 1980-90; chief med. services VA Hosp., San Juan, 1973-90, dir. renal metabolic lab, 1973-90; prof., vice chmn. dept. medicine Emory U. Sch. Medicine, 1990—; chief med. svcs. and clin. affairs Atlanta VA Med. Ctr.; mem. nat. adv. bd. gen. medicine, B study sect. Nat. Inst. Arthritis, Metabolism and Digestive Diseases NIH; mem. bd. sci. counselors, sci. advisors com. Nat. Heart, Lung and Blood Inst., Nat. Insts. Health. Author: La Voz Sostenida, 1984, Palm Beach Blues, 1986, Por Amor al Arte, 1989; film critic for El Reportero, 1983-86, El Mundo, 1987-90; contbr. over 200 med. rsch. articles to sci. jours.; editor or co-editor of 11 books on renal phamacology, nephrology, physiology; mem. editl. bd. U. P.R. Press, numerous profl. jours.; editor-in-chief Am. Jour. of Med. Scis., 1994—. Mem. health com. Poplar Dem. Com., P.R., 1982-84; mem. Com. 500th Anniversary of Discovery Am., P.R., 1987-92; mem. com. on human rights Inst. of Medicine, Washington, 1987-92. Recipient Lederle Internat. award, 1966-67, Faculty Scholar award Macy Faculty, 1979-80, Grand Mobil prize medicine Mobil Oil Corp., 1981, Disting. Alumnus award Temple Med. Sch., 1988, Presdl. award Nat. Kidney Found, 1988, Donald W. Seldin medal 1994, Disting. Physician award P.R. Hosps. Assn., 1988, Orden del Cafetal award Municipality of Yauco, 1989; named one of Outstanding Med (medicine) P.R. C. of C., 1976, Fed. Supr. Employee of Yr., Fed. Execs. Assn., P.R., 1977. Fellow ACP, AAAS, Coun. for High Blood Pressure Rsch., Am. Heart Assn. (hypertension rsch. coun.; mem. Inst. Medicine NAS, Am. Soc. Nephrology (legis. liaison com., chmn. audit com. 1988), So. Soc. Clin. Investigation (sec.-treas. 1983-85, pres. 1985-86, Founders medal 1990), Am. Soc. for Clin. Investigation, Nat. Kidney Found. (chmn. sci. adv. bd. 1987-89, Donald W. Seldin medal, chmn. pub. policy com. 1992-94, pub. svc. medal), L.Am. Soc. Nephrology (v.p. 1987-91, pres. elect 1991-94, pres. 1994-96), Inter-Am. Soc. Hypertension Assn. (bd. govs., chmn. 8th Sci. Congress 1989), U.S. Pharmacopeial Convention Cardio Renal Drugs Com., Assn. Am. Physicians, Inst. Medicine, Consortium of Southeastern Hypertension Ctrs. (bd. dirs.), Alpha Omega Alpha. Achievements include contributions in field of kidney physiology and pathophysiology; contributions in treatment of clinical disturbances of blood composition, clinical use of diuretics, mechanisms of the development of hypertension. Office: VA Med Ctr Med Svc 1670 Clairmont Rd Decatur GA 30033-4004

MARTINEZ-O'FERRALL, JOSÉ A., public health physician, retired air force officer; b. San Juan, P.R., Oct. 30, 1936; s. Jose I. Martinez and Basilia O'Ferrall; m. Ana C. Carrillo, Dec. 27, 1964; children: Ana Celeste, Rebeca Beatriz, Jose Nicolas. BS in Math., U. P.R., 1955, MD, 1959; MPH, U. Calif., Berkeley, 1967; grad., Flight Surgeon Sch., Brooks AFB, Tex., 1960, Sch. Aerospace Medicine, Brooks AFB, Tex., 1969, Air War Coll., Maxwell AFB, Ala., 1973. lectr., presenter in field. Intern Mercy Hosp., Buffalo, 1960; commd. capt. USAF, 1960, advanced through grades to col., 1975; chief of aviation medicine Ben Guerir Air Base, Morocco, 1960-61; chief of profl. svcs. and aviation medicine Zaragoza Air Base, Spain, 1961-64; chief of aerospace medicine Davis-Monthan AFB, Tucson, 1964-66; amb. health clinic med. dir. Bien Hoa, Vietnam, 1969-70; resident in preventive and aerospace medicine Brooks AFB, San Antonio, 1967-69, Scott AFB, Belleville, Ill., 1968-69; hosp. comdr., med. dir. Altus AFB, Altus, Okla., 1970-72; command surgeon, dir. base med. svcs. USAF So. Command, Albrook AFB, Canal Zone, 1973-76; team chief USAF Med. Inspection, Norton AFB, Calif., 1976-78; comdr., med. dir. USAF Med. Ctr., Clark Air Base, The Philippines, 1978-80; dep. surgeon USAF Air Tng. Command, Randolph AFB, Tex., 1980-81; vice comdr. Wilford Hall USAF Med. Ctr., Lackland AFB, Tex., 1981-85; hosp. comdr., med. dir. Laughlin AFB, Del Rio, Tex., 1985-88; med. cons. USAF Mit. Pers. Ctr., Randolph AFB, 1988-90; ret., 1990; preventive medicine cons. Al-Hada Armed Forces Hosp., Taif, Saudi Arabia, 1990-95; prev. medicine cons. Al-Hada Armed Forces Hosp., Taif, Saudi Arabia, 1991-95; apptd. by USAF Surgeon Gen. to represent U.S. Medicine in the Air Forces of Ams., Ecuador, Dominican Republic, Bolivia, Chile, Argentina and Colombia; lectr. in field. Contbr. numerous articles to med. jours. Decorated Legion of Merit with oak leaf cluster, Bronze Star with V for valor, Bronze Star, Air Medal with oak leaf cluster, Meritorious Svc. medal, Air Force Commendation medal; Gallantry Cross with palm (Vietnam); Republic of Vietnam Campaign medal; Vietnamese Honor medal; Vietnam Svc. medal; recipient George Washington medal Freedom Found., 1971, 73; scholar U. P.R., 1952-59; fellow NIH, summer 1956. Fellow Am. Coll. Preventive Medicine (assoc.), Aerospace Med. Assn. (assoc.); mem. AMA, Assn. Mil. Surgeons U.S., Soc. Hosp. Epidemiology Am., U.S.-Mex. Border Health Assn., Soc. USAF Flight Surgeons, Air Force Assn., Fed. Med. Exec. Inst. (life), Soc. Med. Grads. U. P.R. Sch. Medicine, Phi Chi Med. Fraternity. Home: 10602 Benchmark Way San Antonio TX 78213-1945

MARTINEZ-PONS, MANUEL, psychology educator; b. Dominican Republic, Apr. 19, 1940; s. Manuel and Alsacia (Gorsd) Martinez. BGS, U. Nebr., 1973, PhD, 1977, MS, 1975; PhD, CUNY, 1988. Contbr. articles to profl. jours. Home: 453 Beach 138th St Belle Harbor NY 11694 Office: Brooklyn Coll Sch Of Edn Brooklyn NY 11210

MARTÍNEZ-SOLANAS, GERARDO ENRIQUE, reporting service reviser, writer; b. La Habana, Cuba, July 21, 1940; came to U.S., 1961; s. Gerardo Martínez-Alvarez and Carolina del Carmen (Solanas) Martinez; m. Estela Riquelme, July 24, 1966 (div. Dec. 1979); children: Carlos Enrique, Enrique Alejandro; m. Silvia Raquel Yankelevich, July 31, 1981. BA in Polit. Sci., CUNY, 1981, MA in Econ., 1983. Reference clk. UN, N.Y.C., 1961-69, asst. libr., 1969-75, office supr., 1975-79, verbatim reporter, 1979-89, reviser, 1989-94, chief reviser, 1994—; mem. spl. meeting mission UN Gen. Assembly, Geneva, 1989; chef d'equip mission outer space com. UN, Vienna, 1994. Author: (short stories) Two Tales and Two Legends, 1963, Omega, 1997, Democracy in Action, 1997. Del. Directorio del Partido Demócrata Cristiano de Cuba, Miami, Fla., 1991, Caracas, Venezuela, 1993. Recipient 1st prize Círculo de Escritores y Poetas Iberoamericanos de N.Y., 1967, 1st prize U.S. Chess Fedn., 1972. Mem. U.S. Power Squadrons, Am. Legion (vice comdr. Post 33 1987-88). Roman Catholic. Avocations: chess (Atlantic Amateur Chess Championship 1972), boating, numismatics. Home: The Landings 5530 NE 26th Ave Ft Lauderdale FL 33308

MARTINEZ-TABONE, RAQUEL, school psychologist supervisor; b. Santurce, P.R., Mar. 28, 1944; d. Santos and Amelia (Guzman) Gonzalez; m. Fernando Martinez, Oct. 13, 1962 (div. Mar. 1968); 1 child, Stuart Andrew; m. Francis J. Tabone, July 9, 1980; children: Francis N., Christopher M.; grandchildren (wards): Amanda Marie Martinez, Andrea Amelia Martinez. BA, Lehman Coll., 1973, MS, 1977; PD, Fordham U., 1985; MA, Yeshiva U., 1988; MEd, Bank Street Coll., 1990; PhD, Yeshiva U., 1994. Cert. elem. tchr., sch. psychologist, supr. and sch. adminstr., N.Y.; ordained interfaith minister, 1990. Elem. sch. tchr. N.Y.C. Bd. Edn., Bronx, 1973-84, sch. psychologist, com. on spl. edn., 1985-94, supr. sch. psychologists, 1994—; adj. prof. NYU, 1992-94. Mem. Nat. Assn. Sch Psychologists (cert.), Coun. Exceptional Children, Orthopsychiat. Assn. Home: 17 Ritchie Dr Yonkers NY 10705-2543 Office: NYC Bd Edn 1887 Bathgate Ave Bronx NY 10457-6216

MARTING, MICHAEL G., lawyer; b. Cleve., Nov. 5, 1948. BA summa cum laude, Yale U., 1971, JD, 1974. Bar: Ohio 1974. Assoc. Jones, Day, Reavis & Pogue, Cleve., 1974-83, ptnr., 1984—. Mem. ABA, Union Club, Cleve. Racquet Club, Kirtland Country Club, Tavern Club (treas., sec., trustee local chpt. 1985-88). Avocations: fly fishing, birdshooting, big game hunting, squash, golf. Office: Jones Day Reavis & Pogue N Point 901 Lakeside Ave E Cleveland OH 44114-1116

MARTINI, RICHARD K., theatrical producer; b. Bergenfield, N.J., Mar. 11, 1952; s. John F. and June L. (Fenton) M.; m. Susan C. Weaving, Aug. 1, 1981. BA, St. Francis Coll., Loretto, Pa., 1974; MEd, U. S.C., 1975. V.p. Am. Theatre Prodns., N.Y.C., 1975-81; pres. Edgewood Orgn., N.Y.C., 1981-86; pres., owner KL Mgmt., N.Y.C., 1986—; owner, operator Martini Entertainment, Inc., N.Y.C., 1991—. Mem. League of Am. Theatres and Producers. Home: 201 E 37th St New York NY 10016-3159 Office: Martini Entertainment Co 1501 Broadway Ste 1401 New York NY 10036-5601

MARTINI, ROBERT EDWARD, wholesale pharmaceutical and medical supplies company executive; b. Hackensack, N.J., 1932. BS, Ohio State U., 1954. With Bergen Brunswig Corp., Orange, Calif., 1956-92, v.p., 1962-69, exec. v.p., 1969-81, pres., 1981-92, CEO, 1990-97; chmn. Bergen Brunswig Corp., Orange, 1992—; chmn. exec. com. Bergen Brunswig Corp. Capt. USAF, 1954.

MARTINI, WILLIAM J., former congressman; b. Passaic, N.J.; m. Gloria Martini; children: William Jr., Marissa. Degree, Villanova U., 1968; JD, Rutgers U., 1972. Elected mem. City Coun. of Clifton, N.J., Passaic County Bd. Chosen Freeholders, U.S. House of Reps., 1994-96. Pres. Nicholas Martini Found.; trustee United Way of Passaic County, Ctr. Italian Am. Culture, Passaic Valley Coun. Boy Scouts of Am. Office: 1064 Pompton Ave Cedar Grove NJ 07009*

MARTINO, DONALD JAMES, composer, educator; b. Plainfield, N.J., May 16, 1931; s. James Edward and Alma Ida (Renz) M.; m. Mari Rice, Sept. 5, 1953 (div. June 1968); 1 child, Anna Maria; m. Lora Harvey, June 5, 1969; 1 child, Christopher James. B.Mus., Syracuse U., 1952; M.F.A., Princeton, 1954; MA (hon), Harvard U., 1983. Instr. music Princeton, 1957-59; asst. prof. theory music Yale, 1959-66, assoc. prof., 1966-69; chmn. dept. composition New Eng. Conservatory Music, Boston, 1969-80; Irving Fine prof. music Brandeis U., 1980-82; prof. music Harvard U., 1983—, Walter Bigelow Rosen prof. music, 1989-93; Walter Bigelow Rosen prof. emeritus, 1993—; tchr. composition and theory Yale Summer Sch. of Music and Art, summers 1960-63; tchr. composition Berkshire Music Ctr., summers, 1965-67, 69; composer in residence Berkshire Music Ctr., 1973; vis. lectr. Harvard U., 1971; composer in residence Composers' Conf., Johnson, Vt., summer 1979, May in Miami, 1994; Maurice Abravanel vis. disting. composer U. Utah, 1994, Mary Duke Biddle disting. composer Duke U., 1995; composer-in-residence Festival Internat. de Musica de Morelia, Mex., 1996, Composers' Conf., Wellesley, Mass., 1997; master artist-in-residence Atlantic Ctr. for the Arts, 1997. Composer: Separate Songs, 1951; for high voice and piano, Sonata for Clarinet and Piano, 1951, The Bad Child's Book of Beasts, 1952, Suite of Variations on Medieval Melodies, 1952; cello solo, sonata for Violin and Piano, A Set for Clarinet, 1954, Quodlibets for Flute, 1954, Three Songs, 1955, Portraits; a secular cantata for chorus, soloists and orch., 1955, Sette Canoni Enigmatici, 1956, Contemplations for Orch. (commd. by Paderewski Fund), 1956, 24 Tin Pan Alley Tunes, 1956, Quartet for Clarinet and Strings, 1957, After Lennie, 1957, Piano Fantasy, 1958, Trio for violin, clarinet and piano, 1959, Cinque Frammenti, 1961, Two Rilke Songs, 1961, Fantasy-Variations for violin, 1962, Concerto for Wind Quintet (commd. by Fromm Found. and Berkshire Music Center), 1964, Parisonatina Al'Dodecafonia; for cello solo, 1964, Concerto for Piano and Orch. (commd. by New Haven Symphony), 1965, B, a, b, b, it, t; for clarinet, 1966, Strata; for bass clarinet, 1966, Mosaic for grand orch. (commd. by U. Chgo.), 1967, Pianississimo; sonata for piano, 1970, Seven Pious Pieces, 1971, Concerto for Violoncello and Orch., 1972, Augenmusik, 1972, Notturno, 1973 (Naumburg Chamber Music award commn., Pulitzer prize in music 1974), Paradiso Choruses for Chorus, Soloists, Orch. and Tape, 1974 (Paderewski Fund commn., Classical Critics citation Record World mag. 1976), Ritorno for Orch. (Plainfield Symphony commn.), 1975, Triple Concerto for Clarinet, Bass Clarinet and Contrabass Clarinet with Chamber Ensemble (N.Y. State Council on Arts and Andrew W. Mellon Found. commn.), 1977, Impromptu for Roger; piano solo, 1977, Quodlibets II; flute solo, 1980, Fantasies and Impromptus, piano solo (Koussevitzky Found. commn.), 1981, Divertisements for Youth Orch. (Groton, Mass. Arts Ctr. Commn.), 1981, Suite in Old Form, piano solo, 1982, String Quartet (Elizabeth Sprague Coolidge Commn., winner 1st prize Kennedy Ctr. Friedheim Awards 1985), 1983, Canzone e Tarantella, clarinet and cello, 1984, The White Island, for chorus and chamber orchestra (Boston Symphony Centennial Commn.), 1985, Concerto for Alto Saxophone and Chamber Orch. (Nat. Endowment Consortium commn.), 1987, From the Other Side, Divertimento for Flute, Cello, Percussion and Piano (commd. by Flederman New Music Ensemble for the Australian Bicentennial, 1988), 12 Preludes (commd. Meet the Composer-Readers Digest), 1990, 15, 5, '92 AB for Carinet solo, 1992, Three Sad Songs, 1993, Viola and Piano (Elizabeth Sprague Coolidge commn.), Concerto for Violin and Orchestra (Nat. Endowment Commn.), 1997; numerous others; contbr. articles to profl. jours. Recipient BMI Student Composer awards, 1952, 53; Bonsall fellow, 1953-54; Kosciuszko scholar, 1953-54; Nat. Fedn. Music Clubs award, 1953; Kate Neal Kinley fellow U. Ill., 1954-55; Fulbright grantee Florence, Italy, 1954-56; Pacifica Found. award, 1961; Creative Arts citation Brandeis U., 1963; Morse Acad. fellow, 1965; Nat. Inst. Arts and Letters grantee, 1967; Guggenheim fellow, 1967-68, 73-74, 82-83; Nat. Endowment on Arts grantee, 1973, 76, 79, 89; Mass. Council on Arts grantee, 1973, 79, 89; Pulitzer prize in music, 1974; recipient Kennedy Ctr. Friedheim Awards 1st prize, 1985, Mark M. Horblit award Boston Symphony Orch., 1987, Paul Revere award for mus. autography Music Publ. Assn., 1990, 91, 92. Mem. AAAS, AAAL, Coll. Music Soc., Am. Composers Alliance, Broadcast Music Inc., Am. Music Ctr., Internat. Soc. Contemporary Music (a founder New Haven chpt. 1964, dir. U.S. sect. 1961-64), Am. Soc. U. Composers (founding mem., exec. com. 1966-66, trustee 1965—), Internat. Clarinet Soc. (bd. dirs.). Office: Harvard U Dept Music Cambridge MA 02138

MARTINO, FRANK DOMINIC, union executive; b. Albany, N.Y., Apr. 9, 1919; s. Benedetto and Rosina (Esposita) M.; m. Phyllis E. Higgins, June 15, 1963; children—Michael M., Lisa R. Student, Rutgers U., Cornell U., Oxford U. Timekeeper N.Y.C. R.R., 1937-41; chem. operator Sterling Drug Co., 1946-56; internat. rep. Internat. Chem. Workers Union, Akron, Ohio, 1956-70; internat. v.p. Internat. Chem. Workers Union, 1970-72, sec.-treas., 1972-75, internat. pres., 1975—, Washington rep., dir., 1962-70. Served with USAF, 1941-45. Democrat. Roman Catholic. Office: Internat Chem Workers Union 1655 W Market St Akron OH 44313-7004*

MARTINO, JOSEPH PAUL, research scientist; b. Warren, Ohio, July 16, 1931; s. Joseph and Anna Elizabeth (Kubina) M.; m. Mary Lou Bouquot, May 18, 1957; children: Theresa, Anthony, Michael. A.B., Miami U., Ohio, 1953; M.S., Purdue U., 1955; Ph.D., Ohio State U., 1961. Commd. 2d lt. USAF, 1953, advanced through grades to col., 1973; project engr. armament lab. USAF, Wright-Patterson AFB, Ohio, 1955-58; mathematician Office Sci.

Rsch. USAF, Washington, 1961-62; staff scientist Avionics Lab. USAF, Wright-Patterson AFB, 1972-73; dir. engring. standardization Def. Electronics Supply Ctr. USAF, Dayton, Ohio, 1973-75; ret. USAF, 1975; sr. scientist, rsch. inst. U. Dayton, 1975-93. Author: Technological Forecasting for Decisionmaking, 1972, rev. edit., 1983, 3d edit., 1992, A Fighting Chance-The Moral Use of Nuclear Weapons, 1988, Science Funding: Politics and Porkbarrel, 1992, Research and Development Project Selection, 1995; assoc. editor: Tech. Forecasting and Social Change Jour., 1968—. Fellow IEEE, AAAS, AIAA (assoc.); mem. Inst. for Ops. Rsch. and Mgmt. Sci., Am. Soc. Engring. Mgmt. Roman Catholic.

MARTINO, MICHAEL CHARLES, entertainer, musician; b. Philadelphia, Pa., Sept. 10, 1950; s. Salvatore Joseph and Marie Angela (Langone) M. Grad. high sch., Upper Darby, Pa. Spokesperson/rep. Petosa Accordion Co., Seattle, 1979—; featured TV entertainer Mike Martino Show, Delaware County, Pa., 1987-89; accordion tchr. Drexel Hill, Pa., 1989—; entertainer/host/producer St. Jude's Children's Hosp. Marathon, King of Prussia, Pa., 1973; opening act comedian Morty Gunty Downingtown, Pa., 1973, opening act comedian Morty Gunty, 1973, Pat Cooper, Phila., 1981; guest artist/entertainer Internat. Platform Assn. Conv., Washington, 1979; nite club performer Glen Mills, Pa., 1989; actor TV commls., Elkton, Md., 1979, Halloween Spl. KYW-TV, Phila., 1986; performed radio contest jingle Sta. KISS 100 radio, Media, Pa., 1992. Author: (movie script) Forever Fiftys, 1990; composer popular songs; directed, produced, starred video Forever Fiftys; composed theme song Forever Fiftys, (movie theme) That First September; creator, performer Suspended Triple Bellows Shake Technique for the Accordion, 1994; composer (ballad) Through the Music, Through the Words I Sing, 1995. Recipient citation U.S. Ho. Reps., 1989, Proclamation Mike Martino Day Mayor Ward, Del. County, 1988, Danny Thomas Hon. award St. Jude's Hosp., Del. County, 1973, Mayor's Svc. award Upper Darby, Pa., 1994. Roman Catholic. Avocations: antique cars, dogs. Home: 2530 Stoneybrook Ln Drexel Hill PA 19026-1610

MARTINO, PETER DOMINIC, software company executive, military officer; b. N.Y.C., Sept. 21, 1963; s. Rocco Leonard and Barbara Italia (D'Iorio); 1 child, Elizabeth Marie. BS, U.S. Naval Acad., 1985. Cert. cash manager, 1992. Commd. ensign USN, 1985, advanced through grades to lt., 1989, resigned, 1990; with USNR, 1990—; from v.p. mktg. to exec. v.p., COO XRT, Inc., Wayne, Pa., 1990-93, pres., 1993—, CEO, 1996—, also bd. dirs., 1993—; founder, dir. XRT Europe, Ltd., 1994—; founder, dir., pres Four Star Software, Inc., Wayne, 1994—; bd. dirs. Nat. Kidney Found. Delaware Valley. Sustaining mem. Rep. Nat. Com., 1981—; mem. Chester County Rep. Party, 1993-94; coun. mem. Phoenixville Borough Coun., 1993, Rep. committeeman, 1996—; bd. mem. Nat. Kidney Found. Delaware Valley, 1997—. Mem. Treasury Mgmt. Assn., Naval Acad. Alumni Assn., Naval Acad. Athletic Assn., Naval Submarine League, World Affairs Coun. Phila., Pyramid Club (Phila.), Avalon Yacht Club, Lincoln Club (Chester County Rep. Party). Roman Catholic. Avocations: sailing, boating, computers, art collecting, music. Office: XRT Inc 989 Old Eagle School Rd Wayne PA 19087-1704

MARTINO, ROBERT LOUIS, computational scientist and engineer, researcher; b. Derby, Conn.; s. Pasquale Theodore and Louise Mary (Bartomioli) M.; m. Alfreda Helen Guarente, Aug. 28, 1971. BS, Northeastern U., 1971; MS, U. Md., 1973, PhD, 1982. Elec. engr. Goddard Space Flight Ctr., NASA, Greenbelt, Md., 1970-71; electronics engr. NIH, Bethesda, Md., 1973-89; mem. adj. grad. sch. faculty Johns Hopkins U., Balt., 1982—; chief computational sci. and engring. sect. NIH, 1989-93, chief computational bioscience and engring. lab., 1993—; mem. computer sci. program com. Johns Hopkins U., 1985—; NIH rep. Nat., Multi-Agy. High-Performance Computing and Comm. Program, Bethesda, 1992—; mem. program com. Symposium on Frontiers of Massively Parallel Computing, 1993-96. Author: (with others) High Performance Computational Methods for Biological Sequence Analysis, 1996, Parallel and Distributed Computing Handbook, 1995; contbr. articles to profl. jours. Recipient Disting Svc. award HHS, 1994; Grad. fellow U. Md., 1971-73. Mem. IEEE, Sigma Xi, Tau Beta Pi, Eta Kappa Nu. Achievements include the adaptation of high-performance parallel supercomputing to computationally intensive problems in basic and clinical biomedical research; application of concepts and technology of computer science and electrical engineering to biomedical applications for the advancement and understanding of the fundamentals of biological systems and medical practices and for the development of new and improved methods of health care. Home: 7996 Aladdin Dr Laurel MD 20723 Office: NIH Bldg 12A Rm 2033 12 South Dr MSC 5624 Bethesda MD 20892-5624

MARTINO, ROBERT SALVATORE, orthopedic surgeon; b. Clarksburg, W.Va., May 31, 1931; s. Leonard L. and Sarafina (Foglia) M.; m. Lenora Cappellanti, May 22, 1954; children: Robert S. Jr., Leslie F. Reckziegal. AB, W.Va. U., 1953, postgrad., 1955-56, BS in Medicine, 1958; MD, Northwestern U., 1960. Diplomate Am. Bd. Orthopaedic Surgery; lic. Ill., Calif., Ind. Intern Chgo. Wesley, 1960-61; resident dept. orthopaedic surgery Northwestern U., 1961-65, Chgo. Wesley Meml., 1961-62, Am. Legion Hosp. for Crippled Children, 1962-63, Cook County Hosp., Chgo., 1964, 64-65; orthopaedic surgeon Gary, Ind., 1965-67; orthopaedic surgeon Merrillville, Ind., 1967—; fellow Nat. Found. Infantile Parralysis, 1956, Office of Vocat. Rehab., Hand Surgery, 1965; chief of staff St. Mary Med. Ctr., 1976, chief of surgery, 1974-85; chief of staff Gary Treatment Ctr./Ind. Crippled Children's Svcs., 1974-84; adj. asst. prof. anatomy Ind. U., 1978, clin. asst. prof. orthopaedic surgery, 1980, others; mem. Zoning Bd., 1989-90. Chmn. Planning Bd. Town of Dune Acres, 1992-96; bd. dirs. United Steel Workers Union Health Plan, 1994—, St. Mary's Med. Ctr., Hobart, Ind.; com. on Health Care Reform. Capt. U.S. Army, 1953-56. Mem. Ind. Med. Soc., Ill. Med. Soc., Chgo. Med. Soc., Lake County Med. Soc., AMA, Ill. Orthopaedic Soc., Ind. Orthopaedic Soc., Mid-Am. Orthopaedic Assn., Tri-State Orthopedic Soc., Clin. Orthopaedic Soc. Home: Dune Acres 22 Oak Dr Chesterton IN 46304-1016

MARTINO, ROCCO LEONARD, computer systems executive; b. Toronto, Ont., Can., June 25, 1929; s. Domenic and Josephine (DiGiulio) M. BSc, U. Toronto, 1951, MA, 1952; PhD, Inst. Aerospace Studies, 1955, DSc, Neumann Coll., 1993; m. Barbara L. D'Iorio, Sept. 2, 1961; children: Peter Domenic, Joseph Alfred, Paul Gerard, John Francis. Dir., Univac Computing Svc. Ctr., Toronto, 1956-59; pres. Mauchly Assos. Can. Ltd., Toronto, 1959-62, v.p. Mauchly Assocs., Inc., Ft. Washington, Pa., 1959-61; mgr. advanced systems Olin Mathieson Chem. Corp., N.Y.C., 1962-64; dir. advanced computer systems Booz, Allen & Hamilton, N.Y.C., 1965-70; pres., chmn. bd. Info. Industries, Inc. and subs.'s, Wayne, Pa., 1965-70; chmn. bd. XRT, Inc., Wayne, Pa., 1970—; chmn. Cyber Fone, Inc., 1996—; chmn. bd., CEO CyberFone, Inc.; chmn. Internat. Found. for Cath. Health Care; chmn. bd. MBF Computer Ctr. for Handicapped Children; mem. bd. St. Joseph's U., Phila., Gregorian U. Found., N.Y., vice chmn. bd., 1990—; mem. exec. com. Gregorian U., N.Y. and Rome, 1987—, bd. dirs. 1984—, pontifical circle, 1985—, active, 1982—; assoc. prof. math. U. Waterloo, 1959-62, prof. engring., dir. Inst. Systems and Mgmt. Engring., 1964-65; adj. assoc. prof. NYU, 1963-64, adj. prof. math., 1964-65, 66; lectr. on computers mgmt.; chmn. Gov. Ill. Task Force, 1970-71, Ill. Bd. Higher Edn. Task Force, 1971-72, Computer-Use Task Force FCC, 1972-73, Computer-Use Planning Task Force U.S. Postal Svc., 1973-74. Trustee Gregorian Found., N.Y.C. and Rome, 1984—; bd. dirs. St. Joseph's U., 1987—, Cath. League Religious and Civil Rights, 1988-91; chmn. bd. dirs. MBF Ctr. Disabled Children, 1985—; founder Vatican Observatory, 1988—, bd. dirs. Tucson, Rome, 1990—. Mem. Assn. Computing Machinery, Ops. Rsch. Soc. Am., Nat. Italian Am. Found. (bd. dirs. 1991—), Profl. Engrs. Ont., Computing Soc. Can., ITEST (bd. dirs.), Union League Phila., Lions, Overbrook Golf and Country Club, Yacht of Sea Isle City Club (commodore 1973-74, trustee 1975-86, chmn. 1983-86), Commodores Club, Mid-Atlantic Yacht Racing Assn. (commodore 1979-81, sec. 1981-83, officer 1983—), Order St. Gregory the Great (papal knight 1991—), Legatus (bd. dirs. 1988, ea. regional v.p. 1992), Equestrian Order Holy Sepulchre (knight 1986, knight comdr. 1989, knight grand cross 1995), KC, Order of Malta, Knights of Malta (knight 1988, knight commdr. 1989), Cath. Campaign for Am. (nat. coun. 1992). Author: Resources Management, 1968, Dynamic Costing, 1968, Project Management, 1968, Information Management: The Dynamics of MIS, 1968, MIS-Management Information Systems, 1969, Decision Patterns, 1969, Methodology of MIS, 1969, Personnel Information Systems, 1969, Integrated Manufacturing Systems, 1972, APG-Virtual Application Systems, 1981; contbr. numerous articles on mgmt., computers and planning in profl. publs.; designer, developer Application Program Generator computer system, 1974-75, integrated treasury systems; developer cash mgmt. and on-line internat. trading systems, 1984, local area network systems fault tolerant and disaster tolerant systems for real-time fin. transactions, comml. paper trading systems for global networks.

MARTINS, EVELYN MAE, theatre owner; b. Salinas, Calif., June 12, 1929; d. Earl Baldwin and Esther Martine (Harding) Andersen; m. Nolan Anthony Martins, Aug. 20, 1946 (dec. June 1982); children: Dennis, Noelyn, Antonette, Darrin. Owner Skyview Drive-In Theatres, Salinas, 1948—. Mem. Nat. Assn. Theatre Owners, Showest (Calif. Woman Exhibitor of Yr. 1976), Variety Club, Jr. Women's Club (publicity dir. 1965-67), Optimist Youth Found. (treas. 1966-68). Republican. Roman Catholic. Avocation: golf. Home and Office: Skyview Drive-In Theatres 201 Harrison Rd Salinas CA 93907-1612

MARTINS, HEITOR MIRANDA, foreign language educator; b. Belo Horizonte, Brazil, July 22, 1933; came to U.S., 1960; s. Joaquim Pedro and Emilia (Miranda) M.; m. Teresomja Alves Pereira, Nov. 1, 1958 (div. 1977); children—Luzia Pereira, Emilia Pereira; m. Marlene Andrade, Jan. 11, 1984. A.B., U. Federal de Minas Gerais, 1959; Ph.D., U. Federal de Minas Gerais, 1962. Instr. U. N.M., Albuquerque, 1960-62; asst. prof. Tulane U., New Orleans, 1962-66; assoc. prof. Tulane U., 1966-68; prof. dept. Spanish and Portuguese Ind. U., Bloomington, 1968—; chmn. dept. Ind. U., 1972-76; vis. prof. U. Tex., Austin, 1963, Stanford U. 1968. Author: poetry Sirgo nos Cabelos, 1961; essay Manuel de Galhegos, 1964; essays Oswald de Andrade e Outros, 1973; critical anthology Neoclassicismo, 1982; Essays Do Barroco a Guimarães Rosa, 1983; editor: essays Luso-Brazilian Literary Studies. Social Sci. Research Council grantee, 1965; Fulbright-Hays Commn. grantee, 1966; Ford Found. grantee, 1970, 71. Mem. MLA, Renaissance Soc. Am., Am. Comparative Lit. Assn., Am. Assn. for 18th Century Studies. Home: 1316 S Nancy St Bloomington IN 47401-6050 Office: Indiana U Dept Spanish and Portuguese Bloomington IN 47405

MARTINS, NELSON, physics educator; b. Santos, Brazil, Oct. 18, 1930; s. Aniceto and Angelica Martins; m. Maria Lucia, Jan. 8, 1959 (div. Sept. 1983); children: Flavia, Paulo. BS in Physics, Mackenzie U., São Paulo, Brazil, 1958; D in Physics, Pontifica U., Campinas, Brazil, 1977. Cert. physicist. Dir. engring. Mackenzie U., 1971-73, dir. Exact Sci., 1983-90; gen. dir. Ednl. Found., Barretos, Brazil, 1973-76; chief physics dep. Engring. Sch., Araraquara, Brazil, 1991; chief physics dept. U. Santo Amaro, São Paulo, 1990-92; dir. CCET Ctr. Exact Scis. and Tech., São Paulo, 1992-95. Author: (with others) Electricity and Magnetism, 1973, Dimensional Analysis, 1980, Dynamics, 1982. Mem. Am. Assn. Physics Tcrhs., Brazil Soc. Physics. Office: Araraquara Engring Sch, Ave Brazil 782, São Paulo SP 14801-050, Brazil

MARTINS, NILAS, dancer; b. Copenhagen, 1967. Tng., Royal Danish Ballet Sch. Featured in ballets (John Neumaier) Romeo and Juliet, (August Bourronville) Conservatoriet, A Folk Tale, Napoli, (Glen Tetley) Firebird, (Robbins) The Concert, Conservatoriet, Dances at a Gathering, Fanfare, The Four Seasons, Glass Pieces, The Goldberg Variations, Mother Goose, Opus 19, The Dreamer, Robbins with Twyla Tharp) Brahms/ Handel, (Balanchine) Cortege Hongrois, Who Cares?, Apollo, Chaconne, Coppelia, Divertimento No. 15, Duo Concertant, The Four Temperaments, Haieff Divertimento, Jewels, A Midsummer Night's Dream, The Nutcracker, Scotch Symphony, Serenade, Sonatina, La Sonnambula, Stars and Stripes, Stravinsky Violin Concerto, Swan Lake, Symphony in Three Movements, Tschaikovsky Suite No. 3, Union Jack, Vienna Waltzes, Western Symphony, Orpheus, (Martins) Delight of the Muses, Fearful Symmetries, Jazz, Jeu de Cartes, Sleeping Beauty, Tanzspiel, The Waltz Project, X-Ray; also appeared in Ray Charles in Concert with the N.Y.C. Ballet, N.Y.C. Ballet's Balanchine Celebration, 1993. Office: New York City Ballet NY State Theater Lincoln Ctr Plz New York NY 10023*

MARTINS, PETER, ballet master, choreographer, dancer; b. Copenhagen, Oct. 27, 1946; came to U.S., 1967, naturalized, 1970; m. Lise La Cour (div. 1973); 1 child, Nilas; m. Darci Kistler, 1991. Pupil of Vera Volkova and Stanley Williams with Royal Danish Ballet. With N.Y.C. Ballet, 1967—, tchr., 1975, ballet master, 1981-83, co-ballet master-in-chief, 1983-89; ballet master-in-chief, 1989—; Tchr. Sch. Am. Ballet, 1975; artistic adviser Pa. Ballet, 1982—. Mem. Royal Danish Ballet, 1965-67, prin. dancer (including Bournonville repertory), 1967; guest artist N.Y.C. Ballet, 1967-70, prin. dancer, 1970-83; guest artist regional ballet cos. U.S., also Nat. Ballet Can., Royal Ballet, London, Grand Theatre Geneva, Paris Opera, Vienna State Opera, Munich State Opera, London Festival Ballet, Ballet Internat., Royal Danish Ballet; TV appearance in series of Balanchine works, 1974; also has appeared on PBS Dance in America series including A Choreographer's Notebook: Stravinsky Piano Ballets by Peter Martins, 1984; choreographed Broadway musicals including Dream of the Twins (co-choreographer) 1982, On Your Toes, 1982, Song and Dance, 1985; works choreographed include Calcium Light Night, 1977, Tricolore (Pas de Basque sect.), 1978, Rossini Pas de Deux, 1978, Tango-Tango (ice ballet), 1978, Dido and Aeneas, 1979, Sonate di Scarlatti, 1979, Eight Easy Pieces, 1980, Lille Suite, 1980, Suite from Histoire du Soldat, 1981, Capricio Italien, 1981, The Magic Flute, 1981, Symphony No. 1, 1981, Delibes Divertissement, 1982, Piano-Rag-Music, 1982, Concerto for Two Solo Pianos, 1982, Waltzes, 1983, Rossini Quartets, 1983, Tango, 1983, A Schubertiad, 1984, Mozart Violin Concerto, 1984, Poulenc Sonata, 1985, La Sylphide, 1985, Valse Triste, 1985, Eight More, 1985, We Are the World, 1985, Eight Miniatures, 1985, Ecstatic Orange, Tanzspiel, 1988, Jazz, 1993, Symphonic Dances, 1994, Barber Violin Concerto, 1994, Mozart Piano Concerto (No. 17), 1994, X-Ray, 1995; author: (autobiography) Far from Denmark, 1982. Recipient Dance mag. award 1977, Cue's Golden Apple award 1977, award of merit Phila. Art Alliance, 1985, Liberty award N.Y.C., 1986, H.C. Andersen Ballet prize, Royal Danish Theatre, 1988. Office: NY State Theater NYC Ballet 20 Lincoln Center Plz New York NY 10023-6913*

MARTINSON, IDA MARIE, nursing educator, nurse, physiologist; b. Mentor, Minn., Nov. 8, 1936; d. Oscar and Marvel (Nelson) Sather; m. Paul Varo Martinson, Mar. 31, 1962; children—Anna Marie, Peter. Diploma, St. Luke's Hosp. Sch. Nursing, 1957; B.S., U. Minn., 1960, M.N.A., 1962; Ph.D., U. Ill., Chgo., 1972. Instr. Coll. St. Scholastica and St. Luke's Sch. Nursing, 1957-58, Thornton Jr. Coll., 1967-69; lab. asst. U. Ill. at Med. Ctr., 1970-72; lectr. dept. physiology U. Minn., St. Paul, 1972-82; asst. prof. Sch. Nursing U. Minn., 1972-74, assoc. prof. rsch., 1974-77, prof., dir. rsch., 1977-82; prof. dept. family health care U. Calif., San Francisco, 1982—, chmn. dept., 1982-90; vis. rsch. prof. Nat. Taiwan U., Def. Med. Ctr., 1981; vis. prof. nursing Sun Yat-Sen U. Med. Scis., Guang Zhou, Republic of China, Ewha Women's U., Seoul, Korea; vis. prof. nursing Frances Payne Bolton Sch. Nursing, Case Western Res. U., Cleve., 1994—; chair, prof. dept. health scis. Hong Kong Poly. U., 1996—. Author: Mathematics for the Health Science Student, 1977; editor: Home Care for the Dying Child, 1976, Women in Stress, 1979, Women in Health and Illness, 1986, The Child and Family Facing Life Threatening Illness, 1987, Family Nursing, 1989, Home Health Care Nursing, 1989; contbr. chpts. to books, articles to profl. jours. Active Am. Cancer Soc. Recipient Book of Yr. award Am. Jour. Nursing, 1977, 80, 87, 90, Children's Hospice Internat. award, 1988, Humanitarian award for pediatric nursing, 1993; Fulbright fellow, 1991. Mem. ANA, Coun. Nurse Rschrs., Am. Acad. Nursing, Inst. Medicine, Sigma Xi, Sigma Theta Tau. Lutheran. Office: U Calif Family Health Care Nursing San Francisco CA 94143-0606 *The challenge of quality health care to all of society and the critical role nursing has to play in order to achieve this goal has motivated me throughout my professional life. The richness of talent in this country spurs me on.*

MARTINSON, JACOB CHRISTIAN, JR., academic administrator; b. Menomonie, Wis., Apr. 15, 1933; s. Jacob Christian and Matilda Kate (Wisner) M.; m. Elizabeth Smathers, Apr. 29, 1962; children—Elizabeth Anne, Kirsten Kate. BA, Huntingdon Coll., Ala., 1954, LLD (hon.), 1993; MDiv, Duke U., 1957; DDiv, Vanderbilt U., 1972; grad., Inst. Ednl. Mgmt., Harvard U., 1981. Ordained elder United Methodist Ch. Minister Trinity United Meth. Ch., Lighthouse Point, Fla., 1960-67; sr. minister First United Meth. Ch., Winter Park, Fla., 1967-71; supervising instr. Vanderbilt U. Div. Sch., Nashville, 1971-72; pres. Andrew Coll., Cuthbert, Ga., 1972-76, Brevard Coll., N.C., 1976-85, High Point (N.C.) U., 1985—; bd. dirs. First Union Nat. Bank, High Point, chmn. 1989; lectr. St. Mary's Theol. Soc., U. St. Andrews, Scotland. Bd. advisors Uwharrie coun. Boy Scouts Am. Glen Slough scholar Vanderbilt U., 1971; hon. fellow Westminster Coll., Oxford, Eng., 1994. Mem. Nat. Assn. Schs. and Colls. United Meth. Ch. (bd. dirs. 1982-85, 87-90, chmn. fin. com.), So. Assn. Colls. and Schs. (commn. on colls.), Ind. Coll. Fund. N.C. (trustee), N.C. Ctr. Ind. Higher Edn. (bd. dirs.) Brevard C. of C. (pres. 1979), High Point C. of C. (chmn. 1992), Piedmont Ind. Coll. Assn. (chmn. 1991-93), Carolinas Intercollegiate Athletic Conf. (pres. 1991-93), Rotary, Phi Theta Kappa. Methodist. Avocation: mountain hiking. Home: 1109 Rockford Rd High Point NC 27262-3607 Office: High Point U Office of Pres High Point NC 27262-3598

MARTINUZZI, LEO SERGIO, JR., banker; b. Newton, Mass., Aug. 1, 1928; s. Leo Sergio and Jessica (Stewart) M.; m. Helen Renfrew Gibson, Oct. 26, 1957; children: John James, Georgiana Gibson, Samuel Stewart. B.A., Harvard U., 1950; B.Litt., Oxford U., 1952. With Chase Manhattan Bank, N.Y.C., 1956-81; asst. treas. Chase Manhattan Bank, 1960, asst. v.p. Japanese brs., 1961-64, v.p. Japanese brs., 1964-68, marketing exec. internat. staff, 1968-72, sr. v.p., 1971-81; corporate devel. officer Chase Manhattan Corp., 1972-75, group exec. info. services, 1975-81; chmn. Chase Econometric Assocs. Inc., 1975-80; sr. v.p. strategic planning Squibb Corp., 1981-87, cons., 1988-91; chmn. Strategic Dimensions, Inc., 1990—. Trustee Internat. Found. for St. Catherine's Coll., Oxford. Lt. (j.g.) USNR, 1952-56. Mem. Coun. on Fgn. Rels. Home: 336 Galleon Dr Naples FL 34102-7638

MARTLAND, T(HOMAS) R(ODOLPHE), philosophy educator; b. Port Chester, N.Y., May 29, 1926; s. Thomas Rodolphe and Anne Elizabeth (Newbury) M.; BS magna cum laude, Fordham U., 1951; MA, Columbia U., 1955, PhD, 1959; m. Agatha Murphy, Apr. 3, 1952; children: David Allen, Luke Thomas. Asst. prof. Lafayette Coll., Easton, Pa., 1959-65; assoc. prof. So. Ill. U., Carbondale, 1965-66; assoc. prof. philosophy U. Albany (N.Y.), 1966-84, prof., 1984-97, dir. religious studies program, 1980-87; dir. philosophy grad. studies program, 1988-91; disting. Jeannette K. Watson vis. prof. of religion, Syracuse U., 1987; dir. Master of Arts in Liberal Studies Program, 1995-97; Served to lt. (s.g.) USN, 1944-47, 51-53. Faculty Exchange Guest scholar 1976-77, rsch. fellow, 1967, 68, 71, 87; Jones Fund award Lafayette Coll., 1962-63, Signum Laudis award for excellence in tchg. and rsch., 1986. Mem. Am. Philos. Assn., Am. Soc. Aesthetics (steering com. 1985-88), Internat. Assn. Philosophy and Lit. (exec. com. 1976-81). Author: Religion as Art: An Interpretation, 1981; The Metaphysics of William James and John Dewey, 1969; editorial bd. Jour. Comparative Lit. & Aesthetics, 1982-91; guest editor Annals of Scholarship, 1982. Home: RR 1 Box 33 East Ryegate VT 05042-9710 Office: Dept Philosophy U Albany Albany NY 12222

MARTO, PAUL JAMES, retired mechanical engineering educator, consultant, researcher; b. Flushing, N.Y., Aug. 15, 1938; s. Peter Joseph and Natalie Janet (Verrinoldi) M.; m. Mary Virginia Indence, June 10, 1961; children: Terese V. Marto Sanders, Paul J. Jr., Wayne T., Laura C. BS, U. Notre Dame, 1960; SM, MIT, 1962, ScD, 1965. Asst. prof. Naval Postgrad. Sch., Monterey, Calif., 1965-69, assoc. prof., 1969-77, prof., 1977-85, disting. prof., 1985-96, chmn. dept. mech. engring., 1978-86, dean rsch., 1990-96, disting. prof. emeritus, 1996—; cons. Modine Mfg. Co., Racine, Wis., 1986—. Editor: Power Condenser Heat, 1981; regional editor N.Am. Jour. of Enhanced Heat Transfer, 1993—; contbr. articles to profl. jours. Lt. USN, 1965-67. Recipient Rear Adm. John J. Schieffelin award Naval Postgrad. Sch., 1976, Alexander von Humboldt U.S. Sr. Scientist award Humboldt Stiftung, Fed. Republic Germany, 1989-90, Disting. Civilian Svc. award Sec. of Navy, 1996. Fellow ASME (assoc. tech. editor Jour. of Heat Transfer 1984-90); mem. Am. Soc. Naval Engrs., Am. Soc. for Engring. Edn., Sigma Xi. Avocations: walking, tennis, music. Office: Naval Postgrad Sch Dept Mechanical Engring Code ME/MX Monterey CA 93943

MARTOCCHIO, LOUIS JOSEPH, lawyer, educator; b. Hartford, Conn., May 12, 1966; s. Louis Joseph and Mary Noel (Higgins) M.; m. Jodie Meheran, Jan. 4, 1992. BS in Bus. Econs., So. Conn. State U., 1988; JD, U. Bridgeport, 1991. Bar: Conn. 1991. Atty. Carswell Law Offices, Bridgeport, Conn., 1991-92, Moynahan, Ruskin, Mascolo & Minnella, Waterbury, Conn., 1993—; prof. Morse Sch. Bus., Hartford, Conn., 1992-96; bd. dirs. Camelot Property, South Windsor; legal cons. Lobo Enterprises, Southington, Conn., 1994—. Recipient Univ. award U. Bridgeport, 1991. Mem. ABA, Conn. Bar Assn., Conn. Trial Lawyers Assn., Hartford Bar Assn., Waterbury Bar Assn. also Office: Capitol Pl Ste 604 21 Oak St Hartford CT 06106

MARTON, EVA, opera singer; b. Budapest, Hungary, June 18, 1943; m. Zoltan Marton; children: Zoltan, Diana. Student, Liszt Acad., Budapest. Debut Budapest State Opera, 1968-72; performed with Frankfurt Opera, 1972-77, Hambrug State Opera, 1977-80, Maggio Musicale Fiorentino, Vienna State Opera, La Scala Milan, Met. Opera, N.Y., Lyric Opera, Chgo., Grand Opera, Houston, San Francisco Opera, Convent Garden, London, Teatro Liceo, Barcelona, Munich State Opera, Berlin, Paris, Sydney, Teatro Colon Buenos Aires, Bayreuth Festival, Salzburg Festival, Area of Verona, others; roles include Manon Lescaut, Tosca, Turandot, Aida Elisabetta in Don Carlo, Leonora in Forza del destino and in Il Trovatore, Fedora, Maddalena in A Chenire, Wally, Gioconda, Leonore in Fidelio, Salome, Ariadne, Helene in Agyptische Helene, Chrysothemis in Electra, Empress in Die Frau ohne Schatten, Vensu and Elisabeth in Tannhäuser, Elsa and Ortrud in Lohengrin, Sieglinde and Brüunnhilde in the Ring, Isolde, others; rec. include Turandot, Tosca, La Fanciulla del West, A Chenier, Fedora, La Gioconda, Violanta, Tiefland, La Wally, Semirama, Bluebeards Castle, Mefistofele, Electra, Salome, Die Walkuere, Siegfrid, Götterdämmerung, Gurrelider, Forza del destino, Tristan und Isolde, Puccini Arias, Wagner arias, Songs by Bartok and Liszt, others. Office: Orgn Int Opera et Concert, 19 rue Vignon, F-75008 Paris France*

MARTON, LAURENCE JAY, clinical pathologist, educator, researcher; b. Bklyn., Jan. 14, 1944; s. Bernard Dov and Sylvia (Silberstein) M.; m. Marlene Lesser, June 27, 1967; 1 child, Eric Nolan. BA, Yeshiva U., 1965, DSc (hon.), 1993; MD, Albert Einstein Coll. Medicine, 1969. Intern Los Angeles County-Harbor Gen. Hosp., 1969-70; resident in neurosurgery U. Calif.-San Francisco, 1970-71, resident in lab. medicine, 1973-75, asst. research biochemist, 1973-74, asst. clin. prof. depts. lab. medicine and neurosurgery, 1974-75, asst. prof., 1975-78, assoc. prof., 1978-79, prof., 1979-92, asst. dir. div. clin. chemistry, dept. lab. medicine, 1974-75, dir. div., 1975-79, acting chmn. dept., 1978-79, chmn. dept., 1979-92; dean med. sch. U. Wis., 1992-95, prof. pathology and lab. medicine and oncology, 1992—; prof. dept. human oncology U. Wis., Madison, 1993-95; interim vice chancellor Ctr. Health Scis., U. Wis., 1993-94. Co-editor: Polyamines in Biology and Medicine, 1981; Liquid Chromatography in Clinical Analysis, 1981; Clinical Liquid Chromatography, vol. 1, 1984, vol. 2, 1984. Served with USPHS, NIH, 1971-73. Recipient Rsch. Career Devel. award Nat. Cancer Inst., Disting. Alumnus award Albert Einstein Coll. Medicine, 1992. Mem. Am. Assn. Cancer Rsch., AAAS, Acad. Clin. Lab. Physicians and Scientists, Am. Investigative Pathology, Am. Soc. Clin. Pathologists, Soc. Analytical Cytology, Alpha Omega Alpha. Jewish. Avocations: photography, art, music, travel. Home: 5810 Tree Line Dr Fitchburg WI 53711-5826 Office: U Wis Med Sch McArdle Lab Cancer Rsch 1400 University Ave Madison WI 53706-1526

MARTON, MICHAEL, cinematographer; b. Berlin, Germany, Dec. 20, 1942; came to U.S., 1970; s. Alfred Freiherr von Schellerer and Käthe Marie (Hampel) Marton; m. Constance E. Kheel, June 24, 1969 (div. 1975); 1 child, Dunja; m. Ketzel Levine, May 22, 1987 (div. 1992); m. Terry Johnson, June 15, 1996. Diploma in Photography, Lette Haus, Berlin, 1960. Asst. cameraman Sta. ZDF-TV, Mainz, Fed. Republic Germany, 1962-65, Gerard Vandenberg, throughout Europe, 1965-68; ind. cinematographer Europe and U.S., 1968-72, throughout U.S., 1972—; cinematographer corp. and indsl. clients. Cinematographer, dir., prodr., editor: (video documentaries) Stonewall Joe, 1974, Arvilla, 1975, Winterlillies, 1976, A Matter of Size, 1976, Mary Lou at Saratoga, 1981, American Trap, 1982, I Don't Matter I Don't Care, 1983 (U.S. Film and Video award 1984), Henry Brant on the Nature of Music, 1983, The Unsettled Ashes, 1984, Watch Me Now, 1985 (Golden Ring award 1986), Expectations, 1987 (Blue Ribbon award N.Y. Film and Video Festival 1987), Noch ist Polen Nicht Verloren (in coop. with

Känguruh-Film, Berlin), 1992; (with Harold Beckmann) Volga Dreams, 1993; Three in America, 1995; co-dir.: (with Harald Beckmann) Angel from Moscow, 1996, How to Recolonize East Prussia, 1997. Bd. Govs. N.Y. Found. for the Arts, N.Y.C., 1987. Recipient Creative Artists Pub. Service Program award, 1976, 77, 78, N.Y. Humanities award N.Y. Council for the Humanities, 1978, N.Y. Found. for the Arts award, 1985, Telly award, 1997, Communicator Excellence award, 1996; Guggenheim fellow, 1980. Avocations: reading, travel. Home and Office: Michael Marton Prodns 670 Americana Dr 4A Annapolis MD 21403

MARTONE, FREDERICK J., judge; b. Fall River, Mass., Nov. 8, 1943. BS, Coll. Holy Cross, 1965; JD, U. Notre Dame, 1972; LLM, Harvard U., 1975. Bar: Mass. 1972, Ariz. 1974, U.S. Dist. Ct. Mass. 1973, U.S. Dist. Ct. Ariz. 1974, U.S. Ct. Appeals (1st cir.) 1973, U.S. Ct. Appeals (9th cir.) 1974, U.S. Supreme Ct. 1977. Law clk. to Hon. Edward F. Hennessey Mass. Supreme Judicial Ct., 1972-73; pvt. practice Phoenix, 1973-85; assoc. presiding judge Superior Ct. Ariz., Maricopa County; judge Superior Ct. Ariz., Maricopa County, Phoenix, 1985-92; justice Supreme Ct. Ariz., Phoenix, 1992—. Editor notes and comments Notre Dame Lawyer, 1970-72; contbr. articles to profl. jours. Capt. USAF, 1965-69. Mem. ABA, Ariz. Judges Assn., Maricopa County Bar Assn. Office: Supreme Ct Arizona 1501 W Washington St Phoenix AZ 85007-3231

MARTONE, JEANETTE RACHELE, artist; b. Mineola, N.Y., June 5, 1956; d. John and Mildred Cecilia (Loehr) M. BFA, SUNY, Purchase, 1978. One woman shows include Ariel Gallery, N.Y.C., 1990, La Mantia Gallery, Northport, N.Y., 1994-96, Inter-Media Arts Ctr., Huntington, N.Y., 1996; exhibited in group shows from 1980 to 1996 including Harbor Gallery, Cold Spring Harbor, 1980, Huntington Coun. Arts, 1986, Pindar Gallery, N.Y.C., 1987, Mills Pond House, Smithtown, N.Y., 1987, Suffolk County Exec. Offices, Hauppage, N.Y., 1988, La Mantia Gallery, Northport, N.Y., 1990, Nassau County Office Cultural Affairs, 1991, Ward-Nasse. Gallery, N.Y.C., 1991, Monsterrat Gallery, N.Y.C., 1991, Priscilla Redfield Roe Gallery, Bellport, N.Y., 1991, L.I. U., Brookville, 1992, Northport B.J. Spoke Gallery, Huntington, N.Y., 1992, Fischetti Gallery, N.Y., 1992, Artists Space, N.Y.C., 1992, N.Y. Botanical Gardens, Bronx, N.Y., 1993, Visions Gallery, Albany, L.I. U., Brookville, N.Y., 1994, Goodman Gallery, Southampton, N.Y., 1994, B.J. Spoke Gallery, Huntington, N.Y., 1994-95, Islip Art Mus., East Islip, N.Y., 1994, L.I. MacArthur Airport, Ronkonkoma, N.Y., 1995. Recipient Award of Excellence Gold medal Art League of Nassau County, 1993, Best in Show award Nat. League Am. PEN Women Artists, 1990, 92, Windsor and Newton award for oil Arts Coun. East Islip, N.Y., 1989, award of excellence Art League of Nassau County, 1987, 88, many best in shows including 1st Ann. Juried Art Exhibit, Brookhaven Arts and Humanities Coun., Farmingville, N.Y., 1996, Supervisor's award Bablylon Citizens Coun. Arts Juried Exhbn., 1994, Bob Jones Glad Hand Press award Stamford Art Assn., 1995, Faber Biren Nat. Color award Stamford Art Assn., 1995. Mem. Catherine Lorillard Wolfe Art Club (Frank B. and Mary Anderson Cassidy Meml. award 1992, Award for Oil 1987), Allied Artists of Am. (John Young Hunter Meml. award 1993, Antonio Cerino Meml. award 1990), Hudson valley Art Assn., Knickerbock Artists of Am., Nat. Art League. Avocations: travel, reading, volunteer work. Home: 47 Summerfield Ct Deer Park NY 11729-5642

MARTONE, PATRICIA ANN, lawyer; b. Bklyn., Apr. 28, 1947; d. David Andrew and Rita Mary (Dullmeyer) M. BA in Chemistry, NYU, 1968, JD, 1973; MA in Phys. Chemistry, Johns Hopkins U., 1969. Bar: N.Y. 1974, U.S. Dist. Ct. (so. and ea. dists.) N.Y. 1975, U.S. Ct. Appeals (2d cir.) 1975, U.S. Ct. Appeals (1st cir.) 1981, U.S. Ct. Appeals (fed. cir.) 1984, U.S. Patent and Trademark Office 1983, U.S. Supreme Ct. 1984, U.S. Dist. Ct. (ea. dist.) Mich. 1985, U.S. Dist. Ct. (no. dist.) Calif. 1995. Tech. rep. computer timesharing On-Line Systems, Inc., N.Y.C., 1969-70; assoc. Kelley Drye & Warren, N.Y.C., 1973-77; assoc. Fish & Neave, N.Y.C., 1977-82, ptnr., 1983—; adj. prof. NYU Sch. Law, 1990—; participating atty. Cmty. Law Offices, N.Y.C., 1974-78; atty. Pro Bono Panel U.S. Dist. Ct. (so. dist.) N.Y., 1982-84; lectr. Practising Law Inst., N.Y.C., 1995, Aspen Law & Bus., 1990-95, Franklin Pierce Law Sch., 1992—, Lic. Exec. Soc., 1995; mem. panel arbitration Am. Arbitration Assn.; chmn. bd. dirs. N.Y. Lawyers for the Pub. Interest, 1996—, bd. chair 1996—; dir. Legal Svcs. N.Y.C., 1991-95; mem. adv. coun. Engelberg Ctr. Innovation Law & Policy, NYU Sch. Law, 1996—. Mng. editor NYU Law Sch. Rev. Law and Social Change, 1972-73. Contbr. articles to profl. jours. Recipient Founder's Day award NYU Sch. Law, 1973; NSF grad. trainee John Hopkins U., 1968-69; NYU scholar, 1964-68. Mem. ABA, Assn. Bar City N.Y. (mem. environ. law com. 1978-83, trademarks, unfair competition com. 1983-86), Fed. Bar Council, Fed. Cir. Bar Assn., Am. Chem. Soc., Licensing Execs. Soc., Intellectual Property Law Assn., N.Y. Univ. Club. Office: Fish & Neave 1251 Avenue Of The Americas New York NY 10020-1104

MARTONI, CHARLES J., dean; b. Pitts., Aug. 24, 1936; s. John and Virginia (Caputo) M. A.A., Community Coll. Allen County, 1969; B.S., California State Coll. (Pa.), 1971, M.A., 1977; M.S., Duquesne U., 1976, M.Ed., 1972; Ph.D., U. Pitts., 1988. Cert. counselor, nat. and Pa. Asst. dir. fin. aid Boyce Campus Community Coll. Allen County, Monroeville, Pa., 1971-73, dir. fin. aid, 1973-76, dir. fin. aid and counseling, 1976-80, dean of students, 1980—; mem. exec. bd. Tri-State Conf. on Steel. Mayor Swissvale, Pa., 1982-90; pres. Coun. Swissvale, 1990, Mon Valley Initiative. With U.S. Army, 1958-60. John Hart scholar, 1970; named Outstanding Alumnus, Boyce Campus, Community Coll. Allen County, 1978. Mem. Pa. Personnel and Guidance Assn., Pa. Mayors Assn., Nat. Assn. Student Personnel Adminstrs., Am. Assn. Counseling and Devel., Nat. Cert. Counselors. Democrat. Roman Catholic. Home: 7114 Church St Pittsburgh PA 15218-2434 Office: City Hall Swissvale PA 15218

MARTONOSI, ANTHONY NICHOLAS, biochemistry educator, researcher; b. Szeged, Hungary, Nov. 7, 1928; came to U.S., 1957; s. Antal and Anna (Zsoter) M.; m. Mary Alice Gouvea, May 2, 1959; children: Mary Anne, Anthony, Margaret, Susan. MD, U. Med. Sch., Szeged, 1953. Asst. prof. dept. physiology Med. Sch., Szeged, 1955-57; rsch. fellow Mass. Gen. Hosp., Boston, 1957-59; rsch. assoc. Retina Found., Boston, 1959-62, asst. dir. dept. muscle rsch., 1962-65; assoc. prof. biochemistry St. Louis U. Sch. Medicine, 1965-69, prof., 1969-79; prof. biochemistry SUNY Health Sci. Ctr., Syracuse, 1979—; Albert Szent-Gyorgyi Prof., U. Med. Sch., Szeged, Hungary, 1994; adj. prof. Kwangju Inst. of Sci. and Tech., Korea, 1995—; vis. scientist dept. biochemistry U. Birmingham, Eng., 1963-64. Editor: The Enzymes of Biological Membranes, Vols. 1-4, 1976, 2d edit., 1985; Membranes and Transport, Vols. 1-2, 1982; contbr. over 180 articles to sci. publs.; mem. editorial adv. bd. Biochimica et Biophysica Acta, 1988—. Recipient Established Investigator award Am. Heart Assn., 1961-66; rsch. grantee USPHS, NIH, 1959—, NSF, 1963—, Muscular Dystrophy Assn., 1975—. Mem. Am. Soc. Biochemists and Molecular Biologists. Roman Catholic. Home: 110 Stanwood Ln Manlius NY 13104-1412 Office: SUNY Health Sci Ctr 766 Irving Ave Syracuse NY 13210-1602

MARTORANA, BARBARA JOAN, secondary education educator; b. N.Y.C., Oct. 18, 1942; d. Samuel and Joan Renee (Costello) M. BA, St. John's U., Jamaica, N.Y., 1970, MS in English Edn., 1972; advanced cert. computers in edn., L.I. U., 1988, profl. diploma in edn. adminstrn., 1990. Cert. sch. dist. adminstr., sch. adminstr. and supr., tchr. English grades 7-12, N.Y. Exec. sec. Am. Petroleum Inst., N.Y.C., 1960-65; exec. asst. to v.p. Goldring, Inc., N.Y.C., 1965-67; exec. asst. Rsch. Inst. for Cath. Edn., N.Y.C., 1967-69; English tchr. St. Martin of Tours Sch., Amityville, N.Y., 1970-77, Oceanside (N.Y.) Jr. H.S., 1977-78, Freeport (N.Y.) H.S., 1979—; rec. sec. Freeport (N.Y.) Tchr. Ctr. Policy Bd., 1986-89; co-chair Middle States Steering Com., Freeport, 1988-90; chair Freeport (N.Y.) H.S. Shared Decision Team, 1992-93; workshop facilitator L.I. Writing Project, Garden City, N.Y., 1993—, co-leader Summer Insts. Co-author: (textbooks) Writing Competency Practice, 1980, Writing Competency Practice-Revised and Expanded, 1989. With Seaford (N.Y.) Rep. Club, 1975—. Mem. ASCD, Nat. Coun. Tchrs. English (conf. on English edn.), N.Y. State English Coun., L.I. Writing Project. Avocations: reading, writing, traveling. Office: Freeport HS 50 S Brookside Ave Freeport NY 11520-3144

MARTORANA, SEBASTIAN VINCENT, educator, educational consultant; b. Farnham, N.Y., Jan. 7, 1919; s. Francis and Jennie (Mancuso) M.; m. Carrie Mae Stephenson, Sept. 20, 1947; children: Vincenne (Mrs. Alfred Kirmss), Francis Stephen, John Charles. B.S., N.Y. State Coll. at Buffalo, 1939; postgrad., U. Buffalo, 1940; M.A., U. Chgo., 1946, Ph.D., 1948. Prof. Wash. State Coll., 1948-53; dean Ferris State Inst., 1953-55; specialist community colls. U.S. Office Edn., Washington, 1955-57; chief state and regional orgns. U.S. Office Edn., 1957-63; asst. commr. for higher edn. planning N.Y. State Bd. Regents, 1963-65; vice-chancellor for community colls., provost tech. edn. SUNY, 1965-72; sr. rsch. assoc. Ctr. Study Higher Edn., prof. higher edn. Pa. State U., 1972-89, prof. emeritus, 1989; mem. nat. bd. inservice edn. project Edn. Commn. States, 1976-82; pres., chmn. bd. Assoc. Cons. in Edn., 1976-94; lectr. in field; edn. cons., ind. contractor, 1955—, Nova Sooouthea. U., 1972—, Walden U., 1993—. Author: (with D Grant Morrison) Criteria for Establishing Two Year Colleges, 1961, State Formulas for the Support of Public Two Year Colleges, 1962, (with E. Hollis) State Boards Responsible for Higher Education, 1960, College Board of Trustees, 1963, (with C. Blocker, L. Bender) The Political Terrain of American Postsecondary Education, 1975, (with E. Kuhns) Managing Academic Change, 1975, (with Gary McGuire) State Legislation Relating to Community and Junior Colleges, 1975, (with L. Nespoli), 1976, Regionalism in American Postsecondary Education: Concepts and Practices, 1978, Regionalism: Study, Talk, and Action, 1978, (with E. Kuhns) Quality Beyond the Campus, 1983, (with W. D. Smutz) State Legislation Relating to Community and Junior Colleges, 1979, (with W. Piland) Designing Programs for Community Groups, 1984; editor: (with W. Toombs, D. Breneman) Graduate Education and Community Colleges, 1976, (with E. Kuhns) Qualitative Methods for Institutional Research, 1982, (with J. Broomall) State Legislation on Affecting Community, Jr. and 2-Year Technical Colleges, 1981, (with P. Corbett) State Legislation Affecting Community, Jr. and 2-Year Technical Colleges, 1982, (with P. Garland) State Legislation Affecting Community, Jr. and Two-Year Technical Colleges, 1985, 86, 87, 88, 89, (with T. Kelley and L.A. Nespoli) Politics, Law and Economics of Higher Education, 1987; mem. editorial bd. Community Coll. Rev., 1972-86; mem. editorial adv. bd. Jour. Edn. Finance, 1972-86. Pres. Wakefield Forest Civic Assn., Annandale, Va., 1958-59, Pearse Rd. Civic Assn., Schenectady, 1966-67; Trustee Coll. Entrance Exam. Bd., 1966-70, Washington Internat. Coll., 1974-80; lay adv. bd. Notre Dame High Sch., Schenectady, 1968-72; bd. human resources Nat. Acad. Scis., 1971-72; mem. Pres. Nat. Adv. Commn. on Higher Edn., 1969. Served with USAAF, 1942-45. Decorated Legion of Merit; recipient Distinguished Alumnus award State U. N.Y. Coll. at Buffalo, 1959, Distinguished Service award HEW, 1960, Award of Merit N.Y.S. Jr. Coll. Assn., 1972, Outstanding Reservist, Air Univ., 1974, Outstanding Publ. award Nat. Council Univ. and Coll. Profs./Am. Assn. Community and Jr. Colls., 1982, 86, Disting. Svc. award Nat. Coun. Univ. and Coll. Profs./Am. Assn. Community and Jr. Coll Assn., 1985; named to Community Coll. Founders Hall of Fame, 1984. Danforth Found. grantee, 1974; Ford Found. grantee, 1978; grantee Fund for Improvement of Postsecondary Edn., 1982. Mem. NEA, Nat. Coun. State Dirs. Comty. and Jr. Colls. (founding mem., pres. 1968, 72), Am. Assn. Higher Edn., Am. Ednl. Rsch. Assn., Assn. Instnl. Rsch., Am. Assn. Comty. and Jr. Colls. (dir. 1977-80, Nat. Leadership award 1988), Nat. Soc. Study Edn., Nat. Assn. Coll. and Univ. Attys. (founding mem.), Nat. Coun. Coll. and Univ. Profs. Comty. and Jr. Colls. (pres. 1979, bd. dirs. 1987-89), Pa. Higher Edn. Assn., Res. Officers Assn., Air Force Assn., KC, Sons of Italy, Italic Studies Inst. (adv. coun. mem.), Ret. Officers Assn., Phi Delta Kappa. Home: Box 256 Rural Delivery 1 Centre Hall PA 16828 Office: 400 Charlotte Bldg University Park PA 16802-6107

MARTORI, JOSEPH PETER, lawyer; b. N.Y.C., Aug. 19, 1941; s. Joseph and Teresa Susan (Fezza) M. BS summa cum laude, NYU, 1964, MBA, 1968; JD cum laude U. Notre Dame, 1967. Bar: D.C. 1968, U.S. Dist. Ct. D.C. 1968, U.S. Dist. Ct. Ariz. 1968, U.S. Ct. Appeals (9th cir.) 1969, U.S. Supreme Ct. 1977. Assoc. Sullivan & Cromwell, N.Y.C., 1967-68, Snell & Wilmer, Phoenix, 1968-69; pres. Goldmar Inc., Phoenix, 1969-71; ptnr. Martori, Meyer, Hendricks & Victor, P.A., Phoenix, 1971-85; ptnr. Brown & Bain, P.A., Phoenix, 1985-94, chmn. corp. banking & real estate dept., 1994—; chmn. bd. dirs. ILX, Inc., 1994-96; bd. dirs. Firstar, Met. Bank, Phoenix, Red Rock Collection Inc., Phoenix; chmn. ILX Inc., Varsity Clubs Am. Inc. Author: Street Fights, 1987; also articles, 1966-70. Bd. dirs. Men's Arts Coun., Phoenix, 1972—; trustee Boys' Clubs Met. Phoenix, 1974—; consul for Govt. of Italy, State of Ariz., 1987-97. Mem. ABA, State Bar Ariz., Maricopa County Bar Assn., Lawyers Com. for Civil Rights Under Law (trustee 1976—), Phoenix Country Club, Plaza Club (founding bd. govs. 1979-90). Republican. Roman Catholic. Office: ILX Inc 2777 E Camelback Rd Phoenix AZ 85016-4302

MARTS, TERRI LOUISE, management executive; b. Wilkinsburg, Pa., June 8, 1958; d. Robert Jackson and Margaret Elaine (Frescura) Gebrosky; m. Norman Vincent Marts, Sept. 27, 1980. BS in Bus. Adminstrn., U. Pitts., 1980; MBA, Robert Morris Coll., 1985. Clk. Westinghouse Electric Corp., Pitts., 1977-79, pers. rep., 1980-81, in quality, mktg. and human resources, 1981-85; quality engr. Westinghouse Energy Systems, Pitts., 1985-89, mgr. employee svcs., 1989-91, mgr. total quality and nuclear quality assurance, 1991-93; asst. dir. human resources Westinghouse Corp. Hdqs., Pitts., 1993-95; mng. dir. Westinghouse Source W, Pitts., 1995—; faculty mem. Human Resource Planning Soc., N.Y.C., 1992-95; nat. spkr. Am. Soc. Quality Control, 1985-90. Bd. dirs. Jr. Achievement, Pitts., 1995-97. Recipient Am. Legion award, 1970. Mem. Quality Network (sponsorship com. 1992-95), Women in Comm. Avocations: reading, travel, gardening, church activities. Home: 5974 Kemerer Hollow Rd Export PA 15632 Office: Westinghouse Electric Corp 11 Stanwix St Pittsburgh PA 15222-1312

MARTTILA, JAMES KONSTANTIN, pharmacy administrator; b. Soudan, Minn., Oct. 25, 1948; s. Walter Konstantin and Verena (Oliver) M.; m. Kathleen A. Meyerle, Dec. 27, 1980; 1 child, Andrew. BS in Pharmacy, U. Minn., 1971, PharmD, 1972; MBA, Coll. St. Thomas, St. Paul, 1984. Lic. pharmacist, Minn. Prof. Coll. Pharmacy U. Minn., Mpls., 1973-86; dir. pharmacy, adminstr. Mayo Med. Ventures Mayo Found. Med. Edn., Research, Rochester, Minn., 1987—; cons. pharmacy Pharm. Cons. Svc., Mpls., 1975-86; chief operating officer Pharm. Svc. Corp., Mpls., 1975-87. Fellow Am. Soc. Cons. Pharmacists; mem. Am. Soc. Hosp. Pharmacists, Am. Pharm. Assn. (Schwartz award 1979). Office: Mayo Med Ventures Mayo Clinic 200 1st St SW Rochester MN 55902-3008

MARTUCCI, VINCENT JAMES, composer, pianist; b. Medford, Mass., Oct. 21, 1954; s. Vincent James Sr. and Grace Alice (Giorgio) M.; m. Elizabeth Nicoll Lawrence, Sept. 20, 1981; children: Katharine Amalia, James Lawrence. Student, Berklee Coll. Music, Boston, 1974-75; BA in Music, Colby Coll., 1977; student, Hal Galper, N.Y.C., 1978-80, Dave Holland, Woodstock, N.Y., 1982-84. Lectr. music Alfred (N.Y.) U., 1978-80; registrar, instr. Creative Music Studio, Woodstock, 1980-82; owner, composer, performer Vinnie Martucci Prodns., West Hurley, N.Y., 1987—; performer, composer, 1977—; free-lance composer, producer recordings and TV, 1986—; tchr. SUNY, New Paltz, 1991; cons. synthesis and audio technique, 1985—; mem. U.S. Embassy tour concert series, Bogota, Colombia, 1991; participant conf. Internat. Assn. Jazz Educators, Boston, 1994. Composer, performer The Dolphins, North Am., South Am., Europe, Canada, including Newport Jazz at Saratoga, North Sea Jazz Festival, JVC Jazz Festival at Nice, France, The Hague in Holland, Jazz Mecca Festival in Holland, Pori Jazz Festival, Finland, Levercusen Jazz Festival Germany, Brubeck Family Project Tours, and many others, 1987—; performed with Hubert Laws, Nick Brignola, Livingston Taylor, Rory Block; arranger radio concert series Karl Berger Composer, 1985; co-author, arranger Adventures of Comander Crumbcake - TV series, 1987; composer: (rec.) Malayan Breeze, 1991, network theme redesign pkg. lifetime med. TV, 1988; travel channel, 1990, CNN-Daily Menus, 1991; composer, performer, arranger underscore CBS's As the World Turns, 1993—, NBC's Another World, 1993—, Guiding Light; co-composer: (rec.) Old World/New World, 1991, Ain't I a Woman, 1992; author instructional tape series Arranging and Recording Electronic Instruments, 1987—; co-prodr., performer, engr. music for theatrical prodns. McCarter Theatre, Princeton, Asolo Theatre, Sarasota, Fla.; co-prodr., music for theatre prodn. Having Our Say, 1995—; performer, music dir. numerous live TV and radio performances; music dir. for Eileen Fulton star of As the World Turns, 1996-97; author: (book series) Introduction to Jazz Keyboards, Introduction to Blues Keyboards, Introduction to Rock Keyboards, 1997. Recipient 2d pl. jazz composition Billboard Mag., 1988. Mem. ASCAP, AFTRA, Am. Fedn. Musicians. Avocations: photography, bicycling, swimming. Home and Office: Vinnie Martucci Prodn 29 Pleasant Ridge Dr West Hurley NY 12491

MARTUZA, ROBERT L., neurosurgeon; b. Wilkes-Barre, Pa., July 1, 1948. BA, Bucknell U., Lewisburg, Pa., 1969; MD, Harvard U., 1973. Diplomate Am. Bd. Neurol. Surgery. Instr. surgery Harvard Med. Sch., Boston, 1980-81, asst. prof., 1981-86, assoc. prof., 1986-91; prof., chmn. dept neurosurgery Georgetown U., Washington, 1991—; Dir. Georgetown Brain Tumor Ctr., Washington, 1993—, Mass. Gen. Hosp. Neurofibromatosis Clinic, Boston, 1990-91; chair Decade of the Brain Task Force, Chgo., 1994—. Contbr. articles to profl. jours. Recipient Von Recklinghanson award Nat. NF Found., N.Y.C., 1989. Mem. Am. Acad. Neurol. Surgeons, Soc. Neurol. Surgery (Grass award), Am. Assn. Neurol. Surgeons, Congress Neurol. Surgeons. Achievements include development of genetically engineered viruses for brain tumor therapy; first development of replication-competent viral vectors for tumor therapy; localization of NF2 gene defects to chromosome 22. Office: Georgetown U Dept Neurosurgery 3800 Reservoir Rd NW Washington DC 20007-2113*

MARTY, JOHN, state senator, writer; b. Evanston, Ill., Nov. 1, 1956; s. Martin E. and Elsa Louise (Schumacher) M.; m. Connie Jaarsma, Nov. 29, 1980; children: Elsa, Micah. BA in Ethics, St. Olaf Coll., 1978. Rschr. Minn. Ho. of Reps., St. Paul, 1980-82, com. adminstr. com. criminal justice, 1982-84; corp. found. grant adminstr., 1984-86; mem. Minn. State Senate, St. Paul, 1987—. Author Minn. Govt. Ethics Law, campaign fin. reform, DWI (driving while intoxicated) laws. Dem. Farm Labor gubernatorial candidate, 1994.

MARTY, LAWRENCE A., magistrate; b. Leigh, Nebr., June 17, 1926. Student Wayne State U., 1944-46, Creighton Sch. Law, 1946-48; J.D., U.Wyo., 1954. Bar: Wyo. 1954. Sole practice, Green River, Wyo., 1954-67; ptnr. Mart & Clark, Green River, 1967-74; ptnr. Marty & Ragsdale, Green River, 1975—; judge Green River Mcpl. Ct., 1956-58; U.S. Magistrate Dist. Wyo., 1958—. Alt. del. Rep. Nat. Conv., 1964. Mem. ABA, Wyo. Bar Assn., Sweetwater County Bar Assn. Office: 20 E Flaming Gorge Way Green River WY 82935-4210

MARTY, MARTIN EMIL, religion educator, editor; b. West Point, Nebr., Feb. 5, 1928; s. Emil A. and Anne Louise (Wuerdemann) M.; m. Elsa Schumacher, 1952 (dec. 1981); children: Frances, Joel, John, Peter, James, Micah, Ursula; m. Harriet Lindemann, 1982. MDiv, Concordia Sem., 1952; STM, Luth. Sch. Theology, Chgo., 1954; PhD in Am. Religious and Intellectual History, U. Chgo., 1956; LittD (hon.), Thiel Coll., 1964; LHD (hon.), W.Va. Wesleyan Coll., 1967, Marian Coll., 1967, Providence Coll., 1967; DD (hon.), Muhlenberg Coll., 1967; LittD (hon.), Thomas More Coll., 1968; DD (hon.), Bethany Sem., 1969; LLD (hon.), Keuka Coll., 1972; LHD (hon.), Willamette U., 1974; DD (hon.), Wabash Coll., 1977; LLD (hon.), U. So. Calif., 1977, Valparaiso U., 1978; LHD (hon.), St. Olaf Coll., 1978, De Paul U., 1979; DD (hon.), Christ Sem.-Seminex, 1979, Capital U., 1980; LHD (hon.), Colo. Coll., 1980; DD (hon.), Maryville Coll., 1980, North Park Coll. Sem., 1982; LittD (hon.), Wittenberg U., 1983; LHD, Rosary Coll., 1984; LHD (hon.), Rockford Coll., 1984; DD (hon.), Va. Theol. Sem., 1984; LHD (hon.), Hamilton Coll., 1985, Loyola U., 1986; LLD (hon.), U. Notre Dame, 1987; LHD (hon.), Roanoke Coll., 1987, Mercer U., 1987, Ill. Wesleyan Coll., 1987, Roosevelt U., 1988, Aquinas Coll., 1988; LittD (hon.), Franklin Coll., 1988, U. Nebr., 1993; LHD (hon.), No. Mich. U., 1989, Muskingum Coll., Coe Coll., Lehigh U., 1989, Hebrew Union Coll. and Governors State U., 1990, Whittier Coll., 1991; Calif. Luth. U., 1993; DD (hon.), St. Xavier Coll. and Colgate U., 1990, Mt. Union Coll., 1991, Tex. Luth. Coll., 1991, Aurora U., 1991, Baker U., 1992; LHD (hon.), Luth. U., 1993; LHD, Calif. Luth. U., 1993, Midland Luth. Coll., 1995; DD, Hope Coll., 1993, Northwestern Coll., 1993; LHD (hon.), George Fox Coll., 1994, Drake U., 1994, Centre Coll., 1994, Fontbonne Coll., 1996; DD, Yale U., 1995. Ordained to ministry Luth. Ch., 1952. Pastor Washington, 1950-51; asst. pastor River Forest, Ill., 1952-56; pastor Elk Grove Village, Ill., 1956-63; prof. history of modern Christianity Div. Sch. U. Chgo., 1963—, Fairfax M. Cone Disting. Service prof., 1978—; assoc. editor Christian Century mag., Chgo., 1956-85, sr. editor, 1985—; co-editor Ch. History mag., 1963—; pres. Park Ridge (Ill.) Ctr.: An Inst. for Study of Health, Faith and Ethics, 1985-89; dir. fundamentalism project Am. Acad. Arts & Scis., 1988—; dir. The Pub. Religion Project, 1996—. Author: A Short History of Christianity, 1959, The New Shape of American Religion, 1959, The Improper Opinion, 1961, The Infidel, 1961, Baptism, 1962, The Hidden Discipline, 1963, Second Chance for American Protestants, 1963, Church Unity and Church Mission, 1964, Varieties of Unbelief, 1964, The Search for a Usable Future, 1969, The Modern Schism, 1969, Righteous Empire, 1970 (Nat. Book award 1971), Protestantism, 1972, You Are Promise, 1973, The Fire We Can Light, 1973, The Pro and Con Book of Religious America, 1975, A Nation of Behavers, 1976, Religion, Awakening and Revolution, 1978, Friendship, 1980, By Way of Response, 1981, The Public Church, 1981, A Cry of Absence, 1983, Health and Medicine in the Lutheran Tradition, 1983, Pilgrims in Their Own Land, 1984, Protestantism in the United States, 1985, Modern American Religion, The Irony of it All, Vol. 1, 1986, An Invitation to American Catholic History, 1986, Religion and Republic, 1987, Modern American Religion. The Noise of Conflict, Vol. 2, 1991, (with R. Scott Appleby) The Glory and the Power, 1992; editor: (with Jerald C. Brauer) The Unrelieved Paradox: Studies in the Theology of Franz Bibfeldt, 1994 (with Micah Marty) Places Along the Way, 1994, Our Hope for Years to Come, 1995, Modern American Religion, Under God, Indivisble, Vol. 3, 1996, The One and the Many, 1997; editor (jours.) Context, 1969—, Second Opinion, 1990; sr. editor The Christian Century, 1956—; contbr. articles to religious publs. Chmn. bd. regents St. Olaf Coll.; dir. The Pub. Religion Project, 1996—. Sr. scholar-in-residence The Park Ridge Ctr., 1989—. Fellow Am. Acad. Arts and Scis. (dir. fundamentalism project 1988-94), Soc. Am. Historians; mem. Am. Phil. Soc., Am. Soc. Ch. History (pres. 1971), Am. Cath. Hist. Assn. (pres. 1981), Am. Acad. Religion (pres. 1987-88), Am. Antiquarian Soc. Office: 919 N Michigan Ave Ste 540 Chicago IL 60611-1601 Office: Christian Century Mag 407 S Dearborn St Ste 1405 Chicago IL 60605

MARTYL (MRS. ALEXANDER LANGSDORF, JR.), artist; b. St. Louis, Mar. 16, 1918; d. Martin and Aimee (Goldstone) Schweig; m. Alexander Langsdorf, Jr., Dec. 31, 1941; children: Suzanne, Alexandra. A.B., Washington U., St. Louis, 1938. instr. art dept. U. Chgo.; artist in residence Tamarind Inst., U. N.Mex., Albuquerque, 1974. One-man shows include, Calif. Palace of Legion of Honor, 1956, Chgo. Art Inst., 1949, 76, Feingarten Galleries, N.Y.C., Beverly Hills and Chgo., 1961, 62, 63, St. Louis, 1962, Feingarten Gallery, N.Y.C., 1963, Los Angeles, 1964, Kovler Gallery, Chgo., 1967, Washington U., St. Louis, 1967, U. Chgo. Oriental Inst. Mus., 1970, Deson&Zaks Gallery, 1973, Fairweather-Hardin Gallery, 1977, 81, 83, Ill. State Mus., 1978, Fermilab, 1985, 91, Bklyn. Mus., 1986, Oriental Inst. Mus., 1987, Gibbes Art Mus., Charleston, S.C., 1988, Fairweather-Hardin Gallery, 1988, Tokyo Internat. Art Expo, 1990, State of Ill. Art Gallery, Chgo., 1990, Expo Navy Pier, Chgo., 1993, Printworks Gallery Ltd., Chgo., 1997; represented in permanent collections, Met. Mus. Art, Chgo. Art Inst., Pa. Acad. Fine Arts, Ill. State Mus., Bklyn. Mus., DuSable Mus., Chgo., Los Angeles County Mus., Whitney Mus. Am. Art, Davenport (Iowa) Municipal Mus., St. Louis Art Mus., Washington U., U. Ariz., Arnot Gallery, Elmira, N.Y., Greenville (S.C.) Mus., Nat. Coll. Fine Arts, Hirshhorn Mus. and Sculpture Gallery, Rockford (Ill.) Mus. Recipient 1st prize City Art Mus., St. Louis, 1943, 44; Armstrong prize Chgo. Art Inst., 1947; William H. Bartels award, 1953; Frank Logan medal and prize, 1950; Walt Disney purchase award Los Angeles Museum; purchase prize Portrait of America competition, Colo. Springs Fine Arts Center, 1961; honor award for mural AIA, 1962, Outstanding Achievement award in the Arts YWCA, 1986; named Artist of Year Am. Fedn. Arts, 1958. Mem. Chgo. Network, Arts Club (Chgo.), Quadrangle Club (Chgo.). Unitarian. *To be an artist means devoting a lifetime to an intensely difficult activity—one that requires concentration and skill. I've spent my time learning the power of color, line, shape and meaning. I like to think that I have opened out experiences people cannot reveal by themselves.*

MARTZ, CLYDE OLLEN, lawyer, educator; b. Lincoln, Nebr., Aug. 14, 1920; s. Clyde O. and Elizabeth Mary (Anderson) M.; m. Ann Spieker, May 29, 1947; children: Robert Graham, Nancy. AB, U. Nebr., 1941; LLB, Harvard U., 1947. Bar: Colo. 1948, U.S. Ct. Appeals (D.C. cir.) 1968, U.S. Supreme Ct. 1969. Prof. U. Colo., Boulder, 1947-58, 60-62; jud. adminstr. State of Colo., Denver, 1959-60; ptnr. Davis, Graham & Stubbs, Denver, 1962-67, 69-80, 81-87, of counsel, 1988—; asst. atty. gen. U.S. Dept. Justice, Washington, 1967-69; solicitor U.S Dept. Interior, Washington, 1980-81; exec. dir. dept. natural resources State of Colo., 1987; adj. prof. U. Denver,

1961-79, U. Colo., Boulder, 1988—; cons. Pres. Materials Policy Commn., 1951; mem. Colo. Adv. Bd. Bur. Land Mgmt., 1967-69. Author: Cases and Materials on Natural Resources Law, 1951, Water for Mushrooming Populations, 1954; co-author: American Law of Property, 1953, Water and Water Rights, 1963; editor, co-author: American Law of Mining, 1960. Co-chmn. Jud. Reorganization Commn., 1961-63; elder Presbyn. Ch., Boulder; pres. Rocky Mountain Mineral Found., 1961-62, others. Comdr. USN, 1942-58, PTO, with Res. Decorated Silver Star, Bronze Star, Letter of Commendation. Mem. ABA (chmn. natural resources sect. 1985-86), Fed. Bar Assn., Colo. Bar Assn. (chmn. water sect. 1957, chmn. mineral sect. 1961, award of merit 1962), Order of Coif, Phi Beta Kappa. Democrat. Avocations: horticulture, woodworking, mountaineering, skiing. Home: 755 6th St Boulder CO 80302-7416 Office: Davis Graham & Stubbs 370 17th St Ste 4700 Denver CO 80202-5647

MARTZ, JOHN ROGER, lawyer; b. Buffalo, June 13, 1937; s. George Albert and Dorothy (Dinsbier) M.; m. Charlotte Gail Lemberes, July 22, 1966; children: Teresa Gail, Nicole Jackie. BS, U.S. Mil. Acad., 1960; MS in Engring., Purdue U., 1964; JD, U. San Francisco, 1980. Bar: Nev. 1980. Commd. 2d lt. U.S. Army, 1960; nuclear engr. Army Nuclear Power Program, 1964-66; with Spl. Forces in Okinawa, Vietnam, Thailand, Korea, Taiwan,, Philippines, 1966-72; elec. engr. Armed Forces Radiobiology Rsch. Inst. and Def. Nuclear Agy., 1972-75; advisor N.G., Calif. and Nev., 1975-80; ret. U.S. Army, 1980; atty. Henderson & Nelson, Reno, 1980-85; pvt. practice Reno, 1985—. Decorated Bronze Star, Combat Inf. badge; recipient Joint Svc. Commendation medal U.S. Dept. Def., 1975. Mem. Nev. State Bar Assn., Washoe County Bar Assn. Avocations: running, hiking, fishing, motorcycling. Office: 440 Ridge St Reno NV 89501-1718

MARTZ, JUDY, state official; b. Big Timber, Mont., July 28, 1943; m. Harry; children: Justin, Stacey. Owner, operator Martz Disposal Svc.; skater U.S. World Speed Skating Team, Japan, 1963, U.S. Olympic Team, Innsbruck, Austria, 1964; exec. dir. U.S. High Altitude Speed Skating Ctr., Butte, Mont., 1985-89; field rep. Senator Conrad Burns, 1988; lt. gov. State of Mont., 1996; coach Mont. Amateur Speed Skating Assn.; bd. dirs. Youth Hockey Assn.; pres. adv. bd. U.S. Internat. Speed Skating Assn. Bd dirs. St. James Cmty. Hosp., Legion Oasis HUD Housing Project. Named Miss Rodeo Mont., 1963; inducted Butte Sports Hall of Fame, 1987. *

MARTZ, LAWRENCE STANNARD, periodical editor; b. Bklyn., Apr. 2, 1933; s. Lawrence Stannard Martz and Jean Lee Bailey; m. Anne-Sophie Uldall, May 28, 1955; children: Geoffrey Stannard, Jenny-Anne Horst-Martz. AB, Dartmouth Coll., 1954; postgrad., U. Edinburgh, 1955. Reporter The Pontiac (Mich.) Press, 1955-56, The Detroit News, 1956-59; copy editor The Wall St. Jour., N.Y.C., 1959-60; bus. writer/editor to asst mng. editor, editor internat. editions Newsweek Mag., N.Y.C., 1961-93; contbg. editor Newsweek Mag., 1993—; editor World Press Rev. Mag., 1993—. Co-author: Ministry of Greed, 1988; author: Making Schools Better, 1992. Recipient J.C. Penney-Mo. award for bus. writing, U. Mo. Sch. of Journalism, 1969, Silver Gavel award ABA, 1990, Media award N.Y. State Bar Assn., 1986. Mem. Am. Soc. Mag. Editors, Overseas Press Club of Am. (bd. govs. 1994—). Office: World Press Rev 200 Madison Ave New York NY 10016-3903

MARTZ, LOUIS LOHR, English literature educator; b. Berwick, Pa., Sept. 27, 1913; s. Isaiah Louis Bower and Ruth Alverna (Lohr) M.; m. Edwine Montague, June 30, 1941 (dec. 1985); children: Frederick, Louis, Ruth Anne; m. Barbara Stuart, May 5, 1990; children: Olivia, Andrew. AB, Lafayette Coll., 1935, LittD (hon.), 1960; PhD, Yale U., 1939; LHD (hon.), De Pauw U., 1983; LittD (hon.), Siena Coll., 1984. Instr. English Yale U., 1938-44, asst. prof., 1944-48, assoc. prof., 1948-54, prof., 1954-57, Douglas Tracy Smith prof. English and Am. lit., 1957-71, Sterling prof. English, 1971-84, prof. emeritus, 1984—, chmn. dept., 1956-62, 64-65, dir. div. humanities, 1959-62, 80, dir. Beinecke Rare Book and Manuscript Libr., 1972-77, acting master Saybrook Coll., 1978-79, chmn. coll. seminar program, 1968-71, acting dir. Ctr. Brit. Art, 1981; vis. prof. English Georgetown U., 1985-91; vis. prof. English Emory U., 1986-88. Author: The Later Career of Tobias Smollett, 1942, The Poetry of Meditation, 1954, The Paradise Within, 1964, The Poem of the Mind, 1966, The Wit of Love, 1969, Poet of Exile (Milton), 1980, Thomas More: The Search for the Inner Man, 1990, From Renaissance to Baroque: Essays on Literature and Art, 1991; editor: Pilgrim's Progress, 1949, The Meditative Poem, 1963, Milton: Critical Essays, 1966, Anchor Anthology of 17th Century Verse, Vol. I, 1969, (with R. Sylvester) Thomas More's Prayer Book, 1969, Marlowe's Hero and Leander, 1972, (with F. Manley) Thomas More's Dialogue of Comfort, 1976, (with Aubrey Williams) The Author in His Work, 1978, H.D. (Hilda Doolittle) Collected Poems, 1912-1944, 1983, George Herbert and Henry Vaughan, 1986, H.D. Selected Poems, 1988, George Herbert, 1994, Quetzacoatl (D.H. Lawrence), 1995, Henry Vaughan, 1995; mem. editl. bd. Yale Editl. Prose works of John Milton; chmn. Yale Editl. Works of Thomas More; contbr. articles, revs. to Brit. and Am. jours. Recipient Christian Gauss prize, 1955; Guggenheim fellow, 1948-49, 81, Rockefeller fellow, 1966-67, NEH fellow, 1977-78. Mem. Am. Acad. Arts and Sci., Amici Thomae Mori, Renaissance Soc. Am., Brit. Acad., Elizabethan Club, Yale Club (N.Y.C.), Athenaeum Club (London), Phi Beta Kappa, Kappa Delta Rho. Home: 60 Old Quarry Rd Guilford CT 06437-3707 Office: 200994 Yale Sta New Haven CT 06520

MARUMOTO, WILLIAM HIDEO, management consultant; b. L.A., Dec. 16, 1934; s. Harry Y. and Midori Mary (Koyama) M.; m. Jean Masako Morishige, June 14, 1959; children: Wendy H. Vlahos, Todd M., Lani M. Moore, J. Tamiko Smith. BA, Whittier Coll., 1957; postgrad., U. Oreg., 1957-58. Dir. alumni rels. Whittier (Calif.) Coll., 1958-65; assoc. dir. alumni and devel. UCLA, 1965-68; v.p. planning and devel. Calif. Inst. of the Arts, L.A., 1968-69; sr. cons. Peat, Marwick & Mitchell, L.A., 1969; asst. to sec. HEW, Washington, 1969; spl. asst. Pres. of U.S., Washington, 1970-73; pres. The Interface Group Ltd., Washington, 1973-89; chmn. The Interface Group Ltd./Boyden, Washington, 1989—; mng. dir. ptnr. Boyden, Washington, 1992—; lectr. on career strategy, planning and diversity, 1973—; mem. White House Pers. Task Force, 1981-88, White House Conf. on Small Bus., 1986. Trustee Whittier Coll., 1978—, Japanese Am. Nat. Mus., 1989—, Mex. Am. Legal Def. and Ednl. Fund, 1989-93, Wolf Trap Found. for Performing Arts, 1995—, Coun. for Advancement and Support Edn., 1980-84; chmn. Nat. Japanese Am. Meml. Found., 1994-97, chmn., 1995—; chmn. Leadership Edn. for Asian Pacifics, Inc., 1994-97; bd. dirs. Congl. Asian Pacific Am. Caucus Inst., 1997—; mem. assocs. coun. George Washington U. Sch. Bus. and PUb. Mgmt., 1997—. Named one of Am.'s Top 150 Exec. Recruiters, Harper & Rowe Pubs., 1992, 94, One of 500 Most Influential Asian Americans, Ave. Avenue Mag., 1996, Most Influential Asian Am. in Washington, Asian Week, 1997. Mem. Assn. Exec. Search Cons. (bd. dirs. 1994-97), U.S. Nat. Assn. Corp. and Profl. Recruiters, Employment Mgmt. Assn., Congl. Country Club. Republican. Methodist. Home: 8808 Brook Rd McLean VA 22102-1509 Office: Boyden 2425 M St NW Ste 250 Washington DC 20037

MARUOKA, JO ANN ELIZABETH, information systems manager; b. Monrovia, Calif., Jan. 1, 1945; d. John Constantine and Pearl (Macovei) Gotsinas; m. Lester Hideo Maruoka, Nov. 8, 1973 (div. Aug. 1992); stepchildren: Les Scott Kaleohano, Lee Stuart Keola. BA with honors, UCLA, 1966; MBA, U. Hawaii, 1971. Office mgr. and asst. R. Wenkam, Photographer, Honolulu, 1966-69; computer mgmt. intern and sys. analyst Army Computer Sys. Command, Honolulu, 1969-78; reservations mgr. Hale Koa Hotel, Honolulu, 1978-79; equal employment opportunity specialist U.S. Army Pacific Hdqs., Honolulu, 1979-80, computer specialist, 1980-87, supervisory info. sys. mgr., chief plans and programs, 1987—; bd. dirs. High Performance Computing and Comm. Coun., Tiverton, R.I.; pacific v.p. Fedn. Govt. Info. Processing Couns., Washington, 1992-95. Mem. Nat. and Hawaii Women's Polit. Caucus, Honolulu, 1987—; advisor Fed. Women's Coun. Hawaii, Honolulu, 1977—. Recipient EEO Excellence award Sec. of Army, 1989, Pacific Fed. Mgr. award Honolulu-Pacific Fed. Exec. Bd., 1990, Info. Resources Mgmt. award Interagy. Com. on Info. Resources Mgmt., 1991, Lead Dog Leadership award Fedn. Govt. Info. Processing Couns., 1993; named One of Fed. 100 (Execs.) of Yr., Fed. Computer Week, 1996. Mem. NAFE, Nat. Women's Polit. Caucus, AAUW, LWV, Armed Forces Comm.-Electronics Assn. (Hawaii chpt., Internat. award for Info. Resources Mgmt. Excellence 1992), Assn. U.S. Army (Pacific Fed. Mgr. award 1990), Federally Employed Women (advisor Aloha and Rainbow chpts. 1977—), Army Signal Corps Regimental Assn., Hawaii Intergovt. Info. Processing Coun. (pres. 1988-89, svc. award 1989). Democrat. Avocations: travel, reading, tai chi, support of performing arts. Office: US Army Pacific Hdqrs APIM-PR Fort Shafter HI 96858

MARUPUDI, SAMBASIVA RAO, surgeon, educator; b. Chintalapudi, India, July 1, 1952; came to U.S., 1976; s. Venkateswarlu and Nagendramma (Gaddipati) M.; m. Usha Nandipati, Mar. 25, 1976; children: Neena, Neelima. MB, BS, Guntur (India) Med. Coll., 1974. Diplomate Am. Bd. Surgery, Am. Bd. Colon and Rectal Surgery. Rotation intern St. Clare's Hosp., Schenectady, 1976-77; resident in gen. surgery. St. Agnes Hosp., Balt., 1977-78, Franklin Square Hosp., Balt., 1978-82; fellow in colon and rectal surgery U. Tex. Health Scis. Ctr., Houston, 1982-83; pvt. practice, Amarillo, Tex., 1983—; clin. asst. prof. dept. surgery Tex. Tech U Health Scis. Ctr., Amarillo, 1984—. Fellow ACS, Am. Soc. Colon and Rectal Surgeons, Internat. Coll. Surgeons; mem. AMA, Tex. Med. Assn., Potter-Randall County Med. Soc. Democrat. Hindu. Office: 3501 Soncy Rd Ste 103 Amarillo TX 79119-6405

MARUSHIGE-KNOPP, YUKA, food scientist; b. Kyoto, Japan, Feb. 15, 1964; came to U.S., 1964; d. Keiji and Yasuko (Nakamura) Marushige; m. Thomas Karl Knopp, Dec. 16, 1989 (div. Dec. 1996). BS in Human Nutrition, Ohio State U., 1986, MS in Food Sci., 1987. Assoc. project leader product R&D Ross Products divsn. Abbott Labs., Columbus, Ohio, 1987-89, project leader product R&D, 1989-90, clin. rsch. monitor med. nutritional rsch., 1990-92, project leader divsn. quality assurance, 1992-95, project leader Abbott Internat. quality assurance, 1995-97, inventory planner, 1997—. Contbr. articles to profl. jours. Active, Hospice at Riverside and Grant. Univ. fellow Ohio State U., 1986-87. Mem. Inst. Food Technologists, Ohio Valley Inst. Food Technologists, Kappa Omicron Nu, Zeta Tau Alpha. Avocations: running, cooking, gardening, travel. Office: Ross Products Divsn Abbott Labs 625 Cleveland Ave Columbus OH 43215-1754

MARUSKA, EDWARD JOSEPH, zoo administrator; b. Chgo., Feb. 19, 1934; s. Edward M.; m. Nancy; children—Donna, Linda. Student, Wright Coll., Chgo., 1959-61; D.Sc. (hon.), Xavier U., 1986, U. Cin., 1989. Keeper hoofed animals Lincoln Park Zoo, Chgo., 1956-62; head keeper Children's Zoo, 1959-62; gen. curator Cin. Zoo, 1962-68, dir., 1968—; lectr. biol. sci. U. Cin.; numerous TV appearances. Recipient Cin. Conservation Man of Year award, 1973, Ambassador award Cin. Conv. and Visitors Bur., 1974. Fellow Am. Assn. Zool. Parks and Aquariums (pres. 1978-79); mem. Am. Soc. Ichthyologists and Herpetologists, Whooping Crane Conservation Assn., Internat. Union Zoo Dirs., Langdon Club, Cin. Naturalists Soc. Office: Zool Society of Cin 3400 Vine St Cincinnati OH 45220-1333

MARUVADA, PERESWARA SARMA, engineering executive, researcher; b. Rajahmundry, India, Jan. 1, 1938; emigrated to Can., 1964; s. Ramakrishnamma and Meenakshi (Karra) M.; m. Kamakshi Karra, Nov. 28, 1963; children: Venkata Rao, Siva Prasad. B.E. with honors, Coll. Engring., Kakinada, India, 1958; M.E. with distinction, Indian Inst. Sci. (Bangalore), 1959; M.A.Sc., U. Toronto, 1966, Ph.D., 1968. Sr. teaching fellow Indian Inst. Tech., Kharagpur, India, 1959-61; lectr. M.A. Coll. Tech., Bhopal, India, 1961-64; researcher Institute de Recherche d'Hydro-Que., Varennes, Que., 1969-75, program mgr., 1975-81, group mgr., 1981-83, research mgr., 1983-87, sr. researcher, 1987—. Contbr. articles to profl. jours.; patentee in field. Recipient Platinum Jubilee Alumni award Indian Inst. Sci., 1985. Fellow IEEE (exec. chmn. 1996 IEEE/PES Transmission and Distbn. Conf.); mem. Internat. Conf. on Large High Voltage Electric Systems (chmn. study com. 36 on power sys. electromagnetic compatibility), Que. Order Engrs. Home: 817 de Serigny, Boucherville, PQ Canada J4B 5C5 Office: Institut de Recherche d'Hydro-Que, 1800 Montee Sainte-Julie, Varennes, PQ Canada J3X 1S1

MARUYAMA, KARL SATORU, graphic designer; b. Honolulu, Sept. 13, 1958; s. Wallace Shigeru and Evelyn (Kimoto) M.; m. Amanda Cadwalader Worrall Engels, Nov. 23, 1991; 1 child, Christina Masae. BFA, U. Hawaii, 1981. Designer Jack Hough Assoc., Stamford, Conn., 1982-83; v.p. Tom Fowler Inc., Stamford, 1983—. Recipient 1st Place award Nat. Bus. Inst., 1989, Excellence award Print Regional Ann., 1992, Best in Typography award Print Mag., 1992, Excellence award Am. Corp. Identity, 1992. Mem. Am. Inst. Graphic Arts, Conn. Art Dirs. Club (Excellence award 1990, 92, Silver award 1991, 95, Gold award 1993). Avocations: skiing, technology. Office: Tom Fowler Inc 9 Webbs Hill Rd Stamford CT 06903-4427

MARVEL, L. PAIGE, lawyer; b. Easton, Md., Dec. 6, 1949; d. E. Warner Marvel and Louise Harrington Harrison; m. Robert H. Dyer, Jr., Aug. 9, 1975; children: Alex W. Dyer, Kelly E. Dyer. BA magna cum laude, Notre Dame Coll., 1971; JD with honors, U. Md., 1974. Bar: Md. 1974, U.S. Dist. Ct. Md. 1974, U.S. Tax Ct. 1975, U.S. Ct. Appeals (4th cir.) 1977, U.S. Supreme Ct. 1980, U.S. Ct. Claims 1981, D.C. 1985. Assoc. atty. Gabris & Schwait, Balt., 1974-76; shareholder Garbis & Schwait, Balt., 1976-85, Garbis, Marvel & Junghans, Balt., 1985-86, Melnicove, Kaufman, Weiner, Smouse & Garbis, Balt., 1986-88; ptnr. Venable, Baetjer and Howard LLP, Balt., 1988—; bd. dirs. Loyola/Notre Dame Libr., Inc.; mem. U. Md. Law Sch. Bd. Vis., 1995—; mem. adv. com. U.S. Dist. Ct. Md., 1991-93. Coeditor procedure dept. Jour. Taxation, 1989—; contbr. chpts. to books, articles to profl. jours. Active Women's Law Ctr., 1974-85, Md. Dept. Econ. and Community Devel. Adv. Comm., 1978-80. Recipient Recognition award Balt. is Best Program, 1981,. Fellow Am. Bar Found., Am. Coll. Tax Counsel (regent); mem. ABA (sect. taxation coun. dir. 1989-92, vice-chair com. ops. 1993-95, Disting. Svc. award), Am. Law Inst. (advisor Ali restatement of law third), Md. Bar Assn. (taxation sect. chair 1982-83, bd. dirs. 1988-90, 96—, Disting. Svc. award), Md. Bar Found., Balt. Bar Assn. (mem.-at-large exec. coun.), J. Edgar Murdock Am. Inns of Ct., Serjeant's Inn, Rule Day Club. Avocations: golf, music, travel. Home: 7109 Sheffield Rd Baltimore MD 21212-1628 Office: Venable Baetjer & Howard LLP 2 Hopkins Plz Baltimore MD 21201-2930

MARVEL, THOMAS STAHL, architect; b. Newburgh, N.Y., Mar. 15, 1935; s. Gordon Simis and Madelyn Emigh (Jova) M.; m. Lucilla Wellington Fuller, Apr. 19, 1958; children—Deacon Simis, Jonathan Jova, Thomas Stahl. AB, Dartmouth Coll., 1956; MArch, Harvard U., 1962. Registered architect, N.C., P.R., Mass., N.Y. Designer Synergetics, Inc., Raleigh, N.C., 1958; designer IBEC Housing, N.Y.C., 1959; ptnr., architect Torres-Beauchamp-Marvel, San Juan, P.R., 1960-85, Marvel-Flores-Cobian, San Juan, P.R., 1985-97; ptnr. Thomas S. Marvel Architects, San Juan, P.R., 1997—; prof. Sch. Architecture, U. P.R., Rio Piedras, 1967-89. Author: Antonin Nechodoma, Architect, 1994; co-author: Parish Churches of Puerto Rico, 1984. Works include Am. Embassy, Guatemala, 1973, U.S. Courthouse and Fed. Office Bldg., V.I., 1976, City Hall, Bayamon, P.R., 1978, Mcpl. Baseball Stadium, Bayamon, 1975, Am. Embassy, Costa Rica, 1986. Bd. dirs. St. John's Sch., San Juan, 1976-93. Recipient 1st award for regional coll. design U. P.R., Utuado, 1983; Harvard Grad. Sch. Design Julia Amory Appleton travelling fellow, 1962, Henry Klumb prize, 1991. Fellow AIA (bd. dirs. 1993-96, Design award for Fla. Caribbean region 1981, 84-85, 90-91); mem. P.R. Coll. Architects, Acad. Arts and Scis. Roman Catholic. Club: Harvard (N.Y.C.). Home: Del Valle 450 San Juan PR 00915 Office: Thomas S Marvel Architects 161 Calle San Jorge Santurce San Juan PR 00911-2018

MARVEL, WANDA FAYE, home health clinical consultant; b. Price, Utah, Nov. 10, 1951; d. Albert Jr. and Hazel A. Marvel; m. John M. Robinsin Jr. ADN, Westark Community Coll., 1978; BSN, U. Mo., 1986, MSN, 1993. Cardiac nurse Bapt. Med. Ctr., Little Rock, 1978-79; ICU staff nurse Ellis Fischel Cancer Ctr., Columbia, Mo., 1982-84; staff nurse emergency svc., med. ICU U. Mo., Columbia, 1984-87; head nurse surgery dept. Ellis Fischel Cancer Ctr., Columbia, 1987-89; rsch. asst. U. Mo., Columbia, 1988-89; asst. dir. Columbia Regional Hosp. Home Health, 1990-92; area v.p. HealthCor, Inc., Dallas, 1993-94, clin. cons., 1995—; guest lectr. Columbia Coll. RN Completion, 1989; clin. instr. Cen. Meth. Coll., Fayette, Mo., 1987; bd. dirs. Carpe Diem Hospice, Inc. Vol. Hospice Cen. Mo., Columbia, 1990; bd. dirs. Hospice Found., Columbia, 1990-91; mem. risk mgmt. advisory com. City of Columbia, 1996—. Recipient Grad. Nurse Assn. scholarship U. Mo., 1989, Nursing Fund scholarship, 1989, Superior Grad. Achievement award, 1990. Mem. AAUW, ANA, Grad. Nurses Assn. (pres. 1988-89), Oncology Nurses Soc., Emergency Nurses Assn. (chmn. govtl. 1988), Sigma Theta Tau. Avocations: reading, knitting, snow skiing, snorkeling.

MARVIN, CHARLES RODNEY, JR., lawyer; b. Elizabeth, N.J., Feb. 26, 1953; s. Charles Rodney Sr. and Doris Marie (Richards) M.; m. Carol Ann Welteroth, Aug. 30, 1975; children: Kathryn, Kristin, Cynthia, Gregory. BA in Econs., Mich. State U., 1975; JD, Boston U., 1978; LLM in Mil. Law, Judge Advocate Gen. Sch., 1987; LLM in Govt. Contracts, George Washington U., 1995. Bar: N.J. 1982, U.S. Dist. Ct. N.J. 1982, U.S. Ct. Mil. Appeals 1982, U.S. Ct. Appeals (fed. cir.) 1994, D.C. 1996. Nuclear missile officer U.S. Army, Schwaebisch Gmund, Germany, 1979-82; mil. prosecutor U.S. Army, Fort Sill, Okla., 1983-86; sr. def. counsel U.S. Army Trial Def. Svc., Ft. Polk, La., 1987-89; trial counsel, chief protest br. U.S. Army Contract Appeals Divsn., Arlington, Va., 1990-94; of counsel Venable, Baetjer, Howard & Civiletti, Washington, 1994—. Mem. ABA (vice-chair, bid protest com., pub. contract law sect. 1992-93), FBA, Bd. Contract Appeals Bar Assn. (bd. govs. 1993-96), Fed. Cir. Bar Assn., John Carroll Soc., Nat. Contract Mgmt. Assn. Roman Catholic. Avocations: musical composing, adult education, golf. Office: Venable Baetjer et al 1201 New York Ave NW Ste 1000 Washington DC 20005-3917

MARVIN, DAVID KEITH, international relations educator; b. Lincoln, Nebr., Apr. 8, 1921; s. Henry Howard and Alma (Wright) M.; m. Frances Parks Cash, Dec. 14, 1946; children: Margaret Elaine, Keith Wright, Martha Jean. B.A., U. Nebr., 1943; M.A., Northwestern U., 1955, Ph.D., 1957. Mem. UNRRA, Austrian Mission, 1946; vice consul Am. Fgn. Service, Peiping, 1947-50; 2d sec. London, 1950-53; consul Dar-es-Salaam, 1953; Ford Found. fellow Tanganyika, 1956-58; vis. asst. prof. Northwestern U., 1958; asst. prof. San Francisco State U., 1958-62, assoc. prof., 1962-67, prof., 1967—, asst. chmn. social sci. div., 1960-64, chmn. dept. internat. relations, 1964-70, 77-78, 80-84, prof. emeritus, 1986—; vis. prof. U. Calif. at Berkeley, 1967. Author: Emerging Africa in World Affairs, 1965. Chmn. North Coastside Community Council, 1962-64; Bd. dirs. Diablo Valley Edn. Project. Served with inf. AUS, 1943-46. Fellow African Studies Assn.; mem. Phi Beta Kappa. Office: 467 Urbano Dr San Francisco CA 94127-2862

MARVIN, JAMES CONWAY, librarian, consultant; b. Warroad, Minn., Aug. 3, 1927; s. William C. and Isabel (Carlquist) M.; m. Patricia Katharine Moe, Sept. 8, 1947; children: Heidi C., James Conway, Jill C., Jack C. B.A., U. Minn., 1950, M.A., 1966. City librarian Kaukauna, Wis., 1952-54; chief librarian Eau Claire, Wis., 1954-56; dir. Cedar Rapids (Iowa) Pub. Library, 1956-67, Topeka Pub. Library, 1967-92; ALA-Rockefeller Found. vis. prof. Inst. Library Sci. U. Philippines, 1964-65; vis. lectr. dept. librarianship Emporia (Kans.) State U., 1970-80; chmn. Kans. del. to White House Conf. on Libraries and Info. Services, Gov.'s Com. on Library Resources, 1980-81; mem. Kans. Libr. Adv. Commn., 1992—. Served with USNR, 1945-46. Mem. ALA, Iowa Libr. Assn. (past pres.), Kans. Libr. Assn., Philippine Libr. Assn. (life), Mountain Plains Libr. Assn. Home: 40 SW Pepper Tree Ln Topeka KS 66611-2055

MARVIN, OSCAR MCDOWELL, retired hospital administrator; b. Statesville, N.C., Apr. 12, 1924; s. Oscar McDowell and Gladys (Early) M.; m. Jane Everitt Krauss, June 16, 1951 (div. 1975); children: Frederick McDowell, Elizabeth Anne, Robert Doyle; m. Marcia Ann Benefiel Jackson, Dec. 2, 1977; children: Jonathan Paul, Katherine Susanne. A.B., U. N.C., 1948; M.B.A., U. Chgo., 1953; M.S., U. Louisville, 1971. Foreman Hanes Dye & Finishing Co., Winston-Salem, N.C., 1948-51; adminstrv. resident N.C. Bapt. Hosp., Winston-Salem, 1952-53; asst. adminstr. City Meml. Hosp., Winston-Salem, 1953-55, N.C. Med. Care Commn., Raleigh, 1955-57; hosp. adminstr., missionary Bd. World Missions, Presbyn. Ch. U.S., Yodogawa Christian Hosp., Osaka, Japan, 1957-60; asst. adminstr. City Memphis Hosp., 1960-62, adminstr., 1962-68; exec. dir. Louisville Med. Ctr., Inc., 1968-93, Med. Ctr. Commn. Jefferson County, 1982-93; lectr. dept. preventive medicine U. Tenn., 1963-68; assoc. prof. Coll. Pharmacy, 1965-68; organizer N.C. chpt. Hosp. Accts., 1954, pres., 1955-56; treas. Memphis Hosp. Coun., 1963, v.p., 1964, pres., 1965; sec. Memphis Inst. Medicine and Religion, 1966-68; sec.-treas. Assn. Coop. Hosp. Laundries, 1970-71; bd. dirs. Nat. Assn. Hosp. Hospitality Houses, Inc., 1986-93, v.p., 1990-91; sec., bd. dirs. Louisville Med. Ctr. Fed. Credit Union, 1974-92, Med. Ctr. Hospitality House, Inc., 1988-93. Contbr. articles to profl. jours. Mem. Memphis Mayor's Com. to Employ Handicapped, 1963; chmn. hosp. divsn. Shelby United Neighbors, Memphis, 1965; trustee Med. Benevolence Found., 1971; pres. Jefferson County Assn. Children with Learning Disabilities, 1973-74, bd. dirs., 1997—; pres. Ky. Assn. Children with Learning Disabilities, 1974-78; sec., bd. dirs. Butchertown Neighborhood Assn., 1992-96. Served with AUS, 1942-45. Mem. Am. Coll. Health Care Execs., Sigma Nu. Presbyterian (deacon, elder). Clubs: Rotary, Belles 'n Beau's Square Dance (pres. 1983-84). Home: 225 Bramton Rd Louisville KY 40207-3419

MARVIN, ROY MACK, foundry executive; b. Aberdeen, Wash., May 4, 1931; s. Merrill McKinley and Jennie Marie (Larsen) M.; B.S., Lewis and Clark Coll., 1954; A.S., Grays Harbor Coll., 1951; m. Diane Valeri MacKenzie, Nov. 26, 1955. Acct., Pope, Loback & Co., Portland, Oreg., 1953-54, 56-59; controller Ranch Homes, Inc., Beaverton, Oreg., 1959-61; controller, Precision Castparts Corp., Portland, Oreg., 1961-70, treas., 1967-93, dir., 1967—, v.p. fin., 1970-80, v.p. adminstrn., 1980-96, sec., 1983-96, dir. Physicians Assn. Clackamas County, Providence, Milwaukie, Oreg. Bd. dirs. Dwyer Hosp., 1970-79, 84-86; mem. exec. com. Greater Portland Bus. Group on Health; mem. Clackamas County Econ. Devel. Commn., 1984-91, dep. Oreg. Bus. Coun., 1982-90; bd. dirs Boys and Girls Aid Soc. Oreg., 1990—. Served with U.S. Army, 1954-56. C.P.A., Oreg. Mem. Nat. Assn. Accts. (past pres. Portland chpt.), Planning Execs. Inst. (past pres. Portland chpt.), AICPA, Fin. Execs. Inst., Oreg. Soc. C.P.A.s, Associated Oreg. Industries (bd. dirs., vice chmn. 1992-94), Assoc. Oreg. Indus. Pol. Action Com., (pres. 1991, trustee), North Clackamas C. of C. (pres. 1973), Oreg. Metals Industry Coun. (pres. 1991-94). Republican. Presbyterian. Club: Multnomah Athletic. Office: Precision Castparts Corp 4650 SW Macadam Ave Ste 410 Portland OR 97201-4253

MARVIN, URSULA BAILEY, geologist; b. Bradford, Vt., Aug. 20, 1921; d. Harold Leslie and Alice Miranda (Bartlett) Bailey; m. Lloyd Burton Chaisson, June 28, 1944 (div. 1951); m. Thomas Crockett Marvin, Apr. 1, 1952. BA, Tufts Coll., 1943; MA, Harvard/Radcliffe Coll., 1946; PhD, Harvard U., 1969. Rsch. asst. dept. geology U. Chgo., 1947-50; mineralogist Union Carbide Corp., N.Y.C., 1952-58; instr. dept. geology Tufts U., Medford, Mass., 1958-61; geologist, sr. staff Smithsonian Astrophys. Obs., Cambridge, Mass., 1961—, fed. womens program coord., 1974-77; vis. prof. dept. geology Ariz. State U., Tempe, 1978; lectr. geology Harvard U., 1974-92; trustee Tufts U., 1975—, U. Space Rsch. Assn., Columbia Md., 1979-84, chmn., 1982-83; sec.-gen. Internat. Commn. on History Geol. Scis., 1989-96, v.p. for Ams., 1996—. Author: Continental Drift, 1973; contbr. chpt.: Astronomy from Space, 1983, The Planets, 1985; assoc. editor Earth in Space, Am. Geophys. Union, 1988-90; contbr. articles to profl. jours. Mem. Lunar and Planetary Sci. Coun., Houston, 1987-91; chair antarctic meteorite working group Lunar and Planetary Inst., Houston, 1993—. Recipient Antarctic Svc. medal NSF, 1983, Sustained Superior Achievement award SAO, 1988, 93, 96, Lifetime Achievement award Women in Sci. and Engring., 1997; Asteroid Marvin named in her honor Minor Planet Bur. of Internat. Astron. Union, 1991, Marvin Nunatak (mountain peak rising through the Antarctic ice sheet) named in her honor U.S. Bd. on Geog. Names, 1992. Fellow AAAS, Meteoritical Soc. (pres. 1975-76), Geol. Soc. Am. (chmn. history of gology divsn. 1982-83, History of Geology award 1986); mem. Assn. Women in Sci., Am. Geophys. Union, History of Earth Scis. Soc. (pres. 1991), Sigma Xi (pres. Harvard-Radcliffe chpt.1971-72). Avocations: birding. Office: Harvard-Smithsonian Ctr for Astrophysics 60 Garden St Cambridge MA 02138-1516

MARVIN, WILBUR, real estate executive; b. Jamaica, N.Y., Apr. 8, 1921; s. Benjamin and Rose L. (Salmow) M.; m. Shirley G. Marvin, Mar. 18, 1945 (div. 1977); children: Michael F., Anne E. Marvin Swanson, Richard A.; m. Livia Seigho, Feb. 1980. BA, Harvard U., 1941; postgrad., U.S. Naval Acad., 1945-46. V.p. Third & Laurel Corp., N.Y.C., 1946-52; pres. Comml. Properties Devel. Corp., Baton Rouge, 1953—; bd. trustees Internat. Coun. Shopping Ctrs., N.Y.C. Contbr. articles to profl. jours. Comdr. USN, 1941-45. Decorated Purple Heart. Mem. Masons (bd. dirs.), Temple B'Nai Israel, Temple B'Nai Brith. Democrat. Jewish. Avocation: tennis. Home: 18835

Beaconwoods Dr Baton Rouge LA 70817-1808 Office: Comml Properties Devel Corp 1906 Beaumont Dr PO Box 1693 Baton Rouge LA 70821 Office: Guaynabo S Ctr PO Box 8459 SR 20 KM 3 5 Santurce PR 00910

MARVIN, WILLIAM GLENN, JR., former foreign service officer; b. Dobbs Ferry, N.Y., Oct. 30, 1920; s. William Glenn and Charlotte (Linden) M.; m. Sheila Wells, June 6, 1945 (dec.); children: Sally Marvin Lockhart, William Glenn III (dec.), Wells.; m. Suzanne Franzon, Oct. 16, 1982. Student, U. Calif., Berkeley, 1938-40; B.S., Harvard U., 1942; M.A., Stanford U., 1948. European rep. Hoover Instn., 1948-49; polit. scientist Stanford Research Inst., 1949-52; commd. fgn. service officer Dept. State, 1952; vice consul Algiers, 1952-55; consul Berlin, 1955-60; consul, prin. officer Fort de France, Martinique, 1964-66; econ. sec. CENTO, Ankara, Turkey, 1974-76; consul gen. Bordeaux, France, 1977-80; ret., 1980. Served to capt. U.S. Army, 1942-46. Mem. U.S. Fgn. Service Assn., Assn. Bordeaux-L.A. Clubs: Connetablie de Guyenne, Ordre de Tursan.

MARVIT, ROBERT CHARLES, psychiatrist; b. Lynn, Mass., Jan. 23, 1938. BS summa cum laude, Mass. Coll. Pharmacy, 1960; MD, Tufts U., 1964; M.Sc., Harvard U., 1970. Intern New Eng. Med. Ctr., Pratt Diag. Hosp., 1964-65; resident in psychiatry, neuropsychol. medicine Mass. Gen. Hosp., Boston, 1967-70; pvt. practice medicine, specializing psychiatry Honolulu, 1970—; prof. pub. health U. Hawaii, Honolulu, 1974-78, adj. prof. Sch. Pub. Health, 1978—; forensic advisor Hawaii Mental Health Div., 1977—; dir. Health Info. Sys. Office, Dept. Health, 1976-80; cons. in field; lectr. in field. Contbr. articles to profl. jours. Served with USPHS, 1965-67 to lt. comdr. Recipient Alpha Omega Alpha Research award Tufts U., 1963. Fellow Am. Coll. Preventive Medicine, Internat. Soc. Social Psychiatry of Am. Pub. Health Assn., Am. Psychiat. Soc.; mem. Am. Acad. Psychiatry and the Law, Hawaii Psychiat. Soc., AAAS, Harvard Med. Soc., Boston Soc. Neurology and Psychiatry, Hawaii Neurol. Soc., Internat. Soc. Neurosci., Am. Acad. Forensic Psychiatry, Alpha Omega Alpha. Home: 929 Pueo St Honolulu HI 96816-5234 Office: 1314 S King St Ste 759 Honolulu HI 96814-1942

MARWEDEL, WARREN JOHN, lawyer; b. Chgo., July 3, 1944; s. August Frank and Eleanor (Wolgamot) M.; m. Marilyn Baran, Apr. 12, 1975. BS in Marine Engring., U.S. Merchant Marine Acad., 1966; JD, Loyola U., Chgo., 1972. Bar: Ill. 1972, U.S. Dist. Ct. (no. dist.) Ill. 1972, U.S. Supreme Ct. 1974. With U.S. Merchant Marines, 1966-70; ptnr. Keck, Mahin & Cate, Chgo. Served to lt. (j.g.) USNR. Mem. ABA (Ho. of Dels. 1989—), Ill. Bar Assn., Chgo. Bar Assn., Maritime Law Assn. Club: Propellor (Chgo.) (pres. 1982). Avocations: boating, reading, history. Office: Keck Mahin & Cate 77 W Wacker Dr Chicago IL 60601

MARX, ANNE (MRS. FREDERICK E. MARX), poet; came to U.S., 1936, naturalized, 1938; d. Jacob and Susan (Weinberg) Loewenstein; m. Frederick E. Marx, Feb. 12, 1937; children: Thomas J., Stephen L. Student, U. Heidelberg, U. Berlin. mem. staffs N.Y.C. Writers Conf., 1965, Iona Coll., 1964, 65, 70, Wagner Coll., 1965, Poetry Workshop, Fairleigh Dickinson U., 1962, 63, 64, Poetry Soc. Am. Workshop, 1970-71, 78-79; Bronxville Adult Sch. Lecture Series, 1972; bd. dir. poetry series Donnell Library Ctr. (N.Y. Pub. Library), 1970-74; poetry day chmn. Westchester County, 1959—; Poetry Day Workshop, Ark., 1966, 70, Ark. Writers Conf., 1971, South and West Conf., Okla., 1972; vis. poet So. U., 1979; tchr., poetry readings, Jakarta, Indonesia, summer 1979; poetry workshop leader Scarsdale Cultural Ctr., 1981-82; conv. speaker Nat. Fedn. State Poetry Socs., 1974, 81, 82; condr. symposium Immigrant Voices, Pa. State U., 1986; judge Chapbook Award Nat. Federation of Poetry Socs., 1994, 1996-97; judge various nat. poetry contests; ongoing project: Selected Poems from Half a Century, 1997—. Poet; more than 1500 poems published in nat. mags., anthologies, lit. jours. and newspapers; Author: Ein Buechlein, 1935, Into the Wind of Waking, 1960, The Second Voice, 1963, By Grace of Pain, 1966, By Way of People, 1970, A Time to Mend; selected poems, 1973; A Conversation with Anne Marx; 2 hour talking book for blind, 1974; Hear of Israel and Other Poems, 1975, 40 Love Poems for 40 Years, 1977, Face Lifts for All Seasons, 1980, 45 Love Poems for 45 Years, 1982, Holocaust: Hurts to Healings, 1984, German edit. Wunden und Narben, 1986; A Further Semester, 1985, Love in Late Season (New Poems by Anne Marx), 1993; co-editor: Pegasus in the Seventies, 1973; contbr. to American Women Poets Discuss Their Craft, 1983, The Courage to Grow Old, 1989, A Collection of Essays by Ballantine Books, 1989; nat. editor poetry recs., Lamont Library at Harvard, stas. WFAS, WRNW, WEVD, WRVR, Voice of Am., The Pen Woman, 1986-88, Christian Sci. Monitor Anthology of Poems, 1989, Canadian Anthology, 1991, Irish Anthology, 1991. Recipient Am. Weave Chapbook award 1960, Nat. Sonnet 1959, 67, 81, award World Order Narrative Poets, 1981-85 1959, 67, prizes Nat. Fedn. Women's Clubs 1959, 60, Nat. Fedn. State Poetry Socs. 1962, 65, 66, 73, 80-83, South and West Publn. award 1965, Greenwood prize Eng. 1966, 2d Ann. Viola Hayes Parsons award 1977, award Delbrook Center Advanced Studies 1978, 1st prize Nat. Essay Competition, 1990, N.Y. State Outstanding Writer award, 1991; named Poet of the Year N.Y. Poetry Forum, 1981; winner Chapbook competition Crossroads Press, 1984, Ann. Writer's Digest award, 1983-90; recipient N.Y. State 1st prize for Poetry, 1995. Mem. Poetry Soc. Am. (life, exec. bd. 1965-70, v.p. 1971-72, 2 fellowships, Cecil Hemley Meml. award 1974), Poetry Soc. Gt. Britain, Nat. League Am. Pen Women (pres. Westchester county br. 1962-64, North Atlantic regional chmn. 1964-66, nat. letters bd. 1972-74, biennial poetry workshop leader, nat. poetry editor 1974-78, N.Y. State lit. chmn. 1979-80, N.Y. State pres. 1982-84, 2d nat. v.p. 1984-86, nat. editor Pen Woman mag. 1986-88, contbg. editor 1990—, Biennial Book award 1976, Biennial awards (4), 1982, (2), 1984, Writer of Yr. 1991, N.Y. State Poetry award 1996), Acad. Am. Poets, Poet Soc. Pa., Composers, Authors and Artists Am., Inc. (poetry editor mag. 1973-78), Poets and Writers, Inc., N.Y. Poetry Forum (life). Subject of story "An American by Choice, A Poet's Credo" pub. in The PEN Woman mag., Nov. 1988, The Courage to Grow Old, 1989, N.Y. Times interview "Finding Poetry in All of Life's Events," 1993; collected works N.Y. Pub. Libr.: Anne Marx Archives, 1992, early German material added to collection, 1994. *To be undeterred is the key to any achievement that is important to our lives. Undeterred by detractors asserting that one's goal is impossible to reach. Undeterred by blame or praise. Undeterred by demands of custom and fashion. Undeterred by all but the most essential bonds of family and friends. Undeterred even by the knowledge that there will be no greatness at the end of the long climb - only the satisfaction that we have tried to bring out the best that is in us, that we have added to our years that special ingredient we needed most to add zest to existence.*

MARX, DAVID, JR., lawyer; b. Chgo., Nov. 15, 1950. BA cum laude, Amherst Coll., 1972; JD, Syracuse U., 1975. Bar: N.Y. 1976, Ill. 1986. Ptnr. McDermott, Will & Emery, Chgo. Mem. ABA, Chgo. Bar Assn. Office: McDermott Will & Emery 227 W Monroe St Fl 31 Chicago IL 60606-5016

MARX, GERTIE FLORENTINE, anesthesiologist; b. Frankfurt am Main, Germany, Feb. 13, 1912; came to U.S., 1937, naturalized, 1943; d. Joseph and Elsa (Scheuer) M.; m. Eric P. Reiss, Sept. 26, 1940 (dec. 1968). Student, U. Frankfurt, Germany, 1931-36; M.D., U. Bern, Switzerland, 1937. Diplomate: Nat. Bd. Med. Examiners, Am. Bd. Anesthesiology. Intern, resident in anesthesiology Beth Israel Hosp., N.Y.C., 1939-43; adj. anesthesiologist Beth Israel Hosp., 1943-50, assoc. anesthesiologist, 1950-55; attending anesthesiologist Bronx Municipal Hosp. Center, 1955-95; attending anesthesiologist Bronx VA Hosp., 1966-72, cons., 1972-84; asst. prof. anesthesiology Albert Einstein Coll. Medicine, 1955-60, assoc. prof., 1960-70, prof., 1970-95, prof. emeritus, 1995—. Author: (with Orkin) Physiology of Obstetric Anesthesia, 1969; assoc. editor: Survey Anesthesiology, 1957-83; editor: Parturition and Perinatology, 1973, Clinical Management of Mother and Newborn, 1979, (with G. M. Bassell) Obstetric Analgesia and Anesthesia, 1980, Obstetric Anesthesia Digest, 1981—; cons. editor Internat. Jour. Obstetric Anesthesia, 1991—; contbr. articles to profl. jours. Recipient Nils Lofgren award, 1990, Coll. medal Royal Coll. Anaesthetists, 1993. Fellow Am. Coll. Anesthesiology, N.Y. Acad. Medicine, Am. Coll. Obstetricians and Gynecologists; mem. AMA, Am. Soc. Anesthesiologists (Disting. Svc. award 1988), N.Y. State Soc. Anesthesiologists, Am. Soc. Regional Anesthesia (Disting. Svc. award 1990), Bronx County Med. Soc., N.Y. Acad. Scis. Home: 129 Pomperaug Woods Southbury CT 06488-1873 Office: Albert Einstein Coll Medicine Dept Anesthesiology Bronx NY 10461 *I have devoted my professional life to easing the discomfort of childbirth and dare to hope that my efforts have helped to improve the outcome of pregnancy for mother and baby.*

MARX, JOHN NORBERT, chemistry educator; b. Columbus, Ohio, Oct. 31, 1937; s. John Norbert and Cecelia Evelyn (Noziska) M.; m. Charmaine Prudence Mueller, Dec. 27, 1968 (div. 1974); m. Patricia Colleen Loyd, Dec. 21, 1974; children: Ruth Elizabeth, Samuel John Loyd. BS, St. Benedict's Coll., Atcheson, Kans., 1962; PhD, U. Kans., 1965. Postdoctoral assoc. Cambridge (Eng.) U., 1965-66, Johns Hopkins U., Balt., 1966-67; asst. prof. Tex. Tech. U., Lubbock, 1967-74, assoc. prof. dept. chemistry, 1974—. Contbr. articles to profl. jours. Asst. scoutmaster Boy Scouts Am., Lubbock, 1990—. Rsch. grantee Robert A. Welch Found., Houston, 1968—. Mem. Am. Chem. Soc. (treas. South Plains sect. 1983—). Avocations: science fiction, book collecting, computer programming, camping. Office: Tex Tech U Dept Chem Biochemistry Lubbock TX 79409

MARX, KATHRYN, photographer, author; b. N.Y.C., June 4, 1950; d. Arthur and Emilie (Hyman) M. Freelance journalist, photographer N.Y. Newsday, N.Y. Daily News, Village Voice, Soho News, 1974-82, Infinito Mag., Italy, 1986; photographer Photo-Reporter, Paris, 1986, Editions Paris-Musées, 1992; columnist Photographies Mag., 1995—, Aram Dervent's Fatal, 1996. Photography exbhns. include Le Grand Palais, Paris, 1991, U.S. Embassy, Brussels, 1990, Carnavalet Mus., Paris, 1992, N.Y. Pub. Libr., 1992, Mus. Modern Art, Paris, 1994, Galerie Monde de L'Art, Paris, 1995, Aram Dervent's Fatal, 1996, Galerie Jean-Pierre Lambert, Paris, 1997, Month of Photography, Paris, 1997; contbr. articles to profl. jours. Rape crisis counselor St. Vincents Hosp., N.Y.C., 1981-83; active ACLU, N.Y.C., 1974-76; mem. Plan Internat. Foster Program, R.I., 1992—. Grantee Acad. Am. Poets, 1982, Eastman Kodak Co., Paris, N.Y., 1992-96, Fuji Film France, Paris, 1991-94, Sernam Corp., Paris, 1992-97. Mem. Author's Guild, Author's League of Am. Democrat. Avocations: painting, sculpture, yoga, birds, philosophy. Home: 61 Jane St New York NY 10014-5107 Office: 77 rue Notre Dame Des Champs, 75006 Paris France

MARX, MORRIS LEON, academic administrator; b. New Orleans, May 21, 1937. BS in Math., Tulane U., 1959, MS in Math., 1963, PhD, 1964. Asst. prof. math. Vanderbilt U., 1966-69, assoc. prof., 1969-77, dir. grad. studies in math., 1970-72; prof. math., chmn. dept. U. Okla., 1977-81, assoc. dean coll. of arts and scis., 1981-84, interim dean coll. of arts and scis., 1984-85; vice chancellor acad. affairs, prof. math. U. Miss., 1985-88; pres., prof. math. U. West Fla., Pensacola, 1988—. 1st lt. U.S. Army, 1964-65, capt., 1965-66. Office: U West Fla 11000 University Pkwy Pensacola FL 32514-5732*

MARX, NICKI DIANE, sculptor, painter; b. L.A., Oct. 3, 1943; d. Donald F. and Ruth H. (Ungar) M. Undergrad., U. Calif., Riverside, 1965, U. Calif., Santa Cruz, 1973. Represented by Lumina Gallery, Taos, N.Mex., Fred Kline Gallery, Santa Fe, N.Mex. One-woman shows include Palm Springs Desert Mus., 1977, Julie Artisans Gallery, N.Y.C., 1975, Phoenix Art Mus., 1975, Weston Gallery, Carmel, Calif, 1981, Kirk de Gooyer Gallery, L.A., 1982, Rocklands Gallery, Monterey, Calif., 1983, Fetish Gallery, Taos, 1988, Fenix Gallery, Taos, 1991, Earthworks, 1993, Lamberts, 1994, Stables Gallery, Taos, 1995, Fred Kline, 1995, Sun Cities Mus. Art, Ariz., 1996, others; group exhbns. include E.P. Smith Gallery, Santa Cruz, 1994, Lumina Gallery, Taos, 1994, Cafe Gallery, Albuquerque, 1991, Bareiss Gallery, Taos, 1990, Ctr. for Contemporary Art, Santa Fe, 1989, Jordan Gallery, Taos, N.Mex., 1988, 89, Stables Art Gallery, Taos, 1988, 94, Albuquerque State Fair Grounds, 1986, San Francisco Mus. Modern Art, 1977, 78, The Elements Gallery, Greenwich, Conn., 1977, Pacific Design Ctr., L.A., 1976, Lester Gallery, Inverness, Calif., 1976, numerous others; work included in sixteen invitational shows; represented in pub. collections IBM, Milford, Conn., N.Y.C., San Jose, Calif., Bank of Am., San Francisco, The Continental Group, Inc., Stamford, Conn., Cedars-Sinai Hosp., L.A., Farm Bur. Fedn., Sacramento, Calif., Sherman Fairchild Sci. Ctr., Stanford, Calif., Palm Springs (Calif.) Desert Mus., Univ. Mus., Ariz. State U. at Tempe, Mills Coll. Art Gallery, Berkeley, Calif.; exhibited in pvt. collections of Estate of Eugene Klein, Estate of Louise Nevelson, Estate of Georgia O'Keeffe, Fritz Scholder, Ray Graham, Bunny Horowitz, Sue and Otto Meyer, Burt Sugarman, Craig Moody, Paul Pletka, others; subject of numerous articles in jours. and mags. MacDowell Colony fellow, 1975; recipient Adolph and Esther Gottleib Found. grant, 1985. Studio: PO Box 1135 Ranchos De Taos NM 87557-1135

MARX, OWEN COX, lawyer; b. Grosse Pointe, Mich., Oct. 17, 1947; s. Leo A. and Anne (Cox) M.; m. Patricia Windschill, Aug. 14, 1971; children: Patrick Cox, Molly Simser, Anne Windschill. BA, Coll. of St. Thomas, St. Paul, 1969; JD, Cath. U., Washington, 1972. Bar: Minn. 1972, N.Y. 1973. Law clk. to presiding justice Minn. Supreme Ct., St. Paul, 1972-73; assoc. Mudge, Rose, Guthrie & Alexander, N.Y.C., 1973-75; assoc. Dorsey & Whitney, Mpls., 1975-78, ptnr., 1979-86; ptnr., head London office Dorsey & Whitney, 1986-90; ptnr. Dorsey & Whitney, N.Y.C., 1990—; bd. dirs. Bush Mfg. Co., Detroit, Off Site Tech. Inc., Detroit, OFLA Receivables Corp., San Diego. Mem. Internat. Bar Assn., Minn. Bar Assn., Mpls. Athletic Club, N.Y. Athletic Club. Republican. Roman Catholic. Home: 136 E 79th St New York NY 10021-0328 Office: Dorsey & Whitney 350 Park Ave New York NY 10022-6022

MARX, PAUL BENNO, author, social service administrator, missionary; b. Saint Michael, Minn., May 8, 1920; s. George and Elizabeth Marx. PhD in Family Sociology, Cath. U. Am., 1957. Ordained priest Roman Cath. Ch., 1947. Worldwide prolife missionary; founder, exec. dir. Human Life Ctr., 1972-80; founder, chmn. bd., pres. Human Life Internat., 1980—; prof. sociology S. John's U., Collegeville, Minn., 1957-80. Author: Virgil Michel and the Liturgical Movement, 1957, The Mercy Killers, 1971, The Death Peddlers: War on the Unborn, 1972, Japanese edit., 1972, Spanish edit., 1973, Death without Dignity: Killing for Mercy, 1983, And Now Euthanasia. . ., 1985, Confessions of a Prolife Missionary, 1988, Fighting for Life, 1989, The Flying Monk, 1991; contbr. numerous chpts. to books and articles to jours.; founder (quars.) The Internat. Rev. Natural Family Planning, Human Life Issues, Sorrow's Reward, (bi-monthlies) Escoge la Vida!, Seminarians for Life International; (monthly) Pro-Family Parish Notes. Mem. Internat. Fedn. for Family Life Promotion, Japan Found. for Family Life Promotion. Home: 4 Family Life Front Royal VA 22630*

MARX, RICHARD BENJAMIN, lawyer; b. N.Y.C., June 17, 1932; s. Samuel and Veronica (Baer) M.; m. Doriann Belzer, Nov. 28, 1992; children: Jennifer, Bruce. BA, Hobart Coll., 1954; JD, NYU, 1957. Bar: N.Y. 1958, Fla. 1965, U.S. Dist. Ct. (so. dist.) Fla., U.S. Dist. Ct. (no. dist.) Fla., U.S. Ct. Appeals (2d, 5th, 8th, 9th, and 11th cirs.), U.S. Supreme Ct. Sole practice Miami, 1965—. Named one of top 25 criminal attys. in U.S. Town & Country mag., Miami, 1985. Mem. ABA, Dade County Bar Assn., Nat. Assn. Criminal Def. Attys., Acad. Fla. Trial Lawyers, Dade County Trial Lawyers Assn. Clubs: Jockey, Palm Bay, Grove Isle (Miami). Office: 1221 Brickell Ave Ste 1010 Miami FL 33131-3258

MARX, SHARON ROSE, health facility administrator; b. Ferndale, Mich., Dec. 11, 1951; d. William Bernard and Evelyn Grace (Culbert) M. Student, U. Mich., 1970-72; BSN, U. Tex., Galveston, 1975; MS, U. Colo., Denver, 1984. RNC, cert. ob/gyn. nurse practitioner. Staff nurse John Sealy Hosp., Galveston, 1975, Harper Grace Hosp., Detroit, 1975-77, Hutzel Hosp., Detroit, 1977-79; office nurse Sellers & Sanders Clinic, New Orleans, 1979-82; clin. mgr. Rocky Mountain Hosp., Denver, 1982-83; clin. nurse specialist William Beaumont Hosp., Royal Oak, Mich., 1985-89; dir. maternal, child health Botsford Gen. Hosp., Farmington Hills, Mich., 1989-92; dir. women's and children's svcs. McLaren Regional Med. Ctr., Flint, Mich., 1992—; rsch. coord. maternal child health demonstration project Mich. Dept. Pub. Health, Royal Oak, 1985. Bd. dirs. March of Dimes, Flint, 1993—, Children's Wish Fund, Flint, 1992—; mem. task force on children Flint Focus Coun./Focus on Children, 1994. March of Dimes ednl. grantee, 1993. Mem. Mich. Orgn. Nurse Execs., Perinatal Assn. of Mich. (bd. dirs. 1985-86), Assn. Women's Health, Obstetric and Neonatal Nursing (membership coord. Mich. sect. 1993-95, chpt. coord. Detroit 1986-88). Avocations: gardening, fishing. Home: 6036 W Dodge Rd Clio MI 48420-8508 Office: McLaren Regional Med Ctr 401 S Ballenger Hwy Flint MI 48532-3638

MARX, THOMAS GEORGE, economist; b. Trenton, N.J., Oct. 25, 1943; s. George Thomas and Ann (Szymanski) M.; m. Arlene May Varga, Aug. 23, 1969; children: Melissa Ann, Thomas Jeffrey, Jeffrey Alan. BS summa cum laude, Rider Coll., 1969; PhD, U. Pa., 1973. Fin. analyst Am. Cyanamid Co., Trenton, 1968; economist FTC, Washington, 1973; econ. cons. Foster Assocs. Inc., Washington, 1974-77; sr. economist GM, Detroit, 1977-79, mgr. indsl. econs., 1980-81, dir. econs. policy studies, 1981-83; dir. corp. strategic planning group GM, 1984-86, gen. dir. market analysis and forecasting, 1986-88, gen. dir. econ. analysis, 1988-90, gen. dir. issues mgmt. on industry govt. rels. staff, 1990-96; dir. econ. issues and analysis corp. affairs staff GM, Detroit, 1996—; mem. faculty Temple U., 1972-73, U. Pa., 1972-73; adj. prof. Wayne State U., 1981—, U. Detroit, 1988—. Assoc. editor Bus. Econs., 1980—; mem. editorial bd. Akron Jour. Bus. and Econs., 1981-90; contbr. articles to profl. jours. Served with USAF, 1961-65. Mem. Nat. Econs. Club, Am. Econ. Assn., Nat. Assn. Bus. Economists, Detroit Area Bus. Economists (v.p.), Econ. Soc. Mich., So. Econ. Assn., Western Econ. Assn., Planning Forum, Assn. Pub. Policy Analysts, Pi Gamma Mu, Beta Gamma Sigma. Roman Catholic. Home: 3312 Bloomfield Park Dr West Bloomfield MI 48323-3514 Office: GM Corp 3044 W Grand Blvd Detroit MI 48202-3037

MARZETTI, LORETTA A., government agency executive, policy analyst; b. N.Y., Mar. 13, 1943; d. Lawrence Arthur and Josephine (Palazzo) M.; m. Gerald Oren Miller, July 12, 1986. AB in Sociology, Cath. U. Am., 1965. Chief info. svcs. br., OARM EPA, Washington, 1985-88, dir. comm., analysis and budget divsn. Office Solid Waste, 1988-95, dir. comms., info., resources mgt. divsn. Office Solid Waste, 1995-96; ret., 1996. Avocations: aerobics, exercise, walking, European travel, hiking. Home: 3088 S Woodrow St Arlington VA 22206-2115

MARZIO, PETER CORT, museum director; b. Governor's Island, N.Y., May 8, 1943; s. Francis and Katherine (Mastroberte) M.; m. Frances Ann Parker, July 2, 1979; children: Sara Lon, Steven Arnold. B.A. (Neva Miller scholar), Juniata Coll., Huntingdon, Pa., 1965; M.A., U. Chgo., 1966, Ph.D. (univ. fellow, Smithsonian Instn. fellow), 1969. Research asst. to dir., then historian Nat. Mus. History and Tech., Smithsonian Instn., 1969-73, assoc. curator prints, 1977-78, chmn. dept. cultural history, 1978; dir., chief exec. officer Corcoran Gallery Art, Washington, 1978-82; dir. Mus. Fine Arts, Houston, 1982—; instr. Roosevelt U., Chgo., 1966-68; assoc. prof. U. Md., 1976-77u; adv. coun. Anthrop. Film Ctr., Archives Am. Art; mem. adv. bd. Smithsonian Inst. Press; bd. dirs. First Interstate Bank of Tex. Author: Rube Goldberg: His Life and Works, 1973, The Art Crusade, 1976, The Democratic Art: An Introduction to the History of Chromolithography in America, 1979; editor: A Nation of Nations, 1976. Mem. adv. council Dumbarton Oaks, 1979-86; trustee, mem. exec. com., pres. Texart 150, Tex. Commn. on the Arts, Tex. Assn. for Promotion of Art, 1990-91. Sr. Fulbright fellow Italy, 1973-74. Mem. Print Council Am., Am. Print Council, Dunlap Soc., Assn. Art Mus. Dirs. (pres. 1988-89), Am. Assn. Mus. (exec. com.), Am. Fedn. of the Arts (trustee), Young Pres. Orgn. Club: Cosmos (Washington). Home: 101 Westcott St Houston TX 77007 Office: Mus Fine Arts 1001 Bissonet St PO Box 6826 Houston TX 77005

MARZLUF, GEORGE AUSTIN, biochemistry educator; b. Columbus, Ohio, Sept. 29, 1935; s. Paul Bayhan and Opal Faun (Simmons) M.; children: Bruce, Julie, Philip, Glenn. BS, Ohio State U., 1957, MS, 1960; PhD, Johns Hopkins U., 1964. Postdoctoral fellow U. Wis., Madison, 1964-66; asst. prof. biochemistry Marquette U., Milw., 1966-70; assoc. prof. Ohio State U., Columbus, 1970-75, prof., 1975—, chmn. dept. biochemistry, 1985—. Contbr. articles to profl. jours. Mem. Genetics Soc. Am., Am. Soc. Microbiology, AAAS, Am. Soc. Biochemists and Molecular Biologists. Office: Ohio State U Dept of Biochemistry 484 W 12th Ave Columbus OH 43210-1214

MARZLUFF, WILLIAM F., medical educator; b. Washington, May 7, 1945. BA in Chemistry magna cum laude, Harvard Coll., 1967; PhD in Biochemistry, Duke U., 1971; postdoc. student in Biology, Johns Hopkins U., 1971-74. From asst. prof. to prof. chemistry Fla. State U., Tallahassee, 1974-84, prof. chemistry, 1984-91; prof., dir. program molecular biology, biotech. U. N.C., Chapel Hill, 1991—; cons. physiology course MBL, Woods Hole, 1976; istr. sci. summer and math. camp Fla. State U., 1985, dir. program molecular biophysics, 1986-91; acting chmn. dept. biochem. and biophysics, U. N.C., 1994—; mem. rsch. com. Fla. Divsn. Am. Cancer Soc., 1977-91, chmn. summer rsch. fellowship subcom., 1979-83, 90-91; mem. site visit team NIH, 1980-88, ad hoc mem. molecular cytology study sect., 1982-85, ad hoc mem. molecular biology study sect., 1982-83, 86, 88, 89, mem. molecular biology study sect., 1989-91, chmn. molecular biology study sect., 1991-93; mem. cell biology panel NSF, 1987-89, mem. rev. panel biological ctrs., 1987-90; lectr. in field. Co-editor: Histone Genes: Organization and Expression, 1984; mem. editl. bd. Gene Expression; contbr. over 80 articles to profl. pubs. MBL fellow, 1975, NIH fellow; recipient Career Devel. award USPHS, 1975-80, tchg. award Program Med. Scis., 1978. Address: 5116 Green Meadows Rd Hillsborough NC 27278*

MARZULLI, JOHN ANTHONY, JR., lawyer; b. Orange, N.J., Jan. 3, 1953; s. John Anthony Sr. and Ruth Eileen (Dyer) M.; m. Penelope Bennett, Dec. 13, 1986; children: Emily Mooers, John A. III, Peter Bennett. BA magna cum laude, Middlebury Coll., 1975; JD, NYU, 1978. Bar: N.J. 1978, N.Y. 1979. Law clk. to chief judge U.S. Dist. Ct., N.J., 1978-80; assoc. atty. Shearman & Sterling, N.Y.C., 1980-87, pntr., 1988—. Contbg. author: Corporate Restructuring, 1990, European Corporate Finance Law, 1990. Mem. ABA, N.Y. State Bar Assn., N.J. Bar Assn., Order of Coif, Phi Beta Kappa. Office: 599 Lexington Ave New York NY 10022-6030

MASAI, MITSUO, chemical engineer, educator; b. Kobe, Hyogo, Japan, Sept. 30, 1932; s. Ei-ichi and Fumiko (Kimoto) M.; m. Rei Yamamura, May 1960; 1 child, Yohsuke. BS, Osaka U., 1956; PhD, Tokyo Inst. Tech., 1969. Researcher Showa Oil Co., Ltd., Tokyo, 1956-62; rsch. assoc. Tokyo Inst. Tech., 1962-69; from assoc. prof. to prof. catalysis Kobe U., 1969-96, emeritus prof., 1996—; prof. Fukui U. Tech., 1996—. Contbr. articles to profl. jours. Mem. Chem. Soc. Japan, Catalysis Soc. Japan (achievement award 1991), Japan Petroleum Inst., Soc. Chem. Engrs., Surface Sci. Soc. Japan, Camerata Muti Club. Avocations: classical music, audio, photography, visiting art museums. Home: Rokken-cho 2-2-406, Nishinomiya 662, Japan Office: Kobe U Faculty Engring, Rokkodai Nada, Kobe 657, Japan

MASCARA, FRANK, congressman; b. Belle Vernon, Pa., Jan. 19, 1930; married; 4 children. BS, Calif. U. Pa., 1972. Pub. acct., 1956-75; contr. Washington County, 1974-80; chmn. Wash. Bd. County Commrs., 1980-94; mem. 104th Congress 20th Pa. dist., 1995—. Office: US House Reps 314 Cannon HOB Washington DC 20515-3820

MASCETTA, JOSEPH ANTHONY, principal; b. Canonsburg, Pa., Sept. 2, 1931; s. Joseph Alphonso and Amalia (Ciavarra) M.; m. Jean Verrone, June 18, 1960; children: Lisa Marie, Linda Jo, Lori Jean. BS, U. Pitts., 1954; MS, U. Pa., 1963; cert. advanced study, Harvard U., 1970. Cert. tchr. math., phys. scis., adminstr. secondary sch., Pa. Tchr. chemistry Canonsburg High Sch., 1956-59; tchr. chemistry Mt. Lebanon High Sch., Pitts., 1959-75, chair sci. dept., 1967-75; coord. secondary curriculum Mt. Lebanon Sch. Dist., Pitts., 1975-81; prin. Mt. Lebanon Sr. High Sch., Pitts., 1981-91; ret., 1991; vis. team mem. Mid. States Assn. Colls. and Schs., Phila., 1967-78, chair vis. teams, 1981—, Pa. state adv. com., 1988-91; mem. sch. bd. and edn. commn. St. Patrick Sch., Canonsburg, 1972-85; regional dir. Pa. Jr. Acad. Sci., Pitts., 1976-82; ednl. cons. Pitts. area schs., 1992—; mem. quality edn. com. Pitts. Diocese, 1995—. Author: Modern Chemistry Review, 1968, Chemistry the Easy Way, 1989, revised, 1995, Barron's SAT II, Chemistry, 1994; contbg. author: (ency.) Barron's Student Concise Ency., 1988, rev. 1994, Barron's New Student's Concise Ency., 1993. Recipient Outstanding Tchr. award Spectroscopy Soc., 1973; grantee NSF, 1961, 62-63, 63, 67, 69-70, 73; sci. fellow GE, 1959. Mem. ASCD, Nat. Assn. Secondary Sch. Prins. (cert. recognition 1991), Pa. Assn. Curriculum & Supervision (exec. bd. dirs. 1985-87, regional pres. 1987), Western Pa. Assn. Curriculum & Supervision (v.p. 1983-85, pres. 1985-87, exec. bd. dirs. 1989—), Phi Delta Kappa. Roman Catholic. Avocations: painting, writing. Home: 451 Mcclelland Rd Canonsburg PA 15317-2258

MASCHAK-CAREY, BARBARA JEAN, clinical nurse specialist; b. Johnstown, Pa., July 20, 1947; d. Stephen Daniel and Ernestine Agnes (LaBuda) Maschak; m. Francis X. Carey, Dec. 3, 1977; children: Justin Francis, Lisa Jean. RN, Mercy Hosp. Sch. Nursing, Johnstown, Pa., 1968; BSN, U. Pa., 1972, MSN, 1980, postgrad. cert. diabetes educator Am. Assn. Diabetes Educators, clin. nurses specialist, ANA. Staff nurse med. nursing dept. Hosp. U. Pa., Phila., 1968-72, staff nurse med. intensive care unit, 1972-73, primary nurse provider med. diabetes, cardiac, ambulatory, 1973-80, staff devel. instr. for diabetes and hypertension edn., 1975-80, coord. of diabetes edn. program, 1975-85, chairperson patient edn. com., 1985-88, diabetes clin. nurse specialist, 1980—; adj. clin. preceptor grad. program. Sch. Nursing U. Pa., 1980—; rsch. nurse coord. diabetes control and complications trial U. Pa. Med. Ctr., 1985-93, trial coord. Epide,iology of Diabetes Intervention and Complications Study, 1994—; mem. endocrine adv. panel U.S. Pharmacopoeia Conv., Inc., 1991—, ind. cons., 1992; ind. cons. Windemere Comms., Inc., 1992, Becton Dickenson Corp., 1992; reviewer Diabetes Educator, 1989—; mem. faculty pump therapy symposiumMinimed Technologies, Princeton, N.J., 1991, 93; mem. faculty clin. edn. program Four Seasons Hotel, 1990; developer, coord., lectr. dept. med. nursing Hosp. U. Pa., 1983-84; cons. Met. Home Health Svc. Corp., 1985-86; mem. facilty 1st ann. conf. men.-surg. and geriatric nursing Am. jour. Nursing Chgo., 1989, Phila. Dietetic Assn., Del. chpt. Soc. Nutrition Edn., 1989, Clin. edn. program Md. cad. Family Physicians, Annapolis, 1990, clin. edn.program N.J. affiliate, 1990, clin. edn. program Phila. dept. health physicians Phila. County Med. Soc., 1990; lectr., presenter in field. Co-author: Goals for Diabetes Education; contbr. articles to profl. jours. Recipient Alleyen Von Son award for Outstanding Teaching Tool Am. Assn. Diabetes Edn., 1984. Mem. Am. Assn. Diabetes Educators, Am. Diabetes Assn. (Outstanding Health Care Profl. Educator award 1993, mem. com. on sci. and med. programs 1984-86, task force for profl. membership 1986-87, ad hoc reviewer of health edn. abstracts 1987, bd. dirs. 1986-89, facilty on conf. recognition 1988-89, reviewer tng. 1988-90, sec. coun. edn. 1989-91, edn. program rev. panel 1991-93, ADA applications reviewer 1987—, program chair coun. edn. 1992-93, profl. sect. adv. panel 1992-94, chairperson edn. coun. 1992, program co-chair, presenter Post-Grad. Course, Boston 1994, assoc. editor 1995—), Am. Diabetes Assn. Pa. Affiliate, Inc. (transition com. 1989-90, profl. edn. com.1990-91, exec. com. 1991, chmn. profl. activities com. 1991, bd. dirs. 1990-92, assoc. editor 1995—), Am. Diabetes Assn. Phila. Affiliate, Inc. (mem. various coms. including exec. com. 1979-89, chmn. diabetes educators coun. 1983-89, active speakers bur. 1979—, profl. edn. com. 1991, pres. Phila chpt. 1990-92, pres. 1990), Sigma Theta Tau. Home: 461 W Abbottsford Ave Philadelphia PA 19144-4766 Office: Hosp of the U Pa 3400 Spruce St Philadelphia PA 19104

MASCHERONI, ELEANOR EARLE, investment company executive; b. Boston, June 6, 1955; d. Ralph II and Eleanor Forbes (Owens) Earle; m. Mark Mascheroni, May 30, 1981; children: Olivia Forbes, Isabella Starbuck, Rex Owens. AB, Brown U., 1977. Dept. adminstr. Sotheby Parke Benet, N.Y.C., 1978-79; asst. dir. devel. Inst. Architecture and Urban Studies, N.Y.C., 1979-81; assoc. in pub. rels. Prudential Securities Inc., N.Y.C., 1981-84, asst. v.p. pub. rels., 1984-86, assoc. v.p. pub. rels., 1986-87, v.p., mgr. pub. rels., 1987-89, 1st v.p., dir. pub. rels., 1989-91, 91-95; v.p. pub. rels. Scudder, Stevens & Clark, N.Y.C., 1991—, prin., 1996—. N.Y. Alumnae bd. govs. St. Timothy's Sch., Stevenson, Md., 19877-94. Democrat. Episcopalian. Avocations: running, photography.

MASCHO, GEORGE LEROY, education educator emeritus; b. Warsaw, N.Y., Feb. 5, 1925; s. Clayton Leroy and Dorothy Emma (Bailey) M. B.Ed., SUNY, Geneseo, 1948; M.A., Stanford U., 1950; Ed.D., Ind. U., 1961. Tchr. Ontario (N.Y.) Jr. High Sch., 1948-49, Burris Lab. Sch., Muncie, Ind., 1950-61; mem. faculty Ball State U., Muncie, 1961-85; prof. edn. Ball State U., 1967-85, prof. emeritus, 1985—. Contbr. articles to profl. jours. Bd. dirs., treas. United Day Care Center, 1977—; mem. nat. com. developing Head Start program, 1965-66; vol. tutor Hui Malama Adult Literacy Svcs., 1988—; corr. sec. Maui Sr. Citizen Planning and Coordinating Coun., 1987-88; chmn. community ctr. planning com. Pukalani Community Assn., 1989. With inf. U.S. Army, 1943-46. Mem. Nat. Assn. Edn. Young Children, Ind. Assn. Edn. Young Children (chmn. legis. com. 1968-70), Assn. Childhood Edn., Hawaii State Ret. Tchrs. Assn. (chmn. planning com. conv. 1991), Maui Ret. Tchrs. Assn. (dir. 1985—, v.p. 1987-88, 88-89), Maui Sr. Citizen Planning/Coordinating Coun. (corr. sec. 1987-89), AARP, Hawaii, Hawaii State Ret. Tchrs. Assn. (Maui rep. 1989-90), Ind. Arabian Horse Assn. (dir. 1968-73), Am. Contract Bridge League, Pukalani Bridge Club (treas. 1993—), Phi Delta Kappa. Home: 2792 Aina Lani Dr Makawao HI 96768-8404 *To educate is to work with the future. All educators attempt to motivate, provide stimulating environments, prod and inspire students to reach just a bit higher than they would have reached had such contact not been made. If I attain that goal, my life is worthwhile.*

MASCI, JOSEPH RICHARD, medical educator, physician; b. New Brunswick, N.J., Nov. 27, 1950; s. Joseph Nicholas and Delfina (Musa) M.; m. Elizabeth Bass, May 21, 1993; 1 child, Jonathan Samuel. BA, Cornell U., 1972; MD, NYU, 1976. Diplomate Am. Bd. Internal Medicine, Am. Bd. Infectious Diseases. Instr. medicine Boston U. Sch. Medicine, 1979-80; instr. medicine Mt. Sinai Sch. Medicine, N.Y.C., 1982-84, asst. prof. clin. medicine, 1984-88, asst. prof. medicine, 1988-90, assoc. prof. medicine, 1990—; assoc. dir. medicine Elmhurst (N.Y.) Hosp. Ctr., 1987—; peer reviewer NIH, 1994—. Author: Primary and Ambulatory Care of the HIV-Infected Adult, 1992, Outpatient Management of HIV-Infection, 1996. Fellow Am. Coll. Angiology, Am. Coll. Chest Physicians; mem. ACP, Am. Soc. Microbiology, Assn. Program Dirs. Internal Medicine. Office: Elmhurst Hosp Ctr 79-01 Broadway Elmhurst NY 11373-1329

MASEK, BARRY MICHAEL, accountant; b. Beatrice, Nebr., Nov. 18, 1955; s. Charles Joseph and Patricia Anne (Hynek) M.; m. Mary Ellen McNamara, Nov. 27, 1981; children: Katherine Marie, Caroline Christine, Amanda Elizabeth. BS in Acctg., U. Nebr., 1979. CPA, Nebr., Ill. Staff asst. Arthur Andersen LLP, Chgo., 1979-81, sr. acct., 1981-84, mgr. acctg. and auditing, 1984-89, sr. mgr. auditing and fin. cons., 1989-93, ptnr., 1993—. Mem. Am. Inst. CPA's, Nebr. State Soc. CPA's, Ill. State Soc. CPA's. Roman Catholic. Avocations: golf, tennis, basketball, theatre, church choir. Home: 1024 S Hamlin Ave Park Ridge IL 60068-4368 Office: Arthur Andersen LLP 33 W Monroe St Chicago IL 60603-5300

MASEK, MARK JOSEPH, laboratory administrator; b. Joliet, Ill., June 13, 1957; s. Glenn James and Helen Margaret (Gleason) M.; m. Theresa Marie Norton, Oct. 24, 1987. BJ, U. Ill., 1979. Reporter The Daily Illini, Champaign, 1976-79, Joliet Herald-News, 1978-79; columnist, editor Elgin (Ill.) Daily Courier-News, 1979-88; editor The Daily Herald, Arlington Heights, Ill., 1988-90; publs. mgr. Argonne (Ill.) Nat. Lab., 1990—. V.p. Recycle Now-Joliet, 1991—; active City of Joliet Environ. Commn., 1993-96; bd. dirs. Will County Habitat for Humanity, 1994—. Recipient 1st pl. pub. svc. award Ill. AP Editor's Assn., 3d pl. pub. svc. award, 1980, 2d pl. columns award No. Ill. Newspaper Assn., 1982, 1st pl. columns award Nat. Newspaper Assn., 1982. Mem. Soc. Profl. Journalists, Mensa. Democrat. Roman Catholic. Office: Argonne Nat Lab 9700 Cass Ave Argonne IL 60439-4803

MASELLI, JOHN ANTHONY, food products company executive; b. N.Y.C., Feb. 18, 1929; s. Anthony and Livia M.; m. Brigitta Degenkolb, Dec. 26, 1948; children: Elisa, John A. Jr. BS in Chemistry, CCNY, 1947; MS in Chemistry, Fordham U., 1949, PhD in Chemistry, 1952. Dir. research and devel. Standard Brands, Stamford, Conn., 1952-64; mgr. product devel. M&M/Mars, Hackettstown, N.J., 1964-67; pres. OZ Food Corp., Chgo., 1967-79; v.p. tech. Nabisco Brands, East Hanover, N.J., 1979-85; v.p. corp. research and devel. RJR Nabisco, Winston-Salem, N.C., 1985-87; sr. v.p. tech. Planters LifeSavers Co., Winston-Salem, 1987-91, cons., 1991—; bd. dirs. Cultor Food Scis. (Finland), N.C. Biotech. Ctr., Sci-Works, Winston Salem. Patentee in field. Bd. dirs. Chgo. Boy's Club, 1975-79, YMCA, Wilton, Conn. 1980-84. Mem. AAAS, ACS, Inst. Food Tech., Am. Soc. Bakery Engrs., Indsl. Biotechnology Assn., Indsl. Research Inst. Republican. Avocations: sailing, photography, music. Home: 529 Knob View Pl Winston Salem NC 27104-5107

MASER, DOUGLAS JAMES, lawyer; b. Canton, Ohio, Nov. 21, 1951; s. David James and Mardell Margaret (Getz) M.; m. Gloria A. Bishop, Oct. 19, 1996; 1 child, Courtney Leigh. BA, Ohio State U.; JD, Capital U., Columbus, Ohio. Bar: Ohio 1976, U.S. Dist. Ct. (so. dist.) Ohio 1977. Asst. pros. atty. Franklin County Pros. Attys. Office, Columbus, 1975-80; assoc. Janes and Jack Law Offices, Columbus, 1980-85; pvt. practice Columbus, 1985-88; ptnr. Day, Ketterer, Raley, Wright & Rybolt, Columbus, 1988-95; dep. adminstr. med. mgmt. & cost containment Ohio Bur. Worker's Compensation, Columbus, 1995—; legis. cons. Ohio Assn. Chiefs Police, Columbus, 1983-86, Franklin County Bd. Mental Health, Columbus, 1988-90, Ohio Fire Chiefs Assn., Columbus, 1985-90. Dir. Upper Arlington (Ohio) Civic Assn., 1994; mem. Bd. Social Concern, Upper Arlington Luth. Ch., 1993-94; col. Ohio Army Nat. Guard/112 Med. Brigade, 1994-95. 1st lt. U.S. Army, 1977. Mem. ABA, Ohio State Bar Assn., Columbus Bar Assn., Athletic Club Columbus. Republican. Avocations: computer simulations, war gaming, bicycling, hiking, swimming. Office: Ohio Bur Workers Comp 30 W Spring St Columbus OH 43215-2241

MASER, FREDERICK ERNEST, clergyman; b. Rochester, N.Y., Feb. 26, 1908; s. Herman A. and Clara (Krumm) M.; m. Anne S. Spangeberg, Aug. 3, 1933; m. Mary L. Jarden, Dec. 25, 1959. AB, Union Coll., Schenectady, N.Y., 1930; MA, Princeton U., 1933; MDiv, Princeton Theol. Sem., 1933; DD, Dickinson Coll., 1957; LL.D. (hon.), McKendree Coll., 1964. Ordained to ministry Methodist Ch., 1933. Pastor Alice Focht Meml. Ch., Birdsboro, Pa., 1933-38, Central Ch., Frankford, Phila., 1938-45, St. James Ch., Olney, Phila., 1945-53; dist. supt. Northwest dist. Phila. Meth. Ann. Conf., 1953-58; pastor Old St. George's Ch., Phila., 1958-67; on sabbatical leave Europe, 1967-68; acting dean students Conwell Sch. Theology, 1968-69; dir. pub. relations Eastern Pa. Conf. United Meth. Ch., 1969-72; exec. sec. World Meth. Hist. Soc., 1971-74; cons. commn. on archives and history United Meth. Ch., 1974—; Tipple lectr. Drew U., Madison, N.J., 1977; spl. lectr. N.Am. sect. World Meth. Hist. Soc., Ashbury Sem., Wilmore, Ky., 1984—; rep. from Northeast Jurisdiction to TV Radio and Film Commn. Meth. Ch., 1952-60; exec. com. Am. Hist. Socs. of Meth. Ch., 1952-68; vice chmn. N.E. Jurisdictional Hist. Socs., 1948; chmn. div. evangelism Pa. Council Chs., 1953-58; mem.-at-large TV, Radio and Film Commn. Meth. Ch., 1960-64; del. Phila. Ann. Conf. to Jurisdictional Conf. of Meth. Ch., 1952; leader ministerial del. to Gen. Conf. Meth. Ch., Mpls., 1956; del. 9th World Conf. of Methodism, Lake Junaluska, 1956, 10th Conf., Oslo, 1961, 12th Conf., Denver, 1971, 13th Conf., Dublin, 1976, 14th Conf., Hawaii, 1981; dir. pub. relations Phila. Meth. ann. conf., 1961-68; exec. sec. World Meth. Hist. Soc., 1971-74. Author: The Dramatic Story of Early American Methodism, 1965, The History of Methodism in Central Pennsylvania, 1971, The Human Side of the Mother of Methodism, 1973, Challenge of Change: The Story of a City's Central Church, 1982, Robert Strawbridge, First American Methodist Circuit Rider, 1983, The Story of John Wesley's Sisters or Seven Sisters in Search of Love, 1988, The Wesley Sisters, 1990, Unfolding the Secret of History, 1991, Theories of the Atonement and the Final Solution, 1993, Sara Teasdale, A Returning Comet, 1993, John Wesley and the Indians of Georgia, 1995, The Little Known Appearances of Jesus, 1996; co-author: Proclaiming Grace and Freedom, 1984, Christina Rossetti, 1991, United Methodism in America, A Compact History, 1992; mem. editorial bd. Meth. History, 1971-75; editor in chief Jour. Joseph Pilmore, 1968; mem. editorial bd., author History American Methodism, 1964, Ency. World Methodism, 1974, Second Thoughts on John Wesley, 1977, Affectionately, your Brother, 1994, The Little Known Appearences of Jesus-A Fantasy, 1996, The Story of Captain Webb, 1996; contbr. articles to religious jours. Trustee George Ruck Trust, 1958-82; mem. adv. council Wesley Theol. Sem., Washington, 1960-72. Recipient St. George's Gold medal award for disting. svc. to Meth. Ch., 1967, Citation Temple U., 1971, (with Mary L. Maser) Phyllis Goodhart award Bryn Mawr Coll. Libr., 1988, cert. appreciation for disting. contbns. to field of Meth. history Commn. on Archives and History of United Meth. Ch., honoree for life-long commitment to Wesley studies The Charles Wesley Soc., 1992. Mem. Pa. Acad. Fine Arts, Colonial Phila. Hist. Soc. (bd. dirs. 1956-64), Ch. History Soc., Union League, Wesley Soc. (life, honored for disting. contbn. in field of rsch.), Philobiblon Club, Princeton Club, Phi Beta, Phi Alpha. Home: Heritage Towers Apt 634 200 Veterans Ln Doylestown PA 18901-3450 *Life offers many honors but the older I grow, the more I realize that the highest honor is to have one's name written in the Lamb's Book of Life.*

MASEY, JACK, exhibition designer; b. N.Y.C., June 10, 1924; s. Max and Anna Masey; m. Mary Lou Leach, Dec. 27, 1959. Student, Cooper Union, 1941-43; B.F.A., Yale, 1950. Pres. MetaForm Inc., N.Y.C., 1979—; co. project mgr. for design of La. Pavilion, World Expo., New Orleans, 1984, Statue of Liberty Exhibit, N.Y.C., 1986; project mgr. for design Johnstown (Pa.) Flood Mus., 1988, Ellis Island Immigration Mus., N.Y.C., 1990; co. project mgr. for design of Nat. D-Day Mus., New Orleans, 1994, Harry S. Truman Mus., Independence, Mo., 1994; lectr. Sch. Art and Architecture, Yale U., 1968-69. Cartoonist Esquire mag, 1946; exhibits officer, USIS, New Delhi, 1951-55; designer U.S. Pavilion, Kabul Internat. Fair, 1956; dir. design Am. Nat. Exhbn., Moscow, 1959, chief, East-West exhibits br. USIA, Washington, 1960-67; chief design U.S. Pavilion, Montreal (Que., Can.) World's Fair, 1967, dep. commr. gen. for planning and design Osaka (Japan) World Expn., 1970; dir. design Am. Revolution Bicentennial Commn., Washington, 1971-73; dir. design and exhbns. Am. Revolution Bicentennial Adminstrn., 1974-77, design dir. Internat. Communication Agy., Washington, 1977—; designer: Medicine-U.S.A. exhbn. for, USSR exchange program, 1962, Tech.-Books exhbns., 1963. Served with AUS, 1943-45, ETO. Recipient Meritorious Service award USIA, 1959, Superior Service award, 1964, Superior Honor award, 1967, 75; award of excellence Fed. Design Council, 1975; Outstanding Achievement award, 1979; award of excellence Soc. Fed. Artists and Designers, 1971; Gold medal Art Dirs. Club, 1965; cert. of excellence Am. Inst. Graphic Arts, 1964; two Fed. Design Achievement awards for Contributions to Excellence in Design, U.S. Govt., 1984, Presdl. awards for Statue of Liberty Exhibit, 1986, for Ellis Island Immigration Mus., 1990. Home: 131 E 66th St Apt 3A New York NY 10021-6129 Office: 15 E 26th St New York NY 10010-1505

MASH, DONALD J., college president; b. Oct. 12, 1942; m. Julia Larson (div.); children: Maria, Christina, Donnie (dec.). BS in Edn., Ind. U. Pa., 1960; MA in Geography, U. Pitts., 1966; PhD, Ohio State U., 1974. Teaching fellow U. Pitts., 1964-65; instr. geography U. Pitts.-Bradford, 1965-68; dean for student svcs. Ohio Dominican Coll., 1968-75; v.p. for student affairs George Mason U., Fairfax, Va., 1975-85, exec. v.p. adminstrn., 1985-88; pres. Wayne (Nebr.) State Coll., 1988—. Office: Wayne State Coll Office of Pres Wayne NE 68787

MASHECK, JOSEPH DANIEL, art critic, educator; b. N.Y.C., Jan. 19, 1942; s. Joseph Anthony and Dorothy Anna (Cahill) M. A.B., Columbia U., 1963, M.A., 1965, Ph.D., 1973. Editorial researcher Bollingen Found.-Princeton U. Press, 1967-69; lectr. liberal studies Maidstone Coll. Art, Kent, Eng., 1968-69; preceptor in art history Columbia U., 1970-71; instr. art history Barnard Coll., 1971-73, asst. prof., 1973-82; lectr. visual and environ. studies Harvard U., Cambridge, Mass., 1983-86; assoc. prof. art history Hofstra U., Hempstead, N.Y., 1987-94, prof., 1994—; coord. grad. program in humanities, curatorial cons. Hofstra Mus., Hempstead, N.Y. Author: Historical Present: Essays of the 1970s, 1984, Smart Art (Point 1), 1984, Modernites: Art-Matters in the Present, 1993, Building-Art: Modern Architecture Under Cultural Construction, 1993; editor: Marcel Duchamp in Perspective 1975, Van Gogh 100, 1996. Bd. dirs. Crosby St. Project, N.Y., 1995-96. Nat. Endowment Arts fellow, 1972-73, 75-76; Guggenheim fellow, 1977-78. Mem. AAUP, Coll. Art Assn., Internat. Assn. Art Critics, United Arts Club (Dublin). Roman Catholic. Democrat. Office: Hofstra U Dept Fine Arts and Art History Calkins Hall Hempstead NY 11550-1090

MASHIN, JACQUELINE ANN COOK, medical sciences administrator; b. Chgo., May 11, 1941; d. William Hermann and Ann (Smidt) Cook; m. Fredric John Mashin, June 7, 1970; children: Joseph Glenn, Alison Robin. BS, U. Md., 1984. Cert. realtor. Adminstrv. asst. CIA, Washington, 1963-66; asst. to mng. dir. Aerospace Edn. Found., Washington, 1966-74; exec. asst. to asst exec. dir. Air Force Assn., Washington, 1974-79; v.p., ptnrship. owner Discount Linen Store, Silver Spring, Md., 1979-81; asst. regional polit. dir. Office of Pres.-elect, Washington, 1980-81; confidential asst. to dir. Office of Personnel Mgmt. (US), Washington, 1981-83; spl. asst. to dep. dir. Office of Mgmt. and Budget, Washington, 1983-86; dir. internat. communications and spl. asst. to commr. Dept. of the Interior, Washington, 1986-89, cons., 1989-93; with Washington Hosp. Ctr., 1993—. Pres. Layhill Civic Assn., Silver Spring, Md., 1980; state chmn. Md.'s Reagan Youth Delegation, Annapolis, Md., 1980; state treas., office mgr. Reagan-Bush State Hdqrs. of Md., Silver Spring, 1980; mem. Women's Com. Nat. Symphony Orch. Mem. Air Force Assn. (life), Aux. Salvation Army (life), Am. League Lobbyists, Internat. Platform Assn., U.S. Capital Hist. Soc., Women's Nat. Rep. Club (N.Y.C.), Indian Springs Country Club. Republican. Avocations: golf, horseback riding, collecting wine glasses, Hibel plates, lithos and Lalique crystal. Home and Office: 2429 White Horse Ln Silver Spring MD 20906-2243

MASI, DALE A., research company executive, social work educator; b. N.Y.C.; d. Alphonse E. and Vera Avella; children: Eric, Renee, Robin. BS, Coll. Mt. St. Vincent; MSW, U. Ill.; D Social Work, Cath. U. Lectr. Sch. Social Svcs., Ipswitch, Eng., 1970-72; project dir. occupational substance abuse program, asso. prof. Boston Coll. Grad. Sch. Social Work, 1972-79; dir. Office Employee Counseling Svc., Dept. Health/Human Svcs., Washington, 1979-84; pres. Masi Research Cons., Inc., 1984—; prof. U. Md. Grad. Sch. Social Work, 1980—; adj. prof. U. Md. Coll. Bus. and Mgmt., 1980—; mem. IBM Mental Health Adv. Bd., 1990-95; cons. IBM, Toyota, Mobil Chm., The Washington Post, U.S. Ho. Reps., U.S. Postal Svc., White Hous, WHO, Bechtel Corp., other orgns. in pub. and pvt. sector; bd. advisors Employee Assistance mag. and Nat. Security Inst.; USIA Ampart lectr. on alcohol, drugs and AIDS in the workplace. Author: Human Services in Industry, Organizing for Women, Designing Employee Assistance Programs, Drug Free Workplace, AIDS Issues in the Workplace: A Response Model for Human Resource Management, The AMA Handbook for Developing Employee Assistance and Counseling Programs, Evaluating Your Employee Assistance and Managed Behavioral Care Program, Internat. Employee Assistance Anthology; also over 40 articles. Fulbright fellow, 1969-70; AAUW postdoctoral fellow; NIMH fellow, 1962-64; recipient award Employee Assistance Program Digest; named to Employee Assistance Program Hall of Fame. Mem. AAUW, NASW (Internat. Rhoda G. Sarnat award 1993), Acad. Cert. Social Workers, Employee Assistance Profls. Assn. (nat. individual achievement award 1983), Fulbright Assn. (nat. bd.). Democrat. Roman Catholic. Office: 500 23rd St NW Apt 202 Washington DC 20037-2830

MASI, EDWARD A., computer company executive; b. Medford, Mass., May 7, 1947; s. Joseph Carl and Rita Olivine (Metras) M.; m. Kristine Ann Lauderbach Masi, Jan. 24, 1970. BSME, Tufts U., 1969. Mktg. sales IBM, Boston, 1969-76; commercial analysis IBM, Westchester, N.Y., 1976-78; mktg. mgr. IBM, Bethesda, Md., 1978-80; region mgr. mktg. sales Cray Rsch., Calverton, Md., 1980-87; exec. v.p. mktg. Mpls., 1988-92; corp. v.p., gen. mgr. Intel Corp., Beaverton, Oreg., 1992. Mem. Am. Electronics Assn. (vice chair 1991-92). Avocations: tennis, scuba diving. Office: Intel Enterprise Servers Group Server Sys Product Divsn 5200 NE Elam Young Pkwy Hillsboro OR 97124-6463

MASIELLO, ANTHONY M. (TONY MASIELLO), mayor; b. 1947; s. Dan and Bridget M.; married; 1 child, Kimberly; m. Kathleen McCue; 1 child, Ariel Lynn. BS, Canisius Coll.; LHD (hon.), Medaille Coll. Mem. North Dist. Buffalo Common Coun., councilman-at-large, coun. majority leader; mem. N.Y. State Senate, 1980—; mayor City of Buffalo. Office: Office of the Mayor 201 City Hall 65 Niagara Sq Buffalo NY 14202-3331*

MASIELLO, ROCCO JOSEPH, airlines and aerospace manufacturing executive; b. N.Y.C., Jan. 9, 1922; s. Joseph and Armanda (Mansueti) M.; m. Rita Elizabeth Amoruso, Feb. 19, 1945; children: Richard, Robin, Janet. Student, CCNY, 1946-48, Hofstra U., 1951-54. Registered profl. engr., Maine. With Pan. Am. World Airways, N.Y.C., 1950-59; v.p. maintenance and engring. U.S. Air Group, Pitts., 1959-72, Am. Airlines, Tulsa, 1973-82; sr. v.p. ops. Am. Airlines, Dallas, 1982-86; founder, exec. v.p. USAfrica Airways, 1990-94, also bd. dirs; founder The Reston Group; aerospace cons., prin. R.J. Masiello and Assocs. Mem. Soc. Automotive Engr., Royal Aero. Soc. Roman Catholic.

MASIN, MICHAEL TERRY, lawyer; b. Montreal, Jan. 28, 1945; came to U.S., 1954; s. Frank J. and Sonia (Ellmann) M.; m. Joanne Elizabeth Combé, June 4, 1966; 1 child, Courtney. BA, Dartmouth U., 1966; JD, UCLA, 1969. Bar: Calif. 1969, D.C. 1970. Assoc. O'Melveny & Myers, Los Angeles, 1969-76; ptnr. O'Melveny & Myers, Washington, 1976-91; mng. ptnr. O'Melveny & Myers, N.Y.C., 1991—; bd. dirs. Trust Co. West, L.A., GTE Corp., Stamford, Conn., vice chmn., 1993-95, vice chmn., pres. internat., 1995; bd. dirs. Compana Anonima Nacional Telefonos de Venezuela, Brit. Columbia Telephone, The Travelers Group, Inc. Mem. bus. com. bd. trustees Mus. Modern Art; trustee Carnegie Hall; mem. dean's adv. com. Dartmouth Coll., U.S.-Can. Pvt. Sector Adv. Coun. of Inter-Am. Devel.; bd. mem. China Am. Soc. Mem. ABA, Coun. on Fgn. Rels., The Brook, Calif. Club. Republican. Methodist. Office: GTE Corp 1 Stamford Forum Stamford CT 06904

MASINTER, EDGAR MARTIN, investment banker; b. Huntington, W.Va., Jan. 2, 1931; s. Ralph Leon and Gazella (Schlossberg) M.; m. Margery Flocks, July 8, 1962; children: Robert Andrew, Catherine Diane. BA, Princeton U., 1952; LLB, Harvard U., 1955. Bar: D.C. 1955, N.Y. 1958. Assoc. Simpson Thacher & Bartlett, N.Y.C., 1957-65, ptnr., 1966-95; ptnr. The Bridgeford Group, N.Y.C., 1996-97; exec. dir., mem. The Beacon Coun., The Beacon Group, N.Y.C., 1997—; bd. dirs. IBJ Schroder Bank & Trust Co.; spl. advisor Princeton U. Investment Co., Nassau Capital. V.p. bd. dirs. Grand St. Settlement, N.Y.C.; v.p. bd. regents The Mercersburg (Pa.) Acad.; mem. ethics com. Whitney Mus. Am. Art. With U.S. Army, 1955-57. Office: The Beacon Group 280 Park Ave New York NY 10017-1216

MASKELL, DONALD ANDREW, contracts administrator; b. San Bernadino, Calif., June 22, 1963; s. Howard Andrew Maskell and Gloria Evelyn (Iglesias) White. BA, U. Puget Sound, 1985. Adminstrv. asst. State of Wash., Kent, 1986-87; data analyst Boeing Co., Seattle, 1987-93, engring. contract requirements coord., 1993—, requirements support specialist. Mem. Elks. Republican. Presbyterian. Avocations: travel, computers, golf, theater, history.

MASKET, EDWARD SEYMOUR, television executive; b. N.Y.C., Mar. 3, 1923; s. Isadore and Jennie (Bernstein) M.; m. Frances Ellen Rees, June 11, 1958 (div.); children: Joel Daniel, Johanna Rees Bettaeib, Kate Isobel Smiley. BS, CCNY, 1942; LLB, JD, Harvard U., 1949. Bar: N.Y. 1949. Atty., dir. bus. affairs, v.p. bus. affairs ABC, 1951-68; v.p. to exec. v.p. Columbia Pictures TV, Burbank, Calif., 1968-81; sr. v.p. adminstrn. Universal TV, 1982-86, exec. v.p. adminstrn., 1986-90; exec. v.p. adminstrn. MCA TV Group, 1990-93; TV cons., 1993—. Served as 2d lt. AUS, 1942-46, PTO. Mem. Motion Picture Pioneers, Phi Beta Kappa. Avocation: tennis, golf. Office: Paramount Pictures Corp 5555 Melrose Ave Los Angeles CA 90038-3112

MASLACH, CHRISTINA, psychology educator; b. San Francisco, Jan. 21, 1946; d. George James and Doris Ann (Cuneo) M.; m. Philip George Zimbardo, Aug. 10, 1972; children: Zara, Tanya. B.A., Harvard-Radcliffe Coll., 1967; Ph.D., Stanford U., 1971. Prof. psychology U. Calif.-Berkeley, 1971—. Author: Burnout: The Cost of Caring, 1982; co-author: Influencing Attitudes and Changing Behavior, 1977, Maslach Burnout Inventory (rsch. scale), 1981, 2d edit., 1986, 3d edit., 1996, Experiencing Social Psychology, 1979, 2d edit., 1984, 3d edit., 1993, Professional Burnout, 1993, The Truth About Burnout, 1997. Recipient Disting. Teaching award, 1987, Best Paper award Jour. Orgnl. Behavior, 1994. Fellow AAAS, APA, Am. Psychol. Soc., Soc. Clin. and Exptl. Hypnosis (Henry Guze rsch. award 1980), We. Psychol. Assn. (pres. 1989); mem. Soc. Exptl. Social Psychology. Democrat. Office: U Calif Tolman Hall #1650 Dept Psychology Berkeley CA 94720-1650

MASLACH, GEORGE JAMES, former university official; b. San Francisco, May 4, 1920; s. Michael J. and Anna (Pszczolkowska) M.; m. Doris Anne Cuneo, Mar. 12, 1943; children: Christina, James, Steven. A.A., San Francisco Jr. Coll., 1939; B.S., U. Calif., 1942. Staff mem. radiation lab. Mass. Inst. Tech., 1942-45, Gen. Precision Labs., 1945-49; research engr. Inst. Engring. Research, 1949-52, asst. dir., 1956-58; assoc. prof. U. Calif., Berkeley, 1952-58, prof., 1958-72, dean Coll. Engring., 1963-72, provost profl. schools and colls., 1972-81, vice-chancellor research and acad. services,

1981-83; internat. cons. edn. and econ. devel., 1982—; adv. aeros. research and devel. NATO, 1960-78, U.S. Naval Acad. Rev. Bd., 1966-75, Dept. Commerce Tech. Adv. Bd., 1964-69, Ford Found. and Am. Soc. Engring. Edn., 1966-78. Mem. ASME, AAAS, Sigma Xi. Home: 265 Panoramic Way Berkeley CA 94704-1831

MASLAND, LYNNE S., university official; b. Boston, Nov. 18, 1940; d. Keith Arnold and Camilla (Puleston) Shangraw; m. Edwin Grant Masland, Sept. 19, 1960 (div. 1975); children: Mary Conklin, Molly Allison; m. Steven Alan Mayo, July 1, 1995. Student, Mt. Holyoke Coll., South Hadley, Mass., 1958-60; BA, U. Calif., Riverside, 1970; MA, U. Calif., 1971; PhD, U. B.C., Vancouver, Can., 1994. Asst. pub. rels. dir. Inter-Am. U., San German, P.R., 1963-64; asst. to dir. elem. edn. Govt. of Am. Samoa, Pago Pago, 1966-68; project dir., cons. Wash. Commn. for Humanities, Seattle, 1976-80; exec. editor N.W. Happenings Mag., Greenbank, Wash., 1980-84; media specialist Western Wash. U., Bellingham, 1984-88; dir. pub. info. Western Wash. U., 1988—; cons. William O. Douglas Inst., Seattle, 1984, Whatcom Mus. History and Art, Bellingham, 1977; instr. U. Nebr., Omaha, 1972-86, Western Wash. U., 1972-86; asst. adj. prof. Fairhaven Coll/. 1995—. Editor: The Human Touch: Folklore of the Northwest Corner, 1979, Proceedings: The Art in Living, 1980, Reports to the Mayor on the State of the Arts in Bellingham, 1980-81; contbr. numerous articles to profl. jours. Pres. LWV, Whatcom County, Bellingham, 1977-79; bd. dirs. N.W. Concert Assn., 1981-83, Wash. State Folklife Coun., 1985-90; docent Nat. Gallery, Washington, 1969; bd. dirs. Sta. KZAZ, nat. pub. radio, Bellingham, 1992-93. Univ. grad. fellow U. B.C., 1990-94. Mem. Am. Comparative Lit. Assn., Nat. Assn. Presswomen, Wash. Press Assn. (pres. 4th Corner chpt. 1987-88, Superior Performance award 1986), Can. Comparative Lit. Assn., Internat. Comparative Lit. Assn., Philological Assn. of Pacific Coast, Coun. for Advancement and Support Edn. (Case Dist. VIII Gold award for Media Rels.), Rotary (bd. dirs. 1992-94). Episcopalian. Avocations: boating, gardening, travel, piano. Office: Western Wash U High St Bellingham WA 98225

MASLANSKY, CAROL JEANNE, toxicologist; b. N.Y.C., Mar. 3, 1949; d. Paul Jeremiah and Jeanne Marie (Filiatrault) Lane; m. Steven Paul Maslansky, May 28, 1973. BA, SUNY, 1971; PhD, N.Y. Med. Coll., 1983. Diplomate Am. Bd. Toxicology; cert. gen. toxicology. Asst. entomologist N.Y. State Dept. Health, White Plains, 1973-74; sr. biologist Am. Health Found., Valhalla, N.Y., 1974-76; rsch. fellow N.Y. Med. Coll., Valhalla, 1977-83, Albert Einstein Coll. Medicine, Bronx, N.Y., 1983; copr. toxicologist Texaco, Inc., Beacon, N.Y., 1984-85; prin. GeoEnviron. Cons., Inc., White Plains, N.Y., 1982-97, Maslansky GeoEnviron. Inc., Prescott, Ariz., 1997—; lectr. in entomology Westchester County Parks and Preserves, 1973-96, lectr. toxicology and hazardous materials, 1985—. Author: Air Monitoring Instrumentation, 1993, Health and Safety at Hazardous Waste Sites, 1997, (with others) Training for Hazardous Materials Team Members, 1991 (manual, video) The Poison Control Response to Chemical Emergencies, 1993. Mem. Harrison (N.Y.) Vol. Ambulance Corps., 1986-91, Westchester County (N.Y.) Hazardous Materials Response Team, 1987-96. Monsanto Fund Fellowship in Toxicology, 1988-90; grad. fellowship N.Y. Med. Coll., 1977-83. Mem. AAAS, Nat. Environ. Health Assn., N.Y. Acad. Sci., Am. Coll. Toxicology, Am. Indsl. Hygiene Assn., Environ. Mutagen Soc. Achievements include participation in development of genetic toxicity assays to identify potential carcinogens; rsch. on air monitoring instrumentation at hazardous materials sites, health and safety for hazardous waste site workers, environmental and chemical toxicology, genetic toxicology.

MASLIN, HARVEY LAWRENCE, staffing service company executive; b. Chgo., Oct. 22, 1939; s. Jack and Shirley Maslin; m. Marcia Silberman, Aug. 21, 1960; children: Elaine, Shelley, Bonnie. BS, U. Ariz., 1961, JD, 1964. Bar: Ariz., 1964, Calif., 1966, U.S. Dist. Ct., 1964, 66. Ptnr. Maslin, Rotundo & Maslin, Sherman Oaks, Calif., 1966-67; gen. counsel Western Temporary Svcs., Inc., San Francisco, 1967-71, v.p., 1972-78, sr. v.p., sec., 1979-84; pres., chief oper. officer Western Staff Svcs., Inc., Walnut Creek, Calif., 1985-95, vice chmn. bd. dirs., chief adminstrv. officer, 1996—; dir. Western Staff Svcs., USA, Western Staff Svcs., U.K. Ltd., London, Western Staff Svcs. Pty Ltd., Melbourne, Australia, Western Staff Svcs. (N.Z.) Ltd., Auckland, Western Svc. A/S, Copenhagen, Denmark, Western Svc./ Kontorsvc. A/S Oslo, Western Svc., Inc., Zurich, Western Video Images, Inc., San Francisco. Mem. Rep. Presidential Task Force, Washington, 1981. Mem. Nat. Assn. Temporary and Staffing Svcs. (bd. dirs.), Calif. Bar Assn., Ariz. Bar Assn., Phi Alpha Delta. Office: Western Staff Svcs Inc Exec Offices 301 Lennon Ln Walnut Creek CA 94598-2418

MASLIN, JANET, film critic; b. N.Y.C., Aug. 12, 1949; d. Paul and Lucille (Becker) M.; m. Benjamin Cheever; children: John, Andrew. BA in Math., U. Rochester, 1970. Film and music critic The Boston Phoenix, 1972-76; film critic Newsweek, N.Y.C., 1976-77; dep. film critic The N.Y. Times, N.Y.C., 1977-93, chief film critic, 1993—. Office: The NY Times 229 W 43rd St New York NY 10036-3913*

MASLOW, MELANIE JANE, physician; b. N.Y.C., Mar. 11, 1952; d. Morris and Rosalie (Kaufman) Schwartz; m. James Edward Maslow, June 17, 1973 (div. 1977); m. David Tice, Sept. 12, 1985. B.A., Barnard Coll., 1973; M.D., NYU, 1977. Diplomate Am. Bd. Internal Medicine. Intern NYU Med. Ctr.-Manhattan VA Hosp., N.Y.C., 1977-78, resident, chief resident, 1978-81, fellow, 1981-83; co-physician-in-charge infectious disease L.I. Coll. Hosp., Bklyn., 1983-87, co-chief infectious diseases, 1987-92; asst. chief infectious diseases VA Med Ctr., N.Y.C., 1992—; clin. asst. prof. medicine NYU Med. Sch., 1992—. Fellow ACP; mem. Am. Soc. for Microbiology, Infectious Diseases Soc. Am., N.Y. Acad. Sci. Democrat. Jewish. Office: VA Med Ctr 423 E 23rd St New York NY 10010-5050

MASLOW, WILL, lawyer, association executive; b. Kiev, Russia, Sept. 27, 1907; came to U.S., 1911, naturalized, 1924; s. Saul and Raeesa (Moonves) M.; m. Beatrice Greenfield, Dec. 21, 1933; children: Laura, Catha. A.B., Cornell U., 1929; J.D., Columbia U., 1931. Bar: N.Y. 1932, U.S. Supreme Ct. 1932. Reporter N.Y. Times, 1929-31; assoc. Arthur Garfield Hays, 1931-34; assoc. counsel Dept. Investigation, N.Y.C., 1934-36; trial atty., trial examiner NLRB, 1937-43; dir. field operations Pres.'s Com. Fair Employment Practice, 1943-45; gen. counsel Am. Jewish Congress, 1945—, exec. dir., 1960-72; Faculty N.Y. Sch. Social Research, 1948-60; adj. prof. Coll. City N.Y., 1965-84. Editor: Boycott Report, 1977-94, Radical Islamic Fundamentalism Update, 1995—. Trustee Meml. Found. for Jewish Culture; bd. dirs. Interracial Council for Bus. Opportunity, A. Philip Randolph Inst. Mem. World Jewish Congress (exec. com.), ACLU (dir. 1963-72), Am. Jewish Congress (Stephen Wise laureate 1972), Phi Beta Kappa. Home: 401 E 86th St New York NY 10028-6403 Office: 15 E 84th St New York NY 10028-0458

MASNARI, NINO ANTONIO, electrical engineer, educator; b. Three Rivers, Mich., Sept. 20, 1935; s. Antonio and Giovanna (Lupato) M.; m. Judy E. Guild, June 29, 1957; children: Michael A., Jeffrey P., Maria L. BSEE, U. Mich., 1958, MSEE, 1959, PhD, 1964. Electronics engr. R $ D ctr. GE, Schenectady, N.Y., 1967-69; lectr., rsch. assoc. U. Mich., Ann Arbor, 1964-67, assoc. prof. elec. engring., 1969-76, prof., 1976-79, dir. elec. physics lab., 1975-79; prof. elec. engring. N.C. State U., Raleigh, 1979—, dept. head, 1979-88, dir. Advanced Electronic Materials Processing Ctr., 1988-96, dean engring., 1996—; cons. in field. Raytheon predoctoral fellow 1962. Fellow IEEE; mem. Am. Soc. Engring. Edn., Matl. Rsch. Soc., Sigma Xi, Phi Kappa Phi, Tau Beta Pi, Eta Kappa Nu. Achievements include patent for Process for Manufacturing Inertial Confinement Fusion Targets and Resulting Product.

MASO, MICHAEL HARVEY, managing director; b. N.Y.C., Aug. 9, 1951; s. James and Goldie (Aronowitz) M.; m. Lisa Marie Coady, Sept. 13, 1987; children: Alexander Peter, Graham Emanuel. BA, SUNY, Stony Brook, 1972; postgrad., Cornell U., 1973-76. Gen. mgr. Roundabout Theatre Co., N.Y.C., 1972-73; bus. mgr. P.A.F. Playhouse, Huntington, N.Y., 1976-78; pres. Taos (N.Mex.) Arts Mgmt., 1978-80; mng. dir. Ala. Shakespeare Festival, Anniston, 1980-82, Huntington Theatre Co., Boston, 1982—; sec. League of Resident Theatres, 1985-89, v.p., 1988-93; trustee, treas. StageSource, Boston, 1986-95; trustee Mass. Advocates for Arts, Scis. and Humanities, Boston, 1992—; trustee Arts Boston, 1995—. Chair theater advancement panel NEA, Washington, 1988, panelist/challenge grant, 1989; chair Cultural & Sci. Dirs. Group, Boston, 1993—; trustee Arts Boston, 1995—. Avocations: reading, running. Office: Huntington Theatre Co 264 Huntington Ave Boston MA 02115-4606

MASON, ANTHONY GEORGE DOUGLAS, professional basketball player; b. Miami, Fla., Dec. 14, 1966; s. Mary Mason; 1 child, Antoine. Grad., Tenn. State U., 1988. Basketball player, forward N.J. Nets, 1989-90, Tulsa Fast Breakers, 1990-91, Denver Nuggers, 1990, L.I. Surf, 1991, N.Y. Knickerbockers, 1991-96; forward Charlotte Hornets, 1996—. Recipinet Miller Genuine Draft NBA 6th Man award, 1995. Office: Charlotte Hornets 100 Hive Dr Charlotte NC 28217*

MASON, BARBARA E. SUGGS, educator; b. Champaign, Ill., July 9, 1952; d. Raymond Eugene and Hester Barbara (Nelson) Suggs; m. Frederick A. Mason, May 7, 1988. B of Music Edn., Northwestern U., 1974; MS in Music Edn., U. Ill., 1976, M of Music, 1985. Cert. music tchr. K-12, supervisory endorsement, voice performance and lit., Ill. Gen. music specialist Oak Park (Ill.) Sch. Dist. 97, 1976-82; tchr. for the gifted performing arts unit Champaign Community Schs., 1985-86; choral dir. Evanston (Ill.) Twp. H.S., 1986-87, dist. curriculum leader for gen. music, 1990-95; coord. for mid. level edn. Oak Park Sch. Dist. 97, 1995—; adj. instr. Elmhurst Coll., 1990-95; curriculum cons. Office of Cath. Edn. Black History Com., Chgo., 1992—; acad. task team mem. Quigley Preparatory Sem., Chgo, 1993; curriculum cons., presenter Dept. of Mus. Edn., Art Inst. of Chgo., 1992; chmn. dist. comprehensive arts grant com. Dist. 97, Oak Park, 1992—. Bd. dirs. Oak Park and River Forest Children's Chorus, 1991-95; mem. arts fund com. Oak Park Area Arts Coun., 1993-95, bd. dirs., 1997. Grad. coll. fellowship U. Ill., 1984-85; recipient Award of Merit Those Who Excel Program Ill. State Bd. of Edn., 1993. Mem. NEA, ASCD, Nat. Middle Sch. Assn., Music Educators Nat. Conf., Ill. Alliance for Arts Edn. (svc. award selection com. 1993), In-and-About Chgo. Music Educators Club, Mu Phi Epsilon, Phi Delta Kappa. Roman Catholic. Office: Oak Park Sch Dist 97 970 Madison St Oak Park IL 60302-4430

MASON, BARRY JEAN, retired banker; b. Big Spring, Tex., June 3, 1930; s. Vernon E. and Irene E. (Owen) M.; m. Alexana Petroff, Aug. 31, 1958; children: Scott Alexander, Lydia Claire. B.S., U. Tex., 1957; B.F.T., Am. Inst. Fgn. Trade, 1958; postgrad., Advanced Mgmt. Program Harvard, Auspices U. Hawaii, 1968. Trainee First Nat. City Bank, N.Y., Hong Kong, 1959-60; asst. accountant First Nat. City Bank, N.Y., Toyko, Japan, 1960-63; asst. mgr. First Nat. City Bank, N.Y., 1963-66; mgr. First Nat. City Bank, N.Y., Hong Kong, 1966-67; resident v.p. First Nat. City Bank, N.Y., 1967-68, Tokyo, 1968-69; v.p. First Nat. City Bank, N.Y., Japan, Korea, Okinawa, 1969; v.p. Republic Nat. Bank Dallas, 1969-70, sr. v.p., 1970-72, exec. v.p., 1972-83; chmn., chief exec. officer Republic Bank Las Colinas, 1983-87; sr. advisor Sumitomo Trust and Banking Co. Ltd., 1989-91; mem. adv. bd. PEFCO. Trustee Am. Sch. Japan; bd. advisers Internat. Sch. Hong Kong. Served with AUS, 1948-49; Served with USNR, 1952-53; Served with USMCR, 1953-55. Mem. Bankers Assn. for Fgn. Trade (past dir.), Am. Bankers Assn. Clubs: Hong Kong, T Bar M Racquet. Home: 7730 Yamini Dr Dallas TX 75230-3231

MASON, BERT E., podiatrist; b. Ryderwood, Wash., Mar. 17, 1944; s. Jean Grenette and Bette Evelyn (Phillips) M. BA with honors, U. Calif., San Diego, 1971; B in Basic Med. Sci., Calif. Coll. Podiatric Medicine, 1975; D Podiatric Medicine, Calif. Coll. Podiatric Med., 1977. Diplomate Am. Bd. Podiatric Surgery, Am. Bd. Podiatric Orthopedics, Am. Acad. Pain Mgmt. Pvt. practice Fairfield, Calif., 1977-79; chief podiatry sect., dir. podiatric residency VA Med. Ctr., Huntington, W.Va., 1983-87; pvt. practice San Diego, 1987-89; chief podiatry svc., dir. podiatric residency program VA Med. Ctr., Huntington, W.Va., 1993—; asst. prof. podiatric surgery Ohio Coll. Podiatric Medicine, Cleve., 1984-87, 1993—; asst. prof. dept. surgery and community medicine Marshall U. Sch. Medicine, Huntington, 1985-87; v.p. Smith Hanna Med. Group; assoc. prof. of podiatric medicine, Coll. of Podiatric Medicine, Osteo. U. and Health Scis., De Moines, 1993—. Alumni mem. scholarship com., U. Calif., San Diego, 1988—. Maj. U.S. Army, 1979—, chief Podiatry Sect. Ft. Knox, Ky., Ireland Army Hosp. 1980-83, Individual Augmentee Health Svcs. Command, 1983—. Luth. Hosp. Soc. scholar, 1968. Fellow Am. Coll. Foot Surgeons, Am. Coll. Foot Orthopedics, Am. Assn. Hosp. Podiatrists; mem. AAAS, Am. Podiatric Med. Assn., Am. Acad. Pain Mgmt. (diplomate), West. Va. Podiatry Group (pres.), U. Calif. San Diego Alumni Assn. (bd. dirs.). Republican. Avocations: mountain climbing, golf. Office: VA Med Ctr Dept Podiatry Huntington WV 25704

MASON, BOBBIE ANN, novelist, short story writer; b. Mayfield, Ky., May 1, 1940; d. Wilburn A. and Christianna (Lee) M.; m. Roger B. Rawlings, April 12, 1969. BA, U. Ky., 1962; MA, SUNY, Binghamton, 1966; PhD, U. Conn., 1972. Asst. prof. English Mansfield (Pa.) State Coll., 1972-79. Author: Nabokov's Garden, 1974, The Girl Sleuth: A Feminist Guide to the Bobbsey Twins, Nancy Drew and Their Sisters, 1976, 2d edit., 1995, Shiloh and Other Stories, 1976 (Ernest Hemingway award Nat. Book Critic's Circle award nominee, Am. Book award nominee, PEN Faulkner award nominee), In Country, 1985, Spence + Lila, 1988, Love Life, 1989, Feather Crowns, 1993 (Nat. Book Critic's Circle award nominee, So. Book award); comtbr. regularly to the New Yorker, 1980—; contbr. fiction to the Atlantic, Redbook, Paris Rev., Mother Jones, Harpers, N.Am. Rev., Va. Quar. Rev., Story, Ploughshares, So. Rev., Crazyhorse; contbr. works Best American Short Stories, 1981, The Pushcart Prize, Best of the Small Presses, 1983, 86, Best American Short Stories, 1983. Recipient O. Henry Anthology awards, 1986, 88; grantee Pa. Arts Coun., 1983, 89, Nat. Endowment Arts, 1983, Am. Acad. and Inst. Arts and Letters, 1984; Guggenheim fellow, 1984. Office: Internat Creative Mgmt 40 W 57th St New York NY 10019-4001

MASON, BRIAN HAROLD, geologist, curator; b. N.Z., Apr. 18, 1917; came to U.S., 1947, naturalized, 1953; s. George Harold and Catherine (Fairweather) M. M.Sc., U. New Zealand, 1938; Ph.D., U. Stockholm, 1943. Lectr. geology Canterbury Coll., N.Z., 1944-47; prof. mineralogy Ind. U., 1947-53; chmn. dept. mineralogy Am. Mus. Natural History, N.Y.C., 1953-65; research curator Dept. Mineral Scis. Smithsonian Instn., Washington, 1965—. Author: Principles of Geochemistry, 3d edit, 1967, Meteorites, 1962, The Literature of Geology, 1958, (with L. G. Berry) Mineralogy, 1959, (with W.G. Melson) The Lunar Rocks, 1970, Victor Moritz Goldschmidt: Father of Modern Geochemistry, 1992. Fellow Mineral. Soc. Am., Geol. Soc. Am.; mem. Geochem. Soc., Royal Soc. N.Z., Swedish Geol. Soc. Office: Smithsonian Instn Dept Mineral Scis Washington DC 20560

MASON, BRUCE, advertising agency executive; b. Chgo., Dec. 20, 1939; s. William G. and Maryellen (Robb) M.; m. Diana Albery, Sept. 14, 1963; children: Jennifer, Kristin, Amy. BA, St. John's U., 1961; MBA, U. Chgo., 1963. Account exec. Leo Burnett, Chgo., 1965-69; with Foote Cone & Belding, Chgo., 1969—, dir. account mgmt., 1979-81, gen. mgr., 1981-87, pres. cen. region, 1987-88, chmn. cen. region, 1988, chmn. bd., chief exec. officer, 1991—; chmn., CEO True North Comm., Chgo.; bd. dirs. Foote, Cone & Belding, 1987—. Capt. U.S. Army, 1963-65. Mem. Am. Assn. Advt. Agys. (reg. bd. 1987—). Office: True North Comm Inc 101 E Erie St Chicago IL 60611-2897*

MASON, CHARLES ELLIS, III, magazine editor; b. Boston, Oct. 31, 1938; s. Charles Ellis, Jr. and Ada Brooks (Trafford) M. B.A., Yale U., 1960. Loan officer State St. Bank, Boston, 1963-68; assoc. editor Sail mag., Boston, 1968-74; exec. editor Sail mag., 1974—. Author: (with Buddy Melges) Sailing Smart, 1983; editor: Best of Sail Trim, 1976, Best of SAIL Navigation, 1981. Mem. exec. com. Sierra Club Greater Boston Group, 1992. Served with USNR, 1960-62. Home: 16 Joy St Boston MA 02114-4140 Office: Sail Publs 84 State St Boston MA 02109-2202

MASON, CHERYL WHITE, lawyer; b. Champaign, Ill., Jan. 16, 1952; d. John Russell and Lucille (Birden) White; m. Robert L. Mason, Oct. 9, 1972; children: Robert L. II and Daniel G. BA, Purdue U., 1972; JD, U. Chgo., 1976. Bar: Calif. 1977. Assoc. O'Melveny & Myers, L.A., 1976-81, 84-86, ptnr., 1987—; exec. dir. Public Counsel, L.A., 1981-84; bd. dirs. Calif. Pub. Policy Inst. Chmn. State Bar, Legal Svcs. Trust Fund, 1987; trustee L.A. County Bar, 1985-88; bd. dirs. Challengers Boys and Girls Club, L.A., 1990—, Western Ctr. Law and Poverty, L.a., 1991-94. Mem. ABA (co-chair environ. litigation commn. 1992-94, lawyer rep. 9th cir. jud. conf. 1993-94), Calif. Women Lawyers, L.A. County Bar Assn., Women Lawyers L.A., Black Women Lawyers L.A., Langston Bar Assn. Democrat. Office: O'Melveny & Myers 275 Battery St San Francisco CA 94111-3305

MASON, CRAIG WATSON, corporate planning executive; b. Stamford, Conn., June 4, 1954; s. Harry Leeds and Alice Henrietta (Watson) M.; m. Lisa Ellen Boe, Aug. 30, 1980; children: Katherine Anne, Whitney Elizabeth, Lindsey Allison. BA in English, Yale U., 1976. Brand asst. Procter & Gamble Co., Cin., 1976-77; sales trainee Procter & Gamble Co., St. Louis, 1977; asst. brand mgr. Procter & Gamble Co., Cin., 1978-79, Instant Folger's brand mgr., 1979-82, Biz and Mr. Clean brand mgr., 1982-83; dir. brand mgmt. Beecham Products USA, Pitts., 1983-87, dir. bus. planning, 1987-88, dir. bus. and logistics planning, 1988-89; dir. bus. and logistics planning SmithKline Beecham Consumer Brands, 1989-93; dir. N.Am. planning Smith Kline Beecham Consumer Healthcare, 1994—. Editor: The Insiders Guide to the Colleges, 1975; contbr. articles to profl. jours. Class agt. Yale Alumni Fund, 1976—; trustee Peters Twp. (Pa.) Pub. Libr., 1986-90; vestryman St. David's Ch., 1997—. Mem. Rolling Hills Country Club, Yale Club of N.Y.C. Republican. Episcopalian. Avocations: photography, travel. Home: 230 King Richard Dr Mc Murray PA 15317-2535 Office: SmithKline Beecham 100 Beecham Dr Pittsburgh PA 15205-9774

MASON, DEAN TOWLE, cardiologist; b. Berkeley, Calif., Sept. 20, 1932; s. Ira Jenckes and Florence Mabel (Towle) M.; m. Maureen O'Brien, June 22, 1957; children: Kathleen, Alison. BA in Chemistry, Duke U., 1954, MD, 1958. Diplomate Am. Bd. Internal Medicine, Am. Bd. Cardiovasc. Diseases, Nat. Bd. Med. Examiners. Intern, then resident in medicine Johns Hopkins Hosp., 1958-61; clin. assoc. cardiology br., sr. asst. surgeon USPHS, Nat. Heart Inst., NIH, 1961-63, asst. sect. dir. cardiovascular diagnosis, attending physician, sr. investigator cardiology br., 1963-68; prof. medicine, prof. physiology, chief cardiovascular medicine U. Calif. Med. Sch., Davis-Sacramento Med. Center, 1968-82; dir. cardiac ctr. Cedars Med. Ctr., Miami, Fla., 1982-83; physician-in chief Western Heart Inst., San Francisco, 1983—; chmn. dept. cardiovascular medicine St. Mary's Med. Ctr., San Francisco, 1986—; co-chmn. cardiovascular-renal drugs U.S. Pharmacopeia Com. Revision, 1970-75; mem. life scis. com. NASA; med. rsch. rev. bd. VA, NIH; vis. prof. numerous univs., cons. in field; mem. Am. Cardiovascular Splty. Cert. Bd., 1970-78. Editor-in-chief Am. Heart Jour., 1980—; contbr. numerous articles to med. jours. Recipient Research award Am. Therapeutic Soc., 1965; Theodore and Susan B. Cummings Humanitarian award State Dept.-Am. Coll. Cardiology, 1972, 73, 75, 78; Skylab Achievement award NASA, 1974; U. Calif. Faculty Research award, 1978; named Outstanding Prof. U. Calif. Med. Sch., Davis, 1972. Fellow Am. Coll. Cardiology (pres. 1977-78), A.C.P., Am. Heart Assn., Am. Coll. Chest Physicians, Royal Soc. Medicine; mem. Am. Soc. Clin. Investigation, Am. Physiol. Soc., Am. Soc. Pharmacology and Exptl. Therapeutics (Exptl. Therapeutics award 1973), Am. Fedn. Clin. Research, N.Y. Acad. Scis., Am. Assn. U. Cardiologists, Am. Soc. Clin. Pharmacology and Therapeutics, Western Assn. Physicians, AAUP, Western Soc. Clin. Research (past pres.), Phi Beta Kappa, Alpha Omega Alpha. Republican. Methodist. Club: El Marcero Country. Home: 44725 Country Club Dr El Macero CA 95618-1047 Office: Western Heart Inst St Mary's Med Ctr 450 Stanyan St San Francisco CA 94117-1079

MASON, EDWARD EATON, surgeon; b. Boise, Idaho, Oct. 16, 1920; s. Edward Files and Dora Bell (Eaton) M.; m. Dordana Fairman, June 18, 1944; children—Daniel Edward, Rose Mary, Richard Eaton, Charles Henry. B.A., U. Iowa, 1943, M.D., 1945; Ph.D. in Surgery, U. Minn., 1953. Intern, resident in surgery Univ. Hosps., Mpls., 1945-52; asst. prof. surgery U. Iowa, 1953-55, asso. prof., 1956-60, prof., 1961-91, prof. emeritus, 1991—, chmn. gen. surgery, 1978-91; cons. VA Hosp.; trainee Nat. Cancer Inst., 1949-52. Author: Computer Applications in Medicine, 1964, Fluid, Electrolyte and Nutrient Therapy in Surgery, 1974, Surgical Treatment of Obesity, 1981; developer gastric bypass and gastroplasty for treatment of obesity; contbr. articles profl. jours. Served to lt. (j.g.) USNR, 1945-47. Fellow ACS; mem. AMA, Am. Surg. Assn., Western Surg. Assn., Soc. Univ. Surgeons, Internat. Soc. Surgery, Ctrl. Surg. Assn., Soc. Surgery Alimentary Tract, Am. Thyroid Assn., Am. Soc. Bariatric Surgery, Sigma Xi, Alpha Omega Alpha. Republican. Presbyterian. Home: 5 Melrose Cir Iowa City IA 52246-2013 Office: University Hosp Dept of Surgery Iowa City IA 52242 *Continuity of interest and planning weaves the daily decisions into a whole cloth that does more than cover one's imperfections.*

MASON, ELLSWORTH GOODWIN, librarian; b. Waterbury, Conn., Aug. 25, 1917; s. Frederick William and Kathryn Loretta (Watkins) M.; m. Rose Ellen Maloy, May 13, 1951 (div. Oct. 1961); children: Kay Iris Maurice, Joyce Iris Lande; m. Joan Lou Shinew, Aug. 16, 1964; 1 son, Sean David. B.A., Yale U., 1938, M.A., 1942, Ph.D., 1948; L.H.D., Hofstra U., 1973; Diploma, Inst. Children's Lit., 1996. Cert. Christian Writer's Guild, 1997. Reference asst. Yale Library, 1938-42; export license officer Bd. Econ. Warfare, 1942-43; instr. English Williams Coll., 1948-50; instr. humanities div. Marlboro (Vt.) Coll., 1951-52; serials libr. U. Wyo. Libr., 1952-54; reference libr. Colo. Coll. Libr., Colorado Springs, 1954-58; lectr., libr. Colo. Coll., 1958-63; prof., dir. libr. svcs. Hofstra U., Hempstead, N.Y., 1963-72; prof., dir. U. Colo. Librs., Boulder, 1972-76; freelance writer children's lit., 1995—; adj. prof. U. Ill., Urbana, 1968; pres. Mason Assocs., Ltd., 1977—; rsch. assoc. U. Calif.-Berkeley, 1965; vis. lectr. Northwestern U., 1961, Colo. Coll., 1965, Syracuse U., 1965-68, Elmira Coll., 1966, Columbia U., 1966-68, U. Ill., 1972, Lincoln U., 1969, U. B.C. (Can.), 1969, U. Toronto, 1970, U. Tulsa, 1971, 76, Rutgers U., 1971, Colgate U., 1972, Simmons Coll., 1972, U. Oreg., 1973, Hofstra U., 1974, U. N.C., 1976, U. Ala., 1976, Ball State U., 1977, U. Lethbrige, Can., 1977, U. Ariz., 1981, Ariz. State U., 1981, Victoria U., New Zealand, 1983, U. Canterbury, New Zealand, 1983, U. Nev. Las Vegas, 1992, Remember Pearl Harbor Assn., 1993, 94; libr. cons., 1958—, libr. value engr., 1992—. Editor: (with Stanislaus Joyce) The Early Joyce, 1955, Xerox U.M. edit., 1964, (with Richard Ellmann) The Critical Writings of James Joyce, 1959, 2d edit., 1989, Critical Commentary on A Portrait of the Artist as a Young Man, 1966; translator: Recollections of James Joyce (S. Joyce), 1950, Essais de J. Joyce, 1966, Escritos Criticos de James Joyce, (Portuguese edit.), 1967, (Spanish edit.), 1973, 75, James Joyce's Ulysses and Vico's Cycle, 1973, Kritische Schriften v. James Joyce, 1975, Mason on Library Buildings, 1980, (with Walter and Jean Shine) A MacDonald Potpourri, 1988, The University of Colorado Library and Its Makers, 1876-1972, 1994; contbr. Contemporary Authors, 1988—; editor: Colorado College Studies, 1959-62; editor and compiler: Focus on Robert Graves, 1972-88; adv. editor: Focus on Robert Graves and His Contemporaries, 1988—; editor: The Booklover's Bounty, 1977—; mem. editorial bd. Serial Slants, 1957-59, The Serials Librarian, 1977—, Choice, 1962-65, Coll. and Rsch. Librs., 1969-72. Mem. exec. bd. U. Ky. Libr. Assocs., 1991-94; exec. bd. Concerned Christians in Ky., 1993—. Served with USNR, 1943-46. Recipient Harry Bailly spkr.'s award Assn. Colls. of Midwest, 1975; fellow Coun. on Libr. Resources, 1969-70; grantee Am. Coun. Learned Socs., Edn. Facilities Labs., Hofstra U., U. Colo.; named Ky. Col., 1993. Mem. ALA (councillor-at-large 1961-65), Colo. Libr. Assn. (pres. so. dist. 1960-61), Bibliog. Soc. Am., Libr. Assn. (London), N.Z. Libr. Assn., MLA, Pvt. Librs. Assn., Alcuin Soc. Vancouver, Conf. Editors Learned Jours., N.Z. Royal Forest and Bird Protection Soc., Colo. Book Collectors (founder, pres. 1975-86—), Inst. Vio Studies, Concerned Christians in Ky. (exec. bd. 1993—), James Joyce Found. (chmn. sect. on translation from Joyce, 2d Internat. James Joyce Symposium, Dublin 1969), Black America's PAC, Caxton Club, Archons of Colophon, Ghost Town Club, Alpha Sigma Lambda, Sigma Kappa Alpha (pres. 1969-70). Home: 736 Providence Rd Lexington KY 40502-2267 also: 39 Discovery Dr, Whitby New Zealand

MASON, FRANK HENRY, III, automobile company executive, leasing company executive; b. Paris, Tenn., Nov. 16, 1936; s. Frank H. and Dorothy (Carter) M.; children—Robert C., William C. B.E.E., Vanderbilt U., 1958; M.S. in Indsl. Mgmt., MIT, 1965. With Ford Motor Co., 1965-71, asst. controller Ford Brazil, Sao Paulo, Brazil, 1971-74, mgr. overseas financing dept., Dearborn, Mich., 1974-76, asst. controller engine div., 1976-78, mgr. facilities and mgmt. services, 1978-81; controller Ford Motor Credit Co., Dearborn, 1981-87; dir. finance Ford Fin. Services Group, Dearborn, 1987-89; exec. v.p., chief fin. officer U.S. Leasing, Internat., San Francisco, 1989-92; ret. 1992. Served to lt. USN, 1958-63.

MASON, FRANKLIN ROGERS, automotive executive; b. Washington, June 16, 1936; s. Franklin Allison and Jeannette Morgan (Rogers) M.; m.

Aileen Joan Larson, July 29, 1961; children: William Rogers, Elisa Ellen. BS in Engring, Princeton U., 1958; MBA, Northwestern U., 1960. With Ford Motor Co., 1960-75, finance mgr., Portugal, 1969-72; fin. analysis mgr. Ford subs. Richier S.A., France, 1972-75; sr. v.p. finance Raymond Internat. Inc., Houston, 1975-86; chief fin. officer Quanex Corp., Houston, 1986-87; group v.p., chief fin. officer Gulf States Toyota, Inc., Houston, 1987—. With arty. U.S. Army, 1960. Mem. Princeton U. Alumni Assn., Univ. Club, Racquet Club. Republican. Episcopalian. Home: 5765 Indian Cir Houston TX 77057-1302 Office: Gulf States Toyota Inc 7701 Wilshire Place Dr Houston TX 77040-5346 *Business is people, and success is dependent on good communication with people. Effective communication must be accompanied by fairness, consistency, patience, and a willingness to compromise.*

MASON, GEORGE HENRY, business educator, consultant; b. Chgo., Sept. 11, 1929; s. Robert De Main and Dorothy Wills (Belden) M.; m. Constance Eleanor Wolcott, May 14, 1960. AB, Kenyon Coll., 1955; MBA, Cornell U., 1957; MF, Duke U., 1983. CFA. Investment officer Travelers Ins. Co., Hartford, Conn., 1957-88; exec.-in-residence U. Hartford, West Hartford, 1989—; mng. dir. Heaphy Trust Group, Springfield, Mass.; mem. bus. bd. adv. Sustainable Forest Sys. Corp., Incline Village, Nev.; vis. prof. Jagiellonian U., Cracow, Poland, spring 1996. Co-author: Timberland Investments, 1992. Mem. Assn. Investment Mgmt. and Rsch., Hartford Soc. Fin. Analysts, Cornell Club, Internat. Soc. Tropical Foresters. Republican. Avocations: skiing, golf, writing. Office: U Hartford 200 Bloomfield Ave Hartford CT 06117-1545

MASON, GEORGE ROBERT, surgeon, educator; b. Rochester, N.Y., June 10, 1932; s. George Mitchell and Marjorie Louise (Hooper) M.; m. Grace Louise Bransfield, Feb. 4, 1956; children: Douglas Richard, Marcia Jean, David William. BA, Oberlin Coll., 1955; MD with honors, U. Chgo., 1957; PhD in Physiology, Stanford U., 1968. Diplomate: Am. Bd. Surgery (examiner 1977-80, dir. 1980-86), Bd. Thoracic Surgery. Teaching asst. pathology U. Chgo., 1954-56; rotating intern U. Chgo. Clinics, 1957-58; tchg. asst. surgery, NIH postdoctoral fellow, USPHS fellow surgery Stanford U., 1960-62; from asst. resident in surgery to sr. and chief resident in surgery Stanford U. Hosps., 1962-66; mem. faculty Stanford Med. Sch., 1965-71, assoc. prof., 1970-71; prof., chmn. dept. surgery U. Md. Med. Sch., Balt., 1971-80; also prof. physiology; prof., chmn. dept. surgery U. Calif., Irvine, 1980-89; chief surgical svc. Hines (Ill.) VA Hosp., 1990-95; prof. surgery and thoracic cardiovascular surgery Loyola U. Med. Ctr., 1990—; chmn. dept. thoracic and cardiovasc. surgery Loyola U. Med. Ctr., Maywood, Ill., 1995-97; mem. residency review com. for surgery, 1981-87. Contbr. to profl. jours., med. textbooks. Served to capt. M.C., USAF, 1958-60. Giannini fellow Stanford U., 1966-67; recipient Markle scholarship in acad. medicine, 1968-74. Mem. ACS, Am. Assn. Thoracic Surgeons, Am. Coll. Chest Physicians, Am. Physiol. Soc., Am. Gastroent. Assn., Pacific Coast Surg. Assn., Assn. Acad. Surgery, Ctrl. Surg. Soc., So. Surg. Soc., Chgo. Surg. Soc., Am. Surg. Assn., Western Surg. Assn., Soc. Thoracic Surgeons, Ill. Thoracic Surg. Soc. (pres. 1994-95), Halsted Soc., Chesapeake Vascular Soc., Soc. Internat. Chirurgie, Soc. Clin. Surgery, Soc. for Surgery Alimentary Tract, Soc. Univ. Surgeons. Home: PO Box 3877 Oak Brook IL 60522-3877 Office: EMS LUMC Rm 6250 Bldg 110 2160 S 1st Ave Maywood IL 60153-3304

MASON, GREGG C., orthopedic surgeon, researcher; b. Schenectady, N.Y., July 28, 1958; s. George and Maureen (Murphy) M.; m. Dina Marie Sokolokiski, June 16, 1990. BS in Chemistry magna cum laude, Allegheny Coll., 1980; MD, U. Pitts., 1984. Diplomate Am. Bd. Orthop. Surgery, Nat. Bd. Med. Examiners. Gen. surgery intern U. Colo./U. Colo. Med. Ctrs., Denver, 1984-85; orthopaedic rsch. fellow U. Pitts., 1985-86, resident in orthopaedic surgery, 1986-89; with USNH, Okinawa, Japan, 1989-92; pvt. practice, Erie, 1992—; active staff St. Vincent Med. Ctr., St. Vincent Surgery Ctr., Hamot Med. Ctr., Union City Meml. Hosp.; lectr. in field. Contbr. articles to profl. jours. Mem. Chancellor's Circle, U. Pitts. Comdr. M.C. USNR, 1980—. Recipient Outstanding Student Rsch. award U. Pitt. Sch. Medicine, 1984, Harold Henderson Sankey Orthop. award, 1984; rsch. grantee Competitive Med. Rsch. Fund., Presbyn.-Univ. Hosp. of Pitts., 1986-87, U. Pitts. Rsch. Devel. Fund, 1986-87. Disting. Alden scholar 1977, 78, 79, 80, Sandra Doane Turk scholar, 1979, Armed Svcs. Health Professions scholar, 1981-84. Fellow Mil. Soc. Orthop. Surgeons; mem. AMA, Am. Acad. Orthop. Surgeons (tchg.seal 1993), Pa. Orthop. Soc. (Best Rsch. Paper 1987, 88), Erie Orthop. Soc., U. Pitts. Med. Ctr. Orthop. Alumni., Am. Orthop. Soc. of Sports Medicine (Cabaud award 1988), Ea. Orthop. Assn. (Founders award 1988), Phi Beta Kappa. Office: Orthopaedic Surgeons Inc 204 W 26th St Erie PA 16508-1806

MASON, GREGORY WESLEY, JR., secondary education educator; b. Chgo., Jan. 21, 1963; s. Gregory Wesley and Diana (Burton) M.; m. LaTanya Yvonne Brown, June 8, 1991; 1 child, Gregory Arthur. BS, Ill. State U., 1986; MEd, U. Ill., Chgo., 1996. Cert. secondary tchr., Ill. Instr. City Coll. Chgo., 1986-89; instr. project alert Roosevelt U., Chgo., 1989-91, counselor project upward bound, 1991-93; tchr. math. Bowen High Sch., Chgo., 1993-95, chmn. profl. planning adv. com., 1994-95; tchr. math. Whitney M. Young Magnet H.S., Chgo., 1995—; instr. Ill. Math. and Sci. Acad., Aurora, summers 1993-96. Named Outstanding Young Men of Am., 1985. Mem. ASCD, Nat. Coun. Tchrs. Maths., Ill. Coun. Tchrs. Maths., Ill. Coun. for Coll. Attendance (bd. dirs. 1993—), Benjamin Banneker Assn., Masons, Phi Delta Kappa. Avocations: swimming, chess, reading, stock trading, computers. Home: 2729 W 84th St Chicago IL 60652-3909 Office: Whitney M Young Magnet HS 211 S Laflin St Chicago IL 60607-5305

MASON, HENRY LLOYD, political science educator; b. Berlin, Germany, Nov. 4, 1921; came to U.S., 1940, naturalized, 1943; s. Hugo L. and Maria (Werner) M.; m. Mathilde Jessé, Jan. 23, 1946; children—Monica (Mrs. Robert Mimeles), Paul. B.A., Johns Hopkins, 1942; Ph.D., Columbia, 1951. Mem. faculty Tulane U., New Orleans, 1952—, prof. polit. sci., 1961—, chmn. dept., 1966-75, 87-88; vis. assoc. prof. Columbia, 1958; Fulbright prof. U. Innsbruck, 1958-59, Free U. Berlin, 1965; vis. prof. U. Amsterdam, 1973-74. Author: The Purge of Dutch Quislings, 1952, The European Coal and Steel Community, 1955, Toynbee's Approach to World Politics, 1959, Mass Demonstrations Against Foreign Regimes, 1966, University Government, 1972. Bd. dirs. Urban League Greater New Orleans, 1961-69. Served to 1st lt., M.I. AUS, 1942-46, ETO. Mem. AAUP (mem. nat. council 1966-69 1st nat. v.p. 1984-86), Internat. Studies Assn. (pres. so. region 1972-73), So. Polit. Sci. Assn. (mem. exec. council 1973-76). Home: 1821 Upperline St New Orleans LA 70115-5547

MASON, HENRY LOWELL, III, lawyer; b. Boston, Feb. 10, 1941; s. Henry Lowell and Fanny Crowninshield (Homans) M.; m. Elaine Bobrowicz, June 7, 1969. AB, Harvard U., 1963, LLB, 1967. Bar: Ill. 1967. Assoc. Leibman, Williams, Bennett, Baird & Minow, Chgo., 1967-72; assoc. Sidley & Austin, 1972-73, ptnr., 1973—. Republican. Office: Sidley & Austin 1 First Natl Plz Chicago IL 60603-2003

MASON, HERBERT WARREN, JR., religion and history educator, author; b. Wilmington, Del., Apr. 20, 1932; s. Herbert Warren and Mildred Jane (Noyes) M.; m. Jeanine Young, June 25, 1982; children from previous marriage: Cathleen, Paul, Sarah. AB, Harvard U., 1955, AM, 1965, PhD, 1969. English tchr. Am. Sch. Paris, 1959-60; asst. prof. St. Joseph's Coll., Gorham, Maine, 1960-62; vis. lectr. Simmons Coll., Boston, 1962-63; vis. lectr. in Islamic Hist. Tufts U., Medford, Mass., 1965-66; teaching fellow in English Harvard U., Cambridge, Mass., 1962-66, teaching fellow in Islamic Hist., 1966-67; translator Bollingen Found., N.Y.C., 1968-72; prof. History and Religion Boston U., 1972—. Author: Reflections on the Middle East Crisis, 1970, Two Statesmen of Medieval Islam, 1971, Gilgamesh, 1971 (Nat. Book award nomination), The Death of al-Hallaj, 1979, Moments in Passage, 1979, (novel) Summer Light, 1980; translator: La Passion d'al-Hallaj, 4 vols., Bollingen Series (Louis Massignon), 1983, abridged 1 vol., 1994, A Legend of Alexander, 1986, Memoir of a Friend: Louis Massignon, 1988, Testimonies and Reflections, 1989, al-Hallaj, 1995; co-editor Humaniora Islamica; contbr. articles, essays, reviews, fiction, reviews and poetry to popular fiction mags. Sec. Inter-racial Riverside Assn., Cambridge, Mass., 1965-67; trustee Bd. Charity of Edward Hopkins, Boston Athenaeum. Fellow Soc. for Values in Higher Edn.; mem. PEN (bd. dirs. Delos chpt.), Medieval Acad. Am., Am. Oriental Soc., Am. Acad. Religion, Mark Twain Soc., Inst. Internat. des Recherches Louis Massignon in Paris (dir. edn., v.p.), Am. Acad. Poetry, Japan Poetry Mus. (Iwate-Ken). Home: 30 Common St Phillipston MA 01331-2935 Office: Boston U 745 Commonwealth Ave Boston MA 02215-1401

MASON, JACKIE, comedian, actor; b. Sheboygan, Wis., June 9, 1934. Stand-up comedian; performances include (theater) A Teaspoon Every Four Hours, 1969, The World According to Me! (one man show, Tony, Emmy and Ace awards 1987), Brand New, Politically Incorrect, 1994; (films) Operation Delilah, 1966, The Stoolie, 1972, The Jerk, 1979, History of the World Part I, 1981, The Perils of P.K., 1986, Caddyshack II, 1988; TV appearances in Steve Allen, Ed Sullivan, Jack Paar, Garry Moore, Perry Como and Merv Griffin Shows, Johnny Carson, Arsenio Hall, Late Night with David Letterman; (TV series) Chicken Soup, The Jackie Mason Show; (TV movies) The Best of Times; (TV specials) Jackie Mason on Broadway (Emmy award for writing in a variety or music program 1988); records include The World According to Me!, Brand New. Recipient special Tony award, 1987, Emmy award for The Simpsons, 1991. Office: care William Morris Agy 1325 Avenue Of The Americas New York NY 10019-6026*

MASON, JAMES ALBERT, museum director, university dean; b. Eureka, Utah, 1929; married, 1956; 3 children. BA, Brigham Young U., 1955, MA, 1957; EdD, Ariz. State U., 1970. Cons., clinician in fine arts, 1955—; former chmn. dept. music Brigham Young U., Provo, dean Coll. Fine Arts and Communications, 1982-93; dir. Mus. of Art Brigham Young U., 1993-96; retired, 1996; vis. prof., lectr. Ind. U., Northwestern U., Cin. Coll.-Conservatory, U. Tex., Central Conservatory, Beijing, Internat. Soc. Music Edn., Warsaw; chmn. nat. symposium Applications of Psychology to the Teaching and Learning of Music; chmn., bd. dirs. The Barlow Endowment for Music Composition; co-founder, 1st pres. Utah Valley Symphony Orch.; past condr. Utah Valley Youth Orch.; bd. trustees Utah Opera Co.; commr. Utah Centennial of Statehood. Editor: The Instrumentalist, Orch. News, Utah Music Educator, Research News column, Jour. Research in Music Edn. Bd. dirs. Presser Found. Mem. Music Educators Nat. Conf. (past nat. pres., council), Nat. Music Council (past bd. dirs.), Am. Music Conf. (past bd. dirs.).

MASON, JAMES MICHAEL, biomedical laboratories executive; b. Kingsport, Tenn., Mar. 19, 1943; s. William Tilson and Mary Thelma (Epperson) M; m. Linda Kaye Hussung, June 14, 1969. BS, U. Memphis, 1966; PhD, U. Tenn., 1972. Instr. Health Sci. Ctr., U. Tenn., Memphis, 1972-74, asst. prof. pathology, 1974-84, assoc. prof. pathology, 1984-89; dir. paternity evaluation and histocompatibility testing Lab. Corp. Am., Burlington, N.C., 1989—, asst. v.p., 1992-95, assoc. v.p., 1995—; HLA cons. Roche Biomed. Labs., Burlington, 1986-89; blood bank dir. Regional Med. Ctr. at Memphis, 1977-89. Contbr. articles to profl. jours. Rsch. grantee NIH, U. Tenn., 1973-76; recipient Astra Pharm. award Soc. of Perinatal Obstetrics. Fellow Assn. of Clin. Scientists; mem. Am. Assn. of Blood Banks (chmn. transp. immunology com. 1989-92), Internat. Soc. Forensic Hemogenetics, Nat. Child Support Enforcement Assn., Am. Soc. for Histocompatibility and Immunogenetics, Human Identity Trade Assn. (pres. 1993, chmn. stds. com. 1994—), Kiwanis. Presbyterian. Achievements include patents for cryopreservation of platelets and a temperature regulated hybridization chamber; research in T-lymphocyte counting in neoplastic disease, pathogenesis of SIDS, automated reading of HLA reactions for paternity testing, innovative approaches to DNA analysis in parentage and identity testing. Home: 50 Driftwood Ct Gibsonville NC 27249-3318 Office: Laboratory Corp of America 1447 York Ct Burlington NC 27215-3361

MASON, JAMES OSTERMANN, public health administrator; b. Salt Lake City, June 19, 1930; s. Ambrose Stanton and Neoma (Thorup) M.; m. Lydia Maria Smith, Dec. 29, 1952; children: James, Susan, Bruce, Ralph, Samuel, Sara, Benjamin. BA, U. Utah, 1954, MD, 1958; MPH, Harvard U., 1963, DPH, 1967. Diplomate Am. Bd. Preventive Medicine. Intern Johns Hopkins Hosp., Balt., 1958-59; resident in internal medicine Peter Bent Brigham Hosp.-Harvard Med. Service, Boston, 1961-62; chief infectious diseases Latter-day Saints Hosp., Salt Lake City, 1968-69; commr. Health Services Corp., Ch. of Jesus Christ of Latter-day Saints, 1970-76; dep. dir. health Utah Div. Health, 1976-78, exec. dir., 1979-83; chief epidemic intelligence service Ctr. Disease Control, Atlanta, 1959, chief hepatitis surveillance unit epidemiology br., 1960, chief surveillance sect. epidemiology br., 1961, dep. dir. bur. labs., 1964-68, dep. dir. of Ctr., 1969-70; dir. Ctrs. for Disease Control, Atlanta; adminstr. Agy. for Toxic Substances and Disease Registry, 1983-89; acting asst. sec. health HHS, Washington, 1985, asst. sec. for health, acting surgeon gen., 1989-90, asst. sec. for health, 1990-93; asst. prof. dept. medicine and preventive medicine U. Utah, Salt Lake City, 1968-69; assoc. prof., chmn. div. community medicine, dept. family and community medicine U. Utah, 1978-79; v.p. planning, devel., prof. preventive medicine and biometrics Uniformed Svcs. U. Health Scis., 1993-94; 2nd quorum of Seventy LDS Ch., 1994—; physician, cons. to med. services Salt Lake VA Hosp., 1977-83; clin. prof. dept. family and community medicine, U. Utah. Coll. Medicine, 1979-83, clin. prof. dept. pathology, 1980-83; clin. prof. community health Emory U. Sch. Medicine, 1984-86; chmn. joint residency com. in preventive medicine and pub. health Utah Coll. Medicine, 1975-80; mem. Utah Cancer Registry Research Adv. Com., 1976-83; mem. adv. com. Utah Ctr. Health Stats., 1977-79; chmn. bd. Hosp. Coop. Utah, 1977-79; chmn. exec. com. Utah Health Planning and Resource Devel. Adv. Group, 1977-79; chmn. Utah Gov.'s Adv. Com. for Comprehensive Health Planning, 1975-77; mem. recombinant DNA adv. com. NIH, 1979-83; mem. Gov.'s Nuclear Waste Repository Task Force, 1980-83, chmn., 1980-82; bd. dirs. Utah Health Cost Mgmt. Found., 1980-83; mem. adv. com. for programs and policies Ctrs: for Disease Control, 1980; mem. com. on future of local health depts., Inst. Medicine, 1980-82; mem. exec. com., chmn. tech. adv. com. Thrasher Research Found., 1980-89; mem. Robert Wood Johnson Found. Program for Hosp. Initiatives in Long-Term Care, 1982-84; mem. sci. and tech. adv. com. UNDP-World Bank-WHO Spl. Programme for Research and Tng. in Tropical Diseases, 1984-89; mem. Utah Resource for Genetic and Epidemiologic Research, 1982-85, chmn. bd., 1982-83; U.S. rep. WHO Exec. Bd., 1990-93. Author: (with H.L. Bodily and E.L. Updyke) Diagnostic Procedures for Bacterial, Mycotic and Parasitic Infections, 5th edit., 1970; (with M.H. Maxell, K.H. Bousfield and D.A. Ostler) Funding Water Quality Control in Utah, Procs. for Lincoln Inst., 1982; contbr. articles to profl. jours. Mem. nat. scouting com. Boy Scouts Am., 1974-78. Recipient Roche award U. Utah, 1957, Wintrobe award U. Utah, 1958, Disting. Alumni award U. Utah, 1973, Adminstr. of Yr. award Brigham U., 1980, spl. award for outstanding pub. svc. Am. Soc. Pub. Adminstrn. 1984, Disting. Svc. medal USPHS, 1988, LDS Hosp. Deseret Found. Legacy of Life award, 1992, Gorgas Medal and Scroll, 1993. Mem. Inst. Medicine of NAS, AMA, Am. Pub. Health Assn. (task force for credentialing of lab. personnel 1976-78, program devel. bd. 1979-81), Utah State Med. Assn. (trustee 1979-83), Utah Acad. Preventive Medicine (pres. 1982-83), Utah Pub. Health Assn. (pres. 1980-82, Beatty award 1979), Sigma Xi, Alpha Epsilon Delta, Phi Kappa Phi, Alpha Omega Alpha, Delta Omega. Mem. LDS Ch. Lodge: Rotary. Office: LDS 47 E South Temple Salt Lake City UT 84150-1005 also: Africa Area Adminstrv Office, PO Box 1218, Lonehill 2062, South Africa

MASON, JAMES TATE, surgeon; b. Seattle, June 17, 1913; s. James Tate and Laura (Whittlesey) M.; m. Margaret Elisabeth Thomas, Jan. 10, 1942; children—Laura Mason Foster, Anne Mason Curti, James Tate, Mary Mason, Paul. Student, U. Wash., 1936; M.D., U. Va., 1940. Diplomate: Am. Bd. Urology (trustee 1974-80, pres. 1979-80, exec. sec. 1980-84). Intern Bellevue Hosp., N.Y.C., 1940-41; resident Lahey Clinic, Boston, 1942-43, U. Mich., 1946-49; practice medicine, specializing in urologic surgery Seattle, 1949-83; staff Mason Clinic, Virginia Mason, Univ., Harborview hosps., all Seattle; clin. prof. urology U. Wash., Seattle, 1974-83, emeritus clin. prof., 1983—. Contbr. articles to profl. jours. Bd. dirs. Virginia Mason Hosp., 1956-79, pres., 1975-78; trustee Virginia Mason Research Found., Seattle, 1960-79, King County (Wash.) chpt. Boys' Clubs Am., 1965-76, Seattle Art Mus., 1978-88, Seattle Hist. Soc., 1979-86. Served to comdr. M.C., USNR, 1941-46. Fellow A.C.S.; Mem. Am. Urol. Assn. (pres. Western sect. 1968-69, exec. com. assn. 1973-76, nat. pres. 1984-85), Am. Assn. Clin. Urologists, AMA, Am. Assn. Genitourinary Surgeons, Pacific Coast Surg. Assn., SAR (pres. chpt. 1957-58). Clubs: University, Seattle Tennis. Home: 3825 E Mcgraw St Seattle WA 98112-2428 Office: U Wash Med Sch Seattle WA 98195 *Family and friends are the greatest treasures a person may have. One must try in every way to live up to their expectations.*

MASON, JOHN LATIMER, engineering executive; b. Los Angeles, Nov. 8, 1923; s. Zene Upham and Edna Ella (Watkins) M.; m. Frances Howe Draeger, Sept. 1, 1950 (dec. June 1951); m. Mary Josephine Schulte, Nov. 26, 1954; children: Andrew, Peter, Mary Anne, John Edward. B.S. in Meteorology, U. Chgo., 1944; B.S. in Applied Chemistry, Calif. Inst. Tech., 1947, M.S. in Chem. Engring., 1948, Ph.D., 1950. Registered profl. engr., Calif. Engr. AiResearch Mfg. Co., Los Angeles, 1950-60; dir. engring. AiResearch Mfg. Co. div. Garrett Corp., Los Angeles, 1960-72; v.p. engring. Garrett Corp., Los Angeles, 1972-87; v.p. engring. and tech. Allied-Signal Aerospace Co., Los Angeles, 1987-88, cons., 1989-96; chmn. tech. adv. com. Indsl. Turbines Internat., Inc., Los Angeles, 1972-81, bd. dirs., 1980-88; adj. prof. engring. Calif. State U., Long Beach, 1992—; mem. tech. adv. bd. Tex. Ctr. for Superconductivity, U. Houston, 1989—; chair Calif. Coun. Sci. and Tech. Panel on Transp. R&D Ctr., 1993-94; bd. dirs. San Juan Capistrano Rsch. Inst., 1995— ; cons. Capstone Turbine Corp., 1994—. Patentee in field. Chmn. energy and environment com. FISITA Coun., 1990-94. 1st lt. USAAF, 1943-45, PTO. Fellow AIAA (assoc.). Soc. Automotive Engrs. (bd. dirs. 1984-87, 90-93, pres.-elect 1989-90, pres. 1990-91), Performance Rev. Inst. (chmn. 1990-91, bd. dirs. 1992-93); mem. AAAS, NAS (com. on alternative energy R&D strategies 1989-90), Office Sci. and Tech. Policy (Nat. Critical Techs. panel 1992-93), Inst. Medicine of NAS (com. on health effects of indoor allergens 1992-93), Nat. Acad. Engring., U.S. Advanced Ceramics Assn. (chmn. tech. com., bd. dirs. 1985-88), Am. Chem. Soc., Am. Ceramic Soc., Caltech Assocs., Sigma Xi.

MASON, JOHN MILTON (JACK MASON), judge; b. Mankato, Minn., Oct. 31, 1938; s. Milton Donald and Marion (Dailey) M.; m. Vivian McFerran, Aug. 25, 1962; children: Kathleen, Peter, Michael. BA cum laude, Macalester Coll., 1960; JD, Harvard U., 1963. Bar: Minn. 1963, U.S. Supreme Ct. 1970. Assoc. Dorsey & Whitney, Mpls., 1963-68, ptnr., 1969-71, 73-95; solicitor gen. State of Minn., St. Paul, 1971, chief dep. atty. gen., 1972-73; U.S. magistrate judge Dist. of Minn., St. Paul, 1995—. Bd. dirs. Macalester Coll., St. Paul, 1971-77, St. Paul Chamber Orch., 1979-88, U. Minn. Hosps. and Clinics, St. Paul, 1979-83, Mpls. Bd. Edn., 1973-80, Minn. Chorale, 1990-95, MacPhail Ctr. for Arts, 1990-96, Ordway Music Theatre, 1991—; mem. nat. adv. bd. Concordia U. Lang. Villages, 1996—. With USAF, 1957, with Res., 1957-65. Mem. Harvard Law Sch. Assn. (pres. Minn. sect. 1980-81). Avocations: classical piano, bicycling, accordion, German, French, Spanish and Italian languages. Home: 2849 Burnham Blvd Minneapolis MN 55416-4331 Office: 610 Federal Cts Bldg 316 N Robert St Saint Paul MN 55101-1423

MASON, JON DONAVON, military career officer, physician; b. Storm Lake, Iowa, Nov. 17, 1951; s. Donavon Dexter and Lois (Christensen) M.; m. Cherral Westerman, Feb. 10, 1979; children: Emily, Jonathan. BS with honors, U.S. Naval Acad., 1974; MD, Tulane U., 1978. Diplomate Am. Bd. Pediat., Am. Bd. Emergency Medicine; cert. FLEX. Intern pediat. medicine Oakland (Calif.) Naval Regional Med. Ctr., 1978-79, resident pediat. medicine, 1979-81; staff pediatrician Yokosuka, Japan, 1981-85, Newport, R.I., 1985-87; resident emergency medicine Naval Hosp., San Diego, 1987-90, staff physician, 1990-91; dept. head emergency dept. Naval Hosp., Rota, Spain, 1991-94; clin. dir. emergency medicine Naval Med. Ctr., Portsmouth, Va., 1994—; emergency medicine faculty Naval Med. Ctr., San Diego, 1990-91. Contbr. articles to profl. jours. Decorated Naval Def. medal USN, 1970, Combat Action ribbon USN, 1990, Kuwaiti Liberation medal USN, 1991, navy Commendation medal USN, 1994. Fellow Am. Acad. Pediat. (sect. on emergency pediat.), Am. Coll. Emergency Medicine. Avocations: music, reading. Home: 1709 Ladysmith Mews Virginia Beach VA 23455 Office: Naval Med Ctr Portsmouth VA 23708

MASON, JOSEPH See BUSHINSKY, JAY

MASON, LEON VERNE, financial planner; b. Lawrence, Kans., Jan. 13, 1933; s. Thomas Samuel and Mabel Edith (Hyre) M.; divorced; children: Mark Verne, Kirk Matthew, Erik Andrew. BS in Engring. with honors, U. Kans., 1955; MS in Mgmt. with honors, U. Colo., 1970. Engr., Pittsburg Des Moines Steel Co., 1955-56; with IBM, 1958-93 , sr. engr., San Jose, Calif., 1975-77, Boulder, Colo., 1977—; sr. engr. on loan, dir. capital campaign Vols. of Am., 1980-81; with exec. mgmt. IBM, 1985-87, cons. 1988—. Pres., Boulder Interfaith Housing; dir. Golden West Manor, 1978-84, pres., 1983-84; dir. Ret. Sr. Vol. Program, 1979-86; chmn. elders 1st Christian Ch., Boulder, 1977-79. Served with USAF, 1955-57; col. Res. Cert. fin. planner; registered profl. engr.; chmn. trustees 1st Christian Ch., 1989, 93; supervisory faculty Regis U., 1988-95, pres. Mason & Assoc. Bus. Cons., 1988—. Mem. Internat. Assn. Fin. Planners, Am. Soc. Quality Control, Soc. Mfg. Engrs., Inst. CFPs, Kiwanis. Home: 5577 N Fork Ct Boulder CO 80301-3548

MASON, LUCILE GERTRUDE, fundraiser, consultant; b. Montclair, N.J., Aug. 1, 1925; d. Mayne Seguine and Rachel (Entorf) M. AB, Smith Coll., 1947; MA, NYU, 1968, 76. Editor ABC, N.Y.C., 1947-51; asst. casting dir. Compton Advt., Inc., N.Y.C., 1951-55, dir. and head casting, 1955-65; conf. mgr. Camp Fire Girls, Inc., N.Y.C., 1965-66; exec. dir. Assn. of Jr. Leagues of Am. Inc., N.Y.C., 1966-68; dir. div. pub. affairs Girl Scouts U.S.A., N.Y.C., 1969-71; dir. pub. rels. YWCA of City of N.Y., 1971-73; dir. community rels. and devel. Girl Scout Coun. of Greater N.Y., N.Y.C., 1973-76; dir. devel. Montclair Kimberley Acad., Montclair, N.J., 1976-78, Ethical Culture Schs., N.Y.C. and Riverdale, N.Y., 1978-80; pres. Lucile Mason & Assocs., Montclair, 1980-83; devel. officer founds. Fairleigh Dickinson U., Rutherford, N.J., 1983-85; dir. devel. Whole Theatre, Inc., Montclair, 1985-86, YMWCA of Newark & Vicinity, 1986-88; v.p. adminstrn. and fin. devel. Inst. Religion and Health, N.Y.C., 1988-90; dir. corp. and found. rels. Upsala Coll., East Orange, N.J., 1990-91; pres. Lucile Mason & Assocs., Montclair, 1991—. Vol. bd. counselors Smith Coll., 1964-74, chmn. theatre com., mem. exec. com., 1969-74; trustee Citizens Com. Presby Meml. Iris Gardens of Montclair, 1992—; trustee Friends of Barnet, 1994-95; v.p. Neighborhood Ctr., Inc., Montclair, 1987-95, 97—; mem. fund devel. com. Girl Scout Coun. Greater Essex County, 1986-92. Mem. Am. Women in Radio and TV (pres. N.Y.C. chpt. 1955-56), Community Agys. Pub. Rels. Assn. (membership chmn. 1973-76), Nat. Soc. Fund Raising Execs. (bd. dirs. N.J. chpt 1983-86, mem. awards com. 1994, co-chair awards com. N.J. Conf. on Philanthropy 1995), Pub. Rels. Soc. Am., Smith Coll. Club of Montclair (bd. dirs. 1986-90). Avocations: collecting pewter, gardening, concerts, plays. Home and Office: 142 N Mountain Ave Montclair NJ 07042-2350

MASON, MARILYN GELL, library administrator, writer, consultant; b. Chickasha, Okla., Aug. 23, 1944; d. Emmett D. and Dorothy (O'Bar) Killebrew; m. Carl L. Gell, Dec. 29 1965 (div. Oct. 1978); 1 son, Charles E.; m. Robert M. Mason, July 17, 1981. B.A., U. Dallas, 1966; M.L.S., N. Tex. State U., Denton, 1968; M.P.A., Harvard U., 1978. Libr. N.J. State Libr., Trenton, 1968-69; head dept. Arlington County Pub. Libr., Va., 1969-73; chief libr. program Metro Washington Coun. Govts., 1973-77; dir. White House Conf. on Librs. and Info. Svcs., Washington, 1979-80; exec. v.p. Metrics Rsch. Corp., Atlanta, 1981-82; dir. Atlanta-Fulton Pub. Libr., Atlanta, 1982-86, Cleve. Pub. Libr., 1986—; trustee Online Computer Library Ctr., 1984—; Evalene Parsons Jackson lectr. div. librarianship Emory U., 1981. Author: The Federal Role in Library and Information Services, 1983; editor: Survey of Library Automation in the Washington Area, 1977; project dir.: book Information for the 1980's, 1980. Bd. visitors Sch. Info. Studies, Syracuse U., 1981-85, Sch. of Libr. and Info. Sci. , U. Tenn.-Knoxville, 1983-85; trustee Coun. on Libr. Resources, Atlant, 1992—. Recipient Disting. Alumna award N. Tex. State U., 1979. Mem. ALA (mem. council 1986—), Am. Assn. Info. Sci., Ohio Library Assn., D.C. Library Assn. (pres. 1976-77). Home: 12427 Fairhill Rd Cleveland OH 44120-1015 Office: Cleve Pub Libr 325 Superior Ave E Cleveland OH 44114-1205

MASON, MARSHA, actress, director, writer; b. St. Louis; d. James and Jacqueline M.; m. Gary Campbell, 1965 (div.); m. Neil Simon, Oct. 25, 1973 (div.). Grad., Webster (Mo.) Coll. Performances include cast broadway and nat. tour Cactus Flower, 1968; other stage appearances include The Deer Park, 1967, The Indian Wants the Bronx, 1968, Happy Birthday, Wanda June, 1970, Private Lives, 1971, You Can't Take It With You, 1972, Cyrano de Bergerac, 1972, A Doll's House, 1972, The Crucible, 1972, The Good Doctor, 1973, King Richard III, 1974, The Heiress, 1975, Mary Stuart, 1982, Amazing Grace, 1995, Night of the Iguana, 1996; one-woman show off-

Broadway, The Big Love, Perry St. Theatre, 1988, Lake No Bottom, Second Stage, 1990, Escape From Happiness, With Naked Angels, 1994; film appearances include Blume in Love, 1973, Cinderella Liberty, 1973 (recipient Golden Globe award 1974, Acad. award nominee), Audrey Rose, 1977, The Goodbye Girl, 1977 (recipient Golden Globe award 1978, Acad. award nominee), The Cheap Detective, 1978, Promises in the Dark, 1979, Chapter Two, 1979 (Acad. award nominee), Only When I Laugh, 1981 (Acad. award nominee), Max Dugan Returns, 1982, Heartbreak Ridge, 1986, Stella, 1988, Drop Dead Fred, 1990, I Love Trouble, 1994, Nick of Time, 1995, Two Days in the Valley, 1996; TV appearances include PBS series Cyrano de Bergerac, 1974, The Good Doctor, 1978, Lois Gibbs and the Love Canal, 1981, Surviving, 1985, Trapped in Silence, 1986, The Clinic, 1987, Dinner at Eight, 1989, The Image, 1990, Broken Trust, 1994, series Sibs, 1991; dir. (plays) Juno's Swans, 1987, Heaven Can Wait; dir. ABC Afternoon Spl. Little Miss Perfect, 1988; Frasier, 1997. Office: care Internat Creative Mgmt 8942 Wilshire Blvd Beverly Hills CA 90211-1934

MASON, MARSHALL W., theater director; b. Amarillo, Tex., Feb. 24, 1940; s. Marvin Marshall and Lorine (Chrisman) M. B.S. in Speech, Northwestern U., 1961. Prof. Ariz. State U., 1994—; chief drama critic New Times, Phoenix, 1994-96. Founder, artistic dir. Circle Repertory Co., 1969-87, guest artistic dir., Ctr. Theater Group, 1988; dir. Broadway prodns. Redwood Curtain, 1993, The Seagull, 1992, Solitary Confinement, 1992, Burn This, 1987, As Is, 1985 (Drama Desk award, Tony nomination), Passion, 1983, Angels Fall, 1983 (Tony nomination), Fifth of July, 1981 (Tony nomination), Talley's Folly, 1980, (Pulitzer Prize, N.Y. Drama Critics Circle award, Tony nomination), Murder at the Howard Johnsons, 1979, Gemini, 1977, Knock Knock, 1976 (Tony nomination); Off-Broadway prodns. Sympathetic Magic, 1997, Robbers, 1997, Cakewalk, 1996, A Poster of the Cosmos/The Moonshot Tape, 1994, The Destiny of Me, 1992, Sunshine, 1989, Talley and Son, 1985, Childe Byron, 1980, Hamlet, 1979, Serenading Louie, 1976 (Obie award), Knock Knock, 1976 (Obie award), The Mound Builders, 1975 (Obie award), Battle of Angeles, 1974 (Obie award), The Sea Horse, 1974, The Hot L Baltimore, 1973 (Obie award); dir. numerous prodns. including Who's Afraid of Virginia Woolf?, Tokyo, 1985, Talley's Folly, 1982, London, Home Free! and The Madness of Lady Bright, 1968, London, Nat. Tour Sleuth, 1988, Summer and Smoke, 1988, Whisper in the Mind, 1990; dir. numerous TV prodns. including Picnic, 1986, Kennedy's Children, 1982, The Fifth of July, 1983. Recipient Vernon Rice award, 1975, Drama Desk award, 1977, Margo Jones award, 1977, Outer Critics Circle award, 1978, Theatre World award, 1979, Shubert's Vaughan award, 1980, Obie award for Sustained Achievement, 1983, Inge Festival award for lifetime achievement, 1990, Last Frontier award, 1994, Erwin Piscator award, 1996. Mem. Soc. Stage Dirs. and Choreographers (pres. 1983-85), Dirs. Guild Am., Actors Equity Assn. Address: 1948 E Ellis Circle Mesa AZ 85203

MASON, NANCY TOLMAN, state agency director; b. Buxton, Maine, Mar. 14, 1933; d. Ansel Robert and Kate Douglas (Libby) M. Grad., Bryant Coll., Providence, R.I., 1952; BA, U. Mass., Boston, 1977; postgrad., Inst. Governmental Services, Boston, 1985, The Auditor's Inst., 1988. Asst. to chief justice Mass. Superior Ct., Boston, 1964-68; community liaison Action for Boston Community Devel., Boston, 1968-73; mgmt. cons. East Boston Community Devel. Assn., Boston, 1973-78; asst. dir. Mass. Office of Deafness, Boston, 1978-86; dir. of contracts Mass. Rehab. Commn., Boston, 1986—; cons. Jos. A Ryan Assocs., Boston and Orleans, Mass., 1981-86, Radio Sta. WFCC, Chatham, Mass., 1987-91. Author: Bromley-Heath Security Patrols, 1974, Reorganization of East Boston Community Development Corporation, 1976, How to Start Your Own Small Business, 1981. Bd. dirs. Deaf-Blind Contact Ctr., Boston, 1988-91; vol. Am. Cancer Soc., Winchester, Mass., 1986-93, Tax Equity Alliance Mass., 1994. Recipient Good Citizen award DAR, 1950, Community Svc. award Northeastern U., 1986, Gov.'s citation for outstanding performance, 1993; named to Outstanding Young Women of Am., 1965. Mem. NOW, NAFE, Mass. State Assn. Deaf, MRC Statewide Cen. Office Dirs. (chair 1995—). Democrat. Episcopalian. Avocations: reading, music, bridge, swimming, sign language. Office: Mass Rehab Commn 27 Wormwood St Boston MA 02210-1625

MASON, PERRY CARTER, philosophy educator; b. Houston, Sept. 24, 1939; s. Lloyd Vernon and Lorraine (Carter) M.; m. Judith Jane Fredrick, June 11, 1960; children—Gregory Charles, Nicole Elizabeth. B.A., Baylor U., Waco, Tex., 1961; B.D., Harvard U., 1964; M.A., Yale U., 1966, Ph.D., 1968. Asst. prof. philosophy Carleton Coll., Northfield, Minn., 1968-73, assoc. prof. philosophy, 1973-80, prof. philosophy, 1980—, v.p. for planning and devel., 1988-89, v.p. for external rels., 1989-91. Contbr. articles to profl. publs. Fellow Soc. for Values in Higher Edn.; mem. Minn. Philos. Soc., Am. Philos. Assn. Democrat. Home: 8629 Hall Ave Northfield MN 55057-4884 Office: Carleton College One North College St Northfield MN 55057

MASON, PHILLIP HOWARD, aircraft company executive, retired army officer; b. Cash, Va., Mar. 13, 1932; s. Phillip Howard and Mary Armisted (Hogg) M.; m. Frances Murray Gallogly, Mar. 3, 1962 (dec. 1996); children: Mary Catherine, Patrick Howard, Susan Frances, Sheryl Ann. B.S. in B.A., magna cum laude, St. Benedicts, 1966; M.B.A., Shippensburg State Coll., 1976; postgrad., U.S. Army Command and Gen. Staff Coll., 1965-66, U.S. Army War Coll., 1975-76. Enlisted in U.S. Army, 1948, advanced through grades to brig. gen., 1980; bn. comdr. 1st Bn., 1st ADA U.S. Army, Ger., 1971-73, sec. gen. staff 32d Army Air Def. Command, 1974; systems coordinator ODCSRDA, Dept Army U.S. Army, Washington, 1975; project mgr. AD Command and Control Redstone Arsenal, Ala., 1976-78; comdr. 11th ADA Bde Fort Bliss, Tex., 1978-79; project mgr. STINGER Redstone Arsenal, 1979-83; dir. combat support system ODCSRDA, Dept. Army Washington; ret. U.S. Army, 1983; v.p. bus. devel. Sanders Assocs., Nashua, N.H., 1984-90; project mgr. Hughes Aircraft Co., 1990—. Decorated Disting. Svc. medal, Legion of Merit with oak leaf cluster, Bronze star, Meritorious Svc. medal with two oak leaf clusters, Joint Svcs. Commendation medal, Army Commendation medal. Home: PO Box 272 Amherst NH 03031-0272 Office: 1100 Wilson Blvd Ste 2000 Arlington VA 22209-2297

MASON, RICHARD CLYDE, landscape architect; b. Omaha, Mar. 20, 1948; s. Raymond C. and Sue (Elmore) M. Student Austin Coll., 1966-70; B.B.A., So. Meth. U., 1971; postgrad N. Tex. State U., 1971-72; MLA Tex. A&M U., 1989. Auditor, Dallas Fed. Res. Bank, 1972-73; br. office mgr. Neuhaus & Taylor, archs., 1974-76; auditor Lawhon, Thomas, Holmes & Co., Dallas, 1976-78; controller, dir. Mason Johnston & Assocs., Inc., Dallas, 1979-89; exec. dir. Springside Landscape Restoration, Poughkeepsie, N.Y., 1990-91; dist. landscape arch. Tex. Dept. Transp., 1992—. Mem. Nat. Assn. Accts. (past pres. North Dallas chpt., nat. com. cmty. rels.), Tex. State Hist. Assn., Tex. Hist. Found. (life mem.), Dallas Hist. Soc., Dallas Mus. Art, Am. Soc. Landscape Archs. Methodist. Home: 6412 La Cadena Dr El Paso TX 79912-2500 Office: 212 N Clark Dr El Paso TX 79905-3106

MASON, RICHARD J., lawyer; b. Syracuse, N.Y., June 16, 1951. BA with high honors, U. Ill., 1973; MBA, U. Chgo., 1980; JD, U. Notre Dame, 1977. Bar: Ill. 1977. Ptnr., mem. exec. com. Ross & Hardies, Chgo., 1995—; adj. prof. law Kent Coll. Law, Inst. Tech., Chgo., 1984—. Bd. dirs. Ill. Farm Legal Assistance Found., 1985-88. Mem. ABA (chmn. bus. bankruptcy subcom. on use and disposition of property under the bankruptcy code 1989—), Am. Bankruptcy Inst., Ill. State Bar Assn. (mem. banking and bankruptcy law sect. coun. 1986-88), Chgo. Bar Assn. (mem. bankruptcy and reorgn. com. 1978—), Comml. Law League. Office: Ross & Hardies 150 N Michigan Ave Ste 2500 Chicago IL 60601-7524

MASON, ROBERT (BURT MASON), lawyer; b. Ft. Worth, Aug. 17, 1948; s. Joe Lennard and Eugenia (Moss) M. BS, Tex. A&M U., 1970; MS, U. Ark., 1976; JD, St. Mary's U., San Antonio, 1979. Bar: Tex. 1979, Alaska 1979. Lawyer Pletcher, Slaybaugh, Anchorage, 1979-81, lawyer, prin., 1981-83; sole practitioner Anchorage, 1983-87; ptnr. Mason & Griffin, Anchorage, 1987—; legal advisor Dist 49A Lions Dist. and Found., Anchorage, 1990—. Capt. USAF, 1970-76, S.E. Asia. Mem. VFW, Lions (bd. dirs. 1990-93, chmn. 1984-94, v.p. 1994-95, pres. 1995-96, drug awareness chmn. 1990-95, Dist. Lion of Yr. 1990-91), Elks, Am. Legion. Home: 18642 Stillwater Dr Eagle River AK 99577-7928 Office: Mason & Griffin 1600 A St Ste 101 Anchorage AK 99501-5146

MASON, ROBERT MCSPADDEN, technology management educator, consultant; b. Sweetwater, Tenn., Jan. 16, 1941; s. Paul Rankin and Ruby May (McSpadden) M.; m. Betty Ann Durrence (div. 1980); children: Michael Dean, Donald Robert; m. Marilyn Killebrew Gell, July 17, 1981. SB, MIT, 1963, SM, 1965; PhD, Ga. Inst. Tech., 1973. Tech. staff mem. Sandia Labs., Livermore, Calif., 1965-68; rsch. scientist Ga. Inst. Tech., Atlanta, 1971-75, sr. rsch. scientist, 1975; prin. Metrics, Inc., Atlanta, 1975-80; pres. Metrics Rsch. Corp., Atlanta, 1980-86, Cleve., 1986—; adj. prof. Weatherhead Sch. Mgmt. Case Western U., 1987-88, vis. prof., 1988-91, prof. for practice of tech. mgmt., 1991-95; dir. Ctr. Mgmt. Sci. and Tech., 1988-96. Co-author: Library Micro Consumer, 1986; co-editor: Information Services: Economics, Management, and Technology, 1981, Management of Technology V: Technology Management in a Changing World, 1996; co-author: The Impact of Office Automation on Clerical Employment, 1985-2000, 1985; Am. editor Technovation, 1994—; contbr. article series "Mason on Micros" to Libr. Jour., 1983-86, articles to various profl. publs. Mem. Internat. Assn. for Tech. Mgmt. (newsletter editor 1992-93, program chair internat. conf., 1996, pres. 1996—). Republican. Presbyterian. Avocations: flying, skiing, sailing, scuba diving, photography. Home: 12427 Fairhill Rd Cleveland OH 44120-1015 Office: Weatherhead Sch Mgmt Case Western Res U Cleveland OH 44106-7235

MASON, SCOTT MACGREGOR, entrepreneur, inventor, consultant; b. N.Y.C., Feb. 11, 1923; s. Gregory Mason and Mary Louise Turner; m. Mildred Davidson, Mar. 13, 1949 (div. 1970); children: Alan Gregory, Phoebe Louise, Caleb; m. Virginia Frances Perkins, May 5, 1970 (dec. 1990). AB, Princeton U., 1943; MS, NYU, 1947. Control chemist Firestone Tire & Rubber Co., Akron, Ohio, 1943-44; R & D chemist Am. Cyanamid Co. Rsch. Labs., Stamford, Conn., 1948-52; mgr. stearate dept. Warwick Chem. div. Sun Chem. Corp., Wood River Junction, R.I., 1952-58; cons., Stonington, Conn., 1958-59; instr. Williams Meml. Inst., New London, Conn., 1959-63; NSF fellow Brown U., Providence, 1963-64; tchr. Moses Brown Sch., Providence, 1964-70; owner, mgr. Innoventures, Wakefield, R.I., 1970—; cons. Greene Plastics Corp., Canonchet, R.I., 1972-80, Dorette Inc., Pawtucket, R.I., 1982-83. Patentee in field. Trustee Pine Point Sch., Stonington, 1956-62, pres. bd., 1959-61. With AUS, 1944-46, ETO. Named Tchr. of Week, Sta. WICE, Providence, 1967; summer rsch. fellow NSF, U. R.I., 1960. Mem. AAAS, N.Y. Acad. Scis. Avocations: tennis, fishing, snorkeling, photography, music. Office: Innoventures PO Box 369 Wakefield RI 02880-0369

MASON, STEPHEN OLIN, academic administrator; b. Fresno, Calif., July 11, 1952; s. Olin James and Mary Edna (Moyer) M. BA, Bridgewater (Va.) Coll., 1974; MEd, James Madison U., 1979; PhD, Loyola U., Chgo., 1991. Asst. to the dir. student ctr. Bridgewater Coll., 1974-76; guidance counselor Woodlawn Elem. Sch., Sebring, Fla., 1976-77; asst. dean for student devel. Bridgewater Coll., 1977-81; dir. student life Roger Williams Coll., Bristol, R.I., 1981-83; assoc. dean for residential svcs. Dickinson Coll., Carlisle, Pa., 1983-84; v.p., dean student affairs Westmar Coll., LeMars, Iowa, 1984; rsch. assoc. to pres. Elmhurst (Ill.) Coll., 1986-87; v.p. student affairs Felician Coll., Chgo., 1987-88; dean students Huntingdon Coll., Montgomery, Ala., 1988-90; dir. devel. McPherson (Kans.) Coll., 1990-94, v.p. fin. svcs., 1994—. Participant ARC Blood Drive, 1978-79; mem. allocations com. United Way, Carlisle, 1984; mem. adv. bd. LeMars chpt. Siouxland Coun. for Alcoholism and Drug Abuse, 1984; site coord. for coat drive Mental Health Greater Chgo., 1985; dir-at-large Bridgewater Coll. Alumni Bd., 1987-93; v.p. McPherson Habitat for Humanity, 1993, 94, bd. dirs., 1993-96, pres., 1994; bd. dirs. McPherson Mus. and Arts Found., 1992-94, Assn. Brethren Caregivers, 1993—. Mem. Am. Assn. for Higher Edn., Assn. for Study of Higher Edn., Coun. for Advancement and Support of Edn. Avocations: calligraphy, community theatre, barbershop singing, spelunking. Home: 424 N Carrie St Mc Pherson KS 67460-3712 Office: Mc Pherson Coll 1600 E Euclid St Mc Pherson KS 67460

MASON, STEVEN CHARLES, forest products company executive; b. Sarnia, Ont., Can., Feb. 22, 1936. B.S., MIT, 1957. Pres. div. Mead Corp., Dayton, Ohio, 1978-79, group v.p., 1979-82, sr. v.p. ops., 1982, pres., chief oper. exec., 1990-92, vice chmn., 1992—, chmn., CEO, 1992—. Office: Mead Corp Courthouse Plz NE Dayton OH 45463

MASON, THEODORE W., lawyer; b. June 17, 1943. AB, Yale U., 1965; JD, U. Pa., 1972. Bar: Pa. 1972, Fla. 1987. Ptnr. Morgan, Lewis & Bockius LLP, Phila. Treas., bd. dirs. Nat. Adoption Ctr. Mem. Nat. Assn. Bond Lawyers (steering com. workshop, enforcement com.). Office: Morgan Lewis & Bockius LLP 2000 One Logan Sq Philadelphia PA 19103

MASON, THOMAS ALBERT, lawyer; b. Cleve., May 4, 1936; s. Victor Lewis and Frances (Speidel) M.; m. Elisabeth Gun Sward, Sept. 25, 1965; children: Thomas Lewis, Robert Albert. AB, Kenyon Coll., 1958; LLB, Case-Western Res. U., 1961. Bar: Ohio 1961. Assoc. Thompson, Hine and Flory, Cleve., 1965-73, ptnr., 1973—. Trustee Cleve. YMCA, 1975-94. Capt. USMCR, 1962-65. Mem. ABA, Am. Coll. Real Estate Lawyers, Am. Land Title Assn. (lender's counsel group), Mortgage Bankers Assn. of Met. Cleve., Ohio Bar Assn., Cleve. Bar Assn., Am. Coll. Mortgage Attys., Nat. Assn. Indsl. and Office Pks., The Country Club, Union Club of Cleve. Republican. Episcopalian. Avocations: tennis; golf. Home: 23375 Duffield Rd Cleveland OH 44122-3101 Office: Thompson Hine & Flory LLP 3900 Key Ctr 127 Public Sq Cleveland OH 44114-1216

MASON, THOMAS ALEXANDER, historian, educator, author; b. Port Huron, Mich., Oct. 29, 1944; s. Frank Hallgren and Charlotte (Hamilton) M.; m. Christine Huguette Guyonneau, Aug. 11, 1984; 1 child, Charlotte Guyonneau. BA in History with highest honors, Kenyon Coll., 1966; MA, U. Va., 1970, PhD, 1975. Asst. prof. history Pembroke (N.C.) State U., 1976-79; assoc. editor Papers of James Madison, U. Va., 1979-86, acting editor, 1986-87; dir. publs. Ind. Hist. Soc., 1987—. Author: Serving God and Mammon: William Juxon, 1582-1663, 1985; exec. editor: Traces of Indiana and Midwestern History, 1989—; editor: Documentary Editing, 1989-93, Mag. of Albermarle County History, 1984-86; co-editor: Papers of James Madison, congl. series, vols. 14-16, 1983-89, presdl. series, vol. 1, 1984; project dir.: Papers of Lew Wallace, 1992—; mem. editl. bd. Jour. of the Early Republic, 1991-95, Ency. of Indpls., 1990-94; contbr. articles to encys. and scholarly jours. Served with USMC, 1966-68. Mem. Am. Assn. for State and Local History, Am. Hist. Assn., N.Am. Conf. on Brit. Studies, So. Hist. Assn., Assn. Documentary Editing (dir. publs. 1995—, Disting. Svc. award 1993), Hist. Soc. of the Episcopal Ch. (sec. 1995—, bd. dirs. 1993—), English-Speaking Union U.S. (chmn. region VI 1996—, bd. dirs. 1995—, pres. Indpls. br. 1989-96, Lily Dabney scholar 1972), Raven Soc., Rotary (Indpls.), Athletic Club (Indpls.), Colonnade Club (Charlottesville), Royal Commonwealth Soc. (London), Omicron Delta Kappa (faculty sec. Va. cir. 1984-86), Alpha Delta Phi. Episcopalian. Home: PO Box 20331 Indianapolis IN 46220-0331 Office: Ind Hist Soc 315 W Ohio St Indianapolis IN 46202-3210

MASON, WILLIAM A(LVIN), psychologist, educator, researcher; b. Mountain View, Calif., Mar. 28, 1926; s. Alvin Frank and Ruth Sabina (Erwin) M.; m. Virginia Joan Carmichael, June 27, 1948; children: Todd, Paula, Nicole, Hunter. B.A., Stanford U., 1950, M.S., 1952, Ph.D., 1954. Asst. prof. U. Wis.-Madison, 1954-59; research assoc. Yerkes Labs. Primate Biology, Orange Park, Fla., 1959-63; head dept. behavioral sci. Delta Primate Research Ctr., Tulane U., Covington, La., 1963-71; prof. psychology, research psychologist U. Calif., Davis, 1971—, leader behavioral biology unit Calif. Primate Rsch. Ctr., 1972-96; bd. dirs. Jane Goodall Inst., 1978-92, Karisoke Rsch. Ctr., 1980-86. Mem. Editorial bd. Animal Learning and Behavior, 1973-76, Internat. Jour. Devel. Psychobiology, 1980-92, Internat. Jour. Primatology, 1980-90; contbr. numerous articles to profl. jours., chpts. to books. With USMC, 1944-46. USPHS spl. fellow, 1963-64. Fellow AAAS, APA (pres. divsn. 6 1982, disting. sci. contbn. award 1995), Am. Psychol. Soc., Animal Behavior Soc.; mem. Internat. Primatological Soc. (pres. 1976-80, 81-84), Am. Soc. Primatologists (pres. 1988-90, disting. primatologist award), Internat. Soc. Devel. Psychobiology (pres. 1971-72, Best Paper of Yr. award 1976), Sigma Xi. Home: 2809 Anza Ave Davis CA 95616-0257 Office: U Calif Regl Primate Rsch Ctr Davis CA 95616

MASON, WILLIAM CORDELL, III, hospital administrator; b. Montgomery, Ala., June 7, 1938; s. William C. and Sibyl (Evans) M.; m. Mona Holloway, Jan. 5, 1957 (div. June 1992); children: Michael C., Rebecca Mason Malone, Stephen E., Holly M.; m. Juliette Baldwin Woodruff, Apr. 17, 1993. B.S., U. Southwestern La., 1961; M. Hospital and Health Care, Trinity U., 1971. Hosp. rep. Eaton Labs., Norwich, N.Y., 1962-66; fgn. service officer U.S. Dept. State, Manila and Saigon, 1966-69; chief exec. officer Bapt. Hosp. of East Africa, Mbeya, Tanzania, 1971-74, Bapt. Hosp., Bangalore, India, 1974-78; chief operating officer Bapt. Med. Ctr., Jacksonville, Fla., 1978-84, vice chmn., CEO, 1984-95; vice chmn. bd. dirs., CEO Bapt./St. Vincent's Health Sys. Inc., Jacksonville, Fla., 1995—; mem. adj. faculty U. No Fla. Jacksonville, 1985—; cons. So. Bapt. Fgn. Mission Bd., Richmond, Va., 1980-85; bd. dirs. Sun Bank of North Fla., N.A., SunHealth Corp., sec. exec. com., 1990-94. Contbr. articles to profl. jours. Chmn. deacons Hendricks Ave. Bapt. Ch., Jacksonville, 1984-85, Calvary Bapt. Ch., Bangalore, 1976-77; treas. Karnataka State Bapt. Conv., Bangalore, 1975-77; trustee Jacksonville Symphony Orch.; bd. dirs. U. No. Fla.Assn. Vol. Hosps., 1986, Med. Assistance Program Internat., 1986-87, United Way, 1990; chmn. Greater Jacksonville Area Hosp. Coun., 1985, Mayor's Health Econ. Devel. Coun., 1986-87, Greater Jacksonville U.S. Savs. Bond Campaign, 1987; mem. adv. coun. Jacksonville U. Sch. Bus., 1986-88; chmn. area devel. coun. So. Bapt. Fgn. Mission Bd., 1987-91. Fellow Am. Coll. Hosp. Execs.; mem. Am. Hosp. Assn., Fla. Hosp. Assn. (trustee 1982, 83-85, 86), Fla. Hosp. Assn. (chmn. 1992-93, trustee 1994—), Healthcare Exec. Study Soc., Jacksonville C. of C. (vice chmn. exec. com. 1988-89, chmn. health econ. devel. 1992-95, chmn. cornerstone econ. devel. initiative), Epping Forest Yacht Club (bd. govs. 1990—), Beta Sigma Gamma, Rotary. Avocations: golf, boating, reading. Home: 947 Greenridge Rd Jacksonville FL 32207-5203 Office: St Vincent's Health Sys Inc 1301 Riverplace Blvd Ste 1700 Jacksonville FL 32207-9023

MASORO, EDWARD JOSEPH, JR., physiology educator; b. Oakland, Calif., Dec. 28, 1924; s. Edward Joseph and Louise Elizabeth (DePaoli) M.; m. Barbara Weikel, June 25, 1947. AB, U. Calif., Berkeley, 1947, PhD, 1950. Asst. prof. physiology Queen's U., Kingston, Ont., Can., 1950-52; asst. prof., then assoc. prof. Tufts U. Sch. Medicine, 1952-62; research assoc. prof., then research prof. physiology and biophysics U. Wash., 1962-64; prof. physiology and biophysics, chmn. dept. Med. Coll. Pa., 1964-73; prof. physiology, chmn. dept. U. Tex. Health Sci. Center, San Antonio, 1973-91, prof., 1991-96; dir. Aging Rsch. and Edn. Ctr., 1992-96; prof. emeritus, 1996—; cons. coun. basic sci. Am. Heart Assn., 1965-67; chmn. metabolic discussion group Fed. Am. Soc. Exptl. Biology, 1969-73; mem. aging rev. com. Nat. Inst. on Aging, 1981-84, chmn. bd. sci. counselors, 1985-89; chmn. Gordon Conf. on Biology of Aging, 1983; mem. bd. sci. advisors Human Nutrition Inst., Internat. Life Sci. Inst., 1989-92; mem. rsch. com. Am. Fedn. Aging Rsch., 1988—; vis. prof. U. Pisa, 1993; Wellcome vis. prof. basic med. scis., 1992-93. Author: Physiological Chemistry of Lipids in Mammals, 1967; co-author: Acid-Base Regulation: Its Physiology and Pathophysiology, 1971, 2d edit., 1977; editor sct. 24 Internat. Ency. Pharmacology and Therapeutics, 1974; mem. editorial bd. Jour. Lipid Rsch., 1967-83, Jour. Gerontology, 1979-91, Exptl. Gerontology, 1984—, Proc. Soc. Exptl. Biol. Medicine, 1986-92, Physiol. Rev., 1988-94; editor Jour. Gerontology: Biol. Scis., 1991-95, Handbook Physiol. Aging, 1995; editor for biol. scis. Exptl. Aging Rsch., 1980-88; co-editor Aging: Clinical and Experimental Research, 1989—; contbr. articles to profl. jours. Served with USNR, 1943-46. Recipient Christian R. and Mary F. Lindback Disting. Teaching award Med. Coll. Pa., 1967, Golden Apple award Student Am. Med. Assn., 1966, 71, Achievement award Allied Signal, 1989, Rsch. Achievements in Gerontology, U. Pisa, 1991, Irving Wright award Am. Fedn. Aging Rsch., 1995, Glenn Found. award, 1995. Fellow AAAS (coun. 1970—), Gerontol. Soc. Am. (chmn. biol. sci. sect. 1978-79, v.p. 1978-79, Kleemeir award 1990, pres.-elect 1992-93, pres. 1994-95); mem. AAUP, Am. Physiol. Soc. (chmn. endocrinology and metabolism sect. 1981-82), Soc. Exptl. Biology and Medicine (coun. 1987-91), Am. Soc. Biochemistry and Molecular Biology, N.Y. Acad. Scis., Phila. Physiol. Soc. (pres. 1966-67). Office: U Tex Dept Physiology Health Sci Ctr San Antonio TX 78284

MASOTTI, LOUIS HENRY, management educator, consultant; b. N.Y.C., May 16, 1934; s. Henry and Angela Catherine (Turi) M.; m. Iris Patricia Leonard, Aug. 28, 1958 (div. 1981); children: Laura Lynn, Andrea Anne; m. Ann Randel Humm, Mar. 5, 1988. AB, Princeton U., 1956; MA, Northwestern U., 1961, PhD, 1964. Fellow Nat. Ctr. Edn. in Politics, 1962; asst. prof. polit. sci. Case Western Res. U., Cleve., 1963-67, assoc. prof., 1967-69, dir. Civil Violence Rsch. Ctr., 1968-69; sr. Fulbright lectr. Johns Hopkins U. Ctr. Advanced Internat. Studies, Bologna, Italy, 1969-70; assoc. prof. Northwestern U., Evanston, Ill., 1970-72, prof. polit. sci. and urban affairs, 1972-83, dir. Ctr. Urban Affairs, 1971-80, dir. Program in Pub. and Not-for-Profit Mgmt., Kellogg Sch. Mgmt., 1979-80, prof. mgmt. and urban devel. Kellogg Sch. Mgmt., 1983-94, dir. Real Estate Research Ctr. Kellogg Sch. Mgmt., 1986-88; cons. to numerous publs., govt. agys., real estate firms, and corps.; vis. assoc. prof. U. Wash. summer 1969; exec. dir. Mayor Jane Byrne Transition Com., Chgo., 1979; vis. prof. Stanford Sch. Bus., 1989-92, UCLA Sch. Mgmt., 1989-92; prof., dir. real estate mgmt. program U. Calif. Grad. Sch. Mgmt., Irvine, 1992—, bd. dirs. MHC, Inc., Tucker Properties Corp., Facilities Mgmt. Internat. Author: Education and Politics in Suburbia, 1967, Shootout in Cleveland, 1969, A Time to Burn?, 1969, Suburbia in Transition, 1973, The New Urban Politics, 1976, The City in Comparative Perspective, 1976, co-editor: Metropolis in Crisis, 1968, 2d edit., 1971, Riots and Rebellion, 1968, The Urbanization of the Suburbs, 1973, After Daley: Chicago Politics in Transition, 1981, Downtown Development, 1985, 2d edit., 1987; editor Edn. and Urban Soc., 1968-71, Urban Affairs Quar., 1973-80; sr. editor Econ. Devel. Quar., 1986-92; vice chmn. bd. Illinois Issues jour., 1986-92, BOMA Office mag., 1990-95. Rsch. dir. Carl Stokes for Mayor of Cleve., 1967; mem. Cleveland Heights Bd. Edn., 1967-69; devel. coordinator for high tech. State of Ill.-City Chgo., 1982-83; advisor to various congl., gubernatorial and mayoral campaigns, Ohio, Ill., N.J., Calif.; cons. urban devel. issues corps. developers, govt. agys. and news media. Lt. USNR, 1956-59. Fellow Homer Hoyt Inst. for Advanced Real Estate Studies; recipient Disting. Service award Cleve. Jaycees, 1967; numerous fed. and found. research grants, 1963—. Mem. Urban Land Inst., Nat. Coun. Urban Econ. Devel., Internat. Assn. Corp. Real Estate Execs., Internat. Devel. Rsch. Coun., Nat. Assn. Indsl. Office Properties (bd. dirs.), Lambda Alpha Internat. Home: 2810 Villa Way Newport Beach CA 92663-3729

MASOVER, GERALD KENNETH, microbiologist; b. Chgo., May 12, 1935; s. Morris H. and Lillian (Perelgut) M.; m. Bonnie Blumenthal, Mar. 30, 1958 (dec. 1992); children: Steven, Laurie, David; m. Lee H. Tower, Mar. 25, 1995. BS, U. Ill., Chgo., 1957, MS, 1970; PhD, Stanford U., 1973. Registered pharmacist, Calif., Ill. Owner, operator Robert Pharmacy, Chgo., 1960-68; rsch. assoc. Stanford U. Med. Sch., Palo Alto, Calif., 1974-80; assoc. rsch. cell biologist Children's Hosp., Oakland, Calif., 1980-83; rsch. microbiologist Hana Biologics, Berkeley, Calif., 1983-86; pharmacist various locations, 1970—; quality control sect. head Genentech, Inc., South San Francisco, 1986-90, quality control sr. microbiologist, 1990—. Contbr. articles to profl. jours., chpts. to books. 1st Lt. USAR, 1957-66. NSF predoctoral fellow, 1970-73; NIH rsch. grantee, 1974-78. Mem. Soc. In Vitro Biology, Internat. Orgn. for Mycoplasmology, Parenteral Drug Assn., Am. Soc. Microbiology, Sigma Xi. Jewish. Achievements include patents on triphasic mycoplasmatales detection method; triphasic mycoplasmatales detection device. Home: 4472 24th St San Francisco CA 94114-3522 Office: Genentech Inc 460 Point San Bruno Blvd South San Francisco CA 94080-4918

MASRI, JANE MARTYN, finance and operations administrator; b. Devon, Pa., July 1, 1962; d. George William Jr. and Rosanna (Blessey) Martyn; m. Bashar F. Masri, Sept. 23, 1989; children: Tamara, Dina. BA, Bucknell U., 1984. Lic. pvt. pilot. Program coord. Universal Structures, Washington, 1985; adminstrv. mgr. Linton, Mields, Reisler & Cottone, Washington, 1985-89; v.p. fin. and adminstrn. Am. Hwy. Users Alliance, Washington, 1989—; exec. v.p. Diversified Resources Corp., Falls Church, Va., 1992—; bd. dirs. Internat. Student House, Washington, fin. com.; asst. to bd. trustees Automotive Safety Found., Washington, 1989—. Assoc. mem. Mus. for Women in Arts, Washington, 1995-97; mem. Bucknell U. Alumni Assn., Lewisburg, 1984—; mem. Nat. Trust for Hist. Preservation. Mem. Am. Mgmt. Assn., Aircraft Owners and Pilots Assn., Pi Beta Phi. Avocation: private pilot. Home: 2237 Kings Garden Way Falls Church VA 22043 Office: Am Hwy Users Alliance 1776 Massachusetts Ave NW Washington DC 20036-1904

MASRI, MERLE SID, biochemist, consultant; b. Jerusalem, Palestine, Sept. 12, 1927; came to U.S., 1947; s. Said Rajab and Fatima (Muneimné) M.; m. Maryjean Loretta Anderson, June 28, 1952 (div. 1974); children: Kristin Corinne, Allan Eric, Wendy Joan, Heather Anderson. BA in Physiology, U. Calif., Berkeley, 1950; PhD in Mammalian Physiology and Biochemistry, U. Calif. Berkeley, 1953. Rsch. asst. Dept. Physiology, Univ. Calif., Berkeley, 1950-53; predoctoral fellow Baxter Labs., Berkeley, 1952-53; rsch. assoc. hematology Med. Rsch. Inst., Michael Reese Hosp., Chgo., 1954-56; sr. rsch. biochemist Agrl. Rsch. Svc., USDA, Berkeley, 1956-87; supervisory rsch. scientist Agrl. Rsch. Svc., USDA, N.D. State U. Sta., Fargo, N.D., 1987-89; pvt. practice as cons. Emeryville, Calif., 1989—; lectr. numerous confs. Contbr. articles to profl. jours. and books. Recipient Spl. Svc. and Merit awards USDA, 1966, 76, 77, Superior Svc. award USDA, 1977. Mem. AAAS, Am. Chem. Soc., Am. Oil Chemists Soc., Am. Assn. Cereal Chemists, N.Y. Acad. Scis., Inst. Food Technologists, Commonwealth Club Calif., Internat. Platform Assn., Sigma Xi. Achievements include patents for detoxification of aflatoxin in agricultural crops, improved dyeability of cotton fabrics and reduced dye and electrolyte discharge in plant effluent, new closed-circuit raw wool scouring technology to conserve water and energy and control pollution, synthesis and use of polymers for wastewater treatment, and for enzyme immobilization, toxic heavy metals removal and textile finishing treatment, non-polluting new technology for scouring raw wool in a closed circuit with water recycling and re-use and waste effluent control; studied chlorination of water in food processing operations and water re-use and recycle and the generation of mutagens and means of improving disinfection efficiency and reducing mutagen formation; discovered new methods and reagents for protein and amino acid residue modification and analysis, new mammalian metabolic pathways; developed other non-polluting textile finishing treatments. Home: 9 Commodore Dr Emeryville CA 94608-1652

MASS, M. F., allergist, immunologist; b. Phila., Feb. 24, 1945; s. Edward I. and Pearl (Markovitz) M.; m. Marilyn Halpern, June 12, 1966; children: Ellis, David. Student, U. Fla., 1963; BA, Brandeis U., 1966; MD, U. Fla., 1970; postgrad., U. Colo., Albany, N.Y., 1972, U. Colo., Denver, 1975. Intern Albany (N.Y.) Med. Ctr., 1970-71, residency, 1971-72; sr. residency U. Colo. Med. Ctr., Denver, 1972-73, postgrad. fellow/allergy-immunology, 1973-75; assoc. clin. professor of medicine U. Fla., Jacksonville, Fla., 1977—; dir. Osteoporosis Diagnostic Lab. Meml. Med. Ctr., Jacksonville; chmn. Duval County Environ. Protection Bd., 1995-97; past chmn. dept. medicine Meml. Med. Ctr., Jacksonville; sec. S.E. Regional Am. Coll. Rheumatology. Inventor skin chamber. Chmn. Duval County Environ. Protection Bd. Maj. USAF, 1975-77. Health Professions scholar U. Fla. Fellow Am. Coll. Physicians, Am. Acad. Allergy and Immunology, Am. Coll. Allergy; mem. Am. Coll. Rheumatology (sec. S.E. region), Duval County Med. Soc. (v.p., pres.-elect). Office: 3636 University Blvd S Ste B2 Jacksonville FL 32216-4223 also: 1895 Kingsley Ave Ste 401 Orange Park FL 32073-4453

MASSA, CONRAD HARRY, religious studies educator; b. Bklyn., Oct. 27, 1927; s. Harry Frederick and Josephine W. (Lepold) M.; m. Anna W. Rossi, Aug. 19, 1951; children: Stephen Mark, Barbara Ann. A.B. with honors, Columbia U., 1951; M.Div., Princeton Theol. Sem., 1954, Ph.D., 1960; HHD, Lafayette Coll., 1987. Ordained to ministry Presbyn. Ch., 1954. Pastor Elmwood Presbyn. Ch., East Orange, N.J., 1954-57; asst. prof. homiletics Princeton Theol. Sem., 1957-61; sr. pastor Old First Ch., Newark, 1961-66, Third Presbyn. Ch., Rochester, N.Y., 1966-78; dean acad. affairs Princeton Theol. Sem., 1978-94, dean emeritus, 1994—, Charlotte W. Newcombe prof., 1978-95, Charlotte W. Newcombe prof. emeritus, 1995—; 1st moderator Synod of the Northeast, United Presbyn. Ch.; vis. prof. St. Bernard's Roman Cath. Sem., Rochester, 1968-70; keynote speaker 11th ann. conf. Inst. Theology, Yonsei U., Seoul, Republic of Korea, 1991. Author articles and book revs. Trustee Lafayette Coll., Easton, Pa., 1982-93. Served with U.S. Army, 1946-47. Mem. Acad. Homiletics, Am. Acad. Religion. Home: 14691 Blackbird Ln Fort Myers FL 33919-8346 *I have learned to try to understand all events and persons in terms of their relationships to other things, persons and events. While it is sometimes fruitful to isolate a particular and study it in its solitude, nothing and no one really exists in such isolation. This has become a guiding principle in my continued research and growth in those areas of greatest interest - religion, education and society.*

MASSA, SALVATORE PETER, psychologist; b. Queens, N.Y., Aug. 5, 1955; s. Joseph and Marie Massa; AAS, Orange County Community Coll., 1975; BA in Psychology, Queens Coll., 1977; MA, St. John's U., 1978, profl. diploma, 1979, PhD, 1985; m. Patricia Louise Kathryn Kelley, Mar. 12, 1979; children: Kathryn Kelley, Kristopher Kelley, KayLynn Kelley, Patrick Kelley, Grace Kelley, Frank Kelley. Lic. psychologist, N.Y.; nat. cert. sch. psychologist. Intern psychologist Sagamore Children's Psychiat. Hosp., Melville, N.Y., 1978-79; habilitation supr. Suffolk Child Devel. Center, Smithtown, N.Y., 1979; staff psychologist Cumberland Mental Health Center, Bklyn., 1979-81; asst. program dir., dir. clin. services Rhinebeck (N.Y.) Country Sch., 1981-87; cons. psychologist Brookwood Ctr., 1985-86, Anderson Sch., 1987-89, Renssalaer Columbia Greene BOCES, 1987—; chmn. Com. on Spl. Edn., 1991—, Com. on Presch. Edn., 1991—; sch. psychologist Red Hook Cen. Sch. Dist., cons. psychologist Rhinebeck Cen. Sch. Dist., 1986-90, chmn. profl. conf. com., 1986-87, Anderson Sch., 1987-88; cons. Columbia County Advocacy and Resource Ctr., Rehab. Programs, Inc., 1989; adj. prof. Marist Coll., Poughkeepsie, N.Y., 1989—. Head football coach YMCA winter league, 1979-81; asst. football coach Rhinebeck Country Sch., 1982; coach Germantown Little League, Germantown Winter Basketball League. Recipient public service award for vol. work Middletown State Hosp., 1975; spl. recognition award Internat. Council Psychology, 1981; cert. sch. psychology, N.Y. Mem. Am. Psychol. Assn. (divs. pediatric psychology, psychotherapy, sch. psychology, neuropsychology), Eastern Psychol. Assn., Internat. Council Psychologists, Hudson Valley Psychol. Assn., Nat. Assn. Sch. Psychologists, Nat. Soc. Autistic Children. Democrat. Roman Catholic. Contbr. papers to profl. confs.; co-author study on relaxation tng. in residential treatment.

MASSACHI, ALBERT (DAVID MASSACHI), financial strategist; b. Tehran, Iran; came to U.S., 1975; BS, UCLA, 1979. Assoc. broker, sales rep. Charles H. Ellis Realtors, L.A., 1980-81; rep. Equitable Life/Equico Securities, New Hyde Park, N.Y., 1982-90; pres. Group Plan Svcs., Fin. Plans Svcs., Fin. Instns. Cons., Great Neck, N.Y., 1992—, Fin.-Tech. Internat., Great Neck, N.Y., 1992—. Author: books on sci. and logic., resolution of paradoxes; contbr. articles to profl. jours. Achievements include research in economic and financial problems, resulted in innovations and definitive macro-economic, macro-financial, and other system-solutions.

MASSAD, STEPHEN ALBERT, lawyer; b. Wewoka, Okla., Dec. 20, 1950; s. Alexander Hamilton and Delores Jean (Razook) M.; m. Amy S. Massad, Jan. 13, 1979; children: Caroline, Sarah, Margaret. AB, Princeton U., 1972; JD, Harvard U., 1975. Bar: Tex. 1975. Assoc. Baker & Botts, Houston, 1975-82, ptnr., 1983—. Office: Baker & Botts 3000 One Shell Plz 910 Louisiana St Houston TX 77002-4916

MASSALSKI, THADDEUS BRONISLAW, material scientist, educator; b. Warsaw, Poland, June 29, 1926; came to U.S., 1959; s. Piotr and Stanislawa (Andrukaniec) M.; m. Sheila Joan Harris, Sept. 19, 1953; children: Irena, Peter, Christopher. B.Sc., Birmingham (Eng.) U., 1952, Ph.D., 1954, D.Sc., 1964; fellow, Inst. Study Metals, U. Chgo., 1954-56; D.Sc. (h.c.), Warsaw (Poland) U., 1973. Lectr. Birmingham U., 1956-59; head. metal physics group Mellon Inst., Pitts., 1959-75; staff fellow Mellon Inst., 1961—; prof. metal physics and materials sci. Carnegie-Mellon U., 1968—; vis. prof. U. Buenos Aires, 1962, Calif. Inst. Tech., 1962, Stanford, 1963, U. Calif., 1964, 66, Inst. Physics, Bariloche Argentina, 1966, 70, Harvard, 1969; exchange prof. Krakow (Poland) U., 1968; vis. scientist Nat. Bur. Standards, 1980-81; NAVSEA prof. Naval Postgrad. Sch., Monterey, Calif; chmn. bd. govs. Acta Metallurgica, Inc., 1992—. Co-author: Structure of Metals, 3d edit, 1966, Advanced Physical Metallurgy, 1965; co-editor Progress in Materials Science, 1969—, Metall. Transactions, 1991—; editor-in-chief ASM/NIST Phase Diagram Program, 1980—; author papers and articles on alloy theory, crystallography, metal physics, meteorites. Guggenheim fellow Oxford U., 1965-66; recipient Alexander von Humboldt prise, 1991. Fellow Am. Soc. Metals (gold medal 1993), Am. Phys. Soc., The Metals Soc. (gold medal 1995), Brit. Inst. Metals, Brit. Inst. Physics, AIME (Hume-Rotherly prize 1989); mem. Polish Acad. Sci. (fgn.), German Acad. Sci. (fgn.), Phys. Soc. Home: 900 Field Club Rd Pittsburgh PA 15238-2127 Office: Carnegie Mellon U 3303 Wean Hall Pittsburgh PA 15213

MASSARE, JOHN STEVE, medical association administrator, educator; b. Rochester, N.Y., Feb. 16, 1949; s. Peter Anthony and Clara Marie (Skill) M.; 1 child, John Simon. BA in Biol. Scis., SUNY, Oswego, 1970; MS in Physiology, SUNY, Brockport, 1973; postgrad., Ind. U., 1976-80. With Carnation Co., 1970-71; lab. instr. SUNY, Brockport, 1972-73; sales rep. Bausch and Lomb Corp., Rochester, 1973-76; assoc. instr. Ind. U., Bloomington, 1976-80; with CIBA Vision Corp., Atlanta, 1981-91, mgr. profl. svcs., 1986-91; exec. dir. Contact Lens Assn. Ophthalmologists, New Orleans, 1992—; adj. instr. Tulane U. Sch. Medicine, New Orleans, 1994—. Contbr. articles to profl. jours. Recipient Assoc. Inst. of Yr. award Ind. U., 1978, 79, Silver Javal Pin Internat. Contact Lens Coun., 1994; Robert C. Ezell fellow, 1979. Mem. Am. Assn. Soc. Execs., Contact Lens Soc. Am. (assoc., v.p. edn. fund com. 1990-92, bd. dirs. 1990-91). Avocations: reading, golf, personal computers, swimming. Office: Contact Lens Assn 523 Decatur St Ste 1 New Orleans LA 70130-1057

MASSARO, JOSEPH JAMES, secondary school educator; b. Buffalo, Dec. 28, 1950; s. James Vincent and Mary Frances (Valentine) M.; m. Nanette Gayle Tharette, Aug. 7, 1976 (div.); 1 child, Jeffrey Matthew. AS, Genesee C.C., 1975; BS in Health and Phys. Edn., SUNY, Brockport, 1976; MEd, SUNY, Buffalo, 1988. Cert. health and phys. edn. tchr., N.Y. Tchr. aide West Seneca (N.Y.) Sr. H.S., 1977-79; health instr. Royalton Hartland H.S., Middleport, N.Y., 1979—, varsity wrestling coach, 1979—, jr. varsity softball coach, 1982-83, jr. varsity soccer coach, 1992, athletic dir., 1993-94; prin., English tchr. Brockport Migrant Edn. Program, 1986-88; health tchr. Lockport (N.Y.) Sr. H.S., 1990, 92, 94; nutrition instr. Cornell Coop. Extension, Lockport, summer 1993. Chmn. Cmty. Chem. Intervention Group, Middleport, 1979-83; advisor SADD, Middleport, 1986-92. Named Wrestling Coach of Yr., Channel 7, Buffalo, 1988; recipient Sportsmanship award Niagara Frontier Ofcls. Assn., 1988. Mem. ASCD, N.Y. State Tchrs. United, N.Y. State Fedn. Health Edn., Assn. for Advancement of Health Edn., Am. Youth Soccer Orgn. (bd. dirs. 1992-95), Rotary Internat. Republican. Roman Catholic. Avocations: physical fitness, camping, fishing, woodworking, gardening. Office: Royalton Hartland Ctrl Sch 54 State St Middleport NY 14105-1116

MASSÉ, MARCEL, Canadian government minister; b. Montreal, June 23, 1940; m. Josee M'Baye; 4 children. BA, U. Montreal, 1958; LLB, McGill U., 1961; PhB in Econs., Oxford U., 1966; Diploma in Internat. Law, U. Warsaw, Poland, 1962; Diplomas in Internat. Affairs, Econs., Spanish, German and Italian, École des hautes études commerciales de Montréal. Econ. adviser Privy Coun. Office, Ottawa, ON, Can., 1971-73; dep. minister fin. Province of N.B., Fredericton, Can., 1973-74, chmn. Cabinet Secretariat, 1974-77; dep. sec. to Cabinet Fed.-Provincial Rels., Ottawa, 1977-79; dep. sec. to Cabinet Privy Coun. Office, Ottawa, 1979, sec. to Cabinet and clk., 1979-80; pres. Can. Internat. Devel. Agy., Hull, 1980-82, 89-93; undersec. state for external affairs Ottawa, 1982-85; sec. to Cabinet Intergovtl. Affairs, Ottawa, 1993; pres. Queen's privy coun. for Can., min. intergovtl. affairs, min. pub. svc. renewal Govt. of Can., Ottawa, 1993-96; pres. Treasury Bd. of Can., min. infrastructure, Ottawa, 1996—; bd. dirs. for Can. IMF, Washington, 1985-89; mem. Parliament Hull-Aylmer Constituency, 1993—. World Univ. Service scholar in internat. law, 1961; Rhodes scholar, 1963; Nuffield Coll. scholar in econs. Oxford U., 1966. Office: 9th Flr East Tower, 140 O'Connor St, Ottawa, ON Canada K1A 0R5

MASSENGALE, MARTIN ANDREW, agronomist, university president; b. Monticello, Ky., Oct. 25, 1933; s. Elbert G. and Orpha (Conn) M.; m. Ruth Audrey Klingelhofer, July 11, 1959; children: Alan Ross, Jennifer Lynn. BS, Western Ky. U., 1952; MS, U. Wis., 1954, PhD, 1956; LHD (hon.), Nebr. Wesleyan U., 1987; DS (hon.), Senshu U., Tokyo, 1995. Cert. profl. agronomist, profl. crop scientist. Research asst. agronomy U. Wis., 1952-56; asst. prof., asst. agronomist U. Ariz., 1958-62, assoc. prof., assoc. agronomist, 1962-65, prof., agronomist, 1965-76, head dept., 1966-74, assoc. dean Coll. Agr. assoc. dir. Ariz. Agr. Expt. Sta., 1974-76; vice chancellor for agr. and natural resources U. Nebr., 1976-81; chancellor U. Nebr.-Lincoln, 1981-91, interim pres., 1989-91; pres. U. Nebr., 1991-94, pres. emeritus, 1994, found. disting. prof. and dir., 1994—; chmn. pure seed adv. com. Ariz. Agrl. Expt. Sta.; past chmn. bd., pres. Mid-Am. Internat. Agrl. Consortium; coord. com. environ. quality EPA-Dept. Agrl. Land Grand U.; past chmn. bd. dirs. Am. Registry Cert. Profls. in Agronomy, Crops and Soils; bd. dirs. Ctr. for Human Nutrition, Agronomic Sci. Found., U. Nebr. Found.; mem. exec. com. U. Nebr. Tech. Park, LLC. Chmn. NCAA Pres.'s Commn., 1988-91; distbn. revenue com., standing com. on appointments North Ctrl. Assn. Commn. on Insts. Higher Edn., 1991; trustee Nebr. State Hist. Soc.; bd. govs. Nebr. Sci. and Math. Initiative; active Knight Found. Commn. on Intercollegiate Athletics. Named Midlands Man of Yr., 1982, to We. Ky. U. Hall of Disting. Alumni, 1992, DeKalb Crop Sci. Disting. Career award, 1996, Outstanding Educator Am., 1970; recipient faculty recognition award Tucson Trade Bur., 1971, Ak-Sar-Ben Agrl. Achievement award, 1986, Agrl. Builders Nebr. award, 1986, Walter K. Beggs award, 1986, hon. state farmer degrees Ky., Ariz., Nebr. Future Farmers Am. Assns. Fellow AAAS (sect. chmn.), Crop Sci. Soc. Am. (past dir., pres. 1972-73, past assoc. editor), Fellow, Am. Soc. Agronomy (past dir., vis. scientist program, past assoc. editor Agronomy Jour., past chmn. bd. dirs., Disting. Svc. award 1984); mem. Am. Grassland Coun., Ariz. Crop Improvement Assn. (bd. dirs.), Am. Soc. Plant Physiology, Nat. Assn. Colls. and Tchrs. Agr., Soil and Water Conservation Soc. Am., Ariz. Acad. Sci., Nebr. Acad. Sci., Agrl. Coun. Am. (bd. dirs., issues com.), Coun. Agrl. Sci. and Tech. (bd. dirs. budget and fin. 1979-82, 94—), Nat. Assn. State Colls. and Land Grant Univs. (chmn. com. on info. tech. 1987-94, exec. com. 1990-92, bd. dirs. 1992-94)), Edn. Engring. Professions (mem. commn.), Coll. Football Assn. (chmn., bd. dirs. 1986-88), Am. Assn. State Coll. and Univs. (task force instl. resource allocation), Assn. Am. Univs. Rsch. Librs. (steering com. 1992-94), Nebr. C. of C. and Industry, Nebr. C.C. Assn. (hon.), Lincoln C. of C., Nebr. Vet. Med. Assn. (hon.), Sigma Xi, Phi Kappa Phi, Gamma Sigma Delta, Alpha Zeta, Phi Sigma, Gamma Alpha, Alpha Gamma Rho, Phi Beta Delta, Golden Key Nat. Honor Soc. Office: U Nebr 220 Keim Hall Lincoln NE 68583

MASSEY, ANDREW JOHN, conductor, composer; b. Nottingham, Eng., May 1, 1946; came to U.S., 1978; s. Henry Louis Johnson and Margaret (Park) M.; m. Sabra Ann Todd, May 29, 1982; children: Colin Sebastian, Robin Elizabeth. BA, Oxford U., 1968, MA, 1981; MA, Nottingham U., 1969. Asst. condr. The Cleve. Orch., 1978-80; assoc. condr. New Orleans Symphony, 1980-86, San Francisco Symphony, 1985-88; music dir. Fresno (Calif.) Philharmonic, 1986-93, R.I. Philharmonic, Providence, 1986-91; music dir. Toledo Symphony Orch., 1991—, also condr.; vis. scholar Brown U., Providence, 1986—. Composer incidental music (stage prodns.) Murder in the Cathedral, 1968, King Lear, 1971, A Midsummer Night's Dream, 1972. Avocations: trees, computers, astrology, philosophy of Karl Popper. Office: care Toledo Symphony Two Maritime Plz Toledo OH 43604-1868

MASSEY, CHARLES KNOX, JR., advertising agency executive; b. Durham, N.C., Jan. 16, 1936; s. Charles Knox and Louise (Southerl) M.; m. Mary Ann Keith, Aug. 27, 1960; children: Elizabeth, Knox, Louise. BS in Bus. Adminstrn, U. N.C., 1959. Vice pres. C. Knox Massey & Assoc., Inc., advt. agy., Durham, N.C., 1959-64; account exec. Tucker Wayne & Co., advt. agy., Atlanta, 1964-78; pres. Tucker Wayne & Co., advt. agy., 1978-88, Tucker Wayne/Luckie & Co., Atlanta, 1988-95; chmn., CEO West Wayne, Inc., Atlanta, 1996—. Trustee The Lovett Sch., Atlanta, Inst. for the Arts and Scis., U. N.C., Chapel Hill. Mem. Piedmont Driving Club (pres. 1990-92), Coral Beach and Tennis Club (Bermuda), Highlands (N.C.) Country Club. Episcopalian. Home: 67 Brighton Rd NE Atlanta GA 30309-1518 Office: West Wayne Inc 1100 Peachtree St NE Ste 1800 Atlanta GA 30309-4518

MASSEY, DONALD E., automotive executiv. CEO Don Massey Cadillac. Office: Don Massey Cadillac Inc 40475 Ann Arbor Rd E Plymouth MI 48170-4576*

MASSEY, DONALD WAYNE, Episcopal minister, small business owner; b. Durham, N.C., Mar. 7, 1938; s. Gordon Davis and Lucille Alma (Gregory) M.; m. Violet Sue McIlvain, Nov. 2, 1958; children: Kimberly Shan (dec.), Leon Dale, Donn Krichele, Anthony Donn Prestarri. Student, U. Hawaii, 1959, U. Ky., 1965, 66, U. Va., 1970, Piedmont C.C., 1982. Head microfilm sect. Ky. Hist. Soc., Frankfort, 1961; dir. microfilm ctr. U. Ky., Lexington, 1962-67; dir. photog. svcs. and graphics U. Va., Charlottesville, 1967-73; pres. Micrographics II, Charlottesville, Va. & Charleston, S.C., 1973—; owner Roseraie Nursery Ctr., 1988—; instr. U. Va. Sch. Continuing Edn., 1971-72, Central Va. Piedmont Community Coll., 1976; cons. Microform Systems and Copying Centers; owner Massland Farm, Shadwell, Va.; basketball coach Rock Hill Acad., 1975-77; chaplain Cedars Nursing Home, Charlottesville, 1992-94; chaplain Colonnades Charlottesville, Va., 1992—, Our Lady Peace Charlottesville, 1996—. Pub.: Micropublishing Series, 18th Century Sources for Study of English Lit. and Culture, Women Authors 18th and 19th Centuries, 1993, Va. Colonial History, 1994—, Theology in the 18th and 19th Centuries, 1995; author: Episcopal Churches in the Diocese of Virginia, 1989, A Catechism for Children, 1995, A Guide to Colonial Churches in Virginia, 1996, The Christian Philosophy of Patrick Henry, In Memoriam to the Rt. Rev. William Meade, Third Bishop of Virginia, 1996, Jamestown, the Beginning of the Church in Virginia, 1996, Christ Episcopal Church, Monticello Parish, Charlottesville, Va. The First 100 years, 1924-1924, 1996, Ministry in Nursing Homes and Health Care Centers, 1997. Chmn. bd. dirs. Park St. Christian Ch., 1970, 75; pres., Rock Hill Acad. Aux., 1975-76; pres. bd. Workshop V for handicapped, Charlottesville, Va., 1972-73; bd. chmn. Park St. Christ Ch., 1969-73; mem. Emmanuel Episc. Ch., Greenwood, Va., Grace Episc. Ch., Cismont, Va.; pres. region XV Episc. Diocese of Va.; chalice bearer St. Luke's Chapel Simeon, Va., Christ Ch., Charlottesville, 1992, lay eucharistic min., 1993—; lay reader eucharistic minister Christ Episcopal Ch., Charlottesville, Va.; chaplain Cedars Nursing Home, Charlottesville, 1991—; rep. Senatorial Inner Circle, 1990, George Bush Rep. Task Force, 1990; eucharistic min. Grace Episc. Ch., Cismont, 1996—. With USMCR, 1957-63. Named Ky. Col.; recipient Key award Workshop V. Mem. Am. Libr. Assn., Va. Libr. Assn. Soc. Reprodn. Engrs., Nat. Microfilm Assn. (libr. rels. com. 1973—), Va. Microfilm Assn. (pres. 1971-72, v.p. 1973-74, program chmn. ann. conf. 1974, Pioneer award 1973, Fellow award 1976), Ky. Microfilm Assn. (Outstanding award 1967, pres. 1964-67), Assn. for Info. and Image Mgmt., Va. Gamebird Assn., Thoroughbred Owners and Breeders Assn., Am. Rose Soc., Thomas Jefferson Rose Soc. (charter), Nat. Rifle Assn. Contbg. editor Va. Librarian, 1970-71, Micro-News Va. Microfilm Assn., 1970-71, Plant & Print Jour., 1983-85; contbr. articles to profl. publs. Home and Office: 3304 Keswick Rd Keswick VA 22947

MASSEY, HENRY P., JR., lawyer; b. Montclair, N.J., Sept. 2, 1939. AB, Cornell U., 1961, JD with distinction, 1968. Bar: Calif. 1969. Assoc. Jackson, Tufts, Cole & Black, San Francisco, 1968-72, ptnr., 1973-82; ptnr. Wilson Sonsini Goodrich & Rosati, Palo Alto, Calif., 1982—. Bd. editors Cornell Law Rev., 1967-68. Mem. ABA (sects. on corp., banking and bus. law, taxation law), State Bar Calif. (mem. corps. com. bus. law sect. 1979-82), Order of Coif, Phi Kappa Phi. Office: Wilson Sonsini Goodrich & Rosati 650 Page Mill Rd Palo Alto CA 94304-1001

MASSEY, JAMES EARL, clergyman, educator; b. Ferndale, Mich., Jan. 4, 1930; s. George Wilson and Elizabeth (Shelton) M.; m. Gwendolyn Inez Kilpatrick, Aug. 4, 1951. Student U. Detroit, 1949-50, 55-57; BTh, BRE, Detroit Bible Coll., 1961; AM, Oberlin Grad. Sch. Theology, 1964; postgrad. U. Mich., 1967-69; DD, Asbury Theol. Sem., 1972, Ashland Theol. Sem., 1991, Huntington Coll., 1994; Hum. D. Tuskegee U., 1995; DD Warner Pacific Coll., 1995; LittD Anderson U., 1995, DD Washington and Jefferson Coll., 1997; postgrad. Pacific Sch. Religion, 1972, Boston Coll., 1982-83. Ordained to ministry Church of God, 1951. Assoc. minister Ch. of God, Detroit, 1951-53; sr. pastor Met. Church of God, Detroit, 1954-76, pastor-at-large, 1976; speaker Christian Brotherhood Hour, 1977-82; prin. Jamaica Sch. Theology, Kingston, 1963-66; campus minister Anderson Coll., Ind., 1969-77, asst. prof. religious studies, 1969-75, assoc. prof., 1975-80, prof. N.T. and homiletics, 1981-84; dean of chapel and univ., prof. religion and society Tuskegee U., Ala., 1984-89; dean, prof. preaching and bibl. studies Anderson (Ind.) Sch. of Theology, 1989-95, dean emeritus and disting. prof.-at-large, 1995—; chmn. Commn. on Higher Edn. in the Ch. of God, 1968-71; vice chmn. bd. publs. Ch. of God, 1968-78; dir. Warner Press, Inc. Author: When Thou Prayest, 1960; The Worshipping Church, 1961; Raymond S. Jackson, A Portrait, 1967; The Soul Under Siege, 1970; The Church of God and the Negro, 1971; The Hidden Disciplines, 1972; The Responsible Pulpit, 1973; Temples of the Spirit, 1974; The Sermon in Perspective, 1976; Concerning Christian Unity, 1979; gen. editor: Christian Brotherhood Hour Study Bible, 1979; Designing the Sermon, 1980; co-editor Interpreting God's Word for Today, 1982; editor Educating for Service, 1984; The Spiritual Disciplines, 1985, The Bridge Between, 1988, Preaching From Hebrews, 1992, The Burdensome Joy of Preaching, 1996; mem. editl. bd. The Christian Scholar's Rev. Leadership mag.; mem. editorial bd., contbg. editor Vol. I New Interpreter's Bible, 1990—; contbg. editor Preaching mag.; sr. editor Christianity Today Mag. Mem. Corp. Inter-Varsity Christian Fellowship; bd. dirs. World Vision. Served with AUS, 1951-53. Rsch. scholar Christianity Today Inst. Mem. Nat. Assn. Coll. and Univ. Chaplains, Nat. Com. Black Churchmen, Nat. Negro Evang. Assn. (bd. dirs. 1969-86). Office: 201 Mill Stream Ln Anderson IN 46011-1916

MASSEY, LEON R., professional society administrator; b. Grand Island, Nebr., Jan. 16, 1930; s. James Moore and Iva Pearl (Richardson) M.; m. Jean M. Nielsen, June 17, 1951; children: Dean R., Maureen L. Student, U. Colo., 1948-49; BA, U. Nebr., 1955; postgrad., N.Y. Inst. Fin., 1963. Salesman consumer products Union Carbide Corp., Memphis, 1956-57, Greenville, Miss., 1957-58, Albuquerque, 1958-61, Dallas, 1962-63; regional sales mgr. GC Electric div. Textron Corp., Dayton, Ohio, 1963-64; account exec. Merrill Turben Co., Dayton, 1964-66; with Nat. Electric Contractors Assn., Dayton, 1967-72, Denver, 1972-83, exec. sec., 1967-83, also bd. dirs. Rocky Mountain chpt.; pres. RLM's Assocs., Englewood, Colo., 1983—; instr. adult edn. Wayne State U., Dayton, 1964-66. City councilman City of Greenwood Village, Colo., 1986-90; pres. Cherry Creek Civic Assn., 1979-80, bd. dirs. 1973-74; bd. dirs. Assn. Operating Rm. Nurses, Cherry Creek Village Water Dist., 1992-95; bd. dirs. Goldsmith Gulch Sanitation Dist., 1990—, pres., 1992—; active Dem. Party, 1960. With USAF, 1950-54, Korea. Mem. Am. Soc. Assn. Execs. (cert., bd. dirs.), Colo. Soc. Assn. Execs. (life, pres. 1979), Civitan Club, Masons, Phi Kappa Psi. Office: RLM Assocs 4935 E Greenwich Ln Highlands Ranch CO 80126

MASSEY, LEWIS, state official; b. Gainesville, Ga.; s. Abit and Kayanne M.; m. Amy Massey; children: Chandler, Cameryn. BBA in Finance, U. Ga. Mem. campaign staff Ct. Appeals Judge Robert Benham; mgr. reelection campaign Gov. Joe Frank Harris; dir. election campaigns various first time candidates apptd. by Gov. Joe Frank Harris; spl. asst. Gov. Joe Frank Harris; campaign mgr. Pierre Howard for Lt. Gov.; chief of staff Lt. Gov. Pierre Howard; v.p. Bank South Securities Corp.; sec. of state. State of Ga., 1996—. Elder Peachtree Presbyn. Ch.; mem. bd. dirs. Am. Cancer Soc., Eagle Ranch Home For Boys. Recipient Blue Key ALumnus of the Yr. award U. Ga., Outstanding Young Alumnus Bus. Sch. U. Ga. Office: Office of Sec of State State Capitol Rm 214 Atlanta GA 30334*

MASSEY, RICHARD WALTER, JR., investment counselor; b. Birmingham, Ala., May 19, 1917; s. Richard Walter and Elizabeth (Spencer) M.; m. Ann Hinkle, Sept. 4, 1959; children—Richard Walter, Dale Elizabeth. B.S., U. Va., 1939, M.A., Birmingham-So. Coll., 1954; Ph.D., Vanderbilt U., 1960. Owner, mgr. Massey Bus. Coll., Birmingham, Ala., 1946-56; asst. to chancellor Vanderbilt U., 1959-60; chmn. dept. econs. Birmingham-So. Coll., 1960-66; investment trust officer 1st Nat. Bank of Birmingham, 1966-67; prof. econs. U. Ala., Tuscaloosa, 1967-68; v.p., dir. investment rsch. Sterne, Agee & Leach, Inc., Birmingham, 1968-75; pres. Richard W. Massey & Co., Inc., Investment Counsel, Birmingham, 1975—. Served to maj. U.S. Army, 1941-46. Mem. Country Club of Birmingham. Home and Office: 1304 Kingsway Ln Birmingham AL 35243-2174

MASSEY, ROBERT UNRUH, physician, university dean; b. Detroit, Feb. 23, 1922; s. Emil Laverne and Esther Elisabeth (Unruh) M.; m. June Charlene Collins, May 28, 1943; children: Robert Scott, Janet Charlene. Student, Oberlin Coll., 1939-42, U. Mich. Med. Sch., 1942-43; M.D., Wayne State U., 1946. Intern, resident in internal medicine Henry Ford Hosp., Detroit, 1946-50; assoc. Lovelace Clinic, Albuquerque, 1950-68; chmn. dept. medicine Lovelace Clinic, 1958-68, bd. govs., 1957-68; dir. med. edn. Lovelace Found. for Med. Edn. and Research, 1960-68; clin. assoc. U.

N.Mex. Sch. Medicine, 1961-68; prof. medicine U. Conn. Sch. Medicine, Farmington, 1968—; assoc. dean for grad edn. U. Conn. Sch. Medicine, 1968-71, dean Sch. Medicine, 1971-84, currently prof. emeritus dept. community medicine and health care, acting univ. v.p. for health affairs, 1975-76; chief staff Newington (Conn.) VA Hosp., 1968-71; trustee Am. Assn. Med. Clinics, 1966-68; exec. com., regional adv. group Conn. Regional Med. Program, 1971-76; trustee, v.p. Capitol Area Health Consortium, 1974-78, pres., 1980-81. Editor-in-chief Conn. Medicine, 1986—; editor Jour. of the History of Medicine and Allied Scis., 1987-91. Bd. dirs. Health Planning Coun., Inc., 1974-76; bd. dirs. Hartford Inst. for Criminal and Social Justice, 1976-80, Conn. Easter Seal Soc., 1977-85, Hospice Inst. Edn., Tng. and Rsch., 1979-81. With AUS, 1955-57; maj. Res. Fellow ACP; mem. Am. Group Practice Assn. (accreditation commn. 1968-78), Assn. Am. Med. Colls., Am. Assn. History of Medicine, Hartford County Med. Assn., AMA, Conn., Hartford med. socs., Am. Osler Soc., Beaumont Med. Club, Soc. Med. Adminstrs., Twilight Club (Hartford), Sigma Xi, Alpha Omega Alpha. Roman Catholic. Office: U Conn Sch Medicine Farmington CT 06032

MASSEY, STEPHEN CHARLES, auctioneer; b. London, May 9, 1946; s. Charles Dudley and Sheila Florence (Browne) M.; divorced; 1 child, Sarah Louise. Grad. high sch., U.K. Cataloguer books and manuscripts Christie's, London, 1964-75; sr. dir. rare books and manuscripts dept. Christie's, N.Y.C., 1975—. Fellow Pierpont Morgan Libr.; mem. The Grolier Club, The Old Book Table. Avocations: cinema, reading, running, music, forestry. Office: Christie's Intl Inc 502 Park Ave New York NY 10022-1108

MASSEY, THOMAS BENJAMIN, educator; b. Charlotte, N.C., Sept. 5, 1926; s. William Everard and Sarah (Corley) M.; m. Bylee Hunnicutt Massey, July 10, 1968; children: Pamela Ann, Caroline Forest. A.B., Duke U., 1948; M.S., N.C. State U., 1953; Ph.D., Cambridge U., 1968. Assoc. dean students Ga. Inst. Tech., Atlanta, 1950-58; lectr. U. Md. Univ. Coll., 1960-66, asst. dir. London, 1966-69, dir. Toyko, 1969-71, dir. Heidelberg (Fed. Republic of Germany), 1971-76, vice chancellor, 1976-78, chancellor, 1978-88, pres., 1988—; bd. dirs. Internat. Univ. Consortium for Telecommunications in Learning, 1983—. Served with USN, 1943-46. Mem. Am. Assn. Adult and Continuin Edn., Nat. Univ. Continuing Edn. Assn., Am. Psychol. Assn., Am. Assn. Higher Edn., Internat. Confs. on Improving Univ. Teaching (chmn. 1975—). Office: U Md Univ Coll University Blvd at Adelphi Rd College Park MD 20742-1600

MASSEY, VICKIE LEA, radiologist; b. Lebanon, Mo., Mar. 10, 1961; d. Don Delano and Virginia Lea (Woodrum) M.; m. Michael Rosenblum (div. Dec. 1995); children: Aaron David Rosenblum, Daryl Lea Rosenblum. BA in Biology, U. Mo., Kansas City, 1984, MD, 1985. Diplomate Am. Coll. Radiology, Am. Coll. Therapeutic Radiology. Intern St. Mary's Health Ctr., St. Louis, 1985-86; resident Meml. Sloan-Kettering Cancer Ctr., N.Y.C., 1986-89; asst. prof. U. Mich., Ann Arbor, 1989-91; radiation oncologist Therapeutic Radiologists Inc., Kansas City, Mo., 1991—; clin. asst. prof. U. Kans., Kansas City, 1993—, U. Mo., Kansas City, 1993—. Contbr. articles to profl. jours. Knight Health Profl. scholar, 1979-80. Mem. AMA, Am. Assn. Women Radiologists, Am. Coll. Radiology, Am. Soc. Therapeutic Radiology and Oncology, Radiol. Soc. N.Am., Am. Soc. Clin. Oncologists, S.W. Oncology Group, Mo. State Med. Soc., Radiation Therapy Oncology Group, Kansas City Clin. Oncology Program, Kansas City. S.W. Clin. Soc. Home: 805 W 51st St Kansas City MO 64112 Office: Trinity Luth Hosp 3030 Baltimore Ave Kansas City MO 64108-3404

MASSEY, VINCENT, biochemist, educator; b. Berkeley, NSW, Australia, Nov. 28, 1926; s. Walter and Mary Ann (Mark) M.; m. Margot Grunewald, Mar. 4, 1950; children: Charlotte, Andrew, Rachel. BSc with honors, U. Sydney, Australia, 1947; PhD, U. Cambridge, Eng., 1953; DSc (hon.), U. Tokushima, 1994. Mem. research staff Henry Ford Hosp., Detroit, 1955-57; lectr. to sr. lectr. U. Sheffield, 1957-63; prof. Med. Sch. U. Mich., Ann Arbor, 1963-95, J. Lawrence Oncley Disting. U. prof., 1995—; permanent guest prof. U. Konstanz, 1975—; mem. fellowship rev. panel NIH, 1965-69, mem. biochemistry study sect., 1972-76, chmn. 1974-76; mem. biochemistry and biophysics rev. panel NFS, 1980-84. Contbg. author numerous books.; co-editor Flavins and Flavoproteins, 1982; contbr. numerous articles, chiefly on oxidative enzymology, to profl. jours. Recipient Alexander von Humboldt U.S. Sr. Scientist award, 1973-74, 86; Imperial Chem. Industries Research fellow, 1953-55. Fellow Royal Soc. London; mem. NAS, Biochem. Soc., Am. Soc. Biochemistry and Molecular Biology (membership com. 1970, nominating com. 1978-80, chmn. 1979-80, chmn. program com. 1992-93), Am. Chem. Soc. (exec. bd. divsn. biol. chemistry 1975-77). Home: 2536 Bedford Rd Ann Arbor MI 48104-4008 Office: U Mich Med Sch Dept Biol Chemistry Ann Arbor MI 48109

MASSEY, WALTER EUGENE, physicist, science foundation administrator; b. Hattiesburg, Miss., Apr. 5, 1938; s. Almor and Essie (Nelson) M.; m. Shirley Streeter, Oct. 25, 1969; children: Keith Anthony, Eric Eugene. BS, Morehouse Coll., 1958; MA, Washington U., St. Louis, 1966, PhD, 1966. Physicist Argonne (Ill.) Nat. Lab., 1966-68; asst. prof. physics U. Ill., Urbana, 1968-70; assoc. prof. Brown U., Providence, 1970-75, prof., dean of Coll., 1975-79; prof. physics U. Chgo., 1979-93; dir. Argonne Nat. Lab., 1979-84; v.p. for rsch. and for Argonne Nat. Lab. U. Chgo., 1984-91; dir. NSF, Washington, 1991-93; sr. v.p. acad. affairs U. Calif. System, 1993-95; mem. NSB, 1978-84; cons. NAS, 1973-76. Contbr. articles on sci. edn. in secondary schs. and in theory of quantum fluids to profl. jours. Bd. fellows Brown U., 1980-90, Mus. Sci. and Industry, Chgo., 1980-89, Ill. Math. and Sci. Acad., 1985-88; bd. dirs. Urban League R.I., 1973-75. NAS fellow, 1961, NDEA fellow, 1959-60, AAAS fellow, 1962. Mem. AAAS (bd. dirs. 1981-85, pres.-elect 1987-88, pres. 1988-89, chmn. 1989-90), Am. Phys. Soc. (councillor-at-large 1980-83, v.p. 1990), Sigma Xi. Office: Morehouse Coll 830 Westview Dr SW Atlanta GA 30314-3773

MASSEY, WILLIAM LLOYD, federal agency administrator, lawyer; b. Malvern, Ark., Oct. 19, 1948. BA cum laude, Ouachita Bapt. U., 1970; JD, U. Ark., 1973; ML, Georgetown U., 1985. Bar: Ark. 1973, D.C. 1992, U.S. Supreme Ct. 1985, U.S. Ct. Appeals (8th cir.) 1973, U.S. Ct. Appeals (D.C. cirs. 1985), U.S. Dist. Ct. (ea. and we. dists.) Ark. 1973. Assoc. Youngdahl & Larrison, Little Rock, 1973-76; chief atty. Ctrl. Ark. Legal Svcs., Little Rock, 1976-77, dir., 1977-78; law clk. to Hon. Richard S. Arnold U.S. Ct. Appeals (8th cir.), 1978-80; legis. asst. U.S. Senator Dale Bumpers, Washington, 1980-81, chief counsel, legis. dir., 1989-91; ptnr. Mayer, Brown & Platt, Washington, 1991-93; commr. FERC, Washington, 1993—. Contbr. articles to profl. publs. Mem. ABA, D.C. Bar Assn., Ark. Bar Assn., Fed. Energy Bar Assn. Democrat. Presbyterian. Office: Commr FERC 888 1st St NE Washington DC 20426-0001*

MASSEY, WILLIAM S., mathematician, educator; b. Granville, Ill., Aug. 23, 1920; s. Robert R. and Alma (Schumacher) M.; m. Ethel Heap, Mar. 14, 1953; children—Eleanor, Alexander, Joan. Student, Bradley U., 1937-39; B.S., U. Chgo., 1941, M.S., 1942; Ph.D., Princeton, 1948. Mem. research dept. Princeton, 1948-50; from asst. prof. to prof. Brown U., 1950-60; prof. math. Yale, 1960—, Erastus L. Deforest prof. math, 1964-82, Eugene Higgins prof. math., 1983-91, Eugene Higgins prof. math. emeritus, 1991—, chmn. dept. math., 1968-71. Author: Algebraic Topology: An Introduction, 1967, Homology and Cohomology Theory, 1978, Singular Homology Theory, 1980, A Basic Course in Algebraic Topology, 1991; mem. editorial staff math. jours. Served as officer USNR, 1942-46. Fellow Am. Acad. Arts and Scis.; mem. Am. Math. Soc. Achievements include research in algebraic topology, differential topology, homotopy theory, fibre bundles. Home: 64 N Lake Dr Hamden CT 06517-2420 Office: Yale U Math Dept PO Box 208283 New Haven CT 06520-8283

MASSEY, WILLIAM WALTER, JR., sales executive; b. Lawrenceburg, Tenn., Sept. 21, 1928; s. William Walter and Bess Ann (Brian) M.; m. Virginia Claire Smith, Aug. 16, 1952; children: William Walter III, Laura Ann, Lynn Smith, Lisa Claire. BBA, U. Miami, Fla., 1949; BFA, U. Fla., 1969. Exec. v.p., dir. Massey Motors, Inc., Jacksonville, Fla., 1950—; v.p., dir. Atlantic Discount Co. Inc., Jacksonville, 1954-64; pres. Owners Surety Corp., Jacksonville, 1959—, General Svcs. Corp., Jacksonville, 1960-69, Owners Guaranty Life, Phoenix, Ariz., 1960-64, Securities Guaranty Life, Phoenix, Ariz., 1961-64, Fla. Properties, Inc., Jacksonville, 1961-64, Chi-Cha, Inc., Jacksonville, 1965-70, Univ. Square Properties, Jacksonville, 1969-80; v.p., bd. dir. Southside Country Day School, Jacksonville, 1963-68; bd. dirs. Southside Atlantic Bank, Jacksonville, 1965-93. Exhibited in group shows at Internat., N.Y., 1970, Ball State U., 1972. Lt. USAF, 1950-1952. Mem. Ponte Vedra Club, River Club, Epping Forest Club, Sigma Chi. Methodist. Avocations: music, painting, writing.

MASSIE, ANN MACLEAN, law educator; b. South Bend, Ind., Sept. 17, 1943; d. John Allan and Gladys Sherill (Wilkie) MacLean; m. Kent Belmore Massie, Aug. 25, 1973; children: Allan Barksdale, Laura Sherrill. BA, Duke U., 1966; MA in English, U. Mich., 1967; JD, U. Va., 1971. Bar: Ga. 1971. Assoc. Alston, Miller & Gaines, Atlanta, 1971-73, Long and Aldridge, Atlanta, 1974-76; staff atty. regional office FTC, Atlanta, 1973-74; law clk. to Hon. J. Harvie Wilkinson III U.S. Ct. Appeals (4th cir.), Charlottesville, Va., 1984-85; adj. prof. law Washington & Lee U., Lexington, Va., 1985-88, asst. prof. law, 1988-93; assoc. prof. law Washington & Lee U., Lexington, 1993—. Contbr. articles to law jours. Deacon Waynesboro (Va.) Presbyn. Ch., 1986-88; bd. dirs., v.p. Hosp. Aux., Waynesboro, 1986-88; elder Lexington Presbyn. Ch., 1995—. Named Prof. of Yr., Women Law Students Orgn., 1993. Mem. Am. Soc. Law, Medicine and Ethics, Hastings Ctr., Choice in Dying. Avocations: reading, walking, swimming, skiing, cultural events. Home: PO Box 1076 Lexington VA 24450-1076 Office: Washington and Lee U Sch of Law Lexington VA 24450

MASSIE, ANNE ADAMS ROBERTSON, artist; b. Lynchburg, Va., May 30, 1931; d. Douglas Alexander and Annie Scott (Harris) Robertson; m. William McKinnon Massie, Apr. 30, 1960; children: Anne Harris, William McKinnon, Jr. Grad., St. Mary's Coll., Raleigh, N.C., 1950; BA in English, Randolph Macon Woman's Coll., 1952. Tchr. English E.C. Glass High Sch., Lynchburg, 1955-60; juror Ctrl. Va. Watercolor Guild, 1996. Represented in permanent collections at Hotel de Ville, Rueil-Malmaison, France, Randolph Macon Woman's Coll., Lynchburg Coll., Va. Episcopal Sch., Va. Sch. of Arts, Va. State Bar Assn., Richmond, St. John's Episcopal Ch. Bd. dirs. Lynchburg Hist. Found., 1968-81, 91-95, pres., 1978-81; bd. dirs. Lynchburg Fine Arts Ctr., 1992—; bd. dirs. Point of Honor Mus., 1988—, chmn. collections com., 1989—; bd. dirs. Amazement Sq. Children's Mus., 1996; trustee Va. Episcopal Sch., Lynchburg, 1983-89. Mem. Am. Watercolor Soc. (signature, Dolphin fellow 1993, Gold medal Honor 1993), Nat. Watercolor Soc. (signature, Artist's Mag. award), Nat. League Am. Pen Women (pres. 1987, Best in Show 1994), Knickerbocker Artists (signature, Silver medal Watercolor 1993), Watercolor USA Honor Soc., Watercoloer West (signature), Catharine Lorrilard Wolfe Art Club (signature), Southern Watercolor Soc. (signature), Va. Watercolor Soc. (artist mem., Best in Show 1992, chmn. exhbns. 1986, pres. 1995-96), Nat. Arts Club, Artists' Fellowship, Colonial Dames Am. (chmn. 1987-90), Hillside Garden Club (pres. 1974-76), Jr. League (editor 1953-72), Lynchburg Art Club (bd. dirs. 1995—, chmn. 1981-4), Antiquarian Club. Episcopalian. Avocations: book club, gardening, tennis, skiing. Home: 3204 Rivermont Ave Lynchburg VA 24503-2028

MASSIE, ROBERT JOSEPH, publishing company executive; b. N.Y.C., Mar. 19, 1949; s. Franklin Joseph and Genevieve Helen (Savarese) M.; m. Barbara Ellen Batchelder, Apr. 16, 1982; children—David Chance, Caroline Courtenay, Laura Brett. B.A., Yale U., 1970; M.B.A., Columbia U., 1974, J.D., 1974; Diploma, U. d'Aix en Provence, France, 1969. Bar: D.C. 1974. Assoc. Covington & Burling, Washington, 1975-79; mgmt. cons. McKinsey & Co., N.Y.C., 1979-82; v.p. Harlequin Enterprises, Toronto, Ont., Can., 1982-84, exec. v.p. overseas div., 1984-89; exec. v.p. Direct Mktg., 1989-90; pres., chief exec. officer Gale Rsch., Inc., Detroit, 1990-92; dir. Chem. Abstracts Svc., Columbus, Ohio, 1992—; chmn. bd. dirs. Harlequin Mondadori, Milan, Italy, 1985-88; bd. dirs. Harlequin Hachette, Paris, Cora Verlag, Hamburg, Fed. Republic Germany, Mills & Boon, Sydney, Australia, Harlenik Ltd., Athens, Greece. Contbr. articles to law jours. Bd. dirs. Columbus Symphony Orch., Ctr. of Sci. and Industry, Columbus. Harlan Fiske Stone scholar, 1974. Office: Am Chem Soc Chem Abstracts Srvcs PO Box 3012 Columbus OH 43210-0012

MASSIE, ROBERT KINLOCH, author; b. Lexington, Ky., Jan. 5, 1929; s. Robert K. and Mary (Kimball) M.; m. Suzanne L. Rohrbach, 1954 (div. 1990); children: Robert Kinloch, Susanna, Elizabeth; m. Deborah L. Karl, 1992; 1 child, Christopher. BA, Yale U., 1950; BA (Rhodes scholar), Oxford U., 1952. Reporter Collier's mag., N.Y.C., 1955-56; writer, corr. Newsweek mag., N.Y.C., 1956-62; writer USA-1 mag., N.Y.C., 1962, Sat. Eve. Post, N.Y.C., 1962-65; Ferris prof. journalism Princeton U., 1977, 85; Mellon prof. humanities Tulane U., 1981. Author: Nicholas and Alexandra, 1967, Journey, 1975 (Christopher award 1976), Peter the Great: His Life and World, 1980 (Am. Book award nomination 1981, Pulitzer Prize for biography 1981), Dreadnought: Britain, Germany, and the Coming of the Great War, 1991, The Romanovs: The Final Chapter, 1995. Served to lt. (j.g.) USNR, 1952-55. Mem. PEN, Authors Guild Am. (v.p. 1985-87, pres. 1987-91), Soc. Am. Historians. Address: 52 W Clinton Ave Irvington NY 10533

MASSIER, PAUL FERDINAND, mechanical engineer; b. Pocatello, Idaho, July 22, 1923; s. John and Kathryn (Arki) M.; m. Miriam Parks, May 1, 1948 (dec. Aug. 1975); children: Marilyn Massier Schwegler, Paulette Massier Holden; m. Dorothy Hedlund Wright, Sept. 12, 1978. Cert. engring., U. Idaho (so. br.), 1943; BSME, U. Colo., 1948; MSME, MIT, 1949. Engr. Pan-Am. Refining Corp., Texas City, Tex., 1948; design engr. Maytag Co., Newton, Iowa, 1949-50; research engr. Boeing Co., Seattle, 1951-55; sr. research engr. and supr. dep. sect. mgr. Jet Propulsion Lab. Calif. Inst. Tech., Pasadena, 1955-84, task mgr., 1984-88, mem. tech. staff, 1989-94. Contbr. articles to profl. jours. Mem. Arcadia High Sch. Music Club, 1966-71. Served with U.S. Army, 1943-46. Recipient Apollo Achievement award NASA, 1969, Basic Noise Rsch. award NASA, 1980, Life Mem. Svc. award Calif. PTA, 1970, Layman of Yr. award Arcadia Congl. Ch., 1971, Mil. Unit Citation award, 1946. Fellow AIAA (assoc., Sustained Svc. award 1980-81), Am. Biog. Inst. Rsch. Assn., Internat. Biographical Assn.; mem. N.Y. Acad. Scis., Planetary Soc., Sigma Xi, Tau Beta Pi, Pi Tau Sigma, Sigma Tau. Congregationalist. Achievements include reduction of cooling requirements for rocket engines, experimental evaluation of heat transfer from thermally ionized gases, design of supersonic diffusers for rocket engine testing, reduction of noise from aircraft jet engines. Avocations: travelog and documentary film production and presentations, genealogy and history research, antiques, collecting sheet music. Home: 1000 N 1st Ave Arcadia CA 91006-2533

MASSION, WALTER HERBERT, anesthesiologist, educator; b. Eitorf, Ger., June 4, 1923; came to U.S., 1954; s. Rudolf and Margarethe (Polch) M.; m. Rose Marie Kumin, July 15, 1956; children: Birgit, Stuart, Iris. BS, U. Cologne, Ger., 1948; MD, U. Heidelberg, 1951, U. Bonn, 1951. Diplomate German Bd. Anesthesiology. Intern U. Zurich Hosps., 1951-52; trainee WHO Anesthesiology Centre, Copenhagen, 1952-53; asst. prof. physiology U. Basel, Switzerland, 1953-54; postdoctoral fellow U.S. Nat. Acad. Sci., Rochester, N.Y., 1954-56; asst. prof. anesthesiology U. Okla. Med. Ctr., Oklahoma City, 1957-61, assoc. prof., 1961-67; prof. anesthesiology, physiology and biophysics U. Okla. Health Sci. Ctr., Oklahoma City, 1967-88, prof. emeritus, 1988; prin. investigator NATO Collaborative Rsch. Project, Oklahoma City and Homburg, 1988-95. Editor: Hemorrhage/Anesth. Requirements, 1974, Multiple Trauma, 1984, Critical Care Cardiology, 1988; contbr. over 125 articles to profl. jours. Hon. consul Fed. Republic Germany, Oklahoma City, 1980-95. Grantee WHO, 1953, U.S. Nat. Acad. Scis., 1954, NIH, 1959-88; Fulbright scholar, 1985; named Newsmaker of the Yr., Okla. Press Assn., 1964, Alexander von Humboldt prize, 1974; decorated Order of Merit 1st class Fed. Republic Germany, 1990. Avocations: gardening, chamber music, travel. Office: Univ Okla Health Sci Ctr PO Box 26901 Oklahoma City OK 73126

MASSIS, BRUCE EDWARD, library director, media executive, consultant; b. N.Y.C., Jan. 2, 1948; s. Louis and Paula (Cooper) M.; children: Eric John, Heather Lyn. BA in English, CUNY, 1973; MLS, Queens Coll., 1974; MA in English, Adelphi U., 1992. Dir. libr. svcs. JGB Cassette Libr., N.Y.C., 1974—; v.p. In Touch Networks, Inc., N.Y.C., 1991—; adj. libr. faculty, Adelphi U., 1995—; cons. various librs., internationally, 1979—. Author: Voice Painting, 1993; editor: Libraries for the Blind: An International Approach, 1982, International Guide to Large Print, 1985, Interlibrary Loan of Alternative Format Materials, 1993, Serving Print Impaired Library Patrons, 1996. Pres., bd. trustees Deer Park (N.Y.) Pub. Libr., 1991—. 3rd class petty officer USN, 1968-72. Mem. ALA (internat. rels. com. 1986—), Internat. Fedn. Libr. Assns. (sect. pres. 1979-81), Dramatists Guild (assoc.), Authors League (assoc.), Acad. Am. Poets (assoc.). Avocations: writing, music, painting, travel, reading. Office: Jewish Guild for the Blind c/o In Touch Networks Inc 15 W 65th St New York NY 10023-6601

MASSLER, HOWARD ARNOLD, lawyer, corporate executive; b. Newark, July 22, 1946; s. Abraham I. and Sylvia (Botwin) M.; children: Justin Scott, Jeremy Ross. BA, U. Pa., 1969; JD, Rutgers U., 1973; LLM in Taxation, NYU, 1977. Bar: N.J. 1974, U.S. Dist. Ct. N.J. 1974, D.C. 1975, U.S. Ct. Appeals (D.C. cir.) 1975, N.Y. 1977, U.S. Dist. Ct. (we. dist.) N.Y. 1977, U.S. Tax Ct. 1977. Counsel house banking, currency and housing com., chmn. sub-com. U.S. Ho. Reps., Washington, 1974-76; tax atty. Lipsitz, Green, Fahringer, Roll, Schuller & James, N.Y.C. and Buffalo, 1977-79; pvt. practice Mountainside, N.J., 1979-89; pres. Bestway Products Inc., A.A. Records Inc., Servor Corp., 1979-85; pres., chief exec. officer, chmn. bd. Bestway Group Inc., Dover, Del., 1985-91; gen. ptnr. 26/27 Law Drive Assocs., 1988—; ptnr. Shonageri, Pearce & Massler, Hackensack, N.J., 1989-90, Mott, Pearce, Williams & Lee, Hackensack and Washington, 1990-91, Pearce & Massler, Hackensack, N.J., 1991-97; prodn. staff asst. DECCA House Ltd., London, 1968; chief exec. officer Basura Pub., Inc. (affiliated with BMI), 1974-80; arbitrator U.S. Dist. Ct. N.J., 1985—; adj. prof. law Seton Hall U., Newark, N.J., 1988-89, N.J. Inst. for Continuing Legal Edn., 1986; lectr. N.J. Inst. for Continuing Legal Edn., 1986—; assoc. dir. United Jersey Bank/Franklin State Bank, 1987—; del. adv. com. on indsl. trade and econ. devel. U.S./China Joint Sessions, Beijing, People's Republic of China, 1988. Author: QDROs (Tax and Drafting Considerations), 1986, 2nd. ed., 1987; contbr. West's Legal Forms, Vol. 7., 2d edit., 1987, 3d edit., 1993; Domestic Relations with Tax Analysis, Contemporary Matrimonial Law Issues: A Guide to Divorce Economics and Practice; tax author: Matthew Bender, NYCP-Matrimonial Actions and Equitable Distribution Actions, 1988; tax author, tax editor: Matthew Bender, Alimony, Child Support & Counsel Fees-Award, Modification and Enforcement, 1988, 2d edit., 1989, 3d edit., 1991, Matthew Bender, Valuation & Distribution of Marital Property, 1988, 89, 91, 92, 94, 95; contbg. author: How to Make Legal Fees Tax Deductible, 1988, Closely Held Corporations, Forms and Checklists, Buy-Sell Agreement Forms with Tax Analysis, 1988, The Encyclopedia of Matrimonial Practice, 1991, 4th edit., 1995; author: New York Practice Guide: Negligence, Tax Law of Compensation for Sickness and Injury, 2d edit., 1992; contbg. editor Pensions and Ins. Problems, 1984—, Taxation, 1984—, Fair$hare, 1984—, Law & Bus., Inc., 1984—; staff contbr., N.J. Law Jour., 1986—; contbr. articles to law revs. and profl. jours. Bd. dirs., legal counsel western N.Y. chpt. Nat. Handicapped Sports and Recreation Assn., 1977-79; counsel Union County, N.J., 1984-85; candidate Springfield (N.J.) Twp. Commn., 1986. Mem. ABA, N.J. Bar Assn. (vice chmn. taxation comm. family law section 1987—), N.Y. Bar Assn. (taxation com., subcom. on criminal and civil penalties), D.C. Bar Assn., Erie County Bar Assn. (sec. taxation com. 1977-79, continuing edn. lectr. taxation 1977—), Essex County Bar Assn. (tax com. 1981—), Union County Bar Assn. (chmn. tax com. 1984—). Republican. Avocation: Sports Car Club Am. formula Ford racing. Home: PO Box 4360 Warren NJ 07059-4360 Office: 95 Mt Bethel Rd Warren NJ 07059

MASSMAN, RICHARD ALLAN, lawyer; b. Beaumont, Tex., Aug. 19, 1943; s. Irwin Massman and Sylvia (Schmidt) Schwartz; m. Barbara Elaine Kessler; children: Jason Todd, Karen Faye. BS cum laude, U. Pa., 1965; JD cum laude, Harvard U., 1968. Bar: Tex. 1968; cert. in taxation, Tex. Bd. Legal Specialization. Assoc. Coke & Coke, Dallas, 1968-70; assoc. Johnson & Wortley, P.C. (formerly Johnson & Gibbs, P.C.), Dallas, 1970-71, ptnr., 1971-88, shareholder, 1988-94; of counsel Johnson & Wortley P.C., Dallas, 1994-95; sr. v.p., gen. counsel Hunt Consolidated, Inc., Dallas, 1994—; lectr. So. Meth. U., Dallas, 1973. Bd. dirs. Martin Luther King Jr. Community Ctr., Dallas, 1979-81, Jewish Fedn. Greater Dallas, 1980-83, 89—; mem. exec. com. Dallas regional bd. Anti-Defamation League, 1979—, chmn., 1990-92; chmn. Dallas Civil Svc. Bd., 1983; trustee Greenhill Sch., Dallas, 1985-92, vice chmn., 1990-92. Mem. Tex. State Bar (chmn., sec. taxation 1983-84), Dallas Bar Assn. (chmn., sec. taxation 1978), Dallas Petroleum Club, Columbian Club. Office: Hunt Consolidated Inc Fountain Pl 20th Fl 1445 Ross Ave Dallas TX 75202-2812

MASSOF, ROBERT WILLIAM, neuroscientist, educator; b. Minn., Jan. 2, 1948; m. Darcy Rood; children: Eric, Allison. BA, Hamline U., 1970; PhD, Ind. U., 1975. Postdoctoral fellow in ophthalmology Johns Hopkins U. Sch. Medicine, Balt., 1975-76, instr. ophthalmology, 1976-78, from asst. prof. to assoc. prof., 1978-91, prof. ophthalmology, 1991—, prof. neurosci., 1994—, prof. computer sci., 1994—; vis. prof. Taiwan U., Taipei, 1983, Warsaw Acad. Medicine, Poland, 1987, Robert Y. Garrett Meml. Lecture, Lancaster, Pa., 1988, Albert Einstein Coll. Medicine, N.Y.C., 1989, Ohio State U., Columbus, 1991, Mayo Clinic, Rochester, Minn., 1993; guest lectr. in field. Mem. editl. bd. Clin. Vision Scis., N.Y.C., 1985—, Eye Care Technology/Computers in Eye Care, Folsom, Calif., 1992—; patentee in field (3); contbr. articles to profl. jours. Recipient Manpower award, 1989, Tech. Transfer award NASA, 1993, Popular Mechanics Design and Engring. award, 1994, EyeCare Tech. Lifetime Acheivement award, 1995, Richard E. Hoover Svc. award, 1995. Fellow Optical Soc. Am. (chmn. edn. coun. 1993-95, bd. dirs. 1993-95), Am. Acad. Optometry; mem. Assn. Rsch. in Vision and Ophthalmology. Office: Johns Hopkins Univ Lions Vision Ctr 550 N Broadway Fl 6 Baltimore MD 21205-2020

MASSOLO, ARTHUR JAMES, banker; b. N.Y.C., July 21, 1942; s. Silvio Libro and Josephine Louise (Oneto) M.; A.B., Hamilton Coll., 1964; J.D., U. Chgo., 1967; m. Karen Irene Clasen, Mar. 7, 1970; 1 son, Arthur Reab. Vol. Peace Corps, 1967-68; with 1st Nat. Bank of Chgo., 1969—, beginning as trainee, sucessively rep. in Indonesia, gen. mgr. Italy, area head Latin Am. in Panama, sr. v.p. and head corp. personnel, 1979-81, sr. v.p., head Internat. Banking div., 1981-85; pres., chief exec. officer Banco Denasa de Investimento S.A., Brazil, 1985-87; also bd. dirs.; sr. v.p. Internat. Asset Enhancement, 1987-89, corp. sr. v.p. asset mgmt., 1990-94, corp. sr. v.p. of Latin Am., 1995-96; head of the Northea. United States For First Chgo. NBD Corp., 1996-97; entrepreneur Scandinavian Pharmaceuticals, 1997—; founding dir. Banco Latino Americano de Exportaciones Panama; chmn., bd. dirs. Link Unlimited. Past trustee Hamilton Coll. Mem. Ill. Bar Assn., Phi Beta Kappa. Office: Brandstrupsvej 4, Copenhagen Denmark

MASSON, GAYL ANGELA, airline pilot; b. L.A., Feb. 5, 1951; d. Jack Watson and Margaret Jean (Evans) M.; 1 child, Athena. BFA, U. So. Calif., 1970, MA, 1972, MPA, 1975, PhD, 1976. Lic. airline transport, seaplane, glider pilot, flight instr., flight engr. Pilot Antelope Valley Land Investment Co., Century City, Calif., 1972; ROTC flight instr. Claire Walters Flight Acad., Santa Monica, Calif., 1973; flight instr. Golden West Airways, Santa Monica, 1974; co-pilot Express Airways, LaMoore Naval Air Sta., Calif., 1975-76; charter pilot, instr. Shaw Airmotive, Orange County Airport, Calif., 1976; flight engr. Am. Airlines, Dallas, 1976-79, co-pilot, 1979-86, capt., 1986—; accident prevention counselor FAA, 1993—. Contbr. articles to profl. publs. Participant Powder Puff Derby, Angel Derby, Pacific Air Race and others. First woman type-rated on Boeing 747, also type-rated on DC-10, DC-9, Boeing 767, Boeing 757, Airbus-310. Mem. Airline Pilots Assn., Internat. Soc. Women Airline Pilots (charter), Ninety-Nines (past v.p. Smo Bay chpt.), Aerospace Med. Assn., Aerospace Human Factors Assn. Avocations: oil paint, viticulture.

MASSON, ROBERT HENRY, paper company executive; b. Boston, June 27, 1935; s. Robert Louis and Henrietta Hill (Worrell) M.; m. Virginia Lee Morton, Dec. 28, 1957; children: Linda Anne, Kenneth Morton, Robert Louis, II. B.A. in Econs. (Travis and Woods award), Amherst Coll., 1957; M.B.A., Harvard U., 1964. Fin. staff Ford Motor Co., Dearborn, Mich., 1964-68; mktg. services div. controller Ford Motor Co., 1968-70; pres. Knutson Constrn. Co., Mpls., 1970-72; v.p. fin., treas. Ellerbe, Inc., Bloomington, Minn., 1972-77; fin. dir. CirTech, Inc., Mpls., 1973-77; v.p. fin. transp. div. PepsiCo, Inc., Tulsa, 1977; corp. v.p., treas. PepsiCo., Inc., Purchase, N.Y., 1978-80; v.p., treas. Combustion Engring., Inc., Stamford, Conn., 1981-86, v.p. fin. and venture devel., 1986-87, v.p. venture fin. and internat. ops., 1988-90; v.p., CFO Parsons & Whittemore, Inc., Rye Brook, N.Y., 1990—; adv. bd. Shawmut Bank, 1988—. Author: (with others) The Management of Racial Integration in Business, 1964. Pres. North Georgtown Homeowner's Assn., Birmingham, Mich., 1968-70, U.S. Presdl.

Advance Man, 1972-76; trustee Naval Aviation Mus. Found., 1987—, Hebron Acad., 1993—; elder Presbyn. Ch. of Old Greenwich, 1992—. Served to lt. USN, 1957-62; lt. comdr. Res. Mem. Am. Forest and Paper Assn. (fin. com. 1991—), Fin. Execs. Inst. (com. on corp. fin. 1981—), Fairchester Treas. Group (pres. 1986), Lucas Point Homeowner's Assn. (pres. 1986-87), Theta Delta Chi. Clubs: Wayzata Yacht (dir.-treas. 1973-77), Riverside Yacht (asst. treas. 1985-87). Office: Parsons & Whittemore Inc 4 International Dr Rye Brook NY 10573-1065

MASSURA, EDWARD ANTHONY, accountant; b. Chgo., July 1, 1938; s. Edward Matthew and Wilma C. (Kussy) M.; m. Carol A. Barber, June 23, 1962; children: Edward J., Beth Ann, John B. BS, St. Joseph's Coll., Rensselaer, Ind., 1960; JD, DePaul U., 1963. Bar: Ill. 1963; CPA, Mich., Ill., others. Tax acct. Arthur Andersen LLP, Chgo., 1963—, ptnr., 1973—; dir. tax div. Arthur Andersen LLP, Detroit, 1974-84; dep., co-dir. internat. tax Arthur Andersen & Co., Detroit, 1983-84, ptnr.-in-charge internat. trade customs practice, 1983-88. Co-author: West's Legal Forms, 2d. edit., 1984; contbr. numerous articles to bus. jours. Bd. dirs. Arts Found. of Mich., Detroit, 1982-95, treas., 1982-93; bd. dirs. Ctr. for Internat. Bus. Edn. and Rsch., Wayne State U. Mem. AICPA, Internat. Fiscal Assn. (v.p. Eastern Gt. Lakes region), Assn. for Corp. Growth, Mich. Assn. CPAs, Mich. Dist. Export Coun. (chmn. 1985-92), Detroit Internat. Tax Group (founder,co-moderator), Licensing Exec. Soc., World Trade Club of Detroit, Bus. Assn. Mexico and Mich, Inc., Orchard Lake Country Club, Renaissance Club Detroit, Skyline Club, Fairlane Club, Butterfield Country Club. Office: Arthur Andersen LLP 500 Woodward Ave Detroit MI 48226-3423

MASSY, WILLIAM FRANCIS, education educator, academic administrator; b. Milw., Mar. 26, 1934; s. Willard Francis and Ardys Dorothy (Digman) M.; m. Sally Vaughn Miller, July 21, 1984; children by previous marriage: Willard Francis, Elizabeth. BS, Yale U., 1956; SM, MIT, 1958, PhD in Indsl. Econs., 1960. Asst. prof. indsl. mgmt. MIT, Cambridge, 1960-62; from asst. prof. to prof. bus. adminstrn. Stanford U., Calif., 1962—, assoc. dean Grad. Sch. Bus., 1971, vice provost for research, 1971-77, v.p. for bus. and fin., 1977-88, v.p. fin., 1988-91; prof. edn., dir. Stanford Inst. Higher Edn. Research, Calif., 1988—; sr. v.p. P.R. Taylor Assocs., 1995—; cons. assoc. Coopers & Lybrand L.L.P., 1995—; bd. dirs. Diebold, Inc., Bijur Lubricating Corp., 1979-95; mem. univ. grants com. Hong Kong, 1990—; mem. coun. Yale U., 1980-95; mgmt. cons.; mem. Stanford Mgmt. Co., 1991-93. Author: Stochastic Models of Buying Behavior, 1970, Marketing Management, 1972, Market Segmentation, 1972, Planning Models for Colleges and Universities, 1981, Endowment, 1991, Resource Allocation in Higher Education, 1996; mem. editl. bd. Jour. Mktg. Rsch., 1964-70, Harcourt, Brace Jovanovich, 1965-71; contbr. articles to profl. jours. Bd. dirs. Palo Alto-Stanford chpt. United Way, 1978-80, Stanford U. Hosp., 1980-91, MAC, Inc., 1969-84, EDUCOM, 1983-86. Ford Found. faculty research fellow, 1966-67. Mem. Am. Mktg. Assn. (bd. dirs. 1971-73, v.p. edn. 1976-77), Inst. Mgmt. Scis. Office: Stanford U PO Box 5156 Stanford CA 94309

MAST, FREDERICK WILLIAM, construction company executive; b. Quincy, Ill., Jan. 3, 1910; s. Christian Charles and Jessie Minnie (Pape) M.; B.S., U. Ill., 1933; m. Kathryn Mary Boekenhoff, Sept. 15, 1932 (dec. Jan. 17, 1975); children—Robert Frederick, Janet (Mrs. James Austin Jones), Susan (Mrs. Edward Hoskins Wilson), Linda (Mrs. William Frederick Bohlen), Teresa Ann (Mrs. Charles Edward Connell); m. 2d, Elaine Ellen Thies Driver, Feb. 14, 1976. Hwy. engr. Adams County (Ill.) Hwy. Dept., Quincy, 1929-33; jr. engr. Ill. Div. Hwys. Rd. Office, Springfield, 1933-35, asst. hwys. architect, 1935-39; estimator Jens Olesen & Sons Constrn. Co., Waterloo, Iowa, 1939-41, v.p., 1941-54, exec. v.p., 1954-65, pres., 1965-76, chmn. bd., 1970-80; owner Frederick W. Mast & Assos., Waterloo, 1946-60; pres. Broadway Bldg. Co., 1951—, Kimball Shopping Center, Inc., 1964-78; dir. First Fed. Savs. Bank of Waterloo, 1957-78, Nat. Bank of Waterloo, 1958-79. Mem. Council Constrn. Employers, Washington, 1968-72, chmn., 1969; ofcl. U.S. del. to Soviet Union under U.S./USSR Exchanges Agreement, 1968-69; del. 8th and 9th sessions bldg., civil engrng. and public works com. ILO, Geneva, 1971, 77; sr. builder specialist Tech. for the Am. Home Exhibit USIA, USSR, 1975; mem. Nat. Def. Exec. Res., assigned to Fed. Emergency Mgmt. Agy., 1969-89. Mem. Iowa Bldg. Code Council, Des Moines, 1947-50; mem. Bd. Zoning Adjustment, Waterloo, 1947-59; mem. City Plan and Zoning Commn., Waterloo, 1955-78; chmn. Community Devel. Bd., City of Waterloo, 1959-70; fin. chmn. Black Hawk County Republican Central Com., 1958-60; chmn. Waterloo-Cedar Falls Symphony Orch. endowment fund dr., 1977-79, St. Francis Health Care Found., 1980-86; chmn. bd. dirs. St. Francis Hosp., 1976-78; chmn. contractors adv. com. Iowa Coll. Found., 1972-73. Served to col., C.E., AUS, 1941-46. Decorated Legion of Merit; recipient Disting. Service award Waterloo C. of C., 1962; Ky. Col. Registered architect, Ill., Iowa. Mem. Asso. Gen. Contractors Am. (dir. 1956—, mem. exec. com. 1959-62, 66-72, nat. pres. 1968, SIR award Nev. chpt. 1970), Master Builders Iowa (pres. 1952, hon. mem. 1981), Am. Inst. Constructors, Contractors Mut. Assn. Washington (dir. 1971-83, chmn. exec. com. 1971-73), Iowa Engrng. Soc., Nat. Soc. Profl. Engrs., Soc. Am. Mil. Engrs., Waterloo Tech. Soc., Amvets, Am. Legion, Phi Eta Sigma, Sigma Phi Epsilon, Tau Beta Pi, Tau Nu Tau, Theta Tau. Roman Catholic. Clubs: Sunnyside Country. Lodges: Elks, Kiwanis. Home: 3309 Inverness Rd Apt F Waterloo IA 50701-4650 Office: PO Box 575 Waterloo IA 50704-0575

MAST, KANDE WHITE, artist; b. St. Louis, Mar. 10, 1950; d. Elliott Maxwell and Mary (Barritt) W. Student, U. Mo., 1968-70, Longview Community Coll., Kansas City, Mo., 1970-71. Portrait painter, free-lance artist Albany, N.Y., 1973-74, Kansas City, 1974—; dir., tchr. Studio Kande, Sch. Fine Arts, Kansas City, 1983-86; founder, exec. dir. Art Ctr. Kansas City, 1986-90; behavioral foster parent, 1989—, master foster parent, 1992—; mem. psychiat. diversion team, mental health rev. team Ja. County Divsn. Family Svcs., 1992-95. Portrait painter and free-lance artist. Pres., bd. dirs. Advocates for Children, Inc., 1996—; vol. Ozanam Home for Boys, Kansas City, 1987—, mem. adv. bd., 1991—; behavioral foster parent, 1989—, master foster parent, 1992—; mem. psychiat. diversion/mental health rev. team J.A. County divsn. Family Svcs., 1992-95. Named Foster Parent of Yr., 1992. Mem. Nat. Mus. Women in the Arts, Greater Kansas City Art Assn. Home and Office: 10243 Cedarbrooke Ln Kansas City MO 64131-4209

MAST, STEWART DALE, retired airport manager; b. Kalamazoo, May 10, 1924; s. Virgil S. and S. Louise (Rippey) M.; m. Judy Jo Bolton; children: Peter S., Frances Ann Mast Adams; m. May 20, 1979. Student, U. Mich., 1942-43; grad., Spartan Sch. Aerospace, Tulsa, 1946, Argubright Bus. Coll., Battle Creek, Mich., 1947. Mgr. Mcpl. Airport, Battle Creek, 1948-60; airport dir. Mitchell Field, Milw., 1961-66; mgr. Tampa (Fla.) Internat. Airport, 1966-89, ret.; pres. Mich. Assn. Airport Mgrs., 1958; bd. dirs. The Summit Ministries, Inc., Manitou Springs, Colo., 1980—. Past mem. aviation coun. Milw. . of C.; past mem. bd. rev. Boy Scouts Am., Milw.; bd. dirs. Sun'n Fun Aviation Found., Inc., Lakeland, Fla., 1992—, Sun'n Fun EAA Fly-in, Inc., Lakeland, Fla., 1994—. 1st lt. USAAF, 1943-45. Recipient Community Leadership award Greater Tampa C. of C., 1979. Mem. Am. Assn. Airport Execs. (past bd. dirs., pres.'s award 1979), Southeastern Airport Mgrs. Assn., Fla. Assn. Airport Mgrs. Avocations: aviation philately, photography.

MASTANDREA, LINDA LEE, lawyer; b. Chgo., June 10, 1964; d. Robert Anthony and Dorothy Jean (Kilpatrick) M. BA in Speech Comm., U. Ill., 1986; JD, IIT, 1994. Bar: Ill. 1995. Account rep. Health Chgo. HMO, Lisle, Ill., 1986-87; peer counselor Peninsula Ctr. Ind. Living, Newport News, Va., 1988-89; program mgr. Progress Ctr. Ind. Living, Oak Park, Ill., 1990-91; atty. pvt. practice, Ill., 1995—; pub. spkr., Ill., 1991—. Athlete rep. Atlanta Paralympics, 1993-96; v.p. athlete's adv. com., assoc. bd. Rehab. Inst. Chgo., 1992—. Named Athlete of Yr. Colo. Sports Coun., Denver, 1994, Outstanding Woman in Sports YWCA DuPage Dist., DuPage County, Ill., 1995; recipient IOC Pres. Disabled Athlete award U.S. Sports Acad., Mobile, Ala., 1995, USCPAA Female Athlete of Yr., 1995. Mem. U.S. Cerebral Palsy Athletic Assn. (v.p. 1994—), Nat. Italian Bar Assn., Justinian Soc. Lawyers, Chgo. Bar Assn. Avocation: wheelchair track world-record holder 200, 400, 800 and 1500 meters. Home: 266 Michigan St Elmhurst IL 60126-2709

MASTEN, CHARLES C., federal agency administrator; b. Albany, Ga., Apr. 20, 1943; s. Charles C. and Sophia L. (Wynn) M.; m. Betty Dodson, June 25, 1966; children: Deborah Denise, Mia Tereon, Kelle Marie, Stephan John. BS Bus. Adminstrn., Albany State Coll., 1965; MBA, U. Ark., 1976; degree mgmt. law enforcement execs., FBI Exec. Devel. Inst., 1991. Asst. nat. bank examiner comtroller of currency U.S. Treasury, Atlanta, 1969-71; cashier Citizens Trust Bank, Atlanta, 1971-72; spl. agt. FBI, Memphis, 1973-77; supervisory spl. agent FBI, Little Rock, 1978-85; supervisory spl. agent FBI, Washington, 1985-87, unit chief, 1987-91; dep. inspector gen. U.S. Dept. Labor, Washington, 1991-94, inspector gen., 1994—. Lt. USN, 1966-69, Vietnam. Mem. Assn. Govt. Accts. Roman Catholic. Avocations: jogging, gardening. Office: Dept of Labor Office of the Inspector General 200 Constitution Ave NW Ste S Washington DC 20210-0001*

MASTER-KARNIK, PAUL JOSEPH, art museum director; b. N.Y.C., Nov. 20, 1948; s. Charles Oldrich and Evelyn Theresa (Donnelly) K.; m. Susan Irene Master, Aug. 19, 1973. BA, Rutgers U., 1970, MA, 1971, PhD, 1978. Cert. in mus. studies, 1979. Faculty Rutgers U., New Brunswick, N.J., 1974-78; art critic Newhouse Publs., N.Y.C., 1976-80; faculty NYU, N.Y.C., 1980-83; dir. N.J. Ctr. for Visual Arts, Summit, 1981-84, DeCordova Mus. & Sculpture Pk., Lincoln, Mass., 1984—; bd. dirs. UrbanArts, Inc., Boston, 1988—, Mus. Coun. of N.J., Trenton, 1982-84; adv. bd. Archives of Am. Art, Boston, 1985—; vis. com. Sch. Mus. Fine Arts, Boston, 1987-90. Author: Exhibition Catalogues, 1982—. Recipient Outstanding Svc. award Inst. Mus. Svcs., 1988; Art Critic fellow NEA, 1980, Burns-Marvin fellow Rutgers U., 1971-73. Mem. Assn. Art Mus. Dirs. Office: DeCordova Mus & Sculpture 51 Sandy Pond Rd Lincoln MA 01773-2600

MASTERMAN, JACK VERNER, insurance company executive; b. Calgary, Alta., Can., Aug. 8, 1930; s. Lawrence Arthur and Mary F.G. (Robinson) M.; m. Isabel Christine Kaitting, June 25, 1954 (dec. 1990); children: Christine, Lawrence, Sheila, Keith. B.Com. with honors, U. Man., Can., 1953. With Mut. Life Assurance Co. Can., Waterloo, Ont., 1953—, v.p. ops., 1972-75, v.p. individual ins. and annuities, 1975-78, exec. v.p., 1978-82, pres., chief operating officer, 1982-85, pres., chief exec. officer, 1985-89, chmn., chief exec. officer, 1989-92, also bd. dirs., 1980—. Mem. United Ch. of Can. Office: Mut Life Assurance Co Can, 227 King St S, Waterloo, ON Canada N2J 4C5

MASTERS, BETTIE SUE SILER, biochemist, educator; b. Lexington, Va., June 13, 1937; d. Wendell Hamilton and Mildred Virginia (Cromer) Siler; m. Robert Sherman Masters, Aug. 6, 1960; children: Diane Elizabeth, Deborah Ann. B.S. in Chemistry, Roanoke Coll., 1959, D.Sc. (hon.), 1983; Ph.D. in Biochemistry, Duke U., 1963. Postdoctoral fellow Duke U., 1963-66, advanced research fellow, 1966-68, assoc. on faculty, 1967-68; mem. faculty U. Tex. Health Sci. Ctr. (Southwestern Med. Sch.), Dallas, 1968-82; assoc. prof. biochemistry U. Tex. Health Sci. Ctr. (Southwestern Med. Sch.), 1972-76, prof., 1976-82, research prof. surgery, dir. biochem. burn research, 1979-82; prof. biochemistry, chmn. dept. Med. Coll. Wis., Milw., 1982-90; Robert A. Welch prof. chemistry, dept. biochemistry U. Tex. Health Sci. Ctr., San Antonio, 1990—; mem. pharmacology-toxicology rsch. rev. com. Nat. Inst. Gen. Med. Scis., NIH, 1975-79; mem. bd. sci. counselors Nat. Inst. Environ. Health Scis., 1982-86, chmn., 1984-86; mem. adv. com. on biochemistry and endocrinology Am. Cancer Soc., 1989-92, chmn., 1991-92; mem. phys. biochemistry study sect. NIH, 1989-90; vis. scientist Japan Soc. for Promotion Sci., 1978. Mem. editl. bd. Jour. Biol. Chemistry, 1976-81, 96—, Archives Biochemistry and Biophysics, 1991—; contbr. chpts. to books and articles, revs. and abstracts to profl. jours. Recipient Merit award Nat. Heart, Lung and Blood Inst., 1988-97, grantee, 1970—; recipient Excellence in Sci. award Fedn. Am. Socs. for Exptl. Biology, 1992; postdoctoral fellow Am. Cancer Soc., 1963-65, advanced rsch. fellow Am. Heart Assn., 1966-68, established investigator, 1968-73; rsch. grantee NIH, 1970—, Nat. Heart Lung Blood Dist., 1970—, Nat. Inst. Gen. Med. Scis., 1980—, Robert A. Welch Found., 1971-82, 90—. Mem. AAAS, Inst. Medicine NAS, Am. Soc. Biochemistry and Molecular Biology (nominating com. 1983, coun. 1985-86, awards com. 1992—, fin. com. 1993—, publs. com. 1994—), Am. Soc. Pharmacology and Exptl. Therapeutics (exec. com. drug metabolism divsn. 1979-81, chmn. exec. com. 1993-94, bd. publs. trustees 1982-87), Am. Soc. Cell Biology, Am. Chem. Soc., Internat. Union Biochemistry and Molecular Biology (nominating com. 1994-97, chair U.S. nat.com. 1997—), Sigma Xi, Alpha O. Office: U Tex Health Sci Ctr Dept Biochemistry 7703 Floyd Curl Dr San Antonio TX 78284-6200

MASTERS, EDWARD E., association executive, former foreign service officer; b. Columbus, Ohio, June 21, 1924; s. George Henry and Ethel Verena (Shaw) M.; m. Allene Mary Roche, Apr. 2, 1956; children: Julie Allene, Edward Ralston. Student, Denison U., 1942-43; BA with distinction, George Washington U., 1948; MA, Fletcher Sch. Law and Diplomacy, 1949. Joined U.S. Fgn. Service, 1950; intelligence research analyst Near East Dept. State, 1949-50; resident officer Heidelberg, Germany, 1950-52; polit. officer embassy Karachi, Pakistan, 1952-54; Hindustani lang. and area tng. U. Pa., 1954-55; consul, polit. officer Madras, India, 1955-58; intelligence research specialist South Asia Dept. State, 1958-60; chief Indonesia-Malaya br. Dept. State (Office Research Asia), 1960-61, officer-in-charge Thailand affairs, 1961-63; grad. Nat. War Coll., 1964; counselor for polit. affairs Am. embassy, Djakarta, 1964-68; country dir. for Indonesia Dept. State, 1968-70; dir. Office East Asian Regional Affairs, 1970-71; minister Am. embassy, Bangkok, Thailand, 1971-75; ambassador to Bangladesh, 1976-77, to Indonesia, 1977-81; adj. prof. diplomacy Fletcher Sch. Law and Diplomacy, 1981-82; sr. v.p. Natomas Co., 1982-84; pres. Nat. Planning Assn., 1985-92, Edward Masters & Assocs., Washington, 1992—, U.S.-Indonesia Soc., 1994—. Mem. Am. Fgn. Svc. Assn., Phi Beta Kappa, Omicron Delta Kappa, Pi Gamma Mu, Delta Phi Epsilon, Cosmos Club. Home: 4525 Garfield St NW Washington DC 20007-1165

MASTERS, JOHN CHRISTOPHER, psychologist, educator, writer; b. Terre Haute, Ind., Oct. 25, 1941; s. Robert William and Lillian Virginia (Decker) M.; m. Mary Jayne Capps, June 6, 1970; children—Blair Christopher, Kyle Alexander. A.B., Harvard Coll., 1963; Ph.D., Stanford U., 1967. Asst. prof. Ariz. State U., Tempe, 1968-69; from asst. prof. to prof. U. Minn., Mpls., 1969-79; assoc. dir. Inst. Child Devel., 1974-79; Luce prof. pub. policy and the family, prof. psychology Vanderbilt U., Nashville, 1979-87, interim chair dept. psychology, 1986-88; pres. Profl. Mgmt. Group, Inc., 1991—; dir. Master Ventures, 1989—, Master Travel, 1989—. Assoc. editor: Child Development, 1973-76, Behavior Therapy: Techniques and Empirical Findings, 1974, 79, 88; editor: Psychol. Bull., 1987-89. Fellow Am. Psychol. Assn.; mem. Soc. for Research in Child Devel., Internat. Soc. for Study of Behavioral Devel., Assn. for Public Policy and Mgmt. Home: 555 Crosswinds Dr Mount Juliet TN 37122-5064

MASTERS, JON JOSEPH, lawyer; b. N.Y.C., June 20, 1937; s. Arthur Edward and Esther (Shady) M.; m. Rosemary Dunaway Cox, June 16, 1962; children: Brooke Alison, Blake Edward. B.A., Princeton U., 1958; J.D., Harvard U., 1964. Bar: N.Y. 1965, U.S. Dist. Ct. (so. dist.) N.Y. 1965, U.S. Ct. Appeals (2d cir.) 1965. Cons. asst. to under sec. Dept. Army, 1961; mem. policy planning staff asst. sec. for internat. security affairs Dept. Def. Washington, 1962; mem. Pres. Johnson's Spl. Polit. Research Staff, Washington, 1964; assoc. Shearman & Sterling, N.Y.C., 1965-68, 69; mem. staff Bedford-Stuyvesant D & S Corp., Bklyn., 1968-69; v.p., sec., gen. counsel, dir. Baker, Weeks & Co., Inc., N.Y.C., 1969-76; ptnr. Christy & Viener, N.Y.C., 1976-96; prin. Lear, Yavitz & Assocs., N.Y.C., 1996—; vice chmn. Robb Peck McCooey Specialist Corp., N.Y.C., 1996—; mem. exec. com. bd. dirs. Robb, Peck, McCooey Fin. Svcs. Corp., N.Y.C., 1996—; mem. SEC adv. com. broker-dealer compliance, 1972-74; legal advisor NACD Blue Ribbon Commn. on CEO and Dir. Performance Evaluation, 1994; chmn. bd. Clear and Present Prodns., 1992-93; bd. dirs. Harris & Harris Group Inc., 1992—. Mem. implementation com. Econ. Devel. Task Force of N.Y. Urban Coalition, 1968; mem. bd. Internat. Social Service, Am. Br., Inc., 1978-83, pres., 1979-83; bd. dirs. The Arts Connection, 1979-85; mem. steering com. N.Y. Lawyers Alliance for Nuclear Arms Control, 1983-96. Served with USN, 1958-61. Mem. ABA, Assn. Bar City N.Y. (com. mcpl. affairs 1977-80), N.Y. State Bar Assn. Home: 520 E 86th St New York NY 10028-7535 Office: 20 Broad St Fl 27 New York NY 10005-2601

MASTERS, JUDITH ANNE, elementary school educator; b. Fowler, Calif., Mar. 5, 1947; d. Thomas Clayton and Sarah Lois (Pearce) Hollingshead; m. Elmer Ray Masters, Aug. 5, 1966; children: Heather, Kimbereley, Paul, Aaron, Stacie. AA, Coll. of the Sequoias, Visalia, Calif., 1966; BA, So. Calif. Coll., 1975; MEd, Azusa Pacific U., 1987; M of Childhood Edn., Sch. of Bible Theology Sem., San Jacinto, Calif., 1988. Cert. elem. tchr., Calif. Dir. adult edn. Tranquility (Calif.) Sch. Dist., 1975-77; tchr. kindergarten Oliveview Christian Sch., Sylmar, Calif., 1977-79; tchr. kindergarten through 4th grades Hemet (Calif.) Unified Sch. Dist., 1979—; instr., cons./rschr. Sch. of Bible Theology Sem., 1979—; cons. So. Calif. Theol. Sem., Stanton, 1992; mem. English textbook com. Hemet Unified Sch. Dist., 1983-84. Author: (children's books) Samson the Seasick Seagull, 1978, Elephant, Tiger, Kangaroo, 1980. Dir. Women's Missionary Coun., Riverside County, Calif., 1980-81; solicitor Am. Cancer Soc., Riverside County, 1984-85. Mem. NEA, Calif. Tchrs. Assn. (polit. action rep. 1992-93), Hemet Tchrs. Assn. (polit. action rep., sch. site rep. 1992-93). Republican. Mem. Assembly of God Ch. Avocations: knitting, reading, sewing, singing, travel. Home: 1400 E Menlo Ave Sp 36 Hemet CA 92544 Office: Hemet Unified Sch 2350 W Latham Ave Hemet CA 92545-3654 also: Romana Elem Sch 41051 Whittier Ave Hemet CA 92544-6312

MASTERS, LEE, broadcast executive; married; 2 children. Student, Temple U. Various positions including programmer, sta. mgr., owner radio stas.; exec. v.p., gen. mgr. MTV; pres., CEO E! Entertainment TV, 1990—; conf. co-chair CTAM '96. Mem. Nat. Cable TV Assn. (Vanguard award for programmers 1995, pub. affairs com., co-chair state and local govt. com.). Office: E! Entertainment TV Inc 5670 Wilshire Blvd Los Angeles CA 90036-5679

MASTERS, ROGER DAVIS, government educator; b. Boston, June 8, 1933; s. Maurice and S. Grace (Davis) M.; m. Judith Ann Rubin, June 6, 1956 (div. 1984); children—Seth J., William A., Katherine R.; m. Susanne R. Putnam, Aug. 25, 1984. B.A., Harvard U., 1955; M.A., U. Chgo., 1958, Ph.D., 1961; M.A. (hon.), Dartmouth Coll., 1974. Instr. dept. polit. sci. Yale U., 1961-62, asst. prof., 1962-67; assoc. prof. dept. govt. Dartmouth Coll., Hanover, N.H., 1967-73; prof. Dartmouth Coll., 1973—, John Sloan Dickey Third Century prof., 1980-85, chmn. dept., 1986-89, Nelson A. Rockefeller prof., 1991—; cultural attache Am. Embassy, Paris, 1969-71; chmn. France-Am. Commn. Ednl. and Cultural Exch., 1969-71; vis. lectr. Yale U. Law Sch., 1988-89, Vt. Law Sch., 1993, 94; sect. editor Social Sci., Info., 1971; chmn. exec. com. Gruter Inst. Law and Behavioral Rsch., 1995—. Author: The Nation Is Burdened, 1967, The Political Philosophy of Rousseau, 1968, The Nature of Politics, 1989, Beyond Relativism, 1993, Machiavelli, Leonardo, and the Science of Power, 1996; editor: Rousseau's Discourses, 1964, Rousseau's Social Contract, 1978; co-editor: Ostracism: A Social and Biological Phenomenon, 1986, Collected Writings of J.J. Rousseau, 1990—, Primate Politics, 1991, The Sense of Justice, 1992, The Neurotransmitter Revolution, 1994; editor Gruter Inst. Reader in Biology, Law, and Human Social Behavior, 1992—. Served with AUS, 1955-57. Fulbright fellow Institut d'Etudes Politiques, Paris, 1958-59; joint Yale U.-Social Sci. Rsch. Coun. fellow, 1964-65; Guggenheim fellow, 1967-68; fellow Hastings Ctr. for Ethics and Life Scis., 1973-78. Mem. AAAS, Am. Polit. Sci. Assn., Assn. Polit. and Life Sci. (coun.), Am. Soc. for Legal and Polit. Philosophy, Gruter Inst. for Law and Behavioral Rsch. (adv. bd.), Internat. Soc. Human Ethology, Human Behavior Evolution Soc. Home: PO Box 113 South Woodstock VT 05071-0113 Office: Dartmouth Coll Dept Govt Hanover NH 03755

MASTERS, RONALD G., dentist, educator; b. Hannibal, Mo., Jan. 24, 1947; s. Gilbert D. and Beulah E. (Lewton) M.; m. Mary Jane Boulware; children: Alex, Jake, Jessica, Anna. AB in Zoology and Microbiology, Ind. U., 1969; DDS, U. Mo., 1974. From dental student to LTJG USNR, Camp Lejeune, N.C., 1970-74, lt., 1974-76; tchr. sci. Hazelwood (Mo.) Sch. Dist., 1969-70; med. lab. technician Downtown Hosp, Branch of Rsch. Hosp., Kansas City, Mo., 1971-74; pvt. practice, 1976-83; chief of dental svc. State Hosp. Number 1, Fulton, Mo., 1980-84; staff dentist, dir. dental programs for geriatrics and long term care VA Med. Ctr., Houston, 1984—; clin. asst. prof. stomatology, gen. and cmty. dentistry U. Tex. Dental Branch, Houston, 1991—. Contbg. editor for gerodontics Huffington Ctr. forAging, Baylor Coll. Medicine, Home Page/Internet. Mem. ADA, Greater Houston Dental Soc., Assn. Mil. Surgeons U.S. Home: 14 Martins Way Sugar Land TX 77479-2484 Office: VA Med Ctr 2002 Holcombe Blvd Houston TX 77030-4211

MASTERS, WILLIAM HOWELL, physician, educator; b. Cleve., Dec. 27, 1915; s. Francis Wynne and Estabrooks (Taylor) M.; children: Sarah Worthington, William Howell III. BS, Hamilton Coll., 1938, ScD (hon.), 1973; MD, U. Rochester, 1943; ScD (hon.), 1975. Diplomate Am. Bd. Obstetricians and Gynecologists; cert. Am. Assn. Sex Educators, Counselors and Therapists. Intern obstetrics and gynecology St. Louis Maternity and Barnes Hosp., 1943, asst. resident, 1944; intern pathology Washington U. Sch. Medicine, St. Louis, 1944; asst. resident gynecology Barnes Hosp., 1944, intern internal medicine, 1945, resident gynecology, 1945-46; resident obstetrics St. Louis Maternity Hosp., 1946-47; mem. faculty Washington U. Sch. Medicine, 1947—, assoc prof. clin. obstetrics and gynecology, 1964-69, prof., 1969—; dir. Reproductive Biology Research Found., 1964-73; co-dir. Masters & Johnson Inst. (formerly Reproductive Biology Research Found.), 1973-80, chmn. bd., 1981—; asso. physician St. Louis Maternity Barnes and St. Louis Children's hosps.; asso. physician Washington U. Clinics; asst. attending physician Jewish Hosp., St. Louis. Meml. Hosp. Author: (with Virginia E. Johnson) Human Sexual Response, 1966, Human Sexual Inadequacy, 1970, The Pleasure Bond, 1975, Homosexuality in Perspective, 1979, (with Kolodny et al) Textbook of Sexual Medicine; editor: (with V.E. Johnson and R.C. Kolodny) Ethical Issues in Sex Therapy and Research, Vol. 1, 1977, Vol. 2, 1980. Bd. dirs. St. Louis Family and Childrens Service, Planned Parenthood Assn., St. Louis Health and Welfare Council. Served to lt. (j.g.) USNR, 1942-43. Recipient Paul H. Hoch award Am. Psychopathol. Assn., 1971, award SECUS, 1972, Disting. Svc. award Am. Assn. Marriage and Family Counselors, 1976, award fo rdisting. achievement N=Modern Medicine, 1977, award Am. Assn. Sex. Educators, Counselors and Therapists, 1978; Paul Harris fellow, 1976. Mem. Gerontol. Soc., Am. Fertility Soc., Internat. Fertility Assn., Endocrine Soc., Am. Coll. Obstetricians and Gynecologists, N.Y. Acad. Sci., Soc. Sci. Study Sex, AAAS, Comprehensive Med. Soc., Pan Am. Med. Assn., Internat. Soc. for Research in Biology Reprodn., Am. Geriatric Soc., Am. Soc. Cytology, Soc. for Study Reprodn., AMA, Eastern Mo. Psychiat. Soc. (hon.), Authors Guild, Alpha Omega Alpha, Alpha Delta Phi. Episcopalian. Address: 4970 E Oakmont Dr Tucson AZ 85718-1730

MASTERSON, CARLIN See GLYNN, CARLIN

MASTERSON, CHARLES FRANCIS, retired social scientist; b. N.Y.C., Nov. 3, 1917; s. Frank Joseph and Harriett Geneva (Whittaker) M.; m. Vivian Ethel Reppke, May 8, 1954; children by previous marriage: Michael Charles, Susan Masterson Forrest. A.B., L.I. U., 1938; M.A., Columbia U., 1939, Ph.D., 1952. Dir. pub. relations Poly. Prep., Bklyn., 1946-49, Bklyn. C. of C., 1949-50, N.Y.C. Mission Soc., 1950-53; spl. asst. White House, Washington, 1953-56, Rumbough Co., N.Y., 1957-60, Nat. Safety Council, 1960-62; exec. dir. Office of Trustees, 1962-77; sr. assoc. Clark, Phipps, Clark & Harris, 1978-80; now ret. Author: World History, 1949, History of Asia, 1950. Mem. Pub. Rels. Soc. Am., Nat. Inst. Social Scis., N.Y.C. Mission Soc. (bd. dirs.), U.S. Com. for UN (bd. dirs.), Phi Delta Kappa. Presbyterian (elder). Club: Internat. Lawn Tennis. Home: 9801 Shore Rd Brooklyn NY 11209-7655

MASTERSON, JAMES FRANCIS, psychiatrist; b. Phila., Mar. 25, 1926; s. James Francis and Evangeline (O'Boyle) M.; m. Patricia Cooke, Jan. 28, 1950; children: James F., Richard K., Nancy. BS, U. Notre Dame, 1947; MD, Jefferson Med. Sch., Phila., 1951. Diplomate Am. Bd. Psychiatry, Am. Bd. Neurology. Intern Phila. Gen. Hosp., 1951-52; resident in psychiatry Payne Whitney Clinic, N.Y. Hosp., N.Y.C., 1952-55, chief resident, 1955-56, dir. adolescent OPD, 1956-66, head adolescent program, 1968-75, asst. attending psychiatrist, 1956-60, assoc. attending psychiatrist, 1960-70, attending psychiatrist, 1970—, dir. The Symptomatic Adolescent Research Project, 1957-67; dir. Masterson Group, P.C. for Study and Treatment Personality Disorders, N.Y.C., 1977—. Author: Psychotherapy of the Borderline Adolescent, Psychotherapy of the Borderline Adult, Countertransference, Narcissistic Personality Disorder, The Real Self, The Psychiatric Dilemma of Adolescence, The Test of Time: From Borderline Adolescent to Functioning Adult; contbr. articles to profl. jours. Fellow Am. Psychiat. Assn., Am. Coll. Psychoanalysts; mem. AMA, Am. Coll. Psychoanalysis, N.Y. Soc. Adolescent Psychiatry (founder, past pres.), N.Y. County Med. Soc. Office: 60 Sutton Pl S New York NY 10022-4168

MASTERSON, JOHN PATRICK, retired English language educator; b. Chgo., Mar. 15, 1925; s. Michael Joseph and Delia Frances (Dolan) M.; m. Jean Frances Wegrzyn, Aug. 18, 1956; children: Mary Beth, Michael, Maureen, Laura. B.A., St. Mary of the Lake, 1947; M.A., De Paul U., 1952; Ph.D., U. Ill., 1961. Chmn. English dept. De Paul U., Chgo., 1964-67, head humanities div., 1967-70, prof. English, 1970, dean Coll. Liberal Arts and Scis., 1970-76, prof. mgmt., 1976-80, 82-87, prof. emeritus, 1988—, dean Grad. Sch., 1980-82; cons. in field. Recipient award Shell Oil Co., 1968, Via Sapientiae award De Paul U., 1987; fellow adminstrn. program Am. Coun. Edn. Roman Catholic. Home: 1922 Belleview Ave Westchester IL 60154-4345

MASTERSON, KLEBER SANDLIN, former organization executive, retired naval officer; b. San Jon, N.Mex., July 12, 1908; s. John Patrick and Lela (Johnson) M.; m. Charlotte Elizabeth Parker, Oct. 3, 1931 (dec. 1986); 1 son, Kleber Sandlin, Jr. Student, U. N.Mex., 1925-26; B.S., U.S. Naval Acad., 1930; grad., U.S. Naval Postgrad. Sch., 1939, Naval War Coll., 1953. Commd. ensign U.S. Navy, 1930, advanced through grades to vice adm., 1964; assigned various ships, 1930-41; main battery asst. U.S.S. Arizona, Pearl Harbor; gunnery officer U.S.S. Pennsylvania, to 1944; staff research and devel. div., bur. ordnance Navy Dept., Wash., 1944-46; mem. staff CINCLANT FLT, 1946-47; comdr. Destroyer Div. 102, 1947-48; head ammunition br. Bur. Naval Ordnance, 1950-52; comdg. officer U.S.S. Lenawee, 1953-54; comdr. Naval Adminstrv. Unit, also asst. comdr. operations, field command Armed Forces Spl. Weapons Project, 1954-56; comdg. officer U.S.S. Boston, 1956-57; dir. guided missile div. Office Chief Naval Operations, exec. mem. navy ballistic missile com., 1958-60; comdr. Cruiser Div. 1, 1960-61; asst. chief naval operations devel. Office Chief Naval Operations, 1961; dep. chief Bur. Naval Weapons, 1961-62, chief, 1962-64; comdr. 2d Fleet and comdr. Striking Fleet Atlantic, 1964-66; dir. Weapons Systems Evaluation Group, Office of Sec. of Def., Washington, 1966-69; ret. Weapons Systems Evaluation Group, Office of Sec. of Def., 1969; pres. Navy Relief Soc., 1969-73. Decorated D.S.M., Legion of Merit, Navy Commendation; commandeur del'Ordre National du Mérite (France). Mem. U.S. Naval Acad. Alumni Assn., U.S. Naval Inst. Navy Hist. Found. Club: Army Navy Country (Arlington, Va.). Home: 3440 S Jefferson St Apt 360 Falls Church VA 22041-3128

MASTERSON, KLEBER SANLIN, JR., physicist; b. San Diego, Sept. 26, 1932; s. Kleber Sandlin and Charlotte Elizabeth (Parker) M.; m. Sara Ann Cooper, Dec. 21, 1957; children: Thomas Marshall, John Cooper. BS in Engring., U.S. Naval Acad., 1954; MS in Physics, USN Postgrad. Sch., 1960; PhD in Physics, U. Calif., San Diego, 1963; student Advanced Mgmt. Programs, Harvard Bus. Sch., 1981-82. Commd. ensign USN, 1954, advanced through grades to rear adm., 1979; comdg. officer USS Preble, Pearl Harbor, Hawaii, 1969-71; mgr. antiship missile def. project USN, Washington, 1974-77, exec. asst. to sec. of Navy, 1977-79, asst. dep. comdr. Naval Sea Systems Command, 1979-81, chief Studies, Analyses and Gaming Agy., 1981-82; ret. USN, 1982; prin. Booz, Allen and Hamilton, Inc., Arlington, Va., 1982-87; v.p. Booz, Allen and Hamilton, Inc., Arlington, 1987-92; sr. v.p. Sci. Applications Internat. Corp., 1992-94; pres. The Riverside Group, Ltd., 1994—; Washington area mgr. The Nettleship Group Inc., 1995—; bd. control U.S. Naval Inst., Annapolis, Md., 1971-82; bd. dirs. Mil. Ops. Rsch. Soc., 1984-90, pres., 1988-89. Editor: Book of Navy Songs, 1954; contbr. articles on plasma and theoretical nuclear physics, computer science, radars, ops. rsch. to profl. publs. Mem. Am. Phys. Soc., U.S. Naval Acad. Alumni Assn. (pres. Washington chpt. 1989-90), U.S. Naval Acad. Found. (trustee 1991—), Sigma Xi. Achievements include development of NELIAC computer program and Strategic Simulation Methodology. Home and Office: The Riverside Group Ltd 101 Pommander Walk Alexandria VA 22314-3844

MASTERSON, MARY STUART, actress; b. N.Y.C., June 29, 1966; d. Peter and Carlin Glynn Masterson. Theatre appearances include Alice in Wonderland, 1982, Been Taken, 1985, The Lucky Spot, 1987, Lily Dale, 1987; TV movies include Love Lives On, 1985, City in Fear, 1980, Lily Dale, 1996; films: The Stepford Wives, 1975, Heaven Help Us, 1984, At Close Range, 1985, My Little Girl, 1986, Gardens of Stone, 1987, Some Kind of Wonderful, 1987, Mr. North, 1988, Chances Are, 1989, Immediate Family, 1989, Funny About Love, 1990, Fried Green Tomatoes, 1991, Married To It, 1993, Benny and Joon, 1993, Bad Girls, 1994, Radioland Murders, 1994, Heaven's Prisoners, 1996, Bed of Roses, 1996. Office: Creative Artists Agency 9830 Wilshire Blvd Beverly Hills CA 90212-1804

MASTERSON, MICHAEL RUE, journalist, educator, editor; b. Harrison, Ark., Dec. 10, 1946; s. Rue B. and Elaine H. (Hammerschmidt) M.; m. Kathleen Bowling, Aug. 29, 1969 (div. 1988); children: Brandon Lee, Anna Kathleen; m. Ruthie Louette Laws, Mar. 20, 1993. Student, U. N.Mex., 1965-68; BA, U. Cen. Ark., 1971. Editor The Daily Independent, Newport, Ark., 1971-73; exec. editor Sentinel-Record, Hot Springs, Ark., 1973-80; staff writer L.A. Times, 1980; investigative reporter Chgo. Sun-Times, 1981; spl. projects editor WEHCO Media (daily newspapers), Little Rock, 1982-86; investigative team leader Ariz. Republic, 1986-89; Kiplinger Program endowed chair, prof. journalism Ohio State U., Columbus, 1989-94; investigative projects editor The Asbury Park (N.J.) Press, 1994—; instr. journalism Garland Community Coll., 1974-75; adj. faculty mem. U. Ark., 1996. Co-author: (text) Excellence in Reporting, 1987; contbg. editor, cons. Two River Times, Monmouth, N.J., 1993-94; supr. edtl. enhancement program Am. Pub., 1996—. With USCGR, 1968-73. Recipient Nat. Headliner awards Press Club Atlantic City, 1971, 89, Robert F. Kennedy awards and honors, 1972, 74, 77, 80, Freedom of Info. and Investigative Reporting awards Ark. chpt. Soc. Profl. Journalists, 1974, honor awards, 1975, award for editorial Freedom Found. Valley Forge, 1974, Mass Media Gold Medallion NCCJ, 1974, Paul Tobenkin Meml. awards Columbia Grad. Sch. Journalism, 1975, 85, 88, 89, Disting. Svc. awards Sch. Journalism U. Ark. Little Rock, ann. 1979-84, citation Roy Howard Pub. Svc. Awards, 1978, cert. of merit ABA, 1980, 84, 95, Nat. Assn. Black Journalists reporting prize, 1985, Don Bolles award for outstanding investigative reporting, 1987, 88, Best of West Journalism awards, 1987, 88, Congl. Achievement award Nat. Congress Am. Indians, 1987, Clarion journalism award, 1988, George Polk award for nat. reporting, 1989, Heywood Broun Meml. awards, 1984, 87, hon. mention, 1975; finalist Pulitzer Prize Nat. Reporting 1988, Specialized Reporting 89; Ark. Journalist of Yr., 1986; journalism awards IRE, 1979, 82, Best of Best medal, 1979; Alicia Patterson journalism fellow, 1976-77; NEH Ethics fellow Yale U., 1979; edn. fellow Poynter Inst. Media Studies, 1993; finalist First Journalist in Space Program, 1986. Mem. Investigative Reporters and Editors (bd. dirs. 1984-89), Soc. Profl. Journalists, Nat. Headliners Club. Home: 16553 Ranchero Rd Springdale AR 72764 Office: Northwest Ark Times 212 N East Ave Fayetteville AR 72701-5225 *To call attention to the events, predicaments and inequities in the neighborhood in hopes at least one person who follows will somehow benefit from my having once been here.*

MASTERSON, PATRICIA O'MALLEY, publications editor, writer; b. Worcester, Mass., May 15, 1952; d. Paul Francis and Dorothy M. (O'Malley) M. BFA, Emerson Coll., 1974; MA, Goddard Coll., 1980. Reporter, photographer Patriot Newspaper, Webster, Mass., 1975-78; pub. relations dir. Mt. Pleasant Hosp., Lynn, Mass., 1980-84; pubs. editor Ocean Spray Cranberries, Inc., Plymouth, Mass., 1984-89; mktg. comms. coord. Groundwater Tech., Norwood, Mass., 1989-93; pres. O'Malley Masterson Comm., Belmont, Mass., 1993—; freelance writer newspaper and mag. articles, 1974—. Mem. adv. bd. Ad. Com. mag.; contbr. numerous articles to newspapers, mags.; stringer Hanover (Mass.) Mariner Newspaper, 1987-91. Bd. dirs. YWCA, Cambridge, Mass., 1982-86; elected Nat. Alumni Assn., Emerson Coll., 1994-97, chair student rels. com., 1995—; judge Coop. Info. Fair, 1992; mem. publicity com. Healthworks, United Way, 1987; pres. Softball Leagues, Abington, Mass., 1991-92; vol. Rosie's Homeless Shelter, Boston, 1987-93. Recipient Amy England award YWCA, 1986, Green Eyeshade award Internat. Assn. Bus. Communicators, 1987, Yankee Ingenuity award Internat. Assn. Bus. Communicators, 1991, Employee Pub. 2d Place award Cooperative Info. Fair, 1987, 88, Membership Mag. award Cooperative Info. Fair, 1988; named One of Outstanding Young Women in Am. Jaycees, 1983, MVP Northeast Regional Women's Softball Championship, 1995. Mem. Internat. Assn. Bus. Communicators (ann. internat. conf. planning bd. 1993-94, accredited 1993—, mem. accreditation bd. 1995—), South Shore Ad Club (publicity com., newsletter com., 9th Wave award 1987, 89, 92, judge 9th Wave awards 1994), Coop. Communicators Assn. (1st pl. employee publ. award 1987, 3rd pl. mag. award 1989). Avocations: sports, writing fiction, flute. Home: 14A Exchange St Millis MA 02054

MASTERSON, PETER, actor, director; b. Houston, June 1, 1934; s. Carlos Bee and Josephine Yeager (Smith) M.; m. Carlin Glynn, Dec. 29, 1960; children: Carlin Alexandra, Mary Stuart, Peter Carlos. BA in History, Rice U., 1957. Appeared in Broadway plays Marathon '33, 1963, Blues for Mr. Charlies, 1964; title role in Trial of Lee Harvey Oswald, 1967; appeared in The Great White Hope, 1968, That Championship Season, 1974, The Poison Tree, 1975, (films) The Exorcist, 1972, Man on a Swing, 1973, The Stepford Wives, 1974; playwright The Best Little Whorehouse in Texas, 1978; dir. Broadway prodns. The Best Little Whorehouse in Texas, 1978 (Drama Desk award for Best Dir. of Musical 1978); co-dir., co-writer The Best Little Whorehouse Goes Public, 1994; dir. off-Broadway prodns. The Cover of Life, 1994, The Young Man from Atlanta (Pulitzer prize 1995); screenwriter The Best Little Whorehouse in Texas, 1980; prodr. (TV film) City in Fear, 1980; dir. films The Trip to Bountiful, 1985, Blood Red, 1986, Full Moon in Blue Water, 1987, Night Game, 1988, Convicts, 1989, Arctic Blue, 1993, Lily Dale, 1996, The Only Thrill, 1997. Mem. AFTRA, SAG, Actors Equity Assn., Soc. Stage Dirs. and Choreographers, Writers Guild Am., Actors Studio, Dirs. Guild Am., Seawanhaka Club, Corinthian Yacht Club, Tex. Corinthian Yacht Club.

MASTERSON, WILLIAM A., judge; b. N.Y.C., June 25, 1931; s. John Patrick and Helen Audrey (O'Hara) M.; m. Julie Dohrmann Cosgrove; children: Mark, Mary, Timothy, Barbara. BA, UCLA, 1953, JD, 1958. Bar: Calif., U.S. Supreme Ct. Assoc. Sheppard, Mullin, Richter & Hampton, L.A., 1958-62; ptnr., 1962-79; ptnr. Rogers & Wells, 1979-83, Skadden, Arps, Slate, Meagher & Flom, 1983-87; judge L.A. Superior Ct., 1987-92, justice Ct. Appeal, 1993—. Author, editor: Civil Trial Practice: Strategies and Techniques, 1986. With inf. U.S. Army, 1953-55. Fellow Am. Coll. Trial Lawyers; mem. Order of Coif. Office: Ct Appeal 300 S Spring St Los Angeles CA 90013-1230

MASTNY-FOX, CATHERINE LOUISE, administrator, consultant; b. New Rochelle, N.Y., June 4, 1939; d. Louis Francis and Catherine Marie (Haage) Kacmarynski; m. Vojtech Mastny, July 25, 1964 (div. Oct. 1987); m. Richard K. Fox, Oct. 10, 1993; children: Catherine Paula (dec.), John Adalbert (dec.), Elizabeth Louise. BA magna cum laude, Coll. New Rochelle, 1961; MA, Columbia U., 1963, PhD, 1968. Lectr. in history various colls., N.Y. and Calif., 1968-71; researcher, writer H. W. Wilson Co., N.Y.C., 1971-81; contbg. editor Columbia U. Press, N.Y.C., 1972-74; v.p., exec. dir. Internat. Mgmt. and Devel. Inst., Washington, 1978-84, exec. dir., spl. asst. to chmn., 1986-91; v.p. Meridian House Internat., Washington, 1984-85; dir. corp. devel. Washington Music Ensemble, 1991—, also bd. dirs.; cons. in field; panelist NEH, Washington, 1983; internat. advisor Global Nomads, Washington, 1990—. Contbg. author: The American Book of Days, 1978, World Authors, 1970-1971, 1980; contbg. editor: Columbia Ency., 3d edit., 1975. Fulbright Found. grantee, 1961-62; fellow Woodrow Wilson Found., 1962-63, Walter L. Dorn, 1963-64, Konrad Adenauer fellow, 1965-66. Democrat. Roman Catholic. Avocations: travel, classical music, hiking, art collecting, gardening. Home: 5102 Wyoming Rd Bethesda MD 20816-2267

MASTRANTONIO, MARY ELIZABETH, actress; b. Lombard, Ill., Nov. 17, 1958; d. Frank A. and Mary D. (Pagone) M. Student, U. Ill., 1976-78. Actress: (stage prodns.) Copperfield, 1981, Oh, Brother, 1981, Amadeus, 1982, Sunday in the Park with George, 1983, The Human Comedy, 1984, Henry V, 1984, Measure for Measure, 1985, The Knife, 1987, Twelfth Night, (feature films) Scarface, 1983, The Color of Money, 1986 (Acad. award nomination 1986), The January Man, 1989, The Abyss, 1989, Fools of Fortune, 1990, Class Action, 1991, Robin Hood: Prince of Thieves, 1991, Consenting Adults, 1992, White Sands, 1992, Three Wishes, 1995; (TV movie) Mussolini: The Untold Story, 1985, Two Bits, 1995. Office: Internat Creative Mgmt 8942 Wilshire Blvd Beverly Hills CA 90211-1934

MASTRION, GUY, secondary school principal. Prin. Longwood Mid. Sch., Middle Island, N.Y. Recipient Blue Ribbon Sch. award U.S. Dept. Edn., 1990-91. Office: Longwood Mid Sch 41 Yaphank Middle Island Rd Middle Island NY 11953-2369*

MASTROIANNI, LUIGI, JR., physician, educator; b. New Haven, Nov. 8, 1925; s. Marion (Dallas) M.; m. Elaine Catherine Pierson, Nov. 4, 1957; children: John James, Anna Catherine, Robert Luigi. AB, Yale U., 1946; MD, Boston U., 1950, DSc (hon.), 1973; MA (hon.), U. Pa., 1970. Diplomate Am. Bd. Ob-gyn. and Reproductive Endocrinology and Infertility. Intern, then resident ob.-gyn. Met. Hosp. N.Y., 1950-54; fellow rsch. Harvard Med. Sch. and Free Hosp. for Women, Boston, 1954-55; instr. dept. ob-gyn. Sch. of Medicine Yale U., New Haven, 1955-56, asst. prof. ob.-gyn. dept., 1956-61; prof. U. Calif., L.A., 1961-65; chief ob-gyn Harbor Gen. Hosp., L.A., 1961-65; William Goodell prof. ob.-gyn., chmn. dept. U. Pa. Sch. of Medicine, Phila., 1965-87, William Goodell prof. ob.-gyn. dept., dir. human reproduction div., 1987-96. Contbr. numerous articles to profl. jours. Recipient Squibb prize Pacific Coast Fertility Soc., 1965, Christian R. and Mary Lindback award, 1969, Gold medal Barren Found., 1977, King Faisal prize in medicine, 1989, Pub. Recognition award Assn. Profls. of Gynecology and Obstets., 1990, Disting. Svc. award Soc. Study Reproduction, 1992, Axel Munthe award, 1996. Mem. ACS, Am. Gyneol. and Obstet. Soc., Am. Gynecol. Club, Am. Soc. for Reproductive Medicine, Am. Physiol. Soc., Am. Coll. Obs.-Gyns., Inst. Medicine of NAS, Soc. Gynecology Investigation, Soc. for Exptl. Biology and Medicine, Endocrine Soc., Soc. for Study Reproduction (Disting. Svc. award 1992), Pacific Coast Fertility Soc. (hon.), Cen. Assn. Ob-Gyns. (hon.), Tex. Assn. Ob.-Gyns. (hon.), N.C. Gynecol. Soc. (hon.), Assn. Profs. Ob-Gyns., Brazilian Fertility Soc. (hon.), Italian Soc. Ob-Gyns. (hon.). Argentina Fertility Soc. (hon.), Peruvian Fertility Soc. (hon.), Sociedad Espanola de Fertilidad (hon.), Israel Soc. Ob-Gyn. (hon.), Uruguan Soc. Sterility and Fertility (hon.), Inst. Medicine, Sigma Xi, Alpha Omega Alpha. Home: 561 Ferndale Ln Haverford PA 19041-1614 Office: Hosp U Pa 3400 Spruce St Philadelphia PA 19104

MASUBUCHI, KOICHI, marine engineer, educator; b. Otaru, Hokkaido, Japan, Jan. 11, 1924; s. Yosaku and Tomi (Ota) M.; m. Fumiko Kaneno, Oct. 24, 1949. BS, U. Tokyo, 1946, MS, 1948, PhD, 1959. Rsch. engr. Transp. Tech. Rsch. Inst., 1948-58; vis. fellow, cons. Battelle Meml. Inst., Columbus, Ohio, 1958-62; rsch. assoc., fellow, tech. adviser Battelle Meml. Inst., 1963-68; chief welding mechanics sect., welding div. Ship Rsch. Inst., 1962-63; assoc. prof. naval architecture MIT, Cambridge, 1968-71, prof. ocean engring. and materials sci., 1971-89, Kawasaki prof. engring., 1989—. Author: Materials for Ocean Engineering, 1970, Analysis of Welded Structures, 1980; co-author 2 books on residual stresses in weldments; contbr. tech. papers to profl. lit. Recipient Disting. Svc. award Transp. Tech. Rsch. Inst., Ministry Transp., Japan, 1959, Spl. award Min. of Fgn. Affairs, Japan, 1986, Order of Sacred Treasure Gold Royr with Neck Ribbon award Japanese Govt., 1995. Fellow Am. Welding Soc. (life, R.D. Thomas Meml. award 1977, established Prof. Masubuchi/Shinsho Corp. award 1991), Am. Soc. Metals Soc.; mem. Japan Welding Soc. (guest), Soc. Naval Architects and Marine Engrs., Soc. Naval Architects Japan, Sigma Xi. Home: 34 Hamilton Rd Apt 205 Arlington MA 02174-8277 Office: MIT Rm 5-219 Cambridge MA 02139

MASUDA, YOSHINORI, systems analyst; b. Kasai, Hyogo, Japan, Apr. 6, 1953; came to U.S., 1977, naturalized, 1993; s. Saburo and Mitsuyo (Masuda) M. BL, Kobe U., Japan, 1977; MBA, U. San Francisco, 1980. Gen. mgr. Kotobuki Trading Co., San Francisco, 1980-85; distbn. analyst Kikkoman Internat. Inc., San Francisco, 1986-87, mgr. mgmt. info. system, 1987-88, mgr. electronic data interchange, 1988-93, mgr. distbn./customer svc./electronic data interchange, 1993—. Mem. Japanese C. of C. No. Calif. Govt. Rels., Beta Gamma Sigma. Avocations: skiing, scuba diving, travel. Home: 480 Wellesley Ave Mill Valley CA 94941-3540 Office: Kikkoman Internat Inc 50 California St Ste 3600 San Francisco CA 94111-4760

MASUR, HENRY, internist; b. N.Y.C., Mar. 8, 1946; s. Jack and Barbara (Forsch) M.; m. Grace Masur, Jan. 14, 1979; children: Carrie, Jack, Julia. AB, Dartmouth Coll., 1968; MD, Cornell U., 1972. Diplomate Am. Bd. Internal Medicine, Am. Bd. Infectious Diseases. Asst. prof. Cornell Med. Coll., N.Y.C., 1978-82; asst. chief critical care medicine NIH, Bethesda, Md., 1982-83, dep. chief critical care medicine, 1983-89, chief critical care medicine, 1989—; clin. prof. George Washington U. Med. Sch., Washington. Mem. Am. Soc. Clin. Investigation, Assn. Am. Physicians. Office: NIH 9000 Rockville Pike Bethesda MD 20814-1436

MASUR, KURT, conductor; b. Brieg, Silesia, Germany, July 18, 1927. Grad., Nat. Music Schule, Breslau, Germany, 1944, Leipzig Conservatory, 1946-48; hon. degree, U. Mich., Cleve. Inst. Music, Leipzig U., Westminster Choir Coll., Hamilton Coll. Repetiteur and conductor Halle Nat. Theatre, 1948-51; conductor Erfurt City Theatre, 1951-53, Leipzig City Theatre, 1953-55, Dresden Philharm., 1955-58; gen. music dir. Mecklenburg Staatstheater, 1958-60; mus. dir. Komische Oper Berlin, 1960-64; chief conductor Dresden Philharm., 1967-72; conductor Leipzig Gewandhaus Orch., since 1970; mus. dir. New York Philharmonic, N.Y.C., since 1991; conductor London Philharm. Orch., 1989-92; prof. Leipzig Acad. Music, 1975—; hon. guest conductor The Israel Philharm. Orch., 1992. Tours include Europe, South Am., Japan, U.S., Can., Middle East; recordings include: Symphonies by Mendelssohn, Brahms, Bruckner, Beethoven, Schumann, Tchaikovsky, Prokofiev's Piano Concertos, Beethoven's Missa Solemnis. Office: care NY Philharmonic Avery Fischer Hall 10 Lincoln Center Plz New York NY 10023-6912 also: Gewandhaus zu Leipzig, Augustusplatz 8, O-7010 Leipzig Germany*

MASUR, RICHARD, actor. Appeared in films Whiffs, 1975, Semi-Tough, 1977, Who'll Stop The Rain, 1978, Hanover Street, 1979, Scavenger Hunt, 1979, Heaven's Gate, 1980, I'm Dancing as Fast as I Can, 1982, The Thing, 1982, Under Fire, 1983, Risky Business, 1983, Nightmares, 1983, The Mean Season, 1985, My Science Project, 1985, Heartburn, 1986, The Believers, 1986, Rent-A-Cop, 1988, Shoot to Kill, 1988, License to Drive, 1988, Far From Home, 1989, Flashback, 1990, My Girl, 1991, Encino Man, 1992, The Man Without a Face, 1993, Six Degrees of Separation, 1993, My Girl 2, 1994, Forget Paris, 1995, Multiplicity, 1996, TV films Walking Through The Fire, 1979, Fallen Angel, 1981, Adam, 1983, The Burning Bed, 1984, Obsessed With a Married Woman, 1985, Wild Horses, 1985, Adam: His Song Continues, 1986, When The Bough Breaks, 1986, The George McKenna Story, 1986, Settle the Score, 1989, It, 1990, Always Remember I Love You, 1990, cable TV film And The Band Played On, 1993, miniseries John Steinbeck's East of Eden, 1981, Roses Are for The Rich, 1987. Office: Susan Smith & Assocs 121 N San Vicente Blvd Beverly Hills CA 90211*

MASUREL, JEAN-LOUIS ANTOINE NICOLAS, investment company executive; b. Cannes, France, Sept. 18, 1940; s. Antoine and Anne-Marie (Gallant) M.; children: Anne-Sophie, Aude. Grad., Ecoles des Hautes Etudes Commerciales, 1962; M.B.A., Harvard U., 1964. With Morgan Guaranty Trust Co., N.Y.C., 1964-80; v.p., gen. mgr. Morgan Guaranty Trust Co., Paris, 1975-78; sr. v.p. Morgan Guaranty Trust Co., 1978-80; sr. exec. v.p. Banque de Paribas, 1980-82; dep. pres. Banque Pays-Bas, 1982-83; mng. dir. Moët-Hennessy, 1983-87, Moët-Hennessy-Louis Vuitton, 1987-89; pres. Arcos Investissement S.A., 1989—, Hediard S.A., 1991-95; bd. dirs. Peugot S.A., Soc. des Bains de Mer (SBM) Monaco. Bd. govs. Am. Hosp., Paris; hon. chmn., dir. Harvard Bus. Sch. Club France. Address: 31 rue Raynouard, 75016 Paris France

MASYS, DANIEL RICHARD, medical school director; b. Columbus, Ohio, Mar. 6, 1949; s. Paul John and Jane Marie (Mollenauer) M.; m. Linda Suzanne Bross, June 2, 1974; 1 child, Christopher. AB in Biochemistry, Princeton U., 1971; MD, Ohio State U., 1974. Diplomate Am. Bd. Internal Medicine. Staff hematologist, oncologist U.S. Naval Hosp., San Diego, 1980-84; chief ICRDB br. NIH, Bethesda, Md., 1984-86; dir. Lister Hill Nat. Ctr. Nat. Libr. Medicine, Bethesda, Md., 1986-94; dir. informatics and assoc. clin. prof. Sch. Medicine U. Calif., San Diego, 1994—. Assoc. editor Acad. Medicine jour., 1988-91. Mem. high performance computing White House Office of Sci., Washington, 1991-94; rep. Fed. Networking Coun., Washington, 1991-94. Capt. USPHS, 1984-94. Fellow ACP, Am. Coll. Med. Informatics (exec. com. 1989-92); mem. Am. Med. Informatics Assn. (bd. dirs. 1992-95, assoc. editor jour. 1993—, Pres.'s award 1992), Alpha Omega Alpha. Office: Univ of Calif San Diego Sch of Medicine 9500 Gilman Dr Rm 1317 La Jolla CA 92093-5003

MATALON, VIVIAN, theatrical director; b. Manchester, Eng., Oct. 11, 1929; came to U.S., 1977; s. Moses and Rose (Tawil) M. Student, Munro Coll., Jamaica (W.I.) Coll., Neighborhood Playhouse, N.Y.C. Prof. acting Brandeis U., 1977-78; prof. acting and direction SUNY, Stony Brook, 1985-86. Dir. Broadway prodns. After the Rain, Noel Coward in Two Keys, P.S. Your Cat is Dead, Morning's at Seven (Tony award, Drama Desk award 1980), Brigadoon, The American Clock, The Corn is Green, The Tap Dance Kid (Tony nomination 1984); London West End Prodns. include Season of Goodwill, The Chinese Prime Minister, The Glass Menagerie, Suite in Three Keys, After the Rain, Two Cities, Girlfriend, I Never Sang for My Father, Small Craft Warnings, The Gingerbread Lady, Bus Stop, Morning's at Seven; dir. Ah Wilderness, Stratford (Ont., Can.) Festival, 1993, Our Town, Stratford, 1994, The Heiress, Chichester (Eng.) Festival, 1990; television prodns. Private Contentment, Am. Playhouse, Morning's at Seven, Showtime. Home: PO Box 24 Margaretville NY 12455*

MATARAZZO, JOSEPH DOMINIC, psychologist, educator; b. Caiazzo, Italy, Nov. 12, 1925; (parents Am. citizens); s. Nicholas and Adeline (Mastroianni) M.; m. Ruth Wood Gadbois, Mar. 26, 1949; children: Harris, Elizabeth, Sara. Student, Columbia U., 1944; BA, Brown U., 1946; MS, Northwestern U., 1950, PhD, 1952. Fellow in med. psychology Washington U. Sch. Medicine, 1950-51; instr. Washington U., 1951-53, asst. prof., 1953-55; rsch. assoc. Harvard Med. Sch., assoc. psychologist Mass. Gen. Hosp., 1955-57; prof., head med. psychol. dept. Oreg. Health Scis. U., Portland, 1957-96, prof. behavioral neurosci., 1996—; mem. behavioral medicine study sect. NIH; mem. nat. mental health adv. coun. NIMH; mem. bd. regents Uniformed Svcs. U. Health Scis., 1974-80. Author: Wechsler's Measurement and Appraisal of Adult Intelligence, 5th edit., 1972, (with A.N. Wiens) The Interview: Research on its Anatomy and Structure, 1972, (with Harper and Wiens) Nonverbal Communication, 1978; editor: Behavioral Health: A Handbook of Health Enhancement and Disease Prevention, 1984; editorial bd.: Jour. Clin. Psychology, 1962-96; cons. editor: Contemporary Psychology, 1962-70, 80-93, Jour. Community Psychology, 1974-81, Behavior Modification, 1976-91, Intelligence: An Interdisciplinary Jour, 1976-90, Jour. Behavioral Medicine, 1977—, Profl. Psychology, 1978-94, Jour. Cons. and Clin. Psychology, 1978-85; editor: Psychology series Aldine Pub. Co, 1964-74; psychology editor: Williams & Wilkins Co, 1974-77; contbr. articles to psychol. jours. With USNR, 1943-47; capt. Res. Recipient Hofheimer prize Am. Psychiat. Assn., 1962. Fellow AAAS, APA (pres. 1989-90, divsn. health psychology 1978-89, mem. coun. reps. 1982-91, bd. dirs. 1986-90, Ann. Disting. Profl. Contbn. award 1991); mem. Western Psychol. Assn., Oreg. Psychol. Assn., Am. Assn. State Psychology Bds. (pres. 1963-64), Nat. Assn. Mental Health (bd. dirs.), Oreg. Mental Health Assn. (bd. dirs., pres. 1962-63), Internat. Coun. Psychologists (bd. dirs. 1972-74, pres. 1976-77), Am. Psychol. Found. (pres. 1994—). Home: 1934 SW Vista Ave Portland OR 97201-2455 Office: Oreg Health Scis U Sch Medicine 3181 SW Sam Jackson Park Rd Portland OR 97201-3011

MATARÉ, HERBERT F., physicist, consultant; b. Aachen, Germany, Sept. 22, 1912; came to U.S., 1953; s. Josef P. and Paula (Broicher) M.; m. Ursula Krenzien, Dec. 1939; children: Felicitas, Vitus; m. Elise Walbert, Dec. 1983; 1 child, Victor B. BS in Physics, Chemistry and Math., Aachen U. Geneva, 1933; MS in Tech. Physics, U. Aachen, 1939; PhD in Electronics, Tech. U. Berlin, 1942; PhD in Solid State Physics summa cum laude, Ecole Normale Supérieure, Paris, 1950. Asst. prof. physics & electronics Tech. U. Aachen, 1936-45; head of microwave receiver lab. Telefunken, A.G., Berlin, 1939-46; mgr. semicondr. lab. Westinghouse, Paris, 1946-52; founder, pres. Intermetall Corp., Düsseldorf, Fed. Republic Germany, 1952-56; head semicondr. R &

D, corp. rsch. labs. Gen. Telephone & Electronics Co., N.Y.C., 1956-59; dir. rsch. semicondr. dept. Tekade, Nürnberg, Fed. Republic Germany, 1959-61; head quantum physics dept. rsch. labs. Bendix Corp., Southfield, Mich., 1961-64; tech. dir., acting mgr. hybrid microelectronics rsch. labs. Lear Siegler, Santa Monica, Calif., 1963-64; asst. chief engr. advance electronics dept. Douglas Aircraft Co., Santa Monica, 1964-66; tech. dir. McDonnell Douglas Missile Div., 1964-69; sci. advisor to solid state electronics group Autonetics (Rockwell Internat.), Anaheim, Calif., 1966-69; pres. Internat. Solid State Electronics Cons., L.A., 1973—; prof. electronics U. Buenos Aires, 1953-54; vis. prof. UCLA, 1968-69, Calif. State U., Fullerton, 1969-70; dir. Compound Crystals Ltd., London, 1989—; cons. UN Indsl. Devel. Orgn. to 15 Indian insts. and semiconductor cos. with confl. talks at India Inst. Tech., New Delhi and Bombay, 1978. Author: Receiver Sensitivity in the UHF, 1951, Defect Electronics in Semiconductors, 1971, Conscientious Evolution, 1978, Energy, Facts and Future, 1989, (with P. Faber) Renewable Energies, 1993; patentee first European transistor, first vacuum growth of silicon crystals with levitation, growth of bicrystals, first low temperature transistor with bicrystals, optical heterodyning with bicrystals, first crystal TV transmission link, first color TV transmission over fiber with LEDs and bicrystals, liquid phase epitaxy for LEDs and batch process for III-V-solar cells; contbr. over 100 articles to profl. jours. Fellow IEEE (life); mem. AAAS, IEEE Nuclear Plasma Scis. Soc., IEEE Power Engring. Soc., Inst. for Advancement of Man (hon.), Am. Phys. Soc. (solid state div.), Electrochem. Soc., Am. Vacuum Soc. (thin film div.), Materials Rsch. Soc., N.Y. Acad. Scis. (emeritus). Avocations: astrophysics, biology, classical music, piano. Home: 23901 Civic Center Way Apt 130 Malibu CA 90265-4881 Office: ISSEC PO Box 2661 Malibu CA 90265-7661

MATASAR, ANN B., former dean, business and political science educator; b. N.Y.C., June 27, 1940; d. Harry and Tillie (Simon) Bergman; m. Robert Matasar, June 9, 1962; children—Seth Gideon, Toby Rachel. AB, Vassar Coll., 1962; MA, Columbia U., 1964, PhD, 1968; M of Mgmt. in Fin., Northwestern U., 1977. Assoc. prof. Mundelein Coll., Chgo., 1965-78; prof., dir. Ctr. for Bus. and Econ. Elmhurst Coll., Elmhurst, Ill., 1978-84; dean Roosevelt U., Chgo., 1984-92; prof. Internat. Bus. and Fin. Walter E. Heller Coll. Bus. Adminstrn. Roosevelt U., 1992—; dir. Corp. Responsibility Group, Chgo., 1978-84; chmn. long range planning Ill. Bar Assn., 1982-83; mem. edn. com. Ill. Commn. on the Status of Women, 1978-81. Author: Corporate PACS and Federal Campaign Financing Laws: Use or Abuse of Power?, 1986; (with others) Research Guide to Women's Studies, 1974. Contbr. articles to profl. jours. Dem. candidate 1st legis. dist. Ill. State Senate, no. suburbs Chgo., 1972; mem. Dem. exec. com. New Trier Twp., Ill., 1972-76; rsch. dir., acad. advisor Congressman Abner Mikva, Ill., 1974-76; bd. dirs. Ctr. Ethics and Corp. Policy, 1985-90. Named Chgo. Woman of Achievement Mayor of Chgo., 1978. Fellow AAUW (trustee ednl. found. 1992-97, v.p. fin. 1993-97); mem. Am. Polit. Sci. Assn., Midwest Bus. Adminstrn. Assn., Acad. Mgmt., Women's Caucus for Polit. Sci. (pres. 1980-81), John Howard Assn. (bd. dirs. 1986-90), Am. Assembly of Coll. Schs. of Bus. (bd. dirs. 1989-92, chair com. on diversity in mgmt. edn. 1991-92), North Ctrl. Assn. (commr. 1994-97), Beta Gamma Sigma. Democrat. Jewish. Avocations: jogging, biking, tennis, opera, crosswords. Office: Roosevelt U Coll Bus Adminstrn Dept Fin 430 S Michigan Ave Chicago IL 60605-1301

MATASOVIC, MARILYN ESTELLE, business executive; b. Chgo., Jan. 7, 1946; d. John Lewis and Stella (Butkauskas) M. Student, U. Colo. Sch. Bus., 1963-69. Owner, pres. UTE Trail Ranch, Ridgway, Colo., 1967—; pres. MEM Equipment Co., Mokena, Ill., 1979—; sec./treas. Marlin Corp., Ridgway, 1991—, v.p., sec.-treas., 1991—, pres., 1994—; sec.-treas. Linmar Corp., Mokena, 1991-93, pres., 1994—; ptnr. Universal Welding Supply Co., New Lenox, Ill., 1964-90; v.p. OXO Welding Equipment Co, Inc., New Lenox, 1964-90; ptnr. Universal Internat., Mokena, Ill., 1990—; ind. travel agt. Ideal Travel Concepts, Mokena, Ill., 1994—. Co-editor newsletters. U.S. rep. World Hereford Conf., 1964, 68, 76, 80, 84, 96. Mem. Am. Hereford Assn. (charter, bd. dirs. 1989-94, historian 1990-92, v.p. 1992, pres.-elect 1993, pres. 1994), Am. Hereford Women (charter, pres. 1994, bd. dirs. 1994-96), Am. Agri-Women, Colo. Hereford Aux., Ill. Hereford Aux. (v.p. 1969-70), U. Colo. Alumni Assn., Ill. Agri-Women, Las Vegas Social Register. Avocations: showing cattle, computers, travel.

MATAXIS, THEODORE CHRISTOPHER, consultant, lecturer, writer, retired army officer, educator; b. Seattle, Aug. 17, 1917; s. Chris P. and Edla (Osterdahl) M.; m. Helma Mary Jensen, Aug. 27, 1940; children: Shirley Jeanne (Mrs. J. L. Slack), Theodore Christopher, Kaye Louise (Mrs. Vernon P. Isaacs, Jr.). B.A., U. Wash., 1940; student, Def. Services Staff Coll., India, 1950-51, Army War Coll., 1957-58; M.A. in Internat. Relations, George Washington U., 1965. Commd. 2d lt. U.S. Army, 1940, advanced through grades to brig. gen., 1967; inf. bn. comdr. Europe, World War II; regt. comdr. Korea, 1952-53; mem. Gov. Harriman's Presdl. Mission to Establish Mil. Aid Program India, 1962; mil. asst., speech writer for chmn. Joint Chiefs of Staff, 1962-64; sr. adviser II Vietnamese Army Corps. Pleiku, 1964-65; dep. comdr. 1st Brigade, 101st Airborne Div., 1966, asst. div. comdr. 82d Airborne Div., 1967; chief army sect. Army Mission/MAAG Iran, 1968-70; asst., acting div. comdr. Americal Div. Vietnam, 1970; chief mil. equipment delivery team Cambodia, 1971-72; ret., 1972; ednl. and systems mgmt. cons. Republic of Singapore, 1972-74; asst. supt., comdt. cadets Valley Forge Mil. Acad., Wayne, Pa., 1975-83; dir. AZED Assocs., Ltd., Southern Pines, N.C., 1983—; faculty Am. Mil. U., 1993—. Author: (with Seymour Goldberg) Nuclear Tactics, 1958, (chpt.) International Affairs in South West Asia, 1984, American Military Encyclopedia; also numerous mil. and hist. articles. Mem. adv. council Com. for Free Afghanistan. Decorated D.S.M., Silver Star, D.F.C., Bronze Star with 3 oak leaf clusters with V, Commendation medal with 3 oak leaf clusters and V, Joint Services Commendation medal, Purple Heart with oak leaf cluster, Legion of Merit with 2 oak leaf clusters, Air medal with V and 30 oak leaf clusters, Combat Inf. Badge with 2 stars (U.S.); Nat. Order 5th class; Distinguished Service Order; 4 Gallantry crosses; Honor medal 1st class; Air medal Vietnam; Def. medal Order of Republic Cambodia; Chapel of Four Chaplains-Legion of Honor. Mem. Oral History Assn., Soc. Study Mil. History, U.S. Commn. on Mil. History, Mil. Order World Wars (life), Am. Coun. for Study Islamic Socs., The Federalist Rsch. Inst. (bd. dirs.), Am. Legion, VFW, Airborne Assn. (life), 70th Divsn. Assn. (life), Assn. U.S. Army, Nat. Rifle Assn. (endowment mem.), 82d Airborne Divsn. Life Assn. (life), Am. Security Coun. (spkrs. bur.), Ends of the Earth, Scabbard and Blade (adv. coun. nat. soc.), Freedom Medicine (adv. bd.), Def. Policy Coun., Nat. Policy Forum, Am. Immigration Control (mem. adv. bd.). Clubs: Elks (Southern Pines), Army Navy (Washington); Tanglin (Singapore). Office: AZED Assocs Ltd PO Box 1643 Southern Pines NC 28388-1643

MATAYOSHI, CORALIE CHUN, lawyer, bar association executive; b. Honolulu, June 2, 1956; d. Peter J. and Daisy (Look) Chun; m. Ronald F. Matayoshi, Aug. 8, 1981; children: Scot, Kelly, Alana. BA, U. Calif., Berkeley, 1978; JD, U. Calif., San Francisco, 1981. Bar: Hawaii 1981, U.S. Dist. Ct. Hawaii 1981. Trial atty. U.S. Dept. Justice Antitrust, Washington, 1981-84; assoc. Chun, Kerr, & Dodd, Honolulu, 1984-86; exec. dir. Hawaii Inst. of CLE, Honolulu, 1987-90, Hawaii State Bar Assn., Honolulu, 1990—; arbitrator Ct. Annexed Arbitration Program, Honolulu, 1992—; corp. sec. Keola Film Group, Honolulu, 1992; adv. bd. Channel 2 TV Action Line, Honolulu, 1993—. Contbr. chapters to books. Bd. dirs. Neighborhood Justice Ctr., 1994—. Office: Hawaii State Bar Assn 1136 Union Mall Ph 1 Honolulu HI 96813-2711

MATCHETT, JANET REEDY, psychologist; b. Chgo., Sept. 2, 1926; d. Joseph Franklin and Minnie Mae (Burr) Reedy; m. Russell W. Kemerer, Jan. 20, 1949 (div. Aug. 1974); children: Brian Lee, Pamela Ann, Patricia Lynn, Bruce Reed, Bryce Jason; m. Charles Ernest Matchett, Nov. 17, 1984. BS summa cum laude, U. Pitts., 1974; MEd, Indiana U. of Pa., 1977, Ednl. Specialist, 1978; postgrad., U. Akron, U. Pitts., Pa. State U., Duquesne U. Lic. psychologist, Pa.; cert. sch. psychologist, Pa., Ohio, W.Va., nationally. Tchr. adult edn. Greensburg (Pa.)-Salem Sch., 1963-70; tchr. cons. Peterson Sys., Inc., Greensburg, 1967-75, Ednl. Self-Devel., Inc., Greensburg, 1975-78; sch. psychologist Columbiana Bd. Edn., Lisbon, Ohio, 1979, Struthers (Ohio) City Schs., 1979-80; instr. Monroeville (Pa.) Sch. Bus., 1983; sch. psychologist Cmty. Mental Health Ctr. Beaver County, Rochester, Pa., 1983-84, South Side Area Sch. Dist., Hookstown, Pa., 1984-87, Blackhawk Sch. Dist., Beaver Falls, Pa., 1984—; instr. Pa. State U., New Kensington, 1984-86; substitute tchr. Greensburg (Pa.)-Salem Sch. Dist., 1975-83, long range plannign com., 1981-82; cons. Allegheny E. Mental Health/Retardation Ctr., Monroeville, Pa., 1981-83, Westmoreland County Cmty. Coll., Youngwood, Pa., 1981-83; sch. psychologist Wetzel County Schs., New Martinsville, W. Va., 1981; com. action team, strategic planning com. Blackhawk Sch. Dist., Beaver Falls, 1991-95. Vol. Adelphi House, 1978; chmn. drug/alcohol abuse prevention program, City of Greensburg, 1981; troop leader Girl Scouts Am.; asst. den mother Boy Scouts Am.; ch. sch. tchr. United Meth. Ch., Greensburg; Bible sch. program vol. United Ch. of Christ, Greensburg; chmn. PTO, Greensburg. Mem. NEA, NASP, Assn. Sch. Psychologists Pa., Western Pa. Assn. Sch. Psychologists, Beaver County Sch. Psychologists Assn., Blackhawk Edn. Assn., Alpha Sigma Lambda. Republican. Avocations: reading, swimming, sewing, hiking, motorcycling, lecturing. Home: 48 W Manilla Ave Pittsburgh PA 15220-2838

MATCHETT, WILLIAM H(ENRY), English literature educator; b. Chgo., Mar. 5, 1923; s. James Chapman and Lucy H. (Jipson) M.; m. Judith Wright, June 11, 1949; children: David H., Katherine C., Stephen C. BA with highest honors, Swarthmore Coll., 1949; MA, Harvard U., 1950, PhD, 1957. Teaching fellow Harvard U., Cambridge, Mass., 1953-54; instr. English lit. U. Wash., Seattle, 1954-56, asst. prof., 1956-61, assoc. prof., 1961-66, prof., 1966-82, prof. emeritus, 1982—. Author: The Phoenix and the Turtle, 1965, Fireweed, 1980; numerous poems; co-author: Poetry: From Statement to Meaning, 1965; editor: Modern Lang. Quar., Seattle, 1964-82. Mem. Soc. Friends. Home: 1017 Minor Ave Apt 702 Seattle WA 98104-1303

MATEJU, JOSEPH FRANK, hospital administrator; b. Cedar Rapids, Iowa, Oct. 18, 1927; s. Joseph Frank and Adeline (Smid) M. B.A., U. N.Mex., 1951; M.A., N.Mex. State U., 1957. Sr. juvenile probation officer San Diego County, 1958-64; adminstr. Villa Solano State Sch., Hagerman, N.Mex., 1965-67; state coordinator on mental retardation planning N.Mex. Dept. Hosps. and Instns., Santa Fe, 1969-70; adminstr. Los Lunas (N.Mex.) Hosp. and Tng. Sch., 1968-69, 70-85; pres. Intercare. Bd. dirs. Mountain-Plains region Deaf-Blind Program. Served with USAAF, 1946-47. Fellow Am. Assn. Mental Deficiency; fellow Am. Coll. Nursing Home Adminstrs.; mem. Am. Assn. Retarded Children, Albuquerque Assn. Retarded Citizens, N.Mex. Hosp. Assn., Pi Gamma Mu. Home: 405 Fontana Pl NE Albuquerque NM 87108-1168

MATEKER, EMIL JOSEPH, JR., geophysicist; b. St. Louis, Apr. 25, 1931; s. Emil Joseph and Lillian (Broz) M.; m. Lolita Ann Winter, Nov. 25, 1954; children: Mark Steven, Anne Marie, John David. BS in Geophys. Engring., St. Louis U., 1956, MS in Rsch. Geophysics, 1959, PhD in Seismology, 1964. Registered geologist and geophysicist, Calif. Assoc. prof. geophysics Washington U., St. Louis, 1966-69; mgr. geophys. rsch. Western Geophys. Co. of Am., Houston, 1969-70; v.p. R & D Western Geophys. Co. of Am., 1970-74; pres. Litton Resources Sys., Houston, 1977, Litton Westrex, Houston, 1974-79; pres. Aero Svc. divsn. Western Geophys. Co. of Am., 1974-87, v.p., 1974-90; v.p. Western Atlas Internat., Inc., Houston, 1987—, pres. Aero Svc. divsn., 1987-90, v.p. tech. Western Geophysics divsn., 1990-93; pres. Western Atlas Software divsn. Western Atlas Internat. Inc., Houston, 1993-94, sr. v.p. tech., 1994—; mem. State of Calif. Bd. Registration for Geophysicists, Sacramento, 1974—, State of Calif. Bd. Registration for Geologists, Sacramento, 1974—. Author: A Treatise on Modern Exploration Seismology, 2 vols., 1965; contbr. articles to profl. jours.; asst. editor Geophysica, 1969-70. Baseball mgr. Westchester High Sch., 1969-74; soccer coach Spring Forest Jr. High Sch., Houston, 1974; bd. dirs. St. Agnes Acad., Houston, 1977-82, pres. bd. dirs., 1996-97; pres. Strake Jesuits Booster Club, Houston, 1977-78. 2nd lt. U.S. Army, 1951-54. Recipient St. Louis U. Alumni award, 1976. Mem. AAAS, Am. Geophys. Union, Seismological Soc. Am., Geophys. Soc. Houston, European Assn. Exploration Geophysicists, Soc. Exploration Geophysicists (chmn. 1974). Roman Catholic. Avocations: racquetball, golf, literature, running, fishing. Home: 419 Hickory Post Ln Houston TX 77079-7430 Office: Div Western Atlas Internat 10205 Westheimer Rd Houston TX 77042-3115

MATELAN, MATHEW NICHOLAS, software engineer; b. Stephenville, Tex., Aug. 21, 1945; s. Mathew Albert and Mary Frances (Hardwick) M.; m. Lois Margaret Waguespack, Apr. 5, 1975; children: Evelyn Nicole, Eleanor Gillian. BS in Physics, U. Tex., Arlington, 1969; MS in Computer Engring., So. Meth. U., 1973, PhD in Computer Sci., 1976. Sr. aerospace engr. Gen. Dynamics, Ft. Worth, 1969-75; sys. engr. Lawrence Livermore (Calif.) Labs., 1975-76; group mgr. Gen. Dynamics, Ft. Worth, 1976-78; computer R&D mgr. United Techs./Mostek, Carrollton, Tex., 1978-82; chief sys. arch. Honeywell Comm., Dallas, 1982-83; pres., CEO, chmn., co-founder Flexible Computer Corp., Dallas, 1983-90; chief arch. Matelan Software Sys., Dallas, 1991-94; chief engr. Expertware, Santa Clara, Calif., 1991-94; chief tech. officer Learn Techs. Interactive, N.Y.C., 1994—; cons. Bendix Flight Controls Divsn., Teterboro, N.J., 1974-75; founding dir. Picture Telephone, Boston, 1984-86, Spectrum Digital, Washington, 1984-86; adv. bd. Axavision, N.Y.C., 1993—. Contbr. articles to profl. jours. Libr. automation bd. So. Meth. U., Dallas, 1985-86. Devel. grantee U.S. Energy Dept., 1975, NASA, 1985. Mem. IEEE (sr. mem.), Assn. for Computing Machinery. Avocations: traveling, music, skiing, aviation. Home: 3969 Courtshire Dr Dallas TX 75229 Office: Learn Techs Interactive 3530 Forest Ln S 61 Dallas TX 75234

MATELES, RICHARD ISAAC, biotechnologist; b. N.Y.C., Sept. 11, 1935; s. Simon and Jean (Phillips) M.; m. Roslyn C. Fish, Sept. 2, 1956; children: Naomi, Susan, Sarah. BS, MIT, 1956, MS, 1957, DSc, 1959. USPHS fellow Laboratorium voor Microbiologie, Technische Hogeschool, Delft, The Netherlands, 1959-60; mem. faculty MIT, 1960-70, assoc. prof. biochem. engring., 1965-68; dir. fermentation unit Jerusalem, 1968-77; prof. applied microbiology Hebrew U., Hadassah Med. Sch., Jerusalem, 1968-80; vis. prof. dept. chem. engring. U. Pa., Phila., 1978-79; asst. dir. rsch. Stauffer Chem. Co., Westport, Conn., 1980, dir. rsch., 1980-81, v.p. rsch., 1981-88; sr. v.p. applied scis. IIT Rsch. Inst., Chgo., 1988-90; proprietor Candida Corp., Chgo., 1990—. Editor: Biochemistry of Some Foodborne Microbial Toxins, 1967, Single Cell Protein, 1968, Jour. Chem. Tech. and Biotech., 1972—; contbr. articles to profl. jours. Mem. Conn. Acad. Sci. Engring., 1981—; mem. vis. com., dept. applied biol. sci. MIT, 1980-88; mem. exec. com. Coun. on Chem. Rsch., 1981-85. Fellow Am. Inst. Med. and Biol. Engring.; mem. AICE, AAAS, SAR, Am. Chem. Soc., Am. Soc. Microbiology, Soc. for Gen. Microbiology U.K., Inst. Food Technologists, Soc. Chem. Ind. (U.K.) Union League, Sigma Xi. Home: 150 W Eugenie St # 46 Chicago IL 60614-5839 Office: 175 W Jackson Blvd Chicago IL 60604

MATELIC, CANDACE TANGORRA, museum studies educator, consultant, museum director; b. Detroit, Aug. 21, 1952; d. Paul Eugene and Madeline Marie (Tangora) M.; m. Steven Joseph Mrozek, Sept. 17, 1983 (div. Sept. 1987); 1 child, Madeline Rose. BA, U. Mich., 1974; MA, SUNY, Oneonta, 1977; postgrad., SUNY, Albany. Interpretive specialist Living History Farms, Des Moines, 1978-80; mgr. adult edn. Henry Ford Mus./Greenfield Village, Dearborn, Mich., 1981-82, mgr. interpretive tng., 1982-84; dir., prof. mus. studies Cooperstown grad. program SUNY, Oneonta, 1986-94; exec. dir. Mission Houses Mus., Honolulu, 1994-96, Historic St. Mary's City, Md., 1997—; faculty mem. St. Mary's Coll., 1997—; cons. history mus., 1979—; lectr., tchr. nat. and regional confs., workshops, seminars, 1979—; grant reviewer Nat. Endowment for the Humanities and Inst. for Mus. Svc., Washington, 1982—. Author: (with others) Exhibition Reader, 1992; co-author: A Pictorical History of Food in Iowa, 1980, Survey of 1200-Plus Museum Studies Graduates, 1988; contbr. articles and videos on mus. interpretation and tng., 1979—; author conf. proceedings. Trustee Motown Hist. Mus., 1989—; bd. dirs. Hawaii Youth Opera Chorus, 1996. Mem. Am. Assn. State and Local History (sec., bd. dirs. 1988-93, program chmn. ann meeting 1988, mem. edn. com. 1996—, co-chair task force on edn. and tng. 1994-96), Assn. Living Hist. Farms and Agrl. Mus. (bd. dirs. 1980-88, pres. 1985, John T. Schlebecker award Lifetime Disting. Svc. 1996), Midwest Open Air Mus. Coordinating Coun. (founder, bd. dirs., pres. 1978-80), Am. Assn. Museums (mus. studies com. 1986-94), Internat. Coun. Museums, Nat. Trust for Hist. Preservation, Hawaii Museums Assn. (bd. dirs.), Honolulu Rotary. Democrat. Roman Catholic. Office: Historic St Mary's City PO Box 39 Saint Marys City MD 20686

MATER, GENE P., communications consultant; b. N.Y.C., Nov. 27, 1926; s. Albert and Anne (Lande) M.; m. Jeanne M. Blanc, Mar. 7, 1947 (dec.); children: Richard L., Gene A., Philip E. (dec.). Student, Bklyn. Poly. Inst., 1943-44. Editor news agy., various newspapers Fed. Republic of Germany, 1946-48; reporter, county editor, city editor San Bernardino (Calif.) Sun-Telegram, 1949-53; copy editor, makeup editor, asst. night editor, news editor N.Y. World-Telegram & Sun, N.Y.C., 1953-59; news dir. Radio Free Europe, Munich, 1959-65; exec. v.p., sec. Radio Free Europe Fund, Inc., N.Y.C., 1965-70; spl. asst. to pres. Broadcast Group, CBS, Inc., N.Y.C., 1970-72, v.p., asst. to pres., 1972-80, sr. v.p., 1981-83; sr. v.p. CBS News, N.Y.C., 1983-84, v.p. internat. affairs, 1984-85; spl. asst. to dir. Commn. Bicentennial U.S. Constn., 1986; v.p. broadcasting Internat. Media Fund, 1990-95; cons. developing independent media Ctrl. and Ea. Europe, Russia, Ukraine, Belarus, 1990—; cons. comms. The Freedom Forum, Internat. Rsch. & Exchs. Bd., Williamsburg Charter Found., 1987—; guest columnist on comms. issues Washington Journalism Rev., other publs.; mem. U.S. Commn. on Broadcasting to the People's Republic of China, 1992. Mem. adv. bd. World Press Freedom Com., Ohio State Awards, Ctr. for the Book, Libr. of Congress, 1981-85; trustee Radio and Television News Dirs. Found. With AUS, 1944-46. Home: 4001 9th St N Apt 708 Arlington VA 22203-1960

MATER, MAUD, federal agency administrator, lawyer. BA in English, Case Western Reserve U., 1969, JD, 1972. Asst. gen. counsel Fed. Home Loan Mortgage Corp., 1976-78, assoc. gen. counsel, 1978-79, v.p., dep. gen. counsel, 1979-82, v.p., gen. counsel, 1982-84, sr. v.p., gen. counsel, sec., 1984—. Mem. ABA, Am. Corp. Counsel Assn., Am. Arbitration Assn. (dir.), Fed. Bar Assn., Ohio Bar, D.C. Bar, The Conf. Bd., Large Law Dept. Coun., Washington Met. Corp. Counsel Assn. Office: Fed Home Loan Mortgage Corp 8200 Jones Branch Dr Mc Lean VA 22102-3107

MATERA, FRANCES LORINE, elementary educator; b. Eustis, Nebr., June 28, 1926; d. Frank Daniel and Marie Mathilda (Hess) Daiss; m. Daniel Matera, Dec. 27, 1973; children: Richard William Post, Mary Jane Post Craig. BS in Edn., Concordia Tchrs. Coll., Seward, Nebr., 1956; MEd, U. Oreg., 1963; Luth. tchrs. diploma, Concordia Tchrs. Coll., Seward, 1947. Elementary tchr. Our Savior's Luth. Ch., Colorado Springs, Colo., 1954-57; tchr. 5th grade Monterey (Calif.) Pub. Schs., 1957-59; tchr. 1st grade Roseburg (Oreg.) Schs., 1959-60; tchr. several schs. Palm Springs (Calif.) Unified Sch. Dist., 1960-73; tchr. 3rd grade Vista del Monte Sch., Palm Springs, Calif., 1973-93; ret., 1993. Named Tchr. of the Yr., Palm Springs Unified Schs. Mem. Kappa Kappa Iota (chpt. and state pres.).

MATERA, RICHARD ERNEST, minister; b. Hartford, Conn., July 13, 1925; s. Charles Carlo and Philomena Antoinette Cecile (Liberatore) M.; m. Marylynn Olga Beuth, Sept. 3, 1949; children: Thomas Charles, Nancy Jean Matera Dye. Student, Trinity Coll., Hartford, 1943, Biarritz Am. U., France, 1945; BA magna cum laude, Colgate U., 1949; MDiv, Andover Newton Theol. Sch., 1953; DD, Calif. Christian U., 1981. Ordained to ministry Bapt. Ch., 1952. Dir. youth work Quincy Point (Mass.) Congl. Ch., 1949-50; pastor, dir. vacation ch. sch. Panton and Addison (Vt.) chs., 1950; min. Thompson (Conn.) Hill Ch., 1950-51, Waldo Congl. Ch., Brockton, Mass., 1951-54, Cen. Congl. Ch., Orange, Mass., 1954-59; sr. min. 1st Congl. United Ch. of Christ, Berea, Ohio, 1959-71, St. Paul Community Ch., Homewood, Ill., 1971-76; interim min. United Ch. Christ, Chgo., 1978—; pres. Millers River Coun. Chs., 1957-58; mem. dept. ch. world responsibility Mass. Coun. Chs., 1957-59; chmn. internat. affairs com. of state social action com. United Ch. of Christ, 1962-63, del. Gen. Synod, Chgo., mem. peace priority task force Western Res. Assn., 1967-70, mem. commn. on ch. and ministry Ohio conf., 1968-71, chmn. dept. ch. and community Western Res. Assn. Coun., Cleve., 1969-70, mem. peace and internat. rels. com., 1973; mem. ad hoc com. on Vietnam Greater Cleve. Coun. of Chs. of Christ, 1966-68; probation officer DuPage County Probation Dept., Wheaton, Ill., 1985-86; interim min. Chgo. area, 1978—, Sauk Village United Ch. of Christ, 1978-80, Steger 1st Congregation, 1981-83, Forest Park, 1986-88, River Grove Grace, 1989-91, Mont Clare Congregation, 1990-92, St. Nicolai, Chgo., 1992-96. Contbr. poetry to anthologies including Tears of Fire, 1994, A Break in the Clouds, 1994. Capt. Cleve. United Fund, 1961-63, Colgate Fund Dr., 1963; trustee Cleve. Union, 1961-63, Berea United Fund, 1963-69; mem. Berea Coun. on Human Rels., 1965-71, U.S. com. Christian Peace Conf., Prague, Czechoslovakia, 1967—, Nat. Arbor Day Found.; del. Action Conf. on Nat. Priorities, Washington, 1969; bd. dirs., mem. ecumenical mission com. Community Renewal Soc., Chgo., 1972-76; bd. dirs. Respond Now, Chicago Heights, Ill., 1972-78; mem. Pres.'s Coun., Chgo. Theol. Sem., 1973-81; pres. Mended Hearts Inc., Downers Grove, Ill., 1989-90. With U.S. Army Med. Corps., 1943-46, ETO. Austen Colgate scholar, 1946-49; recipient Harvard Book prize, 1942; name inscribed on The Wall of Liberty, Battle of Normandy Found., Normandy, France, 1994. Fellow Profl. Assn. Clergy, Acad. Parish Clergy; mem. Smithsonian Instn., Audubon Soc., Internat. Fellowship of Reconciliation, Internat. Soc. Poets, Nat. Libr.Poetry, Steinway Soc. Chgo., Planetary Soc., Jacques Cousteau Soc., Antique Automobile Club, Hupmobile Club, Cadillac Club, Phi Beta Kappa, Beta Theta Pi. Democrat. Avocations: drawing, poetry, astronomy, piano, working out at health club. Home and Office: 5 E Memorial Rd Bensenville IL 60106-2541 *From world philosophers, I have gleaned this: While borders stand, we are in prehistory. When all borders are gone, human history will begin.-Yevtushenko A person only has the right to do that which he agrees should become universal law.-Kant Do to others as you want them to do to you.-Hebrew tchg. The human race is now capable of and ready for the above.*

MATERNA, JOSEPH ANTHONY, lawyer; b. Passaic, N.J., June 13, 1947; s. Anthony E. and Peggy Ann Materna; m. Dolores Corio, Dec. 14, 1975; children: Jodi, Jennifer, Janine. BA, Columbia U., 1969, JD, 1973. Bar: N.Y. 1975, Fla. 1977, U.S. Dist. Ct. (ea. and so. dists.) N.Y. 1977, U.S. Supreme Ct. 1977, U.S. Tax Ct. 1978, U.S. Ct. of Claims 1978. Trusts and estates atty. Chadbourne Parke Whiteside & Wolff, N.Y.C., 1973-76, Dreyer & Traub, N.Y.C., 1976-80, Finley Kumble Wagner Heine Underberg & Casey, N.Y.C., 1980-85; ptnr., head trusts and estates dept. Newman Tannenbaum Helpern Syracuse & Hirschtritt, N.Y.C., 1985-90, Shapiro Beilly Rosenberg Albert & Fox, N.Y.C., 1990—; lectr. in field. Contbr. articles to profl. jours. Chmn. planned giving com., mem. bd. govs. Arthritis Found. N.Y. Chpt., N.Y.C., 1980—; mem. bd. trustees Cath. Interracial Coun., N.Y.C., 1992—; mem. bequests and planned gifts com. Cath. Archdiocese of N.Y., N.Y.C., 1988—. Recipient Planned Giving award Arthritis Found.-N.Y. Chpt., N.Y.C., 1994, Discovery Alliance award Arthritis Found.-N.Y. Chpt., N.Y.C., 1995; named Accredited Estate Planner, Nat. Assn. Estate Planners, Marietta, Ga., 1995. Mem. Fla. Bar (trusts and estate com.), N.Y. State Bar Assn. (com. on estates and trusts), Bar Assn. of the City of N.Y. (com. on surrogate's ct.), N.Y.C. Estate Planning Coun. (lectr., author), N.Y. County Lawyers Assn. (mem. com. on trusts and estates 1979—), Queen County Bar Assn. (mem. com. trusts and estates 1990—), Am. Judges Assn. (civil ct. arbitrator N.Y.C.), Am. Arbitration Assn. (panel of arbitrators), Richmond County Bar Assn. (com. on surrogates ct.), Columbia Coll. Alumni Assn. of Columbia U. (class pres. 1969—). Republican. Roman Catholic. Home: 155 Johanna Ln Staten Island NY 10309 Office: Shapiro Beilly Rosenberg Albert & Fox 225 Broadway New York NY 10007-3001

MATERNA, THOMAS WALTER, ophthalmologist; b. Passaic, N.J., Oct. 24, 1944; s. Anthony and Ann (Popowich) M.; m. Jorunn Pauline Aronsen, Aug. 18, 1973; children: Richard C., Barbara L. BA, Coll. Holy Cross, Worcester, Mass., 1966; MD, SUNY, N.Y.C., 1971; MBA, Rutgers U., Newark, 1990. Diplomate Am. Bd. Ophthalmology. Intern N.Y. Hosp.-Cornell U. Med. Ctr., N.Y.C., 1971-72; resident N.Y. Eye and Ear Infirmary, N.Y.C., 1975-78; pvt. practice ophthalmology San Francisco, 1986; ophthalmologist N.J. Eye Physicians & Surgeons, Newark; pres., CEO, US Try Zub Ent., Inc., Newark, Bizmore Internat., Inc., Luiv, Ukraine. Com. mem. N.J. Sch. for the Arts, Montclair, 1991—. Lt. USN, 1972-74, comdr. USNR, 1974—. Fellow ACS, Am. Acad. Ophthalmology; mem. Rotary, Army-Navy Club. Democrat. Roman Catholic. Avocations: coin collecting, rare document collecting, tennis, art history. Home: 87 Lorraine Ave Montclair NJ 07043-2304 Office: NJ Eye Physicians and Surgeons 20 Ferry St Newark NJ 07105-1420

MATERSON, RICHARD STEPHEN, physician, educator; b. Phila., Feb. 11, 1941; s. Alfred Lawrence and June Eileen (Slakoff) M.; m. Rosa Maria Navarro, Aug. 22, 1964; children: Lisa Gail, Lawrence Mark. MD, U.

Miami, Coral Gables, Fla., 1965. Diplomate Am. Bd. Phys. Medicine and Rehab. Intern Walter Reed Gen. Hosp., Washington, 1965-66; resident Letterman Gen. Hosp., San Francisco, 1966-68; chief phys. medicine and rehab. Tripler Gen. Hosp., Honolulu, 1968-72; asst. prof. phys. medicine and rehab. Ohio State U., Columbus, 1972-76; assoc. clin. prof. phys. medicine and rehab. Baylor Coll. Medicine, Houston, 1976-93, prof., 1997—; pres. Materson MD, PA, Houston, 1976—; sr. v.p. for med. affairs, med. dir. Nat. Rehab. Hosp., Washington, 1990-96; prof. neurology George Washington U. Med. Ctr., Washington, 1994-97; med. v.p. Meml. Healthcare Sys., 1997—; med. dir. Dept. Phys. Medicine and Rehab., Meml. Hosp. SE, Houston, 1978-90, Ctr. for Sports Medicine and Rehab., 1987-90, Electromyography Lab., 1978-90. Co-author: Physical Medicine and Rehabilitation, 1977, 2d rev. edit., 1980, The Practice of Rehabilitation Medicine, 1982; co-editor: Management of Persons with Stroke, 1993; contbg. author: Practice of Medicine, 1978. Trustee Meml. Hosp. System, Houston, 1986-90, Nat. Rehab. Hosp., Washington, 1990-96; host family Experiment in Internat. Living, 1985, 86, 87. Served to maj. U.S. Army, 1965-72. Fellow Am. Acad. Phys. Medicine and Rehab. (pres. 1986-87, Distng. Pub. Svc. award, 1992, Walter J. Zeiter lectr., 1994), Am. Assn. Electrodiagnostic Medicine; mem. AMA (del. 1978-93), Phys. Medicine and Rehab. Edn. and Rsch. Found. (founder, pres. 1982-90, bd. dirs. 1983—), Houston Acad. Phys. Medicine and Rehab. (pres. 1979-80), Am. Acad. Pain Mgmt. (chmn. bd. advisors 1989-90), Internat. Wine and Food Soc., Knights of Vine (master comdr. 1982—), Confrerie des Chevaliers du Tastevin, Chaine des Rotisseurs. Jewish.

MATES, ROBERT EDWARD, mechanical engineering educator; b. Buffalo, May 19, 1935; s. Cyril S. and Ruth Elizabeth (Dougan) M.; m. Gail Paxson, June 5, 1960; children: Robert E., Elisabeth, Steven,. BS, U. Rochester, 1957; MS, Cornell U., 1959, PhD, 1963. Instr. Cornell U., Ithaca, N.Y., 1958-61; asst. prof. SUNY, Buffalo, 1962-65, assoc. prof., 1965-69, chmn. mech. and aero. engring., 1967-70, 79-82, prof. mech. engring., 1969—, dir. Ctr. Biomed. Engring., 1989-96. Editor various symposium proceedings; contbr. articles to profl. jours. NIH spl. rsch. fellow, 1970-71, 78-79, H.R. Lissner award Am. Soc. of Mechanical Engineers, 1995. Fellow ASME (chmn. winter ann. meeting com. 1989-93, mem.-at-large bd. comm. 1988-93, v.p. bd. comm. 1994—), Am. Inst. for Med. and Biol. Engring. (founding, chmn. acad. coun. 1996-97); mem. AAUP, Biomed. Engring. Soc. (bd. dirs. 1991-94, chmn. awards com. 1991-92, mem. pub. bd. 1992-94), Am. Soc. Engring. Edn., Am. Heart Assn. Office: SUNY Dept Mech & Aero Engr 337 Jarvis Hall Buffalo NY 14260

MATES, SUSAN ONTHANK, physician, medical educator, writer, violinist; b. Oakland, Calif., Aug. 8, 1950; d. Benson and Lois (Onthank) M.; m. Joseph Harold Friedman, Dec. 10, 1978; children: Rebecca, Deborah, William. Student, Juilliard Sch. Music, 1967-69; BA magna cum laude with distinction, Yale Coll., 1972; MD, Albert Einstein Coll. Medicine, 1976. Cert. Am. Bd. Internal Medicine, Nat. Bd. Med. Examiners. Intern Boston City Hosp., 1976-77; fellow in gen. medicine Coll. of Physicians and Surgeons-Columbia U., N.Y.C., 1977-78; resident/fellow in infectious diseases Montefiore Hosp., Bronx, 1978-82; asst. prof. medicine Brown U., Providence, 1982-85, asst. prof. biochemistry, 1985-86, clin. assoc. prof. medicine, 1993—; staff mem., former dir. R.I. State Tuberculosis Clinic R.I. Dept. Health, Providence, 1986—; cons. tuberculosis program R.I. Dept. Health, Providence, 1987—; judge short story contest Providence Jour., 1994; contbg. editor Pushcart Prize, Pushcart Press, 1995, 96. Author: (fiction) The Good Doctor, 1994 (Iowa Short Fiction award 1994); contbr. stories to revs. and jours. (Pushcart prize 1994, John Simmons Short Fiction award); symposium scholar Lit. and Medicine for the 21st Century, Brown U., 1997. Recipient Recognition award for young scholars AAUW, 1985, Clin. Investigator award NIH, 1984, R.I. Found. award, 1983; McDowell Colony fellow, 1995, Yaddo fellow, 1996; Symposium scholar in lit. and medicine Brown U., 1997. Mem. Am. Med. Women's Assn., Poets and Writers, Alpha Omega Alpha. Home: 52 Bluff Rd Barrington RI 02806-4314 Office: R I State TB Clinic 877 Chalkstone Ave Providence RI 02908-4728

MATHAY, JOHN PRESTON, elementary education educator; b. Youngstown, Ohio, Jan. 27, 1942; s. Howard Ellsworth and Mary Clara (Siple) M.; m. Sandra Elizabeth Rhoades, June 9, 1973 (div. Jan. 1986); children: Elizabeth Anne, Sarah Susannah; m. Judith Anne Matthy, June 19, 1988; 1 child, Andrew Micah. B History, Va. Mil. Inst., Lexington, 1964; Cert. Teaching, Cleve. State U., 1972; postgrad., Mich. State U., 1964-65; MEd, Westminster Coll., New Wilmington, 1986. Cert. asst. supt., elem. tchr., elem. prin., high sch. prin. Cabinet maker Artisian Cabinet, Orwig Cabinets, Cleve. and Howland, Ohio, 1970-72; tchr. Urban Community Sch., Cleve., 1972-73, Pymatuning Valley Schs., Andover, Ohio, 1973—; cross country coach, 7th and 8th grade track coach, Andover. Bd. mem. Badger Sch. Bd., Kinsman, Ohio; trustee Kinsman Libr.; trustee, elder Kinsman Presbyn. Ch. Capt. U.S. Army Res., 1966-69. Martha Holden Jennings Found. scholar, Cleve., 1976. Mem. ASCD, Pymatuning Valley Edn. Assn. (pres. 1975-76, 91-92, 94-95), Ohio Edn. Assn., Am. Legion, Rotary (pres. 1991-92, sec. 1992-93, treas. 1995—, Paul Harris fellow), Masons (jr. deacon 1984-85, 32d deg., York Rite commandery), Ashtabula County Antique Engine Club, Phi Delta Kappa. Republican. Presbyterian. Avocations: sailing, skating, ham radio, fishing, reading. Home: 8424 Main St Kinsman OH 44428-9332 Office: Pymatuning Valley Schs W Main St Andover OH 44003

MATHAY, MARY FRANCES, marketing executive; b. Youngstown, Ohio, July 26, 1944; d. Howard E. and Mary C. (Siple) M.; m. Thomas Stone Withgott, Dec. 20, 1969 (div. June 1973). BA in English Lit. and Composition, Queens Coll., 1967; grad. in bus., Katharine Gibbs Sch., 1968. Corp. mktg. mgr., assoc. Odell Assocs., Inc., Charlotte, N.C., 1973-90; dir. pub. rels. and spl. events Charlotte (N.C.)-Mecklenburg Arts and Sci. Coun., 1990-92; pres. Mathay Comm., Inc., Charlotte, 1992-96; pub. rels. mgr. The Mktg. Consortium, 1996—; speakers bur. chmn. Hospice at Charlotte, Inc., 1980-83; pub. rels. and advt. dir. "Chemical People" program PBS, Charlotte, 1983-84. Author: Legacy of Architecture, 1988; editor: Mint Mus. Antiques Show Mag., 1980, editorial advisor Crier, 1987-92; producer Charlotte's Web, 1977. Bd. dirs. Jr. League of Charlotte, Inc., 1978-79, mem., 1968—; bd. dirs. ECO, INc., Charlotte, 1979-86, Arthritis Patient Svcs., 1996—; bd. dirs. Queens Coll. Alumni, Charlotte, 1984-87, 97—, planned giving chmn., 1997—; bd. dirs. Learning How, Inc., Charlotte, 1988-91, Arthritis Patient Svcs.; bd. dirs. on adolescent pregnancy Mecklenburg County Coun., 1986-88; vol. tchr. ABLE Ctr. Piedmont C.C., 1987-90; vol. comm. com. Am. Cancer Soc., 1994-96, Charlotte-Mecklenburg Edn. Found., 1992-94, Charlotte-Mecklenburg Sr. Ctrs., 1994—. Mem. Pub. Rels. Soc. Am. (bd. dirs. 1989—, pres. 1995), Charlotte Pub. Rels. Soc. (bd. dirs. 1986-89, 92-93), Olde Providence Racquet Club, Tower Club. Republican. Presbyterian. Avocations: fgn. travel, tennis.

MATHENY, ADAM PENCE, JR., child psychologist, educator, consultant, researcher; b. Stanford, Ky., Sept. 6, 1932; s. Adam Pence and Dorotha (Steele) M.; m. Ute I. Debus, July 10, 1962 (div.); m. Mary P. Tolbert, June 24, 1967 (div.); children—Laura Steele, Jason Gaverick. B.S., Columbia U., 1958; Ph.D., Vanderbilt U., 1962. Sr. human factors engr. Martin Aerospace div., Balt., 1962-63; instr. Johns Hopkins U. Med. Sch., 1963-65; staff fellow Nat. Inst. Child Health and Human Devel., 1965-67; from asst. prof. to prof. pediatrics U. Louisville Med. Sch., 1967-86, assoc. dir. to dir. Louisville Twin Study, 1986—. mem. review panel NIH, 1991-95. Served with USN, 1951-55. Fellow Internat. Soc. Twin Research, Am. Psychol. Assn., Am. Psychol. Soc.; mem. Soc. Research Child Devel., AAAS, Behavior Genetics Assn., Internat. Soc. Behavior Devel., Internat. Soc. Infant Study, Phi Beta Kappa, Sigma Xi. Co-author: Genetics and Counseling in Medical Practice, 1969; contbr. articles to profl. jours.

MATHENY, CHARLES WOODBURN, JR., retired army officer, retired civil engineer, former city official; b. Sarasota, Fla., Aug. 7, 1914; s. Charles Woodburn Sr. and Virginia (Yates) M.; m. Jeanne Felkel, July 12, 1942; children: Virginia Ann, Nancy Caroline, Charles Woodburn III. BSCE, U. Fla., 1936; grad., Army Command and Gen. Staff Coll., 1944. Lic. comml. pilot. Sanitary engr. Ga. State Dept. Health, 1937-39; civil engr. Fla. East Coast Ry., 1939-41; commd. 2d lt. F.A., USAR, 1936, 2d lt. F.A. U.S. Army, 1942, advanced through grades to col., 1955; comdr. 351st Field Arty. Bn., 1945, commr., 33rd Field Arty. Bn., 1st Inf. Divsn., 1946, artillery staff officer, 1947; gen. staff G-3 Plans Dept. Army, 1948-51; qualified Air Force liaison pilot, 1951; qualified Army aviator airplanes and helicopters, 1952; aviation officer 25th Inf. Div., Korea, 1952-53; sr. Army aviation advisor Korean Army, 1953; dep. first dir. combat devel. dept., first dep. commandant Army Aviation Sch., Ft. Sill, Okla., 1954-55; dep. dir. research, dep. dir. dept. tactics Arty. Sch., Ft. Sill, 1955-57; aviation officer 7th U.S. Army, Germany, 1957-58; Munich sub area comdr. So. Area Command, Europe, 1958-59, qualified sr. army aviator, 1959, dep. chief staff for info. So. Area Command, 1960; Mich. sector comdr. VI Army Corps, 1961-62; ret., 1962; asst. dir. Tampa (Fla.), Dept. Pub. Works 1963-77, asst. to dir., 1977-81, ret., 1981. During World War II, Germany Commd., 351st field artillery Battalion in combat and occupation, 1945, also 33d field artillery battalion, 1st Infantry Divsn., in occupation, 1946. Inititator tact use of helicopters in Army and army warrant officer aviator program, 1949, army combat units equipped with helicopter mobility, 1950; pilot 1st combat observation mission in army helicopter, Korea, 1952; organizer, comdr., helicopter pilot 1st Army combat ops. using helicopter mobility to support inf. and engr. front line units 25th Inf. Div., Korea, 1952; pilot 100 combat observation missions, Korea, 1952-53; author 1st state legis. to establish profl. sch. civil engring. for state of Fla., 1974. Contbr. numerous articles on tactical use of helicopter aerial vehicles to mags. Mem. troop com. Boy Scouts Am., 1965-73; active various community and ch. activities; patron Tampa Art Mus., 1965-83, Tampa Community Concert Series, 1979-82; bd. dirs. Tampa YMCA, 1967-71, Fla. Easter Seal Soc., 1978, Easter Seal Soc. Hillsborough County, 1971-84, hon. bd. dirs. 1984—, treas., 1973-76, pres., 1977. Decorated Bronze Star with oak leaf cluster, Air medal with three oak leaf clusters, Recipient of the Eagle Scout award, 1928; named to U. Fla. Student Hall of Fame, 1936. Mem. ASCE (pres. West Coast br., dir. Fla. sect. 1973, Engr. of Yr. award West Coast br. Fla. sect. 1979, life mem. 1980), Am. Soc. Profl. Engrs., Fla. Engring. Soc., Am. Pub. Works Assn. (pres. West Coast br. Fla. chpt. 1972, exec. com. Fla. chpt. 1972-77, v.p. 1977, pres. 1978), Ret. Officers Assn., Army Aviation Assn., SAR, Fla. Blue Key, Alpha Tau Omega. Episcopalian. Lodge: Kiwanis. Home: 4802 W Beachway Dr Tampa FL 33609-4836

MATHENY, EDWARD TAYLOR, JR., lawyer; b. Chgo., July 15, 1923; s. Edward Taylor and Lina (Pinnell) M.; m. Marion Elizabeth Shields, Sept. 10, 1947; children: Nancy Elizabeth, Edward Taylor III.; m. Ann Spears, Jan. 14, 1984. B.A., U. Mo., 1944; J.D., Harvard, 1949. Bar: Mo. 1949. Pvt. practice Kansas City, 1949-91; ptnr. firm Blackwell, Sanders, Matheny, Weary & Lombardi, 1954-91, of counsel, 1992—; pres. St. Luke's Hosp., Kansas City, 1980-95. Author: The Presence of Care (History of St. Luke's Hospital, Kansas City), 1997. Pres. Cmty. Svc. Broadcasting of Mid-Am., Inc., 1971-72; chmn. Citizens Assn. Kansas City, 1958; chmn. bd. dirs. St. Luke's Found., Kansas City, 1980-95; trustee U. Kansas City, 1980-96, Kansas City Cmty. Found., 1983-94, Eye Found., Kansas City, 1990—, H&R Block Found., Kansas City, 1996—, Jacob L. and Ella C. Loose Found., Kansas City, 1996—. Mem. Kansas City Bar Assn., Mo. Bar, River Club, Mission Hills Country Club, Phi Beta Kappa, Sigma Chi (Balfour Nat. award 1944). Episcopalian (chancellor Diocese West Mo. 1971-89). Home: 2510 Grand Blvd Kansas City MO 64108-2678 Office: 2300 Main St Kansas City MO 64108-2416

MATHENY, RUTH ANN, editor; b. Fargo, N.D., Jan. 17, 1918; d. Jasper Gordon and Mary Elizabeth (Carey) Wheelock; m. Charles Edward Matheny, Oct. 24, 1960. B.E., Mankato State Coll., 1938; M.A., U. Minn., 1955; postgrad., Universidad Autonoma de Guadalajara, Mex., summer 1956, Georgetown U., summer, 1960. Tchr. in U.S. and S.Am., 1938-61; asso. editor Charles E. Merrill Pub. Co., Columbus, Ohio, 1963-66; tchr. Confraternity Christian Doctrine, Washington Court House, Ohio, 1969-70; assoc. editor Jr. Cath. Messenger, Dayton, Ohio, 1966-68; editor Witness Intermediate, Dayton, 1968-70; editor in chief, assoc. pub. Today's Cath. Tchr., Dayton, 1970—; editor in chief Catechist, Dayton, 1976-89, Ednl. Dealer, Dayton, 1976-80; v.p. Peter Li, Inc., Dayton, 1980—. Editorial collaborator: Dimensions of Personality series, 1969—; co-author: At Ease in the Classroom; author: Why a Catholic School?, Scripture Stories for Today: Why Religious Education?. Mem. Bd. Friends Ormond Beach Library. Mem. Nat. League Am. Pen Women, Nat. Coun. Cath. Women, Cath. Press Assn., Nat. Cath. Ednl. Assn., 3d Order St. Francis (eucharistic minister 1990—). Home: 26 Reynolds Ave Ormond Beach FL 32174-7143 Office: Peter Li Inc 330 Progress Rd Dayton OH 45449-2322 *In a world that is constantly changing, a strong religious faith is a dependable compass through which we are able to stay on a positive, forward course.*

MATHENY, SAMUEL COLEMAN, academic administrator; b. Stanford, Ky., Dec. 2, 1941; s. Samuel Ferdinand and Elsie Elizabeth (Coleman) M. BA, Emory U., 1963; MD, U. Ky., 1967; MPH, UCLA, 1974. Dist. health officer Alhambra Health Dist., L.A. County Health Svcs., 1975-77; chmn. U. Soc. Calif., Divsn. Family Medicine, L.A., 1977-81; assoc. dir. Santa Monica (Calif.) Residency, 1981-83; prof. dept. family medicine U. So. Calif., L.A., 1992-93; chmn. dept. family practice U. Ky. Coll. Medicine, Lexington, 1993—. Capt. USPHS, 1968-71, 93-96. Mem. Assn. Depts. Family Medicine (treas. 1996—). Office: U Ky Coll Medicine Dept Family Practice Clinic Lexington KY 40536

MATHENY, TOM HARRELL, lawyer; b. Houston; s. Whitman and Lorene (Harrell) M. BA, Southeastern La. U., 1954; JD, Tulane U., 1957; LLD (hon.), Centenary Coll., 1979, DePauw U.; LHD (hon.), Oklahoma City U. Bar: La. 1957. Ptnr. Matheny & Pierson, Hammond, La., 1957—; gen. counsel First Guaranty Bank, 1960-83; trust counsel, chmn. bd. 1st Guaranty Bank, Hammond; v.p. Edwards & Assocs., So. Brick Supply, Inc.; faculty Southeastern La. U., Holy Cross Coll., New Orleans; lectr. Union Theol. Sem., Law Sci. Acad.; mem. com. on conciliation and mediation of disputes World Peace through Law Ctr.; Matheny lectr. in humanities series Southwestern U., Hammond, La. Chmn. advancement com. Boy Scouts Am., Hammond, 1960-64, mem. dist. coun., 1957-66, mem. exec. bd. Istrouma coun., 1966—, adv. com. to dist. area coun.; past pres. Tangipahoa Parish Mental Health Assn.; pres. La. Mental Health Assn., 1989—; mem. La. Mental Health Advocacy Svc.; co-chmn. La. Mental Health Advocacy Bd.; sec. Chep Morrison Scholarship Found.; mem. men's com. Japan Internat. Christian U. Found; chmn. speakers com., mem. com. on community action and crime prevention, La. Commn. on Law Enforcement and Adminstrn. Criminal Justice; campaign mgr. for Dem. gov. La., 1959-60, 63-64; bd. dirs. La. Moral and Civic Found., Tangipahoa Parish ARC, 1957-67, Hammond United Givers Fund, 1957-68, La. Coun. Chs., Southeastern Devel. Found., La. Mental Health Assn.; bd. dirs. Wesley Found., La. State U., 1965-68, 70—, chmn. bd.; trustee Centenary Coll., 1964-70, Scarritt Coll., 1975-81; pres., bd. trustees Lallie Kemp Hosp. Found., 1994—; hon. trustee John F. Kennedy Coll.; del. world conf. Nat. Assn. Conf. Lay Leaders, London, 1966, Denver, 1971, Dublin, 1976, Hawaii, 1981, del. to gen. confs., 1968, 70, 72; mem. Common Cause. Recipient Man of Yr. award Hammond, 1961, 64, also La. Jaycees, 1964, Layman of Yr. award La. Ann. Conf. United Meth. Ch., 1966, 73, Disting. Alumnus award Southeastern La. U., 1981, W.L. "Bill" May Outstanding Christian Bus. award La. Moral and Civic Found., 1986; scholarship named in his honor United Meth. Found. for Christian Higher Edn., Centenary Coll. and Dillard U., 1997. Fellow Harry S. Truman Libr. Inst (hon.); mem. ABA (com. on probate), La. Bar Assn. (past gen. chmn. com. on legal aid, com. prison reform), 21st Jud. Dist. Bar Assn. (past sec.-treas., v.p. 1967-68, 71), Comml. Law League Am. (past mem. com. on ethics), La. Alumni Coun. (pres. 1963-65), Acad. Religion and Mental Health, La. Assn. Claimant Compensation Attys., Southeastern La. U. Alumni Assn. (dir., pres. 1961-62, dir. spl. fund 1959-62, dir. Tongipahoa chpt.), Tulane Sch. Law Alumni Assn., Am. Assn. for Family and Marriage Therapy, Internat. Soc. Barristers, Internat. Soc. Valuers, Assn. Trial Lawyers Am., Am. Judicature Soc., Law-Sci. Inst., World Peace Through Law Acad. (com. on conciliation), Acad. Polit. Sci., Am. Acad. Polit. and Social Sci., Internat. Acad. Law and Sci., Internat. Platform Assn., UN Assn. Am. Trial Lawyers Assn., La. Hist. Assn., Friends of Cabildo, Gideons Internat., Hammond Assn. Commerce (dir. 1960-65), Intern Soc. Barristers, Intern Assn. Valuers, La. Mental Health Assn. (pres.-elect), Masons (33 degree), La. Lawyers' Club, Demolay (dist. dep. to supreme coun. 1964—, Legion of Honor), Kiwanis (v.p., dir., Layman of Yr. award 1972), Rotary, Phi Delta Phi, Phi Alpha Delta. Democrat. Methodist. Lodges: Masons, Scottish Rite (33 degree), Demolay (dist. dep. to supreme council 1964—, Legion of Honor), Kiwanis (v.p., dir., Layman of Yr. award for La., Miss. and West Tenn. 1972), Rotary. Home: PO Box 221 Hammond LA 70404-0221 Office: PO Box 1598 401 E Thomas St Hammond LA 70404

MATHER, ANN, international entertainment company executive; b. Stockport, Cheshire, Eng., Apr. 10, 1960; came to U.S., 1993; d. Robert Joseph and Theresa (Westhead) M. MA, Cambridge (Eng.) U., 1981. CPA. Sr. Peat Marwick, London, 1981-84; sr. fin. analyst Paramount Pictures, London, 1984-85; European contr. Paramount Pictures, Amsterdam, 1985-87; mgr. strategic planning Paramount Pictures, N.Y.C., 1987-88; pres. art import/export Santa Fe Galleries, London/Santa Fe/San Diego, 1988-89; dir. fin., Europe Polo Ralph Lauren, Paris, 1989-91; European contr. life ins. div. AIG, Paris, 1991-92; dir. fin. and adminstrn. Europe internat. film distbn. div. The Walt Disney Co., Paris, 1992-93; v.p. fin. and adminstrn., world internat. film distbn. div. The Walt Disney Co., Burbank, Calif., 1993—. Contbr. Descanso Gardens, La Canada, Calif., 1996. Recipient award for land values paper Royal Soc. Chartered Surveyors, 1981. Mem. Women in Film, Fin. Execs. Inst. (chmn. profl. devel. com.). Avocations: skiing, horseback riding, travel, literature, film. Office: Buena Vista Internat The Walt Disney Co 500 S Buena Vista St Burbank CA 91521-0001

MATHER, BETTY BANG, musician, educator; b. Emporia, Kans., Aug. 7, 1927; d. Read Robinson and Shirley (Smith) Bang; m. Roger Mather, Aug. 3, 1973. MusB, Oberlin Conservatory, 1949; MA, Columbia U., 1951. Instr. U. Iowa, Iowa City, 1953-58, asst. prof., 1959-65, assoc. prof., 1965-73, prof., 1973-96, prof. emeritus, 1996—; editor Romney Press; vis. instr. U. Iowa, Iowa City, 1952-53. Rec. artist; author: Interpretation of French Music from 1675-1775, 1973, (with David Lasocki) Free Ornamentation for Woodwind Instruments from 1700-1775, 1976 (with David Lasocki) The Classical Woodwind Cadenza, 1978, The Art of Preluding, 1984 (with Dean Karns) Dance Rhythmns of the French Baroque, 1987, (with Gail Gavin) The French Noel, 1996. Mem. Nat. Flute Assn. (v.p. 1986-87, pres. 1987-88, chmn. bd. dirs. 1988-89). Home: 308 4th Ave Iowa City IA 52245-4613

MATHER, BRYANT, research administrator; b. Balt., Dec. 27, 1916; s. Leon Bryant and Julia (Ferguson) M.; m. Katharine Selden Kniskern, Mar. 27, 1940 (dec. Feb. 1991). Grad., Balt. City Coll., 1934; A.B. in Geology, Johns Hopkins, 1936, postgrad., 1936-38; postgrad., Am. U., 1938-39; D.Sc. (hon.), Clarkson U., 1978. Curator mineralogy Field Mus. Natural History, 1939-41; with U.S. Army Corps Engrs., 1941—; geologist Central Concrete Lab., U.S. Mil. Acad., 1941-42, Mt. Vernon, N.Y., 1942-43; supervisory research civil engr., chief engring. scis. br., concrete lab. (Waterways Expt. Sta.), Vicksburg, Miss., 1946-65; asst. chief concrete lab. (Waterways Expt. Sta.), 1965-66, chief, 1966-76, acting chief structures lab., 1978-80, chief lab., 1980-92, dir. structures lab., 1992—; rsch. assoc. Fla. Dept. Agr. and Consumer Svcs., Gainesville, 1968—; Miss. Mus. Natural Scis., 1979—, Miss. Ent. Mus. Miss. State U., 1985—, Am. Mus. Natural History, N.Y.C., 1979—; mem. Sr. Exec. Assn., 1980—; mem. U.S. Com. of Internat. Commn. Large Dams, 1959—; lectr. Purdue U., 1961, Old Master lectr., 1991; lectr. U. Notre Dame, 1964, MIT, 1966, Clemson U., 1967; Henry M. Shaw lectr. N.C. State U., 1967, U. Wis., 1978—, U.Tex., 1987, Okla. State U., 1987, Johns Hopkins U., 1991, Utah State U., 1995; Stanton Walker lectr. U. Md., 1969; Edgar Marburg lectr. ASTM, 1970; mem. 4th, 5th, 6th and 7th Internat. Symposia Chemistry Cement, Internat. Symposium Movement Water in Porous Bodies, Paris, 1964. Co-author: Butterflies of Mississippi, 1958; Editor: Handbook for Concrete and Cement, 1942, 49, also quar. supplements, 1949—. Recipient Meritorious Civilian Svc. award, 1965, Exceptional Civilian Svc. award, 1968, with laurel-leaf cluster, 1991, Civilian of Yr. award C.E., 1992, Disting. Rsch. award Aggregates Found. for Tech., Rsch. and Engring., 1995. Fellow AAAS, ASTM (sec. com. C-9 1952-60, chmn. 1960-66, chmn. com. C-1 1968-74, chmn. com. E-39 1973-75, dir. 1970-73, v.p. 1973-75, pres. 1975-76, Award of Merit 1959, Sanford E. Thompson award 1961, Frank E. Richart award 1972, William T. Cavanaugh award 1990), Transp. Rsch. Bd., NAS-NRC (chmn. concrete divsn. 1963-69, chmn. curing com. 1970-76, hon. mem. concrete divsn. and concrete coms. 1987, Roy W. Crum Disting. Svc. award 1966, 2d Disting. Lectr. 1993), Inst. Concrete Technologists (Eng., hon. 1982); mem. NAE, ASCE (hon. mem. 1988), Entomol. Soc. Am., Am. Concrete Inst. (pres. 1964, Henry C. Turner medal 1973, Charles S. Whitney medal 1974, Robert E. Philleo award 1992, Delmar L. Bloem award 1990, hon. mem.), Entomol. Soc. Md., Mich. Entomol. Soc., Meteoritical Soc., Natural Hist. Soc. Md., Orleans County (Vt.) Hist. Soc., Lepidopterists Soc., Miss. Acad. Sci., Miss. Gem and Mineral Soc., Am. Mus. Natural History (hon. mem. 1968, hon. patron 1974), So. Lepidopterists Soc., Soc. Ky. Lepidopterists, Mining Metall. and Petroleum Engrs. (Legion of Honor), Mencken Soc., Phi Beta Kappa, Sigma Xi. Home: 213 Mount Salus Dr Clinton MS 39056-5007 Office: US Army Engr Waterways Expt Sta Structures Lab 3909 Halls Ferry Rd Vicksburg MS 39180-6133 *The production of hydraulic-cement concrete—a synthetic sedimentary rock, may be the human race's most successful attempt to reproduce an activity previously engaged in only by God; and we have done it better; there are more varieties and there is better uniformity.*

MATHER, DENNIS BRYAN, wholesale insurance company executive; b. Balt., Dec. 3, 1949; s. Nelson Arthur and Dorothy E. (Langham) M.; m. Cindi Lynn Gastner, May 7, 1977; children: James Bryan, Christopher Todd. BS in Bus., Towson (Md.) State U., 1972; MBA, U. Balt., 1981. CLU, ChFC. Agt. Morgan Fin. Group, Balt., 1972-74, supr., 1974-79, v.p., 1979-83; pres., CEO The Mather Cos., Cockeysville, Md., 1983—. Coach Caroll Manor Recreation Coun., Phoenix, Md., 1990—, v.p., 1992. With USCGR, 1967-73. Mem. Nat. Assn. Life Underwriters, Nat. Assn. Health Underwriters (bd. dirs.), Gen. Agts. and Mgrs. Assn., Am. Soc. CLU (bd. dirs., v.p., pres. Balt. chpt. 1986, instr. 1990), Million Dollar Round Table (life), Nat. Assn. Ind. Life Agts., Mass Mktg. Inst. Republican. Presbyterian. Avocations: golf, softball, baseball and soccer coaching. Office: The Mather Cos 10540 York Rd Cockeysville MD 21030-2300

MATHER, ELIZABETH VIVIAN, health care executive; b. Richmond, Ind., Sept. 19, 1941; d. Willie Samuel and Lillie Mae (Harper) Fuqua; m. Roland Donald Mather, Dec. 26, 1966. BS, Maryville (Tenn.) Coll., 1963; postgrad., Columbia U., 1965-66. Tchr. Richmond Community Schs., 1963-67, Indpls. Pub. Schs., 1967-68; systems analyst Ind. Blue Cross Blue Shield, Indpls., 1968-71, Ind. Nat. Bank, Indpls., 1971; med. cons. Ind. State Dept. Pub. Welfare, Indpls., 1971-78, cons. supr., 1978-86; systems analyst Ky. Blue Cross Blue Shield, Louisville, 1988-89; contracts specialist Humana Corp., Louisville, 1989—. Active Rep. Cen. Com. Montgomery County, Crawfordsville, 1976-86, Centenary Meth. Ch., adminstrv. bd., 1990. Mem. DAR (treas. 1963-66, sec. 1978-86). Avocations: designing and sewing clothes. Home: 6106 Partridge Pl Floyds Knobs IN 47119-9427 Office: Humana Corp 500 W Main St Louisville KY 40202-2946

MATHER, GEORGE ROSS, clergy member; b. Trenton, N.J., June 1, 1930; s. Samuel Wooley and Henrietta Elizabeth (Deardorff) M.; m. Doris Christine Anderson, June 28, 1958; children: Catherine Anne Mather-Grimes, Geoffrey Thomas. BA, Princeton U., 1952; MDiv, Princeton Theol. Sem., 1955; DD, Hanover Coll., 1986. Ordained to Ministry, 1955. Asst. pastor Abington (Pa.) Presbyn., 1955-58; pastor 1st Presbyn. Ch. Ewing, Trenton, 1958-71; sr. pastor 1st Presbyn. Ch. Ft. Wayne, Ind., 1971-86; pastor 3d Presbyn. Ch. Ft. Wayne, Ind., 1987-95. Author: Frontier Faith: The Story of the Pioneer Congregations, 1992; co-editor: On the Heritage Trail, 1994; contbr. articles to profl. jours. Pres. Allen County Libr. Trustees, Ft. Wayne, Allen County Libr. Found., Ft. Wayne, Clergy United for Action, Ft. Wayne; trustee Hanover (Ind.) Coll.; chmn. Bicentennial Religious Heritage Commn., 1994; bd. dirs. Smock Found., 1971-85. Mem. Ind. Religious History Assn. (bd. dirs.), Allen County Ft. Wayne Hist. Soc. (bd. dirs.), The Quest Club (pres.). Avocations: tennis, travel, hiking, canoeing. Home: 6669 Quail Ridge Ln Fort Wayne IN 46804-2875

MATHER, JOHN CROMWELL, astrophysicist; b. Roanoke, Va., Aug. 7, 1946; s. Robert Eugene and Martha Belle (Cromwell) M.; m. Jane Anne Hauser, Nov. 22, 1980. BA, Swarthmore (Pa.) Coll., 1968; PhD, U. Calif., Berkeley, 1974; DSc (hon.), Swarthmore Coll., 1994. NAS/NRC rsch. assoc. NASA/Goddard Inst. for Space Studies, N.Y.C., 1974-76; lectr. in astronomy Columbia U., N.Y.C., 1975-76; astrophysicist NASA/Goddard Space Flight Ctr., Greenbelt, Md., 1976—, head infrared astrophysics br., 1988-89, 90-93, sr. scientist, 1989-90, 93—, study scientist Cosmic Background Explorer Satellite,, 1976-82, project scientist COBE, 1982—, prin. investigator FIRAS on COBE, 1976—; chmn. external adv. bd. Ctr. for Astrophys. Rsch. in the Antarctic, U. Chgo., 1992—; mem. lunar astrophysics mgmt. ops. working group NASA Hdqrs., Washington, 1992; study scientist Next Generation Space Telescope, 1995—. Contbr. over 50 articles to profl. jours.

Recipient Nat. Space Achievement award Rotary, 1991, Laurels award Aviation Week and Space Tech., 1992, Space Sci. award AIAA, 1993, John Scott award City of Phila., 1995, Rumford prize Am. Acad. Arts and Scis., 1996; Goddard fellow, 1994—. Fellow Am. Phys. Soc.; mem. Am. Astron. Soc. (Dannie Heineman prize astrophysics 1993), Internat. Astron. Union, Sigma Xi. Democrat. Unitarian. Achievements include proposed Cosmic Background Explorer Satellite, led team to successful launch in 1989, measured spectrum of cosmic microwave background radiation to unprecedented accuracy. Office: NASA/Goddard Space Flight Code G85 Greenbelt MD 20771

MATHER, JOHN RUSSELL, climatologist, educator; b. Boston, Oct. 9, 1923; s. John and Mabelle (Russell) M.; m. Amy L. Nelson, 1946; children: Susan, Thomas, Ellen. BA, Williams Coll., 1945; BS in Meteorology, MIT, 1947, M.S., 1948; Ph.D. in Geography-Climatology, Johns Hopkins U., 1951. Rsch. assoc., climatologist Lab. Climatology, Seabrook, N.J., 1948-54; prin. rsch. scientist Lab. Climatology, Centerton, N.J., 1954-63; pres. Lab. Climatology, C.W. Thornthwaite Assoc., Centerton, 1963-72; asst. prof. Johns Hopkins U., 1951-53; assoc. prof. climatology Drexel Inst. Tech., Phila., 1957-60; prof. geography U. Del., Newark, 1963—; chmn. dept. geography U. Del., 1966-89; state climatologist Del., 1978-92; vis. lectr. geography U. Chgo., 1957-61; vis. prof. U.S. Mil. Acad., 1989. Author 2 books on applied climatology, 1 book on water resources; co-author biography of C.W. Thornthwaite; U.S. editor joint U.S.-USSR book on global change; contbr. numerous articles to tech. jours. Fellow AAAS; mem. Am. Meteorol. Soc., Assn. Am. Geographers (v.p. 1990-91, pres. 1991-92), Am. Geog. Soc. (councilor 1981—, sec. 1982—), Am. Water Resources Assn., Tau Beta Pi, Phi Kappa Phi. Contributed to concept of potential evapotranspiration, its measurement, use in climatic water balance; moisture factor in climate; application of climatic water balance to studies in agr., hydrology, applied climatology. Home: 378 Daretown Rd Elmer NJ 08318-2728 Office: U Del Dept Geography Newark DE 19716

MATHER, MILDRED EUNICE, retired archivist; b. Washington, Iowa, July 25, 1922; d. Hollis John and Delpha Irene (Cummings) Whiting; m. Stewart Elbert Mather, Aug. 7, 1955; children: Julie Marie, Thomas Stewart (dec.). Cert. bus sch., Burlington and Des Moines (Iowa), 1941, 1947; cert., Stenotype Inst., 1948. Typist Burlington Willow-Weave, 1941-42, Burlington Basket Co., 1942; clk. typist U.S. Dept. War, Washington, 1942-43; supr. internat. conf. Dept. State, Washington, 1949-52; bookkeeper Iowa Wesleyan Coll., Mt. Pleasant, 1952-55; clk. typist Herbert Hoover Presdl. Libr., West Branch, Iowa, 1964-69; archives technician Herbert Hoover Presdl. Libr., West Branch, 1964-72, archivist, libr., 1972-92. WAC, 1943-46. Mem. Order of Eastern Star (worthy matron). Republican. Home: 79 Eisenhower St West Branch IA 52358-9403

MATHER, RICHARD BURROUGHS, retired Chinese language and literature educator; b. Baoding, Hebei, China, Nov. 11, 1913; s. William Arnot and Grace (Burroughs) M.; m. Virginia Marjorie Temple, June 3, 1939; 1 dau., Elizabeth Temple. B.A., Princeton U., 1935; B.Th., Princeton Theol. Sem., 1939; Ph.D. in Oriental Langs, U. Calif., Berkeley, 1949. Ordained to ministry United Presbyterian Ch. U.S., 1939; pastor Belle Haven (Va.) Presbyterian Ch., 1939-41; asst. prof. Chinese U. Minn., Mpls., 1949-57; assoc. prof. Chinese U. Minn., 1957-64, prof., 1964-84; mem. Am. Council Learned Socs. Com. on Study of Chinese Civilization, 1979-81. Author: Shih-shuo hsin-yu, A New Account of Tales of the World, 1976, The Poet Shen Yueh (441-513), the Reticent Marquis, 1988; contbr. articles on medieval Chinese lit. and religion. Guggenheim fellow, 1956-57; Fulbright Hays grantee, 1956-57, 63-64; Am. Council Learned Socs. grantee, 1963-64. Mem. Am. Oriental Soc. (pres. 1980-81), Assn. Asian Studies, Chinese Lang. Tchrs. Assn. Democrat. Home: 2091 Dudley Ave Saint Paul MN 55108-1415

MATHER, ROGER FREDERICK, music educator, writer; b. London, England, May 27, 1917; came to U.S., 1938; s. Richard and Marie Louise (Schultze) M.; m. Dorothea Meinen, Sept. 11, 1943 (div. Sept. 1971); children: Arielle Diane, Christopher Richard; m. Betty Louise Bang, Aug. 3, 1973. BA with honors, Cambridge U., 1938; MSc, MIT, 1940; MA in Metallurgy, U. Cambridge, 1941. Registered profl. engr., Ohio, Mich., Pa. Rsch. metallurgist Inland Steel Co., East Chicago, Ind., 1940-42; chief metallurgist Willys-Overland Motors, Toledo, 1942-46, Kaiser-Frazer Corp., Willow Run, Mich., 1946-50; project mgr. U.S. Steel Corp., Pitts., 1950-61; dir. rsch. engring. Mine Safety Appliances Co., Pitts., 1961-62; rsch. staff Du Pont Co., Wilmington, Del., 1962-63; chief nuclear power tech. br. NASA, Cleve., 1963-73; adj. prof. music U. Iowa, Iowa City, 1973-96; instr. pub. speaking and stage fright U. Iowa, 1983-85, Kirkwood C.C., Iowa City, 1983-85; cons. Miyazawa Flutes, U.S.A., Coralville, Iowa, 1985-90; lectr. U. Toledo; Mich. state examiner Registration of Profl. Engrs.; condr. numerous workshops, clinics, classes, and flute recitals regionally, nationally, and abroad. Author: The Art of Playing the Flute, 1980, 2d vol., 1981; author chpts. in Woodwind Anthology and Fluting and Dancing; pub., exec. editor The Romney Press, 1980—; contbr. poems to Nothing Left Unsaid, Through the Looking Glass, 100 Words, Perceptions, Journey Between Stars; contbr. numerous articles to sci. and music jours. Mem. Nat. Flute Assn. (life, coms.), Nat. Assn. Coll. Wind and Percussion Instrs., Internat. Soc. Poets (Disting. Mem., Internat. Poet of Month), The Pa. Assn., Mensa. Episcopalian. Avocations: high fidelity sound reproduction, photography. Home: 308 4th Ave Iowa City IA 52245-4613

MATHER, RUTH ELSIE, writer; b. Waverly, Wash., Feb. 14, 1934; d. James Orrin and Leona Ezthelda (Mather) Tallman; m. Mike Nicholas Dakis, Apr. 20, 1958 (div. Nov. 1971); children: Cynthia Michelle, Martin Nicholas; m. Fred Junior Morgan, Nov. 20, 1971. BA with highest honors, Brigham Young U., 1961, MA, 1965; postgrad., U. Miss., 1977-78. Cert. secondary tchr., Idaho, cert. elem. tchr. and secondary tchr. grades 7-14, Calif. Tchr. English Iglesia Jesucristo Rama Roma, Mexico City, 1955-56; English tchr. Lemhi County Schs., Leadore, Idaho, 1962-66; English instr. Yonsei U., Seoul, Republic of Korea, 1973-74, U. Md. Far East Divsn., Seoul, 1975-77, Boise (Idaho) State U., 1978-79, Coll. of the Redwoods, Eureka, Calif., 1980-81; writer hist. video scripts History West Pub. Co., Oklahoma City, 1990—; screenwriter Frontier Images, Canyon Country, Calif., 1994—; cons. on hist. video for PBS, A La Carte, San Francisco, 1994-95, guest expert on Secrets of the Gold Rush-PBS, 1995. Author: Hanging the Sheriff: A Biography of Henry Plummer, 1987, John David Borthwick: Artist of the Gold Rush, 1989, Gold Camp Desperadoes: Study of Crime & Punishment on Frontier, 1990, Vigilante Victims, 1991; contbr. short stories, book revs., articles to encys. and profl. jours. Local campaign dir. Dem. Party, Arcata, Calif., 1969-70. Mem. Nat. Outlaw and Lawman Assn., Western Outlaw and Lawman Assn. Avocations: reading, hiking. Office: History West Pub Co PO Box 23133 Oklahoma City OK 73123

MATHER, STEPHANIE J., lawyer; b. Kansas City, Mo., Dec. 5, 1952; d. Edward Wayne and H. June (Kunkel) M.; m. Miles Christopher Zimmerman, Sept. 23, 1988. BA magna cum laude, Okla. City U., 1975, JD with honors, 1980. Lawyer Pierce, Couch, Hendrickson, Johnston & Baysinger, Okla. City, Okla., 1980-88, Manchester, Hiltgen & Healy, P.C., Okla. City, 1989-90; sr. staff counsel Nat. Am. Ins. Co., Chandler, Okla., 1990—; asst. v.p. Lagere & Walkingstick Ins. Agy., Inc., Chandler, Okla., 1993—. Co-chair Lincoln County Dem. Party, 1991-92, 95-97; v.p. Lincoln County Dem. Women, 1992-95, pres., 1995-97; bd. dirs. Lincoln County Partnership for Children, 1994—, Gateway to Prevention and Recovery, 1996-97. Mem. Okla. Bar Assn. (editor, bd. editors, 1992—), Lincoln County Bar Assn. (mem. libr. bd. 1990—), Lincoln County Profl. Women, Alpha Phi (treas. Ctrl. Okla. Alumnae 1997—). Democrat. Avocations: reading, geneology, ranching, cooking. Home: PO Box 246 Chandler OK 74834-0246 Office: Nat Am Ins Co PO Box 9 Chandler OK 74834-0009

MATHERLEE, THOMAS RAY, health care consultant; b. Dayton, Ohio, Sept. 18, 1934; s. Dennis R. and Eleanor E. Matherlee; BS in Bus. Adminstrn. Findlay Coll., 1958; MBA, U. Chgo., 1960; m. Ann Deverka; children: Michael, Jennifer, Craig, Brent, Brian. Adminstrv. resident Shannon Hosp., San Angelo, Tex., 1959-60; asst. adminstr. Richland Meml. Hosp., Olney, Ill., 1960-61; adminstrv. asst., then adminstr. Forsyth Meml. Hosp., Winston-Salem, N.C., 1961-68; exec. dir. Gaston County (N.C.) Hosp., 1968-70; exec. dir. Gaston Meml. Hosp., Inc., Gastonia, 1970-80, pres., 1981-85; sr. v.p. Vol. Hosps. of Am. Inc., Washington, 1986-87, exec. v.p., Irving, Tex., 1987-90; pres. AMA Svcs., Inc., 1990-94; sr. v.p. The Hunter Group, 1994—; cons. Sch. Pastoral Care N.C. Bapt. Hosp., Winston-Salem, 1967-68; mem. sub-area adv. coun. Health Systems Agy., 1975-80; adj. faculty Sch. Community and Allied Health, U. Ala.-Birmingham, 1980-85; bd. dirs. Joint Commn. on Accreditation of Healthcare Orgns., 1986-90, treas., audit and fin. com. chmn., mem. exec. com. Dir. Olney Ill. CD, 1960-61; mem. fin. com. Piedmont coun. Boy Scouts Am., 1970; mem. adv. bd. Gastonia Wesleyan Youth Chorus, 1972; mem. joint com. nursing edn. N.C. State Bd. Edn. and Bd. Higher Edn., 1969-71; mem. adminstrv. bd. First United Meth. Ch., Gastonia, 1972-74; bd. dirs. Gaston County Heart Assn., 1968-70, Forsyth County Cancer Soc., 1964-65; trustee N.C. Hosp. Edn. and Research Found., 1966-71, pres., 1970-71; trustee N.C. Blue Cross and Blue Shield, Inc., 1971-77, Southeastern Hosp. Conf., 1971-72, 73-81, mem. edn. com., 1978—, mem. program com., 1975-76. Named Boss of Yr., Nat. Secs. Assn., 1970-71. Fellow Am. Coll. Healthcare Execs.; mem. MGMA, N.C. Hosp. Assn. (life; trustee 1966-72, pres. 1970-71, chmn. council govt. liaison 1978-81, Disting. Service award 1985), N.C. League Nursing, Am. Hosp. Assn. (ho. of dels. 1973-78, 83-85, speaker ho. of dels. 1985, trustee 1975-78, 83-85, chmn. bd. trustees 1984), Gastonia C. of C. (health affairs com. 1969-72). Lodge: Kiwanis. Contbr. articles on hosp. adminstrn. to profl. jours.

MATHERN, TIM, state senator, social worker; b. Edgeley, N.D., Apr. 19, 1950; s. John J. and Christina Mathern; m. Lorene Mathern, Feb. 12, 1971; children: Rebecca, Tonya, Joshua, Zachary. BA, N.D. State U., 1971; MSW, U. Nebr., Omaha, 1980. Dir. of devel. Cath. Family Svc., Fargo, N.D., 1972—; mem. N.D. Senate, Bismarck, 1986—, mem. legis. mgmt. com., 1993—, asst. minority leader, 1992-96, senate minority leader, 1996—, also mem. jud. stds. com.; mem. political subdivsn. com., N.D., 1995-97. Mem. Fargo-Cass County Econ. Devel. Corp., 1993—; bd. dirs. Prairieland Home Health Care; mem. exec. com. N.D. Dem. NPL Party, 1996—. Named Legislator of Yr., Red River Valley Mental Health Assn., 1989, 91, Legislator of Yr., N.D. Children's Caucus, 1993. Mem. NASW (Social Worker of Yr. award 1987), Mental Health Assn. Democrat. Roman Catholic. Home: 406 Elmwood Fargo ND 58103-4315 Office: 2537 S University Fargo ND 58103-5736

MATHERS, THOMAS NESBIT, financial consultant; b. Bloomington, Ind., Apr. 22, 1914; s. Frank Curry and Maud Esther (Bowser) M.; m. Helen M. Curtis, Oct. 23, 1943 (dec.); children: Mary, Abigail. A.B., Ind. U., 1936, LL.B., 1939; M.B.A., Harvard U., 1941. Bar: Ind. 1939. Research asst. No. Trust Co., 1941-43; legal asst. Chgo. Ordnance Dist., 1943-44; employee to ptnr. Woodruff Hays & Co., Chgo., 1944-51; pres. Security Counselors, Inc., Chgo., 1951-62; pres. Mathers & Co., Chgo., 1962-75, chmn. bd., 1975-85, vice chmn., 1985-91; bd. dirs. Lincoln Income Fund, 1978—, Lincoln Convertible Securities Fund, 1986—; pres. Mathers Fund, 1965-75, chmn. bd., 1975-85, vice chmn., 1985-91; v.p., bd. dirs. OFC Corp. Meadowood Project, 1991—. Trustee Beloit Coll., 1970—. Recipient Disting. Alumni Service award Ind. U., 1979. Mem. Ind. U. Disting. Alumni Assn. (past pres.). Republican. Presbyterian. Clubs: Union League, Econ. of Chgo, Westmoreland Country, Mich. Shores, Investment Analysts Chgo. (past pres.). Home: 115 Bertling Ln Winnetka IL 60093-4202

MATHERS, WILLIAM HARRIS, lawyer; b. Newport, R.I., Aug. 27, 1914; s. Howard and Margaret I. (Harris) M.; m. Myra T. Martin, Jan. 17, 1942; children: William Martin, Michael Harris, John Grinnell, Myra Tutt, Ursula Fraser. A.B., Dartmouth Coll., 1935; J.D., Yale U., 1938. Bar: N.Y. 1940. With Milbank, Tweed & Hope, 1938-48; mem. Milbank, Tweed, Hope & Hadley, 1948-57; v.p., sec., dir. Yale & Towne Mfg. Co., Stamford, Conn., 1957-60; ptnr. Chadbourne & Parke, 1960-75, counsel, 1983—; exec. v.p., gen. counsel, sec., dir. United Brands Co., 1975-82. Mayor, trustee Village of Cove Neck, N.Y., 1950-82; trustee Barnard Coll., 1958-69. Served as pvt. to maj. U.S. Army, 1942-46. Mem. ABA, N.Y. State Bar Assn., Nassau County Bar Assn., Assn. of Bar of City of N.Y., New Eng. Soc. in City of N.Y., Casque and Gauntlet, Corbey Court, Piping Rock Club, Seminole Golf Club, N.Y. Yacht Club, Cold Spring Harbor Beach Club, Phi Beta Kappa, Psi Upsilon. Home: Gordon Farm RR 1 Box 83 Sutton VT 05867-9721 Office: 30 Rockefeller Plz New York NY 10112

MATHES, STEPHEN JOHN, plastic and reconstructive surgeon, educator; b. New Orleans, Aug. 17, 1943; s. John Ernest and Norma (Deutsch) M.; m. Jennifer Tandy Woodbridge, Nov. 26, 1966; children: David, Brian, Edward. BS, La. State U., 1964; MD, La. State U., New Orleans, 1968. Diplomate Am. Bd. Surgery, Am. Bd. Plastic Surgery (dir. 1993—). Asst. prof. surgery Wash. U., St. Louis, 1977-78; assoc. prof. U. Calif., San Francisco, 1978-84, prof. surgery, 1984, prof. surgery, anatomy and cell biology, 1984-85, also bd. dirs. craniofacial anomalies; head plastic surgery sect. U. Mich., Ann Arbor, 1984-85, prof. surgery, 1984-85; prof. surgery, head plastic and reconstructive surgery div. U. Calif., San Francisco, 1985—. Author: (textbook) Clinical Applications for Muscle and Musculocutaneous Flaps, 1983 (Best Med. Book award Physician's category, Am. Med. Writer's Assn., 1983); contbr. articles to profl. jours. Recipient 1st prize plastic surgery scholarship contest, Plastic Surgery Edn. Found., 1981, 83, 84, 86; grantee NIH, 1982-85, 86—. Fellow ACS; mem. Am. Assn. Plastic Surgery, Plastic Surgery Research Council (pres.-elect 1986), Am. Soc. Surgery of Hand, Soc. Univ. Surgeons. Republican. Episcopalian. Avocations: gardening, tennis. Home: 30 Trophy Ct Burlingame CA 94010-7434 Office: U Calif San Francisco Dept Surgery San Francisco CA 94143-0932

MATHES, STEPHEN JON, lawyer; b. N.Y.C., Mar. 18, 1945; s. Joseph and Beatrice M.; m. Michele Marshall, Oct. 22, 1972 (div. 1992); children: Aaron, Benjamin; m. Maria McGarry, Dec. 19, 1992; 1 child, Sara. BA, U. Pa., 1967, JD, 1970. Bar: N.Y. 1971, Pa. 1972, U.S. Dist. Ct. (ea. dist.) Pa. 1971. U.S. Ct. Appeals (3d cir.) 1972, U.S. Ct. Appeals (5th cir.) 1985, U.S. Ct. Appeals (4th cir.) 1985, U.S. Supreme Ct. 1978. Law clk. U.S. Ct. Appeals (3d cir.), Phila., 1970-71; asst. dist. atty. Office of Phil. Dist. Atty., Phila., 1975; assoc. Dilworth, Paxson, Kalish & Kauffman, Phila., 1971-74, 76-77, sr. ptnr., 1977-91, mem. exec. com., 1987-90, co-chmn. litigation dept., 1987-91; ptnr., mem. mng. com. Hoyle, Morris & Kerr, Phila., 1992—; bd. dirs. The Levitt Found., 1990—, sec., 1991—. Bd. dirs., exec. com. Acad. Vocal Arts, 1993—, mem. exec. com. Mem. ABA, Pa. Bar Assn., Phila. Bar Assn., Thanatopsis Soc., Racquet Club, Germantown Cricket Club. Home: 199 Lynnebrook Ln Philadelphia PA 19118-2706 Office: Holye Morris & Kerr One Liberty Pl Ste 4900 Philadelphia PA 19103

MATHESON, ALAN ADAMS, law educator; b. Cedar City, Utah, Feb. 2, 1932; s. Scott Milne and Adele (Adams) M.; m. Milicent Holbrook, Aug. 15, 1960; children—Alan, David Scott, John Robert. B.A., U. Utah, 1953, M.S., 1957, J.D., 1959; postgrad. asso. in law, Columbia U. Bar: Utah 1960, Ariz. 1975. Asst. to pres. Utah State U., 1961-67; mem. faculty Ariz. State U., Tempe, 1967—; prof. law Ariz. State U., 1970—, dean, 1978-84; bd. dirs. Ariz. Center Law in Public Interest, 1979-81; bd. dirs. DNA Navajo Legal Services, 1984—. Pres. Tri-City Mental Health Citizens Bd., 1973-74. Served with AUS, 1953-55. Mem. Utah Bar Assn., Ariz. Bar Assn., Maricopa County Bar Assn., Phi Beta Kappa, Order of Coif. Democrat. Mormon. Home: 720 E Geneva Dr Tempe AZ 85282-3737 Office: Coll Law Ariz State U Tempe AZ 85287

MATHESON, MICHAEL J., federal official. BA, Stanford U., 1965; student, Stanford Law Sch., 1968. Atty. Wilmer, Cutler, & Pickering, Washington, 1968-69; gen. counsel USAF, 1969-72; atty.legal affairs bur. U.S. Dept. of State, Washington, 1972-76, asst. legal advisor, 1976-83, dep. legal advisor, 1983-89, prin. dep. legal advisor, 1989-96. Recipient Tom C. Clark award Fedn. Bar Assn., 1991. Mem. Phi Betta Kappa. Office: Dept of State 2201 C St NW Washington DC 20520-7512

MATHESON, NINA W., medical researcher. Prof., dir. William H. Welch Med. Libr., Balt., 1985-94; prof. emeritus Jouns Hopkins U., Balt., 1994—. Named Disting. prof. nursing Vanderbilt Sch. Nursing, 1976-82. Office: Johns Hopkins Univ William H Welch Medical Libr 720 Rutland Ave Baltimore MD 21205-2109*

MATHESON, SCOTT MILNE, JR., lawyer; b. Salt Lake City, July 18, 1953; s. Scott Milne and Norma (Warenski) M.; m. Robyn Kuida, Aug. 12, 1978; children: Heather Blair, Briggs James. AB, Stanford U., 1975; MA, Oxford U., Eng.; JD, Yale U., 1980. Bar: D.C., 1981, Utah 1986. Assoc. Williams & Connolly, Washington, 1981-85; assoc. prof. law U. Utah, 1985-91; dep. atty. Salt Lake County Attys. Office, 1988-89; vis. assoc. prof. JFK Sch. Govt. Harvard U., Cambridge, Mass., 1989-90; assoc. dean law U. Utah, 1990-93, prof. law, 1991—; U.S. atty. Dist. Utah, 1993—; mem. adv. com. on rules of evidence Utah Supreme Ct., 1987-93, Utah Constitutional Revision Commn., 1987-93, adv. com. on the local rules of practice, U.S. Dist. Ct. Utah, 1993—; bd. dirs. Scott M. Matheson Leadership Forum, 1990-93. Contbr. articles to profl. jours. Chair U.N. Day for State of Utah, 1991; mem. Univ. Com. on Tanner Lectures on Human Values U. Utah, 1993—, Honors Program Adv. Com. U. Utah, 1986-87, 1987-88, Adv. Bd. Hinckley Inst. Politics U. Utah, 1990-93; trustee Legal Aid Soc. of Salt Lake, 1986-93, pres., 1987; trustee TreeUtah, 1992-93; campaign mgr. Matheson for Gov., 1976, 1980; vol. state dir. Clinton/Gore '92. Recipient Up'n Comers award Zions Bank, 1991, Faculty Achievement award Burlington Resources Found., 1993; named one of Outstanding Young Men of Am., 1987, 1988; Rhodes scholar. Mem. ABA, Assn. Am. Law Schs. (chair sect. on mass com. law 1993), Utah State Bar, Salt Lake County Bar Assn. (exec. com. 1986-92), Golden Key Nat. Honor Soc. (hon. 1990), Phi Beta Kappa.

MATHESON, WILLIAM LYON, lawyer, farmer; b. Coeburn, Va., Dec. 5, 1924; s. Julius Daniel and Ruth Steele Lyon M.; m. Katrina B. Hickox; children: Katherine, William Lyon, Alline, Thornton; m. Marjorie H. Anderson, Nov. 26, 1977. Student, Emory U., 1946-47; AB, Mercer U., 1944; LLB, U. Va., 1950. Bar: N.Y. 1951. Assoc. firm Patterson, Belknap & Webb, N.Y.C., 1950-57; assoc. Wertheim & Co. (investments), N.Y.C., 1957-58; ptnr. Webster & Sheffield, N.Y.C., 1959-65; pvt. practice N.Y.C., 1965-92; chmn. bd. Mich. Energy Resources Co., Monroe, 1959-89, Mercom Inc. (cable TV), 1984-91. Bd. dirs. Madison Sq. Boys' Club, N.Y.C., 1958-76, assoc. mem. bd. dirs., 1977-91; trustee Police Athletic League, N.Y.C., 1962—. Served to lt. (j.g.) USN, 1942-46. Mem. Links Club (N.Y.C.), Piping Rock Club (Locust Valley, N.Y.), Meadow Brook Club (Jericho, N.Y.), Seminole Golf (North Palm Beach, Fla.), Jupiter Island Club (Hobe Sound, Fla.). Democrat. Home: 430 S Beach Rd Hobe Sound FL 33455-2702 also: Sunset Hill Heather Ln Mill Neck NY 11765

MATHEU, FEDERICO MANUEL, university chancellor; b. Humacao, P.R., Mar. 17, 1941; s. Federico Matheu-Baez and Matilde Delgado-Vazquez; m. Myrna Delgado-Miranda, May 30, 1963; children: Federico Antonio, Rosa Myrna, Alfredo Javier, David Reinaldo. B.S. in Chem. Engring, U. P.R., 1962; Ph.D. in Phys. Chemistry, U. Pitts., 1971. Chem. engr. Commonwealth Oil Refining Co., 1962-63; mem. adminstrv. staff and faculty U. P.R., 1963-78, dir. Humacao Coll., 1976-78; chancellor San German campus Inter Am. U. P.R., 1978-91; exec. dir., gen. coun. on edn. Commonwealth of P.R., Hato Rey, 1991-96; chancellor U. Metropolitena-Ana G. Méndez U. System, 1996—; cons. in field. Author papers, reports in field. Named Disting. Educator P.R. Jaycees, 1974. Mem. Colegio de Quimicos P.R., Am. Chem. Soc., Sci. Tchrs. Assn. P.R. (pres. 1975-76), P.R. Acad. Arts and Scis., Phi Delta Kappa, Phi Tau Sigma. Home: Parque de Villa Caparra Zuania St G-4 Guaynabo PR 00966 Office: Gen Coun on Edn PO Box 5429 San Juan PR 00906-5429

MATHEW, MARTHA SUE CRYDER, retired education educator; b. Hallsville, Ohio, Feb. 21, 1928; d. Earl and Minnie Ada (Hough) Cryder; m. Guy Wilbur Mathew, Mar. 25, 1949; children: John G., Jeffrey Bruce. BS, Ohio No. U., 1966. Cert. tchr., Ohio. Tchr. Immaculate Conception Sch., Celina, Ohio, 1961-64, Zane Trace Local Sch., Chillicothe, Ohio, 1964-93; ret., 1993; mem. Juvenile Ct. Rev. Bd., Ross County, Chillicothe. Vol. ARC; band mem. Cicleville Pumpkin Show. Named Educator of Yr., Zane Trace Local, Ross County, 1993. Mem. Order Ea. Star (Worthy Matron 1976, 88, Evergreen chpt. 169, Adelphi), Ladies Oriental Shrine (treas., sec., v.p., pres.), Delta Kappa Gamma (com.). Republican. Methodist. Home: 8995 State Route 180 Kingston OH 45644-9585

MATHEW, PORUNELLOOR ABRAHAM, molecular biologist, educator; b. Alleppey, Kerala, India, Dec. 13, 1952; came to U.S., 1987; s. Porunelloor and Mary (Philipose) Abraham; m. Annamma Abraham Mathew, July 30, 1981; children: Anoop, Anisha. BS, U. Kerala, India, 1974; MS, U. Poona, India, 1979, PhD, 1987. Govt. of India fellow Ahmednagar (India) Coll., 1980-81, lectr., 1981-87; Am. Cancer Soc. postdoctoral fellow N.J. Med. Sch., Newark, 1987-88; Robert Welch postdoctoral fellow U. Tex. Southwestern Med. Ctr., Dallas, 1988-90, asst. instr., 1990-91, instr., 1991-92, asst. prof. pathology, 1993—. Author: Current Topics in Cell Biology, 1992; contbr. articles to profl. jours. Mem. AAAS. Avocation: sports.

MATHEWS, ANNE JONES, consultant, library educator and administrator; b. Phila.; d. Edmond Fulton and Anne Ruth (Reichner) Jones; m. Frank Samuel Mathews, June 16, 1951; children: Lisa Anne Mathews-Bingham, David Morgan, Lynne Elizabeth Bietenhader-Mathews, Alison Fulton Sawyer. AB, Wheaton Coll., 1949; MA, U. Denver, 1965, PhD, 1977. Field staff Intervarsity Christian Fellowship, Chgo., 1949-51; interviewer supr. Colo. Market Rsch. Svcs., Denver, 1952-64; reference libr. Oreg. State U., Corvallis, 1965-67; program dir. Ctrl. Colo. Libr. Sys., Denver, 1969-70; inst. dir. U.S. Office of Edn., Inst. Grant, 1979; dir. pub. rels. Grad. Sch. Librarianship and Info. Mgmt. U. Denver, 1970-76, dir. continuing edn., 1977-80, from assoc. prof. to prof., 1977-85; dir. office libr. programs, office ednl. rsch., improvement U.S. Dept. Edn., Washington, 1986-91; dir. Nat. Libr. Edn., Washington, 1992-94; cons. Acad. Ednl. Devel., Washington, 1994—; vis. lectr. Simmons Coll. Sch. Libr. Sci., Boston, 1977; cons. USIA, 1984-85, mem. book and libr. adv. com., 1981-91; faculty assoc. Danforth Found., 1974-84; speaker in field; mem. secondary sch. curriculum com. Jefferson County Pub. Schs., Colo., 1976-78; mem. adv. com. Golden H.S., 1973-77; mem. adv. coun. White House Conf. on Librs. and Info. Svcs., 1991; del. Internat. Fedn. Libr. Assn., 1984-93. Author, editor 6 books; contbr. articles to profl. jours., numerous chpts. to books. Mem. rural librs. and humanities program Colo. planning and resource bd. NEH, 1982-83; bd. mgrs. Friends Found. of Denver Pub. Libr., 1976-82; pres. Faculty Women's Club, Colo. Sch. Mines, 1963-64; bd. dirs. Jefferson County Libr. Found., 1997—. Mem. ALA (visionary leaders com. 1987-89, coun. mem. 1979-83, com on accreditation 1984-85, orientation com. 1974-77, 83-84, pub. rels. com.), Am. Soc. Info. Sci. (pub. rels. chmn. 1971), Mountain Plains Libr. Assn. (profl. devel. com. 1979-80, pub. rels. and publs. com. 1973-75, continuing edn. com. 1973-76), Colo. Libr. Assn. (pres. 1974, bd. dirs. 1973-75, continuing edn. com. 1976-80), Assn. Libr. & Info. Sci. Edn. (communication com. 1978-80, program com. 1977-78), Cosmos Club (Washington). Avocations: travel, reading, antique collecting, mus. & gallery activities. Home: 492 Mount Evans Rd Golden CO 80401-9626

MATHEWS, BARBARA EDITH, gynecologist; b. Santa Barbara, Calif., Oct. 5, 1946; d. Joseph Chesley and Pearl (Cieri) Mathews; AB, U. Calif., 1969; MD, Tufts U., 1972. Diplomate Am. Bd. Ob-Gyn. Intern, Cottage Hosp., Santa Barbara, 1972-73, Santa Barbara Gen. Hosp., 1972-73; resident in ob-gyn Beth Israel Hosp., Boston, 1973-77; clin. fellow in ob-gyn Harvard U., 1973-76, instr., 1976-77; gynecologist Sansum Med. Clinic, Santa Barbara, 1977—; faculty mem. ann. postgrad. course Harvard Med. Sch.; bd. dirs. Sansum Med. Clinic, vice chmn. bd. dirs., 1994-96; dir. ann. postgrad course UCLA Med. Sch. Bd. dirs. Meml. Rehab. Found., Santa Barbara, Channel City Club, Santa Barbara, Music Acad. of the West, Santa Barbara, St. Francis Med. Ctr., Santa Barbara; mem. citizen's continuing edn. adv. council Santa Barbara C.C.; moderator Santa Barbara Cottage Hosp. Cmty. Health Forum. Fellow ACS, Am. Coll. Ob-gyn.; mem. AMA, Am. Soc. Colposcopy and Cervical Pathology (dir. 1982-84), Harvard U. Alumni Assn., Tri-counties Obstet. and Gynecol. Soc. (pres. 1981-82), Phi Beta Kappa. Clubs: Birnam Wood Golf (Santa Barbara). Author: (with L. Burke) Colposcopy in Clinical Practice, 1977; contbg. author Manual of Ambulatory Surgery, 1982. Home: 2105 Anacapa St Santa Barbara CA 93105-3503 Office: 317 W Pueblo St Santa Barbara CA 93105-4355

MATHEWS, DAVID, foundation executive; b. Grove Hill, Ala., Dec. 6, 1935; s. Forrest Lee and Doris (Pearson) M.; m. Mary Chapman, Jan. 24, 1960; children: Lee Ann Mathews Hester, Lucy Mathews Heegaard. A.B., U. Ala., 1958; Ph.D., Columbia U., 1965; LL.D., U. Ala., 1969, Mercer U., 1976; L.H.D., William and Mary Coll., 1976, Med. U. S.C., 1976, Samford U., 1978, Transylvania U., 1978, Stillman Coll., 1980, Miami U., 1982; H.H.D., Birmingham-So. Coll., 1976, Wash. U., St. Louis, 1984; L.H.D., Ctr. Coll., 1985; L.L.D., Ohio Wesleyan U., 1987, Lynchburg Coll., 1987; L.H.D., U. New Eng., 1988. Exec. v.p. U. Ala., 1968-69, pres., 1969-80, prof. history, 1977-81; pres., chief exec. officer Charles F. Kettering Found.,

Dayton, Ohio, 1981—; sec. HEW, Washington, 1975-77; dir. Birmingham br. Fed. Res. Bank of Atlanta, 1970-72, chmn., 1973-75; mem. council SRI Internat., 1978-85; chmn. Council Public Policy Edn., 1980—. Contbr. articles to profl. jours. Trustee Judson Coll., 1968-75, Am. Univs. Field Staff, 1969-80; bd. dirs. Birmingham Festival of Arts Assn., Inc., 1969-75; mem. Nat. Programming Council for Public TV, 1970-73, So. Regional Edn. Bd., 1969-75, Ala. Council on Humanities, 1973-75; vice chmn. Commn. on Future of South, 1974; mem. So. Growth Policies Bd., 1974-75; mem. nat. adv. council Am. Revolution Bicentennial Adminstrn., 1975; mem. Ala. State Oil and Gas Bd., 1975, 77-79; bd. dirs. Acad. Ednl. Devel., 1975—, Ind. Sector, 1982-88, ; chmn. Pres.'s Com. on Mental Retardation, 1975-77; chmn. income security com. aging com. Health Ins. Com. of Domestic Council, 1975-77; bd. govs. nat. ARC, 1975-77; bd. govs., bd. visitors Washington Coll., 1982-86 ; trustee John F. Kennedy Center for Performing Arts, 1975-77, Woodrow Wilson Internat. Center for Scholars, 1975-77; fed. trustee Fed. City Council, 1975-77; bd. dirs. A Presdl. Classroom for Young Americans, Inc., 1975-76; trustee Tchrs. Coll., Columbia U., 1977—, Nat. Found. March of Dimes, 1977-83, Coun. om Learning, 1977-84, Miles Coll., 1978—; mem. nat. adv. bd. Nat. Inst. on Mgmt. Lifelong Edn., 1979-84; mem. Ala. 2000, 1980—; spl. adviser Aspen Inst., 1980-84; mem. bd. trustees Gerald R. Ford Found., 1988—, bd. visitors Mershon Ctr. Ohio State U., 1988-91. Served with U.S. Army, 1959-60. Recipient Nicholas Murray Butler medal Columbia U., 1976, Ala. Adminstr. of Year award Am. Assn. Univ. Adminstrs., 1976, Educator of Year award Ala. Conf. Black Mayors, 1977, Brotherhood award NCCJ, 1979. Mem. Newcomen Soc. Am., Phi Beta Kappa, Phi Alpha Theta, Omicron Delta Kappa, Delta Theta Phi. Home: 6050 Mad River Rd Dayton OH 45459-1508 Office: Charles F Kettering Found 200 Commons Rd Dayton OH 45459-2788*

MATHEWS, EDWIN LEE, retired baseball player. Baseball player Boston Braves, 1952, Milw. Braves, 1953-65; baseball player Atlanta Braves, 1966-67, coach, 1971, mgr., 1972-74; baseball player Detroit Tigers, 1968. Named to Baseball Hall of Fame, 1978, Nat. League All-Star Team, 1953, 55-62; mem. World Series Champions, 1957, 68. Office: c/o Nat Baseball Hall Fame PO Box 570 Cooperstown NY 13326-0570

MATHEWS, HARRY BURCHELL, poet, novelist, educator; b. N.Y.C., Feb. 14, 1930; s. Edward James and Mary (Burchell) M.; m. Niki de Saint Phalle, June 6, 1949 (div. 1964); 2 children; m. Marie Chaix, July 29, 1992. BA cum laude, Harvard Coll., 1952. Faculty Bennington (Vt.) Coll., 1978-80; vis. lectr. Hamilton Coll., Clinton, N.Y., 1979, Columbia Coll., N.Y.C., 1982-83; vis. writer Brown U., Providence, R.I., 1988, Temple U., Phila., 1990, Magdalene Coll., Cambridge, U.K., 1992; founding dir. Shakespeare & Co., Lenox, Mass.; lectr. in field, nat., internat. colls, art ctrs., instns. Author: The Conversions, 1962, Tlooth, 1964, The Sinking of the Odradek Stadium, 1975, Country Cooking and Other Stories, 1980, Cigarettes, 1987, 20 Lines A Day, 1988, The Orchard, 1988, The Way Home, 1988,, The American Experience, 1991, Singular Pleasures, 1993, The Journalist, 1994; (poetry) The Ring, Poems 1956-69, 1970, The Planisphere, 1974, Trial Impressions, 1977, Selected Declarations of Dependence, 1977, Armenian Papers: Poems 1954-84, 1987, Out of Bounds, 1989, A Mid-Season Sky: Poems 1954-89, 1991, (in French) Le savoir des rois: poèmes à perverbes, 1976, Ecrits français, 1990; (essays) Immeasurable Distances: The Collected Essays, 1981; trans.: A Man in a Dream (Georges Perec) 1975, The Laurels of Lake Constance (Marie Chaix) 1977, The Life: Memoirs of a French Hooker (Jeanne Cordelier), 1978, Blue of Noon (Georges Bataille), 1978, Chronicles of Ellis Island (Georges Perec) 1981, The Dust of Suns (Raymond Roussel) 1991, various jour. articles; pub., co-editor Locus Solus, 1960-62; Paris editor The Paris Review, 1989—; contbr. poems, stories to anthologies, articles, criticisms, reviews to profl. jours. Recipient award Fiction Writing Am. Acad. Inst. Arts and Letters, N.Y., 1991; grantee Deutsche Akademische Austausch Dienst, Berlin, 1991; fiction writing grantee NEA, 1982. Mem. Ouvroir de Littérature Potentielle (Paris). Avocations: music making, back-country skiing, hiking, cooking.

MATHEWS, JACK WAYNE, journalist, film critic; b. L.A., Dec. 2, 1939; s. Walter Edwin and Dorothy Helen (Friley) M.; m. Lucinda Lucille Herbert, Nov. 5, 1971; children: Darren Brady, Shelby Kay. BA, San Jose (Calif.) State Coll., 1965; MS, UCLA, 1966. Reporter Riverside (Calif.) Press, 1967-69; mktg. exec. Riverside Raceway, 1969-75; columnist, editor Rochester (N.Y.) Democrat & Chronicle, 1975-78; columnist, film critic Detroit Free Press, 1978-82, USA Today, L.A., 1982-85; columnist L.A. Times, 1985-89, film editor, 1989-91; film critic Newsday, L.I., 1991—; co-host Cinema, PBS, 1995—; juror Montreal World Film Festival, 1993. Author: The Battle of Brazil, 1987. Mem. N.Y. Film Critics Cir. Democrat. Office: NY Newsday 2 Park Ave New York NY 10016-5675 also: Newsday Inc 235 Pinelawn Rd Melville NY 11747-4226

MATHEWS, JESSICA TUCHMAN, policy researcher, columnist; b. N.Y.C., July 4, 1946; d. Lester Reginald and Barbara (Wertheim) Tuchman; m. Colin D. Mathews, Feb. 25, 1978; children: Oliver Max Tuchman, Jordan Henry Morgenthau; stepchildren: Zachary Chase, Hilary Dustin. AB magna cum laude, Radcliffe Coll., 1967; PhD, Calif. Inst. Tech., 1973. Congrl. sci. fellow AAAS, 1973-74; profl. staff mem. Energy and Environment subcom. House Com. on Interior and Insular Affairs, Washington, 1974-75; dir. issues and rsch. Udall Presdl. campaign, 1975-76; dir. Office of Global Issues NSC staff, Washington, 1977-79; mem. editorial bd. The Washington Post, 1980-82; v.p., dir. rsch. The World Resources Inst., Washington, 1982-92; dep. to undersec. for global affairs U.S. Dept. State, Washington, 1993; sr. fellow Coun. on Fgn. Rels., Washington, 1993-97; columnist Washington Post, 1991-97; pres. Carnegie Endowment Internat. Peace, Washington, 1997—; mem. numerous adv. panels Office Tech. Assessment, NAS, AAAS, EPA; bd. dirs. Population Ref. Bur., Washington, 1988-93; adv. com. Air Products Corp. Bd. dirs., Joyce Found., Chgo., 1984-91, Inter-Am. Dialogue, 1991—, Radcliffe Coll., 1992-96, Carnegie Endowment for Internat. Peace, Washington, 1992-97, Rockefeller Bros Fund, N.Y.C., 1992-96, Brookings Instn., Washington, 1995—, Surface Transp. Policy Project. Named Disting. fellow Aspen Inst. Mem. Coun. Fgn. Rels., Fedn. Am. Scientists (bd. dirs. 1985-87, 88-92), Trilateral Commn., Inst. for Internat. Econs. (adv. com.). Democrat. Jewish. Office: Carnegie Endowment Internat Peace 2400 N St NW Washington DC 20037-1153

MATHEWS, JOAN HELENE, pediatrician; b. Manchester, N.H., Feb. 3, 1940; d. John Barnaby and Helen A. Wlodkoski; m. Ernest Stephen Mathews, June 1, 1965; 3 children. BS, U. N.H., 1961; MD, Columbia U., 1965. Diplomate Am. Bd. Pediatrics. Med. intern Roosevelt Hosp., N.Y.C., 1965-66; pediatric resident Babies Hops. Columbia Presbyn. Med. Ctr., N.Y.C., 1966-68, pediatric endocrine fellow Babies Hosp., 1968-70; instr. clin. pediat. Columbia U. Coll. Physicians and Surgeons, N.Y.C., 1973-77; asst. prof. pediat. Cornell U. Med. Coll., N.Y.C., 1977-81; clin. instr. pediat. Harvard Med. Sch., Boston, 1985—; clin. assoc. children's svc. Mass. Gen. Hosp., Boston, 1985—. Fellow Am. Acad. Pediat.; mem. Phi Beta Kappa. Office: 777 Concord Ave Cambridge MA 02138-1053

MATHEWS, JOHN DAVID, electrical engineering educator, research director, consultant; b. Kenton, Ohio, Apr. 3, 1947; s. John Joseph and Mary (Long) M.; m. Monica Susan Mathews; children: John Todd, Debra Juanita, Erinn Robin, Alex David. BS in Physics with honors, Case Western Res. U., 1969, MS in Elec. Engring. and Applied Physics, 1972, PhD in Elec. Engring. and Applied Physics, 1972. Lectr. dept. elec. engring. and applied physics Case Western Res. U., Cleve., 1969-72, asst. prof., 1975-79, assoc. prof., 1979-85, prof., 1985-87; prof. dept. elec. engring. Pa. State U., University Park, 1987—, dir. Communications and Space Scis. Lab. Coll. Engring., 1988-94; dir. Comm. & Space Scis. Lab. Ctr. of Excellence, Coll. Engring., University Park, Pa., 1994—; vis. scientist Nat. Astronomy and Ionosphere Ctr., Case Western Res. U., Arecibo, P.R., 1972-75; adj. asst. prof. dept. elec. engring. Pa. State U., 1978-86, dir. artist-in-residence program Coll. Engring., 1990-92; mem. Arecibo adv. bd. and visiting com. Cornell U., 1989-92, chmn., 1991-92; cons. to engring. svc. group and laser engring. group Lawrence Livermore Nat. Labs., 1979-87; cons. Nat. Astronomy and Ionosphere Ctr. Arecibo Obs., 1980—; cons. engr., 1975—; presenter, speaker numerous profl. meetings. Contbr. articles to profl. jours. including Jour. Atmos. Terr. Physics, Jour. Geophys. Rsch., Radio Sci., Leonardo, Icarus, and others. Fulbright scholar, Sweden, 1996-97. Achievements include research on observations of narrow sodium and narrow ionization layers using lidar, incoherent scatter radar, and rocket-based techniques, on tidal, acoustic-gravity wave, and electrodynamic processes as observed in the motions of ionospheric E region meteoric ion layers, on electron concentration configurations during geomagnetic storms, and on detection and correction of coherent interference in incoherent scatter radar data processing, UHF radar meteor observations, and meteor physics. Office: Pa State U Communications & Space Scis Lab 316 Electrical Engineering E University Park PA 16802-2707

MATHEWS, KENNETH PINE, physician, educator; b. Schenectady, N.Y., Apr. 1, 1921; s. Raymond and Marguerite Elizabeth (Pine) M.; m. Alice Jean Elliott, Jan. 26, 1952 (dec.); children: Susan Kay, Ronald Elliott, Robert Pine; m. Winona Beatrice Rosenburg, Nov. 8, 1975. AB, U. Mich., 1941, MD, 1943. Diplomate Am. Bd. Internal Medicine, Am. Bd. Allergy and Immunology (past. sec.). Intern, asst. resident, resident in medicine Univ. Hosp., Ann Arbor, Mich., 1943-45, 48-50; mem. faculty dept. medicine med. sch. U. Mich., 1950—, assoc. prof. internal medicine, 1956-61, prof., 1961-86, prof. emeritus, 1986—, head div. allergy, 1967-83; adj. mem. Scripps Clinic and Research Found., La Jolla, Calif., 1986—; past chmn. residency rev. com. for allergy and immunology, past chmn. allergy and immunology rsch. com. NIH. Co-author: A Manual of Clinical Allergy, 2d edit, 1967; editor: Jour. Allergy and Clin. Immunology, 1968-72; contbr. numerous articles in field to profl. jours. Served to capt. M.C. AUS, 1946-48. Recipient Disting. Service award Am. Acad. Allergy, 1976; Faculty Disting. Achievement award U. Mich., 1984. Fellow Am. Acad. Allergy (past pres.), A.C.P. (emeritus); mem. Am. Assn. Immunologists (emeritus), Ctrl. Soc. Clin. Rsch. (emeritus), Am. Fedn. Clin. Rsch., Alpha Omega Alpha, Phi Beta Kappa. Home: 7080 Caminito Estrada La Jolla CA 92037-5714

MATHEWS, LINDA MCVEIGH, newspaper editor; b. Redlands, Calif., Mar. 14, 1946; d. Glenard Ralph and Edith Lorene (Humphrey) McVeigh; m. Thomas Jay Mathews, June 15, 1967; children—Joseph, Peter, Katherine. B.A., Radcliffe Coll., 1967; J.D., Harvard U., 1972. Gen. assignment reporter Los Angeles Times, 1967-69, Supreme Ct. corr., 1972-76, corr., Hong Kong, 1977-79, China corr., Peking, 1979-80, op-ed page editor, 1980-81, dep. nat. editor, 1981-84, dep. fgn. editor, 1985-88, editorial writer, 1988-89, editor L.A. Times mag., 1989-92; sr. producer ABC News, 1992-93; nat. editor N.Y. Times, 1993—; corr. Wall St. Jour., Hong Kong, 1976-77; lectr.; freelance writer. Author: (with others) Journey Into China, 1982; One Billion: A China Chronicle, 1983. Mem. Women's Legal Def. Fund, 1972-76; co-founder, pres. Hong Kong Montessori Sch., 1977-79; bd. dirs. Ctr. for Childhood. Mem. Fgn. Corrs. Club Hong Kong. Office: NY Times 229 W 43rd St New York NY 10036-3913

MATHEWS, MARY KATHRYN, retired government official; b. Washington, Apr. 20, 1948; d. T. Odon (dec.) and Kathryn (Augustine) M. Student, Pa. State U., 1966-68; BBA, Am. U., 1970, MBA, 1975. Personnel mgmt. specialist, coordinator coll. recruitment program, GSA, Washington, 1971-75, adminstrv. officer, 1975-78; personnel mgmt. specialist Office of Personnel Mgmt., Washington, 1978; employee devel. specialist Office Sec. Transp., Washington, 1978-80, dep. chief departmental services and spl. programs div., 1980-81; asst. dir. adminstrv. div. Farm Credit Adminstrn., Washington, 1981-84; dir. adminstrv. div. Farm Credit Adminstrn., McLean, Va., 1984-86; chief adminstrv. services div. Farm Credit Adminstrn., McLean, 1987-88; dep. staff dir. for mgmt. U.S. Commn. Civil Rights, Washington, 1988-90, asst. staff dir. for mgmt., 1990-91, asst. staff dir. for congl. affairs, 1991-94, staff dir., 1994-97; ret., 1997; chief spl. programs staff and homebound handicapped employment program GSA, Washington, 1973-74; mem. task force Presdl. mgmt. intern program U.S. Office Pers. Mgmt., Washington, 1977-78; coord. mgmt. devel. program for women Office Sec. Transp., Washington, 1979-81. Vol. mentor, speaker Alexandria Commn. on Women. Mem. Exec. Women in Govt. (treas. 1993-94, v.p. 1994-95, pres. 1995-96, bd. dirs.), Small Agy. Coun. (exec. com. 1990-91, 94—, chmn. micro agy. group 1990-91), Internat. Alliance (bd. dirs. 1996—), Nat. Trust Hist. Preservation, Nat. Assn. Mus. Women in Arts (charter), Delta Gamma (rush advisor 1971-73, pres. bd. dirs. local chpt. house corp. 1972-73). Avocations: antiques, classical music. Home: 405 S Royal St Alexandria VA 22314-3717

MATHEWS, MICHAEL STONE, investment banker; b. Ohio, Oct. 23, 1940; s. Robert Green and Dallas Victoria (Stone) M.; m. Cecilia Aall, May 13, 1967; children: Brandon, Mark, Alexander. AB, Princeton U., 1962; JD, U. Mich., 1965. Bar: N.Y. 1966. Assoc. White & Case, N.Y.C., 1965-69; v.p. Smith Barney Harris Upham & Co., N.Y.C., 1969-77; sr. v.p. Scandinavian Securities Corp., N.Y.C., 1977-79; sr. v.p. DNC Am. Banking Corp., N.Y.C., 1979-89; pres. DNC Capital Corp., 1986-89; ptnr. Bradford Assocs., 1989-92; mng. dir. Westgate Capital Co., 1993—; bd. dirs. Petroleum Geo-Svcs., Holo Pak Technols., Inc., Intermetrics, Ltd., Zombie. Home: 193 Elm Rd Princeton NJ 08540-2520 Office: 41 E 57th St New York NY 10022-1908

MATHEWS, PAUL JOSEPH, allied health educator; b. Washington, Aug. 17, 1944; s. Paul Joseph and Ruth Irene (O'Malley) M.; m. Loretta Jeanne Calvo; children: Heather Marie, Amy Elizabeth, Timothy Hunter. AS, Quinnipiac Coll., 1971, BS, 1975; MPA, U. Hartford, 1978; EdS, U. Mo., Kansas City, 1989. Registered respiratory therapist; lic. respiratory therapist, Kans. Instr., clin. coord. New Britain (Conn.) Gen. Hosp., 1971-74; instr. Quinnipiac Coll., Hamden, Conn., 1974-76; chief respiratory therapy dept. Providence Hosp., Holyoke, Mass., 1974-80, dir. cardiology/neurology, 1977-80, asst. dir. planning, 1980-81; asst. prof. U. Kans. Sch. Allied Health, Kansas City, 1981-88, assoc. prof. respiratory care edn., 1988—, chmn. dept. respiratory care edn., 1981-93, assoc. prof. phys. therapy Grad. Sch., 1992—; U. Kans.; adj. assoc. prof. Ctr. on Aging U. Kans. Med. Ctr., 1987—; hon. prof. U. Costa Rica, San Jose, 1987—; cons. FDA, 1988, NIH, 1988, 89, SUNY, Stony Brook, 1990, USPHS, 1994, 95, 97. Mem. editl. bd. Nursing, 1989—, Neonatal Intensive Care, 1990—, Jour. Respiratory Care Edn., 1993—, Respiratory Therapy, 1988—, Respiratory Therapy Intern, 1991—; author audio tapes in field; contbr. articles to profl. jours., chpts. to books. Recipient Creative Achievement award Puritan-Bennett Corp., 1984, 85, A. Gerald Shapiro award N.J. Soc. for Respiratory Care, 1990; internat. fellow Project HOPE, 1987, 92. Fellow Coll. Critical Care Medicine, Soc. Critical Care Medicine; mem. Am. Assn. Respiratory Care (bd. dirs. 1984-87, v.p. 1987, pres.-elect 1988, pres. 1989, life), Am. Coll. Chest Physicians, Soc. Critical Care Medicine, N.Y. Acad. Scis., Midwest Bioethics Ctr., Sigma Xi, Lambda Beta, Phi Lambda Theta. Avocations: scuba diving, reading, travel. Home: 8844 Hemlock Dr Overland Park KS 66212-2946 Office: U Kans Med Ctr 39th and Rainbow Blvd Kansas City KS 66103

MATHEWS, ROBERT C.H., state agency executive. Chmn. Metro. Nashville Airport Auth. Office: Metro Nashville Airport Authority 1 Terminal Dr Ste 501 Nashville TN 37214-4110*

MATHEWS, RODERICK BELL, lawyer; b. Lawton, Okla., Mar. 12, 1941; s. James Malcolm and Sallie Lee (Bell) M.; m. Karla Kurbjin, Apr. 26, 1980; children: Roderick Bell Jr., Andrew Crittenden, Malcolm Timothy. BA, Hampden Syndey Coll., 1963; LLB, U. Richmond, 1966; postgrad., U. Mich., 1991. Bar: Va. 1966. Assoc. Christian, Barton, Parker, Epps & Brent, Richmond, Va., 1966-72; ptnr. Christian, Barton, Epps, Brent & Chappell, Richmond, 1972-88; sr. v.p., corp. legal and govt. affairs officer Trigon Blue Cross & Blue Shield, 1989-96. Trustee, mem. exec. com. Children's Hosp., Richmond, 1980—. Mem. ABA (ho. of dels. 1984-88, state del. Va. 1988-93, bd. govs. 1993-96, exec. com. 1995-96), Am. Bar Found., Am. Bar Endowment (bd. dirs.), Am. Judicature Soc. (bd. dirs.), Va. Bar Found., Va. State Bar (pres. 1987-88). Avocations: travel, fly fishing, photography, skiing. Office: Mail Drop 02H 2015 Staples Mill Rd # 02H Richmond VA 23230-3108

MATHEWS, SHARON WALKER, artistic director, secondary school educator; b. Shreveport, La., Feb. 1, 1947; d. Arthur Delmar and Nona (Frye) Walker; m. John William (Bill) Mathews, Aug. 14, 1971; children: Rebecca, Elizabeth, Anna. BS, La. State U., 1969, MS, 1971. Dance grad. asst. La. State U., Baton Rouge, 1969-71, choreographer, 1975-76; 6th grade tchr. East Baton Rouge Parish, 1971-72, health phys. edn. tchr., 1972-74; dance instr. Magnet High Sch., Baton Rouge, 1975—; artistic dir. Baton Rouge Ballet Theatre, 1975—; dance dir. Dancers' Workshop, Baton Rouge, 1971—; choreographer Baton Rouge Opera, 1989-94. Named Dance Educator of Yr., La. Alliance for Health, Physical Edn., Recreation and Dance, 1986-87. Mem. Southwestern Regional Ballet Assn. (bd. dirs. 1981—, treas., exec. bd. dirs. 1989-92), La. Assn. for Health, Phys. Edn., Recreation and Dance (dance chairperson 1995). Republican. Baptist. Office: Baton Rouge Ballet Theater 10745 Linkwood Ct Baton Rouge LA 70810-2901

MATHEWS, WALTER GARRET, columnist; b. Covington, Va., Sept. 23, 1949; s. Kenneth G. and Betsy (Waid) M.; m. MaryAnne Stevens, June 24, 1978; children: Colin, Evan. BS in Econs., Va. Poly. Inst. and State U., 1971. News editor/columnist Daily Telegraph, Bluefield, W.Va., 1972-87; columnist Evansville (Ind.) Courier, 1987—. Author: Folks I, 1979, Folks II, 1984, Hey Batta, Batta, 1996. With U.S. Army, 1971-77. Avocations: juggling, coaching boys baseball. Home: 7954 Elna Kay Dr Evansville IN 47715-6210 Office: Evansville Courier 300 E Walnut St Evansville IN 47713-1938

MATHEWSON, CHRISTOPHER COLVILLE, engineering geologist, educator; b. Plainfield, N.J., Aug. 12, 1941; s. George Anderson and Elsa Rae (Shrimpton) M.; m. Janet Marie Olmsted, Nov. 2, 1968; children: Heather Alexis, Glenn George Anderson. BSCE, Case Inst. Tech., 1963; MS in Geol. Engring., U. Ariz., 1965, PhD in Geol. Engring., 1971. Registered profl. engr., Tex., Ariz., geologist, Oreg., Alaska. Officer, lt. Nat. Ocean Survey, 1965-71; prof. Tex. A&M U., College Station, 1981—; cons., speaker in field. Author: Engineering Geology, 1981 (C.P. Holdredge award); contbr. articles to profl. publs. Chmn. College Station Planning and Zoning Commn., 1973-81. Fellow Geol. Soc. Am. (chmn. engring. geology divsn. 1986-87, Meritorious Svc. award 1991); mem. Assn. Engring. Geologists (editor bull. 1981-88, pres. 1988-89, C.P. Holdredge award 1981, F.T. Johnston Svc. award 1995), Am. Geol. Inst. (pres. 1991-92), Nat. Coal Coun., Internat. Assn. Engring. Geologists (chmn. U.S. nat. com. 1995—). Office: Tex A&M Univ Dept Geol College Station TX 77843-3115 *Commitment and dedication to the mission will lead to its successful completion regardless of the odds.*

MATHEWSON, GEORGE ATTERBURY, lawyer; b. Paterson, N.J., Mar. 31, 1935; s. Joseph B. and Christina A. (Atterbury) M.; m. Ann Elizabeth, July 31, 1975; 1 child, James Lemuel. AB cum laude, Amherst Coll., 1957; LLB, Cornell U., 1960; LLM, U. Mich., 1961. Bar: N.Y. 1963. Atty. office spl. legal assts., trial atty. FTC, Washington, 1963-65; regional atty. N.Y. State Dept. Environ. Conservation, Liverpool, 1972-73; pvt. practice, Syracuse, N.Y., 1967-72, 73—; adj. instr. bus. law Onondaga Community Coll., Syracuse, 1979-84. Bd. dirs. South Side Businessmen, 1971-72, 88-91, v.p., 1992, pres., 1993; elder Onondaga Hill Presbn. Ch., 1979, 82-85; dir. Manlius C. of C., 1995. Mem. ABA, ATLA, Fed. Bar Assn., N.Y. State Bar Assn. (state and county bar assn. coms.), Kiwanis (bd. dirs. Onondaga club 1988-89, v.p. 1989, pres. 1989-91). Patentee safety device for disabled airplanes. Office: 4302 S Salina St Syracuse NY 13205-2065 also: 224 Fayette St Manlius NY 13104-1804

MATHEWSON, HUGH SPALDING, anesthesiologist, educator; b. Washington, Sept. 20, 1921; s. Walter Eldridge and Jennie Lind (Jones) M.; m. Dorothy Ann Gordon, 1943 (div. 1952); 1 child, Jane Mathewson Holcombe; m. Hazel M. Jones, 1953 (div. 1978); children: Geoffrey K., Brian E., Catherine E. Brock, Jennifer A. Jehle; m. Judith Ann Mahoney, 1979 (div. 1990). Student, Washburn U., 1938-39; A.B., U. Kans., 1942, M.D., 1944. Intern Wesley Hosp., Wichita, Kans., 1944-45; resident anesthesiology U. Kans. Med. Ctr., Kansas City, 1946-48; pvt. practice specializing in anesthesiology Kansas City, Mo., 1948-69; chief anesthesiologist St. Luke's Hosp., Kansas City, 1953-69; med. dir., sect. respiratory therapy U. Kans. Med. Ctr., 1969-92, assoc. prof., 1969-92, prof., 1975-92, prof. anesthesiology emeritus, respiratory care edn., 1992—; examiner schs. respiratory therapy, 1975—; oral examiner Nat. Bd. Respiratory Therapy; mem. Coun. Nurse Anesthesia Practice, 1974-78; prof. phys. therapy edn., 1993—. Author: Structural Forms of Anesthetic Compounds, 1961, Respiratory Therapy in Critical Care, 1976, Pharmacology for Respiratory Therapists, 1977; contbr. articles to profl. publs.; mem. editorial bd. Anesthesia Staff News, 1975-84; assoc. editor: Respiratory Care, 1980—, cons. editor, 1980—, editor-in-chief Respiratory Mgmt., 1989-92. Trustee Kansas City Mus., Kansas City Conservatory of Music, 1993—. Served to lt. comdr. USNR, 1956. Recipient Bird Lit. prize Am. Assn. Respiratory Therapists, 1976. Mem. Mo. Soc. Anesthesiologists (pres. 1963), Kans. Soc. Anesthesiologists (pres. 1974-77), Kans. Med. Soc. (council), Phi Beta Kappa, Sigma Xi, Lambda Beta (hon.). Office: Kans Med Ctr 39th and Rainbow Blvd Kansas City KS 66160-7604

MATHEWSON, MARK STUART, lawyer, editor; b. Pana, Ill., Mar. 6, 1950; s. Raymond Glenn and Frances (King) M.; m. Barbara Jean Siegert, Oct. 30, 1980; children: Margie, Molly. BA, U. Wis., Madison, 1978; JD, U. Ill., 1984; MA, U. Iowa, 1985. Bar: Ill. 1985. Reporter Ill. Times, Springfield, 1985; asst. prof. Culver Stockton Coll., Canton, Mo., 1986-87; pvt. practice Pana, Ill., 1987-88; mng. editor Ill. State bar Assn., Springfield, 1988—; mem. adv. bd. West Pub. Editors Exchange, Eagan, Minn., 1993-95. Home: RR 1 Box 2 Athens IL 62613-9787 Office: Illinois State Bar Assn Illinois Bar Journal Illinois Bar Ctr Springfield IL 62701

MATHIAS, CHARLES MCCURDY, lawyer, former senator; b. Frederick, Md., July 24, 1922; s. Charles McCurdy and Theresa McElfresh (Trail) M.; m. Ann Hickling Bradford, Nov. 8, 1958; children: Charles Bradford, Robert Fiske. B.A., Haverford Coll., 1944; student, Yale U., 1943-44; LL.B., U. Md., 1949. Bar: Md. 1949, U.S. Supreme Ct. 1954. Asst. atty. gen. of Md., 1953-54; city atty. City of Frederick, 1954-59; mem. Md. Ho. of Dels., 1958, 87th-90th Congresses from 6th Dist. Md., U.S. Senate from Md., 1969-87; ptnr. Jones Day Reavis and Pogue, Washington, 1987-93; chmn. bd. First Am. Bankshares, 1993—; Milton Eisenhower vis. prof. Johns Hopkins U., 1987—. Served from seaman to capt. USNR. Decorated Order of Merit (Federal Republic of Germany), Legion of Honor (France), Order of Orange Nassau (The Netherlands), Order of Brit. Empire (Eng.). Republican. Episcopalian. Office: 1450 G St NW Ste 700 Washington DC 20005-2001

MATHIAS, CHRISTOPHER JOSEPH, physician, educator, researcher, consultant; b. Mangalore, India, Mar. 16, 1949; arrived in the U.K., 1972; s. Elias Salvadore and Hilda Frances (Lobo) M.; m. Rosalind Margaret Jolleys, July 31, 1977; children: Sarah, James, Timothy. MB, BChir, Bangalore U., India, 1972; PhD, U. Oxford, Eng., 1976; DSc, U. London, 1995. Hon. rsch. officer, registrar Dept. Neurology, Oxford, 1972-76; sr. house officer dept. medicine Royal Postgrad. Med. Sch., London, 1976-77; registrar dept. medicine, Portsmouth and renal unit Southampton (Eng.) U., 1977-79; Wellcome Trust sr. clin. rsch. fellow St. Mary's Hosp. and Med. Sch., London, 1979-84; Wellcome Trust sr. lectr. St. Mary's Hosp. and Med. Sch. and Nat. Hosp. Inst. Neurology, London, 1984-91; prof. neurovascular medicine St. Mary's/Imperial Coll., Sch. Medicine, Nat. Hosp., Inst. Neune, 1991—; chmn. rsch. com. World Fedn. Neurology on Autonomic Disorders, 1993—; chmn. sci. panel European Fedn. Neurol. Soc., 1994—; guest lectr. Thailand Neurol. Soc., 1995; Nimmo vis. prof. U. Adelaide , Australia, 1996; mem. sci. com. Internat. Spinal Rsch. Trust, 1996. Co-editor (with M. Weber) Book on Mild Hypertension, 1984, (with P. Sever) Concepts in Hypertension, 1989, (with Sir Roger Bannister) Autonomic Failure: A Textbook of Clinical Disorders of the Autonomic Nervous System, 3d edit., 1992; contbr. chpts to books and articles to profl. jours.; found. editor-in-chief Clin. Autonomic Rsch. Official Jour. Am. Autonomic Soc., Brit. Clin. Autonomic Rsch. Soc., 1991—; mem. editl. bd. various internat. med./sci. jours. Named Rhodes scholar U. Oxford, 1972-75, Dr. J. Thomas lectr. St. Johns Med. Coll., U. Bangalore, 1988, Lord Florey Meml. lectr. U. Adelaide, 1991, Sir Hugh Cairns Meml. lectr., Adelaide, 1996; recipient Prof. Ruitinga award and vis. professorship U. Amsterdam, The Netherlands, 1988. Fellow Royal Coll. Physicians (London, Brit. Petroleum lectr. 1992), Royal Soc. Medicine; mem. Am. Antonomic Soc. (bd. dirs.), Royal Coll. Physicians and Surgeons (licentiate Glasgow and Edninburg), Assn. Physicians Gt. Britain, Physiol. Soc., Assn. Brit. Neurologists, Brit. Pharm. Soc., Clin. Autonomic Rsch. Soc. (chmn. 1987-90, found. sec. 1982-86), Brit. European and Internat. Hypertension Soc., Royal Instn. Movement Disorders Soc. Avocations: gardening, watching cricket and football, observing human and canine behavior. Home: Meadowcroft West End Ln, Stoke Poges Bucks SL2 4NE, England Office: St Marys Hosp Imperial Coll Sch Medicine, Neurovascular Medi Unit Praed St, London W2 1NY, England

MATHIAS, EDWARD JOSEPH, merchant banker; b. Camden, N.J., Nov. 11, 1941; s. Edward Joseph and Zelma (Pollack) M.; m. Ann Robyn Rafferty, Aug. 3, 1968; 1 child, Ellen Susannah. BA, U. Pa., 1964; MBA, Harvard U., 1971. Mng. dir. T. Rowe Price Assocs., Inc., Balt., 1971-93; mng. dir., co-founder Carlyle Group Merchant Bank, Washington, 1994—; bd. dirs. Ovation, Inc. U.S. Office Supply Pathogenesis, SIRROM Capital; spl. ltd. ptnr. Trident Capital. Bd. overseers Sch. Arts and Scis. U. Pa.; chmn. bd. visitors Kogod Sch. Bus. Adminstrn., Am. Univ. Lt. USN, 1964-69. Mem. Harvard Club, Univ. Club (N.Y.C.), Columbia Country Club (Chevy Chase, Md.), Robert Trent Jones Golf Club (Manassas, Va.), Coral Beach Club (Bermuda), The Brook (N.Y.C.), Ctr. club (Balt.), Met. Club, Talbot Country Club (Easton, Md.). Republican. Home: 5120 Cammack Dr Bethesda MD 20816-2902 Office: The Carlyle Group 1001 Pennsylvania Ave NW Washington DC 20004-2505

MATHIAS, JOSEPH SIMON, metallurgical engineer, consultant; b. Bombay, India, Oct. 28, 1925; came to U.S., 1948, naturalized, 1954; s. Pascal Lawrence and Dulcine Applina (De Souza) M.; m. Anna Katherine Elliott, Nov. 10, 1956. BS, U. Bombay, 1944, BA, 1946; PhD, Lehigh U., Bethlehem, Pa., 1954; M in Engring., U. Calif., Berkeley, 1951. Rsch. assoc. Lehigh U., 1951-54; chief metallurgist Superior Metals, Inc., Bethlehem, Pa., 1954-56; mgr. process metall. rsch. Foote Mineral Co., Easton, Pa., 1956-59; mgr. materials rsch., then group mgr. physics and materials Sperry Univac Co., Blue Bell, Pa., 1959-67; dir. rsch. Sperry Univac Co., 1967-79, dir. mfg. and systems hardware rsch., 1979-86, v.p. rsch. and tech., 1986-93; program dir. NSF, Washington; cons. Nat. Inst. Stds. and Tech./Advanced Tech. Program, Gaithersburg, Md., 1993—; mem. program com. Internat. Magnetic Conf., 1969, 70; cons. in field. Author. Fellow Am. Inst. Chemists, N.Y. Acad. Scis.; mem. IEEE (sr.), Coun. Arts and Sci. Franklin Inst., Riverton Country Club, Rotary (bd. dirs.), Sigma Xi. Lodge: Rotary (dir.). Patentee in field. Home: 105 Thomas Ave Riverton NJ 08077-1134 Office: NIST/ATP Bldg A 101 Rm 309 Gaithersburg MD 20899

MATHIAS, LESLIE MICHAEL, electronic manufacturing company executive; b. Bombay, Dec. 17, 1935; came to U.S., 1957; s. Paschal Lawrence and Dulcine (D'Souza) M.; m. Vivian Mae Doolittle, Dec. 16, 1962. BSc, U. Bombay, 1957; BS, San Jose (Calif.) State U., 1961. Elec. engr. Indian Standard Metal, Bombay, 1957; sales engr. Bleisch Engring. and Tool, Mt. View, Calif., 1958-60; gen. mgr. Meadows Terminal Bds., Cupertino, Calif., 1961-63; prodn. mgr. Sharidon Corp., Menlo Park, Calif., 1963-67, Videx Corp., Sunnyvale, Calif., 1967-68, Data Tech. Corp., Mt. View, 1968-69; pres. L.G.M. Mfg., Inc., Mt. View, 1969-83; pvt. practice plating cons. Los Altos, Calif., 1983-87; materials mgr. Excel Cirs., Santa Clara, Calif., 1987-91, 93—, acct. mgr., 1991-93, materials mgr., 1993—. Social chmn. Internat. Students, San Jose, 1958-59. Mem. Nat. Fedn. Ind. Bus., Calif. Cirs. Assn., Better Bus. Bur., Purchasing Assn., U.S. C. of C. Roman Catholic. Avocations: computer hacker, electronics, reading, med. jours. Home: 20664 Mapletree Pl Cupertino CA 95014-0449

MATHIAS, REUBEN VICTOR (VIC MATHIAS), real estate executive, investor; b. Copperas Cove, Tex., Mar. 5, 1926; s. Alvin E. and Ella L. (Teinert) M.; m. Helen I. Thoresen, Jan. 28, 1950; children: Mona, Mark, Matt. B.B.A., U. Tex., 1950. Cert. Chamber Exec. Dist. mgr. W.A. Shaeffer Pen Co., Youngstown, Ohio, 1950-51; mgr. Cen-Tex Fair, Temple, Tex., 1951-52; dir. info. Tex. Assn. Soil Conservation Suprs., Temple, 1952-53; mgr. membership dept. Austin (Tex.) C. of C., 1953-56, chief exec. officer, 1956-82; dir. corp. devel. Hardin Corp., Austin, 1983-86; real estate and investments, 1987-92; pres. Tex. Travel Industry Assn., Austin, 1992-96; v.p. Austin Tours, Inc.; sec. Longhorn Caverns, Inc.; chmn. bd., instr. Inst. for Orgn. Mgmt., U. Houston. Contbr. monthly editorial Thoughts While Thinking to Austin Mag., 1961-82. Pres. Austin USO Council, 1958-59; v.p. Beautify Tex. Council, 1975-77; founding pres. Discover Tex. Assn., 1969-70; chmn. Central Tex. Blood Donor Fund, 1979. Served with U.S. Army, 1944-46. Mem. Am. C. of C. Execs., Tex. C. of C. Execs. (pres. 1965), Rotary (pres. Austin 1985-86). Lutheran. Home: 3100 Mistywood Cir Austin TX 78746-7861 *You can find happiness only by giving it to others. Much of my life has been devoted to community building through voluntary action. The fact that my career has allowed me to stay in one community has made it possible for me to make and carry out long-term plans, both for the community and personally.*

MATHIAS, SEAN GERARD, author, director; b. Swansea, South Wales, U.K., Mar. 14, 1956; s. John Frederick and Anne Josephine (Harding) M. Author: (plays) Cowardice, 1983, Infidelities, 1985, A Prayer for Wings, 1985, Poor Nanny, 1989, Swansea Boys, 1990, Language, 1991, (film) The Lost Language of Cranes, 1990, (novel) Manhattan Mourning, 1988; dir. (plays) Exceptions, 1988, Bent, 1990, Talking Heads, 1991, Noel and Gertie, 1991, Uncle Varya, 1991, Indiscretions, 1995 (Tony nomination - Direction of a Play). Bd. mem. West End Cares, 1990; trustee Ian Charleson Trust, London, 1990. Recipient Gold medal Lamda, 1972, Fringe First award Edinburgh Festival, 1985. Office: Jonathan Altaras Assocs Ltd, 2, Goodwins Ct, London WC2 4LL, England*

MATHIES, ALLEN WRAY, JR., physician, hospital administrator; b. Colorado Springs, Colo., Sept. 23, 1930; s. Allen W. and Esther S. (Norton) M.; m. Lewise Austin, Aug. 23, 1956; children: William A., John N. BA, Colo. Coll., 1952; MS, Columbia U., 1956, PhD., 1958; MD, U. Vt., 1961. Rsch. assoc. U. Vt., Burlington, 1957-61; intern L.A. County Hosp., 1961-62; resident in pediatrics L.A. Gen. Hosp., 1962-64; asst. prof. pediatrics U. So. Calif., L.A., 1964-68, assoc. prof., 1968-71, prof., 1971—, assoc. dean, 1969-74, interim dean, 1974-75, dean, 1975-85, head physician Communicable Disease Svc., 1964-75; pres., CEO Huntington Meml. Hosp., Pasadena, Calif., 1985-94; pres., CEO So. Calif. Healthcare Sys., Pasadena, 1992-95, pres. emeritus, 1995—; bd. dirs. Pacific Mut. Contbr. articles to med. jours. Bd. dirs. Occidental Coll. With U.S. Army, 1953-55. Mem. Am. Acad. Pediatrics, Infectious Disease Soc. Am., Am. Pediatric Soc., Soc. Pediatric Rsch. Republican. Episcopalian. Home: 314 Arroyo Dr South Pasadena CA 91030-1623 Office: Huntington Meml Hosp PO Box 7013 Pasadena CA 91109-7013

MATHIESON, ANDREW WRAY, investment management executive; b. Pitts., June 11, 1928; s. Andrew Russell and Margaret (Wray) M.; m. Helen Fricke, Dec. 5, 1953; children—Margaret Adele Conver, Andrew Fricke, Peter Ferris. B.S. in Mech. Engring, Bucknell U., 1950; M.S. in Indsl. Adminstrn, Carnegie-Mellon U., 1952. With elevator div. Westinghouse Electric Corp., 1955-63; dist. mgr. Westinghouse Electric Corp., Cleve., 1960-62; asst. group v.p. constrn. group Westinghouse Electric Corp., Pitts., 1962-63; with T. Mellon and Sons, Pitts., 1963-71; v.p., gov. T. Mellon and Sons., 1967-71; v.p. Richard K. Mellon and Sons, Pitts., 1971-78; exec. v.p. Richard K. Mellon and Sons, 1978—; dir. Gen. Re Corp, Gen. Re Europe Ltd., Mellon Nat. Corp. Trustee, vice-chmn. Richard King Mellon Found., R.K. Mellon Family Found.; bd. dirs. St. Margaret Meml. Hosp., Pitts., 1966—, pres., 1976-81; exec. com. Allegheny Conf. Cmty. Devel., 1976. With USNR, 1952-55. Episcopalian. Clubs: Duquesne (Pitts.) (bd. dirs. 1986, pres. 1989), Fox Chapel Golf (Pitts.) (dir. 1974); Laurel Valley Golf (Ligonier, Pa.), Rolling Rock (Ligonier, Pa.) (v.p., gov.); University (N.Y.C.). Home: 14 The Trillium Pittsburgh PA 15238-1929 Office: Richard K Mellon & Sons 500 Grant St Ste 4106 Pittsburgh PA 15219-2502

MATHILE, CLAYTON LEE, corporate executive; b. Portage, Ohio, Jan. 11, 1941; s. Wilbert and Helen (Good) M.; m. Mary Ann Maas, July 7, 1962; children: Cathy, Tim, Mike, Tina, Jennie. BA, Ohio No. U., 1962, DBA (hon.), 1991; postgrad., Bowling Green State U., 1964. Acct. GM, Napoleon, Ohio, 1962-63; acct. Campbell Soup Co., Napoleon, 1963-65, buyer, 1965-67, purchasing agt., 1967-70; gen. mgr. The Iams Co., Dayton, Ohio, 1970-75, v.p., 1975-80, chief exec. officer, 1980-90, chmn., 1990—, also dir.; mem. Pet Food Inst.; bd. dirs. Midwest Group, Cin., Bush Bros. Co., Knoxville, Tenn. Author: A Business Owner's Perspective on Outside Boards. Trustee Chaminade-Julienne High Sch., Dayton, 1987—, U. Dayton; mem. adv. bd. coll. bus. Ohio No. U., Ada, 1987—, also trustee. Named Best of Best Ctr. for Values Rsch., Houston, 1987. Mem. Am. Mgmt. Assn., Am. Agt. Assn. Roman Catholic. Avocations: traveling, swimming, golf. Officer: The Iams Company 7250 Poe Ave Dayton OH 45414-2572*

MATHIS, JACK DAVID, advertising executive; b. La Porte, Ind. Nov. 27, 1931; s. George Anthony and Bernice (Bennethum) M.; student U. Mo., 1950-52; BS, Fla. State U., 1955; m. Phyllis Dene Hoffman, Dec. 24, 1971; children: Kane Cameron, Jana Dene. With Benton & Bowles, Inc., 1955-56; owner Jack Mathis Advt., 1956—; cons. films, including That's Action!, 1977, Great Movie Stunts: Raiders of the Lost Ark, 1981, The Making of Raiders of the Lost Ark, 1981, An American Legend: The Lone Ranger, 1981; Heroes and Sidekicks: Indiana Jones and the Temple of Doom, 1984, The Republic Pictures Story, 1991, The Making of The Quiet Man, 1992, Roy Rogers: King of the Cowboys, 1992, Cliffhangers: Adventures from the Thrill Factory, 1993, The Making of Sands of Iwo Jima, 1993, Gene Autry: Melody of the West, 1994. Mem. U.S. Olympic Basketball Com. Recipient citation Mktg. Research Council N.Y., inducted Ill. Basketball Hall of Fame. Mem. Alpha Delta Sigma. Author: Valley of the Cliffhangers, Republic Confidential, Valley of the Cliffhangers Supplement. Office: PO Box 3580 Barrington IL 60011-3580

MATHIS, JOHN PRENTISS, lawyer; b. New Orleans, Feb. 10, 1944; s. Robert Prentess and Lena (Horton) M.; m. Karen Elizabeth McHugh, May 31, 1966; children: Lisa Lynne Kirkpatrick, Andrew P. BA magna cum laude, So. Meth. U., Dallas, 1966; JD cum laude, Harvard U., 1969. Bar: Calif. 1970, D.C. 1975, U.S. Ct. Appeals (D.C. cir.) 1972, U.S. Ct. Appeals (5th cir.) 1975, U.S. Ct. Appeals (3rd cir.) 1980, U.S. Supreme Ct. 1982. Assoc. Latham & Watkins, Los Angeles, 1969-71; spl. asst. to gen. counsel, FPC, Washington, 1971-72; gen. counsel Calif. Pub. Utilities Commn., San Francisco, 1972-74; assoc. Baker & Botts, Washington, 1974-76, ptnr., 1976-92; ptnr. Hogan & Hartson, Washington, 1992—. Mem. ABA (litigation sect., chmn. energy litigation com. 1985-89, div. dir. 1989-90, chmn. legis. com. 1990-94, rep. to coord. group energy law 1992—), Fed. Energy Bar Assn., Harvard U. Law Sch. Assn. D.C. (past pres.). Republican. Methodist. Clubs: Harvard U., Congl. Country, Met. (Washington). Home: 9400 Turnberry Dr Potomac MD 20854 Office: Hogan & Hartson 555 13th St NW Ste 1200W Washington DC 20004-1109

MATHIS, JOHNNY, singer; b. San Francisco, Sept. 30, 1935; s. Clem and Mildred Mathis. Student, San Francisco State Coll. Recordings include: Wonderful Wonderful, It's Not for Me to Say, Chances Are, Someone, Twelfth of Never, A Certin Smile, Wild Is The Wind, Misty, Maria, The Best of Everything, Small World; albums include: Johnny Mathis, 1956, Wonderful, Wonderful, 1957, Warm, 1957, Good Night, Dear Lord, 1958, Johnny's Greatest Hits, 1958, Swing Softly, 1958, Merry Christmas, 1958, Open Fire, Two Guitars, 1959, More Johnny's Greatest Hits, 1959, Heavenly, 1959, Faithfully, 1959, The Rhythms and Ballads of Broadway, 1960, Johnny's Mood, 1960, I'll Buy You a Star, 1961, Portrait of Johnny, 1961, Live It Up, 1962, Rapture, 1962, Johnny's Newest Hits, 1963, Johnny, 1963, Romantically, 1963, The Sounds of Christmas, 1963, I'll Search My Heart, 1964, Tender is the Night, 1964, The Wonderful World of Make Believe, 1964, This is Love, 1964, Ole, 1965, The Sweetheart Tree, 1965, So Nice, 1966, Sings, 1967, Up Up and Away, 1967, Love is Blue, 1968, Those Were the Days, 1968, People, 1969, The Impossible Dream, 1969, Love Theme/Romeo & Juliet, 1969, Give Me Your Love For Christmas, 1969, Raindrops Keep Fallin' On My Head, 1970, Close To You, 1970, Bacharach & Kaempfert, 1970, Love Story, 1970, You've Got a Friend, 1971, The First Time Ever I Saw Your Face, 1972, Song Sung Blue, 1972, Me and Mrs. Jones, 1973, Killing Me Softly With Her Song, 1973, I'm Coming Home, 1973, The Heart of a Woman, 1974, Feelings, 1975, When Will I See You Again, 1975, I Only Have Eyes for You, 1976, Hold Me, Thrill Me, Kiss Me, 1977, You Light Up My Life, 1978, That's What Friends Are For, 1978, The Best Days Of My Life, 1979, Mathis Magic, 1979, Different Kinda Different, 1980, Friends in Love, 1982, A Special Part of Me, 1984, Johnny Mathis Live, 1984, Right From the Heart, 1985, Christmas Eve With Johnny Mathis, 1986, The Hollywood Musicals, 1986, Once In A While, 1988, In The Still of the Night, 1989, In a Sentimental Mood: Mathis Sings Ellington, 1990, Better Together, 1991, How do you Keep the Music Playing, 1992, Music of Johnny Mathis: A Personal Collection, 1993, Open Fire, Two Guitars, 1994, (with others) Johnny Mathis, 1996; appeared in films Lizzie, 1957, A Certain Smile, 1958; tours of Europe, Africa, Australia, S.Am., Orient, Can., British Isles; rec. artist, Columbia Records, Mercury Records, 1964-67. Avocations: cooking, golf. Office: care Rojon Prodns Inc PO Box 2066 Burbank CA 91507-2066 also: Columbia Records 2100 Colorado Ave Santa Monica CA 90404*

MATHIS, LUSTER DOYLE, college administrator, political scientist; b. Gainesville, Ga., May 5, 1936; s. Luster and Fay Selena (Wingo) M.; m. Rheba Burch, June 5, 1958; children—Douglas James, Deborah Jane. A.B., Berry Coll., 1958; M.A., U. Ga., 1958, Ph.D. (Univ. Alumni Found. fellow), 1966. Asst. prof. polit. sci. Brenau Coll., Gainesville, 1960-61; asso. prof. Calif. Baptist Coll., 1961-62, Belmont Coll., Nashville, 1962-64; asso. prof., head dept. polit. sci. W.Ga. Coll., Carrollton, 1965-68; prof. W.Ga. Coll., 1969-75, head dept., 1969-71, chmn. div. grad. studies, 1970-73; assoc. dean, 1972-75; research asso., asst. editor Papers of Thomas Jefferson Princeton U., 1968-69; v.p., dean of coll. Berry Coll., Mt. Berry, Ga., 1975-93, v.p. acad. affairs, 1993—; cons. Citizens Com. on Ga. Gen. Assembly. Co-author: Courts as Political Instruments, 1970. Mem. Ga. Democratic Charter Commn., 1974-75; mem. consumer adv. com. Floyd Med. Center, 1978-80. Nat. Hist. Publs. Commn. fellow, 1968-69. Mem. Am. Assn. Higher Edn., Am. Conf. Acad. Deans, Ga. Polit. Sci. Assn. (pres. 1968-69), Conf. Acad. Deans of the So. States, Kiwanis. Democrat. Baptist. Office: Berry Coll Dept Acad Affairs Mount Berry GA 30149

MATHIS, MARK JAY, lawyer; b. N.Y.C., Aug. 25, 1947; s. Meyer and Beulah (Nechemias) M.; m. Marylin Gail Goodman, Aug. 14, 1971; children: Alison Leigh, Brian Todd. BS, MIT, 1969; JD, U. Pa., 1972. Bar: D.C. 1973. Assoc. Arent, Fox, Kintner, Plotkin & Kahn, Washington, 1972-75; minority counsel Com. on D.C. U.S. Ho. of Reps., 1975-76; atty. Chesapeake & Potomac Telephone Cos., Washington, 1977-81, gen. atty., 1982-83, v.p., gen. counsel, 1984-89; v.p., assoc. gen. counsel Bell Atlantic Network Svcs., Washington, 1988-89, v.p., gen. counsel, 1990-91; v.p., dep. gen. counsel, sec. Bell Atlantic Corp., Phila., 1992; v.p., gen. counsel Bell Atlantic NSI, Arlington, Va., 1993—. Office: Bell Atlantic NSI 8th Fl 1320 N Court House Rd Fl 8 Arlington VA 22201-2508

MATHIS, SHARON BELL, author, elementary educator, librarian; b. Atlantic City, Feb. 26, 1937; d. John Willie and Alice Mary (Frazier) Bell; m. Leroy F. Mathis, July 11, 1957 (div. Jan. 1979); children: Sherie, Stacy, Stephanie. B.A., Morgan State Coll., 1958; M.L.S., Catholic U. Am., 1975. Interviewer Children's Hosp. of D.C., Washington, 1958-59; tchr. Holy Redeemer Elementary Sch., Washington, 1959-65, Charles Hart Jr. High Sch., Washington, 1965-72; spl. edn. tchr. Stuart Jr. High Sch., Washington, 1972-74; librarian Benning Elementary Sch., Washington, 1975-76; librarian Friendship Ednl. Ctr. (now Patricia R. Harris Ednl. Ctr.), 1976-95, ret., 1995; writer-in-charge children's lit. div. D.C. Black Writers Workshop; writer-in-residence Howard U., 1972-73. Author: Brooklyn Story, 1970, Sidewalk Story, 1971 (Council on Interracial Books for Children award 1970), Teacup Full of Roses, 1972 (Outstanding Book of Yr. award New York Times 1972), Ray Charles, 1973 (Coretta Scott King award 1974), Listen for the Fig Tree, 1974, The Hundred Penny Box, 1975 (Boston Globe-Horn Book Honor book 1975, Newbery Honor Book 1976), Cartwheels, 1977, Red Dog Blue Fly: Football Poems, 1991 (Children's Book of Yr. award Bank St. Coll. 1992), Red Dog Blue Fly: An American Bookseller (Pick of the List 1995), Running Girl: The Diary of Ebonee Rose, 1997. Mem. bd. advisers lawyers com. D.C. Commn. on Arts, 1972. Nominated Books for Brotherhood list NCCJ, 1970; recipient D.C. Assn. Sch. Librs. award 1976, Arts and Humanities award Archdiocese of Washington Black Secretariat, 1978; Weekly Reader Book Club fellow Bread Loaf Writers Conf., 1970, MacDowell Colony fellow, 1978. Roman Catholic. *My success is due to the glorious African blood which flows throughout my body—and to the dignity, intelligence, strength, pride, efforts, and faith of my very creative parents—and all other Black people who have helped me.*

MATHIS, TERANCE, professional football player; b. Detroit, June 7, 1967. Student, U. N.Mex. Wide receiver, kick returner N.Y. Jets, 1990-93, Atlanta Falcons, 1994—. Named to Sporting News Coll. All-Am. 1st Team, 1989; selected to Pro Bowl, 1994. Office: c/o Atlanta Falcons One Falcon Pl Suwanee GA 30174*

MATHIS, WILLIAM LOWREY, lawyer; b. Jackson, Tenn., Dec. 19, 1926; s. Harry Fletcher and Syrene (Lowrey) M.; m. Marilyn Jayne Cason, Sept. 10, 1949; children: Amanda Jayne Miller, Amy Susan Webb, Peter Andrew, Perry Alexander, Anne Lowrey Mandigo. B.M.E., Duke U., 1947; J.D., George Washington U., 1951. Bar: D.C. bar 1951, Fla. bar 1972, Va. bar 1977. Examiner U.S. Patent Office, 1947-52; mem. firm Swecker & Mathis, Washington, 1952-61, Burns, Doane, Swecker & Mathis, Alexandria, Va., 1961—; adj. prof. law Georgetown U. Law Center, 1974—. Co-author: Trademark Litigation in the Trademark Office and Federal Courts, 1977; also chpt. in Handbook of Modern Marketing, 2d edit., 1986. Mem. Am., D.C. bar assns., Am. Intellectual Property Law Assn., Order of Coif. Roman Catholic. Home: 3709 Chanel Rd Annandale VA 22003-2024 Office: George Mason Bldg Washington and Prince Sts Alexandria VA 22313

MATHISON, IAN WILLIAM, chemistry educator, academic dean; b. Liverpool, Eng., Apr. 17, 1938; came to U.S., 1963; s. William and Grace (Almond) M.; m. Mary Ann Gordon, July 20, 1968; children: Mark W., Lisa A. B. Pharm., U. London, 1960, Ph.D., 1963, D. Sci., 1976. Lic. pharmacist, Gt. Britain. Research assoc. U. Tenn. Ctr. for Health Scis., Memphis, 1963-65, asst. prof., 1965-68, assoc. prof., 1968-72, prof., 1972-76; medicinal chemistry prof. Ferris State U., Big Rapids, Mich., 1977—, dean, prof., 1977—; external examiner U. Sci., Malaysia, 1978-79; mem. Mich. dept. Mental Health Pharmacy Facilities Rev. Panel, Lansing, 1978-90, Quality Assurance Commn., 1979-90; cons. in field. Mem. editorial bd.: Jour. Pharm. Sci., 1981-86 ; contbr. articles to profl. jours.; sr. inventor, patentee in field. Marion Labs. awardee, 1965-74; NSF grantee, 1968-72; Beecham Co. grantee, 1974-79. Fellow Royal Inst. Chemistry, Royal Soc. Chemistry; mem. Am. Pharm. Soc., Am. Chem. Soc., Am. Assn. Coll. Pharmacy (bd. dirs. 1988-90), Nat. Assn. Retail Druggists (edn. adv. com. 1989-94), Royal Pharm. Soc. Gt. Britain, Nat. Assn. Chain Drug Stores (ednl. adv. com. 1993—). Home: 820 Osborn Cir Big Rapids MI 49307-2536 Office: Ferris State U 901 S State St Big Rapids MI 49307-2251

MATHOG, ROBERT HENRY, otolaryngologist, educator; b. New Haven, Apr. 13, 1939; s. William and Tiby (Gans) M.; m. Deena Jane Rabinowitz, June 14, 1964; children: Tiby, Heather, Lauren, Jason. AB, Dartmouth Coll., 1960; MD, NYU, 1964. Diplomate Am. Bd. Facial Plastic and Reconstructive Surgery. Intern Duke Hosp., Durham, N.C., 1964-65; resident surgery Duke Hosp., 1965-66, resident otolaryngology, 1966-69; practice medicine, specializing in otolaryngology Mpls., 1971-77, Detroit, 1977—; chief of otolaryngology Hennepin County Med. Center, Mpls., 1972-77; asst. prof. U. Minn., 1971-74, asso. prof., 1974-77; prof., chmn. dept. otolaryngology Wayne State U. Sch. Medicine, 1977—; chief otolaryngology Hennepin County Hosp., Mpls., 1972-77, Harper-Grace Hosps., Detroit, 1977—, Detroit Receiving Hosp., 1977-92; cons. staff VA Hosp., Allen Park, Minn., 1977—, Children's Hosp., Detroit, 1977—, Hutzel Hosp., Detroit, 1966; mem. adv. coun. Nat. Inst. Deaf and Other Communicable Disorders NIH, 1992-96; chief otolaryngology, head and neck surgery June Hosp., 1994-95. Author: Otolaryngology Clinics of North America, 1976, Textbook of Maxillofacial Trauma, 1983; editor in chief Videomed. Edn. Systems, 1972-75; editor: Atlas of Craniofacial Trauma, 1992; contbr. articles to med. jours. Bd. dirs. Bexer County Hearing Soc., 1969-71; adv. coun. WIDCB, 1993. Maj. USAF, 1969-71. Recipient Valentine Mott medal for proficiency in anatomy, 1961, Recognition award Wayne State Bd. Govs. Faculty, 1993; Deafness Rsch. Found. grantee, 1979-81, NIH grantee, 1986, 92, 96. Fellow ACS, Am. Acad. Otolaryngology, Head and Neck Surgery (Cert. award 1976, Cert. of Appreciation 1978), Am. Soc. Head and Neck Surgery, Triological Soc. (v.p. 1995-96), Am. Otol. Soc., Am. Acad. Facial Plastic and Reconstructive Surgery (v.p. 1980), Am. Neurotology Soc.; mem. AMA, Am. Laryngol. Soc. (coun. 1994—), Am. Laryngol. Assn., Mich. Med. Soc., Am. Head and Neck Soc., Soc. Univ. Otolaryngologists (pres. 1995), Assn. Acad. Depts. Otolaryngology, Assn. Rsch. Otolaryngology (pres. 1981). Home: 27115 Wellington Rd Franklin MI 48025-1329 Office: 27177 Lahser Rd Ste 203 Southfield MI 48034-8468 Also: Wayne State U Sch Med 540 E Canfield St Detroit MI 48201-1928

MATHUES, THOMAS OLIVER, retired automobile company executive; b. Dayton, Ohio, Jan. 26, 1923; s. John Leslie and Florence (Killen) M.; m. Patricia McFarland, May 20, 1944 (dec. Feb. 1992); children: Thomas P., Rebecca, John, Jennifer; m. Mary Nell Galloway, Apr. 15, 1993. Student, Grove City Coll., 1944-45, U. Ill., 1945-46; B.M.E., Gen. Motors Inst., 1947; postgrad., Harvard U. Bus. Sch., 1976. With Inland div. Gen. Motors Corp., Dayton, 1940-78; gen. mgr. Inland div. Gen. Motors Corp., 1966-78; v.p. mfg. staff Gen. Motors, Warren, Mich., 1978-81, v.p. current engring. and mfg. services staff, 1981-85. Served with USNR, 1944-46. Mem. Soc. Automotive Engrs., Commonwealth Yacht Club (Grand Rivers, Ky.), Country Club of Paducah (Ky.), Phi Gamma Delta. Mem. Christian Ch. (Disciples of Christ). Patentee in field. Home: 1930 Sledd Creek Rd Gilbertsville KY 42044-8814

MATHUR, RUPA AJWANI, former state official, risk management consultant; b. Khairpur, Sind, India, Nov. 2, 1939; came to U.S., 1980; d. Menghraj Lalchand and Giani Ajwani; m. Ramesh Saran Mathur, Mar. 2, 1967; children: Sanjay Saran, Seema. BA with honors, Bombay U., 1962, LLB, 1965. CPCU. Lawyer High Ct., Bombay; with GM, U.K., Lindus & Horton, U.K.; welfare staff Brit. High Commn., Africa, 1977-78; English tchr. Thailand, 1978-80; ins. specialist, analyst Met. Transit Authority, Houston, 1980-83; ins. analyst Coastal Corp., Houston, 1983-84; dir. ins. and employee benefits Houston Ind. Sch. Dist., 1984-88; dir. risk mgmt. and benefits Harris County, Houston, 1988-94; dir. State Risk Mgmt., Austin, 1994—; owner Rupa Mathur & Assocs. Inc., Sugar Land, Tex.; bd. dirs. Surplus Line; owner Health Environ. and Risk Mgmt. Co. (HER Inc.); team leader risk mgmt. del. People to People, Ea. Europe and Russia, 1993, China, 1994; instr. CPCU and accredited advisor ins. courses U. Houston Sch. Inst. Mktg. and Fin., 1985-88; speaker in field. Author: Managing Occupational Injury Costs, 1993; contbr. articles to profl. jours. Chmn. Multi Cultural Soc., Ft. Bend County, Tex., 1992, Indian Cmty.-Equal Opportunity, Houston, 1990; bd. dirs. Children at Risk, Ft. Bend Sch. Dist., 1990, mem. task force Multi Culture Ctr., 1993; co-founder Internat. Gourmet Club, 1976; sec.-treas. Internat. Ladies Club, 1976; tchr. English, YMCA, Thailand, 1976; founder Indian Am. Orgn. for Equal Opportunity; bd. dirs. India Culture Ctr., 1993-94, Surplus Lines Stamping. Recipient Honor award Tex. Safety Assn., 1993, Woman on the Move award Houston Post and KPRC/Channel 2, 1993. Mem. Profl. Women in Govt., Risk and Ins. Mgrs. Soc. (com.), Pub. Risk and Ins. Mgmt. Assn. (past pres. Tex. chpt., mem. internat. com.), World Safety Orgn. (cert. safety exec., appreciation award 1991, Concerned Safety Profl. award 1993), CPCU's (edn. com.), State and Local Govt. Benefits Assn., Nat. Safety Coun. (safety awards), Profl. Devel. Inst. (past officer), Internat. Hospitality Coun. (bd. dirs.), People to People Orgn. (Austin chpt.). Avocations: travel, reading, writing, painting, fishing. Home: 3802 Point Clear Missouri City TX 77459

MATHWICH, DALE F., insurance company executive; b. 1934. Student, U. Wis., 1954. Agent Am. Family Mutual Ins. Co., Madison, Wis., 1955—; dist. mgr. Am. Family Mutual Ins. Co., Rockford, Ill., 1960-60; state dir. Am. Family Mutual Ins. Co., 1970-79, v.p. mktg., 1982-85, exec. v.p., 1985-86, pres., chief oper. officer, 1986-89, now chmn. bd., CEO. Office: Am Family Ins Group 6000 American Pkwy Madison WI 53783-0001

MATIA, PAUL RAMON, federal judge; b. Cleve., Oct. 2, 1937; s. Leo Clemens and Irene Elizabeth (Linkert) M.; m. Nancy Arch Van Meter, Jan. 2, 1993. BA, Case Western Res. U., 1959; JD, Harvard U., 1962. Bar: Ohio 1962, U.S. Dist. Ct. (no. dist.) Ohio 1969. Law clk. Common Pleas Ct. of Cuyahoga County, Cleve., 1963-66, judge, 1985-91; asst. atty. gen. State of Ohio, Cleve., 1966-69; adminstrv. ast. to atty. gen. State of Ohio, Columbus, 1969-70; senator Ohio State Senate, Columbus, 1971-75, 79-83; ptnr. Hadley, Matia, Mills & MacLean Co., L.P.A., Cleve., 1975-84; judge U.S. Dist. Ct. (no. dist.) Ohio, 1991—. Candidate Lt. Gov. Rep. Primary, 1982, Ohio Supreme Ct., 1988; vice chmn. exec. com. Cuyahoga County Rep. Orgn., Cleve., 1971-84. Named Outstanding Legislator, Ohio Assn. for Retarded Citizens, 1974, Watchdog of Ohio Treasury, United Conservatives of Ohio, 1979; recipient Heritage award Polonia Found., 1988. Mem. FBA, Am. Judicature Soc., Ohio Bar Assn., Cleve. Bar Assn. (President's award 1988), Cuyahoga County Bar Assn., Club at Society Ctr. Avocations: skiing, gardening, travel. Office: US Dist Ct 201 Superior Ave E Cleveland OH 44114-1201

MATIAS, PATRICIA TREJO, secondary education educator; b. Havana, Cuba; came to U.S., 1967; d. Juan Mario and Maria (Rexach) Trejo; m.

Miguel Matias, Mar. 20, 1972; children: Michael George, Mark Patrick. BA in French/Spanish, Ga. Coll., 1973; MAT in Spanish Edn., Ga. State U., 1985, EdS in Fgn. Lang. Edn., 1991. Cert. Spanish tchr., Ga. Spanish lead tchr. Wheeler High Sch., Marietta, Ga., 1980—; mem. adv. bd. So. Conf. Lang. Teaching, Ga., 1987—; part-time instr. Kennesaw State Coll., 1991—. VIP guest svc. goodwill amb. Olympics Games Com., Atlanta, 1995-96. Mem. AAUW, ASCD, Am. Assn. Tchrs. Spanish and Portuguese, Profl. Assn. Ga. Educators, Fgn. Lang. Assn. Ga., Kappa Delta Pi, Sigma Delta Pi (hon.). Avocations: golf, travel, gardening, tennis. Office: Wheeler High Sch 375 Holt Rd Marietta GA 30068-3560

MATICH, MATTHEW P., secondary school English educator; b. San Pedro, Calif., June 30, 1962. B Fine and Comm. Arts, Loyola Marymount U., 1985; MEd, Nat. U., 1995; grad., Am. Sch. X-Ray, L.A., 1992. Cert. secondary sch. English tchr., Calif. Records retention clk. Starkist Foods, Terminal Island, Calif., 1979-83; producer, newswriter KMET Radio, Hollywood, Calif., 1981-83, 85-86; news dir., broadcaster KXLU Radio, L.A., 1983-87; instr., counselor Columbia Sch. Broadcasting, Hollywood, 1985-88; radio reporter KRTH Radio, L.A., 1987-88; radio producer Transtar Radio Network, Hollywood, 1987-88; deck crew/customer svc. Catalina Island (Calif.) Express, Avalon, 1989-91; substitute tchr. L.A. Unified Sch. Dist., 1989-92; English tchr., head coach football and track San Pedro (Calif.) H.S., 1992—, head coach freshman/sophomore football and track coach, 1993—; founder, mem. adv. bd. Acad. Athletes (now Extracurricular Academics), San Pedro, 1994—; founder local ethnic tribute/holiday Burrito Day in L.A., 1983—; instr. ESL San Pedro/Narbonne Adult Sch., 1996—. Writer, prodr. radio program The Bluez Shift, 1983-87, poetry: It Can't Be, 1996. Mem. San Pedro Pirate Boosters, 1987. Mem. United Tchrs. L.A., Am. Fedn. Tchrs., Nat. Coun. Tchrs. English, Calif. Assn. Tchrs. English, Dalmation Am. Club, Elks Club (scholarship com. 1990). Avocations: travel. Home: 2731 S Averill Ave San Pedro CA 90731-5632 Office: San Pedro HS 2731 Averillain San Pedro CA 90731

MATIJEVIC, EGON, chemistry educator,; b. Otocac, Croatia, Apr. 27, 1922; came to U.S., 1957; s. Grgur and Stefica (Spiegel) M.; m. Bozica Biscan, Feb. 27, 1947. Diploma in chem. engring., U. Zagreb, 1944, PhD in Chemistry, 1948, Dr. Habil. in Phys. Chemistry, 1952; DSc (hon.), Lehigh U., 1977, M. Curie-Sklodowska U., Lublin, Poland, 1990; DSc. (hon.), Clarkson U., 1992. Instr. chemistry U. Zagreb, Yugoslavia, 1944-47; sr. instr. phys. chemistry U. Zagreb, 1949-52, privat dozent in colloid chemistry, 1952-54, dozent in phys. and colloid chemistry, 1955-56, on leave, 1956-59; rsch. assoc. Inst. Cinematography, Zagreb, 1948; rsch. fellow dept. colloid sci. U. Cambridge, Eng., 1956-57; vis. prof. Clarkson Coll. Tech., Potsdam, N.Y., 1957-59; assoc. prof. chemistry Clarkson Coll. Tech., Postdam, N.Y., 1960-62; prof. Clarkson U., Postdam, 1962-86, disting. univ. prof., 1986—; assoc. dir. Inst. Colloid and Surface Sci. Clarkson Coll. Tech., 1966-68; dir. inst., 1968-81, chmn. dept. chemistry, 1981-87; vis. prof. Japan Soc. for Promotion Sci., 1973, U. Melbourne, Australia, 1976, Sci. U. Tokyo, 1979, 84; vis. scientist U. Leningrad, USSR, 1977; Internat. Atomic Energy Agy. adviser Buenos Aires, Argentina, 1978, 80; fgn. guest Inst. Colloid and Interface Sci. Sci. U. Tokyo, 1982; lectr. in field; mem. adv. com. Univs. and Space Research Assn.; referee NATO Advanced Study Inst. Author: (with M. Kesler) General and Inorganic Chemsitry for Senior High Schools, 11 edits., including Croatian, Macedonian, Hungarian, Italian, 1943-63; translator: Einfuhrung in die Stochiometrie (Nylen and Wigern), 1948; editor: (with Alter J. Weber) Adsorption from Aqueous Solution, 1968, Surface and Colloid Science, vols. 1-15, 1969-92; contbr. numerous articles to profl. publs. Recipient Gold medal Am. Electroplaters Soc., 1976; guest of honor 56th and 63rd Colloid and Surface Sci. Symposiums, Blacksburg, Va., 1982, Seattle, 1989. Mem. Am. Chem. Soc. (councilor div. colloid and surface chemistry 1982-87, chmn. 1969-70, Kendall award 1972, Langmuir Disting. Lectureship award 1985, Ralph K. Iler award 1993), Kolloid Gesellschaft (hon. life, Thomas Graham award 1985), Internat. Assn. Colloid Interface Sci. (pres. 1985-87), Chem. Soc. Japan, Inst. Colloid and Interface Sci. of Sci. of Tokyo (hon.), Phalanx Soc., Croatian Acad. Scis. and Arts (fgn.), Am. Ceramic Soc. (hon.), Materials Rsch. Soc. Japan (hon.), Acad. Ceramics (Italy), Croatian Chem. Soc. (Bozo Tezak medal 1991), Sigma Xi (Clarkson Coll. Tech. chpt. award 1972, nat. lectr. 1987-89). Roman Catholic. Office: Ctr Advanced Materials Proc Clarkson U Dept Chem Potsdam NY 13699-5814

MATIN, A., microbiology educator, consultant; b. Delhi, India, May 8, 1941; came to U.S., 1964, naturalized, 1983; s. Mohammed and Zohra (Begum) Said; m. Mimi Keyhan, June 21, 1968. BS, U. Karachi, Pakistan, 1960, MS, 1962; PhD, UCLA, 1969. Lectr. St. Joseph's Coll., Karachi, 1962-64; research assoc. UCLA, 1964-71; sci. officer U. Groningen, Kerklaan, The Netherlands, 1971-75; from asst. prof. to full prof. microbiology and immunology Stanford U., Calif., 1975—; prof. Western Hazardous Substances Rsch. Ctr. Stanford U., 1981—; cons. Engenics, 1982-84, Monsanto, 1984-86, Chlorox, 1992-93; chmn. Stanford Recombinant DNA panel; mem. Accreditation Bd. for Engring. and Tech.; mem. internat. adv. com., Internat. Workshop on Molecular Biology of Stress Response: Meml. Found., Banaras U. and German Min. of Rsch., mem. panel Yucca Mountain Microbial Activity, Dept. of Energy, mem. study sect.; participant DOE, NABIR program draft panel; convenor of microbiol. workshop and confs.; rev. panel DOE environ. mgmt. program; mem. rev. panel DOE NABIR program, mem. Stanford Biosafety Panel; keynote spkr., adv. bd. several internat. confs. Mem. editl. bd. Jour. Bacteriology, Ann. Rev. Microbiol.; reviewer NSF and other grants; contbr. numerous publs. to sci. jours. Fulbright fellow, 1964-71; recipient rsch. awards NSF, 1981-92, Ctr. for Biotech. Rsch., 1981-85, EPA, 1981—, NIH, 1989-92, U.N. Tokten, 1987, DOE, 1993—, Dept. Agrl., 1995—. Mem. AAAS, AAUP, Am Soc. for Microbiology (Found. lectr. 1991-93), Soc. Gen. Microbiology, Soc. Indsl. Microbiology, No. Soc. Indsl. Microbiology (bd. dirs.), Biophys. Soc., Am. Chem. Soc. Avocations: reading, music, hiking. Home: 690 Coronado Ave Stanford CA 94305-1039 Office: Stanford U Fairchild Sci Bldg Dept Microbiology & Immunology Stanford CA 94305-5402

MATJASKO, M. JANE, anesthesiologist, educator; b. Harrison Twp., Pa., 1942. MD, Med. Coll. Pa., 1968. Diplomate Am. Bd. Anesthesiology (bd. dirs.). Resident in anesthesiology Md. Hosp., Balt., 1968-72; prof., chmn. anesthesiology U. Md., Balt.; appt. U. Md. Hosp., Balt. Mem. Am. Soc. Anesthesiologists, Assn. Univ. Anesthesiologists, Am. Bd. Anesthesiology Dirs. Office: U Md Hosp Dept Anesthesiology 22 S Greene St Baltimore MD 21201-1544

MATKOWSKY, BERNARD JUDAH, applied mathematician, educator; b. N.Y.C., Aug. 19, 1939; s. Morris N. and Ethel H. M.; m. Florence Knobel, Apr. 11, 1965; children: David, Daniel, Devorah. B.S., CCNY, 1960; M.E.E., NYU, 1961, M.S., 1963, Ph.D., 1966. Fellow Courant Inst. Math. Scis., NYU, 1961-66; mem. faculty dept. math. Rensselaer Poly. Inst., 1966-77; John Evans prof. applied math., mech. engring. & math. Northwestern U., Evanston, Ill., 1977—, chmn. engring. sci. and applied math. dept., 1993—; vis. prof. Tel Aviv U., 1972-73; vis. scientist Weizmann Inst. Sci., Israel, summer 1976, summer 1980, Tel Aviv U., summer 1980; cons. Argonne Nat. Lab., Sandia Labs., Lawrence Livermore Nat. Lab., Exxon Research and Engring. Co. Editor Wave Motion—An Internat. Jour., 1979—, Applied Math. Letters, 1987—, SIAM Jour. Applied Math., 1976-95, European Jour. Applied Math., 1990-96, Random and Computational Dynamics, 1991—, Internat. Jour. SHS, 1992—, Jour. Materials Synthesis and Processing, 1992—; mem. editl. adv. bd. Springer Verlag Applied Math. Scis. Series; contbr. chpts. to books, articles to profl. jours. Fulbright grantee, 1972-73; Guggenheim fellow, 1982-83. Fellow Am. Acad. Mechanics; mem. AAAS, Soc. Indsl. and Applied Math., Am. Math. Soc., Combustion Inst., Am. Phys. Soc., Am. Assn. Combustion Synthesis, Conf. Bd. Math. Scis. (coun., com. human rights of math. scientists), Com. Concerned Scientists, Soc. Natural Philosophy, Sigma Xi, Eta Kappa Nu. Home: 3704 Davis St Skokie IL 60076-1745 Office: Northwestern U Technological Institute Evanston IL 60208

MATLACK, GEORGE MILLER, radiochemist; b. Pitts., June 14, 1921; s. Allyn Wolcott and Mildred Narcissa (Miller) M.; m. Meredith Mildred Madsen, Sept. 4, 1943; children—Nancy, Christine, Martin, Allyn. AB, Grinnell Coll., 1943; MS, State U. Iowa, 1947, PhD, 1949. Prin. chemist Iowa Geol. Survey, Iowa City, 1943-46; rsch. asst. State U. Iowa, 1946-49; sect. leader, analytical chemistry Los Alamos (N.Mex.) Nat. Lab., 1949-82, assoc. group leader analytical chemistry div., 1983-90, mem. team for devel. remote sensing of dinosaur bones by radiometric methods, 1988-95, sr. adv. analytical chemistry divsn., 1990-95. Contbr. articles to profl. jours. Pres., Los Alamos Choral Soc., 1961-62, Los Alamos Sinfonietta, 1967-69. Fellow Am. Inst. Chemists, AAAS; mem. Am. Chem. Soc., Am. Nuclear Soc., N.Y. Acad. Scis., Iowa Acad. Scis., Four-Fifths Mus. Soc. Lodges: Masons, Eastern Star. Home: 254 San Juan St Los Alamos NM 87544-2635 Office: Los Alamos Nat Lab Chemistry Div MS-G740 PO Box 1663 Los Alamos NM 87545-0001

MATLEY, BENVENUTO GILBERT (BEN MATLEY), computer engineer, educator, consultant; b. Monroe, La., Sept. 8, 1930; s. Welcome Gilbert and Lucette Marie (Renaud) M.; m. Patricia Jean McWilliams, June 21, 1959; children: Elizabeth, Katherine, John, Stephen, Richard, David. AB, San Diego State U., 1960; MBA, U. So. Calif., 1964; EdD, Nova U., 1980. Cert. data processor. Mathematician, engr. various data processing and computing firms, San Diego and L.A., 1956-64; sr. computer systems engr. Nortronics div. Northrop Corp., Hawthorne, Calif., 1964-69; prof. data processing and math. Ventura (Calif.) Coll., 1969—; lectr. in mgmt. and computer sci. West Coast U., L.A., 1982—; software cons, ednl. cons., Ventura, 1972—. Author: Principles of Elementary Algebra: A Language and Equations Approach, 1991; sr. author: National Computer Policies, 1988; contbr. chpts. to books, articles to profl. jours. Active Ventura County coun. Boy Scouts Am., 1979-82; cons. Calif. Luth. U., Thousand Oaks, Calif., 1989. Lt. (j.g.) USNR, 1952-55, Europe. Mem. IEEE Computer Soc. (Disting Visitor 1988-91), Assn. for Computing Machinery, Math. Assn. Am. Avocation: writing. Office: Ventura Coll 4667 Telegraph Rd Ventura CA 93003-3872

MATLIN, MARLEE, actress; b. Morton Grove, Ill., Aug. 24, 1965; m. Kevin Grandalski, Aug. 29, 1993. Attended William Rainey Harper Coll. Appeared in films Children of a Lesser God (Acad. award for best actress), 1986, Walker, 1987, Linguini Incident, 1990, The Player, 1992, Hear No Evli, 1993; TV film: Bridge to Silence, 1989, Against Her Will: The Carrie Buck Sotry, 1994; TV series: Reasonable Doubts, 1991-93; guest of Picket Fences, 1993, 94-96 (Emmy nomination, Guest Actress-Drama Series, 1994), Seinfeld, 1993 (Emmy nomination Guest Actress-Comedy Series, 1994); appeared in: (TV film) Dead Silence, 1997, It's My Party, 1996, Snitch, 1997. Recipient Golden Globe award Hollywood Fgn. Press Assn., 1987, named Best Actress. Office: care ICM 8942 Wilshire Blvd Beverly Hills CA 90211-1934

MATLOCK, CLIFFORD CHARLES, retired foreign service officer; b. Whittier, Cal., Nov. 6, 1909; s. William Holl and Clara Louisa (Wallace) M.; m. Nina Stolypin, Nov. 6, 1934 (dec. Dec. 1969); m. Elisabeth Thompson Scobey, May 3, 1971. A.B., Stanford U., 1932; A.M., Harvard U., 1940, certificate pub. adminstrn. (Littauer fellow), 1940. Economist USDA, 1938-41, U.S. Treasury, 1941-42; economist, adminstr. Bd. Econ. Warfare, Fgn. Econ. Adminstrn., 1942-45; econ., polit. officer Dept. State, 1946-62; polit. adviser European coordinating com. Dept. State, London, 1949-50; polit. officer U.S. delegation North Atlantic Council, London, 1950-52; polit. officer, then dir. plans and policy staff Office U.S. spl. rep. in Europe, Paris, 1952-53; spl. asst. Am. ambassador, Tehran, 1955-57; spl. asst. econ. affairs asst. sec. state for Far Eastern affairs, also alternate to Dep. Asst. Sec., 1959-62, ret.; acting dep. asst. Sec. of State, 1959; spl. asst. for polit. and econ. affairs to asst. adminstr. East Asia AID, Dept. of State, 1962-68, dir. East Asia tech. adv. staff, 1966-68, cons. Bur. for East Asia, 1968-71; coordinator interdisciplinary Devel. Cycles Research Project, 1971-76, prin., 1977-84; U.S. del. Econ. Commn. for Asia and Far East (UN), Tokyo, Japan, 1962; U.S. del. to devel. assistance com. Orgn. for Economic Cooperation and Devel., Paris, France, 1962; Member U.S. delegation Colombo Plan Consultative Com., Seattle, 1958, London, 1964; Member Development Assistance Group, Orgn. Econ. Coop. and Development, Washington, 1960; U.S. alternate rep. UN Econ. Commn. for Asia and Far East, Bangkok, 1960; adviser, mem. U.S. del. bds. govs. Internat. Monetary Fund, Internat. Bank for Reconstrn. and Devel., Tokyo, Japan, 1964; exec. com. SE Asia Devel. Adv. Group, 1965-70. Author: Man and Cosmos: A Theory of Endeavor Rhythms, 1977; draftsman of American Credo (in support of Truman Doctrine, now in U.S. Archives, H.S. Truman Libr.), 1947. Recipient Superior Honor award AID, 1968. Mem. Fgn. Service Assn., Diplomatic and Consular Officers Ret., Phi Beta Kappa. Clubs: Metropolitan (Washington), Harvard (Washington); Harvard of Western N.C. Home: Rte 1 Box 388 Waynesville NC 28786

MATLOCK, (LEE) HUDSON, civil engineer, educator; b. Floresville, Tex., Dec. 9, 1919; s. Lee Hudson Sr. and Charlie Mary (Stevenson) M.; m. Harriett Nadine Kidder, Nov. 28, 1942 (dec. Jan. 1996); children: John Hudson, David Kidder; m. Catherine Wahrmund, Mar. 16, 1997. BSCE, U. Tex., 1947, MSCE, 1950. Registered profl. engr., Tex. From instr. to prof. U. Tex., Austin, 1948-78, chmn. dept. civil engring., 1972-76, prof. emeritus civil engring., 1995—; v.p. R & D Earth Tech. Corp., Long Beach, Calif., 1978-85; civil engring. cons. Kerrville, Tex., 1985—; cons. Shell, Mobil, Chevron, Conoco and others, 1958—. Contbr. numerous tech. papers and sponsored rsch. reports to profl. publs. 1st lt. AC, U.S. Army, 1941-45. Recipient Disting. Achievement award Offshore Tech. Conf., Houston, 1985; named Disting. Engring. Grad. Coll. Engring. U. Tex.-Austin, 1986. Fellow ASCE (J. James R. Croes medal 1968), Tau Beta Pi; mem. NAE. Methodist. Avocations: flying, fishing, gardening. Home and Office: HC 5 Box 574-655 Kerrville TX 78028-9034

MATLOCK, JACK FOUST, JR., diplomat; b. Greensboro, N.C., Oct. 1, 1929; s. Jack Foust and Nellie (McSwain) M.; m. Rebecca Burrum, Sept. 2, 1949; children: James, Hugh, Nell, David, Joseph. A.B. summa cum laude, Duke U., 1950; M.A., Columbia U., 1952; cert., Russian Inst., 1952; LLD (hon.), Greensboro Coll., 1989, Albright Coll., 1992, Conn. Coll., 1993. Instr. Dartmouth, 1953-56; fgn. service officer Dept. State, 1956-91; assigned Washington, 1956-58, Am. Embassy, Vienna, Austria, 1958-60; Am. consul. gen. Munich, Germany, 1960-61; assigned Am. Embassy, Moscow, 1961-63, Accra, Ghana, 1963-66; assigned Am. Consulate, Zanzibar, 1967-69, Am. Embassy, Dar es Salaam, Tanzania, 1969-70, Sr. Seminar in Fgn. Policy, Dept. State, 1970-71; country dir. for USSR State Dept., 1971-74; minister-counselor, dep. chief mission Am. Embassy, Moscow, 1974-78; diplomat-in-residence Vanderbilt U., Nashville, 1978-79; dep. dir. Fgn. Service Inst., Washington, 1979-80; chargé d'affaires ad interim Am. Embassy, Moscow, 1981; ambassador to Czechoslovakia, 1981-83; spl. asst. to pres., sr. dir. European and Soviet Affairs Nat. Security Council, 1983-87; U.S. ambassador to the Soviet Union, Moscow, 1987-91; sr. rsch. fellow Columbia U., N.Y.C., 1991-93, Kathryn and Shelby Collum Davis prof. Practice Internat. Diplomacy, 1993-96; George F. Kennan prof. Inst. for Advanced Study, Princeton, N.J., 1996—. Author: Autopsy on an Empire: The American Ambassador's Account of the Collapse of the Soviet Union, 1995; compiler, editor: Index to J.V. Stalin's Works, 2d edit., 1971. Mem. Am. Acad. Diplomacy, Coun. on Fgn. Rels., Century Assn. N.Y. Home: 2913 P St NW Washington DC 20007-3069 also: 63 Battle Rd Princeton NJ 08540-4901 Office: Inst for Advanced Study Princeton NJ 08540

MATLOCK, JOHN HUDSON, science administrator, materials engineer; b. San Angelo, Tex., Nov. 23, 1944; s. Lee Hudson Jr. and Harriett (Kidder) M.; m. Kathe Lynne Reep, Sept. 3, 1966; children: Michelle, Joseph. B. Engring. Sci., U. Tex., 1967, MSME, 1969, PhD in Material Sci. and Engring., 1970; MBA, So. Ill. U., Edwardsville, 1976. Registered profl. engr., Mo., Wash., Oreg. Sr. rsch. engr. Monsanto Co., St. Peters, Mo., 1970-72, rsch. specialist, 1972-74, supt. tech. svcs., 1974-79; sr. staff engr. Mostek Corp., Carrollton, Tex., 1979-80, mgr. material tech. group, 1980-83; v.p. tech. SEH Am., Inc., Vancouver, Wash., 1983-90, exec. v.p., 1990-96; exec. v.p. Komatsu Silicon Am., Hillsboro, Oreg., 1996, pres., CEO, 1997—; bd. dirs. Wash. Tech. Ctr., 1991—; mem. vis. com. Engring. Coll., U. Wash., Seattle, 1985-94, mem. indsl. adv. bd. Material Sci. and Engring., 1988—; mem. engring. adv. bd. Wash. State U., Pullman, 1984-96, adj. lectr., 1985; bd. dirs. Wash. Higher Edn. Telecomms., 1985-90; adj. prof. mech. engring., mem. grad. faculty Oreg. State U., Corvallis, 1985-90; adj. asst. prof. physics So. Ill. U., Edwardsville, 1973-76. Contbr. approximately 40 articles on silicon crystal growing and the effect of silicon properties on electronic devic performance to profl. and trade jours. Mem. bd. trustees 1st Ch. of God, Vancouver, 1988-91, tchr. adult ch. sch., 1986-91; mem. sch. bd. Kingsway Christian Sch., Vancouver, 1990-91. Mem. Electrochem. Soc., Metall. Soc., AIME, Am. Soc. for Materials, Materials Rsch. Soc., ASTM, Tau Beta Pi, Pi Tau Sigma, Phi Kappa Phi, Beta Gamma Sigma. Home: 10916 NE 30th Ave Vancouver WA 98686-4346

MATNEY, WILLIAM BROOKS, VII, electrical engineer, marine engineer; b. Detroit, June 14, 1935; s. William Brooks VI and Maurine (Huff) M.; m. Carolyn Weaver, Dec. 29, 1959; children: C. Melinda Matney Levin, William Brooks VIII, James Richard, Robert Weaver. BSEE, Marine Engring., U.S. Naval Acad., 1957. Commd. ensign USN, 1957, advanced through grades to lt. j.g., 1962; div. officer aircraft carrier USS Bon Homme Richard, 1957-59; combat, info. officer attack transport USS Paul Revere, 1959-62; design engr. gen. svcs. dept. Exxon Co. USA, Houston, 1962-70; constrn. engr. mktg. dept. Exxon Co. USA, Dallas, 1970-80; oil prodn. engr. prodn. dept. Exxon Co. USA, Ventura, Calif., 1980-85; underground tank engr. mktg. dept. Exxon Co. USA, Houston, 1985-89, coord. regulatory compliance mktg. dept., 1989-92; mgr. aboveground tank svcs. Tanknology Corp. Internat., Houston, 1992-94; v.p. Engring. Tanknology, 1994-96; founder, prin. Storage Tank Advisors, 1996—; instr. Occupl. and Environ. Safety divsn. Tex. Engring. Extension Svc., Tex. A&M U. System, 1996—; expert witness, Assoc. Tech. Adv. Svc. for Attorneys, 1995—; work group leader underground tank certification Am. Petroleum Inst., Washington, 1991-92; committeeman leak detector group U.S. EPA, Washington, 1991-92; chmn. Energy Week Symposium, Houston, 1995—; tank cons. Environ. Fuel Systems. Speaker OSHA safety rules Nat. Safety Coun., 1990; contbr. articles to profl. jours. Trustee Ind. Sch. Dist., Richardson, Tex., 1979-80; hon. life mem. Tex. PTA, 1974—, Calif. PTA, 1982—. Guest of Astronauts, Nat. Space and Aeronautics Agy., 1970. Mem. Nat. Assn. Corrosion Engrs., Am. Contract Bridge League (cert. dir., Regional Master award), Environ. Info. Assn. (underground tank task force leader 1992-95, sec. Tex. chpt. 1990-92). Southern Baptist. Achievements include invention and development of silent ship tracking method (at sea), flood control device, cathodic protection applications. Home: 1503 Anvil Dr Houston TX 77090-2113

MATOIAN, JOHN, broadcasting company executive. Dir. devel. Highgate Pictures/Learning Corp. Am., 1979-84; v.p. devel. Scholastic Prodns., 1984-86; head made-for-TV movies CBS, 1986-88; v.p. internat. program devel. CBS Entertainment, 1988-92, sr. v.p. motion pictures for TV and mini-series, 1992-94; pres. Fox Entertainment Group Fox Broadcasting Co., 1994—; pres. HBO Pictures, L.A. and N.Y.C., 1997—. Office: HBO 2049 Century Park E Ste 3600 Los Angeles CA 90067*

MATON, ANTHEA, education consultant; b. Burnley, Lancashire, England, Feb. 1, 1944; d. William Douglas Newton-Dawson and Beatrice Joan (Simpson) Bateman; m. K.F. Edward Asprey, Nov. 13, 1965 (div. 1978); children: George William Edward, Mariana Alexandra Beatrice; m. Paul Nicholas Maton, Mar. 23, 1978; 1 child, Petra Beatrice Suzanne. Tchg. cert., higher diploma, tchg. diploma; postgrad., U. Okla. Clin. instr. radiotherapy Hammersmith Hosp., London, 1970-75; prin. sch. radiotherapy Royal Free Hosp., London, 1977-80, acting supt., 1979-80; head of careers Putney High Sch. for Girls, London, 1981-83; head of physics St. Andrews Episc. High Sch., Bethesda, Md., 1984-88; vis. fellow Am. Assn. Physics Tchrs., 1988-89; nat. coord. project scope, sequence, and coordination Nat. Sci. Tchrs. Assn., 1989-91; exec. dir. Edn. Commections, Oklahoma City, 1991—, dir. exhbn. on art and physics, 1994—; vis. faculty physics Western Wash. U., 1995; vis. faculty Okla. Sch. Sci. and Math. 1995—; organizer U.S.-Soviet H.S. Physics Student Exch. and Visit, 1989; conducted numerous workshops on sci. curriculum reform and assessment reform, 1987—; faculty USA Physics Olympiad Team, 1986, 89; physics tchr. St. Andrews Episc. H.S., 1984-88, Putney H.S. for Girls, 1980-83, tchr. med. ethics, 1982-83; tchr. physics, anatomy and physiology, radiobiology Royal Free Hosp., 1977-80, contemporary physics edn. project, 1989—. Lead author Prentice Hall Sci., 1993; contbr. articles to profl. jours. Mem. Nat. Mus. Women Arts (charter), Women's Philharm. (charter); apptd. to scientific adv. bd. OMNIPLEX Sci. Mus., Okla. City; cons. Sta. WGBH, Boston, Smithsonian, Am. Mus. of Moving Image, UCLA, Del. Edn. Dept., Ark. Project Advise, Newcastle (Del.) Sch. Dist. Named one of Today's Leaders Okla. Edn. Equity Roundtable, 1992. Mem. NAFE, ASCD, AAUW (pub. policy chair 1995-96), NOW (coord. metro chpt. 1992-95, treas. Okla. state chpt. 1993-95), Nat. Sci. Tchrs. Assn., Am. Assn. Physics Tchrs., N.Y. Acad. Scis., Assn. for Sci. Edn., Soc. Radiographers U.K., Soc. Radiographers Radiotherapy. Avocations: gender and science, drawing, writing poetry, singing, making wood cuts. Home and Office: 1804 Dorchester Dr Oklahoma City OK 73120-4706

MATOS, CRUZ ALFONSO, environmental consultant; b. N.Y.C., Mar. 6, 1929; s. José and Gertrudes (Manzanares) M.; m. Aurelia Santos, Dec. 13, 1963; children: Miguel, Veronica, Monica, Angélica. B in Engring. Sci., Oxford U., 1957, M in Engring. Sci., 1958; DSc (honoris causa) U. Met., P.R., 1995. Pres., CEO Fischer & Porter de P.R., 1964-69; asst. sec. dept. pub. works Govt. of P.R., 1969-70, exec. dir. Environ. Quality Bd., 1970-73, sec. dept. natural resources, 1973-75, cabinet mem., 1970-75; UN chief tech., dir. Inst. Marine Affairs, Trinidad and Tobago, 1975-79; UN Devel. Program regional rep. Trinidad and Tobago, Barbados, Surinam and Dutch West Indies, 1978-80, UN chief tech. adviser South Pacific, dir. CCOP/SOPAC, Suva, Fiji, 1980-89, ret.; advisor to pres. P.R. Senate for natural resources, the environ. and energy, 1993—; advisor to exec. dir. UN Environ. Program for L.Am. and Caribbean, 1994—; mem. various adv. panels and overseas mission U.S. NAS; mem. U.S. Nat. Commn. on Environment, Consejo Consultive Recursos Naturales y Ambientales (apptd. Gov. P.R.), Consejo Consultivo del Programa de Patrimonio Natural de Puerto Rico, Com. Sobre Política Publica Energetica P.R., Consejo Asesor Sobre Energia. Contbr. articles to sci. jours. and mags. Trustee, Conservation Found., U.S., bd. dirs., World Wildlife Fund-U.S.A.; mem. bd. dirs. Caribbean Environment and Devel. Inst., Caribbean Natural Resources Inst. Served with U.S. Army, 1952-54. Recipient Boriquen Conservation award, 1971. Office: PO Box 7627 Playa Cerro Gordo Vega Alta PR 00692

MATOY, ELIZABETH ANNE, personnel executive; b. Stillwater, Okla., Sept. 11, 1946; d. Ray Roland and Helen Louise (Springer) Matoy; m. Michael D. Banks; children: Heather Anne, Kirsten Sue, Aaron Christian, Kendra Jeanne Carlson. BA, U. Ill., Chgo., 1968; MSM, Frostburg (Md.) State Coll., 1975. Publs. mgr. Forum Press, Stillwater, Okla., 1982-84; editor centennial histories project Okla. State U., 1984-88, assoc. pers. dir., 1988-91, pers. dir., 1991—; owner, pub. Prairie Imprints, Stillwater, 1985-92; cons. Active Corps of Execs., Frostburg, Md., 1975-77. Editor: DAC in Oklahoma, 1984; also editor for Payne County (Okla.) Historical Soc., 1980-90. Pres. LaVale (Md.) Vol. Fire Dept. Aux., 1972-77; bd. dirs. Morgantown, W.Va. Shawnee Girl Scouts Council, 1975-77; mem. allocations com. Cumberland, Md. United Way, 1975-77; bus. mgr. Stillwater Sylvia Stapley Day Camp Girl Scouts, 1982-84. Recipient Bronze Pelican award Archdiocese of Tulsa, 1990, Sr. Profl. Human Resources award Human Resources Cert. Inst., 1992. Mem. Payne County Hist. Soc. (sec. 1980-82, historian 1986), Okla. Colls. Univs. Pers. Assn., Stillwater Rotary Club. Republican. Methodist. Home: 210 E Greenvale Ct Stillwater OK 74075-1662 Office: Okla State U Dept Pers Stillwater OK 74076-0481

MATROS, LARISA GRIGORYEVNA, medical philosophy researcher; b. Odessa, Ukraine, USSR, Jan. 30, 1938; d. Grigory Lyvovich and Eva Michailovna (Bulkach) Akselrod; m. Yury Shaevich Matros, July 25, 1960; 1 child, Elena. M in law, State U., Odessa, 1963; PhD, State U., Novosibirsk, USSR, 1972. Lawyer Roskulttorg Trading Co., Novosibirsk, 1962-64; researcher Inst. Clin. and Exptl. Medicine, Novosibirsk, 1975-81; researcher, philosophy cons., coordinator Presidium of USSR (Siberian Branch) Acad. Med. Scientists, Novosibirsk, 1982—; chief philosophy dept. Siberian Med. Acad., 1988-91; freelance writer, rschr., 1992—; lectr. in field, Novosibirsk, 1975. Author: The Right to Be Healthy, 1979, Social Aspects of the Problem of Health, 1992; contbr. articles, short stories, lit. revs. poems and essays to profl. jours. anthologyes. Recipient Hon. Diploma Internat. Poetic Competition, 1993, 96, award of excellence 23rd Internat. Congress of Art and Comm., San Francisco, 1996, Am. Biog. Inst. World Lifetime Achievement award, 1996. Fellow Soviet Sociol. Assn. (inspection com. chairwoman 1970-78), Internat. Biographical Assn. (life); mem. Am. Biographical Inst. Rsch. Assn. (dep. gov. 1995—), Internat. Platform Assn., Soviet Philos. Seminars (medicine divsn. sec. 1984-92), P.E.N., Internat. Pushkin Soc. Home: 14963 Green Circle Dr Chesterfield MO 63017-7826

MATSA, LOULA ZACHAROULA, social services administrator; b. Piraeus, Greece, Apr. 16, 1935; came to U.S., 1952, naturalized 1962; d. Eleftherios Georgiou and Ourania E. (Fraguiskopoulou) Papoulias; student Pierce Coll., Athens, Greece, 1948-52; BA, Rockford Coll., 1953; MA, U. Chgo., 1955; m. Ilco S. Matsa, Nov. 27, 1953; 1 child, Aristotle Ricky. Diplomate clin. social worker. Marital counselor Family Soc. Cambridge, Mass., 1955-56; chief unit II, social service Queen's (N.Y.) Children's Psychiat. Ctr., 1961-74; dir. social services, supr.-coord. family care program Hudson River Psychiat. Ctr., Poughkeepsie, N.Y., 1974-91; supr. social work Harlem Valley Psychiat. Ctr., Wingdale, N.Y., 1991-93; supr. social work Hudson River Psychiat. Ctr., 1993—; field instr. Adelphi, Albany and Fordham univs., 1969—. Fulbright Exch. student, 1952-53; Talcott scholar, 1953-55. Mem. NASW, Internat. Platform Assn., Internat. Coun. on Social Welfare, Acad. Cert. Social Workers, Assn. Cert. Social Workers, Bd. Certified Clin. Social Workers, N.Y. Certified Social Workers, Pub. Employees Fedn., Pierce Coll. Alumni Assn. Democrat. Greek Orthodox. Contbr. articles to profl. jours.; instrumental in state policy changes in treatment and court representation of emotionally disturbed and mentally ill. Home: 81-11 45th Ave Elmhurst NY 11373-3553

MATSCH, RICHARD P., judge; b. Burlington, Iowa, June 8, 1930. A.B., U. Mich., 1951, J.D., 1953. Bar: Colo. Asst. U.S. atty. Colo., 1959-61; dep. city atty. City and County of Denver, 1961-63; judge U.S. Bankruptcy Ct., Colo., 1965-74; judge U.S. Dist. Ct. for Colo., 1974-94, chief judge, 1994—; mem. Judicial Conf. of the U.S., 1991-94, mem. com. on criminal law, 1988-94; mem. bd. dirs. Fed. Judicial Ctr., 1995—. Served with U.S. Army, 1953-55. Mem. ABA, Am. Judicature Soc. Office: Byron White Court House 1823 Stout St Denver CO 80257-1823*

MATSEN, FREDERICK ALBERT, III, orthopedic educator; b. Austin, Tex., Feb. 5, 1944; s. Frederick Albert II and Cecilia (Kirkegaard) M.; m. Anne Lovell, Dec. 24, 1966; children: Susanna Lovell, Frederick A. IV, Laura Jane Megan. BA, U. Tex., Austin, 1964; MD, Baylor U., 1968. Intern Johns Hopkins U., Balt., 1971; resident in orthopaedics U. Wash., Seattle, 1971-74, acting instr. orthopaedics, 1974, asst. prof. orthopaedics, 1975-79, assoc. prof. orthopaedics, 1979-82, prof., 1982-85, 86—, adjunct prof. Ctr. Bioengring., 1985—, dir. residency program orthopaedics, 1978-81, vice chmn. dept. orthopaedics, 1982-85, acting chmn. dept. orthopaedics, 1983-84, prof., chmn. dept. orthopaedics, 1981—; mem. Orthopaedic Residency Rev. Com., Chgo., 1981-86. Author: Compartmental Syndromes, 1980; editor: The Shoulder, 1990; contbr. articles to profl. jours., chpts. to textbooks; assoc. editor Clin. Orthopaedics, Jour. Orthopaedic Rsch., 1981—. Lt. comdr. USPHS, 1969-71. Recipient Traveling fellowship Am. Orthopaedic Assn., 1983, Nicholas Andry award Assn. Bone and Joint Surgery, 1979, Henry Meyerding Essay award Am. Fracture Assn., 1974. Mem. Am. Shoulder and Elbow Surgeons (founding, pres. 1991—), Am. Acad. Orthopaedic Surgeons (bd. dirs. 1984-85), Orthopaedic Rsch. Soc., Western Orthopaedic Assn., Phi Beta Kappa. Office: U Wash Dept Orthopaedics RK-10 1959 NE Pacific St Seattle WA 98195-0004

MATSEN, JOHN MARTIN, academic administrator, pathologist; b. Salt Lake City, Feb. 7, 1933; s. John M. and Bessie (Jackson) M.; m. Joneen Johnson, June 6, 1959; children: Marilee, Sharon, Coleen, Sally, John H., Martin K., Maureen, Catherine, Carl, Jeri. BA, Brigham Young U., 1958; MD, UCLA, 1963. Diplomate Am. Bd. Pediatrics, Am. Bd. Pathology, Spl. Competence in Med. Microbiology. Intern UCLA, 1963-65; resident L.A. County Harbor/UCLA, Torrance, Calif., 1965-66; USPHS fellow U. Minn., Mpls., 1966-68, asst. prof., 1968-70, assoc. prof., 1971-74, prof., 1974; prof. U. Utah, Salt Lake City, 1974—, assoc. dean, 1979-81, chmn. Dept. of Pathology, 1981-93, univ. v.p. health scis., 1993—; pres. Associated Regional and Univ. Pathologists, Inc., Salt Lake City, 1983-93, chmn. bd. dirs., 1993—. Author over 200 publs. in field. Recipient Sonnenwirth Meml. award Am. Soc. Microbiology, 1993. Mem. Acad. Clin. Lab. Physicians and Scientists (pres. 1978-79), Assn. of Pathology Chmn. (pres. 1990-92). Mem. LDS Church. Home: 410 South 10 West Farmington UT 84025-2203 Office: U Utah Health Scis Ctr 50 N Medical Dr Salt Lake City UT 84132-0001

MATSLER, FRANKLIN GILES, higher education educator; b. Glendive, Mont., Dec. 27, 1922; s. Edmund Russell and Florence Edna (Giles) M.; m. Lois Josephine Hoyt, June 12, 1949; children—Linda, Jeanne, David, Winfield. B.S., Mont. State U., Bozeman, 1948; M.A., U. Mont., Missoula, 1952; Ph.D., U. Calif. at Berkeley, 1959. Tchr. Missoula County (Mont.) High Sch., 1949-51, Tracy (Calif.) Sr. Elem. Schs., 1952-53, San Benito County (Calif.) High Sch. and Jr. Coll., 1953-55; grad. asst. U. Calif. at Berkeley, 1955-58; asst. prof. Humboldt State Coll., Arcata, Calif., 1958-62; asso. prof. Humboldt State Coll., 1962-63, asst. exec. dean, 1958-63; chief specialist higher edn. Calif. Coordinating Council for Higher Edn., Sacramento, 1963-68; exec. dir. Ill. Bd. Regents, Springfield, 1968-84; prof. higher edn. Ill. State U., Normal, 1968—, Regency prof. higher edn., 1984—; chancellor Ill. Bd. Regents, 1995-96. Bd. dirs. Ill. Edn. Consortium, 1972-76; bd. dirs. Central Ill. Health Planning Agy., 1970-76, Springfield Symphony Orch. Assn.; pres. Bloomington/Normal Symphony Soc., 1988-90. Served to 1st lt. AUS, 1943-46. Mem. Nat. Assn. Sys. Heads (exec. v.p. 1985-92), Am. Assn. State Colls. and Univs. Assn. for Instl. Rsch., Phi Delta Kappa, Lambda Chi Alpha. Home: 2005 Woodfield Rd Bloomington IL 61704-2452 Office: Illinois State U 539 DeGarmo Hall Normal IL 61761

MATSON, MERWYN DEAN, educational consultant; b. Forest City, Iowa, Aug. 6, 1937; s. Archie Alvin and Henrietta (Wittgreve) M.; m. Audrey Christine Gaydos, Apr. 9, 1988; children: Candace, Kevin, Shaunna, Dan, Cathy, Mindy, Lisa, Matthew. AB, Northwest Nazarene Coll., 1959; MEd, Oreg. State U., 1963; EdM, U. Oreg., 1962. Cert. tchr., sch. counselor, sch. psychologist, Iowa. Elem. sch. guidance coord. Pottawattami County Schs., Council Bluffs, Iowa, 1969-70; sch. psychologist Hancock County Schs., Garner, Iowa, 1970-71; dir. career edn. Mason City (Iowa) Pub. Schs., 1971-73; regional dir. Am. Coll. Testing Inc., Springfield, Mo., 1973-84; Midwest regional dir. career planning svcs. Am. Coll. Testing Inc., Lincolnshire, Ill., 1984-86; Mountains/Plains regional dir. career planning svcs. Am. Coll. Testing Inc., Aurora, Colo., 1986-94, West region dir. elementary/secondary svcs., 1995-96, West region dir. postsecondary bus. svcs., 1996—. Mem. AARP, Am. Counseling Assn., Rotary Club of Conifer. Lutheran. Home: 30095 Kennedy Gulch Rd PO Box 1433 Conifer CO 80433 Office: Am Coll Testing Program 3131 S Vaughn Way Ste 218 Aurora CO 80014-3507 *Personal philosophy: Service above self. He profits most who serves best.*

MATSON, PAMELA ANNE, environmental science educator; b. Eau Claire, Wis., Aug. 3, 1953. BS, U. Wis., 1975; MS, Ind. U., 1980; PhD, Oreg. State U., 1983. Prof. U. Calif., Berkeley, 1993—. MacArthur fellow, 1995; recipient award for excellence in environ. health rsch. Lovelance Inst., Albuquerque, 1995. Mem. Am. Acad. Arts & Scis., Nat. Acad. Sci. Specializes in the interactions between the biosphere and the atmosphere; pioneereed research into the role of land-use changes on global warming, analyzing the effects of greenhouse gas emissions resulting from tropical deforestization; investigating the effects of intensive agriculture on the atmosphere, especially the effects of tropical agriculture and cattle ranching, and is finding ways in which agricultural productivity can be expanded without increasing the level of greenhouse gasses. Office: U Calif Dept Sci Policy and Mgmt Dept Environ Science Berkeley CA 94720-3110

MATSON, ROBERT EDWARD, educator, leadership consultant; b. Chauncey, Ohio, Dec. 2, 1930; s. William I. and Mary Royal (Rivers) M.; m. Mary Athearn, June 27, 1954; children—Laurie, Jeanne, Scott. B.S., Ohio U., 1956, M.Ed., 1957; Ed.D., Ind. U., 1961. Dean men Carroll Coll., Wis., 1961-65; v.p. student affairs Kent State U, Ohio, 1965-70; pres. Ricker Coll., 1970-74; sr. prof. Fed. Exec. Inst., Charlottesville, Va., 1974-80, acad. dean, 1980-82, dir., 1982-87, sr. prof., dir. emeritus, 1987-89; prof., dir. leadership edn. program Ctr. Pub. Svc., U. Va., Charlottesville, 1989—, dir. Inst. Govt., 1994-96. Served to 1st. lt. U.S. Army, 1953-55; Korea. Recipient Sweeney Acad. award Internat. City and County Mgrs. Assn., 1993. Methodist. Office: U Va Ctr for Pub Svc 918 Emmet St N Charlottesville VA 22903-4829

MATSON, VIRGINIA MAE FREEBERG (MRS. EDWARD J. MATSON), retired special education educator, author; b. Chgo., Aug. 25, 1914; d. Axel George and Mae (Dalrymple) Freeberg; m. Edward John Matson, Oct. 18, 1941; children: Karin (Mrs. Donald H. Skadden), Sara M. Drake, Edward Robert, Laurence D., David O. BA, U. Ky., 1934; MA, Northwestern U., 1941. Spl. edn. tchr. area high schs., Chgo., 1934-42, Ridge Farm, 1944-45; tchr. h.s. Pub. Schs. Lake County, Ill., 1956-59; founder Grove Sch., Lake Forest, Ill., 1958-87, ret., 1987; instr. evening sch. Carthage Coll., 1965-66. Author: Shadow on the Lost Rock, 1958, Saul, the King, 1968, Abba Father, 1970 (Friends Lit. Fiction award 1972), Buried Alive, 1970, A School for Peter, 1974, A Home for Peter, 1983, Letters to Lauren, A History of the Methodist Campgrounds, Des Plaines, 1985; contbr. many articles to profl. publs. Mem. Friends of Lit. Dem. Recipient Humanitarian award Ill. Med. Soc. Aux. Home: 4133 Mockingbird Ln Suffolk VA 23434-7186

MATSON, WESLEY JENNINGS, educational administrator; b. Svea, Minn., June 25, 1924; s. James and Ettie (Mattson) M.; m. Doris Cragg; 1 child, James Jennings. BS with distinction, U. Minn., 1948; MA, U. Calif., Berkeley, 1954; EdD, Columbia U., 1960. High sch. tchr. Santa Barbara County Pub. Schs., Santa Maria, Calif., 1948-50; instr. U. Calif., Berkeley, 1950-54, Columbia U., N.Y.C., 1954-55; lectr. Fordham U., N.Y.C., 1955-56; asst. prof. U. Md., College Park, 1956-59; prof., asst. dean U. Wis., Milw., 1959-72; dean emeritus Winona (Minn.) State U., 1972-88; vis. prof. U. P.R., Rio Peidras, Western Wash. U., Bellingham, San Diego State U., U. Minn., Mpls., U. Hawaii; adj. faculty St. Olaf Coll., Northfield, Minn., 1990-95; cons. U.S. Dept. Edn., Washington, Ill., Wis.; bd. regents Wis. Dept. Pub. Instruction; examiner Nat. Coun. Accreditation Tchr. Edn., North Ctrl. Assn., Chgo. Editorial bd.: Jour. Instructional Psychology; contbr. articles to profl. jours. Exec. com. Minn. Alliance of the Arts, Mpls.; mem. Minn. Com. Certification Stds., St. Paul; bd. dirs. Ft. Snelling Meml. Chapel Found.; apptd. by Minn. Supreme Ct. to Minn. Bd. CLE, 1996—. Decorated Bronze star; recipient Disting. Service award Wis. Assn. Tchr. Edn., 1972. Mem. Minn. Assn. Colls. for Tchr. Edn. (pres. 1983-85, hon. life award of merit 1985), Nat. Assn. Tchr. Educators (exec. com. 1970-72), Nat. Edn. Assn. (life), Assn. Higher Edn., Minn. Edn. Assn., Minn. Hist. Soc., U. Minn. Alumni Soc. (Outstanding Educator award 1984), Rotary, Phi Delta Kappa, Kappa Delta Pi, Alpha Sigma Phi. Home: 6615 Lake Shore Dr S Minneapolis MN 55423-2218

MATSUDA, FUJIO, technology research center administrator; b. Honolulu, Oct. 18, 1924; s. Yoshio and Shimo (Iwasaki) M.; m. Amy M. Saiki, June 11, 1949; children: Bailey Koki, Thomas Junji, Sherry Noriko, Joan Yuuko, Ann Mitsuyo, Richard Hideo. BSCE, Rose Poly. Inst., 1949; DSc, MIT, 1952; DEng (hon.), Rose Hulman Inst. Tech., 1975. Rsch. engr. MIT, 1952-54; rsch. asst. prof. engring. U. Ill., Urbana, 1954-55; asst. prof. engring. U. Hawaii, Honolulu, 1955-57; assoc. prof. U. Hawaii, 1957-62, chmn. dept. civil engring., 1960-63, prof., 1962-65, 74-84, dir. engring. expt. sta., 1962-63, v.p. bus. affairs, 1973-74, pres., 1974-84, exec. dir. Rsch. Corp., 1984-94; pres. Japan-Am. Inst. Mgmt. Sci., Honolulu, 1994-96, also bd. dirs., ret., 1996; dir. Hawaii Dept. Transp., Honolulu, 1963-73; v.p. Park & Lee, Ltd., Honolulu, 1956-58; pres. SMS & Assocs., Inc., 1960-63; pvt. practice structural engring., 1958-60; bd. dirs. C. Brewer & Co., Ltd., First Hawaiian Bank, First Hawaiian, Inc., Pacific Internat. Ctr. for High Tech. Rsch., Rehab. Hosp. of Pacific, Kuakini Health Sys., Japanese Cultural Ctr. of Hawaii; mem. Airport Ops. Coun. Internat., 1968-73; pres. Pacific Coast Assn. Port Authorities, 1969; mem. sci. bd. Dept. Army, 1978-80; mem. U.S. Army Civilian Adv. Group, 1978—; mem. exec. com. on sponsored rsch. MIT, 1991-94; mem. Rose-Hulman Inst. Tech. Com. on the Future, 1992-94. Bd. dirs. Aloha United Way, 1973-76, Kuakini Med. Ctr., 1987-89; trustee Kuakini Health Sys., 1984-86, bd. dirs., 1986-89; trustee Nature Conservancy, 1984-89, Hawaiian Cmty. Found. Recipient Honor Alumnus award Rose Poly. Inst., 1971, Disting. Svc. award Airport Ops. Coun. Internat., 1973, Disting. Alumnus award U. Hawaii, 1974, 91; named Hawaii Engr. of Yr., 1972. Mem. NAE, NSPE, ASCE (Parcel-Sverdrup Engring. Mgmt. award 1986), Social Sci. Assn., Western Coll. Assn. (exec. com. 1977-84, pres. 1980-82), Japan-Am. Soc. Honolulu (trustee 1976-84, adv. council 1984—), Japan-Hawaii Econ. Coun., World Sustainable Agr. Assn., Beta Gamma Sigma, Sigma Xi, Tau Beta Pi.

MATSUI, DOROTHY NOBUKO, elementary education educator; b. Honolulu, Jan. 9, 1954; d. Katsura and Tamiko (Sakai) M. Student, U. Hawaii, Honolulu, 1972-76, postgrad., 1982; BEd, U. Alaska, Anchorage, 1979, MEd in Spl. Edn., 1986. Clerical asst. U. Hawaii Manoa Disbursing Office, Anchorage, 1974-76; passenger service agt. Japan Air Lines, Anchorage, 1980; bilingual tutor Anchorage Sch. Dist., 1980, elem. sch. tchr., 1980—; facilitator for juvenile justice courses Anchorage Sch. Dist., Anchorage Police Dept., Alaska Pacific U., 1992-93; mem. adv. bd. Anchorage Law-Related Edn. Advancement Project. Vol. Providence Hosp., Anchorage, 1986, Humana Hosp., Anchorage, 1984, Spl. Olympics, Anchorage, 1981, Municipality Anchorage, 1978, Easter Seal Soc. Hawaii, 1975. Mem. NAFE, NEA, Alaska Edn. Assn., Smithsonian Nat. Assoc. Program, Nat. Space Soc., Smithsonian Air and Space Assn., World Aerospace Edn. Orgn., Internat. Platform Assn., Nat. Trust for Hist. Preservation, Nat. Audubon Soc., Planetary Soc., Cousteau Soc., Alaska Coun. for the Social Studies, Alaska Coun. Tchrs. Math., World Inst. Achievment, U.S. Olympic Soc., Women's Inner Circle Achievement, U. Alaska Alumni Assn., World Wildlife Fund, Japanese-Am. Nat. Mus., Alpha Delta Kappa (treas. Alpha chpt. 1988-92, corr. sec. 1993-96, sgt. at arms 1996—). Avocations: reading, sports, psychology. Office: Anchorage Sch Dist 7001 Cranberry St Anchorage AK 99502-7145

MATSUI, JIRO, importer, wholesaler, small business owner; b. Honolulu, Hawaii, Apr. 5, 1919; s. Juro and Tsuta (Murai) M.; m. Barbara Toshiko Tanji; children: Kenneth Jiro, Alan Kiyoshi, Carol Ritsu. BA, U. Hawaii, 1949. Owner Honolulu Aquarium and Pet Supply, Honolulu, 1946-77, Bird House, Honolulu, 1957-61; owner, pres., chmn. Petland, Inc., Honolulu, 1961—, Pets Pacifica, Inc., Honolulu, 1977—, Global Pet Industries, Honolulu, 1975—; organizer, coord. first Pet Consumer Show in U.S., 1979, pres. 1979-82; first Internat. Pet Show; cons. Japan Pet Product Mfr. Assn. Fair, Japan, 1981—. Pres. Waikiki Vets. Club, Kapahulu, Oahu, Hawaii, 1948-66, Waiawa (Oahu) Farmers, 1948-88; sr. adv. com. plants and animals State of Hawaii, 1974—. Sgt. U.S. Army, 1941-46. Decorated Bronze Star; named retailer of yr. Retail Merchants of Hawaii, 1993. Mem. Am. Pet Soc. (pres. 1979-82, chmn. 1989-92), World Wide Pet Supply Assn. (bd. dirs. 1974-93, pres. 1989-90, Edward B. Price award 1982), Honolulu C. of C. (bd. dirs. 1974—), Merchants of Hawaii. Avocations: fishing, gardening,. Office: Pets Pacifica Inc 94-486 Ukee St Waipahu HI 96797-4211

MATSUI, ROBERT TAKEO, congressman; b. Sacramento, Sept. 17, 1941; s. Yasuji and Alice (Nagata) M.; m. Doris Kazue Okada, Sept. 17, 1966; 1 child, Brian Robert. AB in Polit. Sci, U. Calif., Berkeley, 1963; JD, U. Calif., San Francisco, 1966. Bar: Calif. 1967. Practiced law Sacramento, 1967-78; mem. Sacramento City Council, 1971-78, vice mayor, 1977; mem. 96th-105th Congresses from 5th Calif. dist., 1979—; ranking minority mem., mem. ways and means subcom. on oversight; dep. chair Dem. Nat. Com., 1995—; chmn. profl. bus. forum Dem. Congl. Campaign Com.; congl. liaison nat. fin. council Dem. Nat. Com.; mem. adv. council on fiscal policy Am. Enterprise Inst. chmn. Profl. Bus. Forum of the Dem. Congl. Co. and Com.; congl. liaison Nat. Fin. Council, Dem. Nat. Com.; mem. Am. Enterprise Inst. Adv. Council on Fiscal Policy. Named Young Man of Yr. Jr. C. of C., 1973; recipient Disting. Service award, 1973. Mem. Sacramento Japanese Am. Citizens League (pres. 1969), Sacramento Met. C. of C. (dir. 1976). Democrat. Clubs: 20-30 (Sacramento) (pres. 1972), Rotary (Sacramento). Office: US Ho of Reps 2308 Rayburn HOB Washington DC 20515-0505*

MATSUMORI, DOUGLAS, lawyer; b. Salt Lake City, Oct. 22, 1947. BS, U. Utah, 1973; JD, Harvard U., 1976. With Ray, Quinney & Nebeker P.C., Salt Lake City. Mem. Utah State Bar, Phi Beta Kappa. Office: Ray Quinney & Nebeker Ste 400 PO Box 45385 79 S Main St Salt Lake City UT 84111-0385

MATSUMOTO, GEORGE, architect; b. San Francisco, July 16, 1922; s. Manroku F. and Ise (Nakagawa) M.; m. Kimi Nao, Dec. 15, 1951; children—Mari-Jane, Kiyo-Ann, Kei-Ellen, Kenneth Manroku, Miye-Eileen. Student, U. Calif. at Berkeley, 1938-42; B.Arch., Washington U., 1944; M.Arch., Cranbrook Acad. Art, 1945. Designer Heathers Garden Devel. Co., Calif., 1941-42; designer with George F. Keck, Chgo., 1943-44; sr. designer, planner Saarinen & Swanson, Birmingham, Mich., 1945-46; sr. designer Skidmore, Owings & Merrill, Chgo., 1948; partner Runnells, Clark, Waugh, Matsumoto, Kansas City, Mo., 1946-47; practice architecture Okla., 1948-61, N.C., 1948-61, San Francisco, 1962-92; pres. George Matsumoto and assocs., San Francisco, 1992-93; retired, 1993; instr. U. Okla., 1947-48; prof. N.C. State Coll., 1948-61, U. Calif. at Berkeley, 1961-67. Important works include libraries, office bldgs., schs., recreation ctrs., chs., govt. bldgs., pvt. residences, med. research labs. and offices. Bd. dirs. Young Audiences, Oakland Mus. Assn., Oakland Arts Coun., Friends of Oakland Park and Recreation, East Bay Agy. for Children. Recipient over 50 archtl. awards and prizes. Fellow AIA (dir. chpt.), Internat. Inst. Arts and Letters; mem. Mich. Soc. Architects, Assn. Coll. Sch. Architecture, Raleigh Council Architects, San Francisco Planning and Urban Renewal Assn., Nat. Council Archtl. Registration Bds., Calif. Assn. Architects, Bldg. Research Inst., Japanese-Am. Citizens League. Home: 1170 Glencourt Dr Oakland CA 94611-1405

MATSUMOTO, TERUO, surgeon, educator; b. Fukuoka City, Japan, Jan. 2, 1929; came to U.S., 1956, naturalized, 1964; s. Yoshinari and Fumie (Hayashi) M.; m. Mary L. Cousino, July 29, 1961; children: Louisa Michi, Maria Chieko, Monica Mieko, Nelson Tateru. M.D., Kyushu U., 1953, Ph.D., 1956. Diplomate: Am. Bd. Surgery, Am. Bd. Gen. Vascular Surgery. Intern Cook County Hosp., Chgo., 1956-57; surg. resident Med. Coll. Ohio, Toledo, 1957-61; commd. capt. U.S. Army, 1961, advanced through grades to lt. col., 1965; gen. surgeon U.S. Army Camp Zama Hosp., Japan, 1961-65; chief surg. service U.S. Army Camp Zama Hosp., 1962-65, chief gen. surgery sect., 1962-65; chief dept. exptl. surgery Walter Reed Army Inst. Research, 1965-68, dir. U.S. Army Surg. Research, Pacific, 1968; assoc. prof. surgery Hahnemann Med. Coll. and Hosp., Phila., 1969-72; prof. surgery Hahnemann U., Phila., 1973—; chmn. dept. surgery Hahnemann U., 1975-90, dir. divsn. vascular surgery, 1990—; pres. med. staff Hahnemann Med. Coll. and Hosp., 1979-81; mem. sci. rev. com. NIH, cons. field reader for Office of Orphan Products Devel., FDA, 1986. Editor Emergency Surgery, Jour. Internat. Surgery, Jour. Critical Care Medicine, Jour. Internat. Cardiovascular Surgery; contbr. to profl. jours. and books. Recipient Sir Henry Wellcome medal and prize, 1965, gold medal Southeastern Sug. Congress, 1968, Outstanding Achievement award U.S. Army Sci. Conf., 1969, Golden Apple award Student AMA, 1972. Fellow Southeastern Surg. Congress, ACS, Am. Coll. Angiology, Am. Assn. for Surgery of Trauma, Pan Am. Med. Assn., Assn. Surgery for Alimentary Tract, AMA, Japanese Coll. Surgeons, Internat. Cardiovascular Surgery, Soc. Vascular Surgery, AOA, Phila. Acad. Surgery, Pan Pacific Surg. Congress, Soc. Surg. Chairmen; mem. Council Cardiovascular Surgery, Soc. Surg. Oncology. Home: 1116 Sandringham Rd Bala Cynwyd PA 19004-2023 Office: Hahnemann U Med Sch Philadelphia PA 19102

MATSUO, FUMISUKE, physician, educator; b. Iida, Japan, Dec. 24, 1942; came to U.S., 1969; s. Riichi and Utako (Sasaki) M.; m. Ruth Ann Smith, May 24, 1975; children: Jocelyn, Bryan. MD, Kyoto (Japan) Prefectural U. Medicine, 1968. Asst. prof. U. Iowa, Iowa City, 1975; asst. prof. U. Utah, Salt Lake City, 1975-79, assoc. prof., 1979-87, prof., 1987—; dir. EEG Lab. Univ. Hosp., Salt Lake City, 1975—. Contbr. articles to profl. jours. Fellow Am. Acad. Neurology, Am. Clin. Neurophysiology Soc.; mem. AMA, Soc. Neuroscis., Am. Epilepsy Soc., Epilepsy Assn. Utah (bd. dirs. 1978-81, 87-89), Western EEG Soc. (bd. dirs. 1983-86, sec.-treas. 1989-90, pres. 1991-92). Home: 1353 S 1900 E Salt Lake City UT 84108-2219 Office: U Utah Med Ctr 50 N Medical Dr Salt Lake City UT 84132-0001

MATTA, RAM KUMAR, aeronautical engineer; b. Karachi, India, May 9, 1946; came to U.S., 1967, naturalized, 1976; s. Madhavdas Lalchand and Damyanti (Ahuja) M.; m. Renee M. Verhoff, Dec. 1988. B.Tech., Indian Inst. Tech., New Delhi, 1967; M.S., U. Minn., 1969, Ph.D., 1973; MS in Mgmt., Stanford U., 1988. Acoustics engr. and mgr. Aircraft Engine Group, Gen. Electric Co., Evendale, Ohio, 1973-77, sr. engr. cycle systems and performance, 1977-84, mgr. advanced programs, 1983-84, mgr. CFM56-5 systems engring. and product improvements, 1984-87, gen. mgr. CFM56-5C and advanced programs, 1988-92, program gen. mgr. GE45/CFMXX, dir. CFM advanced programs, 1992-93; bus. interface Gen. Electric Corp. Rsch. and Devel., 1993—. Contbr. articles to profl. publs.; patentee in field. Exec. mem., vol. Minn. Internat. Ctr., Mpls., 1970-72; chmn. Citizens Com. for Community Devel., Forest Park, Ohio, 1975-76. Recipient Pres.'s Gold medal Indian Inst. Tech., 1967, Profl. Performance award, 1975, Mgmt. award, 1979, 87; Merit scholar Indian Inst. Tech., 1967; Sloan fellow Stanford U., 1987-88. Mem. AIAA, Sigma Gamma Tau. Home: 1010 Lamplighter Rd Schenectady NY 12309-1159 Office: GE CR&D MD KW-D281 PO Box 8 Schenectady NY 12301-0008

MATTAR, PHILIP, institute director, editor; b. Haifa, Palestine, Jan. 21, 1944; came to U.S. 1961; m. Evelyn Ann Keith, June 20, 1971; 1 child, Christina. MPhil, Columbia U., 1977, PhD, 1981. Exec. dir. Inst. for Palestine Studies, Washington, 1984—; assoc. editor Jour. Palestine Studies, Washington, 1985—; adj. lectr. history Yale U., 1981; adj. prof. history Georgetown U., 1990, 91, 94. Author: Mufti of Jerusalem, 1988, 2d edit., 1991; co-editor: Encyclopedia of the Modern Middle East, 1996; contbr. articles to profl. jours., including Fgn. Policy, Middle East Jour., Middle Ea. Studies. Mem. adv. com. Human Rights Watch/Middle East. Vis. scholar Columbia U., 1984; Fulbright-Hays Rsch. fellow, 1978. Mem. Middle East Studies Assn., Middle East Inst. Avocations: jogging, chess, reading, travel. Office: Inst for Palestine Studies 3501 M St NW Washington DC 20007-2624

MATTATHIL, GEORGE PAUL, communications specialist, consultant; b. Kottayam, India, May 12, 1957; came to U.S., 1985; s. Paul and Annamma M. Bs, U. Kerala (India), 1973-78; MS, Indian Inst. Tech., 1978-82. Project engr. Tekelec, Calabasas, Calif., 1986-89; sr. systems analyst Security Pacific Automation, L.A., 1989-90; sr. design. engr. Telenova, Camarillo, Calif., 1990-91; cons. Raynet, Menlo Park, Calif., 1991, Larse, Santa Clara, Calif., 1991—, NEC, 1992—, Level One Comm., Sacramento, 1994—, DigitalLink, 1994—, Verilink, San Jose, 1994—, Telebit, Sunnyvale, 1995—, Hitachi, San Jose, 1995—, C-Cor Electronics, Fremont, 1996, Xylan, Calabasas, Calif., 1996—, GoDigital Telecomm., Fremont, 1996—. Nat. Sci. Talent scholar, India, 1975-80. Mem. IEEE, Profl. and Tech. Cons. Assn., Assn. Computing Machinery, Software Forum, Soc. Telecom. Cons. Avocations: photography, biking. Office: Silicom Inc PO Box 2264 Cupertino CA 95015-2264

MATTAUCH, ROBERT JOSEPH, electrical engineering educator; b. Rochester, Pa., May 30, 1940; s. Henry Paul and Anna Marie (Mlinarcik) M.; m. Frances Sabo, Dec. 29, 1962; children: Lori Ann, Thomas J. BS, Carnegie Inst. Tech., Pitts., 1962; MEE, N.C. State U., Raleigh, 1963, PhD, 1967. Asst. prof. elec. engring. U. Va., Charlottesville, 1966-70, assoc. prof. elec. engring., 1970-76, prof. elec. engring., 1976-83, Wilson prof. elec. engring., 1983-86, Standard Oil Co. prof. sci. and tech., 1986-89, chmn. dept. elect. engring., 1987-95, BP Am. prof. sci. and tech., 1989-95; Commonwealth prof., founding chair dept. elec. engring. Va. Commonwealth U., Richmond, 1995—; cons. The Rochester Corp., Culpeper, Va., 1983-88, Milltech Corp., Deerfield, Mass., 1985. Patentee: infrared detector; solid state switching capacitor; thin wire pointing method, whiskerless Schottky diode, controlled in-situ etch back growth technique. Bd. dirs. U. Va. Patent Found. Recipient Excellence in Instruction of Engring. Students award Western Electric, 1980. Fellow IEEE (Centennial medal 1984); mem. Eta Kappa Nu (recipient Oustanding Prof. in Elec. Engring. 1975), Sigma Xi, Tau Beta Pi. Office: Va Commonwealth U Dept Elec Engring PO Box 843072 Richmond VA 23284-3072

MATTEA, KATHY, vocalist, songwriter; m. Jon Vezner, Feb. 14, 1988. Student, W.Va. U. Former mem. bluegrass band. Albums include Walk the Way the Wind Blows, 1986, Untasted Honey, 1987, Willow in the Wind, 1989, Kathy Mattea: A Collection of Hits, 1990, Time Passes By, 1991 (Best country video award Houston Internat. Film Festival 1991), Lonesome Standard Time, 1992, Good News, 1993 (Grammy award, Best Southern Gospel, Country Gospel or Bluegrass Gospel album, 1994), Walking Away a Winner, 1994, Love Travels, 1997. Recipient Best Single award, 1988 (Eighteen Wheels and a Dozen Roses), Song of the Yr. award, 1988 (Eighteen Wheels and a Dozen Roses), Top Female Vocalist award, 1989, Song of the Yr. award., 1989 (Where've You Been) Acad. Country Music, Best Female Vocalist award Country Music Assn., 1989, 90, Best Female Vocalist Radio & Records Country Readers Poll, 1990, Song of the Yr. award (Where've You Been) Country Music Assn., 1990, Best Country Vocal Female Grammy award, 1991, Grammy nomination, Best Country

Vocal Collaboration for "Romeo" with Dolly Parton, Tanya Tucker, Billy Ray Cyrus, Pam Tillis & Mary-Chapin Carpenter, 1994. Address: care Titley & Assocs 900 Division St Nashville TN 37203-4111

MATTERN, DAVID BRUCE, elementary education educator; b. Harrisburg, Pa., Sept. 3, 1952; s. Kenneth Gordon and Betty Jane (Fisher) M.; m. Sheryl Lynn Young, Nov. 30, 1974; children: Melissa Ann, Marcia Lynn. BA in Elem. Edn., Cen. Coll., 1974; MS in Edn. Adminstrn., Iowa State U., 1982. Cert. elem. educator, edn. adminstr. Elem. tchr. Ringrose Elem. Sch., Wentworthville, N.S.W., Australia, 1975-77; tchr. 3rd-6th grade Lovejoy Elem. Sch., Des Moines, 1977-82, tchr. fifth grade, 1983—, asst. prin., 1991—; coord. gifted and talented program Des Moines Pub. Schs., 1979-88, curriculum specialist, 1988—; mem. Des Moines Math. Adv. Bd., 1983-84. Diaconate mem. Park Ave Christian Ch., Des Moines, 1979-96, chmn., 1988-90, 94-95. Mem. Iowa Coun. Tchrs. Math., Nat. Coun. Tchrs. Math., ASCD. Republican. Avocations: softball, tennis, basketball, swimming, travel. Home: 4309 Beaver Hills Dr Des Moines IA 50310-6300

MATTERN, DONALD EUGENE, retired association executive; b. Mapleton Depot, Pa., Feb. 11, 1930; s. John Franklin and Lizzie May (Fiss) M.; m. Anna Mae Bard, Nov. 24, 1951; children: Debra Jeanne, Cynthia Ann, James Franklin. BA, Pa. State U., 1951; MBA, U. Pa., 1955. Exec. trainee Fed. Res. Bank Phila., 1953-55; from asst. cashier to cashier Cumberland County Nat. Bank, New Cumberland, Pa., 1955-63; v.p. 1st Nat. Bank State Coll., Pa., 1963-64; asst. v.p., v.p., sr. v.p., sec. Hamilton Bank, Lancaster, Pa., 1964-86; sec., v.p. Nat. Cen. Fin. Corp., 1972-83; exec. dir. Mfr.'s Assn. Berks County, 1986-95; mem. adv. bd. Berks campus Pa. State U., 1987-92. Treas., bd. dirs. Reading-Berks Human Rels. Coun., 1967-70; v.p. bd. dirs. local chpts. Ams. Competitive Enterprise Sys., 1970-92; past bd. dirs., past pres., past gen. campaign chmn. United Way Berks County; trustee, former chmn. bd. Comty. Gen. Hosp., Reading, 1967—; bd. dirs. Nat. Coun. on Alcoholism, 1967-68, Reading Ctr. City Devel. Fund, 1976—, Greater Berks Devel. Fund, 1984-89, Reading Mus. Found., 1985—, Luth. Home Topton, 1990—, Berkshire Health Plan, 1992-96, Highlands at Wyomissing, 1995—, Congregation Coun. Advent Luth. Ch., various terms 1965—, Reading New Futures Project, Inc., 1988-91, Pub. Edn. Found. for Berks County, 1991-96; mem. exec. bd. Hawk Mountain coun. Boy Scouts Am., 1970—; mem. N.E. Pa. Synod Endowment Investment Fund Com., 1985—, treas., bd. dirs. Housing Opportunities, in Met. Environment, 1968-73. 1st lt. USAF, 1951-53. Mem. Masons, Shriners. Republican. Lutheran. Home: 20 Birchwood Rd Reading PA 19610-1908

MATTERN, DOUGLAS JAMES, electronics reliability engineer; b. Creede, Colo., May 19, 1933; s. John A. and Ethel (Franklin) M.; student San Jose (Calif.) City Coll., San Jose State U., 1956-58; m. Noemi E. Del Cippo, May 4, 1963. Reliability engr. Intersil, Sunnyvale, Calif., 1973-80; sr. engr. Data Gen. Corp., Sunnyvale, 1981-87; staff engr. Apple Computer, 1987—. Sec. Gen. World Citizens Assembly, San Francisco, 1975-86; dir. World Citizens Internat. Registry, U.S. Ctr., San Francisco, 1976—, World Citizen Diplomats, Palo Alto, Calif., 1988—; del. Peoples Congress, Paris, 1980—; pres. Assn. World Citizens, San Francisco, 1989—; pres. World Citizens Found., 1991—; chmn. World Citizens Assembly, San Francisco, 1995. Served with USN, 1951-55. Author resolution To End the Arms Race; contbg. author: Building a More Democratic United Nations, 1991; editor World Citizen Newsmag., 1973—; contbr. 45 articles to profl. jours. Mem. Nat. Electron Microscopy Assn., Union of Concerned Scientists Promoting Enduring Peace. Home: 2671 South Court St Palo Alto CA 94306-2462 Office: 55 New Montgomery St Ste 224 San Francisco CA 94105-3421

MATTERS, CLYDE BURNS, former college president; b. Fargo, N.D., Nov. 10, 1924; s. Lester H. and Pearl Lila (Burns) M.; m. Anna R. Skeels, Mar. 24, 1948; children—Cynthia (Mrs. Charles V. Carroll), Richard B. B.S., Whitworth Coll., Spokane, Wash., 1950, M.Ed., 1951; Ph.D., U. Wash., 1960; L.H.D. (hon.), Hastings Coll., 1985. Tchr. Spokane Pub. Schs., 1950-51; prof. Whitworth Coll., 1950-57, 70-72; research assoc. U. Wash., 1957-60; asst. supt. schs. King County, Wash., 1960-63; program adviser Ford Found., West Africa, 1963-70; pres. Hastings (Nebr.) Coll., 1972-85; pres. Nebr. Ind. Coll. Found.; mem. nexus com. Presbyn. Coll. Union; pres. Assn. Ind. Colls. and Univs. Nebr. Resident camp dir. Spokane YMCA, 1952-57, bd. dirs., 1970-72; bd. dirs. United Good Neighbors, Spokane County, 1969-70; trustee Synod of Alaska N.W. Found., 1995—. With AUS, 1943-46. Decorated Bronze Star. Mem. Assn. Ind. Colls. and Univs. (pres. Nebr. 1979-80), Phi Delta Kappa. Presbyterian (elder). Lodge: Kiwanis. Home: 4415 E 51st Ln # 3 Spokane WA 99223-7888

MATTES, MARTIN ANTHONY, lawyer; b. San Francisco, June 18, 1946; s. Hans Adam and Marion Jane (Burge) M.; m. Catherine Elvira Garzio, May 26, 1984; children: Nicholas Anthony, Daniel Joseph, Thomas George. BA, Stanford U., 1968; postgrad., U. Chgo., 1968-69, U. Bonn, Fed. Republic Germany, 1971; JD, U. Calif., Berkeley, 1974. Bar: Calif. 1974, U.S. Ct. Appeals (D.C., 5th and 9th cirs.) 1978, U.S. Dist. Ct. (no. dist.) Calif. 1979, U.S. Dist. Ct. (ea. dist.) Calif. 1991. Asst. legal officer Internat. Union Conservation of Nature and Natural Resources, Bonn, 1974-76; staff counsel Calif. Pub. Utilities Commn., San Francisco, 1976-79, legal advisor to pres., 1979-82, adminstrv. law judge, 1983, asst. chief adminstrv. law judge, 1983-86; ptnr. Graham & James, San Francisco, 1986—; mem. adv. group. to Calif. Senate Subcom. on Pub. Utilities Commn. Procedural Reform, 1994. Mng. editor Ecology Law Quar., 1973-74; contbr. articles to profl. publs. Mem. Conf. Calif. Pub. Utility Counsel (treas. 1988-90, v.p. 1990-91, pres. 1991-92), Internat. Coun. Environ. Law, San Francisco Bar Assn. Office: Graham & James 1 Maritime Plz Ste 300 San Francisco CA 94111-3406

MATTESON, CLARICE CHRIS, artist, educator; b. Winnipeg, Man., Can., Sept. 2, 1918; came to U.S., 1922; d. Sergis and Nina (Balter) Alberts; m. D.C. Matteson, 1956 (dec. 1976); children: Kemmer, Gretchen. BA, Met. State U., 1976; MA in Liberal Studies, Hamline U., 1986; PhD in Humanities, LaSalle U., 1995. Mem. Orson Welles' staff, Hollywood, Calif., 1945-46; owner Hilde-Gardes Co., L.A., 1947-56; instr. art North Hennepin C.C., Brooklyn Park, Minn., 1975-81; prodr., host Accent on Art TV Program, St. Paul, 1979—; instr. art Lakewood C.C., U. Minn., Normandale C.C., Bloomington (Minn.) Sch. Dist., Mpls. Sch. Dist., St. Paul Sch. Dist., 1981—. Exhibited in group shows at Mpls. Inst. Art, 1994-95, Govs. 1006 Soc., 1994—; represented in permanent collections Richard James Gallery, Mpls., Gallery 416, Mpls.; corr. Schaumberg (Ill.) Newspapers, 1962-68; prodr., host TV series Kids Art, Mpls.-St. Paul, 1995; prodr. series program Internat. Cafe Internet Arts, 1996—; patentee plastic products. Active Minn. Orch. (WAMSO), Mpls., 1972—, vol. Recipient award for creative leadership Minn. Assn. for Continuing Adult Edn., 1977, Gold Cup award Bloomington Cable, 1989, Gov.'s Letter of Commendation, 1994, Popular Music award ASCAP, 1996, honored by Met. State U., 1997; Park Cable TV grantee, 1982, Minn. Humanities Commn. grantee, 1985. Mem. ASCAP (award 1996), AAUW (dir. arts com. 1989-90, bd. dirs. 1990-92), Am. Pen Women (v.p. Minn. chpt. 1994—), Am. Composers Forum, Minn. Artists Assn., Minn. Territorial Pioneers (bd. dirs. 1995—), Internat. Alliance for Women in Music, St. Paul Neighborhood Network, N.Y. Neighborhood Network. Avocations: tennis, dancing, writing children's books, composing liturgical music. Home and Office: 2119 Sargent Ave Saint Paul MN 55105-1126

MATTESON, THOMAS T., academic administrator; s. Ruth (Cole) M.; m. Dorothy Johnston, Apr. 10, 1965; children: Juliet M., Jeffrey C. BS, U.S. Coast Guard Acad., 1957; MS, Naval Post Grad. Coll., 1969; postgrad., Air War Coll., 1976-77. Tng. officer USCG Air Sta., Miami, Fla., 1962-63; RCC contr. 9th dist. U.S. Coast Guard Acad., Cleve., 1963-65; asst. ops. officer air sta. U.S. Coast Guard Acad., Port Angeles, Wash., 1965-68; exec. officer Aviation Tng. Ctr. hdqrs. USCG, Washington, 1973-76; commdg. officer air sta. USCG, Borinquen, P.R., 1977-79; chief aviation br. hdqrs. USCG, Washington, 1979-81, chief, officer pers. divsn. hdqrs., 1981-82; chief ops. divsn. 8th dist. USCG, New Orleans, 1982-84; chief staff 8th dist. U.S. Coast Guard Acad., New Orleans, 1984-85, chief office of boating safety hdqrs., 1985-87, chief office pers. hdqrs., 1987-89; supt. U.S. Coast Guard Acad., New London, Conn., 1989-93, U.S. Merchant Marine Acad., Kings Point, N.Y., 1993—. Office: Dept Transp Merchant Marine Acad Kings Point NY 11024-1699

MATTESON, WILLIAM BLEECKER, lawyer; b. N.Y.C., Oct. 20, 1928; s. Leonard Jerome and Mary Jo (Harwell) M.; m. Marilee Brill, Aug. 26, 1950; children: Lynn, Sandra, Holly. B.A., Yale U., 1950; J.D., Harvard U., 1953. Bar: N.Y. 1954. Clk. to judge Augustus N. Hand U.S. Ct. Appeals, 1953-54; clk. to U.S. Supreme Ct. Justice Harold H. Burton, 1954-55; asso. firm Debevoise & Plimpton (and predecessors), N.Y.C., 1955-61; partner Debevoise & Plimpton (and predecessors), 1961—, Debevoise & Plimpton (European office), Paris, 1973-78; presiding ptnr., 1988-93; lectr. Columbia U. Law Sch., 1972-73, 78-80. Trustee Peddie Sch., Hightstown, N.J., 1968-73, Kalamazoo Coll., 1972-77, Miss Porter's Sch., Farmington, Conn., 1977-83, N.Y. Inst. Spl. Edn., 1981—, Salk Inst., La Jolla, Calif., 1994—, vice-chair, 1994-96, Statue of Liberty Ellis Island Found., 1996—, Hartford Found., 1996—; active USA Bus. and Industry Adv. Com. to the Orgn. for Econ. Coop. and Devel., Paris, 1986—; chmn. Worldwide Bus. and Industry Adv. Com., 1994-96; vice chmn. U.S. Coun. for Internat. Bus., 1990—. Mem. ABA, FBA, Internat. Bar Assn., N.Y. State Bar Assn., Assn. of Bar of City of N.Y. (chmn. securities regulation com. 1968-71), Harvard U. Law Sch. Assn. N.Y.C. (trustee 1968-73), Coun. Fgn. Rels., Union Club, River Club, Sky Club, Links Club, Sankaty Head Club. Home: 291 Llwyds Ln Vero Beach FL 32963 Office: Debevoise & Plimpton 875 3rd Ave New York NY 10022-6225

MATTESSICH, RICHARD VICTOR (ALVARUS), business administration educator; b. Trieste, Venezia-Julia, Italy, Aug. 9, 1922; s. Victor and Gertrude (Pfaundler) M.; m. Hermine Auguste Mattessich, Apr. 12, 1952. Mech. engr., Engring. Coll., Vienna, Austria, 1940; Diplomkaufmann, Hochschule für Welthandel, Vienna, 1944; Dr.rer.pol., Hochschule für Welthandel, 1945; Accademico Ordinario, Accademia Italiana di Economia Aziendale, Bologna, 1980—; corr. mem., Austrian Acad. Scis., Vienna, 1984—. Research fellow Austrian Inst. Econ. Research, Vienna, 1945-47; instr. Rosenberg Coll., St. Gallen, 1947-52; dep. head Mt. Allison U., Sackville, Can., 1953-59; assoc. prof. U. Calif.-Berkeley, 1958-67; prof. econs. Ruhr U., Bochum, W. Ger., 1966-67; prof. indsl. adminstrn. U. Tech., Vienna, 1976-78; prof. bus. adminstrn. U. B.C., Vancouver, 1967-87, Arthur Andersen & Co. Disting. chair, 1980-87, prof. emeritus, 1988—; Vis. prof. Free U., Berlin, 1965, U. Social Scis., St. Gallen, Switzerland, 1965-66, U. Canterbury, 1970, Austrian Acad. Mgmt., 1971, 73; mem. bd. nominations Acctg. Hall of Fame, Columbus, Ohio, 1978-87; bd. govs. Sch. Chartered Accountancy, Vancouver, 1981-82; bd. dirs. Can. Cert. Gen. Accts. Research Found., 1984-90; internat. adv. bd. CGA Rsch. Found., 1993—. Author: Accounting and Analytical Methods, 1964, Simulation of the Firm Through a Budget Computer Program, 1964, Instrumental Reasoning and Systems Methodology, 1978, Critiqie of Accounting, 1995, Foundational Research in Accounting: Professional Memoirs and Beyond, 1995; editor: Modern Accounting Research History, Survey and Guide, 1984, 89, 92, Accounting Research in the 1980s and Its Future Influence, 1991, French transl., 1993, others; mem. editl. bd. Theory and Decision Libr., Jour. Bus. Adminstrn., Economia Azlendale, Praxiology, Acctg., Bus. and Fin. History. Sec.-treas. Internat. House, U. B.C., 1969-70; bd. dirs. Can. Cert. Gen. Accts. Research Found., 1984-90. Served to lt. Orgn. Todt., 1944-45. Recipient Gold medal and Lit. award AICPA, 1972, Haim Falk award Can. Acad. Acctg. Assn., 1991;Ford Found. fellow, 1961-62; Disting. Erskine fellow U. Canterbury, 1970; Killam sr. fellow U. B.C., 1971-72. Fellow Accademia Italiana di Economia Aziendale (accademico ordinario 1980—); mem. Inst. Chartered Accts., Am. Acctg. Assn. (lit. award 1972, 73), Schmalenbach Gesellschaft, Verb. d. Hochschullehrer für Betriebswirtschaft (exec. adv. council 1976-78), Inst. Chartered Accts. of B.C. (bd. of govs. 1981-82), Austrian Acad. Scis. (corr.), Acad. Acctg. Historians (life) (hon. prof. Inst. Univ. Franc de Vitoria, U. Madrid). Office: U BC, Dept Bus Adminstrn, Vancouver, BC Canada V6T 1Z2 *Cautious optimism is the best long-run optimization strategy.*

MATTEUCCI, DOMINICK VINCENT, real estate developer; b. Trenton, N.J., Oct. 19, 1924; s. Vincent Joseph and Anna Marie (Zoda) M.; BS, Coll. of William and Mary, 1948; BS, Mass. Inst. Tech., 1950. Registered profl. engr., Calif.; lic. gen. bldg. contractor, real estate broker; m. Emma Irene DeGuia, Mar. 2, 1968; children: Felisa Anna, Vincent Eriberto. Owner, Matteucci Devel. Co., Newport Beach, Calif.; pres. Nat. Investment Brokerage Co., Newport Beach. Home: 2104 Felipe Newport Beach CA 92660-4040 Office: PO Box 10474 Newport Beach CA 92658-0474

MATTHAU, CHARLES MARCUS, film director; b. N.Y.C., Dec. 10, 1964; s. Walter and Carol M. BA, U. So. Calif., 1986. Pres. The Matthau Co., L.A., 1986—. Dir. motion picture Doin' Time on Planet Earth, 1990 (Saturn award Coun. Film Orgns., Silver Scroll award Acad. Sci. Fiction); dir., prodr. TV show Mrs. Lambert Remembers Love, 1993 (Golden Angel award Best TV Spl. 1993, Golden Medal award Best Drama Prodn. 1993, Grand award The Houston Internat. Film Festival); dir., prodr. motion picture The Grass Harp, 1996 (recipient Best Dir. Family Film awards 1996); dir. over 50 feature shorts. Nat. spokesperson Am. Lung Assn., L.A., 1989—; active Action on Smoking and Health, Washington, 1986—. Recipient Cine award, Coun. Non-Theatrical Events, Washington, 1985, Golden Seal award, London Amateur Film Festival, 1986. Mem. Dirs. Guild Am., Am. Film Inst., Acad. Sci.-Fiction, Fantasy and Horror Films.

MATTHAU, WALTER, actor; b. N.Y.C., Oct. 1, 1920; s. Milton and Rose (Berolsky) M.; m. Carol Grace Marcus, Aug. 21, 1959; children—David, Jenny, Charles. Ed. pub. schs., N.Y.C. Broadway appearances include: Anne of a Thousand Days, 1948, The Liar, 1949, Season in the Sun, 1950, Fancy Meeting You Again, 1951, Twilight Walk, 1951 (N.Y. Drama Critics award), One Bright Day, 1951, In Any Language, 1952, The Grey-Eyed People, 1952, The Ladies of the Corridor, 1953, Will Success Spoil Rock Hunter, 1955, Once More with Feeling, 1958 (N.Y. Drama Critics award), Once There Was a Russian, 1960, A Shot in the Dark, 1961 (Antoinette Perry award), My Mother, My Father and Me, 1963, The Odd Couple, 1964 (Antoinette Perry award); motion pictures include A Guide for the Married Man, Secret Life of An American Wife, Mirage, Charade, The Kentuckian, 1955, The Indian Fighter, 1955, Slaughter on Tenth Avenue, 1957, Ride A Crooked Trail, A Face in the Crowd, 1957, No Power on Earth, Middle of the Street, Onion Head, 1958, Voice in the Mirror, 1958, Bigger Than Life, King Creole, 1958, Island of Love, Strangers When We Meet, 1960, The Gangster Story, 1960, Where's The Action, 1962, Lonely Are the Brave (Film Daily award), 1962, Fail-Safe, 1964, Goodbye Charlie, 1964, The Odd Couple, 1966, The Fortune Cookie (Academy award), 1966, Candy, 1968, Hello Dolly!, 1968, Cactus Flower, 1969, A New Leaf, Plaza Suite, Kotch, 1971, Pete 'n Tillie, 1972, Charley Varrick, Laughing Policeman, The Front Page, The Sunshine Boys, 1975, The Bad News Bears, The Taking of Pelham, One Two Three, California Suite, 1978, Casey's Shadow, 1978, House Calls, 1978, I Ought To Be In Pictures, Little Miss Marker, 1979, Hopscotch, 1979, First Monday in October, 1981, Buddy Buddy, 1981, The Survivors, Movers and Shakers, 1984, Pirates, 1986, Couch Trip, 1987, The Little Devil, 1988, J.F.K., 1991, Dennis the Menace, 1993, Grumpy Old Men, 1993, I.Q., 1994, The Odd Couple 2, 1995, The Grass Harp, 1995, Grumpier Old Men, 1995, I'm not Rappaport, 1996, Out to Sea, 1997; TV films include: Incident in a Small Town, 1994. Served with USAAF, 1941-45, ETO. Office: The Matthau Co. 1999 Avenue Of The Stars Ste 2100 Los Angeles CA 90067-6022*

MATTHEI, EDWARD HODGE, architect; b. Chgo., Dec. 21, 1927; s. Henry Reinhold and Myra Beth (Hodge) M.; m. Mary Nina Hoffmann, June 30, 1951; children: Edward Hodge, Suzanne Marie, Christie Ann, Laura Jean, John William. B.S. in Archtl. Engring. U. Ill., 1951. Registered architect, Ariz., Fla., Ill., Mich., N.Y., Wis. Dir. health facilities planning and constrn. Child & Smith (architects and engrs.), Chgo., 1951-60; sr. v.p. health facilities planning Perkins & Will, Chgo., 1960-74; ptnr. firm Matthei & Colin Assoc., Chgo., 1974-96; planning and archtl. design cons. Chgo., 1996—; com. chmn. Am. Nat. Standards Inst., 1983-89; lectr. 1st Internat. Conf. on Rehab. of Handicapped, Beijing, 1986, Design USA, Novosibirsk and Moscow, USSR, 1990. Editor: Inland Architect, 1956-58; prin. works health facilities projects, med. ctr. master plans including Augustana Hosp. and Health Care Ctr., Chgo., Mercy Hosp., Davenport, Iowa, Westlake Cmty. Hosp., Chgo., Highland Park (Ill.) Hosp., Ctrl. DuPage Hosp., Winfield, Ill., Nebr. Meth. Hosp., Omaha, Rockford (Ill.) Meml. Hosp., U. Ala. Med. Ctr., Birmingham, U. Calif. Sch. Medicine, Irvine, Kent Hall, U. Chgo., Holy Cross Hosp., Chgo., Wis. Cancer Ctr. Second v.p. Nat. Easter Seal Soc., 1978; mem. bd. dirs. St. Scholastica H.S., Chgo., 1973-83, 86-96; mem. Welfare Coun. Greater Met. Chgo., 1965-72; chair profl. adv. coun. Nat. Easter Seal Soc., 1988-89. With AUS, 1946-47. Recipient Leon Chatelain award for barrier-free environ. Nat. Easter Seals Soc., 1979, Disting. Svc. award, 1990, Am. Nat. Standards Inst., 1987, Speedy award Paralyzed Vets. Am., 1993. Fellow AIA (Disting. Svc. award Chgo. chpt. 1988); mem. Am. Hosp. Assn., Am. Assn. Hosp. Planning, Internat. Hosp. Fedn., Nat. Center Barrier Free Environ. (dir.), Builders Assn. Chgo., Chgo. Assn. Commerce and Industry. Home: 1437 W Glenlake Ave Chicago IL 60660-1801 Office: Matthei & Colin Assocs 332 S Michigan Ave Chicago IL 60604-4434

MATTHES, GERALD STEPHEN, advertising agency executive; b. Hamburg, Germany, Aug. 31, 1938; Brit. subject; came to U.S., 1964, naturalized 1977; s. Stanley Rutter and Gerda Elena (Spiro) M.; m. Betsy Durkin (div. 1981); 1 child, Peter Charlton; m. Margaret Emily Secher; children: Christopher Stanley, Lydia Janet. Undergrad. edn., Gt. Britain; M in Communications, Advt. and Mktg., London Coll., 1963. Acct. exec. Press and Gen. Publicity, Ltd., London, 1959-61, Dudley, Turner and Vincent, Ltd., London, 1961-64; v.p., mgmt. supr. Doyle, Dane, Bernbach, N.Y.C., 1964-79; sr. v.p. internat. Bozell, N.Y.C., 1980—; cons. Robert P. Gersin Assoc., 1979. Contbr. articles to profl. jours. Recipient Gold Medal award Direct Mail Assn. Great Britain, 1963. Democrat. Mem. Charismatic Episcopal Ch. Home: 709 Kensington Ln Bloomfield Hills MI 48304-3743 Office: Bozell Worldwide Inc 1000 Town Ctr Ste 1500 Southfield MI 48075-1217

MATTHEWS, BETTY PARKER, special education educator; b. Port Arthur, Tex., Dec. 9, 1929; d. Clarence G. and Florence (Sudduth) Parker; m. Paul A. Matthews, Mar. 25, 1955; children: Michael A., Scott P., Lisa M. Alexander. BS, La. Coll., 1975; MEd, Northwestern U., 1981. Specialist in edn. La., 1984; cert. elem. tchr., mentally retarded, learning disabled, ednl. cons., generic mild/moderate, assessment tchr., ednl. diagnostician, child search coord., La. 3d grade tchr. Rapides Parish Sch. Bd., Alexandria, La., 1975-76, tchr. spl. edn., 1976-81, assessment tchr., 1981-93; ednl. diagnostician Rapides Parish Sch. Bd., Alexandria, 1993—; ednl. cons. Briarwood Psychiatric Hosp., Alexandria, La., 1986-93, Crossroads Psychiat. Hosp., Alexandria, 1993-96; adj. prof. La. State U., Alexandria, 1990—. Dir. children's Bible study 1st Bapt. Ch., Pineville, La., 1985—. Mem. La. Ednl. Diagnosticians Assn. (regional rep. 1987-88, treas. 1988-90, Pres.'s Svc. award 1990-91, La. Assessment Tchr. of Yr. 1993), Coun. Exceptional Children, Reading Coun., Alpha Delta Kappa, Phi Delta Kappa, Epsilon Sigma Alpha (state pres., regional sec.). Home: 3050 Rigolette Rd Pineville LA 71360-7219

MATTHEWS, BRIAN W., molecular biology educator; b. Mount Barker, Australia, May 25, 1938; came to U.S., 1967; s. Lionel A. and Ethlinda L. (Harris) M.; m. Helen F. Denley, Sept. 7, 1963; children: Susan, Kristine. BS, U. Adelaide, Australia, 1959, BS with honors, 1960, PhD, 1964, DSc, 1986. Mem. staff Med. Rsch. Coun., Cambridge, Eng., 1963-66; vis. assoc. NIH, Bethesda, Md., 1967-69; prof. molecular biology U. Oreg., Eugene, 1969—, chmn. dept. physics, 1985-86, dir. Inst. Molecular Biology, 1980-83, 90-92; Drummond lectr. U. Calgary (Can.), 1995; advisor NSF, Washington, 1975-77; investigator Howard Hughes Med. Inst., 1989—; mem. U.S. Nat. Commn. for Crystallography, Washington, 1980-86, 88-90. Rsch. fellow Alfred P. Sloan Found., 1971, Guggenheim fellow, 1977; recipient Career Devel. award NIH, 1973, Faculty Excellence award Oreg. Bd. Edn., 1984, Discovery award Med. Rsch. Found. Oreg., 1987, Reed Coll. Vollum award, 1994. Mem. NAS, AAAS, Crystallographic Assn., Am. Chem. Soc., Protein Soc. (pres. 1995-97). Office: U Oreg/HHMI Inst Molecular Biology Eugene OR 97403

MATTHEWS, BRUCE RANKIN, professional football player; b. Arcadia, Calif., Aug. 8, 1961. BS in Indsl. Engring., U. So. Calif., 1983. Center, guard Houston Oilers, 1983—. Named NFL All-Pro Team Guard by Sporting News, 1988-90, 92, Leader, 1993. Played in Pro Bowl, 1988-93. Office: Houston Oilers 8030 El Rio St Houston TX 77054-4184*

MATTHEWS, CHARLES SEDWICK, petroleum engineering consultant, research advisor; b. Houston, Mar. 27, 1920; s. Charles James and Zadoc Coleman (Sedwick) M.; m. Miriam Loraine Ormerod, June 2, 1945; children—Joan Gail, Wendy Loraine. B.S. in Chem. Engring., Rice U., 1941, M.S. in Chem. Engring., 1943, Ph.D. in Chemistry, 1944. Registered profl. engr., Tex. Engr. Shell Devel. Co., San Francisco, 1944-48; research engr. Shell Devel. Co., Houston, 1948-56; dir. research Shell Devel. Co., 1967-72; chief reservoir engr. Shell Oil Co., Houston, 1965; mgr. engring. Shell Oil Co., 1972-73, sr. petroleum engring. cons., 1973-89; mem. engring. adv. com. Rice U., Houston, 1973-77; cons. Dept. Energy, Washington, 1974-78, mem. adv. com., 1975-79; spl. asst. Nat. Petroleum Council, Washington, 1981-83; mem. reserves com. Am. Petroleum Inst. Author: Pressure Buildup and Flow Tests in Wells, 1967; contbr. articles to profl. jours.; patentee in field. Chmn. Tex. Engrs. for Conservation, Houston, 1973. Recipient Disting. Alumnus award Rice U., 1994. Mem. NAE, Soc. Petroleum Engrs. (hon. mem., Lester Uren award 1975, disting. author, disting. lectr. 1968, Disting. lectr. emeritus 1986), Phi Beta Kappa, Sigma Xi, Tau Beta Pi, Phi Lambda Upsilon. Republican. Methodist. Clubs: Houston, Meyerland (treas. 1982-85). Avocations: swimming; fishing. Home: 5307 S Braeswood Blvd Houston TX 77096-4149

MATTHEWS, CLARK J(IO), II, retail executive, lawyer; b. Arkansas City, Kans., Oct. 1, 1936; s. Clark J. and Betty Elizabeth (Stewart) M.; children: Patricia Eleanor, Pamela Elaine, Catherine Joy. B.A., So. Meth. U., 1959, J.D., 1961. Bar: Tex. 1961. Trial atty. Ft. Worth Regional Office, SEC, 1961-63; law clk. to chief U.S. dist. judge No. Dist. Tex., Dallas, 1963-65; atty. Southland Corp., Dallas, 1965-73; v.p., gen. counsel Southland Corp., 1973-79, exec. v.p., chief fin. officer, 1979-83, sr. exec. v.p., chief fin. officer, 1983-87, exec. v.p., chief fin. officer, 1987-91, pres., chief exec. officer, 1991—. Mem. ABA, Tex., Dallas, Bar Assns., Am. Judicature Soc., Alpha Tau Omega, Pi Alpha Delta. Methodist. Club: DeMolay. Home: 7005 Stefani Dr Dallas TX 75225-1747 Office: Southland Corp 2711 N Haskell Ave Dallas TX 75204

MATTHEWS, CRAIG GERARD, gas company executive; b. Bklyn., Mar. 8, 1943; m. Carol O. Olsen, Sept. 10, 1971; children: Kenneth C., Bradford P., Melinda M. BCE, Rutgers U., 1965; MS in Indsl. Mgmt., Polytech. Inst. Bklyn., 1971. Trainee Bklyn. Union Gas Co., 1965, pres., COO, 1996—. Bd. dirs. Poly. U., Bklyn. Philharm., Salvation Army, Regional Planning Assn., Greater Jamaica Devel. Corp., Pub. Utility Reports, Neighborhood Housing Svcs., Bklyn. Coll. Adv. Bd. Mem. Bklyn. C. of C. (bd. dirs., chmn.), Am. Gas Assn. Republican. Presbyterian. Home: 17 Wynwood Rd Chatham NJ 07928-1755 Office: Bklyn Union Gas Co 1 Metrotech Ctr Brooklyn NY 11201-3831

MATTHEWS, DANE DIKEMAN, urban planner; b. Memphis, Dec. 19, 1950; d. Neil Jude and Virginia Ann (Turnbull) Dikeman; m. John Wesley Matthews, Dec. 28, 1971. BA with distinction, U. Okla., 1972, M of Regional and City Planning, 1974. Planner Hudgins, Thompson & Ball, Inc., Tulsa, 1975-76; econ. devel. planner Tulsa Metro. Area Planning Commn., 1976-77; planner II Tulsa Met. Area Planning Commn., 1977-80; prin. regional planner Indian Nations Coun. Govts., Tulsa, 1980—. Project dir. Kendall-Whittier Neighborhood Master Plan, 1992. Bd. dirs. Met. Tulsa Urban League, 1993-95, Parkside Cmty. Mental Health Ctr., Tulsa, 1986—; bd. dirs., chair house com. Arts and Humanities Coun., Tulsa, 1991—; divsn. chair Tulsa Area United Way, 1988-96. Recipient Spl. Recognition award Downtown Tulsa Unltd., 1988. Mem. Am. Inst. Cert. Planners (cert.), Am. Planning Assn. (Okla. chpt. pres. 1988-89, Master Plan award 1992, Outstanding Profl. Planner 1991), Phi Beta Kappa. Democrat. Episcopalian. Avocations: cooking, reading, raising dogs. Office: INCOG 201 W 5th St Ste 600 Tulsa OK 74103-4278

MATTHEWS, DAVID, clergyman; b. Indianola, Miss., Jan. 29, 1920; s. Albert and Bertha (Henderson) M.; m. Lillian Pearl Banks, Aug. 28, 1951; 1 dau., Denise. A.B., Morehouse Coll., Atlanta, 1950; student, Atlanta U., 1950, Memphis Theol. Sem., 1965, Delta State U., Cleveland, Miss., 1969, 71, 72; D.D. (hon.), Natchez (Miss.) Jr. Coll., 1973, Morris Booker Meml. Coll., 1988. Ordained minister Nat. Baptist Conv. U.S.A., 1946; pastor chs. in Miss., 1951—, Bell Grove Baptist Ch., Indianola, 1951—, Strangers Home, Greenwood, 1958—; tchr., chmn. dept. social sci. Gentry H.S., Indianola, 1958-83; moderator Sunflower Bapt. Assn., 1957—; v.p. Gen. Bapt. Conv. Miss., 1958—, former lectr., conv. congress religious edn.; v.p. Nat. Bapt. Conv. U.S.A., 1971-94; del. to Nat. Coun. Chs., 1960, supr. oratorial contest, 1976; pres. Gen. Missionary Bapt. State Conv. Miss., 1974—. Mem. Sunflower County Anti-Poverty Bd., 1965-71, Indianola Bi-Racial Com., 1965—; mem. Gov.'s Advisory Com.; col. on staff Gov. Finch, 1976-80; mem. budget com. Indianola United Fund, 1971—; chmn. bd. Indianola FHA, 1971—; trustee Natchez Jr. Coll.; mem. Miss. Gov.'s Research and Devel. Council, 1984—; apptd. mem. So. Govs. Ecumenical Coun. Infant Mortality, 1987. Served with U.S. Army, 1942-45, PTO. Recipient citation Morehouse Coll., 1950, citation Miss. Valley State Coll., 1956; J.H. Jackson Preaching award Midwestern Baptist Laymen Fellowship, 1974; Gov.'s Merit award, 1975. Mem. NEA, Miss., Indianola Tchrs. Assns., Am. Bible Soc. (adv. coun. 1991—, student reform theol. sem. centennial edn. 1990—). Democrat. Home: PO Box 627 Indianola MS 38751-0627 *I have learned not to seek honors and success but to become so involved in worthwhile works that I lose myself and by such actions success and honors have come.*

MATTHEWS, DAVID FORT, military weapon system acquisition specialist; b. Lancaster, N.H., Sept. 25, 1944; s. Clinton Fort and Mabel Sawin (Oaks) M.; m. Eva Mae Horton, Nov. 10, 1990. BA, Vanderbilt U., 1966; MA, Mid. Tenn. U., 1973. Cert. acquisition mgr. Rsch. and devel. officer U.S. Army Rsch. Inst., Washington, 1974-77; exec. officer 194th Maintenence Battalion-Camp Humphreys, Korea, 1978-79; career program mgr. U.S. Army Mil. Pers. Ctr., Washington, 1979-82; logistics staff officer Dep. Chief of Staff Logistics, Washington, 1982-83; team chief Chief of Staff Army Study Group, Washington, 1983-85; logistics div. chief Multiple Launch Rocket System Project Office, Huntsville, Ala., 1985-88; comdr. Ordanance Program Div., Riyadh, Saudi Arabia, 1988-90; project mgr. Army Tactical Missile System, Huntsville, 1990-94; sr. lectr. weapon systems acquisition Naval Postgrad. Sch., Monterey, Calif., 1994—. Decorated Legion of Merit, Bronze Star; recipient award as project mgr. of yr. Sec. of Army, 1991. Mem. Am. Ordinance Assn., Am. Def. Prepardness Assn., Assn. U.S. Army. Avocations: spectator sports, water skiing, reading, scuba diving. Home: 83 High Meadow Ln Carmel CA 93923 Office: Naval Postgrad Sch Monterey CA 93943

MATTHEWS, DONALD ROWE, political scientist, educator; b. Cin., Sept. 14, 1925; s. William Procter and Janet Burch (Williams) M.; m. Margie C. Richmond, June 28, 1947 (div.); children: Mary, Jonathan; m. Carmen J. Onstad, July 7, 1970 (div.); children: Christopher, Amy. Student, Kenyon Coll., 1943, Purdue U., 1944-45; A.B. with high honors, Princeton, 1948, M.A., 1951, Ph.D., 1953; Dr. hon. causa, U. Bergen, 1985. Instr. Smith Coll., Northampton, Mass., 1951-53; asst. prof. govt. Smith Coll., 1953-57; lectr. polit. sci. U. N.C., Chapel Hill, 1957-58; assoc. prof. U. N.C., 1958-63, prof., 1963-70; research prof. Inst. for Research in Social Sci., 1963-70; sr. fellow in govtl. studies Brookings Instn., Washington, 1970-73; prof. polit. sci. and research assoc. Inst. for Research in Social Sci., U. Mich., Ann Arbor, 1973-76; prof. polit. sci. U. Wash., Seattle, 1976—, chmn. dept. polit. sci., 1976-83; guest prof. U. Bergen, Norway, 1980; fellow Ctr. for Advanced Study in the Behavioral Scis., 1964-65; cons. to U.S. Commn. on Civil Rights, 1958-60, NBC News, 1966-68, Ford Found., 1967-68, U.S. Ho. of Reps., 1970-72, others; faculty lectr. U. Wash., 1989. Author: The Social Background of Political Decision-Makers, 1954, U.S. Senators and Their World, 1960, (with James Prothro) Negroes and the New Southern Politics, 1966, Perspectives on Presidential Selection, 1973, (with William Keech) The Party's Choice, 1976, (with James Stimson) Yeas and Nays: A Theory of Decision-Making in the U.S. House of Representatives, 1975; Contbr. articles to profl. jours. Served with USNR, 1943-46. Recipient Sr. Award for Research in Govtl. Affairs Social Sci. Research Council, 1962; Ford Found. fellow, 1969-70; Guggenheim fellow, 1980-81. Fellow Am. Acad. Arts and Scis.; mem. Am. Polit. Sci. Assn. (treas. 1970-72, v.p. 1985-86), Pacific N.W. Polit. Sci. Assn. (pres. 1977-78), Western Polit. Sci. Assn. (pres. 1979-80), So. Polit. Sci. Assn., Midwestern Polit. Sci. Assn., Inter-Univ. Consortium for Polit. Research (exec. com. 1970-72). Democrat. Home: 2125 1st Ave #1301 Seattle WA 98121 Office: U Wash Polit Sci Box 353530 Seattle WA 98195

MATTHEWS, EDWARD E., insurance company executive; b. 1931. AB, Princeton U., 1953; MBA, Harvard U., 1957. With Morgan Stanley & Co., 1957-73; exec. v.p. fin., vice chmn. bd. dirs. Am. Internat. Group, Inc., N.Y.C., from 1973, now vice chmn. fin., also bd. dirs. With U.S. Army, 1953-55. Office: Am Internat Group Inc 70 Pine St New York NY 10270-0002*

MATTHEWS, EDWIN SPENCER, JR., lawyer; b. Spokane, Wash., May 31, 1934; s. Edwin Spencer and Dorothy Chace (Ehrhardt) M.; m. Marie-Claude Paris, Dec. 19, 1959 (div. 1982); children: Nadia, Sylvie, Clarissa; m. Patricia L. Sills Barnes, Dec. 22, 1983; children: Paxton, Gillian. AB magna cum laude, Harvard U., 1956; Diplome d'Etudes Francaises, Institut de Tourraine, Tours, France, 1958; LLB, Yale U., 1962. Bar: N.Y. 1963, Calif. 1979, U.S. Supreme Ct. 1992; Conseil Juridique (France) 1965-79. Assoc. Coudert Bros., N.Y.C., 1962-65; assoc. Coudert Freres, Paris, 1965-69, ptnr., 1969-79; ptnr. Coudert Bros., San Francisco, 1979-80, N.Y.C., 1980—. Trustee Sierra Club Legal Def. Fund, San Francisco, 1984—; bd. dirs. Friends of Earth Found., N.Y.C., 1979-85; bd. dirs. Friends of Earth Inc., Washington, 1970-85, pres., 1979-80. With U.S. Army, 1957-58. Mem. Assn. of Bar of City of N.Y. (com. on housing and urban devel. 1964-65, com. on capital representation), Am. Alpine Club, Harvard Club, N.Y. Athletic Club. Democrat. Avocations: ocean sailing, carpentry, mountain climbing, sculling. Home: 11 Harrison St New York NY 10013-2837 also: PO Box 493 Washington Depot CT 06794-0493 Office: Coudert Brothers 1114 Avenue Of The Americas New York NY 10036-7703

MATTHEWS, ELIZABETH WOODFIN, law librarian, law educator; b. Ashland, Va., July 30, 1927; d. Edwin Clifton and Elizabeth Frances (Luck) Woodfin; m. Sidney E. Matthews, Dec. 20, 1947; 1 child, Sarah Elizabeth Matthews Wiley. BA, Randolph-Macon Coll., 1948, LLD (hon.), 1989; MS in Libr. Sci., U. Ill., 1952; PhD, So. Ill. U., 1972; LLD, Randolph-Macon Coll., 1989. Cert. law libr., med. libr., med. libr. III. Libr. Ohio State U., Columbus, 1952-59; libr., instr. U. Ill., Urbana, 1962-63, lectr. Grad. Sch. Libr. Sci., 1964; libr., instr. Morris Libr. So. Ill. U., Carbondale, 1964-67, classroom instr. Coll. Edn., 1967-70, med. libr., asst. prof. Morris Libr., 1972-74, law libr., asst. prof., 1974-79, law libr., assoc. prof., 1979-85, law libr., prof., 1985-92, prof. emerita, 1993—. Author: Access Points to Law Libraries, 1984, 17th Century English Law Reports, 1986, Law Library Reference Shelf, 1988, 2d edit., 1992, 3d edit., 1996, Pages and Missing Pages, 1983, 2d edit., 1989, Lincoln as a Lawyer: An Annotated Bibliography, 1991. Mem. AAUW (pres. 1976-78, corp. rep. 1978-88), Am. Assn. Law Librs., Mid Am. Assn. Law Librs., Beta Phi Mu, Phi Kappa Phi. Methodist. Home: 811 S Skyline Dr Carbondale IL 62901-2405 Office: So Ill U Law Libr Carbondale IL 62901

MATTHEWS, ESTHER ELIZABETH, education educator, consultant; b. Princeton, Mass., June 20, 1918; d. Ralph Edgar and Julia Ellen (Cronin) M. BS in Edn., Worcester State Coll., 1940; EdM, Harvard U., 1943, EdD, 1960. Tchr. various Mass. schs., 1942-47; guidance dir. Holden (Mass.) Pub. Schs., 1947-53, Wareham (Mass.) Pub. Schs., 1954-57; counselor Newton (Mass.) High Sch., 1957-60, head counselor, 1960-66; assoc. prof. edn. U. Oreg., 1966-70, prof. edn., 1970-80, prof. emerita, 1980—; vis. prof. U. Toronto, Ont., Can., summer 1971; lectr. on edn. Harvard U., 1963-66; cons. in field; lectr. various colls. and univs. Author book chpts.; contbr. numerous articles to profl. jours. and papers to conf. proc. Mem. ACD (Recognition for Contbn. to Promote Human Rights 1987), World Future Soc., Nat. Vocat. Guidance Assn. (pres. 1974-75, chair nat. com. 1966-67, sec. 1967-68, bd. trustees 1968-71, editl. bd. Vocat. Guidance Quar. 1966-68), Oreg. Pers. and Guidance Assn. (Leona Tyler award 1973, Disting. Svc. award 1979), Oreg. Career Devel. Assn. (Disting. Svc. award 1987, Esther E. Matthews Ann. award for outstanding contbn. to career devel. in Oreg. established in her honor 1993). Home: 832 Lariat Dr Eugene OR 97401-6438

MATTHEWS, EUGENE EDWARD, artist; b. Davenport, Iowa, Mar. 22, 1931; s. Nickolas Arthur and Velma (Schroeder) M.; m. Wanda Lee Miller, Sept. 14, 1952; children: Anthony Lee, Daniel Nickolas. Student, Bradley U., 1948-51; BFA, U. Iowa, 1953, MFA, 1957. Prof. fine arts grad. faculty U. Colo., Boulder, 1961-96, prof. fine arts emeritus, 1996—, dir. vis. artists program, 1985-96; vis. artist Am. Acad. Rome, 1989. One-man shows include U. Wis., Milw., 1960, Brena Gallery, Denver, 1963, 65, 67, 70, 74, 76, 78, 80, 83, 88, Colorado Springs Fine Arts Ctr., 1967, Sheldon Art Gallery, U. Nebr., 1968, Denver Art Mus., 1972, James Yu Gallery, N.Y.C., 1973, 77, Dubins Gallery, L.A., 1981, Galeria Rysunku, Poznan, 1983, CU. Art Galleries, U. Colo., Boulder, 1996; exhibited in numerous group shows U.S., Europe, Africa, Asia; internat. watercolor exhbn. New Orleans, 1983, Louvre, Paris, Met. Mus. of Art, N.Y.C., Internat. Art Ctr., Kyoto, Japan, Mus. of Modern Art, Rijeka, Yugoslavia, Taipei Fine Arts Mus., Taiwan, Republic of China, Internat. Watercolor Biennial-East/West, Champaign, Ill., 1997; represented in permanent collections Nat. Mus. Am. Art, Washington, Denver Art Mus., Butler Inst. Am. Art, Chrysler Art Mus., others. Recipient Penello d'Argento award Acitrezza Internazionale, 1958, S.P.Q.R. Cup of Rome, Roma Olimpionica Internazionale, 1959, Gold medal of honor Nat. Arts Club, N.Y.C., 1969, Bicentennial award Rocky Mountain Nat. Watercolor Exhbn., 1976, Am. Drawings IV Purchase award, 1982, others; fellow in painting Am. Acad. Rome, 1957-60, U. Colo. Creative Rsch. fellow, 1966-67. Mem. Watercolor U.S.A. Honor Soc. (charter). Home: 720 Hawthorn Ave Boulder CO 80304-2140

MATTHEWS, FRANCIS RICHARD, lawyer; b. Calgary, Alta., Can., Aug. 19, 1920; s. Charles Curtice and Grace (Cathro) M.; m. Joyce Winter Jarvis, Nov. 10, 1944; children: James Richard, Frances Elizabeth, Michael John. B.Com., U. Alta., 1941, LL.B., 1948. Bar: Called to Alta. bar 1949, created Queen's Counsel 1963. Assoc. firm Mackimmie, Matthews, Calgary, 1949-54; ptnr. Mackimmie, Matthews, 1954-87, of counsel, 1987—; dir. Murphy Oil Co. Ltd., Ranger Oil Ltd. Served to lt. Royal Canadian Naval Vol. Res., 1941-45. Mem. Calgary Philharmonic Orchestra Soc. (bd. govs., pres. 1955-56, 61-62), Calgary C. of C., Can., Alberta bar assns., Soaring Assn. Can., Delta Kappa Epsilon. Mem. Anglican Ch. Clubs: Calgary Petroleum, Ranchmen's. Home: 720 13th Ave SW Apt 1810, Calgary, AB Canada T2R 1M5 Office: Gulf Canada Sq 7th Fl, Calgary, AB Canada T2P 2M2

MATTHEWS, GEORGE TENNYSON, history educator; b. Bklyn., May 27, 1917; s. George Tennyson and Olive Beulah (Richardson) M.; m. Mildred G. Byars (dec. 1962); m. Margie R. Kresge (dec. 1989); children: Mildred, Gregory; 1 stepchild, Christopher J. Kresge. AB, Columbia U., 1939, MA, 1941, PhD, 1953. Instr., then asst. prof. history Columbia U., 1946-59, chmn. contemporary civilization staff, 1953-59, asst. to dean Columbia Coll., 1951-59; mem. faculty Oakland U., Rochester, Mich., 1959—; prof. history Oakland U., 1960-85, prof. emeritus, 1985—, dist. prof. emeritus, 1988—, chmn. dept., 1960-62, assoc. dean humanities, then dean Coll. Arts and Scis., 1962-73, vice provost, 1973-79, pres., 1979-81; dir. honors coll. Oakland U., Rochester, Mich., 1991; Hill Family Found. lectr. MacAlister Coll., St. Paul, 1954. Author: Royal General Farms in 18th Century France, 1958, News and Rumor in Renaissance Europe, 1959; also articles, revs.; Editor: Man in Contemporary Society, 2 vols, 1957, Contemporary Civilization in the West, 2 vols, 1956. With USAAF, 1941-45. Mem. Soc. French Hist. Studies (treas. 1967-74), Am. Hist. Assn., Phi Beta Kappa (past chpt. treas.). Democrat. Home and Office: 2900 Heidelberg Dr Rochester Hills MI 48309-2301

MATTHEWS, GERTRUDE ANN URCH, retired librarian, writer; b. Jackson, Mich., July 16, 1921; d. Charles P.A. and Amy (Granville) Urch; student Albion Coll., 1940-41; AA, Jackson Jr. Coll., 1939; BS, MS in Library Arts, U. Mich., 1959; m. Geoffrey Matthews, June 30, 1942 (dec.). Adult services librarian Jackson, Mich., 1959-63; asst. dir., librarian Franklin Sylvester Library, Medina, Ohio, 1963-81, dir. older adults facility library, 1977-93. Pres., Hist. Soc., 1966-67; active Dollars for Scholars Com., 1966-86; mem. Bicentennial Com.; officer diocesean leval Episcopal Ch.; mem. vestry St. Paul's Ch., Medina, 1981-84. Mem. ALA, Ohio Library Assn., AAUW (dir., Community Service award 1985, Woman of Yr.), LWV (dir.). Republican. Contbr. articles to profl. and popular publs.; weekly newspaper columnist, 1958-81; bookreviewer The Nat. Librarian. Home: Friendship Village Apt A158 2645 E Southern Ave Tempe AZ 85282-2038

MATTHEWS, GILBERT ELLIOTT, investment banker; b. Brookline, Mass., Apr. 24, 1930; s. Martin W. and Charlotte (Cohen) M.; m. Anne Lisbeth Barnett, Apr. 20, 1958 (div. 1975); children: Lisa Joan, Diana Kory (dec. 1995); m. Elaine Rita Siegal Pulitzer, Jan. 2, 1978; 1 child, Jennifer Rachel. AB, Harvard U., 1951; MBA, Columbia U., 1953. Chartered fin. analyst. Dept. mgr. Bloomingdale's, N.Y.C., 1953, 56-60; security analyst Merrill Lynch, N.Y.C., 1960; investment banker Bear, Stearns & Co., N.Y.C., 1960-95, gen. ptnr., 1979-85; mng. dir. Bear, Stearns & Co. Inc., 1985-86, sr. mng. dir., 1986-95; sr. mng. dir. Sutter Securities Inc., San Francisco, 1995—; bd. dirs. Oak Industries, Inc., Waltham, Mass. Served as lt. (j.g.) USN, 1953-56. Mem. N.Y. Soc. Security Analysts. Democrat. Jewish. Home: 3362 Clay St San Francisco CA 94118-2007 Office: Sutter Securities Inc One Sansome St Ste 3950 San Francisco CA 94104

MATTHEWS, JACK (JOHN HAROLD MATTHEWS), English educator, writer; b. Columbus, Ohio, July 22, 1925; s. John Harold and Lulu Emma (Grover) M.; m. Barbara Jane Reese, Sept. 16, 1947; children: Cynthia Ann Matthews Warnock, Barbara Ellen Matthews, John Harold. B.A., Ohio State U., 1949, M.A., 1954. Clk. U.S. Post Office, Columbus, 1950-59; prof. English Urbana Coll., Ohio, 1959-64; prof. English Ohio U., Athens, 1964-77, disting. prof., 1977—. Author: Bitter Knowledge, 1964 (Ohioana fiction award 1964), Hanger Stout, Awake!, 1967, The Charisma Campaigns, 1972 (nominee NBA Fiction award), Sassafras, 1983, Crazy Women, 1985, Booking in the Heartland, 1986 (Ohioana non-fiction award 1986), Ghostly Populations, 1986, Memoirs of a Bookman, 1989, Dirty Tricks, 1990, On The Shore of That Beautiful Shore (play), 1991, An Interview with the Sphinx (play), 1992, Storyhood As We Know It and Other Tales (stories), 1993, Booking Pleasures, 1996, others. Served with USCG, 1943-45. Recipient numerous ind. artist awards Ohio Art Council, Major Artist award, 1989-90; Guggenheim fellow, 1974-75. Mem. Phi Beta Kappa. Home: 4314 Fisher Rd Athens OH 45701-9333 Office: Ohio U Dept English Athens OH 45701

MATTHEWS, JACK, psychologist, speech pathologist, educator; b. Winnipeg, Man., Can., June 17, 1917; s. Samuel and Ellen (Walker) M.; m. Hannah Miriam Polster, Aug. 16, 1942; children: Rachel Sophia, Rebecca. A.B., Heidelberg Coll., 1938, D.Sc., 1976; M.A., Ohio U., 1940; Ph.D., Ohio State U., 1946; student, Vanderbilt U., 1942-43. Asst. dir. speech clinic Purdue U., 1946-48; dir. speech clinic, asst. prof. psychology and speech U. Pitts., 1948-55, dir. speech clinic, dir. div. psychol. services, asso. prof. psychology, 1950-55, prof., chmn. speech dept., 1955—, dean humanities, 1967-68, pres. univ. senate, 1969-72; bd. dirs. Community Hearing Coun., Pitts. Hearing Soc.; pres. Am. Bd. Examiners Speech Pathology and Audiology, 1966-67; sec. Speech and Hearing Found., 1964-68; mem. Edn. Commn. States, Nat. Adv. Com. on Handicapped Children; bd. trustees City Theatre, 1985—, Western Pa. Sch. for Deaf, 1980—, v.p. 1982-92. Asst. editor: Jour. Speech and Hearing Disorders, 1952-54; editorial bd., 1965-69, Speech Monographs, 1951-53, 56-65, Jour. Communications, 1961-64, Deafness, Speech and Hearing pubs.; cons. editor: Today's Speech, 1968- 70, ERIC, 1975—; Contbr. articles to profl. jours. Served as sgt. AC Psychol. Research Unit USAAF, 1942-45. Mem. AAAS, APA, AAUP, Am. Speech and Hearing Assn. (pres. 1963-64, assoc. editor jours. 1959-62), Am. Assn. Cleft Palate Rehab. (pres. 1957-59), Speech Assn. (adminstrv. coun., rsch. bd. 1966-69, chmn. 1967-69), Am. Assn. Mental Deficiency, Soc. Psychol. Study Social Issues, Pa. Speech Assn. (pres. 1959-60), Assn. for Comm. Adminstrn. (exec. com. 1978-81), Sigma Xi, Pi Kappa Delta, Alpha Psi Omega, Tau Kappa Alpha, Sigma Alpha Eta. Home: Longwood at Oakmount Ch 53 500 Route 909 Verona PA 15147-3851

MATTHEWS, JAMES SHADLEY, lawyer; b. Omaha, Nov. 24, 1951; s. Donald E. and Lois Jean (Shadley) M.; m. Mary Kvaal, May 3, 1991; 1 child, Katherine. BA cum laude, St. Olaf Coll., 1973; JD, U. Ill., 1976; MBA, U. Denver, 1977. Bar: Minn. 1976, U.S. Dist. Ct. Minn. 1978. With Northwestern Nat. Life Ins. Co., Mpls., 1978-89; v.p., asst. gen. counsel Northwestern Nat. Life Ins. Co., 1985-89; ptnr. Lindquist & Venum, Mpls., 1990—; sr. v.p., gen. counsel Washington Square Capital, Inc., 1989; bd. dirs., sec. NWNL Health Network, Inc., St. Paul, 1987-89; pub. dir. Minn. Health Reins. Assn., 1992-94; speaker to profl. orgns., 1984—. Mem. ABA, Nat. Health Lawyers Assn., Am. Acad. Hosp. Attys., Minn. Bar Assn. (chmn. health law sect. 1986-87). Office: Lindquist & Vennum 4200 IDS Ctr 80 S 8th St Minneapolis MN 55402-2100

MATTHEWS, JAY ARLON, JR., publisher, editor; b. St. Louis, Apr. 13, 1918; s. Jay Arlon and Mary (Long) M.; student San Jose State Coll., 1939-41, U. Tex., 1946-47; BLS St. Edward's U., 1994; m. May Clark McLemore, Jan. 16, 1944; children—Jay Arlon III, Emily Cochrane, Sally McLemore. Asst. dir. personnel Adj. Gen.'s Dept. Tex., 1947-53, dept. adj., 1957-65, mil. support plans officer, 1965-69, chief emergency operations, 1965-71; pub. Presidial Press, Mil. History Press. Past Dir. Civil Def., Austin; mem. adv. bd. Confed. Research Center, Hill Jr. Coll.; mil. historian 65th Legislature, Tex., 1977-78. Served with AGC, Tex. N.G., 1946—, brig. gen. ret., 1973. Named to Tex. Nat. Guard Hall of Honor, 1990. Fellow Co. Mil. Historians (gov. 1981-84); mem. Austin (state v.p. 1951-52), U.S. Jaycees (chmn. nat. security com. 1952-53), N.G. Assn. U.S. (chmn. publicity 81st Gen. Conf.), Instituto Internationale de Historia Militar (hon. life), Mil. Order World Wars (comdr. Austin chpt. 1980). Episcopalian. Club: Exchange (pres. Austin chpt. 1982-83). Editor: Mil. History of Tex. and S.W. Quar., 1961-88; editor emeritus Mil. Hist. of the West, 1989. Home: 1807 Stamford Ln Austin TX 78703-2939 Office: 407-B E 6th St Ste 200 Austin TX 78701

MATTHEWS, JEFFREY ALAN, physicist; b. Lansdale, Pa., Apr. 1, 1962; s. Gerald and Idella Laura (Camburn) M. BS in Physics cum laude, Ursinus Coll., 1984. Teaching asst. physics dept. U. Del., Newark, 1984-85; physicist Army Material Systems Analysis Activity, Aberdeen Proving Ground, Md., 1986—. Disaster capt. ARC, Harford County, Md., 1992-95, alt. disaster coord., 1994-95, disaster coord., 1995—; EMT-A Abingdon (Md.) Vol. Fire Co., 1992-94. Recipient Red Cross Svc. award, 1992, 95. Mem. Sigma Xi, Sigma Pi Sigma. Avocations: model railroading, writing, poetry. Home: 1426 Saint Michael Ct Edgewood MD 21040-2197

MATTHEWS, JOHN FLOYD, writer, educator; b. Cin., Apr. 8, 1919; s. Floyd L. and Helen (Orth) M.; m. Maurine Zollman, Mar. 4, 1945 (dec. 1959); children—Lauralee Alice, Caroline Elaine (dec.); m. Brenda Martin, Aug. 27, 1966. Student, Wooster Coll., 1935-37, Northwestern U., 1937; B.A., U. Cin., 1940, postgrad., 1940-41; postgrad., Columbia U., 1943, New Sch. for Social Research, 1944-45. Lectr. New Sch. for Social Research, 1948-50; lectr., chmn. faculty Dramatic Workshop and Tech. Inst., N.Y.C., 1950-52; lectr. in playwriting CCNY, 1947-63; asst. prof. dramatic lit. and history Brandeis U., 1952-59, assoc. prof., 1959-67, Schulman prof., 1967-71, chmn. dept. theatre, 1955-58, prof. Am. studies, 1971—, chmn. dept. Am. studies, 1973-74, Richter prof. Am. Civilization and Instns., 1972-84, prof. emeritus, 1984—; vis. critic Yale Sch. Drama, 1965; mem. Seminar in Am. Studies, Circle Cultural de Royaumont, France, 1965; founding mem. Brandeis Creative Arts Awards Commn. Network radio actor, writer, producer, 1939-45, screenwriter, Warner Bros., 1945; author: plays, including The Scapegoat, 1950, Michael and Lavinia, 1956, Barnum, 1962; books The Old Vic In America, 1946, El Greco, 1952, Shaw's Dramatic Criticism, 1959, George Bernard Shaw, 1969, Reflections on Abortion, 1976; contbr. fiction to lit. mags.; cons., play doctor for script and prodn. problems of numerous Broadway and off-Broadway plays and musicals including Anastasia, The First Gentleman, others; TV scriptwriter for maj. networks, 1955-64; screenwriter, MGM, United Artists, Asso. Screen Prodns., Toronto, Ont., Can., 1958-64; Contbg. editor: Library of Living Painters, 1949-51, Dictionary of the Arts, 1946, Ency. World Biography, 1970. Mem. Westport (Conn.) Democratic Town Com., 1959-64; mem. Newton (Mass.) Republican City Com., 1977—, Mass. Rep. Platform Com., 1978; bd. dirs. Newton Taxpayers Assn., 1979-81, 86-91. Recipient Arts of the Theatre Found. award, 1950. Mem. Brit. Drama League, The Nat. Trust, English Speaking Union, Trustees of Reservations. Episcopalian. Home: 5 Tudor Close, Dean Court Rd, Rottingdean BN1 7DF, England

MATTHEWS, KATHLEEN SHIVE, biochemistry educator; b. Austin, Tex., Aug. 30, 1945; d. William and Gwyn Shive; m. Randall Matthews. BS in Chemistry, U. Tex., 1966; PhD in Biochemistry, U. Calif., Berkeley, 1970. Post doctoral fellow Stanford (Calif.) U., 1970-72; mem. faculty Rice U., Houston, 1972—, chair dept., 1987-95, Wiess prof., 1989-96, Stewart Meml. chair, 1996—; mem. BBCB study sect. NIH, Bethesda, Md., 1980-84, 86-88, BRSG adv. com., 1992-94; mem. adv. com. on rsch. programs Tex. Higher Edn. Coord. Bd., Austin, 1987-92; mem. undergrad. edn. initiative rev. panel Howard Hughes Rsch. Inst., Bethesda, 1991, mem. rsch. resources rev. panel, 1995. Mem. editl. bd. Jour. Biol. Chemistry, 1988-93, assoc. editor, 1994—; contbr. 130 reviewed papers. Fellow AAAS; mem. Am. Soc. Biochemistry and Molecular Biology (nominating com. 1993-94, 96-97), Phi Beta Kappa. Office: Rice Univ Dept Biochemistry & Cell Biology PO Box 1892 Houston TX 77251

MATTHEWS, L. WHITE, III, railroad executive; b. Ashland, Ky., Oct. 5, 1945; s. L. White and Virginia Carolyn (Chandler) M.; m. Mary Jane Hanser, Dec. 30, 1972; children: Courtney Chandler, Brian Whittlesey. BS in Econs, Hampden-Sydney Coll., 1967; MBA in Fin. and Gen. Mgmt, U. Va., 1970. Cons. fin. Chem. Bank, N.Y.C., 1970-72, asst. sec., 1972-74, asst. v.p., 1974-75, v.p., 1976-77; treas. Mo. Pacific Corp., St. Louis, 1977-82; v.p. fin. Mo. Pacific R.R. Co. subs. Mo. Pacific Corp., St. Louis, 1979-82; v.p., treas. Union Pacific Corp. and Union Pacific R.R. Co., N.Y.C., 1982-87; sr. v.p. fin. Union Pacific corp., Bethlehem, Pa., 1987-92, exec. v.p. fin., 1992—; mem. coun. of fin. execs. The Conf. Bd.; mem. nat. adv. bd. Chase Bank of N.Y.; bd. dirs. Union Pacific Corp., Bethlehem, Pa. Trustee Pilot Funds, St. Louis.

MATTHEWS, LARRYL KENT, mechanical engineering educator; b. Lubbock, Tex., Sept. 18, 1951; s. Morrison Arliss and Juanita Ruby (Parr) M.; m. Marie Elizabeth Twist, May 15, 1972. MS, N.Mex. State U., 1975; PhD, Purdue U., 1982. Test engr. Sandia Nat. Labs., Albuquerque, 1976-81; rsch. dir., educator N.Mex. State U., Las Cruces, 1982—, assoc. dean for rsch.; cons. Sandia Nat. Labs., 1985-89, ISOTEC, Santa Fe, N.Mex., 1986-88; bd. dirs. Waste-Mgmt. Edn. Rsch. Consortium, Las Cruces, 1990—. Author: (with Gabe Garcia) Laser and Eye Safety in the Laboratory, 1994; contbr. articles to Jour. Solar Energy, Internat. Jour. Exptl. Heat Transfer, ASME Jour. Solar Engring., Internat. Jour. Heat and Mass Transfer, Intech mag., Jour. Quantitative Specifications and Radiol. Transfer. Mem. AAAS, ASME, Am. Astron. Soc., Soc. de Ingenieros (founder), Pi Tau Sigma. Democrat. Methodist. Achievements include develoment of multiple-head radiometer for large pool-fire environments, of CSMP (Circum Solar Measurement Package) for contentrating solar applications, and the LODS (Laser Optical Displacements System) for measuring large and small 2-D structural displacements. Office: NMex State U Engring Rsch Ctr PO Box 30001 Las Cruces NM 88003-3449

MATTHEWS, LEONARD SARVER, advertising executive, consultant; b. Glendean, Ky., Jan. 6, 1922; s. Clell and Zetta Price (Sarver) M.; m. Dorothy Lucille Fessler; children: Nancy, James, Douglas. B.S. summa cum laude, Northwestern U., 1948. With Leo Burnett Co., Inc., Chgo., 1948-75; v.p., dir. Leo Burnett Co., Inc., 1958-59, v.p. charge mktg. services, 1959-61, exec. v.p., 1961-69, pres., 1970-75; asst. sec. commerce for domestic and internat. bus., 1976; pres., exec. com., dir. Young and Rubicam, 1977-78; pres. Am. Assn. Advt. Agys., 1979-89; co-founder Matthews & Johnston, Stamford, Conn., 1989-92; chmn. Next Century Media, 1992—; bd. dirs. Digital Gen. Systems, San Francisco; adv. bds. Adcom, Carlsbad, Calif., Ambient Capital, Beverly Hills, Calif., Scripps Capital, San Diego. Served as ensign USCGR, 1942-46. Mem. Advt. Coun. (life bd. dirs.), Sky Club (N.Y.C.), Pine Valley Golf Club (N.J.), Rancho Santa Fe Golf (Calif.), Georgetown Club (Washington), Delta Sigma Pi, Beta Gamma Sigma. Republican. Lutheran. Office: PO Box 2629 Rancho Santa Fe CA 92067-2629

MATTHEWS, LLOYD, government official; married; 5 children. With Revenue Can.; founder Matthews Group of Cos.; owner Lumber World, Metal World, Offshore Supplies Internat., Matthews Investments Inc.; mem. House of Assembly, St. John's North, 1993—; minister of health Dept. Health, St. John's, Nfld., 1994—. Trustee Sch. Bd.; provincial treas., v.p. Nfld. and Labrador Sch. Trustees Assn.; founding chmn. Children's Wish Found. of Can., Nfld., pres., chmn. nat. bd. to date; founding chmn. St. John's Clean and Beautiful; bd. dirs. YM/YWCA, VOCM Cares Found.;

mem. St. John's Bd. Trade, others. Office: Dept Health, PO Box 8700 Sta A Confed Bldg W Blk, Saint Johns, NF Canada A1B 4J6

MATTHEWS, MILDRED SHAPLEY, scientific editor, freelance writer; b. Pasadena, Calif., Feb. 15, 1915; d. Harlow and Martha (Betz) Shapley; m. Ralph Vernon Matthews, Sept. 25, 1937; children:: June Lorrain, Bruce Shapley, Melvin Lloyd, Martha Alys. AB, U. Mich., 1936. Rsch. asst. Calif. Inst. Tech., Pasadena, 1950-61; bilingual editor, rsch. asst. Astron. Obs. Merate-Milan and Trieste, Italy, 1960-70; rsch. asst. Lunar-Planetary Lab., editor space sci. series U. Ariz., Tucson, 1970-96; retired, 1996. Contbr. articles to Sky and Telescope, Astronomia. Recipient Masursky Meritorious Svc. award div. planetary sci. Am. Astron. Soc., 1993. Avocation: classical music concerts, especially opera. Home: 1600 Milvia St Berkeley CA 94709

MATTHEWS, NORMAN STUART, department store executive; b. Boston, Jan. 13, 1933; s. Martin W. and Charlotte (Cohen) M.; m. Joanne Banks, June 11, 1956; children: Gary S., Jeffrey B., Patricia A. B.A., Princeton U.; M.B.A., Harvard U. Ptnr. Beacon Mktg. and Advt. Assocs., N.Y.C., 1956-71; sr. v.p. Broyhill Furniture Co., Lenoir, N.C., 1971-73, E.J. Korvettes, N.Y.C., 1973-78; chmn., chief exec. officer Gold Circle Stores, Columbus, Ohio, 1978-82; vice chmn. Federated Dept. Stores, Cin., from 1982, pres., chief oper. officer, 1987-88, retail cons., 1988—; dir. Progressive Corp., Cleve., Loehmann's, N.Y.C., Finlay Fine Jewelry, N.Y.C., Lechters Inc., N.J., Toys 'R' Us, Paramus, N.J. Office: 650 Madison Ave New York NY 10022-1029

MATTHEWS, ROGER HARDIN, lawyer; b. Greensboro, N.C., Sept. 16, 1948; s. Shuford Roger and Jacqueline (Hardin) M.; m. Jane Elizabeth Dougan, Aug. 7, 1982; children: Christopher Hardin, Marielle Aimée. AB, Harvard U., 1970, JD, 1974. Bar: Mass. 1974. Assoc. Ropes & Gray, Boston, 1974-84, ptnr., 1984—. Mem. ABA (employee benefits com., tax sect.), Boston Bar Assn. (co-chmn. Employee Retirement Income Security Act com. 1985-88). Avocation: piano. Office: Ropes & Gray 1 International Place Boston MA 02110-2624

MATTHEWS, ROWENA GREEN, biological chemistry educator; b. Cambridge, Eng., Aug. 20, 1938 (father Am. citizen); d. David E. and Doris (Cribb) Green; m. Larry Stanford Matthews, June 18, 1960; children: Brian Stanford, Keith David. BA, Radcliffe Coll., 1960; PhD, U. Mich., 1969. Instr. U. S.C., Columbia, 1964-65; postdoctoral fellow U. Mich., Ann Arbor, 1970-75, asst. prof., 1975-81, assoc. prof. biol. chemistry, 1981-86, prof. 1986—, assoc. chmn., 1988-92, G. Robert Greenberg disting. prof., 1995—, chair biophysics rsch. divsn., 1996—; mem. phys. biochemistry study sect. NIH, 1982-86; mem. adv. coun. Nat. Inst. Gen. Med. Scis., NIH, 1991-94; adv. bd. NATO, 1994-96. mem. editorial adv. bd. Biochem. Jour., 1984-92, Arch. Biochemistry, Biophysics, 1992—, Biochemistry, 1993—, Jour. Bacteriology, 1995—. Contbr. articles to profl. jours. Recipient Faculty Recognition award U. Mich., 1984, Merit award Nat. Inst. Gen. Med. Scis., 1991—; NIH grantee, 1978—; NSF grantee, 1992—. Mem. AAAS, Am. Soc. Biochem. and Molecular Biol. (program chair 1995, chair human resources 1996—), Am. Chem. Soc. (program chmn. biochemistry div. 1985, sec. biochemistry div. 1990-92, chair 1994-96), Phi Beta Kappa, Sigma Xi. Avocations: bicycling, snorkeling, cross country skiing, cooking, gardening. Office: U Mich Biophysics Rsch Divsn 4024 Chemistry 930 N University Ave Ann Arbor MI 48109-1001

MATTHEWS, STEVE ALLEN, lawyer; b. Columbia, S.C., Oct. 11, 1955; s. Philip Garland and Vernecia Neely (Wilson) M.; m. Caroline Elizabeth FitzSimons, Sept. 26, 1987; children: Philip Garland II, Nathalie FitzSimons, Caroline Salley. BA in History, U. S.C., 1977; JD, Yale U., 1980. Bar: S.C. 1980, D.C. 1982. Assoc. Boyd, Knowlton, Tate & Finlay, Columbia, 1980-81, Dewey, Ballantine, Bushby, Palmer & Wood, Washington, 1981-85; spl. counsel to asst. atty. gen. Civil Rights Div. U.S. Dept. Justice, Washington, 1985-86, dep. asst. atty. gen. for jud. selection, Office of Legal Policy, 1986-88; exec. asst. to U.S. Atty. Gen., 1988; mem. Sinkler & Boyd P.A., Columbia, 1988—. Mem. Federalist Soc., Party of the Right, Euphradian Soc., Nat. Assn. Bond Lawyers (bd. dirs. 1995-96), Am. Coll. Bond Counsel (bd. dirs.), Collegiate Network, Inc. (chmn. bd. dirs.). Office: Sinkler & Boyd PA 1426 Main St Columbia SC 29201-2834

MATTHEWS, SIR STUART, aviation industry executive; b. London, May 5, 1936; came to U.S., 1974; s. Bernard De Lides and Daisy Vera (Woodcock) M.; student, Hatfield Coll. Advanced Tech., 1958; m. Kathleen Hilary Adams, Jan. 12, 1974; children: Anthony, Caroline, Joanna. Apprentice, de Havilland Aircraft Ltd., Hatfield, 1952-53; aircraft project design engr. Hawker Siddeley Aviation Ltd., Hatfield, 1953-64; with mktg. dept. Brit. Aircraft Co., Bristol, 1964-67; gen. mgr. planning Brit. Caledonian Airways, London, 1967-74; v.p. N.Am. div. Fokker-VFW Internat., Washington, 1974-80; pres., chief exec. officer Fokker Aircraft USA, Alexandria, Va., 1980-93, chmn. 1993-94, Aircraft Fin. and Trade, Alexandria, 1984-94; pres., CEO Flight Safety Found., Alexandria, Va., 1994—; chmn. asso. mem. group Commuter Airlines Assn. Am., 1979-80. Chmn. Flight Safety Found.; mem. adv. bd. Am. Security Bank. Fellow Royal Aero. Soc. (chartered engr.), Inst. Transp. (charter); mem. AIAA, Royal Order of Orange Nassau (The Netherlands) (knight), Netherlands/Am. C. of C. (bd. dirs.), Alexandria C. of C. (bd. dirs.). Clubs: Aero, Nat. Aviation (Washington), Royal Air Force Club (London), Wings (N.Y.C., mem. bd. govs.), Lions (pres. Engleside, Va. 1977-78), Rotary Internat., Mt. Vernon Yacht Club (commodore). Home: 9439 Mt Vernon Cir Alexandria VA 22309-3221 Office: Flight Safety Found 601 Madison St Alexandria VA 22314-1756

MATTHEWS, THOMAS MICHAEL, energy company executive; b. Luling, Tex., May 20, 1943; s. Chester Raymond and Mary Lucille (Stutts) M.; m. Sherry Dianne Klein, May 25, 1968; children: Stephanie Dianne, Leslie Michelle. BSCE, Tex. A & M U., 1965; postgrad., U. Okla., 1967, UCLA, 1975, Stanford U., 1988, Columbia U., 1993. Staff engr. Exxon Co. USA, Houston, New Orleans, 1965-69; project engr. Exxon Co. USA, L.A., 1974-76; div. engr. Exxon Co. USA, Houston, 1969-74; engring. mgr. Exxon Co. USA, Anchorage, 1976-78; v.p. Exxon Gas, Houston, 1978-81, Tenn. Gas/Tenneco, Houston, 1981-86; pres. Tenn. Gas/Tenneco, 1986-89; v.p., gen. mgr. Texaco USA, Houston, 1989—; pres. Texaco Gas, 1990-93; pres., CEO Texaco Refining & Mktg., Inc.; v.p. Texaco, Inc.; pres. NGC Corp., 1996—; dir. Offshore Tech. Ctr., Tex. A & M U., 1987-89, adv. coun.; bd. dirs. Inroads, Inc. Contbr. articles to profl. jours.; inventor in field. Pres., chmn. Ponderosa Forest Community Council, Houston, 1980-85; mem. PTO, Scenic Pk. Sch., Anchorage, 1976-78. Mem. NSPE (bd. dirs.), Soc. Petroleum Engrs., Soc. Ga. Assn., Am. Petroleum Inst., Natural Gas Supply Assn., Gas Rsch. Inst., Petroleum Club, Northgate Forest Country Club. Republican. Lutheran. Avocations: snow skiing, golf, reading, running, singing. Home: 17402 Ridge Top Dr Houston TX 77090-2021 Office: Texaco USA 1111 Bagby St Houston TX 77002-2551

MATTHEWS, WANDA MILLER, artist; b. Barry, Ill., Sept. 15, 1930; d. Harry Leonard and Gladys (Smith) Miller; m. Eugene Edward Matthews, Sept. 14, 1952; children: Anthony Lee, Daniel Nicholas. BFA, Bradley U., Peoria, Ill., 1952; MFA, U. Iowa, 1957. Spl. services artist U.S. Army, Ft. Riley, Kans., 1954-55; research asst. printmaking U. Iowa, 1956-57; travel Italy and Europe, 1957-60. Producing, and exhibiting printmaker, Boulder, Colo., 1961—; one-woman exhbns. include, Lehigh U., Bethlehem, Pa., 1973, Gettysburg (Pa.) Coll., 1973, U. Colo., 1976, U. N.D., 1976, Jane Haslem Gallery, Washington, 1982, Am. Ctr. Gallery, Belgrade, Yugoslavia, 1982, Oxford Gallery (Eng.), 1982, U. Colo., Boulder, 1985, U. Northern Colo., Greeley, 1985, The Printerly Image: Wanda Miller Matthews 1951-1991, Arvada (Colo.) Ctr. for the Arts and Humanities, 1991, Jane Haslem Gallery, Washington, 1990, Barry (Ill.) Pub. Libr., 1995; group exhbns. include USIS Gallery, Naples, Italy, 1960; Nat. Invitational Print Exhbn., Otis Art Inst., L.A., 1962, 63, Brit. Internat. Print Biennale, Bradford, Eng., 1970, 79, Invitational Graphics, Minot (N.D.) State Coll., 1972, Printmaking Now, W. Tex. Mus., Lubbock, 1973, ColorPrint U.S.A., Tex. Tech U., Lubbock, 1974, 78, Nat. Invitational Print Show, Central Wash. State Coll., Ellensburg, 1975, 11th Internat. Exhbn. Graphic Art, Ljubljana, Yugoslavia, 1975, 6th, 7th, 8th, 10th Internat. Print Biennales, Cracow, Poland, 1976, 78, 80, 84, Internat. Book Fair, Leipzig, E.Ger., 1977, New Talent in Printmaking, 1980, Associated Am. Artists, N.Y.C. and Phila., 1980, Rockford Internat. Biennale, Ill., 1985, Western States Invitational, Portland Art Mus., Oreg., 1985, 40th Am. Colorprint Soc. Exhbn., Jenkintown, Pa., 1985, Premio Internzionale Biella per l'incisione, Italy, 1976, 80, 87, Small Graphic Forms, Poland, 1987, 4X4X4: Sixteen Contemporary Printmakers from the Four Corner States, Utah State U., 1987, 3d Internat. Biennial Print Exhbt.: 1987, Taipei, Taiwan, 1987-88, CSP Exch. Show, Brandts Klaedefabrik, Odense, Denmark, 1989, Am. Self Portraits in Prints (traveling exhbn.) Ind. U., Bloomington, 1990, Am. Prints: Last Half of 20th Century Jane Haslem Gallery, Washington, 1993, Juniper Gallery, Napa, Calif., 1993, Boston Archtl. Ctr., 1994, Am. Inst. Architecture, Washington, 1994, U. N.H., 1994, others; represented in permanent collections, Portland Art Mus. (Oreg.); Boston Pub. Library, Bytow Nat. Museum (Poland), L.A. County Mus., Nat. Collection Fine Arts, Washington, Phila. Mus. Art, Library of Congress, Coll. Bd. Collection of Prints by Am. Artists, N.Y.C., Honolulu Acad. Art, others. Recipient numerous awards including: Purchase prize Prints 1962 Nat. Exhbn., State U. Coll., Potsdam, N.Y., 1962, Prints 10th ann. print exhbn., 1970; purchase prize Dublin Nat. Print and Drawing competition Dulin Gallery Art, Knoxville, Tenn., 1968, 81, 22d ann. nat. exhbn. Boston Printmakers, 1970; recipient purchase award Graphics '71, Nat. Print and Drawing Exhbn., Western N.Mex. U., Silver City, 1971, Soc. Am. Graphic Artists, Nat. Exhbn., N.Y.C., 1979, Benton Spruance prize Print Club Phila., 1971, Am. Colorprint Soc. Drabkin Meml. award medallion, 1981, 1st Pl. in Color Prints Ybor Nat. Print Competition, 1985, Leila Sawyer Meml. award 97th ann. exhbn. Nat. Assn. Women Artists, 1986, Cash award Nat. Print Biennial, Silvermine Guild Arts Ctr., 1996, Juror's Spl. Mention award Beyond Boundaries Internat. Print Exhbn., 1996, Purchase award 66th Nat. Print Exhbn. Soc. Am. Graphic Artists, 1997; Tiffany grantee, 1957-58, 58-59. Mem. Calif. Soc. Printmakers, Print Club Phila., Soc. Am. Graphic Artists, The Boston Printmakers. Home: 720 Hawthorn Ave Boulder CO 80304-2140

MATTHEWS, WENDY SCHEMPP, psychologist, researcher; b. Bridgeport, Conn., Feb. 4, 1945; d. Harry Edward and Julie Schempp; m. Robert J. Matthews, Aug. 16, 1969 (div. June 1984); 1 child, Avery. BA, Beaver Coll., 1966; MA, Cornell U., 1971, PhD, 1975; cert., Université de Paris, 1972. Rsch. assoc. Harvard U., Cambridge, Mass., 1977-78; jr. fellow N.J. Div. Human Svcs., Trenton, 1978; clin. assoc. prof. U. of Medicine & Dentistry of N.J., New Brunswick, 1979—; dir. children's ctr. Contemporary Psychology Inst., Skillman, N.J., 1983-87; pediatric psychologist N.J. Div. Youth & Family Svcs., Trenton, 1987—; pvt. practice Princeton, N.J., 1987—. Author: He & She: How Children Develop Their Sex Role Identity, 1977; contbr. articles to profl. jours.

MATTHEWS, WESTINA LOMAX, finance and banking executive; b. Chillicothe, Ohio, Nov. 8, 1948; d. Wesley Smith and Ruth (Fields) M. BS, U. Dayton, 1970, MS, 1974; PhD, U. Chgo., 1980. Tchr. Mills Lawn Elem. Sch., Yellow Springs, Ohio, 1970-75; program officer The Chgo. Community Trust, sr. program officer, 1983-85; v.p. philanthropic programs, sec. Merrill Lynch Found., N.Y.C., 1985—, dir. philanthropic programs, 1997—, trustee, 1993—. Bd. dirs. Arthur Ashe Inst.; trustee N.Y. Theol. Sem., Wilberforce U. Postdoctoral fellow Northwestern U., 1980-81, U. Wis., 1981-82. Office: Merrill Lynch & Co 225 Liberty St New York NY 10281-1008

MATTHEWS, WILLIAM D(OTY), lawyer, consumer products manufacturing company executive; b. Oneida, N.Y., Aug. 25, 1934; s. William L. and Marjorie L. (Doty) M.; m. Ann M. Morse, Aug. 4, 1956; children: Judith Anne, Thomas John. AB, Union Coll., 1956; LLB, Cornell U., 1960. Bar: N.Y. 1960, D.C. 1962. Atty. divsn. corp. fin. SEC, Washington, 1960-62; assoc. Whitlock, Markey & Tait, Washington, 1962-69; gen. counsel Oneida (N.Y.) Ltd., 1973-86, from v.p. to exec. v.p., 1977-86, also dir., chmn., CEO, 1986—; bd. dirs. N.Y. State Bus. Coun.,Coyne Textile Svcs.; trustee Oneida Savs. Bank. Alderman City of Oneida, 1972-79; mem. Madison County Bd. Suprs., 1984-86. Presbyterian. Home: 621 Patio Circle Dr Oneida NY 13421-1820 Office: Oneida Ltd Adminstrn Bldg Kenwood Station Oneida NY 13421-2808

MATTHEWS, WILLIAM EDMUND, newspaper and travel magazine publisher; b. Shelbyville, Ky., Apr. 30, 1930; s. Robert Foster and Zerelda Tribble (Baxter) M.; m. Else Vivien Bender Jorgensen, June 13, 1952; children: Lisa Gaines, William E. II, Ellen Matthews Oetinger, Bland Ballard. BA, U. Mich., 1952. Info. specialist C.I.A., Washington, 1953-61; owner, pubr. The Shelby Sentinel, Shelbyville, Ky., 1961-68; pres., gen. mgr. Newspapers Inc., Shelbyville, Ky., 1968-73; pres. Landmark Community Newspapers, Shelbyville, Ky., 1973-76; pubr./gen. mgr. Scripps Howard Community News, Cin., 1976-82; v.p., editor Mid-Continent Devel. & Tourism, Huntingburg, Ind., 1982-93, pres., editor, 1993—; editor The Huntingburg Press, 1987—, pub., 1993—. Editor/pubr.: The Relentless Reds, 1976, The Royal Reds, 1977. 2d lt. U.S. Army, 1952. Mem. Ky. Press Assn. (pres. 1977), Ky. Weekly Newspaper Assn. (pres. 1975), Rotary. Christian Ch. (Disciples of Christ). Avocation: gardening. Home: 467 Cove Rd Shelbyville KY 40065-8924 Office: The Huntingburg Press 423 E 4th St Huntingburg IN 47542-1339

MATTHEWS, WILLIAM PROCTER, English educator; b. Cin., Nov. 11, 1942; s. William P. and Mary Elizabeth (Sather) M.; m. Marie Murray Harris, May 4, 1963 (div. 1973); children: William, Sebastian. B.A., Yale U., 1965; M.A., U. N.C., Chapel Hill, 1966. Instr. English Wells Colls., Aurora, N.Y., 1968-69; asst. prof. Cornell U., 1969-74; asso. prof. U. Colo., 1974-78; prof. English U. Wash., Seattle, 1978-83, CCNY, 1983—; bd. dirs. Asso. Writing Programs, 1977-80, pres., 1979-80; mem. lit. panel Nat. Endowment Arts, 1976-79, chmn., 1978-79. Author: Ruining the New Road, 1970, Sleek For the Long Flight, 1972, Sticks and Stones, 1975, Rising and Falling, 1979, Flood, 1982, A Happy Childhood, 1984, Foreseeable Futures, 1987, Blues If You Want, 1989, Curiosities, 1989, Selected Poems and Translations, 1992, Time and Money, 1995 (Nat. Book Critics' Cir. award 1995), The Mortal City: 100 Epigrams of Martial, 1995. Fellow Nat. Endowment Arts, 1974, 83, Guggenheim Found., 1980-81, Ruth Lilly prize, 1997. Mem. Poetry Soc. Am. Office: CCNY Dept English New York NY 10038

MATTHEWS, WYHOMME S., music educator, college administrator; b. Battle Creek, Mich., July 22, 1948; d. Woodrow R. and LouLease (Graham) Sellers; m. Edward L. Matthews, Apr. 29, 1972; children: Channing DuVall, Triston Curran, Landon Edward, Brandon Graham. AA, Kellogg C.C., 1968; MusB, Mich. State U., 1970, MA, 1972, MusM, 1972. Cert. elem. and secondary tchr., Mich. Tchr., vocal music dir. Benton Harbor (Mich.) Pub. Schs., 1971-72, dir. vocal music, 1972; dir. edn. head start program Burlington (N.J.) County, 1972-73; pvt. music tchr., 1973-89; tchr. Southeastern Jr. H.S., 1986-87, W.K. Kellogg Jr. H.S., 1987-89; chair visual and performing arts dept. Kellogg C.C., Battle Creek, Mich., 1989—; 1972; part-time instr. Kellogg C.C., 1973-89, dir. Eclectic Chorale, 1994—, dir., organizer Kellogg C.C. Eclectic Chorale Sacred Cultural Festival, 1979—, judge various contests; presenter in field. Pres. Dudley Elem. Sch., 1981-85; active Battle Creek Pub. Schs. PTA, Pennfield Pub. Schs. PTA, Mt. Zion African Meth. Episc. Ch. Mich. State U. fellow, 1971; recipient Outstanding Cmty. Svc. award, 1975. Mem. Mich. Music Tchr. Assn., Nat. Music Tchrs. Assn., Battle Creek Music Tchrs. Assn., Battle Creek Morning Music Club (bd. dirs.), Nat. Leadership Acad., Battle Creek Cmty. Concert Assn. Home: 466 Alton Ave Battle Creek MI 49017-3212 Office: Kellogg CC 450 North Ave Battle Creek MI 49017-3306

MATTHIAS, JOHN EDWARD, English literature educator; b. Columbus, Ohio, Sept. 5, 1941; s. John Marshall and Lois (Kirkpatrick) M.; m. Diana Clare Jocelyn, Dec. 27, 1967; children—Cynouai, Laura. BA, Ohio State U., 1963; MA, Stanford U., 1966; postgrad., U. London, 1967. Asst. prof. dept. English U. Notre Dame, Ind., 1966-73, assoc. prof., 1973-80, prof., 1980—; vis. fellow Clare Hall, Cambridge U., 1966-77, assoc., 1977—; vis. prof. dept. English, Skidmore Coll., Saratoga Springs, N.Y., 1975, U. Chgo., 1980. Author: Bucyrus, 1971, Turns, 1975, Crossing, 1979, Five American Poets, 1980, Introducing David Jones, 1980, Contemporary Swedish Poetry, 1980, Bathory and Lermontov, 1980, Northern Summer, New and Selected Poems, 1984, The Battle of Kosovo, 1987, David Jones: Man and Poet: A Gathering of Ways, 1991, Reading Old Friends, 1991, Swimming at Midnight, 1995, Beltane at Aphelion, 1995. Recipient Columbia U. Transl. award, 1978, Swedish Inst. award, 1981, Poetry award Soc. Midland Authors, 1984, Ingram Merrill Found. award, 1984, 90; Woodrow Wilson fellow, 1963, Lily Endowment fellow, 1993; Fulbright grantee, 1966. Mem. AAUP, PEN, Poets and Writers, Poetry Soc. Am. (George Bogin Meml. award 1990), London Poetry Secretariat. Office: U Notre Dame Dept English Notre Dame IN 46556

MATTHIES, FREDERICK JOHN, architectural engineer; b. Omaha, Oct. 4, 1925; s. Fred. J. and Charlotte Leota (Metz) M.; m. Carol Mae Dean, Sept. 14, 1947; children—John Frederick, Jane Carolyn Matthies Godding. BSCE, Cornell U., 1947; postgrad., U. Nebr., 1952-53. Diplomate Am. Acad. Environ. Engrs.; registered profl. engr., Iowa, Nebr. Civil engr. Henningson, Durham & Richardson, Omaha, 1947-50, 52-54; sr. v.p. devel. Leo A. Daly Co., Omaha, 1954-90; cons. engr., 1990—; lectr. in field; mem. dist. export coun. U.S. Dept. Commerce, 1981-83. Contbr. articles to profl. publs. Mem. Douglas County Rep. Cen. Com., Nebr., 1968-72; bd. regents Augustana Coll., Sioux Falls., S.D., 1976-89; bd. dirs. Orange County Luth. Hosp. Assn., Anaheim, Calif., 1961-62, Nebr. Humanities Coun., 1988—, Omaha-Shizuoka City (Japan) Sister City Orgn.; trustee Luth. Med. Ctr., Omaha, 1978-82; mem. adv. bd. Marine Mil. Acad., Harlingen, Tex. 1st lt. USMCR, 1943-46, 50-52, Korea. Fellow ASCE, Instn. Civil Engrs. (London, Euro Engr. European Econ. Commn.); mem. NSPE, Am. Water Works Assn. (life), Air Force Assn., Am. Legion, VFW, The Omaha Club. Lutheran. Home: 337 S 127th St Omaha NE 68154-2309

MATTHIESEN, LEROY THEODORE, bishop; b. Olfen, Tex., June 11, 1921; s. Joseph A. and Rosa (Englert) M. BA, Josephinum Coll., Columbus, Ohio, 1942; MA, Cath. U., Washington, 1961; LittD, Register Sch. Journalism., Denver, 1962. Ordained priest Roman Cath. Ch., 1946. Editor West Tex. Cath., Amarillo diocese, from 1948; prin. Alamo Cath. High Sch, from 1969; pastor St. Francis parish, from 1972; ordained bishop of Amarillo, Tex., 1980—. Office: 1800 N Spring St PO Box 5644 Amarillo TX 79117-5644*

MATTHIESSEN, PETER, author; b. N.Y.C., May 22, 1927; s. Erard A. and Elizabeth (Carey) M.; m. Patricia Southgate, Feb. 8, 1951 (div.); m. Deborah Love, May 8, 1963 (dec. Jan. 1972); children: Lucas C., Sara C., Rue, Alexander F.L.; m. Maria Eckhart, Nov. 28, 1980. Student, The Sorbonne, Paris, 1948-49; B.A., Yale U., 1950. Author: Race Rock, 1954, Partisans, 1955, Wildlife in America, 1959, Raditzer, 1960, The Cloud Forest, 1961, Under the Mountain Wall, 1963, At Play in the Fields of the Lord, 1965, The Shorebirds of North America, 1967 (Gold medal Phila. Acad. Scis.), Oomingmak: The Expedition to the Musk Ox Island in the Bering Sea, 1967, Sal Si Puedes, 1969 (Christopher medal), Blue Meridian, 1971, The Tree Where Man Was Born, 1972, Far Tortuga, 1975, The Snow Leopard, 1978 (nat. book award), Sand Rivers, 1981 (John Burroughs medal), In the Spirit of Crazy Horse, 1983, Indian Country, 1984, Nine-Headed Dragon River, 1986, Men's Lives, 1986, On the River Styx and Other Stories, 1989, Killing Mister Watson, 1990, African Silences, 1992, Baikal: Sacred Sea of Siberia, 1992, Shadows of Africa, 1992, East of Lo Monthang: In the Land of Mustang, 1995. Trustee N.Y. Zool. Soc., 1965-78. AAAL grantee, 1963. Mem. AAAS, Am. Acad. Arts and Letters.

MATTHIS, EVA MILDRED BONEY, college official; b. Magnolia (Waycross), N.C., Aug. 18, 1927; d. James Horace and Eva Alice (Merritt) Boney; m. George Clifton Matthis, Aug. 31, 1949; 1 child, George Clifton Jr. AA, Louisburg Coll., 1946; BS, East Carolina U., 1969, MLS, 1971. Advt. mgr. Efirds, Wilmington, N.C., 1946-49; advt. acct. Lenoir Co. News, 1950; syn. aviation instrument instr. Serv-Air Aviation, Kinston, N.C., 1951-57; advt. account exec. Kinston Free Press, 1959-64; libr. Caswell Ctr., 1965-66; history tchr. North Lenoir High Sch., 1969-70; libr. Sampson Elem. Sch., 1970-72; head libr. media program Lenoir C.C., Kinston, 1972-76, dean, learning resources, 1976-89, dean, mktg. instl. devel., learning resources, 1989-91, dean, instl. advancement, 1991, v.p. instrnl. svcs.; alumni rep. East Carolina U. LS SACS Self-study, Greenville, 1987-89. Family editor: Heritage of Lenoir County, 1981. Developer Heritage Place, local history mus., 1988; pres. Jr. Women's Club, Kinston, 1960; dist. dir. N.C. Jr. Women's Club, 1961; mem. Kinston Mayor's All-Am. City Com., 1988, co-chair, 1996-97 ; rep. Lenoir County Bicentennial Com., Kinston, 1987; staff-parish chmn. Queen Street United Meth. Ch., 1988-90, mem. bishop's coun., 1988-90, com. chmn., 1988-90, chmn. fin. com., 1992—, bldg. com., 1992-94, Sunday Sch. tchr., mem. adminstrv. bd., 1984—; mem. Kinston Mus. com., 1990-92, Fireman Mus. com., 1992-93; chair archtl. survey, Lenoir county, 1993. Named Scouting Family of Yr., 1970; recipient merit award N.C. Hist. Soc., 1989, Excellence award Kinston C. of C., 1985, Educators Office Pers. Lenoir C.C., Adminstr. of Yr. award, 1990. Mem. N.C. C.C. Learning Resources Assn. (life, pub. info. officer 1989-92, exec. bd., dist. II 1986-89, Achievement award 1992, Hon. Mention Libr. Jour. LIbr. of Yr. 1991), Librs. of Lenoir County (pres. 1985, 92), Lenoir County Hist. Assn. (v.p., exec. bd.), Coun. on Resource Devel., Hist. Lenoir County-Kinston Celebration, East Carolina U. Alumni Assn., Phi Beta Kappa, Delta Kappa Gamma (yearbook editor). Avocations: basketmaking, reading, gardening, grandmothering. Home: PO Box 6340 Kinston NC 28501-1440 Office: Lenoir C C PO Box 188 Kinston NC 28502-0188

MATTICE, HOWARD LEROY, education educator; b. Roxbury, N.Y., Sept. 23, 1935; s. Charles Pierce and Loretta Jane (Ellis) M.; m. Elaine Grace Potts, Feb. 4, 1956; children: Kevin, Stephen. BA, King's Coll., 1960; MA, L.I. U., 1965, NYU, 1969; cert., CUNY, 1972; EdD, NYU, 1978. Cert. tchr. N.Y., clin. educators trainer, Fla. Dept. Edn. Social studies tchr. N.Y.C. Bd. Edn., 1961-90, mid. and jr. H.S. asst. prin., 1970-72, 73-75; assoc. prof. edn. and history Clearwater (Fla.) Christian Coll., 1990-92, chmn. divsn. of edn., prof. edn. and history, 1992—; adj. lectr. history S.I. C.C., CUNY, 1969-75; curriculum writer N.Y.C. Bd. Edn., 1985; program reviewer Fla. Dept. Edn., Tallahassee, 1994—; item writer GED Testing Svc., Washington, 1988-92; mem. So. Assn. Colls. and Schs. Accreditation Team H.S., 1995—. Chmn. bd. New Dorp Christian Acad., S.I., 1973-90; chmn. bd. deacons New Dorp. Bapt. Ch., S.I., 1981-90. Mem. ASCD, Assn. Tchr. Educators, Nat. Coun. Social Studies, So. Assn. Colls. and Schs. (h.s. accreditation review team 1995—). Avocations: reading, traveling, gardening. Office: Clearwater Christian Coll 3400 Gulf To Bay Blvd Clearwater FL 33759-4514

MATTILA, MARY JO KALSEM, elementary and art educator; b. Canton, Ill., Oct. 26, 1944; d. Joseph Nelson and Bernice Nora (Milbauer) Kalsem; m. John Peter Mattila, Jan. 27, 1968. BS in Art, U. Wis., 1966; student, Ohio State U., 1972, Drake U., 1981; MS in Ednl. Adminstrn., Iowa State U., 1988. Cert. tchr., prin., supr., adminstr., art tchr., secondary tchr., Iowa. Tchr. 2d grade McHenry (Ill.) Pub. Schs., 1966-67, Wisconsin Hts. Schs., Black Earth, Wis., 1967-69; substitute tchr. Columbus (Ohio) City Schs., 1969-70; elem. art tchr. Southwestern City Schs., Columbus, 1972-73; adminstrv. intern Ames, Iowa, 1984-86; lead tchr. at Roosevelt Sch. Ames Cmty. Schs., 1986-87, art vertical curriculum chair, 1983-89, art educator, elem. and spl. edn., 1973—. Author articles. Active LWV, Ames, 1982—; fundraiser Altrusa, Ames, 1992—. Recipient Very Spl. Svc. award for Disting. Svc. in Very Spl. Arts, Gov. of Iowa, 1984. Mem. ASCD, NEA, Nat. Assn. Elem. Sch. Prins., Nat. Art Edn. Assn. Avocations: collecting old stoneware jugs, growing orchids, reading. Home: 2822 Duff Ave Ames IA 50010-4710 Office: Ames Cmty Schs 120 S Kellogg Ave Ames IA 50010-6719

MATTINGLY, J. VIRGIL, JR., federal lawyer; b. Leonardtown, Md., Oct. 18, 1944. BBA in Acctg., George Washington U., JD. Sr. atty. Fed. Res. Bd., Washington, 1974-79, asst. gen. counsel, 1979-81, assoc. gen. counsel, 1981-85, dep. gen. counsel, 1985-89, gen. counsel, 1989—. With JAGC, U.S. Army, 1970-74. Office: Fed Res Bd Bd Govs 20th & C Sts NW Washington DC 20551*

MATTINGLY, L. SHARON, elementary principal; b. Henderson, Ky., July 16, 1953; d. George Muir Jr. and Ida Mae (Slaughter) M. AS, Henderson C.C.; BA in Elem. Edn. Adminstrn. & Supervisn., U. Evansville; MA in Elem. Edn., Western Ky. U. Elem. tchr. Henderson County Sch., 1975-95, prin., 1995—. Home: 5371 US 41 Alternate Henderson KY 42420

MATTINGLY, MACK F., former ambassador, former senator, entrepreneur; b. Anderson, Ind., Jan. 7, 1931; m. Carolyn Longcamp, 1957; children: Jane, Anne. BS, Ind. U., 1957. Acct. supr. IND, Arvin, Ind., 1957-59; mktg. mgr. IBM Corp., Ga., 1959-79; owner, pres. M's Inc., Ga., 1975-80; U.S. senator from Ga., 1981-87; asst. sec. gen. def. support NATO, Brussels,

1987-90; amb. to Seychelles Dept. State, 1992-93; spkr./author econ., def., fgn. policy, entrepreneur, 1993—; mem. U.S. Senate Com. Appropriations, chmn. legis and mil. constrn. subcoms.; mem. energy and water devel., agt. rural devel., treasury, postal svc. and gen. govt., mil. constrn. legis. subcoms., U.S. Senate com. Banking, Housing and Urban Affairs, chmn. rural housing, econ. policy subcoms.; mem. select com. ethics, 1981-83, joint econ. com., 1983-87; chmn. Rep. Com. on Coms., mem. Rep. Senate Leadership, 1985-87,. Holocaust Commn.; U.S. del. GATT, Geneva, 1982. Author 40 U.S. Sen. Bills, Amendments and Resolutions. Del. Atl. Sgt.-at-Arms, Rep. Nat. Convs., Del. Georgian Rep. Party Convs., 1964-90; chmn. 8th Dist. Goldwater for Pres., 1964, Ga. 8th Congl. Dist., Cand. U.S. Congress, 8th Dist., 1966; mem. Ga. Rep. Party State Ctrl. Com., State Exec. Com., vice chmn. state party, 1968-75, chmn. Ga. Rep. Party, 1975-77; elected 1st Rep. U.s. Senator from Ga. since 1871, 1980; bd. dirs. U.S. Nat. Chamber Found., 1990, Bus. Leadership Coun., Color Graphics, Inc., First Fed. Savs. Bank; hon. mem. bd. dirs. M.L. King Jr. Fed. Holiday Commn. With USAF, 1951-55. Recipient Southeast Father of Yr. award 1984, Ga. Wildlife Fed. Conservationist of Yr. award 1985, Selective Svc. System Dist. Svc. Gold medal 1985, Watchdog of Treasury award 1981-86, Nat. Taxpayers Union Taxpayers Best Friend award 1981-86, NFIB's Guardian of Small Bus. award 1981-86, Am. Security Coun. award 1981-86, Sec. Def. medal for Outstanding Pub. Svc. 1988. Mem. Brunswick Golden Isle C. of C., Am. Legion. Episcopalian.

MATTIS, LOUIS PRICE, pharmaceutical and consumer products company executive; b. Balt., Dec. 12, 1941; s. Louis Wadsworth and Sara Helene (Myers) M.; m. Patricia Diane Brown, Nov. 29, 1963; children—Louis Wadsworth, Deborah Cook. A.B. in Internat. Affairs, Lafayette Coll., Easton, Pa., 1962; M.B.A., Tulane U., 1964. V.p., gen. mgr. Warner Lambert Co., Manila, 1971-74; regional dir. Warner Lambert Co., Hong Kong, 1974-76; region pres. Warner Lambert Co., Sydney, Australia, 1976-79; exec. v.p. Americas-Far East Richardson-Vicks, Inc., 1979-81, pres. Americas-Far East, 1981-84, exec. v.p., 1985-87; group v.p. Sterling Winthrop Inc., N.Y.C., 1987-88, chmn., pres., CEO, 1988-94; dir. Solomon Bros. Fund, 1992—. Mem. Gov. Ctr. for Creative Leadership, 1989—. Mem. Sea Island Golf Club (Ga.), Shek-o Golf Club, Turnberry Golf Club, Ocean Forest Golf Club, Snowmass Club. Avocations: skiing, golf, woodworking. Home: Cottage 221 Sea Island GA 31561 Office: PO Box 31073 Sea Island GA 31561-1073

MATTISON, DONALD ROGER, dean, physician, military officer; b. Mpls., Apr. 28, 1944; s. Milford Zachary and Elizabeth Ruth (Davey) M.; m. Margaret Rose Libby, Jan. 28, 1967; children: Jon, Amy. BA cum laude in Chemistry and Math., Augsburg Coll., Mpls., 1966; MS in Chemistry, MIT, 1968; MD, Columbia U., 1973. Resident in ob-gyn Presbyn. Hosp., N.Y.C., 1973-75, 77-78; commd. rsch. assoc. USPHS, 1975, advanced through grades to comdr., 1984; rsch. assoc. Nat. Inst. Child Health and Human Devel., NIH, Bethesda, Md., 1975-77, med. officer then chief pregnancy rsch. br., 1978-84; assoc. prof. ob-gyn. U. Ark., Little Rock, 1984-87; prof. U. Pitts., 1987-90, assoc. prof. toxicology, 1984-88, prof., 1988-90, dean Grad. Sch. Pub. Health, prof., 1990—; mem. Bd. Environ. Studies and Toxicology, NRC, NAS, 1988—; mem. sci. adv. bd. Hawaii Heptachlor Edn. and Rsch. Found., 1987—; mem. sci. adv. panel Semicondr. Industry Assn., 1987—; mem. portfolio team United Way Allegheny County and Western Pa., 1990—; mem. pre-screening com. Magee-Women's Hosp., Pitts., 1990—; mem. steering com. Pa. Dept. Health, Harrisburg, 1990—; mem. com. Inst. Medicine, NAS, 1989-91; cons. Women's Vietnam Health Study Protocol Devel., New England Rsch. Inst., 1986-90. Mem. editorial bd. Pediatric Pharmacology, 1980-87, Reproductive Toxicology, 1987—, Devel. Pharmacology and Therapeutics, Switzerland, 1987—, Reproductive Scis., The Info. Netork, 1989—, Methods in Toxicology, 1989—; guest editor Jour. Symposium on Reproductive Toxicology, Am. Jour. Indsl. Medicine, 1983; contbr. numerous articles, abstracts, letters and editorials to profl. publs. Recipient Am. Chem. Soc. medal Minn. sect. Am. Chem. Soc., 1966, Assn. Am. Publs. award, 1983. Mem. APHA, Soc. Risk Analysis (editorial bd. jour. 1988—), Pitts. chpt. Soc. Risk Analysis, Am. Assn. Cancer Rsch., N.Y. Acad. Sci., Am. Coll. Toxicology, Am. Fertility Soc., Soc. Gynecologic Investigation, Soc. Toxicology. Avocations: photography, computer sciences, house restoration, cross country skiing. Office: U Pitts Grad Sch Pub Health 130 Desoto St Pittsburgh PA 15213-2535

MATTOCKS-WHISMAN, FRANCES, nursing administrator, educator; b. Cedar Vale, Kans., Dec. 20, 1945; d. Thomas Emerson and Lavonna Laura (Myers) McKinney; m. Jim L. Whisman, Nov. 6, 1981; stepchildren: Toni Zweigart, Gay Asbell, Jenny Watts, Beth Whisman. Diploma, William Newton Sch. Nursing, Winfield, Kans., 1966; student, Tulsa Jr. Coll., Cen. State U., Edmond, Okla., Graceland Coll., Lamoni, Iowa, 1989—. RN; cert. operating room nurse. Operating room nurse Hillcrest Med. Ctar., Tulsa, 1968-72, 74-76; office mgr. Myra A. Peters, M.D., 1972-76; pvt. duty nurse Homemakers Upjohn, Inc., Tulsa, 1976-77; staff nurse, head nurse, insvc. instr. Doctors Med. Ctr., Inc., Tulsa; co-dir. Sch. Surg. Tech. Tulsa County Area Vo-Tech. Sch., 1981-89; asst. dir. transplantation/retrievals Tulsa chpt. ARC, 1989; staff nurse, infection control coord. Wetumka (Okla.) Gen. Hosp., 1989-91; dir. nurses Bristow (Okla.) Meml. Hosp., 1991-93; br. mgr. Columbia Homecare of Okla., Sapulpa, Okla., 1993-96; br. supr. Sapulpa and Mannford offices Doctors Homecare, 1994-95; orthopaedic program ngr. Columbia Homecare and Columbia Tulsa Regional Med. Ctr., 1996—; instr. Wes Watkins Area Vo-Tech. Sch., Wetumka, 1989-90; cons. ARC, Tulsa chpt. Transplantation, 1990. Contbr. articles to profl. jours. Active ARC. Mem. NEA, Nat. Assn. Orthopedic Nurses, Nat. League for Nursing, Am. Vocat. Assn., Okla. Vocat. Assn., Okla. Edn. Assn., Concerned Oklahomans for Nurse Edn., Assn. Operating Rm. Nurses, Infections Control. Nurses. Home: 1418A E 71st St Tulsa OK 74136 Office: Columbia Homecare-Okla 1418A E 71st St Tulsa OK 74136

MATTOON, HENRY AMASA, JR., advertising and marketing consultant, writer; b. Waterbury, Conn., Jan. 14, 1914; s. Henry A. and Sarah Currie (Hallock) M.; m. Dorothy Ann Teeter, Sept. 13, 1934; children: Ann Brooks Wofford, David Scott, Sara Halsey, Judith Scott Conn. BS, Yale U., 1935. Mail boy, then copywriter, copy supr. Compton Advt. Inc., N.Y.C., 1935-44; v.p., creative dir. Compton Advt. Inc., 1944-50; v.p., chmn. plans bd. Ruthrauff & Ryan, Inc., 1950-52; v.p., creative dir. Dancer-Fitzgerald-Sample, Inc., 1952-54; pres., dir. Reach, Yates & Mattoon, Inc., 1954-56; chmn. mktg. plans bd. McCann-Erickson, Inc., 1956-57, v.p., assoc. creative dir., 1957-62; v.p., gen. mgr. McCann-Erickson, Inc., Los Angeles, 1962-65; sr. v.p. and mgr. McCann-Erickson, Inc., Houston, 1965-68; v.p., dir. advt., pub. relations and sales promotion Yardley of London, Inc., 1968-69; ptnr. Walter Weintz & Co., Inc., Stamford, Conn., 1969-70; prin. Otto Man Associs., Inc., Weston, Conn., 1970-93; exec. v.p. Mktg. Lab, Inc., Danbury, Conn., 1985—, also bd. dirs. Contbr., columnist profl. jours. and mags. Mem. Yale Club of N.Y., Crow Canyon Country Club, Knights of Malta, Chi Phi. Republican. Episcopalian. Home: 675 Doral Dr Danville CA 94526-6206

MATTOON, PETER MILLS, lawyer; b. Bryn Mawr, Pa., Oct. 22, 1931; s. Harold Gleason and Marguerite Jeanette (Mills) M.; m. Mary Joan Henley, June 27, 1953; children: Pamela M. Zisselman, R. Stephen, Peter H., Philip P. AB, Dartmouth Coll., 1953; LLB, Harvard U., 1959. Bar: Pa. 1960. Assoc. Ballard Spahr Andrews & Ingersdoll, Phila., 1959-67, ptnr., 1967—; mem. adv. bd. PNC Bank, Phila. Emeritus trustee The Episcopal Acad., Merion, Pa., 1970—, former chmn.; trustee, v.p. Widener Meml. Found., Lafayette Hill, Pa., 1972—; trustee, vice chmn. Widener U., Chester, Pa., 1984—; trustee Thomas Jefferson U., Phila., 1989—; chmn., overseer Widener U. Law Sch., Wilmington, 1979—. Served to lt USN, 1953-56. Mem. Greater Phila. C. of C. (dir.). Office: Ballard Spahr Andrews & Ingersoll 1735 Market St Ste 51 Philadelphia PA 19103-7501

MATTOX, KENNETH LEON, surgeon, educator, medical scientist; b. Ozark, Ark., Oct. 25, 1938. BS, Wayland Coll., 1960; MD, Baylor U., 1964. Diplomate Am. Bd. Surgery, Am. Bd. Thoracic Surgery. Intern surgery VA Hosp., Houston, 1964-65; resident in gen. surgery, asst. instr. Baylor U., Houston, 1967-71, resident in thoracic surgery, 1971-72, asst. instr. thoracic surgery, 1971-73, instr. surgery, 1973-74, asst. prof. surgery, 1974-78, assoc. prof. surgery, 1978-84, prof. surgery, 1984—; aeromed. cons. Dept. Army, Natick (Mass.) Labs., 1967-70; dep. surgeon in chief, dir. emergency surg. services, chief thoracic surgery service Ben Taub Gen. Hosp., Houston, 1973-90, chief surgery, chief staff, 1990—, surg. tech. adv. bd. 1982-90; surg. cons. Tex. Inst. for Research and Rehab., Houston, 1973-96; attending surgeon VA Hosp., Houston, 1973—, active staff Meth. Hosp., Houston, 1973—, Women's Hosp., Houston, 1973-82; courtesy staff St. Luke's Hosp., Houston, 1973—, Tex. Children's Hosp., Houston, 1973—; clin. prof. Uniformed Services U. for the Health Scis., Bethesda, Md., 1983—; sr. cardiac surgeon Baylor heart team King Faisal Specialist Hosp. and Research Ctr., Riyadh, Saudi Arabia, 1979, 80, 81, 83; active various coms. Baylor Coll. Medicine, Houston, vice chmn. dept. surgery; operating room com., profl. activities tng. fund com., critical care com., others Harris County Hosp. Dist., 1979—; Curtis Artz Meml. lectr. Am. Coll. Surgeons, 1985; emergency med. services adv. council Tex. Dept. Health, 1983-95; mem. task force for state health coordinating council for regionalization specialized health services State of Tex., 1985-86; chmn. categorization sub-com. emergency med. services com. Houston-Galveston Area Council, 1978-82. Sr. editor Trauma, 1987; editor Complications in Trauma, 1993; edtl. cons. Chest, Med. Instrumentation, JAMA, Jour. Trauma; edtl. adv. bd. Emergency Medicine, 1975-92, Emergency Medicine Ann., Emergency Dept. News; assoc. editor thoracic trauma Current Concepts in Trauma Care, 1975-87; edtl. com. Tex. Medicine; reviewer Ann. Surgery, Ann. Thoracic Surgery, Am. Jour. Surgery; referee Med. Principles & Practice, contbr. over 400 sci. articles, chpts. and editorials to med. books and jours. Disaster physician Harris County Sheriff's Dept., 1973-82; pres. Emergency Medicine Found., 1982-83; mem. Houston area disaster and emergency med. system com. Greater Houston Hosp. Council, 1985—; trustee Wayland Bapt. U., 1984—; bd. dirs. Child Abuse Prevention Ctr., 1982-85. Served to capt. U.S. Army, 1965-67. Named one of Outstanding Young Men of Am., 1968; recipient Disting. Alumni award Wayland Bapt. U., 1986. Mem. Am. Assn. for the Surgery Trauma (bd. mgrs. 1985—, recorder, program chmn. 1990-93, pres.-elect 1995, pres. 1995-96), Am. Assn. Thoracic Surgery, Am. Coll. Cardiology (chmn. tech. exhibitor 1979-80), Am. Coll. Chest Physicians (bd. govs. 1986-90, gov. from Tex. 1986-91, Most Outstanding Motion Picture 1975, pulmonary surgery com. 1978, postgrad. med. edn. com. 1979—), Am. Coll. Emergency Physicians (bd. dirs. Tex. div. 1973-78, Cert. Appreciation 1975), Am. Coll. Surgeons (med. device com. 1980-85, chmn. 1983-85, com. on trauma 1983-89, bd. govs. 1985-91, others), AMA (Physician Recognition award 1972, 73), Am. Surg. Assn., Am. Trauma Soc. (founder, sec. 1974, v.p. 1975, Harris unit pres. Tex. div. 1975-76, state bd. dirs., nat. bd. dirs. 1973-82, 1988—, others), Assn. for Acad. Surgery, Assn. for Advancement Med. Instrumentation (bd. dirs. 1980-86, chmn. bd. stds. 1979-84, pres. elect 1987-88, pres. 1988-89), Am. Nat. Stds. Inst. (rep. med. device stds. bd.), Harris County Med. Soc. (alt. del. Tex. Med. Assn. 1982—, emergency med. svcs. com. 1973—, chmn. hosp. subcom. 1973-75, disaster subcom. 1973-78), Houston Surg. Soc. (pres.-elect 1995-96, pres. 1996), Internat. Cardiovascular Soc., Internat. Coll. Angiology, Michael E. DeBakey Internat. Surg. Soc. (program chmn. 1980, 82, 84, bd. dirs. 1978—, sec.-treas. 1987—, others), Pan Pacific Surg. Assn., Soc. Thoracic Surgery, Soc. Univ. Surgeons, Soc. Vascular Surgery, So. Surg. Assn., So. Thoracic Surg. Assn., Am. Coll. Surgeons (1st v.p. south Tex. chpt. 1983-84, pres. 1984-85), SW Surg. Congress (budget and fin. com. 1976-80), Tex. Med. Assn. (trauma com. 1975-94, interspecialty com. 1985—, alt. del. 1982-94), Tex. Surg. Soc., Univ. Assn. for Emergency Medicine (program. chmn. 1976-79, pres. 1979-80, exec. com. 1976-83, pres. 1979-80, emergency dept. design and function 1974-75, James Mackenzie award 1980), Tex. Collegiate Acad. Sci., Tex. Acad. Sci., Aerospace Med. Assn., Tex. Inst. Rehabilitation and Research (utilization rev. com.), TexPac (Harris County Med. Soc. exec. com. 1983), Alpha Chi, Sigma Tau Delta. Office: 1 Baylor Plz Houston TX 77030-3411

MATTRAN, DONALD ALBERT, management consultant, educator; b. Chgo., July 8, 1934; s. George Charles and Lucille Alice (Boule) M.; m. Betty Elena Flores, July 18, 1953 (div. Mar. 1988); children: Donald, Julie, Kimberly, Guy, Christy; m. Rose Lynn Castellano, May, 1988. B.Mus., U. Mich., 1957, M.Mus., 1960. Tchr. Van Buren Schs., Belleville, Mich., 1957-61; asst. prof. U. N.H., Durham, 1961-65, Boston U., 1965-66; assoc. prof. Hartt Sch. Music, West Hartford, Conn., 1966-82, dean, 1971-80; dir. Syracuse U. Sch. Music, N.Y., 1982-83; dean Sch. Fine and Performing Arts Montclair State Coll, Upper Montclair, N.J., 1983-87; pres. Sales Consultants of Sarasota (Fla.) Inc., 1987—; cons. Music div. Kaman Corp., Bloomfield, Conn.; cons., evaluator Nat. Assn. Schs. of Music and Joint Commn. Theater and Dance Accreditation; guest condr. Hartford Symphony Orch., Hartt Opera Theatre, All-State Festivals, 1976-83, Soc. New Music, Syracuse, N.J. Sch. Arts Orch., 1985-87. Co-author: (with Mary Rasmussen) A Teacher's Guide to the Literature of Woodwind Instruments, 1966; condr.: rec. Concerto for Cello and Jazz Band, 1972. Chmn. adv. com. Prodigy Inc., Syracuse, 1982-86; trustee Conn. Opera Assn., 1977-80; bd. advs. Watkinson Sch. Creative Arts Program, Hartford, 1977-80; mem. humanities adv. com. N.J. Dept. Higher Edn., 1984—; mem. multi-disciplinary panel N.J. State Council on Arts, 1985-87; mem. adv. com. on auditions Met. Opera Nat. Council, 1984-87; mem. adv. com. Frank and Lydia Bergen Found., 1986-87. Mem. Nat. Assn. Schs. Music (exec. bd., sec. 1978-81). Home: Apt 204 888 Boulevard Of The Arts Sarasota FL 34236-4827 Office: 1343 Main St Ste 600 Sarasota FL 34236-5637

MATTSON, FRANCIS OSCAR, retired librarian and rare books curator; b. Boston, Aug. 17, 1931; s. Frans Oscar and Catherine (Carr) M. BA, Boston U., 1957, MA, 1959; MS, Sch. Library Sci., Simmons Coll., 1967. Cert. librarian. Teaching fellow Boston U., 1958-60; instr. Tufts U., Medford, Mass., 1960-64, State Coll. at Salem, Mass., 1964-65; librarian Boston Pub. Library, 1965-68, N.Y. Pub. Library, N.Y.C., 1969-95; curator rare books N.Y. Pub. Library, 1981-88, chief spl. collections cataloging unit, 1988-93, curator Berg Collection of English and Am. Lit., 1991-95; mem. adv. com. Small Press Ctr., 1984-88; mem. adv. bd. Biblion, 1990—. Book rev. editor Printing History, 1983-86, contbg. editor Am. Book Collector, 1984-88. Staff sgt. USAF, 1952-56. Mem. Bibliog. Soc. of U. Va. (life), Am. Printing History Assn. (program chmn. ann. confs. 1983, 84, bd. dirs. 1985-90), Manuscript Soc. (trustee 1977-80, 83-86), Assn. Internationale de Bibliophilie, Browning Inst. (sec. bd. dirs. 1975-90), Soc. for Preservation New Eng. Antiquities (life), Grolier Club, Players Club. Home: PO Box 515 Midtown Sta New York NY 10018

MATTSON, JAMES STEWART, lawyer, environmental scientist, educator; b. Providence, July 22, 1945; s. Irving Carl and Virginia (Lutey) M.; m. Carol Sandry, Aug. 15, 1964 (div. 1979); children: James, Birgitta; m. Rana A. Fine, Jan. 5, 1983. BS in Chemistry, U. Mich., 1966, MS, 1969, PhD, 1970; JD, George Washington U., 1979. Bar: D.C. 1979, Fla. 1983, U.S. Dist. Ct. D.C. 1979, U.S. Dist. Ct. (so. dist.) Fla. 1984, U.S. Ct. Appeals (D.C. cir.) 1979, U.S. Ct. Claims 1985, U.S. Supreme Ct. 1985, U.S. Ct. Appeals (11th cir.) 1985, U.S. Ct. Appeals (5th cir.) 1987, U.S. Ct. Appeals (fed. cir.) 1990. Staff scientist Gulf Gen. Atomic Co., San Diego, 1970-71; dir. R & D Ouachita Industries, Inc., Monroe, La., 1971-72; asst. prof. chem. oceanography Rosenstiel Sch. Marine & Atmospheric Sci., U. Miami (Fla.), 1972-76; phys. scientist NOAA, Washington, 1976-78; mem. profl. staff & congl. liaison Nat. Adv. Commn. on Oceans and Atmosphere, 1978-80; ptnr. Mattson & Pave, Washington, Miami and Key Largo, Fla., 1980-86, Mattson & Tobin, Key Largo, 1987—; adj. prof. law U. Miami, 1983-93; cons. Alaska Dept. Environ. Conservation, 1981-91. Author: (with H.B. Mark) Activated Carbon: Surface Chemistry and Adsorption from Solution, 1971; editor (with others): Computers in Chemistry and Instrumentation, 8 vols., 1972-76; The Argo Merchant Oil Spill: A Preliminary Scientific Report, 1977, (with H.B. Mark) Water Quality Measurement: Modern Analytical Techniques, 1981; contbr. articles to profl. jours. Candidate dist. 120 Fla. Ho. of Reps., 1994. Fellow Fed. Water Pollution Control Adminstrn., 1967-68; recipient Spl. Achievement award U.S. Dept. Commerce, 1976-77; Regents Alumni scholar U. Mich., 1963. Mem. ABA, Am. Chem. Soc. (chmn. Symposium on Oil Spill Indentification 1971), Am. Trial Lawyers Assn., Order of Coif. Office: Mattson & Tobin PO Box 586 Key Largo FL 33037-0586

MATTSON, JOY LOUISE, oncological nurse; b. Moline, Ill., Feb. 1, 1956; d. Norman O. and Jeannette (Squier) M.; m. Duncan F. Crannell, Sept. 9, 1988. BA magna cum laude, Bates Coll., 1977; MTS, Harvard U., 1982; BSN magna cum laude, Rutgers U., Newark, 1988; MLS, Rutgers U., 1993. RN, N.J. Staff nurse oncology Muhlenberg Reg. Med. Ctr., Plainfield, N.J., 1987-88; staff nurse St. Lawrence Rehab. Ctr., Lawrenceville, N.J., 1988-89; clin. rsch. asst. G.H. Besselaar Assocs., Princeton, N.J., 1990-91; med. writer Convatec, Skillman, N.J., 1991-92, G.H. Besselaar Assocs., Princeton, N.J., 1992-94; clin. safety assoc. Pfizer Inc., N.Y.C., 1994—. Mem. Phi Beta Kappa. Home: 5 Tudor City Pl Apt 508 New York NY 10017-6861

MATTSON, RICHARD HENRY, neurologist, educator; b. Waterbury, Conn., May 9, 1931; s. George F. and Edith O. (Curtiss) M.; m. Elena Mary Hill, June 13, 1954; children: Richard Jr., Gail Mattson-Gates, Catherine Mattson-Fimmers. BS, Yale U., 1953, MA (hon.), 1967; MD, Boston U., 1957; MS, U. Minn., 1962. Intern Wilford Hall USAF Hosp., San Antonio, 1957-58, chief neurology, cons. to surgeon gen., 1962-67; resident in neurology Mayo Clinic., Rochester, Minn., 1958-62; asst. clin. prof. neurology U. Tex. Med. Br., Galveston, 1964-67; asst. chief and chief of neurology VA Med. Ctr., West Haven, Conn., 1967-92; from asst. prof. to prof. neurology Yale U. Sch. Medicine, New Haven, 1967—, dir. med. studies dept. neurology, 1985—, dir. residency tng. program dept. neurology, 1985-96, dir. clin. neurosci. curriculum, 1990—, vice-chmn. for acad. affairs, 1995—; dir. NIH Yale Epilepsy Program Project, 1985—; cons. VA Ctrl. Office, 1967-92, NIH, 1974-78, various pharm. cos. Author: Antiepileptic Drugs, 1995, and other related books; contbr. articles to profl. jours. Recipient H.V. Jones award Mayo Found., 1962, Best Clin. Trial award Internat. League Against Epilepsy, 1988, Amb. award, Internat. League Against Epilepsy, 1990. Fellow Am. Acad. Neurology, Am. EEG Soc.; mem. Am. Neurol. Assn., Am. Epilepsy Soc. (pres. 1986-87, William G. Lennox award 1994, Hans Berger Lecture award 1997, Novarits Ebilectology prize 1997), Begg Honor Soc. Avocations: Sailing, gardening.

MATTSON, STEPHEN JOSEPH, lawyer; b. Abilene, Tex., Oct. 11, 1943; s. Joseph Martin and Dorothy Irene (Doyle) M.; m. Lynn Louise Mitchell, Mar. 13, 1965; children: Eric, Laura. BA (hon.), U. Ill., 1965, JD (hon.), 1970. Bar: Ill., 1970, U.S. Dist. Ct. (no. dist.) Ill. 1970. Assoc. Mayer, Brown & Platt, Chgo., 1970-77, ptnr., 1978—. Mem. ABA, Ill. State Bar Assn., Chgo. Bar Assn., Fed. Energy Bar Assn., Order of Coif. Office: Mayer Brown & Platt 190 S La Salle St Chicago IL 60603-3410

MATTSSON, AKE, psychiatrist, physician; b. Stockholm, May 30, 1929; came to U.S., 1956, naturalized, 1964; s. Erik H. and Thyra (Bergtsson) M.; m. Margareta Fürst, Jan. 5, 1953; children: Erik, Peter, Nicholas. B.M., Karolinska Inst., Stockholm, 1950, M.D., 1955. Intern Vanderbilt U. Med. Sch., Nashville, 1955-56; resident in pediatrics and child psychiatry Karolinska Hosp., Stockholm, 1958-60; fellow in child devel. Case Western Res. U. Med. Sch., 1957-58, resident in psychiatry and child psychiatry, 1960-64, asst. prof. psychiatry, 1964-70; prof. psychiatry and pediatrics U. Va. Med. Sch., 1970-77, U. Pitts Med. Sch., 1977-78; prof. psychiatry and pediatrics, dir. div. child and adolescent psychiatry N.Y. U. Med. Sch., 1978-85, rsch. prof. psychiatry, 1985—; prof. psychiatry U. Va. Med. Sch., 1985-91; prof. psychiatry and pediatrics, dir. div. child and adolescent psychiatry Med. Sch., East Carolina U., Greenville, N.C., 1991—. Contbr. numerous articles to med. jours. Served with Swedish Navy, 1948-59. Fulbright-Hays grantee, 1975. Mem. Am. Psychiat. Assn., Am. Psychoanalytical Assn., Am. Psychosomatic Soc., N.Y. Psychiat. Soc., Am. Soc. Adolescent Psychiatry, Am. Acad. Child Adolescent Psychiatry, N.Y. Acad. Scis. Office: East Carolina U Med Sch Dept Psychiatry Greenville NC 27858

MATTURRO, ANTHONY, lawyer; b. N.Y.C., May 11, 1933; s. Gerardo and Linda (D'Elia) M.; m. Jean Knakal, Jun. 23, 1962; children: Gina, Anthony. BA, Queens Coll., 1955; JD, St. John's U., 1960. Bar: N.Y. 1962, U.S. Dist. Ct. (ea. and so. dist.) N.Y. 1963, U.S. Ct. Appeals (2d cir.) 1965, U.S. Supreme Ct. 1965, D.C. 1990. Sr. staff atty. Royal Globe Ins. Co., N.Y.C., 1962-69; ptnr. Rivkin, Radler et al, Nassau, N.Y., 1969-92, Matturro & Hirsch, Nassau, N.Y., 1992—. 1st. lt. USMC, 1955-57. Mem. ABA, N.Y. State Bar Assn., Nassau County Bar Assn., D.C. Bar Assn., Am. Inns of Ct. (master). Republican. Roman Catholic. Home: 54 2nd Ave Massapequa Park NY 11762 Office: Matturro & Hirsch 1 Old Country Rd Ste 318 Carle Place NY 11514-1807

MATUG, ALEXANDER PETER, lawyer; b. Chgo., May 25, 1946; s. Alexander J. and Marianne (Paszek) M.; m. Jeanne Marie Buker, Aug. 16, 1969; children: Alexander W., Krista E., Thomas E. BA, St. Mary's Coll., Minn., 1968; JD, Loyola U., Chgo., 1972. Bar: Ill. 1972, U.S. Dist. Ct. (no. dist.) Ill. 1972. Pvt. practice, Palos Heights, Ill., 1972—. Bd. dirs. Am. Heritage, Sertoma, Palos Heights, 1991—; profl. adv. bd. Sertoma Speech and Hearing Ctr., Palos Hills, Ill., 1991—. Mem. Ill. Bar Assn., S.W. Suburban Bar Assn. Roman Catholic. Office: 7110 W 127th St Ste 250 Palos Heights IL 60463-1571

MATULEF, GIZELLE TERESE, secondary education educator; b. Budapest, Jan. 17, 1945; came to the U.S., 1948; d. Louis and Gizelle Beke; m. Gary Matulef, Mar. 21, 1975; 1 child, Margaret. AA in Bus., Phoenix (Ariz.) Coll., 1964; BS in Edn., No. Ariz. U., 1966; MA, Ind. U., 1970, PhD in Comparative Lit., 1983. Cert. secondary teaching credential, Calif., C.C. instr. credential, Calif. Bus. instr. Drake Bus. Coll., N.Y.C., 1973, Cerro Coso Coll., Ridgecrest, Calif., 1973-74; English and bus. instr. Sawyer Bus. Coll., Westwood, Calif., 1974-75; bus. instr. Sierra Sands Adult Sch., Ridgecrest, 1975-82; Indian edn. dir. Sierra Sands Unifed Sch. Dist., Ridgecrest, 1980-82; sch. improvement program dir. Murray Jr. High Sch., Ridgecrest, 1982-89; English and econs. instr. Trona (Calif.) High Sch., 1989-92; tng. dir. High Desert Experience Unlimited Career Counseling, Ridgecrest, 1991-92; substitute tchr. Sierra Sands Unified Sch. Dist., Ridgecrest, 1993-96; archives asst. Albert Michelson Mus., Naval Weapons Ctr., China Lake, Calif., 1976-77, editorial asst. Tech. Info. Dept., 1977-78. Contbr. articles to profl. jours. Active PTA, Ridgecrest Schs., 1983-93, Music Parents Assn., Ridgecrest, 1985-93. Recipient fellowship Ind. U., Bloomington, 1966-69. Mem. AAUW (pres. China Lake/Ridgecrest br. 1992-96), NEA. Avocations: Hungarian culture, drama, classical music, cinema history. Home: 1028 Las Flores Ave Ridgecrest CA 93555

MATUS, WAYNE CHARLES, lawyer; b. N.Y.C., Mar. 10, 1950; s. Eli and Alma (Platt) M.; m. Marsha Rothblum, Jan. 16, 1982; children: Marshall Scott, Scott Adam. BA, Johns Hopkins U., 1972; JD, NYU, 1975. Law clk. Superior Ct. D.C., 1975-76; assoc. Marshall, Bratter, Greene, Allison and Tucker, N.Y.C., 1976-79; assoc. Christy & Viener, N.Y.C., 1979-83, ptnr., 1984—; faculty ABA-Am. Law Inst., 1988; neutral mediator Supreme Ct. comml. divsn. 1st jud. dist. State of N.Y. Unified Ct. Sys. Mem. Assn. Bar City of N.Y. (com. on computer law 1985-88, chmn. com. on state cts., subcom. on motion practice 1982-84, com. product liability 1994—), N.Y. State Bar Assn. (comml. and fed. litigation sect., com. on complex civil litigation 1990—), N.Y. Litigators Club (steering com. 1985—), Johns Hopkins U. Alumni Assn. (bd. dirs. met. N.Y. chpt. 1987—, v.p. 1988—, mem. nat. alumni coun. 1996—). Office: Christy & Viener 620 5th Ave New York NY 10020-2402

MATUSOW, NAOMI C., state legislator; b. Nashville, Oct. 31, 1938; m. Gene R. Matusow; children: Gary, Jason. BA cum laude, Vanderbilt U.; MA in Counseling and Guidance, NYU; JD, Pace U. Bar: N.Y. 1981. Editl. asst. Golden Press; tchr. math. N.Y.C. pub. schs., guidance counselor; pvt. practice as lawyer Armonk, 1981-90, White Plains, 1990-92; mem. N.Y. State Assembly, 1992—, mem. various coms. mem. econ. devel. tng., environ. conservation, local govt., consumer affairs, tourism, arts, sports devel., spkrs. steering coms.; assoc. Westchester Land Trust; bd. dirs. Juvenile Diabetes Found.; chair Hudson River Valley Task Force, Women's Bus. Devel. subcom. Mem. NOW, Nat. Women's Polit. Caucus, N.Y. State Women's Bar Assn., Westchester Assn. Women Bus. Owners. Office: NY State Assembly State Capitol Albany NY 12224 also: 125-131 Main St Mount Kisco NY 10549

MATUSZAK, ALICE JEAN BOYER, pharmacy educator; b. Newark, Ohio, June 22, 1935; d. James Emery and Elizabeth Hawthorne (Irvine) Boyer; m. Charles Alan Matuszak, Aug. 27, 1955; children: Matthew, James. BS summa cum laude, Ohio State U., 1958, MS, 1959; postgrad., U. Wis., 1959-60; PhD, U. Kans., 1963. Registered pharmacist, Ohio, Calif. Apprentice pharmacist Arensberg Pharmacy, Newark, 1953-58; rsch. asst. Ohio State U., Columbus, 1958, lab. asst., 1958-59; rsch. asst. U. Wis., Madison, 1959-60, U. Kans., Lawrence, 1960-63; asst. prof. U. of the Pacific, Stockton, Calif., 1963-67, assoc. prof., 1971-78, prof., 1978—; vis. fgn. prof. Kobe-Gakuin U., Japan, 1992. Contbr. articles to profl. jours. Recipient Disting. Alumna award Ohio State U. Coll. Pharmacy, 1994; NIH grantee, 1965-66. Fellow Am. Pharm. Assn. (chmn. basic scis. 1990); mem. Am.

Assn. Colls. of Pharmacy (chmn. chemistry sect. 1979-80, bd. dirs. 1993-95), Am. Inst. History of Pharmacy (exec. coun. 1984-88, 90-92, 92-95, chmn. contributed papers 1990-92, pres.-elect 1995-97, pres. 1997—, cert. of commendation 1990), Am. Chem. Soc., Internat. Fedn. Pharmacy, Acad. Pharm. Rsch. Sci. (pres. 1993-94), Coun. Sci. Soc. Pres., U.S. Adopted Names Coun., U.S. Pharmacopeial Conv., Clan Irwin Assn., Sigma Xi, Rho Chi, Phi Lambda Sigma, Phi Kappa Phi, Kappa Epsilon (Unicorn award, award of merit 1995), Lambda Kappa Sigma, Delta Zeta. Democrat. Episcopalian. Avocation: collecting historical pharmacy artifacts. Home: 1130 W Mariposa Ave Stockton CA 95204-3021 Office: U of the Pacific Sch of Pharmacy Stockton CA 95211

MATUSZEK, JOHN MICHAEL, JR., environmental scientist, educator, consultant; b. Worcester, Mass., Nov. 30, 1957; s. John Michael and Felicia Martha (Shandruk) M.; m. Roberta Eva Coonan, Nov. 30, 1957; children: Debra-Jane Y., John Michael III, Kevin P., Jennifer R. BS in Chemistry with distinction, Worcester Poly. Inst., 1957; PhD in Nuclear Chemistry, Clark U., 1962. Dept. mgr. Teledyne Isotopes, Westwood, N.J., 1964-71; rsch. scientist in nuclear chemistry, radioactive waste mgmt., radiological health, environ. radioactivity and radiation N.Y. State Health Dept., Albany, 1971—; adj. prof. Rensselaer Poly. Inst., Troy, N.Y., 1977—; prof. SUNY, Albany, 1996—. Lt. comdr. USPHS, 1962-64. Avocations: skiing, music. Home: 82 McGuffey Ln Delmar NY 12054-4206 Office: NY State Dept Health Empire State Plz PO Box 509 Albany NY 12201-0509

MATUSZKO, ANTHONY JOSEPH, research chemist, administrator; b. Hadley, Mass., Jan. 31, 1926; s. Joseph Anthony and Katherine (Narog) M.; m. Anita Colley, Oct. 26, 1956; children—Martha, Mary, Stephen, Richard. BA, Amherst Coll., 1946; MS in Chemistry, U. Mass., 1951; PhD in Chemistry, McGill U., 1953. Demonstrator in chemistry McGill U., Montreal, Que., Can., 1950-52; from instr. to assoc. prof. chemistry Lafayette Coll., Easton, Pa., 1952-58; head fundamental process div. Naval Propellant Lab., Indian Head, Md., 1958-62; program mgr. in chemistry Air Force Office Sci. Research, Washington, 1962-89; cons., Annandale, Va., 1989—. Contbr. articles to tech. jours. Patentee in field. Pres. Forest Heights PTA, Md., 1967. Served with U.S. Army, 1946-48. Named Hon. Fellow in Chemistry, U. Wis.-Madison, 1967-68, recipient Superior Performance award USAF, Outstanding Career Svc. award U.S. Govt. Fellow AAAS, Am. Inst. Chemists (life); mem. Am. Chem. Soc., Cosmos Club, Sigma Xi. Home: 4210 Elizabeth Ln Annandale VA 22003-3654

MATYJASZEWSKI, KRZYSZTOF, chemist, educator; b. Konstantynow, Poland, Apr. 8, 1950; came to U.S., 1985; s. Henryk and Antonina (Styss) M.; m. Malgorzata Kowalska, July 15, 1972; children: Antoni, Maria. BS, MS, Tech. U., Moscow, 1972; PhD, Polish Acad. Scis., Lodz, 1976; DSc, Lodz Poly., 1985. Postdoctoral fellow U. Fla., 1977-78; rsch. assoc. Polish Acad. Scis., 1978-84, CNRS, France, 1984-85; asst. prof. chemistry Carnegie Mellon U., Pitts., 1985-89, assoc. prof., 1989-93, prof., 1993—, head dept. chemistry, 1994—; invited prof. U. Paris, 1985; vis. prof. U. Freiburg, 1988, U. Paris, 1990, 97, U. Bayreuth, 1991, U. Strasbourg, 1992, U. Bordeaux, 1996; cons. Dow Corning, Midland, Mich., 1988-89, Arco, Phila., 1990-92, GE, Schenectady, 1992—, Amoco, Naperville, Ill., 1994—, Reilly Ind., Indpls., 1994—, Air Products, Allentown, Pa., 1994—. Author 3 books; mem. editorial bd. Macromolecules, Macromolecular Synthesis, Jour. Polymer Sci., Jour. Macromolecular Sci.-Pure and Applied Chemistry, Jour. Inorganic and Organometallic Polymers, Macromolecular Reports; contbr. chpts. to books, more than 300 articles to profl. jours.; 15 patents in field. Recipient award Polish Acad. Sci., 1981, Presdl. Yount Investigator award NSF, 1989. Mem. Am. Chem. Soc. (Carl S. Marvel award 1995), Internat. Union of Pure and Applied Chemistry (corr. mem. polymer nomenclature). Achievements include research in synthesis of well defined macromolecules via living and controlled polymerizations; organometallic polymers. Home: 9 Queens Ct Pittsburgh PA 15238 Office: Carnegie Mellon U 4400 5th Ave Pittsburgh PA 15213-2617

MATZ, KENNETH H., JR., newscaster; b. Phila., Oct. 25, 1945; s. Kenneth H. and Kathryn (Beddall) M.; m. Phyllis Ann Walton, Mar. 9, 1991; 1 child, Justin T. BBA, Lebanon Valley Coll., 1969. Radio news anchor WIBG, KYW, Phila., 1969-77; TV news anchor WITI-TV, Milw., 1977-79, KGO-TV/ABC, San Francisco, 1979-81, KTTV-TV/Metromedia, L.A., 1981-84, WMAR-TV, Balt., 1984-89, WCIX-TV/CBS, Miami, Fla., 1989-92, WCAU-TV/NBC, Phila., 1992—. Vol. host Muscular Dystrophy Assn. Telethon, Milw., 1978-80, Children's Miracle Network Telethon, Balt., 1984-89; hon. bd. dirs. Nazareth Hosp., 1995—; bd. dirs. Pa. AP Broadcasters Assn., 1975-77. With USAR, 1969-76. Recipient award Am. Heart Assn., March of Dimes, Nat. Kidney Found., Disting. Journalism award Soc. Profl. Journalists, 1988. Mem. NATAS (Emmy award for Investigative Report 1991, for Best Regularly Scheduled Daily News Program 1983, 84, Emmy award nomination for Outstanding News Feature Series, 1992, 94, for Outstanding Pub. Affairs Program, 1994, for Outstanding Individual Achievement, 1995). Avocations: scuba diving, wine, tennis. Home: 1311 Rutland Ln Wynnewood PA 19096 Office: WCAU-TV City at Monument Philadelphia PA 19131

MATZ, ROBERT, internist, educator; b. N.Y.C., Aug. 5, 1931; s. Milton and Celia (Wachovsky) M.; m. Lita Selma Freed, Dec. 24, 1955 (dec. July 1982); children: Jessica, Jonathan, Daniel; m. Bette Lynn Becker, Aug. 4, 1983. BA cum laude, NYU, 1952, MD, 1956. Diplomate Am. Bd. Internal Medicine. Intern Bronx (N.Y.) Mcpl. Hosp. Ctr., 1956-57, resident, 1957-60; assoc. dir. medicine Morrisania Hosp., Bronx, 1964-77; dir. medicine North Cen. Bronx Hosp., 1977-91, pres. med. bd., 1987-89, med. dir., 1989-91; med. dir. quality assurance and risk mgmt. Mt. Sinai Med. Ctr., N.Y.C., 1991—, attending physician, 1991—; prof. medicine Mt. Sinai Sch. Medicine, N.Y.C., 1991—; asst. prof. Albert Einstein Coll. Medicine, Bronx, 1967-71, assoc. prof., 1971-79, prof., 1979-91; cons. N.Y.C. Health and Hosp. Corp., 1983-91; mem. health adv. com. to pres. Borough of Bronx, 1987-91. Dept. editor Cardiovascular Revs. and Reports, 1985—; contbr. articles to med. jours., chpts. to books. Mem. physicians action network Amnesty Internat., 1979—. Capt. M.C., U.S. Army, 1960-62, Korea. Fellow ACP; mem. AMA, N.Y. Heart Assn., N.Y. Diabetes Assn. (v.p. 1977-83), Soc. Urban Physicians, Am. Diabetes Assn. (pres. elect chpt. 1987-89, pres. N.Y. downstate affiliate 1989-91), Harvey Soc., Hastings Hist. Soc., Phi Beta Kappa, Beta Lambda Sigma. Democrat. Jewish. Avocations: collecting antique postcards, coins, philately, travel. Home: 32 Buena Vista Dr Hastings On Hudson NY 10706-1104 Office: Mt Sinai Hosp 19 E 98th St New York NY 10029-6501

MATZEDER, JEAN MARIE ZNIDARSIC, lawyer; b. Kansas City, Mo., Jan. 27, 1948; d. August J. and Cecelia (Frick) Znidarsic; m. John August Matzeder, June 12, 1971; 1 child, Melanie. BA, St. Mary Coll., Leavenworth, Kans., 1970; JD, U. Mo., 1980. Bar: Mo. 1980, Tex. 1982. Assoc. Stinson Mag & Fizzell, Kansas City, 1980-81, Vinson & Elkins, Houston, 1981-85; asst. regulatory counsel C.E., Kansas City, 1985-88; assoc. Craft Fridkin Shaffer & Rhyne, Kansas City, 1988-90, Polsinelli, White Vardeman & Shalton, Kansas City, 1991-94; ptnr. Shaffer, Spies & Matzeder, P.C., Kansas City, Mo., 1994-96, Hardwick Law Firm, PC, Kansas City, 1996—. Treas. Sion Alliance, Kansas City, 1990-91; mem. MENSA. Mem. ABA, Mo. Bar Assn., Tex. Bar Assn., Assn. Women Lawyers, Bench and Robe Soc. Home: 200 NW Hemlock St Lees Summit MO 64064-1444 Office: Hardwick Law Firm 1044 Main St Kansas City MO 64105-2102

MATZEK, RICHARD ALLAN, library director; b. Milw., Nov. 18, 1937; s. Robert Edward and Alice Elizabeth (Mudroch) M.; m. Ann Lynne Erickson, Aug. 24, 1963; 1 child, John Kensel. BA, Marquette Univ., 1959; MALS, U. Wis., 1960. Asst. libr. Marquette U., Milw., 1962-63; asst. libr. dir. Sacred Heart Univ., Bridgeport, Conn., 1963-66, libr. dir., 1966-77; libr. dir. Nazareth Coll., Rochester, N.Y., 1977—. Editor (book rev. sect.) Religious Book Rev., 1968-80, (publ. series) Libr. Adminstrn. and Mgmt. Assn., 1988-92; contbr. articles to profl. jours. Bd. trustees St. Bernard's Inst., Rochester, 1989—, treas., 1996—. Fellow Rotary Internat., 1974; recipient Cert. Spl. Thanks Libr. Adminstn. and Mgmt. Assn., 1992. Mem. ALA, N.Y. Libr. Assn. (councilor-at-large, Spirit of Librarianship award 1994), Rochester Regional Libr. Coun. (chair, coun. 2000). Avocations: golf, tennis, bridge, travel. Office: Nazareth Coll of Rochester 4245 East Ave Rochester NY 14618-3703

MATZKE, FRANK J., architect, consultant; b. Akron, Ohio, Jan. 28, 1922; s. Frank G. and Erna (Weibel) M.; m. Shirley Elizabeth Hall, Nov. 27, 1952 (div. Dec. 1966); children: Kim Elizabeth, Karla Jo. Student, State Tchrs. Coll. at Buffalo, 1940-41; B.Arch., Rensselaer Poly. Inst., 1951. Registered architect, N.Y., Md. Field rep., project architect W. Parker Dodge Assos., Rensselaer, N.Y., 1951-54; sr. architect div. architecture N.Y. State Dept. Pub. Works, Albany, 1954-58; assoc. architect State U. N.Y., Albany, 1958-62; dep. mgr. planning State U. Constrn. Fund, Albany, 1962-68; dep. gen. mgr. State U. Constrn. Fund, 1968-72; assoc. commr. for project mgmt. Pub. Bldgs. Service, GSA, Washington, 1972-75; acting asst. commr. for constrn. mgmt. Pub. Bldgs. Service, GSA, 1974-75; exec. dir. Ill. Capital Devel. Bd., 1975-76; v.p. for tech. and programs Nat. Inst. Bldg. Scis., Washington, 1978-83; mem. Bldg. Research Adv. Bd., Washington, 1976-79; chmn. Mgmt. Resource Council, 1974-75; cons. to pub. agys., colls. and univs. on methods to expedite design and constrn. of phys. facilities. Contbr. articles to profl. jours. Chmn. Johnsburg Planning Bd., 1962-65; nat. ski patrolman, 1953-73, past patrol leader O.C. Ski Club Ski Patrol; bd. dirs. Bldg Rsch. Inst., 1973-75, Town Ctr. Coop., Inc., 1980-82. 1st lt. inf., AUS, 1942-46, PTO. Decorated Bronze Star. Fellow AIA (pres. Ea. N.Y. chpt 1959-60, dir. 1960-63, mem. nat. commn. on architecture for education 1966-72, chmn. nat. com. on architects in govt. 1975, medal for excellence 1951), N.Y. State Assn. Architects (dir. 1966-69); mem. VFW, Wilderness Soc., Sierra Club, Smithsonian Assocs., Natural Resources Def. Coun., Am. Rivers, Nature Conservancy, Environ. Def. Fund, Mil. Order of Caraboa, Nat. Order of Battlefield Commissions, 31st Inf. "Dixie" Divsn. Soc., 124th Inf. Rgt. Assn., Am. Legion, North Fla. Cruising Club, Sigma Xi (ret. assoc.), Tau Beta Pi, Sigma Phi Epsilon. Address: 24 Andalusia Ct Saint Augustine FL 32086-7647

MATZKE, GARY ROGER, pharmacist; b. Sturgeon Bay, Wis., July 13, 1950; s. Erwin Walter and Alice (Logerquist) M.; m. Cindy Claire Boxwell, Apr. 11, 1981; children: Megan, Jonathon, Jason, Christina, Alicia. BS in Pharmacy, U. Wis., 1973; PharmD, U. Minn., 1977. Asst. prof. Wayne State U. Sch. Pharmacy, Detroit, 1977-80; asst. prof. U. Minn., Mpls., 1980-84, assoc. prof., 1984-87, prof., 1987-89; prof., vice chmn. U. N.C., Chapel Hill, 1989-91; prof., dir. clin. scientist program Sch. of Pharmacy U. Pitts., 1991—; co-dir. The Drug Evaluation Unit, Mpls., 1981-89. Editor: Pharmacotherapy: A Pathophysiologic Approach, Pharmacotherapy: A Patient Focused Approach; contbr. over 150 articles to profl. jours. Fellow Am. Coll. Clin. Pharmacy, Am. Coll. Clin. Pharmacology; mem. Am. Soc. for Clin. Pharmacology and Therapeutics, Am. Soc. Nephrology, Internat. Soc. Nephrology, Internat. Soc. for Study of Xenobiotics. Avocations: golf, running. Office: U Pitts Sch Pharmacy 724 Salk Hall Pittsburgh PA 15261-1907

MATZNER, CHESTER MICHAEL, writer; b. N.Y.C.; s. Sigmund Simon and Rose (Greenberg) M. BS in Physics, L.I. U., 1949; MA in English, Bklyn. Coll., 1954. Tchr. English N.Y.C. Bd. Edn., 1954-59; jr. chemist Nat Synthetic Rubber Co., Louisville; with S. Matzner & Co., N.Y.C. and Mt. Vernon; internat. trade cons. N.Y.C.; fgn. and UN corres. Can. Mil. Jour., Montreal, 1959-79; fgn. corres. The Soldier Illustrated, Manhattan, Kans., 1958-59. Author (plays) Whither Youth?, 1987, Mystic Lady, 1988, The Deceased (?) Embezzler, 1989, Ship Aswirl, 1992, (screenplay) A Warrior's Journey, 1992, (songs) On The Road, (musical drama) Henri Christophe, (poetry) The Red-Haired Dancer & Other Poems; producer (documentary films) Margaret Corbin, America's First Heroine, 1989, Caribbeana, 1991, The Pageant of America, 1992, Circus-Time, The World Dances; (short films) Waiting, Beauty's Passing Parade, (song collection) On The Road, Songs You Love To Sing, 1994; (ballets) Dance of the Waters, 1994, The Austrian Officers, 1994; (documentary films) The Cardinal Mindszenty Story, 1994; contbr. various mil. jours. County committeeman N.Y. Dem. County Com., 1991. Mem. Am. Fedn. Tchrs., Dramatists Guild, Inc., Authors League of Am., Song Writers Guild of Am., Mus. of Modern Art, Finnish-Am. C. of C. (charter mem.). Avocations: reading, travel, ethnology, archaeology. Office: c/o Dramatists Guild Inc 234 W 44th St New York NY 10036-3909

MAU, WILLIAM KOON-HEE, financier; b. Honolulu, Apr. 25, 1913; s. Wah Hop and Mau (Ho Shee) M.; m. Jean Lau, Oct. 17, 1936; children—Milton, Cynthia, Lynette, Leighton, Letitia. Ed. pub. schs., Hawaii; LL.D., Pacific U., 1969. Chmn. bd., chief exec. officer Am. Security Bank, Honolulu, 1958-69; pres. Tropical Enterprises, Ltd. and Ambassador Hotel of Waikiki, Honolulu, Top of Waikiki Revolving Restaurant, Honolulu, 1955—; owner, developer Waikiki Bus. Plaza, Waikiki Shopping Plaza, Aloha Motors Properties; pres. Empress Ltd., Hong Kong, 1962-70, Aloha Motors, Inc. Vice chmn. Hawaii Bd. Land Natural Resources, 1959-63; Bd. dirs. Chinese Cultural Found., Hawaii, 1960—, Aloha United Fund, 1966—, Am. Nat. Red Cross, 1965—; past mem. exec. bd. Boy Scouts Am.; trustee Kauikeolani Children's Hosp., 1959-61. Recipient Golden Plate award Am. Acad. Achievement Bd. Govs., 1969; Wisdom Hall of Fame award of honor, 1969; named Bus. Man of Year Hawaii Bus. and Industry mag., 1966. Mem. Am., Hawaii bank assns., Newcomen Soc. N.Am., Am. Bd. Arbitration, Downtown Improvement Assn., United Chinese Soc., Tsung Tsin Assn., Hawaii Visitors Bur., Hawaii Islanders, Hawaii Pub. Links Golf Assn., Chinese C. of C. (dir., auditor 1959-62). Home: 3938 Monterey Pl Honolulu HI 96816-3922 Office: Waikiki Bus Plaza 2270 Kalakaua Ave Honolulu HI 96815-2519

MAUBERT, JACQUES CLAUDE, headmaster; b. Provins, France, May 19, 1932; s. Jean Pierre and Simone Jeanne (Bocqueho) M.; m. Micheline Josephine Lathuille, June 16, 1956; children: Eric, Sandrine. MA, Dakar U., Senegal, 1969; CAPES, U. Bordeaux (France), 1971. Tchr. French Ministry Edn., Morocco, 1952-62; tchr. French Ministry Edn., Senegal, 1962-73, councellor, 1973-75; councellor French Ministry Edn., Togo, 1975-77; headmaster French Ministry Edn., LeMans, France, 1977-79; headmaster Lycee Francais of San Francisco French Ministry Edn., 1979-85; headmaster French Ministry Edn., Sannois, France, 1985-86; headmaster Lyceum Kennedy French Ministry Edn., N.Y.C., 1986—; mem. presdl. Commn. Reform for Teaching French in Africa, Dakar, 1973-78; pedagogic councellor U. Benin, Togo, 1975-77. Author: French Literature for 11th Grade, 1975. Pres. Union des Francais de l' Etranger, San Francisco, 1983-85. Decorated officer The Acad. Palms (France). Roman Catholic. Avocations: swimming, tennis, classical music, jazz, opera. Home: 245 E 54th St Apt 28R New York NY 10022-4725 Office: Lyceum Kennedy 225 E 43rd St New York NY 10017-4701

MAUCH, JEANNINE ANN, elementary education educator; b. Scribner, Nebr., Apr. 17, 1944; d. Oscar Herman Frederick and Viola Fredricka (Backhus) M. BS in Luth. Teaching, Concordia Coll., 1966, MEd, 1988. Cert. tchr., Nebr. Tchr. 1st, 2d, 3d and 4th grades St. Paul Luth. Ch., Perham, Minn., 1966-68; tchr. 3d and 4th grades Wheat Ridge (Colo.) Luth. Ch., 1968-70; tchr., prin. St. Mark Luth. Ch., Yonkers, N.Y., 1970-86; tchr. 3d, 4th and 5th grades Zion Luth. Ch., Plainview, Nebr., 1987—. Recipient 25-Yr. Svc. plaque Zion Luth. Ch., Plainview, 1992, others. Mem. Luth. Edn. Assn. Avocations: travel, craft shows, punch embroidery. Home: PO Box 218 Plainview NE 68769-0218

MAUCH, ROBERT CARL, gas industry executive; b. Cleve., Dec. 7, 1939; s. Otto Herman and Clara (Lapple) M.; m. Rita Marie Szucs, Aug. 25, 1964 (div. Jan. 1980); children: David Otto, Martin Leslie, Karolyn Leigh; m. Drusilla Ann Tesch, Feb. 18, 1989. AMP, Harvard U., 1983; MS, U. Calif., Berkeley, 1965; BSChemE, Cleve. State U., 1962. V.p., gen. mgr., LP gas divsn. Amerigas Inc., Valley Forge, Pa., 1978-83; v.p. UGI Corp., Valley Forge, 1978-87, sr. v.p., 1987-90; dir. Ansutech, Inc., Valley Forge, 1981-82, Matheson Gas Products, Inc., Valley Forge, 1981-82; pres., dir. AP Propane Inc., Valley Forge, 1983-90, Amerigas Propane, Valley Forge, 1983-96; pres., CEO, dir. AmeriGas Inc., Valley Forge, 1991-96, Petrolane, Inc., Valley Forge, 1993-96, Amerigas, Inc. subs. UGI Corp., Valley Forge, 1990-96, AmeriGas Propane Inc. (gen. ptnr. AmeriGas Ptnrs. L.P.); chmn., CEO The Anthem Group, 1996—. Bd. govs. Pa. Economy League, Phila., 1985-91; mem. World Affairs Coun., Phila., 1980-95. Mem. Nat. Propane Gas Assn. (bd. dirs., exec. com., pres. 1978-95), Waynesborough C. of C., Propane Vehicle Coun. (chmn. 1994—). Lutheran. Avocations: tennis, reading, skiing, hunting, weight training. Office: Amerigas Inc PO Box 965 Valley Forge PA 19482-0965

MAUCK, HENRY PAGE, JR., medical and pediatrics educator; b. Richmond, Va., Feb. 3, 1926; s. Henry Page and Harriet Hutcheson (Morrison) M.; m. Janet Garrett Horsley, May 14, 1955; children—Henry Page III, John Waller. B.A., U. Va., 1950, M.D., 1952. Diplomate: Am. Bd. Internal Medicine. Intern Henry Ford Hosp., Detroit, 1952-53; resident Med. Coll. Va., Richmond, 1953-56; asst. prof. medicine and pediatrics Med. Coll. Va., 1961-66, assoc. prof., 1966-72, prof., 1972—; fellow in cardiology Am. Heart Assn., 1956-57; cons. cardiology Langley Field Air Force Hosp., Hampton, Va., McGuire's VA Hosp., Richmond. Contbr.: chpt. to Autonomic Control of Cardiovascular System, 1972; contbr. articles to sci. jours. Served with U.S. Army, 1944-46. Fellow ACP, Am. Coll. Cardiology (former gov. Va.); mem. Am. Physiol. Soc., So. Soc. Clin. Investigation, Am. Fedn. Clin. Research, So. Soc. Clin. Research. Presbyterian. Home: 113 Oxford Cir W Richmond VA 23221-3224 Office: Med Coll Va PO Box 281 Richmond VA 23202-0281

MAUCK, WILLIAM M., JR., executive recruiter, small business owner; b. Cleve., Mar. 30, 1938; s. William M. and Elizabeth Louise (Stone) M.; m. Paula Jean Mauck, Aug. 15, 1959 (div. Mar. 1983); children: Brian, David; m. Jeanne Lee Mauck, May 21, 1987. BS in Bus., Ind. U., 1961. Sales engr. Inland Container Corp., Louisville, 1961-69; sales mgr. Dixie Container Corp., Knoxville, Tenn., 1969-70, gen. mgr., 1970-75; v.p., ptnr. Heidrick & Struggles, Inc., Houston, 1975-81; pres. Booker & Mauck, Inc., Houston, 1981-85; ptnr. Ward Howell Internat. Inc., Houston, 1985-88; prin. William M. Mauck, Jr., Houston, 1988—; owner Pepe Engring., Inc., Houston, 1990—; mem. adv. bd. Women's Sports Found., N.Y.C., 1985-96. Adv. bd. Women's Sports Found., N.Y.C., 1985-96. Mem. Plaza Club (Houston) (chmn. bd. govs. 1987-88), Sertoma Club (Knoxville 1972-75) (pres. 1974-75). Republican. Methodist. Home: 5203 Norborne Ln Houston TX 77069-1537 Office: 9950 Cypresswood Dr Ste 300 Houston TX 77070-3400

MAUCKER, EARL ROBERT, newspaper editor, newspaper executive; b. St. Louis, Sept. 20, 1947; s. Robert Buffem and Linette (Meloy) M.; m. Betsy Ann Johnson, May 21, 1977; children: Eric Robert, Michael Earl. BA in Mass Communications, So. Ill. U., 1972. Reporter Alton (Ill.) Telegraph, 1969-73; reporter, city editor, news editor, asst. mng. editor Rockford (Ill.) Morning Star, 1973-79; mng. editor Springfield (Mo.) Daily News, 1979-80; mng. editor Ft. Lauderdale (Fla.) Sun-Sentinel, 1990-95, v.p. editorial, 1995—. Sgt. SUAF, 1966-69. Mem. Am. Soc. Newspapers Editors, Fla. Soc. Newspapers Editors, Associated Press Mng. Editors Assn. (bd. dirs. 1989-93). Home: 11160 SW 1st St Coral Springs FL 33071-8175 Office: Sun-Sentinel 200 E Las Olas Blvd Fort Lauderdale FL 33301-2248*

MAUDERLY, JOE LLOYD, pulmonary toxicologist; b. Strong City, Kans., Aug. 31, 1943; s. Joseph Park and Violet May (Cox) M.; m. Cheryl Gaines, Jan. 31, 1965; children: Laurie Jean, Jameson Lynn. BS, Kans. State U., 1965, DVM, 1967. Respiratory physiologist Inhalation Toxicology Research Inst., Albuquerque, 1967-89, supr. pathophysiology group, 1976-89, dir., 1989-96; rsch. prof. medicine U. N.Mex., Albuquerque, 1988—, clin. prof. pharmacy, 1990—; cons. in field; dir. external affairs Lovelace Respiratory Rsch. Inst., 1996—; mem. EPA Clean Air Scientific Adv. Com., 1992-96, chair, 1997—. Assoc. editor Fundamental Applied Toxicology, 1989-94; contbr. articles to profl. jours., chpts. to books. Served to capt. USAF, 1967-69. Mem. Am. Thoracic Soc. (chmn. assembly of environ. and occupational health 1991-93, long-range planning com. 1991-94, sci. adv. com. 1993-96, editl. bds., inhalation toxicology and exptl. lung rsch.), Am. Physiol. Soc., Am. Vet. Med. Assn., N.Mex. Vet. Med. Assn., Soc. of Toxicology, Exptl. Aircraft Assn. Republican. Home: 4517 Banff Dr NE Albuquerque NM 87111-2829 Office: Inhalation Toxicology Rsch Inst PO Box 5890 Albuquerque NM 87185-5890

MAUDLIN, ROBERT V., economics and government affairs consultant; b. Washington, June 8, 1927; s. Cecil V. and Eva Jane (Wright) M.; m. Carole M. Jackson, Sept. 3, 1949; children: Lynda C., David V., Tim W.E. Student, MIT, 1945; BS, Am. U., 1951. Ptnr. C.V. & R.V. Maudlin, Washington, 1952-72, owner, 1972—; mng. dir. Bur. Applied Econs., Washington, 1960—; sec. Nat. Assn. Scissors and Shears Mfrs., 1970—; exec. dir. Joint Govt. Liaison Com., 1973-81; mem. Industry Sector Adv. Com. U.S. Dept. Commerce and U.S. Trade Rep., Washingotn, 1975—. Author econ. and statis. reports. Pres. Forest Hills Citizens Assn., Washington, 1964; chmn. Boy Scouts Am., Washington, 1972. Served to 2d lt. C.E., AUS, 1945-47. Republican. Home: 2906 Ellicott Ter NW Washington DC 20008-1023 Office: CV & RV Maudlin 1511 K St NW Washington DC 20005-1401

MAUER, ALVIN MARX, physician, medical educator; b. LeMars, Iowa, Jan. 10, 1928; s. Alvin Milton and Bertha Elizabeth (Marx) M.; m. Theresa Ann McGivern, Dec. 2, 1950; children: Stephen James, Timothy John, Daria Maureen, Elizabeth Claire. B.A., State U. Iowa, 1950, M.D., 1953. Intern Cin. Gen. Hosp., 1953-54; resident in pediatrics Children's Hosp. Cin., 1954-56; fellow in hematology dept. medicine U. Utah, Salt Lake City, 1956-59; dir. div. hematology Children's Hosp. Cin., prof. dept. hematology, 1959-73; prof. dept. pediatrics U. Cin. Coll. Medicine, 1959-73; prof. pediatrics U. Tenn. Coll. Medicine, Memphis, 1973—, prof. medicine, 1983—, chief med. oncology/hematology; dir. cancer program U. Tenn. Coll. Health Scis.; dir. St. Jude Children's Research Hosp., Memphis, 1973-83; mem. hematology study sect. NIH; mem. clin. cancer investigation rev. com. Nat. Cancer Inst.; mem. com. on maternal and infant nutrition NRC. Author: Pediatric Hematology, 1969; editor: The Biology of Human Leukemia, 1990. Served with U.S. Army, 1946. Mem. Am. Soc. Hematology (pres. 1980-81), Assn. Am. Cancer Insts. (pres. 1980), am. Acad. Pediatrics (com. on nutrition), Am. Assn. Cancer Edn., Am. Soc. Clin. Investigation, Am. Fedn. Clin. Rsch., Assn. Am. Physicians, Am. Pediatric Soc., Cen. Soc. Clin. Investigation, Cen. Soc. Clin. Rsch., Internat. Soc. Hematology (pres. 1988-90, chmn. 1992-96, bd. councilors 1992-96), Am. Cancer Soc. (pres. Tenn. divsn. 1992-93), Midwest Soc. Pediat. Rsch., N.Y. Acad. Scis., Soc. Pediat. Rsch., Am. Assn. Cancer Rsch., Phi Beta Kappa, Sigma Xi, Alpha Omega Alpha. Democrat. Roman Catholic. Office: U Tenn Memphis Cancer Ctr N327 Van Vleet Bldg 3 S Dunlap St Memphis TN 38103-4907

MAUGHAN, DERYCK C., investment banker. Degree earned, King's Coll., Univ. of London, 1969. With Treasury Dept., United Kingdom, from 1969, Salomon Bros. Inc., 1983—; mng. dir. Salomon Bros. Inc, 1976-91, Tokyo, until 1991; COO Salomon Bros. Inc, N.Y.C., 1991-92, chmn., CEO, 1992—. Office: Salomon Bros Inc 7 World Trade Ctr New York NY 10048-1102

MAUGHAN, WILLARD ZINN, dermatologist; b. Riverside, Calif., Apr. 21, 1944; s. Franklin David and Martha Charlotte (Zinn) M.; m. Rona Lee Wilcox, Aug. 20, 1968; children: Julie Anne, Kathryn Anita, Willard Wilcox, Christopher Keith. Student, Johns Hopkins U., Balt., 1962-64; BS, U. Utah, 1968, MD, 1972. Diplomate Am. Bd. Dermatology. Intern Walter Reed Army Med. Ctr., Washington, 1972-73; fellow Mayo Clinic, Rochester, Minn., 1976-79; pvt. practice Ogden, Utah, 1979—. Contbr. articles to profl. jours. Commr. Boy Scouts Am., Weber County, Utah, 1980-84, dist. chmn., 1993-94, assoc. mem. bd. dirs. Trapper Trails coun., 1995—; pres. Am. Cancer Soc., Weber County, 1985-86. Maj. U.S. Army, 1971-76. Recipient Dist. award of merit Boy Scouts Am., 1985, Silver Beaver award 1994. Fellow ACP, Am. Acad. Dermatology, Royal Soc. Medicine (London); mem. N.Y. Acad. Scis., Kiwanis Club, Alpha Omega Alpha, Phi Sigma Iota. Republican. Mormon. Avocations: woodcarving, camping. Home: 2486 W 4550 S Roy UT 84067-1944 Office: 3860 Jackson Ave Ogden UT 84403-1943

MAUKE, OTTO RUSSELL, retired college president; b. Webster, Mass., Jan. 26, 1924; s. Otto G. and Florence (Giroux) M.; m. Leah Louison, June 18, 1950. A.B., Clark U., 1947, A.M., 1948; Ph.D. (Kellogg fellow), U. Tex., 1965. Tchr. history, acad. dean Endicott Jr. Coll., Beverly, Mass., 1948-65; acad. dean Cumberland County Coll., Vineland, N.J., 1966-67; pres. Camden County Coll., Blackwood, N.J., 1967-87, pres. emeritus. Served with U.S. Army, 1943-46, PTO. Home: 2119 E Lakeview Dr Sebastian FL 32958-8519

MAUL, KEVIN JAY, financial consultant; b. York, Pa., Jan. 11, 1968; s. Peter Henry Jr. and Patricia Louise (Young) M. BA, Shippensburg U., 1990; MA, U. Va., 1992. Economist USDA Econ. Rsch. Svc., Washington, 1991-92; fin. cons. Coopers & Lybrand LLP, Washington, 1992—. Author: The Handbook of Mortgage Banking, 1993. Mem. Am. Econ. Assn.

Lutheran. Avocations: music, travel, gardening, stamp collecting. Home: 909-A S Rolfe St Arlington VA 22204 Office: Coopers & Lybrand LLP 1751 Pinnacle Dr Mc Lean VA 22102-3833

MAULDIN, ROBERT RAY, banker; b. China Grove, N.C., Jan. 15, 1935; s. Raymond Ray and Hazel Inez (Luther) M.; m. Patricia Crain Jarman, Aug. 29, 1959; children—John Clayton, Patricia Crain, Elizabeth Jarman, Anne Luther, Katherine Purnell. Student, N.C. State U., 1953-54; B.S., U. N.C., 1959. Trainee, asst. trust officer Nations Bank, Charlotte, 1959-62; cashier Bank of York, S.C., 1962-65; v.p. Colonial Am. Nat. Bank, Roanoke, Va., 1965-69; exec. v.p. Peoples Bank & Trust Co., Rocky Mount, N.C., 1969-81; pres. Peoples Bank & Trust Co., 1981-85, chmn., chief exec. officer, 1985-90; chmn., CEO Centura Banks Inc., 1993—. Pres. Rocky Mount United Cmty. Svcs., 1974-75; mem. Rocky Mount City Schs. Bd., 1979-83, Commn. for Competitive N.C., 1994—; trustee N.C. Wesleyan Coll., 1993—, Va. Episc. Sch., 1993—; bd. dirs. N.C. Citizens Assn., N.C. Pub. TV Found., Global Tranpark Found., N.C. Partnerships for Children, N.C. Cmty. Found.; chmn. bd. Carolinas Gateway Partnership; mem. adv. bd. Kenan Flaglar Bus. Sch. U. N.C., 1994—. Mem. Am. Inst. Banking, N.C. Young Bankers (pres. 1974-75), N.C. Bankers Assn. (dir. 1984-95), Robert Morris Assocs., Rocky Mount C. of C. (dir. 1975-80, pres. 1978-79), Kiwanis (pres. Rocky Mount 1976-77), Chi Phi. Presbyn. Home: 109 Essex Ct Rocky Mount NC 27803-1207 Office: Centura Bank 134 N Church St Rocky Mount NC 27804-5401

MAULDING, BARRY CLIFFORD, lawyer; b. McMinnville, Oreg., Sept. 3, 1945; s. Clifford L. and Mildred (Fisher) M.; m. Reva J. Zachow, Dec. 27, 1965; children: Phillip B., John C. BA in Psychology, U. Oreg., 1967, JD, 1970. Bar: Oreg. 1970. Sec., gen. counsel Alaska Continental Devel. Corp., Portland, also Seattle, 1970-75; gen. counsel Alaska Airlines, Seattle, 1975-84; dir. legal services, corp. sec. Univar Corp., Seattle, 1984-91; v.p., gen. counsel, corp. sec. Prime Source Corp., Seattle, 1991—; dir. Alaska N.W. Properties, Inc., Seattle. Mem. editorial bd. Oreg. Law Rev. Trustee Good Neighbor Found., Seattle. Republican.

MAULE, CHARLES GOUGH, retired industrial engineer, educator; b. Pine Bluff, Ark., Dec. 1, 1929; s. Charles Andrew, Jr. and Ruby Lucille (Gough) M. Dorla Jeann Wright, June 10, 1949; children: Charles Richard, Michael Lewis. BS in Mech. Engring., Ariz. State U., 1963; MS in Indsl. Engring., Okla. State U., 1972. Registered profl. engr., Okla. Enlisted USAF, 1948, advanced through grades to lt. col., ret., 1977; ext. engr. Okla. State U. Ctr. for Local Govt., Stillwater, 1977-83, asst. dir., 1983-93, retired, 1993; computer acquisition cons. Grady County, Chickasha, Okla., 1989, Wagoner County (Okla.) assessor's office, 1990. Author: County Treasurer Handbook, 1989, 90, 91, 92, County Purchasing Handbook, 1989, 90, 91, 92. Mem. CAP, Stillwater, 1978-90 (comdr. 1988-90), Exch. Club, Stillwater, 1980-92. Recipient Meritorious Svc. Medal USAF, 1977. Mem. NSPE, Equipment Maintenance Coun. (v.p. 1988, 90, Silver Wrench award 1990), Okla. Soc. Profl. Engrs., Masons, Shriners. Republican. Baptist. Avocations: fishing, golf, bird watching, traveling. Home: 4802 W Crestview Stillwater OK 74074 Office: Okla State U Ctr Local Govt Tech 3rd Fl CITD Stillwater OK 74078

MAULE, JAMES EDWARD, legal educator, lawyer; b. Phila., Nov. 26, 1951; s. Edward Randolph George and Jennie Elisabeth (Zappone) M.; m. Susan Margaret Noonan, June 26, 1982 (div. May 1988); children: Charles Edward, Sarah Margaret; m. Susan K. Garrison, Apr. 7, 1990 (div. 1991). BS cum laude, U. Pa. Wharton Sch., 1973; JD cum laude, Villanova U., 1976; LLM with highest honors, George Washington U., 1979. Bar: Pa. 1976, U.S. Tax Ct. 1986. Atty.-adv. Office of Chief Counsel to IRS, Legis. and Regulations Div., Washington, 1976-78; atty.-adv. judge U.S. Tax Ct., Washington, 1978-80; asst. prof. law Dickinson Sch. Law, 1981-83, lectr. and tax program chmn. continuing legal edn., 1981-83; assoc. prof. Villanova Sch. Law, 1983-86, prof., 1986—; lectr. continuing legal edn. Pa. Bar Inst. Harrisburg, Continuing Legal Edn. Satellite Network, Inc., 1988—; Nat. Merit scholar, 1969-73; lectr. state and local taxes Georgetown U. Law Ctr. Inst., 1992—. Recipient Dist. Author award BNA Tax Mgmt., 1993. Mem. ABA (chair and reporter phaseout Eliminate Project Tax Simplification and Restricting Com., section on taxation, cons., ex-officio mem. subcom. on state law, S Corp. com., chmn. subcom. on comparison of partnerships, mem. task force on pass-through entities, tax sect., chmn. subcom. manuscripts and unpubl. teaching material, com. teaching tax), Phila. Bar Assn. (lectr. tax sect. state and local tax CLE program 1991, fed. income taxes 1992—), Order of Coif, Beta Alpha Psi. Club: Friars Sr. Soc. (Phila.). Author: Cases and Materials in Federal Income Taxation, 1981, 16th edit., 1996, Materials in Partnership Law and Taxation, 1985, 6th edit., 1991, Materials in Partnership Taxation, 1987, 9th edit. 1996, Materials in Introduction to Taxation, 1987, 2d edit. 1988, Cases and Materials in Introduction to the Taxation of Business Entities, 1992, 4th edit. 1996, Materials in Taxation of Fundamental Wealth Transfers, 1986, 2d edit. 1988, Materials in Tax Consequences of Disposition of Property, 1983, 3d edit., 1985, Materials and Problems in Taxation of Property Disposition I, 1987, 2d edit. 1989, Materials in Tax Planning for Real Estate, 1986, Materials in Estate and Gift Tax, 1983, 3d edit., 1985, Materials in Taxation of Real Estate Transactions, 1986, 2d edit., 1988, 3d edit., 1992, Taxation of Residence Transactions, 1985, S Corporations: State Law & Taxation, 1989, supp. 1989, 90, 91, 92, 93, Materials and Problems in Computer Applications in the Law, 1990, 6th edit., 1995, Materials in Tax Policy, 1990, Materials and Problems in Computer Applications in Tax Law, 1991, 6th edit., 1996, Better That 100 Witches Should Live, 1995, (with A Clay) Preparing the 1065 Return, 1992, 93; author Continuing Legal Edn. Publs., 1981-96; contbg. author: Federal Tax Service, Tax Practice Series; contbr. articles to profl. jours. and monographs, chpts. to books; author and developer Computer Assisted Legal Edn. Programs in Taxation; owner, author, editor TaxJEM Inc. (computer assisted tax law instruction); owner JEMBook Pub. Co.; cons. and prin. author ABA Section of Taxation Model S Corporation Income Tax Act and Commentary, 1989; author, editor Report of the Subcommittee on Comparison of S Corporations and Partnerships, 1990, 91; case and comment editor Villanova Law Rev., 1975-76; columnist, mem. editorial adv. bd. S Corps. Jour., 1987-91; columnist, mem. editl. adv. bd. Jour. of Ltd. Liability Cos., 1994—. Home: 219 Comrie Dr Villanova PA 19085-1402 Office: Villanova U Sch Law Villanova PA 19085

MAULIK, NILANJANA, medical educator; b. Dec. 22, 1960; s. P.N. Ghosh; m. G. Maulik. BS in Chemistry, St. Xavier's Coll., 1981; MS in Biochemistry, U. Coll. Sci., 1983, PhD in Biochemistry, 1990. Asst. prof. dept. surgery U. Conn. Sch. Medicine, Farmington, 1994—; lectr. in field. Jr. Rsch. fellow U. coll. Sci., Calcutta, India, 1983-85, Sr. Rsch. fellow, 1985-90, Postdoctoral fellow U. Conn. Sch. Medicine, 1992-92, Am. Heart fellow, 199294; Nat. Merit scholar, 1978; recipient Young Investigator award Am. Coll. Angiology, 1992, Internat. Soc. Angiology, 1994. Mem. Am. Soc. Biochemistry amd Molecular Biology, Am. Heart Assn. (cardiovascular coun.), N.Y. Acad. Sci. Internat. Soc. Heart Rsch., Soc. Biol. Chemists, Indian Sci. Congress Assn. (life). Office: U Conn Sch Medicine Dept Surgery Farmington CT 06030-1110

MAULION, RICHARD PETER, psychiatrist; b. Rosario, Argentina, Sept. 2, 1949; s. Peter Henry and Vivien Ormsby (Gough) M.; divorced; 1 child, Maximillian. BS, Colegio Salesiano San Jose, Rosario, ARgentina, 1967; MD, U. Nacional de Rosario, 1980. Diplomate Am. Bd. Psychiatry and Neurology, Am. Acad. Psychoanalysis, Am. Acad. Addiction Medicine, Am. Acad. Pain Mgmt., Am. Bd. Forensic Examiners, Am. Bd. Quality Assurance and Utilization Rev. Physicians, Am. Bd. Disability Analysts, Am. Acad. Experts in Traumatic Stress. Intern Kans. U., Kansas City, 1981-82; resident in psychiatry Tulane U., New Orleans, 1983-86, fellow in psychoanalytic medicine, 1984-87; pvt. practice gen. psychiatry Covington, La., 1986-87; pvt. practice psychiatry Ft. Lauderdale, 1987—; founder, med. dir. The Rose Inst., Ft. Lauderdale, Fla., 1988—; sec. med. exec. com., chmn. quality assurance com., The Retreat Hosp., Sunrise, Fla., 1994—; med. dir. Anxiety and Depression prog., CPC Ft. Lauderdale Hosp., 1989-90; med. dir. Acad. Medicine and Psychology, Ft. Lauderdale, 1988-89, CEPHAS Prog., HSA Greenbrier Neurobiologic. Hosp., Covington, La., 1986-87, chief med. staff, 1987; clin. instr. psychiatry Tulane U. Med. Ctr., 1986-87; pres. med. exec. com., chief med. staff, chmn. quality assurance com. Retreat Hosp., 1992—; workshop speaker; radio program host The Rose Institute Hour; lectr. in field; cons. in field. Host ednl.-cmty. svc. radio program The Rose Inst. Hour, 1995—. Mem. pub. health com. for the Health and Human Svcs. Bd., Dist. 10; mem. alochol, drugs and mental health com.. Fellow Am. Acad. Psychoanalysis, Am. Bd. Forensic Examiners, Interam. Coll. Physicians and Surgeons; mem. AMA, Am. Psychiat. Assn., Am. Acad. Psychoanalysis, Am. Soc. Clin. Hypnosis, Fla. Med. Assn. (Med. Speaker of Yr. award, 1st pl. radio, 2nd pl. t.v., 1990, del. 1993—), Fla. Psychiat. Soc. (coun. mem. 1993-94), Broward County Psychiat. Soc. (med. exec. com., pres. 1994-95), Broward County Med. Assn. (chmn. physicians recovery network com., bd. dirs.), Broward County Psychiat. Soc. (pres. 1993—), M.I.N.D. Home: PO Box 350033 Fort Lauderdale FL 33335-0033

MAULL, GEORGE MARRINER, music director, conductor; b. Phila., Oct. 14, 1947; s. Frederick Dunlap and Helen Norbury (Jordan) M.; m. Marcia Eileen Korn, Aug. 13, 1984. MusB, U. Louisville, 1970, MusM, 1972; postgrad., Julliard Sch. Music, 1976-78. Condr. Louisville Ballet Co., 1971-75; asst. condr. Opera Orch. N.Y., N.Y.C., 1976-78, N.J. Symphony Orch., Newark, 1979-80; music dir., condr. Bloomingdale Chamber Orch., N.Y.C., 1980-83, N.J. Youth Symphony, Summit, 1980-97, Philharm. Orch. N.J., Warren, 1987—. Conducting debut Carnegie Hall, N.Y.C., 1989; condr. in Eng., Belgium, The Netherlands, Poland, Romania, Hungary, Germany; featured in WNET mini-documentary Art Effects: Young and Noteworthy, 1988. Named Disting. Alumnus, U. Louisville, 1994. Mem. Am. Fedn. Musicians, Am. Symphony Orch. League (conducting fellow 1978, Nat. Cert. Merit 1980), Condr's. Guild. Episcopalian. Home: 79 Stone Run Rd Bedminster NJ 07921-1711 Office: Philharm Orch of NJ PO Box 4064 Warren NJ 07059-0064

MAULSBY, ALLEN FARISH, lawyer; b. Balt., May 21, 1922. A.B., Williams Coll., Williamstown, Mass., 1944; LL.B., U. Va., 1946. Bar: Md. 1947, N.Y. 1950. Law clk. to judge U.S. Circuit Ct. Appeals 4th Circuit, 1946-47; assoc. firm Cravath Swaine & Moore, N.Y.C., 1947-57; ptnr. Cravath Swaine & Moore, 1958-95. Vestryman St. James' Episcopal Ch., N.Y.C., 1962-68, 80-85, warden, 1986-87; trustee Greer-Woodycrest Child Care, 1961-82; bd. dirs. Episc. Ch. Found., 1973-86. Mem. Am. Bar Found., N.Y. Bar Found., Am. Coll. Trial Lawyers, Am. Bar Assn., N.Y. State Bar Assn., Fed. Bar Assn., Assn. Bar City N.Y., N.Y. County Lawyers Assn. Office: Cravath Swaine & Moore Worldwide Pla 825 8th Ave New York NY 10019-7416

MAUMENEE HUSSELS, IRENE E., ophthalmology educator; b. Bad Pyrmont, Germany, Apr. 30, 1940. MD, U. Gottingen, 1964. Cert. Am. Bd. Ophthalmology, Am. Bd. Med. Genetics. Rsch. asst. U. Hawaii, 1968; vis. geneticist Population Genetics Lab., 1968-69; fellow dept. medicine Johns Hopkins U., 1969-71; ophthalmology preceptorship Wilmer Inst. Johns Hopkins Hosp., 1969-71, from asst. prof. to assoc. prof. Wilmer Ophthalmology Inst., 1972-87; prof. ophthalmology and pediatrics Wilmer Ophthalmology Inst., 1972—; dir. Johns Hopkins Ctr. Hereditary Eye Disease, Wilmer Inst., 1979—; cons. John F. Kennedy Inst. Visually & Mentally Handicapped Children, 1974—; dir. Low Vision Clinic, Wilmer Inst., 1977-88; vis. prof. French Ophthalmology Soc., Paris & French Acad. Medicine, 1988; advisor Nat. Eye Inst. Task Forces, 1976, 81. Mem. AMA, Am. Soc. Human Genetics, Am. Acad. Ophthalmology, Assn. Rsch. Vision & Ophthalmology, Internat. Soc. Genetic Eye Disease, Am. Ophthal. Soc., Pan Am. Assn. Ophthalmology. Achievements include research in nosology and management in ophthalmic and general medical genetics; population genetics; computer application to genetic analysis; molecular genetics; over 200 publications on human genetics and eye diseases. Office: Johns Hopkins Ctr Hereditary Eye Diseases 600 N Wolfe St # 517 Baltimore MD 21205-2110

MAUN, MARY ELLEN, computer consultant; b. N.Y.C., Dec. 18, 1951; d. Emmet Joseph and Mary Alice (McMahon) M. BA, CUNY, 1977, MBA, 1988. Sales rep. N.Y. Telephone Co., N.Y.C., 1970-76, comml. rep., 1977-83, programmer, 1984-86; systems analyst Telesector Resources Group, N.Y.C., 1987-89, sr. systems analyst, 1990-95; pres. Sleepy Hollow (N.Y.) Techs., Inc., N.Y., 1995—. Corp. chmn. United Way of Tri-State Area, N.Y.C., 1985; recreation activities vol. Pioneers Am., N.Y.C., 1982—; active Sleepy Hollow Hist. Soc. Recipient Outstanding Community Service award, Calvary Hosp., Bronx, N.Y., 1984. Mem. N.Y. Health and Racquet Club, Road Runners. Democrat. Avocations: antique restoration, classical music, skiing, running. Office: Sleepy Hollow Techs Inc 3 Farrington Ave Sleepy Hollow NY 10591-1302

MAUNDER, ADDISON BRUCE, agronomic research company executive; b. Holdrege, Nebr., May 13, 1934; s. Addison Haynes and Marie Sophia (Luebs) M.; m. Katherina Marlene Blum, Sept. 8, 1978; children: Lynda Diane, Christopher Allen. B.Sc., U. Nebr., 1956; M.Sc., Purdue U., 1958, Ph.D., 1960; DSc (hon., U. Nebr., 1991. With DeKalb AgResearch, Inc., Lubbock, Tex., 1960—, sorghum breeder, 1960-61, dir. sorghum research, 1961-76, v.p. sorghum research, 1976-78, v.p. rsch. AgResearch, Inc., Lubbock, Tex., 1978-82; v.p. DeKalb-Pfizer Genetics, DeKalb, Ill., 1982-89; v.p. agronomic research DeKalb Plant Genetics, DeKalb, Ill., 1989-91; sr. v.p. DeKalb Genetics Corp., DeKalb, Ill., 1991—; bd. dirs. Diversity Mag., Washington, 1984-95; adj. prof. Tex. Tech. U., 1992—. Contbr. 11 chpts. to books and more than 70 articles to profl. jours. Mem. deans adv. com. Tex. Tech. U., Lubbock, 1983-86; chmn. external rev. INTSORMIL of AID, Lincoln, Nebr., 1980—; bd. dirs. Tex. Tech. U. Rsch. Found., 1986-92; mem. Nat. Plant Genetic Resources Bd., 1991-92, Na.t Plant Variety Protection Bd., 1991-94. Recipient Gerald Thomas award Tex. Tech. U., 1974, Prodn. award Grain Sorghum Producers Assn., 1985, Genetics and Plant Breeding award for Industry, 1987, Indsl. Agronomy award, 1988, Purdue Disting. Alumni award, 1997. Fellow AAAS, Am. Soc. Agronomy (bd. dirs. 1991-92), Crop Sci. Soc. Am. (bd. dirs. 1991-92, pres. 1995-96); mem. Sigma Xi, Alpha Zeta. Republican. Achievements include development of plant products (150 hybrids) emphasizing improved drought and insect resistence as well as nutritional quality.

MAUPIN, ARMISTEAD JONES, lawyer; b. Raleigh, N.C., Nov. 10, 1914; s. Alfred McGhee and Mary Armistead (Jones) M.; m. Diana Jane Barton, May 16, 1942 (dec.); children: Armistead Jones, Anthony Westwood, Jane Stuart; m. Cheryl Leigh Erhard, July 31, 1982. A.B., U. N.C., 1936; J.D., George Washington U., 1940. Bar: N.C. 1939. Ptnr. Maupin, Taylor & Ellis., Raleigh. Pres. Occoneechee coun. Boy Scouts Am., 1962-64; pres. Carolina Charter Corp., 1976-80, 93—; former chancellor Episcopal Diocese of N.C.; former sr. warden Christ Ch. Parish; vice chmn. Am. Battle Monuments Commn., 1981-90. Comdr. USNR, WWII, PTO. Decorated chevalier French Legion of Honor. Fellow Am. Bar Found.; mem. ABA (ho. of dels. 1960-72), N.C. State Bar (coun. 1955-60, pres. 1959-60), Soc. of Cincinnati (v.p. gen. 1968-70, pres. gen. 1971-74, pres. N.C. soc. 1964-67), Carolina Country Club, Circle Club, Triangle Fox Hounds Club. Republican. Episcopalian. Home: 2005 Banbury Rd Raleigh NC 27608-1121 Office: Highwoods Tower One 3200 Beech Leaf Ct Raleigh NC 27604-1063

MAUPIN, ARMISTEAD JONES, JR., writer; b. Washington, May 13, 1944; s. Armistead Jones and Diana Jane (Barton) M. BA, U. N.C., 1966. Reporter News and Courier, Charleston, S.C., 1970-71, AP, San Francisco, 1971-72; account exec. Lowry Russom and Leeper, Pub. Rels., San Francisco, 1973; columnist Pacific Sun mag., San Francisco, 1974; publicist San Francisco Opera, 1975; serialist San Francisco Chronicle, 1976-77, 81, 83; commentator Sta. KRON-TV, San Francisco, 1979; serialist San Francisco Examiner, 1986. Author: (novels) Tales of the City, 1978, More Tales of the City, 1980, Further Tales of the City, 1982, Babycakes, 1984, Significant Others, 1987, Sure of You, 1989, (omnibus) 28 Barbary Lane, 1990, (omnibus) Back to Barbary Lane, 1991, Maybe the Moon, 1992; librettist musical Heart's Desire, 1990; exec. prodr. (TV program) Armistead Maupin's Tales of the City, 1993; contbr. articles to N.Y. Times, L.A. Times, others. Lt. (j.g.) USN, 1967-70, Vietnam. Recipient Freedom Leadership award Freedoms Found., Valley Forge, Pa., 1972, Comms. award Met. Elections Com. L.A., 1989, Exceptional Achievement award ALA, 1990, Best Dramatic Serial award Royal TV Soc., 1994, Peabody award 1994, Outstanding Miniseries award, Gay and Lesbian Alliance Against Defamation, 1994, Best Miniseries award Nat. Bd. of Rev., 1994. Office: Harper Collins 10 E 53rd St New York NY 10022-5244 address: c/o Amanda Urban International Creative Mgnt 40 W 57th St New York NY 10019

MAUPIN, ELIZABETH THATCHER, theater critic; b. Cleve., Oct. 21, 1951; d. Addison and Margaret (Thatcher) M.; m. Jay Edward Yellen, Dec. 29, 1995. BA in English, Wellesley (Mass.) Coll., 1973; M in Journalism, U. Calif., Berkeley, 1976. Editorial asst. Houghton Mifflin Co., Boston, 1973-74; intern Washington bureau McClatchy Newspapers, 1975; reporter, movie critic Times-Standard, Eureka, Calif., 1976-78; theater and movie critic Chronicle-Telegram, Elyria, Ohio, 1978-79; movie and restaurant critic Ledger-Star, Norfolk, Va., 1979-82; feature writer Va.-Pilot and Ledger-Star, Norfolk, 1982-83; sr. theater critic Orlando (Fla.) Sentinel, 1983—. Fellow Nat. Arts Journalism program Columbia U., 1995-96. Fellow Nat. Critics Inst.; mem. Am. Theatre Critics Assn. (exec. com. 1993—, chair 1996—). Office: Orlando Sentinel 633 N Orange Ave Orlando FL 32801-1300

MAUPIN, STEPHANIE ZELLER, French language educator; b. St. Louis, Apr. 16, 1946; d. Robert H. and Pernelle (Santhuff) Zeller; 1 child, Britt. BEd., U. Mo., 1967; MAT in Communication Arts, Webster Coll., St. Louis, 1977, postgrad., 1979-87, St. Louis U., 1986—. Cert. tchr., Mo. Tchr. Mehlville Sch. Dist., St. Louis County, 1967—; tchr. French and English, Oakville High Sch., Mehlville Sch. Dist., 1971—; adj. faculty Webster U., St. Louis, 1980, St. Louis U., 1982—, mentor tchr. 1988-89, Nat. Louis U., 1992—; adj. faculty U. Mo., St. Louis, 1993—; cons. Living on the Edge broadcasting series; speaker in field. Dir. in charge exchange program St. Louis-Lyon Sister Cities Corp.; founder St. Louis-St. Louis du Sénégal Sister cities Corp., 1991. NEH Fellow; Rockefeller Found. Fgn. Language Tchrs. fellow, 1987, Fulbright High Sch. Exch. Tchr., 1990-91 recipient Agnes Garcia-Ponty Meml. award, 1991. Mem. NEA, MLA, NEH Fng. Lang. Tchrs. Fellowship (advocate for Mo., 1995), Nat. Coun. Tchrs. of English, Arts and Edn. Council, African Lit. Assn., The French Soc., Am. Assn. Tchrs. French (dir.), African Studies Assn. Network for Women in Adminstrn., Fgn. Lang. Tchrs. Assn. (pres. 1992-94), Assn. Supervision and Curriculum Devel., Internat. Edn. Consortium, NE Conf. Teaching Fgn. Lang. (adv. bd.), Cen. States Conf. Teaching Fgn. Lang. (adv. bd.), Fgn. Language Assn. Mo., Internat. Platform Assn., Webster U. Alumni Assn., Fgn. Lang. Tchrs. St. Louis, Ind. State Fgn. Language Conf., African Lit. Assn. Conf., Phi Sigma Iota. Presentor: Mo. State Dept. Edn. Fgn. Lang. Assn. Conf., Nat. Conf. Tchr. English, NE Conf. Teaching Fgn. Lang., Fulbright Tchr. Exchange, 1991, 92. Home: 5608 Duchesne Parque Dr Saint Louis MO 63128-4176 Office: 5557 Milburn Rd Saint Louis MO 63129-3514

MAURER, ADAH ELECTRA, psychologist; b. Chgo., Oct. 26, 1905; d. Frank Ulysses and Mary Louise (Meng) Bass; m. Harry Andrew Maurer, June 14, 1937 (div. 1947); children: Douglas, Helen. BS, U. Wis., 1927; MA, U. Chgo., 1957; PhD, Union Inst., 1976. Lic. sch. psychologist, Calif. Tchr. pub. schs. Chgo., 1927-61; psychologist pub. schs. Calif., 1962-71; pvt. practice marriage, family and child counselor Berkeley, Calif., 1965-75; organizer, chief exec. officer End Violence Against the Next Generation, Inc., Berkeley, 1972—; lectr. U. Calif., Davis, 1965-68; bd. dirs. Nat. Ctr. for Study Cpl. Punishment & Alternatives in Schs. Temple U., Phila.; liaison People Opposed to Paddling Students, Houston, 1981—; v.p. Nat. Coalition to Abolish Cpl. Punishment in Schs., Columbus, Ohio, 1987—; cons. Calif. State Dept. Social Svcs., 1988. Author: Paddles Away, 1981, 1001 Alternatives, 1984, (with others) The Bible and the Rod, 1983, Think Twice, 1985; editor: (newsletter) The Last? Resort, 1972—; contbr. numerous articles to profl. jours. Sponsor End Phys. Punishment of Children Worldwide. Recipient Disting. Humanitarian award Calif. State Psychol. Assn., Presdl. award Nat. Assn. Sch. Psychologists, 1988, Donna Stone award Nat. Commn. for Prevention of Child Abuse, 1988, commendation Giraffe Project, 1988, award in recognition of pioneering efforts in banning corporal punishment in nation's schs. Nat. Coalition to Abolish Corporal Punishment in Schs., Achievement award Child, Youth and Family Svcs. Am. Psychol. Assn., 1994. Fellow Am. Psychol. Assn. (Lifetime Career Achievement award 1995); mem. Hemlock Soc. Avocations: hiking, gardening. Home and Office: 977 Keeler Ave Berkeley CA 94708-1440

MAURER, BEVERLY BENNETT, school administrator; b. Bklyn., Aug. 23, 1940; d. David and Minnie (Dolen) Bennett; m. Harold M. Maurer, June 12, 1960; children: Ann Maurer Rosenbach, Wendy Maurer Rausch. BA, Bklyn. Coll., 1960, postgrad., 1961; postgrad., U. Richmond, 1980-90, Va. Commonwealth U., 1980-90. Cert. tchr., N.Y., Va. Math. tchr. Col. David Marcus Jr. High Sch., Bklyn., 1960-61, Pomona (N.Y.) Jr. High Sch., 1967-68; math. tchr. Hebrew day sch. Rudlin Torah Acad., Richmond, Va., 1969-80, asst. prin., 1980-86, prin., 1986-89; dir. edn. Jewish Community Day Sch. Ctrl. Va., Richmond, 1990-93; ednl. cons., 1993—; owner East Coast Antiques; propr. East Coast Antiques. Developed talented and gifted program, pre-admission program for children at Med. Coll. Va., 1982. Bd. dirs. Jewish Comty. Ctr., Richmond, 1980s; bd. dirs. Aux. to Med. Coll. Va., Richmond, 1980s, Aux. to U. Nebr. Med. Ctr., 1994—, Uta Hallee, 1994-97. Recipient Master Tchr. award Rudlin Torah Acad., 1983. Mem. Jewish Community Day Sch. Network, Anti-Defamation League, Jewish Women's Club. Avocations: collecting contemporary and art nouveau glass, world travel.

MAURER, C(HARLES) F(REDERICK) WILLIAM, III, museum curator; b. Jersey City, July 12, 1939; s. William and Daisy L. (Knight) M.; m. Shon Hooker, June 6, 1964; children: Melissa, Adam. BA, Va. Mil. Inst., 1961; MA in Humanities, Manhattanville Coll., 1988; cert. mus. studies, NYU, 1990. Adminstrv. sec. Marshall Libr., 1961-62; v.p. Morse, Maurer & Kopple, Englewood Cliffs, N.J., 1965-72; v.p. instl. sales HMM&K, Englewood Cliffs, 1972-78, v.p., 1972-78; v.p. Maurer & Kopple, Englewood Cliffs, 1978-84, pres., 1984-88; exec. v.p. Foodservice, div. M&H Co., Purchase, N.Y., 1978-90; curator Blackledge-Kearney House, Palisades Interstate Pk. Commn., Alpine, N.J., 1990-94, George Washington's Hdqs. at Tappan, Tappan, N.Y., 1994-95; dir. Gomez Mill House, Marlboro, N.Y., 1995—. Author: Third Continental Dragoons Diary, 1776-1784, 1979. Pres. Park Ridge (N.J.) Bd. Health, 1980-83, councilman, 1984-90. Maj., inf., U.S. Army, 1962-64. Mem. Co. Mil. Historians, Pascack Hist. Soc. (pres. 1978-80), Bergen County Historic Sites Adv. Bd. Methodist. Home: 3 Tulip Ct Park Ridge NJ 07656-1421

MAURER, DAVID L., lawyer; b. Evansville, Ind., Oct. 31, 1945; s. John G. Jr. and Mildred M. (Lintzenich) M.; m. Diane M. Kaput, Aug. 11, 1973; children: Eric W., Kathryn A. BA magna cum laude, U. Detroit, 1967, Cert. in Teaching, 1971; JD, Wayne State U., 1975. Bar: Mich., U.S. Dist. Ct. (ea. and we. dist.) Mich., U.S. Ct. Appeals (6th cir.) Cin. Law clk. Mich. Ct. Appeals, Detroit, 1976, Supreme Ct. Mich., Lansing, 1977-78; asst. U.S. atty. civil div. U.S. Dept. Justice, Detroit, 1978-81; assoc. to ptnr. Butzel, Long, Gust, Klein & Van Zile, Detroit, 1981-85; ptnr. Pepper, Hamilton & Scheetz, Detroit, 1985—; guest lectr. Practicing Law Inst., 1988—, Nat. Bus. Inst., 1989—, U. Mich. Law Sch., U. Detroit Law Sch., 1990, Hazardous Waste Super Conf., 1986-87. Co-author: Michigan Environmental Law Deskbook, 1992; contbr. articles to profl. jours. and chpts. in books. Mem. Energy & Environ. Policy Com., 1988—, chairperson, 1989-90; mem. Great Lakes Water Resources Commn., 1986. Mem. State Bar Mich. (environ. couns. 1986-91, sec., treas., chairperson-elect, chairperson 1991-93). Office: Pepper Hamilton & Scheetz 100 Renaissance Ctr Ste 3600 Detroit MI 48243-1101

MAURER, GERNANT ELMER, metallurgical executive, consultant; b. Sayre, Pa., May 5, 1949; s. Elmer L. and Joyce F. (Fox) M.; m. Suzanne Walker Berry, Aug. 19, 1972. BES, Johns Hopkins U., 1971; PhD, Rensselaer Poly. Inst., 1976. Materials engr. Spl. Metals Corp., New Hartford, N.Y., 1976-80, mgr. R & D, 1981-84, dir. R & D, 1985-87, v.p. tech., 1987—; founding v.p. Splty. Metals Processing Consortium, pres., 1992-93; chmn. Internat. Symposium on Superalloys, 1984-88. Co-editor: Superalloys, 1980, 2d edit., 1988; contbr. tech. papers to profl. jours.; inventor various superalloys. Dir. devel. com. Munson William Proctor Inst., Utica, N.Y., 1988-89. Fellow Am. Soc. for Metals (trustee 1992-95); mem. The Metall. Soc., Am. Vacuum Soc. (bd. dirs. metall. div. 1988), Utica Area C. of C. (bd. dirs. 1986-89), Wash. State U. (adv. materials engring. adv. bd. 1993—), Yahnundasis Club. Avocations: golf, fly fishing, art, photography, metal working. Home: 27 Sherman Cir Utica NY 13501-5808 Office: Spl Metals Corp Middle Settlement Rd New Hartford NY 13413

MAURER, GILBERT CHARLES, media company executive; b. N.Y.C., May 24, 1928; s. Charles and Mildred (Petite) M.; m. Ann D'Espinosa. A.B., St. Lawrence U., 1950; M.B.A., Harvard U., 1952. With Cowles Communications, Inc., N.Y.C., 1952-71, Look Mag., 1952-62; pub.

Venture mag., 1963-67; pres. Family Circle mag., 1967-69, v.p., dir. corporate planning, exec. com., 1969-71, also dir.; sr. v.p., dir. F.A.S. Internat., Inc., 1971-73; v.p. mag. div. Hearst Corp., 1973-74, exec. v.p., 1974-76, pres. mag. div., 1976-90, also dir.; exec. v.p. The Hearst Corp., 1985—, chief operating officer, 1990—. Mem. N.Y. adv. bd. Salvation Army, 1979—; trustee Whitney Mus. Am. Art, 11983—, pres., 1994—; mem. vis. com. Medill Sch. Journalism Northwestern U., 1985-94, chmn., 1989-94; bd. dirs. Boys and Girls Club Am., 1986—; mem. bd. mgrs. N.Y. Bot. Garden, 1989. Mem. Mag. Pubs. Assn. (bd. dirs., chmn. 1979-81). Clubs: Harvard (N.Y.C.), Metropolitan (N.Y.C.). Office: The Hearst Corp 959 8th Ave New York NY 10019-3737

MAURER, HAROLD MAURICE, pediatrician; b. N.Y.C., Sept. 10, 1936; s. Isador and Sarah (Rothkowitz) M.; m. Beverly Bennett, June 12, 1960; children: Ann Louise, Wendy Sue. A.B., N.Y. U., 1957; M.D., SUNY, Bklyn., 1961. Diplomate Am. Bd. Pediatrics, Am. Bd. Pediatric Hematology-Oncology. Intern pediatrics Kings County Hosp., N.Y.C., 1961-62; resident in pediatrics Babies Hosp., Columbia-Presbyn. Med. Center, N.Y.C., 1962-64; fellow in pediatric hematology/oncology Columbia-Presbyn. Med. Center, 1966-68; asst. prof. pediatrics Med. Coll. Va., Richmond, 1968-71; asso. prof. Med. Coll. Va., 1971-75, prof., 1975—, chmn. dept. pediatrics, 1976-93; dean U. Neb. Coll. Medicine, Omaha, 1993—; chmn. Intergroup Rhabdomyosarcoma Study; exec. com. Pediatric Oncology Group; mem. cancer clin. investigation rev. com. NIH. Editor: pediatrics, 1983, Rhabdomyosarcoma and Related Tumors in Children and Adolescence, 1991; mem. editorial bd. Am. Jour. Hematology, Journal Pediatric Hematology and Oncology, Medical and Pediatric Oncology, 1984—; contbr. articles to profl. jours. Mem. Youth Health Task Force, City of Richmond., Gov.'s Adv. Com. on Handicapped.; mem. nat. com. on childhood cancer Am. Cancer Soc., bd. dirs. Va. div. Served to lt. comdr. USPHS, 1964-66. NIH grantee, 1974—. Mem. Am. Acad. Pediatrics (com. oncology-hematology), Am. Soc. Hematology, Soc. Pediatric Rsch., Am. Pediatric Soc., Va. Pediatric Sc. (exec. com.), Assn. Med. Sch. Pediatric Dept. Chmn., Internat. Soc. Pediatric Oncology, Am. Soc. Clin. Oncology, Va. Hematology Soc., Am. Assn. Cancer Rsch., Am. Cancer Soc., Am. Soc. Pediatric Hematology (v.p. 1990-91, pres. 1991-93), Sigma Xi, Coun. Deans AAMC, Gov.'s Blue Ribbon Commn., Alpha Omega Alpha. Republican. Jewish. Home: 9822 Ascot Dr Omaha NE 68114-3848 Office: U Neb Coll Medicine 600 S 42nd St Omaha NE 68198-1002

MAURER, JEFFREY STUART, finance executive; b. N.Y.C., July 9, 1947; s. Herbert and Phoebe Maurer; m. Wendy S. Nemerov. BA, Alfred U., 1969; MBA, NYU, 1975; JD, St. John's U., 1976. With U.S. Trust Co. N.Y., 1970—, pres., 1990; COO U.S. Trust Co., N.Y.C., 1994—. Trustee Alfred (N.Y.) U., 1984; mem. adv. bd. Salvation Army Greater N.Y., 1987; bd. dirs., treas. Children's Health Fund, N.Y.C., 1988; bd. dirs. Hebrew Home Aged, Riverdale, N.Y., 1992; mem. Citizens Budget Commn. and Bankers Roundtable. Mem. ABA, N.Y. State Bar Assn., Nassau County Bar Assn., N.Y. State Bankers Assn. (chmn. trust div. 1987-88), Am. Bankers Assn. (chmn. trust div. 1992-93), Glen Head Country Club. Jewish. Avocations: skiing, golf. Office: US Trust Co NY 114 W 47th St New York NY 10036-1510

MAURER, JOHAN FREDRIK, religious denomination administrator; b. Oslo, Mar. 23, 1953; came to U.S., 1957; s. Harald and Erika Elfreide (Schmitz) M.; m. Judith Marshall Van Wyck, Aug. 9, 1980; children: Luke Van Wyck, Eliot Heyerdahl. BA in Russian, Carleton U., Ottawa, Ont., Can., 1976; postgrad., Earlham Coll., 1983—. Asst. dir., dir. Beacon Hill Friends House, Boston, 1977-80; field sec. Friends World Com. for Consultation, Wilmington, Ohio, Richmond, Ind., 1983-93; coord. Right Sharing of World Resources, Wilmington and Richmond, 1986-93; gen. sec. Friends United Meeting, Richmond, 1993—; mem. Europe com. Nat. Coun. Chs., N.Y.C., 1985—; recorded min. Ind. Yearly Meeting of Friends, Muncie, 1989—; mem. U.S. Ch. Leaders, Chgo., 1993—; mem. bd. advisors Earlham Coll. Sch. Religion, Richmond, 1993—; keynote speaker numerous denominational events, 1982—. Editor Quaker Life, 1994—; contbr. numerous articles to religious publs. Mem., mem. steering com. Social Action Ministries Greater Boston, 1978-80; mem. Boston 350 Com., 1979-80; bilingual vol. Jewish Family and Children's Svcs., Boston, 1978-80. Mem. Quaker U.S.-USSR Com., Soc. for Internat. Devel., Bible Assn. Friends, World Hunger Edn. Svc. (assoc.), Richmond Ministerial Assn., Evangs. for Social Action. Avocations: correspondence, computers, reading, walking. Office: Friends United Meeting 101 Quaker Hill Dr Richmond IN 47374-1926

MAURER, JOHN RAYMOND, internist, educator; b. Des Moines, Dec. 24, 1953; s. Raymond Leinen and Mary Angela (Heartney) M.; m. Carolyn Gutai, June 23, 1978; children: Karen, Lisa, Tim, Kristin. BS, U. Iowa, 1975, MD, 1979. Diplomate Am. Bd. Internal Medicine. Intern Blodgett - St Mary's Hosp., Grand Rapids, Mich., 1979-80; resident in internal medicine Blodgett - St. Mary's Hosp., Grand Rapids, Mich., 1980-83; chief resident medicine Blodgett Meml. Med. Ctr., Grand Rapids, 1982-83, attendant dept. internal medicine, 1983—, also trustee; assoc. clin. prof. Mich. State U., East Lansing, 1983—; med. dir. Blodgett Regional Poison Ctr., Grand Rapids, 1985-94; chief staff Blodgett Meml. Med. Ctr., Grand Rapids, 1995-96; trustee, treas. Ctr. Health Affair, Grand Rapids, 1997—. Chair physician campaign United Way, Grand Rapids, 1992-93. Mem. Am. Soc. Internal Medicine, Am. Coll. Physician, Mich. Soc. Internal Medicine (pres. 1990-91). Home: 7538 Lime Hollow SE Grand Rapids MI 49546 Office: Blodgett Meml Med Ctr 1900 Wealthy St SE Grand Rapids MI 49506-2969

MAURER, LAWRENCE MICHAEL, acting school administrator, educator; b. Bklyn., Oct. 2, 1935; s. Charles and Ethel (Ryan) M.; married Mar. 20, 1970 (div. 1971); 1 child, Lalaine; m. Carol Schneider, July 27, 1971. B of Vocat. Edn., San Diego State U., 1976; MS in Sch. Adminstrn., Nat. U., 1981. Cert. sch. adminstr., tchr., c.c. educator, Calif. Commd. ensign USN, 1953; advanced through grades to chief, 1969, ret., 1972; tchr. San Diego County Office Edn., 1972—, acting vice prin., 1989—; bd. dirs. Multi-cultural Affairs Com., San Diego, 1991—, Self Esteem Devel. C.C., San Diego, 1990—, Vocat. Edn. Commn., San Diego, 1986—; cons. Vocat. Edn. in Ct. Schs., San Diego, 1986—; adj. prof. U. Calif., San Diego; mentor tchrs. in technology San Diego Office Edn., 1996—. Organizer Dem. party. Named Excellent Tchr. of Yr. Corp. for Excellence in Pub. Edn., 1992, mentor Tchr.-Tech., 1996; vocat. grantee, 1988. Mem. ASCD (bd. dirs.), Nat. Vocat. Educators, Calif. Reading Assn., Calif. Ct. Sch. Adminstrs. Avocation: civil rights activist. Home: 98-80 Magnolia Ave Santee CA 92071 Office: San Diego County Office Edn 6401 Linda Vista Rd San Diego CA 92111-7319

MAURER, MARC MORGAN, federation administrator, lawyer; b. Des Moines, June 3, 1951; s. Fred V. and June Jeraldine (Davis) M.; m. Patricia Ann Schaaf; children: David Patrick, Dianna Marie. Student, Orientation and Adjustment Ctr. of Iowa Commn. Blind; grad. cum laude, U. Notre Dame, 1974; JD, U. Ind., 1977. Bar: Ind. 1977, Ohio 1978, Iowa 1978, Md. 1979, U.S. Supreme Ct. 1981. Former auto mechanic; dir. sr. legal assistance project Advocates for Basic Legal Equality, Toledo, Ohio, 1977-78; lawyer rates and routes div. Office of Gen. Counsel CAB, Washington, 1978-81; pvt. practice Balt., 1981—; v.p. Nat. Fedn. of the Blind Inc., 1971, elected pres., 1973, 75, Nat. Fedn. of the Blind Md., 1984-86; pres. Nat. Fedn. of the Blind, 1986—. Bd. dirs. various tenants and community assns. Avocations: books, barbecue. Office: Nat Fedn Blind 1800 Johnson St Baltimore MD 21230-4914

MAURER, PAUL HERBERT, biochemist, educator; b. N.Y.C., June 29, 1923; s. Joseph and Clara (Vogel) M.; m. Miriam Esther Merdinger, June 27, 1948; children—Susan Gail, David Mark, Philip Mitchell. B.S., City Coll. N.Y., 1944; Ph.D., Columbia, 1950. Research biochemist Gen. Foods Corp., Hoboken, N.J., 1944-46; instr. City Coll. N.Y., 1946-51; research asso. Coll. Phys. and Surg., Columbia, 1950-51; asst. research prof. Sch. Medicine, U. Pitts., 1951-54, asso. prof. immunochemistry, 1954-60; asso. prof. microbiology Seton Hall Coll. Medicine, 1960-62; prof. microbiology N.J. Coll. Medicine, 1962-66; prof., chmn. dept. biochemistry Jefferson Med. Coll., Phila., 1966-93, prof. pathology, biochemistry and molecular biology emeritus, 1993—; mem. allergy and infectious diseases tng. grant com. NIH, 1961-66; mem. commn. on albumin Protein Fedn.; mem. NRC com. on plasma; chmn. Transplantation Biology and Immunology Com. NIAID, 1986—. Asso. editor: Immunochemistry, 1964, Science, 1966; Contbr. profl. jours. Served with USNR 1946-48. Recipient Research Career award Nat. Inst. Allergy and Infectious Diseases, 1962-66, Chemistry medal City Coll. N.Y., 1944. Mem. Am. Chem. Soc., N.Y. Acad. Scis., Biochem. Soc. (London), Harvey Soc., Am. Assn. Immunologists, Am. Soc. Biol. Chemistry, AAAS, Societe de Chimie Biologique (France), Soc. Exptl. Biology and Medicine, Sigma Xi. Home: 8470 Limekiln Pike Apt B517 Wyncote PA 19095-2712 Office: Jefferson Med Coll Dept Pathology 1020 Locust St Philadelphia PA 19107-6731

MAURER, RICHARD MICHAEL, investment company executive; b. Bethlehem, Pa., June 4, 1948; s. Richard Thomas and Anna Theresa (Bold) M.; m. Karen Coe, June 13, 1970; children: Christopher Coe, Mark Emerson. Student, Pa. State U., 1966-68; BS, Point Park Coll., 1971; MBA, U. Pitts., 1982. CPA Pa. Staff acct. Price Waterhouse, Pitts., 1972-74, tac acct., 1974, sr. tax acct., 1974-77, tax mgr., 1977-78; dir. taxes The Hillman Co., Pitts., 1978-85; pres. Maurer Ross & Co., Inc., Pitts., 1985—; co-mng. ptnr. Wesmar Ptnrs,, Pitts., 1985—; bd. dirs. Gateway Additive Co., Inc., Pitt Penn Oil Co., Pitt Penn Distbn. Co., Springdale Splty. Plastics, Inc., M & R Distbn. Co., Am. Home Improvement Products, Inc., S2 Golf Inc., Maurer Ross & Co., Inc., Maurer & Ross, Inc. With U.S. Army, 1970-76. Mem. AICPA, Assn. Corp. Growth, Pa. Inst. CPAs, Rotary (past dir., past pres.), Oakmont Country Club, Duquesne Club, Lake Nona Golf Club, Rivers Club. Office: Three Gateway Ctr Pittsburgh PA 15222

MAURER, ROBERT DISTLER, retired industrial physicist; b. St. Louis, July 20, 1924; s. John and Elizabeth J. (Distler) M.; m. Barbara A. Mansfield, June 9, 1951; children: Robert M., James B., Janet L. B.S., U. Ark., 1948, LL.D., 1980; Ph.D., MIT, 1951. Mem. staff MIT, 1951-52; with Corning Glass Works, N.Y., 1952-89; mgr. physics research Corning Glass Works, 1963-78, research fellow, 1978-89. Contbr. articles to profl. jours., chpts. to books. Served with U.S. Army, 1943-46. Recipient Indsl. Physics prize Am. Inst. Physics, 1978, L.M. Ericsson Internat. prize in telecommunications, 1979, Indsl. Rsch. Inst. Achievement award, 1988, Optical Soc. Am./IEEE Leos Tyndall award, 1987, Disting. Alumni award U. Ark, 1994, Am. Innovator award U.S. Dept. Commerce, 1995. Fellow IEEE (Moris N. Liebmann award 1978), Am. Ceramic Soc. (George W. Morey award 1976), Am. Phys. Soc. (New Materials prize 1989); mem. NAE, Nat. Inventors Hall of Fame. Patentee in field. Home: 6 Roche Dr Painted Post NY 14870-1225 Office: Corning Inc Sullivan Park Corning NY 14830

MAURER, THEODORE A., advertising executive. Vice chmn., COO Commonhealth USA, Little Falls, N.J.; chmn,, CEO Health Learning Sys., Little Falls, N.J. Office: Health Learning Systems 150 Clove Rd PO Box 422 Little Falls NJ 07424

MAURER, YOLANDA TAHAR, publisher; b. Tuuis-Tunisia, North Africa, Oct. 8, 1922; d. Joseph Tahar and Oro (Sidi) Tahar; m. William S. Maurer, Jan. 5, 1966; 1 child, Larry. Columnist Ft. Lauderdale News, 1948-65; pub. Pictorial Life, 1965-71; edtl. writer Ft. Lauderdale News, 1971-80; pub., 1980-86. Author: The Best of Broward, 1986, Ode To the City, 1995. Bd. mem. Miami City Ballet, Performing Arts Ctr., 1985-89, Fla. Philharm. Orch., Opera Guild Ft. Lauderdale. Recipient First Prize Fla. Mag., Fla. Newspaper Assn., 1958, George Washington award Freedoms Found., 1975; named Woman of Yr., Am. Cancer Soc., 1983, Woman of Style and Substance, Philharm. Soc., 1996, Woman of Yr., Women in Comms., 1967, 83. Republican. Avocations: writing, reading, computers, cooking. Home: 1811 SE 14th St Fort Lauderdale FL 33316 Office: Lauderdale Life 11 NE 12th Ave Fort Lauderdale FL 33301-1603

MAURICE, DON, personal care industry executive; b. Peoria, Ill., Aug. 29, 1932; s. Imajean (Webster) Crayton; m. Cindalu Jackson, Aug. 31, 1990. Student, Loma Linda U., 1984-86; cert. paralegal studies, Calif. State U., San Bernardino, 1994. Lic. hair stylist, skin therapist; cert. paralegal, notary pub. Owner 2 schs. in advanced hair designs, San Diego, 1962-64, D & M Enterprises, Advt. Agy., 1964-78; now cons. D&M Enterprises Advt. Agy.; dist. mgr. AqRo Matic Co. Water Purification Systems, San Diego, 1972-75; profl. sales educator Staypower Industries, San Diego, 1972-76, 3d v.p., 1975-76; regional bus. cons. Estheticians Pharmacology Rsch., Garden Grove, Calif., 1975-81; owner, operator Don Maurice Hair Designs, Hemet, Calif., 1980-83; dir., operator Hair Sytles by Maurice, Loma Linda, Calif., 1984-88; owner, pres. Grooming Dynamics, Redlands, Calif., 1988—; bus. cons. Yogurt Place, Paradise Valley, Ariz., 1978-79, others; regular guest Channel 6/Channel 8, San Diego, 1968-78; cons. infomercial Pre-Paid Legal Svcs., Inc., 1994—. Author: The New Look For Men, 1967, The Art of Men's Hair Styling, 1968 (accepted by Library of Congress), Baldness, To Be or Not To Be, 1989. Promoter Spl. Olympics, Hemet, 1981. Sgt. U.S. Army, 1950-53, Korea. Decorated Purple Heart, 1952; named Leading Businessman in His Profession, Union and Evening Tribune, 1969. Mem. Internat. Platform Assn., Christian Businessmen's Assn. Avocations: writing, sculpting, art, sports, music. Office: Grooming Dynamics PO Box 1279 Loma Linda CA 92354-1279

MAURO, RICHARD FRANK, lawyer, investment manager; b. Hawthorne, Nev., July 21, 1945; s. Frank Joseph and Dolores D. (Kreimeyer) M.; m. LaVonne M. Madden, Aug. 28, 1965; 1 child, Lindsay Anne. AB, Brown U., 1967; JD summa cum laude, U. Denver, 1970. Bar: Colo. 1970. Assoc. Dawson, Nagel, Sherman & Howard, Denver, 1970-72; assoc. Van Cise, Freeman, Tooley & McClearn, Denver, 1972-73, ptnr., 1973-74; ptnr. Hall & Evans, Denver, 1974-81, Morrison & Forester, Denver, 1981-84; of counsel Parcel, Mauro, Hultin & Spaanstra, P.C., Denver, 1984—, pres., 1988-90, of counsel, 1992—; pres. Sundance Oil Exploration Co., 1985-88; exec. v.p. Castle Group, Inc., 1992—; adj. prof. U. Denver Coll. Law, 1981-84. Symposium editor: Denver Law Jour., 1969-70; editor: Colorado Corporation Manual; contbr. articles to legal jours. Pres. Colo. Open Space Coun., 1974; mem. law alumni coun. U. Denver Coll. Law, 1988-91. Francis Wayland scholar, 1967; recipient various Am. jurisprudence awards. Mem. ABA, Colo. Bar Assn., Denver Bar Assn., Colo. Assn. Corp. Counsel. (pres. 1974-75), Am. Arbitration Assn. (comml. arbitrator), Order St. Ives, Denver Athletic Club (bd. dirs. 1986-89). Home: 2552 E Alameda Ave No 128 Denver CO 80209-3320 Office: 475 17th St Ste 750 Denver CO 80202-4017

MAURY, SAMUEL L., association executive; m. Frances Morrow Nabers; 2 children. BS, U. Pitts., LLB. Bar: Ala., Pa. With law dept. U.S. Steel Corp., 1965-67; with govtl. rels. for 7 state southern region U.S. Steel Corp., Birmingham, Ala., 1968-74, asst. to gen. counsel, 1974-75; gen. atty. U.S. Steel Corp., Washington, 1977-82; exec. dir. The Bus. Roundtable, Washington, 1983-94, pres., 1994—. With USAF. Office: The Bus Roundtable 1615 L St NW Ste 1100 Washington DC 20036-5624

MAUS, JOHN ANDREW, computer systems engineer; b. Whittier, Calif., July 13, 1945; s. Kenneth Waring and Bertha Estella (Eckman) M.; M. Diana Barba, April 16, 1977 (div. May 1, 1983); m. Colette An Moschelle, Nov. 23, 1985; stepchildren: BreAnn, Adam; children: Steven Andrew, Terra An. BA in Physics, U. Calif., Riverside, 1963-67; MS in Physics, San Diego State U., 1967-70. Cert. data processor, 1983. Programmer, analyst San Diego State Found., 1970-72; instr. bus. San Diego State U., 1971-73; systems programmer San Diego State U., San Diego, 1971-74; data processing mgr. M.H. Golden Co., San Diego, 1974-79; computer systems engr. Hewlett-Packard Co., Spokane, Wash., 1979-84, sr. systems engr., 1984-86, network systems engr., 1986-89, sr. tech. cons., 1989-93; UNIX high availability cons. Hewlett-Packard Co., Spokane, 1994—; physics lab. asst. USDA Salinity Lab., Riverside, 1965-67; underwater acoustics programmer Naval Undersea Ctr., San Diego, 1967-70; programmer San Diego Inst. Pathology, 1972-76; adv. com. Computer Sci. Bus. Applications North Idaho Coll., 1989—; mem. career network U. Calif., Riverside, 1990—; dist. tech. com. Nine Mile Falls (Wash.) Sch., 1994—. Author: INTEREX Conference Proceedings, 1989; co-author: Chemical Physics Letters, 1971, Electronic and Atomic Collisions, 1971. Merit badge counselor Spokane chpt. Boy Scouts Am., 1983—. Mem. Assn. Computing Machinery (founder Spokane chpt., chpt. chmn. 1980-82, service award 1981). Avocations: internat. travel, skiing, horses. Home: 12417 W Sunridge Dr Nine Mile Falls WA 99026-9311 Office: Hewlett-Packard Co 1121 N Argonne Rd Ste 121 Spokane WA 99212-2686

MAUSEL, PAUL WARNER, geography educator; b. Mpls., Jan. 2, 1936; s. Paul George and Esther Victoria (Sundstrom) M.; m. Jean Frances Kias, July 2, 1966; children: Paul Brandon, Catherine Suzanne, Justin Thomas. BA in Chemistry and Geography, U. Minn., 1958, MA in Geography, 1961; PhD, U. N.C., 1966. Asst. prof. geography Eastern Ill. U., Charleston, 1965-70, assoc. prof., 1970-71; assoc. prof. geography Ind. State U., Terre Haute, 1971-75, prof., 1975—, dir. Remote Sensing Lab., 1975-89, Geog. Inf. Systems, 1989—; rsch. geographer Lab. Applications of Remote Sensing Purdue U., West Lafayette, Ind., 1972-73; soils geographer cons. U. Mo. at Columbia, summer 1974; lectr. in field; grants, contracts with EPA, NSF, Nat. Park Svc., Dept. Energy, Stnnis Space Ctr./ITD, Oak Ridge Nat. Lab., U.S. Forest Svc., NASA, USDA, USFWS, The Nature Conservancy. Contbr. articles to profl. jours., Chpts. to textbooks. NSF fellow, 1978; recipient research award Ind. State U., 1983. Mem. Assn. Am. Geographers, Am. Soc. Photogrammetry and Remote Sensing (Meritorious Svc. award 1988, 96). Home: 7400 E Old Maple Ave Terre Haute IN 47803-9627

MAUSKOPF, SEYMOUR HAROLD, history educator; b. Cleve., Nov. 11, 1938; s. Philip and Dora (Trompeter) M.; m. Josephine Mary Album, Aug. 9, 1964; children: Deborah, Philip, Alice. A.B., Cornell U., 1960; Ph.D., Princeton U., 1966. Instr. history Duke U., Durham, N.C., 1964-66, asst. prof., 1966-72, assoc. prof., 1972-80, prof., 1980—, dir. program in sci. tech. and human values, 1979-84; dir. Focus Interdisciplinary programs Duke U., Durham, 1995—. Author: Crystals and Compounds, Molecular Structure and Composition in Nineteenth Century French Science, 1976, (with M.R. McVaugh) The Elusive Science; Origins of Experimental Physical Research, 1915-1940, 1980; editor: The Reception of Unconventional Science by the Scientific Community, 1979, Chemical Sciences in th e Modern World, 1993. NSF postdoctoral fellow, 1971-72; NSF grantee, 1974, 92-93; Am. Philos. Soc. travel grantee, 1979; Nat. Endowment for Humanities summer stipend, 1982; Edelstein internat. fellow in history chem. scis. and tech. Beckman Ctr. U. Pa. and Hebrew Univ., Jerusalem, 1988-89. Mem. History Sci. Soc. (exec. com. treas. 1979-83, coun. 1993-95). Jewish. Office: Duke U PO Box 90719 Bldg Durham NC 27708-0719

MAUTZ, KARL EMERSON, engineering executive; b. Columbia, Mo., Sept. 30, 1957; s. Wayne Albert Mautz and Imogene (Embrey) Whitten; m. Pamela Dawn Quillen, Mar. 12, 1988; children: Alyssa Mae, Brandon Tyler. BS in Chemistry, U. Tex., El Paso, 1979, BS in Geology, 1983; MS in Chemistry, Ariz. State U., 1985, PhD, 1987. Process engr. Motorola, Inc., Mesa, Ariz., 1980-87; mem. tech. staff Motorola, Inc., Austin, Tex., 1988—; cons. Motif, Inc., Portland, Oreg., 1994. Contbr. articles to profl. jours.; patentee in field of semiconductor processes; numerous patents pending; development of 300MM wafer process tool technology. Mem. recycling com. Homeowners Assn., Austin, 1992. Mem. Electrochem. Soc., Am. Chem. Soc. Achievements include five patents for semiconductor processes. Office: Motorola Inc 505 Barton Springs Rd Austin TX 78704-1245

MAUZ, HENRY HERRWARD, JR., retired naval officer; b. Lynchburg, Va., May 4, 1936; s. Henry Herrward and Rene C. (Ball) M.; m. Margaret Catherine O'Neill, June 6, 1959; children: Sheila, David, Lynn, Daniel. BS, U.S. Naval Acad., 1959; BSEE, U.S. Naval Postgrad. Sch., 1965; MBA, Auburn U., 1970. Commd. ensign USN, 1959, advanced through grades to adm., 1992, various ships and shore duty assignments, 1977-80; strategy and concepts officer Office of Chief Naval Ops. Washington, 1980-82; comdg. officer USS England, San Diego, 1980-82, chief of staff Carrier Group One, 1982-83; ops./readiness officer SHAPE Belgium, 1983-85; comdr. Cruiser/Destroyer Group 12 Mayport, Fla., 1985-86; ops./plans officer to comdr. in chief Pacific Fleet, Pearl Harbor, Hawaii, 1986-88; comdr. Seventh Fleet Yokosuka, Japan, 1988-90; dep. chief Office Naval Op.s, Washington, 1991-92; comdr. in chief U.S. Atlantic Fleet, 1992-94; ret. USN, 1994. Decorated D.S.M. with four gold stars, Def. Superior Svc. medal, Legion of Merit, Bronze Star with combat V device. Mem. U.S. Naval Inst., U.S. Naval War Coll. Found., Naval Hist. Found., Monterey Peninsula Country Club, Army-Navy Country Club. Avocations: golfing, skiing. Home: 1608 Viscaino Rd Pebble Beach CA 93953-3303

MAUZY, MICHAEL PHILIP, environmental consultant, chemical engineer; b. Keyser, W.Va., Nov. 14, 1928; s. Frank and Margery Ola (Nelson) M.; m. Nancy Shepherd Watson, Mar. 27, 1949; children: Michael P. Jr., Jeffrey A., Rebecca A. BSChemE, Va. Poly. Inst., 1950; MSChemE, U. Tenn., 1951. Registered profl. engr., Va., Ill. With Monsanto Co., St. Louis, 1951-71, dir. engring. and mfg., 1968-71; mgr. comml. devel. Kummer Corp., Creve Coeur, Mo., 1971-72; mgr. labs. Ill. EPA, Springfield, 1972-73, mgr. water pollution control, 1973-74, mgr. environ. programs, 1974-77, dir., 1977-81; v.p. Roy F. Weston, Inc., West Chester, Pa., 1981-88, Vernon Hills, Ill., 1988-93, Albuquerque, 1993—; also bd. dirs. Roy F. Weston, Inc., West Chester, Pa.; bd. dirs. DeTox Internat. Corp., St. Charles, Ill.; provider Congl. testimony, 1974-81; presenter various workshops, symposia and seminars, 1974—. Contbr. articles on environ. mgmt. to profl. publs., 1974—. Mem. Ohio River Valley Water Sanitary Commn., Cin., 1976-81. 1st lt. U.S. Army, 1951-53. Recipient Environ. Quality award Region V, U.S. EPA, Chgo., 1976, Disting. Svc. award Cons. Engrs. Coun. of Ill., 1978, Ill. award Ill. Assn. Sanitary Dists., 1979, Clarence W. Klassen award Ill. Assn. Water Pollution Control Ops., 1984. Mem. Am. Pub. Works Assn., Am. Inst. Chem. Engring., Water Pollution Control Assn., Am. Mgmt. Assn. Avocations: reading, travel, home improvements.

MAUZY, OSCAR HOLCOMBE, lawyer, retired state supreme court justice; b. Houston, Nov. 9, 1926; s. Harry Lincoln and Mildred Eva (Kincaid) M.; m. Anne Rogers; children: Catherine Anne, Charles Fred, James Stephen. BBA, U. Tex., 1950, JD, 1952. Bar: Tex. 1951. Practiced in Dallas, 1952-87; pres. Mullinax, Wells, Mauzy & Baab, Inc. (P.C.), 1970-78; mem. Tex. Senate from 23d Dist., 1967-87, chmn. edn. com., 1971-81, chmn. jurisprudence com., 1981-87, pres. pro tempore, 1973; justice Tex. Supreme Ct., 1987-93; pvt. practice Austin, 1993—; Mem. Tex. Adv. Commn. Intergovtl. Relations, Nat. Conf. State Legislators, Edn. Commn. of the States, Am. Edn. Finance Assn., 1971-87. Vice chmn. judiciary com. Tex. Constl. Conv., 1974; nat. committeeman Young Democrats, 1954. Served with USNR, 1944-46. Home: 5000 Crestway Dr Austin TX 78731-5404

MAVES, MICHAEL DONALD, medical association executive; b. East St. Louis, Ill., Oct. 14, 1948. BS, U. Toledo, 1970; MD, Ohio State U., 1973; MBA, U. Iowa, 1988. Lic. physician, Iowa, Mo., Ill., D.C.; diplomate Am. Bd. Otolaryngology. Rsch. fellow Ohio State U. Coll. Medicine, Columbus, 1977; fellow head and neck surgery Columbia-Presbyn. Med. Ctr., N.Y.C., 1978, U. Iowa Hosps. and Clinics, Iowa City, 1980-81; asst. prof. otolaryngology, head and neck surgery Ind. U. Sch. Medicine, Indpls., 1981-84; asst. prof. otolaryngology, head and neck surgery U. Iowa Hosps. and Clinics, Iowa City, 1984-87, assoc. prof., 1987-88; chmn. dept. otolaryngology St. Louis U. Sch. Medicine, St. Louis, 1988-94; exec. v.p. Am. Acad. Otolaryngology, Head and Neck Surgery, Alexandria, Va., 1994—; lectr. in field. Contbr. articles to profl. jours. Capt. U.S. Army, 1974-76. Recipient numerous awards including Honor award and Pres.'s award Am. Acad. Otolaryngology-Head and Neck Surgery; named one of Best 1000 Physicians in U.S., 1992, 94, One of Best 400 Cancer Doctors in Am., Good Housekeeping, 1992. Fellow ACS; mem. AMA (RBRVS update com.), Am. Cancer Soc., others. Office: Am Acad Otolaryngology One Prince St Alexandria VA 22314

MAVRINAC, ALBERT ANTHONY, political scientist, educator, lawyer; b. Pitts., Nov. 24, 1922; s. Anthony and Mary Theresa (Kvaternik) M.; AB, U. Pitts., 1943; MA, 1950; student Columbia, summer 1948; PhD, Harvard U., 1955; AM, Colby Coll., 1960; JD, U. Maine, 1990; Fulbright scholar, Inst. Superieur de Philosophie, U. Louvain (Belgium), 1950-51; Carnegie fellow law and polit. sci., Harvard Law Sch., 1961-62; m. Marilyn Parks Sweeney, July 3, 1954; children: Georgia Ireland Lindfors, Susan Edwards Mullen, Sarah Clay, Emily Gregor, Anthony John. Labor relations specialist Office Mil. Govt., Hesse, Germany, 1946-48; lectr. polit. sci. U. Pitts., 1948-50; instr. Wellesley Coll., 1953; teaching fellow Harvard, 1953-55, instr., 1955-57, lectr., 1958, Allston Burr sr. tutor, 1956-58; Fulbright prof. univs Rennes and Montpellier (France), 1958-59; prof. govt. Colby Coll., Waterville, Maine, 1958-78, Charles A. Dana prof. govt., 1978-92, Charles A. Dana prof. govt. emeritus, 1992—, chmn. dept. history and govt., 1958-79, chmn. dept. govt., 1979-82, acting dean students, 1970-71; adj. prof. Sch. Bus. & Entrepreneurship Nova-SE U., 1973—; assoc. Daviau, Jabar & Batten Law

Firm, Waterville, 1990-91; fellow Duke, summer 1960; assoc. dir. Insts. Communism and Am. Constitutionalism Am. U., summer 1963; project specialist Ford Found. and Inst. Pub. Adminstrn. for Egyptian Adminstrn., also adviser Govt. UAR, 1965-67; spl. asst. for legislation to gov. Maine, 1968-69; faculty fellow NASA, 1969; chief party Inst. Pub. Adminstrn. Adv. Group to Nat. Inst. Administrn., Vietnam, 1971-72; chmn. Nat. Fulbright-Hays Scholarship Screening Com. for France, 1976; Nat. Endowment for Humanities fellow Princeton U., summer 1977; lectr., cons. in field. Com. chmn. Gov. Maine Task Force Govt. Reorgn., 1967-68; founding mem. No. Kennebec Valley Community Action Com., 1965; mem. Maine Council Humanities and Pub. Policy, 1975-79; mem. U.S. del. to Madrid meeting European Security and Coop., 1980-82; active numerous Democratic campaigns in Maine, also nat. campaigns. chmn. Maine for Muskie, 1970. Served to 1st lt. AUS, 1943-46; ETO. Decorated Bronze Star, Combat Inf. badge; recipient Toppan prize Harvard, 1955. Mem. Am., New Eng. (past pres.) polit. sci. assns., Am. Soc. Polit. and Legal Philosophy, Am. Soc. Pub. Adminstrn. Roman Catholic. Author monographs, articles. Home: 47 Winter St Waterville ME 04901-7336

MAVROS, GEORGE S., clinical laboratory director; b. Adelaide, Australia, Oct. 14, 1957; came to U.S., 1970; s. Sotirios George and Angeliki (Korogiannis) M.; m. Renee Ann Cuddeback, June 24, 1979. BA in Microbiology, U. South Fla., 1979, MS in Microbiology, 1987; MBA, Nova U., 1991; PhD in Health Sci. Mgmt., LaSalle U., 1995. Cert. lab. dir. Nat. Certifying Agy. for Clin. Lab. Pers.; diplomate Am. Coll. Health Care Execs. Med. technologist Jackson Meml. Hosp., Dade City, Fla., 1979-81; microbiology supr. HCA Bayonet Point-Hudson Med. Ctr., Hudson, Fla., 1981-82, dir. labs., 1982-88; lab. mgr., adminstrv. and tch. dir. Citrus Meml. Hosp., Inverness, Fla., 1988—; lab. cons. HCA Oak Hill Hosp., Spring Hill, Fla., 1983-84; cons. lab. info. systems Citation Computer Systems, St. Louis, 1983—, Hosp. Corp. of Am., Nashville, 1986; instr. Microbiology Pasco Hernando Com. Coll., New Port Richey, Fla., 1986-88, Inst. Biolog. Scis. Cen. Fla. Community Coll., Lecanto, 1989—; bd. dirs. Gulf Coast chpt. Clin. Lab. Mgrs. Assn., Tampa, Fla., 1987, pres., 1987-89. Parish pres. Greek Orthodox Ch. of West Cen., Inverness, Fla.; chmn. Bayonet Point Hosp. Good Govt. Group, Hudson, 1986-88. Mem. APHA, Am. Mgmt. Assn., Am. Soc. Microbiology, Am. Soc. Clin. Pathologists (cert. in lab. mgmt.), Am. Soc. Med. Technologists (cert.), Fla. Soc. Med. Technologists, Clin. Lab. Mgmt. Assn. (pres. Gulf Coast chpt. 1988-90), Am. Assn. Clin. Chemists, Am. Acad. Microbiology (cert.), Fla. State Bd. Clin. Lab. Pers. (chmn. 1994). Democrat. Clubs: Greek Orthodox Youth Am. (Clearwater, Fla.). Lodges: Order of DeMolay, Sons of Pericles (sec.). Home: 6 Byrsonima Ct W Homosassa FL 34446-4610 Office: Citrus Meml Hosp 502 W Highland Blvd Inverness FL 34452-4720

MAVROVIC, IVO, chemical engineer; b. Fiume, Italy, Dec. 5, 1927; came to U.S., 1959; s. Janko and Milica (Gregorina) M.; m. Erna Gallian, oct. 14, 1955; 1 child, Paul. BSChemE, U. Zagreb, Yugoslavia, 1952, MSChemE, 1955. Registered profl. engr, N.Y. Chem. engr. Dorr-Oliver, Milan, Italy, 1956-59, Chemico, N.Y.C., 1960-65; cons. N.Y.C., 1965-77; pres. UTI/UTI Constrn. Inc., Hackensack, N.J., 1977—. Patentee in field; contbr. articles to profl. jours. Mem. AICE. Roman Catholic. Office: UTI/UTI Constrn Inc 2 University Plaza Dr Hackensack NJ 07601-6202

MAWARDI, OSMAN KAMEL, plasma physicist; b. Cairo, Dec. 12, 1917; came to U.S., 1946, naturalized, 1952; s. Kamel Ibrahim and Marie (Wiennig) M.; m. Betty Louise Hosmer, Nov. 23, 1950. B.S., Cairo U., 1940, M.S., 1945; A.M., Harvard U., 1947, Ph.D., 1948. Lectr. physics Cairo U., 1940-45; asst. prof. Mass Inst. Tech., 1951-56, asso. prof., 1956-60; prof. engring., dir. plasma research program Case Inst. Tech., Cleve., 1960-88; dir. Energy Research Office, Case Western Res. U., 1977-82; pres. Collaborative Planners, Inc.; mem. Inst. Advanced Study, 1969-70; also cons. Contbr. articles to profl. jours. Trustee Print Club Cleve., Cleve. Inst. Art. Recipient Biennial award Acoustical Soc. Am., 1952; CECON medal of achievement, 1979. Fellow AAAS, Acoustical Soc. Am., Am. Phys. Soc., IEEE (Edison lectr. 1968-69, Centennial award 1984, Cleve. sect. Engr. of Yr. 1994); mem. N.Y. Acad. Scis., Sigma Xi, Eta Kappa Nu. Home: 15 Mornington Ln Cleveland OH 44106 Office: 2490 Lee Rd Cleveland OH 44118-4125 *I never cease to be amazed that the goals I really believe in invariably materialize.*

MAWBY, RUSSELL GEORGE, retired foundation executive; b. Grand Rapids, Mich., Feb. 23, 1928; s. Wesley G. and Ruby (Finch) M.; m. Ruth E. Edison, Dec. 16, 1950; children: Douglas, David, Karen. B.S. in Horticulture, Mich. State U., 1949, Ph.D. in Agrl. Econs., 1959, LL.D. (hon.), 1972; M.S. in Agrl. Econs, Purdue U., 1951, D.Agr. (hon.), 1973; L.H.D. (hon.), Luther Coll., Decorah, Iowa, 1972, Alma (Mich.) Coll., 1975, Nazareth Coll., 1976, Madonna Coll., 1983, N.C. Central U., 1986; LL.D. (hon.), N.C. A&T State U., Greensboro, 1974, Tuskegee Inst., 1978, Kalamazoo Coll., 1980; D.P.A. (hon.), Albion Coll., 1976; D.C.L. (hon.), U. Newcastle, Eng., 1977; D.Sc. (hon.), Nat. U. Ireland, 1980; D.Pub. Service (hon.), No. Mich. U., 1981; D.H.L. (hon.), So. Utah State Coll., 1983; HHD (hon.), Grand Valley State U., 1988; ScD (hon.), Calif. State U., 1989; LLD (hon.), Adrian Coll., 1990; LittD (hon.), Olivet Coll., 1991. Ext. specialist Mich. State U., East Lansing, 1952-56; asst. dir. coop. ext. svc. Mich. State U., 1956-65; dir. div. agr. W.K. Kellogg Found., Battle Creek, Mich., 1965-66; mem., trustee W.K. Kellogg Found., 1967—, v.p. programs, 1966-70, pres., 1970-82, chmn., CEO, 1982-95, chmn. emeritus, 1995—; bd. dirs. Kellogg Co., Detroit br. Fed. Res. Bank Chgo., 1980-85, J.M. Smucker Co., 1983—; fellow Inst. for Children, Youth and Families Mich. State U., 1993; hon. fellow Kellog Coll., U. Oxford, Eng., 1990; mem. chancellor's ct. of benefactors U. Oxford, Eng., 1991; Disting. Vis. Prof. Inst. for Children, Youth and Families and Coll. of Edn., Mich. State U., 1996—. Trustee Youth for Understanding, 1973-79, Mich. State U. Coll. of Agr. and Natural Resources Alumni Assn., 1977-80, pres. 1978-79; trustee Arabian Horse Trust, 1978-90 (emeritus 1990—), Starr Commonwealth, 1987— (chmn. bd. trustees 1993-95), Found. Ctr., 1988-94 (chmn. bd. trustees 1989-94), Mich. Non-profit Assn., 1990-94 (chmn. bd. trustees 1990-94, emeritus 1994—), Mich. State U., 1992-96 (chmn. bd. trustees 1995); founding chmn. Coun. of Mich. Founds., 1972-74, chmn. emeritus 1994—; bd. dirs. Coun. on Founds., 1978-84, Mich.'s Children, 1995—; mem. Joint Coun. on Food and Agrl. Scis., USDA, 1984-88; mem. Com. on Agrl. Edn. in Secondary Schs., NRC, 1985-88, Gov.'s Task Force on Revitalization of Agr. Through Rsch. and Edn., 1986; mem. rural bus. partnership adv. bd. Mich. Dept. Commerce, 1989-90, Mich. Coop. Ext. Svc. Study Com., 1989; mem. pres.'s adv. coun. Clemson U., 1987-95; steering com. Econ. Devel. Forum of Calhoun County, Mich., 1991—; mem. policy bd. Calhoun County Cmtys. in Schs., 1995—; mem. Lt. Gov.'s Children's Commn., State of Mich., 1995-96; mem. leadership adv. coun. Olivet Coll., 1995—; trustee Battle Creek Community Found., 1996—, Mich. 4-H Found., 1996—; scholar-in-residence Ind. U. Ctr. on Philanthropy, 1996—; mem. State Officers compensation Commn., State of Mich., 1996—. With AUS, 1953-55. Ind. U. Ctr. on Philanthropy scholar-in-residence, 1996; decorated knight 1st class Royal Order St. Olaf Norway; knight's cross Order of Dannebrog 1st class Denmark; comdr.'s medal Order of Finnish Lion Finland; recipient Disting. Service award U.S. Dept. Agr., 1963, Disting. Alumni award Mich. State U., 1971, Nat. Alumni award 4-H Clubs, 1972, Disting. Eagle Scout award Boy Scouts Am., 1973, Meritorious Achievement award Fla. A&M U., 1973, Nat. Ptnr. in 4-H award Dept. Agr. Ext. Svc., 1976; named hon. fellow Spring Arbor (Mich.) Coll., 1972; recipient Walter F. Patenge medal for pub. service Coll. Osteo. Medicine, Mich. State U., 1977, Disting. Service award Coll. Agr. and Natural Resources, 1980, Seaman A. Knapp Meml. lectr. U.S. Dept. Agr., 1983; recipient George award for cmty. svc. City of Battle Creek, 1986, Disting. Service award Rural Sociol. Soc., 1986, Centennial Alumnus award for Mich. State U. Nat. Assn. State Univs. and Land Grant Colls., 1988, Pres.'s award Clemson U., 1989, Disting. Citizen award Southwest Mich. Coun. Boy Scouts Am., 1989, Disting. Svc. award 1890 Land-Grant Colls. and Univs., 1990, Vol. of Yr. award Clemson U., 1990, Disting. Grantmaker award Coun. on Founds., 1992, Disting. Svc. award Nat. Assn. Homes and Svcs. for Children, 1992, Merit award Nat. Soc. Fund Raising Execs. West Mich. chpt., 1992, Red Rose award Rotary Club of Battle Creek, 1993, George W. Romney award Nat. Soc. Fund Raising Execs. Greater Detroit chpt., 1993, Director's award Arabian Horse Assn. of Mich., 1994, Disting. Svc. award Mich. Hort. Soc., 1994, Michiganian of Yr. The Detroit News, 1995, Gerald G. Hicks Child Welfare Leadership award Mich. Fedn. Private Child and Family Agys., 1995, Leon Bradley Humanitarian for Youth award No. Area Assn., Detroit, 1995, award of Honor Am. Hosp. Assn., 1995. Mem. Mich. Soc. Architects (hon.), Am. Agrl. Econ. Assn., Mich. State U. Alumni Assn. (bd. dirs. 1984-88), Alpha Gamma Rho (dir. 1976-82, grand pres. 1980-82, Man of Year Chgo. Alumni chpt. 1976, Hall of Fame 1986), Alpha Zeta, Phi Kappa Phi (Disting. Mem. award Mich. State U. 1978), Epsilon Sigma Phi (certificate of recognition 1974, Nat. Friend of Ext. 1982), Gamma Sigma Delta, Delta Sigma Pi (hon. mem., 1995). Home: 8400 N 39th St Augusta MI 49012-9713 Office: Heritage Tower 25 Michigan Ave W Ste 1701 Battle Creek MI 49017-7023

MAWHINNEY, KING, insurance company executive; b. Richmond, Va., Sept. 13, 1947; s. John A. and Ellen E. (King) M.; m. Jeanne Dale Smothers, June 8, 1976 (div. Oct. 1984); m. Cathryn C. Morley, Nov. 15, 1986. AB, Davidson Coll., 1971; MA, Pacific Lutheran U., 1973; MEd, U. Tex., 1992. CLU; ChFC; FLMI; ALHC; registered health underwriter, registered employee benefits cons.;assoc. customer svc., health ins. assoc., devel. mgr. Prudential Ins. Co., Newark, 1977-80; sr. sales rep. USAA Life Ins. Co., San Antonio, 1980-81, sales tng. adminstr., 1981-82, dir. procedures and tng., 1983-85, dir. group/bus. sales, 1985-86, sr. dir. USAA Ednl. Services, 1986-88, exec. dir. life sales, FSD Mktg., 1989-90, asst. v.p. life sales, 1990-91; asst. v.p. health sales Life Gen. Agy., 1991-92, asst. v.p. health ins., 1992-94, v.p. health ins., 1994—. Mem. choir Alamo Heights Presbyterian Ch., 1981-83, deacon, 1982-83; mem. Univ. United Meth. Ch., 1991—, mem. adminstrv. bd., 1992-93; mem. bd. gov's. San Antonio Estate Planners Coun., 1988-92; with U.S. Olympic Festival, 1993; chmn. Dreams for Youth Project; bd. dirs. Boysville, Inc., 1991—, pres., 1997. Capt. U.S. Army, 1972-77; Korea. Mem. Life Office Mgmt. Assn. (coun. mem. 1988-91, 93-97, chmn. soc. com. 1988-91), Davidson Coll. Alumni Assn. (chpt. pres. 1983-94), San Antonio Chpt. C.L.U. (bd. dirs., v.p. programs, v.p. fin., v.p. adminstrn., pres.-elect, pres.), FLMI Soc. So. Cen. Tex. (chpt. pres. 1986, bd. dirs. 1987-88), Leadership San Antonio (class XVII 1991-92), Phi Kappa Phi, Sigma Nu, Kappa Delta Pi. Republican. Avocations: sports cards, walking. Home: 23744 Up Mountain Trl San Antonio TX 78255-2000 Office: USAA Life Ins Co 9800 Fredericksburg Rd San Antonio TX 78288-0001

MAX, CLAIRE ELLEN, physicist; b. Boston, Sept. 29, 1946; d. Louis William and Pearl (Bernstein) M.; m. Jonathan Arons, Dec. 22, 1974; 1 child, Samuel. AB, Harvard U., 1968; PhD, Princeton U., 1972. Postdoctoral rschr. U. Calif., Berkeley, 1972-74; physicist Lawrence Livermore (Calif.) Nat. Lab., 1974—; dir. Livermore br. Inst. Geophysics and Planetary Physics, 1984-93, dir. univ. rels., 1993—; mem. Math.-Sci. Network Mills Coll., Oakland, Calif.; mem. com. on fusion hybrid reactors NRC, 1986, mem. com. on internat. security and arms control NAS, 1986-89, mem. com. on phys. sci., math. and applications NRC, 1991-94, mem. policy and computational astgrophys. panels, astron. and astgrophys. survey NRC, 1989-91; mem. sci. steering com. W.M. Keck Obs., 1992-96, mem. adaptive optics sci. team, 1994—. Editor: Particle Acceleration Mechanisms in Astrophysics, 1979; contbr. numerous articles to sci. jours. Fellow AAAS, Am. Phys. Soc. (exec. com. divsn. plasma physics 1977, 81-82); mem. Am. Astron. Soc. (exec. com. divsn. high energy astrophysics 1975-76), Am. Geophys. Union, Internat. Astron. Union, Phi Beta Kappa, Sigma Xi. Rsch. interests include adaptive optics and laser guide stars for astronomy; astrophys. plasmas. Avocations: violin, skiing. Office: Lawrence Livermore Nat Lab PO Box 808 7000 East Ave L-413 Livermore CA 94550-9900

MAX, ERNEST, surgeon; b. Vienna, Austria, Mar. 3, 1936; m. Silvia Neger, Mar. 18, 1964; children: Yvette Rosa, Oliver Fredrick. MD, U. Chile, 1961. Diplomate Am. Bd. Surgery, Am. Bd. Colon and Rectal Surgeons, Am. Bd. Laser Surgery. Intern Hosp. San Borja, Santiago, Chile, 1960-61, resident, 1962-63; fellow in gen. surgery, colon and rectal surgery Lahey Clinic Found., Boston, 1969-70; resident Sinai Hosp., Balt., 1971-72, The Western Pa. Hosp., Pitts., 1972-74; resident in colon and rectal surgery Hermann Hosp., Houston, 1974-75; staff Hermann Hosp., 1975—, Park Plz. Hosp., 1975—, Meml. Hosp. Southwest, 1975—, Meml. NW Hosp., 1975—, Diagnostic Ctr. Hosp., 1975—, The Methodist Hosp., 1976—, Meml. City Hosp., 1976—, Woman's Hosp., 1976—, HCA Spring Br., 1976—, Houston NW Med. Ctr., 1976—, Sam Houston Meml. Hosp., 1977—, St. Luke's Episcopal Hosp., 1981—, Cypress Fairbanks, 1983—; chief of staff Meml. Hosp., 1983; staff HCA Med. Ctr., 1986—, Meml. Hosp. Southeast, 1994—; CEO Colon and Rectal Clinic PA, 1989—; clin. assoc. prof. surgery Baylor Coll. Medicine; clin. instr. surgery U. Tex. Med. Sch., Houston. Author: (with others) Current Diagnosis, 1971. Recipient Walter A. Fansler Travel Edn. award Am. Soc. Colon and Rectal Surgeons, 1974, Harriet Cunningham award Tex. Med. Assn., 1988, Best of the Best award Tex. Med. Assc., 1989; The Purdue Fredrick fellow Am. Soc. Colon and Rectal Surgeons, 1974. Mem. Am. Coll. Surgeons, Tex. Med. Soc., Harris County Med. Soc., Tex. Soc. Colon and Rectal Surgeons (pres. 1982-83), Am. Soc. Laser Medicine and Surgery, Internat. Soc. Univ. Colon and Rectal Surgeons, Lahey Clinic Alumni Assn., Am. Soc. Colon and Rectal Surgeons, Tex. Gulf Coast Colon and Rectal Surgical Soc. (sec. treas. 1992—), Colombian Soc. Colo-Proctology (hon. mem.). Office: Colon & Rectal Clinic PA 6550 Fannin St Ste 2307 Houston TX 77030-2723

MAXA, RUDOLPH JOSEPH, JR., journalist; b. Cleve., Sept. 25, 1949; s. Rudolph Joseph and Christine Marie (Kimpel) M.; m. Kathleen Ann Zolciak, June 19, 1971 (div. 1988); children: Sarah Lynn, Alexander. BS in Journalism cum laude, Ohio U., 1971. Reporter Washington Post, 1971-83; sr. writer The Washingtonian, 1983-92; daily commentator Cable News Network, 1980-82; chief Washington bur. Spy mag., 1992-94; weekly travel columnist Am. On-Line, 1995-96; talk show host Sta. WRC; lectr. on journalism; columnist Ocean Drive mag., 1993—, Spectrum Mag., 1996—; host Pub. Radio Internat.'s Savvy Traveler show, 1997—. Contbg. editor Worth Mag., 1995—. Recipient John Hancock award for excellence in bus. and fin. writing, 1972, writing excellence 1st place award for best regular column Fla. Mag. Assn., 1995. Office: 1746 N St NW Washington DC 20036-2907

MAXEINER, CLARENCE WILLIAM, lawyer, construction company executive; b. Sioux City, Iowa, Mar. 24, 1914; s. Frank A. and Dora A. (Olson) M.; m. Julie Frazer, Sept. 8, 1937; children: Martha Ann, Jay Frank, Mary Katherine, Nancy Carol; m. Rosalie F. Steele, May 29, 1974. Student, Columbia Coll., 1933-34, Columbia U. Law Sch., 1938-39; A.B., Grinnell Coll., 1936; J.D., U. Calif.-Berkeley, 1941. Bar: Calif. 1941. Ptnr. Thelen, Marrin, Johnson & Bridges, San Francisco and Los Angeles, 1941-60; sr. v.p., gen. counsel, dir. J.H. Pomeroy & Co., Inc. (and affiliated cos.), San Francisco, 1959-65; v.p., gen. counsel Dillingham Corp. (and affiliated cos.), Honolulu, 1966—; sr. v.p., gen. counsel, sec., dir., mem. exec. com. Dillingham Corp. (and affiliated cos.), 1968-71, spl. counsel, 1971—. Chmn. equipment fund com. Sonoma State Hosp., 1956-65; bd. overseers Grinnell Coll., 1964; bd. dirs. Del Monte Forest Found., Calif. Autism Found. Mem. ABA, San Francisco Bar Assn., State Bar Calif., Am. Judicature Soc., Hawaii State Bar (assoc.), Columbia, U. Calif. law schs. assns., Phi Beta Kappa, Phi Delta Phi. Congregationalist. Clubs: Commonwealth of Calif. (San Francisco), The Family (San Francisco). Home: 4071 Sunset Ln Pebble Beach CA 93953-3049

MAXEY, NIGEL AARON, publisher; b. Rock, W.Va., Nov. 29, 1945; s. Aaron Burr and Ruth Aretta (Wiley) M.; m. Linda Sharon Boyd, Oct. 29, 1971. BA, Concord Coll., 1969; MA, W.Va. U., 1987. Reporter Princeton (W.Va.) Times, 1963-64, mng. editor, 1965; editor Mail Order Bus. Mag., Bluefield, W.Va., 1972-77; pub. Small Pub. Mag., Pineville, W.Va., 1993—; with W.Va. Dept. Human Svcs., Pineville, 1970—. Author: How to Successfully Publish and Market Your Own Book, 1996, Publishing 101, 1996, Government Open for Business-Working People Not Served, 1997. Home: PO Box 1620 Pineville WV 24874-1620 Office: 92 C Cedar Ave Pineville WV 24874

MAXFIELD, GUY BUDD, lawyer, educator; b. Galesburg, Ill., May 4, 1933; s. Guy W. and Isabelle B. Maxfield; m. Carol Tunick, Dec. 27, 1970; children—Susan, Stephen, Kim. A.B. summa cum laude, Augustana Coll., 1955; J.D., U. Mich., 1958. Bar: N.Y. 1959. Assoc. White & Case, N.Y.C., 1958-63; prof. law NYU, 1963—. Mem. ABA, Am. Law Inst., N.Y. State Bar Assn. Author: Tennessee Will and Trust Manual, 1982, Federal Estate and Gift Taxation, 7th edit. 1997, Florida Will and Trust Manual 1984, Tax Planning for Professionals, 1986; contbr. articles to profl. jours. Trustee Acomb Found., Newark, 1974—. Served with U.S. Army, 1958-64. Fellow Am. Coll. Tax Counsel; mem. ABA, Am. Law Inst., N.Y. State Bar Assn., Phi Beta Kappa, Order of Coif. Office: NYU Sch Law 40 Washington Sq S New York NY 10012-1005

MAXFIELD, JOHN EDWARD, retired university dean; b. Los Angeles, Mar. 17, 1927; s. Chauncey George and Rena Lucile (Cain) M.; m. Margaret Alice Waugh, Nov. 24, 1948; children—Frederick George (dec.), David Glen, Elaine Rebecca, Nancy Catherine, Daniel John. B.S., Mass. Inst. Tech., 1947; M.S., U. Wis., 1949; Ph.D., U. Oreg., 1951. Instr. U. Oreg., 1950-51; mathmatician U.S. Naval Ordnance Test Sta., China Lake, Calif., 1949-56, head computing br., 1956-57, head math. div., 1957-60; lectr. UCLA, 1951-60; head prof. dept. math. U. Fla., 1960-67; prof., chmn. dept. math. Kans. State U., 1967-81; dean Grad. Sch. and univ. research La. Tech. U., 1981-92, dean emeritus, 1992—; ret. La. Tech. U., 1992. Mem. Am. Math. Soc., Math. Assn. Am., Soc. Indsl. and Applied Math., Sigma Xi. Home: 209 E Louisiana Ave Ruston LA 71270-4471

MAXFIELD, PETER C., state legislator, law educator, lawyer; b. 1941. AB, Regis Coll., 1963; JD, U. Denver, 1966; LLM, Harvard U., 1968. Bar: Colo. 1966, Wyo. 1969. Trial atty. Dept. Justice, 1966-67; assoc. Hindry, Erickson & Meyer, Denver, 1968-69; asst. prof. U. Wyo. Coll. Law, 1969-72, assoc. prof., 1972-76, prof., 1976-96, dean, 1979-87, prof. emeritus, 1996—; vis. assoc. prof. U. N.Mex., 1972-73; Raymond F. Rice Disting. prof. U. Kans., 1984; Chapman Vis. Disting. prof., U. Tulsa, 1987; vis. prof. U. Utah, 1992. Coord. Wyo. State Planning, 1988-89; spl. asst. Gov. Wyo. 1989-90; Dem. nominee U.S. Ho. Reps., 1990; mem. Wyo. Environ. Quality Coun., 1991-93; mem. Wyo. Senate, Laramie, 1993-97. Mem. Order St. Ives, Omicron Delta Kappa, Pi Delta Phi. Author: (with Bloomenthal) Cases and Materials on the Federal Income Taxation of Natural Resources, 1971, 72, 77; (with Houghton) Taxation of Mining Operations, 1973, 76; (with Trelease and Dietrich) Natural Resources Law on American Indian Lands, 1977. Home: 3501 Grays Gable Rd Laramie WY 82070 Office: U Wyo Coll Law PO Box 3035 Laramie WY 82071-3035

MAXIMOS (MAXIMOS DEMETRIOS AGHIORGOUSSIS), bishop; b. Callimassia, Chios, Greece, Mar. 5, 1935; s. Evanghelos G. and Lemonia G. (Rythianou) A. Licentiate, Patriarchal Sch. Theology, Halki, 1957; Baccalaureate, U. Louvain, Belgium, 1964, Th.D., 1964. Ordained to ministry Greek Orthodox Ch., 1957; chaplain U. Louvain, 1957-64; pastor chs. Brussels, Rome, Brookline, Mass., Manchester and Newport, N.H., 1960-78; observer-del. II Vatican Council, 1964-65; chaplain Holy Cross Sem., Brookline, 1967-76; prof. systematic theology Holy Cross Sch. Theology, Brookline, 1967-79, Christ Savior Sem., Johnstown, Pa., from 1979; bishop Greek Orthodox Diocese Pitts., 1979—; mem. Orthodox-Roman Cath. Consultation, from 1967; v.p. Nat. Council Chs. Christ U.S., 1979-81; ecumenical officer Greek Orthodox Archdiocese N. and S. Am., 1978-79, chmn. synodal coms. ecumenical affairs, spiritual renewal and youth, from 1979. Author articles in field. Mem. Orthodox Theol. Soc. Am., AAUP, Christian Assos. Pitts., Pa. Council Chs., W.Va. Council Chs., Helicon Cultural Soc. Office: Greek Orthodox Diocese Pittsburgh 5201 Ellsworth Ave Pittsburgh PA 15232-1421 *My ministry is such that it requires a total commitment to its goals, but first of all a total commitment to Christ. In my childhood, I was fortunate to be guided by excellent parents and grandparents, who gave me not only the necessary security and stability, but also the inspiration to imitate their personal commitment to the Lord. I fully trust in the grace of the Lord, but I also have always accepted my responsibility for everything I have done.**

MAXIMOVICH, MICHAEL JOSEPH, chemist, consultant; b. Akron, Ohio, Mar. 3, 1932; s. Michael Stephen and Josephine Anna (Salzwimmer) M. BS, Kent State U., 1958, MS, 1964. Rsch. chemist PPG Industries, Barberton, Ohio, 1964-69; sr. devel. engr. Goodyear Chems., Akron, 1969-80; sr. rsch. chemist Polymer Industries, Stanford, Conn., 1980-82, Mooney Chems., Cleve., 1982-84; cons. All-Chem Techs., Lakewood, Ohio, 1984—. Pres. St. Mary Holy Name Soc., Akron, 1978-80, Akron Deanery Holy Name Soc., 1978-80; del. Cleve. Holy Name Soc., 1978-80. With USN, 1950-54. Mem. Am. Chem. Soc., Assn. Cons. Chemists and Chem. Engrs. Republican. Roman Catholic. Achievements include patents for liquid phase hydrofluorination of alkynes, for polyglycol carbonates using CO2 and catalysts, for water borne styrene-acrylates; first proof of the mechanism of the Schmidt Reaction of Substituted Acetophenones. Home and Office: 1060 Nathan St Akron OH 44307

MAXMAN, SUSAN ABEL, architect; b. Columbus, Ohio, Dec. 30, 1938; d. Richard Jack Abel and Gussie (Brenner) Seiden; children: Andrew Frankel, Thomas Frankel, Elizabeth Frankel; m. William H. Maxman; children: Melissa, Abby, William Jr. Student, Smith Coll., 1960; MArch., U. Pa., 1977; HHD, Ball State U., 1993, U. Detroit Mercy, 1997. Registered profl. architect, Pa., Ohio, N.J., N.Y., Md., W.Va., Va., Maine, Mo. Project designer Kopple Sheward & Day, Phila., 1978-80; ptnr. Maxman & Sutphin, Phila., 1980-83; prin. Susan Maxman Architects, Phila., 1984—; chmn. bd. overseers Grad. Sch. Fine Arts U. Pa.; bd. dirs. Found. Arch. Works include design of Women's Humane Soc. Animal Shelter, Bensalem, Pa. (Northeastern Sustainable Energy Assn.'s Comml. Bldg. award, 1994, Metal Constrn. Assn. award 1995), Camp Tweedale-Freedom Valley, Girl Scouts USA (AIA honor award, 1991), restoration Vernon House (honorable mention Remodeling Mag.), Germantown, Robert Lewis House (McArthur award 1985), Phila., Restoration Pennock Farmstead (Grand Prize Nat. Trust Historic Preservation 1995), Julia DeBurgos Biligual Middle Sch., Phila., Feasibility Study and renovations Old Main Complex, Kutztown U., Pa., Chestnut Hill Nat. Bank, Phila., Nat. Environ. Edn. Ctr. at John Heinz Nat. Wildlife Refuge, Tinicum. Mem. Eco-Efficiency Task Force Pres. Coun. Sustainable Devel., Urban Land Inst.; bd. dirs. Alliance to Save Energy, Preservation Alliance, Taliesin. Recipient Disting. Dau. Pa. award Gov. Tom Ridge, 1995, Excellence citation Engring. News Record, Shattering the Glass Ceiling award Women's Nat. Dem. Club, Mayor's commendation City Phila., citation Pa. Ho. Reps.; named to Pa. Honor Roll of Women, Pa. Commn. for Women, 1996, named 1 of Pa.'s Best 50 Women in Bus. 1996. Mem. AIA (nat. pres. 1993), Pa. Women's Forum, Forum Exec. Women, Carpenter's Co. Phila. Avocations: swimming, gardening. Office: 123 S 22nd St Philadelphia PA 19103-4335

MAXON, DON CARLTON, construction company executive, mining company executive; b. Downers Grove, Ill., Dec. 23, 1914; s. Norman T. and Agnes M. (Matteson) M.; m. Mary T. Quirk, June 14, 1941; children: Maureen, Don, Paul, Anne, Lee; m. Ella Luanne Roy, Dec. 10, 1971; 1 stepchild, Tom Roy. Student pub. schs., Barrington, Ill. Founder, pres. Maxon Constrn. Co., Barrington, 1936, Gen. Mining & Devel. Co., Santa Fe, N.Mex., 1967—, U.S. Communities S.A. Panama, 1974, Taipei, Taiwan, 1986—, Carson City, NA, 1989—, Bonanza Mines Internat., Carson City, NA, 1987; rancher; internat. fin. cons. Fiduciary Banks, London, Paris, Geneva, mem. pres.'s club. Pres. Johnson and Kennedy; mem. Pockets of Poverty Commn.; founder City of Streamwood, Ill., 1954, City of Green Valley, Ariz., 1963. With Seabees, USN, 1942-45. Recipient awards for designing family communities of Streamwood, Barrington Woods, Ill. and Trout Valley, Ill., Parents' mag., 1953, 59, 60; Tenn. Squire. Mem. Nat. Assn. Home Builders (Nat. Homes Pres.'s Land Planning first place award 1954), Gov.'s Club Ariz. Democrat. Roman Catholic. Rsh. on methods for testing and extracting gold from complex ores and rsch. to create the finest possible environment for quality of life and sci. applications of all disciplines needed for a self contained city of 150,000 population; builder U.S. Gypsum Co. Rsch. Village, Barrington. Home: 2586 E Avenida De Maria Tucson AZ 85718-3056

MAXSON, LINDA ELLEN, biologist, educator; b. N.Y.C., Apr. 24, 1943; d. Albert and Ruth (Rosenfeld) Resnick; m. Richard Dey Maxson, June 13, 1964; 1 child, Kevin. BS in Zoology, San Diego State U., 1964, MA in Biology, 1966; PhD in Genetics, U. Calif. and San Diego State U., 1973. Instr. biology San Diego State U., 1966-68; tchr. gen. sci. San Diego Unified Sch. Dist., 1968-69; instr. biochemistry U. Calif., Berkeley, 1974; asst. prof. zoology, dept. genetics and devel. U. Ill., Urbana-Champaign, 1974-76, asst. prof. dept. genetics, devel. and ecology, ethology & evolution, 1976-79, assoc. prof., 1979-84, prof., 1984-87, prof. ecology, ethology and evolution, 1987-88; prof., head dept. biology Pa. State U., State College, 1988-94; assoc. vice-chancellor acad. affairs/dean undergrad. acad. affairs, prof. ecology and evolutionary biology U. Tenn., Knoxville, 1995—; exec. officer biology programs Sch. Life Scis., U. Ill., 1981-86, assoc. dir. acad. affairs, 1984-86, dir. campus honors program, 1985-88; vis. prof. ecology and evolutionary biology U. Calif., Irvine, 1988; mem. adv. panel rsch. tng. groups behavioral biol. scis. NSF, 1990-94. Author: Genetics: A Human Perspective, 3d edit., 1992; edtl. bd. Molecular Biology Evolution, Amphibia/Reptilia; exec. editor Biochem. Sys. & Ecology, 1993—; contbr. numerous articles to scientific jours. Recipient Disting. Alumni award San Diego State U., 1989, Disting. Herpetologist award Herpetologists' League, 1993. Fellow AAAS; mem. Am. Men and Women in Sci., Am. Genetics Assn. (coun. 1994-96), Soc. for Study of Amphibians and Reptiles (pres. 1991), Internat. Herpetol. Com., Soc. Study Evolution, Soc. Systematic Biology, Soc. Molecular Biology and Evolution (sec. 1992-95, treas. 1992-94), Am. Soc. Ichthyologists and Herpetologists, Am. Soc. Zoologists, Herpetologists League, Phi Beta Kappa. Home: 409 Boxwood Sq Knoxville TN 37919-6628 Office: U Tenn 505 Andy Holt Twr Knoxville TN 37996-0154

MAXTED, WILLIAM C., dean; b. Rome, N.Y., Oct. 12, 1928; m. Claire Cody Maxted (wid. 1995); children: William C., Jr., Ann Marie, Gerard Edward. BS cum laude, Georgetown U., 1950; MD cum laude, Georgetown U. Sch. of Medicine, 1954. Diplomate Am. Bd. Urology. Intern Mercy Hosp., Buffalo, N.Y., 1954-55; asst. resident in pediatrics Georgetown Med. Ctr., Washington, 1957-58, resident in urology, 1958-61, instr. in surgery, 1961-65, asst. prof. of surgery, 1965, assoc. prof. of surgery, 1969-79, prof. surgery, 1979—, dir. divsn. urology, 1976-89, chief of urology, 1976-89, acad. dean, 1989—; cons. for urology to chief, Aeromed. Stds. Divsn., Office of Aviation Medicina, FAA, 1972-90; cons. FDA, 1979-90, VA, 1976—, Dept. of Army, Walter Reed Army Hosp., 1979-80, Dept. of Navy, Nat. Naval Med. Ctr., Bethesda, Md., 1979-90, others; numerous coms., speaker. Mem. Georgetown Clin. Soc. (sec.-treas., v.p. and pres. 1971-75), Washington Urology Soc. (pres. 1978-79), Am. Urologic Assn., Mid-Atlantic Sect. of Am. Urologic Assn., Am. Coll. Surgeons, Soc. Univ. Urologists, Alpha Omega Alpha, others. Office: Office of Acad Dean Georgetown U Sch Medicine Washington DC 20037

MAXWELL, ANDERS JOHN, investment banker; b. San Francisco, Oct. 3, 1946; s. John L. and Deborah A. M.; divorced; children: Lauren A., Colin A., Ian W., Erin C., Ryan N. BArch, U. Calif.-Berkeley, 1969; MBA, U. Pa., 1971. Analyst Gen. Electric Co., 1971-73; v.p. Gen. Electric Credit Corp., Stamford, Conn., 1973-83; mng. dir. Dean Witter Reynolds Inc., N.Y.C., 1983-87; v.p. Kidder Peabody & Co., Inc., N.Y.C., 1987-88; prin. L.F. Rothschild & Co., N.Y.C., 1988; v.p. Smith Barney, Harris Upham & Co., Inc., 1989-91, Lazard Frères & Co., N.Y.C., 1991-92; ptnr. Benedetto, Gartland & Greene, N.Y.C., 1992-94; v.p., gen. mgr. GE Capital Corp., Stamford, Conn., 1994-96; dir. Smith Barney Inc., N.Y.C., 1997—. Served to capt. U.S Army, 1971. Office: Smith Barney Inc 390 Greenwich St Fl 5 New York NY 10013-2309

MAXWELL, ARTHUR EUGENE, oceanographer, marine geophysicist, educator; b. Maywood, Calif., Apr. 11, 1925; s. John Henry and Nelle Irene (Arnold) M.; m. Colleen O'Leary, July 1, 1988; children: Delle, Eric, Lynn, Brett, Gregory, Sam Wade, Henry Wade. BS in Physics with honors, N.Mex. State U., 1949; MS in Oceanography, Scripps Instn. Oceanography, 1952, PhD in Oceanography, 1959. Jr. rsch. geophysicist Scripps Instn. Oceanography, La Jolla, Calif., 1950-55; head oceanographer Office Naval Rsch., Washington, 1955-59, head br. geophysics, 1959-65; assoc. dir. Woods Hole (Mass.) Oceanographic Instn., 1965-69, dir. rsch., 1969-71, provost, 1971-81; prof. dept. geol. scis., dir. Inst. Geophysics U. Tex., Austin, 1982-94, prof. emeritus dept. geol. sci., 1994—; bd. dirs. Palisades Geophys. Inst. Corp.; chmn. bd. govs. planning com. deep earth sampling, 1968-70, chmn. exec. com. deep earth sampling, 1971-72, 78-79, 91-92; mem. joint U.S./USSR com. for coop. studies of the world ocean NAS/NRC, 1973-80, chmn. U.S. nat. com. to Internat. Union Geodesy and Geophysics, 1976-80, vice chmn. outer continental shelf/environ. studies rev. com., 1986-93; chmn. U.S. nat. com. on geology NAS, 1979-83, chmn. geophysics rsch. bd. geophysics study com., 1982-87; nat. sea grant rev. panel NOAA, 1982-85, 90—; mem. vis. com. Rosenstiel Sch. Marine and Atmospheric Studies U. Miami, 1982-86, dept. physics N.Mex. State U., 1986-94; acad. adv. com. Com. Exch. CIA, 1983-96; mem. Gulf of Mexico Regional Marine Rsch. Bd., 1992-96. Editor: The Sea, Vol. 4, Parts I and II, 1970; editorial adv. bd. Oceanus, 1981-92; contbr. articles to profl. jours. Chmn. tech. adv. com. Navy Thresher Search, 1963; mem. Mass. Gov.'s. Adv. Com. on Sci. and Tech., 1965-71. With USN, 1942-46, PTO. Recipient Meritorious Civilian Svc. award Chief Naval Rsch., 1958, Albatross award AMSOC, 1959, Superior Civilian Svc. award Assn. Sec. of Navy, 1963, Disting. Civilian Svc. award Sec. of Navy, 1964, Disting. Alumni award N.Mex. State U., 1965, Bruun Meml. Lecture award Intergovtl. Oceanographic Commn., 1969, Outstanding Centennial Alumnus award N. Mex. State U., 1988. Fellow Am. Geophys. Union (pres. 1976-78, pres. oceanography sect. 1970-72); mem. Marine Tech. Soc. (charter, pres. 1981-82), Cosmos Club. Achievements include research in heat flow through the ocean floor, in structure and tectonics of the sea floor. Home: 8115 Two Coves Dr Austin TX 78730-3122 Office: U Tex Inst for Geophysics 8701 N Mo Pac Expy Austin TX 78759-8345

MAXWELL, BARBARA SUE, systems analyst consultant, educator; b. Bklyn., Feb. 22, 1950; d. Vincent and Esther Alice (Hansen) M. BA in Math Edn., Rider Coll., 1972; postgrad., Montclair State U., 1973. Cert. secondary tchr., N.J. Math tchr. Westwood (N.J.) H.S., 1973-80; programmer Prudential Ins. Co., Roseland, N.J., 1980-81; programmer, analyst Grand Union, Paramus, N.J., 1981-82; cons. Five Techs., Montvale, N.J., 1987-90; project mgr. Info. Sci., Inc., Montvale, 1982-84, cons., project mgr., 1987-90; pres. B. Maxwell Assoc., Inc., Westwood, N.J., 1990—; guest spkr. Info. Sci., Best of Am., Computer Assocs. B.A.C. Contbr. articles to profl. jours. Mem. Westwood Heritage Soc. Mem. NAFE, APA (v.p. N.J. chpt. 1996), Human Resource Sys. Profls., N.J. Info., Am. Payroll Assn. Republican. Lutheran. Avocations: travel, reading, gardening, hiking.

MAXWELL, BRYCE, engineer,educator; b. Glen Cove, N.Y., July 26, 1919; s. Howard W. and Helen (Young) W.; m. Margurite Kulsar, June 5, 1953 (dec. 1974); children: Bryce Jr., Margaret H., Stephen H. B.S. in Engring, Princeton, 1943, M.S. in Engring, 1948. Rsch. assoc. Princeton U., 1948-53, asst. prof., 1953-57, assoc. prof., 1957-66, asst. dean Sch. Engring., 1962-66, prof. chem. engring. Sch. Engring., 1966-68, prof. chem. engring. for polymer studies, chmn. polymer materials program, 1968-85, prof. emeritus, 1985—; pres. Maxwell Instrument Inc., 1992—; bd. dirs. U.S. Rubber Reclaiming Co., Inc., Vicksburg, Miss., 1962-80; cons. several chem. cos. Founding editor: Transactions of the Society of Rhealogy, 1957; editl. adv. bd.: Jour. of Polymer Sci. and Polymer Sci. and Engring., 1960-85; contbr. more than 100 articles to profl. publs.; patentee 30 patents in field. Trustee Plastics Inst. Am. Served with USNR, 1943-46. Recipient Honor Scroll N.J. Inst. Chemists, 1981. Mem. ASME (life), ASTM, Soc. Rheology, Soc. Plastics Engrs. (gold medal and internat. award in plastics sci. and engring. 1976, fellow 1992), Sigma Xi. Achievements include research and publication in polymer viscoelastic behavior, polymer melt rheology; inventor elastic melt extruder, orthogonal rheometer, melt elasticity tester. Home: Rossmoor 686A Yarborough Way Jamesburg NJ 08831-2012

MAXWELL, CARLA LENA, dancer, choreographer, educator; b. Glendale, Calif., Oct. 25, 1945; d. Robert and Victoria (Carbone) M. Student, Bennington Coll., 1963-64; B.S., Juilliard Sch. Music, 1967. Mem. Jose Limón Dance Co., N.Y.C., 1965; prin. dancer Jose Limón Dance Co., 1969—, acting artistic dir., 1977-78, artistic dir., 1978—; lectr., tchr. in field. Soloist, Louis Falco Dance Co., 1967-71, Harkness Festival at N.Y.C. Delacorte Theater, from 1964, artist-in-residence, Gettysburg Coll., 1970, Luther Coll., Decorah, Iowa, 1971, U. Idaho, 1973, guest tchr., performer, Centre Internat. de la Danse, Vichy, France, 1976; choreographer: Function, 1970, Improvisations on a Dream, 1970, A Suite of Psalms, 1973, Homage to José Linón, Place Spirit, 1975, Aadvark Brothers; Schwartz and Columbo Present Please Don't Stone The Clowns, 1975, Blue Warrier, 1975, Sonata, 1980, Keeping Stil, Mountain, 1987; featured in Carlota, Dances For Isadora, La Malinche, Comedy, The Moor's Pavane, The Winged, There Is A Time, The Shakers, Brandenburg Concerto No. 4, Trnaslucence, Caviar, Missa Brevis, Day on Earth, Two Ecstatic Themes, A Choreographic Offering, The Exiles, Sacred Conversations; toured East and West Africa, 1969. N.Y. State Cultural Council grantee, 1971; recipient Dance Mag. award, 1995. Home: 7 Great Jones St New York NY 10012-1135 Office: Jose Limon Dance Ctr 611 Broadway Fl 9 New York NY 10012-2608*

MAXWELL, DAVID E., academic executive, educator; b. N.Y.C., Dec. 2, 1944; s. James Kendrick and Gertrude Sarah (Bernstein) M.; children: Justin Kendrick, Stephen Edward. BA, Grinnell Coll., 1966; MA, Brown U., 1968, PhD, 1974. Instr. Tufts U., Medford, Mass., 1971-74, asst. prof., 1974-78, assoc. prof. Russian lang. and lit., 1978-89, dean undergrad. studies, 1981-89; pres. Whitman Coll., Walla Walla, Wash., 1989-93; dir. Nat. Fgn. Lang. Ctr., Washington, 1993—; chmn. steering com. Coop. Russian Lang. Program, Leningrad, USSR, 1981-86, chmn. 1986-90; cons. Coun. Internat. Ednl. Exchange, 1974—, bd. dirs., 1988-92, 93-94, vice chair, 1991-92, cons. Internat. Rsch. Exchanges, 1976—; mem. adv. bd. Israeli Lang. Policy Inst. Contbr. articles to scholarly jours. Fulbright fellow, 1970-71, Brown U., 1966-67, NDEA Title IV, 1967-70; recipient Lillian Leibner award Tufts U., 1979; citation Grad. Sch. Arts & Scis., Brown U., 1991. Mem. MLA, Am. Coun. Edn. (commn. on internat. edn., pres.'s coun. on internat. edn.), Am. Assn. Advancement of Slavic Studies, Am. Assn. Tchrs. Slavic and E. European Langs., Assn. Am. Colls., Am. Assn. Higher Edn., Am. Coun. Tchg. Fgn. Langs., Brown U. Alumni Assn., Phi Beta Kappa. Democrat. Avocations: tennis, running, music. Office: Nat Fgn Lang Ctr 1619 Massachusetts Ave NW Washington DC 20036-2213

MAXWELL, DAVID OGDEN, former government official and financial executive; b. Phila., May 16, 1930; s. David Farrow and Emily Ogden (Nelson) M.; m. Joan Clark Paddock, Dec. 14, 1968. BA, Yale U., 1952; LLB, Harvard U., 1955. Bar: Pa. 1955, D.C. 1955. From assoc. to ptnr. Obermayer, Rebmann, Maxwell & Hippel, Phila., 1959-67; ins. commr. State of Pa., 1967-69, adminstrn. and budget sec., 1969-70; gen. counsel HUD, Washington, 1970-73; pres., CEO Ticor Mortgage Ins. Co., 1973-81; CEO Fed. Nat. Mortgage Assn., Washington, 1981-91; bd. dirs. Corp. Ptnrs., L.P., Fin Security Assurance Holdings, Ltd., Potomac Electric Power Co., Salomon, Inc., SunAm., Inc.; trustee Enterprise Found., European Inst., Urban Inst., Brookings Instn. Bd. dirs. Sta. WETA-TV; mem. trustees coun. Nat. Gallery Art. With USNR, 1955-59. Home: 3525 Springland Ln NW Washington DC 20008-3119 Office: 5335 Wisconsin Ave NW Ste 440 Washington DC 20015-2030

MAXWELL, DELORES YOUNG, elementary school principal; b. Kansas City, Kans., Dec. 8, 1948; d. Edward and Zelma (Starks) Young; m. Donald L. Maxwell, Sept. 26, 1969; children: Dominique N., Donald E. BA in Elem. Edn., Cen. Mo. State U., 1971; MA in Elem. Edn., Webster Coll., 1977; Edn. Spec. in Elem. Adminstrn., Cen. Mo. State U., 1987. Cert. reading, adult basic edn., Mo. Tchr. Kansas City (Mo.) Sch. Dist., 1972-81, lang. specialist, chpt. I liaision, 1981-83, instrnl. asst., 1983-86, elem. prin., 1986—; bd. dirs. Nat. Coun. Youth Leadership; presenter Nat. Assn. of Partners in Edn., Washington, 1988. Active NAACP, Kansas City, Mo., 1970-73, Peple United to Serve Humanity, Kansas City, 1985-88, v.p. women's com., chmn. aucion com.; attendance, code conduct com. Grandview (Mo.) Sch. Dist., 1986; chmn. fund raising com. Kans. City Chpt. Jack n' Jill Assn., 1988-92; chmn. svcs. to youth, co-chmn. project lead chaplain, com. mem. by laws com. Jackson County Mo. Chpt. Links Inc., 1988—, fundraising com. Elect Emanuel Cleaver Mayor Kansas City, Mo., 1991; active Palestine Missionary Bapt. Ch., 1973. Sch. Recipient Small Grant Partnership award Kansas City Sch. Dist., 1990-91, 91-92, 92-93. Mem. ASCD, Am. Fedn. Tchrs. (chmn. grievance com., mem. exec. bd. 1972-86), Internat. Reading Assn., Kansas City Adminstrs. Assn. (chmn. legis. com. 1987—), Mo. Assn. Elem. Sch. Prins. (Mo. dist. rep. legis. com. 1986—), Kans. City Assn. Elem. Sch. Prins. (pres. elect 1988, pres. 1989-90, bd. mem. 1990), Greater Kansas City Leadership Acad. U. Mo. (bd. mem.), Phi Delta Kappa. Democrat. Avocations: reading, sewing, traveling, visiting museums. Office: Kansas City Sch Dist 1211 Mcgee St Kansas City MO 64106-2416

MAXWELL, DIANA KATHLEEN, early childhood education educator; b. Seminole, Okla., Dec. 16, 1949; d. William Hunter and ImoJean (Mahurin) Rivers; m. Clarence Estel Maxwell, Jly 3, 1969; children: Amanda Hunter, Alexandra Jane. BS, U. Md., 1972; M of Secondary Edn., Boston U., 1974; PhD, U. Md., 1980. Cert. tchr., counselor, Tex. Tchr. Child Garden Presch., Adelphi, Md., 1969-71; tchr., dir. PREP Edn. Ctr., Heidelberg, Germany, 1972-74; tchr. N.E. Ind. Schs. Larkspur, San Antonio, 1974-77, 89-90, Headstart, Boyds, Md., 1978; dir., founder First Bapt. Child Devel. Ctr., Bryan, Tex., 1982-84; instr. English lang. Yonsei Med. Ctr., Seoul, Republic of Korea, 1985-87; asst. prof. Incarnate Word Coll., San Antonio, 1987-89; tchr. kindergarten Fairfax County Pub. Schs., Kings Park, Va., 1990-94; tchr. Encino Park, San Antonio, Tex., 1994-95; lectr. U. Tex., San Antonio, 1995-96; multi-age tchr. Ft. Sam Houston Elem. Sch., San Antonio, 1996—; cons. Sugar N'Spice Child Devel. Ctr., Kilgore, Tex., 1980-90; bd. dirs. Metro Area Assn. for Childhood Edn. Internat., 1991-93. Author: (book revs.) Childhood Education, 1979, 80, 92. Block chairperson March of Dimes, 1991, 92, 93, Am. Heart Assn., Fairfax, Fa., 1991, 92, Am. Diabetes Assn., Fairfax, 1992; judge speaking com. Burke Optomists, 1992, 931 judge writing competition N.E. Ind. Sch. Dist., 1996; sec. Cole H.S. Cougar Club, Ft. Sam Houston, San Antonio, 1996-97; Bible tchr. 1st Bapt. Ch., Alexandria, Va., 1992-94; tchr. kindergarten Trinity Bapt. Ch., San Antonio, 1995—. Named one of Outstanding Young Women of Am., 1983; Md. fellow State of Md., 1978, 79; grantee San Antonio, 1990, Springfield, 1991. Mem. ASCD, Internat. Reading Assn., Assn. Profl. Tchr. Educators, Edn. Internat., Assn. for Childhood Edn. Internat. (v.p., pres.-elect), Tex. Assn. Childhood Edn., Bexar County and Surrounding Areas Assn. Childhood Edn. Avocations: oriental brush painting, singing, collecting butterflies, children/teacher advocate. Home: 106 Artillery Post Rd San Antonio TX 78234 Office: U Tex Divsn Edn 6900 North Loop 1604 San Antonio TX 78249-0616

MAXWELL, DONALD MALCOLM, college president, minister; b. Watford, Eng., Apr. 6, 1934; s. Arthur S. and Rachel Elizabeth (Joyce) M.; m. Eileen J. Bolander, Aug. 25, 1955; children: Wendy E. Maxwell Henderson, D. Kevin. BA in Theology and Biblical Langs., Pacific Union Coll., 1956; MA in Systematic Theology, Andrews U., 1958; PhD in Biblical Studies New Testament, Drew U., 1968. Ordained to ministry Seventh-Day Adventist Ch., 1960. Pastor No. Calif. Conf. Seventh-Day Adventists, Oakland, Calif., 1956-64; instr. in religion Union Coll., Lincoln, Nebr., 1964-65; prof. in religion Walla Walla Coll., College Place, Wash., 1965-78, v.p. acad. affairs, 1978-83; pres. Pacific Union Coll., Angwin, Calif., 1983—. Bd. trustees St. Helena Hosp., Deer Park, Calif., 1983—, Rio Lindo Acad., Healdsburg, Calif., 1983—; bd. dirs., membership com. Adventist Health Sys./West, Roseville, Calif., 1983—. Rockefeller fellow, 1967-68; Drew U. scholar, 1967-68; named Tchr. of Yr., Wash. State Auto Assn., 1971. Mem. Soc. Biblical Lit., Rotary. Avocations: golf, boating, gardening. Office: Pacific Union Coll 1 Angwin Ave Angwin CA 94508-9713

MAXWELL, DONALD STANLEY, publishing executive; b. L.A., May 30, 1930; s. Harold Stanley and Margaret (Trenam) M.; m. Martha Helen Winn, Dec. 5, 1952; children: Sylvia Louise, Cynthia Lynn, Bruce Stanley, Bradley Erl, Walter James, Wesley Richard, Amy Bernice. Student, Long Beach City Coll., 1948-50; BBA, Woodbury Coll., 1956; D of Bus. Adminstrn. (hon.), Woodbury U., 1991. CPA. Ptnr. Robert McDavid & Co. (CPAs), L.A., 1955-61; controller Petersen Pub. Co., L.A., 1961-68; v.p. fin. Petersen Pub. Co., 1969; controller L.A. Times, 1969-79; v.p. Los Angeles Times, 1977-79, v.p. fin., 1979-81; asst. treas. Times Mirror Co., 1971-82, v.p., controller, 1982-87, v.p., chief acctg. officer, 1987-93, v.p., 1993, exec. dir. fin. program, 1993-95; ret., 1995. Trustee Woodbury U., 1981—, chmn. bd. trustees, 1984-87. Served with AUS, 1950-52. Mem. Fin. Execs. Inst. (dir. 1979-82, pres. L.A. chpt. 1973-74), Internat. Newspaper Fin. Execs. (dir. 1978-82, pres. 1980-81), Am. Inst. CPAs, Calif. Soc. CPAs, Am. Horse Council, Internat. Arabian Horse Assn., Arabian Horse Assn. So. Calif., Friendly Hills Country Club. Republican. Baptist. Home: 2160 Le Flore Dr La Habra CA 90631-8020

MAXWELL, J. DOUGLAS, JR., chemical service company executive; b. Glen Cove, N.Y., Sept. 26, 1941; s. John Douglas M. and Marie Elise (Powers) Cummings; m. Hanne Agnete Kristensen, June 6, 1970; children: Scott Rogers, Samuel Douglas, Whitney Bodil. BA, Williams Coll., 1963; MBA, L.I.U., 1970. With Photocircuits Corp., Glen Cove, 1963-70; mgr. epuipment mktg. Chemco Techs., Inc., Glen Cove, 1970-76, treas., 1976-79, mng. dir., 1979-84, pres., 1984-89, also bd. dirs.; chmn. bd. dirs., chief exec. officer Empower Inc., Glen Cove, 1990—; dir. Kellmorgen Corp., Stamford, Conn., Slater Electric Corp., Glen Cove, First Nat. Bank L.I., Glen Head. Bd. dirs., v.p. Glen Cove Boys & Girls Club, 1970; bd. dirs., treas. L.I. Coun. on Alcoholism, Mineola, 1980; trustee Green Wood Cemetery, Bklyn., 1984, Green Vale Sch., Glen Head, 1986. Home: Cherry Ln Glen Head NY 11545-2216 Office: Chemco Tech Inc Charles St Glen Cove NY 11542-2957

MAXWELL, JACK ERWIN, manufacturing company executive; b. Cleve., July 17, 1926; s. Fred A. and Gertrude F. (Haug) M.; m. Martha Jane Miller, Dec. 28, 1966; children by previous marriage: Laura Jane, Fredric, Elizabeth Grant, Carla Moore, Linda Hanson. B.S., Case Inst. Tech., 1949; M.B.A., Harvard U., 1952. Indsl. engr. Lincoln Electric Co., Cleve., 1952-53; mgr. purchase analysis Ford Motor Co., Dearborn, Mich., 1953-57; v.p. Booz, Allen & Hamilton, Inc., Detroit, 1957-69; v.p. corp. devel. Am. Motors Corp., Detroit, 1969-71; v.p. adminstrn. Am. Motors Corp., 1971-76, v.p. non-automotive subsidiaries, 1976-79, v.p. diversified ops., 1979-80; chmn., pres. Wheel Horse Products, Inc., South Bend, Ind., 1974-80; chmn. Ingersoll Products Corp., Chgo., 1980-86; pres. Wellmax, Inc., 1976—. Served with USNR, 1944-46. Mem. Case Inst. Tech. Alumni Assn., Harvard Bus. Sch. Alumni Assn., Tau Beta Pi, Theta Tau. Clubs: Detroit Athletic, Economics, Chicago, Old Club. Home: 3541 Bradway Blvd Bloomfield Hills MI 48301-2409 Office: Ste 330 6905 Telegraph Rd Bloomfield Hills MI 48301-3160

MAXWELL, J.B., financial and marketing consultant; b. Clarksburg, W.Va., Sept. 30, 1944; s. J.B. and Martha (Hornor) M.; m. Valerie Ronson, Oct. 13, 1983; 1 child, Jennifer. BS, Salem (W.Va.) Coll., 1967; M of Mktg., Harvard U., 1970. Lic. in real estate sales, ins., secutities; registered commodity rep.; accredited mgmt. cons. and fin. planner; registered fin. planner, investment adv.; accredited asset mgmt. specialist. Exec. v.p. Textron Inc., Providence, 1968-71; pres. Martech Inc. and 6 other cos., Portland, Maine, 1968—; v.p. E.F. Hutton Co., Portland, 1976-83; 1st v.p. fin. planning Dean Witter Reymonds, Boston, 1983-90; pres. Planning Svcs. Corp., Boston, 1990-92; 1st v.p. Gruntal & Co., Inc., Boston, 1992—; Author handbooks, booklets and articles. Contbr. Portland Coll. Art, 1980-93. Bd. dirs. Wellness Inst., Boston, 1990-91. Recipient Bronze award Nat. Acad. Scis., 1962. Mem. Internat. Assn. for Fin. Planning, Am. Mgmt. Assns., Am. Mktg. Assn., Inst. Mgmt. Cons., World Affairs Coun., Nat. Assn. Security Dealers (formerly br. office mgr.), Boston C. of C., Rotary Internat. Avocations: golf, woodworking, travel, literature. Home: 9279 McCormack Sta Boston MA 02209-9279 Office: Gruntal & Co Inc One Post Office Sq Boston MA 02109-3400

MAXWELL, JOE, state senator; b. Kirksville, Mo., Mar. 17, 1957; s. Robert E. and Molly B. Maxwell; m. Sarah Maxwell; children: Megan, Shannon. BS in Secondary Edn., Social Studies, U. Mo., 1986, JD, 1990. Farmer Rush Hill, Mo., 1976-78; ptnr., operator Maxwell Svc., Laddonia, Mo., 1978-84; rural mail carrier U.S. Postal Svc., Rush Hill, 1980-84; out-state field coord. Travis Morrison's Campaign for State Auditor, Mo., 1986; Mo. state field coord. Richard Gephardt for Pres., 1986-87; atty. Mexico, Mo., 1992—; mem. Mo. Senate, 1990-94, 1994—; mem. Senate Appropriations, Commerce and Environment, Edn., Judiciary, Labor and Indsl. Rels., Pub. Health and Welfare coms.; vice chair Elections, Pensions and Vet.'s Affairs coms. Assoc. editor-in-chief Mo. Jour. of Dispute Resolution, 1989. Mem. Am. Legion, 1982—, adj. Post 510, 1982-84; mem. Young Dem. Clubs Mo., 1982—, jud. coun. Young Dems. Am., 1985, pres., 1984-87, 9th Congl. Dist. chmn., 1982; mem. Laddonia Bapt. Ch., 1975—, Sunday Sch. tchr., 1990-91, pulpit com.; bd. dirs. Handi-Shop Inc., Mexico, 1981-84, chmn. mfg. and mktg. com., 1982-84; bd. dirs. Boy Scouts Am. Troop 94, 1980-82. Recipient St. Louis Globe Dem. award for outstanding achievement, 1979, Cert. of Appreciation, Troop 94, Boy Scouts Am., 1982, Mo.'s Outstanding Male Young Dem. award, 1987, George B. Freeman award for outstanding svc., 1987, Appreciation award Mo. Bar, 1992, Mo. Ho. of Reps. Resolution # 624 for exceptional svc. Mo., 1987, Mo. State Senate Resolution # 382 for exceptional svc. Mo., 1987; named one of Outstanding Young Men of Am., 1983, 85. Mem. Moose, Jaycees (Laddonia chpt. pres. 1978-79, coord. Laddonia Area Blood Drive, coord. Laddonia City Clean-up Day, chmn. Mexico Soybean Festival 1989, chmn. Lenten Breakfast 1990, Presdl. award of honor 1979), Kappa Delta Pi, Golden Key Nat. Honor Soc. Office: State Senate Rm 329 Capitol Bldg Jefferson City MO 65101

MAXWELL, MARILYN JULIA, elementary education educator; b. Flint, Mich., Apr. 3, 1933; d. Clement Daniel and Gwendoline Mae (Evans) Rushlow; m. Dewey Theodore Maxwell, Apr. 22, 1965; 1 child, Bruce Dewey. Student, Baldwin-Wallace Coll., 1951-53; BS, U. Tenn., 1954-56, MEd, 1962. Cert. elem. edn. tchr.; lang. devel. specialist. Elem. tchr. Guy Selby Sch., Flint, Mich., 1956-58, Henry L. Barger Sch., Chattanooga, Tenn., 1958-63, Dept. of Def. Sch., Seville, Spain, 1963-65, Loma Vista Elem. Sch., Lompoc, Calif., 1965-66, Crestview Elem. Sch., Lompoc, 1966-68, LaHonda Elem. Sch., Lompoc, 1969—; lang. arts mentor tchr. Lompoc Unified Schs., 1985-86. Mem. Internat. Reading Assn., Nat. Coun. Tchrs. of Math., Calif. Tchrs. of English to Speakers of Other Langs., Nat. Trust for Hist. Preservation, Am. Fedn. Tchrs. Home: 4219 Centaur St Lompoc CA 93436-1229 Office: LaHonda Elem Sch 1213 N A St Lompoc CA 93436-3514

MAXWELL, NEAL A., church official; m. Colleen Hinckley; four children. B in Polit. Sci., M in Polit. Sci., U. Utah, LLD (hon.); LLD (hon.), Brigham Young U.; LittD (hon.), Westminster Coll.; HHD (hon.), Utah State U., Ricks Coll. Legis. asst. U.S. sen. Wallace F. Bennett, Utah; exec. v.p. U. Utah, Salt Lake City; various ch. positions including bishop Salt Lake City's Univ. Sixth Ward, mem. gen. bd. youth orgn., adult correlation com. and one of first Regional Reps. of the Twelve; elder Ch. Jesus Christ Latter Day Sts., Asst. to the Council of Twelve, 1974-76, mem. of Presidency of First Quorum of the Seventy, 1976-81, mem. Coun. of Twelve Apostles, 1981—. Mem. Quorum of the Twelve Ch. of Jesus Christ of Latter-Day Saints, Salt Lake City. Recipient Liberty Bell award Utah State Bar, 1967; named Pub. Adminstr. of Yr. Inst. Govt. Service Brigham Young U., 1973. Office: LDS Church Quorum of the Twelve 47 E South Temple Salt Lake City UT 84150-1005

MAXWELL, PATRICIA ANNE, writer; b. Winn Parish, La., Mar. 9, 1942; d. John Henry and Daisy Annette (Durbin) Ponder; m. Jerry Ronald Maxwell, Aug. 1, 1957; children: Jerry Ronald Jr., Richard Dale, Delinda Anne, Katherine Leigh. GED, 1960. Author (as Patricia Maxwell): Secret of Mirror House, 1970, Stranger At Plantation Inn, 1971, The Bewitching Grace, 1974, Notorious Angel, 1977, Night of the Candles, 1978, numerous others; (as Elizabeth Trehearne): Storm At Midnight, 1973; (as Patricia Ponder); Haven of Fear, 1977, Murder For Charity, 1977; (as Maxine Patrick): The Abducted Heart, 1979, numerous others; (as Jennifer Blake): Love's Wild Desire, 1977, Golden Fancy, 1980, Embrace and Conquer, 1981, Royal Seduction, 1983, others. Recipient Frank Waters award for fiction excellence, 1997, Frank Waters award for Writing Excellence, 1997, Hist. Romance Author of Yr. award Romantic Times Mag., 1985; inducted into Romance Hall of Fame, 1995. Mem. Nat. League Am. Penwomen, Romance Writers of Am. (charter, Golden Treasure award 1987), Novelists, Inc. Home: PO Box 9218 Quitman LA 71268-9218

MAXWELL, RAYMOND ROGER, accountant; b. Parmer County, Tex., Jan. 7, 1918; s. Frederick W. and Hazel Belle (Rogers) M.; m. Jeanne Hollarn, June 16, 1945 (dec. Dec. 1987); children: Donald R., Bruce Edward, Sabrina G. Ed.B., Western Ill. State Tchrs Coll., 1941; MBA in Acctg., U. Fla., 1949; postgrad., UCLA, 1965-68. CPA, Fla., Calif. Asst. to bus. mgr. Western Ill. State Tchrs. Coll., Macomb, 1939-41; apprentice acct. Charles H. Lindfors, CPA, Ft. Lauderdale, Fla., 1946-48; acct./auditor Frederic Dunn-Rankin & Co. CPA, Miami, Fla., 1948-49; CPA staff Charles Costar, CPA, Miami, 1951; resident auditor/CPA prin. Raymond R. Maxwell CPA, Ft. Lauderdale, 1951-56; supt. pub. instrn. Broward County, Ft. Lauderdale, 1956-61; staff asst. in fin. North Am. Aviation, Inc., El Segundo, Calif., 1961-65; tchr. Calif. Polytechnic, 1967; acctg. prin. Raymond R. Maxwell, CPA, Whittier, Calif., 1968—; tchr. Calif. State U., Fullerton, 1989; part-time rsch. asst. UCLA, 1965, teaching asst., 1966, 67; instr. Calif. Poly., 1967. Active precinct election bds., Whittier, L.A. County, 1989; 1st reader First Ch. of Christ, Scientist, Whittier, 1990-92, 96—, exec. bd., 1989, exec. bd. chmn., 1993, participant Bible Explorations, 1991-92. 1st lt. USAAF, 1942-46. Named Eagle Scout. Republican. Avocations: dancing, swimming, computers. Office: 8235 Painter Ave Whittier CA 90602-3108 *One, with God, is a majority.*

MAXWELL, RICHARD ANTHONY, retail executive; b. N.Y.C., Apr. 1, 1933; s. Arthur William and Mary Ellen (Winestock) M.; m. Jacqueline Ann Creamer, Oct. 27, 1962. Student NYU, 1957-58, Acad. Advanced Traffic, 1959. Import ops. mgr. Associated Merchandising Corp., N.Y.C., 1950-52, 56-65; v.p. Associated Dry Goods Corp., N.Y.C., 1965-86, sr. v.p. mktg., 1980-82, exec. v.p. mktg., 1982-86; pres. A.D.G. Export Mktg., Florence, Italy, 1982-86; pres. Assoc. Dry Goods Ltd., Hong Kong, 1983-86; pres. Inter Textyle Corp., 1987-89; with Matol Botanical Internat., Ltd.; exec. v.p. Matol World Corp., Montreal, Can., 1992-94; dir. Matol Botanical New Zealand, 1994-96; v.p. internat. opers. L'Aprina Internat., Inc., 1994-96; chief internat. officer Camelot Concept Co., Montreal, Can., 1995-96; CFO Showcase Prodns., Phoenix, Ariz., 1996; exec. v.p. Harmony House Internat., Phoenix, 1996—; mem. industry sector adv. com. Dept. Commerce, 1984-93. Mem. shippers adv. com. Nat. Maritime Coun. Served with USAF, 1952-56. Recipient Silver medal for contbns. to trade expansion Republic of China, 1980; appt. to rank of comdr. in Order of Merit in recognition of improvement of trade between Italy and U.S., Republic of Italy, 1985. Mem. Am. Assn. Exporters and Importers (past pres., dir.), Shippers Conf. Greater N.Y. (past pres., dir.), Nat. Retail Mchts. Assn. (vice chmn. fgn. trade com.), Nat. Com. Internat. Trade Documentation (past vice chmn. gen. bus. com.), Transp. Assn. Am., Italy-Am. C. of C. (past pres., dir.), Am. Soc. of Italian Legion of Merit (dir.). Home and Office: 2408 Stag Run Blvd Clearwater FL 34625-1832

MAXWELL, RICHARD CALLENDER, lawyer, educator; b. Mpls., Oct. 7, 1919; s. Bertram Wayburn and Blossom (Callender) M.; m. Frances Lida McKay, Jan 27, 1942; children—Richard Callender, John McKay. B.S.L., U. Minn., 1941, LL.B., 1947; LL.D. (hon.), Calif. Western U., 1983; LLD (hon.), Southwestern U., 1993. Assoc. prof. U. N.D., 1947-49; assoc. prof. U. Tex., 1949-51, prof., 1951-53; counsel Amerada Petroleum Corp., 1952-53; prof. UCLA, 1953-81; dean UCLA (Sch. Law), 1959-69, Connell prof., 1979-81, Connell prof. emeritus, 1981—; Chadwick prof. Duke U. Sch. Law, 1981-89, Chadwick prof. emeritus, 1989—; vis. prof. Columbia U., 1955; vis. Alumni prof. U. Minn., 1970-71; Fulbright lectr. Queen's U., No. Ireland, 1970; vis. Ford Found. prof. U. Singapore, 1971; Thompson prof. U. Colo., 1982; vis. prof. Hastings Coll. Law, 1976, Duke U., 1979-80, U. Tex., 1985; pres. Minn. Law Rev., 1946; chmn. Council Legal Edn. Opportunity, 1971-72; pres. Assn. Am. Law Schs., 1972; chmn. adv. com. law Fulbright Program, 1971-74, chmn. adv. com. U.K., 1974-77; mem. com. on gas prodn. opportunities NRC, 1977-78; mem. law sch. editorial and adv. bd. West Pub. Co., 1971-94. Author: (with S. A. Riesenfeld) Cases and Materials on Modern Social Legislation, 1950, (with H.R. Williams and C.J. Meyers) Cases on Oil and Gas Law, 1956, 6th edit., (with Stephen F. Williams, Patrick H. Martin, Bruce M. Kramer), 1992, (with S. A. Riesenfeld) California Cases on Security Transactions, 1957, 4th edit. (with S.A. Riesenfeld, J.R. Hetland, W.D. Warren), 1991; West Coast editor Oil and Gas Reporter, 1953—. Mem. Los Angeles Employee Relations Bd., 1971-74; bd. dirs. Constl. Rights Found., 1963-81; trustee Calif. Western U., 1979-81; bd. visitors Duke U. Sch. Law, 1973-79, chmn. bd. Pvt. Adjudication Ctr., 1984-89; bd. visitors Southwestern U. Sch. Law, 1981—. Served to lt. comdr. USNR, 1941-46. Recipient Disting. Tchg. award UCLA, 1977, Duke Law Sch., 1986, UCLA medal, 1982, Clyde O. Martz Tchg. award Rocky Mountain Mineral Law Found., 1994. Mem. ABA (com. on youth edn. for citizenship 1975-79, spl. com. on public understanding about the law 1979-84), Order of Coif. (nat. exec. com. 1980-86). Office: Duke U Sch Law Durham NC 27708-0362

MAXWELL, ROBERT EARL, federal judge; b. Elkins, W.Va., Mar. 15, 1924; s. Earl L. and Nellie E. (Rexstrew) M.; m. Ann Marie Grabowski, Mar. 29, 1948; children—Mary Ann, Carol Lynn, Ellen Lindsay, Earl Wilson. Student, Davis and Elkins Coll., LLD (hon.), 1984; LL.B., W.Va. U., 1949; LLD (hon.), Davis and Elkins Coll., 1984. Bar: W.Va. 1949. Practiced in Randolph County, 1949, pros. atty., 1952-61; U.S. atty. for No. Dist. W.Va., 1961-64; judge U.S. Dist. Ct. (no. dist.) W.Va., Elkins, 1965—, Temp. Emergency Ct. of Appeals, 1980-89; past chmn. budget com. Jud. Conf. U.S.; former mem. exec. com. Nat. Conf. Fed. Trial Judges; former mem. adv. bd. W.Va. U. Mem. bd. advisors W.Va. U., past chmn.; bd. advisors Mary Babb Randolph Cancer Ctr. Recipient Alumni Disting. Svc. award Davis and Elkins Coll., 1969, Religious Heritage Am. award, 1979, Outstanding Trial Judge award W.Va. Trial Lawyers Assn., 1988, Order of Vandalia award W.Va. U., Outstanding Alumnus award, 1992, Tenured Faculty Mem. Recognition award Bd. Govs., Def. Trial Coun., W.Va., 1992, Cert. of Merit, W.Va. State Bar, 1994, Justitia Officium award Coll. of Law, W.Va. U., 1994. Mem. Nat. Conf. Federal Trial Judges, Dist. Judges Assn. 4th Cir. (past pres.), Moose (life), Lions (life), Beta Alpha Beta (merit award), Elkins-Randolph County C. of C. (citizen of yr. 1994). Office: US Dist Ct No Dist PO Box 1275 Elkins WV 26241-1275

MAXWELL, ROBERT HAWORTH, agriculture educator, university administrator; b. Earlham, Iowa, Oct. 8, 1927; s. Charles Erich and Mildred Grace M.; m. Betty Ruth Michener, Dec. 24, 1950; children: Robert Steven, Daniel Guy, Timothy Charles, Kristen Kimuli. Student, Earlham Coll., 1946-48; BS in Farm Ops., Iowa State U., 1950, MS in Agrl. Edn., 1964; PhD in Agrl. Edn., Cornell U., 1970. Cert. tchr., Iowa. Farm operator Iowa, 1952-60; instr. Earlham Coll., Richmond, Ind., 1960-62; tchr. vocat. agr. Earlham (Iowa) Community Sch., 1963-64; asst. prof. agrl. edn. W.Va. U., Morgantown, 1964-68, assoc. prof. agrl. edn., 1970-75, prof. agrl. edn., 1975-79, asst. dean coll. agr. & forestry, acting chmn. divsn. animal & vet. scis., 1980, assoc. dean coll. agr. & forestry, chmn. divsn. internat. agr. & forestry, 1980-84, interim dean coll. agr. & forestry, interim dir. W.Va. agrl. & forestry experiment sta., 1984-85, dean coll. agr. & forestry, dir. W.Va. agrl. & forestry experiment sta., 1985-93; prof. agr., coord. internat. agr. U. W.Va., Morgantown, 1994-95, assoc. provost for ext. and pub. svc., dir. coop. ext. svc., 1995—; vocat. agr. tchr. Dexfield Community Schs., Redfield, Iowa, 1958-60; grad. asst. dept. edn. Cornell U., 1969-70; contract AID agrl. edn. advisor Kenya Ministry Edn., 1960-62, 64-68, spl. asst. dir. manpower devel. divsn. Tanzania Ministry Agr., 1975-79; dir. Allegheny Highlands Project, 1970-75; bd. dirs. Northeast Regional Ctr. Rural Devel., W.Va. U. Rsch. Corp.; lectr. in field. Author: (with others) Agriculture for Primary School series, 1979, 82, 85; editor Empire State Vo-Ag Teacher Jour., 1969-70; pub. papers and reports; contbr. articles to profl. jours. Unit leader United Way, Elkins, W.Va., 1970-75, Morgantown, 1979-93. With U.S. Army, 1950-52. Named Disting. West Virginian Gov. W.Va., 1993; recipient Commemorative medal U. Agr., Nitra, Slovakia, 1993; named to W.Va. Agriculture and Forestry Hall of Fame, 1995. Mem. AAAS, Am. Assn. Agrl. Edn., Am. Farmland Trust (life), Am. Soc. Agrl. Conss. (Meritorious Svc. award 1994), Am. Soc. Agrl. Conss. Internat. (cert., bd. dirs.), Nat. Assn. Colls. and Tchrs. Agr., Nat. Peace Inst., World Future Soc., Soc. Internat. Devel., Assn. Internat. Agrl. and Extension Educators (pres.-elect, pres. 1994, Outstanding Svc. 1991), Assn. Internat. Agr. and Rural Devel. (Outstanding Svc. 1992), Coun. Agrl. Sci. and Tech., Northeast Regional Assn. Agrl. Experiment Sta. Dirs. (Svc. Commendation 1993), UN Assn. of the USA, Soil and Water Conservation Soc. (life), Kenya Assn. Tchrs. Agr. (life), Tanzanian Soc. Agr. Edn. and Extension (life), W.Va. Shepherd's Fedn., W.Va. Poultry Assn., W.Va. Cattlemen's Assn., W.Va. Farm Bur., Iowa Farm Bur., W.Va. Grassland Coun., W.Va. Horticultural Soc., Agriculture and Forestry Hall of Fame Found. W.Va. (past pres.), Upshur Livestock Assn. (life), Morgantown Rotary Club, Iowa State U. Alumni Assn. (life), Cornell U. Alumni Assn. (life), W.Va. U. Alumni Assn. (life), FFA Alumni Assn. (life), Phi Delta Kappa, Gamma Sigma Delta, Alpha Zeta, Phi Mu Alpha (life). Mem. Soc. of Friends. Home: 4009 Cedar Ct Morgantown WV 26505-2823 Office: W Va Univ Coll Agriculture & Forestry Evansdale Campus PO Box 6108 Morgantown WV 26506-6108

MAXWELL, ROBERT WALLACE, II, lawyer; b. Waynesburg, Pa., Sept. 6, 1943; s. Robert Wallace and Margaret M.; m. Mamie Lee Payne, June 18, 1966; children—Virginia, Robert William. B.S. magna cum laude, Hampden-Sydney Coll., 1965; J.D. with honors, Duke U., 1968. Bar: Ohio 1968. Assoc. Taft, Stettinius & Hollister, Cin., 1968-75, ptnr., 1975-88; ptnr. Keating, Muething & Klekamp, 1988— ; part-time instr. U. Cin. Sch. Law, 1975-76. Bd. dirs. Contemporary Arts Ctr. of Cin; bd. dirs. Cin. Ballet Co.; elder Wyoming First Presbyterian Ch. Mem. ABA, Am. Assn. Mus. Trustees. Republican. Home: 535 Larchmont Dr Cincinnati OH 45215-4215 Office: Keating Muething & Klekamp 1 E 4th St Cincinnati OH 45202-3717

MAXWELL, SARA ELIZABETH, psychologist, educator, speech pathologist, director; b. DuQuoin, Ill., Jan. 23; d. Jean A. (Patterson) Green; m. David Lowell Maxwell, Dec. 27, 1960 (div. Mar. 1990); children: Lisa Marina, David Scott. BS, So. Ill. U., 1963, MS, 1964, MSEd, 1965; MEd, Boston Coll., 1982; attended, Harvard U., 1983; PhD, Boston Coll., 1992. Cert. and lic. speech/lang. pathologist, early childhood specialist, guidance counselor, sch. adjustment counselor, EMT. Clin. supr. Clin. Ctr. So. Ill. U., Carbondale, 1964-65, grad. clin. instr., 1965-66; speech/lang. pathologist, sch. adjustment counselor Westwood (Mass.) Pub. Schs., 1967-93; grad. faculty Emerson Coll., Boston, 1979-81; cons. Mass. Dept. Mental Health, Boston, 1979-82; grad. clin. supr. Robbins Speech/Hearing Ctr., Emerson Coll., Boston, 1979-82; cons. Westwood Nursery Preschs., 1986-93; devel. and clin. staff psychologist S. Shore Mental Health Ctr., Hingham and Quincy, Mass., 1989-93; emergency svcs. team and respite house manager S. Shore Mental Health Ctr., Quincy, Mass., 1990-93; pvt. practice Twin Oaks Clin. Assocs., Westwood, Mass, 1986-88, S. Coast Counseling Assocs., Quincy, 1989-93; dir. Exceptional Edn. Program, 1996—; cons. local collaboratives and preschs., Westwood, 1980-83; profl. workshops presenter Head Start, 1980; predoctoral intern in clin. psychology S. Shore Mental Health Ctr., Quincy, 1985-86; program specialist speech, lang., learning Broward County (Fla.) Schs., 1993—; adj. prof. grad. sch. of psychology Nova Southeastern U., 1995—; presenter Head Start, ASHA, CEC, APSC, IALP and other profl., nat. and state confs., 1980-93; invited del. to Sino-Am. Conf. on Exceptionality, Beijing Normal U., People's Republic of China, 1995. Contbr. articles to profl. jours., chpts. to textbooks. Mem. adv. coun. Westwood Bd. Health, 1977-80; emergency med. technician Westwood Pub. Schs. Athletic Dept., 1981. Vocat. Rehab. fellow So. Ill. U., 1964; Merit scholar Perry County, Ill., 1959-64, Gloria Credi Meml. scholar So. Ill. U., 1964. Mem. Am. Speech & Hearing Assn. (nat. schs. com., nat. chairperson Pub. Sch. Caucus 1985-87), Am. Psychol. Assn., Assn. Psychiat. Svcs. for Children, Coun. Exceptional Children, Internat. Assn. of Logopedics, Rio Vista Civic Assn., Boston Coll. Alumni Assn., Harvard Club. Episcopalian. Avocations: squash, sailing, skiing. Office: Nova Southeastern U Ctr for Psychol Studies College Ave Fort Lauderdale FL 33314-7721

MAXWELL, W(ILBUR) RICHARD, management consultant, retired; b. Troy, Ohio, June 20, 1920; s. Wilbur D. and Gertrude (McDowell) M.; m. Roberta Mae Kennedy, June 29, 1942; children: Douglas R., Jean Ann. Student, Ohio Wesleyan U., 1938-41; BS, Richmond Profl. Inst. of Coll. William and Mary, 1955. Sec. Troy C. of C., 1948-50, Va. C. of C., 1950-55; asst. to pres./chmn. bd. Reynolds Metals Co., 1955-64; v.p., dir. Reynolds Fgn. Sales Inc., 1964-68; pres. Nat. Better Bus. Bur., 1968-70; pres., chief exec. officer Jr. Achievement, Inc., Stamford, Conn., 1970-82; instr. Richmond Profl. Inst., part-time 1955-57; sponsor-trustee U. Va. Grad. Bus. Sch., 1963-72. Pres. Lancaster County Libr., 1984-85, Rappahannock Gen. Hosp. Found., 1988-90, Northern Neck Vocat.-Tech. Edn. Ctr., 1991-93; bd. dirs. Rappahannock Gen. Hosp., 1988-90, Richmond (Va.) Cmty. H.S., 1989-91; chmn. Northumberland County (Va.) Econ. Devel. Commn., 1994-97. Civilian specialist USAAF, USN, 1942-46. Recipient Albert Schweitzer award Hugh O'Brien Youth Fedn., 1982; inducted Jr. Achievement Profl. Hall of Fame, 1986. Mem. Indian Creek Yacht and Country Club (v.p., 1991-93, bd. dirs. 1991-93). Home: PO Box 1090 Kilmarnock VA 22482-1090

MAXWELL, WILLIAM HALL CHRISTIE, civil engineering educator; b. Coleraine, County Londonderry, Northern Ireland, Jan. 25, 1936; came to U.S., 1958, naturalized, 1967; s. William Robert and Catherine Dempsey (Christie) M.; m. Mary Carolyn McLaughlin, Sept. 28, 1960; children: Katrina, Kevin, Wendy, Liam. B.Sc., Queen's U., Belfast, No. Ireland, 1956; M.Sc., Queen's U., Kingston, Ont., Can., 1958; Ph.D., U. Minn., 1964. Registered profl. engr., Ill. Site engr. Motor Columbus AG, Baden, Switzerland, 1956; teaching asst. Queen's U., 1956-58; research asst. to instr. U. Minn., Mpls., 1959-64; asst. prof. civil engring. U. Ill., Urbana, 1964-70, assoc. prof., 1970-82, prof., 1982-96, prof. emeritus, 1997—; chmn. program com. First Internat. Conf. on New/ Emerging Concepts for Rivers, Chgo., 1996. Editor: Water Resources Management in Industrial Areas, 1982; Water for Human Consumption, Man and His Environment, 1983; Frontiers in Hydrology, 1984. Vestryman, Emmanuel Meml. Episcopal Ch., Champaign, Ill., 1977-80. State exhibitor Ministry Edn., Stormont, No. Ireland, 1953-56; Queen's U. Found. scholar, Belfast, 1954-56; R.S. McLaughlin travelling fellow Queen's U., 1958-59. Fellow ASCE (com. chmn. 1982-83), Internat. Water Resources Assn. (editor-in-chief Water Internat. 1986-93, sr. editor 1994—, mem. publs. com. 1980—, v.p. U.S. geog. com. 1986-91, chmn. awards com. 1995—, bd. dirs. 1995—, Editl. award 1994); mem. Internat. Assn. for Hydraulic Research, Am. Geophys. Union. Avocations: camping, fishing, home construction, oil painting. Home: 1210 Devonshire Dr Champaign IL 61821-6527 Office: U Ill Dept Civil Engring 205 N Mathews Ave Urbana IL 61801-2350

MAXWELL, WILLIAM LAUGHLIN, industrial engineering educator; b. Phila., July 11, 1934; s. William Henry and Elizabeth (Laughlin) M.; m. Judith Behrens, July 5, 1969; children: Deborah, William, Judith, Keely. BMechE, Cornell U., 1957, PhD, 1961. Andrew Schultz Jr. prof. dept. indsl. engring. Cornell U., Ithaca, N.Y., 1961—. Author: Theory of Scheduling, 1967. Recipient Disting. Teaching award Cornell Soc. Engrs., 1968. Fellow Inst. Indsl. Engrs.; mem. Ops. Rsch. Soc., Soc. Mfg. Engrs. Home: 106 Lake Ave Ithaca NY 14850-3537 Office: Cornell U Dept Indsl Engring Ithaca NY 14850

MAXWELL, WILLIAM STIRLING, retired lawyer; b. Chgo., May 2, 1922; s. W. Stirling and Ethel (Bowes) Maxwell Reincke. A.B. with distinction, U. Mich., 1947, postgrad., 1946-49, J.D., 1949. Bar: Ill. 1949, U.S. Ct. Mil. Appeals 1951, U.S. Supreme Ct. 1952. Assoc. Sidley & Austin, Chgo., 1949-60, 61, ptnr., 1962-84; now ret.; sr. legis. counsel U.S. Treasury, Washington, 1960-61. Trustee Mid-North Animal Shelter Found., Chgo., 1971—. Mem. Order of Coif, Phi Beta Kappa. Republican. Episcopalian. Clubs: Law, Legal (Chgo.). Home: PO Box 1268 Goldendale WA 98620-1268

MAXWORTHY, TONY, mechanical and aerospace engineering educator; b. London, May 21, 1933; came to U.S., 1954, naturalized, 1961; s. Ernest Charles and Gladys May (Butson) M.; m. Emily Jean Parkinson, June 20, 1956 (div. 1974); children: Kirsten, Kara; m. Anna Barbara Parks, May 21, 1979. BS in Engring. with 1st class honors, U. London, 1954; MSE, Princeton U., 1955; PhD, Harvard U., 1959. Research asst. Harvard U., Cambridge, Mass., 1955-59; sr. scientist, group supr. Jet Propulsion Lab., Pasadena, Calif., 1960-67, cons., 1968—; assoc. prof. U. So. Calif., Los Angeles, 1967-70, prof., 1970—, Smith Internat. prof. mech. and aero. engring., 1988—, chmn. dept. mech. engring., 1979-89; cons. BBC Rsch. Ctr., Baden, Switzerland, 1972-82, J.P.L., Pasadena, Calif., 1968-80; lectr. Woods Hole Oceanographic Inst., Mass., summers 1965, 70, 72, 83; Forman vis. prof. aeronautics Technion Haifa, 1986; vis. prof. U. Poly., Madrid, 1988, Inst. Superiore Tech., Lisbon, 1988, Swiss Fed. Inst. Tech., Lausanne, 1989; assoc. prof. IMG, U. Joseph Fourier, Grenoble, 1980—, Ecole Superieure Physics and Indsl. Chemistry, Paris, 1995-97; Shimizu vis. prof. Stanford U., 1996—. Mem. editorial bd. Geophys. Fluid Dynamics, 1973-79, 88-96, Dynamic Atmospheric Oceans, 1976-83, Phys. Fluids, 1978-81, Zeitschrift fuer Angewandte Mathematik und Physik, 1987-96; contbr. articles to profl. jours. Recipient Humboldt sr. scientist award, 1981-93; fellow Cambridge U., 1974, 93—, Australian Nat. U., 1978, Nat. Ctr. Atmospheric Rsch., 1976; Glennon fellow U. Western Australia, 1990, F.W. Mosey fellow, 1993; sr. Queen's fellow in marine scis. Commonwealth of Australia, 1984. Fellow Am. Phys. Soc. (chmn. exec. com. fluid dynamics divsn. 1974-79, Otto Laporte award 1990); Mem. NAE, ASME, Am. Meteorol. Soc., Am. Geophys. Union, European Geophys. Soc. Office: U So Calif Dept Mech Engring Exposition Park Los Angeles CA 90089-1453

MAY, ARTHUR W., university president; b. St. John's, Nfld., Can., June 29, 1937; s. William J. and Florence (Dawe), M.; m. Sonia Susan Streeter, Aug. 18, 1958; children—Stephen J., Heather E., Maria S., Douglas W. BSc with honors, Meml. U., St. John's, 1958; MSc, Meml. U., 1964; PhD, McGill U., Montreal, Que., Can., 1966; D of Univ. (hon.), U. Ottawa, 1988; DSc (hon.), Meml. U. Nfld., 1989; LLD (hon.), Brock U., 1992. Sci. adviser internat. fisheries Dept. Fisheries, Ottawa, Ont., Can., 1971-73; dir. Nfld. biol. sta. Dept. Fisheries, St. John's, 1973-75; dir. gen. resource services Dept. Fisheries, Ottawa, 1975-78; asst. dep. minister Atlantic Dept. Fisheries and Oceans, Ottawa, 1978-82; dep. minister Dept. Fisheries and Oceans, 1982-86; pres. Natural Sci. and Engring. Rsch. Coun. Canada, 1986-90; pres., vice chancellor Meml. U. Nfld., St. Johns, 1990—; v.p. Internat. Coun. for Exploration of Seas, Copenhagen, 1977-79; mem. Task Force on Atlantic Fisheries, Ottawa, 1982, Nat. Adv. Bd. Sci. and Tech., 1988-90, 94-95; Canadian rep. to NATO Sci. Conf., 1990—. Contbr. articles to profl. jours. Served to sub. lt. Can. Navy, 1955-58. Decorated officer Order of Can.; recipient Gov.-Gen.'s medal Nfld. Dept. Edn., 1954, Meml. U. Nfld., 1958; named Alumnus of Yr., Meml. U. Nfld., 1983. Mem. N.W. Atlantic Fisheries Orgn. (pres. 1977-80). Anglican. Avocations: gardening; philately. Home: 20 Baker St, Saint Johns, NF Canada A1A 5A7 Office: Meml Univ Nfld, Office of the Pres, Saint Johns, NF Canada A1C 5S7

MAY, BEVERLY, elementary school educator; b. Marshall, Tex., Sept. 11, 1939; d. Carl Glendon and Omie Louise (Berry) Brewster; m. William Raymond May, Sept. 19, 1958; children: William Jr., Karri, David. BS in Elem. Edn., U. Houston, 1969, MEd, 1978. Cert. elem. tchr., profl. reading specialist, profl. supr., Tex. Clerical, secretarial Houston Ind. Sch. Dist., 1957-64, tchr. grades 2, 3, 7, elem. reading ctr., 1969-90, ret., 1990; ednl. materials rep. World Book/Childcraft, Houston, 1975-90; reading cons. Region IV Edn. Svc. Ctr., Houston, 1977-83; supr. reading lab. downtown campus U. Houston, 1985; clk. sec. Houston Ind. Sch. Dist., 1957-64, tchr. grades two, three, seven Elem. Reading Ctr., 1969-90; pvt. reading skills and study skills specialist, 1975—; cons., presenter workshops in field. clerical/secretarial (1957-64). gr 2,3,7, elem. reading center, 1969-90. Participant TV-Radio broadcast ministries workshop 1st Bapt. Ch., Houston, 1988. Mem. Tex. State Reading Assn., Tex. Retired Tchrs. Assn., Inspirational Writers Alive, Soc. Children's Book Writers and Illustrators, Internat. Reading Assn., Greater Houston Area Reading Coun. Home: 2102 Du Barry Ln Houston TX 77018-5060

MAY, CECIL RICHARD, JR., academic adminstrator; b. Memphis, June 13, 1932. BA in biblical langs. magna cum laude, Harding U., MA in New Testament, MTh; LLD (hon.), Freed-Hardeman U., 1984. Min. Holly Springs, Miss., 1954-57, Ripley, Miss., 1957-59; min. Pine Bluff Ch., Ctrl. Acad. Ch., Miss., 1959-60; dist. scout exec. Yocona Area Coun. Boy Scouts Am., Oxford, Miss., 1959-60; min. Ashland, Miss., 1961, Fulton, Miss., 1962-67; min. Eastside Campus Ch., Portland, Oreg., 1967-69; Bible tchr. Columbia Christian Coll., Portland, 1967-69; min. Vicksburg, Miss., 1969-76; dean Internat. Bible Coll., Florence, Ala., 1977-80; pres. Magnolia Bible Coll., Kosciusko, Miss., 1980—; lectr. in field. Editor: Preacher Talk; assoc. editor: Magnolia Messenger; contbr. articles to profl. jours. Elder Vicksburg (Miss.) Ch., 1971-76, South Huntington St. Ch., Kosciusko, 1981—; active Boy Scouts Am., 1954-76; com. chair Kosciusko-Attala County C. of C., 1992; bd. dirs. Am. Cancer Soc., 1971-74, fin. campaign chmn., 1971; bd. dirs. Miss. Econ. Coun., 1985-86, 89-92, area vice-chmn., 1991-92; chmn. Attala County Med. Study Task Force, 1991-92. Mem. Nat. Assn. Ind. Coll. and Univs., Miss. Assn. Ind. Colls. (bd. dirs.), Evang. Theol. Soc., Miss. Assn. Colls. (bd. dirs.), Rotary Club (bd. dirs. 1983-85, pres. 1985-86). Office: Magnolia Bible Coll PO Box 1109 Kosciusko MS 39090-1109

MAY, CLIFFORD DANIEL, newspaper editor, journalist; m. Lou Ann Brunwasser; children: Miranda Rose, Evan Phillip Barr. Cert. in Russian lang. and lit., U. Leningrad, 1972; BA, Sarah Lawrence Coll., 1973; M Journalism, Columbia U., 1975, M Internat. Affairs, 1975. Assoc. editor Newsweek, 1975-78; roving fgn. corr. Hearst Newpapers, 1978-79; sr. editor Am. edit. Geo mag., 1979-80; gen. editor Sunday Mag., Washington corr. N.Y. Times, 1980-89; chief West Africa bur. N.Y. Times, Abidjan, Ivory Coast, 1984; assoc. editor Rocky Mountain News, Denver, 1989—; spl. corr. CBS Radio News, Bill Moyers' Jour./Internat. Report-PBS-TV, 1970's; host, prodr. Roundtable, Sta. KRMA, Colo.; freelance writer, 1979-89. Contbg. editor World Press Rev. Mag.; host, prodr. roundtable Sta. KRMA, Denver, 1994—; host Race for the Presidency TCI News, 1995-96. Avocations: downhill skiing, outdoor activities. Office: Rocky Mountain News 400 W Colfax Ave Denver CO 80204-2607

MAY, DAVID A., protective services official, public official; b. Buffalo, N.Y., May 23, 1947; s. Arthur F. M.; m. Mary E. Beer, Oct. 6, 1973; children: Jordan D., Jared R. AAS in Bus. Adminstrn., Niagara County C.C., Sanborn, N.Y., 1983; BS in Pub. Adminstrn., Empire State Coll., 1988; MA in Orgn. Mgmt., U. Phoenix, 1996. V.p. Simpson Security, Inc., Niagara Falls, N.Y., 1973-78; lt. Niagara Falls (N.Y.) Police Dept., 1986—. Bd. mem. Nat. Conf. Christians and Jews, 1984-90, ARC, 1986-89, Music Sch. of Niagara, 1987-90, Niagara Falls Little Theatre, chmn., 1994; pres. Niagara Cmty. Ctr., Niagara Falls, 1987, Niagara Falls (N.Y.) Sch. Bd., 1988, Niagara Falls (N.Y.) Meml. Day Assn., 1990, 91, 93; lt. gov. N.Y. State Kiwanis, 1989; mem. Niagara Co. Lrgis., 1994. Recipient Svc. award Fellowship House Found., Niagara Falls, 1986; named Civic Leader of Yr., Niagara Cmty. Ctr., Niagara Falls, 1990. Mem. Kiwanis Club North Niagara Falls (pres. 1987, Kiwanian of the Yr. 1991), Lasalle Am. Legion (vice commdr. 1975), Lasalle Sportsmens Club (fin. sec. 1989). Avocations: playing tennis, golfing, amateur historian. Home: 3024 Macklem Ave Niagara Falls NY 14305-1832

MAY, DONALD ROBERT LEE, ophthalmologist, retina and vitreous surgeon, educator, academic administrator; b. Spring Valley, Ill., Nov. 26, 1945; s. Reo Georg and Edna Antoinette (Klein) M.; m. Jane N. Sakauye, Nov. 12, 1988. BS in Liberal Arts and Scis. with high honors, U. Ill., 1968, MD, 1972. Diplomate Am. Bd. Ophthalmology, Nat. Bd. Med. Examiners. Med. student rsch. fellow Dept. Ophthalmology U. Ill. Eye and Ear Infirmary, Chgo., 1971-72; intern rotating internal medicine Northwestern U. Sch. Medicine Meml. Hosps., Chgo., 1972-73; resident Ophthalmology U. Ill. Eye and Ear Infirmary, Chgo., 1973-76, instr. dept. Ophthalmology, 1974-77, attending surgeon dept. Ophthalmology, 1976-77; fellow in Diabetic Retinopathy study, Diabetic Retinopathy Vitrectomy study, and Retina and Vitreous Surgery U. Ill. Eye and Ear Infirmary, 1976-77; founder and dir. Retina/Vitreous/Ocular Trauma Svc. of the USAF dept. Ophthalmology, Wilford Hall USAF Medical Ctr., Lackland AFB, Tex., 1977-79; asst. prof. Ophthalmology, founder, dir. Retina/Vitreous/Ocular Trauma Svc. U. Calif. Davis Sch. Medicine, Calif., 1979-81; assoc. prof. of Ophthalmology, dir. Retina/Vitreous/Ocular Trauma Svc. U. Calif. Sch. Medicine, Davis, 1981-84; prof. Ophthalmology Tulane U. Sch. Medicine, New Orleans, 1984-89, dir. med. student edn., dept. of Ophthalmology, 1985-89; dir. Ophthalmology Tulane U. Sch. Medicine div., Charity Hosp., New Orleans, 1985-89; prof. Tex. Tech. U. Health Scis. Ctr., Lubbock, Tex., 1989—; chmn. dept. ophthalmology and visual scis. Tex. Tech. U. Health Scis. Ctr., Lubbock, 1989-94; prof. dept. health orgn. mgmt. Tex. Tech U. Health Scis. Ctr., Lubbock, 1993—, assoc. dean Sch. Medicine, 1994—; co-investigator in the Intraocular Gentamicin Prophylaxis Study, Govt. Erskine Hosp., Madurai, So. India, 1975, Dept. Ophthalmology, Audie Murphy VA Hosp., San Antonio, 1977-79, Martinez VA Hosp., Calif., 1979-84, VA Hosp., New Orleans, 1984-89, VA Med. Ctr., Alexandria, La., 1985-89, VA Med. Ctr., Big Spring, Tex., 1989-93, VA Ctr., Lubbock, Tex., 1989-92; cons. People's Republic China, 1980, 82, 85, 96, Japan, 1982, 83, 85; vis. prof. Germany, 1984, Switzerland, 1987; 1st v.p. U.S. Eye Injury Registry, 1990-92, pres.-elect, 1992-94, pres. 1994-96; founder, med. dir. Tex. Eye Injury Registry, 1991—. Contbg. editor Ocutome/Fragmatome Newsletter, 1978-81; assoc. editor Vitreoretinal Surgery and Tech., 1989—; mem. editl. bd. Jour. Eye Trauma, 1996—; contbr. articles to profl. jours.; appeared in numerous TV and radio programs. Mem. coms. Sch. Medicine, U. Calif., Davis, Tulane U. Sch. Medicine, New Orleans, Am. Acad. Ophthalmology, San. Francisco, Sch. Medicine Tex. Tech. U. Health Scis. Ctr., U. Med. Ctr., Lubbock. Maj. USAF, 1973-80. Decorated Air Force Commendation medal. Mem. ACS, AMA, Am. Acad. Ophthalmology, Assn. Rsch. in Vision and Ophthalmology, Chinese Am. Ophthal. Soc. (charter mem.), Christian Med. Soc., So. Med. Assn. (vice chmn. sec. ophthalmology 1995-96, chmn. sec. ophthalmology 1996-97), So. Retina Study Group (steering com. 1987-89), Tex. Med. Assn. (com. continuing edn. 1993-96), Tex. Ophthal. Assn. (chair edn. com. 1990-93, coun. 1990-93, nominating com. 1991-93), Tex. Tech. Rsch. Found. (bd. dirs. 1993—), The Pan-Am. Assn. Ophthalmology, The Retina Soc., The Vitreous Soc. (charter mem.), World Eye Found. (bd. dirs. 1982—), Soc. Med. Cons. to Armed Forces, Sigma Xi (sec. Tex. Tech. chpt. 1990-91). Republican. Lutheran. Avocations: farming, travel, photography, cycling, hiking. Home: PO Box 1678 Lubbock TX 79408-1678 Office: Tex Tech U Health Scis Ctr Sch Medicine Dept Ophthalmology Vis Scis Office of Dean Lubbock TX 79430 *If we are to survive as a free society, we must each accept responsibility. The individual must function on the premise that personal rewards come with the investment of hard, honest work and not as a right mediated by government at the expense of others. Our legislative* *bodies must enact laws for the common good and not for individual self-interest. Our judicial systems must provide for the just enforcement of our laws. Our leadership must be the watchdog to ensure the indivdual has the opportunity to life without unreasonable danger, the freedom to follow one's dreams, and the ability to pursue happiness through individual achievement. Security comes with the contribution of all who are able.*

MAY, EDGAR, former state legislator, nonprofit administrator; b. Zurich, Switzerland, June 27, 1929; came to U.S., 1940, naturalized, 1954; s. Ferdinand and Renee (Bloch) M. B.J. with highest distinction, Northwestern U., 1957; student, New Eng. Culinary Inst., 1996—. Reporter, acting editor Bellows Falls (Vt.) Times, 1951-53; reporter Fitchburg (Mass.) Sentinel, 1953; part time reporter Chgo. Tribune, 1955-57; reporter Buffalo Evening News, 1958-61; dir. pub. welfare projects State Charities Aid Assn., 1962-64; mem. President's Task Force on War Against Poverty, 1964; spl. asst. to dir., asst. dir. Office Econ. Opportunity, 1964; spl. adviser to Ambassador Sargent Shriver, 1968-70; cons. Ford Found., 1970-75; mem. Vt. Ho. of Reps., 1975-82; mem. Vt. Senate, 1983-91, chmn. com. appropriations; project dir. Vt. Jud. Mgmt. Study, 1992; COO Spl. Olympics Internat., Washington, 1993-96. Author: The Wasted Americans, 1964. With AUS, 1953-55. Recipient Page One award Buffalo Newspaper Guild, 1959, Walter O. Bingham award, 1959; Pulitzer prize for local reporting, 1961; Merit award Northwestern U. Alumni Assn., 1962. Office: 1325 G St NW Washington DC 20005-3104

MAY, ELAINE, actress, theatre and film director; b. Phila., Apr. 21, 1932; d. Jack Berlin; m. Marvin May (div.); 1 child, Jeannie Berlin; m. Sheldon Harnick, Mar. 25, 1962 (div. May 1963). Ed. high sch., studied Stanislavsky method of acting withMarie Ouspenskaya. Stage and radio appearances as child actor; performed with Playwright's Theatre, in student performance Miss Julie, U. Chgo.; appeared with improvisational theatre group in night club The Compass, Chgo., 1954-1957, (with Mike Nichols) appeared N.Y. supper clubs, Village Vanguard, Blue Angel, also night clubs other cities; TV debut on Jack Paar Show, 1957; also appeared in Omnibus, 1958, Dinah Shore Show, Perry Como Show, Laugh Line, Laugh-In, TV spls.; comedy albums include Improvisations to Music, An Evening with Mike Nichols and Elaine May, Mike Nichols and Elaine May Examine Doctors; weekly appearance NBC radio show Nightline; appeared (with Mike Nichols) NBC radio show, N.Y. Town Hall, 1959, An Evening with Mike Nichols and Elaine May, Golden Theatre, N.Y.C., 1960-61; theater appearances include The Office, N.Y.C., 1966, Who's Afraid of Virginia Woolf?, Long Wharf Theatre, New Haven, Conn., 1980; dir. plays The Third Ear, N.Y.C., 1964, The Goodbye People, Berkshire Theater Festival, Stockbridge, Mass., 1971, various plays at Goodman Theatre, Chgo., 1983; dir., author screenplay, actress film A New Leaf, 1972; dir. films The Heartbreak Kid, 1973, Mikey and Nicky, 1976 (writer, dir. remake 1985), Ishtar, 1987 (also writer); appeared in films Luv, 1967, California Suite, 1978 (Acad. award Best Supporting Actress 1978), In The Spirit, 1990; co-author screenplay Heaven Can Wait, 1978, Birdcage, 1996; author plays A Matter of Position, 1962, Not Enough Rope, 1962, Adaptation, 1969, Hot Line, 1983, Better Part of Valor, 1983, Mr. Gogol and Mr. Preen, 1991, (one act) Death Defying Acts, 1995; stage revue: (with Mike Nichols) Telephone, 1984; co-recipient (with Mike Nichols) Grammy award for comedy performance, Nat. Acad. Recording Arts & Scis., 1961. Office: care Julian Schlossberg Castle Hill Productions 1414 Avenue Of The Americas New York NY 10019-2514

MAY, ERNEST MAX, charitable organization official; b. Newark, July 24, 1913; s. Otto Bernard and Eugenie (Morgenstern) M.; m. Harriet Elizabeth Dewey, Oct. 12, 1940; children: Ernest Dewey, James Northrup, Susan Elizabeth. BA, Princeton, 1934, MA, 1935; PhD in Organic Chemistry, U. Chgo., 1938; LittD (hon.), Montclair State Coll., 1989. With Otto B. May, Inc., Newark, 1938-73; successively chemist, gen. mgr. Otto B. May, Inc., 1938-52, pres., 1952-73; trustee Youth Consultation Service Diocese of Newark, 1952-59, 61-66, 68—; pres., 1971-75; dir. Cone Mills Corp., 1961-73, mem. exec. com., 1968-71; tech. adviser to spl. rep. trade negotiations, 1964-67. Councilman, Summit, N.J., 1963-70; mem. Summit Environ. Com., 1971-75, chmn., 1974-75; pres. Family Svc. Assn. Summit, 1959-61, Mental Health Assn. Summit, 1954, Summit Coun. Chs. Christ, 1962-63; mem. exec. com. Christ Hosp., Jersey City, 1971—, v.p., chmn., 1974—; chmn. Summit Hwy. Adv. Com., 1976-94; trustee, organizer Summer Organic Chemistry Inst., Choate Sch., Wallingford, Conn.; mem. Union County Mental Health Bd., 1973-76; bd. dirs. N.J. Mental Health Assn., 1974-81; trustee Montclair (N.J.) State Univ., 1975-85, vice-chmn., 1976-80, chmn., 1980-83; adviser applied prof. psychology Rutgers U., 1976—; mem. Nat. commn. on Nursing, 1980-83; adviser dept. music Princeton U.; trustee Assn. for Children in N.J., 1975—, Citizen's Com. on Biomed. Ethics in N.J., 1984-95, N.J. Health Decisions, 1995-97; advisor Nat. Exec. Svcs. Corps Health Care Consulting Group, 1994—. Fellow Am. Inst. Chemists; mem. Am. Chem. Soc., Sweiss Chem. Soc., German Chem. Soc., Synthetic Organic Chem. Mfrs. Assn. (bd. govs. 1952-54, 63-70, v.p. 1966-68, chmn. internat. comml. rels. com. 1968-73, hon. mem.), Vol. Trustees Not-for-Profit Hosps. (trustee 1986-88, 94—), Met. Opera (N.Y.), Chemists Club (N.Y.), Beacon Hill Club (Summit, N.J.), Nassau Club (Princeton), N.J. Hosp. Assn. (coun. on edn. 1990-91), Sigma Xi. Republican. Episcopalian (vestry 1950-60). Home: 57 Colt Rd Summit NJ 07901-3004 also: State Rd Chilmark MA 02535 *To live right and help others live right too, each in his own way.*

MAY, ERNEST RICHARD, historian, educator; b. Ft. Worth, Tex., Nov. 19, 1928; s. Ernest and Rachel (Garza) M.; m. Nancy Caughey, Dec. 15, 1950 (div. Feb. 1982); children: John Ernest, Susan Rachel, Donna LaRee; m. Susan B. Wood, June 22, 1988. A.B., UCLA, 1948, M.A. (Native Sons of Golden West fellow in history), 1949, Ph.D. (Univ. fellow), 1951; M.A. (hon.), Harvard U., 1959. Lectr. history Los Angeles State Coll., 1950; mem. hist. sect. Joint Chiefs of Staff, 1952-54; instr. history Harvard U., 1954-56, asst. prof., 1956-59, assoc. prof., 1959-63, prof., 1963—, Charles Warren prof. history, 1981—; Allston Burr sr. tutor Harvard U. (Kirkland House), 1960-66; mem. Harvard U. (Inst. Politics), 1967—, dir. inst., 1971-74, dean of coll., 1969-71, assoc. dean faculty arts & scis., 1970-71; mem. Council on Fgn. Relations. Author: The World War and American Isolation, 1914-17, 1959, The Ultimate Decision, The President as Commander in Chief, 1960, Imperial Democracy, The Emergence of America as a Great Power, 1961, The American Image, 4 vols, 1963, (with John W. Caughey) A History of the United States, 1964, (with editors of Life) The Progressive Era, 1964, War, Boom and Bust, 1964, From Isolation to Imperialism, 1898-1919, 1964, (with John W. Caughey and John Hope Franklin) Land of the Free, 1966, American Imperialism; A Speculative Essay, 1968, Lessons of the Past: The Use and Misuse of History in American Foreign Policy, 1973, The Making of The Monroe Doctrine, 1975, (with Dorothy G. Blaney) Careers for Humanists, 1981; author: A Proud Nation, 1983, Knowing One's Enemies: Intelligence Assessment before the Two World Wars, 1984, (with Richard E. Neustadt) Thinking in Time; The Uses of History for Decision Making, 1986 (Gravemeyer prize 1987), American Cold War Strategy: NSC 68, 1994, (with Philip D. Zelikow) The Kennedy Tapes: Inside the White House during the Cuban Missile Crisis, 1997; author also numerous articles. Chmn. bd. control John Anson Kittredge Trust. Served as lt. (j.g.) USNR, 1951-54. Guggenheim fellow, 1958-59; faculty research fellow Social Sci. Research Council, 1959-61; fellow Center for Advanced Study Behavioral Scis., 1963-64; fellow Woodrow Wilson Internat. Center, 1983. Mem. Mass. Hist. Soc., Am. Hist. Assn., Soc. Historians Am. Fgn. Relations (pres. 1982-83), AAUP, Am. Acad. Arts and Scis. Episcopalian. Club: Belmont Hill. Office: History Dept Harvard U Cambridge MA 02138

MAY, FELTON EDWIN, bishop; b. Chgo., Apr. 23, 1935; s. James Albert May and Florine C. (Felton) May Caruthers; m. Phyllis Elizabeth Henry, June 22, 1963; children: Daphne Endrea, Felton Edwin II. B.A., Judson Coll., 1962; M.Div., Crozer Theol. Sem., 1970; DD, Lycoming Coll., 1989, Lebanon Valley Coll., 1989, Wesley Coll., Dover, Del., 1990, Rust Coll., 1996. Ordained deacon United Meth. Ch., 1962, elder, 1970. Asst. pastor St. James Meth. Ch., Chgo., 1961-63; pastor Maple Park United Meth. Ch., Chgo., 1963-68; assoc. exec. dir. Meth. Action Program, Wilmington, Del., 1968-70, Ezion-Mt. Carmel United Meth. Ch., Wilmington, 1970-75; dist. supt. Peninsula Conf., United Meth. Ch., Easton, Md., 1975-81; coun. dir. Peninsula Conf., United Meth. Ch., Dover, 1981-84; bishop United Meth. Ch., Harrisburg, Pa., 1984-90; spl. assignment Coun. of Bishops, Washington, 1990-91; bishop United Meth. Ch., Harrisburg, 1991-96; chairperson United Meth. Shalom Communities Com., 1992, Pan Meth. Commn., 1993; co-chair Coalition of Religious Leaders, Harrisburg, Pa. Author: Developmental Evangelism (workbook), 1979; co-contbr. articles to mags.; co-author church sch. curriculum. Mem. Atty.'s Grievance Com., Annapolis, 1979-81; bd. govs. Wesley Sem., Washington, 1975—; bd. govs. Wesley Theol. Sem., 1996—; bd. dirs. Boy Scouts Am., Dover, 1981-83, Wesley Coll., 1972-83, Wilmington Parking Authority, 1974, Del. Health and Social Svc. Commn., Dover, 1972; mem. Del. Civil Rights Com., Wilmington, 1970; trustee Lycoming Coll., Lebanon Valley Coll., Camp David Chapel, Sibley Meml. Hosp., 1996—, Africa U., Zimbabwe, 1996—; com. Camp David, Md. With U.S. Army, 1957-59. Avocations: oil painting; tennis; plants; travel. Home: PO Box 76058 Washington DC 20013 Office: United Meth Ch Washington Area 110 Maryland Ave NE Ste 311 Washington DC 20002-5622

MAY, FRANCIS HART, JR., retired building materials manufacturing executive; b. Dunkirk, Ind., Apr. 2, 1917; s. Francis Hart and Agnes (Elabarger) M.; m. June Breen, Aug. 31, 1940; children: Francis Hart, John Joseph, Marcia Ann. A.B., U. Notre Dame, 1938; M.B.A., Harvard, 1940. Mgr. war contracts div. Owens-Ill. Glass Co., Toledo, 1940-44; v.p., sec. Glass Fibers, Inc., Toledo, 1946-54; v.p., sec., treas. L-O-F Glass Fibers Co., Toledo, 1955-58; v.p., gen. mgr. Johns-Manville Fiber Glass, Inc., 1959-60; asst. v.p. finance Johns-Manville Corp., N.Y.C., 1960-61; v.p. fin., dir. Johns-Manville Corp., 1962-70, exec. v.p. fin. and adminstrn., 1971-79, vice-chmn. bd., 1979-80, spl. projects, 1980-82, ret., 1982. Served with inf. AUS, 1944-46. Mem. Fin. Execs. Ins., Dolphin Head Golf Club (Hilton Head Island, S.C.). Home: 8330 E Quincy Ave J-103 Denver CO 80237 Home (summer): PO Box 955 Cooperstown NY 13326-5955 Home (winter): 29 China Cockle Ln Hilton Head Island SC 29926-1908

MAY, FRANK BRENDAN, JR., lawyer; b. Bronx, N.Y., Oct. 17, 1945; s. Frank Brendan and Margaret (Borza) M.; m. Mary Frances Fitzsimmons, June 19, 1976; children: David Brendan, Brian Christopher. BA in Econs., NYU, 1973, postgrad., 1973-75; JD, John Marshall Law Sch., Chgo., 1978. Bar: Ill. 1979, U.S. Dist. Ct. (no. dist.) Ill. 1979, U.S. Ct. Appeals (7th cir.), 1979, U.S. Supreme Ct. 1995. Legal intern criminal div. Cook County State's Atty.'s Office, Chgo., 1977-78; legal intern juvenile div. DuPage County State's Atty.'s Office, Wheaton, Ill., 1978; sr. assoc. atty. Lillig, Kemp & Thorness, Ltd., Oak Brook, Ill., 1978-81; v.p., gen. counsel Coldwell Banker, Oak Brook, 1981-90, Prudential Preferred Properties, Des Plaines, Ill., 1991—; arbitrator 18th Jud. Cir. Ct., Dupage County, Ill., 1993—. Sgt. USAF, 1963-67. NYU Coun. scholar, 1971-73; David Davis Meml. scholar, 1970-71. Mem. ABA (real estate sect.), Ill. State Bar assn. (real estate sect.), DuPage county Bar Assn. (real estate law com., lic. Ill. real estate broker 1994), Medinah Country Club (mem. legal/bylaws com. 1997, mem. clubhouse com. 1997), Ill. Assn. Realtors (chmn. large brokers com. 1996-97, mem. exec. com. 1996-97, mem. lic. law rewrite task force). Avocations: golf, music, gourmet cooking, wine collector. Home: 2064 Stonebridge Ct Wheaton IL 60187-7177 Office: Prudential Pref Properties 2700 S River Rd Ste 415 Des Plaines IL 60018-4108

MAY, GERALD WILLIAM, university administrator, educator, civil engineering consultant; b. Kenya, Jan. 2, 1941; s. William and Ruth (Koch) M.; m. Mary Joyce Pool, July 27, 1963; children: Erica Ruth, Christian William, Heidi Clara. B.S., Bradley U., 1962; M.S., U. Colo., 1964, Ph.D., 1967. Registered profl. engr., N.Mex. Civil engr. Ill. Hwy. Dept., Peoria, summer 1959-63; instr. U. Colo., Boulder, 1964-67; from asst. to prof. engring. U. N.Mex., Albuquerque, 1967-77, prof. of civil engring, 1977—; dean Coll. Engring., U. N.Mex., Albuquerque, 1980-86; pres. U. N.Mex., Albuquerque, 1986-90; dir. accident study program, Albuquerque, 1970-75, cons. to corps., govtl. agys. Contbr. articles to profl. jours., chpts. to books. Recipient Borden Freshman award Bradley U., 1958. Mem. ASCE (pres. N.Mex. sect. 1982-83), Am. Soc. Engring. Edn. (Outstanding Young Faculty award 1973), Nat. Soc. Profl. Engrs., Sigma Xi, Chi Epsilon, Tau Beta Pi, Phi Eta Sigma. Office: Univ N Mex Civil Engring Dept Albuquerque NM 87131

MAY, GITA, French language and literature educator; b. Brussels, Sept. 16, 1929; came to U.S., 1947, naturalized, 1950; d. Albert and Blima (Sieradska) Jochimek; m. Irving May, Dec. 21, 1947. BA magna cum laude, CUNY-Hunter Coll., 1953; MA, Columbia U., 1954, PhD, 1957. Lectr. French CUNY-Hunter Coll., 1953-56; instr. Columbia U., 1956-58, asst. prof., 1958-61, assoc. prof., 1961-68, prof., 1968—, chmn., 1983-93, mem. senate, 1979-83, 86-88, chmn. Seminar on 18th Century Culture, 1986-89; lecture tour English univs., 1965. Author: Diderot et Baudelaire, critiques d'art, 1957, De Jean-Jacques Rousseau à Madame Roland: essai sur la sensibilité préromantique et révolutionaire, 1964, Madame Roland and the Age of Revolution, 1970 (Van Amringe Disting. Book award), Stendhal and the Age of Napoleon, 1977; co-editor: Diderot Studies III, 1961; mem. editl. bd. 18th Century Studies, 1975-78, French Rev., 1975-86, Romanic Rev., 1959—; contbg. editor: Deuvres complétes de Diderot, 1984, 95; gen. editor: The Age of Revolution and Romanticism: Interdisciplinary Studies, 1990—; contbr. articles and revs. to profl. jours. Decorated chevalier and officer Ordre des Palmes Acad.; recipient award Am. Coun. Learned Socs., 1961, award for outstanding achievement CUNY-Hunter Coll., 1963; Fulbright rsch. grantee, 1964-65; Guggenheim fellow, 1964-65, NEH fellow, 1971-72. Mem. AAUP, MLA (del. assembly 1973-75, mem. com. rsch. activities 1975-78, mem. exec. coun. 1980-83), Am. Assn. Tchrs. of French, Am. Soc. 18th Century Studies (pres. 1985-86, 2nd v.p. 1983-84, 1st v.p. 1984-85), Soc. Française d'Etude du Dix-Huitième Siècle, Soc. Diderot, Am. Soc. French Acad. Palms, Phi Beta Kappa. Home: 404 W 116th St New York NY 10027-7202

MAY, HAROLD EDWARD, chemical company executive; b. N.Y.C., Oct. 18, 1920; s. Charles Edward and Mollie (Flax) M.; m. Margaret June Hochman, June 27, 1943; children: Charles S., Michael E., Suzanne E. A.B., Columbia U., 1941, B.S. in Mech. Engring, 1942. With E.I. duPont de Nemours & Co., Inc., 1942—; v.p. materials and logistics E.I. duPont de Nemours & Co., Inc., Wilmington, Del., 1977-82, sr. v.p. corp. staff, 1982-85; ret. E.I. duPont de Nemours & Co., Inc., 1985. Recipient Illig medal Columbia U., 1942. Mem. Phi Beta Kappa, Tau Beta Pi. Jewish. Home: 36 Southridge Dr Kennett Square PA 19348-2714

MAY, HENRY STRATFORD, JR., lawyer; b. Greensboro, N.C., May 12, 1947; s. Henry Stratford and Doris (Richardson) M.; m. Jean Eros, May 5, 1979; children: Henry Stratford III, Benjamin Alexander. BA, U. Tex., 1969, JD, 1971. Bar: Tex. 1972, U.S. Ct. Appeals (D.C. cir.) 1974, U.S. Supreme Ct. 1977, U.S. Ct. Appeals (5th and 11th cirs.) 1981, U.S. Dist. Ct. (so. dist.) Tex. 1985. Law clk. to judge U.S. Ct. Appeals (D.C. cir.), Washington, 1972-73; assoc. Vinson & Elkins, Houston, 1973-79, ptnr., 1979—, head energy sect., 1990—; adj. prof. U. Houston Law Sch., 1994—. Author: Natural Gas Contracts. Mem. ABA, Tex. Bar Assn. Republican. Home: 3606 Del Monte Dr Houston TX 77019-3016 Office: Vinson & Elkins 3400 First City Tower 1001 Fannin St Houston TX 77002-6706

MAY, J. PETER, mathematics educator; b. N.Y.C., Sept. 16, 1939; s. Siegmund Henry and Jane (Polachek) M.; m. Maija Bajars, June 8, 1963; children: Anthony D., Andrew D. BA, Swarthmore Coll., 1960; PhD, Princeton U., 1964. Instr. Yale U., New Haven, 1964-65, asst. prof., 1965-67; assoc. prof. U. Chgo., 1967-70, prof., 1970—, chmn. dept. math., 1985-91, chmn. coun. on teaching, 1991—; mem. Inst. Advanced Study, Princeton, 1966; vis. prof. Cambridge U., Eng., 1971-72, 1977. Author: Simplicial Objects in Algebraic Topology, 1967, The Geometry of Iterated Loop Spaces, 1972, E-infinity Ring Spaces and E-infinity Ring Spectra, 1977, Equivariant Homotopy and Cohomology Theory, 1996; co-author: The Homology of Iterated Loop Spaces, 1976, H-infinity Ring Spectra and Their Applications, 1986, Equivariant Stable Homotopy Theory, 1987, Rings Modules and Algebras in Stable Homotopy Theory; also numerous articles and monographs. NSF grantee, 1967—; Fulbright fellow, 1971-72; fellow Nat. Research Council, Eng., 1977. Mem. AAUP, Am. Math. Soc. Office: U Chgo Dept Math 5734 S University Ave Chicago IL 60637-1514

MAY, JACKSON CAMPBELL, real estate developer, writer; b. Danville, Ky., June 19, 1936; s. Earl Campbell and Emma Lee (Fleming) M.; m. De Lena Inez Courtney, Nov. 26, 1965 (div. 1981); children: Jackson Campbell II (dec.), Geoffrey Courtney; m. Juanita Lucielee Sarver, June 16, 1984; children: Winston Augustus, Emmalee Annabella. BS, U.S. Mil. Acad., 1958. Commd. 1st lt. U.S. Army, 1958, with airborne, ranger and mountain sects. 82d Airborne Divsn., 1958-61; founder The May Cos., Gainesville, Fla., 1961—; Bd. dirs. First City Bank, Gainesville, Nat. Apt. Devel. Coun.; internat. explorer, safari photographer, mountain climber, 1950—; founder Pub. Partnerships for Investment, U.S., Germany, Italy; presenter numerous seminars. Contbr. articles to profl. jours. Patron Jacksonville Symphony, Hippodrome State Theatre, Performing Arts Ctr. U. Fla., World Wildlife Fund; advisor dept. classics U. Fla. Named to Honorable Order Ky. Cols. Mem. Alumni Assn. U. Fla., Gator Boosters U. Fla., Assn. Grads. West Point, Chevaliers du Tastevin (Palm Beach), Explorers Club (N.Y.), Gainesville Country Club, Gator Hunt Club, The Heritage Club (Gainesville), Lodge and Bath Club (Ponte Vedra Beach), Mensa, River Club (Jacksonville), Safari Club Internat., The Seminole Club (Jacksonville), Poinciana Club (Palm Beach), Societe de Bons Vivants, Sports Car Club Am., Univ. Club (Orlando), Soc. Colonial Wars, Circumnavigators Club (N.Y.), Am. Mus. Nat. History, Cousteau Soc., Ducks Unltd., Smithsonian. Republican. Baptist. Avocations: mountaineering, arctic and underwater exploration, photography, automobiles, writing. Office: The May Cos PO Box 140600 Gainesville FL 32614-0600

MAY, JAMES M., medical educator, medical researcher; b. Oklahoma City, Aug. 20, 1947; married; 2 children. BS, Yale Coll., 1969; MD, Vanderbilt U., 1973. Diplomate Am. Bd. Internal Medicine, Am. Bd. Endocrinology and Metabolism. Intern Vanderbilt U., Nashville, 1973-74, assoc. prof. medicine, 1986—, assoc. prof. molecular physiology and biophysics, 1993—; resident in medicine Johns Hopkins Hosp., Balt., 1974-75; fellow in endocrinology U. Wash., Seattle, 1975-78; asst. prof. medicine Med. Coll. Va., Richmond, 1978-83, assoc. prof. medicine, 1983-86; mem. award com. dept. medicine Vanderbilt U., 1992—; mem. awards com. Summer Diabetes Program, Diabetes Rsch. and Tng. Ctr., 1994—. Mem. editl. bd. Metabolism, 1996—; contbr. articles to profl. jours. Recipient Nat. Rsch. Svc. award NIH, 1975-78, grantee, 1993, 95; recipient Poncin Fund award, 1975-78. Mem. Am. Diabetes Assn. (pres. Va. affiliate 1985-86, chmn. rsch. com. Tenn. affiliate 1990-92, Rsch. award 1996), Am. Fedn. Clin. Rsch. (sec.-treas. So. sect. 1983-86, nat. councilor 1983-88, pres.- elect and pres. 1986-88), Am. Soc. Clin. Investigation, So. Soc. Clin. Investigation, Alpha Omega Alpha. Office: Vanderbilt U Med Ctr Divsn Endocrinology & Diabetes 715 Med Rsch Bldg II Nashville TN 37232-6303

MAY, JERRY RUSSELL, psychologist; b. Seattle, Apr. 24, 1942; s. Harold Russell May and Anne Margret (Jones) DeGolier; m. Carolyn Marlene May; children: Darin, Christopher, Laurel. Student, Sorbonne U., Paris, 1961-62; BA, Western Wash. U., 1966; PhD, Bowling Green State U., 1974. Prof. psychiatry sch. medicine U. Nev., Reno, 1974-90, dean admissions and student affairs sch. medicine, 1977—; cons. VA Med. Ctr., Reno, 1974-90, U.S. Olympic Sports Medicine Program, Colorado Springs, Colo., 1977—; pvt. practice clin. psychology, mgmt. cons., Reno, 1977—; team psychologist U.S. Ski Team, Park City, Utah, 1977-92; chmn. U.S. Olympic Psychology Com., Colorado Springs, 1985-92; mem. U.S. Olympic Sports Medicine Coun., Colorado Springs, 1985-92; team psychologist U.S. Sailing Team, 1992—. Author/editor: Sports Psychology: The Psychological Health of the Athlete, 1987; contbr. articles to profl. jours., chpts. to books. Chair West Coast Group on Student Affairs, 1981-82, 96-97. Served to lt. USN, 1968-71. Recipient Disting. Alumni award Western Wash. U., 1993, Bowling Green State U., 1995. Fellow APA; mem. No. Nev. Assn. Cert. Psychologists (pres. 1979-82), Am. Assn. Med. Colls., Nev. Psychol. Assn. Office: U Nev Sch Medicine Reno NV 89557

MAY, JOHN ANDREW, petrophysicist, geologist; b. Lawrence, Kans., July 4, 1952; s. Donald Lawrence and Marie Jean (McCartney) M.; m. Aurelia Angela Szyfer, Nov. 23, 1988; children: Sean, Thomas, Daniel, Krystyna. BS in Geology, U. Kans., 1974. Sr. geologist Cities Svc. Oil Co., Tulsa, 1974-80; div. geologist Exxon, Denver, 1980-85; mgr. exploration systems Sci. Software-Intercomp, Denver, 1985-88; sr. staff geologist Kerr-McGee, Houston, 1985—; mem. quality assurance com. Internat. MWD Soc., Houston, 1994—. Mem. Am. Assn. Petroleum Geologists (cert., Cert. of Merit award 1993), Soc. Petroleum Engrs., Soc. Profl. Well L.A. (publs. com. 1995—), Okla. SPWLA (pres. 1993-94, v.p. tech. 1994-95). Democrat. Roman Catholic. Achievements include mapping of Natuna D-Alpha Reef complex in South China Sea; development of Environ and Calc numerical petrophysical models. Avocations: computers, travel, camping. Home: 99 Tree Crest Cir The Woodlands TX 77381 Office: Kerr McGee 3 Northpoint Dr Houston TX 77060-3232

MAY, JOHN RAYMOND, clinical psychologist; b. Rahway, N.J., Jan. 31, 1943; s. John Y. and Aline (Eichorn) M.; BA in Psychology, Colgate U., 1965; PhD in Clin. Psychology, U. N.C., 1970; m. Brenda Lee Berg, June 17, 1967; children: Stacey Anne, John Jeffrey. Clin. intern U. Wis. Med. Center, 1967-68; staff psychologist to chief, clin. services div. Nat. Security Agy., Ft. Meade, Md., 1969-72, cons., 1972-92; pvt. practice clin. psychology, Columbia, Md., 1972—; exec. dir. Psychol. Health Svcs., Inc., Columbia, 1976-84, 93—; exec. dir. Columbia Psychol. Services, 1984-91, Cmty. Counseling Assocs., 1991—; co-dir. Columbia Addictions Ctr., 1994—; adj. prof. Loyola Coll., 1970-72. Recipient Wallach award U. N.C., 1969, Humanitarian award Citizens Against Spousel Assault, 1989; USPHS fellow, 1966-69; VA fellow, 1965-66. Mem. Am. Psychol. Assn., Md. Psychol. Assn. (exec. council, various coms. 1977-91, treas. 1985-88, pres.-elect 1988, pres. 1989-90, past pres. 1990-91, Outstanding Profl. Contbn. to Psychology award 1993), Am. Bd. Sexology (diplomate), Assn. Advancement of Psychology, Am. Soc. Clin. Hypnosis, Am. Assn. Sex Educators, Counselors and Therapists (cert. sex therapist), Anxiety Disorders Assn. Am., Howard County Psychol. Soc. (pres. 1975-76). Co-author films on mental health tng., articles in profl. jours. and manuals. Home: 6264 Cardinal Ln Columbia MD 21044-3802 Office: 10774 Hickory Ridge Rd Columbia MD 21044-3646

MAY, JOSEPH LESERMAN (JACK), lawyer; b. Nashville, May 27, 1929; s. Daniel and Dorothy (Fishel) M.; m. Natalie McCuaig, Apr. 12, 1957 (dec. May 1990); children: Benjamin, Andrew, Joshua, Maria; m. Lynn Hewes Lance, June 10, 1994. BA, Yale U., 1951; JD, NYU, 1958; postgrad., Harvard Bus. Sch., 1969. Bar: Tenn. 1959. Prodr. Candied Yam Jackson Show, 1947-51; with CIA, 1951-55; pres. Nuweave Socks, Inc., N.Y.C., 1955-59, May Hosiery Mills, Nashville, 1960-83, Athens Hosiery Mills, Tenn., 1966-83; v.p. Wayne-Gossard Corp., Chattanooga, 1972-83; pvt. practice law Nashville, 1984—; bd. dirs. Convertible Holdings, Princeton, N.J., World Income Fund, Princeton, Merrill Lynch Growth Fund; adv. group Civil Justice Reform Act U.S. Dist. Ct., 1991; adv. bd. Asian Strategies Group, 1994. Bd. dirs. Vanderbilt Cancer Ctr., 1994—; pres. Jewish Cmty. Ctr., 1969; chmn. Guardianship and Trust Corp., 1994-96; trustee Tenn. Hist. Soc., 1996—. With USN, 1947-53, U.S. Army, 1954. Mem. Tenn. Bar Assn., Nashville Bar Assn., Tenn. Hist. Soc. (trustee 1996), Eagle Scout Assn., Belle Meade Country Club, Shamus Club, Old Oak Club, Yale Club N.Y., Rotary (pres. Nashville 1971). Home: 2136 Golf Club Ln Nashville TN 37215-1224 Office: Box 190628 424 Church St Ste 2000 Nashville TN 37219-0628

MAY, KENNETH NATHANIEL, food industry consultant; b. Livingston, La., Dec. 24, 1930; s. Robert William and Mary Hulda (Caraway) M.; m. Patsy Jean Farr, Aug. 4, 1953; children: Sherry Alison (dec.), Nathan Elliott. BS in Poultry Sci., La. State U., 1952, MS in Poultry Sci., 1955; PhD in Food Tech., Purdue U., 1959, DAgr, 1988. Asst. prof. U. Ga., Athens, 1958-64, assoc. prof., 1964-67, prof., 1967-68; prof. Miss. State U., State College, 1968-70; dir. rsch. Holly Farms Poultry, Wilkesboro, N.C., 1970-73, v.p., 1973-85, pres., 1985-88, chmn., CEO, 1989; bd. dirs. Hudson Foods, Inc., Embrex, Inc., Alcide Corp.; adj. prof. N.C. State U., 1975. Contbr. over 60 articles to profl. jours.; patentee treatment of cooked poultry. Bd. trustees Appalachian State U., 1987-94, chmn., 1989-90. Recipient Industry Service award Poultry and Egg Inst. Am., 1971, Meritorious Service award, Ga. Egg Commn., 1964, Disting. Service award Agribus. N.C., 1986; named to Am. Poultry Hall of Fame, 1992. Fellow Poultry Sci. Assn.; mem. Nat. Poultry Hist. Soc. (bd. dirs. 1982-83), Inst. Food Technologists. Methodist. Avocations: reading, stained glass.

MAY, LINDA KAREN CARDIFF, safety engineer, nurse; b. San Mateo, Calif., Oct. 26, 1948; d. Leon Davis and Jane Vivian (Gallow) Cardiff; m. Donald William May, Dec. 7, 1969 (div. Feb. 1988); children: Charles David, Andrew William. Student in nursing So. Ill. U., 1969, Ill Wesleyan U., 1989; AAS, Parkland Coll., 1977; BS in Pub. Health and Safety Engring. with honors, U. Ill., Urbana, 1987; RN, BSN, Lakeview Coll., 1990. RN, Ill., Ind., Mo., N.Mex., Tex., Wis.; registered profl. nurse; nat. registered EMT, Ill.; OSHA accredited instr. constrn. safety and health. Indsl. nurse

C.S. Johnson Co., Champaign, Ill., 1978-79; safety dir. Solo Cup Co., Urbana, Ill., 1979-84; safety engr. Clinton Nuclear Power Plant, Ill. Power Co., 1984-86, occupational safety and health specialist Danville Vet.'s Med. Ctr., 1986—; with LKM Health and Safety Cons., Inc., Champaign, Ill. Mem. Champaign County Crime Prevention Coun., 1978-83, bd. dirs., 1980-82; active Champaign County Task Force on Arson, 1981—, Mercy Hosp. Aux., Covenant Hosp Auxiliary, 1977—. Ill. State Gen. Assembly scholar, 1967. Mem. AACN, APHA (mem. occupational health and safety sect.), Am. Soc. Safety Engrs. (vice chair Ctrl. Ill. sect. 1985-86), Am. Nuclear Soc. (mem. biology and medicine divsn., mem. radiopharm. and isotope product stds. com.), Am. Assn. Occupational Health Nurses, Nat. Registery EMT, Ill. Environ. Health Assn., Ill. Soc. Pub. Health Educators, Associated Ill. Milk, Food and Environ. Sanitarians, Pre-Hosp. Care Providers Ill., Ill. EMTs Assn., N.Y. Acad. Sci, U. Ill. Alumni Assn. (life), Parkland Coll. Almuni Assn. (life, bd. dirs. 1987—, v.p. 1992—), Parkland Coll. Found. Bd. (alumni assn. liason bd. dirs. 1993), Ill. Wesleyan U. Alumni Assn., Lakeview Coll. Nursing Alumni Assn., Eta Sigma Gamma. Methodist. Home: PO Box 3954 Champaign IL 61826-3954

MAY, MARGRETHE, allied health educator; b. Tucson, Ariz., Oct. 6, 1943; d. Robert A. and Margrethe (Holm) M. BS in Human Biology, U. Mich., 1970, MS in Anatomy, 1986. Cert. surg. technologist. Surg. technologist Hartford (Conn.) Hosp., 1965-68, U. Mich. Hosps., Ann Arbor, 1968-70; asst. operating room supr. U. Ariz. Med. Ctr., Tucson, 1971-72; coord. operating room tech. program Pima Coll., Tucson, 1971-76; prof., coord. surg. tech. and surg. first asst. programs Delta Coll., University Center, Mich., 1978—; commr. Commn. on Accreditation of Allied Health Ednl. Programs, Chgo., 1994—, Coun. Accreditation and Unit Recognition, 1994-96. Editor: Core Curriculum for Surgical Technology, 3d edit., 1990, Core Curriculum for Surgical First Assisting, 1993; contbr. articles to profl. jours. Mem. Assn. Surg. Technologists (bd. dirs. 1987-89, pres.-elect 1989-90, pres. 1990-91, on-site visitor program accreditation 1974—, chmn. exam writing com. 1981, liaison coun. on cert. co-chmn. 1977, chmn. 1978, sec.-treas. 1979, chmn. accreditation review com for edn. in surg. tech. 1994—), Am. Soc. Law, Medicine and Ethics, Mich. Assn. Allied Health Professions (sec. 1994—), Nat. Network Health Career Programs in Two-Year Colls. Avocations: international health care issues and allied health education. Home: 2506 Abbott Rd Apt P-2 Midland MI 48642-4876 Office: Delta Coll Allied Health Divsn University Center MI 48710

MAY, MARY LOUISE, elementary education educator; b. Highland, Ill., Nov. 9, 1946; d. Cecil S. and Marie (Papp) Harmon; 1 child, Alesia Lovellette. BS, So. Ill. U., Edwardsville, 1973. Elem. tchr. Edwardsville Sch. Dist. 7, 1974—; presenter math. confs., 1990—. Mem. ASCD, Ill. Edn. Assn., Ill. Coun. Tchrs. Math., Edwardsville Edn. Assn. (v.p. 1990-95, pres. 1995—), Illini Tchrs. Whole Lang., Delta Kappa Gamma, Beta Sigma Phi (pres. laureate chpt.). Avocations: reading, writing, golf, counted cross-stitch, walking. Home: 16 Dorset Ct Edwardsville IL 62025-3920 Office: Woodland Sch 59 S State Route 157 Edwardsville IL 62025

MAY, MELVIN ARTHUR, computer software company executive; b. Cortez, Colo., Oct. 22, 1940; s. Everett James and Viola Christina (Lair) M.; m. Dale Charlene Kelly, Oct. 3, 1963; children: Diana, Michael. A.A., Pueblo Coll., 1959; B.S., U. Colo., 1961. Accountant Haskins & Sells (C.P.A.'s), San Diego, Denver, and Colorado Springs, Colo., 1961-68; asst. to v.p., treas. Holly Sugar Corp., Colorado Springs, 1968-69, asst. treas., 1970-71, treas., 1972-82, v.p., 1977-82; v.p. fin. Cibar, Inc., Colorado Springs, 1982-86, chief operating officer, 1983-86, sr. v.p. fin., 1986-87; ret., 1987. Served with USMCR, 1963-64. Mem. NRA. Home: 637 Dexter St Colorado Springs CO 80911-2539

MAY, MICHAEL LEE, magazine editor; b. Dayton, Ohio, Oct. 13, 1959; s. John William and Sarah (Allen) M. BA, Earlham Coll., 1982; MS, U. Conn., 1984; PhD, Cornell U., 1990. Assoc. editor Am. Scientist, Rsch. Triangle Park, N.C., 1991—. Contbr. articles to profl. jours. Mem. Nat. Assn. Sci. Writers, Sigma Xi. Avocations: bicycling, bird watching. Office: Am Scientist PO Box 13975 Research Triangle Pk NC 27709-3975

MAY, PHILIP ALAN, sociology educator; b. Bethesda, Md., Nov. 6, 1947; s. Everette Lee and Marie (Lee) M.; m. Doreen Ann Garcia, Sept. 5, 1972; children: Katrina Ruth, Marie Ann. BA in Sociology, Catawba Coll., 1969; MA in Sociology, Wake Forest U., 1971; PhD in Sociology, U. Mont., 1976. NIMH predoctoral fellow U. Mont., Missoula, 1973-76; dir. health stats. and rsch. Navajo Health Authority, Window Rock, Ariz., 1976-78; asst. prof. U. N.Mex., Albuquerque, 1978-82, assoc. prof., 1982-89, prof., 1989—, dir. Ctr. on Alcoholism, Substance Abuse and Addictions, 1990—; mem. fetal alcohol syndrome study com., Inst. of Medicine/Nat. Acad. Scis., 1994-95; cons. various govt. agys., 1976—; dir. Nat. Indian Fetal Alcohol Syndrome Prevention Program, Albuquerque, 1979-85; mem. adv. bd. Nat. Orgn. on Fetal Alcohol Syndrome, Washignton, 1990—; rsch. assoc. Nat. Ctr. for Am. Indian and Alaska Native Mental Health Rsch., 1986—. Contbr. chpts. to books and articles to profl. jours. Mem. Ctrl. United Meth. Ch., Albuquerque, 1980-90, First United Meth. Ch., Albuquerque, 1990—. Lt. USPHS, 1970-73. Recipient Spl. Recognition award U.S. Indian Health Svc., 1992, award Navajo Tribe and U.S. Indian Health Svc., 1992, Human Rights Promotion award UN Assn., 1994, Program award for Contbns. to Mental Health of Am. Indians, U.S. Indian Health Svc., 1996. Mem. APHA, Am. Sociol. Assn., Population Ref. Bur., Coll. on Problems of Drug Dependence. Home: 4610 Idlewilde Ln SE Albuquerque NM 87108-3422 Office: U NMex CASAA 2350 Alamo Ave SE Albuquerque NM 87106-3202

MAY, PHYLLIS JEAN, financial executive; b. Flint, Mich., May 31, 1932; d. Bert A. and Alice C. (Rushton) Irvine; m. John May, Apr. 24, 1971. Grad. Dorsey Sch. Bus., 1957; cert. Internat. Corr. Schs., 1959, Nat. Tax Inst., 1978; MBA, Mich. U., 1970. Registered real estate agt; lic. life, auto and home ins. agent. Office mgr. Comml. Constrn. Co., Flint, 1962-68; bus. mgr. new and used car dealership, Flint, 1968-70; contr. various corps., Flint, 1970-75; fiscal dir. Rubicon Odyssey Inc., Detroit, 1976-87, Wayne County Treas.'s Office, 1987-93; exec. fin. officer Grosse Pointe Meml. Ch., 1993—; acad. cons. acctg. Detroit Inst. Commerce, 1980-81; pres. small bus. specializing in adminstrv. cons. and acctg., 1982—; supr. mobile svc. sta., upholstery and home improvement businesses; owner retail bus. Pieces and Things. Pres. PTA Westwood Heights Schs., 1972; vol. Fedn. of Blind, 1974-76, Probate Ct., 1974-76; mem. citizens adv. bd. Northville Regional Psychiat. Hosp., 1988, sec. 1989-90, pres. La'Renaissance Condominium Assn., Atlantic City, N.J.; Recipient Meritorious Svc. award Genesee County for Youth, 1976, Excellent Performance and High Achievement award Odyssey Inc., 1981. Mem. NAFE (bd. dirs.), Am. Bus. Women's Assn. (treas. 1981, rec. sec. 1982, v.p. 1982-83, Woman of Yr. 1982), Womens Assn. Dearborn Orch. Soc., Dearborn Community Art Ctr., Mich. Mental Health Assn., Internat. Platform Assn., Guild of Carillonneurs in N.Am., Pi Omicron (officer 1984-85). Baptist.

MAY, RONALD ALAN, lawyer; b. Waterloo, Iowa, Sept. 8, 1928; s. John W. and Elsie (Finlayson) M.; m. Naomi Gray, Aug. 18, 1950 (div. Feb. 1974); children: Sarah, Jonathan, Andrew, Rachel; m. Susan East Gray, May 9, 1975. B.A., U. Iowa, 1950; LL.B., Vanderbilt U., 1953. Bar: Ark. 1953. Atty. Daggett & Daggett, Marianna, 1953-57, Wright, Lindsey & Jennings, Little Rock, 1957-84; sr. ptnr. Wright, Lindsey & Jennings, 1984-96, of counsel, 1996—; Editor: Automated Law Research, 1972, Sense and Systems in Automated Law Research, 1975; contbg. editor Fifty State Construction Lien and Bond Law, 1992, Fifty State Public Construction Contracting, 1996; assoc. editor Jour. Irreproducible Results. Editor: Automated Law Research, 1972, Sense and Systems in Automated Law Research, 1975. Pres. Spl. Com. on Pub. Edn., Ark. Assn. for Mental Health, Friends of Library, Central Ark. Radiation Therapy Inst.; chmn. Ark. Cancer Research Ctr., 1990-92; bd. dirs. Nat. Assn. for Mental Health, Ark. State Hosp., Gaines House, State Bd. Architects; bd. dirs. State Bd. Bar Examiners, chmn. 1987-88, Ark. ethics com., 1991-93; trustee Mus. Sci. and Natural History, Little Rock, chmn., 1973; mem. profl. adv. bd. sch. architecture U. Ark., 1990—, mem. profl. adv. bd. sch. urban studies and design, 1993—. Served with AUS, 1946-47. Mem. ABA (chmn. sci. and tech. sect. 1975-76), Ark., Pulaski County Bar Assns., Internat. Assn. Def. Counsel, Am. Inns of Ct. (Master of the Bench), Assn. for Computing Machinery, Order of Coif, Phi Beta Kappa. Republican. Episcopalian. Clubs: Capital. Home: 821 N Ash St Little Rock AR 72205-2051 Office: Wright Lindsey & Jennings 200 W Capitol Ave Ste 2200 Little Rock AR 72201-3627

MAY, SCOTT C., special education educator; b. Seattle, Mar. 21, 1964; s. Kenneth Gordon and Susan Catherine (Carter) M. BS, Syracuse U., 1986, MS in Emotional Disturbance and Autism, 1989; postgrad., U. Melbourne, Australia, 1995—. Cert. spl. edn. tchr., N.Y., Hawaii, Alaska, Pa. Resident advisor Syracuse (N.Y.) U.; dir. after sch. program, lead tchr. Jowonio Sch., Syracuse, 1986-90; spl. edn. tchr. Lanai High & Elem., Lanai City, Hawaii, 1990-92; rschr. in tchr. tng., 1992-95; resource tchr. Mendenhall River Elem. & Dzantik I Heeni Middle Sch., Juneau, Alaska, 1996—; instr. U. Alaska S.E., 1997; mem. U.S. Spl. Edn. Delegation to Russia and the Czechoslovaka Republic. Advocate inclusive environments handicapped students' programs. Mem. ASCD, Assn. for Persons With Severe Handicaps, Coun. for Exceptional Children. Home: PO Box 33802 Juneau AK 99803-3802 Office: 10014 Crazy Horse Dr Juneau AK 99801-8529

MAY, STEPHEN, writer, former government official; b. Rochester, N.Y., July 30, 1931; s. Arthur J. and Hilda (Jones) M. Grad., Wesleyan U., 1953; LL.B., Georgetown U., 1961. Bar: N.Y. 1963. Exec. asst. to Rep. and Senator Kenneth B. Keating, 1955-64; asso., mem., then ptnr. Branch, Turner & Wise, Rochester, 1965-81; city councilman-at-large Rochester, 1966-73; mayor, 1970-73; chmn. and commr. N.Y. State Bd. Elections, Albany, 1975-79; asst. sec. for legis. and Congl. relations Dept. Housing and Urban Devel., 1981-88; lectr. and freelance writer for newspapers and mags., 1988—; Vice chmn. Temporary State Commn. on Powers of Local Govt., 1970-73; mem. 20th Century Fund Task Force on Future of N.Y.C., 1979, Nat. Adv. Commn. Higher Edn. for Police Officers, 1977-79, Joint Com. Assn. Bar City N.Y. and Drug Abuse Council on N.Y. Drug Law Evaluation, 1977-78; chmn. Rochester Interfaith Com. on Israel, 1973-81; del.-at-large Republican Nat. Conv., 1972; mem. N.Y. State Crime Control Planning Bd., 1970-73. Contbr. numerous articles on Am. art, culture and hist. preservation to newspapers and periodicals. Bd. dirs. Police Found., 1970-81, Nat. Com. for Labor Israel, 1977-81, Empire State Report, 1974-81, Inst. Mediation and Conflict Resolution, 1973-81. Served with U.S. Army, 1953-55. Mem. Phi Beta Kappa. Home and Office: 4101 Cathedral Ave NW Washington DC 20016-3585 also: 270 Mount Pleasant Rd Union ME 04862-3003

MAY, TIMOTHY JAMES, lawyer; b. Denver, Aug. 3, 1932; s. Thomas Henry and Helen Frances (O'Conner) M.; m. Monica Anita Gross, Aug. 24, 1957; children: Stephanie, Maureen, Cynthia, Timothy, Anthony. BA, Cath. U. Am., 1954; LLB, Georgetown U., 1957, LLM, 1960. Bar: D.C. 1957, U.S. Supreme Ct. 1961. Law clk. to judge U.S. Ct. Appeals, D.C. Cir., 1957-58; assoc. Covington & Burling, Washington, 1958-61; cons. Exec. Office of Pres. U.S., Washington, 1961-62; chief counsel subcom. on stockpile Armed Svcs. Com., U.S. Senate, Washington, 1962-63; mng. dir. Fed. Maritime Commn., Washington, 1963-66; gen. counsel U.S. Post Office Dept., Washington, 1966-69; sr. ptnr. Patton Boggs, L.L.P., Washington, 1969—. Bd. dirs. Legal Aid Soc. D.C., 1984—, Coun. for Ct. Excellence, Washington, 1985—; chmn. bd. regents Cath. U. Am., 1988-93, trustee, 1993—. Fellow Am. Bar Found.; mem. ABA (House of Dels.), Fed. Bar Assn., Bar Assn. of D.C. (pres. 1991-92), Congl. Country Club (bd. govs. 1992—, sec. 1994—, mem. exec. com. Nat. Christian Leadership Conf. for Israel), Met. Club, Indian Creek Country Club, Bal Harbour Club, Knight of Malta. Democrat. Roman Catholic. Home: 3828 52nd St NW Washington DC 20016-1924 Office: Patton Boggs LLP 2550 M St NW Washington DC 20037-1301

MAY, WALTER GRANT, chemical engineer; b. Saskatoon, Sask., Can., Nov. 28, 1918; came to U.S., 1946, naturalized, 1954; s. George Alfred and Abigail Almira (Robson) M.; m. Mary Louise Stockan, Sept. 26, 1945 (dec. 1977); children: John R., Douglas W., Caroline O; m. Helen Dickerson, 1988. B.Sc., U. Sask., Saskatoon, 1939, M.Sc., 1942; Sc.D., M.I.T., 1948. Registered profl. engr., Ill. Chemist British Am. Oil Co., Moose Jaw, Sask., 1939-40; asst. prof. U. Sask., 1943-46; with Exxon Research & Engring. Co., Linden, N.J., 1948-83; sr. sci. adv., 1976-83; prof. U. Ill., 1983-90, prof. emeritus, 1990—; with Advanced Research Projects Agy., Dept. Def., 1959-60; industry based prof. Stevens Inst. Tech., 1968-74, Rensselaer Poly. Inst., 1975-77. Recipient Process Indsl. Div. award ASME, 1972. Fellow Am. Inst. Chem. Engrs.; mem. Am. Inst. Chem. Engrs. (Chem. Engring. Practice award 1989), Nat. Acad. Engring. Home: 916 W Clark St Champaign IL 61821-3328 Office: U Ill Dept Chem Engring 1209 W California Ave Urbana IL 61801-3705

MAY, WILLIAM FREDERICK, manufacturing executive; b. Chgo., Oct. 25, 1915; s. Arthur W. and Florence (Hartwick) M.; m. Kathleen Thompson, June 14, 1947; children: Katherine Hartwick (Mrs. Edward W. Bickford), Elizabeth Shaw. BS, U. Rochester, 1937; grad. Advanced Mgmt. Program, Harvard, 1950; D in Engring., Clarkson U.; LLD, Okla. Christian Coll.; LHD, Livingstone U.; LLD, Lafayette U. Research worker E.I. Du Pont de Nemours Co., 1937-38; with Am. Can Co., 1940-80, mgr., 1957-58, v.p., 1958-64, exec. v.p., 1964-65, vice chmn. bd. dirs., 1965, chmn. bd. dirs., chief exec. officer, 1965-80; mem. exec. com. Am. Can Co., Greenwich, Conn., 1960—; bd. dirs. U.S. Surgical & Catalyst Energy Corp., Phibro-Salomon Corp.; dean Grad. Sch. Bus. Adminstrn., NYU, 1980-84; chmn. and chief exec. officer Statue of Liberty Found., 1984—. Bd. dirs. Lincoln Ctr.; trustee Am. Ditchley Found., Am. Mus. Natural History, Taft Inst. Govt., Columbia-Presbyn. Hosp., U. Rochester; mem. corp. Poly. Inst. N.Y.; chmn. pub. policy council Advt. Council. Mem. Nat. Order of Merit (France, officier), River Club, Econ. Club, Round Hill Club, Meguntic ook Golf Club, Golf Phi Beta Kappa, Alpha Delta Phi. Episcopalian. Home: 35 Lauder Ln Greenwich CT 06831-3707 Office: Statue of Liberty Found 52 Vanderbilt Ave New York NY 10017-3808

MAYBAY, DUANE CHARLES, recycling systems executive; b. Ft. Dodge, Iowa, Oct. 5, 1922; s. John H. and Florabel (Hibbard) Lungren; m. Mary Tribble Parrish, Dec. 18, 1947 (div. Oct. 1972); children: Tina Biggs, Karen Woodward. BA in Mktg., U. Wis., 1948. Product engr. Gates Rubber Co., Denver, 1948-50; asst. dir. sales & mktg. Hi-C divsn. Hi-C and Snow Crop Divsn. Minute Maid Corp., N.Y.C., 1951-63; mktg. dir. Knudsen Foods, L.A., 1963-70; owner Mountain Foods, Altadena, Calif., 1970-76, Maybay Recycling Sys., Irvine, Calif., 1976-84; pres. Resource Recovery Sys., Irvine, 1984—. Served to lt. col. U.S. Army Air Corps, 1943-45, Italy. Avocation: antiques. Home: 104 Pergola Irvine CA 92612-1704 Office: Resource Recovery Sys PO Box 17426 Irvine CA 92623

MAYBERRY, JULIUS EUGENE, realty company owner, investor; b. Qulin, Mo., July 3, 1935; s. Julius E. and Mabel L. (Gunnells) M.; m. Nettie Sue Burden, Dec. 8, 1953; children: Michael Eugene, Cynthia E. Copeland, Karen Sue Mayberry-Lee. AS, Ga. Mil. Acad., 1973; postgrad., Augusta Coll., 1976. Enlisted U.S. Army, 1957, advanced through grades to first sgt., 1973, ret., 1979; salesperson TIPS Realty Co., Augusta, Ga., 1979—, owner, broker, 1984—. Scoutmaster Boy Scouts of Am., Ft. Gordon, Ga., 1961-67. Decorated Bronze medal, Purple Heart. Mem. Augusta Bd. Realtors, Multiple Listing Service Augusta. Republican. Baptist. Lodge: Optimist (v.p. 1987). Avocation: golf. Office: TIPS Realty Co 2327 Lumpkin Ct Augusta GA 30906-3090

MAYCOCK, IAN DAVID, oil executive; b. St. Helens, Lancashire, Eng., Dec. 8, 1935; s. Joseph and Lilian (Hewitt) M.; m. Katherine Ella Bennett, May, 1968; children: Alison, Fiona, Colin, Andrew. BSc in Geology with honors, St. Andrews (Scotland) U., 1957; MSc in Geology, Queens U., Kingston, Ont., Can., 1959; PhD in Geology, Reading (Eng.) U., 1962. Field geologist Ont. Dept. Mines, 1957, Texaco Can., 1958-59; subsurface rsch. geologist Sask. (Can.) Dept. Mineral Resources, 1962-64; geologist Conoco, U.K., U.S., Middle East, 1964-73; exploration mgr. Zapata Exploration, London, 1973-80; pres. Hunt United, London, 1980-86; v.p. exploration Yemen Hunt Oil Co., Dallas, 1986-88; sr. v.p. exploration Hunt Oil Co., Dallas, 1989—. Queens/St. Andrews exchange scholar St. Andrews U., 1957; Thayer Linsdley rsch. fellow Queens U., 1958. Mem. Am. Assn. Petroleum Geologist, Soc. Econ. Paleontologists and Mineralogists, Dallas Petroleum Club. Avocations: fishing, photography. Office: Hunt Oil Co Fountain Pl 1445 Ross Ave Dallas TX 75202-2812

MAYCOCK, JOSEPH FARWELL, JR., lawyer; b. Buffalo, June 8, 1930; s. Joseph Farwell and Annie (Richmond) M.; m. Margaret Shaw, May 25, 1968; children—Suzannah, Mary, John. B.A., Hamilton Coll., 1952; J.D., U. Mich. Law Sch., 1955. Bar: Mich. Assoc. Miller, Canfield, Paddock & Stone, Detroit, 1958-68, ptnr., 1968-95, of counsel, 1995—. Contbr. articles to profl. jours. Mem. adv. bd. Small Bus. Council of Am., Columbia Ga., Washington, 1983—. Served with U.S. Army, 1955-57. Mem. ABA, Mich. Bar Assn., Detroit Bar Assn., Mich. Employee Benefits. Republican. Episcopalian. Clubs: Country of Detroit. Office: Miller Canfield Paddock & Stone 150 W Jefferson Ave Detroit MI 48226-4415

MAYDA, JARO, lawyer, educator, author, consultant; b. Brno, Czechoslovakia; came to U.S., 1949, naturalized, 1955; s. Francis and Maria (Hornova) M.; m. Maruja del Castillo, 1967; children by previous marriage: Jaro II, Maria Raquel, Pavel. Dr. Juris Utriusque, Masaryk U., Brno, 1945; J.D. (Rockefeller fellow 1955-56), U. Chgo., 1957. Legal counsel export div. Skodaworks, Pilsen-Prague, 1946-48; vis. prof. polit. sci. Denison U., Granville, Ohio, 1949-50, Ohio State U., Columbus, 1950-51; asst. prof. law and polit. sci. U. Wis.-Madison, 1951-56; mem. faculty U. P.R., Rio Piedras, 1957—; prof. law and public policy U. P.R., 1958-85, research prof., 1985-89; dir. Inst. Policy Studies and Law, 1972-75, spl. asst. to pres., 1972; Fulbright research prof. Inst. Comparative Law, U. Paris, 1967-68; fellow Woodrow Wilson Internat. Ctr. for Scholars (Smithsonian Instn.), 1971; Bailey lectr. La. State U., 1969; lectr. Am. specialist program Dept. State, 1960, Fed. Office of Environ., Berlin, 1983, UN Ctr. for Formation in Environ. Scis., Madrid, 1983, Grad. Sch. Bus. Adminstn., IESA, Caracas, Venezuela, 1987, U.S. Info. Agy. (German Democratic Republic, Czechoslovakia, Poland), 1988; Fulbright prof. Sch. Applied Econs., Dakar, Senegal, 1980; dep. sec. gen. 42d Conf. Internat. Law Assn., 1947; cons. Internat. Assn. Legal Sci., UNESCO, 1972—, FAO, 1974—, UN Environ. Program, 1977—, UN Econ. and Social Commn. for Asia and Pacific, 1977-78, UN Econ. Commn. for Europe, 1981, World Bank, 1994; mem. adv. com. Govt. of Columbia, 1974, Govt. of Honduras, 1977, Govt. of St. Vincent and the Grenadines, 1983, AID, Haiti, 1985, Mozambique, Guinea-Bissau; 1991, Chile, 1992, China, 1993, São Tomé & Principe, 1994; mem., policy adv. Gov.'s Study Group P.R. and Sea, 1972; research assoc. Ctr. Energy and Environ. Research, U. P.R.-U.S. Dept. Energy, 1977-88; adviser P.R. Environ. Quality Bd., 1984-86; mem. com. environ. policy and law Internat. Union Conservation Nature, 1972-78; mem. adv. com. Internat. Juridicial Orgn., Rome, 1991—; adv. panel on Ecosystem Data Handbook, NSF, 1976-77; mem. Internat. Council Environ. Law, Bonn, Ger., 1974—; U.S. rapporteur X Internat. Congress Comparative Law, Budapest, 1978; reporter on comparative legislation Congress on Forest Mgmt. and Environment, Madrid, 1984, Environ. Penal Law Internat. Symposium, San Juan, P.R., 1991, Globalization and Environment Conf. on Wider Caribbean, San Juan, 1994, NATO Advanced Rsch. Workshop on integrated assessment, Durham, N.C., 1995; lectr. Academia Istropolitana, U. Bratislava, 1994, Internat. Seminar on Environ. Impact, Moscow, 1995, Izmir, 1996. Author: Introduction to Law, 1959, 74, Environment and Resources: From Conservation to Ecomanagement, 1967, Francois Geny and Modern Jurisprudence, 1978, Policy Research and Development: Outline of a Methodology, 1979, UNEP Manual on Environ. Legis., 1979; also articles, manuals; translator: law treatises; mem. editorial bd.: Am. Jour. Comparative Law, 1958-78; dir.: U. P.R. Law Rev, 1958-62; contbr. to Ency. Environ. Law, Berlin, 1987, 93. Home: R Pedro de Ornelas 12-B, P-9050 Funchal Madeira, Portugal

MAYDEN, BARBARA MENDEL, lawyer; b. Chattanooga, Sept. 18, 1951; d. Eugene Lester Mendel and Blanche (Krugman) Rosenberg; m. Martin Ted Mayden, Sept. 14, 1986. AB, Ind. U., 1973; JD, U. Ga., 1976. Bar: Ga. 1976, N.Y. 1980. Assoc. King & Spalding, Atlanta, 1976-79, Willkie Farr & Gallagher, N.Y.C., 1980, Morgan Lewis & Bockius, N.Y.C., 1980-82, White & Case, N.Y.C., 1982-89; spl. counsel Skadden, Arps, Slate, Meagher & Flom, N.Y.C., 1989-95; of counsel Bass, Berry & Sims PLC, Nashville, 1996—; lectr. Vanderbilt U. Sch. Law, Nashville, 1995-97. Mem. U. Ga. Bd. Visitors, Athens, 1986-89. Fellow Am. Bar Found. (life); mem. ABA (chair young lawyers div. 1985-86, house of dels. 1986—, commr. commn. on women 1987-91, commr. commn. opportunities for minorities in profession 1986-87, chmn. assembly resolutions com. 1990-91, select com. of the house 1989-91, membership com. of the house 1991-92, chair com. on rules and calendar 1996—, bd. govs. 1991-94, chair bd. govs. ops. com., exec. com. 1993-94, mem. task force long range fin. planning 1993-94), Nat. Assn. Bond Lawyers (bd. dirs. 1985-86), Bond Attys.' Workshop (chmn. 1986), N.Y. State Bar Assn. (mem. ho. of dels. 1993-95), Assn. of Bar of City of N.Y. (internat. human rights com. 1986-89, 2d century com. 1986-90, com. women in the profession, 1989-92), N.Y. County Lawyers Assn. (com. spl. projects, chair com. rels with other bars). Democrat. Jewish. Home: 4414 Herbert Pl Nashville TN 37215-4544 Office: Bass Berry & Sims PLC 2700 First Am Ctr Nashville TN 37238-2700

MAYER, ALLAN, magazine editor, writer; b. N.Y.C., Mar. 15, 1950; s. Theodore H. and Phyllis (Zwick) M. BA, Cornell U., 1971. Staff reporter Wall Street Jour., N.Y.C., 1972-73; assoc. editor, gen. editor Newsweek mag., N.Y.C., 1973-77; fgn. corr. Newsweek mag., London, 1977-80; sr. editor Newsweek mag., N.Y.C., 1980-82; editl. dir. Arbor House Pub., N.Y.C., 1986-88; sr. editor Simon & Schuster, N.Y.C., 1988-89; editor-in-chief Buzz mag., L.A., 1990-95, editor-in-chief, pub., 1996—. Author: Madam Prime Minister, 1980, Gaston's War, 1987. Recipient award Overseas Press Club, 1974, nat. mag. award Am. Soc. Mag. Editors, 1978, William Allen White award City and Regional Mag. Assn., 1995-96. Mem. Writers Guild Am.

MAYER, ANDREW MARK, librarian, journalist; b. N.Y.C., Feb. 9, 1947; s. Richard J. and Helen A. (Aberson) M.; m. Hyacinth P. Franklin, Jan. 19, 1972 (div. May 1976); m. Carmen Mercedes Zapata-Gomez, Feb. 28, 1988; 1 child, Andrew Charles. Student, Hillsdale Coll., 1964-67; BA in History, George Washington U., 1968, MA in History, 1971; postgrad., Georgetown U., 1977; proofreading, copyediting cert., NYU, 1992. Researcher Glaverbel S.A., Brussels, 1966; libr. asst. rsch. Washington Post Co., 1969-73, asst. libr. rsch., 1973-87, night coord. rsch. newsroom, 1987-92; rsch. libr. Bituminous Coal Operators Assn., Washington, 1971; researcher, editor to author Donald Neff Washington, 1981-84; pres. cons. Latin Am. Rsch. Assn., Washington, 1984; libr., researcher Ctr. for Strategic Internat. Studies, Washington, 1986-87; libr. pub. rels. Sawyer/Miller Group, N.Y.C., 1992; libr. newspaper N.Y. Law Pub. Co., N.Y.C., 1994; rsch. analyst Ctr. for Pub. Comm., N.Y.C., 1994—; v.p. R. J. Mayer & Co., N.Y.C., 1984—; book reviewer Small Press Pub., R.I., 1992—, Army Times Pub. Co., Washington, 1972-75; freelance writer Washington Post Co., 1976—. Active McGovern for Pres. campaign, Washington, 1972; researcher Dem. Nat. Com., Washington, 1971; active U.S. Holocaust Meml. Mus., Washington, 1992—. Mem. Am. Hist. Assn. (writer for hist. convs. 1976—), Modern Hist. Soc., Spl. Librs. Assn., Phi Alpha Theta. Jewish. Avocations: tennis, dramatic arts, music, literature, soccer. Home: 181 Roosevelt Ave Staten Island NY 10314-4152 Office: 181 Roosevelt Ave Staten Island NY 10314-4152

MAYER, CARL JOSEPH, lawyer, town official; b. Boston, Apr. 23, 1959; s. Arno Joseph and Nancy Sue (Grant) M. AB magna cum laude, Princeton U., 1981; JD, U. of Chgo., 1986; LLM, Harvard U., 1988. Bar: N.J. 1986, Mass. 1988, N.Y. 1989, D.C. 1989. Writer for Ralph Nader Washington, 1981-83; law clk. to presiding justice U.S. Dist. Ct., Wilmington, Del., 1986-87; asst. prof. Hofstra Law Sch., Hempstead, N.Y., 1989-94; atty. Milberg, Weiss, Bershad, Hynes and Lerach, N.Y.C., 1995—; cons. U.S. Senate Com., Washington, 1988-89. Co-author: Public Domain, Private Dominion, 1985; contbr. articles to profl. jours. Town committeeman, Princeton, N.J. NYU fellow, 1988-89. Mem. ABA, N.Y. Bar Assn., N.J. Bar Assn., Mass. Bar Assn. Avocations: marathon running, squash, tennis. Home: 58 Battle Rd Princeton NJ 08540-4902 Office: Milberg Weiss Bershad Hynes & Lerach One Pennsylvania Plz New York NY 10019

MAYER, DENNIS THOMAS, biochemist, educator; b. Lexington, Mo., Jan. 3, 1901; s. August John and Agatha (Gavin) M.; m. Virginia Louise Miller, May 8, 1937; children—Dennis T., David R., Michael J. Student, U. Ill., 1923-25; A.B., U. Mo., 1931, M.A., 1933, Ph.D., 1938. Agt. U.S. Dept. Agr., 1937-42; mem. faculty U. Mo. at Columbia, 1937—, prof. agrl. biochemistry, 1952—, dir. research in physiology and biochemistry reprodn., 1942—, dir. interdisciplinary reproductive biology tng. program, 1966, chmn. dept. agrl. chemistry, dir. grad. studies, 1968-71, prof. emeritus, 1971—.

Contbr. articles to profl. jours. Mayer lecture series designated by U. Mo. in his honor, 1987. Mem. Am. Soc. Biol. Chemists, Soc. for Exptl. Biology and Medicine, Am. Soc. Animal Sci., N.Y. Acad. Scis., Mo. Acad. Sci., Phi Beta Kappa, Sigma Xi, Gamma Sigma Delta. Home: 3812 Cedar Ln Columbia MO 65201-6502

MAYER, DONNA MARIE, management information systems manager; b. Cicero, Ill., Apr. 21, 1949; d. Edward J. and Valerie I. (Laskowski) Veverka; m. Scott H. Mayer, Jan. 30, 1971; 1 child: Marie. BS in Math., U. Ill., 1971; MBA, U. Calif., Irvine, 1975. Rsch. asst. U. Ill., Urbana, 1969-71; office mgr., tax preparer H & R Block, Calif., 1972; campus stats. info. coord., project mgr., sys. analyst U. Calif., Irvine, 1972-80; project mgr. Northrop, Hawthorne, 1980-83; cons. self-employed Ill., 1971—; tax cons. in field, 1972—; guest spkr. in field. Statis. info. coord.: Mgmt. Info. Systems, 1972-83, info. coordination, 1979, Student & Workload Computerized Estimation System Model, 1973-80. Campus statis. info. coord. U. Calif., Irvine, 1972-80; cmty. fund raising for charities, Panhellenic Scholarship Fund; pres. Alpha Xi Delta Long Beach Alumnae, v.p., treas., sec., 1977-80, mem., 1968—; charity funding U.S. Navy Wives Club, Nuclear U.S. Navy Wives membership recognition, 1973; fall festival com. Friends of Danada Forest Preserve, Ill., 1989-96; mem. PTA, Ill., 1990-97; mem. Girl Scouts USA, 1958-67, 71-72, 90-97, leader, 1971-72, 90-95; ch. organist, 1963-71, 71-77. James scholar U. Ill., 1967—, Dean's list U. Ill., 1967-71; recipient Silver award for Excellence in Income Tax Preparation, 1972, Good Sportsmanship award, 1979, U. Calif. Employee Scholarship award, 1973-75. Mem. AAUW (corp. del. U. Calif. Irvine 1976-79, Nat. Leadership award 1979, univ. del. nat. conv. 1979, hon. bd. dirs. scholarship com. 1975-81), LWV (state budget com. vice chmn. 1975-76, state study com. 1976-78, bd. treas. Orange Coast League 1979-80, treas. 1977-79, com. chmn. 1975-81), Northrop Mgmt. Group, U. Calif. Faculty Club, Am. Statis. Assn., Acad. of Mgmt., Calif. Women in Higher Edn., Assn. Systems Mgmt., Assn. Computing Machinery, Grad. Sch. Mgmt. Alumnae, U. Calif. Alumnae Assn., U. Ill. Alumnae Assn., Internat. Toastmistress Clubs (area. coun. bd. dirs. 1978-80, coun. treas. 1979-80, Speech Contest award 1979, pres., v.p. 1978-79, treas., sec. 1977-78, parliamentarian com. chmn., recording sec. 1978-79, Internat. Mag. recognition 1979, regional rep. 1980), Panhellenic Coun. (bd. dirs. 1969-71, scholarship chmn. 1969-71), Naperville H.S. Alumnae. Avocations: computers, financial and economic data analysis, collectibles, study of various interests, youth and charity activities. Home: 601 N Arboretum Cir Wheaton IL 60187-8707

MAYER, FOSTER LEE, JR., toxicologist; b. Fletcher, Okla., Nov. 17, 1942; s. Foster Lee Sr. and Annis Lucille (Edwards) M.; m. Anita June Poarch, Aug. 31, 1962 (div. Nov. 1981); children: Sunie K., Carolyn Elizabeth; m. Kathleen Joyce Stecher, July 14, 1983. BS in Biology and Chemistry, Southwestern Okla. State U., 1965; MS in Wildlife Biology, Utah State U., 1967, PhD in Toxicology, 1970. Instr. Utah State U., Logan, 1969-70; research sect. leader U.S. Fish and Wildlife Service Columbia (Mo.) Fish Research Lab., 1970-73, asst. chief biologist, 1973-74, chief biologist, 1974-80, research scientist, 1980-84; sect. chief U.S. EPA, Gulf Breeze, Fla., 1984-85; br. chief EPA, Gulf Breeze, Fla., 1985-91, sr. rsch. scientist, 1991—; expert witness U.S. Fish and Wildlife Service, 1973-84. Author: Manual of Acute Toxicity-Freshwater, 1986, Acute Toxicity Handbook-Estuarine, 1987, also book chpts.; editor: Aquatic Toxicity and Hazard Evaluation, 1977; contbr. numerous articles to profl. jours. Instr. 4-H Club, Columbia, Mo., 1978-80. Mem. Am. Chem. Soc., Am. Fisheries Soc. (chpt. pres. 1976, sect. pres. 1979), Soc. Environ. Toxicology and Chemistry (editor 1982-87, bd. dirs. 1985-88), Soc. Toxicology (editl. bd. 1981-90, 95—), Am. Inst. Fishery Rsch. Biologists, ASTM, NRA, Sigma Xi. Republican. Baptist. Avocations: hunting, fishing, boating, wood carving, scrimshawing. Office: EPA Sabine Island Gulf Breeze FL 32561

MAYER, FRANK D., JR., lawyer; b. Dec. 23, 1933. BA, Amherst Coll., 1955; student, Cambridge U.; JD, U. Chgo., 1959. Bar: Ill. 1959. Ptnr. Mayer, Brown & Platt, Chgo. Mem. ABA, Chgo. Bar Assn., Order of Coif, Phi Beta Kappa. Office: Mayer Brown & Platt 190 S La Salle St Chicago IL 60603-3410

MAYER, GEORGE MERTON, elementary education educator; b. Ellisburg, N.Y., July 11, 1936; s. Carlton Scott and Florence Geraldine (Allen) M.; m. Charlotte Anne Dawley, Aug. 31, 1963; children: Linda Sue Mayer Randall, Brian Keith, Amanda Leanne. AA, Erie County Tech. Inst., 1957; BA in Edn., SUNY, Buffalo, 1966, MEd, 1973. Cert. tchr., N.Y. Lab. tech. Sylvania Electric Co., Buffalo, 1957-58; sch. driver, mechanic Ransomville (N.Y.) Bus Lines, 1959-66; coach driver Lockport (N.Y.) and Grand Island Transit Bus Lines, 1966-87; tchr. Thomas Marks Sch., Wilson, N.Y., 1965-82; tchr. remedial math. Wilson Sch. Dist., 1982—; coach wrestling Wilson High Sch., 1977-88, coach jr. varsity football, 1972. Lay leader, mem. choir Ransomville United Meth. Ch., 1960-90; co-chmn. Niagara County Foster Parents, 1980-93; bd. dirs. Town of Porter Recreation Commn. With USNG, 1955-58, USAR, 1958-62. Mem. Wilson Tchrs. Assn., N.Y. State United Tchrs. Assn., N.Y. State Foster and Adoptive Assn. Republican. Avocations: music, electronics, sports, woodworking. Home: 2470 Youngstown Lockport Rd Ransomville NY 14131-9644 Office: W H Stevenson Elem Sch 3745 Ransomville Rd Ransomville NY 14131-9768 also: Thomas Marks Elem Sch PO Box 648 Wilson NY 14172-0648

MAYER, HALDANE ROBERT, federal judge; b. Buffalo, N.Y., Feb. 21, 1941; s. Haldane Rupert and Myrtle Kathleen (Gaude) M.; m. Mary Anne McCurdy, Aug. 13, 1966; children: Anne Christian, Rebecca Paige. B.S., U.S. Mil. Acad., 1963; J.D., Coll. William and Mary, 1971. Bar: Va. 1971, U.S. Ct. Appeals (4th cir.) 1972, U.S. Dist. Ct. (ea. dist.) Va. 1972, U.S. Ct. Mil. Appeals, U.S. Army Ct. Mil. Rev. 1973, D.C. 1980, U.S. Supreme Ct. 1977, U.S. Ct. Claims 1984. Law clk. U.S. Ct. Appeals (4th cir.), Richmond, Va., 1971-72; atty. McGuire Woods & Battle, Charlottesville, Va., 1975-77; spl. asst. to chief justice U.S. Supreme Ct., Washington, 1977-80; atty. Baker & McKenzie, Washington, 1980-81; acting spl. counsel U.S. Merit Systems Protection Bd., Washington, 1981-82; judge U.S. Claims Ct., Washington, 1982-87, U.S. Ct. Appeals (Fed. cir.), Washington, 1987—; adj. prof. U. Va. Sch. Law, 1975-77, 92-94, George Washington U. Law Sch., 1992—. Bd. dirs. William and Mary Law Sch. Assn., 1979-85. Served to maj. AUS, 1963-75, lt. col. res. ret. Decorated Bronze Star, two Army Commendation medals, Meritorious Service medal. Mem. West Point Assn. Grads., Army Athletic Assn., West Point Soc. D.C., Omicron Delta Kappa. Office: US Ct Appeals for Fed Cir 717 Madison Pl NW Washington DC 20439-0002

MAYER, HENRY MICHAEL, mass transit consultant; b. Wauwatosa, Wis., Oct. 20, 1922; s. Henry and Rose (Daas) M.; m. Colleen C. Reisner, July 25, 1944; children: Michael, Michele, David, Jennifer. B.S. in Bus. Adminstrn., Marquette U., 1947. With Milw. Transit System, 1947-83, exec. asst., 1959-67, v.p., gen. mgr., 1967-75; pres., mng. dir. Milw. Transport Services, Inc., 1975-83; cons., 1983—; lectr., cons., author, mass transit. Lt. USNR, 1943-46, PTO. Named to Pub. Transit Hall of Fame. Mem. Inst. Transp. Engrs., Alpha Sigma Nu. Originator bus service using pvt. shopping centers as park-ride lots for freeway express service to downtown. Home: 9995 W North Ave Apt 350 Milwaukee WI 53226-2513

MAYER, HERBERT CARLETON, JR., computer consultant; b. Newton, Mass., Aug. 2, 1922; s. Herbert Carleton and Elsie Marie (Hauser) M.; m. Maryetta Brodkord, Aug. 21, 1948; children: Judith Marie, Christine Louise. BS, Parsons Coll., 1943; MS, U. Iowa, 1947; PhD, U. So. Calif., 1975. Instr. math. U. Idaho, Moscow, 1947-48, U. Utah, Salt Lake City, 1949-51; edn. adminstr. Gen. Electric co., Richland, Wash., 1951-59; systems engr., univ. industry specialist IBM, Chgo., 1959-81; assoc. prof. mgmt. info. systems Wash. State U., Pullman, 1980-82; assoc. prof. U. Wis.-Parkside, Kenosha, 1982-85, Eastern Wash. U., Cheney, 1985-90; adj. prof. mgmt. U. Tex., El Paso, 1976-78. Pres. Tri-City Heights Assn., Kennewick, Wash., 1956-58, PTA, Kennewick, 1957-58; v.p. Kennewick Sch. Bd., 1958-59, pres., 1959. Mem. Math. Assn. Am., Internat. Assn. Computing in Edn., Am. Soc. Engring. Edn., Data Processing Mgmt. Assn. (bd. dirs., sec. Spokane chpt. 1988, v.p. edn. Spokane chpt. 1989, v.p. student chpt. 1990), Manito Lions Spokane (membership chmn. 1991-92, program chmn. 1992-93, v.p. 1993—), Phi Delta Kappa (found. chmn. Spokane chpt. 1992-94). Home: 3334 S Bernard St Spokane WA 99203-1636

MAYER, IRA EDWARD, gastroenterologist; b. Bklyn., July 31, 1951; s. Elias M. and Mollie (Taxerman) M.; m. Celeste Ann Sivak, Mar. 13, 1976; children: Madelaine Rose, Amanda Beth. BS, Bklyn. Coll., 1972; MD, N.Y. Med. Coll., 1975. Diplomate Am. Bd. Internal Medicine, Am. Bd. Gastroenterology, Nat. Bd. Med. Examiners. Asst. resident in internal medicine N.Y. Med. Coll., 1975-76; resident in internal medicine Met. Hosp. Ctr., N.Y.C., 1976-78; fellow Digestive Diseases div. Emory U., Atlanta, 1978-80; assoc. attending gastroenterologist Maimonides Med. Ctr., Bklyn., 1980—, chmn. patient care com., 1984—; clin. instr. medicine SUNY Health Sci. Ctr., Bklyn., 1980-81, instr. medicine, 1981-83, clin. asst. prof. medicine, 1983—. Author: (with others) Digestive Diseases, 1983, Medicine, 1983; contbr. articles to profl. jours. Fellow ACP, Am. Coll. Gastroenterology; mem. Am. Gastroent. Assn., Am. Soc. for Gastrointestinal Endoscopy, N.Y. Acad. Scis., N.Y. Acad. Gastroenterolgy, N.Y. Soc. for Gastrointestinal Endoscopy, Med. Soc. for the State of N.Y. Jewish. Office: 2560 Ocean Ave Brooklyn NY 11229-4521

MAYER, JAMES HOCK, mediator, lawyer; b. Neptune City, N.J., Nov. 1, 1935; s. J. Kenneth and Marie Ruth (Hock) M.; m. Carol I. Keating, Sept. 20, 1958 (div. Feb. 1981); children: Craig, Jeffrey; m. Patrisha Renk, Mar. 28, 1981. AB with distinction, Dartmouth Coll., 1957; JD, Harvard U., 1964. Bar: Calif. 1965, U.S. Dist. Ct (no. dist., so. dist.) Calif. 1965, U.S. Ct. Appeals (9th cir.) 1965, U.S. Supreme Ct. 1974. Assoc. Pillsbury, Madison & Sutro, San Francisco, 1964-72, ptnr., 1973—; ind. mediator, 1992—. Rear adm. USNR, 1957-93. Rufus Choate scholar Dartmouth Coll., 1956-57. Mem. Newcomen Soc., Navy League, Naval Order of U.S., Harvard Club. Office: 101 W Broadway Ste 1800 San Diego CA 92101-8219

MAYER, LLOYD D., allergist, immunologist, physician, medical educator; b. Bklyn., Nov. 6, 1921; s. Morris and Leonore (Sullivan) M.; m. Marie Faith Puntney, Feb. 2, 1957 (dec. Sept. 1981); children: Michael, Fredrick, Loren, Lee; m. Carol Smith, Dec. 21, 1985. BA, U. Louisville, Ky., 1941, MD, 1944. Diplomate Am. Bd. Internal Medicine, Am. Bd. Internal Medicine Alergy, Am. Bd. Allergy and Immunology. Rotating intern Coney Island Hosp., Bklyn., 1944-45; resident in contagious diseases Kingston Ave Hosp., Bklyn., 1945-46; resident in pathology Long Island Coll. Hosp., Bklyn., 1946-47; resident in medicine Montefiore Hosp., Pitts., 1947-48; teaching fellow in allergy U. Pitts., 1948-49; resident in medicine VA Hosp., Pitts., 1949-50; instr. in allergy medicine U. Pitts., 1950-52; staff St. Joseph Hosp., Good Samaritan Hosp.; staff Ctrl. Baptist Hosp., chmn. dept. internal medicine, 1972-74; staff Humana Hosp.; clin. prof. medicine, allergy U. Ky. Med. Ctr., Lexington, Ky., 1962—; cons. in allergy medicine VA Hosp.; chmn. respiratory therapy com. Good Samaritian Hosp., Ctrl. Baptist Hosp., 1970-74; chmn. nursing care com. Ctrl. Baptist Hosp., 1979;bd. dirs. Allergy Clinic, VA Hosp., Adult Allergy Clinic, U. Ky. Med. Ctr. 1994—. Contr. to profl. jours. Lt. US Army, 1941-46. Recipient cert. Appreciation Coll. Allied Health and Nursing Eastern Ky. U., Am. Acad. Family Practice award, 1979. Fellow Am. Coll. Physicians, Am. Acad. Allergy, Am. Coll. Allergists; mem. AMA, Fayette County Med. Soc., Ky. State Med. Assn., Ky. Thoracic Soc. (sec. 1962), Am. Assn. Cert. Allergists, Mason (pres. 1961), Scottish Rite Masonic Shriner (pres. 1962). Home: 470 Woodlake Way Lexington KY 40502-2570 Office: 470 Woodlake Way Lexington KY 40502-2570

MAYER, MORRIS LEHMAN, marketing educator; b. Demopolis, Ala., Dec. 14, 1925; s. Lehman M. and Anne (Rochotsh) M.; m. Judith Marian Morton, Dec. 22, 1957; children: Susan Morton, Elizabeth Anne. B.S. in Bus. Adminstrn, U. Ala., 1949, DHL (hon.), 1994; M.S. in Retailing, N.Y. U., 1950; Ph.D. in Bus. Orgn, Ohio State U., 1961. Buyer Goldblatts Dept. Store, Chgo., 1951-55; mem. faculty U. Ala., 1955—, prof., 1960—, chmn. dept. mktg., 1969-74, dir. Hess Inst. Retailing, 1985-92, Bruno prof. mktg., 1986-92; Bruno prof. mktg. emeritus, 1992—; instr. Ohio State U., Columbus, 1956-60; cons. Mgmt. Horizons Co., Columbus, 1966-70, N.C.R. Co., Dayton, Ohio, 1967-75. Co-author: Modern Retailing, 1978, 6th edit., 1993, Retailing, 1981, 5th edit., 1993. Served with AUS, 1944-46, 50-51. Recipient Teaching Excellence award Burlington No. Found., 1986, Distinctive Image award Jewish Childrens Regional Svc. Bd., 1997, Circle of Honor award Duect Selley Edn. Found., 1997; Ford Found. fellow, 1962-63, So. Mktg. fellow, 1986; named to U. Ala. Bus. Faculty Hall of Fame, 1995, Retail Patronage Acad. Hall of Fame, 1995; Morris Mayer Endowed scholarship established 1992; Morris L. Mayer award established U. Ala., 1993; Morris L. Mayer Outstanding Sutdent award established Sales and Mktg. Execs., 1993, others. Mem. Am. Mktg. Assn. (Morris L. Mayer Outstanding Mem. award estab. Birmingham chpt. 1993), So. Mktg. Assn. (pres.), Ala. Retail Assn. (bd. dirs.), Am. Coll. Retail Assn. (pres., Hall of Fame 1992, Mortar Bd., Beta Gamma Sigma, Eta Mu Pi, Pi Sigma Epsilon, Omicron Delta Kappa, Zeta Beta Tau (chpt. trustee). Jewish (temple trustee). Home: 1321 Montclair Cir Tuscaloosa AL 35404-4241 Office: U Ala PO Box 870225 Tuscaloosa AL 35487-0225

MAYER, NANCY J., state official; b. Phila., June 9, 1937; d. Benjamin and Florence Hannah (Altshuler) Rosenstein; m. Edward C. Leand, Sept. 6, 1958 (div. 1970); children: Judith, Marjorie; m. William L. Mayer, June 16, 1971. BA in Am. Hist., Barnard Coll., 1958; MAT in Am. Hist., Brown U., 1972; JD, Northeastern U., 1982. Assoc. firm Tillinghast, Collins & Graham, Providence, 1982-84; chief legal cunsel R.I. Dept. Bus. Regulation, Providence, 1986-92; treas., general treas. State of R.I., 1992—; candidate R.I. Senate, 1978, 80. Mem. R.I. adv. com. U.S. Commn. on Civil Rights; mem. R.I. Partnership of Sci. and Tech.; mem. AGing 2000 Health Care for Srs. Com., adv. com. U.S. Com. on Civil Rights (R.I. Chpt.). Mem. Nat. Assn. State Treas. (v.p.). Republican. Jewish. Avocations: tennis (former nationally and regionally ranked player), cycling, jogging, writing, duplicate bridge. Office: Treasury Dept 102 State St Providence RI 02908-5021*

MAYER, PATRICIA JAYNE, financial officer, management accountant; b. Chgo., Apr. 27, 1950; d. Arthur and Ruth (Greenberger) Hersh; m. William A. Mayer Jr., Apr. 30, 1971. AA, Diablo Valley Coll., 1970; BSBA, Calif. State U., Hayward, 1975. Cert. mgmt. acct. Staff acct., auditor Elmer Fox Westheimer and Co., Oakland, Calif., 1976; supervising auditor Auditor's Office County of Alameda, Oakland, 1976-78; asst. acctg. mgr. CBS Retail Stores doing bus. as Pacific Stereo, Emeryville, Calif., 1978-79; contr. Oakland Unified Sch. Dist., 1979-84; v.p. fin., CFO YMCA, San Francisco, 1984-96; v.p. fin. customer segments Charles Schwab & Co., San Francisco, 1996—; instr. acctg. to staff YMCA, San Francisco, 1984-96, CBS Retail Stores, 1978-79. Draft counselor Mt. Diablo Peace Ctr., Walnut Creek, Calif., 1970-72; dep. registrar of voters Contra Costa County Registrar's Office, Martinez, Calif., 1972-77. Mem. Fin. Execs. Inst. (bd. dirs. San Francisco chpt.), Inst. Mgmt. Accts. (pres.-elect Diablo Valley chpt. 1995—, pres. 1995-96), Dalmatian Club No. Calif., Dalmation Club Am. Democrat. Jewish. Avocations: showing and breeding Dalmatians, playing Tex. Hold 'Em poker tournaments. Office: Charles Schwab & Co 101 Montgomery St San Francisco CA 94104-4122

MAYER, PATRICIA LYNN SORCI, mental health nurse, educator; b. Chgo., July 22, 1942; d. Ben and Adonia (Grenier) Sorci; 1 child, Christopher David Mayer. AGS with high honors, Pima Community Coll., Tucson, 1983; BSN with honors, U. Ariz., 1986, MS in Nursing, 1987. RN, Ariz.; cert. addictions counselor, chem. dependency therapist; lic. pvt. pilot. Nurse educator Tucson. Contbr. articles to profl. jours. Mem. Nat. Nurses Soc. on Addictions, Phi Kappa Phi, Sigma Theta Tau, Pi Lambda Theta, Golden Key.

MAYER, RAYMOND RICHARD, business administration educator; b. Chgo., Aug. 31, 1924; s. Adam and Mary (Bogdala) M.; m. Helen Lakowski, Jan. 30, 1954; children: Mark, John, Mary, Jane. B.S., Ill. Inst. Tech., 1948, M.S., 1954, Ph.D., 1957. Indsl. engr. Standard Oil Co., Whiting, Ind., 1948-51; orgn. analyst Ford Motor Co., Chgo., 1951-53; instr. Ill. Inst. Tech., Chgo., 1953-56; asso. prof. Ill. Inst. Tech., 1958-60; asst. prof. U. Chgo., 1956-58; Walter F. Mullady prof. bus. adminstrn. Loyola U., Chgo., 1960—. Author: Financial Analysis of Investment Alternatives, 1966, Production Management, 1962, rev. edit., 1968, Production and Operations Management, 1975, rev. edit., 1982, Capital Expenditure Analysis, 1978. Served with USNR, 1944-46. Ingersoll Found. fellow, 1955-56; Machinery and Allied Products Inst. fellow, 1954-55; Ford Found. fellow, 1962. Mem. Acad. Mgmt., Am. Econ. Assn., Am. Statis. Assn., Am. Inst. for Decision Scis., Nat. Assn. Purchasing Mgmt., Polish Inst. Arts and Scis. in Am., Alpha Iota Delta, Alpha Kappa Psi, Beta Gamma Sigma. Home: 730 Green Bay Rd Winnetka IL 60093-1912 Office: 820 N Michigan Ave Chicago IL 60611-2103

MAYER, RICHARD DEAN, mathematics educator; b. Ft. Wayne, Ind., May 26, 1930; s. Lester Blyle and Velma Lucille (Maulsby) M.; m. Patsy Jean Hartwell, Aug. 31, 1952; children—Susan, Joann, John. B.S., Purdue U., 1952, M.S., 1954; Ph.D., U. Wash., 1959. Teaching asst. Purdue U., 1952-54, U. Wash., 1954-59; asst. prof. math. Idaho State U., 1959-61, assoc. prof. math., chmn. dept., 1961-67; prof. math. SUNY, Oswego, 1967-91, prof. math. emeritus, 1991—, chmn. dept., 1967-74; rsch. engr. Boeing Airplane Co., Seattle, summer, 1959, Carter Oil Co., Billings, Mont., summer, 1960. Mem. Ctrl. Oreg. Flyfishers (pres. 1996, 97), Math. Assn. Am., Am. Math. Soc., Sigma Xi, Sigma Pi Sigma, Delta Rho Kappa, Pi Mu Epsilon, Kappa Mu Epsilon. Avocations: handball. Home: 23040 Chisholm Trl Bend OR 97702-9664

MAYER, RICHARD EDWIN, psychology educator; b. Chgo., Feb. 8, 1947; s. James S. and Bernis (Lowy) M.; m. Beverly Linn Pastor, Dec. 19, 1971; children: Kenneth Michael, David Mark, Sarah Ann. BA with honors, Miami U., Oxford, Ohio, 1969; MS in Psychology, U. Mich., 1971, PhD in Psychology, 1973. Vis. asst. prof. Ind. U., Bloomington, 1973-75; asst. prof. psychology U. Calif., Santa Barbara, 1975-80, assoc. prof., 1980-85, prof., 1985—, pres., chmn. dept., 1987-90; vis. scholar Learning Rsch. and Devel. Ctr., U. Pitts., 1979, Ctr. for Study of Reading, U. Ill., 1984. Author: Foundations of Learning and Memory, 1979, The Promise of Cognitive Psychology, 1981, Thinking, Problem Solving, Cognition, 1983, 2d edit., 1992, BASIC: A Short Course, 1985, Educational Psychology, 1987; editor: Human Reasoning, 1980, Teaching and Learning Computer Programming, 1988; editor jours. Instructional Sci., 1983-87, Educational Psychologist, 1983-89. Sch. bd. officer Goleta (Calif.) Union Sch. Dist., 1981—. NSF grantee, 1975-88. Fellow APA (divsn. 15 officer 1987—, G. Stanley Hall lectr. 1988), Am. Psychol. Soc.; mem. Am. Ednl. Rsch. Assn. (divsn. C officer 1986-88), Psychonomic Soc. Democrat. Jewish. Avocations: computers, hiking, bicycling, reading, dogs. Office: U Calif Dept Of Psychology Santa Barbara CA 93016

MAYER, ROBERT ANTHONY, college president; b. N.Y.C., Oct. 30, 1933; s. Ernest John and Theresa Margaret (Mazura) M.; m. Laura Wiley Christ, Apr. 30, 1960. BA magna cum laude, Fairleigh Dickinson U., 1955; MA, NYU, 1967. With N.J. Bank and Trust Co., Paterson, 1955-61; mgr. advt. dept. N.J. Bank and Trust Co., 1959-61; program supr. advt. dept. Mobil Oil Co., N.Y.C., 1961-62; asst. to dir. Latin Am. program Ford Found., N.Y.C., 1963-65; asst. rep. Ford Found., Brazil, 1965-67; asst. to v.p. adminstrn., 1967-73; officer in charge logistical services Ford Found., 1968-73; asst. dir. programs N.Y. Community Trust, N.Y.C., 1973-76; exec. dir. N.Y. State Council on the Arts, N.Y.C., 1976-79; mgmt. cons. N.Y.C., 1979-80; dir. Internat. Mus. Photography, George Eastman House, Rochester, N.Y., 1980-89, mgmt. cons., 1989-90; pres. Cleve. Inst. of Art, 1990—. Mem. editorial adv. bd.: Grants mag., 1978-80; author: (plays) La Borgia, 1971; Alijandru, 1971, They'll Grow No Roses, 1975. Mem. state program adv. panel NEA, 1977-80; mem. Mayor's Com. on Cultural Policy, N.Y.C., 1974-75; mem. pres.'s adv. com. Bklyn. campus, L.I. U., 1978-79; bd. dirs. Fedn. Protestant Welfare Agys., N.Y.C., 1977-79, Arts for Greater Rochester, 1981-83, Garth Fagan's Dance Theatre, 1982-86; trustee Internat. Mus. Photography, 1981-89, Lacoste Sch. Arts, France, 1991-96, sec., 1994-96; mem. dean's adv. com. Grad. Sch. Social Welfare, Fordham U., 1976; mem. N.Y. State Motion Picure and TV Devel. Adv. Bd., 1984-87, N.Y. State Martin Luther King Jr. Commn., 1985-90, Cleve. Coun. Cultural Affairs, 1992-94; chmn. Greater Cleve. Regional Transit Authority Arts in Transit Com., 1992-95. Recipient Nat. award on advocacy for girls Girls Clubs Am., 1976. Mem. Nat. Assembly Art Agys. (bd. dirs. 1977-79, 1st vice chmn. 1978-79), Alliance Ind. Colls. Art (bd. dirs. 1983-91, vice chmn. 1986-87, sec. 1987-89), N.Y. State Assn. Museums (bd. councilors 1983-86, pres. 1986-89), Assn. Ind. Colls. Art and Design (bd. dirs. 1991—, exec. com. 1991-93, 96—). Home: 20201 N Park Blvd Apt 101 Shaker Heights OH 44118-5024 Office: Cleve Inst Art 11141 East Blvd Cleveland OH 44106-1710

MAYER, ROBERT SAMUEL, physician; b. Detroit, Jan. 13, 1962; s. Jack J. and Beatrice (Susskind) M.; m. Sherry J. Weinstein-Mayer, June 15, 1986; children: Aimee, Rachel, Elana. BS, Northwestern Univ., 1984, MD, 1986. Diplomate Am. Bd. Indep. Medical Examiners, Diplomate Am. Bd. Electrodiagnostic Medicine, Am. Bd. Physical Medicine & Rehabilitation. Residency Rush-Marianjoy-Oak Forest, Chgo., 1987-90; internship medicine Rush-Presbyn. St. Luke's Medical Ctr., Chgo., 1986-87; residency program dir. Rush-Marianjoy Residency in Physical Medicine & Rehab., 1996—, assoc. residency program dir., 1994-96; medical dir. Employee Health Svcs., 1994—, Ill. Mcpl. Retirement Fund, Oak Brook, Ill., 1992—; medical dir. rehabilitation svcs. Vencor Hosp. Chgo., Northlake, Ill., 1991-93; physiatrist Rehabilitation Medicine Clinic, Wheaton, Ill., 1990—; asst. prof. dept. physical medicine & rehabilitation Rush Medical Coll., Chgo., 1991—; instr. Loyola Univ. Stritch Sch. Medicine, Maywood, Ill., 1990-91; medical records com. Rush-Presbyn. St. Luke's Medical Ctr., 1993; com. edn. appraisal Rush Medical Coll., Chgo.,1992-95; chair edn. com. Am. Medical Student Assn., 1985-86; medical cons. Met. Life Ins., 1992-94; cons. medical dir. Physical Medicine & Rehab. Health Care Compare Corp., Downers Grove, Ill., 1990-94; attending physician RPSLMC, Chgo., 1991—, Grant Hosp., Chgo., 1991—, Westlake Hosp., Melrose Park, Ill., 1991—, Oak Park Hosp., 1990%; cons. physician Marianjoy Rehab. Ctr., Wheaton, 1990—; lectr. in field. Contbr. numerous articles to profl. jours. Rsch. adv. com. United Cerebral Palsy Assn., 1991. Recipient Elkins award Am. Bd. PM&R, 1990, Best Doctor in Am. award Woodward/White, 1996, Innovation grant Nat. Inst. Disability & Rehabilitation Rsch., 1992. Fellow Am. Acad. Physical Medicine & Rehab., Am. Assn. Electrodiagnostic Medicine, Assn. Spine, Sports, Occupational Rehab.; mem. AMA, Assn. Acad. Physiatrists, Chgo. Medical Soc., Ill. State Medical Soc. Office: Rehab Medicine Clinic 1725 W Harrison St Chicago IL 60612-3828

MAYER, ROBERT WALLACE, emeritus finance educator; b. Mt. Pulaski, Ill., Apr. 17, 1909; s. Edward Otto and Minnie Laura (Clark) M.; m. Nella Coryell DeAtley, AUg. 2, 1933 (dec.); children: nancy (Mrs. Donald G. Wyatt), Anne (Mrs. Robert M. Shannon, dec.), Caroline (Mrs. Chester R. Keller), Melinda. B.S., U. Ill., 1930, M.S., 1931, Ph.D., 1933. Cert. ofcl. U.S. Track and Field Fedn. Statistician Libby McNeill & Libby, Chgo., 1929, Commonwealth Edison Co., Chgo., 1930; from instr. to asst. prof. Lehigh U., 1933-42; sr. economist WPB, Washington, 1942-45; asso. prof. econs. U. Ill., Urbana, 1945-52; prof. U. Ill., 1952-57, prof. finance, 1957-77, prof. emeritus, 1977—, vice chmn. dept. econs., 1953-57; vis. prof. fin. Ill. State U., Normal, 1978-79; Exec. sec. Combined (Brit.-Am.) Steel Com., 1943-45; cons. Rand Corp., 1951-53. Author Stemma, 1984m Bios Didaskalos, 1991; contbr. articles to profl. jours. Mem. Am. Finance Assn, Midwest Finance Assn. (pres. 1967-68), Am. Econ. Assn., Chgo. Fin. Writers Assn., SAR, U. Ill. Varsity Assn. (hon.), Beta Gamma Sigma, Phi Kappa Phi, Alpha Kappa Psi, Tau Kappa Epsilon. Republican. Presbyterian. Club: Kiwanian (pres. 1969-70). Home: 17 Greencroft Dr Champaign IL 61821-5117 Office: U Ill Dept Econ Urbana IL 61801

MAYER, SUSAN MARTIN, art educator; b. Atlanta, Oct. 25, 1931; d. Paul McKeen and Ione (Garrett) Martin; m. Arthur James Mayer, Aug. 9, 1953; 1 child, Melinda Marilyn. Student, Am. U., 1949-50; BA, U. N.C., Greensboro, 1953; postgrad., U. Del., 1956-58; MA, Ariz. State U., 1966. Artist-in-residence Armed Forces Staff Coll., Norfolk, Va., 1968-69; coord. of edn. Huntington Art Gallery U. Tex., Austin, 1970—, mem. art faculty, 1971—. Co-editor: Museum Education: History, Theory and Practice, 1989; author various mus. publs.; contbr. articles to profl. jours. Recipient award Austin Ind. Sch. Bd., 1985. Mem. Nat. Art Edn. Assn. (bd. dirs. 1983-87, award 1987, 91), Tex. Art Edn. Assn. (mus. edn. chair 1982-83, legis. rep. 1988—, Mus. Educator of Yr. 1986), Tex. Assn. Mus. (mus. edn. chair), Austin Visual Arts Assn., Am. Assn. Mus. Office: U Tex Art/Art History Dept Austin TX 78712

MAYER, VICTOR JAMES, earth system science educator; b. Mayville, Wis., Mar. 25, 1933; s. Victor Charles and Phyllis (Bachhuber) M.; m. Mary Jo Anne White, Nov. 25, 1965; children: Gregory, Maribeth. BS in Geology, U. Wis., 1956; MS in Geology, U. Colo., 1960, PhD in Sci. Edn.,

1966. Tchr. Colo. Pub. Schs., 1961-65; asst. prof. SUNY Coll., Oneonta, 1965-67; asst. prof. Ohio State U., Columbus, 1967-70, assoc. prof., 1970-75, prof. ednl. studies, geol. scis. and natural resources, 1975-95, prof. emeritus, 1995—, coord. earth sys. edn. program, 1991—; co-organizer symposium at 29th Internat. Geol. Congress; internat. sci. edn. assistance to individuals and orgns. in Japan, Korea, Taiwan, Russia, and Venezuela; dir. NSF Insts., program for leadership Earth Sys. Edn., 1990-95; dir. Korean Sci. Tchrs. Insts., 1986-88, 95; keynote spkr. U.S.A. rep. Internat. Conf. on Geoscis. Edn., Southampton, Eng., 1993; co-convenor Second Internat. conf. on Geosci. Edn., Hilo, Hawaii, 1997; disting. vis. prof. SUNY, Plattsburg, 1994. Contbr. articles to profl. jours. Served with USAR. Vis. rsch. scholar Hyogo U., Japan, 1996; named Disting. Investigator, Ohio Sea Grant Program, 1983. Fellow AAAS (chmn. edn. 1988-89), Ohio Acad. Sci. (v.p. 1978-79, exec. com. 1993-94, outstanding univ. educator 1995); mem. Nat. Sci. Tchrs. Assn. (bd. dirs. 1984-86), Sci. Edn. Coun. Ohio (pres. 1987-88), Sigma Xi, Phi Delta Kappa. Roman Catholic. Avocation: photography. Home: 111 W Dominion Blvd Columbus OH 43214-2607 Office: Ohio State U Dept Geol Scis 125 S Oval Mall Columbus OH 43210-1308

MAYER, WILLIAM EMILIO, investor; b. N.Y.C., May 7, 1940; s. Emilio and Marie Mayer; m. Katherine Mayer, May 16, 1964; children: Kristen Elizabeth, William Franz. BS, U. Md., 1966, MBA, 1967. Pres., chief exec. officer First Boston Corp., N.Y.C., 1967-91; dean Coll. Bus. & Mgmt. U. Md., College Park, 1992-96; ptnr. Devel. Capital, 1996—; bd. dirs. Chart House Enterprises, Inc., TechnoServe, Am. Trading & Prodn. Corp., Hambrecht & Quist, Inc., Johns Manville Corp., Premier, Inc., Colonial Mut. Fund Group. Bd. dirs. U. Md. Found., College Park; bd. adminstrs. Tulane U.; trustee Cancer Rsch. Inst. 1st lt. USAF, 1961-65. Mem. Annapolis Yacht Club, Manhasset Bay Club (N.Y.), Univ. Club (N.Y.C.), Mashomack Fish & Game Club, Met. Club. Home: 172 Long Neck Point Rd Darien CT 06820-5816 Office: U Md Coll Bus and Mgmt Van Munching Hall College Park MD 20742

MAYERI, BEVERLY, artist, ceramic sculptor, educator; b. N.Y.C., Nov. 2, 1944; d. Bernard and Cora (Wisoff) Howard; m. Earl Melchior Mayeri, Sept. 1, 1968; 1 child, Rachel Theresa. BA, U. Calif., Berkeley, 1967; MA in Art and Sculpture, San Francisco State U., 1976. tchr., seminar conductor, lectr. Dominican Coll., San Rafael, Calif., 1978, Sonoma State U., Rohnert Park, Calif., 1978, NYU, 1987, Calif. State U., 1989, Creative Growth, Oakland, Calif., 1990, Acad Art Coll., 1990, Foothill Coll., Los Altos Hills, 1990, Natsoulas Gallery, 1992, U. Minn., Mpls., 1993, Sonoma Stae U., Rohnert Park, Calif., 1994, Mendocino (Calif.) Art Ctr., 1995, Fresno State U., 1996, CCAC, Oakland, Calif., 1996, Edinboro (Pa.) U., 1997. Artist: solo exhibitions include Palo Alto (Calif.) Cultural Ctr., 1979, Ivory/Kimpton Gallery, San Francisco, 1981, 83, Garth Clark Gallery, N.Y., 1985, 87, Esther Saks Gallery, Chgo., 1988, 90, Dorothy Weiss Gallery, San Francisco, 1990, 92, 94, 96, San Jose Inst. Contemporary Art, 1990, Robert Kidd Gallery, Birmingham, Mich., 1993; group exhibitions include San Francisco Mus. of Art, Northern Calif. Clay Routes: Sculpture Now, 1979, Smithsonian Instn., Renwick Gallery, 1981, Ivory Kimpton Gallery, San Francisco, 1982, Prieto Meml. Gallery, Mills Coll., Oakland, Calif. 1982, Crocker Art Mus., San Francisco, 1983, Euphrate Gallery, De Anza Coll., Cupertino, Calif., 1984, 88, Fisher Gallery, U. So. Calif., L.A., traveled to Pratt Inst., N.Y.C., 1984, Arts Commn. Gallery, San Francisco, 1984, Signet Arts Gallery, St. Louis (two person show), 1984, Garth Clark Gallery, N.Y., 1985, Robert L. Kidd Gallery, Birmingham, Mich., Animals Contemporary Vision, Major Concepts: Clay, 1986, Fresno (Calif.) Arts Ctr. and Mus., 1987, Canton (Ohio) Art Inst., 1991, Soc. for Contemporary Crafts, Pitts., 1992, Triton Mus. of Art, Santa Clara, Calif., 1992, Nat. Mus. of History Taipei, Taiwan, 1993, Lew Allen Gallery, Santa Fe, New Mex., 1993, Perimeter Gallery, 1995, Duane Reed Gallery, St. Louis, 1997; works in pub. and private collections include: Nat. Mus. History, Taipei, Canton Art Inst., Long Beach (Calif.) Parks and Recreation, L.A. Arts Commn., Mr. and Mrs. Eric Lidow, L.A., Alfred Shands, Louisville, Mrs. Audrey Landy, Atlanta, Karen Johnson Boyd, Racine, Wis., Alan and Esther Saks, Chgo., Gloria and Sonny Kamm. Founder Marin Women Artists, Marin County, Calif., 1974-84. Recipient fellowship visual artist NEA, Washington, 1982, 88; grantee: Marin Arts Coun., 1987, Virgina A. Groot Found., 1991. Avocations: painting, hiking, skiing, gardening, environmentalist. Office: Dorothy Weiss Gallery 256 Sutter St San Francisco CA 94108-4409

MAYERS, DANIEL KRIEGSMAN, lawyer; b. Scarsdale, N.Y., July 10, 1934; s. Chauncey Maurice and Helen P. (Kriegsman) M.; m. Karen E. Silverman, Sept. 30, 1956, children: Peter D., Leslie H. Shroyer. AB, Harvard U., 1955, LLB, 1960. Bar: D.C. 1961, U.S. Supreme Ct. 1961. Law clk. to Justice Felix Frankfurter, U.S. Supreme Ct., Washington, 1960-61; spl. asst. U.S. Dept. Justice, Washington, 1961-62; assoc. Wilmer Cutler & Pickering, Washington, 1962-65, ptnr., 1967—; exec. asst. to undersec. U.S. State Dept., Washington, 1965-66; vis. com. Harvard Law Sch., Cambridge, Mass., 1982-89, chmn., 1986-89; bd. dirs. Legal Action Ctr., N.Y.C., 1982—; chmn. Washington Ednl. TV Assn., 1993-97. Pres. Nat. Symphony Orch., Washington, 1987-89; chmn. Sidwell Friends Sch., Washington, 1979-81; mem. Ams. for Peace Now, 1991—, Fed. City Coun., Washington, 1981—; trustee Found. for Nat. Capital Area, 1997—; counsel, dir. Ctr. for Nat. Policy, Washington, 1984-93. With U.S. Army, 1955-57. Recipient Sears prize Harvard Law Sch., 1959. Mem. ABA, Met. Club, Woodstock Country Club. Democrat. Jewish. Avocations: tennis; fishing. Home: 3222 Woodland Dr NW Washington DC 20008-3547 Office: Wilmer Cutler & Pickering 2445 M St NW Washington DC 20037-1435

MAYERS, EUGENE DAVID, philosopher, educator; b. N.Y.C., July 30, 1915; s. Sylvester and Estelle (Weinstein) M.; m. Odette Julia Marguerite Gilchriest, Dec. 30, 1950; children: David Allan, Marilyn Anne, Judith Odette, Peter Michael. AB, Yale U., 1936, LLB, 1940; PhD, Columbia U., 1956. Bar: N.Y. State bar 1941. With Nat. Bur. Econ. Research, N.Y.C., 1941, Office Gen. Counsel, Navy Dept., 1946; mem. faculty Carleton Coll., Northfield, Minn., 1950-61, Columbia, 1959-60, Mills Coll., Oakland, Calif., 1961-63; prof. philosophy Calif. State U., Hayward, 1963-92, prof. emeritus, 1992—; chmn. dept. philosophy Calif. State U., 1963-73, acting head div. humanities, 1966-67; adj. prof. Calif. State U., 1996—. Author: Some Modern Theories of Natural Law, 1957; Contbr. articles to profl. jours. Served to capt. (field artillery) AUS, 1941-46, 51-52; lt. col. judge adv. gen. USAR ret. Fellow Soc. Values in Higher Edn.; mem. AAUP, Am. Philos. Assn. (chmn. conf. dept. chmn. Pacific divsn. 1973-75, Pacific divsn. exec. com. 1976-80, chmn. exec. com. 1978-80), Am. Soc. Polit. and Legal Philosophy, Pacific Coast Theol. Soc. (sec. 1984-86), Internat. Assn. Philosophy Law and Social Philosophy, Am. Acad. Religion, Soc. Advancement Am. Philosophy, Soc. Study Process Philosophies (Pacific Coast rep. 1987—). Home: 3191 Frye St Oakland CA 94602-4040 Office: Calif State U Dept Philosophy Hayward CA 94542

MAYERS, JEAN, aeronautical engineering educator; b. N.Y.C., June 8, 1920; s. Lou and Ida (Edrich) M.; m. Reva Lee Bookbinder, May 20, 1945; children: Eileen, Laurence. B.Aero. Engring., Poly. Inst. Bklyn., 1942, M.Aero. Engring., 1948. Research asst. aero. engring. Poly. Inst. Bklyn., 1946-48; aero. research scientist, structures research div. NACA, Langley Field, Va., 1948-56; successively prin. engr., engring. sec. head, engring. dept. head Sperry Utah Co. div. Sperry Rand Corp., 1956-61; vis. asso. prof. Stanford U., 1961-63, mem. faculty, 1963—, prof. aero. engring., 1967-83, prof. emeritus, 1984—, vice chmn. dept. aero. and astronautics, 1966-71; vis. prof. Technion-Israel Inst. Tech., Haifa, 1970; Naval Air Systems Command Research prof. U.S. Naval Acad., 1978-79; Sci. adviser U.S. Army, 1962-74; cons. to govt. and industry, 1962—; mem. ad hoc vis. com. on aero. engring. curricula Engrs. Council for Profl. Devel., 1969-70. Author articles, reports in field. ARC vol. USN Hosp., Bethesda, Md., 1992—. Lt. comdr. USNR, 1942-46. Recipient U.S. Army Outstanding Civilian Service medal, 1972. Asso. fellow Am. Inst. Aero. and Astronautics (asso. editor jour. 1967-70); mem. Aircraft Owners and Pilots Assn., Naval Res. Assn., Ret. Officers Assn., Am. Soc. Engring. Edn., Sigma Xi. Home: 4550 N Park Ave Apt 909 Chevy Chase MD 20815-7238

MAYERS, STANLEY PENROSE, JR., public health educator; b. Phila., Nov. 9, 1926; s. Stanley Penrose and Margaret Amelia (Thorpe) M.; m. Virginia Lee Lytle, Aug. 25, 1951 (dec. Oct. 1990); children: Douglas Lytle, Kenneth Stanley, Daniel John, Andrew William; m. Patricia Ann Harne Hulsey, Mar. 6, 1993. BA, U. Pa., 1949, MD, 1953; MPH, Johns Hopkins U., 1958. Diplomate Am. Bd. Preventive Medicine. Intern Phila. Gen. Hosp., 1953-54; resident Arlington County Health Dept., Va., 1954-55; health dir. Henry-Martinsville-Patrick Health Dist., Martinsville, Va., 1955-57; regional dir. Va. State Health dept., Richmond, 1958-59; dist. state health officer N.J. State Dept. of Health, Trenton, 1959-62; asst. prof. and asst. dean Johns Hopkins Sch. Hygiene and Pub. Health, Balt., 1962-65; dir. Arlington County Dept. of Human Resources, Arlington, Va., 1965-71; prof. Health Planning and Adminstrn. Program Pa. State U., Univ. Pk., Pa., 1971-74, 88—; prof. in charge Pa. State U., Univ. Park, Pa., 1974-78; chmn. Pa. State U., Univ. Pk., Pa., 1979-88; assoc. dean undergrad. studies Coll. Health and Human Devel. Pa. State U., Univ. Pk., 1989-92, assoc. dean acad. studies Coll. Health and Human Devel., 1992-95; faculty assoc. Johns Hopkins U. Sch. Medicine, Balt., 1965-75; clin. assoc. prof. Georgetown U. Sch. Medicine, Washington, 1965-71; cons. VA, 1985—. Author numerous reports, articles and surveys on pub. health. Mem. Arlington Optimist Club, 1979-72, pres. 1970-71; bd. dirs. Centre County Family Planning Svcs., Bellefonte, Pa., 1972-79. With USN, 1945-46. Recipient Outstanding Achievement award Dept. Community Medicine, Georgetown U. Sch. Medicine, 1968, Saubel award Coll. of Human Devel., Pa. State U., 1985. Fellow Am. Coll. Preventive Med., Am. Pub. Health Assn. (chmn. membership com. health officer's sect. 1968-70, mem. nominating com. health adminstrn. sect. 1970-72, chmn. com. to draft a statement on local health agy. responsibilities 1973-74); mem. AMA, Arlington County Med. Soc. (Wellborn award 1971), Centre County Med. Soc. (pres. 1978), Med. Soc. Va., Met. Washington Health Officers Assn. (sec. 1967-71), Am. Assn. Pub. Health Physicians (pres. Va. chpt. 1970-71), Pa. Med. Soc. (mem. Ho. of Dels. for Centre County 1974-76, 81—, treas. 1973-74, 85—, sec. 1974-76, v.p. 1976, pres. elect 1977, pres. 1978), University Club (State College, Pa.), Phi Beta Kappa. Episcopalian. Avocations: fishing, boating, hiking. Home: 648 Wiltshire Dr State College PA 16803-1450 Office: Pa State U Human Devel Bldg Rm 201 University Park PA 16802 *Never attempt to promote something or someone that you do not believe in yourself.*

MAYERSON, HY, lawyer; b. Phila., June 29, 1937; s. Henry and Gertrude Mayerson; m. June 13, 1964 (div. 1973); children: Merrie Joy, Benjamin, Erin Megan, Stephnie Dawn; m. Colleen Koos. BS, Temple U., 1958, JD, 1961. Bar: Pa. 1961, Phila. Ct. Common Pleas 1962, Pa. Supreme Ct. 1968, U.S. Ct. Appeals (3d cir.) 1980, U.S. Ct. Appeals (4th cir.) 1986, U.S. Dist. Ct. (ea. dist.) Pa. Pvt. practice Phila., 1961-65; sr. ptnr. Hy Mayerson Law Offices, 1965-81, Mayerson, Schniper & Gerasimowicz, Spring City, Pa., 1981-87, Mayerson, Gerasimowicz & Munsing, Spring City, 1987-91, Mayerson, Munsing, Corchin & Rosato, P.C., Spring City, 1991-95; pvt. practice The Mayerson Law Offices, P.C., Spring City, 1995—; coord. Nat. Forklift Litigation, 1978-91; lead counsel Agent Orange Product Liability Litigation. Contbr. articles to profl. jours. Mem. ATLA (emeritus chair sect. on Indsl. & Agrl. Eqipment, Product Liability adv.bd.), Pa. Trial Lawyers Assn. Home: Sky Farm Birchrunville PA 19421 Office: Rt 724 Spring City PA 19475

MAYERSON, PHILIP, classics educator; b. N.Y.C., May 20, 1918; s. Theodore and Clara (Fader) M.; m. Joy Gottesman Ungerleider, Nov. 25, 1976 (dec. Sept. 9, 1995); children: Miriam Mayerson, Clare Mayerson, Peter Ungerleider, Steven Ungerleider, Jeanne Ungerleider, Andrew Ungerleider. AB, NYU, 1947, PhD, 1956. With Puritan Fed. Clothing Stores, N.Y.C., 1935-42; instr. NYU, 1948-56, asst. prof., 1956-60, assoc. prof., 1960-66, prof. classics, 1966—, vice dean, 1969-71, acting dean, 1971-73, dean Washington Sq. and U. Coll. Arts and Scis., 1973-78. Author: The Ancient Agricultural Regime of Nessana and the Central Negeb, 1961, Classical Mythology in Literature, Art and Music, 1971, Monks, Martyrs, Soldiers and Saracens, 1994; contbr. articles in field to profl. jours. Served with USN, 1942-45. Rockefeller Found. grantee, 1956-57; Am. Council of Learned Socs. fellow, 1961-62. Mem. Am. Philological Assn., Am. Schs. of Oriental Rsch. Home: 720 Walton Ave Mamaroneck NY 10543 Office: 100 Washington Sq E New York NY 10003-6688

MAYERSON, SANDRA ELAINE, lawyer; b. Dayton, Ohio, Feb. 8, 1952; d. Manuel David and Florence Louise (Tepper) M.; m. Scott Burns, May 29, 1977 (div. Oct. 1978); 1 child, Katy Joy. BA cum laude, Yale U., 1973; JD, Northwestern U., 1976. Bar: Ill. 1976, U.S. Ct. Appeals (7th cir.) 1976, U.S. Dist. Ct. (no. dist.) Ill. 1977, U.S. Dist. Ct. Md. 1989, U.S. Ct. Appeals (5th cir.) 1994. Assoc. gen. counsel JMB Realty Corp., Chgo., 1979-80; assoc. Chatz, Sugarman, Abrams et al, Chgo., 1980-81; ptnr. Pollack, Mayerson & Berman, Chgo., 1981-83; dep. gen. counsel AM Internat., Inc., Chgo., 1983-85; ptnr. Kirkland & Ellis, Chgo., 1985-87; ptnr., chmn. bankruptcy group Kelley Drye & Warren, N.Y.C., 1987-93; ptnr., chmn. N.Y. bankruptcy group McDermott, Will & Emery, N.Y.C., 1993—; examiner Interco chpt. 11, 1991. Bd. dirs. Jr. Med. Rsch. Inst. coun. Michael Reese Hosp., Chgo., 1981-86; mem. met. div. Jewish Guild for Blind, 1990-92; mem. nat. legal afffairs com. Anti-Defamation League, 1990—; mem. lawyers' exec. com. United Jewish Appeal. Fellow Branford Coll., Yale U., 1993—. Mem. ABA (bus. bankruptcy com. 1976—, sec. 1990-93, chair avoiding powers subcom. 1993-96, chair claims trading subcom. 1997—), Ill. State Bar Assn. (governing council corp. and securities sect. 1983-86), Chgo. Bar Assn. (current events chmn. corp. sect. 1980-81), 7th Cir. Bar Assn., Yale Club (N.Y.C.). Democrat. Jewish. Office: McDermott Will & Emery 50 Rockefeller Plz New York NY 10020-1605

MAYES, BERNARD DUNCAN, broadcast journalist, educator, dramatist; b. London, Oct. 10, 1929; came to U.S., 1957; s. Reginald Harry and Nellie (Drew) M. BA, Cambridge (Eng.) U., 1952, MA, 1954. Ordained to ministry Eng. Episc. Ch., 1958. Reporter BBC, London, 1954-79, Hollywood, Calif., 1965-70; reporter ABC, Sydney, Australia, 1970-84, CBC, Toronto, Ont., 1970-75, Radio New Zealand, Wellington, 1970-80; mem. summer faculty Stanford (Calif.) U., 1970-84; mgr. Sta. KQED-FM, San Francisco, 1969-71; founding chmn. Nat. Pub. Radio, Washington, 1969-71; exec. v.p. Sta. KQED-TV, San Francisco, 1971-73; pres. Trans Pacific Consortium, San Francisco, 1980-87; mem. faculty U. Va., 1984—; dir. U. Va. Ctr. Modern Media Studies, Charlottesville, 1987—, chmn. rhetoric and comms. studies dept., 1993-95, asst. dean Coll. Arts and Scis., 1991—; sr. cons. Corp. for Pub. Broadcasting, Washington, 1978-84. Author: Getting It Across, 1957, This is Bernard Mayes in San Francisco, 1986; audio dramatist The Odyssey, Agammemnon and Antigone; actor (audio drama prodns.) The Hobbit, Lord of the Rings; producer documentary USA 200; reader Blackstone Audio Books. Founder Ctr. for Suicide Prevention, San Francisco, 1961-70, The Parsonage Episc. Study Ctr., San Francisco, 1981; chmn. media com. Campaign to End Homophobia, Boston, 1987; bd. dirs. Cerebral Palsy Assn., 1975-77, Heartland Project; mem. Lesbian and Gay Task Force. Recipient Scripts award Nat. Endowment for Arts., Washington, 1985. Fellow Brown Coll.; mem. Bay Area Suicide Prevention Assn. (pres. 1975-77). Democrat. Avocation: writing. Office: U Va Modern Media Studies Brown Coll Charlottesville VA 22903-3102 also: 217 South St Sausalito CA 94965-2530

MAYES, FRANK GORR, management consultant; b. Kellogg, Idaho, Nov. 27, 1930; s. Gilford H. and Rose (Gorr) M.; m. Pamela Ruth Healy, Apr. 20, 1968; 1 child, Matthew A. B.S., Northwestern U., 1952; M.S., NYU, 1953. Supr. mdse. engring. Marshall Field & Co., Chgo., 1953-58; product mgr. Topco Assocs., Inc., Skokie, Ill., 1959-66, dir. grocery, 1966-72, v.p. grocery, 1972-80, sr. v.p. non-perishables, 1980-88, sr. v.p., planning and devel., 1989-96; lectr. mktg. Northwestern U., Chgo., 1956-73. Mem. Am. Mktg. Assn. Office: Mayes Consulting 9400 W Foster Ave Ste 212 Chicago IL 60656-2862

MAYES, GLENN, social worker; b. Aug. 23, 1955; s. Johnny and Lillie (Hopper) M. BS, Cameron U., 1977; MSW, U. Okla., 1984. Cert. profl. healthcare quality; lic. social worker, Okla.; bd. cert. diplomate clin. social worker. Dir. spl. svcs. Jim Taliaferro C.M.H.C., Lawton. Mem. NASW (S.W. chpt. br. chmn. nominations and leadership com.), Nat. Assn. Healthcare Quality, Acad. Cert. Social Workers. Home: 6112 NW Birch Ave Lawton OK 73505-4442

MAYES, ILA LAVERNE, minister; b. Eldorado, Okla., Dec. 23, 1934; d. Thomas Floyd and Irene Elizabeth (Buchanan) Jordan; m. Forrest Clay Mayes, July 2, 1954; children: Barbara, Marian, Cynthia, Janice. BA, U. Tex., 1973; MSW, U. Mich., 1976; MDiv, Austin Presbyn. Sem., 1986. Ordained to ministry Presbyn. Ch. (U.S.A.), 1986; cert. social worker. Pastor First Presbyn. Ch., Childress, Tex., 1986—; med./social worker Childress Regional Med. Ctr., Tex., 1996—; mem. Austin Sem. Alumni Bd., 1991-94, Synod of the Sun Evangelism Com., Denton, 1990-93, Transition Coordinating Agy., 1991—. Chmn. ARC, Childress, 1990; bd. dirs. Am. Cancer Soc., Childress, 1988-89. Mem. AAUW, Mortarboard, Rotary Internat., Alpha Chi, Alpha Lambda Delta. Home: 309 Avenue B SE Childress TX 79201-5429 Office: First Presbyn Ch 311 Commerce St Childress TX 79201-4525 *You and I live in a wonderful tension between the past and the future. As our Faith in God helps us to reinterpret the past and reshapes our future, we grow and change. I like that.*

MAYES, MAUREEN DAVIDICA, physician, educator; b. Phila., Oct. 16, 1945; d. David M. and Marguerite Cecilia (Fineran) M.; m. Charles William Houser, Dec. 18, 1976; children: David Steven, Edward Charles. BA, Coll. Notre Dame, 1967; MD, Ea. Va. Med. Sch., 1976; MA in Pub. Health, U. Mich., Ann Arbor, 1994. Diplomate Am. Bd. Internal Medicine, Am. Bd. Rheumatology. Resident in internal medicine Cleve. Clinic Found., 1977-79, fellow in rheumatology, 1979-81; asst. prof. medicine W.Va. U., Morgantown, 1981-85; asst. prof. medicine Wayne State U., Detroit, 1985-90, assoc. prof. medicine, 1990-97, prof. medicine, 1997—; dir. scleroderma unit Wayne State U., Detroit, 1991—; prin. investigator Scleroderma Registry NIH, 1994—. Contbr. articles to profl. jours. Pres. bd. United Scleroderma Found., 1988-89, pres. med. adv. bd., 1997—; bd. trustees Arthritis Found., Mich. Robert Wood Johnson scholarship EVMS, 1972, NIH fellow, 1993-94, NIAMS Sr. Rsch. fellowship, 1994; recipient Lower award Cleve. Clinic Found., 1981. Fellow Am. Coll. Rheumatology (mem. ctrl. region coun. 1995—), Am. Coll. Physicians; mem. Am. Fedn. Clin. Rsch., Mich. Rheumatism Soc. Office: Wayne State U Hutzel Hosp 4707 Saint Antoine St Detroit MI 48201-1427

MAYES, PAUL EUGENE, engineering educator, technical consultant; b. Frederick, Okla., Dec. 21, 1928; s. Robert Franklin and Bertha Ellen (Walter) M.; m. Lola Mae Davis, June 4, 1950; children: Gwynne Ellen, Linda Kay, Stuart Franklin, Patricia Gail, Steven Lee, David Thomas. BS in Elec. Engring., U. Okla., 1950; MS in Elec. Engring., Northwestern U., 1952, PhD, 1955. Rsch. asst. Northwestern U., Evanston, Ill., 1950-54; asst. prof. U. Ill., Urbana, 1954-58, assoc. prof., 1958-63, prof., 1963-93, prof. emeritus, 1994—; tech. cons. TRW, Redondo Beach, Calif., Walter Gee and Assocs., San Jose, Calif. Author: Electromagnetics for Engineers, 1965; contbr. articles to profl. jours.; inventor in field. Fellow IEEE. Avocations: woodworking, hiking, camping. Home: 1508 Waverly Dr Champaign IL 61821-5002 Office: U Ill 1406 W Green St Urbana IL 61801-2918

MAYES, WENDELL WISE, JR., broadcasting company executive; b. San Antonio, Mar. 2, 1924; s. Wendell Wise and Dorothy Lydia (Evans) M.; m. Mary Jane King, May 11, 1946; children: Cathey, Sarah, Wendell Wise, III. Student, Schreiner Inst., 1941-42, U. Tex. at Austin, 1942, Daniel Baker Coll., 1946; B.S., Tex. Tech. Coll., 1949. Program dir., sta. mgr. Sta. KBWD, Brownwood, Tex., 1949-57; mgr. Sta. KCRS, Midland, Tex., 1957-63; pres. Sta. KCRS, 1965-84, chmn., 1984-96; pres. Sta. KNOW, Austin, Tex., 1970-81; pres. Stas. KVIC and KAMG, Victoria, Tex., 1970-84, chmn., 1984—; chmn. Sta. KCRS-FM, Midland, 1984-96; pres. Sta. KCSW, San Marcos, 1976-81; sec.-treas. Sta. KSNY-AM-FM, Snyder, 1952-94; mem. bd. mgrs. Sta. KLBJ/KHHT-AM-FM, Austin, 1991—; lectr. Coll. Communications, U. Tex., Austin, 1978-81. Pres. Tex. Broadcast Edn. Found., 1973-76; chmn. bd. Am. Diabetes Assn., 1974-77; mem. Nat. Diabetes Adv. Bd., 1977-84; v.p. Internat. Diabetes Fedn., 1980-88, pres.-elect, 1988-91, pres., 1991-94; mem. Tex. Diabetes Coun., 1983-86, chmn., 1983-86; bd. regents Tex. Tech. U., 1985-91, chmn., 1987-88. With USNR, 1943-46. Recipient Addison B. Scoville award Am. Diabetes Assn., 1977, first Wendell Mayes Jr. award, 1986, Josiah K. Lilly award, 1991, Harold Rifkin award, 1994, Masaji Takeda medal Kobe, Japan Colloquium Med. Sci., 1994; named to Tex. Tech. Mass Comm. Hall of Fame, 1978, Hall of Fame Tex. affiliate Am. Diabetes Assn., 1994; named Disting. Alumnus Tex. Tech. U., 1981, Disting. Engr., 1985. Mem. Tex. Assn. Broadcasters (pres. 1964, named Pioneer Broadcaster of Year 1978), Nat. Assn. Broadcasters (dir. 1969-72), Am. Council on Edn. in Journalism (dir. 1977-80), Broadcast Edn. Assn. (dir. 1973-77), AP Broadcasters (bd. dirs. 1988-91), Tex. Tech. Elec. Engring. Acad. Episcopalian (vestryman 1966-69, 86-88; sr. warden 1988). Home: 2834 Montebello Rd #1 Austin TX 78746 Office: Wendell Mayes Stas 1907 N Lamar Blvd Austin TX 78705-4992

MAYESH, JAY PHILIP, lawyer; b. Davenport, Iowa, July 22, 1947; s. Samuel and Dorothy (Katz) M.; m. Leslie Helene Haupt, June 1969; children: Stacey Janet, Beth Valerie. BA, U. Wis., 1969; JD, Columbia U., 1972. Bar: N.Y. 1973, U.S. Dist. Ct. (so. dist.) N.Y. 1973, U.S. Ct. Appeals (2d cir.) 1974. Assoc. Stroock & Stroock & Lavan, N.Y.C., 1972-80, ptnr., 1981—, mem. exec. com., 1990—; instr. Cardozo Trial Advocacy program, 1988—. Editor Product Liability Law and Strategy, 1984. Harlan Fiske Stone scholar Columbia U., 1971. Mem. ABA, N.Y. State Bar Assn., Phi Beta Kappa. Office: Stroock & Stroock & Lavan 180 Maiden Ln New York NY 10038-4925

MAYFIELD, JEREMY, professional race car driver; b. Owensboro, Ky., May 27, 1969; m. Christina Mayfield. raced go-karts, Owensboro, 1982-86, competed Nashville Motor Raceway, 1990-92, ran ARCA Series, 1993; profl. race car driver NASCAR Winston Cup, 1993—. Named Rookie of Yr. and Most Improved Driver, Ky. Motor Speedway, 1986, ARCA Rookie of Yr., 1993. Office: Jeremy Mayfield Fan Club PO Box 2365 Cornelius NC 28031

MAYFIELD, RICHARD HEVERIN, lawyer; b. Washington, Sept. 29, 1921; s. Robert Edwin and Helen May (Benton) M.; m. Caroline C. Mayfield; children: Elinor D., Nancy L., Anne W. A.B., Swarthmore Coll., 1943; LL.B., Harvard U., 1948. Bar: D.C., Md. Asso. firm McKenney, Flannery & Craighill (name later changed to Craighill, Mayfield & Fenwick & Cromelin), Washington, 1948-54; partner McKenney, Flannery & Craighill (name later changed to Craighill, Mayfield, Fenwick & Cromelin), 1954—. Editor: Will Forms and Clauses, 1969, Trust Forms and Clauses, 1975. Bd. govs. Beauvoir Sch., 1961-67, chmn., 1967. Served with AUS, 1943-46. Fellow Am. Coll. Trust and Estates Counsel; mem. Washington Estate Planning Coun., Barrister Club (sec. 1959), Lawyers Club, Columbia Country Club, Farmington Country Club, Masons, Shriners. Home: 5 E Kirke St Bethesda MD 20815-4216 Office: 4910 Massachusetts Ave NW Washington DC 20016-4300

MAYFIELD, ROBERT CHARLES, university official, geography educator; b. Abilene, Tex., Oct. 15, 1928; s. Percy Anderson and Fay (Hicks) M.; m. Loraine Poindexter, Sept. 3, 1952; children: Julie Barnes, Jennifer Manley, Mark Stanley, Malcolm Randall. B.A., Tex. Christian U., 1952; M.S., Ind. U., 1953; Ph.D., U. Wash., 1961. Chmn. geography dept. Tex. Christian U., Ft. Worth, 1960-64, U. Tex., Austin, 1967-71; Chmn. geography dept. Boston U., 1972-77, acad. v.p. external programs, 1977-83, provost, 1979-84; cons. Coun. for Econ. Action, Boston, 1980—; adj. prof. U. Tex., Austin, 1987—; lectr. U.S. Info. Svc., Bangladesh, 1994; lectr. U. Tex. Seminars for Adult Growth and Enrichment, 1995-97. Editor, contbg. author: Man, Environment and Space, 1972. Served with USAF, 1946-49. Research fellow Nat. Acad. Sci. No. India, 1957-58; Fulbright-Hays fellow Office Edn., Bangalore, Mysore, India, 1966-67; research grantee Agrl. Devel. Council, 1968. Mem. Assn. Am. Geographers.

MAYFIELD, T. BRIENT, IV, media and computer executive; b. Athens, Tenn., Mar. 31, 1947; s. Thomas Brient III and Alma Ruth (Bolton) M.; m. N. Katherine Rodgers, Dec. 7, 1974 (div. Mar. 1984); children: Brittany Alexander, Blair Ashton, Katherine Thomas; m. Margaret L. Reeves, Oct. 3, 1987. BS, U. Tenn., 1969. Project mgr. Mayfield Dairy Farms, Athens, 1969-70; v.p. fin. 13-30 Corp., Knoxville, Tenn., 1970-72; exec. v.p. Computer Concepts Corp., Knoxville, 1970-77, pres., 1977-85; pres. Resource Optimization Inc., Knoxville, 1986—; co-founder Whittle Communications LP, Knoxville, 1970, v.p., pub., 1987-92. Bd. dirs. Results Edn. Fund, Washington,, 1990—. Republican. Avocations: flying, music. Home: 5108 Buckhead Trl Knoxville TN 37919-8903 Office: Resource Optimization Inc 531 S Gay St Ste 1212 Knoxville TN 37902-1520

MAYHEW, AUBREY, music industry executive; b. Washington, Oct. 2, 1927; s. Aubrey and Verna June (Hall) M.; m. Carol de Onis, May 10, 1962 (div. 1971); children: Lawrence Aubrey, Michael Aubrey, Parris Mitchell,

Casey Aran. Student, Wilson Tchs. Coll., 1948. Dir. Sta. WWVA, Wheeling, W.Va., 1947-54, Sta. WCOP, Boston, 1954-56; asst. to pres. MGM Records, N.Y.C., 1957-58; v.p. mktg. Capitol Records, Los Angeles, 1958-60; prodr., dir. Sta. KCAM-TV Prodns., Nashville, 1981—; pres., founder John F. Kennedy Meml. Ctr., 1968; authority on John F. Kennedy life and memorabilia. Author: (books) Commandants Marine Corps, 1953, World Tribute to John F. Kennedy, 1965; composer (music) Touch My Heart, 1966 (Broadcast Music, Inc. award, 1967); record producer, artist mgmt., 1947—; music pub., 1954—; developed careers numerous entertainers including Johnny Paycheck, Jeannie C. Riley, Bobby Helms. Served to cpl. U.S. Army Signal Corps, 1945-48. Named Govs. Aide, Nashville, 1978. Mem. Country Music Assn., Broadcast Music Inc., Manuscript Soc., N.Y. Numismatic Soc., Gospel Music Assn. Republican. Episcopalian. Avocations: collector, historian, author. Home: 827 Meridian St Nashville TN 37207-5856 Office: Amcorp Music Group 827 Meridian St Nashville TN 37207-5856

MAYHEW, DAVID RAYMOND, political educator; b. Putnam, Conn., May 18, 1937; s. Raymond William and Jeanie (Nicholson) M. B.A., Amherst Coll., 1958; Ph.D. (Delancey K. Jay dissertation prize 1964), Harvard U., 1964. Teaching fellow Harvard U., 1961-63; instr., then asst. prof. polit. sci. U. Mass., Amherst, 1963-67; vis. asst. prof. Amherst Coll., 1965-66; mem. faculty Yale U., 1968—, prof. polit. sci., 1977—, chmn. dept., 1979-82, Alfred Cowles prof. govt., 1982—. Author: Party Loyalty Among Congressmen, 1966, Congress: The Electoral Connection, 1974 (Washington Monthly ann. polit. book award 1974), Placing Parties in American Politics, 1986, Divided We Govern, 1991. Recipient Richard E. Neustadt prize 1992; Woodrow Wilson fellow, 1958-59, vis. fellow Nuffield Coll., Oxford, 1978, Guggenheim fellow, 1978-79, Hoover Nat. fellow, 1978-79, Sherman Fairchild fellow, 1990-91, fellow Ctr. for Advanced Study in Behavioral Scis., 1995-96. Fellow Am. Acad. Arts and Scis.; mem. Am. Polit. Sci. Assn. (nat. council 1976-78, Congl. fellow 1967-68), So. Polit. Sci. Assn., New Eng. Polit. Sci. Assn. Home: 100 York St Apt 5C New Haven CT 06511-5611 Office: Yale U Polit Sci Dept Box 208301 New Haven CT 06520-8301

MAYHEW, ERIC GEORGE, cancer researcher, educator; b. London, Eng., June 22, 1938; came to U.S., 1964; s. George James and Doris Ivy (Tipping) M.; m. Barbara Doe, Sept. 28, 1966 (div. 1976); 1 child, Miles; m. Karen Caruana, Apr. 1, 1978 (div. 1994); children: Ian, Andrea: m. Ludmila Khatchatrian, June 29, 1995. BS, U. London, 1960, MS, 1963; PhD, 1967; DSc, U. London, 1993. Rsch. asst. Chester Beatty Rsch. Inst., London, 1960-64; cancer rsch. scientist Roswell Pk. Meml. Inst., Buffalo, 1964-68, sr. cancer rsch. scientist, 1968-72, assoc. cancer rsch. scientist, 1979-93, dep. dir. exptl. pathology, 1988-93; assoc. rsch. prof. SUNY, Buffalo, 1979-93; prin. scientist The Liposome Co., Princeton, N.J., 1993—; ad-hoc mem. NIH study sects., 1982-94. Editor jour. Selective Cancer Therapeutics, 1989-91; contbr. articles to Jour. Nat. Cancer Inst., Cancer Rsch. and many other profl. jours. Grantee NIH, Am. Heart Assn., and pvt. industry, 1972-93. Mem. Am. Assn. Cancer Rsch., N.Y. Acad. Sci. Achievements include development of liposomes for drug delivery and patents for new chemical entities and liposome delivery. Office: The Liposome Co Princeton Forestal Ctr One Research Way Princeton NJ 08540

MAYHEW, HARRY EUGENE, physician, educator; b. St. Clair, Mich., Apr. 16, 1933; s. Eugene Nelson and Viola Erma (Danneels) M; m. Eunice Yvonne Brown, June 23, 1950; children: Dawn Boers, Timothy, Stephen, Elise Couch, Betheny Campbell, Heidi Reimer. Student, Port Huron Jr. Coll., 1951-53; MD, U. Mich., 1958. Diplomate Am. Bd. Family Practice. Intern St. Joseph Hosp., Flint, Mich., 1958-59; pvt. practice St. Clair, Mich., 1959-73; asst. dir. family practice residency Sparrow Hosp., Lansing, Mich., 1974-76; asst. prof. dept. family practice Coll. Human Medicine, Mich. State U., 1974-76; prof., chmn. dept. family medicine Med. Coll. Ohio, Toledo, 1976-97; cons. Residency Assistance Program Acad. Family Physicians, Kansas City, Mo., 1978-95; adv. bd. Salvation Army. Co-editor: Critical Issues in Family Practice: Cases and Commentaries, 1982, Basic Procedures in Family Practice, 1984, Genital Urinary Problems in the Male Patient, 1989. Mem. AMA, Soc. Tchrs. Family Medicine, Assn. Depts. Family Medicine, Coun. Acad. Socs., Assn. Depts. Family Medicine Bd., Coun. Acad. Soc. Bd., Taos Country Club, Alpha Omega Alpha. Baptist. Office: Med Coll Ohio Dept Family Medicine PO Box 10008 Toledo OH 43699-0008

MAYHEW, KENNETH EDWIN, JR., transportation company executive; b. Shelby, N.C., Sept. 27, 1934; s. Kenneth Edwin and Evelyn Lee (Dellinger) M.; m. Frances Elaine Craft, Apr. 7, 1957; 1 dau., Catherine Lynn Prince. A.B., Duke U., 1956. CPA, N.C. Sr. auditor Arthur Andersen & Co., Atlanta, 1956-58, 60-63; controller Trendline, Inc., Hickory, N.C., 1963-66; with Carolina Freight Corp., Cherryville, 1966-93; treas., 1969-74; v.p. Carolina Freight Carriers Corp., Cherryville, 1971-72, exec. v.p., 1972-85, pres., chief oper. officer, 1985-89, dir., 1968-93, chmn., pres., CEO, 1989-93; pres., dir. Robo Auto Wash Shelby Inc., 1967-73, Robo Auto Wash Cherryville, Inc., 1968-73; dir. Cherryville Nat. Bank, Kenmar Bus. Group, Inc. Mem. Bus. Adv. Bd., Fuqua Sch. Bus., Duke U.; bd. dirs., vice-chmn. Gaston Meml. Hosp.; trustee Pfeiffer Coll. With AUS, 1958-60. Mem. AICPA, Am. Trucking Assn. (dir., v.p.), N.C. Trucking Assn. (dir., chmn.), Gaston County C. of C. (v.p. pub. affairs), Lions (pres. Cherryville 1972-73), Phi Beta Kappa, Omicron Delta Kappa, Phi Eta Sigma. Methodist. Home: 507 Spring St Cherryville NC 28021-3540

MAYHEW, LAWRENCE LEE, electronics company executive; b. Santa Paula, Calif., Mar. 17, 1933; s. Paul Donald and Lucille Frances (Winkler) M.; m. Kathleen Joan McCown, Feb. 6, 1955; children: Taryn Lee, Jeffrey Park, Kimberly Anne. BS, Calif. State Poly. U., 1961. Design engr. Tektronix Inc., Beaverton, Oreg., 1961-65; ops. mgr. Tektronix Inc., Netherlands, 1965-69; div. gen. mgr. Tektronix Inc., Beaverton, 1969-73; div. v.p. Tektronix Inc., 1973-78, group v.p., 1978-82; pres., chief exec. officer Data I/O Corp., Redmond, Wash., 1982-90; ret. Lt. USNR, 1953-58. Mem. IEEE (sr.), Am. Electronics Assn. (dir., chmn. 1981). Republican. Avocations: gardening, sailing, woodworking, wine.

MAYHEW, WILLIAM A., judge; b. Pueblo, Colo., July 21, 1940; s. Wilbren D. and Dorothy L. (Holloway) M.; m. Marianne J., May 8, 1971; children: Lance, Kevin, Christie. AA, Modesto Jr. Coll., 1959; BS, UCLA, 1961, JD, 1964. Bar: Calif. 1965, U.S. Ct. Appeals (9th cir.) 1965, U.S. Dist. Ct. (no., ea. dists.) Calif. 1965. Dep. atty. gen. State Calif., 1964-67; ptnr., pvt. practice Thompson, Mayhew & Michel (now Thompson, Meede & Nielsen), 1968-82; prof. law Miss. Coll. Sch. Law, 1982-86; atty. Sarhad & Mayhew, Turlock, Calif., 1986-88; mng. ptnr. Borton, Petrini & Conron, Modesto, Calif., 1988-94; judge Stanislaus County Mcpl. Ct., Modesto, 1994-95, Stanislaus County Superior Ct., Modesto, 1995—; assoc. prof. Coll. Law U. Toledo, 1975-76; lecturer in field. Bd. editors UCLA Law Review; contbr. articles to profl. jours. Mem. Turlock H.S. Bd. Trustees, 1989-94, pres., 1992; usher, progress com. St. Francis Episcopal Ch.; mem. standing com. Episcopal Diocese San Joaquin Diocesan Conv., 1991-95; vice chancelor Episcopal Bishop of San Joaquin, 1990-94. Maj. JAGC, Calif. Army N.G., 1966-77. Mem. Am. Bd. Trial Advocates (nat. bd. dirs., advocate, chair western regional conf. 1987, Miss. chpt., sec.-treas. 1985), Turlock Rotary Club, Order of Coif. Republican. Office: Stanislaus County Superior Ct PO Box 1011 Modesto CA 95353-1011

MAYHUE, RICHARD LEE, dean, pastor, writer; b. Takoma Park, Md., Aug. 31, 1944; s. J. Richard Mayhue and Myrtle Lorraine (Hartsell) Lee; m. Lois Elaine Nettleingham, June 18, 1966; children: Lee, Wade. BS, Ohio State U., 1966; MDiv, Grace Theol. Seminary, Winona Lake, Ind., 1974, ThM, 1977, ThD, 1981. Ordained pastor. Asst. pastor Grace Brethren Ch. of Columbus (Ohio), 1975-77; asst. prof. New Testament and Greek, Grace Theol. Seminary, Winona Lake, 1977-80; assoc. pastor Grace Cmty. Ch., Sun Valley, Calif., 1980-84, 89—; sr. pastor Grace Brethren Ch., Long Beach, Calif., 1984-89; sr. v.p., dean, prof. systematic theology and pastoral mins. The Master's Seminary, Sun Valley, 1989—; bd. dirs. Grace Theol. Sem., 1987-89. Author: (booklets) The Biblical Pattern for Divine Healing, 1979, Snatched Before the Storm, 1980, (books) Divine Healing Today, 1983, How to Interpret the Bible for Yourself, 1986, A Christian's Survival Guide, 1987, Unmasking Satan, 1988, Spiritual Intimacy, 1990, Spiritual Maturity, 1992, The Healing Promise, 1994, What Would Jesus Say About Your Church?, 1995; contbr., editor: Rediscovering Expository Preaching, 1992, Rediscovering Pastoral Ministry, 1994; contbr. New Am. Std. Study Bible, 1997; contbr., assoc. editor MacArthur Study Bible, 1997; contbr. articles to profl. jours. Lt. USN, 1966-71, Vietnam. Recipient Bronze Star with Combat V USN, 1969. Mem. Evang. Theol. Soc., Nat. Fellowship Grace Brethren Ministers (pres. 1988), Far West Region Evang. Theol. Soc. (pres. 1995), Slavic Gospel Assn. (bd. dirs. 1993—). Avocation: N gauge model railroading. Office: The Master's Seminary 13248 Roscoe Blvd Sun Valley CA 91352-3739

MAYHUGH, JOEL OGDEN, JR., financial executive; b. Little Rock, Nov. 9, 1941; s. Joel Ogden Sr. and Jessie Olin (Hall) M.; m. Caroline Elizabeth Boellner, Nov. 5, 1966; 1 child, Katherine Elizabeth. BA in Social Scis., U. Little Rock, 1969. Sales rep. Kraft Foods, Little Rock, 1964-66, 68-72; sr. fin. cons. Merrill Lynch, Little Rock, 1972-92; asst. v.p. Merrill Lynch, Hot Springs, Ark., 1992—. Co-chmn. North Little Rock Port Authority, 1982; pres. Ark. affiliate Am. Diabetes Assn., Little Rock, 1980, North Little Rock Kiwanis Club, 1977; bd. dirs. YMCA, North Little Rock, 1983. With U.S. Army, 1966-68. Named Outstanding Kiwanian of Yr. Kiwanis Club, 1976, Outstanding Stock Broker in the U.S. Money Mag., 1987. Mem. Hot Springs Jazz Soc., Little Rock C. of C. (bd. dirs. 1977-78), Hot Springs C. of C., North Hills Country Club (greens com. 1975-76), Ark. State Golf Assn., Ark. Fly Fishing Assn., Ark. Wilde Life Assn., Ducks Unltd., Merrill Lynch Presidents Club. Baptist. Avocations: golf, boating, cooking, fly fishing, duck hunting. Home: 1340 Rock Creek Rd Hot Springs National Park AR 71913-9283 Office: Merrill Lynch Inc PO Box 205 Hot Springs National Park AR 71951-0205

MAYLAND, KENNETH THEODORE, economist; b. Miami, Fla., Nov. 17, 1951; s. Herbert and Vera (Bob) M; m. Gail Fern Bassok, Apr. 14, 1984. BS, MIT, 1973; MS, U. Pa., 1976, PhD, 1979. Cons. economist Data Resources, Inc., Lexington, Mass., 1973; economist, then chief economist First Pa. Bank, Phila., 1973-89; sr. v.p., chief economist Soc. Nat. Bank, Cleve., 1989-94; sr. v.p., chief fin. economist Key Corp., Cleve., 1994-96, sr. v.p., chief economist, 1996—; econs. instr., Chartered Fin. Aanalysts Assn., Phila, 1984—; econ. adv. com. Phila. Econ. Devel. Coalition, 1984-86; chmn. econ. adv. com. Pa. Bankers Assn., Harrisburg, 1982-84; mem. Gov.'s Econ. Adv. Com., Ohio, 1989—. Contbr. semi-monthly periodical Money Markets, 1981-85, quar. periodical Regional Report, 1980-89, Econ. Viewpoint biweekly periodical, 1989—, Regional Rev. quarterly periodical, 1989—. Mem. curriculum adv. com. Widener U., 1986-89. Mem. Am. Bankers Assn. (econ. adv. com. 1990-93), Internat. Econ. Roundtable (vice chmn. 1987-88, chmn. 1988-90), Nat. Assn. Bus. Economists (New Face for the Eighties award 1979), Phila. Coun. Bus. Economists (pres. 1982-84), Cleve. Bus. Economist Club (sec.-treas. 1990-91, v.p. 1991-92, pres. 1992-93). Avocations: fishing, badminton, gardening, camping. Home: 3237 Fox Hollow Dr Cleveland OH 44124-5426 Office: Key Corp 127 Public Sq Cleveland OH 44114-1216

MAYNARD, CHARLES DOUGLAS, radiologist; b. Atlantic City, Sept. 11, 1934; m. Mary Anne Satterwhite; children—Charles D., Deanne, David. B.S., Wake Forest U., 1955, M.D., 1959. Diplomate Am. Bd. Radiology (trustee, sec.-treas., v.p. 1992-94, pres. 1994-96). Intern U.S. Army Hosp., Honolulu, 1959-60; resident N.C. Baptist Hosp., 1963-66; dir. Nuclear Medicine Lab., 1966-77; asst. dean admissions Bowman Gray Sch. Medicine, 1966-71, asso. dean student affairs, 1971-75, prof. radiology, chmn. dept., 1977—; guest examiner Am. Bd. Radiology. Author: Clinical Nuclear Medicine, 1969; mem. editorial bd. Academic Radiology, Yearbook of Diagnostic Radiology, Contemporary Diagnostic Radiology. Mem. Leadership Winston-Salem, Triad Leadership Network; bd. dirs. Downtown Devel. Corp., 1995—, Winston-Salem Bus., Inc., 1995—. Mem. AMA, Soc. Nuclear Medicine (past pres.), Am. Coll. Radiology (past bd. chancellors, past chmn. commn. on nuclear medicine), Radiol. Soc. N.Am. (sec.-treas.), Assn. Univ. Radiologists, Soc. Chairmen Radiology Depts. (past pres.), Acad. Radiology Rsch. (v.p. 1995—), Am. Bd. Radiology (bd. trustees 1987—, pres. 1994-96), Am. Bd. Med. Specialists, Greater Winston-Salem C. of C. (bd. dirs.). Office: Medical Center Blvd Dept Radiology Winston Salem NC 27157

MAYNARD, DONALD NELSON, horticulturist, educator; b. Hartford, Conn., June 22, 1932; s. Harry Ashley and Elsie Frances (Magnuson) M.; m. Adrienne A. Taylor; 1 child, David Nelson. BS, U. Conn., 1954; MS, N.C. State U., 1956; PhD, U. Mass., 1963. Instr. plant sci. U. Mass., Amherst, 1956-62, asst. prof., 1962-67, assoc. prof., 1967-72, prof., 1972-79, asst. dean, 1974-75, prof. emeritus, 1979—; prof. vegetable crops U. Fla., Gainesville, 1979—; chmn. dept. U. Fla., 1979-85; cons. Greenleaf, Inc., Hackensack, N.J., SRD Rsch., Logan, Utah. Assoc. editor Jour. Am. Soc. Hort. Sci., 1976-80, 89-91, HortSci, 1975-80, 89—. Recipient Aid to Edn. award Gulf Oil Corp., 1965. Fellow Am. Soc. for Hort. Sci. (Environ. Quality Rsch. award 1975, Marion W. Meadows award 1977, pres. 1996-97, chmn. bd. 1997—, So. region pres. 1996-97); mem. Sigma Xi, Phi Kappa Phi, Alpha Zeta, Phi Tau Sigma. Republican. Episcopalian. Home: 5551 Contento Dr Sarasota FL 34242-1836 Office: U Fla Gulf Coast Rsch Edn Ctr Bradenton FL 34203

MAYNARD, E. ROSE, retired school health services coordinator; b. Mosquero, N.Mex., Feb. 7, 1934; d. E.H. and Eudora M. (Freeland) McGlothlin; m. Bob Maynard, Aug. 2, 1952; children: Michael, Michele, Mark. BSN with hons., Calif. State U., L.A., 1971, MA, 1974. CPNP, RN, Calif. Sch. nurse ABC Unified Sch. Dist., Cerritos, Calif., 1970-86, pediatric nurse practitioner, 1977-86; dept. chmn. health svcs. Lancaster (Calif.) Sch. Dist., 1986-92, pediatric nurse practitioner, 1986-96, DATE coord., 1990-96, coord. health svcs., 1992-96; ret., 1996; presenter Ednl. Conf., Hawaii, 1982; PASS Project Replicator, CSNO and NASN, Calif., 1987-91; presenter Calif. Sch. Bd. Ann. State Conf., San Jose, 1994. Coord. Calif. State Contest, 1985. CPR/FA instr. ARC, Quartz Hill, Calif., 1986—; mem. Tobacco Task Force, Am. CA Soc., Palmdale, Calif., 1989—. Fellow Nat. Assn. Pediat. Nurses; mem. Calif. Sch. Nurses Assn. (bd. dirs. so. sect. 1991-93), Nat. Assn. Sch. Nurses, Assn. Calif. Sch. Adminstrs., Alpha Gamma Sigma. Republican. Avocations: travel, exercise, reading, family activities.

MAYNARD, JOAN, education educator; b. Louisa, Ky., Oct. 18, 1932; d. Macon Scott and Jeanette (Thompson) Chambers; m. Frank Maynard Jr., June 15, 1951 (dec. Oct. 1988); children: Mark Steven, Julia Beth Maynard McFann, Robert Blake. BA, Wittenberg U., 1977; MEd, Wright State U., 1980, Wright State U., 1984. Tchr., reading specialist Mechanicsburg (Ohio) Exempted Village Schs., 1976—; pres. TOTT Publs. Inc., Bellbrook, Ohio, 1988—; rep. Career Edn., Mechanicsburg, 1981-88, mem. Thompson Grant Com., Mechanicsburg, 1987-88. Author: Mud Puddles, 1988, Mud Pies, 1989. Vol. Mechanicsburg Schs. Levy, 1980, 82, 88, Congl. Race, Campaign County, Ohio, 1982, 84, 86; cons. Urbana U., Ohio, 1988-90, 91, 92, 93; tutor Laubach Lit. Action, Urbana, 1989-90, 91-93, 94. Recipient Thompson grant, 1982, 88, 92. Mem. AAUW (edn. chmn. Champaign County chpt. 1988-89, treas. 1989-90), Internat. Reading Assn., Champaign County Reading Coun. (treas. 1990-91), Midwestern Assembly Lit. Young People (treas. 1989-93), Kappa Delta Pi. Avocations: collecting children's lit. books, travel, reading. Home: 1546 Parkview Rd Mechanicsburg OH 43044-9779 Office: Exempted Village Schs 60 High St Mechanicsburg OH 43044-1003

MAYNARD, JOHN RALPH, lawyer; b. Seattle, Mar. 5, 1942; s. John R. and Frances Jane (Mitchell) Maynard Kendryk; m. Meridee J. Sagadin, Sept. 10, 1995; children: Bryce James, Pamela Ann. BA, U. Wash., 1964; JD, Calif. Western U., San Diego, 1972; LLM, Harvard Law, 1973. Bar: Calif. 1972, Wis. 1973. Assoc. Whyte & Hirschboeck, Milw., 1973-78, Minahan & Peterson, Milw., 1979-91, Quarles & Brady, Milw., 1991—. Bd. dirs. Am. Heart Assn., 1979-82. Mem. Wis. Adv. Coun. to U.S. SBA, 1987-89. Served to lt. USN, 1964-69. Mem. ABA, Harvard Club (Wis.), Yacht Club (Milw.). Republican. Home: 809 E Lake Forest Ave Milwaukee WI 53217-5377 Office: Quarles & Brady 411 E Wisconsin Ave Milwaukee WI 53202-4409

MAYNARD, JOHN ROGERS, English educator; b. Williamsville, N.Y., Oct. 6, 1941; s. Atherton Rogers and Olive (Fisher) M.; m. Florence Michelson, July 1, 1967 (div. 1980); 1 child, Alex Stevens; m. Ursula Krammer, Oct. 17, 1992 (div. 1995). BA, Harvard U., 1963, PhD, 1970. Asst. prof. Harvard U., Cambridge, Mass., 1969-74, NYU, N.Y.C., 1974-76, assoc. prof., 1976-84, prof. English, 1984—, chmn. English dept., 1983-89; chmn. Faculty Council NYU, 1983-84; vis. prof. U. Venice, Italy, 1991. Author: Brownings Youth, 1977 (Wilson prize 1977), Charlotte Bronte and Sexuality, 1984, Victorian Discourses on Sexuality and Religion, 1993, Browning Re-Viewed, 1997; editor: (with Lockridge and Stone) Nineteenth Century Lives, 1989, (with Bloom) Shankman's Anne Thackeray Ritchie: Journals and Letters, (with Munich) Victorian Literature and Culture, 1991—. Organizer, Concord Sq. Assn., Boston, 1972-74. NEH grantee, 1972-73; Guggenheim fellow, 1979-80. Mem. MLA, PEN, Browning Inst. (bd. dirs.), Signet Soc., Fly Club, Andiron Club (pres. 1983-84). Democrat. Avocation: bicycling. Home: 39 Schermerhorn St Brooklyn NY 11201-4825 Office: NYU Dept of English 19 University Pl New York NY 10003-4556

MAYNARD, KENNETH IRWIN, medical educator, researcher; b. San Fernando, Trinidad, Jan. 17, 1963. Student, Howard U., 1982; BSc with honors, Univ. Coll., London, 1986, MSc, 1987, PhD, 1991. Postdoctoral rsch. assistantship Univ. Coll., London, 1991; postdoctoral rsch. fellow Stroke Rsch. Lab. Neurosurg. Svc. Mass. Gen. Hosp., Harvard Med. Sch., Boston, 1991-93, postdoctoral rsch. fellow neurophysiology lab. Neurosurg. Svc., 1993—; tchg. fellow dept. neurobiology Harvard Med. Sch., Boston, 1992, instr. in surgery, 1995—. Ad hoc reviewer Jour. Vascular Rsch., 1991, Neurosci. Letters, 1995, Vision Rsch., 1996; contbr. articles to profl. jours.; presenter in field. Mem. parish pastoral coun. St. Joseph's Cath. Ch., Boston, 1992-95, chmn. stewardship commn., 1996—; advisor regional com. ctrl. region on stewardship for Archdiocese of Boston, 1995—. Fellow Am. Heart Assn. (mem. stroke coun., minority scientist devel. award 1996); mem. AAAS, Soc. for Neurosci. (NINDS travel fellow for minority neuroscientists 1995), Am. Assn. Neurosurg. Surgeons (adj. assoc. mem. joint sect. on cerebrovascular surgery 1995), Congress of Neurosurg. Surgeons, Internat. Soc. of Cerebral Blood Flow and Metabolism (jr. mem., Young Scientist Bursary award 1993). Office: Mass Gen Hosp Dept Neurosurgery Edwards 414 32 Fruit St Boston MA 02114-2620

MAYNARD, NANCY GRAY, biological oceanographer; b. Middleboro, Mass., Apr. 18, 1941; d. Thomas LaSalle and Clara (Gray) M.; m. Conrad Dennis Gebelein, Jan., 1969 (div. 1977); 1 child, Jennifer Lynn. BS, Mary Washington Coll., 1963; MS, U. Miami (Fla.), 1968, PhD, 1974. Rsch. assoc. Bermuda Biol. Sta., Ferry Reach, 1972-75; rsch. fellow Lamont-Doherty Geol. Obs. Columbia U. (CLIMAP), 1972-75; post-doctoral fellow Div. Engring., Applied Physics Harvard U., Cambridge, Mass., 1975-76; field coord. environ. studies Alaska Outer Continental Shelf Office U.S. Dept. Interior, Anchorage, 1976-78; with oil spills sci. support Nat. Oceanic and Atmospheric Adminstrn., Alaska and S.E. U.S., 1978-81; policy analyst Exec. Office Pres. U.S. Office Sci. and Technology Policy, Washington, 1982-83; fellow Dept. of Commerce Sci. and Tech., 1982-83; staff dir. Bd. Ocean Sci. and Policy NAS, Washington, 1983-85; resident rsch. assoc. Nat. Rsch. Coun. Scripps Instn. Oceanography and Jet Propulsion Lab NASA, 1985-87; br. head Oceans and Ice Br. Goddard Space Flight Ctr. NASA, Greenbelt, Md., 1987-88, assoc. chief rsch. Lab. for Oceans, 1988-89; asst. dir. for environment Exec. Office of Pres. Office Sci. and Tech. Policy, Washington, 1989-93; dep. dir. sci. div. NASA Mission to Planet Earth HQ, Washington, 1993—. Contbr. numerous articles profl. jours. Recipient Pub. Svc. Commendation USCG, 1979. Mem. AAAS, Assn. Women in Sci., The Oceanography Soc., Am. Geophys. Union, Women's Aquatic Network (bd. dirs.), Corp. Bermuda Biol. Sta. Rsch. Office: NASA Mission Planet Earth Sci Divsn 300 E St SW Washington DC 20024-3210

MAYNARD, PARRISH, ballet dancer; b. Epernay, France. Student, San Francisco Ballet Sch., 1978-80. Dancer Am. Ballet Theatre II, N.Y.C., 1983-85; soloist Joffrey Ballet, N.Y.C., 1986-88; mem. corps de ballet Am. Ballet Theatre, N.Y.C., 1988-92, soloist, 1992—; guest artist Australian Nat. Ballet, 1993, English Nat. Ballet, 1993. Created role of narrator in Ulysses Dove's Serious Pleasures; performed in dances including (with Joffrey Ballet) The Clowns, A Midsummer Night's Dream, Monotones I, (with Am. Ballet Theatre) La Bayadere, Etudes, Drink to Me Only With Thine Eyes, Giselle, Romeo and Juliet, The Sleeping Beauty, Swan Lake, Symphonic Variations, Moondance, La Sylphide, The Nutcracker. Office: Am Ballet Theatre 890 Broadway New York NY 10003-1211*

MAYNARD, ROBERT HOWELL, lawyer; b. San Antonio, Feb. 15, 1938; s. William Simpson Sr. and Lillian Isabel (Tappan) M.; m. Joan Marie Pearson, Jan. 6, 1962; children: Gregory Scott, Patricia Kathryn, Alicia Joan, Elizabeth Simms. BA, Baylor U., 1959, LLB, 1961; LLM, Georgetown U., 1965. Bar: Tex. 1961, D.C. 1969, Ohio 1973. Trial atty. gen. litigation sect. lands div. U.S. Dept. Justice, Washington, 1964-65; spl. asst. to solicitor U.S. Dept. Interior, Washington, 1965-69; legis. asst. U.S. Senate, Washington, 1969-73; ptnr., dept. head Smith & Schnacke, Dayton, Ohio, 1973-83; dir. Ohio EPA, Columbus, Ohio, 1983-85; ptnr., environ. policy and strategy devel., tech. law Vorys, Sater, Seymour and Pease, Columbus, 1985—. Trustee Ohio Found. for Entrepren. Edn., Business Technology Ctr., Episcopal Cmty. Svcs. Found., 1990-96, Industry Tech. Coun. Ctrl. Ohio. USNR, 1962-65. Episcopalian. Office: Vorys Sater Seymour & Pease PO Box 1008 52 E Gay St Columbus OH 43216-1008

MAYNARD, STEVEN HARRY, writer; b. San Diego, July 4, 1954; s. Harry Clark and Ruby Kristina (Odna). BA in Communications, U. Wash., 1976; MA in Theology, Fuller Theol. Seminary, 1979. Religion writer, gen. news reporter Walla Walla (Wash.) Union-Bulletin, 1979-84; religion writer Houston Chronicle, 1984-87; religion/ethics/values reporter The News Tribune, Tacoma, Wash., 1987—. Recipient Mng. Editors award Tex. Associated Press, 1984, Wilbur award Religious Pub. Relations Council, 1981. Mem. Religion Newswriters Assn. Office: 1950 S State St Tacoma WA 98405-2817

MAYNARD, TERRELL DENNIS, minister; b. Paducah, Ky., Dec. 10, 1944; s. Claude and Euda (Finley) M.; m. Mary Jacqueline Chappell, Sept. 3, 1965; children: Terrell Geoffrey, Christopher Dennis. BA, Bethel Coll., 1966; MDiv, Memphis Theol. Sem., 1969. Pastor Cumberland Presbyn. Ch., Searcy, Ark., 1969-72, Hohenwald, Tenn., 1972-76; pastor Swan Cumberland Presbyn. Ch., Centerville, Tenn., 1972-76, Elliottsville Presbyn. Ch., Alabaster, Ala., 1976-94, 1st Cumberland Presbyn. Ch., Jackson, Tenn., 1994—; pres. Bd. Christian Edn., Memphis, 1976-85; chair Gen. Assembly's Exec. Com., Memphis, 1987-93. Bd. dirs., pres. Shelby Emergency Assistance, Montevallo, Ala., 1990-94; bd. dirs. Developing Ala. Youth Found., Alabaster, 1989-94, Shelby County Hosp. Authority, Alabaster, 1993-94, Area Relief Ministry, Jackson, 1996—. Recipient Disting. Alumni award Bethel Coll., McKenzie, Tenn., 1992; named Outstanding Vol. Shelby County Chpt. ARC, Alabaster, 1989. Mem. Assn. Cumberland Presbyn. Ch. Educators. Avocations: fishing, golf, huntung, reading, college basketball. Home: 139 Paddock Pl Jackson TN 38305-7718 Office: 1st Cumberland Presbyn Ch 1730 Us Highway 45 Byp Jackson TN 38305-4415

MAYNARD, VIRGINIA MADDEN, charitable organization executive; b. New London, Conn., Jan. 29, 1924; d. Raymond and Edna Sarah (Madden) Maynard; B.S., U. Conn., 1945; postgrad. Am. Inst. Banking, 1964-66, Cornell U., 1975. With Nat. City Bank (now Citibank), N.Y.C., 1954-79, asst. cashier, 1965-69, asst. v.p., 1969-74, v.p. internat. banking group, 1974-76, comptroller's div., 1976-79; v.p. First Women's Bank, N.Y.C., 1979-80; Internat. Fedn. Univ. Women rep. UN, 1982—. Trustee fellowships endowment fund AAUW Ednl. Found., Washington, 1977-80, Va. Gildersleeve Internat. Fund Univ. Women, Inc. (pres., 1987-93, dir. 1994—). Mem. AAUW (fin. chmn. N.Y.C. br. 1976-79, bylaws chmn. 1979-83, adminstr. Meml. Fund 1983-92, dir., 1992-94, 96—, Woman of Achievement 1976). Republican. Congregationalist. Home: 601 E 20th St New York NY 10010-7622

MAYNE, KENNY, sports anchor; b. Sept. 1, 1959. Student, Wenatchee (Wash.) Valley C.C.; BA in Broadcasting, U. Nev.-Las Vegas, 1982. Reporter Sta. KLVX-TV, Las Vegas, 1982; reporter Sta. KSTW-TV, Tacoma/Seattle, 1982-89, prodn. asst., 1982-83, news writer, 1983-86, weekend sports anchor, news reporter, 1986-89; freelance reporter, field prodr. SportsCenter ESPN, 1990-94, SportSmash anchor, 1994—, SportsNight reporter, 1994—, SportsCenter anchor, 1994—; host RPM 2Night ESPN2, 1994—; football player, free agt. Seattle Seahawks, 1982. Office: c/o ESPN ESPN Pla Bristol CT 06010

MAYNE, LUCILLE STRINGER, finance educator; b. Washington, June 6, 1924; d. Henry Edmond and Hattie Benham (Benson) Stringer; children: Patricia Anne, Christine Gail, Barbara Marie. BS, U. Md., 1946; MBA, Ohio State U., 1949; PhD, Northwestern U., 1966. Instr. fin. Utica Coll., 1949-50; lectr. fin. Roosevelt U., 1961-64; lectr. fin. Pa. State U., 1965-66, asst. prof., 1966-69, assoc. prof., 1969-70; assoc. prof. banking and fin. Case-Western Res. U., 1971-76, prof., 1976-94, prof. emerita, 1994—, grad. dean Sch. Grad. Studies, 1980-84; sr. economist, cons. FDIC, 1977-78; cons. Nat. Commn. Electronic Fund Transfer Sys., 1976; rsch. cons. Am. Bankers Assn., 1975, Fed. Res. Bank of Cleve., 1968-70, 73; cons. Pres.'s Commn. Fin. Structure and Regulation, 1971, staff economist, 1970-71; analytical statistician Air Materiel Command, Dayton, Ohio, 1950-52; asst. to promotion mgr. NBC, Washington, 1946-48; expert witness cases involving fin. instns. Assoc. editor: Jour. Money, Credit and Banking, 1980-83, Bus. Econs., 1980-85; contbr. articles to profl. jours. Vol. Cleve. Soc. for Blind, 1979—, Benjamin Rose Inst., 1995—; mem. policyholders nominating com. Tchrs. Ins. and Annuity Assn./Coll. Retirement Equities Fund, 1982-84, chairperson com., 1984; bd. dirs. Women's Cmty. Found., 1994-96. Grad. scholar Ohio State U., 1949; doctoral fellow Northwestern U., 1963-65. Mem. Midwest Fin. Assn. (pres. 1991-92, bd. dirs. 1975-79, officer 1988-93), Phi Kappa Phi, Beta Gamma Sigma. Episcopalian. Home: 3723 Normandy Rd Cleveland OH 44120-5246 Office: Case Western Res U Weatherhead Sch Mgmt U Circle Cleveland OH 44106-7235

MAYNE, WILEY EDWARD, lawyer; b. Sanborn, Iowa, Jan. 19, 1917; s. Earl W. and Gladys (Wiley) M.; m. Elizabeth Dodson, Jan. 5, 1942; children—Martha (Mrs. F.K. Smith), Wiley Edward, John. S.B. cum laude, Harvard, 1938; student, Law Sch., 1938-39; J.D., State U. Iowa, 1939-41. Bar: Iowa bar 1941. Practiced in Sioux City, 1946-66, 75—; mem. Shull, Marshall, Mayne, Marks & Vizintos, 1946-66, Mayne and Berenstein, 1975-87, Mayne & Mayne, 1988—; spl. agt. FBI, 1941-43; Mem. 90th-93d Congresses, 6th Dist. Iowa; mem. judiciary com., agr. com. Commr. from Iowa Nat. Conf. Commrs. Uniform State Laws, 1956-60; chmn. grievance commn. Iowa Supreme Ct., 1964-66; del. FAO, 1973; chmn. Woodbury County Compensation Bd., 1975-80. Chmn. Midwest Rhodes Scholar Selection Com., 1964-66; pres. Sioux City Symphony Orch. Assn., 1947-54, Sioux City Concert Course, 1982-85; vice chmn. Young Republican Nat. Fedn., 1948-50; bd. dirs. Iowa Bar Found., 1962-68. Served to lt. (j.g.) USNR, 1943-46. Fellow Am. Coll. Trial Lawyers; mem. ABA (ho. of dels. 1966-68), Iowa Bar Assn. (pres. 1963-64), Sioux City Bar Assn., Internat. Assn. Def. Counsel (exec. com. 1961-64), Harvard Club (N.Y.C.), Capitol Hill Club, Sioux City Country Club, Masons (Scottish Rite/33 deg.). Home: 2728 Jackson St Sioux City IA 51104-3623 Office: Pioneer Bank Bldg 701 Pierce St Ste 400 Sioux City IA 51101-1036

MAYNES, CHARLES WILLIAM, foundation administrator; b. Huron, S.D., Dec. 8, 1938; s. Charles William and Almira Rose (Summers) M.; m. Gretchen Schiele, July 17, 1965; children: Stacy Kathryn, Charles William. BA, Harvard U., 1960; MA, Oxford (Eng.) U., 1962. UN polit. affairs ofcl. Dept. State, Washington, 1962-65; chief monetary economist AID, Laos, 1965-67; econ. officer Am. Embassy, Moscow, 1968-70; sec. Carnegie Endowment Internat. Peace, 1971-76; sr. legis. asst. to Sen. Fred R. Harris, 1972; mem. issues Sargent Shriver's Vice-Presdl. campaign, 1972; mem. Carter-Mondale Transition team, 1976-77; asst. sec. for internat. orgn. affairs Dept. State, 1977-80; editor Fgn. Policy mag., 1980-97; mem. Clinton-Gore Transition team, 1992-93; pres. Eurasia Found., Washington, 1997—; mem. Coun. Fgn. Rels., Internat. Inst. Strategic Studies, Washington Inst. Internat. Affairs, UN Assn., Overseas Devel. Coun., Nat. Acad. Pub. Adminstrn.; adv. com. European Inst., Lincoln U. Ctr. Pub. Policy and Diplomacy, Overseas Devel. Coun., Nat. Inst. Citizen Participation and Negotiation, U. Calif. Inst. Global Conflict and Cooperation, UN Assn., others. Contbr. articles to profl. jours. Recipient Meritorious Service award Dept. State; congl. fellow Rep. F. Bradford Morse, 1971, Sen. Fred R. Harris, 1971; Rhodes scholar. Mem. Phi Beta Kappa. Democrat. Office: Eurasia Found 1527 New Hampshire Ave NW Washington DC 20036-1206 Home: 3914 Leland St Chevy Chase MD 20815-5036

MAYO, BERNIER L., secondary school principal. Headmaster St. Johnsbury (Vt.) Acad. Recipient Blue Ribbon Sch. award U.S. Dept. Edn., 1990-91. Office: St Johnsbury Acad 7 Main St Saint Johnsbury VT 05819-2699

MAYO, CLYDE CALVIN, organizational psychologist, educator; b. Robstown, Tex., Feb. 2, 1940; s. Clyde Culberson and Velma (Oxford) M.; m. Jeanne Lynn McCain, Aug. 24, 1963; children: Brady Scott, Amber Camille. BA, Rice U., 1961; BS, U. Houston, 1964, PhD, 1972; MS, Trinity U., 1966. Lic. psychologist, Tex. Mgmt. engr. LWFW, Inc., Houston, 1966-72, sr. cons., 1972-78, prin., 1978-81; ptnr. Mayo, Thompson, Bigby, Houston, 1981-83, founder Mgmt. and Personnel Systems, Houston, 1983—; counselor Interface Counseling Ctr., Houston, 1976-79; dir. Mental Health HMO Group, 1985-87; instr. St. Thomas U., Houston, 1979—, U. Houston Downtown Sch., 1972, U. Houston-Clear Lake, 1983-88, U. Houston-Central Campus, 1984—; dir. mgmt. devel. insts. U. Houston Woodlands and West Houston, 1986-1991, adj. prof. U. Houston, 1991—. Author: Bi/Polar Inventory of Strengths, 1978, LWFW Annual Survey of Manufacturers, 1966-1981. Coach, mgr. Meyerland Little League, 1974-78, St. Belles Softball, 1979-80, S.W. Colt Baseball, 1982-83, Friends of Fondren Library of Rice U., 1988—; charter mem. Holocaust Mus. Mem. Soc. Indsl. Organizational Psychologists, Tex. Indsl. Orgnl. Psychologists (founder, bd. dirs. 1995—), Houston Psychol. Assn. (membership dir. 1978, sec. 1984), Tex. Psychol. Assn., Am. Psychol. Assn., Houston Area Indsl. Orgnl. Psychologists (bd. dirs. 1989-92), Forum Club, Found. Contemporary Theology. Methodist. Club: Meyerland (bd. dirs. 1988-92, pres. 1991). Home: 8723 Ferris Dr Houston TX 77096-1409 Office: Mgmt and Personnel Systems 4545 Bissonnet St Bellaire TX 77401-3121

MAYO, ELIZABETH BROOM, lawyer; b. Jackson, Miss., Aug. 20, 1948; d. Harmon W. and Elizabeth (Kehoe) Broom; m. Gerald E. Mayo, Aug. 30, 1980; stepchildren: Sharon E. Parker, Gerald E. Jr. AB, Spring Hill Coll., 1970; JD, Washington U., 1973; LLM in Taxation, Capital U., 1989. Bar: Ohio 1973, S.C. 1995. Assoc. Schottenstein, Zox & Dunn, Columbus, Ohio, 1973-75, ptnr., 1982-89; 2d v.p. underwriting Midland Mut. Life Ins. Co., Columbus, 1975-80; dir. fin. svcs. Nationwide Ins. Cos., Columbus, 1980-82; ptnr. Porter, Wright, Morris & Arthur, Columbus, 1989—, mem. directing ptnrs. com., 1989-93, mem. compensation com., 1990-94, chair healthcare practice group; of counsel Novit, Scarminach & Williams P.A., Hilton Head Island, S.C., 1996—. Active Ohio Arts Coun., 1991—, vice chair, 1994—; active Franklin County Pvt. Industry Coun., Columbus, 1990-96, vice chair, 1994-95; active Recreation and Parks Commn., Columbus, 1990—, chmn., 1993-95; active Met. Human Svcs. Commn., Columbus, 1987-94, chmn., 1991-92, SEIF/Family Arts Ctr., Hilton Head Island, S.C. Fellow Am. Coll. Trusts and Estates Counsel; mem. ABA, S.C. Bar Assn., Ohio Bar Assn., Columbus Bar Assn., Nat. Health Lawyers Assn., Capital Club. Office: Porter Wright Morris & Arthur 41 S High St Columbus OH 43215-6101 also: Novit Scariminach Williams 52 New Orleans Rd Hilton Head Island SC 29928

MAYO, GEORGE WASHINGTON, JR., lawyer; b. Waycross, Ga., Dec. 23, 1946; s. George Washington Sr. and Perrie R. (Ling) M.; m. Katherine Louise Boland, Nov. 15, 1977; children—Regan L.B., Taylor L.B. A.B., Emory U., 1967; J.D., U. Va., 1973. Bar: Va. 1973, D.C. 1974. Assoc., Hogan & Hartson, Washington, 1973-80, ptnr., 1980—. Contbr. articles to prof. jours. Bd. dirs. Vietnam Vets. Meml. Fund, Inc., 1978—, Earth Conservation Corps., 1990—, dean's coun. Emory U., 1994—. Served to 1st lt., U.S. Army, 1969-71, Vietnam. Mem. ABA, D.C. Bar Assn., Order of Coif. Democrat. Methodist. Club: Met. (Washington), City (Washington). Home: 26 Holly Leaf Ct Bethesda MD 20817-2652 Office: Hogan & Hartson 555 13th St NW Washington DC 20004-1109

MAYO, JOAN BRADLEY, microbiologist, healthcare administrator; b. Ada, Okla., Oct. 24, 1942; d. Samuel S. and Norene (Parker) Bradley; m. Harry D. Mayo III, Sept. 30, 1967. BA, Drake U., 1964; MS in Microbiology, NYU, 1978; MBA in Mgmt., Fairleigh Dickinson U., 1989. RN, N.J. Technologist clin. labs. St. John's Episc. Hosp., Bklyn., 1964-66; supr. Med. Tech. Sch. Bklyn.-Cumberland Med. Ctr., 1966-71; clin. instr., technologist SUNY Downstate Med. Ctr., Bklyn., 1970-73; supr. bacteriology lab. Meml. Sloan-Kettering Cancer Ctr., N.Y.C., 1973-82, mgr. microbiology labs., 1982-87; dir. infection control svc. N.Y.C. Health and Hosp. Corp./Harlem Hosp. Ctr., 1987-95; mgr. infection control dept. Atlantic Health System/The Mountainside Hosp., Montclair, N.J., 1995—; mem. com. for prevention of bloodborne diseases N.Y.C. Health and hosp. Corp., 1990-95. Contbr. articles to profl. publs. Active Friends of Harlem Hosp., 1988—, North Bergen (N.J.) Action Group, 1987—. Mem. Am. Soc. Microbiology, Am. Pub. Health Assn., Assn. Practitioners in Infection Control, Delta Mu Delta, Alpha Kappa Alpha. Avocations: writing, travel, reading. Home: 7855 Boulevard E North Bergen NJ 07047-5938 Office: The Mountainside Hosp One Bay Ave Montclair NJ 07047

MAYO, LOUIS ALLEN, corporation executive; b. Durham, N.C., Nov. 27, 1928; s. Louis Allen and Amy Earl (Overton) M.; student Calif. State Poly. Coll., 1948-50; BA in Criminology, Calif. State Coll., Fresno, 1952; MA in Pub. Adminstrn., Am. U., 1960, PhD in Pub. Adminstrn., 1983; postgrad. U. So. Calif., 1960-62; m. Emma Jean Minshew, Oct. 31, 1953 (div.); children: Louis Allen III, Robert Lawrence, Carolyn Jean; m. 2d, Myrna Ann Smith, Feb. 16, 1980 (div.). Spl. agt. U.S. Secret Svc., Treasury Dept., L.A., 1956-58, 60-63, White House, Washington, 1958-60, 63-66; program mgr. law enforcement Office Law Enforcement Assistance, Justice Dept., 1967-68; acting chief Rsch. Ctr., rsch. program mgr. Nat. Inst. Law Enforcement and Criminal Justice, 1968-74; alternate assoc. mem. Fed. Coun. on Sci. and Tech., White House, 1973-74; dir. tng. and testing div. Nat. Inst. Justice, 1975-87; pres. Murphy, Mayo & Assocs., Alexandria, Va., 1987—; lectr. criminology Armed Forces Inst. Tech., 1954-55; professorial lectr. Am. U., 1974-82; adj. prof. August Vollmer U., 1990-95. 2d lt. to 1st lt. USAF, 1952-56. Mem. Am. Police Assn. (pres., co-founder), Internat. Assn. Chiefs of Police, Am. Soc. Pub. Adminstrn. (nat. chmn. sect. on criminal justice adminstrn. 1975-76), Acad. Criminal Justice Scis., Police Exec. Rsch. Forum, Soc. Police Futurists Internat., Am. Soc. Indsl. Security, Pi Sigma Alpha. Methodist. Home and Office: 5200 Leeward Ln # 101 Alexandria VA 22315-3944

MAYO, ROBERT PORTER, banker; b. Seattle, Mar. 15, 1916; s. Carl Asa and Edna Alberta (Nelson) M.; m. Marian Aldridge Nicholson, Aug. 28, 1942; children: Margaret Alice, Richard Carl, Carolyn Ruth (Mrs. Gregory Brown), Robert Nelson. A.B. magna cum laude, U. Wash., 1937, M.B.A., 1938. Research asst., auditor Wash. State Tax Commn., 1938-41; economist U.S. Treasury, 1941-47, asst. dir. office of tech. staff, 1948-53, chief debt div. analysis staff, 1953-59; asst. to sec. Treasury Dept., 1959-60; v.p. Continental Ill. Nat. Bank & Trust Co. of Chgo., 1960-69; chmn. Boye Needle Co., 1963-67; staff dir. Pres. Commn. on Budget Concepts, 1967; dir. U.S. Bur. of Budget, 1969-70; counsellor to Pres. U.S., 1970; pres. Fed. Res. Bank of Chgo., 1970-81; trustee Instnl. Liquid Assets and Assoc. Goldman Sachs Funds, CNA Income Shares; dir. Chgo. Tokyo Bank, Duff and Phelps Utilities Income Fund. Trustee YMCA, Chgo.; bd. dirs. Exec. Svc. Corps, Chgo. Mem. Comml. Club Chgo., Econ. Club Chgo., Perico Bay (Fla.) Club, Bartlett-on-the-Greens Homeowner's Assn., Phi Beta Kappa. Presbyterian.

MAYOCK, ROBERT LEE, internist; b. Wilkes-Barre, Pa., Jan. 19, 1917; s. John F. and Mathilde M.; m. Constance M. Peruzzi, July 2, 1949; children: Robert Lee, Stephen Philip, Holly Peruzzi. B.S., Bucknell U., 1938; M.D., U. Pa., 1942. Diplomate Am. Bd. Internal Medicine. Intern Hosp. U. Pa., Phila., 1943-44; resident Hosp. U. Pa., 1944-45, chief med. resident, 1945-46, attending physician, 1946—; chief pulmonary disease Phila. Gen. Hosp., 1955-72, chief pulmonary disease sect., 1959-72, sr. cons. pulmonary disease sect., 1972—; asst. prof. clin. medicine U. Pa., 1949-59, assoc. prof., 1959-70, prof. medicine, 1970-87, prof. emeritus, 1987—; mem. med. adv. com. for Tb Commonwealth of Pa., 1965-74, mem. med. adv. com. on chronic respiratory disease, 1974-92, chmn. adv. com., 1981-90; mem. subsplty bd. pulmonary disease Am. Bd. Internal Medicine, 1965-76; nat. bd. dirs. Am. Lung Assn., 1983-92, local bd. dirs., 1961, local pres., 1966-69, dir. at large, 1983—. Contbr. articles in field to med. jours. Served to capt. U.S. Army, 1952-54. Fellow ACP, Am. Coll. Chest Physicians (regent 1972-79), Phila. Coll. Physicians; mem. AMA, Am. Thoracic Soc., Am. Fedn. Clin. Rsch., Am. Heart Assn., Pa. Lung Assn. (dir. 1976—), N.Y. Acad. Scis., Pa. Med. Soc., Phila. County Med. Soc., Physiology Soc. Phila., Laennec Soc. Phila., Merion Cricket Club, Westmoreland Club, Swiftwater Res., Sigma Xi. Home: 244 Gypsy Ln Wynnewood PA 19096-1113 Office: U Penn Ravdin Bldg 3rd Fl Ste F Philadelphia PA 19104

MAYOL, RICHARD THOMAS, advertising executive, political consultant; b. Springfield, Ill., Oct. 30, 1949; s. Richard McFaren and Marjorie (Maddex) M. AA, Springfield Coll., 1969; BS, U. Tulsa, 1972. Co-owner First Tuesday Inc., Phoenix, 1976-85; pres. Mayol and Assocs., Phoenix, 1985—; CEO New West Policy Group, Prescott, Ariz., 1993—; cons. Dem. candidates, Dem. candidates ballot issues, corp. pub. policy Western U.S., Nev. Dem. Party, Ariz. Dem. Party, Del Webb Corp., Prop. 102, McDowell Mt. Preserve Initiative. Mem. Phoenix Film Commn., 1985—. Mem. Am. Assn. Polit. Cons., Phoenix Grand Prix Commn. Avocations: photography, writing, horseback riding. Home and Office: 348 Moreland Cir Prescott AZ 86303-4035 also: 223 Union St Prescott AZ 86303-3813

MAYOR, ALFRED HYATT, editor; b. Boston, June 4, 1934; s. Alpheus Hyatt and Virginia (Sluder) M.; m. Brunhilde Hillmann, Feb. 16, 1966. AB, Harvard U., 1956, MA, 1957, PhD, 1961. Editorial asst. Newsweek mag., N.Y.C., 1961-62; sub-editor Reuters Ltd., London, 1962-64, Internat. Herald Tribune, Paris, 1964; sr. editor Holiday mag., N.Y.C., 1964-68; mng. editor Corinthian Editions, N.Y.C., 1968; assoc. editor Am. Heritage Press, N.Y.C., 1969-71; exec. editor Antiques mag., N.Y.C., 1972—. Author: (book) Parliament's Passport to London, 1968. Advisor Brookgreen Gardens, Murrells Inlet, S.C., 1984; trustee Hispanic Soc. Am., N.Y.C., 1986. Mem. 7th Rgt. Rifle Club. Avocations: photography, small repair jobs. Office: Antiques Mag 575 Broadway New York NY 10012-3230

MAYOR, RICHARD BLAIR, lawyer; b. San Antonio, Mar. 27, 1934; s. E. Allan and Elizabeth Ann (Hastings) M.; m. Heather Donald, July 28, 1956; children: Diana Boyd, Philip Hastings. BA, Yale U., 1955; postgrad., Melbourne U., Australia, 1955-56; JD, Harvard U., 1959. Bar: Tex. 1960. Assoc. Butler and Binion, Houston, 1959-67, ptnr., mem. exec. com., 1967-82; founding, sr. ptnr. Mayor, Day, Caldwell & Keeton, L.L.P., Houston, 1982—; bd. dirs., founder Internat. Ctrs. Arbitration. Trustee, chmn. exec. com. Contemporary Arts Mus., Houston, 1972-78; trustee Houston Ballet Found., 1983-88. Fulbright scholar, 1955-56. Fellow Tex. Bar Found.; mem. ABA, Am. Law Inst., Tex. Bar Assn., Ramada Club, Houstonian Club, Houston Club, Phi Beta Kappa. Office: Mayor Day Caldwell & Keeton LLP 700 Louisiana St Ste 1900 Houston TX 77002

MAYORA-ALVARADO, EDUARDO RENE, lawyer, law educator; b. Guatemala, Guatemala, Apr. 20, 1957; s. Eduardo Alfredo Mayora-Dawe and Adelaida (Alvarado) De Mayora; m. Alicia Bascunana, June 18, 1983; children: Javier Eduardo, Santiago, Jose Andres, Sebastian. JD, U. Rafael Landivar, Guatemala, 1980; LLM, Georgetown U., U.S.A., 1982; Diploma (2) in Principles Econ. Sci., U. Francisco Marroquin, Guatemala, 1991. Bar: Guatemala, 1980; cert. notary. Assoc. Mayora & Mayora, Guatemala, 1980-81, ptnr., 1982—; prof. bus. law and principles of law U. Francisco Marroquin, Guatemala, 1984-87, prof. bus. law and principles of law Sch. of Econs., 1986-88, prof. constitutional law, dean Sch. of Law, 1989—, prof. principles of pvt. and pub. law, 1993; bd. dirs. Financiera De Inversion S.A., Guatemala; alternate dir. Seguros Alianza S.A., Guatemala; mem. bd. trustees U. Francisco Marroquin, 1989—; vis. prof. Pontificia U. Catolica, Porto Alegre, Brazil, 1994, Montpellier U. Sch. Law, France, 1995. Co-author: El Desafio Neoliberal, 1992; author; (essay) El Drama De La Arena Movediza, 1993 (Charles Stillman award 1993); contbr. to profl. jours. Mem. Guatemala Bar Assn. (author articles Bar Law Jour. 1990—m v.p. ethics bd. 1985-86), Assn. De Amigos Del Pais, Fundacion Para La Cultura (v.p. 1994), Inst. Guatemalteco De Derecho Notarial, Rotary Club, Phi Delta Phi, Guatemala Country Club. Roman Catholic. Avocations: reading, sailing, golf. Office: Mayora & Mayora, Ruta 6, 9-21 4th Flr, Zona 4 01004 Guatemala City Guatemala also: PO Box 661447 Miami FL 33166

MAYORAS, DONALD EUGENE, corporate executive, speaker, consultant, educator; b. Danville, Ill., Aug. 25, 1939; s. Andrew John and Katherine Ann (Shelato) M.; m. JoAnna Marie Kacmer, June 9, 1962; children—Tyler, Stacie. B.S. in Edn., Purdue U., 1962; postgrad., Northwestern U., 1968-71; M.B.A., So. Ill. U., 1977. Regional mgr. Pacific Intermountain Express, Akron, Ohio, 1972-74; v.p. United Van Lines, Fenton, Mo., 1974-78; pres. Bekins Van Lines, L.A., 1978-83; pres., chief exec. officer Sun Carriers, Inc., Holliston, Mass., 1983-90, chmn. bd. dirs.; vice chmn., chief exec. officer Builders Transport, Camden, S.C., 1990-91; chmn., CEO Truckload Holding Inc., Ida Grove, Iowa, 1995—; CEO Mau Trucking, Inc., Ida Grove, 1995—, Cloverleaf Transp., Inc., Chester, N.Y., 1997—. Trustee Ross Ade Found., West Lafayette, Ind., 1962—. Capt. U.S. Army, 1962-68; Europe, Vietnam. Decorated Bronze Star. Mem. Am. Trucking Assn. (v.p. 1983-91, trustee Found. 1983-91), Nat. Spkrs. Assn., Nat. Coun. Logistics, Nat. Pvt. Truck Coun., Purdue U. Alumni Assn., Nat. Def. Transp. Assn., Aronomink Golf Club (Newton Sq., Pa.), Orange County Golf Club, Delta Nu Alpha, Beta Gamma Sigma, Omicron Delta Kappa. Republican. Roman Catholic. Avocations: golf, antiques, classic automobiles.

MAYPOLE, JOHN FLOYD, real estate holding company executive; b. Chgo., May 17, 1939; s. John James and Althea Floyd M.; m. Anne White, 1961; children: Cynthia, John, Kimberly. B.A. in Econs, Yale U., 1961. With Arthur Andersen & Co., 1961-62, 65-66; mgr. corp. acctg. Interpace Corp., 1966, asst. treas., 1967-68, treas., 1968-70, treas., controller, 1970-73, v.p. fin., 1973-77, sr. v.p., 1977-80, exec. v.p., 1980-81, pres., 1981-83; pres., chief operating officer Clevepak Corp., 1983-84; mng. ptnr. Peach State Real Estate Holding Co., Toccoa, Ga., 1984—; bd. dirs. Dan River Mills, Blodgett Corp., Briggs Industries Inc., also chmn., Bell Atlantic Corp., Mass. Mut. Life Ins. Co., Davies, Turner & Co., Coating Technologies Internat., Inc. Bd. adjustment Borough of Mountain Lakes, N.J., 1971-81, chmn., 1980-81. Served with USMC, 1962-65. Mem. Yale Club (N.Y.C.), Rockaway River Country Club, Laurel Oak Country Club. Republican. Office: PO Box 1223 Toccoa GA 30577-1421

MAYR, ERNST, retired zoologist, philosopher; b. Kempten, Germany, July 5, 1904; came to U.S., 1931; s. Otto and Helene (Pusinelli) M.; m. Margarete Simon, May 4, 1935; children: Christa E., Susanne. Cand. med., U. Greifswald, 1925; Ph.D., U. Berlin, 1926; Ph.D. (hon.), Uppsala U., Sweden, 1957; D.Sc. (hon.), Yale U., 1959, U. Melbourne, 1959, Oxford U., 1966, U. Munich, 1968, U. Paris, 1974, Harvard U., 1980, Guelph U., U. Cambridge, 1982, U. Vt., 1984; DSc (hon.), U. Mass., 1993; PhD (hon.), U. Vienna, 1994; DPhil (hon.), U. Konstanz, 1994; DSc (hon.), U. Bologna, 1995. Asst. curator zool. mus. U. Berlin, 1926-32; mem. Rothschild expdn. to Dutch New Guinea, 1928, expdn. to Mandated Ty. of New Guinea, 1928-29, Whitney Expdn., 1929-30; research asso. Am. Mus. Natural History, N.Y.C., 1931-32; asso. curator Am. Mus. Natural History, 1932-44, curator, 1944-53; Jesup lectr. Columbia U., 1941; Alexander Agassiz prof. zoology Harvard U., 1953-75, emeritus, 1975—; dir. Mus. Comparative Zoology, Harvard U., 1961-70; Messenger lectr. Cornell U., 1985; Hitchcock prof. U. Calif., 1987; hon. fellow Ctr. for Philosophy of Sci., U. Pitts. Author: List of New Guinea Birds, 1941, Systematics and the Origin of Species, 1942, Birds of the Southwest Pacific, 1945, Birds of the Philippines, (with Jean Delacour), 1946, Methods and Principles of Systematic Zoology, (with E. G. Linsley and R. L. Usinger), 1953, Animal Species and Evolution, 1963, Principles of Systematic Zoology, 1969, Populations, Species and Evolution, 1970, Evolution and the Diversity of Life, 1976, (with W. Provine) Evolutionary Synthesis, 1980, Biologie de l'Evolution, 1981, The Growth of Biological Thought, 1982, Toward a New Philosophy of Biology, 1988, One Long Argument, 1991; editor: Evolution, 1947-49, This is Biology, 1997. Pres. XIII Internat. Ornith. Congress, 1962. Recipient Leidy medal, 1946, Wallace Darwin medal, 1958, Brewster medal Am. Ornithologists Union, 1965, Daniel Giraud Elliot medal, 1967, Nat. Medal of Sci., 1970, Molina prize Accademia delle Sci., Bologna, Italy, 1972, Linnean medal, 1977, Gregor Mendel medal, 1980, Balzan prize, 1983, Darwin medal Royal Soc., 1987, Disting. Scientist award UCLA, 1993, Salvin Godman medal, 1994, Japan prize, 1994, Benjamin Franklin medal 1995. Fellow Linnaean Soc. N.Y. (past sec. editor), Am. Ornithol. Union (pres. 1956-59), N.Y. Zool. Soc.; mem. NAS, Am. Philos. Soc., Am. Acad. Arts and Scis., Am. Soc. Zoologists, Soc. Systematic Zoology (pres. 1966), Soc. Study Evolution (sec. 1946, pres. 1950); hon. or corr. mem. Royal Soc., Royal Australian, Brit. ornithol. unions, Zool. Soc. London, Soc. Ornithol. France, Royal Soc. New Zealand, Bot. Gardens Indonesia, S. Africa Ornithol. Soc., Linnean Soc. London, Deutsche Akademie der naturforsch Leopoldina, Accad. Naz. dei Lincei, Royal Soc., Academie des Sci., Ctr. for Philosophy of Sci. (Pitts.), Russian Acad. Sci., Berlin - Brandenburgische Akademie. Office: Harvard U Mus Comparative Zoology 26 Oxford St Cambridge MA 02138-2902

MAYRON, MELANIE, actress, writer; b. Phila., Oct. 20, 1952. Ed., Am. Acad. Dramatic Arts, N.Y.C. Writer Tribeca Prodns. Appearences include (films) Harry and Tonto, 1974, Car Wash, 1976, The Great Smokey Road Block, 1976, Gable and Lombard, 1976, Girl Friends, 1978 (British Acad. award nomination), You Light Up My Life, 1977, Heart Beeps, 1981, Missing, 1982, Sticky Fingers (also co-writer, co-producer), 1988, Checking Out, 1989, My Blue Heaven, 1990, Drop Zone, 1994; (TV movies) Hustling, 1975, The New Love Boat, 1977, Katie: Portrait of a Centerfold, 1978, The Best Little Girl in the World, 1981, Will There Really Be a Morning?, 1983; (TV miniseries) Wallenberg: A Hero's Story, 1985, Playing for Time, 1980, The Boss's Wife, 1986, Other Women's Children, 1993, Ordeal in the Arctic, 1993; (TV series) thirtysomething (Emmy award for best supporting actress in a drama series, 1989), dir. 2 episodes; dir.: Tribeca, 1993, Freaky Friday, 1995, The Baby-Sitters Club, 1995; author (anthology): Stepping Back.

MAYROSE, MONA PEARL, critical care nurse, flight nurse, educator; b. Levittown, N.J., Nov. 3, 1961; d. William Joseph and Sarah (Tanne) Tillis; m. Alan Gary Mayrose, Nov. 1, 1987; 1 child, Kattey; stepchildren: Dale, Brian. BA, NYU, 1982; MSN, Pace U., 1986. Cert. critical care nurse, trauma nurse, staff devel. nurse; instr. ACLS and critical care. Nursery nurse No. Westchester Hosp. Ctr., Mt. Kisco, N.Y., 1987-88; ICU nurse Meth. Hosp., Houston, 1988-89; dir. nursing Golden Age and Winslow Nursing Homes, Houston, 1989; hospice case mgr. Vis. Nurse Assn., Houston, 1989-91; critical care charge nurse Woodlands (Tex.) Meml. Hosp., 1990-92; commd. 1st lt. USAF, 1992, advanced through grades to capt., 1992; charge nurse surg. ICU 59th Med. Wing USAF, Lackland AFB, Tex., 1992-94, critical care educator, 1994-95; flight nurse 23d Aeromed. Evacuation Squadron, Pope AFB, N.C., 1996—; participant Operation Joint Endeavor NATO Implementation Force, Tuzla AB, Bosnia-Herzegovina, 1996—. Mem. AACN (bd. dirs. San Antonio chpt.), Nat. Nurses Staff Devel. Orgn., Air Force Assn., Officers Club, Assn. Mil. Surgeons U.S., Aerospace Med. Assn., Sigma Theta Tau. Jewish. Avocations: quilting, reading, holistic healing. Home: 853 Foxcroft Dr Fayetteville NC 28311

MAYS, GEORGE WALTER, JR., educational technology educator, consultant, tutor; b. Decatur, Ill., July 1, 1926; s. George Walter Sr. and Ida May (Lookabaugh) M.; children: Richard, Steven, John, James. BS in Edn., U. Ill., Champaign, 1950, MS in Edn., 1952; BSEE, U. md., 1960; cert., Calif. State U., Carson, 1987. Tchr. math. and physics Mahomet (Ill.) High Sch., 1950-52, prin., 1952-55; br. chief engring studies Nat. Security Agy., Ft. Meade, Md., 1955-62; sr. engr. Jet Propulsion Lab., Pasadena, Calif., 1962-71; tchr. math.-sci., chair Aviation High Sch., Redondo Beach, Calif., 1971-82; tchr. math. and physics, dept. chair Redondo Union High Sch., 1982-89; cons. edn. tech. Apple Valley, Calif., 1989—; math. coord. Sci. and Tech. Ctr., Apple Valley, Calif., 1990—; part-time instr. electronics Pasadena City Coll., 1962-72, Pepperdine U., 1975-76, math. Victor Valley Coll., 1991—. Author: Educational Technology Application Notes, 1989-90. With USN, 1944-46. Recipient Appollo Achievement award NASA, 1969. Mem. IEEE (life), Calif. Tchrs. Assn. (WHO award 1988-89), Nat. Coun. Tchrs. of Math., Computer Using Educators, Apple Valley Country Club, Victor Valley Aero Club. Avocations: reading, sports, computer usage, flying. Home and Office: 13458 Sunset Dr PO Box 1930 Apple Valley CA 92307-0037

MAYS, GLENDA SUE, retired education educator; b. Freer, Tex., July 18, 1938; d. Archie Richard and Helen Hildred (Morgan) Cox; m. Dewey William Mays, Sept. 7, 1963; children: Rose Marie, Teresa Sue, Frank Dewey. BS, Tex. Tech. U., 1959, MA, 1961; PhD, North Tex. State U., 1969. Cert. tchr., supr., prin. Tchr. Lubbock (Tex.) Pub. Schs., 1959-61, Amarillo (Tex.) Pub. Schs., 1961-62, Austin (Tex.) Pub. Schs., 1962-63; curriculum intern/rsch. asst., elem. coord. U. Tex. at Austin, Hurst, Tex., 1963-65; asst. prof. McMurry U., Abilene, Tex., 1965-67; assoc. prof. Dallas Bapt. U., 1968-71; reading resource tchr., dept. chair Ft. Worth (Tex.) Ind. Sch. Dist., 1971-74, reading specialist, 1974-82, instructional specialist, 1982-

95, ret., 1995; spkr. lang. acquisition and reading 7th World Congress in Reading, Hamburg, Germany, 1978. Advisor/writer (English textbook): McDouglas Littel Language, 1985-86; writer: Bilingual Stories for Ft. Worth Ind. Sch. Dist., 1979-80; contbr. poems to anthologies. Patron Kimbell Mus. Art, Ft. Worth, 1994—; mem. Nat. Cancer Soc., Ft. Worth, 1980—. Fulbright-Hays scholar, Kenya, Africa, 1970; grantee in fgn. langs. Nat. Endowment Arts U. Ark., 1987, Ft. Worth Ind. Sch. Dist. Study grantee U. London, 1978. Fellow ASCD, NEA, Tex. State Tchrs. Assn., Ft. Worth Edn. Assn., Internat. Reading Assn. (hostess 1st Tex. breakfast 1969), Nat. Geog. Soc., Smithsonian Instn., Libr. of Congress, Ft. Worth Reading Assn., Nat. Coun. for Social Studies spkr. social studies symposium N.Y.C. 1970, Tex. Elem. Prins. and Suprs. Assn. (sec. 1971-72). Avocations: travel, reading, music, writing, antique collecting. Home: 1225 Clara St Fort Worth TX 76110-1009

MAYS, LESTER LOWRY, broadcast executive; b. Houston, July 24, 1935; s. Lester T. and Virginia (Lowry) M.; m. Peggy Pitman, July 29, 1959; children: Kathryn Mays Johnson, Linda Mays McCaul, Mark P., Randall T. BS in Petroleum Engring., Tex. A&M U., 1959; MBA, Harvard U., 1962. Comml. recorder San Antonio; with Sta. KTTU-TV, Tucson, Sta. KOKI/KTFO-TV, Tulsa, Sta. WMPI/WJTC-TV, Mobile and Pensacola, Okla., Sta. WAWS-TV, Jacksonville, Fla., Sta. KSAS-TV, Wichita, Kans., Sta. KLRT/KASN-TV, Little Rock, Sta. WFTC-TV, Mpls., Sta. WFTC-TV, WLMT/WMTU-TV, WLMT/WMTU TV, Memphis, Sta. WXXA, Albany, Sta. WQUE-AM-FM, New Orleans, Clear Channel Sports, Des Moines, Okla. News Network, Oklahoma City, Va. News Network, Stas. KJYO and KTOK, Oklahoma City, Sta. KEBC, Oklahoma City, Sta. WELI, New Haven, Sta. WKCI-WAVZ, New Haven, Sta. KPEZ, Austin, Tex., Stas. KHYS, KALO, KBXX, KMJQ, KPRC, KSEV and KYOK, Houston and Point Arthur, Tex., KMOD & KAKC, Tulsa, KTAM & KORA, Bryan and College Station, Tex., WHAS & WAMZ, Louisville; with radio and TV broadcasting WOAI, KQXT, and KAJA, San Antonio; pres., CEO Clear Channel Comms., Inc., San Antonio; past chmn. bd. CBS Radio Affiliates Bd. Bd. dirs., trustee Tex. Rsch. Pk.; bd. dirs., mem. exec. com. United Way; chmn. United Way San Antonio and Bexar County, 1995; regent emeritus Tex. A&M U. Sys.; trustee Tex. Rsch. and Tech. Found.; mem. deve. bd. U. Tex. Health Sci. Ctr.; adv. dir. Permanent Univ. Fund Tex. Mem. Nat. Assn. Broadcasters (past chmn. joint bd.), Greater San Antonio C. of C. (past chmn.), Rotary. Home: 400 Geneseo Rd San Antonio TX 78209-6127 Office: Clear Channel Comms., Inc PO Box 659512 San Antonio TX 78265-9512

MAYS, M. DOUGLAS, state legislator, financial consultant; b. Pittsburg, Kans., Aug. 18, 1950; s. Marion Edmund and Lilliemae Ruth (Norris) M.; m. Lena M. Krog, June 10, 1971; children: Jessica, Aaron. BFA, Pittsburg State U., 1972; postgrad., Washburn U., 1973—. Registered rep. Waddell & Reed, Inc., Topeka, 1981-83, Paine Webber Jackson & Curtis, Topeka, 1983-85, Columbian Securities, Topeka, 1985-87; commr. securities State of Kans., Topeka, 1987-91; pres. Mays & Assocs., Topeka, 1991—; mem. Kans. Ho. Reps., Topeka, 1993—, asst. majority leader, 1997—; adminstrv. law judge various securities proceedings, 1987—; with securities and commodities fraud working group U.S. Dept. Justice, 1988-90; with penny stock task force SEC, 1988-90; del. Commonwealth Secretariat Symposium Comml. Crime, Cambridge, Eng., 1989; securities arbitrator, 1991—. Rep. precinct committeeman Shawnee County, Kans., 1976—, county chmn., 1978-82; mem. 2d Dist. Rep. State Com., Kans., 1976-86, 92—; mem. Kans. Rep. State Com., 1976-87; Senate steering com. Kassebaum for Senate campaign, 1978; chmn., mgr. Hoferer for Senate campaign, 1984; campaign coord., dir. fin. Hayden for Gov., 1986; mem. pub. bldg. commn. City of Topeka, 1985-86, bldg. and fire appeals bd. , 1986-89, dep. mayor, 1987-88; mem. Topeka City Coun., 1985-89; exec. bd. Topeka/Shawnee County Interngovtl. Coun., 1986-89; adv. bd. Topeka Performing Arts Ctr., 1989-90; active Topeka/Shawnee County Met. Planning Commn., 1992—, chmn., 1994-97. Mem. North Am. Securities Adminstrs. Assn. (chmn. enforcement sect. 1988-89, pres.-elect, bd. dirs. 1989-90, pres. 1990-91), Nat. Assn. Securities Dealers, Nat. Futures Assn. (bd. arbitrators), Internat. Orgn. Securites Commns. (inter-Am. activities consultative com. 1990, pres.'s com. 1990, del. 1990). Methodist. Home: 1920 SW Damon Ct Topeka KS 66611-1926 Office: Kans Ho Reps State Capitol Topeka KS 66612

MAYS, WILLIE HOWARD, JR. (SAY HEY KID), former professional baseball player; b. Westfield, Ala., May 6, 1931; s. William Howard and Ann M.; m. Mae Louise Allen, Nov. 27, 1971; 1 adopted son, Michael. Baseball player Birmingham Black Barons, 1948-50, Trenton Inter-State League, 1950-51, Mpls. Millers, Am. Assn., 1951, N.Y. Giants, 1951-57, San Francisco Giants, 1958-72, N.Y. Mets, 1972-73; with Bally's Park Place, Atlantic City, 1980—; pub. rels. exec. San Francisco Giants, 1986—. Author: Willie Mays: My Life In and Out of Baseball, 1966, Say Hey: The Autobiography of Willie Mays, 1988. Served with AUS, 1952-54. Named Most Valuable Player Nat. League, 1954, 65; named Player of Yr. Sporting News, 1954, Baseball Player of Decade Sporting News, 1970, Male Athlete of Yr. AP, 1954, Rookie of the Yr., 1951, Most Exciting Playin Sport Sporting News, 1954, All-Star Game, 1954-73; recipient Hickok belt, 1954, Golden Bat award to commemorate 600 home runs, Gold Glove award (12 times), 1st Commissioner's award, 1970, Golden Plate awarded to America's Captains of Achievement by Am. Acad. Achievement, 1976, Spirit of Life award City of Hope, 1988, Sportsman of Decade, Cong. Racial Equality, 1991, Legendary Star award HBO Video; inducted into Ala. Sports Hall of Fame, Baseball Hall of Fame, 1979, Black Hall of Fame, 1973, Calif. Sports Hall of Fame. Holder 3d place in major league homeruns (660); lifetime batting average of .302; signed lifetime pub. rels. contract with San Francisco Giants, 1993. Office: care San Francisco Giants Candlestick Park San Francisco CA 94124

MAYSENT, HAROLD WAYNE, hospital administrator; b. Tacoma, Wash., June 26, 1923; s. Wayne L. Shivley and Esther Pierce M.; m. Marjorie Ellen Hodges, June 13, 1953; children: Jeffrey, Nancy, Brian, Gregory. BA, U. Wash., 1950; MS in Hosp. Adminstrn. with distinction, Northwestern U., 1954. Adminstrv. resident Passavant Meml. Hosp., 1953-54, adminstrv. asst., 1954-55; research asso. hosp. adminstrn. Northwestern U., Evanston, Ill., 1954-55; with Lankenau Hosp., Phila., 1955-72; dir. Lankenau Hosp., 1963-67, exec. dir., 1967-72; exec. v.p. Rockford (Ill.) Meml. Hosp., 1972-75, pres., 1975-91; pres. Rockford Meml. Corp., 1983-91, pres. emeritus, 1991—; pres. The Rockford Group, 1983-91; tchg. assoc. Rockford Sch. Medicine, U. Ill., 1974-89, adj. assoc. prof., 1989-92; mem. Ill. Health Facility Planning Bd., 1980-92; chmn. bd. Ill. Hosp. Joint Ventures, Inc., 1977-78, Vol. Hosps. Am. Midwest Partnership, 1985-89. Contbr. articles to profl. jours. Chmn.-elect Coll. Healthcare Execs., 1988-89, chmn., 1989; coach, adminstr. Broomal (Pa.) Little League, 1962-72; bd. dirs. Community Health Assn., 1964-70, Rockford Med. Edn. Found., 1972-87, Tri State Hosp. Assembly, 1978-80, Rockford Coun. 100, 1987-91, exec. com. 1987-91. With AUS, 1942-46. Recipient Malcolm T. MacEachern award Northwestern U., 1954, Laura G. Jackson Alumni Assn. award, 198, Disting. Svc. award Ill. Hosp. Assn., 1989. Fellow Am. Coll. Hosp. Adminstrs. (Ill. regent 1979-84, dist. bd. govs. 1984-88, gov. 1984-88, chmn. elect 1988-89, chmn. 1989-90, past chmn. 1990-91); mem. Am. Hosp. Assn. (com. on vols. 1976-80, coun. patient svcs. 1980-82, ho. of dels. 1977-84, rep. Am. Acad. Pediatrics com. on hosp. care 1983-85), Pa. Hosp. Assn. (bd. dirs. 1965-68), Ill. Hosp. Assn. (trustee 1973-79, sec. 1974-76, chmn. elect 1977, chmn. bd. trustees 1978, named Outstanding Leader in Hosp. Industry 1978, Disting. Svc. award 1989). Office: Rockford Meml 2400 N Rockton Ave Rockford IL 61103-3655

MAYTHAM, THOMAS NORTHRUP, art and museum consultant; b. Buffalo, July 30, 1931; s. Thomas Edward and Margaret (Northrup) M.; m. Daphne Chace, Dec. 30, 1960 (div.); 1 child, T.F. Gifford; m. Gloria Maytham, June 11, 1994. BA in Art History, Williams Coll., Williamstown, Mass., 1954; MA in Art History, Yale U., 1956; cert. in German, Colby Coll., 1954. Intern Wadsworth Atheneum, 1955; rsch. asst. Yale U., 1956; head dept. paintings Boston Mus. Fine Arts, 1957-67; assoc. dir., acting dir. Seattle Art Mus., 1967-74; dir. Denver Art Mus., 1974-83; art cons., pub. Artadvisors LLC, Denver, 1983—; mus. accreditation program evaluator Am. Assn. Museums; past trustee, mem. exhbns. adv. com. Am. Fedn. Arts, N.Y.; past mem. mus. program panel, grants reviewer Nat. Endowment for Arts, Washington; reviewer Nat. Endowment for Humanities, Washington; mem. adv. panel, grants reviewer Nat. Mus. Act, Smithsonian Instn.; past mem. policy panel and adv. com., econ. impact of arts study Colo. Coun. Arts and Humanities; co-founder Consortium of Rocky Mountain Regional Conservation Ctr., U. Denver; founder dirs. assn. Denver cultural agys.; del. Inter-Am. Museums Conf., Oaxaca, Mexico; co-founder United Arts Fund, Seattle; mem. art adv. com. Airport Art Program, Port of Seattle; vis. faculty Leadership Denver program, Pres.'s Leadership class U. Colo.; cons. Aspen Ctr. Visual Arts, Sangre de Cristo Arts Ctr., Pueblo, Western States Arts Found., Santa Fe, BBHC, Cody, Wyo.; lectr. museums, colls., corporate groups and art assns. Exhbns. organized include Ernst Ludwig Kirchner Retrospective, Seattle, Pasadena and Boston museums, 1968-69, Am. Painting from the Boston and Met. Museums, Nat. Gallery, St. Louis and Seattle museums, 1970-71; contbr. articles to profl. jours.; presenter TV programs on collections and exhbns. Boston Pub. TV, WGBH-TV. Trustee Internat. Exhbns. Found., Washington. Recipient Gov.'s Arts award Seattle Airport Art Program, 1972, Denver Art mus., award Downtown Denver Inc., 1978. Mem. Assn Art Mus. Dirs. (officer, trustee, ops. com. sec., future directions. com. chmn.). Office: Artadvisors LLC 3882 S Newport Way Denver CO 80237-1246

MAZA, MICHAEL WILLIAM, newspaper editor, columnist; b. Detroit, June 19, 1947; s. Frank Michael and Irene (Boiczuk) M.; m. Cynthia Jeanne Nash, Apr. 8, 1972 (div. Apr. 1985); 1 child, Lydia Anne; m. Jean Ann Zinsmaster, Mar. 1, 1987. BA, U. Detroit, 1969. Reporter, editor Detroit Free Press, 1969-70, Detroit News, 1970-77; film, theater critic, arts editor Ariz. Republic, Phoenix, 1979-87; assst. arts editor Dallas Morning News, 1987-89; book columnist "Help Yourself" Dallas Morning News/KRT Newswire, Dallas, Washington, 1989—; mng. editor Dallas Life Mag., 1989-95; mng.editor Guide, Dallas, 1995—; Ariz. corr. People weekly mag., N.Y.C., 1983-84; Detroit corr. New Times, mag., N.Y.C., 1974-75. Avocations: running, ceramics, travel. Office: Dallas Morning News 508 Young St Dallas TX 75202-4808

MAZANKOWSKI, DONALD FRANK, Canadian government official; b. Viking, Alta., Can., July 27, 1935; s. Frank and Dora (Lonowski) M.; m. Lorraine Poleschuk, Sept. 6, 1958; children: Gregory, Roger, Donald. Student, pub. schs., 1987; PhD in Engring (hon.), N.S. Inst. Tech.; LLD (hon.), U. Alta., 1993. MP Ho. of Commons, 1968—, chmn. com. transp., 1972-74, mem. com. govt. ops., 1976-77, mem. com. trans. and communication, 1977-79; min. of transp., min. responsible for Can. Wheat Bd. Govt. of Can., 1979-80, min. of transp. (re-drafted Nat. Transp. Act), 1984-86, dep. prime min., 1986—, govt. house leader, 1986-88, pres. Privy Coun., 1986-91, pres. Treas. Bd., 1987-88, min. responsible for privatization and regulatory affairs, 1988-91, min. of agriculture, 1988-91, min. of fin., 1991-93; chmn. Inst. of Pharmaco Econs.; mem. bd. govs. U. Alta; bd. dirs. Gulf Can. Resources, Power Corp. Can., Power Fin. Corp., Great West Life Assurance, The Investors Group, Can. Utilities Ltd., Shaw Comms. Inc., Weyerhaeuser Co., Greyhound Can. Transp. Corp., Golden Star Resources. Mem. Royal Can. Legion (life). Roman Catholic. Club: Vegreville Rotary (past dir.). Lodge: KC.

MAZE, THOMAS H., engineering educator; b. St. Paul, June 1, 1952; s. Robert O. and Viola A.E. (Schultz) M.; m. Leslie Foster Smith, Aug. 2, 1979; children: Lauren L. Simonds, Julie W. Simonds. BS in Civil Engring., Iowa State U., 1975; M of Engring., Urban and Pub. Systems, U. Calif., Berkeley, 1977; PhD in Civil Engring., Mich. State U., 1982. Asst. prof. dept. civil engring. Wayne State U., 1979-82; assoc. prof. sch. civil engring. and environ. sci. U. Okla., Norman, 1982-87; prof. dept. civil and construction engring. Iowa State U., Ames, 1988—, prof. in-charge transp. planning program, 1987—, dir. ctr. for transp. rsch. and edn., ext. and applied rsch., 1988—; assoc. dir. inst. urban transp., transp. rsch. ctr. Ind. U., Bloomington, 1987—; dir. Midwest Transp. Ctr., U.S. Dept. Transp.'s Univ. Transp. Ctr. Fed. Region VII, 1990-96. Mem. ASCE, Am. Pub. Transit Assn., Its Am. (founding, instl. issues com., CVO com.), Am. Pub. Works Assn. (adj. workshop faculty mem. 1986-91, exec. coun. inst. equipment svcs. 1991—), Coun. Univ. Transp., Transp. Rsch. Bd. (mem. various coms., chair 8th equipment mgmt. conf. 1990), Inst. Transp. Engrs. (assoc. mem. dept. 6 standing com., chmn. various coms., pres. U. Fla. student chpt. 1976-79), Chi Epsilon (faculty advisor U. Okla. 1985-87), Sigma Xi. Office: Ctr Transp Rsch & Edn ISU Rsch Park 2625 N Loop Dr Ste 2100 Ames IA 50010-8615

MAZEK, WARREN F(ELIX), academic administrator, economics educator; b. Pitts., Oct. 14, 1938; s. Felix Frank and Josephine Catherine (Sethner) M.; m. Nancy Lee Metcalfe, June 18, 1960 (div. Jan. 1982); children: Thomas W., Erika A., Laura J., Michael M.; m. Susan Chapman, Apr. 24, 1982; 1 child, Marissa C. AB, Washington and Jefferson Coll., 1960; MA, Ind. U., 1962; PhD, U. Pitts., 1965. Asst. prof. econs. Coll. Wooster, 1965-67; asst. prof. Fla. State U., 1967-70, assoc. prof., 1970-75, prof., 1975-86, dean coll. Social Scis., 1973-86; prof., asst. supt. acad. affairs U.S. Merchant Marine Acad., Kings Point, N.Y., 1986—. Cons. on econ. loss to legal firms, 1974—; vestryman Christ Ch., Manhasset, 1991-96; chmn. Big Bend chpt. March of Dimes, Tallahassee, 1981-83. Recipient faculty research award Fla. State U., 1973-74; Resources of the Future dissertation fellow, 1964; Richard K. Mellon fellow Am. Council for Edn., 1975. Mem. Am. Assn. Higher Edn., Am. Econs. Assn., Regional Sci. Assn., Conf. Fed. Degree Granting Insts., Assn. Acad. Affairs Adminstrs. Episcopalian. Home and Office: US Merchant Marine Acad Kings Point NY 11024

MAZEL, JOSEPH LUCAS, publications consultant; b. Paterson, N.J., Oct. 1, 1939; s. Joseph Anthony and Anne (Kidon) M.; children: Joseph William, Jeanne Eileen; m. Joyce Virginia Kronenberger, Feb. 14, 1992. B.M.E., Newark Coll. Engring., 1960. Mech. engr. Austin Co., Roselle, N.J., 1960-61; engr. Western Electric Co., Newark, Atlanta, 1961-62; asst. assoc., sr. editor Factory mag. McGraw-Hill Publs. Co., N.Y.C., 1962-71, editor-in-chief, sr. editor 33 Metal Producing mag., Newark, Summit, N.J. and N.Y.C., 1971-85, chmn. editorial bd., 1980-82; pub. rels. account supr. Hammond Farrell Inc., N.Y.C., 1985-87; mgr. corp. publs. Siemens Corp., Iselin, N.J., 1987-92; pres. Mazel Editorial Assocs., 1992—; group editor Inst. Mgmt. and Adminstrn., Inc. N.Y.C., 1993—; guest lectr. Writers Conf., N.J. Inst. Tech., 1972-83; mem. editorial adv. com. Tech. and Soc. publ., 1981-85; mem. property maintenance com. Borough of Fair Lawn (N.J.), 1995-97; mem. employment assist. response network St. Catharine's Ch., Glen Rock, N.J., 1993—. Mem. N.G., 1963-69. Recipient Apolloneer award Gen. Electric Co., 1966; Jesse H. Neal cert. of merit, 1977, 79, 83; Jesse H. Neal Editorial Achievement award, 1979; Disting. Alumni award for Outstanding Achievement, N.J. Inst. Tech., 1979, Steuben Wise Old Owl award U.S. Steel Corp. Mem. Soc. Profl. Journalists, Nat. Assn. Purchasing Mgmt., Am. Soc. Engring. Mgmt., Am. Prodn. and Inventory Control Soc., Inc., Materials Handling and Mgmt. Soc., Coun. of Logistics Mgmt., Inst. Indsl. Engrs., Sigma Delta Chi. Lodge: KC (grand knight 1967-68, trustee 1968-71); Pitts. Press; Deadline. Home: 40-22 Tierney Pl Fair Lawn NJ 07410-5141

MAZELIS, MENDEL, plant biochemist, educator, researcher; b. Chgo., Aug. 31, 1922; s. Jacob and Anna (Brvarnick) M.; m. Noreen Beimer, Mar. 24, 1969; 1 son, Jacob Russell. B.S., U. Calif.-Berkeley, 1943, Ph.D., 1954. Jr. research biochemist U. Calif.-Berkeley, 1954-55; research assoc., instr. U. Chgo., 1955-57; assoc. chemist Western Regional Research Lab., Albany, Calif., 1957-61; asst. prof. U. Calif.-Davis, 1961-64, assoc. prof., 1964-73, prof., 1973-91, prof. emeritus, 1991—. Served to lt. (j.g.) USN, 1943-46. Mem. Am. Soc. Plant Physiologists, Am. Soc. Biochemists and Molecular Biologists, Biochem. Soc. London, Phytochem. Soc. N.Am., Phytochem. Soc. Europe, Inst. Food Technologists. Office: U Calif Dept Food Sci/Tech Davis CA 95616

MAZER, NORMA FOX, writer; b. N.Y.C., May 15, 1931; d. Michael and Jean (Garlen) Fox; m. Harry Mazer, Feb. 12, 1950; children: Anne E., Joseph D., Susan R., Gina B. Author: I, Trissy, 1971, A Figure of Speech, 1973 (Nat. Book award nominee 1974); Saturday, the Twelfth of October, 1975 (Lewis Carroll Shelf award 1976); Dear Bill, Remember Me? and Other Stories, 1976 (N.Y. Times Notable Book 1976, ALA Notable Book 1976, Sch. Library Jour. Best Books of Yr. 1976, Christopher award 1976, Lewis Carroll Shelf award 1977); (with Harry Mazer) The Solid Gold Kid, 1978 (ALA Best Books for Young Adults 1978, Internat. Reading Assn. Children's Choice, 1979, ALA 100 Best of the Best award 1968-93); Up in Seth's Room, 1979 (ALA Best Books for Young Adults 1979, SLJ Best Books of Yr. 1979, ALA Best of the Best Books, 1970-83); Mrs. Fish, Ape and Me, The Dump Queen, 1980 (German Children's Literature prize 1982, List of Honor Austrian Children's Books 1983); Taking Terri Mueller, 1981 (Edgar award 1982, Calif. Young Readers' Medal 1985), Summer Girls, Love Boys and Other Short Stories, 1982, When We First Met, 1982 (Iowa Teen award 1985); Someone to Love, 1983 (ALA Best Books for Young Adults 1983), Downtown, 1984 (ALA Best Books for Young Adults 1984, N.Y. Times Notable Book 1984), Supergirl The Novel, 1984, Three Sisters, 1986, A, My Name Is Ami (Internat. Reading Assn. Children's Choice, 1987), 1986, B, My Name is Bunny, 1987, After the Rain, 1987 (Newbery Honor Book, ALA Notable Book, Sch. Library Jour. Best Books 1987, ALA Best Books for Young Adults 1987, Canadian Children's Book Coun. Choice 1988, Assn. Booksellers for Children Choice, 1988, Horn Book Fanfare Book 1988), Silver, 1988 (ALA Best Books for Young Adults, 1988, Iowa Teen award 1990-91, ALA 100 Best of the Best award 1980-93), (with Harry Mazer) Heartbeat, 1989 (Internat. Reading Assn. Children's Choice 1990, Literature prize ZDF Germany); editor: Waltzing on Water, 1989, C, My Name Is Cal, 1990, D, My Name Is Danita, 1991, Babyface, 1991 (Am. Booksellers pick of list 1991, Internat. Reading Assn. Tchr.'s Choice), E, My Name Is Emily, 1991, (with Harry Mazer) Bright Days, Stupid Nights, 1992 (Am. Bookseller Pick of List 1992), Out of Control, 1993 (Am. Booksellers Pick of the List 1993, ALA Best Books for Young Adults 1994), Missing Pieces 1995 (Am. Booksellers Pick of List 1995); contbr. short stories, essays and articles to numerous anthologies, collections and mags. including Redbook, Playgirl, Voice, Ingenue, English Jour., The Writer, Alan Review, Scope, Young Miss. Home: 7626 Brown Gulf Rd Jamesville NY 13078-9636

MAZLISH, BRUCE, historian, educator; b. N.Y.C., Sept. 15, 1923; s. Louis and Lee (Reuben) M.; m. Neva Goodwin, Nov. 22, 1988; children from previous marriage: Anthony, Jared, Cordelia, Peter. B.A., Columbia U., 1944, M.A., 1947, Ph.D., 1955. Instr. history U. Maine, 1946-48, Columbia U., 1949- 50, Mass. Inst. Tech., 1950-53; dir. Am. Sch. in Madrid, Spain, 1953-55; mem. faculty Mass. Inst. Tech., 1955—, prof. history, 1965—, chmn. history sect., 1965-70, head dept. humanities, 1974-79. Author: (with J. Bronowski) The Western Intellectual Tradition, 1960, The Riddle of History, 1966, In Search of Nixon, 1972, James and John Stuart Mill: Father and Son in the 19th Century, 1975, 2d edition, 1988, The Revolutionary Ascetic, 1976, Kissinger, The European Mind in American Policy, 1976, The Meaning of Karl Marx, 1984, A New Science: The Breakdown of Connections and the Birth of Sociology, 1989, The Leader, the Led and the Psyche, 1990, The Fourth Discontinuity: The Co-Evolution of Humans and Machines, 1993; Editor: Psychoanalysis and History, 1963, rev. edit., 1971, The Railroad and the Space Program: An Exploration in Historical Analogy, 1965, (with Ralph Buultjens) Conceptualizing Global History, 1993, (with Les Marx) Progress: Fact or Illusion, 1996. Bd. dirs. Rockefeller Family Fund, 1987—; v.p. Mount Desert Festival of Chamber Music, 1985—; bd. dirs. Toynbee Prize Found., 1992—. Served with inf. and OSS, AUS, 1943-45. Recipient Toynbee prize, 1986-87. Fellow Am. Acad. Arts and Scis. Clubs: Cambridge Tennis, Badminton and Tennis; Harbor (Seal Harbor, Maine). Home: 11 Lowell St Cambridge MA 02138-4725 Office: MIT 77 Massachusetts Ave Cambridge MA 02139-4301

MAZO, MARK ELLIOTT, lawyer; b. Phila., Jan. 12, 1950; s. Earl and Rita (Vane) M.; m. Fern Rosalyn Litman, Aug. 19, 1973; children: Samantha Lauren, Dana Suzanne, Ross Elliott, Courtney Litman. AB, Princeton U., 1971; JD, Harvard U., 1974. Bar: D.C. 1975, U.S. Dist. Ct. D.C. 1975, U.S. Claims Ct. 1975, U.S. Ct. Appeals (D.C. cir.) 1976, U.S. Supreme Ct. 1979. Assoc. Jones, Day, Reavis & Pogue, Washington, 1974-79; assoc. Crowell & Moring, Washington, 1979-81, ptnr., 1981-90; ptnr. Hogan & Hartson, L.L.P., Washington and Paris, 1990—. Contbr. articles to profl. jours. White House intern Exec. Office of Pres., Washington, 1972. Capt. USAR, 1971-79. Mem. ABA, Harvard Law Sch. Assn., D.C. Bar Assn., Columbia Country Club, Princeton Club (N.Y.C.), Colonial Club, City Club, Phi Beta Kappa. Republican. Home: 3719 Cardiff Rd Chevy Chase MD 20815-5943 Office: Hogan & Hartson LLP 555 13th St NW Washington DC 20004-1109 Office: Hogan & Hartson LLP, 12 rue de la Paix, 75002 Paris France

MAZO, ROBERT MARC, chemistry educator, retired; b. Bklyn., Oct. 3, 1930; s. Nathan and Rose Marion (Mazo) M.; m. Joan Ruth Spector, Sept. 5, 1954; children: Ruth, Jeffrey, Daniel. B.A., Harvard U., 1952; M.S., Yale U., 1953, Ph.D., 1955. Research assoc. U. Chgo., 1956-58; asst. prof. Calif. Inst. Tech., 1958-62; assoc. prof. U. Oreg., Eugene, 1962-65; prof. chemistry U. Oreg., 1965-95; prof. emeritus, 1996; head chemistry dept. U. Oreg., 1978-81, dir. Inst. Theoretical Sci., 1964-67, 84-87, assoc. dean Grad. Sch., 1967-71; program dir NSF, 1977-78; Alfred P. Sloan fellow, NSF Sr. Postdoctoral fellow, vis. prof. U. Libre de Bruxelles, Belgium, 1968-69; vis. prof. Technische Hochschule Aachen, Weizmann Inst., Rehovoth, Israel, 1981-82, U. New South Wales, Australia, 1989. Author: Statistical Mechanical Theories of Transport Processes, 1967; also research articles. NSF Postdoctoral fellow U. Amsterdam, Netherlands, 1955-56. Mem. Am. Phys. Soc., AAAS, AAUP. Home: 2460 Charnelton St Eugene OR 97405-3214 Office: U Oreg Inst Theoretical Sci Eugene OR 97403

MAZRUI, ALI AL'AMIN, political science educator, researcher; b. Mombasa, Kenya, Feb. 24, 1933; came to U.S., 1960; s. Al'Amin Ali and Safia (Suleiman) M.; m. Molly Vickerman, 1962 (div. 1982); children: Jamal, Al'Amin, Kim Abubakar; m. Pauline Uti, Oct. 1991; children: Farid Chinedu, Harith Ekenechukwu. B.A. with distinction, U. Manchester, Eng., 1960, M.A., Columbia U., 1961; D.Phil., Oxford U., 1966. Lectr. Makerere U., Kampala, Uganda, 1963-65, prof. polit. sci., head dept. polit. sci., 1965-73; dean faculty social scis. Faculty Social Scis., Makerere U., Kampala, Uganda, 1967-69; prof. polit. sci. U. Mich., Ann Arbor, 1974-91, prof. Ctr. Afroam. and African Studies, dept. polit. sci., 1974-91; Andrew D. White prof.-at-large Cornell U., Ithaca, 1986-92; research prof. polit. sci. U. Jos, Nigeria, 1981-86; Albert Schweitzer prof. humanities SUNY, Binghamton, 1989—; Albert Luthuli prof.-at-large U. Jos (Nigeria), 1991—; sr. scholar, Andrew D. White prof.-at-large emeritus Cornell U, Ithaca, 1992—; dir. Inst. Global Cultural Studies SUNY, Binghamton, 1991—; Ibn Khaldun prof.-at-large Sch. Islamic and Social Scis., Leesburg, Va.; Reith lectr. BBC, London, 1979; vis. prof. various univs. including U. London, U. Chgo., Oxford U., U. Pa., Ohio State U., Manchester U., Harvard U., Nairobi U., UCLA, Northwestern U., U. Singapore, Colgate Coll., U. Australia, Stanford U., U. Cairo, Sussex U., U. Leeds, 1965—; mem. bank's coun. African advisers, World Bank, Washington, 1988-91. Author: Towards A Pax Africana: A Study of Ideology and Ambition, 1967, The Anglo-African Commonwealth: Political Friction and Cultural Fusion, 1967, On Heroes and Uhuru-Worship: Essays on Independent Africa, 1967, Violence and Thought: Essays on Social Tensions in Africa, 1969, Cultural Engineering and Nation-Building in East Africa, 1972, World Culture and the Black Experience, 1974, The Political Sociology of the English Language: An African Perspective, 1975, Soldiers and Kinsmen in Uganda: The Making of a Military Ethnocracy, 1975; co-editor: (with Robert I. Rotberg) Protest and Power in Black Africa, 1970, (with Hasu Patel) Africa in World Affairs: The Next Thirty Years, 1973; editor: The Warrior Tradition in Modern Africa, 1978, Africa since 1935 Volume III Unesco General History of Africa, 1973-93, (with Alamin M. Mazrui) The Political Culture of Language Swahili, Society and the State, 1996—; sr. editor: (with T.K. Levine) The Africans: A Reader, 1986; author: The Trial of Christopher Okigbo, 1971, A World Federation of Cultures: An African Perspective, 1976; Africa's International Relations: The Diplomacy of Dependency and Change, 1977, Political Values and the Educated Class in Africa, 1978, The African Condition: A Political Diagnosis, 1980, (with Michael Tidy) Nationalism and New States in Africa, From About 1935 to the Present, 1984; narrator, presenter: The Africans: A Triple Heritage, 1986, Cultural Forces in World Politics, 1990; mem. editl. bd. various profl. jours., 1963—; contbr. articles to profl. publs. Fellow Ctr for Advanced Study in Behavioral Scis., Palo Alto, Calif., 1972-73; sr. fellow Hoover Instn. on War, Revolution and Peace, Stanford, Calif., 1973-74, Mich. Soc. Fellows, 1978-82. Fellow Internat. Assn. Mid. Ea. Studies, Ghana Acad. Arts and Scis. (hon.); mem. African Studies Assn. (exec. bd. 1975-80, pres. 1978-79, Disting. Africans award 1995), Internat. Congress African Studies (v.p. 1978-85), Internat. Polit. Sci. Assn. (v.p. 1970-73), World Order Models Project (dir. African sect. 1968-83), Royal African Soc. (v.p.), Royal Commonwealth Soc., United Kenya Club (Nairobi), Athenaeum Club (London). Office: SUNY Inst Global Cultural Studies Off Schweitzer Chair PO Box 6000 Binghamton NY 13902-6000

MAZUMDER, JYOTIRMOY, mechanical and industrial engineering educator; b. Calcutta, India, July 9, 1951; came to U.S., 1978; s. Jitendra Mohan and Gouri (Sen) M.; m. Aparajita, June 17, 1982; children: Debashis, Debayan. B in Engring., Calcutta U., 1973; diploma, PhD, Imperial Coll., London U., 1978. Rsch. scientist U. So. Calif., L.A., 1978-80; asst. prof. mechanical and indsl. engring. U. Ill., Urbana, 1980-84, assoc. prof., 1984-88, prof., 1988-96; Robert H. Lurie Prof. Engring. U. Mich., Ann Arbor, 1996—; co-dir. ctr. laser aided material processing U. Ill., 1990-96; dir. Quantum Laser Corp., Edison, N.J., 1982-89; pres. Laser Scis., Inc., Urbana, 1988—; vis. scholar physics dept. Stanford (Calif.) U., 1990. Author: (with others) Laser Welding; co-editor: Laser Materials Processing, 1984, 88; contbr. numerous articles to profl. jours. Fellow Am. Soc. of Metals and Laser Inst. of Am. (life, sr. editor Jour. Laser Application); mem. Am. Inst. Metallurgical Engrs. (phys. mets. com. 1980—), Optical Soc. Am. Achievements include non-equilibrium synthesis of Ni-Cr-Al-Hf alloy by laser; patentee: weld pool visualization system for measurement of free surface deformation. Office: U Mich Dept Mech Engring & Mechs 2250 GG Brown Ann Arbor MI 48109-2125

MAZUR, ALLAN CARL, sociologist, engineer, educator; b. Chgo., Mar. 20, 1939; s. Joseph and Esther (Markowitz) M.; m. Minnette Albrecht, Jan. 21, 1968; children—Julie Elizabeth, Rachel Lee. B.S., Ill. Inst. Tech., 1961; M.S., UCLA, 1964; Ph.D., Johns Hopkins U., 1969. Research engr. North Am. Aviation Co., Los Angeles, 1961-64; instr. polit. sci. Mass. Inst. Tech., 1966-67; ops. research analyst Lockheed Missile & Space Corp., Sunnyvale, Calif., 1967-68; asst. prof. sociology Stanford U., 1968-71; mem. faculty Syracuse U., N.Y., 1971—; prof. pub. affairs Syracuse U., 1992—. Author: Dynamics of Technical Controversy, 1981, Global Social Problems, 1991, Rashomon at Love Canal, 1997; co-author: Biology and Social Behavior, 1972; contbr. articles to profl. jours. Fellow AAAS; mem. Am. Sociol. Assn. Jewish. Home: 246 Scottholm Ter Syracuse NY 13224-1738 Office: Syracuse U Maxwell Sch Syracuse NY 13244

MAZUR, ERIC, physicist, educator; b. Amsterdam, The Netherlands, Nov. 14, 1954; came to U.S., 1982; s. Peter and Hélène E.C. (Contamine) M.; m. Angela B.Romijn, July 14, 1984; children: Natalie I., Marc, Sophie B. BA in Physics and Astronomy, U. Leiden, 1975, MS in Physics, 1977, PhD, 1981. Research fellow Harvard U., Cambridge, Mass., 1982-84, asst. prof., 1984-88, assoc. prof., 1988-90; prof. physics and Gordon McKay prof. applied physics Harvard U., 1990—; cons. N.E. Rsch. Assocs., Woburn, Mass., 1985-89. Contbr. articles to profl. jours. Recipient Presidential Young Investigator award, 1988. Fellow. Am. Phys. Soc., Optical Soc. Am. Avocation: photography. Office: Harvard U 29 Oxford St Cambridge MA 02138-2901

MAZUR, JAY J., trade union official. BA in Indsl. Relations, CUNY, 1965; MA in Labor Studies, Rutgers U., 1977. Dir. orgn. local 40 Internat. Ladies Garment Workers Union, N.Y.C., 1955-59, dir. orgn. local 23, 1959-64, asst. mgr. local 23-25, 1964-77, mgr. sec. local 23-25, 1977-83, gen. sec.-treas., 1983-86; pres. Unite, N.Y.C., 1986—; v.p. exec. council AFL-CIO, Washington, 1986—, N.Y. State exec. council, Albany; mem. exec. council Indsl. Union Dept., Washington, 1984—; mem. exec. bd. Fiber, Fabric and Apparel Coalition, Washington, 1986—; bd. dirs. Occupational Health Legal Rights Fund, Washington. V.p. Nat. Immigration Refugee and Citizenship Forum, Washington; bd. dirs. Regional Plan Assn., N.Y.C., 1983, Spl. Contbn. Fund NAACP, Balt., 1987. Avocations: music, jogging, gardening. Office: Unite 1710 Broadway New York NY 10019-5254*

MAZUR, LEONARD L., pharmaceutical company executive; b. Ansbach, Germany, Jan. 23, 1945; came to U.S., 1949; s. Walter and Maria (Zatwarnitsky) M.; m. Helena Maria Olijnyk, Nov. 1966; children: Maria, Michael, Irene. BA, Temple U., 1968, MBA, 1975. Mktg. mgr. Cooper Labs., Inc., Fairfield, N.J. and Palo Alto, Calif., 1971-81; dir. product mgmt. Knoll Pharm. Corp. divsn. BASF, Whippany, N.J., 1981-84; v.p. ICN Pharm. Corp., Costa Mesa, Calif., 1984-88; pres., COO Chantal Pharm. Corp., L.A., 1988-89; exec. v.p. Medicis Pharm. Corp., N.Y.C., 1989-93; vice chmn. Cabot Labs., Inc., N.Y.C., 1994-96; chmn., CEO Genesis Pharm., Inc., Mountain Lakes, N.J., 1996—; ptnr. Mazier Ptnrs. LLC, Morristown, N.J., 1995—. Patentee in field. Mem. adv. bd. Manor Jr. Coll., Jenkintown, Pa., 1972-78; ind. observer Referendum for Independence, Ukraine, 1991. Roman Catholic. Home: 32 Arden Rd Mountain Lakes NJ 07046-1503

MAZUR, MICHAEL, artist; b. N.Y.C., Nov. 2, 1935; s. Burton Boris and Helen (Isaacs) M.; m. Gail Lewis Beckwith, Dec. 28, 1958; children: Daniel Isaac, Kathe Elizabeth. BA, Amherst Coll., 1958; BFA, Yale U., 1959, MFA, 1961. Asst. prof. fine arts Brandeis U., Waltham, Mass., 1965-76; instr. RISD, 1962-65; vis. prof. Yale U. Sch. Art and Arch., 1972, 81, Queens Coll., CUNY, 1973, U. Calif., Santa Barbara, 1974-75, Boston U., 1982, Mass. Coll. Art, 1994, 95; lectr. Mus. Fine Arts, Boston, Brown U., U. Calif., Berkeley, New Sch. for Social Rsch., Bennington Coll., U. Iowa, Boston U., 1994-95, Katonah Mus., N.Y. Studio Sch., 1994; vis. lectr. Carpenter Ctr., Harvard U., 1976, 78, 89, 92, 94, 95, 97, others; illustrator Fleur du Mal, 1984, The Inferno of Dante, Farrar, Strans & Giroux, 1994, Genesis, 1996; co-chair bd. Fine Arts Work Ctr., Provincetown, Mass., 1996—. Exhibited in one-man shows at Kornblee Gallery, N.Y.C., 1960, 63, 66, Boris Mirski, Boston, 1963, 65, Phila. Print Club, 1964, Silvermine Guild, 1964, Fla. State U., 1966, Shoemaker Gallery Juniata Coll., 1966, Alpha Gallery, Boston, 1967, 68, 74, OGL Gallery, Los Angeles, Calif., 1968, Rose Art Mus., Brandeis U., 1969, A.A.A. Gallery, 1969, Inst. Contemporary Art, Boston, 1970, Terry Dintenfass, N.Y.C., 1974, 76, Picker Gallery, Colgate U., 1973, Trinity Coll., 1976, Ohio State U., 1975, Robert Miller Gallery, N.Y.C., 1977, 80, Harkus-Krakow, Boston, 1977, 79, 80, Pace Gallery, N.Y.C., 1980, John Stoller, Mpls., 1981, 85, 88, 91, William and Mary Coll., 1981, Ronald Greenberg, St. Louis, 1981, Janus Gallery, L.A., 1982, 84, 88, Barbara Mathes Gallery, N.Y.C., 1984, 86, Barbara Krakow Gallery, Boston, 1984, 86, 89, 91, 93, 95, 97, Art Club Chgo., 1985, Beaver Coll., 1985, Joe Fawbush, N.Y., 1987, 88, Jan Turner Gallery, L.A., 1988, Butler Gallery, Houston, 1989, Mary Ryan Gallery, N.Y.C., 1990, 94, 95, 96, 97; exhibited group shows at, Mus. Modern Art, 1964, 75, Bklyn. Mus., 1960, 62, 64, 66, 76, 80, 84, 86, Fogg Art Mus., 1966, 76, 94, Art. Inst. Chgo., 1964, Pa. Acad., 1966, 93, Phila. Mus., 1966, 88, Boston Mus. Fine Arts., 1967, 68, 76, 77, 80, 88, 90-91, 92, DeCordova Mus., Lincoln, Mass., 1965-67, 75, 86, 87, Whitney Mus. Am. Art, 1965, 81, 90, 92, Nat. Inst. Arts and Letters, 1965, 74, 80, 86, Sivermine Guild, 1965, Print Biennial of Americas, Santiago, Chile, 1965, Paris Biennale, 1969, Venice Biennale, 1970, Finch Coll. Mus., 1971-72, 2d and 3d Biennial Graphic Art, Cali, Colombia, N.A.D. Ann., 1974, Butler Inst., Youngstown, Ohio, 1974, Ball State U., 1974, America-1976, Sense of Place, Met. Mus., N.Y.C., 1979, 80, Montreal Mus. Fine Arts, 1977, Palais Royale, Brussels, 1979, Claude Bernard, Paris, 1980, Alan Frumkin, N.Y.C., 1981, 82, Madison Art Ctr., 1989, Nat. Gallery of Art, Washington, 1990, Pratt Mus., N.Y.C., 1990, Nat. Mus. Am. Art, 1997; traveling exhbns. include, Bicentennial Exhbn., 1976, State Arts Councils, Iowa, Kans., Mo., Nebr., 1973, Am. Monotypes, Smithsonian Instn., 1977; represented in permanent collections, Met. Mus., N.Y.C., Mus. Modern Art, Smith Coll. Art Mus., Library Congress, Fogg Art Mus., Art Inst. Chgo., Whitney Mus., Los Angeles County Art Mus., Mus. R.I. Sch. Design, Oreg. Art Mus., U. Maine, Mpls. Inst., Pa. State U., Toledo Art Mus., Phila. Art Mus., U. Ohio Westminster Found., Boston Mus. Fine Arts, Boston Pub. Library, Bklyn. Mus., Addison Gallery, Andover Acad., Yale Art Gallery, Montreal Mus. Fine Arts; (Recipient 2d prize Soc. Am. Graphic Artists 1963, Nat. Inst. Arts and Letters award 1965). Co-founder Artists Against Racism and the War, 1968; bd. dirs. Artists Found., co-chair, 1995—; bd. dirs. Fine Arts Work Ctr., Provincetown, Mass.; mem. Mass. Coun. on Arts and Humanities; mem. Pennell com. Libr. of Congress, 1983-93; founder, dir. Art for Nuc. Weapons Freeze, 1983-84, New Provincetown Print Project, 1990-95. Grantee Tiffany Found., 1964, Tamarind Lithography Workshop, 1968; Guggenheim Found. fellow, 1964-65; winner numerous purchase awards. Home: 5 Walnut Ave Cambridge MA 02140-2706 also: 561 Commercial St Provincetown MA 02657-1724

MAZUR, PETER, cell physiologist, cryobiologist; b. N.Y.C., March 3, 1928; s. Paul M. and Adolphia (Kaske) M.; m. Drusilla Stevens, May 28, 1953 (dec. May 1982); 1 child, Timothy Stevens; m. Sara Jo Bolling, June 16, 1984. A.B. magna cum laude, Harvard U., 1949, Ph.D., 1953. NSF postdoctoral fellow, Princeton U., N.J., 1957-59; research staff biology div. Oak Ridge Nat. Lab., 1959—, group leader fundamental and applied cryobiology, 1966—, sci. dir. biophysics and cell physiology, biology div., 1974-75, corporate fellow, 1985; chmn. ORNL Corp. Fellows Coun., 1995-96; mem. vis. com. biology Harvard U. Bd. Overseers 1972-77; adj. prof. U. Tenn.; mem. Space Sci. Bd. of Nat. Acad., 1975-77. Contbr. articles to prof. jours. Served to capt. USAF, 1953-57. Recipient Author of Yr. award Martin-Marietta Energy Systems, 1985, Disting. Svc. award Am. Assn. Tissue Banks, 1993, R & D 100 award R & D Mag., 1993; Lalor fellow Harvard U., 1952, John Harvard fellow, 1951. Sigma Xi Nat. lectr., 1980. Fellow AAAS; mem. Soc. for Cyrobiology (pres. 1973-74, bd. govs., 1979-96), Phi Beta Kappa. Club: Cosmos (Washington). Current work: Cryobiology mechanisms of freezing injury in living cells and tissues. Subspecialties: Cell biology; Biophysics (biology). Home: 125 Westlook Cir Oak Ridge TN 37830-3856 Office: Oak Ridge Nat Lab Life Scis Divsn PO Box 2009 Oak Ridge TN 37831-8080

MAZUR, RHODA HIMMEL, community volunteer; b. Bklyn., July 4, 1929; d. Morris and Gussie (Nadler) Himmel; m. Marvin Irwin Mazur, June 7, 1952; children: Jody, Amy, Leslie, Eric. Student, CCNY, CUNY. Bd. dirs. Newport News Social Svcs. Adv. Bd., 1979-84, Gov.'s Commn. Status Women, Richmond, 1981-84, Coun. Jewish Fedns., N.Y.C., 1985-87, Nat. Coun. Christians and Jews, 1985-89; v.p. Anti-Defamation League Regional Bd., Richmond, 1983-85, bd. dirs., 1985—; pres. Newport News Hadassah, 1984-85, United Jewish Cmty. Va. Peninsula Inc., Newport News, 1985-88; active Newport News Task Force on Emergency Housing, 1984-85; chair fin. com. Peninsula Peace Edn. Ctr., Newport News, 1984-85; mem. adv. bd. Friends of the Homeless, Inc., 1987—, pres., 1993—; mem. adv. bd. Associated Marine Inst., 1988-92; mem. social svcs. com. United Jewish Cmty. Va. Peninsula, 1995—; cmty. activist. Recipient Young Leadership award Jewish Fedn. Newport News, 1968, Brotherhood citation Nat. Conf. Christians and Jews, 1984. Democrat. Avocations: hand crafts, reading, music, photography. Home: 114 James River Dr Newport News VA 23601-3604

MAZUREK, JOSEPH P., state attorney general, former state legislator; b. San Diego, July 27, 1948; B.A., U. Mont., 1970, J.D., 1975; m. Patty Mazurek; 3 children. Bar: Mont. 1975; atty. Gough, Shanahan, Johnson, and Waterman, Helena, Mont.; mem. Mont. Senate from 23d Dist., 1981-92; Senate pres., 1991-92; atty. gen., State of Mont., 1993—; mem. Revenue Oversight Com., 1983-92; chmn. Senate Judiciary Com.; assoc. editor Mont. Law Rev., 1974-75. Served with U.S. Army, 1970-72. Mem. ABA, Beta Gamma Sigma, Phi Delta Phi, Phi Delta Theta. Office: Justice Bldg PO Box 201401 215 N Sanders 3rd Fl Helena MT 59620*

MAZURSKY, PAUL, screenwriter, theatrical director and producer; b. Bklyn., Apr. 25, 1930; s. David and Jean (Gerson) M.; m. Betsy Purdy, Mar. 12, 1953; children—Meg, Jill. B.A., Bklyn. Coll., 1951. Actor, star, TV and Films, 1951—, including film Deathwatch, Miami Rhapsody, 1995; night club comedian, 1954-60; writer Danny Kaye Show, 1963-67; co-writer film I Love You, Alice B. Toklas, 1968; writer, dir. films Bob & Carol & Ted & Alice, 1969, Alex in Wonderland, 1970, Blume in Love, 1972, Harry & Tonto, 1973, Next Stop, Greenwich Village, 1976, An Unmarried Woman, 1977-78, Willie & Phil, 19679-80, Tempest, 1982, Moscow on the Hudson, 1984; writer, prodr., dir. films Down and Out in Beverly Hills, 1986, Moon Over Parador, 1988; co-scriptwriter, prodr., dir. film Enemies, A Love Story, 1989, Scenes From a Mall, 1990, The Pickle, 1992, Faithful, 1995. Office: ICM care Ken Kamins 8942 Wilshire Blvd Beverly Hills CA 90211-1934*

MAZZA, THOMAS CARMEN, lawyer; b. Erie, Pa., Feb. 14, 1940; s. Carmen J. and Helen (Fronius) M.; m. Lois Bigbie, June 12, 1993; children: Elizabeth Williamson Burnette, Thomas Denholm. BA, Yale U., 1961, LLB, 1964. Bar: N.Y. 1965; U.S. Ct. Appeals (2nd cir.) 1965, U.S. Dist. Ct. (so. and ea. dists.) N.Y. 1976, U.S. Ct. Appeals (11th cir.) 1980, U.S. Dist. Ct. (no. dist.) N.Y. 1982, U.S. Supreme Ct. 1982. Assoc. Dewey Ballantine, N.Y.C. and Brussels, 1964-72; ptnr. Dewey Ballantine, N.Y.C., 1972—. Vestryman Trinity Parish, N.Y.C., 1976-83, 86-93, 94—; bd. dirs. St. margaret's House Housing Corp., N.Y.C., 1994—. Fellow Am. Coll. Investment Counsel; mem. ABA, N.Y. State Bar Assn., Assn. Bar City of N.Y., Collectors Club N.Y. (gov. 1989—, pres. 1993—). Episcopalian. Avocations: music, philately. Office: Dewey Ballantine 1301 Avenue Of The Americas New York NY 10019-6022 also: The Collectors Club Inc 22 E 35th St New York NY 10016-3806

MAZZAFERRI, ERNEST LOUIS, physician, educator; b. Cleve., Sept. 27, 1936; s. Joseph and Nanetta (Marinelli) M.; m. Florence Mildred Marolt, Nov. 23, 1957; children: Patricia Marie Atchison, Michael Louis, Sharon Lynne Brown, Ernest Louis. BS cum laude, John Carroll U., 1958; MD, Ohio State U., 1962. Diplomate Am. Bd. Internal Medicine, Am. Bd. Endocrinology and Metabolism. Intern Ohio State U. Hosps., Columbus, 1962-63; resident Ohio State U. Hosps., 1963-64, 66-68; asst. prof. medicine Ohio State U., 1968-70, assoc. prof., 1973-76, prof., 1976-79, dir. div. endocrinology and metabolism, 1975-78; acting dean U. Nev., Reno, 1979-81; prof., chmn. dept. medicine U. Nev., 1978-84, prof. physiology, 1982-84; prof., chmn. dept. medicine, prof. physiology Ohio State U., Columbus, 1984—; pres. Dept. of Medicine Found., 1986—; chmn. bd. Ohio State Practice Group, 1996—. Author: Endocrinology Case Studies, 3d edit., 1985, Internal Medicine Pearls, 1993; editor: Textbook of Endocrinology, 3d edit., 1986, Contemporary Internal Medicine, 1988, 3d edit., 1990, Advances in Endocrinology and Metabolism, Vol. 6, 1995, Endocrine Tumors, 1993; mem. sci. adv. bd. Western Jour. Medicine, 1993; mem. editl. bd. Jour. Lab. Clin. Medicine, 1987—, Hosp. Practice; contbr. articles to profl. jours. Chmn. Gov.'s Com. on Radiation Fallout in Nev., 1980-84, hosp. ethics com. Ohio State U.; mem. Sec. of Energy Dose Assessment Adv. Com., 1980-84, Agy. for Health Care Policy, Rsch. Cataract Guideline Com., 1991-92. Lt. col. USAF, 1964-72; col. USAR. Decorated Air Force Commendation medal, Meritorious Svc. medal. Fellow ACP (master, gov. for Nev. 1984-85, chmn. clin. efficacy assessment program com. 1992-95, mem. health and pub. policy com., edn. policy com.); mem. Am. Bd. Internal Medicine (Endocrinology and Metabolism, 1996—), AMA, Am. Thyroid Assn., Am. Diabetes Assn. (pres. Ohio affiliate 1988-89), Endocrine Soc., Am. Clin. and Climatol. Assn., Ctrl. Soc. Clin. Rsch., Am. Coll. Clin. Endocrinology (bd. dirs. 1995-96), Alpha Omega Alpha. Republican. Roman Catholic. Achievements include research in thyroid cancer. Home: 2481 Slate Run Columbus OH 43220-2850 Office: Ohio State U Means Hall 1655 Upham Dr Columbus OH 43210-1251 *Success, like every other human experience, is relative, measured against shifting standards and subject to the scrutiny of time. One must strike a fine balance—self certainty against external review—that permits the full expression of new ideas enriched by the best and time-worn thoughts of others.*

MAZZAFERRI, KATHERINE AQUINO, lawyer, bar association executive; b. Phila., May 14, 1947; d. Joseph William and Rose (Aquino) M.; m. William Fox Bryan, May 5, 1984 (separated); 1 child, Josefa Mazzaferri Bryan; 1 stepchild, Patricia M. Bryan. BA, NYU, 1969; JD, George Washington U., 1972. Bar: D.C., 1972. Trial atty. EEOC, Washington, 1972-75; dir. litigation LWV Edn. Fund, Washington, 1975-78; dep. asst. dir. for advt. practices FTC, Washington, 1978-80, asst. dir. for product liability, 1980-82, asst. dir. for advt. practices, 1982; exec. dir., v.p. pub. svcs. activities corp. D.C. Bar, Washington, 1982—; bd. dir. regulatory analysis project U.S. Regulatory Coun.; mediator D.C. Mediation Svc., 1982; vis. instr. Antioch Law Sch., Washington, 1985; mem. Bd. of Women's Bar Assn. Found., 1990-93; mem. FBA Meml. Found., 1991—. Recipient Superior Service award FTC, 1979. Mem. ABA (rep. of the homeless project steering com. 1988-90), D.C. Bar, Womens Legal Def. (pres. 1972-73, bd. dirs. 1971-75, 76-79), FBA Meml. Found. Home: 5832 Lenox Rd Bethesda MD 20817-6070 Office: DC Bar 1250 H St NW Fl 6 Washington DC 20005-3952

MAZZARELLA, DAVID, newspaper editor; b. 1938. With AP, Lisbon, N.Y.C., Rome, 1962-70, Daily American, Rome, 1971-75, Gannett News, D.C., 1976-77, The Bridgewater, Bridgewater, N.J., 1977-83; now editor USA Today, Arlington, Va. Office: USA Today 1000 Wilson Blvd Arlington VA 22209-3901*

MAZZARELLA, JAMES KEVIN, business administration educator; b. Phila., Sept. 22, 1955; s. Samuel Charles and Rosemary C. (Queenan) M. BA, St. Joseph's U., 1977; MBA, La Salle U., 1981; MA, Temple U., 1987; PhD, Columbia-Pacific U., 1987; DBA, Pacific-Western U., 1988; cert. in acctg., Thomas Edison State Coll., 1994; BS, SUNY, 1996. Asst. mgr. Olney Oil & Burner Co., Phila., 1977-80; data processing Craig Fuel Co., Phila., 1980-84; supr. M. Kelley Son's Inc., Phila., 1984-86; adj. instr. Holy Family Coll., Phila., 1987-88, instr., 1989, asst. prof., 1989—; adj. instr. Phila. (Pa.) Coll. Textiles, 1984-86, La Salle U., Phila., 1985—, Rosemont (Pa.) Coll., 1988-91. Mem. Am. Econs. Assn., Am. Fin. Assn., Am. Statis. Assn., Nat. Assn. Bus. Econs., Am. Risk and Ins. Assn., Inst. Mgmt. Accts., Math. Assn. Am., Fin. Mgmt. Assn., Prodn. and Ops. Mgmt. Soc., Midwest Fin. Assn., Western Econs. Assn. Internat., Ea. Econ. Assn., Ea. Fin. Assn., Am. Mgmt. Assn., So. Fin. Assn., Multinat. Fin. Soc., Am. Math. Soc., Am. Law and Econs. Assn. Roman Catholic. Home: 5101 N Fairhill St Philadelphia PA 19120-3126 Office: Holy Family College Grant & Frankford Ave Philadelphia PA 19114

MAZZARELLA, ROSEMARY LOUISE, business administration executive; b. Phila., Aug. 20, 1959; d. Samuel Charles and Rosemarie Claire Mazzarella. BA, La Salle U., 1985, MS in Orgnl. Devel. & Mgmt., 1991. Materials mgmt. exec. Sun Refining & Mktg. Co., Phila., 1979-91; purchasing asst. Children's Seashore House, Phila., 1992-94; adminstr. FMC Corp., Phila., 1994—. Vol. Child Abuse Prevention Com. Greater Phila., 1992, Walnut Street Theatre, Phila., 1992; vol. tutor Ctr. for Literacy, Phila., 1992. Mem. Assn. Behavior Analysis (sustaining), Alpha Epsilon. Avocations: theatre, art, writing.

MAZZARESE, MICHAEL LOUIS, executive coach, consultant; b. S.I., Jan. 25, 1941; s. Louis John and Helen Ermenia (Mazzei) M.; m. Maureen Ann Starace, Oct. 3, 1970; children: Lauren, Adrienne. BA, St. Joseph's Sem. and Coll., 1962; MS, CUNY, 1971, profl. dipl., 1973; PhD, Fordham U., 1980. Tchr. high sch. N.Y. and Maine, 1963-73; prof. CUNY, 1973-78; asst. dir. med. edn. St. Barnabas Med. Ctr., Livingston, N.J., 1978-79; staff supr. AT&T, Bedminster, N.J., 1979-84; mgr. Johnson and Johnson, New Brunswick, N.J., 1984-86; dir. EQUICOR, N.Y.C., 1986-87; exec. dir. Dun and Bradstreet, Murray Hill, N.J., 1987-92; v.p. Hoechst Celanese Corp., Somerville, N.J., 1992-94; pres. Mazzarese & Assocs., Westfield, N.J., 1994—. Translator: Letters from Paris (Teilhard J. Chardin), 1966. Recipient Excellence in Human Resources Devel. award Brigham Young U., 1985. Mem. Am. Psychol. Assn., Am. Soc. Tng. and Devel., Am. Evaluation Assn., Am. Evaluation and Rsch. Assn., Soc. Human Resource Mgmt., Human Resources Planning Soc. Home: 330 Benson Pl Westfield NJ 07090-1302 Office: Mazzarese & Assocs 213 Scotch Plains Ave Westfield NJ 07090-1302

MAZZATENTA, ROSEMARY DOROTHY, school administrator; b. Phila., Sept. 17, 1932; d. John and Mary Aida (Perrucci) M. BS in Edn., U. Pa., 1953, MS in Edn., 1956. Cert. tchr., prin., Pa. Tchr. Haverford Twp. (Pa.) Sch. Dist., 1953-54; tchr. Sch. Dist. Phila., 1954-63, cons., 1963-65, elem. sch. prin., 1965-72, asst. dir. pre-kindergarten Head Start, 1965-80, dir. child care, 1980-86, dir. pre-kindergarten Head Start, parent coop. nurseries, 1986—, dir. Even Start program, 1986—; dir. Head Start Learning Ctr., 1993—. dir. Southeastern Pa. unit ARC, 1969—; mem. Phila. Fellowship Commn., 1957—; bd. dirs. Delaware Valley Child Care Coun., 1982—. Decorated Legion of Honor Chapel of 4 Chaplains, 1975; recipient award of excellence Del. Valley Assn. Edn. Young Children, 1995. Mem. Nat. Assn. Edn. Young Children (award of excellence 1995), Alumnae Club Phila. (past pres.), Edn. Alumni Assn. (past pres., award of distinction 1970), Sons of Italy (charter mem. Columbus forum, Pres.'s award 1985, Outstanding Svc. award 1997), Soroptomists (Woman of Distinction 1993), Kappa Delta Epsilon, Pi Lambda theta, Phi Delta Kappa (Svc. Key 1995). Avocations: travel, reading, needlepoint. Office: Pre-Kindergarten Head Start 13th at Spring Garden St Philadelphia PA 19123

MAZZE, EDWARD MARK, marketing educator, consultant; b. N.Y.C., Feb. 14, 1941; s. Harry Alan and Mollie (Schneider) M.; m. Sharon Sue Hastings, Sept. 9, 1967; children—Candace, Thomas. B.B.A., City U. N.Y., 1961, M.B.A., 1962; Ph.D., Pa. State U., 1966. Lectr. bus. adminstrn. CCNY, 1961-62; bus. cons., 1961—; pres., dir. JET Corp., East Orange, N.J., 1976-79; instr. bus. Pa. State U., 1963-66; assoc. prof. mktg. U. Detroit, 1966-68; assoc. prof., dir. spl. programs W.Va. U., 1968-70; prof. bus. adminstrn., coordinator mktg. program Va. Poly. Inst. and State U., Blacksburg, 1970-75; v.p. adminstrv. services, dean Sch. Bus., Seton Hall U., South Orange, N.J., 1975-79; dean sch. bus. adminstrn. Temple U., Phila., 1979-86, prof. mktg. and internat. bus., 1979-93; dean Belk Coll. Bus. Adminstrn., prof. mktg. U. N.C.-Charlotte, Charlotte, 1993—; chmn. bd. William Penn Bank, Phila., 1985-87; bd. dirs. Technitrol, Inc.; mem. dist. export coun. U.S. Dept. Commerce, 1978-80, 83-93; mem. panel trustees U.S. Bankruptcy Ct., 1984-96. Author: International Business: Articles and Essays, 1963, Readings in Organization and Management, 1965, Marketing in Action, 1963, Case Histories in Sales Management, 1965, Sales Management: Theory and Practice, 1965, International Marketing Adminstration, 1967, Introduction to Marketing, 1970, Marketing in Turbulent Times: The Challenges and the Opportunities, 1975, Personal Selling: Choice Against Chance, 1976; mem. editorial bd. Jour. Econs. and Bus., 1976-80, Indsl. Mktg. Mgmt., 1977—, Jour. Internat. Bus. Studies, 1978-82, Jour. Acad. Mktg. Sci., 1980-91, Jour. Mktg. Edn., 1985-94, Jour. Global Mktg., 1987—; contbr. articles to profl. and trade jours. Trustee Phila. Home Care, 1984-89, Manor Coll., 1985-92, Thomas A. Edison State Coll. Found., 1987-89, Delaware Valley Coll. Sci. and Agr., 1991—, Pa. Inst. Tech., 1992-93; chmn. econ. devel. adv. com. Village South Orange, 1977-80; mem., vice-chmn. Bd. Suprs. Doylestown Twp., 1980-81. Ford. Found. fellow, 1962-63. Mem. Am. Mktg. Assn., Acad. Internat. Bus., Nat. Assn. Corp. Dirs., Acad. Mktg. Sci., City Club, Tower Club, Beta Gamma Sigma, Alpha Kappa Psi, Pi Sigma Epsilon, Pi Kappa Alpha. Home: 6805 Linkside Ct Charlotte NC 28277-0394 Office: Univ NC Charlotte NC 28223

MAZZE, ROGER STEVEN, medical educator, researcher; b. N.Y.C., May 14, 1943; s. Harry Alan and Mollie (Schneider) M.; m. Rochelle Linda March, Dec. 28, 1969; children—Aaron, Rebekkah. B.A., Queens Coll., 1965, M.A., 1967; Ph.D., U. Ill., 1971. Fellow in social psychiatry Brandeis U., Waltham, Mass., 1971; chmn. urban studies Fordham U., N.Y.C., 1970-75; from assoc. to full prof. epidemiololgy and social medicine Einstein Coll. Medicine, N.Y.C., 1975-87, exec. dir. Diabetes Research and Tng. Ctr., 1980-88; sr. v.p. research and devel. Internat. Diabetes Ctr., Mpls., 1988—; clin. prof. U. Minn. Med. Sch., 1988—; v.p. Inst. for Rsch. and Edn., Health Sys. Minn., Mpls., 1993—; adv. bd. Nat. Diabetes Info. Clearinghouse, Washington, 1980-84, Pa. Diabetes Acad., Harrisburg, 1982—; co-dir. WHO Coll. Ctr. in Diabetes Care, Edn. and Computer Sci., Mpls., 1988—. Author: Narcotics, Knowledge and Nonsense, 1977, Professional Education in Diabetes, 1983, Frontiers of Diabetes Research, 1990, Staged Diabetes Management, 1995; editor: Practical Diabetes, 1987-89; contbr. articles to profl. jours. Active Internat. Diabetes Fedn., European Assn. for Study of Diabetes; chmn. Am. Diabetes Assn. Named Disting. vis. Scientist CDC, 1983-84; Hoechst lectr. Australian Diabetes Soc., 1985, 87, Japanese Diabetes Assn., 1983, 88, 93, 94, Polish Diabetes Assn., 1993, 94, 95, 96; named Best Spkr. of Yr., Soc. for Clin. Chemistry, 1991, Minn. Med. Alley award for excellence in rsch. and devel., 1995; grantee NIH, 1977—, ADA, 1991—, Juvenile Diabetes Found., 1992—. Mem. Am. Diabetes Assn. (chmn.), Itnernat. Diabetes Fedn., European Assn. for Study Diabetes. Home: 5870 Boulder Bridge Ln Excelsior MN 55331-7969 Office: Internat Diabetes Ctr 3800 Park Nicollet Blvd Minneapolis MN 55416-2527

MAZZEO-MERKLE, LINDA L., legal administrator; b. Washington, Apr. 6, 1947; d. Robert Clifton Shreeves II and Esther A. (Harrison) Shreeves; m. John T. Mazzeo; children: Christina L., Regina L. Hodges. Lic. real estate, Prince Georges C.C., Largo, Md., 1972. Various secretarial positions, 1964-65, 67-72; real estate saleswoman, 1973-74; div. sec. Prince Georges C.C., 1974-75; real estate saleswoman Harvest Realty Inc., Clinton, Md., 1974-75; legal adminstr., property mgr., investment mgr. firm Tucker, Flyer, Sanger, Reider & Lewis P.C., Washington, 1975-84; legal adminstr. Anderson, Heibey, Nauheim & Blair, Washington, 1984-85; v.p. fin. and adminstrn. Barnes, Morris, Pardoe & Foster, Inc., Washington, 1985-93; former CFO, chief adminstrv. officer Barnes, Morris & Pardoe, Inc.; legal adminstr. Payne, Negroni & Winston, Washington, 1994-95, Buckmaster & Assocs., Washington, 1996—; with Md. Corp.; pres. Lawtabs Inc. Del. Corp.; cons., speaker. Mem. Assn. Legal Adminstrs. (chmn. new adminstrs. and gen. adminstrn. sect. 1984-85), ABA (assoc.). Home: 4100 N River St Mc Lean VA 22101-5814 Office: 22101 Office 1250 24th St NW Washington DC 20008

MAZZIA, VALENTINO DON BOSCO, physician, educator, lawyer; b. N.Y.C., Feb. 17, 1922; s. Alexander Lloret and Francesca M.; m. Rosana Sgarlata, Sept. 2, 1974; children: Lisa Mitchell, Donald Mitchell, Christopher Mitchell. B.S. cum laude, CCNY, 1943; M.D., NYU, 1950; postgrad., U. So. Calif. Sch. Law, 1973-74; J.D., U. Denver, 1978. Bar: Colo. 1978, U.S. Dist. Ct. Colo. 1978, Calif. 1979, U.S. Dist. Ct. (So. dist.) Calif. 1979, U.S. Supreme Ct. 1982, Ala. 1984, U.S. Dist. Ct. Ala. 1984, N.Y. 1987; diplomate: Am. Bd. Anesthesiology., Am. Bd. Law in Medicine. Intern Kings County Hosp., Bklyn., 1950-52; resident N.Y. Hosp., N.Y.C., 1952-54; asst. prof. Cornell U. Med. Coll., N.Y.C., 1952-61; prof. anesthesiology, chmn. dept. Coll. Medicine NYU, N.Y.C., 1961-72, prof. anesthesiology, chmn. dept. Postgrad. Med. Sch., 1961-72, prof. anesthesiology Coll. Dentistry, 1962-72; dir., attending anesthesiologist Univ. Hosp., N.Y.C., 1961-72; vis.-in-charge, dir. anesthesia service Bellevue Hosp. Center, N.Y.C., 1961-72; cons. N.Y. VA Hosp., Manhattan State Hosp., 1961-72; dir. anesthesiology Los Angeles County/Martin Luther King Jr. Gen. Hosp., 1971-73; chief anesthesiology Kern County Gen. Hosp., Bakersfield, Calif., 1973; practice medicine specializing in anesthesiology Bakersfield, Los Angeles; solo practice Las Vegas; staff 35 hosps., 1973-75; prof. anesthesiology U. Colo. Health Scis. Center and Dental Sch., Denver, 1976-83; clin. prof. U. Colo. Health Scis. Center and Dental Sch., 1984-88; clin. dir. operating room for anesthesiology Univ. Hosp., 1976-82; vis. prof., chmn. anesthesiology Charles R. Drew Post Grad. Med. Sch., Los Angeles, 1971-73; vis. prof. anesthesiology UCLA, 1972; asst. med. examiner, cons. forensic anesthesiology Office of Chief Med. Examiner, N.Y.C., 1962-73; dep. coroner, asst. med. examiner County Coroner's Office, Los Angeles, 1973-82; of counsel Cunningham Bounds Yance Crowder & Brown, Mobile, Ala. Co-author: Practical Anesthesiology, 1962—; contbr. chpts. to books, articles to profl. jours. Served with USAAF, 1943-45, to med. dir. USPHS Res., 1945-95. Fellow Am. Coll. Anesthesiology, N.Y. Acad. Medicine, Am. Coll. Chest Physicians, Am. Osteo. Coll. Anesthesiologists, Am. Coll. Legal Medicine; mem. Harvey Soc., Assn. Trial Lawyers Am., Ala. Trial Lawyers Assn., Phi Beta Kappa, Sigma Xi, Alpha Omega Alpha. Club: New York Athletic (life). Office: 120 E 87th St Apt P14D New York NY 10128-1119 also: 1601 Dauphin St Mobile AL 36604-1305 *When one's progress appears to be blocked by circumstances or people, change location or vocation. Persistence always wins.*

MAZZILLI, PAUL JOHN, investment banker; b. White Plains, N.Y., Dec. 4, 1948; s. Philip Joseph and Sara (Bialick) M.; m. Sharon Pickett, May 23, 1986; children: Meredith Paige, Nicholas Parker. BS in Indsl. Engring., Syracuse U., 1970; MBA, Columbia U., 1973. Lic. real estate agt., N.Y. Budget analyst The Pentagon, Washington, 1972; mgr. planning and analysis Xerox Corp., White Plains, 1973-75; mgr. planning and analysis Morgan Stanley & Co., Inc., N.Y.C., 1975-78, dir. planning and analysis, 1979-80, exec. asst. to oper. com., 1981-82, new product specialist, 1982-83, v.p. hedging products, 1984-85, prin. pension svcs. group, 1986-87, head stategy group for Employee Stock Ownership Plan, 1988-91, head of Equity Derivatives Corp. Svc. Group, 1992-93; prin. Equity Capital Markets Svcs., 1993—; pres. Wall St. Planning Group, N.Y.C., 1979-80; adj. prof. fin. Mercy Coll., Dobbs Ferry, N.Y., 1977-79; mem. tax rev. bd. Town of Greenburgh, N.Y., 1972-77. Coun. mem. Jr. Achievement N.Y., 1976-78; elected Westchester County Rep. Com., 1970-75. Capt. USAFR, 1970-76. Mem. Nat. Assn. Securities Dealers (registered rep.), Columbia U. Alumni Assn. (rep. 1979-80), Columbia Bus. Sch. Alumni Assn. (bd. dirs., v.p. 1978-81), Sleepy Hollow Country Club, Shattemuc Yacht Club (Ossining, N.Y.). Home: Tower Hill Rd Scarborough NY 10510 Office: Morgan Stanley & Co Inc 1585 Broadway New York NY 10036-8200

MAZZO, KAY, ballet dancer, educator; b. Evanston, Ill., Jan. 17, 1946; d. Frank Alfred and Catherine M. (Hengel) M.; m. Albert C. Bellas, 1978; children: Andrew, Kathryn. Student, Sch. Am. Ballet, 1959-61. Profl. debut in ballets U.S.A. 1961, touring Europe with co., performing for Pres. Kennedy at White House, 1961, joined N.Y.C. Ballet, 1962-80, soloist, 1965-69, prin. ballerina, 1969-80, prin. roles in world premiere of ballets including Tschaikowsky Suite No. #3, 1970, PAMTGG, 1971, Stravinsky Violin Concerto, 1972, Scherzo A La Russe, 1972, Duo Concertant, 1972, Sheherazade, 1975, Union Jack, 1976, Vienna Waltzes, 1977, Davidsbundlertanze, 1980; ballet tchr. Sch. Am. Ballet, 1980—; appeared as guest artist in leading roles with numerous cos. including Boston Ballet, Washington Ballet, Berlin Ballet, Geneva Ballet; appeared on TV in U.S., Can., Fed. Republic Germany. Recipient Mademoiselle Merit award 1970. Office: Sch Am Ballet 70 Lincoln Center Plz New York NY 10023-6548*

MAZZOCCO, ANGELO, language educator; b. Cerreto di Vastogirardi, Isernia, Italy, May 13, 1936; came to U.S., 1954, naturalized, 1957; s. Giuseppe and Ida (Rotolo) M.; m. Elizabeth Hunt Davis, Oct. 7, 1990; children: Michael Ray, Marco Angelo. BS, BA, Ohio State U., 1959, MA, 1963; PhD in Romance Langs. and Lits., U. Calif., Berkeley, 1973. Instr. Spanish John Carroll U., Cleve., 1962-65; teaching asst. Italian U. Calif., Berkeley, 1966-69; asst. prof. Italian No. Ill. U., DeKalb, 1970-75; asst. prof. Spanish and Italian Mt. Holyoke Coll., South Hadley, Mass., 1975-78, assoc. prof., 1978-83, prof., 1983—, chair dept., 1981-84, 93-96; chair romance langs. and lits., 1989-93; assoc. Columbia U. Renaissance Seminar. Author: Linguistic Theories in Dante/Humanists, 1993; contbr. chpts. in books and articles to profl. jours. Travel grantee Am. Coun. Learned Socs., 1985, Gladys Krieble Delmas Found. Rsch. grantee, 1993-94, 96-97; Italian-Am. traveling fellow U. Calif., 1969-70, NEH Italian Humanism summer sem. fellow, 1981, NEH/NSF award, 1995-98. Mem. MLA (N.E. chpt., exec. com. Medieval and Renaissance Italian Lit. 1981-85, assembly del. 1985-87), Am. Assn. Tchrs. Italian, Dante Soc. Am. (coun. assoc. 1985-90, coun. 1994—), Medieval Acad. Renaissance Soc. Am., Internat. Assn. Neo-Latin Studies, Internat. Assn. History Lang. Soc., Assn. Internat. Sudi di Lingua e Letteratura Italiana, Internat. Soc. Classical Tradition, Am. Boccaccio Assn. (v.p. 1982-83), Am. Assn. Italian Studies, Nat. Assn. Scholars. Office: Mt Holyoke Coll Dept Spanish Italian South Hadley MA 01075

MAZZOCCO, GAIL O'SULLIVAN, nursing educator; b. Bklyn., Aug. 5, 1942; d. John F. and Marie A. (Saleski) O'S.; m. Victor E. Mazzocco, Jan. 5, 1973; children: Victor, Diane, Denise, Michelle, Mark. Diploma, Mass. Gen. Hosp., 1963; BSN, U. Md., 1972, MS, 1974, EdD, 1988. Staff nurse Meml. Hosp., Cumberland, Md., 1964-67; area supr. Meml. Hosp., Cumberland, 1967-69; clin. specialist Sacred Heart Hosp., Cumberland, 1974-75; asst. prof. U. Md. Sch. Nursing, 1977—, acting chair RN to BSN program/acting dir. statewide program, 1994-95; coord. We. Md. Outreach Sites, 1995—; bd. dirs., pres. Allegany Cmty. Coll. Found. Contbr. chpt. to book. Mem. Md. Nurses Assn. (Dist. 1 Nurse of Yr. 1986, Nurse Educator of Yr. 1991), Nat. League for Nursing, Sigma Theta Tau, Phi Kappa Pi (Faculty Mentor award 1994). Home: 9 Warfield Pl Cumberland MD 21502-7433

MAZZOLA, ANTHONY THOMAS, editor, art consultant, designer, writer; b. Passaic, N.J., June 13, 1923; s. Thomas and Jennie (Failla) M.; m. Michele Morgan, Nov. 18, 1967; children: Anthony Thomas II, Marc Eden, Alisa Morgan. Grad., Cooper Union Art Sch., N.Y.C., 1948. Art dir. Street & Smith Publs., N.Y.C., 1948, Town and Country mag. (pub. by Hearst Corp.), N.Y.C., 1948-65; editor-in-chief Town and Country mag. (pub. by Hearst Corp.), 1965-72, Harpers Bazaar, 1972-92; pres. Anthony Mazzola Design Corp., N.Y.C., 1963—; creative cons. Hearst Mags., 1992—; editorial dir. 125 Great Moments of Harper's Bazaar, 1991-94, Town & Country 150th Anniversary, 1994—; cons. designer United Nations Childrens' Fund, Assn. Jr. Leagues Am., Columbia Pictures Corp., Sells Spltys., Gen. Foods, Paramount Pictures, Princess Marcella Borghese, Inc., Huntington Hartford, Ltd., N.Y. World's Fair, 1965. Exhibited, Art Dirs. Club. N.Y., ann. exhbns., 1948—. Served with AUS, 1943-46. Decorated Bronze Star, Knight Officer of Order of Merit Italy; recipient Cert. of Merit awards N.Y. Art Dirs. Club; medal Art Dirs. Club N.Y.C., 1955. Office: Town & Country 150th Anniversary 1790 Broadway New York NY 10019-1412

MAZZOLA, CLAUDE JOSEPH, physicist, small business owner; b. Newton, Mass., May 24, 1936; s. Gradinola and Anne (Cicconi) M.; m. Helen Alamanos, July 25, 1965; children: Peppina, Jean-Claude. BS in Physics, Boston Coll., 1959; postgrad. in Physics, MIT, 1961-62. Jr. engr. Lab. for Electronics, Boston, 1959-61; scientist AVCO R&D, Wilmington, Mass., 1961-62; engr. Space Scis., Waltham, Mass., 1962-63, BBN, Cambridge, Mass., 1963-72; staff engr. Edo, College Point, N.Y., 1972-82; engr. Sperry, Great Neck, N.Y., 1982-89; sole proprietor Namlak, Mamaroneck, N.Y., 1989—. Author: Active Sound Absorption, 1993; patentee Magnetic Storage Device (floppy disc), 1963; developer sound absorption system for aircraft cabins; contbr. articles to profl. jours., papers to sci. confs. and meetings. Mem. IEEE. Republican. Roman Catholic. Avocations: jogging, skiing, sailing, foreign travel. Home: 106 Lawn Ter Mamaroneck NY 10543-4023 Office: Namlak PO Box 804 Mamaroneck NY 10543-0804

MAZZOLA, JOHN WILLIAM, former performing arts center executive, consultant; b. Bayonne, N.J., Jan. 20, 1928; s. Roy Stephen and Eleanor Burnett (Davis) M.; m. Sylvia Drulie, Mar. 7, 1959; children: Alison, Amy. AB, Tufts U., 1949; LLD, Fordham U., 1952. Bar: N.Y. 1956. Mem. firm Milbank, Tweed, Hadley & McCloy, N.Y.C., 1952-64; sec., exec. v.p. Lincoln Center for Performing Arts, N.Y.C., 1964-68; gen. mgr., chief exec. officer Lincoln Center for Performing Arts, 1969-70, mng. dir., chief exec. officer, 1970-77, pres., chief exec. officer, 1977-84; cons. performing arts ctrs. in U.S. and abroad, also motion pictures, non-profit orgns. Bd. dirs. various charitable orgns.; mem. adv. bd. U. S.C. Koger Arts Ctr. With CIC, U.S. Army, 1953-55. Decorated cavaliere ufficiale Ordine al Merito della Repubblica Italiana; Ordre des Arts et des Lettres France; Benjamin Franklin fellow Royal Soc. Arts. Mem. Watch Hill Yacht Club, Misquamicut Club (R.I.). Episcopalian. Home: 12 Beekman Pl New York NY 10022-8059

MAZZONE, A. DAVID, federal judge; b. Everett, Mass., June 3, 1928; s. A. Marino and Philomena M.; m. Eleanor G. Stewart, May 10, 1951; children: Margaret Clark, Andrew David, John Stewart, Jan Eleanor, Martha Ann, Robert Joseph, Carolyn Cook. B.A., Harvard U., 1950; J.D., DePaul U., 1957. Bar: Ill. 1957, Mass. 1959, U.S. Supreme Ct. 1964. Asst. dist. atty. Middlesex County, Mass., 1961; asst. U.S. atty. Mass., 1961-65; partner firm Moulton, Looney & Mazzone, Boston, 1965-75; asso. justice Superior Ct., Boston, 1975-78; U.S. dist. judge, now sr. judge Boston, 1978—. Served with U.S. Army, 1951-52. Mem. ABA, Mass. Trial Lawyers Assn., Am. Law Inst., Mass. Bar Assn., Boston Bar Assn., Middlesex Bar Assn., Fed. Bar Assn. Democrat. Roman Catholic. Office: US Dist Ct 90 Devonshire St Rm 2001 Boston MA 02109-4501*

MAZZUCELLI, COLETTE GRACE CELIA, author, university administrator, educator; b. Bklyn., Nov. 26, 1962; d. Silvio Anthony and Adeline Marie (De Ponte) M. BA, U. Scranton, 1983; MA in Law and Diplomacy, Fletcher Sch. Law & Diplomacy, 1987; PhD, Georgetown U., 1996. Instr. Georgetown U., Washington, 1990-96; rsch. fellow Inst. fuer Europaeische Politik, Deutsche Gesellschaft fuer Auswaertige Politik, Bonn, Deutsch-Franzoesisches Inst., Ludwigsburg; asst. ratification process Treaty European Union German Fgn. Minstry, Maastricht; cons. Jean Monnet Coun., Washington, 1994—; Civic Edn. Project lectr. Budapest Inst. Grad. Internat. and Diplomatic Studies, 1995—; lectr. U.S. Info. Svc. Speakers Program in Europe, 1994—; active IPSA Rsch. Com. on European Unification; internat. program dir. Budapest Inst. Grad. Internat. and Diplomatic Studies; instr. in-house tng. in negotiations Hungarian Fgn. Ministry, Hungarian Del. Ministry Def. to NATO Accession Talks. Author: France and Germany at Maastricht Politics and Negotiations to Create the European Union, 1997; asst. editor: The Evolution of an International Actor: Western Europe's New Assertiveness, 1990; author: Monnet Case Studies in European Affairs, 1995; contbr.: Dimensions of German Unification, 1994. Swiss Univ. grantee, 1984-85; Pi Gamma Mu scholar, 1985, Rotary grad. scholar, 1987-88, Fulbright scholar, 1991; Jean Monnet Coun. dissertation fellow, 1991, European Commn. fellow, 1992, Robert Bosch Found. fellow, 1992-93. Mem. Am. Polit. Sci. Assn., Civic Edn. Project Alumni Assn. (co-founder 1997), Deutsche Atlantische Gesellschaft, European Cmty. Studies Assn., Robert Bosch Found. Alumni Assn. (exec. com. 1994-96), The Fletcher Club of N.Y. (bd. dirs.), Alpha Sigma Nu (student pres. 1984), Pi Gamm Mu (chpt. sec. 1982-84, Frank C. Brown scholarship medal 1984), Phi Sigma Tau (founder Scranton chpt.), Phi Alpha Theta, Pi Sigma Alpha, Alpha Mu Gamma, Delta Tau Kappa. Avocations: chess, swimming, karate, poetry writing. Home: 1864 74th St Brooklyn NY 11204-5752 Office: Budapest Inst Grad Internat and Diplomatic Studies, Kçniszi út. 1-7, 1092 Budapest Hungary

MCADAM, PAUL EDWARD, library administrator; b. Balt., Jan. 30, 1934; s. Joseph Francis Jr. and Irene Cecile (Heineck) McA. BA in Romance Langs., Johns Hopkins U., 1955, MA, 1956; MLS, Drexel U., 1970. Libr. Free Libr. Phila., 1969-81; br. mgr. Phila. City. Inst. Libr., 1974-81; dir. Am. Libr., Paris, France, 1981-85; libr. collection devel., libr. tech. svcs. Catonsville (Md.) C.C., 1986-89; assoc. v.p. learning resources Carroll C.C., Westminster, Md., 1989—; mem. adv. bd. Coop. Librs. Ctrl. Md., Annapolis, 1992-96, State Libr. Resource Ctr., Balt., 1994-95, Renew, 1995—; del. Internat. Fedn. Libr. Assns., 1993, 95. Vol. MPT, Walters Art Gallery, Md. Film Arts Festival. 1st lt. U.S. Army, 1956-58. Mem. ALA (mem. membership com. 1996—), Coll. Air Consortium, Congress Resource Dirs., Md. Libr. Assn. (membership chair 1993-96, awards chair 1996-97), Consortium Md. C.C. Libr. Dirs. (treas. 1993—), Beta Phi Mu (Sigma chpt.). Democrat. Home: 524 Academy Rd Baltimore MD 21228-1814 Office: Carroll Cmty Coll 1601 Washington Rd Westminster MD 21157-6944

MCADAM, WILL, electronics consultant; b. Wheeling, W.Va., Oct. 22, 1921; s. Will and Elizabeth Margaret (Wickham) McA.; m. Evelyn Virginia Warren, Sept. 22, 1945; children: Elizabeth Ruth, Margaret Evelyn. BSEE, Case Inst. Tech., 1942; MSEE, U. Pa., 1959. Registered control engr., Calif. Rsch. technologist Leeds & Northrup Co., Phila., 1945-57; head elec. sect. R&D dept. Leeds & Northrup Co., North Wales, Pa., 1957-68, assoc. dir. rsch. ops., 1968-75, mgr. devel. and engring. adv. devel., 1977-79, prin. scientist rsch. dept., 1979-82, ret., 1982; cons. in electronics, 1982—. Contbr. articles to profl. jours., chpts. to handbooks; 30 patents in field. 1st lt. AUS, 1942-45, ETO. Decorated Bronze Star. Fellow IEEE (life; chmn. subcom. on elec. and high frequency measurements 1957-59, com. indsl. electronic and control instruments 1961-65, Prize Paper award 1958), Eta Kappa Nu, Tau Beta Pi. Republican. Presbyterian. Avocations: amateur radio, woodworking/cabinetmaking, hiking, bicycling. Home: PO Box 470 Worcester PA 19490-0470

MCADAMS, HERBERT HALL, II, banker; b. Jonesboro, Ark., June 6, 1915; s. Herbert Hall I and Stella (Patrick) McA.; children by previous marriage: Judith (Mrs. Walter A. DeRoeck), Sandra (Mrs. Robert C. Connor), Herbert Hall III, Penny (Mrs. Tim Hodges); m. Shelia Wallace, Nov. 27, 1970; children: Nicole Patrick., Kara (Mrs. John C.) Kratzer, Anne (Mrs. Randy) Bynum. BS, Northwestern U., Evanston, Ill., 1937; postgrad., Harvard U., 1937-38, Loyola U., Chgo., 1938-39; JD with honors, U. Ark., 1940; LLD (hon.), Ark. State U., 1984. Bar: Ark. 1940, U.S. Dist. Ct. Ark., U.S. Supreme Ct. 1944, U.S. Ct. Appeals (8th cir.) 1944, U.S. Ct. Claims 1944,. Chmn. bd., CEO Citizens Bank and Citizens Bancshares Corp., Jonesboro, 1958-95, Union Nat. Bank, Little Rock, 1970-93, Union Ark. Corp., 1980-93; bd. dirs. Worthen Bank Corp., 1993-95; McAdams-Frierson chair bank mgmt. Ark. State U., 1987; bd. dirs. 1st Ark. Devel. Fin. Corp., Systematics, Inc. Pres. Jonesboro Sch. Dist., 1948-50, Bapt. Med. Ctr. Sys. Real Estate Corp., 1977—; state chmn. Citizen's Com. on Edn., 1950; mem. Ark. Indsl. Devel. Commn., 1965-73, chmn., 1967-72; trustee Ark. Children's Hosp., 1972-75, Bapt. Med. Ctr. Sys., 1975-77, Bapt. Found., 1975; bd. govs. Ark. State Fair and Livestock Show Assn., 1976—; mem. Bapt. Med. Ctr. Sys. Corp. Fifty for Future; founder, chmn. bd. govs. Ark. State U. Found.; bd. dirs. Nat. Children's Eye Care Found., 1987—, numerous others. Served USN. Decorated Purple Heart; recipient Rector Meml. award Fifty for the Future, 1987; named Outstanding Alumnus U. Ark., 1984. Mem. ABA (uniform laws com. 1961-66, mem. tax sect. 1954—), Ark. Bar Assn., Ark. Coun. Econ. Edn., Craighead (Ark.) County Bar Assn. (past pres.), Pulaski (Ark.) County Bar Assn., Greater Little Rock C.of C. (dir.), Sales and Mktg. Execs. (top mgmt. honoree 1972), Sigma Nu. Methodist. Clubs: Country of Little Rock, Capital, Little Rock. Lodge: Rotary. Home: 47 Edgehill Rd Little Rock AR 72207-5461 Office: Union Nat Bldg 124 W Capitol Ave Ste 1700 Little Rock AR 72201-3737

MCADAMS, JAMES GLEN (), federal official. BA in Psychology, Davidson Coll., 1970; JD cum laude, U. Miami, 1981. Asst. U.S. atty. U.S. Attys. Office (so. dist.) Fla., Miami, 1982-88, chief narcotivs divsn., 1989-92, acting U.S. atty., 1992, mng. asst. U.S. atty., 1992-94; sr. litigation counsel U.S. Attys. Office (so. dist.) Fla., 1994-95; counsel for intelligence policy Dept. Justice, Washington, 1995—. Office: US Dept Justice Office Intelligence Policy 10th & Pennsylvania Ave NW Washington DC 20530

MCADAMS, JOHN P., lawyer; b. Phila., June 5, 1949; s. Eugene P. and Mary (Miller) McA.; m. Anne Christina Connelly, Sept. 5, 1970; children: Emily Lane, Anne Connelly. BA, U. N.C., 1971; JD, Wake Forest U., 1976. Bar: Fla. 1976, N.C. 1976, U.S. Dist. Ct. (mid. dist.) Fla. 1977. Assoc. Carlton, Fields, Ward, Emmanuel, Smith & Cutler, Tampa, Fla., 1976-82, ptnr., 1982—. Contbg. editor: The Developing Labor Law, 1983, Employee Duty of Loyalty, 1995; contbr. articles to profl. jours. Pres. Hillsborough Community Mental Health Ctr., Tampa, 1983; trustee City of Temple Ter. (Fla.) Pension Plan, 1985-89; pres. Hyde Park Preservation, Inc., Tampa, 1993; bd. dirs. Tampa Lighthouse for the Blind, 1997. Mem. ABA, ABA Equal Rights & Responsibilities Com., Fla. Bar Assn. (exec. coun. labor sect. 1987-89). Republican. Episcopalian. Home: 820 S Delaware Ave Tampa FL 33606-2915 Office: Carlton Fields PO Box 3239 Tampa FL 33601-3239

MCAFEE, JOHN GILMOUR, nuclear medicine physician; b. Toronto, Ontario, Can., June 11, 1926; came to U.S., 1952; s. Robert Duncan and Susan Jane (Damery) McA.; m. Joan Weber, Feb. 11, 1952 (dec. 1978); children: Paul Clifton, Carol Joan, David Robert. MD, U. Toronto, 1948. Rotating intern Victoria Hosp., London, Ont., Can., 1948-49; resident in radiology Victoria Hosp., London, Ont., 1950-51; resident in internal medicine Westminster Hosp., London, 1949-50; resident in radiology Johns Hopkins Hosp., Balt., 1951-52, fellow, 1952-53; instr. radiology Johns Hopkins Sch. Medicine, Balt., 1953-55, asst. prof. radiology, 1955-58, assoc. prof. radiology, 1958-65; prof., chmn. radiology SUNY Health Sci. Ctr., Syracuse, 1965-73, dir. div. nuclear medicine, 1973-78, dir. div. radiological scis., 1978-90; prof. div. nuclear medicine George Washington U. Med. Ctr., Washington, 1990-92; sect. chief, dept. nuclear medicine Clin. Ctr., NIH, Bethesda, Md., 1992-95; cons. in nuclear medicine, 1995—; chmn. radiology tng. com. NIH, Bethesda, Md., 1970-73; bd. dirs. Am. Bd. Nuclear Medicine, L.A., 1973-80; cons. editl. bd. Jour. Nuclear Medicine, N.Y.C., 1975—; chmn. subcom. nuclear medicine DOE, Gaithersburg, Md., 1987-88; trustee Rsch. and Edn. Fund, 1990-96; mem. radiopharms. adv. bd. U.S. Pharmacopeial Conv., 1990-95. Author, editor: (with others) Differential Diagnosis in Nuclear Medicine, 1984; assoc. editor: Year Book of Nuclear Medicine, 1993-95; contbr. articles to profl. jours. NIH grantee, 1961-92. Fellow Royal Coll. Physicians, Am. Coll. Nuclear Physicians; mem. Soc. Nuclear Medicine (Paul C. Aebersold award 1979, Georg Charles De Hevesy Nuclear Medicine Pioneer award 1989), Radiol. Soc. N.Am., Am. Roentgen Ray Soc., Assn. Univ. Radiologists. Avocations: sailing, jazz, organ, yachting, swimming. Home: 3203 Winnett Rd Bethesda MD 20815-3201

MC AFEE, WILLIAM, government official; b. Port Royal, Jan. 25, 1910; s. French and Willietta (Anderson) McA. B.A., Coll. of Wooster, 1932; M.A. in Am. History, Pa. State U., 1941; student, Oxford, Eng., summer 1937. Wooster in India rep. on faculty Ewing Christian Coll., Allahabad, India, 1932-35; tchr. pub. high schs. and prep. sch. Pa., 1935-42; joined State Dept., 1946; country specialist (Office Chinese Affairs), 1946-50; coordinator current intelligence (Bur. Intelligence and Research), 1950-56, spl. asst. to dir., 1956-60, dir. ops. staff, 1960-66, asst. dep. dir. coordination, 1966-72, dep. dir. coordination, 1972-80, dep. asst. sec. intelligence coordination, 1980—; dir. (Office of Intelligence Liaison), 1981-86, ret.; adviser Griffin Econ. Aid Mission to S.E. Asia, 1950. Served to lt. col. AUS, 1942-46, CBI. Decorated Legion of Merit; Order Brit. Empire; Precious Tripod Chinese Nationalist Govt.; recipient Superior Honor award State Dept., 1964, Disting. Honor award, 1980. Mem. Am. Fgn. Service Assn., Delta Sigma Rho. Home: 4433 Brandywine St NW Washington DC 20016-4419

MCAHREN, ROBERT WILLARD, history educator; b. Sioux City, Iowa, Dec. 3, 1935; s. Willard Calvin and Winifred Mae (Small) McA. B.A., So. Meth. U., 1958; Ph.D., U. Tex.-Austin, 1967. Instr. history Washington & Lee U., Lexington, Va., 1966-67, asst. prof. history, 1967-70, assoc. prof. history, 1970-75, prof. history, 1975—, asst. dean coll., 1971-73, assoc. dean coll., 1973-77, head dept. history, 1988—. Editor (with David D. Van Tassel) document collection with interpretive introduction; European Origins of American Thought, 1969. Mem. Phi Beta Kappa. Democrat. Avocations: orchid growing; model railroading. Office: Washington and Lee U Dept Of History Lexington VA 24450

MC ALEECE, DONALD JOHN, mechanical engineering educator; b. Detroit, May 26, 1918; s. Joseph Patrick and Kathryn (DeLeeuw) McA.; m. Margaret Ann Mull, Nov. 25, 1954; children: Stephen, Donald, Michele Denise. Diploma, machinist-toolmaker apprentice program, Gen. Electric Co., 1940; BS, Purdue U., 1952; MA, Ball State U., 1968; postgrad., U. S.C., 1990, 91. With Gen. Electric Co., Fort Wayne, Ind., 1936-66; mem. faculty Purdue U., Ft. Wayne campus, 1966-88, prof. mech. engring. tech., 1966-88, prof. emeritus, 1988—; tchr. Ind. U.-Purdue U., Fort Wayne, Ind. Vocation Tech. Coll., Fort Wayne, fall 1988; vis. prof. U. Ark., Little Rock, 1989, Trident Tech. Coll., Charleston, S.C., 1989—; assisted devel. job tng. program and minority intro. to engring. and tech. ind. U.-Purdue U., Ft. Wayne, summer 1986, 87; design engr., advanced safety rsch. Ford Motor Co., Dearborn, Mich., 1972; Job placement cons. Outreach office Nat. Alliance Businessmen, Fort Wayne, 1968; indsl. engr. cons. Am. Hoist & Derric Co., Ft. Wayne, 1969; cons. Franklin Electric Co., 1970, Wayne Home Equipment divsn. Scott & Fetzer, 1979; intern Harvester Co., 1977; engring. cons. Dana Corp., Ft. Wayne, 1984; mem. tech. Accreditation Commn., Accreditation Bd. Engring. and Tech., 1980-82, program evaluator, 1988; statis. process control cons. Gen. Motors Corp., Ft. Wayne, 1986. Mem. editorial cons. bd. Indsl. Press, Inc., 1982-84. Scout master, com. Boy Scouts Am. With AUS, 1946-47. Ednl. Profl. Devel. Act grantee, 1971; Soc. Mfg. Engrs. grantee, 1982; named Eagle Scout Boy Scouts Am. Mem. Am. Soc. Engring. Edn., Am. Tech. Edn. Assn., Soc. Auto Engrs., Inc. (faculty advisor student br. Trident Coll. 1991-97, Ind. U.-Purdue br. 1971-88, elec. vehicle com. 1980-95, svc. award 1982, Ralph R. Teetor award 1972, outstanding faculty adv. svc. award 1974), Soc. Am. Mil. Engrs., ASME (life, chmn. program com. 1971-75), ASHRAE (nat. engring. coun. prof. devel. accreditation team), S.C. Tech. Edn. Assn. Robotics Internat. of Soc. Mfg. Engrs. (life cert.), GE Co. Quarter Century Club (Ft. Wayne), GE Apprentice Alumni Assn., Eagle Scout Assn. (scoutmaster, com. BSA 1968-72), Pi Tau Sigma. Baptist (deacon 1968-72). Lodges: Masons, Shriners. Home: Apt 2B 7910 Crossroads Dr North Charleston SC 19406-9438

MCALEER, JOHN JOSEPH, English literature educator; b. Cambridge, Mass., Aug. 29, 1923; s. Stephen Ambrose and Helen Louise (Collins) McA.; m. Ruth Ann Delaney, Dec. 28, 1957; children: Mary Alycia, Saragh Delaney, Seana Caithlin, John Joseph, Paul Bernard, Andrew Stephen. AB, Boston Coll., 1947, MA, 1949; PhD, Harvard U., 1955. Teaching fellow Boston Coll., 1947-48, English and Latin instr., 1948-50; Dexter fellow in Europe Harvard U., 1952, teaching fellow gen. edn., 1953-55; from asst. prof. to prof. Boston Coll., 1955—; vis. fellow Durham (Eng.) U., 1988-89. Author: Ballads and Songs Loyal to the Hanoverian Succession, 1962, Theodore Dreiser: A Biography, 1968, Artist and Citizen Thoreau, 1971, (with M. Tjader) Notes on Life: The Philosophical Writings of Theodore Dreiser, 1974, Rex Stout: A Biography, 1977, Justice Ends at Home: The Early Crime Fiction of Rex Stout, 1977, (with others) Rex Stout: An Annotated Primary and Secondary Bibliography, 1980, (with Billy Dickson) Unit Pride, 1981, Royal Decree: Conservations with Rex Stout, 1983, Ralph Waldo Emerson: Days of Encounter, 1984, Queens Counsel: Conversations with Ruth Stout, 1986, Coign of Vantage, 1988; editor-in-chief: Rex Stout Jour., 1979—, Thorndyke File, 1981-95, Best Sellers, 1965-85, Shakespeare newsletter, 1959-71, Armchair Detective, 1978-82; cons. editor: Dreiser Studies, 1971—. Mem. adv. bd. Walden Woods Project, 1990—, Parents Choice, 1980—. Sgt. U.S. Army, 1942-46. Recipient Cath. Press Assn. award, 1969, New Eng. Hist. Soc. award, 1985, Humanities award Boston Coll. Alumni Assn., 1991, Ignatian medal Boston Coll., 1995; permanent mem. Soc. of Fellows, Durham (Eng.) U., 1988—. Mem. Thoreau Soc. (pres., dir. 1971—), Mystery Writers Am. (v.p., dir. 1979-89, Edgar Allan Poe award 1978), R. Austen Freeman Soc. (pres. 1981—), Edith Wharton Soc., Jane Austen Soc. (Burke award 1991), Internat. Dreiser Soc. (founding mem. 1991—), Trollope Soc., Boston Authors Club (pres., dir. 1982-96), Tavern Club (Boston), Baker St. Irregulars, Patrick O'Brian Soc. (pres. 1995—). Democrat. Roman Catholic. Avocations: swimming, bibliopoly, genealogy, philately, gardening. Home: 121 Follen Rd Lexington MA 02173-5942 Office: Boston Coll Dept English McGuinn 530 Chestnut Hill MA 02167

MCALEER, WILLIAM HARRISON, software venture capitalist; b. Pitts., Feb. 14, 1951; s. William Kearns and Helen (Harrison) McA.; m. Colleen

McGinn, Aug. 9, 1975; children: William F., Lindsay J. BS, Cornell U., 1973, MBA, 1975. CPA, Wash. Sr. acct. KPMG-Peat Marwick, Seattle, 1975-78; v.p., controller Westin Hotels, Seattle, 1978-87; v.p. finance, CFO Ecova Corp., Seattle, 1987-88; v.p. fin., CFO, sec. Aldus Corp., Seattle, 1988-95; mng. dir. Voyager Capital, Seattle, 1995—; bd. dirs. Apex PC Solutions, Truevision Corp., Four Gen Corp., Primus Comm. Corp. Pres., dir. Seattle Jr. C. of C., 1977-82; bd. dirs. Big Bros. King County, Seattle, 1994—. Mem. Fin. Execs. Ins., Software Pubs. Assn., Wash. Software Assn., Wash. Soc. CPAs, Cornell Alumni Club, Sand Point Country Club. Avocations: hiking, travel, golfing, boating, gardening. Home: 3530 W Laurelhurst Dr NE Seattle WA 98105-5358 Office: Voyager Capital 10900 NE 4th St Ste 2300 Bellevue WA 98004-5841

MCALHANY, TONI ANNE, lawyer; b. Decatur, Ind., May 1, 1951; d. Robert Keith and Evelyn L. (Fisher) McA. BA, Ind. U., 1973; JD, Valparaiso U., 1976. Bar: Mich. 1976, Ind. 1982, Ill. 1986, U.S. Dist. Ct. (no. dist.) Ind. 1989. Asst. prosecutor Ottawa County Prosecutor's Office, Grand Haven, Mich., 1976-81; assoc. Hann, Doss & Persinger, Holland, Mich., 1981-82, Romero & Thonert, Auburn, Ind., 1982-85; ptnr. Dahlgren & McAlhany, Berwyn, Ill., 1985-88, Colbeck, McAlhany & Stewart, Angola, Ind. & Coldwater, Mich., 1988—; atty. Angola Housing Authority, 1989—. Bd. dirs. Child and Family Svcs., Ft. Wayne, Ind., 1983, Fillmore Ctr., Berwyn, 1986-88, Altrusa, Coldwater, 1989-92. Mem. ATLA, State Bar Mich., State Bar Ind., State Bar Ill., Branch County Bar Assn., Steuben County Bar Assn. Avocations: traveling, horseback riding. Office: Colbeck McAlhany & Stewart 215 W Maumee St Angola IN 46703-1424

MC ALISTER, LINDA LOPEZ, educator, philosopher; b. Long Beach, Calif., Oct. 10, 1939; d. Manuel Lee and Elena Maria (Sherwood) McAlister; AB, Barnard Coll., 1962; postgrad. Coll. City N.Y., 1963-64; PhD, Cornell U., 1969. Mem. faculty, adminstr. Bklyn. Coll., 1968-77, CUNY. Grad. Center, 1970-77; prof. humanities, dean campus Imperial Valley campus San Diego State U., 1977-82; prof. philosophy, campus dean U. South Fla., Ft. Myers, 1982-85; spl. asst. to vice chancellor for acad. programs State Univ. System Fla., 1985-87; prof. Women's Studies and Philosophy U. South Fla., Tampa, 1987—, chair women's studies, 1996—; Fla. state coordinator Am. Council Edn. Nat. Identification Project, 1983-86. Franz Brentano Found. grantee, 1968-72; Fulbright-Hays research grantee, 1973-74. Mem. Am. Philos. Assn., Nat. Women's Studies Assn., Soc. Women in Philosophy, Internat. Assn. von Philosophinnen (founding). Author: The Development of Franz Brentano's Ethics, 1982; gen. editor Hypatia: A Journal of Feminist Philosophy, 1990—; editor Hypatia's Daughters: 1500 Years of Women Philsophers, 1996; contbr. articles to profl. jours. Editor and translator: Psychology From an Empirical Standpoint (Franz Brentano), 1973; Sensory and Noetic Consciousness (Franz Brentano), 1980; editor: The Philosophy of Brentano, 1976; translator: On Colour (Ludwig Wittgenstein), 1977, SWIP-L Electronic Mail Forum for Feminist Philosophy, 1992—, Film Criticism: Radio, Print and Electronic Media, 1990—. Office: U South Fla HMS 413 4202 E Fowler Ave Tampa FL 33620-9900

MCALISTER, MICHAEL HILLIS, architect; b. Bakersfield, Calif., May 22, 1945; s. Doyle R. and Mary E. McAlister. AA, Bakersfield Coll., 1967; BArch, Calif. Polytech. U., 1971. Planning technition Bakersfield City Hall, 1963; carpenter Del Webb Corp., Kern City, Calif., 1964; architectural draftsman Goss & Choy Architects, Bakersfield, 1965-67; architect, v.p. D.G.C. & Assocs., Bakersfield, 1971-80; dir. architecture, v.p. N.B.A. & Assocs., Architects, Bakersfield, 1980-83; architect, pres. Michael H. McAlister, A.I.A., Bakersfield, 1983—; nepthrology design cons. for various treatment groups and hosps., 1987—. Commr., architectural advisor Historic Preservation Commn., Bakersfield, 1986-87; bd. dirs. Camp Fire Coun., Kern County, Calif., 1980-84. Recipient Architectural Pub. Bldg. Hist. award Beautiful Bakersfield Com., City of Bakersfield's City Coun. and Hist. Preservation Commn., 1985, 87, Exterior Environ. Design Excellence Bakersfield C. of C., 1988, Comml. Design Excellence award, 1984, Design Excellence and Beautification award City of Taft, Calif., 1989, Design Excellence award State of Nev., 1992. Mem. AIA (Calif. Coun., Golden Empire chpt.). Avocations: horseback riding, art and sculpture. Office: 5030 Office Park Dr Ste B Bakersfield CA 93309-0612

MCALISTER, ROBERT BEATON, lawyer; b. N.Y.C., Oct. 5, 1932; s. Richard Charles and Martha Olive (Weisenbarger) McA.; widowed; children: Michael, Peter, Betsy. AB, Kenyon Coll., 1954; JD, U. Mich., 1957. Ptnr. Alexander, Ebinger, Fisher, McAlister & Lawrence, Columbus, Ohio, 1957-85; supt. Ohio Div. Savs. & Loan Assns., Columbus, 1985; ptnr. Baker & Hostetler, Columbus, 1985—, chmn. litigation dept., 1988-93. Exec. com. mem. Ohio Dem. Party, Columbus, 1967-74; active Dem. Nat. Com., Washington, 1972-76; counsel Gov. Richard F. Celeste, Columbus, 1982-90, Senator John Glenn, Washington, 1986-94. With USAF, 1968-64. Fellow Ohio Bar Found., Columbus Bar Found.; mem. Capital Club (Columbus). Democrat. Episcopalian. Home: 5571 Sutterton Ln Westerville OH 43081-5228 Office: Baker & Hostetler 65 E State St Columbus OH 43215-4213

MCALLISTER, CHARLES JOHN, nephrologist, medical administrator; b. Bklyn., Dec. 1, 1947; s. John Anthony and Lillian Marceline McAllister; m. Diane Dolores, Aug. 22, 1970; children: Jill, Kelly, Myles. BS magna cum laude, St. Francis Coll., 1969; MD with honors, SUNY, Buffalo, 1973. Pres. Nephrology Assocs., Clearwater, Fla., 1978—; v.p. med. affairs Vivra Renal Care, Laguna Hills, Calif., 1992—; chief of medicine Morton Plant Hosp., Clearwater, 1991-92; v.p. med. affairs Vivra Renal Care; med. dir. VRC, Clearwater, Palm Harbor. Contbr. articles to sci. and profl. jours. Comdr. USNR, 1981-90. Republican. Roman Catholic. Avocation: coaching soccer. Home: 1001 S Keene Rd Clearwater FL 34616-4633 Office: Nephroogy Assocs 1124 Lakeview Rd Clearwater FL 33756-3524

MCALLISTER, EDWARD WILLIAM CHARLES, educator; b. Bronx, May 3, 1941; s. Charles Irving and Elaine Madeline (Yates) McA.; m. Shirley Ann Burlingame, Aug. 14, 1965; children: Kathleen, Jonathan, E. Bruce, Brian. BS, SUNY, Albany, 1963, MS, 1965, PhD, 1971. Tchr. Voorheesville (N.Y.) High Sch., 1963-64; instr. Jr. Coll. Albany, 1965-66; prof. Russell Sage Coll., Troy, N.Y., 1967—; exec. dir. Capital Area Chriatian Counseling Svc., Inc., Delmar, N.Y., 1976-94. Contbr. articles to profl. jours. Republican. Evangelical. Office: Russell Sage Coll Troy NY 12180

MCALLISTER, (RONALD) ERIC, pharmaceutical executive, physician; b. Halifax, N.S., Can., Apr. 15, 1942; s. (James) Ronald and Barbara Hope (Curry) McA.; m. Carol M. Browne, Feb. 8, 1967 (div. July 1981); children: Natasha Naomi, Neil Eric; m. Suzanne Yee, Apr. 8, 1989; 1 child, Petra Camille Mei-Fong. BSc with honors, Dalhousie U., Halifax, 1962, MSc, 1963, MD, 1976; DPhil, Oxford (Eng.) U., 1967. Asst. prof. Dalhousie U., 1968-76; intern Sunnybrook Med. Ctr. U. Toronto, Can., 1976-77; med. practitioner Murakami Clinic, Hope, B.C., Can., 1977-78; physician in pvt. practice San Leandro, Calif., 1978-84; assoc. med. dir. Syntex Corp., Palo Alto, Calif., 1984-87; med. dir. G.D. Searle & Co., Skokie, Ill., 1987-89; exec. med. dir. Bristol-Myers Squibb Co., Princeton, N.J., 1989-90; v.p. clin. affairs Cholestech Corp., Hayward, Calif., 1990-92; pvt. practice medicine, prin. investigator Ukiah, Calif., 1992—; clin. assoc. divsn. family practice U. Calif., San Francisco, 1986-87. Contbr. articles to profl. jours. Rhodes scholar, 1963-65. Avocations: back-country skiing and hiking, photography, personal computers, travel. Home: 1225 Vista Verde Rd Ukiah CA 95482-7554 Office: 1165 S Dora St E-1 Ukiah CA 95482-6353

MC ALLISTER, GERALD NICHOLAS, retired bishop, clergyman; b. San Antonio, Feb. 23, 1923; s. Walter Williams and Leonora Elizabeth (Alexander) McA.; m. Helen Earle Black, Oct. 2, 1953; children—Michael Lee, David Alexander, Stephen Williams, Elizabeth. Student, U. Tex., 1939-42, Va. Theol. Sem., 1948-51; D.D. (hon.), Va. Theol. Sem., 1977. Rancher, 1946-48; ordained deacon Episcopal Ch., 1953, priest, 1954; deacon, priest Ch. of Epiphany, Raymondville, Ch. of Incarnation, Corpus Christi, St. Francis Ch., Victoria, all Tex., 1951-63; 1st canon Diocese of W. Tex., 1963-70; rector St. David's Ch., San Antonio, 1970-76; consecrated Episcopal bishop of Okla., Oklahoma City, 1977-89, ret., 1989; bishop-in-residence Episcopal Theol. Sem., Austin, Tex., 1990-93; trustee Episcopal Theol. Sem. of S.W., 1961—, adv. bd., 1974—; mem. Case Commn. Bd. for Theol. Edn., 1981-82; pres. Tex. Council Chs., 1966-68, Okla. Conf. Chs., 1980-83; bd. dirs. Presiding Bishop's Fund for World Relief, 1972-77, Ch. Hist. Soc., 1976—; chmn. Nat. and World Mission Program Group, 1973-76; mem. Structure of Ch. Standing Commn., 1979, mem. standing com. on Stewardship/Devel., 1979-85; founder Chaplaincy Program, Bexar County Jail, 1968; mem. governing bd. nat. council Ch. of Christ, 1982-85; chmn. standing commn. on stewardship Episcopal Ch., 1983-85; v.p., trustee The Episc., Episc. Theol. Sem. of Soutwest, 1987—, chmn. bd. trustees, 1993—. Author: What We Learned from What You Said, 1973, This Fragile Earth Our Island Home, 1980. Bd. dirs. Econ. Opportunity Devel. Corp., San Antonio, 1968-69; mem. exec. com. United Way, 1968-70, vice-chmn., 1970. Served with U.S. Mcht. Marines, 1942; to 1st lt. USAAF, 1942-45. Recipient Agudas Achim Brotherhood award, 1968. Address: 507 Bluffestates San Antonio TX 78216-7930

MCALLISTER, KENNETH WAYNE, lawyer; b. High Point, N.C., Jan. 3, 1949; s. John Calhoun and Ruth Welch (Buie) McA.; m. Susan Lee Haralson, May 22, 1992; children: Katherine Owen, Kenneth Grey. B.A., U. N.C., 1971; J.D., Duke U., 1974. Bar: N.C. 1974, U.S. Dist. Ct. for Middle dist. N.C. 1974, U.S. Ct. Appeals for 4th circuit 1980, U.S. Supreme Ct. 1980. Ptnr. firm Fisher, Fisher & McAllister, High Point, 1974-81; former U.S. atty. for middle dist. N.C. U.S. Dept. Justice, Greensboro, from 1981; exec. v.p., gen. counsel Wachovia Corp., Winston-Salem, N.C.; bd. of visitors Wake Forest U. Sch. of Law, 1988-96, U. N.C. at Chapel Hill, 1989-93, Duke U. Law Sch., 1996—. Pres. High Point Drug Action Coun., 1977-78; chmn. High Point Rep.Com., 1976-78, 88-89; mem. adv. bd. Salvation Army, High Point, 197-79; bd. dirs. Sch. of Nursing Found., U. N.C., Chapel Hill, 1993—. John Motley Morehead scholar Morehead Found., 1967; Arthur Priest scholar Phi Delta Theta, 1971. Mem. High Point Country Club, Phi Beta Kappa. Republican. Presbyterian. Home: 1902 La Vista Dr High Point NC 27265-9685 Office: Wachovia Corp 100 N Main St Winston Salem NC 27101-4047

MCALLISTER, WILLIAM HOWARD, III, newspaper reporter, columnist; b. Durham, N.C., Nov. 6, 1941; s. William Howard, Jr. and Dorothy Fisk (Tillett) McA.; m. Rena Catherine Farrell, June 13, 1965; children: William Howard IV, Christopher F., Jonathan T., Benjamin J. B.A. in Polit. Sci, U. N.C., Chapel Hill, 1964, M.A. in Journalism, 1966. Cecil Prince research asst. U. N.C., 1965; reporter The Virginian-Pilot, Norfolk, 1964-67; reporter, city editor Virginian-Pilot, 1972-75; reporter Wall St. Jour., San Francisco, 1968-72; reporter Washington Post, 1975-78, Va. editor, 1978-86, nat. reporter, 1986—, columnist stamp and coin sect., 1987—; TV cons. Ford Found., 1969-72. Capt. USNR, 1966-93. Decorated Navy Commendation medal, Meritorous Svc. medal, Gold Star; recipient Lidman prize for philatelic writing, 1990. Mem. Kappa Tau Alpha. Presbyterian. Home: 4140 Lenox Dr Fairfax VA 22032-1111 Office: 1150 15th St NW Washington DC 20071-0001

MCALPINE, ANDREW, production designer. Prodn. designer: (films) Sid and Nancy, 1986, Aria, 1987, Straight to Hell, 1987, High Season, 1988, Stormy Monday, 1988, For Queen and Country, 1989, The Rachel Papers, 1989, Slipstream, 1989, The Piano, 1993, The Tool Shed, 1993. Office: Sandra Marsh Mgt 9150 Wilshire Blvd Ste 220 Beverly Hills CA 90212-3429*

MCALPINE, FREDERICK SENNETT, anesthesiologist; b. Monessen, Pa., June 16, 1929; s. Karl Sennett and Kathryn Helen (Schuerhoff) McA.; m. Barbara Ellen Adams, June 23, 1956; children: Christopher, Daniel, Karen. AB with honors, St. Vincent Coll., Latrobe, Pa., 1950; MD, U. Pitts., 1954. Diplomate Am. Bd. Anesthesiology. Rotating intern U.S. Naval Hosp., Bethesda, Md., 1954-55; resident in anesthesia Mass. Gen. Hosp., Boston, 1955-57, chief resident anesthesia, 1957; asst. chief anesthesia Bethesda Naval Hosp., 1957-60; staff anesthesiologist Lahey Clinic, Boston, 1960-95, chmn. dept. anesthesiology, 1971-82, sr. staff anesthesiologist, 1962-95; retired, 1995. Contbr. chpts. to books. Del. Am. Soc. Anesthesiologists, 1970-74. Lt. comdr. USN. Mem. Mass. Med. Soc. (sr. physicians program 1996—). Republican. Roman Catholic. Home: 49 Arnold Rd Wellesley MA 02181-2819 Office: Lahey Clinic Med Ctr 41 Mall Rd Burlington MA 01805-0001

MCALPINE, PHYLLIS JEAN, genetics educator, researcher; b. Petrolia, Ont., Can., Aug. 29, 1941; d. Archie S. and Jessie Mae (Cran) McA. BS with honors, U. Western Ont., London, Can., 1963; M.A., U. Toronto, Ont., Can., 1966; Ph.D., U. London, U.K., 1970. Postdoctoral fellow Queen's U., Kingston, Ont., 1970-72; postdoctoral fellow Coll. Hosp. Med. Sch., London, Eng., 1972; rsch. assoc. U. Man., Winnipeg, Can., 1972-74, from asst. to assoc. prof. genetics, 1974-84, acting dir. div. human genetics, 1982-84, prof., 1984—, head dept. human genetics, 1993—; mem. sci. staff Health Scis. Ctr., Winnipeg, 1975—. Contbr. articles to profl. jours. Pres. Manitoba Opera Assn. Guild, Winnipeg, 1976-78. Recipient Gold medal in Zoology U. Western Ontario, 1963. Fellow Can. Coll. Med. Geneticists; mem. Genetics Soc. Can., Am. Soc. Human Genetics, AAAS. Avocation: performing arts. Office: U Manitoba, Dept of Human Genetics, Winnipeg, MB Canada R3E 0W3

MCAMIS, EDWIN EARL, lawyer; b. Cape Girardeau, Mo., Aug. 8, 1934; s. Zenas Earl and Anna Louise (Miller) McA.; m. Malin Eklof, May 31, 1959 (div. 1979); 1 child, Andrew Bruce. AB magna cum laude, Harvard U., 1956, LLB, 1959. Bar: N.Y. 1960, U.S. Dist. Ct. (so. dist.) N.Y. 1962, U.S. Supreme Ct. 1965, U.S. Ct. Appeals (2d and 3d cirs.) 1964, U.S. Ct. Appeals (D.C. cir.) 1981. Assoc. law firm Webster, Sheffield & Chrystie, N.Y.C., 1959-61, Regan Goldfarb Powell & Quinn, N.Y.C., 1962-65; assoc. law firm Lovejoy, Wasson, Lundgren & Ashton, N.Y.C., 1965-69, ptnr., 1969-77; ptnr. Skadden, Arps, Slate, Meagher & Flom, N.Y.C., 1977-90, spl. ptnr., pro bono, 1990-93; adj. prof. law Fordham U., 1984-85, Benjamin N. Cardozo Sch. Law, N.Y.C., 1985-90. Bd. dirs. Aston Magna Found. for Music, Inc., 1982-93, Cmty. Rsch. Initiative N.Y., 1988-89; mem. Lambda Legal and Edn. Fund, 1991-95. With U.S. Army, 1961-62. Mem. ABA, Selden Soc. Home: 4110 Kiaora St Coconut Grove FL 33133

MCANDREW, PAUL JOSEPH, JR., lawyer; b. Kalona, Iowa, Mar. 8, 1957; s. Paul Joseph and Virginia (Krowka) McA.; m. Lola Maxine Miller, Mar. 1, 1975; children: Stephanie, Susan, Rose, Paul Joseph III, Bridget. BA with honors, U. Iowa, 1979, JD with high distinction, 1983. Bar: Iowa 1983, U.S. Dist. Ct. Iowa 1985, U.S. Claim Ct. 1985. Law clk. to chief judge U.S. Dist. Ct. (so. dist.) Iowa, Des Moines, 1983-85; ptnr. Meardon, Sueppel, Downer & Hayes, Iowa City, 1985—. Recipient Hancher-Finkbine award, 1979, 2 Am. Jurisprudence awards Lawyers Co-Operative Pub. Co., Rochester, N.Y., 1982, 83. Mem. ABA, ATLA, Iowa Bar Assn. (chmn. worker's compensation sect. 1993-95), Iowa Trial Lawyers Assn. (rep. bd. govs. 1993—), Johnson County Bar Assn., Iowa Assn. Workers Compensation Attys. (rep. bd. govs. 1993—). Democrat. Roman Catholic. Avocations: jogging, biking, golf, travel. Home: 620 Scott Park Dr Iowa City IA 52245-5140 Office: Meardon Sueppel Downer Hayes 122 S Linn St Iowa City IA 52240-1802

MCANDREWS, JAMES PATRICK, retired lawyer; b. Carbondale, Pa., May 11, 1929; s. James Patrick and Mary Agnes (Walsh) McA.; m. Mona Marie Steinke, Sept. 4, 1954; children: James P., George A., Catherine McAndrews Lawlor, Joseph M., Anne Marie, Michael P., Edward R., Daniel P. B.S., U. Scranton, 1949; LL.B., Fordham U., 1952; grad., Real Estate Inst., NYU, 1972. Bar: N.Y. 1953, Ohio 1974. Assoc. James F. McManus, Levittown, N.Y., 1955; atty. Emigrant Savs. Bank, N.Y.C., 1955-68; counsel Tchrs. Ins. and Annuity Assn., 1968-73; assoc. Thompson, Hine & Flory, 1973-74; ptnr. Thompson, Hine & Flory, Cleve., 1974-84, Benesch, Friedlander, Coplan & Aronoff, Cleve., 1984-94; mem. law faculty Am. Inst. Banking, N.Y.C., 1968-69; mem. faculty Lakeland C.C. 1st lt. USAF, 1952-54. Fellow Am. Bar Found. (life); mem. Am. Coll. Real Estate Lawyers (gov. 1983-86, treas. 1986-88, chmn. membership devel. com. 1985-87), Ohio Land Title Assn. (life, trustee 1985-88), Bar Assn. Greater Cleve. (past chmn. real estate sect.). Roman Catholic. Home: 6638 Duneden Ave Cleveland OH 44139-4048

MCANELLY, ROBERT D., physiatrist, researcher; b. Austin, Tex., Jan. 31, 1958; s. Robert C. and Betty J. McAnelly; m. Suzanne Marie Blickhan, Aug. 18, 1990. BS in Engring., Calif. Inst. Tech., 1979, BS in Physics, 1980; MD, U. Tex., 1987. Diplomate Am. Bd. Phys. Medicine and Rehab. Aerospace engr. Vought Corp., Dallas, 1980-82; resident U. Kans., Kansas City, 1987-91, chief resident, 1990-91; asst. prof. U. Tex. Health Scis. Ctr., San Antonio, 1991-94; dir. movement analysis lab. U. Tex., San Antonio, 1994—; staff physician, univ. liaison Warm Springs Rehab. Hosp., San Antonio, 1993-94. Contbr. chpt. Physical Medicine and Rehabilitation, 1996, Cancer Rehabilitation, 1994. Mem. Assn. Acad. Psysiatrists (mem. com. 1993—), N.Am. Soc. Gait and Clin. Movement Analysis, Paralyzed Vets. Am. Avocations: gardening, music. Office: U Tex Health Sci Ctr 7703 Floyd Curl Dr San Antonio TX 78284-6200

MCANIFF, EDWARD JOHN, lawyer; b. N.Y.C., June 29, 1934; s. John Edward and Josephine (Toomey); m. Jane Reiss, June 11, 1960; children: John E., Maura T., Anne T. Annick, Jane A., Peter J., Kathleen A. AB magna cum laude, Holy Cross Coll., 1956; LLB cum laude, NYU, 1961. Bar: N.Y. 1962, Calif. 1963, D.C. 1976. Law clk. to Justice A.T. Goodwin Supreme Ct. Oreg., Salem, 1961-62; assoc. then ptnr. O'Melveny & Myers, L.A., 1962—; adj. prof. Sch. Law Stanford U., 1974-75, 94—, Boalt Hall Law Sch., 1992—, UCLA Law Sch., 1996—; fgn. law counsel Freehill, Hollingdale & Page, Sydney, 1981-82; bd. dirs. Mellon Bank Corp. Bd. dirs. L.A. Master Chorale, 1979-81, 87—, pres., 1992-96, chmn., 1996—; trustee Music Ctr. L.A. County, 1992—, mem. exec. com., 1992—; bd. dirs. Music Ctr. Found., 1992—. Capt. USNR, 1956-87. Mem. Valley Hunt Club. Republican. Home: 3315 San Pasqual St Pasadena CA 91107-5436 Office: O'Melveny & Myers 400 S Hope St Ste 1711 Los Angeles CA 90071-2801

MCANIFF, NORA P., publishing executive. BA, CUNY. Pub. People Weekly, N.Y.C., 1994—. Office: People Magazine Time Inc Rockfeller Ctr New York NY 10020-1393*

MCANINCH, JACK WELDON, urological surgeon, educator; b. Merkel, Tex., Mar. 17, 1936; s. Weldon Thomas and Margaret (Canon) McA.; m. Barbara B. Buchanan, Dec. 29, 1960 (div. Aug. 1972); m. Burnet B. Sumner, Dec. 29, 1987; children: David A., Todd G., Brendan J. BS, Tex. Tech U., 1958; MS, U. Idaho, 1960; MD, U. Tex., 1964. Diplomate Am. Bd. Urology (trustee 1991-97, pres. 1996-97). Commd. capt. U.S. Army, 1964-66, advanced through grades to col., 1977, ret., 1977; col. USAR; intern then resident Letterman Army Med. Ctr., San Francisco, 1964-69; chief urol. surgery San Francisco Gen. Hosp., 1977—; prof. urol. surgery U. Calif., San Francisco, 1977—. Editor: Urogenital Trauma, 1985, Urologic Clinics of North America, 1989, Smith's General Urology, 1995; section editor: Early Care of the Injured Patient, 1990, Traumatic and Reconstructive Urology, 1996. Col. US Army, 1964-72. Recipient Disting. Alumnus award Tex. Tech U., 1994; named Disting. Alumnus U. Idaho, 1997. Fellow ACS (gov. 1992-97); mem. Am. Urol. Assn. (pres. we. sect. 1992-93, bd. dirs. 1990—, pres. 1996-97), Genitourinary Reconstructive Surgeons (pres.), Am. Assn. Surgery Trauma (v.p.), Soc. Univ. Urologists, Am. Bd. Urology (pres. 1996-97). Office: San Francisco Gen Hosp Dept Urology 1001 Potrero Ave San Francisco CA 94110-3518

MC ANINCH, ROBERT DANFORD, philosophy and government affairs educator; b. Wheeling, W.Va., May 21, 1942; s. Robert Danford and Dorothy Elizabeth (Goudy) McA.; 1 child, Robert Michael; m. Helen M. Perry, June 5, 1993. AB, West Liberty State Coll., 1969; MA, W.Va. U., 1970; MA, Morehead State U., 1975; postgrad. U. Hawaii, U. Ky. Engring. technician Hydro-Space Rsch., Inc., Rockville, Md., 1965-66; prof. govt., philosophy Prestonsburg (Ky.) Community Coll., 1970—; v.p. Calico Corner, Inc.; dir. Chase-Options, Inc., Medisin, Inc. Bd. dirs. Big Sandy Area Community Action Program, Inc., 1973-76; chmn. Floyd County Solid Waste, Inc.; mem. War on Drug Task Force. Served with AUS, 1962-65. Recipient Great Tchr. award Prestonsburg Community Coll., 1971; named Ky. col., 1977. Mem. Am. Polit. Sci. Assn., Am. Philos. Soc., Ky. Philosophy Assn., Ky. Assn. Colls. and Jr. Colls. Achievements include designed Cosmic ray chamber, artificial human circulatory system, Wilson type cloud chamber, TOTO 1, 2. Home: Bert Combs Dr Prestonsburg KY 41653

MCARDLE, RICHARD JOSEPH, academic administrator; b. Omaha, Mar. 10, 1934; s. William James and Abby Marie (Menzies) McA.; m. Katherine Ann McAndrew, Dec. 27, 1958; children: Bernard, Constance, Nancy, Susan, Richard. B.A., Creighton U., 1955, M.A., 1961; Ph.D., U. Nebr., 1969. Tchr. pub. high schs. Nebr., 1955-65; grad. asst. romance langs. U. Nebr., 1965-66, instr. fgn. lang. methods, 1966-69; chmn. dept. edn. Cleve. State U., 1969-70; chmn. dept. elem. and secondary edn. U. North Fla., 1971-75; dean Coll. Edn. Cleve. State U., 1975-87, prof. edn., 1987-89, spl. asst. to pres. for campus planning, 1989-91, vice provost for strategic planning, 1991-92, acting provost, v.p. for acad. affairs, 1992-94, vice provost for strategic planning, 1994-96, prof. edn., 1996—; cons. in field. Author articles related to issues in tchr. edn. Mem. ASCD, World Future Soc., Am. Assn. Higher Edn., Phi Delta Kappa. Office: Office of Provost Academic Affairs Cleve State U Cleveland OH 44115

MCARTHUR, ELDON DURANT, geneticist, researcher; b. Hurricane, Utah, Mar. 12, 1941; s. Eldon and Denise (Dalton) McA.; m. Virginia Johnson, Dec. 20, 1963; children: Curtis D., Monica McArthur Bennion, Denise, Ted O. AS with high honors, Dixie Coll., 1963; BS cum laude, U. Utah, 1965, MS, 1967, PhD, 1970. Postdoctoral rsch. fellow, dept. demonstrator Agrl. Rsch. Coun. Gt. Britain, Leeds, Eng., 1970-71; rsch. geneticist Intermountain Rsch. Sta. USDA Forest Svc., Ephraim, Utah, 1972-75; rsch. geneticist Shrub Scis. Lab., Intermountain Rsch. Sta. USDA Forest Svc., Provo, Utah, 1975-83, project leader, chief rsch. geneticist, 1983-97; project leader, chief rsch. geneticist Rocky Mountain Rsch. Sta., USDA Forest Svc., Provo, Utah, 1997—; adj. prof. dept. botany and range sci. Brigham Young U., Provo, 1976—. Author more than 270 rsch. papers; contbr. chpts. to books; editor symposium procs. Named USDA Forest Svc. Superior Scientist, 1990, Disting. Scientist, 1996; Sigma Xi grantee, 1970, NSF grantee, 1981, 85, 96, Coop. State Rsch., Svc. grantee, 1986, 91. Mem. Soc. Range Mgmt. (pres. Utah sect. 1987, Outstanding Achievement award 1992), Botan. Soc. Am., Soc. Study Evolution, Am. Genetic Assn., Shrub Rsch. Consortium (chmn. 1983—), Intermountain Consortium for Aridlands Rsch. (pres. 1991—). Mormon. Avocations: hiking, cycling, basketball. Home: 555 N 1200 E Orem UT 84097-4350 Office: USDA Forest Svc Shrub Scis Lab 735 N 500 E Provo UT 84606-1856

MC ARTHUR, GEORGE, journalist; b. Valdosta, Ga., July 15, 1924; s. George and Ann (Johnson) McA.; m. Eva Kim, Sept. 17, 1979. B.A. in Journalism, U. Ga., 1948. With AP, 1948-69; corr. AP, Korea, 1950-54, Paris, 1954-60; bur. chief AP, Cairo, 1960-63, Manila, 1963-65; corr. AP, Saigon, 1966-68; bur. chief AP, 1968-69; with Los Angeles Times, 1969-83; bur. chief Los Angeles Times, Saigon, 1970-75; corr. for Southeast Asia Los Angeles Times, Bangkok, 1975-79; diplomatic corr. U.S. News & World Report, 1983-85. Served with USNR, 1943-45. Recipient citation for fgn. reporting Overseas Press Club, 1973. Mem. Sigma Delta Chi. Clubs: Fgn. Corrs. (Hong Kong); Glen Arven Country (Thomasville, Ga.); River Bend Country (Gt. Falls, Va.). Address: 506 E Creek Ct Vienna VA 22180-3578

MC ARTHUR, JANET WARD, endocrinologist, educator; b. Bellingham, Wash., June 25, 1914; d. Hyland Donald and Alice Maria (Frost) McA. A.B., U. Wash., 1935, M.S., 1937; M.B., Northwestern U., 1941, M.D., 1942; ScD (hon.), Mt. Holyoke Coll., 1962. Diplomate: Am. Bd. Internal Medicine. Intern Cin. Gen. Hosp., 1941-42, asst. resident in medicine, 1942-43; asst. resident, rsch. fellow in medicine H.P. Walcott fellow clin. medicine Mass. Gen. Hosp., Boston, 1943-47, assoc. physician, 1959-84, assoc. children's svc., 1968-84; instr. Harvard U., 1955-57, asst. prof., 1960-64, assoc. prof., 1964-73, prof., 1973-84, prof. emeritus, 1984—; clin. prof. medicine Boston U. Sch. Medicine, 1984—; adj. prof. Sargent Coll. Allied Health Scis. Boston U., 1982—; mem. reproductive biology study sect. NIH, 1974-78, Com. on Population Studies, 1980-84; co-dir. Vincent Meml. Rsch. Lab., 1977-79; sr. scientist U. London, 1985-86. Author: (with others) Functional Endocrinology from Birth Through Adolescence, 1952; editor: (with Theodore Colton) Statistics in Endocrinology, 1970; contbr. articles to profl. jours. Fellow ACP; mem. AMA, AAAS, Endocrine Soc., Am. Soc. Reproductive Medicine, Boston Obstetrical Soc., Phi Beta Kappa, Sigma Xi, Alpha Omega Alpha. Home: 865 Central Ave Apt F-505 Needham MA 02192 Office: Boston U 635 Commonwealth Ave Fl 4 Boston MA 02215-1605

MCARTHUR, JOHN HECTOR, business educator; b. Vancouver, B.C., Can., Mar. 31, 1934; came to U.S., 1957; s. Hector and Elizabeth Lee

(Whyte) McA.; m. Netilia Ewasiuk, Sept. 15, 1956; children: Jocelyn Natasha, Susan Patricia. B in Commerce, U. B.C., 1957; MBA, Harvard U., 1959, DBA (hon.), 1962; LLD (hon.), Simon Fraser U., 1982, Queens U., 1985, Middlebury Coll., 1988, U. Western Ont., 1992; hon. degree, U. B.C., Spain, 1996, U. Navarra, Spain, 1989. Prof. dean. Sch. Bus. Adminstrn. Harvard U., Cambridge, Mass., 1980-95; sr. advisor World Bank Group, 1996—; bd. dirs. AES Corp., BCE, Inc., Rohm and Haas Co., Inc., Springs Industries, Inc., Cabot Corp., Glaxo Welcome Plc.; cons. numerous cos. and govt. agys. in Can., Europe, Asia and U.S. Home: 140 Old Connecticut Path Wayland MA 01778-3202 Office: Harvard Univ Sch Bus Adminstrn Boston MA 02163

MCATEE, PATRICIA ANNE ROONEY, medical educator; b. Denver, Apr. 20, 1931; d. Jerry F. and Edna E. (Hansen) Rooney; m. Darrell McAtee, Sept. 4, 1954; 1 son, Kevin Paul. BS, Loretto Heights Coll., 1953; MS, U. Colo., 1961; PhD, Union of Univs., 1976. Supr. St. Anthony Hosp., Denver, 1952-55; pub. health nurse, edn. dir. Tri-County Health Dept., Colo., 1956-58; adminstr. sch. health program Littleton (Colo.) Pub. Schs., 1958-60; asst. prof. community health, acad. adminstr. continuing edn. U. Colo., 1968-70; project dir. Western Interstate Commn. for Higher Edn., 1972-74; asst. prof. pediatrics, project co-dir. Sch. Medicine U. Colo., 1975—; mem. profl. svcs. staff Mead Johnson & Co., 1981—; cons. Colo. Safety Coun.; treas. Vista Nueva Assocs. Editor: Pediatric Nursing, 1975-77. Chmn. bd. dirs. Found. for Urban and Neighborhood Devel.; mem. Arapahoe Health Planning Coun. Mem. NAS, APHA, Inst. Medicine, Nat. Bd. Pediatric Nurse Practitioners and Assocs. (pres.), Nat. Assn. Pediatric Nurse Practitioners (v.p.), Am. Acad. Polit. and Social Scientist, Nat. League Nursing, Western Soc. Rsch., Am. Sch. Health Assn., Sigma Theta Tau. Home: 877 E Panama Dr Littleton CO 80121-2531 Office: 4200 E 9th Ave Box C-219 Denver CO 80262

MCATEER, J. DAVITT, federal agency administrator; m. Kathryn Grace Lough; 5 children. BA, Wheeling Coll., 1966; JD, W.Va. U., 1970. Solicitor of safety United Mine Workers Am., 1972-76; with Ctr. for Law and Social Policy, Washington, 1976-84; exec. dir. Occupl. Safety and Health Law Ctr., Sheperdstown, W.Va., 1984-94; asst. sec. of labor Mine Safety and Health Adminstrn., Arlington, Va., 1994—; acting solicitor of labor U.S. Dept. Labor, Washington, 1996—. Office: US Dept Labor 200 Constitution Ave NW Washington DC 20210-0001

MCAULAY, ALASTAIR D., electrical and computer engineer, educator; b. May 9, 1938; came to U.S., 1967; s. John and Martha (Hune) McA.; m. Carol Julia Saggs, May 27, 1967; 1 child, Alexander. BA with honors, Cambridge U., Eng., 1961, MA with honors, 1964; PhD, Carnegie Mellon U., 1974. Program mgr. ctrl. rsch. lab. Tex. Instruments, Dallas, 1980-88; chair computer sci./computer engring., NCR disting. prof. Wright State U., Dayton, Ohio, 1988-92; chair elec. engring. & computer sci. dept., Chandler Weaver prof. Lehigh U., Bethlehem, Pa., 1992—. Author: Optical Computer Architectures, 1991; patentee in field. Fellow Internat. Soc. Optical Engrs.; mem. IEEE (sr.). Home: 3971 Lilac Rd Allentown PA 18103 Office: Lehigh U 19 Memorial Dr W Bethlehem PA 18015-3006

MCAULEY, BRIAN D., communications executive; m. Jane McAuley; children: Beth, Christian, Tricia, Mary. BBA, Adelphi U. CPA. Mgr. Deloitte & Touche; sr. v.p., dir. Millicom Inc., 1982-86; co-founder, pres., CEO Nextel Comm., Inc., Rutherford, N.J., 1987-95; vice-chmn. bd. Nextel Comm., Inc., Rutherford, 1996—. Chmn. endowment fund com. Archdiocese of Newark, fin. coun. mem., investment and audit com.; bd. dirs. Nat. Alliance for Bus. Office: Nextel Comm Inc 201 State Rt 17 Rutherford NJ 07070-2574

MCAULEY, SKEET, artist; b. Monahans, Tex., Mar. 7, 1951; s. George Clifford and Thelma Lee (Martin) McA.; m. Karen Suzanne Gee, June 25, 1994. BA, Sam Houston State U., 1976; MFA, Ohio U., 1978. Instr. photography Spring Hill Coll., Mobile, Ala., 1978-79, Tyler (Tex.) Jr. Coll., 1979-81; assoc. prof. photography U. N.Tex., Denton, 1981-93; featured in numerous articles and publs. One-person exhibits include Christopher Grimes Gallery, Santa Monica, Calif., 1995, Lowinsky Gallery, N.Y.C., 1993, U.S. Golf Assn. Mus., Far Hills, N.J., 1993, Dallas Mus. Art, 1992, Moody Gallery, Houston, 1992, Tyler Mus. of Art, 1992, The Heard Mus., Amherst, Mass., 1991, Calif. Mus. Photography, Riverside, 1991, Etherton/Stern Gallery, Tucson, Ariz., 1991, The Albuquerque Mus., 1990; group exhibits include Cleve. Mus. Art, 1994, Virginia Beach Ctr. for Arts, 1994, others, San Francisco Mus. Modern Art, 1996, Whitney Mus. Am. Art, N.Y.C., 1996; author: Sign Language: Contemporary Southwest Native America, 1989. Grantee Polaroid Copr., 1988, Nat. Endowment for the Arts Individual Artist fellowship, 1984, 86. Mem. Soc. Photographic Education (bd. dirs. 1990-93). Democrat. Office: 3516 Madera Ave Los Angeles CA 90039-1930

MCAULIFFE, EUGENE VINCENT, retired diplomat and business executive; b. Boston, Oct. 25, 1918; s. Thomas Joseph and Charlotte Philippine (Metzger) McA.; m. Winifred Marie Gallivan, Aug. 17, 1946; children: Eugene Vincent Jr., Paul, Lawrence, Marie, Stephen, Terence, Patricia, John. AB cum laude, Boston Coll., 1940; postgrad., Boston U., 1940-42, Nat. War Coll., 1962-63. Spl. agt. Mass. Bonding & Ins. Co., Boston, 1940-42; vice consul, exec. sec. Office of High Commn. for Germany, Berlin, 1948-54; with U.S. Dept. State, Washington, 1954-58, 63-68; 1st sec. Am. Embassy, Mexico City, 1958-62; minister, dep. chief of mission Am. Embassy, Madrid, 1968-70; ambassador Am. Embassy, Budapest, Hungary, 1975-76; minister counselor, internat. advisor SHAPE, Casteau, Belgium, 1970-72; minister counselor, dep. chief of mission U.S. Mission to NATO, Brussels, 1972-75; asst. sec. def. for internat. security affairs Dept. Def., Washington, 1976-77; pres. United Tech. (Europe) Inc., Brussels, 1977-83. Capt. U.S. Army, 1942-47. Decorated Bronze Star, Croix de Guerre, Belgian Govt., 1945. Mem. Am. Fgn. Svc. Assn., Acad. Polit. Sci., Assn. Diplomatic Studies, SHAPE Officers Assn., Nat. War Coll. Alumni Assn., Boston Coll. Alumni Assn., Boston Latin Sch. Assn., Internat. Inst. Strategic Studies (London), Fgn. Affairs Retirees New Eng. (pres. 1985-86), Ambs. Coun. World Affairs Boston, DACOR House. Roman Catholic. Home: 80 Flint Locke Dr Duxbury MA 02332-4807

MCAULIFFE, JANE DAMMEN, Middle Eastern and Islamic studies educator. BA in Classics and Philosophy, Trinity Coll., 1968; MA in Religious Studies, U. Toronto, 1979, PhD in Islamic Studies, 1984. Asst. prof. dept. religious studies U. Toronto, 1981-86, assoc. prof. dept. Middle East and Islamic studies, 1992—, chair dept. study of religion, dir. Ctr. Study of Religion, 1992—; from asst. prof. to assoc. prof. history of religions and Islamic studies Candler Sch. Theology Emory U., Atlanta, 1986-92, assoc. dean Candler Sch. Theology, 1990-92; appointed Vatican Commn. for Religious Rels. with Muslims, 1994. Author: Qur'anic Christians: An Analysis of Classical and Modern Exegesis, 1991, 'Abbasid Authority Affirmed: The Early Years of al-Mansur, vol. 28, 1995; contbr. articles to profl. jours. Danforth Found. fellow, 1976-80, NEH Summer fellow, 1979-80, Charles Gordon Heyd fellow, 1980-81, Social Scis. and Humanities Rsch. Coun. doctoral fellow, 1981-84, Postdoctoral fellow, 1984-86, CASA II fellow, 1986, NEH Summer Faculty Travel fellow, 1989, NEH Rsch. fellow, 1992, Mellon fellow, 1994, Guggenheim fellow, 1996. Mem. Am. Soc. Study of Religion, Am. Acad. Religion, Am. Oriental Soc., Can. Soc. Study of Religion, Mid. East Studies Assn. (Thesis award 1985), Oriental Club Toronto, Soc. Values in Higher Edn. Office: U Toronto Dept & Ctr Religion, 123 Saint George St, Toronto, ON Canada M5S 2E8

MCAULIFFE, JOHN F., retired judge; b. Washington, Nov. 4, 1932; m. Barbara McAuliffe, Nov. 4, 1955; children: John M., Mary K. JD, Am. U., 1955. Assoc. judge Cir. Ct. for Montgomery County, Md., 1972-85; judge Md. Ct. Appeals, Annapolis, 1985-92. Office: 50 Maryland Ave Rockville MD 20850-2320

MC AULIFFE, MICHAEL F., bishop; b. Kansas City, Mo., Nov. 22, 1920. Student, St. Louis Prep. Sem., Cath. U. Ordained priest Roman Cath. Ch., 1945; consecrated bishop, 1969; bishop diocese of Jefferson City Jefferson City, Mo., 1969—. Office: Chancery Office 605 Clark Ave PO Box 417 Jefferson City MO 65102*

MCAULIFFE, RICHARD L., church official; m. Janet Bettinghaus; children: Brian, Andrea Stephenson. Student, Carleton Coll.; MBA, Harvard U. Exec. v.p., treas., CFO Harris Bankcorp, Harris Trust and Savs. Bank, 1960-90; mng. agt. Resolution Trust Corp., 1990—; treas. Evang. Luth. Ch. in Am., Chgo., 1992—; pres. Grace Luth. Ch., Glen Ellyn, Ill., Evang. Luth. Ch. Am. Ch. Coun.; treas. English Synod and Christ Sem.-Seminex, AELC; bd. dirs./com. mem. Christian Century Found., Luth. Gen. Healthcare Sys.; active Luth. Social Svcs. Ill. Office: Evang Luth Ch Am 8765 W Higgins Rd Chicago IL 60631-4101*

MCAULIFFE, STEVEN JAMES, federal judge; b. 1948. BA, Va. Mil. Inst., 1970; JD, Georgetown U., 1973. Capt. appellate coun. U.S. Army Judge Advocate Gens. Corps, 1973-77; asst. atty. gen. Office N.H. Atty. Gen., 1977-80; ptnr. Gallagher, Callahan, Gartrell, P.A., Concord, N.H., 1980-92; fed. judge U.S. Dist. Ct. (N.H. dist.), Concord, 1992—. Trustee Univ. System of N.H., 1986-94; bd. dirs. N.H. Med. Malpractice Stabilization Res. Fund Trust, 1987-92, Office Pub. Guardian, 1980-92, Challenger Ctr. for Space Sci. Edn.; active N.H. Dem. Leadership Coun., 1988-92. Capt. U.S. Army, 1970-77, USAR, 1977-80, N.H. Army NG, 1980-88. Fellow N.H. Bar Found.; mem. ABA, N.H. Bar Assn. (pres. 1991-92, pres.-elect 1990-91, v.p. 1989-90, mem. ex-officio N.H. Supreme Ct. com. profl. conduct 1989-90, mem. ethics com. 1984-86), Nat. Conf. Bar Pres., Merrimack County Bar Assn., D.C. Bar Assn., U.S. Supreme Ct. Hist. Soc., N.H. Jud. Coun. (vice-chmn. 1991-92), Aircraft Owners and Pilots Assn., N.H. Hist. Soc., Concord Country Club. Office: US Dist Ct PO Box 1498 55 Pleasant St Rm 216 Concord NH 03301-3938*

MCAUSLAND, RANDOLPH M. N., arts administrator; b. Phila., Oct. 9, 1934; s. John Randolph and Helen (Neal) McA.; m. Marilynn Kemp, July 10, 1965 (div. 1976); children: Andrew, Sean; m. Jane E. Tribbey, May 9, 1986. AB, Princeton U., 1957. Copy editor Wall Street Journal, N.Y.C., 1960-61; editor, publisher Stowe Reporter, 1961-63; consulting editor Interpub. Group Cos., 1963-67; creative dir. The Progress Group, N.Y.C., 1967-70, gen. mgr., 1970-75; dir. mktg. Billboard Pubs., N.Y.C., 1975-77; asst. to pres. Macmillan Mag., Stamford, Conn., 1977-80; editor The New Satirist, New Canaan, Conn., 1980-82; pres. Design Pubs. Inc., N.Y.C., 1983-89; dir. Design Arts Program, NEA, Washington, 1989-90; dep. chmn. programs NEA, Washington, 1990-93; writer, arts cons. Richmond, Va., 1993-94; founder, dir. Design History Found., N.Y.C., 1988-89. Author: Supermarkets: History of an American Institution, 1980; contbr. articles to profl. jours. Bd. dirs. Hand Wodkshop, Richmond, 1993-94, Richmond Choral Soc., 1994, Worldesign Found., 1994—, Fla. Friends Librs., 1995—, Fla. Ctr. for the Book. With U.S. Army, 1957-60. Recipient Commendation N.Y.C. Police Dept., 1971, Pres. Cup Am. Comedy Club N.Y., N.Y.C., 1974, Bronze Apple award Indsl. Design Soc., 1987, Disting. Svc. award NEA, 1991-92. Mem. Am. Ctr. For Design (hon.), Coalition Ind. Scholars, Ivy Club. Home: 2708 NE 37th Dr Fort Lauderdale FL 33308-6327

MCAVITY, JOHN GILLIS, museum director, association executive, museologist; b. St. John, N.B., Can., Oct. 30, 1950; s. J. Patrick H. and Catharine A. (McNeill) McA. B.A., U. N.B., 1972. Cert. assn. exec. Asst. curator Kings Landing Mus., Fredericton, N.B., Can., 1972-73; provincial mus. adviser N.B. Mus., St. John, Can., 1973-76; exec. dir. Ont. Mus. Assn., Toronto, Can., 1976-81, Can. Mus. Assn., Ottawa, Ont., Can., 1981—; bd. dirs. internat. mus. Mgmt. Com., Internat. Coun. Mus. Editor INTERCOM News, 1997—. V.p. St. John Heritage Trust, 1974-76; exec. com. Can. Club, St. John, 1975, English Speaking Union, St. John, 1974-76; vol. fundraiser Kidney Found., Can.; bd. dirs. Centretown Citizens Corp.; founding dir. Mus. Found. Can., 1994—. Mem. Am. Assn. Museums, Am. Assn. for State and Local History (awards com. 1981-84, nominations com. 1985), Mus. Found. Can. (founding dir. 1994—), Inst. Assn. Execs. (chmn. postal com., bd. dirs. Ottawa chpt., cert.), Assn. Cultural Execs. (bd. dirs. 1988-92, apptd. to senate 1995), Quaco Hist. and Libr. Soc. (hon. life), Tourism Industry Assn. Can. (bd. dirs.), Assn. Museums N.B. (founding mem.), Ont. Assn. Art Galleries (bd. dirs. 1986-90), Can. Soc. Copyright Consumers, Can. Soc. Assn. Execs. (bd. dirs. 1993-96), Can. Art Mus. Dirs. Orgn., Shefford Heritage Co-op (membership chair 1992-95). Anglican. Home: 300 Cooper St Apt 41, Ottawa, ON Canada K2P 0G7 Address (summer): 29 Kingshurst Ln, East Riverside-Kingshurst, Saint John, NB Canada E2H 1T3

MCAVOY, BRUCE RONALD, scientist, consultant; b. Jamestown, N.Y., Jan. 30, 1933; s. George Harold and Agda Amelia (Martinson) McA. BS in Physics, U. Rochester, 1954. Jr. engr. Westinghouse Air Arm Div., Balt., 1956-57, assoc. engr., 1957-58; rsch. engr. Westinghouse Rsch. Ctr., Pitts., 1958-69; sr. rsch. engr. Westinghouse R & D Ctr., Pitts., 1969-78, fellow engr., 1978-84, adv. scientist, 1984—; adv. bd. mem. Nat. Ctr. Physical Acoustics, U. Miss., 1987-88. Editor spl. issue IEEE Trans. Microwave Theory Tech., Ultrasonics Symposium procs., 1976-96; mem. editl. bd. jour. Microwave and Guided Wave Letters, 1990. With U.S. Army, 1954-56. Fellow IEEE (awards and recognition com. 1989—, def. R&D policy com. 1989-91, Centennial medal 1984, tech. program com. Internat. Microwave Symposium 1986—); mem. DAV (life), Ultrasonic, Rerroelectric and Frequency Control Soc. of IEEE (pres. 1986-87), Electromagnetics Acad., Microwave Theory and Techniques Soc. (chmn. microwave acoustics tech. com. 1988—). Republican. Lutheran. Home: 926 Ivy St Pittsburgh PA 15232-2651

MCAVOY, JOHN JOSEPH, lawyer; b. Worley, Idaho, June 28, 1933; s. Earl Francis and Florence Jewel (Mitchell) McA.; m. Joan Marjorie Zeldon, Sept. 20, 1964; children: Jason, Jon. B.A., U. Idaho, 1954, LL.B., 1958; LL.M., Yale U., 1959. Bar: Idaho 1958, U.S. Supreme Ct. 1962, N.Y. 1963, U.S. Tax Ct. 1969, D.C. 1976. Asst. prof. law George Washington U., Washington, 1959-62; staff atty. stockpile investigating subcom. Armed Forces Com. U.S. Senate, Washington, 1962; assoc. White & Case, N.Y.C., 1963-71, ptnr., 1972-95; of counsel Lukas, McGowan, Nace & Gutierrez, 1995—; assoc. Bus. Mediation Assocs., 1995—; adj. prof. Washington Coll. Law, Am. U., Washington, 1990. Bd. dirs. N.Y. Civil Liberties Union, 1975-77; chmn. due process com. ACLU, 1971-75. Served with U.S. Army, 1954-56. Mem. Assn. of Bar of City of N.Y., D.C. Bar Assn. (ethics com. 1982-88, vice chmn. 1986-87, chmn. 1987-88), Phi Beta Kappa, Phi Alpha Delta. Democrat. Avocations: swimming, bicycling, fgn. travel. Office: Lukas McGowan Nace & Gutierrez 1111 19th St NW Washington DC 20036-3603

MCAVOY, ROGERS, educational psychology educator, consultant; b. Webster Springs, W.Va., Dec. 28, 1927; s. Ellis McLaughlin and Carolyn (McIntosh) McA.; m. Anne T. Limpe, Dec. 19, 1956 (div.); children: Carol Ann, Philip Ellis, Karen Lynelle; m. Irma Jean Tingler, July 7, 1973. BA, Fairmont State Coll., 1951; MA, W.Va. U., 1954; PhD, Ind. U., 1966. Tchr. biology Petersburg (W.Va.) High Sch., 1951-53; asst. dir. admissions Marshall U., Huntington, W.Va., 1953-55; registrar Glenville (W.Va.) State Coll., 1955-56; rsch. asst., asst. to dean Ind. U., Bloomington, 1956-61; asst. prof. ednl. psychology W.Va. U., Morgantown, 1961-65, assoc. prof., 1967-72, prof., 1973—, chmn. dept., 1966-77; cons. state and county ednl. systems, W.Va., others, 1965-89; cons. follow through program Stanford Rsch. Inst., 1969-72. Contbr. articles to profl. jours. Mem. Phi Delta Kappa (Disting. Svc. award 1982, 25-yr. svc. award 1990). Avocations: writing, book collecting, restoring houses, photography, reading. Office: WVa U 608 Allen Ave Morgantown WV 26505-5618

MCAVOY, THOMAS JAMES, federal judge; b. 1934. AB, Villanova U., 1960; JD, Union U., 1964. Bar: N.Y. 1964, U.S. Dist. Ct. (no. dist.) N.Y. 1964. Assoc. Hinman, Howard & Kattell, Binghamton, N.Y., 1964-69, Kramer, Wales, & McAvoy, Binghamton, 1969-84, McAvoy & Hickey, P.C., Binghamton, 1984-85; from judge to chief judge U.S. Dist. Ct. (no. dist.) N.Y., Binghamton, 1986—. With USMC, 1958. Office: US Dist Ct/No Dist NY 225 Fed Bldg 15 Henry St Binghamton NY 13901-2723*

MCBATH, DONALD LINUS, osteopathic physician; b. Chgo., May 19, 1935; s. Earl and Phyllis (Michalski) McB.; m. Ruth Southerland, Jan. 18, 1956; children: Donald L. Jr., Donna Ruth McBath Bassett, Daniel P. BA in Polit. Sci., U. Fla., 1957, BS in Pre Med., 1962; DO, Kansas City (Mo.) Coll. Osteopathy and Surgery, 1969; MA, St. Leo Coll., 1981. Diplomate Nat. Bd. Examiners; cert. family practice Am. Osteo. Bd. Family Physicians, Correctional Health Profl. Med. Med. dir. various orgns., Dade City, Fla., 1971; chief of staff Jackson Meml. Hosp., Dade City, Fla., 1969—; past chief of staff, med. dir. East Pasco Med. Ctr., Zephyrills, Fla.; med. dir. Pasco County, Hernando County Prison Sys/.Fla.; bd. dirs. East Pasco med. Ctr., Zephrillis; mem. adv. bd. Prudential Health Plan; trustee, pres., exe.c com. Fla. Osteo. Med. Assn.; sports physician Pasco Comprehensive H.S.; med. examiner FAA; Dade City grand marshall, past chmn. adv. coun.; pres., trustee East Pasco Med. Ctr. Found.; assoc. prof. clin. sci. Nova Southeastern U. Health Scis., Miami, Fla. Trustee St. Leo (Fla.) Coll.; adv. dir. First Union Nat. Bank Fla., Dade City; com. chmn. Hall of Fame Bowl, Pasco County, Fla., 1987. Recipient Pump Handle award Pasco County Health Authority, 1988, Outstanding Contbn. award H.R.S. Pasco County Pub. Health Unit, 1988, Outstanding Svc. award Fla. Interscholastic Athletic Adminstrs. Assn., 1994; named Gen. Practitioner of Yr., Fla. Acad. Gen. Practice, 1990-91. Fellow Am. Coll. Osteo. Family Physicians; mem. Am. Osteo. Assn. (nat. program conv. chmn., conv. com., exhibit adv. com., mem. ho. of dels., coun. on predoctoral edn.), Fla. Soc. Am. Coll. of Gen. Practitioners (nat. conv. com., bd. dirs. 1989-90, pres. 1991-92), Rotary (Dade City chpt. past pres., Paul Harris fellow). Roman Catholic. Avocations: sports. Home and Office: McBath Med Ctr 13925 17th St Dade City FL 33525-4603

MCBAY, ARTHUR JOHN, toxicologist, consultant; b. Medford, Mass., Jan. 6, 1919; s. Arthur and Virginia (Davito) McB.; m. Avis Louise Botsford, Aug. 24, 1946; children: John, Robert. BS, Mass. Coll. Pharmacy, 1940, MS, 1942; PhD, Purdue U., 1948. Diplomate Am. Bd. Forensic Toxicology; cert. toxicol. chemist Am. Bd. Clin. Chemistry; registered pharmacist, Mass. Asst. prof. chemistry Mass. Coll. Pharmacy, Boston, 1948-53, asst. in legal medicine, dept. legal medicine, 1953-63; lectr. legal medicine Harvard U.; toxicologist, criminalist, cons. Mass. State Police Chemistry Lab., 1955-63; instr. Northeastern U., 1962-63; assoc. prof. toxicology Law-Medicine Inst. Boston U., 1963-69, assoc. prof. pharmacology Med. Sch., 1963-69; supr. lab. Mass. Dept. Pub. Safety, Boston, 1963-69; assoc. prof. pathology and toxicology U. N.C., Chapel Hill, 1969-73, prof., 1973-89, prof. emeritus pharmacy and pathology, 1989—; chief toxicologist Office Chief Med. Examiner, Chapel Hill, 1969-89; mem. task force on alcohol, other drugs and transp. NRC; cons. toxicology resource com. Coll. Am. Pathologists, 1975-95, Bur. Med. Devices and Diagnostic Products, FDA, 1975-91, N.C. Drug Authority, 1971-75; dir. Mass. Alcohol Project, 1968-69. Mem. editl. bd. Jour. Forensic Scis., 1981-95; bd. editors Yearbook of Pathology, 1981-91; contbr. numerous articles on toxicology to profl. jours. Served to capt. USAAF, 1943-45. Fellow Am. Acad. Forensic Scis.; mem. Internat. Assn. Forensic Toxicologists, Nat. Safety Coun. (exec. bd. com. on alcohol and drugs 1981-91), Am. Pharm. Assn. (sec., treas. sci. sect. 1954-57), Soc. Forensic Toxicologists (dir. 1978), Am. Chem. Soc., Sigma Xi, Rho Chi, Phi Lambda Upsilon. Democrat. Roman Catholic. Home: V-306 Carolina Meadows Chapel Hill NC 27514

MCBEAN, SHARON ELIZABETH, church administrator; b. Chgo., July 15, 1937; d. Archibald Lewis Jr. and Mary Elizabeth (Rees) McBean; children: Debra Sue Sanders, Catherine Leigh Sanders Ferguson. BA cum laude, La Roche Coll., 1977; MS in Edn., Duquesne U., 1978. Adminstrv. asst. 1st Presbyn. Ch., Santa Barbara, Calif., 1988-89, bus. mgr., 1989—; deacon 1st Presbyn. Ch., Santa Barbara, 1987-89. Mem. adv. bd. Valle Verde Retirement Cmty., also chmn. health svcs. com. Mem. AAUW, Presbyn. Ch. Bus. Adminstrn. Assn., Nat. Assn. Ch. Bus. Adminstrs. (cert.).

MCBEATH, ANDREW ALAN, orthopedic surgery educator; b. Milw., Mar. 4, 1936; s. Ivor Charles and Lida McBeath; m. Margaret McBeath; children: Craig Matthew, Drew Alan. BS, U. Wis., 1958, MD, 1961. Diplomate Am. Bd. Orthopaedic Surgery (oral examiner). Intern, resident Hartford (Conn.) Hosp., 1961-63; resident in orthopedic surgery U. Iowa, Iowa City, 1963-66; asst. prof. div. orthopedic surgery div. surgery U. Wis., Madison, 1968-72, assoc. prof., 1972-79, prof., 1979—, Frederick J. Gaenslen prof., 1980, acting chmn. div., 1972-75, chmn. div., 1975—. Contbr. over 70 articles, chpt. to books. Capt. M.C., USAF, 1966-68. Mem. AMA, Am. Acad. Orthopaedic Surgeons, Orthopaedic Rsch. Soc., Am. Orthopaedic Assn., Hip Soc., Wis. Orthopaedic Soc., Rotary, Alpha Omega Alpha. Avocations: bicycling, skiing, reading. Office: U Wis Div Orthopedic Surg 600 Highland Ave #G5/361 Madison WI 53792-0001

MCBEATH, GERALD ALAN, political science educator, researcher; b. Mpls., Sept. 13, 1942; s. Gordon Stanley and Astrid Elvira (Hjelmeir) McB.; m. Jenifer Huang, June 7, 1970; children: Bowen, Rowena. BA, U. Chgo., 1963, MA, 1964; PhD, U. Calif., Berkeley, 1970. Vis. asst. prof. polit. sci. Rutgers Coll., New Brunswick, N.J., 1970-72; asst. prof. John Jay Coll., CUNY, N.Y.C., 1972-74, 75-76; assoc. prof. Nat. Chengchi U., Mucha, Taipei, Taiwan, 1974-75; prof. U. Alaska, Fairbanks, 1976—, acting dean coll. liberal arts, 1991-93, dir. faculty devel., 1990-92; cons. Inst. Social and Econ. Rsch., Anchorage, 1976-77; contract rschr. Alaska Dept. Natural Resources, Alaska Dept. Edn., Nat. Inst. Edn., others; staff dir. task force on internat. trade policy Rep. Conf., U.S. Senate. Sr. author: Dynamics of Alaska Native Self-Government, 1980; author monograph: North Slope Borough Government and Policymaking, 1981; jr. author: Alaska's Urban and Rural Governments, 1984; sr. editor Alaska State Government and Politics, 1987; co-author: Alaska Politics and Government, 1994 (Am. Assn. State & Local History Commendation cert. 1995); author: The Alaska State Constitution, 1997; editor: Alaska's Rural Development, 1982. Mem. bd. edn. Fairbanks North Star Borough, 1986-95, pres. 1989-90, 93-94, treas., 1991-93. Recipient Emil Usibelli Disting. Svc. award 1993; Chiang Ching-Kuo Found. fellow, 1995-97; named Outstanding Faculty Mem., Assn. Students U. Alaska, Fairbanks, 1979, Alumni Assn. U. Alaska, Fairbanks, 1981; grantee Nat. Inst. Edn., 1980-83, Alaska Coun. on Sci. and Tech., 1982-84, Spencer Found., 1987-88, Chiang Ching-Kuo Found., 1995-97. Mem. Asian Studies on Pacific Coast (program chmn. 1983, bd. dirs. 1982-83), Assn. Asian Studies, Western Polit. Sci. Assn. (mem. editl. bd. Western Govtl. Rschr.), Am. Polit. Sci. Assn., Fairbanks N. Star Borough Bd. Edn. Democrat. Home: 1777 Red Fox Dr Fairbanks AK 99709-6625 Office: U Ala Dept Polit Sci Fairbanks AK 99775

MCBEE, MARY LOUISE, state legislator, former academic administrator; b. Strawberry Plains, Tenn., June 15, 1924; d. John Wallace and Nina Aileen (Umbarger) McB. BS, East Tenn. State U., 1946; MA, Columbia U., 1951; PhD, Ohio State U., 1961. Tchr. East Tenn. State U., Johnson City, 1947-51; asst. dean of women, 1952-56, 57-60, dean of women, 1961-63; dean of women U. Ga., Athens, 1963-67; world campus afloat adminstr., 1966-67, assoc. dean of students, 1967-72, dean of students, 1972-74, asst. v.p. acad. affairs, 1974-76, assoc. v.p. acad. affairs, 1976-86, v.p. acad. affairs, 1986-88; now mem. Ga. Gen. Assembly; bd. dirs. Ga. Nat. Bank, Athens, 1989—. Author: College Responsibility for Values, 1980; co-author: The American Woman: Who Will She Be?, 1974, Essays, 1979,, 2d edit. 1981. Bd. dirs. Salvation Army, Athens, 1978—, United Way, Athens. Fulbright scholar, The Netherlands, 1956-57. Mem. Athens C. of C. (bd. dirs.). Democrat. Methodist. Avocations: gardening, tennis, hiking. Home: 145 Pine Valley Pl Athens GA 30606-4031 Office: GA House of Reps State Capitol Atlanta GA 30334

MCBEE, ROBERT LEVI, retired federal government official, writer, consultant; b. Braymer, Mo., Aug. 25, 1927; s. Calvin Levi and Wavah E. (Tripp) McB.; m. Lucymae A. Armijo, June 13, 1959; children: Martin Christopher, Mark Antony Christian, Mathew Alfonso Calvin. BA, Westminster Coll., Fulton, Mo., 1952. Editor Take-Off Smoky Hill AFB, Salina, Kans., 1947-58; publicity writer Westminster Coll., Fulton, Mo., 1950-52; advt. mgr. Battenfeld Grease and Oil Corp., Kansas City, Mo., 1952-53; asst. to advt. mgr. Ash Grove Lime and Cement Co., Kansas City, Mo., 1953-57; publicity dir. Am. Campaign Svcs., Kansas City, Mo., 1957; freelance writer Chelan, Wash., 1957-58; reporter Kansas City (Mo.) Times Star, 1958-61; assoc. editor Bailey Publs., Independence, Mo., 1961-63; editor Nat. Cath. Register, Denver, 1963-64; mng. editor Pleasant Hill (Mo.) Times, 1964-67; community affairs specialist Region 7 Job Corps, Kansas City, Mo., 1967-69; pub. info. officer Region 7 Office Econ. Opportunity, Community Svc. Adminstrn., Kansas City, Mo., 1969-81; pub. affairs specialist Kansas City Dist. Army C.E., 1981-85; chief community rels. Fifth U.S. Army, San Antonio, 85-88; acting dir. Chgo. Regional Office Pub. Affairs Dept. Vet. Affairs, 1989-90, asst. dir., 1988-94; acting dir. dept. vets. affairs Chgo. Regional Office Pub. Affairs, 1989-91. Sec., asst. treas. Kansas City Area Transp. Authority, 1965-70; pres. Pleasant Hill (Mo.) C. of C., 1966-67; sec. City Planning and Zoning Comm., Pleasant Hill, 1966; bd. dirs. Cath. Info. Svcs., Kansas City, 1966-72; adv. trustee Rsch. Med. Ctr.,

Kansas City, 1967-82. Mem. Westminster Coll. Alumni Coun. (life), Pi Delta Epsilon, Eta Sigma Phi, Kappa Alpha. Democrat. Roman Catholic. Avocation: reading.

MCBEE, SUSANNA BARNES, journalist; b. Santa Fe, Mar. 28, 1935; d. Jess Stephen and Sybil Elizabeth (Barnes) McBee; m. Paul H. Recer, July 2, 1983. AB, U. So. Calif., 1956; MA, U. Chgo., 1962. Staff writer Washington Post, 1957-65, 73-74, 77-79, asst. nat. editor, 1974-77; asst. sec. for public affairs HEW, 1979; articles editor Washingtonian mag., 1980-81; assoc. editor U.S. News & World Report, 1981-86; news editor Washington Bur. of Hearst Newspapers, 1987-89, asst. bur. chief, 1990—; Washington corr. Life mag., 1965-69; Washington editor McCall's mag., 1970-72. Bd. dirs. Washington Press Club Found., 1992-95. Recipient Penney-Missouri mag. award, 1969, Hall of Fame award, Soc. Profl. Journalists 1996; Sigma Delta Chi Pub. Svc. award, 1969, Hearst Eagle award, 1994. Mem. Nat. Press Club, Cosmos Club. Home: 5190 Watson St NW Washington DC 20016-5329 Office: 1701 Pennsylvania Ave NW Washington DC 20006-5805

MCBIRNEY, BRUCE HENRY, lawyer; b. L.A., June 16, 1954; s. Bruce H. and Gretta (Doyle) McB.; m. Joanne Stillman McBirney, May 31, 1980; children: James Stillman, Esther Kathleen. BA summa cum laude, Loyola Marymount U., L.A., 1976; JD, U. Calif., Berkeley, 1979. Bar: Calif. 1979, U.S. Dist. Ct. (ctrl. dist.) 1979. Mem. Thorpe & Thorpe, L.A., 1979-95, mng. ptnr., 1991, pres., 1992-94, dir., 1992-95, v.p., 1994-95; shareholder, dir., v.p. McBirney & Chuck, L.A., 1995—. Named Scholar of Yr. Loyola Marymount U., L.A., 1976, assoc. editor Calif. Law Review, Berkeley, 1977-79, Eagle Scout Boy Scouts Am., 1968. Mem. Bldg. Owners and Mgrs. Assn., L.A. Serra Club, L.A. County Bar Assn., State Bar Calif. Office: McBirney & Chuck 611 W 6th St Ste 2500 Los Angeles CA 90017-3102

MCBRAYER, LAURA JEAN H., school media specialist; b. Bremen, Ga., July 11, 1944; d. Robert Byron Holloman and Ruth Mildred (McGukin) McLaughlin; m. Dennis Durrett McBrayer; children: Keith, Dana, Scott, Leah. BA in English, West Ga. Coll., 1966, MEd, 1977, M in Media, 1982. Cert. media tchr., secondary English tchr., Ga. English tchr. Bremen (Ga.) H.S., 1966-72, Villa Rica (Ga.) H.S., 1974-75, Ctrl. H.S., Carrollton, Ga., 1975-78; libr., English tchr. Mt. Zion (Ga.) H.S., 1979-80; media specialist West Haralson Jr. H.S., Tallapoosa, Ga., 1980-86, Bremen H.S./Sewell Mid. Sch., Bremen, 1986—. Mem., past sec. West Ga. Regional Libr. Bd., 1988—; sec. Warren P. Sewell LIbr. Bd., Bremen, 1989—, Haralson County Libr. Bd., 1988—; mem. choir First Bapt. Ch., Bremen, 1987-92; mem. centennial com. Dem. Party, Haralson County, 1989—. Mem. ALA, Ga. Libr. Media Assn., Ga. Libr. Assn., Ga. Assn. for Instrnl. Tech., Phi Delta Kappa (Tchr. of Yr. 1977). Avocations: photography, reading, walking, movies, music. Home: 623 Laurel St Bremen GA 30110-2129 Office: Sewell Mid-Bremen HS Media Ctr 504 Laurel St Bremen GA 30110-2128

MCBRIDE, ANGELA BARRON, nursing educator; b. Balt., Jan. 16, 1941; d. John Stanley and Mary C. (Szcpepanska) Barron; m. William Leon McBride, June 12, 1965; children: Catherine, Kara. BS in Nursing, Georgetown U., 1962; LHD (hon.), 1993; MS in Nursing, Yale U., 1964; PhD, Purdue U., 1978; D of Pub. Svc. (hon.), U. Cin., 1983; LLD (hon.), Ea. Ky. U., 1991; DSc(hon.), Med. Coll. of Ohio, 1995. Asst. prof., rsch. asst. inst. Yale U., New Haven, 1964-73; assoc. prof., chairperson Ind. U. Sch. Nursing, Indpls., 1978-81, 80-84, prof., 1981-92, disting. prof., 1992—; assoc. dean rsch. Ind. U. Sch. Nursing, 1985-91, interim dean, 1991-92, univ. dean, 1992—. Author: The Growth and Development of Mothers, 1973, Living with Contradictions, A Married Feminist, 1976, How to Enjoy A Good Life With Your Teenager, 1987; editor: Psychiatric-Mental Health Nursing: Integrating the Behavioral and Biological Sciences, 1996 (Best Book award 1996). Recipient Disting. Alumna award Yale U., Disting. Alumna award Purdue U., Univ. Medallion, U. San Francisco, 1993; Kellog nat. fellow; Am. Nurses Found. scholar. Fellow APA (nursing and health psychology award divsn. 38 1995), Am. Acad. Nursing (past pres.), Nat. Acads. Practice; mem. Midwest Nursing Rsch. Soc. (Disting. Rsch. award 1985), Soc. for Rsch. in Child Devel., Inst. of Medicine, Nat. Acad. Scis., Sigma Theta Tau Internat. (past pres., mentor award 1993, disting. lectr., 1995—). Home: 744 Cherokee Ave Lafayette IN 47905-1872

MCBRIDE, BARRY CLARKE, microbiology and oral biology educator, research microbiologist; b. Victoria, B.C., Can., June 22, 1940; s. Clarke Fyfe and Phyllis Frankie (Whitchelo) McB.; m. Barbara Elizabeth Insley, Oct. 12, 1963; children—Christopher, David. B.Sc., U. B.C., Vancouver, Can., 1963; M.Sc., U. B.C., 1965; Ph.D., U. Ill., 1970. Asst. prof. oral biology and microbiology U. B.C., 1970-75, assoc. prof., 1976-80, prof., head dept. oral biology, 1981-86, head dept. microbiology, 1986-89, dean faculty sci., 1990—; mem. Med. Research Council, 1973-79, vis. scientist, 1979, vis. prof., 1982-84; sci. officer Dental Scis. Grants Com., 1981-86. Assoc. editor Oral Microbiology and Immunology; contbr. articles to profl. jours. Rsch. grantee Med. Rsch. Coun., 1971—. Mem. Internat. Assn. Dental Research, Can. Assn. Dental Research (pres. 1990), Am. Soc. Microbiology, Sigma Xi. Avocations: mountaineering; kayaking; sailing. Office: U BC, Faculty of Sci, Vancouver, BC Canada V6T 1Z4

MCBRIDE, DONNA JANNEAN, publisher; b. Kansas City, Kans., July 3, 1940; d. Donald Merle and Hazel Frances (Williams) McBride; life ptnr. Barbara Grier, 1972. AB, Central Coll., 1962; MLS, U. Mo.-Columbia, 1969. Tchr., Pilot Grove (Mo.) H.S., 1961-62; corr. Bus. Men's Assurance Co., Kansas City, Mo., 1962-66; acctg. clk. Prudential of Eng., Sydney, Australia, 1966-67; head tech. processes Kansas City Pub. Library (Mo.), 1967-77; customer rep. C.L. Systems, Inc., Newtonville, Mass., 1977-80; dir. support services Leon County Pub. Library, Tallahassee, 1980-82; v.p., CFO The Naiad Press, Inc., Tallahassee, 1982—; dir. The Naiad Press, 1976—, Sappho's Libr., 1983—. Mem. ALA, Nat. Gay Task Force, Am. Booksellers Assn., Nat. Women's Studies Assn., NOW. Home: RR 1 Box 3565 Alligator Point FL 32346 Office: The Naiad Press Inc PO Box 10543 Tallahassee FL 32302-2543

MC BRIDE, GUY THORNTON, JR., college president emeritus; b. Austin, Tex., Dec. 12, 1919; s. Guy Thornton and Imogene (Thrasher) McB.; m. Rebekah Jane Bush, Sept. 2, 1942; children: Rebekah Ann, William Howard, Ellen McBride McCarty. B.S. in Chem. Engring., U. Tex., 1940; Sc.D., MIT, 1948; D.P.S. (hon.), Regis Coll., 1979; D.Engring. (hon.), Colo. Sch. Mines, 1984. Registered profl. engr., Tex. La., N.Y., Colo. Instr. chem. engring. Mass. Inst. Tech., 1942-44, research assoc., 1946-48; job engr. Standard Oil Co. Calif., 1944-46; asst. prof. chem. engring Rice Inst., 1948-55, assoc. dean students, 1950-57, dean, 1957-58, assoc. prof., 1955-58; cons. Tex. Gulf Sulphur Co., 1950-58, asst. mgr. research dept., 1958-59, mgr., 1959-60, v.p., mgr. research, 1960-63; v.p. Tex. Gulf Sulphur Co. (Phosphate div.), 1963-70, gen. mgr., 1966-70; pres. Colo. Sch. Mines, Golden, 1970-84; ret.; dir. Halliburton Co., Kerr-McGee Corp., Hercules, Inc.; hon. dir. Texasgulf Inc. Fellow Am. Inst. Chem. Engrs.; mem. Am. Chem. Soc., Nat. Soc. Profl. Engrs., Sigma Xi, Phi Lambda Upsilon, Tau Beta Pi. Club: Mile High (Denver). Home: 2615 Oak Dr Apt 13 Lakewood CO 80215-7182

MCBRIDE, JOHN ALEXANDER, retired chemical engineer; b. Altoona, Pa., Mar. 29, 1918; s. Raymond E. and Carolyn (Tinker) McB.; m. Elizabeth Anne Vogel, Aug. 28, 1942; children: Katherine M. Harris, Susan McBride Malick, Carolyn McBride Nafziger. A.B., Miami U., Oxford, Ohio, 1940; M.Sc., Ohio State U., 1941; Ph.D., U. Ill., 1944. Registered profl. engr., Calif. Various positions in research and devel. dept. Phillips Petroleum Co., 1944-58, 59-65; dir. chem. tech. Phillips Petroleum Co. (Atomic energy div.), 1963-65; chief applications engring. Astrodyne, Inc., 1958-59; dir. div. materials licensing AEC, 1965-70; v.p. E.R. Johnson Assocs., Inc., Fairfax, Va., 1970-92; asst. gen. mgr. Nuclear Chems. & Metals Corp., 1970-71; Adviser U.S. del. 3d Internat. Conf. Peaceful Uses Atomic Energy, 1964. Mem. AIChE (chmn. nuclear engring. divsn. 1986, Robert E. Wilson award 1991), Am. Chem. Soc., Alpha Chi Sigma, Phi Kappa Tau. Achievements include publications and patents on petrochemical products and processes, solid propellant rockets, irradiated fuel reprocessing, radioactive waste fixation and disposal. Home: 1727 Sherman Ave Canon City CO 81212-4354 Address: PO Box 1482 Canon City CO 81215-1482

MCBRIDE, JONATHAN EVANS, executive search consultant; b. Washington, June 16, 1942; s. Gordon Williams and Martha Alice (Evans) McB.; BA, Yale U., 1964; m. Emilie Evans Dean, Sept. 5, 1970; children: Webster Dean, Morley Evans. Account exec. Merrill Lynch & Co., Washington, 1968-72; v.p. dept. mgr. Lionel D. Edie & Co., N.Y.C., 1972-76; v.p., exec. search cons. Simmons Assocs., Inc., Washington, 1976-79; pres. McBride Assocs., Inc., Washington, 1979—. Bd. dirs. Yale U. Alumni Fund, 1974-79; bd. trustees Sidwell Friends Sch., Washington, 1996—. Served to lt. USNR, 1964-68. Clubs: Yale (N.Y.C.); Met. (Washington); Chevy Chase (Md.). Office: 1511 K St NW Washington DC 20005-1401

MCBRIDE, KENNETH EUGENE, lawyer, title company executive; b. Abilene, Tex., June 8, 1948; s. W. Eugene and I. Jean (Wright) McB.; m. Peggy Ann Waller, Aug. 7, 1969 (div. 1980); m. Katrina Lynne Small, June 1, 1985; children: Katherine Jean, Kellie Elizabeth. BA, Central State U., 1971; JD, Oklahoma City U., 1974. Bar: Okla. 1974. Assoc. Linn, Helms & Kirk, Oklahoma City, 1974-76; city atty. City of Edmond (Okla.), 1976-77; v.p., gen. counsel Am. First Land Title Ins., Oklahoma City, 1977-81; pres. Am. First Abstract Co., Norman, Okla., 1981-90, Lawyers Title of Oklahoma City, Inc., 1990—; CEO Am. Eagle Title Ins. Co., 1994—; pres. Okla. Land Title Assn., 1987-88, LT Exch. Corp., 1996—; bd. dirs. Okla City Met. Assn. Realtors. Bd. dirs. Norman Bd. Adjustment, 1982-85, Leadership Okla., Inc., 1986-94, pres., 1989-90, 93-94. Fellow Okla. Bar Found.; mem. ABA, Okla. Bar Assn. (bd. dirs. Real Property Sect. 1992-94), Oklahoma County Bar Assn., Oklahoma City Met. Assn. Realtors, Oklahoma City Real Property Lawyers Assn., Leadership Norman Alumni. Democrat. Presbyterian. Avocation: sailing. Office: Lawyers Title Oklahoma City Inc 1141 N Robinson Ave Oklahoma City OK 73103-4929

MCBRIDE, MATTHEW GORDON, broadcasting executive; b. Halifax, N.S., Can., Mar. 31, 1960; s. Richard Thomas McBride and Mary Agnes (Keller) Boudreau; m. Caroline A. Hamaura, Oct. 28, 1989; children: Chelsea, Ryan. Diploma in Bus. Adminstrn., Open U., B.C., Can., 1996. Announcer CFBV Radio, Smithers, B.C., 1982-83; morning host CHTK Radio, Prince Rupert, B.C., 1983-84; afternoon host CHAB Radio, Moose Jaw, Sask., Can., 1984-85; mid-day host CHFM-FM Radio, Calgary, Alta., Can., 1985-87; mid-day host, asst. music dir. CKKS-FM Radio, Vancouver, B.C., Can., 1987-91; music dir., asst. programmer CKZZ-FM Radio, Vancouver, 1991-95; gen. mgr. CKMM-FM Radio, Winnipeg, Man., Can., 1995-97; CEO Craig Radio, 1997—. Prodr.; (music albums) The New Beat of Christmas, 1991 (BCAB award 1991), The New Beat of Christmas 2, 1992 (CAB award 1993). With Can. Navy, 1977-81. Mem. Royal Can. Legion. Office: CKMM-FM Radio, 1700-155 Carlton St, Winnipeg, MB Canada R3X 1H8

MCBRIDE, MICHAEL FLYNN, lawyer; b. Milw., Mar. 27, 1951; s. Raymond Edward and Marian Dunne McBride; m. Kerin Ann O'Brien, Mar. 23, 1991. BS in Chem. and Biology, U. Wis., 1972, JD, 1976; MS in Environ. Engr. Sci., Calif. Inst. Tech., 1973. Bar: Wis. 1976, D.C. 1976. Assoc. LeBoeuf, Lamb, Greene & MacRae, Washington, 1976-84, ptnr., 1985—. Mem. Fed. Energy Bar Assn., Assn. for Transp. Law, Logistics and Policy (v.p., energy tranps., law inst. com. 1990, co-chmn. 1991—, pres. 1994-95, editor ATLLP Jour.), Chantilly Nat. Golf and Country Club. Roman Catholic. Avocations: golf, reading, travel. Home: 6648 Byrns Pl McLean VA 22101-4419 Office: LeBoeuf Lamb Greene & MacRae LLP 1875 Connecticut Ave NW Washington DC 20009-5728

MCBRIDE, NANCY ALLYSON, child resource center administrator; b. Lakewood, Ohio, June 15, 1952; d. Harold Jackson and Mary Alice (Inman) McB. BA in Psychology magna cum laude, Oakland U., 1977. Program dir. Alternative Lifestyles, Inc., Pontiac, Mich., 1975-77; youth counselor Creative Outlooks Counseling Ctr., Pontiac, Mich., 1977-78; chief probation officer 47th Dist. Ct., Farmington Hills, Mich., 1978-80; exec. dir. Kids in Distress, inc., Wilton Manors, Fla., 1980-81; program coord. Adam Walsh Ctr., Ft. Lauderdale, Fla., 1981-87; regional trainer Home Box Office, Inc., Atlanta, 1987-90; exec. dir. Nat. Ctr. for Missing and Exploited Children/Fla. Br., Lake Park, Fla., 1990—; adj. instr. Nova U., Ft. Lauderdale, 1985-87, 90—, Broward C.C., Ft. Lauderdale, 1986-87; cons. 5 maj. TV prodns., Ft. Lauderdale, 1983-87; instr. Inst. for Nonprofit Orgn. and Mgmt., Denver, 1986-87; instr. victims svcs. cert. program Palm Beach Atlantic Coll., West Palm Beach, Fla., 1993-94. Author: (rsch. project) Child Abuse & Neglect: The Plight of the 2nd Class Citizen, 1977. Tutor Laubach Literacy Tng., Chgo., 1972; vol Erie Neighborhood House, Chgo., 1970, 72, student intern Macomb County Youth Svcs., Warren, Mich., 1977; family aide Family Focus, Birmingham, Mich., 1976-77. Recipient plaque 2d Conf. Missing Children, Chgo., 1987, Guardian Ad Litem Program, Ft. Lauderdale, 1982, Cmty. Svc. award Consortium for Human Devel., Troy, Mich., 1980, Spl. Plaque award John and Reve Walsh, 1992. Democrat. Avocations: swimming, reading, creative writing. Office: Nat Ctr - Florida 9176 Alternate A1A Ste 100 Lake Park FL 33403-1445

MCBRIDE, RODNEY LESTER, investment counselor; b. Denver, Sept. 1, 1941; s. Laurence Thomas and Harriet Alvina (Primmer) McB.; m. Nancy Faye Davenport, Mar. 21, 1964 (div. June 1984); children: Douglas L., Cheryl L.; m. Judy Winslow, Nov. 7, 1992; stepchildren: Mark P. Winslow, Scott C. Winslow. BS in Mktg., U. Colo., 1963; MBA, U. Calif., Berkeley, 1976. Chartered investment counselor Investment Counsel Assn. Am., Fin. Analyst Fedn. Indsl. salesman Fibreboard Corp., San Diego and San Francisco, 1963-66; investment counselor Shuman, Agnew & Co., San Francisco, 1966-71; investment counselor, co-founder capital counseling svc. Bank of Am., San Francisco, 1971-75; investment counselor Scudder, Stevens and Clark, San Francisco, 1975-76; sr. v.p., office mgr. Crocker Investment Mgmt. Corp., Los Angeles, 1977-84; sr. v.p., dir. portfolio mgmt., chmn. equity strategy com. Crocker Investment Mgmt. Corp., San Francisco, 1984-86; mng. dir., sr. portfolio mgr., chmn. equity strategy com., chmn. core equity com., chmn. internat. asset allocation com. Chancellor Capital Mgmt., Inc. (formerly Citicorp Investment Mgmt. Corp.), N.Y.C., 1986-94; mng. dir., sr. portfolio mgr., chmn. equity strategy com. Furman Selz Capital Mgmt., N.Y.C., 1994—. Pres., coach Palos Verdes (Calif.) Basketball Assn., 1982-83; mem. 2d Congregational Ch.; bd. dirs. Greater N.Y. couns. Boy Scouts Am. Mem. L.A. Soc. Fin. Analysts (sec., bd. dirs. 1984, treas. 1983, chmn. seminar com. 1982-83), N.Y. Soc. Fin. Analysts, Assn. Investment Mgmt. and Rsch. (chartered fin. analyst), Western Pension Conf., U. Colo. Alumni Assn., U. Calif. Alumni Assn., Stanwich Country Club, Round Hill Country Club, Alpha Kappa Psi (treas. 1963). Republican. Avocations: golf, tennis, volleyball, duck hunting, fishing. Home: 148 Clapboard Ridge Rd Greenwich CT 06831-3351 Office: Furman Selz Capital Mgmt 230 Park Ave New York NY 10169

MCBRIDE, THOMAS DWAYNE, manufacturing executive; b. Brownwood, Tex., Feb. 13, 1947; s. Thomas Alfred and Eula Faye (Harvey) McB.; m. Peggy Anne Kimbrough McBride, Oct. 14, 1967; children: Jeffery Dwayne, Stacy Anne. AS, Crowder Coll., Neosho, Mo., 1967; BS in Mech. Engring., U. Mo., Rolla, 1970; MBA in Mgmt., U. Akron, 1978. Registered profl. engr., Ohio. Engring. supr. Babcock & Wilcox, Barberton, Ohio, 1972-79; mgr. engring. Bendix Corp., South Beloit, Ill., 1979-83; mgr. sales engring. Bendix/Warner & Swasey, Worcester, Mass., 1983-84, mgr. Product Engring., 1984-86; program mgr. Design Tech. Corp., Billerica, Mass., 1986-87; mgr. engring. Netco, Inc., Haverhill, Mass., 1987-88; dir. engring. The Nelmor Co., North Uxbridge, Mass., 1988-95; tech. mgr. Lawrence (Mass.) Pumps Inc., 1995-96, ops. mgr., 1996—; tech. and bus. cons. Micromation, Inc., Altoona, Pa., 1988-90. Inventor: Granulator Knife, 1991, 94, Bin Deflector, 1991; author: Society of Manufacturing Engineers, 1992. 1st lt. U.S. Army, 1970-72. Recipient Curator's scholarship U. Mo., 1967. Mem. Soc. Plastics Engrs., Environ. Industry Assn. (co-chairperson Wastec divsn. subcom. on safety standards for size reduction equipment 1995—). Mem. Trinity Ch. Avocations: golf, genealogy, religious history. Home: 36 Deerfield Rd Shrewsbury MA 01545-3707 Office: Lawrence Pumps Inc 371 Market St Lawrence MA 01843-1528

MC BRIDE, THOMAS FREDERICK, lawyer, former university dean, government official; b. Elgin, Ill., Feb. 8, 1929; s. Thomas Wallace and Sarah Rosalie (Pierce) McB.; m. Catherine Higgs Milton, Aug. 23, 1975; children: Matthew (dec.), Elizabeth, John, Raphael, Luke. BA, NYU, 1952; LLB, Columbia U., 1956. Bar: N.Y. 1956, D.C. 1966, U.S. Supreme Ct. 1963, Calif. 1989. Asst. dist. atty. N.Y. County, 1956-59; trial atty. organized crime sect. Dept. Justice, 1961-65; adviser to Home Ministry, Govt. India, 1964; ofcl. Peace Corps, 1965-68; dep. chief counsel select com. on crime Ho. of Reps., 1969-70; assoc. dir., staff dir. Police Found., 1970-73; assoc. spl. prosecutor Watergate, 1973-75; dir. bur. enforcement CAB, 1975-77; insp. gen. U.S. Dept. Agr., Washington, 1977-81, U.S. Dept. Labor, Washington, 1981-82; assoc. dean Stanford Law Sch. (Calif.), 1982-89; mem. Pres.'s Commn. Organized Crime, 1983-86, Calif. Council on Mental Health, 1986-90; dir. environ. health and safety Stanford U., 1990-92; counselor U.S. Dept. Energy, Washington, 1993-95. Served with AUS, 1946-47. Mem. D.C. Bar Assn. Home and Office: 837 Cedro Way Stanford CA 94305-1034

MCBRIDE, WANDA LEE, psychiatric nurse; b. Dayton, Ohio, Dec. 13, 1931; d. Owen Francis Staup and Ruby Madonna (Campbell) Inscore; m. Richard H. McBride, July 28, 1951 (div. Mar. 1966); children: Kathleen Kerns, Kimberlee Haley. Diploma, Christ Hosp. Sch., Cin., 1953; student, U. Cin., 1954-55. Cert. psychiat. mental health nurse ANA. Various health-care positions, 1953-66; from supr. 4 acute male units to supr. outpatient dept. Cen. Ohio Psychiat. Hosp., Columbus, 1966-77; supr. hosp., head nurse urology and respiratory diseases flr. St. Anthony Hosp., Okla., 1977-83; shift supr. and coord. child program Willowview Hosp., Spencer, Okla., 1983-88; adminstrv. nursing supr. Grant Ctr. of Deering Hosp., Miami, 1988—, assessment specialist, 1995—; disabilities case mgr. Kemper Nat. Svcs., Plantation, Fla., 1996—; clin. nurse Savannas Hosp., Pt. St. Lucie, Fla., 1997. Mem. Gov.'s Com. for Mental Health and Retardation, 1963-66, Logan County Mental Health League, Ohio, 1963-66. Named Nurse of Yr., 1983-90. Mem. Nat. League for Nursing, Mental Health League (past pres.), Lioness Club (past pres.). Republican. Episcopalian. Avocations: orchid growing, classical music, cooking, fishing, camping. Home: 1 Cartagesa Port Saint Lucie FL 34952

MCBRIDE, WILLIAM BERNARD, treasurer; b. N.Y.C., May 22, 1931; s. William and Nora (Hughes) McB.; m. Lorraine Barry, May 27, 1956; children: Mary, William, Stephen, Anne. BS, Fordham U., 1952; MBA, Baruch Sch., 1963. CPA, N.Y. Staff auditor Touche, Ross, Bailey & Smart (CPAs), N.Y.C., 1952-58; asst. v.p. Bankers Trust Co., N.Y.C., 1959-67; treas. Kidde, Inc., Saddle Brook, N.J., 1967-87; v.p. Kidde, Inc., 1974-87; cons. Hanson Industries, other cos., Iselin, N.J., 1987—. Mem. AICPA, N.Y. State Soc. CPAs. Home and Office: 243 Sunset Ave Ridgewood NJ 07450-2420

MC BRIDE, WILLIAM LEON, philosopher, educator; b. N.Y.C., Jan. 19, 1938; s. William Joseph and Irene May (Choffin) McB.; m. Angela Barron, July 12, 1965; children: Catherine, Kara. A.B., Georgetown U., 1959; postgrad. (Fulbright fellow), U. Lille, 1959-60; M.A. (Woodrow Wilson fellow), Yale U., 1962, PhD (Social Sci. Rsch. Coun. fellow), 1964. Instr. philosophy Yale U., New Haven, 1964-66, asst. prof., 1966-70, assoc. prof., 1970-73; lectr. Northwestern U., Evanston, Ill., summer 1972; assoc. prof. Purdue U., West Lafayette, Ind., 1973-76, prof., 1976—; lectr. Korcula Summer Sch., Yugoslavia, 1971, 73. Author: Fundamental Change in Law and Society, 1970, The Philosophy of Marx, 1977, Social Theory at a Crossroads, 1980, (with R.A. Dahl) Demokrati og Autoritet, 1980, Sartre's Political Theory, 1991, Social and Political Philosophy, 1994; editor: (with C.O. Schrag) Phenomenology in a Pluralistic Context, 1983, Sartre and Existentialism, 8 vols., 1997. Decorated chevalier Ordre des Palmes Académiques. Mem. AAUP (pres. Purdue chpt. 1983-86, pres. Ind. conf. 1988-89), Am. Philos. Assn. (chmn. com. on internat. coop. 1992-95, bd. dirs. 1992-95), N.Am. Soc. Social and Polit. Philoophy (v.p. 1997—), Am. Soc. Polit. and Legal Philosophy, Soc. Phenemonology and Existential Philosophy (exec. co-sec. 1977-80), Sartre Soc. N.Am. (chmn. bd. dirs. 1985-88, 91-93), Am. Soc. Philosophy in the French Lang. (pres. 1994-96). Home: 744 Cherokee Ave Lafayette IN 47905-1872 Office: Purdue U Dept Philosophy West Lafayette IN 47907-1360

MCBRIEN, RICHARD PETER, theology educator; b. Hartford, Conn., Aug. 19, 1936; s. Thomas Henry and Catherine Ann (Botticelli) McB. AA, St. Thomas Sem., 1956; BA, St. John Sem., 1958, MA, 1962; STD, Gregorian U., 1967. Assoc. pastor Our Lady of Victory Ch., West Haven, Conn., 1962-63; prof., dean of studies Pope John XXIII Nat. Sem., Weston, Mass., 1965-70; prof. theology Boston Coll., Newton, Mass., 1970-80, dir. inst. of religious edn. and pastoral ministry,, 1975-80; prof. theology U. Notre Dame, Ind., 1980—, chmn. dept., 1980-91; cons. various dioceses and religious communities in the U.S. and Can., 1965—; vis. fellow John F. Kennedy Sch. Govt. Harvard U., Cambridge, 1976-77; mem. Council on Theol. Scholarship and Research Assn. of Theol. Schs., 1987-91. Author: Do We Need Church?, 1969, Catholicism, 2 vols., 1980, rev. edit., 1994 (Christopher award 1981), Caesar's Coin: Religion and Politics in America, 1987, Report on the Church: Catholicism after Vatican II, 1992, Responses to 101 Questions on the Church, 1996, Inside Catholicism, 1996; editor: Encyclopedia of Religion, 1987, Harper Collins Encyclopedia of Catholicism, 1995. Recipient Best Syndicated Weekly Column award Cath. Press Assn. of U.S. and Can., 1975, 77, 78, 84. Mem. Cath. Theol. Soc. of Am. (pres. 1973-74, John Courtney Murray award 1976), Coll. Theology Soc., Am. Acad. Religion. Office: Univ of Notre Dame Dept Theology Notre Dame IN 46556

MCBROOM, DIANE CRAUN, accountant, horse trainer; b. Gettysburg, Pa., Jan. 2, 1962; d. Edward Kenneth and Suzanne (Catchings) Craun; m. Stephen Cushing, June 3, 1993; children: Emily, Michael Ross. AAS, Piedmont Va. C.C., 1983; BA in Environ. Sci. with distinction, U. Va., 1985, MS in Taxation with distinction, 1990. CPA, Va., Md.; notary public, Va. Rsch. asst. U. Va. Hosp., Charlottesville, 1980-86; instr. The Miller Sch. of Albemarle, Charlottesville, 1986-88; adj. prof. U. Va., Charlottesville, 1987-90; tax assoc. Deloitte & Touche, N.Y.C., 1990-91, Coopers & Lybrand, Roanoke, Va., 1991-92; acct. Owl Hollow Farm, Floyd, Va., 1992—; horse trainer Owl Hollow Farm, Floyd, 1980—. Asst. editor: (instrnl. book) Lotus 1-2-3, 1987; editor BRCTA Newsletter, 1996-97, USCTA Area II Newsletter, 1997—. Leader Jr. Achievement, Roanoke, 1991-92; exec. dir. Boy Scouts Am., Charlottesville, 1986-90. Edmund P. Berkely scholar Commonwealth of Va., 1982. Mem. AICPA, Va. Soc. CPAs, U.S. Equestrian Team, U.S. Combined Tng. Assn., U.S. Dressage Fedn., Am. Horse Shows Assn. Republican. Episcopalian. Avocations: riding, reading, hiking, investing, photography. Home and Office: Owl Hollow Farm RR 4 Box 212 Floyd VA 24091-9117

MCBROOM, NANCY LEE, insurance executive; b. Tulsa, Nov. 7, 1925; d. Lee Webster and Dora Irene (Londigan) Adams; m. Robert B. McBroom, Jan. 22, 1945 (dec. Aug. 1969); children: Dacia Adams, Rene McBroom, Robert McBroom. Student, John Brown U., 1941-42, Little Rock Bus. Coll., 1941-42. Profl. horse trainer, judge, breeder N.C., Va. and Calif., 1955-75; owner Stombock's West, Inc., Del Mar, Calif., 1968-74; agt. Mut. Omaha Ins. Co., San Diego, 1978-84; owner, broker McBroom Ins. Svcs., San Diego, 1984—; dir. Dependent's Riding Program, USMC, Camp LeJeune, N.C., 1963-66. Author: Handbook for Riding Instructors, 1963. Mem. com. Civitan Fund Raiser for Spl. Olympics, 1986. Mem. Nat. Assn. Securities Dealers, Rancho Bernardo C. of C. (com. 1986). Republican. Lodge: Soroptomist Internat. (mem. com. Women Helping Women 1985-86). Avocations: music, tennis, swimming, horseback riding, hiking, travel. Home: 12093 Caminito Campana San Diego CA 92128-2061 Office: McBroom Ins Svcs Ste 110-b 16776 Bernardo Center Dr San Diego CA 92128-2534

MCBROOM, THOMAS WILLIAM, SR., utility manager; b. Atlanta, Mar. 29, 1963; s. William Ralph and Ethel Irene (Bradley) McB.; m. Susan H.; 1 child, Thomas William Jr. B in Mech. Engring., Ga. Tech., 1985, MS in Mech. Engring., 1987; JD, Ga. State U., 1992, MBA, 1992. Bar: Ga. 1993, D.C. 1994, U.S. Tax Ct. 1993, U.S. Supreme Ct. 1996; registered profl. engr., Ga.; lic. comml. pilot and flight instr. Mfg. engr. AT & T Techs., Norcross, Ga., 1985-86; energy systems engr. Atlanta Gas Light Co., 1987-89, sales engr., 1989-90, dir. power systems markets, 1991-94, sr. corp. planning analyst, 1994-95, mgr. major accounts, 1995-97, dir. major accts., 1997—. Mem. Leadership Coweta, 1996, Coverdell Rep. Leadership Inst., 1997; del. Ga. 3d Congl. Dist. Rep. Conv., 1997, Ga. Rep. Conv., 1997; parliamentarian Coweta County Rep. Conv., 1997; vice chmn. state ho. dists. Coweta County Rep. Com., 1997-99. Mem. ASHRAE, Ga. Bar Assn., Ga. Soc. Profl. Engrs. (treas. 1990-91, sec. 1991-92, pres. 1992-93, Young Engr. of Yr. 1991), Coverdell Leadership Inst., 1997—, Newnan-Coweta C. of C. (transp. com. 1996, cmty. devel. com. 1997), Toastmasters Internat. (treas. 1996—), Phi Delta Phi (exchequer 1991). Home: 15 Culpepper Way Newnan GA 30265-2217 Office: Ga Natural Gas Co PO Box 698 Newnan GA 30264

MCBRYDE, JAMES EDWARD, state legislator; b. Santa Monica, Calif., Sept. 23, 1950; s. Edward James McBryde and Barbara Jean (Fowler) Mallon; m. Kimberly Anne Benoit, Nov. 28, 1987; children: Sarah Joy, Natalie Marie, Elizabeth Anne, Rebecca Christine. BS, Cen. Mich. U., 1972. Sales rep. Laconia (N.H.) Shoe Co., 1977-78, The McBryde Shoe Co., Petoskey, Mich., 1978-79, The Sheboygan (Wis.) Co., 1979-85, The Timberland Co., Hampton, N.H., 1985-90; mem. Mich. Ho. of Reps., 1991—. Chmn. Isabella County Criminal Justice Com., Mt. Pleasant, Mich., 1985-86, 1989-90, 91, Isabella County 911 Governing Bd., Mt. Pleasant, 1989-90, Campaign Search Com., Isabella County, 1988, 90, 92, 94, 96; county commr. Isabella County Bd. Commrs., 1985-90, vice chmn., 1985-86, 89-90; first vice chmn. Isabella County Rep. Com., 1989-90; rep. Mich. Rep. State Com., Lansing, 1989-90; active Isabella County Farm Bur. Named Legislator of Yr. Mich. Sheriff's Assn., 1994; recipient Star award for Legis. Achievement Mich. Dep. Sheriff's Assn., 1994, 96. Mem. Mich. and Isabella County Right to Life, Mt. Pleasant Lions Club. Republican. Presbyterian. Avocations: reading, biking, running. Office: PO Box 164 Mount Pleasant MI 48804-0164

MCBRYDE, JOHN HENRY, federal judge; b. Jackson, Oct. 9, 1931; m. Betty Vinson; children: Rebecca McBryde Dippold, Jennifer, John Blake. BS in Commerce, Tex. Christian U., 1953; LLB, U. Tex., 1956. Bar: Tex. 1956, U.S. Ct. Appeals (5th cir.) 1958, U.S. Dist. Ct. (no. dist.) 1958, U.S. Dist. Ct. (ea. dist.) 1989, U.S. Supreme Ct. 1972. Assoc. Cantey, Hanger, Johnson, Scarborough & Gooch, Ft. Worth, 1956-62; ptnr. Cantey & Hanger and predecessor firm, Ft. Worth, 1962-69, McBryde, Bennett and predecessor firms, Ft. Worth, 1969-90; judge U.S. Dist. Ct. (no. dist.) Tex., Ft. Worth, 1990—. Fellow Am. Bar Found. (life), Tex. Bar Found. (life), Am. Coll. Trial Lawyers. Office: US Dist Ct US Courthouse Rm 401 501 W 10th St Fort Worth TX 76102-3637

MCBRYDE, NEILL GREGORY, lawyer; b. Durham, N.C., Jan. 11, 1944; s. Angus M. and Priscilla (Gregory) McB.; m. Margaret McPherson, Aug. 1, 1970; children: Margaret Courtauld, Neill Gregory Jr. AB cum laude, Davidson Coll., 1966; JD with high honors, U. N.C., 1969. Bar: N.C. 1969, Ga. 1972. Assoc. King & Spalding, Atlanta, 1971-76; ptnr. Fleming, Robinson, Bradshaw & Hinson, Charlotte, N.C., 1977-81, Helms, Mulliss & Johnston, Charlotte, 1981-86, Smith Helms Mulliss & Moore, Charlotte, 1986-90, Moore & Van Allen PLLC, Charlotte, 1990—; lectr. in field, conductor workshops in field. Author, editor: First Union National Bank of North Carolina Will Book, 1986; contbr. to profl. jours. Elder and Deacon Myers Park Presbyn. Ch., Charlotte, 1980-86, 92-95; dir. sec. Presbyn. Home for Aged, Charlotte, 1978-82; trustee Charlotte Latins Schs., Inc., 1980-86, 87-93. Fellow Am. Coll. Trust and Estate Counsel (mem. bd. regents, sec.), Am. Coll. Tax Counsel; mem. ABA, Ga. Bar Assn., N.C. Bar Assn. (probate and fiduciary law sect.), Order of Coif, Phi Beta Kappa, Omicron Delta Kappa. Republican. Avocations: tennis, golf, fishing. Office: Moore & Van Allen PLLC Nations Bank Corp Ctr 100 N Tryon St Fl 47 Charlotte NC 28202-4000

MCBRYDE, THOMAS HENRY, lawyer; b. New Albany, Miss., Oct. 26, 1925; s. Henry Thornton and Mary Catherine (Davis) McB.; m. Barbara White, Dec. 28, 1946; children: Elise, William Henry, John Thomas. B.S., U.S. Mil. Acad., 1946; LL.B., U. Va., 1952. Bar: Va. 1952, N.Y. 1959. Commd. 2d lt. U.S. Army, 1946, advanced through grades to capt., 1950; assigned to Japan, ETO and U.S.; instr. law U.S. Mil. Acad., 1956-57; resigned, 1957; asst. counsel N.Y. State Banking Dept., 1960-61; assoc. Rogers & Wells and predecessors, N.Y.C., 1957-60, 61-65, ptnr., 1965-93, sr. counsel, 1993—; chief counsel N.Y. State Joint Legis. Com. to Revise Banking Law, 1962-65, minority counsel, 1965-66; mem. comml. panel Am. Arbitration Assn., 1976—; mem. adv. com. supervision mut. instns. Office N.Y. Banking Supt., 1966-67. Mem. Assn. Grads. U.S. Mil. Acad., Order of Coif, Am. Yacht Club. Republican. Episcopalian. Home: 4812 NW 62d St Gainesville FL 32606 Office: Rogers & Wells 200 Park Ave Ste 5200 New York NY 10166-0005

MCBURNEY, ELIZABETH INNES, physician, educator; b. Lake Charles, La., Dec. 24, 1944; d. Theodore John and Martha (Caldwell) Innes; divorced, 1980; children: Leanne Marie, Susan Eleanor. BS, U. Southwestern La., 1965; MD, La. State U., 1969. Diplomate Am. Bd. Internal Medicine, Am. Bd. Dermatology. Intern Pensacola (Fla.) Edn. Program, 1969-70; resident in internal medicine Boston U. and Carney Hosps., 1970-72; resident in dermatology Charity Hosp., New Orleans, 1972-74; staff physician Ochsner Hosp., New Orleans, 1974-80; assoc. head of dermatology Ochsner Clinic, New Orleans, 1974-80; clin. asst. prof. Sch. Medicine La. State U., New Orleans, 1976-79, clin. assoc. prof., 1979-90, clin. prof., 1990—; clin. asst. prof. Sch. Medicine Tulane U., New Orleans, 1976-88, clin. assoc. prof., 1988-91, clin. prof., 1991—; mem. staff Northshore Regional Med. Ctr., Slidell, La., 1985—, Slidell Meml. Hosp., 1988—, chmn. CME courses, 1988—; regional dir. Mycosis Fungoides Study Group, Balt., 1974-94. Contbr. articles to profl. jours. Bd. dirs. Slidell Art Coun., 1988—, Camp Fire, New Orleans, 1979-83, Cancer Assn. New Orleans, 1978-83; juror Art in Pub. Places, Slidell, 1989. Fellow ACP; mem. Am. Soc. Dermatologic Surgery (treas. 1991-94, bd. dirs. 1988-91, pres. elect 1995-96, pres. 1996-97), Am. Acad. Dermatology (bd. dirs. 1994—), Am. Bd. Laser Medicine & Surgery (bd. dirs. 1991-96), La. Dermatologic Soc. (pres. 1989-90), St. Tammary Med. Soc. (pres. 1988), Phi Kappa Phi, Alpha Omega Alpha. Avocations: reading, gardening, fine art, music, film. Office: 1051 Gause Blvd Ste 460 Slidell LA 70458-2950

MCBURNEY, MARGOT B., librarian; b. Lethbridge, Alta., Can.; d. Ronald Laurence Maness and R. Blanche (Lott) Hart; children: Margot Elisabeth McBurney Lane, James Ronald Gordon. B.A. with honours, Principia Coll., 1953; M.Sc. in L.S, U. Ill., 1969. Sec. Marshall Brooks Library, Principia Coll., Elsah, Ill., 1966-69; reference librarian Marshall Brooks Library, Principia Coll., 1969-70; systems analyst trainee in library systems U. Alta. Library, Edmonton, 1970-71; undergrad. reference librarian U. Alta. Library, 1971-72, editor periodicals holdings list, 1972-73, serials cataloguer, 1973-74, head acquisitions div., 1974-77; chief librarian Queen's U. Library, Kingston, Ont., Can., 1977-90. Editor: Am. Soc. Info. Sci. Western Can. chpt. Proceedings, 1975, 76. Mem. ALA, Am. Soc. Info. Sci. (councilor-at-large 1976-79, past chmn. chpt.), Assn. Research Libraries (dir. 1978-81, chmn. task force on library edn. 1980-83), Can. Assn. Info. Sci., Can. Assn. Research Libraries, Can. Library Assn., Council on Library Resources (PETREL com. 1981-84), Phi Alpha Eta, Beta Phi Mu.

MCCABE, CHARLES LAW, retired manufacturing company executive, management consultant; b. Port Deposit, Md., Oct. 13, 1922; s. Joshua Burton and Adah (Law) McC.; m. Ingrid Alice Koebel, Dec. 21, 1949; children: Chad, Sigrid Christina, Ingrid Lisa. B.S., Dickinson Coll., 1943; M.S., Carnegie Mellon U., 1947, Sc.D., 1948. Mem. faculty Carnegie Mellon U., Pitts., 1951-65, prof., 1959-65; dean Grad. Studies, Carnegie Mellon U., 1962-65, v.p. research, 1964-65; pres. Koebel Diamond Tool Co., Detroit, 1966-70, Teledyne Firth Sterling, Pitts., 1970-75; gen. mgr. v.p. High Tech. Materials div. Cabot Corp., Kokomo, Ind., 1975-82; v.p. Cabot Corp., Boston, 1982-87; pres. High St. Assocs., Boston, 1988—. Author: (with C.L. Bauer) Metals, Atoms and Alloy, 1964. Past trustee Dickinson Coll.; active fund drives United Way. Served with AUS, 1945-46. Fellow Am. Soc. Metals (Pitts award 1961); mem. AIME, Grosse Pointe Club, Naples Yacht Club (dir. 1995—), Pt. Royal Club (Naples). Episcopalian.

MCCABE, EDWARD R. B., academic administrator, educator, physician; b. Balt., Mar. 26, 1946. BA in Biology, Johns Hopkins U., 1967; PhD in Pharmacology, U. So. Calif., 1972, MD, 1974. Diplomate Am. Bd. Pediatrics. Resident in pediatrics U. Minn. Hosps., Mpls., 1974-76; pediatric metabolism fellow Sch. Medicine U. Colo., Denver, 1976-78, instr., assoc. prof. pediatrics Sch. Medicine, 1978-86; assoc. prof. genetics Baylor Coll. Medicine, Houston, 1986-94; prof., chmn. dept. pediatrics Sch. Medicine UCLA, 1994—; physician-in-chief UCLA Children's Hosp.; mem. med. genetics residency rev. com. Accreditation Coun. Grad. Med. Edn., 1993—; chmn. conf. gaucher disease NIH, Bethesda, Md., 1994-96, mem. NICHD coun., Bethesda, 1995—. Editor Biochem. and Molecular Medicine, 1990—. Mem. sci. adv. bd. Hereditary Disease Found., L.A., 1995—; chmn. Basil O'Connor Award March Dimes, White Plains, N.Y., 1997—. Mem. Am. Acad. Pediatrics (chmn. com. genetics Elk Grove Village, Ill. 1987-91, co-founder, chmn. sect. genetics Elk Grove, 1990, 93-95), Am. Bd. Med. Genetics (diplomate, pres. Washington 1995-96), Am. Soc. Human Genetics, Am. Fedn. Clin. Rsch., Am. Pediatric Soc., Am. Soc. Biochemistry and Molecular Biology, Soc. Pediatric Rsch. (E. Mead Johnson award, 1993), Phi Kappa Phi (L.A.), Sigma Xi (L.A.), Alpha Omega Alpha (L.A.). Achievements include first to describe the Continguous Gene Syndrome, Complex Glycerol Kinase Deficiency; first to extract DNA from blood in newborn screening blotters; first to set up molecular genetic diagonosis for sickle cell disease as part of newborn screening; developement of concept of molecular genetic triage of bacterial infection. Office: UCLA Sch Medicine Dept Pediatrics 22-412 MDCC 10833 Le Conte Ave Los Angeles CA 90095-1752*

MC CABE, GERARD BENEDICT, retired library administrator; b. N.Y.C., Jan. 22, 1930; s. Patrick Joseph and Margaret Irene (McDonald) McC.; m. Jacqueline L. Maloney, Aug. 3, 1963 (dec. 1987); children: Theresa Marie, Rebecca Mary. B.A. in English, Manhattan Coll., 1952; A.M. in Library Sci. (scholar), U. Mich., 1954; M.A. in English, Mich. State U., 1959. Asst. acquisitions dept. U. Nebr. Library, Lincoln, 1954-56; chief bibliog. acquisitions dept. Mich. State U. Library, East Lansing, 1956-58; librarian Inst. Community Devel. and Service, Mich. State U., 1958-59; acquisitions librarian U. S. Fla., Tampa, 1959-66; asst. dir. planning and devel. U. S. Fla., 1967-70; assoc. dir. U. Ark. Library, Fayetteville, 1966-67; dir. univ. libraries Va. Commonwealth U., Richmond, 1970-82; dir. libraries Clarion U. of Pa., 1982-95; ret., 1995; libr. cons., Wilmington, N.C., 1995—. Editor: The Smaller Academic Library: A Management Handbook, 1988, Operations Handbook for Small Academic Library, 1989, Academic Libraries in Urban and Metropolitan Areas, 1992; co-editor ann. pub. Advances in Libr. Adminstrn. and Orgn., vols. 1-12, Insider's Guide to Libr. Automation: Essays of Practical Experience, 1993, Acad. Librs.: Their Rationale and Role in Am. Higher Edn., 1995, Introducing and Managing Academic Library Automation Projects, 1996; contbr. articles to profl. jours. Mem. ALA, Southeastern Library Assn., Bibliog. Soc. Am. Home and Office: PO Box 4793 Wilmington NC 28406-1793 *Consideration for others is a guiding principle for my personal and professional behavior. I, as a librarian, must have concern for those I serve. Their needs are my first and only interest, not success, not notoriety, only their service and their satisfaction.*

MCCABE, JAMES PATRICK, library director; b. Phila., May 24, 1937; s. Felix and Josephine (Murtaugh) McC. BA, Niagara U., 1963; MA, U. Mich., 1964, MA in LS, 1965, PhD, 1968. Libr. dir. Allentown Coll., Center Valley, Pa., 1968-89; acting libr. dir. Muhlenberg Cedar Crest Colls., Allentown, Pa., 1989-90; dir. univ. libr. Fordham U., N.Y.C., 1990—. Author: Critical Guide to Catholic Reference Books, 3d edit., 1989. Bd. dirs. Pa. Shakespear Festival, Center Valley, 1990—. Office: Fordham U Libr Bronx NY 10458

MCCABE, JOHN CHARLES, oral surgeon; b. Bklyn., July 27, 1950; s. Vincent James and Helen Cecelia (Byrne) McC.; m. Barbara Ann Carr-Dolan, Jan. 27, 1996; children: Sean Michael, Jacqueline Carr. BA, Manhattan Coll., 1972; DDS, Columbia U., 1985, MD, 1990. Diplomate Am. Bd. Oral and Maxillofacial Surgery. Attending physician Presbyn. Hosp., N.Y.C., 1990—; asst. prof. Columbia U., N.Y.C., 1990—, dir. anesthesia and pain control Sch. Dental and Oral Surgery, 1990—; attending surgeon VA Med. Ctr., Bronx, N.Y., 1992—. Asst. scoutmaster Boy Scouts Am., Yorktown Heights, N.Y., 1995—. Fellow Am. Assn. Oral and Maxillofacial Surgeons; mem. AMA, Am. Cleft Palate Assn., N.Y. State Soc. Oral and Maxillofacial Surgeons (Oral Surgery award 1985), N.Y. State Assn. Cleft Palate Ctrs. (bd. dirs.). Roman Catholic. Avocations: guitar, photography, drawing, skiing, hiking. Office: Columbia-Presbyn Med Ctr 620 W 168th St # 8 New York NY 10032-3702

MC CABE, JOHN CHARLES, III, writer; b. Detroit, Nov. 14, 1920; s. Charles John and Rosalie (Dropiewski) McC.; m. Vija Valda Zarina, Oct. 19, 1962 (dec. 1984); children—Linard Peter, Sean Cahal and Deirdre Rose (twins); m. Rosina Lawrence, June 8, 1987. Ph.B., U. Detroit, 1947; M.F.A. in Theatre, Fordham U., 1948; Ph.D. in English Lit, Shakespeare Inst., U. Birmingham, Eng., 1954. Instr. theatre Wayne State U., 1948-51, CCNY, 1955; mem. faculty N.Y. U., 1956-68, prof. dramatic art, chmn. dept., 1962-68; chmn. dept. drama and theatre arts Mackinac Coll., Mackinac Island, Mich., 1968-70; founder The Sons of the Desert (group devoted to works Laurel and Hardy), 1963. Profl. actor, 1928—, producer-dir., Milford (Pa.) Playhouse, summers, 1948-53, prodr., N.Y.U. Summer Theatre, Sterling Forest, N.Y., 1963-65, author-in-residence, Lake Superior State Coll., Sault Ste. Marie, Mich., 1970-86; author: Mr. Laurel and Mr. Hardy, 1961, rev. edit., 1986, George M. Cohan: The Man Who Owned Broadway, 1973, The Comedy World of Stan Laurel, 1974, Laurel & Hardy, 1975, (with G.B. Harrison) Proclaiming the Word, 1976, Charles Chaplin, 1978, Grand Hotel: Mackinac Island, 1987, Babe: The Life of Oliver Hardy, 1990, The High, 1992, Cagney, 1997; ghostwriter of James Cagney's autobiography, Cagney by Cagney, 1976, Cagney, 1997. Served with USAAF, 1943-45, ETO. Mem. Shakespeare Assn. Am., Actors Equity Assn., Catholic Actors Guild Am., Baker St. Irregulars. Clubs: The Players (N.Y.C.), The Lambs (N.Y.C.). Home: British Landing PO Box 363 Mackinac Island MI 49757-0363 *At fourteen I learned from the Jesuits that one who knows both the function and beauty of an English sentence will be blessed life-long.*

MCCABE, JOHN L., lawyer; b. Chgo., Oct. 17, 1941. BA, U. Notre Dame, 1963; LLB, Harvard U., 1966. Bar: Ill. 1967, Colo. 1967. Ptnr. Davis, Graham & Stubbs, Denver. Office: Davis Graham & Stubbs PO Box 185 370 17th St Ste 4700 Denver CO 80201-0185

MCCABE, ROBERT HOWARD, college president; b. Bklyn., Dec. 23, 1929; s. Joseph A. and Kathryn (Greer) McC.; m. Arva Moore Parks, June 1992. BEd, U. Miami (Fla.), 1952; MS, Appalachian State U., Boone, N.C., 1959; PhD, U. Tex., Austin, 1963; LLD (hon.), Barry U., 1986, U. Miami, 1990, Fla. Internat. U., 1990. Asst. to pres. Miami-Dade C.C. (Fla.), 1963-65, v.p., 1965-67, exec. v.p., 1969-80, pres., 1980-95 pres. Essex County Coll., Newark, 1967-69; sr. fellow League for Innovation in the C.C., 1995—; exec. com. So. Regional Edn. Bd., Atlanta, 1981-83; trustee Coll. Bd., chmn., 1988-90; vice chair The Miami Coalition for a Drug-Free Cmty., 1989-93. Recipient Disting. Svc. award Fla. Congl. Del., 1983, Spirit of Excellence award The Miami Herald, 1988, Harold W. McGraw Jr. prize in Edn., 1991, The Coll. Bd. medal, 1995; named Outstanding Grad., Coll. Edn., U. Tex., 1982, named one of the 18 Most Effective Chief Exec. Officer in Am. Higher Edn. Bowling Green U., 1988; Disting. Svc. award, Dade County, Fla., 1983; Kellogg fellow, 1962-63, MacArthur fellow John D. and Catherine T. MacArthur Found., 1992. Fellow League for Innovation in the C.C. (dir. exec. com. 1985—, disting. svc. award 1995); mem. Am. Assn. C.C. (bd. dirs. 1991—, disting. svc. award 1995), Am. Assn. Higher Edn. (dir. 1973-75), Am. Assn. for Environ. Edn. (pres. 1970-73), Am. Coun. on Edn., Commn. on Higher Edn. Issues, Higher Edn. Consortium, Am. Coun. Edn. (bd. dir. 1983-85, 92—), Southeast Fla. Edn. Consortium (chmn. bd. 1981-83). Episcopalian. Author: Man and Environment, 1971; contbr. articles to profl. jours.; editor Jour. Environ. Edn.; cons. editor Change Mag., 1980—. Home: 1601 S Miami Ave Miami FL 33129

MCCABE, SHARON, humanities and art educator; b. Flint, Mich., Sept. 6, 1947. AA, Pasco Hernando C.C., New Port Richey, Fla., 1988; BA in Art, U. South Fla., 1990, MA in Art, gifted endorsement, 1992, MLA in Humanities, 1996. Cert. gifted edn. tchr., Fla. Tchr. art Hernando County Schs., Spring Hill, Fla., 1990—; prof. humanities and art Pasco Hernando C.C., 1992—. Recipient numerous art awards, 1982—. Office: PHCC Humanities Dept 10230 Ridge Rd New Port Richey FL 34654-5129

MCCABE, STEVEN LEE, structural engineer; b. Denver, July 11, 1950; s. John L. and M. Leora (Shaw) McC.; m. Ann McCabe, Aug. 10, 1974; 1 child, Stephanie A. BSME, Colo. State U., 1972, MSME, 1974; PhD in Civil Engring., U. Ill., 1987. Registered profl. engr., Colo., Kans., Okla. Engr. Pub. Svc. Co. of Colo., Denver, 1974-77; sr. engr. R.W. Beck and Assocs., Denver, 1977-78; engr., project engr. Black & Veatch Cons. Engrs., Kansas City, Mo., 1978-81; asst. prof. civil engring. U. Kans., Lawrence, 1985-91, assoc. prof., 1991—, tchg. fellow, 1994—; vis. prof. structural engring. Norwegian Inst. Tech., Trondheim, 1995-96. Contbr. articles to profl. jours. Named Fulbright scholar U.S. Govt. to Norway, 1995-96, Ill. fellow, 1981-82; grantee Am. Inst. Steel Constrn., 1990-91, NSF, 1989-91, 91—, Civil Engring. Rsch. Found., 1991—; recipient Mech. Coupler Industry Testing Consortium Funding, 1992-95, Structural Rsch. Paper award Am. Concrete Inst., 1996. Mem. ASME (pressure vessels and piping divsn. honor paper award 1989, cert. of recognition for svc. 1993), ASTM, ASCE (assoc. editor Jour. Structural Engring. 1992-94), ACI (pres. Kans. chpt. 1992), IEEE Computer Soc., Am. Soc. Engring. Edn., Earthquake Engring. Rsch. Inst., Com. Euro-Internat. du Beton, Sigma Xi, Sigma Tau, Pi Tau Sigma, Phi Kappa Phi, Chi Epsilon. Republican. Roman Catholic. Achievements include development of relationships for bond and anchorage of reinforcing bars in conrete, industry specifications for headed reinforcing bars, improved damage mechanics techniques for prediction of earthquake effects on structures, seismic design criteria for power plants; research on inelastic cyclic behavior of reinforcing bars and mechanical couplers, on structural dynamics and earthquake engineering as well as computational mechanics, on the evaluation of response and damage and predictions of reserve capacity in structures and members subjected to earthquake strong ground motion, on use of finite element analysis for the response of structures and machines to various types of loading. Office: U Kans 2015 Learned Hall Lawrence KS 66044-7526

MCCABE, THOMAS EDWARD, lawyer; b. Washington, Jan. 22, 1955; s. Edward Aeneas and Janet Isabel McCabe; m. Kelly Marie McCarthy; children: Edward Charles, Benjamin Patrick, Adrienne Marie, Therese Eileen, Luke Stevens, Nicholas Joseph. AB, Georgetown U., 1977; MBA, U. Notre Dame, 1981, JD, 1981. Bar: D.C. 1982, U.S. Dist. Ct. D.C. 1983, U.S. Ct. Appeals (D.C. cir.) 1983, Va. 1989, U.S. Supreme Ct. 1990. Law clk. U.S. Dist. Ct. Judge Hon. Charles R. Richey, Washington, 1981-82; assoc. Reavis & McGrath, Washington, 1982-84, Venable Baetjer Howard & Civiletti, Washington, 1984-85, McCarthy & Durrette, Washington, 1985-88; ptnr. McCarthy & Burke, Washington, 1988-91; sr. v.p., gen. counsel, sec. GRC Internat., Inc., Vienna, Va., 1992—. Republican. Roman Catholic. Office: GRC Internat Inc 1900 Gallows Rd Vienna VA 22182-3865

MCCAFFERTY, JAMES ARTHUR, sociologist; b. Columbus, Ohio, Jan. 1, 1926; s. James A. and Marjorie Agatha (Gilchrist) McC.; m. Jane Roush, June 13, 1948 (dec. Oct. 1984); children: Lucinda Jane Martin, James Stanley Thomas, Bridget Anne Roush Green; m. Carolyn Ring Bradley, Nov. 7, 1987 (div. Apr. 1992); m. Irma Mae Prosser Nicholson, May 28, 1993 (dec. Nov. 1996). BS, Ohio State U., 1948; MA, 1954; postgrad. Am. U. Social rsch. analyst Ohio State Dept. Pub. Welfare, 1948-51; criminologist U.S. Bur. Prisons, Washington, 1951-63; asst. chief divsn. info. systems Adminstrv. Office of U.S. Cts., Washington, 1963-77, chief statis. analysis and reports divsn., 1977-86, ret.; vis. lectr. American U., 1959, 62-64; adj. instr. Fordham U., 1978-89. Editor: Capital Punishment, 1972; contbr. articles on criminology to profl. jours. Life mem. Md. State PTA; past pres. Potomac area coun. Camp Fire Girls of U.S., 1966-67; v.p. Prince George's County (Md.) Coun. of PTAs, 1964-65; chmn. Prince George's County Youth Commn., 1970-72; past pres. Hypoglycemia Assn., 1991-93, past pres. Interfaith Cmty. Action Coun., Inc. Cpl. USAAF, 1944-46. Mem. AAUP, Md. Soc. SAR (past pres., trustee), Am. Sociol. Assn., Am. Correctional Assn. (life), Assn. Correctional Rsch. and Info. Mgmt., Am. Statis. Assn., Prince George's County Geneal. Soc. (past pres.), Ohio Geneal. Soc. (life, Nat. Capital Buckeye chpt., co-editor newsletter), Judicature Soc., Md. State Beekeepers Assn. (life), DAV (life), Sons of Union Vets. Civil War (life, past camp comdr), Am. Legion (life). Presbyterian. Home: 613 Rosier Rd Fort Washington MD 20744-5554

MCCAFFERTY, JOHN MARTIN, real estate executive, commodities trader; b. Detroit, May 28, 1956. AA, Northwestern Mich. Coll., 1976; BS with honors, No. Mich. U., 1978; BSBA with honors, U. Denver, 1982. Staff acct. Patrick J. McCafferty & Co. CPA's, Traverse City, Mich., 1978-81; investment analyst Beaumont Investment Co., Traverse City, 1982-84; v.p. Beaumont/McCafferty Devel. Group, Traverse City, 1984-89; pres. Mitchell Creek Investors, Traverse City, 1985-9; v.p. McCafferty Real Estate Group, Traverse City, 1985-88; mng. ptnr. J.M. McCafferty & Assocs. L.L.C., 1996—. Kenneth M. Good scholar Opportunity Found., 1982. Mem. Nat. Assn. Realtors, Mich. Assn. Realtors, Traverse City Bd. Realtors. Republican. Roman Catholic. Avocations: weight training, skiing, offshore powerboat racing. Home: 10281 E San Remo Blvd Traverse City MI 49684-6808 Office: PO Box 1427 Traverse City MI 49685-1427

MCCAFFREE, BURNHAM CLOUGH, JR., retired naval officer; b. San Diego, Sept. 28, 1931; s. Burnham Clough and Elisabeth Cory (Woodhull) McC.; m. Erlend Elizabeth Carlton, June 19, 1954; children: Elizabeth Anne McCaffree Antanitus, Debora Lynn McCaffree Hagwood. BS in Naval Engring., U.S. Naval. Acad., 1954. Commd. ensign USN, 1954, advanced through grades to rear adm., 1983, served on six ships, mem. staffs Atlantic Fleet and Pacific Fleet, until 1970; comdg. officer USS Johnston, U.S. Atlantic Fleet, Charleston, S.C., 1970-72; action officer, sr. navy planner Office Chief Naval Ops., Washington, 1972-76, dir. mobile logistic support forces, amphibious, mine and spl. warfare div., 1982-84, asst. dep. chief naval logistics, 1986-87, dir. logistics plans div., 1987-88; comdg. officer USS Shreveport, U.S. Atlantic Fleet, Norfolk, Va., 1976-78; chief staff, comdr. amphibious group 2 U.S. Atlantic Fleet, Norfolk, 1978-80, comdr. amphibious squadron 2, 1980-82; comdr. amphibious force U.S. 7th Fleet, Okinawa, Japan, 1984-86; ret., 1988; mem. adj. rsch. staff Inst. Def. Analyses, Alexandria, Va., Ctr. Naval Analyses, Alexandria, Va., 1989—. Decorated Legion of Merit with 4 gold stars, Meritorious Service Medal, others. Mem. U.S. Naval Inst., U.S. C. of C. (assoc.). Episcopalian. Home: 3620 Buckwood Ct Annandale VA 22003-1951

MCCAFFREY, ANNE INEZ, author; b. Cambridge, Mass., Apr. 1, 1926; d. George H. and Anne (McElroy) McC.; m. Wright Johnson, Jan. 14, 1950 (div. Aug. 1970); children: Alec Anthony, Todd, Georgeanne. B.A. cum laude, Radcliffe Coll., 1947; student, U. City of Dublin, 1970-71. Copywriter, layout designer Liberty Music Shops, N.Y.C., 1948-50; copywriter, sec. Helena Rubinstein, N.Y.C., 1950-52. Author: Restoree, 1967, Dragonflight, 1968, Decision at Doona, 1969, Ship Who Sang, 1969, Mark of Merlin, 1971, Dragonquest: Being the Further Adventures of the Dragonriders of Pern, 1971, Ring of Fear, 1971, To Ride Pegasus, 1973, Cooking Out Of This World, 1973, A Time When, 1975, Dragonsong, 1976, Kilternan Legacy, 1975, Dragonsinger, 1977, Dinosaur Planet, 1977, Get Off the Unicorn, 1977, White Dragon, 1978, Dragondrums, 1979, Crystal Singer, 1981, The Worlds of Anne McCaffrey, 1981, The Coelura, 1983, Moreta: Dragonlady of Pern, 1983, Dinosaur Planet Survivors, 1984, Stitch in Snow, 1984, Killashandra, 1985, The Girl Who Heard Dragons, 1985, The Year of the Lucy, 1986, Nerilka's Story, 1986, The Lady, 1987, People of Pern, 1988, Dragonsdown, 1988, Renegades of Pern, 1989, (with Jody-Lynn Nye) The Dragonlover's Guide to Pern, 1989, The Rowan, 1990, Pegasus in Flight, 1990, (with Elizabeth Moon) Sassinak, 1990, (with Nye) The Death of Sleep, 1990, All the Weyrs of Pern, 1991, Generation Warriors, 1991, Damia, 1991, (with Margaret Ball) The Partnership, 1991, (with Nye) Crisis at Doona, 1991, Damia, 1992, (with Mercedes Lackey) The City Who Fought, 1993, (with Elizabeth Ann Scarborough) Powers That Be, 1993, Chronicles of Pern: First Fall, 1993, Lyon's Pride, 1994, (with Nye) The Ship Who Won, 1994, (with Scarborough) Power Lines, 1994, Dolphins of Pern, 1994, (with Scarborough) Power Play, 1995, Freedom's Landing, 1995, Black Horses for The King, 1996, Red Star Rising, 1996; editor: Alchemy and Academe, 1970; anthology: The Girl Who Heard Dragons, 1991; dir. musical Brecks Mill Cronies, 1962-65. Recipient Hugo award, 1967, Nebula award, 1968, E.E. Smith award, 1975, Ditmar award, 1979, Gandalf award, 1979, Eurocon/Streso award, 1979, Balrog award, 1980, Golden PEN award, 1981, Sci. Fiction Book Club award, 1986, 89, 91, 92, 93, 94. Mem. PEN (Ireland), Sci. Fiction Writers Am. (sec.-treas. 1968-70), Authors' Guild. Office: Dragonhold Underhill, Timmore Ln Newcastle, Wicklow Ireland

MCCAFFREY, BARRY RICHARD, federal official, retired army officer; b. Taunton, Mass., Nov. 17, 1942; s. William Joseph and Mary Veronica (Curtin) McC.; m. Jill Ann Faulkner, June 8, 1964; children: Sean, Tara, Amy. BS, U.S. Mil. Acad., 1964; MA, Am. U., 1971; postgrad., Command and Gen. Staff Coll., Ft. Leavenworth, Kans., 1976, Army War Coll., Carlisle Barracks, Pa., 1982. Commd. 2d lt. U.S. Army, 1964, advanced through grades to full gen., 1994; co. comdr. 7st Cav. Div., Vietnam, 1968-69; assoc. prof. dept. social sci. U.S. Mil. Acad., West Point, N.Y., 1972-75; bn. comdr. 3d Inf. Div., Germany, 1979-81, chief ops. br., 1976-77; div. chief staff, then brigade comdr. 9th Inf. Div., Ft. Lewis, Wash., 1983-84; comdr. 3d brigade 9th Inf. Div., Ft. Lewis, 1984-86; asst. comdt. U.S. Army Inf. Sch., Ft. Benning, Ga., 1986-88; dep. U.S. mil. rep. NATO, Brussels, 1988-89; div.

comdr. 24th Inf. Div., Ft. Stewart, Saudi Arabia, Ga., 1990-92; asst. to chmn. Joint Chiefs of Staff, Washington, 1992-93; dir. strategic plans and policy directory The Joint Staff, Washington, 1993-94; dir. Nat. Drug Control Policy, Washington, DC, 1995—; mem. Pres. Cabinet U.S. So. Command, Quarry Heights, Panama, 1995—. Contbr. articles to mil. publs. Decorated D.S.C. with oak leaf cluster, Silver Star with oak leaf cluster, Purple Heart with two oak leaf clusters, Def. Disting. Svc. Medal, Disting. Svc. Medal with two oak leaf clusters. Mem. Legion of Valor. Roman Catholic. Avocations: hunting, reading military history. Office: Office Nat Drug Control Policy 750 17th St NW Washington DC 20006-4607

MCCAFFREY, JUDITH ELIZABETH, lawyer; b. Providence, Apr. 26, 1944; d. Charles V. and Isadore Frances (Langford) McC.; m. Martin D. Minsker, Dec. 31, 1969 (div. May 1981); children: Ethan Hart Minsker, Natasha Langford Minsker. BA, Tufts U., 1966; JD, Boston U., 1970. Bar: Mass. 1970, D.C. 1972, Fla. 1991. Assoc. Sullivan & Worcester, Washington, 1970-76; atty. FDIC, Washington, 1976-78; assoc. Dechert, Price & Rhoads, Washington, 1978-82, McKenna, Conner & Cuneo, Washington, 1982-83; gen. counsel, corp. sec. Perpetual Savs. Bank, FSB, Alexandria, Va., 1983-91; ptnr. Powell, Goldstein, Frazer & Murphy, Washington, 1991-92, McCaffrey & Raimi, P.A., 1992—. Contbr. articles to profl. jours. Mem. edn. com. Bd. Trade, Washington, 1986-92. Mem. ABA (chairperson subcom. thrift instns. 1985-90), Fed. Bar Assn. (exec. com., banking law com. 1985-91), D.C. Bar Assn. (bd. govs. 1981-85), Women's Bar Assn. (pres. 1980-81), Zonta Club of Naples (dir. 1994—). Episcopalian. Avocations: golf, travel, tennis, sailing, reading. Home: PO Box 2081 Naples FL 34106-2081 Office: McCaffrey & Raimi PA 5811 Pelican Bay Blvd Ste 206-A Naples FL 34108-2752

MCCAFFREY, ROBERT HENRY, JR., retired manufacturing company executive; b. Syracuse, N.Y., Jan. 20, 1927; s. Robert Henry and May Ann (McGuire) McC.; m. Dorothy Anne Evers, Sept. 22, 1956; children: Michael Robert, Kathleen Mary. BS, Syracuse U., 1949. Sales asst. Sealright Corp., Fulton, N.Y., 1949-50; with TEK Hughes div. Johnson & Johnson, Metuchen, N.J., 1950-67, gen. sales mgr., 1958-59, v.p. sales, 1959-62, pres., 1962-67; gen. mgr. med. div. Howmet Corp., N.Y.C., 1967-70; group v.p. Howmedica, Inc., 1970-73, sr. v.p., 1973-74, exec. v.p., also bd. dirs., 1974-76; pres., CEO C.R. Bard, Inc., Murray Hill, N.J., 1976-78, chmn. bd. dirs., CEO, 1978-89, chmn. bd., 1989-91, also bd. dirs.; chmn. exec. com. C.R. Bard, Inc., Murray Hill, 1991—; bd. dirs. Summit and Elizabeth Trust, Summit Bancorp, Thomas & Betts Corp. Trustee Found. for Univ. Medicine and Dentistry N.J., 1987-90, Syracuse U., 1979—, chmn. corp. adv. council, 1974-75. With AUS, 1945-46. Mem. Orthopedic Surg. Mfrs. Assn., Health Industry Mfrs. Assn. (bd. dir., chmn. 1982-83), N.Y. Sales Execs. Club, Algonquin Club (Boston), Baltusrol Golf Club (Springfield, N.J.), Oyster Harbors Club (Osterville, Mass.), Sigma Chi. Republican. Roman Catholic. Avocations: reading, skiing, golf. Office: C R Bard Inc 1200 Technology Park Dr Billerica MA 01821-4139

MCCAFFREY, WILLIAM THOMAS, financial services company executive; b. N.Y.C., July 7, 1936; s. Daniel and Alice (Dineen) McC.; m. Mary Margaret Timms, June 25, 1960; children: Ann, William E., Christine. BS, NYU, 1970; MS in Bus., Columbia U., 1972. Dir. pub. The Equitable Fin. Cos., N.Y.C., 1968-71, asst. v.p. communications, 1972-74, v.p., office of the pres., 1975-77, v.p. corp. devel., 1977-79, v.p., personnel dir., 1980-84, sr. v.p. pers. and adminstrn., 1984-85, exec. v.p. corp., 1986-87, exec. v.p., chief adminstrv. officer, 1988-96, sr. exec. v.p., COO, 1996—, chmn. benefits com., 1986—; bd. dirs. Equitable Variable Life Ins. Co., N.Y.C., Equitable Life Assurance Soc. U.S., Innovir, All Faiths Cemetery, U.S. Assist. Bd. dirs. Equitable Found., 1987—, Bronx-Lebanon Hosp.; project mgr. Grace Commn., Washington, 1982—; chmn. bd. trustees Xavier U., New Orleans, 1986—; chmn. bd. Outreach, N.Y.C. Sgt. U.S. Army, 1957-58. Mem. West Side Tennis Club (Forest Hills, N.Y.) (gov. 1988—). Avocations: tennis, photography. Home: 89-25 63rd Ave Flushing NY 11374-2836 Office: Equitable 787 7th Ave New York NY 10019-6018

MCCAGHY, CHARLES HENRY, sociology educator; b. Eau Claire, Wis., Apr. 29, 1934; s. Elmer and Anna Josephine (Soha) McC.; m. M. Dawn Ysebaert, June 10, 1961. B.B.A., U. Wis., 1956, M.S., 1962, Ph.D, 1966. Instr. sociology U. Conn., 1964-66; asst. prof. sociology Case Western Res. U., Cleve., 1966-70; assoc. prof. sociology Bowling Green State U., Ohio, 1970-76, prof., 1976-94, prof. emeritus, 1994—; vis. scholar Australian Inst. Criminology, 1984. Author: Deviant Behavior: Crime, Conflict and Interest Groups, 1976, 4th edit., 1996, Crime in American Society, 1980, 2d edit., 1987. Lt. (j.g.) USN, 1956-59. Mem. Am. Sociol. Assn., Am. Soc. Criminology (treas. 1978-82), Soc. for Sci. Study of Sex. Office: 221 Williams St Bowling Green OH 43402-3259

MCCAHILL, BARRY WINSLOW, public affairs official; b. Glen Ridge, N.J., May 25, 1947; s. William Francis and Frances (Elliott) McC.; m. Margaret Anne Bonnes, Feb. 8, 1980; children: Jennifer, Kimberly, Erin, Meghan; 1 stepchild, Rob White. BA in English, U. Va., 1969, postgrad., 1974-76. USCG lic. master. Account exec. Whyte Berry Price, Advt. & Pub. Rels., Washington, 1967-69; publs. mgr. Nat. Telephone Coop. Assn., Washington, 1972-74; visual info. specialist U.S. Customs Svc., Washington, 1974-76; pub. affairs specialist IRS, Washington, 1976-79; mgr. radio and TV news Nat. Hwy. Traffic Safety Adminstrn., U.S. Dept. Transp., Washington, 1979-85, dep. dir. Office Pub. and Consumer Affairs, 1985-96; ret., 1996; sr. counselor Strat@Comm, Inc., Washington, 1996—. Co-creator Vince & Larry crash dummies pub. svc. campaigns The Ad Council. Loaned exec. Combined Fed. Campaign United Way, Washington, 1983. 1st lt. U.S. Army, 1969-72. Recipient Blue Pencil award Nat. Assn. Govt. Communicators, 1975, 88, Adminstrs. award for exceptional achievement Nat. Hwy. Traffic Safety Adminstrn., 1983, Adminstr.'s Leadership award, 1995, Sec.'s Honor award Sec. of Treasury, 1983, Sec.'s award for meritorious achievement Sec. of Transp., 1985, Spl. Recognition awards, 1995, 96, Sec. Transp. Way To Go awards, 1995, 96, Disting. Career Svc. award, 1996. Mem. Washington Automotive Press Assn., Old Dominion Morgan Horse Assn. (pres.), Cobbosseecontee Yacht Club (Manchester, Maine), Pi Kappa Alpha. Avocations: boating, Morgan horses. Home: 4832 Heron Neck Ln Fairfax VA 22033-4406 Office: Strat@Comm Inc 818 Connecticut Ave NW Washington DC 20006-2702

MCCAIG, JEFFREY JAMES, transportation company executive; b. Moose Jaw, Sask., July 5, 1951; s. John Robert and Anne Shorrocks (Glass) McC.; m. Marilyn Graves, July 7, 1983; children: Robbert Angus, Scott Thomas, Christa Mae. Student, Can. Jr. Coll. Lausanne, Switzerland, 1970; AB, Harvard Coll., 1973; LLB, Osgoode Hall Law Sch., Can., 1976; MSc in Mgmt., Leland Stanford Jr. U., 1984. Assoc. MacKimmie Matthews, 1976-81; owner, sr. officer Jeffery J. McCaig Profl. Corp., 1981-83; v.p. planning and corp. devel. Trimac Corp., Calgary, Alta., Can., 1983-87; exec. v.p. Trimac Ltd., Calgary, Alta., Can., 1987-90, pres., 1990-94, pres., CEO, 1994—; chmn. Bovar, Inc., Calgary, 1994—; bd. dirs. Bovar, Inc., chmn. bd. dirs. Trimac Corp., Greyhound Can. Transp. Corp., Richland Petroleum Corp., Conf. Bd. Can., ATA Found., Parks Found. Mem. Law Soc. Alta., Young Pres.'s Orgn., Calgary Golf and Country Club, Calgary Petroleum Club, Glencoe Club, 400 Club. Home: 708 Riverdale Ave SW, Calgary, AB Canada T2S OY3 Office: Trimac Corp, 800 5 Ave SW Ste 2100, Calgary, AB Canada T2P 5A3

MCCAIG, JOHN ROBERT, transportation executive; b. Moose Jaw, Sask., Can., June 14, 1929; m. Ann McCaig; children: Jeffrey, JoAnn, Melanie. Grad. pub. sch., Moose Jaw. Various positions Maccam Transport Ltd., 1947-52, gen. mgr., 1952-60; pres. Trimac Transp. Ltd. and H.M. Trimble & Sons Ltd., 1961-68, Westburne Internat. Industries Ltd., 1969-70; chmn. Trimac Corp., Calgary, Alta., Can., 1970-72, 80—; pres. Trimac Ltd., Calgary, Alta., 1972-80; CEO Trimac Corp., Calgary, Alta., 1972-94; chmn. Trimac Corp., Calgary, 1994—; bd. dirs. Banister Found., Inc., Chauvco Resources Ltd., Computalog, Inc., Cameco Corp., Brookfield Properties Corp. Past pres. Jr. Achievement So. Alta, Calgary; campaign chmn. Western Orthopaedic and Arthritis Found., Calgary. Mem. Calgary Petroleum Club, Ranchmen's Club, Calgary Golf and Country Club, Glencoe Club. Avocations: golf, skiing. Office: Trimac Corp, 800 5th Ave SW Ste 2100, Calgary, AB Canada T2P 3T6

MCCAIN, ARTHUR WILLIAMSON, JR., retired pension investment consultant; b. N.Y.C., Apr. 15, 1934; s. Arthur Williamson and Marion Wilmer (Vinsonhaler) McC.; m. Margaret Bain Dale, Nov. 3, 1956; children: Robert Williamson, Elizabeth Dale, Scott Lamar. BA in Philosophy magna cum laude, Washington and Lee U., 1956. Various positions as fin. mgr., auditor and trainee GE, 1958-73; comptr. GE Investment Corp., Stamford, Conn., 1973-87; mgr. master custody, cons. Chase Manhattan Bank N.A., N.Y.C., 1987-90; v.p., cons. InterSec Rsch. Corp., Stamford, 1990-96; speaker Investment Mgmt. Inst., Greenwich, Conn., 1990-96, Inst. for Internat. Rsch., N.Y.C., 1990-96. Mem. Pension East Assn., Stamford, 1982-87; founder, mem. Peer Group-Large Plan Sponsors, Stamford, 1982-87; sec. Internat. Performance Forum, 1992-96; deacon Greenfield Hill. Congl. Ch., Fairfield, Conn., 1987-91, treas., 1992-97. Capt. arty. U.S. Army, 1956-61. Mem. Phi Beta Kappa. Republican. Avocations: singing, tennis, reading. Home and Office: 212 Brookbend Rd Fairfield CT 06430-3833

MCCAIN, BETTY LANDON RAY (MRS. JOHN LEWIS MCCAIN), political party official, civic leader; b. Faison, N.C., Feb. 23, 1931; d. Horace Truman and Mary Howell (Perrett) Ray; student St. Marys Jr. Coll., 1948-50; AB in Music, U. N.C., Chapel Hill, 1952; MA, in Music Columbia U., 1953; m. John Lewis McCain, Nov. 19, 1955; children: Paul Pressly III, Mary Eloise. Courier, European tour guide Ednl. Travel Assocs., Plainfield, N.J., 1952-54; asst. dir. YWCA, U. N.C., Chapel Hill, 1953-55; chmn. N.C. Democratic Exec. Com., 1976-79 (1st woman); mem. Dem. Nat. Com., 1971-72, 76-79, 80-85, chmn. sustaining fund, N.C., 1981, 88-91, mem. com. on Presdl. nominations (Hunt Commn.), 1981-82, mem. rules com., 1982-85, mem. cabinet Gov. James B. Hunt, Jr., sec. dept. cultural resources 1993—; mem. Winograd Commn., 1977-78; pres. Dem. Women of N.C., 1971-72, dist. dir., 1969-72; pres. Wilson County Dem. Women, 1966-67; precinct chmn., 1972-76; del. Dem. Nat. Conv., 1972, 88; mem. Dem. Mid-term Confs., 1974, 78, mem. judicial council Dem. Nat. Com., 1985-89; dir. Carolina Tel. & Tel. Co. (now Sprint), 1981-97 (1st woman). Sunday sch. tchr. First Presbyn. Ch., Wilson, 1970-71, 86-88, 90-92, mem. chancel choir, 1985—, deacon, 1986-92, elder, 1992-95, chmn. fin. com., 1990-91; treas. Wilson on the Move, 1990-92; mem. Council on State Goals and Policy, 1970-72, Gov.'s Task Force on Child Advocacy, 1969-71, Wilson Human Relations Commn., 1975-78, chmn. Wilson-Greene Morehead scholarship com., 1986-89; mem. career and personal counseling service adv. bd. St. Andrews Coll.; charter mem. Wilson Edn. Devel. Council; active Arts Council of Wilson, Inc., N.C. Art Soc., N.C. Lit. and Hist. Assn.; regional v.p., bd. dirs. N.C. Mental Health Assn.; pres., bd. dirs., legis. chmn. Wilson County Mental Health Assn.; bd. dirs. U. N.C. Ctr. Pub. TV, 1993—, Country Doctor Mus., 1968-93, Wilson United Fund; bd. govs. U. N.C., 1975-81, 85-93, personnel and tenure com., 1985-91, chmn. budgets and fin. com. 1991-93; bd. regents Barium Springs Home for Children; bd. dirs., pres. N.C. Mus. History Assocs., 1982-83, membership chair, 1987-88; co-chmn. Com. to Elect Jim Hunt Gov., 1976, 80, co-chmn. senatorial campaign, 1984; mem. N.C. Adv. Budget Com., 1981-85 (1st woman); chmn. State Employees Combined Campaign N.C., 1993; bd. visitors Peace Coll., Wake Forest U. Sch. Law, U. N.C., Chapel Hill; co-chmn. fund drive Wilson Community Theatre; state bd. dirs. N.C., Am. Lung Assn., 1985-88; bd. dirs. Roanoke Island Commn. 1994—, USS/NC Battleship Commn., 1993—. Recipient state awards N.C. Heart Assn., 1967, Easter Seal Soc., 1967, Community Service award Downtown Bus. Assocs., 1977, award N.C. Jaycees, 1979, 85, Women in Govt. award N.C. and U.S. Jaycettes, 1985, Alumni Disting. Svc. award U. N.C., Chapel Hill, 1993, Flora Mac Donald Scottish Heritage award, 1995, Carpathian award N.C. Equity, 1995; named to Order of Old Well and Valkyries, U. N.C., 1952; named Dem. Woman of Yr., N.C., 1976. Mem. U. N.C. Chapel Hill Alumni Assn. (dir.), St. Marys Alumni Assn. (regional v.p.), AMA Aux. (dir., nat. vol. health services chmn., aux. liaison rep. AMA Council on Mental Health, aux. rep. Council on Vol. Health Orgns.), N.C. (pres., dir., parliamentarian) med. auxs., UDC (historian John W. Dunham chpt.), DAR, N.C. Found. for Nursing (bd. dirs. 1989-92), N.C. Agency Pub. Telecoms.(bd. dirs. 1993—), Info. Resources Mgmt. Commn. N.C. (bd. dirs. 1993—), N.C. Symphony (bd. dirs. 1993—), N.C. Soc. Internal Medicine Aux. (pres., bd. dirs. N.C. Equity), N.C. Sch. Arts (bd. trustees 1993—), Pi Beta Phi. The Book Club (pres.), Little Book Club , Wilson Country Club. Contbg. editor History of N.C. Med. Soc. Home: 1134 Woodland Dr Wilson NC 27893-2122

MCCAIN, JOHN SIDNEY, III, senator; b. Panama Canal Zone, Aug. 29, 1936; s. John Sidney and Roberta (Wright) McC.; m. Cindy Hensley, May 17, 1980; children: Doug, Andy, Sidney, Meghan, Jack, Bridget. Grad. U.S. Naval Acad., 1958; grad., Nat. War Coll., 1973-74. Commd. ensign U.S. Navy, 1958, capt., navy pilot, 1977; prisoner of war Hanoi, Vietnam, 1967-73; dir. Navy Senate Liaison Office, Washington, 1977-81; mem. 98th-99th Congress from 1st Ariz. Dist.; U.S. senator from Ariz., 1987—, mem. armed svcs. com., commerce, sci. and transp. com., Indian affairs com., nat. rep. senatorial com. Bd. dirs. Community Assistance League, Phoenix, 1981-82. Decorated Legion of Merit; decorated Silver Star, Bronze Star, Purple Heart, D.F.C., Vietnamese Legion of Honor. Mem. Soc. of the Cin., Am. Legion, VFW. Republican. Episcopalian. Office: US Senate Office 241 Russell Washington DC 20510*

MCCAIN, MARGARET, province official. Lt. gov. Govt. New Brunswick, Fredericton, Can. Office: Office of Lt Gov, 736 King St PO Box 6000, Fredericton, NB Canada E3B 5H1

MCCALEB, GARY DAY, university official; b. Anson, Tex., Nov. 2, 1941; s. Victor Earl and Vivian (Day) McC.; m. Sylvia Ravanelli, June 5, 1964; children: Cara Lee Cranford, Bryan Day. BA, Abilene Christian Coll., 1964; MBA, Tex. A&M U., 1975, PhD, 1979. Asst. dir. alumni rels. Abilene (Tex.) Christian U., 1964-65, dir. alumni rels., 1965-69, dir. coll. rels., 1969-73, asst. acad. dean, 1978-80, v.p. pub. rels., 1980-83, v.p., dean campus life, 1983-91, v.p., 1991—; asst. dir. devel. Tex. A&M U., Bryan, 1973-75; leader internat. travel and goodwill groups; U.S. rep. to world exec. com. Internat. Union Local Authorities, 1996—. Coun. mem. City of Abilene, 1985-90, mayor, 1990—; bd. dirs. Taylor County Am. Cancer Soc., 1972-73; mem. adv. bd. United Way of Abilene, 1979-83, dir. pub. svc. divsn., 1987, chmn. consortium on drug and alcohol abuse, 1989; bd. dirs. Civic Abilene, Inc., 1981-83; treas. Abilene Task Force on Drug and Alcohol Abuse, 1984-86; active March of Dimes; mem. Tex. Sci. and Tech. Coun., 1997—. Recipient Polit. Courage award John Ben Shepperd Pub. Leadership Forum, Austin, Tex., 1993, Tex. Urban Leadersip award U. Tex.-Arlington Sch. Urban and Pub. Affairs, 1995. Mem. Nat. League Cities (nat. steering com. on fin., adminstrn. and intergovtl. rels. 1989-90, adv. bd. 1994, bd. dirs. 1992-94), U.S. Conf. Mayors, Internat. Mcpl. Consortium (chmn. 1994-95), Tex. Mcpl. League (legis. policy com. Houston 1986, resolutions com. Dallas 1988, v.p. region 6 1988-89, bd. dirs. 1989-90, pres. 1992), Abilene C. of C. (aviation com. 1981, 94). Republican. Mem. Ch. of Christ. Avocations: art, baseball, jogging. Office: City of Abilene PO Box 60 Abilene TX 79604-0060

MCCALEB, JOE WALLACE, lawyer; b. Nashville, Dec. 9, 1941; s. J.W. McCaleb and Majorie June (Hudson) DePriest; m. Glenda Jean Queen, June 26, 1965. BA, Union U., 1964; JD, Memphis State U., 1970; MSEL cum laude, Vt. Law Sch., 1995. Bar: Tenn. 1971, U.S. Dist. Ct. (mid. dist.) Tenn. 1977, U.S. Ct. Appeals (6th cir.) 1984, U.S. Supreme Ct. 1978. Law clk. to presiding justice Tenn. Supreme Ct., Memphis, 1970-71; staff atty. Tenn. Dept. of Pub. Health Bur. Environ. Svcs., Nashville, 1971-77; pvt. practice Hendersonville, Tenn., 1977-94, 96—. Chmn. Hendersonville Recycling Com., 1990-91. Mem. ABA, Tenn. Bar Assn., Sierra Club (chmn. local chpt. 1980-81, chmn. mid.-Tenn. group 1989-90, 93-94, chmn. water quality com., co-chmn. forestry com.), Tenn. Environ. Coun. (v.p. 1987-88, conservation adv. 1991-92), Hendersonville Exch. Club (sec. 1983, pres. 1985-86). Democrat. Avocations: wilderness backpacking, photography, forestry, environmental protection. Home and Office: 100 Colonial Dr Hendersonville TN 37075-3205

MCCALEB, MALCOLM, JR., lawyer; b. Evanston, Ill., June 4, 1945. BA, Colgate U., 1967; JD, Northwestern U., 1971. Bar: Ill. 1971. Ptnr. Keck, Mahin & Cate, Chgo., 1985-95, Foley & Lardner, Chgo., 1995—. Chmn. Northfield (Ill.) Village Caucus, 1981-82, active, 1977-82, Northfield Zoning Commn., 1985-88; pres. bd. dirs. Vols. Am., 1977-79; active Northfield Sch. and Park Bd. Caucus, 1980-87. Mem. Chgo. Bar Assn., Bar Assn. 7th Fed. Cir., Patent Law Assn. Chgo., Internat. Trademark Assn. Office: Foley & Lardner 330 N Wabash Ave Ste 3300 Chicago IL 60611-3603

MCCALL, BILLY GENE, charitable trust executive; b. Ellerbe, N.C., Mar. 28, 1928; s. Arthur Hall and Letha Belle (Anderson) McC.; m. Betty Sue Berryhill, Aug. 20, 1949; children: Stephen Andrew, Kathryn Elaine McCall Manson. BS magna cum laude, Clemson U., 1950, HHD (hon.), 1991. Adminstrv. resident Charlotte Meml. Hosp., N.C., 1951-53; asst. adminstr. Anderson Meml. Hosp., S.C., 1953-54; field rep. hosp. and child care divs. The Duke Endowment, Charlotte, 1954-62, dir. mgmt. service, 1962-66, asst. exec. dir., 1966-70, assoc. exec. dir., 1970-77, exec. dir., 1977-80, asst. sec., 1966-80, dep. exec. dir., sec., 1980-86, dep. exec. dir., 1987-90, exec. dir., 1990-92; ret., 1992; bd. dirs., mem. exec. com. SunHealth Alliance, Inc., 1992-95; chmn. Commn. on Profl. and Hosp. Activities, Ann Arbor, Mich., 1977-78; mem. N.C. Med. Care Commn., Raleigh, 1977-89; mem. adv. bd. Kate B. Reynolds Health Care Trust, Winston-Salem, N.C., 1977-91, 96—. Past pres. Presbyn. Home at Charlotte; bd. dirs. United Way of Cen. Carolinas, Charlotte; adv. bd. Queens Coll., Charlotte; bd. visitors Davidson Coll., N.C., Lineberger Cancer Ctr., U. N.C., Chapel Hill; past pres., bd. dirs. Charlotte-Mecklenburg Sr. Ctrs., N.C. With U.S. Army, 1946-47, 50-51, PTO. Fellow Am. Coll. Healthcare Execs. (hon.); mem. Am. Hosp. Assn., N.C. Hosp. Assn., S.C. Hosp. Assn., Carmel Country Club. Democrat. Presbyterian. Home: 7724 Cooper Ln Charlotte NC 28217-2387

MC CALL, CHARLES BARNARD, health facility executive, educator; b. Memphis, Nov. 2, 1928; s. John W. and Lizette (Kimbrough) McC.; m. Carolyn Jean Rosselot, June 9, 1951; children: Linda, Kim, Betsy, Cathy. B.A., Vanderbilt U., 1950, M.D., 1953. Diplomate: Am. Bd. Internal Medicine (pulmonary diseases). Intern Vanderbilt U. Hosp., Nashville, 1953-54; clin. assoc., sr. asst. surgeon USPHS, Nat. Cancer Inst., NIH, 1954-56; sr. asst. resident in medicine U. Ala. Hosp., 1956-57, chief resident, 1958-59; fellow chest diseases Nat. Acad. Scis.-NRC, 1957-58; instr. U. Ala. Med. Sch., 1958-59; asst. prof., then assoc. prof. medicine U. Tenn. Med. Sch., 1959-69, chief pulmonary diseases, 1964-69; mem. faculty U. Tex. System, Galveston, 1969-75, prof. medicine med. br., 1971-73; assoc. prof. medicine Health Sci. Center, Southwestern Med. Sch., Dallas, 1973-75, also assoc. dean clin. programs, 1973-75; dir. Office Grants Mgmt. and Devel., 1973-75; dean, prof. medicine U. Tenn. Coll. Medicine, 1975-77, Oral Roberts U. Sch. Medicine, Tulsa, 1977-78; interim assoc. dean U. Okla. Tulsa Med. Coll., 1978-79; clin. prof. medicine U. Colo. Med. Sch., Denver, 1979-80; prof. medicine, assoc. dean U. Okla. Med. Sch., 1980-82; exec. dean and dean U. Okla. Coll. Medicine, 1982-85; v.p. patient affairs, prof. medicine U. Tex. M.D. Anderson Cancer Ctr., 1985-94; chief of staff VA Med. Center, Oklahoma City, 1980-82; cons. in field; physician cons. Fla. Cancer Network, M.D. Anderson Cancer Ctr., Orlando. Contbr. articles to med. jours. Fellow ACP, Am. Coll. Chest Physicians; mem. AMA, Am. Thoracic Soc., So. Thoracic Soc. (pres. 1968-69), Am. Fedn. Clin. Rsch., Sigma Xi, Alpha Omega Alpha. Baptist. Home: 17056 Crossgate Dr Jupiter FL 33477-5851

MCCALL, CLYDE SAMUEL, JR., petroleum engineer; b. Memphis, May 29, 1931; s. Clyde Samuel and Marguerete (Rogers) McC.; m. Patricia Dean Boswell, Sept. 5, 1989; children: Clyde Samuel III, Amy Woolsey McDonald, John Porter Boswell, Vivienne Boswell Mays (Mrs. Robert Clayton Mays), Elise Boswell, Edith Annlouise Boswell. BS in Commerce, Washington and Lee U., 1953; BS in Petroleum Engring., U. Tex.-Austin, 1959. Registered profl. engr., Tex. Engr. to sr. petroleum engr. Amoco Prodn. Co., Andrews and Midland, Tex., 1959-69; cons. petroleum engr., Midland, Tex., 1969-73; petroleum engr. James A. Lewis Engring., Dallas, 1973-81, exec. v.p. 1974-76, pres., 1977-81; exec. v.p. McCord-Lewis Energy Svcs., Dallas, 1981-83; petroleum cons., pres. Cenesia Petroleum Corp., 1983—. With U.S. Army, 1954-56. Mem. Soc. Petroleum Engrs., Ind. Petroleum Assn. Am., Soc. Ind. Profl. Earth Scientists, Kappa Alpha Order, Idlewild Club, Terpsichorean Club, Steeplechase Club, Dallas Petroleum Club, Brook Hollow Golf Club, Confriere des Chevalier du Tastavin., Commanderie de Bordeaux. Address: 2 Energy Sq 4849 Greenville Ave Ste 648 Dallas TX 75206-4124

MCCALL, DANIEL THOMPSON, JR., retired judge; b. Butler, Ala., Mar. 12, 1909; s. Daniel Thompson and Caroline Winston (Bush) McC.; m. Mary Edna Montgomery, Apr. 3, 1937; children: Mary Winston McCall Laseter, Daniel Thompson III, Nancy McCall Poynor. A.B., U. Ala., 1931, LL.B., 1933, LL.D. (hon.), 1981. Bar: Ala. 1933, U.S. Supreme Ct. 1960. Practice law Mobile, 1933-60; ptnr. Johnston, McCall & Johnston, 1943-60; cir. judge Mobile County, 1960-69; assoc. justice Supreme Ct. Ala., 1969-75; dir. Title Ins. Co., 1959-69; pres. Jr. Bar Ala., 1937. Author McCall Reprot on U. Ala. Hosps. Elected to Mobile County Bd. Sch. commrs., 1950-56, 58-60; co-founder, trustee Julius T. Wright Sch. Girls, 1953-63; dir. U. Ala. Law Sch. Found., Ala. Bar. Commrs., 1957-60; trustee U. Ala., 1965-79, nat. alumni pres., 1963, pres. Mobile chpt., 1961, Disting. Alumnus award, 1995. Lt. USNR, World War II. Named to Ala. Acad. of Hon.; recipient Dean's award, U. Ala. Law Sch., 1974, Julius T. Wright Sch. Disting. Svc. award, 1979, M.O. Beale Scroll Merit, 1979, U.M.S. Preparator Sch. Outstanding Alumnus award, 1980. Mem. ABA, Ala. Bar Assn. (grievance com. 1954-57), Mobile Bar Assn. (pres. 1953), Am. Judicature Soc., Farrah Law Soc. (charter), Cumberland Law Sch. Order Jurisprudence, Inst. Jud. Adminstrn., Nat. Trust Hist. Preservation, Hist. Mobile Preservation Soc., Navy League U.S. (co-founder, pres. Mobile chpt. 1963-65), Am. Legion, Ala. Hist. Soc., Res. Officer's Assn. U.S., 40 and 8, U. Tuscaloosa Club, Omicron Delta Kappa, Phi Delta Phi, Sigma Nu. Democrat. Episcopalian. Home: 2253 Ashland Place Ave Mobile AL 36607-3242

MCCALL, DAVID WARREN, retired chemistry research director, consultant; b. Omaha, Dec. 1, 1928; s. H. Bryron and Grace (Cox) McC.; m. Charlotte Marion Dunham, July 30, 1955; children—William Christopher, John Dunham. B.S., U. Wichita, 1950; M.S., U. Ill., 1951, Ph.D., 1953. Mem. tech. staff AT&T Bell Labs, Murray Hill, N.J., 1953-62; head dept. phys. chemistry AT&T Bell Labs, Murray Hill, NJ, 1962-69, asst. chem. dir., 1969-73, chem. dir., 1973-91; dir. environ. chemistry rsch. AT&T Bell Labs, Murray Hill, N.J., 1991-92; chmn. bd. trustees Gordon Rsch. Confs.; mem. adv. bd. Chem. Abstract Svcs.; chmn. Nat. Commn. on Super-conductivity; chmn. panels on advanced composites, electronic packaging and shipboard pollution control NRC, mem. Naval Studies Bd. Trustee Matheny Sch. Hosp. Fellow AAAS, Am. Phys. Soc., Royal Soc. Chemistry London; mem. NAE, AICE, Am. Chem. Soc. (Barnes award 1992). Home: 12 Polo Club Rd Far Hills NJ 07931-2467

MCCALL, DOROTHY KAY, social worker, psychotherapist; b. Houston, July 18, 1948; d. Sherwood Pelton Jr. and Kathryn Rose (Gassen) McC. BA, Calif. State U., Fullerton, 1973; MS in Edn., U. Kans., 1978; PhD, U. Pitts., 1989. Lic. social worker; cert. alcoholism counselor, N.Y. State. Counselor/intern Ctr. for Behavioral Devel., Overland Park, Kans., 1976-77; rehab. counselor Niagra Frontier Voc. Rehab. Ctr., Buffalo, 1978-79; counselor/instr. dept. motor vehicles Driving While Impaired Program N.Y. State, 1979-80; alcoholism counselor Bry Lin Hosp., Buffalo, 1979-81; instr. sch. social work U. Pitts., 1984, 91; alcohol drug counselor The Whale's Tale, Pitts., 1984-86; sole practice drug and alcohol therapy Pitts., 1986—; faculty Chem. People Inst., Pitts., 1987-89; guest lectr. sch. social work U. Pitts., 1982-87, 89; educator, trainer Community Mental Health Ctr., W.Va., 1986-87, Tenn., 1986; trainer Tri-Cmty. Sch. Sys., Western Pa., 1984-87; cons. Battered Women's Shelter, Buffalo, 1980, Buffalo Youth and Alcoholism Abuse program, 1980; lectr. in field. Mem. Spl. Adv. Com. on Addiction, 1981-83; bd. dirs. Chem. People, Task Force Adv. Com., 1984-86; bd. dirs. Drug Connection Hot Line, 1984-86; mem. Coalition of Addictive Diseases, 1984—; co-founder Greater Pitts. Adult Children of Alcoholics Network, 1984; mem. adv. bd. Chem. Awareness Referral and Evaluation System Duquesne U., 1988-93. Recipient Outstanding Achievement award Greater Pitts. Adult Children of Alcoholics Network, 1987, Disting. Svc. award Pa. Assn. for Children of Alcoholics, 1993; Nat. Inst. Alcohol Abuse tng. grantee, 1981; U. Pitts. fellow, 1983. Mem. NASW, Pa. Assn. for Children of Alcoholics (bd. dirs. 1987—, v.p. 1990-94, Disting. Svc. award 1993), Employee Assistance Profls.. Assn. Inc., Am. Soc. for Clin. Hypnosis, Nat. Assn. for Children of Alcoholics, Inst. for Noetic Scis., Internat. Soc. for Study of Subtle Energies and Energy Medicine. Democrat. Avocations: perfumery, film, reading, drawing, playing the recorder. Office: 673 Washington Rd Pittsburgh PA 15228-1917

MCCALL, DUKE KIMBROUGH, clergyman; b. Meridian, Miss., Sept. 1, 1914; s. John William and Lizette (Kimbrough) McC.; m. Marguerite Mullinnix, Sept. 1, 1936 (dec. 1983); children: Duke, Douglas H., John Richard,

Michael W.; m. Winona Gatton McCandless, Feb. 2, 1984. BA, Furman U., Greenville, S.C., 1936; MDiv, So. Bapt. Sem., Louisville, 1938; PhD, So. Bapt. Sem., 1943; LLD (hon.), Baylor U.; DD (hon.), Furman U., U. Richmond, Stetson U.; LittD, Georgetown Coll. Ordained to ministry, Bapt. Ch., 1937. Pastor Broadway Bapt. Ch., Louisville; pres. New Orleans Bapt. Theol. Sem., 1943-46; exec. sec. So. Bapt. Exec. Com., Nashville, 1946-51; pres. So. Bapt. Theol. Sem., Louisville, 1951-82; chancellor So. Bapt. Theol. Sem., 1982-92; pres. Bapt. World Alliance, Washington, 1980-85; chmn. bd. dirs. Covenant Life Ins. Co., 1989-90. Author: God's Hurry, 1948, Passport to the World, 1951, Broadman Comments, 1957, 2nd edit., 1958, A Story of Stewardship, 1996; editor: What is the Church. Recipient E.Y. Mullins Denominational Svc. award. Avocations: golf; boating. Home: 3534 Lantern Bay Dr Jupiter FL 33477

MC CALL, JERRY CHALMERS, government official; b. Oxford, Miss., June 30, 1927; s. E. Forrest and Mariada (Huffaker) McC.; m. Margaret Denton, Nov. 28, 1952; children: Betsy, Lynn, Kim. B.A., U. Miss., 1951, M.A., 1951; M.S., U. Ill., 1956, Ph.D., 1959. Teaching asst. dept. math. U. Miss., 1950-51, instr. math., 1952-53, prof. math., 1973-76, exec. vice chancellor, 1973-76; rsch. assoc. U. Ill., 1953-57; applied sci. rep. IBM, Springfield, Ill., 1957-58; mgr. IBM, Bethesda, Md., 1966-68, Huntsville, Ala., 1968-71, Owego, N.Y., 1971-72; exec. v.p. Midwest Computer Service, Inc., Decatur, Ill., 1958-59; mem. sci. staff computation lab. Army Ballistic Missile Agy., Huntsville, 1959-60; asst. to dir. Marshall Space Flight Ctr., NASA, Huntsville, 1960-63, dep. dir. rsch. and devel. ops., 1963-66; dir. info. rsch. Miss. Test Facility NASA, Bay St. Louis, 1972-73; pres. 1st State Bank and Trust Co., Gulfport, Miss., 1976-77; dir. Nat. Data Buoy Ctr., Miss., 1977—; pres. McKool, Inc., Gulfport, Miss., 1982-94, Am. Mini Storage, Gulfport, 1985—, Am Crane Rentals, Inc., 1985-89, Cool-Power, Inc., 1988-93; head math. dept. St. Bernard Coll., Cullman, Ala., part-time, 1960-65; asso. prof. math. U. Ala., Huntsville, 1960-62; pub. speaker, 1960-63; chmn. incorporators First State Bank & Trust Co., Gulfport, Miss., 1973-76; tech. cons. Gen. Electric Co., 1974-75. Editor: (with Ernst Stuhlinger) Astronautical Engineering and Science, 1963, From Peenemunde to Outer Space, 1963. Mem. Miss. Criminal Justice Standards Commn., 1974-75; mem. Miss. Marine Resources Council, 1974-76; bd. dirs. U. Miss. Found.; bd. advisers Sch. Engring., U. Miss., 1965-73; mem. indsl. advisors U. New Orleans; chmn. founders U. Ala. Research Inst., Huntsville, 1960-62. Mem. Am. Judicature Soc. (lay mem.), U. Miss. Alumni Assn. (dir. 1966-73). Home: PO Box 7092 Gulfport MS 39506-7092 Office: Nat Data Buoy Ctr Bldg 1100 Stennis Space Center MS 39529

MCCALL, JOHN PATRICK, college president, educator; b. Yonkers, N.Y., July 17, 1927; s. Ambrose V. and Vera E. (Rush) McC.; m. Mary-Berenice Morris, June 15, 1957; children: Claire, Anne, Ambrose, Peter. AB, Holy Cross Coll., 1949; MA, Princeton U., 1952, PhD, 1955; DHL, Knox Coll., Galesburg, Ill., 1993. Instr. Georgetown U., 1955-57, asst. prof. English, 1957-62, asso. prof., 1962-66; prof. U. Cin., 1966-82, head dept. English, 1970-76, sr. v.p., provost, 1976-82; pres. Knox Coll., 1982-93, pres. emeritus and prof. emeritus English, 1993—; vol. Peace Corps, Turkmenistan, 1993-95; vis. prof. Turkmen State U., 1994-95; vice chmn. Gov.'s Task Force on Rural Ill., 1986; pres. Associated Colls. Ill., 1986-88; chmn. Associated Colls. of M.W., 1991-92; mem. edn. com. Ill. Bd. Higher Edn., 1985, 90; mem. rural libr. panel, State of Ill., 1992. Author: Chaucer Among the Gods: the Poetics of Classical Myth, 1979; contbr. articles to profl. jours.; research in medieval lit. and Chaucer's poetry. With Signal Corps, U.S. Army, 1952-54. Am. Coun. Learned Socs. fellow, 1962-63; John Simon Guggenheim Meml. Found. fellow, 1975; Fulbright grantee, 1962. Mem. Medieval Acad. Am. MLA, AAUP. Democrat. Roman Catholic. Home: 1404 3d St New Orleans LA 70130

MC CALL, JULIEN LACHICOTTE, banker; b. Florence, S.C., Apr. 1, 1921; s. Arthur M. and Julia (Lachicotte) McC.; m. Janet Jones, Sept. 30, 1950; children: Melissa, Alison Gregg, Julien Lachicotte Jr. BS, Davidson Coll., 1942, LLD (hon.), 1983; MBA, Harvard U., 1947. With First Nat. City Bank, N.Y.C., 1948-71, asst. mgr. bond dept., 1952-53, asst. cashier, 1953-55, asst. v.p., 1955-57, v.p., 1957-71; 1st v.p. Nat. City Bank, Cleve., 1971-72, pres., 1972-79, chmn., 1979-85, chief exec. officer, from 1979, also bd. dirs.; pres. Nat. City Corp., 1973-80, chmn., chief exec. officer, 1980-86, also bd. dirs., cons.; bd. dirs. Acme Steel Co.; mem. fed. adv. coun. Fed. Res. Bd., 1984-87. Trustee St. Luke's Hosp., United Way Services, Boy Scouts Am., Playhouse Sq. Found., Cleve. Mus. Natural History. Served with AUS, 1942-46, Africa, ETO. Mem. Pepper Pike Club, Chagrin Valley Hunt Club, Kirtland Country Club (Ligonier, Pa.), Mountain Lake Club (Lake Wales, Fla.), Rolling Rock Club. Home: Arrowhead 115 Quail Ln Chagrin Falls OH 44022 Office: 30195 Chagrin Blvd Ste 104W Pepper Pike OH 44124-5703

MCCALL, THOMAS DONALD, marketing communications company executive; b. Syracuse, N.Y., Jan. 4, 1958; s. Donald Andrew and Ann Catherine (Lamb) McC.; m. Vicki Lynne Russ; children: Pamella Jean Lanty, Jamie Lynne Lanty, Kathleen Marchand, Matthew Thomas Owen. BS, SUNY, Brockport, 1980. Dir. comm. and pub. rels. Cazenovia (N.Y.) Coll., 1984-86; mgr. corp. pub. rels. Oneida (N.Y.) Silversmiths Ltd., 1986-90; account supr. Eric Mower and Assocs., Syracuse, 1990-91, sr. account supr., 1991-92, mgmt. supr., 1992-94; ptnr. Eric Mower and Assocs., Rochester, N.Y., 1994—; bd. mem. Pub. Rels. Soc. Am.-Ctrl. N.Y. Chpt., Syracuse, 1991-93. Bd. mem. Boys and Girls Club Syracuse, 1994-95; bd. deacons First Presbyn. Ch., Liverpool, N.Y., 1995-97. Recipient Prism award Pub. Rels. Soc. Am., Rochester, N.Y., 1992, 93, 94. Home: 5473 Saltbox Ln Clay NY 13041 Office: Eric Mower & Assocs 350 Linden Oaks Rochester NY 14625-2807

MCCALL, TINA, critical care nurse; b. Searcy, Ark., Sept. 15, 1960; d. Junior Lee and Doris (Weaver) Barger; m. Todd McCall, Sept. 4, 1981; children: Morgan, Christian. BSN, U. Cen. Ark., Conway, 1982; student, Webster U., Little Rock. Cert. critical care nurse. Cardiac ICU staff nurse St. Vincent Infirmary, Little Rock; asst. head nurse in oncology St. Bernards Hosp., Jonesboro, Ark.; staff devel. instr. Doctors Hosp., Little Rock, nursing dir. intensive care; head nurse intermediate care unit St. paul Med. Ctr., Dallas; asst. divisional dir. med. surg. critical care Arlington (Tex.) Meml. Hosp., staff nurse critical care, adminstrv. coord., 1993—. Mem. AACCN, Am. Heart Assn., Sigma Theta Tau. Home: 934 Rio Vista Ln Arlington TX 76017-1753

MCCALL, WILLIAM CALDER, oil and chemical company executive; b. Hoquiam, Wash., Feb. 1, 1906; s. Dougall Hugh and Hughena (Calder) McC.; m. Marian Hall, Mar. 22, 1946; children—Ernest, Robert. Student U. Oreg., 1924-28; LHD Lewis & Clark Coll., 1992. Asst. sales mgr. Anaconda Sales Co., Chgo., 1932-39; chmn. McCall Oil & Chem. Corp., Portland, Oreg., 1939—, Gt. Western Chem. Co., Portland, 1975—; dir. Oreg. Bank, Portland, King Broadcasting Co., Seattle. Pres. Oreg. Art Mus., Portland; trustee Lewis and Clark Coll., Portland; exec. v.p. Oreg. Symphony Soc.; dir. Oreg. Health Scis. Found., Good Samaritan Hosp. Found., Portland. Republican. Episcopalian. Clubs: Eldorado Country (Indian Wells, Calif.) (pres. 1978-79); Arlington (Portland); Pacific-Union (San Francisco); Los Angeles Country, Vintage (Palm Desert, Calif.), Waverley Country, Rainier (Seattle). Office: McCall Oil and Chem Corp 808 SW 15th Ave Portland OR 97205-1907

MCCALLA, JON P., federal judge; b. 1947; m. Mary R. McCalla; children: Marjorie Katherine, Elisabeth Clair. BS, U. Tenn., 1969; JD, Vanderbilt U., 1974. Law clk. to Hon. Bailey Brown U.S. Dist. Ct. (we. dist.) Tenn., 1974-75; assoc. Armstrong, Allen, Braden, Goodman, McBride & Prewitt, 1975-80; ptnr. Armstrong, Allen, Prewitt, Gentry, Johnson & Holmes, 1980-87, Heiskell, Donelson, Bearman, Adams, Williams & Kirsch, 1987-92; fed. judge U.S. Dist. Ct. (we. dist.) Tenn., Memphis, 1992—. Mem. Fed. Bar Assn., Tenn. Bar Assn., Memphis Bar Assn. Office: US Dist Ct 167 N Main St Ste 907 Memphis TN 38103-1828

MCCALLION, HAZEL, mayor; b. Port Daniel, Can.; m. Samuel McCallion; children—Peter, Linda, Paul. Formerly office mgr. Can. Kellogg Co.; mayor City of Mississauga, Ont., Can., 1978—; mem. com. on transp. of dangerous goods Minister of Transport. Dep. reeve City of Streetsville, 1968, mayor, 1970-73; chmn. Mississauga Taxicab Authority, Mississauga Planning com., Mississauga Sign Com.; vice chmn. adv. com. on local govt. mgmt.; chmn. provincial mcpl. subcom. on transp. of dangerous goods; bd. dirs. Credit Valley Hosp.; 3d v.p. World Conf. of Mayors, 1989. Paul Harris fellow Rotary Internat., 1983. Mem. Streetsville C. of C. (former pres.), Assn. Municipalities Ont. (past pres.), Can. Fedn. Municipalities (bd. dirs.), Can. Jaycees (gov.); hon. mem. Polish Alliance Can., Mississauga Real Estate Bd. (hon.), Alpha Delta Kappa. Club: Mississauga Kinsmen (hon. mem.). Office: City of Mississauga, 300 City Centre Dr, Mississauga, ON Canada L5B 3C1

MCCALLUM, BENNETT TARLTON, economics educator; b. Poteet, Tex., July 27, 1935; s. Henry DeRosset and Frances (Tarlton) McC.; m. Sally Jo Hart, June 3, 1961. B.A., Rice U., 1957, B.S. in Chem. Engring., 1958, Ph.D., 1969; M.B.A., Harvard U., 1963. Chem. engr. Petro-Tex Chem. Corp., Houston, 1958-61; lectr. U. Sussex, Eng., 1965-66; asst. prof. to prof. U. Va., Charlottesville, 1967-80; prof. econs. Carnegie-Mellon U., Pitts., 1981-86, H.J. Heinz prof. econs., 1986—; cons. Fed. Res Bd., Washington, 1974-75; rsch. assoc. Nat. Bur. Econ. Rsch., Cambridge, Mass., 1979—; adviser Fed. Res. Bank Richmond, Va., 1981—. Author: Monetary Economics, 1989, International Monetary Economics, 1996; co-editor Am. Econ. Rev., 1988-91, Carnegie-Rochester conf. series on pub. policy, 1995—; contbr. more than 100 articles to profl. publs. NSF grantee, 1977-86; vis. scholar Internat. Monetary Fund, Washington, 1989-90, Bank of Japan, 1993, Victoria U. Wellington and Res. Bank of New Zealand, 1995. Fellow Econometric Soc.; mem. Am. Econ. Assn. Home: 219 Gladstone Rd Pittsburgh PA 15217-1111 Office: Carnegie-Mellon U Grad Sch Indsl Adminstrn 206 Pittsburgh PA 15213

MC CALLUM, CHARLES ALEXANDER, university official; b. North Adams, Mass., Nov. 1, 1925; s. Charles Alexander and Mabel Helen (Cassidy) McC.; m. Alice Rebecca Lasseter, Dec. 17, 1955; children: Scott Alan, Charles Alexander III, Philip Warren, Christopher Jay. Student, Dartmouth Coll., 1943-44, Wesleyan U., Middletown, Conn., 1946-47; DMD, Tufts U., 1951; MD, Med. Coll. Ala., 1957; DSc (hon.), U. Ala., 1975, Georgetown U., 1982, Tufts U., 1988, Chulalongkorn U., Thailand, 1993, U. Medicine and Dentistry, N.J., 1993. Diplomate Am. Bd. Oral Surgery (pres. 1970). Intern oral surgery Univ. Hosp., Birmingham, Ala., 1951-52, resident oral surgery, 1952-54, intern medicine, 1957-58; mem. faculty U. Ala. Sch. Dentistry, 1956-96, prof., chmn. dept. oral surgery, 1959-65, dean sch., 1962-77; prof., dept. surgery U. Ala. Sch. of Medicine, 1965-96; v.p. for health affairs, dir. U. Ala. Med. Center, Birmingham, 1977-87; pres. U. Ala., Birmingham, 1987-93, chief sect. oral surgery Sch. Dentistry, 1958-65, 68-69; prof., 1959-93, disting. prof., 1993—; mem. nat. adv. dental rsch. coun. NIH, 1968-72; mem. Joint Commn. on Accreditation of Hosps., 1980-91, vice chmn., 1985, chmn., 1986-88. Fellow Am. Coll. Dentists, Internat. Coll. Dentists; mem. ADA (council on dental edn. 1970-76), Am. Assn. Dental Schs. (pres. 1969), Ala. Acad. of Honor, AMA, Am. Soc. Oral Surgeons (trustee 1972-73, pres. 1975-76), Southeastern Soc. Oral Surgeons (pres. 1970), Inst. of Medicine of Nat. Acad. of Scis., Assn. Acad. Health Ctrs. (chmn. bd. dirs. 1984-85), Omicron Kappa Upsilon, Phi Beta Pi. Home: 2328 Garland Dr Birmingham AL 35216-3002 Office: Univ Ala 107 MJH Birmingham AL 35294-2010

MC CALLUM, CHARLES EDWARD, lawyer; b. Memphis, Mar. 13, 1939; s. Edward Payson and India Raimelle (Musick) McC.; m. Lois Ann Gowell Temple, Nov. 30, 1985; children: Florence Andrea, Printha Kyle, Chandler Ward, Sabra Nicole Temple. B.S., MIT, 1960; J.D., Vanderbilt U., 1964. Bar: Mich., Tenn. 1964. Assoc. Warner Norcross & Judd LLP, Grand Rapids, Mich., 1964-69, ptnr., 1969—, mng. ptnr., 1992-97; rep. assemblyman State Bar Mich., 1973-78; dir. Rsch. and Tech. Inst. West Mich., 1986-96, chmn., 1989-91; lectr. continuing legal edn. programs; chmn., bd. dirs. Butterworth Ventures, 1987-96; mem. West Mich. World Trade Week Com., 1988—, chmn., 1990-91; mem. Mich. Dist. Export Coun., 1990—, chmn., 1992—. Chmn. Grand Rapids Area Transit Authority, 1976-79, mem., 1972-79; regional v.p. Nat. Mcpl. League, 1978-86, mem. coun., 1971-78; pres. Grand Rapids Art Mus., 1979-81, 96—, trustee, 1976-83, 94—; chmn. Butterworth Hosp., 1979-87, trustee, 1977-87; chmn. Butterworth Health Corp., 1982-89, dir., 1982—, vice chmn., 1989-91, sec., 1991—; vice chmn. Citizens Com. for Consolidation of Govt. Svcs., 1981-82. Woodrow Wilson fellow, 1960-61; Fulbright scholar U. Manchester, Eng., 1960-61. Mem. ABA (com. on law firms bus. law sect. 1982-94, chmn. com. on law firms bus. law sect. 1994—, mem. fed. regulation of securities com. 1982—, mem. internat. bus. law com.), Am. Law Inst., Tenn. Bar Assn., Mich. Bar Assn. (mem. coun. bus. law sect. 1983-89, sect. chmn. 1988-89, ex-officio coun. bus. law sect. 1989—, chmn. takeover laws subcom. 1986-88, co-chmn. internat. bus. law com., internat. law sect. 1988-89), Grand Rapids Bar Assn., Internat. Bar Assn., Grand Rapids C. of C. (pres. 1975, bd. dirs. 1970-76), Univ. Club, Peninsular Club, Order of Coif, Sigma Xi. Home: 110 Bittersweet Ln NE Ada MI 49301-9552

MCCALLUM, JAMES SCOTT, lieutenant governor, former state senator; b. Fond du Lac, Wis., May 2, 1950; s. George Duncan and Marilyn Joy (Libke) McC.; m. Laurie Ann Riach, June 19, 1979; children: Zachary Scott, Rory Duncan, Cara. BA, Macalester Coll., 1972; MA, Johns Hopkins U., 1974. Mem. Wis. State Senate, Madison, 1977-87; lt. gov. State of Wis., Madison, 1987—. Chmn. Fond du Lac County Reps., 1974-76, Wis. Safe Kids Project; mem. resolutions com. Wis. State Rep. Conv., 1977; presdl. appointee to Internat. Trade Adv. Group, 1988-89, U.S. EPA Nat. Adv. Coun. for Environ. Policy and Tech., 1991—; chmn. Gov.'s Conf. on Small Bus. and Gov.'s Com. on Econ. Issues and Safe Kids Project; chair Nat. Conf. of Lt. Govs., 1991—. Named one of Outstanding Young Men Am., Jaycees, 1976; recipient Presdl. award Honor, Jaycees, 1976; Toll Fellow, 1987. Office: State of Wis Office of Lt Gov 22 E State Capitol Madison WI 53702-0001*

MCCALLUM, LAURIE RIACH, lawyer, state government; b. Virginia, Minn., Aug. 19, 1950; d. Keith Kelvin and Maybelle Louella (Hanson) Riach; m. J. Scott McCallum, June 19, 1979; children: Zachary, Rory, Cara. BA, U. Ariz., 1972; JD, So. Meth. U., 1977. Bar: Wis. 1977. Consumer atty. Office of Commr. of Ins., Madison, Wis., 1977-79; asst. legal counsel Gov. of Wis., Madison, Wis., 1979-82; mng. ptnr. Petri and McCallum Law Firm, Fond du Lac, Wis., 1979-80; exec. dir. Wis. Coun. on Criminal Justice, Madison, 1981-82; commr. Wis. Pers. Commn., Madison, 1982—, chairperson, 1988—; mem. gov.'s jud. selection com. Supreme Ct., 1993; dir. State Bar Labor Law Sect., Madison, 1988-91; faculty U. Wis. Law Sch., Madison, 1992, 93. Chair vol. com. Wis. Spl. Olympics, Madison, 1981; dir. Off-the-Square Club, Madison, 1981, Met. Madison YMCA, Madison, 1982-88. Republican. Avocations: piano, tennis, youth sports. Office: State Pers Commn Ste 1004 131 West Wilson St Madison WI 53703-3233

MCCALLUM, RICHARD WARWICK, medical researcher, clinician, educator; b. Brisbane, Australia, Jan. 21, 1945; came to U.S., 1969; MD, BS, Queensland U., Australia, 1968. Rotating intern Charity Hosp. La., New Orleans, 1969-70; resident in internal medicine Barnes Hosp., Washington, 1970-72; fellow in gastroenterology Wadsworth VA Hosp., L.A., 1972-74, chief endoscopic unit, dept gastroenterology, 1974-76; dir. gastrointestinal diagnostic svcs. Yale-New Haven Med. Ctr., New Haven, 1979-85; asst. prof. medicine UCLA, 1974-76; asst. prof. medicine Yale U., New Haven, 1977-82, assoc. prof., 1982-85; prof., chief div. gastroenterology, hepatology and nutrition U. Va., Charlottesville, 1985-95, Paul Janssen prof. medicine, 1987-96; prof. medicine and physiology U. Kans. Med. Ctr., Kansas City, 1996—, chief div. gastroenterology and hepatology, 1996—, dir. Ctr. for Gastrointestinal Motility Disorders, 1996—; dir. GI Motility Ctr., U. Va. Health Sci. Ctr., 1990096. Fellow ACP, Am. Coll. Gastroenterology, Royal Australasian Coll. Physicians, Royal Australian Coll. Surgeons; mem. Australian Gastroenterology Soc., Am. Fedn. Clin. Rsch., Am. Assn. Study Liver Diseases, Am. Soc. Gastrointestinal Endoscopy, Am. Soc. for Clin. Investigation, Am. Gastroenterology Assn., Soc. for Chemical Investigation (pres. southern region 1996-98). Office: U Kans Med Ctr Dept Internal Medicine 3901 Rainbow Blvd Kansas City KS 66160-0001

MCCALLUM, SCOTT, state official; b. Fond du Lac, Wis.; m. Laurie McCallum; children: Zachary, Rory, Cara. BA, Macalester Coll.; MA in Internat. Studies, Johns Hopkins U. Property developer Fond du Lac; mem. Wis. State Senate; lt. gov. State of Wis.; dir. Workplace Child Care Clearinghouse; chair Repeat Offenders Task Force State of Wis., Trauma and Injury Prevention Task Force; coord. Gov.'s Conf. on Small Bus.; presdl. appointee to Internat. Trade Policy Adv. Com.; past chair Nat. Conf. of Lt. Govs.; gov.'s appointee to Nat. Aerospace States Assn. Office: Lt Gov Rm 22 East State Capitol Madison WI 53702*

MCCALLY, CHARLES RICHARD, construction company executive; b. Dallas, Oct. 5, 1958; s. Richard Holt and Elizabeth Ann (Webster) McC.; m. Shirley Elizabeth Avant, Aug. 18, 1979 (div.); children: Charles Richard Jr., Meredith Holt; m. Judy Lynn Tackett, June 24, 1993. BSME, So. Meth. U., 1981. Engr. McCally Co., Dallas, 1977-83; owner, v.p. DRT Mech. Corp., Dallas, 1983-95; owner McCally Svc. Co., Inc., Dallas, 1995—. Active Young Reps., Dallas, 1980—. Mem. NSPE, ASME, ASHRAE, Am. Soc. Plumbing Engrs. (membership com. 1983-89), Tex. Soc. Profl. Engrs., So. Meth. U. Alumni Assn., SMU Mustang Club, Bent Tree Country Club (Dallas), Oaktree Country Club (Garland, Tex.) (bd. dirs. 1986-89), Sigma Chi. Avocations: tennis, boating, traveling, camping. Home: 4832 Sandestin Dr Dallas TX 75287 Office: McCally Svc Co Inc 2850 Congressman Ln Dallas TX 75220-1408

MCCAMBRIDGE, JOHN JAMES, civil engineer; b. Bklyn., Oct. 27, 1933; s. John Joseph and Florence Josita (McDonnell) McC.; m. Dorothy Antoinette Cook, Mar. 17, 1962; children: Sharon J., John S., Patrick J., Kathleen C. BCE, Manhattan Coll., 1955; MS, Vanderbilt U., 1958; postgrad., UCLA, 1963-66. Civil engr. Raymond Concrete Pile Co., N.Y.C., 1955; commd. 2d lt. USAF, 1955, advanced through grades to col., 1972; exec. sec. Defense Com. On Rsch., Washington, 1971-73, DOD-NASA Supportive Rsch. Tech. Panel, Washington, 1972-74; asst. dir. Def. Rsch. and Engring. (for Life Scis.) Office Sec. Def., Washington, 1974-75; dir. Air Force Life Support Systems Program Office, Wright Patterson AFB, Ohio, 1975-79; retired USAF, 1979; prin. Booz, Allen & Hamilton, Inc., Bethesda, Md., 1979-86; v.p. Espey, Huston & Assoc., Inc., Falls Church, Va., 1986-90; mng. prin. JMC Cons. Group, McLean, Va., 1990—; chmn. air panel on NBC Def., NATO, Evere, Belgium, 1970-71; def. dept. rep. to physics survey com., Nat. Acad. Scis., Washington, 1971. Contbr. articles to profl. jours. Decorated Legion of Merit with oak leaf cluster. Fellow Aerospace Med. Assn. (exec. coun. 1972-73), Inst. Hazardous Materials Mgmt. (chmn. 1988-94); mem. Coun. Engring. and Sci. Splty. Bds. (exec. com. 1995—), Acad. Cert. Hazardous Materials Mgrs. (pres. 1984-86), Survival and Flight Equipment Assn. (nat. sec. 1977-78), The Washington Assembly, River Bend Golf and Country Club, Fairfax Hunt Club, Black Tie Club, Tower Club, KC, Sigma Xi, Chi Epsilon. Republican. Roman Catholic. Office: JMC Cons Group 9200 Falls Run Rd Mc Lean VA 22102-1028

MC CAMERON, FRITZ ALLEN, retired university administrator; b. Nacogdoches, Tex., Oct. 8, 1929; s. Leland Allen and Gladys (Turner) Mc C.; m. Jeannine Young, June 11, 1957; 1 child, Mary Hartley. B.B.A., Stephen F. Austin State Coll., 1950, M.A., 1951; Ph.D., U. Ala., 1954. C.P.A., La. Asso. prof. La. State U., 1959-62, prof., 1962-67, chmn. dept. accounting, 1967-71, asst. vice chancellor, 1971-73, dean continuing edn., 1973-95; ret., 1995; cons. in field. Author: FORTRAN Logic and Programming, 1968, Cobol Logic and Programming, rev. edit, 1970, 5th edit., 1985, FORTRAN IV, 1970, rev. edit., 1974, 3d edit., 1977. Mem. Am. Inst. C.P.A.'s, La. Soc. C.P.A.'s, Am. Accounting Assn. Home: 930 Rodney Dr Baton Rouge LA 70808-5867

MC CAMMON, DAVID NOEL, retired automobile company executive; b. Topeka, Nov. 6, 1934; s. Noel F. and Freda E. McC.; m. Valerie L. Palliaer, May 18, 1968; children: Jeff, Mark, Scott. B.S. in Bus. Adminstrn, U. Nebr., 1957; M.B.A. (Baker scholar), Harvard U., 1962. With Ford Motor Co., Dearborn, Mich., 1957—; contr. Ford div. Ford Motor Co., 1970-71, asst. corp. contr., 1971-77, exec. dir. bus. strategy, 1977-78, v.p. corp. strategy analysis, 1979-84, v.p., contr., 1984-87, v.p. fin., treas., 1987-94, v.p. fin., 1995-97; ret., 1997. Served with U.S. Army, 1957-58. Club: Harvard Bus. Sch. (Detroit). Office: Ford Motor Co The American Rd Dearborn MI 48126-2798

MCCAMMON, JAMES ANDREW, chemistry educator; b. Lafayette, Ind., Feb. 8, 1947; s. Lewis Brown and Jean Ann (McClintock) McC.; m. Anne Elizabeth Woltmann, June 6, 1969. BA magna cum laude, Pomona Coll., 1969; MA, Harvard U., 1970, PhD, 1976. Research fellow Harvard U., Cambridge, Mass., 1976-78; asst. prof. U. Houston, 1978-81, M.D. Anderson prof. chemistry, 1981-94, dir. Inst. for Molecular Design, 1987-94, prof. biochemistry, 1989-94, adj. prof. chemistry, 1995—; adj. prof. molecular physiology and biophysics Baylor Coll. Medicine, Houston, 1986-94, adj. prof. biochemistry, 1992-94; Joseph E. Mayer chair theoretical chemistry U. Calif., San Diego, 1995—, prof. pharmacology, 1995—. Author: Dynamics of Proteins and Nucleic Acids, 1987. Recipient Tchr.-scholar award Camille and Henry Dreyfus Found., George H. Hitchings award Burroughs-Wellcome Fund, 1987, Computerworld Smithsonian Info. Tech. Leadership award for Breakthrough Computational Sci., 1995; named Alfred P. Sloan Rsch. fellow, 1980. Fellow Am. Phys. Soc.; mem. AAAS, Am. Chem. Soc., Biophys. Soc., Protein Soc., Phi Beta Kappa. Achievements include development of the molecular dynamics simulation method for proteins and nucleic acids, of the thermodynamic cycle perturbation method for studying molecular recognition, and of the Brownian dynamics method for simulating diffusion-controlled reactions. Office: U Calif San Diego Dept Chemistry La Jolla CA 92093-0365

MCCAN, JAMES LAWTON, education educator; b. Plymouth, Ind., Aug. 10, 1952; s.Jean F. and Mildred P. (Hayn) McC.; m. Carolyn G. Splain, Jan. 16, 1971; children: Kendra, Brittany. B of Phys. Edn., Purdue U., 1974; MS in Edn., 1981, PhD, 1983. Tchr. reading and English Waynetown (Ind.) Mid. Sch., 1974-75, Yorkville (Ill.) H.S., 1979-80; reading specialist Purdue U., West Lafayette, Ind., 1983-89; program chair Basic Skills Advancement Ind. Voc-Tech. Coll., Lafayette, 1989-91; asst. prof., coord. student teaching Hillsdale (Mich.) Coll., 1991-95; dir. Student Achievement Zone, South Bend, Ind., 1995-96; asst. prof. Nova Southeastern U., Ft. Lauderdale, Fla., 1996—. Contbr. articles and poetry to jours. Mem. DARTEP, Internat. Reading Assn., Mich. Reading Assn. Avocations: reading, music. Home: 6737 College Ct Davie FL 33317 Office: Nova Southeastern U Dept Edn & Behaviorial Scis Fort Lauderdale FL 33314

MCCANDLESS, BARBARA J., auditor; b. Cottonwood Falls, Kans., Oct. 25, 1931; d. Arch G. and Grace (Kittle) McCandless; m. Allyn O. Lockner, 1969. BS, Kans. State U., 1953; MS, Cornell U., 1959; postgrad. U. Minn., 1962-66, U. Calif., Berkeley, 1971-72. Cert. family and consumer scientist; enrolled agt. IRS. Home demonstration agt. Kans. State U., 1953-57; teaching asst. Cornell U., 1957-58, asst. extension home economist in marketing, 1958-59; consumer mktg. specialist, asst. prof. Oreg. State U., 1959-62; instr. home econs. U. Minn., 1962-63, research asst. agrl. econs., 1963-66; asst. prof. U. R.I., 1966-67; assoc. prof. family econs., mgmt., housing, equipment dept. head S.D. State U., 1967-73; asst. to sec. Dept. Commerce and Consumer Affairs, S.D., 1973-79, tax cons., 1980-91, revenue auditor, 1991—. Mem. Nat. Council Occupational Licensing, dir., 1973-75, v.p., 1975-79. Mem. Am. Agrl. Econs. Assn., Am. Assn. Family and Consumer Scis., Am. Coun. Consumer Interests, Assn. Govt. Accts., Inst. Internal Auditors, Nat. Coun. on Family Rels., LWV, Kans. State U. Alumni Assn., Pi Gamma Mu. Research on profl. and occupational licensing bds. Address: 2114 SW Potomac Dr Topeka KS 66611-1445

MCCANDLESS, BRUCE, II, aerospace engineer, former astronaut; b. Boston, June 8, 1937; s. Bruce and Sue McCandless; m. Alfreda Bernice Doyle, Aug. 6, 1960; children: Bruce III, Tracy. BS, U.S. Naval Acad., 1958; MSEE, Stanford U., 1965; MBA, U. Houston, Clear Lake, 1987. Commd. ensign USN, 1958, advanced through grades to capt., 1979, naval aviator, 1960, with Fighter Squadron 102, 1960-64; astronaut Johnson Space Ctr., NASA, Houston, 1966-90; mem. Skylab 1 backup crew Johnson Space Center, NASA, Houston, mem. STS-11 shuttle crew, mem. STS-31 Hubble Space Telescope deployment crew; ret. USN, 1990; prin. staff engr. Lockheed Martin Astronautics, Denver, 1990—. Decorated Legion of Merit; recipient Def. Superior Service medal, NASA Exceptional Service medal, NASA Spaceflight medal, NASA Exceptional Engring. Achievement medal, Collier Trophy, 1985, Haley Space Flight award AIAA, 1991. Fellow Am. Astron. Soc.; mem. IEEE, U.S. Naval Inst., Nat. Audubon Soc., Houston Audubon Soc. (past pres.). Episcopalian. Achievements include executing 1st untethered free flight in space using Manned Maneuvering Unit. Office:

Lockheed Martin Astronautics MS DC3005 PO Box 179 Denver CO 80201-0179

MCCANDLESS, J(ANE) BARDARAH, retired religion educator; b. Dayton, Ohio, Apr. 16, 1925; d. J(ohn) Bard and Sarah Catharine (Shuey) McC. BA, Oberlin Coll., 1951; MRE, Bibl. Sem., N.Y.C., 1953; PhD, U. Pitts., 1968. Dir. Christian edn. Wallace Meml. United Presbyn. Ch., Pitts., 1953-54, Beverly Heights United Presbyn. Ch., Mt. Lebanon, Pa., 1956-61; instr. religion Westminster Coll., New Wilmington, Pa., 1961-65, asst. prof., 1965-71, assoc. prof., 1971-83, prof. religion, 1983-94, prof. emeritus, 1994—, chair dept. religion and philosophy, 1988-92; leader Christian edn. workshops Presbytery of Shenango, Presbyn. Ch. (U.S.A.), 1961—, Synod of Trinity, 1972, 76. Author: An Untainted Saint...Ain't, 1978; contbr. articles to profl. jours., Harper's Ency. Religious Edn. Mem. session New Wilmington Presbyn. Ch., 1977-79. Mack grantee Westminster Coll., 1962-63, Faculty rsch. grantee, 1972, 78, 90. Mem. Religious Edn. Assn., Assn. Profs. and Researchers in Religious Edn. (mem. exec. com. 1978-80), Soc. for Sci. Study Religion, Phi Beta Kappa, Pi Lambda Theta.

MCCANLES, MICHAEL FREDERICK, English language educator; b. Kansas City, Mo., Mar. 8, 1936; s. Martin and Dorothy (Kaysing) McC.; m. Penelope A. Mitchell, May 27, 1967; children—Christopher, Stephanie, Jocelyn. B.S., Rockhurst Coll., 1957; M.A., U. Kans., 1959, Ph.D., 1964. Instr. dept. English U. Cin., 1962-64; asst. prof. Marquette U., 1964-68, assoc. prof., 1968-76, prof., 1976—. Author: Dialectical Criticism and Renaissance Literature, 1975, The Discourse of Il Principe, 1983, The Text of Sidney's Arcadian World, 1989, Jonsonian Discriminations: The Humanist Poet and the Praise of True Nobility, 1992; contbr. articles to profl. jours. Guggenheim fellow, 1978-79. Home: 2640 N 89th St Milwaukee WI 53226-1808 Office: Dept English Marquette U Milwaukee WI 53233 *As educator, scholar, and citizen I try to encourage in the public domain the same qualities of open-mindedness, secular tolerance of multiple viewpoints, and critical judgement of these viewpoints that I encourage among my students and colleagues.*

MCCANN, CLARENCE DAVID, JR., special events coordinator, museum curator and director, artist; b. Mobile, Ala., Apr. 30, 1948; s. Clarence David and Theresa (Pope) McC.; m. Brenda Clemens (div. 1979); 1 child, Nathan; m. Robin Chiavaroli, 1980; children: Angela, John. BFA, U. South Ala., 1970; MFA, U. Cin., 1972; grad. cert., Mus. Mgmt. Inst., Berkeley, Calif., 1982. Art instr. Spring Hill Coll., Mobile, 1972-75, U. South Ala., Mobile, 1975-76; mem. staff, asst. registrar Fine Arts Mus. of South, Mobile, 1977-78, registrar, 1978-81, curator collection, 1981-84, asst. dir., 1985-86, 88-91, acting dir., 1986-88, mus. curator, 1988-91; asst. mgr. spl. events coord. City of Mobile, 1991—; adj. lectr. U.S. Ala., 1990-91, adj. lectr. Bishop State Community Coll., 1991—. Author: (catalogues) The Ripening of American Art: Duveneck and Chase, 1979, The Artists of Barbizon: The Boone Collection, 1983, Enisled Visions: The Southern Nontraditional Folk Artist, 1987, The Acquisitive Eye: Selections From The Collection of James M. Younger, 1990. Pres. Contemporary Artists Consortium of Mobile, 1979-81. Recipient various painting awards Allied Arts Coun., Mobile, 1974; U. Cin. fellow, 1972. Mem. Am. Assn. Mus., Ala. Mus. Assn., Southeastern Mus. Assn. Democrat. Home: 9080 Rawhide Ct Semmes AL 36575-7275 Office: Office of Spl Events 2900 Dauphin St Mobile AL 36606-2420

MCCANN, DENNIS JOHN, columnist; b. Janesville, Wis., July 25, 1950; s. Thomas G. and Jean E. (Skelly) McC.; m. Barbara Jo Bunker, Sept. 11, 1971. BA, U. Wis., 1974. Reporter WMIR Radio, Lake Geneva, Wis., 1974, Janesville (Wis.) Gazette, 1975-78, 79-83; reporter, columnist Milw. Jour. Sentinel, 1983—; reporter Daily Herald, Arlington Heights, Ill., 1978. Contbg. author: Best of the Rest, 1993. Recipient Writing awards Milw. Press Club, Wis. Newspaper Assn., Newspaper Farm Editors. Avocations: golf, running. Office: The Milw Jour Sentinel 333 W State St Milwaukee WI 53203-1305

MCCANN, EDWARD, investment banker; b. San Diego, June 22, 1943; s. Edward F. and Anna Marie (McKay) McC.; m. Sara Sheffield Hall, Nov. 15, 1980; children: Sheffield Hall, Henry Howland, Edward Brewster. BS, U.S. Naval Acad., 1965, MSEE, 1965; postgrad., MIT, 1970. Staff mem. Rsch. Lab. Electronics MIT, Cambridge, Mass., 1968-70; program mgmt. exec. Westinghouse Corp. Rsch. Lab., Churchill, Pa., 1971-73; chief planner Chevron Shipping Co., San Francisco, 1973-77, div. mgr., 1977-79; corp. planning and acquisition staff exec. Standard Oil Co. Calif., San Francisco, 1979-83; dir. strategic planning, def. sector Sperry Corp., N.Y.C., 1983-85, with merger team, 1986; v.p. corp. fin. Eberstadt Fleming Inc., N.Y.C., 1986-88; sr. v.p. investment banking, dir. aerospace and tech. group Robert Fleming Inc., London and N.Y.C., 1988-90; prin. investment banking Hambrecht & Quist, Inc., N.Y.C., 1990-97; mng. dir., head tech. investment banking Advest Inc., Boston, 1997—; bd. dirs. Am. Def. Preparedness Assn., 1986-92, L.I. Biol./Cold Spring Harbor Lab., 1988—. Mem. long-range planning coun. United Way, L.I., 1983-86; treas. Oyster Bay Youth and Family Counseling Agy., 1984-86; trustee Oyster Bay Community Found., 1984—. Recipient class prize systems engring. and naval weaponry, S.R. and Daus. of Am. Colonists awards, 1965. Mem. Coun. Fgn. Rels., Soc. Naval Architects and Marine Engrs., Am. Soc. Naval Engrs., Assn. Old Crows, Navy League, Assn. Naval Aviators, Naval Acad. Alumni Assn., Am. Def. Preparedness Assn. (bd. dirs. 1988-92), Bohemian Club, Seawanhaka Corinthian Yacht Club, Cold Spring Harbor Beach Club. Episcopalian. Home: 398 West Neck Rd Lloyd Harbor NY 11743-1620 Office: Advest Inc 100 Federal St Fl 29 Boston MA 02110-1802

MCCANN, ELIZABETH IRELAND, theater, television and motion picture producer, lawyer; b. N.Y.C., Mar. 31, 1931; d. Patrick and Rebecca (Henry) McC. BA, Manhattanville Coll., 1952, PhD hon., 1983; MA, Columbia U., 1954; LLD, Fordham U., 1966; ArtsD (hon.), Manhattanville Coll., 1987; LitD (hon.), Marymount Coll., 1993. Bar: N.Y. 1966. Assoc. firm Paul, Weiss, Rifkind, Wharton & Garrison, N.Y.C., 1965-66; assoc. numerous theater mgmts. Robert Joffrey, Hal Prince, Saint Suber, Maurice Evans, 1956-68; mng. dir. Nederlander Orgn., N.Y.C., 1968-76; pres. McCann & Nugent Prodns., Inc., N.Y.C., 1976-86; bd. dirs. City Ctr. Music and Dance, Marymount Coll. Prodr.: (play) My Fat Friend, 1975, Dracula (Tony award 1977), The Elephant Man, 1978 (Tony award, Drama Critics award 1978, Drama Desk award 1978, Outer Critics Circle award 1978, Obie award 1978), Night and Day, 1979, Home, 1980 (Adelco award 1980), Amadeus, 1980 (Tony award 1980, Drama Desk award 1980), Morning's At Seven, 1980 (Tony award 1980), Piaf, 1981, Rose, 1981, The Dresser, 1981, Mass Appeal, 1981, The Life and Adventures of Nicholas Nickleby, 1981 (Tony award 1981, Drama Critics Circle award 1981), Good, 1982, All's Well That Ends Well, 1983, The Glass Menagerie, 1983, Total Abandon, 1983, Painting Churches, 1983, The Lady and the Clarinet, 1983, Cyrano de Bergerac/Much Ado About Nothing, 1984, Pacific Overtures, 1984, Leader of the Pack, 1985, Les Liaisons Dangereuses, 1987 (Drama Critics Circle award 1987), Stepping Out, 1987, Orpheus Descending, 1989, Nick & Nora, 1991, Three Tall Woman, 1995, A Midsummer Nights Dream, 1995, Who's Afraid of Virginia Woolf?, 1996; TV show Piaf, 1981, Morning's At Seven, 1982, Philobolus Dance Theatre, 1982; assoc. prodr. Orpheus Descending, 1990. Recipient Entrepreneurial Woman award Women Bus. Owners of N.Y., 1981, 82; recipient James J. and Jame Hoey award for Interracial Justice, 1981, Spl Drama League award for co-producing the Life and Adventures of Nicholas Nickleby on Broadway, 1982, Dr Louis M. Spadero award Fordham Grad. Sch. Bus., 1982.

MC CANN, FRANCES VERONICA, physiologist, educator; b. Manchester, Conn., Jan. 15, 1927; d. John Joseph and Grace E. (Tuttle) Mc C.; m. Elden J. Murray, Sept. 20, 1962 (dec. Nov. 1975). AB with distinction and honors, U. Conn., 1952, PhD, 1959; MS, U. Ill., 1954; MA (hon.), Dartmouth Coll., 1973. Investigator Marine Biol. Lab., Woods Hole, Mass., 1952-62; instr. physiology Dartmouth Med. Sch., Hanover, N.H., 1959-61, asst. prof., 1961-67, assoc. prof., 1967-73, prof., 1973—; adj. prof. biol. scis. Dartmouth Coll., 1974—; mem., cons. physiology study sect. NIH, 1973-77, mem. biomed. rsch. devel. com., 1978-82, chmn. 1979; cons. Hayer Inst., 1979—; cons. staff Hitchcock Hosp., Hanover, 1980—, sr. staff rsch. Norris Catton Cancer Ctr., 1980—; mem. NRC, 1982-86; chmn. Symposium on Comparative Physiology of the Heart, 1968. Editor: Comparative Physiology of the Heart: Current Trends, 1965; contbr. numerous articles to profl. jours. Trustee Lebanon Coll., 1970-73, Montshire Mus. Sic., Hanover, 1975—, Hanover Health Coun., 1976, Lebanon Coll., 1978—; incorporator Howe Libr., 1975—; active LWV, 1980—, Conservation Coun., 1983—, Hist. Soc., 1975—, N.H. Lakes Asson., 1992—; pres. Armington Lake Assn., 1991—. Nat. Heart Inst. fellow, 1959; NIH rsch. grantee, 1959—, Nat. Heart Inst., 1960, N.H. Heart Assn., 1964-65, Vt. Heart Assn., 1966—. Mem. AAAS, Am. Assn. Advancement of Lab. Animal Care, Am. Physiol. Soc., Soc. Gen. Physiologists, Biophys. Soc., Am. Heart Assn. (coun. basic sci., exec. coun. Dallas chpt. 1982-86), Soc. Neurosci. Marine Biol. Lab., LWV, Sigma Xi, Phi Kappa Phi. Avocations: sailing, hiking, reading, keyaking, skiing. Office: Dartmouth Med Sch Lebanon NH 03756

MCCANN, GAIL ELIZABETH, lawyer; b. Boston, Aug. 25, 1953; d. Joseph and Ruth E. (Lagerquist) McC.; m. Stanley J. Lukasiewicz. AB, Brown U., 1975; JD, U. Pa., Phila., 1978. Bar: R.I. 1978, Mass. 1984, U.S. Dist. Ct. R.I. 1978, U.S. Dist. Ct. Mass. 1990. Ptnr. Edwards & Angell, Providence, 1978—. Bd. dirs. Pembroke Ct. Assocs. Coun., Providence, AAA South Ctrl. New Eng., Warwick, R.I., Caritas House, Inc.; mem. R.I. adv. coun. New Eng. Legal Found. Mem. R.I. Bar Assn., Assoc. Alumni of Brown U. (past pres.). Avocations: hiking, travel, aerobics. Office: Edwards & Angell 2700 Hospital Trust Tower Providence RI 02903

MCCANN, JACK ARLAND, former construction and mining equipment company executive, consultant; b. Chestnut, Ill., Apr. 16, 1926; s. Keith Ogden and Miriam Imogene McC.; m. Marian Adele Gordon, Mar. 31, 1956; 1 child, Christopher John. A.B., Bradley U., 1950. Mgr. Washington Office, R.G. LeTourneau Inc., 1950-58; mgr. def. and spl. products Westinghouse Air Brake Co., 1958-64, mgr. nat. accounts, 1964-67, mng. dir. Belgian plant and European mktg., 1967-70; gen. sales mgr. WABCO div. Am. Standard Inc., Peoria, Ill., 1970-73, v.p. mktg., 1973-80, v.p. staff, 1980-82; ret., 1982; now cons. Vestryman St. Francis-in-Valley Episcopal Ch., Green Valley Ariz.

MCCANN, JEAN FRIEDRICHS, artist, educator; b. N.Y.C., Dec. 6, 1937; d. Herbert Joseph and Catherine Brady (Ward) Friedrichs; m. William Joseph McCann, May 14, 1960; children: Kevin, Brian, Maureen McCann Breslin, William, James, Denis Gerard, Kathleen. Student, Caton-Rose Inst. Fine Arts, 1955-57; AAS, SUNY, Farmingdale, 1959; BS, SUNY-Empire State Coll., Binghamton, 1986; MA summa cum laude, Marywood Coll., 1987, MFA in Art summa cum laude, 1989; completed Kellogg Leadership Progam, Sch. Mgmt., SUNY, Binghamton, 1992; PhD, Nova Coll., 1995. Dir. ArtSpace Gallery, Owego, N.Y., 1992-94; substitute art tchr. Owego-Apalachin Sch. Dist., Owego, 1968-88; tutor, evaluator SUNY-Empire State Coll., 1987—; v.p. bd. dirs. Tioga County Coun. on Arts, 1990-91, pres., 1992-95; demonstrator for various schs., ednl. TV and county museums. One woman shows include IBM, Owego, 1972, Tioga County Hist. Soc. Mus., Owego, 1975, Nat. Hist. Ct. House, 1982, Visual Arts Ctr., Scranton, Pa., 1989-90, ArtSpace Gallery, 1991, MacDonald Art Gallery of Coll. Misericordia, Dallas, Pa., 1992, Plaza Gallery, Binghamton, 1992, Artist Guild Gallery, Binghamton, 1993, Wilson Gallery, Johnson City, N.Y., 1994, Countryside Gallery, Owego, N.Y., 1996; exhibited in numerous group shows, including IBM, Owego, 1970, Roberson Ctr., Binghamton, 1972, Arnot Art Mus., Elmira, 1974, 89, 92, Nat. Exhibits at Arena, Binghamton, 1974-76, Riise Gallery, St. Thomas, 1975-78, Pennino's Gallery, Burlington Vt., 1975-77, Visual Arts Ctr., Scranton, Pa., 1987, Grand Concourse Gallery, Albany, N.Y., 1987, Tioga County Hist. Soc. Mus., 1990, ArtSpace Gallery, 1990, Contemporary Gallery, Scranton, 1992, 96; art represented in numerous pvt. collections including those of Pres. George Bush, Congressman Matt McHugh, Senator Tom Libous, also pub. collections. Bd. dirs. Birthright of Owego, 1993—. Recipient N.Y. State Artisans award, 1982, Nat. Strathmore Silver award, 1989, 1st pl. in Graphic Arts award Jericho Arts Coun., 1994. Mem. Nat. mus. Women in Arts (charter), Kappa Pi (pres. Zeta Omicron chpt. 1987-89, life). Avocations: travel, read, visit museums. Home: 23 Paige St Owego NY 13827-1617

MCCANN, JOHN FRANCIS, financial services company executive; b. South Orange, N.J., Nov. 30, 1937; s. Frank Charles and Dorothy Marie (Devaney) McC.; m. Mary Ellen Howland, Aug. 4, 1962; children: Sean Francis, Maureen Ellen, Darragh Siobain, Kevin Patrick. Student, LaSalle Mil. Acad., 1951-55, U. Notre Dame, 1955-57, Niagara U., 1959-61, U. Pa., 1984-86. V.p., sales mgr. Imco Container Co., N.Y.C., 1962-68; vice-pres., sales mgr. Eastman Dillon, Union Securities Co., N.Y.C., 1968-72; sr. v.p., sales mgr. Faulkner, Dawkins & Sullivan, N.Y.C., 1972-75; sr. v.p., br. mgr. Faulkner, Dawkins & Sullivan, Chatham, N.J., 1975-77; sr. v.p. Shearson Loeb Rhoades, Chatham, N.J., 1977-83; exec. v.p. Shearson Am. Express, N.Y.C., 1983-84; exec. v.p., dir. Shearson Lehman Bros., N.Y.C., 1984-92, divisional dir. Philanthropic Found., 1989-92; pres. Smith Barney Shearson, N.Y.C., 1993—; bd. dirs. The Robinson-Humphrey Co., Inc., South Atlantic Group, Smith Barney; pres. Great Atlantic Group, 1994—. Fund raiser Riverview Hosp. Found., Red Bank, N.J., 1983; regional dir. Am. Express Found., N.Y.C., 1985—, Shearson Lehman Bros. Philanthropic Found. Mem. N.Y. Stock Exch. (arbitrator 1982—), Securities Industry Assn., Nat. Assn. Securities Dealers (dist. com. 1988-91), Navesink Country Club, Monmouth Beach Bath and Tennis Club, Beacon Hill Club (Summit, N.J.). Republican. Roman Catholic. Avocations: golf; tennis; travel; reading. Home: 135 Bingham Ave Rumson NJ 07760-1852 Office: Smith Barney 151 Bodman Pl Red Bank NJ 07701-1070

MC CANN, JOHN JOSEPH, lawyer; b. N.Y.C., Feb. 4, 1937; s. John and Katherine (McKeon) Mc C.; m. June M. Evangelist, Oct. 16, 1965; children: Catherine Anne, John Bernard, Robert Joseph, James Patrick. AB, Fordham U., 1958; LLB, Columbia U., 1961. Bar: N.Y. 1962, N.J. 1974, Fla. 1994. Ptnr. Donovan Leisure Netwon & Irvine, N.Y.C.; mem. legal adv. com. N.Y. Stock Exch., 1989-92. Mem. ABA (chmn. bus. law sect. 1992-93), Am. Law Inst., Am. Coll. Investment Counsel (pres. 1984-85), Am. Arbitration Assn. (bd. govs. 1985-96), Tiro A Segno Club, Canoe Brook Golf and Country Club. Roman Catholic. Office: Donovan Leisure Newton & Irvine 30 Rockefeller Plz New York NY 10112

MCCANN, MICHAEL F., industrial hygienist; b. Toronto, Jan. 19, 1943; s. Jack Francis McCann and Bertha Alice (Singleton) Maher; m. Lois Kaggen, Sept. 26, 1984. BSc with honors, U. Calgary, 1964; PhD in Chemistry, Columbia U., 1972. Cert. in comprehensive practice in indsl. hygiene. Sci. tchr. St. Anne's Episc. Sch., Bklyn., 1971-72; sr. technical writer, product safety coord. GAF Corp., N.Y.C., 1973-75; dir. Art Hazards Resource Ctr. Found. for Community of Artists, N.Y.C., 1975-77; founder, pres., exec. dir. Ctr. for Safety in Arts (formerly Ctr. Occupational Hazards), N.Y.C., 1977-96; indsl. hygiene cons., 1975—; adj. faculty N.Y. State Sch. Indsl. and Labor Rels., Cornell U., N.Y.C., 1978, 79; lectr. environ. scis., Sch. Pub. Health, Columbia U., N.Y.C., 1981-92; instr., U. Man., Winnipeg, Can., 1982, 83, adviser, task force on toxicity of art materials, Am. Soc. Testing and Materials, 1980-82; mem. ad hoc com. on heal hazards of arts and crafts materials, Can. Dept. Nat. Health and Welfare, 1981—; mem. adv. bd., Mt. Sinai Occupational Health Clinic, N.Y.C., 1987-95. Author: Health Hazards Manual for Artists, 1975, 4th edit., 1994, Artist Beware, 1979, 2d edit., 1992, Lights! Camera! Safety, 1991, Art Safety Procedures for Art Schools and Art Departments, 1992, School Safety Procedures for Art and Industrial Art Programs, 1994; sr. assoc. editor ILO Ency. of Occupational Health and Safety, 1995-97; writer, narrator videotape Art Safety: Hazards and Precautions, 1988; contbr. articles on art materials hazards to various publs.; editor profl. publs. Presenter testimony on labeling of art materials, U.S. Ho. of Reps., 1980, N.Y. State Assembly, 1981. Mem. APHA, Am. Acad. Indsl. Hygiene, Am. Indsl. Hygiene Assn., Am. Chem. Soc. (chem. health and safety divsn.), N.Y. Com. Occupl. Safety and Health (exec. bd. 1977-87, 94—, treas. 1980-85). Avocations: science fiction, computers.

MCCANN, RICHARD EUGENE, lawyer; b. Billings, Mont., Aug. 14, 1939; s. Oakey O. and Edith May (Miller) McC.; m. Mona N. Miyagishima, Apr. 27, 1964; children: Tami, Todd (dec.), Jennifer. BA magna cum laude, Rocky Mountain Coll., 1965; JD with highest honors, U. Mont., 1972. Bar: Mont. 1972, Washington 1977, Alaska 1982. Law clk. to Judge W. Jameson U.S. Dist. Ct., Billings, 1972-73; assoc. Crowley, Haughey, Hansen, Toole & Dietrich, Billings, 1973-77; assoc. Perkins Coie, Seattle, 1977-80, ptnr., 1981—. Contbr. articles to profl. jours. Trustee Rocky Mountain Coll., Billings, 1973-77. Served with USMC, 1957-61. Mem. ABA, Mont. Bar Assn., Wash. Bar Assn., Alaska Bar Assn. Office: Perkins Coie 1201 3rd Ave Fl 40 Seattle WA 98101-3099

MCCANN, SAMUEL MCDONALD, physiologist, educator; b. Houston, Sept. 8, 1925; s. Samuel Glenn and Margaret (Brokaw) McC.; m. Barbara Lorraine Richardson; children: Samuel Donald, Margaret, Karen Elizabeth. Student, Rice U., Houston, 1942-44; M.D., U. Pa., 1948. Intern in internal medicine Mass. Gen. Hosp., Boston, 1948-49; resident Mass. Gen. Hosp., 1949-50; mem. faculty U. Pa. Sch. Medicine, 1952-65, prof. physiology, 1964-65, acting chmn. dept., 1963-64; prof., chmn. physiology U. Tex. Southwestern Med. Sch., Dallas, 1965-85, dir. neuropeptide div., 1985-95, prof. internal medicine, 1995; endowed prof. Pennington Biomed. Rsch. Ctr. La. State U., Baton Rouge, 1995—; cons. Schering Corp., Bloomfield, N.J., 1958; mem. gen. medicine B study sect. NIH, 1965-67, endocrinology study sect., 1967-69, population research com., 1974-76, reproductive biology study sect., 1978-82, chmn. reproductive biology study sect., 1980-82, neurology study sect., 1985-86. Mem. editl. bd. Endocrinology, 1963-68, 72-77, Neuroendocrinology, 1967-76, editor, 1985-92; mem. editl. bd. Ann. Rev. Physiology, 1974-79, Soc. Exptl. Biology and Medicine, 1976-85, 91-96, Am. Jour. Physiology, 1980-85; editor: Endocrine Physiology, Pioneers in Neuroendocrinology; co-editor Neuroimmuno Modulation, 1993—; contbr. articles to profl. jours., chpts. to books. Recipient Spencer Morris prize U. Pa. Med. Sch., 1948, Lindback award for distinguished teaching, 1965, Oppenheimer award for research in endocrinology, 1966, Hartman award Soc. Study of Reproduction, 1986. Mem. Endocrine Soc. (exec. council 1985-88, Fred Conrad Koch award 1979), Am. Physiol. Soc. (council 1979-81), Soc. for Exptl. Biology and Medicine (coun. 1979-83, pres. 1995—), Soc. Clin. Investigation, N.Y. Acad. Scis., Nat. Acad. Scis., Am. Acad. Arts and Scis., Neuroendocrine Discussion Group (chmn. 1965), Internat. Neuroendocrine Soc. (council 1972-79, pres. 1984-88), Internat. Soc. Neuroimmunomodulation (sec. gen. 1990-96, pres. 1996—). Office: La State U Pennington Biomed Rsch Ctr 6400 Perkins Rd Baton Rouge LA 70808-4124

MCCANN, SUSAN LYNN, elementary education educator; b. Forest Hills, N.Y., Feb. 11, 1947; d. Henry August and Frances Susan (Kleist) Kupsch; m. Kevin Daniel McCann, June 28, 1970; children: Christopher, Megan. BS in Edn., St. John's U., 1968, MS in Edn., 1971. Elem. tchr. Bellmore (N.Y.) Schs., 1968-76, Massapequa (N.Y.) Schs., 1987—; pvt. tutor, Massapequa, 1968—; mem., chair N.Y. State Sch. Com., Massapequa, 1990—; chair Shared-Decision-Making, Massapequa, 1994-96, Ptnrs. in Reading, Massapequa, 1992-93. Chmn. cultural arts Birch Lane PTA, Massapequa, 1986-90; chmn. Earthday com. Unqua Sch., Massapequa, 1991—; vol. Am. Heart Assn., Bohemia, N.Y., 1991—, Nancy Waters Meml. Run, Seaford, N.Y., 1982-92; cmty. outreach chmn. Massapequa Fedn. Tchrs., 1995—. Recipient Cmty. Svc. Merit cert. Massapequa Bd. Edn., 1995, Nat. Lifetime award PTA, 1995, Disting. Svc. award Unqua PTA, 1997. Mem. Am. Fedn. Tchrs., N.Y. State United Tchrs. (gifts of the heart award 1994, cmty. svc. award 1995), Massapequa Fedn. Tchrs. (coord. pub. rels. 1996—). Avocations: cooking, baking, cross-country skiing, reading. Office: Massapequa Schs Merrick Rd Massapequa NY 11758

MCCANN, VONYA B., federal agency administrator. BA, U. Calif., L.A., 1976; MPP, U. Calif., Berkeley, 1979, JD, 1980. Bar: D.C. Law clk. Commr. Tyrone Brown, Fed. Comm. Commn.; policy analyst Nat. Telecom.; ptnr. Arent, Fox, Kintner, Plotkin and Kahn; U.S. coord., dep. asst. sec. internat. comm. & info. policy Dept. State, 1994—, amb., 1994—. Office: Dept of State Internat Comm & Info Policy Bur 2201 C St NW Washington DC 20520-0001*

MCCANN-TURNER, ROBIN LEE, child, adolescent analyst; b. Spokane, Wash., Sept. 27, 1945; d. Robert Allen McCann and Mary Lavelle Wilson; m. C. F. Turner, Sept. 10, 1975. BA, U. Mont., 1967; MSW, Wash. U., 1969; cert. child-adolescent psychoanalysis, Hampstead Ctr., London, Eng., 1979; postgrad., St. Louis Psychoanalytic Inst., 1997. Asst. clin. prof., child and adolescent medicine St. Louis U. Med. Sch., 1984—, Cardinal Glennon Children's Hosp., 1984—; pvt. practice; mem. faculty St. Louis Psychoanalytic Inst., 1982—, chmn. child study group, 1994—, dir. child devel. project, 1994—; mem. ho. of dels. U. Mont., Missoula, 1990—. Mem. APA, NASW, Assn. Child Psychoanalysis, Am. Psychoanalytic Assn. Office: 141 N Meramec Ave Ste 208-209 Clayton MO 63105-3750

MCCARD, HAROLD KENNETH, aerospace company executive; b. Corinth, Maine, Dec. 18, 1931; s. Fred Leslie and Ada (Drake) McC.; m. Charlotte Marie Despres, June 29, 1957; children: Robert Fred, Renee Glen. BEE, U. Maine, Orono, 1959; MEE, Northeastern U., 1963; MS in Mgmt., MIT, 1977. Engr. Avco Systems div. Textron, Wilmington, Mass., 1959-60, group leader, 1960-62, section chief, 1962-65, dept. mgr., 1965-72, dir./staff dir., 1972-77, chief engr., 1977-79, v.p. ops., 1979-82, v.p., gen. mgr., 1982-85; pres. Textron Def. Systems (formerly Avco Systems div./Avco Systems Textron), Wilmington, Mass., 1985-95; sr. v.p. ops. Textron, Inc., Providence, 1995—. Mem. AIAA (Leadership in Quality Mgmt. award 1991), Nat. Indsl. Security Assn. (bd. dirs. 1986—), Electronics Industry Assn. (bd. dirs. 1993—, bd. dirs. govt. div. 1989—), Am. Def. Preparedness Assn. (exec. com.). Avocations: golf, tennis, skiing. Home: 15 Buttonwood Dr Andover MA 01810 Office: Textron Inc 40 Westminster St Providence RI 02903-2525

MCCARDELL, JAMES ELTON, retired naval officer; b. Daytona Beach, Fla., Jan. 22, 1931; s. J. Elton and Margaret Almira (Payne) McC.; m. Nancy Ann Chandler, July 9, 1955; children: Jenise, Patrick. Student, U. Fla., 1948-50; B.A., U.S. Naval Postgrad. Sch., 1965. Commd. ensign US Navy, 1952, advanced through grades to rear adm., 1980; exec. officer USS Forrestal, 1972-73; dep. chief of staff Air Readiness Staff, Chief Naval Res., New Orleans, 1973-76; comdg. officer NAS, Key West, Fla., 1976-78; chief of staff Staff of Chief Naval Res., New Orleans, 1978-80; def. and naval attache U.S. Embassy, Brasilia, Brazil, 1981-83; dir. Inter-Am. Def. Coll., Fort L.J. McNair, Washington, 1983-85; ret., 1985. Decorated Legion of Merit with cluster, Bronze Star medal, Air medal with 12 clusters, Def. Disting. Service medal, Def. Superior Performance medal. Republican. Roman Catholic. Home: PO Box 719 Pass Christian MS 39571-0719 *The absolute measure of successful leadership has always been reflected by performance of subordinates in the achievement of unit goals.*

MCCARGAR, ELEANOR BARKER, portrait painter; b. Presque Isle, Maine, Aug. 30, 1913; d. Roy Morrill and Lucy Ellen (Hayward) Barker; m. John Albert McCargar, Feb. 18, 1947; children: Margaret, Lucy, Mary. Cert. elem. sch. tchg., Aroostook State Normal Sch., Presque Isle, 1933; student, Acadia U., 1935-36; B of Sociology, Colby Coll., 1937; summer student, Harvard U., 1939; postgrad., Cambridge Sch. Art, 1939; studied portrait painting with Kenneth Washburn, Thomas Leighton, Marion Ridelstein, Jean Henry, 1957-67. Ltd. svc. credential in fine and applied arts and related techs. Calif. C.C. Tchr. sci. and geography Limestone (Maine) Jr. H.S., 1937-41; ins. claim adjuster Liberty Mut. Ins. Co., Boston, 1941-42, Portland, Maine, 1943; ARC hosp. worker 20th Gen. Hosp., Ledo, Assam, India, 1944-45; portrait painter Burlingame and Apple Valley, Calif., 1944—. Commns. include more than 650 portraits in 10 states and fgn. countries. Recipient M. Grumbacher Inc. Merit award for outstanding contbn. to arts, 1977; named Univ. of Maine Disting. Alumnus in Arts, 1981. Avocations: canoeing, camping, travel, studying.

MCCARGAR, JAMES GOODRICH, diplomat, writer; b. San Francisco, Apr. 20, 1920; s. Jesse B. and Addie May (Goodrich) McC.; m. Geraldine Claudia Cooper-Key, Aug. 2, 1948 (div. 1954); m. Emanuela Butculescu, Dec. 22, 1973. BA, Stanford U., 1942. Commd. Fgn. Svc. Officer, 1942; Dept. State, Moscow, 1942, 43; Vladivostok, 1942-43, Santo Domingo, 1943-44; sec. of legation, chief polit. sect. Budapest, Hungary, 1946-47; vice consul Genoa, Italy, 1948; chief div. Southeastern European Affairs Office of Policy Coordination, Washington, 1948-50; sec. of embassy, mem. U.S. Del. to Allied Coordinating Com., Paris, 1950-53; asst. to v.p. Free Europe Com., Inc., N.Y.C., 1955; European dir. polit. ops. Free Europe Com., Inc., Paris, 1956-58; cons. to pres. Free Europe Com., Inc., 1959-60, 71-76; spl. asst. to chmn. NEH, Washington, 1978-82; U.S. del. UNESCO confs., 1978, 80, 82; alt. rep. U.S.-Japan Friendship Commn., 1979-82; U.S. del. U.S.-Mexico Commn. on Cultural Coop., 1980, Sem. on Funding of Culture, Madrid, 1982; cons. BBC-TV, London, 1984, Nat. Dem. Inst. Internat. Affairs, Washington, 1984, African-Am. Labor Ctr., Washington, 1984-85, Am. Inst. Free Labor Devel., Washington, 1985, Dept. Internat. Affairs, AFL-CIO, Washington, 1986-95, Free Trade Union Inst., Washington, 1993-95; editorial adv. Interco Press, Washington, 1988-96; panelist internat. conf.

Hungary and the World 1956, Budapest, 1996; bd. dirs. Ams. for Universality of UNESCO, Washington. Author: A Short Course in the Secret War, 1963, rev. edit., 1988, 3d edit., 1992, El Salvador and Nicaragua: The AFL-CIO Views on the Controversy, 1985; co-author: Three-Cornered Cover, 1972, Lost Victory, 1989, Ferenc Nagy: Smallholder or Statesman?, 1995; contbr. articles and book revs., 1940-70; ghostwriter, 1964-96. Co-founder, sec. Ams. Abroad for Kennedy, Paris, 1960. Ensign USNR, 1944-46. Recipient Cert. of Appreciation Internat. Ctr. for Free Trade Unions in Exile, 1958, Fed. Outstanding Performance award NEH, 1979, 81; decorated Knight First Class Royal Norwegian Order St. Olav, 1983, Silver Medallion of the Hungarian Parliament, 1991, Officer's Cross Order of the Hungarian Republic, 1992, Officer's Cross Order of Merit of the Rep. of Poland, 1993. Mem. Polish Inst. Arts and Scis. Am. (elected), Diplomatic and Consular Officers Retired, Chevaliers du Tastevin (France), Vets. of OSS (hon.), Authors' Guild. Democrat. Home and Office: 4201 Cathedral Ave NW Washington DC 20016-4901

MCCARL, HENRY N., economics and geology educator; b. Balt., Jan. 24, 1941; s. Fred Henderson and Mary Bertha (Yaeger) McC.; m. Louise Becker Rys, June 8, 1963 (div. 1986); children: Katherine Lynne, Patricia Louise, Fredrick James; m. Mary Frederica Rhinelander, Jan. 31, 1987; 1 stepchild, Francesca C. Morgan. BS in Earth Sci., MIT, 1962; MS in Geology, Pa. State, 1964, PhD in Mineral Econ., 1969. Cert. profl. geologist. Market rsch. analyst Vulcan Materials Co., 1966-69; asst. prof. econs., asst. prof. geology U. Ala., Birmingham, 1969-72, assoc. prof. econs., 1973-77, assoc. prof. econs. and geology, 1978-91, prof. econs. and geology, 1991-95, prof. econs., edn. and geology, 1995—, dir. Ctr. for Econ. Edn., Sch. Bus., 1987—, prof. econs., edn., geology, 1995—; chief econs. div. Ala. Energy Mgmt. Bd., Montgomery, 1973-74; sr. lectr. in energy econs. Fulbright-Hays Program, Bucharest, Romania, 1977-78; mng. dir. McCarl & Assocs., Birmingham, 1969—; vis. fellow Grad. Sch. Arts and Scis., Harvard U., Cambridge, Mass., 1987. Co-author: (book) Energy Conservation Economics, 1986; Introduction to Energy Conservation, 1987; contbr. articles to profl. jours. Mem. Zoning Bd. of Adjustments, Birmingham, 1974-79, Birmingham Planning Commn., 1974-86, chmn. 1980-86; dist. commr. Boy Scouts Am., Birmingham, 1988-94. Mem. SAR (nat. trustee 1996-97, nat. soc. sec. fin. com. 1995-97, Birmingham chpt. pres. 1994-96, Ala. soc. pres. 1995-96), Soc. Mining Engrs. of AIME (bd. dirs. 1978-80), Am. Inst. Profl. Geologists (sect. pres. 1981-83), Mineral Econs. and Mgmt. Soc. (pres. 1992-93), Ala. Geol. Soc., Nat. Assn. Econ. Educators, St. Andrews Soc. of Mid-South (sec. 1996). Democrat. Episcopal. Avocations: hunting, woodworking, collections, art collections. Home: 1828 Mission Rd Birmingham AL 35216-2229 Summer home: 1828 Mission Rd Vestavia Hls AL 35216-2229 Office: U Ala Sch Bus Dept Econs Birmingham AL 35294-4460

MCCARLEY, GEORGE DAVID, management executive; b. Franklin, Ga., Oct. 25, 1953; s. Earl Robertson and Almadge Elizabeth (Barnes) McC. BBA, Jacksonville State U., 1975; cert. in design engring., U.S. Army, 1976. Supr. Milliken & Co. Inc., La Grange, Ga., 1976-79; mgmt. engr. Ops. Mgmt. Group, Atlanta, 1979-83; mgmt. cons. Kerry Meg, Inc., Gulf Shores, Ala., 1983-86; pres. McCarley & Assocs., Inc., Roanoke, Ala., 1986—; cons. Dow Badische, Anderson, S.C., 1979, GE, 1981, Carrier Corp., 1982, DuraCell, 1983, Woolworths Australia Ltd., Sydney, 1983—, Steel Warehouse Cos., South Bend, Ind., 1985—, Walker Machine and Foundry, Roanoke, Va., 1985—, Steel Joist Ind., Lafayette, La., 1986—, Wilson Mktg., Inc., 1990—, Murray Ohio Mfg. Co., 1990—, Ciba Geigy, Inc., 1991—, Bapt. Hosp. Systems, Birmingham, 1994—, Jim Walter Resources, 1996—; affiliated with Ga. Tech. Southea. Inst. of Tech.; acting gen. mgr. Fairmont Foundry Co., Inc., 1989. Trumpeter 16 classical music recordings La Grange Symphony Orch., 1989—; contbr. writer Voice of the People, featured performer Ga. Musician of the Year Award Banquet; software developer Beta Testor, Datastream Software Sys., Microsoft. Mgr., pres. La Grange Symphony Orch., 1983; active ARC, United Way; founder, chmn. Ronald Hyche Scholarship Found., 1992—, Randolph County Ala. Indsl. Devel. Bd.; foreman Fed. Jury, 1994. 1st lt. C.E., USAR, 1975-83. Mem. NRA (life), Jacksonville State U. Nat. Alumni Assn. (gov. 1987—, chmn. athletic status com. 1990-91), Nat. Geog. Soc., Quail Unltd., Grey Echelon (ret. col. 1982), Gun Owners of Am. Washington, No. Am. Hunting Club, Gamecock club. Republican. Baptist. Avocations: music, tennis, running, outdoor sports, wildlife habitat management. Home and Office: 105 Chestnut St Roanoke AL 36274-1301

MCCARRICK, EDWARD R., magazine publisher. Pub. Life Mag., N.Y.C. Office: Life Time Inc Time & Life Bldg 1271 Avenue Of The Americas New York NY 10020-1300*

MC CARRICK, THEODORE EDGAR, archbishop; b. N.Y.C., July 7, 1930; s. Theodore Egan and Margaret (McLaughlin) McC. Student, Fordham U., 1950-52; AB, St. Joseph's Sem., 1954, AM, 1958; MA, Cath. U., 1960, PhD, 1963; LLD, Mt. St. Vincent Coll., 1967; STD, Inter-Am. U., 1969; STD (hon.), Niagara U., 1982; LHD (hon.), St. John's U., 1974, St. Peter's Coll., 1987. Ordained priest Roman Cath. Ch., 1958. Asst. chaplain Cath. U. Am., Washington, 1959-61, dean students, 1961-63, asst. to rector, dir. univ. devel., 1963-65, instr. dept. sociology, 1961-65; domestic prelate, 1965; pres. Cath. U. P.R., 1965-69; assoc. dir. edn. Archdiocese of N.Y., 1969-71; sec. to Cardinal-Archbishop N.Y., 1971-77; titular bishop of Rusubisir, aux. bishop N.Y., 1977-81; 1st bishop Diocese of Metuchen, N.J., 1981-86; 4th archbishop Newark, 1986—; mem. policy bd. Washington Consortium, Peace Corps, 1962-63, Pontifical Commn. for Migrants and Refugees, 1987; chmn. U.S. Bishops Com. on Migration, 1986-89, 92-95; mem. Nat. Coun. for Spanish-Speaking People, 1961-65; chmn. Gov.'s Commn. for Higher Edn. in P.R., 1968, P.R. Adv. Coun. on Tech. and Vocat. Edn., 1968-69. Mem. Fed. Commn. for Study of Migration and Econ. Devel., 1989; Episcopal promoter Apostleship of the Sea, 1989-92; chmn. com. aid to ch. in Ctrl. and Ea. Europe, Nat. Conf. Cath. Bishops, 1992-96, chmn. internat. policy com., 1996—; sec.-treas. Papal Found., 1988-96, pres., 1996—. Named knight grand cross Holy Sepulchre. Clubs: K.C, Am. Assn. Knights Malta (chaplain 1978-82). Office: PO Box 9500 171 Clifton Ave Newark NJ 07104-9500

MCCARROLL, JEANNE LOUISE, association executive; b. Boston, June 29, 1946; d. William Collyer and Barbara (Bailey) Smith; m. Harry Stephen Newman, June 9, 1968 (div. 1977); children: Michael Stephen, Catherine Louise; m. Fred Michael McCarroll, May 18, 1991. BSBA, Am. U., 1968. Bookkeeper Am. Pharm. Assn., Washington, 1968-69; bus. mgr. Soc. Photog. Scientists and Engrs., Washington, 1969-73; controller Nat. Ctr. for Vol. Action, Washington, 1973-75; fin. officer Bur. Rehab., Washington, 1975-79; acting dir. bus. affairs Assn. Am. Med. Colls., Washington, 1979-88, dir. fin. svcs., 1988-93, asst. v.p. admin. svcs., 1993—. Treas. Potomac Valley Civic Assn., 1975-77; pres. Franconia Commons Homeowners Assn., Alexandria, Va., 1982-88. Mem. Am. Soc. of Assn. Execs. Office: Assn Am Med Colls 2450 N St NW Washington DC 20037-1167

MCCARROLL, KATHLEEN ANN, radiologist, educator; b. Lincoln, Nebr., July 7, 1948; d. James Richard and Ruth B. (Wagenknecht) McC.; m. Steven Mark Beerbohm, July 10, 1977 (div. 1991); 1 child, Palmer Brooke. BS, Wayne State U., 1974; MD, Mich. State U., 1978. Diplomate Am. Bd. Radiology. Intern/resident in diagnostic radiology William Beaumont Hosp., Royal Oak, Mich., 1978-82, fellow in computed tomography and ultrasound, 1983; radiologist, dir. radiologic edn. Detroit Receiving Hosp., 1984—, vice-chief dept. radiology, 1988-96, chief dept. radiology, 1996—; pres.-elect med. staff Detroit Receiving Hosp., 1992-94, pres., 1994-96; mem. admissions com. Wayne State U. Coll. Medicine, Detroit, 1991—; trustee Detroit Med. Ctr., 1996—; officer bd. dirs. Dr. L. Reynolds Assoc., P.C., Detroit, 1991-94, 96—; presenter profl. confs.; assoc. prof. radiology Wayne State U. Sch. Medicine, Detroit, 1995—. Editor: Critical Care Clinics, 1992; mem. editorial bd. Emergency Radiology; contbr. articles to profl. publs. Mem. AMA, Am. Coll. Radiology (Mich. chpt. sec. 1995—), Radiol. Soc. N.Am., Assn. Univ. Radiologists, Am. Roentgen Ray Soc., Am. Soc. Emergency Radiologists (bd. dirs. 1996—), Mich. State Med. Soc., Wayne/Oakland County Med. Soc., Phi Beta Kappa. Avocations: travelling, skiing, reading. Office: Detroit Receiving Hosp 3L-8 4201 Saint Antoine St Detroit MI 48201-2153

MCCARRON, JOHN FRANCIS, columnist; b. Providence, Jan. 20, 1949; s. Hugh Francis and Katherine Anne (Brooks) McC.; m. Janet Ann Velsor, Sept. 3, 1971; children: Veronica, Catherine. BS in Journalism, Northwestern U., 1970, MS in Journalism, 1973. Gen. assignment reporter Chgo. Tribune, 1973-80, urban affairs writer, 1980-91, fin. editor, 1991-92, editorial bd. columnist, 1992—. Contbr. to Planning mag., World Book Ency., Preservation mag. Lt. USNR, 1970-72. Recipient Editors award AP, 1983, 84, Ann. Journalism award Am. Planning Assn., 1983, Heywood Broun award Am. Newspaper Guild, Washington, 1989, Peter Lisagor award Soc. Profl. Journalists, 1994. Home: 1425 Noyes St Evanston IL 60201-2639 Office: Chicago Tribune Chicago IL 60611

MCCARRON, ROBERT FREDERICK, II, orthopedic surgeon; b. Hot Springs, Ark., Oct. 31, 1952; s. Robert Frederick and Irene (Shanks) McC.; m. Vicki Lynn Nichols, June 10, 1977; children: Elizabeth, Jennifer. BS, La. Tech. U., 1974; MD, U. Ark., 1977. Diplomate Am. Bd. Orthopedic Surgery. Intern U. Ark., Little Rock, 1977-78; resident Tex. Tech U., Lubbock, 1978-82, instr. dept. orthopedics, 1983-84, asst. prof., 1984-88; trauma fellow Kantonspittal, Basel, Switzerland, 1982; spine fellow St. Vincent's Hosp., Melbourne, Australia, 1983; pvt. practice orthopedic surgery Conway (Ark.) Orthopaedic and Sports Medicine Clinic, P.A., 1988—; cons. physician U. Cen. Ark., Conway, 1989; chief of surgery Conway Regional Med. Ctr., 1991-94; presenter, exhibitor in field. Contbr. articles to profl. publs. Bd. dirs. Clifton Day Care Ctr., chmn. 1994-95; pres. Conway Regional Physician Hosp. Orgn., 1996, sec., 1995. Fellow Am. Acad. Orthopedic Surgeons, Am. Orthopedic Foot and Ankle Soc.; mem. Ark. Med. Soc., Faulkner County Med. Soc., Ark. Orthopedic Soc., Conway Area C. of C., Sigma Nu. Republican. Mem. Christian Ch. (Disciples of Christ). Avocations: reading, racquetball, basketball, computering, trumpet. Office: Conway Orthopaedic Clinic 525 Western Ave Ste 202 Conway AR 72032-4980

MCCARTER, CHARLES CHASE, lawyer; b. Pleasanton, Kans., Mar. 17, 1926; s. Charles Nelson and Donna (Chase) McC.; m. Clarice Blanchard, June 25, 1950; children—Charles Kevin, Cheryl Ann. BA, Principia Coll., 1950; JD, Washburn U., 1953; LLM, Yale U., 1954. Bar: Kans. 1953, U.S. Supreme Ct. 1962, Mo. 1968. Asst. atty. gen. State of Kans., 1954-57; lectr. law sch. Washburn U., 1956-57; appellate counsel FCC, Washington, 1957-58; assoc. Weigand, Curfman, Brainerd, Harris & Kaufman, Wichita, 1958-61; gen. counsel Kans. Corp. Commn., 1961-63; ptnr. McCarter, Frizzel & Wettig, Wichita, 1963-68, McCarter & Badger, Wichita, 1968-73; pvt. practice law St. Louis, 1968-76; ptnr. McCarter & Greenley, St. Louis, 1976-85; mng. ptnr. Gage & Tucker, St. Louis, 1985-87, Husch and Eppenberger, St. Louis, 1987-89; McCarter & Greenley, 1990—; prof. law, assoc. dir. law sch. Nat. Energy Law and Policy Inst. Tulsa U., 1977-79; prof. law, coach nat. moot ct. coll. of law Stetson U. Coll., St. Petersburg, Fla., 1980-84; mem. govtl. adv. coun. Gulf Oil Corp., 1977-81 ; legal com. Interstate Oil Compact Commn. Co-author: Missouri Lawyers Guide; assoc. editor Washburn U. Law Rev., 1952-53; contbr. articles to profl. jours. Chmn. Wichita Human Rels. Devel. Adv. Bd., 1967-68; bd. dirs. Peace Haven Assn.; active St. Louis estate planning coun., 1987—, bequests and endowment com. Salvation Army, 1995—, YMCA endowment com., 1996—. With USNR, 1944-46. Recipient Excellent Prof. award U. Tulsa , 1979; vis. scholar Yale U., 1980. Mem. ABA (sect. real property, probate and trust law), Kans. Bar Assn., Mo. Bar Assn., Am. Legion, VFW, Native Sons and Daus. Kans (pres. 1957-58), Kappa Sigma, Delta Theta Phi, Principia Dads Club (bd. dirs.). Republican. Office: 1 Metropolitan Sq Ste 2160 Saint Louis MO 63102-2733

MC CARTER, JOHN ALEXANDER, biochemistry educator; b. Wareham, Eng., Jan. 25, 1918; emigrated to Can., 1919; s. Alexander and Helen T. (McKellar) McC.; m. Patricia Jocelyn St. John, Dec. 27, 1941; children: David G., Robert M., Patricia L., William A. B.A., U. B.C., 1939, M.A., 1941; Ph.D., U. Toronto, 1945. Research officer NRC Can. Atomic Energy Project, Chalk River, Ont., 1945-48; asso. prof. Dalhousie U., Halifax, Can., 1948-50; prof. Dalhousie U., 1950-65; prof. biochemistry, dir. Cancer Research Lab., U. Western Ont., London, 1965-83; prof. dept. biochemistry and microbiology U. Victoria, B.C., Can., 1980-83; Mem. Med. Research Council Canada, 1961-67; research adv. group Nat. Cancer Inst. Canada, 1967-72. Contbr. articles to profl. jours. Fellow Brit. Empire Cancer Campaign, 1959-60. Fellow Royal Soc. Can.; mem. Can. Biochem. Soc. (pres. 1966-67), Alpha Omega. Research on tumor virology. Home: 3171 Henderson Rd, Victoria, BC Canada V8P 5A3

MC CARTER, JOHN WILBUR, JR., museum executive; b. Oak Park, Ill., Mar. 2, 1938; s. John Wilbur and Ruth Rebecca McC.; m. Judith Field West, May 1, 1965; children: James Philip, Jeffrey John, Katherine Field. A.B., Princeton U., 1960; postgrad., London Sch. Econs., 1961; M.B.A., Harvard U., 1963. Cons., assoc., v.p. Booz Allen and Hamilton, Inc., Chgo., 1963-69; White House fellow Washington, 1966-67; dir. Bur. Budget and Dept. Fin., State of Ill., Springfield, 1969-73; v.p. DeKalb AgResearch, Ill., 1973-78, dir., 1975-86, exec. v.p., 1978-80, pres., 1981-82; pres., chief exec. officer DeKalb-Pfizer Genetics, 1982-86; pres. DeKalb Corp., 1985-86; sr. v.p. Booz Allen & Hamilton Inc., 1987-97; pres., CEO Field Mus., Chgo., 1996—; bd. dir. A.M. Castle & Co., W.W. Grainger, Inc., Harris Insight Funds. Trustee Chgo. Pub. Television, 1973—, chmn., 1989-96, trustee Princeton U., 1983-87, U. Chgo., 1993—. Office: Field Museum Roosevelt Rd/Lake Shore Dr Chicago IL 60605-2496

MCCARTER, P(ETE) KYLE, JR., Near Eastern studies educator; b. Oxford, Mich., July 9, 1945; s. Pete K. and Mary Ann (Hudson) McC.; m. Susan J.F. McCarter; children: Robert, David, Mary. BA, U. Okla., 1967; MDiv, McCormick Theological Seminary, Chgo., 1970; PhD, Harvard U., 1974. Asst. prof. religious studies U. Va., Charlottesville, 1974-79, assoc. prof., 1979-82, prof., 1982-85; William Foxwell Albright prof. of Bibl. and near eastern studies Johns Hopkins U., Balt., 1985—, chmn. dept. near eastern studies, 1991—, assoc. dean sch. arts. and scis., 1987-90; vis. lectr. on bibl. Hebrew Harvard U., Cambridge, Mass., 1978-79; vis. assoc. prof. Dartmouth Coll., Hanover, N.H., 1979; fellow Ctr. for Advanced Studies, U. Va., 1980-82. Author: The Antiquity of the Greek Alphabet and the Early Phoenician Scripts, 1975, I Samuel: A New Translation with Introduction, Notes, and Commentary 1980, II Samuel: A New Translation with Introduction, Notes, and Commentary, 1984, Recovering the Text of the Hebrew Bible: An Introduction fo Textual Criticism, 1986. Mem. Soc. Bibl. Lit., Am. Schs. Oriental Research (pres. 1988-90), Bibl. Colloquium, Colloquium for Bibl. Research. Democrat. Presbyterian. Avocations: squash, fly fishing. Office: Johns Hopkins U 124 Gilman Hall 34th and Charles St Baltimore MD 21218*

MC CARTER, THOMAS N., III, investment counseling company executive; b. N.Y.C., Dec. 16, 1929; s. Thomas N., Jr. and Suzanne M. (Pierson) McC.; student Princeton U., 1948-51. Sales exec. Mack Trucks, Inc., N.Y.C., 1952-59; ptnr. Kelly, McCarter, D'Arcy Investment Counsel, N.Y.C., 1959-62; v.p., sec., dir. D'Arcy, McCarter & Chew, N.Y.C., 1962-66; v.p., dir. Trainer, Wortham & Co., Inc., N.Y.C., 1967-71, exec. v.p., 1971-75; chmn. bd., dir. Island Security Bank Ltd., 1976-78; pres. Knottingham Ltd., N.Y.C., 1976-84; gen. ptnr. W.P. Miles Timber Properties, New Orleans, 1974—; exec. v.p., Yorke McCarter Owen & Bartels, Inc., N.Y.C., 1985-89, also bd. dirs.; fins. cons. Laidlaw Holdings, Inc., 1990-92; pres., bd. dirs., Mentor Mgmt. Group, Inc. N.Y.C., 1986-90; chmn. bd. dirs. Ramapo Land Co., Sloatsburg, N.Y., 1990—, Stillrock Mgmt. Inc., N.Y.C., 1992-96, chmn. bd. dir., Pendragon Tech., 1996—, DIR., Hyseq Inc.; bd. dirs. Parock Group Inc. Chmn. bd. trustees Christodora Found., Inc., N.Y.C., 1970-93; charter trustee Dalton Sch., N.Y.C., 1968-76, v.p., 1972-76; pres., trustee Civil War Libr. and Mus., Phila., 1985-92; chmn. bd. trustees ASPCA, 1984-95; chmn. Loyal Legion Found., N.Y.C.; trustee Children's Aid Soc. N.Y.C., 1973-94, Joffrey Ballet, Found. for Am. Dance, 1973-77; pres., trustee N.Y.C. Marble Cemetery Assn.; mem. Nat. Com. for Preservation of the U.S. Treasury Bldg., 1988-92; trustee Nat. Symphony Orch., Washington, 1990-94. Chartered investment counselor. Mem. Loyal Legion U.S. (comdr. N.Y. State 1964-66, nat. comdr. in chief 1977-81). Clubs: Racquet and Tennis, Brook, Links, River, St. Nicholas Soc., Pilgrims of U.S. (N.Y.C.), Meadow (Southampton, N.Y.), Ivy (Princeton, N.J.). Republican. Home: 188 E 64th St New York NY 10021-7451 Office: 188 E 64th St New York NY 10021

MCCARTER, WILLIAM J., JR., broadcasting executive; b. Phila., June 10, 1929; s. William J. and Julia R. (Miller) McC.; m. Emma Linda Warner, Jan. 19, 1952; children—Julianne, William J. II, Amy, James Andrew. B.A., Lafayette Coll., 1951; postgrad., Temple U. Sch. Communication, 1957-58. Dir. WFIL-TV, Phila., 1953-57; program dir. WHYY-TV, Phila., 1957-62; program devel. officer Nat. Ednl. Television, N.Y.C., 1962-64; pres., gen. mgr. WETA-TV/FM, Washington, 1964-71, WTTW-TV, Chgo., 1971—; lectr. U. Pa., Am. U., Northwestern U.; TV cons. Govt. V.I.; pres. Eastern Ednl. TV Network, 1968-71. Mem. Pres.'s Commn. on Human Rights, 1968; telecommunications adviser to mayor of Washington.; Trustee St. John's Coll., Washington; bd. mgrs. Pub. Broadcasting Service, mem. Chgo. com. bd. dirs. Served to 1st lt. AUS, 1951-53. Decorated Bronze Star medal, Purple Heart.; Recipient Bd. Govs.' award Washington Acad. Television Arts and Scis., 1971. Mem. Nat. Acad. Televison Arts and Scis. (v.p. 1967-69), Washington Acad. Television Arts and Scis, pres. 1966-68), Public TV Mgrs. Council, Nat. Assn. Ednl. Broadcasters (dir. 1970-72, vice chmn. 1970-72), Radio and TV Corrs. Assn., Chgo. Council Fgn. Relations (dir.). Clubs: National Press (Washington), International (Washington); Mid-Am. (Chgo.), Union League (Chgo.). Office: Sta WTTW-TV 5400 N Saint Louis Ave Chicago IL 60625-4623

MCCARTHY, ABIGAIL QUIGLEY, writer, columnist, educator; b. Wabasha, Minn., Apr. 16, 1915; d. Stephen Michael and Mary Cecelia (O'Leary) Quigley; m. Eugene Joseph McCarthy, June 25, 1945 (separated 1970); children: Ellen Anne, Mary Abigail, Michael Benet, Margaret Alice. BA, Coll. St. Catherine, 1936; MA, U. Minn., 1942; postgrad., U. Chgo., Middlebury Sch. of Eng.; hon. doctorates, Trinity Coll., Cath. U. Am., 9 others. Tchr. Mandan (N.D.) High Sch., 1936-39; asst. prof. Eng. Coll. St. Catherine, St. Paul, 1939-46; columnist Commonweal Mag., N.Y.C., 1974—, RNS, N.Y. Times Syndicate, 1992-94; bd. dirs. Nat. Com. Study of Electorate, Dreyfus Corp., dir. emeritus; pres. Herald Comms., Ltd.; past chmn. bd. Carroll Pub. Co.; Poynter lectr. Ind. U.; Collition lectr. U. Pacific; Audenshaw lectr. Chgo. U.; lectr. Harvard U., Fordham U., Bryn Mawr U., Georgetown U., Hunter U., U. So. Calif., U. Scranton, Boston Coll., Clarke Coll., Stephens U., Trinity U., others. Author: (memoir) Private Faces/Public Places, (novels) Circles, A Washington Story, One Woman Lost; co-author Minnesota Women, At the Edge of Hope, ER: First Lady Without Precedent, Why Catholic?. Founding pres. Clearinghouse Women's Issues; mem. first adv. com. Women's Equity Action League and Women's Polit. Caucus; former mem. Bishops' Com. Edn., Ecumenism; former v.p. Ch. Women United, USA; bd. dirs. Nat. Conf. Interracial Justice. Mem. Wash. Ind. Writers Orgn. (mem. adv. bd.), Cosmos Club, Phi Beta Kappa. Office: 2126 Connecticut Ave NW Washington DC 20008-1729*

MCCARTHY, ALBERT HENRY, human resources executive; b. Worcester, Mass., May 17, 1944; s. Albert H. and Rosemary (Sheehan) McC.; m. Ann F. Arseneault, 1965; children: Erin Marie, Caitlin Ann. BA in Sociology, Coll. Holy Cross, Worcester, Mass., 1968, Cert. Indsl. Rels., 1975; postgrad., Assumption Coll., Worcester, Mass. Recruiter Data Gen. Corp., Southborough, Mass., 1972-73, personnel adminstr., 1973-74, personnel supr., 1974-76; New Eng. dist. personnel mgr. Digital Equip. Corp., Waltham, Mass., 1976-78; mgr. staffing systems and programs Honeywell Info. System, Inc., Waltham, Mass., 1978-80; dir. human resources NEC Info. Systems, Inc., Boxborough, Mass., 1980-84, v.p. human resources, 1984-93; v.p. human resources Simplex Time Recorder Co., Gardner, Mass., 1993—; speaker, panelist Japan External Trade Orgn./Bus. Wk. Symposium, 1989; bd. trustees Mt. Wachusett C.C., 1996—. author: Personel Journal, 1989, 91, Bureau of Business Practice, Sales Manager's Guide, 1993. Bd. trustees Mount Wachusett C.C., 1996—. Recipient Best Practice: Recruitment Category Peronnel Recruitment Program award Human Resource Exec. mag., 1992. Mem. Internat. Assn. Corp. and Profl. Recruiters (co-pres. Boston chpt. 1992-95, bd. dirs. 1994-95), Soc. Human Resource Mgmt. (Yoder Heneman Creative Application award 1990), N.E. Human Resources Assn., Boxborough Bus. Assn. (founding mem.), Human Resource Exec. Forum (founding mem.), Greater Gardner C. of C. (bd. dirs. 1996—), Soc. for Human Resource Mgmt. (nominee Award for Profl. Excellence 1993). Home: 466 Burncoat St Worcester MA 01606-1418 Office: Simplex Time Recorder Co Simplex Plz Gardner MA 01441-0001

MCCARTHY, BRIAN NELSON, marketing and distribution company executive; b. Detroit, May 24, 1945; s. Andrew Nelson and Ruth Elizabeth (Hill) McC.; married, 1991 (div. 1996); children: Amanda Lang, Kelly Elizabeth, Meghan Virginia; m. Shannon Headley, Sept. 7, 1991; 1 child, Conner Michael. BS in Engring. Sci., Oakland U., Rochester, Mich., 1966; MBA, Harvard U., 1972. Engr. Gen. Motors Corp., Pontiac, Mich., 1965-67; co-owner Sound Wave Systems, Costa Mesa, Calif., 1971-78; chief fin. officer, controller A&W Gershenson Co., Farmington, Mich., 1972-75; chief op. officer Devel. Group, Southfield, Mich., 1975-81; chief exec. officer Brichard & Co., San Francisco, 1982-87; pres., chief exec. officer Watermark Corp., Sausalito, Calif., 1987-95; chief exec. officer Indian Wells Water Co., Inc., 1996—, chief exec. officer Watermark Corp., Ssusalito, Calif., 1995—. Lt. USNR, 1967-70, Rear Adm. supply corps, Res. Recipient Navy Achievement medal, Joint Commendation medal; decorated Navy Commendation medal with gold star, Meritorious Svc. medal with two gold stars, Def. Meritorious Svc medal with oak leaf cluster, others. Mem. Navy Supply Corps Assn. (bd. dirs. 1987—), Internat. Bottle Water Assn., Calif. Bottle Water Assn., Harvard Bus. No. Calif. Club, Commonwealth Club. Republican. Office: Indian Wells Water Co 1 Gate 6 Rd Ste 201 Sausalito CA 94965

MCCARTHY, CAROLYN, congresswoman. LPN. Mem. 105th Congresses from 4th N.Y. dist., 1996—; mem. house edn. and workforce com., house small bus.; subcom. postsecondary edn., tng., and life-long learning, employer-employee rels.

MCCARTHY, CATHERINE THERESE, elementary educator; b. Escanaba, Mich., Apr. 22, 1950; d. Robert Francis and Mary Frances (Koebel) Groos; m. J. Michael McCarthy III, Apr. 25, 1970; children: John Kevin, Sean Michael, Ryan Patrick. BS, Nazareth Coll., Kalamazoo, 1972; MA, Western Mich. U., 1981. Cert. continuing edn. tchr., Mich. Substitute presch. and kindergarten tchr. Am. Nursery Sch. and Kindergarten in Japan, Naka Meguro, Japan, 1972-73; tchr. ESL, English Lang. Edn. Coun., Kanda, Japan, 1972-73; substitute tchr. Kalamazoo County Schs., Kalamazoo, 1973-74, 85-86; elem. tchr. St. Monica Sch., Kalamazoo, 1974-82; owner, mgr. Yarn Mcht., Kalamazoo, 1985-86; elem. tchr. Parchment Sch. Dist., Kalamazoo, 1986—; mem. edn. adv. bd. Nazareth Coll., 1976-82. Mem. edn. commn., Sunday sch. tchr. St. Ambrose Ch., Parchment, Mich., 1976-84; asst. coach Am. Yough Soccer Orgn., Kalamazoo, 1982-84, 86-87; mem. Kalamazoo Women's Network, 1982-86. Excellence in Edn. incentive grantee, 1992; recipient Parchment Educator of Yr. award, 1992-93. Mem. NEA, Mich. Edn. Assn. (rep. bargainers coun. 1989-91, coordinating coun. 1990, baraginers assembly 1990—), Parchment Edn. Assn. (v.p., pres., sec., bargainer 1988-92), Kalamazoo Weavers Guild (edn. chmn. 1984-89, newsletter editor 1993-94, 95, sec. 1995-96, pres. 1996-97). Home: 6886 Springbrook Ln Kalamazoo MI 49004-9665 Office: Northwood Elem Sch 5535 Keyes Dr Kalamazoo MI 49004-1581

MCCARTHY, CORMAC, writer; b. Providence, R.I., July 20, 1933; s. Charles Joseph and Gladys (McGrail) McC.; m. Lee Holleman, 1961 (div.); 1 child, Cullen; m. Anne deLisle, 1967 (div.). Author: (novels) The Orchard Keeper, 1965 (William Faulkner Found. award 1965), Outer Dark, 1968, Child of God, 1974, Suttree, 1979, Blood Meridian, or The Evening Redness in the West, 1985, All the Pretty Horses, 1992 (Nat. Book award for fiction 1992, Nat. Book Critics Circle award for fiction 1993), The Crossing, 1994; (teleplays) The Gardner's Son, 1977; (plays) The Stonemason: A Play in Five Acts, 1994. Ingram-Merrill Found. creative writing grantee, 1960, Am. Acad. Arts and Letter traveling fellow, 1965-66, Rockefeller Found. grantee, 1966, Guggenheim fellow, 1976, MacArthur Found. grantee, 1981; recipient Jean Stein award Am. Acad. and Inst. Arts and Letters, 1991. Address: 1011 N Mesa El Paso TX 79902

MC CARTHY, D. JUSTIN, emeritus college president; b. Brockton, Mass.; s. Denis Joseph and Jane Vincent (Dempsey) McC.; m. Rose Mary Hoye; children: Daniel Justin, Rosemary, John Emmet, Vincent Joseph. B.S., Bridgewater State Coll., 1938, Ed.M., 1939; Ed.D., Harvard U., 1955; LL.D. (hon.), Framingham State Coll., 1985. Tchr., prin. Hanover (Mass.) Pub. Schs.; tchr., asst. prin. Belmont (Mass.) Elem. Schs.; dean instrn. U. Maine, Farmington, 1947-48; extension lectr. U. Maine, Orono, 1947-48; supr. student teaching U. Mass. at Amherst, 1948-55; supr., asst. dir. div. state colls. Mass. State Colls., 1955-56, dir. div. state colls., 1956-61; pres.

Framingham (Mass.) State Coll., 1961-85; assoc. in edn. Harvard Grad. Sch. Edn., 1980-83; past sr. advisor Nat. Commn. on the Role and Future State Colls. and Univs. Contbr.: articles to profl. jours. including Harvard Educational Review. Chmn. evaluation Nat. Coun. Accreditation Tchr. Edn., Mass. Bd. Coll. Authority, New Eng. Assn. Colls.and Secondary Schs.; past pres. New Eng. Tchr. Prep. Assn.; former mem. 1202 Commn. Higher Edn. Mass. Mem. Assn. Supervision and Curriculum Devel. (past pres.), Phi Delta Kappa, Kappa Delta Pi (hon.). Address: 302 Washington St Box 1209 Duxbury MA 02331

MC CARTHY, DANIEL CHRISTOPHER, JR., manufacturing company executive; b. St. Paul, May 10, 1924; s. Daniel Christopher and Isobel Beatrice (Wilmot) McC.; m. Gail Lloyd Allen, Mar. 9, 1951. B.Mech. Engring. with distinction, Cornell U., 1949. Mgr. profit planning Ford div. Ford Motor Co., 1949-56; dir. mfg. staff Chrysler Corp., 1956-58; controller Chrysler Internat., Geneva, Switzerland, 1958-59; exec. v.p. Pratt & Whitney Co., 1959-61, pres., 1961-64; v.p. bus. equipment group Litton Industries, Orange, N.J., 1964-65; pres. Monroe Internat., Inc. div., 1965-67; founder, v.p., dir. Keene Corp., 1967-74; founder, pres. Gale Corp., 1974-80; founder, chmn. Porta-Fab Corp., 1980-88, Norwood Mfg. Corp., 1980-88; pres., sole proprietor Gale Assocs., cons. and investments, Montclair, N.J., 1982—; founder, dir. Am. Mobile Systems, Inc., 1982-90; cons., dir. JJI Lighting Group Inc., 1980—, M.H. Koomey subs. Maritime Group, AS, 1991-93; gen. ptnr. Fiduciary Capital Mgmt., L.P., 1989—; founder, vice chmn. Glenco Holdings Inc., 1992-94. Mem. Cornell U. Council. Served with inf. AUS, 1942-46. Mem. ASME, Tau Beta Pi, Phi Kappa Phi, Pi Tau Sigma, Psi Upsilon. Home and Office: Gale Assocs 78 Lloyd Rd Montclair NJ 07042-1729

MCCARTHY, DANIEL WILLIAM, management consultant; b. Syracuse, N.Y., Apr. 15, 1952; s. William Cornelius and Ruth Francis (Geller) McC.; m. Mary Coleen Kisil, Jan. 17, 1987; children: Katherine M., Kevin D., Patrick W. BA in Polit. Sci., SUNY, Geneseo, 1974; MBA, NYU, 1982. Asst. buyer Abraham & Straus, Bklyn., 1976-78; buyer Lord & Taylor, N.Y.C., 1978-80; cons. Touche Ross, Newark, 1982-87; sr. mgr. Deloitte & Touche, N.Y.C., 1987-93; dir. Coach Leatherware, N.Y.C., 1993-94; prin. Greenvale Consulting Group, Poughkeepsie, N.Y., 1994—. Author: Point of Sale - Current Trends and Beyond, 1986; contbr. articles to profl. jours. Mem. Town of Poughkeepsie Hist. Planning Commn., Town of Washington Hist. Soc. Mem. Nat. Retail Fedn., Inst. Mgmt. Cons. Roman Catholic. Avocations: wine collecting, ballet, gardening, home renovation, investing.

MCCARTHY, DAVID JEROME, JR., law educator; b. Hartford, Conn., July 19, 1935; s. David Jerome and Flora Emily (Edmondo) McC.; m. Mary Elizabeth McGlynn, Aug. 13, 1960; children: Emilie Anne, Mary Theresa, Carolyn Elizabeth, Katherine Margaret. AB cum laude, Fairfield (Conn.) U., 1957; LLB, Georgetown U., 1960, LLM, 1962, LLD (hon.), 1983. Bar: Conn. 1960, D.C. 1962. Law clk. U.S. Ct. Appeals D.C. Cir., 1960-61; law clk. to Judge John A. Danaher, 1961-62; atty. Appellate sect. civil div. U.S. Dept. Justice, Washington, 1962-63; dir. D.C. Bail Project, 1963-65; adj. prof. law Georgetown U., 1964-65, assoc. prof., 1965-68; prof. Georgetown U., Washington, 1968-96, Carmack Waterhouse Prof. State & Local Govt. Law, 1996—; asst. dean Georgetown U., 1965-68, assoc. dean, 1968-70, dean, 1975-83, exec. v.p. Law Ctr. Affairs, 1975-83, mem. adv. bd. Health Policy Inst., 1982-88; chmn. exec. com. D.C. Pretrial Services Agy., 1966-87; mem. exec. com. Assn. Am. Law Schs., 1981-83, chmn. accreditation com., 1984-86, chmn. accreditation regulations rev. com., 1986-90; mem. Nat. Chamber Found. Task Force on Products Liability, 1978-81; chmn. Nat. Commn. on Taxes and the IRS, 1979-81; mem. Joint Com. on Clin. Legal Edn. Guidelines, Am. Bar Assn.-Am. Assn. Law Schs., 1977-80, Gov.'s Commn. for Modernization of Md. Exec. Br., 1966-67; counsel Md. Gov.'s Fiscal Rev. Com., 1984-86; mem. adv. bd. Nat. Inst. for Citizen Edn. in Law, 1976-86. Author: Local Government Law in a Nutshell, 1975, 4th edit., 1995; co-author: Local Government Law: Cases and Materials, 4th edit., 1992, supplement, 1995; contbr. articles to profl. jours., chpts. to books. Chmn. bd. dirs. Jesuit Internat. Vols., 1986-89. Recipient Profl. Achievement award Fairfield U. Alumni, 1965, 83. Mem. Am. Law Inst. Democrat. Roman Catholic. Home: 12612 Orchard Brook Ter Potomac MD 20854-2326 Office: Georgetown U Law Ctr 600 New Jersey Ave NW Washington DC 20001-2075

MCCARTHY, DENIS, artist, educator; b. N.Y.C., Feb. 21, 1935; s. Patrick and Carmel McCarthy. Cert. in fine art, The Cooper Union, 1963; B.F.A., Yale U., 1966, M.F.A., 1966. Instr. in drawing Sch. Visual Art, N.Y.C., 1967-72, NYU, 1976-78; prof. fine art Hunter Coll., N.Y.C., 1971—; vis. lectr. Fordham U., Md. Inst., 1979. One-man shows include: Stable Gallery, N.Y.C., 1970, 55 Mercer Gallery, N.Y.C., 1978, N.Y. State Coll., Old Westbury, 1980; exhibited in group shows: Stable Gallery, 1969, Whitney Mus., N.Y.C., 1969, Reese Palley, N.Y.C., 1970, O.K. Harris, N.Y.C., 1972, Warren Benedek Gallery, N.Y.C., 1973, Whitney Mus., N.Y.C., 1973, Aldrich Mus., Ridgefield, Conn., 1973, Paula Cooper Gallery, N.Y.C., 1974, Michael Wyman Gallery, Chgo., 1974, U. Maine, Portland, 1975, Automation House, N.Y.C., 1976, Hundred Acres Gallery, N.Y.C., 1977, NYU, 1977, N.Y. Acad. Scis., 1978. Home: 147 Spring St New York NY 10012-3860

MC CARTHY, EUGENE JOSEPH, writer, former senator; b. Watkins, Minn., Mar. 29, 1916; s. Michael John and Anna (Baden) McC.; m. Abigail Quigley, June 1945; children—Ellen, Mary, Michael, Margaret. A.B., St. John's U., Collegeville, Minn., 1935; A.M., U. of Minn., 1939. Tchr. pub. schs., 1935-40, 45; prof. econ. edn. St. John's U., 1940-42; civilian tech. work with Mil. Intelligence Div., War Dept., 1944; instr. sociology and econs. St. Thomas Coll., St. Paul, 1946-48; mem. 81st-85th Congresses from 4th Minn. dist., 1949-59, mem. ways and means com.; U.S. senator from Minn., 1959-70; mem. senate finance, fgn. relations and govt. ops. coms.; Adlai Stevenson prof. polit. sci. New Sch. for Social Research, 1973-74; syndicated columnist, 1977—; dir. Harcourt Brace Jovanovich, Inc. Author: Frontiers in American Democracy, 1960, Dictionary of American Politics, 1962, A Liberal Answer to the Conservative Challenge, 1964, The Limits of Power, 1967, The Year of the People, 1969, Other Things and The Aardvark, 1970, Up 'Til Now, 1987; also, The Hard Years, 1975, Mr. Raccoon and His Friends, 1977, America Revisited, 1978, Ground Fog and Night, 1979, The Ultimate Tyrany, 1980, Gene McCarthy's Minnesota, 1982, Complexities and Contraries: Essays of Mild Discontent, 1982, The View from Rappahannock, 1984; co-author: A Political Bestiary, 1978, Up 'Til Now, 1987, Required Reading, 1988, 89, The View from Rappahannock II, 1989, Colony of the World, 1993. Roman Catholic. Office: 271 Hawlin Rd Woodville VA 22749-1721

MC CARTHY, FRANK MARTIN, oral surgeon, surgical sciences educator; b. Olean, N.Y., Aug. 27, 1924; s. Frank Michael and Joan (Quinn) McC.; m. Julia Richmond, Nov. 24, 1949; children: Robert Lee, Joan Lee. B.S., U. Pitts., 1943, D.D.S., 1945, M.D., 1949; M.S. in Oral Surgery, Georgetown U., 1954; Sc.D. (hon.), St. Bonaventure U., 1956. Med. intern Mercy Hosp., Pitts., 1949-50; practice oral surgery L.A., 1954-75; teaching fellow Georgetown U., 1952-53; rsch. fellow NIH, 1953-54; prof. oral surgery U. So. Calif. Sch. Dentistry, 1966-75, prof., chmn. sect. anesthesia and medicine, 1975-90, prof. emeritus, 1990—, chmn. dept. surg. scis., 1979-84, assoc. dean adminstrv. affairs, 1977-79, asst. dean hosp. affairs, 1979-84; dir. anesthesiology U.So. Calif. oral surgery sect. L.A. County Hosp., 1958-89; clin. supr., lectr. dental hygiene program Pasadena City Coll., 1992—; v.p. Am. Dental Bd. Anesthesiology, 1984-89; lectr. in field; mem. adv. panel on dentistry sect. anesthesizing agts. Nat. Fire Protection Assn., 1971-79; mem. Am. Nat. Standards Com., 1974-86, 95—; cons. in field. Author: Emergencies in Dental Practice, 1967, rev., 1972, 79, Medical Emergencies in Dentistry, 1982, Safe Treatment of the Medically Compromised Patient, 1987, Essentials of Safe Dentistry for the Medically Compromised Patient, 1989; mem. editorial bd.: Calif. Dental Assn. Jour; contbr. articles to profl. publs. Bd. councilors Sch. Dentistry, U. So. Calif., 1972-75. Served as lt., M.C. USNR, 1950-52. Fellow Internat. Assn. Oral Surgeons (founder), Am. Coll. Dentists, Internat. Coll. Dentists; mem. ADA (editorial bd. jour.), Am. Dental Soc. Anesthesiology (Heidbrink award 1977), Am. Assn. Oral-Max Surgeons (chmn. anesthesia com. 1971), So. Calif. Soc. Oral Surgeons (pres. 1974), Calif., Los Angeles County dental assns., Delta Tau Delta, Psi Omega, Phi Rho Sigma, Omicron Kappa Upsilon. Home and Office: 480 S Orange Grove Blvd Apt 11 Pasadena CA 91105-1752

MCCARTHY, G. DANIEL, lawyer; b. Butte, Mont., Mar. 23, 1949; s. George Denis and Mary Agnes (Kiely) McC.; m. Carolyn M. Scully, June 19, 1976; children: Brendan, Katie, Kelly, Sean. BA, U. Dayton, 1971; JD, U. Notre Dame, 1974; AMP, Harvard U., 1994. Bar: Md. 1974, D.C. 1975, U.S. Ct. Appeals (D.C. cir.) 1976, Pa. 1977, N.Y. 1985, U.S. Ct. Appeals (10th cir.) 1985. Assoc. Bilger & Blair, Washington, 1974-77, 79-80; asst. U.S. atty. U.S. Dist. Ct. (ea. dist.) Pa., Phila., 1977-78; assoc. Abourezk, Shack & Mendenhall, Washington, 1980-83; atty. AT&T, N.Y.C., 1983-85; sr. v.p., gen. counsel and sec. AT&T Credit Corp., Morristown, N.J., 1985-89; sr. v.p., gen. counsel, sec., chief risk mgmt. officer. AT&T Capital Corp., Morristown, 1990-96; v.p., gen. counsel, sec. Compaq Capital Corp., Woodbridge, N.J., 1996—; vis. lectr. Marymount Coll., Arlington, Va., 1979-83; bd. dirs. AT&T Credit Corp., AT&T Capital Ltd., NCR Credit Corp., Eaton Fin. Corp., AT&T Comml. Fin. Corp., AT&T Capital Svcs. Corp., AT&T Systems Leasing Corp., AT&T Capital Holdings Internat., Inc. Mem. ABA, D.C. Bar Assn. Avocation: golf, fly fishing. Home: 82 Van Doren Ave Chatham NJ 07928-2253 Office: Compaq 100 Woodbridge Ctr Dr Woodbridge NJ 07095-1125

MCCARTHY, GERALD MICHAEL, electronics executive; b. Chgo., June 13, 1941; s. John J. and Hannah (Naughton) McC.; m. Margaret-Mary O'Neill, June 20, 1964; children: John, Michael, Gerald Jr., Kevin. BS, Loyola U., Chgo., 1963; MBA, U. Chgo., 1976. Order dept. rep. Zenith Electronics Corp., Chgo., 1965-66, supr. sales plans, 1967-69, asst. mgr. product devel. TV, 1970-71, product mgr. B&W TV, 1971-72, nat. sales tng. mgr., 1972-74, dir. TV product planning, 1974-79, v.p. sales western div., 1979-82, exec. v.p. sales-consumer products, 1982-83; pres. Zenith Sales Co., Chgo., 1983-96, Zenith Radio Can., Ltd., 1983—; sr. v.p., mem. office of the pres. Zenith Electronics Corp., Chgo., 1991; corp. exec. v.p. Zenith Electronics Corp., 1993-96; chmn. video divsn. Consumer Electronics Mfrs. Assn., Glenview, Ill., 1995-96. Trustee Resurrection Health Care Corp., Chgo., 1983—, Jr. Achievement Chgo., 1983—. Served to 1st lt. U.S. Army, 1963-65. Mem. Electronics Industries Assn. (bd. govs. 1983-96). Avocations: fishing, golf. Home: 1745 Dartmouth Ln Deerfield IL 60015-3946

MCCARTHY, HAROLD CHARLES, retired insurance company executive; b. Madelia, Minn., Dec. 5, 1926; s. Charles and Merle (Humphry) McC.; m. Barbara Kaercher, June 24, 1949; children: David, Susan. B.A., Carleton Coll., Northfield, Minn., 1950; postgrad. With Federated Mut. Ins. Co., Owatonna, Minn., 1950-67; with Meridian Mut. Ins. Co., Indpls., 1967-91; exec. v.p., then exec. v.p., gen. mgr. Meridian Mut. Ins. Co., 1972-75, pres., 1975-90, bd. dirs., past chmn. bd., 1990-91; past pres. North Meridian Bus. Group; past pres., chmn. bd. Meridian Ins. Group, Inc.; chmn. bd., dir. Meridian Life Ins. Co.; past chmn., exec. com., bd. dirs. Ind. Ins. Inst.; mem. adv. bd. Harbor Fed. Savs. Bank. Former mem. Met. Devel. Commn., Corp. Community Council; bd. dirs. Meth. Health Found., Family Services Assn., Boy Scouts Am.; trustee Butler U. With USNR, 1944-46. Named Sagamore of the Wabash. Mem. Nat. Assn. Ind. Insurers (past chmn. bd. govs.) Indpls. C. of C. (bd. dirs.), Ind. C. of C. (bd. dirs.), Skyline Club, Legacy Golf & Tennis Club. Republican. Methodist. Office: 2955 N Meridian St Indianapolis IN 46208-4714

MCCARTHY, J. THOMAS, lawyer, educator; b. Detroit, July 2, 1937; s. John E. and Virginia M. (Hanlon) McC.; m. Nancy Irene Orrell, July 10, 1976. BS, U. Detroit, 1960; JD, U. Mich., 1963. Bar: Calif. 1964. Assoc. Julian Caplan, San Francisco, 1963-66; prof. law U. San Francisco, 1966—; vis. prof. law Univ. Coll., Dublin, summer 1975; vis. prof. law U. Calif., Berkeley, 1976-77, Davis, 1979-80; vis. prof. law Monash U., Melbourne, Australia, 1985; cons. in field; mem. Trademark Rev. Commn., 1986-88. Author: McCarthy on Trademarks and Unfair Competition, 5 vols., 4th edit., 1996; (with Oppenheim and Weston) Federal Antitrust Laws, 1981, McCarthy on Rights of Publicity and Privacy, 1987, McCarthy's Desk Encyclopedia of Intellectual Property, 2d edit., 1995; mem. editl. bd. Trademark Reporter. Recipient Rossman award Patent Office Soc., 1979, Jefferson medal N.J. Intellectual Property Assn., 1994. Mem. Am. Intellectual Property Law Assn. (Watson award 1965), Internat. Assn. for Advancement of Teaching and Rsch. in Intellectual Property, Am. Law Inst. (adv. com. on restatement of law of unfair competition), IEEE.

MC CARTHY, JEAN JEROME, retired physical education educator; b. St. Paul, Sept. 11, 1929; s. Joseph Justin and Florence (Quirin) McC.; m. Norma Louise Shermer, July 30, 1955; children: Patrick J., Anne L., Kevin M. BS, U. Minn., 1956, PhD, 1986; MS, Wash. State U., 1958. Teaching asst. Wash. State U., 1956-57, U. Minn., 1957-59, adminstrv. asst., 1959-60; asst. prof. phys. edn. U. South Fla., 1960-62; asst. prof. phys. edn. Mankato State U., 1962-71, assoc. prof., 1971-86, prof. 1986-91, ret. 1991, baseball coach, 1962-77; cons. AAU. Contbr. articles to profl. jours. Mem. Minn. Gov.'s Phys. Fitness Adv. Com. Served with USAF, 1950-54. Recipient Outsanding Faculty award Mankato State U., 1979; named Region 2 Coach of Yr., NCAA, 1971, Outstanding Educators Am., 1970; named to Mankato State U. Athletic Hall of Fame, 1993; U. Minn. Grad. Sch. fellow, 1959-60; Lilly Found. scholar, 1974—; Rsch. Consortium fellow. Mem. AAHPER, Minn. Assn. Health, Phys. Edn. Recreation and Dance, Phi Delta Kappa, Phi Epsilon Kappa (scholarship award 1972), Phi Kappa Phi. Roman Catholic.

MCCARTHY, JOANNE MARY, reading specialist. AB in Hist., Emmanuel Coll., 1967; MEd in Elem. Edn., Boston State Coll., 1969; EdD in Reading, Boston U., 1990. Cert. elem. tchr., sch. psychologist, hist. tchr., guidance counsleor, cons. tchr. reading, supr. reading, elem. prin., social studies tchr., English tchr., supr., dir., Mass. With dept. of def. Nat. Security Agy., 1967-68; tchr. St. Gregory's Sch., Dorchester, Mass., 1969-74; ednl. coord., tchr. Boston Children's Svcs., 1974-75; testing diagnostician Duxbury (Mass.) Pub. Schs., 1975-76; reading tchr. Duxbury High Sch., 1975-81; reading specialist Chandler Sch. and Duxbury Elem. Sch., 1981—; adult literacy program vol. Odwin Learning Ctr., Dorchester, 1990-92. Presenter in field. Exec. bd. mem. Boston U. Sch. Edn. Alumni Assn. Mem. ASCD, Nat. Coun. Tchrs. of English, Internat. Reading Assn., Assn. Childhood Edn. Internat., Duxbury Tchrs. Assn., Greater Boston Reading Coun., Mass. Tchrs. Assn., New England Assn. Tchrs. of English, Pi Lambda Theta.

MCCARTHY, JOHN, computer scientist, educator; b. Boston, Sept. 4, 1927; s. Patrick Joseph and Ida McC.; children: Susan Joanne, Sarah Kathleen, Timothy Talcott. B.S., Calif. Inst. Tech., 1948; Ph.D., Princeton U., 1951. Instr. Princeton U., 1951-53; acting asst. prof. math. Stanford U., 1953-55; asst. prof. Dartmouth Coll., 1955-58; asst. and asso. prof. communications scis. M.I.T., Cambridge, 1958-62; prof. computer sci. Stanford U., 1962—, Charles M. Pigott prof. Sch. Engring., 1987-94. Served with AUS, 1945-46. Recipient Kyoto prize, 1988, Nat. medal of Sci. NSF, 1990. Mem. NAS, NAE, Am. Acad. Arts and Scis., Assn. for Computing Machinery (A.M. Turing award 1971), Am. Math. Soc., Am. Assn. Artificial Intelligence (pres. 1983-84). Home: 885 Allardice Way Stanford CA 94305-1050 Office: Stanford U Dept Computer Sci Stanford CA 94305

MC CARTHY, JOHN EDWARD, bishop; b. Houston, June 21, 1930; s. George Gaskell and Grace Veronica (O'Brien) McC. Student, St. Mary's Sem., Houston, 1949-56; M.A., St. Thomas U., Houston, 1979. Ordained priest Roman Catholic Ch., 1956; served various Houston Cath. parishes; exec. dir. Nat. Bishops Com. for Spanish speaking, 1966-68; asst. dir. Social Action Office, U.S. Cath. Conf., 1967-69; exec. dir. Tex. Cath. Conf., Houston, 1973-79; ordained aux. bishop Diocese of Galveston-Houston, 1979-86; installed third bishop of Austin, 1986—; Bd. dirs. Nat. Center for Urban Ethnic Affairs, Mexican-Am. Cultural Center, Sisters of Charity of the Incarnate Word, Houston, from 1981, St. Thomas U., Houston, from 1980. Mem. Cath. Conf. for Urban Ministry. Democrat. Office: Chancery N Congress &16th PO Box 13327 Austin TX 13327

MCCARTHY, JOSEPH HAROLD, consultant, former retail food company executive; b. Derby, Conn., Dec. 21, 1921; s. Joseph Harold and Kathryn (Feeley) McC.; m. Jean K. Ryan, June 7, 1947; children: Timothy J., Maureen, Barbara, Richard, Joseph Harold. B.S. in Econs., Villanova U., 1944. Sr. v.p. First Nat. Stores Inc., Boston, 1947-76, Grand Union Co., Elmwood Park, N.J., 1976-80; exec. v.p., chief oper. officer Great Atlantic and Pacific Tea Co., Inc., Montvale, N.J., 1980-90, ret., 1990; cons. Great Atlantic and Pacific Tea Co., Inc., North Chatham, Mass., 1990-92. Served to capt. USMC, 1943-46, PTO; served to capt. USMC, 1951-52, Korea. Home: 2030 Imperial Golf C Blvd Naples FL 34110 Office: 38 Captains Walk North Chatham MA 02650-1041

MC CARTHY, JOSEPH MICHAEL, historian, educator; b. Lynn, Mass., Oct. 2, 1940; s. Joseph Donald and Johanna (Downing) Mc C.; AB, St. John's Sem., 1961, postgrad., 1961-63; AM, Boston Coll., 1968, PhD, 1972; m. Kathleen Theresa Wright, July 30, 1966; children: Joanna, Kristenmarie, Erika, Joseph Michael. Tchr., Bishop Fenwick H.S., Peabody, Mass., 1964-67; fin. adminstr. Boston Coll., 1967-71; lectr. in edn. Boston Coll., 1971-74, vis. prof., 1990; prof. edn., dir. leadership programs Suffolk U., 1973—; adj. lectr. Merrimack Coll., 1975, Boston U., 1973; prin. Ednl. Mgmt. Svcs., 1976-96; gen. editor Garland Pub., 1979-92; bd. dirs. Inst. for Study of Academia, 1992-94. Recipient Hearn scholarship, 1959-61, fellowship, 1961-63. Mem. Am. Hist. Assn., Soc. for Medieval and Renaissance Philosophy, Soc. Romanian Historians, East European Rsch. Inst., Phi Alpha Theta, Phi Delta Kappa. Author: An International List of Articles on the History of Education, 1977; Guinea-Bissau and Cape Verde Islands, 1977; Humanistic Emphases in the Educational Thought of Vincent of Beauvais, 1976; Pierre Teilhard de Chardin, 1981; assoc. editor The Urban and Social Change Rev., 1969-72; asst. editor occasional papers series The Bureaucrat, Inc., 1974-76; contbr. to numerous scholarly jours. Home: 344 West St Duxbury MA 02332-3609 Office: Suffolk U Beacon Hill Boston MA 02114

MCCARTHY, KAREN P., congresswoman, former state representative; b. Mass., Mar. 18, 1947. BS in English, Biology, U. Kans., 1969, MBA, 1985; MEd in English, U. Mo., Kansas City, 1976. Tchr. Shawnee Mission (Kans.) South High Sch., 1969-75, The Sunset Hill (Kans.) Sch., ., 1975-76; mem. Mo. House of Reps., Jefferson City, Mo., 1977-94; cons. govt. affairs Marion Labs., Kansas City, Mo., 1986-93; congresswoman, Mo. 5th Dist. U.S. Congress, Washington, D.C., 1995—; rsch. analyst pub. fin. dept. Stearn Bros. & Co., 1984-85, Kansas City, Mo.; rsch. analyst Midwest Rsch. Inst., econs. and mgmt. scis. dept., Kansas City, 1985-86. Del. Dem. Nat. Conv., 1992, Dem. Nat. Party Conf., 1982, Dem. Nat. Policy Com. Policy Commn., 1985-86; mem. Ho. Commerce Com. Energy and Power, Telecom., Trade and Consumer Protection; co-chair Dem. Caucus Task Health Care Reform. Recipient Outstanding Young Woman Am. award, 1977, Outstanding Woman Mo. award Phi Chi Theta, Woman of Achievement award Mid-Continent Coun. Girl Scouts U.S., 1983, 87, Annie Baxter Leadership award, 1993; named Conservation Legislator of Yr., Conservation Fed. Mo., 1987. Fellow Inst. of Politics; mem. Nat. Inst. of Politics; mem. Nat. Conf. on State Legis. (del. on trade and econ. devel. to Fed. Republic of Germany, Bulgaria, Japan, France and Italy, mem. energy com. 1978-84, fed. taxation, trade and econ. devel. com. 1986, chmn. fed. budget and taxation com. 1987, vice chmn. state fed. assembly 1988, pres.-elect 1993, pres. 1994), Nat. Dem. Inst. for Internat. Affairs (instr. No. Ireland 1988, Baltic Republics 1992, Hungary 1993). Office: US House Reps 1232 Longworth Bldg Washington DC 20515-2505

MC CARTHY, KATHRYN A., physicist; b. Lawrence, Mass., Aug. 7, 1924; d. Joseph Augustine and Catherine (Barrett) McCarthy. A.B., Tufts U., 1945, M.S., 1946; Ph.D., Radcliffe Coll., 1957; D.Sc. (hon.), Coll. Holy Cross, 1978; D.H.L. (hon.), Merrimack Coll., 1981. Instr. physics Tufts U., 1946-53, asst. prof., 1953-59, assoc. prof., 1959-62, prof., 1962-95, emerita, 1995—, dean Grad. Sch., 1969-74, provost, sr. v.p., 1973-79; research fellow in metallurgy Harvard, 1957-59, vis. scholar, 1979-80; research assoc. Baird Assocs., 1947-49, 51, Boston U. Optical Research Lab., summer 1952; assoc. research engr. U. Mich., summer 1957-58; dir. Mass. Electric Co., State Mut. Assurance Co. Trustee Southeastern Mass. U., 1972-74, Merrimack Coll., 1974-83, Coll. Holy Cross, 1980—; corporator Lawrence Meml. Hosp., 1975—, dir., 1978—, chmn., 1991. Fellow Optical Soc. Am., Am. Phys. Soc.; mem. Soc. Women Engrs. (sr.), Phi Beta Kappa, Sigma Xi. Roman Catholic. Home: 1580 Massachusetts Ave Apt 5D Cambridge MA 02138-2926 Office: Tufts U Dept Physics 4 Colby St Medford MA 02155-6013

MCCARTHY, KEVIN BART, lawyer; b. Washington, May 7, 1948; s. Frank Jeremiah and Frances Patricia (Bilderback) McC.; m. Patrice Borders, Apr. 3, 1971; children: Kevin Patrick, Charles Ryan, Molly Virginia, Bridget Louise, Moira Patrice. BBA, U. Notre Dame, 1970; JD, Ind. U., Indpls., 1973. Bar: Ind. 1973, U.S. Dist. Ct. (so. dist.) Ind. 1973, U.S. Ct. Appeals (7th cir.) 1974, Ill 1976, U.S. Dist. Ct. (cen. dist.) Ill. 1985, U.S. Ct. Appeals (6th cir.) 1985. Bail commr. Mcpl. Ct. Marion County, Indpls., 1972-73; asst. regional counsel Fed. Hwy. Adminstrn., Homewood, Ill., 1973-75; 1st asst., chief counsel Ill. Dept. Transp., Springfield, 1975-77; counsel com. on interstate and fgn. commerce, subcom. on transp. and commerce Ho. Reps., Washington, 1977-79, asst. counsel com. on pub. works and transp., 1979-82, counsel com. on pub. works and transp., 1982; pvt. practice law Springfield, 1982-87; acting U.S. trustee Dept. Justice, Springfield, 1987-88; U.S. trustee Dept. Justice, Indpls., 1988—; pvt. practice Indpls. and Springfield. Mem. Ill. State Bd. Agrl. Advisors, 1987-88. Mem. Ill. Bar Assn., Ind. Bar Assn. Home: 5619 Surrey Hill Rd Indianapolis IN 46226-1561

MCCARTHY, KEVIN JOHN, lawyer; b. N.Y.C., Apr. 8, 1941; s. Vincent Patrick and Mary (H.) McC.; m. Marianne Pitts, Nov. 5, 1966; children: Mary Rita, Kevin, Colin. BS, U. Md., 1963; JD, U. Md., Balt., 1966. Bar: Md. 1966, U.S. Dist. Ct. Md. 1966, U.S. Ct. Appeals (4th cir.) 1966, U.S. Supreme Ct. 1972, D.C. 1976, U.S. Dist. Ct. D.C. 1976, U.S. Ct. Appeals (D.C. cir.) 1976. Law clk. Cir. Ct. for P.G. County, Upper Marlboro, Md., 1964-66; assoc., ptnr. Sasscer, Clagett & Channing, Upper Marlboro, Md., 1966-76; ptnr. O'Malley, Miles & McCarthy, Upper Marlboro, Md., 1976-86, McCarthy, Bacon & Costello, Landover, Md., 1986—; arbitrator Am. Arbitration Assn., Washington, 1972—. Contbg. author: Maryland Civil Patter Jury Instructions, 1975, 2d edit., 1984, 3d edit., 1993. Named The Best Lawyers in Am., Woodward/White. Fellow Am. Bar Found., Md. Bar Found.; mem. Internat. Assn. Ins. Counsel, Fedn. Ins. and Corp. Counsel, Def. Rsch. Inst., Am. Trial Lawyers Assn., Md. Trial Lawyers Assn., Assn. Def. Trial Attys. Avocations: golf, racquetball, coaching soccer and lacrosse. Office: McCarthy Bacon & Costello 4640 Forbes Blvd Lanham Seabrook MD 20706-4323

MCCARTHY, MARK FRANCIS, lawyer; b. Boston, July 8, 1951; s. William Alfred and Martha Louise (Blodgett) McC.; m. Karen Marie Umerley; children: Kevin Francis, Daniel Henry. AB in Theology, Georgetown U., 1973, JD, 1976. Bar: Ohio 1976. Assoc. Sweeney, Mahon, & Vlad, Cleve., 1976-80; ptnr. Arter & Hadden, Cleve., 1980—; atty. asst. to bd. pres. Bd. Cuyahoga County Commrs., Cleve., 1976-80; adj. prof. Case Western Reserve Law Ctr., Cleve., 1986—. Active Greater Cleve. Growth Assn. Leadership Cleve., 1979-80; pres. bd. trustees Parmadale, Parma, Ohio. Mem. Ohio Assn. Civil Trial Attys. (chmn. product liability sect. 1989—), Fedn. Ins. & Corp. Counsel, Ct. of Nisi Prius, Rowfant Club. Democrat. Roman Catholic. Avocations: book collecting, fly fishing, upland shooting. Home: 404 Regatta Dr Avon Lake OH 44012-2910 Office: Arter & Hadden 1100 Huntington Bldg 925 Euclid Ave Cleveland OH 44115

MCCARTHY, MARY FRANCES, hospital foundation administrator; b. Washington, Apr. 16, 1937; d. Joseph Francis and Frances (Oddi) McGowan; m. Charles M. Sappenfield, Dec. 14, 1963 (div. June 1990); children: Charles Ross, Sarah Kathleen; m. Daniel Fendrich McCarthy, Jr., Aug. 25, 1990. BA, Trinity Coll., Washington, 1958; cert. in bus. adminstrn., Harvard U.-Radcliffe Coll., 1959; MA, Ball State U., Muncie, Ind., 1984. Systems engr. IBM, Cambridge, Mass., 1959-61; editl. asst. Kiplinger Washington Editors, 1961-63; feature writer pub. info. dept. Ball State U., 1984-85, coll. editor Coll. Bus., 1985-86, coord. alumni and devel., 1986-88, dir. major gift clubs and donor rels., 1988-90; dir. devel. Sweet Briar (Va.) Coll., 1990-91; adminstr. St. Mary's Hosp. and Med. Ctr. Found., Grand Junction, Colo., 1991—. Editor: A History of Maxon Corporation, 1986, Managing Change, 1986, Indiana's Investment Banker, 1987; assoc. editor Mid-Am. Jour. Bus., 1985-86. Participant Leadership Lynchburg, 1990, Jr. League; mem. Sr. Companions Bd., Grand Junction, 1992—; mem. Mesa County Healthy Cmtys. Steering Com., 1992—; mem. Mesa County Health Assessment, 1994—; regional dir. IX, Assn. for Healthcare Philanthropy, 1996—. Recipient Golden Broom award Muncie Clean City, 1989; svc. of distinction award Ball State U. Coll. Bus., 1990. Mem. Coun. for Advancement and Support of Edn., Assn. of Healthcare Philanthropy (regional 9 cabinet 1992—), Nat. Soc. Fundraising Execs. (cert., Colo. chpt. bd. dirs. 1994—). Republican. Avocations: biking, walking, cross-country skiing, gardening. Office: St Marys Hosp/Med Ctr Found 2635 N 7th St Grand Junction CO 81501-8209

MCCARTHY, MICHAEL JOSEPH, communications company executive; b. Davenport, Iowa, Oct. 21, 1944; s. Thomas Patrick and Mary Elizabeth (McCabe) McC.; m. Monica Catherine Martin; children: Michael, Maureen. BA, U. Notre Dame, 1966; MSc, London Sch. Econs., 1968; JD, George Washington U., 1973. Speech writer Office of Telecommunications Policy, Office of Pres. of U.S., Washington, 1972-73; assoc., ptnr. Dow, Lohnes & Albertson, Washington, 1973-85; sr. v.p., sec., gen. counsel A.H. Belo Corp., Dallas, 1985—. Author fiction books. Trustee Dallas Bar Found., 1987; bd. dir. N. Tex. Commn. Home: 6138 Aberdeen Ave Dallas TX 75230-4208 Office: A H Belo Corp 400 S Record St Dallas TX 75202-4841

MCCARTHY, MICHAEL SHAWN, health care company executive, lawyer; b. Evergreen Park, Ill., May 16, 1953; s. Martin J. and Margaret Anne (McNeill) McC.; m. Jane F. Alberding, Oct. 28, 1988; children: Caroline Margaret, Nicholas Michael, Claire Patricia. BA, Georgetown U., 1975; MS, U. Ill., 1976; JD, Loyola U., 1980. Bar: Ill. 1980, U.S. Dist. Ct. (no. dist.) Ill. 1980. V.p., sec., gen. counsel Luth. Gen. Health Care System, Park Ridge, Ill., 1980-85, sr. v.p., sec., gen. counsel, 1985-91, sr. v.p. corp. svcs., sec., gen. counsel, 1990-93; chmn., CEO Parkside Sr. Svcs., LLC, Park Ridge, Ill., 1993—; bd. dirs. Cath. Lawyers Guild; chmn. bd. trustees Lake Forest Acad. Mem. ABA, Am. Assn. for Preferred Providers Orgn., Ill. Hosp. Assn., Ill. Pub. Health Assn., Chgo. Bar Assn. Roman Catholic. Avocations: golf, travel. Home: 269 Locust Rd Winnetka IL 60093-3608 Office: Parkside Sr Svcs LLC 205 W Touhy Ave Park Ridge IL 60068

MCCARTHY, PATRICE ANN, lawyer; b. New Haven, Jan. 23, 1957; d. Robert Edmund and Faith Arline (Augur) McC.; m. Donald Allen Kirshbaum, Oct. 25, 1986; children: Lynn Anne, Sara. BA, Mt. Holyoke Coll., 1978; JD, U. Conn., 1981. Bar: Conn. 1981, U.S. Dist. Ct. Conn. 1981. Staff assoc. Conn. Conf. Municipalities, New Haven, 1981-83; legal counsel Conn. Assn. Bds. Edn., Hartford, 1983-88, gen. counsel, assoc. exec. dir. for govt. rels., 1988-91; dep. dir., gen. counsel, 1991—. Editor: Conn. Manual Bd. Policy Regulations and By-laws, 1987; contbr. articles to profl. jours. Mem. ABA, Nat. Sch. Bds. Assn. Coun. Sch. Attys. (bd. dirs. 1990-94), Am. Soc. Pub. Adminstrn. (coun. 1988—), Nat. Orgn. for Legal Problems in Edn., Conn. Bar Assn., Conn. Sch. Attys. Coun. (pres. 1988-89), Conn. Pub. Employers Labor Rels. Assn. (bd. dirs. 1985-88), Mt. Holyoke Club (v.p. 1986-88, pres. 1990-94). Office: Conn Assn Bds Edn 81 Wolcott Hill Rd Hartford CT 06109-1242

MCCARTHY, PATRICK, magazine publishing executive. Joined Women's Wear Daily, 1977; reporter Women's Wear Daily, D.C.; bur. chief Women's Wear Daily, London, Paris; editor Women's Wear Daily, N.Y.C., 1985-88, exec. editor, 1988-92; editor W, N.Y.C., 1985-88, exec. editor, 1988-92; exec. v.p. Fairchild Publs., N.Y.C., 1992-97; chmn., editl. dir., 1997—. Recipient Eugenia Sheppard award for fashion journalism CFDA, 1994. Office: Fairchild Publs c/o Alyssa Schaier Seven West 34th St New York NY 10001

MCCARTHY, PATRICK A., English language educator; b. Charlottesville, Va., July 12, 1945; s. Thomas Blair and Virginia Rose (Feuerstein) McC.; children: Keely, Cailin, Brendan. BA, U. Va., 1967, MA, 1968; PhD, U. Wis., Milw., 1973. Asst. prof., English U. Miami, Coral Gables, Fla., 1976-81, assoc. prof., 1981-84, prof., 1984—; dir. grad. studies English dept. U. Miami, 1986-95; manuscript cons. various univ. presses. Author: The Riddles of Finnegans Wake, 1980, Olaf Stapledon, 1982, Ulysses: Portals of Discovery, 1990, Forests of Symbols: World, Text, and Self in Malcolm Lowry's Fiction, 1994; editor: Critical Essays on Samuel Beckett, 1986, Critical Essays on James Joyce's Finnegans Wake, 1992, Malcolm Lowry's La Mordida: A Scholarly Edition, 1996; co-editor: The Legacy of Olaf Stapledon, 1989, Joyce/Lowry: Critical Perspectives, 1997. Travel grantee Am. Coun. Learned Socs., 1977; recipient Max Orovitz summer stipend U. Miami, 1980, 82, 85, 90, 92, gen. rsch. support grant, 1990, 92, 93, 97. Mem. MLA, Assn. Lit. Scholars and Critics, South Atlantic MLA, Internat. James Joyce Found., Am. Coun. Irish Studies. Office: U Miami Dept English Coral Gables FL 33124

MCCARTHY, PAUL FENTON, aerospace executive, former naval officer; b. Boston, Mar. 3, 1934; s. Paul Fenton and Jane Gertrude (O'Connor) McC.; m. Sandra Williams, June 20, 1959; children: Paul Fenton III, Susan Stacy. B.S. in Marine and Elec. Engring., Mass. Maritime Acad., 1954; M.S. in Mgmt., U.S. Naval Postgrad. Sch., 1964; D of Pub. Adminstrn. (hon.), Mass. Maritime Acad., 1987. Commd. ensign U.S. Navy, 1954, advanced through grades to vice adm., 1985; 7 command tours have included Aircraft Carrier USS Constellation, Carrier Group One, Task Force Seventy; commdr. U.S. 7th Fleet, 1980-82; dir. R & D USN, Washington, 1980-83; negotiator Naval Air, Incidents at Sea Agreement, Moscow, 1980; ret., 1990; cons. in field Alexandria, Va., 1990-92; pres. McCarthy and McCarthy, Ltd.; v.p., chief engr., dep. gen.mgr. McDonnell Douglas Aerospace, St. Louis, 1992-95, v.p. processes and sys. integration, 1995—; Mem. engring adv. coun. Fla. State U. Trustee Naval Mus., 1990; bd. visitors Mass. Maritime Acad., 1993. Decorated D.S.M., Legion of Merit, D.F.C., also by govts. of South Vietnam, Korea, Japan. Mem. Mass. Maritime Acad. Alumni Assn., Soc. Exptl. Test Pilots, Naval Inst., Nat. Soc. Profl. Engrs. (mem. industry adv. group). Episcopalian. Avocations: research, development and acquisition, aircraft and missile systems, financial management. Home: 16475 Saddle Creek Rd Chesterfield MO 63005-4443

MCCARTHY, PAUL LOUIS, pediatrics educator; b. Springfield, Mass., Aug. 9, 1941; s. Alfred Lawrence and Minnie Josephine (Vivian) McC.; m. Barbara Jean Burns, Nov. 30, 1963; children: Paul, Scott, Brian. BA, Dartmouth Coll., 1963; MD, Georgetown U., 1969; MA (in privatum), Yale U., 1982. Diplomate Am. Bd. Pediatrics, Am. Bd. Pediat. Rheumatology. Pediat. intern Children's Hosp., Buffalo, 1969-70, pediat. resident, 1970-72; fellow in ambulatory pediatrics Children's Hosp. Med. Ctr., Boston, 1972-74; asst. prof. pediat. Yale U. Sch. Medicine, New Haven, 1974-78, assoc. prof., 1978-82, prof., 1982—, head gen. pediat., 1985—; Morrison lectr. Geisinger Clinic, Danville, Pa., 1990. Author: Evaluation and Management of Febrile Children, 1985; author 4 monographs; contbr. numerous articles to med. jours., chpts. to books. Fellow Am. Acad. Pediatrics; mem. Ambulatory Pediatric Assn. (pres. 1989-90, Armstrong award 1991), Soc. for Pediatric Rsch., Am. Pediatric Soc. Achievements include research in clinical judgment in acute illnesses in children. Avocations: reading, walking. Office: Yale U Sch of Medicine 333 Cedar St New Haven CT 06510-3206

MCCARTHY, ROBERT EMMETT, lawyer; b. Bklyn., May 26, 1951; s. John Joseph and Leona Mary (Hart) McC.; m. Elizabeth Anne Naumoff, May 20, 1978; children: John Philip, Emily Jane. BS in Fgn. Studies, Georgetown U., 1973, MS in Fgn. Studies, JD, 1978. Bar: N.J. 1978, U.S. Dist. Ct. (ea. and so. dists.) N.Y. 1979. Assoc. Patterson, Belknap et al, N.Y.C., 1978-84; gen. counsel MTV Networks Inc., N.Y.C., 1984-86; v.p., counsel/communications Viacom Internat., N.Y.C., 1986-87; exec. v.p. Nelson Vending Tech., Ltd., N.Y.C., 1987-89; exec. v.p., gen. counsel Cateret Savs. Bank FA, Morristown, N.J., 1989-91; cons. McCarthy Comms., Elizabeth, N.J., 1991-95; sr. v.p., gen. counsel Time, Inc., N.Y.C., 1996—; cons. UN Ctr. on Transnat. Corps., N.Y.C., 1979; exec. dir. Spl. Master Reapportionment of N.J., 1982; term mem. Council Fgn. Relations, N.Y.C., 1980-84. Founder, pres. Elizabeth (N.J.) Dem. Assn., 1980; coordinator Florio for Gov., Union County, N.J., 1981. Mem. ABA, N.Y. State Bar Assn., N.J. State Bar Assn., N.Y. County Lawyers Assn., Assn. Bar City N.Y. Roman Catholic. Home: 3 Woods Ln Chatham NJ 07928 Office: Time Inc 33rd Fl 1271 Avenue Of The Americas New York NY 10020-1300

MCCARTHY, ROGER LEE, mechanical engineer. AB in Philosophy with high distinction, U. Mich., 1972, BSME summa cum laude, 1972; MS in Mech. Engring., MIT, 1973, MechE, 1975, PhD in Mech. Engring., 1977. Registered profl. engr., Calif., Ariz. Project engr. machine design and devel. engring. div. Proctor & Gamble, Inc., Cin., 1973-74; program mgr. Spl. Machinery Group Foster-Miller Assocs., Inc., Waltham, Mass., 1976-78; prin. design engr. Failure Analysis Assocs., Inc., Menlo Park, Calif., 1978—; chmn. bd. dirs., 1988—; CEO The Failure Group, Inc., Menlo Park, 1988-96, chief tech. officer, 1996—. Co-contbr. numerous articles to profl. jours. Mem. Pres.' Commn. on Nat. Medal od Sci., 1992-94. NSF fellow, 1972-75. Mem. Am. Soc. Metals, ASME, Soc. Automotive Engrs., Am. Welding Soc., Am. Soc. for Testing and Materials, Human Factors Soc., ASHRAE, Nat. Fire Protection Assn., Phi Beta Kappa, Sigma Xi (James B. Angell scholar). Office: Failure Group Inc PO Box 3015 149 Commonwealth Dr Menlo Park CA 94025

MCCARTHY, SEAN MICHAEL, air force officer, pilot; b. Tacoma, Feb. 8, 1971; s. Lawrence Joseph and Mary Ann (Kramer) McC. BS with distinction, USAF Acad., Colorado Springs, 1993. Cadet USAF Acad., Colorado Springs, 1989-93; commd. 2d lt. USAF, 1993; student pilot Undergrad. Pilot Tng., Del Rio, Tex., 1993-94; A-10 pilot USAF, Osan Air Base, Korea, 1995-96; air liaison officer 2d Infantry Divsn. USAF, Korea, 1997—; summer intern Def. Mapping Agy., Alexandria, Va., 1992. Mem. Nat. Geographic Soc. (Dr. John Oliver LaGorce award 1993). Avocations: weight lifting, cycling, swimming, model building. Home: 1717 Devon Ave Linwood NJ 08221-2210 Office: PSC 3 Box 4321 APO AP 96266-0143

MC CARTHY, THOMAS PATRICK, magazine publisher; b. Elizabeth, N.J., Mar. 17, 1928; s. Thomas Joseph and Genevieve Elizabeth (Duffy) McC.; m. Joan Ellen Bodet, Jan. 16, 1954; children: Kathleen E., Patricia E., Thomas Patrick. BA, Seton Hall U., East Orange, N.J., 1955. Salesman, Joseph Davis Plastics Co., Kearney, N.J., 1955-57; nat. accounts mgr. ESB Corp., N.Y.C., 1957-65, Bekins Van & Storage Co., N.Y.C., 1965-67; nat. sales mgr. Traffic Mgmt. mag., N.Y.C., 1967-74; pub. Traffic Mgmt. mag., Boston, 1974—; v.p. Traffic Mgmt. mag., 1980-83; pres. Am. Resource Devel. Group, 1983-86, Land-Air-Sea-Transp. Pub. Co., N.Y.C., 1983-95; ptnr. PROMATE Energy Systems, Inc., Marshfield, Mass., 1994—; pres. Transp. Mktg. Cons., Marshfield, Mass. Served with AUS, 1950-53. Mem. Bus. Publ. Advt. Assn., Assn. R.R. Advt. Mgrs., Sales & Mktg. Council Am. Trucking Assn. • Roman Catholic. Clubs: Lions, K.C. Home: 57 Salt Meadow Waye Marshfield MA 02050-2427 Office: 233 Sandy Hill Dr Bldg 2 Marshfield MA 02050-2732

MCCARTHY, TIMOTHY MICHAEL, career non-commissioned officer; b. Mpls., July 18, 1944; s. Howard Allen and Elonora H. (Joa) McC.; m. Kang Suk Yi, Jan. 7, 1969; 1 child, Sony Srithai. AAS in Gen. Mgmt., El Paso C.C., 1995. With U.S. Army, 1965-95; platoon sgt. B Co., 143rd Signal BN, Frankfurt, Germany, 1979-81; discom platoon sgt., 1st sgt. 143d Signal Bat., Frankfurt, 1981-82; 1st sgt. 501st Signal Bat., Clarksville, Tenn., 1983-84; divsn. chief signal NCO 101st Airborne Divsn., Clarksville, 1984-85; bat. ops. sgt. 102nd Signal Bat., Frankfurt, 1986-87; sgt. maj. 7th Signal Brigade, Mannheim, Germany, 1987-88; command sgt. maj. 72d Signal Bat., Karlsruhe, Germany, 1988-90, 7th Signal Bridgade, Karlsruhe, 1990-93, Comm.-Electronics Command, Ft. Monmouth, N.J., 1993-95; ret. U.S. Army, 1995; asst. instr. Jr. ROTC Allendale-Fairfax (S.C.) H.S. Jr. ROTC, 1995. Mem. Noncommissioned Officers Assn. (life, chpt. chmn.), Knights of the Square Table, Assn. of the U.S. Army (life), Armed Forces Comm. Electronics Assn., Signal Corps Regimental Assn. Democrat. Roman Catholic. Avocations: golf, running, skiing. Home: 3534 Biltmore Pl Augusta GA 30906-4577 Office: Allendale-Fairfax HS Jr ROTC Rte 2, Box 222 Fairfax SC 29827-0222

MCCARTHY, VINCENT PAUL, lawyer; b. Boston, Sept. 25, 1940; s. John Patrick and Marion (Buckley) McC.; children: Vincent, Sybil, Hope. AB, Boston Coll., 1962; JD, Harvard U., 1965. Bar: Mass. 1965. Ptnr. Hale and Dorr LLP, Boston, 1965—; sr. ptnr. Hale and Dorr, Boston, 1976—. Bd. dirs., sec. Robert F. Kennedy Action Corps, Inc.; bd. dirs. Boston Alcohol Detoxification Project, Inc.; mem. Mass. Gov.'s Adv. Coun. on Alcoholism, Boston, 1984—, Gov.'s Jud. Nominating Com., 1991—; chmn. Mass. Housing Partnership Fund; past chmn. Boston Ctr. for Arts; mem. adv. coun. Harvard Internat. AIDS Inst.; trustee, sec. Franklin Square House; past pres. Mass. Assn. for Mental Health; bd. dirs., past sec.-treas. Human Rights Campaign Found. Recipient Vols. of Am. Outstanding Svc. award, 1989. Mem. ABA (Pro Bono Publico award 1987), Mass. Bar Assn., Boston Bar Assn. (Pub. Svc. award 1995).

MC CARTHY, WALTER JOHN, JR., retired utility executive; b. N.Y.C., Apr. 20, 1925; s. Walter John and Irene (Trumbl) McC.; m. Linda Lyon, May 6, 1988; children by previous marriage: Walter, David, Sharon, James, William. B.M.E., Cornell U., 1949; grad., Oak Ridge Sch. Reactor Tech., 1952; D.Eng. (hon.), Lawrence Inst. Tech., 1981; D.Sc. (hon.), Eastern Mich. U., 1983; LHD, Wayne State U., 1984; LLD, Alma (Mich.) Coll., 1985. Engr. Public Service Electric & Gas Co., Newark, 1949-56; sect. head Atomic Power Devel. Assos., Detroit, 1956-61; gen. mgr. Power Reactor Devel. Co., Detroit, 1961-68; with Detroit Edison Co., 1968-90, exec. v.p. ops., 1975-77, exec. v.p. divs., 1977-79, pres., chief operating officer, 1979-81, chmn., chief exec. officer, 1981-90; bd. dirs. Comerica Bank Calif., Energy Conversion Devices Inc. Author papers in field. Past chmn., bd. dirs. Inst. Nuclear Power Ops.; trustee Monterey Inst. of Internat. Studies. Fellow Am. Nuclear Soc., Engring. Soc. Detroit; mem. ASME, NAE. Methodist.

MCCARTIN, THOMAS JOSEPH, advertising executive; b. Rockville Centre, N.Y., Sept. 6, 1957; s. John Francis and Agnes (Farrell) McC.; m. Louise Ann Cuccurullo, Mar. 10, 1990; children; Thomas Joseph, Sean Cody. BS in Mktg., N.Y. Inst. Tech., 1979. Bus. devel. officer Mfrs. Hanover Trust, N.Y.C., 1981-83; asst. sec. Dollar Dry Dock Savs. Bank, N.Y.C., 1983-84; sr. v.p. IMC Mktg. Group, N.Y.C., 1984-86; pres. McCartin & Kunin, Inc., N.Y.C., 1986-95, M&K West, Phoenix, 1993-95; exec. v.p. Lipman, Richmond, Greene Advt., N.Y.C., 1995—; bd. dirs. Delta Dental of N.Y., N.Y.C. Mem. NRA, Distributive Edn. Clubs Am. (life), Direct Mktg. Assn., Bus. Coun. N.Y. State, Sierra Club, Vet. Corps of Arty. Conservative. Roman Catholic. Avocations: hunting, camping. Office: Lipman Richmond Greene Advt 470 Park Ave S New York NY 10016-6819

MCCARTNEY, CHARLES PRICE, retired obstetrician-gynecologist; b. Barnesville, Ohio, Aug. 18, 1912; s. Jesse Thomas and Carrie (Price) McC.; m. Phyllis Helen Graybill, Sept. 27, 1940; children—Marilyn B., Ann E. B.S., U. Chgo., 1942, M.D., 1943. Diplomate: Am. Bd. Obstetricians and Gynecologists. Intern U. Chgo. Clinics, 1943-44, resident, 1947-50; mem. faculty U. Chgo. Med. Sch., 1950-71, prof. obstetrics and gynecology, 1960-71, Mary Campeau Ryerson prof., 1967-71; clin. prof. obstetrics and gynecology U. Ill., 1971-80, prof. emeritus, 1980—; attending gynecologist and obstetrician Chgo. Lying-In Hosp., 1950—. Mem. Cook County Com. Maternal Welfare, 1965—. Served to maj., M.C. AUS, 1944-46. Fellow Am. Gynecol. Soc.; mem. Am. Gynecol. and Obstetrical Soc., Chgo. Gynecol. Soc. (pres. 1967), Chgo. Med. Soc. (councillor 1960—, pres. 1973, chmn. bd. trustees 1973), Am. Coll. Obstetricians and Gynecologists (chmn. Ill. sect. 1965—), Cen. Assn. Obstetricians and Gynecologists. Home: 916 Thornwood Dr Saint Charles IL 60174-5018

MCCARTNEY, JAMES HAROLD, retired newspaper columnist, educator, journalist; b. St. Paul, July 25, 1925; s. Floyd Allen and Cora Jeanette (Heilig) McC.; m. Jule Ann Graham, Jan. 19, 1952 (div. 1983); children: Robert, Sharon; m. Molly Kathleen Bowers, Sept. 8, 1984. BA, Mich. State U., 1949; MSJ, Northwestern U., 1951. Reporter South Bend (Ind.) Tribune, 1949-50; reporter Chgo. Daily News, 1952-60, Washington corr., 1960-66, city editor, 1966-68; Washington corr. Knight-Ridder Newspapers, Miami, Fla., 1968-90, columnist, 1985-96; lectr. Georgetown U., 1990—. With U.S. Army, 1943-45, ETO. Mem. Nat. Press Club, Gridiron Club (pres. 1987). Avocation: golf. Home: 4456 Springdale St NW Washington DC 20016-2716

MCCARTNEY, JAMES ROBERT, psychiatrist; b. Elmira, N.Y., Jan. 6, 1932; s. James L. and Edith T. (Tufs) McC; m. Lois McCartney; 4 children. BA, Ohio Wesleyan U., 1952; MD, Columbia U., 1955; MA (ad Eundem)(hon.), Brown U., 1989. Diplomate Nat. Bd. Med. Examiners, Am. Bd. Psychiatry and Neurology, Am. Bd. Geriatric Psychiatry. Intern Boston City Hosp. for Medicine, 1955-56; resdient in psychiatry Elizabeth's Hosp., Washington, 1958-59; assoc. attending psychiatrist then attending psychiatrist North Shore U. Hosp., 1964-80, dir. tng. and edn. dept. psychiatry, 1972-79, chief of liaison svcs., 1973-80, assoc. dir., 1978-80; attending psychiatrist Meadowbrook Hosp., 1961-64; assoc. attending psychiatrist Nassau Hosp., 1964-71; on staff Butler Hosp., 1980—; psychiatrist-in-chief The Miriam Hosp., Providence, 1980—; adv. bd. Mental Health Assn. of Providence County, 1972-80; cons. impaired physician com. R.I. Med. Soc., 1981—; asst. prof. psychiatry Brown U., Providence, 1980-88, assoc. prof., 1988—. Contbr. articles to profl. jours. Capt. U.S. Army, 1956-58. Fellow ACP, Am. Psychiat. Assn., Acad. of Psychosomatic Medicine; mem. AMA, R.I. Med. Soc., Am. Psychosomatic Soc., Assn. for Acad. Psychiatry, Providence Med. Assn., Am. Assn. Gen. Hosp. Psychiatrists, Gerontol. Soc. of Am., Am. Geriatrics Soc. Office: Miriam Hosp 164 Summit Ave Providence RI 02906-2853

MCCARTNEY, N. L., investment banker; b. Jameson, Mo., Oct. 12, 1923; m. Helen M. Walsh, Feb. 11, 1950; children: Patricia, Deborah, Patrick. BS, U. Md., 1956; MBA, Syracuse U., 1959; MPA, George Washington U., 1963. Enlisted U.S. Army, 1944, advanced through grades to col., ret., 1972; dir. S.W. Mo. Health Care Foun., Springfield, 1974-88; pres. Resource Mgmt. Co., Springfield, 1988-96; exec. v.p. Spencer and Assocs., Springfield, 1990-94, Mo. Adv. Capital, 1995-97; instr. Southwest Mo. State U., Springfield, 1972-82. Pres. S.W. Mo. Adv. Coun. Govts., Ozarks Crime Prevention Coun., 1983-93, Vis. Nurse Assn.; mayor of Springfield, 1993-95. Mem. Rotary. Methodist. Home: 1233 E Loren St Springfield MO 65804-0041 Office: PO Box 389 Springfield MO 65801-0389

MCCARTNEY, (JAMES) PAUL, musician; b. Liverpool, Eng., June 18, 1942; s. James and Mary Patricia (Mohin) McC.; m. Linda Eastman, Mar. 12, 1969; 4 children. Hon., Univ. Sussex, Brighton, 1988. With John Lennon and George Harrison in groups Quarrymen, Moondogs, Silver Beatles, 1956-62, also with Ringo Starr in group The Beatles, 1962-70, solo performer and with group, Wings, 1970-80, The Paul McCartney World Tour, 1989; film appearances include: A Hard Day's Night, 1964, Help!, 1965, Let It Be, 1970, Give My Regards to Broad Street, 1984, Get Back, 1991; TV appearances include Magical Mystery Tour, 1967, James Paul McCartney, 1973, Wings Over the World, 1979; producer animated film The Oriental Nightfish, 1978; composer numerous songs including (with John Lennon) Please Please Me, I Want To Hold Your Hand, All My Loving, Can't Buy Me Love, I Saw Her Standing There, Love Me Do, Yesterday, Michelle, She's a Woman, Here, There and Everywhere, Good Day Sunshine, Penny Lane, She's Leaving Home, Fool on the Hill, Back in the USSR, Martha My Dear, Blackbird, Helter Skelter, Hey Jude, Let It Be, The Long and Winding Road, Get Back, (solo) Maybe I'm Amazed, My Love, Live and Let Die, Band on the Run, Silly Love Songs, Another Day, No More Lonely Nights, With a Little Luck; rec. artist: (albums with The Beatles) Meet the Beatles, Introducing the Beatles, Hard Day's Night, Help!, Rubber Soul, Revolver, Sgt. Pepper's Lonely Hearts Club Band, Magical Mystery Tour, The Beatles, Yellow Submarine, Abbey Road, Hey Jude, Let It Be; solo albums include McCartney, 1970, Ram, 1971, Red Rose Speedway, 1973, Band on the Run, 1973, Venus and Mars, 1975, Wings Over America, 1975, Wings at the Speed of Sound, 1976, London Town, 1978, Wings Greatest, 1978, Back to the Egg, 1979, McCartney II, 1980, Tug of War, 1982, Press to Play, 1986, All The Best, 1987, Flowers in the Dirt, 1989, Jet, 1989, Tripping the Live Fantastic,1990, Unplugged/The Official Bootleg, 1991, Off the Ground, 1993, Paul is Live, 1993, Flaming Pie, 1997; composer The Liverpool Oratorio, 1991. Decorated Order of Brit. Empire, 1965; recipient Acad. award (with Beatles) for Best Original Song Score, Let It Be, 1970, 5 Grammy awards with Beatles, 2 solo, 1 with Wings, Ivor Novello award for outstanding services to Brit. music, 1989; named to Rock and Roll Hall of Fame, 1988, Lifetime Achievement award, 1990. •

MC CARTNEY, RALPH FARNHAM, lawyer; b. Charles City, Iowa, Dec. 11, 1924; s. Ralph C. and Helen (Farnham) McC.; J.D., U. Mich., 1950; B. Sci., Iowa State U., 1972; m. Rhoda Mae Huxsol, June 25, 1950; children: Ralph, Julia, David. Bar: Iowa 1950. Mem. firm Miller, Heuber & Miller, Des Moines, 1950-52, Frye & McCartney, Charles City, 1952-73, McCartney & Erb, Charles City, 1973-78; judge Dist. Ct. Iowa, Charles City, 1978-87; chief judge 2d. Judicial Dist., 1987-92; sr. judge Ct. Appeals, 1992—; mem. jud. coordinating com. Iowa Supreme Ct. Chmn. Supreme Ct. Adv. Com. on Adminstrn. of Clks. Offices; mem. Iowa Ho. of Reps., 1967-70, majority floor leader, 1969-70; mem. Iowa Senate, 1973-74. Bd. regents U. Iowa, Iowa State U., U. No. Iowa, Iowa Sch. for Deaf, Iowa Braille and Sight Saving Sch. Served with AUS, 1942-45. Mem. Iowa Judges Assn. Home: 1828 Cedar View Dr Charles City IA 50616-9129 Office: Cty Chambers Courthouse Charles City IA 50616

MCCARTNEY, RHODA HUXSOL, farm manager; b. Floyd County, Iowa, June 30, 1928; d. Julius Franklin and Ruth Ada (Carney) Huxsol; m. Ralph Farnham McCartney, June 25, 1950; children: Ralph, Julia, David. AA, Frances Shimer, 1948; BA, U. Iowa, 1950. Mng. dir. McCartney-Huxsol Farms, Charles City, Iowa, 1969—; prin. trustee J.F. Huxsol Trusts, Charles City, Iowa, 1984—. Pres. Nat. 19th Amendment Soc., Charles City, 1991—; mem. Terace Hill Commn., Des Moines, 1988-94; bd. dirs. Iowa Children and Family Svcs., Des Moines, 1963-68; mem. Iowa Arts Coun., Des Moines, 1974-78. Mem. AAUW, Iowa LWV, PEO. Congregationalist. Avocations: church work, gardening, travel. Home: 1828 Cedar View Dr Charles City IA 50616-9129 Office: McCartney-Huxsol Farms 117 N Jackson St Charles City IA 50616-2002

MCCARTNEY, ROBERT CHARLES, lawyer; b. Pitts., May 3, 1934; s. Nathaniel Hugh and Esther Mary (Smith) McC.; m. Janet Carolyn Moore, June 16, 1956; children: Ronald K., Sharon S., Carole J. AB, Princeton U., 1956; JD, Harvard U., 1959. Bar: D.C. 1959, Pa. 1960, U.S. Dist. Ct. (we. dist.) Pa. 1960, U.S. Ct. Appeals (3d dist.) 1960, U.S. Supreme Ct. 1966. Assoc. Eckert, Seamans, Cherin & Mellott, Pitts., 1959-64, ptnr., 1965-93, mem. exec. com., 1991-93, of counsel, 1993—; sec., gen. counsel Ryan Homes, Inc., 1969-93; bd. dirs., v.p. Prism Fiber Optics, Inc., 1996—; bd. dirs. United Meth. Found. of Western Pa., 1971—, v.p., 1981-85, chmn., 1985-86; gen. counsel Rimoldi of Am., Inc., 1989—. Solicitor North Pitts. Cmty. Devel. Corp., 1968-76, alt. dir., 1968-80; mem. McCandless Twp. Govt. Study Commn., 1973-74; solicitor, asst. sec. McCandless Indsl. Devel. Authority, 1972—; mem. exec. com. Princeton U. Alumni Coun., 1966-70, 76-85, vice chmn., 1981-83, chmn., 1983-85, co-chair Spl. Com. for 250th Anniversary of Princeton U., 1994-97; trustee Otterbein Coll., 1975-83, Pa. S.W. Assn., 1992-96, Pitts. Cultural Trust, 1992—; corp. bd. North Hills Passavant Hosp., 1976—; chmn. conf.-wide endowment program United Meth. Conf. Western Pa., 1985-87; bd. dirs. Pitts. Civic Light Opera Assn., 1986—, v.p., 1987-92, pres., 1992—; gen. counsel, dir. The Ireland Inst. Pitts., 1991—, vice chmn., 1996—; mem. No. Ireland Partnership, 1991—. Princeton fellow Harvard U., 1956-59. Mem. ABA, Pa. Bar Assn., Internat. Bar Assn., Allegheny County Bar Assn., Princeton U. Alumni Assn. West Pa. (pres. 1976-78), Duquesne Club, Princeton Club, Nassau Club. Republican. Home: 9843 Woodland Rd Pittsburgh PA 15237-4362 Office: Eckert Seamans Cherin & Mellott 600 Grant St Ste 42 Pittsburgh PA 15219-2703

MCCARTT, SUSAN STOCKTON, medical, surgical nurse; b. Ft. Smith, Ark., July 24, 1957; d. Charles E. and Betty Lou (Yakley) Stockton; m. John Foster McCartt, July 4, 1979; 1 child, Michael. Diploma in nursing, Westark Community Coll., Ft. Smith, 1975. Staff nurse Sparks Regional Med. Ctr., 1977-81; dialysis nurse St. Mary's Hosp., Enid, Okla., 1982-83; staff nurse Available Med. Care, Ft. Smith, 1983-87; home health/Hospice nurse Area Agy. on Aging, Ft. Smith, 1987-88; admitting nurse Crawford Meml. Hosp., Van Buren, Ark., 1988-89; coord. Indsl. Medicine Ctr., Van Buren, 1989-91, Ambulatory Surgery Ctr. Crawford Meml. Hosp., Van Buren, 1991-92, Crawford Meml. Pretesting Ctr., 1992-95; office nurse Dr. Rebecca Floyd, 1995—. Pres., sec. Parkview Elem. PTA; vol. Good Samaritan Health Clinic; bd. dirs. Western Ark. Jr. Tennis Assn.; pres. Van Buren Sr. H.S. Baseball Booster Club; med. coord. Crawford County chpt. Am. Cancer Soc. Mem. Ark. River Valley Indsl. Health Assn. (sec.-treas.).

MC CARTY, BRUCE, architect; b. South Bend, Ind., Dec. 28, 1920; s. Earl Hauser and Hazel (Beagle) McC.; m. Julia Elizabeth Hayes, Apr. 5, 1945; children: Bruce Hayes, Douglas Hayes, Sarah Elizabeth. B.A., Princeton U., 1944; B.Arch., U. Mich., 1949. Ptnr. Painter, Weeks & McCarty, 1955-65, Bruce McCarty & Assocs., 1965-70; pres. McCarty Bullock Holsaple (Architects, Planners, Engrs., Inc.), Knoxville, Tenn., 1970-84; pres., chmn. McCarty Holsaple McCarty (Architects), Knoxville, Tenn., 1984—; Mem. Knox County Met. Planning Commn., 1967-72; master architect planner 1982 World's Fair, 1976-82; prin. architect Knoxville Waterfront Master Plan, 1989. Works include residential, pub. and instnl. architecture. Trustee Dulin Gallery of Art, 1969-74; bd. dirs., co-founder East Tenn. Cmty. Design Ctr., 1970-80; bd. dirs. Knoxville Beautification Bd., 1984-87, 89-91, Knoxville Arts Coun., 1984-87; exec. com. Mayor's Waterfront Task Force,

1989; chair Design Tenn., 1992-95. 2d lt. USAAF, 1942-45. Recipient AIA EFL 1st honor for Humanities Bldg. U. Tenn.; Prestressed Concrete Inst. award for Mountain View Parking Garages; AIA regional awards for Humanities Bldg., Clarence Brown Theatre, Townview Terrace Housing, U. Tenn., Pedestrian Bridge, Art and Architecture Bldg., St. Johns Luth. Ch.; State of Tenn. Competition winner for U. Tenn. Art and Architecture Bldg., 1975; Mayor's award for Arts, 1975, 82; U. Tenn. Chancellor's assoc.; E. Tenn. chpt. AIA Gold medal, 1996; named to Leadership Knoxville, 1994—. Fellow AIA; mem. Tenn. Soc. Architects (pres. 1972), Knoxville C. of C. (dir. 1965-69). Presbyterian (elder). Office: Mc Carty Holsaple Mc Carty Inc Nations Bank Ctr 550 W Main Ave Knoxville TN 37902-2567

MCCARTY, DENNIS L., insurance executive; b. Des Moines, Aug. 27, 1937; s. Francis L. McCarty and Edna V. (Olson) Hall; m. Jane Umsted, Sept. 5, 1970; children: Cindy, Adam. BS, Drake U., 1966. CLU, ChFC. Patrolman Des Moines Sheriff's Dept., 1966-69; capt. Johnston (Iowa) Police Dept., 1970-73; sales rep. Travelers Ins. Co., Des Moines, 1973-75, agy. supr., 1975-76; regional mktg. dir. Old Am. Ins. Co., Kansas City, Mo., 1976-79, regional v.p., 1979-87, v.p., 1987—. Sgt. U.S. Army, 1954-62. Mem. VFW, Amvets (pub. rels. officer State of Iowa 1964-65), Shriners, Masons, Scottish Rite, Am. Soc. CLU & ChFC. Avocations: golf, boating.

MCCARTY, DONALD JAMES, retired education educator; b. Ulster, Pa., July 17, 1921; s. James Leonard and Louise (Golden) McC.; m. Mary Elizabeth Donahue, Aug. 23, 1951; children: Mary Louise, Donald James, Kevin, Maureen. B.S. cum laude, Columbia U., 1949; M.A., Tchrs. Coll., Columbia U., 1950; Ph.D., U. Chgo., 1959. Jr. high sch. tchr. Brookings, S.D., 1950-51; sr. high sch. tchr. Toms River, N.J., 1951- 52, Brookings, 1952-53; supt. schs. Colman, S.D., 1953-56; staff assoc. U. Chgo., 1956-59; prof. ednl. adminstrn. Cornell U., Ithaca, N.Y., 1959-66; dean U. Wis. Sch. Edn., Madison, 1966-75; prof. ednl. adminstrn. U. Wis. Sch. Edn., 1975-95. Author: (with Charles E. Ramsey) The School Managers: Power and Conflict in American Public Education, 1971, The Dilemma of the Deanship, 1980; also articles. Served to maj. USAAF, 1939-46. Mem. Nat. Coun. Profs. Ednl. Adminstrn. Home: 2926 Harvard Dr Madison WI 53705-2206

MCCARTY, FREDERICK BRIGGS, electrical engineer; b. Dilley, Tex., Aug. 11, 1926; s. John Frederick Briggs and Olive Ruth (Snell) Briggs McCarty; m. Doris Mary Cox, May 3, 1950 (div. 1970); children: Mark Frederick, David Lambuth, Jackson Clare; m. Nina Lucile Butman, Aug. 17, 1973. B.S.E.E., U. Tex., 1949. Registered profl. engr., Calif. Design engr. Gen. Electric Co., Schenectady, N.Y., 1949-51; sr. design engr. Convair, Ft. Worth, Tex., 1951-55; sr. engr. Aerojet Gen., Azusa, Calif., 1955-61; sr. engrng. specialist Garrett Corp., Torrance, Calif., 1961-91; v.p., founder Patio Pacific, Inc., Torrance, 1973-84; owner, operator Textiger Co., Torrance, 1980-91; cons., 1991—. Author computer software, Textiger word processor, Tiger Tools, Big Mag and Roundrot generator synthesizers. Designer superconducting acyclic motor for U.S. Navy and various high speed elec. machines for aerospace and transp. Patentee in field. Served with USNR, 1944-46, PTO. Mem. IEEE (sr. life), Tau Beta Pi, Eta Kappa Nu. Democrat. Home and Office: 1366 Stonewood Ct San Pedro CA 90732-1550

MCCARTY, HARRY DOWNMAN, tool manufacturing company executive; b. Balt., Aug. 30, 1946; s. H. Downman and Melissa (Dunham) McC.; m. Helen Hilliard, May 13, 1948; children: Cormac Downman, Henning Hilliard. BA, Johns Hopkins U., 1968. Math. instr. Gilman Sch., Balt., 1970-71; sales mgr. Balt. Tool Works Inc., Balt., 1971-79, pres., 1979—; bd. dirs. Tool Ins. Co., Ltd., Hamilton, Bermuda. Co-chmn. Robert Nicolls scholarship fund Friends Sch., Balt., 1986-89. 1st lt. U.S. Army, 1968-70. Recipient Barton Cup winner for campus leadership, Johns Hopkins U., 1968, 1st Team All-Am.-Lacrosse, 1968. Mem. Hand Tools Inst. (bd. dirs. 1985-86, 90-92, 96—), Am. Hardware Mfg. Assn., Am. Supply and Machinery Mfg. Assn., Specialty Tools and Fastener Distbn. Assn., Am. Soc. Metals, Forging Industry Assn., Md. Club, L'Hirondelle Club (bd. dirs. 1989-92), ODK Hon. Soc. Republican. Episcopalian. Avocations: tennis, squash, platform tennis, flyfishing. Office: Balt Tool Works Inc 110 E West St Baltimore MD 21230-4314

MCCARTY, LESLIE PAUL, pharmacologist, chemist; b. Detroit, May 30, 1925; s. Leslie Evart and Ruth Winifred (Clouse) McC.; m. Marie-Jeanne Beullay, May 8, 1976; children: Michael, Patricia, Maureen, Brian. BS, Salem Coll., 1947; MSc, Ohio State U., 1949; PhD, U. Wis., 1960. Diplomate Am. Bd. Toxicology. Rsch. chemist Upjohn Co., Kalamazoo, 1949-55; rsch. leader Dow Chem. Co., Midland, Mich., 1960-92. Contbr. articles to profl. jours.; patentee in field. Served with USNR, 1943-45. Mem. Am. Soc. Pharmacology and Exptl. Therapeutics, Sigma Xi. Avocations: amateur radio, gardening, woodworking. Home: 4588 Flajole Rd Midland MI 48642-9261

MCCARTY, MACLYN, medical scientist; b. South Bend, Ind., June 9, 1911; s. Earl Hauser and Hazel Dell (Beagle) McC.; m. Anita Alleyne Davies, June 20, 1934 (div. 1966); children: Maclyn, Richard E., Dale, Colin; m. Marjorie Steiner, Sept. 3, 1966. AB, Stanford U., 1933; MD, Johns Hopkins U., 1937; ScD (hon.), Columbia U., 1976, U. Fla., 1977, Rockefeller U., 1982, Med. Coll. Ohio, 1985, Emory U., 1987, Wittenberg U., 1989; MD (hon.), U. Cologne, Fed. Republic Germany, 1988; LHD (hon.), Mount Sinai Sch. of Medicine, 1995. House officer, asst. resident physician Johns Hopkins Hosp., 1937-40; assoc. Rockefeller Inst., 1946-48, assoc. mem., 1948-50, mem., 1950-81, prof., 1957-81, v.p., 1965-78, physician in chief to hosp., 1961-74, prof. emeritus, 1981—; research in streptococcal disease and rheumatic fever; Cons. USPHS, NIH. Author: The Transforming Principle: Discovering That Genes are Made of DNA, 1985. Mem. distbn. com. N.Y. Community Trust, 1966-74; chmn. Health Research Council City N.Y., 1972-75; Mem. bd. trustees Helen Hay Whitney Found; chmn. bd. dirs. Pub. Health Research Inst. of N.Y., 1985-92. Served with Naval Med. Research Unit, Rockefeller Hosp. USNR, 1942-46. Fellow medicine N.Y. U. Coll. Medicine, 1940-41; NRC fellow med. scis. Rockefeller Inst., 1941-42; Recipient Eli Lilly award in bacteriology and immunology, 1946, 1st Waterford Biomed. Rsch. award, 1977, Wolf Found. prize in medicine, Israel, 1990, Lasker Spl. Pub. Health award, 1994. Mem. Am. Soc. for Clin. Investigation, Am. Assn. Immunologists, Soc. Am. Bacteriologists, Soc. for Exptl. Biology and Medicine (pres. 1973-75), Harvey Soc. (sec. 1947-50, pres. 1971-72), N.Y. Acad. Medicine (Acad. medal 1979, John Stearns award for lifetime achievement in medicine 1993), Assn. Am. Physicians (Kober medal 1989), Nat. Acad. Scis. (Kovalenko medal 1988), Am. Acad. Arts and Scis., N.Y. Heart Assn. (1st v.p. 1967, pres. 1969-71), Am. Philos. Soc. Home: 400 E 56th St New York NY 10022-4147 Office: Rockefeller U 66th St and York Ave New York NY 10021

MC CARTY, PERRY LEE, civil engineering educator, research director; b. Grosse Pointe, Mich., Oct. 29, 1931; s. James C. and Alice C. (Marsom) McC.; m. Martha Davis Collins, Sept. 5, 1953; children: Perry Lee, Cara L., Susan A., Kathleen R. BSCE, Wayne State U., 1953; MS in San. Engring, Mass. Inst. Tech., 1957; ScD, MIT, 1959; DEng (hon.), Colo. Sch. Mines, 1992. Field engr. Edwin Orr Co., Dearborn, Mich., 1951-52; engr. Pate & Hirn, Detroit, 1952-53; field engr. Hubbell, Roth & Clark, Detroit, 1953; instr. civil engring. Wayne State U., 1953-54; field engr. George Jerome & Co., Detroit, 1954; engr. Civil Engrs., Inc., Detroit, 1956; assoc. Rolf Eliassen Assos., Winchester, Mass., 1958-61; asst. prof. san. engring. Mass. Inst. Tech., 1958-62; mem. faculty Stanford U., 1962—, prof. civil engring., 1967-75, Silas H. Palmer prof., 1975—, chmn. dept. civil engring., 1980-85; dir. Western Region Hazardous Substance Rsch. Ctr., 1989—; chmn. Gordon Rsch. Conf. Environ. Scis., 1972; vice chmn. environ. studies bd. NRC-NAS, 1976-80, mem. com. on phys. scis., math. and resources, 1985-88, bd. on radioactive waste mgmt., 1989-96, mem. com. geoscis., environment, resources, 1994-97. Co-author: Chemistry for Environmental Engineering, 4th edit., 1994. Served with AUS, 1954-56. Recipient Tyler Prize for Environ. Achievement, 1992, Harrison P. Eddy award Am. Soc. Civil Engrs., 1962, 77, Clarke Prize for Achievement in Water Scis. and Tech., 1997; NSF faculty fellow, 1968-69. Fellow AAAS (Clarke prize Outstanding Achievement in Water Sci. and Tech. 1997), Am. Acad. Microbiology; mem. NAE, Am. Water Works Assn. (hon. 1981, life 1987, chmn. water quality divsn. 1972-73, trustee rsch. divsn. 1980-85, Best Paper award 1985, A.P. Black Rsch. award 1989), Am. Soc. for Microbiology, Water Pollution Control Fedn. (hon. 1989, Thomas Camp award 1975, Harrison L. Huber rsch. prize 1964, Simon W. Freese Environ. Engring. award 1979, James R. Croes medal 1995), Assn. Environ. Engring. Profs. (Disting. Faculty award 1966, Engring.-Sci. award 1979, Outstanding Publ. award 1985, 88, Founders award 1992), Am. Soc. Engring. Edn. (vice chmn. environ. engring. divsn. 1968-69), Internat. Assn. Water Pollution Rsch. and Control, Sigma Xi, Tau Beta Pi (fellow 1957-58). Home: 823 Sonoma Ter Stanford CA 94305-1024 Office: Stanford U Civil Engring Dept Stanford CA 94305-4020

MCCARTY, RICHARD CHARLES, psychology educator; b. Portsmouth, Va., July 12, 1947; s. Constantine Ambrose and Helen Marie (Householder) McC.; m. Sheila Adair Miltier, July 12, 1965; children: Christopher Charles, Lorraine Marie, Ryan Lester, Patrick James. BS in Biology, Old Dominion U., 1970, MS in Zoology, 1972; PhD in Pathobiology, Johns Hopkins U., 1976. Rsch. assoc. NIMH, Bethesda, Md., 1976-78; asst. prof. U. Va., Charlottesville, 1978-84, assoc. prof., 1984-88, prof., 1988—, chair psychology, 1990—, chair Coun. of Grad. Depts. Psychology, 1996-97. Co-editor: Stress: Molecular Genetic and Neurobiological Advances, 1996; mem. editl. bd. Behavioral and Neural Biology, 1985-90, Physiology and Behavior, 1989—; editor-in-chief of Stress, 1995—; sec. gen. 6th Symposium on Stress, 1995; contbr. articles to profl. jours. Lt. comdr. USPHS, 1976-78. Recipient Rsch. Scientist Devel. award NIMH, 1985-90; sr. fellow Nat. Heart Lung Blood Inst., NIH, 1984-85. Fellow Soc. Behavioral Medicine, Acad. Behavioral Med. Rsch., Am. Psychol. Soc., Am. Inst. Stress, Coun. for High Blood Pressure Rsch., AHA; mem. Internat. Soc. for Investigation of Stress (exec. bd. 1996—). Roman Catholic. Avocations: sports, gardening. Office: U Va Dept Psychology 102 Gilmer Hall Charlottesville VA 22903

MCCARTY, RICHARD EARL, biochemist, biochemistry educator; b. Balt., May 3, 1938; s. Maclyn and Anita (Davies) McC.; m. Kathleen Connolly, June 17, 1961; children—Jennifer A., Richard E., Jr., Gregory P. A.B., Johns Hopkins U., 1960, Ph.D., 1964. Postdoctoral assoc. Pub. Health Research Inst., N.Y.C., 1964-66; asst. prof. Cornell U., Ithaca, N.Y., 1966-72, assoc. prof., 1972-77, prof., 1977-90, prof., chmn., 1981-85; dir. biotech. program Cornell U., Ithaca, 1988-90; prof., chmn. Johns Hopkins U., Balt., 1990—; interim dean Sch. of Arts and Scis., Johns Hopkins U., 1997—; mem. panel NSF, Washington, 1984-86; panel mgr. Photosynthesis and Respiration Program, USDA, Nat. Rsch. Initiative Competitive Grants Program, 1994. Author: (with D. Wharton) Experiments and Methods in Biochemistry, 1972; mem. editl. bd. Jour. Biol. Chemistry, 1978-88, 95—, assoc. editor, 1981-82; mem. editl. bd. Biochemistry, 1996; contbr. articles to profl. jours. Recipient Career Devel. award NIH, 1968-73, Charles F. Kettering award for Excellence in Photosynthesis Am. Soc. Plant Physiologists, 1994. Mem. AAAS, Am. Soc. Biochemistry and Molecular Biology, Am. Soc. Plant Physiologists. Home: 2204 Dalewood Rd Lutherville Timonium MD 21093-2701 Office: Johns Hopkins U Dept Biology 3400 N Charles St Baltimore MD 21218-2608

MCCARTY, RICHARD JOSEPH, consulting engineer; b. Warren, Ohio, Apr. 15, 1948; s. Ralph Edward and Ann Katheerine (Nelms) McC.; m. Cathy Rae Reid, May 12, 1970 (div.); children: Michelle Rae, Erica Ann; m. Nora Elaine Jennings, Dec. 5, 1981; 1 child, Trillion Nora. BA, Hiram Coll., 1991; MBA, Baldwin-Wallace Coll., 1993; postgrad., Nova U., 1993—; PhD, Am. Coll. Metaphys. Theology, 1995-96; postgrad., Am. Inst. Hypnosis, 1997—. Cert. K-12 tchr., adult tchr., spl. edn. tchr., Ohio. Engr. United Telephone Co., Warren, Ohio, 1969-70; cons. engr. Henkels & McCoy, Inc., Blue Bell, Pa., 1970-78, Lambic Telecom, Inc., N.Y.C., 1978-83; regional mgr. Lambic Telecom, Inc., Warren, Ohio, 1985-88; v.p. McAreg Enterprises, Inc., Pocono Lakes, Pa., 1983-84; computer instr. Trumbull County Joint Vocat. Sch., Warren, 1988-90; pres., adminstr. Trillion Inst., Warren, 1990-91; cons. engr. E.G. Keller and Assocs., Elkhart, Ind., 1991-97, Harris-McBurney Co., Jackson, Mich., 1997—; spkr. Steelworkers Reemployment Challenger, Youngstown, Ohio, 1990-92; edn. cons. to GM Corp. for Warren City Schs. state and fed. programs, 1994-95. Contbr. articles to profl. publs. Democrat. Avocations: coin collecting, art. Home: 1932 W Market St Warren OH 44485-2643 Office: EG Keller & Assocs PO Box 964 Elkhart IN 46515-0964

MC CARTY, ROBERT LEE, lawyer; b. New London, Conn., Mar. 1, 1920; s. Robert Patrick and Lyda (Griser) McC.; m. Eileen Joan Noone, Sept. 1, 1945; children: Michael N., Patrick J., Charles Barry. B.S., Bowdoin Coll., 1941; LL.B., Yale U., 1948; LL.M., Georgetown U., 1953. Bar: D.C. 1948, U.S. Supreme Ct 1953, Va. 1976. Assoc. Northcutt Ely, 1948-54; mem. Ely, McCarty & Duncan, 1955-60; ptnr. McCarty and Wheatley, 1961-67, McCarty & Noone, 1968-80, McCarty, Noone & Williams, 1981-87, Heron, Burchette, Ruckert & Rothwell, Washington, 1987-90, Ritts Brickfield & Kaufman, Washington, 1990-92, Brickfield, Burchette & Ritts, Washington, 1993—; mem. Adminstrv. Conf. U.S., 1972-74; mem. edn. appeals bd. U.S. Dept. Edn., 1978-83. Contbr. chpts. to books. Pres. bd. dirs. Belle Haven Citizens Assn., 1959-60. Served with USAAF, 1942-46; Served with USAF, 1951-53; col. Res. Decorated D.F.C. (2), Air medal with 3 oak leaf clusters, Army Commendation medal. Fellow Am. Bar Found.; mem. ABA (chmn. sect. adminstrv. law 1966-67), (sect. del. to ho. dels. 1968-70), Fed. Bar Assn., D.C.Bar Assn., Va. Bar Assn. Roman Catholic. Clubs: University (Washington), Belle Haven Country (Va.). Home: 2108 Woodmont Rd Alexandria VA 22307-1155 Office: 8th Flr West Tower 1025 Thomas Jefferson St NW Washington DC 20007-5201 *If you are to be satisfied with your product, there is no substitute for work.*

MCCARTY, ROGER LELAND, chemical company official; b. Coos Bay, Oreg., Apr. 6, 1953; s. James Cleo and Dorothy Jean (Beach) McC.; m. Marsha Lee Peterson, Dec. 18, 1976; children: Margie, Heather, Aura Lee, Becky, Allison, Katy, Chelsea, Lori. BSChemE, Brigham Young U., 1977; MBA, Keller Grad. Sch. Mgmt., Chgo., 1981. Registered engr.-in-tng., Mich. Missionary LDS Ch., Washington, 1972-74; with mktg. devel. program Dow Chem. Co., Denver, 1977-78; sales rep. organic chems. Dow Chem. Co., Chgo., 1978-82; from sr. sales specialist to mgr. product mktg. Dow Chem. Co., Houston, 1982-88; mgr. product mktg. Dow Chem. Co., Midland, Mich., 1988-89, mgr. bus. rsch. chems. and performance products dept., 1989-92, group mktg. mgr. new ventures, strategy facilitator, 1989-92, sr. econ. planning assoc. value-based mgmt., 1992-95; sr. VBM strategy devel. mgr. Dow Chem. Co., Midland, 1995-96, bus. devel. mgr. specialty chems. new bus., 1997—; sales trainer Dow Chem. Co., Houston, 1987-88; presenter in mktg. strategy field. Author: Value Based Strategy Development Guide Book, 1989-94; contbr. articles to profl. jours. Mem. Coos Bay Mayor's Adv. Coun., 1970-71; pres. men's group LDS Ch., Elgin, Ill., 1979-82; mem. stake high coun., Houston, Ill., 1979-82, 89-94, mem. Midland State Presidency, 1995—; explorer leader Boy Scouts Am., Houston, 1985-87; mem. Music Soc. Chorale, 1993-96, Camarata Singers, 1995, LDS choir dir., 1992-94; music and computer vol. elem. sch., Midland, 1989-90. Mem. AIChE (sec.-treas. mktg. divsn. 1989-90, bd. dirs. 1986-89, nat. program dir. 1985-89, mem. nat. program com. 1985-89), Gas Processors Assn. (mem. com. 1987-88). Republican. Avocations: music, drama, sports, dancing, reading. Home: 1200 Wakefield Dr Midland MI 48640-2733 Office: Dow Chem Co Larkin Ctr Midland MI 48674

MCCARTY, THOMAS JOSEPH, publishing company executive; b. Waltham, Mass., June 10, 1938; s. Raymond Anthony and Mary Agatha (Riley) McC; m. Colette Ann Koechley, Aug. 3, 1963; children: Matthew Thomas, Brendan James, Sarah Katherine. BA, Holy Cross Coll., 1960; cert., Harvard U., 1961. Various mgmt. positions Oxford U. Press, N.Y.C., 1960-71, mgr. ops., 1971-79, dir. distbn., 1980-81, v.p. distbn., 1982-84, v.p. distbn. and info. systems, 1985-88, sr. v.p., 1988-90; sr. v.p.,gen. mgr. Oxford U. Press, Cary, N.C. ops., 1990—; chmn., bd. advs. Carolina Pub. Inst. U. N.C., Chapel Hill. Trustee N.C. Symphony Found.; mem. adv. bd. Sch. Info. and Libr. Sci., U. N.C., Chapel Hill;; bd. dirs. Shakti for Children Found., English Speaking Union of Rsch. Triangle; mem. N.C. Mus. Art. Mem. Assn. Am. Pubs., Am. Mgmt. Assn., Capital City Club (Raleigh, N.C.), MacGregor Downs Country Club (Cary), Carolina Club, U. N.C. Faculty Club (Chapel Hill). Office: Oxford U Press Inc 2001 Evans Rd Cary NC 27513-2009

MCCARTY, W(ILLARD) DUANE, obstetrician, gynecologist, physician executive; b. Alliance, Ohio, Dec. 15, 1930; s. Willard Raymond and Louise L. (Allmon) McC.; m. Frances Ann Rings, Dec. 5, 1959; children: Susan L., James A., Rebecca Ann, Sharon L. BS in Chemistry, Biology, Mt. Union Coll., 1952; MD, Ohio State U., 1956, MMS, 1961. Diplomate Am. Bd. Ob-Gyn; bd. cert. in Addictionology. Intern, Univ. Hosps. Ohio State Univ., 1956-57; resident in ob-gyn. Ohio State U. Hosps., Columbus, 1957-61, instr. ob-gyn., 1960-61; assoc. ob-gyn. Lovelace Clinic, Albuquerque, 1963-86; chmn. ob-gyn. Lovelace-Bathan Hosp., Albuquerque, 1967-70; clin. assoc. prof. dept. ob-gyn., Sch. Medicine Univ. New Mex., Albuquerque, 1970-86; v.p., med. dir. Lovelace Health Plan, Albuquerque, 1972-84; clin. dir. Vista Pathways-Vista Sandia Hosp., Albuquerque, 1986-87; field rep., cons. Joint Comm. Accreditation of Hosps.-Ambulatory Care, Chgo., 1975-86; cur. rep. group practice Med. Group Mgmt. Assn., Chgo., 1978-82; v.p. bd. trustees Lovelace Health Plan-Lovelace FDN, Albuquerque, 1970-85; mem. Instl. Rsch. Rev. Bd.; bd. trustees N.Mex. Med. Soc.; pres., CEO N.Mex. Monitored Treatment Program; mem. The Lovelace Inst. Bus. Leaders Coun.; bd. dirs. Lovelace Inst.; mem. instrl. rsch. rev. bd. Lovelace Respiratory Rsch. Inst. Author, rschr.: Recurrent Abortion, 1963 (MMS award). Founding dir. Profl. Stds. Rev. Orgn., Albuquerque, 1974; counselor Alcoholics Anonymous, Albuquerque, 1988—; trustee, mem. exec. com., core edn. com. Menual Presbyn. Sch., Albuquerque, New Mexichords Barbershop Chorus, exec. com. Recipient Tchr.-Leader award N.Mex. Ob-Gyn. Soc., 1981. Fellow Am. Coll. Ob-Gyn., Am. Fertility Soc., Am. Coll. Physician Execs.; mem. AMA, Am. Acad. Med. Dirs. (founding trustee 1975—), Am. Soc. Addiction Medicine (cert.), N.Mex. Med. Soc. (continuing edn. com. 1990—, physician aid com. 1984—, sec.-treas. monitor treatment program, pres., CEO 1995-96), S.W. Ob-Gyn. Soc. (pres. 1981-82), Presbyn. Men (John Knox fellow, exec. com., v.p. for missions 1992-94), N.Mex. Med. Soc. Republican. Avocations: barber-shop quartet singing, photography, travel, gardening, Bible study. Home: 610 Graceland Dr SE Albuquerque NM 87108-3335

MCCARUS, ERNEST NASSEPH, retired language educator; b. Charleston, W.Va., Sept. 10, 1922; s. Nasseph Mitchell and Della (Saad) McC.; m. Adele Najib Haddad, Sept. 10, 1955; children: Peter Kevin, Carol Ann. Student, Morris Harvey Coll., 1939-40; A.B., U. Mich., 1945, M.A., 1949, Ph.D., 1956. Translation team capt. Allied Translators and Interpreters' Service, Allied Hqrs., Tokyo, Japan, 1946-47; mem. English Lang. Inst. staff U. Mich., 1948-52, mem. univ. expdn. to Near East, 1951, instr. univ., 1952-56, asst. prof. Arabic, 1956-61; dir. Fgn. Service Inst., Field Sch. Arabic Lang. and Area Study, U.S. Dept. State, Beirut, Lebanon, 1958-60; asso. prof. dept. Near Eastern studies U. Mich., 1961-67, prof., 1967-95, chmn. dept., 1969-77, dir. Center for Arabic Study Abroad, 1974-83, dir. U. Mich. Center for Near Eastern and North African Studies, 1983-92, assoc. dir. Ctr for Mid. Eastern and North African Studies, 1995—, prof. emeritus, 1995—. Author: Grammar of Kurdish of Sulaimania, Iraq, 1958, (with H. Hoenigswald, R. Noss, J. Yamagiwa) A Survey of Intensive Programs in the Uncommon Languages, 1962, (with A. Yacoub) Elements of Contemporary Arabic, 1962, 3d edn., 1966, (with Raji Rammuny) First Level Arabic: Elementary Literary Arabic for Secondary Schools, 1964, Teacher's Manual to Accompany First Level Arabic, 1964, (with Jamal J. Abdullah) Kurdish Basic Course - Dialect of Sulaimania, Iraq, 1967, Kurdish Readers, Vol. I Newspaper Kurdish, Vol. II. Kurdish Essays, Vol. III Kurdish Short Stories, 1967, A Kurdish-English Dictionary, 1967, (with P. Abboud) Elementary Modern Standard Arabic, 1983, (with R. Rammuny) Word Count of Elementary Modern Literary Arabic Textbooks, 1969, (with P. Abboud, E.T. Abdel-Massih, S. Altoma, W. Erwin, R. Rammuny) Modern Standard Arabic Intermediate Level, 1971, (with R. Rammuny) A Programmed Course in Modern Literary Arabic Phonology and Script, 1974; editor: Language Learning, Vol. VII, 1956-57, Language Learning, Vol. XIII, 1963, An-Nashra, 1967-74, Contemporary Arabic Readers, Vols. I-V, 1962-66, The Development of Arab-American Identity, 1994; contbr. articles to scholastic jours. Served with AUS, 1942-46. Rockefeller fellow, 1951. Mem. Mich. Linguistic Soc. (pres. 1962-63), Am. Assn. Tchrs. Arabic (pres. 1973, exec. coun. 1979-81, 89-92), Middle East Studies Assn. (bd. dirs. 1973-75), Linguistic Soc. Am., Am. Oriental Soc., Linguistic Circle N.Y., Arabic Linguistic Soc. (pres. 1992). Home: 1400 Beechwood Dr Ann Arbor MI 48103-2940

MCCASKEY, EDWARD W., professional football team executive; b. Phila., Apr. 27; m. Virginia Halas; 11 children. Student, U. Pa., 1940. Mgr. merchandising Nat. Retail Tea and Coffee Assn., Chgo.; exec. v.p. Mdse. Services, Inc., Chgo.; account exec. E.F. McDonald Co., Chgo.; v.p., treas. Chgo. Bears, 1967-83, chmn. bd. dirs., 1983—. Served to capt., AUS. also: Chicago Bears Halas Hall 250 Washington Rd Lake Forest IL 60045-2459*

MCCASKEY, MICHAEL B., professional football team executive; b. Lancaster, Pa., Dec. 11, 1943; s. Edward B. and Virginia (Halas) McCaskey; m. Nancy McCaskey; children: John, Kathryn. Grad., Yale U., 1965; PhD, Case Western Res. U. Tchr. UCLA, 1972-75, Harvard U. Sch. Bus., Cambridge, Mass., 1975-82; pres., chief exec. officer Chgo. Bears (NFL), 1983—. Author: The Executive Challenge: Managing Change and Ambiguity. Named Exec. of Yr. Sporting News, 1985. Office: Chgo Bears Halas Hall 250 Washington Rd Lake Forest IL 60045-2459*

MCCASLIN, RICHARD BRYAN, history educator; b. Atlanta, Feb. 21, 1961; s. Jerry L. and Ann Elizabeth (Sharman) McC.; m. Jana Dawn Maryovich, Apr. 5, 1979; 1 child, Christina Michele. BA, Delta State U., 1982; MA, La. State U., 1983; PhD, U. Tex., 1988. Tchg. asst. La. State U., 1982-83, grad. asst. La. Bus. Rev., 1983; tchg. asst. U. Tex., Austin, 1983-87, rsch. assoc., 1984-87; rsch. asst. prof. U. Tenn., Knoxville, 1988-90; asst. prof. history High Point (N.C.) U., 1990-94, assoc. prof., 1994—; instr. Pellissippi State C.C., 1988-89, Roane State C.C., 1989; adj. prof. Corpus Christi (Tex.) State U., 1989; lectr. East Tenn. Hist. Soc., 1990; rsch. cons. Huston-Tillotson Coll., 1985-86, Tex. Senate, 1986-89, Nat. Pk. Svc., 1989-90; assoc. historian Futurepast: History Co., Spokane, Wash., 1987-89; presenter Southwestern Social Sci. Assn., AAAS, Soc. for Mil. History. Author: (with Earnest F. Gloyna) Commitment to Excellence: One Hundred Years of Engineering Education at The University of Texas at Austin, 1986, Andrew Johnson: A Bibliography, 1992, Portraits of Conflict: A Photographic History of South Carolina in the Civil War, 1994, Tainted Breeze: The Great Hanging at Gainesville, Texas, October 1862, 1994 (Tullis prize Tex. State Hist. Assn., commendation AASLH), Remembered Be Thy Blessings: High Point University—The College Years, 1924-1991, 1995, Portraits of Conflict: A Photographic History of North Carolina in the Civil War, 1997; contbr. chpt. to: 100 Years of Science and Technology in Texas: A Sigma Xi Centennial Volume, 1986; columnist Greensboro News and Record, 1993-94; referee Southwestern Hist. Quar., 1990—; asst. editor, then assoc. editor Papers of Andrew Johnson, U. Tenn., 1988-90; contbr. articles and book revs. to various profl. publs. U. Tex. dissertation fellow, 1987-88, Clara H. Driscoll fellow in Tex. history Daus. of Republic of Tex., 1985-87; James H. and Minnie M. Edmonds Ednl. Found. scholar, 1983-85, Colonial Dames Am. grad. scholar, 1987. Mem. So. Hist. Assn. (presenter), Soc. Civil War Historians, Tex. State Hist. Assn. (presenter), Hist. Soc. N.C. Episcopalian. Home: 714 Ferndale Blvd High Point NC 27262 Office: High Point Univ Dept History and Polit Sci High Point NC 27260

MCCASLIN, TERESA EVE, human resources executive; b. Jersey City, Nov. 22, 1949; d. Felix F. and Ann E. (Golaszewski) Hrynkiewicz; m. Thomas W. McCaslin, Jan. 22, 1972 (div.). BA, Marymount Coll., 1971; MBA, L.I. U., 1981. Adminstrv. officer Civil Service Commn., Fed. Republic Germany, 1972-76; personnel dir. Oceanroutes, Inc., Palo Alto, Calif., 1976-78; mgr., coll. relations Continental Grain Co., N.Y.C., 1978-79, corp. personnel mgr., 1979-81, dir. productivity, internal cons., 1981-84; dir., human resources Grow Group, Inc., N.Y.C., 1984-85, v.p. human resources, 1985-86, v.p. adminstrn., 1986-89; corporate v.p. human resources Avery Dennison Corp., Pasadena, Calif., 1989-94, Monsanto Co., St. Louis, 1994-97; v.p. human resources Continental Grain Co., N.Y.C., 1997—; adv. bd. St Johns Mercy Med. Ctr., Goodwill Industries of Mo., St. Louis U. Internat. Sch. Bus. Bd. advisers St. John's Mercy Med. Ctr., Goodwill Industries of Mo., St. Louis U. Grad. Sch. Internat. Bus. Mem. Am. Mgmt. Assn., Human Resources Coun. Roman Catholic. Avocations: skiing, tennis, traveling. Office: Continental Grain Co 277 Park Ave New York NY 10172

MCCAUGHEY ROSS, ELIZABETH P. (BETSY MCCAUGHEY), state official; b. Oct. 20, 1948; d. Albert Peterkin; m. Thomas McCaughey, 1972 (div. 1994); children: Amanda, Caroline, Diana. BA, Vassar Coll., 1970; MA, Columbia Univ., 1972, PhD, 1976. Public policy expert Manhattan Inst., N.Y.C.; lt. gov. State of N.Y., 1995—; asst. prof. Vassar Coll., 1979, Columbia U., 1980-84; chmn. Governor's Medicaid Task Force, 1994.

Author: From Loyalist to Founding Father, 1980, Government By Choice, 1987; also articles including an article in The New Republic (Nat. Mag. award for Pub. Policy 1995). Recipient Bancroft Dissertation award, Richard B. Morris prize; Woodrow Wilson fellow, Herbert H. Lehman fellow, Honorary Vassar fellow, John Jay fellow, Post Doctoral Rsch. fellow NEH, 1984, John M. Olin fellow Manhattan Inst., 1993, sr. fellow Ctr. Study of the Presidency. Republican. Office: Office of Lt Governor Executive Chamber State Capitol Rm 326 Albany NY 12224

MCCAULEY, BRUCE GORDON, financial consultant; b. St. Louis; s. William Maurice and Evylin Adele (Halbert) McC.; m. Barbara Allen Stevens, Mar. 16, 1945 (dec.); children: David S., Sharon; m. Gwen Crumpton Cummings, Nov. 25, 1967. Student, U. Mo., 1939-41, Yale U., 1944; BS in Engring., U. Calif., Berkeley, 1948, MBA, 1949, MS in Indsl. Engring., 1952. Registered profl. engr., N.Y., Calif., Hawaii. Asst. purchasing agt. Curtis Mfg. Co., St. Louis, 1941-43; teaching asst. U. Calif., Berkeley, 1948-49, asst. prof. mech. engring., 1950-56, chmn. indsl. engring. inst., 1954-55; design engr. Standard Oil Co. of Calif., 1949-50; sr. ptnr. McCauley & Dunmire, San Francisco, 1952-56; v.p. Shand & Jurs Co., Berkeley, 1956-58, dir., 1957-60, exec. v.p., 1958-60; asst. to pres. Honolulu Star-Bulletin, 1960-62; gen. mgr. Christian Sci. Pub. Soc., Boston, 1962-69; gen. mgr., sec. N.Y. Daily News Inc., N.Y.C., 1969-74, v.p., 1971-73, sr. v.p., 1973-75, asst. to pres., 1974-75, dir., 1971-75; v.p. Daseke & Co. Inc., Westport, Conn., 1975-77, sr. v.p., 1977-86, mgr. West Coast office, 1978-86; vis. scholar Principia Coll., Elsah, Ill., 1988-91; pres., dir. Rossmoor Mut. 48 Corp., Walnut Creek, 1994—. Bd. dirs. Better Bus. Bur., N.Y.C., 1973-77, N.Y.C. Conv. and Visitors Bur., 1974-77, Albert Baker Found., 1979-90, Asher Found., 1983-93, Sopac Energy Corp., 1986-92. Capt. USAAF, 1943-46, PTO. Mem. ASME (life), Am. Inst. Indsl. Engrs. (life), Nat. Assn. Accts., Nat. Soc. Profl. Engrs., U. Calif. Alumni Assn., Principia Alumni Assn., Sigma Xi, Tau Beta Pi, Beta Gamma Sigma, Pi Mu Epsilon. Christian Scientist. Club: Rossmoor Golf (Walnut Creek). Lodges: Masons (32 deg.), Kiwanis. Home: 3266 Ptarmigan Dr Apt 3B Walnut Creek CA 94595-3149

MCCAULEY, FLOYCE REID, psychiatrist; b. Braddock, Pa., Dec. 30, 1933; d. John Mitchel and Irene (Garner) Reid; m. James Calvin McCauley, July 15, 1955; children: James Stanley, Lori Ellen. BS in Nursing, U. Pitts., 1956; D.O., Coll. Osteopathic Medicine, Phila., 1972. Bd. eligible in child and adult psychiatry. Intern Suburban Gen. Hosp., Norristown, Pa., 1972-73; resident in adult psychiatry Phila. State Hosp. and Phila. Mental Health Clinic, 1973-75; fellow Med. Coll. of Pa. and Ea. Pa. Psychiat. Inst., Phila., 1975-78; Chief child psychiatry inpatient unit Med. Coll. Pa., Phila., 1978-80; med. dir. Carson ValleySch., Flourtown, Pa., 1980-82; dir. outpatient psychiat. clinic Osteopathic Med. Ctr. Phila., 1980-86; staff psychiatrist Kent Gen. Hosp., Dover, Del., 1986-89; psychiat. cons. Del. Guidance Svcs. for Children, Dover, 1986-91; clin. dir. children's unit HCA Rockford Ctr., Newark, 1991-93; with Kid's Peace Nat. Hosp. for Kids in Crisis, 1993-95, Pa. Found., Sellersville, 1995—; mem. Mental Health Code Rev. Com. for Del., 1991; inducted into the Chapel of Four Chaplains, Phila., 1983; psychiat. cons. Seaford (Del.) Br. of New Eng. Fellowship for Rehab., 1991-93, Cath. Charities Day Treatment Program for 3-6 Yr. Olds, Dover, Del., 1990—; cons. Del. Guidance Day Treatment Program, 1990—; staff psychiatrist Kids Peace Nat. Hosp. for Kids in Crisis, 1993-95, Penn Found., 1995—. Mem. Mayor's Com. for Mental Health, Phila., 1983. Mem. Am. Osteopathic Assn. Democrat. Methodist. Avocations: sewing, decorating, knitting, playing classical guitar, drawing, painting, gardening.

MCCAULEY, JANE REYNOLDS, journalist; b. Wilmington, Del., Oct. 22, 1947; d. John Thomas and Helen (Campbell) McC. BA, Guilford Coll., 1969. Writer Nat. Geographic Soc., Washington, 1975-80, writer, editor, 1980-90; former owner Unique Native Crafts. Author of 15 children's books; co-author award-winnnig travel books. Mem. Children's Book Soc. of Am., Washington Ind. Writers, Am. Quilters' Soc. (exec. editor).

MCCAULEY, LISA FRANCINE, secondary education educator; b. New Haven, Feb. 15, 1966; d. Fred and Elaine Carolyn (Webb) McC. AA, Mt. Sacred Heart Coll., Hamden, Conn., 1988; BA in History, So. Conn. State U., 1989, MS in History, 1992. Cert. secondary edn. grades 7-12, Conn. Tchr. St. Lawrence Sch., West Haven, Conn., 1989-95, Wilbur Cross High Sch., New Haven, Conn., 1996—; adj. prof. So. Conn. State U., New Haven, 1993—. Vol. Conn. Spl. Olympics, New Haven, 1989—; dist. coord. Nat. History Day, Conn. Hist. Soc., Hartford, 1993—. Recipient cert. for dedicated svcs. and encouragement of student participation Conn. Hist. Soc., Hartford, 1992, cert. appreciation Jr. Achievement, Wallingford, Conn., 1992; named Outstanding Tchr. of Merit Conn. Hist. Soc., 1997. Mem. AAUP, Nat. Cath. Edn. Assn., Conn. Coun. for the Social Studies, Conn. and New Haven Hist. Socs., Conn. Geographic Alliance, Conn. Humanities Coun. Roman Catholic. Avocations: musician, reading. Home: 392 State St Apt 11-A North Haven CT 06473

MC CAULEY, R. PAUL, criminologist, educator; b. Highspire, Pa., Jan. 13, 1943; s. Paul Herbert and Frances Vaden (Harper) McC.; m. Gail Lee Gummo, Jan. 30, 1965; 1 child, Brent Clayton. A.S., Harrisburg Area Community Coll., 1968; B.S., Va. Commonwealth U., 1969; M.S., Eastern Ky. U., 1971; Ph.D. (fellow), Sam Houston U., 1973; certificate Home Office Detective Tng. Course, Eng., 1967. Diplomate Am. Coll. Forensic Examiners. Police officer Highspire Police, 1964-69; adminstr. Burns Internat. Security Services Inc., 1969-71; prof. police sci. and adminstrn., dir. grad. studies in adminstrn. of justice U. Louisville, 1973-82; prof., chmn. dept. criminology Indiana U. of Pa., 1982—; co-founder Sempas Security and Safety Technologies, 1980; advisor Reagan Presdl./Congressional Task Force on Criminal Justice, 1980; mem. staff So. Police Inst., 1973-82, Nat. Crime Prevention Inst., 1973-82; researcher, ptnr. McShan Assocs., 1974-85; cons. U.S. Congress Com. on Emergency Communications, 1967. Co-author: The Criminal Justice System, 1976, 3d edit., 1984; co-founder, editor: Criminal Justice Policy Rev., 1984-86; contbr. chpts. to books, articles to profl. jours.; patents. Active Metro Child Abuse Program, Crime Clinic of Greater Harrisburg, 1965-74; mem. Lower Swatara Twp. Police Civil Service Commn., 1967-69. Served with USMC, 1962-66. Recipient Mayor's Citation, City of Louisville, 1982, Gold medal Educator of the 1980's; honoree Silliman Coll., Yale U., 1984; Fulbright scholar, lectr., Australia, 1987. Mem. Acad. Criminal Justice Scis. (exec. bd. 1980-83, pres. 1985), Navy League (award for disting. community service). Home: 4620 Lucerne Rd Indiana PA 15701-8950 Office: Indiana U of Pa 204 Walsh Hall Indiana PA 15705 *One's philosophy, spirit, and drive contributes more to his relative success than do economic resources, social position, planning, or timing.*

MCCAUSLAND, THOMAS JAMES, JR., brokerage house executive; b. Cleve., Nov. 27, 1934; s. Thomas James and Jean Anna (Hanna) McC.; m. Kathryn Margaret Schacht, Feb. 9, 1957; children: Thomas James III, Andrew John, Theodore Scott. BA in Econs., Beloit (Wis.) Coll., 1956. V.p. A.G. Becker & Co., Inc., Chgo., 1959-74; v.p. The Chgo. Corp., 1974-76, sr. v.p., dir., 1976-83, exec. v.p., 1983-90, vice chmn., 1991—; pres. The Chgo. Corp. Internat., 1990—; also bd. dirs. The Chgo. Corp.; bd. dirs. Chicorp, Inc., The Founders Fund, Naples, Fla.; bd. dirs., treas. The LaSalle St. Coun., Chgo. v.p. Hospice the North Shore, Evanston, Ill., 1986-90; bd. dirs. McCormick Theol. Sem., Chgo., 1971-79, Presbyn. Home, Evanston, 1968-74; trustee Beloit Coll., 1987-90. Lt. USN, 1956-59. Mem. Securities Industry Assn. (investment mgmt. com. 1979-82), Union League, United Presbyn. Found. (trustee, vice-chmn. 1980-86), Skokie Country Club (bd. dirs. 1983-85, pres. 1993), Pelican Bay Club (Naples, Fla.), Royal Poinciana Golf Club (Naples). Republican. Avocations: travel, Am. history, golf. Office: The Chgo Corp 208 S La Salle St Chicago IL 60604

MCCAW, JOHN E., JR., professional sports team executive. Co-founder, bd. dirs. McCaw Comm., McCaw Cellular Comm., Inc.; owner, bd. dirs. Seattle Mariners, 1992; co-chmn. Orca Bay Sports and Entertainment, Vancouver, B.C. Office: Vancouver Canucks, 800 Griffiths Way, Vancouver, BC Canada V6B 6G1*

MCCAWLEY, AUSTIN, psychiatrist, educator; b. Greenock, Scotland, Jan. 17, 1925; came to U.S., 1954; s. Austin and Anna Theresa (McBride) McC.; m. Gloria Klein, Feb. 15, 1958; children: Joseph, Tessa. MBCHB, U. Glasgow, 1948. Diplomate Am. Bd. Psychiatry and Neurology; DPM Royal Coll. London. Intern Glasgow Royal Infirmary, Scotland, 1948; resident Inst. Living, Harford, Conn., 1954-57, clin. dir., 1960-66; med. dir. Westchestor br. St. Vincent's Hosp., N.Y.C., 1966-72; dir. psychiatry St. Francis Hosp., Hartford, 1972-88; prof. psychiatry U. Conn. Med. Sch., Farmington, 1983-93; pvt. practice, West Hartford, Conn., 1988—; dir. psychiatry Kaisor, 1996—; dir. psychiatry Kaiser Permanente of Conn., 1996—. Co-author: The Physician, 1983; contbr. articles to profl. jours. Chmn. Bd. Mental Health, State of Conn., 1981-84, Search Com. for Commr. Mental Health, Conn., 1981; mem. Gov.'s Spl. Task Force on Mental health Policy, Conn., 1982. With RAF, 1948-50. Fellow Am. Psychiat. Assn., Am. Coll. Psychiatry (charter fellow, founder); mem. Conn. Psychiat. Soc. (pres. 1978-79), Hartford Golf Club. Democrat. Roman Catholic. Avocations: music, golf. Home: 128 Westmont St West Hartford CT 06117-2926 Office: 18 N Main St West Hartford CT 06107-1919

MCCAY, THURMAN DWAYNE, university administrator; b. Wynne, Ark., Sept. 2, 1946; s. Thurman Ellis and Vetra Marcella (Jones) McC.; m. Mary Helen Johnston, Oct. 3, 1985; children: Audra Lee, Leesa Marie. BS in Physics, Auburn U., 1968, MS in Engring., 1969, PhD in Engring. and Math., 1974; postgrad. mgmt. sci. program, Air Force Inst. Tech., Wright-Petterson AFB, Ohio, 1985. Rsch. engr. gas diagnostics sect. aerospace projects br. ARO, Inc., Arnold Air Force Station, Tenn., 1973-78; sr. rsch. phys. scientist, plume tech. br. Air Force Rocket Propulsion Lab., Edwards AFB, Calif., 1978-81; sr. aerospace engr., br. chief, chief propulsion divsn. NASA, George G. Marshall Center, Ala., 1981-86; prof. engring. sci. and mechanics, adj. prof. engring. U. Tenn. Space Inst., Tullahoma, 1986—, v.p., 1993—; tchr. Auburn U., 1970-72, Calif. State U., Fresno, 1980, U. Ala., Huntsville, 1985, U. Tenn. Space Inst., 1986—; bd. dirs. Tenn. Valley Aerospace Region; mem. rev. bd. NASA Lewis Rocket Thruster Rsch. Program, Dept. of Def. Fellowship Program, Indsl. Laser Handbook; mem. nat. adv. bd. NASA Enring. Rsch. Ctr. for Propulsion, Pa. State U., NASA Ctr. for Advanced Space Propulsion, U. Tenn. Space Inst./Calspan. Reviewer Jour. Spacecraft and Rockets, Jour. Propulsion and Power, Jour. Thermophysics and Heat Transfer, Jour. Heat Transfer; contbr. articles to profl. jours.; patentee in field. Maj. U.S. Army, 1972-73. NRC rsch. fellow, 1980-84. Assoc. fellow AIAA (liquid propulsion tech. com. 1984-88, assoc. editor Jour. Propulsion and Power 1988-91); mem. Am. Soc. Metals, Am. Welding Soc., Laser Inst. Am. (chmn. ICALEO 1994), Am. Soc. Engring. Edn. Roman Catholic. Avocation: tennis. Office: Univ Tenn Vice Pres Office UT Space Inst Tullahoma TN 37388 Office: B H Goethert Pkwy MS01 Tullahoma TN 37388-8897

MCCHESNEY, ROBERT MICHAEL, SR., political science educator; b. Effingham, Ill., Oct. 5, 1942; s. J.D. and Helen Grace (Russell) McC.; m. Laraine Freeman, Aug. 28, 1965; children: Robert M. Jr., Todd Patrick, Jennifer Laraine, Grant Russell, Brent Steven. BA, U. Southwestern La., 1964; MA, U. Va., 1967, PhD, 1969. Asst. instr. U. Va., Charlottesville, 1967-68; chmn. dept. polit. sci. U. Cen. Ark., Conway, 1971-76, dean coll. scis. and humanities, 1976-82, v.p. for acad. affairs, 1982-89, disting. prof., 1989-90; provost U. Montevallo, Ala., 1990-92; pres. U. Montevallo, 1992—; v.p. Survey Rsch., Inc., Conway, 1989-92; spl. cons. U. Ark. System, Little Rock, 1989. Mem. Carmichael Found., Conway, 1975-79; exec. bd. Quapaw coun. Boy Scouts Am., Little Rock, 1982-88; Birmingham Area Coun., 1995—. Capt. Med. Svc. Corps U.S. Army, 1968-71. Grantee State Justice Inst./Adminstrv. Office of Cts., Ark., 1989. Mem. Ark. Polit. Sci. Assn. (pres. 1975), Ala. Coun. Univ. and Coll. Pres. (chmn. 1993-95), So. Com. Colls. and Schs. (exec. coun.), Conway C. of C., Montevall C. of C., Rotary (pres. Conway Club 1987-88, Paul Harris fellow 1986), Phi Beta Kappa, Phi Kappa Phi, Alpha Chi, Golden Key, Phi Alpha Theta, Phi Eta Sigma, Blue Key. Mormon. Avocations: hunting, fishing, golfing. Office: U Montevallo Station 6001 Montevallo AL 35115

MCCHESNEY, ROBERT PEARSON, artist; b. Marshall, Mo., Jan. 16, 1913; s. John and Ruby (Pearson) McC.; m. Mary Ellen Fuller, Dec. 17, 1949. Student, Sch. Fine Arts, Washington U., 1931-34, Otis Art Inst., Los Angeles, 1936-37. Represented by Adrianne Fish, San Francisco, Annex Galleries, Santa Rosa, Calif., Robert Green Fine Arts, Mill Valley, Calif.; instr. art Calif. Sch. Fine Arts, San Francisco, 1949-51, Santa Rosa Jr. Coll., 1957-58; trustee San Francisco Art Inst., 1965-67. One-man shows include San Francisco Mus. Modern Art, 1949, 53, San Francisco Art Inst., 1957, 20th Century West, 1965, Bolles Gallery, N.Y., 1962, Nev. Mus., 1994, also others; one-man retrospective Fresno (Calif.) Mus. Art, 1996; group shows include Art Inst. Chgo., 1947, 3d Biennial Sau Paulo, Brazil, 1955, Whitney Annual, 1955, Corcoran, 1957, Provincetown, 1957, Chgo., 1959, Osaka, Japan, 1970, Whitney, 1980, Robert Green Fine Arts, Mill Valley, Calif., also others; represented in permanent collections, Fresno Art Mus., Art Inst. Chgo., Worcester (Mass.) Art Mus., Whitney Mus., N.Y., San Francisco Mus. Modern Art, Utah State Mus., Nev. Art Mus., Laguna Beach Art Mus., others; executed mural San Francisco Social Svcs. Bldg., 1978; author: Robert McChesney: An American Painter-Biography, 1996. Address: 2955 Sonoma Mountain Rd Petaluma CA 94954-9559 *The desert wilderness, which I truly love to be in as much as possible, has influenced me a great deal. Of course, the artist is no different from anyone else in that he is influenced by everything around him visually and psychologically, but he has the ability to digest this, you might say, and then transform it into art.*

MCCHESNEY, S. ELAINE, lawyer; b. Bowling Green, Ky., Sept. 14, 1954; d. Kelsey H. McChesney and Lorraine (Carter) Durey; m. Paul Boylan; children: Michael, Jessica, Andrew. AB summa cum laude, Western Ky. U., 1975; JD, Harvard U., 1978. With Bingham Dana & Gould, Boston, 1978—, ptnr., 1985—; chair joint MBA/BBA bar com. on jud. appts., 1988-89, 90-91; trial practice advisor moot ct. exercises Harvard Law Sch.; moot ct. judge Harvard Law Sch., Boston U., Suffolk U. Author: (with Gordon and Rainer) Massachusetts Civil Practice: Discovery, 1996; bd. editors Mass. Lawyer's Weekly, 1987-88; panelist, speaker in field; contbr. articles to profl. jours. Treas., bd. dirs. St. Paul's Nursery Sch., Dedham, Mass., 1990-95; parent rep. Charles River Sch., Dover, Mass., vol. numerous coms.; vol. Am. Heart Found., March of Dimes; vol. street canvassing on zoning issues. Mem. ABA (labor law sect. subcom. individual rights in the workplace 1982—, comml. banking or fin. transactions litigation 1982), Mass. Bar Assn., Boston Bar Assn. (coun. 1994—, law sch. liaison com. 1984-85, IOLTA com., co-chair ann. mtg.), Women's Bar Assn. (editor calendar 1988-92). Office: Bingham Dana & Gould 150 Federal St Boston MA 02110

MCCHRISTIAN, JOSEPH ALEXANDER, international business executive; b. Chgo., Oct. 12, 1914; s. Robert Lee and Lillian (Alexander) McC.; BS in Mil. Sci., U.S. Mil. Acad., 1939; grad. Command and Gen. Staff Coll., 1942, Armed Forces Staff Coll., 1951, Army War Coll., 1955, Army Lang. Sch., 1956; m. Dempsie Catherine Van Fleet, Sept. 26, 1940; children: Joseph Alexander, Anne, Lillian. Enlisted U.S. Army, 1933, commd. 2d lt., 1939, advanced through grades to maj. gen., 1961; various assignments 1933-44; successively armored inf. bn. comdr., asst. chief staff plans and ops., chief staff 10th Armored Div., ETO, 1944-45; asst. chief staff intelligence Hdqrs. 3d U.S. Army, Germany, 1945-47; dep. dir. intelligence U.S. Forces, Austria, 1947-48; comdg. officer 2d Bn., 3d Inf., "The Old Guard", Ft. McNair, D.C., 1948-49; spl. asst. to chief JUSMAG, Greece, 1949-50; S3 dept. tactics U.S. Mil. Acad., 1951-53, comdg. officer 1st Regt., U.S. Corp Cadets, 1953-54; U.S. Army attache, Greece, 1956-60; comdg. officer 1st Armored Regt. (tng.), also comdg. officer U.S. Army Tng. Ctr., Armor, Ft. Knox, Ky., 1960-61; chief Western div. Office Asst. Chief Staff-Intelligence, Dept. Army, 1962-63; asst. chief staff intelligence Hdqrs. U.S. Army Pacific, 1963-65; chief Army, Navy, Air Force and Marine Corps Intelligence, Hdqrs. U.S. Mil. Assistance Command, Vietnam, 1965-67; comdg. gen. 2d Armored Div., also III Corps, Ft. Hood, Tex., 1967-68; asst. chief of staff for intelligence Dept. Army, 1968-71; v.p. Overseas Basic Industries, Fla., 1972-74; v.p., gen. mgr. Société des Eaux, Athens, Greece, 1972-74; v.p. Ulen Mgmt. Co., Fla., 1972-75, Van Fleet Estates, Inc., Fla., 1970-77. Commr., Town of Jupiter Island (Fla.), 1975-83. Decorated D.S.M. with oak leaf cluster, Silver Star, Legion of Merit, Bronze Star with 3 oak leaf clusters, Air medal, Army Commendation, Am. Def., Am. Campaign, ETO Campaign with 3 bronze stars, WWII Victory, Nat. Def. with bronze oak leaf cluster, Vietnam Svc. with 4 oak leaf cluster, Vietnam Campaign, Combat Inf. badge; Croix de Guerre with gold star and bronze star (France); comdr. Royal Order King George 1st, also Disting. Svc. medal (Greece); Nat. Order 5th class and Disting. Svc. Order 1st class (Republic Vietnam); Mil. Merit medal, Chung Mu (Korea), Grand Cross of Mil. Merit with white ribbon (Spain), Medal of Metz (France). Mem. Mil. Order World Wars, Alumni Assn. U.S. Mil. Acad. Clubs: Army and Navy (Washington); Hobe Sound Yacht, Jupiter Island Club (Hobe Sound, Fla.); Ends of the Earth. Home: 365 South Beach Rd Hobe Sound FL 33455-2428

MCCLAIN, BENJAMIN RICHARD, music educator, educational administrator; b. Highland Park, Mich., May 20, 1931; s. Benjamin Richard and Julia (Hockett) McC.; m. Tahlia Helen Ruth Carter, Feb. 9, 1952 (div.); children: Terrence, Gerald, Sharalyn, Marilyn; m. Shirley Ann Brown, June 16, 1982; stepchildren: Keith, Sheila, Kenneth Hall. BMus, U. Mich., 1959, MusM, 1967, PhD, 1972. Cert. tchr., Mich., Fla., Wash. Jr. high sch. tchr. Inkster (Mich.) Pub. Schs., 1959-62; high sch. tchr. Dearborn Heights (Mich.) Pub. Schs., 1962-67, attendance officer, 1967-68, asst. high sch. prin., 1968-69; high sch. prin. Robichaud High Sch., Dearborn Heights, 1969-72; cons. State Dept. of Edn., Lansing, Mich., 1973-74; prof. Fla. Atlantic U., Boca Raton, 1974-79; academic dean Fla. Meml. Coll., Miami, 1979-80; prof. U. North Fla., Jacksonville, 1980-82, Gonzaga U., Spokane, Wash., 1982-85; with Seattle Pub. Schs., 1985-88; CEO MELT and Assocs., 1985-88; prof. Valdosta (Ga.) State U., 1988—. Editorial bd. The Western Jour. of Black Studies, 1984; contbr. numerous articles to profl. jours. Co-chmn. Athletic Booster Club, Boca Raton, 1977. Recipient Lafayette Allen Sr. Disting. Svc. award, 1973; Mott fellowship U. Mich., 1971-72, Regents Alumni scholarship, 1949-53. Mem. NAACP, Nat. Community Edn. Assn. (human rels. chair), Kiwanis, Phi Delta Kappa, Kappa Alpha Psi. Democrat. Baptist. Avocations: church choir, organist, piano accompanist. Office: Valdosta State Univ EDL Dept Valdosta GA 31698

MCCLAIN, DENNIS DOUGLAS, advertising executive; b. Portsmouth, Va., Aug. 9, 1948; s. Merl Lane and Bonnie May (Herrick) McC.; m. Claudia Trammell, Oct. 6, 1979; children: Matthew, Cameron. A.B.J., Henry Grady Sch. Journalism, U. Ga., 1970. Account supr. Leber Katz Ptnrs., 1974-76, group account supr., 1976-78, dir. creative svcs., 1978-81, exec. v.p. creative svcs., 1981—; pres. Southwest Bozell, 1985—; chmn., exec. creative dir. The Bloom Agy., 1983-85. Named Alumni of Yr. Henry Grady Sch. Journalism, U. Ga., 1983. Office: Temerlin McLain Inc 201 E Carpenter Frwy Irving TX 75062

MCCLAIN, GREGORY DAVID, minister; b. Anderson, S.C., June 6, 1957; s. Lemuel David and Mary Josephine (Hawkins) McC.; m. Anne Leigh Blackwell, May 21, 1983; children: Jonathan David, Sean Gregory. AS, Anderson Coll., 1977; BA, Erskine Coll., 1979; MDiv, Southeastern Bapt. Theol. Sem., Seminary, Wake Forrest, N.C., 1982; D of Ministry, Wesley Theol. Sem., Washington, 1996. Ordained Boulevard Bapt. Ch., 1983. Chaplain extern Bapt. Med. Ctr., Columbia, S.C., 1982; assoc. pastor First Bapt. Ch., South Boston, Va., 1983-86; minister Corrottoman Bapt. Ch., Lancaster, Va., 1986-93, Colonial Beach (Va.) Bapt. Ch., 1993—; pres. Dan River Bapt. Pastors, Halifax, Va., 1984-85; preacher-jr. high weekend, Va. Bapt. Gen. Assn., 1986, faculty youth week, 1984-88; v.p. Lancaster Ministerial Assn., 1987-88. Active CROP walk, South Boston, Va., 1984-85; coach youth soccer, South Boston, 1985, Westmoreland County, Va., 1995, 96; merit badge counselor Boy Scouts Am., Lancaster, 1990-93; mem. Lancaster Ednl. Task Force, 1988. Mem. Ruritan Club (chaplain 1990-93). Office: Colonial Beach Bapt Ch PO Box 27 Colonial Beach VA 22443-0027 *The Kingdom of God exists wherever God is king.*

MCCLAIN, LEE BERT, corporate lawyer, insurance executive; b. East Chicago, Ill., Jan. 1, 1943; s. Wilson C. and Ida (Dapra) M.; 1 child, Adam. BS, Purdue U., 1966; MBA, Loyola U., Chgo., 1968, JD, 1975. Bar: Ill. 1975. Divsn. contr. Armour-Dial, Chgo., 1970-73; mgr. corp. planning Spiegel Inc., Chgo., 1973-76; with Kemper Group, Long Grove, Ill., 1976—, employee rels. officer, 1978-81, gen. counsel, corp. sec., mgr. govt. affairs, 1986-91; ptnr., co-chair ins. practice group Wildman, Harold, Allen & Dixon, Chgo., 1991-96; of counsel, CEO, pres. Arbella Capital, Mass., 1996—; chair Supreme Ct. Ill. Atty. Disciplinary Commn. Inquiry Bd., 1990, 91; bd. dirs. Arbella Ins. Group, Mass.; bd. dirs. Preferred Am. Ins. Co., Iowa. Mem. staff Presdl. Commn. on Drunk Driving, 1982. Sgt. U.S. Army, 1968-70, Vietnam. Decorated Bronze Star. Mem. ABA (nat. commn. on minorities 1990-93), Ill. Bar Assn., Chgo. Bar Assn., Fedn. Ins. & Corp. Counsel. Avocations: tennis, jazz. Office: Wildman Harold Allen & Dixon 225 W Wacker Dr Chicago IL 60606-1224

MCCLAIN, MARILYN RUSSELL, university student counselor; b. Laurelton, N.Y., Aug. 18, 1956; d. Russell H. and Lillian A. (Yarbrough) McC.; 1 child, Amy Lynne Roberts. BS in Social Work, Harding U., 1977; MA in Adult Edn., Okla. State U., 1997. Career counselor Foothills Vo-Tech Sch., Searcy, Ark., 1977-78; social worker Dept. Social Svcs., Tulsa, Okla., 1978-79; owner, operator, instr. Spl. Deliveries Childbirth Preparation Ctr., Tulsa, 1980-85; mgr. One Hour Moto Photo, Tulsa, 1986-89; area mgr. Mervyn's, Tulsa, 1989-92; health scis. student counselor Rogers U., Claremore, Okla., 1992—; student counselor for health scis. Rogers U., Claremore, 1996—; primary advisor Adult Students Aspiring to Prosper, Claremore, Okla., 1993—; pres. RSC Staff Assn., 1995—; parent educator Parenting Ptnrs., Claremore, 1994—. Sec. Oologah-Talala Sch. Found., 1994-95, pres., 1995—; mem. statue and hotel coms. Rogers County Hist. Soc., Claremore, 1994—; mem. planning com. Leadership Claremore, 1994—; mem. Oologah PTA, 1990—. Mem. Okla. Acad. Advising Assn. (comm. com. 1994—), Am. Assn. for Adult and Continuing Edn. Republican. Avocations: needlework, reading, piano. Home: 3612 N Oaklawn Dr Claremore OK 74017-1828 Office: Rogers Univ 1701 W Will Rogers Blvd Claremore OK 74017

MCCLAIN, PAULA DENICE, political scientist; b. Louisville, Jan. 3, 1950; d. Robert Landis and Mabel (Molock) McC.; stepdau. of Annette Williams McClain; m. Paul C. Jacobson, Jan. 30, 1988; children: Kristina L., Jessica A. BA, Howard U., Washington, 1972; MA, Howard U., 1974, PhD, 1977; postgrad., U. Pa., 1981-82. Asst. prof. dept. polit. sci. U. Wis., Milw., 1977-82; assoc. prof. and prof. pub. affairs Ariz. State U., Tempe, 1982-91; prof. govt. and fgn. affairs U. Va., Charlottesville, 1991—, chair govt. and fgn. affairs, 1994-97. Co-author: Can We All Get Along? Racial and Ethnic Minorities in American Politics, 1995, Race, Place and Risk: Black Homicide in Urban America, 1990; editor: Minority Group Influence, 1993; co-editor: Urban Minority Administrators, 1988. Mem. Nat. Conf. Black Polit. Scientists (pres. 1989-90), Am. Polit. Sci. Assn. (mem. coun. 1985-87, v.p. 1993-94), So. Polit. Sci. Assn. (exec. coun. 1992-95). Office: U Va Dept Govt 232 Cabell Hall Charlottesville VA 22901

MCCLAIN, SYLVIA NANCY, voice educator, classical vocalist; b. Worthington, Minn., July 16, 1943; d. Walter Deming and Naomi Leona (Deters) Grimm.; m. Joseph T. McClain (div. Feb. 1994); children: Raimund, Hermine. MusB with honors, Ind. U., 1966, MusM with honors, 1969; D of Musical Arts with commendation, U. Tex., Austin, 1989. Apprentice artist Santa Fe (N.Mex.) Opera, 1968-69; performing singer various concert and opera venues, Germany, 1970-78; asst. prof. dept. music Howard Payne U., Brownwood, Tex., 1992, 94; asst. prof. voice dept. fine arts Southwestern U., Georgetown, Tex., 1986-91; assoc prof., chair voice dept. sch. music Hardin-Simmons U., Abilene, Tex., 1992—. Performer: (recital) Portraits of Women in Songs of Hugo Wolf. Vol. cons. Leadership of Edn. in Arts Professions, Austin, 1990-92; co-founder, Austin Lyric Opera, 1983-92. Fulbright scholar, Stadtliche Hochschule für Musik, Stuttgart, Germany, 1969-70. Mem. AAUW, Nat. Assn. Tchrs. of Singing, Phi Kappa Lambda, Mu Phi Epsilon. Democrat. Methodist. Avocations: aerobics, reading, computers. Home: 457 Merchant Abilene TX 79603

MCCLAIN, THOMAS E., communications executive; b. East Liverpool, Ohio, July 26, 1950; s. Thomas E. and Helen Marie (Polinski) McC. BA, Case Western Reserve, Cleve., 1972; MA, Kans. State U., 1973. With intergovtl. rels. Ohio EPA, Columbus, 1974-77; legis. liaison Ohio Consumers Counsel, Columbus, 1977-80; dep. dir. Ohio Consumers Counsel, 1980-81; press sec. Ohio Atty. Gen., Columbus, 1982-83; asst. dir. Pub. Utilities Commn., Columbus, 1983; with instnl. rels. dept. Battelle Project Mgmt. Div., Chgo., 1983-84; mgr. instl. rels. Battelle Project Mgmt. Div., 1984-86; mgr. comms. Battelle, Columbus, 1986-88, dir. corp. comms., 1989-95, v.p. corp. comms., 1995—; sec. devel. bd. Children's Hosp., Columbus, 1990—. Vol. Ohio Youth Commn., Columbus, 1975-76; active ARC-Cen. Ohio chpt., 1986-87. Warren Lahr scholar Case Western Reserve U., 1971-72. Mem. Rotary (chmn. program com. 1991-93, bd. dirs. 1994-95, 2d v.p. 1996—). Presbyterian. Avocations: basketball, golf, travel. Home: 2689

Camden Rd Upper Arlington OH 43221-3221 Office: Battelle 505 King Ave Columbus OH 43201-2696

MCCLAIN, WILLIAM ANDREW, lawyer; b. Sanford, N.C., Jan. 11, 1913; s. Frank and Blanche (Leslie) McC.; m. Roberta White, Nov. 11, 1944. AB, Wittenberg U., 1934; JD, U. Mich., 1937; LLD (hon.), Wilberforce U., 1963, U. Cin., 1971; LHD, Wittenberg U., 1972. Bar: Ohio 1938, U.S. Dist. Ct. (so. dist.) Ohio 1940, U.S. Ct. Appeals (6th cir.) 1946, U.S. Supreme Ct. 1946. Mem. Berry, McClain & White, 1937-58; dep. solicitor, City of Cin., 1957-63, city solicitor, 1963-72; mem. Keating, Muething & Klekamp, Cin., 1972-73; gen. counsel Cin. Br., SBA, 1973-75; judge Hamilton County Common Pleas Ct., 1975-76; judge Mcpl. Ct., 1976-80; of counsel Manley, Burke, Lipton & Cook, Cin., 1980—; adj. prof. U. Cin., 1963-72, Salmon P. Chase Law Sch., 1965-72. Exec. com. ARC, Cin., 1978—; bd. dirs. NCCJ, 1975—. Served to 1st lt. JAGC, U.S. Army, 1943-46. Decorated Army Commendation award; recipient Nat. Layman award, A.M.E. Ch., 1963; Alumni award Wittenberg U., 1966; Nat. Inst. Mcpl. Law Officers award, 1971, Ellis Island Medal of Honor, 1997. Fellow Am. Bar Found.; mem. Am. Judicature Soc., Cin. Bar Assn., Ohio Bar Assn., ABA, Fed. Bar assn., Nat. Bar Assn., Alpha Phi Alpha, Sigma Pi Phi. Republican. Methodist. Clubs: Bankers, Friendly Sons of St. Patrick Lodge: Masons (33 deg.). Home: 2101 Grandin Rd Apt 904 Cincinnati OH 45208-3346

MCCLAIN, WILLIAM THOMAS, lawyer; b. Louisville, June 4, 1926; s. George Lee and Catherine (Spalding) McC.; m. Wanda Barry, Feb. 28, 1949; children: Nina, Catherine, Ann, William, Mary. BS in Metall. Engring., U. Ky., 1948; JD, Loyola U., New Orleans, 1958. Bar: Ill. 1960, D.C. 1988. Engr. Shell Oil Co., Deer Park, Tex., 1948-55; asst. prof. U. Houston, 1951-55; sales engr. Pacific Valves, Inc., New Orleans, 1955-58; assoc. Wier, Greene & Nelson, New Orleans, 1958, Amoco Corp., Chgo., 1959-86, Finnegan, Henderson, Farabow, Garrett & Dunner, Washington, 1987—. With USN, 1944-46. Mem. ABA (chmn. 1987—), Am. Intellectual Property Law Assn. (dir., treas. 1986-90). Republican. Avocations: golf, tennis, reading. Office: Finnegan Henderson Farabow and Dunner LLP 1300 I St NW Washington DC 20005-3314

MCCLAMROCH, N. HARRIS, aerospace engineering educator, consultant, researcher; b. Houston, Oct. 7, 1942; s. Nathaniel Harris and Dorthy Jean (Orand) McC.; m. Margaret Susan Hobart, Aug. 10, 1963; 1 child, Kristin Jean. B.S., U. Tex., 1963, M.S., 1965, Ph.D., 1967. Prof. dept. elec. engring. and computer sci. U. Mich., Ann Arbor, 1967—, chair dept. aerospace engring., 1992-95; research engr. Cambridge U., Eng., 1975, Delft U., Netherlands, 1976, Sandia Labs., Albuquerque, 1977, C.S. Draper Lab., Cambridge, Mass., 1982. Author: State Models of Dynamic Systems, 1980; contbr. numerous articles to profl. jours. Chmn. U. Mich. Faculty Senate, 1987-88. Fellow IEEE (pres.-elect Control Sys. Soc. 1997, editor Transactions on Automatic Control 1989-92); mem. AAAS, Control System Soc. (pres. 1998). Home: 4056 Thornoaks Dr Ann Arbor MI 48104-4254 Office: U Mich Dept Aerospace Engring Ann Arbor MI 48109

MCCLANAHAN, CONNIE DEA, pastoral minister; b. Detroit, Mar. 1, 1948; d. Manford Bryce and Dorothy Maxine (Keely) McC. BA, Marygrove Coll., 1969; MRE, Seattle U., 1978; D Ministry, St. Mary Sem. and U., Balt., 1988. Cert. in spiritual direction, youth ministry, advanced catechist. Campus minister Flint (Mich.) Newman Ctr., 1970-80; coord. religious edn. Blessed Sacrament Ch., Burton, Mich., 1981-84; pastoral assoc. Good Shepherd Cath. Ch., Montrose, Mich., 1984-90; pastor Sacred Heart Ch., Flint, 1990—; music min. New Light Prayer Cmty., Flint, 1979—; co-chaplain Dukette Cath. Sch., Flint, 1991—; ind. spiritual dir., 1988—; rep. Diocesan Regional Adult Edn., 1993-96; mem. Nat., State and Lansing Diocese Catholic Campus Ministry Assns., 1970-80; mem. campus ministry task force Interfaith Metro. Agy. for Planning, 1974-76; mem. Lansing Diocesan Liturgical Commn., 1977-80; mem. Flint Cath. Urban Ministry, 1977-80, 90—, co-chair, 1992-94; mem. Flint Cath. Healing Prayer Team, 1977-84; coord. nat. study week Cath. Campus Ministry Assn., 1978; mem. steering com. All-Mich. Cath. Charismatic Conf., 1984-86; convener Diocesan Lay Ministry Com. on Cert./Continuing Edn./Spirituality, 1985-86; mem. Diocesan Com. to Update Catechist Formation Handbook, 1989-91; mem. Diocesan All Family Conf. Steering Com., 1990-91; mem. Lansing Diocese svc. com. of Cath. Charismatic Renewal, 1979-85, 95—, chair, 1996—. Mem. Assn. Cath. Lay Ministers (co-chair Region III 1986-87), Profl. Pastoral Ministers Assn. (co-chair 1988-90), Nat. Assn. Lay Ministry. Roman Catholic. Avocations: guitar, singing, leather crafting, reading. Office: Sacred Heart Ch 719 E Moore St Flint MI 48505-3905

MCCLANAHAN, LARRY DUNCAN, civil engineer, consultant; b. Franklin, Ky., July 30, 1938; s. Ernest William McClanahan and Anne Isabel (Henderson) McClanahan Hodges; m. Betty Jane Marquess, Mar. 16, 1963; children: Michael Curtis, Marta Suzette Stinson, Meredith Angela. BSCE, Tenn. Poly. Inst., 1965; MSCE, Tenn. Tech. U., 1974. Registered profl. engr., Tenn., Ky., Ala. Sr. civil engr. Tenn. Bur. Aero., Nashville, 1965-67; airport planning engr. FAA, Memphis, 1967-68; assoc. R. Dixon Speas & Assocs., Atlanta, 1968-70; prin. Larry D. McClanahan & Assocs., Nashville, 1970—; pres. Agtech-Ky., Inc., Franklin, Ky., 1984-87. Pres. Nannie Perry Sch. PTA, Hendersonville, Tenn., 1975, Woodlands Homeowners Assn., 1992-93; v.p. Jackson Park Cmty. Assn., Nashville, 1985-86, pres., 1986-87, 90-94; chmn. bd. dirs. Hendersonville Mcpl. Airport Authority, 1973-75; geneal. mem. Nashville Met. Pub. Records Commn., 1992—, chmn., 1992—; mem. subarea 4 citizens adv. com. Metro Planning Commn., 1993-94; alt. chmn. Citizens Postal Adv. Com. for Jere Baxter Sta. of U.S. Post Office, 1993-94. Recipient Sustained Superior Service award FAA, 1968. Mem. ASCE (chmn. landing area subcom. 1969-71), SAR (sec., registrar Tenn. Soc. 1985-90, state v.p. 1999-91, pres.-elect 1992, pres. 1992-93, founding pres. Sumner chpt. 1990-91, alt. nat. trustee 1993-94, nat. trustee, v.p. gen. so. dist. 1994-95, historian gen., 1997—, chmn. nat. Americanism com. 1994-95, mem. 1995—, mem. nat. exec. com. 1995-96, chmn. bldg. growth com. 1995—, mem. membership nt. hdqs., DAR liaison, mem. congress planning, history, nat. nominating coms. 1994-95, chmn. state host com. nat. congress for 2002, Disting. Svc. cert. 1986, Meritorious Svc. medal 1987, Florence Kendall medal and award 1991, Liberty medal with 4 oak leaf clusters 1994, Patriot medal 1993, Silver Good Citizenship medal 1995, Minuteman award 1997), Soc. Boonesborough, McClanahan Family Assn., Clan McLennan, Clan Henderson (convenor 1994—), No. Neck of Va. Hist. Soc., Gen. Soc. Colonial Wars (dep. gov. Tenn. 1993-94, gov. Tenn 1994—), Knights of Sovereign Mil. Order of Temple of Jerusalem & Knight Comdr., 1996, Freolac Club, Order of Engrs., Masons, St. Andrew Priory (treas. 1996), Wine Club Nashville, Middle Tenn. Scottish Soc. Republican. Baptist. Avocations: geneology, history, travel, basketball and baseball (amateur coach). Home: 1119 Winding Way Rd Nashville TN 37216-2213 Office: 203A Point East Dr Nashville TN 37216-1400

MCCLANAHAN, LELAND, academic administrator; b. Hammond, Ind., Mar. 14, 1931; s. Alonzo Leland and Eva (Hermanson) McC.; m. Lavaughn Adell Meyrer, June 5, 1954; children: Lindel, Loren. Diploma, Ctrl. Bible Coll., 1954; PhBB, Nat. Postgrad. Bible Acad., 1969; BA, Southwestern Coll., 1973; MA, Fla. State Christian Coll., 1964, ThD, 1970; PhD, Faith Bible Coll. and Sem., Ft. Lauderdale, Fla. and Marina, Lagos, Nigeria, 1969; MA, Bapt. Christian U., 1988; PhD, Freedom U., 1989; ThD, Bapt. Christian U., 1989, DLitt, 1990, PsyD, 1991; PhD, Hawaii U., 1995; DEd, Bapt. Christian U., 1992, D in Bus. Adminstrn., 1993; DD (hon.), Internat. Evangelism Crusades, 1969, Trinity Union Coll., 1991; LLD, La. Bapt. U., 1994; StD, PhD, Trinity Internat. U., 1994; HHD (hon.), La. Bapt. U., 1995; LittD (hon.), Cambridge Theol. Sem., 1995; PhD, LittD, PsyD, DBA, LLD, EdD, U. Hawaii, 1995; LittD(hon.), The Messianic Coll. of Rabbinical Studies. Diplomate Nat. Bd. Christian Clin. Therapists; ordained pastor, Christian Ch., 1950. Founder, pastor Evangel Temple, Griffith, Ind., 1954-73, Abundant Life Temple, Cocoa, Fla., 1974-77; mgr. ins. divsn. United Agys., Cocoa, Fla., 1979-81; assoc. pastor Merritt Assembly of God, Merritt Island, Fla., 1982-85, Palm Chapel, Merritt Island, 1987-89, 1990-93; founder Hawaii U., Merritt Island Offices, Merritt Island, Fla., 1990—; chancellor Hawaii U. Merritt Island Offices, 1995—; dir. Fla. Hawaii U. Schs.; founder, dir. Griffith Youth Ctr., 1960-70, Todd Nursery Sch., Griffith, 1971-73; founder, chancellor Ind. Bible Coll., Griffith, 1971-73; dir. Chapel Counseling Ctr., Merritt Island, 1990-94; mem. national accreditation com. Hawaii U. Author: Is Divine Healing For Today?, 1989, Truths From the Gospel of St. John, 1991, An Outline of the Revelation, 1993, Numbers in the Bible, 1994, An Outline of the Acts of the Apostle, 1995; author 142 coll. courses and books. Recipient Disting. Svc. award U.S. Jaycees, 1966; named Hon. Lt. Col., Gov. Guy Hunt, 1988. Fellow Am. Biog. Inst. (life); mem. Internat. Platform Assn., Order of Internat. Fellowship (life), Am. Inst. Clin. Psychotherapists, Am. Assn. christian Counselors, Nat. Christian Counseling Assn. (assoc., lic.), Internat. Assn. Pastoral Psychologists (lic.), Order of St. John, Knight of Malta (comdr. 1990). Republican. Avocations: reading, walking, watching sports, watching television adventures, weight lifting. Office: Hawaii U Meritt Island Offices 670 N Courtenay Pkwy Ste 15 Merritt Island FL 32953-4770

MCCLANE, ROBERT SANFORD, bank holding company executive; b. Kenedy, Tex., May 5, 1939; s. Norris Robert and Ella Addie (Stockton) McC.; m. Sue Nitschke, Mar. 31, 1968; children: Len Stokes McClane Brown, Norris Robert. BS in Bus. Adminstrn., Trinity U., San Antonio, 1961. With Ford Motor Co., Detroit, 1961-62; with Frost Nat. Bank, San Antonio, 1962—, mem. staff, 1962-68, v.p., 1968-78; exec. v.p. Cullen/Frost Bankers, Inc., 1976—, pres., dir., 1985—; bd. dirs. Frost Nat. Bank, San Antonio. Crusade chmn. Baxar County chpt. Am. Cancer Soc., 1974; bd. dirs. Bexar County ARC, 1969-72; sr. warden St. Luke's Episopal Ch., San Antonio, 1980; trustee Alamo Pub. Telecomms. Coun., San Antonio, 1981-88, Trinity U., 1990—; chmn. San Antonio Econ. Devel. Found., 1987-89, exec. com. 1985-91. Mem. Greater San Antonio C. of C. (chmn. leadership San Antonio 1975-76, bd. dirs. exec. com. 1994—, chmn. 1996), Trinity U. Alumni Assn. (pres. 1968-69, disting. alumnus 1987), San Antonio German Club, Order Alamo, Tex. Cavaliers, Argyle Club, Town Club, Plaza Club (bd. dirs. 1973-92). Episcopalian. Office: Cullen/Frost Bankers Inc 100 W Houston St San Antonio TX 78205-1400

MCCLARD, JACK EDWARD, lawyer; b. Lafayette, La., May 13, 1946; s. Lee Franklin and Mercedes Cecile (Landry) McC.; m. Marilyn Kay O'Gorman, June 3, 1972; 1 child, Lauren Minton. BA in Hist., Rice U., 1968; JD, U. Tex., 1974. Bar: Va. 1974, U.S. Dist. Ct. (ea. and we. dists.) Va. 1974, D.C. 1981, U.S. Dist. Ct. D.C. 1981, N.Y. 1985, U.S. Dist. Ct. (so. and ea. dists.) N.Y. 1985, U.S. Ct. Appeals (4th cir.) 1978, U.S. Ct. Appeals (D.C. cir.) 1980, U.S. Ct. Appeals (5th cir.) 1993, Tex. 1996. Assoc. Hunton & Williams, Richmond, Va., 1974-81; ptnr. Hunton & Williams, Richmond, 1981—. Contbr. articles to profl. jours. Served to lt. (j.g.) USN, 1968-71. Mem. ABA, Va. Bar Assn., Richmond Bar Assn., Va. Trial Lawyers Assn., 5th Cir. Bar, John Marshall Inns of Ct. Democrat. Episcopalian. Avocations: bridge, gardening. Home: 100 Trowbridge Rd Richmond VA 23233-5724 Office: Hunton & Williams Riverfront Plz E Tower 951 E Byrd St Richmond VA 23219-4040

MCCLARON, LOUISIANNA CLARDY, retired secondary school educator; b. Clarksville, Tenn., Dec. 12, 1929; d. Abe and Chinaster (Simpson) Clardy; m. Joe Thomas McClaron, July 17, 1965. BS, Tenn. State U., 1952; MA, Ohio State U., 1956; EdS, Tenn. State U., 1977; PhD, Vanderbilt U., 1981. Cert. secondary tchr., sch. adminstr., supr., Tenn. Tchr. Madison County Bd. Edn., Normal, Ala., 1952-58, Metro Nashville Bd. Edn., 1958-94; ret., 1994; presenter workshops in field. Treas. Patterson Meml. United Meth. Ch., 1980. Mem. NEA (ret.), Tenn. Ret. Tchrs. Assn., Metro Nashville Ret. Tchrs. Assn., Les Nevvettes Social Club (pres.), Woodbine Cmty. Orgn. (sec.), Delta Pi Epsilon (former v.p. Omega chpt., now pres.), Alpha Kappa Alpha, Alpha Delta Omega Chpt. Found. (housing treas.).

MC CLARREN, ROBERT ROYCE, librarian; b. Delta, Ohio, Mar. 15, 1921; s. Dresden William Howard and Norma Leona (Whiteman) McC.; m. Margaret Aileen Weed, May 31, 1947; children: Mark Robert, Todd Adams. Student, Antioch Coll., 1938-40; AB, Muskingum Coll., 1942; MA in English, Ohio State U., 1951; MS in L.S., Columbia, 1954; DLitt (hon.), Rosary Coll., 1989. Registration officer VA, Cin., 1946-47; instr. English Gen. Motors Inst., 1949-50; head circulation dept. Oak Park Public Library, Ill., 1954-55; acting head librarian Oak Park Public Library, 1955; head librarian Crawfordsville Public Library, Ind., 1955-58, Huntington Public Library, also Western Counties (W.Va.) Regional Public Library, W.Va., 1958-62; dir. Ind. State Library, 1962-67; system dir. North Suburban Library System, 1967-89; system dir. emeritus, 1990—; cons. libr. Chgo. Pub. Libr. Found., 1990; del. White House Conf. on Librs., 1979; instr. U. Wis., summer 1964, Rosary Coll., 1968-80, U. Tex., summer 1979, 82, No. Ill. U., 1980; pres. W.Va. Libr. Assn., 1960; mem. Gov. Ind. Commn. Arts, 1964-65, Ill. State Libr. Adv. Com., 1972-79, 87-89, chmn., 1975-79, vice chmn., 1988-89; bd. dirs. Ill. Regional Libr. Coun., 1972-82, pres., 1977; chmn. adv. commn. Nat. Periodical System, Nat. Commn. on Librs. and Info. Sci., 1978-81; treas. Ill. Coalition Libr. Advs., 1982-89. Contbr. articles to profl. jours. Served to 1st lt. AUS, 1942-46, 51-52; maj. Res. Named Ill. Librarian of Yr., 1978; recipient Sagamore of Wabash (Ind.), 1966. Mem. ALA (councilor 1966-68, 74-78, treas. 1968-72, endowment trustee 1972-78, mem. publ. bd. 1972-75, pres. reference and adv. svc. div. 1975-76, Melville Dewey award 1989, Honor Roll of Legis. and Libr. Champions 1996), Ill. Libr. Assn. (pres. 1981, Robert R. McClarren Legis. award 1989), Am. Libr. Trustee Assn. (v.p. 1976-77), Assn. Spl. and Coop. Libr. Agys. (pres. 1978-79, Exceptional Achievement award 1982), Ohio Hist. Soc., Am. Philatelic Soc. Home: 1560 Oakwood Pl Deerfield IL 60015-2014 Office: 200 W Dundee Rd Wheeling IL 60090-4750

MCCLARY, JAMES DALY, retired contractor; b. Boise, Idaho, July 19, 1917; s. Neil Hamaker and Myrtle (Daly) McC.; m. Mary Jane Munger, Feb. 2, 1939; children: Pamela, John. Student, Boise Jr. Coll., 1934-36, AA, 1957; AB, Stanford U., 1938; LLD, Gonzaga U., 1976. Laborer to supt. Morrison-Knudsen Co., Inc., Boise, 1932-42, project mgr., asst. dist. mgr., 1942- 47; gen. mgr. Mexican subs. Morrison-Knudsen Co., Inc., 1947-51, asst. to gen. mgr., 1951-53, asst. gen. mgr., 1953-60, dir., 1955-78, v.p., 1956-60, exec. v.p., 1960-72, chmn. bd., 1972-78; mem., vice chmn. Idaho Permanent Bldg. Fund Adv. Council, 1961-64, chmn., 1964-71. Treas. Idaho Rep. Cen. Com., 1964-70; presdl. elector, 1968; trustee Boise Jr. Coll., 1960-83, vice chmn., 1967-73, chmn., 1973-83; bd. dirs. Boise State U. Found., Inc., 1964-91, pres., 1970-81; bd. dirs. AGC Edn. and Rsch. Found., 1974-91, pres., 1974-90; elector Hall of Fame for Great Ams., 1976—; trustee St. Alphonsus Regional Med. Ctr., 1976-82, vice chmn., 1981-82. Recipient George Washington medal of honor Freedoms Found., Valley Forge, Pa., 1977, Disting. Alumnus award Boise State U., 1988, Silver medallion, 1996; decorated Chevalier and Legion of Honor, Order of DeMolay; named Disting. Alumnus of Yr. Boise State U. Alumni Assn., 1971, Ky. Col. Fellow ASCE, Am. Inst. Constructors; mem. Internat. Rd. Fedn. (bd. dirs. 1972-78, vice chmn. 1977-78), Soc. Am. Mil. Engrs., Assoc. Gen. Contractors Am. (bd. dirs. 1958—, mem. exec. com. 1961-78, pres. 1972), Cons. Constructors Coun. Am., Newcomen Soc., Conf. Bd. (sr. mem.), Idaho Assn. Commerce and Industry (bd. dirs., chmn. 1974-77, Harwood award 1994), Moles (hon., mem. award for Outstanding Achievement in Constrn. 1978), Hillcrest Country Club (bd. dirs. 1965-67, 69, pres. 1967), Arid Club (mem. exec. com. 1966), Ariz. Club (Scottsdale), Ariz. Country Club (Phoenix), Univ. Club (Mexico City), Stanford Club (Washington). Episcopalian. Home: 4903 Roberts Rd Boise ID 83705-2805

MCCLATCHY, J. D., editor, writer, educator; b. Bryn Mawr, Pa., Aug. 12, 1945; s. J. Donald and Mary Jane (Hayden) McC. BA summa cum laude, Georgetown U., 1967; PhD, Yale U., 1974. Instr. English dept. LaSalle Coll., Phila., 1968-71; asst. prof. English dept. Yale U., New Haven, Conn., 1974-81, lectr. English dept., 1983, 86-87; writer-in-residence CCNY, 1982; writer-in-residence Poetry Ctr. 92d St. YMCA, N.Y.C., 1983-84, workshop leader Poetry Ctr., 1982-91; lectr. Creative Writing program, English dept. Princeton U., 1981-87, 89-93; editor The Yale Rev., New Haven, 1991—; poet-in-residence Southampton Writers Conf., 1988; lectr. MFA Parsons/New Sch., 1989, English dept. Rutgers U., 1989, writing divsn. Columbia U., 1989, 92; vis. prof. English dept. UCLA, 1990, 92; selection com. Conn. Poetry Cir. Author: (poetry) Scenes from Another Life, 1981, (London 1983), Lantskip, Platan, Creatures Ramp'd, 1983, Stars Principal, 1986, Kilim, 1987, The Rest of the Way, 1990; librettist: A Question of Taste, 1989, Mario and the Magician, 1994, Orpheus Decending, 1994, Emmeline, 1996; editor: The Yale Review, 1991—, (books) Anne Sexton: The Artist and Her Critics, 1978, For James Merrill: A Birthday Tribute, 1986, Recitative: Prose by James Merrill, 1986, Poets on Painters: Essays on the Art of Painting by Twentieth Century Poets, 1988, The Vintage Book of Contemporary American Poetry, 1990, Woman in White: Selected Poems of Emily Dickinson, 1991, The Vintage Book of Contemporary World Poetry, 1996; assoc. editor Four Quarters, 1968-71; contbg. editor Am. Poetry Review; poetry editor The Yale Review, 1981-91; trans. articles, contbr. poems, stories, articles, reviews to various jours. Bd. dirs. Ingram Merrill Found., 1986—; chancellor The Acad. of Am. Poets, 1996—. Recipient gold medal Vergilian Acad., 1967, O. Henry award, 1972, prize Am. Acad. Poets , 1972, Chase Going Woodhouse Poetry prize, 1976, Michener award, 1982, Gordon Barber Meml. award Poetry Soc. Am., 1984, Eunice Tietjens Meml. prize Poetry Mag., 1985, Witter Bynner Poetry prize Am. Acad. and Inst. Arts and Letters, 1985, award in lit., 1991, Oscar Blumenthal prize Poetry Mag., 1988, Levinson prize, 1990, Melville Cane award Poetry Soc. Am., 1991, Literary Lion N.Y. Pub. Libr., 1992; grantee Ingram Merrill Found., 1979, Conn. Commn. Arts, 1981; fellow NEA, 1987, John Simon Guggenheim Meml. Found., 1988; fellow lit. Acad. Am. Poets, 1991; artist resident Djerassi Found., 1988; Woodrow Wilson fellow 1967-68; Yale U. fellow, 1971-72; Ethel Boise Morgan fellow, 1972-74; artist's fellow N.Y. Found. Arts, 1986; artist resident Yaddo, 1991, MacDowell Colony, 1991. Mem. Am. Acad. Poets (chancellor 1996), Phi Beta Kappa, Alpha Sigma Nu. Home: 15 Grand St Stonington CT 06378-1340 Office: The Yale Review Yale Univ PO Box 208243 New Haven CT 06520-8243

MCCLATCHY, JAMES B., editor, newspaper publisher; b. Sacramento; s. Carlos K. and Phebe (Briggs) McC.; m. Susan Brewster; children: Carlos F., William B. B.A., Stanford U.; M.S., Columbia U. Reporter Sacramento Bee; reporter, editor Fresno Bee, Calif.; pub. McClatchy Newspapers, Sacramento.; past pres., dir. InterAm. Press Assn. Trustee Nat. Ctr. Internat. Schs. Mem. Am. Press Inst. (bd. dirs.). Office: McClatchy Newspapers 21st & Q Sts Sacramento CA 95813

MCCLAUGHERTY, JOHN LEWIS, lawyer; b. Bluefield, W.Va., Feb. 13, 1931; s. William N. and N. Louisa (Shelton) McC.; m. Sallie H. Fredeking, June 27, 1953; children: Martha M. Nepa, John W. BS, Northwestern U., 1953; LLB, W.Va. U., 1956. Bar: W.Va. 1956, U.S. Dist. Ct. (so. dist.) W.Va. 1956, U.S. Ct. Appeals (4th cir.) 1956, U.S. Supreme Ct. 1975, U.S. Ct. Mil. Appeals 1957. Assoc. Jackson & Kelly, Charleston, W.Va., 1959-65, ptnr., 1965-86; mng. ptnr. Jackson & Kelly, Charleston, 1986—; mem. Nat. Conf. Commrs. on Uniform State Laws, Chgo., 1977—; pres. Ea. Mineral Law Found., Morgantown, W.Va., 1983-84; dir. Wesbanco South Hills, Charleston. Contbr. articles to profl. jours., chpts. to books. Pres. W.Va. Symphony Orch., Charleston, 1982—; trustee Am. Symphony Orch. League, Washington, 1991—, W.Va. Wesleyan Coll., Buckhannon, 1989-94; dir. Charleston Renaissance Corp., 1989—. 1st lt. USAF, 1956-59. Named Coal Lawyer of the Yr. Nat. Coal Lawyers Conf., 1983, Mayor's Award for Arts Vol., Fund for the Arts, Charleston, 1990; listed in The Best Lawyers in America. Fellow Am. Bar Found. (life); mem. ABA, W.Va. Bar Found. (pres. 1992—), Am. Judicature Soc., W.Va. Bar Assn. (pres. 1995-96), Kanawha County Bar Assn. (pres. 1980-82, Outstanding Achievement award for meritorious svc. to the legal profession and the cmty. 1995), W.Va. State C. of C. (chmn. workers compensation and unemployment compensation com., bd. dirs., exec. com. mem.), Kiwanis, Masons, Shriners, Order of Coif. Democrat. Methodist. Home: 3 Bendcrest Pl Charleston WV 25314-1510 Office: Jackson & Kelly PO Box 553 1600 Laidley Twr Charleston WV 25322

MCCLAVE, DONALD SILSBEE, professional society administrator; b. Cleve., May 7, 1941; s. Charles Green and Anne Elizabeth (Oakley) McC.; m. Christine Phyllis Mary Tomkins, Feb. 19, 1966; children: Andrew Green, Susan Elizabeth (dec.). BA, Denison U., 1963. Mktg. rsch. officer Bank of Calif., San Francisco, 1966-70; v.p. Cen. Nat. Bank, Chgo., 1970-75; v.p. First Interstate Bank, Portland, Oreg., 1975-77, sr. v.p., 1977-79, exec. v.p., 1979-86; pres., chief exec. officer Portland Met. C. of C., 1987—; instr. Grad. Sch. Mktg. and Strategic Planning, Athens, 1982-84, Pacific Coast Sch. Banking, Seattle, 1976-78. Pres. Oreg. Episc. Sch. Bd., Portland, 1983-84; pres. Assn. Oreg. Industries Found., Salem, 1984-85; pres., co-chmn. Japan-Am. Conf. Mayors and C. of C., Portland, 1985, trustee, 1991—, exec. com., 1992—; trustee YMCA of Columbia-Willamette, 1990-92, Portland Student Svcs. Corp., 1991-93; mem. METRO Urban Growth Mgmt. Adv. Com., 1989-92; mem. adv. com. Downtown Housing Preservation Partnership Adv. Com., 1989-94; mem. City of Portland Mayoral Transition Team, 1992, Mayor's Bus. Roundtable, 1993—; bd. dirs. Oreg. Trail chpt. ARC, 1994-95, Tri-Met, 1994—, chair fin. com., 1995-97, bd. chair, 1997—. Avocations: reading, travel, golf, model building. Office: Portland Met C of C 221 NW 2nd Ave Portland OR 97209-3999

MCCLEARY, BENJAMIN WARD, investment banker; b. Washington, July 9, 1944; s. George William and Nancy (Grim) McC.; m. Dierdre Marsters, May 6, 1967 (div. 1977); children: Benjamin, Katherine; m. Jean Muchmore, Oct. 15, 1984. AB, Princeton U., 1966. With Chemical Bank, N.Y.C., 1969-81; trainee, asst. sec., asst. v.p., v.p. Chemical Bank; sr. v.p. Lehman Bros. Kuhn Loeb, N.Y.C., 1981-83; mng. dir. Shearson Lehman Bros., 1983-87, Shearson Lehman Hutton Internat., London, 1987-88, Shearson Lehman Hutton, Inc., N.Y.C., 1988-89; ptnr. McFarland Dewey & Co., N.Y.C., 1989—; dir. Detrex Corp., Detroit, Harvel Plastics, Easton. Lt. (j.g.) USN, 1966-69. Office: McFarland Dewey & Co 230 Park Ave Rm 1450 New York NY 10169-1499

MCCLEARY, ELLIOTT HAROLD, magazine editor; b. Dixon, Ill., Sept. 12, 1927; s. Harold Elliott and Ruth C. (LieVan) McC.; m. Ann Roberts Morgan, Aug. 18, 1962 (div. 1976); children: Bryan, Heather; m. Patricia Mary Sherburne McCabe, Feb. 10, 1996. BA in English, Beloit Coll., 1952. Asst. editor Popular Mechs. mag., Chgo., 1952-56, Rotarian Mag., Evanston, Ill., 1956-65; editor-in-chief Today's Health mag., Chgo., 1966-69; freelance writer, editor Evanston, 1969-78, 81-82; sr. editor Rand McNally, Skokie, Ill., 1978-81; sr. editor Consumers Digest mag., Chgo., 1983-85, exec. editor, 1986—. Author: New Miracles of Childbirth, 1974; co-author: American Medical Association Book of Heartcare, 1982. With U.S. Army, 1946-48. Mem. Am. Soc. Journalists and Authors (pres. Midwest chpt. 1980, 93-95). Avocation: photography. Home: 2747 Meadowlark Ln Evanston IL 60201-4937

MCCLEARY, HENRY GLEN, geophysicist; b. Casper, Wyo., June 4, 1922; s. Raymond and Wyoma N. (Posey) McCleary Grieve; m. Beryl Tenney Nowlin, May 28, 1950; children: Gail, Glenn, Neil, Paul. Geol. Engr., Colo. Sch. Mines, 1948. From geophysicist to party chief seismic Amoco, various locations, 1948-53; exploration mgr. Woodson Oil Co., Fort Worth, 1953-60; resident mgr. NAMCO, Tripoli, Libya, 1961-62; chief geophysicist to staff geophys. assoc. Amoco Internat. Oil Co., 1963-68, Cairo, London and Buenos Aires, 1963-72, Chgo., 1972-82, Denver, 1982-84, Houston, 1984-86; internat. geophys. cons., 1986—. Served with USN, 1943-46. Named Hon. Admiral Tex. Navy, 1968. Mem. Soc. Exploration Geophysicists, Soc. Petroleum Engrs., AAAS, Houston Gem and Mineral Soc., Profl. Oil People, Sigma Alpha Epsilon, Theta Tau. Republican. Episcopalian. Clubs: Adventurers, Meml. Forest (Houston). Home: 232 Warrenton Dr Houston TX 77024-6226

MCCLEARY, LLOYD E(VERALD), education educator; b. Bradley, Ill., May 10, 1924; s. Hal and Pearl McC.; m. Iva Dene Carter, June 13, 1971; children: Joan Kay, Victoria Lea, Karen Ann. Student, Kans. U., 1941-42; B.S., U. Ill., 1948, M.S., 1950, D.Ed., 1956; postgrad., Sorbonne, Paris, 1946. Tchr., asst. prin. Portland (Oreg.) Public Schs., 1949-51; asst. prin. Univ. High Sch., Urbana, Ill., 1951-52; prin. Univ. High Sch., 1953-56; asst. supt. Evanston Twp. (Ill.) High Sch., 1956-60; assoc. Roosevelt U., 1957-69; mem. faculty U. Mich., summers, 1958-59; prof. ednl. adminstrn. U. Utah, 1969—, chmn. dept., 1969-74; assoc. CFK Ltd. Found., 1971-76; dir. projects in Latin Am. for AID, World Bank, Ford Found., Bolivian Govt.; dir. Nat. Sch. Prin. Study, 1976-79, 86-89, res. project Families in Edn., 1992-94; edn. rep. to Utah People to People Program; Keynoter Asian Conf. Edn., 1985; edn. adviser Office of the Queen, Jordan, 1985-86; advisor Nat. Commn. on Standards in the Principalship; U.S. del. Conf. on Status Children, Senegal, 1994, Yr. of the Family, Malta, 1993; J. Lloyd Trump lectr., New Orleans, 1994. Author: Organizational Analysis X-Change, 1975, Politics and Power in Education, 1976, The Senior High School Principalship, 1980, Educational Administration, Today, 1984, High School Leaders and Their Schools, vols. 1 and 2, 1990, Leadership, 1996; editor Western Hemisphere Edn. Sch. Orgn., 1989—. Served with inf. AUS, 1941-46. Decorated Bronze Star with oak leaf cluster, Army Commendation medal; S.D. Shankland fellow, 1956; Grantee Ford Found., 1968, 72, AID, 1966, 67, 70, 72, 74, 76, CFK Ltd.,

1970-74, Rockefeller Family Found., 1979-80, U.S. Dept. State, 1981, 86-87, U.S. Dept. Def., 1986—; recipient Hatch Prize, 1988-89. Mem. Nat. Assn. Secondary Sch. Prins. (cert. of merit 1978, scholar-in-residence fall 1989, grantee 1969, 77, 86—), Assn. Supervision and Curriculum Devel., Nat. Assn. Elem. Sch. Prins., Phi Delta Kappa, Kappa Delta Pi. Methodist. Home: 1470 Wilton Way Salt Lake City UT 84108-2549 Office: U Utah 339 MBH Salt Lake City UT 84112

MCCLELLAN, BENNETT EARL, producer; b. Sedalia, Mo., Nov. 20, 1952; s. G. Earl and Ruth E. (McQueen) McC.; m. Gail Jones, Sept. 5, 1981; children: Ian Michael, Elizabeth Gayle. MBA, Harvard U., 1981; MFA in Film and TV, UCLA, 1989. Writer, dir. Old Globe Theater, San Diego, 1973-76; artistic dir. Genesis Theater, San Diego, 1977-79; cons. McKinsey & Co., L.A., 1981-87, Arthur D. Little Media & Entertainment Group, Cambridge, Mass., 1987-89; prodn. exec. Hanna-Barbera Prodns., 1990-91; gen. mgr. L.A. Philharmonic Assn., 1992-94, Nicktoons/Games Animation, Studio City, Calif., 1995—. Producer: (TV series) Good News, Bad News, 1988. Paramount fellow Paramount Pictures, 1989; named Outstanding Grad. Student UCLA Alumni Assn., 1990. Mem. Hollywood Radio and TV Soc. (Internat. Broadcasting award 1989), Acad. TV Arts and Scis. Office: Tune N Toonz 209 S Holliston Ave Pasadena CA 91106

MC CLELLAN, CATHARINE, anthropologist, educator; b. York, Pa., Mar. 1, 1921; d. William Smith and Josephine (Niles) McClellan; m. John Thayer Hitchcock, June 6, 1974. A.B. magna cum laude in Classical Archaeology, Bryn Mawr Coll., 1942; Ph.D. (Anthropology fellow), U. Calif. at Berkeley, 1950. Vis. asst. prof. U. Mo. at Columbia, 1952; asst. prof. anthropology U. Wash., Seattle, 1952-56; anthrop. cons. USPHS, Arctic Health Research Center, Alaska, 1956; asst. prof. anthropology, chmn. dept. anthropology Barnard Coll., Columbia U., 1956-61; asso. prof. anthropology U. Wis. at Madison, 1961-65, prof., 1965-83, prof. emeritus, 1983—, John Bascom prof., 1973; vis. lectr. Bryn Mawr (Pa.) Coll., 1954; vis. prof. U. Alaska, 1973, 87. Assoc. editor: Arctic Anthropology, 1961; editor, 1975-82; assoc. editor: The Western Canadian Jour. of Anthropology, 1970-73. Served to lt. WAVES, 1942-46. Margaret Snell fellow AAUW, 1950-51; Am. Acad. Arts and Scis. grantee, 1963-64; Nat. Mus. Can. grantee, 1948-74. Fellow Am. Anthrop. Assn., Royal Anthrop. Inst. Gt. Britain and Ireland, AAAS, Arctic Inst. N.Am.; mem. Am. Ethnol. Soc. (sec.-treas. 1958-59, v.p. 1964, pres. 1965), Kroeber Anthrop. Soc., Am. Folklore Soc., Am. Soc. Ethnohistory (exec. com. 1968-71), Sigma Xi. Various archaeol. and ethnographic field investigations in Alaska and Yukon Territory in Can.

MCCLELLAN, EDWIN, Japanese literature educator; b. Kobe, Japan, Oct. 24, 1925; came to U.S., 1952; s. Andrew and Teru (Yokobori) McC.; m. Rachel Elizabeth Pott, May 28, 1955; children: Andrew Lockwood, Sarah Rose. M.A., U. St. Andrews, Scotland, 1952; Ph.D., U. Chgo., 1957. Instr. English U. Chgo., 1957-59, asst. prof. Japanese lang. and lit., 1959-63, asso. prof., 1963-65, prof., 1965-70, Carl Darling Buck prof., 1970-72, chmn. dept. Far Eastern langs. and civilizations, 1966-72; prof. Japanese lit. Yale U., 1972-79, Sumitomo prof. Japanese studies, 1979—, chmn. dept. East Asian langs. and lits., 1973-82, 88-91, chmn. council humanities, 1975-77, chmn. council East Asian studies, 1979-82; vis. lectr. Far Eastern langs. Harvard U., spring 1965; mem. adv. coun. dept. Oriental studies Princeton U., 1966-71; mem. Com. to Visit East Asian Studies, Harvard U., 1982-88; mem. Am. adv. com. Japan Found., 1985-95; mem. bd. Coun. for Internat. Exch. Scholars, 1981-84. Translator: Kokoro (Natsume Soseki), 1957, Grass on the Wayside (Soseki), 1969, A Dark Night's Passing (Naoya Shiga), 1976, Fragments of a Past (Eiji Yoshikawa), 1992; author: Two Japanese Novelists: Soseki and Toson, 1969, Woman in the Crested Kimono, 1985; mem. bd. editors Jour. Japanese Studies, 1986—; contbr. articles to profl. jours. Bd. trustees Society Japanese Studies U. Wash., 1992—; mem. Com. on Emerson-Thoreau Medal and Am. Acad. Award for Humanistic Studies Am. Acad. Arts and Scis., 1995—. Recipient Kikuchi Kan prize for contbn. to study of Japanese lit., Tokyo, 1994, Noma Lit. Translation prize, 1995. Mem. Am. Acad. Arts and Scis. Home: 641 Ridge Rd Hamden CT 06517-2516

MCCLELLAN, JAMES HAROLD, electrical engineering educator; b. Guam, Oct. 5, 1947; s. Harold James McClellan and Esther Mary (Rosenbach) Matkin; m. Carolyn Frances Monjure, May 31, 1969; children—Amy, Scott. B.S., La. State U., 1969; M.S., Rice U., 1972, Ph.D., 1973. Research staff Lincoln Lab., Lexington, Mass., 1973-75; asst. prof. MIT, Cambridge, 1975-78, assoc. prof., 1978-82; tech. cons. Schlumberger Well Services, Austin, Tex., 1982-87, Ga. Inst. of Tech., 1987—; cons. Lincoln Lab., 1975-82, Lawrence Livermore Nat. Lab., Calif., 1979-82, Schlumberger, 1988-89, MathWorks, Inc., Natick, Mass., 1990—. Author: Number Theory in Digital Signal Processing, 1979, Computer-Based Exercises for Signal Processing, 1994. NSF fellow, 1971-73. Fellow IEEE; mem. Speech and Signal Processing Soc. of IEEE, Tau Beta Pi, Eta Kappa Nu. Home: 5169 Sandlewood Ct Marietta GA 30068-2875 Office: Ga Inst Tech Sch of Elec Engring Atlanta GA 30332-0250

MCCLELLAN, LARRY ALLEN, educator, writer; b. Buffalo, Nov. 3, 1944; s. Edward Lurelle McClellan and Helen (Denison) Greenlee; m. Diane Eunice Bonfoey, Aug. 19, 1973; children: Kara E., Seth C. Student, U. Ghana, 1964-65; BA in Psychology, Occidental Coll., 1966; MTh, U. Chgo., 1969, D Ministry, 1970. Ordained to ministry Presbyn. Ch. (U.S.A.), 1970. Prof. of sociology and community studies Govs. State U., University Park, Ill., 1970-86; interim pastor Presbyn. Ch. (U.S.A.), Chgo. area, 1980-86; sr. pastor St. Paul Community Ch., Homewood, Ill., 1986-96; adj. prof. Govs. State U., University Park, Ill., 1987-96; dir. South Met. Regional Leadership Ctr., Govs. State U., University Park, Ill., 1996—; newspaper columnist Star Publs. Chgo., 1993—; trustee Internat. Coun. Community Chs., 1989-91, pres., 1991-93. Author: Local History South of Chicago, 1988; developer social simulation games; contbr. articles to profl. pubs. Mayor Village of Park Forest South (name now University Park), Ill., 1975-79; co-organizer S. Region Habitat for Humanity, Chgo. area, 1989; pres. S. Suburban Heritage Assn., Chgo. area, 1988-91. Fellow Layne Found., 1966-70, NEH, 1979. Mem. Urban Affairs Assn., Am. Acad. Religion, Assn. for Sociology of Religion, Am. Assn. State and Local History, Ill. State Hist. Soc. (Spl. Achievement award 1989), Chgo. Hist. Soc., South Suburban Ministerial Assn. (pres. 1989-91). Office: Govs State U So Met Regl Leadership Ctr University Park IL 60466

MCCLELLAN, MARY ANN, pediatrics nurse, educator; b. Mar. 29, 1942. BS, Tex. Woman's U., 1964; MN, U. Wash., 1968-69; cert., U. Tex., 1976. Cert. family life educator. Charge nurse Baylor U. Med. Ctr., Dallas, 1964-65; pub. health staff nurse Dallas County Health Dept., Dallas, 1965-68; supervising nurse Okla. State Dept. Health, Oklahoma City, 1969-70, maternal-child health nurse cons., 1971; asst. prof. U. Okla. Coll. Nursing, Oklahoma City, 1971-72; from instr. to asst. prof. Harris Coll. Nursing Tex. Christian U., Ft. Worth, 1972-75; asst. prof. continuing edn. U. Okla. Coll. Nursing, Oklahoma City, 1976-79, asst. prof. baccalaureate program, 1979—, mem. grad. faculty, 1991—; cons. and lectr. in field. Contbr. chpts. to books, articles to profl. jours. Mem. Okla. Family Resources Coalition, Nat. Assn. of Pediatric Nurse Assocs. and Practitioners (Okla. chpt.), So. Early Childhood Assn., Okla. Early Childhood Assn., Sigma Theta Tau., Phi Kappa Phi. Office: U Okla Coll Nursing PO Box 26901 Oklahoma City OK 73126

MCCLELLAN, ROGER ORVILLE, toxicologist; b. Tracy, Minn., Jan. 5, 1937; s. Orville and Gladys (Paulson) McC.; m. Kathleen Mary Dunagan, June 23, 1962; children: Eric John, Elizabeth Christine, Katherine Ruth. DVM with highest honors, Wash. State U., 1960; M of Mgmt, U. N.Mex., 1980. diplomate Am. Bd. Vet. Toxicology, cert. Am. Bd. Toxicology. From biol. scientist to sr. scientist Gen. Electric Co., Richland, Wash., 1957-64; sr. scientist biology dept. Pacific N.W. Labs., Richland, Wash., 1965; scientist med. research br. div. biology and medicine AEC, Washington, 1965-66; asst. dir. research, dir. fission product inhalation program Lovelace Found. Med. Edn. and Research, Albuquerque, 1966-73; v.p., dir. research adminstrn., dir. Lovelace Inhalation Toxicology Research Inst., Albuquerque, 1973-76, pres., dir., 1976-88; chmn. bd. dirs. Lovelace Biomedical and Environ. Research Inst., Albuquerque, 1988; pres., CEO Chem. Industry Inst. Toxicology Research, Triangle Park, N.C., 1988—; mem. research com. Health Effects Inst., 1981-92; bd. dirs. Toxicology Lab. Accreditation Bd., 1982-90, treas., 1984-90; adj. prof. Wash. State U., 1980—, U. Ark., 1970-88; clin. assoc. U. N.Mex., 1971-85, adj. prof. toxicology, 1985—; adj. prof. toxicology and occupational and environ. medicine Duke U., 1988—; adj. prof. toxicology U. N.C. Chapel Hill, 1989—; adj. prof. toxicology N.C. State Univ., 1991—; mem. dose assessment adv. group U.S. Dept. Energy, 1980-87, mem. health and environ. research adv. com., 1984-85; mem. exec. com. sci. adv. bd. EPA, 1974-95, mem. environ. health com., 1980-83, chmn., 1982-83, chmn. radionuclide emissions rev. com., 1984-85, chmn. Clean Air Sci. Adv. Com., 1987-92, chmn. rsch. strategies adv. com., 1992-94; mem. com. on toxicology NAS-NRC, 1979-87, chmn., 1980-87; bd. dirs. Lovelace Anderson Endowment Found.; mem. com. risk assessment methodology for hazardous air pollution NAS-NRC, 1991-94, com. biol. effects of Radon NAS NRC, 1994—; mem. com. on environ. justice Inst. of Medicine, 1996—; pres. Am. Bd. Vet. Toxicology, 1970-73; mem. adv. council Ctr. for Risk Mgmt., Resources for the Future, 1987—; council mem. Nat. Council for Radiation Protection, 1970—; bd. dirs. N.C. Assn. Biomedical Rsch., 1989-91, N.C. Vet. Medical Found., 1990-95, pres., 1993-94; bd. govs. Rsch. Triangle Inst., 1994—. Contbr. articles to profl. jours. Editorial bd. Jour. Toxicology and Environ. Health, 1980—, assoc. editor, 1982—; editorial bd. Fundamental and Applied Toxicology, 1984-89, assoc. editor, 1987-89; editorial bd. Toxicology and Indsl. Health, 1984—; editor CRC Critical Revs. in Toxicology, 1987—; assoc. editor Inhalation Toxicology Jour., 1987—; mem. edit. bd. Regulatory Toxicology and Pharmacology, 1993—. Recipient Herbert E. Stokinger award Am. Conf. Govtl. Indsl. Hygienists, 1985, Alumni Achievement award Wash. State U., 1987, Disting. Assoc. award Dept. Energy, 1987, 88, Arnold Lehman award Soc. Toxicology, 1992; co-recipient Frank R. Blood award Soc. Toxicology, 1989. Fellow AAAS, Am. Acad. Vet. and Comparative Toxicology, Soc. Risk Analysis; mem. Am. Chem. Soc., Inst. Medicine (elected), NAS, Radiation Research Soc. (sec.-treas. 1982-84, chmn. fin. com. 1979-82), Health Physics Soc. (chmn. program com. 1972, Elda E. Anderson award 1974), Soc. Toxicology (v.p.-elect to pres. 1987-90; inhalation specialty sect. v.p. to pres. 1983-86; bd. publs. 1983-86, chmn. 1983-85), Am. Assn. Aerosol Research (bd. dirs. 1982-94, treas. 1986-90, v.p. to pres. 1990-93), Am. Vet. Med. Assn., Gesellschaft fur Aerosolforschung, Sigma Xi, Phi Kappa Phi, Phi Zeta. Republican. Lutheran. Home: 1111 Cuatro Cerros Trl SE Albuquerque NM 87123-4149 also: 2903 Bainbridge Dr Apt Q Durham NC 27713-1448 Office: Chem Industry Inst Toxicology PO Box 12137 Research Triangle Park NC 27709*

MC CLELLAN, WILLIAM MONSON, library administrator, retired; b. Groton, Mass., Jan. 7, 1934; s. James Lewis and Ruth Caldwell (Monson) McC.; m. Jane Muir, Sept. 3, 1955; children—Jennifer, Anne, Margaret, Amy. B.A., Colo. Coll., 1956, M.A., 1961; A.M. in L.S, U. Mich., Ann Arbor, 1959. Music librarian U. Colo., Boulder, 1959-65; dir. Music Library, U. Ill., Urbana, 1965-97; cons. music library resources and services to colls. and univs.; co-dir. Inst. Music Librarianship, Kent State U., 1969. Editor: Music Library Assn. Notes, 1977-82; Contbr. articles to profl. jours. Council on Library Resources fellow, 1976-77. Mem. Internat. Assn. Music Librs., Music. Libr. Assn. (pres. 1971-73, conf. panelist, chmn. stats. subcom. 1990-93). Home: 1701 Gentry Sq Ln #108 Champaign IL 61821-5956 *To commit myself daily to giving and opening myself to others in all professional and other contexts.*

MCCLELLAND, EMMA L., state legislator; b. Springfield, Mo., Feb. 26, 1940; m. Alan McClelland; children: Mike, Karen. BA, U. Mo., 1962. Dir. field office, corp. divsn. Mo. Sec. of State, St. Louis; committeewoman Gravis Township; mem. St. Louis County Rep. Cent. Com., Mo. Rep. State Com.; mem. Mo. State Ho. Rep., 1991—, mem. appropriations, edn., budget, mcpl. corps., rules, joint rules and bills perfected and printed coms. Bd. dirs. Epworth Children's Home, Family Support Network; elder Webster Groves Presbyn. Ch.; mem. Leadership St. Louis. Recipient Silver Svc. award Nat. Soc. Autistic Children, Outstanding Svc. award Am. Assn. Mental Deficiency, Spl. Leadership award for govt. YWCA of St. Louis, Spirit of Enterprise award Mo. C. of C. Mem. Webster Groves C. of C., Pi Lambda Theta. Republican. Presbyterian. Home: 455 Pasadena Ave Webster Grvs MO 63119-3126 Office: Mo Ho of Reps State Capitol Building Jefferson City MO 65101-1556

MCCLELLAND, JAMES LLOYD, psychology educator, cognitive scientist; b. Cambridge, Mass., Dec. 1, 1948; s. Walter Moore and Frances (Shaffer) McC.; m. Heidi Marsha Feldman, May 6, 1978; children: Mollie S., Heather Ann. BA in Psychology, Columbia U., 1970; PhD in Cognitive Psychology, U. Pa., 1975. Asst. prof. dept. psychology U. California, San Diego, 1974-80, assoc. prof., 1980-84; assoc. prof. Carnegie-Mellon U., Pitts., 1984-85, prof. psychology, 1985—, prof. computer sci., 1987—, acting head psychology, 1989-90, co-dir. Ctr. for Neural Basis of Cognition, 1994—; adj. prof. neurosci. U. Pitts., 1995—; vis. scientist dept. psychology and Ctr. Cognitive Sci., MIT, 1982-84; vis. scholar dept. psychology Harvard U., 1982-84; mem. com. on basic rsch. in behavioral and social scis. NRC, 1985, rev. panel for cognition, emotion and personality NIMH, 1983-87, behavioral scis. rsch. br. assessment panel, 1987-88, Cognitive Functional Neurosci., 1995—, chair 1997—; co-organizer NSF workshop on connectionism and cognitive sci., 1986. Author: (with others) Parallel Distributed Processing: Explorations in the Microstructure of Cognition, Vols. I, II, 1986; co-author: A Handbook of Models, Programs, and Exercises, 1988; contbr. numerous articles, reports, book chpts. to profl. publs.; sr. editor Cognitive Sci., 1988-91; mem. editorial bd. Perception and Psychophysics, 1977-82, Jour. of Verbal Learning and Verbal Behavior, 1980-84, Cognitive Sci., 1983-88, Cognitive Neuropsychology, 1983—, (book series) Computational Approaches in Cognitive Sci., 1983—, Cognitive Psychology, 1984—, Jour. Exptl. Psychology: General, 1984-87, Lang. and Cognitive Processes, 1988—, Neural Computation, 1989—. Recipient William W. Cumming prize Columbia U., 1970, Rsch. Scientist Career Devel. award NIMH, 1981-86, 87—; NSF fellow, 1970-73, grantee, 1976-79, 80-84, 86-87, 88—; grantee Office Naval Rsch., 1982-87. Fellow AAAS, APA (Disting. Sci. Contbn. award 1996); mem. Cognitive Sci. Soc. (governing bd. 1988—, chmn. 1991), Psychonomics Soc., Internat. Assn. for Study Attention and Performance (governing bd. 1986—, lectr. 1986), Soc. Exptl. Psychologists (Warren medal 1993), Soc. for Neuroscience, Phi Beta Kappa. Office: Ctr Neural Basis of Cognition 115 Mellon Inst 4400 5th Ave Pittsburgh PA 15213-2617

MCCLELLAND, NORMAN P., food products executive. Ceo., chmn. Shamrock Foods Co., Phoenix, Ariz., 1949—. Office: Shamrock Foods Co 2228 N Black Canyon Hwy Phoenix AZ 85009-2707*

MC CLELLAND, ROBERT NELSON, surgeon, educator; b. Gilmer, Tex., Nov. 20, 1929; s. Robert Hilton and Verna Louise (Nelson) McC.; m. Connie Logan, May 5, 1958; children: Robert Christopher, Alison, Julie. B.A., U. Tex., Austin, 1952; M.D., U. Tex., Galveston, 1954. Diplomate Am. Bd. Surgery. Rotating intern U. Kans. Med. center, 1954-55; resident in gen. surgery Parkland Hosp., Dallas, 1957-59, 60-62; instr. surgery Southwestern Med. Sch., U. Tex., Dallas, 1962-63; asst. prof. Southwestern Med. Sch., U. Tex., 1963-67, asso. prof., 1967-71, prof., 1971—, Alvin Baldwin prof. surgery, 1977—; examiner Nat. Bd. Med. Examiners. Editor Audio Jour. Rev. Gen. Surgery, 1971-82, Selected Readings in Gen. Surgery, 1974—; contbr. numerous articles to profl. jours., chpts. to books. Served to capt. M.C. USAF, 1955-57. Fellow ACS (mem. grad. edn. com.); mem. AMA, Am. Surg. Assn., Western Surg. Assn., Soc. Surgery of Alimentary Tract, Am. Gastroent. Assn., Southwestern Surg. Soc., So. Surg. Assn., Dallas Soc. Gen. Surgeons (pres. 1987-88), Tex. Surg. Soc., Tex. Med. Assn., Dallas County Med. Soc., Soc. Internatale de Chiurgie (bd. dirs. Am. chpt.), Phi Beta Kappa, Alpha Omega Alpha. Republican. Lutheran. Home: 3601 Potomac Ave Dallas TX 75205-2110 Office: 5323 Harry Hines Blvd Dallas TX 75235-7208

MCCLELLAND, TIMOTHY REID, baseball umpire; b. Jackson, Mich., Dec. 12, 1951; s. Richard Nathan and Geraldine Betty (Donaldson) McC.; m. Sandra Ann Seltz; children: Cole, Molly, Maggie. BS, Mich. State U., 1974, MA, 1975. Umpire Fla. State League of Minor League Baseball, Lakeland, 1976-77, So. League of Minor League Baseball, Montgomery, Ala., 1978, P.R. Baseball League, 1979, 80, Am. Assn. Minor League Baseball, Wichita, Kans., 1979-82, Am. League of Profl. Baseball, N.Y.C., 1983—. Mentor Valley H.S., West Des Moines, 1993-94; playing Santa Claus to orgns. Mem. Major League Umpires Assn. Mem. Lutheran Ch. Mo. Synod. Umpire Major League All-Star Game, Houston, 1986, Am. League Championship Series, Boston, Oakland, Calif., 1988, World Series of Profl. Baseball, Toronto, Can., Phila., 1993, Am. League Championship Series, Cleve., Seattle, 1995. Home: 5405 Woodland Ave West Des Moines IA 50266-7259 Office: Am League Profl Baseball 350 Park Ave New York NY 10022-6022

MCCLELLAND, W. CLARK, retail company financial executive; b. Detroit, Feb. 6, 1939; s. Fauvia McClelland; m. Marjorie Mele; children: Michael, Troy, Cory, Deborah. Grad., Elizabethtown Coll., 1965. Acct. Coopers and Lybrand, Phila., 1967-70; treas., chief fin. officer Heilig Meyers Corp., Richmond, Va., 1970-74; dir., chief fin. officer Gas Spring Corp., Montgomeryville, Pa., 1974-75; exec. v.p., CFO Hechinger Co., Landover, Md., 1975—. Mem. AICPA, Nat. Capital Group Fin. Execs. Inst. Office: Hechinger Co 1801 Mccormick Dr Upper Marlboro MD 20774-5326

MCCLELLAND, WILLIAM CRAIG, paper company executive; b. Orange, N.J., Apr. 21, 1934; s. William N. and Pauline (Lee) McC.; m. Alice Garrett, Dec. 28, 1956; children: Suzanne, Alice Elizabeth, Heather. BS in Econs., Princeton U., 1956; MBA, Harvard U., 1965. Salesman, branch mgr. PPG Industries, Cleve. and Erie, Pa., 1960-63; pres. Watervliet Paper Co. div. Hammermill Paper Co., Mich., 1969-73; product, mktg. mgr. Hammermill Paper Co., Erie, Pa., 1965-69, v.p., 1973-80, sr. v.p., 1980-83, exec. v.p., dir., 1983-85, pres., CEO, 1985-88, also bd. dirs.; sr. v.p. Internat. Paper Co., 1986-87, exec. v.p., 1987-88, also bd. dirs.; exec. v.p. Union Camp Corp., Wayne, N.J., 1988-89, chmn., pres., COO, 1989—, now chmn., CEO, 1996—; bd. dirs. Quaker State Corp., PNC Fin. Corp., Allegheny Ludlum Corp. Mem. Coun. Fellows, Behrend Coll. of Pa. State U., 1980-88; dir. Pitts. Theol. Seminary, 1988—. Lt. (j.g.) USN, 1956-59. Home: 7 Ridge Crest Rd Saddle River NJ 07458-3107*

MCCLENAHAN, MARY TYLER FREEMAN, civic and community volunteer; b. Richmond, Va., Apr. 6, 1917; d. Douglas Southall and Inez Virginia (Goddin) Freeman; m. Leslie Cheek Jr., June 3, 1939 (dec. Dec. 1992); children: Leslie III, Richard Warfield, Elizabeth Cheek Morgan; m. John Lorimer, Aug. 14, 1993. AB, Vassar Coll., 1937; LHD (hon.), St. Paul's Coll., 1977, Washington and Lee U., 1983, Va. Commonwealth U., 1993, Hollins Coll., 1993; HHD (hon.), U. Richmond, 1985. Author: (religious booklet) Death, The Key to Life, 1982, (hist. booklet, with Alonzo T. Dill) A Visit to Stratford and the Story of the Lees, 1986; (biographical booklet) Douglas Southall Freeman: Reflections By His Daughter, His Research Associates and a Historian, 1986; contbr. articles to mags. Active Robert E. Lee Meml. Assn., Stratford, Va., 1964-95, hon. dir., 1995—; dame, bd. govs. Order of Hosp. St. John, N.Y.C., 1984—; bd. dirs. Maymont Found., 1982—, Va. Cmty. Devel. Corp., 1989—, Trees for Richmond, 1991—, Caucus for Future Ctrl. Va., 1992—, (hon.) Va. League Planned Parenthood (Outstanding Svc. award), 1952—; bd. dirs., exec. com. Richmond Renaissance, 1982-96; former bd. dirs., chair, mem. adv. bd. Coun. Am.'s First Freedom; trustee Va. Union U., Richmond, 1985—, Va. Hist. Soc. (hon.), Black History Mus. and Cultural Ctr. of Va., Hist. Richmond Found.; chair, founder Richmond Better Housing Coalition, 1989—; vice chair Conserve Va.; mem. pres.'s coun. So. Environ. Law Ctr.; adv. bd. ARC, 1992—, Christian Children's Fund, 1993-95; adv. com. Girl Scouts U.S., Va; mem. nat. com. Jefferson Poplar Forest Fund. Recipient Mary Mason Anderson Williams Preservation award Assn. Preservation Va. Antiquities, 1977, Barbara Ransome Andrews disting. vol. award Jr. League Richmond, 1982, Fair Housing award Housing Opportunities Made Equal, 1983, Brotherhood award Nat. Conf. Christians and Jews, 1983, Human Rels. award, 1984, Ten Outstanding Women award YWCA-Richmond, 1986, Sallie Wilson Peake Meml. award Housing Opportunities Made Equal, 1987, Charlotte J. Washington cmty. svc. award Richmond Urban League, 1988, Archtl. medal Am. Inst. Architects, 1991, Liberty Bell award Richmond Bar Assn., 1991, Faith in Action award Va. Coun. Churches, 1992, Outstanding Citizen award Civitan Club, 1992, Hope award Nat. Multiple Sclerosis, 1994; named Richmonder of Yr. STYLE mag., 1990, Va. Women Hall Fame Va. Coun. on Status Women, 1991. Mem., founder, chair (hon.) Richmond Urban Forum; mem. Women's Club of Richmond, Cosmopolitan Club, The Acorn Club of Phila., Hroswitha Club, James River Garden Club, Va. Writer's Club, Richmond First Club (Good Govt. award, 1987), Omicron Delta Kappa, Phi Beta Kappa. Democrat. Episcopalian. Avocations: writing, literature, hist. preservation, gardening, urban devel. Home: 4703 Pocahontas Ave Richmond VA 23226

MCCLENDON, EDWIN JAMES, health science educator; b. Troy, Okla., Dec. 3, 1921; s. Charles Wesley and Mattie (Reed) McC.; m. Ruby Wynona Scott, May 5, 1950; children: Edwin James Jr., Melody Jan, Joy Renee. B.S., Okla. East Central State U., 1946; M.Ed., U. Okla., 1954; Ed.D., Wayne State U., Detroit, 1964. Instr. U. Okla., Norman, 1946-47; head speech dept., tchr. Wewoka High Sch., Okla., 1947-49; assoc. dir. Tb Control, Oklahoma City, 1949-51; dir. sch health project Okla. Dept. Health and Edn., Oklahoma City, 1951-54; assoc. dir. Tb Control, Wayne County, Mich., 1954-56; dir. sch. health Wayne County, Mich., 1956-63; dir. secondary edn. Wayne County Intermediate Sch., Detroit, 1963-67; supt. schs. Highland Park, Mich., 1967-68; v.p. Highland Park Coll., Mich., 1968-69; asst. supt. health Mich. Dept. Edn., Lansing, 1969-71; prof., chmn. health edn. U. Mich., Ann Arbor, 1971-88, prof. health behavior and pub. health, 1971-88, prof. emeritus, 1988—; cons. pub. health care, 1985—; cons. WHO, 1978-89, dir. field study for Western Pacific, 1981; health field study of Arabic states, 1979-80; cons., Papua, New Guinea, Japan, Korea, Philippines, 1983-84, Fiji and Malaysia, 1987-88. Author Drug Education-A Teacher's Guide, 1969, Maxi Minds in Mini Cages, The Gifted, 1972, HEalthful Living for Today and Tomorrow, 1981, Health and Wellness, 1987, Evaluation Study of Growing Healthy, 1993; contbr. 60 articles to profl. publs. Chmn. bd. dirs. Am. Cancer Soc., Detroit, 1977-78, mem. nat. pub. edn. com., 1969-83, hon. life mem., 1980—; mem. adv. coun. alcohol abuse NIH, 1976-80; pres. Plymouth-Canton Sch. Bd., 1974-78, 82-91; Tax Rev. Bd., Plymouth, Mich., 1980-85; chmn. Jr. Red Cross S.E. Mich., 1969-73; chmn., cons. Polio Plus immunization campaign, WHO, Rotary Internat; bd. dirs. ARC S.E. Mich., 1992—, exec. com., 1993—, mem. health, safety, youth and internat. coms. Served with USN, 1942-46. Decorated Bronze Star; recipient Disting. Health Edn. award Cen. Mich. U., 1978; adminstrn. bldg. Plymouth-Canton (Mich.) schs. dedicated E. J. McClendon Edn. Ctr., 1992. Fellow Am. Pub. Health Assn., Am. Sch. Health Assn. (pres. 1970-71, Disting. Service award 1962, William A. Howe award 1976), Am. Cancer Soc. (hon. life mem., bd. dirs.), Royal Soc. Health; mem. NEA, AAUP, Mich. Sch. Health Assn. (hon. life mem., Disting. service award 1967, Golden Anniversary award 1985), Am. Social Health Assn. (dir.), Nat. Assn. Curriculum and Devel., Am. Venereal Disease Assn., Alliance Advancement Health Edn., Soc. Pub. Health Edn., Soc. Sex Educators and Counselors, Nat. Council for Internat. Health, Am. Assn. for WHO, Soc. Native Am. Indians, Rotary (pres. 1989-91), Phi Delta Kappa. Democrat. Methodist. Home and Office: 40742 Crabtree Ln Plymouth MI 48170-2742

MCCLENDON, FRED VERNON, real estate professional, business consultant, equine and realty appraiser, financial consultant; b. Vernon, Tex.; s. Guy C. and Lexie M. (Johnson) Mc C.; m. Dorothy J. Seibert, June 1943 (div. 1953); children: Cathy, Kent, Tracy; m. Ethel R. Cherry, Sept. 15, 1959; children: Tess, Rob, J.T. Assoc. in Commerce, Hannibal La Grange Coll., 1947; BBA, Baylor U., 1949; MBA, Harvard U., 1951, postgrad. in law, 1951; postgrad. in banking, Colo. U., 1951-52; postgrad., Denver U., 1951-52. Lic. ins. agt., Tenn.; cert. real estate broker, Tenn.; sr. cert. valuer. Asst. cashier U.S. Nat. Bank, Denver, 1951; gen. mgr. Nat. Paper Band Co., Denver, 1952-53; personnel mgr. Houston Fire & Casualty Co., Ft. Worth, 1954-56; gen. sales mgr. City Lincoln/Mercury, Dallas, 1957-58; owner INS-Bank Personnel Agy., Dallas, 1959-61; mng. ptnr. Allen & Mc Clendon Ins., Dallas, 1959-63; owner, broker Mc Clendon Real Estate, Dallas, 1959-63; pres. Mc Clendon Realty Co., Hampton, Tenn., 1961—; gen. mgr. Eagle Nest Ranch, Roan Mountain, Tenn., 1963-88, Mile High Ranch, Roan Mountain, 1988—; pres. FMV Appraisal Co., Hampton, 1988—; cons. Gen. Adjustments Bur., 1981—, Debourdieux Corp., 1985—, Wachesaw Corp., 1985—, Hidden Lakes Devel. Corp., various ins. cos. and law firms in U.S. and Can., IRS, U.S. Marshals Svc., U.S. Customs, 1993—; exec. cons. El Dorado Ranch, 1991—; cons. IRS; lectr. to lodges and assns.; gen. ptnr. Flexnet Investments, Ltd., Dallas, 1988—; pres. Bus. Realty Internat. Cons., Roan Mountain, Tenn., 1990—; exec. v.p. OmniVue, Inc., S.C., 1992—; chmn. AmeriFund Ventures, Inc., Tenn., 1995—; pres. U.S. Med-Am. Fin. Svcs., 1995—. Contbr. articles to profl. jours. Recipient W.T. Grant fellow Harvard U., 1950-51. Mem. Am. Quarter Horse Assn. (life), Australian Appaloosa Assn., Appaloosa Horse Club U.S., Tenn. Walking Horse

Breeders Assn., Am. Paint Horse Assn., Am. Soc. Equine Appraisers, Am. Horse Coun., Am. Soc. Appraisers (Accredited sr. appraiser, bd. examiners 1990—), Internat. Real Estate Inst., Nat. Assn. Real Estate Appraisers, Environ. Assessment Assoc. (cert. insp. 1991—), Appraisers Assn. Am. (cert. sr. appraiser). Republican. Mem. Seventh Day Adventists. Avocations: boating, travel, fishing, swimming. Home: Mile High Ranch PO Box 190 Roan Mountain TN 37687-0190 Office: FMV Appraisal Co PO Box 330 Hampton TN 37658-0330

MCCLENDON, SARAH NEWCOMB, news service executive, writer; b. Tyler, Tex., July 8, 1910; d. Sidney Smith and Annie Rebecca (Bonner) McClendon; 1 child, Sally Newcomb Mac Donald. Grad., Tyler Jr. Coll., U. Mo. Mem. staff Tyler Courier-Times and Tyler Morning Telegraph, 1931-39; reporter Beaumont (Tex.) Enterprise; Washington corr. Phila. Daily News, 1944; founder McClendon News Svc., Washington, 1946—; talk show host Ind. Broadcasters Network; lectr. Faneuil Hall, Boston, Poor Richard's Club, Phila., Cobo Hall, Detroit, Chautauqua Instn., N.Y., Comstock Club, Sacremento, others; adv. to Senior Beacon; v.p. Nat. Press Club, hostess Study Group, 1991—. Author: My Eight Presidents, 1978 (1st prize), Mr. President, Mr. President! My Fifty Years of Covering the White House, 1996; contbr. articles to mags. including Esquire, Penthouse, Diplomat; TV appearances include Merv Griffin Show, Tomorrow, Inside the White House, PBS, NBC Meet the Press, KUP Show, NBC Today Show, C-Span, CNN, Fox Morning News, Late Night with David Letterman, Michael Jackson Show (L.A. radio). Mem. VA Adv. Bd. on Women Vets, def. adv. com. Women in the Svcs.; army advisor, mem. task force Women in the Army Policy Rev.; bd. dir. Sam Rayburn Libr., In Our Own Way, So. Poverty Relief Orgn. Served with WAC. Recipient Woman of Achievement award Tex. Press Women, 1978, 2d prize Nat. Fedn. Press Women, 1979, Headliner award Women in Comm., 1st Pres. award for Journalism in Washington, Nat. Fedn. Press Women, Pub. Rels. award Am. Legion, Bob Considine award, 1990, Am. Woman award Women's Rsch. Edn. Inst., 1991. Mem. DAR (Nat. Constn. award 1990), U. Mo. Alumni Assn. (chpt. pres.), Women in Comm. (Margaret Caskey award), Am. Legion (post comdr.), Nat. Woman's Party (v.p.), Nat. Coun., Soc. Profl. Journalists (Hall of Fame Washington chpt.), Nat. Press Club (v.p.), Am. Newspaper Women's Club (pres.), Capitol Hill First Friday Club (pres.). Club: Capitol Hill First Friday (pres.). *After covering eleven presidents, I still feel that I am my own self, honest and owned by no one. I believe that journalism is a public trust and that I must uphold that public trust.*

MC CLENDON, WILLIAM HUTCHINSON, III, lawyer; b. New Orleans, Feb. 19, 1933; s. William H. and Eleanor (Eaton) McC.; m. Eugenia Mills Slaughter, Feb. 6, 1960; children: William Hutchinson, IV, Virginia Morris, Eleanor Eaton, Bryan Slaughter. B.A., Tulane U., 1956, LL.B., 1958. Bar: La. 1958, U.S. Supreme Ct. 1964. Atty. Humble Oil & Refining Co., 1958-60; with firm Taylor, Porter, Brooks & Phillips, Baton Rouge, 1960—; ptnr. Taylor, Porter, Brooks & Phillips, 1966—; instr. comml. law and negotiable instruments Am. Inst. Banking, 1963-74; lectr. movable Property La. Bar Assn. Bridging the Gap Inst., 1965; lectr. La. State U. LAw Sch. and Real Estate Seminar chmn., 1972, 74, 76, 80, 82, 85, 87, 95, La. Soc. of Profl. Surveying, 1989, La. Soc. CPA's, 1991, Banking Seminar, 1995; adj. prof. La. State U. Legal Negotiation, 1983—. Contbr. articles to legal jours. Bd. dirs. Cancer Soc. Baton Rouge, 1968-71; trustee Episcopal High Sch., 1976-78; mem. Dean's council Tulane U. Law Sch., 1984-88. Served to capt. AUS. Mem. ABA, Am. Judicature Soc., La. Bar Assn. (chmn. sect. trust estates, probate and immovable property law 1969-70, Meml. award article 1987), Baton Rouge Bar Assn. (chmn. title standards com. 1968-69), Tulane Alumni Assn. Greater Baton Rouge (pres. 1968-69), Baton Rouge Green (bd. dirs. 1991-93), Hilltop Aboretum (bd. dirs. 1993-95), La. Civil Svc. League (pres. 1992-94), La. Tulane Law Alumni (treas., 2d v.p. 1964-65), Kappa Alpha. Republican. Episcopalian (vestry, sr. warden 1975, 81, 84, diocesan standing com. 1985-89). Clubs: Baton Rouge Assembly (treas. 1983); Toastmasters (Baton Rouge) (pres. 1970), Baton Rouge Country (Baton Rouge), Camelot (Baton Rouge); Pickwick (New Orleans). Lodge: Rotary (bd. dirs. Baton Rouge club 1972). Home: Oakland at Gurley 6165 Highway 963 Ethel LA 70730-3615 Office: 451 Florida St Fl 8 Baton Rouge LA 70801-1700

MC CLENNEN, LOUIS, lawyer, educator; b. Cambridge, Mass., May 29, 1912; s. Edward F. and Mary (Crane) Mc C.; m. Miriam Jacobs, Apr. 25, 1969; children by previous marriage: Adams, James, Helen, Persis, Crane, Emery. AB cum laude, Harvard U., 1934, JD, 1937. Bar: Mass. 1937, Ind. 1940, Ariz. 1946. Practice in Boston, 1937-39, Indpls., 1940-42, Phoenix, 1946—; now pres. McClennen & Fels, P.C.; adj. prof. law (fed. taxation) Ariz. State U., 1974-80, pres. Law Soc., 1981-83. Author: (with others) Arizona Estate Tax, 1953, (with J.T. Melczer Jr.) Arizona Income Tax Regulations, 1954; contbr. articles to profl. mags. Pres. Ariz. Bd. Edn., 1965-69; trustee No. Ariz. Mus.; past pres., bd. dirs. Maricopa County Legal Aid Soc., Phoenix Symphony Assn.; v.p., bd. dirs. Phoenix United Fund; sec., bd. dirs. Phoenix Country Day Sch.; bd. dirs. Ariz. Acad.; regional dir. Harvard Alumni Assn. Maj. USAAF, 1942-46. Mem. ABA, Ariz. Bar Assn., Maricopa County Bar Assn. (dir., past v.p.), Harvard Law Sch. Assn. (v.p.) Lawyers Club Phoenix (pres.), Phoenix Country Club, Eastward Ho Country Club (Chatham, Mass.). Unitarian. Home and Office: 5311 N La Plaza Cir Phoenix AZ 85012-1415

MC CLENNEY, BYRON NELSON, community college administrator; b. San Antonio, Dec. 14, 1939; s. Thomas B. and Lorene Holley McC.; children: Mark Nelson, Don Alan; m. Kay McCullough, May 17, 1986. BS, U. Tex., 1961, MEd, 1963, EdD, 1969. Asst. dean evening divsn. San Antonio Coll., 1966-68; dean instrn. McLennan C.C., Waco, Tex., 1968-70; dean instrn. Eastfield Coll., Dallas County, Tex., 1970-71, pres., 1971-78; pres. Parkersburg (W.Va.) C.C., 1978-81, San Antonio C.C. Dist., 1981; chancellor Alamo C.C. Dist., 1982-86; pres. C.C. Denver, 1986—; cons. Ctr. for Higher Edn. Mgmt. Sys. Author: Management for Productivity, 1980. NDEA fellow, 1965-66; recipient Disting. Alumni award U. Tex. Coll. Edn., 1982-83, Thomas J. Peters Nat. Leadership award League for Innovation, 1989. Mem. Am. Assn. Cmty. and Jr. Colls. (chmn. pres.'s acad. 1983-84, mem. urban commn. 1987-90), Commn. on Instns. of Higher Edn., Rotary (past dist. gov.). Presbyterian. Club: Rotary (past dist. gov.). Office: Community Coll Denver PO Box 173363 Denver CO 80217-3363*

MCCLENON, JOHN RAYMOND, chemistry educator; b. Grinnell, Iowa, May 1, 1937; s. Raymond Benedict and Erika (Weber) McC.; m. Mary Alice Thornton, June 7, 1959; children: Anne Jeanette, Marca Kay, Maureen. B.A., Grinnell Coll., 1959; Ph.D., UCLA, 1964. Asst. prof. Milton Coll., Wis., 1963-65; asst. prof. chemistry Sweet Briar (Va.) Coll., 1965-72, assoc. prof., 1972-76, prof., 1976-82, Charles A. Dana prof., 1982—; head FBN Microcomputing, Lynchburg, Va., 1980—, Johnny McClenon Big Band, Lynchburg, Va., 1978—. Editor: (newsletter) Macintosh User's Group, Sweet Briar Coll. Chmn. ACLU local chpt., 1966-75; prin. clarinettist Lynchburg Symphony, Va., 1976—. Mem. Am. Chem. Soc., AAUP (chmn. Sweet Briar chpt. 1982-83). Democrat. Unitarian. Home: 712 Riverside Dr Lynchburg VA 24503-1327 Office: Sweet Briar Coll PO Box 73 Sweet Briar VA 24595-0073

MCCLIMON, TIMOTHY JOHN, lawyer; b. Clinton, Iowa, July 17, 1953; s. Leonard James and Celeste Margaret (Borman) McC.; m. Suzanne Berman, Jan. 30, 1994. BA magna cum laude, Luther Coll., 1975; MS, St. Cloud State U., 1976; JD, Georgetown U., 1986. Bar: N.Y. 1987. Asst. dir. student activities St. Cloud (Minn.) State U., 1975-76; performing arts coordinator Western Ill. U., Macomb, 1976-79; program specialist Nat. Endowment for the Arts, Washington, 1979-82, program adminstr., 1982-86, law clk., 1985-86; assoc. Webster and Sheffield, N.Y.C., 1986-88; v.p. AT&T Found., N.Y.C., 1988-96, exec. dir., 1996—; adj. prof. NYU, 1990—; bd. dirs. Marie Cunningham Dance Found., N.Y.C., Second Stage Theatre, N.Y.C., Theatre Comms. Group, N.Y.C., Field Papers, Inc., N.Y.C., Performance Space 122, N.Y.C.; speaker Confs. on Arts Mgmt., 1979—; cons. NEA, Washington, 1986—; mem. mayor's cultural affairs adv. commn. City of N.Y.C., 1992-94. Author: (textbook chpt.) Audiences and the Arts, 1981; contbr. articles to Jour. of Law and the Arts, 1986, other publs., 1989—. Recipient Eagle Scout award Boy Scouts Am., 1967, Faculty award Blue Key Nat. Honor Frat., 1979. Mem. N.Y.C. Bar Assn. (com. mem. 1987-92), ABA (com. mem. 1986-88), N.Y. State Bar Assn., Vol. Lawyers for the Arts. Avocations: photography, tennis, bicycling, traveling, reading. Home: Penthouse 2-C 222 Riverside Dr New York NY 10025-6809 Office: AT&T Found Ste 3100 1301 Avenue Of The Americas New York NY 10019-6022

MCCLINTIC, FRED FRAZIER, simulation engineer; b. Chester, Pa., Aug. 15, 1948; s. Fred F. and Maxene Mary (Felter) McC.; m. Janet Mary DeVitis, May 23, 1970; children: Shannon Janet, Sharon Marie. BS in Engring., Widener U., Chester, Pa., 1970; MS in Indsl. Engring., Tex. A&M U., 1972. Ops. rsch. analyst U.S. Army Civil Svc., Ft. Knox, Ky., 1970-78; prof. wargaming U.S. Army War Coll., Carlisle, Pa., 1978-83, tech. dir. dept. wargaming, 1978-83; pres. McClintic Wargaming Inc., Media, Pa., 1983-85; sr. assoc. CACI, Mechanicsburg, Pa., 1985-86; lead scientist Computer Scis. Corp., Moorestown, N.J., 1986-89; mgr. rsch. and devel. Lockheed Martin, Orlando, Fla., 1989—. Author: The Armor Development Plan, 1976-78; (wargames) McClintic Theater Model, 1979, VII Corps Model, 1981, Warrior Preparation Model, 1983, TACAIR, 1975. Mem. TAu Beta Pi, Sigma Pi Sigma, Alpha Pi Mu, Phi Kappa Phi, Alpha Chi. Roman Catholic. Achievements include tech. leadership in Army, Navy and Air Force interactive simulations, models and wargames; designing and setup of USAF Warrior Preparations Ctr. Models derived from work include JTLS, JESS, CBS, JOINTWARS, and others; lead scientist for Enhanced Naval Wargaming System. Home: 1491 Warner Dr Chuluota FL 32766-8816

MCCLINTIC, HOWARD GRESSON, foundation executive; b. Pitts., Feb. 27, 1951; s. Stewart and Pamela Mary (Gresson) McC.; m. Katherine Davis Foss, Sept. 14, 1948; children: Margaret Gresson, Katherine Davis, Henry Stewart. BA in Polit. Sci./Econs., George Washington U., 1973. Legis. asst. U.S. Sen. Howard H. Baker, Washington, 1973-75; assoc. cons. Energy Decisions, Inc., Washington, 1975-78; energy policy analyst Chem. Sys., Inc., N.Y.C., 1978-80; sr. cons. Coal Use Group, Inc., Washington, 1980-83; staff officer NAS, Washington, 1983-87; exec. dir. The Jefferson Energy Found., Washington, 1987—; spl. cons. NAS, 1973-74, Law Offices of Dudley & Warner, N.Y.C., 1979, Internat. Bus. Counsellors, Washington, 1982, Japan Nat. Oil Co., Washington, 1983. Co-editor: NAS Com. Rept., Oceans in Year 2000, 1974, staff coord. reprts., 1984, 86; exec. prodr. energy films, 7-part PBS series, 1997—, Clean Cities: The Future of Alternatively Fueled Vehicles, sponsored by U.S. Energy Dept. and GM; Everything Starts with Energy, Energy Policy on Trial, Future Energy Sources, Double Jeopardy, Access to Public Lands and Waters, Nuclear Waste and the West, White Price Cheap Oil?, The Emerging National Energy Strategy. Co-founder Decade Soc., Washington, 1979-83; coord. Washingtonians for Bush, 1983; chmn. subcom. U.S. Dept. Energy, 1988; assoc. mem. Naval War Coll. Found. Mem. Am. Energy Assurance Coun. (advisor 1988—), Internat. Assn. Energy Economists, Atlantic Coun. U.S. (participant energy study 1989), Rolling Rock Club, Mid-Ocean Club (Bermuda), Gibson Island Club, Chevy Chase Club, Potomac Boat Club. Republican. Episcopalian. Avocations: skiing, golf, tennis, sailing. Home: 5115 Palisade Ln NW Washington DC 20016-5337 Office: The Jefferson Energy Found Connecticut Ave NW 12th Fl Washington DC 20036-9999

MC CLINTOCK, ARCHIE GLENN, lawyer; b. Sheridan, Wyo., Mar. 26, 1911; s. James Porter and Martie E. (Glenn) McC.; m. Ina Jean Robinson, May 27, 1939 (dec. 1974); children: Ellery, Jeffry, Kathleen. B.A., U. Wyo., 1933, LLB with honor, 1935. Bar: Wyo. 1935, Calif. 1982. Pvt. practice law Cheyenne, Wyo., 1935-73, 81-83, 87—; justice Wyo. Supreme Ct., Cheyenne, 1973-81; atty. gen. State of Wyo., 1982-87; semi-ret.; adj. prof. law U. Wyo., 1988, 90-92. Mem. Wyo. Fair Employment Practices Commn., 1965-71. Served with USNR, 1944-45. Mem. Wyo. State Bar (pres. 1950-51), Am. Judicature Soc., Order of Coif (hon. mem.) Sigma Nu. Democrat. Club: Elks. Home: 1211 Richardson Ct Cheyenne WY 82001-2424

MCCLINTOCK, DONNA MAE, social worker; b. Confluence, Pa., Aug. 4, 1954; d. Everett and Mayalene (Newcomer) McC. AA, Garrett Community Coll., 1974; BS, Frostburg State U., 1976; MSW, W.Va. U., 1983. ACSW; lic. clin. social worker, Md. Dir. job readiness program, vocat. counselor Western Md. Consortium, Oakland, 1979-83; social worker Thomas B. Finan Ctr., Cumberland, 1983-84; coord. geriatric edn. svcs., social worker Garrett County Health Dept., Oakland, 1984—. Group leader Alzheimer's/Dementia Support Group, Oakland, 1987—. Mem. NASW, We. Md. Geriatric Social Workers, Garrett and Allegany County Social Work Caucus, Garrett County Bus. and Profl. Women's Club, W.Va. U. Alumni Assn. Lutheran. Avocations: travel, reading. Office: Garrett County Health Dept 253 N 4th St Oakland MD 21550-1334

MCCLINTOCK, EUGENE JEROME, minister; b. San Diego, Calif., Jan. 25, 1924; s. Alberta Jerome and Gladys Elizabeth (Wilsie) McC.;m. Lena LaVerne Brown, Feb. 16, 1947; children: Nathan-Calvin, Joseph, Mark. Student, Caldwell Seminary, 1942-45; BTh, Pentecostal Bible Inst., 1951. Ordained to ministry United Pentecostal Ch. Pastor United Pentacostal Ch., Twin Falls, Idaho, 1945-47, 1st Pentecostal Ch., Aberdeen, Miss., 1949-60, Dupo (Ill.) Pentecostal Ch., 1960-64, Calvary Apostolic Ch., Mt. Vernon, Ill., 1964-79; gen. sec. Sunday sch. United Pentecostal Ch., St. Louis, 1979-82, gen. dir. Sunday sch., 1982—; part time instr. Pentecostal Bible Inst., Tupelo, Miss., 1950-60. Author: Achieving Excellence in the Sunday School, Vols. I, II, III, IV, 1992; editor Christian Educator, 1982-94. Active ministerial fellowship, Aberdeen, Miss., 1950-60, Dupo, 1960-64, Mt. Vernon, 1964-79. Avocations: golf, photography, travel, writing. Office: United Pentecostal Ch Internat 1968 Graystone Dr Saint Charles MO 63303-4662

MCCLINTOCK, GEORGE DUNLAP, lawyer; b. Pocatello, Idaho, Nov. 30, 1920; s. George Dunlap and Jessie (McCabe) McC.; m. Aileen McHugh, Sept. 19, 1945; children—Jessie Kelly, Catharine, George, Jane Wyatt, Michael, Anne. A.B. cum laude, Dartmouth Coll., 1942; LL.B., Harvard U., 1948. Bar: Minn. 1948. Ptnr. Faegre & Benson, Mpls., 1948-90; dir. Merchants Bank, Rugby, N.D.; trustee Douglas Rees Trust, 1966—, Paul R. Held Testamentary Trusts, 1980—. Trustee, mayor City of Woodland, Minn., 1970-79; exec. bd., Viking council Boy Scouts Am., Mpls., 1959-74, pres., 1966-67; gen. campaign chmn. United Way of Mpls., 1972, bd. dirs., 1973-81, pres., 1976; trustee Convent of Visitation Sch., St. Paul, 1975-81; trustee North Meml. Med. Ctr., Robbinsdale, Minn., 1959-75; trustee, sec. Minn. Med. Found., Mpls., 1982-90. Served to lt. USNR, 1942-46. Recipient Disting. Eagle Scout award Boy Scouts Am., 1982. Mem. Mpls. Club (governing com. 1983-89, pres. 1987), Woodhill Country Club (trustee 1985-94). Republican. Presbyterian. Avocations: golf; waterfowl hunting. Office: care Faegre & Benson 2200 Norwest Ctr 90 S 7th St Minneapolis MN 55402-3903

MCCLINTOCK, RICHARD POLSON, dermatologist; b. Lancaster, N.H., Dec. 16, 1933; s. Richard P. and Dorothy Grace (Ramsey) McC.; m. Barbara Wyatt, June 1959 (div. Mar. 1970); children: Peter, Pamela; m. Mary Joy Fitzgerald, Mar. 21, 1970; children: Wayne, Patrick. BA, Dartmouth U., 1956; MD, Harvard U., 1960. Diplomate Am. Bd. Dermatology, Am. Bd. Dermatopathology. Intern in medicine U. N.C., Chapel Hill, 1960-61; resident in dermatology Stanford U., Palo Alto, Calif., 1964-67; pvt. practice Ukiah, Calif., 1967—; clin. instr. dermatology Stanford U., Palo Alto, 1967-78, clin. asst. prof., 1978-86, assoc. clin. prof., 1986-92, lectr., 1992—; mem. hosp. staff Ukiah Valley Med. Ctr., chief of staff, 1974. Contbr. articles to profl. jours. Trustee Found. for Med. Care for Mendocino and Lake Counties, 1990-94, pres., 1992-94. Lt. Med. Corps, USN, 1961-64. Mem. San Francisco Dermatol. Soc., Pacific Dermatol. Assn., Am. Acad. Dermatology, Calif. Med. Soc., Mendocino Lake County Med. Soc., Internat. Soc. Dermatopathology. Office: 723 S Dora St Ukiah CA 95482-5335

MCCLINTOCK, WILLIAM THOMAS, health care administrator; b. Pittsfield, Mass., Oct. 23, 1934; s. Ernest William and Helen Elizabeth (Clum) M.; m. Wendolyn Hope Eckerman, June 22, 1963; children: Anne Elizabeth, Carol Jean, Thomas Daniel. BA, St. Lawrence U., Canton, N.Y., 1956; MBA, U. Chgo., 1959, MHA, 1962. Prodn. planner Corning Glass Works, Corning, N.Y., 1959-60; adminstrv. resident Highland Hosp., Oakland, Calif., 1961-62; adminstrv. asst. Univ. Hosps. of Cleve., 1962-65; asst. adminstr. Presbyn. Hosp., Whittier, Calif., 1965-68; regional asst. Kaiser Found. Hosps., Oakland, Calif., 1968-70; assoc. dir., exec. dir. Conn. Hosp. Planning Commn., New Haven, 1970-75; project dir., lectr. sch. health studies U. N.H., Durham, 1975-77; regional mgr. Tex. Med. Found., Austin, 1977-81; adminstr. Schick Shadel Hosp., Fort Worth, 1981-87; mgmt. cons. George S. May Internat. Co., Park Ridge, Ill., 1987-88; mgr. Nat. Ctr. Rsch. Programs Am. Heart Assn., Dallas, 1988-89; adminstr. Ambulatory Svcs. Health Care of Tex., Ft. Worth, 1990-92; CEO Boundary Community Hosp. & Nursing Home, Bonners Ferry, Idaho, 1992—. 1st lt. U.S. Army, 1957. Fellow Am. Coll. Health Care Execs., Am. Coll. Addiction Treatment Adminstrs.; mem. Am. Hosp. Assn. (life), Am. Heart Assn. (mem. bd. dirs. Idaho/Mont. affiliate 1993—), Idaho Hosp. Assn. (bd. dirs. 1995—), Unity Lodge No. 9, F&AM, N.Y. Republican. Presbyterian. Avocations: book collections, gardening, photography. Home: County Rd 62C PO Box 1226 Bonners Ferry ID 83805-1226 Office: 6640 Kaniksu St Bonners Ferry ID 83805-7532

MC CLINTON, DONALD G., diversified holding company executive; b. Pitts., June 30, 1933; s. Donald K. and Ethel M. McC.; m. Jane Ann Knoebel, Apr. 12, 1958; children: Catherine, D. Scott. B.S., Miami U., Oxford, Ohio, 1955. Audit mgr. Arthur Andersen & Co., Cleve., 1955-62; mgr. accounting E. Ohio Gas Co., Cleve., 1962-66; exec. v.p. Nat. Industries, Inc., Louisville, 1966-79; pres. Yellow Cab Co., Louisville, 1979-94; owner, chmn. bd. Interlock Industries, Inc., 1982-94; pres. Skylight Thoroughbred Tng. Ctr., Inc., 1994—; bd. dirs. Bank of Louisville, Cartenders Heathcorp, Clifton Ctr.; trustee Jewish Hosp. Health Care Systems, Inc., 1983—. Mem. Louisville-Jefferson County Bicentennial Commn., 1976-77; mem. coun. treas. Old Kentucky Home. coun. Boy Scouts Am., 1976-94; mem. Citizens at Large Jefferson County Budget Com., 1978-84; bd. overseers Bellarmine Coll., 1978-84; bd. dirs. Ky. Derby Festival, 1978—, Jewish Hosp., Louisville, 1980-86; trustee Spalding U., 1985-91. Mem. Fin. Execs. Inst. Home: 6205 Deep Creek Dr Prospect KY 40059-8606 Office: Skylight Thoroughbred Tng Ctr Inc PO Box 4 Goshen KY 40026

MCCLINTON, JAMES LEROY, city administrator; b. Longview, Wash., Oct. 14, 1949; s. James Delmer and Norma Jean (Ammons) McC.; m. Carmen Lassaphine Amador, Nov. 7, 1983; children: James Andrew, Ian Tyler, Kevin Riley. AA, SUNY, Albany, 1973; BA, Upper Iowa U., 1974; MA, Calif. State U., Carson, 1984; PhD, Calif. Coast U., 1985. Cert. mgr. Inst. Cert. Profl. Mgrs. Non-commd. officer USCG, various locations, 1967-72, commd. officer, 1972-89; comdr. (ret.) USCG; bur. mgr. adminstrv. svcs. Charleston (S.C.) County Sheriff's Office, 1989—; spkr. pro tem S.C. Criminal Justice Acad., Columbia, 1989—; mem. auditor selection com. Charleston County Govt., 1989—, computer users action com., 1989—; mem. various coms. County Govt. and Sheriff's Office, Charleston, 1989—. Editor (newsletter) The Badge, 1989—; contbr. articles to profl. jours. Mem. Charleston Police Pipes and Drums, 1994—; grad. Leadership S.C., 1993, Leadership Charleston, 1997. Recipient Achievement award Nat. Assn. Counties, Washington, 1993, 96, Golden Pen award The Post and Courier Newspaper, Charleston, 1996. Mem. ASPA, S.C. Law Enforcement Officers Assn. Republican. Avocations: bagpipes, writing.

MCCLINTON, WENDELL C., religious organization administrator; b. Waco, Tex., Jan. 10, 1933; s. Clyde E. and Gertrude (Cotton) McC.; m. Beverly A. Harrison, Oct. 19, 1954; children: Kent, Jana, Lori, Meg. BBA, Baylor U., 1960. Exec. dir. Gideons Internat., Nashville.

MCCLOSKEY, GUY CORBETT, Buddhist religious leader; b. Akron, Ohio, Aug. 15, 1943; s. Burr Clark McCloskey and Rose (Brody) Marlin; m. Doris Jean Dye, Aug. 1, 1971; children: Brian, Vincent, Mary. Dir. adminstrn. Nichiren Shoshu of Am., Santa Monica, Calif., 1967-78; regional dir. Nichiren Shoshu Soka Gakkai of Am., Washington, 1978-91; corp. v.p. Soka Gakkai Internat.-USA, Santa Monica, 1991—; sr. vice gen. dir. Soka Gakkai Internat.-USA, Chgo., 1991—, also bd. dirs.; bd. dirs. Boston Rsch. Ctr. for the 21st Century. With U.S. Army, 1965-67. Office: Sokai Gakkai Internat-USA 1455 S Wabash Ave Chicago IL 60605-2806

MCCLOSKEY, JAY P., prosecutor. Asst. U.S. atty. Dept. Justice, Bangor, Maine; U.S. atty. Dept. Justice, Portland, Maine, 1993—. Office: US Attys Office East Tower 6th Fl 100 Middle St Portland ME 04101-4100

MCCLOSKEY, J(OHN) MICHAEL, association administrator; b. Eugene, Oreg., Apr. 26, 1934; s. John Clement and Agnes Margaret (Studer) McC.; m. Maxine Mugg Johnson, June 17, 1965; stepchildren: Claire, Laura, James, Rosemary Johnson. BA, Harvard U., 1956; JD, U. Oreg., 1961. N.W. rep. Sierra Club, Eugene, 1961-65; asst. to pres. Sierra Club, San Francisco, 1965-66, conservation dir., 1966-69, exec. dir., 1969-85; chmn. Sierra Club, Washington, 1985—, acting exec. dir., 1986-87; vice-chmn. Commn. on Environ. Law and Policy (Internat. Union for Conservation of Nature), Gland, Switzerland, 1978-88; mem. Pres.'s Commn. on Agenda for 1980's, Washington, 1979-80; co-chmn. OSHA-Environ. Conf., Washington, 1983-87; vice chmn. Am. Com. on Internat. Conservation, 1988-90; mem. Internat. Union for Conservaton of Nature Commn. Nat. Parks and Protected Areas, 1988—; mem. adj. faculty Sch. Natural Resources, U. Mich., 1988—. Contbr. articles to profl. jours. Bd. dirs. Nat. Resources Coun. Am., 1988-94, vice chmn., 1989-91, chmn., 1992-93, chmn. advocacy forum, 1989-91; bd. dirs. Ind. Sector, 1990-96, Mineral Policy Ctr., 1988—, Coalition for Environmentally Responsible Economies, 1989—; mem. steering com. Blueprint for Environ., 1987-88; nominated candidate Oreg. Ho. of Reps., 1962. Recipient award Calif. Conservation Coun., 1969, John Muir award Sierra Club, 1979, UN Environ. Program Global 500 award, 1992. Mem. Harvard Club, Explorers Club (N.Y.C.). Democrat. Office: Sierra Club 408 C St NE Washington DC 20002-5818

MC CLOSKEY, ROBERT, artist; b. Hamilton, Ohio, Sept. 15, 1914; s. Howard Hill and Mabel (Wismaier) McC.; m. Margaret Durand, Nov. 23, 1940; children: Sarah, Jane. Student, Vesper George Sch., N.Y.C., NAD; Litt.D. (hon.), Miami U., Oxford, Ohio, 1962, Mt. Holyoke Coll., South Hadley, Mass., 1967, U. Maine, 1990; hon. degree, Bowdoin Coll., 1991. Artist, illustrator, host, Am. Songfest, Weston Woods bicentennial film.; Executed bas-reliefs, Hamilton Municipal Bldg., Ohio, 1935; author: Lentil, 1940, Make Way for Ducklings, 1941 (bronze ducklings sculpted by Nancy Schön installed Boston Pub. Garden, 1987, replicas placed in Moscow Park, 1991), Homer Price, 1943, Blueberries for Sal, 1948, Centerburg Tales, 1951, One Morning in Maine, 1952, Time of Wonder, 1957, Bert Dow, Deep Water Man, 1963. Recipient numerous awards including President's award for creative work NAD, 1936; recipient numerous awards including Prix de Rome Am. Acad. in Rome, 1939, Caldecott medal for most disting. picture book for children published in 1941, 1942, Caldecott medal for Time of Wonder, 1958, Regina medal Cath. Library Assn., 1974; hon. by. ALA, 1991. Fellow Am. Acad. Rome; mem. P.E.N., Authors League Am.

MCCLOW, ROGER JAMES, lawyer; b. St. Johns, Mich., July 23, 1947; s. Jack Gordon and Madalene V. (Mahaffy) McC.; m. Suzanne Terese Posler, July 13, 1978. BA in Polit. Sci. with distinction, U. Mich., 1969; JD magna cum laude, Wayne State U., 1976. Bar: Mich. 1977, U.S. Dist. Ct. (ea. dist.) Mich. 1977, U.S. Ct. Appeals (6th cir.) 1985, U.S. Ct. Appeals (8th cir.) 1987, U.S. Supreme Ct. 1988. Assoc. Miller, Cohen, Martens & Sugerman, Detroit, 1977-81, Klimist, McKnight & Sale, P.C., Southfield, Mich., 1981-83; ptnr. Klimist, McKnight, Sale, McClow & Canzano, P.C., Southfield, 1983—. Bd. dirs. Hemid (Sr. Citizen's Agy.), Detroit, 1982—; tutor Children's Ctr., Detroit, 1990-93; vol. Hospice Legal Aid, Detroit, 1991—; mem. gun safety com. Alliance for Greater, Safer Detroit, 1993-95. Mem. State Bar Mich. (coun. mem., labor law and employment sect. 1992-96), Detroit Bar Assn., Oakland County Bar Assn., Assn. Trial Lawyers Am., Mich. Trial Lawyers Assn., Indsl. Rels. Rsch. Assn., Phi Sigma Alpha. Democrat. Avocations: antiques, tennis, guitar. Office: Klimist McKnight Sale McClow & Canzano 400 Galleria Officentre Ste 11 Southfield MI 48034-8473

MCCLUNG, A(LEXANDER) KEITH, JR., lawyer; b. Gallipolis, Ohio, Sept. 13, 1934; s. Alexander Keith and Florence (Juhling) McC.; m. Sandra B. Foley, Aug. 17, 1957; children: Alexander Keith III, Martha E. AB, W.Va. U., 1956; JD, Harvard U., 1959. Bar: W.Va. 1959, Md. 1970, Mich. 1972. Assoc. Jackson, Kelly, Holt & O'Farrell, Charleston, W.Va., 1959-69; assoc. counsel Comml. Credit Corp., Balt., 1969-70, v.p., counsel, 1973-82, gen. atty., 1982-85; sr. gen. atty. Comml. Credit Co., Balt., 1985-89, sr. v.p., gen. counsel, 1989—; v.p., counsel McCullagh Leasing, Inc., Roseville, Mich., 1970-73; bd. dirs. Travelers Bank; trustee Roland Park Found.; mem. adv. coun. Coll. Arts and Sci., W.Va. U. Lt. U.S. Army, 1961-62. Mem. ABA (subcom. uniform comml. code, com. equipment leasing). Democrat.

Home: 13 Devon Hill Rd Baltimore MD 21210-2210 Office: Comml Credit Co 300 Saint Paul St Baltimore MD 21202-2103

MCCLUNG, J(AMES) DAVID, corporate executive, lawyer; b. Lamesa, Tex., July 16, 1943; s. Jack Weldon Sr. and Ruby (Brown) McC.; m. Linda Nelson, Feb. 12, 1966; children: LeEtta McClung Felter, Dennis, Pamela McClung Frazier, Jennifer McClung Gottschalk. Student, N.E. La. State Coll., 1961-62, McNeese State Coll., 1963; BSBA cum laude, Bethany Nazarene Coll., 1965; postgrad., U. Okla., 1967-68; JD cum laude, Baylor U., 1973. Bar: Tex. 1973, U.S. Dist. Ct. (no. dist.) Tex. 1975, U.S. Ct. Appeals (5th cir.) 1974. Assoc. Jackson & Walker, Dallas, 1973-76; exec. v.p. Austin Industries, Inc., Dallas, 1976-88; pres., chief exec. officer, chmn. bd. Green Internat., Inc., Denver, 1988—; arbitrator Am. Arbitration Assn., 1978—; bd. dirs. Green Holdings, Inc., Denver; chmn. bd. Green Construction Co., Green Mining, Inc., Green Alaska, Inc., GEM Investors, Inc., Green Overseas Corp., Northland Maintenance Co., Northland Alaska, Inc., Green Investments, Inc., Denver, 1988—; pres. Triton Marine Cons., 1994. Contbr. articles to profl. jours. Trustee So. Nazarene U., Bethany, Okla., 1978-86; mem. gen. bd. Ch. of the Nazarene, Kansas City, 1985-89, sec. Commn. Report, 1989. Capt. USAF, 1965-71, Vietnam. Decorated 6 Air medals; recipient Young Grads. award of merit Baylor U., 1983, Outstanding Alumni award So. Nazarene U., 1989, Disting. Svc. award Ch. of the Nazarene, 1989. Mem. ABA, Tex. Bar Assn., The Beavers. Republican. Avocations: dark room photography, fishing. Home: 13318 Tropicana Dr Houston TX 77041-6579

MC CLUNG, JIM HILL, light manufacturing company executive; b. Buena Vista, Ga., Nov. 8, 1936; s. Jim Hill and Marjorie (Oxford) McC.; m. Jo Patrick, July 5, 1958; children—Jim Hill, Karen Mareese. B.A., Emory U., 1958; M.B.A., Harvard U., 1964. With Lithonia Lighting div. Nat. Svc. Industries, Inc., Conyers, Ga., 1964—; now pres., assoc. dir. Lithonia Lighting div. Nat. Svc. Industries, Inc. Served with USAF, 1958-62. Mem. Illuminating Engring. Soc. N.Am. (vice chmn. lighting rsch. and edn. fund), Nat. Elec. Distbrs. Assn. (mfrs. bd.), Nat. Elec. Mfrs. Assn. (nat. lighting bur., bd. dirs., vice chmn.), Intelligent Bldgs. Inst. (bd. dirs.), Lighting Rsch. Inst. (bd. dirs.), Elec. Mfrs. Club, World Pres.'s Orgn. Methodist. Office: Lithonia Lighting Div PO Box A Conyers GA 30207-0067

MCCLUNG, KENNETH AUSTIN, JR., training executive, performance consultant; b. Decatur, Ga., Apr. 11, 1947; s. Kenneth Austin Sr. and Marianne (Conklin) McC.; m. Christina June Palensar, Mar. 21, 1975. BA, North Ga. Coll., 1969; MS, EdD, U. So. Calif., 1976. Commd. 2d lt. U.S. Army, 1969, advanced through grades to maj., 1980; col. USAR; cons. in field Suffern, N.Y., 1980-81; sr. ptnr. Instrl. Design Group, Inc., Morristown, N.J., 1981—; bd. dirs. Nat. Productivity Ctr., Boulder, Colo., LTI, Inc., Washington; author/mgr. more than 150 mgmt., sales, and tech. tng. programs for major corps.; performance cons. to sr. corp. mgmt. Author: Microcomputers for Medical Professionals, 1984, Microcomputers for Legal Professionals, 1984, Microcomputers for Investment Professionals, 1984, Microcomputers for Insurance Professionals, 1984, Personal Computers for Executives, 1984, French edit. 1985; co-author: Sales Training Handbook, 1989. Mem. ASTD, Internat. Soc. for Performance Improvement (pres. N.J. chpt. 1986-88, N.E. regional cons. 1989-90, nat. nomination chmn. 1990-91, nat. emerging tech. chmn. 1991-92). Avocations: sailing, tennis, bicycling, rock climbing, skiing. Office: Instrnl Design Group Inc 144 Speedwell Ave Morristown NJ 07960-3850

MC CLUNG, LELAND SWINT, microbiologist, educator; b. Atlanta, Tex., Aug. 4, 1910; s. Joe Baker and Roxie Buelah (Swint) McC.; m. Ruth Wilhelmien Exner, Dec. 25, 1944. A.B., U. Tex., 1931, A.M., 1932; Ph.D., U. Wis., 1934. Research bacteriologist Am. Can Co., Maywood, Ill., 1934-36; instr. in fruit products and jr. bacteriologist Coll. Agr., U. Calif., 1936-37; instr. research medicine George Williams Hooper Found. for Med. Research, U. Calif., 1937-39; asst. prof. Ind. U., Bloomington, 1940-44; assoc. prof. Ind. U., 1944-48, prof., chmn. dept. bacteriology, 1946-66, prof. microbiology, 1966-81, prof. emeritus, 1981—, asst. dir. div. biol. scis., 1965-68; sec. pub. health and nutrition sect. 5th Pacific Sci. Congress. Author: (with Elizabeth McCoy), 2 vols.) The Anaerobic Bacteria and Their Activities in Nature and Disease: A Subject Bibliography, 1939, supplement, 1941; The Anaerobic Bacteria: Their Activities in Nature and Disease: The Literature for 1940-75 (7 vols.), 1982; contbr. articles to sci. jours. John Simon Guggenheim Meml. Found. fellow, 1939-40; rsch. fellow in bacteriology Harvard Med. Sch., 1939-40. Fellow AAAS, Am. Acad. Microbiology (gov. 1961-67, 76-77), Ind. Acad. Sci.; mem. Am. Soc. Microbiology (hon., archivist 1960-82), Soc. Am. Bacteriologists (editl. bd. Jour. Bacteriology 1953-57, archivist 1953-60, chmn. com on edn. 1958-61, Chas. A. Behrens award Ind. br. 1981, Barnett Cohen award Md. br. 1984), Am. Inst. Biol. Scis. (gov. bd. 1968-74), Inst. Food Tech., Nat. Assn. Biology Tchrs. (pres. 1965), Soc. Indsl. Microbiology, Sigma Xi, Phi Sigma, Gamma Alpha, Alpha Epsilon Delta. Office: Ind U Dept Biology Jordan Hall # 138 Bloomington IN 47405-6801

MCCLUNG, RICHARD GOEHRING, lawyer; b. Butler, Pa., June 26, 1913; s. Frank A. and Mary A. (Goehring) McC.; m. Jean Barrett Coffin, Dec. 1, 1951 (dec.); children: Jean C., Mary G., Priscilla B. A.B., Princeton U., 1935; LL.B., Yale U., 1939; cert., Harvard U. Bus. Sch., 1937. Bar: N.Y. 1940. Pvt. practice N.Y.C., 1940—; with Carter, Ledyard & Milburn, 1946—, ptnr., 1948, of counsel, 1983—. Served to comdr. USNR, 1942-46. Home: 101D Lewis St Greenwich CT 06830-6606 Office: 2 Wall St New York NY 10005-2001

MCCLURE, ANN CRAWFORD, lawyer, judge; b. Cin., Sept. 5, 1953; d. William Edward and Patricia Ann (Jewett) Crawford; m. David R. McClure, Nov. 12, 1983; children: Kinsey Tristen, Scott Crawford. BFA magna cum laude, Tex. Christian U., 1974; JD, U. Houston, 1979. Bd. cert. in family law and civil appellate law Tex. Bd. Legal Specialization. Assoc. Piro and Lilly, Houston, 1979-83; pvt. practice El Paso, Tex., 1983-92; ptnr. McClure and McClure, El Paso, 1992-94; justice Eighth Ct. of Appeals, El Paso, 1995—; former mem. Tex. Bd. Law Examiners, Bd. Disciplinary Appeals; mem. Family Law Specialization Exam Com., 1989-93. Contbr. articles to profl. jours.; past editor The Family Law Forum; contbg. editor: Texas Family Law Service; mem. editl. bd. Tex. Family Law Practice Manual, 1982-93. Mem. State Bar Tex. (dir. family law sect. 1987-91, treas. 1993-94, vice chmn. 1995-96, chmn.-elect 1996-97, chmn. 1997-98), dir. appellate and advocacy sect. 1991-95, treas. 1996-97, sec. 1997-98), Tex. Acad. Family Law Specialists (past dir.). Democrat. Presbyterian.

MCCLURE, BROOKS, management consultant; b. N.Y.C., Mar. 8, 1919; s. Walter Harsha and Angelica (Mendoza) McC.; m. Olga Beatrice Gallik, Oct. 15, 1949; 1 child, Karen. AB summa cum laude, U. Md.; disting. grad., U.S. Naval War Coll. N.Y. corr. Western Press Ltd., Australia, 1939-42; copy editor Washington Eve. Star, 1946-51; joined U.S. Fgn. Service, 1951; information officer, attache embassy Copenhagen, 1951-53; press attache embassy Vienna, 1953-55; information officer, attache embassy Cairo, 1956-57, Seoul, 1957-60, Bonn, 1960-63; policy officer Europe USIA, 1963-66; pub. affairs officer 1st sec. embassy, Copenhagen, 1967-72; spl. asst. policy plans and nat. security council affairs, internat. security affairs Dept. Def., 1972-76; internat. security adviser USIA, 1976-77; program coordinator Crisis Assessment Staff, Dept. Commerce, 1977-78; dir. ops. Internat. Mgmt. Analysis and Resources Corp., 1978-81, v.p., 1982—; sec. Cross-Continent Assocs. Ltd., 1994—; various spl. assignments, Europe, Middle East, Asia, Africa; lectr. FBI Acad., Fgn. Svc. Inst., Inter-Am. Def. Coll., Army War Coll., Navy War Coll. Contbg. author: Modern Guerrilla Warfare, 1962, Dynamics of Terrorism, 1977, International Terrorism in Contemporary World, 1978, Corporate Vulnerability and How to Assess it: Political Terrorism and Business, 1979, Business and the Middle East, 1981, Political Terrorism and Energy, 1981; Contbr. articles profl. jours.; author report to Senate Judiciary Com. on internat. terroism and hostage def. measures; testifier on internat. security, hostage behavior, def. of Alaskan pipeline, FBI charter U.S. Senate, 1975-79. With AUS, 1942-46, ETO. Mem. Am. Fgn. Svc. Assn., Assn. for Diplomatic Studies, Nat. Press Club, DACOR, Phi Kappa Phi, Alpha Sigma Lambda. Home: 6204 Rockhurst Rd Bethesda MD 20817-1756 Office: IMAR Corp PO Box 34528 Bethesda MD 20827-0528

MCCLURE, DANIEL M., lawyer; b. Enid, Okla., Feb. 5, 1952; s. Larry M. and Marie Dolores (Sarver) McC.; m. Judy Lynn Pinson, Jan. 3, 1976; children: Andrew Mead, Mark William, Kathleen Claire. BA with highest hons., U. Okla., 1974; JD cum laude, Harvard U., 1978. Bar: Tex. 1978, U.S. Dist. Ct. (so. dist., ea. dist.) Tex. 1979, U.S. Ct. Appeals (5th cir., 11th cir.) 1981. Assoc. Fulbright & Jaworski, Houston, 1978-86, ptnr., 1986—. Fellow Tex. Bar Found.; mem. ABA, Nat. Health Lawyers Assn., Nat. Assn. R.R. Trial Counsel, Tex. Bar Assn., Houston Bar Assn. (cert. civil trial law), Harvard Law Sch. Assn. Avocation: tennis. Home: 2 Long Timbers Ln Houston TX 77024-5445 Office: Fulbright & Jaworski 1301 Mckinney St Houston TX 77010-3031

MCCLURE, DONALD EDWIN, electrical construction executive, consultant; b. Pasadena, Calif., Mar. 13, 1934; s. Robert Wirt and Edna Buela (Williamson) McC.; m. Diana Lee Myrick, Feb. 9, 1958; children: Scott Patrick, Christopher Daniel. BS in Bus. Adminstrn., San Diego State U., 1957. Lic. gen. engring., bldg., elec. Elec. estimator Calif. Electric Works, San Diego, 1953-57; v.p. JCS Elec., San Diego, 1958-61; owner, proprietor McClure Electric, San Diego, 1961-63; chief estimator Am. Electric Contracting Corp., La Mesa, Calif., 1963-65; pres. Cal Pacific Electric Inc., San Diego, 1965-69; v.p., sec., dir. Am. Elec. Contracting, La Mesa, 1969-79; v.p. Steiny and Co., Inc., San Diego, 1979—; cons. constrn., expert witness Don E. McClure, San Diego, 1987—. Active Nat. Rep. Com., Washington, 1984—. Mem. Am. Subcontractors Assn., Singing Hills Tennis Club, San Diego State U. Alumni Assn., Am. Legion, Friendly Sons' of St. Patrick, Kappa Sigma Alumni Assn. Presbyterian. Avocations: skiing, tennis, fly fishing, deep sea fishing, boating, golf. Office: 1083 N Cuyamaca St El Cajon CA 92020-1803

MC CLURE, DONALD STUART, physical chemist, educator; b. Yonkers, N.Y., Aug. 27, 1920; s. Robert Hirt and Helen (Campbell) McC.; m. Laura Lee Thompson, July 9, 1949; children: Edward, Katherine, Kevin. B.Chemistry, U. Minn., 1942; Ph.D., U. Calif., Berkeley, 1948. With war research div. Columbia U., 1942-46; mem. faculty U. Calif., Berkeley, 1948-55; group leader, mem. profl. staff RCA Labs., 1955-62; prof. chemistry U. Chgo., 1962-67; prof. chemistry Princeton (N.J.) U., 1967-91, prof. emeritus, 1991—; vis. lectr. various univs.; cons. to govt. and industry. Author: Electronic Spectra of Molecules and Ions in Crystals, 1959, Some Aspects of Crystal Field Theory, 1964; also articles. Guggenheim fellow Oxford (Eng.) U., 1972-73; Humboldt fellow, 1980; recipient Irving Langmuir prize, 1979. Fellow Am. Acad. Arts and Scis., Nat. Acad. Scis.; mem. Am. Chem. Soc., Am. Phys. Soc. Home: 23 Hemlock Cir Princeton NJ 08540-5405

MCCLURE, FREDERICK DONALD, investment banker, lawyer; b. Ft. Worth, Feb. 2, 1954; s. Foster Donald and Mayme Nell (Barnett) McC.; m. Harriet Elizabeth Jackson, Dec. 17, 1977; children: Lauren Elizabeth, Frederick Donald. BS, Tex. A&M U., 1976; JD, Baylor U., 1981. Bar: Tex. 1981, U.S. Dist. Ct. (so. dist.) Tex. 1982, U.S. Ct. Appeals (5th cir.) 1982. Agrl. asst. to U.S. Senator John Tower, Washington, 1977-79, legis. dir., 1983-84; assoc. Reynolds, Allen & Cook, Houston, 1981-83; assoc. dep. atty. gen. Dept. Justice, Washington, 1984-85; spl. asst. to pres. for legis. affairs White House, Washington, 1985-86, asst. to pres legis. affairs, 1989-92; mng. dir. First S.W. Co., Dallas, Tex., 1992-94; sr. v.p. Pub. Strategies, Inc., 1995—; bd. regents The Tex. A & M U. Sys., 1995—; bd. dirs. Alex Lee, Inc. Mem. Tex. Real Estate Rsch. Adv. Com., College Station, 1979-92; mem. Adv. Coun. on Tech.-Vocat. Edn., Austin, 1975-77; mem. bd. vis. U.S. Naval Acad., 1992-95, chmn., 1994; bd. dirs. Mcpl. Adv. Coun. Tex., 1993. Named Disting. Alumnus Tex. A&M, 1991; Outstanding Young Alumnus Baylor U., 1991. Mem. State Bar Tex., Former Students Assn. of Tex. A&M (v.p. 1985-89, 93-95), Future Farmers Am. (nat. sec. 1973-74), Tex. Future Farmers Am. (state pres. 1972-73), Phi Alpha Delta, Phi Kappa Phi, Alpha Zeta (dir. 1985-93), Alpha Gamma Rho. Republican. Baptist. Home: 6722 Lakehurst Ave Dallas TX 75230-5206 Office: 200 Crescent Ct Ste 1065 Dallas TX 75201-7836

MCCLURE, GEORGE MORRIS, III, lawyer; b. Danville, Ky., Nov. 12, 1934; s. George Morris Jr. and Helen Louise (McCormack) McC.; m. Judith DeGolier Selee, July 6, 1957 (div. Jan. 1969); 1 child, George Morris IV; m. Patricia Moberly, Dec. 11, 1971; children: Joseph Scott Kirk, Patrick Spencer McClure. AB, Princeton U., 1956; JD, Denver U., 1963. Bar: Colo. 1963, Ky. 1970, U.S. Dist. Ct. (ea. dist.) Ky. 1970. Assoc. Yegge, Hall, Schulenberg, Denver, 1963-65; sole practitioner Denver, 1965-67; assoc. Zarlengo, Mott & Carlin, Denver, 1967-69, James G. Sheehan, Danville, Ky., 1970-71; sole practitioner Danville, 1971-72, 72—; county atty. Boyle County, Danville, 1972—. Adv. div. Cmty. Theatre, Danville, 1984—. 1st lt. USMC, 1956-59. Mem. ABA, Ky. Bar Assn. Democrat. Avocations: golf, fishing, amateur radio, flying, gardening. Office: Boyle County Court House 321 W Main St Danville KY 40422-1848

MCCLURE, GROVER BENJAMIN, management consultant; b. Houstonia, Mo., Oct. 15, 1918; s. Grover B. and Sue F. (Cook) McC. B.A., U. Richmond, 1939. Pres. internat. div. Richardson-Merrell, N.Y.C., 1954-62; pres. Europe and Africa divs. Paris, 1960-81; exec. v.p. Richardson-Vicks, Inc., Wilton, Conn., 1981-85; cons. New Canaan, Conn., 1985—; bd. dirs. Northrup & Johnson Cannes, France. Served to lt. comdr. USNR, 1941-46. Republican. Presbyterian. Clubs: Silver Springs (Ridgefield, Conn.). Avocations: tennis, golf, travel, yachting. Home and Office: 12 Saint Johns Pl New Canaan CT 06840-4528

MCCLURE, JAMES FOCHT, JR., federal judge; b. Danville, Pa., Apr. 6, 1931; s. James Focht and Florence Kathryn (Fowler) McC.; m. Elizabeth Louise Barber, June 14, 1952; children: Holly McClure Kerwin, Kimberly Ann Pacala, Jamee McClure Sealy, Mary Elizabeth Hudec, Margaret McClure Persing. AB, Amherst Coll., 1952; JD, U. Pa., 1957. Bar: D.C. 1957, Pa. 1958, U.S. Dist. Ct. D.C. 1957, U.S. Dist. Ct. (ea. and mid. dist.) Pa. 1958, U.S. Ct. Appeals (3d cir.) 1959. Atty., advisor Dept. State, Washington, 1957-58; assoc. Morgan, Lewis & Bockius, Phila., 1958-61; atty. Merck & Co., Inc., N.Y.C., 1961-65; ptnr. McClure & McClure, Lewisburg, Pa., 1965-77, McClure & Light, Lewisburg, 1978-84; pres., judge Ct. Common Pleas, 17th Jud. Dist. Pa., Lewisburg, 1984-90; dist. judge U.S. Dist. Ct. (mid. dist.) Pa., Williamsport, Pa., 1990—; dist. atty. Union County, Lewisburg, 1974-75. Pres. bd. sch. dirs. Lewisburg Area Sch. Dist., 1969-74. Cpl. U.S. Army, 1952-54. Mem. Pa. Bar Assn., Union County Bar Assn., Bucknell U. Golf Club, Susquehanna Valley Chorale, Order of Coif, Phi Beta Kappa. Republican. Presbyterian. Office: US Dist Ct Federal Bldg PO Box 1448 240 W 3d St Williamsport PA 17703-1448

MC CLURE, JAMES J., JR., lawyer, former municipal executive; b. Oak Park, Ill., Sept. 23, 1920; s. James J. and Ada Leslie (Baker) McC.; m. Margaret Carolyn Phelps, Apr. 9, 1949; children: John Phelps, Julia Jean, Donald Stewart. BA, U. Chgo., 1942, JD, 1949. Bar: Ill. 1950. Ptnr. Gardner, Carton & Douglas, Chgo., 1962-91, of counsel, 1991—; mem. Oak Park Plan Commn., 1966-73; mem. Northeastern Ill. Planning Commn., 1973-77, pres., 1975-77; pres. Village of Oak Park, 1973-81, Oak Park Exch. Congress Inc., 1981—. Pres. United Christian Community Svcs., 1967-69, 71-73, Erie Neighborhood House, 1953-55, Oak Park-River Forest Community Chest, 1967; moderator Presbytery Chgo., 1969; mem. Gov.'s Spl. Com. on MPO, 1978-79; bd. dirs. Leadership Council of Met. Open Communities, 1981—, sec., 1990—; bd. dirs. Met. Planning Coun., 1982-93, honorary dir., 1993—; bd. dirs. Community Renewal Soc., 1982-91, v.p., 1984-88, treas. 1988-91; chmn. Christian Century Found., 1981—; bd. trustees McCormick Theol. Sem., 1981—, chmn. bd. 1987-90. hon. trustee, 1990—; mem. ch. vocations unit, 1987-92, vice chair 1990; mem. gen. assembly coun. Presbyn. Ch. U.S.A., 1987-90; bd. dirs. Oak Park Edn. Found., 1991-96, Oak Park River Forest Community Found., 1991—; mem. Vision 2000 (Oak Park) Coordinating Com., 1995. With USNR, 1942-46. Recipient Disting. Citizen award Oak Park, 1976; Silver Beaver award; Disting. Eagle Scout award Boy Scouts Am., Carl Winters Cmty. Svc. award Oak Park Rotary Club, 1996, William Staczak award Oak Park Edn. Found., 1997, Rita Johnson award Oak Park Family Svc. and Mental Health Ctr., 1997, Public Svc. award U. Chgo. Alumni Assn., 1997. Mem. ABA, Am. Coll. Trust and Estate Counsel, Ill. Bar Assn., Chgo. Bar Assn., Am. Law Inst., Lambda Alpha. Clubs: Univ. (Chgo.). Home: 200 S Maple Ave Oak Park IL 60302-3026 Office: Gardner Carton & Douglas 321 N Clark St Chicago IL 60610 *Love of God, love of family, awareness of both the uniqueness and the contribution of every other human being, a sense of the wholeness of life with my religious faith, my profession of law, my family and my community service each playing an important part and complimenting each other.*

MCCLURE, LUCRETIA WALKER, medical librarian; b. Denver, Jan. 2, 1925; d. Oscar W. and Rachel E. (Stander) Low; m. Arnold L. McClure, May 26, 1946 (dec. Oct. 1992); children: John N., Paul W. BJ, U. Mo., 1945; MA in Librarianship, U. Denver, 1964. Cataloging/serials libr. Edward G. Miner Libr., U. Rochester, N.Y., 1964-68, readers svcs. libr., 1968-72, assoc. libr., 1972-78, med. libr., assoc. prof. med. bibliography, 1979-93, med. libr. emerita, 1993—; bd. dirs. Friends of Nat. Libr. of Medicine, Bethesda, Md., 1991—. Editor Bull., Edward G. Miner Libr., 1979-93; editor IFLA sect. Biol. and Med. Scis. Librs., 1993—; contbr. articles to profl. jours. Recipient Disting. Svc. award U. Rochester, 1992. Fellow Med. Libr. Assn. (chair Upstate N.Y. and Ont. chpt. 1969, parliamentarian 1993—, pres. 1990-91, bd. dirs., fin. chair 1981-83, Marcia C. Noyes award 1996, Pres.'s award 1995), Assn. Acad. Health Scis. Libr. Dirs. (pres. 1985-86), Internat. Fedn. Libr. Assns., Acad. Health Info. Profls. (Disting. mem.). Home: 164 Elmore Rd Rochester NY 14618-3651

MCCLURE, ROGER JOHN, lawyer; b. Cleve., Nov. 22, 1943; s. Theron R. and Colene (Irwin) McC. BA, Ohio State U., 1965, JD cum laude, 1972; MA, Northwestern U., 1966. Bar: U.S. Ct. Appeals (D.C. cir.) 1974, U.S. Supreme Ct. 1978, Va. 1983, Md. 1983, Ohio, U.S. Ct. Appeals (4th, 5th & 10th cirs.). Asst. atty. gen. State of Ohio, Columbus, 1972; trial atty. FTC, Washington, 1972-76; sr. assoc. Law Offices of A.D. Berkeley, Washington, 1976-81; pvt. practice, Alexandria, Va., 1981-86; pres. Roger J. McClure, P.C., Alexandria, 1987—; del. Va. Gen. Assembly, 1992—; adj. prof. Antioch Sch. Law, Washington, 1982-84; host talk show Sta. WRC Radio, 1987-93, Sta. WPGC, 1993-94. Co-author: Winning the Syndication Game, 1988, Advanced Estate Planning in Virginia, 1997; bd. editors Ohio State U. Law Rev., 1970-72; contbr. numerous articles to profl. jours. Bd. dirs. No. Va. Cmty. Found., 1995—. Served with U.S. Army, 1967-69. Decorated Bronze Star; Masters Fellow Esperti Peterson Inst., 1996—. Mem. D.C. Bar Assn. (real estate steering com. 1982-84, chmn. antitrust divsn. 1975-76), No. Va. Apt. Assn. (bd. dirs. 1988—, 1st v.p. 1987-88, pres. 1988-89), Nat. Network Estate Planning Attys., Dulles Area Transp. Assn. (bd. dirs.). Avocation: sailing. Office: 500 N Washington St Alexandria VA 22314-2314

MCCLURE, WILLIAM OWEN, biologist; b. Yakima, Wash., Sept. 29, 1937; s. Rexford Delmont and Ruth Josephine (Owen) McC.; m. Pamela Preston Harris, Mar. 9, 1968 (div. 1979); children: Heather Harris, Rexford Owen; m. Sara Joan Rorke, July 27, 1980. BSc, Calif. Inst. Tech., 1959; PhD, U. Wash., 1964. Postdoctoral fellow Rockefeller U., N.Y.C., 1964-65; rsch. assoc. Rockefeller U., 1965-68; asst. prof. U. Ill., Urbana, 1968-75; assoc. prof. U. So. Calif., L.A., 1975-79; prof. biology, prof. neurology U. So. Calif., 1979—; v.p. sci. affairs Nelson Rsch. & Devel. Co., Irvine, Calif., 1981-82; acting v.p. rsch. & devel. Nelson Rsch. & Devel. Co., 1985-86; dir. program. neurol. info. sci. U. So. Calif., 1982-92, dir. program in psychobiology, 1991—; dir. cellular biology U. So. Calif., 1979-81, dir. neurobiology, 1982-88, dir. prog. psychobiology, 1991—; cons. in field; dir. Marine & Freshwater Biomed. Ctr., U. So. Calif., 1982-83; co-dir. Baja Calif. Expedition of the R/V Alpha Helix, 1974, others; chmn. Winter Conf. on Brain Rsch., 1979, 80, others; lectr. in field; sci. adv. bd. Nelson R & D, 1972-91; mem. bd. commentators Brain and Behavioral Scis., 1978—. Editor or author 3 books; co-editor: Wednesday Night at the Lab; patentee in field; mem. editorial bd. Neurochem. Rsch., 1975-81, Jour. Neurochemistry, 1977-84, Jour. Neurosci. Rsch., 1980-86; contbr. over 100 articles to profl. jours. Bd. dirs. San Pedro and Peninsula Hosp. Found., 1989—, Faculty Ctr., U. So. Calif., 1991-95, San Pedro Health Svcs., 1992—. Scripps Inst. fellow, 1958, NIH fellow, 1959-64, 64-65, Alfred P. Sloan fellow, 1972-76, others; recipient rsch. grants, various sources, 1968—; Intersci. Rsch. Inst. fellow, 1989. Mem. AAAS, Am. Soc. Neurochemistry, Soc. for Neurosci., Am. Soc. Biol. Chemistry and Molecular Biology, Internat. Soc. Neurochemistry, Assn. Neurosci. Depts. and Programs, Univ. Park Investment Group, Bay Surgical Soc., N.Y. Acad. Scis. Republican. Presbyterian. Avocations: computing, travel. Home: 30533 Rhone Dr Palos Verdes Peninsula CA 90275-5742 Office: U So Calif Dept Biol Scis Los Angeles CA 90089

MCCLURE, WILLIAM PENDLETON, lawyer; b. Washington, May 25, 1925; s. John Elmer and Helen Newsome (Pendleton) McC.; children: Marilyn Alexander, Helen Pendleton, Elizabeth Ruffin, Melinda Geoghegan. B.S., U. Pa., 1949; J.D., George Washington U., 1951, LL.M., 1954; postgrad., The Hague (Netherlands) Acad. Internat. Law, 1952. Bar: D.C. 1951. Sr. ptnr. McClure & Trotter, Washington, 1952-91, McClure, Trotter & Mentz, Washington, 1991-93, McClure, Trotter & Mentz, chartered, Washington, 1993-95; ptnr. White & Case, Washington, 1995—. Chmn. D.C. div. Crusade Against Cancer, Am. Cancer Soc., 1966, 67. Served from pvt. to 1st lt., inf. U.S. Army, 1943-46, PTO. Mem. Am. Bar Assn., Bar Assn. D.C., Am. Judicature Soc., Order of Coif, Phi Delta Phi, Phi Delta Theta. Clubs: Metropolitan (Washington), Columbia Country (Washington), Nat. Press (Washington). Home: 9505 Brooke Dr Bethesda MD 20817-2207 Office: 601 13th St NW Ste 600 S Washington DC 20005-3807

MCCLURE-BIBBY, MARY ANNE, former state legislator; b. Milbank, S.D., Apr. 21, 1939; d. Charles Cornelius and Mary Lucille (Whittom) Burges; m. D.J. McClure, Nov. 17, 1963 (dec. Apr. 1990); 1 child, Kelly Joanne Kyro; m. John E. Bibby, May 1, 1993. BA magna cum laude, U. S.D., 1961; postgrad., U. Manchester, Eng., 1961-62; M of Pub. Adminstrn., Syracuse (N.Y.) U., 1980. Staff asst. U.S. Senator Francis Case, Washington, 1959-61; sec. to lt. gov. State of S.D., Pierre, 1963, with budget office, 1964; exec. sec. to pres. Frontier Airlines, Denver, 1963-64; tchr. Pub. High Schs., Pierre and Redfield, S.D., 1965-66, 68-70; mem. S.D. State Senate, Pierre, 1975-89, pres. pro tem, 1979-89, vice chmn. coun. of state govts., 1987, chmn. coun. of state govts., 1988; spl. asst. to Pres. Bush for intergovernmental affairs, 1989-92; exec. dir. S.D. Bush-Quayle Campaign, 1992. Vice chmn. sch. bd. Redfield Ind. Sch. Dist., 1970-74. Fulbright scholar, 1961-62, Bush Leadership fellow, 1977-80. Mem. Phi Beta Kappa. Republican. Congregationalist. Home: 822 8th Ave Brookings SD 57006-1315

MCCLURG, DOUGLAS P., lawyer; b. Cleve., Feb. 17, 1949; s. Donald Wayne and Helen Mildred (Tulin) McC.; m. Christie Jene Cobourn, Aug., 1976; children: Kelly Cobourn, Douglas Paul, Jr., Lauren Christie. BA, U. Fla., 1973, JD, 1976. Bar: Fla. 1976, U.S. Ct. Appeals (11th cir.) 1981, U.S. Dist. Ct. (mid. dist.) Fla. 1976. Assoc., shareholder Mahoney, Hadlow & Adams, Jacksonville, Fla., 1976-81; shareholder Smith & Hulsey, Jacksonville, Fla., 1981-84; ptnr. Holland & Knight, Tampa, 1984-92; shareholder Hill, Ward & Henderson, Tampa, 1992—; chmn. Bankruptcy/UCC com. of Bus. Law Section of The Fla. Bar, 1984-85, chmn. Legislation Com. Bus. Law Sect., 1986-87, pres., chmn. Tampa Bay Bankruptcy Bar Assoc., 1989-91. Trustee The Tampa Mus. of Art, 1991-92, pres. The Tampa Club, 1992, Exec. Com. mem. Young Life of Tampa, 1994-85; trustee U. Fla. Law Ctr. Assn., 1996—, Gulf Ridge coun. Boy Scouts Am., 1996—. Decorated Bronze Star (with Vdevice), Purple Heart (with Oak Leaf Cluster). Mem. Ye Mystic Krewe of Gasparilla, The Tampa Yacht and Country Club. Republican, Episcopalian. Avocation: competitive shooting, gun collecting, hunting, camping. Office: Hill Ward & Henderson 101 E Kennedy Blvd Ste 3700 Tampa FL 33602-5151 Home: 2721 Terrace Dr Tampa FL 33609

MCCLURG, JAMES EDWARD, research laboratory executive; b. Bassett, Nebr., Mar. 23, 1945; s. Warren James and Delia Emma (Allyn) McC. B.S., N.E. Wesleyan U., 1967; Ph.D., U. Nebr., 1973. Instr., U. Nebr. Coll. Medicine, Omaha, 1973-76, research instr., 1973-76, clin. asst. prof. Med. Ctr., 1984—; v.p., tech. dir. Harris Labs., Inc., Lincoln, Nebr., 1976-82, exec. v.p., 1982-84, pres., chief exec. officer, 1984—; bd. dirs. Lincoln Mut. Life Ins. Co., Lincoln Gen. Hosp. (chmn.), Unemed Corp., Lincoln, Harris Labs. Ltd, Belfast No. Ireland. Mem. editorial bd. Clin. Rsch. Practices and Drug Regulatory Affairs, 1984. Contbr. articles to profl. jours. Trustee Univ. Nebr. Found.; mem. Commn. on Human Rights, Lincoln, 1982-85; com. mem. Nebr. Citizens for Study Higher Edn., Lincoln, 1984; chmn. U. Nebr. Found. Recipient ann. research award Central Assn. Obstetricians and Gynecologists, 1982. Mem. Am. Assn. Lab. Accreditation (bd. dirs.). Republican. Clubs: Century (pres. Nebr. Wesleyan U. 1983-84), Nebraska (Lincoln). Lodge: Rotary. Avocation: boating. Office: Harris Labs Inc PO Box 80837 Lincoln NE 68501-0837

MCCLUSKEY, EDWARD JOSEPH, engineering educator; b. N.Y.C., Oct. 16, 1929; s. Edward Joseph and Rose (Slavin) McC.; m. Lois Thornhill, Feb. 14, 1981; children by previous marriage: Edward Robert, Rosemary, Therese, Joseph, Kevin, David. AB in Math. and Physics, Bowdoin Coll., Brunswick, Maine, 1953, BS, MS in Elec. Engring., 1953; ScD, MIT, 1956; doctor honoris causa Inst. Nat. Polytech. de Grenoble, 1994. With Bell Telephone Labs., Whippany, N.J., 1955-59; assoc. prof. elec. engring. Princeton, 1959-63, prof., 1963-66, dir. Computer Center, 1961-66; prof. elec. engring. and computer sci. Stanford (Calif.) U., 1967—, dir. Digital Systems Lab., 1969-78; dir. Center for Reliable Computing, 1976—; tech. advisor High Performance Systems, 1987-90. Author: A Survey of Switching Circuit Theory, 1962; Introduction to the Theory of Switching Circuits, 1965; Design of Digital Computers, 1975; Logic Design Principles with Emphasis on Testable Semicustom Circuits, 1986. Editor: Prentice-Hall Computer Engineering Series, 1988-90; assoc. editor: IRE Transactions on Computers, 1959-65; editorial bd. IEEE Design and Test, 1984-86; assoc. editor, IEEE Trans. Computer Aided Design, 1986-87. Patentee in field. Fellow AAAS, IEEE (pres. computer soc. 1970-71, Centennial medal 1984, Emanuel Piore award 1996), Assn. Computing Machinery (assoc. editor jour. 1963-69); mem. IEEE Computer Soc. (Tech. Achievement award 1984, Taylor L. Booth Edn. award 1991), Am. Fedn. Info. Processing Socs. (dir., exec. com.), Internat. Fedn. Info. Processing (charter), Japan Soc. Promotion of Sci. Office: Stanford U Ctr for Reliable Computing Gates 2A Stanford CA 94305-4055

MCCLUSKEY, JEAN LOUISE, civil and consulting engineer; b. Pitts., Jan. 8, 1947; d. Matthew Ralph McCluskey Sr. and Violet (Banas) Fontaine. BS in Civil Engring., Northeastern U., 1969; MA in Urban Affairs, Boston U., 1974; postgrad., MIT, 1984. Registered profl. engr., N.Y., Maine, Mass. Staff engr. Metcalf & Eddy, Inc., Boston, 1969-74, project planner/engr., 1974-75, 76-79; sr. environ. engr. Exxon Co. USA, Pelham, N.Y., 1975-76; environ. engr. Stone and Webster Engring. Corp., Boston, 1979-84, project mgr., 1984-89, v.p., 1989-94, dir. project mgmt., 1991-93; also bd. dirs. Stone & Webster Engring. Corp., Boston; pres. Stone & Webster Civil & Transp. Svcs., Inc., 1993-94; v.p., area mgr. Parsons, Brinckerhoff, Quade & Douglas, Inc., Boston, 1995—. Mem. Hull (Mass.) Fin. Com., 1985-88; mem. adv. com. Hull H.S., 1989-95; trustee New Eng. Aquarium, 1993-96, South Shore Charter Sch., 1994-96; mem. govt. affairs com., chair Am. Cons. Engrs. Coun. New. Eng., 1995-96, bd. dirs., 1996—. Recipient Outstanding Woman award Cambridge (Mass.) YWCA, 1986; fellow MIT, 1984. Mem. Water Environ. Fedn., Greater Boston C. of C. (bd. dirs. 1992-94), Chi Epsilon. Roman Catholic. Office: 120 Boylston St Boston MA 02116-4611

MCCLUSKEY, MATTHEW CLAIR, physical chemist; b. New Kensington, Pa., Jan. 2, 1957; s. John J. and Carole Sue (Hilliard) McC.; m. Cornelia Mary Sanders, Sept. 26, 1981. BS, Ohio State U., 1985; PhD, U. Va., 1990. Post-doctoral fellow in chemistry Dept. Energy Lawrence Berkeley Lab., Berkeley, 1990-92; cons. Annapolis Rsch. Assocs., Fontana, Calif., 1991—; historic ho. preservationist The Ridge, Manchester, Ohio, 1992—; pres., founder YogaWorks, 1994—; cons. Hopewell Farm, 1993—. Contbr. articles to profl. jours. Mem. Inter-Tribal Indian Coun., 1993—. Home: 5151 Us Highway 52 Manchester OH 45144-9753

MCCOBB, JOHN BRADFORD, JR., lawyer; b. Orange, N.J., Oct. 14, 1939; s. John Bradford and Dorothea Joyce (Hoffman) M.; m. Maureen Kelly, Oct. 6, 1973; 1 dau., Carrie Elizabeth. A.B., Princeton U. cum laude, 1961; J.D., Stanford U., 1966; LL.M., NYU, 1973. Bar: Calif. 1967. Assoc., IBM, Armonk, N.Y., 1966-1974, gen. counsel, Tokyo, 1974-77, lab. counsel, Endicott, N.Y., 1977-79, sr. atty., White Plains, N.Y., 1979-81, regional counsel, Dallas, 1981-83; counsel, sec. IBM Instruments, Inc., Danbury, Conn., 1983-87; area counsel European Labs, Hursley, England, 1987-90; counsel govtl. programs IBM, Washington, 1990—. Trustee Princeton-in-Asia, Inc., 1970-86 . Princeton-in-Asia-teaching fellow at Chinese Univ. of Hong Kong, 1963-65. Mem. ABA, State Bar of Calif., Phi Beta Kappa. Contbr. articles to profl. jours. Office: IBM 1301 K St NW Washington DC 20005-3317

MCCOID, DONALD JAMES, bishop; b. Wheeling, W.Va., Dec. 31, 1943; s. Roy Conrad and Alberta Virginia (Sturm) McC.; m. Saundra Ernette Piisila, Oct. 20, 1973; children: Kimberly, Elizabeth. AB, West Liberty (W.Va.) State Coll., 1965; MDiv, Luth. Theol. Sem., Phila., 1968; DD (hon.), Thiel Coll., 1983. Ordained to ministry Evang. Luth. Ch. in Am., 1968. Pastor St. Luke's Luth. Ch., Monessen, Pa., 1968-72; assoc. pastor St. John's Luth. Ch. Highland, Pitts., 1972-74; area Luth. coord. Western Pa.—W.Va. synod, Luth. Ch. Am., Clarksburg, W.Va., 1974-77; sr. pastor Trinity Luth. Ch., Latrobe, Pa., 1977-87; bishop Southwestern Pa. synod, Evang. Luth. Ch. in Am., Pitts., 1987—; bd. dirs. Pa. Coun. Chs., Harrisburg. Bd. dirs. Religious Leadership Forum, Pitts., 1988—, Luth. Svcs. in Am., 1997—; mem. exec. com. Christian Assocs. S.W. Pa., Pitts., 1988—, chair coun., 1994—. Office: Evang Luth Ch in Am SW Pa Synod 9625 Perry Hwy Pittsburgh PA 15237-5555

MCCOLL, HUGH LEON, JR., bank executive; b. Bennettsville, S.C., June 18, 1935; s. Hugh Leon and Frances Pratt (Carroll) McC.; m. Jane Bratton Spratt, Oct. 3, 1959; children: Hugh Leon III, John Spratt, Jane Bratton. B.S. in Bus. Adminstrn, U. N.C., 1957. Trainee NCNB Nat. Bank, Charlotte, 1959-61, officer, 1961-65, v.p., 1965-68, sr. v.p., 1968, div. exec., 1969, exec. v.p., 1970-73, vice chmn. bd., 1973-74, pres., 1974-83, also dir.; chmn., CEO NationsBank Corp., Charlotte, 1983—; bd. dirs. Sonoco Products Inc., Hartsville, S.C., CSX Corp., Richmond, Va., Jefferson-Pilot Corp., Greensboro, N.C. Trustee Heineman Found., Charlotte, 1976—, Queens Coll., Charlotte; bd. visitors Grad. Sch. Bus. U. N.C. at Chapel Hill; chmn. Charlotte Uptown Devel. Corp., 1978-81, 85. 1st lt. USMCR, 1957-59. Mem. Bankers Roundtable (mem. trialateral commn.), Am. Bankers Assn., N.C. Bankers Assn. (pres. 1974). Democrat. Presbyterian. Office: NationsBank Corp 100 N Tryon St Fl 57 Charlotte NC 28202-4000*

MCCOLLAM, WILLIAM, JR., utility company executive; b. New Orleans, Mar. 15, 1925; s. William and Marie (Mason) McC.; m. Hope Flower Joffrion, Apr. 20, 1947; children: Ellendale McCollam Hoffman, William Cage, Stephen Mason. B.S., La. State U., 1943; B.S. in Engring., U.S. Mil. Acad., 1946; M.S. in Civil Engring., MIT, 1954. Registered profl. engr., N.Y. Commd. 2d lt. U.S. Army, 1946; advanced through grades to lt. col. U.S Army; resigned U.S. Army, 1961; with Ark. Power and Light Co., Little Rock, 1961-70, exec. asst., 1961-64; v.p. Ark Power and Light Co., Little Rock, 1964-68; sr. v.p. Ark. Power and Light Co., Little Rock, 1968-70; exec. v.p. New Orleans Pub. Service, 1970-71, pres., 1971-78; pres. Edison Electric Inst., Washington, 1978-90, pres. emeritus, 1990—; cons. energy mgmt. Washington, 1990—; bd. dirs. McDermott Internat., Inc., New Orleans, Burns and Roe Enterprises, Inc., Oradell, N.J.; trustee Thomas Alva Edison Found., Detroit, 1978-89; past chmn. S.W. Power Pool, Little Rock, 1973-74, Nat. Elec. Reliability Coun., Princeton, N.J., 1975-78; bd. dirs., exec. com. U.S. Mem. Com., World Energy Coun., Washington, 1978-94. Past pres. Greater New Orleans area C. of C., 1974-75; former dir. Loyola U., New Orleans, 1975-78; pres.'s council Tulane U., 1982-86. Named to La. State U. Alumni Hall of Distinction, 1985; recipient U.S. Energy award in recognition of outstanding contbn. to world energy coun., 1991. Mem. La. Soc. Profl. Engrs. (A.B. Paterson award 1975). Republican. Episcopalian. Clubs: Chevy Chase, Metropolitan (Washington); Boston, New Orleans Country. Home: 2411 Tracy Pl NW Washington DC 20008-1628 Office: Edison Electric Inst 701 Pennsylvania Ave NW Washington DC 20004-2608

MCCOLLEY, ROBERT MCNAIR, history educator; b. Salina, Kans., Feb. 2, 1933; s. Grant and Alice Elizabeth (McNair) McC.; m. Diane Laurene Kelsey, Aug. 30, 1958; children: Rebecca, Susanna, Teresa, Margaret, Carolyn, Robert Lauren. B.A., Harvard U., 1954, M.A., 1955; Ph.D., U Calif.-Berkeley, 1960. Instr. to prof. history U. Ill., Urbana, 1960-97; mem. Com. for Advanced Placement Test in Am. History, 1987-90, chmn. 1988-90. Author: Slavery and Jeffersonian Virginia, 1964 (Dickerson award 1964); editor: Federalists, Republicans and Foreign Entanglements, 1969; editor: Henry Adams, John Randolph, 1995; co-editor: Refracting America, 1993; mem. editorial bd. Jour. Early Republic, 1981-85, Va. Mag. of History and Biography, 1994-97; mem. editorial bd. Ill. Hist. Jour., 1984-93, chair, 1991-93; classical recs. reviewer Fanfare mag., 1989—. Mem. Am. Hist. Assn., Soc. Historians of Early Republic (pres. 1982), Orgn. Am. Historians, Va. Hist. Soc., Ill. Hist. Soc. (bd. dirs. 1978-81, 92-95, pres. 1997—), Chgo. Hist. Soc., Cliff Dwellers. Episcopalian. Home: 503 W Illinois St Urbana IL 61801-3927 Office: U Ill Dept History 810 S Wright St Urbana IL 61801-3611

MC COLLISTER, JOHN CHARLES, writer, clergyman, educator, executive producer; b. Pitts., June 1, 1935; s. John Charles and Caroline Jesse (Hall) Mc C.; m. Beverly Ann Chase, Aug. 6, 1960; children: Beth Ann, Amy Susan, Michael John. BA, Capital U., 1957; MDiv, Luth. Theol. Sem., Columbus, Ohio, 1961; PhD, Mich. State U., 1969. Ordained to ministry Luth. Ch., 1961. Pastor Zion Luth. Ch., Freeland, Mich., 1961-65, Bethlehem Luth. Ch., Lansing, Mich., 1965-71; prof. religion and Greek Olivet (Mich.) Coll., 1970-74; prof. religion and philosophy Bethune-Cookman Coll., Daytona Beach, Fla., 1974-76; prof. religion and philosophy Embry-Riddle Aero. U., 1976-82, dir. profl. programs, 1979-80; cons. to pres., 1980-82; pres. Wright Advt. Co., Daytona Beach, 1975-76; CEO New Arran Prodns., Inc., Daytona Beach, 1993—, Yongestreet Prodns., Ormond Beach, Fla., 1986; arbitrator Fed. Mediation and Conciliation Svc., 1978; spl. master Fla. Pub. Employees Rels. Commn., 1975—; mgmt. cons. Hoover Ball and Bearing, Charlotte, Mich.; pres. Am. Writers Inst., 1982—. Host: Open Phone Forum, radio sta. WROD, Daytona Beach, 1974-76; author: A Philosophy of Flight, 1981, So Help Me, God, 1981, The Christian Book of Why, 1983, Problem Solving for Executives, 1984, The Sky is Home, 1986; co-author: The Sunshine Book, 1979, Day by Day, 1990; editor and compiler: A Child is Born, 1972, Portraits of the Christ, 1974, Writing for Dollars, 1995; ; contbr. articles to various mags. Vol. probation officer, Mich., 1961-71, hearing officer, 1970-74; commr. Mich. Dept. Commerce, 1969-72; speaker Nat. Lincoln Day Observance, Washington, 1982; internat. adviser Han Nam U., Taejon, Republic of Korea, 1989. Recipient Outstanding Am. award Daytona Beach Jaycees, 1974. Mem. Am. Arbitration Assn. Home and Office: 26 Lazy Eight Dr Daytona Beach FL 32124-6775

MCCOLLOM, HERBERT FORREST, JR., audiologist; b. Ridley Park, Pa., Sept. 7, 1931; s. Herbert Forrest and Dorothy Mae (Allison) McC.; m. Joan Elizabeth Fleming, June 16, 1956; children: Geoffrey, Mark. BA, Pa. State U., 1953; MEd, Franklin & Marshall, 1959. Cert. clin. competence in audiology, clin. competence in speech-lang. pathology. Tchr. Elizabethtown (Pa.) Schs., 1955-58; itinerant hearing clinician Lancaster (Pa.) County Supt. of Schs., 1958-64; audiologist, exec. dir. Hearing Conservation Ctr., Lancaster, 1966-77; pvt. practice in audiology Hearing Svcs. of Lancaster, 1977—. Co-author: Hearing Aid Dispensing Practice, 1984; contbr. articles to profl. jous. With U.S. Army, 1953-55. John F. Steinman scholarship Steinman Found., 1964. Fellow Acad. of Dispensing Audiologists (pres. 1986-87, jour. editor 1993-95), Am. Acad. Audiology, Pa. Acad. of Audiology, Am. Speech-Lang.-Hearing Assn. Republican. Avocations: writing, photography, Asian cooking. Office: Hearing Svcs of Lancaster 202 Butler Ave Lancaster PA 17601-6306

MC COLLOM, KENNETH ALLEN, retired university dean; b. Sentinel, Okla., June 17, 1922; s. Walter William and Irene Pearl (Allen) McC.; m. Katherine Tompkins, Jan. 4, 1944; children: Alan Tompkins, Neal Norman. B.S., Okla. State U., 1948; M.S., U. Ill., 1949; Ph.D., Iowa State U., 1964. Engr. Phillips Petroleum Co., Bartlesville, Okla., 1949-51, 54-57; sect. chief, br. mgr. Phillips Petroleum Co. (Atomic Energy div.), Idaho Falls, Idaho, 1951-54, 57-62; project leader Ames (Iowa) Lab. Research Reactor, 1962-64; prof. elec. engring. Okla. State U., Stillwater, 1964-68; asst. dean engring. Okla. State U., 1968-73, assoc. dean engring., 1973-77, dean engring., architecture and tech., 1977-86; adminstrv. judge, mem. atomic safety and licensing bd. panel Nuclear Regulatory Commn., 1976—; cons. AEC; mem. Okla. State Bd. Registration for Profl. Engrs. and Land Surveyors, 1986-92, chmn. 1991-92; mem. Nat. Council for Examiners of Engring. and Surveying, 1986-92. Patentee in field. Asst. condr. Idaho Falls Civic Symphony Orch., 1958-60; bd. mem., Cub Pack leader, asst. scoutmaster Boy Scouts Am., 1960-72; campaign chmn. Stillwater United Fund, 1971-72. Served with AUS, 1942-46, ETO. Recipient Disting. Alumnus award elec. engring. dept. U. Ill., Profl. Devel. citation in engring. Iowa State U., Disting. Svc. award Nat. Coun. for Examiners of Engring. and Surveying, 1992. Fellow Am. Soc. Engring. Edn. (Chester F. Carlson award 1973, Outstanding Engr. in Okla. 1990); mem. IEEE (life, Centennial Medallion award 1993), Am. Nuclear Soc. (chmn. Okla. sect. 1974-75), Nat. Profl. Engrs. Soc. (nat. dir. 1975-78), Okla. Profl. Engrs. Soc. (adminstrv. v.p. 1974-75, exec. v.p. 1975-76, pres. 1976-77). Pres.'s Disting Scholarship established in his name Okla. State U. Home: 1107 W Knapp Ave Stillwater OK 74075-2712

MCCOLLOUGH, MICHAEL LEON, astronomer; b. Sylva, N.C., Nov. 3, 1953; s. Stribling Mancell and Vivian Hazel (Bradley) McC. B.S., Auburn U., 1975, M.S., 1981; PhD, Ind. U., 1989. Lab. instr. Auburn (Ala.) U., 1974-75, grad. asst., 1975-77, lab. technician, 1977-78; assoc. instr. Ind. U., Bloomington, 1978-86; ops. astronomer Computer Scis. Corp., Balt., 1988-90, sci. planning and scheduling system dep. br. chief, 1990-92; data processing and distbn. mgr. U.S. ROSAT Sci. Data Ctr., 1992-93; asst. system mgr. BATSE Data Analysis System, 1993—; vis. lectr. Okla. State U., 1986-87; vis. asst. prof. U. Okla., 1987-88. Recipient Achievement award Space Telescope Sci. Inst., 1990, 91, Pub. Svc. Group Achievement award NASA, 1991, Cert. Recognition, 1991, 93. Mem. Am. Astron. Soc., Royal Astron. Soc., Astron. Soc. Pacific, Am. Phys. Soc., Sigma Xi (assoc.), Sigma Pi Sigma. Baptist. Home: 201 Water Hill Rd Apt G13 Madison AL 35758-2919 Office: NASA/MSFC Code ES84 Huntsville AL 35812

MCCOLLUM, ALLAN LLOYD, artist; b. L.A., Aug. 4, 1944; s. Warren Whiting and Elizabeth Ann (Hinton) McC. One-man shows include Jack Glenn Gallery, Corona Del Mar, Calif., 1971, 72, Nicholas Wilder Gallery, L.A., 1973, 74, Cusack Gallery, Houston, 1973, Douglas Drake Gallery, Kansas City, 1975, 79, 83, Claire S. Copley Gallery, L.A., 1977, Julian Pretto & Co., N.Y.C., 1979, 87, 88, 89, 90, Galerie Yvon Lambert, Paris, 1980, 88, 90, Artists Space, N.Y.C., 1980, 112 Workshop, N.Y.C., 1980, Dioptre, Geneva, 1981, Hal Bromm Gallery, N.Y.C., 1981, Galerie Nicole Gonet, Lausanne, France, 1982, Health Gallery, Atlanta, 1982, Ben Shahn Galleries William Patterson Coll., Wayne, N.J., 1982, Marian Goodman Gallery, N.Y.C., 1983, Rhona Hoffman Gallery, Chgo., 1984, 85, 86-87, Richard Kuhlenschmidt Gallery, L.A., 1984, 89, 90, Diane Brown Gallery, N.Y.C., 1984, 86, 87, 89, Lisson Gallery, London, 1985, 87, 91, Cash/Newhouse Gallery, N.Y.C., 1985, 86, Gallery Nature Morte, N.Y.C., 1985, Heath Gallery, Atlanta, 1985, Tex. Gallery, Houston, 1985, Kuhlenschmidt Simon Gallery, L.A., 1985, 86, Guttenbergstrasse 62, Stuttgart, 1986, Inst. Contemporary Art U. Pa., Phila., 1986, Portikus, Frankfurt, Germany, 1988, John Weber Gallery, N.Y.C., 1988, 89, 90, 92, Centre d'Art Contemporain, Geneva, Switzerland, 1993, Castello Di Rivara, Turin, Italy, 1993, Modulo Centro Difusor De Arte, Lisbon, Portugal, 1993, Kohji Ogura Gallery, Nagoya, Japan, 1993, Galerie Franck & Schulte, Berlin, 1993, Studio Trisorio, Naples, Italy, Shiraishi Contemporary Art Inc., Tokyo, 1993, Mus. Haus Esters, Krefeld, Germany, 1994, S.L. Simpson Gallery, Toronto, Can., 1994, others; exhibited in group shows at Los Angeles County Mus. Art, L.A., 1971, 87, Seattle Art Mus., 1972, Detroit Inst. Arts, 1973, Whitney Mus. Am. Art, N.Y.C., 1975, 85, 89, 89-90, L.A. Inst. Contemporary Art, 1977, Pratt Inst. Gallery, N.Y.C., 1982, Mus. Fine Arts, Mus. N.Mex., Santa Fe, 1983, Nexus Contemporary Art Ctr., Atlanta, 1985, New Mus. Contemporary Art, N.Y.C., 1986, Padigolione d'Arte Contemporanea, Milan, Italy, 1986-87, Moderna Museet, Stockholm, 1987, Israel Mus., Jerusalem, 1987, 90, Sidney Janis Gallery, N.Y.C., 1987, 88, Milw. Art Mus., 1987-88, Internat. Ctr. Photography, N.Y.C., 1988, 89, 90, Mus. Contemporary Art, L.A., 1989, Nat. Mus. Am. Art, Washington, 1989, Galeria 57, Madrid, 1990, Mus. Contemporary Art, Chgo., 1990, La Gerenne Lemot Getigne, Paris, 1991, Carnegie Mus. Art, Pitts., 1991-92, Mus. Modern Art, N.Y.C., 1992, Museo National de Arte Reina Sofia, Madrid, 1992, Lillehammer Art Mus., Norway, 1993, Lieu D'Art Contemporain, France, 1993, numerous others; represented in permanent collections Met. Mus. Art, N.Y.C., Mus. Modern Art, N.Y.C., Mus. Fine Arts, Boston, Mus. Modern Art, San Francisco, Los Angeles County Mus. Art, Mus. Contemporary Art, L.A., Denver Art Mus., Art Inst. Chgo., Detroit Inst. Arts, Mus. Fine Arts, Houston, Hirshhorn Mus., Washington, Seattle Art Mus., Newark (N.J.) Mus., Long Beach (Calif.) Mus. Art, Springfield (Mo.) Mus. Fine Art, John & Mable Ringling Mus. Art, Sarasota, Fla., Nelson Gallery Art, Kansas City, Santa Fe Mus. Art, Grey Art Gallery NYU, N.Y.C., Weatherspoon Art Gallery, Greensboro, N.C., Washington U., St. Louis, Cin. Art Mus., Van Abbe Mus., Eindhoven, The Netherlands, Louisiana Mus. Modern Art, Humlebaek, Denmark, Inst. Valenciano de Arte Moderno, Valencia, Spain, Mus. Boymans van Beunigen, Rotterdam, The Netherlands, New Tokyo Met. Mus., Ctr. Georges Pompidou, Paris, Musee National d'Art Moderne, Paris, Sprengel-Mus., Hannover, Germany, Rooseum, Malmo, Sweden, Le Consortium, Dijon, France, Fonds Regional d'Art Contemporain Bourgogne, KunstMuseum Wolfsburg, Germany, Ctr. d'art Contemporain, Geneva, Musée d'art Contemporain et Moderne, Geneva. Short Term Activities Fellowships grantee NEA, 1973; Individual Visual Artist fellow NEA, 1988. Democrat. Studio: 17 White St Apt 2B New York NY 10013-2485

MCCOLLUM, ALVIN AUGUST, real estate company executive; b. L.A., Jan. 20, 1920; s. Nile Clarkson and Ida Martha (Kuhlman) McC.; m. Maxine Eleanor Seeberg, July 29, 1944; children: Robert Michael, James Alan, Patricia Kathleen. BA, UCLA, 1941; postgrad., U.S. Naval Acad., 1946, Southwestern U., 1949-50. Exec. v.p., dir. Strout Realty, N.Y.C., 1948-61, Del E. Webb Corp., Phoenix, 1961-67; pres., dir. Sahara Nev. Corp., Las Vegas, 1964-67, Devel. Svcs., Inc., Scottsdale, Ariz., 1967-69; pres., chmn. Recreation Leisure Land, Inc., Scottsdale, 1969-71; asst. pres., dir. A.J. Industries, Inc., L.A., 1971-74; pres., dir. Carefree (Ariz.) Ranch, Inc., 1974-76; pres., bd. dir. Cons. Internat., Scottsdale, 1976—; chmn. CEO Greenway Environ. Svs., Inc., Gilbert, Ariz., 1992—; pres., bd. dirs. Combined Assets, Inc., Westlake Village, Calif., First Realty Fin., Inc., L.A., Corp. Capital Resources, Inc., Westlake Village. Bd. dirs. Admiral Nimitz Found., Fredericksburg, Tex., 1970—, Boys Club Las Vegas, 1964-68, United Fund, Las Vegas, 1966; co-chmn. NCCJ, Las Vegas, 1966; elder Presbyn. Ch. USA, 1954—. Lt. USN, 1943-48, PTO. Mem. Masons, Shriners, Am. Legion, Mt. Shadows Country Club (bd. dirs. 1962-64). Avocations; golf, swimming, camping, sailing. Home: 215 N Power Rd # 180 Mesa AZ 85205 Office: Greenway Environ Svcs Inc 644 E Southern Ave Ste 204 Mesa AZ 85204-4934

MCCOLLUM, BETTY, state legislator; b. July 12, 1954; m. Douglas McCollum; 2 children. BS in Edn., Coll. St. Catherine. Retail store mgr. Minn.; mem. Minn. Ho. Reps., 1992—, mem. edn. com., environ. and natural resources com., mem. gen. legis. com., vet. affairs and elections com., mem. transportation and transit com., asst. majority leader, chair legis. commn. on econ. status of women, mem. rules and adminstrv. legis. com. Mem. St. Croix Valley Coun. Girl Scouts, Greater East Side Boy Scouts. Democrat. Home: 2668 4th Ave E North Saint Paul MN 55109-3116 Office: Minn Ho of Reps State Office Bldg 100 Constitution Ave Ste 501 Saint Paul MN 55155-1201*

MCCOLLUM, CLIFFORD GLENN, college dean emeritus; b. South Gifford, Mo., May 12, 1919; s. William Henry and Aultie V. (Westfall) McC.; m. Alice Elizabeth Erickson, Aug. 18, 1940; children: Eric Edward, Lisa Buren. Student, Central Coll., 1935-37; B.S., U. Mo., 1939, M.A., 1947, Ed.D., 1949. Tchr. pub. schs. Monett, Mo., 1938-39, Poplar Bluff, Mo., 1939-41, Boonville, Mo., 1941-42; asst. prof. sci. U. No. Iowa, 1949-55, assoc. prof., 1956-59, prof., 1959-84, prof. emeritus, 1984—, head dept. sci., 1957-68; dean U. No. Iowa (Coll. Natural Scis.), 1968-84, dean emeritus, 1984—; prof. State U. N.Y. at Oneonta, 1955-56; Dir., instl. rep. Central States Univs., Inc.; cons. Coronet Instrnl. Films; cons. on sci. curricula to pub. schs. and colls.; speaker in field. Contbr. articles to profl. jours. Served with USAAF, 1943-46. Fellow AAAS (nat. committeeman 1964-67), Iowa Acad. Sci. (pres. 1979-80); mem. Am. Inst. Biol. Scis., Nat. Assn. Biology Tchrs. (regional dir. 1963-65), Nat. Assn. Research in Sci. Teaching, Nat. Sci. Tchrs. Assn., Sigma Xi, Phi Delta Kappa. Home: 2002 Chapel Hill Rd Columbia MO 65203-1916 *My personal response to the philosophical conditions in which we live today is one of preparing to live rather consistently with crises. It is my conviction that the mood of our time is toward a growing pessimism, and much of this is associated with the concomitants of a galloping technology. Yet we are not willing at this point to give up our human condition to the natural evolution that would result from basic environmental mechanisms. We will still try to condition that destiny.*

MCCOLLUM, GARY WAYNE, government official; b. Mineral Wells, Tex., Apr. 14, 1939; s. Buster Len and Edna Sue (Fowler) McC.; m. Sonja Dru Woodham, May 27, 1960 (div. 1973); children: Scott, Greg, Cynthia; m. Barbara Jean Millican, Sept. 16, 1978. BS in Biology, East Tex. State U., 1962, MS in Biology, 1963. Quarantine control officer Lunar Receiving Lab., Apollo Program to Moon, NASA Johnson Space Ctr., Houston, 1969-71; mgr. med. surveillance office Apollo Flight Crew Health Stabilization Program, Houston, 1971-72, Skylab Flight Crew Health Stabilization Program, Houston, 1972-74; life scis. ground ops. mgr. NASA Life Sci. Project Div., Houston, 1974-78, discipline mgr., 1978-83; payload integration mgr. NASA Space Shuttle Program Office, Houston, 1983-88; program mgr. NASA Hdqs. Office Space Sci. & Applications, Washington, 1988-93, NASA Hdqs. Office Life & Microgravity Scis. & Applications, Washington, 1993-95; engring. rsch. tech. discipline mgr. space sta. program office NASA Johnson Space Ctr., Houston, 1995-96, life scis. discipline mgr., 1996—; successful completion as hdqtrs. payloads program mgr. of STS-40/Spacelab Life Scis.-I mission, 1991, STS-47/Spacelab-J, coop. mission with Japan, 1992, STS-58/Spacelab Life Scis.-2 mission, 1993, STS-65/Internat. Microgravity Lab.-2 mission, 1994. 1st lt. USAF, 1963-66. Recip. Disting. Alumnus Award, East Texas State U., 1994. Mem. AIAA (sr.), Sr. Exec. Assn., Delta Tau Delta. Avocations: all sports, travel. Office: NASA Johnson Space Ctr Mail Code OZ4 Houston TX 77058

MC COLLUM, IRA WILLIAM, JR. (BILL MC COLLUM), congressman; b. Brooksville, Fla., July 12, 1944; s. Ira William and Arline Gray (Lockhart) McC.; m. Ingrid Mary Seebohm, Sept. 25, 1971; children: Douglas Michael, Justin Randolph, Andrew Lockhart. BA, U. Fla., 1965, JD, 1968. Bar: Fla. 1968. Ptnr. Pitts, Eubanks & Ross (P.A.), Orlando, Fla., 1973-80; mem. 97th-102nd Congresses from 5th Dist. Fla., 1981-92, 103d-105th Congresses from 8th Dist. Fla., 1993—; ranking minority mem., mem. banking and fin. svcs. subcom. on fin. instns. supervision, mem. regulation and deposit ins. com., chmn. judiciary subcom. on crime, mem. select com. on intelligence; vice chair House Rep. Conf. 101st-103d Congresses. Chmn. Rep. Exec. Com. Seminole County, Fla., 1976-80; county chmn.'s rep. 5th Dist. Fla. State Rep. Exec. Com., 1977-80; co-chmn. rep. platform com., 1992. With USN, 1969-72. Mem. Fla. Bar, Naval Res. Assn., Res. Officers Assn., Orange County Bar Assn. (exec. coun. 1975-79), Am. Legion, Mil. Order World Wars, Fla. Blue Key, Phi Delta Phi, Omicron Delta Kappa, Kiwanis. Episcopalian. Office: 2266 Rayburn HOB Washington DC 20515

MCCOLLUM, JAMES FOUNTAIN, lawyer; b. Reidsville, N.C., Mar. 24, 1946; s. James F. and Dell (Frazier) McC.; m. Susan Shasek, Apr. 26, 1969; children: Audra Lynne, Amy Elizabeth. BS, Fla. Atlantic U., 1968; JD, Fla. State U., 1972. Bar: U.S. Ct. Appeals (5th cir.) 1973, Fla. 1972, U.S. Ct. Appeals (11th cir.) 1982. Assoc. Kennedy & McCollum, 1972-73; prin. James F. McCollum, P.A., 1973-77, McCollum & Oberhausen, P.A., 1977-80, McCollum & Rhoades, Sebring, Fla., 1980-86; pres. Highlands Devel. Concepts, Inc., Sebring, 1982—; sec. Focus Broadcast Communications, Inc., Sebring, 1982-87; mng. ptnr. Highlands Investment Service. Treas. Highlands County chpt. ARC, 1973-76; vestryman St. Agnes Episcopal Ch., 1973—, chancellor, 1978—; mem. Fla. Sch. Bd. Atty.'s Assn., 1974—, bd. dirs., 1989—, pres., 1995-96; mem. Com. 100 of Highlands County, 1975-83, bd. dirs., 1985-87, chmn., 1991-92; chmn. Highlands County High Speed Rail Task Force; chmn. bd., treas. Ctrl. Fla. Racing Assn., 1976-78; chmn. Leadership Sebring; life mem., past pres. Highlands Little Theatre, Inc.; bd. dirs. Palms of Sebring Nursing Home, 1988-90, Palms Estate Mobile Home Park, Sebring Airport Authority, 1988-90, treas., 1988, chmn. indsl. com., 1988, vice-chmn., 1989-90, chmn., 1990-91, Highlands County High Speed Rail Task Force, 1986-89; bd. dirs. Highlands County Family YMCA, 1985-93, pres. Sebring br., 1992-93, chmn. bldg. com., 1992-94. Recipient ARC citation, 1974, Presdl. award of appreciation Fla. Jaycees, 1980-81, 82, 85, Outstanding Svc. award Highlands Coun. of 100, 1988, Most Valuable Player award Highlands Little Theatre, Inc., 1986, Zenon Significant Achievement award, 1991; named Jaycee of Year, Sebring Jaycees, 1981, Outstanding Local Chpt. Pres., U.S. Jaycees, 1977. Outstanding Service award Highlands Council of 100, 1988. Mem. ABA, ATLA, Comml. Law League Am., Am. Arbitration Assn. (comml. arbitration panel), Nat. Assn. Retail Credit Attys., Fla. Bar (jour. com.), Highlands County Bar Assn. (past chmn. legal aid com.), Fla. Sch. Bd. Attys. Assn. (dir. 1989—, v.p. 1993-94, pres. 1994-95), Greater Sebring C. of C. (dir. 1982-89, pres. 1986-

87, chmn. transp. com. 1986—, Most Valuable Dir. award 1986, 87), Fla. Jaycees (life mem. internat. senate 1977—), Lions (bd. dirs. 1972-73, v.p. 1994—, Disting. award 1984). Republican. Episcopalian. Office: 129 S Commerce Ave Sebring FL 33870-3602

MCCOLLUM, JEAN HUBBLE, medical assistant; b. Peoria, Ill., Oct. 21, 1934; d. Claude Ambrose and Josephine Mildred (Beiter) Hubble; m. Everett Monroe Patton, Sept. 4, 1960 (div. Jan. 1969); 1 child, Linda Joanne; m. James Ward McCollum, Jan. 2, 1971; 1 child, Steven Ward. Student, Bradley U., Ill. Cen. Coll. Stenographer Caterpillar Tractor Co., Peoria, 1952-53, supr. stenographer pool, 1953-55, adminstrv. sec., treas., 1955-60, sec., asst. dept. mgr., 1969-71; med. staff sec. Proctor Cmty. Hosp., Peoria, 1978-82; med. asst. Drs. Taylor, Fox and Morgan, Peoria, 1982-84; freelance med. asst. Meth. Hosp. and numerous physicians, Peoria, 1984-89; office mgr. Dr. Danehower, McLelland and Stone, Peoria, 1989—. Vol. tutor Northmoor Sch., Peoria, 1974-78; bd. dirs., mem. exec. com., com. chmn. Planned Parenthood, Peoria, 1990-92. Recipient Outstanding Performance award Proctor Hosp., 1981, also various awards for svc. to schs., ch. and hosps. for mentally ill. Mem. Nat. Wildlife Fedn., Mensa Internat. (publs. officer, editor 1987-89), Mothers League (treas. 1977), Willow Knolls Country Club (social com. 1989-90), Nature Conservancy, World Wildlife Fund, Forest Park Found., Jacques Cousteau Soc., Wilderness Soc. Methodist. Avocations: socializing, reading, travel, theatre, yoga. Home: 2822 W Pine Hill Ln Peoria IL 61614-3256

MCCOLLUM, JOHN MORRIS, tenor; b. Coalinga, Calif., Feb. 21, 1922; s. Fay James and Ingabord Telette (Mason) McC.; m. Mary Margaret Wilson, Jan. 23, 1944; children: Kristi Elizabeth, Timothy James. Student, Coalinga Coll., 1939-40; B.A. in Journalism, U. Calif. at Berkeley, 1947; student voice and acting, Am. Theatre Wing, 1951-53. Reporter, city editor Coalinga Record, 1947-50; editor agrl. news U. Calif. Coll. Agr., 1950-51; prof. music and chmn. voice faculty U. Mich.; dir. U. Mich. div. Nat. Music Camp; faculty Aspen Music Festival and School, 1963-76. Concert and opera singer, 1951—, soloist, Fifth Ave. Presbyn. Ch., N.Y.C., 1953-56, debut, Town Hall, N.Y.C., 1952, with, Boston Symphony Orchestra, Tanglewood, Mass., summer 1952, engagements with Symphony Orchestras in, N.Y.C., Chgo., Phila., San Francisco, Cleve., Washington, St. Louis, Detroit, New Orleans, Toronto, London, Mexico; with opera companies of, Boston, Washington, Toronto, Ft. Worth, Central City, Colo., also, NBC-TV, music festivals and oratorio societies, European debut, Festival of Two Worlds, Spoleto, Italy, summer 1958, Santa Fe Opera Co., leading tenor, N.Y.C. Opera Co., performing mem., Music Assos. of Aspen. (Recipient award Atwater Kent Auditions 1950, Am. Theatre Wing award 1952). Mem. Rep. Ctrl. Com., Fresno County, Calif., 1950; pres. Ann Arbor Civic Theatre, 1987-88; mem. Sarasota County Rep. exec. com.; mem., bd. dirs. Sarasota Concert Assn.,; bd. dirs. Univ. Mich. Alumni Club. Mem. U. Calif. Alumni Assn., Nat. Assn. Tchrs. Singing, Am. Acad. Tchrs. Singing, Alpha Tau Omega, Sigma Delta Chi, Pi Kappa Lambda. Episcopalian (lay reader). Clubs: Rotary (pres. 1977, Paul Harris fellow), Ann Arbor Golf and Outing (pres. 1979), The Meadows Country Club (Sarasota, Fla.). Home: 3380 W Chelmsford Ct Sarasota FL 34235-0947

MCCOLLUM, ROBERT WAYNE, physician, educator; b. Waco, Tex., Jan. 29, 1925; s. Robert Wayne and Minnie (Brown) McC.; m. Audrey Talmage, Oct. 16, 1954; children: Cynthia, Douglas Scott. A.B., Baylor U., 1945; M.D., Johns Hopkins, 1948; D.P.H., London Sch. Hygiene and Tropical Medicine, 1958; MA (hon.), Yale U., 1965, Dartmouth Coll., 1985. Intern pathology Columbia-Presbyn. Med. Center, N.Y.C., 1948-49; intern internal medicine Vanderbilt Hosp., Nashville, 1949-50; asst. resident internal medicine Yale-New Haven Med. Center, 1950-51; mem. faculty Yale Sch. Medicine, 1951-81, prof. epidemiology, 1965-81, chmn. dept. epidemiology and public health, 1969-81; dean Sch. Medicine Dartmouth Coll., Hanover, N.H., 1982-90, prof. epidemiology, 1982-95, dean emeritus, 1990—; prof. emeritus, 1995—; assoc. physician Yale-New Haven Hosp., from 1954; v.p. Dartmouth-Hitchcock Med. Ctr., 1983-90; cons. WHO, 1962-79; surgeon gen. U.S. Army, from 1960. Contbr. articles on epidemiology and control infectious diseases to profl. jours. Bd. sci. advisers Merck Inst., 1981-85; trustee Mary Hitchcock Meml. Hosp., Hanover, 1982-90. Capt. M.C., AUS, 1952-54. Mem. Assn. Tchrs. Preventive Medicine, Am. Epidemiological Soc., Internat. Epidemiological Assn., Infectious Diseases Soc. Am., Conn. Acad. Sci. and Engring., Am. Coll. Epidemiology. Office: Dartmouth Med Sch Dartmouth-Hitchcock Med Ctr Lebanon NH 03756

MCCOMAS, DAVID JOHN, science administrator, space physicist; b. Milw., May 22, 1958; s. Harrold James and Hazelyn (Melconian) McC.; m. Richelle Wolff, May 30, 1981; children: Random A., Koan I., Orion G. BS in Physics, MIT, 1980; MS in Geophysics and Space Physics, UCLA, 1985, PhD in Geophysics and Space Physics, 1986. Mem. staff Los Alamos (N.Mex.) Nat. Lab., 1980-91, sect. leader space plasma and planetary physics, 1991-92, group leader space and atmospheric scis., 1992—; mem. strategic planning com. earth and space scis. divsn. Los Alamos Nat. Lab, 1986; mem. advanced composition explorer phase A study team NASA, 1988-89, mem. space physics data system steering com., 1990-91, mem. inner magnetosphere imaging study team, 1991-94; mem. com. solar-terrestrial rsch. Nat. Rsch. Coun., 1991-94, mem. com. space sci. tech. planning Aeronautics and Space Engring. Bd./space studies bd., 1992, mem. task group rsch. prioritization future space sci. space studies bd., 1994—. Assoc. editor Jour. Geophys. Rsch.-Space Physics, 1993-94; contbr. over 200 sci. papers to profl. jours. Grad. fellow Inst. Geophysics and Planetary Physics, 1983-84. Fellow Am. Geophysical Union (Macelwane medal 1993). Office: Los Alamos Nat Lab MS-D466 Los Alamos NM 87545

MC COMIC, ROBERT BARRY, real estate development company executive, lawyer; b. Selmer, Tenn., Nov. 6, 1939; s. Richard Donald and Ila Marie (Prather) McC.; children: Thomas Christopher, Robert Geoffrey. BS, Union U., 1961; LLB, Tulane U., 1964; postgrad. in law, U. Freiburg, W. Ger., 1964-65, Hague (Netherlands) Internat. Acad. Law, 1965. Bar: Tenn. 1964, N.Y. 1966, Calif. 1971. Assoc. Donovan Leisure Newton & Irvine, N.Y.C., 1965-68; assoc. gen. counsel Avco Corp., Greenwich, Conn., 1968-70; exec. v.p., pres., CEO Avco Community Developers, Inc., 1973-82; chmn., CEO R.B. McComic, Inc., 1982-92, McComic Consolidated, Inc., 1992—; bd. dirs. CDC Small Bus. Fin. Corp. Pres. emeritus U. Calif. San Diego Found. Honoree Human Relations Inst. Am. Jewish Com., 1981, Kellog's Celebrity Tribute, 1988. Mem. ABA, Calif. Bar Assn., San Diego County Bar Assn., Assn. of Bar of City of N.Y., San Diego Bldg. Industry Assn., San Diego Yacht Club, Order of Coif, Sigma Alpha Epsilon, Omicron Delta Kappa, Lambda Alpha. Home: 2032 Via Casa Alta La Jolla CA 92037-5732 Office: McComic Consolidated Inc 750 B St Ste 3140 San Diego CA 92101-8105

MCCONAHEY, STEPHEN GEORGE, securities company executive; b. Fond du Lac, Wis., Nov. 8, 1943; s. George and Charlotte McC.; m. Kathleen Louise Litten, Aug. 19, 1967; children: Heather, Benjamin. BS, U. Wis., 1966; MBA, Harvard U., 1968. Assoc. McKinsey & Co., Washington, 1968-72; White House fellow Washington, 1972-73; program adminstr. Dept. Transp., Washington, 1973-75; spl. asst. to Pres. Gerald Ford The White House, 1975-77; underwriter, ptnr. Boettcher & Co., Inc., Denver, 1977-80, mgr. pub. fin., 1980-82, mgr. corp. fin., 1982-84, pres., chief exec. officer, 1984-86, chmn. bd., 1986-87; chmn. bd. Boettcher Investment Corp., Denver, 1987-90; sr. v.p. for corp. and internat. devel. Kemper Corp., Chgo., 1991—; exec. v.p. Kemper Fin. Svcs., Inc., Chgo., 1991—; pres., COO EVEREN Capital Corp., Chgo., 1994—; chmn. oper. com. EVEREN Securities, Chgo., 1994—; trustee Amli Properties, Ill. Inst. Tech. Trustee Denver Symphony Assn., 1986; chmn. Greater Denver Corp., 1987; bd. dirs. The Denver Partnership; bd. fellows U. Denver. Served with USAR, 1968-74. Mem. Young Presidents Orgn., Greater Denver C. of C. (bd. dirs.), Denver Club, Colo. Harvard Bus. Sch. Club (Denver), Cherry Hills Country Club (Englewood, Colo.), Castle Pines Country Club (Castle Rock, Colo.), Chgo. Club. Home: 1050 E Green Oaks Dr Littleton CO 80121-1325 Office: EVEREN Securities Inc 77 W Wacker Dr Chicago IL 60601

MC CONAHEY, WILLIAM MCCONNELL, JR., physician, educator; b. Pitts., May 7, 1916; s. William McConnell and Charlotte Maude (Hixson) McC.; m. Adrienne Parsons Magness, June 15, 1940; children: William McConnell III, Meredith McConahey Pollak, Peter Magness. A.B., Washington and Jefferson Coll., 1938; M.D., Harvard U., 1942; M.S., U. Minn., 1948. Resident internal medicine Mayo Clinic, 1946-48, asst. to staff, 1949, mem. staff internal medicine and endocrinology, 1949-85, emeritus staff, 1986—; cons. internal medicine St. Mary's, Rochester Methodist hosps., 1949-85; chmn. dept. endocrinology Mayo Clinic, 1967-74; prof. medicine Mayo Grad. Sch. Medicine U. Minn., 1966-73, prof. medicine Mayo Med. Sch., 1973—. Author articles in field. Served with M.C. AUS, 1943-45; now col. Res. (ret.). Decorated Silver Star, Bronze Star; recipient Disting. Alumni Service award Washington and Jefferson Coll., 1978. Fellow ACP; mem. Am. Thyroid Assn. (Disting. Service award 1973, pres. 1976), Endocrine Soc., Am. Diabetes Assn., Am. Fedn. Clin. Investigation, AMA, Central Soc. Clin. Research, Zumbro Valley Med. Soc., Am. Assn. Clin. Endocrinologists (Disting. Clinician award 1997), Minn. Med. Assn., Phi Beta Kappa, Sigma Xi. Home: 1122 6th St SW Rochester MN 55902-1950

MCCONKEY, JAMES RODNEY, English educator, writer; b. Lakewood, Ohio, Sept. 2, 1921; s. Clayton Delano and Grace (Baird) McC.; m. Gladys Jean Voorhees, May 6, 1944; children: Lawrence Clark, John Crispin, James Clayton. BA, Cleve. Coll., 1943; MA, Western Res. U., 1946; PhD, U. Iowa, 1953. Teaching fellow, instr. Cleve. Coll., 1945-46; teaching asst. U. Iowa, Iowa City, 1949-50; asst. prof. Morehead State Coll., Ky., 1950-54, assoc. prof., 1954-56; asst. prof. Cornell U., Ithaca, N.Y., 1956-62, assoc. prof., 1962-67, prof., 1967-87, Goldwin Smith prof. English lit., 1987-92; Goldwin Smith prof. emeritus, 1992—; dir. Morehead Writers Workshop, 1951-56, Antioch Seminar in Writing and Pub., Yellow Springs, Ohio, 1957-59. Author: The Novels of E.M. Forster, 1957, Night Stand, 1965, Crossroads, 1968, Journey to Sahalin, 1971, The Tree House Confessions, 1979, Court of Memory, 1983, To a Distant Island, 1984; editor: The Structure of Prose, 1963, Chekhov and Our Age, 1985, Kayo: The Authentic and Annotated Autobiographical Novel From Outer Space, 1987, Rowan's Progress, 1992, Stories From My Life With the Other Animals, 1993, The Anatomy of Memory, 1996. Served with U.S. Army, 1943-45. Guggenheim fellow, 1970; Eugene Saxton Meml. Trust Fund fellow, 1962; recipient Nat. Endowment of Arts essay award, 1968, Am. Acad. and Inst. Arts and Letters award in lit., 1979. Democrat. Home: 402 Aiken Rd Trumansburg NY 14886-9733 Office: Cornell Univ Goldwin Smith Hall Dept English Ithaca NY 14853

MC CONKIE, GEORGE WILSON, education educator; b. Holden, Utah, July 15, 1937; s. G. Wilson and Mabel (Stephenson) McC.; m. Orlene Carol Johnson, Sept. 6, 1962; children: Lynnette Mooth, Heather Usevitch, April Rhiner, Faline Coffelt, George Wilson, Bryce Johnson, Camille, Elissa, Esther, Bryna, Ruth, Anna May, Cynthia, Thomas Oscar. A.A., Dixie Jr. Coll., 1957; B.S., Brigham Young U., 1960, M.S., 1961; Ph.D., Stanford U., 1966. Asst. prof. edn. Cornell U., 1964-70, assoc. prof., 1970-75, prof., 1975-78, chmn. dept. edn., 1977-78; prof. U. Ill., Champaign, 1978—, chmn. dept. ednl. psychology, 1993-94, 95—; sr. scientist Ctr. for Study of Reading, 1978—, Beckman Inst., 1989—; rsch. fellow Cath. U. Leuven, Belgium, 1991-92. Contbr. articles to profl. publs. Recipient Outstanding Sci. Contbn. award Soc. for Sci. Study of Reading, 1995; NIMH spl. fellow, 1991-92; grantee U.S. Office Edn., 1970-73, Nat. Inst. Edn., 1974-77, NIMH, 1974-84, NICHHD, 1983-89, 91-95, AT&T, 1986-89, NSF, 1989-91, CIA, 1991—, Army Rsch. Lab., 1996—, Yamaha Motor Corp., 1997—. Fellow Am. Psychol. Assn.; mem. Am. Ednl. Research Assn., Am. Psychol. Soc., Psychonomic Soc., Cognitive Sci. Soc. Mem. Ch. of Jesus Christ of Latter-day Saints. Home: 2605 Berniece Dr Champaign IL 61821-7225 Office: Beckman Inst for Advanced Sci and Tech 405 N Mathews Ave Urbana IL 61801-2325

MCCONNAUGHEY, BAYARD HARLOW, biology educator; b. Pitts., Apr. 21, 1916; s. Harlow Alexander and Hattie (Cherryman) McC.; m. Evelyn Irene Shirek, June 12, 1950; children: William B., Edward A., John, Rebecca, Diane. BA with highest honors, Pomona Coll., 1938; MA, U. Hawaii, 1941; PhD, U. Calif., Berkeley, 1946. From asst. prof. to prof. U. Oreg., Eugene, 1949-86, prof. emeritus, 1986—; assoc. prof. U. Indonesia, 1963-66; prof. biology World Campus Afloat Semester at Sea, World Cruise, 1974, 88. Author: Introduction to Marine Biology, 1990; contbr. articles to profl. jours. Tech. sgt. U.S. Army, 1942-44. Rsch. fellow Scripps Inst. Oceanography, LaJolla, Calif., 1948. Mem. Phi Beta Kappa, Sigma Xi. Democrat. Unitarian. Home: 1653 Fairmount Blvd Eugene OR 97403-1791

MCCONNAUGHEY, GEORGE CARLTON, JR., lawyer; b. Hillsboro, Ohio, Aug. 9, 1925; s. George Carlton and Nelle (Morse) McC.; m. Carolyn Schlieper, June 16, 1951; children: Elizabeth, Susan, Nancy. B.A., Denison U., 1949; LL.B., Ohio State U., 1951, J.D., 1967. Bar: Ohio 1951. Sole practice Columbus; ptnr. McConnaughey & McConnaughey, 1954-57, McConnaughey, McConnaughey & Stradley, 1957-62, Laylin, McConnaughey & Stradley, 1962-67, George, Greek, King, McMahon & McConnaughey, 1967-79, McConnaughey, Stradley, Mone & Moul, 1979-81, Thompson, Hine & Flory (merger McConnaughey, Stradley, Mone & Moul with Thompson, Hine & Flory), Cleve., Columbus, Cin., Dayton and Washington, 1981-93; ret. ptnr. Thompson, Hine & Flory, Columbus, 1993—; bd. dirs. N.Am. Broadcasting Co. (Sta. WMNI and WBZX Radio); asst. atty. gen. State of Ohio, 1951-54. Pres. Upper Arlington (Ohio) Bd. Edn., 1967-69, Columbus Town Meeting Assn., 1974-76; chmn. Ohio Young Reps., 1956; U.S. presdl. elector, 1956; trustee Buckeye Boys Ranch, Columbus, 1967-73, 75-81, Upper Arlington Edn. Found., 1987-93; elder Covenant Presbyn. Ch., Columbus. With U.S. Army, 1943-45, ETO. Fellow Am. Bar Found., Ohio Bar Found., Columbus Bar Found.; mem. ABA, Ohio Bar Assn., Columbus Bar Assn., Am. Judicature Soc., Scioto Country Club, Athletic Club, Rotary, Masons. Home: 1993 Collingswood Rd Columbus OH 43221-3741 Office: Thompson Hine & Flory One Columbus 10 W Broad St Columbus OH 43215-3418

MCCONNELL, ADDISON MITCHELL, JR. (MITCH MCCONNELL, JR.), senator, lawyer; b Tuscumbia, AL, Feb. 20, 1942; s. Addison Mitchell and Julia (Shockley) McC.; children: Eleanor Hayes, Claire Redmon, Marion Porter; m. Elaine Chao, Feb. 6, 1993. B.A. with honors, U. Louisville, 1964; J.D., U. Ky., 1967. Bar: Ky. 1967. Chief legis. asst. to Senator Marlow Cook, Washington, 1968-70; sole practice Louisville, 1970-74; dep. asst. U.S. atty. gen. Washington, 1974-75; judge Jefferson County, Louisville, 1978-85; U.S. Senator from Ky., 1985—, chmn. select com. on ethics 104th Congress; mem. agr., nutrition, and forestry com., appropriations com., labor and human resources com., rules and adminstrn. com. Chmn. Jefferson County Republican Com., 1973-74; co-chmn. Nat. Child Tragedies Coalition, 1981; chmn., founder Ky. Task Force on Exploited and Missing Children, 1982; mem. Pres.'s Partnership on Child Safety. Recipient commendation Nat. Trust on Hist. Preservation in U.S., 1982, Conservationist of Yr. award League Ky. Sportsmen, 1983, cert. of appreciation Am. Correctional Assn., 1985. Mem. Ky. Assn. County Judge Execs. (pres. 1982), Nat. Inst. Justice (adv. bd. 1982-84). Republican. Baptist. Avocations: fishing; cooking. Office: 361A Russell Office Bldg Washington DC 20510-1702*

MCCONNELL, CALVIN DALE, clergyman; b. Monte Vista, Colo., Dec. 3, 1928; s. Roy and Leota Fern (Taylor) McC.; m. Mary Caroline Bamberg, Sept. 2, 1952 (dec. Apr. 1986); children: David William, Mark Andrew; m. Velma Duell, Dec. 17, 1988. B.A., U. Denver, 1951; M.Div., Iliff Sch. Theology, 1954; S.T.M., Andover Newton Theol. Sem., 1967. Ordained to ministry United Meth. Ch.; pastor Meth. Ch., Williams, Calif., 1955-58, 1st United Meth. Ch., Palo Alto, Calif. and Stanford U. Wesley Found., 1958-61; chaplain and asst. prof. religion Willamette U., Salem, Oreg., 1961-67; pastor Christ United Meth. Ch., Denver, 1968-72; pastor 1st United Meth. Ch., Boulder, Colo., 1972-79, Colorado Springs, Colo., 1979-80; bishop United Meth. Ch., Portland Area, 1980-88, Seattle Area, 1988-96; retired, 1996.

MCCONNELL, DAVID M., secondary school principal. Prin. Kennebunk (Maine) High Sch. Recipient Blue Ribbon Sch. award U.S. Dept. Edn., 1990-91. Office: Kennebunk H S 89 Fletcher St Kennebunk ME 04043-1904

MCCONNELL, DAVID MOFFATT, lawyer; b. Chester, S.C., June 12, 1912; s. Harvey Elzaphon and Elizabeth (Simpson) McC.; m. Ona Altman, Dec. 31, 1952; children: David Moffatt, Lynn Torbit, Joseph Moore. B.S. summa cum laude, Davidson Coll., 1933; student, Harvard. Grad. Bus. Sch., 1933-34, Law Sch., 1934-35; J.D., Georgetown U., 1939, LL.M., 1940; LLD (hon.), Mex. Acad. Internat. Law, 1987. Bar: S.C. 1936, D.C. 1945, N.C. 1946, U.S. Supreme Ct 1946. With firm Henry & Henry, Chester, 1936; counsel com. govt. reorgn. U.S. Senate, 1937-38; spl. atty. to chief counsel Internal Revenue Service, 1938-41; practice in Charlotte, N.C., 1946—; v.p., gen. counsel Belk Stores, Charlotte, 1946-76; gen. counsel Leggett Stores, 1946-76; dir. So. Nat. Bank, Lumberton, N.C., also chmn. Charlotte bd., 1970-76; U.S. ambassador to UN, 1968-69; Spl. adviser UN Econ. and Social Council; mem. U.S. delegation Fed. Republic Germany Marshall Plan, 1967. Chmn., sec. N.C. Bd. Elections, 1952-62; chmn. exec. com. Mecklenburg County (N.C.) Democratic Party, 1952-57; mem. nat. platform com. Dem. Party, 1964-72; elector U.S. Electoral Coll., 1948, 52; Donor McConnell Collection Tibetan Art to Baton Rouge Arts Mus., 1965; bd. dirs. emeritus Billy Graham Evangelistic Assn.; bd. visitors Davidson Coll., 1972-76; trustee Erskine Coll., Due West, S.C., 1954-58, bd. advisers, 1968-72; trustee Robert Lee Stowe, Jr. Found., Henderson Belk Found. Served to col. U.S. Army, 1940-46, CBI; brig. gen. N.C. State Militia. Decorated Legion of Merit with oak leaf cluster; Order Cloud with banner (Republic China); knight comdr. Order of the Knights of Malta. Fellow Mexican Acad. Internat. Law; mem. Am., N.C., 26th Jud. Dist. bar assns., St. Andrews Soc., Newcomen Soc., Phi Beta Kappa, Kappa Alpha. Presbyterian. Clubs: Mason (Charlotte) (Shriner), Charlotte Country (Charlotte), City (Charlotte), University (Washington). Home: 920 Granville Rd Charlotte NC 28207-1832

MCCONNELL, DAVID STUART, insurance agent, retired federal executive; b. Charlotte, Mich., Dec. 5, 1935; s. Russell and Beatrice (Martin) McC.; m. Marchelle Elizabeth Wiltshire, June 10, 1960; children: Marchelle Kern, Martin. BA, Olivet Coll., 1957; grad., Union Theol. Sem., Union Sch. Sacred Music, N.Y.C., 1958, 62. Position classifier U.S. Dept. State, Washington, 1961-62; rsch. specialist U.S. Nat. Interdepartmental Seminar, Washington, 1962-66; head East Asia sect. Am. Specialist Program, 1966-68; asst. to acad. advisor U.S. Bd. Fgn. Scholarships, Washington, 1968-69; desk officer Near East br. Bur. Ednl. and Cultural Affairs, Washington, 1969-72; coord. for multi-regional seminars U.S. Office Internat. Visitors, Washington, 1972-87; head internat. visitor programs for Andean nations U.S. Info. Agy., Washington, 1978-87; agt. Liberty Nat. Life Ins., 1994-95; ind. ins. agt. McConnell Ins. Agy., 1996—. Compiler: Problems of Development and Internal Defense, 1966. Mem. 3 cabinet subcoms. on narcotics, Washington, 1973-78; coord. narcotics U.S. Bur. Ednl. and Cultural Affairs, 1973-78, U.S. Info. Agy., Washington, 1978; mem. Montgomery County Econ. With U.S. Army, 1958-61. Grantee (9) White House Spl. Action Office for Drug Abuse Prevention, Ford Found., 1973. Home and Office: RR 3 Box 152 Carrollton MS 38917-9424

MCCONNELL, E. HOY, II, advertising executive; b. Syracuse, N.Y., May 14, 1941; s. E. Hoy and Dorothy R. (Schmitt) McC.; m. Patricia Irwin, June 26, 1965; children: E. Hoy, III, Courtney. BA in Am. Studies magna cum laude, Yale U., 1963; MBA in Mktg, Harvard Bus. Sch., 1965. With Foote, Cone & Belding, 1965-76; v.p. account supr. Foote, Cone & Belding, Chgo., 1971-72, 74-76, Phoenix, 1972-74; with D'Arcy-MacManus & Masius, Chgo., 1976-85, sr. v.p., dir. client services, then vice chmn., 1978-80, pres., 1980-84, chmn., 1984-85; mng. dir. D'Arcy Masius Benton & Bowles, Chgo., 1986-96, also bd. dirs.; sr. v.p., account dir. Leo Burnett Co., Chgo., 1996—. Bd. dirs. Evanston (Ill.) United Way, 1980-83, Evanston Youth Hockey Assn., 1980-89, pres. 1981-83; bd. dirs. Off-the-Street Club, 1980-90, Bus. Profl. People for Pub. Interest, 1981-83, 96—, v.p. 1984-89, pres. 1990-95; bd. dirs. Harvard Bus. Sch. Club, 1990-92; mem. Chgo. Coun. on Fgn. Rels., 1989—. Mem. Am. Assn. Advt. Agys. (gov.-at-large Chgo. coun. 1984, sec. 1986, vice chmn. 1987, chmn. 1988-89), BBB Chgo. (mem. advt. rev. bd.), Tavern Club, Glen View Country Club (bd. dirs. 1992-96), Dairymen's Country Club, Chgo. Club (membership comm. 1994-96), Yale Club Chgo. (bd. dirs. 1996—). Democrat. Unitarian. Home: 2703 Colfax St Evanston IL 60201-2035 Office: Leo Burnett Co 35 W Wacker Dr Chicago IL 60601-1614

MCCONNELL, EDWARD BOSWORTH, legal organization administrator, lawyer; b. Greenwich, Conn., Apr. 3, 1920; s. Raymond Arnott and Anna Bell (Lee) McC.; m. Jeanne M. Rotton (dec. 1984); children: Annalee, Marilyn, Edward, Barbara, William; m. Florence M. Leonard, (dec. 1991); stepchildren: Susan L. Little, William R. Leonard, Molly M. Leonard. A.B., U. Nebr., 1941, LL.B., 1947; M.B.A. with distinction, Harvard U., 1943. Bar: Nebr. 1947, N.J. 1950. Mem. faculty Rutgers U. Sch. Bus. Adminstrn., Newark, 1947-53; assoc. firm Toner, Speakman and Crowley, Newark, N.J., 1949-50; adminstrv. asst. and law sec. to Chief Justice of N.J., 1950-53; adminstrv. dir. Cts. of N.J., Trenton, 1953-73; also standing master Supreme Ct., 1953-73; pres. Nat. Center for State Cts., Williamsburg, 1973-90, bd. dirs., 1980-90, pres. emeritus, 1990—, cons. on ct. mgmt., 1990—; mem. U.S. Dept. Justice Coun. on Role of Cts. in Am. Soc., 1978-83; mem. adv. com. Dispute Resolution Policy Study, Social Sci. Rsch. Inst., U. So. Calif., 1975-79, Civil Litigation Rsch. Project, U. Wis. and U. So. Calif., 1979-83, nat. judg. edn. program to promote equality for men and women in the cts., 1980—; mem. Nat. Inst. Criminal Justice Task Force, Urban Consortium, 1979-83; participant Access To Justice Colloquium, European Univ. Inst., Florence, Italy, 1979; nat. adv. coun. Ctr. Adminstrn. Justice, Wayne Stae U., 1973-77; nat. project com. State Jud. Info. Sys. Project SEARCH Group, 1973-76; lectr. Inst. of Local and State Govt. Wharton Sch. U. Pa., 1955-65, Appellate Judges Seminar, Inst. Jud. Adminstrn., NYU, 1962-75; vis. expert UN Asia and Far East Inst., Tokyo, 1971; mem. Cts. Task Force Nat. Adv. Commn. Criminal Justice Standards and Goals, 1971-73; nat. adv. com. D.C. Ct. Mgmt. Project, 1966-70; trustee Inst. Ct. Mgmt., 1969-73, 84-86; chmn. Nat. Conf. Ct. Adminstrv. Officers, 1956; mem. nat. task force on gender bias in cts. Nat. Assn. Women Judge's 1985-90; mem. adv. bd. Nat. Ctr. for Citizen Participation in Admisntrn. of Justice, 1984-90; mem. Nat. Commn. Trial Ct. Performance Standards, 1991-95. Mem. adv. com. on article III Commn. on the Bicentennial of the Constitution, 1989-91; adv. com. Judicary Leadership Coun., 1990-95. Maj. C.E., AUS, 1943-46. Decorated Bronze Star medal; recipient Warren E. Burger award for greatest contbn. to improvement of ct. adminstrn. Inst. for Ct. Mgmt., 1975, Herbert Lincoln Harley award for efficient adminstrn. justice Am. Judicature Soc., 1973, Glenn R. Winters award for outstanding service in jud. adminstrn. Am. Judges Assn., 1974, Tom C. Clark award for outstanding contbns. to field of ct. adminstrn. Nat. Conf. Met. Cts., 1983, Award of Merit Nat. Assn. Ct. Mgmt., 1987, Spl. award, Nat. Assn. Women Judges, 1989, Paul C. Reardon award for disting. svc. Nat. Ctr. for State Cts., 1991, Alumni Achievement award U. Nebr., 1991. Fellow Nat. Acad. Pub. Adminstrn. (mem. panel on evaluation budget decentralization project of fed. cts. 1989-91, chmn. panel long range planning in fed. cts. 1991-92, mem. panel for study of fed. trial ct. adminstrv. structure 1995-96—); mem. ABA (fellow-at-large, coun. mem. 1960-66, 71-80, house of dels., 1977-80, chmn. com. on oversight and goals 1975-76, chmn. com. on jud. compensation jud. adminstrn. div. 1984-89, chmn. jud. adminstrn. div. 1976-77, sect. of litigation task force on excess litigiousness in Am. 1986-88, task force on reduction of litigation cost and delay, jud. adminstrn. dir. 1984-94, chmn. 1991-94, mem. long range planning com. 1989-94), N.J. Bar Assn., Nebr. Bar Assn., Kingsmill (Va.) Golf, Tennis and Yacht Clubs, Order of Coif (hon.), Delta Upsilon, Sigma Delta Phi, Phi Delta Phi.

MCCONNELL, ELLIOTT BONNELL, JR., oil company executive; b. Elizabeth, N.J., June 2, 1928; s. Elliott Bonnell and Mildred A. (Snibbe) McC.; m. Sara Gerber, Aug. 16, 1952; children: Marilyn McConnell Huston, James D. A.B., Duke U., 1951; M.S., Pa. State U., 1953; postgrad. Advanced Mgmt. Program, Harvard U., 1973. Exploration mgr. Mobil Oil Corp., U.S. and Can., 1953-69; v.p. land and exploration Gen. Crude Oil Co., Houston, 1969-79; pres. Pennzoil Internat., Houston, 1979-81; exec. v.p. exploration and prodn. Santa Fe Energy Co. subs. Santa Fe S.P. Corp., Houston, 1981-86, petroleum cons.; commr. Tex. Dept. Licensing and Regulation, 1997—. Chmn. Appraisal Rev. Bd., Aransas County, 1989-92; pres. Key Allegro Property Owners Assn., 1989-92; chmn. Rockport Redistricting Commn., 1991, Rockport Charter Rev. Commn., 1991; commr. Aransas County, 1993-96. Republican. Clubs: Rockport Country. Avocation: tennis.

MCCONNELL, HARDEN MARSDEN, biophysical chemistry researcher, chemistry educator; b. Richmond, Va., July 18, 1927; s. Harry Raymond and Frances (Coffee) McC.; m. Sophia Milo Glogovac, Oct. 6, 1956; children: Hunter, Trevor, Jane. BS, George Washington U., 1947; PhD, Calif. Inst. Tech., 1951; DSc (hon.), U. Chgo., 1991, George Washington U., 1993. NRC fellow dept. physics U. Chgo., 1950-52; research chemist Shell Devel. Co., Emeryville, Calif., 1952-56; asst. prof. chemistry Calif. Inst. Tech., 1956-58, prof. chemistry and physics, 1963-64; prof. chemistry Stanford U., Calif., 1964-79, Robert Eckles prof. chemistry, 1979—, chmn. dept., 1989—; founder Molecular Devices Corp., 1983—; cons. in field. Contbr. numerous articles to profl. publs.; patentee (in field). Pres. Found. for Basic Rsch. in Chemistry, 1990—; hon. assoc. Neurosci. Rsch. Program. Recipient Calif. sect. award Am. Chem. Soc., 1961, award in pure chemistry Am. Chem. Soc., 1962, Harrison Howe award, 1968, Irving Langmuir award in chem. physics, 1971, Pauling medal Puget Sound and Oreg. sects., 1987, Peter Debye award in phys. chemistry, 1990; Am. Achievement award George Washington U., 1971; Disting. Alumni award Calif. Inst. Tech., 1982, Sherman Fairchild Disting. scholar, 1988; Dickson prize for sci. Carnegie-Mellon U., 1982, Wolf prize in chemistry, 1984, ISCO award, 1984; Wheland medal U. Chgo., 1988; Nat. Medal Sci., 1989, Brucker prize, 1995. Fellow AAAS, Am. Phys. Soc.; mem. Nat. Acad. Scis. (award in chem. scis. 1988), Am. Acad. Arts and Scis., Am. Soc. Biol. Chemists, Internat. Acad. Quantum Molecular Scis., Am. Chem. Soc. (Award in Surface Chemistry 1997), Biophysical Soc., Internat. Coun. on Magnetic Resource in Biol. Systems, Brit. Biophysical Soc. Office: Stanford U Dept Chemistry Stanford CA 94305

MCCONNELL, J. DANIEL, sports marketing professional; b. Noblesville, Ind., Oct. 5, 1944; s. John Worley and Nadine Lillian (McFarlin) McC.; m. Jane Brantlinger, June 29, 1968. AB in English/Journalism, Ind. U., 1966, MS in Bus., 1968. Asst. to pres. Ind. U. Found., Bloomington, 1966-67; legis. liaison Dept. Health, Edn. and Welfare, Washington, 1968; dir. pub. rels. Cummins Engine Co., Columbus, Ind., 1970-72; dir. investor comm. Commins Engine Co., Columbus, Ind., 1972-75, dir. exec. recruiting, 1975-77; prin., CEO The McConnell Co. Pub. Rels., Seattle, 1977-93; sr. v.p., group dir. Elgin DDB, Seattle, 1993—; founder The Mountain Summit Internat. Symposium, 1987—; co-founder College Baseball Classic Found., 1990—; bd. dirs. Great Adventures Ltd., Jersey, U.K. Bd. dirs. Child Haven, Seattle, 1985-91, Internat. Snow Leopard Trust, Seattle, 1991-95, Pacific Crest Outward Bound Sch., Portland, Oreg., 1992—; trustee Seattle Ctrl. C.C., 1992—. Capt. U.S. Army, 1968-70. Mem. Pub. Rels. Soc. (Hoosier chpt. bd. dirs. 1975-77, Puget Sound bd. dirs. 1995—). Avocations: snow skiing, mountaineering, racquetball, sailing. Office: Elgin DDB 1008 Western Ave Ste 601 Seattle WA 98104-1058

MCCONNELL, JAMES GUY, lawyer; b. Hinsdale, Ill., Sept. 24, 1947; s. William F. and Virginia (Brown) McC.; m. Linda McConnell; children: Colin, Nicholas, Joanna, Cameron, Gabriel. BS in Journalism, Iowa State U., 1969; JD, Northwestern U., 1973. Bar: Ill. 1973, U.S. Dist. Ct. (no. dist.) Ill. 1973, U.S. Ct. Appeals (7th cir.) 1973, U.S. Supreme Ct. 1977. Assoc. Rooks, Pitts & Poust, Chgo., 1973-80, ptnr., 1980-85; ptnr. Bell, Boyd & Lloyd, Chgo., 1985-88, Freeborn & Peters, Chgo., 1990-96, Goldstein & Fluxgold, Chgo., 1996—; adj. prof. Kent Coll. Law Ill. Inst. Tech., Chgo., 1978-83. Author: Comparative Negligence Defense Tactics, 1985; contbg. editor jour. Hazardous Waste & Toxic Torts Law & Strategy. Mem. Dist. 102 Sch. Bd., LaGrange Park, Ill., 1975-76; mem. Dist. 106 Sch. Bd., Bannockburn, Ill., 1989-92. Mem. ABA, Ill. Bar Assn., Chgo. Bar Assn., Soc. Trial Lawyers. Clubs: Legal of Chgo., Law of Chgo. Office: Goldstein & Fluxgold Plaza & McConnell LLC 33 N Dearborn St Ste 1015 Chicago IL 60602-3105

MC CONNELL, JOHN DOUGLAS, retail corporation executive, owner; b. Dimboola, Victoria, Australia, May 13, 1932; s. William Thomas and Ada Maud (Gardner) McC.; came to U.S., 1964; BA, Melbourne U., 1954; PhD, Stanford U., 1967; m. Gloria Ann Revak, Oct. 12, 1968; children: Joanne Patricia, Meredith Lorraine. Asst. to mng. dir. Automotive & Gen. Industries Ltd., Melbourne, 1954-59; mgr. Eagle M.R. Svc. Pty. Ltd., Melbourne, 1959-64; dir. mgmt. systems SRI Internat., Washington, 1975-77, dir. mgmt. econs. Europe and Middle East, 1977-78, dir. mgmt. svcs. group, Menlo Park, Calif., 1978-80, dir. Food and Forest Products Ctr., 1980-83; v.p. Sungene Techs. Corp., Palo Alto, 1983-85; dir. fin. svcs. ctr. SRI Internat., 1986-87, prin., 1987-91, Menlo Park; pres., CEO, owner Remnant World Inc., San Jose, 1991—; vis. lectr. U. Bradford (Eng.); lectr. San Francisco State U. Contbr. articles to profl. mags. Life gov. Royal Victorian Inst. Blind, 1957—; mem. exec. bd. Stanford Area Council Boy Scouts Am., 1974-94. Decorated comdr. The Most Venerable Order of St. John of Jerusalem; recipient Silver Beaver award, 1986; Alfred P. Sloan Fellow, 1964-65; GE fellow, 1966. Fellow Australian Inst. Mgmt., Advt. Inst. Australia; mem. Royal Scottish Country Dance Soc. Presbyterian. Clubs: St. Andrews Soc. San Francisco, The Queen's, Army and Navy. Lodge: Masons. Home: 4174 Oak Hill Ave Palo Alto CA 94306-3720 Office: Remnant World Inc 5158 Stevens Creek Blvd San Jose CA 95129-1019

MCCONNELL, JOHN EDWARD, electrical engineering company executive; b. Minot, N.D., July 28, 1931; s. Lloyd Waldorf and Sarah Gladys (Mathis) McC.; m. Carol Claire Myers, July 4, 1952 (dec. Feb. 1989); children: Kathleen Anne, James Mathis, Amy Lynn; m. Heidi Banziger, Sept. 29, 1990. Registered profl. engr., Pa. B.S. in Mech. Engring., U. Pitts., 1952; M.S., Drexel Inst. Tech., 1958. With mktg. and design depts. for turbomachinery Westinghouse Electric Corp., Lester, Pa., 1954-60, 63-67, Pitts., 1960-63; mgr. power generation equipment activities in U.S., ASEA Inc., White Plains, N.Y., 1967-79; regional mgr. power equipment activities Middle Atlantic and Southeastern U.S. regions, 1967-79, mgr. turbine generator dept., 1980-83, mgr. internat. ops. Power Systems div., 1983-84, mgr. transmission substas. dept., 1984-85; mgr. Eastern U.S. ops. ASEA Power Systems Inc., 1985-86, mgr. eastern ops. measurements div. GEC, 1986-91; mgr. eastern region Protection and Control div. GEC Alsthom T&D Inc., 1991—; adviser on energy matters to U.S. congressman 1968-74; speaker and author on energy and electric power topics. Served to 1st lt., C.E., U.S. Army, 1952-54. Mem. IEEE (sr.; energy com., past chmn. subcom. cogeneration, mem. power sys. relay com.), IEEE Power Engring. Soc. (sr.; past chmn. chpts. public affairs subcom.), ASME. Republican. Contbr. numerous articles on energy and electric power to industry publs.; developer analytical techniques for power systems performance characteristics and econs. of cogeneration systems. Home: 173 Remington Rd Ridgefield CT 06877-4324 Office: GEC Alsthom T&D Inc 4 Skyline Dr Hawthorne NY 10532 *1) If it doesn't produce revenue, is it worthwhile? 2) Problem solving begins with careful listening. 3) Keep people informed. If they don't know, they'll assume the worst. 4) The truth is the most credible explanation you'll find.*

MCCONNELL, JOHN THOMAS, newspaper executive, publisher; b. Peoria, Ill., May 1, 1945; s. Golden A. and Margaret (Lyon) McC.; 1 child, Justin. B.A., U. Ariz., 1967. Mgr. Fast Printing Co., Peoria, 1970-71; mgmt. trainee Quad-Cities Times, Davenport, Iowa, 1972-73; asst. gen. mgr., then v.p., gen. mgr. Peoria Jour. Star, 1973-81, pub., 1981—, pres., 1987—. Bd. dirs. Peoria Downtown Devel. Council, Peoria Devel. Corp.; past trustee Methodist Hosp., Peoria. Served with USAR, 1967-69. Named Young Man of Year Peoria Jaycees, 1979. Mem. Peoria Advt. and Selling Club, Peoria C. of C. Congregationalist. Club: Peoria Country. Office: Peoria Jour Star Inc 1 News Plz Peoria IL 61643-0001

MCCONNELL, JOHN WESLEY, real estate-resort developer, corporate executive; b. Steubenville, Ohio, Dec. 3, 1941; m. Clare Yenchochic; 5 children. BS, U. Steubenville, 1967. Various corp. fin. positions Diamond Shamrock Corp., 1967-76, asst. treas., 1976-81, v.p. fin. and adminstrn. coal co., 1981-83, v.p. fin. and adminstrn., 1983-85, exec. v.p., COO, 1985-86; sr. v.p., CFO, treas. Fairfield Communities, Inc., Little Rock, 1986-90, pres., COO, 1990-91, pres., CEO, 1990—, also bd. dirs. With U.S. Army, 1962-64. Avocation: golf. Office: Fairfield Communities Inc 11001 Executive Center Dr Little Rock AR 72211-4316

MCCONNELL, JOHN WILLIAM, JR., lawyer; b. Bessemer, Ala., Apr. 17, 1921; s. John W. and Elizabeth (Sheridan) McC.; m. Margaret B. Snider, Jan. 7, 1944; children—Margaret E. (Mrs. John Evans), Rebecca L. (Mrs. A.D. Braden), Catherine L., John W. III. A.B., U. Ala., 1942, M.A., 1946; LL.B., Yale, 1948. Bar: Ala. 1948, D.C. 1977. Atty. Inge, Twitty, Armbrecht & Jackson, Mobile, Ala., 1948-56, Armbrecht, Jackson, McConnell & DeMouy, 1956-65; dir. U.S. Peace Corps, Nigeria, 1965-68; v.p. legal Sea-Land Service, Inc., Menlo Park, N.J., 1968-76; also dir., of counsel Haight, Gardner, Poor & Havens, Washington, 1977-94; Atty. for Reynolds v. Sims on legislative reapportionment, U.S. Supreme Ct., 1963-64. Mem. Ala. Dem. Exec. Com., 1963-65. Served to capt. AUS, 1943-46, 50-52. Mem. ABA, Ala. Bar Assn., D.C. Bar Assn., Maritime Law Assn. Methodist. Home: 926 Seagull Dr Mount Pleasant SC 29464-4145

MCCONNELL, LORELEI CATHERINE, library director; b. Port Jefferson, N.Y., Dec. 5, 1938; d. Alvin and Mary (McConnell) Philibert; m. Thomas McConnell, Jan. 20, 1962; children: Catherine, Michael. BA, Drew U., 1960; MLS, Rutgers U., 1963. Reference libr. Irvington (N.J.) Pub. Libr., 1963-90, dir., 1990—; founder Irvington Literacy Program, 1986, dir., 1986-90. Mem. ALA, N.J. Libr. Assn. (mem. exec. bd. 1990-93, N.J. Libr. of Yr. 1993-94), Irvington (N.J.) C. of C. (exec. bd. 1992—, Civic award 1996), Internat. Primal Assn., Beta Phi Mu. Home: 563 Park St Montclair NJ 07043-2027 Office: Irvington Pub Libr Civic Sq Irvington NJ 07111 *The world would be a better place if we could find ways to reward and honor every single person who works hard and does the right thing.*

MCCONNELL, MICHAEL, opera company director; b. Charlotte, N.C., Dec. 25, 1954; s. Jackson McConnell and Patsy Anne (King) White. MusB, Coll. Conservatory of Music, U. Cin., 1976, postgrad., 1979. Adj. lectr. Cin. Coll. Conservatory, 1980-81; resident stage dir. Opera Memphis, 1982-84; exec. dir. Lyric Opera Cleve., 1984-94; dir. opera Cleve. Inst. Music, 1991-95; stage dir. Fla. State Opera, Tallahassee, 1995—; dir. opera workshop Baldwin-Wallace Conservatory, Berea, Ohio, 1987-91; frequent panelist opera-music theater NEA. With prodn. staff Santa Fe Opera, Opera Theatre St. Louis, Edinburgh Festival, Opera Memphis, others; stage dir. Opera Theatre St. Louis, Opera Memphis, Opera Theatre Rochester, Memphis Playhouse on Sq., Human Race Theatre, Miss. Opera, Cin. Opera, Skylight Opera Theatre, Cleve. Inst. Music, Cin. Coll. Conservatory Music, Cleve. Orch., Opera Theatre of Lucca (European debut), others; contbr. articles to profl. jours. Mem. OPERA Am. (bd. dirs. 1993—), Actor's Equity Assn. Office: Fla State U School of Music Tallahassee FL 32306-2098

MCCONNELL, MICHAEL ARTHUR, lawyer; b. Ft. Worth, Jan. 15, 1947. BA, Loyola U., New Orleans, 1969; JD, U. Tex., 1975. Bar: Tex. 1976, U.S. Dist. Ct. (no. dist.) Tex. 1976, U.S. Dist. Ct. (ea. dist.) Tex. 1981, U.S. Dist. Ct. (we. dist.) Tex. 1982, U.S. Dist. Ct. (so. dist.) Tex. 1989, U.S. Ct. Appeals (5th cir.) Tex. 1980, U.S. Ct. Appeals (10th cir.) 1987. Briefing atty. U.S. Dist. Ct. Hon. Eldon B. Mahon, Ft. Worth, 1976-77; assoc. atty. Cantey, Hanger, Gooch, Munn and Collins, Ft. Worth, 1977-81, ptnr., 1981-83; judge no. dist. U.S. Bankruptcy Ct., Ft. Worth, 1983-86; ptnr. Kelly, Hart & Hallman, Ft. Worth, 1986-88, Jackson & Walker, Ft. Worth, 1988-95. Sgt. USAF, 1969-73. Mem. Nat. Conf. Bankruptcy Judges, Assn. Former Bankruptcy Judges. Office: McConnell Goodrich & Lenox 303 Main St Ste 220 Fort Worth TX 76102-4000

MCCONNELL, ROB, jazz musician, composer; b. Ont., Can., 1935. Hon. doctorate, St. Francis Xavier U., Nova Scotia, Can. Mem. The Boss Brass, 1968—; mem. faculty staff, head of the profl. instrumental program Grove Sch. Music, Van Nuys, Calif., 1988—. Recs. include All in Good Time (Grammy award for Best Big Band Album of Yr. 1984), Brassy & Sassy, Overtime, Don't Get Around Much Anymore, Mel Tormeé-Rob McConnell and The Boss Brass, Trio Sketches, Our 25th Year, The Brass is Back, Mutual Street, Sabia, 1990, Overtime, 1994, Rob McConnell & The Boss Brass, 1995. Recipient 4 Juno awards, 7 Juno nominations, Toronto Musician's award, 1994; named Best Arranger Nat. Assn. Jazz Educators. Office: Concord Jazz Inc PO Box 845 Concord CA 94522*

MCCONNELL, ROBERT CHALMERS, former city official; b. Santa Fe, Aug. 7, 1913; s. Chalmers and Mary (Foree) McC.; m. Colleen Alford, Feb. 3, 1948; 1 dau., Julie. B.A., U. N.Mex., 1935; LL.B., George Washington U., 1939. Bar: N.Mex. bar 1941, U.S. Supreme Ct. bar 1947. Law clk. to U.S. circuit judge, 1939-40; asst. dist. atty. N.Mex., 1940-41, 45-47, adminstrv. asst. to congressman from, 1947-57, 57-61; spl. asst. to asst. sec. interior, 1961-62; asst. to sec. for congl. liaison Dept. Interior, Washington, 1962-67; asst. sec. for adminstrn. Dept. Interior, 1967-69; mayor City of Redington Beach, Fla., 1971-72; partner McConnell-Wilroy Cons., St. Petersburg, Fla., 1976-77. Mgr. Madeira Beach (Fla.) Little League Baseball; pres. Gulf Beaches Little League; chmn. bd. govs. Redington Beach Assn., 1977-79; chmn. Chaves County Dem. Com., 1946-48, The Biog. History of N.Mex. With CIC, AUS, 1941-45. Recipient Distinguished Service award U.S. Dept. Interior, 1967. Mem. Sigma Chi. Club: Rotary. Home: 15849 Redington Dr Redington Beach FL 33708-1743

MCCONNELL, ROBERT EASTWOOD, architect, educator; b. Spokane, Wash., July 15, 1930; s. Robert Ervie and Alma (Eastwood) Mc C.; m. Beverly Ann Vincent, Sept. 12, 1953; children: Kathleen Ann, Karen Eileen, Terri Lynn. B in Archtl. Engring., Wash. State U., 1952; MArch, Mass. Inst. Tech., 1954. Project architect John W. Maloney (Architect), Seattle, 1956-62; asst. prof. architecture Ariz. State U., Tempe, 1962-66; asso. prof. Ariz. State U., 1966-67; prof. U. Kans., Lawrence, 1967-69; prof., head dept. art and architecture U. Idaho, Moscow, 1969-71; prof. U. Ariz., Tucson, 1971-92; dean Coll. Architecture U. Ariz., 1971-77; prof. emeritus, dean emeritus U. Ariz., Tucson, 1992—, acting assoc. dean, 1994; partner McConnell & Peterson, Architects, Tempe, 1963-66; pvt. practice architecture, 1962-96. Author, project dir.: Land Use Planning for Ariz., Ariz. Acad, 1974; Contbr. articles to profl. jours. Chmn. Idaho Gov.'s Awards Program in Arts and Humanities, 1970; project dir. Rio Salado Conceptual Study, Phoenix, 1966; bd. dirs. Tucson Regional Plan, 1972-79. Served with USAF, 1954-56. Fellow AIA (awards 1969, 76, pres. So. Ariz. chpt. 1975-76, bd. dirs. 1971-77); mem. AIA Ariz. (mem. coun. of dels. 1971-77, chmn. honor awards jury 1975), Phi Kappa Phi, Scarab, Tau Beta Pi, Sigma Tau. Home: 7001 N Edgewood Pl Tucson AZ 85704-6924 Office: U Ariz Coll Architecture Tucson AZ 85721

MCCONNELL, WILLIAM THOMPSON, commercial banker; b. Zanesville, Ohio, Aug. 8, 1933; s. William Gerald and Mary Gladys McC.; m. Jane Charlotte Cook, Aug. 25, 1956; children: Jennifer Wynne, William Gerald. BA, Denison U., 1955; MBA, Northwestern U., 1959. Pres. Park Nat. Bank, Newark, Ohio, 1979-83, pres., chief exec. officer, 1983-93; chmn., chief exec. officer Park Nat. Bank, Newark, 1993—; also bd. dirs. Park Nat. Bank, Newark, Ohio; pres., chief exec. officer Park Nat. Corp., Newark, 1987-94, chmn., CEO, 1994—; bd. dirs. Freight Svcs., Inc., Newark, Consol. Computer Ctr., Newark. Mem. Newark Area C. of C. (past pres., dir. 1977-83), Ohio Bankers Assn. (pres., chmn. 1981-83). Office: Park Nat Bank PO Box 3500 Newark OH 43058-3500

MCCONOMY, JAMES HERBERT, lawyer; b. Pitts., Mar. 24, 1937; s. Murray Michael and Catherine Elizabeth (Herbert) McC.; m. Jeanne Margaret Cronin, Sept. 3, 1960 (div. Apr. 1989); children: Margaret Jeanne, Michael Murray; m. Roberta L. Cavanaugh, June 30, 1989. AB cum laude, Harvard U., 1959, LLB, 1962. Bar: Pa. 1963, U.S. Ct. Appeals (3d cir.) 1972, U.S. Supreme Ct. 1977. Ptnr. Reed, Smith, Shaw & McClay, Pitts., 1962-92; mng. ptnr. Titus & McConomy, Pitts., 1992—. Fellow Am. Coll. Trial Lawyers; mem. ABA, Pa. Bar Assn. (chmn. comml. litigation sect. 1986—), Allegheny County Acad. Trial Lawyers. Roman Catholic. Clubs: Duquesne, Harvard-Yale-Princeton (Pitts.). Avocations: photography, travel. Home: 1117 Harvard Rd Pittsburgh PA 15205-1726 Office: Titus & McConomy Four Gateway Ctr 20th Fl Pittsburgh PA 15222

MCCOOK, KATHLEEN DE LA PEÑA, university educator; b. Chgo.; d. Frank Eugene and Margaret L. (de la Peña) McEntee; m. Philip G. Heim, Mar. 20, 1972 (div.); 1 child, Margaret Marie; m. William Woodrow Lee McCook, Oct. 12, 1991; stepchildren: Cecilia, Billie Jean, Nicole. B.A., U. Ill.; M.A., Marquette U., U. Chgo.; Ph.D., U. Wis.-Madison. Reference librarian Elmhurst Coll. Library, Ill., 1971-72; dir. pub. services Rosary Coll. Library, River Forest, Ill., 1972-76; lectr. U. Wis., Madison, 1976-78; asst. prof. library sci. U. Ill., Urbana, 1978-83; dean, prof. La. State U. Sch. Library and Info. Sci., Baton Rouge, 1983-90; dean grad. sch. La. State U., 1990-92; dir. Sch. Libr. and Info. Sci. U. South Fla., 1993—. Author: (with L. Estabrook) Career Profiles, 1983, (with William E. Moen) Occupational Entry, 1989, Adult Services, 1990, (with Gary O. Rolstad) Developing Readers' Advisory Services, 1993, Toward a Just and Productive Soc., 1994, Opportunities in Library and Information Science, 1997; contbr. essays to books, articles to profl. jours. Chmn. Equal Rights Amendment Task Force, Ill., 1977-79; mem. Eugene McCarthy campaign, U. Ill., Chgo., 1968; mem. La. Gov.'s Comm. for Women, 1985-88; bd. dirs. La. Endowment for Humanities, 1991-92. Recipient Disting. Alumnus award U. Wis., 1991; Bradshaw scholar Tex. Woman's Univ., 1994. Mem. ALA (com. chmn. 1980—, editor RQ jour. 1982-88, Pub. Librs. Jour. 1989-90, Am. Librs. adv. com. 1994-96, Equality award 1987, Adult Svc. award 1991), Assn. for Libr. and Info. Sci. Edn. (com. chmn. 1981—, pres. 1987-88), Fla. Libr. Assn. (bd. dirs. 1995—, Transformer award 1996), Tampa Bay Libr. Consortium (bd. dirs. 1994—), Women Libr. Workers, Ruskin Civic Assn. (sec. 1997—), Ill. Libr. Assn. (treas. 1981-83), Beta Phi Mu. Democrat. Roman Catholic. Avocation: reading. Office: U South Fla Sch Libr and Info Sci 4202 E Fowler Ave # 1040 Tampa FL 33620-9900

MCCOOMB, LLOYD ALEXANDER, transportation executive; b. Edmonton, Alta., Can., Sept. 22, 1945. BASc, U. Toronto, Ont., Can., 1968, PhD, 1981; SM, MIT, 1970. With mil. engring. bd. Can. Armed Forces, 1964-74; sr. devel. officer Transport Devel. Agy. Transport Can., 1974-83; dir. stats. and forecasts Air Adminstrn., Ottawa, Ont., Can., 1983-86; from dir. gen. mktg. to dir. gen. safety and tech. svcs. Airports Group, Ottawa, 1986-94; airport gen. mgr. Toronto-Leser B. Pearson Internat. Airport, 1994-96; exec. v.p. airport devel. Greater Toronto Airports Authority, 1996—. Office: Lester B Pearson Intl Airport, Transport Canada PO Box 6003, Toronto, ON Canada L5P 1B5

MCCOPPIN, PETER, symphony orchestra conductor; b. Toronto, Ont., Can.; m. Roswitha McCoppin, 1975. BMus in Performance Art, U. Toronto; studied conducting with, Erich Leinsdorf, Prof. Hans Swarosky, Lovro von Maticic, Seriu Celibidache. Formed chamber choir Toronto, 1970-75; condr. orchestral program, prof. conducting Cleve. Inst. Music, 1975-78; guest condr. Alta. Ballet Co., Nat. Ballet Can., major orchs. Can.; music. advisor, condr. Vancouver (B.C.) Symphony Orch., 1988-89, now guest condr.; music dir. Victoria (B.C.) Symphony Orch., 1989—, Charlotte (N.C.) Symphony Orch., 1993—. Guest condr. Thunder Bay (Ont.) Symphony, Syracuse (N.Y.) Symphony; condr. Shanghai Symphony, Ctrl. Philharmonic, Beijing, Tokyo Symphony, Osaka Philharmonic, Gunma Symphony, Sapporo Symphony, Nat. Symphony Mex., Rochester Philharmonic, Buffalo Philharmonic, Tucson Symphony, most major orchs. in Can.; concerts with KBS Symphony, Korea; host B.C. TV Knowledge Network Classic Theatre, TV spls., radio programs. Office: Victoria Symphony Orch, 846 Broughton St Lower Level, Victoria, BC Canada V8W 1E4*

MCCORD, DON LEWIS, surgeon; b. Vernon, Tex., Aug. 25, 1929; s. Thomas Garfield and Dola (Cavender) McC.; m. Gayle McCord, Mar. 4, 1972; children: Daniel Lindsey, Elizabeth Ann, Melissa Ann Mares, Nicole Pryor. BS in Chemistry, Abilene Christian U., 1949; MD, U. Tex., 1953. Diplomate Am. Bd. Surgery. Intern U. Hosp., Ann Arbor, Mich., 1953-54; resident in surgery U.S. Naval Hosp., Oakland, Calif., 1955-59; asst. chief of surgery U.S. Naval Hosp., Corpus Christi, Tex., 1959-62; pvt. practice Hamilton, Tex., 1962-74; group practice Clifton, Tex., 1974-86; pvt. practice Med. City, Dallas, 1986—, sect. chief gen. surgery, 1990-92; cons. in surgery Hamilton (Tex.) Gen. Hosp., 1988-96, De Leon (Tex.) Hosp. Lt. comdr. USN, 1954-62. Fellow ACS; mem. AMA, Tex. Med. Assn., Dallas County med. Soc., Dallas Soc. Gen. Surgeons, Flying Physicians Assn., Alpha Omega Alpha. Republican. Avocation: flight instructor. Office: 7777 Forest Ln Ste C-608 Dallas TX 75230-2505

MC CORD, GUYTE PIERCE, JR., retired judge; b. Tallahassee, Sept. 23, 1914; s. Guyte Pierce and Jean (Patterson) McC.; student Davidson Coll., 1933-34; B.A., J.D., U. Fla., 1940; m. Laura Elizabeth Mack, Dec. 16, 1939; children: Florence Elizabeth, Guyte Pierce III, Edward LeRoy. Bar: Fla. 1940. Summer ranger Yosemite Nat. Park, 1936-39; rsch. aide to Fla. Supreme Ct., summer 1940; legal practice in Tallahassee, 1940-60; dep. commr. Fla. Indsl. Commn., 1946-47; pros. atty. Leon County, 1947-48; asst. gen. counsel Fla. Public Service Commn., 1949-60; judge 2d Jud. Circuit Fla., Tallahassee, 1960-74; judge Ct. Appeal 1st Dist. Fla., 1974-83, chief judge, 1977-79; mem. Fla. Senate Pres.'s Council on Criminal Justice 1972; mem. appellate ct. rules com. Fla. Supreme Ct., 1977-78, mem. appellate ct. structure commn. 1978-79. Pres., Murat House Assn., Inc., 1967-69; bd. dirs. Fla. Heritage Found., 1969-70, mem. exec. com., 1965-69; mem. Andrew Jackson staff of Springtime Tallahassee, 1973-74, 84-86, Andrew Jackson, 1987. Served to comdr. USNR, 1942-46, 52-53. Mem. Ret. Officers Assn., ABA, Fla. Bar, Tallahassee Bar Assn. (hon.), Fla. Conf. Circuit Judges (sec.-treas. 1970, chmn. 1972), Fla. State U. Pres. Club, Phi Delta Phi, Sigma Alpha Epsilon. Presbyterian (elder 1960—, ch. trustee 1981-86). Club: Kiwanis (dir. 1958-59). Home: 502 S Ride Tallahassee FL 32303-5164 Office: PO Box 4121 Tallahassee FL 32315-4121

MCCORD, JAMES RICHARD, III, chemical engineer, mathematician; b. Norristown, Ga., Sept. 2, 1932; s. Zachariah Thigpen Houser Jr. and Neilie Mae (Sumner) McC.; m. Louise France Manning, Oct. 1956 (div. 1974); children: Neil Alexander, Stuart James, Valerie France, Kent Richard. Student, Abraham Baldwin Agrl. Coll., Tifton, Ga., 1949-50; BChE with honors, Ga. Inst. Tech., 1955; postgrad., U. Pitts., 1955-56, Carnegie Inst. Tech., 1956-57; MS, MIT, 1959, PhD in Math, 1961. Asst. chem. engr. TVA, Wilson Dam, Ala., 1951-54; assoc. engr. Westinghouse Electric Corp., Pitts., 1955-57; rsch. asst. ops. rsch. MIT, Cambridge, Mass., 1957-59; tchg. asst. dept. math. MIT, Cambridge, 1959-61, rsch. assoc. dept. math., 1961-62, asst. prof., postdoctoral fellow dept. chem. engring., 1962-64, rsch. assoc., 1957-62; sr. engr., project analyst Esso Research and Engring. Co., Florham Park, N.J., 1964-68; asst. prof. Emory U., Atlanta, 1968-71; pvt. practice math. cons. Atlanta, 1971-80; instr. in math. Ga. So. Coll., Statesboro, 1980-81; inventory control Lovett & Tharpe, Inc., Dublin, Ga., 1981-84; Norristown-Adrian, farmer, businessman, 1984—. Contbr. numerous articles to sci. and math. jours. WEBELOS den leader Boy Scouts Am., Dunwoody, Ga., 1969-70; mem., vol. worker Key Meml. Found., Adrian-Norristown, Ga., 1965—. Mem. AIChE, Ga. Tech. Alumni Assn., MIT Alumni Assn., Sigma Xi, Tau Beta Pi. Republican. Methodist. Avocations: music, fishing, gardening, mathematical puzzles. Home and Office: Rt 1 Box 58C Adrian GA 31002-9461

MCCORD, JEAN ELLEN, secondary art educator, coach; b. Ilion, N.Y., Oct. 20, 1952; d. Harold Shepard and Marian Alice (Bernier) Shepard; m. Colin McCord, May 10, 1977 (div. Sept. 1993). AA, Mohawk Valley C.C., Utica, N.Y., 1972; BA, SUNY, New Paltz, 1975, postgrad., 1976-77. Cert. art educator, N.Y. Jr. kindergarten tchr. Norfolk (Va.) Naval Base, 1978-79; jr. kindergarten and art tchr. Sunnybrook Day Sch., Virginia Beach, Va., 1979-81; tchr. art Fisher Elem. Sch., Mohawk, N.y., 1982-84, Mechanicstown Sch., Middletown, N.Y., 1984-88, Middletown (N.Y.) Start Ctr., 1986-87, tchr. synergetic edn., Middletown Tchr. Ctr., 1986-87; pvt. portfolio tutor Middletown, 1989-91; tchr. art Middletown Elem. Summer Sch., 1989—, Middletown H.S., 1987—; sec. of policy and exec. bds. Middletown Tchr. Ctr., 1988-91, chmn. policy and exec. bds., 1991-92; mem. Bicentennial of Edn. com.; advisor NAt. Art Honor Soc., 1989—; coord. After Sch. Program for Youth at Risk, 1995—, tchr., 1992-94. Actress, vocalist, designer in regional theatre, 1970—; artistic designer sch. plays and Creative Theatre Group; writer, dir. for local cabarets and charities; local muralist and portraitist, 1990—; designer sets for Off Broadway prodns. in N.Y.C. incl. Mother Posture, Seedless Grapes, The Pelican, New Village Prodns. benefit for AIDS, 1st Theatre Mus. Village, Monroe, N.Y. County svc. coord. Orange County Youth-In-Govt. (adv. 1988—), Goshen, N.Y., 1991-93; Odyssey of the Mind Coach, 1984-92;. Named for outstanding set design Times Herald Record, 1994; honored by Bd. Edn. Outstanding Educator, 1992. Episcopalian. Avocations: theatrical design, singing, calligraphy. Home: 638 Route 211 E Middletown NY 10940-1718 Office: Middletown City Schs Wisner Ave Middletown NY 10940

MC CORD, KENNETH ARMSTRONG, consulting engineer; b. Balt., May 4, 1921; s. William Ellermeyer and Bertha (Turnt) McC.; m. Carol Blanton, Oct. 12, 1946; children—Thomas B., Kenneth Armstrong, William C., David M., Jean E. B. Engring., Johns Hopkins U., 1941. Registered profl. engr., Md., Va., N.J., D.C., Del. registered profl. surveyor, Md., Del. registered profl. planner, N.J. Ret. ptnr. Whitman, Requardt and Assos., Balt.; gen. ptnr. B&H Investments, Manassas, Va. Served with C.E. U.S. Army, 1942-46. Decorated Silver Star, Croix de Guerre France. Fellow ASCE; mem. NSPE, Am. Water Works Assn., Am. Cons. Engrs. Coun., Water Pollution Control Fedn., L'Hirondelle Club. Democrat. Presbyterian. Home: 1010 W Wind Ct Baltimore MD 21204-6738

MCCORD, WILLIAM CHARLES, retired diversified energy company executive; b. San Antonio, Apr. 1, 1928; s. Sam Byard and Helen (Schoepfer) McC.; div.; children: Kathleen McCord Burnett, Martha McCord Pennington, Billy, Helen McCord Curry, Elizabeth McCord Baker, Richard, Douglas, James, Quannah, Korrin Li, Minta Ann Tilden; m. Kay Moran; stepchildren: Heather Moran, Caitlin Moran, James Moran Jr. B.S. in Mech. Engring, Tex. A & M U., 1949. With Enserch Corp. (formerly Lone Star Gas Co.), 1949—, dir. bldg. mgmt., 1965-67; v.p. Enserch Corp. (Dallas div.), 1967, sr. v.p. operations, 1968-70, pres., prin. exec. officer, 1970-77, chmn., pres., 1977-91, chmn., chief exec. officer, 1991-93; sr. v.p. Nipak, Inc., chem. subsidiary, Dallas, 1991-93; ret., 1993; bd. dirs. Enserch Corp., Pool Energy Svcs. Co., Lone Star Techs., Inc. Past pres., mem. exec. bd. Circle Ten council Boy Scouts Am.; mem. nat. exec. bd. Boy Scouts Am.; bd. dirs., former chmn. Tex. Research League, Dallas Citizens Council, State Fair Tex. Mem. Tau Beta Pi. Baptist. Office: 4925 Greenville Ave Dallas TX 75206-4026

MCCORISON, MARCUS ALLEN, librarian, cultural organization administrator; b. Lancaster, Wis., July 17, 1926; s. Joseph Lyle and Ruth (Mink) McC.; m. Janet Buckbee Knop, June 10, 1950; children: Marcus Allen II, Judith McC. Gove, Andrew Buckbee, Mary McC. Rosenbloom, James Rice, Peter Gardner. AB, Ripon Coll., 1950; MA, U. Vt., 1951, LittD (hon.), 1992; MS, Columbia U., 1954; LHD (hon.), Assumption Coll., Worcester, Mass., 1987, Coll. of the Holy Cross, 1992; LittD (hon.), Clark U., 1992. Librarian Kellogg-Hubbard Library, Montpelier, Vt., 1954-55; chief of rare books dept. Dartmouth Coll. Library, Hanover, N.H., 1955-59; head spl. collections dept. State U. Iowa Libraries, 1959-60; libr. Am. Antiquarian Soc., Worcester, Mass., 1960-91, editor Procs., 1960-67, dir., 1967-89, pres., 1989-92, pres. emeritus, 1993—; cons. Christie, Manson & Woods, Internat., 1993-96, A.W. Mellon Found., 1994-95, Libr. Congress, Hist. Soc. of Pa., 1996; mem. N.Am. steering com. 18th Century Short Title Catalogue, 1977—; mem. Com. for a New Eng. Bibliography, 1968-90, treas., 1970-77; mem. adv. com. Eleutherian Mills-Hagley Found., 1971-74, 87-89; mem. adv. coun. Princeton U. Libr., 1988-92; bd. govs. Rsch. Librs. Group, 1980-91, chmn. preservation com., 1982-85, chmn. governance com., 1989-91, chmn. Writings of James Fenimore Cooper, 1991—. Author: Vermont Imprints 1778-1820, 1963, The 1764 Catalogue of the Redwood Library, 1965; contbr.: The Pursuit of Knowledge in the Early American Republic, 1976, Publishing and Readership in Revolutionary France and America, 1993; editor: History of Printing in America by Isaiah Thomas, 1970; mem. editorial bd.: History of the Book in America, 1993—. Trustee Fruitlands Mus., 1978-89, Old Sturbridge Village, 1981-92, Hist. Deerfield, Inc., 1991—; mem. bd. mgrs. Lewis Walpole Libr., Yale U., 1995—; nat. trustee Newbury Libr., 1995—. With USNR, 1944-46, U.S. Army, 1951-52. Recipient Samuel Pepys medal Ephemera Soc., London, 1980, Disting. Alumni award Ripon Coll., 1989, Columbia U. Sch. Libr. Svc., 1992. Fellow Pilgrim Soc.; mem. Am. Antiquarian Soc., Mass. Hist. Soc., Coll. and Rsch. Librs. Assn. (chmn. rare books sect. 1965-66), Bibliog. Soc. Am. (pres. 1980-84, del. to ACLS 1985—), Vt. Hist. Soc. (hon., trustee 1956-66), Worcester Hist. Mus. (exec. com. 1967-80), Ind. Rsch. Librs. Assn. (chmn. 1972-73, 78-80), Ctr. for Rsch. on Vt. (assoc.), N.E. Am. Soc. 18th Century Studies (pres. 1978-79), Colonial Soc. Mass., Club of Odd Vols., Grolier Club (councillor 1979-82, 83-84), Zamorano Club, Roxburghe Club (San Francisco), Century Assn. Democrat. Congregationalist. Home and Office: 3601 Knightsbridge Close Worcester MA 01609-1161

MCCORKLE, HORACE JACKSON, physician, educator; b. Center Point, Tex., Feb. 5, 1905; s. Homer Thomas and Helen Hart (Cason) McC.; m. Marion Fisher, June 10, 1939; children—Alan, Donald, Malcolm, Douglas, Jeanette. M.D., U. Calif., 1934. Intern San Francisco City and County Hosp., 1933-34; surgeon U. Calif. Med. Sch., 1938—, prof. surgery, 1953—. Mem. Am., Pan Pacific, Western, Pacific Coast surg. assns., Internat. Surg. Soc., Pan Am. Med. Soc., Soc. Exptl. Biology and Medicine, Soc. Univ. Surgeons, Am. Gastroenterol. Assn., Nu Sigma Nu, Kappa Delta Rho. Home: 35 San Fernando Way San Francisco CA 94127-1503

MCCORKLE, ROBERT ELLSWORTH, agribusiness educator; b. Salinas, Calif., Apr. 3, 1938; s. Stanley Heard and Muriel Eugenia (Vosti) McC.; m. Mary E. McCorkle, June 26, 1965; children: Bonnie Kathleen, Robyn Krystyna. BSc in Farm Mgmt., Calif. Poly. State U., San Luis Obispo, 1960; MSc in Agrl. Econs., U. Calif., Davis, 1962; postgrad., U. Wis., 1969, Oreg. State U., 1966. Rsch. statistician U. Calif., Davis, 1960-62; asst. prof. agrl. bus. Calif. Poly. State U., San Luis Obispo, 1962-66, dir. internat. edn., 1970-74, asst. prof. agrl. mgmt., 1969-76, prof. agribus., 1976—; chief farm mgmt. officer Ministry Agr., Lusaka, Zambia, 1967-69; dir., owner McCorkle Farms, Inc., Willows, Calif., 1970—; vis. prof. Mich. State U., U.S. AID, Washington, 1984-85; dir., owner McCorkle Trucking, Glenn, Calif., 1988—; agrl. economist U.S. AID-Redso ESA, Nairobi, Kenya, 1984-85. Author: Guide for Farming in Zambia, 1968. Pres. Cabrillo Property Owners Assn., Los Osos, Calif., 1976-78; vol. Atty. Gen.'s Adv. Com., Calif., 1972-74; bd. dirs. Nat. Alpha Zeta Found. U.S. Peace Corps strategy grantee, Washington, 1976—. Mem. Am. Agrl. Econs. Assn., Am. Soc. Farm Mgrs. and Rural Appraisers, Western Agrl. Econs. Assn., Calif. Poly. Farm Mgmt. Club, Calif. Poly. Alumni Assn., Blue Key, Alpha Zeta (founding mem., sr. advisor Delta chpt., nat. high coun. chronicler, treas., bd. dirs.), Nat. Alpha Zeta Found. (bd. dirs.). Republican. Episcopalian. Avocations: hunting, fishing. Office: Calif Poly State U San Luis Obispo CA 93407

MCCORMAC, BILLY MURRAY, physicist, research institution executive, former army officer; b. Zanesville, Ohio, Sept. 8, 1920; s. Samuel Dennis and Phyllis (Murray) M.; m. Dorothy Boros, 1948; children: Norene Leslie, Candace Elizabeth, Lisbeth Phyllis; m. Diana Root, 1968; children: Billy Murray II, Samuel Dennis Root. B.S., Ohio State U., 1943; M.S., U. Va., 1956, Ph.D. in Nuclear Physics, 1957. Commd. 2d lt. U.S. Army, 1943; advanced through grades to lt. col.; physicist U.S. Army (Office Spl. Weapons Devel.), 1957-60; scientist U.S. Army (Office of Chief of Staff), 1960-61; physicist U.S. Army (Def. Atomic Support Agy.), 1961-62, chief electromagnetic br., 1962-63; ret., 1963; sci. advisor rsch. inst. Ill. Inst. Tech., 1963, dir. div. geophysics rsch. inst., 1963-68; sr. cons. scientist Lockheed Rsch. Labs., Palo Alto, Calif., 1968-69, mgr. Radiation Physics Lab., 1969-74, mgr. Electro-optics Lab., 1974-76, mgr. solar and optics physics, 1976-89, staff exec. physical and electronic scis., 1989-92; Chmn. radiation trapped in earth's magnetic field Adv. Study Inst., Norway, 1965, chmn. aurora and airglow, Eng., 1966, Norway, 1968, Can., 1970, chmn. physics and chemistry of atmospheres, France, 1972, Belgium, 1974, chmn. earth's particles and fields, Germany, 1967, Calif., 1969, Italy, 1971, Eng., 1973, Austria, 1975; chmn. Shuttle Environment and Ops.-I, Washington, 1983, -II, Houston, 1985; chmn. Space Station in 21st Century, Reno, 1986, Space Station I, Washington, 1988. Editor Jour. Water, Air and Soil Pollution, Geophysics and Astrophysics Monographs; editor-in-chief Natural Sinks CO2, 1991, Quantification of Sinks and Sources, 1993, Acid Reign Proceedings, 1996. Fellow AIAA (assoc., mem. publ. com. 1981—, v.p. publs. 1987-91); mem. AAAS, Am. Astron. Soc. (sr.), Am. Phys. Soc., Am. Geophys. Union, Marine Tech. Soc. Home: 1312 Cuernavaca Cir Mountain View CA 94040

MC CORMAC, JOHN WAVERLY, judge; b. Zanesville, Ohio, Feb. 8, 1926; s. Samuel D. and Phyllis (Murray) McC.; m. Martha Ann Cunningham, June 22, 1952; children: Michael Paul, John Mark, James Samuel. B.S., Muskingum Coll., 1951; J.D., Capital U., 1961. Bar: Ohio 1961. Fire protection engr. Ohio Insp. Bur., 1951-60; pvt. practice Columbus, 1961-65; prof. law Capital U., Columbus, 1965-66, 71-74; dean Law Sch. Capital U., 1966-71; judge 10th Dist. Ct. Appeals, 1975-92; prof. law Ohio State U., Columbus, 1993—; mem. staff cons. rules adv. com. Supreme Ct. Ohio; chmn. adv. bd. Vols. in Probation, 1972-74; chmn. ohio Jud. Conf., 1982-84; commr. Ohio Dispute Resolution Com., 1989-96, chmn., 1993-95; chief justice Ohio Ct. Appeals Assn., 1989-91. Author: Ohio Civil Rules Practice, 1970, 2nd edit., 1992, Anderson's Ohio Civil Practice, Vol. 1, 1971, Vol. 2, 1976, Vol. 3, 1977, Wrongful Death in Ohio, 1982. Served with USNR, 1943-46. Fellow Ohio Bar Assn. Found.; mem. League Ohio Law Schs. (pres. 1969-70), ABA, Ohio Bar Assn. (council of dels. 1973-77), Columbus Bar Assn. (bd. govs. 1968-72, sec.-treas. 1973-74, pres. 1975-76), Am. Judicature Soc., Phi Alpha Delta. Republican. Club: Masons (33 deg.). Home: 395 Longfellow Ave Columbus OH 43085-3024

MC CORMAC, WESTON ARTHUR, retired educator and army officer; b. Tacoma, Mar. 5, 1911; s. Jesse Carney and Jessie (Myron) McC.; BA, Golden Gate U., MBA, 1968; diploma Nat. War Coll., 1956; MPA, U. So. Calif., 1972; MA, Calif. Poly. State U., 1975. m. Mary Jeanne Rapinac, Sept. 5, 1941. Account exec. Merrill, Lynch, Pierce, Fenner & Beane, Tacoma, Seattle, 1929-40; commd. lt. U.S. Army, 1940, advanced through grades to col., 1946; asst. chief of staff 7th Army G 1, 1952-54; comdg. officer 35th F.A. Group, Germany, 1956-58; dep. chief of staff V Corps, 1958-60, asst. chief of staff G 1, Pacific, 1962-65; ret., 1966; prof. bus., dept. chmn. Calif. Poly. State U., San Luis Obispo, 1968-80, ret., 1980. Decorated Legion of Merit with 2 oak leaf clusters, Silver Star, Bronze Star medal, Commendation medal with oak leaf cluster. Fellow Fin. Analysts Fedn.; mem. Los Angeles Soc. Fin. Analysts. Home: 16732 Lew Allen Cir Riverside CA 92518-2909

MCCORMACK, DENNIS K., clinical psychologist; m. Nancy K. McCormack; children: Kelly, Karen. BA in Math., Calif. Western U., 1969; MA, U.S. Internat. U., 1971, PhD in Leadership and Human Behavior, PhD in Psychology, 1974, 78. Diplomate Internat. Council Profl. Counseling and Psychotherapy, Am. Inst. Counseling and Psychotherapy, Internat. Acad. Health Care Profls. Pvt. practice family therapist Coronado, Calif., 1974-92; chief psychologist, Trauma Svc. Group Winn Army Cmty. Hosp., Ft. Stewart, Ga.; supervisory clin. psychologist Winn Army Cmty. Hosp., 1994—; chief Family Therapy Winn Army Hosp., 1994—, acting chief Psychology and Psychiatry svcs., 1994—; guest spkr. at numerous clubs, lodges and local orgns. Contbr. articles to profl. jours. Mem. Sr. Citizen Adv. Com., 1982—, Land Use Adv. Com., Coronado, 1979-80; chmn. Coronado Planning Commn., 1978-83, St. Paul's United Meth. Ch., 1978-81, personnel com., 1978-81, mem. adminstrv. bd., 1983—; pres. Coronado Coordinating Council, 1983—; mem. adv. bd. Mil. Affairs Com., 1984—; bd. dirs. Vietnam Vets. Leadership Program, 1984—, Coronado Hosp. Found., 1988—; mem. Southbay Chember Exec. Com., 1986—, Coronado Visitor Promotion Bd., 1986—. Fellow Internat. Council of Sex Edn. and Parenthood of Am. U., Am. Bd. Med. Psychotherapists (clin. assoc.), S.D. Acad. Psychologists (chmn. membership com. 1988—), Coronado C. of C. (pres. 1986—). Office: PO Box 577 Richmond Hill GA 31324-0577

MCCORMACK, DONALD PAUL, newspaper consultant; b. Brockton, Mass., Jan. 15, 1926; s. Everett G. and Esther (Lufkin) McC.; m. Petronella Ruth Seger, Apr. 28, 1951; 1 son, Christopher Paul. B.A., U. Pitts., 1949. Corr. U.P.I., 1949-52; asst. city editor Pitts. Sun-Telegraph, 1952-56; pub. relations exec., 1956-64; copy reader N.Y. News, 1964-67, editorial writer, 1967-72, chief editorial writer, 1972-82; cons., 1982—. With USAAF, 1944-46, Pa. N.G., 1952-57. Home and Office: PO Box 3539 Westport CT 06880-8539

MCCORMACK, ELIZABETH J., foundation administrator; b. Mar. 7, 1922; m. Jerome I. Aron, Dec. 23, 1976. BA, Manhattanville Coll., 1944; PhD, Fordham U., 1966. Headmistress Acad. Sacred Heart, Greenwich, Conn., 1954-58; asst. to pres. Manhattanville Coll., Purchase, N.Y., 1958-62, acad. dean, 1962-66, pres., 1966-74; asst. to pres. Rockefeller Bros. Fund, N.Y.C., 1974-76; philanthropic advisor Rockefeller Family & Assocs., N.Y.C., 1976—. Trustee Alliance Capital, N.Y., 1984—, Am. Acad. in Rome, N.Y.C., 1990—, Asian Cultural Coun., N.Y.C., 1980; supervisory dir. Arrow Ventures, N.V., N.Y.C., 1983—; bd. dirs. United HealthCare Corp., 1991—; overseer Meml. Sloan-Kettering Cancer Ctr., Inc., N.Y.C., 1979—, mgr., 1980—; trustee emeritus Swarthmore (Pa.) Coll., 1980—. Mem. Am. Acad. Arts and Scis., Century Assn., Coun. on Fgn. Rels. Office: Rockefeller Found 30 Rockefeller Plz Rm 5600 New York NY 10112*

MC CORMACK, FRANCIS XAVIER, lawyer, former oil company executive; b. Bklyn., July 9, 1929; s. Joseph and Blanche V. (Dengel) Mc C.; m. Margaret V. Hynes, Apr. 24, 1954; children: Marguerite, Francis Xavier, Sean Michael, Keith John, Cecelia Blanche, Christopher Thomas. AB cum laude, St. Francis Coll., Bklyn., 1951; LLB, Columbia U., 1954. Bar: N.Y. 1955, Mich. 1963, Calif. 1974, Pa. 1975. Assoc. Cravath, Swaine & Moore, N.Y.C., 1956-62; sr. atty. Ford Motor Co., 1962-64, asst. gen. counsel, 1970-72; v.p., gen. counsel, sec. Philco-Ford Corp., 1964-72; v.p., gen. counsel Atlantic Richfield Co., 1972-73, sr. v.p., gen. counsel, 1973-94. Editor Columbia U. Law Rev., 1954. Decorated commendatore Ordine al Merito (Italy); Stone scholar Columbia U., 1954. Mem. Calif. Club, Chancery Club, Annandale Golf Club. Home and Office: 975 Singingwood Dr Arcadia CA 91006-1924

MC CORMACK, FRED ALLEN, state social services administrator; b. Bklyn., June 10, 1930; s. Frank J. and Rhea (Del Castro) Mc C.; m. Ellen Anne Lockwood, June 19, 1954 (div.); children: Mary Lee, Lynn Anne, Rosemarie, Fred A., Julie Ellen, Rhea Michelle, Claire Eileen; m. Elin Howe, Jan. 1994. BS, Seton Hall U., 1953; MSW, U. Conn., 1955. Social worker Montrose (N.Y.) VA Hosp., 1955-61; adminstr., dir. Tappan Zee Mental Health Ctr., North Tarrytown, N.Y., 1957-62; supr. social worker Orange County Mental Health Clinic, Goshen, N.Y., 1961-62; dir. Sweetwater Counseling Svc., Rock Springs, Wyo., 1962-65; asst. supt., dir. geriatric program Manteno (Ill.) State Hosp., 1965-68; dir. Tacoma Comprehensive Mental Health Ctr., 1968-69; cons. Dept. Instns. Wash., 1968-69, Laurel Haven Sch., Ballwin, Mo., 1977-78; supt. W.G. Murray Children's Ctr., Centralia, Ill., 1969-71, Elisabeth Ludeman Ctr., Park Forest, Ill., 1971-76; dir. San Luis Valley Mental Health Ctr., Alamosa, Colo., 1976-77, Monroe Devel. Ctr., Rochester, N.Y., 1977-80, Suffolk Devel. Ctr., Melville, N.Y., 1980-85; assoc. commr. N.Y. State Office Mental Retardation and Devel. Disabilities, Albany, 1985-93; ret., 1993; part-time tchr. Western Wyo. Jr. Coll., 1963-65, Prairie State Coll., Chicago Heights, Ill., 1965-68, Green River C.C., 1968-69; instr. Adams State Coll., Alamosa, 1977; cons. Snohomish Community Action Coun., Everett, Wash., 1969. Past mem. citizens adv. bd. Sch. Dist. 162, Matteson, Ill.; chmn. Park Forest Sr. Citizens Commn., State Employees Federated Appeal, United Way Rochester, 1978-80, L.I., 1984-85; past bd. dirs. Gavin Found., Park Forest; bd. Jones Cmty. Ctr., Chicago Heights, Four County Devel. Disabilities Conf.; vol. Prescott Spl. Olympics, 1993, 94, 95, 96; advisor Prescott Oasis. Recipient cert. of merit Nat. Assn. Physically Handicapped, Dir. of Yr. award N.Y. State Family Care Providers Assn., 1984. Fellow Am. Assn. Mental Deficiency (pres. Ill. chpt. 1972); mem. NASW, Acad. Cert. Social Workers. Home: 1408 Myers Holw Prescott AZ 86301-5145

MCCORMACK, JOHN JOSEPH, JR., insurance executive; b. Morristown, N.J., Aug. 22, 1944; s. John Joseph and Marion Loretta (Smith) McC.; m. Judith Gail Harvey, July 20, 1968; children—Brendan, Matthew, Margaret. B.B.A., St. Bonaventure U., 1966. Group underwriter Tchrs. Ins. and Annuity Assn.-Coll. Retirement Equities Fund, N.Y.C., 1966-71, benefit plan counselor, 1971-72, asst. adv. officer, 1972-73, adv. officer, 1973-74, asst. v.p., 1974-75, 2d v.p., 1975-78, v.p., 1978-80, sr. v.p., 1980-83, exec. v.p., 1983—; trustee Am. Psychol. Assn. Ins. Trust, Washington, 1980-90, chmn., 1985-86, trustee investment com., 1990—; trustee Employee Benefit Research Inst., Washington, 1983—, treas., 1986-90. Mem. pres.'s coun. St. Bonaventure U., 1986—, chmn., 1986-89, trustee, 1996—; bd. visitors Ctr. for Study Future Mgmt., 1987-92; trustee Coll. and Univ. Pers. Assn. Found., 1992-94; bd. govs. Investment Co. Inst., 1994—. Roman Catholic. Office: Tchrs Ins & Annuity Assn Am 730 3rd Ave New York NY 10017-3206

MCCORMACK, MARK HUME, lawyer, business management company executive; b. Chgo., Nov. 6, 1930; s. Ned and Grace (Wolfe) McC.; m. Nancy Ann Breckenridge, Oct. 9, 1954 (div.); children: Scott, Todd, Leslie; m. Betsy Nagelsen. BA, William and Mary Coll., 1951; LLB, Yale U., 1954. Assoc. Arter and Hadden, Cleve., 1957-63; ptnr. Arter and Hadden, 1963—; pres., chief exec. officer Internat. Mgmt. Group, Cleve., 1964—. Author: The World of Professional Golf, 1967, Arnie, The Evolution of a Legend, 1967, Arnie, The Man and the Legend, 1967 (British edit.), Arnie, What They Did Not Teach You in Harvard Business School, 1984, Terrible Truth About Lawyers, 1987, What They Still Don't Teach You at Harvard Business School, 1989. Served with U.S. Army, 1955-56. Mem. Cleve. Bar Assn., Author's Guild, Royal and Ancient Club (St. Andrews, Scotland), Union Club, Pepper Pike Club, The Club (Cleve.), Isleworth Club, Deepdale Club, All England Club, Theta Delta Chi. Office: Internat Mgmt Group 1 Erieview Plz Ste 1300 Cleveland OH 44114-1715*

MCCORMACK, PATRICIA SEGER, independent press service editor, journalist; b. Pitts., June 11, 1927; d. Arthur John and Anne Irene (McCaffrey) Seger; m. Donald P. McCormack, Apr. 28, 1951; 1 son, Christopher Paul. B.A., U. Pitts., 1949; certificate, A.P. Inst. Seminar, 1967. News editor weekly newspapers Mt. Lebanon, Pa., 1950-52; med. editor Pitts. Sun Telegraph, 1952-57; med. sci. editor INS, N.Y.C., 1958-59; columnist, family, health and edn. editor UPI, 1959-84, sr. editor, 1987-90. Mem. Boy of Year selection com. Boys Clubs Am., 1966; mem. Coty Fashion award jury, 1965-72, nat. selection com. Century III Leader Scholarship Competition Nat. Assn. Secondary Sch. Prins., 1986. Recipient Biennial Media award Family Service Assn. Am., 1965, Freedom Found. medal; 1st place Sci. Writing award Am. Dental Assn., 1976; Nat. Media award United Negro Coll. Fund, 1977; John Swett award for disting. educating reporting Calif. Edn. Assn., 1981. Mem. AAAS, Nat. Assn. Sci. Writers (life), Edn. Writers Assn., Women's Forum Inc. (N.Y.C.), Nat. Fedn. Press Women (Comm. Achievement medal 1993), Conn. Press Club (v.p., Communicator of Achievement 1993), Conn. Women's Forum. Home and Office: PO Box 3539 Westport CT 06880-8539

MCCORMACK, RICHARD THOMAS FOX, government official, former ambassador; b. Bradford, Pa., Mar. 6, 1941; s. C.H. and Ruth N. (Fox) McC.; m. Karen L. Hagstrom, Oct. 18, 1980; children: Charlotte Louise, Justin Randall, Elizabeth Caroline. B.A., Georgetown U., 1963; Ph.D., U. Fribourg (Switzerland), 1966. With Peace Corps, 1966-67; sr. staff mem. Pres.' Adv. Council on Exec. Orgn., White House, Washington, 1969-71; with Am. Enterprise Inst., 1975-77; dep. asst. sec. for internat. econ. affairs Dept. Treasury, 1974; mem. staff U.S. Senate, 1979-81; asst. sec. state for econ. and bus. affairs U.S. Dept. State, Washington, 1982-85; ambassador Orgn. Am. States U.S. Dept. State, 1985-89, undersec. of state for econ. affairs, 1989-91; candidate in primary elections for U.S. Congress, 1972, 74; cons. Office Telecommunications Policy, 1971, Coun. on Internat. Econ. Policy, 1972, Office Spl. Trade Rep., 1975, Exec. Office of the Pres., Washington; guest scholar Woodrow Wilson Ctr. Smithsonian Instn., Washington, 1991-92; bus. advisor Am. companies, cons. U.S. Govt. on Internat. Econ. Affairs, 1992—. Author: Asians in Kenya, 1971, The Twilight War, 1979, Economic Reforms for Israel's Economy, 1991, Managing Japan's Financial Crisis, 1992. Recipient Superior Honor award Dept. State, 1987, Sec. of State's Disting. Svc. award, 1991; decorated Legion of Honor (France). Mem. Internat. Inst. Strategic Studies, Econ. Club N.Y. Republican. Home: 1601 Walden Dr Mc Lean VA 22101

MCCORMACK, ROBERT CORNELIUS, investment banker; b. N.Y.C., Nov. 7, 1939; m. Mary Lester, Dec. 14, 1963; children: Robert Cornelius Jr., Walter, Scott. BA, U. N.C., 1962; MBA, U. Chgo., 1968. V.p. Dillon Read & Co. Inc., 1968-81; mng. dir. Morgan Stanley & Co., Inc., Chgo., 1981-87; dep. asst sec. def. prodn. support U.S. Dept. Def., Washington, 1987-88, dep. under sec. def. indsl. and internat. programs, 1988-89; acting dep. under sec. of def. acquisition U.S. Dept. Def., 1989-90; asst. sec. Navy fin. mgmt. U.S. Dept. Def., Washington, 1990-93; founding ptnr. Trident Capital L.P., Chgo., 1993—. Served to lt. USNR, 1963-66. Office: Trident Capital LP 190 S La Salle St Ste 2760 Chicago IL 60603-3412

MCCORMACK, STANLEY EUGENE, financial consultant; b. Olney, Ill., Oct. 15, 1949; s. Donald Eugene and Patricia Louise (Dickerson) McC.; m. Janis Eileen Bush; m. Jeffrey Daniel, Erin Louise, Evan Stuart. Student, DePauw U., 1967-68, Ohio State U., 1968-71; MS in Fin. Svc., The Am. Coll., 1991, MS in Mgmt., 1996. CLU; chartered fin. cons. Ins. agt. Art Holtzman Assocs., Rochester, N.Y., 1973-75, ins. sales mgr., 1975-82; fin. cons., pres. Associated Fin. Cons., Rochester, 1983—; instr. Am. Coll., Rochester, 1988. Moderator Webster (N.Y.) Bapt. Ch., 1985-88, mem. fin. com., 1994—, chmn. long range planning and growth com.; pres. Parkwood Park Assn., Webster, 1987-90; com. mem. Rep. Com., Webster, 1978-81; mem. fin. com. Webster Swim Assn., 1993-95, treas., 1989-91. Mem. Am. Soc. Chartered Life Underwriters and Chartered Fin. Cons., Internal Assn. Fin. Planners (bd. dirs. 1989-95, v.p. chmn. symposium 1990, pres. 1993-94, pres. adv. bd. 1994—), Estate Planning Coun. Rochester, Phi Delta Theta. Avocations: voice, bridge, furniture building. Home: 622 Fairmont Dr Webster NY 14580-8967

MCCORMACK, THOMAS JOSEPH, retired publishing company executive; b. Boston, Jan. 5, 1932; s. Thomas Joseph and Lena Carolyn (Allen) McC.; m. Sandra Harriet Danenberg, Aug. 21, 1964; children: Daniel Aaron, Jed Charles (dec.), Jessie Ann. Student, U. Conn., 1950-51; A.B. summa cum laude (James Manning scholar), Brown U., 1954; postgrad. (G.H. Palmer scholar, Woodrow Wilson fellow), Harvard U., 1956. Writer radio news WSTC, Stamford, Conn., 1957-59; editor Doubleday & Co., Inc., N.Y.C., 1959-64, Harper & Row, N.Y.C., 1964-67; edn. editor New Am. Library, N.Y.C., 1967-69; dir. trade dept. St. Martin's Press, N.Y.C., 1969-70; pres. St. Martin's Press, 1970-87, chief exec. officer, editorial dir., 1970-96, chmn., 1987-97; pres., chmn. bd. St. James Press, Ltd., London, 1973-79; dir. Prudential-Bache Govt. Securities Trust; dir. Prudential-Bache High Yield Mcpls., Inc., Prudential-Bache Tax Free Money Fund, Inc., Prudential-Bache High Yield Fund, Inc.; v.p., treas. Sandra D. McCormack, Inc. (Interior Designer.); chmn., chief exec. officer Tor Books, N.Y.C., 1987-96; exec. com. Holtzbrinck GmbH, Stuttgart, Germany, 1995-97. Author: Afterwords, Novelists on Their Novels, 1969, The Fiction Editor, the Novel and the Novelist, 1988; (play) American Roulette, 1969. Mem. Play Devel. Coun., Manhattan Theater Club, 1995—, Dramatists Gild, 1997—. With AUS, 1954-56. Mem. Assn. Am. Pubs. (dir. 1973-76, freedom to read com. 1974-77, Curtis Benjamin award 1997, LMP Lifetime Achievement award 1997), Phi Beta Kappa. Clubs: The Players (N.Y.C.), Century Assn. (N.Y.C.). Home: 50 Central Park W New York NY 10023-6028 Office: St Martin's Press Inc 175 5th Ave New York NY 10010-7703

MCCORMALLY, KEVIN JAY, editor; b. Boston, Mar. 13, 1950; s. John Patrick and Marguerite Louise (Wichert) McC.; m. Anne Louise Long, May 27, 1972; children: Niamh Anna, Patrick Henry. BA with honors, U. Iowa, 1972. Area editor Burlington (Iowa) Hawk Eye, 1969-70; city editor Daily Iowan, Iowa City, 1971-72; press sec. U.S. Rep. Edward Mezvinsky, Washington, 1972-77; assoc. editor Changing Times Mag., Washington, 1977-85, sr. editor, 1985-90; exec. editor Kiplinger's Personal Fin. Mag. (formerly Changing Times), Washington, 1991—; commentator Nightly Bus. Report PBS. Author: Successful Tax Planning, 1988, Sure Ways to Cut Your Taxes, 1989-94, Cut Your Taxes, 1996, 97; co-author: A Term to Remember, 1977; editor: Get More for Your Money, 1981. Mem. Nat. Press Club (best consumer journalism award 1986, 88), Sigma Delta Chi. Democrat. Roman Catholic. Avocations: photography, camping. Home: 161 D St SE Washington DC 20003-1809 Office: Kiplingers Personal Fin Mag 1729 H St NW Washington DC 20006-3904

MCCORMICK, BARNES WARNOCK, aerospace engineering educator; b. Waycross, Ga., July 15, 1926; s. Barnes Warnock and Edwina (Brogdon) McC.; m. Emily Joan Hess, July 18, 1946; 1 dau., Cynthia Joan. B.S. in Aero. Engring, Pa. State U., 1948, M.S., 1949, Ph.D., 1954. Research assoc. Pa. State U., University Park, 1949-54, assoc. prof., 1954-55, prof. aero. engring., 1959-92, Boeing prof. aero. engring., 1985-92, prof. emeritus, cons., 1992—, head dept. aerospace engring., 1969-85; assoc. prof., chmn. aero. dept. Wichita U., 1958-59; chief aerodynamics Vertol Helicopter Co., 1955-58; mem. Congl. Adv. Com. Aeros., 1984-86; U.S. coord. flight vehicle integration panel Adv. Group for Aerospace R&D, 1988—; cons. to industry. Author: Aerodynamics of V/Stol Flight, 1967, Aerodynamics, Aeronautics and Flight Mechanics, 1979, 2d edit., 1995; co-author: (with M.P. Papadakis) Aircraft Accident Reconstruction and Litigation, 1996; contbr. articles to profl. jours. Served with USNR, 1944-46. Recipient joint award for achievement in aerospace edn. Am. Soc. Engring. Edn.-Am. Inst. Aeros. and Astronautics, 1976. Fellow Am. Inst. Aeros. and Astronautics (assoc.); mem. ASEE, Am. Helicopter Soc. (tech. council, hon. fellow), Sigma Xi, Sigma Gamma Tau, Tau Beta Pi. Club: Masons. Patentee in field. Home: 611 Glenn Rd State College PA 16803-3475 Office: Pa State U Coll Engring University Park PA 16802

MCCORMICK, DAVID ARTHUR, lawyer; b. McKeesport, Pa., Oct. 26, 1946; s. Arthur Paul and Eleanor Irene (Gibson) McC. BA, Westminster Coll., 1967; JD, Duquesne U., 1973; MBA, U. Pa., 1975. Bar: Pa. 1973, D.C. 1978, U.S. Ct. Appeals (3d cir.) 1977, U.S. Ct. Appeals (4th and D.C. cirs.) 1980, U.S. Supreme Ct. 1980. Asst. commerce counsel Penn Cen. R.R., Phila., 1973-76; assoc. labor counsel Consol. Rail Corp., Phila., 1976-78; atty. Dept. Army, Washington, 1978—. Author various geneal. and hist. works; contbr. articles to profl. jours. Mem. Pa. Bar Assn., Phila. Bar Assn., D.C. Bar Assn., Assn. Transp. Practitioners, Soc. Cin. (Del. chpt.), SAR

(Pitts. chpt.), Am. Legion, Res. Officers Assn., Masons, Phi Alpha Delta. Presbyterian.

MCCORMICK, DONALD BRUCE, biochemist, educator; b. Front Royal, Va., July 15, 1932; s. Jesse Allen and Elizabeth (Hord) McC.; m. Norma Jean Dunn, June 6, 1955; children: Susan Lynn, Donald Bruce, Michael Allen. B.A., Vanderbilt U., 1953, Ph.D., 1958; postdoctoral fellow, U. Calif., Berkeley, 1958-60. Asst. prof. Cornell U., 1960-63, assoc. prof., 1963-69, prof. nutrition, biochemistry and molecular biology, biol. scis., 1969-79, Liberty Hyde Bailey prof. nutritional biochemistry, 1978-79; chmn. dept. biochemistry Emory U., Atlanta, 1979-94, Fuller E. Callaway prof. biochemistry, 1979—; exec. assoc. dean sci. Emory U. Sch. Medicine, 1985-89; vis. lectr. U. Ill, 1963; Wellcome vis. prof. U. Fla., 1986, Med. Coll. Pa., 1989; Hurley lectr. U. Calif., Davis, 1992; O'Dell lectr. U. Mo., Columbia, 1993; biochem. cons. Interdeptl. Com. on Nutrition for Nat. Def., Spain, 1958; mem. and chmn. nutrition study sect. NIH, 1977-81; mem. diet and health com., dietary guidelines implementation com., vice chmn. food and nutrition bd. NRC, Inst. Medicine, NAS; exec. com., chmn. dept. med. biochemistry, Council Acad. Soc., Am. Assn. Med. Colls., 1984-87. Author: (with others) Spain: Nutrition Survey of the Armed Forces, 1958, Molecular Associations in Biology, 1968, Flavins and Flavin Enzymes, 1968, Flavins and Flavoproteins, 1980, 82, 84, 88, 89, 91, Comprehensive Biochemistry, Vol. 21, 1971, Riboflavin, 1974, Metal Ions in Biological Systems, Vol. 1, 1974, Present Knowledge in Nutrition, 1976, 84, 90, Natural Sulphur Compounds, 1979, Vitamin B6, Metabolism and Role in Growth, 1980, Ann. Rev. of Nutrition, Vol. 1, 1981, Vol. 9, 1989, Mechanisms of Enzymatic Reactions: Stereochemistry, 1986, Chemical and Biological Aspects of Vitamin B6 Catalysis, Part A, 1984, Biochemistry of Vitamin B6, 1987, Textbook of Clinical Chemistry, 1986, 94, Fundamentals of Clinical Chemistry, 1987, 95, Vitamins and Biofactors in Life Science, 1992, Encyclopedia of Food Science, 1993, Encyclopedia of Molecular, Biology and Molecular Medicine, 1996, 97, Modern Nutrition in Health and Disease, 1988, 94, New Trends in Biological Chemistry, 1990, Chemistry and Biochemistry of Flavins, 1991, Encyclopedia of Human Biology, 1991, Liver, 1994, Molecular Biology and Biotechnology, 1995; editor: Vitamins and Hormones, Vitamins and Coenzymes, Ann. Rev. of Nutrition. Recipient award Bausch and Lomb, 1950, award Mead Johnson, 1970, award Osborne and Mendel, 1978, award Ga. Nutrition Coun., 1989; Westinghouse Sci. scholar, 1950; fellow NIH, 1957-58, 58-60; Guggenheim fellow, 1966-67. Fellow AAAS; mem. Am. Soc. Biochemistry and Molecular Biology, Am. Inst. Nutrition (pres. 1991), Soc. Exptl. Biology and Medicine, Am. Chem. Soc., Am. Inst. Biol. Sci., Biophysics Soc., Fedn. Am. Socs. Exptl. Biology (bd. dirs., LSRO scientific steering group), Microbiol. Soc., Photobiol. Soc., N.Y. Acad. Sci., Protein Soc., Sigma Xi. Home: 2245 Deer Ridge Dr Stone Mountain GA 30087-1129 Office: Emory U Dept Biochemistry Atlanta GA 30322

MCCORMICK, DONALD E., librarian, archivist; b. Hartford, Conn., 1941. BA, Trinity Coll., 1963; MLS, Columbia U., 1967. Drama libr. N.Y. Pub. Libr., N.Y.C., 1965-72, sound recording libr., 1972-73, asst. chief libr., 1973-85, sound archive curator, 1985—. Mem. Assn. Recorded Sound Colls. (past pres. 1988-90), Assoc. Audio Archives (chmn. 1990-94), Music Libr. Assn. Office: NY Pub Libr for Performing Arts 40 Lincoln Center Plz New York NY 10023-7486

MCCORMICK, DONNA LYNN, social worker; b. Austin, Minn., Aug. 13, 1944; d. Raymond Alois and Grace Eleanor (Hayes) Schrom; m. James Michael McCormick, Jan. 15, 1972. BA in Psychology, Coll. St. Catherine, 1966. Caseworker Phila. County Bd. Pub. Assistance, 1968-70; sr. social worker San Francisco Dept. Human Svcs., 1986—. Mem. AAUW, Coll. St. Catherine Alumnae Assn., Emily's List, Nat. Trust Hist. Preservation, Nat. Mus. Women in Arts, Met. Opera Assn. Democrat. Avocations: reading, walking, wine tasting, letter writing, opera. Home: 168 17th Ave San Francisco CA 94121 Office: San Francisco Dept Human Svcs PO Box 7988 San Francisco CA 94120

MC CORMICK, EDWARD ALLEN, foreign language educator; b. Fairfax County, Va., July 1, 1925; s. Jesse Allen and Elizabeth (Hord) McC.; m. Diana Festa, Mar. 1, 1952 (div. Aug. 1973); children: Allen Sergio, Marco Kevin, Carlo Brian; m. Marie Parrice, Apr. 2, 1974 (div. Apr. 1980); m. Phyllis van Slyck, June 10, 1980 (div. May 1985); 1 son, Andrew Stuart; m. Ping Tsai, Mar. 19, 1993. A.B., Randolph-Macon Coll., 1948; Ph.D., U. Berne, Switzerland, 1951; M.A. (hon.), Dartmouth, 1965. Instr. German Princeton U., 1952, asst. prof. German, 1954-58; instr. German U. Mich., 1952-53, Harvard U., 1953-54; asst. prof. German Brown U., 1958-59; mem. faculty Dartmouth, 1959—; prof. German, German and comparative lit., dir. comparative lt. Queens Coll., CUNY, 1966-70; prof. German and comparative lit. Queens Coll., CUNY (Grad. Ctr.), 1970—, exec. officer comparative lit., 1970-74, exec. officer German, 1980-92; retired, 1992. Author: Whitman's Leaves of Grass in deutscher Übertragung, 1953, (with F.G. Ryder) Lebendige Literatur, 1960, 2d edit., 1974, 3d edit., 1986, Theodor Storm's Novellen, 1964; editor: Lessing's Laokoon, 1962, (J.E. Schlegel) On Imitation, 1965, Germans in America, 1983; gen. editor: Studies in European Thought, 1990—; also articles in jours., encys. Served with 82d Airborne Div. AUS, 1943-46, ETO. Recipient Princeton Bicentennial Preceptorship, 1954-58; Dartmouth Faculty fellow, 1963. Mem. MLA, Am. Comparative Lit. Assn., Am. Assn. Tchrs. German. Home: 309 Calzada De Bougainville Marathon FL 33050-2513

MCCORMICK, EDWARD JAMES, JR., lawyer; b. Toledo, May 11, 1921; s. Edward James and Josephine (Beck) McC.; m. Mary Jane Blank, Jan. 27, 1951; children: Mary McCormick Krueger, Edward James III, Patrick William, Michael J. B.S., John Carroll U., 1943; J.D., Western Res. U., 1948. Bar: Ohio 1948, U.S. Supreme Ct. 1980. Mem. teaching staff St. Vincent Hosp. Sch. Nursing, 1951-67. Pvt. practice 1948—; Trustee Toledo Small Bus. Assn., 1950-75, pres., 1954-55, 56-58, 67-68; trustee Goodwill Industries Toledo, 1961-74, chmn. meml. gifts com., mem. exec. com., 1965-70; trustee Lucas County unit Am. Cancer Soc., 1950-61, sec., 1953, v.p., 1954-56, pres., 1957-58; founder, incorporator, sec., trustee Cancer Cytology Research Fund Toledo, Inc., 1956-79; trustee Ohio Cerebral Palsy Assn., 1963-70; incorporator, sec., trustee N.W. Ohio Clin. Engring. Ctr., 1972-74; trustee Friendly Ctr., 1973-83, Ohio Blind Assn., 1970-79; founder-incorporator, trustee, sec. Western Lake Erie Hist. Soc., 1978-85; mem. Toledo Deanery Diocesan Coun. Cath. Men; asst. gen. counsel U.S. Power and Sail Squadrons; life mem. China, Burma and India Vets. Assn., Inc. 1st lt. U.S. Army, 1942-46, USAR, 1946-52. Named Outstanding Young Man of Yr., Toledo Jr. C. of C., 1951; Man of Nation, Woodmen of World, Omaha, 1952. Fellow Ohio State Assn.; mem. ABA, Ohio Bar Assn. (chmn. Am. citizenship com. 1958-67, mem. pub. rels. com. 1967-72, estate planning, probate and trust law com.), Toledo Bar Assn. (chmn. pub. rels. com. 1979, mem. grievance com. 1974-92, chmn. probate, estate planning and trust law com. 1986-90, Disting. Svc. award in memory Robert A. Kelb, Esq. 1993), Lucas County Bar Assn. (chmn. Am. citizenship com.), Assn. Trial Lawyers Am., Am. Judicature Soc., Am. Arbitration Assn., Conf. Pvt. Orgns. (sec.-treas.), Toledo C. of C., Toledo Yacht Club (mem. com. 1970-71), Toledo Torch Club, Blue Gavel, Elks (grand esteemed leading knight 1964-65, mem. grand forum 1965-70), Lions (trustee, legal advisor Ohio Eye Research Found. 1956-70; pres. 1957-58, chmn. permanent membership com. 1961-85, hon. mem. 1984, pres. 1957, A.B. Snyder award 1979), Ky. Col. Office: 2828 W Central Ave Ste 10 Toledo OH 43606-3078

MCCORMICK, FLOYD GUY, JR., agricultural educator, college administrator; b. Center, Colo., July 3, 1927; s. Floyd Guy and Gladys (Weir) McC.; m. Constance P. Slane; children: Angela Lynn, Craig Alan, Kim Ann, Robert Guy. BS, Colo. State U., 1950, MEd, 1959; PhD, Ohio State U., 1964. Tchr. vocat. agr. State of Colo., 1956-62; asst. prof. agrl. edn. Ohio State U., 1964-67; mem. com. agr. edn. com. edn. in agr. and natural resources Nat. Acad. Scis., 1967-69; prof. agrl. edn., head dept. U. Ariz., 1967-89, prof. emeritus, dept. head emeritus, 1990—; cons. in-svc. edn., div. vocat. edn. Ohio Dept. Edn., 1963-64; vis. prof. Colo. State U., 1973, U. Sierra Leone, Njala Univ. Coll., 1989; external examiner U. Sierra Leone, 1984, 85, 87; adv. trustee Am. Inst. Cooperatives, Washington, 1985-88; mem. Nat. Coun. Vocat. and Tech. Edn. in Agr., Washington, 1985-88. Co-author: Teacher Education in Agriculture, 1982, Supervised Occupational Experience Handbook, 1982; author: The Power of Positive Teaching, 1994, also instrl. units, tech. bulls., articles in profl. jours.; spl. editor: Agrl. Edn. mag., 1970-74. Trustee Nat. FFA Found. Served with USNR, 1945-46. Named hon. state farmer Colo., 1958, Ariz., 1968, Am. farmer, 1972; recipient Centennial award Ohio State U., 1970, E.B. Knight award NACTA Jour., 1980, Regional Outstanding Tchr. award Nat. Assn. Coll. Tchrs. Agr., 1989, also fellow, 1988, VIP citation Nat. FFA Assn., 1990, Diamond Anniversary award Ohio State U., 1992. Mem. Am. Vocat Assn. (mem. policy com. agrl. edn. divsn. 1976-79, v.p. divsn. 1985-88, chmn. membership com. 1980-83, sec. agrl. edn. divsn. 1983-86, pres. 1985-88, outstanding svc. awrd 1989), Nat. Vocat. Agr. Tchrs. Assn. (life, Outstanding Svc. award Region I 1974, 83, 96), Am. Assn. Tchr. Educators in Agr. (disting. lectr. 1984, editor newsletter 1975-76, pres. 1976-77, Disting. Svc. award 1978, 88, Rsch. award western region rsch. 1988), Alpha Zeta, Alpha Tau Alpha (hon.), Gamma Sigma Delta, Phi Delta Kappa, Epsilon Pi Tau. Home: 6933 E Paseo San Andres Tucson AZ 85710-2203

MCCORMICK, HUGH THOMAS, lawyer; b. McAlester, Okla., Nov. 24, 1944; s. Hugh O. and Lois (McGucken) McC.; m. Suzanna G. Weingarten, Dec. 5, 1975; 1 child, John B. BA, U. Mich., 1968; JD, Rutgers U., 1977; LLM in Taxation, Georgetown U., 1980. Bar: N.Y. 1977, D.C. 1979, Maine 1981. Atty. office chief counsel interpretative divsn. IRS, Washington, 1977-81; assoc. Perkins, Thompson, Hinkley & Keddy, Portland, Maine, 1981-83; assoc. LeBoeuf, Lamb, Leiby & MacRae, N.Y.C., 1983-88, counsel, 1989-91; ptnr. LeBoeuf, Lamb, Greene & MacRae, L.L.P., N.Y.C., 1992—; dir. Ins. Tax. Conf., 1993—, v.p., sec., 1996—. Mem. bd. contbrs. and advisors Jour. of Taxation of Investments; contbr. articles to profl. jours. Trustee U.S. Team Handball Found., N.J., 1985-95. Fellow Am. Bar Found.; mem. ABA (chmn. com. on taxation of ins. cos. 1989, chmn. subcom. sect. of taxation 1989-96, mem. torts and ins. practice sect., sect. on taxation), D.C. Bar Assn. Democrat. Home: 555 Pelham Manor Rd Pelham Manor NY 10803-2525 Office: LeBoeuf Lamb Greene MacRae LLP 125 W 55th St New York NY 10019-5369

MC CORMICK, JAMES CHARLES, leasing and financial services company executive; b. Cleve., Jan. 23, 1938; s. Michael Patrick and Agnes Christine (Mortensen) McC.; m. Claire A. Maskaly, Nov. 28, 1963 (div. June 1978); children: Kelly, Shannon.; m. Patricia A. Lelko, May 28, 1982. B.S. in Acctg., Regis Coll., Denver, 1960. C.P.A. Accountant Ernst & Ernst, Allentown, Pa., 1963-73; treas. Fuller Co., Catasauqua, Pa., 1973-82; asst. controller GATX Corp., Chgo., 1982-93, dir. internal audit, 1993—. Vol. Chgo. council Boy Scouts Am. Served with USNR, 1960-63. Mem. AICPA, Fin. Execs. Inst. Home: 835 Arbor Ln Glenview IL 60025-3233

MCCORMICK, JAMES EDWARD, oil company executive; b. Providence, Nov. 5, 1927; s. James Edward and Edna Josephine (Smith) McC.; m. Catherine Sullivan, Aug. 30, 1952. AB in Geology, Boston U., 1952. Engr. trainee Sun Oil Co., Beaumont, Tex., 1953-54; jr. geologist Sun Oil Co., Houston, 1954-67, exploration mgr., 1967-70; regional mgr. geology Sun Oil Co., Dallas, 1970-71, exploration program mgr., 1971-74, div. mgr. strategy planning, 1974-77, v.p. internat. exploration and prodn., 1977-86, pres. exploration and prodn., 1986-88; pres. Oryx Energy, Dallas, 1988-92; bd. dirs. Dallas Nat. Bank, Tesco Corp., B.J. Svcs. Co., Lone Star Tech., Dallas, Snyder Oil Co., Ft. Worth, Tex. Bd. dirs. United Way Met. Dallas, 1986-92; mem. Dallas Citizens Council, 1986-88. Served as sgt. USAF, 1945-48. Mem. Am. Assn. Petroleum Geologists, N.Y. Acad. Scis., Nat. Ocean Industries Assn. (bd. dirs. 1986-92), Northwood Country Club, Las Colinas Country Club, Energy Club, Dallas Petroleum Club. Roman Catholic. Clubs: Northwood Country, Las Colinas Country. Office: McCormick Enterprises 5949 Sherry Ln # 98 Dallas TX 75225-6532

MCCORMICK, JAMES HAROLD, academic administrator; b. Indiana, Pa., Nov. 11, 1938; s. Harold Clark and Mary Blanche (Truby) McCormick; m. Maryan Kough Garner, June 7, 1963; children: David Harold, Douglas Paul. BS, Indiana U. of Pa., 1959; MEd, U. Pitts., 1961, EdD, 1963, postdoctoral, 1966; postdoctoral, Columbia U., U. Mich., 1966-67, Harvard U., 1982. Tchr. Punxsutawney (Pa.) Area Joint Sch. Dist., 1959-61; adminstr. Baldwin-Whitehall Schs., Pitts., 1961-64; grad. asst. U. Pitts., 1962-63; asst. supt. instrn. Washington (Pa.) City Schs., 1964-65; prof. dept. edn. and psychology, asst. dean acad. affairs, acting dean acad. affairs, acting dean tchr. edn., asst. to pres., v.p. adminstrn. and fin. Shippensburg (Pa.) U., 1965-73; pres. Bloomsburg (Pa.) U., 1973-83, pres. emeritus, 1983—; chancellor Pa. State System Higher Edn., Harrisburg, 1983—; Falk intern in politics, 1959; mem. adv. bd. Pa. Ednl. Policy Seminar, Nat. Ctr. for Study Sport in Soc.; mem. Gov.'s Econ. Devel. Partnership Bd.; mem. higher edn. adv. coun. pa. State Bd. Edn.; past commr. Edn. Commn. of the States. Contbr. articles profl. jours. Named One of 10 Outstanding Young Men of Yr., Pa. Jr. C. of C.; recipient Young Leader in Edn. award Phi Delta Kappa, 1981, Disting. Alumnus award Indiana U. Pa., 1981, Outstanding Alumni award Bloomsburg U., 1984, Outstanding Alumnus award U. Pitts., 1985, Adler award Pa. Edn. assn., 1992; selected CIVITAS Prague mission, 1995, Presdl. Lectures, Kuwait U., 1993. Mem. Am. Assn. State Colls. and Univs. (pa. state rep. 1988-93, former chmn. acad. and student pers. com., mem. com. on state rels. and task force on ednl. equity, chmn. policies and purposes com. 1996), Am. Coun. on Edn. (commn. on women in higher edn.), Nat. Assn. Sys. Heads, (exec. com., past pres.), Commn. State Colls. and Univs. (mem. and past chmn. govt. rels. and student rels. coms.), Assn. Governing Bds. (adv. coun.), Am. Assn. for Affirmative Action, Am. Assn. Higher Edn., Am. Assn. Sch. Adminstrs., Am. Assn. Univ. Adminstrs. (Tosney Leadership award 1993), Pa. Assn. Colls. and Univs. (bd. dirs., chair 1982), Pers. Assn., Bloomsburg Area C. of C. (pres. 1983), Rotary (bd. dirs. through 1992), Phi Delta Kappa. Home: 2991 N Front St Harrisburg PA 17110 Office: Pa State Sys Higher Edn Dixon Univ Ctr 2986 N 2nd St Harrisburg PA 17110-1201

MCCORMICK, JAMES HILLMAN, retired broadcast executive; b. Montgomery, Ala., Sept. 10, 1921; s. James Hillman and Odessa (Garrett) McC.; m. Myra Sage, May 20, 1945; children: James Hillman III, Carol. BA in Cinema, U. So. Calif., 1947; postgrad., So. Meth. U., 1974. Theatre mgr. Malco Theatres, Memphis, 1940-41; prodn. asst. So. Film Svc. U. Ga., Athens, Ga., 1947-48; sales exec. Columbia Pictures, Atlanta, 1948-50, Warner Bros., Atlanta, 1950-54; Memphis mgr., Atlanta mgr., ea. sales mgr. CBS, N.Y., 1954-64; divsn. mgr. CBS, Dallas, 1964-71; v.p. Viacom Internat., Dallas, 1971-86; prin. James H. McCormick Broadcast Counselor, Dallas, 1986-89; bd. dirs. Tex. Enfield, Inc., Victoria, 1989-91; nat. v.p. Colosseum Motion Picture Salesmen, 1953-54; mem. founding group which established Viacom as world leader in comms. and entertainment, 1971-86; bd. mem. Assn. Broadcasting Execs. Tex., 1967. Author: Smart Selling--An Advertising/Media Guide; prodn. mgr. The School That Learned to Eat (U.S. Documentary award Edinbergh Film Festival, 1948). Charter mem. Cowboy Hall of Fame, Western Heritage Ctr., Oklahoma City, 1965—; mem. Dallas Mus. Art, 1967—; mem. Tex. State Hist. Assn. Sgt. U.S. Army, 1942-45. Recipient Lifetime Achievement award TV Program Conf., 1986, Rep. Presdl. Legion of Merit, 1993. Mem. Acad. TV Arts and Scis., Internat. Radio and TV Soc., Nat. Assn. TV Program Execs. (charter), Tex. Assn. Broadcasters, TV Program Conf. (bd. dirs. 1968-69), Cinema Circulus, Broadcast Pioneers, Northwood Club, Kiwanis Internat., Alpha Delta Sigma, Delta Kappa Alpha, Pi Kappa Alpha. Republican. Presbyterian. Avocations: oil painting, tennis, western art. Home: 7318 Kenshire Ln Dallas TX 75230-2432 Office: PO Box 515987 Dallas TX 75251-5987 *A persistence of vision, when strengthened by your own enthusiasm, will provide your days with much happiness. Always remember, however, that nothing ever happens in this old world until the sale is made.*

MCCORMICK, JOHN HOYLE, lawyer; b. Pensacola, Fla., July 30, 1933; s. Clyde Hoyle and Orrie Brooks (Frink) McC.; m. Patricia McCall, Dec. 27, 1974. BS, U. Fla., 1955; JD, Stetson U., 1958. Bar: Fla. 1958. Ptnr. McCormick, Drury & Scaff, Jasper, Fla., 1958-74; county atty., 1973—; sr. ptnr. McCormick, Drury & Scaff, Jasper, 1974-91; pvt. practice Jasper, 1991—; county judge, Hamilton County, Fla., 1960-72; local counsel So. Ry. System, 1968—, CSX, Ry., 1972—; atty. Hamilton County Devel. Authority, 1970-91; bd. dirs. 1st Fed. Savs. Bank Fla.; bd. dirs., v.p., atty. Hamilton County Bank. Mayor City of White Springs, Fla., 1959; pres. Hamilton County C. of C., Jasper, 1961. Mem. Phi Delta Phi. Democrat. Methodist. Lodges: Masons. Avocations: gardening, motorhome camping, college football. Home: 403 SE 2nd Ave Jasper FL 32052-3242 Office: 215 NE 2nd St Jasper FL 32052-2015 Address: PO Drawer O Jasper FL 32052-0695

MCCORMICK, JOHN OWEN, retired comparative literature educator; b. Thief River Falls, Minn., Sept. 20, 1918; s. Owen Charles and Marie Antoinette Beauchemin (Smith) McC.; m. Helen Manuel, 1942; m. Mairi Clare MacInnes, 1954; children: Jonathan, Peter, Antoinette, Fergus. B.A. magna cum laude, U. Minn., 1941; M.A., Harvard U., 1947, Ph.D., 1951. Dean, lectr. Salzburg Seminar in Am. Studies, 1951-52; lectr., prof. Free U., Berlin, 1952-59; prof. comparative lit. Rutgers U., 1959-87, prof. emeritus, 1987—; vis. prof. Nat. U. Mexico, 1961-62, Hachioji (Tokyo) seminar, 1979; Christian Gauss Seminar lectr. Princeton, 1969; resident fellow Sch. Letters of Ind. U., 1970. Author: The Middle Distance: a Comparative History of American Imaginative Literature, 1919-32, 1971, The Complete Aficionado, 1967, (with Mairi MacInnes McCormick) Versions of Censorship, 1962, Der moderne amerikanische Roman, 1960, Amerikanische Lyrik, 1957, Catastrophe and Imagination, 1957, Fiction as Knowledge, 1975, George Santayana: A Biography, 1987, Wolfe, Malraux, Hesse, 1987; editor: (with G. Core) Sallies of the Mind: Essays of Francis Fergusson, 1997. Served with USNR, 1941-46. Recipient prize for non-fiction Longview Found., 1960, Am. Acad. and Inst. Arts and Letters award, 1988; Gugenheim fellow, 1964-65, 79-80, Bruern fellow Leeds (Eng.) U., 1975-76, NEH fellow, 1983-84, hon. fellow U. York, 1992. Mem. Taurino Club, Harvard Club.

MCCORMICK, KATHLEEN ANN KRYM, geriatrics nurse, computer information specialist, federal agency administrator; b. Manchester, N.H., June 27, 1947. BSN, Barry Coll., 1969; MSN, Boston U., 1971; MS, U. Wis., 1975, PhD, 1978. Capt. nurse officer USPHS; COSTEP nurse USPHS, Staten Island, N.Y., 1968; staff nurse, instr. USPHS, Brighton, Mass., 1970; staff nurse Mercy Hosp., Miami, 1969, St. Elizabeth's Hosp., Brighton, 1970-71; clin. nurse specialist Boston U. Hosp., 1970-71; clin. nurse specialist, instr. U. Wis., Madison, 1971-72; asst. rsch. to chief nursing clin. ctr., dept. Nursing NIH, Bethesda, 1978-83; rsch. nurse, co-dir. inpatient geriatric continence project, Lab. Behavioral Scis., Gerontology Rsch. Ctr. Nat. Inst. Aging, Balt., 1983-88, dir. nursing rsch., 1988-91; dir. office forum quality and effectiveness health care Agy. Health Care Policy and Rsch., Rockville, Md., 1991-93; sr. sci. adviser Agy. Health Care Policy and Rsch., 1993—; adj. asst. prof. Cath. U., Washington, 1979, 82; faculty assoc. U. Md., Balt., 1979-81; ad hoc reviewer biomed. rsch. grants NIH, 1979-80, divsn. nursing rsch. and tng. HRA, 1979-82; instr. Found. Advanced Edn. in Scis., 1981-82; exec. com. Bat. Inst. Aging Liaison Ctr. Nursing Rsch., 1986-91; Surgeon Gen.'s rep. Sec. Alzheimer's Task Force, 1989—; Surgeon Gen. alternate to Bd. Regents Nat. Libr. Medicine, 1989—; co-chair panel guidelines for urinary incontinence in adult, 1990-91; speaker. Editor: Nursing Outlook, 1988-90; mem. editorial staff Mil. Medicine, 1985-93; assoc. editor: Internat. Jour. Tech. and Aging, 1985-87. Recipient award Jour. Acad. Sci., 1965, travel award NSF, 1973, J.D. Lane Jr. Investigator award USPHS Profl. Assn., 1979, Excellence in Writing award Nat. League Nursing/Humana, 1983, award Spl. Recognition Rsch., U. Pa. Sch. Nursing, 1986, Federal Svc. Nursing award, 1987, Surgeon Gen.'s medallion, 1989,; grantee U. Wis. Grad. Sch., 1977, Upjohn Co., 1977; Queen's Vis. scholar Royal Adelaide (Austrailia) Hosp., 1990. Fellow Am. Acad. Nursing, Royal Coll. Nursing (Australia), Coll. Am. Med. Informatics, Gerontologic Soc. Am. (clin. med. sect., computer program coord. 1985-87, clin. medicine rep. publs. com., Nurse of Yr. 1992), Nat. Acad. Scis. Inst. Medicine; mem. ANA (sec., editor newsletter coun. nurse rschrs. 1980-85, vice chairperson exec. com. coun. computer applications in nursing 1984-86), AACN (strategic planning com. 1987-89, Disting. Rsch. award 1986), Am. Lung Assn./Am. Thoracic Soc. (cert. appreciation mid.-Md. chpt. 1982, 83, 84, chairperson 1983-84, nominating com. 1989, nat. rsch. rev. com.), Am. Med. Informatics Assn., Inst. Medicine, Acad. Medicine, Am. News Women's Club, Internat. Med. Informatics Assn. (working group 8, program com. 1984—), Assn. Mil. Surgeons (sustaining mem. award 1982), Commd. Officers Assn., Met. Area Nursing Rsch. Consortium, Md. Lung Assn. (awards and grants subcom. 1978, 92, v.p. exec. bd. dirs. 1980-87), Capital Spkrs. Club (10 M), Lambda Sigma, Sigma Delta Epsilon (Eloise Gerry grant-in-aid fellow 1979-80), Sigma Theta Tau (grantee 1976). Office: US Agy Health Care Policy Rsch 2101 E Jefferson St Rockville MD 20852-4908

MC CORMICK, KENNETH DALE, retired editor; b. Madison, N.J., Feb. 25, 1906; s. John Dale and Ida Pearl (Wenger) McC.; children: Dale, Kevin; m. Anne Hutchens, 1968; 1 son, John Bradley. A.B., Willamette U., 1928. With Doubleday and Co., Inc., 1930-92, successively clk., mgr., bookshop, promotion mgr. pub. house, reader in editorial dept., chief asso. editor, 1938, editor in chief, 1942-71, v.p., 1948-71, sr. cons. editor, 1971-92; lectr. on books. Contbr. to Publishers' Weekly. Democrat. Conglist. Clubs: Century Assn, Coffee House, Dutch Treat. Home: 670 W End Ave New York NY 10025-7313

MCCORMICK, KENNETH L., pediatrics educator, researcher. BS in Chem. Engring., U. Pa., 1970; MD, U. Rochester, 1974. Diplomate Am. Bd. Pediatrics, Am. Bd. Pediatric Endocrinology. Intern in pediatrics U. Hosp. Cleve., Case Western Reserve U., 1974-75, resident in pediatrics, 1975-76; instr., rsch. and clin. fellow in pediat. metabolism/diabetes Brown U., Rhode Island Hosp., Providence, 1976-79; asst. prof. pediatrics U. Rochester (N.Y.), 1979-85, assoc. prof. pediatrics, 1985-88; assoc. prof. pediatrics SUNY Health Sci. Ctr., Syracuse, 1988-92; assoc. prof. pediatrics, dir. metabolism and diabetes Med. Coll. of Wis., Milw., 1993—. Mem. editl. bd. Endocrinology, 1993—; reviewer Metabolism, Am. Jour. Diseases in Children, Endocrinology, Am. Jour. of Physiology; contbr. articles and revs. to profl. jours., chpts. to books. NIH fellow, 1978-79; Grantee Kroc Found., 1981-83, NIH, 1982-87, 93—, Wilson Found., 1984-85, Upjohn Co., 1985, Hendricks Found., 1989-90, Squibb Novo, 1994-95, Am. Heart Assn., 1995—. Mem. Am. Diabetes Assn. (bd. dirs. Rochester affiliate 1980-88, grantee 1994-96, Rsch. award 1995), Endocrinology Soc. Office: Med Coll of Wis Dept Endocrinology 8701 W Watertown Plank Rd Milwaukee WI 53226-3548

MCCORMICK, MARIE CLARE, pediatrician, educator; b. Haverhill, Mass., Jan. 7, 1946; d. Richard John and Clare Bernadine (Keleher) McC.; m. Robert Jay Blendon, Dec. 30, 1977. BA magna cum laude, Emmanuel Coll., 1967; MD, Johns Hopkins Medical Sch., 1971; ScD, Johns Hopkins, 1978; MA, Harvard, 1991. Diplomate Am. Bd. Pediatrics. Pediatric resident, fellow Johns Hopkins Hosp., Balt., 1971-75; rsch. fellow Johns Hopkins Hosp., 1972-75; asst. prof. U. Ill. Schs. Medicine & Pub. Health, Chgo., 1975-76; pediatrics instr. Johns Hopkins Medical Sch., Balt., 1976-78; asst. prof. healthcare orgn. Johns Hopkins Sch. Hygiene & Pub. Health, 1978-81; asst. prof. pediatrics U. Pa., Phila., 1981-86, assoc. prof. pediatrics, 1986-87; assoc. prof. pediatrics Harvard Medical Sch., Boston, 1987-91; prof., chair. maternal & child health Harvard Sch. Pub. Health, 1992—; prof. pediatrics Harvard Medical Sch., 1992—, 1st Sumner and Esther Feldberg prof. maternal/child health, 1996—; adj. assoc. prof. pediatrics U. Pa., 1987-92; active attending physician, Johns Hopkins Hosp., 1976-81, asst. physician Children's Hosp. Phila., 1981-84, assoc. physician, 1984-86, sr. physician, 1986-87, assoc. pediatrician Brigham & Women's Hosp., 1987,88—; vis. prof. Wash. U., St. Louis, 1993; editorial bds. Health Svcs. Rsch., 1985-94, Pediatrics in Review, 1986-91, Pediatrics, 1993—; adv. coun. Ctr. Perinatal & Family Health Brigham & Women;s Hosp., 1991—; cons. to numerous coms., orgns. and bds. Contbr. articles to profl. jours. Adv. The David and Lucile Packard Found., 1993-95; bd. dirs. Family Planning Coun. S.E. Pa., 1984-87; chair com. child health Mayor's Commn. Phila., 1982-83. Named Henry Strong Denison scholar Johns Hopkins Sch. Medicine, 1971, Leonard Davis inst. Health Econs. fellow U. Pa. 1984, First Sumner and Esther Feldberg prof. maternal and child health, 1996; recipient Johns Hopkins U. Soc. Scholars award, 1995, Ambulatory Pediat. Assn. Rsch. award, 1996—. Fellow Am. Acad. Pediatrics; mem. AAAS, Ambulatory Pediatrics Assn. (Rsch. award 1996), Soc. Pediatric Rsch. (sr.), Am. Pediatric soc., Am. Pub. Health Assn., Internat. Epidemiological Assn., Assn. Health Svcs. Rsch., Eastern Soc. Pediatric Rsch., Soc. Pediatric Epidemiologic Rsch., Assn. Tchrs. Maternal and Child Health, Mass. Med. Soc., Norfolk Dist. Med. Soc., Mass. Pub. Health Assn., Johns Hopkins U. Soc. Scholars. Office: Harvard Sch Pub Health 677 Huntington Ave Boston MA 02115-6028

MCCORMICK, MICHAEL, history educator; b. Tonawanda, N.Y., Nov. 7, 1951; s. Jerome Anthony and Barbara Ann (Bowman) Mc.; m. Magda Jabbour, May 21, 1988; children: Thomas Kennedy III, Elena Sylvie. Grad., Cath. U. Louvain, Belgium, 1971, diploma in Medieval History, 1972, PhD, 1979. Rsch. assoc. Dictionary Medieval Latin Belgian Nat. Com., Louvain, 1976-79; rsch. assoc. Byzantine studies Dumbarton Oaks, Washington, 1979-87; from asst. prof. to prof. dept. history Johns Hopkins U., Balt., 1979-91;

prof. Harvard U., Cambridge, Mass., 1991—. Author: Les Annales du haut Moyen âge, 1975, Index Scriptorum Operumque Latino-Belgicorum Medii aevi, XIIe siecle, 1977, vol. 2, 1979, Eternal Victory, Triumphal Rulership in Late Antiquity Byzantium and the Early Medieval West, 1986, 500 Unknown Glosses from the Palatine Virgil, 1992; editl. bd. Bulletin Codicologique, 1978-91, Am. Jour. Philology, 1982-88; bd. editors Speculum Anniversary Monographs, 1989-91. Guggenheim Meml. Found. fellow, 1985-86; Am. Coun. Learned Socs. grantee, 1987. Mem. Medieval Acad. Am. Roman Catholic. Office: Harvard U Dept History Robinson Hall Cambridge MA 02138

MCCORMICK, MICHAEL JERRY, judge; b. Fort Lewis, Wash., Oct. 17, 1945; s. Thaddeus Charles and Geraldine (Fogle) McC.; m. Kathleen Karen Kelley, Sept. 2, 1967; children: Patrick Kelley, Karen Michelle. BA, U. Tex.-Austin, 1967; JD, St. Mary's U., 1970. Bar: Tex. 1970. Briefing atty. Tex. Ct. Criminal Appeals, 1970-71; asst. dist. atty., Travis County, Tex., 1971-72; exec. dir. Tex. Dist. and County Attys. Assn., Austin, 1972-80; judge Tex. Ct. Criminal Appeals, Austin, 1981—, presiding judge 1988—; dir. Tex. Ctr. for Judiciary, 1983; vice-chmn. Tex. Commn. on Sentencing, 1984; mem. Tex. Jud. Budget Bd., 1983. Pres. Joslin P.T.A., 1981-82. Served with U.S. Army, 1966-72. Named Rosewood Gavel Outstanding Jurist, St. Mary's U. Sch. Law, 1984, Disting. Law Grad., 1992. Mem. State Bar Tex., Tex. Dist. and County Attys. Assn. Episcopalian. Author: Branch's Annotated Penal Code, 3d edit., Criminal Forms and Trial Manual, 10th edit., Texas Justice Court Deskbook, Texas Constables' Civil Process Handbook. Office: Tex Ct Criminal Appeals PO Box 12308 Austin TX 78711-2308

MCCORMICK, RICHARD, telecommunications company executive; b. Fort Dodge, Iowa, July 4, 1940; s. Elmo Eugene and Virgilla (Lawler) McC.; m. Mary Patricia Smola, June 29, 1963; children: John Richard, Matthew David, Megan Ann, Katherine Maura. B.S. in Elec. Engring., Iowa State U., 1961. With Bell Telephone Co., 1961-85; N.D. v.p., CEO Northwestern Bell Telephone Co., Fargo, 1974-77; asst. v.p. human resources AT&T, Basking Ridge, N.J., 1977-78; sr. v.p. Northwestern Bell, Omaha, 1978-82, pres., CEO, 1982-85; exec. v.p. U S West Inc., Englewood, Colo., 1985-86, pres., COO, 1986-90, pres., CEO, 1990-91, chmn., pres., CEO, 1992—; bd. dirs. Norwest Corp., United Airlines Corp. Mem. Phi Gamma Delta. Office: U S West Inc 7800 E Orchard Rd Ste 200 Englewood CO 80111-2526

MCCORMICK, RICHARD ARTHUR, priest, religion educator, writer; b. Toledo, Oct. 3, 1922; s. Edward J. McCormick. BA, Loyola U., Chgo., 1945, MA, 1950, hon. degree, 1989; STD, Gregorian U., Rome, 1957; hon. degree, U. Scranton, 1975, Wheeling Coll., W.Va., 1976, Jesuit Sch. Theology, Berkeley, Calif., 1982, Siena Coll., 1985, U. Louvain, 1986, Coll. Holy Cross, 1986, Seattle U., 1987, Fordham U., 1988, Xavier U., 1988, U. San Francisco, 1989, Georgetown U., 1990, Cath. Theol. Union, 1991. Joined S.J., Roman Cath. Ch., 1940, ordained priest, 1953. Prof. moral theology Jesuit Sch. Theology, Chgo., 1957-73; Rose F. Kennedy prof. Christian ethics Georgetown U., Washington, 1974-86; John A. O'Brien prof. U. Notre Dame, Ind., 1986—; rsch. assoc. Woodstock Theol. Ctr., Washington, 1974-86; past mem. Ethics Adv. Bd., HEW; mem. Cath. Commn. on Intellectual and Cultural Affairs; lectr. in field. Author: Ambiguity in Moral Choice, 1973, Notes on Moral Theology, 1965 through 1980, 1980, Notes on Moral Theology 1981-1984, 1984, Health and Medicine in the Catholic Tradition, 1984, The Critical Calling: Moral Dilemmas Since Vatican II, 1989, Corrective Vision: Explorations in Moral Theology, 1994; co-author: (with Paul Ramsey) Doing Evil to Achieve Good, 1978; contbr. to numerous books, articles to Christianity and Crisis, New Cath. World, other religious jours.; co-editor: (with Charles E. Curran) Readings in Moral Theology I: Moral Norms and Catholic Tradition, 1979, Readings in Moral Theology II: The Distinctiveness of Christian Ethics, 1980, Readings in Moral Theology III: Morality and Authority, 1981, Readings in Moral Theology IV: The Use of Scripture in Moral Theology, 1982, Readings in Moral Theology V: Official Catholic Social Teaching, 1986, Readings in Moral Theology VI: Dissent in the Church, 1988, Readings in Moral Theology VII: The Natural Law, 1990, Readings in Moral Theology VIII: Dialogue about Catholic Sexual Teaching, 1993, Readings in Moral Theology IX: Feminist Ethics and the Catholic Moral Tradition, 1996; former assoc. editor Am. mag.; editorial advisor Theology Digest, Hosp. Progress jours.; mem. editorial bd. Jour. Religious Ethics, Jour. Contemporary Health Law and Policy. Former trustee U. Detroit, Fairfield U. Recipient Henry Knowles Beecher award Hastings Ctr., 1988; Inst. Soc., Ethics and Life Scis. fellow. Mem. Am. Acad. Arts and Scis., Cath. Theol. Soc. Am. (past pres., Cardinal Spellman award 1969), Am. Soc. Christian Ethics (past bd. dirs.), Am. Hosp. Am. (spl. bioethics com.), Nat. Hospice Orgn. (bioethcis com.), Cath. Health Assn. (bioethics com.), Am. Fertility Soc. (ethics com.). Office: U Notre Dame Dept Theology Notre Dame IN 46556

MC CORMICK, RICHARD PATRICK, history educator; b. N.Y.C., Dec. 24, 1916; s. Patrick Austin and Anna (Smith) McC.; m. Katheryne Crook Levis, Aug. 25, 1945; children: Richard Levis, Dorothy Irene. BA, Rutgers U., 1938, MA, 1940, LittD (hon.), 1982; PhD, U. Pa., 1948. Historian, Phila. Q.M. Depot, 1942-44; instr. U. Del., 1944-45; mem. faculty Rutgers U., 1945—, univ. historian, 1948—; dean Rutgers Coll., 1974-77, Univ. prof. history, 1977-82, Univ. prof. emeritus, 1982—; research adviser Colonial Williamsburg, 1953-61; Fulbright lectr. Cambridge (Eng.) U., 1961-62; Commonwealth lectr. U. London, 1971; chmn. N.J. Hist. Commn., 1967-70. Author: Experiment in Independence, 1950, History of Voting in N.J, 1953, N.J. From Colony to State, 1964, Second American Party System, 1966, Rutgers: a Bicentennial History, 1966, The Presidential Game, 1982, The Black Student Protest Movement at Rutgers, 1990; co-author: The Case of the Nazi Professor, 1989. Mem. N.J. Tercentenary Commn., 1958-60, Am. Revolution Bicentennial Commn., 1971-74. Social Sci. Research Council fellow, 1956-57. Mem. Am. Hist. Assn., Soc. Historians of Early American Republic (pres. 1988-89), N.J. Hist. Soc. (pres. 1950-57), Phi Beta Kappa. Home: 938 River Rd Piscataway NJ 08854-5504 Summer: 42 Julien Rd Harwich Port MA 02646

MCCORMICK, ROBERT JUNIOR, company executive, former government official; b. Boone, Iowa, Aug. 1, 1929; s. Ivyl Robert and Darlene Adel (Bowes) McC.; m. Shirley May Zerbe, Dec. 24, 1950; children: Elaine, Kathleen, Michael, Tara McCormick Wieting, Tammy McCormick Kirby. Grad., Flying Sch., Williams Field, Ariz., 1951, Parachute Jump Sch., 1964, Armed Forces Staff Coll., Norfolk, Va., 1966, Def. Systems Mgmt. Coll., Ft. Belvoir, Va., 1975; B.S., Tex. Tech. U., 1963; cert., Harvard U. Def. Studies Program, 1984. Served as enlisted man USAF, 1948-51, commd. 2d lt., 1951, advanced through grades to col., 1971; pilot USAF, U.S., Japan, Korea, Europe, Vietnam; exec. officer to Gen. George Brown 7th Air Force, Saigon, Vietnam, 1969-70; mil. asst. to asst. sec. of Air Force for research and devel. USAF, Washington, 1970-74; ret. USAF, 1975; exec. officer NASA, Washington, 1976-80; adminstrv. asst. to sec. of Air Force USAF, Washington, 1980-94; mem. U.S. Sr. Exec. Service, 1979—; pres. McCormick Ltd., Fairfax, Va. Decorated Air Force Legion of Merit, 1972, 74, Bronze star, Air medal, Meritorious Svc. medal, Air Force Exceptional Civilian Svc. medal, 1985, 88, others; recipient Exceptional Svc. medal NASA, 1980, Presdl. Meritorious Rank, 1989, Dept. Def. Disting. Civilian Svc. medal, 1994. Mem. ASME, DAV, Air Force Assn., Am. Def. Preparedness Assn., Order of Daedalians, St. Andrews Soc. Washington, Mil. Order of Carabao, Chevaliers du Testevin. Club: Army-Navy Country (Fairfax, Va.). Office: 4035 Hadley Ln Fairfax VA 22032-1308

MCCORMICK, ROBERT MATTHEW, III, newspaper executive; b. N.Y.C., Dec. 31, 1938; s. Robert Matthew Jr. and Rita Patricia (McGuinness) McC.; m. Janet Severin Ahrens, Apr. 27, 1957; children: Susan Anne Heisler, Mary Teresa Berrier, Robert M. IV, Mark P. BA, Georgetown U., 1960; grad. advanced mgmt. program, Harvard U., 1978. Various sales and mktg. positions The Washington Post, 1962-76, v.p. sales, 1976-82; exec. v.p. Chgo. Sun-Times, 1982-83; sr. v.p., sales and mktg. San Francisco News Agy., 1984-86, pres., CEO, 1987-93; exec. v.p. South Jersey Pub. Co., Atlantic City, 1994—; pub. Press of Atlantic City. Bd. dirs. Noyes Mus., 1995—, United Way of Atlantic County, 1997—; mem. governance bd. Success by 6, 1996—. Mem. Newspaper Assn. Am., Burning Tree Club, Atlantic City Country Club. Home: 222 Arlington Ave Linwood NJ 08221-2303

MCCORMICK, ROBERT WILLIAM, court reporting educator; b. Hornell, N.Y., Sept. 7, 1949; s. Charles F. and Catherine M. (Bulock) McC.; m. Rose A. Belden, Dec. 29, 1970; children: Tara R., Erin R., Nicole L. AAS in Court Reporting, SUNY, Alfred, 1969; BS in Bus. Edn., SUNY, Albany, 1971, MS in Bus. Edn., 1974; MA in Theology, Colgate Rochester Divinity Sch, 1988. Cert. reporting instr. Prof. ct. reporting SUNY, Alfred; deacon St. Ann's Roman Catholic Ch., Hornell, N.Y.; chaplain-on-call St. James Mercy Hosp., Hornell. Series editor for ct. and realtime reporting theory textbooks.

MCCORMICK, ROD, sculptor, art educator; b. Battle Creek, Mich., Sept. 2, 1952; s. Rodney Lawrence and Joan (Kaminski) McC.; m. Barbara Mail, Dec. 29, 1985; children: Anna, Sonya. BFA, Tyler Sch. Art, 1974; MFA, RISD, 1978. Sculptor and metalsmith, Phila., 1974—; vis. prof. Kent State U., Ohio, 1978-79; assoc. prof. U. Arts, Phila., 1981—, chmn. crafts dept., 1993-94, 95-96. One-man shows include Owen Patrick Gallery, Phila., 1990, U. Arts, 1993; exhibited in group shows at Phila. Mus. Art, 1990, Pa. State U., 1991, Meredith Gallery, Balt., 1991, Leo Kaplan Modern Gallery, N.Y.C., 1992, Paley Design Ctr., Phila., 1993, Peter Joseph Gallery, N.Y.C., 1994, Md. Art Place, Balt., 1996, Pentimenti Gallery, Phila., 1996, Stedman Gallery-Rutgers, Camden, N.J., 1997. Recipient Young Americans Metal exhbn. award Am. Craft Mus., 1980; grantee Nat. Endowment Arts, 1990, Pa. Coun. Arts, 1991. Mem. Soc. N.Am. Goldsmiths, Internat. Sculpture Ctr. Home: PO Box 29578 Philadelphia PA 19144 Office: University of the Arts 320 S Broad St Philadelphia PA 19102-4901

MCCORMICK, STEVEN THOMAS, insurance company executive; b. Phila., Dec. 18, 1955; s. Howard C. and Ruth Marion (Stahl) McC.; m. Helene Mary Trommler, Nov. 21, 1981; children: Matthew Thomas, Bria Helene. BBA, U. Ky., 1978; gen. ins cert., Ins. Inst. Am., 1980. Cert. adminstrv. mgr., purchasing mgr., ins. agt., Ky., 1980. Supr. trainee Ky. Farm Bur. Ins. Cos., Louisville, 1978-79, supr. micrographics dept., 1979-83, supr. adminstrv. svcs., 1983-85, mgr. adminstrv. svcs., 1985-89; asst. v.p. ops. and legis. agt., 1989—. Named to Hon. Order Ky. Cols., Outstanding Employee of Yr., Nat. Assn. of Mut. Ins. Cos., 1986; recipient Cert. of Excellence, Jefferson County Bd. Edn. Mem. Adminstrv. Mgmt. Soc. (internat. top recruiter 1985, chpt. pres. 1988, internat. dir. area 7 1990-91, internat. v.p. profl. devel. 1992-93), Acad. Adminstrv. Mgmt. (mem. bd. regents 1991-92, internat. v.p. 1992-93, internat. pres. 1993-94), U. Ky. Alumni Assn., Sigma Nu. Republican. Home: 706 Elsmere Cir Louisville KY 40223-2764 Office: Ky Farm Bur Ins Cos PO Box 20700 Louisville KY 40250-0700

MCCORMICK, SUSAN KONN, retired publishing executive; b. Cleve., Dec. 13, 1953; d. Frank Andrew and Mary Lou (Dunn) K.; m. Michael F. McCormick, May 25, 1985; 1 child, Amanda. BS, Ind. U., 1976; MBA, Stanford U., 1983. CPA, N.Y. Acct. Deloitte Haskins & Sells, Indpls., 1975-77; fin. analyst GM, N.Y.C., 1977-83; exec. Brown Bros. Harriman, N.Y.C., 1983-84; v.p. Bankers Trust Co., N.Y.C., 1984-85; treas. Scholastic, Inc., N.Y.C., 1985—; now ret. Mem. AICPA, N.Y. State Soc. CPA's, Risk Ins. Mgmt. Soc., Stanford U. Alumni Assn., N.Y. Treas.'s Club.

MC CORMICK, THOMAS JULIAN, art history educator; b. Syracuse, N.Y., Nov. 14, 1925; s. Thomas Julian and Doris (Rafferty) McC.; m. Margaret Emily Dorkey, Mar. 23, 1957; children: Sarah Elizabeth, Martha Dorcas. AB, Syracuse U., 1948, AM, 1949; MFA, Princeton U., 1953, PhD, 1971. Research asst. Va. Mus. Fine Arts, Richmond, 1953-54; instr. Smith Coll., Northampton, Mass., 1954-56; dir., asst. prof. Robert Hull Fleming Mus., U. Vt., 1956-58; assoc. prof., chmn. art dept. Wells Coll., Aurora, N.Y., 1958-60; assoc. prof., dir. Art Gallery, Vassar Coll., Poughkeepsie, N.Y., 1960-70; Wright-Shippee prof. Wheaton Coll., Norton, Mass., 1970-79; A. Howard Meneely prof. Wheaton Coll., 1981-82, prof., 1979-91, prof. emeritus, 1991—, chmn. art dept., 1970-79, 90-91; Frederic Lindley Morgan prof. archtl. design U. Louisville, 1991; vis. assoc. prof. Williams Coll., 1969; lectr. Worcester (Mass.) Art Mus., 1978; vis. prof. Sch. Architecture, Canterbury, Eng., 1985-86. Author: Charles-Louis Clérisseau and the Genesis of Neo-Classicism, 1990; contbr. articles to profl. jours., exhbn. catalogs. Bd. dirs. Dutchess County (N.Y.) Landmarks Assn., 1968-70, Olana State Historic Site, 1968-70. With AUS, 1944-46, ETO. Corning Mus. Glass fellow, 1954; Fulbright sr. research fellow Gt. Britain, 1966-67, Yugoslavia, 1976-77. Fellow Soc. Antiquaries (London); mem. Coll. Art Assn., Archeol. Inst. Am., Soc. Archtl. Historians (book rev. editor Jour. 1958-65, dir. 1960-63), Am. Soc. for Eighteenth Century Studies, Delta Kappa Epsilon. Episcopalian. Clubs: Princeton (N.Y.C.); Club of Odd Vols. (Boston). Home: 18 Still St Brookline MA 02146-3444

MCCORMICK, TIMOTHY BRIAN BEER, lawyer; b. Northampton, Mass., May 16, 1959; s. Brian Beer and Margaret Ann McCormick; m. Lee Hillary Kadis, Sept. 2, 1979 (div. June 1991); m. Virginia Lee Kostner, June 30, 1991 (div. May 1995); 1 child, Cameron A.; m. Jill Ann Knowland, Apr. 23, 1997. BA, U. Calif., Berkeley, 1984; JD, Am. U., 1987. Bar: Calif. 1987, U.S. Dist. Ct. (no. dist.) Calif. 1987, U.S. Ct. Appeals (9th cir.) 1987, U.S. Dist. Ct. (ea. dist.) Calif., 1991, U.S. Dist. Ct. (ctrl. dist.) Calif. 1994. Staff asst. Office of Lt. Gov., Sacramento, 1982-83; cons. Calif. Rep. Party, Sacramento, 1984; rsch. asst. Nat. Right to Work Found., Springfield, Va., 1985-86; assoc. Graham & James, San Francisco, 1987-93, McPharlin & Mahl, San Jose, Calif., 1993-94; ptnr. McPharlin & Sprinkles, San Jose, 1994-95; v.p., assoc. coun. Fidelity Nat. Title Ins. Co., Walnut Creek, Calif., 1995-96; prin. Mediation and Arbitration Offices of Timothy B. McCormick, Piedmont, Calif., 1996—; judge pro tem Santa Clara County Superior Ct., 1993—. Comments editor Adminstrv. Law Jour., 1986-87. Treas., Hom for Mayor, San Francisco, 1995; mem. Rep. State Cen. Com. of Calif., 1983-85, assoc. mem., 1985—, mem. exec. com., 1983-84; gen. coun. Asian Am. Polit. Edn. Found., 1992—. Mem. ABA (litigation sect.), Santa Clara County Bar Assn., Bar Assn. San Francisco, Engring. and Utility Contractors Assn. (legis. com. 1991-95, co-chair, 1994-95). Avocations: skiing, bicycling, cooking, scuba diving. Home: 235 Park View Ave Piedmont CA 94610-1041

MCCORMICK, WILLIAM EDWARD, environmental consultant; b. Potters Mills, Pa., Feb. 9, 1912; s. George H. and Nellie (Mingle) McC.; m. Goldie Stover (dec.), June 6, 1935; children: John F. (dec.), Kirk W. B.S., Pa. State U., 1933, M.S., 1934. Tchr., Centre Hall (Pa.) High Sch., 1934-37; chemist Willson Products, Inc., Reading, Pa., 1937-43; indsl. hygienist Ga. Dept. Pub. Health, Atlanta, 1946; mgr. indsl. hygiene and toxicology B.F. Goodrich Co., Akron, Ohio, 1946-70; mgr. environ. control B.F. Goodrich Co., 1970-73; mng. dir. Am. Indsl. Hygiene Assn., Akron, 1973-83; exec. sec. Soc. Toxicology, 1976-83; chmn., treas. Envirotox Mgmt., Inc., 1983-93; pres. WRC Environmental, 1996—; mem. exec. com. rubber sect. Nat. Safety Coun., 1955-73, gen. chmn., 1971-72; mem. environ. health com. Chlorine Inst., 1968-73; mem. food, drug and cosmetic chems. com. Mfg. Chemists Assn., 1960-73, chmn., 1967-69, also mem. occupational health com., 1965-73; mem. adv. com. on heat stress U.S. Dept. Labor, 1973; mem. Nat. Adv. Com. Occupational Safety and Health, 1983-85; pres. Am. Indsl. Hygiene Found., 1984, trustee, 1982-89. Contbr. articles to profl. jours. Served to capt. USPHS, 1943-46. Recipient Borden award Am. Indsl. Hygiene Assn., 1993. Mem. AAAS, Am. Chem. Soc., Soc. Toxicology, Am. Indsl. Hygiene Assn. (pres. 1964, charter), Indsl. Hygiene Roundtable (charter), Am. Acad. Indsl. Hygiene (charter), Mason (33 degree), Shriner. Republican. Episcopalian. Home and Office: 419 Dorchester Rd Akron OH 44320-1315

MCCORMICK, WILLIAM THOMAS, JR., electric and gas company executive; b. Washington, Sept. 12, 1944; s. William Thomas and Lucy Valentine (Offutt) McC.; m. Ann Loretta du Mais, June 13, 1969; children: Christopher, Patrick. B.S., Cornell U., 1966; Ph.D., M.I.T., 1969. Mem. staff Inst. for Def. Analysis, Arlington, Va., 1969-72; mem. staff Office of Sci. and Tech., Exec. office of the Pres., Washington, 1972-73; sr. staff mem. Energy Policy Office, The White House, 1973-74; chief sci. and energy tech. br. Office Mgmt. and Budget, Exec. Office of the Pres., 1974-75; dir. commercialization U.S. Energy Research and Devel. Adminstrn., 1975-76; v.p. policy and govt. relations Am. Gas Assn., 1976-78; v.p., asst. to chmn. Am. Natural Resources Co., Detroit, 1978-80; exec. v.p. Mich. Wis. Pipeline Co., Am. Natural Resources System, Detroit, 1980-82; pres. Am. Natural Resources Co., Detroit, 1982-85; chmn., chief exec. officer Consumers Power Co., Jackson, Mich., 1985-92, chmn., 1992—; chmn., CEO CMS Energy Corp.; bd. dirs. Bancorp. Prin. author, editor: Commercialization of Synthetic Fuels in the U.S, 1975. Bd. dirs. Detroit Symphony, St. John Hosp. Alfred P. Sloan scholar, 1962-66. Mem. Econ. Club Detroit (bd. dirs.), Greater Detroit C. of C. (bd. dirs.), Econ. Alliance Mich. (bd. dirs.). Roman Catholic. Clubs: Cosmos (Washington); Detroit Athletic, Country of Detroit, Detroit. Office: Consumers Power Co 212 W Michigan Ave Jackson MI 49201-2236 also: CMS Energy Corp 330 Town Center Dr Ste 1100 Dearborn MI 48126*

MCCOTTER, JAMES RAWSON, lawyer; b. Denver, May 19, 1943; s. Charles R. and Jane M. (Ballantine) McC.; m. Carole Lee Hand, Sept. 5, 1965; children: Heidi M., Sage B. BA, Stanford U., 1965; JD, U. Colo., 1969. Bar: Colo. 1969, D.C. 1970, U.S. Dist. Ct. Colo. 1969, U.S. Ct. Appeals (10th and D.C. cirs.) 1970, U.S. Ct. Appeals (5th cir.) 1972, U.S. Supreme Ct. 1974. Law clk. U.S. Ct. Appeals (10th cir.), Denver, 1969-70; assoc. Covington & Burling, Washington, 1970-75; assoc. Kelly, Stansfield & O'Donnell, Denver, 1975-76, ptnr., 1977-86; assoc. gen. counsel Pub. Svc. Co. Colo., 1986-88; sr. v.p., gen. counsel, corp. sec., 1988-93; of counsel LeBoeuf, Lamb, Greene & MacRae, Denver, 1993-94, v.p. law and adminstrn., El Paso Natural Gas Co., Tex., 1994-95, v.p., dep. gen. counsel, 1997—. Editor in chief U. Colo. Law Rev., 1968-69 (Outstanding Achievement award 1969). Dem. precinct committeeman, Denver, 1983-84; bd. dirs. Sewall Rehab. Ctr., Denver, 1979-84, Opera Colo., 1987-95; dir., vice chmn. Denver Civic Ventures, Inc., 1988-94; mem. law alumni bd. U. Colo., 1988-91; bd. dirs. Colo. Coun. on Econ. Edn., Found. for Denver Ctr. for Performing Arts Complex, 1991-94. Recipient Disting. Achievement award U. Colo. Law Sch., 1989; named to Outstanding Young Men Am., U.S. Jaycees, 1971; Storke scholar U. Colo., Boulder, 1967. Mem. ABA, Colo. Bar Assn. (adminstrv. law com. 1979-84), Fed. Energy Bar Assn. (chmn. com. on environment 1982-83), Tex. Bar Assn., Coronado Country Club (El Paso), Univ. Club, Denver Country Club, Order of Coif, El Paso C. of C. Episcopalian. Home: 1036 Broadmoor Dr El Paso TX 79912-2004 Office: El Paso Natural Gas Co PO Box 1492 El Paso TX 79978-0001

MCCOUBREY, R. JAMES, advertising executive; b. Grand Mere, Que., Can., Sept. 1, 1944; s. James Addison and Margaret G. F. (Scarratt) McC.; m. Annette L. Hebert, Sept. 16, 1972; children: James Andrew, Matthew Alexander. B. of Commerce, McGill U., 1966, MA, 1967. With brand mgmt. Procter and Gamble, Toronto, Ont., Can., 1967-69; asst. mgr. Young and Rubicam, Montreal, Que., 1969-72; dir. client svcs. Young and Rubicam, Toronto, 1972-74, mgr., 1974-77, pres., 1977-80; area dir. Americas Young and Rubicam, N.Y.C., Toronto, 1980-82; gen. mgr. Europe Young and Rubicam, London, 1982-83; group and area dir. Young and Rubicam, N.Y.C., 1983-85; chmn. Young and Rubicam, Toronto, 1985-90; exec. v.p. Young and Rubicam, N.Y.C., 1984; area dir. Young and Rubicam, Africa, Australia, New Zealand and Can., 1984-90; pres., chief exec. officer Telemedia Inc., North York, Ont., Can., 1990—, Telemedia Communications USA Inc, Charlotte, Vt., 1991-97; pres. Scotchblock Investment Inc., 1996—; chmn. Inst. Can. Advt., Toronto, 1981-82; bd. dirs. Greyhound Transp. Can. Dir. Coun. for Bus. and the Arts in Can.; chmn. regional divsn. McGill Univ. Twenty-First Century Fund, chair person, Lansing Bldg. Group, Reitmans Inc. Mem. Can. Assn. Broadcasters (bd. dirs., chmn.), Young Pres. Orgn. (past chmn.), Mag. Assn. Can. (chmn. 1992-94), Royal Can. Yacht Club, Mt. Royal Club. Anglican. Home: 54 Bernard Ave, Toronto, ON Canada M5R 1R5

MCCOUBREY, SARAH, artist and art educator; b. New Haven, Conn., Sept. 5, 1956; d. John Walker and Betty (Morse) McC.; m. Michael Crockett Olmsted, Sept. 12, 1987; 1 child, Emily Crockett Olmsted. BA, U. Pa., 1979, BFA in Painting, 1979, MFA in Painting, 1981. Instr. Phila. C.C., 1984-87, Drexel U. Sch. of Art, Phila., 1983-87, No. Va. C.C., Annandale, Va., 1988-89, Geo. Washington U., Washington, 1989-90, Corcoran Sch. of Art, Washington, 1990-91; asst. prof. Syracuse (N.Y.) U. Coll. of Visual and Performing Arts, 1991—. Artist: solo exhibitions: The More Gallery, Phila., 1985, Leslie Cecil Gallery, N.Y.C., 1989, Recent Paintings, Comfort Gallery, Haverford, Pa., 1990, Recent Paintings Robert Brown Contemporay Art, Washington, 1990, Recent Paintings, Robert Brown Gallery, Washington, 1994, Robert Brown Contemporary Art, Washington, 1996, Morris Gallery Mus. Am. Art, Pa. Acad. Fine Arts, 1996—; selected group exhibits New Talent Show, Marion Locks Gallery, Phila., 1981, New Figurative Painting, Univ. City Arts League, Phila., 1982, Forty first Award Exhibition of the Cheltenham Art Ctr., Phila., 1982, The More Gallery, Phila., 1985, 86, 88, Art in City Hall, Phila. Urbanscape, Phila. City Hall, Twentieth Juried Exhibition, Allentown (Pa.) Art Mus., 1986, Four Contemporary Artists, 1987, Landscape Transformed, The Dimock Gallery, George Washington U., Washington, 1988, Collectors Exhibition, Ark. Art Ctr., Little Rock, 1989, 90, Bauhaus, Charles St., Balt., 1990, Evidence of Man, Gallery 10, Washington, Back to Basics, Washington, 1991, Cheekwood Nat. Contemporary Painting Competition, Fine Arts Ctr., Nashville (Merit award), 1991, Perspective VI, Am. Soc. Architectural Perspectivists, Security Pacific Gallery, Seattle, AIA Nat. Conv., Boston, Gwenda Jay Gallery, Chgo., 1992, Matrilineage: Women, Art and Change, Altered Space, Syracuse, 1993, Patricia Shea Gallery, Santa Monica, Calif., 1993, Women's Art Works 4: Work on Paper, Shoestring Gallery, Rochester, N.Y., Nat. Women's Hall of Fame, Seneca Falls, N.Y., 1994 (Hon. Mention), Everson Mus., Syracuse, 1994, Erector Square Gallery, New Haven, Conn., 1995, Wright State U. Galleries, Dayton, Ohio, 1996, F.A.N. Gallery, Phila. Milton Avery fellow, 1996. Recipient Elizabeth Greenshields Found. Grant award, 1981, McDowell Colony fellowship, 1990, Md. State Arts Coun. Individual Artist award, 1990; grantee NEA, 1989. Hon. Mention Vietnam Women's Meml. Competition, 1990. Home: 7027 Woodchuck Hill Rd Fayetteville NY 13066 Office: Syracuse Univ Dept Found Sch Art and Design Syracuse NY 13200

MC COVEY, WILLIE LEE, former professional baseball player; b. Mobile, Ala., Jan. 10, 1938; s. Frank and Ester (Jones) McC. Baseball player, minor league, 1955-59; baseball player, minor league San Francisco Giants, 1959-73, 77-80, active in pub. rels., 1981-86, spl. asst. to the pres., 1986—; baseball player San Diego Padres, 1974-76; coach Oakland Athletics, 1976-81. Named Nat. League Rookie of Year, 1959, Most Valuable Player, 1969; Home Run Champion, 1963, 68, 69; Runs Batted In Leader, 1968, 69; Comeback Player of Year, 1977; 8th on All-Time Major League List of Career Home Runs; All-Time Nat. League leader in grand slam home runs; mem. Nat. League All-Star Team, 1963, 66, 68-71; inducted into Baseball Hall of Fame, 1986. Office: care San Francisco Giants Candlestick Park San Francisco CA 94124-3998*

MCCOWN, HALE, retired judge; b. Kansas, Ill., Jan. 19, 1914; s. Ross S. and Pauline (Collins) McC.; m. Helen Lanier, July 15, 1938; children: Robert B., William L., Mary Lynn. AB, Hastings Coll., 1935; LLB, Duke U., 1937. Bar: Oreg. 1937, Nebr. 1942. With firm Carey, Hart, Spencer & McCulloch, Portland, 1937-42; pvt. practice Beatrice, Nebr., 1942-65; ptnr. McCown, Baumfalk & Dalke; justice Supreme Court Nebr., 1965-83. Author articles in legal jours. Served to lt. USNR, 1943-45. Recipient Disting. Alumnus award Hastings Coll., 1981, Charles S. Murphy award Duke U., 1986, Legal Pioneer award Nebr. Bar Found., 1996. Fellow Am. Coll. Trial Lawyers, Am. Coll. Trust and Estate Counsel; mem. ABA (legal ethics com. 1957-62), Nebr. Bar Assn. (chmn. ho. dels. 1955-56, pres. 1960-61), Am. Law Inst. (mem. council 1969—), Am. Judicature Soc. Presbyterian.

MCCOY, BERNARD ROGERS, television anchor; b. Cortland, N.Y., Dec. 24, 1955; s. Donald Richard and Vivian Alicia (Rogers) McC.; m. Joanne Louise Lohr, Apr. 29, 1989; children: Emily Louise, Marjan Alicia. BS in Journalism, U. Kans., 1979; postgrad., Mich. State U. Mgmt. trainee Garney Constrn. Co., Kansas City, Mo., 1979-80; reporter, anchor Sta. WIBW-AM-FM-TV, Topeka, 1979-80, Sta. KCTV-TV, Kansas City, 1980-89; anchor Sta. WKBD-TV, Detroit, 1989-93, WILX-TV, NBC, Lansing, Mich., 1993—; chmn. Earthwork Environ. Adv. Bd., Southfield, Mich., 1989—. Bd. dirs. Judson Ctr.; celebrity fundraiser Salvation Army, Detroit, 1989, March of Dimes, Detroit, 1989, hon. co-chair Mid-Mich. WalkAmerica, 1996; celebrity fundraiser Cancer Soc., Detroit, 1989, The Sanctuary, Royal Oak, Mich., 1989; mem. YMCA, 1991—; mem. Sparrow Hosp. Children's Miracle Network Com., 1996, Mid-Mich. Environ. Action Coun., 1996; project coord. News-10 Computer Edn., 1996. Recipient Spot News awards Mo. Broadcasters Assn., 1987, Kansas City Press Club, 1987, Kans. Broadcasters Assn., 1987, Disting. Environ. Reporting awards Detroit Audubon Soc., 1991, Mich. Audubon Soc., 1992, Ben East award Mich. United Conservation Clubs, 1991, 93, Mich. Outstanding Individual Reporting award UPI, 1991, Emmy award for Outstanding Reporting in Mich.,

1994. Mem. Nat. Acad. of TV Arts and Scis. (bd. dirs. Mich. chpt.), Nat. Geo. Soc., Soc. Environ. Journalists (charter, planner nat. conf.). Avocations: back-packing, golf, fishing, tennis, running. Office: WILX-TV PO Box 30380 Lansing MI 48909-7880*

MCCOY, EDWARD FITZGERALD, social services facility administrator; b. Enid, Okla., July 11, 1938; s. Leonard Edward and Florence Wortman (Fitzgerald) McC.; m. Patricia Jean Semon, Sept. 11, 1970 (div. July 1986); children: Mary Clare, Leonard Edward II, Edward Fitzgerald Jr. BA in Polit. Sci., Park Coll., 1961; MA in Rehab. of Blind, Western Mich. U., 1969; postgrad., U. Md., 1971-74. Sales mgr. St. Joseph (Mo.) Surg. Supply, 1961-63; house master Nebr. Sch. for Blind, Nebraska City, 1963-65; dir. recreation Mo. Sch. for Blind, St. Louis, 1965-68; orientation and mobility specialist Montgomery County Pub. Schs., Rockville, Md., 1969-76; child find specialist Montgomery County Pub. Schs., Rockville, Mo., 1976-77, diagnostic prescriptive resource tchr., 1977-78; exec. dir. Fla. Lions Conklin Ctr. for Multihandicapped Blind, Daytona Beach, Fla., 1978—. Charter mem. Planned Giving Coun. Ctrl. Fla.; mem. East Ctrl. Fla. Radio Reading Svc.; mem. bd. counselors Bethune-Cookman Coll.; chmn. Fla. divsn. Blind Svcs. Statewide Rehab. Adv. Coun., 1993—, chmn., 1996-97. Named to Ky. Cols., 1991; Western Mich. U. fellow, 1968-69; acad. leave grantee Montgomery County Pub. Sch., 1973-74. Mem. Fla. Assn. for Edn. and Rehab. of the Blind and Visually Impaired (pres. 1992-94), Nat. Soc. Fund Raising Execs. (cert.), Nat. Coun. Pvt. Agys. for the Blind and Visually Impaired, Nat. Accreditation Coun. for Agys. Serving Blind (team chmn.), Fla. Assn. Agys. Serving Blind (pres. 1985-87, treas. 1994—), Nat. Rehab. Assn., Am. Assn. Workers for Blind (pres. Washington chpt. 1977-78), Daytona Beach C. of C. (leadership coun.), Halifax Rowing Assn., Lions (pres. Daytona Beach Club 1982-83, chmn. sight conservation com. 1985—). Democrat. Roman Catholic. Avocations: camping, cooking, water sports. Home: 640 N Nova Rd Apt 115 Ormond Beach FL 32174-4408 Office: Conklin Ctr Multihandicapped Blind 405 White St Daytona Beach FL 32114-2925

MCCOY, EILEEN CAREY, academic dean; b. Jersey City; d. James Bernard and Nan (Dalton) Carey; m. Thomas James McCoy (dec.); children: Thomas James III, Mary Eileen McCoy Whang. BA, Coll. St. Elizabeth, Convent Station, N.J., 1954; MA, Fairleigh Dickinson U., 1969, EdD, 1983; postgrad., Harvard U., 1985. Mem. faculty County Coll. Morris, Dover, N.J., 1970-75; dir. cmty. rels. Raritan Valley Community Coll., Somerville, N.J., 1977-79, dean continuing, community edn. and svcs., 1979-95; dean Evening Coll. and Extension Site, 1995—. Author: The Community Education Component of the Community College: New Jersey in Comparative Perspective, 1983. Mem. Morris County Bd. Freeholders, 1975-77, Branchburg Twp. Rep. Mcpl. Com., 1996—; founding chmn. Somerset County Commn. on Women, 1985-88; mem. adv. coun. Somerset County Office on Aging, 1987—; bd. dirs. Rolling Hills Girl Scout Coun., 1991-93, Irish Am. Pub. Action Com., 1993, pres., 1994—; bd. advisors Somerset County United Way; mem. mcpl. com. Montgomery Twp., 1993-95; bd. dirs. Edn. Found. Bridgewater-Raritan, 1993—. Recipient Righteous Gentile award Jewish Fedn. Somerset, Hunterdon and Warren Counties, 1989, Somerset County Tercentennial award, 1989, Woman of Achievement award Rolling Hills Girl Scout Coun., 1991. Mem. Nat. Coun. Continuing Edn. and Community Svc. (bd. dirs. and region rep. 1987—, Person of Yr. region 2 1989), Greater Somerset County C. of C. (v.p. and bd. dirs. 1988-92, Outstanding Woman in Business and Industry 1982), Rotary (pres. Branchburg, N.J., club 1989-90). Republican. Roman Catholic. Office: Raritan C C Box 3000 Somerville NJ 08876-1262

MC COY, FRANK MILTON, concert pianist, educator, lecturer; b. El Centro, Calif., s. Henderson C. and Annie (Lee) McC.; A.B. (Rotary scholar), San Francisco State Coll., 1949, MA, 1960; postgrad. U. Wash., 1952-53, U. Calif. at Santa Barbara, 1957-58, U. So. Calif., 1961-65, U. Valencia (Spain), summer 1967; PhD Walden U., 1980; studied piano under Jean Le Duc, 1947-49, Madame Berthe Poncy-Jacobsen, 1952-53, Amparo Iturbi, 1960-62, Oria Kenah, Gladys Fawcette, Charles Shatto. Grad. asst. Sch. Music, U. Wash., Seattle, 1952-53; tchr. music edn. San Diego City Schs., 1953-54, El Centro Pub. Schs., 1954-57; counselor Social Service Center, Calexico, Calif., 1955-59; prof. piano and English Compton Coll., 1971-73; chmn. dept. music Portola Jr. H.S., L.A., 1985; personal rep. Odyssey Internat. Attractions. Piano, soloist All Am. Chorus tour 1956; 1st Am. to concertize on islands of St. Pierre and Miguelon, 1960; made concert tours Europe, Can., Latin Am., U.S., North Africa, Carribean, Middle East, USSR, China, Hong Kong; TV appearance CBC, 1965; appeared in Ebony mag., Sepia mag.; music critic Gilmore Piano Festival, Kalamazoo, Mich., 1994; adjudicator piano div. Southwestern Youth Music Festival, 1964; mem. bd. adjudicators Nat. Piano Playing Auditions, 1965; music-drama critic Post-Press Newspapers; founder, chmn. Annie Lee McCoy-Chopin Meml. Piano Award, 1975—; Mem. Founders Ch. of Religious Sci.; master tchr. in music L.A. City Schs., 1983-84. Bd. dirs. El Centro Cmty. Concert Assn. Recipient Leona M. Hickman award U. Wash., 1953, Mayor Tom Bradley commendation, 1991. Mem. Music Educators Nat. Conf., Nat. Guild Piano Tchrs., Am. Guild Mus. Artists, Music Critics Assn. North Am., Southeast Symphony Assn. (bd. dirs.), Internat. Platform Assn., Greater L.A. Press Club, Kiwanis (Angelus Mesa chpt. L.A.). Author: Black Tomorrow: A Portrait of Afro-American Culture, 1976 (children's book) Fruits and Vegetables A.B.C. Book; Playlet: Music Masters, Old and New, 1966, We, Too, Are Americans, 1977; music critic L.A. Sentinel, 1988—. Home: 234 S Figueroa St Apt 431 Los Angeles CA 90012-2509

MC COY, FREDERICK JOHN, retired plastic surgeon; b. McPherson, Kans., Jan. 17, 1916; s. Merle D. and Mae (Tennis) McC.; m. Mary Bock, May 17, 1972; children: Judith, Frederick John, Patricia, Melissa, Steven. B.S., U. Kans., 1938, M.D., 1942. Diplomate: Am. Bd. Plastic Surgery (dir. 1973-79, chmn. 1979). Intern Lucas County Hosp., Toledo, 1942-43; resident in plastic surgery U. Tex. Med. Sch., Galveston, 1946; preceptorship in surgery Grand Rapids, Mich., 1947-50; practice medicine specializing in plastic and reconstructive surgery Kansas City, Mo., 1950-93; staff St. Mary's Hosp., 1950-83, St. Joseph's Hosp., 1950—, N. Kansas City Meml. Hosp., 1955—; mem. staff, chief plastic surgery Kansas City Gen. Hosp. and Med. Center, 1952-72, Children's Mercy Hosp., 1954-93, Research Hosp., 1950—, St. Luke's Hosp., 1951—, Baptist Hosp., 1958—, Menorah Hosp., 1950—; chief div. plastic surgery Truman Med. Ctr., 1972-91; chmn. maxillo-facial surgery U. Kansas City Sch. Dentistry, 1950-57; assoc. prof. surgery U. Mo. Med. Sch., Kansas City, 1964-69; clin. prof. surgery U. Mo. Med. Sch., 1969—; pres. McCoy Enterprises, Kansas City, Mo. Contbr. articles to, profl. jours.; editor: Year Book of Plastic and Reconstructive Surgery, 1971-88. Bd. govs. Kansas City Mus., 1959-93, pres., 1973-74. Served to maj. M.C. U.S. Army, 1943-46. Mem. ACS (pres. Mo. chpt. 1973), AMA, Am. Acad. Pediatrics, Am. Soc. Plastic and Reconstructive Surgeons (sec. 1969-73, dir. 1973-76, pres. 1976, chmn. bd. 1977, Spl. Achievement award 1988), Am. Soc. Pediatric Plastic Surgeons, Pan Pacific Surg. Soc., Singleton Surg. Soc. (v.p. 1965), Am. Assn. Plastic Surgeons (founding mem. plastic surgery rsch. coun.), Internat. Soc. Aesthetic Plastic Surgery, Am. Soc. Aesthetic Plastic Surgery, Jackson County Med. Soc. (pres. 1964-65), Kansas City Southwest Clin. Soc. (pres. 1971), Mo. Med. Assn. (v.p. 1975), Internat. Coll. Surgeons (v.p. 1969), Royal Soc. Medicine (London), Kansas City C. of C., Conservation Fedn. Mo., Natural Sci. Soc. (founder, chmn. 1973), Citizens Assn. Kansas City, Explorer's Club, Mission Hills Country Club, Boone and Crocket Club, Phi Delta Theta, Nu Sigma Nu. Republican. Mem. Christian Ch. Home: 5814 Mission Dr Shawnee Mission KS 66208-1139 Office: 500 Nichols Rd Ste 401 Kansas City MO 64112-2013

MCCOY, GEORGIA SIDERIS, magazine editor, writing consultant; b. S.I., N.Y., Aug. 28, 1958; d. George Nicholas and Mary (Paulos) Sideris; m. Thomas O. McCoy; 1 child, Michael. BA in English magna cum laude, Wagner Coll., 1980. Editorial asst. Woman's Day Mag., N.Y.C., 1980-81, rsch. editor, 1981-85; freelance writer N.Y.C., 1985-87; rschr. Good Food Mag., N.Y.C., 1987-88; copy chief New Woman Mag., N.Y.C., 1988-96. amed Outstanding Mem., Women in Comms., 1984. Mem. NOW, Sierra ub, Holy Trinity Fellowship. Democrat. Greek Orthodox. Avocations: king, biking, travel, theater, museums.

MCCOY, GERALD LEO, superintendent of schools; b. Worthington, Minn., Dec. 4, 1936; s. Lawrence Joseph and Mildred Alice (Burns) McC.; m. Louise Marie Budde, Oct. 17, 1959; children: Susan, Peggy, Mary, Paul. BS, Mankato State U., 1960; MEd, U. Ill., 1963; EdD, U. Minn., 1978. Cert. English and speech tchr., prin., supt., Minn. Tchr. English, Springfield (Ill.) Schs., 1960-63; from tchr. English to prin. Burnsville (Minn.) Schs., 1964-73, asst. supt., 1974-80; supt. Eden Prairie (Minn.) Schs., 1980—; policy bd. Ctr. for Applied Rsch. and Edn. Improvement, Mpls., 1990-92; bd. dirs. Minn. Coun. for Quality, Mpls. Mem. Fairview Ridges Planning Bd., Burnsville, 1977-80; bd. dirs. Eden Prairie Found., 1980-88; trustee Fairview Southdale Hosp., Edina, Minn., 1987—. Recipient Outstanding Svc. award Eden Prairie Found., 1988, Cmty. Contbns. award Minn. Cmty. Edn. Assn., 1990, Disting. Alumnus award Mankato State U., 1996; fellow Bush Exec. Fellows Program, 1983-84. Mem. ASCD, Am. Assn. Sch. Adminstrs., Minn. Assn. Sch. Adminstrs. (Minn. Supt. of Yr. award 1989), West Metro Assn. Sch. Adminstrs. (past pres.), Eden Prairie C. of C. (pres. 1980-88, Outstanding Svc. award 1987), Rotary, Lions, Optimists (Optimist of Yr. award Eden Prairie 1986), Phi Kappa Phi, Phi Delta Kappa. Avocations: fishing, hunting. Office: Eden Prairie Schs 8100 School Rd Eden Prairie MN 55344-2233

MCCOY, HELEN THOMAS, civilian military employee; m. W.L. McCoy; 1 child, Kendra. BA in Math., Bennett Coll.; MPA, George Washington U. Mathematician Naval Space Surveillance Sys., Dahlgren, Va., 1967; dep. comptroller Def. Logistics Agy., 1990-93, acting comptroller, 1993; asst. sec. U.S. Army Fin. Mgmt. and Comptroller, 1994—. Mem. St. Bapt. Ch. Sr. Choir. Mem. Am. Soc. Mil. Comptrollers, Am. Assn. Budget and Program Analysts. *

MCCOY, JERRY JACK, lawyer; b. Pitts., Aug. 4, 1941; s. Norris and Martha (Jack) McC.; m. Alexandra Armstrong; children: MadeleineRena, Allison Norah, Jonathan Howard. BS, W.Va. U., 1963; LLB, Duke U., 1966; LLM in Taxation, N.Y.U., 1967. Bar: D.C. 1968, N.Y. 1967. Assoc. Silverstein & Mullens, Washington, 1968-72, ptnr., 1973-92; of counsel Reid and Priest, N.Y.C., Washington, 1992-94; sole practitioner Washington, 1994—; adj. law faculty George Washington U., Washington, 1977-87, U. Miami, Fla., 1983—, Law Ctr. Georgetown U., 1996—. Exec. editor Tax Mgmt., Estates Gifts and Trusts series, Washington, 1972-92; co-editor Charitable Gift Planning News, Dallas, 1983—; contbr. articles to profl. jours. Mem. Am. Law Inst., Am. Coll. Trust and Estate Counsel, Am. Coll. Tax Counsel, ABA. Democrat. Jewish. Home: 3560 Winfield Ln NW Washington DC 20007 Office: PO Box 66491 1050 Connecticut Ave NW Washington DC 20035-6491

MC COY, JOHN BONNET, banker; b. Columbus, Ohio, June 11, 1943; s. John Gardner and Jeanne Newlove (Bonnet) McC.; m. Jane Deborah Taylor, Apr. 21, 1968; children: Tracy Bonnet, Paige Taylor, John Taylor. B.A., Williams Coll., 1965; M.B.A., Stanford U., 1967; LLD (hon.), Williams Coll., 1991; D of Bus. Adminstrn. (hon.), Ohio State U., 1993; LLD (hon.), Kenyon Coll., 1994. With Banc One Corp., Columbus NA, Columbus, Ohio, 1970—, banking officer, 1970-73, v.p., 1973-77, pres., 1977-83; pres., chief operating officer Banc One Corp., Columbus, Ohio, 1983-84, pres., chief exec. officer, 1984-87, chmn., chief exec. officer, 1987—, also bd. dirs.; pres., COO Banc One Corp., Columbus, Ohio, 1983-84, pres., CEO, 1984-87, chmn. CEO, 1987—, also bd. dirs.; pres. Bank One Trust Co., 1979-81; bd. dirs. Cardinal Health, Inc., Fed. Nat. Mortgage Assn., Ameritech Corp., Tenneco Inc.; fed. adv. coun. Fed. Res. Sys., 1991-93. Active Boy Scouts Am.; trustee, chmn. bd. dirs. Kenyon Coll.; trustee Stanford U., Battelle Meml. Inst.; bd. dirs. Sr. PGA Tour; pres. Columbus Area Growth Found.; chmn. Capitol South Urban Redevel. Corp. Capt. USAF, 1967-70. Recipient Ernest C. Arbuckle award Stanford U., 1994. Mem. Columbus C. of C. (past chmn., trustee), Am. Bankers Assn., Bankers Roundtable (bd. dirs. 1989-94), Assn. Bank Holding Cos., Young Pres. Orgn. (chmn. Columbus chpt. 1982-83), Cypress Point Club, Seminole Golf Club, Links Club N.Y.C. Episcopalian. Office: Banc One Corp 100 E Broad St Columbus OH 43215-3607*

MCCOY, JOHN JOSEPH, lawyer; b. Cin., Mar. 15, 1952; s. Raymond F. and Margaret T. (Hohmann) McC. BS in Math. summa cum laude, Xavier U., 1974; JD, U. Chgo., 1977. Bar: Ohio 1977, D.C. 1980. Ptnr. Taft, Stettinius & Hollister, Cin., 1977—; lectr. Greater Cin. C. of C., 1984. Pro bono rep. Jr. Achievement Greater Cin., 1978; fund raiser Dan Beard coun. Boy Scouts Am., 1983; fund raising team leader Cin. Regatta, Cin. Ctr. Devel. Disorders, 1983; account mgr. United Appeal, Cin., 1984; mem. green areas trust adv. com. Village of Indian Hill, 1994—. Mem. ABA, Ohio State Bar Assn. (banking, comml. and bankruptcy law com., corp. law com., fed. ct. practice com.), Cin. Bar Assn. (fed. cts., common pleas cts. and negligence law coms., trustee Vol. Lawyers for the Poor Found. 1994—, chmn. 1996-97), Cin. Inn. of Ct. (barrister 1984-86), Cin. Athletic Club (pres. bd. trustees 1986-89, nominating com. 1989—). Home: 6700 Wyman Ln Cincinnati OH 45243-2730

MCCOY, LARRY, journalist; b. Frankfort, Ind., Sept. 30, 1937; s. Lavon James and Ethel Marie (Smith) McC.; m. Irene Theresa Kristoff, July 2, 1960; children: Julie, Jack. BS, Ind. U., 1959, AB, 1962. Writer UPI, Chgo., 1960-64; editor, sr. editor ABC News, N.Y.C., 1964-69; editor Radio Free Europe, Munich, 1969-71, sr. editor, asst. news dir., 1973-80; writer CBS News Radio, N.Y.C., 1971-73, editor, asst. bur. mgr., news dir., 1980—. Contbr. articles to opinion/editorial pages in newspaper. Office: CBS News Radio 524 W 57th St New York NY 10019-2902

MC COY, LEE BERARD, paint company executive; b. Ipswich, Mass., July 27, 1925; d. Damase Joseph and Robena Myrtle (Bruce) B.; student U. Ala., Mobile, 1958-60; m. Walter Vincent de Paul McCoy, Sept. 27, 1943; children: Bernadette, Raymond, Joan, Richard. Owner, Lee's Letter Shop, Hicksville, L.I., N.Y., 1950-56; mgr. sales adminstrn. Basila Mfg. Co., Mobile, Ala., 1957-61; promotion mgr., buyer Mobile Paint Co., Inc., Theodore, Ala., 1961—. Curator, Shepard Meml. Libr., 1972—; bd. dirs. Monterey Tour House, Mobile, 1972-78, Old Dauphin Way Assn., 1977-79, Friends of Mus., Mobile, 1978—, Miss Wheelchair Ala., 1980—; del. Civic Roundtable, 1977-78, bd. dirs., 1980-81, 1st v.p., 1980-81, pres., 1981-82; pres.'s Com. Employment of Handicapped, 1981—; chmn. Mobile, Nat. Yr. Disabled Persons, 1982; chmn. Mobile, Internat. Decade Disabled Persons, 1983—; mem. Nat. Project Adv. Bd., 1983—, Nat. Community Adv. Bd., 1983—, World Com. for Decade of Disabled Persons, 1983—; v.p. Bristol Sister City Soc.; active Mobile Area Retarded Citizens, Am. Heart Assn.; mem. City of Mobile Cultural Enrichment Task Force, 1985—, Mobile United Recreation and Culture Com.; dir. Culture Mobile, 1986—; v.p., bd. dirs. Joe Jefferson Players, 1986; co-chmn. Brit. Faire, 1983; chmn. Mobile Expo, 1990, Culture & Recreation Com. Mobile United, 1989, steering com., 1990. Recipient Honor award Civic Roundtable, 1979, 80; Service award Women's Com. of Spain Rehab. Center, State of Ala., 1980; award Nat. Orgn. on Disability, 1983, Gayfer's Outstanding Career Woman award, 1988; Golden Rule award JC Penney, 1993. Mem. Spectromatic Assos., Nat. Paint Distbrs., Hist. Preservation Soc., Color Mktg. Group, English Speaking Union (v.p., pres. 1992, 94, 95, 96, 97), U.S. C. of C. (chmn. local cultural enrichment task force 1986), Toastmasters (pres. 1995-96, area gov. 1997), The Nat. Mus. of Women of the Arts, Washington (charter), Internat. Platform Assn. Methodist. Republican. Clubs: Quota (charter mem. Mobile chpt., dir. 1977—, pres. 1978-80, chmn. numerous coms., recipient Service award Dist. 8, 1979, Internat. award for serving club objectives, 1980, editor Care-Gram, Weekly newsletter for nursing homes 1980—), Bienville; writer 10 books; lectr., worldwide traveler. Home: 1553 Monterey Pl Mobile AL 36604-1227 Office: 4775 Hamilton Blvd Theodore AL 36582-8523

MCCOY, LINDA KORTEWEG, media specialist; b. Passaic, N.J., Oct. 12, 1948; d. Christian Adrian and Irene (Morse) Korteweg; m. Rudolph William, Aug. 1, 1970; children: Jill Ann, Lori Lynn. BA in Math. Edn., William Paterson, 1970, BA in Acctg., 1987, MA in Ednl. Media, 1993. Cert. math. tchr. grades 7-12, media specialist grades K-12, supr., N.J. Math. tchr. Woodrow Wilson Middle Sch., Clifton, N.J., 1970-71; media specialist Schs. 5, 11, 13, Clifton, 1971-78, Schs. 2 & 5, Clifton, 1984-93, Clifton High Sch., 1993—; adj. math. tchr. Tombrock Coll., West Patterson, N.J., 1970-72; adv. bd. Grove Hill Nursery Sch., Clifton, 1984-86; tchr's adv. bd. Clifton (N.J.) Bd. Edn., 1992-93. Treas. Advs. for Quality Edn., Clifton, 1990-93; exec. bd. Clifton (N.J.) Concert Choir Parents, 1992-96; mem. Middlestates Evaluation Com., 1995; chair Task Force for Coll. Preparation, 1996-97, tech. com. dist., 1995—. Recipient NSF computer study grant St. Peter's Coll., 1970-71, tel cable grant for tech. study at the Sparkman Ctr., Colo., Internet Access for H.S. Media Ctrs. grant, 1995, N.J. Gov.'s Tchr. Recognition award N.J. State Bd. Edn., Trenton, 1992. Mem. NEA, N.J. Edn. Assn., Clifton Tchrs. Assn., N.J. Libr. Assn., Ednl. Media Assn. N.J., Assn. for Ednl. Comm. and Tech., Pi Lambda Theta, Kappa Delta Pi. Avocations: computers, sewing. Home: 82 Mountainside Ter Clifton NJ 07013-1177 Office: Clifton High Sch 333 Colfax Ave Clifton NJ 07013-1701

MC COY, LOIS CLARK, emergency services professional, retired county official, magazine editor; b. New Haven, Oct. 1, 1920; d. William Patrick and Lois Rosilla (Dailey) Clark; m. Herbert Irving McCoy, Oct. 17, 1943; children: Whitney, Kevin, Marianne, Tori, Debra, Sally, Daniel. BS, Skidmore Coll., 1942; student Nat. Search and Rescue Sch., 1974. Asst. buyer R.H. Macy & Co., N.Y.C., 1942-44, assoc. buyer, 1944-48; instr. Mountain Medicine & Survival, U. Calif. at San Diego, 1973-74; cons. editor Search & Rescue Mag., 1975; cons. editor, Rescue Mag., 1988-97; editor Press On Newsletter, 1992—. coord. San Diego Mountain Rescue Team, La Jolla, Calif., 1973-75; exec. sec. Nat. Assn. for Search and Rescue, Inc., Nashville and La Jolla, 1975-80, comptr., 1980-82; disaster officer San Diego County, 1980-86, Santa Barbara County, 1986-91, ret. Contbr. editor Rescue Mag., 1989-97, editor-in-chief Response! mag., 1982-86; editor Press On! Electronic mag., 1994—; mem. adv. bd. Hazard Montly, 1991—; cons. law enforcement div.; Calif. Office Emergency Svcs., 1976-77; pres. San Diego Com. for Los Angeles Philharmonic Orch., 1957-58. Bd. dirs. Search and Rescue of the Californias, 1976-77, Nat. Assn. for Search and Rescue, Inc., 1980-87, pres., 1985-87, trustee, 1987-90, mem. Calif. OES strategic com., 1992-96; CEO Nat. Inst. For Urban Search, 1989—; mem. Gov.'s Task Force on Earthquakes, 1981-82, Earthquake Preparedness Task Force, Seismic Safety Commn., 1982-85. Recipient Hal Foss award for outstanding service to search and rescue, 1982, Diamond Safety award for outstanding work in emergency services, 1996. Mem. IEEE, Armed Forces Comm. and Electronics Assoc., Nat. Assn. for Search & Rescue (life, Svc. award 1985), San Diego Mountain Rescue Team (hon. life), Santa Barbara Amateur Radio Club. Episcopalian. Author: Search and Rescue Glossary, 1974; contbr. to profl. jours. Office: PO Box 91648 Santa Barbara CA 93190-1648

MCCOY, MARILYN, university official; b. Providence, Mar. 18, 1948; d. James Francis and Eleanor (Regan) McC.; m. Charles R. Thomas, Jan. 28, 1983. BA in Econs. cum laude, Smith Coll., 1970; M in Pub. Policy, U. Mich., 1972. Dir. Nat. Ctr. for Higher Edn. Mgmt. Systems, Boulder, Colo., 1972-80; dir. planning and policy devel. U. Colo., Boulder, 1981-85; v.p. adminstrn. and planning Northwestern U., Evanston, Ill., 1985—; bd. dirs. Pegasus Funds. Co-author: Financing Higher Education in the Fifty States, 1976, 3d edit., 1982. Bd. dirs. Evanston Hosp., 1988—, Met. Family Svcs., Chgo., 1988—, Mather Found., 1995—. Mem. Am. Assn. for Higher Edn., Soc. for Coll. and Univ. Planning (pres., v.p., sec., bd. dirs. 1980—), Assn. for Instnl. Rsch. (pres., v.p., exec. com., publs. bd. 1978-87), Chgo. Network (chmn. 1992-93), Chgo. Econ. Club. Home: 1100 N Lake Shore Dr Chicago IL 60611-1045 Office: Northwestern U 633 Clark St Evanston IL 60208-0001

MCCOY, MARY ANN, state official; b. Duluth, Minn., Oct. 13, 1924; d. Homer Burke and Avis (Woodworth) Hursh; B.A., Grinnell Coll., 1946; postgrad. Laval U., 1946, Mankato State U., 1964-65, U. Minn., 1970-73; m. Charles Ramon McCoy, June 11, 1949; children—Jeffrey, Mary, Jeremy. Cert. neutral mediator Minn. Supreme Ct., 1996—. Exec. trainee Younkers, Inc., Des Moines, 1946; advt. copywriter Des Moines Register & Tribune, 1947; field dir. Duluth (Minn.) Girl Scout Council, 1947-49; with merchandising dept. Dayton's, Inc., Mpls., 1966-75; dir. election and legis. manual div. Office of Sec. of State of Minn., St. Paul, 1975-81; exec. dir. Minn. State Ethical Practices Bd., St. Paul, 1981-95; cons., 1996—. Mem. Minn. Hist. Soc. (life, hon. council), Council on Govt. Ethics Laws (steering com. 1986-89, treas. 1987-88, hon. life), exec. council Minn. Hist. Soc., 1972-81, 82-90 ; mem. Minn. Supreme Ct. Bd. for Continuing Legal Edn., 1981-87; sec. State Rev. Bd. for Nominations to Nat. Register, 1976-89 . Mem. Minn. Assn. Pub. Adminstrs., Am. Judicature Soc., Internat. Assn. Facilitators, Women Historians of Midwest, Am. Assn. State and Local History. Editor, Minn. Legis. Manual, 1975-81.

MCCOY, MILLINGTON F., management recruitment company executive; b. Cape Girardeau, Mo., Jan. 22, 1941; d. Howard Hanscom and Mary Helen (Kinder) Flentge; m. W. David McCoy; 1 child, Daniel Phipps. BA, U. Mo., 1962; Cert. in Bus. Adminstrn. program, Harvard-Radcliffe U., 1963. Field market researcher Procter & Gamble Co., N.Y.C., 1964-65; advt. and market rsch. analyst Gardner Advt. Agy., N.Y.C., 1965-66; v.p. Handy Assocs., N.Y.C., 1966-77; mng. dir. Gould, McCoy & Chadick, Inc., N.Y.C., 1977—; founding mem. Com. of 200; panel of experts boardroom reports, dean's coun. Harvard Divinity Sch. Mem. Phi Beta Kappa. Avocations: dressage, Enneagram. Office: Gould McCoy & Chadick Inc 300 Park Ave New York NY 10022-7402

MCCOY, PATRICIA A., psychology educator, writer, art critic; b. Seattle, Wash., Dec. 20, 1951; d. Robert Wilson and Barbara (Foss) McC. BS, U. Nev., 1974; MA, NYU, 1983; postgrad. in psychoanalysis, Ctr. for Modern Psychoanalytic, Studies, N.Y.; postgrad. in applied linguistics, NYU. Lectr. in English CUNY, N.Y.C., 1984-88, John Jay Coll. of Criminal Justice, N.Y.C., 1988-91; clin. educator August Aichhorn Resdl. Treatment Ctr., N.Y.C., 1991-93, St. Vincent's Hosp. Psychiatry Inpatient, N.Y.C., 1993-95; staff, spl. edn. dist. 75 N.Y.C. Bd. Edn., 1995—; lectr. contemporary art New Arts Program and others, east coast, 1991—; ind. curator, 1987—. Editor: N.A.P. Texts jour., 1993—; contbr. articles to profl. jours., including Jour. Modern Psychoanalysis, Jour. Am. Orthopsychiatry; art critic; curated shows include Lang and O'Hara Gallery, N.Y.C., Sandra Gering Gallery, N.Y.C., 1989, Northampton Gallery, Pa., 1994, La Mama Gallery, N.Y.C., 1994. Grantee N.Y. State Found. for the Arts, 1987, Pa. Coun. for the Arts, 1991, Mid-Atlantic, 1991, Nat. Endowment for the Arts, 1992, Pew Charitable Trust, 1993. Mem. Nat. Soc. Modern Psychoanalysts, Assn. Internat. des Critiques d'Art, Am. Orthopsychiatric Assn., N.Y. State Coun. Humanities.

MC COY, ROBERT BAKER, publisher; b. Arrowsmith, Ill., Mar. 26, 1916; s. Robert Benton and Charlotte (Miller) McC. B.S., Northwestern U., 1950; M.S., 1951; postgrad., U. Ill. extension. Various positions with branches U.S. Govt., 1939-51; mng. editor book dept. Popular Mechanics Mag. Co., Chgo., 1951-60; mng. editor high sch. textbook div. J.B. Lippincott Co., Chgo., 1960-62; owner, pres., chmn. bd. Rio Grande Press Inc. (pubs. nonfiction Western Americana books), Chgo., 1962—; chmn. bd., pres. Rio Grande Press of N.Mex., Inc. Lectr., author articles on Am. Indian, ornithology, travel. Served with AUS, 1941-45. Office: The Rio Grande Press Inc La Casa Escuela PO Box 33 Glorieta NM 87535

MCCOY, SUE, surgeon; b. Charlottesville, Va., Nov. 14, 1935; d. Hulburt Christopher and Evelyn (Savage) McC. AB, Radcliffe Coll., 1957; PhD, Johns Hopkins U., 1964; MD, U. Va., 1980. Diplomate Am. Bd. Surgery. Fellow in physiol. chemistry Johns Hopkins U., Balt., 1964-67; asst. prof. chemistry U. South Fla., Tampa, 1967-69; asst. prof. orthopedics U. Va., Charlottesville, 1969-73, asst. prof. surgery, 1973-78; resident in surgery Hosp. U. Pa., Phila., 1980-83; resident in surgery Cooper Hosp. Rutgers U. Med. Sch., Camden, N.J., 1983-85, asst. prof. surgery, 1985-86; asst. prof. surgery East Tenn. State U., Johnson City, 1986-91, assoc. prof., 1991—. Mem. ACS, Am. Chem. Soc., N.Y. Acad. Sci., Royal Soc. Chemistry, Assn. for Acad. Surgery, Shock Soc., Internat. Soc. Oxygen Transport to Tissue, Am. Fedn. Clin. Rsch., Tenn. Med. Assn., Southeastern Surg. Congress, Assn. for Surg. Edn., Assn. for Women Surgeons, Tenn. Geriatric Assn., Am. Soc. for Parenteral and Enteral Nutrition, Sigma Xi. Achievements include research in hemorrhagic shock, aging, oxygen transport. Home: PO Box 265 Mountain Home TN 37684-0265

MC COY, TIDAL WINDHAM, former government official; b. Gainesville, Fla., Apr. 25, 1945. Grad., U.S. Mil. Acad., 1967; M.A. in Bus. Fin, George Washington U., 1975. Officer U.S. Army, 1967-72; mem. long-range planning and net assessment group Office of Sec. Def., Washington, 1972-73; mem. staff Nat. Security Council, 1973; staff asst. and then dep. asst. to Sec. Def., 1973-77; sci. asst. to asst. sec. for research, engring. and systems Dept. Navy, 1977-78; dir. policy research, office of under sec. for policy Dept. Def., 1978-79; asst. for nat. security affairs to Sen. Jake Garn, 1979-81; asst. sec.

for manpower, res. affairs and installations Dept. Air Force, Washington, 1981-87; asst. sec. for readiness support USAF, Washington, 1987-88; acting sec. and undersec. USAF, 1981-88; sr. assoc. Hecht, Spencer & Assocs., 1988-89; v.p. govt. rels. Thiokol Corp., 1989—. Recipient DOD Outstanding Civil Svc. medal Sec. Defense. Mem. Space Transp. Assn. U.S.A. (dir., chmn. 1996—).

MCCOY, WESLEY LAWRENCE, musician, conductor, educator; b. Memphis, Jan. 27, 1935; s. Harlan Eftin and Gladys (Coggin) McC.; m. Carolyn June Noble, Aug. 26, 1960; children: Jill Laurene McCoy Kurtz, Scott Edward. B.Music Edn., La. State U., 1957, Ph.D., 1970; M of Music Edn, U. Louisville, 1958; M Sacred Music, So. Bapt. Theol. Sem., 1960. Minister of music Beechmont Bapt. Ch., Louisville, 1959-62; also instr. music So. Bapt. Theol. Sem., Louisville; asst. prof. music, dir. bands Carson Newman Coll., Jefferson City, Tenn., 1962-67; asst. prof. music U. S.C., Columbia, 1969-72; asso. prof. music U. Ark., Little Rock, 1972-77; prof. U. Ark., 1977-80, asst. dean for public service Coll. Fine Arts,, 1978-79; condr. Wind Ensemble, River City Community Band, 1972-80, Oklahoma City Youth Symphony, 1985-89; chmn. dept. music Phillips U., Enid, Okla., 1980-82, chmn. fine arts div., 1982-84; minister music 1st United Meth. Ch., Edmond, Okla., 1983—; owner Centre Office, Travel Agts. Internat. French horn player, Knoxville (Tenn.) Symphony Orch., 1962-67, Columbia Philharm. Orch., 1969-72, Ark. Symphony Orch., 1972-80, Enid-Phillips Symphony, 1980-84; contbr. to Ch. Musician, 1974-76, 85-86. Co-chmn. Jefferson County (Tenn.) Com. for Goldwater for Pres., 1962; mem. Pulaski County Republican Com., 1977-81; mem. Oklahoma County Rep. xec. Com., 1995-97; pres. Ctrl. Okla. LSU Alumni, 1997—. Mem. S.C. Music Educators Assn. (pres. coll. div. 1971-73), Ark. Music Edn. Assn. (chmn. rsch. 1975-80), Cen. Okla. La. State U. Alumni Assn. (pres. 1997-98), Phi Mu Alpha, Pi Kappa Lambda, Phi Delta Kappa, Alpha Tau Omega. Republican. Baptist. Home: 1904 Blue Jay Ct Edmond OK 73034-6105 Office: 1331 W Memorial Rd Oklahoma City OK 73114-1423

MCCOY, WILLIAM EARL, JR., economic development training consultant; b. Grand Rapids, Mich., Nov. 19, 1953; s. William Earl and Evelyn (Duke) McC.; m. Allene Denise Garrett, Aug. 20, 1977; children: Erin Nicole, Shannon Michele. BA, Alma Coll., 1975; MPA, Am. U., 1977; CID/CED, Am. Econ. Devel. Coun., 1989. Cert. indsl. and econ. developer; cert. violence interruption educator. Dep. city mgr. City of Benton Harbor, Mich., 1977-79; resident fellow Acad. Contemporary Problems, Columbus, Ohio, 1979-82; country dir. Peace Corps, Maseru, Lesotho, 1982-84; spl. asst. to Africa region dir. Peace Corps, Washington, 1984-85; pres. The McCoy Co., Columbus, 1985—; v.p. Econ. Devel. Council, Lima, Ohio, 1986-89; project dir. Columbus Found., 1989-91; planning, econ. devel., and tng. cons. in pvt. practice Columbus, 1985—; instr. Phoenix Coll. and South Mountain C.C., 1996—; cons. on rsch. Joint Ctr. Polit. Studies, Washington, 1976-77; cons. on small cities Nat. League Cities, Washington, 1978; cons. on urban affairs Ohio State U., Columbus, 1980-81; strategic planning, econ. devel. and tng. cons. City of Dayton, Ohio, 1985—, City of Lima, City of Kettering, Montgomery County, Ohio Commn. on Minority Health, Dayton Pub. Schs., Nat. Black Programming Consortium, Nat. Coun. Black Studies, Nat. Urban Policy Inst., Ctr. for Violence Interruption, Ohio Dept. Alcohol and Drug Addiction Svcs., Ohio Dept. Health, Nat. Women's Resource Ctr., NFL, others. Co-author: Managing Fiscal Retrenchment in Cities, 1980, Housing Problems of Black Mayor Cities, Planning Needs of Small Cities, Black Crime: A Police View. Dir. city drive United Way, Benton Harbor, 1978, Godman Guild, Columbus, 1980, ARC, Lima, 1987, Coun. for Arts Greater Lima, Lima Area Food Bank, 1988; chmn. bd. Lima-Allen County Full Employment Commn.; mem. fin. roundtable U.S. Econ. Devel. Adminstrn., Washington, 1980; mem. econ. devel. com. City of Lima, 1989; mem. Coun. on Urban Econ. Devel. Recipient Econ. Devel. Excellence award Ohio Devel. Assn., 1988, Jobs for Columbus Grads., 1991, PHA Cmtys. United, 1995. Mem. Am. Econ. Devel. Coun., Am. Soc. Pub. Affairs and Adminstrn., Nat. Bus. League, Internat. Traders, Internat. Downtown Assn., Am. Entrepreneurs Assn., Internat. City Mgmt. Assn., Nat. Main St. Network, Rotary, Pi Alpha Alpha. Home: 12 Westerville Sq Westerville OH 43081 Office: The McCoy Co 5918 Sharon Woods Blvd Ste 200 Columbus OH 43229-2665

MCCRABB, DONALD RAYMOND, religious ministry director; m. Catherine Olds; 1 child, Andrew Thomas. BA in Religion, BA in Polit. Sci., Wright State U., 1975; MA in Theology, U. Dayton, 1978; grad. program, Jesuit Renewal Ctr., Milford, Ohio, 1984. Cert. catechetical leader, Roman Cath. Ch. Campus min. Newman Ctr., Wright State U., Dayton, Ohio, 1975-76; grad. asst. U. Dayton, 1976-78; pastoral assoc. St. Raphael Cath. Ch., Springfield, Ohio, 1978-82; Cath. campus min. Cen. State U., Wilberforce U., 1982-85; exec. dir. Cath. Campus Ministry Assn., 1985—; mem. planning com. Cath. Edn. Futures Project, 1985-88; bd. dirs., site visitor Commn. on Cert. and Accreditation, U.S. Cath. Conf., 1986—. Home: 1433 Constance Ave Dayton OH 45409-1807 Office: Cath Campus Ministry Assn 3000 College Park Ave Dayton OH 45469-2515*

MCCRACKEN, ALEXANDER WALKER, pathologist; b. Motherwell, Lanarkshire, Scotland, Nov. 24, 1931; came to U.S., 1968; s. William and Mary Snedden (Walker) McC.; m. Theresa Credgington, June 4, 1960; children: Fiona Jane, Claire Louise. MD, U. Glasgow, Scotland, 1956. Resident in surgery Glasgow Royal Inf., 1956-57; resident in pathology Royal Air Force, U.K., 1957-61, pathologist, 1962-68; fellow in pathology Royal Postgrad. Med. Sch., London, 1961-62; assoc. prof. Med. Sch., U. Tex., San Antonio, 1968-72; prof. Med. Sch., U. Tex., Houston, 1972-73; dir. of microbiology Baylor U. Med. Ctr., Dallas, 1973-81; pres. med. staff, dir. of labs. Meth. Hosps. of Dallas, 1982—; pres. med. staff Meth. Med. Ctr., 1994-95; adj. prof. pathology Baylor U. Coll. Dentistry, Dallas, 1982—; clin. prof. U. Tex. Southwestern Med. Sch., Dallas, 1986—. Author: Pathologic Mechanisms of Human Disease, 1985, Oral and Clinical Microbiology, 1986, Pathology, 1990, (play) Mister Gilbert, 1985, 89. With Royal Air Force, 1957-68. Decorated Gen. Svc. medal. Fellow Royal Coll. Pathologists, Coll. Am. Pathologists; mem. AAAS, AMA, Am. Soc. Microbiology, Tex. Med. Assn., Dallas County Med. Soc., Tex. Soc. Infectious Diseases, Tex. Med. Found., Assn. of Clin. Chemists, Masons. Republican. Anglican. Avocations: theater, music, gardening. Home: 607 Kessler Lake Dr Dallas TX 75208-3943 Office: Lab Physicians Assn 221 W Colorado Blvd Dallas TX 75208-2363

MCCRACKEN, CARON FRANCIS, computer company executive, consultant; b. Detroit, Jan. 12, 1951; d. William Joseph and Constance Irene (Kramer) McC. AS, Mott C.C., 1971; BS, Ctrl. Mich. U., 1973; MA, U. Mich., 1978; postgrad., Wayne State U., 1979-81, 93—. Tchr. Elkton, Pigeon, Bayport (Mich.) High Sch., 1973-74, Davison (Mich.) Jr. High Sch., 1974-75; instr. Mott C.C., Flint, Mich., 1974-78; planning and rsch. specialist Flint Police Dept., 1977-79; campus coord., programmer Systems & Computer Tech. Corp., Detroit, 1981-82, acad. specialist computing systems, 1982-83, mgr. acad. computing systems, 1983-84, mgr. adminstrv. computing systems, 1984-85; communications analyst Fruehauf Corp., Detroit, 1985-86, sr. comms. analyst, 1986-87; account cons. US Sprint Communications Co., Detroit, 1987-89; account mgr. US Sprint Communications Corp., Detroit, 1989-90; sr. mgr. Technology Specialists, Inc., Phila., 1990-91; sr. tech. cons. Digital Mgmt. Group, Detroit, 1991-92; sr. assoc. info. tech. practice, tech. delivery svcs. Coopers & Lybrand, Detroit, 1992—; adv. bd. CONTEL Bus. Networks, Atlanta, 1987. Contbr. articles to profl. jours. Vol. charitable and homeless orgns., including COTS - Coalition on Temporary Shelter, Core Cities, Paint the Town; undergrad. computer lab. cons./student mgr. computer sci. dept. Wayne State U., 1993-95, vol. computer cons. Bus. Sch., 1997—; vol. tech. advisor on 1992 elections project City of Detroit; vol. St. Joseph's Mercy Hosp., Pontiac, Mich., 1995; pres. bd. dirs. Bloomfield Hills Condominium Assn., 1996—; vol. Pub. TV Channel 56 WTVS-Detroit, 1996—, vol., Pub. Radio Sta. WDET-Detroit, 1996—. Mem. Data Processing Mgmt. Assn., Assn. Computing Machinery, Detroit Inst. Arts, Alumni Assn. U. Mich., Alumni Assn. Wayne State U., Smithsonian Instn. (assoc.), Adventure Cycling Assn. (Missoula, Mont.). Avocations: distance bicycling and swimming, golf, personal research, travel. Home: 100 W Hickory Grove H4 Bloomfield Hills MI 48304-2169 Office: Coopers & Lybrand 400 Renaissance Ctr Detroit MI 48243

MCCRACKEN, INA, business executive; b. Highland Park, Mich., Oct. 7, 1939; d. James Howard and Lodaskia (Smoot) Smith; children: Michalene, Colet, Paulet, Pauleta. BA, Mich. State U., 1961, MEd, 1980; Edn. Specialist cert., Wayne State U., 1982, EdD, 1994. Cert. tchr., adminstr., supt., Mich. Pres. Career Mgmt. Systems, Inc., Detroit; instr. Highland Park Bd. Edn. Bus. trainer Detroit Self-Employment Project. Mem. Minority Bus. Inc. (corr. sec.), Nat. Alliance of Black Sch. Educators, Wayne State U. Coll. Edn. Alumni (chmn. bd. govs.), Phi Delta Kappa. Office: PO Box 04721 Detroit MI 48204-0721

MCCRACKEN, JOHN HARVEY, painter, sculptor; b. Berkeley, Calif., Dec. 9, 1934; s. John H. and Marjorie McC.; m. Gail Barringer, May 4, 1991; children: David Gordon, Patrick Daniel. BFA, Calif. Coll. Arts & Crafts, 1962, postgrad., 1962-65. Tchr., U. Calif., Irvine, 1965-66, L.A., 1966-68, Santa Barbara, 1974-85, Sch. Visual Arts, N.Y.C., 1968-69, Hunter Coll., N.Y.C., 1970-71, U. Nev., Reno, 1971-72, Las Vegas, 1972-75. One man shows include: Robert Elkon Gallery, N.Y.C., 1966, 67, 68, 72, 73, Galerie Ileana Sonnabend, Paris, 1969, Sonnabend Gallery, N.Y.C., 1970, Ace Gallery, L.A., 1985, PS 1, Long Island City, N.Y., 1986, Newport Harbor Art Mus., Calif., 1987, Contemporary Arts Mus., Houston, 1989, Hoffman Borman Gallery, Santa Monica, Calif., 1988, Konrad Fischer Gallery, Düsseldorf, Germany, 1989, Lisson Gallery, London, 1990, 97, Galerie Nordenhake, Stockholm, 1990, Fred Hoffman Gallery, L.A., 1990, Galerie Froment & Putman, Paris, 1991, 96, Sonnabend Gallery, N.Y.C., 1992, Louver Gallery, L.A., 1993-95, 97, Galerie Xavier Hufkens, Brussels, 1993, Galerie Art & Public, Geneva, 1994, Galerie Tanit, Munich, 1995, Hochshule Fur Angwandte Kunst, Vienna, 1995, Kunsthalle Basel, Switzerland, 1995, David Zwirner Gallery, N.Y., 1997; exhibited in group shows at Solomon R. Guggenheim Mus., N.Y.C., 1967, Saatchi Gallery, London, 1985, Venice (Italy) Biennale, 1986, Centro de Arte Reina Sofia, Madrid, 1987, Musee St. Pierre Art Contemporain, Lyon, France, 1988, Solomon R. Guggenheim Mus., N.Y.C., 1989-90, Carnegie Internat., Carnegie Mus. Art, Pitts., 1991, Corcoran Biennal, Washington, 1995; represented in permanent collections at Art Inst. Chgo., Solomon R. Guggenheim Mus., N.Y.C., Mus. Modern Art, N.Y.C., San Francisco Mus. Art, Whitney Mus. Art, N.Y.C., Mus. Contemporary Art, L.A., L.A. County Mus. Art. Grantee, NEA, 1968.

MC CRACKEN, PAUL WINSTON, retired economist, business educator; b. Richland, Iowa, Dec. 29, 1915; s. Sumner and Mary (Coffin) McC.; m. Emily Ruth Siler, May 27, 1942; children—Linda Jo, Paula Jeanne. Student, William Penn Coll., 1937; MA, Harvard U., 1942, PhD, 1948. Faculty Found. Sch., Berea Coll., Ky., 1937-40; economist Dept. Commerce, Washington, 1942-43; fin. economist, dir. research Fed. Res. Bank of Mpls., 1943-48; assoc. prof. Sch. Bus. Adminstrn., U. Mich., 1948-50, prof., 1950-66, Edmund Ezra Day Univ. prof. bus adminstrn., 1966-86, prof. emeritus, 1986—, ret.; chmn. Nat. Bur. Econ. Rsch.; trustee Earhart Found.; mem. pub. oversight bd. AICPA. Author: monographs Can Capitalism Survive?; articles on financial, econ. subjects. Fellow Am. Statis. Assn.; mem. Am. Econ. Assn., Am. Finance Assn., Royal Econ. Soc., Harvard Grad. Soc. (coun.). Presbyn. Clubs: Cosmos (Washington); Harvard (N.Y.C.). Home: 2564 Hawthorne Rd Ann Arbor MI 48104-4032

MC CRACKEN, PHILIP TRAFTON, sculptor; b. Bellingham, Wash., Nov. 14, 1928; s. William Franklin and Maude (Trafton) McC.; m. Anne MacFetridge, Aug. 14, 1954; children—Timothy, Robert, Daniel. B.A. in Sculpture, U. Wash., 1954. Asst. to Henry Moore Eng., 1954. One-man shows: Willard Gallery, N.Y.C., 1960, 65, 68, 70, Seattle Art Mus., 1961, Wash. State Capitol Mus., Olympia, 1964, Art Gallery of Greater Victoria, B.C., 1964, LaJolla (Calif.) Mus. Art, 1970, Anchorage Hist. and Fine Arts Mus., 1970, Tacoma Art Mus., 1980, Kennedy Galleries, N.Y.C., 1985, Lynn McAllister Gallery, Seattle, 1986, 89, Valley Mus. N.W. Art, La Conner, Wash., 1993, Whatcom Mus., Bellingham, Wash., 1994, Schneider Mus. Art, 1994, So. Oreg. State Coll., 1994, others; group shows include: Mus. Art, Ogunquit, Maine, 1957, Chgo. Art Inst., 1958, Detroit Inst. Arts, 1958, Pa. Acad. Fine Arts, 1958, Contemporary Art Gallery, Houston, 1958, DeYoung Meml. Mus., San Francisco, 1960, Los Angeles Mcpl. Art Mus., 1960, Galerie Claude Bernard, Paris, 1960, Phillips Gallery, Washington, 1966, Corcoran Gallery, 1966, Mus. Art, Akron, 1967, Finch Coll., N.Y.C., 1968, Rutgers U., 1968, Whitney Mus. Art, 1978, Portland Art Mus., 1976, Mont. State U., Bozeman, 1979, Brigham Young U., 1980, Bellvue (Wash.) Art Mus., 1986, Lynn McAllister Gallery, 1986, Am. Acad. Arts and Letters, N.Y.C., 1986, Schmidt Bingham Gallery, N.Y.C., 1987, Wash. State Capital Mus., 1987, 89, Cheney-Cowles Mus., Spokane, Wash., 1988, Smithsonian Instn., 1991—, Nat. Mus., Ottawa, Can., 1991-92, Gallery Three-Zero, N.Y.C., 1993, Seattle Art Mus., 1994, SA Gallery Christ Ch., New Zealand, 1996, others; sculptures represented: Norton Bldg., Seattle, Kankakee (Ill.) State Hosp., Swinomish Indian Tribal Center, LaConner, UN Assn., N.Y.C., King County King Dome, Seattle, City Hall, Everett, Wash., others. (Recipient numerous prizes, awards). Address: 401 Guemes Island Rd # B Anacortes WA 98221-9534

MCCRACKEN, ROBERT DALE, anthropologist, writer; b. Fairplay, Colo., Aug. 8, 1937; s. Robert Gerald McCracken and Martha Lucile (Grice) Foster; m. Susan Shihadeh Cline, June 24, 1967 (div. Oct. 1974); 1 child, Bambi Michelle McCracken Metscher. BA in Psychology, U. Colo., 1962, MA in Anthropology, 1965, PhD in Anthropology, 1968; postgrad., Washington U., St. Louis, 1972. Instr. extension ctr. U. Colo., Grand Junction, 1965; instr. dept. anthropology Met. State Coll., Denver, 1966; instr. Colo. Women's Coll., Denver, 1966-67; asst. prof. anthropology Calif. State U., Long Beach, 1968-69; asst. prof. Memphis State U., 1976-78; asst. prof. Sch. Pub. Health UCLA, 1969-71; postdoctoral fellow dept. psychology Washington U., St. Louis, 1971-72; freelance writer, 1972-74; dir. rsch. Colo. Migrant Coun., Denver, 1974-76; asst. prof. U. Tenn., Knoxville, 1978-79; ind. social sci. cons. RDM Assocs., Las Vegas, 1980—; rsch. and field experience at Navajo Urban Relocation Project, U. Colo., Boulder, 1964-67, Navajo Reservation, summers, 1966-71; cons., researcher, presenter in field; dir. rsch. and new programs Colo. Migrant Coun., 1974-75. Contbr. articles to profl. publs. Mem. Nev. Town History Project, Nye County, 1987-96; active with Sioux, Ute, Hopi, Shoshoni, Navajo Native Ams., 1965—, with migrant farmworkers, Colo., 1974-76; educator on sch. nutrition and learning performance West L.A., 1970-71, sci. TV & film prodn., 1986—. Mem. Anthropolical Assn. Avocations: hiking, film research. Home: PO Box 1232 Tonopah NV 89049-1232 Office: 3930 Swenson St Apt 810 Las Vegas NV 89119-7271

MCCRACKEN, STEVEN CARL, lawyer; b. Artesia, Calif., Oct. 29, 1950; s. Glenn A. and Helen V. (Fears) McCracken; m. Susan Lee Waggener, July 29, 1979; children: Casey James, Scott Kevin. BA magna cum laude, U. Calif., Irvine, 1972; JD, U. Va., 1975. Bar: Calif. 1975, U.S. Dist. Ct. (cen. dist.) Calif. 1975, U.S. Ct. Appeals (9th cir.) 1976, U.S. Dist. Ct. (no. dist.) Calif. 1977, D.C. 1979, U.S. Supreme Ct. 1985, U.S. Dist. Ct. (so. dist.) Calif. 1990. Assoc. Gibson, Dunn & Crutcher, L.A., 1975-82; ptnr. Gibson, Dunn & Crutcher, Irvine, Calif., 1983-94; v.p., sec. and gen. counsel Callaway Golf Co., Carlsbad, Calif., 1994-96; exec. v.p., gen. counsel and sec. Callaway Golf Co., Carlsbad, 1996-97, exec. v.p. licensing, chief legal officer, sec., 1997—; lawyer rep. Ninth Cir. Jud. Conf., 1989-91. Editor Va. Law Rev., 1973-75, mng. bd. 1974-75, bd. editors The Computer Lawyer, 1984-96. Mem. ABA (antitrust sect.), Orange County Bar Assn. (bd. dirs. 1988-90, chmn. fed. ct. com. 1988-89, chmn. bus. litigation sect. 1990, sec. 1991, treas. 1992, pres.-elect 1993, pres. 1994). Democrat. Office: Callaway Golf Co 2285 Rutherford Rd Carlsbad CA 92008-8814

MCCRACKEN, THOMAS JAMES, JR., lawyer; b. Chgo., Oct. 27, 1952; s. Thomas J. Sr. and Eileen (Brophy) McC.; m. Peggy A. Jamrok; children: Catherine, Michael, Amanda, Quinn. BA, Marquette U., 1974; JD, Loyola U., 1977. Bar: Ill. 1977, U.S. Dist. Ct. (no. dist.) Ill., U.S. Ct. Appeals (7th cir.) 1984. Asst. state's atty. DuPage County State's Atty.'s Office, Wheaton, Ill., 1977-81; assoc. atty. McCracken & Walsh, Chgo., 1981-84; ptnr. McCracken, Walsh deLaVan & Hetler, Chgo., 1984—; commr. Nat. Conf. of Commns. on Uniform State Laws, 1989—; bd. dirs. Oak Trust and Savs. Bank, Chgo. Contbr. articles to profl. jours. State rep. Ill. Gen. Assembly, Springfield, Ill., 1983-93, state senator, 1993; chmn. Regional Trans. Authority, Chgo., 1993—. Named Top Ten Legislators Chgo. Mag., 1990. Mem. Chgo. Bar Assn., Ill. State Bar Assn. Avocations: skiing, fishing, hunting, coaching children's sports. Office: McCracken Walsh de-LaVan & Hetler 134 N La Salle St Ste 600 Chicago IL 60602-1004

MCCRADY, JAMES DAVID, veterinarian, educator; b. Beaumont, Tex., June 26, 1930; s. James Homer and Lucyle (Ward) McC.; m. Mary Elizabeth McDougald, Sept. 8, 1951; children—David, Diane, Darla. B.S., Tex. A. and M. Coll., 1952, D.V.M., 1958; Ph.D., Baylor U., 1965. Instr., then asst. prof. Tex. A. and M. Coll., 1958-62; dir. animal rsch., instr. Baylor U. Coll. Medicine, 1962-64; mem. faculty Tex A&M U., 1964—; prof., head dept. vet. physiology and pharmacology Tex. A. and M. Coll., 1966-90, prof., dir. spl. programs, 1990—; dir. Russian-Am. Tng. Partnership, 1995—; adj. prof. Baylor Coll., Medicine, M.D. Anderson Hosp. and Tumor Inst. Served with USAF, 1952-54. Mem. AVMA, Tex. Acad. Sci., Am. Physiol. Soc., Sigma Xi, Phi Kappa Phi, Phi Zeta. Research on comparative cardiovascular and respiratory physiology. Home: 511 Olive St Bryan TX 77801-3506 Office: Tex A&M U College Station TX 77843

MCCRAE, KEITH R., medical educator, researcher; b. Springfield, Mass., Dec. 4, 1956; m. Jo Ann; children: Brett, Kristen Ann. BA in Biochemistry summa cum laude, Dartmouth Coll., 1978; MD, Duke U., 1982. Diplomate Am. Bd. Internal Medicine, Am. Bd. Med. Oncology, Am. Bd. Hematology. Resident in internal medicine Duke U. Med. Ctr., Durham, N.C., 1982-85; fellow in hematology and oncology U. Pa., Phila., 1985-89, postdoctoral fellow, 1986-88; co-dir. clin. coagulation lab. U. Pa., 1991-93, dir. clin. coagulation course, 1992-93; rsch. assoc. U. Pa. Sch. Medicine, 1989, lectr. bridge curriculum, 1989-93, asst. prof. medicine, 1990-93, asst. prof. pathology and lab. medicine, 1991-93; lectr. basic curriculum U. Pa. Dental Sch., 1989-92; attending physician Hosp. of U. Pa., 1989-93, Phila. VA Hosp., 1990-93, Temple U. Hosp., 1993—; asst. prof. medicine Temple U. Sch. Medicine, 1993-96, lectr. bridge curriculum, 1993—, assoc. prof. medicine, 1996—; tchg. attending hematology consult svc. U. Pa., 1989-93, tchg. attending hematology oncology inpatient unit, 1992-93; with hematology/oncology outpatient clinic, 1989-93; attending staff mem. hematology consult svc. Temple U. Sch. Medicine, 1993—, attendin staff mem. hematology sickle cell outpatient clinic, 1993—, attending staff mem. gen. internal medicine svc., 1993. Co-author (with M.D. Feldman) Blood: Hemostasis, Transfusion and Alternatives in the Perioperative Period, 1995; jour. reviewer Blood, 1990—, Thrombosis and Haemostasis, 1991—, Annals of Internal Medicine, 1991—, Jour. Biol. Chem., 1992—, Placenta, 1992—, Jour. Exptl. Medicine, 1992—, Platelets, 1992—, Jour. Allergy and Clin. Immunology, 1992—, Cancer Rsch., 1993—, Am. Jour. Hematology, 1993—, Jour. Clin. Oncology, 1994—, Jour. Histochemistry and Cytochemistry, 1994—, Am. Jour. Physiol., 1995—, Thrombosis Rsch., 1995—; contbr. articles to profl. jours., chpts. to books; lectr. in field. Recipient Rsch. award Am. Diabetes Assn., 1995. Mem. AAAS, Am. Heart Assn. (mem. thrombosis coun. 1994—, mem. arteriosclerosclerosis coun. 1994—, mem. southeastern Pa. peer rev. com. B 1995—), Am. Soc. Hematology, Am. Fedn. Clin. Rsch., Phi Beta Kappa. Office: Temple U Sch Medicine Sol Sherry Thrombosis Rsch Ctr 3400 N Broad St Philadelphia PA 19140-5104

MCCRAIN, MICHAEL WILLIAM, accountant, consultant; b. Bklyn., Apr. 25, 1952; s. William Joseph Sr. and Penelope (Malarios) McC.; m. Kathleen Jean O'Donnell, June 9, 1974; children: Michael Walter, Kevin O'Donnell, Christopher William. AS in Computer Sci. with honors, Suffolk County C.C., Selden, N.Y., 1973; BBA in Pub. Acctg. cum laude, Hofstra U., 1975; MS in Bus., Columbia U., 1988. CPA, N.Y. Supervising sr. acct. Peat, Marwick, Mitchell Co., Jericho, N.Y., 1974-79; corp. acctg. mgr. Pall Corp., Glen Gove, N.Y., 1979-81; v.p. CFO North Atlantic Industries, Inc., Hauppauge, N.Y., 1981-88; v.p. fin. Loral Fairchild Sys., Syosset, N.Y., 1988-89; prin. owner, pres. McCrain & Co., Ltd., Smithtown, N.Y., 1989—. Trustee Sachem Schs. Dist., Lake Ronkonkuma, N.Y., 1992-93; v.p. Sachem Athletic Booster Club, Lake Ronkonkuma, 1993-94, pres., 1994-95; vice chairperson Sachem Cmty. Adv. Coun., Lake Ronkonkuma, 1994-95, chairperson, 1995-97. Mem. AICPA, N.Y. Soc. CPAs, Monarch Bus. Group, Beta Gamma Sigma. Avocations: racquetball, skiing, golfing, computers, coaching lacrosse. Office: 1797 Veterans Hwy Ste 12 Central Islip NY 11722-1537

MCCRANK, MICHAEL NEIL, government official; b. Bourlamaque, Que., Can., May 9, 1943; s. Ernest Martin and anna Mary (Amyotte) McC.; married, Aug. 26, 1967; children: Jason, Kelly, Darren, Matthew. BSc, Queen's U., Kingston, Ont., Can., 1966, LLB, 1969. Assoc. Lang, Michener, Toronto, Ont., 1969-73; asst. crown atty. Regional Municipality of Durham, Whitny, Ont., 1973-79; spl. prosecutor Alta. Atty. Gen., Edmonton, Can., 1979-82, dir. spl. prosecutions, 1982-84, asst. dep. min. criminal justice, 1984-90, acting dep., 1989, dep. atty. gen., 1990, dep. min. justice, 1993—; chmn. liaison officers com. Can. Ctr. for Justice. Bd. dirs. Cath. Social Svcs., Edmonton, 1988-92, chmn. bd. dirs., 1992-93; chmn. bd. dirs. Edmonton Cath. Charities, 1994—. Recipient Commemorative medal for 125th Anniversary of Confedn. Can., 1992. Office: Alta Justice Dept, Bowker Bldg 9833 109th St 2d Fl, Edmonton, AB Canada T5K 2E8

MCCRARY, EUGENIA LESTER (MRS. DENNIS DAUGHTRY MCCRARY), civic worker, writer; b. Annapolis, Md., Mar. 23, 1929; d. John Campbell and Eugenia (Potts) Lester; m. John Campbell Howard, July 15, 1955 (dec. Sept. 1965); m. Dennis Daughtry McCrary, June 28, 1969; 1 child, Dennis Campbell. AB cum laude, Radcliffe Coll.-Harvard U., 1950; MA, Johns Hopkins U., 1952; postgrad., Harvard U., 1953, Pa. State U., 1953-54, Drew U., 1957-58, Inst. Study of USSR, Munich, 1964. Grad. asst. dept. Romance langs. Pa. State U., 1953-54; tchr. dept. math. The Brearley Sch., N.Y.C., 1954-57; dir. Sch. Langs., Inc., Summit, N.J., 1958-69; trustee Sch. Langs., Inc., Summit, 1960-69. Co-author: Nom de Plume: Eugenia Campbell Lester, (with Allegra Branson) Frontiers Aflame, 1987. Dist. dir. Ea. Pa. and N.J. auditions Met. Opera Nat. Coun., N.Y.C., 1960-66, dist. dir. publicity, 1966-67, nat. vice chmn. publicity, 1967-71, nat. chmn. public rels., 1972-75, hon. nat. chmn. pub. rels., 1976—; bd. govs., chmn. Van Cortlandt House Mus., 1985-90. Mem. Nat. Soc. Colonial Dames Am. (bd. mgrs. N.Y. 1985-90), Met. Opera Nat. Coun., Soc. Mayflower Desc. (former bd. dirs. N.Y. soc., chmn. house com. 1986-89), Soc. Daus. Holland Dames (bd. dirs. 1982-87, 3d directress gen. 1987-92, directress gen. 1992-96), L'Eglise du St.-Esprit (vestry 1985-88, sr. warden 1988-90), Huguenot Soc. Am. (governing coun. 1984-90, asst. treas. 1990-91, sec. 1991-95, 2d v.p. 1995—), Colonial Dames Am., Daus. of Cin., Colony Club (bd. govs. 1988-96). Republican. Episcopalian. Home: 24 Central Park S New York NY 10019-1629

MCCRAW, LESLIE G., engineering and construction company executive; b. Sandy Springs, S.C., Nov. 3, 1934; s. Leslie Gladstone and Cornelia (Milam) McC.; m. Mary Earle Brown; children: Leslie Gladstone III, James B., John. BSCE, Clemson U., 1956. Registered profl. engr., Del. Design engr. Gulf Oil Corp., Phila., 1956-57; various engrng. and constrn. positions E.I. DuPont Co., Wilmington, Del., 1960-75; v.p., mgr. div. Daniel Constrn. Co., Greenville, S.C., 1975-82, pres., 1982-84; pres., chief exec. officer Daniel Internat., Greenville, 1984-86, Fluor Daniel, Greenville and Irvine, Calif., 1986-88; pres. Fluor Corp., Irvine, 1988-90, vice chmn., chief exec. officer, 1990-91, chief exec. officer, chmn. bd. dirs., 1991—. Bd. dirs. Allergan, N.Y. Life Ins. Co., U.S.-China Bus. Coun.; trustee Hampden-Sydney Coll., Va.; adv. bd. rsch. found., pres.'s adv. coun. Clemson U.; bd. visitors U. Calif. Grad. Sch. Mgmt.; internat. adv. bd. Br.-Am. Bus. Coun. Mem. NAM (bd. dirs.), Bus. Roundtable, Constrn. Industy's Presidents' Forum, Calif. Bus. Roundtable, Palmetto Bus. Forum, Pres.'s Export Coun. Republican. Presbyterian. Office: Fluor Corp Inc 3333 Michelson Dr Irvine CA 92612

MCCRAW, THOMAS KINCAID, business history educator, editor, author; b. Corinth, Miss., Sept. 11, 1940; s. John Carey and Eugenia Olive (Kincaid) McC.; m. Susan Morehead, Sept. 22, 1962; children: Elizabeth Morehead, Thomas Kincaid Jr. BA, U. Miss., 1962; MA, U. Wis., 1968, Ph.D., 1970; MA (hon.), Harvard U., 1978. Tchg. asst. U. Wis., Madison, 1968-69; asst. prof. U. Tex., Austin, 1970-74, assoc. prof., 1974-78; vis. assoc. prof. Bus. Sch., Harvard U., Boston, 1976-78, prof., 1978-89, Straus prof. bus. history, 1989—; dir. research Bus. Sch., Harvard U., 1985-87, co-chmn. bus. govt. and internat. economy unit, 1986-97; ednl. cons. to cos., U.S., Japan, 1977-95. Author: Morgan versus Lilienthal, 1970, TVA and the Power Fight, 1971, Prophets of Regulation, 1984; co-author: Management Past and Present, 1996, Creating Modern Capitalism, 1997; editor: Regulation in Perspective, 1981, American Versus Japan, 1986, The Essential Alfred Chandler, 1988; editor: Bus. History Rev., 1994—; contbr. numerous articles to various publs., chpts. to books. Trustee Bus. History Conf., 1986-95, pres., 1989;

mem. coun. Mass. Hist. Soc., 1987-92. Lt. USN, 1962-66. Recipient Lyons Master's Essay award Loyola U., Chgo., 1969, Younger Humanist award NEH, 1975, Pulitzer prize in history Columbia U., 1985, Thomas Newcomen Book award, 1986; Woodrow Wilson fellow, 1966-67; named to Alumni Hall of Fame, U. Miss., 1986; Newcomen fellowship Harvard U., 1973-74. Mem. Orgn. Am. Historians, Econ. Hist. Assn., Am. Econ. Assn. Democrat. Roman Catholic. Office: Harvard U Bus Sch Soldiers Field Boston MA 02163

MCCRAY, CURTIS LEE, university president; b. Wheatland, Ind., Jan. 29, 1938; s. Bert and Susan McCray; m. Mary Joyce Macdonald, Sept. 10, 1960; children: Leslie, Jennifer, Meredith. B.A., Knox Coll., Galesburg, Ill., 1960; postgrad. U. Pa., 1960-61; Ph.D., U. Nebr., 1968. Chmn. dept. English, Saginaw Valley Coll., University Center, Mich., 1972-73, dean arts and scis., 1973-75, v.p. acad. affairs, 1975-77; provost, v.p. acad. affairs Govs. State U., Chgo., 1977-82; pres. U. North Fla., Jacksonville, 1982-88, Calif. State U., Long Beach, 1988-93, Millikin U., Decatur, Ill., 1993—. Bd. dirs., 1982-88, campaign chmn. Jacksonville United Way, 1987; bd. dirs. Sta. WJCT Channel 7 and Stereo 90, Jacksonville, 1982-88, Jacksonville Art Mus., 1983-88, Meml. Med. Ctr., Jacksonville, 1983-88, Jacksonville Community Council, Inc., 1982-88, Arts Assembly Jacksonville, 1984-88, Jacksonville Urban League, 1985-88; hon. dir. Jacksonville Symphony Assn., 1983; mem. Dame Point Bridge Commn., Jacksonville, 1982; mem. Jacksonville High Tech Task Force, 1982; chmn. SUS High Tech. and Industry Council, 1986-88; mem. state relations and undergrad. edn. com. Am. Assn. State Colls. and Univs., 1985-88. Woodrow Wilson fellow, 1960; Johnson fellow, 1966; George F. Baker scholar, 1956; Ford Found. grantee, 1969; recipient Landee award for excellence in teaching Saginaw State Coll., 1972. Mem. AAUP. Club: Torch. Office: Millikin U 1184 W Main St Decatur IL 62522-2039*

MCCRAY, RICHARD ALAN, astrophysicist, educator; b. L.A., Nov. 24, 1937; s. Alan Archer and Ruth Elizabeth (Woodworth) McC.; m. Sandra Broomfield; children: Julia, Carla. BS, Stanford U., 1959; PhD, UCLA, 1967. Rsch. fellow Calif. Inst. Tech, Pasadena, 1967-68; asst. prof. astronomy Harvard U., Cambridge, Mass., 1968-71; assoc. prof. astrophysics U. Colo., Boulder, 1971-75, prof., 1975—, chmn. Joint Inst. Lab. Astrophysics, 1981-82, chmn. Ctr. for Astrophysics and Space Astronomy, 1985-86; prof. astronomy Nanjing (China) U., 1996—. Contbr. articles to profl. jours. Guggenheim fellow, 1975-76. Mem. NAS, Am. Astron. Soc. (councilor 1980-83, chmn. high energy astrophysics div. 1986-87, Heineman Prize for Astrophysics, 1990), Internat. Astron. Union. Office: U Colo Joint Inst Lab Astrophysics Boulder CO 80309-0440

MCCREADY, KENNETH FRANK, past electric utility executive; b. Edmonton, Alta., Can., Oct. 9, 1939; s. Ralph and Lilian McCready; m. Margaret E. Randall, Sept. 2, 1961; children: John, Janet, Brian. BSc, U. Alta., 1963. Supr. data processing and systems Calgary (Alta.) Power Ltd., 1965-67, supr. rates and contracts, 1967-68, adminstrv. asst. to exec. v.p., 1968-72, asst. mgr. mgmt. cons. div., 1972-75; mgr. mgmt. systems dept., gen. mgr. Montreal Engring. Co., Calgary, 1975-76; v.p. adminstrn. Calgary (Alta.) Power Ltd., 1976-80; sr. v.p. ops. TransAlta Utilities, Calgary, 1980-85, pres., COO, 1985-89, also bd. dirs., 1988-96; pres., CEO TransAlta Corp., 1989-96; CEO TransAlta Energy Corp., 1989-96; pres. K. F. McCready & Assocs. Ltd., Calgary; bd. dirs. PanCan. Petroleum Ltd., Hewlett Packard (Can.) Ltd., ABB Asea Brown Boveri Environment adv. bd., Aurich, Marigold Found. Ltd., Exergy, Inc., San Francisco, Tech. Devel. Corp., Toronto, Computer Modelling Group, Calgary, Internat. Inst. Sustainable Devel., Winnipeg; past chmn. Conf. Bd. Can.; past chmn. bd. Advanced Computing Techs., Inc.; mem. Dow Chem. Corp. Adv. Coun., Midland, Tata Energy Rsch. Inst. adv. bd., Washington. Past dep. chmn. bd. govs. So. Alta. Inst. Tech.; past chair Alta. Round Table on Environment and Econ.; past mem. com. on trade and environment Govt. Can. Internat. Trade Adv.; past pres. Western Electric Power and Light Assn. Mem. Assn. Profl. Engrs., Geologists and Geophysicists of Alta., Ranchmen's Club. Avocations: computers, cycling, photography.

MC CREARY, JAMES FRANKLIN, lawyer, mediator; b. Farmington, Mo., June 15, 1942; s. Frank J. and Bernice E. (Dugal) McCreary; m. Martha Jean Tucker, June 30, 1962; children: James Franklin, III, Jason Tucker, Josh Adam. BSBA, U. Evansville, 1964; JD, Nashville Law Sch., 1969; MBA, Vanderbilt U., 1980. Bar: Tenn. 1969. With Old Nat. Bank, Evansville, Ind., 1960-64; with First Am. Corp., Nashville, 1972-80, exec. v.p., corp. sec., gen. counsel, 1974-80; with First Am. Nat. Bank Nashville (N.A.), 1964-72, 80-86, exec. v.p., 1980-86; ptnr. Borod & Huggins Attys., Memphis, 1986-87; ptnr. Gerrish & Mc Creary, Memphis, 1988, of counsel, 1988-92, dir., 1993—; pres. Met. Fed. Bank, 1988-91; vis. prof. bus. law David Lipscomb U., 1975-77; instr. law and banking Am. Inst. Banking, 1969-75. Mem. Beta Gamma Sigma. Mem. Ch. of Christ. Office: Gerrish & Mc Creary PC 222 2nd Ave N Nashville TN 37201-1649

MCCREDIE, JAMES ROBERT, fine arts educator; b. Chgo., Dec. 31, 1935; s. William and Mareta (Black) McC.; m. Marian Lucille Miles, Sept. 3, 1960; children: Miles William, Meredeth Black. AB in History and Literature summa cum laude, Harvard U., 1958, AM, 1961, PhD, 1963; student, Am. Sch. Classical Studies, Athens, Greece, 1958-59, 61-62. Instr. NYU, 1963-64, asst. prof., 1965-66, assoc. prof., 1967-70, prof., 1970, 78-88, Sherman Fairchild Prof. Fine Arts, 1988—, dep. dir. Inst. Fine Arts, 1967-69, acting dir., 1982-83, dir., 1983—, asst. field dir. Excavations in Samothrace, 1962, field dir., 1963-65, dir. excavations, 1966—; dir. Am. Sch. Classical Studies at Athens, Greece, 1969-77, chmn. mng. com., 1980-90, trustee, 1980—; vis. mem. Inst. Advanced Study, Princeton, N.J., 1977-78; mem. vis. com. dept. classical and near eastern Archeology Bryn Mayr Coll., 1982, dept. european paintings Met. Mus. Art, 1983—, Ctr. Old World Archaeology and Art Brown U., Providence, 1985; mem. adv. bd. Alexander S. Onassis Ctr. for Hellenic Studies NYU, 1990—; cons. in field. Author: Fortified Military Camps in Attica, Hesperia, 1966, Samothrace, 7, The Rotunda of Arsinoe, 1992; mem. adv. bd. Am. Jour. Archaeology, 1969-81; contbr. articles to prof. jours.. Bd. dirs. Hellenic-Am. Union, Athens, 1973-77, vice chmn., 1974-77, U.S. Ednl. Found., Greece, 1969-75; active Pres. Adv. Com. on Cultural Property, 1992-95. Charles Norton fellow, 1961-62; named hon. citizen Community of Samothrace, 1976. Mem. Am. Philos. Soc., Archaeol. Inst. Am. (life, trustee 1972-75, mem. exec. com. 1978-81), Archaeol. Soc. Athens (hon.), Deutsches archaeologisches Inst. (corr.). Home: 30 Battle Rd Princeton NJ 08540-4902 also summer: Palaiopolis GR-680 02, Samothrace Greece Office: NYU Inst Fine Arts 1 E 78th St New York NY 10021-0102

MCCREE, DONALD HANNA, JR., banker; b. Orange, N.J., Sept. 17, 1936; s. Donald Hanna and Elna (Van Houten) McC.; m. Patricia H. Jones, June 13, 1959; children: Donald, Douglas, David. A.B., Dartmouth Coll., 1958. With Mfrs. Hanover Trust Co., N.Y.C., 1960-90; sr. v.p., mgr. Mfrs. Hanover Trust Co. (London br.), 1976-78; sr. v.p., dep. gen. mgr. Mfrs. Hanover Trust Co., N.Y.C., 1978-79, sector exec. v.p. corp. banking, mem. gen. adminstrv. bd., 1980-90; pres., CEO IBJ Schroder Bank and Trust Co., N.Y.C., 1995-96, vice chmn., 1996—. Served with USNR, 1958-60. Mem. Bankers Roundtable, Am. Bankers Assn. (exec. com. comml. lending div.), United Way of N.Y.C. (bd.of dirs.). Club: Whippoorwill, Loblolly. Office: IBJ Schroder Bank & Trust Co 1 State Ste New York NY 10004

MCCREE, PAUL WILLIAM, JR., systems design and engineering company executive; b. St. Louis, Oct. 27, 1926; s. Paul William and Hazel Elfrieda (Wilson) McC.; m. Carolyn Williams, Sept. 7, 1955; children—Brian, Paula, Ross. B.S. in Biochem. Scis., Harvard U., 1950. Mem. tech. staff System Devel. Corp., Santa Monica, Calif., 1956-62, Mitre Corp., Bedford, Mass., 1966-67; prin. engr., equipment div. Raytheon Co., Sudbury, Mass., 1963-66, 67-72; mem. tech. staff MIT Lincoln Labs., Lexington, 1972-76; mgr. Aerospace Systems div. Input Output, Waltham, Mass., 1976-79, tech. dir., 1979-80; mem. tech. staff Mitre Corp., Bedford, Mass., 1980-82; founder, pres. BPR Co., profl. cons. services (sci., engring. and bus. applications of computers), 1981—; sr. mem. tech. staff, mgr. subsystem design and devel. dept. GTE Strategic Systems Div., 1982-84; tech. dir. HH Aerospace and Design Co. Inc., Bedford, 1984-86; prin. engr., mem. tech. staff Raytheon Equipment div. Software Systems Lab., Sudbury, 1986-87; v.p. HH Aerospace and Design Co. Inc., Bedford, 1986-91. Mem. NAACP, Urban League. Served with U.S. Army, 1944. Recipient Black Achiever award Greater Boston YMCA, 1977. Mem. AAAS, IEEE, Math. Assn. Am., Am. Math. Soc., N.Y. Acad. Scis. Democrat. Club: Harvard (Concord); Harvard Faculty (Cambridge). Home: 173 Goodman's Hill Rd PO Box 77 Sudbury MA 01776-0077

MCCREERY, WILLIAM See **RAMSEY, BILL**

MCCREIGHT, JOHN A., management consultant; b. Phila., Jan. 29, 1938; s. John A. and Marion R. (Vetter) McC.; m. Kim Amet Healey; children: Laura, Cindy, Brian, Kimberly. BS in Mgmt. Scis., Northeastern U., 1968. Cert. mgmt. cons. Chief systems devel. AVCO Apollo Systems, Boston, 1964-68; sr. mgmt. cons. Touche, Ross & Co., Detroit, 1968-72, ptnr., Detroit and N.Y.C., 1972-80, nat. dir., mem. exec. com., N.Y.C., 1980-83 mng. dir. Hayes Hill, N.Y.C., 1983; pres. McCreight & Co., Inc. New Canaan, Conn. and Phila., 1983-86; mng. dir. Hay Group, Inc., N.Y.C., 1986-91; pres. McCreight & Co., Inc., New Canaan and Wilton, Conn., 1991—; mem. Presdl. Task Force to Reduce Cost and Improve Effectiveness of USN; dir., officer dep. sec. def. Inst. Mgmt. Cons. Adv. Carnegie Hall Bd. Trustees, NIH, N.Y. Mayor's Office, Salvation Army; past chmn. N.Y. Corp. Fund Raising, NIMH; mem. N.Y. Ireland U.S. Coun.; Served with USNR, 1955-63. Mem. Univ. Club (N.Y.C.). Office: McCreight & Co Inc 487 Danbury Rd Wilton CT 06897-2126

MCCREIGHT, ROBERT EDWIN, federal agency administrator, educator; b. Phila., Jan. 27, 1948; s. Samuel Edwin and Mae (Muffett) McC.; m. Eileen Rose Mellert, June 16, 1973; children: Brian Douglas, David Carter, Adrienne Eileen. BS in History, West Chester U., 1969; MPA, George Washington U., 1978; PhD in Pub. Adminstrn., George Mason U., 1989. Officer employee rels. NIH/HHS, 1978-82; program dir., pers. mgmt. tng. ctr. Office Pers. Mgmt., 1982-84; dep. dir. labor rels. staff USIA, 1984-86; program officer office mgmt. systems and programs, br. mgmt. U.S. Dept. State, Washington, 1986-90, staff analyst polit./mil. affairs br. intelligence and rsch., 1990-91, liaison officer office def. trade controls, br. politico/mil. affairs, 1991-92, project officer office of internat. security ops., br. politico/mil. affairs, 1992-93, treaty officer office arms control compliance and implementation, br. politico/mil. affairs, 1993, policy analyst office exec. dir., br. intelligence and rsch., 1993—; program officer Pol-Mil/WMD Issues Bureau of Intelligence & Rsch., 1997—. Maj. USAR, 1987-94. Mem. Am. Soc. Pub. Adminstrn., Internat. City Mgmt. Assn., Internat. Pers. Mgmt. Assn., Ctr. Study of Presidency. Home: 8624 Cromwell Dr Springfield VA 22151-1209 Office: US Dept State INR/PMA 21st & C St NW Washington DC 20540

MCCRENSKY, EDWARD, international consultant, former organization executive; b. Boston, June 19, 1912; s. Benjamin and Anna (Miller) McC.; m. Louise C. Marshall, Apr. 16, 1942; children: Myron Wilson, Richard Marshall. B.A., Boston Coll., 1933; M.Ed., Boston Tchrs. Coll., 1935; student, Harvard Grad. Sch. Edn., 1940-41. High sch. tchr. Boston, 1936-41; govt. ofcl. U.S. Civil Service Commn., 1941-46; dir. civilian personnel and service Office Naval Research, Washington, 1946-66; chief personnel adminstrn. dept. social and econ. affairs UN, N.Y.C., 1966-68; inter-regional adviser UN, 1968-77; team leader UN, Bangkok, Thailand, 1977-81; internat. cons., 1981—; prof. George Washington U., 1950-68; guest prof. Royal Coll. Sci. and Tech., Strathclyde U., Glasgow, Scotland, 1961; cons. U.S. and internat. orgns.; lectr. human relations and internat. sci. manpower. Author: Wartime Practices in Recruitment, 1946, Scientific Manpower in Europe, 1959, Strategy and Tactics, Professional Recruitment, 1963; Contbr. articles U.S. fgn. jours. Recipient Rockefeller Pub. Service award and fellowship, 1957; Merit citation Nat. Civil Service League, 1955; Distinguished Civilian Service award Navy Dept., 1966. Mem. Soc. Pers. Adminstrn. (pres. 1955-56), Rotary (bd. dirs. Surfside club 1986-89, Paul Harris fellow). Home: 614 7th Ave N Surfside Beach SC 29575-4104 *I have always sought to broaden my experience in work, geographical location and cultural differences by accepting available opportunities for personal growth. I have constantly tried to prepare myself through research, planning, and authorship for improved professional capability.*

MCCRERY, DAVID NEIL, III, lawyer; b. Ames, Iowa, Mar. 7, 1957; s. David Neil Jr. and Judith Ann (Purlee) McC.; m. Katherine Marie Meridith, June 9, 1979; children: Evelyn Judith, David Neil IV. BS in Agr., U. Ill., 1979; JD, So. Ill. U., Carbondale, 1993. Bar: Ill. 1993, U.S. Dist. (ctrl. dist.) Ill. 1993. Dist. mgr. Ralston Purina Co., St. Louis, 1979-83; farmer, businessman McCrery Farms, Monmouth, Ill., 1984-90; grad. rsch. asst. So. Ill. U. Sch. Law, 1991-93; pvt. practice Law Offices David N. McCrery, III, Galesburg, Ill., 1993—. Assoc. del. U.S.-Can. Gt. Lakes Conf., 1984; assoc. bd. dirs. Warren County Soil and Water Dist., Monmouth, 1986; bd. dirs. West Ctrl. Ill. Legal Assistance, 1996—, Head Start Ops. for Presch. Edn.-HOPE, 1996—, Galesburg Youth Athletic Club, 1994—; mem. Ill. Agr. Leadership Program, 1986, 87; judge Teen Ct., Knox County, 1996—. Recipient Outstanding State Dir. award Monmouth Jaycees, 1988. Mem. Knox County Bar Assn. Methodist. Avocations: hunting, fishing, collecting antiques, travel, mission work. Home: 105 N Carlysle Ave Abingdon IL 61410-1403 Office: 311 E Main St Ste 511 Galesburg IL 61401-4834

MCCRERY, JAMES (JIM MCCRERY), congressman; b. Shreveport, LA, Sept. 18, 1949; m. Johnette Hawkins, Aug. 3, 1991; children: Claiborne Scott, Otis Clark. BA, La. Tech. U., 1971; JD, La. State U., 1975. Bar: La. 1975. Pvt. practice Leesville, La., 1975-78; asst. city atty. City of Shreveport, 1979-80; mem. staff U.S. Rep. Buddy Roemer, 1981-84; regional mgr. Ga.-Pacific Corp., 1984-88; mem. 100th-103rd Congresses from 4th (now 5th) La. dist., 1988—; mem. ways and means com. Office: US Ho of Reps 2104 Rayburn Bldg Washington DC 20515

MC CRIE, ROBERT DELBERT, editor, publisher, educator; b. Sarnia, Ont., Can., Oct. 8, 1938; s. Robert Newton and Evelyn May (Johnston) McC.; m. Fulvia Madia, Dec. 22, 1965; children: Carla Alexandra, Mara Elizabeth. B.A., Ohio Wesleyan U., 1960; M.S., U. Toledo, 1964; postgrad., U. Chgo., 1962-63; MA, Hunter Coll., 1994; MPhil, CUNY, 1994, PhD, 1995. Cert. protection profl. Researcher Connective Tissues Research Lab., Copenhagen, 1963; copywriter numerous advt. agys., 1965-70; owner, editor Security Letter, N.Y.C., 1970—; editor, pub. HBJ Publs., N.Y.C., 1973-76; pres. Mags. for Medicine, Inc., N.Y.C., 1972-81; faculty John Jay Coll. Criminal Justice, 1985—, asst. prof., 1986-91, assoc. prof., 1992—; bd. dirs. numerous cos.; cons. in field; speaker at numerous meetings. Editor: Behavioral Medicine, 1978-81, Security Letter Source Book, 1983—, Security Jour., 1989—; contbr. books and articles on security and urban crime and policing. Mem. AAUP, Am. Hist. Assn., Am. Correctional Assn., Am. Soc. Indsl. Security (pres.'s cert. of merit 1990), Nat. Coun. Investigation and Security Svcs. (Duffy Meml. Achievement award 1992), Internat. Security Mmgt. Assn. (Brennan award 1993), Urban History Assn., Internat. Assn. of Profl. Security Cons. Disting. Svc., Accolade, Union League Club, Alpha Tau Omega, Delta Sigma Rho, Pi Delta Epsilon. Presbyterian (deacon). Home: 49 E 96th St New York NY 10128-0782 Office: 166 E 96th St New York NY 10128-2565 also: John Jay Coll Criminal Justice 899 10th Ave New York NY 10019-1029

MCCRIMMON, JAMES MCNAB, language educator; b. Renton, Scotland, June 16, 1908; came to U.S., 1929, naturalized, 1939; s. John and Margaret (Patterson) McCrimmon; m. Barbara Smith, June 10, 1939; children: Kevin M., John M. B.A., Northwestern U., 1932, M.A., 1933, Ph.D., 1937. Asst. instr. English, Northwestern U., 1935; instr. English, U. Toledo, 1936-38, asst. prof., 1938-43, asso. prof., 1943-47; faculty U. Ill., 1947—, chmn. humanities div. Galesburg extension, 1947-49; asso. prof. humanities U. Ill., Urbana, 1949-55, prof., 1955-65; prof. emeritus U. Ill., 1965—, head div. gen. studies, 1954-62, dir. U. High Sch. English project, 1962—; vis. prof. English Fla. State U., 1967-70, lectr., 1970-78. Author: (with MacMinn and Hainds) Bibliography of the Writings of John Stuart Mill, 1945, Writing with a Purpose, 1950, Open Door to Education, (with Louttit and Habberton), 1951, From Source to Statement, 1968. Mem. Nat. Council Tchrs. English, College Conf. Composition and Communication, Phi Kappa Phi. Home: 1330 W Indianhead Dr Tallahassee FL 32301-4763

MCCROHON, CRAIG, lawyer; b. Harvey, Ill., Oct. 17, 1961; s. Maxwell and Nancy McCrohon. BA, Harvard U., 1984, London Sch. Econs., 1988; JD, U. Pa., 1989, MBA, 1989. Bar: Ill. 1989, U.S. Dist. Ct. (no. dist.) Ill. 1989. With Winston & Strawn, Chgo., 1989-91; assoc. Freeborn & Peters, Chgo., 1991—. Editor: Let's Go: USA, 1983. Mem. strategic planning com. Econ. Devel. Commn. City of Chgo., 1991; mem. Cook County Transition Team-Econ. Devel., 1995. Mem. Ill. C. of C. (working group econ. devel. com.), Chgo. Bar Assn. (chmn. com. consumer fin. svcs. 1991-92), Cook County Bar Assn., Bus. Execs. for Econs. Justice (exec. com.), Alliance of Bus. Brokers and Intermediaries (mem. bd. dirs.), Tech. Execs. Roundtable (mem. bd. dirs.), Com. to Lower Utility Bills (chmn. 1984), Dem. Leadership for the Twenty-First Century (mem. bd. dirs. 1993-95), Phi Alpha Delta. Home: 200 E Chestnut St Apt 907 Chicago IL 60611-2317 Office: Freeborn & Peters 311 S Wacker Dr Chicago IL 60606-6627

MCCRONE, ALISTAIR WILLIAM, university president; b. Regina, Can., Oct. 7, 1931. BA, U. Sask., 1953; MSc, U. Nebr., 1955; PhD, U. Kans., 1961. Instr. geology NYU, 1959-61, asst. prof., 1961-64, assoc. prof., 1964-69, prof., 1969-70, supr. Rsch. Ship Sea Owl on L.I. Sound, 1959-64; asst. dir. univ. program NYU, Sterling Forest, 1965-66; resident master Rubin Internat. Residence Hall NYU, 1966-69, chmn. dept. geology, 1966-69, assoc. dean Grad. Sch. Arts and Scis., 1969-70; prof. geology, acad. v.p. U. Pacific, 1970-74, acting pres., 1971; prof. geology, pres. Calif. State U. Sys. Humboldt State U., Arcata, 1974—; mem. sys. exec. coun. Calif. State U. Sys., 1974—, acad. senate Humboldt State U., 1974—, mem. chancellor's com. on innovative programs, 1974-76, trustees' task force on off-campus instrn., 1975-76, presdl. search com. Sonoma State U., 1976-77, exec. com. Chancellor's Coun. of Pres., 1976-79, Presdl. search com. Calif. State U., Chico, 1979-80, adv. group. exec. coun., 1980-81; Calif. state del. Am. Assn. State Colls. and Univs., 1977-80; mem. Commn. on Ednl. Telecomm., 1983-86; chair Calif. State U. Statewide Task Force on Earthquake and Emergency preparedness, 1985-88, 95; chmn., mem. accreditation teams Western Assn. Schs. and Colls.; mem. western sect. Am. Coun. Edn. Adminstrv. Intern Selection Panel, 1973; chair com. on energy and environ. Am. Assn. State Colls. and Univs., 1980-84; chair program com. Western Coll.Assn., 1983-84, panelist, 1983; mem. bd. dirs. Assn. Am. Colls., 1989-93, chair, 1992-93. Contbr. articles to profl. jours.; lectr. on geology Sunrise Semester program CBS Nat. Network, 1969-70; various appearances on local TV stas. Bd. trustees Presbyn. Hosp.-Pacific Med. Ctr., San Francisco, 1971-74; mem. Calif. Coun. for Humanities, 1977-82; mem. local campaign bd. United Way, 1977-83; mem. Am. Friends Wilton Park, 1980—; bd. dirs. Humboldt Convention and Visitors Bur., 1980-87, Redwood Empire Assn., 1983-87; bd. dirs. Calif. State Automobile Assn., 1988—, Am. Automobile Assn., 1990-93; bd. trustees Calif. State Parks Found., 1994—. Shell fellow in geology U. Nebr., 1954-55; Danforth assoc. NYU, 1964. Fellow Calif. Acad. Scis.; mem. AAAS, Geol. Soc. Am., Am. Assn. U. Adminstrs. (nat. bd. 1986-89, 96—), Rotary, St. Andrews Soc. N.Y. (life), Sigma Xi (pres. NYU chpt. 1967-69), Phi Kappa Phi. Avocation: golf. Office: Humboldt State U Univ Campus Arcata CA 95521

MCCRONE, WALTER COX, research institute executive; b. Wilmington, Del., June 9, 1916; s. Walter Cox and Bessie Lillian (Cook) McC.; m. Lucy Morris Beman, July 13, 1957. B Chemistry, Cornell U., 1938, PhD, 1942. Microscopist, sr. scientist Armour Research Found., Ill. Inst. Tech., Chgo., 1944-56; chmn. bd. Walter C. McCrone Assos. Inc., Chgo., 1956-81; sr. research advisor Walter C. McCrone Assos. Inc., 1956-78; pres. McCrone Research Inst., Inc., 1961-94, chmn. bd., 1961-66, emeritus pres. and chmn. bd., 1994—; vis. prof. chem. microscopy Cornell U., 1984—; adj. prof. IIT, 1950—, NYU, 1974—, U. Ill., 1989-95. Author: Fusion Methods in Chemical Microscopy, 1957, The Particle Atlas, 1967, Particle Atlas Two 6 vols., 1973-78, Particle Atlas Three Electronic CD-ROM edit., 1992, Polarized Light Microscopy, 1978, Asbestos Particle Atlas, 1980, Asbestos Identification, 1987, Judgement Day for the Turin Shroud, 1997; editor Microscope Jour., 1962-95; contbr. over 350 articles to profl. jours., chpts. to books. Pres. bd. dirs. Ada S. McKinley Cmty. Svcs., 1962-95, emeritus pres., 1995—; chmn. bd. trustees Vandercook Coll. Music, 1986-95, emeritus pres. 1995—; trustee Campbell Ctr., 1990—. Recipient Benedetti-Pichler award Am. Microchem. Soc., 1970, Anachem award Assn. Analytical Chemists, 1981, cert. of merit Franklin Inst., 1982, Forensic Sci. Found., 1983, Madden Disting. Svc. award Vandercook Coll. Music, 1988, Fortissimo award, 1991, Irving Selikoff award Nat. Asbestos Coun., 1990, Founder's Day award Calif. Assn. Criminalists, 1990, Roger Green award, 1991, Pub. Affairs award Chgo. Pub. Schs., 1993, Disting. Svc. award USAF AFTAC program. Mem. Am. Chem. Soc. (Pub. Affairs award 1993, Disting. Svc. award USAF AFTAC Program 1994), Am. Phys. Soc., Am. Acad. Forensic Sci. (Disting. Svc. award criminalistics sect. 1984), Am. Inst. Conservators Art (hon.), Internat. Inst. Conservators, Australian Micros. Soc., N.Y. Micros. Soc. (hon., Ernst Abbe award 1977), La. Micros. Soc., Can. Micros Soc., Midwest Micros. Soc., Royal Micros Soc. (hon.), Ill. Micros. Soc. (hon.), Quekett Micros. Club, Sigma Xi, Phi Kappa Phi, Phi Lambda Upsilon, Alpha Chi Sigma. Achievements include discovery of highly sensitive polymorphs of HMX and development of a safe prodn. method, improved prodn. method for casting of artillery rounds with TNT; proved the Vinland map to be a modern forgery, 1974, the Turin Shroud to be a medieval painting, 1980; developed the analytical methods for detection and identification of asbestos; first zoning ordinance based on performance stds. instituted in Chgo. Home: 501 E 32nd St Chicago IL 60616-4053 Office: McCrone Rsch Inst 2820 S Michigan Ave Chicago IL 60616-3230

MCCRORY, JOHN BROOKS, retired lawyer; b. St. Cloud, Minn., Oct. 23, 1925; s. John Raymond and Mary Lee (Rutter) McC.; m. Margaret Joan Dickson, Sept. 4, 1954 (dec. Apr. 1957); 1 child, William B.; m. Elizabeth Ann Quick, June 27, 1959; children—John B., Ann Elizabeth. B.A., Swarthmore Coll., 1948; J.D., U. Pa., 1951. Bar: N.Y. 1952, D.C. 1985. Assoc. Donovan, Leisure, Newton, Lumbard & Irvine, N.Y.C., 1951-52; assoc. Nixon, Hargrave, Devans & Doyle, Rochester, N.Y., 1952-62, ptnr., 1963-92; retired, 1992. Author: Constitutional Privilege in Libel Law, 1977-90. Served to lt. comdr. USNR, 1943-47, PTO. Fellow Am. Coll. Trial Lawyers; mem. ABA, Monroe County Bar Assn., N.Y. State Bar Assn., D.C. Bar Assn. Republican. Presbyterian. Home: 210 Whitewood Ln Rochester NY 14618-3226 Office: Nixon Hargrave Devans & Doyle LLP Clinton Sq PO Box 1051 Rochester NY 14603-1051

MCCRORY, PATRICK, mayor; b. Columbus, Oct. 17, 1956; m. Ann Gordon. BA in Polit. Sci. and Edn., Catawba Coll., 1978. With Duke Power Co., N.C., 1978—, now mgr. bus. rels.; mem. Charlotte City Coun., N.C., 1989—, mayor protem, 1993-95, mayor, 1995—. Co-chmn. Charlotte's Fighting Back Commn.; mem. Children Svcs. Network; hon. chmn. Cystic Fibrosis Found., Arthritis Found.; former chmn. United Way Corp. Campaign; former mem. U. N.C.-Charlotte Bus. Adv. Com., Charlotte Bond Campaign, ARC Pers. Recruitment Com.; H.S. basketball ofcl.; former bd. dirs. Drug Free Workplace Alliance Com.; founder Uptown Crime Prevention Coun. Office: Office of the Mayor 600 E 4th St Charlotte NC 28202-2870

MCCRORY, ROBERT LEE, physicist, mechanical engineering educator; b. Lawton, Okla., Apr. 30, 1946; s. Robert Lee Sr. and Marjorie Marie (Garrett) McC.; m. Betsey Christine Wahl, June 14, 1969; children: Katherine Anne, John Damon, George Garrett. BSc, MIT, 1968, PhD, 1973. Physicist Los Alamos Nat. Lab., Albuquerque, 1973-76; scientist, coleader Lab. for Laser Energetics, U. Rochester, N.Y., 1976-77, sr. scientist, 1977—, dir. theoretical dir., 1979-90; dir. Lab. for Laser Energetics, U. Rochester, 1983—; assoc. prof. of physics and astronomy U. Rochester, 1980, prof. of mech. engring., 1983—, exec. dir. of govtl. rels. pres.'s office, 1997—. Author: Laser Plasma Interactions, 1989, Computer Applications in Plasma Science and Engineering, 1991; contbr. articles to profl. publs. Alfred P. Simon scholar, 1964-67; AEC fellow, 1985; recipient Edward Teller medal, 1994. Fellow Am. Phys. Soc. (mem. fellowship com., mem. exec. com. div. plasma physics, Excellence in Plasma Physics award). Office: U Rochester Lab Laser Energetics 250 E River Rd Rochester NY 14623-1212

MC CRORY, WALLACE WILLARD, pediatrician, educator; b. Racine, Wis., Jan. 19, 1920; s. Willard L. and Beulah (St. Clair) McC.; m. Sylvia E. Hogben, Feb. 6, 1943; children—Pamela, Michael, Christine. B.S., U. Wis., 1941, M.D., 1944. Diplomate: Am. Bd. Pediatrics. Rotating intern Phila. Gen. Hosp., 1944-45; resident pediatrics Children's Hosp., Phila., 1945-46; chief resident physician Children's Hosp., 1948-49, asso. pediatrician, 1953-55, sr. pediatrician, 1955-58; provisional asst. pediatrician to out-patients, Lewis Cass Ledyard, Jr. fellow pediatrics N.Y. Hosp., 1949-50, pediatrician-in-chief, 1961-80, sr. pediatrician, chief pediatric nephrology, 1980—; chief pediatric service Univ. Hosp., Iowa City, 1958-61; instr. pathology U. Wis.

Med. Sch., 1942-43; instr. pediatrics U. Pa. Sch. Medicine, 1948-49, instr., research fellow pediatrics, 1950-53, asst. prof., 1953-55, asso. prof., 1955-58; prof. pediatrics, chmn. dept. State U. Iowa Coll. Medicine, 1958-61; prof. pediatrics Cornell U. Med. Coll., 1961—. Pres. Nat. Kidney Found., 1964-66. Served to capt., M.C. AUS, 1946-48. Fellow N.Y. Acad. Medicine, Royal Soc. Medicine; mem. Am. Pediatric Soc., Am. Acad. Pediatrics, Soc. Pediatric Research, Am. Soc. Nephrology, Am. Soc. Pediatric Nephrology, AAAS, Sigma Xi, Alpha Omega Alpha. Home: 171 Salem Rd Pound Ridge NY 10576-1324 Office: NY Hosp Cornell Med Ctr 525 E 68th St New York NY 10021-4873

MCCROSKEY, WILLIAM JAMES, aeronautical engineer; b. San Angelo, Tex., Mar. 9, 1937; s. J. M. and W. Elizabeth McC.; m. Elizabeth W. Wear, Jan. 31, 1960; children: Nancy E., Susan C. BS, U. Tex., 1960; MS, Princeton U., 1962, PhD, 1966. Rsch. assoc. Princeton U., 1966; rsch. engr. U.S. Army Aeromechanics Lab., Moffett Field, Calif., 1966-80; sr. rsch. scientist U.S. Army and NASA Aerophysics Directorate, 1980—; exch. scientist Office Nat. Etudes et Recherches Aérospatiale, Châtillon, France, 1972-73; mem. fluid dynamics panel NATO Adv. Group for Aerospace R & D, 1976-94, chmn., 1989-91. With U.S. Army, 1966-68. Recipient French Medaille l'Aeronautique, 1994, AGARD von Kármán medal, 1995, Nat. Acad. Engring., 1996. Fellow AIAA (Outstanding Engr. San Francisco sect. 1975, fluid dynamics tech com. 1984-88, internat. activities com. 1990—); mem. ASME (Freeman scholar award 1976), Am. Helicopter Soc. (Howard Hughes award 1991). Office: Ames Rsch Ctr N258-1 Moffett Field CA 94035

MCCRYSTAL, ANN MARIE, community health nurse, administrator; b. Jersey City, Jan. 5, 1937; d. Robert W. and Sybilla M. (Koenig) Bouse; m. Hugh K. McCrystal, Sept. 14, 1963; children: Carolyn, Hugh K., Kelly Ann. BSN, U. Miami, 1959. Office mgr., sec.-treas. Indian River Urology Assocs., P.C., Vero Beach, Fla.; chmn. bd. Vis. Nurse Assn. of the Treasure Coast, Vero Beach. Chmn. Vis. Nurse Assn. Treasure Coast Found., 1991, adv. coun. Vis. Nurse Assn. of Am., 1994. Mem. Fla. Nurses Assn., Am. Urol. Assn. Allied, Am. Cancer Soc. (life hon.), Vis. Nurse Assn. Am. (chmn. bd. dirs. 1995—, adv. coun., edn. com., Vol. of Yr. 1991), Sigma Theta Tau. Home: 511 Bay Dr Vero Beach FL 32963-2163

MCCUAIG, IAN CARRUTHERS, fundraising consultant; b. Orillia, Ont., Can., Mar. 5, 1962; came to U.S., 1992; s. Alan Hayes and Elizabeth Louise (Bonnell) McC.; m. Sarah Elizabeth Robertson, July 2, 1994. Student, Royal Conservatory of Music, Toronto, Ont., 1983; BA in Internat. Rels., U. Toronto, 1990; CSPG, Calif. State U., 1997. Cert. specialist planned giving. Devel. cons. UN Assn., Toronto, 1988-89; account exec. Gordon L. Goldie Co., Ltd., Toronto, 1989-92; cons. Marts & Lundy, Inc., San Francisco, 1992-96; sr. dir. Devel. Goodwill, San Francisco, 1996—. Contbr. articles to profl. publs. Nat. sec. Amnesty Internat. Can., Ottawa, Ont., 1986-88; chair human rights com. UN Assn., Toronto, 1988-89; elder Timothy Eaton Meml. Ch., Toronto, 1984-92; deacon Calvary Presbyn. Ch., San Francisco, 1992-96; mem. Dem. Nat. Com. Mem. World Affairs Coun., Nat. Soc. Fundraising Execs. (cert., v.p. Golden Gate chpt., mem. nat. acad.), Internat. Diplomacy Coun., Nat. Com. on Planned Giving Can.-Am. C. of C., St. Francis Yacht Club, Commonwealth Club of Calif. Avocation: sailing. Office: Goodwill 1500 Mission St San Francisco CA 94103-2513

MCCUAN, WILLIAM PATRICK, real estate company executive; b. Muskogee, Okla., Oct. 28, 1941; s. Lee L. and LaRee A. (Beverage) McC.; m. Jill Pamela Thomas, May 5, 1982; children: LaRee, Megan. Student, U. Tulsa, 1961-62; BA in Psychology, Baylor U., 1965; MRE, So. Sem., Louisville, 1967; MS, U. Louisville, 1969; postgrad., U. Md., 1971-73. Prof., asst. dean grad. sch. U. Md., Balt., 1969-73; lobbyist, cons. Washington, 1973-76; chmn. bd. dirs. KMS Group, Inc., Columbia, Md., 1976-84; pres., CEO MDG Cos. of Md., 1985—; CEO MGD Cos. of Naples, Fla., 1992—; chmn. bd. dirs. Tuscasrora Real Estate Corp., Berkeley Springs, W.Va., 1991—; adj. prof. Cmty. Coll., Balt., 1969-72, U. Md. College Park, 1969-71; lectr. Univ. Coll.-Univ. Md., Balt., 1970-71, Howard C.C., Columbia, 1987-88; chmn. Pet Holiday, Inc., Toledo, 1973-94; CEO Uniglobe Columbia Travel Ctr., 1986-94; non-lawyer mem. Atty. Grievance Commn., Md., 1990-96. Contbr. to numerous publs. Chmn., bd. dirs. Concert Soc. Md., 1988—; chmn. United Way, Howard County, Md., 1984, Am. Presdl. Inaugural Com., Md., 1988, Howard County Cmty. Partnerships; fin. chmn. Rep. Ctrl. Com., Howard County, 1988-92; trustee Columbia Found., Howard County; mem. Pres.'s Commn. on Food, Nutrition and Health, Washington, 1970, Howard County Environ. Affairs Bd., Columbia Archives Com.; mem. bus. adv. coun. Howard C.C.; bd. dirs. Congl. Commn. on Mental Health of Children, Washington, 1973-75, Human Svcs. Inst. for Children & Families. Mem. Nat. Assn. Home Builders (bd. dirs. 1979-87, fed. govt. affairs com.), Md. Builders Assn. (pres. 1981-82), Home Builders Assn. Md. (bd. dirs. 1977-82, Award of Honor 1979, Award of Excellence 1980, Presdl. award 1982), Howard County Home Builders Assn. (pres. 1978-80), Howard County C. of C. (pres. bd. dirs. 1984-86). Home: 11838 Farside Rd Ellicott City MD 21042-1526 Office: MDG Bldg 5550 Sterrett Pl Columbia MD 21044-2611

MC CUE, CAROLYN MOORE, retired pediatric cardiologist; b. Richmond, Va., June 26, 1916; d. Thomas Justin and Caroline (Willingham) Moore; m. Howard M. McCue, Jr., Apr. 5, 1941; children—Carolyn McCue Osteen, Howard McDowell. LLB, Wellesley Coll., 1933-35; AB, Leland Stanford U., 1937; MD, Med. Coll. Va., 1941. Intern Wis. Gen. Hosp., Madison, 1941-42; resident in pediatrics Children's Hosp., Phila., 1942-43, Med. Coll. Va., 1946-47; dir. pediatric cardiology Med. Coll. Va., Richmond, 1947-81; prof. pediatrics Med. Coll. Va., 1963-91; clin. dir. pediatric cardiology clinics State of Va., 1958-81. Contbr. articles to profl. jours. Named Va. Laureate, 1982. Fellow Am. Acad. Pediatrics, Am. Coll. Physicians, Am. Coll. Cardiology, A.C.P.; mem. Richmond Acad. Medicine (pres. 1975), Richmond Area Heart Assn. (pres. 1959-60), Phi Beta Kappa, Alpha Omega Alpha. Club: Country of Va. Home: 12 Huntley Rd Richmond VA 23226-3306

MCCUE, GERALD MALLON, architect; b. Woodland, Calif., Dec. 5, 1928; s. Floyd F. and Lenore (Mallon) McC.; m. Barbara Walrond, Sept. 1, 1951; children: Scott, Mark, Kent. BA, U. Calif. at Berkeley, 1951, MA, 1952; MA (hon.), Harvard U., 1977. Ptnr. archtl. firm Milano-McCue, Berkeley, Calif., 1953-54; pres. Gerald M. McCue & Assocs., Berkeley, 1954-70, McCue, Boone, Tomsick, San Francisco, 1970-76; prin. MBT Assocs., San Francisco, 1976-80; faculty U. Calif. at Berkeley, 1954-76; prof. architecture and urban design U. Calif. at Berkeley, 1966-76; chmn. dept. U. Calif. at Berkeley, 1966-71; prof. architecture/urban design, chmn. dept. and assoc. dean Grad. Sch. Design Harvard U., 1976-80, dean, 1980-92; John T. Dunlop prof. housing studies Sch. Design and Kennedy Sch. Govt., Harvard U., 1992-96. Planning and designn commns. executed for variety pub. and pvt. clients with over 30 nat., regional and local design awards. Fellow AIA, Urban Land Inst. Office: Harvard U Grad Sch Design 48 Quincy St Cambridge MA 02138-3000

MCCUE, HOWARD MCDOWELL, III, lawyer, educator; b. Sumter, S.C., Jan. 4, 1946; s. Howard McDowell and Carolyn Hartwell (Moore) McC.; m. Judith Weiss, Apr. 3, 1972; children—Howard McDowell IV, Leigh. A.B., Princeton U., 1968; J.D., Harvard U., 1971. Bar: Mass. 1971, Ill. 1975, U.S. Tax Ct. 1977. Assoc. Hale and Dorr, Boston, 1971-72; assoc. Mayer, Brown & Platt, Chgo., 1975-77, ptnr., 1977—; adj. prof. law master in tax program Chgo. Kent Coll. Law, 1981—. Author: (with others) Drafting Wills and Trust Agreements, 1979, 82, 85, 87, 90; mem. editorial adv. bd. Trusts and Estates mag., 1981—; contbr. articles to profl. jours. Bd. dirs. Art Inst. Chgo., Lawrence Hall Youth Svcs., Northwestern U. Libr. Coun.; bd. dirs., vice chmn. Ravinia Festival Assn. Lt. USN, 1972-75. Princeton U. scholar, 1965. Mem. ABA, Ill. Bar Assn., Chgo. Bar Assn. (fed. tax com., past chmn., exec. coun.), Chgo. Bar Found. (bd. dirs., past pres.), Am. Coll. Tax Counsel, Am. Coll. Trust and Estate Counsel, Harvard Law Soc. Ill., Internat. Acad. Estate and Trust Law, Chgo. Club, Phi Beta Kappa.

MCCUE, JUDITH W., lawyer; b. Phila., Apr. 7, 1948; d. Emanuel Leo and Rebecca (Raffel) Weiss; m. Howard M. McCue III, Apr. 3, 1971; children: Howard, Leigh. BA cum laude, U. Pa., 1969; JD, Harvard U., 1972. Bar: Ill. 1972, U.S. Tax Ct. 1984. Ptnr. McDermott, Will & Emery, Chgo., 1995—; dir. Schawk, Inc., Des Plaines, Ill.; pres. Chgo. Estate Planning Coun. Trustee The Orchestral Assn., 1995—. Fellow Am. Coll. Trust and Estate Counsel (com. chair 1991-94, regent 1993—); mem. Chgo. Bar Assn. (chmn. probate practice com. 1984-85, chmn. fed. estate and gift tax divsn. fed. tax com. 1988-89). Office: McDermott Will & Emery 227 W Monroe St Chicago IL 60606-5016

MCCUE, STEPHEN PATRICK, lawyer; b. Montclair, N.J., June 12, 1956; s. Francis James and Mary Theresa (Carroll) McC.; m. Wendy Ellen York, May 2, 1987; 1 child, Alexander York. BA cum laude, Harvard U., 1978; JD, U. Colo., 1983. Bar: N.Mex. 1983, U.S. Dist. Ct. N.Mex. 1983, Colo. 1985, U.S. Ct. Appeals (10th cir.) 1986), U.S. Supreme Ct. 1986. Assoc. Poole, Tinnin & Martin, Albuquerque, 1983-84; asst. pub. defender N.Mex. Pub. Defender Dept., 1984-86; asst. fed. pub. defender Fed. Pub. Defender-N.Mex., Albuquerque, 1986-93, supervisory asst. fed. pub. defender, 1993-95; sr. litigator, 1995—. Mem. ABA, Nat. Assn. Criminal Def. Lawyers, N.Mex. State Bar (bd. dirs. criminal law sect. 1991—, chair 1993-94), N.Mex. Assn. Criminal Def. Lawyers (bd. dirs. 1996—). Avocations: t'ai chi, jogging. Office: Fed Pub Defender 600 Central SW PO Box 449 Albuquerque NM 87103

MCCUEN, JOHN FRANCIS, JR., lawyer; b. N.Y.C., Mar. 11, 1944; s. John Francis Sr. and Elizabeth Agnes McC.; children: Sarah, Mary, John. AB, U. Notre Dame, 1966; JD, U. Detroit, 1969. Bar: Mich. 1970, Fla. 1970, Ohio 1978. Legal counsel Kelsey-Hayes Co., Romulus, Mich., 1970-77; corp. counsel Sheller-Globe Corp., Toledo, 1977-79; v.p., gen. counsel Sheller-Globe Corp., 1979-86, sec., 1982-87, sr. v.p. gen. counsel, 1986-89; ptnr. Marshall & Melhorn, Toledo, 1989-92; pvt. practice Law Offices John F. McCuen, Toledo, 1992-93; counsel Butzel Long, Ann Arbor, Mich., 1994; v.p. legal Kelsey Hayes Co., Livonia, Mich., 1994—; bd. dirs. K & W Acquisition Group. Trustee Kidney Found. N.W. Ohio, 1979-88, pres., 1984-86. Mem. ABA, Fla. Bar, Mich. Bar, Inverness Club. Home: 2734 Winter Garden Ct Ann Arbor MI 48105-2952 Office: Kelsey Hayes Co 11878 Hubbard St Livonia MI 48150-1733

MCCUEN, JOHN JOACHIM, building company and financial company executive; b. Washington, Mar. 30, 1926; s. Joseph Raymond and Josephine (Joachim) McC.; m. Gloria Joyce Seidel, June 16, 1949; children: John Joachim Jr., Les Seidel. BS, U.S. Mil. Acad., 1948; M of Internatl. Affairs, Columbia U., 1961; grad., U.S. Army War Coll., 1968. Commd. 2d. lt. U.S. Army, 1948, advanced through grades to col.; dir. internal def. and devel. U.S. Army War Coll., Carlisle Barracks, Pa., 1969-72; chief U.S. Def. Liaison Group, Jakarta, Indonesia, 1972-74; chief field survey office U.S. Army Tng. and Doctrine Command, Ft. Monroe, Va., 1974-76; ret. U.S. Army, 1976; mgr. tng. Chrysler Def., Center Line, Mich., 1977-82; mgr. modification ctr. Land Systems div. Gen. Dynamics, Sterling Heights, Mich., 1982-83; mgr. field ops. Land Systems div. Gen. Dynamics, Warren, Mich., 1983-94; pres. Mich. Econ. Devel. Corp., Birmingham, 1994—, The Magic Christmas Tree, Inc., Birmingham, 1994—; pres., CEO Laminar, Inc., Livonia, Mich., 1996—; owner Adventure and Exotic Travel Outfitters, Inc., Birmingham, 1995—; pres. First Internat. Corp., Birmingham, 1995—; ptnr. East West Connection, Birmingham, Mich.; past pres. Energy Resource Mgmt. Sys., Inc., Birmingham; armor advisor 3d Royal Thai Army, Utaradit, 1957-58; U.S. rep. users' com. NATO Missile Firing Installation Crete, Paris, 1964-66; advisor Vietnamese Nat. Def. Coll., Saigon, 1968-69; spkr. on terrorism and counter insurgency. Author: The Art of Counter Revolutionary War-The Strategy of Counter Insurgency, Faber 1966, Stackpole, 1967, Circulo Militar, 1967. Pres. Troy (Mich.) Cmty. Concert Assn., 1985—, bd. dirs., 1992; past pres. Mich. Oriental Art Soc., Birmingham; pres. Grander View Found. Sr. Housing and Nursing, Milford, Mich., 1984—; past 1st reader First Ch. of Christ Scientist, Birmingham, 1989-92; past chmn. region VI N.E. unit Detroit United Way Campaign. Mem. Soc. Logistics Engrs., Nat. Mgmt. Assn., Assn. U.S. Army, Oriental Art Soc. Republican. Avocation: collecting and selling Oriental antiques, lecturing on terrorism and national security. Home: 32863 Balmoral St Beverly Hills MI 48025-3008 Office: Laminar Inc 29200 Vassar St Ste 360 Livonia MI 48152-2116 also: Mich Econ Devel Corp 700 E Maple Rd Ste 203 Birmingham MI 48009

MCCUISTION, PEG OREM, hospice administrator; b. Houston, July 28, 1930; d. William Darby and Dorothy Mildred (Beckett) Orem; m. Palmer Day McCuistion, Sept. 4, 1949 (div. 1960); 1 child, Leeanne E. BBA, Southwest Tex. State, 1963; MBA, George Washington U., 1968; EdD, Wayne State U., 1989. Patient care adminstr. Holy Cross Hosp., Silver Spring, Md., 1968-79; exec. dir. Hospice of S.E. Mich., Southfield, 1979-86, Hospice Austin, Tex., 1987-94; CEO EMBI, Inc., Arlington, Tex., 1994—. Bd. dirs. Cmty. Home for the Elderly, Austin, 1989-92. Fellow Am. Coll. Health Care Execs. (membership com.); mem. Internat. Hospice Inst. (assoc.), Nat. Hospice Orgn. (chair standards and accreditation com.), Tex. Hospice Orgn. (pres. 1993-94), exec. com., standards and ethics com., edn. com., chair legis. com.), Mich. Hospice Orgn. (chair edn. com., bd. dirs.). Office: Embi Inc 511 Chaffee Dr Arlington TX 76006-2009

MCCUISTION, ROBERT WILEY, lawyer, hospital administrator, management consultant; b. Wilson, Ark., June 15, 1927; s. Ed Talmadge and Ruth Wiley (Bassett) McC.; m. Martha Virginia Golden, June 11, 1949 (dec. Nov. 1991); children: Beth, Dan, Jed.; m. Sudola M. Getz, Feb. 12, 1994. A.B. in History and Polit. Sci, Hendrix Coll., Conway, Ark., 1949; J.D., U. Ark., 1952. Bar: Ark. 1952. Practice in Dermott, Ark., 1952-57; dep. pros. atty. 10th Jud. Dist. Ark., 1953-57; bus. mgr. St. Mary's Hosp., Dermott, 1953-56, asst. adminstr., 1956-57; adminstr. Stuttgart (Ark.) Meml. Hosp., 1957-60, Forrest Meml. Hosp., Forrest City, Ark., 1960-68; assoc. adminstr. St. Edward Mercy Hosp., Ft. Smith, Ark., 1968-70; pres. Meml. Med Center, Corpus Christi, Tex., 1970-79; adminstr. Methodist Hosp., Mitchell, S.D., 1979-85, cons., 1985-86; mgmt. cons., owner Creative Leadership Concepts, Arlington, Tex., 1985—; adminstr. Cen. United Meth. Ch., Fayetteville, 1986-91; sec. Ark. Hosp. Adminstrs. Forum, 1958-59, pres., 1959-60; pres. Ark. Hosp. Assn., 1964-65, Areawide Health Planning, 1970; pres. Ark. Conf. Cath. Hosps., 1970; chmn. Twin City Hosp. Council, 1968; v.p. Ark. Assn. Mental Health, 1966-70. Div. chmn. Forrest City United Community Svcs., 1961, Corpus Christi United Way Community Svcs., 1972, DeSoto coun. Boy Scouts Am., Explorer adviser, 1954-57. With USAAF, World War II. Recipient Eminent Leadership award DeSoto Area council Boy Scouts Am., 1956. Mem. Am. Assn. Hosp. Accountants (pres. Ark. chpt. 1957), S.D. Hosp. Assn. (dist. chmn. 1980-81), Mid-West Hosp. Assn. (trustee 1963-65), Am. Coll. Health Execs. (life). Methodist (vice chmn., sec. ofcl. bd. 1957, lay del. S.D. ann. conf. 1980-85). Lodge: Rotary (pres. Forrest City 1964-65). Home and Office: 1101 Briarcreek Dr Arlington TX 76012-1824

MCCULLAGH, GRANT GIBSON, architect; b. Cleve., Apr. 18, 1951; s. Robert Ernest and Barbara Louise (Grant) McC.; m. Suzanne Dewar Folds, Sept. 13, 1975; children: Charles Weston Folds, Grant Gibson Jr. BArch, U. Ill., 1973; MArch, U. Pa., 1975; MBA, U. Chgo., 1979. Registered architect, Ill. Project designer Perkins & Will, Chgo., 1975-77; dir. mktg. The Austin Co., Chgo., 1977-83, asst. dist. mgr., 1983-84, dist. mgr., 1984-88, v.p., 1987-88; chmn., chief exec. officer McClier Corp., Chgo., 1988—. Contbr. articles to various indsl. publs. Bd. dirs. Friends of Prentice Hosp. Fellow AIA; mem. Chgo. Architecture Found. (pres. 1988-91, adv. bd. trustee 1994—), Design/Build Inst. Am. (bd. dirs 1994—, treas. 1995-96, pres. 1997—), Econ. Club, Chgo. Comml. Club, Casino Club, Univ. Club, Indian Hill Country Club. Republican. Episcopalian. Home: 43 Locust Rd Winnetka IL 60093-3725 Office: McClier Corp 401 E Illinois St Chicago IL 60611-4395

MCCULLAGH, JAMES CHARLES, publishing company executive; b. London, Oct. 22, 1941; s. James Christopher and Violet Anne (Smith) McC.; children: Declan, Deirdre. BS, Ind. U. Pa., 1968; MA, Lehigh U., 1970, PhD, 1974. Tchr. Holidaysburg (Pa.) Area High Sch., 1968; teaching asst. Lehigh U., Bethlehem, Pa., 1968-71, doctoral fellow, 1971-73; vis. poet Pa. Council on Arts Inc., Harrisburg, 1974-78; editor Rodale Press Inc., Emaus, Pa., 1979-83, pub., editor dir., group v.p., 1984—; pub. Novii Fermer, USSR, 1991—; pub. dir. Scuba Diving, 1992; sr. v.p. Internat. Mag. Devel.; mng. dir. Rodale Press, Inc., Russia, 1996—; interim dir. DeSilva & Phillips, 1997adr. Author: Bicycle Fitness Book, 1984, Bicycling for Health and Fitness, 1995, Cycling for Health, Fitness and Well-Being, 1995, (poetry) That Kingdom Coming Business, 1984; pub.: Mountain Bike, 1994. Served with USN, 1960-64. Recipient Man of Yr. award Bicycle Mfrs. Assn. Am., Washington, 1983. Mem. Am. Assn. Mag. Editors, Mag. Pubs. Assn., Bicycle Fedn. (bd. dirs. 1980—), Bicycle Inst. Am. (pres. 1993—). Democrat. Roman Catholic. Avocations: cycling, running. Home: PO Box 265A 4040 Lower Saucon Rd RD #1 Hellertown PA 18055

MCCULLEN, JOSEPH T., JR., venture capitalist; b. Phila., Mar. 15, 1935; s. Joseph Thomas and Sara Ellen (Berryman) McC.; m. Eleanor Joan Houder, July 5, 1958; children: Geoffrey, Jennifer, Justin. BA, Villanova U., 1957, PhD (hon.), 1976. Mgr. planning & acquisitions Merck & Co., Inc., Rahway, N.J., 1961-65; sr. v.p., ptnr. Spencer Stuart & Assocs., N.Y.C., 1965-71; spl. asst. to Pres. Richard M. Nixon, Washington, 1971-73; asst. sec. of The Navy, Washington, 1973-77; sr. v.p., sec. New Eng. Mut. Life, Boston, 1977-80; pres. McCullen Ptnrs. Inc., Boston, 1980-86; gen. ptnr. OneLiberty Ventures, Boston, 1986—; bd. dirs. Eastern Telelogic Corp., King of Prussia, Pa., Vt. Microsystems Inc., Winooski, Vt., Netlink, Inc., Framingham, Mass., HealthShare Tech. Inc., Acton, Mass., CellCall, Inc., Lexington, Ky., Brooks Fiber Properties, Inc., Town & Country, Mo., TeleCorp, Inc., Arlington, Va., Gen. Wireless Inc., Dallas, Spectrum Wireless Inc., Mountainside, Calif., K2NET Inc., Waltham, Mass., Brooks Fiber Properties, Inc., St. Louis, Boston, METRONET Comm. Corp., Calgary, Can.; bd. advisors Ctr. for Photonic Rsch. Boston U., 1995—. Mem. selection com. White House Fellows Program, 1979-96; bd. dirs. World Affairs Coun., 1977-95, Boston Ballet, 1978-85, chmn., 1980-85; bd. trustees Goodwill Industries, 1979-95, Boston Biomed. Rsch. Inst., 1989-95; assoc. dir. Pres. Reagan Transition Team, 1980; advisor Pres. Bush Transition Team, 1988. Served with U.S. Navy, 1952-53; lt. U.S. Army, 1958-61. Recipient Disting. Pub. Svc. medals Exec. Office of Pres., 1973, U.S. Dept. Def., 1977. Home: 97 Essex Rd Chestnut Hill MA 02167-1316 Office: One Liberty Ventures One Liberty Sq Boston MA 02109-4825

MC CULLOCH, ERNEST ARMSTRONG, physician, educator; b. Toronto, Ont., Can., Apr. 27, 1926; s. Albert E. and Letitia (Riddell) McC.; m. Ona Mary Morganty, 1953; children: James A., Michael E., Robert E., Cecelia E., Paul A. M.D. with honors, U. Toronto, 1948. Intern Toronto Gen. Hosp., 1949-50, sr. intern, 1951-52; NRC fellow dept. pathology U. Toronto, 1950-51; asst. resident Sunnybrook Hosp., Toronto, 1952-53; pvt. practice specializing in internal medicine Toronto, 1954-67; clin. tchr. dept. medicine U. Toronto, 1954-60, asst. prof. dept. med. biophysics, 1959-64, assoc. prof., 1964-66, prof., 1966, asst. prof. dept. medicine, 1967-68, assoc. prof., 1968-70, prof., 1970—, univ. prof., 1982-91, univ. prof. emeritus, 1991—; mem. grad. faculty U. Toronto (Inst. Med. Sci.), 1968—; dir. Inst. Med. Sci. U. Toronto, 1975-79, asst. dean Sch. Grad. Studies, 1979-82; physician Toronto Gen. Hosp., 1960-67; sr. scientist, sr. physician Ont. Cancer Inst., 1957-91, head divsn. biol. rsch., 1982-89, head divsn. cell and molecular biology, 1989-91, sr. scientist emeritus, 1991-93; vis. prof. U. Tex. Med. Ctr. Anderson Cancer Ctr., Houston, 1992-93, adj. prof., 1993—; cons. Nat. Cancer Plan, 1972—; mem. standing com. on health rsch. and devel. Ont. Coun. Health, 1974-82. Author numerous articles on research in hematology; editorial bd.: Blood, 1969-80, Biomedicine, 1973, Clin. Immunology and Immunopathology, 1972-76; assoc. editor: Jour. Cellular Physiology, 1966-68; editor, 1968-91. Trustee Banting Rsch. Found., 1975-84, hon. sec.-treas., 1958-74, v.p., 1977-79. Decorated officer Order of Can., 1988; recipient William Goldie prize U. Toronto, 1964, Ann. Gairdner award Internat. Gairdner Found., 1969, Starr Medallist award Dept. Anatomy U. Toronto, 1957; Thomas W. Eadie Medal, 1991, Royal Soc. Canada, Nat. Cancer Inst. Can. fellow, 1954-57. Fellow Royal Soc. Can. (pres. Acad. Sci. 1987-90, Thomas W. Eadie Medal 1991), Royal Coll. Physicians and Surgeons Can.; mem. Can. Acad. Sci., Am. Soc. Exptl. Pathology, Am. Assn. Cancer Rsch., Can. Soc. Cell Biology, Can. Soc. Clin. Investigation, Am., Internat. socs. hematology, Internat. Soc. Exptl. Hematology, Inst. Acad. Medicine (charter mem.). Clubs: Badminton, Racquet. Home: 480 Summerhill Ave, Toronto, ON Canada M4W 2E4 Office: 610 University Ave, Toronto, ON Canada M5G 2M9 *Research success depends on associating with agreeable and talented people.*

MCCULLOCH, JAMES CALLAHAN, manufacturing company executive; b. Pittsfield, Mass., Aug. 20, 1947; s. G. Robert and Marion Elizabeth (Callahan) McC.; m. Patricia A. Greene, Dec. 28, 1970; children: William Brennan, Patrick Callahan, Daniel Daly, Peter Brennan, James Callahan II. BS in Commerce, St. Louis U., 1969, MS in Commerce, 1970. With Ford Motor Co., 1970-72; group contr. Chemetron Corp., 1972-80; corp. contr. Six Flags Corp., L.A., 1980-82; v.p. fin. and planning Indsl. Controls Group Allen-Bradley Co., Milw., 1982-86; v.p., chief fin. officer and treas. Sybron Corp., Saddle Brook, N.J., 1986-87, also bd. dirs.; pres. McCulloch Investments, Madison, N.J., 1987—; bd. dirs. Summit Industries, Chgo. Mem. Fin. Exec. Inst., Morris County Golf Club. Republican. Office: McCulloch Investments 14 Main St Ste 200 Madison NJ 07940-1818

MCCULLOCH, RACHEL, economics researcher, educator; b. Bklyn., June 26, 1942; d. Henry and Rose (Offen) Preiss; m. Gary Edward Chamberlain; children: Laura Meressa, Neil Dudley. BA, U. Pa., 1962; MA in Teaching, U. Chgo., 1965, MA, 1971, PhD, 1973; student, MIT, 1966-67. Economist Cabinet Task Force on Oil Import Control, Washington, 1969; instr., then asst. prof. Grad. Sch. Bus. U. Chgo., 1971-73; asst. prof., then assoc. prof. econs. Harvard U., Cambridge, Mass., 1973-79; assoc. prof., then prof. econs. U. Wis., Madison, 1979-87; prof. Brandeis U., Waltham, Mass., 1987—, Rosen Family prof., 1989—, dir. Lemberg Program in Internat. Econs. and Fin., 1990-91, dir. PhD program Grad. Sch. Internat. Econs. and Fin., 1994—; mem. Pres.'s Commn. on Indsl. Competitiveness, 1983-84; mem. adv. coun. Office Tech. Assessment, U.S. Congress, 1979-88; cons. World Bank, Washington, 1984-86; mem. com. on internat. rels. studies with People's Republic of China, 1984-91; rsch. assoc. Nat. Bur. Econ. Rsch., Cambridge, 1985-93; mem. adv. com. Inst. for Internat. Econs., Washington, 1987—; faculty Advanced Mgmt. Network, La Jolla, Calif., 1985-92; mem. com. examiners econs. test Grad. Record Exam. Ednl. Testing Svc., 1990-96, chair, 1992-96; mem. discipline adv. com. for Fulbright scholar awards in econs. Coun. Internat. Exch. Scholars, 1991-93, chair, 1992-93; mem. adv. com. for Fulbright Chairs Program, 1997; cons. Global Economy Project, Edn. Film Ctr., 1993-94; mem. study group on pvt. capital flows to developing and transitional economies Coun. Fgn. Rels., 1995-96. Author: Research and Development as a Determinant of U.S. International Competitiveness, 1978; contbr. articles to profl. jours. and books. Grantee NSF, 1975-79, Hoover Inst., 1984-85, German Marshall Fund of U.S., 1985, Ford Found., 1985-88, U.S. Dept. Edn., 1990-91. Mem. Am. Econ. Assn. (dir. summer program for minority students 1983-84, mem. executive com., 1997—), Internat. Trade and Fin. Assn. (bd. dirs. 1993-95), New England Women Economists Assn. Home: 10 Frost Rd Lexington MA 02173-1904 Office: Brandeis U Dept Econs MS 021 Waltham MA 02254

MC CULLOCH, SAMUEL CLYDE, history educator; b. Ararat, Australia, Sept. 3, 1916; came to U.S., 1936, naturalized, 1944; s. Samuel and Agnes Almond (Clyde) McC.; m. Sara Ellen Rand, Feb. 19, 1944; children: Ellen (Mrs. William Henry Meyer III), David Rand, Malcolm Clyde. A.B. with highest honors in History, UCLA, 1940, M.A. (grad. fellow history), 1942; Ph.D., U. Calif. at Los Angeles, 1944. Asst. U. Calif. at Los Angeles, 1943-44; instr. Oberlin Coll., 1944-45; asst. prof. Amherst Coll., 1945-46; vis. asst. prof. U. Mich., 1946-47; mem. faculty Rutgers U., 1947-60, prof. history, assoc. dean arts and scis., 1958-60; dean coll., prof. history San Francisco State Coll., 1960-63; dean humanities, prof. history U. Calif. at Irvine, 1963-70, prof., 1970-87, prof. emeritus, 1987—, coordinator Edn. Abroad Program, 1975-85, dir. Australian Study Ctr., 1986, 87; vis. summer prof. Oberlin Coll., 1945, 46, U. Calif. at Los Angeles, 1947, U. Del., 1949; Fulbright Research prof. Monash U., Melbourne (Australia) U., 1970; Am. Philos. Soc. grantee, 1970. Author: British Humanitarianism, 1950, George Gipps, 1966, River King: The Mc Culloch Carrying Company and Echura, 1865-1898, 1986, Instant University: A History of U.C.I., 1957-1993, 1995, William McCulloch, 1932-1909, 1997; contbr. numerous articles, revs. to profl. jours.; assoc. editor Jour. Brit. Studies, 1960-68, bd. advisors, 1968-70; bd. corrs. Hist. Studies: Australia and New Zealand, 1949-83. Mem. Calif. Curriculum Commn., 1961-67, Highland Park (N.J.) Bd. Edn., 1959-60. Grantee Am. Philos. Soc., Social Sci. Research Council and Rutgers U. Research Council to Australia, 1951; Fulbright research fellow U. Sydney, Australia, 1954-55; grantee Social Sci. Research Council to Eng., summer 1955. Fellow Royal Hist. Soc.; mem. Am. Hist. Assn., Church, Royal Australian hist. socs., A.A.U.P., Conf. Brit. Studies (exec. sec. 1968-73, pres. 1975-77), English Speaking Union (pres. New Brunswick 1957-59), Phi Beta Kappa, Pi Gamma Mu. Episcopalian (vestry). Home: 2121 Windward Ln

Newport Beach CA 92660-3820 Office: Dept of History Univ of California Irvine CA 92717

MCCULLOCH, WILLIAM LEONARD, trade association administrator; b. Providence, Mar. 11, 1921; s. William Fraser and Elsie Cornelia (Westeberg) McC.; m. Dolores Ione Collier, July 26, 1952; children—William Fraser, II, Bruce Collier. B.S., U.S. Naval Acad., 1945; M.A. in Internat. Relations, Georgetown U., 1958. Commd. 2d lt. USMC, 1944, advanced through grades to brig. gen., 1971; service in Okinawa, China, Korea and Vietnam; comdg. gen. (1st Marine Div.), 1974-75; congl. aide, 1975-76; exec. dir. Am. Assn. Orthotists and Prosthetists, Washington, 1976-86; pres. nat. office Orthotics and Prosthetics, 1986-88; pres. Assn. Communications and Mktg. Svcs., Washington, 1988—; bd. dirs. Hanger Orthopedic Group. Decorated Legion of Merit with 2 stars, Bronze Star. Mem. Am. Soc. Assn. Execs., U.S. Naval Acad. Class of 1945 Assn. (pres. 1979-80), U.S. Naval Acad. Athletic Assn., Ret. Officers Assn., Capitol Hill Club (Washington), Army-Navy Country Club (Arlington, Va.), Marine Meml. Club (San Francisco), Army and Navy Club (pres. Washington chpt.). Republican. Presbyterian. Home and Office: 528 Ft Williams Pky Alexandria VA 22304-1849

MCCULLOH, JOHN MARSHALL, historian; b. Abilene, Kans., Sept. 13, 1943; s. Marshall S. and Gladys Irene (Mobley) McC.; m. Karen Indall, Dec. 26, 1965; children: John Andrew, Katherine Anna Edith. BA, U. Kans., 1965; MA, U. Calif., Berkeley, 1966, PhD, 1971. Acting asst. prof. U. Calif., San Diego, 1971-72, Los Angeles, 1972-73; asst. prof. Kans. State U., Manhattan, 1973-76, assoc. prof., 1976-86, head history dept., 1984-91; prof. Kans. State U., 1986—. Editor: Book, Rabani Mauri Martyrologium. Fellow Woodrow Wilson Found., Alexander Von Humboldt Found., German Acad. Exch. Svc., German Fulbright Commn. Mem. Am. Hist. Assn., Medieval Acad. Am., Am. Soc. Ch. History. Democrat. Episcopal. Home: 1516 Leavenworth St Manhattan KS 66502-4155 Office: Kans State U Dept History Manhattan KS 66506

MCCULLOH, JUDITH MARIE, editor; b. Spring Valley, Ill., Aug. 16, 1935; d. Henry A. and Edna Mae (Traub) Binkele; m. Leon Royce McCulloh, Aug. 26, 1961. BA, Ohio Wesleyan U., 1956; MA, Ohio State U., 1957; PhD, Ind. U., 1970. Asst. to dir. Archives of Traditional Music, Bloomington, Ind., 1964-65; asst. editor U. Ill. Press, Champaign, 1972-77, assoc. editor, 1977-82, sr. editor, 1982-85, exec. editor, 1985—, dir. devel., 1992—; advisor John Edwards Meml. Forum, Los Angeles, 1973—. Mem. Editorial Bd. Jour. Am. Folklore, Washington, 1986-90; co-editor Stars of Country Music, 1975; editor (LP) Green Fields of Ill., 1963, (LP) Hell-Bound Train, 1964, Ethnic Recordings in America, 1982; gen. editor Music in America Life series. Trustee Am. Folklife Ctr., Libr. of Congress, Washington, 1986—, chair, 1996—. Fulbright grantee, 1958-59; NDEA grantee, 1961, 62-63; grantee Nat. Endowment for the Humanities, 1978; Disting. Achievement citation Ohio Wesleyan U. Alumni Assn. Fellow Am. Folklore Soc. (pres. 1986-87), Soc. for Ethnomusicology (treas. 1982-86), Sonneck Soc. (1st v.p. 1989-93), Women in Scholarly Pub., Am. Anthropological Assn. Democrat. Office: U Ill Press 1325 S Oak St Champaign IL 61820-6903

MCCULLOUGH, COLLEEN, author; b. Wellington, N.S.W., Australia, June 1, 1937; m. Ric Robinson, Apr. 13, 1984. Student, U. Sydney, Australia; student Inst. Child Health, London U.; LittD (hon.), Macquarie U., Sydney, 1993. Neurophysiologist Sydney, London, Yale U. Sch. Medicine, 1967-77. Author: Tim, 1974, The Thorn Birds, 1977, An Indecent Obsession, 1981, Cooking with Colleen McCullough and Jean Easthope, 1982, A Creed for the Third Millennium, 1985, The Ladies of Missalonghi, 1987, The First Man in Rome, 1990, The Grass Crown, 1991, Fortune's Favorites, 1993, Caesar's Women, 1996.

MCCULLOUGH, DAVID, author; b. Pitts., July 7, 1933; s. Christian Hax and Ruth (Rankin) McC.; m. Rosalee Ingram Barnes, Dec. 18, 1954; children: Melissa (Mrs. John E. McDonald, Jr.), David, William Barnes, Geoffrey Barnes, Doreen Kane. BA, Yale U., 1955; HLD, Skidmore Coll., 1983, Rensselaer Poly. Inst., 1983; D of Engring. (hon.), Villanova U., 1984; hon. doctorate, Worcester Poly. Inst., 1984; LittD (hon.), Allegheny Coll., 1984; LHD (hon.), Wesleyan U., Middletown, Conn., 1984, Colo. Coll., 1985; LittD (hon.), Middlebury Coll., 1986, U. Indiana at Pa., 1991, U. S.C., 1993; HLD (hon.), U. N.H., 1991; LittD (hon.), U. Pitts., 1994, Union Coll., 1994, Washington Coll., 1994; LHD (hon.), Chatham Coll., 1994. Writer, editor Time, Inc., N.Y.C., 1956-61, USIA, Washington, 1961-64, Am. Heritage Pub. Co., N.Y.C., 1964-70; sr. contbg. editor Am. Heritage mag.; free-lance author, 1970—; Newman vis. prof. American civilization, Cornell U., fall 1989; mem. Bennington (Vt.) Coll. Writers Workshop, 1978-79; scholar-in-residence U. N. Mex., 1979, Wesleyan U. Writers Conf., 1982, 83; mem. adv. bd. Ctr. for the Book, Libr. of Congress. Author: The Great Bridge, 1972, The Path Between the Seas, 1977, The Johnstown Flood, 1968, Mornings on Horseback, 1981, Brave Companions, 1991, Truman, 1992 (Pulitzer Prize for biography 1993), host TV series: Smithsonian World, 1984-88, The American Experience, 1988—. Mem. Harry S. Truman Centennial Commn.; trustee Nat. Trust Hist. Preservation, Harry S. Truman Libr. Inst., Hist. Soc. Western Pa., Jefferson Meml. Found., Boston Pub. Libr.; hon. trustee Carnegie Inst. Recipient N.Y. Diamond Jubilee award, 1973, cert. of merit Mcpl. Art Soc. N.Y., 1973, Nat. Book award for history, 1978, Francis Parkman prize, 1978, 93, Samuel Eliot Morison award, 1978, Cornelius Ryan award, 1978, Civil Engring. History and Heritage award, 1978, L.A. Times prize for biography, 1981, Am. Book award for biography, 1982, Harry S. Truman Pub. Svc. award, 1993, St. Louis Lit. award, 1993, Pa. Gov.'s award for excellence, 1993, Pa. Soc. Gold Medal award, 1994. Fellow Soc. Am. Historians (pres.); mem. ASCE (hon.), Soc. Am. Historians (pres. 1991—). Office: Janklow & Nesbit Associates 598 Madison Ave New York NY 10022-1614

MCCULLOUGH, DAVID L., urologist; b. Chattanooga, 1938. MD, Bowman Gray, 1964. Intern U. Hosps. Case Western Reserve U., Cleve., 1964-65, resident in surgery, 1965-66; fellow urology Baylor U. Coll. Medicine, Houston, 1968-69; resident in urology Mass. Gen. Hosp., Boston, 1969-72; chief urologist N.C. Bapt. Hosp., Winston-Salem, 1983—; prof., chmn. urology Bowman Gray, Winston-Salem; past pres. Am. Bd. Urology. Mem. ACS, AMA, Am. Urol. Assn. (pres.-elect southeastern sect.), Am. Assn. Genitourinary Surgeons (sec.-treas.), Clin. Soc. Urol. Surgeons.

MCCULLOUGH, EDWARD EUGENE, patent agent, inventor; b. Baldwin, N.D., June 4, 1923; s. Elmer Ellsworth and Emma Izelda (Nixon) McC. BA, U. Minn., 1957; postgrad., Utah State U., 1965. Machine designer Sperry Rand Corp., Mpls., 1952-58; patent adminstr. Thiokol Corp., Brigham City, Utah, 1958-86; patent cons. Thiokol Corp., Brigham City, 1986; pvt. practice, 1986—. Inventor 33 patents including instruments for making perspective drawings, apparatus for forming ignition surfaces in solid propellant motors, passive communications satellite or similar article, flexible bearings and process for their manufacture, rocket nozzel support and pivoting system, cavity-shaping machine, among others; patents in field. Pianist Aldersgate Meth. Ch., Brigham City, 1959—. Staff Sgt. U.S. Army, 1949-52. Decorated two battle stars. Avocations: inventing, philosophy, music composition, hiking in the mountains. Home: PO Box 46 784 Highland Blvd Brigham City UT 84302

MC CULLOUGH, HELEN CRAIG, Oriental languages educator; b. Hollywood, Calif., Feb. 17, 1918; d. Everett Emerson and Mabel (Bishop) Craig; m. William Hoyt McCullough, July 19, 1952; 1 son, Dundas Craig. A.B., U. Calif., Berkeley, 1939, M.A., 1952, Ph.D., 1955. Lectr. in history, Asian langs. Stanford (Calif.) U., 1964-69; lectr. Oriental langs. U. Calif., Berkeley, 1969-75, prof., 1975-88, emerita, 1988—; vis. prof. Harvard U., 1978-79. Author: Yoshitsune, 1966, Tales of Ise, 1968, Okagami, The Great Mirror, 1980; (with William H. McCullough) A Tale of Flowering Fortunes, 1980; Brocade by Night, 1985, Kokin Wakashu, 1985, The Tale of the Heike, 1988, Classical Japanese Prose: An Anthology, 1990, Genji and Heike, 1994; translator, author research articles in field of classical Japanese lit. Served with WAVES, 1943-46. Recipient Order of the Precious Crown, Japan, 1996. Mem. Sierra Club. Democrat. Home: 40 Alta Rd Berkeley CA 94708-1204 Office: U Calif Dept East Asian Langs Berkeley CA 94720

MC CULLOUGH, J. LEE, industrial psychologist; b. Bryn Mawr, Pa., Oct. 3, 1945; s. Leo Francis and Margaret Mary (Hart) McC.; AB, Villanova U., 1967; MA, Ohio State U., 1968, PhD, 1971; m. Bonnie R. Goldberg, Jan. 14, 1979. Teaching asst. Ohio State U., 1967-68, rsch. assoc., 1968-69; assoc. O.P.S. Assos., Columbus, 1970-71; assoc., sr. assoc., sr. prin., v.p. Hay Group, N.Y.C., 1971-90, v.p., dir. fin. svcs. cons., 1990-94; prin. William M. Mercer, Inc., N.Y.C., 1994—; adj. prof. Fordham U. Grad. Sch. Bus., 1984-89. Served with AUS, 1972. NSF fellow, 1969; NDEA Title IV fellow, 1970; Univ. Dissertation Year fellow, 1971. Mem. Am., Eastern, Pa., Am. Psychol. Soc., Human Resource Planning Soc., Met. Psychol. Assns. Home: 6 Hereford Dr Princeton Junction NJ 08550-1514 Office: 1166 Avenue Americas 29th Fl New York NY 10036-2708

MC CULLOUGH, JOHN PRICE, retired oil company executive; b. Dallas, May 10, 1925; s. John A. and Alta (McGee) McC.; m. Mary Ann Calvert, Aug. 5, 1946; children: Sherri, Cathryn, Patricia. Student, U. Denver, 1942-43; B.S. in Chem. Engring, U. Okla., 1945; M.S., Oreg. State U., 1948, Ph.D. in Chemistry, 1949. With U.S. Bur. Mines, Bartlesville, Okla., 1949-63, phys. chemist, 1949-57, chief thermodynamics br., 1958-63; mgr. central research div. Mobil Oil Corp., Princeton, N.J., 1963-69, mgr. applied research and devel., 1969-71; gen. mgr. research and devel. Mobil Chem. Co., 1971-78; v.p. environ. health and safety Mobil Research & Devel. Corp., Princeton, N.J., 1978-89; adj. prof. chemistry Okla. State U., Stillwater, 1961-63; vis. fellow Woodrow Wilson Found., 1991-95; dir. Internat. petroleum Industry Environ. Conservation Assn., 1981-89, chmn., 1985-88; dir. Mobil Found., Inc., 1987-89. Co-author: (with Donald Scott) Experimental Thermodynamics, Volume I: Calorimetry of Non-reacting Systems, 1968; contbr. 90 articles on thermodynamics, molecular structure and energetics, environ. and health policy to profl. jours. mem. adv. com. Mercer County (N.J.) C.C., 1968-69; bd. dirs. Chem. Industry Inst. Toxicology, 1977-89, chmn., 1986-88; bd. dirs. United Cmty. Fund, Princeton, 1963-69, Middlesex-Somerset-Mercer Regional Study Coun., 1968-69, 86-89, World Environ. Ctr., 1986-89; mem. adv. bd. Georgetown U. Inst. Health Policy Analysis, 1986-89; trustee Stony Brook-Millstone Watershed Assn., 1989-95, vice chmn., 1991-93, adv. bd., 1996—; trustee Art Mus. Princeton U., 1994—; elder, pres. corp. Nassau Presbyn. Ch., 1995—. Lt. (j.g.) USNR, 1943-54. DuPont fellow, 1947-48; recipient Meritorious Service award U.S. Dept. Interior, 1959, Distinguished Service award, 1962; Am. Chem. Soc. award petroleum chemistry, 1963; Chemtech award, 1977; Huffman award Internat. Calorimetry Conf., 1963. Mem. AAAS, Gordon Rsch. Conf. (trustee, chmn. bd. trustees, mem. coun.), Am. Chem. Soc. (editorial bd. Jour. Chem. and Engring. Data, Jour. Phys. Chemistry, mem. coun. com. on chemistry and pub. affairs 1984-92, chmn. 1987-89), Internat. Calorimetry Conf. (chmn. 1960), Am. Inst. Chemists, Sigma Xi. Home: 30 Boudinot St Princeton NJ 08540-3008

MCCULLOUGH, JOSEPH, college president emeritus; b. Pitts., July 6, 1922; s. Joseph Phillip and Margaret (List) McC.; m. Elizabeth Cramer, Mar. 31, 1945; children—Marjorie Ann, Warren. BFA, Yale U., 1949-50, MFA, 1951; Diploma, Cleve. Sch. Art, 1948; DFA (hon.), U. Evansville, Ind., 1980; DA (hon.), Cleve. Inst. Art, 1996. Instr. San Jose State Coll., Calif., 1948-49; asst. instr. Yale U., New Haven, 1949-51; asst. dir. Cleve. Inst. Art, 1952-54, dir., 1954-74, pres., 1974-88. Artist paintings, nat. regional and local exhbns., 1948—. Chmn. Fine Arts Adv. Com., Cleve. Planning Commn., 1963-91; trustee Mpls. Coll. of Art and Design, 1988—, Sculpture Ctr. Cleve., 1990—; trustee, sec. Access to the Arts, Cleve., 1991-95. Capt. USAAF, 1943-46, ETO. Recipient Cleve. Arts prize Women's City Club, 1971. Mem. Coll. Art Assn. (past dir.), Union Club, Rowfant Club. Home: 20101 North Park Blvd Cleveland OH 44118-5006

MCCULLOUGH, KATHRYN T. BAKER, social worker, utility commissioner; b. Trenton, Tenn., Jan. 5, 1925; d. John Andrew and Alma Lou (Wharey) Taylor; m. John R. Baker, Sept. 30, 1972 (dec. Oct. 1981); m. T.C. McCullough, May 14, 1988. BS, U. Tenn., 1945, MSW, 1954; postgrad., U. Chgo., 1950, Vanderbilt U., 1950-51. Lic. social worker, Tenn.; emeritus diplomate in clin. social work Am. Bd. Examiners. Home demonstration agt., agrl. extension svc. U. Tenn., Hardeman County, 1946-49; Dyer County, 1949-50; dir. med. social work dept. Le Bonheur Children's Hosp., Memphis, 1954-57; chief clin. social worker clinic mentally retarded children U. Tenn. Dept. Pediatrics, Memphis, 1957-59; clin. social worker Children's Med. Ctr., Tulsa, 1959-60; dir. med. social work dept. Coll. of Medicine U. Tenn., Memphis, 1960-69; dir. community svcs. regional med. program Coll. of Medicine, 1969-76; dir. regional clinic program Child Devel. Ctr. Coll. of Medicine, 1976-85; mem. faculty Coll. of Medicine, Coll. of Social Work U. Tenn., Memphis, 1960-85; social worker admissions rev. bd. Arlington Devel. Ctr., Memphis, 1976—. Author 14 books. Active Gibson County Fedn. Dem. Women, 1987—; commr. Dist. I, Gibson Utility Dist., 1990—. Fellow Am. Assn. Mental Retardation (life); mem. NASW, AAUP, Acad. Cert. Social Workers, Tenn. Conf. on Social Welfare, Sigma Kappa Alumni. Mem. Ch. of Christ. Avocations: piano, organ, symphony. Home: 627 Riverside Yorkville Rd Trenton TN 38382-9513

MCCULLOUGH, KEVIN, CNBC anchor, correspondent. CNBC anchor The Money Wheel, Fort Lee, N.J. Office: CNBC The Money Wheel 2200 Fletcher Ave Fort Lee NJ 07024-5005

MCCULLOUGH, LAUREN FINK, aluminum company manager; b. New Kensington, Pa., Sept. 9, 1960; d. David Roy and Lois Ann (Coulson) Fink; m. John P. McCullough, Aug. 2, 1986; children: Joel David, Paul Jacob. BSChemE, Carnegie-Mellon U., 1982, MS in Indsl. Adminstrn., 1986. Cert. mgmt. acct. Chem. engr. Gulf Oil Co., Pitts., 1982-84; staff analyst Alcoa, Pitts., 1986-88; bus. analyst Alcoa Separations Tech., Inc., Warrendale, Pa., 1988-90, contr. membrane products group, 1991; cons. Alcoa, Pitts., 1992-94, mgr., corp. and competitor analysis, 1995; v.p. fin. specialty metals divsn. Alcoa, 1995-96; NA contr. Alcoa Indsl. Chems., Pitts., 1996—. Mem. Nat. Assn. Accts., Inst. Mgmt. Accts. Presbyterian. Office: Alcoa 3450 Park Lane Dr Pittsburgh PA 15275-1122

MCCULLOUGH, M. BRUCE, judge; b. Princeton, N.J., July 26, 1944; s. Malcolm S. and Ruth S. (Strandness) McC.; m. Kathleen M. Ryan, Apr. 12, 1985. BA in Polit. Sci. and Econs., Whitworth Coll., 1966; JD, U. Mich., 1969. Bar: Pa., Fla., D.C. Ptnr. Buchanan Ingersoll P.C., Pitts., 1969-95; judge U.S. Bankruptcy Ct., Pitts., 1995—. Chmn. ARC (southwest Pa., 1994—). With USAR, 1969-75. Mem. Am. Land Title Assn. (lenders counsel), Chartiers Country Club, Duquesne Club, Rivers Club. Avocations: golf, boating, hunting. Office: US Bankruptcy Ct 1000 Liberty Ave Pittsburgh PA 15222-4004

MCCULLOUGH, R. MICHAEL, management consultant; b. Springfield, Ohio, Dec. 31, 1938; s. Jerome Edward and Sara Amelia (Fitzsimmons) McC.; m. Frances P. Kelly, Nov. 24, 1962; children: Jeanne M., Michael F., Colleen T., Brian A., Kathleen H., Christopher E., Brendan P. BSEE, U. Detroit, 1962. Engr. GE Co., Washington, 1962-65; engr., rsch. dir. Booz Allen & Hamilton, Bethesda, Md., 1965-71, ptnr., 1971-73, mng. ptnr., 1973-84; chmn., CEO Booz Allen & Hamilton, New York, N.Y., 1984-91; sr. chmn. Booz Allen & Hamilton, McLean, Va., 1991-96, ret., 1997; bd. dirs. Profl. Svcs. Coun., Washington, pres., 1983-84; bd. dirs. Interstate Hotels, O'Sullivan Corp., Watson Wyeth. Mem. adv. coun. Stanford U., 1985-91; bd. dirs. Wolf Trap Found., 1989—; trustee U. Detroit Mercy, 1990, Nat. Rehab. Hosp., 1996—, U.S.-Panama Bus. Coun., U.S.-Russia Bus. Coun. Mem. Columbia Country Club (Chevy Chase, Md.), Burning Tree Country Club (Bethesda, Md.), Country Club Fla. (West Palm Beach), Robert Trent James Golf Club (Manassas, Va.), Pine Valley (N.J.) Golf Club.

MC CULLOUGH, RALPH CLAYTON, II, lawyer, educator; b. Daytona Beach, Fla., Mar. 28, 1941; s. Ralph C. and Doris (Johnson) McC.; m. Elizabeth Grier Henderson, Apr. 5, 1986; children from previous marriage: Melissa Wells, Clayton Baldwin. B.A., Erskine Coll., 1962; J.D., Tulane U., 1965. Bar: La. 1965, S.C. 1974. Assoc. Baldwin, Haspel, Maloney, Rainold and Meyer, New Orleans, 1965-68; asst. prof. law U. S.C., 1968-71, asso. prof., 1971-75; prof. U. S.C., 2, 1975—; chair prof. of advocacy U. S.C., 1982—, asst. dean Sch. Law, 1970-75, instr. Med. Sch., 1970-79, adj. prof. law and medicine Med. Sch., 1979—; adj. prof. medicine Med. U. of S.C., 1984—; of counsel Finkel, Altman & Bailey, 1978—; adj. prof. pathology Med. U. S.C., 1985—; asst. dean U. S.C. Sch. Law 1970-75. Author: (with J.L. Underwood) The Civil Trial Manual, 1974, 7th supplement, 1987, The Civil Trial Manual II, 1984, 87, (with Myers and Felix) New Directions in Legal Education, 1970, (with Finkel) S.C. Torts II, 1986, III, 1990, IV, 1995; co-reporter S.C. Criminal Code, 1977, S.C. Study Sentencing, 1977. Trustee S.C. dist. U.S. Bankruptcy Ct., 1979—; exec. dir. S.C. Continuing Legal Edn. Program.; bd. visitors Erskine Coll.; reporter S.C. Jury Charge Commn., 1991—. Mem. ABA, La. Bar Assn., S.C. Bar (sec. 1975-76, exec. dir. 1972-76, award of service 1978), New Orleans Bar Assn., Am. Trial Lawyers Assn., Am. Law Inst., Southeastern Assn. Am. Law Schs. (pres.), S.C. Trial Lawyers Assn. (bd. govs. 1984-88), Phi Alpha Delta. Republican. Episcopalian. Club: Forest Lake. Home: PO Box 1799 Columbia SC 29202-1799 Office: U SC Sch Law Columbia SC 29208

MCCULLOUGH, RAY DANIEL, JR., insurance company executive; b. Daytona Beach, Fla., Feb. 28, 1938; s. Ray Daniel and Clarice (Malphurs) McC.; m. Barbara Jean Winchester, Aug. 16, 1963; children—Courtney Ann, Justin Ray. BSBA with honors, U. Fla., 1960. CPA, Fla. Acct. Deloitte Haskins & Sells CPAs, Jacksonville, Fla., 1960-63; with Gulf Life Ins. Co., Jacksonville, 1963-85; v.p., contr. Gulf Life Ins. Co., 1971-85; sr. v.p. fin. Dependable Ins. Group, 1985-88; pvt. practice Jacksonville, 1988—; owner Broilerage Co., 1996—; Mem. bus. adv. council U. Fla., Gainesville, 1979-85. Mem. Am., Fla. Insts. CPAs, Jacksonville Toastmasters Club (pres. 1966), Beta Alpha Psi, Beta Gamma Sigma. Home: 10312 Sylvan Ln W Jacksonville FL 32257-6240 Office: 2700 University Blvd W Ste 1A Jacksonville FL 32217-2120

MCCULLOUGH, RICHARD LAWRENCE, advertising agency executive; b. Chgo., Dec. 1, 1937; s. Francis John and Sadie Beatrice McCullough; m. Julia Louise Kreimer, May 6, 1961; children: Stephen, Jeffery, Julie. BS, Marquette U., 1959. Commd. U.S. Army, 1959, advance through grades to sgt., 1966; account exec. Edward H. Weiss Advt., Chgo., 1960-66; account supr. Doyle Dane Bernbach, N.Y.C., 1966-68; sr. v.p. J. Walter Thompson Co., Chgo., 1969-86; pres. E.H. Brown Advt., Chgo., 1986-97; exec. v.p. Space-Time Media Mgmt., Chgo., 1997—; developer Mktg. with Country Music nat. seminar, 1996. Author: Building Country Radio, 1986, A New Look at Country Music Audiences, 1988, (video) Country Music Marketing, 1989. Bd. dirs. Gateway Found., Chgo., 1976—, chmn., 1988-91; bd. dirs. Catholic Charities, Chgo. Mem. Country Music Assn. (Nashville dir. 1979—, pres. 1983-85, Pres.'s award 1987), Nat. Assn. Rec. Artists and Scis. (Nashville chpt.), North Shore Country Club (Glenview, Ill.), Tower Club, Dairymen's Country Club (Boulder Junction, Wis.), Quail Creek Country Club (Naples, Fla.). Roman Catholic. Home (summer): 2720 Lincoln St Evanston IL 60201-2043 also (winter): St Simone 5633 Turtle Bay Dr Naples FL 34108-2749 Office: Space-Time Media Mgmt Inc 35 E Wacker Dr Chicago IL 60601

MCCULLOUGH, ROBERT WILLIS, former textile executive; b. Monclair, N.J., Sept. 19, 1920; s. Willis G. and Viola (Mock) McC.; m. Margaret Elizabeth Hammons, Aug. 12, 1942; children—Constance Joan, Sandra Margaret, D. Scott, Linda Anne. Student, Phila. Textile Sch.; grad., Brown U., 1943. With Collins & Aikman Corp., N.Y.C., 1946-84; exec. v.p. Collins & Aikman Corp., 1955—, chmn. exec. com., 1961-84; ret.; bd. dirs. parent org. Collins & Aikman; adviser to supt. U.S. Naval Acad. Trustee, past chmn. South Street Seaport Mus.; trustee Brown U., Am. Scottish Found., Textile Research Inst. at Princeton. Served from ensign to lt. comdr. USCGR, 1942-46. Named to Brown U. Hall of Fame. Mem. Am. Arbitration Assn. Clubs: Riverside Yacht, N.Y. Yacht (past commodore; chmn. Am.'s Cup Com.), Storm Trysail, Cruising of Am. Home and Office: 93 Club Rd Riverside CT 06878-2003

MCCULLOUGH, ROY LYNN, chemical engineering educator; b. Hilsboro, Tex., Mar. 20, 1934; s. Roy Lee and Rubye Maye (Ingram) McC.; m. Jamis Carol Petersen, Sept. 5, 1958; children: Catherine Lynne, Amanda Kaye, Roy Lawrence. BS, Baylor U., 1955; PhD, U. N.Mex., 1960. Mem. staff Los Alamos (N.Mex.) Sci. Lab., 1955-60; group leader, sect. head Monsanto Co., Durham, N.C., 1960-69; sr. scientist Boeing Co., Seattle, 1969-71; prof. chem. engring. U. Del., Newark, 1971—, dir.Ctr. for Composite Material, 1990-94. Author: Concepts of Fiber-Resin Composites, 1971; mem. editorial bd. Jour. Composite Sci. and Tech., 1984—; contbr. articles to profl. jours. Mem. Am. Inst. Chem. Engrs., Am. Chem. Soc., Am. Phys. Soc., Am. Soc. Composites. Home: 107 Reynard Dr Landenberg PA 19350-1145 Office: U Del Ctr for Composite Material Newark DE 19716

MCCULLOUGH, V. BETH, pharmacist, educator; b. Harrison, Ark., May 15, 1953; d. A. G. and Willene L. (McLain) McC.; m. David Mark Pearson, Oct. 25, 1980; children: Colin McCullough-Pearson, Emily McCullough-Pearson. BS in Edn. cum laude, Southwest Mo. State U., 1976; BS in pharmacy, U. Mo., 1981. Registered Pharmacist, Mo. Chief pharmacist Mt. Vernon Park Pharmacy, Springfield, Mo., 1981-89; dir. pharmacy Foster Health Care Group, Springfield, 1989-96; chief pharmacy ops. Balanced Care Corp./Foster Health Care Group, Springfield, 1996—; long term care pharmacy cons. Foster Health Care Group, Springfield, 1981-83. Mem. NOW, Springfield, 1982—, assoc. mem. Animal Shelter League of the Ozarks, Nixa, Mo. Mem. Southwest Mo. Humane Soc., Mo. Equine Coun., Mo. Pharmacy Assn., Long Term Care Acad. Avocations: watercolor painting, jewelry making, horse breeding and showing. Home: RR 1 Fordland MO 65652-9801 Office: Foster Health Care Group 426 S Jefferson Ave Springfield MO 65806-2316

MCCULLY, EMILY ARNOLD, illustrator, writer; b. Galesburg, Ill., 1939; d. Wade E. and Kathryn (Maher) Arnold; m. George E. McCully, 1961 (div. 1975); children: Nathaniel, Tad. BA, Brown U., 1961; MA, Columbia U., 1964. Author: How's Your Vacuum Cleaner Working? O'Henry Collection, 1977, A Craving, 1982, (novel) Picnic, 1984 (Christopher award), First Snow, 1985, (novel) Life Drawing, 1986, The Show Must Go On, 1987, School, 1987, You Lucky Duck!, 1988, New Baby, 1988, The Grandma Mix-up, 1988, The Christmas Gift, 1988, Zaza's Big Break, 1989, Grandma's at the Lake, 1990, The Evil Spell, 1990, Speak Up, Blanche!, 1991, Mirette on the Highwire, 1992 (Caldecott medal 1992), Grandma's at Bat, 1993, The Amazing Felix, 1993, My Real Family, 1994, Crossing The New Bridge, 1994, Little Kit, or: The Industrious Flea Circus Girl, 1995, The Pirate Queen, 1995, The Ballot Box Battle, 1996, The Bobbin Girl, 1996; illustrator: Sea Beach Express, 1966, The Seventeenth Street Gang, 1966, Rex, 1967, Luigi of the Streets, 1967, That Mean Man, 1968, Gooney, 1968, Journey From Peppermint Street, 1968 (Nat. Book award 1969), The Mouse and the Elephant, 1969, The Fisherman, 1969, Tales from the Rue Brocca, 1969, Here I Am, 1969, Twin Spell, 1969, Hobo Toad and the Motorcycle Gang, 1970, Slip! Slop! Gobble!, 1970, Friday Night is Papa Night, 1970, Maxie, 1970, Steffie and Me, 1970, The Cat and the Parrot, 1970, Gertrude's Pocket, 1970, Go and Hush the Baby, 1971, Finders Keepers, 1971, Ma n Da La, 1971 (Bklyn. Mus. award 1976, N.Y. Pub. Libr. award 1976), Hurray for Captain Jane!, 1971, Michael Is Brave, 1971, Finding Out With Your Senses, 1971, Henry's Pennies, 1972, Jane's Blanket, 1972, Grandpa's Long Red Underwear, 1972, Girls Can Too!, 1972, The Boyhood of Grace Jones, 1972, Black Is Brown Is Tan, 1973, Isabelle the Itch, 1973, When Violet Died, 1973, That New Boy, 1973, How To Eat Fried Worms, 1973, Jenny's Revenge, 1974, Her Majesty, Grace Jones, 1974, Tree House Town, 1974, I Want Mama, 1974, Amanda, the Panda and the Redhead, 1975, The Bed Book, 1976, My Street's A Morning Cool Street, 1976, Professor Coconut and the Thief, 1977, Martha's Mad Dog, 1977, That's Mine, 1977, Where Wild Willie, 1978, No Help At All, 1978, Partners, 1978, The Twenty-Elephant Restaurant, 1978, What I Did Last Summer, 1978, The Highest Hit, 1978, I and Spraggy, 1978, Edward Troy and the Witch Cat, 1978, My Island Grandma, 1979, Whatever Happened to Beverly Bigler's Birthday?, 1979, Last Look, 1979, Ookie-Spooky, 1979, The Black Dog Who Went Into the Woods, 1980, How I Found Myself at the Fair, 1980, How We Got Our First Cat, 1980, Oliver and Allison's Week, 1980, Pajama Walking, 1981, The April Fool, 1981, I Dance in My Red Pajamas, 1982, The Halloween Candy Mystery, 1982, Go and Mush the Baby, 1982, Mitzi and the Terrible Tyrannosaurus Rex, 1983, Best Friend Insurance, 1983, Mail-Order Wings, 1984, Gertrude's Pocket, 1984, Fifth Grade Magic, 1984, The Ghastly Glasses, 1985, Fourth of July, 1985, The Explorer of Barkham Street, 1985, Wheels, 1986, Lulu and the Witch Baby, 1986, Richard and the Vratch, 1987, Molly, 1987, Molly Goes Hiking, 1987, Jam Day, 1987, The Boston Coffee Party, 1988, The Take-Along Dog, 1989, Selene Goes Home, 1989, The Magic Mean Machine, 1989, It Always Happens to Leona, 1989, The Grandpa Days, 1989, Dinah's Mad, Bad Wishes, 1989, Stepbrother Sabotage, 1990, Lulu Goes to Witch School, 1990, The Day Chubby Became Charles, 1990, The Christmas Present Mystery, 1990, Sky Guys to White Cat, 1991, Meatball, 1991, Leona and Ike, 1991, The Butterfly Birthday,

1991, Yankee Doodle Drumsticks, 1992, One Very Best Valentine's Day, 1992, Meet the Lincoln Lions Band, 1992, Jingle Bells Jam, 1992, In My Tent, 1992, Anne Flies the Birthday Bike, 1993, Amzat and His Brothers, 1993.

MC CUNE, BARRON PATTERSON, federal judge; b. West Newton, Pa., Feb. 19, 1915; s. James Patterson and Lyda Barron (Hammond) McC.; m. Edna Flannery Markey, Dec. 23, 1943; children: Edward M., James H., Barron Patterson. AB, Washington and Jefferson Coll., 1935; LLB, U. Pa., 1938. Bar: Pa. bar 1939. Practiced in Washington, Pa., 1939-64; judge 27th Jud. Dist. Ct. Common Pleas, Washington, Pa., 1964-71; judge U.S. Dist. Ct., Western Dist. Pa., Pitts., 1971-95, sr. fed. judge; ret., 1995. Trustee emeritus Washington and Jefferson Coll.; bd. dirs. emeritus Washington (Pa.) Hosp. Served with USNR, 1942-45. Home: 144 Le Moyne Ave Washington PA 15301

MCCUNE, DAVID FRANKLIN, publisher; b. Trenton, N.J., Jan. 15, 1954; s. George David and Mary Jane McCune; m. Susan Ruth Watt, Apr. 11, 1981; 1 child, Douglas David. BA summa cum laude, Williams Coll., 1975. Free-lance journalist Malmö, Sweden, 1975-80; editor Time Inc., N.Y.C., 1981-83; pres. The Proteus Group Inc., N.Y.C., 1983-87; mktg. dir. Sage Publs. Inc., Newbury Park, Calif., 1988, pres., 1989—. Mem. Soc. for Scholarly Pub., Assn. for Computing Machinery, Young Pres.'s Orgn. Avocations: sailing, skiing. Office: Sage Publications Inc 2455 Teller Rd Thousand Oaks CA 91320-2218

MCCUNE, ELLIS E., retired university system chief administrator, higher education consultant; b. Houston, July 17, 1921; s. Ellis E. and Ruth (Mason) McC.; m. Hilda May Whiteman, Feb. 8, 1946; 1 son, James Donald. Student, Sam Houston State U., 1940-42; B.A., UCLA, 1948, Ph.D., 1957; LHD, Golden Gate U., 1994. Teaching asst. UCLA, 1949-51; from instr. to assoc. prof. polit. sci. Occidental Coll., Los Angeles, 1951-59; chmn. applied politics and econs. curriculum Occidental Coll., 1951-56; asst. prof. Calif. State U., Northridge, 1959-61, assoc. prof., chmn. dept. polit. sci., 1961-63, prof., 1963, dean letters and sci., 1963; dean acad. planning Calif. State Univs. and Colls., 1963-67; pres. Calif. State U., Hayward, 1967-90, pres. emeritus, 1991—; acting chancellor The Calif. State U. System, 1990-91, ret., 1991; cons. govtl. units and agys.; lectr., panelist; mem. Calif. State Scholarship and Loan Commn., 1964-68, chmn., 1967-68; pres. Govtl. Adminstrn. Group Los Angeles, 1959; chair planning com., mem. exec. com., bd. dirs. Eden Med. Ctr. Found., 1994—, pres.-elect, 1995-97, pres., 1997—. Chmn. univs. and colls. div. United Bay Area Crusade, 1969-70, 73-74; bd. dirs. Oakland (Calif.) Museum Assn., 1974-77, 86-88; vice chmn. higher edn. div., East Bay United Way, 1989-90; mem. arts adv. council, 1986-87, devel. com., 1988-89, Bay Area Urban League, bd. trust Calif. Coun. Econ. Edn. No. sect., Emergency Shelter Program Adv. Coun., Hayward Area Hist. Assn., NAACP Hayward chpt.; trustee Calif. Council Econ. Edn.; sec. bd. dirs. Eden Community Found., 1978-79; rsch. fellow Haynes Found, 1957. With USAAF, 1942-46. Mem. Am. Coun. Edn. (adv. com. 1970-72, inst. coll. & univ. adminstrs. 1973-74, bd. dirs. 1985-86), Western Assn. Schs. and Colls. (accrediting commn. sr. colls. and univs. 1974-78, chmn., 1978-82, pres. 1979-81), N.W. Assn. Schs. and Colls. (commn. colls. 1974-80), Assn. Am. Colls. (bd. dirs. 1972-75, vice chmn. 1975-76), Assn. Western Univs. (bd. dirs.), Coun. Postsecondary Accreditation (bd. dirs. 1977-88, exec. com. 1979-88, chmn. 1985-87, immediate past chmn., 1988-89, chmn. com. recognition 1982-84), Am. Assn. State Colls. and Univs. (chmn. accreditation com. 1983-86, com. acad. pers. and acad. freedom 1987-88, com. on acad. affairs 1988-91), Calif. Coun. Edn. (trustee), Western Polit. Sci. Assn. (exec. coun. 1958-61), Hayward C. of C. (dir. 1968-71, 73-76, 77-80, 82-85, 86-90), Regional Assn. East Bay Colls. and Univs. (exec. com. 1974-90, sec. 1975-76, 87-88, vice chmn. 1976-77, 84-85, chmn. 1977-79, 85-86), Rotary, Phi Beta Kappa, Pi Gamma Mu, Pi Sigma Alpha. Club: Bohemian (San Francisco). Home: 17577 Parker Rd Castro Valley CA 94546-1227 Office: Calif State U Pres Emeritus LI 3167 Hayward CA 94542-3053

MC CUNE, JOHN FRANCIS, III, retired architect; b. New Castle, Pa., Oct. 23, 1921; s. John Francis and Alice (Miles) McC.; m. Jeanne Ramsay, Sept. 28, 1946; children—Morgan R., Martha (Mrs. Dennis L. Maddox), David M., William S. Student, Vanderbilt U., 1938-40; B.S. in Architecture, U. Mich., 1943. Draftsman firm Walter E. Bort (Architect), Clinton, Iowa, 1946-47; firm Pope & Kruse (Architects), Wilmington, Del., 1947-54; asso. Pope & Kruse (Architects), 1955-60; partner firm Pope, Kruse & McCune (Architects), Wilmington, 1961-72; owner McCune Assos. (Architects), Wilmington, 1972-81; v.p., prin. architect Diamond/McCune (Architects & Engrs.), Wilmington, 1981-88. Projects include Gander Hill Correctional Facility; renovation of Wilmington Public Bldg, all Wilmington; historic preservation projects include Presbyn. Ch, New Castle, Old Court House, New Castle, Barrett's Chapel, Frederica, Del., Old State House, Dover, Del., Loockerman Hall, Dover. Mem. Hist. Area Commn., New Castle, Del., 1974-88. Mem. AIA (pres. Del. chpt. 1970-71, mem. nat. com. historic resources 1975-88, state preservation coordinator Del. 1975-88), Soc. Archtl. Historians, Assn. for Preservation Tech., ASTM (com.), Nat. Trust Hist. Preservation, Del. C. of C., Nat. Fire Protection Assn. (com. libraries, museums and hist. bldgs. 1975-88), Kappa Sigma. Home: 14011 Antelope Ct Sun City West AZ 85375

MCCUNE, MARY JOAN HUXLEY, microbiology educator; b. Lewistown, Mont., Jan. 14, 1932; d. Thomas Leonard and Anna Dorothy (Hardie) Huxley; m. Ronald William McCune, June 7, 1965; children: Anna Orpha, Heather Jean. BS, Mont. State Coll., 1953; MS, Wash. State U., 1955; PhD, Purdue U., 1965. Rsch. technician VA Hosp., Oakland, Calif., 1956-59; bacteriologist U.S. Naval Radiol. Def. Lab., San Francisco, 1959-61; tchg. assoc. Purdue U., West Lafayette, Ind., 1961-65, vis. asst. prof., 1965-66; asst. prof. Occidental Coll., L.A., 1966-69; asst. rsch. bacteriologist II UCLA, 1969-70; affiliate asst. prof. Idaho State U., Pocatello, 1970-80, from asst. prof. to prof. microbiology, 1980—; instr. U. Calif., Davis, 1964. Contbr. articles to profl. jours. Pres. AK chpt. PEO, Pocatello, 1988-89; chair faculty senate Idaho State U., 1994-95. David Ross fellow Purdue U., 1964. Mem. AAAS, N.Y. Acad. Sci., Idaho Acad. Sci. (trustee 1989-95, v.p. 1992-93, pres. 1993-94), Am. Soc. for Microbiology (v.p. Intermountain br. 1988-89, pres. 1989-90), Idaho Edn. Alliance for Sci. (bd. dirs.), Sigma Xi, Sigma Delta Epsilon. Presbyterian. Home: 30 Colgate St Pocatello ID 83201-3459 Office: Idaho State U Dept Biol Scis Pocatello ID 83209

MCCUNE, THOMAS, construction executive contractor. CEO M. A. Mortenson, Mpls. Office: M A Mortenson PO Box 710 Minneapolis MN 55440*

MC CUNE, WILLIAM JAMES, JR., manufacturing company executive; b. Glens Falls, N.Y., June 2, 1915; s. William James and Brunnhilde (Decker) McC.; m. Janet Waters, Apr. 19, 1940; 1 dau., Constance (Mrs. Leslie Sheppard); m. Elisabeth Johnson, Aug. 8, 1946; children: William Joseph, Heather H.D. SB, MIT, 1937. With Polaroid Corp., Cambridge, Mass., 1939-91, v.p. engring., 1954-69, v.p., asst. gen. mgr., 1963-69, exec. v.p., 1969-75, dir., pres., 1975-83, CEO, 1975-86, chmn. bd., 1982-91, ret., 1991—. Chmn. bd., trustee Mitre Corp.; Trustee Boston Mus. Sci., Mass. Gen. Hosp. Fellow Am. Acad. Arts and Scis.; mem. Nat. Acad. Engring. Office: Polaroid Corp 549 Technology Sq Cambridge MA 02139-3539

MCCURDY, GILBERT GEIER, retired retailer; b. Rochester, N.Y., May 25, 1922; s. Gilbert J.C. and Virginia (Geier) McC.; m. Katherine W. Babcock, Nov. 9, 1946; children—Gilbert Kennedy, Lynda Babcock (Mrs. Hotra). B.A., Williams Coll., 1944. With McCurdy & Co., Inc., Rochester, 1946—; controller, asst. treas. McCurdy & Co., Inc., 1953-55, v.p., 1956-59, exec. v.p., 1959-62, pres., gen. mgr., 1962-80, chief exec. officer, 1969-80, chmn. bd., chief exec. officer, 1980-92, chmn. exec. com. of bd., 1993—; chmn. bd. Frederick Atkins, 1968-70; dir. Chase Lincoln First Bank of Rochester; former dir. Chase Lincoln First Bank of Rochester. Bd. dirs. Pathway Houses of Rochester; former mem. bd. dirs. United Way Rochester and Monroe County; sr. trustee U. Rochester. 1st lt. Signal Corps, AUS, 1943-46. Mem. Rochester C. of C. (pres. 1975). Baptist. Home: 1 Whitney Ln Rochester NY 14610-3551 Office: Midtown Plz Rochester NY 14645

MC CURDY, HAROLD GRIER, psychologist; b. Salisbury, N.C., May 30, 1909; s. McKinnon Grier and Nellie (Curd) McC.; m. Mary Burton Derrickson, Sept. 15, 1937; children: John Derrickson, Ann Lewis. A.B., Duke U., 1930, Ph.D., 1938. Asst. prof. biology High Point Coll., 1931-32; caseworker Fed. Transient Bur., Salisbury, N.C., 1934; prof. psychology Milligan Coll., 1938-41; assoc. prof. to prof. psychology and philosophy Meredith Coll., 1941-48; assoc. prof. to Kenan prof. psychology U. N.C., Chapel Hill, 1948-71; Kenan prof. psychology emeritus U. N.C., 1971—. Author: The Personality of Shakespeare, 1953, reprint, 1973, The Personal World, 1961, Personality and Science, 1965, Barbara, 1966, About Mary, 1989, (poetry) Oblation, 1990, 50 Metaphysical Sonnets for a Rock Age, 1993; contbg. author: Historical Roots of Contemporary Psychology, 1968, Humanistic Psychology, 1981, Foundations of Psychology, 1984; poetry The Chastening of Narcissus, 1970, Novus Ordo Seclorum, 1981, And Then the Sky Turned Blue, 1982, Twenty Four Bagatelles in an Antique Mode, 1989, others. Mem. AAAS, Am. Psychol. Assn., Sigma Xi. Democrat. Methodist. Home: 6 Gooseneck Rd Chapel Hill NC 27514-4600

MCCURDY, HARRY WARD, otolaryngologist; b. Branchton, Pa., Aug. 15, 1918; s. Adam Oscar and Sarah Fern (Hindman) McC.; m. Joan Jacqueline Talty, Dec. 10, 1955; children: Bridget Elizabeth, Peter Adam. A.B., Allegheny Coll., 1940; M.D., U. Pa., 1943. Diplomate: Am. Bd. Otolaryngology. Intern Geisinger Meml. Hosp., Danville, Pa., 1944; resident in otolaryngology Geisinger Meml. Hosp., 1944-45, 48-49; resident in pathology Hamot Hosp., Erie, Pa., 1945-48; mem. staff Geisinger Med. Center, Danville, 1948-50; commd. 2d lt. U.S. Army, 1945, advanced through grades to col., 1962-74; mil. cons. Surgeon Gen., U.S. Army, 1964-74; ret., 1974; exec. v.p. Am. Acad. Otolaryngology-Head and Neck Surgery, Washington, 1974-84; mem. staff Walter Reed Army Hosp.; Mem. resources council Gallaudet Coll., 1975-80; mem. nat. adv. council Sertoma Found., 1976-84; chmn. FDA Panel on Otolaryngologic Med. Devices, 1974-78, cons., 1978-84. Mem. ACS, AMA, Royal Soc. Medicine (U.K.), Am. Acad. Otolaryngology, Mil. Surgeons Assn., Am. Soc. Assn. Execs., Soc. Med. Consultants to Armed Forces, AAAS, Am. Soc. Facial Plastic Surgery, Soc. Mil. Otolaryngologists, Am. Acad. Facial Plastic and Reconstructive Surgery, Am. Laryngol., Rhinol. and Otol. Soc., Anglo-Am. Med. Soc., Am. Audiology Soc., Royal Soc. Health, Osler Med. Soc., Acad. Medicine, Soc. Univ. Otolaryngologists, Am. Council Otolaryngology, Pan-Am. Soc. Bronchoesophagology., Internat. Fedn. Otolaryngol. Socs. (sec. gen. 1981—), Soc. Mil. Cons. to Armed Forces (sec. 1993—). Republican. Methodist. Clubs: Army Navy, Press, Mil. Attaches of London, Les Chevaliers du Tastevin. Home and Office: 6006 Dellwood Pl Bethesda MD 20817-3812

MCCURDY, LARRY WAYNE, automotive parts company executive; b. Commerce, Tex., July 1, 1935; s. Weldon Lee and Eula Bell (Quinn) McC.; m. Anna Jean Ogle, June 2, 1956; children: Michael, Kimberly, Laurie. BBA, Tex. A&M U., 1957. Jr. acct. Tenneco Inc., Houston, 1958-60; sr. acct. Tenneco Oil Co., Houston, 1960-64; acctg. supr. Tenneco Chems., Houston, 1964-69; div. controller Tenneco Chems., Saddle Brook, N.J., 1970-72, corp. controller, 1972-74, v.p., fin., 1974-78; sr. v.p. fin. Tenneco Automotive, Deerfield, Ill., 1978-80; pres. Walker Mfg. Co., Racine, Wis., 1980-81; exec. v.p. N.Am. ops. Tenneco Automotive, Deerfield, 1981-82; v.p. fin. Echlin Inc., Branford, Conn., 1983, pres. chief operating officer, 1983-85; pres., chief exec. officer Moog Automotive Inc., St. Louis, 1985-94; exec. v.p. ops. Cooper Industries, Houston, 1994-97; pres., CEO Echlin, Inc., Branford, Conn., 1997—; bd. dirs. Lear Seating Corp., Mohawk Industries, Inc., Breed Tech., Inc. Trustee Somerset County Coll., Somerville, N.J., 1974-78, Millikin U., Decatur, Ill., 1991—; former mem. bd. dirs. Jr. Achievement, Chgo.; bd. dirs. Sam Houston coun. Boy Scouts Am., 1995—; mem. adv. coun. Tex. A&M U. Engring. Sch., 1995—. Mem. Fin. Execs. Inst., Nat. Assn. Accts., Motor Equipment Mfrs. Assn. (chmn. bd. dirs. 1989). Office: Echlin Inc 100 Double Beach Rd Branford CT 06405-4909

MCCURDY, LAYTON, medical educator; b. Florence, S.C., Aug. 20, 1935; m. Gwendolyn A. McCurdy, 1958; children: Robert Jr., David Barclay. BS, U. N.C., 1956; MD, Med. U. S.C., 1960. Dipplomate Am. Bd. Psychiatry and Neurology (bd. dirs. 1983-91, pres. 1990); lic. psychiatrist, S.C., N.C., Md., Ga., Pa. Resident in psychiatry N.C. Meml. Hosp., Chapel Hill, 1961-64; with psychiatry tng. br. NIMH, Bethesda, Md., 1964-66; asst. prof. dept. psychiatry Sch. Medicine Emory U., Atlanta, 1966-68; prof., chmn. dept. psychiatry and behavioral scis. Med. U. S.C., 1968-82, v.p. med. affairs, dean, 1990—; prof. psychiatry Sch. Medicine U. Pa., Phila., 1982-90; psychiatrist-in-chief Inst. of Pa. Hosp., Phila., 1982-90; vis. colleague Inst. Psychiatry, U. London, 1974-75; nat. adv. mental health coun. NIMH, 1980-83; apptd. Pa. Adv. Com. for Mental Health and Mental Retardation, 1984-87; chmn. consensus panel on panic disorder NIH, 1991. Recipient Disting. Alumnus award Med. U. S.C., 1988, George C. Ham. Soc., 1990; rsch. fellow NIMH, 1974-75. Fellow Am. Coll. Psychiatrists (bd. regents 1987-90, v.p. 1990-93, pres. 1993-94, Bowis award 1997), Am. Psychiat. Assn. (joint commn. pub. affairs 1981-84, chmn. com. on diagnosis and assessment 1988-94), So. Psychiat. Assn. (bd. regents 1977-80, chmn. bd. regents 1979-80), Royal Coll. Psychiatrists (U.K.); mem. AMA, Assn. for Acad. Psychiatry (pres. 1970-72), S.C. Med. Assn., Charleston County Med. Soc. (exec. com.), Waring Libr. Soc. (pres. 1979-80), Cosmos Club (Washington)., Alpha Omega Alpha. Office: Med U SC Coll Medicine 171 Ashley Ave Ste 601 Csb Charleston SC 29425-0001

MCCURDY, MICHAEL CHARLES, illustrator, author; b. N.Y.C., Feb. 17, 1942; s. Charles Errett and Beatrice (Beatson) McC.; m. Deborah Lamb, Sept. 7, 1968; children: Heather, Mark. BFA, Tufts U., 1964, MFA, 1971. Dir. Penmaen Press, Lincoln, Mass., 1968-85; instr. Concord (Mass.) Acad., 1972-75, Wellesley (Mass.) Coll., 1976. Illustrator: The Man Who Planted Trees, 1985, American Tall Tales, 1991, American Buffalo, 1992, The Winged Life: The Poetry of Henry David Thoreau, 1992, The Beasts of Bethlehem, 1992, McCurdy's World, 1992, The Way West: Journal of a Pioneer Woman, 1993, Giants in the Land, 1993, The Gettysburg Address, 1995; author, illustrator: Hannah's Farm, 1988, The Old Man and the Fiddle, 1992; editor, illustrator: Escape From Slavery: The Boyhood of Frederick Douglass in His Own Words, 1994, The Season Sewn, 1996. Mem. Great Barrington (Mass.) Housing Authority, 1990-93. Small press grantee Nat. Endowment Arts, 1978, Mass. Arts and Humanities, 1978. Mem. Soc. Printers, St. Botolph Club. Democrat. Episcopalian.

MC CURDY, PATRICK PIERRE, editor, consultant; b. Angers, France, Sept. 14, 1928; s. Joseph Alexander and Constance Yolande (Hillairet de Boisferon) McC.; m. Eiko Yamada, May 30, 1953; children: Alan J., Wendy C., Alec J., Jeffrey R. B.S. in Chem. Engring., Carnegie Inst. Tech., 1949. Chem. engr. tech. service dept. Humble Oil & Refining Co., Baytown, Tex., 1949-50; chem. engr. Callery Chem. Co., Pa., 1954-56; sr. chem. engr. U.S. Army Engr. R & D Labs., Ft. Belvoir, Va., 1956-60; asst. editor Chem. & Engring. News, Washington, 1960-61, N.Y.C., 1961-62; bur. head Chem. & Engring. News, Frankfurt, Germany, 1962-64, Tokyo, 1964-67; mng. editor Chem. & Engring. News, Washington, 1967-69; editor Chem. & Engring. News, 1969-73; editor in chief Chemical Week, 1973-80, 84-87, editor-in-chief, assoc. pub., 1987-88; dir. communications Am. Chem. Soc., 1988-91, dir. industry rels., 1991-93, editor Today's Chemist at Work, 1989—; cons. American Chemical Soc., 1993—; pub. issues mgr. Dow Chem. Co., Midland, Mich., 1980-82, dir. tech. communications, 1982-84; bd. dirs. Centcom, Ltd. Served to 1st lt. C.E. AUS, 1950-54. Recipient Jesse H. Neal award, 1979, finalist 1985; recipient Carnegie Mellon Univ. Alumni Merit award, 1988. Mem. AIChE, Am. Chem. Soc., Fgn. Corrs. Club Japan, Chemists Club (suburban v.p.), Societe de Chimie Industrielle (bd. dirs. Am. sect., past pres.), Soc. Chem. Industry (Am. sect.), Comml. Devel. Assn., Tokyo Am. Club, Tau Beta Pi, Phi Kappa Phi, Theta Tau, Phi Kappa. Home: 11717 Chauncey Ln Mason Neck VA 22079-4140 Office: 1155 16th St NW Washington DC 20036-4800

MCCURDY, RICHARD CLARK, engineering consultant; b. Newton, Iowa, Jan. 2, 1909; s. Ralph Bruce and Florence (Clark) McC.; m. Harriet Edith Sutton, Sept. 11, 1933; children: Gregor, Richard, Carolyn, Robert. A.B., Stanford U., 1931, E.M., 1933. With engring. and prodn. div. Shell Oil Co., 1933-47; with prodn. mgmt. Shell Caribbean Petroleum Co., 1947-50; gen. mgr. Shell Group Companies, Venezuela, 1950-53; pres. Shell Chem. Co., N.Y.C., 1953-65; dir. Shell Oil Co., mem. exec. com., 1959-69, pres., chief exec. officer, 1965-69; assoc. adminstr. orgn. and mgmt. NASA, Washington, 1970-73; cons. NASA, 1974-82. Trustee United Seamans Service, 1954-70, Stanford U., 1965-70; trustee Hood Coll., 1968-86, trustee emeritus, 1986—, hon. trustee, 1987—; trustee Rensselaer Poly. Inst., 1974-86, hon. trustee, 1986—. Recipient Disting. Service medal NASA, 1972. Mem. Mfg. Chemists Assn. (dir. 1955-65, chmn. bd. 1961-62, chmn. exec. com. 1964-65), Am. Inst. Mining, Metall. and Petroleum Engrs., Am. Phys. Soc., Am. Petroleum Inst., N.Y. Yacht Club, Noroton (Conn.) Yacht Club (commodore), Cruising of Am. (commodore 1980-82), Beta Theta Pi. Home: Contentment Island Darien CT 06820

MC CURLEY, ROBERT LEE, JR., lawyer; b. Gadsden, Ala., Sept. 7, 1941; s. Robert Lee and Nellie Ruth McC.; 1 child, Allison Leah. BS, U. Ala., 1963, JD, 1966. Bar: Ala. 1966, D.C. 1973, U.S. Ct. Mil. Appeals 1966, U.S. Supreme Ct. 1970, U.S. Ct. Appeals (5th cir.) 1972, U.S. Ct. Appeals (11th cir.) 1973, U.S. Ct. Appeals (fed. cir.) 1981. Am. Law Inst. asst. to dir. Fed. Savs. & Loan Ins. Corp., Washington, 1966-67; partner firm Rains, Rains, McCurley & Wilson, Gadsden, Ala., 1967-75; city judge Southside, Ala., 1970-75; dir. Ala. Law Inst.; assoc. dir. U. Ala. Center Public Law and Service, 1981-82; asst. dean Sch. Law U. Ala., 1978-81; panelist White House Conf. on Volunteerism; pres. Gadsden Jaycees, 1972; mem. White House Fifty States Project; Henry Toll fellow Coun. State Govt., 1992. Editor: Divorce, Alimony and Child Support Custody, 3d edit., 1993, Land Laws of Alabama, 5th edit., 1990, The Legislative Process, 6th edit., 1995, Alabama Law Office Practice Deskbook, 7th edit., 1995, Federally Mandated State Legislation, 1990, Alabama Legislation, Cases and Statutes, 3d edit., 1992, Alabama Election Handbook, 7th edit., 1996. Pres. Gadsden Boys Club, 1971; mem. Nat. Dem. Charter Commn., 1974. Mem. ABA, Am. Law Inst. Order of Coif, Scribes, Farrah Law Soc., Commn. Uniform State Laws, Nat. Conf. State Legislatures (exec. com. legal staff sect.), Kiwanis (pres. Tuscaloosa club 1976, gov. Ala. dist. 1984, internat. v.p. 1991-92, trustee Internat. Found. 1994-97, treas. 1996-97), Indian Hills County Club, Univ. Club. Baptist.

MCCURN, NEAL PETERS, federal judge; b. Syracuse, N.Y., Apr. 6, 1926. LL.B., Syracuse U., 1952, J.D., 1960. Bar: N.Y. 1952. Ptnr. Mackenzie Smith Lewis Mitchell & Hughes, Syracuse, 1957-79; judge U.S. Dist. Ct. (no. dist.) N.Y., 1979-88; chief judge U.S. Dist. Ct. (no. dist.), N.Y., 1988-93; sr. judge, 1993—; del. N.Y. State Constl. Conv., 1976; mem. 2d Cir. Jud. Council. Pres. Syracuse Common Coun., 1970-78. Mem. ABA, N.Y. State Bar Assn. (chmn. state constn. com.), Onondaga County Bar Assn. (past pres.), Am. Coll. Trial Lawyers, Am. Judicature Soc. (bd. dirs. 1980-84). Office: US Dist Ct 100 S Clinton St Rm 33 Syracuse NY 13261-9211

MCCURRY, MARGARET IRENE, architect, educator; b. Chgo., Sept. 26, 1942; d. Paul D. and Irene B. McC.; m. Stanley Tigerman, Mar. 17, 1979. BA, Vassar Coll., 1964. Registered architect, Ill., Mass., Mich.; registered interior designer, Ill. Design coord. Quaker Oats Co., Chgo., 1964-66; sr. interior designer Skidmore, Owings & Merrill, Chgo., 1966-77; pvt. practice architect Margaret I, Chgo., 1977-82; ptnr. Tigerman, McCurry, Chgo., 1982—; vis. studio critic Art Inst. Chgo., 1985-86, 88, lectr., 1988, bd. dirs. Archtl. Soc., 1988—, adv. bd. textile dept., 1992—; vis. studio critic U. Ill., Chgo., Miami U., Oxford, Ohio, 1990; juror Internat. furniture awards Progressive Architecture mag., N.Y.C., 1986, advt. awards, 1988; juror design grants Nat. Endowment for Arts, Washington, 1983; NEA Challenge Design Rev., 1992; peer reviewer design excellence program Gen. Svcs. Adminstrn., 1992—; juror, Wis., Minn., Calif., Va., Washington, Pitts., Ky., Conn. Soc. Architects, Detroit, N.Y.C., Memphis, Austin, L.A. chpts. AIA, Am. Wood Coun., Am. Inst. Architecture Students Design Competition, 1993. Contbr. Chgo. Archtl. Club Jour.; designer, contbr. archtl. exhibit Art Inst. Chgo., 1983-85, 93, Chgo. Hist. Soc., 1984, Gulbenkian Found., Lisbon Portugal, 1989, Chgo. Athenaeum, 1990, Gwenda Jay Gallery, 1992, Women of Design Traveling Exhbn., 1992-96; archtl. drawings and models in permanent collection Art Inst. Chgo. and Deutsches Architektur Mus., Frankfurt. Chmn. furniture sect. fundraising auction Sta. WTTW-TV, PBS, Chgo., 1975-76; mem. Chgo. Beautiful Com., 1968-70; pres. alumni coun. Grad. Sch. Design, Harvard U.; bd. mem. Architecture and Design Soc. Art Inst. Chgo., mem. textile adv. bd. textile dept. Loeb fellow Harvard U., 1986-87; recipient Builders Choice Grand award Builders Mag., 1985, Interior Design award Interiors Mag., 1983, Dean of Architecture award Chgo. Design Source and the Merchandise Mart, 1989; inducted into Interior Design Hall of Fame, Interior Design Mag., 1990. Fellow AIA (v.p. bd. dirs. Chgo. chpt. 1984-89, chairperson 1993, nat. design com., lectr. Colo. chpt. 1985, nat. conv. 1988, 97, Monterey Design Conf. 1989, Washington Design Ctr. 1989, Nat. Honor award 1984, Nat. Interior Architecture award 1992, Disting. Bldg. award Chgo. chpt. 1984, 86, 91, 94, Disting. Interior Architecture award 1981, 83, 88, 91, product display Neocon award 1985, 88), Coll. of Fellows AIA, Internat. Interior Design Assn., Chgo. Network, Am. Soc. Interior Designers (Nat. Design award 1992, 94, Ill. chpt. Design award 1994, Ill. chpt. Merit award 1994, v.p. bd. dirs. Chgo. chpt.), Chgo. Archtl. Club, Arts Club Chgo., Womens Athletic Club. Episcopalian. Avocations: drawing, writing, travel, tennis, golf. Office: Tigerman McCurry Archs 444 N Wells St Chicago IL 60610

MCCURRY, MICHAEL DEMAREE, government spokesman, press secretary; b. Charleston, S.C., Oct. 27, 1954; s. William Joseph and Rosemary (Demaree) McC.; Debra Lyn Jones, June 16, 1984; children: William Harry, Marjorie Vera, Christopher Michael. BA, Princeton U., 1976; MA, Georgetown U., 1985. Press sec. Sen. Harrison Williams, Washington, 1976-81, Sen. Daniel P. Moynihan, Washington, 1981-83, Sen. John Glenn, Washington, 1984; pub. affairs dir. ERISA Industry Com., Washington, 1985; press sec. Gov. Bruce Babbitt, Phoenix, 1986-88; dir. comms. Dem. Nat. Com., Washington, 1988-90; sr. v.p. Robinson, Lake, Lerer & Montgomery, Washington, 1990-93; spokesman U.S. Dept. State, Washington, 1993-95; press sec. White House, Washington, 1995—. Mem. coun. St. Paul's United Meth. Ch., Kensington, Md., 1992—. Office: The White House Office Office of the Press Secretary 1600 Pennsylvania Ave NW Washington DC 20500-0005*

MCCUSKER, JOHN, financial executive; b. Bklyn., May 28, 1939; s. John Michael and Helen Frances (Sweeney) McC.; BBA, St. John's U., 1961; m. Brenda Ann Caprio, June 27, 1964; children: John Christian, Joseph Andrew, David Douglas. Sr. acct. Haskins & Sells, N.Y.C., 1961-67; asst. dir. fin. planning Colt Industries, Inc., N.Y.C., 1967-69; dir. fin. planning Shearson Hammill & Co., N.Y.C., 1969-70; dir. fin. analysis The Allen Group, Inc., Melville, N.Y., 1971-73, asst. corp. contr., 1974-76, v.p., contr., 1976-82, v.p. fin., 1983-87, sr. v.p. fin., 1987-96; sr. v.p. fin. Geraghty & Miller, Inc., Melville, N.Y., 1997; pres. McCusker Assocs., Melville , N.Y. Bd. dirs. Nassau-Sufffolk Hosp. Coun., 1983-88, chmn., 1986-89; treas. b. Huntington (N.Y.) Hosp., 1978-86, bd. dirs., 1979—, chmn., 1989-92, Family Svc. League Suffolk County, Huntington, N.Y. Served with U.S. Army, 1963. CPA, N.Y. Mem. AICPAs, N.Y. State Soc. CPAs, Fin. Execs. Inst. Republican. Roman Catholic. Home: 4 Harbor View Dr Huntington NY 11743-6710 Office: 88 Duryea Rd Melville NY 11747-3803

MCCUSKEY, ROBERT SCOTT, anatomy educator, researcher; b. Cleve., Sept. 8, 1938; s. Sidney Wilcox and Jeannette M. (Scott) M.; m. Rebecca Woodworth, July 19, 1958 (div.); children: Geoffrey, Gregory, Michael; m. Margaret A. Krasovich, Apr. 17, 1993. A.B., Western Res. U., 1960, Ph.D., 1965. Instr. anatomy U. Cin., 1965-67, asst. prof., 1967-71, assoc. prof., 1971-75, prof., 1975-78; prof., chmn. anatomy W.Va. U., Morgantown, 1978-86; prof., head dept. cell biology and anatomy U. Ariz., Tucson, 1986—, prof. physiology, 1987—; vis. prof. U. Heidelberg, Fed. Republic Germany, 1981-83, 87-88, 93-95; cons. Hoffmann-La Roche, N.J., 1972-75, Procter & Gamble Co., Cin. 1966-86. Recipient NIH Rsch. Career Devel. award, 1969-74; Humboldt Sr. U.S. Scientist prize, Fed. Republic Germany, 1982, Nishimaru award Japan Microcirculatory Soc., 1987; grantee NIH, NSF, 1966—. Mem. AAAS, Microcirculatory Soc., Am. Assn. Anatomists, Am. Assn. Study Liver Diseases, Rsch. Soc. on Alcoholism, Internat. Soc. Exptl. Hematology, Microscopy Soc. Am. Mem. editorial bd. Microvascular Rsch., 1974-84, Shock, 1993—, Am. Jour. Physiology, 1995—; contbr. numerous articles to profl. jours. Office: Ariz Health Scis Ctr Dept Cell Biology and Anatomy P O Box 245044 Tucson AZ 85724-5044

MCCUTCHAN, GORDON EUGENE, lawyer, insurance company executive; b. Buffalo, Sept. 30, 1935; s. George Lawrence and Mary Esther (De Puy) McC.; m. Linda Brown; children: Lindsey, Elizabeth. B.A., Cornell U., 1956, M.B.A., 1958, LL.B., 1959. Bar: N.Y. 1959, Ohio 1964. Pvt. practice Rome, N.Y., 1959-61; atty., advisor SEC, Washington, 1961-64; ptnr. McCutchan, Druen, Maynard, Rath & Dietrich, 1964-94; mem. office of gen.

counsel Nationwide Mut. Ins. Co., Columbus, Ohio, 1964-94, sr. v.p., gen. counsel, 1982-89; exec. v.p., gen. counsel Nationwide Mut. Ins. Co., 1989-94; exec. v.p. Law and Corp. Svcs., Nationwide Ins. Enterprise, 1994—. Trustee, bd. govs. Franklin U.; trustee Ohio Tuition Trust Authority. Mem. Columbus Bar Assn., Ohio Bar Assn., Am. Corp. Counsel Assn., Assn. Life Inst. Counsel (bd. govs. 1990-94), Fedn. Ins. and Corp. Counsel, Am. Coun. Life Ins. (chair legal sect. 1992-93). Home: 2376 Oxford Rd Columbus OH 43221-4011 Office: Nationwide Mut Ins Co 1 Nationwide Plz Columbus OH 43215-2220 also: Employers Ins Wausau 2000 Westwood Dr Wausau WI 54401-7802

MCCUTCHEN, CHARLES WILLIAM, chemical engineer; b. Wichita Falls, Tex., Nov. 20, 1928; s. William Urlin and Karis (Jameson) McC.; m. Joyce Forse, June 10, 1956; children: David William, Karis Ann. BSChE, MIT, 1949. Engring. trainee Dow Chem. Co., Midland, Mich., 1949; R&D engr. Dow Chem. Co., Freeport, Tex., 1949-68; sr. process engr. Dow Chem. Co., —, —, 1968-79, internal process cons., 1979-86; ret., 1986. Mem. AIChE. Achievements include 4 U.S. patents. Home: 109 Blossom St Lake Jackson TX 77566

MCCUTCHEON, HOLLY MARIE, accountant; b. Pitts., Aug. 14, 1950; d. George and Ruth (Bradburn) Rudawski. Student, Ohio Dominican Coll., 1968-69, Wittenburg U., 1979-81; BS in Acctg. and Fin. magna cum laude, Wright State U., 1983. Cert. mgmt. acct. Acct. Morris Bean & Co., Yellow Springs, Ohio, 1983-86; contr. Speco Aerospace Corp., Springfield, Ohio, 1986-96, AIDA-Dayton (Ohio) Techs. Corp., Dayton, Ohio, 1996—; cons. Glenwood Tng. Ctr., Yellow Springs, 1983-86. Coach City Recreation Youth Soccer, Springfield, 1982-85; mem. st. Raphael Adult Choir, Springfield, 1986-89. Mem. Inst. Mgmt. Accts. (pres. Dayton chpt. 1994-95). Avocations: fishing, golf, tennis, cross country skiing. Office: AIDA-Dayton Techs Corp 3131 S Dixie Dr Ste 401 Dayton OH 45439-2223

MC CUTCHEON, JOHN TINNEY, JR., journalist; b. Chgo., Nov. 8, 1917; s. John Tinney and Evelyn (Shaw) McC.; m. Susan Dart, Feb. 1, 1943; children: Anne McCutcheon Lewis, Mary, John Tinney III. BS, Harvard U., 1939. Reporter City News Bur., Chgo., 1939-40; Reporter Chgo. Tribune, 1940-51, editor column A Line O' Type or Two, 1951-57, editorial writer, 1957-71, editor editorial page, 1971-82, columnist, 1967-70. Pres. Lake Forest (Ill.) Libr., 1970-72. Served with USNR, 1941-46. Mem. Soc. Midland Authors, Am. Soc. Newspaper Editors, Nat. Conf. Editorial Writers, Geog. Soc. Chgo. (pres. 1955-57), Chgo. Zool. Soc. (hon. trustee), Chgo. Hist. Soc. (life trustee), Inter Am. Press Assn. (dir., freedom of press com. 1978-87), Sigma Delta Chi. Clubs: Onwentsia (Lake Forest), Tavern (Chgo.), Wayfarers (Chgo.). Home: PO Box 689 Lake Forest IL 60045-0689 also: 99 Holbert Cove Rd Saluda NC 28773-9502

MCCUTCHEON, STEVEN CLIFTON, hydrologist, environmental engineer; b. Decatur, Ala., Oct. 29, 1952; s. Bernard Clifton and Rosa May (Askenburg) McC.; m. Sherry Lynn Sharp; children: Michael Ian, Alexander Tavis. BS, Auburn U., 1975; MS, Vanderbilt U., 1977, PhD, 1979. Registered profl. engr., La. Hydrologist U.S. Geol. Survey, Bay St. Louis, Miss., 1977-86; environ. engr. U.S. EPA, Athens, Ga., 1986—; adj. asst. prof. Tulane U., New Orleans, 1984-85; panel mem. Nat. Rsch. Coun., Washington, 1989-92; adj. prof. Forestry U. Ga., Athens, 1994—; asst. prof. Clemson (S.C.) U., 1990-97; program evaluator Accreditation Bd. Engring. & Tech., 1992—. Author: Water Quality Modeling, vol. 1, 1989, (with others) Fate and Transport of Sediment-Associated Contaminants, 1989, Water Quality, Handbook of Hydrology, 1993; editor and author: (with others) Manual for Performing Estuarine Waste Load Allocations, 1990, Hydrodynamics and Transport for Water Quality Modeling, 1997; editor Jour. Environ. Engring., 1992-94; mem. editl. bd. Ecol. Engring., 1995—; vice-chair editl. bd. Hazardous Toxic and Radioactive Waste Mgmt., 1996—. Mem. Zoning Commn., St. Tammany Parish, La., 1984-85; vice=chmn. Planning Adv. Bd., St. Tammany Parish, 1985; asst. den leader pack 83 Cub Scouts Am., Athens, 1991-92. Recipient medal and plaque Korea Soc. Water Pollution Rsch. and Control, Seoul, 1986, Engr. of Yr. award in EPA, NSPE, 1992, EPA Sci. Achievement award in Waste Mgmt. Air and Waste Mgmt. Assn., 1995, EPA Sci. Achievement award in Chemistry Am. Chem. Soc., 1997, Richard R. Torrens award Am. Soc. of Civil Engineers, 1994. Mem. ASCE (br. pres. 1983-84, Young Civil Engr. of Yr. award 1984, Torrens award 1994), Am. Geophys. Union, Internat. Soc. Environ. Ethics, Internat. Assn. Water Quality, Internat. Assn. Hydrologic Scis., Water Environ. Fedn., Sigma Xi (chpt. sec. 1982-84, membership com. 1984-85), Phi Kappa Phi, Phi Theta Kappa. Achievements include development of phytoremediation and ecological engineering to clean up federal facilities and response to Exxon Valdez oil spill. Home: 147 Spalding Ct Athens GA 30605-3716 Office: US EPA Nat Exposure Rsch Lab 960 College Station Rd Athens GA 30605-2720

MCDADE, JAMES RUSSELL, management consultant; b. Dallas, Jan. 15, 1925; s. Marion W. and Jeannette (Reneau) McD.; m. Elaine Bushey, Sep. 10, 1955. BSEE, So. Meth. U., Dallas, 1947; MBA, Northwestern U., Evanston, Ill., 1950. Asst. to pres. Davidson Corp., Chgo., 1951-52; asst. to pres. Mergenthaler Linotype Co., Bklyn., 1952-53, comml. works mgr., 1953-56; chief indsl. engr. Tex. Instruments, Inc., Dallas, 1956-57, product gen. mgr., 1958-60, v.p., 1961-64; chmn. bd. McDade Properties Co., Aspen (Colo.), Denver, Dallas, 1964—; bd. dirs. Pitkin County Bank, Aspen; chmn. bd. dirs. Harley-Davidson Tex., Westec Security of Aspen, Aspen Security, Inc. Founding mem. Aspen Art Mus., 1980; mem. Ballet Aspen, 1980—; pres. club Aspen Valley Hosp., 1984—. Served to 1st lt. USAF, 1943-46. Mem. Rep. Senatorial Inner Circle, Am. Mgmt. Assn., Presidents Assn. Avocations: skiing, horseback riding, camping, swimming. Home and Office: 1000 Red Mountain Rd PO Box 9090 Aspen CO 81612-9090

MCDADE, JOE BILLY, federal judge; b. 1937. BS, Bradley U., 1959, MA, 1960; JD, U. Mich., 1963. Staff atty. antitrust divsn. U.S. Dept. Justice, 1963-65; exec. trainee First Fed. Savs. and Loan Assn., 1965; exec. dir. Greater Peoria (Ill.) Legal Aid Soc., 1965-69; ptnr. Hafele & McDade, Peoria, Ill., 1968-77; pvt. practice Peoria, 1977-82; assoc. cir. judge State of Ill., 1982-88; cir. judge Cir. Ct. Ill., 1988-91; fed. judge U.S. Dist. Ct. (ctrl. dist.) Ill., 1991—. Bd. dirs. Peoria (Ill.) Pub. Libr., 1965-77, Peoria YMCA, ARC, Peoria Tri-Centennial; fin. chmn. St. Peters Cath. Ch.; active Peoria Civic Ctr. Authority, 1976-82; pres. Ill. Health Systems Agy., 1978-80, bd. dirs., 1975-82. Mem. Ill. State Bar Assn., Peoria County Bar Assn. (bd. dirs. 1980-82). Office: US Dist Ct 100 NE Monroe St Peoria IL 61602-1003

MCDADE, JOSEPH MICHAEL, congressman; b. Scranton, Pa., Sept. 29, 1931; s. John B. and Genevieve (Hayes) McD.; children: Joseph, Aileen, Deborah, Mark; m. Sarah Scripture, May 1988; 1 child, Jared. B.A. in Polit. Sci. with honors, U. Notre Dame, 1953; LL.B., U. Pa., 1956; LL.D. (hon.), St. Thomas Aquinas Coll., 1968, U. Scranton, 1969, Misericordia Coll. and Kings Coll., 1981, Mansfield State Coll., 1982; H.H.D., Kings Coll. Bar: Pa. bar 1957. Clk. to fed. judge, 1956-57; pvt. practice law Scranton, 1957—, city solicitor, 1962; mem. 88th-105th Congresses from 10th Pa. dist., Washington, D.C., 1963—; mem. appropriations com. Mem. Am., Pa., Lackawanna County bar assns., Scranton C. of C. Republican. Roman Catholic. Clubs: K.C; James Wilson Law (Phila.). Office: US Ho of Reps 2107 Rayburn Ho Office Bldg Washington DC 20515-3810*

MCDADE, LINNA SPRINGER, retired academic program administrator; b. Lincoln, Ill., May 18, 1932; d. Clifford Harry and Lois Mae (Lovett) S.; m. Wesley Dale McDade, June 13, 1951; children: Kimberly Rachel, Chance Linnea, Wesley Dale Jr., Bryan Anthony, Darby Erin. Student, Northwestern U., 1950; AB with honors, U. Ill., 1971. Cert. tchr., Ill. Substitute tchr. Sch. Dist. 116, Urbana, Ill., 1972-74; mng. editor Am. Sociol. Rev., Am. Sociol. Assn., Urbana, 1977-80; asst. to head dept. sociology U. Ill., Urbana, 1980-90; ret., 1990; grants coord. The Reading Group, Urbana, Ill., 1995-96. Chorus mem. Ill. Opera Theatre, 1979-82; pres. Evening Etude Music Club, 1958-60; dir. children's choir 1st Presbyn. Ch., Urbana, 1977, deacon, 1985—, elder, 1989—; co-pres. Washington Sch. PTA, Urbana, 1963-64; bd. dirs. Frances Nelson Health Ctr., Champaign, Ill., 1989-93; vol. fundraising coord. New Hope Jobs, Champaign, 1994—; bd. dirs. Adoption Studies Inst., Washington, 1995-96. Recipient " So Proudly We Hail" Community Svc. award The Exch. Club Urbana, 1990. Mem. Phi Alpha Theta. Avocations: singing, swimming, horseback riding. Home: 2433 County Road 1225 N Saint Joseph IL 61873-9727

MCDANIEL, BOYCE DAWKINS, physicist, educator; b. Brevard, N.C., June 11, 1917; s. Allen Webster and Grace (Dawkins) McD.; m. Jane Chapman Grennell, Aug. 3, 1941; children: Gail P., James G. B.S., Ohio Wesleyan U., 1938; M.S., Case Inst. Tech., 1940; Ph.D., Cornell U., 1943. Staff mem. radiation lab. Mass. Inst. Tech., 1943; physicist Los Alamos Sci. Lab., 1943-46; mem. faculty Cornell U., Ithaca, N.Y., 1945—, prof., 1956-87, assoc. dir. lab. nuclear studies, 1960-67, dir. lab. nuclear studies, 1967-85, Floyd R. Newman prof. nuclear studies, 1977-87, prof. emeritus, 1987—; head accelerator sect. Nat. Accelerator Lab., Batavia, Ill., 1972; mem. high energy physics adv. panel ERDA, 1975-78. Contbr. articles to profl. jours. Trustee Associated Univs., Inc., 1962-75. Vis. fellow Brookhaven Nat. Lab., 1966; Fulbright Research grantee Australian Nat. U., 1953; Guggenheim and Fulbright grantee U. Rome and Synchrotron Lab., Frascati, Italy, 1959-60. Fellow Am. Phys. Soc.; mem. NAS, Univs. Rsch. Assn. (trustee 1971-77, 83-84, chmn. superconducting super-collider bd. overseers 1984-91, mem. 1991-93). Spl. research neutron spectroscopy, gamma ray spectroscopy, high energy photoprodn. K mesons and hyperons, instrumentation for high energy physics, accelerator design and constrn. Home: 318 Savage Farm Dr Ithaca NY 14850

MCDANIEL, CHARLES-GENE, journalism educator, writer; b. Luxora, Ark., Jan. 11, 1931; s. Charles Waite and Edith Estelle (Kelly) McD. B.S., Northwestern U., 1954, M.S. in Journalism, 1955. Reporter Gazette and Daily, York, Pa., 1955-58; sci. writer Chgo. bur. A.P., 1958-79; assoc. prof. journalism dept. Roosevelt U., Chgo., 1979-83, prof., 1984-96, chmn. dept., 1979-93, head faculty of journalism and communication studies, 1993-95, prof. emeritus, 1996—. Contbg. editor Libido; contbr. to anthologies, poems, Ency. Britannica, World Book Ency.; contbr. articles to profl. jours.; Chgo. corr. The Med. Post, Toronto, 1979—. Trustee Roosevelt U., 1985-94; bd. dirs. Internat. Press Ctr. Chgo., 1993-96; mem. Ill. Gay and Lesbian Task Force. Recipient writing awards Erikson Inst. for Early Edn., 1972, writing award AMA, 1974, writing awards Chgo. Inst. for Psychoanalysis, 1971, 73, writing awards Ill. Med Soc., 1972, 73, writing awards ADA, 1975, Am. Psychol. Assn., 1982. Mem. ACLU, Fellowship of Reconciliation, War Registers League, Art Inst. Chgo. (life), Mus. Contemporary Art (charter), Nat. Lesbian and Gay Journalists Assn., Ill. Arts Alliance, Handgun Control Inc. Home and Office: 5109 S Cornell Ave Chicago IL 60615-4215 *That which we achieve for ourselves is for naught unless we have at the same time contributed to a world in which peace and justice prevail.*

MCDANIEL, DAVID HENRY, physician; b. Clarksburg, W.Va., May 12, 1952; s. Hubert Harold and Ada Virginia (Henry) McD.; m. Sheila Marie Travis, Sept. 17, 1994. BS in Chemistry cum laude, W.Va. U., Morgantown, 1974, MD, 1978. Diplomate Am. Bd. Dermatology, 1983. Emergency physician Monongalia Gen. Hosp., Morgantown, 1979-82; dir. Laser Ctr. of Va., Virginia Beach, Va., 1982—; asst. prof. clin. dermatology Ea. Va. Med. Sch., Norfolk, 1991—, asst. prof. clin. plastic surgery, 1992—; command cons., Dept. Plastic Surgery Naval Med. Ctr., Portsmouth, Va., 1994—; pres. The Ctr. for Disfigurement, Virginia Beach, 1993—; adv. coun. mem. Disfigurement Guidance Ctr., Scotland, 1994—; pres. David H. McDaniel Cons., Internat., Virginia Beach, 1995—. Contbr. numerous articles to sci. jours. Fellow Am. Acad. Dermatology, Am. Soc. Laser Medicine and Surgery, Am. Soc. Dermatologic Surgery (com. practice mktg. and pub. rels. 1993-96, chair 1996), Internat. Soc. Dermatologic Surgery; mem. Tidewater Dermatology Soc. (pres. 1987-88), Space Dermatology Found. (founding), Va. Space Bus. Roundtable (charter), Phi Lambda Upsilon. Avocations: nature and wildlife photography, bicycling, gardening, hiking, church and charitable activities. Office: Laser Ctr of Va Ste 113 933 First Colonial Rd Virginia Beach VA 23454

MCDANIEL, DOLAN KENNETH, oil exploration service company executive; b. Clarksville, Ark., June 9, 1935; s. Lowell William and Dana Estelle (Kinney) McD.; m. Letha Patricia Craven, Jan. 2, 1957; children: Laurie McDaniel Holgate, David. BS, Kans. State U., 1957. Field ops. Geophys. Service Inc., various locations, 1957-66; mgr. Rocky Mountains region Geophys. Service Inc., Denver, 1966-70; mgr. N. Latin Am. Geophys. Service Inc., Bogota, Colombia, 1970-72; mgr. land data collection Geophys. Service Inc., Dallas, 1973-77, mgr. marine exploration, 1977, pres., 1977-88; cons. geophys. industry, 1989—; v.p. Tex. Instruments, Dallas, 1978-88. Mem. Soc. Exploration Geophysicists, Dallas Geophys. Soc., Internat. Assn. Geophys. Contractors (bd. dirs. 1982-89). Home and Office: 213 Crooked Creek Dr Richardson TX 75080-2024

MCDANIEL, DONALD HAMILTON, lawyer; b. Washington, Apr. 26, 1948; s. Roy Hamilton and Mildred Dean (Borden) McD.; m. Eva Styron, Dec. 29, 1973; children: Sharon, Michelle. BS, La. State U., 1970; JD, U. Miss., 1973. Bar: Miss. 1973; bd. cert. tax atty., 1987—; bd. cert. estate planning & adminstrn. atty. Atty. IRS, Washington, 1974-77; tax law specialist Bourgeois Bennett Thokey, New Orleans, 1977-81; ptnr. McCloskey Dennery Page, New Orleans, 1981-85, Lemle & Kelleher, New Orleans, 1985—. Author: Estate Planning in Louisiana, 1991. Trustee St. Martins Episcopal Sch., New Orleans, 1993, East Jefferson Hosp. Found., New Orleans, 1995, United Meth. Found., New Orleans, 1995. Mem. ABA, La. State Bar Assn., Miss. State Bar Assn., New Orleans Estate Planning Coun. Avocations: golf, fishing. Office: Lemle & Kelleher LLP 601 Poydras St Ste 2100 New Orleans LA 70130-6021

MCDANIEL, GERALDINE HOWELL, nursing administrator; b. Como, N.C., Feb. 21, 1943; d. Jarvis Littleton and Nell Carson (Daughtley) Howell; m. Paul G. McDaniel; children: Christopher Louis Winstead, Kimberley Ann Winstead. Student, Old Dominion U., 1961-62; diploma, RN, Norfolk (Va.) Gen. Hosp. Sch., 1964. RN, Va.; cert. parish nursing, Wis. Model. Office nurse ob-gyn. Dr. A.R. Garnett, Norfolk, Va., 1964; staff nurse Radford (Va.) Cmty. Hosp., 1965-66, Med. Coll. Va., Richmond, 1965; student health nurse Union Coll., Schenectady, N.Y., 1966-69; DON Confederate Home for Women, Richmond, 1975-80; clin. coord. Catawba (Va.) Hosp. Mental/Geriatric, 1981-86; DON Friendship Manor, Roanoke, Va., 1986-89, Avanté of Roanoke, Va., 1989-92, Va. Vets. Care Ctr., Roanoke, 1992-94; rehab. nurse cons. Mariner Rehab., Chapel Hill, N.C., 1994-96; mem. Task Force to Study How Regulations Affect Patient Outcomes in Long Term Care, Roanoke, 1994. Sunday sch. tchr., com. chairperson, mission trips to Argentina, Mexico, Peru First Bapt. Ch., Roanoke, 1987—; vol. state coord. for parish nursing Va. Bapt. Women's Missionary Union. Mem. ANA (cert. nurse adminstr.), Am. Rehab. Assn. (cert. rehab. RN), Assn. Rehab. Nurses, Va. Bapt. Nurses Fellowship (sec., treas., area rep. 1993—), Noble Dirs. Nurses S.W. Va., Va. Nurses Assn., Va. Dirs. Nurses Long Term Care (past dist. rep.). Baptist. Avocations: parish nurse, volunteering for med. mission trips.

MC DANIEL, JAMES EDWIN, lawyer; b. Dexter, Mo., Nov. 22, 1931; s. William H. and Gertie M. (Woods) McD.; m. Mary Jane Crawford, Jan. 22, 1955; children: John William, Barbara Anne. AB, Washington U., St. Louis, 1957, JD, 1959. Bar: Mo. 1959. Assoc. firm Walther, Barnard, Cloyd & Timm, 1959-60; assoc. firm McDonald, Barnard, Wright & Timm, 1960-63, ptnr., 1963-65; ptnr. firm Barnard, Timm & McDaniel St. Louis, 1965-73; ptnr. firm Barnard & Baer, St. Louis, 1973-82; ptnr. Lashly & Baer, St. Louis, 1982—, prosecuting atty., 1968—; city atty. City of Glendale, Mo., 1996—; bd. dirs. Eden. Theol. Sem., Airtherm Mfg. Co.; lectr. Latvian U., Riga, Inst. Fgn. Rels., Banking in Am., 1992-93. Leader legal del. Chinese-Am. Comparative Law Study, People's Republic China, 1988, Russian-Am. Comparative Law Study, USSR, 1990; trustee, past chmn., past treas. 1st Congl. Ch. St. Louis. With USAF, 1951-55. Fellow Am. Bar Found. (life), St. Louis Bar Found. (life); mem. ABA (ho. of dels. 1976-80, 84-92, state del. 1986-92, chmn. lawyers conf., jud. adminstrn. divsn. 1992-95, 8th cir. rep. standing com. on fed. judiciary 1995-96, mem. standing com. on jud. qualification, tenure and compensation 1996—, mem. bd. govs. 1997—), The Mo. Bar (pres. 1981-82, bd. govs. 1974-83), Mo. Assn. Def. Counsel, Bar Assn. Met. St. Louis (pres. 1972), Internat. Assn. Ins. Counsel, Assn. Def. Counsel St. Louis (past pres.), Phi Delta Phi. Home: 767 Elmwood Ave Saint Louis MO 63122-3216 Office: Lashly & Baer 714 Locust St Saint Louis MO 63101-1603

MCDANIEL, JARREL DAVE, lawyer; b. Clovis, N. Mex., Oct. 17, 1930; s. Raymond Lee and Blanch (Booth) McD.; m. Anne Louise McAllister; children: Jarrel Dave Jr., Julia Anne. A.A., Riverside Coll., 1951; B.A., U. Tex., 1956, LL.B., 1957. Bar: Tex. 1957. Assoc. Vinson & Elkins, Houston, 1957-69, ptnr., 1969-96; of counsel Sheinfeld, Maley & Kay, Houston, 1997—; author, lectr. in field. Served with USAF, 1950-54. Mem. ABA, Am. Coll. Bankruptcy, State Bar Tex., Am. Bankruptcy Inst., Tex. Bd. Legal Specialization in Bankruptcy (mem. adv. com. 1976—). Roman Catholic. Clubs: Houston, Houston Ctr. Home: 1217 Potomac Dr Houston TX 77057 Office: Sheinfeld Maley & Kay PC 1001 Fannin St Houston TX 77002-6706

MCDANIEL, JOHN PERRY, health care company executive; b. Findlay, Ohio, Sept. 4, 1942; s. Oliver Perry and Lorraine (Schraeding) McD.; m. Ellen Rachel Garb, June 18, 1966; children—Celia Lorraine, Michael Perry. BS, Wittenberg U.; MHA, U. Mich.; LHD (hon.), Wittenberg U., 1990. Adminstrv. resident Wilmington Med. Ctr., Del. Hosp., 1965-66, asst. adminstrs., 1966-67; asst. adminstr. Community Hosp., Springfield, Ohio, 1967-68; assoc. adminstr. Md. Gen. Hosp., Balt., 1968-72; pres., chief exec. officer Lutheran Hosp. Md., Inc., Balt., 1972-81, Md. Health Care Systems, Inc., Balt., 1977-81; pres. Washington Hosp. Ctr. and Medlantic Healthcare Group, 1981—; pres. Medlantic Mgmt. Corp., 1983—, now CEO; cons. Westchester Med. Ctr. Found. Inc., White Plains, N.Y., 1980-81; mem. adv. coun. Nat. Ctr. for Therapeutic Riding, Washington, 1983—. Contbr. articles to profl. jours. Mem., bd. dirs. Vol. Hosps. of Am.-Mid. Atlantic, Greater Washington Bd. Trade ; mem. Washington Trustees of Fed. City Coun. Fellow Am. Coll. Hosp. Adminstrs.; mem. Royal Soc. Health, U. Mich. Program in Hosp. Adminstrn. Alumni Assn. (bd. dirs.), Howard County Hist. Soc., Univ. Club (Washington), Econ. Club of Washington. Republican. Avocations: horseback riding and other related sports. Office: Medlantic Healthcare Group 100 Irving St NW Washington DC 20010-2911*

MCDANIEL, JOSEPH CHANDLER, lawyer; b. Covington, Va., Mar. 24, 1950; s. Everts Hardin and Betty (Chandler) McD.; m. Sandra Lee Bonds, Dec. 27, 1976; children: Sean Kenneth, Caitlin Bonds. BA in Philosophy, Ariz. State U., 1974, JD, 1980. Bar: Ariz. 1980, U.S. Dist. Ct. Ariz. 1981; cert. specialist bankruptcy law Ariz. Bd. Legal Specialization, cert. specialist consumer bankruptcy law Am. Bankruptcy Bd. Specialization, cert. specialist bus. bankruptcy law. Law clk. U.S. Bankruptcy Ct., Phoenix, 1980-82; pvt. practice Phoenix, 1982-84; ptnr. McDaniel and Jaburg, P.C., Phoenix, 1984-89, McDaniel and Lee, Phoenix, 1989-91, McDaniel & Gan, P.C., 1991-93, McDaniel & Kaup, P.C., 1993-94, Lerch, McDaniel & Kaup, P.L.C., 1994-96, Lerch, McDaniel, DePrimn & Kaup, P.L.C., 1996—; lectr. in field; mem. Scriveners Com. Local Rules of Ct. for Dist. of Ariz. Bankruptcy Cts., Phoenix, 1980. Author: A Guide to Researching Bankruptcy Law, 1980; editor: (with others) Arizona Civil Remedies, 1982; lectr. in field. Bd. dirs. St. Patrick's Day Parade, 1988-89, Irish Cultural Assn. Phoenix, 1988-89. Mem. ABA (gen. practice sect. bankruptcy com., chmn., sr. vice chmn. membership com. pubs. bd.), Ariz. Bar Assn. (lectr., co-chmn. continuing legal edn. com., bankruptcy sect. 1987-88, chmn. 1988-89, co-chmn. jud. rels. com. 1990-92), Maricopa County Bankruptcy Practitioners (chmn.), Ariz. Bankruptcy Coalition (bd. dirs. 1986—, chair speakers com. 1994-96), Maricopa County Bar Assn., Am. Bankruptcy Inst. Democrat. Roman Catholic. Avocations: computer tech., chess, hiking. Office: Lerch McDaniel et al 2700 N Central Ave Ste 1500 Phoenix AZ 85004-1112

MCDANIEL, KAREN JEAN, university library administrator; b. Newark, Nov. 16, 1950; d. Alphonso Cornell Cotton Jr. and Maude Jean (Smoot) Cotton Bledsoe; m. Rodney McDaniel Sr., Aug. 25, 1971; children: Rodney Jr., Kimberly Renee, Jason Bradley. BSBA, Berea Coll., 1973; MS in Libr. Sci., U. Ky., 1975, postgrad., 1977-78; postgrad., Ky. State U., 1979-83, Ea. Ky. U., 1983. Asst. libr., instr. reference studies Paul G. Blazer Libr.-Ky. State U., Frankfort, 1975-79, asst. libr., instr. cataloging, 1980-83, head cataloging and classification, 1983; program coord. libr. svcs. Ky. Dept. Pub. Advocacy, Frankfort, 1983-85, libr. sr., 1985-87, program coord. state publs., 1987-89; dir. libr. svcs. Paul G. Blazer Libr.-Ky. State U., Frankfort, 1989—; bd. dirs. Solinet; mem. adv. bd. African Am. Ednl. Archives Initiative, Wayne State U.; mem. faculty adv. bd. Ctr. of Excellence for Study of Ky. African Ams.; mem. subcom. on target groups Ky./White House Conf. on Libr. and Info. Svcs. II, chair, 1990-91. Mem. State of Ky. Textbook Commn., 1993—; mem. Nat. Coun. Negro Women; adult membership Girl Scouts Am., 1987—, asst. troop leader, 1991-93; active Frankfort H.S. PTA, 1994—, Hearn Elem. Sch. PTA, 1983-94, Elkhorn Mid. Sch. PTA, 1991—, Friends of Paul Sawyer Libr.; active St. John AME Ch.; mem. bd. Frankfort YMCA, 1995—. Mem. ALA, AAUP, NAACP, Assn. Coll. and Rsch. Librs., Black Caucus of ALA (affirmative action com.), Southeastern Libr. Assn. (planning and devel. com. 1991—, preservation round table 1993—), Land Grant and Tuskegee Libr. Dir.'s Assn. (editor Libline 1993—, vice-chair, chair 1994—), State Assisted Acad. Libr. Coun. Ky. (sec. 1991-92, sec. 1992-93), Ky. Libr. Assn. (sec. acad. sect. 1990-91), Ky. Coun. Archives, Ky. Assn. Blacks in Higher Edn., Alpha Delta Kappa, Delta Sigma Theta. Democrat. African Methodist Episcopalian. Avocations: genealogical research, reading, needlework. Home: 147 Northwood Rd Frankfort KY 40601-1477 Office: Ky State U Paul G Blazer Libr Frankfort KY 40601

MCDANIEL, MICHAEL CONWAY DIXON, bishop, theology educator; b. Mt. Pleasant, N.C., Apr. 8, 1929; s. John Henry and Mildred Juanita (Barrier) McD.; m. Marjorie Ruth Schneiter, Nov. 26, 1953; 1 son, John Robert Michael. B.A., U. N.C., 1951; B.D., Wittenberg U., 1954; M.A., U. Chgo., 1969, Ph.D., 1978; D.D. (hon.), Lenoir-Rhyne Coll., 1983; LL.D., Belmont Abbey Coll., 1984. Ordained to ministry United Lutheran Ch. in America, 1954. Pastor Faith (N.C.) Luth. Ch., 1954-58, Ch. of the Ascension, Savannah, Ga., 1958-60; assoc. dir. evangelism United Luth. Ch. in Am., N.Y.C., 1960-62; sr. pastor Edgebrook Luth. Ch., Chgo., 1962-67; pastor, guest lectr. Wittenberg U., Springfield, Ohio, 1970-71; prof. Lenoir-Rhyne Coll., Hickory, N.C., 1971-82, Raymond Morris Bost disting. prof., 1982, dir., prof. Ctr. for Theology, 1991—; bishop N.C. Luth. Ch. in Am., Salisbury, 1982-87, Evang. Luth. Ch. Am., Salisbury, 1988-91; chmn. humanities div. Lenoir-Rhyne Coll., 1973-82; cons., grant coord. NEH, 1977-79; master tchr. Hickory Humanities Forum, 1981—; chmn. task force on ecumenical and interfaith relationships Commn. Forming a New Luth. Ch., 1983-87; rep. Luth. Orthodox Dialogue In U.S.A., 1983-89;; chmn., cons. bishops governing coun. Evang. Luth. Ch. Am., 1987-89. Author: Welcome to the Lord's Table, 1972. Mem. Englewood Human Relations Council, N.J., 1959-60; pres., bd. trustees Edgebrook Symphony, Chgo., 1965-67; sec. Chgo. Astron. Soc., 1966-67; pres. Community Concerts Assn., Hickory, N.C., 1977-80. Served to sgt. U.S. Army, 1946-48, Korea. Luth. World Fedn. fellow, 1967-69, Mansfield Coll. fellow U. Oxford, 1989; recipient Disting. Alumnus award Trinity Luth. Sem., 1990. Home: 125 42nd Avenue Cir NE Hickory NC 28601-9012 Office: Lenoir-Rhyne Coll Hickory NC 28603 *Since Christian faith is a joyous relationship with God, Christian hope is courageously counting on God's promises, and Christian love a daily adventure. The Christian approaches each aspect of life as An Adventure in Courageous Joy.*

MCDANIEL, MYRA ATWELL, lawyer, former state official; b. Phila., Dec. 13, 1932; d. Eva Lucinda (Yores) Atwell; m. Reuben Roosevelt McDaniel Jr., Feb. 20, 1955; children: Diane Lorraine, Reuben Roosevelt III. BA, U. Pa., 1954; JD, U. Tex., 1975; LLD, Huston-Tillotson Coll., 1984, Jarvis Christian Coll., 1986. Bar: Tex. 1975, U.S. Dist. Ct. (we. dist.) Tex. 1977, U.S. Dist. Ct. (so. and no. dists.) Tex. 1978, U.S. Ct. Appeals (5th cir.) 1978, U.S. Supreme Ct. 1978, U.S. Dist. Ct. (ea. dist.) Tex. 1979. Asst atty. gen. State of Tex., Austin, 1975-81, chief taxation div., 1979-81, gen. counsel to gov., 1983-84, sec. of state, 1984-87; asst. gen. counsel Tex. R.R. Commn., Austin, 1981-82; gen. counsel Wilson Cos., San Antonio and Midland, Tex., 1982; assoc. Bickerstaff, Heath & Smiley, Austin, 1984, ptnr., 1987-96; mng. ptnr. Bickerstaff, Heath, Smiley, Pollan, Kever & McDaniel, Austin, 1996—; mem. asset. mgmt. adv. com. State Treasury, Austin, 1984-86; mem. legal affairs com. Criminal Justice Policy Coun., Austin, 1984-8, Inter-State Oil Compact, Oklahoma City, 1984-86; bd. dirs. Austin Cons. Group, 1983-86; mem. Jud. Efficiency Coun., Austin, 1995-96; lectr. in field. Contbr. articles to profl. jours., chpts. to books. Del. Tex. Conf. on Librs. and Info. Sci., Austin, 1978, White House Conf. on Librs. and Info. Scis., Washington, 1979; mem. Libr. Svcs. and Constrn. Act Adv. Coun., 1980-84, chmn., 1983-84; mem. long range plan task force Brackenridge Hosp., Austin, 1981; clk. vestry bd. St. James Episcopal Ch., Austin, 1981-83, 89-90; bd. visitors U. Tex. Law Sch., 1983-87, vice chmn., 1983-85; bd. dirs. Friends of Ronald McDonald House Ctrl. Tex., Women's Advocacy, Inc., Capital Area Rehab. Ctr.; trustee Episcopal Found. Tex., 1986-89, St. Edward's U., Austin, 1986—, chmn. acad. com., 1988—; chmn. divsn. capital area campaign United Way, 1986; active nat. adv. bd. Leadership Am.; trustee Episcopal Sem. S.W., 1990-96, Assn. Governing Bds. Univs. and Colls., Leadership

Edn. Arts Program, 1995—; adv. bd. mem. Women Basketball Coaches Assn., 1996—. Recipient Tribute to 28 Black Women award Concepts Unltd., 1983; Focus on women honoree Serwa Yetu chpt. Mt. Olive grand chpt. Order of Eastern Star, 1979, Woman of Yr. Longview Metro C. of C., 1985, Woman of Yr. Austin chpt. Internat. Tng. in Communication, 1985, Citizen of Yr. Epsilon Iona chpt. Omega Psi Phi. Master Inns of Ct.; mem. ABA, Am. Bar Found., Tex. Bar Found. (trustee 1986-89), Travis County Bar Assn., Travis County Women Lawyers' Assn., Austin Black Lawyers Assn., State Bar Tex. (chmn. Profl. Efficiency & Econ. Rsch. subcom. 1976-84), Golden Key Nat. Honor Soc., Longhorn Assocs. for Excellence in Women's Athletes (adv. coun. 1988—), Order of Coif (hon. mem.), Omicron Delta Kappa, Delta Phi Alpha. Democrat. Home: 3910 Knollwood Dr Austin TX 78731-2915 Office: Bickerstaff Heath Et Al 1700 Forst Bank Plz 816 Congress Ave Austin TX 78701-2442

MCDANIEL, OLA JO PETERSON, social worker, educator; b. Hot Springs, Ark., Sept. 17, 1951; d. Milton Paul and Ella Floyd (Dickerson) Peterson; m. Daniel Tillman McDaniel, June 11, 1994; 1 child, Cadra Peterson. B Music Edn., Henderson State Coll., Arkadelphia, Ark., 1973; MA in Edn., Lindenwood Colls., St. Charles, Mo., 1983, cert. in Social Studies, 1977. Cert. tchr., Mo., Ark. Mem. faculty Sch. Dist. St. Charles, 1974-84; adj. faculty Garland County C.C., Hot Springs, 1988-90; social worker Ark. Dept. Human Svcs., Hot Springs, 1990-94; substitute tchr. Hot Springs Sch. Dist., 1994-95; tutor St. Michael's Sch., Hot Springs, 1995—; soloist Congr. House of Israel, Hot Springs, 1965-73; cons. scholarships Hot Springs Music Club, 1988; const. student performance Garland County C.C., Hot Springs, 1988. Author, contbr. (learning activities) 3 R's for the Gifted: Reading, Writing, Research, 1982. Vol. Hot Springs Mayorial Campaign, 1993, Dem. Gubernatorial campaign, Hot Springs, 1990; hon. mem. Nat. Steering Com. to Reelect the Pres., Washington, 1995; mem. Dem. Nat. Com., Washington, 1995-97; mem. Pres.' Second Term Com., Washington, 1997; active Hot Springs Mid. Sch. PTO, 1996-97. Recipient Certs. of Appreciation, St. Chrysostom's Am. Episcopal Ch., Hot Springs, 1990, Nat. Mus. Am. Indian, Washington, 1995, award Alpha Chi; cert. of apreciation Nat. Mus. Women in the Arts, 1997. Mem. AAUW, Nat. Mus. Am. Indian, Nat.Mus. Women in Arts, Mid-Am. Sci. Mus., Henderson Alumni Assn., Lindenwood Alumni Assn. Democrat. Roman Catholic. Avocations: advocate of welfare reform, museum volunteer, reading, music. Home: 102 Woodberry Ave Hot Springs National Park AR 71913

MCDANIEL, RICKEY DAVID, senior living executive; b. Rochester, Minn., Apr. 10, 1946; s. Malcolm David and Elaine (Lee) McD.; m. Shelley Ann Sorensen, May 10, 1980; children: Michael, Mathew, Joseph. AA, Rochester Jr. Coll., 1966; BA, Winona State U., 1969. Clin. mgr. St. Mary's Hosp., Rochester, Minn., 1971-74; long term care adminstr. Roderick Enterprises, Inc., Portland, Oreg., 1974-78; regional dir. Roderick Enterprises, Inc., Portland, 1978-80, v.p. ops., 1980-84; pres. Health Sys. Mgmt. and Devel., L.A., 1984-86; ops. dir. Brim Enterprises, Inc., Portland, 1987-88, v.p., 1988-92, sr. v.p., 1992-93; pres. Brim Sr. Living, Inc., Portland, 1993-97; sr. v.p. Encore Sr. Living, LLC, 1997—; bd. dirs. Brim Homestead, Inc., Portland, Dominican Life Care Svcs., Portland, Belmar, Inc., Portland, also v.p. 1989—; pres. Care Mgmt., Inc., A Fla. Employee Leasing Corp., 1991—; developer alzheimer patients care and housing program, 1993. Cpl. USMC, 1969-71. Republican. Lutheran. Avocations: ice hockey, coaching basketball, baseballand hockey. Home: 16492 S Arrowhead Dr Oregon City OR 97045-9287 Office: Brim Inc 305 NE 102nd Ave Portland OR 97220-4170

MCDANIEL, ROBERT STEPHEN, technical professional; b. Nashville, Sept. 26, 1946; s. Robert Stephen and Dorothy (Leahy) McD.; m. Katherine Wood Johnson, May 26, 1972; 1 child, Benjamin C. BS in Chemistry, U. Notre Dame, 1968; PhD in Organic Chemistry, U. Mo., Rolla, 1974. Sr. rsch. chemist Armak Co., McCook, Ill., 1975-79, sect. head process devel., 1979-80; mgr. new products R&D A.E. Staley Mfg. Co., Decatur, Ill., 1980-88; sr. scientist Henkel Corp., Ambler, Pa., 1988-91; mgr. R&D durable spltys. divsn. FiberMark Inc., Quakertown, Pa., 1992—. Contbr. articles to profl. jours. Mem. Tree Bd., Decatur, 1986-88. U. Chgo. Ben May Lab. for Cancer Rsch. fellow, 1974-75. Fellow Sigma Xi; mem. TAPPI (splty. coated papers com. 1994—), Am. Chem. Soc., Pa. Guild Craftsmen (juried). Roman Catholic. Achievements include 12 patents. Avocations: golf, fencing, soap making. Office: FiberMark Inc Durable Spltys Divsn 45 N 4th St Quakertown PA 18951-1239

MCDANIEL, RODERICK ROGERS, petroleum engineer; b. High River, Alta., Can., 1926; s. Dorsey Patton and Daisy (Rogers) McD.; m. Marilyn Bouck, Oct. 16, 1948; children: Nancy, Leslie. BS, U. Okla., 1947. Petroleum reservoir engr. Creole Petroleum Corp., 1947; petroleum reservoir engr. Imperial Oil Ltd., 1948-52, chief reservoir engr., 1952-55; chmn. McDaniel Cons., Calgary, 1955—, PWA Corp, Calgary, 1974-91, Can. Regional Airlines, Calgary, 1991-92; bd. dirs. Honeywell Can. Ltd., Prudential Steel Ltd. Bd. dirs. Calgary Exhbn. and Stampede, 1979-88, hon. bd. dirs., 1988—; dir. Calgary Stampeder Football Team, 1988, Corp. Commissionaires S.A.B. Mem. Assn. Profl. Engrs. Alta and Sask., Can. C. of C. (bd. dirs. 1973), Calgary C. of C. (past pres.), Calgary Petroleum Club (past pres.), Calgary Highlanders (hon. col.), Ranchmen's Club, Calgary Golf and Country Club, Outrigger Club (Honolulu), Mission Hills Country Club. Mem. Progressive Conservative Party. Home: 11 3231 Rideau Ridge Pl SW, Calgary, AB Canada T2S 2T1 Office: McDaniel & Assoc, 2200-255 5th Ave SW, Calgary, AB Canada T2P 3G6

MCDANIEL, SUE POWELL, cultural organization administrator; b. Jefferson City, Mo., Mar. 13, 1946; d. Ernest Gayle and Ruth Angeline (Raithel) Powell; m. Walter Lee Zimmerman, Aug. 14, 1966 (div. 1980); m. Olin Cleve McDaniel, June 23, 1985. BS in Edn., U. Mo., 1968, MEd in Edn., 1977, EdS, 1980, PhD, 1985. Cert. tchr., Mo. Tchr. Jefferson City Pub. Schs., 1968-80; fiscal assoc. Mo. Coordinating Bd. for Higher Edn., Jefferson City, 1980-90; exec. dir. Mo. Women's Coun., Jefferson City, 1990—. Co-author: Missouri Women Today, 1993, Status of the Women, 1994. Mem. Zonta Internat., Lincoln Women in Devel. (pres. 1993—). Avocations: reading, music, drawing, flower garden, photography. Office: Mo Women's Coun PO Box 1684 Jefferson City MO 65102-1684

MCDANIELS, B. T., bishop. Bishop Northeastern Nebr. region Ch. of God in Christ, Omaha. Office: Ch of God in Christ 1106 N 31st Ave Omaha NE 68131-1433*

MCDANIELS, PEGGY ELLEN, special education educator; b. Pulaski, Va., Jan. 4, 1945; d. James H. and Gladys M. (Hurd) Fisher; m. Robert A. McDaniels, Feb. 17, 1973; children: Dawn Marie, Robert C. A Gen. Studies, Schoolcraft Coll., 1976; BA, Ea. Mich. U., 1980, MA, 1985. Cert. adminstr. Woodcock Johnson Psychoednl. Battery Orton-Gillingham Tng. Payroll sec. Otto's Painting and Drywall, West Bloomfield, Mich., 1964-75; office mgr., closing sec. Bing Constrn. Co., West Bloomfield, 1964-75; substitute tchr. Wayne-Westland Schs., Westland, Mich., 1980-83, Farmington (Mich.) Schs., 1980-83; tchr. spl. edn. Romulus (Mich.) Community Schs., 1983-85, Cros-Lex Schs., Croswell, Mich., 1985-87, Pointe Tremble Elem. Sch., Algonac, Mich., 1987—; organizer, recorder Tchr. Assistance Team, Algonac, 1991—. Mem. Coun. Exceptional Children, Learning Disability Assn. (treas. 1988-90), Mich. Assn. Learning Disability Edn., ASCD. Avocations: camping, bicycling, reading. Home: 302 Merritt Midland MI 68640

MCDANIELS, WILLIAM E., lawyer; b. Needham, Mass., July 1, 1941. BA, Williams Coll., 1963; JD, Georgetown U., 1966. Bar: D.C. 1967, Md. 1983. Grad. fellow criminal law, litigation U. Pa., Phila., 1966-68; pub. defender Phila. Pub. Defender's Office, 1966-68; adj. prof. evidence, criminal law, advanced criminal procedure Georgetown U. Law Ctr., Washington, 1970-87; mem. Williams & Connolly, Washington; instr. Nat. Inst. Trial Advocacy, 1975—. Fellow Am. Coll. Trial Lawyers; mem. ABA, Md. State Bar Assn, D.C. Bar. Office: Williams & Connolly 725 12th St NW Washington DC 20005-3901

MC DANNALD, CLYDE ELLIOTT, JR., management consultation company executive; b. N.Y.C., June 29, 1923; s. Clyde E. and Evelyn (Tunison-Morgan) McD.; BA, Columbia Coll., 1948, MBA, 1950; m. Virginia Washington, Apr. 25, 1953; children: Leslie Ann, Clyde Elliott III, Bruce Robert, Bonnie Washington, Brian Christopher (dec.), Laura Leigh. Market rsch. analyst J. Walter Thompson Co., N.Y.C., 1948-50; asst. dir. market rsch. Nat. Lead Co., N.Y.C., 1950-51; product rsch. supr., account exec. Foote, Cone & Belding, Inc., N.Y.C., 1951-52; product mgr., asst. advt. mgr. Am. Safety Razor Corp., N.Y.C., 1953-54; account exec., account supr. Meldrum & Fewsmith, Inc., Cleve., 1954-56; sr. account exec. Young & Rubicam, N.Y.C., 1956-58; exec. asst. to v.p., advt. mgr. Brown & Williamson Tobacco Corp. subs. Brit.-Am. Tobacco Co., Ltd., Louisville, 1959-63; dir. advt. and mktg. svcs., dir. mktg. Miller Brewing Co., Milw., 1963-65; div. gen. mgr., v.p. consumer products, corp. v.p. Revere Copper & Brass Inc., N.Y.C., 1966-71; pres., COO H.H. Pott Distillers Ltd. U.S. subs. H.H. Pott NFGR, N.Y.C., 1972-80, also bd. dirs.; pres., CEO Oxbridge Cons., Inc., N.Y.C., 1981—; ptnr. Hilbert, Peers and Young, Inc., N.Y.C., 1984—; bd. dirs. West Indies Distillers, Ltd., Distilled Spirits Inst., Washington, McFrank & Williams Inc. and Cooperating Cons. Corp., N.Y.C.; vis. prof. mktg. Fairfield U. Sch. Bus., 1975-77. Apptd. to staff Col. Ky. Govs., 1959-63, 92—; mem. Ky. Hwy. Commn. 1960-63, N.Y. Gov.'s Indsl. Com., 1967-72; bd. govs. N.Y. Mil. Acad., 1970-76, trustee, 1975-92. Served from pvt. to capt. Inf. USAAF, 1942-45, ETO. Decorated D.F.C., Air medal with 4 oak leaf clusters; recipient Conspicuous Service Cross State of N.Y. with 5 oak leaf clusters, Valor medal UDC, Knickerbocker Greys City of N.Y., War Cross, Sons of Confederate Vets., Medaille de la France Liberee, Croix de Guerre (Belgium), Roi Leopold III, Battle of Britain, Knight Mil. Order of Malta, Knight Sovereign Mil. Order Temple Jerusalem. Mem. SAR, SR (bd. mgrs. 1988—), Alumni Fedn. Columbia U., Am. Mgmt. Assn., NAM (mktg. com.), Audit Bur. Circulation, Navy League, St. Andrews Soc. State of N.Y., Am. Revolution Round Table, Am. Legion, VFW, N.Y. Soc. Mil. and Naval Officers World Wars, Sons of Confederate Vets., Soc. Colonial Wars, St. George Soc., Sigma Chi (life), Alpha Chi Sigma. Clubs: Columbia U., Explorers, University. Presbyterian. Democrat. Home: 57 Canterbury Ln Wilton CT 06897-4103

MCDARRAH, FRED WILLIAM, photographer, editor, writer, photography reviewer; b. Bklyn., Nov. 5, 1926; s. Howard Arthur and Elizabeth (Swahn) McD.; m. Gloria Schoffel, Nov. 5, 1960; children: Timothy Swann, Patrick James. BA, NYU, 1954. Mem. staff Village Voice Newspaper, N.Y.C., 1959—, picture editor, 1971—; book reviewer ASMP Infinity Mag., 1972-73, Photo Dist. News, 1985-88, The Picture Profl., 1990—. Exhibited in Soho Photo Gallery, 1973, Whitney Mus., 1974, 76-77, Dallas Mus. Art, 1974, San Francisco Mus. Art, 1975, Wadsworth Atheneum, 1975, Sidney Janis Gallery, 1976, Basel (Switzerland) Art Fair, 1976, Alfred Stieglitz Gallery, 1976, Empire State Mus., Albany, N.Y., 1978, Lightworks Gallery, Syracuse, N.Y., 1981, Cape Cod Gallery, Provincetown Mass., 1982, Galleria di Franca Mancini, Pesaro, Italy, 1983, Musée du Quebec, 1987, Anita Shapolsky Gallery, N.Y.C., 1988, Hartnett Gallery U. Rochester, N.Y., 1989, G. Ray Hawkins Gallery, L.A., 1989, Read Gallery Antioch (Ohio) Coll., 1989, Mus. Art/Sci./Industry, Bridgeport, Conn., 1989, N.Y.C. Gallery Queens Mus., 1989, Ctr. Photography, Woodstock, 1989, Frumkin/Adams Gallery, 1990, Musée d'Art Moderne De La Ville de Paris, 1990, Musée d'Art Contemporain, Montreal, 1990, Pollack-Krasner Mus., East Hampton, N.Y., 1990, Found. Cartier, Paris, 1990, Marty Carey Pictures Gallery, Woodstock, N.Y., 1992, Galerie Gilles Ringuet, Belfort, France, 1992, Galerie Contre Jour, Belfort, France, 1992, Galleria La Pescheria, Cesena, Italy, 1994, Whitney Mus. Am. Art, 1995—, Nat. Portrait Gallery, 1996, Candice Perich Gallery, 1996; exhbns. include Jack Kerouac Visions of the Road, Les Rencontres D'Arles, Arles, France, 1991, Jack Kerouac Travelling Writers, Saint-Malo (France) Internat. Festival, 1991, Images of Greenwich Village N.Y. Camera Club, 1992, Walker Art Ctr., Mpls., 1996, M.H. de Young Meml. Mus., San Francisco, 1996; author: The Beat Scene, 1960, The Artist's World in Pictures, 1961, rev. edit. 1988, Greenwich Village, 1963, New York, New York, 1964, Sculpture in Environment, 1967, Museums in New York, 1973, French edit., 1979, 5th edit., 1990, Photography Marketplace, 2d edit., 1977, Stock Photo and Assignment Source Book, 1977, 2d edit., 1984, Kerouac and Friends: A Beat Generation Album, 1984, Japanese edit, 1990, Frommer's Atlantic City and Cape May, 4th edit., 1991, 5th edit., 1993 ; co-author: The New Bohemia, 1967, 2d edit., 1990 Guide for Ecumenical Discussion, 1970, Greenwich Village Guide, 1992, Frommer's Virginia, 1992, 2d edit. 1994, Gay Pride: Photographs from Stonewall to Today, 1994; The Beat Generation: Glory Days in Greenwich Village, editor, 1996: Saturday Rev. Executive Desk Diary, 1962-64; photographer: Personality Posters, Fotofolio (post cards) (polit. and social figures); contbr. articles, picture features to various publs. including N.Y. Mag., Vanity Fair, Entertainment Weekly, Vogue. With U.S. Army, 1944-47. Recipient numerous photography awards including 1st place spot news photo award. N.Y. Press Assn., 1964, 68; recipient 1st place feature photo award N.Y. Press Assn., 1967, 1st place picture story award N.Y. Press Assn., 1969, 2nd place spot news photo award N.Y. Press Assn., 1967, 70, 3d place spot news photo award N.Y. Press Assn., 1965, 3d place feature photo award N.Y. Press Assn., 1965, 3d place picture story award N.Y. Press Assn., 1970, 1st place Best Pictorial Series Nat. Newspaper Assn., 1966, Page One award Newspaper Guild N.Y., 1971, 80; Guggenheim fellow in photography, 1972. Mem. Nat. Press Photographers Assn., N.Y. Press Photographers Assn., Am. Soc. Mag. Photographers, Soc. Photog. Edn., Photog. Hist. Soc. N.Y., Authors Guild, N.Y. Press Club, Am. Soc. Picture Profls., Photog. Soc. Am. Office: 36 Cooper Sq New York NY 10003-7118

MCDARRAH, GLORIA SCHOFFEL, editor, author; b. Bronx, N.Y., June 22, 1932; d. Louis and Rose Schoffel; m. Fred W. McDarrah, Nov. 5, 1960; children: Timothy, Patrick. BA in French, Pa. State U., 1953; MA in French, NYU, 1966. Editorial asst. Crowell-Collier, N.Y.C., 1957-59; exec. asst. to pub. Time Inc., N.Y.C., 1959-61; libr., tchr. N.Y.C. Pub. Schs. and St. Luke's Sch., 1972-76; exec. asst. to pres. Capital Cities Communications Inc., N.Y.C., 1972-76; analyst N.Y.C. Landmarks Preservation Commn., 1976-79; project editor Grosset & Dunlap Inc., N.Y.C., 1979-80; sr. editor Prentice Hall trade div. Simon & Schuster Inc., N.Y.C., 1980-88; pres. McDarrah Media Assocs., N.Y.C., 1988—. Author: Frommer's Guide to Virginia, 1992, 2d edit., 1994-95, Frommer's Atlantic City and Cape May, 1984, 4th edit., 1991, 5th edit., 1993-95, The Artist's World, 2d edit., 1988; co-author: Museums in New York, 5th edit., 1990, Photography Marketplace, 1975 (book rev. sect.), The Beat Generation: Glory Days in Greenwich Village, 1996; co-editor Exec. Desk Diary Saturday Rev., 1962-64; contbg. editor quar. Dollarwise Traveler, Fodor's Cancun, Cozumel, Yucatan Peninsula, Fodor's Arizona; editor book rev. The Picture Profl., 1989—; book reviewer Pub.'s Weekly, 1994—.

MCDAVID, DOUGLAS WARREN, systems consultant; b. San Francisco, Feb. 25, 1947; s. James Etheridge and Elizabeth Rae (Warren) McD.; m. Nancy Kathleen Somers, June 1968 (div. 1982); 1 child, Amy Kemp; m. Carleen Ann Richmond, Feb. 14, 1987; 1 child, Amanda Claire. BA in Sociology, U. Calif., Santa Cruz, 1969; MA in Libr. Sci., San Jose State U., 1972. Libr. Palo Alto (Calif.) City Libr., 1969-81; systems analyst Tymnet (Tymshare), Cupertino, Calif., 1981-84; mgr. systems architecture Tymnet McDonnell Douglas, San Jose, Calif., 1984-86; data modeling cons. Fireman's Fund Ins., Terra Linda, Calif., 1986-87, Bank of Calif., San Francisco, 1988; systems cons. Pacific Bell, San Ramon, Calif., 1989-93; prin. Integrated Info., 1994—; dir. Computer Resources Group, San Francisco; spkr. Entity/Relationship Conf. Internat., Burlingame, Calif., 1991, DAMA Internat. Conf., 1994—; sr. cons. in bus. semantic modeling for object oriented applications IBM Corp., 1994—; 1996 spkr. Bus. Rules Conf. OOPSLA, IBM Object Technology Conf., Ind. Labor & Mgmt. Coun. Assoc. editor: Handbook of Object Technology. Mem. IEEE, Assn. for Computing Machinery, Data Adminstrn. Mgmt. Assn. (San Francisco bd. dirs. 1987-91, Sacramento bd. dirs. 1992, speaker 1991, 92), Data Processing Mgmt. Assn. (speaker 1992), Am. Assn. Artificial Intelligence (speaker 1993). Avocations: golf, gardening, creative writing, investing, swimming. Home and Office: 8611 Kingslynn Ct Elk Grove CA 95624-3135

MC DAVID, GEORGE EUGENE (GENE MC DAVID), newspaper executive; b. McComb, Miss., June 30, 1930; s. O.C. and Inez S. McDavid; m. Betty Ernestine Tinsley, Sept. 24, 1949; children: Carol McDavid, Martha Gene Newman. B.B.A. cum laude, U. Houston, 1965. Owner, publisher Wilk Amite Record, Gloster, Miss., 1949-58; with Houston Chronicle, 1958—, prodn. mgr., 1967-74, v.p. ops., 1974-85, v.p., gen. mgr., 1985-90, pres., 1990—; adv. bd. Am. Press Inst.; past pres. bd. dirs. S.W. Sch. Printing Mgmt. Chmn. Greater Houston chpt. ARC, nat. bd. govs., 1st vice chmn.; mem. pres.'s counsel Houston Bapt. U.; vice-chmn. Sam Houston Boy Scouts Am., United Negro Coll. Fund, Asia Soc. Goodwill Industries, YMCA; bd. dirs., Greater Houston Partnership, Nat. Conf. Christians and Jews, Houston region Am. Cancer Soc.; bd. dirs., pres. Houston Symphony; bd. dirs., v.p. Books of the World; mem. devel. bd. U. Houston; spl. deacon Second Bapt. Ch., Houston. Recipient Franklin award U. Houston, 1961, Disting. Alumnus award, 1990, 1997, Taggart award Tex. Newspaper, 1992, Man of Yr. award NCCJ, 1993; named Outstanding Ex-Citizen Gloster, 1973, Hon. Father of Yr., 1996. Mem. Am. Newspaper Pubs. Assn. (chmn. newsprint com.), So. Newspaper Pubs. Assn. (pres.) Tex. Daily Newspaper Assn. (pres.), Houston C. of C. (Houston Citizen's Community Svc. award 1993), Phi Kappa Phi, Beta Gamma Sigma. Clubs: Houston, Houstonian, Coronado Texas, Pine Forest Country. Home: 403 Hunters Park Ln Houston TX 77024-5438 Office: Houston Chronicle 801 Texas St Houston TX 77002-2906

MCDAVID, JANET LOUISE, lawyer; b. Mpls., Jan. 24, 1950; d. Robert Matthew and Lois May (Bratt) Kurzeka; m. John Gary McDavid, June 9, 1973; 1 child, Matthew Collins McDavid. BA, Northwestern U., 1971; JD, Georgetown U., 1974. Bar: D.C. 1975, U.S. Supreme Ct., 1980, U.S. Ct. Appeals (fed. cir.) 1975, (D.C. cir.) 1976, (5th cir.) 1983, (9th cir.) 1986. Assoc. Hogan & Hartson, Washington, 1974-83, ptnr., 1984—; gen. counsel ERAmerica, 1977-83; mem. antitrust task force Dept. Defense, 1993-94; mem. antitrust coun. U.S. C. of C., 1994—. Contbr. articles to profl. jours. Participant Clinton Administrn. Transition Team FTC. Mem. ABA (antitrust sect., vice chmn. civil practice com. 1986-89, sect. 2 com. 1989-90, chmn. franchising com. 1990-91, coun. mem. 1991-94, program officer 1994—, governing com. of forum on franchising 1991—), ACLU, U.S. C. of C. (antitrust coun. 1995—), Washington Coun. Lawyers, D.C. Bar Assn., Fed. Bar Assn., Womens Legal Def. Fund, Antitrust Coun. C. of C. Democrat. Office: Hogan & Hartson 555 13th St NW Washington DC 20004-1109

MCDAVID, SARA JUNE, librarian; b. Atlanta, Dec. 21, 1945; d. William Harvey and June (Threadgill) McRae; m. Michael Wright McDavid, Mar. 20, 1971. BA, Mercer U., 1967; MLS, Emory U., 1969. Head librarian Fernbank Sci. Ctr., Atlanta, 1969-77; dir. rsch. libr. Fed. Res. Bank of Atlanta, 1977-81; mgr. mem. services SOLINET, Atlanta, 1981-82; media specialist Parkview High Sch., Atlanta, 1982-84; ptnr. Interncontinental Travel, Atlanta, 1984-85; librarian Wesleyan Day Sch., Atlanta, 1985-86; mgr. info. svcs. Internat. Assn. Fin. Planning, Atlanta, 1986-90; dir. rsch. Korn Ferry Internat., Atlanta, 1990-95; rschr. Lamalie Amrop Internat., Atlanta, 1995—; bd. dirs. Southeastern Library Network, Atlanta, 1977-80, vice chmn. bd., 1979-80. Contbr. articles to profl. jours. Pres., mem. exec. com. Atlanta Humane Soc., 1985-86, bd. dirs. aux., 1978-90. Mem. Ga. Library Assn. (v.p. 1981-83), Spl. Libraries Assn. Home: 1535 Knob Hill Dr NE Atlanta GA 30329-3206 Office: Lamalie Amrop Internat 191 Peachtree St NE Ste 800 Atlanta GA 30303-1747

MCDAVID, WILLIAM HENRY, lawyer; b. N.Y.C., May 10, 1946; s. William H. and Margaret B. (Carmody) McD.; m. Sylvia Noin, Dec. 21, 1984; children: Andrew, Madeline, William, Flora. AB, Columbia Coll., N.Y.C., 1968; JD, Yale U., 1972. Assoc. Debevoise & Plimpton, N.Y.C., 1972-81; asst. gen. counsel Bankers Trust Co., N.Y.C., 1981-83, assoc. gen. counsel, 1983-84, v.p., 1984-85, v.p., counsel, 1986-88; gen. counsel Chase Manhattan Corp., N.Y.C., 1988—. Office: The Chase Manhattan Corp Office Gen Coun 270 Park Ave Fl 8 New York NY 10017-2014

MCDERMON, LINDA GARRETT, elementary school educator; b. Nov. 29, 1949; d. Jack Sellars and Ruby (Varner) Garrett; m. John Nathan McDermon, Mar. 6, 1971; children: Jonathan, Daniel. BS in Child Devel., U. N.C., 1981, MS in Early Childhood, 1986. Cert. tchr., mentor, N.C. Tchr. Winston-Salem (N.C.)/Forsyth County Schs., 1982—; coord./coach Odyssey of the Mind program Rural Hall (N.C.) Elem. Sch., 1992-93; participant N.C. Ctr. for Advancement of Teaching, Cullowhee, spring 1993. Past den leader, Tiger Cub coord., pack sec. Cub Scouts/Boy Scouts Am., Rural Hall, 1980-87; sec., active publicity, cultural arts and book fair events Rural Hall Sch. PTA, 1980-82; mem. Frields of Libr. Bd., Rural Hall, 1992-94. Named Dist. Cub Scouter of Yr., Piedmont dist. Boy Scouts Am., 1986, Tchr. of Yr. Rural Hall Sch., 1996, 97. Mem. ASCD, Nat. Coun. Tchrs. English, Nat. Coun. Tchrs. Math., Internat. Reading Assn. (membership chmn. local unit 1987), Nat. Sci. Tchrs. Assn., N.C. Assn. Educators (faculty rep. 1985, 92). Democrat. Avocations: reading, sewing, swimming, sailing, scuba diving. Home: PO Box 250 Rural Hall NC 27045-0250 Office: Rural Hall Elem Sch 275 College St Rural Hall NC 27045-9703

MCDERMOTT, AGNES CHARLENE SENAPE, philosophy educator; b. Hazelton, Pa., Mar. 11, 1937; d. Charles G. and Conjetta (Ranieri) Senape; children: Robert C., Lisa G., Jamie C. B.A., U. Pa., 1956, Ph.D., 1964; postgrad., U. Calif.-Berkeley, 1960-61, U. Amsterdam, Netherlands, 1965, U. Wis., 1967-69. Instr. math. Drexel Inst. Tech., Phila., 1962-63; asst. prof. philosophy SUNY-Buffalo, 1964-65, Hampton Inst., Va., 1966-67; asst. prof. U. Wis.-Milw., 1967-70; assoc. prof. philosophy U. N.Mex., Albuquerque, 1970-80, prof., dean grad. studies, 1981-86; dean in residence Council of Grad. Schs., Washington, 1985-86; provost, v.p. acad. affairs CUNY, CUNY, 1986-89; prof. philosophy CUNY, 1986-91; dean for acad. and student affairs, cons. Albuquerque Acad., 1991-93; ind. cons. Corrales, N.Mex., 1993—; vis. assoc. prof. U. Wash., Seattle, 1974, U. Calif.-Berkeley, 1973-74, U. Hawaii, Honolulu, 1975; vis. prof. U. Calif.-Berkeley, 1980; lectr., panelist. Author: An Eleventh Century Buddhist Logic of 'Exists', 1969, Boethius' Treatise on the Modes of Signifying, 1980; compiler, editor anthology: Comparative Philosophy: Selected Essays, 1983; rev. editor Phil. East West, 1986—; contbr. articles to profl. jours. Vol. Albuquerque Care Alliance, 1988—. AAUW postdoctoral fellow, 1965-66; NEH Younger Humanist fellow, 1971-72; faculty rsch. fellow U. N.Mex., 1978, 79, 80; U. Pa. grad. fellow, 1961-62; S. Fels Found. fellow, 1963-64;U. Pa. tuition scholar; Pa. Hist. Soc. scholar. Mem. N.Y. Acad. Scis., Am. Philos. Soc., Am. Philos. Assn. (exec. com. 1977-80), Assn. Asian Studies (exec. com. 1977-80), Am. Oriental Soc., Western Assn. Grad. Schs. (pres. 1986-87), Phi Beta Kappa, Pi Mu Epsilon. Democrat. Avocations: skiing, fly-fishing.

MC DERMOTT, ALBERT LEO, lawyer; b. Lowell, Mass., Jan. 21, 1923; s. John Thomas and Josephine (Rohan) McD. AB, Boston Coll., 1944; LLB, Georgetown U., 1949. Bar: Mass. 1950, D.C. 1950, U.S. Supreme Ct. 1972. Practice of law Washington, 1950-54; asso. Ingoldsby & Coles, 1950-52, partner, 1952-54; spl. asst. to Sec. Labor, 1954-61; ptnr. law firm McDermott & Russell (and predecessor), 1961-92; Washington rep. Am. Hotel and Motel Assn., 1963-88; adv. bd. Maritime Cargo Transp. conf., Fed. Svc. Impasses Panel, 1972-78; alt. rep. Pres. Nixon's Pay Bd., 1971-73; staff dir. Senate Rules Com., 1994-95, Senate Com. on Govtl. Affairs, 1995-96; sr. counsel senate appropriations com., 1997—. Served as lt. USNR, World War II. Mem. Nat. Acad. Sci. (mem. research council 1957-60), ABA, Bar Assn. D.C. Clubs: Congl. Country, Capitol Hill (Washington); Tavern (N.Y.C.); Rehoboth Country (Del.). Home: 4813 Van Ness St NW Washington DC 20016-2353 Office: US Senate Washington DC 20510

MCDERMOTT, CECIL WADE, mathematics educator, educational program director; b. Parkin, Ark., Aug. 19, 1935; s. Joe E. and Myrtle L. (Davis) McD.; m. Nelda Grace Lyons, June 4, 1961; children: Kevin Scott, Stephen Kyle. BS in Math., U. Ark., 1957; MS in Stats., Purdue U., 1962; EdD in Math. Edn., Auburn (Ala.) U., 1967. Cert. tchr. math., gen. sci., phys. sci., curriculum specialist supr., designated ind. fee appraiser, rsch. analyst. Instr. math. Sikeston (Mo.) H.S., 1957-59; state math. supr. Ark. Dept. Edn., Little Rock, 1959-65; ednl. cons. Auburn U., 1965-67; chmn., prof. math. Hendrix Coll., Conway, Ark., 1967-83; program dir. IMPAC Learning Sys., Inc., Little Rock, 1983—; co-dir. NSF Inst. Tulane U., New Orleans, summers 1967-71; residential appraiser Morrilton (Ark.) Savs. & Loan, summers 1977-82; cons. Okla. Legis. Coun., Oklahoma City, 1987, America 2000 Project, Dallas, 1991; mem. tchr. tng. panel Office Tech. Assessment, 1994; pres. Ark. Intercoll. Conf. Faculty Rep., 1974-84. Author: (audio-tutorial film) Primary School Mathematics, 1975; co-author: Modern Elementary Mathematics, 1978, Landmarks, Rudders and Crossroads, 1993, Modern Job, 1997; designer: (computer courseware) Mathematics/Basic Skills, 1989, 93. Plan coord. Gov.'s Task Force on Telecomm. Planning, 1991-95; mem. Murphy Commn. Tech. Panel, 1997; bd. dirs. Hendrix Coll. Hall of Honor, 1993—. Rsch. grantee U.S. Office Edn., Washington, 1972-73, Rockefeller Found., Little Rock, 1983-85, Ross Found., 1997; recipient Cert. of Merit award Electronic Learning, 1987,

Endowment Scholarship Hendrix Coll., Conway, Ark., 1987; state honoree Nat. Gov.'s Assn., 1997. Mem. Ark. Amateur Union (chmn. state long distance running program 1969-72), Ark. Coun. Tchrs. Math. (chmn. regional conf. 1970), Am. Math. Soc., Math. Assn. Am. (pres. Okla./Ark. 1976-77), Phi Delta Kappa, Phi Kappa Phi, Pi Mu Epsilon. Episcopalian. Avocations: long distance running, creative writing, farming. Home: 1204 Hunter St Conway AR 72032-2716 Office: IMPAC Learning Sys Inc 501 Woodlane Dr Ste 122 Little Rock AR 72201-1024

MCDERMOTT, DYLAN, actor. Appeared in films Hamburger Hill, 1987, Twister, 1988, Steel Manolias, 1989, In The Line Of Fire, 1993, The Cowboy Way, 1994, Miracle on 34th Street, 1994, Destiny Turns On The Radio, 1995, Home For The Holidays, 1995, 'Til There Was You, 1996. Office: Creative Artists Agy 9830 Wilshire Blvd Beverly Hills CA 90212*

MCDERMOTT, EDWARD ALOYSIOUS, lawyer; b. Dubuque, Iowa, June 28, 1920; s. Edward L. and Sarah (Larkin) McD.; m. Naola Spellman, Sept. 1, 1945; children: Maureen, Edward Aloysious, Charles Joseph, Daniel John. B.A., Loras Coll., Dubuque, 1939; J.D., State U., Iowa, 1942; J.D. (hon.), Xavier U., 1962, Loras Coll., 1973. Bar: Iowa 1942, D.C. 1942, Nebr. 1942. Mem. legal dept. Travelers Ins. Co., Omaha, 1942-43, Montgomery Ward & Co., Chgo., 1943-46; atty. firm O'Connor, Thomas & O'Connor, Dubuque, 1946-50; chief counsel sub-com. privileges and elections U.S. Senate, 1950-51; partner firm O'Connor, Thomas, McDermott & Wright, Dubuque, 1951-61; prof. bus. law and econs. Loras Coll., also Clarke Coll., Dubuque; dep. dir. U.S. Office Civil and Def. Moblzn., 1961-62, U.S. Office Emergency Planning, 1961-62; dir. Office Emergency Planning, 1962-65; ptnr. firm Hogan & Hartson, Washington, 1965-88; ret., 1989; U.S. rep. to sr. com. and other coms. NATO, 1962-65; chmn. Pres.'s Exec. Stockpile Com., 1962-65; mem. bd. advisers Indsl. Coll. Armed Forces, 1962-65; mem. Nat. Conf. Uniform Commrs. State Laws, 1959-64; chmn. Nat. CD Adv. Coun., 1962-65; mem. Pres.'s Com. Employment Handicapped, 1962-65, Pres.'s Com. Manpower, 1963-65, Pres.'s Com. Econ. Impact Def. and Rearmament, 1963-65, Pres.'s Sr. Adv. Com. on Govt. Reorgn., 1978-79; chmn. Com. on Assumptions for Nonmil. and Devel. Commn., Alaska, 1964-65; bd. dirs. Mercedes-Benz N.A., 1985—, mem. ops. com., 1986—; mem. adv. com. Office Comptr. Gen. of U.S., 1990—. Del. Democratic Nat. Conv., 1952, 56, 60, 64; trustee, sec. Ford's Theatre, Christ Child Soc., Religious Educators Found., Loras Coll.; mem. fin. council Archdiocese of Washington, 1985-89; chmn. emeritus Lombardi Cancer Inst.; regent emeritus Coll. Notre Dame; trustee emeritus Colgate U.; mem. council Hosp. St. John and St. Elizabeth, London, Maynooth Coll., Ireland; regent emeritus U. Santa Clara, Calif; bd. advisers Lynchburg (Va.) Coll., Iowa Law Sch. Found., Up With People; v.p. Flax Trust, No. Ireland. Decorated knight Holy Sepulchre; recipient Amvets Spl. Silver Helmet award, 1963. Fellow ABA; mem. Fed. Bar Assn., Iowa Bar Assn. (bd. govs. 1956-60), D.C. Bar Assn., Am. Judicature Soc., John Carroll Soc. (pres. 1972), Am. Ireland Fund (bd. dirs.), Friendly Sons St. Patrick (pres. 1978-79), Ireland Club Fla., The City Club (bd. dirs.), 1925 F Street Club, Met. Club (Washington), Delray Beach Club (Fla.), Knights of Malta Fed. Assn. (pres. 1979-82). Democrat. Home: Lake House South 875 E Camino Real Boca Raton FL 33432-6356 Office: Columbia Sq 555 13th St NW Washington DC 20004-1109

MCDERMOTT, FRANCIS OWEN, lawyer; b. Denver, Feb. 25, 1933; s. Paul Harkins and Agnes (Clark) McD.; divorced; children: Diana, Daniel, Christopher, Anthony, Justine; m. Estella Marina Idiaquez, June 6, 1986. JD, Am. U., 1960. Bar: D.C. 1960, U.S. Dist. Ct. D.C., 1960, U.S. Ct. Appeals (D.C. cir.) 1960, u.S. Tax Ct. 1961, U.S. Supreme Ct. 1964. Trial atty. office regional counsel IRS, Washington, 1961-65; mem. profl. staff com. on fin. U.S. Senate, Washington, 1965-68; tax counsel Assn. Am. R.R.s, Washington, 1968-73; assoc. Hopkins & Sutter, Washington, 1973-76, ptnr., 1976—; gen. counsel Inst. Ill., Washington, 1987—. Mem. ABA, Fed. Bar Assn., Nat. Def. Transp. Assn. (v.p., gen. counsel 1974—). Roman Catholic. Avocation: tennis.

MCDERMOTT, JAMES A., congressman, psychiatrist; b. Chicago, Ill., Dec. 28, 1936; children: Katherine, James. BS, Wheaton Coll., 1958; MD, U. Ill., 1963. Intern Buffalo Gen. Hosp., 1963-64; resident in adult psychiatry U. Ill. Hosps., Chgo., 1964-66; resident in child psychiatry U. Wash. Hosps., Seattle, 1966-68; asst. clin. prof. dept. psychiatry U. Wash., Seattle, 1970-83; mem. Wash. Ho. of Reps., 1971-72, Wash. Senate, 1975-87; regional med. officer U.S. Fgn. Svc., 1987-88; mem. 101st-105th Congresses from 7th Wash. dist., 1989—; former chmn. stds. of ofcl. conduct com., mem. ways and means com., ranking minority mem., mem. stds. of ofcl. conduct com.; mem. exec. and edn. com. Nat. Conf. State Legislatures, chair ethics com. Mem. Wash. State Arts Commn., Wash. Coun. for Prevention Child Abuse and Neglect; Dem. nominee for gov., 1980. Lt. comdr. M.C., USN, 1968-70, . Mem. Am. Psychiat. Assn., Wash. State Med. Assn., King County Med. Soc. Democrat. Episcopalian. Office: US Ho of Reps 2349 Rayburn HOB Washington DC 20515*

MCDERMOTT, JAMES ALEXANDER, retired lawyer; b. Tulsa, May 2, 1938; s. Richard Bertram McDermott and Ruth Lamb; m. Renée Rassler, Jan. 1, 1986; children: Melora, Melissa. AB, Princeton U., 1960; JD, U. Mich., 1963. Bar: Ind. 1963. Assoc. Barnes & Thornburg, Indpls., 1963-71, ptnr., 1971-94, counsel, 1994-96; ret., 1997—. Author: Recommended Law Books, 1987. Founder Penrod Soc., Festival Music Soc., Indpls. 1967; rowing commr. X Pan Am. Games, Indpls., 1987. Democrat. Home: 1008 McLary Rd Nashville IN 47448-9176

MCDERMOTT, JOHN E., lawyer; b. Ravenna, Ohio, Oct. 25, 1946. BA, Ohio Wesleyan U., 1968; JD, Harvard U., 1971. Bar: Calif. 1972. Mem. Cadwalwder, Wickersham & Taft, L.A. Mem. ABA, State Bar Calif., Los Angeles County, Phi Beta Kappa. Office: Howrey & Simon 555 S Hope St Los Angeles CA 90017

MC DERMOTT, JOHN FRANCIS, JR., psychiatrist, physician; b. Hartford, Conn., Dec. 12, 1929; s. John Francis and Camilla R. (Cavanaugh) McD.; m. Sarah N. Schemm, Dec. 27, 1958; children: Elizabeth C., John Francis III. A.B., Cornell U., 1951; M.D., N.Y. Med. Coll., 1955. Diplomate in psychiatry and child psychiatry Am. Bd. Psychiatry and Neurology. Intern Henry Ford Hosp., Detroit, 1955-56; resident in psychiatry U. Mich. Med. Center, 1956-58, resident in child psychiatry, 1960-62; practice medicine, specializing in psychiatry and child and adolescent psychiatry Honolulu, 1969-95; instr., asst. prof., asso. prof. psychiatry U. Mich. Sch. Medicine, 1962-69; prof., chmn. dept. psychiatry U. Hawaii Sch. Medicine, 1969-95, prof. emeritus, 1995—; scholar-in-residence Rockefeller Found. Study Ctr., Bellagio, Italy, 1985, 92; chmn. com. cert. in child psychiatry Am. Bd. Psychiatry and Neurology, 1974-78, bd. dirs., 1983-91, chmn. R&D com., 1985-91; sr. vis. scientist dept. exptl. psychology Oxford (Eng.) U., 1993; vis. prof. numerous univs.; cons. numerous mental health clinics and orgns. Co-author: Psychiatry for the Pediatrician, 1970, Childhood Psychopathology, 1972, Mental Health Education in New Medical Schools, 1973, Roles and Functions of Child Psychiatrists, 1976, Psychiatric Treatment of the Child, 1977, New Directions in Childhood Psychopathology, vol. I, 1980, vol. II, 1982, Raising Cain (and Abel Too), 1980: People and Cultures of Hawaii, 1980, Culture Mind and Therapy: An Introduction to Cultural Psychiatry, 1982, Japanese edit., 1984, The Complete Book on Sibling Rivalry, 1987, German edit., 1991; editor Jour. Am. Acad. Child and Adolescent Psychiatry, 1987-97; contbr. over 150 articles to profl. jours.; mem. editorial bds. numerous psychiat. jours. Served with USN, 1958-60. Named Disting. Alumnus N.Y. Med. Coll., 1976. Fellow Am. Psychiat. Assn. (life), Am. Orthopsychiat. Assn., Am. Acad. Child and Adolescent Psychiatry, Am. Coll. Psychiatrists, Pacific Rim Coll. Psychiatrists, World Psychiat. Assn. (chmn. child and adolescent psychiatry 1977-89). Clubs: Outrigger Canoe, Cosmos. Home: PO Box 6840 Kamuela HI 96743 Office: U Hawaii Sch Medicine Dept Psychiatry PO Box 6840 Honolulu HI 96826-1032

MCDERMOTT, JOHN H(ENRY), lawyer; b. Evanston, Ill., June 23, 1931; s. Edward Henry and Goldie Lucile (Boso) McD.; m. Ann Elizabeth Pickard, Feb. 19, 1966; children: Elizabeth A., Mary L., Edward H. BA, Williams Coll., 1953; JD, U. Mich., 1956. Bar: Mich. 1955, Ill. 1956. Assoc. McDermott, Will & Emery, Chgo., 1958-64, ptnr., 1964—; bd. dirs. Patrick Industries Inc. 1st lt. USAF, 1956-58. Mem. ABA, Ill. Bar Assn., Chgo. Bar Assn. Clubs: Commerical of Chgo., Econ. of Chgo., Legal Chgo. (pres. 1981-82), Law Chgo. (pres. 1986-87). Home: 330 Willow Rd Winnetka IL 60093-4130 Office: McDermott Will & Emery 227 W Monroe St Chicago IL 60606-5016

MCDERMOTT, KEVIN J., engineering educator, consultant; b. Teaneck, N.J., Nov. 21, 1935; s. Francis X. and Elizabeth (Casey) McD.; m. Ann McDermott, Aug. 3, 1959; children: Kathleen, Kevin, Donna, Michael. BSEE, N.J. Inst. Tech., 1965; MS Indsl. Engring., Columbia U., 1970; EdD, Fairleigh Dickinson U., 1975. Registered profl. engr., N.J. With Bell Telephone Labs., Murray Hill, N.J., 1960-65, Westinghouse Electic, Newark, 1965-67, Columbia U., NASA, N.Y.C., 1967-70, RCA Corp., N.Y.C., 1970-76, Ramapo (N.J.) Coll., 1976-80; prof. N.J. Inst. Tech., Newark, 1980—; chmn. engring. dept. N.J. Inst. Tech., 1983—; dir. Computer Aided Design/Computer Aided Manufacture Robotics Consortium. Contbr. more than 50 articles to tech. jours. IBM fellow, 1987. Fellow IEEE, Soc. Mech. Engrs.; mem. Inst. Indsl. Engrs. Achievements include research in industrial robot work cells, manufacturing systems, expert systems, analysis of industrial robotics, flexible manufacturing systems, expert and vision systems in compuer aided design and manufacturing.

MCDERMOTT, KEVIN R., lawyer; b. Youngstown, Ohio, Jan. 26, 1952; s. Robert J. and Marion D. (McKeown) McD.; m. Cindy J. Darling, Dec. 11, 1976; children: Ciara, Kelly. AB, Miami U., Oxford, Ohio, 1974; JD, Ohio State U., 1977. Bar: Ohio 1977, U.S. Dist. Ct. (so. dist.) Ohio 1978, U.S. Dist. Ct. (no. dist.) Ohio 1988, U.S. Dist. Ct. (we. dist.) Mich. 1993, U.S. Supreme Ct. 1990, U.S. Ct. Appeals (3rd cir.) 1996, U.S. Ct. Appeals (6th cir.) 1988. Assoc. ptnr. Murphey Young & Smith, Columbus, Ohio, 1977-88; ptnr. Squire Sanders & Dempsey, Columbus, Ohio, 1988-90, Schottenstein Zox & Dunn, Columbus, Ohio, 1990—; adv. bd. mem. Capital U. Legal Asst. Program, Columbus, Ohio, 1988—. Bd. pres. Easter Seal Soc. Ctrl. Ohio, Columbus, 1992-94, bd. mem. 1988-92; pres. Upper Arlington Civic Svc. Commn., Columbus, Ohio, 1988-93. Office: Schottenstein Zox & Dunn 41 S High St Columbus OH 43215-6101

MCDERMOTT, LARRY ARNOLD, newspaper publisher, newspaper editor; b. Parkin, Ark., Apr. 27, 1948; s. John Allen and Ila Mae (Harris) McD.; m. Linda Louis Lancaster, Mar. 20, 1969; children: Marshall, Kelly, Amanda. BS, Ark. State U., 1970. Reporter Jonesboro (Ark.) Sun, 1968-70; reporter AP, Richmond, Va., 1970-71, 72-75, Norfolk, Va., 1975-76; polit. correspondent AP, Lansing, Mich., 1976-78; bur. chief AP, Little Rock, 1978-80, Mpls., 1980-84, Detroit, 1984-87; asst. to the pres. AP, N.Y.C., 1987-88; info. specialist UN Command, Seoul, Republic of Korea, 1971-72; copy editor Korea Times, Seoul, 1971-72; editor, bur. chief Booth Newspapers, Lansing, 1988-90; pub. Bay City (Mich.) Times, 1990-92; exec. editor Springfield Union News, Mass., 1993—; v.p., bd. dirs. Mich. State News, East Lansing, 1990-91. Bd. dirs. Bay Area Econ. Growth Alliance, Bay City, 1990-91. With U.S. Army, 1970-72. Presbyterian. Avocations: fly fishing, golf, camping. Home: 26 Tennyson Dr East Longmeadow MA 01106-2334 Office: Bay City Times 311 5th St Bay City MI 48708-5806 also: Union-News 1860 Main St Springfield MA 01103-1000*

MCDERMOTT, LUCINDA MARY, ecumenical minister, teacher, philosopher, poet, author; b. Lynwood, Calif., June 3, 1947; d. R. Harry and Cathrine Jayne (Redmond) Boand. BA, U. So. Calif., L.A., 1969; MS, Calif. State U., Long Beach, 1975; PhD, Saybrook Inst., San Francisco, 1978. Pres. Environ. Health Systems, Newport Beach, Calif., 1976-90; founder, pres. Forerunner Publs., Newport Beach, 1985—, Life-Skills Learning Ctr., Newport Beach, 1985—; founder, dir. Newport Beach Ecumenical Ctr., 1993—; bd. dirs. Tri Delta Mgmt., The Boand Family Found. Author: Bridges to Another Place, 1972, Honor Thy Self, Vol. I and II, 1973, Hello-My-Love-Good Bye, 1973, Life-Skills for Adults, 1982, Au Courants, 1983, Life-Skills for Children, 1984, Myrika-An Autobiographical Novel, 1989, White Knights and Shining Halos: Beyond Pair Bonding, 1996. Mem. APA, Truthsayer Minstrels (founder, dir. 1996—), Alpha Kappa Delta, Kappa Kappa Gamma.

MCDERMOTT, MOLLY, lay minister; b. Cloquet, Minn., Aug. 19, 1932; d. Harry W. McD.; children: Elizabeth Sanders Hellenbrand, Sarah Sanders, Mary Sanders Day, Margaret Kathleen Sanders Lorfeld. Student, Oreg. State Coll., 1951, U. Minn., Duluth, 1953. Claims specialist Cuna Mut. Ins. Soc., Madison, Wis., 1975—; propr. Molly's Garden. Storyteller, ventriloquist St. Bernard's Parish, liturgical environ. com. Mem. Perennial Soc., Toastmasters, The Rose Soc. (storyteller, ventriloquist). Roman Catholic. Home: 1724 Parmenter St Middleton WI 53562-3153

MCDERMOTT, RENÉE R(ASSLER), lawyer; b. Danville, Pa., Sept. 26, 1950; d. Carl A. and Rose (Gaupp) Rassler; m. James A. McDermott, Jan. 1, 1986. BA, U. So. Fla., 1970, MA, 1972; JD, Ind. U., 1978. Bar: Ind. 1978, U.S. Dist. Ct. (so. and no. dists.) Ind. 1978, U.S. Dist. Ct. Ariz. 1984, U.S. Ct. Appeals (7th cir.) 1979, U.S. Ct. Appeals (9th cir.) 1985. Law clk. to presiding judge U.S. Dist. Ct. (no. dist.) Ind., Ft. Wayne, 1978-80; assoc. Barnes & Thornburg, Indpls., 1980-84, ptnr., 1985-93; pvt. practice Nashville, Ind., 1994—; county atty. County of Brown, Ind., 1994—. Editor in chief Ind. U. Law Jour., 1977-78. Bd. visitors Ind. U. Law Sch., Bloomington, 1979—; bd. dirs. Environ. Quality Control Inc., Indpls. Named one of Outstanding Young Women Am., 1986. Fellow Ind. Bar Found., Am. Bar Found. (life); mem. ABA (bus. sect. coun. 1995—, chmn. environ. controls com. 1991-95, liaison to standing com. on environ. law bus. law sect.), Ind. State Bar Assn. (chmn. young lawyers sect. 1985-86, chmn. environ. law sect. 1989-91), Bar Assn. 7th Fed. Cir., Ind. Mfrs. Assn. (environ. affairs com.), Order of Coif. Avocations: scuba diving, horseback riding, music, reading, hiking. Home and Office: 1008 W McLary Rd Nashville IN 47448-9176

MCDERMOTT, RICHARD T., lawyer, educator; b. Milw., Jan. 30, 1940; s. Richard A. and Sylvia Carmen (Portuondo) McD.; m. Mary Patricia Scanlon, Aug. 24, 1963; children: Richard B., Christina M. BA, Marquette U., 1962; LLB, Fordham U., 1966. Bar: N.Y. 1967. Assoc. Alexander & Green, N.Y.C., 1966-73, ptnr., 1973-86; ptnr. Walter, Conston, Alexander & Green, N.Y.C., 1987-90, Rogers & Wells, N.Y.C., 1990—; adj. prof. law NYU Sch. Law, N.Y.C., 1980—. Author: Legal Aspects of Corporate Finance, 1985, 2d edit., 1995. Fellow Am. Bar Found.; mem. ABA, N.Y. State Bar Assn., Bar Assn. City N.Y., Univ. Club, Woodstock Golf Club (N.Y.). Avocations: foreign relations, golf. Office: Rogers & Wells 200 Park Ave New York NY 10166-0005

MCDERMOTT, ROBERT B., lawyer; b. Washington, June 16, 1927; s. Edward H. and Goldie Lucile (Boso) McD.; m. Julia Wood, Nov. 16, 1950; children: John, Jeanne, Charles; m. Jane S. Whitman, July 31, 1973; m. Sarah Jaicks, Jan. 6, 1996. A.B., Princeton U., 1948; LL.B., Harvard U., 1951. Bar: D.C. 1951, Ill. 1955. Atty. Office Gen. Counsel, Navy Dept., Washington, 1951-52; assoc McDermott, Will & Emery, Chgo., 1954-60, ptnr., 1961-92, chmn., 1986-91, of counsel, 1992—; bd. dirs. The Cherry Corp., Waukegan, Ill., Furst-McNess Co., Freeport, Ill., Maynard Oil Co., Dallas. Trustee Ill. Inst. Tech., Chgo., 1985—, The Mather Found., Evanston, Ill., 1988—; bd. chair Ct. Theatre. Lt. USNR, 1945-46, 52-54. Mem. Chgo. Bar Assn. Clubs: Chicago, Economic, University (Chgo.). Home: 990 N Lake Shore Dr #31E Chicago IL 60611-1353 Office: 227 W Monroe St Chicago IL 60606-5016

MCDERMOTT, THOMAS JOHN, JR., lawyer; b. Santa Monica, Calif., Mar. 23, 1931; s. Thomas J. Sr. and Etha Irene (Cook) McD.; m. Yolanda; children: Jodi Friedman, Kimberly E., Kish S. BA, UCLA, 1953, JD, 1958. Bar: Calif. 1959. Ptnr., Gray, Binkley and Pfaelzer, Los Angeles, 1964-67, Kadison, Pfaelzer, Woodward, Quinn and Rossi, Los Angeles, 1967-87, Rogers & Wells, 1987-93, Bryan Cave, 1993-95, Manatt, Phelps & Phillips, LLP, 1995—. Served with U.S. Army, 1953-56, Korea. Fellow Am. Coll. Trial Lawyers; mem. ABA, UCLA Law Alumni Assn. (pres. 1961-62), Assn. of Bus. Trial Lawyers (pres. 1980-81, mem. exec. com. 9th cir. jud. conf. 1993—, chair 1997), State Bar Calif. (chair litigation sect. 1993-94), Order of Coif. Office: Manatt Phelps & Phillips LLP 11355 W Olympic Blvd Los Angeles CA 90064-1614

MCDERMOTT, WILLIAM THOMAS, accountant, lawyer; b. New Orleans, Jan. 3, 1945; s. William Thomas and Delia Ethel (Belden) McD.; m. Geraldine Dorothy Constantine, Nov. 20, 1965; children: Lisa Anne, Shannon Marie. BSBA, Am. U., 1969, MBA, 1971; JD (with hon.), George Washington U., 1974; grad. exec. mgmt. program, J.L. Kellogg Grad. Sch. CPA, Va.; cert. mgmt. acct.; fellow Life Mgmt. Inst. Ptnr. for tax Ernst & Young, Richmond, Va., 1969—; co-chmn. U. Va. Fed. Tax Conf., Charlottesville, 1981—; apptd. by Gov. of Va. to Commn. on Competitive and Equitable Tax Policy, 1996. Contbr. articles to profl. jours. Past chmn. bd. dirs. Richmond br. Tuckahoe YMCA, 1984; mem. citizens promotion bd. Henrico County Police Dept., Richmond, 1985; bd. dirs. Greater Richmond YMCA, 1983-84, Theater Va., Richmond, 1982—; treas., bd. dirs., mem. exec. com. Arts Coun. of Richmond, 1988-96, Children's Home Soc., Richmond, 1987—. Recipient Cert. Appreciation award Henrico County Police Dept., 1985, Karl B. Wagner Service award Tuckahoe YMCA, 1986. Mem. ABA, AICPA (individual tax com. 1990-93, chmn. interest expense task force 1993-96), Inst. Mgmt. Accts. (nat. v.p. 1991-92, nat. dir. 1987-89, 95—, chmn. nat. ethics com., prin. Va. Coun. 1987-88), Va. Soc. CPAs, D.C. Inst. CPAs, Bull and Bear Club, Hermitage Country Club. Roman Catholic. Home: 1701 Locust Hill Rd Richmond VA 23233-4149 Office: Ernst & Young 901 E Cary St Richmond VA 23219-4057

MC DERMOTT, WILLIAM VINCENT, JR., physician, educator; b. Salem, Mass., Mar. 7, 1917; s. William Vincent and Mary A. (Feenan) McD.; m. Blanche O'Riorden, May 15, 1943 (dec. July 1969); children: Blanche Anne, William Shaw, Jane Travers Hoch; m. Mary Boit Bingham, June 1, 1976 (dec. 1984); m. Frances Weld Gardiner, June 16, 1989 (dec. 1993). A.B., Harvard U., 1938, M.D., 1942. Diplomate: Nat. Bd. Med. Examiners (chmn. surgery test com.), Am. Bd. Surgery. Intern Mass. Gen. Hosp., Boston, 1942; asst. resident surgeon Mass. Gen. Hosp., 1946-49, chief resident surgeon, 1950; practice medicine specializing in surgery Boston, 1951—; mem. staff Mass. Gen. Hosp., 1951—, New Eng. Deaconess Hosp., 1963—; dir. Fifth (Harvard) Surg. Svc. and Sears Surg. Lab. Boston City Hosp., 1963-73; mem. corp. vis. com., 1968—; USPHS fellow dept. biochemistry Sch. Medicine, Yale U., 1949-50; from instr. to prof. surgery Med. Sch. Harvard U., 1951-69, Cheever prof. surgery, 1969-87, prof. surgery emeritus, 1987—, sec. Faculty of Medicine, 1985-87; tutor premed. adv. Cabot House, Harvard Coll., 1989—; vis. prof. pro tem Kings Coll. Hosp. Med. Sch., London, 1960; dir. Harvard Surg. Svc. and Cancer Rsch. Inst., 1973-80; chmn. dept. surgery New Eng. Deaconess Hosp., 1980-85, mem. vis. com., 1987—, bd. dirs. Author six books, over 230 sci. papers; contbr. 12 chapters to books; mem. editorial bd. Jour. Surg. Rsch., 1960-73, Jour. Surg. Oncology, 1970—. Pres. Med. Found., Boston, 1968-70, trustee, 1970-87, hon. trustee, 1987—; bd. trustees Nat. Youth Leadership Forum, 1995—. Maj. M.C. AUS, 1943-46, ETO. Decorated Bronze Star, oak leaf cluster, 5 battle stars; recipient Disting. Alumnus award Harvard U., 1992. Mem. ACS (bd. govs. 1984-90, pres. Mass. chpt. 1980), Soc. Univ. Surgeons, Am. Surg. Assn., Am. Acad. Arts and Scis., New Eng. Surg. Soc. (pres. 1985-86), Boston Surg. Soc. (pres. 1971), Harvard Med. Alumni Assn. (treas. 1965-68, pres. 1975-76, dir. alumni rels. 1987-93, bd. dirs. 1993-95), Harvard Coll. Alumni Assn., Soc. de Chirurgie Internat., Assn. Acad. Surgery, Soc. Surgery Alimentary Tract, Aesculapian Club (pres. 1971), Harvard Club of Boston (bd. govs. 1971-77), Tavern Club, Country Club. Home: 570 Bridge St Dedham MA 02026-4131 Office: New Eng Deaconess Hosp Dept Surgery Boston MA 02215

MCDEVITT, BRIAN PETER, history educator, educational consultant; b. Jersey City, Dec. 29, 1944; s. Bernard Aloysius and Veronica Sabina (Decker) McD.; m. Dorothy Helen Gilligan, Oct. 19, 1968; children: Peter David, Timothy Bernard. BS, Seton Hall U., 1966; MA, Columbia U., 1971. Tchr. history St. Patrick's High Sch., Elizabeth, N.J., 1966-68, Vail Deane High Sch., Elizabeth, N.J., 1968-70; fed. grant writer Alexian Bros. Hosp., Elizabeth, N.J., 1970-72, Union County Coll., Cranford, N.J., 1972-76; prin., owner Ednl. Svcs., Westfield, N.J., 1976—; adj. prof. history Union County Coll., Cranford, N.J., 1976—; adj. prof. classics Montclair (N.J.) State U., 1990—. Author: The Irish Librists, 1988, The Irish Librists and the Scrolls of Aristotle, 1993, A Historian's Thematic Study of Western Civilization, 1994, Evidence of an Ancient Greek Navigation System, 1995, The Irish Librists and The Vatican Library Mystery, 1996, A Definition of Western Civilization, 1997, (video) The Minoans According to Sir Arthur Evans; contbr. articles to profl. jours. N.J. Dept. Higher Edn. grantee. Mem. Trireme Trust U.S.A. (internat. rowing team 1990), Friends of Trireme (London), Soc. Naval Architects and Marine Engrs., Assn. Ancient Historians, Soc. Ancient Greek Philosophy, Assn. Muslim Social Scientists, Westfield United Fund, Westfield P.A.L., Westfield Basketball Assn., Westfield Baseball Assn., Boy Scouts Am. Roman Catholic. Avocations: golfing, rowing, basketball, playing piano, stamp collecting. Home: 607 S Chestnut St Westfield NJ 07090-1369

MCDEVITT, CHARLES FRANCIS, state supreme court justice; b. Pocatello, Idaho, Jan. 5, 1932; s. Bernard A. and Margaret (Hermann) McD.; m. Virginia L. Heller, Aug. 14, 1954; children: Eileen A., Kathryn A., Brian A., Sheila A., Terrence A., Neil A., Kendal A. LLB, U. Idaho, 1956. Bar: 1956. Ptnr. Richards, Haga & Eberle, Boise, 1956-62; gen. counsel, asst. sec. Boise Cascade Corp., 1962-65; mem. Idaho State Legislature, 1963-66; sec., gen. counsel Boise Cascade Corp., 1965-67, v.p. sec., 1967-68; pres. Beck Industries, 1968-70; group v.p. Singer Co., N.Y.C., 1970-72, exec. v.p., 1973-76; pub. defender Ada County, Boise, 1976-78; co-founder Givens, McDevitt, Pursley & Webb, Boise, 1978-89; justice Idaho Supreme Ct., Boise, 1987-97, chief justice, 1993-97; served on Gov.'s Select Com. on Taxation, Boise, 1988-89. Home: 4940 Boise River Ln Boise ID 83706-5706 Office: Idaho Supreme Ct 451 W State St Boise ID 83702-6006

MCDEVITT, HUGH O'NEILL, immunology educator, physician; b. Cin., 1930. M.D., Harvard U., 1955. Diplomate: Am. Bd. Internal Medicine. Intern Peter Bent Brigham Hosp., Boston, 1955-56, sr. asst. resident in medicine, 1961-62; asst. resident Bell Hosp., 1956-57; research fellow dept. bacteriology and immunology Harvard U., 1959-61; USPHS spl. fellow Nat. Inst. Med. Research, Mill Hill, London, 1962-64; physician Stanford U. Hosp., Calif., 1966—; assoc. prof. Stanford U. Sch. Medicine, Calif., 1969-72, prof. med. immunology, 1972—, prof. med. microbiology, 1980—, Burt and Marian Avery Prof. Immunology, 1990—; cons. physician VA Hosp., Palo Alto, Calif., 1968—. Served as capt. M.C., AUS, 1957-59. Mem. NAS, AAAS, Am. Fedn. Clin. Rsch., Am. Soc. Clin. Investigation, Am. Assn. Immunologists, Transplantation Soc., Inst. Medicine, Royal Soc. (fgn.). Office: Stanford U Dept Microbiology Stanford CA 94305

MCDEVITT, SHEILA MARIE, lawyer, energy company executive; b. St. Petersburg, Fla., Jan. 15, 1947; d. Frank Davis and Marie (Barfield) McD. AA, St. Petersburg Jr. Coll., 1966; BA in Govt., Fla. State U., 1968, JD, 1978. Bar: Fla. 1978. Research asst. Fla. Legis. Reference Bur., Tallahassee, 1968-69; adminstr., research assoc. Constitution Revision Commn. Ga. Gen. Assembly, Atlanta, 1969-70; adminstrv. asst., analyst Fla. State Sen., Tallahassee, Fla., 1970-79; assoc. McClain, Walkley & Stuart, P.A., Tampa, Seminole, Fla., 1979-81; govtl. affairs counsel Tampa Electric Co., 1981-82, corp. counsel, 1982-86; sr. corp. counsel Teco Energy, Inc., Tampa, 1986-89, asst. v.p., 1989-92; v.p., asst. gen. counsel, 1992—; mem. Worker's Compensation Adv. Council Fla. Dept. Labor, Tallahassee, 1984-86; mem. bd. visitors Fla. State U. Coll. Law, 1996—; mem. adv. coun. ctr. for ethics U. Tampa, 1997—; Met. Ministries, 1996—; bd. vis. Fla. State U., 1997—. Bd. dirs. Vol. Ctr. Hillsborough County, Tampa, 1984-85; chmn., trustee Tampa Lowry Park Zoo Soc., 1986-94, also legal advisor; bd. dirs. Hillsborough County Easter Seal Soc., 1994-95; mem. Fla. Rep. Exec. Com., Tallahassee, 1974-75, Hillsborough County Rep. Exec. Com., 1974-75; mem. transition team for Fla. Gov. Bob Martinez, 1986-87; mem. Fed. Jud. Adv. Commn., 1989-93. Mem ABA, Fla. Energy Bar Assn., Fla. Bar (vice chmn., then chmn. energy law com. 1984-87, jud. nominating procedures com. 1986-91, jud. adminstrn. selection and tenure com. 1991-93), Hillsborough County Bar Assn. (chmn. law week com. 1990, corp. counsel com. 1986-87, internat. law com. 1994-95), Am. Corp. Counsel Assn. (bd. dirs. Ctrl. Fla. chpt. 1986-87), Tampa Club, Tiger Bay Club, Tampa Yacht and Country Club. Roman Catholic. Avocations: photography, bicycling, reading, boating. Office: TECO Energy Inc PO Box 111 702 N Franklin St Tampa FL 33602

MCDIARMID, LUCY, English educator, author; b. Louisville, Mar. 29, 1947; m. Harris B. Savin, Oct. 13, 1984; children: Emily Clare, Katharine

Eliza. BA, Swarthmore (Pa.) Coll., 1968; MA, Harvard U., 1969, PhD, 1972. Asst. prof. Boston U., 1972-74; from asst. prof. to assoc. prof. Swarthmore Coll., 1974-81; asst. prof. U. Md. Balt. County, Catonsville, 1982-84; prof. Villanova (Pa.) U., 1984—; vis. prof. English Princeton U., 1995; mem. exec. com. Am. Conf. for Irish Studies, 1987-91, v.p., 1995-97, pres., 1997—. Author: Saving Civilization: Yeats, Eliot and Auden Between the Wars, 1984, Auden's Apologies for Poetry, 1990; co-editor: Selected Writings of Lady Gregory, 1995, High and Low Moderns: Literature and Culture, 1889-1939, 1996; contbr. articles to profl. jours. NEH fellow, 1981-82; ACLS grantee, 1976, Bunting Inst. fellow, 1981-82, Guggenheim fellow, 1993-94; vis. fellow N.Y. Inst. Humanities, 1993-95. Mem. MLA (exec. com. Twentieth Century Lit. divsn.), Internat. Assn. for Study Anglo-Irish Lit. (Am. sec.-treas. 1994-96), Phi Beta Kappa. Home: 1931 Panama St Philadelphia PA 19103-6609 Office: Villanova U Dept Of English Villanova PA 19085

MCDILL, THOMAS ALLISON, minister; b. Cicero, Ill., June 4, 1926; s. Samuel and Agnes (Lindsay) McD.; m. Ruth Catherine Starr, June 4, 1949; children: Karen Joyce, Jane Alison, Steven Thomas. Th.B., No. Baptist Sem., Oakbrook, Ill., 1951; B.A., Trinity Coll., 1954; M.Div., Trinity Evang. Div. Sch., 1955, DD, 1989; D.Ministries, Bethel Theol. Sem., 1975. Ordained to ministry Evang. Free Ch. Am., 1949. Pastor Community Bible Ch., Berwyn, Ill., 1947-51, Grace Evang. Free Ch., Chgo., 1951-58, Liberty Bible Ch., Valparaiso, Ind., 1959-67, Crystal Evang. Free Ch., Mpls., 1967-76; v.p., moderator Evang. Free Ch. of Am., 1973-74, chmn. home missions bd., 1968-72, chmn. exec. bd., 1973-90, pres., 1976-90, ret., 1990; min. at large Evang. Free Ch. Am., 1991—. Contbr. articles to publs. Chmn. bd. Trinity Coll., Deerfield, Ill., 1974-76; bd. govs. Trinity Western Coll.; bd. dirs. Trinity Evang. Divinity Sch. Mem. Evang. Free Ch. Ministerial Assn., Evang. Ministers Assn., Nat. Assn. Evangelicals (bd. adminstrn. 1976—, mem. exec. com. 1981-88), Greater Mpls. Assn. Evangelicals (bd. dirs., sec. bd. 1969-73). Home: 4246 Goldenrod Ln N Minneapolis MN 55441-1241 Office: 901 E 78th St Bloomington MN 55420-1334

MC DONAGH, EDWARD CHARLES, sociologist, university administrator; b. Edmonton, Alta., Can., Jan. 23, 1915; came to U.S., 1922, naturalized, 1936; s. Henry Fry and Aletta (Bowles) McD.; m. Louise Lucille Lorenzi, Aug. 14, 1940 (dec.); children: Eileen, Patricia. A.B., U. So. Calif., 1937, A.M., 1938, Ph.D., 1942. Asst. prof. So. Ill. U., Carbondale, 1940-46, asst. to pres., 1942-44; asst. prof. U. Okla., Norman, 1946-47; asst. prof. U. So. Calif., L.A., 1947-49, assoc. prof., 1949-56, prof., 1956-69, head dept., 1958-62, chmn., acad. univ. affairs com., 1963, assoc. dean divsn. social scis. and comms., 1960-63; head dept. sociology U. Ala., 1969-71; chmn. dept. sociology Ohio State U., Columbus, 1971-74, acting dean Coll. Social and Behavioral Scis., 1974—, dean Coll. Social and Behavioral Scis., 1975-78, chmn. coordinating coun. deans Colls. Arts and Scis., 1977-78, prof. emeritus Colls. Arts and Scis., 1981—; Smith-Mundt prof., Sweden, 1956-57; vis. prof. U. Hawaii, summer 1965; cons. Los Angeles and related sch. dists.; mem. Region XV Woodrow Wilson Selection Com., 1961-62. Author: (with E.S. Richards) Ethnic Relations in the U.S, 1953, (with J.E. Nordskog, M.J. Vincent) Analyzing Social Problems, 1956, (with Jon Simpson) Social Problems: Persistent Challenges, 1965, rev., 1969; Assoc. editor: Sociology and Social Research, 1947-69; editorial cons.: Sociometry, 1962-65; Contbr. articles to profl. publs. Served with AUS, 1944-46. Fellow Am. Sociol. Assn. (co-chmn. nat. conf. com. 1963, budget and exec. office com. 1975-78); mem. AAUP, AAAS, Am. Assn. Pub. Opinion Rsch., Alpha Kappa Delta (pres. united chtps. 1965-66), Phi Beta Kappa (chpt. pres. 1959-60), Blue Key, Skull and Dagger. Democrat. Home: 201 Spencer Dr Amherst MA 01002-3365

MCDONAGH, THOMAS JOSEPH, physician; b. N.Y.C., Feb. 29, 1932; s. John and Delia (Lee) McD.; m. Helen Marie Drury, May 18, 1957; children: Kevin T., Eileen D., Thomas J., Brian P., Patricia M. B.S., CCNY; M.D., Columbia U. Diplomate Am. Bd. Internal Medicine, Am. Bd. Preventive Medicine-Occupational Medicine. Intern Bronx Mcpl. Hosp., N.Y., 1957-58, resident, 1958-60; fellow in medicine, trainee in gastroenterology Albert Einstein Coll. Medicine, Bronx, 1960-62; pvt. practice internal medicine Coatesville, Pa., 1962-64; sr. physician Exxon Corp., N.Y.C., 1964-69, asst. med. dir., 1969-79; dir. medicine and environ. health Exxon Chem. Co., Darien, Conn., 1979-80, dir. medicine and environ. affairs, 1980-81; v.p. medicine and occupational health Exxon Corp., Dallas, 1981-97; dir. medicine and environ. health Exxon Co. Internat., Florham Park, N.J., 1983-97; bd. dirs. Nat. Assn. Drug Abuse Problems, N.Y.C., 1981-92; bd. dirs. Nat. Found. Med. Edn., San Francisco, 1983-95. Contbr. articles to med. jours. Chmn. bd. appeals Inc. Village of Bellerose, N.Y., 1977-84, trustee, 1965-77, dep. mayor, 1975-77. Fellow ACP, Am. Coll. Occupational and Environ. Medicine (bd. dirs. 1989-92); mem. AMA. Roman Catholic.

MCDONALD, ALAN ANGUS, federal judge; b. Harrah, Wash., Dec. 13, 1927; s. Angus and Nell (Britt) McD.; m. Ruby K., Aug. 22, 1949; children: Janelle Jo, Saralee Sue, Stacy. BS, U. Wash., 1950, LLB, 1952. Dep. pros. atty. Yakima County, Wash., 1952-54; assoc. Halverson & Applegate, Yakima, 1954-56; ptnr. Halverson, Applegate & McDonald, Yakima, 1956-85; judge U.S. Dist. Ct. (ea. dist.) Wash., Yakima, 1985-95, sr. judge, 1995—. Fellow Am. Coll. Trial Lawyers; Yakima C. of C. (bd. dirs.). Clubs: Yakima Country, Royal Duck (Yakima). Office: US Dist Ct PO Box 2706 Yakima WA 98907-2706

MCDONALD, ALICE COIG, state agency administrator; b. Chalmette, La., Sept. 26, 1940; d. Olas Casimere and Genevieve Louise (Heck) Coig; m. Glenn McDonald, July 16, 1967; 1 child, Michel. B.S., Loyola U., New Orleans, 1962; M.Ed., Loyola U., 1966; cert. rank I sch. adminstrn., Spalding Coll., 1975. Tchr. St. Bernard Pub. Schs., Chalmette, La., 1962-67; counselor, instructional coordinator Jefferson County Schs., Louisville, 1967-77; ednl. adviser Jefferson County Govt., Louisville, 1977-78; chief exec. asst. Office of Mayor, Louisville, 1978-80; dep. supt. pub. instrn. Ky. Dept. Edn., Frankfort, 1980-83, supt. pub. instrn., 1984-88; bd. dirs., com. mem. Ky. Coun. on Higher Edn., 1984-88, Ky. Juvenile Justice com., 1984-88, Ky. Ednl. TV Authority, 1984-88, So. Regional Coun. Ednl. Improvement, 1984-88. Mem. Pres.'s Adv. Com. on Women, 1978-80; active Dem. Nat. Conv., 1972, 76, 80, 84; pres. Dem. Woman's Club Ky., 1974-76, mem. exec. com., 1977-88; bd. dirs. Ky. Found. for Blind; exec. dir. Ky. Govtl. Svcs. Ctr., 1996—. Mem. NEA, Coun. Chief State Sch. Officers, Women in Sch. Adminstrn., Ky. Edn. Assn., River City Bus. and Profl. Women. Home: 6501 Gunpowder Ln Prospect KY 40059-9334 Office: 4th Fl W Acad Bldg Ky State Univ Frankfort KY 40601

MCDONALD, ALONZO LOWRY, JR., business and financial executive; b. Atlanta, Aug. 5, 1928; s. Alonzo Lowry Sr. and Lois (Burrell) McD.; m. Suzanne Moffitt, May 9, 1959; four children. AB in Journalism, Emory U., 1948; MBA with distinction, Harvard U., 1956. Asst. to sales mgr. air conditioning div. Westinghouse Electric Corp., Staunton, Va., 1956-57; Western zone mgr. Westinghouse Electric Corp., St. Louis, 1957-60; assoc. N.Y. office McKinsey & Co., Inc., 1960-64, prin. London office, 1964-66, mng. prin. Zurich Office, 1966-68, mng. dir. Paris Office, 1968-73; mng. dir., chief exec. officer of firm worldwide, 1973-76; dir. N.Y. Office, 1976-77; dep. spl. trade rep., also ambassador in charge U.S. del. Tokyo round of Multilateral Trade Negotiations, 1977-79; acting spl. trade rep. Washington, 1979; asst. to Pres. U.S., White House staff dir., 1979-81; mem. faculty Harvard U. Grad. Sch. Bus. Adminstrn., Boston, 1981; pres. The Bendix Corp., Southfield, Mich., 1981-83; chmn., chief exec. officer Avenir Group, Inc., Birmingham, Mich., 1983—. Mem. Coun. Fgn. Rels.; vestry Am. Cathedral in Paris, 1970-73; vestry, warden St. Joseph of Arimathea Episcopal Ch., Elmsford, N.Y., 1974-77; trustee CED, 1975—; chmn. Williamsburg Charter Found., Washington, 1986-90; chmn. bd. trustees Trinity Forum, Washington, 1991—; mem. dean's adv. coun. Harvard U. Div. Sch., Boston, 1989—; trustee Emory U., 1992—, Carter Ctr., Atlanta, 1994—. With USMCR, 1950-52. Office: 380 N Old Woodward Ave Ste 314 Birmingham MI 48009-5322

MC DONALD, ANDREW J., bishop; b. Savannah, Ga., Oct. 24, 1923; s. James Bernard and Theresa (McGrael) McD. AB, St. Mary's Sem., Balt., 1945, STL, 1948; JCB, Cath. U. Am., 1949; JCD, Lateran U., Rome, 1951. Ordained priest Roman Cath. Ch., 1948. Consecrated bishop, 1972; curate Port Wentworth, Ga., 1952-57; chancellor Diocese of Savannah, 1952-68; vicar gen., from 1968, vice oficialis, 1952-57, oficialis, 1957; pastor Blessed Sacrament Ch., 1963; named papal chamberlain, 1956, domestic prelate, 1959; bishop Diocese of Little Rock, 1972—. Office: Diocese of Little Rock PO Box 7239 2415 N Tyler St Little Rock AR 77217*

MC DONALD, ANDREW JEWETT, securities firm executive; b. Cin., Sept. 7, 1929; s. Matthew Arnold and Jane (Jewett) Mc D. Grad., Hotchkiss Sch., 1947, Yale U., 1951. With Paine, Webber, Jackson & Curtis Inc., Boston, 1955—; dir. Paine, Webber, Jackson & Curtis Inc. (New Eng. region), 1972-73; sr. v.p., dir. Paine, Webber, Jackson & Curtis Inc. (Eastern div.), 1973—; dir. F. W. Paine Found., 1973—; pvt. trustee and investor, 1985—; allied mem. N.Y. Stock Exch., 1971—. Mem. Flight Safety Found., 1971—. Served with USAF, 1951-55. Mem. Am. Farmland Trust (life), Am. Aviation Hist. Soc. (life). Clubs: Aero of New Eng. (Boston), Fed. (Boston), Down Town (Boston), Yale (Boston). Home: 5 Stonehill Dr Stoneham MA 02180-3927

MCDONALD, ANGUS WHEELER, farmer; b. Washington, Apr. 21, 1927; s. John Yates and Dorothy Helen (Bosworth) McD.; m. Mary Joan Montgomery, May 8, 1952 (div. Sept. 1958); children: Mary Ann Hetzer, Paul Yates. BA, Columbia Union Coll., 1974. Farmer, owner Pleasant View Farm, Charles Town, W.Va., 1953—. Presdl. candidate Democratic Party, 1987-88, 92. With U.S. Army, 1946-47. Mem. AARP, Jefferson County Farm Bur., W.Va. State Hort. Soc., No. W.Va. Automobile Club, Am. Legion, The Moose. Avocations: photography, travel, attending historical events. Home and Office: Pleasant View Farm RR 3 Box 142 Charles Town WV 25414-9413

MCDONALD, ARTHUR BRUCE, physics educator; b. Sydney, N.S., Canada, Aug. 29, 1943; s. A. Bruce and Valerie M. (DeRoche) McD.; m. Janet Catherine MacDonald, July 16, 1966; children: Bruce, Heather, Ross, Fraser. BSc in Physics, Dalhousie U., 1964, MSc in Physics, 1965; PhD, Calif. Inst. Tech., 1969. Post doctoral fellow Chalk River (Ont., Can.) Nuclear Labs., 1969-70, research scientist, 1970-82; prof. physics Princeton (N.J.) U., 1982-89; prof. physics Queen's U., Kingston, Ont., Can., 1989—, dir. Sudbury Neutrino Obs. Inst., 1989—; mem. nuclear sci. adv. com. Dept. Energy, NSF, 1987-89; adv. com. Triumf Experiment, 1987-89; mem. subatomic physics rev. com. Natural Sci. and Engring. Rsch. Coun. Can., 1987-89; mem. adv. com. nuclear sci. divsn. Lawrence Berkeley Lab., 1992-95. Fellow Am. Physical Soc.; mem. Can. Assn. Physicists (bd. dirs. 1978-80). Avocations: skiing, swimming. Office: Queens U Stirling Hall, Dept Physics, Kingston, ON Canada K7L 3N6

MCDONALD, BENNA J., nursing educator, critical care nurse; b. Denton, Tex., Aug. 18, 1943; d. Beno C. and Imogene M. (Talkington) Sawyers; children: Russell, Bobbie Sue, Thomas. ADN, Kilgore (Tex.) Coll., 1980; lic. vocat. nurse, Petit Jean Voc.-Tech., Morrilton, Ark., 1973. RN, Tex.; cert. emergency med. technician-paramedic. Dir. edn. Henderson (Tex.) Meml. Hosp. Mem. Am. Heart Assn. (affiliate faculty, safety specialist). Home: 551 CR 223N Henderson TX 75652-3043

MCDONALD, BERNARD ROBERT, federal agency administrator; b. Kansas City, Kans., Nov. 17, 1940; s. Bernard Luther and Mabel McD.; m. Jean Graves, June 7, 1963 (div. 1996); children: Aaron Michael, Elizabeth Kathleen. BA, Park Coll., Parkville, Mo., 1962; MA, Kans. State U., 1964; PhD, Mich. State U., 1968. Prof. math. U. Okla., Norman, 1968-83, chmn. math. dept., 1981-83; program dir. div. math. scis. NSF, Washington, 1983-86, program dir. spl. projects, 1986-88, dep. dir. div. math. scis., 1988—. Author: R-linear Endomorphism, 1983, Geometric Algebra, 1976, Finite Rings, 1974, Ring Theory III, 1980. Mem. Am. Math. Soc., Math. Assn. Am., Soc. Ind. and Applied Math., Assn. Women Math., Sigma Xi. Home: 5016 N 35th St Arlington VA 22207 Office: NSF Div Math Scis 4201 Wilson Blvd Rm 1025 Arlington VA 22230-0001

MCDONALD, BRONCE WILLIAM, community activist, advocate; b. Dayton, Ohio, Mar. 21, 1949; s. Lawrence and Pauline Elizabeth (Macknight) McD. Student, Wright State U., 1968-71, U. Dayton, 1971, Dayton Art Inst., 1967-68. Trainer, cons. Nat. Assn. Youth Orgns. United, Washington, 1971-73; program assoc. Dayton (Ohio) Model Cities, 1973-74; child care worker II Montgomery County Children's Svcs. Bd., Dayton, 1974-78; inventory control Mark Morris Tires, San Francisco, 1979-82; office mgr. Bio-Feedback Internat., San Francisco, 1978-84; speaker, bd. dirs. Dayton Area AIDS Task Force, 1987—, AIDS Found. Dayton, 1988-92; community activist People With AIDS, Dayton, 1987—; co-chair Dayton HIV Prevention Cmty. Planning Group Montgomery County Combined Health Dist.; com. mem. Direct Svcs. Dayton Area AIDS Task Force, 1987-92, speaker bur., 1987-92, edn. com., 1987-92, AIDS Found. Miami Valley, 1992—, speaker bur., 1992—, edn. com., 1992—, Pub. Policy and Conflict Mgmt., Ohio Statewide HIV Prevention Cmty. Planning Group, Ohio Dept. Health, The Prevention Summit: HIV Prevention Cmty. Planning Co-chairs meeting, Ctr. for Disease Control and Prevention, Nat. Alliance of State & Territorial AIDS Dirs., Nat. Minority AIDS Coun., Atlanta, 1995—; hotline vol. Dayton Lesbian & Gay Ctr., 1988—; mem. minority AIDS coalition Montgomery County Health Dept., Dayton, 1987—, minority health and social issues coalition, 1988—; bd. dirs. The African Am. Forum on AIDS, Dayton, 1990—, nat. AIDS awareness program So. Christian Leadership Conf., Dayton, 1993—; speaker numerous orgns. on AIDS; bd. dirs. Miami Valley AIDS Partnership, mem. membership, outreach, and needs assessment coms., 1995—. Founding mem., treas. Dayton Area People with AIDS Coalition, 1987-92, Men of All Colors Together, Dayton, 1988-90; co-chair Regional Cmty. Prevention Coord. Com., 1996—; bd. dirs. Ohio AIDS Coalition, 1997, mem. healing com. the leadership tng. program com., 1996—; co-chair AIDS Prevention Coun., Dayton; mem. bd. State of Ohio HIV Prevention Cmty. Planning Group, mem. cmty. info. com., 1996—; bd. dirs. Dayton Ryan White Consortium, mem. finance com., promotion evaln. com., 1994—, Dayton AIDS Prevention Group, membership com., mktg. com. Recipient Pres.'s Citation, 1989, Ohio AIDS Svc. award Ohio Dept. Health, 1990, Cert. of Merit Ohio Dept. Health, Columbus, 1994, Plaque of Vol. Outstanding Merit Montgomery County Combined Health Dist., Dayton, 1995, Outstanding Vol. Svc. Plaque Ohio Dept. Health, 1995, Man of Yr. award Met. Cmty. Ch., Cmty. Unity Health and Wholeness Project, Dayton, 1995. Mem. Nat. Assn. Black and White Men Together. Avocations: drawing, painting, writing, col. work. Home: 39 Central Ave Apt 323 Dayton OH 45406-5514

MCDONALD, BRYANT EDWARD, physicist, oceanographer; b. Louisville, Nov. 12, 1944; s. Blythe Orman and Mildred Eloise (Poythress) McD.; m. Kathleen Lucille Maiorana, July 27, 1968; children: Leah, Esther. BA, Utah State U., 1966; MA, Princeton U., 1968, PhD, 1971. Computational physicist U.S. Naval Rsch. Lab., Washington, 1971-80, physicist, 1990—; oceanographer Naval Ocean Rsch. & Devel., Bay St. Louis, Miss., 1980-90; cons. Sandia Nat. Lab., Albuquerque, 1985-89, Lawrence Livermore (Calif.) Nat. Lab., 1993—; site review panelist Office of Naval Rsch., Arlington, Va., 1990—. Contbr. articles to profl. jours. PhD thesis com. mem. Pa. State U., State College, 1994, U. Calif., San Diego, 1996; rehab. vol. ARC, Princeton, 1966-68. NSF fellow, 1968. Fellow Acoustical Soc. Am. (mem. tech. com. on underwater acoustics 1993-94, tech. com. acoustic oceanography 1994-95); mem. Am. Geophys. Union. Achievements include first successful computer simulation of ionospheric electrojet turbulence, of sonic boom focusing; theory/computer model for global scale ocean acoustic tomography. Avocations: boating, biking, skiing, hiking. Home: 4708 Randolph Ct Annandale VA 22003-6216 Office: US Naval Rsch Lab mAIL cODE 7104 4555 Overlook Ave SW Washington DC 20375-0001

MCDONALD, CAPERS WALTER, biomedical engineer, corporate executive; b. Georgetown, S.C., Nov. 29, 1951; s. WalBern and Cecilia (Lockwood) McD.; m. Marion E. Kiper, Aug. 23, 1975; child, Adam Capers. BS in Engring. magna cum laude, Duke U., 1974; MS in Mech. Engring., MIT, 1976; MBA, Harvard U., 1983. Registered profl. engr., N.C. Dir. mktg. dept. Becton Dickinson Co., Sunnyvale, Calif., 1978-81; cons. Booz, Allen & Hamilton, San Francisco, 1982-84; v.p. HP Genenchem, S. San Francisco, Calif., 1984-87; bio-analytic systems mgr. Hewlett-Packard Corp., Palo Alto, Calif., 1987; v.p. Orion Instruments, Inc., Redwood City, Calif., 1987-88; v.p. Spectroscopy Imaging Systems, Fremont, Calif., 1988-90, pres., 1990-92; pres., ceo BioReliance Corp., Rockville, Md., 1992—; pres., CEO MAGENTA Corp., Bethesda, Md., 1993—; chmn., dir. MAGENTA Svcs., Ltd., Stirling, Scotland, 1994—; chmn., bd. dirs. BioReliance Holding GmbH, Heidelberg, Germany, 1996—; guest lectr. Weizmann Inst., Rehovot, Israel, 1977, All-Union Cardiology Ctr., Moscow, 1978, Inst. Hematology Munich, 1978, Christ Church (New Zealand) Clin. Sch., 1980, U. Edinburgh, Scotland, 1981; co-founder, chmn. Md. Biosci. Alliance, 1995; bd. dirs. Md. State C. of C., 1996; bd. visitors U. Md. Biotech. Inst., 1996; bd. advisors Md. Partnership for Workforce Quality, 1996. Author: chpt. Flow Cytometry and Sorting, 1979; patentee flow microfluorometer; contbr. articles to profl. jours. Asst. scout master Boy Scouts Am., Georgetown, 1965-66. Duke U. scholar, 1970-74, MIT scholar, 1974-76; NSF fellow, 1974; recipient High Tech. Firm of Yr. award Md. High Tech. Coun., 1995, Leadership in Tech. award Md. High Tech. Coun., 1996, Employer of Yr. award Md. Pvt. Industry Coun., 1996. Mem. N.C. Acad. Scis., Harvard U. Alumni Assn., Duke U. Alumni Assn., MIT Alumni Assn., Rotary, Sigma Xi, Tau Beta Pi, Phi Eta Sigma, Pi Mus Epsilon. Republican. Methodist. Avocations: fresh and salt water fishing, travel. Office: 9900 Blackwell Rd Rockville MD 20850-3301

MCDONALD, CAROLYN ANN, dance educator, choreographer; b. Blytheville, Ark., Aug. 27, 1963; d. Travis Eugene and Barbara Jean (Myers) McD. BA in Dance, U. Calif., Irvine, 1987; postgrad., U. Iowa, 1995—. Instr. dance Kirkwood C.C., Cedar Rapids, Iowa, 1987-90, choreographer, 1987—, artistic dir., 1990-96, 96—; owner, pres. McDonald Arts Ctr., Marion, Iowa, 1988—; instr. dance Coe Coll., Cedar Rapids, 1989—; choreographer color guard dance ensemble Washington H.S., Cedar Rapids, 1996—; cons. Jane Boyd Cmty. House, Cedar Rapids, 1993-94. Avocations: wine tasting, gourmet cooking, flying, gardening. Office: 105 Southview Dr Marion IA 52302-3055

MC DONALD, CHARLES J., physician, educator; b. Tampa, Fla., Dec. 6, 1931; s. George B. and Bertha C. (Harbin) Mc D.; m. Maureen McDonald; children—Marc S., Norman D., Eric S. B.S. magna cum laude, A&T Coll. N.C., 1951; M.S., U. Mich., 1952; M.D. with highest honors, Howard U., 1960. Diplomate: Am. Bd. Dermatology. Rotating intern Hosp. St. Raphael, New Haven, 1960-61; asst. resident in medicine Hosp. St. Raphael, 1961-63; asst. resident in dermatology Yale U., 1963-65, spl. USPHS research fellow, chief resident in dermatology, 1965-66, instr. in medicine and pharmacology, 1966-67, asst. prof. medicine and pharmacology, 1967-68; asst. prof. med. sci. Brown U., 1968-69, assoc. prof., 1969-74, prof., 1974—, dir. dermatology program, 1970-74, head subsect. dermatology, 1974-82, dir. dermatology, 1982—, chair dept. dermatology, 1996—; dir. dermatology Roger Williams Gen. Hosp., 1968-97; physician-in-charge dermatology divsn. R.I. Hosp., 1989-97; mem. com. and task force, chmn. task force on minority affairs Am. Acad. Dermatology, 1975-80; mem. dermatology adv. panel FDA, until 1978, cons., 1978—; mem. pharm. scis. rev. commn. NIH, 1979-83, mem. adv. com. Arthritis, Muscular/Skeletal and Skin Disease Inst., 1993-95; chmn. com. pub. edn., dir., v.p. R.I. divsn. Am. Cancer Soc., 1978-80, pres., 1980-83, bd. dir. nat. soc., 1983—, nat. dir. at large, 1990-95, mem. nat. exec. com., 1991, nat. officer, 1995—; mem. residency rev. com. dermatology ACGME, 1992—; vice chmn. RRC dermatology, 1996—. Dermatology editor Postgrad. Medicine; contbr. numerous articles to med. publs. Trustee Howard U., 1993—, chair health affairs com., 1994—, mem. exec. com., 1994—; bd. dirs. Providence Health Care Found., chmn. mem. adv. com., 1976-87; bd. dirs. Providence Fund for Edn.; bd. dirs. Providence Pub. Libr., 1987-96, sec., 1991-96; mem. R.I. State Bd. Edn., 1970-72. Served to maj. USAF, 1952-56. Recipient Disting. Svc. award Hosp. Assn. R.I., 1971, Disting. Alumni award Howard U. Coll. Medicine, 1983, St. George medal nat. divsn. Am. Cancer Soc., 1992. Mem. AAAS, Am. Dermatol. Assn. (bd. dirs. 1995—), New Eng. Dermatol. Assn. (v.p. 1983-84, pres. 1984-85), R.I. Dermatol. Assn., Noah Worcester Dermatol. Assn. (bd. dirs. 1983-86), Soc. Investigative Dermatology, Am. Fedn. Clin. Rsch., Am. Acad. Dermatology (bd. dirs. 1987-91, Nat. Med. Assn. (chmn. sect. dermatology 1973-75), Am. Soc. Clin. Oncology, New Eng. Dermatology Soc., Dermatology Found. (chmn. sci. com. 1972-76), Assn. Profs. Dermatology (bd. dirs. 1991-94), Sigma Xi, Alpha Omega Alpha, Alpha Kappa Mu, Beta Kappa Chi. Democrat. Office: 593 Eddy St Providence RI 02903-4923

MCDONALD, DARYL PATRICK, lawyer; b. Detroit, Aug. 27, 1950; s. Donald Angus and Rita Martha (Tymoszek) McD.; m. Deborah Ann Wenzinger, Dec. 29, 1972 (div. 1996); children: Andrea, Laura. BA, U. Toledo, 1972; JD, Tulane U., 1975. Bar: Mich. 1975, U.S. Dist. Ct. (we. dist.) Mich. 1975, U.S. Dist. Ct. (ea. dist.) Mich. 1982. Magistrate 93rd Dist. Ct., Munising, Mich., 1976-78; pvt. practice Munising, 1977-82; assoc. Patterson & Patterson, Whitfield, Manikoff, Ternan & White, Bloomfield Hills, Mich., 1982-85, ptnr., 1986; asst. corp. counsel Tecumseh (Mich.) Products Co., 1986-92, corp. counsel, sec., 1993—; city atty., City of Munising, 1978-82. Asst. editor Tulane U. Law Rev., 1973-75. Trustee Munising Meml. Hosp., 1980-82, Tecumseh Cmty. Fund Found., 1992-96, Adrian Symphony Orch., 1993—, Adrian Coll., 1997—. Recipient Oustanding Svc. award Alger County Hist. Soc., Munising, 1982. Mem. ABA, Mich. Bar Assn., Lenawee County Bar Assn., Rotary (sec. Munising 1975-76, sec. Tecumseh 1989-91, pres. 1992-93), Order of Coif. Roman Catholic. Avocations: jogging, reading, family activities. Office: Tecumseh Products Co Legal Dept 100 E Patterson St Tecumseh MI 49286

MC DONALD, DAVID WILLIAM, retired chemist, educator; b. Shreveport, La., Aug. 4, 1923; s. Maxwell Wood and Mary Estelle (Weber) McD.; m. Nell Cullen Welch, July 31, 1948; children: Mason, Thomas, Daniel, David. BS, U. Southwestern La., 1943; PhD, U. Tex., 1951. Chemist Humble Oil & Refining Co., Baytown, Tex., 1943-44, 46-47; rsch. chemist, group leader Monsanto Co., Texas City, Tex., 1951-59; rsch. sect. leader, mgr. Monsanto Co., 1959-67; product adminstr. Monsanto Co., St. Louis, 1967-69, dir. research plastics div., 1969-74; dir. tech. plastics div. Monsanto Co., 1974-80, dir. tech. plans, corp. rsch. and devel. staff, 1980-82; sr. assoc. Pugh-Roberts Assocs., Inc., Cambridge, Mass., 1983-93; mng. cons. PA Consulting Group, Santa Rosa, Calif., 1993—; affiliate prof. tech. mgmt. Washington U., St. Louis, 1983-88; cons. in field, 1982—; vis. lectr., scholar Stanford U., 1989. Served with USNR, 1944-46. Mem. Am. Chem. Soc., Soc. Plastics Engrs., AAAS, Sigma Xi. Episcopalian. Patentee in field. Home and Office: 423 Pythian Rd Santa Rosa CA 95409-6324

MCDONALD, FORREST, historian, educator; b. Orange, Tex., Jan. 7, 1927; s. John Forrest and Myra (McGill) McD.; m. Ellen Shapiro, Aug. 1, 1963; children from previous marriage: Kathy, Forrest Howard, Marcy Ann, Stephen, Kevin. BA, MA, U. Tex., 1949, PhD, 1955; MA (hon.), Brown U., 1962; LHD (hon.), SUNY, Geneseo, 1989. Exec. sec. Am. History Research Ctr., Madison, Wis., 1953-58; assoc. prof. history Brown U., Providence, 1959-63, prof., 1963-67; prof. Wayne State U., Detroit, 1967-76; prof. U. Ala., Tuscaloosa, 1976-87, disting. univ. research prof., 1987—; James Pinckney Harrison prof. Coll. of William and Mary, Williamsburg, Va., 1986-87; presdl. appointee Bd. Fgn. Scholarships, Washington, 1985-87; mem. fellowship selection com. Richard M. Weaver Fellowships, Bryn Mawr, Pa., 1980—. Author: We The People, 1958, Insull, 1962, E Pluribus Unum, 1965, Alexander Hamilton, 1979 (Frances Tavern Book award 1980), Novus Ordo Seclorum, 1985, Requiem, 1988, The American Presidency: An Intellectual History, 1994. Trustee Phila. Soc., North Adams, Mich., 1983-86, 87-90, pres. 1988-90; co-chmn. New Eng. for Goldwater, 1964. Served with USN, 1945-46. Recipient George Washington medal Freedom's Found., Valley Forge, Pa., 1980, Best Book award Am. Revolution Round Table, N.Y., 1986, Richard M. Weaver award Ingersoll Found., 1990, First Salvatori award Heritage Found., 1992, Salavatori Book award Intercollegiate Studies Inst., 1994; Guggenheim fellow, N.Y., 1962-63; Jefferson lectr. NEH, 1987. Republican. Avocations: horticulture, tennis. Office: U Alabama PO Box 870212 Tuscaloosa AL 35487-0212

MCDONALD, GAIL CLEMENTS, government official; b. Ft. Worth, Tex., Mar. 9, 1944; d. Eugene and Cornelia (Nagle) Clements; m. William C. Scott, Aug. 26, 1967 (div. 1976); 1 child, Jill Miriah Scott; m. Danny Lee McDonald, Aug. 6, 1982. BA, Tex. Christian U., Ft. Worth, 1966, MA, 1967. Instr. social sci. Cooke County Jr. Coll., Gainesville, Tex., 1967-69, Langston (Okla.) U., 1969, Tulsa Jr. Coll., 1977-79; instr. humanities Okla. State U., Stillwater, 1971-74; adminstrv. asst. edn. and cultural affairs Gov. David L. Boren, Oklahoma City, 1975-78; legis. aide Sen. David L. Boren, Tulsa, 1979; state assoc. Inst. for Ednl. Leadership, George Washington U., Washington, 1979-81; exec. asst. Commr. Norma H. Eagleton, Okla. Corp. Commr., Oklahoma City, 1990-95; commr. ICC, Washington, 1990—, vice chmn., 1993, chmn, 1993-95; adminstr. St. Lawrence Seaway Devel. Corp. U.S. Dept. Transp., Wahsington, 1995—. Bd. dirs. Okla. Sci. & Arts Found., 1975-83; exec. com. Frontiers of Sci. Found., 1976-80; fundraiser Washington chpt. Spl. Olympics. Named Woman of Yr., Women's Transp. Seminar, 1991. Mem. Nat. Assn. Regulatory Commrs. (transp. com.), Exec. Women in Govt., Conservation Round Table (chmn. 1990), Transp. Table Washington, Toastmasters (pres. 1988), Phi Alpha Theta. Democrat. Episcopalian. Avocations: gardening, bird watching. Office: US Dept Transp St Lawrence Seaway Devel Co 400 7th St SW Ste 5424 Washington DC 20590-0001*

MCDONALD, GREGORY CHRISTOPHER, author; b. Shrewsbury, Mass., Feb. 15, 1937; s. Irving Thomas and Mae (Haggerty) M.; m. Susan Aiken, Jan. 12, 1963 (div. Oct. 1990); children: Christopher Gregory, Douglas Gregory. BA, Harvard U., 1958. bd. dirs. Camaldon Corp. Novelist, critic Boston Globe, 1966-73; author: (novels) Running Scared, 1964, Fletch, 1974, Confess, Fletch, 1976, Flynn, 1977, Love Among the Mashed Potatoes, 1978, Fletch's Fortune, 1978, Fletch Forever, 1978, Who Took Toby Rinaldi?, 1980, Fletch and the Widow Bradley, 1981, The Buck Passes Flynn, 1981, Fletch's Moxie, 1982, Fletch and the Man Who, 1983, Carioca Fletch, Flynn's In, 1984, Fletch Won, Safekeeping, 1985, Fletch, Too, 1986; (non-fiction) The Education of Gregory Mcdonald, 1985, Fletch Chronicle, Vol. 1, Bull's Eye (drama), 1986, A World Too Wide, 1987, Fletch Chronicle, Vol. 2, 1987, Exits and Entrances, 1988, Fletch Chronicle, Vol. 3, 1988, Merely Players, 1988, The Brave, 1991, Son of Fletch, 1993, Fletch Reflected, 1994, Skylar, 1995, Skylar in Yankeeland, 1997; editor: Last Laughs, 1986; dir. Bach Cantata Singers, 1973-80. Mem. vis. com. Boston Mus. Fine Arts, 1970-73, 85—; mem. Lincoln Recreation Com., 1977, 78; mem. Winthrop House Sr. Commons Harvard Coll. 1982—. Recipient Humanitarian of Yr. award Tenn. Assn. Fed. Execs., 1989, Citizen of Yr. award Nat. Assn. Social Workers, 1990, Roger William Straus award NCCJ, 1990, Alex Haley award, 1992. Mem. Authors Guild, Dramatists Guild, Mystery Writers Am. (dir. 1977—, pres. 1985-86, Poe award 1975, 77), Crime Writers Eng., Writers Guild Am., Mass. Chiefs Police Assn., Giles Countians United. Clubs: Harvard (Boston); Overseas Press (N.Y.C.); Hillcrest Country (Pulaski, Tenn.). Office: care Arthur Greene Esq 101 Park Ave New York NY 10178

MCDONALD, JACQUELYN MILLIGAN, parent and family studies educator; b. New Brunswick, N.J., July 28, 1935; d. John P. and Emma (Mark) Milligan; m. Neil Vanden Dorpel; five children. BA, Cornell U., 1957; MA, NYU, 1971; MEd, Columbia U., 1992, EdD, 1993. Cert. in behavior modification, N.J.; cert. tchr. grades K-8, N.J.; cert. family life educator. Instr. Montclair (N.J.) State Coll., 1982-93, Edison C.C., Naples, Fla., 1994—; mem. steering com. Fla. Gulf Coast U. Family Ctr.; parent vol. tng. project coord. Montclair Pub. Schs., 1984-86; coord. Collier County IDEAS for Parenting, Inc., Naples, 1993—; tchr. parenting for teen mothers Crisis Parenting Women's Abuse Shelter; mem. Collier County Teenage Pregnancy Prevention Coalition. Chairperson Interfaith Neighbors Juvenile Delinquency Prevention, N.Y.C., 1960-68; support family Healing the Children, 1970-90; founder The Parent Ctr., Montclair, 1983, Essex County N.J. Fair Housing Coun., 1990. Mem. Pre-Sch. Interagy. Couns., Raven and Serpent Hon. Soc. (pres. 1956). Psi Chi, Kappa Delta Pi. Avocations: swimming, tennis, golf, boating, hiking. Home: 27075 Kindlewood Ln Bonita Springs FL 34134-4370

MCDONALD, JAMES, science foundation executive. Pres. Sci.-Atlanta, Inc. Address: One Technology Pkwy S Norcross GA 30092-2967

MC DONALD, JAMES MICHAEL, JR., research institute consultant; b. Chgo., Jan. 19, 1924; s. James Michael and Gertrude Isabel (Dame) McD.; m. Helen Elizabeth Sharp, Feb. 3, 1948; children: Megan, Melissa, Rebecca. AB cum laude, Syracuse U., 1949; MA, Sch. Advanced Internat. Studies, 1950; postgrad., Bologna Ctr, 1956-57; grad., Nat. War Coll., 1969. Joined U.S. Fgn. Svc., 1950; assigned Germany, 1951-56, Italy, 1956-57, France, 1957-58, Washington, 1958-61, Nicaragua, 1961-65, Dominican Republic, 1969-71; dep. pub affairs officer Rome, 1971-74; chief resource and ops. analysis USIA, Washington, 1974-75; dir. seminar and studies program Battelle Meml. Inst., 1975-83, internat. programs mgr., corp. edn. and tng. advisor, 1983-85, cons., 1985—. Trustee, v.p., past pres. Seattle Opera, Kluckhohn Values Rsch. Ctr. With USAAF, 1943-47. Recipient Superior Honor award USIA, 1975. Mem. Rainier Club, Inst. Current World Affairs. Address: 1278 NW Blakely Ct Seattle WA 98177-4340

MCDONALD, JOHN CECIL, lawyer; b. Lorimor, Iowa, Feb. 19, 1924; s. Cecil F. and Mary Elsie (Fletcher) McD.; m. Barbara Joan Berry, May 8, 1943; children: Mary Elisabeth (Mrs. Dell Richard), Joan Frances (Mrs. Andrew Ackerman), Jean Maurine. Student, Simpson Coll., 1942, So. Ill. U., 1943; J.D., Drake U., 1948. Bar: Iowa 1948, U.S. Ct. Mil. Appeals 1956, U.S. Supreme Ct. 1956. Practiced in Dallas Center, Iowa, 1948—; sr. ptnr. McDonald, Brown & Fagen and predecessor firms, 1971—; county atty. Dallas County, 1958-62; asst. county atty., 1963-69; city atty. Dallas Center, 1956-80. Mem. Simpson Coll. Alumni Council, pres., 1977-80; legal adviser Dallas Community Bd. Edn., 1953-69, pres., mem., 1968-76; nat. adv. com. Cen. Coll.; alt. del. Iowa Coordinating Council for Post-High Sch. Edn.; finance chmn. Dallas County Rep.Cen. Com., 1954-63, chmn., 1963-68; chmn. Iowa 7th Congl. Dist. Rep. Cen. Com., 1968-69, Iowa Rep. Cen. Com., 1969-75; mem. Rep. Nat. Com., 1969-88, mem. exec. com., 1973—; mem. Rule 29 com., com. on reform; mem. Gov. Iowa's inaugural com., 1969, 71, 73, 75, 79; del. Rep. Nat. Conv., 1964, 72, 76, 80, 84, chmn. com. on contests, 1976, 80, 84, 88, chmn. com. on credentials, 1976, 80, 88, mem. com. on arrangements and exec. com. of com. on arrangements, 1976, 80, 84, mem. rules rev. com., 1977-84; chmn. Midwest Rep. State Chairmen's Assn., 1973-75, Nat. Rep. State Chairmen's Adv. Com., 1973-75; hon. co-chmn. Vice Pres.'s Inaugural, 1981; trustee Dallas County Hosp., Perry, Iowa; bd. visitors U.S. Air Force Acad., 1975-78, chmn., 1977-78; trustee Simpson Coll., 1978—; bd. dirs. Iowa Student Loan Liquidity Corp., 1987—; mem. Iowa Coll. Aid Commn., 1989—; mem. Iowa Bd. Regents, 1981-87, pres., 1985-87; bd. dirs. Iowa Public Broadcasting Network, 1981-85; U.S. commr. Am. Battle Monuments Commn., 1982—. Served with USAAF, 1942-46; Col. USAF, 1951-52, ret. Recipient Alumni Achievement award Simpson Coll., 1974; Disting. Service award Drake U., 1978. Mem. ABA, Iowa Bar Assn. (past chmn. spl. com. on mil. affairs, mem. mil. affairs com.), Dallas County Bar Assn. (past pres.), Am. Legion, Farm Bur., Blackfriars, Drake U. Law Sch. Alumni Assn. (class officer), Comml. Club (past pres.) (Dallas Ctr.), Hillcrest Country Club (past pres.) (Adel, Iowa), Des Moines Club, Masons (32 degree), Shriners, Rotary (past pres. Dallas Ctr.), Alpha Tau Omega, Delta Theta Phi, Alpha Psi Omega. Presbyterian. Club: Des Moines. Lodges: Masons (32 deg.), Shriners, Rotary (pas pres. Dallas Ctr.). Home: PO Box 250 Dallas Center IA 50063-0250 Office: McDonald Brown & Fagen PO Box 250 Dallas Center IA 50063-0250

MCDONALD, JOHN CLIFTON, surgeon; b. Baldwyn, Miss., July 25, 1930; s. Edgar Hone and Ethel (Knight) McD.; m. Martha Dennis, Sept. 9, 1956; children: Melissa Lee, Karen Ann, Martha Knight. B.S., Miss. Coll., 1951; M.D., Tulane U., 1955. Diplomate: Am. Bd. Surgery. Intern Confederate Meml. Med. Ctr., Shreveport, La., 1955-56; asst. resident Meyer Meml. Hosp., Buffalo, 1958-62, resident, 1962-63, from asst. attending surgeon to attending surgeon, 1963-68, assoc. dir. surg. research lab., 1965-68; from asst. attending surgeon to attending surgeon Deaconess Hosp., Buffalo, 1965-69, head sect. transplantation, 1966-68; dir. transplantation Charity Hosp. of La., New Orleans, 1969-77, vis. surgeon, 1969-77; clin. asst. surgeon Touro Infirmary, New Orleans, 1969-77; mem. med. staff So. Bapt. Hosp., New Orleans, 1969-77; assoc. mem. dept. surgery Hotel Dieu Hosp., 1969-77; surgeon in chief La. State U. Med. Ctr., Shreveport, 1977—, prof., chmn. dept. surgery, 1977—; asst. prof. surgery SUNY-Buffalo, 1965-68; cons. surgeon various La. Hosps., 1969-77; dir. La. Organ Procurement Program, 1971-77; cons. N.W. La. Emergency Med. Services, 1977—; Buswell research fellow in immunology SUNY-Buffalo, 1963-65, instr. surgery, 1963-65, assoc. prof., 1965-68; assoc. prof. surgery Tulane U. Sch. Medicine, 1969-72, prof., 1972-77, assoc. prof. microbiology and immunology, 1969-77, dir. surg. research labs., 1969-77, dir. transplantation labs., 1969-77, dir. Med. Ctr. Histocampatability Testing Lab., 1969-77. Contbr. articles to med. jours. Served to capt. USAF, 1956-58. Recipient Owl Club award for outstanding teaching Tulane U., 1977; grantee Kidney Found., 1966-67, NIH, 1969—, Schlieder Found., 1970-73, Cancer Assn. Greater New Orleans, 1971-72, La. Regional Med. Program, 1971-73. Mem. AMA, ACS, Am. Assn. Clin. Histocompatability Testing (founding), Am. Assn. Immunologists, Am. Soc. for Artificial Internal Organs, Am. Soc. Transplant Surgeons (founding, pres. 1987), Buffalo Surg. Soc. (sec. 1968), So. Surg. Assn. (Arthur H. Shipley award 1972, treas. 1988-91, sec. 1991-3, pres. 1993-94), Surg. Assn. La. (dir. 1977—, pres. 1983), Am. Assn. for Surgery of Trauma, Transplantation Soc., Southeastern Surg. Congress, Am. Surg. Assn., Halsted Soc. (pres. 1991), Soc. U. Surgeons, La. Med. Soc., Shreveport Med. Soc., United Network for Organ Sharing (pres. 1986-88). Office: La State U Sch of Medicine Dept Surgery Shreveport LA 71130

MCDONALD, JOHN FRANCIS PATRICK, electrical engineering educator; b. Narberth, Pa., Jan. 14, 1942; s. Frank Patrick and Lulu Ann (Hegedus) McD.; m. Karen Marie Knapp, May 26, 1979. BSEE, MIT, 1963; MS in Engring., Yale U., 1965, PhD, 1969. Instr. Yale U., New Haven, 1968-69, asst. prof., 1969-74; assoc. prof. Rensselaer Poly. Inst., Troy, N.Y., 1974-86, prof., 1986—; founder Rensselaer Ctr. for Integrated Electronics, 1980—. Contbr. some 195 articles to profl. publs. Patentee in field. Recipient numerous grants, 1974—. Mem. ACM, IEEE (assoc. editor Transactions on VSLI Design 1995—), Optical Soc., Acoustical Soc., Vacuum Soc., Materials Rsch. Soc. Office: Rensselaer Poly Inst Ctr for Integrated Electronics Troy NY 12181

MCDONALD, JOHN GREGORY, financial investment educator; b. Stockton, Calif., 1937; m. Melody McDonald. BS, Stanford U., 1960, MBA, 1962, PhD, 1967. Mem. faculty Grad. Sch. Bus. Stanford U., Calif., 1968—; now The IBJ prof. fin. Grad. Sch. Bus. Stanford U.; vis. prof. U. Paris, 1972, Columbia Bus. Sch., 1975, Harvard Bus. Sch. 1986; vice chmn., bd. govs. NASD/NASDAQ Stock Market, 1989-90; mem. adv. bd. InterWest Venture Capital; dir. Investment Co. of Am., New Perspective Fund, Inc., Scholastic Corp., Varian, EuroPacific Growth Fund. Contbr. articles to profl. jours. Bd. overseers vis. com. Harvard U. Bus. Sch., Cambridge, Mass., 1994—. Fulbright scholar, Paris, 1967-68. Office: Stanford U Grad Sch Business Stanford CA 94305

MC DONALD, JOHN JOSEPH, electronics executive; b. N.Y.C., Apr. 18, 1930; s. John J. and Margaret (Shanley) McD.; m. Tessa de R. Greenfield, Aug. 22, 1956; children: Kathryn, Elizabeth, Andrew. B.A., Bklyn. Coll., 1951. With Sperry Rand Corp., Blue Bell, Pa., 1954-75; v.p. Sperry Rand Corp., 1972-75; mng. dir. Casio Electronics Ltd., London, 1975-78; pres. Casio Europe Casio Electronics Ltd., 1975-78; pres., CEO Casio, Inc., Dover, N.J., 1978—; also bd. dirs. Casio, Inc., Fairfield, N.J.; chmn. Casio Can. Ltd., 1988-90, pres., chief exec. officer, 1990—; bd. dirs. Casio Mfg. Corp., Casio de Mex. S.A. Served with U.S. Army, 1952-54. Mem. Brit. Inst. Mktg., Am. Mgmt. Assn., Electronic Industries Assn. (bd. govs.), Electronic Industries Found. (trustee 1987—), Consumer Electronics Group (bd. dirs.). Home: PO Box 322 Hope NJ 07844-0322 Office: 570 Mount Pleasant Ave Dover NJ 07801-1620

MC DONALD, JOHN RICHARD, lawyer; b. Connersville, Ind., Aug. 8, 1933; s. Vernon Louis and Thelma (Venham) McD.; m. Mary Alice Boyd, Aug. 17, 1957; children: Anne Elizabeth, John Richard, Colleen Lynn. B.A., U. Ariz., 1957, LL.B., 1960. Bar: Ariz. 1960. Since practiced in Tucson; assoc. Richard N. Roylston, 1961-62; pvt. practice, 1963-65; ptnr. McDonald & Rykken, 1965-68, DeConcini & McDonald (now DeConcini, McDonald, Brammer, Yetwin, Lacy, P.C.), 1968—; mem. adv. bd. Dependable Nurses, Inc., 1994—. Mem. Ariz. Law Rev. Pres., bd. dirs. Comstock Children's Hosp. Found.; v.p. Ariz. Sch. Bds. Assn., 1979, pres., 1981; v.p. All Ariz. Sch. Bd., 1981; v.p., bd. dirs. Tucson Assn. for Blind; trustee Catalina Foothills Sch. Dist., 1976-82; mem. Tucson Com. on Fgn. Rels., 1989—; bd. dirs. Tucson Unified Sch. Dist. Ednl. Enrichment Found., Ariz. Acad., 1981—, Tucson Symphony Soc., 1997—. Mem. Ariz. Bar Assn., Ariz. Law Rev. Assn. (pres. 1994), Pima County Bar Assn. (dir. 1978-86, pres. 1984-85), Nat. Coun. Sch. Attys. (dir. 1992-96), Delta Chi. Republican. Presbyterian. Home: 6151 N Camino Almonte Tucson AZ 85718-3729 Office: 2525 E Broadway Blvd Tucson AZ 85716-5398

MC DONALD, JOHN WARLICK, diplomat, global strategist; b. Coblenz, Germany, Feb. 18, 1922; s. John Warlick and Ethel Mae (Raynor) McD.; m. Barbara Jane Stewart, Oct. 23, 1943 (div.); children: Marilyn Ruth, James Stewart, Kathleen Ethel, Laura Ellen; m. Christel Meyer, Oct. 24, 1970. AB, U. Ill., 1943, JD, 1946; D (hon.), Mt. Mercy Coll., 1989, Teikyo Marycrest U., 1991, Salisbury State U., 1993. Bar: Ill. 1946, U.S. Supreme Ct. 1951. With legal div. Office Mil Govt., Berlin, 1947; asst. dist. atty. U.S. Mil. Govt. Cts., Frankfort, Germany, 1947-50; with Allied High Commn., Bonn, Germany, 1950-52; U.S. mission to NATO and OEEC, Paris, 1952-54; fgn. affairs officer Dept. State, Washington, 1954-55; exec. sec. to dir. ICA, Washington, 1955-59; U.S. econ. coord. for CENTO affairs Ankara, Turkey, 1959-63; chief econ. and comml. sect. Am. Embassy, Cairo, 1963-66; student Nat. War Coll., Washington, 1966-67; dep. dir. office econ. and social affairs Bur. Internat. Orgn. Affairs, Dept. State, 1967-68, dir., 1968-71; coord. UN Multilateral Devel. Programs, Dept. State, 1971-74, acting dep. asst. sec. econ. and social affairs, 1971, 73; dep. dir. gen. ILO, Geneva, 1974-78; pres. INTELSAT Conf. Privileges and Immunities, 1978; U.S. coord. Tech. Coop. among Developing Countries, 1978; rep. with rank of amb. to UN Conf., 1978—; sec. gen. 27th Colombo Plan Ministerial Meeting, 1978; U.S. coord. UN Decade on Drinking Water and Sanitation, 1979; U.S. coord., ambassador Third World Conf. on Indsl. Devel., 1979, World Assembly on Aging, 1980-82; chmn. fed. inter-agy. com. Internat. Yr. of Disabled Persons, 1980-81; U.S. rep. Internat. Youth Yr., 1981-83; coord. multilateral affairs Ctr. Study of Fgn. Affairs, 1983-87; profl. lectr. in law George Washington U. Nat. Law Ctr., 1987-88, lectr. in conflict resolution, multilateral diplomacy and art of negotiation; pres. Iowa Peace Inst., Grinnell, 1988-92; prof. polit. sci. Grinnell Coll., 1989-92; Disting. vis. prof. George Mason U., Fairfax, Va., 1992-93; chmn. Inst. for Multi-Track Diplomacy, Washington, 1992—; mem. Fgn. Affairs Res. Corps., 1993—. Author: The North-Shore Dialogue and the UN, 1982, How to Be a Delegate, 1984, 2nd edit., 1994; co-editor: International Negotiation, 1985, Perspectives on Negotiation, 1986, Conflict Resolution: Track Two Diplomacy, 1987, 2nd edit., 1995, U.S. Soviet Summitry, 1987, US Bases Overseas: Negotiations with Spain, Greece and The Philippines, 1990, Multi-Track Diplomacy, 1991, revised, 1993, 3rd edit., 1996, Defining A U.S. Negotiating Sytle, 1996; contbr. articles on aging, terrorism, water conflict resolution. Bd. dirs. Global Water, 1982—, Touchstone Theatre, 1982-88, World Com.-UN Decade of Disabled Persons, 1987—, Countdown 2001, 1987-93, People-to-People Com. on Disability, 1987, Am. Impact Found., 1987-89, chmn. bd., 1988-89; dir. Am. Assn. Internat. Aging, 1983—, chmn., 1983—; v.p. nat. capital area UN Assn., 1993—, mem., 1978—. Recipient Superior Honor award, 1972, Presdl. Meritorious Service award, 1984; named Patriot of Yr., Kansas City, 1987. Mem. ABA, Am. Fgn. Svc. Assn., U.S. Assn. for Club of Rome, Soc. Profls. in Dispute Resolution, Consortium of Peace Rsch., Edn. and Devel., Cosmos Club, Delta Kappa Upsilon, Phi Delta Phi. Office: IMTD 1819 H St NW Ste 1200 Washington DC 20006-3603

MCDONALD, JOSEPH LEE, insurance broker; b. Bremerton, Wash., Aug. 15, 1931; s. Joseph Okane and Ida Elizabeth (Finholm) McD.; m. Glorietta Maness, Jan. 22, 1954 (dec. 1984); children: Holly Ann Chaffin, Andrew Lee McDonald; m. Beverly Mae Falkner, June 22, 1986. BS, U. Wash., 1954. Various mgmt. positions AT&T, 1956-62; broker, ptnr. McDonald & McGarry Co., Seattle, 1962-84; ptnr., exec. McDonald Ins. Group, Kirkland, Wash., 1984—; v.p., bd. dirs. Chimayo Inc., Seattle, 1990—, Santa Fe Food Corp., Seattle, 1991—. City councilman City of, Bellevue, 1971-75; commr. Water Dist. #97, Bellevue, 1967-71, Lake Hills Sewer Dist., Bellevue, 1965-71; pres. Wash. State Assn. of Sewer Dists., Seattle, 1969. With U.S. Army, 1954-56. Mem. Coll. Club of Seattle, Overlake Golf and Country Club, Western Assn. of Ins. Brokers, Ind. Ins. Agts. Assn., Seattle Master Builders Assn., Nat. Wildlife Fedn., Natures Conservancy, Apt. Assn. of Seattle and King County, Roche Harbor Yacht Club. Avocations: skiing, sailing, tennis. Home: 7235 91st Pl SE Mercer Island WA 98040-5803 Office: McDonald Ins Group 416-6th St South Kirkland WA 98033

MC DONALD, JOSEPH VALENTINE, neurosurgeon; b. N.Y.C., June 7, 1925; m. Carolyn Alice Patricia Petersen, Apr. 30, 1955; children: Judith Katherine McDonald Aquadro, Elizabeth Ann McDonald Iwanicki, Catherine Eleanor McDonald Schneider, Joseph Bede, David Randolph. A.B., Coll. Holy Cross, 1945; M.D., U. Pitts., 1949. Intern St. Vincent's Hosp., N.Y.C., 1949-50; rsch. fellow neuroanatomy Vanderbilt U., 1950-51; gen. surgery asst. resident Cushing VA Hosp., Boston, 1951-52; neurology extern Lenox Hill Hosp., 1952; asst. resident neurosurgery Johns Hopkins Hosp., 1953-55, resident neurosurgeon, 1955-56; practice medicine specializing in neurol. surgery Rochester, N.Y., 1956—; emeritus prof. neurosurgery and neurology U. Rochester Med. Sch. Mem. Soc. Neurol. Surgeons, A.C.S., Am. Assn. Neurol. Surgeons, Congress Neurosurgeons. Home: 800 Allens Creek Rd Rochester NY 14618-3412 Office: Strong Meml Hosp Div Neuro Surg Rochester NY 14642

MCDONALD, MARIANNE, classicist; b. Chgo., Jan. 2, 1937; d. Eugene Francis and Inez (Riddle) McD.; children: Eugene, Conrad, Bryan, Bridget, Kirstie (dec.), Hiroshi. BA magna cum laude, Bryn Mawr Coll., 1958; MA, U. Chgo., 1960; PhD, U. Calif., Irvine, 1975, doctorate (hon.) Am. Coll. Greece, 1988, hon. diploma Am. Archaeological Assn. Teaching asst. classics U. Calif., Irvine, 1974, D Litt (hon.) U. Athens, Greece, 1994, U. Dublin, 1994. instr. Greek, Latin and English, mythology, modern cinema, 1975-79, founder, rsch. fellow Thesaurus Linguae Graecae Project, 1975—; bd. dir. Centrum. Bd. dirs. Am. Coll. of Greece, 1981-90, Scripps Hosp., 1981; Am. Sch. Classical Studies, 1986—; mem. bd. overseers U. Calif. San Diego, 1985—; nat. bd. advisors Am. Biog. Inst., 1982—; pres. Soc. for the Preservation of the Greek Heritage, 1990—; founder Hajime Mori Chair for Japanese Studies, U. Calif., San Diego, 1985, McDonald Ctr. for Alcohol and Substance Abuse, 1984, Thesaurus Linguarum Hiberniae, 1991—; vis. prof. U. Dublin, 1990—; adj. prof. theatre U. Calif., San Diego, 1990, prof. theatre and classics, 1994. Recipient Ellen Browning Scripps Humanitarian award, 1975; Disting. Svc. award U. Calif.-Irvine, 1982, Irvine medal, 1987, 3rd Prize Midwest Poetry Ctr. Contest, 1987; named one of the Community Leaders Am., 1979-80, Philanthropist of Yr., 1985, Headliner San Diego Press Club, 1985, Philanthropist of Yr. Honorary Nat. Conf. Christians and Jews, 1986, Woman of Distinction Salvation Army, 1986, Eleventh Woman Living Legacy, 1986, Woman of Yr. AHEPA, 1988, San Diego Woman of Distinction, 1990, Woman of Yr. AXIOS, 1991; recipient Bravissimo gold medal San Diego Opera, 1990, Gold Medal Soc. Internationalization of Greek Lang., 1990, Athens medal, 1991, Piraeus medal, 1991, award Desmoi, 1992, award Hellenic Assn of Univ. Women, 1992, Academy of Achievement award AHEPA, 1992, Woman of Delphi award European Cultural Ctr. Delphi, 1992, Civis Universitatis award U. Calif. San Diego, 1993, Hypatia award Hellenic U. Women, 1993, Am.-Ireland Fund Heritage award, 1994, Contribution to Greek Letters award Aristotle U. Thessaloniki, 1994, Mirabella Mag. Readers Choice One of 1000 Women for the Nineties, 1994, Order of the Phoenix, Greece, 1994, citations from U.S. Congress and Calif. Senate, Alexander the Gt. award Hellenic Cultural Soc., 1995, made hon. citizen of Delphi and gold medal of the Amphiktuonon, Delphi, Greece, 1995, award European Cultural Ctr. of Delphi, 1995, Women Who Mean Bus. award for Fine Arts San Diego Bus. Jour., 1995. Vol. of Decade Women's International Ctr., 1994, 96. Mem. MLA, AAUP, Am. Philol. Assn., Soc. for the Preservation of the Greek Heritage (pres.), Libr. of Am., Am. Classical League, Philol. Assn. Pacific Coast, Am. Comparative Lit. Assn., Modern and Classical Lang. Assn. So. Calif., Hellenic Soc., Calif. Fgn. Lang. Tchrs. Assn., Internat. Platform Assn., Greek Language Found., Royal Irish Acad., Greece's Order of the Phoenix (commdr. 1994), KPBS Producers Club, Hellenic Univ. Club (bd. dir.). Author: Terms for Happiness in Euripides, 1978, Semilemmatized Concordances to Euripides' Alcestis, 1977, Cyclops, Andromache, Medea, 1978, Heraclidae, Hippolytus, 1979, Hecuba, 1984, Hercules Furens, 1984, Electra, 1984, Ion, 1985, Trojan Women, 1988, Iphigenia in Taurus, 1988, Euripides in Cinema: The Heart Made Visible, 1983; translator: The Cost of Kindness and Other Fabulous Tales (Shinichi Hoshi), 1986, (chpt.) Views of Clytemnestra, Ancient and Modern, 1990, Classics and Cinema, 1990, Modern Critical Theory and Classical Literature, 1994, A Challenge to Democracy, 1994, Ancient Sun/Modern Light: Greek Drama on the Modern Stage, 1990, Star Myths: Tales of the Constellations, 1996; contbr. numerous articles to profl. jours. Avocations: karate, harp (medieval), skiing, diving. Home: PO Box 929 Rancho Santa Fe CA 92067-0929 Office: U Calif at San Diego Dept Theatre La Jolla CA 92093

MCDONALD, MARK DOUGLAS, electrical engineer; b. Princeton, N.J., Aug. 3, 1958; s. James Douglas and Jacquelyn (Milligan) McD.; m. Patricia Joann Watson, Sept. 12, 1980. BSE, Duke U.; MS, N.C. State U. Product engr. Exide Electronics, Raleigh, N.C., 1981-84; rsch. asst. N.C. State U., Raleigh, 1985-86; mem. tech. staff Avantek (Hewlett Packard), Newark, Calif., 1987-90; prin. engr. Nat. Semiconductor, Santa Clara, Calif., 1990-92, engring. project mgr., 1992-95; design engring. mgr. Linear Tech. corp., Milpitas, Calif., 1995—; session chmn. Wireless Symposium, Santa Clara, 1993—, RF and Microwave Applications Conf., Santa Clara, 1992; mem. com. Symposium on VLSI Circuits Program, 1995—. Contbr. articles to profl. jours. Precinct capt. various polit. campaigns, Fremont, Calif., 1988. Mem. IEEE (sr.), Cairn Terrier Club of No. Calif. (asst. chairperson 1995, specialty show chairperson 1996—, bd. govs. 1996—). Achievements include U.S. and foreign patents in area of high-speed analog circuits; designed front-end integrated circuits in first wireless digital European cordless telecomm. transceiver (DECT) for voice comm.; design of first selective frequency trip circuit for parallel uninterruptible power supplies. Office: Linear Tech Corp 1630 Mccarthy Blvd Milpitas CA 95035-7417

MCDONALD, MICHAEL LEE, clinic administrator, retired naval officer; b. Salt Lake City, Oct. 23, 1949; s. Jack Alex and Dorothy Elsie (Mantle) McD.; m. Celia McKean Smoot, June 23, 1975; children: Sarah Lynn, Michelle Elise, AnnMarie, Jeffrey Michael, Matthew David, Emily Jane. BA, U. Utah, 1973; MA, U. Iowa, 1977. Commd. ensign USN, 1975; advanced through grades to comdr., 1991; patient adminstr. Naval Hosp., Great Lakes, Ill., 1977-80, Oakland, Calif., 1980-82; med. recruiter Navy Recruiting Dist., San Francisco, 1982-84; adminstr. Navy Environ. and Preventative Medicine Unit # 7, Naples, Italy, 1984-87; staff officer Navy Med. Commd. Europe, London, 1987-89; healthcare advisor U.S. Naval Forces Europe, London, 1989-91; exec. officer Naval Med. Clinic, Seattle, 1991-93, commdg. officer, 1993-94; officer in charge Branch Med. Clinic, Everett, Wash., 1994-96; ret., 1996, health care cons.,, 1996—. Coach Northshore Little League, Bothell, Wash., 1992, 93; scoutmaster Boy Scouts Am., Dublin, Calif., 1981-85, instl. sponsor, Naples, Italy, 1985-87. Fellow Am. Coll. Healthcare Execs. Mem. LDS Ch. (bishop). Avocations: golf, basketball, English literature, cycling. Home and Office: 19225 4th Dr SE Bothell WA 98012-7013

MCDONALD, MICHAEL SCOTT, lawyer; b. Ft. Stockton, Tex., Feb. 6, 1962; s. Roland R. and Harriett L. McD.; m. Sara; children: Matthew, Michael. BA, U. Tex., El Paso, 1984; JD, U. Tex., Austin, 1987. Bar: Tex. 1987, U.S. Ct. Appeals (5th cir.), U.S. Dist. Ct. (all dists.) Tex. With Littler, Mendelson, Fastiff, Tichy & Mathiason, Dallas, ptnr., shareholder; presenter in field. Co-author, editor: The 1996 Texas Employer; contbg. editor: Covenents Not to Compete-A State by State Survey, 1995, Employee Duty of Loyalty, 1995; contbr. articles to profl. jours. Mem. ABA (litigation sect., labor and employment law sect.), Tex. Bar Assn. (labor and employment law sect.), Tex. Assn. Bus., Dallas Bar Assn. (employment law sect.), mem. exec.com. 1994—), Dallas Young Lawyers Assn. Office: Littler Mendelson Fastiff Tichy & Mathiason 300 Crescent Ct Dallas TX 75201-1876

MCDONALD, MILLER BAIRD, management consultant, columnist, historian; b. Huntsville, Tenn., Feb. 16, 1920; s. Melva Lawson and Bertha Clarence (Baird) McD.; m. Lois Fox, Nov. 30, 1941; 4 children. Ed., Lincoln Meml. U., 1939-40, U. Tenn., 1948-49; cert., Cornell U., 1958, U. Wis., 1967, U. Mich., 1971; B.S., Pacific Western U., 1984, Ph.D., 1985. Admistrv. asst. Home Owners Loan Corp., Washington, 1940-41; personnel officer AEC, Oak Ridge, 1946-51; pers., tng. and intelligence officer AEC, Albuquerque, 1953-59; policy devel. officer FAA, Washington, 1959-60; chief out-service tng. IRS, Washington, 1960-66; dir. mgmt. tng. Sec. Commerce, Washington, 1966-72; pres., cons. to mgmt. Miller McDonald and Assocs., La Follette, Tenn., 1973—, Arlington, Va., 1972—; syndicated columnist County Line, Tenn., 1980—; owner, mgr. County Services Syndicate, 1981—; commr. for human devel. State of Tenn., 1979—; instr. internat. program in taxation Harvard U. Law Sch., 1964-66; instr. U. Ga., 1970, La. State U., 1971; bd. dirs. Wesleyan Found., 1978—; mem. nat. adv. bd. Am. Security Council, 1979—; del. White House Conf. on Aging, 1981—; mem. Gov.'s Conf. on Aging, 1982—. Author: Campbell County Tennessee, 3 vols., 1993, (news series) Our Government, What's Wrong, 1982, also profl. papers.

Mem. Presdl. Task Force on Career Advancement, 1965; charter mem. Statue of Liberty Found., 1983; chmn. Pres. Ford Com. East Tenn., 1976; mem. Senator Baker for Pres. Com., 1979; chmn. Campbell County Republican Exec. Com., Tenn., 1976-80, 2d Congl. dist. Reagan for Pres. Com., 1980, Upper 4th Dist. Reagan-Bush Com., 1984; dir. Tenn. Citizen's Against Govt. Waste (Grace Commn.), 1986—; mem. U.S. Capitol Hist. Soc., 1987—; historian Campbell County, Tenn., 1988—; incorporator, founder, dir. Campbell County Hist. Soc., 1989—, pres. bd., 1991—. Served to col. U.S. Army, 1942-46, 50-53. Decorated Presdl. award for Outstanding Meritorious Svc.; decorated numerous other medals; recipient Superior Performance award AEC, 1960, cert. recognition IRS, 1966, medal Sec. Army, 1971, cert. svc. Dept. Commerce, 1972, cert. merit Tenn. Hist. Commn., 1997, Presdl. Achievement award Rep. Nat. Com., 1982, Tenn. Gov.'s Outstanding Achievement award, 1992, Merit award Tenn. Hist. Commn., 1993, Proclamation Tenn. Ho. of Reps., 1993, award of Merit, Tenn. Libr. Assn., 1994. Mem Nat. Trust Historic Preservation, Inst. Applied Behavioral Sci., NEA, Am. Soc. Tng. and Devel., Adult Edn. Assn., Libr. of Congress Assocs. (charter), Am. Legion, Clan Donald U.S.A., Rotary, Masons. Methodist. Home and Office: 109 Crestview Dr La Follette TN 37766-4822 *Society has lost much because of failure to persist. To be sure you are right and go ahead is the thing. Many of life's goals have been lost simply because one has given up too soon. To have the steadfastness to persist in the face of great odds has largely accounted for what measure of success I have achieved.*

MCDONALD, PATRICK ALLEN, lawyer, arbitrator, educator; b. Detroit, May 11, 1936; s. Lawrence John and Estelle (Maks) Mc D.; m. Margaret Mercier, Aug. 10, 1963; children: Michael Lawrence, Colleen Marie, Patrick Joseph, Timothy, Margaret, Thomas, Maureen. PhB cum laude, U. Detroit, 1958, JD magna cum laude, 1961; LLM (E. Barrett Prettyman Trial scholar, Hugh J. Fegan fellow), Georgetown U., 1962. Bar: D.C. 1961, Mich. 1961, Colo. 1993. Case worker Dept. Pub. Welfare, Detroit, 1958; field examiner NLRB, Detroit, 1961; practiced in Washington, 1961-62; trial cons. NIH, Bethesda, Md., 1962; staff judge adv. USAF, France, 1962-65; ptnr. Monagham, LoPrete, Mc Donald, Yakima & Grenke, Detroit, 1965—; bd. dirs., chmn. Delta Dental Plan of Mich.; chmn. Delta Dental Plan of Ohio; bd. dirs., v.p. Guest House, Lake Orion, Mich., Rochester, Minn., Detroit Athletic Club, Brighton Hosp.; instr. polit. sci. and law U. Md., 1963-65, U. Detroit Law Sch., adj. prof., 1965—. Co-author: Law and Tactics in Federal Criminal Cases, 1963. Mem. Detroit Bd. Edn., 1966-76, pres.; sec., trustee Mt. Elliott Cemetary Assn.; mem. U. Detroit Sports Hall of Fame; mem. adv. bd. Providence Hosp., Southfield, Mich.; exec. bd. U. Detroit Pres.'s Cabinet. Named one of Five Outstanding Young Men of Mich., Outstanding Young Man of Detroit. Mem. ABA, Detroit Bar Assn., State Bar Mich. (commr.), U. Detroit Alumni Assn. (bd. dirs.), Mensa, Blue Key, Alpha Phi Omega (pres. Eta Pi chpt. 1955), Alpha Sigma Nu (v.p. 1960). Home: 13066 Lashbrook Ln E Brighton MI 48116-6002 Office: 1700 N Woodward Ave Bloomfield Hills MI 48304-2249 *In the field of law, as an attorney, professor and arbitrator, I have prayed and attempted to be able in argument, accurate in analysis, correct in conclusion, candid with clients, honest with adversaries, and responsible for obligations assigned to me. I have advocated moderation in all things with the exception of my love for Him who created me.*

MCDONALD, ROBERT BOND, chemical company executive; b. Seattle, Oct. 31, 1936; s. Theodore Day and Elizabeth Wood (Robbins) McD.; m. Eleanore Mary Beca, June 27, 1959; children: James Arthur, Kylie Robbins. BE, Yale U., 1958; MS, U. Wash., 1960. Mng. dir. Gt. Lakes Chem. Corp., Lancaster, Eng., 1976-79; asst. to pres. Great Lakes Chem. Corp., West Lafayette, Ind., 1979-81, v.p., 1981-87, sr. v.p., 1987-94, exec. v.p., COO, pres., CEO, 1994—; also bd. dirs. Gt. Lakes Chem. Corp., West Lafayette, Ind.; v.p. COB Octel Am., Inc.; adv. bd. Inst. for Applied Neurology, Purdue U., deans adv. coun. Krannert Sch. Mgmt.; bd. dirs. Kao-Quaker, Japan, Tetrabrom Tech., Ltd., Israel, Assoc. Octel, U.K., The Lafayette Life Ins. Co., OSCA, Inc., Bio-Lab., Inc. Mem. Tippecanoe County Hist. Assn., Greater Lafayette Mus. Art. Mem. Ind. C. of C. (bd. dirs.), Greater Lafayette C. of C. (bd. dirs. 1987-90), Lafayette Country Club (bd. dirs.). Republican. Episcopalian. Office: Gt Lakes Chem Corp 1 Great Lakes Blvd PO Box 2200 West Lafayette IN 47906

MCDONALD, ROBERT DELOS, manufacturing company executive; b. Dubuque, Iowa, Jan. 30, 1931; s. Delos Lyon and Virginia (Kolck) McD.; m. Jane M. Locher, Jan. 16, 1960 (div. Jan. 1970); children: Jean, Patricia, Maria, Sharon, Rob; m. Marilyn I. Miller, July 4, 1978. BA in Econs., U. Iowa, 1953. With A.Y. McDonald Mfg. Co., Dubuque, 1956—, salesman, 1956-60, sales mgr., 1961-64, mgr. Dubuque wholesale br., 1965-72, v.p., 1971-72, v.p., corp. sec., 1972-83, sr. v.p., corp. sec., 1983-85, pres., 1985-95, chmn. bd., chief exec. officer, 1987—, also bd. dirs., 1964—; bd. dirs. Brock-McVey Co., Lexington, Ky., 1964—, A.Y. McDonald Supply Co., Inc., Dubuque, 1984—; sr. v.p., bd. dirs. A.Y. McDonald Industries, Inc., Dubuque, 1983—; chmn. bd., pres., CEO, bd. dirs. A.Y.M. Inc., Albia, Iowa, 1988—. Trustee, bd. dirs. A.Y. McDonald Mfg. Co. Charitable Found., 1978—, pres., 1982—; bd. dirs. Stonehill Care Ctr., Dubuque, 1984-92, chmn. bd., 1991-92; mem. Stonehill Renovation and Financing Task Force, 1994—; bd. dirs. Dubuque Boys Club, 1989—, Save Iowa's Civil War Monument Restoration Fund, 1995—, Dubuque Bank & Trust Co., 1994—, Dubuque County Hist. Soc., 1996—, Grand Opera House Found.; trustee United Way Svcs., Inc., Dubuque, 1989—; vice chmn. Stonehill Benevolent Found., Dubuque, 1988-92; mem. adv. coun. region VII SBA, Cedar Rapids, 1984—; mem. adv. bd. Jr. Achievement Tri-States, Inc., 1991—, Iowa State Fair Blue Ribbon Found., 1993—. Lt. USNR, 1953-56, Korea. Mem. Am. Mgmt. Assn., Am. Supply Assn., Am. Water Works Assn., Nat. Assn. Mfrs., Dubuque Area C. of C., Am. Legion, Dubuque Shooting Soc., Dubuque Golf and Country Club, Sigma Alpha Epsilon. Republican. Roman Catholic. Home: Fountain Hill 3399 Eagle Point Dr Dubuque IA 52001 Office: AY McDonald Mfg Co PO Box 508 Dubuque IA 52004-0508

MC DONALD, ROBERT EMMETT, company executive; b. Red Wing, Minn., Apr. 29, 1915; s. Mitchell W. and Olivia (Carlson) McD.; m. Marion L. Wigley, Sept. 14, 1946; children: Patricia L., Barbara C. B.B.A., B.E.E., U. Minn., 1940; postgrad., U. Chgo., 1942. Employment interviewer Commonwealth Edison Co., Chgo., 1940-43; supr. accessory maintenance Northwest Airlines, St. Paul, 1946-51; dir. maintenance No. region Braniff Airways, Mpls., 1951-53; mgr. ops., then v.p., mgr. def. div. Univac, St. Paul, 1953-64; pres. Univac div. Sperry Rand Corp., Blue Bell, Pa., 1966-71; exec. v.p. parent co. Univac div. Sperry Rand Corp., 1966-72; pres., COO Sperry Rand Corp., N.Y.C., 1972-79; vice chmn. bd. Sperry Rand Corp., 1979-80; dir. CertainTeed Corp., Valley Forge, Pa., SKF Industries, Phila., 1979-85, Glenmede Corp., Phila.; mgmt. cons. Trustee U. Minn. Found., 1975-85. Served to lt. USNR, 1943-46. Mem. Tau Beta Pi, Eta Kappa Nu, Acacia. Clubs: Phila. Country, Union League (Phila.). Home: 1125 Robin Rd Gladwyne PA 19035-1007

MCDONALD, STANFORD LAUREL, clinical psychologist; b. Lincoln, Nebr., Mar. 14, 1929; s. Laurel C. and Irene Virginia (Frey) McD.; m. Shirley P. Peterson, Apr. 26, 1964; children: Stacia E. V., Jeffrey J.S., Kathleen S., Patricia M. AB, Nebr. Wesleyan U., 1956; MA, U. Nebr., 1959, postgrad., 1958-60; PhD, Fielding Inst., 1974. Licensed clin. psychologist, Ill. Intern Nebr. Psychiat. Inst., Omaha, 1957-58; staff psychologist Presbyn. St. Lukes Hosp., Chgo., 1960-61; sch. psychologist Chgo. Bd. Edn., 1961-65; chief psychologist SPEED Devel. Ctr., Chicago Heights, Ill., 1965-79; pvt. practice psychology Park Forest, Ill., 1980—; cmty. prof. Gov.'s State U., University Park, Ill., 1974—; clin. dir. Dr. Stanford L. McDonald and Assocs., Park Forest, 1980; vis. prof. U. Witwatersrand, Johannesburg, S.A., spring 1996. Contbr. papers for profl. convs. With USMC, 1950-52, Korea. Fellow Am. Orthopsychiat. Assn.; mem. Am. Psychol. Assn., Biofeedback Soc. Ill. (past pres.), N.Y. Acad. Scis., Midwestern Psychological Assn., 1st Marine Divsn. Assn. (life), Zeta Psi, Psi Chi. Avocations: horticulture, automotive design, gourmet cooking. Home: 255 Rich Rd Park Forest IL 60466-1629 Office: 24 Centre Ste 4 Park Forest IL 60466-2032

MC DONALD, STEPHEN LEE, economics educator; b. Arkadelphia, Ark., Aug. 8, 1924; s. Claud Bethel and Ruth Jane (Gresham) McD.; m. Elizabeth Gene Brewer, Aug. 14, 1945; children: Martha Elizabeth Mc Donald Worchel, Kathryn Ann Mc Donald McGlothlin. B.A., La. Poly. Inst., 1947; M.A., U. Tex., 1948, Ph.D., 1951. Asst. prof. U. Tex., Austin, 1950-56, prof. econs., 1961—, Josey prof. in energy studies, 1983-85, Duncan prof. econs., 1985-94; chmn. dept. U. Tex., 1972-76, 78-79, 88-89, emeritus, 1997; sr. fellow Bur. Bus. Rsch., 1990-97; economist Humble Oil & Refining Co., 1956-57; assoc. prof., prof., chmn. dept. La. State U., 1957-61; mem. faculty Stonier Grad. Sch. Banking; staff assoc., Brookings Instn., 1961-63; mem. econs. adv. panel NSF, 1962-64; cons. to govt. and industry, 1957—. Author: Federal Tax Treatment of Income from Oil and Gas, 1963, Petroleum Conservation in the United States, 1971, The Leasing of Federal Lands for Fossil Fuels Production, 1979; mem. editorial bds.: So. Econ. Journal, 1961-64, Energy Jour., 1979-86; contbr. articles to profl. jours. Served with USNR, 1943-46. Recipient Citation for Excellence Am. Bankers Assn.; Ford Found. grantee, 1964; Resources for Future grantee, 1967, 76; Pres. Assocs. award teaching excellence, 1982. Mem. Am. Econ. Assn., So. Econ. Assn. (v.p. 1969-70), Southwestern Econ. Assn. (pres. 1964-65), Internat. Assn. Energy Econs., Gamma Epsilon, Phi Kappa Phi. Democrat. Methodist. Home: 4002 Sierra Dr Austin TX 78731-3914

MCDONALD, SUSAN F., business executive, county official; b. Rockford, Ill., Jan. 18, 1961; d. John Augustus and Jeanne (Reitsch) Floberg; m. Robert Arthur McDonald, June 19, 1981; children: Molly Jeanne, Amanda Elizabeth. AAS in Bus. Mgmt., Colo. Mountain Coll., Glenwood Springs, 1981. Teller, bookkeeper Alpine Bank, Glenwood Springs, 1981-82; teller Macktown State Bank, Rockford, 1982-83; treas., mgr., owner Roscoe (Ill.) Movie House, 1984-94; sales cons. Lou Bachroot, Inc., Rockford, 1992-93; mem. bd. suprs. Winnebago County Bd., Rockford, 1992—; exec. v.p., owner Corp. Svc. Alliance, Machesney Park, Ill., 1993-95; leasing and fleet mgr. Budweiser Motors, Inc., Beloit, Wis., 1994-95; bus. mgr. Finley Oldsmobile GMC, South Beloit, Ill., 1995—. V.p. Roscoe Bus. Assn., 1989, pres., 1990, 91; chair, founder Roscoe Beautification Assn., 1991; mem. county bd. dirs. Winnebago County, 1992—, vice chmn. econ. devel. com., 1993—, chmn. zoning com., 1997—; chmn. econ. devel. environ. com. Winnebago County Bd., 1994—; commr. Winnebago County Forest Preserve, Rockford, 1992—; co-founder, bd. dirs. Very Important Pregnancy, Rockford Meml. Hosp.; bd. dirs. Family Advocate Aux., Rockford, 1987-88; bd. dirs. U. Ill. Extension Svc./Winnebago County, 1994—. Nominated Video Retailer of Yr., Am. Video Assn., 1989, Leadership award, Stateline YWCA, 1989. Republican. Methodist. Avocations: horseback riding, hunting and jumping equestrian activities, golfing, skiing. Office: Finley Oldsmobile GMC 1790 Gardner St South Beloit IL 61080-1424

MCDONALD, THOMAS ALEXANDER, lawyer; b. Chgo., Aug. 20, 1942; s. Owen Gerard and Lois (Gray) McD.; m. Sharon Diane Hirk, Nov. 25, 1967; children: Cristin, Katie, Courtney, Thomas Jr. AB, Georgetown U., 1965; JD, Loyola U., Chgo., 1968. Bar: Ill. 1969, U.S. Dist. Ct. (no. dist.) Ill. 1969. Ptnr. Clausen Miller, PC, Chgo., 1969—. Mem. ABA, Ill. Bar Assn., Chgo. Bar Assn. Office: Clausen Miller PC 10 S La Salle St Chicago IL 60603-1002

MCDONALD, THOMAS PAUL, controller; b. Williamsport, Pa., Aug. 13, 1949; s. Paul Tripp and Ethel Mary (Cowden) McD.; m. Debra Ann Rosamilia, July 17, 1976; children: Kevin, Gail. BS in Acctg., U. Scranton, 1971. CPA, N.Y. Auditor Coopers & Lybrand, N.Y.C., 1971-79; internal audit dir. Ward Foods, N.Y.C., 1979-81; contr. Mallory Randall Corp., N.Y.C., 1981-83, Sullivan & Cromwell, N.Y.C., 1983—. Mem. AICPA, N.Y. State Soc. CPAs. Avocations: golf, coaching recreational sports. Home: 34 Dawson Dr West Caldwell NJ 07006-8128 Office: Sullivan & Cromwell 125 Broad St New York NY 10004-2400

MCDONALD, THOMAS ROBERT, materials technologist, consultant, business owner; b. Denver, Dec. 2, 1945; s. Phillip John and Anne Winslow (Jewell) McD.; m. Mary Kathleen Pfannenstiel, Mar. 6, 1970; children: Michael T., Patrick R. BS in Bus. Fin., U. Colo., 1974. Project materials technician Colo. Dept. Hwys., Denver, 1964-71; pub. works inspector, project mgr. City of Lakewood, Colo., 1971-76; quality control supr., construct materials lab. mgr. Brannan Sand & Gravel Co., Denver, 1976-82; area mgr. Soiltest, Inc., Evanston, Ill., 1982-84; pavement maintenance specialist Western Technologies, Phoenix, 1984-87, Brewer Cote of Ariz., Glendale, 1987-88; sales mgr., estimator Driveway Maintenance of Ariz., Phoenix, 1988-92; owner Pavement Maintenance Info. Source, Mesa, Ariz., 1992—; materials quality control cons. Colo. Dept. Hwys., Denver, 1964-71, Brannan Sand & Gravel, Denver, 1976-82; pavement maintenance cons. Western Technologies, Phoenix, 1984-87, Brewer Cote of Ariz., Glendale, 1987-88, Pavement Maintenance Inf. Source, Mesa, 1992—. Author: (software) Ecopave, 1986, (book) Property Managers Guide to Pavement Maintenance, 1992, Asphalt Estimating, 1995; contbr. articles to property mgmt. and pavement maintenance mags. Mem. Leadership Mesa, 1986. With USN, 1965-68. Recipient Most Innovative Pavement Maintenance Program award FAA, 1986. Mem. ASCE, Bldg. Owners and Mgrs. Assn. (bd. dirs. 1984-93), Multihousing Assn. Ariz. (instr. 1987, 89, 91), Am. Assn. Asphalt Paving Technologists, Internat. Platform Assn., Nat. Assn. Aviation Ofcls., Calif. Assn. Aero. Execs. Achievements include development of a property management training course on pavement maintenance and budgeting; developed effective specification manual for pavement maintenance applications for property managers; develop budgets and cash flow models for pavement maintenance budgets and construction. Office: Pavement Maintenance Info Source PO Box 30567 Mesa AZ 85275-0567

MCDONALD, TIM, professional football player; b. Fresno, Calif., Jan. 6, 1965. Student, U. So. Calif. With St. Louis Cardinals, 1987; safety Phoenix Cardinals (formerly St. Louis Cardinals), 1988-92; with S.F. 49ers, 1993—. Named defense back The Sporting News All-America team, 1985. Played in Pro Bowl, 1989, 1991, 92, 93. Office: San Francisco 49ers 4949 Centennial Blvd Santa Clara CA 95054-1229*

MCDONALD, WARREN GEORGE, accountant, former savings and loan executive; b. Oakland, Calif., Feb. 14, 1939; s. George Daniel and Barbara (Sainsot) McD.; m. Roberta Anne Peterson, Apr. 27, 1968; children: Edward Bruce, Deborah Lynn. B.A., San Francisco State Coll., 1962. CPA, Calif. Ptnr. Main Lafrentz & Co., CPAs, San Francisco, 1969-74; v.p., treas. Imperial Corp. Am., San Diego, 1975-80; v.p. fin. No. Calif. Savs. & Loan, Palo Alto, 1980-82; sr. v.p. fin. Unified Mortgage Co., Santa Clara, Calif., 1982-85; pres. Saratoga Savs., 1985-89; pvt. practice cons. San Francisco, 1989—. Co-author: Power Above The Law, 1990. Served to capt. USCGR. Mem. AICPA, Calif. Soc. CPAs, Inst. Mgmt. Accts., Res. Officers Assn. Home: 1430 Wendy Way Menlo Park CA 94025-6022

MCDONALD, WILLIAM ANDREW, classics educator; b. Warkworth, Ont., Can., Apr. 26, 1913; came to U.S., 1936, naturalized, 1943; s. William Douglas and Jean (Lane) McD.; m. Elizabeth Jackson Anderson, June 28, 1941; children: Susan, Elizabeth. B.A., U. Toronto, 1935, M.A., 1936; Ph.D., Johns Hopkins, 1940. Asst. prof. classics Lehigh U., 1939-43; tech. writer Consol. Vultee Aircraft Co., 1943-44; assoc. prof. classics U. Tex., Austin, 1945-46; prof. classics, chmn. dept. Moravian Coll., Bethlehem, Pa., 1946-48; prof. classics U. Minn., 1948-80, Regents' prof. classical studies, 1973-80; dir. honors div. U. Minn. (Coll. Liberal Arts), 1964-67; dir. Minn. Messenia expdn. in S.W. Greece, 1961-92, dir. grad. center for ancient studies, 1973-78, 85-86; Research prof. Am. Sch. Classical Studies, Athens, 1978-79; excavation staff Johns Hopkins U. at Olynthus, 1938, U. Cin. at Pylos, 1939, 53; dir. Nichoria excavation, 1969-75. Author: Political Meeting Places of Greeks, 1943, Progress into the Past, 1967, (with C.C. Thomas) 2d edit., 1990, (with D. J. Georgacas) Place Names of Southwest Peloponnesus, 1969, (with G. Rapp Jr.) Minnesota Messenia Expedition: Reconstructing A Bronze Age Regional Environment, 1972, (with W.D.E. Coulson and John Rosser) Excavations at Nichoria in Southwest Greece: Dark Age and Byzantine Occupation, 1983, (with N.C. Wilkie) Bronze Age Occupation, 1992. Vogeler Meml. fellow Johns Hopkins, 1936-38; Royal Soc. Can. fellow Am. Sch. Classical Studies, Athens, 1938-39; Guggenheim fellow, 1958-59, 67-68. Mem. Archaeol. Inst. Am. (exec. com. Gold medal for Disting. Archaeol. Achievement 1981), Am. Philol. Assn., Assn. for Field Archaeology (v.p.), Soc. Prof. Archaeologists (dir.). Home: 1666 Coffman St Apt 333 Saint Paul MN 55108-1340 Office: Univ Minn 331 Folwell Hall Minneapolis MN 55455

MCDONALD, WILLIAM HENRY, lawyer; b. Niangua, Mo., Feb. 27, 1946; s. Milburn and Fannie M. McDonald; m. Janice E. Robinson, July 13, 1968; children: Melissa L., Meghan M. BS in Pub. Adminstrn., Southwest Mo. State U., 1968; JD, U. Mo., 1971. Bar: Mo. 1971, U.S. Dist. Ct. (we. dist.) Mo. 1973, U.S. Supreme Ct. 1978, U.S. Ct. Appeals (8th cir.) 1982. Pres. William H. McDonald & Assocs., P.C., Springfield, Mo., 1973—; ptnr. Woolsey, Fisher, Whiteaker & McDonald, P.C., 1973-95. Chmn. blue ribbon task force on Delivery of Mental Health Services to Southwest Mo., Mo. Commn. Continuing Legal Edn.; pres. Tan Oaks Homeowners Assn.; mem. fin. com. Child Adv. Council, Rep. Nat. Com., Mo. Rep. Com., Greene County Nat. Com.; active various Southwest Mo. State U. Clubs; bd. dirs. Greene County div. Am. Heart Assn., Ozarks regional Am. Athletic Union Jr. Olympics; pres., bd. dirs. Springfield Little Theatre; v.p. pub. affairs Springfield Area C. of C., bd. dirs., 1995—. Served to capt. U.S. Army, 1971-73. Named one of Outstanding Young Men Am., 1978, 81, Outstanding Young Men Springfield, 1980. Fellow ABA (life, litigation and torts and ins. sects.); mem. ATLA, Mo. Bar Assn. (chmn. spol. com. on mandatory continuing edn., various coms., Pres.'s award 1986), Greene County Bar Assn. (bd. dirs., chmn. pub. edn. speakers bur.), Met. Bar Assn. St. Louis, Def. Rsch. Inst., Am. Judicature Soc., Am. Bd. Trial Advs., Nat. Bd. Trial Advs., 31st Jud. Cir. Bar Com. (chmn.), Supreme Ct. Hist. Soc., U. Mo.-Kansas City Sch. Law Found., Beta Omega Tau, Kappa Epsilon. Presbyterian. Home: 4857 E Royal Dr Springfield MO 65809-2425

MCDONALD, WILLIAM HENRY, financial executive; b. Ottawa, Ont., Can., Sept. 8, 1924; s. Joseph and Constance Mary (Gordon) McD.; m. D. Gwen Selkirk, July 8, 1950; 1 child, Barbara Elaine. Grad. high sch. Credit and operating mgr. B.F. Goodrich Co., Winnipeg, Man., Can., 1945-49; fin. adminstrn. officer Govt. Can., Ottawa, 1949-55; asst. gen. mgr. mortgages Bank of N.S., 1955-66; mng. dir. Boyd Stott & McDonald Ltd., Toronto, Ont., 1966-79; exec. v.p., dir. Morguard Trust Co., 1966-74; chmn. bd. Can. Comml. Bank, Toronto, 1976-81, chmn. exec. com., 1981-84; chmn. bd. Can. Comml. Bank Mortgage Investment Corp., 1983-84; pres., CEO, dir. Boyd Stott and McDonald Techs., Ltd., 1984—; pres. Thornton McDonald Assocs., Inc. Chmn. bd. govs. J. Douglas Ferguson Hist. Research Found., 1971—. Served with RCNVR, 1943-45. Mem. Can. Paper Money Soc. (hon. pres.), Internat. Bank Note Soc. (life), Can. Credit Inst., Classical & Medieval Numismatic Soc. (exec. sec.). Conservative. Anglican. Office: PO Box 956 Sta B, Willowdale, ON Canada M2K 2T6

MCDONALD-WEST, SANDI M., headmaster, consultant; b. Lowell, Mass., May 8, 1930; d. Walter Allan and Celina Louise (Lalime) MacLean; m. Thomas D. McDonald, Sept. 8, 1951 (div.); children: Todd F. McDonald, Brooke McDonald Killian, Ned M. McDonald, Reid A. McDonald, Heather McDonald Acker. BA, DePauw U., 1951; MA, Fairleigh Dickinson U., 1966; MEd, North Tex. State U., 1980. Cert. in Montessori teaching. Tchr., adminstr. Hudson (Ohio) Montessori Sch., 1966-68, Berea (Ohio) Montessori Sch., 1968-70, Creative Learning Ctr., Dallas, 1970-71; tchr., head of lower sch. The Selwyn Sch., Denton, Tex., 1971-83; tchr., headmaster Cimarron Sch., Enid, Okla., 1983-87; cons. Corpus Christi (Tex.) Montessori Sch., 1987-89, Azlann-Eren Horn Montessori Sch., Denton, 1989-95, Highland Meadow Montessori Acad., Southlake, Tex., 1994—; ednl. dir., pres. Southwestern Montessori Tchg. Ctr., Inc., Denton, 1974—; adj. prof. North Tex. State U., Denton, 1979-80; cons., lectr. Am. Montessori Soc., N.Y.C., 1970—, Japanese Montessori Soc., 1978—, also pub. and pvt. schs., 1972—; chair commn. for accreditation Montessori Accreditation Coun. Tchr. Edn., Denton, 1991—. Developer various Montessori materials; contbr. articles to profl. jours. Mem. Am. Montessori Soc., No. Ohio Montessori Assn. (pres. 1968-70), Assn. Montessori Internat., N.Am. Montessori Tchrs. Assn., Wheat Capital Assn. for Children Under Six (pres. 1986-87), LWV. Mem. Am. Montessori Soc., No. Ohio Montessori Assn. (pres. 1968-70), Assn. Montessori Internat., N.Am. Montessori Tchrs. Assn., Wheat Capital Assn. for Children Under Six (pres. 1986-87), LWV, Concerned Scientists. Avocations: ecology, golf, reading, travel. Home: 2005 Marshall Rd Denton TX 76207-3316

MCDONELL, EDWIN DOUGLAS, information systems executive, consultant, writer; b. Johnson City, N.Y., Aug. 16, 1953; s. Alex Edwin and Loretta Arlene (Terry) McD. BA in English Lit., U. Cin., 1976; MSLS in Info. Sci., Case Western Reserve U., 1978; MBA in Mgmt. Info. Systems, Ind. U., 1983. Assoc. Crowe Chizek & Co., CPAs, Indpls., 1983-88, prin., 1989-92; dir. office automation USA Group, Fishers, Ind., 1992-95; ind. cons. and writer, 1995—; com. chairperson Fin. Mgrs. Soc., Chgo., 1989-92; cons., spkr. Lafferty Group Confs., London, 1992—. Author: (books) Creating a Customer-Driven Retail Bank, 1991, Rebuilding the Retail Bank, 1992, Document Imaging Technology, 1993; contbg. author procs., reports in field; contbg. editor Bank Adminstrn. Inst., Chgo., 1989-91; contbr. articles to profl. jours. Mem. Inst. Mgmt. Cons. (cert.), Beta Gamma Sigma, Sigma Iota Epsilon. Presbyterian. Office: 8403 La Habra Ln Indianapolis IN 46236-8832

MCDONELL, HORACE GEORGE, JR., instrument company executive; b. N.Y.C., Sept. 23, 1928; s. Horace Gustave and Anabel (Armstrong) McD.; m. Eileen Romar, Sept. 6, 1952; children: Victoria (dec.), Diane, Horace. A.B., Adelphi Coll., 1952; postgrad., Harvard U., 1962. Engr. Sperry Gyroscope Co., N.Y.C., 1952; with Perkin-Elmer Corp., Norwalk, Conn., 1963—; mgr. instrument group Perkin-Elmer Corp., 1967-77, v.p., 1966-69, sr. v.p., 1969-77, exec. v.p., 1977-80, pres., 1980-85, chmn., 1985-90, ret., 1990; bd. dirs. Perkin Elmer, Ltd., U.K. UniRoyal, Inc., Perkin Elmer Internat., Inc., Harvey Hubbell, Inc., Ethan Allen Inc.; Mem. adv. task force on export controls U.S. Def. Sci. Bd., 1975—, chmn. instrumentation subcom., 1975—. Mem. Bd. Edn., Ridgefield, Conn., 1969; Bd. dirs. Conn. Sci. Fair.; Trustee, bd. dirs. Danbury (Conn.) Hosp.; trustee Adelphi U.; bd. dirs. Danbury Health Svcs. With AUS, 1946-48. Mem. Sci. Apparatus Maker Assn. (dir., chmn. analytical instrument sect.), Am. Inst. Physics, AAAS, Instrument Soc. Am., Am. Electronics Assn. (bd. dirs. 1984-89, chmn. 1987). Home: 740 Bald Eagle Dr Naples FL 34105-7409 Office: Perkin-Elmer Corp 761 Main Ave Norwalk CT 06859-0002

MCDONELL, KATHERINE MANDUSIC, professional society administrator; b. Mansfield, Ohio, Nov. 8, 1954; d. Sam and Ann Julia (Konves) Mandusic; m. Edwin D. McDonell, Aug. 18, 1979 (div. Dec. 1994). BA, Ohio Wesleyan U.; MA in History and Mus. Studies, Case Western Res.; MBA, Ind. U. Rschr. Conner Prairie Mus., Fishers, Ind., 1978-82; exec. dir./rsch. historian Ind. Med. History Mus./Ind. Hist. Soc., Indpls., 1982-91; asst. dir. for comm. and mktg. Ind. U. Ctr. on Philanthropy, 1991-93; exec. dir. Internat. Roller Skating Assn., Indpls., 1993—. Author: The Journals of William A. Lindsay, 1989; contbg. editor The Encyclopedia of Indianapolis, 1994; contbr. articles to profl. jours. Pres. Altrusa Internat. of Indpls., 1995—; bd. dirs. Nat. Mus. of Roller Skating, Lincoln, 1994—; bd. dirs. Ind. Soc. of Assn. Exec. Found., 1996—. Mem. Am. Soc. of Assn. Execs., Nat. Soc. of Fund Raising Execs. (cert.), Am. Mktg. Assn., Beta Gamma Sigma, Sigma Iota Epsilon, Phi Beta Kappa. Avocations: reading, walking, gourmet cooking, traveling. Office: Roller Skating Assn 7301 Georgetown Rd Ste 123 Indianapolis IN 46268-4157

MCDONELL, ROBERT TERRY, magazine editor, novelist; b. Norfolk, Va., Aug. 1, 1944; s. Robert Meinard and Irma Sophronia (Nelson) McD.; m. Joan Raffeld Hitzig, June 15, 1981; Robert Nicholas Campbell, Thomas Hunter Campbell. Student, U. Calif., Berkeley, 1962-63, San Jose State U., 1963-64; BA in Art, U. Calif., Irvine, 1967. With AP, N.Y.C., 1970-72; reporter Los Angeles Weekly, 1972-73; assoc. editor San Francisco mag., 1974-76, City mag., San Francisco, 1976-77; sr. editor San Francisco mag., 1977, Outside mag., San Francisco, 1978-79; founding editor Rocky Mountain mag., Denver, 1979-80; mng. editor Rolling Stone mag., N.Y.C., 1980-83; asst. mng. editor Newsweek Mag., N.Y.C., 1983-86; founder Smart mag., N.Y.C., 1986-90; editor-in-chief Esquire mag., N.Y.C., 1990-93; editor-in-chief, pub. Sports Afield Mag., N.Y.C., 1994—. Author: California Bloodstock, 1980, paperback edit., 1989; screenwriter: Miami Vice, China Beach. Office: Sports Afield 250 W 55th St New York NY 10019-5201*

MCDONNELL, ARCHIE JOSEPH, environmental engineer; b. N.Y.C., June 3, 1936; s. Patrick and Margaret (O'Reilly) McD.; m. Nancy Carol Schaeffer, June 18, 1966; children: Patrick, Sean. BS in Civil Engring., Manhattan Coll., 1958; MS in Civil Engring., Pa. State U., 1960; PhD in Civil Engring., 1963. Prof. Pa. State U., University Park, 1963-96; asst. dir. Water Resources Rsch. Ctr., Pa. State U., 1969-82; dir. Inst. for Rsch. on Land and Water Resources, Pa. State U., 1982-86, Environ. Resources Rsch.

Inst., Pa. State U., 1986—; bd. dirs. Pa. Environ. Coun., 1989-92, Nat. Assn. State Univs. & Land Grant Colls., 1990-92, chmn. water resources com., 1985-91; mem. rsch. & modeling subcom. EPA Chesapeake Bay Program, 1984-86, sci. & tech. adv. com., 1984—, exec. com., 1988-92; U.S. rep. Internat. Joint Commn., 1976-79, 87-89; mem. Pa. State Conservation Com., 1988-89, water resources policy adv. com. Pa. Dept. Environ. Resources, 1979-82, air & water quality tech. adv. com., 1983—, chmn. water quality subcom., 1986-88; chmn. Northeast Assn. Water Inst. Dirs., 1973-74; mem. exec. com. Nat. Assn. Water Inst. Dirs., 1975-78. Contbr. articles to profl. jours. Fellow U.S. Pub. Health Svc., 1961-62; recipient Commendation cert. Internat. Joint Commn., Conservationist of Yr. award Chesapeake Bay Found., Washington, 1986, Outstanding Rsch. award Pa. State U. Engring. Soc., 1988, Outstanding Profl. Rsch. award Water Pollution Control Assn. Pa., 1990, Karl M. Mason medal Pa. Assn. Environ. Profls., 1991, Gabriel Narutowicz medal Ministry Environ. Protection and Natural Resources, Poland, 1991. Mem. ASCE (chmn. 1972-73, exec. com. 1976-80, J. James R. Croes Rsch. medal 1976, Outstanding Svc. award 1981), Water Environ. Fedn. (co-chmn. 1991—), Fed. Water Pollution Control Fedn., Internat. Assn. Water Pollution Rsch., Am. Soc. Limnology and Oceanography, Chi Epsilon, Sigma Xi, Phi Kappa Phi. Achievements include demonstration of low cost treatment method for renovation of acidmine waters. Office: Pa State U 100 Land Water Research University Park PA 16802-4900

MCDONNELL, BARBARA, health facility administrator. B, Univ. Ill.; M, Univ. Iowa; JD magna cum laude, Univ. Pa. Law Sch. With Sherman & Howard, 1982-87; staff atty. Colo. Ct. Appeals, 1988-89; law clerk Phila.; legal adv. Gov. Romer, dep. dir. policy and rsch., 1989-90; exec. dir. Colo. Dept. Human Svcs., 1991—. Rep. Nursing Adv. bd., team leader Policy Acad. Team on Families & Children At Risk. Office: Dept Human Svcs 1575 Sherman St Denver CO 80203-1702

MCDONNELL, JOHN FINNEY, aerospace and aircraft manufacturing executive; b. Mar. 18, 1938; s. James Smith and Mary Elizabeth (Finney) McD.; m. Anne Marbury, June 16, 1961. BS in Aero. Engring., Princeton U., 1960, MS in Aero. Engring., 1962; postgrad. in bus. adminstrn., Washington U., St. Louis, 1962-66. Strength engr. McDonnell Aircraft Co. (subs. McDonnell Douglas Corp.), St. Louis, 1962, corp. analyst, 1963-65, contract coord., adminstr., 1965-68; asst. to v.p. fin. Douglas Aircraft Co. (subs. McDonnell Douglas Corp.), 1968; v.p. McDonnell Douglas Fin. Corp. (subs. McDonnell Douglas Corp.), 1968-71; staff v.p. fiscal McDonnell Douglas Corp., 1971-75, corp. v.p. fin. and devel., 1975-77, corp. exec. v.p., 1977-80, pres., 1980—, mem. exec. com., 1975—, chmn., 1988—, past CEO, also bd. dirs.; bd. dirs. Ralston Purina Co. Bd. commrs. St. Louis Sci. Ctr.; trustee KETC, Washington U., also chmn. nat. coun. faculty arts and scis. com. Office: McDonnell Douglas Corp PO Box 516 Saint Louis MO 63166-0516*

MCDONNELL, ROSEMARY CYNTHIA, social services administrator; b. Washington, July 31, 1969; d. Joseph Patrick and Judith Ann (Bruscino) McD. BS, Bradley U., Peoria, Ill., 1991; postgrad., Ill. Ctrl. Coll., 1993; psotgrad., DePaul U., Chgo., 1996—. Qualified mental retardation profl. Team leader Community Workshop and Tng. Ctr., Peoria, 1989-92; polit. sci. intern City of Peoria, 1991; undergrad. teaching asst. Bradley U., Peoria, 1991; family support coord. Tazewell County Resource Ctr., Pekin, Ill., 1992-93, early intervention asst., 1993-94; spl. populations programmer Pekin Pk. Dist. Recreation Office, 1994-96; rsch. asst. DePaul U., Chgo., 1996—. Asst. coach Spl. Olympics, Peoria, 1992. Olive B. White scholar Bradley U., 1990. Mem. NOW, Pi Gamma Mu, Phi Alpha Theta. Roman Catholic. Avocations: reading, weight lifting, basketball, history, travel. Home: 235 Indiana St Park Forest IL 60466

MC DONOUGH, GEORGE FRANCIS, JR., retired aerospace engineer, consultant; b. Chgo., July 3, 1928; s. George Francis and Minnie L. (Bartoli) McD.; m. Louise Guthrie, June 4, 1955; children: Michael Neil (dec.), Kathleen Louise, Thomas Charles, Daniel George. B.S., Marquette U., Milw., 1953; M.S., U. Ill., 1956, Ph.D., 1959. Asst. prof. U. Ill., 1959-60; assoc. prof. San Jose (Calif.) State Coll., 1960-61; sr. engr. E.H. Plesset Assos., Los Angeles, 1961-63; sr. scientist United Aircraft Corp., Los Angeles, 1963; with George C. Marshall Space Flight Center, NASA, Huntsville, Ala., 1963-95, dep. dir. data systems lab., 1974-78, dep. assoc. dir. engring., 1978-81, dir. systems dynamics lab., 1981-86, dir. structures and dynamics lab., 1986-88, dep. dir. for space systems, sci. and engring., 1988-89, dir. sci. and engr., 1989—; chmn. NASA Engring. Mgmt. Coun., 1993—; lectr. U. Ala., Huntsville, 1965—. Co-author: Wind Effects on Launch Vehicles, 1970. Chmn. Westbury Civic Assn., 1965-67; mem. Huntsville Air Pollution Control Bd., 1977—, vice-chmn., 1978-80, 87—, chmn., 1980-82, 85-87; mem. adv. coun. Coll. Engring., Marquette U., 1991—; mem. bd. visitors U. Ala., Birmingham, 1993—. With USNR, 1945-47, 51-52. Recipient Superior Performance award NASA, 1964, Superior Achievement award, 1966, Exceptional Svc. medal, 1973, Outstanding Leadership medal, 1982, 88, Group Achievement award, 1982, 84, 87-88, 92, Outstanding Performance rating, 1987-91, Profl. Achievement award Coll. Engring., Marquette U., 1991, Disting. Engring. Alumnus award Marquette U., 1994; named Presdl. Meritorious Exec., 1988, Presdl. Disting. Exec., 1992; dir.'s commendation George C. Marshall Space Flight Ctr., 1973. Mem. ASCE, AIAA, Whitesburg Yacht Club (chaplain 1988-90, fleet capt. 1990-94), Sigma Xi (pres. Huntsville 1972-74). Democrat. Roman Catholic. Home: 1902 Fairmont Rd SE Huntsville AL 35801-1443

MCDONOUGH, JAMES FRANCIS, civil engineer, educator; b. Boston, June 7, 1939; s. John Joseph and Blanche Cecelia (Murphy) McD.; m. Kathryn Ann Hilvert, Mar. 9, 1985; children by previous marriage: John, James, Jennifer. BS in Civil Engring., Northeastern U., 1962, MS in Civil Engring., 1964; PhD, U. Cin., 1968, MBA, 1981. Registered profl. engr., Ohio. Project engr. Fay, Spofford & Thorndike, Boston, 1962; teaching asst. Northeastern U., 1962-64; teaching asst. U. Cin., 1965, instr. civil engring., 1965-68, asst. prof., 1968-74, assoc. prof., 1974-78, William Thoms prof. civil engring., chmn. dept. civil and environ. engring., 1978-86, assoc. dean acad. affairs, 1986-95; interim dean Clermont Coll., 1996—; vis. prof. faculty engring. Kabul U., Afghanistan, 1969-71; vis. prof. N.C. State U., 1971. Contbr. articles to profl. jours. Pres. Greenhills Winton Sports Assn., 1981-83, treas., 1977-81. Recipient Teaching Excellence award U. Cin., 1973-75; Dow Chem. Outstanding Young Faculty award Am. Soc. for Engring. Edn., 1975; Outstanding Engring. Educator award Am. Soc. Engring. Edn.-Western Electric, 1977; Profl. Accomplishment award Acad.-Tech. and Sci. Council Cin., 1979. Fellow Am. Soc. Engring. Edn. (v.p. 1984-86, chmn. sect. 1982-83, v.p. membership affairs 1992—); mem. ASCE (zone sec. 1983, sect. pres. 1982), NSPE (chmn. Ohio state bd. registration for engrs. and surveyors 1987-90), Ohio Soc. Profl. Engrs., Tech. Socs. Coun. Clin. (Disting. Engr. of Yr. award 1993), ASEE (Centennial medal 1993, George Wadlin Disting. Svc. award 1993), NCEES (Profl. Accomplishment award 1993), Sigma Xi, Tau Beta Pi, Chi Epsilon, Beta Gamma Sigma. Home: 5304 Belfast Owensville Rd Batavia OH 45103-9637 Office: 4200 Clermont College Dr Batavia OH 45103-1748

MCDONOUGH, JOHN MICHAEL, lawyer; b. Evanston, Ill., Dec. 30, 1944; s. John Justin and Anne Elizabeth (O'Brien) McD.; m. Susan J. Moran, Sept. 19, 1982; children: John E., Catherine Anne. AB, Princeton U., 1966; LLB, Yale U., 1969. Bar: Ill. 1969, Fla. 1991. Assoc. Sidley & Austin, Chgo., 1969-75, ptnr., 1975—. Bd. dirs. Met. Planning Coun., 1978—, pres., 1982-84; bd. dirs. Ctr. Am. Archeology, 1980-85, chmn., 1982-84; bd. dirs. Leadership Greater Chgo., 1984-90, sec.-treas., 1987-90; bd. dis. Brian Rsch. Found., 1985—, pres., 1989-94. With JAGC, USAR, 1969-75. Mem. ABA, Ill. Bar Assn., Chgo. Bar Assn., Chgo. Club, Racquet Club, Saddle & Cycle Club, Commonwealth Club, Econ. Club, Phi Beta Kappa. Democrat. Episcopalian. Home: 1209 N Astor St Chicago IL 60610-2314 Office: Sidley & Austin 1 First Natl Plz Ste 4400 Chicago IL 60603-2003

MC DONOUGH, JOHN RICHARD, lawyer; b. St. Paul, May 16, 1919; s. John Richard and Gena (Olson) McD.; m. Margaret Poot, Sept. 10, 1944; children—Jana Margaret, John Jacobus. Student, U. Wash., 1937-40; LL.B., Columbia U., 1946. Bar: Calif. 1949. Asst. prof. law Stanford U., 1946-49, prof., 1952-69; asso. firm Brobeck, Phleger & Harrison, San Francisco, 1949-52; asst. dep. atty. gen. U.S. Dept. Justice, Washington, 1967-68; asso. dep. atty. gen. U.S. Dept. Justice, 1968-69; of counsel and ptnr. firm Keatinge & Sterling, L.A., 1969-70; ptnr. Ball, Hunt, Hart, Brown and Baerwitz, 1970-90, Calsmith Ball Wichman Case & Ichiki, L.A., 1990-96; of counsel Calsmith Ball Wichman Case & Ichiki, L.A., 1996—; exec. sec. Calif. Law Revision Commn., 1954-59, mem. commn., 1959-67, vice chmn., 1960-64, chmn., 1964-65; participant various continuing edn. programs. Served with U.S. Army, 1942-46. Mem. ABA, State Bar Calif., Am. Coll. Trial Lawyers. Democrat.

MCDONOUGH, JOSEPH CORBETT, former army officer, aviation consultant; b. N.Y.C., Sept. 30, 1924; s. Joseph Walter and Catherine Loretta (Corbett) McD.; m. Mary Patricia Aaron, June 10, 1945; children—Joseph Corbett, Thomas Michael, Robert Timothy. B.S., U.S. Mil. Acad., West Point, N.Y., 1945; M.A., Georgetown U., Washington, 1957; grad., U.S. Command and Gen. Staff Coll., 1954, Brit. Staff Coll., Camberly, 1958, U.S. Army War Coll., 1965. Commd. 2d lt. U.S. Army, 1945, advanced through grades to maj. gen., 1973, served in Philippine Scouts, 1945-47, served with 82d Airborne Div., 1948-51; served with 40th Inf. Div. U.S. Army, Korea, 1952-53; instr. U.S. Naval Acad., 1954-57; staff and command U.S. Army, Europe, 1958-61; with Office Personnel Mgmt., Dept. Army, Washington, 1961-64; mem. staff Office Under Sec. Army, Washington, 1965-67; bn. and brigade comdr. 1st Calvary Div. U.S. Army, Vietnam, 1967-68; with Joint Chiefs of Staff, Washington, 1968-71; brigade and asst. div. comdr. Vietnam, 1971-72; chief of staff CENTO, Turkey, 1972-73; comdg. gen. 8th Inf. Div. U.S. Army, Germany, 1973-75; U.S. Comdr. Berlin, 1975-78; ret. U.S. Army, 1978; cons. numerous govt. agys., 1978-79; v.p., gen. mgr. Butler Aviation, BWI Airport, Md., 1980-83; v.p. ops. Butler Aviation Internat., 1983-86; cons., 1986-88; exec. v.p. Butler Aviation Internat., 1988-90; cons., 1990—. Decorated D.S.M. with oak leaf cluster, Silver Star, Legion of Merit with oak leaf cluster, D.F.C., Bronze Star, Air medal with 32 oak leaf clusters, Army Commendation medal with 2 oak leaf clusters. Mem. Assn. U.S. Army, Army Aviation Assn. Address: 219 Greenbury Ct Annapolis MD 21401-6302

MCDONOUGH, JOSEPH RICHARD, lawyer; b. Newark, July 7, 1950; s. Richard Thomas and Catherine M. (Burns) McD.; m. Susan H. Fenske, Feb. 17, 1985. BA, Middlebury Coll., 1972; JD, Rutgers U., 1978. Bar: N.J. 1978, U.S. Ct. Appeals (3d cir.) 1983, U.S. Supreme Ct. 1985. Law sec. appellate div. N.J. Superior Ct., 1978-79; assoc. Carpenter, Bennett & Morrissey, Newark; now ptnr. Graham, Curtin & Sheridan, Morristown. Pres. Delbarton Sch. Alumni Assn., Morristown, N.J., 1986-89. Recipient Outstanding Achievement in Oral Advocacy award Internat. Acad. Trial Lawyers, 1978. Mem. ABA, N.J. State Bar Assn., Morris County Bar Assn. Office: Graham Curtin & Sheridan Four Headquarters Plz Morristown NJ 07960

MCDONOUGH, KENNETH LEE, disease management company executive; b. Buffalo, Apr. 7, 1953; s. Sidney Lee and Jeanne Francis (Sheets) McD.; children: Jameson, Laurel, Meghan; m. Connie Kay Staley; stepchildren: Audrey, Kelsie. BS, U. Minn., 1975, MD, 1979, MS, 1986. Diplomate Am. Bd. Quality Assurance and Utilization Rev. Physicians. Resident U. Calif., San Francisco, 1984; med. dir. Indsl. Health and Hygiene Group, Mpls., 1982-86; practice occupational medicine, 1985-92; v.p. Am. Gen. Ins., Dallas, 1986-88; v.p. Mut. of Omaha Ins., Omaha, 1988-91, sr. v.p., 1991-95; dir. med. svcs. Stuart Disease Mgmt. Svcs. Inc., Wilmington, Del., 1995-97; group dir., intervention skills Stuart Disease mgmt. Svcs. Inc., Wilmington, Del., 1997—; asst. clin. prof. dept. preventive medicine and pub. health Creighton U. Sch. Medicine, 1994—; instr. nursing Gustavus Adolphus Coll. Nursing, St. Paul, 1984-86; instr. astronomy Met. State U ., St. Paul, 1982-83; prin. rsch. into cost effectiveness of Dr. Dean Ornish's coronary reversal program in collaboration with Harvard Med. Sch., 1992-95. Author and designer of computer software. Instr. Sci. Mus. of Minn., St. Paul, 1982. Recipient Design Excellence award Seako, Inc., 1987, 3M Creativity award Minn. Mining & Mfg., 1971; recipient acad. scholarships. Mem. Am. Coll. Med. Quality, Am. Coll. Physician Execs., Am. Coll. Occupl. and Environ. Medicine, Am. Acad. Ins. Medicine, Nat. Assn. Managed Care Physicians, Gt. Plains Occupl. Medicine Assn. (nominating com. 1990-91), Am. Lung Assn. Nebr. (bd. dirs. 1995—), Disease Mgmt. Soc., Phi Kappa Phi. Avocations: genealogy, travel, astronomy, computer science, ancient history. Home: 126 Bromley Dr Wilmington DE 19808 Office: Stuart Disease Mgmt Svcs 2711 Centerville Rd Ste 100 Wilmington DE 19808-1643

MCDONOUGH, MAMIE, public relations executive; b. Plainfield, N.J., Mar. 24, 1952; d. Peter J. and Elizabeth (Driscoll) McD. BA, Elmira Coll., 1974; DFA (hon.), Pratt Inst., 1990. Protocol asst. U.S. Dept. State, Washington, 1974-75; staff asst. Office of U.S. V.P., Washington, 1975-77; dir. info. service Rep. Nat. Com., Washington, 1977-79; pres. Festive Occasions, Inc., Washington, 1979-81; staff asst. Office of Dep. Chief of Staff The White House, Washington, 1981-82; sr. ptnr. Britt-McDonough Assocs., Washington, 1982-86; prin. The McDonough Group, Washington and N.Y.C., 1986—; co-author, developer Student/Corp. Jr. Bd. Dirs. Program. Bd. dirs. Jr. League Washington, 1977-90; mem. fin. com. various Rep. congl. campaigns, 1979—. Roman Catholic. Office: 157 E 75th St New York NY 10021-3279

MCDONOUGH, PATRICK DENNIS, academic administrator; b. Virginia, Minn., Jan. 30, 1942; s. James Morris and Vivian S. McDonough; children: Jeffrey, Anne; m. Karen Howe, June 27, 1981. BA cum laude, Moorhead State U., 1964; MA, U. Kans., 1969; PhD, U. Minn., 1972. Asst. prof. theatre Emporia (Kans.) State U., 1966-70; dir. sales, mktg. Guthrie Theater, Mpls., 1971, 72; asst. prof. speech, dir. of forensics Moorhead (Minn.) State U., 1972-73; assoc. prof., mng. dir., chair Marshall Performing Arts Ctr. U. Minn., Duluth, 1973-76; dean fine arts, prof. U. Evansville (Ind.), 1976-81; vice chancellor, prof. U. Wis., Stevens Point, 1981-84; program dir. (edn. and leadership) W.K. Kellogg Found., Battle Creek, Mich., 1984-89; 15th pres., prof. theatre and mgmt. Marietta (Ohio) Coll., 1989-95, exec. dir. McDonough Ctr. for Leadership and Bus.; assoc. vice chancellor planning and analysis Calif. State U. Sys., Long Beach, 1995-97, prof. theatre, 1997—; pres. Emporia chpt. AAUP, 1969; cons. Lexington (Ky.) Children's Theatre, 1979; festival evaluator Am. Coll. Theatre Festival, 4 states, 1975, 76; mem. theatre panel Ind. Arts Commn., Indpls., 1977-79; mem. arts orgn. panel Mich. Arts Bd., Detroit, 1985-89; presenter workshops, conv. programs. Producer, dir. 100 plays and musicals, 1964-84; contbr. articles to profl. publs. Bd. visitors U. Wis., Stevens Point, 1988-90; dist. organizer Eugene McCarthy Presdl. Campaign, Emporia, 1968; mem. leadership commn. Am. Coun. Edn., 1989-94; mem. exec. com. Campus Compact, 1990-95; bd. dirs. numerous civic and arts orgns., 1973-90; chmn. govs. adv. com. on vol. svc., Ohio, 1990-93; mem. leadership studies project U. Md., 1994—. Recipient Disting. Alumnus award Moorhead State U., 1989; grantee Minn. Arts Bd., 1974-76, Ind. Arts Commn., 1976-79. Mem. Am. Assn. Higher Edn., Univ. and Coll. Theatre Assn. (v.p. 1982-83), Marietta Country Club, Stevens Point Country Club, Athletic Club of Columbus. Democrat. Episcopalian. Avocations: travel, international relations, arts. Office: Dept Theatre 1250 N Bellflower Blvd Long Beach CA 90840-0006

MCDONOUGH, PATRICK JOSEPH, JR., lawyer; b. Paterson, N.J., Sept. 13, 1941; s. Patrick Joseph and Margaret Mary (Bohan) McD.; m. Joanne Catherine Hansen, Dec. 26, 1966; children: Patrick Joseph III, Katherine Ann. BS, St. Joseph's U., Phila., 1964; AM, NYU, 1969; JD, Seton Hall Law Sch., Newark, 1976. Bar: N.J. 1978. Tchr. N.J. high schs., Elizabeth, N.J., 1964-69; dist. mgr. AT&T Hdqrs., N.Y.C., 1969-79; spl. asst. and mgr. external affairs, exec. dept., law dept. AT&T Hdqrs., Basking Ridge, N.J., 1981-90; mng. dir. internat. div. AT&T Hdqrs., Morristown, N.J., 1991-96; legis. asst. U.S. Senate, Washington, 1980-81; pvt. practice, 1996—; speaker in field. Author: Are Your Electronic Files Secure?, 1989; co-author: Guide to Prosecution of Telecommunication Fraud, 1989. Mem. exec. bd. Watchung (N.J.) Area Boy Scouts Am., 1985—; chair Utility Adv. Bd., Cranford, N.J., 1976-79; mem. Zoning Bd. Adjustment, Cranford, 1978-79; mem. Union County (N.J.) Com., 1977-79; pres. Cranford (N.J.) Rep. Club, 1977-78. NSF grantee, 1968. Mem. ABA (chmn. computer crime com. 1986—, coun. mem. sci. and tech. sect. 1992-95), N.J. Bar Assn., Summit (N.J.) Bar Assn., Comm. Fraud Control Assn. Home and Office: 93 Pine Grove Ave Summit NJ 07901-2436

MCDONOUGH, REGINALD MILTON, religious organization executive; b. Mt. Vernon, Tex., Aug. 16, 1936; s. J.C. McDonough and Gladys (White) Branch; m. Joan Bird, Aug. 28, 1956; children: Michael Keith, Teri Royce. BS, East Tex. Bapt. U., 1957; MRE, New Orleans Bapt. Theol. Sem., 1960, DEd, 1967; DD, U. Richmond, 1988. Ordained to ministry Bapt. Ch. Minister Bapt. Ch., Arcadia, La., 1959-60; instr. East Tex. Bapt. U., Marshall, 1960-61; minister edn. North End Bapt. Ch., Beaumont, Tex., 1961-64; cons. ch. adminstrn. Bapt. Sun. Sch. Bd., Nashville, 1964-65, supr. ch. adminstrn., 1965-78, dept. dir., 1978-80; exec. v.p. exec. com. So. Bapt. Conv., Nashville, 1981-86; exec. dir. Bapt. Gen. Assn. Va., Richmond, 1987—. Author: Working with Volunteer Leaders in the Church, 1976, Keys to Effective Motivation, 1979, A Church on Mission, 1980; editor monthly mag. Bapt. Program, 1981-86. Recipient Eagle Scout award Boy Scouts Am., 1951, Disting. Alumnus award, New Orleans Bapt. Theol. Sem., 1979, Disting. Achievement award East Tex. Bapt. U. Alumni Assn., 1984. Mem. Soc. Religious Orgns. Mgrs. Avocations: flying, skiing, golfing. Home: 12800 Knightcross Rd Midlothian VA 23113-9608 Office: Va Bapt Gen Bd PO Box 8568 Richmond VA 23226-0568

MC DONOUGH, RICHARD DOYLE, retired paper company executive; b. St. Stephen, N.B., Can., May 8, 1931; s. Kenneth Paul and Mary (Doyle) McD.; m. Caroline Wilkins, July 7, 1956; children: Elizabeth Wilkins, Richard David, Philip Bradford. AB, Dartmouth Coll., 1952. Mgmt. trainee Gen. Electric Co., Lynn, Mass., 1953-56; various fin. positions lamp div. Gen. Electric Co., Monterrey, Mex., 1956-59; controller Mexican subs. Gen. Electric Co., Mexico City, 1959-63; cost supr. Singer Co., N.Y.C., 1964; fin. dir. Singer Co., Clydebank, Scotland, 1965-66; controller Eur. div. Singer Co., London, 1967-69; v.p. ops. Home Furnishings Group, 1969; v.p., corp. contr. Singer Co., N.Y.C., 1970-73; corp. v.p., pres. mail order div. Singer Co., Hanau, Fed. Republic of Germany, 1973-76; v.p. Singer Co., London, 1976-79; sr. v.p., CFO, dir. Bowater Inc., Darien, Conn., 1979-92, vice chmn., CFO, 1992-93, vice chmn., 1993-94, ret., 1994; dir. Xylem Investments, Compensation Resources Group. Mem. Am. Forest and Paper Assn. (fin. com. 1980-94, steering com. 1987-94, vice chmn. 1989-91, chmn. 1991-93), Fin. Execs. Inst., Greenwich Country Club. Republican. Episcopalian. Avocations: scuba, opera. Home: Barons Mead E Point Ln Old Greenwich CT 06870-2403 Office: 25 E Point Ln Old Greenwich CT 06870-2403

MCDONOUGH, RUSSELL CHARLES, retired state supreme court justice; b. Glendive, Mont., Dec. 7, 1924; s. Roy James and Elsie Marie (Johnson) McD.; m. Dora Jean Bidwell, Mar. 17, 1946; children: Ann Remmich, Michael, Kay Jensen, Kevin, Daniel, Mary Garfield. JD, George Washington U., 1949. Bar: Mont. 1950. Pvt. practice Glendive, Mont., 1950-83; judge Gen. Jurisdiction State of Montana, Glendive, 1983-87; justice Mont. Supreme Ct., Helena, 1987-93, ret., 1993. City atty. City of Glendive, 1953-57; county atty. Dawson County, Mon., 1957-63; del. Mont. Constl. Conv., Helena, 1972. 1st lt. AC, U.S. Army, 1943-45, ETO. Decorated DFC. Mem. Mont. Bar Assn. Roman Catholic. Home: 1805 Joslyn St Trlr 131 Helena MT 59601-0113

MCDONOUGH, WILLIAM ANDREW, dean. Dean sch. architecture U. Va., Charlottesville. Office: U Va Dept Architecture 206 Campbell Hall Charlottesville VA 22902*

MCDONOUGH, WILLIAM J., banker; b. Chgo., 1934; married. BS, Coll. of Holy Cross, 1956; MA, Georgetown U., 1962. With Dept. of State, Uruguay, 1961-67; with 1st Nat. Bank of Chgo., 1967-89, asst. v.p. internat. banking dept., 1967-70; v.p., gen. mgr. 1st Nat. Bank of Chgo., Paris, 1970-72; area head, Europe, Middle East and Africa 1st Nat. Bank of Chgo., 1972-73, sr. v.p., head internat. banking dept., 1973-75, exec. v.p., 1975-86, CFO, 1982-89, chmn. asset and liability mgmt. com., until 1989; vice chmn. 1st Chgo. Corp. and 1st Nat. Bank Chgo., 1986-89; exec. v.p., head bank markets group Fed. Res. Bank of N.Y., N.Y.C., 1992-93, pres., CEO, 1993—; vice chmn. fed. open market com. Fed. Res. Sys.; bd dirs. Bank for Internat. Settlements. Bd. dirs. N.Y. Philharm. Orch. Mem. N.Y. Acad. Scis. (mem. coun. on fgn. rels., mem. bd. govs.), Econ. Club of N.Y. (chmn.). Office: Fed Res Bank of NY 33 Liberty St New York NY 10045-1003

MCDORMAND, FRANCES, actress; b. Ill., 1957. Student, Yale U. Sch. Drama. Stage appearances include Awake and Sing!, N.Y.C., 1984, Painting Churches, N.Y.C., 1984, The Three Sisters, Mpls., 1985, N.J., 1991, All My Sons, New Haven, 1986, A Streetcar Named Desire, N.Y.C., 1988, Moon for the Misbegotten, 1992, Sisters Rosensweig, N.Y.C., 1993, The Swan, N.Y.C., 1993; TV appearances include The Twilight Zone, The Equalizer, Spencer: For Hire, Hill Street Blues, (series) Legwork, 1986-87, (TV movies) Scandal Sheet, 1985, Vengeance: The Story of Tony Cimo, 1986, Crazy In Love, 1992; film appearances include Blood Simple, 1984, Crime Wave, 1986, Raising Arizona, 1987, Mississippi Burning, 1988, Chattahoochee, 1990, Darkman, 1990, Miller's Crossing, 1990, Hidden Agenda, 1990, The Butcher's Wife, 1991, Passed Away, 1992, Short Cuts, 1993, Beyond Rangoon, 1995, Fargo, 1996 (Academy award for Best Actress in a Leading Role, 1997), Lone Star, 1996, Paradise Road, 1997. Office: William Morris Agy 1325 Avenue Of The Americas New York NY 10019-6026*

MCDOUGAL, ALFRED LEROY, publishing executive; b. Evanston, Ill., Feb. 12, 1931; s. Alfred L. and Mary (Gillett) McD.; m. Gudrun Fenger, May 7, 1960 (div. 1982); children: Thomas, Stephen; m. Nancy A. Lauter, Mar. 1, 1986. BA, Yale U., 1953; MBA, Harvard U., 1957. Asst. to pres. Rand McNally & Co., Skokie, Ill., 1962-65, mgr. sch. dept., 1965-69; pres. McDougal, Littell & Co., Evanston, Ill., 1969-91, chmn., CEO, 1991-94; dir. Houghton Mifflin Co., Boston, 1994—; CEO Alm Corp., 1994—; chmn. McDougal Family Found.; gov. Yale U. Press, 1995—. Trustee Hadley Sch. for Blind, Winnetka, Ill., 1980-83; chmn. budget com. Evanston United Fund, 1974-76, bd. dirs.; bd. dirs. Evanston YMCA, 1988-94, Youth Job Ctr., 1987-93, chmn., 1989-91, Opportunity Internat., 1994—, Literacy Chgo., 1992—, treas., 1994-96. With U.S. Army, 1953-55. Mem. Assn. Am. Pubs. (exec. com. sch. divsn. 1981—, chmn. 1988-89, 92-94, dir. 1987-89), No. Ill. Assn. (1st v.p. 1984, chmn. 1985). Office: ALM Corp 400 N Michigan Ave Ste 300 Chicago IL 60611-4130

MCDOUGAL, STUART YEATMAN, comparative literature educator, author; b. L.A., Apr. 10, 1942; s. Murray and Marian (Yeatman) McD.; m. Menakka Weerasinghe, Apr. 29, 1967 (div. 1977); children—Dyanthe Rose, Gavin Rohan; m. Nora Gunneng, Aug. 4, 1979; children—Angus Gunneng, Tobias Yeatman. B.A., Haverford Coll., 1964; M.A., U. Pa., 1965, Ph.D., 1970. Lectr. U. Lausanne, Switzerland, 1965-66; asst. prof. Mich. State U., East Lansing, 1970-72; from asst. prof. to prof. English, comparative lit. and film /video U. Mich., Ann Arbor, 1972-85; dir. program in comparative lit. U. Mich., Ann Arbor, 1981-97, asst. to dean spl. projects, 1997—; vis. scholar Senapulli, Brazil, 1996. Author: Ezra Pound and the Troubadour Tradition, 1972 (Bredvold prize 1973), 2d edit. 1993; Made into Movies: From Literature to Film, 1985, 5th edit. 1994. Editor: Dante Among the Moderns, 1985; contbr. articles to profl. jours. Am. Council of Learned Socs. fellow, 1974-75; U. Mich. Rackham Research grantee, 1975-76; Fulbright Assn. sr. lectr., Italy, 1978; recipient Faculty Recognition award, U. Mich., 1987. Fellow Dirs. Guild Am. (summr workshop, 1993), Aegean Inst. Greece (vis. prof. film, 1994); mem. MLA, Am. Comparative Lit. Assn. (sec.-treas. 1983-89, v.p. 1989-91, pres. 1991-93), Internat. Comparative Lit. Assn., Soc. Cinema Studies. Democrat. Office: U Mich Program in Comparative Lit 2015 Tisch Hall Ann Arbor MI 48109

MCDOUGAL, WILLIAM SCOTT, urology educator; b. Grand Rapids, Mich., 1942; s. William Julian and Verna Wilma (Pasma) McD.; m. Mary Stuart Logan, Sept. 19, 1992; 1 child, Molly Katherine. AB, Dartmouth Coll., 1964; MD, Cornell U., 1968. Intern in surgery U. Hosps., Cleve., 1968-69, resident in surgery, 1969-75, attending urologist, 1977-80; postdoctoral fellow in physiology Yale U., New Haven, 1971-72; postdoctoral fellow in surgery Case-Western Res. U., Cleve., 1972-75; chief, burn study div. Inst. Surg. Rsch. Brook Army Med. Ctr., Ft. Sam Houston, 1975-77; instr. surgery U. Tex., San Antonio, 1975-77; asst. prof. urology Case Western Res. U., Cleve., 1977-78, assoc. prof., 1978-80; assoc. prof. Dartmouth Coll., Hanover, N.H., 1980-84, chmn. dept. urology, 1982-84; prof., chmn. dept. urology Vanderbilt U., Nashville, 1984-90; Walter S. Kerr Jr. prof. urology Harvard Med. Sch., 1991—; chief urology Mass. Gen. Hosp., Boston, 1991—. Office: Mass Gen Hosp Dept Urology Fruit St Boston MA 02114

MCDOUGALL, DONALD BLAKE, retired government official, librarian; b. Moose Jaw, Sask., Can., Mar. 6, 1938; s. Daniel Albert and Donela (McRae) McD.; m. Norma Rose Peacock, May 19, 1962. BA, U. Sask.,

1966, BEd, 1966; BLS, U. Toronto, 1969, MLS, U. Alta., 1983, cert. pub. adminstrn. U. Alta., 1990. Classroom tchr., Regina Bd. Edn., Sask., 1960-63, vice prin., 1963-68; asst. chief libr. Stratford Pub. Libr., Ont., Can., 1969, chief. libr., 1970-72; supr. info. svcs. Edmonton Pub. Libr., Alta., Can., 1972, head pub. svcs., 1973-74; legislature libr. Province of Alta., Edmonton, 1974-87; asst. dep. min., legis. libr. Legis. Assembly Alta., 1987-93, ret., 1993. Editor microfilm: Alberta Scrapbook Hansard, 1906-1964, 1976, editor Book: A History of the Legislature Library, 1979, Princess Louise Caroline Alberta, 1988, Canada's Parliamentary Libraries, 1989, Lieutenant-Governors of the Northwest Territories and Alberta, 1876-1991, 1991, Premiers of the Northwest Territories and Alberta, 1897-1991, 1991. Govt. Sask. scholar, 1965; recipient Queen's Silver Jubilee medal Govt. Can., 1977; named Hon. Clk.-At-The-Table, Legis. Assembly Alberta, 1987-93. Mem. Alta. Govt. Libraries Coun. (chmn. 1975), Assn. Parliamentary Librarians in Can. (pres. 1980-82), Edmonton Libr. Assn., Hist. Soc. Alta. (v.p. Edmonton chpt. 1987), Libr. Assn. Alta., Can. Libr. Assn., Beta Phi Mu. Presbyterian. Clubs: Edmonton Jaguar Drivers, Edmonton Scottish Soc. Home: 209 Rhatigan Rd W NW, Edmonton, AB Canada T6R 1A2

MC DOUGALL, DUGALD STEWART, retired lawyer; b. Indpls., May 15, 1916; s. George and Effie (Barclay) McD.; m. Carol Brueggeman, Aug. 1938; children: George, Duncan, Walter, Robert; m. Judith Stephen, Dec. 1967. A.B., U. Chgo., 1935, J.D., 1937. Bar: Ill. 1937. Since practiced in Chgo.; sr. ptnr. McDougall, Hersh & Scott, 1961-87; sec., dir. Aladdin Industries, Inc. Served with USNR, 1942-46. Fellow Am. Coll. Trial Lawyers; mem. ABA, Am. Patent Law Assn., Patent Law Assn. Chgo., Law Club Chgo., Union League (Chgo.). Clubs: Union League (Chgo.); Olympia Fields (Ill.) Country. Office: Theodore R Scott 77 W Wacker Dr Chicago IL 60601

MCDOUGALL, GERALD DUANE, lawyer; b. Hammond, Ind., Sept. 18, 1931; s. John and Carol Maxine (Lind) McD.; m. Ingrid Rosina Kempf, Jan. 26, 1960; children: Manfred, James. JD, Mercer U., 1971. Bar: U.S.V.I. 1972, Colo. 1973, Germany 1973, Tex. 1985. Atty. USVI Dept. Labor, St. Thomas, 1971-72; pvt. practice Denver, 1972-74, 76-84, Heilbronn, Neckar, Germany, 1974-76, Amarillo, Tex., 1985—. Precinct committeeman Rep. Ctrl. Com., Denver, 1978-84. Sgt. U.S. Army, 1951-54, ETO, 61-67, Vietnam. Mem. Nat. Assn. Criminal Defense Lawyers, Tex. Bar Assn., Tex. Criminal Defense Lawyers Assn., Amarillo Bar Assn. Home: 7910 Merchant Dr Amarillo TX 79121 Office: PO Box 50898 Amarillo TX 79159-0898

MCDOUGALL, IAIN ROSS, nuclear medicine educator; b. Glasgow, Scotland, Dec. 18, 1943; came to U.S., 1976; s. Archibald McDougall and Jean Cairns; m. Elizabeth Wilson, Sept. 6, 1968; children: Shona, Stewart. MB, ChB, U. Glasgow, 1967, PhD, 1973. Diplomate Am. Bd. Nuclear Medicine (chmn. 1985-87), Am. Bd. Internal Medicine (gov. 1984-86). Lectr. in medicine U. Glasgow, 1969-76; fellow Harkness-Stanford Med. Ctr., 1972-74; assoc. prof. radiology and medicine Stanford (Calif.) U., 1976-84, prof. radiology and medicine, 1985—. Contbr. numerous articles to sci. jours. Fellow Royal Coll. Physicians (Glasgow), Am. Coll. Physicians; mem. Am. Thyroid Assn., Soc. Nuclear Medicine, Western Assn. for Clin. Research. Office: Stanford U Med Ctr Divsn Nuclear Medicine Stanford CA 94305

MCDOUGALL, JOHN ROLAND, civil engineer; b. Edmonton, Alta., Can., Apr. 4, 1945; s. John Frederick and Phyllis Eirene (Sladden) McD.; m. Susan Carley, July 2, 1971 (div. 1995); children: John Christopher, Jordan Page, Michael Tait; m. Irene Makar, May 15, 1996. BSCE, U. Alta., Edmonton, 1967. Registered profl. engr., Alta. Engr. Imperial Oil Ltd., Calgary, Alta., 1967-69; sr. engr. Imperial Oil Ltd., Edmonton, Alta., 1969-75; treas. McDougall & Secord, Edmonton, 1969-85; v.p. McDougall & Secord, Ltd., 1975-90, pres., 1990—; pres., chief exec. officer Dalcor Cos., Edmonton, 1975-91; chmn. Trade Innoventures, Inc., 1992—; chair engring. mgmt. U. Alta., Edmonton, 1991—; chmn. D.B. Robinson & Assocs., Edmonton; bd. dirs. Edmonton Northlands; chmn. World Trade Centre, Edmonton, 1994—; mem. adv. bd. Royal Trust Corp., 1984-94. Chmn. Edmonton Civic Govt. Assn., 1975-77; mem. Premiers Coun. on Sci. and Tech., 1990. Fellow Can. Acad. Engrs. (bd. dirs. 1992—); mem. Can. Coun. Profl. Engrs. (pres. 1990-91), Assn. Profl. Engrs. Alta. (hon. life, pres. 1980-81), Can. Engring. Manpower Bd. (chmn. 1985-88), Edmonton C. of C. (pres. 1989), Loyal Edmonton Regiment (hon.), Edmonton Club (pres. 1983-84). Anglican. Avocations: skiing, travel, cycling, philately, railroad modeling. Office: U Alta, Faculty Engring, Edmonton, AB Canada T6G 2G8

MCDOUGALL, RONALD ALEXANDER, restaurant executive; b. Chgo., Aug. 12, 1942; s. John A. and Doris E. (Sengstock) McD.; m. Dale O. Ryser, Feb. 1, 1964 (div. July 1969); children: Timothy, Jonathan; m. Carolyn Kay Conley, Aug. 9, 1979; 1 child, Matthew. BBA, U. Wis., 1964, MBA, 1965. With Procter & Gamble, Cin., 1967-68, Sara Lee, Deerfield, Ill., 1969-72, The Pillsbury Co., Mpls., 1972-74, S&A Restaurant Corp., Dallas, 1974-82, Burger King, Miami, Fla., 1982-83; pres., CEO Brinker Internat., Dallas, 1983—; bd. dirs. Brinker Internat., Excel Comm., Inc. With U.S. Army, 1965-67. Mem. Nat. Restaurant Assn., Am. Mgmt. Assn., Bent Tree Country Club, Aerobics Activity Ctr., Employment Policies Inst. Republican. Presbyterian. Avocations: running, cycling, golf. Office: Brinker Internat 6820 Lyndon B Johnson Fwy Dallas TX 75240-6515

MC DOW, JOHN JETT, agricultural engineering educator; b. Covington, Tenn., Jan. 6, 1925; s. Robert Simpson and Lucy Ann (Cocke) McD.; m. Dorothy Virginia Glass, Dec. 22, 1946; children: Ronald Allan, Jane Virginia. Student, Franklin and Marshall Coll., 1944-45; B.S., U. Tenn., 1948; M.S., Mich. State U., 1949, Ph.D., 1957. Registered profl. engr., Tenn., La. Instr. Mich. State U., 1949; instr. Okla. State U., 1949-51, asst. prof. agrl. engring., 1951; assoc. prof. La. Poly. U., 1951-57, prof., 1957-62, head agrl. engring. dept., 1953-62; prof., head dept. agrl. engring. U. Tenn., Knoxville, 1962-73; dean admissions and records U. Tenn., 1973-83, prof. agrl. engring., 1983-92, prof. emeritus, 1992—; cons./collaborator Agrl. Research Service, U.S. Dept. Agr., 1970-76; leader Rotary Internat. Found. Group Study Exchange Team to Philippines, 1984; mem. scholarship selection com. N.Am. Philips Corp., 1976-88. Contbr. articles to profl. jours. Mem. La. Engring. Council, 1955-56; Bd. dirs. Tenn.-Venezuela-Amazonas Partners, 1977-80; vol. Internat. Centennial Olympic Summer Games, Atlanta, 1996. So. Fellowship grantee, 1957. Mem. Am. Soc. Agrl. Engring. (dir. 1973-75), Am. Soc. Engring. Edn. (sec. agrl. engring. div. 1971-72, vice chmn. 1972-73, chmn. 1973-74), Sigma Xi, Tau Beta Pi, Pi Mu Epsilon, Omicron Delta Kappa, Gamma Sigma Delta, Phi Kappa Phi (v.p. 1971-77, nat. pres. elect 1977-80, pres. 1980-83, pres. found. 1974-78). Lodge: Rotary (pres. 1989-90, chmn. dist. scholarship selection com., 1982-87, 88-91). Home: 2008 Walnut Hills Dr Knoxville TN 37920-2946

MCDOWELL, CHARLES EAGER, lawyer, retired military officer; b. Manchester, N.H., Sept. 9, 1923; s. Joseph Curry and Mildred (Eager) McD.; m. Carolyn A. Gibbons, June 21, 1947; children—Robin, Patricia. A.B., Dartmouth Coll., 1947; J.D., U. Va., 1950. Bar: Tex. 1950, Va. 1981, D.C. 1981. With land div. Shell Oil Co., Houston, 1950; commd. lt. (j.g.) USN, 1951, advanced through grades to rear adm., 1976; staff legal officer Comdr. Service Force, U.S. Pacific Fleet; staff judge adv., head internat. law div. Naval War Coll., 1963-66; staff legal officer, comdr. 7th Fleet, 1966-68; sr. Navy mem. ad hoc com., dep. asst. judge adv. gen. Office Judge Adv. Gen. Dept. Def., Washington, 1968-72; staff judge adv. on staff comdr. in chief U.S. Naval Forces, Europe, London, 1972-75; comdg. officer Naval Justice Sch., Newport, R.I., 1975-76; dep. judge adv. gen. Navy Dept., Washington, 1976-78, judge adv. gen., 1978-80; pvt. practice Dumfries, Va., 1981-96. Served to 2d lt. AUS, 1943-46. Decorated D.S.M., Bronze Star, Joint Service Commendation medal, Navy Commendation medal with Combat V, Purple Heart, Combat Inf. badge. Mem. FBA, Tex. Bar Assn., Va. Bar Assn., Judge Advs. Assn., Order of Coif, Chi Phi, Square Dancer Club. Methodist. Home: 1106 Croton Dr Alexandria VA 22308-2008

MCDOWELL, CHARLES R., columnist, news analyst, lecturer; b. Danville, Ky., June 24, 1926; m. Ann Webb, Apr. 26, 1952. BA, Washington & Lee U., 1948; MS in Journalism, Columbia U., 1949; LHD (hon.), Washington & Lee U., 1975; hon. degree, Centre Coll. With Richmond (Va.) Times-Dispatch, 1949-65, Washington corr., columnist, 1965—; panelist PBS Washington Week in Review, 1977—. Author: One Thing After Another, 1960, What Did You Have in Mind?, 1963, Campaign Fever, 1965; author: (with others) Beyond Reagan, 1986; writer, narrator (documentary) Summer of Judgment, 1983, 84; voices (TV series) The Civil War, 1990, Baseball, 1994; commentator weekly TV series The Lawmakers; contbr. articles to profl. jours. Past chmn. Standing Com. Corrs. Recipient Burkett Miller Presdl. award White-Burkett Miller Ctr. Pub. Affairs at U. Va., 1984, Fourth Estate award for lifetime achievement as a journalist, 1996; named to Soc. Profl. Journalists' Washington Hall of Fame, 1992. Mem. Gridiron Club (past pres.). Office: 1214 National Press Building Washington DC 20045-2200

MCDOWELL, DAVID JAMISON, clinical psychologist; b. Pitts., Jan. 11, 1947; s. David Emerson and Auleene Marley (Jamison) McD.; m. Nancy Annis, Jan. 13, 1973; children: Sasha, Christopher. BA, Princeton U., 1968; PhD, U. Maine, 1980. Predoctoral intern clin. psychology Worcester (Mass.) State Hosp., 1976-77, admissions officer, 1979-82; instr. dept. psychology Coll. Holy Cross, Worcester, 1977-78; lectr. dept. psychology and edn. Assumption Coll., Worcester, 1978-79; clin. dir. Milford (Mass.) Assistance Program, 1978-80; asst. prof. psychiatry and pediatrics U. Mass. Med. Ctr., Worcester, 1980-83; clin. dir. Newton-Wellesley-Weston-Needham (Mass.) Multi-Service Ctr., 1983-84; dir. Lancaster (Mass.) Assocs., 1987—; ptnr. Worcester County Counseling Assocs., Bolton, Mass., 1980-87; allied profl. staff St. Vincent Hosp., Worcester, 1985—; clin. cons. Mass. Dept. Youth Svcs., Worcester, 1986-87, 89-90, 94-95; assoc. med. dir. psychiat. disability claims Paul Revere Ins., Co., Worcester, Mass., 1996—; clin. cons. disability ins. industry and health ins. cos.; lectr. in field. Author: (with others) The Mental Health Industry, 1978; contbr. articles to profl. jours. Mental Health fellow U. Maine, 1973-75. Fellow Mass. Psychol. Assn. (legis. com. 1985-86); mem. APA, Soc. for Clin. and Exptl. Hypnosis. Avocations: running, music, reading. Office: Lancaster Assocs PO Box 175 Lancaster MA 01523-0175

MCDOWELL, DONNA SCHULTZ, lawyer; b. Cin., Apr. 23, 1946; d. Robert Joseph and Harriet (Parronchi) Schultz; m. Dennis Lon McDowell, June 20, 1970; children: Dawn Megan, Donnelly Lon. BA in English with honors, Brandeis U., 1968; MEd, Am. U., 1972; CASE with honors, Johns Hopkins U., 1979; JD with honors, U. Md., 1982, MS, Hood Coll., 1995. Bar: Md. 1982. Instr., Anne Arundel & Prince George's C.C., Severna Park and Largo, Md., 1977-78; coll. adminstr. Bowie State Coll. (Md.), 1978-79; assoc. Miller & Bortner, Lanham, Md., 1982-83; sole practice, Lanham, 1983-87; Gaithersburg, Md. 1987—; ednl. cons. Chmn. Housing Hearing Com., Bowie, 1981-83; trustee Unitarian-Universalitst Ch., Silver Spring, Md., 1979-83; bd. dirs. New Ventures, Bowie, 1983, Second Mile (Runaway House), Hyattsville, Md., 1983; officer Greater Laytonsville Civic Assn., 1989—; founding mem. People to Preserve, Laytonsville; mem. Solid Waste Adv. Com., Montgomery County, Md.; election judge. Recipient Am. Jurisprudence award U. Md., 1981. Mem. Montgomery County Bar Assn., Prince George's Bar Assn., Phi Kappa Phi. Democrat. Avocations: gardening, reading, bluebirds. Home: 24308 Hipsley Mill Rd Gaithersburg MD 20882-3132 Office: PO Box 5205 Laytonsville MD 20882-0205

MCDOWELL, EDWARD R. H., chemical engineer; b. Cleve., Aug. 13, 1932; s. Blake and Lois (Held) McD.; m. Joyce Patricia Dudley, June 18, 1955; children: Edward R. H. Jr., James D. BSChemE, Cornell U., 1955; MS, Calif. Inst. Tech., 1960, PhD, 1964. Registered profl. chem. engr., Calif. Instr. Cornell U., Ithaca, N.Y., 1955; assoc. rsch. engr. Calif. Rsch. Corp., El Segundo, 1955-59; instr. Calif. Inst. Tech., Pasadena, 1959-63; rsch. engr. Chevron Rsch. Corp., La Habra, Calif., 1963-66, sr. rsch. engr., 1966-68; sr. engring. assoc. Chevron Oil Field Rsch. Co., La Habra, 1968-74, mgr., 1974-86; gen. ptnr. C. Blake McDowell Ltd. Partnership, Akron, Ohio, 1986—. NSF fellow Calif. Inst. Tech., 1961-63; recipient Engring. Merit award Orange County Engring. Coun., 1985. Fellow Am. Inst. Chem. Engrs. (pres. 1989, v.p. 1988, dir. 1982-84, Civic Achievement award 1983, F.J. & Dorothy Van Anwepen award 1992), Inst. for Advancement of Engring.; mem. Soc. Petroleum Engrs., Am. Assn. Engring. Socs. (bd. govs.), King Harbor Yacht Club (commodore 1990, vice commodore 1989, rear commodore 1988), St. Francis Yacht Club (San Francisco), Transpacific Yacht Club (Long Beach, Calif.), Assn. Santa Monica Bay Yacht Clubs (commodore 1989, vice commodore 1988, rear commodore 1987), Nawiliwili Yacht Club (Lihue, Hawaii), Magic Castle Club, Manhattan Country Club, The Cornell Club (N.Y.C.). Avocations: offshore sailboat racing (winner ULDB70 Season Sailing Championship 1990, 92), magic. Home: 2510 The Strand Hermosa Beach CA 90254-2553

MCDOWELL, ELIZABETH MARY, retired pathology educator; b. Kew Gardens, Surrey, Eng., Mar. 30, 1940; came to U.S., 1971; d. Arthur and Peggy (Bryant) McD. B Vet. Medicine, Royal Vet. Coll., London, 1963; BA, Cambridge U., 1968, PhD, 1971. Gen. practice vet. medicine, 1964-66; Nuffield Found. tng. scholar Cambridge (Eng.) U., 1966-71; instr. dept. pathology U. Md., Balt., 1971-73, asst. prof., 1973-76, assoc. prof., 1976-80, prof., 1980-96, ret., 1996. Co-author: Biopsy Pathology of the Bronchi, 1987; editor: Lung Carcinomas, 1987; contbr. over 120 articles to sci. jours., chpts. to books. Rsch. grantee NIH, 1979-92. Fellow Royal Coll. Vet. Surgeons Gt. Britain and Ireland. Avocations: conservation education, gardening, swimming. Home: 606 W 37th St Baltimore MD 21211

MCDOWELL, EUGENE CHARLES, systems analyst, bioethicist; b. Washington, Jan. 13, 1940; s. Charles Jacob and Voilet Marie (Brown) McD.; m. Jill Perry Huntley, May 4, 1986 (dec. 1989); m. Hendrika Maria Ram, Mar. 21, 1992; step-daughter, Deepa Maria Long. BA, Am. U., 1962; MA, U. Chgo., 1966, 76; adv. cert. in Pub. Adminstrn., U.S. Dept. of Agr. Grad. Sch., 1973; grad. cert., Mastery U., 1995. Rsch. asst. ops. rsch. office Johns Hopkins U., Bethesda, Md., 1958-61; rsch. asst. Rsch. Analysis Corp., McLean, Va., 1961-66, ops. rsch. analyst, 1966-71; ops. rsch. analyst Nat. Bur. Standards, Gaithersburg, Md., 1971-80, mgmt. analyst, 1980-82; ops. rsch. analyst Nat. Oceanic and Atmospheric Adminstrn., Rockville, Md., 1982-87, computer systems analyst, 1987—; mem. bioethics com. and policy subcom. Washington Hosp. Ctr., Washington, 1996—; convenor Symposium on Legis. for Physician-Assisted Suicide, Bethesda, Md., 1996; mem. bioethics adv. pael Superior Ct. of D.C., 1997—. Student condr. Nat. Symphony Orch., Washington, 1960. Pres. Hemlock Soc. Nat. Capital Area, Washington, 1991-93, mem. bd. dirs., 1990-97, Nuclear Free Am., Balt., 1991-94, mem. bd. dirs., 1989—, Garrett Park (Md.) Citizens Assn., 1982-84; originator nuclear-free zone movement in U.S., Garrett Park, Md., 1982; auditor North Bethesda Congress of Citizens Assn., 1982-84; active U. Chgo. Profl. Achievement Award com., Washington, 1977—, chmn. 1982-84. Recipient Spl. Svc. citation Nat. Oceanic and Atmospheric Adminstrn., 1991, U.S. Dept. of Commerce Bronze medal, 1995, Govt. Computer News citation, 1995. Mem. Hemlock Soc. USA (life), AAAS (life), Philos. Soc. Washington (life, bd. dirs. 1996—), Azalea Soc. Am., Metropolitan Washington Bioethics Network (bd. dirs. 1996—), Standards Engring. Soc. (chmn. bd. govs. 1983-84, sr. 1982). Democrat. Unitarian. Avocations: gardening, reading. Home: PO Box 92 Garrett Park MD 20896-0092

MCDOWELL, FLETCHER HUGHES, physician, educator; b. Denver, Aug. 5, 1923; married. BA, Dartmouth Coll., 1943; MD, Cornell U., 1947. From instr. to prof. neurology Cornell U. Med. Coll., N.Y.C., 1968—, assoc. dean, 1970-95, Winifred Masterson Burke prof. rehab. medicine; pres. Winifred Masterson Burke Rsch. Inst., White Plains, 1992—. Mem. Am. Acad. Neurology, Am. Neurol. Assn., Am. Fedn. Clin. Research. Office: Burke Rehab Ctr 785 Mamaroneck Ave White Plains NY 10605-2523

MCDOWELL, JACK BURNS, professional baseball player; b. Van Nuys, Calif., Jan. 16, 1966. Grad., Stanford U. Baseball player Chgo. White Sox, 1987-88, 90-95, N.Y. Yankees, 1995, Cleve. Indians, 1996—. mem. Am. League All-Star Team, 1991-93; Sporting News All-Star Team, 1992, 93; Am. League Complete Games Leader, 1991-92; recipient Cy Young award Baseball Writers Assn. Am., 1993; named Sporting News Pitcher of Yr., 1993. Office: Cleveland Indians 2401 Ontario St Cleveland OH 44115-4003*

MCDOWELL, JENNIFER, sociologist, composer, playwright, publisher; b. Albuquerque; d. Willard A. and Margaret Frances (Garrison) McD.; m. Milton Loventhal, July 2, 1973. BA, U. Calif., 1957; MA, San Diego State U., 1958; postgrad., Sorbonne, Paris, 1959; MLS, U. Calif., 1963; PhD, U. Oreg., 1973. Tchr. English Abraham Lincoln High Sch., San Jose, Calif., 1960-61; free-lance editor Soviet field, Berkeley, Calif., 1961-63; rsch. asst. sociology U. Oreg., Eugene, 1964-66; editor, pub. Merlin Papers, San Jose, 1969—, Merlin Press, San Jose, 1973—; rsch. cons. sociology San Jose, 1973—; music pub. Lipstick and Toy Balloons Pub. Co., San Jose, 1978—; composer Paramount Pictures, 1982-88; tchr. writing workshops; poetry readings, 1969-73; co-producer radio show lit. and culture Sta. KALX, Berkeley, 1971-72. Author: (with Milton Loventhal) Black Politics: A Study and Annotated Bibliography of the Mississippi Freedom Democratic Party, 1971 (featured at Smithsonian Inst. Spl. Event 1992), Contemporary Women Poets, 1977, Ronnie Goose Rhymes for Grown-Ups, 1984; co-author: (plays off-off Broadway) Betsy and Phyllis, 1986, Mack the Knife Your Friendly Dentist, 1986, The Estrogen Party To End War, 1986, The Oatmeal Party Comes To Order, 1986, (plays) Betsy Meets the Wacky Iraqui, 1991, Bella and Phyllis, 1994; contbr. poems, plays, essays, articles, short stories, and book revs. to lit. mags., news mags. and anthologies; rschr. women's autobiog. writings, contemporary writing in poetry, Soviet studies, civil rights movement, and George Orwell, 1962—; writer: (songs) Money Makes a Woman Free, 1976, 3 songs featured in Parade of Am. Music; co-creator mus. comedy Russia's Secret Plot To Take Back Alaska, 1988. Recipient 8 awards Am. Song Festival, 1976-79, Bill Casey Award in Letters, 1980; doctoral fellow AAUW, 1971-73; grantee Calif. Arts Coun., 1976-77. Mem. Am. Sociol. Assn., Soc. Sci. Study of Religion, Poetry Orgn. for Women, Dramatists Guild, Phi Beta Kappa, Sigma Alpha Iota, Beta Phi Mu, Kappa Kappa Gamma. Democrat. Office: care Merlin Press PO Box 5602 San Jose CA 95150-5602

MC DOWELL, JOHN B., bishop; b. New Castle, Pa., July 17, 1921; s. Bernard A. and Louise M. (Hannon) McD. B.A., St. Vincent Coll., 1942, M.A., 1944; M.A., Catholic U. Am., 1950, Ph.D., 1952; Litt.D. (hon.), Duquesne U., 1962; grad., St. Vincent Sem., Latrobe, Pa. Ordained priest Roman Catholic Ch., 1945, consecrated as titular bishop of Tamazuca and aux. bishop of Pitts., 1966—; asst. pastor St. Irenaeus Ch., Oakmont, 1945-49; asst. supt. schs. Diocese of Pitts., 1952-55, supt. schs., 1955-70, vicar for edn., from 1970; now vicar gen.; pastor Epiphany Parish, Pitts., 1969—; ret., 1996; papal chamberlain to Pope Pius XII, 1956, to Pope John XXIII, 1958; domestic prelate to Pope Paul VI, 1964; chmn. ad hoc com. on moral values in our soc. Nat. Conf. Cath. Bishops, from 1973, Bishops Com. for Pastoral on Moral Values, from 1976; mem. Internat. Council for Catechesis, from 1975. Co-author elem. sch. religions series, jr. high sch. lit. series, elem. sci. series and elem. reading series; contbr. ednl. articles to various publs.; former editor: Cath. Educator Mag. Bd. dirs. Western Pa. Safety Council, Duquesne U. Named Man of Yr. in Religion Pitts., 1970, 93, Educator of Yr., United Pvt. Acad. Schs. Assn., 1978, Man of Yr., Pitts. chpt. KC, 1989. Mem. Nat. Cath. Ednl. Assn., Cath. Ednl. Assn. Pa., Omicron Delta Kappa Gamma Circle (hon.). Office: 1817 Redcoach Rd Allison Park PA 15101-3226 also: Chancery Office 111 Blvd Of The Allies Pittsburgh PA 15222-1618

MCDOWELL, JOHN EUGENE, lawyer; b. Toledo, Nov. 22, 1927; s. Glenn Hugh and Evelyn (Millspaugh) McD.; m. Jean Ann Hepler, June 18, 1950; children: Jane Lynn McDowell Thummel, Sheila Lorraine McDowell Laing. BS, Miami U., Oxford, Ohio, 1949; JD, U. Mich., 1952. Bar: Ohio 1952. Assoc. Dinsmore & Shohl, Cin., 1952-59, ptnr., 1959—; bd. dirs. Structural Dynamics Rsch. Corp., Milford, Ohio. Mem. solicitation coms. United Appeal, Cin., NCCJ, Cin., Boy Scouts Am., Cin. Mem. ABA, Ohio Bar Assn., Cin. Bar Assn., Cin. Country Club, Queen City Club, Order of Coif. Democrat. Episcopalian. Office: Dinsmore & Shohl 1900 Chemed Ctr 255 E 5th St Cincinnati OH 45202-4700

MCDOWELL, MALCOLM, actor; b. Leeds, Eng., June 13, 1943; m. Mary Steenburgen, 1980 (div.); 2 children; m. Kelley Kuhr, 1991. Began career with: Royal Shakespeare Co., Stratford, Eng., 1965-66; early TV appearances include: role of Dixon of Dock Green in Z Cars, British TV; other TV appearances: Little Red Riding Hood, Faerie Tale Theatre, Showtime TV, 1983, Gulag, HBO, 1985; stage appearance: Look Back in Anger, N.Y. Stage, 1980, In Celebration, N.Y.C., 1984, Hunting Cockroaches, L.A. Stage, 1987, Another Time - Stage, 1993; films include: Poor Cow, 1967, If..., 1969, Figures in a Landscape, 1970, The Raging Moon, 1971, A Clockwork Orange, 1971, O Lucky Man, 1973, Royal Flash, 1975, Aces High, 1976, Voyage of the Damned, 1977, Caligula, 1977, The Passage, 1978, Time After Time, 1979, Cat People, 1981, Britannia Hospital, 1984, Blue Thunder, 1983, Get Crazy, 1983, Cross Creek, 1983, Sunset, 1987, Buy and Cell, 1989, Class of 1999, 1989, Assassin of the Tsar, 1990, Bopha!, 1993, Milk Money, 1994, The Caller, Star Trek: Generations, 1994, Tank Girl, 1995, (TV) Pearl, 1996-97, Hugo Pool, 1996.

MCDOWELL, MICHAEL DAVID, lawyer, utility executive; b. Lewisburg, Pa., May 10, 1948; s. David Leonard and Mary Ellen (Scallan) McD.; m. Martha LaMantia, Aug. 4, 1973; 1 child, Daniel Joseph. B.S. in Bus. Mgmt., U. Dayton, 1970; J.D., U. Pitts., 1973. Bar: Pa. 1973, U.S. Ct. Appeals (3d cir.) 1974, U.S. Dist. Ct. (we. dist.) Pa. 1975, U.S. Supreme Ct. 1977. Asst. U.S. atty. Dept. Justice, Lewisburg, Pa., 1973-75; assoc. Hirsch, Weise & Tillman, Pitts., 1975-76, Plowman & Spiegel, Pitts., 1976-80; counsel Dravo Corp., Pitts., 1980-86, sr. counsel, 1987; atty. West Penn Power Co., Greensburg, Pa., 1987—; mem. panel of arbitrators Am. Arbitration Assn., 1978-94, Pa. Bur. Mediation, 1983—, Pa. Labor Relations Bd., 1985—. Contbr. articles to profl. jours. Mem. nat. panel consumer arbitrators Better Bus. Bur., 1986—; sr. arbitrator, 1989—. Recipient Dravo Corp. Editorial Achievement awards, 1982, 83, 85, 86; nominated as one of Outstanding Young Men. Am., 1983,84. Fellow Am. Bar Found., Pa. Bar Found.; mem. ABA (Ho. of Dels. 1985-91, exec. coun. sect. labor and employment law 1983-85, exec. council young lawyers div. 1982-84, chmn. YLD Labor Law Com. 1981-83, fellow, 1985—), Pa. Bar Assn. (Ho. of Dels. 1980-94, chmn. special rules subcom. Disciplinary Bd. Study Com. 1983-93, com. on legal ethics and profl. responsibility, 1983—, arbitrator lawyer dispute resolution program 1987—, house com. on rules and calendar 1991-94, Outstanding Young Lawyer award 1984, Spl. Achievement award 1986,), Allegheny County Bar Assn. (profl. ethics com. 1980-94, bd. govs. 1979, 85-91, asst. sec.-treas. 1979, chmn. young lawyers sect. 1978, council professionalism 1988-90, by-laws com. 1990—, award for outstanding leadership and valuable contbns. to bar 1979), Am. Corp. Counsel Assn., Phi Alpha Delta (justice 1972-73, cert. Outstanding Service 1973). Republican. Roman Catholic. Office: West Penn Power Co 800 Cabin Hill Dr Greensburg PA 15601-1650

MCDOWELL, SHERRIE LORRAINE, secondary education educator; b. Manchester, Ky., Apr. 20, 1948; d. Alonzo and Madge Loudean (Christensen) Garrison; m. Gary Lynn McDowell, July 11, 1970; 1 child, Marc Ryan. BA, U. No. Colo., 1970; MA, Lesley Coll., 1989; postgrad., U. Wyo. Cert. tchr., Wyo. Tchr. English St. Mary's Cath. Sch., Cheyenne, Wyo., 1971-72; instr. homebound program Laramie County Sch. Dist., Cheyenne, 1978-84; English instr. Cen. High Sch., Cheyenne, 1984—; Wyo. coach Nat. Tournament of Acad. Excellence, 1988-90; recorder NCTE Conv., Boston, 1996. Mem. NEA (Assembly rep. 1993-96, cadre trainer state level women's leadership tng. program 1995—), AAUW (sec. 1975-77), Wyo. Edn. Assn. (co-chair profl. standards and practices commn. 1995—, chair summer Inst. 1996—), Nat. Coun. Tchrs. English (recorder Boston Conv. 1996), Cheyenne Tchrs. Edn. Assn. (edn. assn. del. 1992—, chair instrnl. issues 1995, co-chair pub. rels. 1988-90, editor ACCENTS 1988-90, sec. 1995—), Wyo. Assn. Tchrs. English (presenter), Wyo. Chautauqua Soc. (pres. 1985-86, bd. dirs. 1984-85), Delta Kappa Gamma (state scholarship chair 1989-90, pres. chpt. 1988-90). Home: 100 Grandview Ct Cheyenne WY 82009-4912 Office: Ctrl High Sch 5500 Education Dr Cheyenne WY 82009-4008

MCDUFFIE, FREDERIC CLEMENT, physician; b. Lawrence, Mass., Apr. 27, 1924; m. Isabel Simpson Wiggin, May 31, 1952; children: Elisabeth Wiggin, Joan Selden, Deborah Howard, Charles Dennett. Grad., Harvard U., M.D. cum laude, 1951. Diplomate Am. Bd. Internal Medicine and Subbd. Rheumatology. Intern Peter Bent Brigham Hosp., Boston, 1951-52; resident Peter Bent Brigham Hosp., 1952-53, 56-57; tng. in phys. chemistry Harvard U., 1953-54; in immunology Columbia Coll. Physicians and Surgeons, 1954-56; asst. prof. internal medicine U. Miss., Jackson, 1957-62; asst. prof. microbiology U. Miss., 1957-64, assoc. prof., 1964-65; cons. medicine and microbiology Mayo Clinic and Mayo Found., Rochester, Minn., 1965; asst. prof. internal medicine and microbiology Mayo Grad. Sch. Medicine, 1965-69, asso. prof., 1969-73; asso. prof. Mayo Med. Sch., 1973, prof. internal medicine and immunology, 1974-79; prof. medicine Emory U., Atlanta, 1979—; vis. investigator Center for Disease Control, Atlanta, 1979-

88; sr. v.p. med. affairs Arthritis Found., Atlanta, 1979-87; dir. Piedmont Hosp. Arthritis Ctr., 1988—; pres. Miss. chpt. Arthritis Found., 1962-63; bd. dirs., mem. exec. com. Miss. chpt. Arthritis Found. (Minn. chpt.), 1974-79, chmn. med. and sci. com., 1975-79, nat. trustee, 1978-79, chmn. nat. research com., 1978-79; trustee Nat. Health Coun., 1984—. Editorial bd. Arthritis and Rheumatism, 1976-81, Jour. Rheumatology, 1974—; editor Jour. Lab. and Clin. Medicine, 1977-79; contbr. articles to profl. jours. Served with U.S. Army, 1943-45. Mem. Am. Assn. Immunologists, Am. Rheumatism Assn., Central Rheumatism Assn. (pres. 1973-74), Central Soc. Clin. Research (council 1977-79), Soc. Exptl. Biology and Medicine, Am. Fedn. Clin. Research, A.C.P., Alpha Omega Alpha. Home: 2025 Peachtree Rd NE Atlanta GA 30309 Office: Ste 205 2001 Peachtree Rd NE Atlanta GA 30309-1476

MCDUFFIE, KEITH A., literature educator, magazine director; b. Spokane, Wash., Feb. 12, 1932; s. Clair L. and Helen Marie (Yaeger) McD.; m. Helen E. Ferry, June 5, 1965 (div. July 1995); children: Anne Leslie, Andrew Keith; m. Pamela Philips Bacarisse, Aug. 10, 1995 (dec. Mar. 1996). BA in English, Gonzaga U., Spokane, 1954; MA in Spanish, Middlebury (Vt.) Coll., 1960, Univ. Complutense, Madrid, Spain, 1960; PhD in Hispanic Lit., U. Pitts., 1969. Prof. U. Mont., 1969-74; Mellon postdoctoral fellow U. Pitts., 1974, prof., chair dept. Hispanic lit., 1975-92, prof. Hispanic lit., 1975—; editor Revista Iberoamericana, Pitts., 1991-96; pres. Univ. Senate, 1995-97. Co-author: Co-Textes: Cesar Vallejo, 1987; co-editor: Texto y Contexto-Actas 19 Congreso del IILI, 1980, En Este Aire de America: Homenaje a Alfredo Roggiano, 1990. With U.S. Army Security Agy., 1954-56. Mellon Predoctoral fellow U. Pitts., 1965, Title VI fellow U.S. Govt., 1966; Spanish Govt. scholar Spanish Govt., 1959-60. Mem. Instituto Internacional de Literatura Iberoamericana (contbg., bd. dirs. 1991-96, exec. dir. 1991-96). Democrat. Home: 220 N Dithridge St Apt 1001 Pittsburgh PA 15213-1425

MC DUFFIE, MALCOLM, oil company executive; b. San Francisco, Nov. 14, 1915; s. William Chester and Mary (Skaife) McD.; m. Mary Sutherland de Surville, Dec. 8, 1951; children: Cynthia de Surville, Duncan de Surville. A.B. in Econs, Stanford U., 1940. With O.C. Field Gasoline Corp., 1940-41, Wilmington Gasoline Corp., 1941-42; with Mohawk Petroleum Corp., 1945-80, pres., dir., 1969-80; dir. Res. Oil & Gas Co., 1973-80, sr. v.p., 1977-80; sp. asst. to pres. Getty Oil Co., Los Angeles, 1980-82. Bd. overseers Huntington Library, Art Gallery and Bot. Gardens, 1972—; bd. dirs. Calif. Inst. Tech. Assos., 1976-82. Mem. Nat. Petroleum Refiners Assn. (Dir. 1970-80), Ind. Refiners Assn. Calif. (pres. 1967-69, 77-78, dir. 1950-80), Rancheros Visitadores. Republican. Episcopalian. Clubs: California (Los Angeles); Bohemian (San Francisco); Valley Hunt (Pasadena, Calif.), Annandale Golf (Pasadena, Calif.); Birnam Wood (Santa Barbara, Calif.), Valley (Montecito, Calif.). Office: 180 S Lake Ave Ste 315 Pasadena CA 91101-2668

MCDUFFIE, MARCIA JENSEN, pediatrics educator, researcher; b. Phila., Apr. 10, 1949; d. John Calvin and Agnes Margaret (Jakob) J.; children: Kathryn Steere, Joanna Steere, Michael. Student, Duke U., 1967-69; BA cum laude with honors in Biochemistry, U. Pa., 1971; MD with honors, U. N.C., 1981. Diplomate Am. Bd. Pediat. Pediat. intern U. Colo. Health Scis. Ctr., Denver, 1981-82, resident in pediat., 1982-84, asst. prof., 1987-93, rsch. mem. Barbara Davis Ctr. for Childhood Diabetes, 1989-93; postdoctoral fellow div. basic immunology dept. medicine Nat. Jewish Ctr. for Immunology and Respiratory Medicine, Denver, 1984-87; assoc. prof. U. Va. Health Scis. Ctr., Charlottesville, 1993—. Assoc. editor Jour. Immunology, 1992-94; mem. editl. bd. Diabetes, 1995—; contbr. articles to profl. jours. Recipient career devel. award Juvenile Diabetes Found., 1992-95; rsch. grantee Juvenile Diabetes Found., 1991-95, 96—, Am. Diabetes Assn., 1994—, NIH, 1996—. Mem. Soc. for Pediatric Rsch., Am. Assn. Immunologists. Office: U Va Health Scis Ctr MR-4 Rm 5116 Charlottesville VA 22908

MCEACHEN, RICHARD EDWARD, banker, lawyer; b. Omaha, Sept. 24, 1933; s. Howard D. and Ada Carolyn Helen (Baumann) McE.; m. Judith Ann Gray, June 28, 1969; children: Mark E., Neil H. BS, U. Kans., Lawrence, 1955; JD, U. Mich., 1961. Bar: Mo. 1961, Kans. 1982. Assoc. Hillix, Hall, Hasburgh, Brown & Hoffhaus, Kansas City, Mo., 1961-62; sr. v.p. First Nat. Bank, Kansas City, Mo., 1962-75; exec. v.p. Commerce Bank Kansas City, Mo., 1975-85, Centerre Bank of Kansas City N.A., 1985-87, Security Bank Kansas City, Kans., 1987-88; exec. v.p., trust officer UMB Overland Park Bank, 1988-93; atty. Ferree, Bunn & O'Grady, Chartered, Overland Park, 1994—. Gov. Am. Royal Assn., Kansas City, Mo., 1970—, amb., 1980—, com. mem., 1995—; bd. dirs. Harry S. Truman Med. Ctr., Kansas City, 1974-86, mem. fin. com., 1975-86, treas., 1979-84, bd. govs., 1986—, mem. bldg. and grounds com., 1993—, mem. pension com., 1976-93, 96—; trustee Clearinghouse for Midcontinent Founds., 1980-87; bd. dirs. Greater Kansas City Mental Health Found., 1963-69, treas., 1964-69, v.p., 1967-69; adv. bd. urban svcs. YMCA, Kansas City, 1976-83; cubmaster Kanza dist. Boy Scouts Am., 1982-83, dist. vice chmn., 1982-83, troop com., 1983-90, treas., 1986-88; bd. dirs. Scout Booster Club, Inc., 1989-94; mem. planned gift com. William Rockhill Nelson Gallery Art, Children's Mercy Hosp. Planned Gift Coun., 1991; mem. adv. com. Legal Assistance Program Avila Coll., 1978-80, adv. coun. Future Farmers Am., 1972-82; mgr. Oppenstein Bros. Found., 1979-85; trustee Village Presbyn. Ch., 1987-90, chmn., 1989-90, elder, 1994-97; bd. dirs. Village Presbyn. Ch. Found., 1987-89, 94-97, chmn., 1996-97, mem. adv. bd., 1997—; bd. dirs. Estate Planning Coun., 1984-86; bd. dirs. Shawnee Mission Med. Ctr. Found., 1988—, fin. com., 1989-92, mem. planned giving com., 1996—. Mem. Nat. Assn. Securities Dealers Inc. (bd. arbitrators), Am. Arbitration Assn. (panel arbitrators), Estate Planning Soc. Kansas City, Mo. Bar Assn., Kans. Bar Assn., Johnson County Bar Assn., Kansas City Met. Bar Assn., Estate Planning Assn. (pres. 1974-75), Kansas City Jr. C. of C. (v.p. 1964-66), Lawyers Assn. Kansas City, Ea. Kans. Estate Planning Coun., Indian Hills Club, Delta Tau Delta Alumni (v.p. Kansas City chpt. 1978-80). Republican. Home: 9100 El Monte St Shawnee Mission KS 66207-2627 Office: One Glenwood Pl 9300 Metcalf Ave Ste 300 Shawnee Mission KS 66212-6319

MCEACHERN, ALEXANDER, electronics company executive; b. Boston, Feb. 18, 1955; s. Alexander William and Elisabeth Helena McEachern; m. Barbara Ruth Pereira, Dec. 18, 1975; children: Alexander Wallis, Ian Wallis. V.p. Mac Systems, 1975-79; dir. R&D Lomac Corp., Santa Clara, Calif., 1979-80; chmn., founder Basic Measuring Instruments, Santa Clara, 1981—; pres. Electrotek Concepts, Inc., 1996—. Author: Handbook of Power Signatures; contbr. articles to profl. jours. Mem. IEEE (sr.). Office: Electrotek Concepts 3250 Jay St Santa Clara CA 95054-3309

MCEACHERN, ALLAN, Canadian justice; b. Vancouver, B.C., Can., May 20, 1926; s. John A. and Blanche L. (Roadhouse) McE.; m. Gloria, July 17, 1953; children: Jean Williams, Joanne Evans. BA, U. B.C., Vancouver, 1949; LLB, U. B.C., 1950. Assoc., sr. ptnr., barrister, solicitor Messrs. Russell & DuMoulin, Vancouver, B.C., 1950-78; chief justice Supreme Ct. B.C., Vancouver, 1979-88, Ct. Appeals B.C., Vancouver, 1988—. Pres. Kats Rugby Club, Vancouver, 1953-64, B.C. Lions Football Club, Vancouver, 1967, 68. 69, We. Football Conf., 1964, Can. Football League, 1967-68, commr. 1967-68. Mem. Can. Bar Assn. (bd. dirs.), Vancouver Bar Assn. (bd. dirs.), Legal Aid Soc. (pres. 1977-78), Law Soc. B.C. (bencher 1971-79). Avocations: sailing, gardening, walking, summer cottage. Home: 1414 W King Edward Ave, Vancouver, BC Canada V6H 2A2 Office: Law Cts, 800 Smithe St, Vancouver, BC Canada V6Z 2E1*

MCEACHRAN, ANGUS, newspaper editor; b. Memphis, Aug. 24, 1939; s. Angus G. and Maxine (Taylor) McE.; m. Ann Blackwell; children: Angus G. 111, Amanda Simmons. Student, George Washington U., 1958-59, Memphis State U., 1959-61. Reporter The Comml. Appeal, Memphis, 1960-63, asst. city editor, 1963-65, metro editor, 1965-69, asst. mng. editor, 1969-77; exec. editor Birmingham (Ala.) Post-Herald, 1977-78, editor, 1978-82; exec. editor The Pitts. Press., 1982-83, editor, 1983-92; editor The Commercial Appeal, Memphis, Tenn., 1993-94, editor, pres., 1994—; corr. N.Y. Times, Wall St. Jour., Newsweek, The Nat. Observer. Mem. Am. Soc. Newspaper Editors, Pa. Soc. Newspaper Editors (bd. dirs.), Sigma Delta. Roman Catholic. Avocations: fishing, hiking, reading, racquetball. Home: 872 River Park Dr Memphis TN 38103-0804 Office: Commercial Appeal 495 Union Ave Memphis TN 38103-3242*

MCEACHRON, DONALD LYNN, biology educator, researcher; b. Erie, Pa., Nov. 8, 1953; s. Karl Boyer and Marjorie (Blalock) McE.; m. Barbara Anne O'Donnell, Aug. 14, 1987; 1 child, Christopher Karl. BA with highest honors, U. Calif., 1977, PhD, 1984. Lab. technician psychiatry VA Med. Ctr., La Jolla, Calif., 1978-82; rsch. technician cell biology U. Tex. Health Sci. Ctr., Dallas, 1983-84; sci. dir. Imaging and Computer Vision Ctr. Drexel U., Phila., 1984-88, vis. asst. prof. dept. biosci., 1986-88, rsch. asst. prof. Biomed. Engrng. and Sci. Inst., 1989-92, rsch. assoc. prof., 1992—, program dir. Enhanced Edn. in Sci. and Engrng., 1994—, acting assoc. dir. Biomed. Engrng. and Sci. Inst., 1995-96, assoc. dir. Biomed. Engrng. and Sci. Inst., 1996-97, assoc. dir. sch. biomed. engrng. sci. and health sys., 1997—, program dir. enhanced edn. sci. engrng., 1994—, assoc. dir.sch. biomed. engrng., sci., health sys., 1997—; cons. Hoffman-LaRoche, Nutley, N.J., 1984-86; mem. adv. bd. BioAutomation, Inc., Bridgeport, Pa., 1988—; project dir. NSF Young Scholar's Project/Drexel U., Phila., 1994—; lectr. U. Pa., Phila., 1986-93, adj. asst. prof. dept. psychiatry, 1993—; vis. asst. prof. dept. psychology Haverford (Pa.) Coll., 1987; adj. asst. prof. Thomas Jefferson U., Phila., 1989—. Editor: Functional Mapping in Biology and Medicine, 1986; contbg. editor Diversity in Biomed. Imaging, 1989, Progress in Imaging in the Neurosciences using Microcomputers and Workstations, 1990; mem. editl. bd. Computerized Med. Imaging and Graphics, 1988—, NeuroImage, 1990. 1st lt. USAR, 1993, capt., 1993—. Regent's fellow U. Calif., 1979. Fellow Internat. Behavioral Neurosci. Soc.; mem. AAAS, Internat. Soc. Chronobiology, N.Y. Acad. Sci., Animal Behavior Soc., Soc. Rsch. on Biol. Rhythms. Republican. Avocations: Am. history, photography. Office: Drexel U Commonwealth Bldg Rm 721 Philadelphia PA 19104

MCELDOWNEY, RENE, health care educator, consultant; b. Denver, Mar. 31, 1956; d. Raymond James and Barbara Louise (McNeal) Polanis; m. George Adams McEldowney Jr., June 1, 1984. AB, Morris Harvey Coll., Charleston, W.Va., 1977; BS, W.Va. State Coll., 1983; MBA, Marshall U., 1987; PhD, Va. Tech. U., 1994. X-ray technologist Charleston Area Med. Ctr., 1977-79, nuc. medicine technologist, 1979-84; asst. to v.p. acad. affairs Marshall U., Huntington, W.Va., 1984-87, mgmt. instr., 1987-89; asst. prof. Auburn (Ala.) U., 1992—; rsch. cons. Netherland Sch. Govt., Das Hagg, Holland, 1990—; physics cons. Health Physics & Assocs., Roanoke, Va., 1991-92. Founder Food Search, Charleston, 1987-89; mem. Score, Huntington, 1988-89; literacy vol. Ala. Literacy Coun., Montgomery, Ala., 1993—; mem. Montgomery Jr. League, 1992—. Recipient scholarship Oxford U., 1991. Mem. ASPA, Am. Acad. Mgmt., Mortar Bd., Kappa Kappa Gamma. Avocations: book collecting, tennis, jogging, classical music. Office: Auburn U 1224 Haley Ctr Auburn AL 36849

MC ELHANEY, JAMES WILSON, lawyer, educator; b. N.Y.C., Dec. 10, 1937; s. Lewis Keck and Sara Jane (Hess) McE.; m. Maxine Dennis Jones, Aug. 17, 1961; children: David, Benjamin. AB, Duke U., 1960; LLB, 1962. Bar: Wis. 1962. Assoc. Wickham, Borgelt, Skogstad & Powell, 1966; asst. prof. U. Md. Law Sch., 1966-69, assoc. prof., 1969-72; vis. prof. So. Meth. U. Sch. of Law, Dallas, 1973-74; prof. So. Meth. U. Sch. of Law, 1974-76; Joseph C. Hostetler prof. trial practice and advocacy Case Western Res. U. Sch. of Law, Cleve., 1976—; mem. faculty Nat. Inst. Trial Advocacy, Boulder, Colo., 1975—; vis. prof. U. Tulsa Coll. Law, summer 1977, 79, Ind. U. Law Sch., summer 1980; cons. to U.S. Atty. Gen. on Justice Dept. Advocacy Tng. Programs, 1979—; lectr. in field. Author: Effective Litigation: Trials, Problems and Materials, 1974, Trial Notebook, 1981, 3rd edit., 1994, Trial Notebook on Tape: The Basics, 1989, Mc Elhaney's Trial Notebook on Tape: Advanced Techniques, 1991, Mc Elhaney's Trial Notebook on Tape: Evidence, Foundations and Objections, 1992, Mc Elhaney's Trial Notebook on Tape: Winning Tactics, 1994, Mc Elhaney's Litigation, 1995; editor-in-chief Litigation mag., 1984-86, sr. editor, 1986—; contbr. columns to Trial Notebook, Litigation, articles to profl. jours. Mem. ABA (mem. coun. on litigation 1987—, author jour. column Litigation), Assn. Am. Law Schs. (chmn. sect. on trial advocacy 1974-76, chmn. sect. on evidence 1978). Office: Case Western Res U 11075 East Blvd Cleveland OH 44106-5409 *The lamp of doctrine is a flickering and unsteady guide; we are led more by facts than obtuse theory.*

MC ELHANEY, JOHN HESS, lawyer; b. Milw., Apr. 16, 1934; s. Lewis Keck and Sara Jane (Hess) McE.; m. Jacquelyn Masur, Aug. 4, 1962; children—Scott, Victoria. B.B.A., So. Meth. U., 1956, J.D., 1958. Bar: Tex. bar 1958. Pvt. practice law Dallas, 1958—; shareholder Locke Purnell Rain Harrell, 1976—; lectr. law So. Meth. U., 1967-76. Contbr. articles to legal jours. Trustee St. Mark's Sch. Tex., 1980-86. Fellow Am. Coll. Trial Lawyers; mem. Am. Bd. Trial Advs., ABA, Tex. Bar Assn., So. Meth. U. Law Alumni Assn. (pres. 1972-73, dir. 1970-73), Town and Gown Club (pres. 1981-82). Presbyterian. Home: 5340 Tanbark Dr Dallas TX 75229-5555 Office: Locke Purnell Rain Harrell 2200 Ross Ave Ste 2200 Dallas TX 75201-2748

MCELHANEY, RICHARD FRANKLIN, quality assurance nursing coordinator; m. Lynne E. Mcelhaney, 1972; children: Richard Franklin Jr., Virginia Lynne. Student, U. of So. Miss., 1963-66; BSN, William Carey Coll., 1974; postgrad., U. South Ala., 1988-90; MSN, U. Mobile, Ala., 1994. RN, Ala., Miss.; cert. nursing adminstr. ANCC. Scrub nurse in surgery So. Bapt. Sch., New Orleans, 1972-74; med. surg. nurse U. South Ala. Med. Ctr., Mobile, 1974; instr. nursing Mobile (Ala.) Infirmary Sch. of Nursing, 1974-75; dir. inservice edn. Springhill Meml. Hosp., Mobile, 1975-76; staff nurse U. South Ala. Med. Ctr., Mobile, 1977, head nurse surgery, asst. dir. nursing, 1977-78, 78-80; nursing supr. surg. unit Singing River Hosp., Pascagoula, Miss.; dir. staff devel., head nurse ICU and psychiat. svcs. Doctors Hosp. of Mobile, 1982-89; quality assurance coord., nurse mgr. Knollwood Pk. Hosp., 1990-92, CQI coord., 1990—, with quality mgmt., 199—. Tech. sgt. USAF, 1966-70. Mem. Nat. Assn. Quality Assurance Profls. (Gulf Coast Coun.), Ala. Org. Nurse Execs., Gulf Coast Assn. for Health Care Quality (treas.), U. Mobile Nursing Honor Soc. (pres.). Republican. Methodist. Home: 1006 Uster Dr Mobile AL 36608-4112 Office: Univ S Ala 5500 Girby Rd Mobile AL 36693-5040

MCELHINNEY, JAMES LANCEL, artist, educator; b. Abington, Pa., Feb. 3, 1952; s. James and Joan Howland (Carpenter) McE.; m. Victoria Maria Dávila, Sept. 12, 1981 (div.). Scholarship student, Skowhegan (Maine) Sch. of Art, 1973; BFA, Temple U., 1974; MFA, Yale U., 1976. Asst. prof. Moore Coll. of Art, Phila., 1977-78, Skidmore Coll., Saratoga Springs, N.Y., 1979-87; adj. instr. UCLA, L.A., 1983, Moore Coll. of Art, Phila., 1983, Tyler Sch. of Art, Phila., 1983-86, Univ. of the Arts, Phila., 1985-89; instr. Milw. Inst. of Art and Design, 1991-93; vis. artist E. Carolina U., Greenville, N.C., 1994—. Artist: (paintings) solo exhbns. include: Peninsula Ctr. for the Fine Arts, Newport News, Va., 1993, Danville (Va.) Mus., 1993, Second Street Gallery, Charlottesville, Va., 1995, F.A.N. Gallery, Phila., 1995, Greenville (N.C.) Mus. Art, 1996, Lee Hansley Gallery, Raleigh, N.C., 1996, Asheville (N.C.) Art Mus., 1996, F.A.N. Gallery, Phila., 1997. Vol. Richmond (Va.) Nat. Battlefield Park, 1991—. Grantee: (painting) NEA, Washington, 1987-88, Ptnrs. in the Arts, Richmond Arts Coun., 1995. Mem. Coll. Art Assn. Home: 109 A N West Ave Ayden NC 28513

MCELHINNY, HAROLD JOHN, lawyer; b. San Francisco, Jan. 5, 1947; s. Harold James and Margaret I. (Mahoney) McE.; m. Mary Ellen McElhinny, June 22, 1968; children: Hannah, Jennifer, William. BA in Polit. Sci., U. Santa Clara, 1970; JD, U. Calif., Berkeley, 1975. Bar: Calif. 1976, U.S. Supreme Ct. 1983. Vol. Peace Corps., Tripoli, Libya, 1968-69; juvenile counselor Santa Clara County (Calif.) Juvenile Hall, 1969-72; law clk. U.S. Dist. Ct., Hartford, Conn., 1975-76; ptnr. Morrison & Foerster, San Francisco, 1976—. Mem. ABA, Calif. State Bar Assn., State Bar Calif. (rev. dept. 1986-89, chair 1988), San Francisco Bar Assn., Am. Intellectual Property Law Assn., Assn. Bus. Trial Lawyers (bd. govs. 1992—). Democrat. Roman Catholic. Office: Morrison & Foerster 425 Market St San Francisco CA 94105

MCELHINNY, WILSON DUNBAR, banker; b. Detroit, July 27, 1929; s. William Dunbar and Elizabeth (Wilson) McE.; m. Barbara Cheney Watkins, June 6, 1952 (dec.); children: David Ashton, Ward Cheney, Edward Wilson, William Dunbar; m. Lisa Lesher, Mar., 1993. BA, Yale U., 1953. With Union and New Haven Trust Co., 1952-63; with Reading Trust Co., Pa., 1963-68, pres., 1968-70; pres. Nat. Central Bank (formerly Reading Trust Co.), Pa., 1970-79, chief exec. officer, 1975-79; chmn. bd. dirs., pres., chief exec. officer Hamilton Bank (formerly Nat. Central Bank), Lancaster, Pa., 1979-81, chmn. bd. dirs., chief exec. officer, 1981-83, chmn. bd. dirs., 1981-90; pres. CoreStates Fin. Corp., Phila., 1983-86, vice chmn., 1986-90; pres., chmn. Hamilton Bank, Lancaster, Pa., 1988-90, also dir.; bd. dirs. Hunt Mfg. Co., Phila., Educators Mut. Life Ins. Co., Reading Eagle Co., Wohlsen Constrn. Co.; chmn. bd. Irex Corp. Bd. dirs. UAI Group LP, Sinking Spring, Pa., Lancaster Health Alliance. Mem. Pa. C. of C. (chmn. 1990-92), Hamilton Club (Lancaster), Lancaster Country Club, The Valley Club. Home and Office: 198 Pinetown Rd Leola PA 17540-9736

MCELLIGOTT, JAMES PATRICK, JR., lawyer; b. Chgo., Jan. 11, 1948; s. James Patrick and Helen Cecelia (Hogan) McE.; children: Michael Sean, Andrew David; m. Trina Reff, Aug. 25, 1985. BA, U. Ill., Urbana, 1970; JD, Harvard U., 1973. Bar: Va. 1974, U.S. Dist. Ct. (ea. and we. dists.) Va. 1974, U.S. Ct. Appeals (4th cir.) 1974, U.S. Supreme Ct. 1979. Research asst. U. Ill., 1970; assoc. McGuire, Woods & Battle, Richmond, 1973-79; ptnr. McGuire, Woods, Battle & Boothe, Richmond, 1979—. Mem. exec. com. Va. Home for Boys, Richmond, 1976—, pres. bd. govs., 1981-83; mem. Leadership Metro Richmond-Met. C. of C., 1984-85; bd. dirs. ARC Greater Richmond Chpt., 1990—, chmn., 1994-95. Mem. ABA, Va. Bar Assn. (exec. com., chmn. pub. rels. com. 1978-82, producer pub. svc. message 1973, Hot Spot award 1973), Richmond Bar Assn., Fed. Bar Assn. (pres. Richmond chpt. 1986), Nat. Sch. Bds. Assn., Coun. of Sch. Attys., Phi Beta Kappa, Phi Kappa Phi, Omicron Delta Epsilon. Home: 203 Cyril Ln Richmond VA 23229-7740 Office: McGuire Woods Battle & Boothe One James Ctr Richmond VA 23219-3229

MC ELRATH, RICHARD ELSWORTH, retired insurance company executive; b. Thompsontown, Pa., Oct. 11, 1932; s. Clayton Ellsworth and Jane Elizabeth (Shoop) McE.; m. Donna Gail Booher, Aug. 18, 1952; children—Leslie Jo, Jennifer Jo, Josie Arlene Elizabeth, Rebekah Clare. B.S. cum laude, Elizabethtown (Pa.) Coll., 1955; M.B.A. cum laude, Harvard U., 1961. Research asst. Harvard U., 1961-62; asst. to pres. Callaway Mills Co., LaGrange, Ga., 1963-65; with Irving Trust Co., N.Y.C., 1965-73; v.p. Irving Trust Co., 1969-73; treas. Tchrs. Ins. Annuity Assn. and Coll. Retirement Equities Fund, 1973-81; v.p. Met. Life Ins. Co., 1982-95; pres., dir. MetLife Funding, Inc., MetLife Credit, Inc., 1984-95. Author articles, case studies. Trustee Elizabethtown Coll.; mem. Society Valley Hosp., Ridgewood, N.J.; mem. Boston Rep. Com., 1961-63, Troup County (Ga.) Rep. Com., 1964-65; bd. dirs. Family Counseling Svc., Ridgewood, 1986-92. Lt. comdr. USNR, 1956-59. Mem. Assn. Gov. Bds. Univs. and Colls. Methodist. Club: Harvard (N.Y.C.). Home: 17 Cedar St Glen Rock NJ 07452-1608

MCELROY, EDWARD J., union officer; b. Providence, Mar. 17, 1941; s. Edward J. Sr. and Clara (Angelone) McE.; m. Edwina Barbara Ricci, Apr. 20, 1963; children: Kathleen, Mary, Stephen, Elizabeth. AB, Providence Coll., 1962. Cert. tchr. Tchr. Lockwood Jr. High Sch., Warwick, R.I., 1962-72; pres. Warwick Tchrs. Union, Warwick, R.I., 1967-69, R.I. Fed. Tchrs., Am. Fed. Tchrs., Providence, 1971-92; v.p. Am. Fed. Tchrs., AFLCIO, Providence, 1974-92; sec. treas. Am. Fed. Tchrs., AFLCIO, Washington, 1992—; pres. R.I. AFLCIO, Providence, 1977-92. Exec. com. mem. R.I. Democratic State Com., Providence, 1976-92; sec. exec. com. United Way So. New England, Providence, 1978-92; devel. commn. R.I. State, 1984-85, mem. Workforce 2000, 1987-92. Recipient Quirk Inst. award Providence Coll., 1980. Mem. Aurora Civic Assn. Democrat. Roman Catholic. Avocations: golf, photography, reading. Office: Am Fed Tchrs AFL CIO 555 New Jersey Ave NW Washington DC 20001-2029

MCELROY, FREDERICK WILLIAM, economics educator, consultant; b. Dublin, Ireland, May 18, 1939; came to U.S., 1963; s. Herbert John and Annie Maureen (McDowell) McE.; m. Kathleen Child, Sept. 8, 1964; children: Dominique, Hugh. BA, Nat. U. of Ireland, Dublin, 1960; MA, U. Coll. Dublin, 1961; PhD, Georgetown U., 1967. Asst. prof. econs. SUNY, Buffalo, 1967-68; asst. prof. econs. Georgetown U., Washington, 1968-71, assoc. prof. econs., 1971-77, prof. econs., 1977—, chair econs. dept., 1994-97; cons. in antitrust cases. Contbr. articles to profl. jours. Trustee, treas. Help the Aged, Washington, 1982-86; bd. dirs. Oxfam-Am., Boston, 1976-79. Mem. Am. Econs. Assn., Phi Beta Kappa, Alpha Sigma Nu. Democrat. Roman Catholic. Avocations: golf, tennis. Home: 5013 Brookdale Rd Bethesda MD 20816-1709 Office: Georgetown U Dept Econs Washington DC 20057

MCELROY, JANICE HELEN, government agency executive; b. Topeka, Kans., Dec. 12, 1937; d. Rudolph Ralph and Josephine Elizabeth (Kern) Jilka; m. James Douglas McElroy, June 25, 1967; children: Helen Elizabeth, Bryan Douglas. BS cum laude, Colo. Coll., Colorado Springs, 1960; MAT, Johns Hopkins U., 1964; PhD, U.S. Internat. U., San Diego, 1970. Biology tchr. Roland Park Country Day Sch., Balt., 1962-63, Edmundston H.S., Balt., 1964; chmn. dept. sci. Bishop's Sch., La Jolla, Calif., 1964-69; instr. Somerset County C.C., Somerville, N.J., 1973-75; instr. Cedar Crest Coll., Allentown, Pa., 1976-82, dir. re-entry program, 1979-82; exec. dir. Resource Devel. Svcs., Allentown, Pa., 1982-86; dir. planning and devel. Montgomery County C.C., Blue, Pa., 1986-88; exec. dir. Pa. Commn. for Women, Harrisburg, 1988-95; editor, pub. Womansword, Allentown, 1996—. Research dir./editor: Our Hidden Heritage: Pennsylvania Women in History, 1983; contbr. articles to profl. jours. Mem. Women's Adv. Bd. Task Force, Lehigh County, Pa., 1981-82, Nat. Child Care Adv. Coun.; chair Gov.'s Conf. on Responses to Workforce 2000, 1990; lay corp. mem. Pa. Blue Shield, 1992; alt. del. Dem. Nat. Conv., 1992; elder, trustee, commr. Presbyn. Ch.; bd. dirs. Women's Polit. Network Pa., 1988—, pres., 1996—; bd. dirs. Coalition Adult Literacy, 1989-95; NGO del. UN Fourth World Conf. Women, Beijing, 1995; founder Leadership Devel. Inst. for Women in State Govt., 1993. Fulbright scholar, 1960; Ford Found. fellow, 1963; NSF fellow, 1965. Mem. AAUW (pres. Pa. divsn. 1984-88, nat. bd. dirs. 1989-93), Nat. Assn. Commns. for Women (nat. bd. dirs. 1991-93), LWV, Delta Epsilon, Phi Beta Kappa, Alpha Lambda Delta, Kappa Kappa Gamma. Avocations: reading, travel, photography. Home: 2826 Crest Ave N Allentown PA 18104-6106 Office: Womansword 3140-B Tilghman St #263 Allentown PA 18104

MC ELROY, JOHN HARLEY, electrical engineering educator; b. Marion, Ohio, June 27, 1936; s. Francis and Alice Marie McElroy; m. Eleonore Hildegard Schmidt, Mar. 18, 1957. B.S. in Elec. Engring, U. Tex., Austin, 1966; M.E.E., Cath. U. Am., 1973, Ph.D., 1978. Instr. guided missles Air Defense Sch. U.S. Army, 1957-63; rsch. asst. Quantum Electronics rsch. Lab U. Texas, Austin, 1963-66; staff Goddard Flight Center, Greenbelt, Md., 1966-79, 80-82; chief communications tech. div. Goddard Flight Center, 1978-79, dep. dir. center, 1980-82; dir. communications programs NASA Hdqrs., Washington, 1979-80; asst. adminstr. NOAA, Washington, 1982-85; dir. spl. projects Hughes Aircraft Co., Los Angeles, 1985-86; v.p. tech. Hughes Communications, Inc., 1986-87; dean Coll. Engring., prof. elec. engring. U. Tex., Arlington, 1987-96, vice provost for rsch. and grad. studies, 1996—; cons. satellite communications and earth observations. Contbr. articles to profl. jours. Served with AUS, 1954-63. Recipient Apollo Achievement award NASA, 1969, Applications Tech. Satellite award, 1975, Earth Resources Satellite award, 1973; named Wernher von Braun Meml. Lectr. Smithsonian Instn. Fellow AIAA, Washington Acad. Scis., IEEE. Home: 5605 Hunterwood Ln Arlington TX 76017 Office: U Tex Arlington PO Box 19019 Arlington TX 76019

MCELROY, LEO FRANCIS, communications consultant, journalist; b. Los Angeles, Oct. 12, 1932; s. Leo Francis and Helen Evelyn (Silliman) McE.; m. Dorothy Frances Montgomery, Nov. 3, 1956 (div. 1981); children: James, Maureen, Michael, Kathleen; m. Judith Marie Lewis, May 30, 1992. BS in English, Loyola U., L.A. 1953. News dir. KFI, KRLA, KABC Radio, L.A., 1964-72; pub. affairs host Sta. KCET, Pub. TV, L.A., 1967-74; v.p. Sta. KROQ AM/FM, L.A., 1972-74; polit. editor Sta. KABC-TV, L.A., 1974-81; pres. McElroy Communications, L.A. and Sacramento, 1981—; pres. sec. Lt. Gov.'s Office, Sacramento, 1982-84; chmn. Calif. AP Broadcasters, 1972-74; cons. State Office Migrant Edn., Sacramento, 1974, Californians for Water, L.A. , 1982, Calif. Water Protection Coun., Sacramento, 1982, Planning and Conservation League, Sacramento, 1984—, Common Cause, Sacramento, 1988—. Author: Uneasy Partners, 1984; author plays: Mermaid Tavern, 1956, To Bury Caesar (Christopher award 1952), 1952, Rocket to Olympus, 1960, The Code of Whiskey King, 1995. State del. Western Am. Assembly on Prison Reform, Berkeley, Calif., 1973;

chmn. State Disaster Info. Task Force; Calif., 1973-74; campaign media cons. statewide issues, various candidates, Sacramento, L.A., 1981—; bd. dirs. Vols. in Victim Assistance, Sacramento, 1984, Rescue Alliance, Sacramento, 1987-92, Mental Health Assn., Sacramento, 1985-89, Leukemia Soc., 1992—. Recipient Gabriel award Cath. Archdiocese, L.A., 1972, Golden Mike award Radio-TV News Assn., L.A., 1973; Hon. Resolution, Calif. State Assembly, Sacramento, 1981. Mem. ASCAP, AFTRA, Screen Actors Guild, Am. Assn. Polit. Cons. Mem. Reform Party. Roman Catholic. Home: 8217 Oakenshaw Way Orangevale CA 95662-2953 Office: McElroy Comm 2410 K St Ste C Sacramento CA 95816-5002 *No gift is greater than the gift of oneself - honestly given, honestly received.*

MC ELROY, WILLIAM THEODORE, lawyer; b. Newark, Jan. 20, 1925; s. William J. and Matilda (Hamilton) McE.; m. Emilie Hoinowski, Jan. 18, 1947; children: Karen L., William J., Ruth P. LL.B. cum laude, Rutgers U., 1950. Bar: N.J. 1949, U.S. Dist. Ct. (fed. dist.) N.J. 1950, U.S. Dist. Ct. (ea. and so. dists.) N.Y. 1986. Assoc. Duggan, Shaw & Hughes, Newark, 1949-50; with McElroy, Connell, Foley & Geiser (and predecessor firms), Newark, 1950-78; ptnr. McElroy, Connell, Foley & Geiser (and predecessor firms), 1956-78; judge Superior Ct. N.J., Morristown, 1978-80; Appellate Div. Superior Ct. N.J., 1980-85; presiding judge part H, 1984-85; ptnr. McElroy, Deutsch & Mulvaney, Morristown, N.J., 1985—. Served with USNR, 1942-45. Fellow Am. Coll. Trial Lawyers; mem. ABA, N.J. Bar Assn. (chmn. civil procedure sect. 1973-74), Essex County Bar Assn., Morris County Bar Assn., Trial Attys. N.J. (Disting. Svc. in cause of justice award 1986).d. Home: 80 Old Farm Rd Basking Ridge NJ 07920-3309 Office: 1300 Mt Kemble Ave PO Box 2075 Morristown NJ 07960

MCELVAIN, DAVID PLOWMAN, retired manufacturing company financial executive; b. Chgo., Oct. 16, 1937; s. Carl R. and Ruth P. (Plowman) McE.; B.B.A., U. Ariz., 1961, M.B.A., 1962; m. Mary Rosalind Hysong, Dec. 20, 1961; children—Jana, Jodi. Consolidation accountant, exec. div. Dresser Industries, Inc., Dallas, 1962-67, corporate fin. controller, 1973-76, dir. fin. services, 1976-78, staff v.p. fin. service and risk mgmt., 1978-82, exec. v.p. fin. services group, 1982-83, pres. fin. services group, 1984-86, v.p. fin., chief fin. officer, 1987-1993; controller crane, hoist & tower div., Muskegon, Mich., 1967-73. Cert. mgmt. acct. Mem. Nat. Assn. Accts., Beta Gamma Sigma, Phi Delta Theta. Episcopalian. Home: 14828 Bellbrook Dr Addison TX 75240

MCELVEEN, JOSEPH JAMES, JR., author, journalist, public broadcasting executive; b. Sanford, Fla., Feb. 23, 1939; s. Joseph James Sr. and Genevieve (Stoll) McE.; m. Mary Louise Young, Aug. 18, 1979; 1 child, Ryan Leighton. BA, Furman U., 1961; MA, U. S.C., 1968. Editor, pub. West Ashley News, Charleston, S.C., 1951-57; reporter, photographer Charleston Post, 1955-57; tchr. English and journalism St. Andrew's Parish High Sch., Charleston, 1961-65; dir. info., prof. journalism Columbia Coll., S.C., 1965-68; prof. journalism U. S.C., Columbia, 1968-79; staff pub. affairs FCC, Washington, 1979-81; dir. pub. affairs adminstrn. Nat. Cable TV Assn., Washington, 1981-87; dir. internal communications Corp. for Pub. Broadcasting, Washington, 1987-92, dir. program adminstrn., 1992—; ombudsman, columnist Alexandria (Va.) Gazette, 1981-88. Author: Introduction to Creative Writing, 1963, Modern Communications, 1964; contbr. chpt. to Dictionary of Literary Biography (Mencken), 1986, Words, words, words: A Journalist's Journey, 1997. Mem. Orgn. of News Ombudsmen, Soc. Profl. Journalists, Mencken Soc. Democrat. Episcopalian. Avocations: photography, reading, desktop pub. Office: Corp for Pub Broadcasting 901 E St NW Washington DC 20004-2037

MCELVEEN, JUNIUS CARLISLE, JR., lawyer; b. Rogersville, Tenn., Feb. 17, 1947; s. Junius Carlisle and Martha Kathleen (Harrison) McE.; m. Mary Wallace Pyles, Sept. 22, 1973; children: Kathryn Carlisle, Sarah Elizabeth. BA cum laude, U. Va., 1969, JD, 1972. Bar: Va. 1972, Calif. 1975, U.S. Dist. Ct. (ea. dist.) Va. 1976, D.C. 1978, U.S. Ct. Appeals (4th cir.) 1978, U.S. Ct. Appeals (Fed. cir.) 1986, U.S. Ct. Appeals (11th cir.) 1990. Rsch. assoc. Atlantic Richfield, Washington, 1972; assoc. Pender & Coward, Norfolk, Va., 1976-77; assoc. Seyfarth, Shaw, Washington, 1977-80, ptnr., 1981-83, Jones, Day, Reavis & Pogue, Washington, 1983—; mem. adv. com., reproductive hazards in the workplace Office of Tech. Assessment, Washington, 1984-86; mem. adv. council Ctr. Environ. Health, U. Conn., 1986-95; mem. editorial bd. The Occupational and Environ. Medicine Report, 1986—, Human and Ecol. Risk Assessment; contbr. articles to legal jours. Elder Kirkwood Presbyn. Ch., Springfield, Va., 1984-86. Served as lt. USN, 1972-75. Mem. ABA, Va. State Bar, State Bar Calif., Phi Beta Kappa, Phi Delta Phi (sec. local chpt. 1971-72, Outstanding Grad. award 1972). Home: 10113 Homar Pond Dr Fairfax VA 22039-1650 Office: Jones Day Reavis & Pogue 1450 G St NW Ste 600 Washington DC 20005-2001

MCELVEEN, WILLIAM HENRY, minister; b. Winston-Salem, N.C., June 7, 1932; s. Adam Ezra and Selma Anita (Adams) McE.; m. Carol Lee Sloan, Aug. 28, 1955; children: Miriam Lee Story, Gregory William, David William. BA, Davidson Coll., 1954; MDiv, Moravian Theol. Sem., 1958, DD (hon.), 1994; MA, Wake Forest U., 1971. Assoc. pastor Home Moravian Ch., Winston-Salem, N.C., 1958-61; pastor Messiah Moravian Ch., Winston-Salem, 1961-70; exec. dir. Bd. Christian Edn. So. Province Moraviah Ch. in Am., Winston-Salem, 1970-80, asst. to pres., 1993—; founding pastor Unity Moravian Ch., Lewisville, N.C., 1980-93; asst. to pres. Provincial Elder's Conf. Moravian Ch. Am. South Province, 1993—. Contbr. articles to profl. jours. Chair Model Cities Com., Winston-Salem, 1970s. Democrat. Avocations: carpentry, electrical wiring, gardening, walking, bicycling. Office: Moravian Church Drawer O Salem Sta Winston Salem NC 27108

MCELVEEN, WILLIAM LINDSAY, broadcasting executive, lecturer; b. Columbia, S.C., Sept. 20, 1950; s. Henry Moody and Dorothy Butler (Sligh) McE.; m. Laurie Wells Boyle, Sept. 8, 1969 (div. 1976); 1 child, Earle Sligh; m. Catharine Elizabeth McCaslin, Aug. 13, 1992; 1 child, Kerry Elizabeth McCaslin. BA in English, Univ. of South, 1972. Acct. exec. Sta. WNOK-FM, Columbia, S.C., 1972-73; mng. dir. Sta. WNOK-FM, Columbia, 1973-79; v.p., gen. mgr. Stas. WNOK-AM-FM, Columbia, 1979-84; pres. Audubon Broadcasting Co., Columbia, 1984-89, Radio South Carolina, Columbia, 1989—; lectr. Internat. Media Fund, Washington, 1993—. Chmn. bd. dirs. Columbia Urban League, 1983-85; bd. dirs. Crimestoppers of Midlands, 1984-88, S.C. Law Inst., Columbia, 1985-88, Helpline of Midlands, 1986-90; gen. campaign chair United Negro Coll. Fund, Columbia, 1985-86; mem. exec. com. United Way of Midlands, Columbia, 1987-88. Mem. Nat. Assn. Broadcasters (bd. dirs. 1988-92, 96—), S.C. Broadcasters Assn. (exec. com., bd. dirs. 1980-87, pres. 1988-92, Hall of Fame inductee 1996), Columbia Advt. Fedn. (pres. 1980-81), Media Club of Columbia (bd. dirs., pres. 1983-84). Presbyterian. Avocations: golf, tennis, travelling. Home: 263 Tombee Ln Columbia SC 29209-0804 Office: Radio SC 1801 Charleston Hwy Cayce SC 29033-2019

MCELVEIN, THOMAS I., JR., lawyer; b. Buffalo, Apr. 19, 1936; s. Thomas I. and Edith Marian (Bowen) McE.; m. Ernesta F. McElvein, June 26, 1965; children—Christopher, Andrew, Kathryn. B.A., Antioch Coll., 1959; J.D., Yale U., 1962. Bar: N.Y. 1962, U.S. Dist. Ct. (we. dist.) N.Y. 1969. atty. Village Akron (N.Y.); dir. Pollack Printing Corp. Mem. N.Y. State Bar Assn., Erie County Bar Assn. Home: 295 Nottingham Ter Buffalo NY 14216-3125 Office: 1500 Liberty Bldg Buffalo NY 14202-3612

MC ELWAIN, JOSEPH ARTHUR, retired power company executive; b. Deer Lodge, Mont., Nov. 13, 1919; s. Lee Chaffee and Johanna (Petersen) McE.; m. Mary Cleaver Witt, Mar. 8, 1945 (dec. June 1992); m. Mary E. McLaughlin, Oct. 9, 1996; children—Lee William and Lori Louise (twins). B.A., U. Mont., 1943, LL.B., 1947. Bar: Mont. 1947. Individual practice law Deer Lodge, 1947-63; Washington legis. counsel Mont. Power Co., Butte, 1954-63, counsel, 1963-65, asst. to pres., 1965-67, v.p., 1967-70, exec. v.p., dir., 1970, then chmn., chief exec. officer, now ret.; dir. Mont. Power Co., First Bank System 1975-84, Devel. Credit Corp. Mont.; MHD Devel. Corp. 1986—; mem. U.S. nat. com. World Energy Conf.; Mont. dir. for U.S. Savs. Bonds, 1980-81; cons. in field. Mem. Mont. Pub. Land Law Rev. Adv. Com. City atty. Deer Lodge, 1950-57, 60-63; mem. Mont. Ho. of Reps., 1949-55, majority floor leader, 1951; mem. Mont. State Senate, 1962-64; state chmn. Republican Central Com., Mont., 1952-54; mem. adv. com. Edison Electric Inst., U. Mont. Found., Missoula, Rocky Mountain Coll., Billings; bd. dirs. Mont. Internat. Trade Commn. Served with AUS, World War II and Korea. Recipient Judstin Miller award, 1947. Mem. Mont., Am. bar assns. Episcopalian. Clubs: Masons, Shriners, Kiwanis. Home: 205 Aspen Loop Butte MT 59701-3968 Office: 40 W Broadway St Butte MT 59701-9222

MCELWEE, DENNIS JOHN, lawyer, former pharmaceutical company executive; b. New Orleans, July 30, 1947; s. John Joseph and Audrey (Nunez) McE.; m. Nancy Lu Travis, Sept. 3, 1976. BS, Tulane U., 1970; JD, U. Denver, 1992, Hague Acad. Internat. Law, 1990-91. Clean room and quality control analyst Sci. Enterprises Inc., Broomfield, Colo., 1975-76; analytical chemist in toxicology Poisonlab. Inc., Denver, 1977; analytical chemist, then dir. analytical quality control program Colo. Sch. Mines Rsch. Inst., 1977-79; dir. quality control, then dir. compliance Benedict Nuclear Pharms. Co., Golden, Colo., 1979-84; pres. MC Projections, Inc., Morrison, Colo., 1985-86, dir. regulatory affairs, Electromedics Inc., Englewood, Colo., 1986-89; pvt. practice 1992—. Author: Mineral Research Chemicals, Toxic Properties and Proper Handling, 2d edit., 1979; contbr. articles to profl. jours. Bd. dirs. Denver Chpt. Cystic Fibrosis Found., 1996. Mem. Colo. Bar Assn., Colo. Criminal Def. Bar, Denver Bar Assn., 1st Judicial Dist. Bar Assn. Recipient Sutton prize in internat. law U. Denver Sch. Law, 1991. Office: 2009 Wadsworth Blvd Ste 200 Lakewood CO 80215-2031

MC ELWEE, JOHN GERARD, retired life insurance company executive; b. Port Bannatyne, Scotland, Dec. 19, 1921; came to U.S., 1925; s. James and Margaret (Fitzgerald) McE.; m. Barbara Sullivan, Mar. 31, 1951; children: Neal, Janet, Sheila, Brian. Attended, Boston Coll., 1939-42, LLB, 1950, LLD (hon.), 1987; grad. advanced mgmt. program, Harvard U., 1960; LLD (hon.), Bentley Coll., 1986. With John Hancock Mut. Life Ins. Co., Boston, 1945-93, asst. sec., 1957-61, 2d v.p., 1961-65, v.p., 1965-71, sr. v.p., sec., 1972-74, exec. v.p., sec., 1974-79, pres., 1979-81, chmn., 1982-86, also bd. dirs., 1976-93; bd. dirs. Data Gen. Corp. Trustee, assoc. Boston Coll.; life trustee Boston Mus. Sci. With USN, 1941-45. Mem. Weston Golf Club, Comml. Club, Knights of Malta. Roman Catholic. Home: 139 Buckskin Dr Weston MA 02193-1131

MCELYEA, JACQUELYN SUZANNE, accountant, real estate consultant; b. Dallas, July 19, 1958; d. Owen Clyde and Mary Lou (Cockerill) Harvey; m. James E. McElyea, June 14, 1983. BBS, Tex. A&M U., 1980. CPA, Tex. Acctg. mgr. Oxford Tex. Devel., Dallas, 1980-81; staff to dir. Price Waterhouse, Dallas, 1981—; bd. dirs. Nat. Assn. Corp. Real Estate, Dallas. Co-author: Real Estate Accounting Reporting, 1995. Bd. dirs. Am. Diabetes Assn., Dallas, 1996-97. Mem. AICPA, Nat. Assn. Real Estate Cos., Tex. Soc. CPAs. Presbyterian. Avocations: animals, cooking. Office: Price Waterhouse 2001 Ross Ave Dallas TX 75201-8001

MCELYEA, ULYSSES, JR., veterinarian; b. Ft. Collins, Colo., Oct. 29, 1941; s. Ulysses and Hazel (Hall) McE.; m. Rexanna Bell, Dec. 29, 1975 (div. 1980). BS in Pharmacy, U. N.Mex., 1963; DVM, Colorado State U., 1967, MS, 1968. Diplomate Am. Bd. Vet. Practicioners; cert. in companion animals. Owner Alta Vista Animal Clinic, Las Cruces, N.Mex., 1970—; bd. dirs. N.Mex. Acad. Vet. Practice, Albuquerque, bd. dirs. state of N.Mex. Bd. Vet. Examiners, v.p., 1989-92, vice chair, 1992, chair, 1992—, Bank of the Rio Grande. Pres. Las Cruces Community Theater, 1974; founder, bd. dirs. Dona Ann Arts Coun., Las Cruces, 1976-80. Capt. U.S. Army, 1968-70. Mem. AVMA, Am. Pharm. Assn., Am. Assn. Feline Practitioners, Am. Soc. Vet. Ophthalmologists, N.Mex. Vet. Med. Assn. (bd. dirs. 1976-82), So. N.Mex. Vet. Assn. (pres. 1974, 84), N.Mex. State U. Athletic Assn. 9bd. dirs. 1976—, pres.-elect 1992-93, pres. 1993-94), N.Mex. State U. Pres.'s Assn. 9bd. dirs. 1988-91), U. N.Mex. Alumni Assn. (bd. dirs. 1976-80). Democrat. Home: 2635 Fairway Dr Las Cruces NM 88011-5044 Office: Alta Vista Animal Clinic 725 S Solano Dr Las Cruces NM 88001-3244

MCENERY, JANET GOLDBERG, lawyer; b. Albany, N.Y., Feb. 6, 1951; m. John T. McEnery; children: Patrick E. McEnery, Margaret Anne McEnery. BA magna cum laude, SUNY, Buffalo, 1972; JD, U. Ill., 1975. Bar: Ill. 1975, Mo. 1976, Fla. 1992, U.S. Dist. Ct. (so. dist.) Ill. 1976, U.S. Dist. Ct. (no. dist.) Ill. 1980, U.S. Dist. Ct. (mid. dist.) Fla. 1994, U.S. Dist. Ct. (so. dist.) Fla. 1995. Law clk. to judge James Foreman U.S. Dist. Ct. (so. dist.) Ill., East Saint Louis, 1975-77; atty., acting supr. NLRB, St. Louis, 1977-80; from assoc. to ptnr. Friedman & Koven, Chgo., 1980-85; ptnr. Sachnoff & Weaver, Chgo., 1986-93; of counsel Levin & Funkhouser Ltd., 1993-94; of counsel to ptnr. Macfarlane, Ferguson & McMullen, 1994—. Co-editor: The Labor Law Handbook, 1984; contbr. articles to publs. Recipient award Ill. Assn. Park Dists., 1984. Mem. ABA (devel. labor law com.), Fla. Bar Assn., Hillsborough County Bar Assn., Hillsborough Assn. for Women Lawyers, Phi Beta Kappa. Jewish. Home: 66 Martinique Ave Tampa FL 33606-4039 Office: 111 E Madison St Ste 2300 Tampa FL 33602-4708

MCENERY, TOM, professional sports team executive; married; three children. BA, MA degress, Santa Clara U. Mayor City of San Jose, Calif., 1983-90; vice-chmn. San Jose Sharks; lectr. Stanford U., 1991-92. Contbr. editl. to L.A. Times, 1995; author: The New City-State: Change and Renewal in America's Cities, California Cavalier; editor: A New Ireland. Presdl. scholar Santa Clara U., 1992-93. Office: San Jose Sharks 525 W Santa Clara St San Jose CA 95113-1520

MCENIRY, ROBERT FRANCIS, education educator; b. Milw., Feb. 22, 1918; s. Frank Michael and Mary (Brown) McE. BA, St. Louis U., 1941, Philosophiae Licentiatus cum laude, 1944, Theologiae Licentiatus cum laude, 1953, PhL, ThL cum laude, 1953; PhD, Ohio State U., 1972. Instr. classics St. Louis U. High Sch., 1944-47, Creighton Prep. Sch., Omaha, 1947-48; asst. prof., chmn. classics Rockhurst Coll., Kansas City, Mo., 1953-58; retreat dir. White House Retreat, St. Louis, 1958-68; assoc. research prof. Creighton U., Omaha, 1972-89; ret., 1989; dir., facilitator Growth for Couples, 1975-89; lectr. Creighton Natural Family Planning Ctr.; facilitator groups Adult Children of Alcoholism and Dysfunctional Families, 1989-93; vis. lectr. San Francisco Sch. Theology, San Anselmo, Calif., 1985; more than 800 presentations (lectrs., papers, workshops and seminars) in 91 cities, 35 states and 12 fgn. countries on value decisions during high anxiety and stress in marriage, family, teaching and learning; exec. dir. Studies Adult Survivors of Abuse, 1993—; tchr., counselor in marriage and family issues. Editor and pub. Interaction Review, 1982-89; editor Scholar and Educator, 1974-76; mem. editorial bd. Counseling and Values, 1976-82; editor (book) Pastoral Counseling, 1977, Premarriage Counseling, 1978; contbr. over 180 articles to profl. jours.; literary agent, 1992—. Mem. Bd. of Pastoral Ministry, Omaha, 1972-78. Research grantee Council for Theol. Reflection, 1975-77; recipient Research award Creighton U., 1977; 1st prize for "Pro and Con" in Queen's Work Play can fest, 1945. Fellow Nat. Acad. Counselors and Family Therapists (editor book rev. 1979-91); mem. APA, Am. Assn. for Religious Values in Counseling (editor newsletter 1982-89, Outstanding Svc. award 1985, Meritorious Svc. award 1989), Phi Delta Kappa (exec. com. 1977-83, del. 1981-83). Avocations: barbershop quartets, photography, Civil War sites, yoga. Home: 3016 Paddock Rd Apt 12B Omaha NE 68124-2942 Office: Creighton U 2500 California St Omaha NE 68131-1676

MCENROE, JOHN PATRICK, JR., retired professional tennis player, commentator; b. Wiesbaden, Fed. Republic of Germany, Feb. 16, 1959; s. John Patrick and Katy McEnroe; m. Tatum O'Neal, Aug. 1, 1986; children: Kevin Jack, Sean. Grad., Trinity Sch., N.Y.C., 1977; student, Stanford U. Winner numerous U.S. jr. singles and doubles titles; winner jr. titles French Mixed Doubles, 1977, French Jr. Singles, 1977, Italian Indoor Doubles, 1978; winner Nat. Coll. Athletic Assn. Intercollegiate U.S. Men's Singles title, 1978; professional tennis player, 1978-93; played on victorious U.S. Davis Cup Team, 1978, 79, 81, 82, 92; winner Stockholm Open, 1978, Benson and Hedges Tournament, 1978, Grand Prix Masters singles and doubles, Wembley, 1978, Grand Prix Masters Tournament, N.Y.C., 1979, New Orleans Grand Prix, 1979, WCT Milan Internat., Italy, 1979, Stella Artois Tournament, London, 1979, U.S. Open Men's Singles Championship, 1979, 80, 81, 84, World Championship Tennis Championship, 1979, 83, Australian Indoor Singles Championship, 1980-83, U.S. Indoor Singles Championship, 1980-83, Wimbledon Singles, 1981, 83, 84, Tournament of Champions, 1981, 83, AT & T Challenge, 1987, Japan Open, 1988, U.S. Hard Court Singles, 1989, Wimbledon Doubles, 1992; tennis sportscaster USA Network, 1993; mem. Men's Seniors' Tour Circuit, 1994. Office: care John P McEnroe Sr Paul Weiss Rifkind Wharton & Garrison 1285 Ave the Americas New York NY 10019-6028*

MCENROE, PATRICK, professional tennis player; b. Manhasset, N.Y., July 1, 1966; s. John Patrick Sr. and Katy McEnroe. Student, U. Stanford. Ranked 12th U.S. Tennis Assn., 1991. Mem. U.S. Davis Cup Team, 1993, 94. Office: care US Tennis Assn 70 W Red Oak Ln White Plains NY 10604-3602*

MCENROE, PAUL, reporter. Gen. assignment reporter, National writer Mpls. Star Tribune, Mpls. Office: Star Tribune 425 Portland Ave Minneapolis MN 55415-1511*

MCENTEE, GERALD W., labor union official; b. Phila., Jan. 11, 1935; four children. B in Econs., LaSalle Coll., 1956; postgrad., Temple U., Harvard U. With Am. Fedn. State County and Mcpl. Employees, 1973—; former leader Dist Coun. 13, Harrisburg, Penn.; union internat. v.p., mem. exec. bd., since 1974; internat. pres. Washington, 1981—. Office: AFSCME 1625 L St NW Washington DC 20036-5601*

MCENTEE, ROBERT EDWARD, management consultant; b. Franklin, N.J., Mar. 22, 1932; s. William J. and Marie C. (Gorman) McE.; m. Ruth M. Kathalynas, Sept. 29, 1956; children—Kathleen, Susan, Jane, Robert, Christopher. B.S., Villanova U., 1953. C.P.A., N.J. With Price Waterhouse, 1955-63; sr. fin., adminstrv. exec. Beecham Inc., West Paterson, N.J., 1963-88; pres. fin. div. Beecham Inc., 1974-88; pres., chief oper. officer Russ Berrie & Co., Inc., Oakland, N.J., 1988-90; pvt. practice cons., 1990—; bd. dirs. Valley Nat. Bancorp, Wayne, N.J. Trustee Archdiocese of Newark, pension bd. Served with U.S. Army, 1953-55. Mem. Am. Inst. C.P.A.s, N.J. Soc. C.P.A.s, Fin. Exec. Inst. Roman Catholic. Home: 398 Autumn Chase Dr Venice FL 34292-3178

MCENTIRE, REBA N., country singer; b. McAlester, Okla., Mar. 28, 1955; d. Clark Vincent and Jacqueline (Smith) McE.; m. Narvel Blackstock, 1989; 1 child, Shelby Steven McEntire Blackstock. Student elem. edn., music, Southeastern State U., Durant, Okla., 1976. Rec. artist Mercury Records, 1978-83, MCA Records, 1984—. Albums include Whoever's in New England (Gold award), 1986, What Am I Gonna Do About You (Gold award), 1987, Greatest Hits (Gold award, Platinum award, U.S., Can.), 1987, Merry Christmas To You, 1987, The Last One To Know (Gold award), 1988, Reba (Gold award 1988), Sweet 16 (Gold award 1989, U.S.), Rumor Has It (Gold award 1991, Platinum award 1992, Double Platinum 1992), Reba Live (Gold award 1990, Gold award 1991, Platinum award 1991), For My Broken Heart, 1991, Forever in Your Eyes, 1992, It's Your Call, 1992, Read My Mind, 1994, Starting Over, 1995, Reba compilation video (Gold award, Platinum award 1992); author: (with Tom Carter) Reba: My Story, 1994; actress: (miniseries) Buffalo Girls, 1995. Spokesperson Middle Tenn. United Way, 1988, Nat. and State 4-H Alumni, Bob Hope's Hope for a Drug Free Am.; Nat. spokesperson Am. Lung Assn., 1990-91. Recipient numerous awards in Country music including Disting. Alumni award Southeastern State U., Female vocalist award Country Music Assn., 1984, 85, 86, 87, Grammy award for Best Country Vocal Performance, 1987, 2 Grammy nominations, 1994, Grammy award, Best Country Vocal Collaboration for "Does He Love You" with Linda Davis, 1994, Entertainer of Yr. award Country Radio Awards, 1994, Female Vocalist award, 1994; named Entertainer of Yr., Country Music Assn., 1986, Female Vocalist of Yr. Acad. Country Music, 1984, 85, 86, 87, 92, Top Female Vocalist, 1991, Am. Music award favorite female country singer, 1988, 90, 91, 92, 93, Am. Music award, 1989, 90, 91, 92, Best Album, 1991, Favorite Female Vocalist, 1994, Favorite Female Vocalist, Peoples Choice Award, 1992, Favorite Female Country Vocalist, 1992, 93, Favorite Female Vocalist, TNN Viewer's Choice Awards, 1993, Favorite Female Country Artist, Billboard, 1994, Favorite Country Album award Am. Music Awards, 1995, Favorite Female Country Vocalist award Am. Music Awards, 1995, Favorite Female Vocalist award People's Choice Awards, 1995, Top Female Vocalist of Yr. award Acad. Country Music, 1995, Entertainer of Yr. award Acad. Country Music, 1995, Favorite Female Vocalist award TNN Viewer's Choice Awards, 1995. Mem. Country Music Assn., Acad. County Music, Nat. Acad. Rec. Arts and Scis., Grand Ol' Opry, AFTRA, Nashville Songwriters Assn. Inc. Avocations: golf, shopping, being with Narvel and Shelby, horse racing, raising horses.

MCERLANE, JOSEPH JAMES, insurance company executive; b. Phila., Mar. 5, 1948; s. Joseph Leo and Theophila Mary (Szymanski) McE.; m. Florence Mary Myhasuk; children: Joan Reardon, Rebecca Ann, Megan Diane, Erin Moira, Joseph James Jr. BA, Villanova U., 1970. CLU; cert. employee benefit specialist. Group sales asst. Metro. Life Ins. Co., Phila., 1970-72; mgr. group bus. svcs. Investors Diversified Svcs., Valley Forge, Pa., 1972-74; from mgr. to dir. to v.p. and divisional mgr. group ins. sales Investors Diversified Svcs., Mpls., 1974-84; pres. Nat. Benefit Resources Group Svcs., Inc., Mpls., 1984—. Mem. sch. bd. Annunciation Sch., Mpls., 1984-87, chmn., 1986-87. Mem. Mass. Mktg. Inst., Self-Insured Inst. Am. (bd. dirs. 1993-96), Sertoma (Mpls. Sertoman of Yr. 1982). Office: Nat Benefit Resources Inc 5402 Parkdale Dr Minneapolis MN 55416-1608

MCEVERS, DUFF STEVEN, lawyer; b. L.A., Apr. 21, 1954; s. Milton Stoddard and Virginia Mary (Tongue) McE.; m. Jeannine Marie Matthews, July 14, 1984; children: Tay Colleen, Reily Maureen. BA, U. So. Calif., 1976; JD, Western State U., 1980. Bar: Calif. 1981, U.S. Dist. Ct. (so. dist.) Calif. 1993, U.S. Dist. Ct. (ctrl. dist.) Calif. 1982, U.S. Ct. Appeals (9th cir.) 1988. Assoc. Donald B. Black Inc., Laguna Beach, Calif., 1981-85; pvt. practice Laguna Beach and Newport Beach, Calif., 1985-88, Assoc. Law Office of Terry J. Coniglio, Inc., Long Beach, Calif., 1988-89; with Barclay Law Corp., 1989-91; pvt. practice Newport Beach and Sonoma, Calif., 1992—; of counsel Walker Law Firm, P.C., Newport Beach, Calif., 1992—. Editor: Law Review, 1979. Mem. Calif. Bar Assn., Breakfast Club Newport Beach, St. Timothy's Men's Club. Office: 1301 Dove St Ste 450 Newport Beach CA 92660-2464

MCEVILLY, JAMES PATRICK, JR., lawyer; b. Phila., July 30, 1943; s. James P. and Virginia Frances (Madden) McE.; m. Joan Elizabeth O'Connor; children: James III, Christopher, Sara, Michael. BS, St. Joseph's U., 1965; JD, Temple U., 1971. Bar: Pa. 1971, U.S. Dist. Ct. (ea. dist.) Pa. 1972, U.S. Ct. Appeals (3d cir.) 1975, U.S. Supreme Ct. 1982. Law clk. to president judge Phila. Mcpl. Ct., 1971-73; assoc. Galfand, Berger, Lurie & March, Phila., 1973-76; asst. dist. atty. Phila. Dist. Atty., 1976-79; prin. McEvilly & Assocs., Feasterville, Pa., 1979—. Editor Temple U. Law Rev., 1971. Mem. Pa. Trial Lawyers Assn., Phila. Bar Assn., Trial Lawyers Am. Home: 1401 Silo Rd Yardley PA 19067-4240 Office: McEvilly & Assocs 1200 Bustleton Pike Ste 1B Feasterville Trevose PA 19053

MCEVILLY, MICHAEL JAMES, civil engineer; b. Newburgh, N.Y., Sept. 29, 1958; s. William George and Mary Elizabeth (Waye) McE.; m. Mary Ellen Hilton, May 23, 1980; children: Melissa Renee, Michael Patrick. BS in Civil Engring., U. Mo., Rolla, 1980, MS in Engring. Mgmt., 1981. Registered profl. engr., Tex. Prodn. engr. Cities Svc. Co., Houston, 1981-84, sr. prodn. engr., 1984-85; sr. constrn. engr. Anadarko Petroleum Corp., Houston, 1985-92, staff constrn. engr., 1992-94, divsn. constrn. supr., 1994—; offshore platform staff Cities Svc. Co., Houston, 1981-85; facilities, pipeline design, fabrication, installation and commissioning Gulf of Mex., onshore Gulf Coast, Alaska and internat. Anadarko Petroleum Corp., Houston, 1985—. Mem. Little League Umpires, Spring, Tex., 1988—. Named Young Engr. of Yr., Tex. Soc. Profl. Engrs., Houston, 1992. Mem. NSPE, ASCE, Am. Welding Soc., Soc. Petroleum Engrs., Am. Soc. Nondestructive Testing, Masters, Warden and Secs. Assn. (sec. 1993—), Order Ea. Star (patron, v.p.), Masons (pres. 1992-93, master, dist. instr., Golden Travel award), Lions Club, Shriners, Elks. Republican. Presbyterian. Achievements include multiple derrick barge (2) lift of a 1700 ton offshore drilling/production platform. Avocations: baseball umpiring, sporting events, coaching youth sports. Home: 5210 Nodaway Ln Spring TX 77379-8048 Office: Anadarko Petroleum Corp 17001 Northchase Dr Houston TX 77060-2141

MCEVOY, LORRAINE K., oncology nurse; b. S.I., N.Y., Mar. 24, 1950; d. Edward Donald and Josephine (Boyle) McMahon; children: Kelly Ann, Kevin Michael. Diploma, St. Vincent's Sch. Nursing, 1970; BSN, Seton Hall

U., 1994; MSN, Kean Coll. N.J., 1997. RN, N.J. Charge nurse Van Dyk's Manor, Ridgewood, N.J., 1977-81; staff nurse St. Joseph's Hosp. and Med. Ctr., Paterson, N.J., 1981-88, nurse mgr. oncology, bone marrow transplant, 1988—, cons., edutor devel. bone marrow and stem cell transplant programs, 1995, 96, 97. Susan G. Komen Breast Cancer Found. grantee, 1997. Mem. Oncology Nursing Soc., Tri-State Bone Marrow Transplant Nurses Assn., Breast Cancer Connection, Sigma Theta Tau. Office: St Joseph's Hosp and Med Ctr 703 Main St Paterson NJ 07503-2621

MCEVOY, MICHAEL JOSEPH, economist; b. Cork, Ireland, Feb. 16, 1963; came to U.S., 1991.; s. Patrick Joseph and Pauline (Heffernan) McE. BA, Univ. Coll., Cork, Ireland, 1984, M in Econ. Sci., 1987; MBA, U. Penn., 1996. Rsch. economist Irish Export Bd., Dublin, Ireland, 1986-87; sr. analyst economist Fixpoint Ltd., London, 1987-91; rsch. assoc. Micra, Inc., Washington, 1991-92; chief economist Embassy of France, Washington, 1992-96; cons. The Tower Group, Boston, 1996—; dir. Fixpoint Ltd., 1989-91. Co-author: (quarterly pub.) European Business: Forecasts, Strategies, Tactics, 1989-91. Mem. Nat. Assn. Bus. Economists, Soc. Govt. Economists, Nat. Economists Club, Am. Film Inst., U.S. Holocaust Meml. Mus., Smithsonian Inst. Roman Catholic. Avocations: golf, tennis, walking. Office: The Tower Group 7 Wells Ave Newton MA 02159

MCEVOY, NAN TUCKER, publishing company executive; b. San Mateo, Calif., July 15, 1919; d. Nion R. and Phyllis (de Young) Tucker; m. Dennis McEvoy, 1948 (div.); 1 child, Nion Tucker McEvoy. Student, Georgetown U., 1975. Newspaper reporter San Francisco Chronicle, 1944-46, N.Y. Herald Tribune, N.Y.C., 1946-47, Washington Post, 1947-48; rep. in pub. rels. John Homes, Inc., Washington, 1959-60; spl. asst. to dir. U.S. Peace Corps, Washington, 1961-64; mem. U.S. delegation UNESCO, Washington, 1964-65; dir. Population Coun., Washington, 1965-70; co-founder, dep. dir. Preterm, Inc., Washington, 1970-74; former chmn. bd. Chronicle Pub. Co., San Francisco, 1975-95, dir. emeritus, 1995—. Mem. nat. bd. dirs. Smithsonian Instn., Washington, 1994—; bd. dirs. Am. Farmland Trust, Trust for Pub. Land; mem. coun. Brookings Instn., Washington, 1994—; mem. U. Calif. San Francisco Found., 1993—; dir. emeritus Nat. Mus. Am. Art; mem. Nat. Coun. Fine Arts Museums; formerly arbitrator Am. Arbitration Assn., Washington. Named Woman of Yr., Washingtonian Mag., 1973. Mem. Am. Art Forum, Burlingame Country Club, The River Club, Commonwealth Club of Calif., World Affairs Coun., Villa Taverna. Avocation: overseeing California olive grove ranch producing fine extra virgin olive oil. Office: 655 Montgomery St Ste 1430 San Francisco CA 94111-2631

MCEVOY, SHARLENE ANN, business law educator; b. Derby, Conn., July 6, 1950; d. Peter Henry Jr. and Madaline Elizabeth (McCabe) McE. BA magna cum laude, Albertus Magnus Coll., 1972; JD, U. Conn., West Hartford, 1975; MA, Trinity Coll., Hartford, 1980, UCLA, 1982; PhD, UCLA, 1985. Bar: Conn., 1975. Pvt. practice Derby, 1984—; asst. prof. bus. law Fairfield (Conn.) U. Sch. Bus., 1986—; adj. prof. bus. law, polit. sci. Albertus Magnus Coll., New Haven, Conn., 1978-80, U. Conn., Stamford, 1984-86; acting chmn. polit. sci. dept. Albertus Magnus Coll., 1980; assoc. prof. law Fairfield U., 1992—; Chmn. Women's Resource Ctr., Fairfield U., 1989-91. Staff editor Jour. Legal Studies Edn., 1989-94; reviewer Am. Bus. Law Assn. jour., 1988—, staff editor, 1995—; sr. articles editor N.E. Jour. of Legal Studies in Bus., 1995-96. Mem. Derby Tercentennial Commn., 1973-74; bd. dirs. Valley Transit Dist., Derby, 1975-77, Justice of Peace, City of Derby, 1975-83; alt. mem. Parks and Recreation Commn., Woodbury, 1995—; mem., treas. Woodbury Dem. Town Com., 1995-96, corr. sec. 1996—. Recipient Best Paper award N.E. Regional Bus. Law Assn., 1990, Best Paper award Tri-State Regional Bus. Law Assn., 1991; Fairfield U. Sch. Bus. rsch. grantee 1989, 91, 92, Fairfield U. rsch. grantee, 1994. Mem. ABA, Conn. Bar Assn., Acad. Legal Studies in Bus., Mensa (coord. SINISTRAL spl. interest group 1977—). Democrat. Roman Catholic. Avocations: running, chess, tennis, swimming. Office: 198 Emmett Ave Derby CT 06418-1258

MC EWAN, LEONARD, former judge; b. Great Falls, Mont., Feb. 17, 1925; s. Leonard Wellington and Olga (Trinastich) McE.; m. Cameon Wolfe, Sept. 2, 1953 (dec. 1977); m. Mary Hurst Amschel, Feb. 20, 1988. B.S., U. Wyo., 1955, J.D., 1957. Bar: Wyo. bar 1957. Practice in Sheridan, 1957-69; municipal judge City Sheridan, 1958-69; justice Wyo. Supreme Ct., Cheyenne, 1969-75; chief justice Wyo. Supreme Ct., 1975; dist. judge Sheridan, Wyo., 1975-85. Trustee Sheridan Coll., 1963-69, Sheridan County YMCA, 1963-68, All-American Indian Days, 1959-63, N. Am. Indian Found., 1960-67. Served with USAAF, 1943-46. Recipient Distinguished Service award Jr. C. of C., 1960. Mem. Wyo. State Bar, Am. Bar Assn., Am. Legion, U. Wyo. Alumni Assn. (bd. dirs. 1962-66), Sigma Alpha Epsilon. Episcopalian. Lodges: Elks, Eagles, Masons, Rotary, Quarterback. Address: PO Box 460 Story WY 82842-0460

MCEWEN, ALEXANDER CAMPBELL, cadastral studies educator, former Canadian government official, surveying consultant; b. Ryde, Isle of Wight, Eng., Aug. 22, 1926; emigrated to Can., 1949; s. Walter Scott and Florence Lilian (Goodall) McE.; m. Patricia Stuart Richards, July 27, 1956 (div. 1988); m. Sherry Lee Wilson, June 13, 1993; children: Ann Florence, Sheila Jean, Laura Susan. LL.B., U. London, 1966, Ph.D., 1979; LL.M., U. East Africa, 1970. Sr. surveyor H. Wheeler Assocs., Toronto, Ont., Can., 1961-62; sec. treas. Assn. Ont. Land Surveyors, Toronto, 1963-64; prin. Survey Tng. Centre, Dar es Salaam, Tanzania, 1964-70; survey cons. Ottawa, Ont., Can., 1970-72; dir. lands and surveys Govt. Nfld., St. John's, 1972-76; commr. Internat. Boundary Commn., Ottawa, Ont., 1976-90; survey adviser Govt. Can., Jesselton, North Borneo, 1954-56, Lagos, Nigeria, 1989-90; tech. expert UN, Victoria, Seychelles, 1958-61; survey cons. Can. Exec. Service Orgn., Kingston, Jamaica, 1981, Quito, Ecuador, 1986; prof. cadastral studies, dept. geomatics engring. U. Calgary, Alta., Can., 1991-96. Author: International Boundaries of East Africa, 1971 In Search of the Highlands, 1988; contbr. articles to profl. jours. Served with Royal Armoured Corp. Mem. Can. Inst. Geomatics (mem. coun. 1977-81, Jim Jones award 1967, 83, 90, Presdl. citation 1981), Western Can. Bd. Examiners for Land Surveyors (registrar, bd. dirs. 1991-96), Assn. Ont. Land Surveyors (sec.-treas. 1963-64), Assn. Nfld. Land Surveyors (bd. examiners 1975-76), Writer's Union Can. Home: 2129 2d Ave NW, Calgary, AB Canada T2N OG8

MCEWEN, ALFRED SHERMAN, planetary geologist; b. Lawrence, Kans., July 22, 1954; s. William Edwin and Miriam (Sherman) McE.; m. Eileen Haney; 1 child, Ian. B.S., SUNY-Syracuse, 1975; B.S. No. Ariz. U., 1981, M.S., 1983; PhD Ariz. State U., 1988. Vol. Peace Corps, Guatemala, Central Am., 1975-77; soil conservationist Soil Conservation Service, USDA, 1978-80; geologist U.S. Geol. Survey, Flagstaff, Ariz., 1981-96, U. Ariz., 1996—. Mem. Galileo, Cassini, Mars Global Surveyor, and Clementine Spacecraft Sci. Teams. Contbr. articles, image processing-color images to profl. jours. Mem. Am. Geophys. Union, Am. Astron. Soc. Home: 4135 E Cooper St Tucson AZ 85711 Office: U Ariz Dept Planetary Scis Lunar and Planetary Lab 1629 E University Blvd Tucson AZ 85721-0092

MCEWEN, JAMES, publishing executive. Pub. Family Cir., N.Y.C. Office: Gruner & Jahr USA Pub Family Cir 110 5th Ave New York NY 10011-5601*

MCEWEN, JEAN, painter; b. Montreal, Que., Can., Dec. 14, 1923; s. William and Elaine (Renaud) McE.; m. Indra Kagis, Sept. 18, 1976; children: Jean Sabin, Marianne Jérémie; children by previous marriage: Isabelle, Domenique. Grad., U. Montreal, 1947. Tchr. U. Concordia, Montreal. One-man exhbns. include, Gallery Godart-Lefort, Montreal, 1962-69, Gallery Montreal, 1963, Gallery Moos, Toronto, 1963-69, Gallery Martha Jackson, N.Y.C., 1963, Mayer Gallery, Paris, 1964, group exhbns. include, Dunn Internat. Exhbn., Tate Gallery, London, 1963; rep. permanent collections, Mus. Modern Art, N.Y.C., Walker Art Center, Mpls., Albright-Knox Art Gallery, Buffalo, Hirshhorn Mus., Smithsonian Instn., Ottawa Mus., Toronto Mus.; commd. for stained glass window, Sir George Williams U., 1966, murals for, Toronto Airport, Plase Arts, Montreal. (Winner Quebec Art competition 1962, recipient Jessie Dow award Montreal Spring Exhbn. 1964), large mural Bank Scotia, Montreal, head office, 1991; major retrospect Mont. Mus. Fine Arts, 1987—. grantee Can. Council, 1977-78. Academician Royal Can. Acad. Arts. Roman Catholic. Address: 3908 Parc Lafontaine Rue, Montreal, PQ Canada H2L 3M6

MCEWEN, LARRY BURDETTE, retired English and theater arts educator, author; b. Clay Center, Nebr., Aug. 4, 1934; s. Gerald E. and Marie L. (Pennington) McE.; m. Charlotte E. Alloway, Feb. 14, 1978; children: Diana J., Sheila J. AB, Augustana Coll., Rock Island, Ill., 1962; MS, Ill. State U., 1968. Cert. tchr., Nebr. Prof. theatre arts Blackburn Coll., Carlinville, Ill., 1969-75; counselor div. vocat. rehab. Nebr. Dept. Edn., Lincoln, 1976-82; tchr. English Hastings (Nebr.) Sr. High Sch., 1983-92; vis. lectr. Mt. Senario Coll., Ladysmith, Wis., 1971, Knox Coll., Galesburg, Ill., 1974, Hastings (Nebr.) Coll., 1976. Author: Much Ado About Shakespeare, 1992, Goose and Fables, 1994, To Honor Our Fathers and Mothers, 1996; author Apple Software; dir. 63 theatrical prodns.; contbr. numerous articles to profl. publs. With USAF, 1951-52. Grad. fellow Ind. U., 1968-69; Quad-City Music Guild scholar, 1961-62. Mem. NEA, Neb. State Edn. Assn., Acad. Computers in Eng., Apple Programmers and Developers Assn., Nat. Apple Users Group, Nat. Coun. Tchrs. English, Alpha Psi Omega, Alpha Phi Omega. Home and Office: 603 E 5th St Hastings NE 68901-5336

MCFADDEN, DAVID REVERE, museum director; b. Devils Lake, N.D., Aug. 28, 1947; BA, U. Minn., 1972, MA, 1978. Assoc. curator Mpls. Inst. Arts, 1976-78, curator, 1978; asst. dir. collections and rsch., curator decorative arts Cooper-Hewitt, Nat. Mus. of Design, N.Y.C., 1978-95; exec. dir. Millicent Rogers Mus., Taos, N.Mex., 1995—; adj. prof. art Cooper-Hewitt-Parsons M.A. program, N.Y.C., 1983—; gov. Decorative Arts Trust; pres. applied arts com. Internat. Coun. Mus., 1993-95; mem. exhbn. com. Am. Fedn. Arts. Author: Scandinavian Modern Design (Wittenborn award 1984), 1983, L'Art de Vivre: Decorative Arts and Design in France 1789-1989, 1989. Decorated knight 1st class Order of the Lion (Finland), 1984; knight commdr. Order of No. Star (Sweden); chevalier des l'Ordre des Arts et des Letrres (France). Recipient Awards of Merit Smithsonian Instn., 1981, 88, 89, Presdl. Design award, 1994; fellow Kress Found., 1973-74. Mem. Worshipful Co. Goldsmiths London. Office: Millicent Rogers Mus PO Box A Taos NM 87571

MCFADDEN, DENNIS, experimental psychology educator; b. Oct. 2, 1940; s. Samuel John and Evelyn (Dinnerson) McF.; m. Nancy L. Wilson, Dec. 28, 1960; children: Tracie Ann, Devin James. BA, Sacramento State Coll., Calif., 1962; PhD, Ind U., 1967. Asst. prof. U. Tex., Austin, 1967-72, assoc. prof., 1972-77, prof., 1977—. Contbr. articles to profl. jours. Recipient Jacob K. Javits Neurosci. Investigator award, 1984-89, Claude D. Pepper award, 1989-91; named Piper Prof., Minnie Stevens Piper Found., 1987. Fellow AAAS, Acoustical Soc. Am.; mem. Assn. for Rsch. Otolaryngology, CHABA (NAS-NRC com. on hearing, bioacoustics and biomechanics), Soc. Neurosci. Office: U Tex Dept Psychology Mezes Hall # 330 Austin TX 78712-1189

MCFADDEN, EDWARD REGIS, JR., pulmonary educator; b. Pitts., Aug. 2, 1936. BA, St. Vincent Coll., 1958; MD, U. Pitts., 1963. Assoc. prof. medicine U. Tex. Med. Br., Galveston, 1972-73; asst. prof. Harvard U., Boston, 1973-77, assoc. prof., 1977-81, 81-84; assoc. prof. MIT div. health sci., Boston, 1979-84; Argyl J. Beams prof. medicine Case Western Res. U., Cleve., 1984—; dir. Airway Disease Ctr. Univ. Hosp., Cleve., 1984-93, respiratory therapy, 1985—, Clin. Research Ctr., 1986—, divsn. pulmonary and critical care medicine, 1993—. Editor-in-chief Airway Diseases, N.Y.C., 1985—; contbr. articles to profl. jours. Recipient George W. Thorn Teaching award Peter Bent Brigham Hosp., Boston, 1980. Fellow ACP; mem. Am. Fedn. Clin. Research, Am. Thoracic Soc., So. Soc. Clin. Investigation, Am. Physiol. Soc., Am. Acad. Allergy and Immunology, Am. Soc. Clin. Investigation, Assn. Am. Physicians. Home: 2706 Landon Rd Cleveland OH 44122-2008 Office: Univ Hosps Cleve 2074 Abington Rd Cleveland OH 44106-5067

MCFADDEN, FRANK HAMPTON, lawyer, business executive, former judge; b. Oxford, Miss., Nov. 20, 1925; s. John Angus and Ruby (Roy) McF.; m. Jane Porter Nabers, Sept. 30, 1960; children—Frank Hampton, Angus Nabers, Jane Porter. B.A., U. Miss., 1950; LL.B., Yale U., 1955. Bar: N.Y. 1956, Ala. 1959. Assoc. firm Lord, Day & Lord, N.Y.C., 1955-58; assoc. firm Bradley, Arant, Rose & White, Birmingham, Ala., 1958-63, partner, 1963-69; judge U.S. Dist. Ct. No. Dist. Ala., Birmingham, 1969-73; chief judge U.S. Dist. Ct. No. Dist. Ala., 1973-81; sr. v.p., gen. counsel Blount, Inc., Montgomery, Ala., 1982-91, exec. v.p. adminstrn. and govt. affairs, 1991, exec. v.p. legal affairs, 1991-93, exec. v.p., gen. counsel, 1993-95; mem. Capell, Howard, Knabe & Cobbs, P.A., Montgomery, 1995—; chmn. Blount Energy Resource Corp., Montgomery, 1983-88. Mem. jud. panel CPR Inst. for Dispute Resolution, 1985—. Served from ensign to lt. USNR, 1944-49, 51-53. Fellow Am. Coll. Constrn. Lawyers; mem. Am. Corp. Counsel Assn. (bd. dirs. 1984-93, chmn. 1989). Office: Capell Howard Knabe 57 Adams Ave Montgomery AL 36104-4001

MC FADDEN, G. BRUCE, hospital administrator; b. Winchester, Va., Feb. 19, 1934; s. S. Donald and Ruth D. McF.; m. Lois F. Richardson, Aug. 22, 1964; children—Christopher, Amy. BS, Va. Poly. Inst., 1953; MHA, Med. Coll. Va. (Va. Commonwealth U.), 1961. Asst. adminstr. Meml. Hosp. at Easton, Md., Inc., 1963-70; v.p. Pa. Hosp., Phila., 1970-75; dir. U. Md. Hosp., Balt., 1975-82; pres. Robert Wood Johnson, University Hosp., 1982-88; exec. dir. N.Y. Health Career Ctr., N.Y.C., 1989-91, N.Y. Regional Transplant Program, N.Y.C., 1991-95; v.p. One Call Med., 1995—; cons. Hosp. Joint Practice Demonstration Project, Nat. Joint Practice Commn. of AMA, ANA; preceptor for programs in health care adminstrn. Med. Coll. Va., Columbia U., N.Y. U., U. Pa., Temple U.; bd. dirs., mem. recognition com. Am. Blood Commn.; bd. dirs., mem. exec. com. Central Md. Health Systems Agy.; chmn. Accreditation Council on Grad. Med. Edn.; chmn. Cen. Jersey Health Care Corp., New Brunswick; bd. dirs. New Brunswick Savs. Bank;. Bd. dirs. Vis. Nurse Soc., Phila., George St. Playhouse, New Brunswick, N.J., Westfield YMCA, N.J.; bd. dirs., vice chmn. Community Nursing Svcs. of Phila.; pres. Robert Wood; mem. Bd. of Edn., Westfield, N.J. Fellow Am. Coll. Hosp. Adminstrs.; mem. Am. Hosp. Assn. (chmn. coun. on human resources, chmn. spl. coms. on mandatory continuing edn., gen. coun.). Home: 585 Trinity Pl Westfield NJ 07090-3305

MC FADDEN, GEORGE LINUS, retired army officer; b. Sharon, Pa., Oct. 16, 1927; s. George Linus and Frances Jane (Byrne) McF.; m. Floretta Theresa McFadden, Nov. 20, 1948; children: Kenneth William, Mark Edward, Mary Kathleen, Robert Bernard, George Linus, William. B.E., U. Omaha, 1961; M.S., George Washington U., 1967; grad., Advanced Mgmt. Program, Harvard U., 1971. Pvt. U.S. Army, 1946, advanced through grades to maj. gen., 1976; comdg. officer (7th inf. div. arty.), Korea, 1969-70; dep. comdg. gen. U.S. Army Security Agy., Arlington, Va., 1972-74; dep. dir. for field mgmt. and evaluation, dep. chief central security service Fort George G. Meade, Md., 1975-78; dep. dir. ops. Nat. Security Agy., 1978-79; comdg. gen. U.S. Army So. European Task Force, Vicenza, Italy, 1979-82; corp. v.p. CompuDyne Corp., 1986-89; sr. v.p. The Abbott Group, Inc., Annapolis, Md., 1989—; dir. Washington Studies and Analysis Group McDonnell Douglas Corp., 1985-86; dir. security affairs Dept. Energy, 1991—. Pres., chmn. bd. Met. Washington chpt. Arthritis Found., 1986-95. Decorated D.F.C., D.S.M., Silver Star, Bronze Star, Purple Heart, others. Roman Catholic.

MCFADDEN, JOHN THOMAS, financial planner, insurance agent, investor; b. Bronx, N.Y., Sept. 12, 1954; s. John W. and Mary Jane (Brown) McF.; m. Marguerite Louise Monaco, June 14, 1975; children: Shannon Louise, Sean Patrick, Kaitlyn Marie. AS in Criminal Justice, Westchester C.C., Vallhalla, N.Y., 1974; BS in Criminal Justice, Iona Coll., 1975. CLU; ChFC; CFP; CFS; Life Underwriter Tng. Coun. Fellow. Security guard Mary Knoll Fathers, Ossining, N.Y., 1972-76; salesman Best Plumbing Supply, Mohegan Lake, N.Y., 1973-76; mgr. sales Cor-Wil Dist., Stormville, N.Y., 1976-81, Martin Plumbing Supply, New Milford, Conn., 1981-82; agt. Mut. of N.Y., Poughkeepsie, 1982-83; owner, prin. McFadden & Assocs., Poughkeepsie, 1983—. Asst. scoutmaster Boy Scouts Am., Pleasant Valley, N.Y., 1993—; bd. dirs. Dutchess County chpt. ARC, 1994—. Mem. Am. Soc. CLU-ChFC, NRA (life), Family Motor Coach Assn., Nat. Assn. Eagle Scouts (life), Million Dollar Round Table (life), Order of the Arrow Lodge (brotherhood 1968—), Nat. Assn. Life Underwriters (pres. local chpt. 1987-89), Good Sam Club (life). Roman Catholic. Avocations: travel, camping, hunting, coin collecting, investing. Home: 22 David Dr Poughkeepsie NY 12601-6501 Office: McFadden & Assocs 22 IBM Rd Ste 204-b Poughkeepsie NY 12601-5455

MCFADDEN, JOHN VOLNEY, retired manufacturing company executive; b. N.Y.C., Oct. 3, 1931; s. Volney and Mary Lucile (McConkie) McF.; m. Marie Linstead, June 27, 1953; children—Deborah, John Scott, David. B.S. in Commerce and Fin, Bucknell U., 1953; J.D., Detroit Coll. Law, 1960. Pres., vice-chmn. MTD Products, Inc., Cleve., 1960-92; pres. MTD Products Inc., Cleve., 1980-91, vice chmn., 1990-92; gen. ptnr. Camelot Ptnrs., Cleve., 1992—; chmn. AC Products Co., Inc., C.E. White Co.; bd. dirs. Nat. Machinery Inc., Fusion Inc., Star Bank, Flambeau Corp.; chmn. bd. dirs. Guaranty Spltys. Inc.; past chmn. financing adv. bd. State of Ohio Devel.; past pres. Cleve. World Trade Assn.; chmn. Parkside Acquisition Ptnrs. Ltd. Trustee, chmn. Fairview Health Svcs. Lt. Supply Corps, USN. Mem. Cleve. Yachting Club. Office: Camelot Ptnrs 20160 Parkside Dr Cleveland OH 44116-1347

MC FADDEN, JOSEPH MICHAEL, academic administrator; b. Joliet, Ill., Feb. 12, 1932; s. Francis Joseph and Lucille (Adler) McF.; m. Norma Cardwell, Oct. 10, 1958; children: Timothy Joseph, Mary Colleen, Jonathan Andrew. B.A., Lewis Coll., 1954; M.A., U. Chgo., 1961; Ph.D., No. Ill. U., 1968. Tchr. history Joliet Cath. High Sch., 1957-60; mem. faculty history dept. Lewis Coll., Lockport, Ill., 1960-70, asso. prof., 1967-70, v.p. acad. affairs, 1968-70; prof. history, dean sch. Nat. and Social Sci., Kearney (Nebr.) State Coll., 1970-74; prof. history, dean Sch. Social and Behavioral Scis., Slippery Rock (Pa.) State Coll., 1974-77; pres. No. State Coll., Aberdeen, S.D., 1977-82, U. S.D., Vermillion, 1982-88, U. St. Thomas, Houston, 1988—. Served with USNR, 1954-56. Roman Catholic. Office: U St Thomas Office of Pres 3812 Montrose Blvd Houston TX 77006-4626

MCFADDEN, JOSEPH PATRICK, insurance company executive; b. Norristown, Pa., Jan. 1, 1939; s. Joseph Patrick and Anna (Brennan) McF.; m. Patricia Ann Burke, Jan. 28, 1961; children: Mary Ann, Linda, Patricia, Joseph, Nancy, Meghan. BA, LaSalle U., 1961. Claim adjuster Allstate Ins. Co., Valley Forge, Pa., 1963-66; various mgmt. positions Valley Forge and Harrison, N.Y., 1966-74; regional claim mgr. Rochester, N.Y., 1974-76, Murray Hill, N.J., 1976-79; zone claim mgr. Bannockburn, Ill., 1979-81; asst. regional mgr. Skokie, Ill., 1981-83; asst. v.p. Northbrook, Ill., 1983-84; regional v.p. Santa Ana, Calif., 1984-86; claim v.p. Northbrook, 1986-91, territorial v.p., 1991—. 1st lt. U.S. Army, 1961-63. Mem. Nat. Auto Theft Bur. (mem. bd. govs. 1986), Nat. Assn. Ind. Insurers (mem. claims com. 1986), Ins. Crime Prevention Inst., Ins. Info. Inst. (mem. adv. panel on legal issues). Roman Catholic. Home: 1005 Ashley Ln Libertyville IL 60048-3813 Office: Allstate Ins Co 2775 Sanders Rd Ste F6B Northbrook IL 60062-6110

MCFADDEN, LEON LAMBERT, artist, inventor; b. St. Paul, Apr. 19, 1920; s. Frank Grover and Irene Manilla Lambert McF.; m. Karyn Flannery, Nov. 6, 1986. Student, several colls., univs., art insts. Prin. McFadden Commercial Studios, 1946-50; with McFadden-Kaump Art Service, 1952-54; pres. McFadden Advt. (merger with Sundial Services, Inc.), 1954-70; mktg. dir. Kinelogic Corp., Mountain View, Calif., 1965-70; dir. rsch. and devel. proprietary patents Sundial Svcs., Inc., 1968-70; art instr. various Calif. community colls., 1972-74; minority bus. cons. VISTA/ACTION, 1974-75; pres., CEO Prometheus Project, Inc., Yreka, Calif., 1975—. Inventor, patentee 18 mechanical tools and devices; prin. artistic works include large assemblage painting of liberty, found image works (represented in White House spl. collection). Served with USN, 1942-46, PTO. Mem. AAAS, Mensa, Artists Equity Assn. Inc., Artists Equity Assn. N.Y., Siskiyou Artists Assn., Sierra Club. Home: 551 N Main St Yreka CA 96097-2524 Office: Liberty Painting Corp 6725 Old Highway 99 S Yreka CA 96097-9760

MCFADDEN, MARY JOSEPHINE, fashion industry executive; b. N.Y.C., Oct. 1, 1938; d. Alexander Bloomfield and Mary Josephine (Cutting) McF.; m. Philip Harari; 1 child, Justine. Ed., Sorbonne, Paris, France, Traphagen Sch. Design, 1957, Columbia, 1959-62; DFA, Internat. Fine Arts Coll., 1984. Pub. relations dir. Christian Dior, N.Y.C., 1962-64; merchandising editor Vogue South Africa, 1964-65, editor, 1965-69; polit. and travel columnist Rand (South Africa) Daily Mail, 1965-68; founder sculptural workshop Vukutu, Rhodesia, 1968-70; spl. projects editor Vogue U.S.A., 1973; pres. Mary McFadden, Inc., N.Y.C., 1976—; ptnr. MMcF Collection by Mary McFadden, 1991—; bd. dirs., advisor Sch. Design and Merchandising Kent State U., Eugene O'Neill Meml. Theatre Ctr.; mem. profl. com. Cooper-Hewitt Mus., Smithsonian Inst., Nat. Mus. of Design. Fashion and jewelry designer, 1973—. Advisor Nat. Endowment for Arts; active local Police Athletic League, We Care About N.Y., CFDA-Vogue Breast Cancer Initiative, Beth Israel Hosp., The Chemotherapy Found. Recipient Am. Fashion Critics award-Coty award, 1976, 78, 79, Audemars Piguet Fashion award, 1976, Rex award, 1977, award More Coll. Art, 1977, Pa. Gov.'s award, 1977, Roscoe award, 1978, Pres.'s Fellows award RISD, 1979, Neiman-Marcus award of excellence, 1979, Design Excellence award Pratt Inst., 1993, award N.Y. Landmarks Conservancy, 1994, NU Breed Fashion award, 1996, Marymount Coll. Fashion award, 1996; named to Fashion Hall of Fame, 1979; fellow RISD. Mem. Fashion Group (bd. dirs. 1981-82), Council of Fashion Designers Am. (past pres., current v.p. bd. dirs.). Office: Mary McFadden Inc 240 W 35th St Fl 17 New York NY 10001-2506

MCFADDEN, NADINE LYNN, secondary education Spanish educator; b. Cleve., May 13, 1947; d. Frank and Helen (Senich) Mancini; m. Francis Joseph McFadden, Aug. 22, 1970; children: Ian Mancini, Kevin Mancini. BS in Edn., Ohio U., 1969; MA in Edn., Kent State U., 1990. Lic. tchr., Ohio. High sch. tchr. Spanish Parma (Ohio) City Schs., 1969—; v.p. Jonah-Kater Distance Learning Inc., 1995—; chaperone European cultural trips Parma City Schs., 1973-76, 80, 92, 95, 96, strategic planning com., 1991-92; chmn. textbook com. Strongsville (Ohio) City Schs., 1990-92; program presenter in-svc. fgn. lang. tchrs., Parma; adj. prof. Fresno Pacific Coll. Mem. NEA, Am. Assn. Tchrs. Spanish and Portuguese, Ohio Modern Lang. Tchrs. Assn., Ohio Edn. Assn., Parma Edn. Assn. Avocations: travel, reading, quilting. Home: 17536 Brandywine Dr Strongsville OH 44136-7034 Office: Parma City Schs Ridge Rd Parma OH 44129

MCFADDEN, NANCY ELIZABETH, lawyer; b. Wilmington, Del., Oct. 20, 1958; d. William P. and Mary Elizabeth (Adams) McF. BA, San Jose State U., 1984; JD, U. Va., 1987. Judicial clk. Hon. John P. Wiese U.S. Claims Ct., Washington, 1987-88; atty. O'Melveny & Myers, Washington, 1988-91; deputy communications dir. Office of Pres.-Elect, Washington, 1992-93; st atty. gen. U.S. Dept. Justice, Washington, 1993, prin. deputy assoc. atty. gen., 1993—; gen. counsel Dept. Transp., Washington, 1996—. Nat. deputy polit. dir. Clinton for Pres. Campaign, 1992, nat. surrogate dir. Clinton-Gore for Pres. Campaign, 1992.

MCFADDEN, PETER WILLIAM, mechanical engineering educator; b. Stamford, Conn., Aug. 2, 1932; s. Kenneth E. and Marie (Gleason) McF.; children: Peter, Kathleen, Mary. B.S. in Mech. Engring, U. Conn., 1954, M.S., 1956; Ph.D., Purdue U., 1959. Registered profl. engr., Ind. Asst. instr. U. Conn., 1954-56, prof. mech. engring., 1971—, dean Sch. Engring., 1971-85, dir. devel., 1985-88, provost, v.p., 1988, exec. asst. to pres., exec. sec. to bd. trustees, 1989—; mem. faculty Purdue U., 1956-71; prof. mech. engring., head Purdue U. (Sch. Mech. Engring.), 1965-71; postdoctoral research Swiss Fed. Inst., Zurich, 1960-61; cons. to industry, 1959—. Mem. ASME, Am. Soc. Engring. Edn. Research in cryogenics, heat transfer, mass transfer. Office: U Conn Gulley Hall U-48 352 Mansfield Rd Storrs Mansfield CT 06268

MC FADDEN, ROBERT DENNIS, reporter; b. Milw., Feb. 11, 1937; s. Francis Joseph and Violet (Charleston) McF.; student U. Wis., Eau Claire, 1955-57; B.S. cum laude, U. Wis., Madison, 1960; m. Judith Marian Silverman, June 20, 1971; 1 son, Nolan Seth. Reporter, Wisconsin Rapids (Wis.) Daily Tribune, 1957-58, Wis. State Jour., Madison, 1958-59, Cin. Enquirer, 1960-61; sr. writer, reporter N.Y. Times, 1961—; mem. adv. coun. St. John's U. dept journalism, 1996—. Co-author: No Hiding Place, 1981; Outrage: The Story Behind the Tawana Brawley Hoax, 1990. Served with U.S. Army, 1960-61, Res., 1961-68. Recipient Byline award N.Y. Press Club, 1973, 74, 80, 87, 89, 92, Page One award Newspaper Guild N.Y., 1978, Spot News award Uniformed Firemen's Assn., 1967, Spot News award L.I. Press Club, 1984, 95, Chancellor's award for Disting. Svc. U. Wis., 1987, Man of Yr. award Alumni N.Y., 1997, Excellence in Local Reporting award N.Y. Newspaper Publ. Assn., 1988, Spot News award N.Y. State Associated Press, 1989, 91, Continuing Coverage award, 1995, In Depth Reporting award, 1989, 91, Feature Writing award, 1996, Ochs Prize in Journalism, 1989, Best News/Feature Story award Internat. Assn. Fire Fighters, 1991, Pulitzer Prize for Spot News Reporting (N.Y. Times team), 1994, (individual) 96, Nat. Spot News award Asian-Am. Journalists Assn., 1994, Comprehensive Reporting award, N.Y. Uniformed Fire Officers Assn., 1995. Mem. N.Y. Soc. Silurians (Spot News Story award 1977, Peter Kihss award 1987, Investigative reporting award 1989, Excellence in Journalism award 1994, gov. 1988—). Office: NY Times 229 W 43rd St New York NY 10036-3913

MCFADDEN, ROBERT STETSON, hepatologist; b. Houston, Mar. 29, 1951; s. David Barnett and Phyllis Reed (Gowell) McF.; m. Addie Elizabeth Hunt, Mar. 23, 1975; children: William Gordon, Elizabeth Stetson. BS in Biology, Baylor U., 1973; MD, U. Tex., Galveston, 1977. Diplomate Am. Bd. Internal Medicine; cert. gastroenterology Am. Bd. Internal Medicine. Intern in internal medicine La. State U. Med. Sch., New Orleans, 1977-78, resident in internal medicine, 1978-81; staff physician clinic Pub. Health Hosp., New Orleans, 1981; fellow gastroenterology U. Ala., Birmingham, 1981-83; fellow hepatology U. Miami, Fla., 1983-84; gastroenterologist Diagnostic Clinic Houston, 1984-87, Oklahoma City Clinic, 1987-92; hepatologist Okla. Transplantation Inst., Oklahoma City, 1993—; cons. gastroenterology Diagnostic Clinic of Houston, 1984-87, Oklahoma City Clinic, 1987-92; cons. liver diseases and liver transplant medicine Okla. Transplant Inst., Oklahoma City, 1993—. Contbr. articles to profl. jours. Mem. ACP, AMA, Am. Assn. for Study of Liver Diseases, Internat. Liver Transplantation Soc., Okla. State Med. Assn. Republican. Baptist. Avocations: Victorian antiques, gardening. Home: 2600 Coffee Creek Edmond OK 73003 Office: Okla Transplantation Inst 3435 NW 56th St Oklahoma City OK 73112-4414

MCFADDEN, THOMAS, academic administrator; b. N.Y.C., Nov. 12, 1935; m. Monica A. Dowdall; children—Monica, David. B.A., Cathedral Coll., 1957; S.T.L., Gregorian U., 1961; S.T.D., Cath. U., 1963. Asst. prof. St. Joseph's Coll., Bklyn., 1963-66; chmn. theology dept. Cathedral Coll., Douglaston, N.Y., 1966-68; asst. prof. Loyola Coll., Balt., 1968-69; prof. St. Joseph's U., Phila., 1970-82, dean Coll. Arts and Scis., 1982-87; acad. v.p. St. John Fisher Coll., Rochester, N.Y., 1987-92; pres. Marymount Coll., Calif., 1992—; vis. prof. Cath. U., Washington, 1967-68, LaSalle U., Phila., summer 1974-79. Author, editor: New Cath. Ency., 1974, 79. Editor, Dictionary of Religion, 3 vols., 1979; editor: Liberation, Revolution and Freedom, 1975, America in Theological Perspective, 1976. Recipient Disting. Teaching award Lindback, 1978, N.Y. State Excelsior award Bd. Examiners, 1991; HEW grantee, 1972; CAPHE grantee, 1985. Mem. AAUP, Coll. Theology Soc. (chmn. pubs. com. 1973-77). Democrat. Roman Catholic. Office: Marymount Coll 30800 Palos Verdes Dr E Rancho Palos Verdes CA 90275-6273

MCFADIN, HELEN LOZETTA, retired elementary education educator; b. Tucumcari, N.Mex., Sept. 7, 1923; d. Henry J. and LaRue Altha (Ford) Stockton; m. John Reece McFadin, July 3, 1946; 1 child, Janice Lynn McFadin Koenig. AB in Edn./Psychology, Highlands U., Las Vegas, N.Mex., 1956; MA in Teaching, N.Mex. State U., 1968; postgrad., U. N.D., 1965, St. Leo's Coll., St. Leo, Fla., 1970. Cert. tchr., K-12 reading/psychology specialist, N.Mex. Tchr. 1st and 2d grades Grant County Schs., Bayard, N.Mex., 1943-44; tchr. 4th grade Durango (Colo.) Pub. Schs., 1946-48; tchr. 2d grade Artesia Pub. Schs., Loco Hills, N.Mex., 1955; tchr. 3d grade Alamogordo (N.Mex.) Pub. Schs., 1957-66, h.s. reading specialist, 1966-72, elem. reading specialist, 1972-77, tchr. 4th grade, 1977-82, reading tchr. 7th grade, dept. chair, 1982-87; ret. N.Mex. State U., Alamogordo, 1987, instr. edn., 1987-90; organizer reading labs. h.s., elem. schs., Alamogordo, 1966-77, designer programs and curriculum, 1957-89; presenter/cons. in field; cons. Mary Kay Cosmetics; rep. Excel Telecomms., Inc. Contbr. articles to profl. jours. Local and dist. judge spelling bees and sci. fairs Alamogordo Pub. Schs., 1987—. Recipient Literacy award Otero County Reading Coun., 1986; inducted in Women's Hall of Fame, Alamogordo Women's Clubs, 1989. Mem. Am. Bus. Women's Assn. (pres. 1986-87, Woman of the Yr. 1988), C. of C., NEA (del. 1957-87, Dedicated Svc. award 1987), N.Mex. Edn. Assn., Internat. Reading Assn. (mem. Spl. League of the Honored 1985, pres. 1975-76), N.Mex. Reading Assn. (bd. dirs. 1988-94, del. to 1st Russian reading conf. 1992, Dedicated Svc. award 1994), Beta Sigma Phi, Kappa Kappa Iota (Disting. Educator Emeritus Cert. of Merit 1988). Republican. Baptist. Avocations: reading, fashion modeling. Home: 2364 Union Ave Alamogordo NM 88310-3848

MCFALL, CATHERINE GARDNER, poet, critic, educator; b. Jacksonville, Fla., July 10, 1952; d. Albert Dodge and Joan (Livingston) McF.; m. Peter Forbes Olberg, Oct. 21, 1978; 1 child, Amanda Olberg. Baccalaureat, U. Paris, 1973; AB magna cum laude, Wheaton Coll., Norton, Mass., 1974; MA, Johns Hopkins U., 1975; PhD, NYU, 1990. Editorial asst., short story editor Ladies' Home Jour., N.Y.C., 1975-77; adminstrv. dir. Poetry Soc. Am., N.Y.C., 1981-83; instr. writing NYU, N.Y.C., 1983-87, asst. dir. Poetics Inst., 1984-86; asst. prof. humanities Cooper Union, N.Y.C., 1990—. Author: Jonathan's Cloud, 1986, Discovery, 1989 (Nation award), Naming the Animals, 1994, The Pilot's Daughter, 1996; contbr. poetry and revs. to mags. including Paris Rev., New Yorker, N.Y. Times, others. MacDowell Colony fellow, 1980, 86, Yaddo fellow, 1981, 84, 91, 93, 97, Nat. Arts Club Poetry scholar Bread Loaf Writers Conf., 1983. Mem. MLA, Poets and Writers, Poetry Soc. Am., Nat. Book Critics Circle.

MCFARLAN, FRANKLIN WARREN, business administration educator; b. Boston, Oct. 18, 1937; s. Ronald Lyman and Ethel Warren (White) McF.; m. Margaret Karen Nelson, Dec. 17, 1971; children: Andrew, Clarissa, Elizabeth. A.B., Harvard Coll., 1959, M.B.A., 1961, D.B.A., 1965. Asst. prof. Harvard Bus. Sch., Boston, 1964-68, assoc. prof., 1968-73, prof. bus. adminstrn., 1973—, sr. assoc. dean, dir. rsch., 1991-95, sr. assoc. dean external rels., 1995—; dir. Providian Corp., Louisville, Pioneer Hy-Bred Corp., Des Moines, Computer Sci. Corp., L.A. Author: (with Richard Nolan) Information Systems Administration, 1973; (with Linda Applegate and James L. McKenney) Corporate Information Management, 4th edit., 1996; editor: (with Richard Nolan) Information Systems Handbook, 1973, Information Systems Research Challenge, 1984; sr. editor MIS Quar., 1986-88. Bd. dirs., pres. Belmont (Mass.) Day Sch., 1982-86; bd. dirs. Dana Hall Sch., Wellesley, Mass., 1982-94, chmn. bd., 1990-93; trustee Mt. Auburn Hosp., 1991—, chmn. bd., 1995—, trustee Care Group, 1996—; trustee Winsor Sch., 1994—. 1st lt. U.S. Army, 1962-67. Republican. Episcopalian. Club: The Country (Brookline, Mass.). Home: 37 Beatrice Cir Belmont MA 02178-2657 Office: Harvard Bus Sch Soldiers Field Rd Boston MA 02163

MCFARLAND, DAVID E., university official; b. Enid, Okla., Sept. 25, 1938; s. Eugene James McF. and Lydia May (Catlin) Lawson; m. Marcia Ruth Lake, Nov. 27, 1958 (div. 1978); children: Jennifer, Jeffrey, Jon, Julie; m., Susan Kaye Siler, Mar. 3, 1979 (div. 1994); 1 child, Matthew Chapple; m. Barbara Ambrogro, Oct. 1994. BS, Wichita State U., 1961, MS, 1964; PhD, U. Kans., 1967. Stress analysis engr. Boeing Co., Wichita, Kans., 1957-64; instr. U. Kans., Lawrence, 1964-67; asst. v.p., dean Wichita State U., 1967-81; dean. sch. tech., Pittsburgh State U., Kans., 1981-85; provost, v.p. acad. affairs Cen. Mo. State U., 1985-88; pres. Kutztown U. of Pa., 1988—. Author: Mechanics of Materials, 1977; Analysis of Plates, 1972. Contbr. articles to tech. jours. Office: Kutztown U of Pa Office of Pres Kutztown PA 19530

MC FARLAND, FRANK EUGENE, university official; b. Ft. Towson, Okla., Sept. 8, 1918; s. Thomas Edward and Sadie Margaret (Gayer) McF.; m. Trudy Hudson Lively, Dec. 20, 1947 (dec.); children—Marsha Lane, Martha Lynne McFarland Cox. B.A. cum laude, Baylor U., 1950; M.A., Columbia U., 1953, Ed.D., 1959; postgrad., U. Tex., 1956, Tex. A. and M. U., 1956. Lic. psychologist, Okla. Counselor Tex. A&M U., College Station, 1950-51; acting dir. counseling Tex. A&M U., 1951, personal and vocat. counselor, 1951-55, instr., 1951-53, asst. prof. psychology, 1953-55, acting dir. testing and research basic div., asst. prof. psychology, 1955-56, dir. testing and research, basic div., assoc. prof., 1956-69; dir. student personnel Coll. Arts and Scis., assoc. prof. Okla. State U., Stillwater, 1959-61; dean student affairs, prof. psychology Okla. State U., 1961-68, prof. edn. Coll. Edn., 1968-73, dir. student services, prof. applied behavioral studies, 1973-84, dir. student svcs., prof. applied behavioral studies emeritus, 1984—; treas., adminstrv. sec. Okla. State U. Emeriti Assn., 1990—. Author: Compilation of Research Studies from 1953-59, 1959, Student Attitudes Toward the Basic Division, 1958; contbr. articles to profl. jours. First v.p. United Fund Stillwater, Inc., 1963-64, pres., 1964-65; cabinet adviser Will Rogers council Boy Scouts Am., 1961-63; mem. Mayor's Com. on Hosp. Adv. Bd., 1963-66; mem. devel. council Baylor U., 1983—; treas., bd. dirs. YMCA Found.; treas. Stillwater YMCA Found., Inc., 1986—. Served with AUS, 1941-45. Decorated Purple Heart with oak leaf cluster, Bronze Star; recipient Okla. State U. Student Senate award of recognition, 1968; Columbia U. faculty fellow, 1952-53. Mem. Am. Psychol. Assn., Okla. Psychol. Assn. (assoc.), Am. Personnel and Guidance Assn., Southwestern Assn. Student Personnel Adminstrs., Okla. Personnel, Guidance and Counseling Assn., Okla. Deans and Counselors Assn., Okla. Edn. Assn. (pres. 1972-73), Omicron Delta Kappa (achievement award for outstanding contbn. to Okla. State U. 1968), Phi Delta Kappa, Kappa Delta Pi, Alpha Chi, Psi Chi, Sigma Epsilon Sigma, Phi Kappa Phi, Omicron Delta Kappa (coll. rep.). Lodge: Rotary. Home: 1224 N Lincoln St Stillwater OK 74075-2749

MC FARLAND, H. RICHARD, food company executive; b. Hoopeston, Ill., Aug. 19, 1930; s. Arthur Bryan and Jennie (Wilkey) McF.; m. Sarah Forney, Dec. 30, 1967. BS, U. Ill., 1952. With Campbell Soup Co., Camden, N.J., 1957-67; mgr. purchasing Campbell Soup Co., 1961-67; dir. procurement Keebler Co., Elmhurst, Ill., 1967-69; v.p. purchasing and distbn. Ky. Fried Chicken Corp., Louisville, 1969-74; v.p. food svcs., sales and distbn. Ky. Fried Chicken Corp., 1974-75; pres., dir. Mid-Continent Carton Co., Louisville, 1974-75, Ky. Fried Chicken Mfg. Corp., Nashville, 1974-75; owner, pres., dir. McFarland Foods Corp., Indpls., 1975—; bd. dirs. Fountain Trust Co., Ind., Covington Svc. Corp., Ind.; pres., bd. dirs. Ky. Fried Chicken Advt., Inc., Ind., 1975-87, exec. coun., 1988-91; mem. exec. coun., nat. franchise coun. Ky. Fried Chicken, 1979-85; bd. dirs. Ky. fried Chicken Nat. Purchasing Coop., 1981-85, chmn. ins. com., 1982-84; chmn. processed foods com. World's Poultry Congress, 1974; dir. nat. advt. coun. Ky. Fried Chicken, 1985-91, exec. com., 1988-90, chmn., 1989-90; mem. devel. com. U. Ill., 1989—. Mem. U. Ill. Found., 1992—, bd. dirs., 1993—; chmn. U. Ill. Nat. Advocates, 1994—; life pres. U. Ill. Sr. Class of '52; bd. dirs. Ind. Fedn. Children and Youth, 1983-84; chmn. campaign Ind. Ky. Fried Chicken March of Dimes, 1978-87; nat. trustee McCormick Theol. Sem., 1993-97. 1st lt. USAF, 1952-54, Korea. Recipient Award of Merit U. Ill. Coll. Agr., 1988, Achievement award U. Ill. Alumni Assn., 1996. Mem. Ky. Restaurant Asns. (bd. dirs. 1970-75), Nat. Broiler Coun. (bd. dirs. 1971-74), Ind. Restaurant Assn., Am. Shorthorn Breeders Assn., Great Lakes Ky. Fried Chicken Franchise Assn. (bd. dirs. 1975-91, 1st v.p. 1978-79, pres. 1979-80), Delta Upsilon. Presbyterian. Clubs: Main Line Ski (Phila.) (pres. 1964); Hillcrest Country. Home: 6361 Avalon Ln Indianapolis IN 46220-5009 Office: 6284 Rucker Rd Ste M Indianapolis IN 46220-4851

MCFARLAND, JAMES W., academic administrator. Dean bus. adminstrn. U. Houston, University Park, until 1988; dean Freeman Sch. Bus. Tulane U., New Orleans, 1988—. Office: Dean School of Business Tulane University 440 Gold Ring 2 Waldenberg New Orleans LA 70118

MCFARLAND, JAMES WILLIAM, real estate development company executive; b. Montgomery, Ala., Sept. 7, 1948; s. Ward Wharton and Frances Adelia (Morrow) McF.; B.S., U. Ala., 1970; m. Miriam Melinda Webster, Feb. 20, 1971; children—James William, Mimi Morrow. Dir. real estate for Ky., Ind. and Tenn., Winn-Dixie Stores, Inc., Louisville, 1970-72; v.p. Ward McFarland, Inc., Tuscaloosa, Ala., 1972—, also dir. Mem. Coun. for Devel. of French in La., 1976—, Friends of Libr., 1975—; commr. Dept. Mental Health, 1987-89; ; Rep. nominee U.S. Congress Ala. 7th Dist., 1986; young churchmen adviser Episcopal Diocese Ala., 1976—, conv. del.; charter investor, chair of real estate U. Ala.; chmn. Ala. Rapid Rail Transit Commn.; vice chmn. La.-Miss.-Ala. Rapid Rail Transit Commn., 1983-84, chmn., 1984—; state advisor Congl. Adv. Com., Am. Security Coun.; sr. warden Christ Episc. Ch., 1984; bd. dirs. Tuscaloosa Kidney Found.; mem. Rep. State Exec. Com., 1991—; commr. Dept. Mental Health State of Ala.; chmn. Tuscaloosa County Reps., 1991—; flotilla staff officer USCG Aux., 1994—. Named hon. citizen of Mobile and New Orleans, hon. mem. mayor's staff, Mobile. Mem. Nat. Assn. Realtors, Tuscaloosa Bd. Realtors, Nat. Small Bus. Assn., U. Ala. Commerce Execs. Soc., U. Ala. Alumni Assn., Nat. Assn. R.R. Passengers, Ala. Assn. R.R. Passengers (pres. 1982, 90, 91), North River Yacht, Kiwanis of Greater Tuscaloosa, Delta Sigma Pi. Flotilla comdr., dists. pub. affairs officer U.S. Coast Guard Aux., 1997. Home: 4714 7th Ct E Tuscaloosa AL 35405-4104 Office: 325 Skyland Blvd E Tuscaloosa AL 35405-4030

MCFARLAND, JANE ELIZABETH, librarian; b. Athens, Tenn., June 22, 1937; d. John Homer and Martha Virginia (Large) McFarland. AB, Smith Coll., 1959; M in Divinity, Yale U., 1963; MS in LS, U. N.C., 1971. Tchr. hist. and religion Northfield Schs., Mass., 1961-62; head librarian reference and circulation Yale Divinity Library, New Haven, Conn., 1963-71; head librarian Bradford (Mass.) Coll., 1972-77; reference librarian U. Tenn., Chattanooga, Tenn., 1977-80; head librarian reference dept Chattanooga-Hamilton County Bicentennial Library, Tenn., 1980-86, acting dir., 1986, dir., 1986—. Mem. Chattanooga Library Assn., Tenn. Library Assn., Southeastern Library Assn., Am. Library Assn., Phi Beta Kappa (treas. 1987, 88). Democrat. Roman Catholic. Avocations: reading, travel, needlework. Home: 1701 Estrellita Cir Chattanooga TN 37421-5754 Office: Chattanooga-Hamilton County Libr 1001 Broad St Chattanooga TN 37402-2620

MCFARLAND, JANET CHAPIN, consulting company executive; b. New Castle, Pa., Jan. 5, 1962; d. Robert Chapin McFarland and Dorothy Jean (Heade) Jost; m. Steven Mitchell Walters, July 30, 1994. BS in Imaging Sci. and Engring., Rochester Inst. Tech., 1985; MBA in Innovation Mgmt. and Mktg., Syracuse U., 1990. Rsch. engr. Shipley Co., Inc., Newton, Mass., 1985-88; mktg. cons. Syracuse (N.Y.) U. Sch. Mgmt., 1988-90; market rsch. coop. AT&T Consumer Comms. Svcs., Basking Ridge, N.J., summer 1989; tech. analyst DynCorp Meridian, Alexandria, Va., 1991-93; dir. studies and analysis Tech. Strategies & Alliances, Burke, Va., 1993-94; pres. ArBar, Inc., Alexandria, Va., 1994—; presenter in field. Mem. Internat. Soc. Optical Engrs., Soc. Mfg. Engrs. (chpt. chair 1995), Beta Gamma Sigma, Alpha Mu Alpha. Office: ArBar Inc 312 S Washington St Ste 5B Alexandria VA 22314-3631

MCFARLAND, JON WELDON, retired county commissioner; b. Wenatchee, Wash., Aug. 23, 1938; s. Charles Edward and Maud Elizabeth (Brennan) McF.; m. Kay Annette Erbes, Apr. 5, 1956; children: Colleen, Michael, Heather. BS in Edn., Eastern Wash. State U., 1961; MS in Personnel Adminstrn., George Washington U., 1966; Grad., Command and Gen. Staff Coll., Fort Leavenworth, Kans., 1970, U.S. Army War Coll., Carlisle Barracks, Pa., 1980. Commd. U.S. Army, 1961, advanced through grades to col., 1981, retired, 1988; ops. officer European Hdqtrs. U.S. Army, Heidelberg, Fed. Republic Germany, 1980-83; commdr. 16th mil. police brigade U.S. Army, Fort Bragg, N.C., 1983-85, provost marshal 18th Airborne Corps, 1983-85; asst. commandant, commdr. of troops U.S. Army Mil. Police Sch., Fort McClellan, Ala., 1985-88; county commr. Columbia County, Wash., 1989-96; dir., owner Mr. Mc's Direct Mktg. Svcs., 1992—; owner, dir. Spectro-Optics of Ea. Wash., Dayton, 1994—; Wash. staff for courthouse security, 1995-96; vice chmn. Southeastern Emergency Med. and Trauma Coun., Wash., 1990-94, chmn., 1995-97; chmn. Columbia County Bd. Commrs., 1990, 96; bd. dirs. Emergency Mgmt. Svcs., Columbia County. Author: History of Civil Disturbance 1960-68, 1969. Bd. dirs. Columbia County Pub. Health Dist., Dayton, 1989-96, chmn., 1995-96; bd. dirs. Project Timothy Pub. Svcs., bd. dirs., Columbia County Health Found., 1989—; vice chmn. Palouse Econ. Devel. Corp., 1990-92, chmn., 1993-95. Decorated Legion of Merit, Bronze Star, numerous others. Mem. Assn. U.S. Army, Wash. State Assn. Counties, U.S. Army War Coll. Found., Kiwanis (bd. dirs. Dayton 1990—). Democrat. Roman Catholic. Avocations: woodworking, pottery, fishing, hunting, travel. Home: RR 3 Box 248 Dayton WA 99328-9792 Office: Columbia County 205 S 4th St Dayton WA 99328-1411

MCFARLAND, KAY ELEANOR, state supreme court chief justice; b. Coffeyville, Kans., July 20, 1935; d. Kenneth W. and Margaret E. (Thrall) McF. BA magna cum laude, Washburn U., Topeka, 1957, JD, 1964. Bar: Kans. 1964. Sole practice Topeka, 1964-71; probate and juvenile judge Shawnee County, Topeka, 1971-73; dist. judge Topeka, 1973-77; assoc. justice Kans. Supreme Ct., 1977-95, chief justice, 1995—. Mem. Kans. Bar Assn., Women Attys. Assn. Topeka. Office: Kans Supreme Ct Kans Jud Ctr 301 W 10th St Topeka KS 66612

MCFARLAND, LESLIE KING, special education educator; b. Canton, Ohio, July 13, 1954; d. John Edward and Nadine Mae (Phillips) King; m. James David McFarland, July 16, 1977. BS in Edn., Bowling Green State U., 1976. Cert. specific learning disabilities, spl. edn. tchr. K-12, developmentally handicapped spl. edn. tchr. K-12, elem. tchr. 1-8, Ohio. Tchr. developmentally handicapped Warren (Ohio) City Schs., 1976—; bd. dirs. McFarland and Son Funeral Svcs., Inc., v.p., 1992—. Mem. Fine Arts Coun. Trumbull County, 1988-95; bd. dirs. Warren Dance Ctr., sec., 1988-90; bd. dirs. Warren Chamber Orch., 1986-92; mem. Trumbull County Women's History Com., 1993—; deacon 1st Presbyn. Ch., 1994. Mem. NEA, Ohio Edn. Assn., Warren Edn. Assn., AAUW (past sec.), Embroiderers' Guild Am. (Western Res. chpt.). Avocations: embroidery, needlepoint, camping, travel. Home: 197 Washington St NW Warren OH 44483-4732

MCFARLAND, MARY A., elementary and secondary school educator, administrator; b. St. Louis, Nov. 12, 1937; d. Allen and Maryann (Crawford) Mabry; m. Gerald McFarland, May 30, 1959. BS in Elem. Edn., S.E. Mo. State U., 1959; MA in Secondary Edn., Washington U., St. Louis, 1965; PhD in Curriculum and Instrn., St. Louis U., 1977. Cert. tchr. elem., secondary, supt., Mo. Elem. tchr. Berkeley Sch. Dist., St. Louis, 1959-64; secondary tchr. Parkway Sch. Dist., St. Louis, 1965-75, social studies coord. K-12, 1975—, dir. staff devel., 1984—; adj. prof. Maryville U., St. Louis, 1990—; cons. pvt. practice, Chesterfield, Mo. Co-author: (text series) The World Around Us, 1990, 3d rev. edit., 1995; contbr. articles to profl. jours. Nat. faculty Nat. Issues Forum, Dayton, Ohio. Mem. ASCD, Social Sci. Edn. Consortium, Nat. Coun. for Social Studies (pres. 1989-90), Mo. Coun. for Social Studies (pres. 1980-81). Democrat. Methodist. Avocations: music, sailing. Office: Parkway Schs Dist Instrnl Svcs 12657 Fee Fee Rd Saint Louis MO 63146-3855

MC FARLAND, NORMAN FRANCIS, bishop; b. Martinez, Calif., Feb. 21, 1922; student St. Patrick's Sem., Menlo Park, Calif.; J.C.D., Cath. U. Am. Ordained priest Roman Catholic Ch., 1946, consecrated bishop, 1970; titular bishop of Bida and aux. bishop of San Francisco, 1970-74; apostolic adminstr. Diocese of Reno, 1974-76; bishop Diocese of Reno-Las Vegas, 1976-87, Diocese of Orange, Calif., 1987—. Office: Marywood Ctr 2811 E Villa Real Dr Orange CA 92867-1932

MCFARLAND, RICHARD M., executive recruiting consultant; b. Portland, Maine, Sept. 10, 1923; s. George Fiske and Phillys C. (Macomber) McF.; BChemE, Rensselaer Poly. Inst., 1944; postgrad. U. Mich., 1946-47; m. Virginia Fitz-Randolph Ripley, Dec. 6, 1947; children: Richard Macomber, Kirk, Jane. Prodn. supr. E. I. duPont, 1947-51; mgr. agrl. chem. market research Brea Chem. (Calif.) subs. Union Oil Co., 1953-55; product mgr. chem. div. FMC Corp., N.Y.C., 1955-59; mgr. mktg. devel. Tex. Butadiene & Chem., N.Y.C., 1959-60; pres. Cumberland Chem. Corp., N.Y.C., 1960-67; gen. mgr. inorganic div. Wyandotte Chem. Co. (Mich.), 1967-69; asso. Heidrick & Struggles, Inc., N.Y.C., 1969-72, v.p., 1972-81; founder, pres. Brissenden, McFarland, Wagoner & Fuccella, Inc. and predecessors, Stamford, Conn., 1981-94 . Ensign USNR, 1943-46, lt. comdr., 1951-53. Mem. Am. Chem. Soc., Lambda Chi Alpha. Clubs: Landmark, Cedar Point Yacht, Nutmeg Curling. Patentee in field. Home: 16 Clover Ln Westport CT 06880-2626

MCFARLAND, RICHARD MACKLIN, retired journalist; b. Blockton, Iowa, Mar. 27, 1922; s. William Harold McFarland and Elsie (Sisson) McFarland Chavannes; m. Jacquelyn Jean Folske, Mar. 22, 1955; children: Bethany Rose, Scott Macklin, Elizabeth Ann McFarland Heyda, Kathryn Belle. BA, U. Iowa, 1944. Newsman UPI, Des Moines, 1944, Chgo., 1945, 46-47; bur. mgr. UPI, Bismarck, N.D., 1944-45, Herrin, Ill., 1945, Sioux Falls, S.D., 1947-49, Milw., 1949-51; legis. reporter UPI, Des Moines, 1947, Pierre, S.D., 1949; Iowa mgr. UPI, Des Moines, 1951-54; NW mgr. UPI, Mpls., 1954-55; Wis. mgr. UPI, Milw., 1956-57, regional exec. sales, 1958-59; bur. mgr. UPI, Chgo., 1960-61; Minn. mgr. UPI, Mpls., 1961-69; Mich. editor UPI, Detroit, 1969-71; Minn. editor UPI, Mpls., 1971-84; bur. mgr.-capitol reporter UPI, St. Paul, 1985-89; bd. dirs. Minn. Press Club, 1981-84. Former deacon, Advent Luth. Ch., Roseville, Minn., 8 yrs; coun. mem. Redeemer Luth. Ch., Bradenton, Fla., 1996—. Served with USN, 1943-44. Avocations: reading, music, fishing, backpacking, golf. Home: 7312 5th Ave NW Bradenton FL 34209-1522

MCFARLAND, ROBERT EDWIN, lawyer; b. St. Louis, July 25, 1946; s. Francis Taylor and Kathryne (Stephens) McF.; m. Jeannine M. Ghekiere, Feb. 26, 1982. B.A., U. Mich. 1968, J.D., 1971. Bar: Mich. 1971, U.S. Dist. Ct. (ea. dist.) Mich. 1971, U.S. Ct. Appeals (6th cir.) 1974, U.S. Supreme Ct. 1975, U.S. Ct. Appeals (D.C.) 1978. Law clk. to chief judge Mich. Ct. Appeals, 1971-72; assoc. William B. Elmer, St. Clair Shores, Mich., 1972-74, James Elsman, Birmingham, Mich., 1974-75; ptnr. McFarland, Schmier, Stoneman & Singer, Troy, Mich. 1975-77; sr. ptnr. McFarland & Bullard, Bloomfield Hills, Mich., 1977-90; sr. ptnr. McFarland & Niemer, Farmington Hills, Mich., 1990-91; shareholder, Foster, Swift, Collins & Smith, P.C., Farmington Hills, Mich., 1992—. Chmn. bd. of govs. Transp. Law Jour., U. Denver Coll. of Law, 1981-83; mem. rulemaking study com. Mich. Pub. Svc. Commn., 1983-84, Motor Carrier adv. bd., 1984-88; mem. bd. of control Intercollegiate Athletics, U. Mich., 1966-68. Served to capt. USAR, 1971-80. Mem. ABA, Transp. Lawyers Assn., Assn. Transp. Law, Logistics and Policy, State Bar Mich. (vice-chmn. transp. law com. adminstrn. law sect. 1990—, sect. coun. adminstrv. law sect. 1994—), Am. Judicature Soc.

MC FARLAND, ROBERT HAROLD, physicist, educator; b. Severy, Kans., Jan. 10, 1918; s. Robert Eugene and Georgia (Simpson) McF.; m. Twilah Mae Seefeld, Aug. 28, 1940; children: Robert Alan, Rodney Jon. B.S. and B.A., Kans. State Tchrs. Coll., Emporia, 1940; Ph.M. (Mendenhall fellow), U. Wis., 1943, Ph.D., 1947. Sci. instr., coach high sch. Chase, Kans., 1940-41; instr. navy radio sch. U. Wis., Madison, 1943-44; sr. engr. Sylvania Elec. Corp., 1944-46; faculty Kans. State U., 1947-60, prof. physics, 1954-60, dir. nuclear lab., 1958-60; physicist U. Calif. Lawrence Radiation Lab., 1960-69; dean Grad. Sch., U. Mo., Rolla, 1969-79, dir. instnl. analysis and planning, 1979-82; prof. physics U. Mo., Rolla, 1969-84, prof. emeritus physics dept., 1985—; v.p. acad. affairs U. Mo. System, 1974-75; Intergovtl. Personnel Act appointee Dept. Energy, Washington, 1982-84; vis. prof. U. Calif., Berkeley, 1980-81; mem. Grad. Record Exams. Bd., 1971-75, chmn. steering com., 1972-73; cons. Well Surveys, Inc., Tulsa, 1953-54, Argonne Nat. Lab., Chgo., 1955-59, Kans. Dept. Pub. Health, 1956-57, cons. in residence Lawrence Radiation Lab., U. Calif., 1957, 58, 59, med. physics U. Okla. Med. Sch., 1971, grad. schs., PhD physics program, Utah State U., 1972; physicist, regional counselor Office Ordnance Research, Durham, N.C., 1955. Contbr. articles to profl. jours. Active Boy Scouts Am., 1952—, mem. exec. bd. San Francisco Bay Area council, 1964-68, Ozark Council, 1986—; chmn. Livermore (Calif.) Library Bond drive, 1964. Mem. Kans. N.G., 1936-40. Recipient Silver Beaver award Boy Scouts Am., 1968, Community Service award C. of C., 1965, Disting. Alumnus award Kans. State Tchrs. Coll., 1969. Fellow Kiwanis Internat., 1992, fellow AAAS, Am. Phys. Soc.; mem. AAUP (chpt. pres. 1956-57), Am. Assn. Physics Tchrs., Mo. Acad. Sci., Mo. Assn. Phys. Sci. Tchrs., Am. Soc. Engring. Edn., Kiwanis (lt. gov. Mo.-Ark. dist. 1984-85, internat. accredited rep. 1985-92, Disting. Lt. Gov. 1985, Tablet of honor award 1997), Sigma Xi, Lambda Delta Lambda, Xi Phi, Kappa Mu Epsilon, Kappa Delta Pi, Pi Mu Epsilon, Gamma Sigma Delta, Phi Kappa Phi. Patentee in field of light prodn., vacuum prodn., controlled thermonuclear reactions. Home: 309 Christy Dr Rolla MO 65401-4073 Office: U Mo Dept Physics Rolla MO 65401 *Continuation of the last hundred years of major progress in the quality of life for the human race will not only require the best of our educational systems and technological talents but a sincere interest in all of us to contribute positively toward our collective well-being.*

MC FARLAND, THOMAS L., book publishing executive; m. Dianne L. McFarland; 2 children. BA in English and Journalism, Westminster Coll.; MA in History of Ideas, Johns Hopkins U. Reporter Intelligencer Jour., Lancaster, Pa., 1957; editor-in-chief Stanwix House, Inc., Pitts., 1958-63; mktg. mgr. Johns Hopkins U. Press, Balt., 1963-67, asst. dir. ops. and mktg.,

1967-73; part-time jours. mgr. & acquisitions editor, asst. dir. ops. and mktg. U. Calif. Press, Berkeley, 1973-79; dir., editor Univ. Press New Eng., Hanover, N.H., 1979—; dep. chmn., dir. European mktg. office several Am. univ. presses, Trevor Brown Assocs., Ltd., London, 1970—; invited speaker Translation Ctr. Columbia U., Buenos Aires, 1989; met with scholarly pubs. univs. sponsored USIA, China, 1985; mem. adv. bd. NAS Press, 1980-89; cons. U. Calgary Press, U. Alta. Press, 1991, U. Tenn. Press, 1989, U. Minn. Press, 1988, U. Colo. Office of Pres., 1987, Duke U. Press Office of Provost, 1978, others; judge New Eng. Book Show, 1990, Sara Josepha Hale Award, 1989—; student, lectr. Graphic Arts Ctr., Dartmouth Coll., Hanover; faculty mem. pub. seminar. Bd. dirs. Opera North, 1992—; pres. Congregl. Ch. Dartmouth Coll., 1985-88, bd. elders, 1985-88; mem. book and author event com. Friends of Hopkins Ctr./Hood Mus. Art, Dartmouth Coll., 1984—, bd. dirs., 1987-89. Mem. AAUP (del. univ. press pub. meeting Soviet Union 1989, pres. 1989-90, bd. dirs. 1975-78, 88-91, chair govt. and found. rels. com. 1989—, chair exec. dir. search com. 1990, chair membership and standards com. 1985, chair annual meeting program com. 1984, numerous panels, workshops). Avocations: community chorus, piano, house and garden projects. Home: 23 Valley Rd Hanover NH 03755-2230 Office: Univ Press Of NE 23 S Main St Hanover NH 03755-2048

MCFARLANE, BETH LUCETTA TROESTER, former mayor; b. Osterdock, Iowa, Mar. 9, 1918; d. Francis Charles and Ella Carrie (Moser) Troester; M. George Evert McFarlane, June 20, 1943 (dec. May 1972); children: Douglas, Steven (dec.), Susan, George. BA in Edn., U. No. Iowa, 1962, MA in Edn., 1971. Cert. tchr. Tchr. rural and elem. schs., Iowa, 1936-50, 55-56; elem. tchr. Oelwein Cmty. Schs., Iowa, 1956-64, jr. high reading tchr., 1964-71, reading specialist, 1971-83; mayor of Oelwein, 1982-89; evaluator North Cen. Accreditation Assn. for Ednl. Programs; mem. planning team for confs. for Iowa Cities, N.E. Iowa, 1985; v.p. N.E. Iowa Regional Council for Econ. Devel., 1986-89; mem. Area Econ. Devel. Com. N.E. Iowa, 1985, Legis. Interim Study Com. on Rural Econ. Devel., 1987-88; mem. policy com. Iowa League Municipalities, 1987-88; bd. dirs. Oelwein Indsl. Devel. Corp., 1982-91, Oelwein Betterment Corp., 1982-94. V.p. Fayette County Tourism Council, 1987-88; Iowa State Steering Com. on Road Use Tax Financing, 1988-89; chmn. bd. govs. Oelwein Community Ctr, 1990-94; chmn. Reorganized LDS Ch. Bldg. and Fin. Com., 1980—, Dist. Ch. Fin. Com., 1992—, Dist. Ch. Revolving Loan Com., 1982—. Named Iowa Reading Tchr. of Yr., Internat. Reading Assn. Iowa, 1978; recipient Outstanding Contbrn. to Reading Council Activities award Internat. Reading Assn. N.E. Iowa, 1978, State of Iowa's Gov.s' Leadership award, 1988. Mem. N.E. Iowa Reading Council (pres. 1975-77), MacDowell Music and Arts Orgn. (pres. 1978-80), Oelwein Bus. and Profl. Women (Woman of Yr. 1983), Oelwein Area Ret. Sch. Pers. (pres. 1994-96), Oelwein Area C. of C. (bd. dirs. 1986-89, Humanitarian award 1987), Delta Kappa Gamma (pres. 1980-82). Republican. Mem. Reorganized Ch. of Jesus Christ of Latter Day Saints. Avocations: hiking, refinishing antiques, gardening, jogging, creative sewing. Home: 512 7th Ave NE Oelwein IA 50662-1326

MC FARLANE, KAREN ELIZABETH, concert artists manager; b. St. Louis, Jan. 2, 1942; d. Nicholas and Bonita Margaret (Fults) Walz; m. Ralph Leo McFarlane, Nov. 30, 1968 (div.); children: Sarah Louise.; m. Walter Holtkamp, June 19, 1982. B.Mus.Ed. (Presser Music Found. scholar), Lindenwood Coll., 1964. Public sch. music tchr. St. Louis County, 1964-66; music asst. Riverside Ch., N.Y.C., 1966-70; dir. music Park Ave. Christian Ch., N.Y.C., 1974-81; also pres. Murtagh/McFarlane Artists, Inc., Cleve., 1976-88; pres. Karen McFarlane Artists, Cleve., 1989—. Mem. Am. Guild Organists, Nat. Assn. Performing Arts Mgrs. and Agts., Inc., Internat. Soc. Performing Arts Adminstrn. Republican. Presbyterian. Office: 12429 Cedar Rd Ste 29 Cleveland OH 44106-3172

MCFARLANE, NEIL, church administrator. Children's dir. The Missionary Church, Fort Wayne, Ind. Office: The Missionary Ch 2122 S Valley Ave Marion IN 46953-2913*

MCFARLANE, WALTER ALEXANDER, lawyer, educator; b. Richlands, Va., May 4, 1940; s. James Albert and Frances Mae (Padbury) McF.; m. Judith Louise Copenhaver, Aug. 31, 1962; children: Brennan Alexander, Heather Copenhaver. BA, Emory and Henry Coll., 1962; JD, T.C. Williams Sch. Law, U. Richmond, 1966. Bar: Va. 1966, U.S. Supreme Ct. 1970, U.S. Ct. Appeals (4th cir.) 1973, U.S. Ct. Appeals (D.C. cir.) 1977, U.S. Dist. Ct. (ea. dist.) Va. 1973. Asst. atty. gen. Office Va. Atty. Gen., Richmond, 1969-73, dep. atty. gen., 1973-90; exec. asst., chief counsel, dir. policy Gov.'s office, Commonwealth Va., 1990-94; supt. Dept. Correctional Edn. Commonwealth of Va., 1994—, acting dir. Dept. Juvenile Justice, 1997—; prof. adj. staff U. Richmond, 1978—. Contbr. articles to profl. jours. Chmn. transp. law com. Transp. Research Bd., Nat. Research Bd. Nat. Acads. Scis. and Engring., Washington, 1977-85, 88-94, chmn. legal affairs com., 1978-85, chmn. environ., archeological and hist. com., 1985-90; mem. State Water Commn., 1994-96; mem. exec. com., bd. govs. Emory and Henry Coll., 1985—; pres. Windsor Forest Civic Assn., Midlothian, Va., 1975-76; bd. dirs. Greater Midlothian Civic League, 1981-86, v.p., 1980; instr. water safety ARC, 1962-87; chmn. bldg. com. Mt. Pisgah United Meth. Ch., 1980-85, pres. men's club, 1980-81; bd. dirs. cen. Va. chpt. Epilepsy Assn. Va., 1988-91, Woodland Pond Civic Assn., 1988-89; mem. State Criminal Justice Svcs. Bd., 1994—. Capt. JAGC, USAF, 1966-69. Recipient J.D. Buscher Disting. Atty. award Am. Assn. State Hwy. and Transp. Ofcls., 1983, John C. Vance legal writing award Nat. Acads. Sci. and Engring., 4th ann. outstanding evening lectr. award Student Body U. Richmond, 1980. Mem. Chesterfield Bar Assn., Richmond Bar Assn. (bd. dirs. 1989-93), Richmond Scottish Soc. (bd. dirs. 1980-82), Emory and Henry Coll. Alumni Assn. (chpt. pres. 1971-73, regional v.p. 1974-77, pres. 1981-83), Meadowbrook Country Club. Home: 9001 Widgeon Way Chesterfield VA 23838-5274 Office: 101 N 14th St Richmond VA 23219-3684

MCFARLIN, DIANE H., newspaper editor; b. Lake Wales, Fla., July 10, 1954; d. Ruffie Denton Hooten and Anna Loraine (Peeples) Huff; m. Henry Briggs McFarlin, Aug. 28, 1976 (div. 1993). BS, U. Fla., 1976. Reporter Sarasota (Fla.) Jour., 1976-77, asst. news editor, 1977-78, city editor, 1978-82; asst. mng. editor Sarasota (Fla.) Herald Tribune, 1983-84, mng. editor, 1985-87; exec. editor Gainesville (Fla.) Sun, 1987-90, Sarasota Herald-Tribune, 1990—; mem. adv. bd. U. Fla. Coll. Journalism and Comm., 1987—. Mem. accrediting coun. Edn. in Journalism and Mass Comms., 1994—. Mem. Am. Soc. Newspaper Editors (com. chair 1992, 94, bd. dirs. 1994—), Fla. Soc. Newspaper Editors (sec.-treas. 1993, v.p. 1994, pres. 1995). *

MCFARLIN, RICHARD FRANCIS, industrial chemist, researcher; b. Oklahoma City, Oct. 12, 1929; s. Loy Lester and Julie Mae (Collins) McF.; m. Clare Jane Burroughs, Apr. 4, 1953; children: Robin Sue McFarlin Godwin, Richard Prescott, Rebecca Lynn McFarlin Bray, Roger Whitsitt. BS, Va. Mil. Inst., 1951; MS, Purdue U., 1953, PhD, 1956. Rsch. chemist Monsanto Chem. Co., St. Louis, 1956-60; supr. inorganic rsch. Internat. Minerals and Chems., Mulberry, Fla., 1961; mgr. Agr. Rsch. Ctr. Armour Agrl. Chem. Co., Atlanta, 1962; v.p. rsch., ops., devel. & adminstrn. div. agri-chems. U.S. Steel, Atlanta, 1986; tech. dir. Lester Labs. Inc., Atlanta, 1986-88; exec. dir. Fla. Inst. Phosphate Rsch., Bartow, 1988-96; ret., 1996; mem. bd. advisors engring. coun. U. South Fla., Lakeland, 1990—, U. Fla., Gainesville, 1991—; mem. bd. advisors Inst. Recyclable Materials La. State U., Baton Rouge, 1990—. Capt. USAR, 1951-61. M. M. Cohn Found. scholar, 1947, L. D. Wall scholar, 1949, O. M. Baldinger scholar, 1950. Presbyterian. Achievements include eight U.S. and foreign patents for selective organic reducing agents, fertilizer processes and selective biocides. Home: 6611 Sweetbriar Ln Lakeland FL 33813-3598

MCFATE, KENNETH LEVERNE, trade association administrator; b. LeClaire, Iowa, Feb. 5, 1924; s. Samuel Albert and Margaret (Spear) McF.; m. Imogene Grace Kness, Jan. 27, 1951; children: Daniel Elliott, Kathryn Margaret, Sharon Ann. BS in Agrl. Engring., Iowa State U., 1950; MS in Agrl. Engring., U. Mo., 1959. Registered profl. engr., Mo. Agrl. sales engr. Ill. No. Utility Co., Aledo, 1950-51; extension agrl. engr. Iowa State U., Ames, 1951-53, rsch. agrl. engr., 1953-56; prof. agrl. engr. U. Mo., Columbia, 1956-86, prof. emeritus, 1986; dir. Mo. Farm Electric Coun., Columbia, 1956-75; exec. mgr. Nat. Farm Electric Coun., Columbia, 1975-86; pres., exec. mgr. Nat. Food and Energy Coun., Columbia, 1986-91, pres. emeritus, 1991; mgr. Electrotechnology Rsch., 1991-93; bd. dirs. Internnat. Congress Agrl. Engrs., Brussels, 1989-94. Editor, author: (with others) Handbook for Elsevier Science, Electrical Energy in World Agriculture, 1989; mem. editl. bd. Energy in Agriculture for Elsevier Sci., Amsterdam, The Netherlands, 1981-88. 2d lt. USAAF, 1943-45. Recipient Outstanding Svc. awards Nat. Safety Coun., 1975, MOFEC, 1976, Nat. 4-H Coun., 1982, Nat. Hon. Extension Frat., 1984, Hon. award Future Farmers Assn., 1991. Fellow Am. Soc. Agrl. Engrs. (George Kable elec. award 1974); mem. Alpha Epsilon, Gamma Sigma Delta. Republican. Presbyterian. Avocations: technical writing, gardening, woodworking. Home: 2223 Concordia Dr Columbia MO 65203-1345

MCFATE, PATRICIA ANN, foundation executive, scientist, educator; b. Detroit, Mar. 19, 1936; d. John Earle and Mary Louise (Bliss) McF.; m. Sidney Norman Graybeal, Sept. 10, 1988. B.A. (Alumni scholar), Mich. State U., 1954; M.A., Northwestern U., 1956, Ph.D., 1965; M.A. (hon.), U. Pa., 1977. Assoc. prof. English, asst. dean liberal arts and scis. U. Ill., Chgo., 1967-74; assoc. prof. English, assoc. vice chancellor acad. affairs U. Ill., 1974-75; assoc. prof. folklore Faculty Arts and Scis., U. Pa., Phila., 1975-81; prof. tech. and soc. Coll. Engring. and Applied Sci., 1975-81, vice provost, 1975-78; dep. chmn. Nat. Endowment for Humanities, Washington, 1978-81; exec. v.p. Am.-Scandinavian Found., N.Y.C., 1981-82, pres., 1982-88; sr. scientist Sci. Applications Internat. Corp., Mc Lean, Va., 1988—, program dir. Ctr. for Nat. Security Negotiations, 1988—; cons. UN, 1994-95; vis. assoc. prof. dept. medicine Rush U., Chgo., 1970-85; bd. dirs. CoreStates Fin. Corp. Author: The Writings of James Stephens, 1979, Uncollected Prose of James Stephens, 1983; exec. producer Northern Stars, 1985, Diego Rivera: I Paint What I See, 1989; contbr. articles in fields of sci. policy and lit. to various jours. Mem. sci. and policy adv. com. Arms Control and Disarmament Agy., 1995—; bd. dirs. Raoul Wallenberg Com. of U.S., Swedish Coun. Am., Santa Fe Stages, Santa Fe Opera. Decorated officer Order of Leopold II Belgium, comdr. Order Icelandic Falcon, comdr. Royal Order of Polar Star (Sweden), comdr. Order of Lion (Finland), comdr. Royal Norwegian Order Merit, Knight 1st class Royal Order Dannebrog (Denmark); U. Ill. Grad. Coll. faculty fellow, 1968; Swedish Bicentennial Fund grantee, 1981. Fellow N.Y. Acad. Scis.; mem. AAAS (chmn. com. on sci., engring. and pub. policy 1984-87, com. on sci. and internat. security 1976-79, 88-93), Coun. on Fgn. Rels., Acad. Scis. Phila. (founding mem., corr. sec. 1977-79), N.Y. Sci. Policy Assn., Am. Women for Internat. Understanding, Cosmpolitan Club (Phila.), Theta Alpha Phi, Omega Beta Pi, Delta Delta Delta.

MC FEATTERS, DALE STITT, retired electric company executive; b. Avella, Pa., Aug. 20, 1911; s. James Dale and Alice Mabel (Stitt) McF.; m. Tirzah McHenry Bigham, Sept. 29, 1938; children: Dale Bigham, Ann Carol McFeatters Koepke, Susan Love. Student, Art Inst. Pitts., U. Pitts. Reporter, feature writer, news commentator, fin. editor Pitts. Press., 1931-45; with Westinghouse Electric Corp., Pitts., 1945-73; dir. employee info., dir. info. services, v.p. Westinghouse Electric Corp., 1945-73. Creator: nationally syndicated cartoon Strictly Business. Mem. Nat. Cartoonists Soc., Nat. Press Club. Republican. Episcopalian. Clubs: Duquesne (Pitts.), Chartiers Country (Pitts.); Rolling Rock (Ligonier, Pa.). Lodge: Masons. Home: 1461 Navahoe Dr Pittsburgh PA 15228-1617

MC FEE, ARTHUR STORER, physician; b. Portland, Maine, May 1, 1932; s. Arthur Stewart and Helen Knight (Dresser) McF.; m. Iris Goeschel, May 13, 1967. B.A. cum laude, Harvard U., 1953, M.D., 1957; M.S., U. Minn., 1966, Ph.D., 1967. Diplomate: Am. Bd. Surgery. Intern U. Minn. Hosp., 1957-58, resident in surgery, 1958-65; asst. prof. surgery U. Tex. Med. Sch., San Antonio, 1967-70; asso. prof. U. Tex. Med. Sch., 1970-74, prof., 1974—; co-dir. surg. ICU Med. Ctr. Hosp., San Antonio, 1968—; spl. cons. on emergency med. care text to AAOS. Contbr. articles to profl. jours. Served with USNR, 1965-67. Fellow ACS; mem. AMA, Am. Assn. History of Medicine, Assn. Acad. Surgery, Tex. Med. Assn., Bexar County Med. Soc., Tex. Surg. Soc., Western Surg. Assn., San Antonio Surg. Soc., Soc. Surgery Alimentary Tract, So. Med. Assn., N.Y. Acad. Scis., Royal Soc. Medicine, So. Surg. Assn., Internat. Surg. Soc., Halsted Soc., J. Bradley Aust Surg. Soc., Am. Surg. Assn. Home: 131 Brittany Dr San Antonio TX 78212-1721 Office: 7703 Floyd Curl Dr San Antonio TX 78284-6200 *Most of my life has been spent in training surgeons. It has been an informative experience.*

MCFEE, RICHARD, electrical engineer, physicist; b. Pitts., Jan. 24, 1925; s. William and Beatrice (Allender) McF.; m. Anne Stauffer, June 26, 1947 (div. 1960); m. 2d., Joanellen Lewis, Dec. 31, 1974. BEE, Yale U., 1947; MS in Physics, Syracuse U., 1949; PhDEE, U. Mich., 1955. Rsch. asst. Syracuse U. Med. Sch., 1947-48; instr. Syracuse U. elec. engring. dept., 1948-49; rsch. assoc. U. Mich. Med. Sch., 1949-51; engr. Electro-Mech. Rsch. Inc., Ridgefield, Conn., 1951-52; mem. tech. staff Bell Telephone Labs., Whippany, N.J., 1952-57; prof. elec. engring. Syracuse U., 1957-82; ind. researcher Union Springs, N.Y., 1982-86, Hawi, Hawaii, 1986—; cons. Arthur D. Little Inc., Cambridge, Mass., 1960-61, cardiovascular study sect. NIH, GE Inc., Crouse Hinds Inc., Syracuse, N.Y., 1970, Stanford U. physics dept., 1974-75. Author numerous articles on electronics, electrocardiography, magnetocardiography, superconductivity, circuit theory, thermodynamics, inertial navigation, elec. measurements, energy conservation, rehab. equipment; patentee in field. Sgt. U.S. Army, 1943-46. Sci. Faculty fellowship NSF, Stanford U., 1970. Fellow IEEE; mem. AAAS, Sigma Xi. Home and Office: PO Box 989 Kapaau HI 96755-0989

MC FEE, THOMAS STUART, retired government agency administrator; b. Delafield, Wis., Nov. 19, 1930; s. Leon Worrick and Margurette Ella (Morris) McFee; m. Mary Virginia Butler, June 7, 1952; children: Richard Stuart, John Worrick, Charles Paxton. BS, U. Md., 1953, postgrad., 1956-60. Mathematician math. computation divsn. David Taylor Model Basin, Navy Dept., Washington, 1956-58; dir. sys. analysis br. ops. rsch. divsn. David Taylor Model Basin, Navy Dept., 1958-62; project leader weapons sys. evaluation group U.S. Dept. Def., 1962-65; tech. asst. to dir. Sci. and Tech. Office, Exec. Office of Pres., White House, 1965-66; dir. sys. devel. HEW, 1967-69, dep. asst. sec. for program sys., planning and evaluation, 1969-71, dep. asst. sec. for mgmt. planning and tech., 1971-77, dep. asst. sec. for mgmt., 1977-78; asst. sec. for pers. adminstrn. HHS, 1978-95. With USAF, 1954-56. Mem. Am. Soc. Pub. Adminstrn., Am. Consortium for Internat. Pub. Adminstrn., Nat. Acad. Pub. Adminstrn. (elected).

MCFEE, WILLIAM WARREN, soil scientist; b. Concord, Tenn., Jan. 8, 1935; s. Fred Thomas and Ellen Belle (Russell) McF.; m. Barbara Anella Steelman, June 23, 1957; children—Sabra Anne, Patricia Lynn, Thomas Hallie. B.S., U. Tenn., 1957; M.S., Cornell U., 1963, Ph.D., 1966. Mem. faculty Purdue U., 1965—, prof. soil sci., 1973—, dir. natural resources and environ. sci. program, 1975-91, head dept. agronomy, 1991—; vis. prof. U. Fla., 1986-87; cons. U.S. Forest Svc., Desert Rsch. Inst. Author articles in field, chpts. in books. Served with USAR, 1958-61. Alpha Zeta scholar, 1957; named Outstanding Agr. Tchr. Purdue U., 1972; recipient Am. Educator award Soil Sci. Soc., 1987. Fellow Am. Soc. Agronomy (pres. 1996-97, resident edn. award 1989), Soil Sci. Soc. Am. (pres. 1991-92); mem. Internat. Soil Sci. Soc., Sigma Xi. Presbyterian. Home: 708 Mccormick Rd West Lafayette IN 47906-4915 Office: Purdue U Dept Agronomy West Lafayette IN 47907

MC FEELEY, JOHN JAY, chemical engineer; b. Bklyn., Aug. 15, 1945; s. John Joseph and Maude May (Irvine) McF.; m. Jacquelyn Anne Ratzin, Oct. 30, 1971; children: Christine, John Jay. BS, Poly. Inst. Bklyn., 1966, MS, 1967, Phd, 1972. Engr. Polaroid Corp., Cambridge, Mass., 1971-72, sr. engr., 1972-74, sr. scientist, 1974-77, prin. engr. research and devel., 1977-79, tech. mgr. chem. engring. devel., 1979-83, sr. mgr. chem. engring., 1983—. Mem. water supply study com. Town of Norfolk (Mass.), 1976-77, mem. adv. bd., 1979-81, mem. bicentennial com., 1975-76, chmn. adv. bd., 1980-81, selectman, 1981-84, chmn., 1983-84; registrar of voters, 1991—, chmn., 1993—; mem. Dem. Town Com., 1981—, vice-chmn., 1988—; mem. Norfolk Community TV, 1989—, pres., 1992-94, 95—. NDEA fellow, 1969-71; NSF fellow, 1968-69, teaching fellow, 1967-68, rsch. fellow, 1966-67. Mem. AAAS, Am. Chem. Soc., Am. Inst. Chem. Engrs., N.Y. Acad. Scis., Lions (pres. 1977-78, 89-90), Tau Beta Pi, Sigma Xi, Omega Chi Epsilon, Phi Lambda Upsilon. Democrat. Roman Catholic. Contbr. articles in field to profl. jours. Home: 10 Chicatabut Ave Norfolk MA 02056-1164 Office: 103 4th Ave Waltham MA 02154-7554

MCFEELY, WILLIAM DRAKE, publishing company executive; b. Port Chester, N.Y., July 15, 1954; s. William Shield and Mary (Drake) McF.; m. Karen Gail Eliason, Aug. 12, 1978; children: Matthew Bensen, Eric Daniel, Laura Mae. BA cum laude, Amherst Coll., 1976. Coll. traveler W.W. Norton & Co., Inc., N.Y.C., 1976-80, asst. sales mgr., 1980-82, editor, 1982—, v.p., 1990-94, bd. dirs., 1990—, pres., 1994—; dir. W.W. Norton & Co., Ltd., 1994—, Liveright Pub. Corp., N.Y.C., 1994—, Nat. Book Co., Scranton, Pa., 1994—. Mem. Pubs. Lunch Club, Seven Bridges Field Club (pres. 1989). Home: 106 Seven Bridges Rd Chappaqua NY 10514 Office: WW Norton & Co 500 5th Ave New York NY 10110

MC FEELY, WILLIAM SHIELD, historian, writer; b. N.Y.C., Sept. 25, 1930; s. William C. and Marguerite (Shield) Mc F.; m. Mary Drake, Sept. 13, 1952; children: William Drake, Eliza, Jennifer. B.A., Amherst Coll., 1952, L.H.D., 1982; M.A., Yale U., 1962, Ph.D., 1966; LD, Washington Coll., 1986. Asst. prof. history and Am. studies Yale U., 1966-69, assoc. prof., 1969-70; dean faculty Mount Holyoke Coll., 1970-73, prof. history, 1970-80, Rodman prof. history, 1980-82, Andrew W. Mellon prof. in the humanities, 1982-86; Richard B. Russell prof. Am. history U. Ga., Athens, 1986-94, Abraham Baldwin prof. of Humanities, 1994-97; tchr. Yale-Harvard-Columbia intensive summer studies program, 1967-69; vis. prof. history Univ. Coll. London, 1978-79, Amherst Coll., 1980-81, U. Mass., 1984-85, John J. McCloy prof., 1988-89 ; cons. to com. on judiciary U.S. Ho. of Reps., 1974. Author: Yankee Stepfather: Gen. O.O. Howard and the Freedmen, 1968, Grant: A Biography, 1981, Frederick Douglass, 1991, Sapelo's People, 1994. Recipient Pulitzer Prize in biography, 1982, Francis Parkman prize, 1982, Lincoln prize, 1992, Avery O. Craven award, 1992; Morse fellow, 1968-69, fellow Am. Coun. Learned Socs., 1974-75, Huntington Library, 1976, 83, Guggenheim fellow, 1982-83, assoc. fellow Charles Warren Ctr., 1991-91, vis. scholar W.E.B. Du Bois Inst., Harvard U., 1992—; NEH grantee, 1986-87. Mem. Am. Hist. Assn., So. Hist. Assn., Assn. Study Afro-Am. Life and History, Orgn. Am. Historians, PEN Ctr., Century Assn., Authors Guild. Home: 35 Mill Hill Rd Wellfleet MA 02667

MC FERON, DEAN EARL, mechanical engineer; b. Portland, Oreg., Dec. 24, 1923; s. Wallace Suitor and Ruth Carolyn (Fessler) McF.; m. Phyllis Grace Ehlers, Nov. 10, 1945; children: David Alan, Phyllis Ann, Douglas Dean, Donald Brooks. Student, Oreg. State Coll., 1942-43; BSME with spl. honors, U. Colo., 1945, MSME, 1948; PhD, U. Ill., 1956. Instr. U. Colo., Boulder, 1946-48; assoc. prof. U. Ill., 1948-58; rsch. assoc. Argonne (Ill.) Nat. Lab., 1957-58; prof. mech. engring., assoc. dean U. Wash., Seattle, 1958-82; prof. emeritus U. Wash., 1983—; cons. to industry, 1959-80. Served with USNR, 1942-46, to comdr. Res., 1946-72. Co-recipient Outstanding Tech. Applications Paper award ASHRAE, 1974; Ednl. Achievement award Soc. Mfg. Engrs., 1970; NSF faculty fellow, 1967-68. Mem. ASME, Am. Soc. Engring. Edn., U.S. Naval Inst. (life), Sigma Xi (nat. dir. 1972-80, nat. pres. 1978), Tau Beta Pi, Sigma Tau, Pi Tau Sigma. Home: 4008 NE 40th St Seattle WA 98105-5422 Office: U Wash Dept Mech Engring Seattle WA 98195 *What matters most in life is what you can do for others.*

MCFERRIN, BOBBY, singer, musician, composer and conductor. Creative chair St. Paul Chamber Orch. Albums: Bobby McFerrin, 1982, The Voice, 1984, Spontaneous Inventions, 1986, Simple Pleasure, 1988, Medicine Music, 1990, (with Chick Corea) Play, 1992, (with Yo Yo Ma) Hush, 1992, (with St. Paul Chamber Orch.) Paper Music, 1995, Bang! Zoom, 1996. Recipient 10 Grammy awards, Emmy award, ACE award. Office: c/o Original Artists 826 Broadway Fl 4 New York NY 10003-4826

MCFERRIN, JAMES HAMIL, lawyer; b. Mobile, Ala., July 26, 1960. BS in Criminal Justice, U. Ala., 1982; JD, Cumberland Sch. of Law, 1987. Bar: Ala. 1987, U.S. Dist. Ct. (no. dist.) Ala. 1987. Pvt. practice, Birmingham, Ala., 1987—; legal dir. Behavioral Health Systems, Birmingham, 1991—, Risk Reduction, Inc., Birmingham, 1991—; mem. task force Birmingham Area C. of C., 1992; mem. task force on utilization rev. State of Ala.; cons., com. chair Ala. Supreme Ct. Author: Informed Consent: A New Standard For Proximate Cause, 1987; rsch. editor Cumberland Law Rev. Recipient Dean's scholarschip Cumberland Law Sch., 1984-87, Book awards Am. Jurisprudence, 1984-87. Mem. Am. Trial Lawyers Assn. (state capt. worker's compensation), Nat. Employment Assn., Ala. Bar Assn., Ala. Trial Lawyers Assn., Birmingham C. of C. Office: 2102 Cahaba Rd Ste A Birmingham AL 35223-1140

MCFERSON, DIAMOND RICHARD, insurance company executive; b. 1937; m. Darlene Moss; 7 children. BA, UCLA, 1959; MA, U. So. Calif., 1972. CPA, CLU. With Ernst & Young; sr. v.p. finance Surety Life Ins. Co., Salt Lake City, New Eng. Life, until 1979; sr. v.p. fin., then exec. v.p. Nationwide Mut. Ins. Co., 1978-88, pres., dir., 1988-96, CEO, 1996—, also chmn. bd. dirs.; also pres. Nationwide Mut. Fire Ins., Nationwide Gen. Ins. Co.; sr. v.p. fin., dir. Nationwide Fin. Svcs. Inc.; sr. v.p. Nationwide Devel. Co.; CEO Nationwide Ins. Enterprise, Columbus, Ohio, 1992—, now chmn., 1996—. Office: Nationwide Mut Ins Co 1 Nationwide Plz Columbus OH 43215-2220*

MCGAFFEY, JERE D., lawyer; b. Lincoln, Nebr., Oct. 6, 1935; s. Don Larsen and Doris (Lanning) McG.; m. Ruth S. Michelsen, Aug. 19, 1956; children: Beth, Karen. B.A., B.Sc. with high distinction, U. Nebr., 1957; LL.B. magna cum laude, Harvard U., 1961. Bar: Wis. 1961. Mem. firm Foley & Lardner, Milw., 1961—, ptnr., 1968—; dir. Wis. Gas Co., Smith Investment Co., WICOR. Author works in field. Chmn. bd. dirs. Helen Bader Found.; former chmn. bd. dirs. Aurora Health Care; vice chmn. legis. Milw. Met. Assn. Commerce; former chmn. Wis. Taxpayers Alliance, sec., treas., 1994—; mem. bd. visitors U. Wis. Med. Sch., Madison; chmn. bd. advisors U. Wis. Nursing Sch., Milw. Mem. ABA (chmn. tax sect. 1990-91), AICPA, House of Del., 1995—, Wis. Bar Assn., Wis. Inst. CPA's, Am. Coll. Tax Counsel (chmn. 1996—, regent), Am. Coll. Trust and Estate Counsel (chmn. bus. planning com. 1994-97), Am. Law Inst., Univ. Club, Milw. Club, Milw. Country Club, Harvard Club N.Y.C., Univ. Club Washington, Phi Beta Kappa, Beta Gamma Sigma, Delta Sigma Rho. Home: 12852 NW Shoreland Dr Thiensville WI 53097-2304 Office: Foley & Lardner 777 E Wisconsin Ave Ste 3600 Milwaukee WI 53202-5302

MCGAGH, WILLIAM GILBERT, financial consultant; b. Boston, May 29, 1929; s. Thomas A. and Mary M. (McDonough) McG.; m. Sarah Ann McQuigg, Sept. 23, 1961; children: Margaret Ellen, Sarah Elizabeth. BSBA, Boston Coll., 1950; MBA, Harvard U., 1952; MS, MIT, 1965. Fin. analyst Ford Motor Co., Dearborn, Mich., 1953-55; mem. staff treas. office Chrysler Corp., Detroit, 1955-64; compt., treas. Canadian divsn. Chrysler Corp., Windsor, 1965-67; staff exec.-fin. Latin Am. ops. Chrysler Corp., Detroit, 1967-68, asst. treas., 1968-75, treas., 1975-76, v.p., treas., 1976-80; sr. v.p. fin., dir. Northrop Grumman Corp., Los Angeles, 1980-88; owner McGagh Assocs., Beverly Hills, Calif., 1988—; bd. dirs. Pacific Am. Income Shares, Inc., Western Asset Trust, Inc. Bd. dirs. Greater L.A. Zoo Assn., John Tracy Clinic (pres. 1994—), Mt. St. Mary's Coll., L.A. Orthop. Hosp. Found. Sloan fellow MIT, 1965. Mem. Fin. Execs. Inst. (pres. Detroit chpt. 1979-80). Clubs: Orchard Lake Country; Harvard (N.Y.C. and Boston); Beach (Santa Monica, Calif.); Los Angeles Country, California (Los Angeles), Eastward Ho Country. (Chatham, Mass.). Home: 2189 Century Hl Los Angeles CA 90067-3516 Office: McGagh Assocs 9601 Wilshire Blvd Ste 623 Beverly Hills CA 90210-5208

MCGANN, JEROME JOHN, English language educator; b. N.Y.C., July 22, 1937; s. John Joseph and Marie Violet (Lecouffe) McG.; m. Anne Patricia Lanni, July 26, 1938; children: Geoffrey, Christopher, Jennifer. BS, Le Moyne Coll., 1959; MA, Syracuse U., 1962; PhD, Yale U., 1966; LHD (hon.), U. Chgo., 1996. From asst. prof. to prof. U. Chgo., 1966-75; prof. Johns Hopkins U., Balt., 1975-80; Dreyfuss prof. humanities Calif. Inst. Tech., Pasadena, 1980-86; John Stewart Bryan prof. English U. Va., Charlottesville, 1987—. Author: Swinburne: An Experiment in Criticism, 1972 (Melville Cane award 1972), The Romantic Ideology, 1983, The Beauty of Inflections, 1985, Social Values and Poetic Acts, 1987, Towards a Literature of Knowledge, 1989, The Textual Condition, 1991, Black Riders: The Visible Language of Modernism, 1993; editor: The New Oxford Book of Verse of the Romantic Period, 1993, Poetics of Sensibility: A Revolution in Literary Style, 1996, Byron: Complete Poetical Works, 7 vols., 1980-93; author, editor 22 scholarly books and 3 poetry books. Fulbright fellow, Fels

Found. fellow, Eng., 1965-66; Guggenheim fellow, Eng., 1970-71, 74-75; NEH fellow, Eng. and Europe, 1975-76, 87-88. Fellow Am. Acad. Arts and Scis.; mem. MLA. Office: U Va Dept English Charlottesville VA 22903

MCGANN, JOHN RAYMOND, bishop; b. Bklyn., Dec. 2, 1924; s. Thomas Joseph and Mary (Ryan) McG. Student, Cathedral Coll. Immaculate Conception, 1944, Sem. Immaculate Conception, Huntington, 1950; LL.D., St. Johns U., 1971; L.H.D., Molloy Coll., 1977; L.L.D., Niagara U., 1983; L.H.L., St. Joseph's Coll., 1983, Adelphi U., 1985, L.I. U., 1997. Ordained priest Roman Cath. Ch., 1950, ordained bishop, 1971. Asst. priest St. Anne's, Brentwood, 1950-57; asst. chaplain St. Joseph Convent, Brentwood, 1950-54; tchr. religion St. Joseph Acad., 1950-54; assoc. Cath. chaplain Pilgrim State Hosp., 1950-57; asst. chancellor Diocese of Rockville Centre, 1957-67, vice chancellor, 1967-71; sec. to Bishop Kellenberg, 1957-59; elevated to papal chamberlain, 1959; sec. to Bishop Kellenberg, 1959-70; apptd. titular bishop of Morosbisdus and aux. bishop Diocese of Rockville Centre, 1970-76, bishop, 1976—; Del. Sacred Congregation for Religious to Marianists, 1973-76; theol. cons. Nat. Conf. Cath. Bishops, Rome, 1974, treas. 1984-87; mem. adminstrv. com., 1977-79; Anglican/Roman Cath. task force on pastoral ministry of bishops, 1978-81, nat. adv. coun. U.S. Cath. Conf., 1969-70, 81-83, treas. 1984-87; mem. health affairs com., 1972-75, adminstrv. bd., 1976-79, sem. admissions bd. Diocese Rockville Centre, 1971-76, diocesan boundary commn., 1971-76, Tri-Conf. Religious Retirement Project, 1985-88; mem. Papal visit, 1986-87; chmn. Nat. Conf. Cath. Bishops region 2, 1988-91, 94—, chmn. religious life and ministry com., 1991-94, mem. bishop's welfare emergency relief com., 1992-93, ad hoc com. on econ. concerns of Holy See, 1993-94. Bd. Diocesan Svcs., Inc., 1971-76; com. that established Consultation Svcs. for Religious, 1972-74; vicar gen. Diocese Rockville Centre, 1971-76, Episc. vicar, Suffolk County, 1971-76; mem. N.Y. State Cath. Conf. Com. on Prison Apostolate, 1971-74, U.S. Bishops' Com. for Apostolate to Laity, 1972-76, Rockville Centre Diocesan Bd. Consultors, 1969-76; Episc. mem. N.Y. State Cath. Com., 1974-78; chmn. N.Y. State Bishops' Com. on Elective Process, 1974—, Com. Religious Studies in Pub. Edn., 1975-79; mem. com. on ednl. concerns, com. on priests senates and couns. N.Y. State Cath. Conf.; bd. dirs. Good Samaritan Hosp., West Islip, N.Y., 1972-76, chmn., 1976—; trustee Cath. Charities Diocese of Rockville Centre, 1971-76; trustee St. Charles Hosp., Port Jefferson, N.Y., 1972-76, chmn., 1976—; pres. Mercy Hosp., St. Francis Hosp., 1976—; chmn. Consolation Residence, 1976—; bd. advisers Sem. Immaculate Conception, 1975—; treas. Nat. Conf. Cath. Bishops U.S. Cath. Conf., 1984-87, ad hoc com. on stewardship, 1988—, tri-conf. commn. on religious life and ministry, 1988-91; mem. Papal Visit, 1986-87, Tri-Conf. Religious Retirement Project., 1985-88; chmn. Nat. Conf. Cath. Bishops/U.S. Cath. Conf. Telecommunications Network Am., 1990-93; mem. adminstrv. bd. Nat. Conf. Cath. Bishops, 1991-93. Office: 50 N Park Ave Rockville Centre NY 11570-4129

MCGANN, LISA B. NAPOLI, language educator; b. West Hartford, Conn., Sept. 7; d. James Napoli; m. Edward Harrison McGann, Jr. BA, Vassar Coll., 1980; MA, Columbia U., 1983, postgrad., 1991-95; MA, Middlebury Coll., 1987. Cert. tchr. French, ESL and Italian, Conn. Cmty. English program coord. Tchrs. Coll., Columbia U., N.Y.C., 1982-83; mgr. English teaching com. Jr. League N.Y., N.Y.C., 1983-84; asst. dir. ESL Fordham U., N.Y.C., 1988-89; ESL instr. Laguardia C.C., CUNY, Long Island City, N.Y., 1983—, Columbia U., 1983—; ESL instr. Yale U., 1988, 89; ESL specialist, tchr. UN, N.Y.C., 1990. Big sister Highland Hts., New Haven, 1976-77; ESL tchr. Boys and Girls Club, Astoria, N.Y., 1992. Recipient awards and scholarships. Mem. Nat. TESOL Soc., Am. Assn. Tchrs. French, Am. Assn. Tchrs. Italian, Italian-Am. Hist. Soc., Nat. Italian Am. Found. (coun.),. The Statue of Liberty-Ellis Island Found., Inc.,. Roman Catholic. Avocations: ballet, reading, travel, real estate, tennis.

MCGANN, MICHELLE, professional golfer. Leader in driving distance, eagles LPGA Tour, 1992, 18th ranked woman, 1992; winner Oldsmobile Classic, 1996, Youngstown-Warren LPGA Classic, 1996, State Farm Rail Classic, 1996. Address: care LPGA 100 International Golf Dr Daytona Beach FL 32124*

MCGANNEY, THOMAS, lawyer; b. San Mateo, Calif., Mar. 12, 1938; s. Daniel James and Mary Irene (West) McG.; m. Mildred Kalik; children—Jennifer, Abigail, Melanie, Juliana. B.A., Stanford U., 1959; LL.B., Harvard U., 1962. Bar: N.Y. 1963, U.S. Dist. Ct. (so. and ea. dists.) N.Y. 1965, U.S. Ct. Appeals (2d cir.) 1966, (3d cir.) 1969, (10th cir.) 1970, U.S. Supreme Ct. 1971, U.S. Ct. Appeals (9th cir.) 1990. Law clk. U.S. Dist. Ct., So. Dist. N.Y., 1962-64; assoc. White & Case, N.Y.C., 1964-72, ptnr., 1973—; adj. prof. NYU Law Sch., 1984-86. Mem. Am. Coll. Trial Lawyers, N.Y. State Bar Assn., ABA, Fed. Bar Council, Assn. Bar City N.Y. Office: White & Case 1155 Ave Of The Americas New York NY 10036-2711

MCGANNON, JOHN BARRY, university chancellor; b. Humboldt, Kans., Apr. 18, 1924; s. Patrick Joseph and Jane Clare (Barry) McG. AB magna cum laude, St. Louis U., 1947, MA, 1952, PhD, 1963. Joined Soc. of Jesus, 1942, ordained priest Roman Catholic Ch., 1955. Dean Coll. Arts and Scis. St. Louis U., 1963-73; v.p. Rockhurst Coll., Kansas City, 1973-77; v.p. for devel. St. Louis U., 1977-90, chancellor, 1990—; cons., examiner North Ctrl. Accrediting Assn., Chgo., 1958-80. Trustee Loyola U., New Orleans, 1988-94, St. Peter's Coll., Jersey City, 1991—, U. San Francisco, 1991—. Mem. Jesuit Advancement Adminstrs. (pres. 1985-87), Coun. for Advancement and Support of Edn., Nat. Soc. Fund Raising Execs., Nat. Coun. for Planned Giving, Rotary. Office: St Louis U 221 N Grand Blvd Saint Louis MO 63103-2006

MCGARR, FRANK JAMES, retired federal judge, dispute resolution consultant; b. 1921. A.B., Loyola U., Chgo., 1942; J.D., Loyola U., 1950. Bar: Ill. 1950. Assoc. firm Dallstream Schiff Stern & Hardin, Chgo., 1952-54; asst. U.S. atty. No. dist. of Ill., 1954-55, first asst. U.S. atty., 1955-58; ptnr. firm McKay Solum & McGarr, Chgo., 1958-69; first asst. atty. gen. State of Ill., 1969-70; judge U.S. Dist. Ct. for No. Ill., 1970-88, chief judge, 1980-86, sr. judge, 1986-88; of counsel Phelan Cahill & Quinlan, Chgo., 1988-96, Foley & Lardner, Chgo., 1996—. Served with USN, 1942-45. Mem. Am. Coll. Trial Lawyers, 7th Cir. Bar Assn., Chgo. Bar Assn. Home: 4146 Venard Rd Downers Grove IL 60515-1908 Office: Foley & Lardner 330 N Wabash Ave Chicago IL 60611-3603

MCGARRELL, JAMES, artist, educator; b. Indpls., Feb. 22, 1930; s. James and Gretchen (Heermann) McG.; m. Anna Harris, June 24, 1955; children: Andrew Rider, Flora Raven. B.A., Ind. U., 1953; M.A., UCLA, 1955. Artist-in-residence Reed Coll., Portland, Oreg., 1956-59; prof. fine arts, dir. grad. painting Ind. U., Bloomington, 1959-80; prof. fine arts Washington U., St. Louis, 1981-93, prof. emeritus, 1993—; artist in residence Dartmouth Coll., 1993. One man exhbns. include Frumkin/Adams Gallery, N.Y.C., 1961, 64, 66, 68, 71, 73, 77, 80, 84, 86, 88, 89, 90, 91, 93, 95, George Adams Gallery, N.Y.C., 1997, Galerie Claude Bernard, Paris, 1967, 70, 74, Galleria Il Fante de Spade, Rome and Milan, 1967, 71, 72, 74, 76, 79, Galeria Gian Ferrari, Milan, 1981, 83, Galerie Simonne Stern, New Orleans, 1989, 91, 94, 95, Struve Gallery, Chgo., 1988, 90, More Gallery, Phila., 1987, 89, Utah Mus. Art, Salt Lake City, 1972, Art Mus. U. N.Mex., Albuquerque, 1982, St. Louis Art Mus., 1985, Art Mus. U. Ariz., Tucson; represented in permanent collections at Mus. Modern Art, Met. Mus. Art, Whitney Mus. Am. Art, Pa. Acad., Phila., Santa Barbara Mus. Art, San Francisco Art Mus., Art Inst. Chgo., Joseph Hirshhorn Mus., Washington, St. Louis Art Mus., Hamburg (Germany) Mus. Art, Centre Georges Pompidou, Paris. Bd. govs. Skowhegan Sch. Painting and Sculpture. Recipient Am. Acad. Arts and Letters Lifetime Achievement award, 1995; Fulbright fellow, 1955-56; Guggenheim Found. fellow, 1965; Nat. Endowment for Arts grantee, 1967, 85. Mem. Coll. Art Assn. (bd. dirs. 1969-73), Academie des Beaux Arts de L'Institut de France, Nat. Acad. Design. Home: PO Box 39 Newbury VT 05051-0039

MCGARRY, CARMEN RACINE, historian, artist; b. Plattsburgh, N.Y., Dec. 15, 1941; d. Allyre Joseph and Annette Cecile (Roy) Racine; sep.; children: Suzanne, John Jr., Annette, Patrick. BA, Coll. St. Rose, 1962. Tchg. cert. Ill.; lic. real estate broker, Ill.; cert. interior designer, Ill. Tchr. Chgo. Bd. Edn., 1962-69; comptr., mgr., broker K&G Bldg. Mgmt., Chgo., 1969-90; rsch. asst. U. Chgo., 1985-89. Designer and creator stained glass windows St. Anne's Shrine, Isle La Motte, Vt., 1995. Mem. Women's History Coalition, Broward County, Ft. Lauderdale, Fla., 1993—; com. mem. County Health Fair, Broward County, 1994—; bd. mem. Hillsboro Lighthouse Com., 1994—; co-chair adv. coun. Area Agy. on Aging, Ft. Lauderdale, 1996—, chmn., 1997—; mem. nominating com. for women's hall of fame Broward County, 1996; rep. for srs. on transp. Disadvantaged Coord. Bd. Broward County. Mem. ASID, Stained Glass Assn. Am., Women's League Hillsboro (bd. mem. 1993—), Broward County Hist. Commn., Palm Beach Hist. Soc., Hillsboro Beach Hist. Commn. (founder, pres.), Deerfield Beach Hist. Soc., Deerfield Beach Rotary (dir. 1996—). Avocations: traveling, writing. Home: 1073 Hillsboro Mile Hillsboro Beach FL 33062

MCGARRY, FREDERICK JEROME, civil engineering educator; b. Rutland, Vt., Aug. 22, 1927; s. William John and Ellen (Dunn) McG.; m. Alice M. Reilly, Oct. 7, 1950 (dec. Jan. 1971); children: Martha Ellen, Alice Catherine, Joan Louise, Carol Elizabeth, Susan Elizabeth, Janet Marian. A.B., Middlebury (Vt.) Coll., 1950; S.B., Mass. Inst. Tech., 1950, S.M., 1953. Faculty MIT, 1950—, prof. civil engring., 1965—, prof. materials sci. and engring., 1974—, head materials div., 1964—, dir. materials research lab., 1964—, assoc. dir. inter-Am. program civil engring., 1961—, dir. summer session, 1983—. Contbr. numerous articles to profl. jours. Recipient Best Paper award Soc. Plastics Industry, 1968, 91. Mem. AAAS, ASTM, Soc. Rheology, Soc. Plastics Engrs., Am. Soc. Metals, Sigma Xi. Home: 90 Bakers Hill Rd Weston MA 02193-1774 Office: Mass Inst Tech 77 Massachusetts Ave Cambridge MA 02139-4301

MCGARRY, JOHN EVERETT, lawyer; b. Madison, Wis., May 11, 1939; s. Daniel E. and Margaret A. (Haas) McG.; m. Kate Wilkinson, Aug. 26, 1961; children: John Eric, Andrew Lawrence. BA, Lehigh U., 1961, BS in Metall. Engring., 1962; LLB, Georgetown U., 1966. Bar: Okla. 1966, Mich. 1968. Atty. Phillips Petroleum Co., Bartlesville, Okla., 1966-67, Price, Heneveld, Huizenga & Cooper, Grand Rapids, Mich., 1967-70; pvt. practice, Grand Rapids, 1970-72; ptnr. McGarry & Waters, Grand Rapids, 1973-78, Varnum Riddering Wierengo & Christenson, Grand Rapids, 1979-84, Varnum Riddering Schmidt & Howlett, Grand Rapids, 1984—. Mem. Opera Grand Rapids, 1984-92, pres., 1991. Mem. Am. Intellectual Property Law Assn. (chair harmonization com. 1993-95). Office: Varnum Riddering Schmidt & Howlett PO Box 352 Bridgewater Pl Grand Rapids MI 49501-0352

MCGARRY, JOHN PATRICK, JR., advertising agency executive; b. Elizabeth, N.J., Nov. 22, 1939; s. John Patrick and Elizabeth (Weber) McG.; m. Gilda R. Spurio, Oct. 24, 1964; children: Victoria Elizabeth, John Patrick, III. BS in Mktg. Econs, Villanova U., 1961. Salesman Exxon Corp., Elizabeth, 1961-64; advt. exec. Young and Rubicam Inc., N.Y.C., 1965-69, sr. v.p., mgmt. supr., 1969-87, pres., mem. ops. com., advt. exec. com., 1987—; vice chmn. Young and Rubicam Advt. Worldwide, N.Y.C., 1990—; chmn. Client Svcs. Worldwide, N.Y.C., 1987—; pres., CEO Young and Rubicam N.Am., N.Y.C., 1992-94; pres. Young & Rubicam Inc., N.Y.C., 1996—; bd. dirs. Caramoor; mem. corp. exec.'s com. Young and Rubicam, 1992. Bd. dirs. New Youth Performing Theatre, Bedford, N.Y., Regional Rev. League, Westchester, 4 A's, Louisville Opera Assn., 1981-83, Dominican Coll., Drop-out Prevention Fund, United Negro Coll. Fund, 1994—; bd. dirs. N.Y. coun. Boy Scouts Am., 1992; head parents fund St. Lawrence U. Mem. Internat. Advt. Assn. (pres. U.S. and Can.), Proprietory Assn. (bd. dirs.), Bedford Club, Golf and Tennis Club, N.Y. Athletic Club, The Roundabout Theater (adv. bd. 1994—). Democrat. Roman Catholic. Home: 465 Cantitoe St Bedford NY 10506-1103 Office: Young & Rubicam Inc 285 Madison Ave New York NY 10017-6401

MCGARRY, MARCIA LANGSTON, community service coordinator; b. Washington, Dec. 9, 1941; d. Emil Sylvester and Bernice B. (Bland) Busey. BS, Morgan State U., 1964. Cert. tchr., law enforcement officer, Fla. Payroll clk., jr. acct. U.S. Dept. Labor, Washington, 1964-65; English tchr., Taiwan, 1968-70; tchr. Monroe County Sch. Bd., Key West, Fla., 1971-81; exec. dir. Monroe Assn. Retarded Citizens, Key West, 1977-79; dep. sheriff Monroe County Sheriff's Dept., Key West, 1979-83, 1986-90; probation/parole officer Fla. State Dept. Corrections, Key West, 1983-91; law enforcement instr. Fla. Keys C.C., 1983-91; cmty. svc. coord. City of Bradenton, 1991—; mem. rev. bd. City of Bradenton Police Dept., 1996—, mem. cmty. rels. com. 1996. Active local polit. campaigns; co-founder day schs. for under-privileged children; former mem. Big Bros./Big Sisters Am., mem. com. 1985-86, former bd. dir., Spouse Abuse, former bd. dirs. Adv. Coun. Orange-Ridge Elem., 1991-93; bd. dirs. mayor's com., chmn. task force Drug Free Communities, 1991-94, bd. dirs. 1996—; bd. dirs. Human Rels. Commn., 1991-93, Drug Free Schs. and Cmty. Adv. Coun., 1991—; former mem. adv. coun. Byrd Edn. Found., Sweet Adelines Internat., 1992-94, commr. 12th Jud. Nominating Commn. 1992—, cons., facilitator Cultural Diversity Conflict Resolution Workshops, Manatee County High Schs. and Bradenton Police Dept.; attendance avd. com. Bayshore High, 1993, multicultural com., 1994, former rep. Women's Forum; former dir. Choir, Lutheran Ch.; founding mem. Comprehensive Neighborhood Support Network; mem. adv. bd. Manatee County Sheriff's Dept., 1994—. Recipient Appreciation cert. Lions Club, 1978, 79, Career Week award Harris Elem. Sch., 1981, Glynn Archer Elem. Sch., 1989, Trainers award Probation/Parole Acad., 1987, cert. of acknowledgement for cmty. svc. AAUW, 1995, Vol. Army for the War on Drugs. Mem. NAFE, Fla. Police Benevolent Assn., Fla. Women in Govt. (mem. Manatee County chpt.), Ecumanical Luth. Ch. of Am. (elected consultation con. Fla. Synod 1989), Key West Profls., Luth. Ch. Women, Delta Sigma Theta (v.p. 1990-91, corr. sec. 1993-95). Office: City of Bradenton Caller Svc 25015 Bradenton FL 34206

MCGARY, BETTY WINSTEAD, minister, counselor, individual, marriage, and family therapist; b. Louisville, June 21, 1936; d. Philip Miller and Mary Jo (Winstead) McG.; married, 1960 (div. 1979); children: Thomas Edward, Mary Alyson, Andrew Philip Pearce. BS, Samford U., 1958; MA, So. Bapt. Theol. Sem., 1961; EdD, U. Louisville, 1988. Ordained to ministry Bapt. Ch., 1986; cert. secondary tchr., Ky., Ga.; lic. profl. counselor, marriage and family therapist, Tex. Min. to youth Broadway Bapt. Ch., Louisville, 1958-60; learning disability and behavior disorders specialist Jefferson County Schs., Muscogee Schs., Cobb County Schs., Louisville, Columbus, Ga., Atlanta, 1964-88; min. to adults South Main Bapt. Ch., Houston, 1986-90; assoc. pastor Calder Bapt. Ch., Beaumont, Tex., 1991-96; pwochotherapist pvt. practice, Beaumont, Tex., 1996—; marriage enrichment cons. Pastoral Inst., Columbus, 1973-76; co-founder and coord. Ctr. for Women in Ministry, Louisville, 1983-86, exec. bd. dirs., 1983-90; cons. Tex. Christian Life Commn., Ft. Worth, 1989-93; co-therapist pvt. practice, Houston, 1989—. Author: (with others) The New Has Come, 1988, A Costly Obedience: Sermons by Women of Steadfast Spirit, 1994; co-editor nat. newsletter Folio: A Newsletter for Southern Bapt. Women in Ministry, 1983-86. Vice-chairperson exec. bd. dirs. handicapped Boy Scouts Am., Houston, 1986-90; mem. leadership coun. Triangle Interfaith Project, Beaumont, 1995—. Recipient citation for Disting. Svc. So. Bapt. Theol. Sem., 1984, Dean's citation Outstanding Achievement U. Louisville, 1988. Mem. The Alliance of Baptists (exec. bd. dirs. 1988-90, v.p. 1990-91), So. Bapt. Women in Ministry (pres. 1988-90, treas. 1995-96), Bapt. Gen. Conv. of Tex. (exec. bd. dirs. 1996—), Leadership Beaumont. Avocations: gardening, interior design, travel. Home: 2107 Bartlett St Houston TX 77098-5305 Office: PO Box 12308 Beaumont TX 77726-2308 *All around us there are new opportunities for creating, ordering, liberating and healing our world. It is our calling and our challenge to be God's partners in this holy purpose.*

MCGARY, RITA ROSE, social worker; b. Frenchville, Me., Sept. 18, 1927; d. Joseph N. and Lula (Labbe) Babin; m. Lawrence E. McGary; children: Philip, Robert, Kathleen. BA in Sociology, Rivier Coll., 1949; MEd, U. Va., 1978; MSW, U. Nev., 1994. Lic. social worker, Nev., nat. cert. counselor, clin. mental health counselor. Tchr. Fort Kent (Me.) H.S., 1949-51; dir., tchr. Nursery Sch., Palembang, Indonesia, 1954-56; tchr. Am. Sch., Asunción, 1963-66; tchr. for homebound Fairfax County Pub. Schs., Fairfax, Va., 1971-74, presenter workshop, cons., case mgr., vis. tchr., 1980-92, sch. social worker, conflict mediator, 1990-92; case mgr. Washoe County Sch. Dist., Reno, 1994—; mediator Fairfax County Family Ct., Fairfax, Va.,1 991-92; case mgr., program coord. Family Resource Ctr., Reno, 1996; social work intern Nev. State Prison, Nev. Women's State Prison, 1993, VA Med. Ctr. and Vet. Ctr., Reno, Nev., 1994, 1994; presenter in field; adj. prof. U. Nev., Reno. Contbr. article to profl. jour. Election worker Dem. Party, Va., 1984; sch. rep. Hisp. Multidisciplinary Team Child Protective Svcs., Fairfax, Va., 1990-92; coord. V.A. Day of Svc. for Homeless, 1994; field exec. Girl Scout Coun. Nation's Capital, Washington, 1975-79. Recipient Excellence in Edn. Dept. of Cmty. Action, Fairfax, Va., 1991. Mem. AAUW, NASW (chair com. sch. social work), NOW, Sch. Social Work Assn. Am., So. Poverty Law Ctr., People for Am. Way, Phi Kappa Phi. Home: 1539 Foster Dr Reno NV 89509-1211

MC GAUGH, JAMES LAFAYETTE, psychobiologist; b. Long Beach, Calif., Dec. 17, 1931; s. William Rufus and Daphne (Hermes) McG.; m. Carol J. Becker, Mar. 15, 1952; children: Douglas, Janice, Linda. BA, San Jose State U., 1953; PhD (Abraham Rosenberg fellow), U. Calif. - Berkeley, 1959; sr. postdoctoral fellow, NAS-NRC, Istituto Superiore di Sanitá, Rome, 1961-62; DSc (hon.), So. Ill. U., 1991. Asst. prof., assoc. prof. psychology San Jose State U., 1957-61; assoc. prof. psychology U. Oreg., 1961-64; assoc. prof. U. Calif., Irvine, 1964-66, founding chmn. dept. psychobiology, 1964-67, 71-74, 86-89, prof., 1966-94; rsch. prof., 1994—; dean Sch. Biol. Sci. U. Calif., Irvine, 1967-70, vice chancellor acad. affairs, 1975-77, exec. vice chancellor, 1978-82, founding dir. Ctr. Neurobiology of Learning and Memory, 1983—; mem. adv. coms. NIMH, 1965-78, Mental Health Coun. NIMH, 1992-95. Author: (with J.B. Cooper) Integrating Principles of Social Psychology, 1963, (with H.F. Harlow, R.F. Thompson) Psychology, 1971, (with M.J. Herz) Memory Consolidation, 1972, Learning and Memory: An Introduction, 1973, (with R.F. Thompson and T. Nelson) Psychology I, 1977, (with C. Cotman) Behavioral Neuroscience, 1980; editor: (with N.M. Weinberger, R.E. Whalen) Psychobiology, 1966, Psychobiology-Behavior from a Biological Perspective, 1971, The Chemistry of Mood, Motivation and Memory, 1972, (with M. Fink, S.S. Kety, T.A. Williams) Psychobiology of Convulsive Therapy, 1974, (with L.F. Petrinovich) Knowing, Thinking, and Believing, 1976, (with R.R. Drucker-Colín) Neurobiology of Sleep and Memory, 1977, (with S.B. Kiesler) Aging, Biology and Behavior, 1981, (with G. Lynch and N. M. Weinberger) Neurobiology of Learning and Memory, 1984, (with N.M. Weinberger and G. Lynch) Memory Systems of the Brain, 1985, Contemporary Psychology, 1985, (with C.D. Woody and D.L. Alkon) Cellular Mechanisms of Conditioning and Behavioral Plasticity, 1988, (with N.M. Weinberger and G. Lynch) Brain Organization and Memory: Cells, Systems and Circuits, 1990, (with R.C.A. Frederickson and D.L. Felten) Peripheral Signaling of the Brain, 1991, (with L. Squire, G. Lynch and N.M. Weinberger) Memory: Organization and Locus of Change, 1991; (with N.M. Weinberger and G. Lynch) Brain and Memory: Modulation and Mediation of Neuroplasticity, 1995; author over 400 sci. papers; founding editor Behavioral Biology, 1972-78, Behavioral and Neural Biology, 1979-94, Neurobiology of Learning and Memory, 1995—, Plasticity in the Central Nervous System; Learning and Memory, 1995, Brain Processes and Memory, 1996. Recipient medal U. Calif., Irvine, 1992; recipient John P. McGovern award, 1996. Fellow AAAS, Am. Acad. Arts and Scis., Soc. Exptl. Psychologists, Am. Psychol. Soc. (William James fellow 1989, pres. 1989-91), Western Psychol. Assn. (pres. 1992-93); mem. NAS (chmn. psychol. secat. 1992-95), APA (chief sci. advisor 1986-88, Sci. Contbn. award 1981), Internat. Brain Rsch. Orgn., Soc. Neurosci., Am. Coll. Neuropsychopharmacology, Brazilian Acad. Sci. (fgn. mem.), Collegium Internat. Neuropsychopharmacologicum, Psychonomic Soc., European Behavioral Pharmacology Soc., Phi Beta Kappa, Sigma Xi. Office: U Calif Dept Psychobiology Ctr Neurobiology Learning Irvine CA 92697-3800

MC GAUGHAN, ALEXANDER STANLEY, architect; b. Phila., May 18, 1912; s. Henry T. and Mable (Colgan) McG.; m. Virginia Storm, July 11, 1936 (dec. Sept. 1989); 1 son, Alexander Stanley; m. Maria R. Drayer, Oct. 27, 1990.. BArch, U. Mich., 1934. Draftsman, designer Pontiac, Mich., 1934-36; architect Resettlement Adminstrn. and Farm Security Adminstrn., 1936-44; labor economist, planner WPB, Washington, 1944-45; housing economist, prodn. engr. Nat. Housing Agy., Washington, 1945-47; indsl. designer Cairns Corp., N.Y.C., also Hugh Johnson Assos., Washington, 1947-50; partner McGaughan & Johnson, Washington, 1950-80; asst. dir. design and constrn. Gallaudet U., Environ. Design Center for the Deaf, 1980-84; univ. architect Am. U., Washington, 1984-87; archtl. cons., 1988—; spl. cons. Nat. Security Resources Bd., Def. Prodn. Adminstrn., HHFA, HUD, Dept. Def.; mem. D.C. Bd. Examiners and Registrars Architects, 1966-73, pres., 1969-72; dir. Mid. Atlantic region Nat. Coun. Archtl. Registration Bds., 1966-73, chmn., 1970-71, chmn. exam. com. on design and site planning, 1972-73. Prin. works include Charred Oak Estates, Md., doctor's residence D.C. Gen. Hosp., housing, Carlisle Barracks, Pa., housing for USAF and U.S. Army C.E., ea. U.S., shopping ctrs., McLean, Va., Greenbelt, Md., Fairfax County, Va., Prince Georges County, Md., Washington pub. schs., Andrew Radar Clinic, Ft. Myer, Va., D.C. Police Acad., 2d, 4th and 5th dist. police hdqrs., Washington; patentee aluminum bldg. systems. Bd. govs. Washington Bldg. Congress, 1968-71, bd. dirs., 1973-76; mem. President's Com. on Employment People with Disabilities, 1974-93; bd. dirs. Nat. Ctr. for Barrier Free Environ., 1974-79. Recipient 1st award for contemporary architecture and land planning Md. Homebuilders, 1962; disting. urban landscape award U.S. Army C.E., 1968; disting. archtl. award, 1969; nat. archtl. award of excellence Am. Inst. Steel Constrn., 1973. Fellow AIA (pres. Washington met. chpt. 1963, chmn. nat. com. archtl. competitions 1966-67, mem. barrier free task force 1974-77, rep. to Am. Nat. Stds. Inst. A 117.1 com. 1977-88); mem. Am. Arbitration Assn. (nat. panel arbitrators), Cosmos Club (bd. mgmt. 1978-80). Home and Office: 2028 Hillyer Pl NW Washington DC 20009-1006

MCGAUGHEY, CHARLES GILBERT, retired research biochemist; b. San Diego, Sept. 8, 1925; s. Gilbert Arthur and Louisa Ellen (Inskeep) McG. BA, U. Calif., Berkeley, 1950; MA, U. So. Calif., 1952. Diplomate Am. Inst. Oral Biology. Scientist radiol. hazards evaluation U.S. Naval Radiol. Def. Lab., San Francisco, 1952; research biochemist VA Med. Ctr., Long Beach, Calif., 1953-81; prin. investigator studies dental caries and oral cancer Oral Diseases Research Lab., 1978-81. Contbr. articles to profl. jours. Grantee Nat. Inst. Dental Research, 1965. Mem. AAAS. Republican. Home: 337 N Winnipeg Pl Long Beach CA 90814-2564

MC GAUGHY, JOHN BELL, civil engineer; b. Norfolk, Va., Nov. 5, 1914; s. John Bell and Frances Vivian (Coleman) McG.; m. Charlotte Edna Schwartz, Jan. 20, 1940 (dec. Dec. 1978); 1 child, John Bell; m. Page Cook Axson, Sept. 26, 1981. Student, U. Va., 1933-35; B.S. in Civil Engring, Duke U., 1938. Asst. to project engr. U.S. Dept. Agr., Farmville, Va., 1936-37; tech. asst. civil engring. sect. U.S. Coast Guard, Norfolk, Va., 1938-39; civil engr. constrn. q.m. U.S. Army, Albrook Field, C.Z., 1939-41; chief mil. design sect. U.S. Engrs. Office, Norfolk, 1941-44; sr. partner McGaughy, Marshall & McMillan (architects and cons. engrs.)(formerly Lublin, McGaughy & Assocs), Norfolk, 1945-65; pres. MMM Design Group (formerly McGaughy, Marshall & McMillan), Norfolk, Washington, Dublin, Ireland, Frankfurt, Fed. Republic Germany, 1965-81, chmn. bd., chief exec. officer, 1981—; spl. cons. Office Coal Research U.S. Dept. Interior; mem. Va. Gov.'s Met. Areas Study Commn.; chmn. faculty Norfolk extension U. Va., 1943-46. Named Va. Engr. of Yr., 1970. Fellow ASCE; mem. Am. Concrete Inst., ASTM, Am. Road Bldg. Assn. (bd. dirs. engring. div. 1966-68), Nat. Soc. Profl. Engrs. (v.p. 1957-59), Va. C. of C., Norfolk C. of C. (bd. dirs. 1960-63), Va. Soc. Profl. Engrs. (past pres.), Engrs. Club Hampton Roads (past pres.), Soc. Am. Mil. Engrs., Va. Engring. Found. (bd. dirs. 1970-72, 90—), Phi Delta Theta, Thelta Tau. Clubs: Cedar Point Golf (Suffolk); Harbor, Norfolk Yacht and Country (Norfolk); Princess Anne Country (Virginia Beach, Va.). Home: 5905 Studeley Ave Norfolk VA 23508-1030 Office: 229 W Bute St PO Box 269 Norfolk VA 23501

MCGAVIC, JUDY L., coal company official; b. Evansville, Ind., June 29, 1944; d. M. Galen and Helen L. (Sims) Barclay; m. Ronald R. McGavic, Aug. 22, 1962; 1 child, Michael D. Student, Ky. Wesleyan Coll., 1965-66, Murray (Ky.) State U., 1968, U. Ky., 1969; B of Liberal Arts, U. Evansville, 1994. Mine clk. Peabody Coal Co., Centertown, Ky., 1973-78, chief mine clk., 1978-81, sr. mine clk., 1981-86, panel technician, 1986, sr. coord. employee rels., 1987-88, employee rels. rep., 1988-92; sr. employee rels. rep. Peabody Coal Co., Lynnville, Ind., 1993-95. Peabody Coal Co. campaign chmn. United Way, 1992, 93, also chmn. blood drive. Mem. NAFE. Avocations: golf, boating, walking, bowling. Home: 7600 Edgedale Dr Newburgh IN 47630-3062

MCGAVRAN, FREDERICK JAEGER, lawyer; b. Columbus, Ohio, Apr. 24, 1943; s. James Holt and Marion (Jaeger) McG.; m. Elizabeth Dowlig, Jan. 5, 1980; children: Sarah Ann, Marian Katherine. BA, Kenyon Coll., 1965; JD, Harvard U., 1972. Bar: Ohio 1972, U.S. Supreme Ct. 1984, Ky.

1992. Assoc. Kyte, Conlan, Wulsin & Vogeler, Cin., 1972-78, Frost & Jacobs, Cin., 1978—. Editor: Sixth Circuit Federal Practice Manual, 1993. Lt. USN, 1965-69. Mem. Fed. Bar Assn. (pres. Cin. chpt. 1984-85, mem. exec. com. Cin. chpt. 1985—), Ohio State Bar Assn. (chmn. com. on fed. cts. 1982-85), Univ. Club of Cin., The Literary Club. Home: 2560 Perkins Ln Cincinnati OH 45208-2723 Office: Frost & Jacobs 2500 PNC Ctr Cincinnati OH 45202

MCGAW, KENNETH ROY, wholesale distribution executive; b. Parry Sound, Ont., Can., Aug. 25, 1926; s. Dalton Earnest and Grace (Crockford) McG. Student, Denison U., 1946-48; BA, Western Res. U., 1949. With Bigelow Carpets, N.Y. and Ohio, 1949-53; representing Frederick Cooper Lamps, Inc., Chgo., 1953—; home furnishing salesman Gates Mills, Ohio, 1958-74, Fort Lauderdale, 1974-77, Dallas, 1978-79; pres. Ken McGaw, Inc., Dallas, 1979—; factory rep. for maj. furniture and furniture accessory mfrs. Bd. dirs. Big Bros. Cleve., 1963-65, Dallas Opera Co., 1981-92; v.p. Nat. Council on Alcoholism, Cleve., 1972-74; chmn. fundraising drive Wholesale div. Dallas Industry for Dallas Opera, 1982-83; ruling elder 1st Presbyterian Ch., Dallas., 1981—. Served to 2d lt. U.S. Army, 1944-46. Mem. Greater Dallas Home Furnishings Assn. (bd. dirs. 1985-86), S.W. Homefurnishings Assn., S.W. Roadrunners Assn., Internat. Homefurnishings Reps. Assn. Lodge: Rotary.

MCGEADY, SISTER MARY ROSE, religious organization administrator, psychologist; b. Hazelton, Pa., June 28, 1928; d. Joseph James and Catherine Cecilia (Mundie) McG. BA in Sociology, Emmanuel Coll., 1955; MA in Clin. Psychology, Fordham U., 1961; DHL (hon.), St. John's U., Queens, N.Y., 1982, Coll. New Rochelle, N.Y., 1991, Fordham U., 1991, Niagara U., 1991, Coll. St. Rose, Albany, N.Y., 1991, DePaul U., 1991. Joined Daus. of Charity St. Vincent De Paul, Roman Cath. Ch., 1946. Dir. Astor Home Clinics, Rhinebeck, N.Y., 1961-66; exec. dir. Nazareth Child Care Ctr., Boston, 1966-71; dir. mental health Cath. Charities Bklyn., 1971-79, assoc. exec. dir., 1987-90; dir. Kennedy Child Study Ctr., N.Y.C., 1979-81; provincial supr. Daus. of Charity St. Vincent DePaul, Albany, 1981-87; pres., chief exec. officer Covenant House, N.Y.C., 1990—; bd. dirs. Cardinal Cooke Health Care Ctr., N.Y.C., Meninger Found., Kans., St. Michael's Coll., Vt., Ctr. for Human Devel., Washington. Author: Catholic Special Education, 1979. Mem. N.Y. State Mental Health Svcs. Coun., Albany, 1983-90, N.Y. State Mental Health Planning Coun., Albany, 1986-91, Cath. Charities USA, 1966—. Recipient svc. award N.Y.C. Dept. Mental Health, 1988, Encouragement award Cath. U. Am., 1991. Home: 75 Lewis Ave Brooklyn NY 11206-7015 Office: Covenant House 346 W 17th St New York NY 10011-5002

MCGEE, DOROTHY HORTON, writer, historian; b. West Point, N.Y., Nov. 30, 1913; d. Hugh Henry and Dorothy (Brown) McG.; *Perhaps her interest and dedication to local history, particularly the town of Oyster Bay, reach back to the First Purchase Deed of Oyster Bay (1653) on which the first joint purchaser was William Washbourne, her ancestor. As to the town of Hempstead, she is descended from early settlers Captain John Seaman and Colonel John Jackson.* ed. Sch. of St. Mary, 1920-21, Green Vale Sch., 1921-28, Brearley Sch., 1928-29, Fermata Sch., 1929-31. Asst. historian Inc. Village of Roslyn (N.Y.), 1950-58; historian Inc. Village of Matinecock, 1966—. Author: Skipper Sandra, 1950; Sally Townsend, Patriot, 1952; The Boarding School Mystery, 1953; Famous Signers of the Declaration, 1955; Alexander Hamilton-New Yorker, 1957; Herbert Hoover: Engineer, Humanitarian, Statesman, 1959, rev. edit., 1965; The Pearl Pendant Mystery, 1960; Framers of the Constitution, 1968; author booklets, articles hist. and sailing subjects. Chmn., Oyster Bay Am. Bicentennial Revolution Commn., 1971—; historian Town of Oyster Bay, 1982—; mem. Nassau County Am. Revolution Bicentennial Commn.; hon. dir. The Friends of Raynham Hall, Inc.; treas. Family Welfare Assn. Nassau County, Inc., 1956-58; dir. Family Service Assn. Nassau County, 1958-69. Recipient Cert. of award for outstanding contbn. children's lit. N.Y. State Assn. Elem. Sch. Prins., 1959; award Nat. Soc. Children of Am. Revolution, 1960; award N.Y. Assn. Supervision and Curriculum Devel., 1961; hist. award Town of Oyster Bay, 1963; Cert. Theodore Roosevelt Assn., 1976. Fellow Soc. Am. Historians; mem. Soc. Preservation L.I. Antiquities (hon. dir.), Nat. Trust Hist. Preservation, N.Y. Geneal. and Biol. Soc. (dir., trustee), Oyster Bay Hist. Soc. (hon., pres. 1971-75, chmn. 1975-79, trustee), Theodore Roosevelt Assn. (trustee), Townsend Soc. Am. (trustee). Republican. Address: PO Box 142 Locust Valley NY 11560-0142 *Through several of her published books, she is able to forward the cause of American history and the local Oyster Bay history. Her many articles and illustrated lectures address this goal, too. Her work as Town Historian, Landmark Preservation and Bicentennial Chairman, including historial re-enactment, writings, contests, etc., has reached all ages and continues to do so.*

MCGEE, HALL THOMAS, JR., newspaper, radio and television executive; b. Charleston, S.C., Aug. 7, 1913; s. Hall Thomas and Gertrude Wyman (Frampton) McG.; m. Margaret Anne Pringle, June 29, 1939; children—Margaret Anne McGee McManes, Hall Thomas, III. B.S., Coll. Charleston, 1935; postgrad., Harvard U. Bus. Sch., 1936. With Eve. Post Pub. Co. and News and Courier Co., Charleston, 1936-87; treas. Eve. Post Pub. Co. and News and Courier Co., 1945-81, v.p., gen. mgr., 1969-84, pres., 1984-87, also dir., 1945—; trustee retirement plan, 1955—; treas., dir. Rochelle Corp., Beaufort, S.C., 1962-75, Aiken Cablevision, Inc., S.C., 1965-83, Banner Corp., Cambridge, Md., 1965-86, Aiken Communications, Inc., 1968-87 , Georgetown Communications, Inc., S.C., 1973-87 , Waynesboro Pub. Co., Va., 1974-82; treas., dir. Portal Communications, Inc., El Paso, Tex., 1974-86, Sangre de Cristo Communications, Inc., Pueblo, Colo., Editors Press Service Inc., N.Y.C., Buenos Aires (Argentina) Herald, Mardel Communications, Inc., Salisbury, Md., 1980-86. Bd. dirs. Charleston YMCA; bd. dirs. treas. Charleston Indsl. Assn., 1964-80; pres., trustee Grant Home, Charleston, 1975-86; trustee Coll. Charleston, 1952-68, Magnolia Cemetery, Charleston, 1970-86, Roper Found., 1988—; elder Second Presbyn. Ch., 1958—. Mem. Am. Newspaper Pubs. Assn. (chmn. taxation com.), So. Newspaper Pubs. Assn. (dir.), S.C. Press Assn. (past pres.), St. Cecilia Soc., S.C. Soc., St. Andrews Soc., Agrl. Soc. S.C., Huguenot Soc. S.C., Rotary (dir. Charleston chpt.), Carolina Yacht Club, Supper Club. Home: 200 Wentworth St Charleston SC 29401-1233 Office: Executive Suites 171 Church St Ste 300 Charleston SC 29401-3165

MCGEE, HAROLD JOHNSTON, academic administrator; b. Portsmouth, Va., Apr. 13, 1937; s. Harold Valentine McGee and Clara Mae (Johnston) Webber; m. Mary Frances Eure, Mar. 22, 1959; children: Harold Johnston, Mary Margaret, Matthew Hayden; m. Linda Gayle Stevens, Apr. 3, 1976; 1 child, Andrew Meade. BS, Old Dominion U., 1959; MEd, U. Va., 1962, EdD, 1968. Tchr. Falls Church (Va.) City Schs., 1959-62; asst. dean, then dean of admissions Old Dominion U., Norfolk, Va., 1962-65; field rep., program officer, sr. program officer U.S. Office Edn. Bur. Higher Edn., Charlottesville, 1965-70; provost Tidewater Community Coll., Portsmouth, 1970-71; founding pres. Piedmont Va. Community Coll., Charlottesville, 1971-75; various offices including dean grad. sch., asst. to pres., v.p. student affairs, v.p. adminstrv. affairs, sec. bd. visitors James Madison U., Harrisonburg, Va., 1975-86; pres. Jacksonville (Ala.) State U., 1986—; bd. dirs. Marine Environ. Scis. Consortium, Dauphin Island, Ala., Gulf South Conf. Conf., chmn. 1990-92; bd. dirs. Birmingham Calhoun County C. of C., vice chmn. 1988-90; chmn. Ala. Coun. Univ. Pres., 1991-93; mem. Gov.'s Tax Reform Task Force, 1991-92; bd. dirs. Trans America Athletic Conf., 1995—, Southland Football League, 1995—. Author: Impact of Federal Support, 1968, The Virginia Project, 1976. Mem. United Way of Calhoun County Ala. 1986-92, Knox Concert Series Adv. Bd., Anniston, Ala., Leadership Ala., Anniston Mus. Natural History Found. Mem. NCAA (coun. 1991-95), ACA, Soc. Coll. and Univ. Planning Am. Assn. Higher Edn., Capital City Club (Montgomery, Ala.), Rotary, Phi Delta Kappa. Episcopalian. Office: Jacksonville State U Office of Pres Jacksonville AL 36265

MCGEE, HENRY ALEXANDER, JR., university official; b. Atlanta, Sept. 12, 1929; s. Henry Alexander and Arrie Mae (Mallory) McG.; m. Betty Rose Herndon, July 29, 1951; children: Henry Alexander, Charles Nelson, Kathy Nan. BChemE, Ga. Inst. Tech., 1951, PhD, 1955; postgrad., U. Wis., 1955-56. Rsch. scientist Army Rocket and Guided Missile Agy. and NASA, Huntsville, Ala., 1956-59; from assoc. prof. to prof. chem. engring. Ga. Inst. Tech., Atlanta, 1959-71; prof. Va. Poly. Inst. and State U., Blacksburg, 1971-94, head dept. chem. engring., 1971-82; assoc. provost for engring. Va. Commonwealth U., Richmond, 1994-95, founding dean engring., 1995—; vis. prof. Calif. Inst. Tech., 1964; dir. chem. and thermal sys. div. NSF, Washington, 1990-93; cons. in field. Author: Molecular Engineering, 1991; editorial adv. bd.: Chemical Abstracts; contbr. numerous articles to profl. publs. Danforth Assoc.; recipient various rsch. grants NSF, NASA, Air Force Office Sci. Rsch.; named one of five Outstanding Young Men of Yr. Atlanta, 1964, Acad. Disting. Engring. Alumni, Ga. Tech., 1994. Fellow AIChE (chmn. nat. program com., mem. editl. bd. jour), AAAS (chmn. sect. on engring. 1985-86), Am. Chem. Soc.; mem. Sigma Xi. Republican. Home: 6 River Court Ln Richmond VA 23233 Office: Va Commonwealth U Richmond VA 23284

MCGEE, HUMPHREY GLENN, architect; b. Hartsville, S.C., June 26, 1937; s. James Gladney and Elizabeth Adams (Williams) McG.; BArch, Clemson U., 1960. Designer, Clark, McCall & Leach, Hartsville-Kingstree, S.C., 1961; Designer prodn. A. G. Odell & Assocs., Charlotte, N.C., 1962; chief designer Clark, McCall & Leach, Hartsville-Kingstree, S.C., 1963; sr. designer LBC & W, Inc., Columbia, S.C., 1965-69, pres., 1969-76, sr. v.p. client services and design, 1976; pres. CEDA, Inc., Columbia, S.C., 1976-86; pres., treas. McGee-Howle & Assocs., Vero Beach, Fla, 1986—. With USAR, 1961-67. Mem. Am. Inst. Architects, Nat. Soc. Interior Designers (award 1972), Am. Soc. Interior Designers (chmn. S.C. chpt. com. on Found. Interior Design Edn. and Rsch. 1976). Published: Who's Who in Interior Design, 1993-95; cited in 100 Designer's Favorite Rooms, 1993, 94, 95. Home: 251 Johns Island Dr Indian River Shores FL 32963-3238 Office: 2801 Ocean Dr Ste 302 Vero Beach FL 32963-2025

MCGEE, JAMES SEARS, historian; b. Houston, July 12, 1942; s. William Sears and Mary Elizabeth (Peterson) McG.; m. Mary Arnall Broach, Aug. 20, 1966; children: Elizabeth, Claude. BA, Rice U., 1964; MA, Yale U., 1966, M in Philosophy, 1968, PhD, 1971. Asst. prof. Ga. So. Coll., Statesboro, 1969-71; asst. prof. history U. Calif., Santa Barbara, 1971-78, assoc. prof., 1978-84, prof., 1984—, chmn. dept., 1990-95. Author: The Godly Man in Stuart England, 1976; editor: The Miscellaneous Works of John Bunyan, Vol. 3, 1987. Named Disting. Tchr. in Soc. Scis., U. Calif., Santa Barbara, 1989; fellow Abraham Found., 1962-63; Woodrow Wilson fellow, 1964-65; recipient summer stipend NEH, 1975. Mem. Royal Hist. Soc., Am. Soc. Ch. History, Am. Hist. Assn., N.Am. Conf. on Brit. Studies. Democrat. Episcopalian. Avocation: gardening. Office: U Calif Dept History Santa Barbara CA 93106

MCGEE, JERRY EDWARD, academic administrator; b. Rockingham, N.C., Nov. 4, 1942; s. Sam McGee and Mary (McKinnon) Caddell; m. Hannah Covington, Aug. 15, 1965; children: Jeremy Ryan, Marcus Samuel. BS, East Carolina U., 1965; MA, Appalachian State U., 1974; EdD, Nova U., 1979; AA (hon.), Richmond C.C., 1993. Insdl. engr. Burlington Inc., Rockingham, 1965-68; program dir. Tri-County Cmty. Action, Laurinburg, N.C., 1968-71; counselor, program dir. Richmond C.C., Hamlet, N.C., 1971-75; exec. asst. to pres. Gardner Webb U., Boiling Springs, N.C., 1975-80; v.p. for devel. Meredith Coll., Raleigh, N.C., 1980-87, Furman U., Greenville, S.C., 1987-92; pres. Wingate (N.C.) U., 1992—; bd. dirs. Bank of Union, Monroe, N.C., First Charter Corp., Concord, N.C.; bd. visitors Johnson C. Smith U., Charlotte, N.C., 1995—; pres. coun. NCAA Divsn. II, 1997—. Dist. gov. Civitan Internat., Western N.C., 1974-75; football referee divsn. I NCAA. With USNG, 1967-73. Democrat. Baptist. Home: 1204 Irongate Dr Monroe NC 28110 Office: Wingate Univ Office of Pres Wingate NC 28174

MC GEE, JOHN FRAMPTON, communications company executive; b. Charleston, S.C., Jan. 9, 1923; s. Hall Thomas and Gertrude (Frampton) McG.; m. Ruth Bouknight Smedley, June 19, 1971; children: Beverly C. McGee Kinder, Catharine F. McGee Mebane, Charles V. Smedley. BS in Bus. and Polit. Sci., Davidson Coll., 1943. With Charleston (S.C.) Post-News and Courier, 1946-62; asst. gen. mgr. State-Record Newspapers, Columbia, S.C., 1962-64, gen. mgr., pres., co-pub., 1964-69; gen. exec. Knight Newspaper, Inc., Miami, Fla., 1969-70; pres., associated pub. Charleston (W.Va.) Daily Mail, 1970-87, pub., 1987-90; pres. Clay Communications, Inc. parent co. Charleston Daily Mail, Raleigh Register, Post-Herald, Beckley (W.Va.), Enquirer-Jour., Monroe, N.C., Shelby (N.C.) Daily Star, Sta. WWAY-TV, N.C., Sta. KFDX-TV, Tex., Sta. KJAC-TV, Tex., Sta. WAPT-TV, Miss., 1970-87; gen. ptnr. McGee Enterprises, Charleston, 1987—; bd. dirs., mem. exec. com. AP, N.Y.C.; bd. dirs. Thomson Newspapers, Inc., N.Y.C. and Toronto, Can., United Nat. Bank, Charleston, W.Va.; mem. adv. bd. Sch. Journalism, W.Va. U.; vis. prof. Grad Sch. Journalism, U. Nairobi, Kenya, 1992, 93, Harare Zimbabwe, 1993, 94; vis. lectr. media matters USIS Wind Hook Namibia, 1994; print media counselor, Namibia, Botswana, 1995. Vice chmn. Charleston Area Med. Ctr., U. Charleston; chmn. bd. visitors Davidson (N.C.) Coll., trustee; mem. gen. exec. bd. Presbyn. Ch., U.S.A., 1974-76; mem. S.C. Commn. for Higher Edn., 1966-69. Capt. inf. U.S. Army, 1943-45. Decorated Purple Heart with one oak leaf cluster, Bronze Star with three oak leaf clusters, Combat Infantry badge, Croix de Guerre with palm (France and Belgium), Presdl. Merit citation, Knight Fellow Knight Found., 1995. Fellow Internat. Press Inst. (bd. dirs. Am. com., mem. UNESCO commn. for free press during S. African elections 1994); mem. So. Newspaper Pubs. Assn. (bd. dirs. 1967-69), W.Va. Press Assn. (pres. 1977-78), New Eng. Soc. S.C. Clubs: Cosmos (Charleston, W.Va.); Edgewood Country of W.Va. Office: McGee Enterprises Bank One Ctr Ste 812 Charleston WV 25301

MC GEE, JOSEPH JOHN, JR., former insurance company executive; b. Kansas City, Mo., Dec. 2, 1919; s. Joseph J. and Margaret (Cronin) McG.; m. Anne Cunningham, Apr. 30, 1949; children: Sally, Peter, Mary, John, David, Julie, Simon. Attended, Rockhurst Coll., Kansas City, Georgetown U. Asst. sec. Old Am. Ins. Co., Kansas City, Mo., 1939-45; v.p. Old Am. Ins. Co., 1946-51, exec. v.p., 1952-55, pres., 1956-87; ins. cons. Kansas City, Mo., 1987-91. Bd. dirs. Truman Med. Ctr., Truman Libr. Inst. for Nat. and Internat. Affairs; trustee emeritus Rockhurst Coll.; pres. McGee Found. Office: 4800 Main St Ste 458 Kansas City MO 64112-2510

MCGEE, MARY ALICE, health science research administrator; b. Winston-Salem, N.C., Oct. 14, 1950; d. C.L. Jr. and Mary Hilda (Shelton) McG. AB, Meredith Coll., 1972. Tchr. Augusta (Ga.) Schs., 1972-73; specialist grants Med. Sch. Brown U., Providence, R.I., 1974-76; profl. basketball player, 1975-76; dir. research adminstn. Med. Sch. Brown U., Providence, 1976-94; tchr., coach Providence Country Day Sch., East Providence, R.I., 1995—. Bd. dirs. Sojourner House, Providence, 1983—, v.p., 1986, 91, treas. 1987-89. Mem. Soc. Rsch. Adminstrs., Nat. Coun. U. Rsch. Adminstrs., R.I. Assn. Women in Edn. Avocations: sports, travel, dogs. Home: 121 Plain St Rehoboth MA 02769-2540 Office: Providence Country Day Sch 660 Waterman Ave East Providence RI 02914-1714

MCGEE, MICHAEL JAY, fire marshal, educator; b. Ft. Worth, June 9, 1952; s. Cecil Carl McGee and Helen Ruth (Peeples) McGee-Furrh; m. Carol Lee Garbarino, Sept. 18, 1982; children: Megan Rose, John Michael, Molly Caitlin. Student, U. Tex., 1970-73, Western Oreg. State U., 1983; AAS in Fire Protection Tech., Colo. Mountain Coll., 1990. Lic. fire suppression systems insp., Colo., vocat. educator, Colo.; cert. hazardous materials technician, Colo., 1992, EMT, Colo.; cert. fire safety hazardous materials instr., evaluator. Driver Massengale Co., Austin, Tex., 1970-73; gen. mgr. Sundae Palace, Austin, 1973-74; staff mem. Young Life, Colorado Springs, Colo., 1970-75; mgr. Broadmoor Mgmt. Co., Vail, Colo., 1974-76; technician Vail Cable Communications, 1976-77; fire marshal Vail Fire Dept., 1977—, fire sci. coord., 1995—, emergency med. program coord., 1996—; v.p. HAZPRO (Hazardous Materials and Fire Safety Consulting Firm), 1996—; dist. rep. Joint Coun. Fire Dist. Colo., 1983-85; co-chmn. Eagle County Hazardous Materials, 1984-85, mem. planning com., 1987-90; mem. accountability com. Eagle County Sch. Dist., 1991-96, mem. budget rev. com., 1991-93, vice chair accountability com. 1992-93, chmn. accountability com., 1993-96; mem. policy rev. com., 1993-96, bldg. coord., team coach Odyssey of the Mind at Eaglevale Elem. Sch., 1995; invited dir. workshops Colo. Dept. Edn. Dist. Accountability Convention, Colo. Springs, 1995. Chmn. Eagle County chpt. ARC, 1980-83, disaster chmn., 1977-80; tng. officer Eagle Vol. Fire Dept., 1988-90; mem. parish coun. St. Mary's Parish, Eagle County, 1989-90; mem. citizen's adv. com. Colo. Mountain Coll., 1990-91, bd. dirs. 1990; bldg. coord., team coach Odessey of the Mind, Eagle Valley Elem. Sch., 1994-95; mem. facilities master planning com. Engle County Sch. Dist., 1996-97. Mem. Internat. Assn. Arson Investigators (Colo. chpt.), Internat. Platform Assn., Nat. Fire Protection Assn., Colo. State Fire Marshals Assn., Colo. State Fire Chiefs Assn. Office: Vail Fire Dept 42 W Meadow Dr Vail CO 81657-5705

MCGEE, WILLIAM HOWARD JOHN, library system coordinator; b. Rochester, N.Y., May 15, 1942; s. William Peter and Cecilia Matilda (Kuhn) McG.; m. Sheila Anne Drumm, Sept. 4, 1965; children: Kathleen Moira, Margaret Frances. BA with honors, U. Toronto, Ont., Can., 1965; MEd, U. Toronto, 1973; MLS, U. Western Ont., London, 1980. Tchr. Mimico (Ont.) High Sch., 1966-67; tchr., libr. Applewood Secondary Sch., Mississauga, Ont., 1967-71; libr. Crestwood Secondary Sch., Peterborough, Ont., 1971-74; libr. cons. Cayman Islands Edn. Dept., Grand Cayman, B.W.I., 1975-79; adminstrv. asst. Lake Erie Regional Libr., London, Ont., 1980-83; chief libr. Ft. Erie (Ont.) Pub. Libr., 1983-86; asst. dir. McAllen (Tex.) Pub. Libr., 1986-89; coord. Hidalgo County Libr. System, McAllen, 1989—; cons. Grand Ct. Libr., Grand Cayman, 1974-79; mem. Tex. State Libr. Task Force, Austin, Tex., 1991-93; adv. coun. Libr. Svcs. Consultation Act, Austin, 1993—. Editor InTraLogue jour., 1980-83; assoc. editor Can. Jour. Info. Sci., 1980. Mem. ALA, Ont. Libr. Assn., Tex. Libr. Assn. (chmn. dist. 4 1994-95, intellectual freedom com. 1995-96), Bibliothecaires Francophones Internat. Roman Catholic. Avocations: gourmet cooking, music, travel, reading. Office: Hidalgo County Libr Sys 4305 N 10th St Ste E McAllen TX 78504-3009

MCGEE, WILLIAM TOBIN, intensive care physician; b. Port Chester, N.Y., May 23, 1957; s. James R. and Mary (Delzotto) McG.; m. Sarah McGrath; children: Erin, Kelly, Mary Kate. BA in Physics, Dartmouth Coll., 1979; MD, N.Y. Med. Coll., 1983. Diplomate Am. Bd. Internal Medicine with spl. qualifications in Critical Care. Resident in internal medicine Baystate Med. Ctr., Springfield, Mass., 1983-86, intensivist, acting dir. surg. ICU, 1990-95; fellow in critical care St. Louis U./St. John's Mercy Med. Ctr., St. Louis, 1986-88; intensivist critical care divsn. Baystate Med. Ctr., Springfield, MA, 1990—. DeWitt Wallace fellow rehab. medicine Rusk Inst. NYU Med. Ctr. Fellow Coll. Chest Physicians; mem. AMA, Soc. Critical Care Medicine, Am. Soc. Parenteral and Enteral Nutrition. Roman Catholic. Avocations: skiing, biking, hiking, sailing, windsurfing. Office: Baystate Med Ctr 759 Chestnut St Springfield MA 01199-1001

MCGEEIN, MARY MARTHA, health care organization executive; b. Toledo, Oct. 26, 1938; d. Andrew John and Gertrude Ceceil (Doyle) McG.; m. Thomas Dale Winkeljohn, Nov. 26, 1959 (div. 1977); children: Ellen T., Mary Beth, Joseph J., Katherine M.; m. Ronald Allan Schnepper, May 21, 1980. RN, Mercy Sch. of Nursing, Toledo, 1959; BSN, Marymount U., 1983; MBA, U. Pa., 1992. Cert. in-patient ob/gyn care/RNC. Nurse Luth. Hosp., Fort Wayne, Ind., 1959-60, Mercy Hosp., Toledo, 1960-62, Holy Cross Hosp., Silver Spring, Md., 1967-83; spl. asst. to pres. for pub. liaison and dir. bus. liaison The White House, Washington, 1983-88; assoc. dir. Nat. Coun. Community Hosps., Washington, 1988-92, v.p., 1992—; bd. dirs. Indigo Inst., Washington; vis. prof. Wharton Sch. U. Pa., Phila., 1992—; grants reviewer Dept. H.H.H./U.S., Washington, 1991—; expert work group mem. U.S. Dept. H.H.S., Washington, 1991—; bd. dirs. Health Care Liability Alliance, Washington, 1993—. Fundraiser Am. Diabetes Assn., Washington, 1988—; vol. mentor No. Va. Women's Ctr., Arlington, Va., 1987—; vol. health care provider Tutwiler (Miss.) Rural Clinic, 1989—; task force mem. Nat. Policy Forum, Washington, 1994—. Mem. Internat. Childbirth Educators, Assn. Women's Health Obstet. and Neonatal Nurses, Sigma Theta Tau. Office: The McGeein Group Nat Coun Comm Hosps 1700 K St NW Washington DC 20006-3817

MCGEER, EDITH GRAEF, neurological science educator emerita; b. N.Y.C., Nov. 18, 1923; d. Charles and Charlotte Annie (Ruhl) Graef; m. Patrick L. McGeer, Apr. 15, 1954; children: Patrick Charles, Brian Theodore, Victoria Lynn. BA, Swarthmore Coll., 1944; PhD, U. Va., 1946; DSc (hon.), U. Victoria, 1987. Research chemist E.I. DuPont de Nemours & Co., Wilmington, Va., 1946-54; research assoc. div. neurological sci. U. B.C., Vancouver, Can., 1954-74; assoc. prof. U. B.C., Vancouver, 1974-76, prof., acting head, 1976-83, prof., head., 1983-89, prof. emerita, 1989—. Author: (with others) Molecular Neurobiology of the Mammalian Brain, 1978, 2d. edit., 1987; editor: (with others) Kainic Acid as a Tool in Neurobiology, 1978, Glutamine, Glutamate, and GABA, 1983; contbr. articles to profl. jours. Decorated officer Order of Can.; recipient Citation Am. Chem. Soc., 1958, Rsch. Prize in Psychiatry Clarke Inst., 1992, Lifetime Achievement spl. award Sci. Coun. B.C., 1995, Hon. Alumnus award, 1996. Fellow Can. Coll. Neuropsychopharmacology; mem. Can. Biochemical Soc., Internat. Brain Research Orgn., Internat. Soc. Neurochemistry, Soc. Neuroscience, Am. Neurochemical Soc. (councilor 1979-83), North Pacific Soc. Neurology and Psychiatry (hon. fellow), Lychnos Soc., Sigma Xi, Phi Beta Kappa. Office: U BC Div Neurol Scis, 2255 Wesbrook Mall, Vancouver, BC Canada V6T 1Z3

MCGEER, JAMES PETER, research executive, consultant; b. Vancouver, B.C., Can., May 14, 1922; s. James Arthur and Ada Alice (Schwenger) McG.; m. Catherine Pearson Deas, June 22, 1948; children: Mary, Allison, James, Thomas. BA, U. B.C., 1944, MA, 1946; MA, Princeton U., 1948, PhD, 1949; DSc, Queens U., Kingston, Ont., Can., 1996. Researcher Alcan R & D, Arvida, Que., Can., 1949-52, group leader, 1952-59, pilot plant dir., 1960-67; dept. head Alcan Smelters, Arvida, Que., Can., 1968-71, asst. div. head, 1972-73; mgr. tech. transfer Alcan Smelter Svcs., Montreal, Que., 1973-77; dir. rsch. Alcan Internat. Ltd., Kingston, Ont., Can., 1978-82, dir. lab., 1983-87; mng. dir. Ont. Ctr. Materials, Kingston, 1988—; chmn. bd. Can. Rsch. Mgmt. Assn., Toronto, Ont., 1990-91, Welding Inst. Can., Mississauga, Ont., 1988-90, Can. U. Ind. Con. Advanced Ceramics, Ottawa, Ont., 1986-88; dir. Metall. Soc., Pitts., 1987-89; Can. Coun. lectr. Am. Soc. Metals, 1985-86; disting. lectr. Can. Inst. Mining Metallurgy, 1987. Contbr. articles to profl. jours. Chmn. bd. Que. Assn. Protestant Sch. Bds., Montreal, 1968-70. Recipient Airey award Can. Inst. for Mining and Metallurgy, 1993, Forum award Xerox Can., 1994. Mem. Anglican Ch. Office: Ontario Ctr Materials Rsch, PO Box 1146, Kingston, ON Canada K7L 4Y5

MCGEHEE, FRANK SUTTON, paper company executive; b. Aug. 15, 1928; s. Clifford G. and Ray (Sutton) McGehee; m. Ann Whitehurst, Mar. 18, 1949; children: Frank Sutton, David Searcy, Ann Lynwood Riley. BA in Econs., U. Ala., 1950. Co-founder, co-chmn. bd. Jacksonville Paper Co. (now UNIJAX), 1950-64; dir. Flagship Banks of Jacksonville; co-founder, co-chmn. bd. Mac Paper Converters, Inc., now chmn. bd., CEO. Trustee, mem. exec. com. Bolles Sch.; past pres., dir. Wolfson Childrens Hosp.; past pres., pres. bd. Ga. Christian Sch. and Home, North Fla. Coun. Boy Scouts Am.; past chmn. Weyerhaeuser Mcht. Coun., Kimberly Clark Mcht. Coun.; active San Jose Ch. of Christ. Mem. Nat. Paper Trade Assn. (dir.), Jacksonville Businessmen Club (sec., dir.), Tournament Players Club (founder), River Club, San Jose Country Club, Sawgrass Country Club, Plantation Country Club. Home: 6750 Epping Forest Way N Jacksonville FL 32217-2688 Office: MAC Papers Inc 3300 Phillipps Hwy PO Box 5369 Jacksonville FL 32247

MC GEHEE, H(ARRY) COLEMAN, JR., bishop; b. Richmond, Va., July 7, 1923; s. Harry Coleman and Ann Lee (Cheatwood) McG.; m. June Stewart, Feb. 1, 1946; children: Lesley, Alexander, Harry III, Donald, Cary. BS, Va. Poly. Inst., 1947; JD, U. Richmond, 1949; MDiv, Va. Theol. Sem., 1957, DD, 1973. Bar: Va. 1949, U.S. Supreme Ct. 1954; ordained to ministry Episcopal Ch., 1957. Spl. counsel dept. hwys. State of Va., 1949-51, gen. counsel employment svc., 1951, asst. atty. gen., 1951-54; rector Immanuel Ch.-on-the-Hill, Va. Sem., 1960-71; bishop Diocese of Mich., Detroit, 1971-90; adv. bd. Nicaraguan Network, Ctr. for Peace and Conflict Studies, Wayne State U.; bd. dirs. Mich. Religious Coalition for Abortion Rights, 1976-84; trustee Va. Theol. Sem., 1978-93; pres. Episc. Ch. Pub. Co., 1978-85. Columnist: Detroit News, 1979-85; weekly commentator pub. radio sta. WDET-AM, Detroit, 1984-90. Mem. Gov.'s Commn. on Status of Women, 1965-66, Mayor's Civic Com., Alexandria, 1967-68; sponsor Nat. Assn. for ERA, 1977-85; pres. Alexandria Legal Aid Soc., 1969-71; bd. dirs. No. Va. Fairhousing Corp., 1963-67; pres. Mich. Coalition for Human Rights, 1980-89; chmn. Citizens' Com. for Justice in Mich., 1983-84; sponsor Farm Labor Orgn. for Children, 1983-85; bd. dirs. Pub. Benefit Corp., Detroit, 1988-90, Mich. Citizens for Personal Freedom, 1989-92, Poverty and Social Reform Inst., Detroit, 1989—, Bread for the World, 1990-94, Ams. United for

Separation of Ch. and State, 1990, ACLU Oakland County, Mich., 1991-94; co-chair Lesbian-Gay Found. Mich., 1991—. 1st lt. C.E., U.S. Army, 1943-46. Named Feminist of Yr., Detroit NOW, 1978; recipient Humanitarian award Detroit ACLU, 1984, Phillip Hart medal Mich. Women's Studies Assn., 1984, Sayre award for justice and peace Episc. Peace Fellowship, 1988, Spirit of Detroit award, 1989, Archbishop Romero award Mich. Labor Com., 1990, Brotherhood award AME Ch., Detroit, 1993, Ira Jayne award Detroit br. NAACP, 1993, Martin Luther King, Jr. award United Ch. of Christ, 1995. Mem. Detroit Econ. Club (bd. dirs.). Home: 1496 Ashover Dr Bloomfield Hills MI 48304-1215 Office: Diocese of Mich 4800 Woodward Ave Detroit MI 48201-1310

MC GEHEE, LARRY THOMAS, university administrator; b. Paris, Tenn., May 18, 1936; s. George Eugene and Margaret Elizabeth (Thomas) McG.; m. Elizabeth Hathhorn Boden, Aug. 26, 1961; children: Elizabeth Hathhorn, Margaret Thomas. BA, Transylvania Coll., 1958; BD, Yale U., 1963, MA, 1964, PhD, 1969. Dir., asst. v.p. for univ. relations U. Ala., 1966-68, exec. asst. to pres., 1968-69, exec. v.p., 1969-71; lectr., assoc. prof. dept. Am. studies, 1969-71, acad. v.p., 1971; chancellor U. Tenn., Martin, 1971-79; spl. asst. to pres. U. Tenn., Knoxville, 1979-82; v.p. coll., prof. religion Wofford Coll., Spartanburg, S.C., 1982—. Danforth fellow Yale U., 1960-66. Home: 1047 Woodburn Rd Spartanburg SC 29302-2867 Office: Wofford Coll 429 N Church St Spartanburg SC 29303-3612

MCGEHEE, THOMAS RIVES, paper company executive; b. Jacksonville, Fla., July 12, 1924; s. Clifford Graham and Ray (Sutton) McG. Student Davidson Coll., 1942-43, BS in Chemistry, U. Ala. 1948; m. Delia Houser, Nov. 3, 1950; children: Delia McGehee II, Thomas R. Jr. V.p. Jacksonville Paper Co., 1948-56, pres., 1956-64, Mac Papers, Inc., Jacksonville, 1964-79, co-founder, chief exec. officer, chmn. bd., 1979—; co-chmn., chief exec. officer Mac Papers Converters, Inc., 1965—, pres., North Fla. TV-47, Inc., 1979-90; pres. Higley Pub. Co., 1968-90; bd. dirs. Barnett Bank of Jacksonville, 1961-89; chmn. exec. com. Sta. WTLV-TV 12, 1972-78; numerous real estate interests. Chmn. and founder Greater Jacksonville Community Found., 1964-84, trustee, 1984-89; trustee Jacksonville U., 1959—, vice chmn., 1962-65, chmn., 1991-92; trustee Regent U., 1996—; mem. U. Fla. Pres.' Coun., U. Fla. Health & Sci. Ctr.; mem. post secondary edn. planning commn. State of Fla., 1987-90; bd. dirs. Dreams Come True, pres. and founder 1984-90, chmn. emeritus, 1990—; bd. dirs. Bapt. Hosp. Found., 1986-90; vice chmn. Every Home For Christ, 1987—; past mem., officer numerous other community orgs. Served with U.S. Army, 1943-46, ETO. Recipient 3 Battle Stars, Fla. Gov.'s award, 1962. Mem. NAM (dir. 1964-66), Asso. Industries Fla. (dir. 1961-63), Nat. Paper Trade Assn., So. Paper Trade Assn., Nat. Assn. Broadcasters, Fla. State C. of C., Phi Gamma Delta (pres. 1948). Republican. Episcopalian. Clubs: River (dir. 1980-83), Fla. Yacht, Timuquana Country, Ponte Vedra, Plantation Country, Blowing Rock Country (bd. dirs. 1991-94). Home: Park Plz Condos Condo 6 505 Lancaster St Jacksonville FL 32204-4136 Office: MAC Papers Inc 3300 Phillips Hwy PO Box 5369 Jacksonville FL 32247

MCGEORGE, RONALD KENNETH, hospital executive; b. Fredericton, N.B., Can., June 7, 1944; s. Hubert Oswald and Ruth Johanna (Kolding) McG.; m. Gail F. Mitchell, July 17, 1970; children: Ronald Millard, Scott, Dacia Gail. BS, Houghton Coll., 1966; diploma in hosp. adminstrn., U. Toronto, Ont., Can., 1969. Adminstrv. counsellor N.S. Hosp. Ins. Commn., Halifax, 1969-70; asst. exec. dir. Izaak Walton Killam Hosp. for Children, Halifax, 1970-72; v.p. Greater Niagara Gen. Hosp., Niagara Falls, Ont., 1972-74; chmn. Council Teaching Hosps.; exec. dir. Halifax Infirmary, 1974-79, Kingston Gen. Hosp., Ont., 1980-90; CEO Dr. Everett Chalmers Hosp., 1990-92; pres., chief exec. officer Region 3 Hosp. Corp., Fredericton, N.B., Can., 1992-95; exec. pastor Moncton Wesleyan Ch., 1995-97; Atlantic Provinces dir. Promise Keepers, 1995; nat. coord. Promise Keepers Can., 1997—; preceptor hosp. adminstrn. U. Ottawa, U. Toronto; chmn. Ont. Council Adminstrn. Teaching Hosps.; cons. in field. Contbr. articles to profl. jours. Chmn., pres. Wesleyan Men, 1st Wesleyan Ch. Named Bus. Alumnus of Yr., Houghton Coll., 1987. Mem. Can. Coll. Health Services Execs. (pres. 1979-80), Assn. Hosp. Adminstrs. N.S. (pres.-elect 1972), N.S. Assn. Health Orgns. (dir.), Ont. Council Adminstrs. of Teaching Hosps. (pres.), Ont. Hosp. Assn. (mem. exec. com., chmn. exec. com. 1989-90), Alumni Assn. of Bethany Bible Coll. (pres.). Home: Steeves Mountain RR # 1, Moncton, NB Canada E1C 8J5 Office: 945 Saint George Blvd, Moncton, NB Canada E1C 8J5

MCGERVEY, JOHN DONALD, physics educator, researcher; b. Pitts., Aug. 9, 1931; s. Daniel Donald and Eleanor (Rogerson) McG.; m. Nancy Ruth Maher, July 6, 1957; children: Anne, Donald, Joan. BS in Math., U. Pitts., 1952; postgrad., U. Chgo., 1952-53; MS in Physics, Carnegie Inst. Tech., 1955, PhD in Physics, 1960. Instr. math. Carnegie Inst. Tech., Pitts., 1957-60; asst. prof. physics Case Western Res. U., Cleve., 1960-65, assoc. prof., 1965-78, prof. physics, 1978—; vis. scientist Kernforschungsanlage, Julich, Fed. Republic Germany, 1972-73, U. der Bundeswehr München, Fed. Republic Germany, 1988, U. Göttingen, Germany, 1994, U. Bristol, Eng., 1996; Sci. Rsch. Coun. vis. fellow U. East Anglia, Norwich, Eng., 1978-79; resident rsch. assoc. Argonne (Ill.) Nat. Lab., 1963; faculty participant Oak Ridge Assoc. Univs., 1974-90; cons. WQED-TV, Pitts., 1994, Glencoe-Merrill Pub., 1992—. Author: Introduction to Modern Physics, 1971, Spanish lang. edit., 1975, 2d edit., 1983, Probabilities in Everyday Life, 1986, paperback edit., 1989, Quantum Mechanics: Concepts and Applications, 1995; newspaper columnist Numbers, 1994—. Pres. Cath. Interracial Coun. of Cleve., 1969-72; bd. dirs. Commn. on Cath. Cmty. Action, Cleve., 1969-78; pres. Project Equality of Ohio, Columbus, 1970-72; mem. Physicians for Social Responsibility, Cleve., 1982—; mem. speakers bur. Union Concerned Scientists, 1992—. NSF fellow, 1952; grantee AEC, 1963-66, NSF, 1969-72, 74-81, 85, 87, 90-96, NASA, 1981-85, Army Rsch. Office, 1986—, OHio Bd. Regents, 1995-97. Mem. AAAS, AAUP (pres. chpt. 1983-84), Am. Phys. Soc., Am. Assn. Physics Tchrs., Cleve. Astron. Soc., Sierra Club, Cleve. Philosophical Club, S. Shore Skeptics, Cleveland Heights Tennis Club, Sigma Xi. Democrat. Roman Catholic. Home: 1819 Wilton Rd Cleveland OH 44118-1628 Office: Case Western Reserve U Dept Physics Cleveland OH 44106

MCGERVEY, TERESA ANN, technology information specialist; b. Pitts., Sept. 27, 1964; d. Walter James and Janet Sarah (Donehue) McG. BS in Geology, Calif. U. Pa., 1986, MS in Earth Sci., 1988. Phys. sci. technician U.S. Geol. Survey, Reston, Va., 1989-90; editor, indexer Am. Geol. Inst., Alexandria, Va., 1990-91; cartographer Def. Mapping Agy., Reston, 1991-93; tech. info. specialist Nat. Tech. Info. Svc., Springfield, Va., 1993—; intern Dept. Mineral Scis., Smithsonian Instn., summers 1985, 1986.

MCGETTIGAN, CHARLES CARROLL, JR., investment banker; b. San Francisco, Mar. 28, 1945; s. Charles Carroll McGettigan and Molly (Fay) McGettigan Pedley; m. Katharine Havard King, Nov. 1, 1975 (div. 1981); m. Meriwether Lewis Stovall, Aug. 6, 1983; 1 child, Meriwether Lewis Fay. AB in Govt., Georgetown U., 1966; MBA in Fin., U. Pa., 1969. Assoc., asst. v.p., v.p. Blyth Eastman Dillon, N.Y.C., 1970-75, 1st v.p., 1975-78, sr. v.p., San Francisco, 1978-80; sr. v.p. Dillon, Read & Co., San Francisco, 1980-83; gen. ptnr. Woodman Kirkpatrick & Gilbreath, San Francisco, 1983-84; prin. corp. fin. Hambrecht & Quist, Inc., San Francisco, 1984-88, mng. dir, founder McGettigan, Wick & Co., Inc., San Francisco, 1988—; gen. ptnr., founder Proactive Ptnrs. L.P., San Francisco, 1990—, Proactive Investment Mgrs., L.P., 1991—; gen. ptnr. Fremont Proactive Ptnrs., L.P., 1991—; bd. dirs. Digital Dictation, Inc., Vienna, Va., NDE Environ. Corp., Austin, Tex., PMR Corp., San Diego, Phoenix Network Inc., Golden, Colo., I.-Flow Corp., Irvine, Calif., Sonex Rsch., Inc., Annapolis, Md., Modtech, Inc., Perris, Calif., Wray-Tech Instruments, Inc., Stratford, Conn.; chmn. Onsite Energy Corp., Carlsbad, Calif.; adv. dir. Chesapeake Ventures, Balt., 1984-94. Trustee St. Francis Meml. Hosp., San Francisco, 1980-86; mem. United San Francisco Rep. fin. com., 1983—, steering com., 1986—; adv. bd. dirs. Leavey Sch. Bus. Adminstrn., Santa Clara U., Calif., 1984-1990. With USN, 1966. Named Confrerie des Chevaliers du Tastevin, 1991. Mem. Soc. Calif. Pioneers, The Brook, Racquet and Tennis Club (N.Y.), The Pacific Union Club, Bohemian Club (San Francisco), San Francisco Golf Club, Burlingame Country Club (Hillsborough, Calif.), Calif. Club (L.A.), Boston Club (New Orleans), Piping Rock Club (Locust Valley, N.Y.), White's (London). Republican. Roman Catholic. Home: 3375 Clay St San Francisco CA 94118-2006 Office: McGettigan Wick & Co Inc 50 Osgood Pl San Francisco CA 94133-4644

MCGHEE, GEORGE CREWS, petroleum producer, former government official; b. Waco, Tex., Mar. 10, 1912; s. George Summers and Magnolia (Spruce) McG.; m. Cecilia Jeanne De Golyer, Nov. 24, 1938; children: Marcia Spruce, George DeGolyer, Dorothy Hart, Michael Anthony, Cecilia Goodrich, Valerie Foster. Student, So. Meth. U., 1928, DCL, 1953; BS, U. Okla., 1933; DPhil (Oxon), (Rhodes scholar), Oxford U., 1937; postgrad., U. London, 1937; LL.D., Tulane U., 1957, U. Md., 1965; D.Sc., U. Tampa, 1969. Registered profl. engr., Tex. Geologist Atlantic Refining Co., 1930-31; geophysicist Continental Oil Co., 1933-34, Compagnie Generale de Geophysique, Morocco, 1935; v.p. Nat. Geophys. Co., 1937-40; partner DeGolyer, MacNaughton & McGhee, Dallas, 1940-41; ind. explorer, producer oil, 1940—; sole owner McGhee Prodn. Co.; chmn. bd. Saturday Rev., 1973-77; Coordinator for aid to Greece and Turkey Dept. State, 1947-49, spl. asst. to sec. state, 1949; asst. sec. for Dept. State (Near Eastern, South Asian, African affairs), 1949-51; mem. various adv. groups to pvt., govtl. orgns., 1940—; U.S. ambassador, chief Am. Mission for Aid to Turkey, 1951-53; sr. adviser N. Atlantic Treaty Council, Ottawa, Can., 1951; mem. bd. Middle East Inst., 1953-58; cons. Nat. Security Council, 1958-59; mem. Pres.'s Com. to study U.S. Mil. Assistance program, 1958-59; chmn. policy planning council, counselor Dept. State, 1961; under-sec. state for polit. affairs, 1961-63; ambassador Fed. Republic of Germany, 1963-68; ambassador-at-large, 1968-69; spl. rep. to chmn. Urban Coalition, 1969-70; chmn. bd. Bus. Council for Internat. Understanding, 1969-73; mem. bd. Fed. City Council, Washington, 1958-61, 70—; pres. Fed. City Council, 1970-74; vice chmn. Japan-U.S. Internat. Adv. Council, 1970-74; chmn. adv. com. on housing and urban devel. Nat. Acad. Scis., 1970-74; bd. dirs. Procter & Gamble Co., Am. Security Bank, Washington, TransWorld Corp., Transworld Airlines.; mem. Am. Council on Germany, 1969—, Fed. City Housing Corp., 1972—; hon. fellow Queen's Coll., Oxford, 1968—; guest lectr. Nat., Air, Naval War Colls., Salzburg Seminar, Austria, 1960. Author: Envoy to the Middle World, 1983, At the Creation of a New Germany, 1989, The U.S.-Turkish-NATO Middle East Connection, 1990, Dance of the Billions, 1990, International Community: A Goal for a New World Order, 1992, Life in Alanya: Turkish Delight, 1992, On the Frontline in the Cold War, 1996; editor: Diplomacy for the Future, 1987, National Interest and Global Goals, 1989; contbr. to profl. publs.; patentee in field. Trustee Thessalonica (Greece) Agrl. and Indsl. Inst. (Am. Farm Sch.), 1949-61; mem. bd. devel. So. Meth. U., 1949-61; bd. dirs. Near East Found., 1956-61, Aspen Inst. Humanistic Studies, 1958—, Atlantic Council, Atlantic Inst. for Internat. Affairs, Resources for Future; vice chmn. bd. dirs. Inst. for Study of Diplomacy, Georgetown U., Washington; trustee or bd. dirs. Com. for Econ. Devel., 1957—, Fgn. Service Edn. Found. and Sch. Advanced Internat. Studies, Johns Hopkins, 1947—, Nat. Civil Service League, 1969-73, Population Crisis Com., 1969—, Population Crisis Found. Tex., 1969-70, Nat. Trust for Historic Preservation, 1971-75, Duke U., 1962—, Vassar Coll., 1959-61, Am. U., 1980—, Asia Found., 1973—, Va. Outdoors Found.; adv. council Renewable Natural Resources Found., 1973-74; bd. dirs., treas. Piedmont Environmental Council; internat. com. YMCA, 1949-61; adv. council dept. Oriental langs. and lits. Princeton, 1949-61; vis. com. Middle Eastern Studies and Summer Sch., Harvard, 1954-61; sponsor Atlantic Inst., 1954-60; chmn. nat. adv. com. Ctr. for Book, Library of Congress, 1980-82; mem. Folger Library Council, 1983-85, Inst. Turkish Studies, 1983-85, Carnegie Coun.; mem. vis. com. Arthur M. Sackler Gallery, Smithsonian Instn.; trustee Am. U., 1981—; mem. German Am. Cultural Fund, 1992—, Circle Nat. Gallery Art, 1991, Carnegie Coun., 1990—, CED subcom. Global Econ. Strategy for U.S., 1991—; bd. dirs. adv. bd. Am.-Turkish Friendship Coun., Nat. Tree Trust, 1992—. Served with USNR, 1943-45; lt. col. USAF Res., 1945-72. Decorated Legion of Merit with 3 battle stars; Order of Cherifien Empire Morocco; recipient Distinguished Service award U.S. Jr. C. of C., 1949, Distinguished Service citation U. Okla., 1952, So. Meth. U. Distinguished Alumnus award, 1955; Andrew Wellington Cordier fellow Columbia U.; named Hon. citizen Ankara, Turkey, 1954. Mem. NAS (pres.'s circle), Am. Assn. Petroleum Geologists, Soc. Exploration Geophysicists (Spl. Commendation award 1992), m. Inst. Mining, Metall. and Petroleum Engrs., English SPeaking Union (chmn. bd. 1970-74), Am. Philos. Soc., Coun. Am. Mbs., Smithsonian Nat. Assocs. (chmn. 1975-78), Sigma Si. Phi Beta Kappa, Cosmos Club, Metro. Club, Washington. Episcopalian. Home and Office: Farmers Delight 36276 Mountville Rd Middleburg VA 20117 also: Turkish Delight, Alanya Turkey

MCGHEE, VICKI GUNTER, home health nurse, pediatrics psychiatry, alcohol and Drug rehabilitation; b. Ga., May 23, 1956; d. James Wesley Gunter and Flora Gunter LeDrew; m. Roger Lane McGhee, Sept. 8, 1984; (div. 1991). Diploma, Pickens Technical Inst., Jasper, Ga., 1975; student, Ga. Bapt. Hosp., Atlanta, 1976; ASN, Floyd Coll., Rome, Ga., 1978; student, Pickens Technical Inst., 1996—. RN, Ga., 1979. Primary staff nurse Woodstock (Ga.) Hosp., Atlanta; home health nurse Med. Personnel Pool, Atlanta; nurse Etowah Nursing Care, Inc., Marietta, Ga., Med. Temps, Marietta, Ga; pvt. duty nurse Acworth, Ga., 1996; pvt. duty contract nurse, Kennesaw, Ga., 1988. Home: Bethesda Trail Box 830 Ball Ground GA 30107

MCGIFF, JOHN C(HARLES), pharmacologist; b. N.Y.C., Aug. 6, 1927; s. John Francis and Rose (Rieger) McG.; m. Sara Leighton Babb, Feb. 8, 1958 (dec.); children: John, Katharine, Sara, Jeremiah, Elizabeth. B.S., Georgetown U., 1947; M.D., Columbia U., 1951; Doctorate Honoris Causa, Copernicus Acad. Medicine, Cracow, Poland, 1987. Diplomate: Am. Bd. Internal Medicine. Intern U. Cin., 1951-52; resident in medicine U. Va. Med. Center, 1952-53; tng. in physiology and pharmacology Columbia Presbyn. Hosp., N.Y.C., 1957-58; mem. faculty U. Pa. Med. Sch., 1961-66; dir. cardiovascular sect. St. Louis U. Med. Sch., 1966-71; dir. clin. pharmacology Med. Coll. Wis., Milw., 1971-75; prof., chmn. dept. pharmacology U. Tenn. Center Health Scis., 1975-79, N.Y. Med. Coll., Valhalla, 1979—; vis. scientist Wellcome Rsch. Labs., Beckenham, Eng., 1975-76; adv. bd. Am. Heart Assn., Kidney Found.; mem. nat. vis. coun. for health sci. faculties Columbia U. Coll. Physicians and Surgeons, 1987; mam. arteriosclerosis hypertension and lipid adv. com. NIH, 1987; cons. in field; chmn. cardiovascular renal study sect. Nat. Heart, Lung and Blood Inst. NIH, 1994. Author articles in books; contbr. articles to profl. jours. Pres. sch. bd. St. Louis Cathedral Sch., 1970. Served as flight surgeon M.C. USMCR, 1955-57, Korea. Recipient Medal of Achievement Copernicus Acad. Medicine, Cracow, Poland, 1984; Terence Cardinal Cooke medal for Disting. Service in Health Care, 1985; CIBA award Am. Heart Assn., 1986, Merit award Nat. Heart, Lung, and Blood Inst. of NIH, 1990; Burroughs Wellcome Fund scholar, 1971-74, Richard Bright award Am. Soc. Hypertension, 1997. Mem. Am. Physiol. Soc., Am. Soc. Pharmacology and Exptl. Therapeutics (Otto Krayer award 1997), Council High Blood Pressure Research (med. adv. bd. 1968), Am. Soc. Clin. Investigation, Brit. Pharmacology Soc. Roman Catholic. Home: 5 Bay Rd East Patchogue NY 11772-6201 Office: NY Med Coll Dept Pharmacology Valhalla NY 10595

MC GIFFERT, DAVID ELIOT, lawyer, former government official; b. Boston, June 27, 1926; s. Arthur Cushman and Elizabeth (Eliot) McG.; m. Enud De Kibedi-Varga, Jan. 21, 1966; children: Laura, Carola.; m. Nelse Greenway, Apr. 9, 1983. Student, U. Calif.-Berkeley, 1944; B.A., Harvard U., 1949, LL.B., 1953; postgrad., Cambridge (Eng.) U., 1950. Bar: D.C. 1954. With firm Covington & Burling, Washington, 1953-55, 57-61; ptnr. Covington & Burling, 1969-77, 81—; lectr. law U. Wis., 1956; asst. to sec. def. for legis. affairs Dept. Def., 1962-65, undersec. army, 1965-69, asst. sec. for internat. security affairs, 1977-81. Served with USNR, 1944-46. Mem. Am. Bar Assn., Council Fgn. Relations, Alpha Delta Phi. Club: Metropolitan (Washington). Home: 3819 Veazey St NW Washington DC 20016-2230 Office: Covington & Burling 1201 Pennsylvania Ave NW PO Box 7566 Washington DC 20044

MC GIFFERT, JOHN RUTHERFORD, retired cultural institute director, retired army officer; b. Jefferson Barracks, Mo., Aug. 5, 1926; s. Stephen Yates and Louise Brockenbrough (Jones) McG.; m. Patricia Ann Clipp, May 2, 1946; children: William Christian, Katherine Louise, Elizabeth Ann, Mary Margaret. Student, Va. Mil. Inst., 1944; B.S., U. Md., 1967; M.S., George Washington U., 1968. Enlisted U.S. Army as pvt., 1945, advanced through grades to lt. gen., 1977; assignments in U.S., Germany, Iceland, Vietnam; dir. of Army Staff Office Chief of Staff Hdqrs. Dept. of Army Washington, 1977-80; comdg. gen. 5th U.S. Army Ft. Sam Houston, Tex., 1980-83; ret. U.S. Army, 1983; adminstr. U. Tex. Inst. Texan Cultures, San Antonio, 1983-85; dir. U. Tex. Inst. Texan Cultures, 1985-91; v.p. downtown ops. U. Tex., San Antonio, 1989-91. Decorated D.S.M., Silver Star, D.F.C., Legion of Merit, Bronze Star, Air medal, others. Mem. Assn. U.S. Army, Field Arty. Assn. Episcopalian. Home: 8926 Willmon Way San Antonio TX 78239-1947

MCGIFFERT, MICHAEL, history educator, editor; b. Chgo., Oct. 5, 1928; s. Arthur Cushman and Elisabeth (Eliot) McG.; m. Genevieve White Mischel, Aug. 13, 1960; m. Elizabeth Eastman, June 19, 1949 (div. 1960). B.A., Harvard Coll., 1949; B.D., Yale U., 1952, Ph.D., 1958; postgrad., Union Theol. Sem., N.Y.C., 1949-50. Instr. history Colgate U., Hamilton, N.Y., 1954-55, 56-60, U. Md., College Park, 1955-56; asst. prof. history U. Denver, 1960-64, assoc. prof., 1964-69, prof. history, 1969-74; editor William and Mary Quar., Inst. Early Am. History and Culture, prof. history, Coll. William and Mary, Williamsburg, Va., 1972—. Author: The Higher learning in Colorado, 1964; editor: The Character of Americans, 1964 (rev. edit.), 1969, Puritanism and the American Experience, 1969, (with Robert A. Skotheim) American Social Thought, 1972, God's Plot: The Paradoxes of Puritan Piety, 1972, God's Plot: Puritan Spirituality in Thomas Shepard's Cambridge, 1994. Faculty rsch. grantee U. Denver, 1970, Coll. William and Mary, 1981-82, 89; rsch. fellow NEH, 1977-78. Mem. Am. Hist. Assn., Orgn. Am. Historians, Confr. of Hist. Jours. (pres.1987-89). Home: 102 Old Glory Ct Williamsburg VA 23185-4914 Office: Inst Early Am History & Culture PO Box 8781 Williamsburg VA 23187-8781

MCGILBERRY, JOE HERMAN, SR., university administrator; b. Mobile, Ala., Aug. 6, 1943; s. Thomas Henry and Yvonne (Jorden) McG.; m. Betty Sue Reynolds, Dec. 20, 1964; children: Joe H. Jr., Michele, Brent. BS, Auburn U., 1965; MS, U. Tenn., 1972; PhD, TEx. A&M U., 1978. Gen. plant asst. Gen. Telephone Fla., Tampa, 1966; systems analyst E.I. DuPont de Nemours & Co., Old Hickory, Tenn., 1966-68; research asst. U. Tenn., Knoxville, 1968-69; advanced materials engr. Union Carbide Corp., Texas City, TX, 1969-70; asst. prof. Tenn. Tech. U., Cookeville, 1970-72, 73-75, 76-77; mgr. prodn. support Fleetguard div. Cummins Engine, Cookeville, 1972-73; assoc. research engr. Tex. A&M U., College Station, 1975-76; mgr. food and fiber ctr. Miss. State Coop. Extension Program, 1978-94, state program leader in cmty. resource devel. coop. ext. svc., 1994-96; adminstrv. support coord. E&CRD, 1997—; cons. Dunlap Industries, U. Tenn. at Nashville, Norwalk Furniture Corp., Teledyne-Stillman, Genco Stamping, Inc., Riley Enterprises; lectr. various seminars and presentations, 1978—. Author numerous articles in field. Mem. Inst. Indsl. Engrs. (sr.), Miss. Indsl. Devel. Coun., Order Engrs., Nat. Assn. County Agrl. Agts., Alpha Phi Mu. Office: Miss State U 203-B Bost Ext Ctr Box 9601 Mississippi State MS 39762

MC GILL, ARCHIE JOSEPH, venture capitalist; b. Winona, Minn., May 29, 1931; s. Archibald Joseph and Anne (Lettner) McG.; m. Jeanne Sullivan, Mar. 17, 1974; children: Archibald Joseph, III, Mark E., Gregory P., Debora, Karen, Susan, Brian. BA in Econs., St. Mary's Coll., Winona, 1956. With IBM Corp., 1956-69; v.p. market ops. IBM Corp., White Plains, N.Y., 1956-69; founder, pres. McGill Assocs., White Plains, 1970-73; dir. market mgmt. AT&T Co., 1973-78, v.p. bus. mktg., 1978-83; pres. Advanced Info. Systems Am. Bell, Inc., 1983; pres., chief exec. officer Rothschild Ventures, Inc., 1983; now pres. Chardonnay, Inc.; dir. various cos. Bd. dirs. Steadman/Hawkins Found. With USAF, 1951-54. Named Mktg. Statesman of Year Sales Execs. Club, 1978.

MCGILL, CATHY BROOME, gifted and talented education educator; b. Gastonia, N.C., Sept. 26, 1945; d. Harold Beeler and Christine (Hicks) Broome; m. Paul Furman McGill, July 5, 1969; children: Paul Bryan, Harold Marcus. BA, Mars Hill Coll., 1967; MA, Appalachian State U., 1968. Tchr. 6th grade Victory Elem., Gastonia, N.C., 1968-69; lang. arts, social studies & music tchr. Northside Mid. Sch., West Columbia, S.C., 1969-71, Fulmer Mid. Sch., West Columbia, 1972-76; tchr. Pine View Elem. Sch., West Columbia, 1978-81; sci. & lang. arts tchr. Heiskell Sch., Atlanta, 1981-82; lang. arts & gifted tchr. Fulmer Mid. Sch., 1982-85; itinerant gifted educator Lex II, West Columbia, 1985—; in-svc. presenter Lex II, 1992-95. Pianist Holland Ave. Baptist Ch., Cayce, S.C., 1970—, vacation Bible sch. dir., 1982-93, youth choir dir., 1982-85; neighborhood solicitor Arthritis Found., Columbia, S.C., 1993-95. Mem. Nat. Assn. for Gifted Children, Palmetto State Tchrs. Assn., Alpha Delta Kappa (chaplain 1993—). Republican. Avocations: music, reading. Home: 100 Sweetgum Dr Cayce SC 29033-1930

MCGILL, CHARLES MORRIS, physician, consultant; b. Seattle, Oct. 25, 1908; s. Robert Allen and Angela Folsom (Chase) McG.; m. Edith Hansen, Nov. 30, 1935; children—Charles Robert, Kenneth Chase. Student Pacific U., 1926-27; B.S., U. Wash., 1931; M.D., Vanderbilt U., 1935; M.P.H., Harvard U., 1945. Diplomate Am. Bd. Occupational Medicine. Commd. med. officer USPHS, 1935, advanced through grades to lt. col., 1947; med. dir. Tacoma Smelter Co., 1945-57; practice medicine specializing in occupational medicine, Tacoma, 1957-62; assoc. prof. occupational medicine U. Wash., Seattle, 1950-60; med. dir. Weyerhaeuser Co., Tacoma, 1960-72; regional med. dir. Western Electric Co., Kent, Wash., 1973-80; dir. employee health Consol. Hosps., Tacoma, 1959—; med. cons. Wash. Pub. Power Supply System, Richland, Wash., 1982—; dir. employee health St. Joseph Hosp., Tacoma, 1976—. Contbr. articles to profl. jours. Fellow Am. Occupational Med. Assn. (bd. dirs. 1963-69), Am. Acad. Occupational Medicine, Am. Pub. Health Assn.; mem. Pierce County Med. Soc., Wash. Med. Assn., AMA. Home: 10124 36th St NW Gig Harbor WA 98335-5814

MCGILL, DAN MAYS, insurance business educator; b. Greenback, Tenn., Sept. 27, 1919; s. John Burton and Jane (Mays) McG.; m. Elaine Kem, June 22, 1952; children: Douglas Russell, Melanie Mays. BA, Maryville Coll., 1940, LLD (hon.), 1982; MA, Vanderbilt U., 1941; PhD, U. Pa., 1947. Assoc. prof. fin. U. Tenn., Knoxville, 1947-48; Julian Price assoc. prof. ins. U. N.C., Chapel Hill, 1948-51; assoc. prof. ins. U. Pa., Phila., 1952-56, Frederick H. Ecker prof. life ins., 1959-90; trustee N.W. Mut. Life Ins. Co., Milw., 1978-90; bd. dirs. NRG Life Reassurance Corp., Phila., 1984-94, Phila. Reins. Corp., 1990—, Independence Blue Cross, 1990—; exec. dir. S.S. Huebner Found., 1954-75, 78-86, chmn., 1965-94; dir. rsch. Pension Rsch. Coun., 1952-90; chmn., mem. governing bd. Leonard Davis Inst. Health Econs., 1967-90; 1st chmn. adv. commn. Pension Benefit Guaranty Corp., 1975-78, mem. 1978-81. Author: An Analysis of Government Life Insurance, 1949, The Fundamentals of Private Pensions, 7th edit., 1996, Legal Aspects of Life Insurance, 1959, Fulfilling Pension Expectations, 1962, Life Insurance, 1967, Preservation of Pension Benefit Rights, 1972, others; editor: (with others) World Insurance Trends, 1959, others. Chmn. bd. pensions Presbyn. Ch. U.S., 1977-78; trustee Presbyn. Found. for Phila., 1996—, Presbyn. Med. Ctr. Phila., 1987-96; chmn. Boettner Inst. Fin. Gerontology, 1993—; mem. retirement bd. Mass. Bay Transp. Authority, 1980-96. Maj. USAAF, 1942-46, 51-52. Recipient Disting. Alumni award Maryville Coll., 1962, Huebner Gold medal award Am. Coll., 1977, Gold medal Internat. Ins. Soc., 1987. Mem. Am. Risk and Ins. Assn. (pres. 1959, Eluzur Wright award 1955, 81), Union League. Republican. Presbyterian. Avocations: music, travel, sports. Home: 50 Belmont Ave Bala Cynwyd PA 19004-2437

MCGILL, ESBY CLIFTON, former college official; b. Omaha, Ark., Jan. 12, 1914; s. James Preston and Celia (Stafford) McG.; m. Ruth Evelyn Jones, Oct. 22, 1932 (dec.); children: Barbara (Mrs. Forrest E. Nelson), Marilyn (Mrs. Joel Pahk); m. Mary Elizabeth Beardsley, July 5, 1978. BS, S.W. Mo. State U., 1940; MS, Okla. State U., 1941; EdD, NYU, 1955. Tchr. public schs. Mo., 1932-33, 35-39; head bus. dept. High Sch. Stillwater, Okla., 1941-42; assoc. prof. in charge of U.S. Naval Radio Sch., Tex. A&M U., College Station, 1942-44; chmn. div. bus. Emporia State U., Kans., 1945-59; chmn. bus. edn. dept. Utah State U., Logan, 1959-60; dean faculties, dir. acad. planning, dir. summer sessions So. Oreg. State Coll., Ashland, 1960-77; dir. summer sessions So. Oreg. State Coll., 1976-79, dir. continuing edn., 1976-78, dir. non-traditional programs, 1978-79; comml. loan officer for Jackson-Josephine Counties Coos, Curry, Douglas Bus. Devel. Corp., Medford, Oreg., 1990-91; cons. curriculum for schs. in cen. states, 1950-69; mem. regional adv. bd. So. Oreg. U., 1st term, 1987-89, 2d term, 1989-91, 3d term, 1991-93, 4th term, 1994—. Author: Communications Typing, 1944, Production Typing, 1955, Business Principles, Organization and Management, 1958, rev., 1963, Briefhand, 1957, manuals in field; also contbr. over 100 articles to profl. jours.; spl. editor: Nat. Bus. Edn. Quar, 1951-55; mem. editorial bd.: Bus. Edn. Forum, 1956-59, Nat. Assn. Bus. Tchr. Tng. Instns.

Bull, 1951-55. Chmn. Downtown Redevel. Com., Ashland, Oreg., 1967-71; bd. dirs. Peter Britt Music and Arts Festival Assn., Jacksonville, Oreg., 1966-69, Ashland Rotary Found., Jackson-Josephine Counties, Oreg. Comprehensive Health Planning Unit. Recipient Founder's Day award NYU, 1956, Man of Yr. award Ashland C. of C., 1965. Mem. NEA, Oreg. Edn. Assn., Nat. Assn. Bus. Tchr. Edn. Instns. (past pres., bd. dirs.), United Bus. Edn. Assn. (past pres., bd. dirs.), Mountain Plains Bus. Edn. Assn. (past pres., bd. dirs.), North Ctrl. Assn. Conf. Summer Schs. and Future Bus. Leaders Am. (past bd. dirs. both), Nat. Office Mgmt. Assn. (hon.), Ashland C. of C. (pres., bd. dirs.), Am. Assn. Colls. Tchrs. Edn. (liaison officer for Oreg. 1970-73), Svc. Corp. Ret. Execs. (chmn. chpt. 269 1985-86, 86-87, 87-88, 88-89), SCORE (alternate dist. rep. Portland dist. 1988-89, dist. rep. Portland dist. 1990-91, asst. regional dir. region 10 1991-92, dir. region 10 States of Alaska, Idaho, Oreg. and Wash., 1993-95, 95-97, nat. treas. 1994-95, Masons, Rotary (past sec., pres. bd. Ashland, gov. internat. dist. 5110, 1983-84, materials chmn. pres. elect tng. program 9 dists. U.S. N.W., Can. S.W. 1990-94, ext. chmn. 1991—, rep. Rotary Internat. Coun. Legislation dist. 5110 1995, Paul Harris fellow), Phi Delta Kappa, Kappa Delta Pi, Delta Pi Epsilon, Pi Omega Pi, Pi Gamma Mu, Sigma Tau Gamma. Home: 1785 Zemke Rd Talent OR 97540-9718

MCGILL, HENRY COLEMAN, JR., physician, educator, researcher; b. Nashville, Oct. 1, 1921; s. Henry Coleman and Thursa (Lowry) McG.; m. Cloace Laurite Ferguson, Sept. 12, 1945; children: Margaret Ann, Laurilynn, Elizabeth Gail. BA, Vanderbilt U., 1943, MD, 1946. Intern Vanderbilt Hosp., Nashville, 1946-47; asst. prof. La. State U. Med. Ctr., New Orleans, 1950-55, assoc. prof., 1955-61, prof., chmn. pathology, 1961-66, U. Tex. Health Sci. Ctr., San Antonio, 1966-72, prof., 1972-91; sci. dir. S.W. Found. for Biomed. Rsch., San Antonio, 1979-92, sr. scientist, 1992-96, sr. scientist emeritus, 1996—. Capt. U.S. Army, 1948-50. Mem. Phi Beta Kappa, Sigma Xi, Alpha Omega Alpha. Contbr. numerous articles to profl. jours. Home: 4102 Fawnridge Dr San Antonio TX 78229-4212 Office: PO Box 760549 San Antonio TX 78245-0549

MCGILL, JAY, magazine publisher. Pub. Country Living, N.Y.C. Office: Country Living Hearst Mags 224 W 57th St New York NY 10019-3212*

MCGILL, JENNIFER HOUSER, non-profit association administrator; b. Abingdon, Va., Mar. 3, 1957; d. Mason L. and Margaret Jane (Powers) H.; m. James B. McGill, July 15, 1978; children: Melissa Diane, Mark James. AA, Va. Highlands C.C., Abingdon, 1978; BA, U. S.C., 1980. Reporter, editor Sumter (S.C.) Daily ITEM, 1980-81; assoc. editor Sandlapper Mag., Columbia, S.C., 1981-82; membership editor Assn. for Edn. in Journalism/Mass Comm., Columbia, 1982-83, adminstrv. asst., 1984-85, exec. dir., 1985—; mem. nat. steering com. Journalist-in-Space Project, Columbia, 1985-86. Mem. Lioness Club (3d v.p. 1990-91, 2d v.p. 1991-92). Avocations: reading, cooking, biking. Office: Assn Schs Journalism & Mass Comm Univ SC Columbia SC 29208-0251

MCGILL, JUDY ANNELL MCGEE, early childhood and elementary educator; b. Kosciusko, Miss., Oct. 16, 1949; d. Reeves and Martha Lee (Thompson) McGee; m. Ronald Eugene McGill, June 5, 1971; 1 child, Thomas Eugene. Student, U. Colo., 1979, James Madison U., 1974; BS, Miss. State U., 1971; MEd, Northeast La. U., 1984. 4th grade tchr. Harrison County Schs., Gulfport, Miss., 1971; 1st and 2d grade tchr. Oktibbeha County Schs., Starkville, Miss., 1971-72; 4th grade tchr. Natchez-Adams (Miss.) County Schs., 1972-74; 2d and 3d grade tchr. Shenandoah County Schs., Woodstock, Va., 1974-78; elem. tchr. Jefferson County Schs., Lakewood, Colo., 1980-81; 7th and 8th grade tchr. Ouachita Parish Schs., Monroe, La., 1982; elem. sch. tchr. Union Parish Schs., Farmerville, La., 1982-85; early childhood and elem. tchr. Ouachita Parish Schs., Monroe, La., 1985-95; master tchr., intern assessor Quachita Parish Schs., Monroe, La., 1993-95; elem. tchr. Scottsboro (Ala.) City Schs., 1995—; in-svc. instr. Natchez-Adams County Schs., 1972-74, Shenandoah County Schs., 1974-78; trainer Sci. Rsch. Assocs., Woodstock, 1978; chairperson curriculum revision Ouachita Parish Schs., 1986-92, staff devel. trainer, 1990-92. Den leader Boy Scouts Am., West Monroe, La., 1986-88; sponsor Young Astronauts Coun. La. Quality in Sci. and Math. grantee, 1994-95, grantee Jr. League Monroe, 1994-95. Mem. NEA, ASCD, Am. Assn. Young Children, Nat. Assn. Edn. Young Children, So. Early Childhood Assn., La. Assn. on Children Under Six (Jane Herrin grantee 1987, v.p., program chair 1988-94), N.E. La. Reading Coun. (chairperson grants 1987-88, Reading Tchr. of Yr. 1987-88), Internat. Reading Assn. Methodist. Avocations: downhill skiing, target shooting, sourdough baking. Home: 106 Colonial Dr Scottsboro AL 35768-2226

MCGILL, MAURICE LEON, financial executive; b. Malden, Mo., Aug. 22, 1936; s. William Howard and Iris (Phillips) McG.; m. Wanda Coral Wirt, Feb. 2, 1957; children—Melany, Melinda, William Shannon. B.S., U. Mo., 1958, M.A., 1959. C.P.A., Mo., Iowa, Ariz. Mgr. Touche, Ross, Bailey & Smart, Kansas City, Mo., 1959-64; fin. v.p., treas. Iowa Beef Packers, Inc., Dakota City, Nebr., 1964-69; exec. v.p., treas. Spencer Foods, Inc., Iowa, 1969-71, also dir.; sr. v.p. Diamond Reo Trucks, Inc., Lansing, Mich., 1971-72; fin. v.p. Ariz. Colo. Land & Cattle Co., Phoenix, 1972-75; ptnr. Touche Ross & Co., Phoenix, 1975-81; exec. v.p. fin. and adminstrn., treas., bd. dirs. IBP, Inc., Dakota City, Nebr., 1981-89; pres., bd. dirs. Wirmac Corp., Garland, Tex., 1989—; bd. dirs. Bluebonnet Savs. Bank, Dallas, Premium Std. Farms, Kansas City, Mo. Mem. AICPA, Iowa Soc. CPAs, Ea. Hills Country Club. Home: 1414 Seminary Rdg Garland TX 75043-1241

MCGILL, ROBERT ERNEST, III, retired manufacturing company executive; b. San Francisco, Apr. 30, 1931; s. Robert Ernest and Madeleine Melanie (Ignace) McG.; m. Daphne Urquhart Driver, Apr. 26, 1958; children: Robert Ernest, Meredith Louise, Christina Elizabeth, James Alexander. B.A., Williams Coll., 1954; M.B.A., Harvard U., 1956. With Morgan Stanley & Co. (investment bankers), N.Y.C., 1956-63; mem. fin. staff Air Products & Chems., Inc., Allentown, Pa., 1963-64; dir. corp. planning and devel. Air Products & Chems., Inc., 1964-68; v.p. Gen. Interiors Corp., N.Y.C., 1968-70; exec. v.p. Gen. Interiors Corp., 1970-73; v.p. fin. Ethan Allen, Inc., Danbury, Conn., 1973-75; v.p. fin., sec. Dexter Corp., Windsor Locks, Conn., 1975-83, sr. v.p. fin. and adminstrn., dir., 1983-89, exec. v.p., 1989-94; dir. Dexter Corp., Windsor Locks, 1989-95; pres. Kettlebrook Ins. Co. Ltd., 1983-93, chmn., 1993-94; pres. Dexter Credit Corp., 1982-88; bd. dirs. The Conn. Surety Corp., Chemfab Corp., CN Bioscis., Inc.; bd. mgrs. Travelers Funds for Variable Annuities; trustee Travelers Mut. Fund. Trustee Colt Bequest, Inc., Assn. des Amis L'Abbaye Valmont, Williamstown Arts Conservation Ctr, 1989-94; resident fellow U. Conn. Sch. Bus.; bd. dirs. Village Ambulance Svc. Home: 295 Hancock Rd Williamstown MA 01267-3005

MCGILL, THOMAS EMERSON, psychology educator; b. Sharon, Pa., Sept. 26, 1930; s. Emerson Dickson and Margaret Hughes (McCallen) McG.; m. Nancy C. Welch, June 14, 1955; children: Michael Howard, Steven Emerson. BA, Youngstown State U., 1954; MA, Princeton U., 1957, PhD, 1958. Instr. psychology Williams Coll., Williamstown, Mass., 1958-59, asst. prof., 1960-64, asso. prof., 1965-69, prof., 1969-91, chmn. dept. psychology, 1976-82, 85-86, Hales prof., 1970-91, prof. emeritus, 1991—; postdoctoral fellow U. Calif., Berkeley, 1959-60; sr. postdoctoral fellow U. Edinburgh, 1964-65, vis. research fellow, 1969-70. Editor: Readings in Animal Behavior, 3d edit, 1977, (with Dewsbury and Sachs) Sex and Behavior, 1977. USPHS grantee, 1960-82; sr. postdoctoral fellow Nat. Acad. Sci., 1964-65. Fellow AAAS; mem. Newfoundland Club N.Am. (dir. 1980-94, pres. 1990-92), Newfoundland Club New Eng. (pres. 1980-82), Sigma Xi. Home: 137 Laura Ln Tiverton RI 02878-4711 Office: Williams Coll Dept Of Psychology Williamstown MA 01267

MCGILL, WARREN EVERETT, lawyer, consultant; b. Brazil, Ind., Sept. 10, 1923; s. Ira and Joyce S. (Wenning) McG.; m. Irene Marie Kish, Aug. 31, 1946; children: Cecelia, Daniel, Nancy, Mary Beth, Mark. BS, Ind. U., 1944, JD with honors, 1945. Bar: Ind. 1945. Assoc. Oare, Thornburg, McGill & Deahl, South Bend, Ind., 1945-60; ptnr. Thornburg, McGill, Deahl, Harman, Carey & Murray, South Bend, 1960-83; ptnr. Barnes & Thornburg, South Bend, 1983-89, of counsel, 1989—; chmn. Probate Code Study Commn., Ind., 1972-90. Editor, co-author: Indiana Land Trust Practice, 1980, Trust Litigation, 1981; asst. editor, co-author: Probate Code 1975 Reform, 1975; author: Special Comment on Indiana Probate Code, 1982. Sec., dir. Michiana Arts and Scis. coun., Inc., South Bend, 1965—; pres. Com. of 100, South Bend, Mishawaka, Ind., 1960-64; community adv. bd. Channel 34 Pub. TV, No. Ind., So. Mich., 1982-86. Recipient Cmty. Achievement citation City of South Bend, 1985, 50 Yr. award Ind. Bar Found., 1996. Fellow Ind. Acad. Law Alumni; mem. ABA, St. Joseph County Bar Assn., Am. Coll. Trust and Estate Counsel (chmn. membership com. 1972-90), Ind. State Bar Assn. (chmn. ho. dels. 1982-83, Presdl. citation 1985), Ind. Bar Found. (pres. 1984-86, bd. dirs. 1984-89), Ind. Continuing Legal Edn. Forum (bd. dirs. 1984-90), Morris Park Country Club (pres. 1978), Summit Club. Avocations: golf, history, travel. Home: 2831 Caroline St South Bend IN 46614-1543 Office: Barnes & Thornburg 600 1st Source Bank Ctr 100 N Michigan St South Bend IN 46601-1610

MCGILL, WILLIAM JAMES, JR., academic administrator; b. St. Louis, Mo., Mar. 25, 1936; s. William James Sr. and Ethel (Williams) McG.; m. Ellen Buck, June 18, 1960; children: Sara Louise, Susan Elizabeth, Alison Marcia. BA, Trinity Coll., 1957; MA, Harvard U., 1958, PhD, 1961, grad. Inst. Ednl. Mgmt., 1989. Instr. history Western Md. Coll., Westminster, 1960-62; asst. prof. history Alma (Mich.) Coll., 1962-68, assoc. prof., 1968-72; dean of coll. Washington & Jefferson Coll., Washington, Pa., 1972-75, prof. history, 1972-84; asst. dir., div. edn. programs NEH, Washington, 1984-86; v.p., dean faculty Lebanon Valley Coll., Annville, Pa., 1986—, acting pres., 1987-88. Author: Maria Theresa, 1972; contbr. 55 articles to profl. jours., 46 book revs., 6 short stories, numerous poems; poetry editor Spitball Mag., 1993—. Assoc. to rector St. Luke's Episc. Ch., Lebanon, Pa., 1986—; priest-in-charge St. George's Episc. Ch., Waynesburg, Pa., 1974-83; actor Washington Theater Wing, 1984-86, Gretna Playhouse, Mt. Gretna, Pa., 1987-90; bd. dirs. Lebanon County United Way, 1987-95, Gretna Prodns., Mt. Gretna, 1986-90, 91-92; trustee Penn Sch. Art and Design, 1992—. Mem. Am. Assn. Higher Edn., Phi Beta Kappa. Avocations: sailing, writing, acting. Home: PO Box 682 Cornwall PA 17016-0682 Office: Lebanon Valley Coll Office Academic Affairs Annville PA 17003

MC GILLEM, CLARE DUANE, electrical engineering educator; b. Clinton, Mich., Oct. 9, 1923; s. Virgil and Starlie (Weaver) McG.; m. Frances Ann Wilson, Nov. 29, 1947; 1 child, Mary Ann. BSEE, U. Mich., 1947; MSE, Purdue U., 1949, PhD, 1955. Rsch. engr. Diamond Chain Co. Inc., Indpls., 1947-51; head functional design U.S. Naval Avionics Ctr., Indpls., 1951-56; head mil. and elec. engring. AC Spark Plug, GM, Flint, Mich., 1956-58; dir. elec. and applied rsch. AC Spark Plug, GM, Milw., 1958-59; program mgr. def. rsch. div. GM, Santa Barbara, Calif., 1959-62; prof. elec. engring. Purdue U., West Lafayette, Ind., 1963-92, assoc. dean engring., 1968-72, prof. emeritus of elec. engring., 1992—; dir. engring. expt. sta. Purdue U., West Lafayette, Ind., 1968-72; bd. dirs. VETRONICS Inc., West Lafayette, 1984—, pres., 1984-87; pres. Tech. Assocs. Inc., West Lafayette, 1977-96. Co-author: Probabilistic Methods of Signal and System Analysis, 1971, Continuous and Discrete Signal and System Analysis, 1974, Modern Communications and Spread Spectrum, 1986. Lt. (j.g.) USN, 1943-46, PTO. Recipient Meritorious Civilian Svc. award USN, 1955. Fellow IEEE (Centennial award 1984, J. Fred Peoples award 1988). Avocation: duplicate bridge, amateur radio. Office: Sch Elec Engring Purdue U West Lafayette IN 47907

MCGILLEY, SISTER MARY JANET, nun, educator, writer, academic administrator; b. Kansas City, Mo., Dec. 4, 1924; d. James P. and Peg (Ryan) McG. BA, St. Mary Coll., 1945; MA, Boston Coll., 1951; PhD, Fordham U., 1956; postgrad., U. Notre Dame, 1960, Columbia U., 1964. Joined Sisters of Charity, Roman Catholic Ch., 1946. Social worker Kansas City, 1945-46; tchr. English Hayden H.S., Topeka, 1948-50, Billings (Mont.) Central H.S., 1951-53; faculty dept. English St. Mary Coll., Leavenworth, Kans., 1956-64; pres. St. Mary Coll., 1964-89, disting. prof. English and Liberal Studies, 1990-96, pres. emeritus, 1996—. Contbr. articles, fiction and poetry to various jours. Bd. dirs. United Way of Leavenworth, 1966-85; mem. Mayor's Adv. Coun., 1967-72; bd. dirs. Kans. Ind. Coll. Fund, 1964-89, exec. com., 1985-86, vice chmn., 1984-85, chmn., 1985-86. Recipient Alumnae award St. Mary Coll., 1969; Disting. Service award Baker U., 1981, Leavenworth Bus. Woman of Yr. Athena award, 1986. Mem. Nat. Coun. Tchrs. of English, Nat. Assn. Ind. Colls. and Univs. (bd. dirs. 1982-85), Kans. Ind. Coll. Assn. (bd. dirs. 1964-89, treas. 1982-84, v.p. 1984-85, chmn. exec. com. 1985-86), Am. Coun. Edn. (com. on women in higher edn. 1980-85), Am. Assn. Higher Edn., Kansas City Regional Coun. for Higher Edn. (bd. dirs. 1965-89, treas. 1984-85, v.p. 1986-88), Ind. Coll. Funds Am. (exec. com. 1974-77, trustee-at-large 1975-76), North Cen. Assn. Colls. and Schs. (exec. commr. Com. on Insts. Higher Edn. 1980-88, vice chair 1985-86, chair 1987-88), Leavenworth C. of C. (bd. dirs. 1964-89), Assn. Am. Colls. (commn. liberal learning 1970-73, com. on curriculum and faculty devel. 1979-82) St. Mary Alumni Assn. (hon. pres. 1964-89), Delta Epsilon Sigma. Democrat. Office: St Mary Coll 4100 S 4th St Leavenworth KS 66048-5082

MCGILLICUDDY, JOAN MARIE, psychotherapist, consultant; b. Chgo., June 23, 1952; d. James Neal and Muriel (Joy) McG. BA, U. Ariz., 1974, MS, 1976; PhD, Walden U., 1996. Cert. nat. counselor. Counselor ACTION, Tucson, 1976; counselor, clin. supr. Behavioral Health Agy. Cen. Ariz., Casa Grande, 1976-81; instr. psychology Cen. Ariz. Coll., Casa Grande, 1978-83; therapist, co-dir. Helping Assocs., Inc., Casa Grande, 1982—, v.p., sec., 1982—; cert. instr. Silva Method Mind Devel., Tucson, 1986—. Mem. Mayor's Com. for Handicapped, Casa Grande, 1989-90, Human Svcs. Planning, Casa Grande, 1985-95. Named Outstanding Am. Lectr. Silva Midn Internat., 1988-96. Mem. ACA. Avocations: jogging, singing. Office: Helping Assocs Inc 1901 N Trekell Rd Casa Grande AZ 85222-1706

MC GILLICUDDY, JOHN FRANCIS, retired banker; b. Harrison, N.Y., Dec. 30, 1930; s. Michael J. and Anna (Munro) McG.; m. Constance Burtis, Sept. 9, 1954; children: Michael Sean, Faith Burtis Benoit, Constance Erin Mc Gillicuddy Mills, Brian Munro, John Walsh. A.B., Princeton, 1952; LL.B., Harvard, 1955. With Mfrs. Hanover Trust Co. subs. Mfrs. Hanover Corp., N.Y.C., 1958-91, v.p., 1962-66, sr. v.p., 1966-69, exec. v.p., asst. to chmn., 1969-70, vice chmn., dir., 1970, pres., 1971-91, chmn., chief exec. officer, 1979-91; chmn. bd., chief exec. officer Chem. Banking Corp., N.Y.C., 1992-93, ret., 1994; bd. dirs. USX Corp., So. Pero Copper Co., Kelso, Inc., Empire Blue Cross and Blue Shield, UAL Corp. Bd. dirs. Nat. Multiple Sclerosis Soc.; trustee, chmn. N.Y. Hosp., N.Y. Pub. Libr.; trustee emeritus Princeton U.; pres. Boy Scouts Am., Greater N.Y. Couns. Lt. (j.g.) USNR, 1955-58. Mem. Bus. Coun., Westchester Country Club (Rye, N.Y.), Blind Brook Club (Port Chester, N.Y.), Princeton Club (N.Y.C.), Augusta Nat. Golf Club (Ga.), Pine Valley Golf Club (N.J.), Laurel Valley Golf Club (Ligonier, Pa.), Seminole Golf Club (north Palm Beach, Fla.), Links Club (N.Y.C.), Sky Club (N.Y.C.). Roman Catholic. Office: Chem Banking Corp 270 Park Ave New York NY 10017-2014

MCGILLIS, KELLY, actress; b. Newport, Calif., July 9, 1957; m. Fred Tillman, Dec. 31, 1988; 3 children. Student, Pacific Conservatory of Performing Arts, Juilliard Sch. Music. Actress: (feature films) Reuben, Reuben, 1983, Witness, 1985, Top Gun, 1986, Made in Heaven, 1987, Promised Land, 1988, The House on Carroll Street, 1988, The Accused, 1988, Winter People, 1989, The Babe, 1992, North, 1994; (TV films) Sweet Revenge, 1984, Private Sessions, 1985, Grand Isle (also prod.), 1991, Bonds of Love, 1993, In the Best of Families: Marriage, Pride and Madness, 1994, Remember Me, 1995; (stage) Hedda Gabler, Roundabout Theatre Company, 1994. *

MCGILLIVRAY, DONALD DEAN, seed company executive, agronomist; b. Muscatine, Iowa, Aug. 28, 1928; s. Walter C. and Pearl E. (Potter) M.; m. Betty J. Anderson, June 24, 1951; children—Ann E., Jean M. B.S. in Agronomy, Iowa State U., 1950. Asst. mgr. Iowa, Minn., Wis. sect. Funk Seeds Internat., Belle Plaine, Iowa, 1965-69, mgr., 1969-70, mgr. hybrid corn ops., Bloomington, Ill., 1970-75, v.p. ops., 1976-82, pres., 1982-88; assoc. Smart Seeds, Inc., 1989—; dir. U.S. Feed Grains Coun., Washington, D.C., 1984-87. Bd. dirs. Ill. Agrl. Leadership Found., Macomb, Ill., 1985—, chmn. bd. 1990—, Ill. Wesleyan Assocs., 1986-89, Ill. 4-H Found., 1996—; adv. bd. Bro-Menn Hosp., pres., 1989-90. Sgt. U.S. Army, 1951-53. Mem. Am. Seed Trade Assn. (bd. dirs. 1978—, div. chmn. 1978-79, 2d v.p. 1986-87, 1st v.p. 1987-88, pres. 1988-89), Am. Seed Rsch. Found. (bd. dirs. 1982-95, pres. 1984-87), Masons.

MCGILLIVRAY, KAREN, elementary school educator; b. Richland, Oreg., Aug. 24, 1936; d. Kenneth Melton and Catharina (Sass) McG. BS in Edn. cum laude, Ea. Oreg. State Coll., 1958; MRE, Pacific Sch. Religion, 1963. Cert. tchr., Oreg. 4th grade tchr. Salem (Oreg.)-Keizer Pub. Schs.; ret., 1995. Contbr. articles, stories to ednl. mags. U.S. Govt. grantee. Mem. NEA (rep. assembly), NEA-Ret. Oreg. (state officer), Oreg. Edn. Assn. (rep. assembly), Oreg. Ret. Educators Assn. (officer), Salem Edn. Assn. (officer), Delta Kappa Gamma (officer), Phi Delta Kappa (officer). Methodist. Home: 325 SW Cedarwood Ave Mcminnville OR 97128-5813

MC GIMPSEY, RONALD ALAN, oil company executive; b. Cleve., June 7, 1944; s. John E. and Muriel N. McGimpsey; m. Linda V. Tiffany, Apr. 20, 1974. BS, Case Inst. Tech., 1966; MS, Case Western Res. U., 1974; grad. exec. program, Stanford U., 1987. With BP Am. Inc. (formerly Standard Oil Co.), Ohio, 1966—; treas. BP Am. Inc. (formerly Standard Oil Co.), 1977-81, v.p. fin., 1981-82, sr. v.p. crude trading and transp., 1982-86; sr. v.p. petroleum products and refining BP Am. Inc. (formerly Standard Oil Co.), Cleve., 1986-89; group contr. BP-London, 1989-91; regional sr. v.p., CFO BP America, Cleve., 1991-92, sr. v.p., fin. officer, 1992-93; CEO BP Australia, Melbourne, 1994—. Chmn. bd. trustees Marymount Hosp., Cleve., 1986-88; adv. bd. Case Inst. Tech. Mem. Bus. Coun. Australia, Australia Inst. of Petroleum (chmn. 1995—). Office: BP Australia, 360 Elizabeth St, Melbourne 3000, Australia

MC GIMSEY, CHARLES ROBERT, III, anthropologist; b. Dallas, June 18, 1925; s. Charles Robert, Jr. and Ellen Randolph (Pitts) McG.; m. Mary Elizabeth Conger, Dec. 20, 1949; children—Charles Robert, Brian Keith, Mark Douglass. Student, Vanderbilt U., 1942-43, U. of South, 1943-44; B.A., U. N.Mex., 1949; M.A., Harvard U., 1954, Ph.D., 1958. Instr. U. Ark., Fayetteville, 1957; asst. prof. U. Ark., 1958-62, assoc. prof., 1962-67, prof. anthropology, 1967-90, prof. emeritus, 1990—, chmn. dept., 1969-72; asst. curator U. Ark. Mus., 1957-59, dir., 1959-83; dir. Ark. Archeol. Survey, 1967-90, dir. emeritus, 1990—; cons. archeology U.S. GAO, 1979-87, U.S.-Internat. Com. on Monuments and Sites; Rep. to Internat. Com. on Archeol. Heritage Mgmt., 1988-95. Author: (with G.R. Willey) Monagrillo Culture of Panama, 1954, Mariana Mesa, 1980, Indians of Arkansas, 1969, Public Archeology, 1972, Archeology and Archeological Resources, 1973, (with H.A. Davis) The Management of Archeological Resources, 1977; assoc. editor Am. Antiquity, 1972-80; Co-editor (with H. A. Davis) Southeastern Museums Conf., 1964-73; Contbr. articles to profl. jours. Mem. Ark. Rev. Com., Historic Preservation Program, 1968-76; collaborator Nat. Park Service, 1971-74, adviser, 1974-77; mem. Com. on Recovery Archeol. Remains, 1971-78; mem. adv. bd. dirs. Red River Mus., 1975-76; mem. adv. bd. Am. Indian Archeol. Inst., 1975-80, Ark. Natural and Cultural Heritage Dept., 1976-90. Served to lt. (j.g.) USNR, 1943-47. Recipient Cert. Recognition State of Ark., 1990; rsch. grantee Am. Philos. Soc., Am. Acad. Arts and Scis., Andean Rsch. Inst., Nat. Park Service, NSF, Smithsonian Instn., Wenner-Gren Found.; rsch. fellow dept. archaeology U. Cambridge, 1985-86, assoc. mem. Darwin Coll., 1985—. Fellow Am. Anthrop. Assn.; mem. Soc. for Am. Archeology (pres. 1974-75, Disting. Svc. award 1975, award for excellence in cultural resource mgmt. 1995), Ark. Archeol. Soc. (editor 1960-83, Preservationist award 1989), Southeastern Mus. Conf. (coun. 1962-71, editor 1964-71), Am. Soc. for Conservation Archeology (founding, award for outstanding contbn. 1980), Soc. Profl. Archeologists (founder, bd. dirs. 1976-79, pres. 1983-84, Seiberling award 1989, presdl. recognition award 1997), Am. Assn. Mus., Am. Assn. for State and Local History (award of merit 1985). Home: 435 Hawthorne St Fayetteville AR 72701-1935 Office: Ark Archeol Survey PO Box 1249 Fayetteville AR 72702-1249

MCGINLEY, EDWARD STILLMAN, II, former naval officer, engineering executive; b. Allentown, Pa., June 9, 1939; s. Edward Stillman and Dorothy Mae (Kandle) McG.; m. Connie Lee Mayo, July 1, 1962; children: Amanda Lee, Edward Stillman III. BS, U.S. Naval Acad., 1961; advanced degree in naval architecture, MIT, 1970; MSA, George Washington U., 1972; cert. exec. program, U. Va., 1981. Commd. ensign USN, 1961, advanced through grades to rear adm., 1990, various positions in submarine engring., 1962-76; repair officer USN, Rota (Spain) and Charleston, S.C., 1976-83; ops. mgr. Mare Island Naval Shipyard, Vallejo, Calif., 1983-87; comdr. Norfolk Naval Shipyard, Portsmouth, Va., 1987-90; maintenance officer U.S. Pacific Fleet, Honolulu, 1990-93; comdr. Naval Surface Warfare Ctr., Washington, 1993-94; vice-comdr. Naval Sea Sys. Command, Washington, 1994-96; sr. engring. duty officer USN, 1994-96, ret., 1996; dir., infrastructure/security Fluor Daniel, Hanford, Wash., 1997—. Contbr. articles to profl. jours. Recipient Environ. award Sec. of Navy, 1987, Productivity Improvement award Inst. Indsl. Engrs., 1988, Quality Improvement award Office Mgmt. and Budget, 1989, Productivity award U.S. Senate, 1990. Mem. Am. Soc. Naval Engrs. (nat. counselor), U.S. Naval Inst., Am. Soc. for Quality Control, Sigma Xi, Tau Beta Pi. Republican. mem. United Church of Christ. Avocations: art, running. Home: 356 Riverwood Dr Richland WA 99352

MCGINLEY, JOSEPH PATRICK, brokerage house executive; b. Phila., Mar. 17, 1947; s. Joseph Robert and Kathaleen (Brennan) McG.; m. Linda L. Irvin, May 15, 1970 (div. 1981); children: Lisa C., Andrew S.; m. Sharon A. Malloy, Sept. 7, 1984; 1 child, Christopher J. BSBA, Villanova U., 1965-69. Sr. v.p. Dean Witter, Phila., 1974—; bd. dirs. Tara Investments Ltd., Phila., Orion Assoc., Phila., Florence Ave. Corp., Phila. Co-founder A Better Chance of Lower Merion; bd. dirs. Phila. City Sail; pres. Friends of the Maya Pa. Mus. Mem. Union League Yacht Club (commodore), Union League of Phila., Cynwyd Club, Corinthian Yacht Club (Phila.). Republican. Roman Catholic. Avocation: yachting. Office: Dean Witter Reynolds 2 Logan Sq Philadelphia PA 19103-2707

MCGINLEY, MORGAN, newspaper editor; b. New London, Conn., Mar. 1, 1942; s. Morgan St. and Elizabeth (Zuccardy) McG.; m. Mary Elizabeth Dowd, Sept. 11, 1971; children: John, Carolyn, Brendan. BA, Colby Coll., 1964. Reporter Providence Jour., 1965; reporter The Day, New London, 1965-75, asst. city editor, 1975-78, night city editor, 1978-81, asst. editorial page editor, 1981-82, editorial page editor, 1982—; writer in residence Emerson Coll., Boston, 1992; presenter editl. writing Wilmington Writers Workshop, 1995. Bd. dirs. Salvation Army, New London, 1976—, Found. Open Govt., Conn., 1993—; chmn. Conn. Coun. on Freedom of Info.; mem. Task Force on Minorities in the Newspaper Bus.; panelist Conn. Pub. TV Fourth Estate Show, 1987—. With U.S. Army, 1965, cpl. Army NG, 1965-70. Fellow Washington Journalism Ctr., 1969, Knight Ctr. Specialized Journalism U. Md., 1991, 94, 95, 96; recipient 2 1st place edit. writing awards New Eng. AP New Execs. Assn., New Eng. Press Assn., 1st place award Soc. Profl. Journalists. Mem. Nat. Conf. Editl. Writers (chmn. minorities com. 1988—, bd. dirs. 1989-90, 92-93, chair mem. 1993-94, mem. editl. mgmt. and ops. com., sec. 1995, treas. 1996, v.p. 1997), New Eng. Soc. Newspaper Editors (bd. govs. 1987—, minority affairs com., pres. 1992, past v.p., treas. and sec.), New Eng. Newspaper Assn. (mem. minority affairs com.), Trout Unltd. (bd. dirs. Thames Valley chpt. 1972—). Episcopalian. Avocations: fly fishing, fly tying. Home: 119 Glenwood Ave New London CT 06320-4302 Office: The Day Pub Co 47 Eugene Oneill Dr New London CT 06320-6306

MCGINN, BERNARD JOHN, religious educator; b. Yonkers, N.Y., Aug. 19, 1937; s. Bernard John and Catherine Ann (Faulds) McG.; m. Patricia Ann Ferris, July 10, 1971; children: Daniel, John. BA, St. Joseph's Sem., Yonkers, N.Y., 1959; Licentiate in Sacred Theology, Gregorian U., Rome, 1963; PhD, Brandeis U., 1970. Diocesan priest Archdiocese N.Y., N.Y.C., 1963-71; prof. U. Chgo., 1969—, Naomi Shenstone Donnelly Prof., 1992—; program coord. Inst. for Advanced Study of Religion, Divinity Sch., U. Chgo., 1980-92. Author: The Calabrian Abbott, 1985, Meister Eckhart, 1986, Foundations of Mysticism, 1991, Growth of Mysticism, 1994, Antichrist, 1994; editor: (series) Classics of Western Spirituality, 1978, (book) God and Creation, 1990. Fellow Medieval Acad. Am. Home: 5701 S Kenwood Ave Chicago IL 60637-1718 Office: U Chgo Divinity Sch 1025 E 58th St Chicago IL 60637-1509

MCGINN, CHERIE M., secondary education educator; b. Oil City, Pa., Feb. 5, 1949; d. Rendall Baxter and Helen Joyce (Kunselman) Agnew; 1 child from previous marriage, Joshua Edward; m. Stephen James McGinn, Jan. 1, 1983; 1 child, Kathleen Erin. BS Clarion State Coll., 1971. Cert. secondary tchr., Md. Grad. asst. Clarion State Coll., Pa., 1971-72; tchr. Montgomery County Pub. Schs., 1972—; chairperson Montgomery Blair

H.S., Silver Spring, Md., 1994—; cons. curriculum, Upper Marlboro, Md., 19; panelist Odyssey 1984, Excellence in Edn., Md. Humanities Coun., Balt., 1984. Vol. reader grant proposal Coun. for Basic Edn., fellow, 1983.91. NEH, Washington, 1984—. NEH fellow, 1989, 92, 95. Mem. Nat. Coun. for Social Studies, U.S. Capitol Hist. Soc., Assn. Supervision and Curriculum Devel., Md. Social Studies Assn., Montgomery County Social Studies Coun., NEA, Md. State Tchrs. Assn., Montgomery County Educators Assn. Democrat. Mem. Unitarian Ch. Home: 14228 Rutherford Rd Upper Marlboro MD 20774-8564 Office: Montgomery Blair HS 313 Wayne Ave Silver Spring MD 20910-5500

MCGINN, MARY JOVITA, lawyer, insurance company executive; b. St. Louis, Apr. 9, 1947; d. Martin J. and Janet (Hogan) McG.; m. Bernard H. Shapiro, Sept. 6, 1971; children: Sara, Colleen, Molly, Daniel. BA, Rosary Coll., River Forest, Ill., 1967; JD, St. Louis U., 1970. Bar: Mo. 1970, Ill. 1971. Atty. tax div. U.S. Dept. Justice, Washington, 1970-73; atty. Allstate Ins. Co., Northbrook, Ill., 1973—; v.p., asst. gen. counsel Allstate Ins. Co., 1980—. Mem. ABA, Am. Coll. Investment Counsel, Assn. Life Ins. Counsel. Roman Catholic. Home: 155 N Buckley Rd Barrington IL 60010-2607 Office: Allstate Ins Co 3075 Sanders Rd Ste G5A Northbrook IL 60062-7119

MCGINN, MAX DANIEL, lawyer; b. Lexington, N.C., July 30, 1942; s. Max Terry and Ethel Mae (Peck) McG.; m. Judith Eaton McBee, June3, 1965; children: Brian, Tracie. BA magna cum laude, Wake Forest U., 1964, JD cum laude, 1967. Bar: U.S. Dist. Ct. (mid. dist.) N.C. 1971, U.S. Supreme Ct. 1977, U.S. Ct. Appeals (4th cir.) 1976, U.S. Dist. Ct. (we. and ea dists.) N.C. 1979. Atty. NLRB, Winston-Salem, N.C., 1967, 1970; ptnr. Brooks, Pierce, McLendon, Humphrey & Leonard, Greensboro, N.C., 1971—. Lt., atty. Judge Adv. Gen.'s Corps, USN, 1967-70. Fellow Am. Coll. of Trial Lawyers; mem. ABA, N.C. Bar Assn. (chmn. Labor and Employment Law sect. 1989). Presbyterian. Avocations: tennis, sports, reading. Home: 3008 Redford Dr Greensboro NC 27408-3116 Office: Brooks Pierce McLendon Humphrey & Leonard 230 N Elm St Greensboro NC 27401-2436

MC GINNES, EDGAR ALLEN, JR., forestry educator; b. Chestown, Md., Feb. 15, 1926; s. Edgar Allen and Emily Frances (Howard) McG.; m. Jean Marie Heidemann, June 23, 1951; children—Jeffrey, Christine, Karen. B.S., Pa. State U., 1950, M.F., 1951; Ph.D., N.Y. State Coll. Forestry, 1955. Research chemist Am. Viscose Corp., 1951-52, research scientist, 1955-60; prof. forestry U. Mo., Columbia, 1960-88; cons. abnormal wood formation. Contbr. articles to profl. jours. Served with AUS, 1944-46. Fellow AAAS (coun. 1970-74), Am. Inst. Chemists, Soc. Am. Foresters, Mo. Acad. Scis. (pres. 1981-82); mem. Am. Chem. Soc., TAPPI, Forest Products Rsch. Soc. chmn. midwest sect. 1986-87), Internat. Assn. Wood Anatomists, Soc. Wood Sci. and Tech. (pres. 1986-87), Kappa Sigma. Club: Cosmopolitan Internat. (Columbia) (pres. 1971-72). Home: 900 Bourn Ave Columbia MO 65203-1457

MCGINNIES, ELLIOTT MORSE, psychologist, educator; b. Buffalo, Sept. 19, 1921; s. Elliott Morse and Mabel Christina (Hussong) McG.; m. Bessie Yeh, Jan. 27, 1967; children: Michelle, Lisa, Amy. BA, SUNY-Buffalo, 1943; MA, Brown U., 1944; PhD, Harvard U., 1948. Teaching fellow Harvard U., 1944-47; asst. prof. U. Ala., 1947-52; assoc. prof., then prof. U. Md., 1952-70; prof., chmn. dept. psychology Am. U., 1970-86, prof. emeritus, 1987— ; vis. scholar U. Calif., Berkeley, 1987-88; Fulbright prof. Nat. Taiwan U. With AUS, 1943. Fellow Am. Psychol. Assn.; mem. Eastern Psychol. Assn., Psychonomic Soc., Sigma Xi. Author: Social Behavior: A Functional Analysis, 1970, The Reinforcement of Social Behavior, 1971, Attitudes, Conflict and Social Change, 1972, Perspectives on Social Behavior, 1994. Office: The Am Univ Dept of Psychology 4400 Massachusetts Ave NW Washington DC 20016-8001

MC GINNIS, ARTHUR JOSEPH, publisher; b. Paterson, N.J., Apr. 5, 1911; s. Arthur L. and Rose (Seyer) McG.; m. Roselind P. Diskon, May 17, 1939; children: Roselind P. (Mrs. Joseph W. Mullen, Jr.), Carolyn M., Kathleen M. (Mrs. A.A. Stein III), Patricia A., Arthur J. B.A., Fordham U., 1932; M.B.A., Harvard, 1934. Traveling auditor, 1934-35; staff statistician Western Union Telegraph Co., 1935-40; assoc. editor Ry. Age, 1940-44, fin. editor, 1944-46; asst. treas. Simmons-Boardman Pub. Corp., 1946-50; mem. White House press corps, Washington, 1950-58; treas., dir. Simmons-Boardman Pub. Corp., 1950-54, exec. v.p., treas., 1954-58, pres., treas., 1958-72, chmn. exec. com., treas., chief exec. officer, 1972—; pub. Am. Builder mag., 1955-61. Trustee Monmouth Med. Center, Long Branch, N.J., 1956—, chmn. devel. com. Roman Catholic. Clubs: N.Y. Athletic (N.Y.C.), Harvard Business (N.Y.C.), Nat. Arts (N.Y.C.); Deal (N.J.) Golf and Country (pres.), Allenhurst (N.J.) Bathing. Home & Office: 345 Hudson St New York NY 10014-4502

MCGINNIS, CHARLES IRVING, civil engineer; b. Kansas City, Mo., Jan. 31, 1928; s. Paul Sherman and Sidney (Bacon) McG.; m. Shirley Ann Meyer, Nov. 5, 1955; children: Gail B., Ann K., James P. B.S., Tex. A&M., 1949; M.Engring., Tex. A & M Coll., 1950; grad., Army Engring. Sch., 1955, Command and Gen. Staff Coll., 1959, Armed Forces Staff Coll., 1962, Army War Coll., 1969. Registered profl. engr., Tex., Mo. Enlisted as pvt. U.S. Army, 1945, advanced through grades to maj. gen., 1976; area engr. Ethiopia and Somali Republic, 1962-65; dist. engr. St. Paul, 1969-71; dir. engring. and constrn. bur. Panama Canal Co., 1971-72, v.p., 1972-74; lt. gov. C.Z., 1972-74; div. engr. southwestern div. C.E., Dallas, 1974-77; dir. civil works Office Chief of Engrs. U.S. Army, Washington, 1977-79; civil engr., 1979—; exec. v.p. Fru-con Corp.; pres. Fruco Engrs., Inc., 1983-87; assoc. dir. Constrn. Industry Inst. U. Tex., 1987-93; sr. lectr. civil engring. dept. U. Tex., Austin, 1992—; mem. vis. com., dept. civil engring. M.I.T., 1978-81; mem. Mississippi River Commn., 1975-77, Bd. Engrs. for Rivers and Harbors, 1975-77. Chmn. Combined Fedn. Campaign coordinating com., C.Z., 1972-74; pres. C.Z. coun. Boy Scouts Am., 1973-74; mem. exec. bd. St. Louis area coun., 1983-87, Capitol area coun., 1987-90; mem. com. mgmt. Balboa YMCA, 1973-74; trustee C.Z. United Way, 1972-74. Decorated D.S.M., Legion of Merit with oak leaf cluster, Joint Svcs. Commendation medal, U.S. Army Commendation with oak leaf cluster, Chuong My medal 1st class Vietnam. Fellow ASCE, Soc. Am. Mil. Engrs. (past pres. Twin Cities post and Panama post); mem. NSPE (chmn. water policy task force 1979-81), Assn. U.S. Army, Mil. Order of the World Wars, Tau Beta Pi, Chi Epsilon. Episcopalian. Address: 10006 Sausalito Dr Austin TX 78759-6106 *The simple four-part philosophy which has well served three generations of my family requires an uncompromising commitment to honesty in all things, industry, concentration on the job and on personal objectives, and economy of all resources, both natural and man-made.*

MCGINNIS, GARY DAVID, chemist, science educator; b. Everett, Wash., Oct. 1, 1940. BS, Pacific Luthera U., 1962; MS, U. Wash., 1968; PhD in Organic Chem., U. Mont., 1970. Prodn. chemist Am. Cyanamid Co., 1964-67; fell. U. Mont., 1970-71; from asst. prof. wood chemistry to assoc. prof. wood sci. Forest Products Utilization Lab. Mich. State U. Mem. Am. Chem. Soc., Forest Products Rsch. Soc., Sigma Xi. Office: Michigan Technology University Institute of Wood Research Houghton MI 49931*

MCGINNIS, JAMES MICHAEL, physician; b. Columbia, Mo., July 12, 1944; s. Leland Glenn and Lillian Ruth (Mackler) McG.; m. Patricia Anne Gwaltney, Aug. 4, 1978; children—Brian, Katherine. A.B., U. Calif., Berkeley, 1966; M.A., M.D., UCLA, 1971; M.P.P., Harvard U., 1977. House officer in internal medicine Boston City Hosp., 1971-72; internat. med. officer HEW, 1972-74; dir. Office for Asia and Western Pacific, 1974-75; state coordinator smallpox eradication program WHO, India, 1974-75; fellow Harvard Center for Community Health and Med. Care, Boston, 1976-77; cons. to sec. HEW, Washington, 1977; dep. asst. sec. for health, dir. office disease prevention HEW, 1977-95, asst. surgeon gen., 1980-95, acting dir. office of rsch. integrity, 1992-93; scholar-in-residence NAS, Washington, 1995—; instr. medicine George Washington U. Med. Sch., 1973-75; adj. prof. pub. policy Duke U., 1979-81; lectr. pub. and internat. affairs Princeton U., 1996—; chair, sec. task force on smoking and health; chair exec. com. HHS Environ. Health Policy Com.; mem. U.S. Japan Leadership program; chair World Bank/European Commn. Task Force on Reconstrn. of Health Sector, Bosnia, 1996-97. Mem. editl. bd. Jour. Med. Edn., 1975-78, Jour. Preventive Medicine, 1987—, Jour. Health Promotion, 1992—; editor-in-chief: Healthy People 2000, Surgeon General's Report on Nutrition and Health, Determining Risks to Health. Served with USPHS, 1972-75, 77—. Recipient Arthur S. Flemming Pub. Svc. award, 1979, USPHS Disting. Svc. medal, 1989, Surgeon Gen.'s medallion, 1995, Fed. Profile in Leadership award, 1989, Wilbur Cohen award, 1995, award for excellence APHA, 1995, Health Leader of Yr. award, 1996. Fellow Am. Coll. Epidemiology, Am. Coll. Preventive Medicine. Office: 330 C St SW Washington DC 20201-0001

MCGINNIS, JOÁN ADELL, retired secondary school educator; b. Erie, Pa., Jan. 20, 1932; d. Roy Hamilton and Sara Zelma (Gorman) Sjöberg; m. Richard H. Edwards, Aug. 6, 1954 (div. 1965); m. George William McGinnis, Dec. 29, 1966 (dec. Apr. 1994). BA, St. Lawrence U., Canton, N.Y., 1953. Cert. tchr., Calif. Spl. proxies Sun Life Assurance Co., Montreal, 1952-53; pvt. sec. Detroit Trust, 1953-54; sec. Meth. Ch., Lancaster, Calif., 1964—; tchr. Sunny Hills H.S., Fullerton, Calif., 1966-97; contr. Mission Viejo (Calif.) Sheet Metal, 1980-81; dept. sec. Fgn. Lang. Dept. Sunny Hills H.S., 1966-80, dept. chair, 1987-89; internat. baccalaureate examiner in Spanish, 1991—, French, 1992—; advanced placement examiner in Spanish, 1990—. Mem. Am. Assn. Tchrs. Spanish and Portuguese, Modern Classical Lang. Assn. Calif., Fgn. Lang. Assn. Orange County (Exptl. Tchr. of Orange County award 1994), Am. Women's Orgn. Republican. Avocations: languages, music, drama. Home: 26382 Estanciero Dr Mission Viejo CA 92691-5401

MCGINNIS, JOHN OLDHAM, lawyer, educator; b. N.Y.C., Mar. 21, 1957; s. John Patrick and Pauline Ruth (Oldham) McG. BA magna cum laude, Harvard U., 1978, JD magna cum laude, 1983; MA, Oxford U., Eng., 1980. Bar: N.Y. 1984. Law clk. to judge U.S. Ct. Appeals (D.C. cir.), Washington, 1983-84; assoc. Sullivan & Cromwell, N.Y.C., 1984-85; atty./advisor Office Legal Counsel, Dept. Justice, Washington, 1985-87, dep. asst. atty. gen., 1987-91; prof. Benjamin N. Cardozo Sch. Law, N.Y.C., 1991—. Contbr. articles to profl. popular jours.; editor Harvard Law Rev., 1982-83. Recipient Paul M. Bator award Federalist Soc., 1997. Home: 21 E 22nd St New York NY 10010-5332 Office: Cardozo Law Sch 55 5th Ave New York NY 10003-4301

MCGINNIS, PATRICK BRYAN, mental health counselor; b. Bellville, Ill., June 17, 1948; s. Raymon Lee and Virginia B. (Wiggins) McG.; 1 child, Patrick Bryan II. BS, Rollins Coll., 1977, MS in Criminal Justice, 1981; MA in Counseling Psychology, Norwich U., 1996. Cert. hypnotherapist, criminal justice addictions profl., criminal justice specialist-master addictions counselor. Ct. liaison officer, probation officer, classification spec. State of Fla. Dept. Corrections, Polk County, 1975-87; victim intervention program coord./therapist Peace River Ctr. for Personal Devel., Inc., Lakeland, Fla., 1987-90; clin. social worker State of Fla. Dept. Corrections/South Fla. Reception Ctr., Miami, 1991-92; counselor CareUnit of Coral Springs' Carepsychcenter, Coral Springs, Fla., 1992-93; psychotherapist Ctr. for Human Potential, Ft. Lauderdale, Fla., 1993—; counselor Unity Counseling Ctr./Unity Ch. of Ft. Lauderdale, 1993-94; vocat. rehab. counselor Fla. Divsn. Vocat. Rehab., Ft. Lauderdale, 1995-97; adjunct faculty Broward C.C., Ft. Lauderdale, Fla., 1996—; counselor Unity of Hollywood Counseling Ctr., 1996—; clin. supr. Spectrum Programs, Ft. Lauderdale, 1997—; clin. supr. Spectrum Programs, Ft. Lauderdale, 1997—. With USAF, 1968-69. Recipient State of Fla. Clinician of Yr. award Fla. Coun. for Cmty. Mental Health, 1990; named Clinician of Yr., Peace River Ctr. for Personal Devel., 1980 Law Enforcement Officer of Yr., Greater Lakeland Area Am. Legion. Home: 8560 NW 20th Ct Sunrise FL 33322-3802 Office: Ctr for Human Potential 1881 NE 26th St Ste 103 Fort Lauderdale FL 33305-1427

MCGINNIS, ROBERT E., lawyer; b. Caldwell, Ohio, May 1, 1931; s. Earl Peregoy and Mary Ethel (Richner) McG.; m. Jane Ann Lindenmeyer, Sept. 12, 1953; children: Sharon Ann, David E. BA, Ohio Weslayan U., 1952; JD, Ohio State U., 1954. Bar: Ohio 1954, Calif. 1956. Asst. judge advocate USAF, 1954-56; sr. ptnr. Luce, Forward, Hamilton, & Scripps, San Diego, 1956—; counsel to pub. utilities, pub. agys., savs. and loan instns., ins. cos. and contractors. Trustee Wesley Meth. Ch., San Diego, Fine Arts Soc., First Meth. Ch., La Mesa, Calif.; counsel Kensington Community Ch.; dir. San Diego Opera Assn., corp. sec., v.p. Mem. Order of Coif. Republican. Mem. United Ch. Christ. Office: Luce Forward Hamilton & Scripps 600 W Broadway Ste 2600 San Diego CA 92101-3391

MC GINTY, JOHN MILTON, architect; b. Houston, Apr. 24, 1935; s. Milton Bowles and Ruth Louise (Dreaper) McG.; m. Juanita Jones, May 4, 1957; children: Christopher Harold, Jacqueline Ruth McGinty Carlson. B.S., Rice U., 1957; M.F.A., Princeton U., 1961. With archtl. firm Barnes, Landes & Goodman, Austin, Tex., 1957-58, Ingram & Harris, Beaumont, Tex., 1958-59; prin. McGinty Partnership, Architects, Inc., Houston, 1961-89, City Assos., Inc., 1979-91, Bovay-McGinty, Inc., engrs. & architects, Houston, 1989-91; co-owner, pres. Am. Constrn. Investigations Inc., Houston, 1991—; instr. archtl. design U. Houston, 1965-67; White House fellow, asst. to Sec. of Interior, 1967-68; vis. prof. architecture Rice U., 1969-70. Named Disting. Alumnus Rice U., 1986. Fellow AIA (mem. U.S. delegation to USSR 1972, pres. Houston chpt. 1973, nat. pres. 1977). Home: HC-02 Box 308 Palacios TX 77465 Office: Am Constrn Investigations Ste 200 602 Sawyer St Houston TX 77007-7510

MCGINTY, KATHLEEN, federal official. Dep. asst. to pres., dir. environ. policy Exec. Office of Pres. of U.S., Washington, 1993-95, chairperson coun. on environ. quality, 1995—. Office: Council on Environ Quality 722 Jackson Pl NW Washington DC 20503-0002*

MCGINTY, MICHAEL DENNIS, air force officer; b. Waukegan, Ill., Sept. 20, 1942; s. Roy Leonard and Betty Jane (Anderson) McG.; m. Karen Lee Dibble, July 2, 1965; children: Shannon, Timothy. BA in Math., U. Minn., 1964; MA in Pub. Adminstrn., Shippensburg U., 1983. Commd. 2d lt. USAF, 1965, advanced through grades to lt. gen., 1996; chief of standarization and evaluation 3d Tactical Fighter Wing, Clark Air Base, The Philippines, 1975-76; ops. officer 9th Tactical Fighter Squadron, Holloman AFB, N.Mex., 1976-78; grad. student Air Command and Staff Coll., Maxwell AFB, Ala., 1979; chief of officer assignments Hdqrs. Tactical Air Command, Langley AFB, Va., 1979-82; grad. student U.S. Army War Coll., Carlisle, Pa., 1983; dep. comdr. for ops. 355th Tactical Tng. Wing, Davis-Monthan AFB, Ariz., 1983-85; chief cols. group Air Force Mil. Pers. Ctr., Randolph AFB, Tex., 1985-87; vice comdr. 10th Tactical Fighter Wing, RAF Alconbury, U.K., 1987-88, comdr., 1988-90; dep. chief of staff for plans and requirements Hdqrs. Air Tng. Command, Randolph AFB, 1990; vice comdr. Air Force Mil. Pers. Ctr., Randolph AFB, 1990-92, comdr., 1992-94; dir. pers. programs, edn. and tng. USAF The Pentagon, Washington, 1994-96, dep. chief of staff, personnel, 1996—. Author: Low Altitude Training for F-4 Aircrews, 1979, Theory Z Management: Can It Be Used Effectively in the Air Force, 1983. Decorated Disting. Svc. medal, Legion of Merit (2), DFC (2), Meritorious Svc. medal (4), Air medal (10). Mem. Air Force Assn., Ret. Officers Assn., Order of Daedalians (flight capt. Tucson club 1984-85), Pi Sigma Alpha. Republican. Roman Catholic. Avocations: running, hiking, camping, outdoor activities. Home: 75 Westover Ave SW Washington DC 20336-5409 Office: Hq USAF/DP 1040 Air Force Pentagon Washington DC 20330-1040

MCGINTY, THOMAS EDWARD, management consultant; b. Holyoke, Mass., Aug. 20, 1929; s. Patrick John and Alice May (Hill) McG.; m. June Theresa Coutu, Jan. 27, 1951; children: Thomas, Michael, Matthew. B.S. in Econs. and Commerce, U. Vt., 1951; M.B.A., NYU, 1957. Chartered fin. analyst. Sr. fin. analyst Moody's Investor Service, 1955-59, Model, Roland and Stone, N.Y.C., 1959-62; with Cleve.-Cliffs Iron Co., 1962-83, v.p. fin., 1971-75, sr. v.p., 1975-83; pres. Belvoir Cons., Inc., 1983—; bd. dirs. Park Ohio Industries. Author: Project Organization and Finance, 1981. Bd. advisers Notre Dame Coll. Served with U.S. Army, 1951-55, Korea. Decorated Bronze Star. Mem. Assn. Investment Mgmt. and Rsch., Cleve. Skating Club, Wilderness Country Club (Naples, Fla.). Roman Catholic. Home: 2705 Belvoir Blvd Cleveland OH 44122-1925 Office: Belvoir Cons 23200 Chagrin Blvd Ste 325 Cleveland OH 44122-5404

MCGIRR, DAVID WILLIAM JOHN, investment banker; b. Glasgow, Scotland, May 19, 1954; came to U.S., 1991; s. Edward McCombie and Diane Curzon (Woods) McG.; m. Margaret Joslin Richardson, May 9, 1981; children: William David, Katherine Joslin, Lucy Ann, Elizabeth Margaret. BSc with honors, U. Glasgow, 1976; MBA, U. Pa., 1978. Assoc. S.G. Warburg & Co. Ltd., London, 1978-80, exec. dir., 1981-86; mng. dir. S.G. Warburg & Co. Inc., N.Y.C., 1991-95, CFO, 1992-95; assoc. Warburg Paribas Becker Inc., N.Y.C., 1980-81; exec. dir. S.G. Warburg Securities, London, 1986-87; CEO S.G. Warburg Securities (Can.) Ltd., Toronto, Ont., Can., 1987-89; COO, CFO Bunting Warburg Inc., Toronto, 1989-91; pres. GAB Robins North Am. Inc., Parsippany, N.J., 1996—, CEO, 1997—; mem. selection com. Thouron Scholarship. Thouron scholar, 1976-78. Mem. Apawamis Club (Rye, N.Y.), Nat. Club (Can.). Avocations: collecting cars, motor racing, family, golf. Office: GAB Robins N Am Inc 9 Campus Dr Parsippany NJ 07054-4408

MCGIVERIN, ARTHUR A., state supreme court justice; b. Iowa City, Iowa, Nov. 10, 1928; s. Joseph J. and Mary B. McG.; m. Mary Joan McGiverin, Apr. 20, 1951; children: Teresa, Thomas, Bruce, Nancy. BSC with high honors, U. Iowa, 1951, JD, 1956. Bar: Iowa 1956. Pvt. practice law Ottumwa, Iowa, 1956; alt. mcpl. judge Ottumwa, 1960-65; judge Iowa Dist. Ct. 8th Jud. Dist., 1965-78; assoc. justice Iowa Supreme Ct., Des Moines, 1978-87, chief justice, 1987—. Mem. Iowa Supreme Ct. Commn. on Continuing Legal Edn., 1975. Served to 1st lt. U.S. Army, 1946-48, 51-53. Mem. Iowa State Bar Assn., Am. Law Inst. Roman Catholic. Avocation: golf. Office: Iowa Supreme Ct State Capital Bldg Des Moines IA 50319*

MCGIVERN, DIANE, nursing educator. PhD, NYU, 1972. RN. Head divsn. nursing NYU, N.Y.C. Fellow AAN. Office: New York Univ Hosp 50 W 4th St Rm 429 New York NY 10012-1106

MCGIVNEY, JOHN JOSEPH, lawyer; b. Boston, Oct. 31, 1956; s. William A. and Mary Angela (Wall) McG.; m. Lynette Mari Ariail, 1995. AB magna cum laude, Boston Coll., 1978, JD cum laude, 1981. Bar: Mass. 1981, U.S. Dist. Ct. Mass. 1982, U.S. Ct. Appeals (1st cir.) 1983, U.S. Supreme Ct. 1990. Assoc. Burns & Levinson, Boston, 1981-87, ptnr., chief appellate sect., 1988-95; ptnr. Tedeschi and Grasso, Boston, 1996, Rubin and Rudman, Boston, 1997—. Sec. Lynnfield (Mass.) Dem. Town Com., 1974-75, chmn., 1976-77. Mem. Mass. Acad. Trial Attys., Mass. Def. Lawyers Assn. (bd. dirs.). Office: Tedeschi and Grasso 100 Summer St Boston MA 02110-2106

MC GLAMERY, MARSHAL DEAN, agronomy, weed science educator; b. Mooreland, Okla., July 29, 1932; s. Walter Gaiford and Bernice (Gardner) McG.; m. Marilyn Hudson, June 2, 1957; children—Paul, Steve. B.S., Okla. State U., 1956, M.S., 1958; Ph.D., U. Ill., 1965. Instr. Panhandle A. and M. Coll., 1958-60; agronomist Agribus. Co., Lawrence, Kans., 1960-61; teaching asst. U. Ill., 1961-63, research fellow, 1963-65, asst. prof. weed sci., 1965-70, asso. prof., 1970-76, prof., 1976—, extension agronomist, 1965—. Served with U.S. Army, 1953-55. NSF fellow, 1963. Mem. Am. Soc. Agronomy, Weed Sci. Soc. Am., Council Agr. and Sci. Tech. Baptist. Home: 35 Lange Ave Savoy IL 61874-9705 Office: 1102 S Goodwin Ave Urbana IL 61801-4730

MCGLAMRY, MAX REGINALD, lawyer; b. Wilcox County, Ga., Sept. 12, 1928; s. Edgar Lee and Allie Bea (Faircloth) McG.; m. Jean Louise Hilyer, Dec. 28, 1950; children: Sharon Kay McGlamry Hendrix, Michael Lee. BS, Auburn U., 1948; LLB cum laude, Mercer U., 1952, JD cum laude, 1970. Bar: Ga. 1953, U.S. Dist. Ct. (mid. dist.) Ga. 1954, U.S. Ct. Appeals (5th cir.) 1964, U.S. Supreme Ct. 1972, U.S. Ct. Appeals (11th cir.) 1981, U.S. Ct. Appeals (4th cir.) 1985, U.S. Dist. Ct. (no. dist.) Calif. 1988, U.S. Dist. Ct. (no. dist.) Ga. 1989. Pvt. practice Columbus, Ga., 1953-64; from ptnr. to officer Swift, Pease, Davidson & Chapman (name changed to Page, Scrantom, Harris, McGlamry, & Chapman, P.C.), Columbus, 1964-85; ptnr. Pope, Kellogg, McGlamry, Kilpatrick & Morrison, Columbus, 1985-90, Pope, McGlamry, Kilpatrick & Morrison, LLP, Columbus, 1990—. Mem. exec. com. Muscogee County Dem. Orgn., Columbus, 1956-60; bd. dirs. Columbus Jr. C. of C. With USN, 1948-49. Am. Coll. Trust & Estate Counsel fellow, 1973, Ga. Bar Found., Inc. fellow, 1983. Mem. ABA, ATLA, State Bar Ga., Ga. Trial Lawyers Assn., Assn. U.S. Army, Metro Columbus Urban League, Inc., Columbus Lawyers Club (pres. 1964-65), Lions (Columbus chpt. pres. 1967-68), Chattahoochee River Club, Green Island Country Club, Phi Kappa Phi, Alpha Epsilon Delta, Phi Alpha Delta, Pi Kappa Alpha. Democrat. Methodist. Avocations: golf, fishing. Home: 2937 Lynda Ln Columbus GA 31906-1337 Office: Pope McGlamry Kilpatrick & Morrison PO Box 2128 2d Fl 318 11th St Columbus GA 31902

MCGLATHERY, JAMES MELVILLE, foreign language educator; b. New Orleans, Nov. 22, 1936; s. Samuel Lyon and Mary Jackson (Garrott) McG.; m. Nancy Judith Beyer, June 1, 1939; children: Samuel Lyon, Daniel Beyer, Andrew James, Benjamin Kim. AB, Princeton U., 1958; AM, Yale U., 1959, PhD, 1964. Instr. German Phillips Andover (Mass.) Acad., 1959-60; lectr. German Harvard U., 1963-64, instr. German, 1964-65; from asst. prof. to assoc. prof. U. Ill. at Urbana-Champaign, 1965-84, prof. German, 1984—, acting dept. head, spring 1985, dept. head, 1985-95; instr. Colby Coll. Summer Lang. Sch., 1964, Harvard U. Summer Lang. Sch., 1965, 66, 70, U. Ill. at Urbanan-Champaign summer session, 1972, 74, 76, 78, 80, 82, 87, 90; lectr. and presenter conf. papers numerous orgns. Author: Mysticism and Sexuality: E. T. A. Hoffmann, Part One: Hoffmann and His Sources, 1981, Desire's Sway: The Plays and Stories of Heinrich von Kleist, 1983, Mysticism and Sexuality: E. T. A. Hoffmann, Part Two: Interpretations of the Tales, 1985, Fairy Tale Romance: The Grimms, Basile, Perrault, 1991, Grimms' Fairy Tales: A History of Criticism on a Popular Classic, 1993; editor: German Source Readings in the Arts and Sciences, 1974, Journal of English and Germanic Philology, 1976, The Brothers Grimm and Folktale, 1988, 91, Music and German Literature: Their Relationship since the Middle Ages, 1992; contbg. author: Reader in German Literature, 1969, Moliére and the Commonwealth of Letters: Patrimony and Posterity, 1975, Fairy Tales as Ways of Knowing: Essays on Märchen in Psychology, Society, and Literature, 1981, Reflection and Action: Essays on the Bildungsroman, 1991; mng. editor: Jour. English and Germanic Philology, 1972—; contbr. articles and book revs. to profl. jours. Full undergrad. tuition scholar Princeton U., 1954-58; undergrad. rsch. assistantship Princeton U., 1956-58; Woodrow Wilson Nat. fellow Yale U., 1958-59, Jr. Sterling fellow Yale U., 1960-61, Nat. Def. Edn. Act fellow in Russian, Yale U., 1961-63; grad. rsch. bd. grantee U. Ill. Urbana-Champaign, 1975, 79, 80, 86, 89, 92. Mem. MLA (exec. com. divsn. comparative studies in 18th century lit. 1984-89), Am. Assn. Tchrs. of German, E. T. A. Hoffmann-Gesellschaft, Heinrich von Kleist-Gesellschaft, N.Am. Heine Soc. Home: 1204 Thomas Dr Champaign IL 61821-1632 Office: U Ill Urbana-Champaign Dept Germanic Langs & Lits 707 S Mathews Ave Urbana IL 61801-3625

MCGLAUCHLIN, TOM, artist; b. Turtle, Wis., Sept. 14, 1934; s. Charles Orion and Frances Lenore (Cadman) McG.; m. Patricia Ann Smith, Aug. 5, 1961; children: Christopher, Jennifer (dec.), Patrick (dec.). BS in Art, U. Wis., 1959, MS in Art, 1960; studied pottery with James McKinnell, 1962. Instr. dept. art and art edn. U. Wis., Madison, 1960-61; instr. art dept. Cornell Coll., Mt. Vernon, Iowa, 1961-64, asst. prof. art dept., 1964-68; assoc. prof., chmn. art dept. Cornell Coll., Mt. Vernon, N.Y., 1968-71; instr. Toledo Mus. Art, 1971-82, prof., dir. glass program, 1982-84. One-man exhbns. include Habatat Gallery, Dearborn, Mich., 1979, Glass Art Gallery, Toronto, 1981, 85, Glass Gallery, Bethesda, Md., 1981, 85, 87, 91, Heller Gallery, N.Y.C., 1983, B.Z. Wagman Gallery, St. Louis, 1983, Running Ridge Gallery, Santa Fe, 1990; selected group exhbns. include Toledo Mus. Art, 1972, 88, Glasmuseum Frauenau, Franenau, Germany, 1977, Habatat Gallery, 1980, 84, The Hand and the Spirit Gallery, Scottsdale, Ariz., 1980, Gallery of Contemporary Crafts, Detroit, 1980, The Naples (Fla.) Art Gallery, 1981, The Craftsman's Gallery, Scarsdale, N.Y., 1981, 84, The Nat. Mus. Modern Art, Kyoto and Tokyo, 1981, Perception Gallery, Houston, 1985, The AirLoft Gallery, Honolulu, 1986, The Corning (N.Y.) Mus. Glass, 1987; selected competitive exhbns. include Everson Mus. Art, Syracuse, N.Y., 1961, 62, Mus. Contemporary Crafts, N.Y.C., 1962, Corning Glass Mus., Met. Mus. Art, N.Y.C., Victoria and Albert Mus., London, Musee Ars Decoratif, Paris; public collections include Toledo Mus. Art, The Smithsonian Collection, Washington, Portland (Oreg.) Art Mus., New Orleans Mus. Art, Mus. Contemporary Crafts, Musee des arts decoratifs de la Ville de Lausanne, Switzerland, Minn. Mus. Art, St. Paul, Kunstmuseum, Dusseldorf, Germany, Corning Glass Mus. Grantee Associated Colls. Midwest, 1966-67; recipient First Jury award Toledo Glass Nat. II, 1968. Mem. Am. Crafts Coun., Internat. Sculpture Soc., Ohio Designer-Craftsmen, Glass Art Soc. Office: The Glass Studio 1940 W Central Ave Toledo OH 43606-3944

MCGLAUGHLIN, THOMAS HOWARD, publisher, retired naval officer; b. Cin., Jan. 12, 1928; s. George Godden and Cordelia (Herrlinger) McG.; m. Moana Maharam-Stone, Jan. 4, 1984. BS in Elec. Engring., U.S. Naval Acad., 1950. Lic. master mariner. Commd. ensign U.S. Navy, 1950, advanced through grades to capt., 1970; White House aide to Pres. John F. Kennedy, Washington, 1960-63; exec. officer USS Prichett, Long Beach, Calif., 1963-65; comdg. officer USS Maddox, Long Beach, 1965-67; exec. officer USS Boston, Boston, 1967-70; chief naval ops. Comdr.-in-Chief, Pacific, Honolulu, 1970-74; chief of staff Mil. Sealift Command, N.Y.C., 1974-79; ret. U.S. Navy, 1979; pres. Falmouth Press, Honolulu, 1983—; marine surveyor R.W. Dickieson Internat., Inc., Honolulu, 1982—; master M.V. Rella Mae, Honolulu, 1981-90, Royal Taipan, Cebu, Philippines, 1990. Hon. police chief Boston Police Dept., 1969. Decorated Bronze Star; recipient medal for Outstanding Svc., Am. Legion, Pitts., 1942. Mem. Nat. Def. Transp. Assn., VFW (life), U.S. Naval Acad. Alumni Assn. (life), The Retired Officers Assn. Republican. Presbyterian. Avocations: flying, scuba diving. Home: The Royal Iolani #1702 581 Kamoku St Honolulu HI 96826-5250 Office: RW Dickieson Internat Inc 46-208 Kahuhipa St Kaneohe HI 96744-3905

MCGLINCHEY, JOSEPH DENNIS, retail corporation executive; b. Lowell, Mass., Mar. 14, 1938; s. Patrick Joseph and Grace E. (Curley) McG.; m. Joan Fitzgerald, Sept. 12, 1964; children: Joseph II, Mark, Christopher, David. BA in Acctg., Bentley Coll., 1965; MBA, Babson Coll., 1971. Internal auditor The Stop and Shop Cos., Inc., Boston, 1962-65, dir. fin. planning and control, 1973-74, corp. controller, 1974-77, v.p., corp. controller, 1977-83, v.p. fin., chief acctg. officer, 1983-86, sr. v.p., chief fin. officer, 1986—; controller Gilchrist Co., Boston, 1969-72; mem. adv. bd. New Eng. region Arkwright Mus. Ins. Co., Norwalk, Conn., 1988-92. Bd. overseers, mem. fin. com. Harvard Cmty. Health Plan, Brookline, Mass., 1985-91; treas. St. Mary's Parish, Randolph, Mass.; mem. gen. bd. Greater Boston YMCA, 1993—, treas., 1995—. Roman Catholic. Home: 360 Beacon St Boston MA 02116-1002 Office: Stop & Shop Cos Inc 1 Quincy Center Plz Quincy MA 02169

MCGLINN, FRANK CRESSON POTTS, lawyer; b. Phila., Nov. 19, 1914; s. John Alexander and Emma Frances (Potts) McG.; m. Louise Cabeen Lea, Sept. 9, 1942; children: Marion McGlinn Lockwood, Louise McGlinn Preston, Alice McGlinn Fetter, Ann Stillwell. AB, U. N.C., 1937; JD, U. Pa., 1940; LLD (hon.), Villanova U., 1970. Assoc. Pepper, Hamilton & Scheetz, Phila., 1945-53; dir. Rep. Fin. Com. of Pa., Phila., 1945-53; v.p., asst. to pres. Al Paul Lefton Co. Advt., Phila., 1953-57; exec. v.p. Fidelity Bank, Phila., 1957-78; sr. v.p. Western Savs. Bank, Phila., 1978-82; exec. v.p. Barra Found., Wyndmoor, Pa., 1982-83; dir. Rittenhouse Trust Co., Phila., 1984—; cons. William Penn Found., 1978-82, Barra Found., 1983-85. Trustee, bd. dirs. Free Libr. Phila., 1948-88, Hist. Soc. Pa., 1978-85; bd. dirs. William Penn Found., 1971-78, Actord Fund Am., 1985—, Walnut St. Theatre, 1969—; mem. Pa. Coun. on the Arts, 1964-71, 79-87; mem. coun. mgrs. Archdiocese of Phila., 1970-89; dir. chmn. ARC, 1949; chmn. cancer Crusade, 1954, Cath. Charities Appeal, 1966; vice chmn. Young Rep. Nat. Com., 1949-51; chmn. Pa. Young Reps., 1949-51; chmn. Rep. Fin. Com., Pa., 1963-65, vice chmn. 1972-76; vice chmn. Rep. Nat. Fin. Com., 1965-77; chmn. NCCJ, Phila., 1961-66, Hon. chmn., 1966-95;. Decorated Purple Heart; knight comdr. Equestrian Order of St. Gregory the Great; recipient Humanitarian award NCCJ, 1967, The Actors Fund Am. medal, 1996. Mem. Merion Cricket Club, Knights of Malta. Republican. Roman Catholic. Avocations: theater, fishing. Home: 729 Millbrook Ln Haverford PA 19041-1210 *Peace-understanding-tolerance in the world can only be achieved through complete freedom of expression and the opportunity to freely question all such expressions. To work toward such a goal is the first step toward one's own success and a better world.*

MCGLOHON, REEVES, education administrator; b. Charlotte, N.C., July 2, 1947; s. Loonis R. and Nan (Lovelace) McG.; m. Peggy Martin; children: Max, Allan, Brooke. AB in Econs., Lenoir Rhyne Coll., 1969; MEd, U. N.C., 1972. Cert. tchr., adminstr., N.C. Tchr. Charlotte (N.C.)/ Mecklenburg Schs., 1969-71; cons. N.C. Dept. Pub. Instrn., Raleigh, 1972-75; exec. asst. Am. Assn. Sch. Adminstrs., Washington, 1975-76; dir. fed. programs N.C. Dept. Pub. Instrn., Raleigh, 1977-82, dep. state supt., 1982-90; asst. supt. Gaston County Schs., Gastonia, N.C., 1991-94; dept. supt. Gaston County Schs., Gastonia, 1995—; bd. dirs. S.E. Regional Edn. Lab., Rsch. Triangle Park, N.C., 1985-90; dir. N.C. Leadership Inst. for Principals, Raleigh, 1979-82. Bd. dirs. Holy Angels, Inc., 1997—, United Way of Gaston Co., 1997. With U.S. Army, 1970-72. Named Top Pub. Mgr. in N.C., Duke U., 1986. Mem. AASPA, Am. Assn. Sch. Adminstrs., Pers. Adminstrs. of N.C., Mt. Holly Rotary Club (pres. 1997), Phi Delta Kappa. Democrat. Baptist. Avocations: golf, gardening. Home: 849 Deerfield Dr Mount Holly NC 28120-1161 Office: Gaston County Schs 943 Osceola St Gastonia NC 28054-5482

MCGLONE, MICHAEL ANTHONY, lawyer; b. New Orleans, Jan. 6, 1951; s. James Godfrey and Dorothy (Barta) McG.; m. Suzanne Blanchard, Nov. 27, 1976; children: Kevin, Kathleen, Meghan. BBA cum laude, Loyola U., New Orleans, 1972, JD, 1975. Bar: La. 1975, U.S. Dist. Ct. (ea. dist.) La. 1975, U.S. Ct. Appeals (5th and 11 cirs.) 1975, U.S. Dist. Ct. (we. dist.) La. 1978, U.S. Dist. Ct. (mid. dist.) La. 1979, U.S. Supreme Ct. 1981. Law clk. to Hon. Herbert W. Christenberry U.S. Dist. Ct., New Orleans, 1975-76; ptnr. Lemle and Kelleher, New Orleans, 1976—. Mem. ABA, ALA, FBA (bd. dirs. New Orleans chpt. 1986—, pres. 1995-96), La. Bar Assn., Southeastern Admiralty Law Inst., New Orleans Bar Assn., Maritime Law Assn., St. Thomas More Inn of Ct. (master barrister), Alpha Sigma Nu, Beta Gamma Sigma. Democrat. Roman Catholic. Home: 4708 N Turnbull Dr Metairie LA 70002-1447 Office: Lemle and Kelleher 601 Poydras St New Orleans LA 70130-6029

MCGLOTHLIN, JAMES W., wholesale distribution executive; b. 1940. Grad., William & Mary Coll. Bar: Va. 1964. CEO United Ctrl. Indsl. Supply Co., Big Rock, Va. Office: United Co Inc PO Box 1280 Bristol VA 24203*

MCGLOWN, BRENDA PRYOR, special education educator; b. Memphis, Tenn., Oct. 31, 1946; d. George and John Ella (Hobbs) Pryor; m. Andrew McGlown III, Dec. 29, 1979; 1 child, Toya Angeliqué. BA, LeMoyne-Owen, 1970; MEd, Memphis State U., 1977. Cert. tchr., Tenn. Tchr. Memphis (Tenn.) City Schs., 1970—; mem. Inservice Com. Spl. Edn., Memphis, 1990-91, Adminstrv. Adv. Com., Memphis, 1992-93. Author: (test) Adaptive Reading Special Needs, 1986-87, (curriculum) Adaptive Social Studies, 1991-92. Mem. Dist. 33 Adv. Bd., Memphis, 1990-92; officer Shelby County Election Commn., Memphis, 1991-92, election official, 1996-97; mem. People's Rescue Mission, South Memphis, 1989-90; vol. Spl. Olympics, 1990. Recipient Tchr. Excellence award Memphis Rotary Club, 1993; named Tchr. of Yr., Coun. of Exceptional Children, 1988; grantee Memphis Rotary Club, 1988-89, 91-92, 96-97. Mem. NEA, Tenn. Edn. Assn., Memphis Edn. Assn., Tenn. Assn. for Children with Learning Disabilities, Zeta Phi Beta Sorority. Avocations: reading, cooking. Home: 5819 W Fox Bend Cv Memphis TN 38115-3804 Office: Grahamwood Elem Sch 3950 Summer Ave Memphis TN 38122-5210

MCGLYNN, BETTY HOAG, art historian; b. Deer Lodge, Mont., Apr. 28, 1914; d. Arthur James and Elizabeth Tangye (Davey) Lochrie; m. Paul Sterling Hoag, Dec. 28, 1936 (div. 1967); children: Peter Lochrie Hoag, Jane Hoag Brown, Robert Doane Hoag; m. Thomas Arnold McGlynn, July 28, 1973. BA, Stanford U., 1936; MA, U. So. Calif., 1967. Cert. secondary tchr., Calif. Rsch. dir. So. Calif. Archives of Am. Art, L.A., 1964-67, Carmel (Calif.) Mus. Art, 1967-69; dir. Triton Mus. Art, Santa Clara, Calif., 1970; archivist, libr. San Mateo County (Calif.) Hist. Soc. Mus., 1972-74; cons. Monterey Peninsula Mus. Art, Calif., 1964—; tchr. art extension Monterey Peninsula Coll., Calif., 1970, San Jose City Coll., 1971; lectr. in field. Author: The World of Mary DeNeale Morgan, 1970, Carmel Art Association: A History, 1987; contbg. author: Plein Air Painters of California, The North, 1986, Orchid Art and The Orchid Isle, 1982, Hawaiian Island Artists and Friends of the Arts, 1989; editor, author of jours. La Peninsula (San Mateo County Hist. Soc.), 1971-75, Noticias (Monterey History and Art Assn.), 1983-88, 95; author of booklets; contbr. articles to profl. jours. Appraiser art work City of Carmel, 1967, City of Monterey, 1981; mem. Friends of Harrison Meml. Libr., Carmel, Friends of Sunset Found., Carmel, Pacific Grove Art Ctr., Monterey Bay Aquarium. Mem. Butte (Mont.) Arts Chateau, Carmel Art Assn. (hon.), Carmel Heritage Soc., Carmel Found., Carmel Residents Assn., Chinese Hist. Soc., Monterey History and Art Assn. (art cons.), Monterey Peninsula Mus. Art (acquisitions bd.), Gallatin County Hist. Soc. (Mont.), Stanford Alumni Assn., Robinson Jeffers Tor House Found. (art cons.), Hawaiian Hist. Soc., Mont. Hist. Soc., Nat. Mus. of Women in Arts, The Westerners, P.E.O., Book Club of Calif. Republican. Avocations: research archives and library. Home and Office: PO Box 7189 Carmel CA 93921-7189

MCGLYNN, JOSEPH LEO, JR., federal judge; b. Phila., Feb. 13, 1925; s. Joseph Leo and Margaret Loretta (Ryan) McG.; m. Jocelyn M. Gates, Aug. 26, 1950; children: Jocelyn, Leo, Timothy, Suzanne, Alisa, Deirdre, Caroline, Elizabeth, Meghan, Brendan. B.S., Mt. St. Mary's Coll., 1948; LL.B., U. Pa., 1951. Bar: Pa. 1952. Asst. U.S. atty. Phila., 1953-60, 1st asst., 1957-60; assoc., then ptnr. Blank Rudenko Klaus & Rome, Phila., 1960-65; judge County Ct. of Phila., 1965-68, Ct. of Common Pleas, 1st Jud. Dist. of Pa., 1968-74, U.S. Dist. Ct. (ea. dist.) Pa., Phila., 1974—; mem. County Bd. Law Examiners, 1961-65, adv. com. bankurptcy rules U.S. Judicial Conf., 1987-93. Mem. bd. mgrs. Phila. Youth Study Ctr., 1961-65. Served with USN, 1943-46, PTO. Mem. Phila. Bar Assn. Office: US Dist Ct 16614 US Courthouse Philadelphia PA 19106

MC GLYNN, SEAN PATRICK, physical chemist, educator; b. Dungloe, Ireland, Mar. 8, 1931; came to U.S., 1952, naturalized, 1957; s. Daniel and Catherine (Brennan) McG.; m. Helen Magdalena Salacz-von Dohnanyi, 4Apr. 11, 1955; children: Sean Ernst, Daniel Julian, Brian Charles, Sheila Ann, Alan Patrick, Shane Joseph. B.S., Nat. U. Ireland, 1951, M.S., 1952; Ph.D., Fla. State U., 1956. Fellow Fla. State U., 1956, U. Wash., 1956-57; mem. faculty La. State U., 1957—, prof. chemistry, 1964—, Boyd prof. chemistry, 1967—, dean Grad. Sch., 1981-82, vice chancellor for research, 1981-91; asso. prof. biophysics Yale U., 1961; Humboldt prof. physics U. Bonn, W.Ger., 1979-80; cons. to pvt. cos. Author: (with others) Molecular Spectroscopy of the Triplet State, 1969, Introduction to Applied Quantum Chemistry, 1971, Photophysics and Photochemistry in the Vacuum Ultraviolet, 1985, The Geometry of Genetics, 1988; editor Wiley-Interscience Monographs in Chem. Physics; contbr. over 400 articles and chpts. to profl. pubs. Fellow Research Corp., 1960-63; Sloan fellow, 1964-68; recipient award Baton Rouge Council Engring. and Sci. Socs., 1962-63; Sr. Scientist award Alexander von Humboldt Found., 1979; Disting. Research medal U. Bologna, Italy, 1979. Mem. Am. Chem. Soc. (S.W. regional award 1967, Fla. sect. award 1970, Coates award 1977), AAAS, Am. Phys. Soc. Research molecular electronic spectroscopy, electronic structure, energy transfer, molecular genetics, bioenergetics, mathematical biology, optoacoustics, optogalvanics. Home: 1056 E Lakeview Dr Baton Rouge LA 70810-4621

MC GOLDRICK, JOHN GARDINER, lawyer; b. Grand View-on-Hudson, N.Y., July 25, 1932; s. Francis Michael and Elizabeth Theresa (Leitner) McG.; m. Cathleen Elinor Cloney, June 5, 1965; children: John Francis, Ann Cathleen. Student, Coll. of Holy Cross, Worcester, Mass., 1950-51; seminarian, S.J., 1951-58; AB, Fordham U., 1957; JD, Georgetown U., 1961. Bar: N.Y. 1962, U.S. Dist. Ct (so. and ea. dists.) N.Y. 1975, U.S. Ct. Appeals (2d cir.) 1975, U.S. Supreme Ct. 1975. Assoc. Lowenstein, Pitcher, Hotchkiss, Amann & Parr, N.Y.C., 1961-66, Kaye, Scholer, Fierman, Hays & Handler, N.Y.C., 1966-69; ptnr. Schulte & McGoldrick, N.Y.C., 1969-81; counsel to Gov. Hugh L. Carey, N.Y., 1981-82; ptnr. Schulte Roth & Zabel LLP, N.Y.C., 1983—; commr. Port Authority N.Y. and N.J., 1982-93, chair audit com., 1985-93; bd. dirs. Com. on Modern Cts., Inc., 1983-94; mem. N.Y.C. Mayor's Com. on Judiciary, 1990-93. Bd. dirs., mem. exec. com. Georgetown U., 1973-79, vice chmn. bd., 1975-79. Fellow Am. Bar Found., Am. Law Inst., N.Y. State Bar Assn. (com. on state constitution 1985-93, chmn. 1987-90, mem. ho. of dels. 1985-91, spl. com. lawyers in pub. svc. 1986-88, com. on fin. 1990-96), Assn. of Bar of City of N.Y. (com. on profl. responsibilities 1974-76, com. on grievances 1976-79, com. profl. discipline 1980, com. 2d century 1982-88, treas., mem. exec. com. 1984-87, com. on govt. ethics 1988-93), Univ. Club. Home: 111 E 80th St New York NY 10021-0334 Office: Schulte Roth & Zabel LLP 900 3rd Ave New York NY 10022-4728

MCGONIGLE, JAMES GREGORY, financial consultant; b. Bklyn., Nov. 17, 1945; s. William John and Helen Bernadette (Dennin) McG.; m. Francine Anne Falango, May 27, 1972; children: MarieElena, Lauren Anne. AAS in Acctg., CUNY, 1972; BS in Fin. summa cum laude, L.I. U., 1980. Cert. fin. planner Internat. Bd. Cert. Fin. Planners. Account exec. Coburn Credit Corp., Rockville Centre, N.Y., 1965-66; asst. credit mgr. UNI-CARD, Greatneck, N.Y., 1966-68; accounts receivable mgr. Granite Leasing Corp., Garden City, N.Y., 1968-73; v.p. Citicorp., N.Y.C., 1973-88; cons. O/E Learning, Inc., Detroit, 1988-90; regional dir. Ednl. Techs., Inc., Troy, Mich., 1989—; adj. faculty Coll. for Fin. Planning, Denver. Vol. Family Svc. Assn., Nassau, N.Y., 1981-84, Better Bus. Bur., Farmingdale, N.Y., 1987—; vol., career advisor L.I. U., Brookville, N.Y., 1990—; treas. W. Tresper Clarke Friends of Arts, 1988-89. Mem. ABA (assoc.), Fin. Mgmt. Assn., Internat. Assn. Fin. Planning, Adelphi Soc. Cert. Fin. Planners, Internat. Assn. Registered Fin. Planners (speaker's bur.), Nat. Assn. Life Underwriters, Nat. Panel Consumer Arbitrators, Nat. Ctr. for Fin. Edn., Inst. Cert. Fin. Planners (bd. dirs. L.I. 1989-92), N.Y. State Assn. Cert. Fin. Planners, Delta Mu Delta. Republican. Roman Catholic. Avocations: bicycling, public speaking, traveling, writing, gardening. Home: 2167 Plum Tree Rd N Westbury NY 11590-6029 Office: 33 Willis Ave Mineola NY 11501-4411

MCGONIGLE, JOHN LEO, JR., civil engineer; b. Pitts., May 2, 1921; s. John L. and Marie (Cannon) McG.; m. Mary Frances McInerney, Oct. 10, 1953; children: Loretta, John III, Maureen, Charles, Thomas, Robert. BS in Civil Engring., Lehigh U., 1942. Registered profl. engr. N.Y., Pa., Conn. Field engr. Bethlehem Steel Corp., N.Y., Boston, 1947-50, resident engr., 1950-57; constrn. mgr. Bethlehem Steel Corp., San Francisco, 1957-67; mgr. estimates Bethlehem Steel Corp., Bethlehem, Pa., 1967-78; project mgr. C. F. Braun, Berkeley Heights, N.J., 1978-83; prin. resident engr. Berger-Lehman Assocs., Rye, N.Y., 1983-93; self-employed project mgmt. cons., 1993—; com. mem. Am. Inst. Steel Constrn., Pitts., 1970-73. Mem. Hanover Twp. (Pa.) Planning Commn. Mem. Am. Soc. Engrs., Lehigh U. Alumni Assn. (pres. San Francisco 1960). Republican. Roman Catholic. Achievements include resident engineer for high level bridges over Passaic River, N.J., Rappahonnock, Va., Missouri River, Annisquam River, Mass., Raritan River, N.J., and Newark Bay; also high rise buildings in Detroit, N.Y., S.I. Ferry Terminal, John Hancock, Boston.

MCGONIGLE, RICHARD THOMAS, lawyer; b. Columbus, Ohio, Jan. 29, 1951; s. Francis Phillip and Mary Lou (Daughtery) McG.; m. Janet Christine Bowser, Aug. 17, 1974; children: Richard K., Michael P., Robin C. BA, St. Leo Coll., 1978; JD, Duquesne U., 1981. Bar: Pa. 1981, Okla. 1986, U.S. Supreme Ct. 1994, U.S. Dist. Ct. (we. dist.) Pa. 1981, U.S. Dist. Cts. (ea., we., and no. dists.) Okla. 1985, U.S. Ct. Appeals (5th and 10th cirs.) 1985. Police officer City of Hilliard, Ohio, 1973-74, City of Virginia Beach, Va., 1974-78; atty. Eckert Seamans Cherin & Mellot, Pitts., 1981-85, Hall, Estill, Tulsa, Okla., 1985-95; of counsel Ronald D. Wood & Assocs., Tulsa, 1995—; faculty mem., co-author seminar materials Nat. Bus. Inst., 1992. Author: (case notes) Duquesne Law Rev., 1979. Pres. Eastwood Lake Homeowners Assn., Owasso, Okla., 1993-96; mem. Associated Builders & Contractors, Inc., Tulsa, 1994. Recipient Acad. Achievement award Franklin County Sheriff's Acad., Columbus, 1973, Honor Grad. award Fraternal Order of Police Assn., Norfolk, Va., 1975, Best Oralist award Mugel Nat. Tax Moot Ct., Buffalo, N.Y., 1980. Mem. ABA, Okla. Bar Assn., Pa. Bar Assn., Tulsa County Bar Assn., Muscogee (Creek) Nation Bar Assn. Republican. Roman Catholic. Avocations: motorcycling, hunting, fishing, camping, reading. Home: 18432 E 90th St N Owasso OK 74055-8019 Office: Ronald D Wood & Assocs 2727 E 21st St Ste 500 Tulsa OK 74114-3536

MC GOON, DWIGHT CHARLES, retired surgeon, educator; b. Marengo, Iowa, Mar. 24, 1925; s. Charles Douglas and Ada Belle (Buhlman) McG.; m. Betty Lou Hall, Apr. 2, 1948; children: Michael, Susan, Betsy, Sarah. Student, Iowa State U., 1942-43, St. Ambrose Coll., Davenport, Iowa, 1943-44; M.D., Johns Hopkins U., 1948. Intern Johns Hopkins Hosp., 1948-49, resident in surgery, 1949-54; cons. in surgery Mayo Clinic, Rochester, Minn., 1957—; Stuart W. Harrington prof. surgery Mayo Med. Sch., 1975-79. Editor-in-chief: Jour. Thoracic and Cardiovascular Surgery, 1977-87; editorial bd.: Circulation, 1970-76, Surgery, 1971-77, Am. Jour. Cardiology, 1969-77, Am. Heart Jour, 1969-76; contbr. numerous articles to profl. jours. Served with USN, 1943-45; with M.C. USAF, 1954-56. Fellow ACS; mem. Am. Assn. Thoracic Surgery (pres. 1983-84), Am. Coll. Cardiology (trustee 1979-83), Am. Surg. Assn., Soc. Clin. Surgery, Soc. Univ. Surgeons, Johns Hopkins Soc. Scholars, Phi Beta Kappa, Alpha Omega Alpha. Presbyterian. Home: 706 12th Ave SW Rochester MN 55902-2028 Office: Mayo Clinic 200 1st St SW Rochester MN 55902-3008

MCGOUGH, DUANE THEODORE, economist, retired government official; b. Rice Lake, Wis., Aug. 3, 1932; s. James Patrick and Josephine Margaret (Huerth) McG.; m. Donna Mae Jones, June 13, 1959. Student, Wis. State Coll., Eau Claire, 1950-52, U. Wis., 1952-54, 56-60; B.S. in Light Constrn. Industry, U. Wis., 1959, M.B.A. in Urban Land Econs., 1962; postgrad., U. So. Calif., 1968-69. Housing mgmt. officer Pub. Housing Adminstrn. Atlanta, 1960-62; program planning analyst Pub. Housing Adminstrn. Phila., 1962-67; program analyst HUD, Washington, 1967-68, 69-70; industry economist HUD, 1970-73, supervisory economist, 1973-77, dir. housing and demographic analysis, 1977-97, govt. tech. rep. ann. housing survey, 1977-83; govt. tech. rep. Am. Housing Survey, 1984-97; acting dep. asst. sec. for econ. affairs (chief economist) HUD, Washington, 1977, 82, 84-85, ret., 1997; U.S. rep housing subcom. UN Econ. Commn. for Europe, Geneva, 1976, 79, 82; HUD rep. Interagy. Com. on Population Rsch., 1978-97, Interagy. Forum on Aging-Related Stats., 1986-97; mem. Fed. Task Force on Household Survey Redesign, 1988-97; mem. policy com. Year 2000Census. Editor: President's Report on Housing Goals, 1974-78, Nat. Housing Prodn. Report, 1980, 82; U.S. Housing Market Conditions Report, 1994-97, FEMA national Emergency Management Program, 1972-97, Housing Consultant, 1997—. With U.S. Army, 1954-56; saxophonist 7th Army Band. Fellow NAt. Inst. Pub. Affairs, 1969; recipient Outstanding Performance award Pub. Housing Adminstrn., Phila., 1966, HUD, 1984, 92, 97, Career Edn. award Nat. Inst. Pub. Affairs, 1968-69, Cert. Spl. Achievement, HUD, 1978, 83, 84, 96, Cert. Superior Svc., HUD, 1988, 95, Cert. Appreciation, Bur. Census, 1990. Mem. Am. Econ. Assn., Am. Real Estate and Urban Econ. Assn., Nat. Economists Club, Lambda Alpha Internat. (v.p. programs 1987-89, chmn. real estate and fin. com. George Washington chpt. 1990-92, dir.-at-large 1992-93). Avocations: music, gardening, rockhounding.

MCGOUGH, WALTER THOMAS, JR., lawyer; b. Pitts., Nov. 7, 1953; s. Walter Thomas and Jane (Fitzpatrick) McG.; m. Rebecca Gai Frazier, June 24, 1978; children: Emily Ann, Walter Thomas III. BA, Princeton U., 1975; JD, U. Va., 1978. Bar: Pa., D.C., U.S. Dist. Ct. (we. dist.) Pa. 1980, U.S. Ct. Appeals (3d cir.) 1983, U.S. Ct. Appeals (6th cir.) 1984, Pa. Supreme Ct. 1978, U.S. Supreme Ct. 1983. Law clk. to judge U.S. Ct. Appeals 3d Cir., Wilmington, Del., 1978-79; law clk. to Hon. William H. Rehnquist U.S. Supreme Ct., Washington, 1979-80; asst. U.S. atty. We. Dist. Pa., 1980-82; assoc. Reed, Smith, Shaw & McClay, Pitts., 1982-86, ptnr., 1987—; assoc. counsel Sen. Select Com. on Secret Mil. Asst. to Iran and the Nicaraguan Opposition, Washington, 1987; mem. lawyers adv. com. U.S. Ct. Appeals (3d cir.), 1987-89, chmn., 1989; atty. Fed. Criminal Justice Def. Panel West Dist. Pa., 1983—. Co-author: federal Appellate Procedure, 3rd Circuit, 1996; contbr. articles to profl. jours. Mem. Allegheny County (Pa.) Bd. Assistance, 1986-90, chmn., 1989-90; bd. visitors H. John Heinz III Pub. Policy and Mgmt., Carnegie-Mellon U., Pitts., 1987—; mem. 3d Cir. Task Force on Rule 11, 1987-89. Mem. Allegheny County Bar Assn. (ethics com. 1983-86, bd. gov.'s 1994—), Allegheny County Acad. Trial Lawyers, Duquesne Club, Ross Mountain Club, World Affairs Coun. Office: Reed Smith Shaw & McClay 435 6th Ave Pittsburgh PA 15219-1809

MCGOVERN, BARBARA ELIZABETH ANN, elementary education educator; b. Newton, Mass., July 24, 1936; d. Joseph and Katherine Frances (Broderick) McG. BS in Edn., Lowell State Tchrs. Coll., 1957; postgrad., Salem State Coll., 1959-64, Andover-Newton Theol. Sem., 1965-68. Cert. tchr., Mass. 2d grade tchr. Thomson Sch., North Andover, Mass., 1957-58; 1st, 4th and 5th grade tchr. Franklin Sch., North Andover, 1958-95, coord. various intergenerational programs, 1970-95, ret., 1995; owner B.E.A.M.S Dreams, North Andover, 1994-95; cons. City of Lawrence Youth Commn., 1993—; panelist Holy Cross Coll., 1993. Camp counselor, 1952-70; tchr. arts and crafts Lawrence Jewish Comty. Ctr., 1954-55; asst. coach 6th-8th grade Girl's Basketball and Softball and Jr. Varsity Softball, 1958-67; sec. Kings Daus., 1958-65; leader Girl Scouts Am., 1960-63; vol. Civil Def., 1965-68; coord. holiday programs Franklin Sch., 1970-93, 95-96, Spl. Friends Program, 1989-95, 96, Hobby Show, 1982-95, 96, Audio Visual com., Pen Pals with City of Lawrence Sch., 1989-95; sec. North Andover PTO, 1970-74, v.p., 1974-79, rep., 1979-84, chair social com., 1972-90; day capt. Ground Observer Corp., Methuen, Mass., 1958-65; softball umpire ASA, 1974-76; supt. Sunday sch. Lawrence St. Congl. Ch., 1958-67, tchr., 1951-57, asst. ch. flower com., 1957-67; leader jr. and sr. pilgrim fellowships, 1957-67, also mem. choir; coach bantam group Pro Bowl, North Reading, Mass., 1990-95; coun. mem. Sch. Improvement, 1985-90; active Matching Families with Shut Ins in Chs., 1994—; mem. Trinitarian Congl. Ch., 1995—, supt. sch., 1996-97; mem. Interfaith Choir, Derry, N.H., 1995—, Meerimac Valley Choral Arts Soc., 1996—; vol. cons. North Andover Sch. Sys., 1995; mem. 350th Anniversary North Andover commn., 1995-96; coord. Carvell chpt. Blind in Merrimack Valley, 1995-96. Recipient citation of recognition Mass. Ho. of Reps., 1988, Congressman Chet Akins, 1988, award Nevins Home, 1988, Point of Light award Eagle Tribine, 1990, Those Who Care award Elder Svcs. of Merrimack Valley, 1990, Living Tribute award Acad. Manor Nursing Home, 1990, plaque Prescott Nursing Home, 1992, Sportsmanship award Lawrence Recreation Women's Softball League, 1989, 90. Mem. AARP, Mass. Intergenerational Network (sec. 1991—), North Andover Tchrs. Assn., Lawrence Sports Club (life, bd. dirs. 1972-73, v.p. 1973-75, pres. 1975-84). Republican. Avocations: softball, ten pin bowling, Mickey Mouse, drawing, painting. Home: 42 York St Andover MA 01810-2601 Office: Franklin Sch Cypress Ter North Andover MA 01845

MCGOVERN, FRANCES, retired lawyer; b. Akron, Ohio, Apr. 18, 1927; d. Bernard Francis and Pauline A. (Menegay) McG. AB, U. Akron, 1948; LLB, Case Western Res. U., 1949; Bar: Ohio 1949, U.S. Dist. Ct. (no. dist.) Ohio 1951, U.S. Supreme Ct. 1963, U.S. Ct. Appeals (6th cir.) 1975. Pvt. practice, Barberton, Ohio, 1949-52; assoc. Motz, Morris, Wilson & Quine, Akron, Ohio, 1952-55; ptnr. Quine & McGovern, Akron, 1955-60, 63-65; atty. Ohio Edison Co., Akron, 1965-78, sr. atty., 1978-88, assoc. gen. counsel, 1988-89. Mem. Ohio Gen. Assembly, 1955-60, chmn. judiciary com., 1959-60; mem., chmn. Ohio Pub. Utilities Commn., 1960-63; mem. Dept. Labor Employment Security Bd., Washington, 1963-68; vice chmn. Charter Commn. Summit County, 1969-70; del., mem. platform com. Dem. Nat. Conv., 1960, del., 1964; trustee N.E. Ohio Coll. Medicine, Rootstown, 1979-81, U. Akron, 1973-82; pres. United Way, 1987-89, also bd. dirs.; sec. Employee Spl. Svcs. Commn., 1974-91; bd. dirs. Med. Edn. Found. of N.E. Ohio U. Coll. Medicine, 1982—, Archbishop Hoban H.S., 1984-90, U. Akron Found., 1973—, Summit County Hist. Soc., 1997—; chmn. county charter com. Akron Regional Devel. Bd., 1990-92; active League Women Voters, Akron Edn. Found., 1993-96, Summit 2000, Progress Through Preservation, 1996—. Author: Written on the Hills-The Making of the Akron Landscape, 1996. Recipient Achievement award Kappa Kappa Gamma, 1962, Akron Beacon Jour., 1968, Disting. Svc. award United Way, Akron, 1969, Disting. Alumni award U. Akron, 1989, others. Mem. Akron Bar Assn. (St. Thomas More award 1997). Democrat. Roman Catholic.

MC GOVERN, GEORGE STANLEY, former senator; b. Avon, S.D., July 19, 1922; s. Joseph C. and Frances (McLean) McG.; m. Eleanor Stegeberg, Oct. 31, 1943; children: Ann, Susan, Teresa, Steven, Mary. BA, Dakota Wesleyan U., 1945; MA, Northwestern U., 1949, PhD, 1953. Prof. history and polit. sci. Dakota Wesleyan U., 1949-53; exec. sec. S.D. Dem. Party, 1953-55; mem. 85th-86th Congresses, 1st Dist. S.D., 1957-61; spl. asst. to Pres., dir. Food for Peace, 1961-62; U.S. senator from S.D., 1963-81, chmn. senate select com. on nutrition and human needs; pres. Middle East Policy Coun.; chmn. Ams. for Common Sense, Washington, 1981-82; guest lectr. Northwestern U., Evanston, Ill., Duke U., Columbia U., Cornell U., Munich, Berlin, and numerous others in U.S. and Europe, from 1981. Author: The Colorado Coal Strike, 1913-14, 1953, War Against Want, 1964, Agricultural Thought in the Twentieth Century, 1967, A Time of War, A Time of Peace, 1968, (with Leonard Guttridge) The Great Coalfield War,

1972, An American Journey, 1974, Grassroots, 1978. Democratic candidate for Pres. U.S., 1972; candidate for presdl. nomination Dem. Party, 1984. Served as pilot USAAF, World War II. Decorated D.F.C. Mem. Am. Hist. Assn. Methodist. Clubs: Mason (33 deg., Shriner), Elk, Kiwanian. *

MCGOVERN, JAMES P., congressman; b. Worcester, Mass., Nov. 20, 1959; m. Lisa Murray. BA, Am. U., 1981, MA in Pub. Administration, 1984. Aide U.S. Senator George McGovern (Dem. South Dakota); spokesman, legis. dir., sr. aide U.S. Congressman Joe Moakley (Dem. South Boston); mem. 105th Congress from 3rd Mass dist., 1997—; elected regional whip 105th Congress from 3rd Mass dist., 1997—; mgr. George McGovern for Pres., 1984; delivered McGovern presdl. nomination speech Dem. Nat. Convention, San Francisco, 1984; leader Congressional Investigation on El Salvador, 1989; mem. U.S. Congresssional House Transportation and Infrastructure Com., 1997—. Candidate for U.S. Congress, 1996; vol. Mt. Carmel House; bd. dirs. Jesuit Internat. Vols. Office: Ho of Representatives 512 Cannon House Office Bldg Washington DC 20515*

MCGOVERN, JOHN HUGH, urologist, educator; b. Bayonne, N.J., Dec. 18, 1924; s. Patrick and Mary (McGovern) McG.; m. Mary Alice Cavazos, Aug. 2, 1980; children by previous marriage: John Hugh, Robert, Ward, Raymond. BS, Columbia U., 1947; MD, SUNY, Bklyn., 1952. Diplomate Am. Bd. Urology. Rotating intern Bklyn. Hosp., 1952-53; asst. resident in surgery Bklyn. VA Hosp., 1953-54; with urology N.Y. Hosp., 1954-56; exchange surg. registrar West London Hosp., Eng., 1956-57; resident in urol. surgery N.Y. Hosp., 1957-58, rsch. asst. pediatric urology, 1958-59, asst. attending surgeon James Buchanan Brady Found., 1959-61, assoc. attending surgeon, 1961-66, attending surgeon, 1966—; asst. in surgery Med. Coll. Cornell U., 1957-59, asst. prof. clin. surgery, 1959-64, assoc. prof., 1964-72, prof., 1972—; attending staff in urology Lenox Hill Hosp., 1969—, in-charge urology, 1969-83; cons. urology Rockefeller Inst., St. Vincent's Hosp., Mercy Hosp., Phelps Meml. Hosp.; chmn. coun. on urology Nat. Kidney Found., 1982. Contbr. articles to profl. jours., chpts. to books. Lt. M.C., U.S. Army, 1942-45. Recipient Conatvoy mos medal Chile, 1975, Tree of Life award Nat. Kidney Found., 1990; named Huesped de Honor, Mimunicipalidad de Guayaquil (Ecuador), 1976; award in urology Kidney Found. N.Y., 1977, Sir Peter Freyer medal, Galway, Ireland, 1980. Fellow N.Y. Acad. Medicine (exec. com. urol. sect. 1968-72, chmn. 1972), ACS (credentials com. 1991—), Am. Acad. Pediatrics (urological); mem. AMA (diagnostic and therapeutic tech. assessment bd. 1991—, diagnostic and therepautic tech. assessment program panel 1991, DATTA panel 1991—), Am. Assn. G.U. Surgeons, N.Y. State Med. Soc. (chmn. urol. sect. 1975), Med. Soc. County N.Y., Am. Urol. Assn. (hon. mem. 1994—, pres.-elect 1988-89, pres. 1989-90, pres. N.Y. sect. 1979-80, N.Y. rep. exec. com. 1982-87, socioecons. com. 1987, chmn. fiscal affairs rev. com. 1987, chmn. awards com. 1990, time and place com. 1989-90), N.Y. State Urol. Soc. (exec. com. 1982—), Pan Pacific Surg. Assn., Am. Assn. Clin. Urologists (pres.-elect 1987-88, pres. 1988-89, bd. dirs. 1984—, mem. interpersonal rels. com. 1975—, govt. rels. com. 1989-90, program com. 1989-90, nominating com. 1989-90), Assn. Am. Physicians and Surgeons, Pan Am. Med. Assn. (diplomate 1981—), Urol. Investigators Forum, Soc. Pediatric Urology (pres.-elect 1979-80, pres. 1980-81), Am. Trauma Soc., Kidney Found. (med. adv. bd. N.Y. sect., trustee, 1979) Société Internationale d'Urologie (exec. com. U.S. sect.); hon. mem. Sociedad Peruana de Urologia, Sociedad Guatemale de Urología, Sociedad Ecuadorians de Urología, Royal Coll. Surgeons (London). Home and Office: 53 E 70th St New York NY 10021-4941

MCGOVERN, JOHN JOSEPH, retired air pollution control executive; b. Pitts., June 21, 1920; s. John J. and Philomene (Henigin) McG.; m. Doris I. Judy, Sept. 25, 1947 (dec. 1986); children: John Joseph (dec.), Joseph Edgar (dec.), Daniel Paul, Michael James, William Patrick, Edward Vernon; m. Patricia E. Carothers, Apr. 1987. B.S., Carnegie Inst. Tech., 1942, M.S., 1944, Sc.D., 1946. Fellow, then sr. fellow Mellon Inst., Pitts., 1945-50; head research services Mellon Inst., 1958-71; dir. ednl. and research services Carnegie-Mellon U., 1971-73, asst. dir. div. sponsored research, 1973; asst. dir. Carnegie-Mellon Inst. Research, 1974-76; info. scientist U. Pitts., 1976—; edn. services mgr. Air Pollution Control Assn., 1979-83, mem. services mgr., 1983-87; now ret.; asst. chief chemist, then chief chemist Koppers Co., Inc., 1950-58. Editor: The Crucible, 1970-76. Mem. Spectroscopy Soc. Pitts. (chmn. 1951), Am. Chem. Soc. (sec. Pitts. 1960, chmn. sect. 1964, dir.), PITTCON (pres. 1951). Club: Chemists (pres. Pitts. 1968-69). Home: 600 Chatham Park Dr P3 Pittsburgh PA 15220-2423

MCGOVERN, MICHAEL BARBOT, lawyer; b. N.Y.C., Mar. 6, 1947; s. Michael Malachy and Annette (Barbot) McG.; m. Christine Anne Beaudet, Sept. 2, 1972; children: Kathleen, Ellen, Maura. AB, Georgetown U., 1969, JD, 1972; LLM (Taxation), George Washington U., 1987. From assoc. to ptnr. Wilkes & Artis, Washington, 1973-79; sole practice Washington, 1980, 84-87; ptnr. Lambert, Griffin & McGovern, Washington, 1981-84, Venable, Baetjer, Howard & Civiletti, Washington, 1987-93, Montedoninco, Hamilton & Altman, D.C., 1994—. Bd. dirs. Hist. Soc. Washington, 1984-93; co-founder, vice-chair, bd. dirs. Greater Bethesda-Chevy Chase Coalition Inc., 1986—; pres. Westmoreland Citizens Assn. Inc., 1988-90; mem. Leadership Washington, 1987—. Capt. USAFR, 1969-82, bd. dirs., Montgomery Co. Historical Soc., 1997—. Recipient Distinguished Service award Fed. Bar Assn., 1978. Mem. ABA, Fed. Bar Assn., D.C. Bar Assn., Md. State Bar Assn., Columbia Country Club (Chevy Chase), Met. Club (Washington), Barristers, John Carroll Soc. Republican. Catholic. Home: 5414 Albemarle St Bethesda MD 20816-1825 Office: Montedonico Hamilton & Altman 5301 Wisconsin Ave NW Ste 400 Washington DC 20015-2015

MCGOVERN, PATRICK J., communications executive. BA in Physics, M.I.T. With Internat. Data Corp., Framingham, Mass., 1964—, chmn., 1976—; with IDG Comm. Inc., Framingham, 1987—, now CEO. Office: Internat Data Group One Exeter Plaza 15th Fl Boston MA 02116*

MCGOVERN, R(ICHARD) GORDON, food company executive; b. Norristown, Pa., Oct. 22, 1926; s. James Joseph and Marion (Stritzinger) McG.; m. Julia Merrow, June 4, 1955; children: Lucinda, Jennifer, Martha, Douglas. Student, Williams Coll., 1944-45, Coll. Holy Cross, 1945-46; AB, Brown U., 1948; MBA, Harvard U., 1950. With Pepperidge Farm, Inc., 1956-80, pres., 1968-80; dir., v.p. Campbell Soup Co., 1976-80, exec. v.p., 1980, pres., 1980-89, ret., 1989; bd. dirs. Merrow Machine Co., Newington, Conn. Lt. USNR, 1944-46, 52-54. Mem. Am. Mktg. Assn., Am. Soc. Bakery Engrs., Grocery Mfrs. Assn. (past. bd. dirs.), Phi Beta Kappa, Sigma Xi, Delta Upsilon. Home: 182 Lounsbury Rd Ridgefield CT 06877-4725

MCGOVERN, THOMAS AQUINAS, retired utility executive; b. N.Y.C., Mar. 2, 1933; s. Thomas Aquinas and Helen Frances (Carroll) McG.; m. Miriam Anne Howley, July 16, 1955; children: Cecilia, Louise, Pamela. BS in History, Coll. of the Holy Cross, 1954; MA in Econs., L.I. U., 1965. Dep. asst. Consol. Edison Co. of N.Y., N.Y.C., 1958-61, supts. asst., 1961-66, asst. supt., 1967-68, supt., 1968-69, staff dir., 1969-70, asst. to exec. v.p., 1970-72, exec. dir., 1972-82, asst. v.p., 1982-89, v.p., 1989-95; sr. assoc. John Hall Co., Danbury, Conn., 1995—; mem. Edison Elec. Inst. Sec. Commn., Washington, 1976-90, Mailers' Tech. Adv. Com., Washington, 1990-91; vice-chmn. Nat. Postal Coun., Washington, 1982—; pres. D.C.K. Mgmt. Corp., N.Y.C., 1982-94; mem. Real Estate Bd. N.Y., N.Y.C., 1988-94. Mem. N.Y.C. (N.Y.) Health and Hosps. Security Adv. Com., 1985; pres. Westchester County Police Meml., White Plains, N.Y., 1987—. With U.S. Army, 1954-56. Recipient Svcs. to Nation and FBI award FBI, N.Y.C., 1984, Svc. to Law Enforcement Community award N.Y. State Chiefs of Police, Albany, N.Y., 1989, Appreciation for Svc. award N.Y. State Fedn. of Police, Briarcliff Manor, N.Y., 1989, Svc. to Orgns. award FBI Marine Corps Assn., Cresskill, N.J., 1989, Svc. to Orgns. award N.Y.C. Honor Legion, Richmond Hill, N.Y. Mem. KC, VFW, Am. Legion, Assn. of U.S. Army, U.S. Naval Inst., FBI Marine Corps Assn., Friendly Sons of St. Patrick, VFW, Pi Gamma Mu. Roman Catholic. Avocations: U.S. mil. history, post card collecting, toy soldier collecting, Royal Doulton china collecting. Office: John Hall & Co PO Box 187 Glen Ridge NJ 07028

MCGOVERN, THOMAS BOARDMAN, physician, pediatrician; b. St. Louis, Sept. 26, 1940; s. John Thomas and Hazel Marie (Boardman) McG.; m. Jane Emly Keyes, June 17, 1967; children: John Thomas, Erin Kathleen, Ann Michal, Robert Andrew. AB, Dartmouth Coll., Hanover, N.H., 1962; MD, U. Mo., Columbia, 1966. Diplomate Am. Bd. Pediatrics, 1976, 89. Maj. USAF, 1966-72; rotating intern M. Co. Gen. Hosp., Indpls., 1966-67; flight med. officer USAF, Korea, Calif., 1967-69; pediatric resident USAF Hosp., K. AFB, Miss., 1969-71; pediatrician USAF, Westover AFB, Mass., 1971-72, partnership, Binghamton, N.Y., 1972-86, Assocs. in Medicine, Johnson City, N.Y., 1986-91, United Med. Assocs., Johnson City, N.Y., 1991—; pediatric dept. chmn. Binghamton Gen. Hosp., 1980-82, sec.-treas. med. staff, 1982-84; pediatric dept. chmn. Lourdes Hosp., Binghamton, 1984-86, 93-95; clin. asst. prof. pediatrics Health Science Ctr., Syracuse, N.Y., 1980—. Cons. pediatrician Handicapped Children's Assn., Johnson City, 1973-78, mem. bd. dirs. 1980-91. Fellow Am. Acad. Pediatrics; mem. N.Y. State Med. Soc., Broome County Med. Soc. (bd. dirs. 1992-93). Republican. Roman Catholic. Home: 4 Cornell Ave Binghamton NY 13903 Office: United Med Assocs PC 601 Riverside Dr Johnson City NY 13790-2549

MCGOVERN, THOMAS JOHN, environmental engineer; b. Rockville Ctr., N.Y., May 31, 1968; s. Thomas Edward and Barbara Ann (Bukoski) McG. BSCE, U. Hartford, 1990; JD, St. Johns Sch. Law, 1995. Engr. Suffolk County Dept. Health Svcs., Farmingville, N.Y., 1988, N.Y.C. Dept. Environ. Protection, 1989; environ. engr. Camp Dresser and McKee, Woodbury, N.Y., 1990—. Contbr. articles to profl. jours.; speaker in field. Mem. ABA, Water Environ. Fedn., Tau Beta Pi, Sigma Xi, Alpha Chi. Home: 24 Sycora Ln Central Islip NY 11722 Office: Camp Dresser & McKee 100 Crossways Park Dr W Woodbury NY 11797-2012

MC GOVERN, WALTER T., federal judge; b. Seattle, May 24, 1922; s. C. Arthur and Anne Marie (Thies) McG.; m. Rita Marie Olsen, June 29, 1946; children: Katrina M., Shawn E., A. Renee. B.A., U. Wash., 1949, LL.B., 1950. Bar: Wash. 1950. Practiced law in Seattle, 1950-59; mem. firm Kerr, McCord, Greenleaf & Moen; judge Municipal Ct., Seattle, 1959-65, Superior Ct., Wash., 1965-68, Wash. Supreme Ct., 1968-71, U.S. Dist. Ct. (we. dist.) Wash., 1971—; chief judge, 1975-87; mem. subcom. on supporting personnel Jud. Conf. U.S., 1981-87, chmn. subcom., 1983, mem. adminstrn. com., 1983-87, chmn. jud. resources com., 1987-91. Mem. Am. Judicature Soc., Wash. State Superior Ct. Judges Assn., Seattle King County Bar Assn. (treas.), Phi Delta Phi. Club: Seattle Tennis (pres. 1968). Office: US Dist Ct US Courthouse 5th Fl 1010 5th Ave Seattle WA 98104-1130

MCGOWAN, GEORGE VINCENT, public utility executive; b. Balt., Jan. 30, 1928; s. Joseph H. and Ethna M. (Prahl) McG.; m. Carol Murray, Aug. 6, 1977; children by a previous marriage: Gregg Blair, Bradford Kirby. BS in M.E., U. Md., 1951; LHD (hon.), Villa Julie Coll., 1991, Loyola Coll., Md., 1992. Registered profl. engr., Md. Project engr. nuclear power plant Balt. Gas & Electric Co., 1967-72, chief nuclear engr., 1972-74, pres., chief operating officer, 1980-87, chmn. bd. dirs.; CEO, 1988-92, chmn. exec. com., 1993—, mgr. corp. staff services, 1974-78, v.p. mgmt. and staff services, 1978-79; bd. dirs. Balt. Life Ins. Co., McCormick & Co., Life of Md., Inc., UNC Inc., Orgn. Resources Counselors, Inc., NationsBank, N.A., GTS Duratek, Scientech, Inc. Bd. dirs. U. Md. Med. Sys., United Way Ctrl. Md., Coll. Bound Found., Md. Pride of Balt.; chmn. Balt. Symphony Orch. Recipient Disting. Alumnus award U. Md. Coll. Engring., 1980, U. Md., 1987, Disting. Marylander award Advt. and Profl. Club Balt., 1992, Disting. Citizen award U. Md., 1991, Disting. Citizen of Yr. award Balt. Coun. Boy Scouts Am., 1991, Disting. Alumnus award Balt. Poly. Inst., 1992, Nat. Multiple Sclerosis Soc. Corp. Honoree, Md. chpt., 1993, Outstanding Vol. Fund Raiser award Nat. Soc. Fund Raising Execs., 1993, Pub. Affairs award Md. Bus. Coun., 1994, United States Energy award, 1995, Jr. Achievement Ctrl. Md. Bus. Hall of Fame, 1996. Mem. ASME (James N. Landis medal 1992), Am. Nuclear Soc., U.S. Energy Assn. of the World Energy Coun., Engring. Soc. Balt. (Founders Day award 1988), Caves Valley Golf Club, The Ctr. Club (pres. bd. govs.), U. Md. M. Club, Talbot Country Club, Annapolis Yacht Club, Md. Club. Presbyterian. Office: Balt Gas & Electric Co PO Box 1475 Baltimore MD 21203-1475

MCGOWAN, HAROLD, real estate developer, investor, scientist, author, philanthropist; b. Weehawken, N.J., June 23, 1909; s. Sylvester and Grace (Kalbfleish) McG.; m. Anne Cecelia McTiernan, Jan. 15, 1938; children—Linda Anne, Harold Charles, Janice Marie. Ed., Bklyn. Poly. U., Pratt Inst., N.Y. U.; student, N.Y. Tech.; ed., Hubbard U. (Eng.); D.Sc., Coll. Fla. Chmn. bd. Atomic Rsch. Inc.; pres. Harold McGowan Builders; owner, developer Central Islip Shopping Center, Central Islip Indsl. Center; developer, builder Brinsley Gardens, Rolling Green, Slater Park, Clover Green, Maple Acres, Wheeler Acres; owner-donor Little League Baseball Pks. Sculptures include: Bless Them; Victory, Eternity, Love and Hate, Triumph; author: Green Flight, (originator) The Thoughtron Theory of Life and Matter, Race with Death across the Sahara, The Incorrigibles, The Frigid Trap, The Shah's Swiss Secret, Another World for Christmas, The Spirit of Christmas in Words and Sculpture, The Making of a Universalist, The Journeyman, $800,000 for Love, Beyond the Visible, Shock after Shock, Christmas Stories, Short Stories, Born Again, You Are Forever, Black Shroud Over Bagdad, The Gold Mine; mural Back to Creation; holder U.S. patent to form one-piece plywood corner units, U.S. patent apparatus for forming one-piece plywood corner units. Hwy. commr., Suffolk County; chmn. Recreation & Parks-Islip; past dir. Suffolk County Girl Scouts; land donor St. John of God R.C. Ch., The Episcopal Ch. of the Messiah, Ctrl. Islip Sch. Dist. Recipient Winston Churchill Medal of Wisdom, 1986, Wisdom Hall of Fame, Beverly Hills, Calif., 1970; Churchill fellow, 1989. Mem. AAAS, IEEE, Explorers Club, Mensa Internat. Avocations: sculpture, art, philanthropy. Address: 28 2nd Ave Central Islip NY 11722-3012 *To become a really whole and successful person, one should recognize the efforts and good will of those living and dead who developed the culture, the fruits of which he enjoys, and repay his benefactors by contributing more to that society than he takes and also by doing good deeds to make the society better than he found it. He must also strive to understand the world and his relationship to it and know that the universe is neither capricious nor mysterious, that miracles do not happen. Everything and every action can only occur within the bounds of the laws of physics, chemistry, biology and communication. He must further realize that he is eternal and the basic purpose of human life is to become aware of and to live by these universal laws. The acme of a person's accomplishments would be his comprehension of the structure of the physical universe, the processes of life, the nature of his mind and his own being and intelligence. Our intellect, like eternity, is unbounded. It is inde*

MC GOWAN, JAMES ATKINSON, business executive, financial consultant; b. De Soto, Mo., Nov. 10, 1914; s. James Electra and Dora Mercer (Atkinson) McG.; m. Barbara Louise Bevan, Apr. 5, 1941; m. Margaret Mercier Johns, Dec. 21, 1974; children: James Michael, John Barrie, Susan Alexandra, Jean Christine. AA, Little Rock Jr. Coll., 1934; BSChemE, Iowa State U., 1936. With Aluminum Co. Am., 1936-79; dist. sales mgr. Aluminum Co. Am., Cleve., 1959-60; gen. mgr. indsl. sales Aluminum Co. Am., Pitts., 1962-67, v.p., 1967-75; exec. v.p. Aluminum Co. Am., 1975-79; v.p. Amcan Trading Co. subs. Am. Can Corp., Pitts., 1980-81; fin. cons.; arbitrator Better Bus. Bus. Mem. AICE, Chem. Mfg. Assn. (dir.), Aluminum Assn., Nat. Assn. Corrosion Engrs., Sigma Chi. Republican. Episcopalian. Clubs: Duquesne, Fox Chapel Golf, Rolling Rock.

MCGOWAN, JOHN EDWARD, JR., clinical microbiology educator, epidemiologist, infectious diseases specialist; b. Poughkeepsie, N.Y., June 30, 1942; s. John Edward and Doris Robinson (Wearne) McG.; m. Linda Kay Hudson, May 28, 1967; 1 child, Angela Kay. B.M.S., Dartmouth Coll., 1965; M.D., Harvard U., 1967. Diplomate Am. Bd. Internal Medicine, Am. Bd. Infectious Diseases, Am. Bd. Pathology in Med. Microbiology. Intern, resident Harvard Service, Boston City Hosp., 1967-69; research fellowship Thorndike Lab. Harvard Med. Sch., 1971-72; instr. Harvard Med. Sch., Boston, 1972-73; asst. prof. Emory Med. Sch., Atlanta, 1973-76, assoc. prof., 1977-81, prof. pathology and medicine, 1982—; prof. epidemiology Emory U. Rollins Sch. Pub. Health, 1992—; dir. microbiology Grady Meml. Hosp., Atlanta, 1982—; chmn. panel on microbial devices FDA, 1992-94. Assoc. editor, Infection Control and Hosp. Epidemiology jour., 1980-92; contbr. 200 sci. articles to profl. jours. Governing bd. Young Singers of Callanwolde, Decatur, Ga., 1981-86; treas. Leafmore Creek-Park Club, Decatur, 1982-84. Sr. surgeon USPHS, 1969-71. Fellow Infectious Diseases Soc. Am. (antimicrobial agts. com. 1980-93, tuberculosis com. 1993—, governing bd. 1995—), So. Soc. for Clin. Investigation, Am. Coll. Epidemiology; mem. Am. Soc. for Microbiology (div. chmn. 1982-84, governing bd. 1984-87), Soc. Hosp. Epidemiologists of Am. (pres. 1981), Am. Hosp. Assn. (panel on infections in hosps. 1989-95). Office: Emory U Rollins Sch Pub Health Dept Epidemiology 442 GCR Atlanta GA 30322

MCGOWAN, JOSEPH ANTHONY, JR., news executive; b. Sheridan, Wyo., May 16, 1931; s. Joseph Anthony and Eda B. (Harris) McG.; m. Patricia Donnette Mitchell, June 7, 1958 (div. 1980); children: Joseph Howard, Colleen Diane; m. Catherine Doris Netick, June 12, 1982; stepchildren: Nancy Malick, Diane Malick, Laura Malick. B.S., U. Wyo. Newsman AP, Miami, Fla., 1960-64; bur. chief AP, New Delhi, India, 1965-68, Lima, Peru, 1968-70, Indpls., 1970-75, Boston, 1975-78, Denver, 1978—; lectr. U. Denver, 1978—, Colo. U., Boulder, 1978—, Northeastern U., Boston, 1975-78. Scoutmaster Boy Scouts Am., Sudbury, Mass., 1977-78. Served with USNR, 1953-55. Named Disting. Alumnus, U. Wyo., 1992; Knight Internat. Press fellow to Pakistan, 1995. Mem. Denver Press Club (bd. dirs. 1989-92), Press Club Boston, Colo. Assn. Commerce and Industry (communications council 1986-89), Sigma Delta Chi (Big Hat award 1983). Republican. Avocations: bird hunting; cross country skiing; fishing, cross country bicycling. Office: AP 1444 Wazee St Ste 130 Denver CO 80202-1326

MCGOWAN, MICHAEL BENEDICT, investment banker; b. Wilkes-Barre, Pa., Jan. 21, 1950; s. John W. and Catherine (Hore) McG.; m. Nancy King, May 24, 1980; children: Nicholas King, Grace Caroline. BArch, U. Ark., 1977; MBA, U. Va., 1981. Architect Cromwell Firm, Little Rock, 1976-79; v.p. Oliver Carr Co., Washington, 1981-85; sr. v.p. Stephens Inc., Little Rock, 1985—. Mem. econ. cluster team Clinton-Gore Transition Team, Washington, 1992. Home: PO Box 22 Turner Mountain Rd Ivy VA 22945 Office: Stephens Inc 111 Center St PO Box 3507 Little Rock AR 72201

MCGOWAN, PATRICK FRANCIS, lawyer; b. N.Y.C., July 23, 1940; s. Francis Patrick and Sonia Veronica (Koslow) M.; m. Patricia Neil, June 6, 1964; children: Susan Claire, Kathleen Anne. BA, Rice U., 1962; JD, U. Tex.-Austin, 1965. Bar: Tex. 1965, U.S. Tax Ct., 1972, U.S. Ct. Appeals (5th cir.) 1969, U.S. Ct. Appeals (fed. cir.) 1993, U.S. Supreme Ct. 1970. Briefing atty. Tex. Supreme Ct., Austin, Tex., 1965-66; ptnr. Strasburger & Price, Dallas, 1966—; pres., chmn. bd. Tex Lex, Inc. Contbr. numerous articles on trademark, copyright and franchise law. Bd. advisors Dallas Ft. Worth Sch. Law. Mem. ABA (forum com. on franchising, trademark and unfair competition com., patent, trademark and copyright law sect.), State Bar Tex. (intellectual property sect., com. continuing legal edn.), Coll. State Bar Tex. (faculty Franchising inst., 1987—, Intellectual Property Inst., 1992—, S.W. Legal Found. Patent Law Inst., 1992—, Practising Law Inst. 1996), Dallas Bar Assn. (dir. intellectual property law section, 1994—), Internat. Anti Counterfeiting Assn., Tex. Law Review Editors Assn., Phi Delta Phi. Office: Strasburger & Price 4300 NationsBank Plz 901 Main St Dallas TX 75202-3714

MCGOWAN, THOMAS RANDOLPH, religious organization executive; b. Balt., Apr. 19, 1926; s. Robert and Mary (Miller) McG.; m. Bernice A. Bernard, May 20, 1967 (dec. Nov. 1981); children: Howard, James, Terry; m. Roedean Olivia Oden, Feb. 9, 1985; children: Karen White, Kevin, Kurt. AA, Oakland Jr. Coll., 1964; postgrad., San Francisco State Coll., 1964-68; BS, U. Md., 1978. Lt. security police Oakland (Calif.) Army Base, 1955-60; chief motor pool San Francisco Procurement Agy., Oakland, 1960-64, contract specialist, 1964-68; contract specialist Harry Diamond Labs., Washington, 1968-79, br. chief procurement divsn., 1972-79; chief procurement directorate Yuma (Ariz.) Proving Ground, 1979-82; dir. ecumenism Roman Cath. Diocese of Oakland, 1983—; dir. African Am. Cath. Pastoral Ctr., Diocese of Oakland, 1991—. Convenor Interreligious Coun. of Oakland, 1988—; trustee Greater Oakland Interfaith Network, 1989-92; mem. East Oakland Renewal Task Force, 1990—; bd. dir. Columbia (Md.) Found., 1972-74, chmn., 1975-79; div. Bd. Cons., Graymoor, N.Y., 1990—; bd. dirs. Thea Bowman Manor, Oakland, 1989—. With U.S. Army, 1944-46. Mem. Knights of Peter Claver, Rotary. Democrat. Avocations: tennis, woodworking. Home: 139 Pinto Dr Vallejo CA 94591-8451

MC GOWIN, WILLIAM EDWARD, artist; b. Hattiesburg, Miss., June 2, 1938; s. William Edward and Emily (Ratliff) Mc G.; m. Claudia DeMonte, May 28, 1977; children: Leah, Jill. BS, U. So. Miss., 1961; MA, U. Ala., 1964. prof. art SUNY, Old Westbury, 1978—, Coll. Old Westbury; mem. faculty Corcoran Gallery Art, 1966-77, head sculpture dept., 1967-74; lectr. in field. One-man shows include Corcoran Gallery Art, Washington, 1962, 71, 75, Martha Jackson Gallery, N.Y.C., 1968, Am. Cultural Ctr., Paris, 1974, Mus. Modern Art, Paris, 1978, Brooks Jackson Gallery, Iolas, N.Y.C., 1978-80, Fendrick Gallery, Washington, 1977-80, U. Colo., New Orleans Contemporary Art Ctr., 1982, Project Studios 1, L.I., N.Y., Cranbrook Acad., Bloomfield Hills, Mich., 1983, Art Park, Lewiston, N.Y., 1984, Gracie Mansion Gallery, N.Y.C., 1985, 86, 89, Mus. Fine Arts, Miami, Jones, Troyer Gallery, Washington, 1987, 89, 91, Boca Raton (Fla.) Mus., 1991, Margulis-Taplin Gallery, Miami, 1993, Paris-New York-Bangkok Gallery, Bangkok, Thailand, 1994, Grey Art Gallery, NYU, 1995; group shows include Contemporary Mus., Houston, Miss. Mus. Art, Whitney Mus., N.Y.C., Detroit Inst. Art, Guggenheim Mus., Speed Mus., Ky., Cologne (Germany) Art Fair, Zurich (Switzerland) Art Fair; represented in permanent collections Phillips Collection, Washington, Indpls. Mus. Art, Addison Mus. Art, Andover, Mass, Corcoran Gallery Art, Nat. Collection Fine Arts, Washington, New Orleans Mus. Art, Whitney Mus. Am. Art, N.Y.C., Guggenheim Mus., N.Y.C., Hirshorn Gallery and Sculpture Garden; permanent commn. U.S. Gen. Svc. Adminstrn., 1979, VA, Indpls., 1985, Percent for Art, N.Y.C., 1992, City of Jubai, Saudi Arabia, 1993, Dallas Rapid Transit Authority, 1994, Queens Co. N.Y. Superior Ct., 1996. Recipient Oscar for painting, 1977, Painting prize 9th Internat. Painting Festival, Cagnes-sur-Mer, France, 1977, Miss. Arts and Letters award for visual arts, 1980; Nat. Endowment for Arts grantee, 1967-68, 79-80, pub. outdoor sculpture grantee, 1977, Cassandra Found. grantee. Home and Office: 96 Grand St New York NY 10013-2660

MCGRADY, CLYDE A., secondary school principal. Prin. A. S. Staley Mid. Sch., Americus, Ga. Recipient Elem. Sch. Recognition award U.S. Dept. Edn., 1989-90. Office: A S Staley Middle Sch 915 N Lee St Americus GA 31709-3047*

MCGRADY, DONALD LEE, retired Spanish language educator; b. Greenhurst, Md., Jan. 17, 1935; s. Francis Guy and Lida Amelia (Ewing) McG.; m. Marina Ignacia Pedroza, Sept. 6, 1958; children: Martha, Sandra, Daniel, Arthur. BA, Swarthmore Coll., 1957; AM, Harvard, 1958; PhD, Indiana Univ., 1961. Instr. U. Tex., Austin, 1961-63, asst. prof., 1963-64; asst. prof. U. Calif., Santa Barbara, 1964-67, assoc. prof., 1967-69; assoc. prof. U. Va., Charlottesville, 1969-71, prof., 1971-94; prof. emeritus, 1994—; vis. assoc. prof. U. Calif., Berkeley, 1969. Author: La Novela Histórica en Colombia, 1877-1959, 1962, Mateo Alemán, 1968, Critical edition of Jorge Isaacs María, 1970, Bibliografía sobre Jorge Isaacs, 1971, Jorge Isaacs, 1972, Critical edition of Cristóbal de Tamariz Novelas en verso, 1974, Critical edition of Lope de Vega's La francesilla, 1981, Edition of Lope de Vega's La bella malmaridada, 1986, Critical edition of Lope de Vega, Fuente Ovejuna, 1993, Critical Edition of Lope de Vega, Peribañez, 1996. Guggenheim fellow Guggenheim Found., N.Y., 1972-73, NEH fellow NEH, Washington, 1976-77. Mem. Asociación Internacional de Hispanistas, Asociación Internacional Siglo de Oro., Comediantes. Home: 530 N 1st St Charlottesville VA 22902-4613

MCGRADY, STEPHANIE JILL, speech communications educator; b. Enid, Okla., May 25, 1950; d. James Monroe and Evelyn Fern (Pursell) Payne; m. Charles Radford, May 10, 1969 (div. 1976); children: Stacy, Steven; m. Ron L. McGrady, Nov. 28, 1992. BA, No. Okla. State U., 1978; MA, Okla. State U., 1979; postgrad., UCLA, Ctrl. State U., Okla. State U., U. LaVerne, U. Calif. Riverside. Lic. tchr., Okla., Calif.; C.C. credential, Calif. Tchr. English, drama, speech, music Crescent (Okla.) Pub. Schs., 1980-86; tchr. English and drama Palmdale (Calif.) H.S., 1986-89, Desert Winds H.S., Lancaster, Calif., 1988-91; tchr. English Highland H.S., Palmdale, 1991-92; instr. speech comm. Antelope Valley Coll., Lancaster, Calif., 1988—; edn. program advisor, Antelope Valley Acad. Ctr. Chapman Univ., Palmdale; tchr. power cons. Antelope Valley Union H.S., Palmdale, 1987-88, reader's theatre cons., Lancaster and Palmdale, 1987-92, mentor tchr., Lancaster, 1991-92, curriculum writer, Lancaster, 1989-92; owner, mgr.

Golden Goose, Palmdale; tchr. ceramics, porcelain dolls. Author: (screenplays) Color Blind, 1988, Forever Yours, 1992; performed stage, TV, movies; directed more than 25 prodns. Bd. dirs. Cedar St. Theatre, Lancaster, 1987-89, mem. adv. bd., 1988-89; bd. dirs. Palmdale Repertory Theatre, 1992, mem. adv. bd., 1994—. Mem. SAG, Am. Fedn. TV Actors. Republican. Avocations: theatre, piano, writing, painting, ceramics.

MCGRATH, ANNA FIELDS, librarian; b. Westfield, Maine, July 4, 1932; d. Fred Elber and Nancy Phyllis (Tarbell) Fields; m. Bernard McGrath (div.); children: Timothy, Maureen, Patricia, Colleen, Rebecca. BA, U. Maine, Presque Isle, 1976; MEd, U. So. Maine, 1979; MLS, U. R.I., 1982. Libr. U. Maine, Presque Isle, 1976-86, assoc. libr. dir., 1986-89, interim libr. dir., 1989-92, dir., 1992-94, spl. collection libr., 1994—. Editor: County: Land of Promise, 1989. Mem. Friends of Aroostook County Hist. Ctr. at Libr., U. Maine-Presque Isle. Mem. Maine Libr. Assn., Friends of Aroostook County Hist. Ctr. at Libr. U. Maine-Presque Isle, Inst. Noetic Scis., Am. Mensa. Office: U Maine Libr 181 Main St Presque Isle ME 04769-2844

MCGRATH, CHERYL JULIA, elementary education educator; b. Milw., Feb. 17, 1947; d. Elmer William and Marjorie (Bleiler) Scherkenbach; m. Robert Edward McGrath, July 25, 1970; children: Edward, Erin, Molly. BA in Edn., Alverno Coll., Milw., 1969. Cert. tchr., Wis. Tchr. grade 1 Greenfield (Wis.) Pub. Schs., 1969-72, St. Lawrence Sch., Wisconsin Rapids, Wis., 1972-80; tchr. grades 7-8 Our Lady Queen of Heaven, Wisconsin Rapids, Wis., 1980-85; substitute work Wisconsin Rapids (Wis.) Pub. Schs., 1987-88, tchr. grade 2, 1988—; bd. mem. Girl Scouts Samoset Coun., Stevens Point, Wis., 1979-84; com. Math Their Way, 1992-94, Report Card, 1990-93, Able Learner, 1990-92, Peer Tutoring, 1989-91, Wisconsin Rapids Pub. Schs. Recipient Advance Religious Cert. award Diocese of Lacrosse, Wis., 1978. Mem. NEA, Wis. Rapids Edn. Assn., Wis. Edn. Assn., Alverno Coll. Alumnae Assn. Republican. Roman Catholic. Avocations: reading, boating, early childhood development, travel, computer programming. Home: 4711 Townline Rd Wisconsin Rapids WI 54494-8988 Office: Wisconsin Rapids Pub Schs 510 Peach St Wisconsin Rapids WI 54494-4663

MCGRATH, DON JOHN, banker; b. Springfield, Ill., June 15, 1948; s. Donald John and Wilma P. (Beck) McG.; m. Patricia Ratti, May 7, 1983. B.S. in Mktg., U. Ill., 1970; M.B.A., Boston U., 1973. Investment officer Banque Nationale de Paris, San Francisco, 1975-76, treas., San Francisco and Los Angeles, 1976-78, v.p. and treas., 1978-80; v.p., treas. Bank of the West, San Francisco, 1980, v.p., CFO, 1980-81, sr. v.p., CFO, 1981-84, sr. exec. v.p., CFO, 1984-87, sr. exec. v.p., COO, 1987-91, pres., COO, 1991-95, pres., CEO, 1996—. Bd. dirs. Commonwealth Club Calif., Nature Conservancy Calif., Dominican Coll. San Rafael, Calif. Mem. Calif. Bankers Assn., Univ. Club, St. Francis Yacht Club (San Francisco), Diablo (Calif.) Country Club. Office: Bank of the West 1450 Treat Blvd Walnut Creek CA 94596-2168

MCGRATH, EUGENE R., utility company executive; b. New York City, 1942. BSME, Manhattan Coll., 1963; MBA, Iona Coll., 1980. With Consol. Edison Co. N.Y., N.Y.C., 1963—, v.p., 1978-82, exec. v.p., 1982-89, pres., COO, 1989-90, chmn. pres., CEO, 1990—, also bd. dirs. Office: Consol Edison Co NY Inc 4 Irving Pl Rm 1610 New York NY 10003-3502

MCGRATH, J. NICHOLAS, lawyer; b. Hollywood, Calif., Feb. 12, 1940; m. Margaret Crowley, Oct. 4, 1980; children: Nicholas Gerald, Molly Inez. BA with honors, Lehigh U., 1962; LLB magna cum laude, Columbia U., 1965. Bar: D.C. 1966, Calif. 1969, U.S. Supreme Ct. 1970, Colo. 1971. Law clk. to presiding justice U.S. Ct. Appeals (D.C. cir.), 1965-66; law clk. to assoc. justice Thurgood Marshall U.S. Supreme Ct., Washington, 1967-68; assoc. Pillsbury, Madison & Sutro, San Francisco, 1968-70; from assoc. to ptnr. Oates, Austin, McGrath, Aspen, Colo., 1970-80; ptnr. Austin, McGrath & Jordan, Aspen, 1980-82; sole practice Aspen, 1982—; chmn. grievance com. Colo. Supreme Ct., 1989, mem. 1984-89. Mem. bd. editors Columbia Law Review, 1964-65. Vice chair Pitkin Co. Home Rule Charter Com., 1976-78; mem. Planning Commn., Town of Basalt, Colo., 1992-93, town trustee, 1993-94; bd. dirs. CLE in Colo., Inc., 1995-96, lectr. nat. and state CLE programs on ethics, litigation and land use subjects; pres. Basalt Children's Recreation Fund, Inc., 1994—; chair Basalt Hwy. 82 Citizens Task Force, 1996—; mem. Aspen-Pitkin Co. Alt. H Hwy 82 Task Force, 1996-97, cmty. forum task force on Pitkin Co. charter, 1997—; bd. dirs. Club 20. Mem. Colo. Bar Assn. (v.p. 1991-92), Assn. Trial Lawyers Am., Pitkin County Bar Assn. (pres. 1977). Democrat. Avocations: skiing, tennis, computers. Office: 600 E Hopkins Ave Ste 203 Aspen CO 81611-2933

MCGRATH, JAMES CHARLES, III, financial services company executive, lawyer, consultant; b. Davenport, Iowa, May 25, 1942; s. James Charles and Genevieve (Clarke) McG.; m. Sherbourne Everett, Apr. 11, 1970. BA, U. Notre Dame, 1964; JD, U. Iowa, 1967. Bar: Iowa 1967, D.C. 1971, U.S. Ct. Mil. Appeals 1974, U.S. Ct. Appeals (D.C. cir.) 1971, U.S. Supreme Ct. 1970. Spl. agt. FBI, Balt., N.Y.C., 1967-71; trial atty. Dept. Justice, Washinton, 1971-75; dir. investigations Am. Express Co., N.Y.C., 1975-77, v.p. corp. security, 1978-82, sr. v.p. security, 1982-89; pres. McGrath Internat., Inc., 1989—; mem. overseas security adv. coun. U.S. State Dept., 1985-88; bd. dirs. Barringer Techs. Inc., New Providence, N.J. Mem. Soc. Former Spl. Agts. FBI, Am. Soc. Indsl. Security (chmn. white collar crime com. 1985-88), Internat. Assn. Credit Card Investigators (exec. adv. bd. 1985-88), Iowa State Bar Assn., D.C. Bar Assn., U.S. C. of C. (white collar crime adv. panel 1979—), Debordieu Club (Georgetown, S.C.), Phi Delta Phi. Office: McGrath Internat Inc PO Box 1384 Georgetown SC 29442-1384

MCGRATH, JAMES EDWARD, chemistry educator; b. Easton, N.Y., July 11, 1934; s. Thomas Augustine and Marguerite Monica (Hiland) McG.; m. Marlene Mary Potter, May 9, 1959; children: Colleen McGrath Kraft, Patricia McGrath Hoover, Matthew, Barbara, Elizabeth McGrath Throckmorton, Joseph. BS in Chemistry, St. Bernadine of Siena Coll., 1956; MS in Chemistry, U. Akron, 1964, PhD in Polymer Sci., 1967. Rsch. chemist rsch. divsn. Rayonier, Inc., Whippany, N.J., 1956-59, Goodyear Tire & Rubber Co., Akron, Ohio, 1959-65; mem. staff Inst. Polymer Sci., U. Akron, 1965-67; sr. rsch. chemist Union Carbide Corp., Bound Brook, N.J., 1967-69, project scientist, 1969-72, rsch. scientist, 1972-74, rsch. scientist, group leader, 1974-75; asst. prof. chemistry Va. Poly. Inst. and State U., Blacksburg, 1975-76, assoc. prof. chemistry, 1976-79, prof. chemistry, 1980-87; dir. Materials Inst. Va. Poly. Inst. and State U., 1987-89, prof. dept. chem., co-dir. polymer materials and interface lab., 1979—, Ethyl prof. polymer chemistry, 1986—, dir. Ctr. for Polymer Adhesives and Composites, 1989—, Univ. disting. prof., 1996—; bd. dirs. ChemFab Inc., N.H.; mem. fire safety report com. NAS/NRC; mem. external adv. com. High Performance Polymers and Ceramics Ctr., Clark Atlanta U. Author, editor: Polyimides: Materials, Chemistry and Characterization, 1989; co-author (with Noshay): Block Copolymers: Overview and Critical Survey, 1977; mem. editl. bd. Jour. Polymer Sci., 1987—, Polymer, 1990—, High Performance Polymeric Polymers, 1990—; adv. bd. Jour. Polymer Sci., 1989—, Advances in Polymer Sci. Capt. U.S. Army, 1957. Recipient H.F. Maric award Polymer divsn. Am. Chem. Soc., 1996; named Va. Scientist of Yr., 1997; named to SPE Plastics Hall of Fame, 1997. Mem. NAS (mem. nat. materials bd. 1992-95), NAE, Soc. Plastics Engrs. (Internat. Rsch. award 1987, Outstanding Achievement award 1992). Republican. Roman Catholic. Avocations: music, tennis, travel. Office: Va Poly Inst Ctr Polymeric Adhesives and Composites 2108 Hahn Hall Blacksburg VA 24061-0344

MCGRATH, JAMES THOMAS, real estate investment company executive; b. N.Y.C., Nov. 10, 1942; s. Thomas James and Mary Ita (Finnegan) McG.; m. Paulette L. Franck, Aug. 16, 1980; 1 child, Tara (dec.). BS in Acctg., Providence Coll., 1964. CPA, N.Y. Sr. auditor Coopers & Lybrand, N.Y.C., 1968-72, mgmt. cons., 1972-74; group controller IU Internat. Corp., Phila., 1974-77; v.p. fin. Taylor Engring. Corp. subs. IU Internat., Detroit, 1977-78; controller Pool Co. subs. Enserch Corp., Houston, 1978-85; sr. v.p. fin., treas. Lone Star Gas Co. subs. Enserch Corp., Dallas, 1985-91; pres. McGrath & Assocs., Inc., Dallas, 1991—. Bd. dirs. ARC, Dallas chpt., 1990-93. Lt. USN, 1964-68. Mem. AICPA, Dallas Athletic Club, St. Vincent de Paul Soc. Republican. Roman Catholic. Avocations: golf, cooking, skiing, scuba diving, sailing. Home and Office: 2838 Colleen Dr Garland TX 75043-1215

MCGRATH, JOHN FRANCIS, utility executive; b. Freeport, N.Y., May 4, 1925; s. John Francis and Catherine Frances (Maune) McG.; m. Catherine Elizabeth Zainor, June 22, 1946; children—Joseph R., Susan M., Martha J., Thomas J. B.S., U.S. Mcht. Marine Acad., 1944; A.B., Muhlenberg Coll., Allentown, Pa., 1948; J.D., St. John's U., Bklyn., 1952; grad. bus. exec. program, U. Minn. Grad. Sch., 1973. Bar: N.Y., 1952, Minn., 1958, Fla.-Emeritus, 1991. Atty. firm Casey, Lane & Mittendorf, N.Y.C., 1953-58; jud. inquiry asst. counsel N.Y. State Supreme Ct., 1957-58; atty. U.S. Steel Corp., Duluth, Minn., 1958-64; with Minn. Power & Light Co., Duluth, 1964-83; sr. v.p. Minn. Power & Light Co., 1978-83, gen. counsel, 1975-83, sec., 1979-88; adj. prof., gen. counsel Coll. St. Scholastica, Duluth; vol. atty. Bay Area Legal Svcs., Tampa, Fla. Bd. dirs. emeritus Duluth Cathedral H.S., 1972, St. Anne's Residence, Duluth, 1963-83; commr. Seaway Port Authority, Duluth, 1966-76, pres., 1970, 75; bd. dirs., sec. Good Samaritan Fund Greater Sun City Center, Fla.; mem. Hillsborough County Bd. Zoning Adjustment, 1992-94. With U.S. Mcht. Marine, 1943-46. Mem. Minn. Bar Assn., St. Louis County Bar Assn. Democrat. Roman Catholic. Home: 2036 Hampstead Cir Sun City Center FL 33573-7350

MCGRATH, JUDITH, broadcast executive; b. Scranton, PA, 1952. Former fashion copywriter Mademoiselle; now pres. MTV, New York, NY. Office: MTV 1515 Broadway New York NY 10036

MCGRATH, KATHRYN BRADLEY, lawyer; b. Norfolk, Va., Sept. 2, 1944; d. James Pierce and Kathryn (Hoyle) Bradley; children: Ian M., James D. AB, Mt. Holyoke Coll., 1966; JD, Georgetown U., 1969. Ptnr. Gardner, Carton & Douglas, Washington, 1979-83; dir. div. investment mgmt. SEC, Washington, 1983-90; ptnr. Morgan, Lewis & Bockius, LLP, Washington, 1990—. Named Disting. Exec. Pres. Reagan, 1987. Mem. Fed. Bar Assn. (exec. council securities law com.). Office: Morgan Lewis & Bockius LLP 1800 M St NW Washington DC 20036-5802

MC GRATH, LEE PARR, public relations executive, author; b. Robstown, Tex.; d. James Carl and Margaret Marden (Russ) Parr; m. Richard J. McGrath, Nov. 5, 1955 (div. 1975); children: John Parr, Margaret Lee, Maureen Alison; m. Robert Lansing Phipps, Jan. 1, 1989. B.A., So. Methodist U., 1955. Book reviewer Dallas Morning News, 1953, New Orleans Times-Picayune, 1956; guest editor Mademoiselle mag., 1952; chmn. bd. McGrath/Power Assocs., N.Y.C., 1973-93; chmn. bd. dirs. McGrath/Crossen Assocs., Richmond, Va., chmn., 1993—; pub. rels. cons. Waldenbooks, Campbell Soup Co., Reebok, N.Y. Times Mag. Group, Citibank. Author: Creative Careers For Women, 1968, Do-It-All-Yourself Needlepoint, 1971, What Is a Father?, 1969, What Is a Mother?, 1969, What Is a Grandmother?, 1970, What Is a Grandfather?, 1970, What is a Brother?, 1971, What Is a Sister?, 1971, What Is a Friend?, 1971, What Is a Pet?, 1971, Celebrity Needlepoint, 1972, Housekeeping With Antiques, 1971. Recipient Prix de Paris Vogue, 1954. Mem. Pub. Rels. Soc. Am., Am. Soc. Journalists and Authors, Cousteau Soc. (bd. dirs.), Cosmopolitan Club, Phi Beta Kappa. Home: Bolan Hall Plantation Ridgeland SC 29936 Office: McGrath/Crossen Assocs 5805 River Rd Richmond VA 23226-3313

MCGRATH, MARY HELENA, plastic surgeon, educator; b. N.Y.C., Apr. 12, 1945; d. Vincent J. and Mary M. (Manning) McG.; m. Richard H. Simon, Apr. 11, 1970; children: Margaret E. Simon, Richard M. Simon. BA, Coll. New Rochelle, 1966; MD, St. Louis U., 1970; MPH, George Washington U., 1994. Lic. surgeon, D.C. Resident in surg. pathology U. Colo. Med. Ctr., Denver, 1970-71, intern in gen. surgery, 1971-72, resident in gen. surgery, 1971-75, chief resident in gen. surgery, 1975-76; resident in plastic and reconstructive surgery Yale U. Sch. Medicine, New Haven, Conn., 1976-77; chief resident plastic and reconstructive surgery Yale U. Sch. Medicine, New Haven, 1977-78; fellow in hand surgery U. Conn.-Yale U., New Haven, 1978; instr. in surgery divsn. plastic and reconstructive surgery Yale U. Sch. Medicine, New Haven, 1977-78, asst. prof. plastic surgery, 1978-80; attending in plastic and reconstructive surgery Yale-New Haven Hosp., 1978-80, Columbia-Presbyn. Hosp., N.Y.C., 1980-84, George Washington U. Med. Ctr., Washington, 1984—, Children's Nat. Med. Ctr., Washington, 1985—; asst. prof. plastic surgery Columbia U., N.Y.C., 1980-84; assoc. prof. plastic surgery Sch. Medicine, George Washington U., Washington, 1984-87, prof. plastic surgery, 1987—; attending physician VA Hosp., West Haven, Conn., 1978-80; attending in surgery Hosp. Albert Schweitzer, Deschapelles, Haiti, 1980; co-investigator Charles W. Ohse Fund, Yale U. Sch. Medicine, 1979; prin. investigator various rsch. grants, 1979-89; historian, bd. dirs. Am. Bd. Plastic Surgery, 1991-95; guest examiner certifying exam., 1986-88, 95-97; specialist site visitor Residency Rev. Com. for Plastic Surgery, 1985, 87, 91, 94; presenter in field; cons. in field; senator med. faculty senate George Washington U., bd. govs. Med. Faculty Assocs. Co-editor: (with M.L. Turner) Dermatology for Plastic Surgeons, 1993; assoc. editor: The Jour. of Hand Surgery, 1984-89, Plastic and Reconstructive Surgery, 1989-95, chmn. nominating com., 1994—; contbr. book chpts.: Problems in General Surgery, 1985, Human and Ethical Issues in the Surgical Care of Patients with Life-Threatening Disease, 1986, Problems in Aesthetic Surgery, Biological Causes and Clinical Solutions, 1986; guest reviewer numerous jours.; contbr. articles, abstracts to profl. jours. Fellow ACS (bd. govs. 1995—, exec. com. 1996—, chmn. adv. coun. for plastic surgery 1995—, chmn. adv. coun. chmns. surgical specialists 1996—); mem. AAAS, AMA, Am. Surg. Assn., Am. Assn. Hand Surgery (exec. sec. 1988-90, rsch. grants com. 1983-86, chmn. edn. com. 1983-88, 1st prize ann. resident contest 1978, numerous other c ms., D.C. chpt. program ann. meeting chmn. 1992, v.p. 1993-94, pres. 1994-95), Am. Assn. Plastic Surgeons (pub. info. com. 1988-89, James Barrett Brown com. 1990-92, rsch. and edn. com. 1992-95), Am. Burn Assn., Am. Soc. for Aesthetic Plastic Surgery (FDA implant task force 1990—, pub. edn. com. 1991-92, sci. rsch. com. 1990—), Am. Soc. Maxillofacial Surgeons, Am. Soc. Plastic and Reconstructive Surgery (chmn. ethics com. 1985-87, chmn. device/tech. evaluation com. 1993-94, bd. dirs. 1994-96, mem. ednl. found. bd. dirs. 1985-96, treas. 1989-92, v.p. 1992-93, pres.-elect 1993-94, pres. 1994-95), Am. Soc. Reconstructive Microsurgery (mem. edn. com. 1992-94), Am. Soc. Surgery of Hand (chmn. 1987 ann. residents' and fellows conf. 1986-87, mem. rsch. com. 1988-90), Assn. Acad. Chmn. Plastic Surgery (mem. prerequesite tng. com. 1990-92, mem. com. aesthetic surgery tng. 1992-94), Assn. Acad. Surgery, D.C. Met. Area Soc. Plastic and Reconstructive Surgeons, Internat. Soc. Reconstructive Surgery, Met. D.C. Soc. Surgery Hand, N.Y. Surg. Soc., Northeastern Soc. Plastic Surgeons (chmn. sci. program com. 1991, chmn. fin. com. 1992-93, treas. 1993-96, pres.-elect 1996-97), Plastic Surgery Rsch. Coun. (chmn. 1990), Surg. Biology Club III, The Wound Healing Soc., Washington Acad. Surgery, Washington Med. and Surg. Soc. Office: George Washington U # 6B-422 2150 Pennsylvania Ave NW Washington DC 20037-3201

MCGRATH, MICHAEL ALAN, state government officer; b. Trenton, N.J., Oct. 27, 1942; s. Lyman Levitt and Ada Frances (Hofreiter) McG.; m. Marsha Louise Palmer, Aug. 6, 1966; children: David Patrick, Stephen Gregory, Christopher Andrew. AA, Daytona Beach Jr. Coll., 1967; BA, Stetson U., 1969. Supr. 1st Trust Co., St. Paul, 1969-72; v.p. Internat. Dairy Queen, Inc., Bloomington, Minn., 1972-84; dir. ops. WISCECO, Inc., Bloomington, 1984; bus. mgr. McGraw-Hill, Inc., Edina, Minn., 1985; pres. Policy Advisors, Inc., Bloomington, 1986; treas. State of Minn., St. Paul, 1987—; mem. State Bd. Investment, State Exec. Coun., 1987—; bd. dirs. Minn. State Retirement Systems, St. Paul; Minn. rep. Pub. Fin. Network, 1989—. Mem. editorial bd. Pension Fund News, 1988-90. Chmn. bd. dirs. Urban Concerns Workshop, Inc., St. Paul, 1984-86; sec. League Minn. Human Rights Commn., Mpls., 1985-86; chmn. sen. dist. 41 Dem. Farm Labor Party, 1984-86, treas. 3d congl. dist., New Hope, Minn., 1986, pres. Dem. Farm Labor Club, Bloomington, 1982-84; bd. dirs. The Learning Ctr., 1996—. With USAF, 1962-66. Mem. Nat. Assn. State Treas. (midwest v.p. 1988-89, sec.-treas. 1990-94, sr. v.p. 1994-95, pres. 1995-96, coun. of state govts., fin. com. 1993-94, long-range planning com. 1995, exec. com. 1995—), Coun. of Instnl. Investors (co-chair 1997—), Govt. Fin. Officers Assn., Nat. Assn. State Auditors, Comptrs. and Treas. (exec. com. 1995—, nat. electronic benefits transfer coun., 1995—). Office: Office of Treasury State Minn 50 Sherburne Ave Ste 303 Saint Paul MN 55155-1470

MCGRATH, PATRICK J., advertising agency executive; b. Bronx, N.Y., May 9, 1934; s. Patrick J. and Mary Clare (Bird) McG.; m. Patricia Barbara Pullets, June 29, 1957; children: James, Maryann, Deann, Brinn, Kristian. B.S., Fordham U., 1956. Product mgr. Vicks Products div. Richardson-Merrell, 1956-60; sr. v.p. Benton & Bowles, 1960-69; pres. Jordan, McGrath, Case & Taylor Inc. (formerly Case & McGrath), 1969—. Office: Jordan McGrath Case & Taylor Inc 445 Park Ave New York NY 10022-2606

MCGRATH, RICHARD PAUL, lawyer; b. Chgo., Aug. 10, 1929; s. John Francis and Helen Leone (Hoyer) M.; m. Luisa Sacco y Artze, Aug. 12, 1956; children: Lisa, Deborah, Holly. BA magna cum laude, Georgetown U., 1951; JD cum laude, Harvard U., 1954. Bar: D.C. 1954, N.Y. 1955, Mass. 1957, Conn. 1960, U.S. Supreme Ct. 1965. Assoc. Hughes, Hubbard, Blair and Reed, 1954-57; corp. counsel Raytheon Co., 1957-60; assoc. Cummings & Lockwood, Stamford, Conn., 1960-63, ptnr., 1963—; gen. counsel, corp. sec. Internat. Exec. Svc. Corps, 1990—, mem. coun., 1990—. Author: Proxy Regulation; mem. editl. bd. Harvard Law Rev., 1952-54; contbr. articles to profl. jours.; panelist law seminars. Past pres. Fairfield County Coun. Boy Scouts Am. Mem. ABA, Conn. Bar Assn. (chmn. corp. law com. 1984-86, fee disputes arbitration com. 1980-84), Pi Gamma Mu, Eta Sigma Phi, Gold Key Soc., Stamford Rotary Club (past pres.), Woodway Country Club (Darien, Conn., bd. govs., sec. 1983-91). Avocations: golf, trap, chess. Office: Cummings & Lockwood 4 Stamford Plz Stamford CT 06904-0120

MCGRATH, THOMAS J., lawyer, writer, film producer; b. N.Y.C., Oct. 8, 1932; m. Mary Lee McGrath, Aug. 4, 1956 (dec.); children: Maura Lee, J. Connell; m. Diahn Williams, Sept. 28, 1974; 1 child, Courtney C. B.A., NYU, 1956, J.D., 1960. Bar: N.Y. 1960. Assoc. Milbank, Tweed, Hadley & McCloy, N.Y.C., 1960-69; ptnr. Simpson, Thacher & Bartlett, N.Y.C., 1970-95; retired, 1995; lectr., writer Practicing Law Inst., 1976—, Am. Law Inst. ABA, 1976-81; bd. dirs. Fast Food Devel. Corp. Author: Carryover Basis Under Tax Reform Act, 1977; contbg. author: Estate and Gift Tax After ERTA, 1982; producer: feature film Deadly Hero, 1977. Bd. dirs. N.Y. Philharm.; trustee Am. Austrian Found., Tanzania Wildlife Fund. With U.S. Army, 1953-54. Fellow Am. Coll. Trust and Estate Coun.; mem. ABA, N.Y. State Bar Assn., Assn. Bar City N.Y. Home: 988 5th Ave New York NY 10021-0143 Office: Simpson Thacher & Bartlett 425 Lexington Ave New York NY 10017-3903

MC GRATH, WILLIAM RESTORE, transportation planner, traffic engineer; b. Stratford, Conn., Oct. 4, 1922; s. Thomas Christopher and Alpha Retta (Perry) McG.; m. Lillian Joyce DeAngelis, Mar. 9, 1945; children: Brian, David, Raymond, Harold, Vincent, Mary, Kevin, Rita, Beverly, Nora, Margaret. B.C.E., Rensselaer Poly. Inst., 1950; diploma, Yale Bur. Hwy. Traffic, 1951. Registered profl. engr. Fla. Mem. faculty Yale Bur. Hwy. Traffic, New Haven, 1951-55; dir. traffic and parking City of New Haven, 1955-63; transp. coordinator Boston Redevel. Authority, 1963-68; commr. dept. traffic and parking City of Boston, 1968-70; v.p. Raymond Parish Pine & Weiner, Tarrytown, N.Y., 1970-79; mgr. traffic and parking Daniel, Mann, Johnson & Mendenhall, 1980-83; ptnr. McGrath, O'Rourke & Assocs., 1983-85; owner/mgr. McGrath Engring., Cape Coral, Fla., 1985-87; transp. planner Lee County Dept. Transp. & Engring., 1987-94; safety coord. 5 counties S.W. Fla. Regional Planning Coun., 1996—; cons. AID, Madras, India, 1963, Dublin, Ireland, 1965; Cons. World Trade Center, Moscow, USSR, 1974. Mem. exec. com. Met. Area Planning Council, Boston, 1965-70, Gov.'s Council on Transp., 1968-70; mem. urban ecology adv. council Inst. Ecology, 1973—. Served with USNR, 1942-45. Mem. NSPE, Inst. Transp. Engrs. (hon., nat. pres. 1973, chmn. equal opportunity com., chmn. U.S. legis. com.), Transp. Rsch. Bd., Fla. Engring. Soc., Sigma Xi, Tau Beta Pi, Chi Epsilon. Roman Catholic. Home: 215 SE 14th Ct Cape Coral FL 33990-1799 Office: SWFRPL 4980 Bayline Dr Fort Myers FL 33917-3909

MCGRATTAN, MARY K., state legislator; b. N.Y.C.. RN, St. Catherine's Hosp. Sch. of Nursing. Mem. town coun. Town of Ledyard, Conn., 1977-83, mayor, 1983-91; pres. Conn. Conf. of Municipalities, 1990-91; mem. Conn. Ho. of Reps., Hartford, 1993—. Mem. Ledyard Dem. Town Com. Address: 13 Lynn Dr Ledyard CT 06339-1312 Office: Conn Ho of Reps State Capitol Hartford CT 06106

MC GRAW, DARRELL VIVIAN, JR., state attorney general; b. Mullens, W.Va., Nov. 8, 1936; s. Darrell Vivian and Julia (ZeKany) McG.; m. Jorea Marple; children: Elizabeth, Sarah, Darrell, Elliott. AB, W.Va. U., 1961, JD, 1964, MA, 1977. Bar: W.Va. 1964. Gen. atty. Fgn. Claims Settlement Commn., U.S. Dept. State, 1964; counsel to gov. State of W.Va., 1965-68; pvt. practice Charleston, Shepherdstown and Morgantown, 1968-76; judge W.Va. Supreme Ct. Appeals, Charleston, 1977-88, chief justice, 1982, 83; atty. gen. State of W.Va., Charleston, 1996—. Served with U.S. Army, 1954-57. Fellow W.Va. U., Nat. Ctr. Edn. in Politics/Ford Found. Fellow Am. Polit. Sci. Assn. Democrat. Office: Office of Atty Gen 1900 Kanawha Blvd E Rm E-26 Charleston WV 25305-0009

MCGRAW, DELOSS HOLLAND, illustrator, painter; b. Okemah, Okla., Feb. 1, 1945. Student, Ea. Ctrl. State Coll., 1963-65, Otis Art Inst., L.A., 1965-67; BA, Calif. State Coll., Long Beach, 1969; MFA, Cranbrook Acad. Art, 1972. Commissioned mural Whittier Inst., La Jolla, Calif., 1989, bronze sculptor Homart Corp., L.A., 1990, sculpture and painting Carlsbad Libr. Ctr., Calif., 1991-94, mural Luce, Forward & Assocs., San Diego, 1992, set design Shakespeare Festival, L.A., 1994; exhibited at The Book in Art, U. Art Mus., Calif. State U., Laguna Beach, 1986, Book as Art, Victoria and Albert Mus., London, 1987; one-man shows include La Maison Visinand, Montreux, Switzerland, 1988, The Death of Cock Robin, DeSaisset Mus., Santa Clara (Calif.) U., 1991, A Mus. in the Making, Scottsdale (Ariz.) Ctr. for Arts, 1991, Calif. Gothic, Mary Ryan Gallery, N.Y., 1994. *

MCGRAW, DONALD JESSE, biologist, historian of science, writer; b. Altadena, Calif., Oct. 27, 1943; s. Jesse E. and Mary L. (Hajostek) McG.; m. Laura Lee Hansen, July 13, 1968; children: Adrienne, Holly, Rachel. BS in Biol. Scis., Calif. State Poly. Coll., 1965; MS, Utah State U., 1967; PhD, Oreg. State U., 1976. Registered microbiologist Am. Acad. Microbiology. Research asst. microbiology Utah State U., 1965-66, teaching asst. food and aquatic microbiology, 1966-67; grad. teaching asst. gen. biology Oreg. State U., 1970-72, instr., 1972-73; tchr. phys. and biol. scis. U.S. Bur. Indian Affairs Boarding Sch., Shonto, Ariz., 1974-75; asst. prof. biology Franklin Coll., Ind., 1975-78; adj. asst. prof. biology Ind. Central U., Indpls., 1977-78; adj. asst. prof. Ind. U.-Purdue U., Columbus, 1978; mem. faculty Yavapai Community Coll., Prescott, Ariz., 1978-79; assoc. dir. Ute Research Lab., Ft. Duchesne, Utah, 1980-81, dir., 1981-82; vis. prof. biology Bard Coll., N.Y., Spring 1984, Coll. St. Thomas, Minn., 1985-87; adj. asst. prof. biology, assoc. provost U. San Diego, 1988—; ranger-naturalist U.S. Nat. Park Svc., summers, 1970-79, 83-86; writer, 1968—; adj. faculty Southwestern Coll., 1989-92. Contbr. numerous articles on history of microbiology and history of antibiotics to sci. publs. Commr. San Diego County Columbian Quincentenary Commn., 1990-93, chmn. edn. com., 1990-93; mem. pres.'s adv. com. San Diego Zool. Soc., 1995—; trustee Quail Bot. Gardens Found., 1995—. Recipient Disting. Alumnus award, Calif. State Poly. U., 1991, Monrovia High Sch., 1991; Eli Lilly doctoral grantee Oreg. State U., 1973-74. Mem. AAAS, History of Sci. Soc., Soc. for Econ. Botany, Cabrillo Hist. Assn. (bd. dirs. 1989-94, vice chair 1992, chair 1993, 94), Alpha Scholastic Honor Soc. of Franklin Coll. (pres. 1976-78), Sigma Xi (sec. San Diego chpt. 1996-97), Beta Beta Beta. Office: U San Diego Office of Provost 5998 Alcala Park San Diego CA 92110-2429

MCGRAW, HAROLD WHITTLESEY, JR., publisher; b. Bklyn., Jan. 10, 1918; s. Harold Whittlesey and Louise (Higgins) McG.; m. Anne PerLee, Nov. 30, 1940; children: Suzanne, Harold Whittlesey III, Thomas Per-Lee, Robert Pearse. Grad., Lawrenceville (N.J.) Sch., 1936; A.B., Princeton U., 1940. With G.M. Basford (advt. agy.), N.Y.C., 1940-41, Brentano's Bookstores, Inc., 1946; with McGraw-Hill Book Co., Inc., N.Y.C., 1947—, successively promotion mgr., dir. co. advt. and trade sales, 1947-55, dir., v.p. charge trade book, indsl. and bus. book depts., co. advt., 1955-61, sr. v.p., 1961-68, pres., chief exec. officer, 1968-74; pres., chief exec. officer McGraw-Hill, Inc., 1974-83, chairman, 1976-88; chairman emeritus, 1988—; bd. dirs. McGraw Hill, Inc., 1954-88. Founder, pres., bd. dirs. Bus. Council Effective Literacy and Bus. Press Ednl. Found. Served as capt. USAAF, 1941-45. Clubs: Bent Pine (Vero Beach); Blind Brook (Purchase, N.Y.); Wee Burn (Darien, Conn.). Home: Watch Tower Rd Darien CT 06820 Office: McGraw-Hill Inc 1221 Ave Of The Americas New York NY 10020-1001

MCGRAW, HAROLD WHITTLESEY, III (TERRY MCGRAW), financial services company executive; b. Summit, N.J., Aug. 30, 1948; s. Harold W. McGraw Jr.; m. Nancy Goodrich, Sept. 22, 1973; children: Harold W. IV, Megan G. BA, Tufts U., 1972; MBA, U. Pa., 1976. Various fin. mgmt. positions GTE; asst. v.p. pension investment GTE Mgmt. Corp; with McGraw-Hill, Inc., N.Y.C., 1980—, asst. v.p. pension investment, 1980-83, dir. corp. planning systems, 1983-84, v.p. corp. planning, 1984-85; also bd. dirs. McGraw-Hill, Inc. and divs./subs., N.Y.C.; group v.p., pub. Transp. group McGraw-Hill Publs. Co., N.Y.C., 1985-86, Transp., Aerospace and Def. group McGraw-Hill Publs. Co., N.Y.C., 1986-87; pres. McGraw-Hill Publs. Co., N.Y.C., 1987-88; pres., McGraw-Hill Fin. Svcs. Co., N.Y.C., 1988—. Bd. dirs. Brunswick Sch., Greenwich, Conn., 1986—, Hartley House, N.Y.C., 1983—. Home: 5 Halter Ln Darien CT 06820-3019 Office: Standard & Poor's Corp 22 Broadway New York NY 10004

MCGRAW, JACK WILSON, government official; b. Balt., May 19, 1943; s. P.W. and Nina (Gwinn) McG.; m. Nancy F. Foster, Aug. 31, 1974; children—David, Mark. B.A., Morris Harvey Coll., 1964; B.Div., Tex. Christian U., 1967. Ordained minister Christian Ch. (Disciples of Christ). Dir. temporary housing HUD, Washington, 1979-82; asst. assoc. dir. Fed. Emergency Mgmt. Agy., Washington, 1982, dep. asst. dir., 1982-83; dep. asst. adminstr. EPA Office Solid Waste and Emergency Response, Washington, 1983-88, acting asst. adminstr.; dep. regional adminstr. EPA Regional Office, Denver, 1988—. Nominee William H. Jump award HUD, 1972, Presdl. Rank award for sr. exec. service. Presbyterian. Avocation: skiing. Home: 8074 S Oneida Ct Englewood CO 80112-3128 Office: EPA Regional Office 999 18th St Denver CO 80202-2499

MCGRAW, JAMES L., retired ophthalmologist, educator; b. Syracuse, N.Y., Sept. 7, 1917; s. John J. and Elizabeth B. (Hemmer) M. A.B., Syracuse U., 1938, M.D., 1941; D.M.S., Columbia U., 1946. Diplomate Am. Bd. Ophthalmology. Intern, Grad. Hosp. U. Pa., 1941-42; resident Inst. Ophthalmology of Presbyn. Hosp., N.Y.C., 1942-46; teaching and research fellow Inst. Ophthalmology, Columbia U. Coll. Physicians and Surgeons, N.Y.C., 1945-46, instr. ophthalmology, 1945-46; clin. instr. ophthalmology SUNYHealth Sci. Ctr. Hosp., Syracuse, N.Y., 1947-54, clin. asst. prof., 1954-57, prof., dept. chmn., 1957-84, prof. emeritus, 1984—; attending ophthalmologist Crouse-Irving Meml. Hosp.; Univ. Hosp. SUNY; cons. VA Hosp. Contbr. articles to profl. jours, papers to profl. orgns. Served to maj. M.C., U.S. Army, 1950-52. Mem. Onondaga County Med. Soc., N.Y. State Med. Soc., AMA, Am. Acad. Ophthalmology (Honor award 1963), Nat. Soc. for Prevention Blindness, Nat. Med. Found. for Eye Care, Am. Bd. Ophthalmology, N.Y. Ophthal. Soc., Inst. Ophthalmology Alumni Assn., N.Y. Eye Bank, Alpha Omega Alpha. Roman Catholic. Club: Skaneateles Country. Home: 3069 E Lake Rd Skaneateles NY 13152-9002 Office: Eye Cons of Syracuse 224 Harrison St Syracuse NY 13202-3052

MCGRAW, LAVINIA MORGAN, retired retail company executive; b. Detroit, Feb. 26, 1924; d. Will Curtis and Margaret Coulter (Oliphant) McG. AB, Radcliffe Coll., 1945. Mem. Phi Beta Kappa. Home: 2501 Calvert St NW Washington DC 20008-2620

MCGRAW, ROBERT PIERCE, publishing executive; b. Bronxville, N.Y., June 13, 1954; s. Harold W. Jr. and Anne (Per-Lee) McG.; m. Dawn A. Watson, Sept. 15, 1979; children: Avery Christine, Dale Per-Lee. AB, Princeton U., 1976. Sales rep. McGraw Hill Book Co., Chgo., 1976-79; editor McGraw-Hill Inc., N.Y.C., 1979-82, editorial dir., 1982-83, gen. mgr., 1983-85, group v.p., 1985-87, exec. v.p., 1987—; bd. dirs. McGraw-Hill Cos.; dep. dir. Med. China Ltd., Hong Kong, 1986—. Republican. Presbyterian. Office: The McGraw-Hill Cos 1221 Ave Of The Americas New York NY 10020-1001

MCGREAL, JOSEPH A., JR., publishing company executive; b. Bklyn., Mar. 6, 1935; s. Joseph A. and Aresta (Noon) McG.; m. Margaret A. Molloy, June 6, 1959; children—Patrick, Pegeen, Joseph. BBA, St. Francis Coll., 1962. Pres. Med./Pharm. Pub. Co., Inc., Manhasset, N.Y., 1995—. Served with U.S. Army, 1955-57. Home: 52 Rockywood Rd Manhasset NY 11030-2513 Office: Med/Pharm Pub Co Inc 29 Park Ave Manhasset NY 11030-2401

MCGREAL, RORY PATRICK, educational administrator; b. Pontefract, Eng., Dec. 21, 1950; came to Can., 1957; s. Thomas and Ellen (Madden) McG.; m. Kathleen Fay, Jan. 13, 1975; children: Donal, Seamus, Sean. BA, McGill U., Montreal, Que., Can., 1975; BEd, Dalhousie U., Halifax, Ont., Can., 1977; cert., Pushkin Inst., Moscow, 1977; MA, Concordia U., Montreal, 1984; postgrad., Nova Southeastern U., 1992—. Tchr. Knob Lake Sch., Schefferville, Que., 1977-79; union pres. Ea. Que. Tchr.'s Assn., Quebec, 1979-80; tchr. Nat. Youth Svcs., Seychelles Islands, 1980-83; lectr. U. Petroleum & Minerals, Dhahran, Saudi Arabia, 1984-86; dir. tech. studies Bahrain U., Manama, 1986-88; profl. officer Meml. U. Nfld. Faculty Assn., St. John's, Can., 1989-90; sch. liaison supr. Contact North, Sudbury, Ont., 1990-93; exec. dir. Tele Edn. N.B., Fredericton, Can., 1993—. Co-author: WWW Instructor's Manual, 1995; contbr. articles to profl. publs., chpt. to book. Mem. edn. com. Can. Network for Advancement of Rsch., Industry and Edn., 1995-96; mem. adv. coun. Learning and Tng. Working Group of Info. Hwy., 1994-95; bd. dirs. Ctr. Internat. Devel. Info. Highway in French 1996—; mem. Premier's Task force Info. Hwy., 1994—. Russian study scholar Can. Office External Affairs, 1977, Killam scholar, 1983. Mem. Can. Assn. Distance Edn., U.S. Distance Learning Assn. Roman Catholic. Avocation: web surfing. Home: 8 Camber Dr, Fredericton, NB Canada E3C 1N6 Office: TeleEdn NB DAEL, 500 Beaverbrook Ct Box 6000, Fredericton, NB Canada E3B 5H6

MCGREEVY, ROBERT MICHAEL, oil company executive, owner; b. Providence, R.I., May 19, 1950; s. Wilfred Barrington and Doris Helen Kenyon; m. Louise Aline Vegiard, Sept. 14, 1974; children: Lacey Aline McGreevy, Ashley Marissa McGreevy. Grad. high sch., Wakefield, R.I. Janitor URI, Kingston, R.I., 1966-69; carpenter/locksmith URI, Kingston, 1969-71; carpenter Bostich, East Greenwich, R.I., 1971-73; fuel delivery Norm's Oil Svc., Narragansett, R.I., 1969-88; pres. Norm's Fuel Co. Ltd., Narragansett, 1988—. Firefighter Kingston Fire Dept., 1965-75. Avocations: computers, baseball, motor sports. Home: 17 Boxwood Ct Wakefield RI 02879-1430 Office: Norms Fuel Co Ltd 330 Great Island Rd Narragansett RI 02882-5622

MC'GREGOR, DONALD THORNTON, newspaper editor, journalist; b. McLennan County, Tex., Mar. 20, 1924; s. Marshall Thornton and Flora Elvira (Welch) McG.; m. Alice Carlene Barnhill, Dec. 21, 1946; children: Alice Diane McGregor Tyrone, Robert Thornton, Donald Wayne. B.A., Baylor U., Waco, Tex., 1947; postgrad., Southwestern Baptist Theol. Sem., Ft. Worth, 1951-52. Agr. reporter Midland (Tex.) Reporter-Telegram, 1948-49; continuity dir. Sta. KCRS, Midland, 1949-50; editorial asso. Bapt. Standard, Dallas, 1952-55; real estate editor Dallas Times Herald, 1959; pub. relations exec. Union Bankers Ins. Co., Dallas, 1955-58; asso. editor Bapt. Standard, 1959-71; editor Calif. So. Bapt., Fresno, 1971-73; publisher Kemp (Tex.) News, Ferris (Tex.) Wheel, also Dawson (Tex.) Herald, 1973-74; asso. editor Bapt. Record, Jackson, Miss., 1974-76, editor, 1976-90; ret., 1990. Chmn. public rels. adv. com. So. Bapt. Conv., 1979-80. Served with AUS, 1943-45; prisoner of war, Germany, 1944-45. Decorated Purple Heart; recipient Distinguished Service award So. Bapt. Conv., 1973. Mem. So. Bapt. Press Assn. (sec.-treas. 1964-68, pres. 1981, chmn. Bapt. press liaison com. 1988-90), Associated Bapt. Press (co-founder and bd. dirs., exec. dir. 1991-94). Home: PO Box 850547 Mesquite TX 75185-0547

MCGREGOR, F. DANIEL, education educator; b. Indiana, Pa., Aug. 8, 1946; s. Ralph Murray and Elaine (Kennedy) McG.; m. Bonnie J. Corridoni; 1 stepchild, Daniel B. McDivitt. BS in Edn., Ind. U., 1972, MEd, 1977; cert. prin., U. Pitts., 1979; cert. supt., Indiana U., 1988. Prin. Blairsville (Pa.) Saltsburg Sch. Dist., 1970-83, Kiski Area Sch. Dist., Vandergrift, Pa., 1984-87; regional coord. Dept. of Edn., Harrisburg, Pa., 1987-91; prof. Elem. Edn. Indiana (Pa.) U., 1991-93; prin. Duquesne Sch. Dist., 1993—; dir. edn. Pa. Dept. Corrections; prof. Westmoreland C.C. Mem. Pa. Congress of Parents and Tchrs. (life).

MCGREGOR, MARTIN LUTHER, JR., lawyer; b. Rossville, Ga., Mar. 25, 1940; s. Martin Luther and Ora Louise (Stanley) McG.; m. Linda Joyce Buehler, June 31, 1978; children: Martin Luther III, James Franklin. BS in Chemistry, U. Ga., 1962; PhD, U. S.C., 1969; JD, Okla. U., 1978. Bar: Tex. 1979, U.S. Patent Office 1978, U.S. Supreme Ct. 1985. Various teaching positions Ga. and S.C., 1966-70; rsch. assoc. Okla. State U., Stillwater, 1971-76; rsch. chemist FMC Corp., Middleport, N.Y., 1976-77; assoc. atty. Baker & Botts, Houston, 1978-85; atty. Norvell & Assocs., Houston, 1985-86; mng. ptnr. Jamison McGregor & Harris, Houston, 1986-89; sr. biotech. specialist Baker & Botts, Houston, 1989-94; head biotech. Gardere & Wynne, L.L.P., Dallas, 1994-95; sec. McGregor & Adler PC, Houston, 1996—; adj. prof. chemistry U. Tex., Arlington, 1995. Mem. editorial bd. Biotech. Law Reports; contbr. articles to profl. jours. Mem. steering com. BioInternat. '93 Found. for the Future, Houston, 1992—, Andrews Campaign, Houston, 1992, Biotech. Industry Orgonizatio, 1997; bd. dirs. Mangum Manor Civic Assn., Houston, 1986. 2d lt. USAR, 1962-65. Named to Order of the Coif, Okla. U., 1978. Mem. AAAS, Houston Intellectual Property Law Assn., Am. Chem. Soc., Am. Arbitration Assn. (panel of patent arbitrators), Biotech. Ind. Orgn. (co-chmn. law 1993—), Assn. Biotech. Cos. (chmn. tech. transfer 1992-93, co-chmn. regulatory and patents 1991-92, gen. counsel S.W. chpt.). Unitarian Universalist. Avocations: camping, soccer coaching, chess. Office: McGregor & Adler PC 5380 W 34th St # 345 Houston TX 77092-6626

MC GREGOR, MAURICE, cardiologist, medical educator; b. South Africa, Mar. 24, 1920; s. Frank and Eleanor (Roechling) McG.; m. Margaret Rigsby Becklake, Mar. 20, 1948; children—James Andrew, Margaret Jane. M.B., B.Ch., U. Witwatersrand, Johannesburg, South Africa, 1942, M.D., 1947. Lectr. U. Witwatersrand, 1950-57; assoc. prof. medicine McGill U., Montreal, Que., Can., 1958-66, prof. medicine, 1966—, prof. emeritus, 1987—, dean medicine, 1967-72, vice prin. health care, 1972-74; physician-in-chief Royal Victoria Hosp., 1974-79, sr. physician, 1980—; dean medicine U. Witwatersrand, Republic of South Africa, 1984-86; chmn. Council for the Evaluation of Health Tech., Que., 1988-94. Contbr. numerous articles to tech. jours. Fellow Royal Coll. Physicians (London, Eng.), Royal Coll. Physicians and Surgeons Can. Research in physiology, physiopathology of coronary circulation in health and disease, health tech., health policy. Home: 532 Pine Ave W, Montreal, PQ Canada H2W 1S6 Office: M4 76 Royal Victoria Hospital, 687 Pine Ave W, Montreal, PQ Canada H3A 1A1

MCGREGOR, RALPH, textile chemistry educator, consultant, researcher, author; b. Leeds, Eng., Feb. 11, 1932; s. Robert and Evelyn (Hutchison) McG.; m. Maureen Mabel McGaul, Aug. 8, 1959; children—Alasdair, Ralph, Francine. B.Sc with 1st class honors, Leeds U. (Eng.), 1953, Ph.D. in Applied Chemistry, 1957, D.Sc., 1979. Chemistry tchr. Roundhay Sch., Leeds, 1956-58; Courtauld research fellow U. Manchester, 1958-59, lectr. in polymer and fiber sci., 1959-68; vis. sr. researcher Ciba A.G., Basel, Switzerland, 1965-66; sr. scientist Fibers div. Allied Corp., Petersburg, Va., 1968-70; from assoc. prof. to prof., Cone Mills Disting. prof. textile chemistry N.C. State U., Raleigh, 1970—; spl. invited prof. Tokyo Inst. Tech., 1986; vis. sr. rsch. Tech. Chem. Lab Swiss Fedn. Inst. Tech., 1993. Recipient LeBlanc medal Leeds U., 1953; research medal Dyers Co., 1976; Perkin travel fellow, 1962; U.S.-Japan NSF Coop. Sci. Program grantee, 1981; N.C. Japan Ctr. fellow. Mem. Am. Chem. Soc., Am. Assn. Textile Chemists and Colorists (Olney medal 1984), Soc. Dyers and Colorists, Fiber Soc., AAUP, Sigma Xi, Phi Kappa Phi, Phi Sigma Iota. Author: Diffusion and Sorption in Fibres and Films, 1974. Contbr. articles to profl. jours. Home: 8276 Hillside Dr Raleigh NC 27612 Office: NC State Univ Box 8301 Raleigh NC 27695

MCGRIFF, FRED (FREDERICK STANLEY MCGRIFF), baseball player; b. Tampa, Oct. 31, 1963. Grad. high sch., Tampa. Baseball player Toronto Blue Jays, 1982-90, San Diego Padres, 1990-93, Atlanta Braves, 1993—. Named to Sporting News All-Star team, 1989, 92, 93; recipient Silver Slugger award, 1989, 92, 93; mem. Nat. League All-Star Team, 1992, 94; Am. League Home Run Leader, 1989; Nat. League Home Run Leader, 1992. Mem. World Series championship team, 1995. Office: Atlanta Braves PO Box 4064 Atlanta GA 30302

MC GRODDY, JAMES CLEARY, retired computer company executive, consultant; b. N.Y.C., Apr. 6, 1937; s. Charles B. and Helen F. (Cleary) McG.; children: Kathleen, Sheila, Christine, James, Aileen. B.S., St. Joseph's U., 1958; Ph.D., U. Md., 1964. With IBM, 1965-96; dir. rsch., sr. v.p. rsch. IBM, Armonk, N.Y., 1989-96; prof. Tech. U. Denmark, 1970-71; chmn. Integrated Surg. Sys., Inc. Contbr. articles to profl. jours.; patentee in field. Recipient Frederik Philips award Inst. of Elec. and Electronics Engrs., 1995. Fellow IEEE, Am. Phys. Soc. (George E. Pake prize 1995); mem. Nat. Acad. Engring. Office: 200 Business Park Dr Ste 307 Armonk NY 10504-1700

MC GRORY, MARY, columnist; b. Boston, 1918; d. Edward Patrick and Mary (Jacobs) McGrory. A.B., Emmanuel Coll. Reporter Boston Herald Traveler, 1942-47; book reviewer Washington Star, 1947-54, feature writer for nat. staff, 1954-81; now syndicated columnist The Washington Post, Universal Press Syndicate. Recipient George Polk Meml. award; Pulitzer prize for commentary, 1975. Office: Washington Post 1150 15th St NW Washington DC 20071-0001*

MCGRUDER, ROBERT, newspaper publishing executive. Exec. editor Detroit Free Press. Office: 321 W Lafayette Blvd Detroit MI 48226

MC GRUDER, STEPHEN JONES, portfolio manager; b. Louisville, Nov. 14, 1943; s. Clement W. and Elizabeth Boyer (Short) McG.; m. Angeline W. Goreau, Mar. 19, 1983; 1 child, Keaton A. BS in Chemistry, Stanford U., 1966; BA in Econs, Claremont Men's Coll., 1966. Chartered fin. analyst. V.p. Surveyor Fund, N.Y.C., 1978-86, The Portfolio Group, N.Y.C., 1986-88, Wafra Investment Adv. Group, N.Y.C., 1988-95, Lord Abbett, N.Y.C., 1995—. Mem. Fin. Analysts Fedn., Univ. Club. Republican. Presbyterian. Office: Lord Abbett & Co 767 5th Ave New York NY 10153-0001

MCGRUDER-HOULIHAN, RUBY LEE, special education educator; b. Clarksdale, Miss., Sept. 9, 1950; d. Saul and Irene (Radiford) McGruder; m. Robert A. Houlihan, July 27, 1974; 1 child, Coleen Tess. BS, U. Mass., 1975; M, So. Conn. State U., New Haven, 1983; 6th Yr. Cert. in Adminstrn./Supervision, 1992; postgrad., Century U., Mex., 1993—. Cert. tchr., Conn., Mass., N.H. Tchr. spl. edn. Bridgeport (Conn.) Schs. System, 1980-90; tchr. spl. edn., cons. Conn. Correctional Dept., Cheshire, 1990-93; owner North Country Alternative Sch., Littleton, N.H., 1993—; tchr. social studies and reading Hill House High, New Haven, Conn., 1988-89. Contbr. articles to profl. jours. Mem. Aging Com., Cheshire, Conn., 1991-92; bd. dirs. Lafayette Arts Coun., 1992. Mem. Soc. for Protection of Forests, Preservation Soc., Hist. Soc. (bd. dirs. 1980-92), Audubon Soc., Women's Pistol Club. Republican. Roman Catholic. Avocations: horseback riding, roller skating, classical music. Home: RR 1 Box 524 Littleton NH 03561-9537 Office: North Country Alternative Sch PO Box 805 Main St Littleton NH 03561

MCGUANE, THOMAS FRANCIS, III, author, screenwriter; b. Wyandotte, Mich., Dec. 11, 1939; s. Thomas Francis and Alice Rita (Torphy) McG.; m. Portia Crockett, Sept. 8, 1962 (div. 1975); 1 child, Thomas Francis; m. Margot Kidder, 1976 (div. 1977); 1 child, Maggie; m. Laurie Buffett, Sept. 19, 1977; 1 child, Anne Buffett; 1 stepchild, Heather. BA, Mich. State U., 1962; MFA, Yale U., 1965; Wallace Stegner fellow, Stanford U., 1966; PhD (hon.), Mont. State U., 1993. Author: The Sporting Club, 1969, The Bushwacked Piano, 1971 (Richard and Hinda Rosenthal Found. award for fiction 1971), Ninety-Two in the Shade, 1973 (Nat. Book award nomination 1974), Panama, 1977, An Outside Chance: Essays on Sport, 1980, Nobody's Angel, 1982, Something to be Desired, 1984, In the Crazies: Book and Portfolio, 1984, To Skin a Cat, 1986, Keep the Change, 1989, An Outside Chance: Classic and New Essays on Sport, 1990, Nothing But Blue Skies, 1992, Sons, 1993, fiction, Fly Fishing and the Search for Innocence: Short Stories on Fly Fishing, 1994, Live Water, 1996; screenwriter: (films) Rancho Deluxe, 1975, Missouri Breaks, 1976, Tom Horn, 1980, Cold Feet, 1989; screenwriter, dir.: (films) Ninety-Two in the Shade, 1975; editor: Best American Sports Writing, 1992; contbr. to Sports Illustrated mag., 1969-73. Wallace Stegner fellow Stanford Univ., 1966-67; recipient Mont. Gov.'s award 1988, N.W. Bookseller's award 1992, Golden Plate award Am. Acad. Achievement, 1993. Mem. Tale Club of N.Y. Address: PO Box 25 Mc Leod MT 59052-0025*

MCGUCKIN, JOHN H., JR., lawyer; b. Bryn Mawr, Pa., Nov. 8, 1946. AB magna cum laude, Harvard Coll., 1968, JD, 1971. Bar: Mass. 1971, Calif. 1973. Assoc. Orrick, Herrington, Rowley & Sutcliffe, 1972-79; sr. counsel legal divsn. Bank Am., 1979-81; exec. v.p., gen. counsel Union Bank Calif., N.A., San Francisco; adj. instr. Hastings Coll. Law U. Calif., 1980-82. Contbr. articles to profl. jours. Mem. ABA, State Bar Calif. (v.p., treas., bd. govs., chmn. subcom. duties and liabilities trustees probate and trust law sect. 1985-86, legal svcs. trust fund commn. 1989-90, minimum CLE com.), Calif. Bankers Assn. (legal affairs com. 1988—), Bar Assn. San Francisco (chmn. probate and trust law sect. 1985, exec. com., vice chmn. corp. law dept. sect. 1985-87), Phi Beta Kappa. Office: Union Bank of Calif NA 400 California St San Francisco CA 94104-1302

MCGUCKIN, WENDY MICHELLE BLASSINGAME, accounting specialist; b. Guymon, Okla., June 11, 1966; d. Ronald Clifford Blassingame and Evelyn Marie (Maddox) Martin; m. Randall Mack McGuckin, Sept. 11, 1993. BS, U. Okla., 1989, postgrad. Tchr. Norman (Okla.) Pub. Schs., 1989-90; pub. rels. coord. Hatfield and Bell, Inc., Norman, 1990-91; fin. cons. Sun Fin. Group, Oklahoma City, 1991; acctg. specialist U. Okla., Norman, 1991—; co-owner EnviroPin; chair awards com. U. Okla. Staff Senate. Environ. activist, Oklahoma City, 1990; vol. Okla. Equine Hosp., 1994. Mem. NAFE, Am. Coll. Healthcare Execs., Okla. Equestrian Trail Riders Assn. Avocations: golf, scuba diving, gourmet cooking, skiing, western riding. Office: Univ Okla 620 Elm Ave Norman OK 73069-8801

MCGUE, CHRISTIE, federal official; b. Colombus, Ohio, Feb. 1, 1949; m. Robert Calt, Nov. 13, 1992. Sr. mgmt. analyst Nuclear Regulatory Comm., Washington, 1973-76; asst. sec., asst. dir. Office of Elec. Power Regulations, asst. dir. Office of Hydropower Licensing Fed. Energy Regulatory Comm., Washington, 1977-85; with Dept. Interior, Washington, 1986-88; dep. exec. dir. Fed. Energy Regulatory Commn., Washington, 1990-93, exec. dir., CFO, 1994—. Office: Fed Energy Regulatory Commn 888 1st St NE Rm 11-j Washington DC 20426-0001

MCGUFF, JOSEPH THOMAS, professional sports team executive; m. Mary Heard; children: Nanch Thomas, Mike, Marianne, John, Elaine, Bill. Sportwriter Kansas City (Mo.) Star, 1948-66, sports editor, 1966-86, v.p., editor, 1986-92, ret., 1992; bd. dirs. Kansas City Royals, 1994—. Author: Winning It All, Why Me? Why Not Joe McGuff. Recipient 6 Outstanding Sports Writer in Mo. awards Sportswriters and Sportscasters Assn.; named Mr. Baseball, Kansas City Baseball Awards Dinner, 1983; named to writers wing Baseball Hall of Fame, 1986. Mem. Baseball Writers and AP Sports Editors (past nat. pres.), Mo. Sports Hall of Fame. Office: Kansas City Royals PO Box 419969 Kauffmann Stadium Kansas City MO 64141-6969

MCGUIGAN, CHARLES JAMES, rehabilitation therapist; b. Maple Shade, N.J., May 8, 1944; s. Charles J. and Frances G. (Abbott) McG.; divorced; 1 child, Richard Holmes. AA, Atlantic C.C., 1977; student, Montclair State Coll., 1977-78, Glassboro State Coll., 1981-83, 88; BA in Social Sci. and History, Thomas A. Edison Coll., 1983. Cert. elem. tchr. N.J., computer specialist Fla., CPR, first aid, team tng., rehab. therapist. Tchr. 4th and 5th grades, track coach St. Nicholas Sch., Atlantic City, 1978-84; tchr. 5th grade, track coach St. Michaels Sch., Atlantic City, 1984-88; security guard Securex, Inc., Tampa, Fla., 1988; resident tng. instr. Upper Pinellas Assn. for Retarded Citizens, Clearwater, Fla., 1988-89; rehab. therapist Gulf Coast Ctr., Ft. Myers, Fla., 1989-95, resdl. counselor, 1995-96; edn. tech III Sch. Union 92, 1996-97; track coach Camden (N.J.) Diocese Office, 1983-88. Author poetry; contbr. to anthologies. Singer with barbershop quartet, musical shows; tchr. creative writing Unity Ch., Ft. Myers, Fla. Recipient Outstanding Citizen award Equal Opportunity Fund, 1975, Liberty Bell award City of Phila., 1976, Outstanding Counselor award Atlantic Human Resource, 1984; named Golden Poet of Yr. World of Poetry, 1991; 95 Presidential Poetry award Iliad Press. Mem. Kappa Delta Pi. Republican. Roman Catholic. Avocations: creative writing, travel, reading, computers, raising chows. Home: 226 Garland St Bangor ME 04401-5539

MCGUIGAN, FRANK JOSEPH, psychologist, educator; b. Oklahoma City, Dec. 7, 1924. BA, UCLA, 1945, MA, 1949; PhD, U. So. Calif., 1950. Instr. Pepperdine Coll., 1949-50; asst. prof. U. Nev., 1950-51; rsch. assoc. Psychol. Corp., 1950-51; rsch. scientist, sr. rsch. scientist, acting dir. rsch. Human Resources Rsch. Office, George Washington U., 1951-55; prof. psychology (Hollins Coll.), Roanoke, Va., 1955-76; chmn. dept. (Hollins Coll.), 1955-76; rsch. prof. (Grad. Sch.); prof. dept. psychology, dep. psychiatry and behavioral scis. (Sch. Medicine); dir. Performance Rsch. Lab., Inst. Advanced Study, U. Louisville, 1976-83; disting. rsch. prof., dir. Inst. Stress Mgmt. U.S. Internat. U., San Diego, 1983—; adj. prof. psychiatry and behavioral scis. U. Louisville Sch. Medicine, 1986—; adj. rsch. prof. N.C. State U., 1970-72; vis. prof. U. Hawaii, summer 1965, U. Calif., Santa Barbara, 1966, Hiroshima Shudo U., 1984; Nat. Acad. Scis. vis. scientist, Hungary, 1975, Bulgaria, 1987; sr. rsch. fellow Naval Health Rsch. Ctr., summer 1991. Author: numerous books in field including The Biological Basis of Behavior, 1963, Contemporary Studies in Psychology, 1972, Cognitive Psychophysiology - Principles of Covert Behavior, 1978, Experimental Psychology: Methods of Research, 6th edit., 1993, Psychophysiological Measurement of Covert Behavior—A Guide for the Laboratory, 1979, Calm Down—A Guide for Stress and Tension Control, 2d edit., 1992, Stress and Tension Control: Procs. of Internat., Interdisciplinary Conf. on Stress and Tension Control, 1980, vol. 2, 1984, vol. 3, 1989; (with Edmund Jacobson) cassettes Self-Directed Progressive Relaxation Training Instructions, 1981, Critical Issues in Psychology, Psychiatry and Physiology, 1986, Biological Psychology--A Cybernetic Science, 1994; editor numerous works in field.; editor, Internat. Jour. Stress Mgmt.; contbr. articles to profl. jours.; mem. editorial bd. Archiv fur Arzneitherapie, Biofeedback and Self-regulation, Activitas Nervosae Superioris. Served with USNR, 1942-46. Recipient award for outstanding contbns. to edn. in psychology Am. Psychol. Found., 1973, Blue medal of honor Union Scientists Bulgaria, 1980, medal of Sechenov USSR Acad. Med. Scis., 1983, medal of Anohkin, 1984, Pres.'s medal U. Hiroshima-Shudo, 1982, medal Okayama U., 1987, medal Tbilisi (USSR) Inst. Physiology, 1989, Edmund Jacobson award for stress mgmt., 1995, Gold medal award for lifetime achievement in application of psychology Am. Psychol. Found., 1995. Fellow APA, Internat. Soc. Rsch. on Aggression; mem. Am. Assn. Advancement of Tension Control (now Internat. Stress Mgmt. Assn.) (exec. dir. 1973-82, pres. 1985-89, exec. dir. 1992—, chmn. bd. dirs.), Pavlovian Soc. (mem. exec. bd. 1973—, pres. 1975-86, editor, chmn. publ. bd. Pavlovian Jour. Biol. Sci.), Am. Physiol. Soc., Biofeedback Soc. Am., Internam. Soc. Psychology, Internat. Congress of Applied Psychology, Psychonomic Soc., Soc. Psychophysiol. Rsch., Bulgarian Soc. for Psychiatry (hon.), Sigma Xi. Office: US Internat U Inst for Stress Mgmt 10455 Pomerado Rd San Diego CA 92131-1717

MCGUINN, MARTIN GREGORY, banker, lawyer; b. Phila., Sept. 9, 1942; s. Martin G. and Rita (Horgan) McG.; m. Ann M. Muldoon, Sept. 17, 1977; children: Patrick J., Christopher M. A.B., Villanova U., 1964, J.D., 1967. Bar: Pa. bar 1967, N.Y. bar 1970. Assoc. Sullivan & Cromwell, N.Y.C., 1970-77; mng. counsel The Singer Co., Stamford, Conn., 1977-80; vice chmn. Mellon Bank, Pitts., 1981—; dir. Master Card Internat., Regl. Industrial Development Corp. SW Penn.; bd. consultors Villanova Law Sch., 1972—, chmn. 1985-87; bd. dirs. Gen. Re Corp. Editor in chief Villanova Law Rev., Vol. 12, 1966-67. Bd. dirs. U. Pitts. Med. Ctr.; trustee Carnegie Mus. of Pitts., Hist. Soc. Western Pa. Mem. ABA, N.Y. State Bar Assn., Pa. Bar Assn., Allegheny County Bar Assn., Am. Law Inst., The Bankers Roundtable, Am. Soc. Corp. Secs. (chmn. 1990-91), Pa. Chamber of Bus. and Industry (bd. dirs.). Home: 714 Amberson Ave Pittsburgh PA 15232-1446 Office: Mellon Bank Corp 1 Mellon Bank Ctr Pittsburgh PA 15258-0001

MCGUINN, MICHAEL EDWARD, III, retired army officer; b. Spartanburg, S.C., Feb. 22, 1925; s. Michael Edward Jr. and Margaret Cordelia (Shackleford) McG.; m. Betty Gay Corn, 1948 (div. 1951); m. Phyllis Fryer, Oct. 7, 1952; childen: Michael Edward IV, Carol Ann McGuinn Branch. Student, Clemson U., 1941-43, 46, Coll. William and Mary, 1962-63. Served with U.S. Navy, PTO, 1943-46; commd. 2d lt. U.S.

Army, 1949, advanced through grades to col., 1971; asst. mil. attache Am. Embassy, Copenhagen, 1958-61; posted to svc. British Army, Longmoor, Eng., 1964-66; served on U.S. Dept. Army Gen. Staff, Washington, 1966-68; comdr. 10th Transp. Bn. U.S. Army, Vietnam, 1968-69; chief transp. div. U.S. Readiness Command, MacDill AFB, Fla., 1969-72; ret. U.S. Army, 1972; state govt. svc. various locations, 1972-82; chief of staff Ga. State Def. Force, an Agy. of the State of Ga., Atlanta, 1987-95. Decorated Legion of Merit (2), Army Commendation medal (2), Naval Commendation medal. Mem. U.S. Army Transp. Mus., The Old Guard of the Gate City Guard. Avocations: military history, photography, home workshop. Home and Office: 6420 Tanacrest Ct NW Atlanta GA 30328-2837 *Since boyhood when a young cadet,I have lived by one code "Duty, Honor and Country". In good times and bad, it has kept me faithful to principles of personal responsibility, personal integrity, and the importance of service to something greater than oneself. The code has never failed our nation nor has it ever failed me.*

MCGUIRE, DIANNE MARIE, psychotherapist; b. Houston, Feb. 22, 1950; d. Sidney A. and Shirley Lee (Ward) Schwartz; m. Walter Fred McGuire, May 7, 1983; children: Christopher C., Emily Nicole, Robert L. AA, San Jacinto Coll., Pasadena, Tex., 1984; BS in Psychology, U. Houston, 1986, MSW, 1988. Cert. social worker, advanced clin. practitioner, trauma resolution therapist, chem. dependency specialist, Tex. Pvt. practice Clear Lake, Pasadena and Deer Park, Tex., 1990—; adj. mem. faculty U. Houston, Clear Lake; presenter in field. Active Multiple Sclerosis Soc. Mem. NASW, Houston Live Stock Show and Rodeo (life), U. Houston Alumni Orgn. (life), U. Houston Clear Lake Alumni Orgn., Psi Chi, Phi Theta Kappa, Alpha Chi. Home: 16910 Pleasant Trace Ct Houston TX 77059-4039 Office: U Houston Clear Lake 2700 Bay Area Blvd Ste 2-529 Houston TX 77058-1002

MC GUIRE, DOROTHY HACKETT, actress; b. Omaha, June 14, 1916; d. Thomas Johnston and Isabel (Flaherty) McG.; m. John Swope, July 18, 1943 (dec.); children: Topo Swope, Mark Swope. Student, Pine Manor Jr. Coll., 1936-38. Stage debut in A Kiss for Cinderella, Omaha, 1933; played stock in Deertrees, Maine; N.Y.C. debut as understudy in Stop-Over, 1938; played role of Emily in Our town, on Broadway, 1938; toured with My Dear Children, 1939; starred in Claudia, 1941; toured in USO prodn. Dear Ruth, Europe, 1945, USO prodn. Tonight at 8:30, 1947, Summer and Smoke, 1950; appeared in Broadway prodn. Legend of Lovers, 1951, Joan at the Stake, 1954, Winesburg, Ohio, 1958, The Night of the Iguana, 1976, Cause Celebre, 1979; film appearances include: Claudia, 1943, A Tree Grows in Brooklyn, 1945, The Enchanted Cottage, 1945, Claudia and David, 1946, The Spiral Staircase, 1946, Gentlemen's Agreement, 1947, Mr. 880, Invitation, 1952, Make Haste to Live, 1954, Three Coins in the Fountain, 1954, Trial, 1955, Friendly Persuasion, 1956, Old Yeller, 1957, This Earth is Mine, 1959, A Summer Place, 1959, The Remarkable Mr. Penny Pincher, The Swiss Family Robinson, 1960, The Dark at the Top of the Stairs, 1960, Susan Slade, 1961, Summer Magic, 1962, The Greatest Story Ever Told, 1965, Flight of the Doves, 1971; film appearances include (voice only) Jonathan Livingston Seagull, 1973; appeared in: TV movie She Waits, 1971, TV prodn Am. Playhouse: I Never Sang For My Father, 1988; radio serial Big Sister, 1937; Juliette in: Romeo and Juliette; Ophelia in Hamlet, 1951; TV appearances include U.S. Steel Hour, 1954, Lux Video Theatre, 1954, Climax, 1954, 56, Play House 90, Another Part of the Forest, 1972, The Runaways, 1975, The Philadelphia Story, 1954, Rich Man Poor Man, 1970, Little Women, 1978, The Incredible Journey of Doctor Meg Laurel, Ghost Dancing, 1983, Love Boat, 1984. Recipient N.Y. Drama Critics Circle award, 1941; named Best Actress by Nat. Bd. Rev., 1955. Mem. Screen Actors Guild, Actors Equity Assn., AFTRA. Office: Raymond J Gertz Acctg Corp 10351 Santa Monica Blvd Los Angeles CA 90025-6908

MCGUIRE, EDWARD DAVID, JR., lawyer; b. Waynesboro, Va., Apr. 11, 1948; s. Edward David and Mary Estelle (Angus) McG.; m. Georgia Ann Charuhas, Aug. 15, 1971; children: Matthew Edward, Kathryn Ann. BS in Commerce, U. Va., 1970; JD, Coll. William and Mary, 1973. Bar: Va. 1973, D.C. 1974, Md. 1990, Pa. 1995, U.S. Dist. Ct. (ea. dist.) Va. 1974, U.S. Dist. Ct. D.C. 1974, U.S. Dist. Ct. Md. 1990, Ct. Appeals (4th cir.) 1974, U.S. Ct. Appeals (D.C. cir.) 1974, U.S. Supreme Ct. 1993. Assoc. Wilkes and Artis, Washington, 1973-78; gen. corp counsel Mark Winkler Mgmt., Alexandria, Va., 1978-80; sr. contracts officer Amtrak, Washington, 1980-81; sr. real estate atty., asst. corp. sec. Peoples Drug Stores, Inc., Alexandria, 1981-88; of counsel Cowles, Rinaldi & Arnold, Ltd., Fairfax, Va., 1989-91; sr. assoc. Radigan, Rosenberg & Holmes, Arlington, Va., 1991; pvt. practice, Annandale, Va., 1992—. Bd. dirs. Dist. XVI Va. Student Aid Found., 1978-85, George Washington dist. Boy Scouts Am., 1986; active William and Mary Law Sch. Assn., bd. dirs., 1983-96, pres., 1987-88, treas., 1990-91. Capt. JAGC, USANG, 1973-79. Mem. ABA, Va. Bar Assn., Va. State Bar, D.C. Bar, Md. State Bar Assn., Fairfax Bar Assn., Arlington County Bar Assn., Va. Trial Lawyers Assn., Nat. Network Estate Planning Attys., William and Mary Alumni Soc. (bd. dirs. D.C. chpt. treas. 1992-94), U. Va. Club of Washington (schs. com. chmn. 1995—, v.p. outreach 1997-98, bd. dirs. 1996—), Rotary (treas. Springfield chpt. 1985-86, sec. 1986-87, pres.-elect 1987, chmn. World Affairs Conf. 1985-88, bd. dirs. 1984-88, 96—Dist. 7610 youth leadership awards chmn. 1994—, Outstanding Rotarian award 1985). Greek Orthodox. Avocations: racquetball, coaching youth sports. Home: 31 W Myrtle St Alexandria VA 22301-2422 Office: 4306 Evergreen Ln Ste 103 Annandale VA 22003-3217

MCGUIRE, FRANK JOSEPH, accountant; b. Boston, June 21, 1944; s. Frank Joseph and Eleanor Anna (Welch) McG.; m. Donna Marie Marone, Apr. 24, 1971; 1 child, Heather Lyn. BS in Acctg., Stonehill Coll., 1966. CPA, Mass. Audit supr. Touche Ross & Co., Boston, 1966-73; corp. dir. internal audit First Nat. Stores, Inc., Somerville, Mass., 1973-77; corp. controller E.R.T., Inc., Concord, Mass., 1978; corp. dir. internal audit Ludlow Corp., Needham, Mass., 1979-81; corp. dir. internal audit KDT Industries, Inc., Newton, Mass., 1981-82, asst. to the pres., 1982-83; prin. Frank J. McGuire, P.C., 1983-86; prin. Nash and McGuire, P.C., 1986-90; prin. Frank J. McGuire, CPA, 1990—. Mem. Am. Inst. CPA's, Mass. Soc. CPA's, Inst. Mgmt. Accts. Democrat. Roman Catholic. Home: 147 Ash St Hopkinton MA 01748-1903 Office: 147 Ash St Hopkinton MA 01748-1903

MCGUIRE, HUNTER HOLMES, JR., surgeon, educator; b. Richmond, Va., Dec. 13, 1929; s. Hunter Holmes and Catharine Skelton (Bemiss) McG.; m. Alice Burwell Reed, Apr. 23, 1960; children: Alice McGuire Massie, Hunter III, William Reed. BA, U. Va., 1951, MD, 1955. Cert. Am. Bd. Surgery. Asst. dean of medicine Med. Coll. Va., Richmond, 1964-76, prof. surgery, 1973—; chief surg. svc. VA Hosp., Richmond, 1976—. Trustee Va. Hist. Soc., Richmond, 1970-90. Lt. USNR, 1956-58. Mem. So. Surg. Assn. (pres. 1994), Med. Soc. Va. (v.p. 1965), Assn. Va. Surgeons (pres. 1994, Disting. Svc. award 1996), Ea. Surg. Soc. (sec. 1975-80), Va. Surg. Soc. (pres. 1976).

MCGUIRE, JAMES CHARLES, aircraft company executive; b. St. Louis, Aug. 8, 1917; s. John Patrick and Anna Beulah (Erbar) McG.; AB, Washington U., St. Louis, 1949, MA (Univ. fellow), 1953, PhD, 1954; m. Eunice Leota Sloop, Mar. 21, 1942 (div. June 1948); 1 child: Judith Lynn; m. Ingrid Elisabeth Getreu, Sept. 16, 1954. Research assoc. Ohio State U., 1953-56; rsch. psychologist Aeromed. Lab., Wright-Patterson AFB, Ohio, 1956-59; group supr. Boeing Airplane Co., Seattle, 1959-61; dept. mgr. Internat. Electric Corp., Paramus, N.J., 1961-62; sr. human factors scientist System Devel. Corp., Santa Monica, Calif., 1962-67; v.p. Booz-Allen Applied Rsch., Saigon, Vietnam, 1967-72; v.p. Assoc. Cons. Internat., Saigon, 1972-75, Bethesda, Md., 1975-78; br. chief Human Factors, System Tech. Devel., 1978-82; prin. staff engr. tech. modernization methodology Douglas Aircraft Co., Long Beach, Calif., 1982-85; program mgr. cockpit automation tech. program, Northrop Aircraft div., Hawthorne, Calif., 1985-87; sect. mgr. aircraft programs human factors engring. dept. Douglas Aircraft Co., Long Beach, 1987-90, sr. staff engr. Crew Systems Tech., 1990-93; prin. engr. tech. McDonnell Douglas Aerospace Transport Aircraft, 1993-94; prin. engr.-scientist, crew sys. tech., advanced transport aircraft devel., McDonnell Douglas Aerospace, 1995—; lectr. Nat. Def. Coll., Vietnamese Armed Forces, Saigon, 1971. Served with AUS, 1940-46. Decorated Bronze Star medal with oak leaf cluster; recipient Tech. Svc. First Class medal Republic South Vietnam Armed Forces, 1968. Mem. Am. Psychol. Assn., IEEE, Computer Soc. of IEEE, Human Factors and Ergonomics Soc., Am. Assn. Artificial Intelligence, Phi Beta Kappa, Sigma Xi. Republican. Home: 23201 Mindanao Cir Dana Point CA 92629-3625 Office: McDonnell Douglas Aerospace Mail code C0071-0011 2401 E Wardlow Rd Long Beach CA 90807-5309

MCGUIRE, JOHN LAWRENCE, pharmaceuticals research executive; b. Kittanning, Pa., Nov. 3, 1942; s. Lawrence F. and Florence G. (Jones) McG.; m. Pamela Hale, Aug. 2, 1969; children—Megan L., Christa H. BS, Butler U., 1965; MA, Princeton U., 1968, PhD, 1969; postgrad., Columbia Sch. Bus., 1981. Asst. in instrn. Princeton U., N.J., 1967-69; pharmacologist Ortho Pharm. Corp., Raritan, N.J., 1969-72, sect. head molecular biology, 1972-75, exec. dir. research, 1975-80, v.p. preclinical research and devel., 1980-88, bd. dirs., 1988-93; sr. v.p. rsch. and devel. worldwide, bd. dirs. R.W. Johnson Pharm. Rsch. Inst., Raritan, N.J., 1988-92; corp. v.p. bus. devel., pharm./diagnostics group Johnson & Johnson, New Brunswick, N.J., 1992—; adj. assoc. prof. dept. medicine M.S. Hershey Sch. Medicine Pa. State U., 1978—; adj. prof. dept. animal sci. Rutgers U., 1983-92; adj. prof. ob-gyn. East Va. Med. Sch., 1987—; adj. prof. ob-gyn. and reproduction endocrinology U. Medicine and Dentistry, N.J., 1988—; cons. NASA, 1985-87. Mem. editorial bd. Ullman's Ency. Indsl. Chemistry, 1987—; contbr. articles to profl. jours.; patentee in field. Mem. exec. bd. Keystone Area council Boy Scouts Am., Harrisburg, Pa., 1975-96, George Washington council, Trenton, N.J., 1980-86, 95—; trustee Raritan Valley Community Coll., N.J., 1986—, vice-chmn., 1990—, United Way of Hunterdon County, N.J., 1983—, pres., 1985-87, Hunterdon Med. Ctr., Flemington, N.J., 1978—, vice chmn., 1984-88, chmn., 1988—; trustee Hunterdon Health Care Sys. Flemington, N.J., 1986—, chmn. 1989—, Atlantic Health Systems Morristown, N.J., 1991-93, vice-chmn., 1992-93, Tri State United Way, N.Y., 1987-94; bd. dirs. Hunterdon County YMCA, N.J., 1982-87; chmn. bd. dirs. Mid Jersey Health Corp., 1986-88; trustee The Pennington (N.J.) Sch., 1995—, pres., 1996—. Recipient Silver Beaver award Boy Scouts Am., 1984; Population Council fellow, 1969. Mem. Am. Soc. Pharmacology and Exptl. Therapeutics, Soc. Exptl. Biology and Medicine, Am. Physiol. Soc., Endocrine Soc., Am. Coll. Ob-Gyn, Am. Soc. Clin. Pharmacology and Therapetics, Licensing Execs. Soc., Biochemistry Soc. Great Britain, Royal Soc. Medicine (U.K.), Am. Chem. Soc. Club: Princeton (N.Y.C.). Home: 10 Clubhouse Dr Whitehouse Station NJ 08889-3351 Office: Johnson & Johnson New Brunswick NJ 08933

MCGUIRE, JOHN MURRAY, chemist, researcher; b. New Bedford, Mass., May 15, 1929; s. Thomas C., Jr. and Mary W. (Murray) McG.; m. Harriet S. Drake, Aug. 5, 1954; children: Joseph P., John M. Jr., Thomas C., David Vincent, James E., M. Catherine. BS in Chemistry, U. Miami, Coral Gables, Fla., 1948, MS in Phys. Chemistry, 1951; PhD in Phys. Chemistry, U. Fla., Gainesville, 1955. Product chemist GE, Waterford, N.Y., 1955-57; sr. rsch. chemist W. R. Grace R & D, Clarksville, Md., 1957-60; sr. chemist, supr. GE, Syracuse, N.Y., 1960-70; engr. advanced materials GE, Decatur, Ill., 1970-71; rsch. chemist EPA, Athens, Ga., 1971-73, supervisory rsch. chemist, 1973-95; ret., 1995; ham radio operator, 1995—. Editorial advisor Biomedical Mass Spectrometry jour., 1974-83; contbr. articles to tech. publs. Decorated knight and knight comdr. of Holy Sepulchre of Jerusalem. Mem. Am. Chem. Soc. (sect. chmn. 1986), Am. Soc. Mass Spectrometry (chmn. environ. com. 1973-75), KC (grand knight Athens 1973-79, state dep. Ga. 1986-87, Ga. master 4th degree 1988-92). Republican. Roman Catholic. Avocations: reading, church work.

MCGUIRE, JOHN W., SR., advertising executive, marketing professional, author; b. Chgo., May 12, 1952; s. Eugene H. Sr. and Marjorie (Bolger) McG.; m. Mary Sue Roper, June 17, 1972 (div. 1977); 1 child, John William Jr.; m. Lynn L. Rembos, June 21, 1984 (div. April 1991); children: Kelly Lynn, Ryan Michael. AA, Chgo. City Colls., 1972; BA, Northeastern Ill., Chgo., 1974. Janitor Bd. of Edn., Chgo., 1970-74; sales rep. Motorola Comms., Inc., Schaumburg, Ill., 1974-76, Pattis Group, Chgo., 1976-77; midwest sales mgr. Harcourt Brace Jovanovich Pub. Co., N.Y.C., 1977-79; account sales mgr. Cosmopolitan Mag. Hearst Pub. Co., N.Y.C., 1979-81; midwest acct. mgr. Psychology Today Mag. Ziff-Davis Pub. Co., N.Y.C., 1981-82; midwest regional mgr. Pennwell Pub. Co., Tulsa, Okla., 1982-84; western regional sales mgr. SN Pub. Co., West Dundee, Ill., 1984-91; western regional sales mgr., midwest regional sales mgr. Jobson Pub. Co., N.Y.C., 1991—. Author: (book) One Man's Life: A Poetic Review, 1995, singer (cassette tapes), designer (creative posters). With USN, 1970. Mem. VFW, Midwest Healthcare Mktg., Arlington Poetry Project. Republican. Roman Catholic. Avocations: writer, scuba, horsemanship, traveling, skydiving. Home: 41w585 Golden Oaks Ln Saint Charles IL 60175-7885

MC GUIRE, JOSEPH WILLIAM, business educator; b. Milw., Mar. 14, 1925; s. William B. and Marion (Dunn) McG.; m. Margaret Drewek, Aug. 20, 1946; children: Laurence, Karen, Eileen, Kevin. Ph.B., Marquette U., 1948, D.B.A. (hon.), 1981; M.B.A., Columbia U., 1950, Ph.D., 1956; LL.D. (hon.), St. Benedict's Coll., 1968. Asst. prof. U. Wash. Coll. Bus. Adminstrn., Seattle, 1954-56; assoc. prof. U. Wash. Coll. Bus. Adminstrn., 1956-61, prof., 1961-63; prof., dean U. Kans. Sch. Bus., 1963-68; dean Coll. Commerce and Bus. Adminstrn., prof. U. Ill., Urbana, 1968-71; v.p. planning U. Calif., Berkeley, 1971-74; prof. adminstrn. U. Calif., Irvine, 1973-95, assoc. dean exec. degree programs, 1990-94, prof. emeritus, 1995—; vis. prof. Netherlands Coll. Econs., Rotterdam, 1957-58, dept. econs. U. Hawaii, 1962-63, Michael Smrfit Grad. Sch. of Bus. Univ. Coll., Dublin, Ireland, 1993, Am. U. of Armenia, 1993; Ford. vi. rsch. prof. Carnegie-Mellon U. Grad. Sch. Indsl. adminstrn., 1987-88; cons. editor Wadsworth Pub. Co., 1964-70, Goodyear Pub. Co., 1973-81, Scott Foresman & Co., 1981-90. Author: Business and Society, 1963, Theories of Business Behavior, 1964, Factors Affecting the Growth of Manufacturing Firms, 1963, Inequality; The Poor and the Rich in America, 1968; Editor, contbr.: Interdisciplinary Studies in Business Behavior, 1962, Contemporary Management: Issues and Viewpoints, 1973. Served with USAAF, 1943-45. Recipient McKenzie awards, 1963, 65. Fellow Am. Acad. Mgmt. (bd. govs. 1967-70), Internat. Acad. Mgmt.; mem. Am. Assn. Collegiate Schs. Bus. (dir. 1970-71), Am. Econ. Assn., AAUP, Am. Inst. Decision Scis., Western Econs. Assn., Western Tax Assn. (dir. 1977-80), Assn. Social Econs. (exec. council 1970-75, pres. 1973-74), Western Acad. Mgmt. (dir. 1975-81, pres. 1980-81), Phi Beta Kappa, Beta Gamma Sigma. Home: 54 Lessay Newport Beach CA 92657-1060

MCGUIRE, MARY JO, state legislator; b. Mpls., 1956. BA in Bus. Adminstrn., Coll. of St. Catherine, 1978; JD, Hamline U., 1988; postgrad., Harvard U., 1995—. Mem. Minn. Ho. of Reps., 1988-94, mem. judiciary com., judiciary fin. divsn., vice chair family and early childhood edn. fin. divsn., mem. govt. ops., chair data practices subcom. Democrat. Home: 1529 Iowa Ave W Saint Paul MN 55108-2128 Office: Minn Ho of Reps State Ho Office Bldg Saint Paul MN 55155

MCGUIRE, MICHAEL FRANCIS, plastic and reconstructive surgeon; b. St. Louis, Oct. 4, 1946; s. Arthur Patrick and Virginia Claribel (Gannon) McG. BA, Columbia U., 1968, MD, 1972. Diplomate Am. Bd. Surgery, Am. Bd. Plastic Surgery. Intern UCLA, 1972-73, resident in gen. surgery, 1973-77, resident in plastic surgery, 1978-80; fellow in plastic surgery rsch. Stanford (Calif.) U., 1977-78; traveling fellow in plastic surgery Gt. Britain, 1980; chief plastic surgery L.A. County-Olive View Med. Ctr., Sylmar, Calif., 1980-85; pvt. practice Santa Monica, Calif., 1980—; chief plastic surgery St. John's Health Ctr., 1990—, chair surg. rev., 1996—; bd. dirs. Calif. Med. Rev., Inc., sec.-treas., 1997—. Charter patron L.A. Music Ctr. Opera, 1983—; sponsoring patron Los Angeles County Art Mus., 1986—; patron Colleague Helpers in Philanthropic Svc., Bel Air, Calif., 1987, 93, 95; pres. Found. for Surg. Reconstrn., 1996—. Fellow ACS, Royal Soc. Medicine; mem. Am. Soc. Plastic and Reconstructive Surgeons (membership chmn. 1997—), Am. Soc. Aesthetic Plastic Surgery, Los Angeles County Med. Assn. (v.p. 1995—), Calif. Med. Assn. (del., exec. com., splty. delegation 1994—), Calif. Soc. Plastic Surgery (exec. com., auditor 1988-89, program chmn. 1990, exec. coun. 1991-94, treas. 1994-97, v.p. 1997—), Am. Assn. Accreditation of Ambulatory Surgery (facilities ops. com. 1995-96, bd. dirs. 1996, treas. 1996—), Alpha Omega Alpha. Democrat. Episcopalian. Avocations: golf, travel, collecting antique Irish glass, opera, modern art. Office: 1301 20th St Ste 460 Santa Monica CA 90404-2054

MC GUIRE, MICHAEL JOHN, environmental engineer; b. San Antonio, June 29, 1947; s. James Brendan and Opal Mary (Brady) McG.; BS in Civil Engring., U. Pa., 1969; MS in Environ Engring., Drexel U., 1972, PhD in Environ. Engring., 1977; diplomate Am. Acad. Environ. Engring.; m. Deborah Marrow, June 19, 1971; children: David, Anna. San. engr. Phila. Water Dept., 1969-73; rsch. assoc. Drexel U., Phila., 1976-77; prin. engr. Brown & Caldwell Cons. Engrs., Pasadena, Calif., 1977-79; water quality engr. Met. Water Dist. of So. Calif., L.A., 1979-84, water quality mgr., 1984-86, dir. water quality, 1986-90, asst. gen. mgr., 1990-92; pres. McGuire Environ. Cons., Inc., Santa Monica, Calif., 1992—; cons. to subcom. on adsorbents, safe drinking water com. Nat. Acad. Scis., 1978-79; cons. mem. Techs. Workgroup USEPA, DBP Reg Neg, 1992-93. Registered profl. engr., Pa., N.J., Calif., Ariz. Mem. Am. Water Works Assn. (Acad. Achievement award 1978, edn. div. chmn. 1982-83, chair taste and odor com. 1993—, Calif.-Nev. sect., chmn. water quality and resources div. 1982-83, governing bd. 1984-87, 89-96, exec. com. 1989-96, chmn. 1991-92, nat. dir. 1993-96, trustee Research Found. 1983-86, nat. v.p. 1994-96, nat. exec. com. 1994-96, Fuller award 1994), Am. Chem. Soc., ASCE, Internat. Water Supply Assn., Internat. Assn. on Water Quality (specialist group on taste and odor control 1982—, chmn. organizing com. 1991, off-flavor symposium 1987-91), Internat. Ozone Assn. (internat. bd. dirs. 1992-95), Sigma Xi, Sigma Nu, Sigma Tau. Editor: (with I.H. Suffet) Activated Carbon Adsorption of Organics From the Aqueous Phase, 2 vols., 1980; Treatment of Water by Granular Activated Carbon, 1983; contbr. articles to profl. jours. Office: McGuire Environ Cons Inc 469 25th St Santa Monica CA 90402-3103

MCGUIRE, MICHAEL WILLIAM, communications executive; b. Pomona, Calif., Aug. 1, 1960; s. Frederick L. and Anna Belle (Crum) McG.; m. Victoria Jean Von Tobel; children: Gordon, Michael Jr. BA in Polit. Sci., U. San Diego, 1984. Spokesman, dir. Congl. affairs Voice of Am., Washington, 1986-88; owner, chief exec. officer McGuire Rsch. Svcs., Las Vegas, Denver and, San Francisco, 1988—; cons. various U.S. and multinat. corps. Cons. various candidates for pub. office, 1988. Mem. Hiwan Golf Club. Home: 34123 Upper Bear Creek Rd Evergreen CO 80439 Office: 1616 Champa St Ste 300 Denver CO 80202-2709

MCGUIRE, PATRICIA A., lawyer, academic administrator; b. Phila., Nov. 13, 1952; d. Edward J. and Mary R. McGuire. BA cum laude, Trinity Coll., 1974; JD, Georgetown U., 1977. Bar: Pa. 1977, D.C. Ct. Appeals 1979. Program dir. Georgetown U. St. Law Clinic, Washington, 1977-82; asst. dean for devel. and external affairs Georgetown U. Law Ctr., Washington, 1982-89; pres. Trinity Coll., Washington, 1989—; adj. prof. law Georgetown U., 1977-82, Georgetown Law Ctr., 1987—; commr. Mid. States Commn. on Higher Edn., 1991—; bd. dirs. Acacia Group. Editor: Street Law Mock Trial Manual, 1984; contbr. articles to profl. jours. Trustee Trinity Coll., 1986—; bd. dirs. Assn. Cath. Colls. and Univs., 1991—, Eugene and Agnes Meyer Found.; mem. adv. bd. Merion Mercy Acad. and Sisters of Mercy, 1990—; bd. dirs. Nat. Assn. Ind. Colls. and Univs.; mem. commn. govt. rels. Am. Coun. Edn. Recipient Daytime Emmy, TV Acad., N.Y.C., 1979-80. Mem. ABA, Assn. Am. Law Schs. (instl. advancement 1985—), Coun. for the Advancement and Support of Edn., Trinity Coll. Alumnae Assn. (pres. 1986-89). Democrat. Roman Catholic. Office: Trinity Coll Office of the President 125 Michigan Ave NE Washington DC 20017-1004

MCGUIRE, RICHARD JOSEPH, retired basketball player; b. Huntington, N.Y., Jan. 25, 1926. Attended, St. John's U., Dartmouth Coll. Basketball player N.Y. Knicks, 1951-54, head coach, 1965-68; basketball player Detroit Pistons, 1958-60, player, head coach, 1959-63; head coach Belmont Abbey, 1957-58, 63-64, Marquette U., 1964-65, 76-77. Named to Basketball Hall of Fame, 1993, All- Am. 2d Team Sporting News, 1944, All NBA 2d Team, 1951; recipient Haggarty award, N.Y.C.; selected Helms Found. All-Am. Office: c/o Basketball Hall Fame PO Box 179 Springfield MA 01101-0179

MCGUIRE, ROGER ALAN, foreign service officer; b. Troy, Ohio, July 1, 1943; s. Charles M. and Mary L. (Coppock) McG.; m. Harriet H. Cooke, July 12, 1969; children: Sara, Casey. BA, Beloit Coll., 1965; MA, U. Wis., 1967. Country desk officer Dept. State, Washington, 1974-78; dep. chief of mission Am. Embassy, Maputo, Mozambique, 1978-80; congl. fellow Am. Polit. Sci. Assn., Washington, 1980-81; polit. officer Am. Embassy, Asuncion, Paraguay, 1981-83, Lusaka, Zambia, 1983-86; dep. dir. Office of West African Affairs Dept. of State, Washington, 1986-88; chief of mission Am. Embassy, Windhoek, Namibia, 1988-90; consul Am. Consulate, Porto Alegre, Brazil, 1990-92; U.S. amb. to Guinea-Bissau, 1992-95; counselor for polit. affairs Am. Embassy, Canberra, Australia, 1995—. Recipient Superior Honor award U.S. Agy. for Internat. Devel., 1969. Mem. Rotary Internat., Phi Beta Kappa. Home and Office: Am Embassy-Canberra Psc 277 Box 18 APO AP 96549-0239

MCGUIRE, TIMOTHY JAMES, lawyer, editor; b. Mount Pleasant, Mich., Mar. 24, 1949; s. James Edward and Anita Matilda (Starr) McG.; m. T. Jean Fannin, May 10, 1975; children: Tracy, Jason, Jeffrey. BA, Aquinas Coll., Grand Rapids, Mich., 1971; JD cum laude, William Mitchell Coll. Law, St. Paul, 1987. Bar: Minn. 1987. Mng. editor Ypsilanti Press, Mich., 1973-75, Corpus Christi Caller, Tex., 1975-77, Lakeland Ledger, Fla., 1977-79, Mpls. Star, 1979-82; mng. editor features and sports Mpls. Star and Tribune, 1982-84, mng. editor, 1984-91, exec. editor, 1991-93, editor, sr. v.p., 1993—; Pulitzer Prize juror, 1988-89, 95-96. Lay preacher at St. Joseph Roman Cath. Ch., Mpls., 1995—. Mem. Am. Soc. Newspaper Editors (bd. dirs. 1992—, chmn. change com. 1994-95, chmn. program com. 1996-97), Minn. State Bar Assn. Roman Catholic. Home: 3645 Rosewood Ln N Minneapolis MN 55441-1127 Office: Star Tribune 425 Portland Ave Minneapolis MN 55415-1511

MCGUIRE, TIMOTHY WILLIAM, economics and management educator, dean; b. Englewood, N.J., Nov. 30, 1938; s. Charles James and Marie (McCarthy) McG.; children: Timothy William Jr., Gretchen Elizabeth, Michael Joseph; m. Nancy Paule Melone, 1991. BS in Indsl. Mgmt., Carnegie Inst. Tech., 1960, MS in Econs., 1961; PhD in Econs., Stanford U., 1968. Staff mem. Coun. Econ. Advisors, 1963-64; rsch. assoc. in econs. Grad. Sch. Indsl. Adminstrn., Carnegie Mellon U., Pitts., 1964-66, asst. prof. econs., 1966-69, assoc. prof., 1969-75, prof., 1975-79, prof. mgmt. and econs., 1982—, dep. dean, 1983-90; prof. social scis. and econs. Dept. Social Scis. Carnegie Mellon U., Pitts., 1981-82; prof. econs., chmn. dept. U. Iowa, Iowa City, 1979-80; dean, Harry B. Miller prof. bus. Charles H. Lundquist Coll. Bus., U. Oreg., Eugene, 1994—; sr. visitor U. Cambridge, Eng., summer, 1970; vice chmn. bd. dirs. Mgmt. Sci. Assocs., Inc., Pitts., Pacific Pension Inst. Contbr. articles to profl. jours. Woodrow Wilson Nat. Hon. fellow Carnegie Inst. Tech., 1960-61; Stanford U. fellow, 1961-62; fellow Ford Found., 1962-63, 70-71. Mem. Internat. Soc. Bayesian Analysis, Am. Econ. Assn., Am. Mktg. Assn., Am. Soc. Quality Control, Inst. Ops. Rsch. & Mgmt. Scis., Soc. Judgment and Decision Making, Western Assn. Collegiate Schs. of Bus. (dir. at large), Am. Statis. Assn., Tau Beta Pi, Omicron Delta Kappa. Home: 3302 Stoney Ridge Rd Eugene OR 97405-7009 Office: Charles Lundquist Coll Bus 1208 U Oreg Eugene OR 97403-1208

MC GUIRE, WILLIAM, civil engineer, educator; b. S.I., N.Y., Dec. 17, 1920; s. Edward Joseph and Phoebe (Sellman) McG.; m. Barbara Weld, Feb. 5, 1944; children—Robert Weld, Thomas Rhodes. B.S. in Civil Engring, Bucknell U., 1942; M.Civil Engring., Cornell U., 1947. Structural designer Jackson & Moreland (engrs.), Boston, 1947-49; faculty Cornell U., Ithaca, 1949—; prof. civil engring. Cornell U., 1960-90, prof. emeritus of civil engring., 1990—; dir. Cornell U. (Sch. Civil Engring.), 1966-68; vis. prof. civil engring. Asian Inst. Tech., Bangkok, Thailand, 1968-70; vis. research engr. Nat. Bur. Standards, 1972; Gledden vis. sr. fellow U. Western Australia, 1973; cons. structural engr., 1951—; vis. prof. U. Tokyo, 1979, U. Strathclyde, 1986. Author: Steel Structures, 1967, (with R.H. Gallagher) Matrix Structural Analysis, 1979. Served to lt. USNR, 1942-45. Recipient Naval Letter of Commendation, award for Outstanding Achievement, Bucknell U., 1987, T.R. Higgins Lectureship award Am. Inst. Steel Constrn., 1992. Fellow ASCE (pres. Ithaca 1964, Norman medal 1962, 94, Hardesty award 1992, honorary mem. 1994); mem. Internat. Assn. Bridge and Structural Engring., Nat. Acad. Engring., Sigma Xi, Chi Epsilon, Kappa Delta Rho. Congregationalist. Home: 121 Simsbury Dr Ithaca NY 14850-1728

MCGUIRE, WILLIAM B(ENEDICT), lawyer; b. Newark, Feb. 14, 1929; m. Joan Glinane, June 3, 1968 (dec. Mar. 1996); children: Joan Ellen, Ralph R., James C., Keith P., Grant W. BS, Fordham U., 1950; JD, Seton Hall U., 1958; LLM in Taxation, NYU, 1963. Bar: N.J. 1958, U.S. Dist. Ct. N.J. 1958, U.S. Supreme Ct. 1971, U.S. Ct. Appeals (3rd cir.) 1980, N.Y. 1982. Chief acct. Hanover Fire Ins. Co., N.Y.C., 1950-58; sr. ptnr. Lum, Biunno &

Tompkins, Newark, 1958-83, Tompkins, Mc Guire & Wachenfeld, 1984—; asst. prosecutor Essex County, N.J., 1964-65; bd. dirs. Ind. Coll. Fund of N.J., St. Peter's Coll., Delbarton Sch.; trustee St. Barnabas Corp., St. Barnabas Med. Ctr. and Irvington Gen. Hosp.; mem. Essex County Ethics Com., 1974-77; mem. com. to review State Commn. of Investigation, 1982. Fellow Am. Coll. Trial Lawyers, Am. Bar Found. (state chmn.), Am. Bd. Trial Advocates, Internat. Acad. Trial Lawyers, Internat. Soc. Barristers; mem. ABA, N.J. State Bar Assn. (trustee 1982-89, sec. 1989-90, treas. 1990-91, 2nd v.p. 1991-92, 1st v.p. 1992-93, pres. elect 1993-94, pres. 1994-95), N.J. State Bar Found. (pres. 1988-89), Essex County Bar Assn. (pres. 1975-76), Internat. Assn. Ins. Counsel, Fedn. Ins. Counsel, Def. Research Inst., Maritime Law Assn. U.S., Am. Arbitration Assn., Trial Attys. N.J., Assn. Fed. Bar N.J. (pres. 1985-88). Roman Catholic. Club: Essex County Country (pres. 1983), Newark. Office: 4 Gateway Ctr 100 Mulberry St Newark NJ 07102-4004

MCGUIRE, WILLIAM DENNIS, health care system executive; b. Glen Ridge, N.J., Sept. 24, 1943; s. John William and Kathleen Mary (Sexton) McG.; B.A., U. Notre Dame, 1965; M.H.A., U. Mich., 1968; m. Nancy Katherine Hoyne, Aug. 13, 1966; children: Kathleen Anne, Colleen Dempsey. Asst. adminstr. U. Wis. Hosps., Madison, 1971-74; adminstr. Children's Med. Ctr., Dayton, Ohio, 1974-79; sr. v.p. Mercy Cath. Med. Ctr., Phila., 1979-80; chief exec. officer Wills Eye Hosp., Phila., 1980-85; pres., chief exec. officer Mercy Health Care System, Scranton, Pa., 1985-89; pres., chief exec. officer Mt. Carmel Health, Columbus, Ohio, 1989-92; pres., chief exec. officer Incarnate Word Health Services, San Antonio, 1992-95; pres., chief exec. officer Catholic Med. Ctr. Bklyn. & Queens, 1996—; adj. faculty dept. health care Trinity U., 1992-95; asst. prof. Ohio State U., 1990-92; asst. clin. prof. Wright State U. Sch. Medicine, Dayton, Ohio, 1978-79; instr. U. Wis., Madison, 1972-73; mem. Wilkes Coll. Health Adminstrn. Adv. Com., 1988-89; bd. dirs. Coll. Misericordia Health Care Task Force, 1988-89; mem. bd. govs. League Vol. Hosps., 1996—, sec., 1997—; mem. bd. govs. Fidelis Care N.Y., 1996—; mem. bd. govs. Queensbrook Ins. Ltd., 1996—, vice chmn., 1996-97, chmn., 1997—. Trustee Community Blood Ctr., 1977-79, Cath. Social Svcs., 1976-79, pres., 1978-79; bd. dirs. Coop. Purchasing Corp., 1974-79; mem. Dayton Pub. Schs. Lay Adv. Com. on Vocat. Edn., 1974-79; pres. Dayton Area Young Adminstrs. Group, 1977; pres. elect Greater Dayton Area Hosp. Assn., 1979; mem. allied health technologies adv. com. Sinclair Community Coll., 1974-79; bd. dirs. Covenant Health System, 1992—, Consolidated Cath. Casualty Risk Retention Group, 1992-95, Cath. Charities, 1996—; active United Hosp. Fund, United Way, ARC. Mem. Am. Coll. Healthcare Execs., Acad. for Cath. Health Care Leadership, Mercy Leadership Group, Nat. Commn. Cath. Health Care Ministry-Resource Devel. Com., 1988-89, Maj. Cath. Hosp. Alliance (sec. 1990-95, chmn.-elect 1995-97, chmn. 1997—), Health Care Fin. Mgmt. Assn., Am. Assn. Univ. Profs. Ophthalmology, Am. Soc. Law and Medicine, Am. Hosp. Assn., Am. Assn. Eye and Ear Hosps. (pres.-elect 1984-85), Health Mgmt. Edn. Assn. (pres. 1987-88), Hosp. Assn. N.Y. State, Greater N.Y. Hosp. Assn. (mem. bd. govs. 1997—), Tex. Hosp. Assn., Ohio Hosp. Assn., Hosp. Assn. Pa., Cath. Health Assn., Am. Pub. Health Assn., Pa. Pub. Health Assn., Del. Valley Hosp. Council, Pa. Emergency Health Svcs. Coun., Del. County Emergency Health Svcs. Coun., Nat. Union Hosp. and Health Care Employees (plan trustee), Pa. Hosps. Ins. Co. Adv. Coun., 1988-89, C. of C., U. Notre Dame Alumni Assn., U. Mich. Alumni Assn., U. Wis. Med. Sch. Alumni Assn., Wills Eye Soc., Sorin Soc., Notre Dame Club (pres. 1971, v.p. 1983-84), Landmark Club, Dominion Country Club. Republican. Roman Catholic. Home: 15 Horseshoe Rd Greenwich CT 06807 Office: Catholic Med Ctr Bklyn & Queens 88-25 153 St Jamaica NY 11432

MC GUIRE, WILLIAM JAMES, social psychology educator; b. N.Y.C., Feb. 17, 1925; s. James William and Anne M. (Mitchell) McG.; m. Claire Vernick, Dec. 29, 1954; children—James William, Anne Maureen, Steven Thomas. BA, Fordham U., 1949, MA, 1950; PhD, Yale U., 1954; PhD (hon.), Eötvös U., Budapest, Hungary, 1990. Postdoctoral fellow U. Minn., 1954-55; assoc. prof. psychology U. Ill., 1958-61; prof. Columbia U., 1961-67, U. Calif., San Diego, 1967-70; vis. prof. London Sch. Econs., 1970-71; asst. prof. Yale U., New Haven, 1955-58, prof., 1971—, chmn. dept. psychology, 1971-73; Mem. adv. panel for sociology and social psychology NSF, 1963-65; mem. review panel for social scis. NIMH, 1968-72, cons., 1974-85. Author: Content and Processes in the Experience of Self, 1988, A Perspectivist Approach to Strategic Planning, 1989, Structure of Attitudes and Attitude Systems, 1989, The Content, Structure, and Operation of Thought Systems, 1991; contbr. to Ency. Brit.; editor Jour. Personality and Social Psychology, 1967-70; cons. editor European Jour. Social Psychology, 1978—, Jour. Applied Social Psychology, 1983—, Jour. Exptl. Social Psychology, 1994—, Comm. Rsch., 1988—. With AUS, 1943-46. Recipient Ann. Social Psychology award AAAS, 1964, Gen. Electric Found. awards, 1963, 64, 66, Disting. Scientist award Soc. Exptl. Social Psychology, 1992; grantee NSF, 1960-79, NIH, 1979—; Fulbright fellow Louvain (Belgium) U., 1950-51, Ctr. for Advanced Study in Behavioral Scis. fellow, 1965-66, Guggenheim fellow, 1970-71, William James fellow Am. Psychol. Soc., 1989—. Fellow APA (pres. divsn. personality and social psychology 1973-74, Disting. Sci. Contbn. award 1988); mem. Am. Sociol. Assn., Am. Assn. Pub. Opinion Rsch., Sigma Xi. Home: 225 Saint Ronan St New Haven CT 06511-2313 Office: Yale U Dept Psychology Box 208205 New Haven CT 06520-8205

MC GUIRE, WILLIAM W., health service organization executive; b. Troy, N.Y., 1948. Grad., U. Tex., 1970, U. Tex., 1974. Chmn., CEO, pres., dir. United Healthcare Corp.; bd. dirs. Minn. Bus. Partnership. Dir. Minn. Orch. Assn., Mpls.; trustee Mpls. Inst. of Arts. Office: United Healthcare Corp 300 Opus Ctr 9900 Bren Rd E Minnetonka MN 55343-9664

MCGUIRK, RONALD CHARLES, banker; b. Balt., Dec. 9, 1938; s. Charles F. and Grace E. (Delcher) McG.; m. Katherine Sauer, Oct. 1, 1960; children: Frank D., Ann E. Student St. John's Coll., Annapolis, Md., 1956-59. Sr. data processing officer 1st Nat. Bank, Balt., 1966-72, v.p. data processing, 1972-76, v.p. mktg., 1976-80, sr. v.p. mktg., 1980-90, sr. v.p. corp. plan, chief of staff to CEO, 1990-94; sr. v.p., corporate sec. First Md. Bancorp, Balt., 1995—. Bd. dirs. North Arundel Hosp., Glen Burnie, Md., 1974—, Internet, Inc., 1990-95, Glen Burnie Urban Renewal Com., 1995—, Annapolis Symphony, 1991-92; mem. adv. bd. Hist. Annapolis Found., 1982-85, dir., 1985-90; chmn. Annapolis Boundary Commn., 1983-84; mem. Anne Arundel County Coun., 1974-82, Anne Arundel County Libr. Bd., 1974-84; pres. Anne Arundel County Scholarship for Scholars/Bd. Edn., 1983-85, treas., 1985-88; mem. Anne Arundel County Charter Rev. Commn., 1986, Anne Arundel County Govt. Salary Commn., 1985, 89; chmn. Anne Arundel County Impact Fee Study Task Force, 1987; pres. Anne Arundel County YMCA, 1987-89, bd. dirs. 1982-87, 89-90; mem. Commn. for Ednl. Excellence, 1988-90; vice chmn. Ft. Meade Coordinating Coun., 1989-91; mem. Exec. Com. Md. Bus.-Industry PAC 1991—, Anne Arundel County Charter and Orgn. Transition Group, 1991; corp. ptnr. Sch. bus. and Mgmt. Morgan State U., 1991-92; trustee Md. Hist. Soc., 1995-96. Mem. Ctr. Club. Democrat. Roman Catholic. Office: 1st Nat Bank Md 25 S Charles St Baltimore MD 21201-3330

MCGUIRK, TERRENCE, former broadcasting company executive; b. Bklyn., Apr. 2, 1925; s. William Edward and Loretta Beatrice (Lanigan) McG.; m. Gloria Helen Geoghan, June 17, 1950; children: Terence F., Sara McGuirk Duncan, Susan McGuirk Blank, Elizabeth McGuirk Magee, Melissa McGuirk Bowman, Bryan, Michelle McGuirk O'Connor. B.S., Fordham U., 1950. Nat. sales mgr. St. WAGA-TV, Atlanta, 1966-68; mgr. Sta. WAGA-TV, Atlanta, 1970-75; eastern sales mgr. Storer TV Sales, N.Y.C., 1968-70; pres., gen. mgr. Sta. WTEN-TV, Albany, N.Y., 1976-82; pres. Knight-Ridder Broadcasting, Inc., 1982-85; ret. Assoc. trustee Siena Coll., Loudonville, N.Y., 1979-83; trustee Meml. Hosp. Found., 1980-83; dir. Albany chpt. ARC, 1987-91. Served with U.S. Army, 1943-46. Mem. Mariner Sands Country Club, Babylon Yacht Club (hon.).

MCGUIRL, MARLENE DANA CALLIS, law librarian, educator; b. Hammond, Ind., Mar. 22, 1938; d. Daniel David and Helen Elizabeth (Baludis) Callis; m. James Franklin McGuirl, Apr. 24, 1965. AB, Ind. U., 1959; JD, DePaul U., 1963; MALS, Rosary Coll., 1965; LL.M., George Washington U., 1978, postgrad. Harvard U., 1985. Bar: Ill. 1963, Ind. 1964, D.C. 1972. Asst., DePaul Coll. of Law Libr., 1961-62, asst. law libr., 1962-65; ref. law librarian Boston Coll. Sch. Law, 1965-66; libr. dir. D.C. Bar Library, 1966-70; asst. chief Am.-Brit. Law Div. Libr. of Congress, Washington, 1970, chief, 1970-90, environ. cons., 1990—; counsel Cooter & Gell, 1992-93; adminstr. Washington Met. Transit Authority, 1994—; libr. cons. Nat. Clearinghouse on Poverty Law, OEO, Washington, 1967-69, Northwestern U. Nat. Inst. Edn. in Law and Poverty, 1969, D.C. Office of Corp. Counsel, 1969-70; instr. law librarianship Grad. Sch. of U.S. Dept. of Agr., 1968-72; lectr. legal lit. Cath. U., 1972; adj. asst. prof., 1973-91; lectr. environ. law George Washington U., 1979—; judge Nat. and Internat. Law Moot Ct. Competition, 1976-78, 90—; pres. Hamburger Heaven, Inc., Palm Beach, Fla., 1981-91, L'Image de Marlene Ltd., 1986-92, Clinique de Beauté Inc., 1987-92, Heads & Hands Inc., 1987-92, Horizon Design & Mfg. Co., Inc., 1987—; dir. Stoneridge Farm Inc., Gt. Falls, Va., 1984—. Contbr. articles to profl. jours. Mem. Georgetown Citizens Assn.; trustee D.C. Law Students in Ct.; del. Ind. Democratic Conv., 1964. Recipient Meritorious Svc. award Libr. of Congress, 1974, letter of commendation Dir. of Pers., 1976, cert. of appreciation, 1981-84. Mem. ABA (facilities law libr. Congress com. 1976-89), Fed. Bar Assn. (chpt. council 1972-76), Ill. Bar Assn., Women's Bar Assn. (pres. 1972-73, exec. bd. 1973-77, Outstanding Contbn. to Human Rights award 1975), D.C. Bar Assn., Am. Bar Found., Nat. Assn. Women Lawyers, Am. Assn. Law Libraries, (exec. bd. 1973-77), Law Librarians Soc. of Washington (pres. 1971-73), Exec. Women in Govt. Home: 3416 P St NW Washington DC 20007-2705

MC GURN, BARRETT, communications executive, writer; b. N.Y.C., Aug. 6, 1914; s. William Barrett and Alice (Schneider) McG.; m. Mary Elizabeth Johnson, May 30, 1942 (dec. Feb. 1960); children: William Barrett III, Elizabeth (Mrs. John J. Hehn), Andrew; m. Janice Ann McLaughlin, June 19, 1962; children: Summers, Martin Barrett, Mark Barrett. AB, Fordham U., 1935, LittD, 1958. Editor Fordham Ram, 1934-35; with N.Y. Herald Tribune, 1935-66; asst. corr. N.Y. Herald Tribune, Rome, 1939, bur. chief, 1946-52, 55-62; reporting staff N.Y. Herald Tribune, 1935-42, 62-66; bur. chief N.Y. Herald Tribune, Paris, 1952-55; acting chief bur. N.Y. Herald Tribune, Moscow, 1958; with, assignments in Morocco, Algeria, Tunisia, Hungary (1956 revolution), Egypt, Greece, Yugoslavia, Poland, Cen. Africa, Gaza Strip. N.Y. Herald Tribune, 1946-62; press attache Am. Embassy, Rome, 1966-68; counselor for press affairs Am. Embassy, Vietnam, 1968-69; U.S. consular officer, sec. appointed by Pres., 1969; dir. U.S. Govt. Press Ctr., Vietnam, 1968-69; White House and Pentagon liaison for State Dept. spokesman Washington, 1969-72; World Affairs commentator USIA, 1972-73; dir. pub. info. U.S. Supreme Ct., Washington, 1973-82; dir. communications Cath. Archdiocese of Washington, 1984-87; pres. Carroll Pub. Co. pub. Cath. Standard and El Pregonero, 1987-91; dir. Our Sunday Vistor Pub. Co., 1988—; mem. Italian-Am. com. to select Italian fellowship winners for study in U.S., 1950-52; mem. U.S. Nat. Cath. Com. on Comm. Policy, 1970-74, White House Com. on Drug Control Info., 1970-72; mem. interdept. com. on U.S. govt. press info. policy, 1970, interdept. U.S. govt. task force to rescue 100 Ams. kidnapped in Jordan, 1970, one-man U.S. Presdl. mission to Cambodia on media news problems, 1970; archivist John Carroll Soc., Washington, 1990—. Author: Decade in Europe, 1959, A Reporter Looks at the Vatican, 1962, A Reporter Looks at American Catholicism, 1967, America's Court, The Supreme Court and The People, 1997; contbg. author: The Best from Yank, 1945, Yank, the GI Story of the War, 1946, Combat, 1950, Highlights from Yank, 1953, Overseas Press Club Cook Book, 1962, I Can Tell it Now, 1964, U.S. Book of Facts, Statistics and Information, 1966, New Catholic Treasury of Wit and Humor, 1967, How I Got that Story, 1967, Heroes for Our Times, 1968, Newsbreak, 1975, Saints for all Seasons, 1978, Informing the People, 1981, The Courage to Grow Old, 1989, Am. Peoples Encyclopedia Yearbook, Close To Glory: Yank Correspondents Untold Stories of World War II, 1992; contbr. articles to profl. jours. Trustee Corrs. Fund, 1965-68; mem. bd. Anglo-Am. Charity Fund in Italy, 1967-68; v.p. Citizens Assn., Westmoreland Hills, Md., 1984-86. Sgt. AUS, 1942-45. Decorated Purple Heart; grand knight Italian Order of Merit; Vietnam Psychol. Warfare medal 1st class; recipient Polk award for outstanding fgn. reporting L.I. U., 1956; named best press corr. abroad Overseas Press Club, 1957; recipient N.Y.C. Fire Dept. Essay Silver Medal, 1924, N.Y. Times Oratorical Contest Bronze Medal, 1930; Christopher award for one of ten most inspiring books of year, 1959; named Man of Year Cath. Inst. Press, 1962, Fordham U. Alumnus of Year in communications, 1963; co-winner ann. Golden Typewriter award N.Y. Newspaper Reporters Assn., 1965, nominated by N.Y. Herald Tribune for Journalism Pulitzer Prize, 1965; outstanding pub. service award N.Y. chpt. Sigma Delta Chi, 1965; recipient Page One award N.Y. Newspaper Guild, 1966, Silurians award, 1966, award N.Y. Newspaper Reporters Assn., 1966, Citation for pub. service N.Y.C. Citizens Budget Commn., 1966, Meritorious Honor award Dept. State, 1972; Ann. Achievement award Fordham U. Club, Washington, 1986. Mem. Fgn. Press Assn. Italy (v.p. 1951-52, pres. 1961-62), SHAPE Corrs. Assn. Paris (treas. 1955), Authors Guild, Am. Fgn. Svc. Assn., Pax Romana Soc. for Cath. Intellectuals (Washington chmn. 1986—, dir. 1994—), Overseas Press Club (pres. 1963-65), Nat. Press Club, Kenwood Club, Cosmos Club, Fordham U. Club Washington (bd. govs. 1990—). Roman Catholic. Home: 5229 Duvall Dr Bethesda MD 20816-1875 *Providing information to our democratic public has been the work of my life both as a foreign correspondent, as a government spokesman, and as a lecturer. The newsman and the person who speaks for government share the same objective of explaining government policy. The spokesman has an added responsibility—to help government policy succeed. The reporter and the spokesman sometimes are at war with one another, but it is a war in behalf of the same beneficiary: the people.*

MCGURN, GEORGE WILLIAM, lawyer; b. Chgo., May 10, 1914; s. George William and Margaret Anna (Gavin) McG.; m. Margaret Mary Daley (dec. Oct. 1967); children: Margaret Mary (dec.), George, Anne, Jane, Mary, Michael, Susan; m. Antoinette Margaret Feuce, Nov. 28, 1970. Student, Clemson U., 1932-34; JD, Ill. Inst. Tech., 1938; LLM, U. Chgo., 1946. Bar: Ill. 1938, U.S. Dist. Ct. (no. dist.) Ill. 1951, U.S. Supreme Ct. 1955, U.S. Ct. Appeals (7th cir.) 1974. Assoc. LaRochelle, Brooks & Beardsley, Chgo., 1938-40; asst. gen. counsel Pabst Brewing Co., Chgo., 1946-48; ptnr. Reum, Casello and McGurn, Chgo., 1948-51; asst. counsel Chgo. Dist. Engr. Office U.S. Army, Chgo., 1951-53; asst. atty. gen. Office of Ill. Atty. Gen., Springfield, Ill., 1953-54; chief counsel and sec. Ill. State Toll Highway Commn., Chgo. and Oak Brook, Ill., 1954-63; ptnr. Healy and McGurn, Chgo. and Oakbrook, 1963-82; ret. Healy and McGurn, 1982-88; counsel Law Offices of Michael McGurn, Warrenville, Ill., 1988—. Editor Chgo.-Kent Law Rev., 1936-38. Rep. committeeman, Elmhurst, Ill., 1960-63. Served to maj. U.S. Army, 1941-46; col. res. ret. Postgrad scholar Chgo.-Kent Coll. Law Ill. Inst. Tech., 1938; recipient Citizenship award Ill. Inst. Tech., 1988. Mem. ABA, Ill. State Bar Assn. (sr. counselor 1988), DuPage County Bar Assn., Rotry (sec. Oak Brook club 1962-63, v.p 1963-64), K.C., Delta Theta Phi (scholarship key). Roman Catholic. Home: 1572 S Prospect St Wheaton IL 60187-7750 Office: McGurn & Assocs Ltd 29w140 Butterfield Rd Warrenville IL 60555-2812

MCGURN, WILLIAM BARRETT, III, lawyer; b. N.Y.C., Apr. 3, 1943; s. Barrett and Mary Elizabeth (Johnson) McG.; m. Catherine Roche, June 17, 1972; children Mary Anne, Edward Johnson. BA, Yale U., 1965; JD, Harvard U., 1972. Bar: D.C. 1973, Paris 1992. Assoc.t Cleary, Gottlieb, Steen & Hamilton, Paris and Washington, 1972-80, ptnr., 1981—. Chmn. Dem. Abroad, France, 1987-89, mem. exec. com., 1989—; gov. Am. Hosp. Paris, 1991—, sec., 1992—. Lt. USNR, 1967-69. Mem. ABA, Am. Club Paris, Am. C. of C. France (bd. dirs. 1996—, sec. 1997—). Democrat. Home: 29 Ave Bosquet, 75007 Paris France Office: Cleary Gottlieb Steen & Hamilton, 41 Ave Friedland, 75008 Paris France

MCGWIRE, MARK DAVID, professional baseball player; b. Pomona, Calif., Oct. 1, 1963; s. John and Ginger McGwire; m. Kathy McGwire; 1 child, Matthew. Student, U. So. Calif. With Oakland Athletics, 1984—; player World Series, 1988, 89, 90. Named Am. League Rookie of Yr. Baseball Writers' Assn. Am., 1987, Sporting News, 1987; recipient Gold Glove award, 1990; named to All-Star team, 1987-92, 95-96; recipient Silver Slugger Award, 1992; Am. League Home Run Leader, 1987; mem. U.S. Olympic Baseball Team, 1984. Office: 7677 Oakport St Ste 200 Oakland CA 94621-1933*

MCHALE, EDWARD ROBERTSON, retired lawyer; b. Chgo., Jan. 24, 1921; s. Edward F. and Martha (Robertson) McH.; m. Helen Louise Lindgren, Aug. 28, 1953; children: Nancy Ellen McHale Kaufman, Sally Jane McHale Cutler, John Robertson. B.S.S., Northwestern U., 1942; LL.B., Harvard U., 1948. Bar: Calif. 1949. Asst. U.S. atty. U.S. atty. So. Dist. Calif., 1949-61, chief tax div., 1954-61; assoc. Mitchell, Silberberg & Knupp, Los Angeles, 1961-64; partner Mitchell, Silberberg & Knupp, 1965-86, mgr. litigation dept, 1978-82; pres. Edward R. McHale, P.C., 1979—; lectr. U. So. Calif. Law Center, 1958-61. Co-author: Handling Federal Tax Litigation, 1961. Served to lt. USNR, 1943-46. Mem. Fed. Bar Assn. (past pres. Los Angeles chpt., past nat. v.p. for 9th Circuit), Assn. Bus. Trial Lawyers (bd. govs. 1981-83), State Bar Calif., Delta Sigma Rho. Lutheran. Clubs: South Hills Country (West Covina); Clan Donnachaidh Soc. Home: 1116 S Serena Dr West Covina CA 91791-3754

MC HALE, JOHN JOSEPH, baseball club executive; b. Detroit, Sept. 21, 1921; s. John Michael and Catherine M. (Kelly) McH.; m. Patricia Anne Cameron, Feb. 15, 1947; children: Patricia Cameron II, John Joseph, Jr., Kevin K., Anne F., Brian F., Mary M. A.B. cum laude, U. Notre Dame, 1947. Profl. baseball player, 1941-42, 45-47; asst. dir. minor league clubs Detroit Tigers Baseball Club, 1948, asst. farm dir., 1948-53, dir. minor league clubs, 1954-55, dir. player personnel, 1956-57, gen. mgr., 1957-58; v.p., gen. mgr. Milw. Braves Baseball Club (became Atlanta Braves Baseball Club 1961), 1957-61, pres., gen. mgr., 1961-67; adminstrv. asst. to commr. baseball N.Y.C., 1967-68; pres. Montreal Expos Baseball Club, 1968-87, dep. chmn., chief exec. officer, 1987—; pres. Japan Sports Systems; dir. Perini Corp. Trustee, Intracoastal Hosp. Corp., West Palm Beach, Fla., 1986—, Schwartz Investment Trust. Mem. Nat. Monogram Club (U. Notre Dame), Assn. Profl. Ball Players Am. (pres.) Harbour Ridge Club, Amelia Island Plantation Club. Address: Harbor Ridge 2014 Royal Fern Ct Palm City FL 34990

MCHALE, KEVIN EDWARD, former professional basketball player; b. Hibbing, Minn., Dec. 19, 1957; m. Lynn McHale; children: Kristyn, Michael. Student, U. Minn., 1976-80. Basketball player Boston Celtics, 1980-93; v.p. basketball ops. Minn. Timberwolves. Named to NBA All Rookie Team, 1981, NBA All-Defensive First Team, 1986-88, All-NBA First Team, 1987, NBA All-Star Game, 1984, 86-91; recipient NBA Sixth Man award, 1984, 85. Played on NBA Championship Team, 1981, 84, 86. Office: Minn Timberwolves Target Ctr 600 1st Ave N Minneapolis MN 55403-1400*

MCHALE, MICHAEL JOHN, lawyer; b. N.Y.C., Apr. 14, 1960; s. Michael Joseph and Mary Beatrice (Graddy) McH. BA, U. of the South, 1982; JD, Samford U., 1985. Bar: Ala. 1986, U.S. Dist. Ct. (no., mid. and so. dists.) Ala. 1986, U.S. Ct. Appeals (11th cir.) 1986, Fla. (cert. admiralty and maritime law) 1991, U.S. Dist. Ct. (mid. and so. dists.) 1991, U.S. Supreme Ct. 1991; cert. admiralty and maritime lawyer Fla. Bar Bd. of Legal Specialization, mediator Fla. Supreme Ct. Assoc. Wagner, Nugent, Johnson, Roth, Romano, Eriksen & Kupfer, West Palm Beach, Fla., 1989-92; ptnr. Whalen & McHale, West Palm Beach, Fla., 1992-95, Daves, Whalen. McHale & Considine, West Palm Beach, Fla., 1995—. Author: Strategic Use of Circumstantial Evidence, 2nd edit., 1991, Evaluating and Settling Personal Injury Claims, 1992, supplement through present, Making Trial Objections, 1993, supplement through present, Expert Witnesses: Direct and Cross Examination, 1993, supplement through present; editor, author: Litigating TMJ Cases, 1993 and yearly supplements. Named one of Outstanding Young Men of Am., 1988. Mem. ABA (mem. admiralty com.), ATLA, Am. Acad. Fla. Trial Lawyers, Maritime Law Assn. U.S., Southeastern Admiralty Law Inst., Fla. Bar (admiralty law com. editl. bd.), Palm Beach Bar Assn., Sigma Nu Phi. Avocation: fishing. Home: 23018-D Oxford Pl Boca Raton FL 33433 Office: Daves Whalen McHale & Considine 301 Clematis St Ste 200 West Palm Beach FL 33401-4601

MCHALE, PAUL, congressman, lawyer; b. Bethlehem, Pa., July 26, 1950; m. Katherine McHale; children: Matthew, Mary, Luke. BA in Govt. sigma cum laude, Lehigh U., 1972, JD, Georgetown U. Law Sch., 1977. Atty. Bethlehem, 1977-82; mem. Pa. Ho. of Reps., 1983-92, 103rd-105th Congresses from 15th Pa. dist., 1993—; mem. nat. security com., mem. sci. com. Infantry officer USMC, Okinawa, Philippines, 1972-74; Maj. USMCR Persian Gulf, 1990-92. Decorated Navy Commendation medal. Mem. Phi Beta Kappa. Democrat. *

MCHALE, ROBERT MICHAEL, lawyer; b. Youngstown, Ohio, Oct. 14, 1932; s. John F. and Elizabeth (Prendergast) M.; children: John F. II, Rachel Anne, Robert M. Jr. Student, St. Mary's Coll., Moraga, Calif., 1950-53; JD, Tulane U., 1956. Bar: La. 1956, U.S. Dist. Ct. (we. dist.) La. 1958, U.S. Ct. Mil. Appeals 1959, U.S. Supreme Ct. 1959, U.S. Ct. Appeals (5th cir.) 1960, U.S. Dist. Ct. (ea. dist.) La. 1963. Ptnr. Rogers, McHale & St. Romain, Lake Charles, La., 1960-70; prin. McHale, Bufkin & Dees, Lake Charles, 1970-94, McHale Schwartzberg, Lake Charles, 1995—; bd. dirs. Cameron (La.) State Bank; chair mineral bd. State of La., 1992-94, 96, chair legal and title controversy commn., 1994-96. Democrat. Roman Catholic. Avocations: horse racing, railroads. Office: 1901 Oak Park Blvd Lake Charles LA 70601-8915

MCHALE, VINCENT EDWARD, political science educator; b. Jenkins Twp., Pa., Apr. 17, 1939; m. Ann Barbara Cotner, Nov. 8, 1963; 1 child, Patrick James. A.B., Wilkes Coll., 1964; M.A., Pa. State U., 1966, Ph.D. in Polit. Sci., 1969. Asst. prof. polit. sci. U. Pa., Phila., 1969-75, dir. grad. studies, 1971-73; assoc. prof. Case Western Res. U., Cleve., 1975-84, prof., 1984—, chmn. dept. polit. sci., 1978—; vis. lectr. John Carroll U., summer 1980, Beaver Coll., spring 1975. Author: (with A.P. Frognier and D. Paranzino) Vote, Clivages Socio-politiques et Developpement Regional en Belgique, 1974. Co-editor; contbr.: Evaluating Transnational Programs in Government and Business, 1980; Political Parties of Europe, 1983; edit. adv. bd. Worldmark Ency. of Nations, 1994—. Contbr. chpts. to books, articles to profl. jours. Project cons. Council Econ Opportunity in Greater Cleve., 1978-81; mem. Morris Abrams Award Com., 1977—. Recipient Outstanding Prof. award Lux chpt. Mortar Bd., 1989, 90; named one of Most Interesting People of 1988, Cleve. Mag.; NSF grantee, 1971-72; HEW grantee, 1976-78; Woodrow Wilson fellow, 1968, Ruth Young Boucke fellow, 1967-68; All-Univ. fellow, 1967-68. Mem. Phi Kappa Phi. Home: 3070 Coleridge Rd Cleveland OH 44118-3556 Office: Case Western Res U Cleveland OH 44106

MCHARG, IAN LENNOX, landscape architect, regional planner, educator; b. Clydebank, Scotland, Nov. 20, 1920; came to U.S., 1946, naturalized, 1960; s. John Lennox and Harriet (Bain) McH.; m. Pauline Crena de Iongh, Aug. 30, 1947 (dec. 1974); children: Alistair Craig, Malcolm Lennox, Ian William, Andrew Maxwell; m. Carol Ann Smyser, May 28, 1977. B.Landscape Architecture, Harvard U., 1949, M.Landscape Architecture, 1950, M.City Planning, 1951; L.H.D. (hon.), Amherst Coll., 1970, Bates Coll., 1978; H.H.D. (hon.), Lewis and Clark Coll., 1970; D.L. (hon.), Heriot-Watt U., Edinburgh, Scotland. Planner Dept. Health, Scotland, 1950-54; prof. dept. landscape architecture and regional planning U. Pa., Phila., 1954-86; disting. sci. lectr. Brookhaven Nat. Lab., 1968; Horace Albright Meml. lectr. U. Calif., Berkeley, 1969, sr. vis. prof., 1986-87; Danz lectr. U. Wash., Seattle, 1971; Brown and Haley lectr. U. Puget Sound, 1971; Found. prof. U. Auckland, 1986; vis. prof. Pa. State U., Harvard U., 1994; Bruce Goff prof. architecture Okla. U., 1994. Prin. works include Ecol. Study for Mpls.-St. Paul Met. Area, San Francisco Met. Area, plan for New Town, Ponchartrain, New Orleans, plan for New Town, Woodlands, Tex., Environ. Park for Tehran, Iran, Amelia Island, Medford, Sanibel, EMAP, Nat. Ecol. Inventory; author: Design With Nature, 1969, Quest for Life, 1996. Recipient B.Y. Morrison medal N.Am. Wildlife Mgmt. Assn., 1971, Creative Arts award Brandeis U., 1972, Pioneer award AICP, Phila. Art Alliance award, 1975, Rene du Bos award, 1986, Alfred La Gasse award, 1987, Nat. Medal of Art, 1990, Richard Neutra medal, 1992, CELA Outstanding Educator award, 1992, Outstanding Achievement award Harvard U., 1992, Thomas Jefferson medal U. Va., 1995. Fellow Royal Soc. Art, Am. Soc. Landscape Architects (Bradford Williams medal 1968, 76, ASLA medal 1984), Inst. Landscape Architects, Royal Inst. Brit. Architects; mem. NAS (com. on sci. in nat. pks. 1991-92), AIA (hon., Allied Professions medal 1972). Office: U Pa Dept Landscape Arch & Regl Plng Philadelphia PA 19104

MC HARGUE, CARL JACK, research laboratory administrator; b. Corbin, Ky., Jan. 30, 1926; s. John David and Virginia (Thomas) McH. B.S. in Metall. Engring., U. Ky., 1949, M.S., 1951, Ph.D., 1953; m. Edith Trovillion, Aug. 28, 1948; children: Anne Odell McHargue Diegel, Carol Virginia, Margaret Katherine McHargue; m. Betty Ford, Sept. 30, 1960. Instr. U. Ky.,

Lexington, 1949-53; with Oak Ridge Nat. Lab., 1953-90, sect. head, 1960-80, program mgr. for materials scis., 1961-88, sr. rsch. staff 1980-90; prof. metall. engring. U. Tenn., Knoxville, 1963—, dir. ctr. materials processing, 1991—; vis. prof. U. Newcastle upon Tyne, Eng., 1987; adj. prof. Vanderfilt U., 1988—. With AUS, 1944-46. Named to Engring. Hall of Distinction, U. Ky., 1995. Fellow Metall. Soc. AIME, Am. Soc. for Metals; mem. Am. Nuclear Soc., Materials Rsch. Soc., Sigma Xi, Tau Beta Pi. Republican. Presbyterian. Contbr. numerous articles in field to profl. jours. Home: 7201 Sheffield Dr Knoxville TN 37909-2414 Office: U Tenn 102 Estabrook Hall Knoxville TN 37996-2350

MCHENRY, BARNABAS, lawyer; b. Harrisburg, Pa., Oct. 30, 1929; s. William Cecil and Louise (Perkins) McH.; m. Marie Bannon Jones, Dec. 13, 1952; children: Thomas J.P., W.H. Davis, John W.H. AB, Princeton U., 1952; LLB, Columbia U., 1957. Bar: N.Y. 1957. Assoc. Lord, Day, & Lord, N.Y.C., 1957-62; gen. counsel The Reader's Digest Assn., Inc., N.Y.C., 1962-85; exec. dir. Wallace Funds, N.Y.C., 1985-86; chmn. N.Y. state orgns., 1986—. Trustee Boscobel Restoration, Inc., 1964, Am. Conservation Assn., 1977, Hudson River Found. for Sci. and Environ. Rsch., Inc., Saratoga Performing Arts Ctr., 1984, Aperture Found., 1986; trustee emeritus Met. Mus. Art, 1980; coun. mem. Villa I Tatti, Harvard Sch. Renaissance Studies, 1982; regent emeritus Smithsonian Instn., 1985; commr. Palisades Interstate Park Commn., 1987; chmn. Hudson River Valley Greenway Coun., 1989. Home: 164 E 72nd St New York NY 10021-4363

MCHENRY, HENRY MALCOLM, anthropologist, educator; b. Los Angeles, May 19, 1944; s. Dean Eugene and Emma Jane (Snyder) McH.; m. Linda Jean Conway, June 25, 1966; children: Lindsay Jean, Annalisa Jane. BA, U. Calif., Davis, 1966, MA, 1967; PhD, Harvard U., 1972. Asst. prof. anthropology U. Calif., Davis, 1971-76, assoc. prof. anthropology, 1976-81, prof. anthropology, 1981—, chmn. dept. anthropology, 1984-88. Fellow Am. Anthrop. Assn., Calif. Acad. Sci.; mem. Am. Assn. Phys. Anthropologists (exec. com. 1981-85), Soc. Study Evolution, Soc. Vertebrate Paleontology, Phi Beta Kappa, Phi Kappa Phi. Democrat. Buddhist. Avocation: winemaker. Home: 330 11th St Davis CA 95616-2010 Office: U of Calif Davis Dept Of Anthropology Davis CA 95616

MC HENRY, MARTIN CHRISTOPHER, physician, educator; b. San Francisco, Feb. 9, 1932; s. Merl and Marcella (Bricca) McH.; m. Patricia Grace Hughes, Apr. 27, 1957; children: Michael, Christopher, Timothy, Mary Ann, Jeffrey, Paul, Kevin, William, Monica, Martin Christopher. Student, U. Santa Clara, 1950-53; MD, U. Cin., 1957; MS in Medicine, U. Minn., 1966. Intern, Highland Alameda County (Calif.) Hosp., Oakland, 1957-58; resident, internal medicine fellow Mayo Clinic, Rochester, Minn., 1958-61, spl. appointee in infectious diseases, 1963-64; staff physician infectious diseases Henry Ford Hosp., Detroit, 1964-67; staff physician Cleve. Clinic, 1967-72, chmn. dept. infectious diseases, 1972-92, sr. physician infectious diseases, 1992—. Asst. clin. prof. Case Western Res. U., 1970-77, assoc. clin. prof. medicine, 1977-91, clin. prof. medicine, 1991—; assoc. vis. physician Cleve. Met. Gen. Hosp., 1970—; cons. VA Hosp., Cleve., 1973—. Chmn. manpower com. Swine Influenza Program, Cleve., 1976. Served with USNR, 1961-63. Named Disting. Tchr. in Medicine Cleve. Clinic, 1972, 90; recipient 1st ann. Bruce Hubbard Stewart award Cleve. Clinic Found. for Humanities in Medicine, 1985, Nightingale Physician Collaboration award Cleve. Clinic Found. Divsn. Nursing, 1995. Diplomate Am. Bd. Internal Medicine. Fellow ACP, Infectious Diseases Soc. Am., Am. Coll. Chest Physicians (chmn. com. cardiopulmonary infections 1975-77, 81-83), Royal Soc. Medicine of Great Britain; mem. Am. Soc. Clin. Pharmacology and Therapeutics (chmn. sect. infectious diseases and antimicrobial agts., 1970-77, 80-85, dir.), Am. Thoracic Soc., Am. Soc. Clin. Pathologists, Am. Fedn. Clin. Rsch., Am. Soc. Tropical Medicine and Hygiene, Am. Soc. Microbiology, N.Y. Acad. Scis. Contbr. numerous articles to profl. jours., also chpts. to books. Home: 2779 Belgrave Rd Pepper Pike OH 44124-4601 Office: 9500 Euclid Ave Cleveland OH 44195-0001

MC HENRY, POWELL, lawyer; b. Cinn., May 14, 1926; s. L. Lee McHenry and Marguerite L. (Powell) Heinz; m. Venna Mae Guerrea, Aug. 27, 1948; children: Scott, Marshall, Jody Lee, Gale Lynn. AB, U. Cinn., 1949; LLB, Harvard U., 1951, JD, 1969. Bar: Ohio 1951, U.S. Ct. Appeals (6th cir.) 1964, U.S. Supreme Ct. 1966. Assoc. Dinsmore, Shohl, Sawyer & Dinsmore, Cinn., 1951-58; ptnr. Dinsmore, Shohl, Coates & Deupree (and predecessors), Cinn., 1958-75; gen. counsel Federated Dept. Stores, Inc., 1971-75; assoc. gen. counsel Procter & Gamble Co., 1975-76, v.p., gen. counsel, 1976-83, sr. v.p., gen. counsel, 1983-91; counsel Dinsmore & Shohl, Cin., 1991—; bd. dirs. Eagle Picher Industries, Inc., 1991—. Mem. com. Hamilton County Pub. Defender, Cinn. With USNR, 1944-46. Recipient award of merit Ohio Legal Center Inst., 1969. Mem. ABA, Ohio Bar Assn., Cin. Bar Assn. (pres. 1979-80, exec. com. 1975-81), Harvard U. Law Sch. Assn. Cin. (pres. 1960-61), Am. Law Inst., Assn. Gen. Counsel (pres. 1986-88), Harvard Club, Western Hill Country Club (bd. dirs. 1964-70, sec. 1966-69, 87-89, treas. 1969-70, 89-90), Queen City Club, Commonwealth Club. Republican. Methodist. Office: Dimsmore & Shohl 1900 Chemed Ctr 255 E 5th St Cincinnati OH 45202-4700

MCHENRY, ROBERT (DALE), editor; b. St. Louis, Apr. 30, 1945; s. Robert Dale and Pearl Lenna (Nalley) McH.; m. Carolyn F. Amundson, Oct. 2, 1971; children: Curran, Zachary. BA in English Lit., Northwestern U., 1966; MA in English Lit., U. Mich., 1967; MBA in Mgmt., Northwestern U., 1987. Proofreader, prodn. editor Ency. Britannica, Inc., Chgo., 1967-69, editor, 1974-75, dir. yearbooks, 1985-86, mng. editor, 1986-90, gen. editor, v.p., 1990-92, editor-in-chief, 1992—. Editor: Documentary History of Conservation in America, 1972, Webster's American Military Biographies, 1978, Liberty's Women, 1980, Webster's New Biographical Dictionary, 1983. Mem. United Ch. of Christ.

MCHOES, ANN MCIVER, technical writer, computer systems consultant; b. San Diego, June 17, 1950; d. Donald Anthony McHoes and Ann Mae McIver; children: A. Genevieve, Katherine Marie. BS in Math., U. Pitts., 1973, MS in Info. Sci., 1986. Tech. writer Westinghouse Electric Corp., Pitts., 1973-79; pres. McHoes & Assocs., Pitts., 1981—; adj. faculty computer sci., Carlow Coll., Pitts., 1992—; cons. Westinghouse Electric Corp., 1988—, PNC Bank, Pitts., 1988—; vis. lectr. Pa. State U., State College, 1990-91; judge Pa. Jr. Acad. Sci., Pitts., 1993—; vol. tutor Greater Pitts. Literacy Coun., 1996-97. Co-author: Understanding Operating Systems, 1991, 2d edit., 1997. Mem. Assn. Computing Machinery, Info. Sys. Security Assn. (chpt. sec. 1991-94, v.p. 1995-96, membership chair 1994—), IEEE Computer Soc., Pa. Mid. Sch. Assn. (conf. exhibit chair 1996-97). Avocations: travel, tennis, music. Office: McHoes & Assocs 2737 Beechwood Blvd Pittsburgh PA 15217-2705

MCHUGH, BETSY BALDWIN, sociologist, educator, journalist, business owner; b. Concord, N.H., 1928; d. Walter Killenbeck and Eliza Alice (Hunt) Slater; m. Michael Joseph McHugh, Dec. 19, 1954; children: Betsy, Michael. MusB in Vocal Music, Syracuse (N.Y.) U., 1954; grad. student, Cornell U. Tchr. pub. schs. Juneau, Alaska, 1966-85; owner, founder Cashé Pub. Co., Tampa, Fla., and Juneau, 1986—, Nikish Ki Lodges and Youth Camps subsidiaries Baldwin Enterprises. Named one of Alaska's Outstanding Educators, Gov. Alaska Woman's Commn., 1985, Uno of Yr., 1993, 94, Internat. Una of Yr., 1993, 94, one of 2000 Most Notable Women, 1994, Better Profl. WOmen, 1993, 94. Mem. Can. Nat. Libr., Nat. Press Club, Bus. Assn. N.Y. State, Libr. of Congress, Can. Bus., D.C. C. of C., Mex. C. of C., Sigma Delta Chi. Avocations: snorkeling, writing, sociology, dancing, music.

MCHUGH, CARIL DREYFUSS, art dealer, gallery director, consultant; b. New Haven, Conn.; d. Irving and Gertrude (Lax) Eisenstein; m. Barney Dreyfuss II (div.); children: Caryn, Barney III (Terry), Andrew, Evan; m. James Marshall McHugh Jr., Dec. 31, 1976. BA, Smith Coll.; MA, Am. U. Libr. archivist, mem. staff art rental Washington Gallery of Modern Art, 1963-67; asst. to curator of prints and drawings Nat. Mus. Am. Art, Washington, 1967-69; dir. Studio Gallery, Washington, 1970-75; dir., ptnr. Parsons-Dreyfuss Gallery, N.Y.C., 1976-80; dir. Frank Marino Gallery, N.Y.C., 1981, Humphrey Fine Art, N.Y.C., 1988-90, Gregory Gallery, N.Y.C., 1995-96; curator Hugo de Pagano Gallery, 1997—; art cons., writer, N.Y.C., 1982-95; arranger exhbns. Nat. Mus. Am. Art, Washington, 1968, 69, USIA, Washington, 1976, Automation House, N.Y.C., 1983. Contbr. essays to catalogs, articles to profl. mags. Bd. dirs. Women's Nat. Dem. Club, Washington, 1972-76, Friends of the Corcoran, Washington, 1972-76, Smith Club of Washington, 1974-76; Sophia Smith Assoc. Smith Coll., Northampton, Mass., 1985, 90, 95. Avocations: reading, hiking, swimming, designing accessories, writing poetry. Home: 241 Central Park West Apt 9C New York NY 10024

MCHUGH, EARL STEPHEN, dentist; b. Colorado Springs, Colo., Feb. 27, 1936; s. Earl Clifton and Margaret Mary (Higgins) M.; m. Joan Bleckwell, Aug. 24, 1957; children: Kevin, Stacey, Julie. BA, Cornell U., 1958; DDS, U. Mo., 1962. Pvt. practice, Kansas City, Mo., 1964—; lectr. U. Mo. Dental Sch., Kansas City, 1988, clin. staff, 1989, 90, 91, 92, 93, 94, 95, 96, ethics seminar faculty staff, addiction in dentistry faculty, 1995; cons. Hallmark, Inc., Kansas City, 1988; adv. dir. Rsch. Hosp., Kansas City. Contbr. articles to profl. jours. Deacon Presbyn. Ch. Prairie Village, Kans., 1982-84; vol. Shawnee Mission Hosp. Kans., 1985-88; lectr. Drug Recovery Program, Kansas City, Kans., 1988-89, 92, 93, 94. Capt. Dental Corp, U.S. Army, 1962-64. Mem. Valley Hope Assn., Audubon Soc. (Ortnithologist of Yr. award Kansas City chpt. 1990), Kans. Ornithol. Soc. (v.p. 1989-90, pres. 1990-91), Internat. Coun. Bird Preservation (Kans. del. 1990, coord. Kans. Breeding Bird Atlas 1992, 93, 94, 95, 96, chmn. Kans. bird records com.), Omicron Kappa Upsilon, Chi Psi.

MCHUGH, EDWARD FRANCIS, JR., lawyer; b. Cambridge, Mass., Sept. 6, 1932; s. Edward Francis and Eleanor (Whelton) McH.; m. Mary Judith Murchison, Sept. 15, 1962; children: Mary, Alexandra, Edward III, Michael. AB, Georgetown U., 1953, LLB, 1958. Bar: Mass., 1958, U.S. Dist. Ct. Mass. 1958, D.C. 1958, U.S. Ct. Appeals (D.C. cir.) 1958. Law clk. U.S. Ct. Appeals (D.C. cir.), Washington, 1958-59; assoc., jr. ptnr, then ptnr. Nutter, McClennen & Fish, Boston, 1959—; gen. counsel Two/Ten Found., Watertown, Mass., 1975-95; counsel, sec. New Eng. Aquarium Corp., Boston, 1987—; gen. counsel and clk. South Shore Health and Ednl. Corp. and South Shore Hosp., 1991—. Editor in chief Georgetown Law Journal, 1958; contbr. to profl. publs. Trustee Notre Dame Acad., Hingham, Mass., 1975-85, Harold Brooks Found., Quincy, Mass., 1987-88; chmn. bd. trustees South Shore Hosp. and South Shore Health and Ednl. Corp., Weymouth, Mass., 1986-88. 1st lt. USAF, 1953-55. Mem. Boston Bar Assn. (coun. 1984-87), Knights of Malta, Hatherly Country Club (pres. 1978-79), Clover Club. Roman Catholic.

MCHUGH, HEATHER, poet; b. Calif., Aug. 20, 1948. BA, Radcliffe Coll., 1970; MA, U. Denver, 1972. Assoc. prof. English SUNY, Binghamton, 1976-82; prof. English, Milliman writer-in-residence U. Wash., Seattle, 1983—; vis. prof. Columbia U., 1987; Holloway lectr. U. Calif., Berkeley, 1987; judge Nat. Poetry Series book award, 1986, 95. Author: (poetry) Dangers, 1977, A World of Difference, 1981, To the Quick, 1987, Shades, 1988, (essays) Broken English: Poetry and Partiality, 1993, Hinge & Sign: Poems, 1968-93, 1994 (Nat. Book award nomination 1994); translator: D'Apres Tout: Poems by Jean Follain, 1981; (with Nikolai Popov) Because the Sea Is Black: Poems by Blaga Dimitrova, 1989. Recipient Harvard U./Pollock prize, 1995, Lila Wallce/Reader's Digest Writer's award, 1996. Office: Univ of Washington Box 354330 Dept of English Seattle WA 98195-4330

MCHUGH, HELEN FRANCES, research administrator, consumption economist; b. Tucson, Aug. 19, 1931; d. James Patrick and Mary Catherine (Hochstatter) McH.; m. Herbert J. Brauer, Mar. 26, 1982. B.S. with distinction, U. Mo.-, Columbia, 1958, M.S., 1959; Ph.D., Iowa State U., 1965. Instr. U. Tex., Austin, 1961-63; asst. prof. U. Tex., 1963-66, asso. prof., 1966-67; asso. prof. Ind. State U., Terre Haute, 1967-69; asso. prof., dept. head Oreg. State U., Corvallis, 1969-73; prof., dean Coll. Home Econs., U. Del., Newark, 1973-75; prof. consumer econs. Colo. Experiment Sta., Colo. State U., Ft. Collins, 1976—; dean Coll. Human Resource Scis. Colo. State U., Ft. Collins, 1976-86, assoc. dir. Colo. Experiment Sta., 1976-86, dep. dir. Colo. Experiment Sta., 1986—; cons. in field. Chmn. policy bd.: Jour. Consumer Research, 1978-80. Recipient Disting. Service award U. Mo. Alumni Assn., 1975. Mem. Am. Econ. Assn., Am. Agrl. Econs. Assn., Am. Assn. of Family and Consumer Scis. (bd. dirs. 1973-75), Assn. Adminstrs. Home Econs. (pres. 1978-79), Western Assn. Agrl. Experiment Sta. Dirs., Great Plains Agrl. Coun. (bd. dirs. 1994-96, chair 1995-96), Sigma Xi, Gamma Sigma Delta, Phi Kappa Phi. Roman Catholic. Office: Colorado State U Agricultural Experimen Fort Collins CO 80523

MCHUGH, JAMES JOSEPH, retired naval officer, retired associate dean; b. Phila., Aug. 12, 1930; s. James Joseph and Patience Mary (McGowan) McH.; m. Rita Marie Huber, May 21, 1960; children: Margaret Marie, James Joseph IV. B.A. (with honors), U. Pa., 1951, LL.B., 1954; M.S. in Internat. Relations, George Washington U., 1972. Bar: Pa. 1955. Commd. ensign U.S. Navy, 1955, advanced through grades to rear adm., 1980; legal officer Naval Air Station, Point Mugu, Calif., 1955-58; staff officer Office Judge Adv. Gen., Washington, 1959-63; staff instr. U.S. Naval Justice Sch., Newport, R.I., 1963-65; counsel Bur. Naval Personnel, Washington, 1965-68; asst. fleet judge adv. to comdr. in chief U.S. Pacific Fleet, 1968-71; spl. counsel to chief naval ops. Washington, 1972-76; officer in charge Naval Legal Service Office, San Francisco, 1976-78; asst. judge adv. gen. Washington, 1978-80; dep. judge adv. gen. Alexandria, Va., 1980-82, judge adv. gen., 1982-84; asst. dean McGeorge Sch. Law, Sacramento, 1984-86, assoc. dean, 1987-93. Decorated D.S.M., Legion of Merit (2), Meritorious Svc. medal (2), Navy Commendation medal. Mem. ABA, Order of Coif (hon.), Phi Beta Kappa. Republican. Roman Catholic. Home: 4704 Olive Oak Way Carmichael CA 95608-5663

MCHUGH, JAMES LENAHAN, JR., lawyer; b. Pitts., June 28, 1937; s. James Lenahan and Annette (Dalton) McH.; m. Mary-Ann Curto, Feb. 16, 1963 (div. 1988); children: Angela Dalton Sherrill, Hillary Lenahan Clagett; m. Rosa Lamoreaux, Sept. 8, 1991. BA, Duquesne U., 1959; LLB, Villanova U., 1962. Bar: D.C. 1963. Law clk. U.S. Dist. Ct. (ea. dist.) Pa., Phila., 1962-63; law clk. to Assoc. Justice Tom C. Clark, U.S. Supreme Ct., Washington, 1963-64; assoc. Steptoe & Johnson, Washington, 1967-70, ptnr., 1970-94; gen. counsel APA, Washington, 1994—; mem. bd. consultors Law Sch., Villanova (Pa.) U., 1973—; dir. Higher Achievement Program, Washington, 1984-87; coord. Washington Lawyers' Project, Robert F. Kennedy Meml. Found., Washington, 1972-75. Editor-in-chief Villanova Law Rev., Vol. VII, 1961-62; chmn. editorial adv. bd. Fed. Comm. Law Jour., 1981-84. Bd. dirs. Columbia Hosp. for Women's Found., Washington, 1985-96, Children's Radio Theatre, Washington, 1983-86; chmn. exec. giving Archbishop's Appeal, Archdiocese of Washington, 1982-84; mem. bd. visitors Ctr. for Study of Orgns. and Mgmt., U. Md. Univ. Coll., 1987-92; bd. dirs. Human Resources Rsch. Orgn., Inc., 1978—; chmn. bd. dirs., 1991—; mem. advisors Inst. for Conflict Analysis and Resolution, George Mason U., 1990-94. Capt. U.S. Army, 1964-67. Mem. ABA (forum com. health law, sect. on tax, antitrust and intellectual property), Nat. Health Lawyers Assn., D.C. Bar Assn., Choral Arts Soc., Order of Coif. Home: 4112 Fessenden St NW Washington DC 20016-4227 Office: APA 750 1st St NE Washington DC 20002-4241

MCHUGH, JAMES T., bishop; b. Orange, N.J., Jan. 3, 1932. Educated at Seton Hall Univ., Immaculate Conception Sem. (Darlington, N.J.), Fordham Univ., Catholic Univ., Angelicum (Rome). Ordained priest, 1957; consecrated bishop, 1988. Asst. dir. Family Life Div., U.S. Cath. Conf., 1965-67, dir., 1967-75; dir. Office for Pro-Life Activities, Nat. Conf. Cath. Bishops, 1972-78; aux. bishop Newark, 1987-89; bishop Diocese of Camden, N.J., 1989—. Home: Marywood PO Box 577 Blackwood NJ 08012 Office: The Chancery PO Box 709 1845 Haddon Ave Camden NJ 08101*

MC HUGH, JOHN LAURENCE, marine biologist, educator; b. Vancouver, B.C., Can., Nov. 24, 1911; came to U.S., 1946, naturalized, 1958; s. John and Annie Margaret (Woodward) McH.; m. Sophie Kleban, Mar. 30, 1979; children by previous marriage—Peter Chadwick, Heather, Jan Margaret. B.A., U. B.C., 1936, M.A., 1938; Ph.D., U. Calif. at Los Angeles, 1950. Summer sci. asst. Fisheries Research Bd. Can., 1929-37, fishery biologist, 1938-41; research asso. Scripps Instn. Oceanography, 1948-51; dir. Va. Fisheries Lab., Gloucester Point, 1951-59; prof. marine biology Coll. William and Mary, 1951-59; chmn. sci. com. Atlantic States Marine Fisheries Commn., 1956-58; chief div. biol. research Bur. Comml. Fisheries, Dept. Interior, 1959-63, asst. dir. for biol. research, 1963-66, dep. dir. bur., 1966-70; acting dir. Office Marine Resources, 1968-70; head NSF Office for Internat. Decade Ocean Exploration, 1970; prof. marine resources SUNY-Stony Brook, 1970-82, prof. emeritus, 1982—; U.S. commr. Inter-Am. Tropical Tuna Commn., 1960-70, sec. commn., 1960-61, 67-68, sec. U.S. sect., 1961-67, head U.S. del., 1967-70; dep. U.S. commr. Internat. Whaling Commn., 1961-67, commr., 1967-73, vice chmn., 1968-71, chmn., 1971-72; mem. U.S. nat. com. Internat. Biol. Program, 1968-70; adv. com. marine resources research to dir.-gen. FAO, 1967-71; mem. U.S. dels. to internat. sci., fishery meetings, 1959-72, NRC, 1963-69; mem. com. on internat. marine sci. affairs policy, ocean affairs bd. Nat. Acad. Scis.-Nat. Acad. Engring., 1971-74, com. on aquatic food resources, food and nutrition bd., 1973-74, vice chmn., 1973; mem. blue ribbon panel to rev. fed. programs on continental shelf. Office Sci. and Tech., Exec. Office Pres., 1971; chmn. select com. to rev. Eastern Pacific Oceanic Conf., Scripps Instn. Oceanography, 1972; mem. steering com., chmn. panel on fisheries, chmn. working group on information needs for effective mgmt. Coastal Zone workshop Woods Hole Oceanographic Instn., 1971-72; hon. mem. Whaling Mus. Soc., Cold Spring Harbor, N.Y., 1972-76; sec. Internat. Marine Archives, Nantucket, Mass., 1973-78; cons. to Nat. Council Marine Resources and Engring. Devel., 1970-71, Smithsonian Instn., 1970-72, Nat. Oceanic and Atmospheric Adminstrn., 1971-73, Riverside Research Inst., N.Y.C., 1971-72, Town of Islip, N.Y., 1974-78; mem. Mid-Atlantic Regional Fishery Mgmt. Council, 1976-79, mem. sci. and statis. com., 1980-84; mem. steering com. Nat. Acad. Sci.-NRC Panel to Review Fishery Research, 1975-76. Author: Fishery Management; contbr. numerous sci. papers, book chpts., articles to profl. lit. Served to capt. Canadian Army, 1941-45. Recipient Disting. Teaching award Marine Scis. Rsch. Ctr. Assocs., 1977, cert. for meritorious svc. Marine Scis. Rsch. Ctr./U. Stony Brook, 1994; fellow Internat. Oceanographic Found., 1955-74; trustee emeritus, 1974—; fellow Woodrow Wilson Internat. Ctr. for Scholars Smithsonian Instn., summer 1971. Mem. AAAS (selection com., Rosenstiel award 1976), Am. Fisheries Soc. (Bronze medal, award of excellence 1984), Nat. Shellfisheries Assn. (citation 1984, hon. mem.), Va. Acad. Scis. (past chmn. biology sect.), Atlantic Estuarine Research Soc. (hon., past pres.), Am. Inst. Fishery Research Biologists, Nat. Shellfisheries Assn. (hon. mem.), Estuarine Research Fedn. (hon. mem.), Sigma Xi, Beta Theta Pi. Home: Vinson Hall Apt 170 6251 Old Dominion Dr Mc Lean VA 22101

MCHUGH, JOHN MICHAEL, congressman, former state senator; b. Watertown, N.Y., Sept. 29, 1948; s. Donald and Jane (O'Neill) McH. BA in Polit. Sci., Syracuse U., 1970; MPA, Nelson A. Rockefeller Grad. Sch. Pub. Affairs, 1977. Asst. city mngr. Watertown, 1968-73; confidential asst. Watertown City Mgrs. Office, 1971-76; chief of research, liaison with local govts. Office of N.Y. State Senator H.D. Barclay, 1976-84; U.S. senator from 46th N.Y. dist., 1984-93, chmn. joint legis. commn. on dairy industry devel., 1987-92; mem. 103rd-105th Congresses from 24th N.Y. dist., 1993—; chmn. govt. reform and oversight subcom. on postal svc., mem. nat. sucurity com. Mem. Legis. Commn. on Modernization of the Tax Code, Nat. Conf. State Legis., Commerce & Econ. Devel. Com., Commerce, Labor and Regulation Com. of the State Fed. Assembly, Coun. State Govt. Eastern Regional Conf. Com. on Fiscal Affairs. Recipient 40 Outstanding Alumni awards Syracuse U., Individual Achievement award N.Y. State Dept. Econ. Devel.; named to Hon. First Citizen, City of Watertown, 1976. Mem. Legis. on State Legislators (nat. conf. state legislators), Nat. Conf. State Legislators (vice chmn. agrl. and internat. trade com. State-Fed. Assembly), Am. Soc. Young Polit. Leaders. Republican. Roman Catholic. Avocations: boating, snow skiing, music. Office: US Ho of Reps 2441 Rayburn Washington DC 20515-3224*

MC HUGH, PAUL R., psychiatrist, neurologist, educator; b. Lawrence, Mass., May 21, 1931; s. Francis Paul and Mary Dorothea (Herlihy) McH.; m. Jean Barlow, Dec. 27, 1959; children: Clare Mary, Patrick Daniel, Denis Timothy. AB, Harvard U., 1952, MD, 1956. Diplomate: Am. Bd. Psychiatry and Neurology. Intern Peter Bent Brigham Hosp., Boston, 1956-57; resident in neurology Mass. Gen. Hosp., 1957-60, fellow in neuropathology, 1958-59; teaching fellow in neurology and neuropathology Harvard, 1957-60; clin. asst. psychiatry Maudsley Hosp., London, Eng., 1960-61; mem. neuropsychiatry div. Walter Reed Army Inst. Research, Washington, 1961-64; asst. prof. psychiatry and neurology Cornell U., N.Y.C., 1964-68; assoc. prof. Cornell U., 1968-71, prof., 1971; dir. electroencephalography N.Y. Hosp., 1964-68; founder, dir. N.Y. Hosp. Bourne Behavioral Rsch. Lab., 1967-68, clin. dir., supr. psychiat. edn., founder, dir. Weschester divsn. dept. psychiatry, 1968-73; prof., chmn. dept. psychiatry U. Oreg. Health Sci. Center, Portland, 1973-75; Henry Phipps prof. psychiatry Johns Hopkins, Balt., 1975—; chmn. dept. psychiatry Johns Hopkins, 1975—, prof. dept. mental hygiene, 1976—; psychiatrist-in-chief Johns Hopkins Hosp., 1975—; dir. Blades Ctr. for Clin. Practice and Rsch. in Alcoholism Johns Hopkins Med. Inst., 1992—; chmn. med. staff Johns Hopkins Hosp., 1983-89, trustee, 1983—; vis. prof. Guys Hosp., London, Eng., 1976; chmn. bio-psychology Study sect. NIH, 1986-89. Author: The Perspectives of Psychiatry, 1983; (with Phillip R. Slavney) Psychiatric Polarities, 1987, Genes, Brain and Behavior, 1990; contbg. author: Cecil-Loeb Textbook of Medicine; mem. editorial bd. Am. Jour. Physiology, Jour. Nervous and Mental Disease, Comprehensive Psychiatry, Medicine, Psychol. Medicine, 1976—, Am. Scholar; contbr. articles to profl. jours. Mem. Md. Gov.'s Adv. Com., 1977-80. Grantee NIH, 1964-68, 67-70, 70-74, 75—; recipient William C. Menninger award ACP, 1987. Fellow Royal Coll. Psychiatry, Am. Psychiat. Assn.; mem. Inst. Medicine-NAS, Am. Neurol. Assn., Am. Physiol. Soc., Harvey Soc., Am. Coll. Neuropsychopharmacology, Am. Psychopath. Assn., Pavlovian Soc., W Hamilton St. Club. Home: 3707 St Paul St Baltimore MD 21218-2403 Office: Johns Hopkins Med Insts Meyer 4-113 600 N Wolfe St Baltimore MD 21205-2110

MCHUGH, RICHARD WALKER, lawyer; b. Sullivan, Ind., Dec. 9, 1952; s. Richard Harrison and Virginia Ann (Robinson) McH.; m. Marsha J. Marshall, May 24, 1975; children: Walker, Cora. BA, Wabash Coll., 1975; JD, U. Mich., 1978. Bar: Mich. 1984, Ky. 1979, U.S. Supreme Ct. 1987. Assoc. Youngdahl Law Firm, Little Rock, 1978-79; staff atty. Legal Aid Soc., Louisville, 1979-84; assoc. gen. counsel Internat. Union UAW, Detroit, 1984-95; pvt. practice, Ann Arbor, Mich., 1995—; dir. Mich. Legal Svcs., Detroit, 1986-91. Mem. ABA (labor co-chmn. com. on state labor and employment law devel. 1996—), Nat. Acad. Social Ins. Democrat. Avocations: fishing, backpacking. Office: 255 E Liberty St Ste 289 Ann Arbor MI 48104-2119

MCILVAINE, JOSEPH PETER, professional baseball team executive; b. Bryn Mawr, Pa., Jan. 18, 1948; s. Joseph Francis and Mary Margaret (Wack) McI.; m. Martha Anne Marmer, Nov. 24, 1973; children: Timothy, Susan, Patrick. BA, St. Charles Borromeo Sem., Phila., 1969. Tchr. Our Mother of Good Counsel, Bryn Mawr, Pa., 1969-72; deliveryman United Parcel Svc., West Chester, Pa., 1972-73; profl. baseball player Detroit Tigers, 1969-73; major league baseball scout Balt. Orioles, 1974-76, Calif. Angels, Anaheim, 1977-78, Milw. Brewers, 1979-80; dir. scouting N.Y. Mets, Flushing, 1980-85, v.p., dir. baseball ops., 1986-90; exec. v.p., gen. mgr. San Diego Padres, 1990-93; former gen. mgr. N.Y. Mets, now exec. v.p. baseball ops.; cons. Athletes for Life, Washington, 1988—; bd. dirs. Major League Scouting Bur., Newport Beach, Calif., Returning Baseball to Inner Cities, L.A. Recipient World Series ring Major League Baseball, Flushing, 1986. Mem. Fla. Diamond Club (pres. 1980-81, Exec. of Yr. award 1984). Avocation: golf. *

MC ILVEEN, WALTER, mechanical engineer; b. Belfast, Ireland, Aug. 12, 1927; s. Walter and Amelia (Thompson) McI.; came to U.S., 1958, naturalized, 1963; M.E., Queens U., Belfast, 1948; H.V.A.C., Borough Polytechnic, London, 1951; m. Margaret Teresa Ruane, Apr. 17, 1949; children: Walter, Adrian, Peter, Anita, Alan. *Walter McIlveen graduated in Mechanical Engineering from the College of Technology, Queens University, Ireland and then completed graduate work at Borough Polytechnic, England and lectured, in Engineering Science at Regent St. Polytechnic, and University of Hartford, CT evening Division. After graduation, he gained valuable experience, as a manufacturer's contract application engineer on industrial and commercial systems and later in Consulting Engineering Services. Mr. McIlveen is a member of the Illuminating Engineering Society; Institution of Electronic and Electrical Engineers; American Society of Heating, Refrigerating and Air Conditioning Engineers; American Society of Mechanical Engineers, and The American Society of Plumbing Engineers.* Mech. engr. Davidson & Co., Belfast, 1943-48; sr. contract engr. Keith Blackman Ltd., London, 1948-58; mech. engr. Fred S. Dubin Assos., Hartford, Conn., 1959-

64; chief mech. engr. Koton & Donovan, West Hartfor, Conn., 1964-66; prin., engr. Walter McIlveen Assos., Avon, Conn., 1966—. Mem. IEEE, ASME, ASHRAE, Illuminating Engring. Soc., Hartford Engring. Club, Conn. Engrs. in Pvt. Practice. Mem. Ch. of Ireland. Home: 3 Valley View Dr Weatogue CT 06089-9714 Office: 195 W Main St Avon CT 06001-3685 *Walter McIlveen P.E. is a registered Professional Engineer and Chairman and President of Walter McIlveen Associates, Inc., consulting engineers. With a current staff of ten, Mr. McIlveen provides quality mechanical-electrical engineers services to architectural, municipal, business and industrial clients. Engineering services provided includes design of plumbing, ventilation, air conditioning, heating and electrical systems for commercial, institutional and industrial buildings. Mr. McIlveen is registered as a Professional Engineer in Connecticut, Florida, Illinois, Massachusetts, Maryland, Maine, New Hampshire, New Jersey, New York, Rhode Island, and Vermont.*

MCILVEEN, WALTER RONALD, architectural engineer; b. London, Sept. 9, 1950; came to U.S., 1959; s. Walter and Margaret Theresa (Ruane) McI.; m. Barbara Lee O'Neill, June 8, 1974 (div. June 1993); life ptnr. Jennifer L. Bistor; 1 child, Daniel Walter. BS in Mech. Engring., Worcester (Mass.) Poly. Inst., 1972; MS in Mech. Engring., Rensselaer Poly. Inst., Hartford, Conn., 1975; MBA, Wayne State U., 1979. Registered profl. engr., Conn., Fla., Tenn., Ga., Mich., Ala. Design engr. Walter McIlveen Assocs., Avon, Conn., 1972-77, project engr., 1977; project engr. Smith Hinchman & Grylls Assocs., Detroit, 1977-78, divsn. discipline head, 1978-81; divsn. mgr. Diaz Seckinger Assocs., Tampa, 1981-84; chief mech. and elec. engr. Archtl. Engring. Inc., Palm Harbor, Fla., 1984—; pres. Archtl. Engrs., Inc., Palm Harbor, 1993—. Mem. ASHRAE, NSPE, Nat. Fire Protection Assn., Nat. Coun. Engring. Examiners, Inc., So. Bldg. Code Congress Internat. Inc., Greater Tampa C. of C. Leadership Tampa. Republican. Roman Catholic. Avocations: tennis, water skiing, stone sculpting, snorkeling. Home: 3526 Shoreline Cir Palm Harbor FL 34684-1743 Office: Archtl Engring Inc 3442 E Lake Rd Palm Harbor FL 34685-2406

MCILWAIN, CARL EDWIN, physicist; b. Houston, Mar. 26, 1931; s. Glenn William and Alma Ora (Miller) McI.; m. Mary Louise Hocker, Dec. 30, 1952; children—Janet Louise, Craig Ian. B.A., N. Tex. State Coll., Denton, 1953; M.S., State U. Iowa, 1956, Ph.D., 1960. Asst. prof. State U. Iowa, 1960-62; assoc. prof. physics U. Calif.-, San Diego, 1962-66; prof. U. Calif., 1966—; mem. space scis. steering com., fields and particles subcom. NASA, 1962-66; mem. anti-submarine warfare panel President's Sci. Adv. Com., 1964-67; mem. com. potential contamination and interference from space expts. Space Sci. Bd., Nat. Acad. Scis.-NRC, 1964-71; mem. advisory com. for radiation hazards in supersonic transports FAA, 1967-71; mem. Fachbeirat Inst. Extraterrestrial Physics, Max Planck Inst., Garching, Fed. Republic Germany, 1977-83, Space Sci. Bd., NRC, 1983-86. Author. Guggenheim fellow, 1968, 72; recipient Space Sci. award Am. Inst. Aeros. and Astronautics, 1970; Computer Art award U.S. Users Automatic Info. Display Equipment, 1971; Sr. U.S. Scientist award Alexander von Humboldt Found., Ger., 1976. Fellow Am. Geophys. Union (John A. Fleming award 1975); mem. Am. Phys. Soc., Am. Astron. Soc. Patentee in field. Home: 6662 Avenida Manana La Jolla CA 92037-6228 Office: Cass, 0424 Univ Calif San Diego La Jolla CA 92093-0424

MCILWAIN, THOMAS DAVID, fishery administrator, marine biologist, educator; b. Pascagoula, Miss., Nov. 15, 1940; s. Julius Coleman and Kathleen (Folsom) McI.; m. Janet Ellen Chapman, Dec. 29, 1962; 1 child, Stacey Lee. BS in Biology and Psychology, U. So. Miss., 1964, MS in Biology, 1966, PhD in Zoology, 1978. Lab. aid U.S. Bur. Comml. Fisheries, Pascagoula, summer 1958; instr. biology U. So. Miss., Hattiesburg, 1964-66; tchr. sci. St. Martin (Miss.) High Sch., 1965-66; rsch. biologist Gulf Coast Rsch. Lab., Ocean Springs, Miss., 1966-67, sect. leader, 1967-78, asst. dir. fisheries, 1978-83, dir., 1989-94; legis. asst. U.S. Congressman Trent Lott, Washington, 1983-84; fishery adminstr. Nat. Marine Fisheries Svc., Pascagoula, Miss., 1994—; fishery cons. Gulf and South Atlantic Fishery Devel. Found., Tampa, Fla., 1984-86, Republic of Honduras, 1990; pres. bd. dirs. Miss.-Ala. Sea Grant Consortium, Ocean Springs, 1991-94. Contbr. numerous articles to profl. jours. Chmn. Harbor Commn., Ocean Springs, 1980—; bd. dirs. Jackson County United Way, Pascagoula, 1991-95, Walter Anderson Art Mus. Fellow Am. Inst. Fish Rsch. Scientists (regional bd. dirs. 1980); mem. Am. Fisheries Soc. (cert. fishery scientist), World Mariculture Soc., Miss. Acad. Scis. (bd. dirs. 1981), U.S. C. of C. (chmn. environ. com. 1990-95), So. Assn. Marine Labs. (pres. 1991-94). Presbyterian. Avocations: sailing, scuba diving, fishing. Office: Nat Marine Fisheries Svc Pascagoula Lab PO Drawer 1207 Pascagoula MS 39568-1207

MCILWAIN, WILLIAM ANTHONY, orthopedic surgeon; b. Waynesboro, Miss., May 29, 1949; s. Robert Lee and Bernice Arley (Taylor) McI.; m. Dian Wymer, June 12, 1971; children: William A., Jr., Cameron Cole, Douglas Graham. BS, U. Tenn., 1970, MD, 1974. Diplomate Am. Bd. Orthopedic Surgery. Chemist Quaker Oats Chemicals, Memphis, 1970-71; intern, resident orthopedic surgery U.S. Army Brooke Army Med. Ctr., San Antonio, 1974-78; orthopedic surgeon, asst. chief orthopaedic surgery 2d Gen. Hosp., Landstuhl, Germany, 1978-80; asst. chief spinal trauma ctr. Armed Forces Europe, Landstuhl, 1979-80; pvt. practice orthopedic surgery Bristol, Tenn., 1980—; pres. Bristol Orthopedic Assocs., 1982—; med. dir. physical therapy dept. Bristol Regional Med. Ctr., 1983—, chmn. dept. surgery, 1984-85; assoc. prof. clin. medicine East Tenn. State U., Johnson City, 1984—. Fellow Am. Acad. Orthopedic Assns., Am. Coll. Surgeons, N. Am. Spine Soc., Arthroscopy Assn. N. Am.; mem. Am. Coll. Physician Execs., Diagnostic Spine Soc. (pres. 1993). Avocations: cars, yardwork, fishing, skiing. Home: 7 S Briarcliff Rd Bristol TN 37620-4560 Office: Bristol Orthopaedic Assocs Office Plz 300E 1 Medical Park Blvd Bristol TN 37620-7430

MC ILWAIN, WILLIAM FRANKLIN, newspaper editor, writer; b. Lancaster, S.C., Dec. 15, 1925; s. William Franklin and Docia (Higgins) McI.; m. Anne Dalton, Nov. 28, 1952 (div. 1973); children: Dalton, Nancy, William Franklin III; m. K. L. Brelsford, June 5, 1978 (div. 1983). B.A., Wake Forest Coll., 1949; postgrad., Harvard, 1957-58. Various positions with Wilmington (N.C.) Star, 1943, Charlotte (N.C.) Observer, 1945, Jacksonville (Fla.) Jour., 1945, Winston-Salem (N.C.) Jour.-Sentinel, 1949-52, Richmond (Va.) Times-Dispatch, 1952-54; chief copy editor Newsday, Garden City, N.Y., 1954-57; day news editor Newsday, 1957-60, city editor, 1960-64, mng. editor, 1964-66, editor, 1967-70; writer-in-residence Wake Forest U., 1970-71; dorm leader Alcoholic Rehab. Ctr., Butner, N.C., 1971; dep. mng. editor Toronto Star, 1971-73; mng. editor The Record, Hackensack, N.J., 1973-77; editor Boston Herald Am., 1977-79; dep. editor Washington Star, 1979-81, exec. mng. editor, 1981; editor Ark. Gazette, 1981-82; founding editor N.Y. Newsday, 1982-84; exec. editor Sarasota (Fla.) Herald-Tribune, 1984-90; sr. editor N.Y. Times Regional Newspaper Group, 1991-92; chmn. Bill Mc Ilwain, Inc., 1993—; Stone Ridge lectr., 1978. Author: The Glass Rooster, 1960, (with Walter Friedenberg) Legends of Baptist Hollow, 1949; collaborator: (with Newsday staff) Naked Came The Stranger, 1969, A Farewell to Alcohol, 1973; contbr. to: Reader's Digest, Harper's, Esquire, Atlantic Monthly. Mem. Pres. Johnson's Commn. on Civil Rights. With USMC, 1944. Mem. Am. Soc. Newspaper Editors, Soc. Nieman Fellows. Home and Office: 305 N Channel Dr Wrightsville Beach NC 28480 *As Fats Waller said, "One never knows, do one?".*

MC INDOE, DARRELL WINFRED, nuclear medicine physician, former air force officer; b. Wilkinsburg, Pa., Sept. 28, 1930; s. Clarence Wilbert and Dorothy Josephine (Morrow) McI.; m. Carole Jean McClain, Aug. 23, 1952; children: Sherri L., Wendy L., Darrell B., Ronald S., Holly B. BS, Allegheny Coll., 1952; MD, Temple U., 1956, MS, 1960. Commd. 2d lt. M.C. U.S. Air Force, 1956, advanced through grades to col., 1971; intern Brooke Army Med. Ctr., San Antonio, 1956-57; resident in medicine Temple U. Med. Ctr., Phila., 1957-60; chief internal medicine and hosp. svcs. Norton AFB, 1960-64; chief internal medicine and hosp. services 7520 U.S. Air Force Hosp., U.K., 1964-68; vis. rsch. fellow Royal Post Grad. Med. Sch., London, 1968-69; chief endocrinology svcs., chmn. dept. nuclear medicine USAF Med. Center, Keesler AFB, Miss., 1969-75; dep. dir. Armed Forces Radiobiology Rsch. Inst., Def. Nuclear Agy., Bethesda, Md., 1975-77; dir. Armed Forces Radiobiology Rsch. Inst., Def. Nuclear Agy., 1977-79; staff physician nuclear medicine br., dept. radiology Nat. Naval Med. Center, Bethesda, 1979-82; sr. lectr. mil. medicine Uniformed U. of Health Scis., Bethesda, 1975-80; asst. prof. radiology/nuclear medicine and rsch. program coord. Uniformed U. of Health Scis., 1980-82; assoc. div. nuclear medicine St. Joseph Hosp., Towson, Md., 1982-91, dir. div. nuclear medicine, 1992—; med. advisor Nev. ops. office Dept. Energy, Las Vegas; cons. in field. Fellow Royal Soc. Medicine, Am. Coll. Nuclear Physicians (regent Ea. USA); mem. Am. Coll. Nuclear Physicians, Air Force Soc. Physicians (bd. govs. 1973-77), Uniformed Services Nuclear Medicine Assn. (pres. 1975), Soc. Nuclear Medicine (pres. Mideastern chpt.), Md. Soc. Nuclear Medicine (pres.-elect), AMA, Health Physics Soc. (dir. Balt., Washington chpt.), Assn. Mil. Surgeons U.S., Soc. Med. Cons.'s to Armed Forces, Alexander Graham Bell Soc. Home: 15510 Foxpaw Trail Woodbine MD 21797 Office: St Joseph Hosp Towson MD 21204

MC INERNEY, DENIS, lawyer; b. N.Y.C., May 31, 1925; s. Denis and Anne (Keane) McI.; m. Mary Irene Murphy, Nov. 14, 1953; children: Kathleen Mc Inerney O'Hare, Denis J., Maura Mc Inerney Romano. BSS, Fordham U., 1948, JD cum laude, 1951, LLD (hon.), 1996. Bar: N.Y. 1951, D.C. 1961. Instr. philosophy Fordham U., 1948-51; assoc. Cahill Gordon & Reindel, N.Y.C., 1951-61, ptnr., 1961-90, sr. counsel, 1991—; vice chmn. Com. Character and Fitness Admission State Bar N.Y., 1st Jud. Dept., 1979-97, chmn. departmental disciplinary com., 1997—; lectr. in field. Co-author: Practitioners Handbook for Appeals to the Appellate Divisions of the State of New York, 1979, Practitioners Handbook for Appeals to the Court of Appeals of the State of New York, 1981. Bd. dirs. Vols. of Legal Svc., Inc., 1985—, Cath. Youth Orgn., 1975—; mem. adv. bd. St. Vincent's Hosp., Westchester, N.Y., 1988—; chmn. bd. visitors Fordham Law Sch., 1989—; trustee Fordham U., 1988-94. Sgt. 82d Airborne Divsn. U.S. Army, 1943-46, ETO. Decorated Knight of Malta, Knight of the Holy Sepulcher; recipient Achievement in Law award Fordham U., 1977. Fellow Am. Coll. Trial Lawyers (state chmn. 1980-82); mem. ABA, N.Y. State Bar Assn., New York County Lawyers Assn. (pres. 1982-84), Fordham U. Law Alumni Assn. (pres. 1968-72, medal of achievement 1975). Roman Catholic. Clubs: Westchester Country, Univ. Office: Cahill Gordon & Reindel 80 Pine St New York NY 10005-1702

MCINERNEY, JAMES EUGENE, JR., trade association administrator; b. Springfield, Mass., Aug. 3, 1930; s. James Eugene and Rose Elizabeth (Adikes) McI.; m. Mary Catherine Hill, July 17, 1963; children: Anne Elizabeth, James Eugene, III. B.S., U.S. Mil. Acad., 1952; M.S. in Engring., Princeton U., 1960; postgrad., Royal Air Force Staff Coll., 1964; M.S. in Internat. Affairs, George Washington U., 1970. Commd. 2d lt. USAF, 1952, advanced through grades to maj. gen., 1976; fighter pilot Korea, Japan and Ger.; comdr. tactical fighter squadron Thailand, 1967; tactical fighter wing Ger., 1971; sr. U.S. adviser Turkish Air Force, 1973; dir. mil. assistance and sales Hdqrs. USAF, 1975-78; comdt. Indsl. Coll. Armed Forces, 1978-79; dir. programs Hdqrs. USAF, 1979-80, asst. dep. chief of staff for programs and evaluation, 1980; dir. legis. liaison McDonnell Douglas Corp., Washington, 1980-83, dir. internat. affairs, 1983-86; v.p. Am. League for Exports and Security Assistance, 1986-89, exec. v.p., 1989-92; v.p. Am. Def. Preparedness Assn., 1992—. Decorated Air Force Cross, D.S.M. (2), Silver Star (3), D.F.C. (7), Bronze Star, Meritorious Service medal (2), Air medal (18), Air Force Commendation medal; Vietnamese Crosses of Gallantry with palm and star; Republic of Korea Cheongsu medal. Mem. Air Force Assn. (citation of honor 1968), Brit.-Am. Bus. Assn.-Washington (pres. 1982-94, chmn. 1994—), Brit.-Am. Bus. Coun. (US-UK) (chmn. 1996—), Am.-Air Mus. in Britain (exec. dir. 1984—). Roman Catholic. Home: 1031 Delf Dr Mc Lean VA 22101-2009

MCINERNEY, JOHN VINCENT, obstetrician and gynecologist; b. Evergreen Park, Ill., July 13, 1957; s. Vincent F. and Kathleen T. McI.; m. Cabrini F. Costello, July 14; children: Patrick, Meghan, Elizabeth, John, Brendan, Molly. DO, Chgo. Coll. Osteo. Medicine, 1983; BS, Loyola U. Chgo., 1979. Diplomate Am. Bd. Osteopathic Medicine, Am. Bd. Ob-Gyn. Intern Chgo. Osteo. Hosp., 1983-84, resident in ob-gyn., 1984-88; obstetrician-gynecologist Assoc. of Edward C. Ryan, Orland Park, Ill., 1988-92, Assoc. of Scott Multack, Downers Grove, Ill., 1992-93; pvt. practice Palos Heights, Ill., 1993—; sr. staff Palos Cmty. Hosp., 1988—; mem. active staff Christ Hosp., 1989—; coord. continuing med. edn. in ob-gyn. Christ Hosp., 1994-96, vice chmn. continuing med. edn. adv. com., 1995—; clin. isntr. Rush Med. Coll., 1990—, Finch. U., Chgo. Med. Sch., 1996—; clin. mentor Chgo. Med. Sch., 1995-96. Chmn. Brother Rice H.S. devel. coun., Chgo., 1995-96, pres. alumni assn., 1992-99; leader Boy Scouts Am. Recipient Chgo. Coll. Osteo. Medicine Alumni Assn. Pres.'s citation, 1994. Fellow Am. Coll. Osteopathic Ob-Gyn. (steering com. on strategic planning, steering com. on managed care malpractice reform 1996-97), Am. Soc. Colposcopy and Cervical Pathology; mem. Chgo. Gynecologic Soc., Am. Assn. Gynecol. Laparoscopists. Roman Catholic. Avocations: exercise, outdoor sports. Home: 9800 S Longwood Dr Chicago IL 60643-1706 Office: 11824 Southwest Hwy Palos Heights IL 60463-1055

MCINERNEY, JOSEPH ALOYSIUS, hotel executive; b. Oak Park, Ill., Sept. 2, 1939; s. Joseph Aloysius and Helene (Mustari) McI.; m. Ruth McClelland, Aug. 29, 1969; children—Joseph A., Susan B. Student, Loyola U., Chgo., 1959-61; B.A. cum laude, Boston Coll., 1974. With Sheraton-Chgo. Hotel, 1961-65, regional dir. franchise ops., 1966-67, dir. franchise devel., 1968-69; gen. mgr. Sheraton-Winston, Salem, 1969-70; v.p., asst. to pres. Sheraton Corp., 1970-73, sr. v.p., dir. franchise ops., 1973-79; sr. v.p. Sheraton Corp., pres. Sheraton Corp. (Franchise div.), 1979-86; pres. Hawthorn Suites, 1986-91; pres., chief exec. officer Travelodge Internat., 1991-92; pres., CEO Forte Hotels, Inc., 1992—; guest lectr. Cornell Hotel Sch., Boston U. Hotel Sch., U. N.H. Hotel Sch., Mich. State U., San Diego State U. Former mem. industry sect. adv. com. U.S. Dept. Commerce, also U.S. trade rep.; mem. adv. bd. Master Sci. degree program in hospitality industry studies at NYU; mem. hospitality adv. bd. N.Mex. State, Calif. Poly. Hosp.; former trustee Boston U. Med. Ctr., Bethune-Cookman Coll.; bd. trustees St. Vincent de Paul Village; exec. com. CEO San Diego Roundtable. Mem. Am. Hotel & Motel Assn. (govtl. affairs com.), Am. Hotel & Motel Ednl. Inst. (chmn.). Office: Forte Hotels Inc 1973 Friendship Dr El Cajon CA 92020-1130

MCINERNEY, JOSEPH JOHN, biomedical engineer, educator; b. Boston, Aug. 13, 1932; s. John Joseph and Anne (Berry) McI.; m. Suzanne Finke, Oct. 20, 1970; children by previous marriage: Joseph, Lynn, Maureen; children by present marriage: Kathleen, John. B.S. in Mech. Engring., Northeastern U., 1960; M.S. in Nuclear Engring., Pa. State U., 1962, Ph.D. in Theoretical Physics, 1964, M.S. in Human Physiology, 1980. Nuclear physicist Knolls Atomic Lab., Schenectady, 1964-76; postdoctoral fellow Sch. Medicine, Pa. State U., Hershey, 1976-79, staff rsch. scientist, 1979—; asst. prof. depts. biomed. engring. and medicine, Pa. State U., State College, 1984-90, assoc. prof., 1990—; referee Am. Nuclear Soc., Hinsdale, Ill., 1966—, Med. Biol. Engring., 1986—; cons. Whitaker Found., Harrisburg, Pa., 1981—, NIH; mem. standard com. Am. Nuclear Soc., Hinsdale, 1966—. Patentee in field. Contbr. articles to profl. jours. Served with USN, 1951-55. NIH fellow, 1976-79; Whitaker Found. grantee, 1979-81; Am. Heart Assn. grantee, 1979-80; NIH grantee, 1976-84, 84—, Pa. Rsch. Corp. grantee, 1983-84, Applied Rsch. Labs. grantee, 1985—. Mem. Am. Nuclear Soc., Am. Heart Assn., AAAS, Am. Physiol. Soc., Am. Fedn. Clin. Rsch., Am. Assn. Physicists in Medicine, IEEE (referee 1986—), Sigma Xi, Pi Tau Sigma. Democrat. Home: 260 Quarry Rd Hummelstown PA 17036-8902 Office: Pa State U Milton S Hershey Med Ctr PO Box 850 Hershey PA 17033-0850

MCINERNY, RALPH MATTHEW, philosophy educator, author; b. Mpls., Feb. 24, 1929; s. Austin Clifford and Vivian Gertrude (Rush) McI.; m. Constance Terrill Kunert, Jan. 3, 2953; children: Cathleen, Mary, Anne, David, Elizabeth, Daniel. BA, St. Paul Sem., 1951; MA, U. Minn., 1952; PhD summa cum laude, Lval U., 1954; DHL, St. John Fisher Coll., 1993, St. Anselm Coll., 1995. Instr. Creighton U., 1954-55; prof. U. Notre Dame, Ind., 1955—, Michael P. Grace prof. medieval studies, 1988—, dir. dept., 1978-85; vis. prof. Cornell U., 1988, Cath. U., 1971, Louvain, 1983, 95; founder Internat. Catholic Univ. Author: (philos. works) The Logic of Analogy, 1961, History of Western Philosophy, vol. 1, 1963, vol. 2, 1968, Thomism in an Age of Renewal, 1966, Studies in Analogy, 1967, New Themes in Christian Philosophy, 1967, St. Thomas Aquinas, 1976, Ethica Thomistica, 1982, History of the Ambrosiana, 1983, Being and Predication, 1986, Miracles, 1986, Art and Prudence, 1988, A First Glance at St. Thomas: Handbook for Peeping Thomists, 1989, Boethius and Aquinas, 1989, Aquinas on Human Action, 1991, The Question of Christian Ethics, 1993, Aquinas Against the Averroists, 1993; (novels) Jolly Rogerson, 1967, A Narrow Time, 1969, The Priest, 1973, Gate of Heaven, 1975, Rogerson at Bay, 1976, Her Death of Cold, 1977, The Seventh Station, 1977, Romanesque, 1977, Spinnaker, 1977, Quick as a Dodo, 1978, Bishop as Pawn, 1978, La Cavalcade Romaine, 1979, Lying Three, 1979, Abecedary, 1979, Second Vespers, 1980, Rhyme and Reason, 1981, Thicker than Water, 1981, A Loss of Patients, 1982, The Grass Widow, 1983, Connolly's Life, 1983, Getting Away with Murder, 1984, And Then There Were Nun, 1984, The Noonday Devil, 1985, Sine Qua Nun, 1986, Leave of Absence, 1986, Rest in Pieces, 1985, Cause and Effect, 1987, The Basket Case, 1987, Veil of Ignorance, 1988, Abracadaver, 1989, Body and Soil, 1989, Four on the Floor, 1989, Frigor Mortis, 1989, Savings and Loan, 1990, The Search Committee, 1991, The Nominative Case, 1991, Sister Hood, 1991, Judas Priest, 1991, Easeful Death, 1991, Infra Dig, 1992, Desert Sinner, 1992, Seed of Doubt, 1993, The Basket Case, 1993, Nun Plussed, 1993, Mom and Dead, 1994, The Cardinal Offense, Law and Ardor, 1995, Let's Read Latin, 1995, Aguinas and Analogy, 1996, The Tears of Things, 1995, Half Past Nun, 1997, On This Rockne, 1997, Penguin Classic Aquinas, 1997; editor The New Scholasticism, 1967-89; editor, pub. Crisis, 1982-96; pub. Catholic Dossier, 1995—. Exec. dir. Wethersfield Inst., 1989-92; bd. govs. Thomas Aquinas Coll., Santa Paula, Calif., 1992—. With USMCR, 1946-47. Fulbright rsch. fellow, Belgium, 1959-60, NEH fellow, 1977-78, NEA fellow, 1983, Fulbright scholar, Argentina, 1986, 87; recipient Aquinas medal, 1992, Maritain medal, 1994, Cardinal Wright award, 1996. Fellow Pontifical Roman Acad. St. Thomas Aquinas; mem. Am. Philos. Assn., Am. Cath. Philos. Assn. (past pres., recipient medals), Am. Metaphys. Soc. (pres. 1992), Internat. Soc. for Study Medieval Philosophy, Medieval Acad., Mystery Writers Am., Authors Guild, Fellowship Cath. Scholars (pres. 1992-95). Home: 51236 Golfview Ct Granger IN 46530-6500 Office: U of Notre Dame Jacques Maritain Ctr 714 Hesburgh Libr Notre Dame IN 46556-5639

MCINNES, DONALD GORDON, railroad executive; b. Buffalo, Nov. 6, 1940; s. Milton Gordon and Blanche Mae (Clunk) McI.; m. Betsy Campbell, Mar. 18, 1967 (dec. Feb. 1995); children: Campbell Gordon, Cody Milton; m. Carol Anne Haverly, Oct. 12, 1996; stepchildren: Molly Caroline, Lawrence Joseph. B.A., Denison U., 1963; M.S., Northwestern U., 1965; cert. in transp. Yale U., 1965. Budget mgr. operating AT&SF R.R. Co., Chgo., 1969-71, asst. trainmaster, San Bernardino, Calif., 1971-73, trainmaster, Temple, Tex., 1973-76, asst. supt., Carlsbad, N.M., 1976-77, supt. eastern divsn., Emporia, Kans., 1977-79, supt. Los Angeles divsn., San Bernardino, Calif., 1979-81, asst. to exec. v.p., Chgo., 1981-82, gen. supt. transp., 1983-87, gen. mgr. transp., 1987, gen. mgr. ea. region, 1988, v.p. adminstrn., 1989, v.p. intermodal, 1989-91, sr. v.p. intermodal, 1991-93, sr. v.p., COO, 1994-95; sr. v.p., COO Burlington No. Santa Fe Corp., 1995—; bd. dirs. AT & SF Railway Co., TTX Corp., leader of group Intermodal Assn. N.Am., 1st chmn., 1991-93. Bd. dirs. Jr. Achievement Ft. Worth, Tex. Christian U., Ft. Worth. Served to 2d lt., USAF, 1965-67; capt. U.S. Army, 1967-69. Decorated Bronze Star. Rivercrest Country Club (Ft. Worth). Republican. Episcopalian. Clubs: Union League (Chgo.), Meadow (Rolling Meadow, Ill.), Pass (Boca Grande, Fla.), Boca Grande Pass Yacht, Lemon Bay Golf (Englewood, Fla.). Home: 429 Rivercrest Dr Fort Worth TX 76107 also: 75 Queen St Falmouth MA 02540 also: PO Box 278 148 Carrick Bend Ct Boca Grande FL 33921 Office: Burlington No Santa Fe Corp PO Box 961034 Fort Worth TX 76161-0034

MC INNES, ROBERT MALCOLM, lawyer, business consultant; b. Pictou, N.S., Can., July 17, 1930; naturalized U.S. citizen, 1964; s. John Logan and Jenny MacKay (Malcolm) McI.; m. June Hughena O'Brien, Apr. 19, 1952; children: Donald, Elizabeth, Susan. B.A., Dalhousie U., Halifax, N.S., 1951, LL.B., 1953; postgrad., Harvard U. Bus. Sch., 1968. Assoc. firm Duquet, MacKay, Weldon & Tetreault, Montreal, Que., Can., 1953-57; with Pickands Mather & Co., Cleve., 1957-69, 71-87; v.p. Pickands Mather & Co., 1971-73, exec. v.p., 1973-83, pres., chief exec. officer, 1983-87; gen. counsel, treas. Diamond Shamrock Corp., 1969-71; group exec. v.p. Cleve. Cliffs Inc., 1987-88; of counsel Arter and Hadden, Cleve., 1988-94; bd. dirs. Brush Wellman Inc., Cliffs Drilling Co. Mem. Mayfield Country Club, Union Club. Republican. Methodist. Home: 32300 Meadow Lark Way Pepper Pike OH 44124-5510

MC INNES, WILLIAM CHARLES, priest, campus ministry director; b. Boston, Jan. 20, 1923; s. William Charles and Mary (Byrne) McI. B.S., Boston Coll., 1946, A.B., 1950, M.A., 1951; S.T.L., Weston Coll., 1958; Ph.D., N.Y. U., 1955. Joined Soc. of Jesus, 1946; ordained priest Roman Cath. Ch., 1957; prof. mktg. and bus. ethics Boston Coll. Sch. Bus. Adminstrn., 1959-63, assoc. dean, 1961-63, dir. honors program, 1963-64, mem. citizens seminar planning com., 1959-63; pres. Fairfield (Conn.) U., 1964-73, prof. urban problems, 1969-72; pres. U. San Francisco, 1972-77, Assn. Jesuit Colls. and Univs., 1977-89; campus min. U. Conn., Storrs, 1990-96; moderator Nat. Jesuit Honor Soc. Boston College, 1997—; vis. fellow Woodstock Theol. Ctr., 1990-91. Past chmn. bd. ABCD (cmty. action agys.); pres. Conn. Assn. for Cmty. Action Programs; founder Fairfield County Cmty. forum, Conn. Charter Oak Coll.; life mem. United Cerebral Palsy Assn. Fairfield County; bd. dirs. Nat. Better Bus. Bur.; vice chmn. Nat. Better Bus. Bur. Found.; mem. adv. com. Conn. Dept. Social Svcs., 1993-96. Served to capt. USAAF, 1942-46, CBI. Mem. Beta Gamma Sigma, Alpha Sigma Nu, Delta Sigma Pi, Phi Kappa Theta, Alpha Epsilon Delta. Home: Jesuit Cmty Boston Coll Chestnut Hill MA 02167

MCINNIS, SCOTT STEVE, congressman, lawyer; b. Glenwood Springs, Colo., May 9, 1953; s. Kohler McInnis and Carol Kreir; m. Lori McInnis; children: Daxon, Tessa, Andrea. BA, Ft. Lewis Coll., 1975; JD, St. Mary's Law Sch., 1980. Atty. Delaney & Balcomb P.C., Glenwood Springs, Colo., 1981—; mem. Colo. Ho. of Reps., 1984-93; majority leader, 1990-93; mem. 103d-105th Congresses from 3d Colo. Dist., 1993—; chmn. agrl. livestock and natural resources com., 1986-90, mem. rules com. Recipient Florence Sabin award, 1984, Guardian of Small Bus. award Nat. Fed. Ind. Bus., 1990, Lee Atwater Leadership award, 1991, and various awards from United Vets. Commn.; named Legislator of Decade and Legislator of Yr by Colo. Ski Country and Colo. Wildlife Found. Mem. Elks, Rotary, Phi Delta Phi. Republican. Roman Catholic. Office: US Ho of Reps 215 Cannon HOB Washington DC 20515-0603*

MCINTIRE, JERALD GENE, investment executive, former municipal official; b. Abilene, Tex., Mar. 16, 1938; s. Andrew Noble and Viola (Richey) McI.; m. Linda Carole Sanders, Aug. 28, 1964 (div. Mar. 1976); children: Chrisitan Tilghman, Ross Andrew, John Patrick Morgan. AA, N.Mex. Mil. Inst., 1958; BA, Ea. N.Mex. U., 1964. Ptnr., officer Ruffino Prodns., Dallas, 1960-64; tchr., drama dir. Roswell (N.Mex.) Pub. Schs., 1966-70; tchr. curriculum Thiokol Chem., Roswell, 1970-74; pvt. bus. mgr. Dallas, 1974-77; career coordinator Soc. Ednl. Reconstrn./Jobs for Progress, Dallas, 1977-82; council asst. City of Dallas, 1982-83, asst. to mayor pro tem, 1983-87, asst. to mayor, 1987-89; pres., chief exec. officer Multinational Investments, Multinational Offshore Venture, M'N'M Antiquities, Grand Caymen, Bahamas, 1990—; ptnr., officer Multi-Nat. Investments, Inc., Dallas, 1980. Con., v.p. Chrysalis Home & Health Care, Dallas, 1985-87; devel. dir., mem. sch. bd. Immaculate Conception Sch, Grand Prairie, Tex., 1983-85; pres. bd. dirs. Hist. Soc. Southeast N.Mex., 1996. Mem. Nat. Assn. Council Assts. Democrat. Jewish. Avocations: gardening, travel, writing, music, riding. Office: Multinational Investments, M N M Antiquities, Grand Cayman Bahamas

MCINTIRE, LARRY VERN, chemical engineering educator; b. St. Paul, June 28, 1943; s. James Lawrence and Lenore Vineal (Converse) McI.; m. Suzanne G. Eskin, June 27, 1997. BChemE, MS, Cornell U., 1966; MA, Princeton U., 1968, PhD, 1970. Registered profl. engr., Tex. Asst. prof. Rice U., Houston, 1970-74, assoc. prof., 1974-78, prof. chem. engring., 1978—, E.D. Butcher prof., 1983—, chmn. dept., 1981-91, chmn. Bioscis. and Bioengring. Inst., 1991—, chmn. rsch. coun., 1988-91, dir. Biomed. Engring. Lab., 1980—, chmn. dept. biomed. engring., 1997—; spke faculty coun., 1994-95; adj. prof. medicine Baylor Coll. Medicine, Houston, 1982—, U. Tex. Med. Sch., Houston, 1982—; chmn. blood/materials working group NIH, Bethesda, Md., 1982-85; mem. surgery and bioengring. study sect. NIH, 1984-88; mem. com. on bioprocessing NRC, 1991-94; chmn. rheology subcom. Internat. Coun. on Thrombosis and Hemostasis, 1985-89. Contbr.

over 200 articles to profl. jours. Recipient Merit award NIH, 1989; NSF fellow Cornell U., Princeton U., 1965-69, NATO-NSF postdoctoral fellow Imperial Coll., London, 1976-77. Fellow Am. Inst. Med. Biol. Engring. (sec., treas. 1993-96, pres. 1997—), AICHE (officer lical sect. 1980-81, 86, Food Pharm. and Bioengring. divsn. award 1992); mem. AAAS, Biomed. Engring. Soc. (bd. dirs. 1992—, pres. 1995-96, Disting. lectr. 1992), N.Am. Soc. Biorheology (v.p. 1992-94, pres. 1994-96), N.Y. Acad. Scis., Am. Heart Assn. (coun. on thrombosis, exec. com. 1994—), Faculty Club Rice U. (bd. dirs., chmn. 1982-84), Sigma Xi (nat. lectr. 1993-96). Presbyterian. Avocations: tennis, squash, classical music, hiking. Office: Rice U Inst Bioscis and Bioengring John W Cox Lab Biomed Engring Houston TX 77251-1892

MCINTOSH, CAROLYN MEADE, retired educational administrator; b. Waynesburg, Ky., Oct. 21, 1928; d. Clarence Hobert and Sarah Letitia (Bentley) Meade; m. Edgar G. McIntosh, Aug. 21, 1948; children: Wayne, Jeanne, Penny, Jimmi, Carol. BS, Miami U., Oxford, Ohio, 1962; MEd, Xavier U., Cin., 1966. Elem. tchr. Ohio, 1961-79; prin. New Richmond (Ohio) Sch. Dist., 1980-91; ret., 1991; tchr. Clermont County Adult Edn. Program, 1970-95, Clermont County dir.of Headstart 1971-72, Clearmont County Rep. to Ohio elem. adminstr., 1985-87, Pres. Clermont and Brown County adminstr., 1988-89. Editor Ret. Tchrs. Newsletter. Pres. New Richmond Bd. Edn.; v.p. U.S. Grant Vocat. Sch. Bd. Edn.; mem. Clermont County Excellence in Edn. Com.; mem. edn. adv. com. Clermont Coll.; mem. adv. bd. Bethany Children's Home; mem. Clermont 2001 Com.; mem. Rep. Ctrl. Com. of Clermont County. Recipient New Richmond Adminstr. of the Yr. award City of New Richmond, 1989; named citizen of yr. Monroe Twp., 1996; selected for sr. leadership charter class, Clermont 2001. Mem. AAUW, ASCD, NAESP, Nat. Sch. Bd. Assn., Ohio Sch. Bd. Assn., Ohio Assn. Elem. Sch. Adminstrs. (all county legis. liaison), Ohio County Ret. Tchrs. Assn., Clermont County Ret. Tchrs. Assn. (pres.), Order Eastern Star, Phi Delta Kappa, Delta Kappa Gamma (pres. chpt.). Baptist.

MCINTOSH, CECILIA ANN, biochemist, educator; b. Dayton, Ohio, Apr. 30, 1956; d. Russell Edward McIntosh and Geraldine Rita (Cochran) Slemp; m. Kevin Smith Schweiker, May 28, 1978 (div. Mar. 1989); children: Katrina Lynn McIntosh Schweiker, Rebecca Sue McIntosh Schweiker. BA in Biology cum laude, U. South Fla., 1977, MA in Botany, 1981, PhD in Biology, 1990. Rsch. assoc. U. South Fla., Tampa, 1981-86, teaching/rsch. asst. dept. biology, 1986-90; postdoctoral fellow dept. biochemistry U. Idaho, Moscow, 1990-93; asst. prof. dept. biol. scis. East Tenn. State U., Johnson City, 1993—; adj. asst. prof. dept. biochemistry Quillen Coll. Medicine, East Tenn. State U., Johnson City, 1995—; sci. mentor U. So. Fla. Ctr. for Excellence, Tampa, 1984-90; rsch. forum judge Coll. Medicine Rsch. Forum, East Tenn. State U., Johnson City, 1994—. Author: (rev. articles) The Molecular Biology of Mitochondria, 1995, Biotechnology of Medicinal and Aromatic Plants, 1991; contbr. rsch. articles to profl. jours. including Plant Physiology, Archives of Biochemistry & Biophysics. Sci. fair judge East Tenn. Regional Sci. Fair, Johnson City, 1994—. Strenghthening program grantee USDA, 1994-95, Seed grantee, 1995-97; rsch. devel. grantee East Tenn. State U. Rsch. Devel. Coun., 1994-96, 97-98. Mem. Am. Assn. Women in Sci., Am. Soc. Plant Physiologists, Phytochem. Soc. N.Am., Sigma Xi (sci. fair workshop coord. Appalachian chpt. 1995—, dissertation award 1991). Achievements include characterization of new enzyme in plant flavonoid biosynthesis; biochemical characterization of plant mitochondrial membrane tricarboxylate and phosphate transporters. Avocations: outdoor activities, sports, mysteries. Office: East Tenn State U Dept Biol Scis Box 70 703 Johnson City TN 37614-0703

MCINTOSH, DAVID M., congressman; b. June 8, 1958; m. Ruthie McIntosh. Grad., Yale Coll., 1980, U. Chgo., 1983. Bar: Ind., U.S. Supreme Ct. Spl. asst. domestic affairs to Pres. Reagan; spl. asst. to Atty. Gen. Meese; liaison Pres.'s Commn. on Privatization; spl. asst. to V.P. Quayle, dep. legal counsel to; exec. dir. Pres.'s Coun. on Competitiveness; sr. fellow Citizens for a Sound Economy; founder Federalist Soc. for Law & Pub. Policy, now co-chmn.; mem. U.S. Ho. of Reps., 105 Congress, Washington, 1995—, mem. Govt. Reform & Oversight Com., chmn. panel's Econ. Growth, Natural Resources and Regulatory Affairs Subcom. Mem. State Bar of Ind. Republican. Office: US House Reps 1208 Longworth Bldg Ofc Bldg Washington DC 20515-1402

MCINTOSH, DECOURCY EYRE, museum director; b. Balt., Dec. 1, 1942; s. David Gregg and Grace (Wright) McI.; m. Susan Reed Bell, Nov. 11, 1967; children: Madeline Eyre, David Gregg. AB, Harvard U., 1965. Program officer Richard King Mellon Found., Pitts., 1969-74; exec. dir. Hist. Savannah (Ga.) Found., 1974-77; mng. dir. Minn. Landmarks, St. Paul, 1977-79; v.p. Mpls. Soc. Fine Arts, 1979-84; exec. dir. Helen Clay Frick Found., Pitts., 1984—, Frick Art & Hist. Ctr., Pitts., 1990—. Editor: (exhbn. catalogues) 19th Century French Drawings from Lyon, 1992, Renaissance & Baroque Bronzes in The Frick Art Museum, 1993, Florentine Drawings of the 17th & 18th Centuries from Lille, 1994; co-author: Collecting in the Gilded Age: Art Patronage in Pittsburgh, 1890-1910, 1997. Trustee Pitts. History & Landmarks, 1984—, Art Svcs. Internat., Alexandria, 1990—; bd. dirs. Pitts. Parks & Playgrounds Fund, 1986—, Preservation Pa., 1991—. Mem. Am. Assn. Mus., Century Assn., Pitts. Golf Club, Walpole Soc. Office: The Frick Art & Hist Ctr 7227 Reynolds St Pittsburgh PA 15208-2919

MCINTOSH, DENNIS KEITH, veterinary practitioner, consultant; b. Newark, June 12, 1941; s. Sheldon Weeks and Enid Nicholson (Casey) McI.; m. Rachel McIntosh; children: Rebecca, Kevin, Jamie. BS in Animal Sci., Tex. A&M U., 1963, BS in Vet. Sci., 1967, DVM, 1968. Asst. county agrl. agt., Cleburne, Tex., 1963-65; owner, operator Park North Animal Hosp., San Antonio, 1970-75, El Dorado Animal Hosp., San Antonio, 1973—; co-chmn. vet. tech. adv. coun. Palo Alto Coll. tchr. Animal Health Tech., San Antonio Coll., 1985-95; pres., mgr. Bexar County Emergency Animal Clinic, Inc., 1978-81; cons. vet. practice mgmt., mktg., client relations; speaker for vet. meetings, assns.; vet. mem. Tex. Bd. Health, 1984-89, chmn. disease control com., personnel com.; mem. environ. health, hosps. com. Team capt. Alamo Roundup Club and Pres.' Club of San Antonio C. of C., 1970-75; mem. Guadalupe County Youth Fair Bd., 1978-80; 1st v.p. No. Hills Lions Club, 1972-73. Served with Vet. Corps, USAF, 1968-70. Recipient Alumnus award Guadalupe County 4-H Club, 1979, Outstanding Service award San Antonio Coll., 1986-87, Outstanding Bus. Ptnrs. award N.E. Ind. Sch. Dist., 1995-96. Mem. Tex. Vet. Med. Assn. (pres., chmn. bd.), Tex. Acad. Vet. Practice (pres.), Am. Assn. Human-Animal Bond Vets., AVMA, Vet. Hosp. Mgrs. Assn., San Antonio C. of C. (Life), Tex. County Agrl. Agts. Assn. (4th v.p. 1964), Delta Soc. (pres. San Antonio chpt. 1989-90). Contbr. articles to profl. jours. Office: 13039 Nacogdoches Rd San Antonio TX 78217-1960

MCINTOSH, ELAINE VIRGINIA, nutrition educator; b. Webster, S.D., Jan. 30, 1924; d. Louis James and Cora Boletta (Bakke) Nelson; m. Thomas Henry McIntosh, Aug. 28, 1955; children: James George, Ronald Thomas, Charles Nelson. BA magna cum laude, Augustana Coll., Sioux Falls, S.D., 1945; MA, U. S.D., 1949; PhD, Iowa State U., 1954. Registered dietitian. Instr., asst. prof. Sioux Falls Coll., 1945-48; instr. Iowa State U., Ames, 1949-53, rsch. assoc., 1955-62; postdoctoral rsch. assoc. U. Ill., Urbana, 1954-55; asst. prof. human biology U. Wis., Green Bay, 1968-72, assoc. prof., 1972-85, prof., 1985-90, emeritus prof., 1990—, writer, cons., 1990—, chmn. human biology dept., 1975-80, asst. to vice chancellor, asst. to chancellor, 1974-76. Author 2 books including American Food Habits in Historical Perspective, 1995; contbr. numerous articles on bacterial metabolism, meat biochemistry and nutrition edn. to profl. jours. Fellow USPHS, 1948-49. Mem. Am. Dietetic Assn., Inst. Food Technologists, Wis. Dietetics Assn., Wis. Nutrition Coun. (pres. 1974-75), Sigma Xi. Avocation, travel. Office: U Wis ES 301 Human Biology 2420 Nicolet Dr Green Bay WI 54311-7003

MCINTOSH, GORDON ANDREW, local government official; b. Verdun, Canada, Jan. 18, 1955; s. Robert Linden and Antoinette Marie (Bujold) McI.; m. Diane Lee, Jan. 31, 1976; children: Andrew William, Christopher Robert. BS, U. Ottawa, 1979; MA, U. Alberta, 1990. cert. local govt. mgr. Supervisor City of Ottawa, Ont., Canada, 1976-79; dir. Dist. Gillam, Manitoba, Canada, 1979-81; dir. corp. svcs. City of Spruce Grove, Alberta, Canada, 1981-89; CEO Peterson Ross Solicitors, Edmonton, Alberta, 1989-91; assoc. George B. Cuff & Assocs., Edmonton, 1986-92; exec. dir. Islands Trust, Victoria, B.C., Canada, 1992—; program dir. local govt. leadership Banff Ctr. Mgmt., Alberta, 1994—; adv. Local Govt. Inst., U. Victoria, 1995—; instr. U. Alberta, 1988—. Author: Municipal Recreation, 1985. Exec. mem. Alberta Recreation, Parks & Wildlife Found., 1988-92; protocol capt. Com. XV Commonwealth Games, Victoria, 1994. Recipient achievement award World Leisure & Recreation Assn., 1986. Mem. Mcpl. Officers Assn. B.C. (profl. award), Soc. Local Govt. Mgrs. Avocations: squash, orchid growing, gardening. Office: Islands Trust, 2d Fl 1627 Fort St, Victoria, BC Canada V8R 1H8

MCINTOSH, HENRY DEANE, cardiologist; b. Gainesville, Fla., July 19, 1921; s. Thomas Irvin and Nelle Deane (Calwell) McI.; m. Harriet Owens, Nov. 6, 1945; children: Thomas Irvin, James Owens, Willa Elizabeth. BS, Davidson Coll., 1943; MD, U. Pa., 1950; DSc (hon.), U. Francisco Martinique, Guatemala de la Asuncion, 1987. Diplomate Am. Bd. Internal Medicine, subspecialty bd. cardiovascular disease. Intern medicine Duke U., Durham, N.C., 1950-51, fellow cardiology, 1952-54, instr. medicine Sch. Medicine, 1954-55, assoc., 1955-57, from asst. prof. to assoc. prof., 1957-62, prof., 1962-70, chief cardiology divsn., 1966-70; asst. resident medicine Lawson VA Hosp., Atlanta, 1951-52; chief resident medicine VA Hosp., Durham, N.C., 1954-55, asst. chief cardiovascular-renal sect., 1955-56; prof., chmn. dept. medicine Baylor Coll. Medicine, Houston, 1970-77, chief sect. cardiology, 1977, adj. prof. medicine, 1977—; chief med. svc. The Meth. Hosp., Houston, 1970-77; clin. prof. medicine U. Fla. Sch. Medicine, Gainesville, 1977—, U. South Fla. Sch. Medicine, Tampa, 1993—; cons. VA Hosp., Durham, 1956-70, Watts Hosp., Durham, 1956-79, Womack U.S. Army Hosp., Ft. Bragg, N.C., 1957-70, Portsmouth (Va.) Naval Hosp., 1957-70, VA Hosp., Houston, 1970-77, Harris County Dist. Hosps., Houston, 1970-77, St. Luke's Episc. Hosp., Houston, 1970-77, Hermann Hosp., Houston, 1970-77, Lakeland (Fla.) Regional Med. Ctr., 1977-92, St. Joseph's Hosp., Tampa, 1992—; med. dir. prevention and rehab. ctr. St. Joseph's Heart Inst., Tampa, 1992—. Editl. bd. Circulation, Heart and Lung, Am. Jour. Cardiology, Am. Jour. Geriatric Cardiology; asst. editor Modern Concepts in Cardiovascular Disease, 1967; editor Baylor Cardiology Series, 1975-77; contbr. 240 articles to profl. jours. Founder, bd. dirs. Heartbeat Internat., Lakeland, Fla., 1983-92, Tampa, Fla., 1992—, pres., 1993-95, chmn. bd. dirs., 1995—. Capt. U.S. Army, 1943-45. Decorated Silver Star; decorated Croix de Guerre with two bronze and one silver star; recipient Disting. Alumni award Duke U. Med. Ctr., 1972, Rotary Internat. Hon. Fellowship, 1985, Paul Harris Fellow, 1986, U.S. Presdl. Citation from Ronald Reagan, Heartbeat Internat., 1986, Disting. Kennedy Lectureship, Univ. Assn. Emergency Medicine, 1986, Disting. Alumni award Davidson Coll., 1988; named hon. prof. West China U. Med. Scis., Chengdu, Sichuan, Kunming Med. Coll., Yunnan, People's Republic of China, 1996. Fellow Am. Coll. Cardiology (Disting. Svc. award 1996, pres. 1974-75, govt. rels. com. 1986-93, prevention com. 1986-90, chair 1987-90, rep. to pub. health svc. objectives for the yr. 2000, 1988-96, Spl. Achievement award Fla. chpt. 1994); mem. AMA, ACP (Laureate award Fla. chpt. 1994), NASPE (continuing med. edn. coun. 1988-91, bldg. com. 1992-94, Disting. Svc. award 1991), Am. Fedn. Clin. Rsch., Soc. Clin. Investigation (Founders award 1984), Assn. Univ. Cardiologists, Am. Clin. and Climatological Soc., Am. Soc. Internal Medicine, Assn. Am. Physicians, Assn. Profs. Medicine, Am. Heart Assn. (v.p. 1977-78, rsch. com. 1986-90, chair sci. sessions com. 1971-73, coun. clin. cardiology 1975-76, Disting. Achievement award coun. clni. cardiology 1986), Coun. Geriat. Cardiology (membership com. 1986—, pres. 1991-92, Disting. Svc. award 1995). Presbyterian. Avocations: jogging, fostering international good will, public education. Office: St Joseph's Heart Inst PO Box 4227 3003 Martin Luther King Blvd Tampa FL 33677-4227

MC INTOSH, JAMES EUGENE, JR., interior designer; b. Dadeville, Ala., Nov. 13, 1938; s. James Eugene and Jessie (Latimer) McI. B.Interior Design, Auburn (Ala.) U., 1961. Designer contract div. Rich's Dept. Store, Atlanta, 1961-64; assoc. William Trapnell & Assocs., Atlanta, 1964-70; dir. Interior Concepts, Inc., Atlanta, 1970-72; dir. design comml. design div. Rich's Dept. Store, 1972-80; v.p. Comml. Interior Designs, Inc., 1980-82; exec. staff Rollins Inc., 1982-85; owner Gene Mc Intosh & Assocs., 1985—. Fellow Am. Soc. Interior Designers (Presdl. citation 1974); mem. Nat. Trust Hist. Preservation, Ala. Hist. Soc., High Mus. Art, Soc. Archtl. Historians.

MC INTOSH, J(OHN) RICHARD, biologist, educator; b. N.Y.C., Sept. 25, 1939; s. Rustin and Millicent Margaret (Carey) McI.; m. Marjorie Rogers Keniston, Aug. 30, 1961; children—Robert K., Elspeth R., Craig T. B.A. in Physics, Harvard U., 1961, Ph.D. in Biophysics, 1968. Instr. in math. and physics Cambridge Sch., Weston, Mass., 1961-63; asst. prof. biology Harvard U., 1968-70; asst. prof. U. Colo., Boulder, 1970-72; assoc. prof. U. Colo., 1972-76, prof., 1977—, chmn. dept. molecular, cellular and devel. biology, 1977-78, dir. Lab for High Voltage Electron Microscopy, 1986—. Mem. editl. bd. Jour. Cell Biology, 1978-82, 86-90, Cell Motility, 1986-87, Jour. Structural Biology, 1990—, Molecular Biology Cell, 1995—; contbr. articles to profl. jours. Recipient Teaching Recognition award U. Colo., 1974, Scholar award Am. Cancer Soc., 1976, 90; Am. Cancer Soc. grantee, 1971-90, NSF grantee, 1970-82, NIH grantee, 1973-78, 80—; Eleanor Roosevelt Internat. Cancer fellow, 1984; Guggenheim fellow, 1990-91. Mem. Am. Soc. Cell Biology (coun. 1977-80, 86-89, pres. 1994), Am. Cancer Soc. (cell biology panel 1983-87, rsch. prof. 1994—), NIH (molecular cytology study sect. 1988-92). Home: 870 Willowbrook Rd Boulder CO 80302-7439 Office: U Colo Dept Molec Devel & Devel Biol Boulder CO 80309-0347

MCINTOSH, JON CHARLES, illustrator; b. Alliance, Ohio, Aug. 8, 1947; s. John Cowles and Lucile Tipple (Ketcham) McI.; 1 child, Forgan Cowles; m. Jean Bogart Goodman, Apr. 24, 1993; stepchildren: Buffy Trott, Hays Spangler Trott. Student, Hobart Coll., 1965-67; BFA, R.I. Sch. of Design, 1974. Pres. McIntosh Ink, Inc., Vineyard Haven, Mass., 1971—; bd. ov overseers New Eng. Conservatory of Music, Boston, 1989-95; bd. dirs. Sail Martha's Vineyard. Illustrator: (book) The Foolish Dinosaur Fiasco, 1978, The Mysterious Zetabet, 1980, The Doctor's Handbook, 1982, Witch Way to The Country, 1995, Witch Way to the Beach, 1997; author, illustrator: Hooked On Golf, 1986. Artwork contbr. Ducks Unltd; art for advt. Bose, Wang, Digital, NASA. Recipient Silver medal V.I. Internat. Film Festival, 1976, Gold medal Soc. of Newspaper Designers, 1985, First place Francis Hatch Advt. Awards, 1987. Mem. Soc. of Illustrators (Silver Funny Bone 1991), The Country Club, The West Chop Club. Republican. Episcopalian. Avocations: musician, ski racing, tennis, fishing, skeet shooting. Office: McIntosh Ink Inc Box 2020 Tisbury Wharf 60 Beach Rd Vineyard Haven MA 02568

MCINTOSH, JOYCE EUBANKS, special education educator; b. Miami, Fla., July 5, 1947; d. Harvey and Lillie Mae (Jones) Eubanks; m. Willie E. McIntosh, Feb. 12, 1968 (dec. Feb. 1987); 1 child, Weldon R. McIntosh. AA, Miami Dade C.C., 1969-71; EdB, U. Miami, 1971-73; MS, Nova U., 1977-86. Asst. classroom spl. edn. resource tchr. Dade County Sch. Dist., Miami, 1969-73, edn. resource tchr., 1973-92, asst. prin., 1992—; class rep. at large U. Alumni Sch. Edn., Coral Gables, Fla., 1989-92; dir. at large U. Miami, Gen. Alumni Bd., 1992. Mem. Missionary Soc., Miami, 1991, The Family Christian Soc., Local/Nat. Alliance of Black Sch. Educators. Cert. Accomplishment Metro Dade County, Miami, Fla., 1974, U. Miami, Coral Gables, Fla., 1990, Miami Dade C.C., Fla., 1969; Cert. Appreciation Kappa Delta Pi, Miami, Fla., 1988. Mem. ASCD, Coun. for Exceptional Tchr. Edn., Miami Mus. Sci. Democrat. Methodist. Avocations: interior decorating, orchid grower, community volunteer.

MCINTOSH, L(ORNE) WILLIAM, marketing executive; b. Kingston, Ont., Can., May 1, 1945; s. Jack Lorne and Lillian (Oaks) McI.; m. Delthyn Lee Johnson, Mar. 11, 1965. BSBA, Lehigh U., 1967, MBA, 1968. Asst. prof. Union Coll., Cranford, N.J., 1968-72; sr. market rsch. analyst Merck, Sharp & Dohme, West Point, Pa., 1972-75, advt. copywriter, 1975-77, product mgr., 1977-80, assoc. dir. advt., 1980-82, dir. licensing and acquisitions, 1982, sr. dir. mktg., 1983-86; exec. v.p. mktg. Medco Containment Svcs., Inc., Fair Lawn, N.J., 1987-88; v.p. mktg. and bus. devel. Boehringer Mannheim Pharms., Rockville, Md., 1988-92; chmn. bd., chief exec. officer Target Mktg. Systems, Inc., Blue Bell, Pa., 1992-93; sr. v.p. bus. devel. and com. ops. Zynaxis, Inc., Malvern, Pa., 1993-95; sr. cons. SmithKline Beecham, Phila., 1995—. Mem. Am. Econ. Assn., Am. Mktg. Assn., Lic. Execs. Soc., Antique Automobile Club Am., Model A Ford Club Am., Vintage Chevrolet Club Am., Beta Gamma Sigma. Avocations: antique automobiles, woodworking, antique furniture restoration, boating, music. Home: 202 Somerset Ct Lansdale PA 19446 Office: SmithKline Beecham One Franklin Plz MC FP1615 PO Box 7929 Philadelphia PA 19101

MCINTOSH, ROBERT EDWARD, JR., electrical engineering educator, consultant, electronics executive; b. Hartford, Conn., Jan. 19, 1940; s. Robert Edward and Natalie Rose (Glynn) McI.; m. Anne Marie Potvin, July 7, 1962; children—Robert Edward III, Edgar J., Michael T., William P., Matthew P. B.S.E.E., Worcester Poly. Inst., 1962; S.M. in Applied Physics, Harvard U., 1964; Ph.D. in Elec. Engring., U. Iowa, 1967. Mem. tech. staff Bell Telephone Labs, North Andover, Mass., 1962-65; asst. prof. elec. engring. U. Mass., Amherst, 1967-70, assoc. prof., 1970-73, prof., 1973-96; disting. univ. prof., 1996—; coord. microwave electronics group U. Mass., Amherst, 1980-87, dir. microwave remote sensing lab., 1981—, acting head dept. elec. and computer engring., 1983-84; treas. Quadrant Engring., Inc., Amherst, 1982-84, 88-91, pres. 1984-87, 91-93, also bd. dirs.; mem. adv. bd. ECE Dept. Worcester Poly. Inst., 1992—. Assoc. editor Radio Sci., 1987-89; contbr. articles to profl. jours. Recipient sr. faculty scholarship award Alumni Coll. Engring., U. Mass., 1984, dept. of ECE Faculty award, 1987, 90, 92, GE Tchg. award, 1988, Univ. Disting. Lectr. award, 1992, Hobart Newell award WPI, 1993; Univ. Faculty Rsch. fellow, 1995; rsch. grantee NSF, NASA, Dept. Energy, Air Force Office Sci. Rsch., Army Rsch. Office, Office Naval Rsch., numerous electronics cos., 1967—. Fellow IEEE (Centennial medal 1984, tech. activities bd. 1984-85, fellows com. 1986-89); mem. Antennas Propagation Soc. (sec.-treas. 1980-83, v.p. 1984, pres. 1985, editor newsletter 1979-81, assoc. editor Trans. 1984-87, editor 1989-92), Geosci. Remote Sensing Soc. (sec.-treas. 1980-83, pres. 1984, Disting. Svc. award 1985, 97), Internat. Radio Sci. Union (U.S. nat. com. 1984-92), Am. Phys. Soc., Nat. Acad. Engring., Am. Geophys. Union. Democrat. Roman Catholic. Avocations: athletics, music, theatre. Office: U Mass Dept Elec Computer Eng Amherst MA 01003

MCINTOSH, ROBERTA EADS, retired social worker; b. Milw., Oct. 1, 1936; d. Robert Howard and Carlene (Rosboro) Eads; m. James Stuart Cameron McIntosh, Sept. 19, 1959; children: Ronald Stuart, Ian Robert, Peter Cameron. BA, Bucknell U., 1958; MS in Social Adminstrn., Case Western Reserve U., 1977. Lic. social worker, Ohio, Fla. Foster care caseworker Monroe County Child Welfare, Rochester, N.Y., 1958-63; group home counselor Betterway, Inc., Elyria, Ohio, 1974-75; group program coord. Elyria YWCA, 1975; caseworker, group home supr. Lorain County Children's Svcs., Elyria, 1977-83; treatment counselor Glenbeigh Adolescent Hosp., Cleve., 1984-86; youth dir. Washington Ave. Christian Ch., Elyria, 1984-85; outreach counselor Spouse Abuse Shelter Religious Community Svcs., Clearwater, Fla., 1986-93; pvt. practice Dunedin, Fla., 1993-97; cons., expert witness in domestic violence. Bd. pres. Elyria YWCA, 1972-75; sec., pres. Community Coordinated Child Care, Lorain County, 1970-72. Named Friend of Guidance Guidance Counselors Assn., 1982, Woman of Interest Elyria YWCA & City of Elyria, 1985. Mem. NASW, Acad. Cert. Social Workers, Fla. Coalition Against Domestic Violence (v.p. bd. 1993-94), Nat. Coalition Against Domestic Violence, Leadership Pinellas, Deaf Svc. Ctr. (bd. dirs. 1991-94), Victim Rights Coalition Pinellas County (v.p. bd. 1992-93), Ctrl. Christian Ch. Christian Womens Fellowship (pres. 1988-9), Delta Zeta. Democrat. Avocations: walking, gardening, reading, grandchildren. Home: 1501 Pleasant Grove Dr Dunedin FL 34698-2341

MCINTOSH, SUSAN KEECH, anthropology educator; b. Dunkirk, N.Y., Feb. 2, 1951; d. S. Elwin and Lucille M. (Stone) Keech; m. Roderick J. McIntosh, June 28, 1976; children: David Alexander, Annick Michelle. Student, Wellesley Coll., 1969-71; BA in Anthropology summa cum laude, U. Pa., 1973; MA in Archaeology, Cambridge U., Eng., 1975; MA in Anthropology, U. Calif., Santa Barbara, 1976, PhD in Anthropology, 1979. Vis. asst. prof. Washington U., St. Louis, 1978-80; from adj. asst. prof. to assoc. prof. anthropology Rice U., Houston, 1980-88, prof., 1988—; master Baker Coll., Rice U., 1984-89, treas. com. masters, 1986-89, chair com. campus climate women, pres.'s commn. women, 1988-89; mem. archaeology panel NSF, 1988-90; co-dir. various excavations and surveys; presdl. appointee U.S. Culture Property Com., 1996—. Author: Excavations at Jenne-jeno, Hambarketolo and Kaniana, 1995, (with R.J. McIntosh) Prehistoric Investigations in the Region of Jenne, Mali, 1980; contbr. articles to profl. jours.; assoc. editor for archaeology Current Anthropology, 1985-87; mem. editl. bd. Jour. World Prehistory, 1987—, Jour. African History, 1989-94, Antiquity, 1993—; contbg. editor Jour. Archaeol. Rsch., 1992—, African Archaeol. Rev., 1995—. Fulbright-Hays grantee, 1973; grantee NSF, 1977—, Nat. Geog. Soc., 1983-92; Thouron Brit.-Am. Exch. fellow, 1973-75; fellow Ctr. for Advanced Study in the Behavioral Scis., Stanford U., 1989-90. Mem. Am. Anthrop. Assn., Soc. Am. Archaeology, Soc. Africanist Archaeologists Am., Prehistoric Soc., West African Archeol. Assn., Société des Africanistes, Panafrican Congress Prehistory, Mande Studies Assn., Phi Beta Kappa. Avocations: classical music, tennis, skiing. Office: Rice U Dept Anthropology PO Box 1892 Houston TX 77251-1892

MCINTOSH, TERRIE TUCKETT, lawyer; b. Ft. Lewis, Wash., July 20, 1944; d. Robert LeRoy and Elda (Perry) Tuckett; m. Clifton Dennis McIntosh, Oct. 13, 1969; children: Alison, John. BA, U. Utah, 1967; MA, U. Ill., 1970; JD, Harvard U., 1978. Bar: N.Y. 1979, Utah 1980. Assoc. Hughes, Hubbard & Reed, N.Y.C., 1978-79; assoc. Fabian & Clendenin, Salt Lake City, 1979-84, shareholder, 1984-86; staff atty. Questar Corp., Salt Lake City, 1986-88, sr. atty., 1988-92, sr. corp. counsel, 1992—; instr. philosophy Douglass Coll. Rutgers U., New Brunswick, N.J., 1971-72; mem. adv. com. civil procedure Utah Supreme Ct., Salt Lake City, 1987—; mem. jud. nominating com. 5th Cir. Ct., Salt Lake City, 1986-88. Mem. Utah State Bar (ethics and discipline screening panel 1989—, vice chair ethics and discipline com. 1996—, co-chair law related edn. com. 1985-86), Women Lawyers of Utah (chair exec. com. 1986-87), Harvard Alumni Assn. Utah (bd. dirs. 1987—), Phi Beta Kappa, Phi Kappa Phi. Office: Questar Corp PO Box 45433 180 E 1st South St Salt Lake City UT 84145

MCINTYRE, ANITA GRACE JORDAN, lawyer; b. Louisville, Ky., Jan. 29, 1947; d. Blakely Gordan and Shirley Evans (Grubbs) Jordan; m. Kenneth James McIntyre, Oct. 11, 1969; children: Abigail, Jordan Kenneth. BA, Smith Coll., 1969; JD, U. Detroit, 1975. Bar: Mich. 1975, U.S. Dist. Ct. (ea. dist.) Mich. 1975, U.S. Dist. Ct. (we. dist.) Mich. 1979, U.S. Ct. Appeals (6th cir.) 1979. Ptnr. Rollins White & Rollins, Detroit, 1975-79; vis. assoc. prof. Detroit Coll. Law, 1979-81; assoc. Tyler & Canham, Detroit, 1981-82; prin. Anita G. McIntyre, P.C., Grosse Pointe, Mich., 1982-87, 91—; of counsel Nederlander Dodge & Rollins, Detroit, 1987-90; assoc. Damm & Smith, P.C., Detroit, 1990-91. Editor, author (case notes) U. Detroit Jour. Urban Law, 1975; contbr. articles to profl. jours. Sec. Berry Subdivsn. Assn., Detroit, 1975-77; pres. Smith Coll. Club Detroit, 1982-86; mem. parents bd. U. Liggett Sch., Grosse Pointe, Mich., 1991-95. Mem. State Bar Mich., Detroit Bar Assn. (family law, debtor-creditor sect. 1980-95), Wayne County (Mich.) Probate Bar Assn., Wayne County Juvenile Trial Lawyers Assn. Episcopalian. Avocations: skiing, swimming, needle point. Office: 15324 Mack Ave Grosse Pointe MI 48224-3349

MCINTYRE, BRUCE HERBERT, media and marketing consultant; b. Takoma Park, Md., Jan. 24, 1930; s. Orrin Raymond and Leila Hazel (Olmsted) McI.; m. Natalie Ann Wolff, Oct. 10, 1953; children: Douglas A., Elizabeth W., Emily O., Catherine N., Jane A. Student, Gannon Coll., 1954-57, U. Akron, 1958-61. Reporter, city editor Erie (Pa.) Times and News, 1949-57; reporter, city editor, asst. to exec. editor Akron (Ohio) Beacon Jour., 1958-67; with Battle Creek (Mich.) Enquirer & News, 1967-71, asst. mng. editor, 1967-68, mng. editor, 1968-71; exec. v.p., editor Oakland Press, Pontiac, Mich., 1971-77; pub. Oakland Press, 1977-95; v.p., pub. div. Capital Cities/ABC Inc., 1987-96; chmn. Great Lakes Media Inc., Birmingham, Mich., 1995-96; lectr. Am. Press Inst., 1968—; journalism juror Pulitzer Prizes, 1972—. Served with AUS, 1951-53; lt. col. Res. ret. Mem. Soc. Profl. Journalists. Episcopalian. Club: Pine Lake Country (Bloomfield, Mich.). Office: McIntyre Media Inc 700 E Maple Rd Ste 303 Birmingham MI 48009-6360

MCINTYRE, CHARLES EARL, insurance executive; b. L.A., Mar. 28, 1944; s. Donald Earl and Helen (Walker) McI.; m. Linda W. McIntyre, Oct. 17, 1969; children: Amanda, Margaret. BA, U. Redlands, Calif., 1966. CLU, ChFC. With Ray C. Watson Co., L.A., 1966-70; dir. human resources Leadership Housing, Newport Beach, Calif., 1970-75; agt. Northwestern Mut. Life, Ft. Lauderdale, Fla., 1975-80, dist. agt., 1980-85, gen. agt.,

1985—. Bd. dirs. Bonnet House, Ft. Lauderdale, 1993-96; bd. advisors Fla. Atlantic U., Ft. Lauderdale, 1994—. Mem. Gen. Agts. and Mgrs. Assn. (pres. 1989-90, Master Agy. award 1987—), Gen. Agts. Assn. (bd. dirs. 1988—), Broward County Life Underwriters, Chartered Life Underwriters Assn. Republican. Episcopalian. Avocations: reading, cards, jogging, travel. Office: Northwestern Mutual Life 2101 W Commercial Blvd Ste 5100 Fort Lauderdale FL 33309-3055

MCINTYRE, DEBORAH, psychotherapist, author; b. Pensacola, Fla., Sept. 11, 1955; d. John Joseph and Mary Cecelia (Campbell) McI.; m. Denis Miller Donovan, Sept. 6, 1985. BA in Psychology, George Mason U., 1976; MA Counseling Psychology, U. West Fla., 1980; AA in Nursing, Pensacola Jr. Coll., 1981. Diplomate Am. Bd. Med. Psychotherapists (fellow); RN, Va., Fla. Child psychotherapist Holly Hall Sch. for Exceptional Children, Vienna, Va., 1975-77; area rep. Youth For Understanding, Vienna, 1976-78; vol. child psychotherapist Children's Resource Ctr. of N.W. Fla., Pensacola, Fla., 1979-80; staff/charge nurse med. surgery Va. Beach Gen. Hosp., 1981-83; intake coord., child and family psychotherapist Psychiatric Inst., Norfolk, Va., 1982-83; head nurse, program coord., child and family therapist Children's Service, Horizon Hosp., Clearwater, Fla., 1983; child and adolescent psychotherapist The Children's Ctr. for Devel. Psychiatry, St. Petersburg, Fla., 1983—; cons., trainer Project Playpen, Juvenile Welfare Bd., St. Petersburg, 1985-87; cons. Early Childhood Coun. of Pinellas County; mem. adv. bd. New Traumatology Ann. Conf.; participant in workshops and seminars for mental health care. Author: (with Denis M. Donovan) Healing the Hurt Child: A Developmental-Contextual Approach, 1990; editl. adv. bd. The New Child Psychiatry; contbr. articles to profl. jours., chpts. to books.; co-originator of developmental-contextual child psychotherapy. Fellow Am. Psychol. Soc. Roman Catholic. Office: Childrens Ctr Devel Psych 6675 13th Ave N Ste 2-A Saint Petersburg FL 33710-5483

MCINTYRE, DONALD CONROY, opera singer, baritone; b. Auckland, New Zealand, Oct. 22, 1934; s. George D. and Hermyn McI.; m. Jill Redington, 1961; 3 children. Student, Auckland Tchrs. Tng. Coll., Guildhall Sch. Music, London; MusD, Auckland U., 1992. Prin. bass Sadler's Wells Opera, London, 1960-67, Royal Opera House-Covent Garden, London, from 1967. Appeared at Bayreuth Festival, 1967-81, 87, 88; frequent internat. guest appearances maj. opera houses including Metropolitan, N.Y.C., La Scala, Milan, Vienna, Paris, Munich, Berlin, Hamburg, Zurich, Chgo., Savonlinna Festival, Sydney, Buenos Aires; roles include: Wotan and Wanderer, Der Ring, Dutchman, Der Fliegende Hollander, Telramund, Lohengrin, Barak, Die Frau ohne Schatten, Pizzaro, Fidelio, Golaud, Pelleas et Melisande, Kurwenal, Tristan and Isold, Gurnemanz, Klingsor and Amfortas, Parsifal, Heyst, Victory, Jochanaan, Salome, Macbeth, Scarpia, Tosca, The Count, Marriage of Figaro, Nick Shadow, The Rake's Progress, Hans Sachs, Die Meistersinger, The Doctor, Woyzeck, Cardillac, Cardillac Hindemith, Kasper, Der Freischütz, Rocco, Fidelio, Prospero, Un Re In Ascolto (Brit. premier), Balstrode, Peter Grimes, Shakloviti, Khovanshchina, Sarastro Zauberflöte; recs. include Pelleas et Melisande, Oedipus Rex, Il Trovatore, Parsifal, The Ring, Damnation of Faust, Messiah Beethoven's 9th, Boris, Lady Macbeth of Mtsensk. Decorated comdr. Order of Brit. Empire; created knight, 1992; recipient Worldwide Fidelio medal Assn. Internat. Dirs. of Opera, 1989, New Zealand Commemoration award, 1990. Home: Foxhill Farm, Jackass Ln, Keston, Bromley, Kent BR2 6AN, England Office: care Ingpen & Williams, 14 Kensignton Ct, London W8 5DN, England also: Org Intl Opera et Concert, 19 rue Vignon F-7, Paris France

MCINTYRE, DOUGLAS ALEXANDER, magazine publisher; b. Erie, Pa., Mar. 16, 1955; s. Bruce Herbert and Natalie Ann (Wolff) McI.; divorced; children: Garrett Wolff, Hunter Garrahan; m. Patricia Yarberry Allen, Apr. 20, 1995. B.A. magna cum laude, Harvard U., 1977. Strategic planner Time Inc., N.Y.C., 1977-81; asst. to pres. Penthouse Internat., N.Y.C., 1981-82; assoc. Veronis, Suhler and Assocs., N.Y.C., 1982-83; gen. mgr. Fin. World, N.Y.C., 1983-84, pres., pub., 1984-95; pres., CEO McIntyre Media Properties, 1996-97; pres. Switchboard, Inc., 1997—; pres. Harvard Advocate Trustees Inc., 1983—; bd. dirs. Oster Comms., Inc.; corps. and founds. subcom. NYU Hosp./Cornell Med. Ctr. Mem. Harvard Club. Episcopalian.

MCINTYRE, ELIZABETH GEARY, Olympic athlete; b. Hanover, N.H., 1965. AB, Dartmouth Coll., 1988. Silver medalist, women's moguls final freestyle skiing Olympic Games, Lillehammer, Norway, 1994. Office: US Olympic Com 1750 E Boulder St Colorado Springs CO 80909-5724*

MCINTYRE, GUY MAURICE, professional football player; b. Thomasville, Ga., Feb. 17, 1961. Student, U. Ga. Offensive guard San Francisco 49ers, 1984-94, Phila. Eagles, 1995—; played in Super Bowl XIX, 1984, XXIII, 1988, XXIV, 1989. Played in Pro Bowl, 1989-93. *

MC INTYRE, HENRY LANGENBERG, former business executive, lawyer; b. St. Louis, Sept. 30, 1912; s. Joseph Shelby and Ida (Langenberg) McI.; m. Winifred Wheeler, Dec. 21, 1934; children: Robert W., Shelby H., Virginia H., Penelope T. A.B., Princeton U., 1933; J.D., Northwestern U., 1936. Bar: Ill. 1936. Practiced in Chgo., 1936-41; sec.-treas. Hiller Helicopters, 1946-52; partner McIntyre & Parker (real estate, mfr. devels.), 1952-58; pres. Pacific Industries, San Francisco, 1958-64; dir. Pacific Intermountain Express, 1960-64; partner McIntyre & Gage, 1965-70; sec.-treas. Bangert & Co., San Francisco, 1971-75. Mem. Palo Alto Planning Comm., 1953-56; chmn. Children's Health Coun., 1954-56; founder Population Resource Center, Princeton, N.J., 1976—; bd. dirs. Palo-Stanford Hosp., 1955-57, Planned Parenthood Fedn. Am., 1958-63, Internat. Planned Parenthood Fedn., 1962-70, Alzheimer's Disease and Related Disorders Assn., Chgo., 1987-92. Served as maj. F.A. AUS, 1942-45. Mem. Phi Beta Kappa, Phi Delta Phi, Order of Coif. Republican. Episcopalian. Clubs: Cottage (Princeton), Cypress Point, Burlingame (Calif.) Country, Eldorado Country (Calif.), Menlo Circus (Calif.). Home: 55 Serrano Dr Atherton CA 94027-3961 also: 47186 Crystal Loop Indian Wells CA 92210

MCINTYRE, JAMES OWEN, insurance executive; b. Cleve., July 21, 1958; s. Owen Eugene and Carole Diane (Saladin) McI.; m. Marina Zeccardi, Dec. 4, 1981; children: Antoinette, Owen, Helen, Robert. BS, Pa. State U., 1980, M of Mgmt., 1992. CLU. Sales rep. Liberty Mutual Ins. Co., Boston, 1982-89; sales mgr. Prudential Ins. Co., Blue Bell, Pa., 1989-94; adv. coun. agents Prudential Ins. Co., Ft. Washington, Pa., 1989; mgr. Del. Valley Fin. Group (agy. of Provident Mutual), Radnor, Pa., 1994-96; sales support and competition cons. Provident Mut. Ins. Co., Valley Forge, Pa., 1996—. Author: Economic Effect of Banks Entering the Insurance and Financial Services Industry, 1992. Mgr. Hatfield Area Little League, Pa., 1991-97; den leader Boy Scouts of Am., Hatfield, Pa., 1994-96. Recipient Pa. Life Roundtable award Pa. Assn. Life Underwriters, 1991. Fellow Life Underwriting Tng. Coun.; mem. Nat. Assn. Life Underwriters, Am. Soc. CLU & ChFC, Gen. Agt. and Mgrs. Assn. Republican. Lutheran. Avocation: golf. Home: 264 Meadow Ln Dr Downingtown PA 19335 Office: Provident Mut Ins Co 1050 Westlakes Dr Berwyn PA 19312-2421

MCINTYRE, JERRY L., lawyer; b. Atlantic City, July 1, 1941. AB, Columbia U., 1963; JD, Fordham U., 1969. Bar: N.Y. 1969, R.I. 1970. Mem. Skolnik, McIntyre & Tate, Providence; com. mem. Family Ct. Bench/Bar Com., 1985—. Pres. town coun., Town of Jamestown, R.I., 1983-89. Fellow Am. Acad. Matrimonial Lawyers; mem. ABA (sect. family law), N.Y. State Bar Assn. (sect. trusts and estates law), R.I. Bar Assn., R.I. Bar Found. Office: Skolnik McIntyre & Tate 321 S Main St Providence RI 02903-7108

MCINTYRE, JOHN ARMIN, physics educator; b. Seattle, June 2, 1920; s. Harry John and Florence (Armin) McI.; m. Madeleine Forsman, June 15, 1947; 1 son, John Forsman. B.S., U. Wash., 1943; M.A., Princeton U., 1948, Ph.D., 1950. Mem. design elec. engring. Carnegie Inst. Tech., Pitts., 1943; radio engr. Westinghouse Elec. Co., Balt., 1944; research asso. Stanford, 1950-57; mem. faculty Yale, 1957-63, asso. prof., 1960-63; prof. physics Tex. A&M U., College Station, 1963-95, emeritus prof., 1995—; asso. dir. Cyclotron Inst., 1965-70. Mem. council Oak Ridge Asso. Univs., 1964-71. Fellow Am. Phys. Soc., Am. Sci. Affiliation (exec. council 1968-73); mem. AAAS. Presbyn. Research and publs. on scintillation counters for gamma ray spectroscopy; determination of nuclear charge distbns. by electron scattering; study of nuclear structure by neutron transfer reactions; devel. variable energy gamma ray beams, gamma ray cameras. Home: 2316 Bristol St Bryan TX 77802-2405 Office: Tex A&M U Dept Physics College Station TX 77843

MCINTYRE, JOHN GEORGE WALLACE, real estate development and management consultant; b. Toronto, Ont., Can., July 26, 1920; s. George Crerar and Gwendolyn Alberta (Wallace) McI.; m. Ruth Elizabeth Wilson, July 26, 1945 (dec.); children: Angus, Heather, Robert, Anne. B of Commerce, U. Toronto, 1941; MBA, Harvard U., 1947. Budget acct. Abitibi Paper Co., Toronto, 1947-51; budget mgr., asst. gen. mgr. Ford of Can., Windsor, Ont., 1951-58, gen. mgr. mfg. ops., 1963-65; asst. mng. dir., mng. dir. Ford of Australia, Melbourne, 1958-63; exec. v.p., pres. Columbia Cellulose Ltd., Vancouver, B.C., Can., 1965-67; v.p. retail devel. and distbn. Hudson's Bay Co., Toronto, 1967-84; pres. Rupert's Land Tng. Co., Hudson's Bay Co. Devels. Ltd.; trustee Internat. Council of Shopping Ctrs., 1970-84; v.p., gen. mgr. Broadcast Ctr. Devel. Project Can. Broadcasting Corp., 1984-88; cons., 1988—. Served to capt. Royal Can. Ordnance Corps., 1942-45, ETO. Address: 53 Widdicombe Hill Blvd Ste 401E, Weston, ON Canada M9R 1Y3

MCINTYRE, LOUISE S., income tax consultant; b. Cin., Jan. 29, 1924; d. George Washington and Bertha (McDaniels) Sullivan; m. Harry McIntyre Jr., Jan. 18, 1947; children: Carol L., Patricia A., Harriet L., Harry J., Brenda R. AA, Mira Costa Coll., Oceanside, Calif., 1972; grad. in auditing, Nat. Tax Practice Inst., 1989. Enrolled agt. Hydraulic testor Paterson Field, Fairfield, Ohio, 1942-45; control clk. Hickam Field, Honolulu, 1945-47; clk.-typist Patterson Field, Fairfield, 1947-49, Camp LeJeune, Jacksonville, N.C., 1951-56; sec., bookkeeper Mission Bowl, Oceanside, 1973-79; income tax cons. Oceanside, 1974—. Mem. Oceanside Human Rels. Commn., 1970; bd. dirs. Armed Forces YMCA, Oceanside, 1969-71, Oceanside Christian Women's Club, 1988-91; bd. dirs. North County Concert Assn. Aux., 1993-96. Mem. Inland Soc. Tax Cons. (bd. dirs. 1988—), Am. Soc. Women Accts. (v.p. 1989-90), Enrolled Agts. Palomar, Nat. Assn. Enrolled Agts., Nat. Soc. Pub. Accts., Calif. Assn. Ind. Accts., Palmquist PTA (hon. life). Avocations: bowling, dancing, crafts, interior decorating, cake decorating. Home: 328 Camelot Dr Oceanside CA 92054-4515

MCINTYRE, MIKE, congressman; b. Lumberton, N.C., Aug. 6, 1956; m. Dee Strickland; children: Joshua, Stephen. BA, U. N.C., 1978, JD, 1981. Atty. Lumberton; mem. 105th Congress from 7th N.C. dist., 1997—; pres. Lumberton Economic Advancement Downtown, Inc.; state chmn. citizenship edn. com. Young Lawyers divsn. N.C. Bar Assn.; mem. focused edn. adv. com. N.C. Law; mem. exec. com. citizen edn. com. Young Lawers divsn. ABA. Columnist For the Family. Vol. Lumberton Recreation Dept., coach; active PTA, Boy Scouts Am., Lumberton Youth Baseball Assn.; elder, deacon, Sunday sch. tchr., clerk of session, chmn. weekday sch. and day care com. First Presbyn. Ch.; chmn. legis. com. Lumberton C. of C., bd. dirs., mem. exec. com.; mem. Lumberton's All-Am. City Del.; mem. Lumberton Commn. Youth and Family; chmn. Robeson County's U.S. Constitution Com. Named one of state's Ten Most Outstanding Young Dems., 1984, 85; recipient Nat. Bicentennial Leadership award, 1988. Mem. Phi Beta Kappa. Democrat.

MCINTYRE, MILDRED JEAN, clinical psychologist, writer, neuroscientist; b. Boston; d. William James and Theodora Grace (Jackson-McCullough) McI. BA, Swarthmore Coll., 1965; MA, Clark U., 1972, PhD, 1975. Lic. psychologist, Mass., Alaska, Hawaii. Ford Found. fellow, 1972, 73. Mem. APA, Internat. Neuropsychol. Soc., Cognitive Neurosci. Soc. Avocations: art, music, travel. Office: PO Box 990124 Boston MA 02199-0124

MCINTYRE, NORMAN F., petroleum industry executive; b. Pangman, Sask., Can., Oct. 21, 1945; s. Donald and Jean (Cruickshank) McI.; m. Lana Jean, June 10, 1967; children: Jason Lee, Spencer James. BSc in Petroleum Engring., U. Wyo., 1971; MS in Mgmt., MIT, 1991. Various positions with Mobil Oil, U.S., Can., to 1982; group mgr. engring. offshore divsn. Petro-Can., 1982-83, gen. mgr. frontier devel. offshore divsn., 1983, v.p. frontier devel., 1983-86, v.p. prodn. devel., 1986-89; sr. v.p. western region Petro-Can. Products, 1989-90; pres. Petro-Can. Resources, Calgary, Alta., Can., 1990-95, exec. v.p., 1995—; chmn., dir. Panarctic Oils Ltd.; dir. Petroleum Transmission Co.. Office: Petro-Canada, 150-6th Ave SW PO Box 2844, Calgary, AB Canada T2P 3E3

MCINTYRE, OSWALD ROSS, physician; b. Chgo., Feb. 13, 1932; m. Jean Geary, June 5, 1957; children—Margaret Jean, Archibald Ross, Elizabeth Geary. A.B. cum laude, Dartmouth Coll., 1953, postgrad, 1953-55; M.D., Harvard U., 1957. Intern U. Pa. Hosp., 1957-58; resident in medicine Dartmouth Med. Sch. Affiliated Hosps., 1958-60; instr. medicine Dartmouth Coll., 1964-66, asst. prof. medicine, 1966-69, assoc. prof., 1969-75, prof., 1976—, James J. Carroll prof. oncology, 1980-95, dir. Norris Cotton Cancer Center, 1975-92, prof. emeritus, 1995—; attending physician VA Hosp., White River Junction, Vt., 1964; cons. in hematology and oncology; acting chmn. dept. medicine Dartmouth-Hitchcock Med. Ctr., 1987-89; chmn. Cancer and Leukemia Group B.; 1990-95. Fellow AAAS; mem. Am. Fedn. Clin. Rsch., Am. Soc. Hematology, Internat. Assn. Study Lung Cancer, Am. Assn. Cancer Rsch., Am. Soc. Clin. Oncology, Assn. Cancer Inst. (pres. 1988-89), New Eng. Cancer Soc. (pres. 1989-90). Home: 34 Lamphire Hill Ln Lyme NH 03768-3109

MCINTYRE, PETER MASTIN, physicist, educator; b. Clewiston, Fla., Sept. 26, 1947; s. Peter Mastin and Ruby Eugenia (Richaud) McI.; m. Rebecca Biek, June 29, 1968; children: Peter B., Colin H., Jana M., Robert J. BS, U. Chgo., 1967, MS, 1968, PhD, 1973. Asst. prof. Harvard U., Cambridge, Mass., 1975-80; group leader Fermilab, Batavia, Ill., 1978-80; assoc. prof. Tex. A&M U., College Station, 1980-84, prof. physics, 1985—, assoc. dean Coll. of Sci., 1990-92; pres. Accelerator Tech. Corp., College Station, 1988—; dir. Tex. Accelerator Ctr., The Woodlands, 1991-93. Prin. author Tex. SSC Site Proposal, 1988. Sloan Found. fellow, 1976-78; recipient IR-100 award Indsl. Rsch. Mag., 1980. Mem. AAAS, Am. Phys. Soc. (pres. Tex. sect. 1990-91). Achievements include Proton-Antiproton Colliding Beams; patents for Continuous Unitized Tunneling System, Gigatron High Power Microwave Amplifier, Gas Microstrip Chamber for Medical Imaging; X-ray Disinfestation of Foods; development of 16 Tesla Superconducting magnets for future hadron colliders; micro-fabricated silicon array for DNA sequencing by hybridization. Home: 611 Montclair Ave College Station TX 77840-2868 Office: Tex A&M U Dept Physics College Station TX 77843

MCINTYRE, RICHARD RAWLINGS, II, elementary school educator; b. Houston, Nov. 20, 1946; s. Richard Rawlings and Emma Ruth (Blossom) McI.; m. Bonnie Antoinette Kimball, Dec. 23, 1973; 1 child, Richard Rawlings III. BA in History, Trinity U., San Antonio, 1969; MEd, Columbus (Ga.) Coll., 1983. Cert. tchr., phys. edn. coach, tech. specialist. Mgmt. trainee Deering Miliken, Manchester, Ga., 1972; tchr. Meriwether County Pub. Schs., Manchester, 1972—; instr. adult edn., Greenville, Ga., 1985-89. Editor newsletter Per Ardua, 1985-91. Coord. Jump Rope for Heart, Am. Heart Assn., Manchester Elem. Sch., 1985—; del. State Dem. Convs.; mem. State Dem. Com., 1990—; pres. Meriwether County Heart Assn, 1991-92. Capt. U.S. Army, 1969-72, Vietnam. Decorated Bronze Star; Nat. Presbyn. scholar, 1965-67. Mem. Meriwether Assn. Educators (past pres., treas., pres. 1996-98), Ga. Assn. Educators (chmn. state spelling bee com. 1987—, legis. contact team and polit. action com.), NEA, Ga. Supporters of Gifted, Warm Springs Merchants Assn. (pres. 1993-95), Jaycees, Clan MacIntyre Assn. (treas. 1994-96), Scottish Am. Mil. Soc. Avocations: Scottish heritage, genealogy, stamps, chess, computers. Home: RR 1 Box 175A Woodland GA 31836-9719 Office: Manchester Elem Sch 203 W Perry St Manchester GA 31816-1347

MCINTYRE, ROBERT WALTER, church official; b. Bethlehem, Pa., June 20, 1922; s. Simon Jesse and Ruth (Young) McI.; m. Edith Jones, Sept. 1, 1944 (dec. Jan. 1953); m. Elizabeth Norman, Nov. 6, 1953; children: Judith McIntyre Keilholtz, Joy McIntyre McCallum, John, James, June McIntyre Brannon. Student, Miltonvale Wesleyan Coll., 1939-43; B.Religion, Marion Coll., 1944, LittD (hon.), 1980, B.A., 1959; postgrad., Ball State U., 1960-61; D.D. (hon.), Ea. Pilgrim Coll., 1969; LLD (hon.), Houghton Coll., 1976; DHL (hon.), Ctrl. Wesleyan Coll., 1988. Ordained to ministry The Wesleyan Ch., 1945. Pastor Marengo, Ohio, 1944-47, Columbus, Ohio, 1947-52, Coshocton, Ohio, 1952-55; exec. sec. dept. youth The Wesleyan Ch., Marion, Ind., 1955-68; editor The Wesleyan Youth, Marion, 1955-68; gen. editor The Wesleyan Ch., editor The Wesleyan Adv., Marion, 1968-73; assoc. editor The Preacher's Mag., Marion, 1973-88; gen. supt. The Wesleyan Ch., Marion, 1973-88; mem. gen. bd. adminstrn. The Wesleyan Ch., 1955-88, mem. Commn. Christian Edn., 1959-73, 76-80, chmn. Commn. Christian Edn., 1976-80, mem. exec. bd., 1968-88; chmn. Commn. on World Missions, 1973-76, Commn. on Publs., 1980-84, Commn. on Extension and Evangelism, 1984-88; spl. asst. to the pres. Ind. Wesleyan U., Marion, 1988-93; denominational rep., bd. adminstrn. Nat. Assn. Evangelicals, 1973-83, exec. com., 1978-80, 81-87, 2d v.p., 1981-82, 1st v.p., 1982-84, pres., 1984-86, mem., 1973—; denominational rep. The Lord's Day Alliance, 1973-76; trustee Marion Coll., Asbury Theol. Sem., 1976—. Author: Ten Commandments for Teen-Agers, 1965; editor: Program Pathways for Young Adults, 1964, Mandate for Mission, 1970; contbr. articles to religious jours. Mem. Christian Holiness Assn. (chmn. social action commn. 1971-73, sec. 1973-76), Wesleyan Theol. Soc., Best Yrs. Fellowship (gen. dir. 1992—), Wesleyan Bible Conf. Assn. (bd. dirs. 1993—). Home: 4613 S Star Dr Marion IN 46953-7303

MCINTYRE, THOMAS, recording industry executive; b. 1948. CFO BMG Entertainment, N.Y.C., 1985—. Office: BMG Entertainment 1540 Broadway New York NY 10036-4039

MC ISAAC, GEORGE SCOTT, business policy educator, government official, former management consultant; b. Auburn, N.Y., July 25, 1930; s. Robert Scott and Agnes Congalton (Aitchison) McI.; m. Betsy Clark, Sept. 11, 1954; children: Ian Scott, Christopher Clark. BS, Yale U., 1952; MS, U. Rochester, 1961. In mfg. mgmt. Eastman Kodak Co., Rochester, N.Y., 1954-62; dir. McKinsey & Co. (Mgmt. Consultants), N.Y.C., Dusseldorf, Ger., Washington, 1962-78; asst. sec. of energy for resource applications U.S. Dept. Energy, Washington, 1978-80; sr. v.p. ops. Schlegel Corp., Rochester, 1980-85; AT&T resident mgmt. fellow; exec. prof. bus. and pub. policy William E. Simon Grad. Sch. Bus. Adminstrn., U. Rochester, 1985—; cons. various govts., mfg. cos., fin. instns., non-profit enterprises. Contbr. articles to bus. jours. Bd. dirs. Rochester Hosp. Corp.; trustee emeritus Internat. Mus. Photography, George Eastman House. Lt. USMC, 1952-54. Clubs: Met. (Washington), Genesee Valley (Rochester). Office: U Rochester Grad Sch Mgmt Carol G Simon Hall Rochester NY 14627

MCISAAC, PAUL ROWLEY, electrical engineer, educator; b. Port Washington, N.Y., Apr. 20, 1926; s. Robert Milton and June Zatella (Barrus) McI.; m. Mary Lou Heldenbrand, Sept. 10, 1949; children—Wendy Lee, Karen Jo, Hugh Paul, Kathleen Anne. B.E.E., Cornell U., 1949; M.S.E., U. Mich., 1950, Ph.D., 1954. Research engr. Microwave Tube div. Sperry Gyroscope Co., Great Neck, N.Y., 1954-59; assoc. prof. elec. engring. Cornell U., 1959-65, prof., 1965—, assoc. dean engring., 1975-80. Served with USN, 1944-46. Rotary Found. fellow, 1951-52. Mem. IEEE, AAAS, Sigma Xi. Office: Cornell University 306 Phillips Hall Ithaca NY 14853-5401

MCIVOR, DONALD KENNETH, retired petroleum company executive; b. Winnipeg, Man., Can., Apr. 12, 1928; s. Kenneth MacIver and Nellie Beatrice (Rutherford) McI.; m. Avonia Isabel Forbes, 1953; children: Gordon, Deborah, Duncan, Donald, Daniel. B.S. with honors in Geology, U. Man., 1950; postgrad., Nat. Def. Coll., 1973. Geophysical trainee seismic crew Imperial Oil Ltd., Alta., 1950, various operational and rsch. positions in exploration, 1950-58; held various positions including asst. to exploration mgr., suprv. exploration planning, mgr. exploration rsch. Imperial Oil Ltd., Calgary, 1958-68; with Jersey Prodn. Rsch. Co. Imperial Oil Ltd., Angola, France and Tulsa, Okla.; asst. mgr., mgr. corp. planning Toronto HO, 1968-69, mgr. exploration, 1970-72, sr. v.p., dir., 1973, exec. v.p., 1975; v.p. oil and gas exploration and prodn. Exxon Corp., 1977-81; dep. chmn., dir. Imperial Oil Ltd., 1981, chmn., chief exec. officer, 1982-85; dir., sr. v.p. Exxon Corp., Dallas, 1985-92; bd. dirs. Nat. Coun. on Econ. Edn.; exec. v.p. Internat. Exec. Svc. Corps. Mem. Can. Soc. Petroleum Geologists, Am. Petroleum Inst., Nat. Coun. Econ. Edn. (dir.). Home: 79 Lukes Wood Rd New Canaan CT 06840

MCKAGAN, DUFF (MICHAEL MCKAGAN), bassist; b. Feb. 5, 1964. Bassist Guns n' Roses, 1985—. Albums with Guns n' Roses include Live Like a Suicide, 1986, Appetite for Destruction, 1987, Guns n' Roses Lies, 1988, Use Your Illusion I, 1991, Use Your Illusion II, 1991, The Spaghetti Incident?, 1993; solo album: Believe in Me, 1993. Office: care Geffen Records 9130 W Sunset Blvd West Hollywood CA 90069-3110*

MCKAIN, MARY MARGARET, musician; b. Spokane, Wash., June 11, 1940; d. Neil Dunn and Elinore (Bien) McK. BA in Music and Police Sci., Calif. State U., L.A., 1968; studied trumpet with Rafael Mendez, Jane Sager, Sidney Lazar, and others. Trumpet player Peter Meremblum Jr. Symphony, 1954-59, Jack Benny at Greek Theater, 1963, Highland Park Symphony, L.A., 1955-66, Beverly Hills (Calif.) Symphony, 1960-66, South East Symphony, Downey, Calif., 1957-70, Santa Monica (Calif.) Elks Club, 1965-70, The Foresters, 1965-69, Latin Am. Symphony, L.A., 1961-63, L.A. Concert Band, Mexican Tipica Orch. Symphony, West Covina (Calif.) Symphony, 1976-79, Monterey Park (Calif.) Band, 1970-81, Calif. Concert Band, 1978-81, L.A. Police Dept. Concert Band, 1956-65, San Fernando Valley (Calif.) Opera, 1955-61, Iturbi on Tour, 1961; leader, trumpet player Pieces of 8 Polka Band, L.A., 1961-96; band leader, dir. Elks 99 Concert Band, 1996—; 1st female dep. marshal, L.A., 1973; part time musician TV series Here Come The Brides, 1972; musician for film E.T., 1983, leader Elks 99 Concert Band; also numerous TV commls., recordings, 1980—. Trumpet player with Peter Meremblum Jr. Symphony, Jack Benny at Greek Theater, Highland Park Symphony, L.A., 1955-66, Beverly Hills (Calif.) Symphony, South East Symphony, Downey (Calif.) Symphony, Santa Monica (Calif.) Elks Club, The Foresters, Latin Am. Symphony, L.A., L.A. Concert Band, Mexican Tipica Orch., W. Covina (Calif.) Symphony, Calif. Concert Band, Monterey Park (Calif.) Band, L.A. Police Dept. Concert Band, San Fernando Valley (Calif.) Opera, 1955-61, Iturbi on tour, 1961; leader, trumpet player with Pieces of 8 Polka Band, L.A., 1961—. Mem. Quartz Hill Town Coun.; active Alads, Sheriff's Relief. Mem. Musicians Local 47 (life), Sons and Daughters Mont. Pioneers (life), Wild Life Fedn., U.S. Humane Soc., Marshals Assn. (sec., dir.), Internat. Police Assn. Avocations: fishing, bicycling, genealog. rsch. Home: 43212 45th St W Quartz Hill CA 93536-5523

MCKANE, DAVID BENNETT, business executive; b. Salem, Mass., July 10, 1945; s. Vernon Wilson and Barbara Inez (Bennett) McK.; m. Wilson Lineburgh Baldwin, Apr. 16, 1977; adopted daughters, Taylor A., Lee and Paige Baldwin. BA, Dartmouth Coll., 1967; MBA, Amos Tuck Sch., 1969. Product mgr. Church & Dwight Co. Inc. (Arm and Hammer Products), N.Y.C., 1969-72; v.p. NTA Inc. N.Y.C., Nanuet, N.Y., 1972-75; v.p., exec. asst. to chmn. Schick Inc., Westport, Conn., 1975-77, sr. v.p., 1977-79, COO, exec. v.p., 1979-84, treas., 1980-84, also bd. dirs.; chmn., CEO A.I. Friedman, Inc., N.Y.C., 1985-87; chmn. McKane Robbins & Co. Inc., N.Y.C. and Westport, 1986—; bd. dirs. Oakhurst Dairy, Portland, Maine. Mem. bd. trustees Greens Farms (Conn.) Acad., 1991—. Mem. New Eng. Soc. in City N.Y., Mass. Mayflower Soc., Union Club (N.Y.C.), Country Club Fairfield, John's Island Club (Vero Beach, Fla.). Episcopalian. Home: 48 Owenoke Park Westport CT 06880-6833

MC KAUGHAN, HOWARD PAUL, linguistics educator; b. Canoga Park, Calif., July 5, 1922; s. Paul and Edith (Barton) McK.; m. Barbara Jean Budroe, Dec. 25, 1943; children: Edith (Mrs. Daniel Skene Santoro), Charlotte (Ms. Charlotte Barnhart), Patricia (Mrs. Stephen B. Pike), Barbara (Mrs. Ronald Chester Bell), Judith (Ms. Judith B. Achilles). AB, UCLA, 1945, MTh, Dallas Theol. Sem., 1946; MA, Cornell U., 1952, PhD, 1957. Mem. linguistic rsch. team Summer Inst. Linguistics, Mexico, 1946-52; asso. dir. Summer Inst. Linguistics, Philippines, also assoc. dir. summer sessions U. N.D., 1952-57, dir. Philippine br., 1957-61; rsch. asst. prof. anthropology U. Wash., 1961-62; rsch. assoc. prof., 1962-63; assoc. prof. linguistics U. Hawaii, 1963-64; prof. linguistics, 1964-88, prof. emeritus, 1988—, chmn. dept., 1963-66, dir. Pacific and Asian Linguistics Inst., 1964, 1966-69, assoc. dean grad. div., 1965-72, dean grad. div., dir. rsch., 1972-79, acting chancellor, 1979, interim vice chancellor acad. affairs, 1981-82, acting dir rsch., 1982-84, acting dean grad. div., 1982-83, dean, 1984-87, dir. rsch. rels., 1987-88; lectr. linguistics U. Philippines, summers, 1954, 60; Fulbright vis.

prof. Philippine Normal Coll.-Ateneo-De La Salle Consortium, Philippines, 1977, De La Salle U., Philippines, 1992; vis. prof. lingustics Bukidnon State Coll., Malaybalay, Philippines, 1993, 94; linguistic cons. Summer Inst. Linguistics, Malaysia branch, 1995—; prin. Wycliffe Sch. Linguistics, summers 1953, 61; vis. prof. Australian Nat. U., Canberra, 1970; adj. prof. linguistics U. Okla., summers 1984, 85, 86; vis. prof., head dept. linguistics Payap U., Chiang Mai, Thailand, 1989-90. Sr. scholar East-West Ctr., Honolulu, 1964; NDEA Maranao-Philippines research grantee, 1963-65; Office of Edn. Hawaii English grantee, 1965-66; NSF Jeh Language of South Vietnam grantee, 1969-70, Maranao Linguistic Studies, 1971-72, numerous other research grants. Mem. linguistic socs. Am., Philippines, Western Assn. Grad. Schs. (pres. 1978), Hawaii, Linguistic Circle N.Y., Philippine Assn. Lang. Tchrs., Hawaii Govt. Employees Assn., Phi Beta Kappa, Phi Kappa Phi. Author (with B. McKaughan): Chatino Dictionary, 1951; (with J. Forster) Ilocano: An Intensive Language Course, 1952; The Inflection and Syntax of Maranao Verbs, 1959; (with B. Macaraya): A Maranao Dictionary, 1967, rev. edit., 1996. Editor: Pali Language Texts: Philippines, 21 vols., 1971; The Languages of the Eastern Family of the East New Guinea Highlands Stock, 1973; Maranao Stories, 1995; Stories from the Darangen, 1995; contbr. articles, chpts. to books, sci. jours. Home: 420 S Hill Rd Mcminnville OR 97128-9105

MC KAY, ALEXANDER GORDON, classics educator; b. Toronto, Dec. 24, 1924; s. Alexander Lynn and Marjory Maude Redfern (Nicoll) McKay; m. Helen Jean Zulauf, Dec. 24, 1964; stepchildren: Julie Anne Stephanie Brott, Danae Helen Fraser. BA, U. Toronto, 1946; MA, Yale U., 1947, Princeton U., 1948; PhD, Princeton U., 1950; LLD (hon.), U. Man., 1986, Brock U., 1990, Queen's U., 1991; DLitt (hon.), McMaster U., 1992, U. Waterloo, 1993. Mem. faculty classics Wells Coll., 1949-50, U. Pa., 1950-51, U. Man., 1951-52, 55-57, Mt. Allison U., 1952-53, Waterloo Coll., 1953-55; mem. faculty McMaster U., 1957-90, prof., chmn. dept. classics, 1962-68, 76-79, dean humanities, 1968-73, mem. faculty senate, 1968-73, 85-87, prof. emeritus, 1990—; Disting. vis. prof. classics U. Colo., 1978; prof. in charge Intercollegiate Center for Classical Studies, Rome, 1975; vis. mem. Inst. Advanced Study, Princeton, 1979, 81; vis. scholar U. Tex., Austin, 1987, Hardt, Vandoeuvres, Geneva, 1988; vis. fellow Trinity Coll., Cambridge, 1988; adj. prof. Miami U., Oxford, Ohio, 1989, 92-95; adj. prof. humanities York U., 1990-96; Disting. vis. lectr. Concordia U., Montreal, 1992-93, Rockefeller Study and Conf. Ctr., Bellagio (Como) Italy, 1993. Author: Naples and Campania: Texts and Illustrations, 1962, Roman Lyric Poetry: Catullus and Horace, 2d edit., 1974, Vergil's Italy, 1970, Cumae and the Phlegraean Fields, 1972, Naples and Coastal Campania, 1972, Houses, Villas and Palaces in the Roman World, 1975, Roman Satire, 1976, Vitruvius, Architect and Engineer, 1978, 2d edit., 1985, Römische Häuser, Villen und Paläste, 1980, Roma Antiqua: Latium and Etruria, 1986; co-author: Selections from Vergil, Aeneid I, IV and VI (Dido and Aeneas), 1988, Festschrift, The Two Worlds of the Poet: New Perspectives on Vergil, 1992, Tragedy, Love, and Change: Roman Poetic Themes and Variations, 1994. Pres., bd. govs. Hamilton Philharm. Orch., 1967-96, Hamilton Chamber Music Soc., 1965-67, Hamilton br. Archtl. Conservancy Ont., 1965-67, Hamilton and Region Arts coun., 1971-72; bd. dirs. Can. Fedn. Humanities, 1980-82; v.p., dir. Internat. Acad. Union, 1978-90; trustee Hamilton Found., 1972-75; bd. govs. Art Gallery Hamilton; bd. govs., dir. Boris Brott Summer Music Festival, 1989—, Montreal Chamber Music Festival, 1997—; presdl. bd. trustees McMaster U. Art Gallery, 1985-91; pres. Sir Ernest MacMillan String Ensemble, 1988-90; mem. adv. bd. Inst. for Classical Tradition, Boston U., 1987-88; v.p., dir. Bach-Elgar Choral Soc., Hamilton, 1992-95. Decorated knight comdr. Order St. John of Jerusalem; officer Order of Can.; recipient Silver Jubilee medal Queen Elizabeth II, 1977, 125th Anniversary medal Can. Confedn.; Woodrow Wilson fellow, 1947-48, Can. Coun. fellow, 1973-74, Killam rsch. fellow, 1979-80, fellow Vanier Coll., York U., 1991-96, vis. scholar, 1996—. Fellow Royal Soc. Can. (hon. editor 1970-83, pres. 1984-87, past pres. 1987-89, Centennial medal 1982); mem. Vergilian Soc. (pres. 1972-74, Hon. Pres. for Life 1988—, chmn. Villa Vergiliana mgmt. com. 1993—), Classical Assn. Mid. West and South award of merit com. 1989-91), Classical Assn. Can. (v.p. 1970-72, 76-78, pres. 1978-80), Ont. Classical Assn. (hon. pres. 1994—), Societas Cumana (trustee 1993-96), The Campanian Soc., Inc. (dir. 1994—), Yale Club (N.Y.C.), Univ. Club (Pitts.), Tamahaac Club (Ancaster), Arts and Letters Club (Toronto), X Club (Toronto), Faculty Club (McMaster). Home: 1 Turner Ave, Hamilton, ON Canada L8P 3K4 Office: McMaster U, Dept of Classics, Hamilton, ON Canada L8S 4M2

MCKAY, CRAIG, film editor. Editor: (films) Scarecrow, 1973, Thieves, 1977, Melvin and Howard, 1980, (with Dede Allen) Reds, 1981 (Academy award nomination best film editing 1981), Swing Shift, 1984, Something Wild, 1986, (with Alan Miller) Crack in the Mirror, 1987, Married to the Mob, 1988, She-Devil, 1989, Miami Blues, 1990, The Silence of the Lambs, 1991 (Academy award nomination best film editing 1991), Shining Through, 1992, (with Elena Maganini) Mad Dog and Glory, 1993, Philadelphia, 1993, (TV movies) Private Sessions, 1985. Address: 345 W 58th St New York NY 10019-1145 also: c/o Paul Hook/ICM 8942 Wilshire Blvd Beverly Hills CA 90211*

MC KAY, DEAN RAYMOND, computer company executive; b. Seattle, Nov. 13, 1921; s. Joseph and Nora (MacDermitt) McK.; m. Jean Davis, Dec. 26, 1942; children: Dean Brian, Bruce Thompson, Robert Joseph. BA, U. Wash., 1944; postgrad., Harvard U., 1955. With IBM Corp., Armonk, N.Y., 1946-82, from br. mgr. to dir. pers. div. data processing, 1957-61, v.p. communications, 1961-69, v.p. corp. ops. and services staff, 1969, mem. mgmt. com., 1970, sr. v.p., 1971, sr. v.p., group exec. data processing mktg., 1972—, sr. v.p. corp. ops. and services staffs, mem. corp. mgmt. com., bd. dir., 1978-82, mem. adv. bd., 1982—; bd. dirs. Marsh & McLennan Cos., Inc., N.Y.C., MCI Communications Corp., Washington, MARCAM, Newton, Mass., Du Pont, Wilmington, Del. Served to lt. (s.g.) Intelligence Corps USNR, 1942-46. Mem. Phi Beta Kappa. Clubs: Ekwanok (Manchester, Vt.); Gulf Stream (Delray Beach, Fla.), Blind Brook (Purchase, N.Y.).

MC KAY, EMILY GANTZ, civil rights professional; b. Columbus, Ohio, Mar. 13, 1945; d. Harry S. and Edwina (Bookwalter) Gantz; BA, Stanford U., 1966, MA, 1967; m. Jack Alexander McKay, July 3, 1965. Pub. info. specialist Community Action Pitts., 1967-68, exec. asst. to manpower dir., 1968-69, rsch. assoc., 1969-70; free-lance cons., 1969-70; pub. rels. and materials specialist Metropolitan Cleve. JOBS Coun., 1971-72; rsch. and mgmt. cons. BLK Group, Inc., Washington, 1970-73; dir. tech. products Am. Tech. Assistance Corp., McLean, Va., 1973-74; rsch. and mgmt. cons. CONSAD Rsch. Corp., Pitts., 1974-76, v.p., 1976-78; spl. asst. to Pres. for planning and eval. Nat. Coun. La Raza, Washington, 1978-82, v.p. rsch., advocacy and legislation, 1981-88, exec. v.p., 1983-88, cons. to the pres., 1988-90, v.p. for instl. devel., 1991-93, sr. v.p. instl. devel., 1993-94; pres. MOSAICA Ctr. for Nonprofit Devel. and Pluralism, 1994—; mem. adv. merit selection panel Superior Ct. D.C., 1987-90; cons. resource devel. New Israel Fund, 1989-91; cons. City of Cleve., Nat. Assn. Cmty. Devel., Nat. Coun. La Raza, 1975-78, Ford Found., 1989, Nat. AIDS Network, 1988-89, Am. Cultural Ctr., Israel, 1990, Nat. Hispana Leadership Inst., 1993; vol. orgnl. cons. SHATIL, Jerusalem and community based groups in Israel, 1987—; guest faculty Union Grad. Sch.; adj. faculty Am. U., Washington, 1995—. Author: numerous nonprofit orgn. devel. tng. materials. Co-chmn. Citizens Adv. Com. to D.C. Bar, 1986-87; mem. Mayor's Commn. Coop. Econ. Devel., 1981-83; non-lawyer mem. bd. govs. D.C. Bar, 1982-85; exec. com., bd. dirs. Indochina Resource Action Ctr., 1982-92; bd. dirs. exec. com. Southeast Asia Resource Action Ctr., 1993-97; co-chmn. Citizens Commn. Adminstrn. Justice, 1982-84; mem. exec. com. Coalition on Human Needs, 1981-88; mem. Washington area steering com. New Israel Fund, 1989-91; co-chmn. adv. com. to Washington dist. office dir. Immigration and Naturalization Svc., 1984-88; chair Refugee Women in Devel., 1987-90, vice chair, 1990-94; mem. nat. adv. bd. Project Blueprint United Way Am., 1992-94, mem. diversity com., 1994-96; vice chair, treas. Fund for the Future of Our Children, 1994—; sec. bd. dirs. New Bosnia Fund, 1995—; bd. advisors Internat. Ctr. for Residential Edn., 1994-96; treas. bd. dir. Mary's Ctr. for Maternal and Child Care, 1995—; treas., bd. dirs. AVODAH: The Jewish Svc. Corps, 1996—; bd. dirs. Nat. Hispana Leadership Inst., 1997—. Ford Found. nat. honors fellow, 1966-67; recipient I. Pat Rios award Guadalupe Ctr., 1988; mem. working group Memorandum of Understanding between HHS and Israeli Ministry of Labour and Social Welfare, 1990-94, chairperson subcom. Youth at Risk, 1992-94. Mem. NAACP, Phi Beta Kappa. Democrat. Home: 3200 19th St NW Washington DC 20010-1006 Office: 1000 16th St NW Ste 604 Washington DC 20036-5743

MCKAY, EUGENE HENRY, JR., food company executive; b. Battle Creek, Mich., June 25, 1929; s. Eugene Henry and Ella Florence (Everest) McK.; m. Beverly June Blakeman, Nov. 6, 1951 (div. 1981); children: Eugene Henry III, John Blakeman, Heather Melinda; m. Janice Lee Rook, 1989. BA, Mich. State U., 1951. Prodn. mgr. Battle Creek Food Co., 1955-60; franchise mgr. Archway Cookies, Inc., 1960-65, v.p., 1965-75, exec. v.p., 1975-85, pres., ptnr., 1985-96, ptnr., chmn., CEO, 1996-97, 1997—. Maj. U.S. Army, 1951-54. Republican. Presbyterian. Office: Archway Cookies Inc 5451 W Dickman Rd Battle Creek MI 49015-1034

MCKAY, JACK ALEXANDER, electronics engineer, physicist; b. Alhambra, Calif., Apr. 3, 1942; s. Gordon Alexander and Helen Leona (Lappin) McK.; m. Emily Gantz, July 3, 1965. BS in Physics, Stanford U., 1964, MSEE, 1967; MS in Physics, Carnegie-Mellon U., 1969, PhD in Physics, 1974. Rsch. physicist Naval Rsch. Lab., Washington, 1974-84; rsch. scientist Phys. Scis. Inc., Alexandria, Va., 1984-91; scientist Rsch. Support Instruments, Hunt Valley, Md., 1991-96; rsch. scientist Utah State U., 1996—; cons. Remote Sensor Concepts, Washington, 1996—. Home: 3200 19th St NW Washington DC 20010-1006 Office: Remote Sensor Concepts 3200 19th St NW Washington DC 20010-1006

MC KAY, JIM, television sports commentator; b. Phila., Sept. 24, 1921; s. Joseph F. and Florence (Gallagher) McManus; m. Margaret Dempsey, Oct. 2, 1948; children: Mary Edwina, Sean Joseph. A.B., Loyola Coll., Balt., 1943, HLD (hon.), 1981. Reporter Balt. Evening Sun, 1946-47; news and sports commentator sta. WMAR- TV, Balt., 1947-50; sports commentator CBS Network, 1950-61; host This is New York, 1958-59; sports commentator for Winter and Summer Olympics, 1960-88; host ABC Wide World of Sports, from 1961; now commentator ABC Sports; chmn. "Maryland Million" Horse Racing Program, 1986—. Author: My Wide World, 1973. Served to lt. USNR, 1943-46. Decorated Officer's Cross Order of Merit (Fed. Republic Germany), 1974; recipient 12 Emmy awards, George Polk Meml. award, 1973, Olympic medal Austria, 1977, Engelhard award Thoroughbred Breeders of Ky., 1978, 90, Humphrey S. Finney award Md. Racing Writers, 1985, Nat. Turf Writers award, 1987, Peabody Award, 1989; named to Sportscasters Hall of Fame, 1987, U.S. Olympic Hall of Fame, 1989. Clubs: Jockey, Balt. Country, Md. Club, Hamilton St., Pinetree (Fla.) Golf Club. Avocations: raising and breeding race horses. Office: ABC Sports 47 W 66th St New York NY 10023-6201*

MCKAY, JOHN, lawyer; b. Seattle, June 19, 1956; s. John Larkin and Kathleen (Tierney) M. BA, U. Wash., 1978; JD, Creighton U., 1982. Bar: Wash. 1982, U.S. Dist. Ct. (we. dist.) Wash. 1982, U.S. Supreme Ct. 1990, U.S. Ct. Appeals (9th cir.) 1990. Ptnr. Lane Powell Spears Lubersky, Seattle, 1982-92, Cairncross & Hempelmann, Seattle, 1992-97; pres. Legal Svcs. Corp., Washington, 1997—. White House fellow, Washington, 1989-90. Mem. ABA (bd. govs. 1991-94), Wash. State Bar Assn. (pres. young lawyers divsn. 1988-89). Republican. Roman Catholic. Avocations: soccer, golf. Office: Legal Svcs Corp 750 1st St NE Washington DC 20002-4241 also: Legal Svcs Corp 750 First St NW Washington DC 20002

MCKAY, JOHN DOUGLAS, lawyer; b. Wheeling, W.Va., Feb. 27, 1960; s. Douglas and Margaret Ann McK.; m. Jennifer Hall, June 13, 1987; children: John Wallace, Megan Diane, Hannah Nadine. BA with distinction, U. Va., 1982; JD, U. Maine, 1985. Bar: W.Va. 1985, Maine 1985, U.S. Dist. Ct. (so. dist.) W.Va. 1985, U.S. Dist. Ct. Maine 1985, U.S. Ct. Appeals (1st cir.) 1986, Va. 1988, U.S. Ct. Appeals (4th cir.) 1988, U.S. Dist. Ct. (we. dist.) Va. 1988, Colo. 1997. Assoc. Petruccelli, Cohen, Erler & Cox, Portland, Maine, 1985-88, Taylor & Zunka, Ltd., Charlottesville, Va., 1988-91; ptnr. McKay & Cattano PLC, Charlottesville, Va., 1991—. Editor (legal newsletter) Equine Law & Bus. Letter, 1990-95; contbr. articles to profl. jours. Elder Westminster Presbyn. Ch. Recipient Best Adv. award U. Maine Sch. of Law, 1988. Mem. Va. State Bar (7th dist. disciplinary com.), Va. Bar Assn., W.Va. State Bar, Charlottesville-Albemarle Bar Assn. (bd. dirs. 1994-96), Thomas Jefferson Inn of Ct. (past pres). Office: McKay & Cattano PLC 408 Park St Charlottesville VA 22902-4738

MCKAY, JOHN JUDSON, JR., lawyer; b. Anderson, S.C., Aug. 13, 1939; s. John Judson and Polly (Plowden) McK.; m. Jill Hall Ryon, Aug. 3, 1961 (div. Dec. 1980); children: Julia Plowden, Katherine Henry, William Ryon, Elizabeth Hall; m. Jane Leahey, Feb. 18, 1982; children: Andrew Leahey, Jennifer McFaddin. AB in History, U. S.C., 1960, JD cum laude, 1966. Bar: S.C. 1966, U.S. Dist. Ct. S.C. 1966, U.S. Ct. Appeals (4th cir.) 1974, U.S. Supreme Ct. 1981, U.S. Dist. Ct. (so. dist.) Ga. 1988, U.S. Ct. Appeals (11th cir.), 1990. Assoc. Haynsworth, Perry, Bryant, Marion & Johnstone, Greenville, S.C., 1966-70; ptnr. Rainey, McKay, Britton, Gibbes & Clarkson, P.A., and predecessor, Greenville, 1970-78; sole practice, Hilton Head Island, S.C., 1978-80; ptnr. McKay & Gertz, P.A., Hilton Head Island, 1980-81, McKay & Mullen, P.A., Hilton Head Island, 1981-88, McKay & Taylor, Hilton Head, 1988-91; pvt. practice, 1991—. Served to lt. (j.g.) USNR, 1961-64; lt. comdr. Res. (ret.). Mem. ABA, S.C. Bar Assn. (pres. young lawyers sect. 1970, exec. com. 1971-72, assoc. mem. grievance and disciplinary com. 1983-87), S.C. Bar, Beaufort County Bar Assn., Hilton Head Bar Assn., Assn. Trial Lawyers Am., S.C. Trial Lawyers Assn., S.C. Bar Found. (pres. 1977), Blue Key, Wig and Robe, Phi Delta Phi. Episcopalian. Clubs: Poinsett (Greenville). Editor-in-chief U. S.C. Law Rev., 1966; contbr. articles to legal jours. Home: 17 Foxbriar Ln Hilton Head Island SC 29926 Office: 203 Watersedge Hilton Head Island SC 29928-3541

MCKAY, KENNETH GARDINER, physicist, electronics company executive; b. Montreal, Que., Can., Apr. 8, 1917; came to U.S., 1946, naturalized, 1954; s. James Gardiner and Margaret (Nicholas) McK.; m. Irene C. Smith, July 25, 1942; children—Margaret Craig, Kenneth Gardiner. B.Sc., McGill U., 1938, M.Sc., 1939; Sc.D, MIT, 1941; D.Eng. (hon.), Stevens Inst. Tech., 1980. Research engr. Nat. Research Council Can., 1941-46; with Bell Telephone Labs., 1946-66, 73-80, dir. solid state device devel., 1957-59, v.p. systems engring., 1959-62, exec. v.p. systems engring., 1962-66, exec. v.p., 1973-80; v.p. engring AT&T, 1966-73; chmn. bd. Bellcomm Inc., 1966-73, Charles Stark Draper Lab., 1982-87; advisor Min. of Transp. and Comms., Republic of China, 1992-95. Trustee Stevens Inst. Tech., 1974-87; bd. govs. McGill U., 1972-77, N.Y. Coll. Osteo. Medicine, 1980-89; mem. vis. com. for engring. Stanford U., 1974-87; mem. sci. and acad. adv. com. U. Calif., 1980-88; mem. Sci. and Tech. Adv. Group, Republic of China, 1982-96. Fellow IEEE, Am. Phys. Soc., N.Y. Acad. Scis.; mem. NAS, NAE (councillor 1970-73), Century Assn. Home and Office: 5 Carolina Meadows # 206 Chapel Hill NC 27514-8522

MCKAY, LAURA L., banker, consultant; b. Watonga, Okla., Mar. 3, 1947; d. Frank Bradford and Elizabeth Jane (Smith) Drew; m. Cecil O. McKay, Sept. 20, 1969; 1 child, Leslie. BSBA, Oreg. State U., 1969. New br. research U.S. Bank, Portland, Oreg., 1969-80; cash mgmt. officer U.S. Bank, Portland, 1980-82, asst. v.p., 1982-87, v.p., 1987-94; founder, cons. LLM Cons., Milw., 1994—. Chmn. Budget Com., North Clackamas Sch. Dist., 1982-84. Mem. Nat. Corp. Cash Mgrs. Assn., Nat. Assn. Bank Women (chmn. Oreg. group 1979-80), Portland Cash Mgrs. Assn., Portland C. of C. Republican. Office: LLM Cons 5686 SE Viewcrest Dr Milwaukie OR 97267-4146

MCKAY, LAURIE MARIE, special education educator; b. Cadillac, Mich., Sept. 10, 1960; d. Leonard Max and Mary Ann (Pierzina) Tykwinski; m. John William McKay, June 27, 1992; 1 child, Abbe Rose; stepchildren: David John, Chad Richard. BA in Psychology, Mich. State U., 1983; cert., Ctrl. Mich. U., 1990; postgrad., Grand Valley State U., 1992—. Cert. tchr. elem. edn., emotionally impaired, Mich. Tchr. spl. edn. Reed City (Mich.) Pub. Schs., 1990-91; instrl. aide Wexford-Missaukee Intermediate Sch., Cadillac, Mich., 1983-89, tchr. spl. edn., 1991—; rep., mem. student assistance program com., CCD instr. grade 4 Wexford-Missaukee Profl. Assn.; water safety instr. ARC, 1995. Cookie mgr. Crooked Tree Girl Scout Coun., Cadillac, 1989. Mem. Mich. Assn. of Tchrs. of Emotionally Disturbed Children, Coun. for Exceptional Children, Wexaucola Reading Coun. Democrat. Roman Catholic. Avocations: cross-country skiing, skating, baking, gardening, swimming. Home: 121 Henderson Pl Cadillac MI 49601-9633 Office: Wexford Missaukee Sch Dist 9905 S 13 Rd Cadillac MI 49601-9352

MCKAY, MICHAEL DENNIS, lawyer; b. Omaha, May 12, 1951; s. John Larkin and Kathleen (Tierney) McK.; m. Christy Ann Cordwin, Apr. 22, 1978; children: Kevin Tierney, Kathleen Lindsay, John Larkin. BA in Polit. Sci. with distinction, U. Wash., 1973; JD, Creighton U., 1976. Bar: Wash. 1976, U.S. Dist. Ct. (we. dist.) Wash. 1978, U.S. Dist. Ct. (ea. dist.) Wash. 1982, U.S. Ct. Appeals (9th cir.) 1982, U.S. Supreme Ct. 1993. Sr. dep. pros. atty. King County, Seattle, 1976-81; ptnr. McKay & Gaitan, Seattle, 1981-89; U.S. atty. we. dist. Wash. Seattle, 1989-93; ptnr. Lane Powell Spears Lubersky, Seattle, 1993-95, McKay, Chadwell & Matthews PLLC, Seattle, 1995—. Bd. dirs. Mental Health North, Seattle, 1982-85, St. Joseph Sch. Bd., 1984-87, Our Lady of Fatima Sch. Commn., 1994—, Creighton U., 1988-90; mem. stadium adv. bd. Seattle Kingdome, 1987-89; state vice chmn. George Bush for Pres., 1988; mem. U.S. Atty. Gen. Adv. Com., 1991-93, vice chmn., 1992; mem. Washington Citizens' Commn. on Salaries for Elected Officials, 1997—. Mem. Creighton U. Alumni Assn. (pres. 1988-90, nat. alumni bd. 1988-92), Wash. Athletic Club, Columbia Tower Club. Republican. Roman Catholic. Avocations: tennis, running, swimming. Office: McKay Chadwell & Matthews PLLC 701 5th Ave Seattle WA 98104-7016

MCKAY, MONROE GUNN, federal judge; b. Huntsville, Utah, May 30, 1928; s. James Gunn and Elizabeth (Peterson) McK.; m. Lucile A. Kinnison, Aug. 6, 1954; children: Michele, Valanne, Margaret, James, Melanie, Nathan, Bruce, Lisa, Monroe. B.S., Brigham Young U., 1957; J.D., U. Chgo., 1960. Bar: Ariz. 1961. Law clk. Ariz. Supreme Ct., 1960-61; assoc. firm Lewis & Roca, Phoenix, 1961-66; ptnr. Lewis & Roca, 1968-74; assoc. prof. Brigham Young U., 1974-76, prof., 1976-77; judge U.S. Ct. Appeals for 10th Cir., Denver, 1977-91, chief judge, 1991-94, sr. judge, 1994—. Mem. Phoenix Community Council Juvenile Problems, 1968-74; pres. Ariz. Assn. for Health and Welfare, 1970-72; dir. Peace Corps, Malawi, Africa, 1966-68; bd. dirs., pres. Maricopa county Legal Aid Soc., 1972-74. Served with USMCR, 1946-48. Mem. ABA, Ariz. Bar Assn., Maricopa County Bar Assn., Am. Law Inst., Am. Judicature Soc., Order of Coif, Blue Key, Phi Kappa Phi. Mem. LDS Ch. Office: US Ct Appeals for 10th Cir Rm 6012 Fed Bldg 125 S State St Salt Lake City UT 84138

MCKAY, NEIL, banker; b. East Tawas, Mich., Aug. 9, 1917; s. Lloyd G. and Rose (McDonald) McK.; m. Olive D. Baird, Nov. 11, 1950; children: Julia B., Lynn B., Hunter L. A.B., U. Mich., 1939, J.D. with distinction, 1946. Bar: Mich. 1946, Ill. 1947. With firm Winston & Strawn, Chgo., 1946-63; partner Winston & Strawn, 1954-63, mem. mgmt. com., 1958-63; with First Nat. Bank of Chgo., 1963-83, from v.p. charge heavy industry lending div., gen. mgr. London br., to exec. v.p., cashier, 1970-75, vice chmn. bd., 1976-83, also dir.; exec. v.p., sec. First Chgo. Corp., 1970-75, vice chmn. bd., 1976-83; also bd. dirs.; bd. dirs. Baird & Warner, Inc., Chgo.; founding dir. Student Loan Mktg. Assn. Mem.: U. Mich. Law Rev; assoc. editor-in-chief: U. Mich. Law Rev., 1942, sr. editor, 1946. Trustee Morton Arboretum; former trustee Kalamazoo Coll. and Ill. Inst. Tech. Served with USNR, 1942-46. Mem. ABA, Ill. Bar Assn., Dunham Woods Riding Club, Chgo. Hort. Soc. (bd. dirs.), Chgo. Club, Mid-Day Club, Geneva Golf Club. Office: 1 First National Plz Rm 2538 Chicago IL 60603

MCKAY, RICHARD JAMES, lawyer; b. Eugene, Oreg., Mar. 16, 1959; s. John H. and Nancy Jean (Hunter) McK.; m. Terrin Lea Few, May 19, 1984; children: K. Hunter, John Crosby. BA, Princeton U., 1981; JD, Stetson Coll. Law, St. Petersburg, Fla., 1984. Bar: Fla. 1984, U.S. Dist. Ct. (mid. dist.) Fla. 1984. Law clk. Judge William Terrell Hodges U.S. Dist. Ct. (middle dist. Fla.), Tampa, 1984-86; ptnr. Hill, Ward & Henderson, Tampa, Fla., 1986-92; ptnr. Tampa Bay Bucaneers, 1992—, gen. mgr.; adj. prof. Stetson Coll. Law, St. Petersburg, 1989-92; mem. NFL Competition Com., 1994—. Office: Tampa Bay Buccaneers One Buccaneer Pl Tampa FL 33607

MC KAY, THOMAS, JR., lawyer; b. Kearny, N.J., Sept. 26, 1920; s. Thomas and Mary (Paterson) McK.; m. Rosemary T. LaMarra, Oct. 5, 1946; children—Thomas III, Barbara Anne, Robert Michael. AB, Rutgers U., 1941; LLB, NYU, 1944. Bar: N.J. 1945, Ill. 1967. Assoc. to Arthur T. Vanderbilt, 1944-47; assoc. firm Toner, Speakman & Crowley, Newark, 1947-50; with McGraw-Edison Co. (and predecessor), 1950-80, sec., gen. counsel, 1967-80, v.p., 1973-80; v.p., gen. counsel, sec. Swift Ind. Corp., Chgo., 1980-84; of counsel Boodell Sears Giambalvo & Crowley, Chgo., 1984-87; securities industry arbitrator pub., 1988—. Vol. legal aid atty. Prairie State Legal Svcs., Inc., St. Charles, Ill., 1987-96. Mem. Am. Arbitration Assn. (comml. and securities law arbitrator). Home: 1435 Hampton Crse Saint Charles IL 60174-1319

MCKAYLE, DONALD COHEN, choreographer, director, writer, dance educator; b. N.Y.C., July 6, 1930; s. Philip Augustus and Eva Wilhelmina (Cohen) McK.; m. Esta Beck, 1954; m. Leah Levin, 1965; children—Gabrielle, Liane, Guy Eylon. Student, CCNY. mem. faculty Bennington Coll., Sarah Lawrence Coll., Conn. Coll., Bard Coll., Neighborhood Playhouse, Juilliard Sch., Martha Graham Sch., Am. Dance Festival; artistic dir., dean Calif. Inst. Arts Sch. of Dance; prof. dance, artistic dir. U. Calif., Irvine. Dancing debut, 1948; dir., 1964—; choreographer, 1950—, for cos. including, Alvin Ailey Am. Dance Theater, Batsheva Dance Co. Israel, Repertory Dance Theater, San Francisco Ballet, Cleve. San Jose Ballet, Dayton Comtemporary Dance Co., Cleo Parker Robinson Dance Ensemble; artistic mentor, resident choreographer Limon Dance Co., 1995; dir., choreographer stage prodns.: Free and Easy, 1961, Trumpets of the Lord, 1963 (Tony award nominee for best dir. and best choreographer 1975), Raisin, 1974 (Tony award nominee for best choreographer 1974), Dr. Jazz, 1975 (Tony award nominee for best choreographer 1975), The Last Minstrel Show, 1978, Evolution of the Blues, 1978-79, Sophisticated Ladies, 1981 (Best Choreographer award Outer Critics Cir. 1981, Tony award nominee for best choreographer 1981); choreographer stage prodns.: The Tempest, 1963-64, Anthony and Cleopatra, 1963-64, As You Like It, 1963-64, Golden Boy, 1964 (Tony award nominee for Best Choreographer, 1965), A Time for Singing, 1966, The Four Musketeers, 1967, I'm Solomon, 1968, Mass., 1972; choreographer films: The Great White Hope, 1968, Bed Knobs and Broomsticks, 1970, Charlie and the Angel, 1972, The Jazz Singer, 1980; T.V. works include: Baseball Ballet, 1963, Amahl and the Night Visitors, 1963, Fan Fare, 1965, Jazz Dance, U.S.A., 1965, The Strolling Twenties, 1965, Ten Blocks of the Camino Real, 1966, The Ed Sullivan Show, 1966-67, The Bill Cosby Special, 1967, Soul, 1968, Soul, 1968, TCB, 1968, The Second Bill Cosby Special, 1968, The Sounds of Summer, 1969, The Leslie Uggams Show, 1969, Dick Van Dyke and the Other, 1969, And Beautiful, 1969, Yesterday, Today and Tomorrow, 1970, The Super Comedy Bowl, 1971, A Funny Thing Happened on the Way to a Special, 1972, The New Bill Cosby Show, 1972-73, Angelitos Negros, 1973, Free to Be You and Me, 1974, Good Times, 1974-78, The Minstrel Man, 1977 (Emmy nominee 1977), The Richard Pryor Special, 1977, Cindy, 1978; choreographer concert works: Games, 1951, Nocturne, 1952, Rainbow Round My Shoulder, 1959, Dist. Storyville, 1962, They Called Her Moses, Incantation, 1968, Migrations, 1972, Album Leaves, 1976, Blood Memories, 1976, and numerous others, (staged club acts and TV specials for Diana Ross, Ann-Margret, Harry Belafonte, Mary Tyler Moore and others. Recipient Drama Logue Critics award Evolution of the Blues, Samuel H. Scripps Am. Dance Festival award, 1992, Capezio award, 1963, Lauds and Laurels profl. achievement award U. Calif. Irvine Alumni Assn., 1992, Disting. Faculty Lectureship award for rsch., 1997, Balasaraswati/Joy Ann Dewey Beinecke Endowed Chair for Disting. Tchg., 1997, Lifetime Achievement award Am. Dance Guild, 1994, Living Legend award Nat. Black Arts Festival, 1994, Balasaraswati, Joy Ann Dewey Beinecke Endowed chair for Disting. Teaching, Am. Dance Festival, 1997.

MCKEACHIE, WILBERT JAMES, psychologist, educator; b. Clarkston, Mich., Aug. 24, 1921; s. Bert A. and Edith E. (Welberry) McK.; m. Virginia Mae Mack, Oct. 30, 1942; children: Linda, Karen. BA, Mich. State Normal Coll., 1942; MA, U. Mich., 1946, PhD, 1949; LLD, Ea. Mich. U., 1957, U. Cin.; ScD, Northwestern U., 1973, Denison U., 1975, Nat. Acad. Edn., 1977, Alma Coll., 1995; DLitt (hon.), Hope Coll., 1985; LHD (hon.), Shawnee State U., 1994. Faculty U. Mich., 1946—, prof. psychology, 1961—, chmn. dept., 1961-71, dir. Center for Research in Learning and Teaching, 1975-83; mem. nat. adv. mental health council NIMH, 1976-80; mem. spl. med. adv. group VA, 1967-72. Author: (with J.E. Milhollaand) Undergraduate Curricula in Psychology, 1961, (with Charlotte Doyle and Mary Margaret Moffett) Psychology, 1966, 3d edit., 1977 (also Spanish edit. and instr.'s manual), Teaching Tips, 9th edit., 1994. Trustee Kalamazoo Coll., 1964-77; trustee-at-large Am. Psychol. Found., 1974-84, 92-96, pres., 1979-82. Officer USNR, 1943-45. Recipient Outstanding Tchr. award U. Mich. Alumni Assn., Am. Coll. Testing-Am. Ednl. Rsch. Assn. award for outstanding rsch. on coll. students, 1973, career contbns. award, 1990, award for disting. teaching in psychology Am. Psychol. Found., 1985. Mem. Am. Psychol. Assn. (sec., dir., pres. 1976-77, Disting. Career Contbn. to Edn. and Tng. in Psychology award 1987, E.L. Thorndike award for outstanding rsch., 1988), Internat. Assn. Applied Psychology (pres. div. ednl. instrn. and sch. psychology 1982-86), Am. Assn. Higher Edn. (dir. 1974-80, pres. 1978), AAUP (pres. U. Mich. chpt. 1970-71), AAAS (chmn. sect. on psychology 1976-77), Sigma Xi. Baptist. Home: 4660 Joy Rd Dexter MI 48130-9706 Office: U Mich Dept Psychology 525 E University Ave Ann Arbor MI 48109-1109

MCKEAGUE, DAVID WILLIAM, district judge; b. Pitts., Nov. 5, 1946; s. Herbert William and Phyllis (Forsyth) McK.; m. Nancy L. Palmer, May 20, 1989; children: Mike, Melissa, Sarah, Laura, Elizabeth, Adam. BBA, U. Mich., 1968, JD, 1971. Bar: Mich. 1971, U.S. Dist. Ct. (we. dist.) Mich. 1972, U.S. Dist. Ct. (ea. dist.) 1978, U.S. Ct. Appeals (6th cir.) 1988. Assoc. Foster, Swift, Collins & Smith, Lansing, Mich., 1971-76, ptnr., 1976-92; sec.-treas. Foster, Swift, Collins & Smith, 1990-92; judge U.S. Dist. Ct., Western Dist. Mich., Lansing, 1992—. Mem. nat. com. U. Mich. Law Sch. Fund, 1980-92; gen. counsel Mich. Rep. Com., 1989-92; mem. adv. coun. Wharton Ctr., Mich. State U., 1996—. Mem. FBA (bd. dirs. Western Mich. chpt. 1991—), Mich. Bar Assn., Ingham County Bar Assn., Country Club Lansing (bd. govs. 1988-92, 96—), The Federalist Soc. for Law and Pub. Studies (lawyers divsn. Mich. chpt. 1996—). Roman Catholic. Office: US Dist Ct 315 W Allegan St Lansing MI 48933-1514

MC KEAN, JOHN ROSSEEL OVERTON, university dean; b. Cortland, N.Y., July 31, 1928; s. Norman Dodge and Janet (Passage) McK.; m. Ruth MacDonald, July 2, 1955; children: Janet, Annalise. B.A., Coll. William and Mary, 1951; M.Ed., Cornell U., 1956, Ed.D., 1961. Tchr. Landon Sch. for Boys, Washington, 1952-53; tchr. Central Sch., Homer, N.Y., 1953-55; asst. prof. history, dean students Allegheny Coll., 1957-67; headmaster Kingswood Sch. for Girls, Cranbrook, Bloomfield Hills, Mich., 1967-68; dean Hobart Coll., 1968-73; v.p. Coll. Kenyon Coll., Gambier, Ohio, 1973-77; dean arts and scis. State U. N.Y. at Canton, 1977-92. Mem. SUNY Coun. Deans Arts and Scis., Nat. Assn. Student Personnel Adminstrs. (pres. Pa. 1958-59), SUNY Coun. Two-Yr. Bus. Adminstrs., Nat. Assn. Student Personnel Adminstrs. (dir. 1959-61), Am. Assn. Higher Edn., Community Coll. Gen. Edn. Assn., Middle States Assn. Colls. and Secondary Schs., Direct Descs. Signers Declaration Independence (pres. gen. Va.), St. Lawrence County Hist. Soc., Geneva Concerts Assn., (dir. 1969-72), Am. Hist. Assn., Round Table, English-Speaking Union, Phi Delta Kappa, Kappa Sigma. Club: Rotarian, St. Andrews Soc. Home: 1184 Jamestown Rd Apt 46 Williamsburg VA 23185-3357

MC KEAN, KEITH FERGUSON, former education educator; b. Beaver Falls, Pa., Aug. 18, 1915; s. Arthur and Eleanor (Ferguson) McK.; m. Catherine Stevenson, Oct. 31, 1942 (div. 1965); children—Kevin, Bruce; m. Joan Sanford Canter, Sept. 26, 1969. AB, Williams Coll., 1938; MA, U. Chgo., 1940; Ph.D. (Rackham fellow), U. Mich., 1950. Instr. U. Toledo, 1940-42; prof. N.C. State U., 1949-62, Elmira Coll., 1962-68; prof. U. No. Iowa, Cedar Falls, 1968-80, prof. emeritus, 1980—; lectr. Morse Mus. Am. Art, 1981—. Author: Cross Currents in the South, 1960, The Moral Measure of Literature, 1961, Critical Approaches to Fiction, 1968, Informative and Persuasive Prose, 1971. Bd. dirs. Winter Park Libr., 1982-86, Friends of Orlando Libr., 1987-90, Winter Park Hist. Assn., 1993-95; mem. evaluation com. Orlando Human Svcs. Coun., 1989-91; pres. Morse Mus. Am. Art Assocs., 1996-97. 1st lt. USAAF, 1942-46. Ford Faculty fellow for postdoctoral study, 1954-55. Mem. AAUP, Univ. Club of Winter Park, Delta Kappa Epsilon. Home: 1272 Sara Ct Winter Park FL 32789-5922 *I am deeply impressed with the part that plain chance plays in one's success or failure. Everything I have achieved that is really desirable was, in large measure, an accident of such things as time or place. Indeed, I might have accomplished far less than I actually have or far more—depending on factors over which I had no control. We are all created equal, in one sense, because all men are created equally dependent on blind chance, and a full realization of this fact can temper foolish pride and guard against excessive self-abasement.*

MCKEAN, ROBERT JACKSON, JR., retired lawyer; b. N.Y.C., Dec. 21, 1925; s. Robert Jackson and Isabel (Murphy) McK.; m. Sally H. Ament; children from previous marriage: Katherine, Douglas, Lauren, Andrew. B.A., Amherst Coll., 1950; LL.B., Harvard U., 1953. Bar: N.Y. 1954. Assoc. Simpson Thacher & Bartlett, N.Y.C., 1953-62, ptnr., 1962-85; pres. Nat. Bldg. Mus., Washington, 1986. Trustee Amherst Coll., Mass., Folger Shakespeare Library, Washington. Served with U.S. Army, 1944-46, ETO. Recipient medal for eminent service Amherst Coll., 1968. Mem. Phi Beta Kappa. Democrat.

MCKEAN, THOMAS WAYNE, dentist, retired naval officer; b. Adams County, Ind., May 18, 1928; s. Gorman F. and Elmira B. (Staley) McK.; m. Marilyn Kimberlin, Aug. 9, 1952; children: Thomas Wayne, Randall K., Dana K. D.D.S., Ind. U., 1953; grad., Naval Dental Sch., 1963. Diplomate: Am. Bd. Oral Surgery. Commd. ensign Dental Corps USN, 1949, advanced through grades to rear adm., 1980; stationed at Naval Tng. Ctr., Great Lakes, Ill., 1953; dental officer U.S.S. Randall, 1953-56; head dental svc., asst. dental officer U.S. Naval Acad./Naval Hosp., Annapolis, Md., 1956-59; dental officer FASRON III; asst. dental officer U.S. Naval Sta., Bermuda, 1959-63; postgrad. student Naval Dental Sch., Bethesda, Md., 1963-64; resident oral and maxillofacial surgery Naval Hosp., Great Lakes, Ill., 1964-66; dental officer U.S.S. America, 1966-68; chief oral surgery Naval Hosp., Orlando, Fla., 1968-70; dir. oral surgery and gen. practice residency tng. programs Naval Regional Med. Ctr., Great Lakes, 1970-74, chmn. dept. dentistry, 1970-74; cons., lectr. U.S. Army, Fort Sheridan, Ill., 1970-74; dir. oral surgery and gen. practice residency tng. programs Naval Regional Med. Ctr., Oakland, Calif., 1974-78; chmn., dept. dentistry Naval Regional Med. Ctr., 1974-78; lectr. oral surgery Letterman Army Med. Ctr., San Francisco, 1974-78; clin. lectr. dept. oral surgery U. of Pacific Sch. Dentistry, San Francisco, 1974-78; comdg. officer Naval Regional Dental Ctr., Pensacola, Fla., 1978-80; lectr. oral surgery Pensacola (Fla.) Jr. Coll., 1978-80; cons., lectr. Dwight D. Eisenhower Army Regional Med. Ctr., Augusta, Ga., 1978-80; insp. gen. dental Bur. Medicine and Surgery, Dept. of Navy, Washington, 1980-81; comdg. officer Naval Regional Dental Ctr., San Diego, 1981-82; insp. gen. Naval Med. Command, Washington, 1983-85; ret. USN, 1985. Contbr. articles to profl. jours. Chmn. bd. trustees UMC, Winter Park, 1992, mem. bd. adminstrs. 1995-96; bd. dirs. Circle of Friends Fla. Hosp. Found., 1989-91, Fla. Hosp. Found., 1991—, chmn. bd., 1995-96; chmn. Fla. Hosp. Shares, 1994—. Decorated Humanitarian Service medal, Legion of Merit with Gold Star, Meritorious Service medal, Nat. Def. Service medal with star, Vietnam Service medal, Republic of Vietnam Campaign medal with device, others; recipient Alumnus of Yr. award Ind. U. Sch.of Dentistry Alumnus Assn., 1988. Fellow Am. Dental Soc. of Anesthesiology, Internat. Coll. Dentists, Am. Coll. Dentists, Internat. Assn. Oral Surgeons; mem. Am. Assn. Oral and Maxillofacial Surgeons, ADA, Western Soc. Oral Surgeons, Assn. Mil. Surgeons U.S. (medal), Fla. Soc. Oral Surgeons, Delta Sigma Delta, Sigma Chi (Significant Sig award 1983). Home: 1309 Temple Grove Ct Winter Park FL 32789-2716

MCKEAND, PATRICK JOSEPH, newspaper publisher, educator; b. Anderson, Ind., June 10, 1941; s. William Dale and Iva Pearl (Shaw) McK. BA, Ind. U., 1963; MA, Ball State U., 1983. Staff writer The St. Petersburg (Fla.) Times, 1963; mng. editor The Anderson (Ind.) Herald, 1968-79; adminstr. analyst Ind. Medicaid Program, Indpls., 1980-81; assoc. prof. Defense Info. Sch., Ft. Ben Harrison, Ind., 1981-89; owner p.m. ink!, Indpls., 1989—; pub. bd. dirs. Student Pub. at Ind. U., Purdue U. at Indpls., 1992—; bd. dirs. Miss Indpls. Scholarship Pageant, Indpls, 1994—. Capt. U.S. Army, 1964-68. Decorated Bronze Star, Army Commendation medal with 1 Oak leaf cluster. Mem. Soc. Profl. Journalists (bd. dirs., pres.), Soc. Newspaper Design, Assn. Educators in Journalism and Mass Comm., Associated Press Mng. Editors Assn., Ind. Collegiate Press Assn. (bd. dirs., exec. dir.), Coll. Media Advisors. Home: 4450 E 56th St Indianapolis IN 46220-5710 Office: Sch of Journalism 902 W New York St Indianapolis IN 46202-5197

MCKECHNIE, MARGARET A., public relations professional; b. Niagara Falls, N.Y., Jan. 7, 1944; d. Donald and Margaret Frances (Hayes) McK. BS in Journalism cum laude, Ohio U., 1966. Pub. rels. asst. The 1st Nat. Bank Cin., 1966-69; assoc. dir. prodn. Computer Image Corp., Denver, 1969-75; comm. mgr. United Bank Denver, 1976-85; dir. corp. comm. Norwest Bank Colo. (formerly United Banks Colo., Inc.), Denver, 1986—. Mem. Pub. Rels. Soc. Am. (Accredited Pub. Rels., bd. dirs. Colo. chpt. 1980-92, pres. 1991, assembly del. 1994-96), Women Comm. (bd. dirs. 1976-80, v.p. fin.). Office: Norwest Bank Colorado 1740 Broadway Denver CO 80274-0001

MCKEE, ALAN REEL, foreign service officer; b. Des Moines, May 23, 1943; s. T. Bonar and Lois Ellen (Reel) McK.; m. Martha Berry, July 16, 1966; children: Alexander, Amanda. BA, Dartmouth Coll., 1964; MA, Tufts U., 1968, MA in Law and Diplomacy, 1969. Country officer for Nigeria Dept. of State, 1972-73, mem. secretariat staff, 1974-75; political officer Am. Consulate, Kaduna, Nigeria, 1970-71, Am. Embassy, Lagos, Nigeria, 1971-72; country officer Norway & Denmark Office No. European Affairs Dept. of State, 1983-85, dep. dir. Office So. African Affairs, 1989-91, dir. Office West African Anglophone & Lusophone Affairs, 1991-93; chief polit.-econ. sect. Am. Embassy, Dakar, Senegal, 1975-78; polit. officer Am. Embassy, Ottawa, Can., 1978-82; congl. fellow Office of Senator Edward M. Kennedy, 1982-83; polit. counselor U.S. Embassy, The Hague, The Netherlands, 1985-89; U.S. consul gen. Johannesburg, South Africa, 1993-96; U.S. Ambassador to Swaziland, 1996—; rsch. intern U.S. AID, Accra, Ghana, 1968. Participant Operation Crossroads Africa, Zimbabwe, 1962. Capt. U.S. Army, 1964-67, Vietnam. Decorated Bronze Star. Mem. Am. Fgn. Svc. Assn. Home: 6611 River Rd, Bethesda. South Africa Office: Ambassador to Swaziland Dept State Mbabane Washington DC 20521-2350

MCKEE, CHRISTOPHER FULTON, astrophysics and astronomy educator; b. Washington, Sept. 6, 1942; m. Suzanne P. McKee; 3 children. AB in Physics summa cum laude, Harvard U., 1963; PhD in Physics, U. Calif., Berkeley, 1970. Physicist Lawrence Livermore (Calif.) Labs., 1969-70, cons., 1970—; rsch. fellow in astrophysics Calif. Inst. Tech., Pasadena, 1970-71; asst. prof. astronomy Harvard U., Cambridge, 1971-74; asst. prof. physics and astronomy U. Calif., Berkeley, 1974-77, assoc. prof., 1977-78, prof., 1978—, Miller Rsch. prof., 1984-85; assoc. dir. Space Scis. Lab., Berkeley, 1978-83, acting dir., 1983-84, dir., 1985—; dir. Theoretical Astrophysics Ctr., Berkeley, 1985. Fannie and John Hertz Found. fellow, 1963-69; Sherman Fairchild Disting. scholar, 1981, Nat. Acad. Scis., 1992. Fellow AAAS, Am. Phys. Soc. (exec. com. astrophysics div. 1986-88); mem. Am. Astron. Soc. (councillor 1981-84), Internat. Astron. Union, Phi Beta Kappa. Office: U Calif Dept Physics Berkeley CA 94720

MCKEE, CHRISTOPHER FULTON, librarian, naval historian, educator; b. Bklyn., June 14, 1935; s. William Ralph and Frances (Manning) M.; m. Ann Adamczyk, 1993; children: Sharon, David B. AB, U. St. Thomas, Houston, 1957; AMLS, U. Mich., 1960. Catalogue libr. Washington and Lee U., Lexington, Va., 1958-62; social sci. libr. So. Ill. U., Edwardsville, 1962-66; book selection officer So. Ill. U., 1967-69, asst. dir., 1969-72; libr. of coll. Grinnell Coll., Iowa, 1972—, Samuel R. and Marie-Louise Rosenthal prof.; Sec. of Navy rsch. chair in naval history Naval Hist. Ctr., Washington, 1990-91; trustee Bibliog. Ctr. Rsch., Denver, 1984-88. Author: Edward Preble, 1972, A Gentlemanly and Honorable Profession: The Creation of the U.S. Naval Officer Corps, 1794-1815, 1991. NEH-Newberry Libr. fellow, 1978-79, Newberry Libr.-Brit. Acad. fellow, 1995-96; recipient U.S. Naval History prize for best pub. article, 1985, John Lyman book award N.Am. Soc. Oceanic History, 1994, Samuel Eliot Morison Disting. Svc. award USS Constitution Mus., Boston, 1992. Mem. Am. Hist. Assn., Navy Records Soc., Soc. for Mil. History, Orgn. Am. Historians, Soc. Historians of Early Republic, U.S. Naval Inst. Home: PO Box 272 Grinnell IA 50112-0272 Office: Grinnell Coll Burling Libr PO Box 805 Grinnell IA 50112-0811

MCKEE, ELLSWORTH, food products executive. CEO McKee Foods, 1996—, chmn. bd. dirs. Office: McKee Foods PO Box 750 10260 Mc Kee Rd Collegedale TN 37315 Office: PO Box 750 Collegedale TN 37315-0750*

MCKEE, FRAN, retired naval officer; b. Florence, Ala., Sept. 13, 1926; d. Thomas W. and Geneva (Lumpkins) McK. BS, U. Ala., 1950; postgrad., Gen. Line Sch., Postgrad. Sch. USN, Monterey, Calif., 1957; MS in Internat. Affairs, George Washington U., 1970, Naval War Coll., 1970; D. in Pub.Adminstrn. (hon.), Mass. Maritime Acad., 1978. Commd. ensign USN, 1950, advanced through grades to rear adm., 1976; (1st woman line officer promoted to rear adm.); svc. in various U.S. locations and in Morocco and Spain; dep. asst. chief for human goals (Bur. Naval Personnel), 1972-73; comdg. officer Naval Security Group Activity Ft. Meade, Md., 1973-76; dir. naval ednl. devel. Staff of Chief Naval Edn. and Tng. Naval Air Sta., Pensacola, Fla., 1976-78; dir. human resource mgmt. div. Office Chief of Naval Ops., Navy Dept. Washington, 1978-81; ret., 1981. Mem. nat. com. Armed Svcs. YMCA of U.S.A., 1981-83; mem. nat. adv. com. Women in Mil. Svc. Meml. Found., 1988—. Decorated Legion of Merit with gold star, Meritorious Svc. medal; recipient DAR Medal of Honor, 1982, Nat. Vets. award, 1993; elected to Ala. Acad. Honor, 1979. Episcopalian. Home: 7420 Adams Park Ct Annandale VA 22003-5722

MC KEE, GEORGE MOFFITT, JR., civil engineer, consultant; b. Valparaiso, Nebr., Mar. 27, 1924; s. George Moffitt and Iva (Santrock) McK.; student Kans. State Coll. Agr. and Applied Sci., 1942-43, Bowling Green State U., 1943; B.S. in Civil Engring., U. Mich., 1947; m. Mary Lee Taylor, Aug. 11, 1945; children—Michael Craig, Thomas Lee, Mary Kathleen, Marsha Coleen, Charlotte Anne. Draftsman, Jackson Constrn. Co., Colby, Kans., 1945-46; asst. engr. Thomas County, Colby, 1946; engr. Sherman County, Goodland, Kans., 1947-51; salesman Oehlert Tractor & Equipment Co., Colby, 1951-52; owner, operator George M. McKee, Jr., cons. engrs., Colby, 1952-72; sr. v.p. engring. Contract Surety Consultants, Wichita, Kans., 1974—. Adv. rep. Kans. State U., Manhattan, 1957-62; mem. adv. com. N.W. Kans. Area Vocat. Tech. Sch., Goodland, 1967-71. Served with USMCR, 1942-45. Registered profl. civil engr., Kans., Okla., registered land Surveyor, Kans. Mem. Kans. Engring. Soc. (pres. N.W. profl. engrs. chpt. 1962-63, treas. cons. engrs. sect. 1961-63), Kansas County Engr's. Assn. (dist. v.p. 1950-51), N.W. Kans. Hwy. Ofcls. Assn. (sec. 1948-49), Nat. Soc. Profl. Engrs., Kans. State U. Alumni Assn. (pres. Thomas County 1956-57), Am. Legion (Goodland 1st vice comdr. 1948-49), The Alumni Assn. U. Mich. (life), Colby C. of C. (v.p. 1963-64), Goodland Jr. C. of C. (pres. 1951-52). Methodist (chmn. ofcl. bd. 1966-67). Mason (32 deg., Shriner); Order Eastern Star. Home: 8930 Suncrest St # 502 Wichita KS 67212-4069 Office: 6500 W Kellogg Dr Wichita KS 67209-2212

MC KEE, JAMES, JR., retired bank executive; b. Utica, N.Y., Aug. 29, 1918; s. James and Marie Roze (Tuller) McK.; m. Doris Elsie Nafis, June 28, 1947; children: James III, Nancy C. (dec.), Peter C., David R., John S. BS, Syracuse U., 1940. Exec. v.p., cashier First Nat. Bank, Richfield Springs, N.Y., 1940-56; with State Bank of Albany, 1956-83, v.p., cashier, 1969-83, sr. v.p., cashier, 1982-83. Co-chmn. United Fund, Clinton County, 1969; treas. Ea. Adirondack Econ. Devel. Commn., 1967-69; treas., mem. bd. mgrs. Parsons Child and Family Ctr., 1971-78, assoc. mem. bd., 1978; mem. Plattsburgh Coll. Found., bd. dirs., 1995—, mem. planned giving commn.; bd. dirs. Champlain Devel. Corp., 1969, New Industries for Clinton County, 1969; trustee Albany Rotary Found., Inc., 1980-85, v.p., 1986-88; trustee Champlain Valley Physicians Hosp., 1969. Maj. C.E., AUS, 1942-46, ETO. Decorated Bronze star. Mem. Norstar Bank Quarter Century Club (pres. 1974-75), Elks, Rotary (treas. dist. 7190 1983-89, mem. Plattsburgh N.Y. 1989—, treas. dist. 7040 1990-91, Paul Harris fellow 1980, Rotarian of Yr. 1988), Albany Rotary (pres. 1974-75), Ft. Orange Club, Alpha Kappa Psi, Delta Kappa Epsilon, Phi Kappa Phi, Beta Gamma Sigma, Beta Alpha Psi. Home: 30 Tanglewood Dr Port Kent NY 12975

MCKEE, JOSEPH FULTON, engineering and construction executive; b. Placerville, Calif., Apr. 28, 1921; s. Joseph Fulton and Pearl Margarite (Varroza) McK.; m. Eva Deane Adcock, Mar. 15, 1949 (dec.); m. Sharon Lucille Ricketts Adamson, Jan. 23, 1982; children—Robert Deane, Reneé E. Hackbarth. B.C.E., U. Santa Clara, 1947. Constrn. engr. Western Contracting Corp., 1947-50; supt., project engr., gen. supt. constrn. Morrison-Knudsen Co., Western U.S., 1950-54; project engr., constrn. mgr. Morrison-Knudsen Co., Western U.S., Morocco, 1954-57; constrn. mgr. Morrison-Knudsen Co., Western U.S., Iran, 1957-60, worldwide, 1960-65; area mgr. Morrison-Knudsen Co., Western U.S., Australia, 1965-73; v.p. Morrison-Knudsen Co., Western U.S., Europe, Africa, Mid-East, 1973-77; sr. v.p. Morrison-Knudsen Co., Western U.S., Tehran, 1977-80, Boise, Idaho, 1981-81; project dir. Cerrejon Coal Project, Colombia, 1981-85; exec. v.p. internat. Morrison-Knudsen Engrs., San Francisco, 1985-86, ret., 1986. Served to lt. C.E., USN, 1943-46. Mem. ASCE, Chi Epsilon, Tau Beta Pi. Republican. Roman Catholic. Office: 4781 River Vista Pl Boise ID 83703-1954

MCKEE, KATHRYN DIAN GRANT, human resources consultant; b. L.A., Sept. 12, 1937; d. Clifford William and Amelia Rosalia (Shacher) G.; m. Paul Eugene McKee, June 17, 1961; children: Scott Alexander, Grant Christopher. BA, U. Calif., Santa Barbara, 1959; grad. Sch. Mgmt. Exec. Program, UCLA, 1979. Cert. compensation and benefits. Mgr. Mattel, Inc., Hawthorne, Calif., 1963-74; dir. Twentieth Century Fox Film Corp., L.A., 1975-80; sr. v.p. 1st Interstate Bank, Ltd., L.A., 1980-93; sr. v.p. and human resources dir. Am.'s Standard Chartered Bank, 1993-95; pres. Human Resources Consortia, Santa Ana, Calif., 1995—; dir. Accordia benefits of Southern Calif., 1991-96, mem. exec. com. H.R. div. of Am. Bankers Assn., 1991-93; bd. dirs. Bank Certification Inst. Am. Bankers Assn., 1992-94; treas. Pers. Accreditation Inst., 1983-86, pres., 1986. Contbr. articles to profl. jours. Pres. GEM Theatre Guild, Garden Grove, Calif., 1984-86; bd. dirs. Vis. Nurses Assn., L.A., 1984-88; bd. dirs. SHRM, 1986-92, treas., 1989, vice-chmn., 1990, chmn., 1991, pres. SHRM Found., 1994, 95; bd. dirs. Laguna Playhouse, 1996—. Recipient Sr. Honor Key award U. Calif., Santa Barbara, 1959, named Outstanding Sr. Woman, 1959; recipient William Winter award Am. Compensation Assn., 1986, Excellence award L.A. Pers. Indsl. Rels. Assn., 1990, Profl. Excellence award SHRM, 1994. Mem. Internat. Assn. Pers. Women (various offices, past nat. pres., Mem. of Yr. 1986), Orgn. Women Execs., U. Calif. Santa Barbara Alumni Assn. (bd. dirs. 1995—). Office: Human Resources Consortia 2700 N Main St Ste 800 Santa Ana CA 92705-6636

MCKEE, KEITH EARL, manufacturing technology executive; b. Chgo., Sept. 9, 1928; s. Charles Richard and Maude Alice (Hamlin) McK.; m. Lorraine Marie Celichowski, Oct. 26, 1951; children: Pamela Ann Houser, Paul Earl. BS, Ill. Inst. Tech., 1950, MS, 1956, PhD, 1962. Engr. Swift & Co., Chgo., 1953-54; rsch. engr. Armour Rsch. Found., Chgo., 1954-62; dir. design and product assurance Andrew Corp., Orland Park, Ill., 1962-67; dir. engring. Rsch. Ctr. Ill. Inst. Tech., Chgo., 1967-80, dir. mfg. prodn. ctr., 1977—; prof. Ill. Inst. Tech., Chgo., 1979—; coord. Nat. Conf. on Fluid Power, Chgo., 1983-88; mem. com. on materials and processing Dept. Def., Washington, 1986—. Author: Productivity and Technology, 1988; editor: Automated Inspection and Process Control, 1987; co-editor: Manufacturing High Technology Handbook, 1987; mng. editor: Manufacturing Competitiveness Frontier, 1977—. Capt. USMC, 1950-54. Recipient outstanding presentation award Am. Soc. of Quality Control, Milw., 1983. Fellow World Acad. Productivity Scis.; mem. ASCE, Am. Def. Preparedness Assn. (pres. Chgo. chpt. 1972—), Am. Assn. Engring. Soc. (Washington) (coor. com. on productivity 1978-88), Inst. of Indsl. Engrs., Soc. Mfg. Engrs. (Gold medal 1991), Am. Assn. for Artificial Intelligence, Robotic Industry Assn. (bd. dir. 1978-81), Assn. for Mfg. Excellence, Soc. for Computer Simulation. Democrat. Roman Catholic. Home: 18519 Clyde Rd Homewood IL 60430-3015 Office: Illinois Inst Tech Mfg Productivity Ctr 3255 S Dearborn St Chicago IL 60616-3793

MCKEE, MARGARET JEAN, federal agency executive; b. New Haven, June 20, 1929; d. Waldo McCutcheon and Elizabeth (Thayer) McKee; A.B., Vassar Coll., 1951. Staff asst. United Rep. Fin. Com., N.Y.C., 1952; staff asst. N.Y. Rep. State Com., N.Y.C., 1953-55; staff asst. Crusade for Freedom (name later changed to Radio Free Europe Fund), N.Y.C., 1955-57; researcher Stricker & Henning Research Assocs., Inc., N.Y.C., 1957-59; exec. sec. New Yorkers for Nixon (name later changed to N.Y. State Ind. Citizens for Nixon Lodge), N.Y.C., 1959-60; asst. to Raymond Moley, polit. columnist, N.Y.C., 1961; asst. campaign com. Louis J. Lefkowitz for Mayor, N.Y.C., 1961; research programmer, treas. Consensus, Inc., N.Y.C., 1962-67; spl. asst. to U.S. Senator Jacob K. Javits, N.Y., 1967-73, adminstrv. asst., 1973-75; dep. adminstr. Am. Revolution Bicentennial Adminstrn., 1976, acting adminstr., 1976-77; chief of staff Perry B. Duryea (minority leader) N.Y. State Assembly, 1978; public affairs cons., 1979-80; dir. govt. relations Gen. Mills Restaurant Group, Inc., 1980-83; exec. dir. Fed. Mediation and Conciliation Service, 1983-86; mem. Fed. Labor Rels. Authority, 1986-89, chmn., 1989-94; mem. Nat. Partnership Coun., 1993-94; bd. dirs. Interam. Life Ins. Co., 1979-86, VNNC, Inc., 1992— (treas.). Mem. N.Y. State Bingo Control Commn., 1965-72, U.S. Adv. Commn. on Public Diplomacy, 1979-82; pres. Bklyn. Heights Slope Young Rep. Club, 1955-56; co-chmn. Bklyn. Citizens for Eisenhower-Nixon, 1956; chmn. 2d Jud. Dist. Assn. N.Y. State Young Rep. Clubs, Inc., 1957-58, vice-chmn., mem. bd. govs., 1958-60, v.p., 1960-62; pres., 1962-64; mem. exec. com. Fedn. Women's Rep. Clubs N.Y. State, Inc., 1960-64, mem. council, 1964-70; mem. exec. com. N.Y. Rep. State Com. 1962-64; co-chmn. spl. assts. Rockefeller for Pres. Nat. Campaign com., N.Y.C., 1964; co-dir. N.Y. Rep. State Campaign Com., 1964; asst. campaign mgr. Kenneth B. Keating for Judge Ct. Appeals, N.Y., 1965; dir. scheduling Gov. Rockefeller campaign, 1966, Sen. Charles E. Goodell campaign, 1970; dir. scheduling and speakers' bur. N.Y. Com. to Re-elect the Pres., 1972; dir. planning and strategy, Conn. Reagan-Bush campaign, Hartford, 1980; mem. annual fund adv. com. Vassar Coll., 1992-96. Mem. bd. govs. Women's Nat. Rep. Club, N.Y.C., 1963-66. Mem. Jr. League of Bklyn. (past (dir.), Exec. Women in Govt. (chmn. 1986), Nat. Women's Edn. Fund (mem. bd.), Am. Newspaper Women's Club, Nat. Soc. Colonial Dames Am. Episcopalian. Club: Vassar (past dir., Bklyn.). Home: 532 S Brooksvale Rd Cheshire CT 06410-3515

MCKEE, MARY ELIZABETH, producer; b. Syracuse, N.Y., Feb. 14, 1949; d. Anthony Henry and Mary (Robards) Krystosik; m. Peter S. Fama, June 27, 1970 (div. Mar. 1973); 1 child, Kiralie Fama; m. Michael R. McKee, Feb. 15, 1975 (Oct. 1978); 1 child, Quinn. BFA, Fla. Internat. U., Miami, 1974; MFA, Memphis State U., 1977. Copywriter announcer Sta. WREC/WZXR Radio, Memphis, 1978-79; creative dir. Cit Neifert & Assoc. Advt., Memphis, 1979-82; promotion dir. Sta. WGNX-TV, Atlanta, 1982-86; program mgr. Sta. WVEU-TV, Atlanta, 1986-90; v.p., sta. mgr. Sta. WHSP-TV, Vineland, N.J., 1990-95; v.p. V Boxes Worldwide, Phila., 1995—, V Box Prodns., Atlantic City, 1995—; adj. prof. Glassboro State U., 1990—; exec. dir. South Jersey Cultural Alliance, Atlantic City, 1997—. Actor in field (Top 10 Memphis Mag. 1979). Vol. Com. to Feed the Hungry, Atlanta, 1988, Tenn. Talking Libr., Memphis, 1982; mem. Greenpeace, 1987—; mem. adv. coun. SES, Easter Seal Soc. N.J. Recipient Merit award Tenn. Talking Libr., 1982; named Best TV Comml. Memphis Advt. Club, 1982; Hair scholar Fla. Internat. U., 1973. Mem. AFTRA, Nat. Assn. Broadcasters, Am. Women in Radio and TV (publicity chmn. 1985-86), Nat. Assn. TV Program Execs., N.J. Broadcasters Assn. (TV chair 1995-96), Broadcast Cable Fin. Mgmt. Assn. South Jersey Stage Co. (exec. bd. 1997—), Chelsea Neighborhood Assn. (exec. bd.), Rotary. Democrat. Roman Catholic. Avocations: writing journals, published poet, running and video production bus., bicycling. Home and Office: 55 S Dover Ave Atlantic City NJ 08401-5912

MCKEE, RICHARD MILES, animal studies educator; b. Cottonwood Falls, Kans., Oct. 8, 1929; m. Marjorie Fisk, June 22, 1952; children: Dave, Richard, Annell, John. BS in Agriculture, Kans. State Coll. Agriculture and Applied Sci., 1951; MS in Animal Husbandry, Kans. State U., 1963; PhD in Animal Science, U. Ky., 1968. Herdsman Moxley Hall Hereford Ranch, Coun. Grove, Kans., 1951-52, 54-55, Luckhardt Farms, Tarkio, Mo., 1955-58; asst. mgr. L&J Cruse Ranch, Cheboygan, Mich., 1958-59; asst. instr., cattle herdsman Kans. State U., Manhattan, 1959-65, from asst. prof. to assoc. prof., 1959-65, prof., departmental teaching coord., 1976—; program participant and/or official judge numerous shows, field days including Kans. Jr. Hereford Field Day, Kans. Jr. Shorthorn Field Day, Better Livestock Day, Kans. Jr. Livestock Assn., Am. Jr. Hereford Assn. Field Day, Cheyenne, Wyo., 1973, Kans. Jr. Polled Hereford Field Day, Am. Jr. Shorthorn Assn., Kans. City, Mo., 1965, Am. Internat. Jr. Charolais Assn. Show, Lincoln, Nebr., 1976, Am. Royal 4-H Livestock Judging Contest, Kans. City, 1975, Jr. Livestock Activities various cattle breed assns. nationwide, 1977-81; served on many breed assn. coms.; judge County Fairs; official judge 14 different Nat. Beef Breed Shows U.S. and Can.; conducted 60 livestock judging and showmanship schs. at county level. Contbr. articles to profl. jours. Deacon 1st Presbyn. Ch., Manhattan, 1969-75, Sunday Sch. tchr., Chancel choir, elder; project leader com. mem. 4-H; foster parent Kans. State U. Football Program. Lt. USMC, 1952-54, Korea. Named Hon. State Farmer of Kans.; Hall of Merit Honoree for Edn. by Am. Polled Hereford Assn., 1985; NDEA scholar U. Ky., 1966-67; Miles McKee Student Enrichment Fund established at Kans. State U. Mem. Am. Soc. Animal Sci., Kans. Livestock Assn. (beef cattle improvement com. 1970-78, cow-calf clinic com. 1973, 74, 75, 76, 77, 78), Nat. Assn. Colls. and Tchrs. Agriculture, Block and Bridle Club, Am. Jr. Hereford Assn. (hon.), FarmHouse, Sigma Xi, Phi Kappa Phi, Alpha Zeta, Gamma Sigma Delta, Alpha Tau Alpha (hon.). Home: 901 Juniper Dr Manhattan KS 66502-3148 Office: Dept of Animal Scis & Industry Kansas State U Manhattan KS 66506

MCKEE, ROGER CURTIS, federal magistrate judge; b. Waterloo, Iowa, Feb. 11, 1931; s. James A. and Leonace (Burrell) McK.; m. Roberta Jeanne Orvis, Sept. 3, 1954; children: Andrea Jane, Brian Curtis, Paul Robert. BA, State Coll. of Iowa, 1955; MA, U. Ill., 1960; JD, U. San Diego, 1968. Bar: Calif. 1970, U.S. Dist. Ct. (so. dist.) Calif. 1969, U.S. Ct. Appeals (9th cir.) 1971. Telegrapher, agt. Ill. Cen. R.R., 1950-55; tng. asst. No. Ill. Gas Co., Aurora, 1959-60; with indsl. rels. dept. Convair div. Gen. Dynamics Corp., San Diego, 1960-68; contract adminstr. and supr. Datagraphix div. Gen. Dynamics Corp., San Diego, 1968-69, asst. counsel, 1969-70; ptnr. Powell & McKee, San Diego, 1970-75, Millsberg, Dickstein & McKee, San Diego, 1975-83; magistrate judge U.S. Dist. Ct. for So. Dist. Calif., San Diego, 1983—; presiding magistrate judge, 1993—. Bd. trustees So. Calif. Presbyn. Homes, L.A., 1979-81; moderator Presbytery of San Diego, 1980. Capt. USNR, 1949-85. Mem. Calif. Bar Assn., Fed. Magistrate Judges Assn., Navy League U.S., Naval Res. Officers Assn., Res. Officers Assn., Dixieland Jazz Soc. (bd. dirs. San Diego chpt. 1984—). Republican. Office: US Cts Bldg 940 Front St San Diego CA 92101-8994

MCKEE, RONALD GENE, vocational education educator; b. Williamsville, Mo., May 5, 1947; s. Enos Elmer and Elsie Mae (Chiles) McK.; m. Sondra Mae Malone, Dec. 1, 1968; 1 child, David. Student, Pearl River C.C., 1992-94, U. Miss., 1994—. Cert. tchr., Miss. Enlisted man, electronics warfare repairman USAF, 1966-73; enlisted man USCG, 1973, advanced through grades to electronics technician 1st class, 1973-87; ret., 1987; tchr. electronics Picayune (Miss.) Vocat.-Tech. Ctr., 1988-95, Pascagoula (Miss.) Vocat.-Tech. Ctr., 1995—. Mem. Vocat. Indsl. Clubs. Am. Avocations: radio-controlled airplanes, oil painting, informal target shooting, amateur radio. Home: 8508 Sundance Dr Gautier MS 39553 Office: Pascagoula HS Vocat-Tech Ctr 2602 Market St Pascagoula MS 39567-5158

MCKEE, THEODORE A., federal judge; b. 1947. B.A., SUNY, Cortland, 1969; J.D. magna cum laude, Syracuse U. Coll. of Law, 1975. Dir. of minority recruitment & admissions SUNY, Binghamton, 1969-72; atty. Wolf, Block, Schorr & Solis-Cohen, Phila., 1975-77; asst. U.S. atty., Eastern Dist. PA, 1977-80, asst. U.S. atty., Eastern Dist. Gen. Crimes Unit, Narcotics and Firearms Unit, then Polit. Corruption Unit; lecturer Rutgers U. Coll. of Law, 1980-91; dep. city solicitor Law Dept., Phila., 1980-83; gen. counsel Phila. Parking Auth., 1983; judge Ct. of Common Pleas, 1st Jud. Dist, PA, 1984-94, judge major felony program, 1986, judge orphans' ct. divsn., 1992; circuit judge Third Circuit, Phila., 1994—; bd. dirs. Diagnostic and Rehab. Ctr. of Phila. Mem. World Affairs Coun., New Directions for Women, Inc.; trustee Edna McConnell Clark Found. Mem. ABA, Nat. Bar Assn., Am. Law Inst., Barristers' Assn. Phila., Temple Inn of Ct., Crime Prevention Assn. (bd. dirs.). Office: 601 Market St Rm 20614 Philadelphia PA 19106-1713*

MCKEE, TIMOTHY CARLTON, taxation educator; b. South Bend, Ind., Mar. 9, 1944; s. Glenn Richard and Laura Louise (Niven) McK.; m. Linda Sykes Mizelle, Oct. 13, 1984; children: Brandon Richard. BS in Bus. Econs., Ind. U., 1970, MBA in Fin., 1973, JD, 1979; LLM in Taxation, DePaul U., 1980. Bar: Ill. 1980, U.S. Dist. Ct. (no. dist.) Ill. 1980; CPA, Ill., Va.; cert. govt. fin. mgr. Procedures analyst Assocs. Corp., South Bend, Ind., 1969-71; asst. dir. fin. Ind. U., Bloomington, Ind., 1971-79; sr. tax mgr. Peat Marwick Mitchell & Co., Chgo., Norfolk, Va., 1979-84; corp. counsel K & K Toys, Norfolk, 1984; assoc. prof. acctg. Old Dominion U., Norfolk, 1985—, chmn. dept., 1994-95, chmn. acctg., fin. and law dept., 1995; computer coord. Peat, Marwick, Mitchell & Co., 1982-84; micro computer cons. Old Dominion U., 1985-91. Contbr. articles to profl. jours. Mem. Friends of Music, Bloomington, 1978, Art Inst., Chgo., 1981; loaned exec. United Way, Chgo., 1981; telethon chmn. Va. Orch. Group, Norfolk, 1983. Mem. Assn. Govt. Accts., Am. Acctg. Assn., Am. Assn. Atty. CPAs, Inc., Am. Tax Assn., Fin. Execs. Inst. (pres. 1995-96), Hampton Rds. Tax Forum, Inst. Internal Auditors, Beta Alpha Psi. Home: 412 Rio Dr Chesapeake VA 23320-7144 Office: Old Dominion U Hughes Hall # 2065 Norfolk VA 23529-0229

MCKEEN, ALEXANDER C., engineering consulting company owner; b. Albion, Mich., Oct. 10, 1927; s. John Nisbet and Janet (Callander) McK.; m. Evelyn Mae Feldkamp, Aug. 18, 1951; Jeffrey, Brian, Andrew. BSME, U. Mich., 1950; MBA, Mich. State U., 1968. Registered profl. engr., Mich. From asst. supt. maintenance to supt. final assembly Cadillac Motor Car divsn. GM, Detroit, 1961-69, asst. dir. reliability, 1969-72; exec. engr. Product Assurance GM, Warren, Mich., 1972-75, asst. dir. engring. analysis, 1975-77, dir. engring analysis, 1977-87; pres., owner Engring. Analysis Assocs., Inc., Bingham Farms, Mich., 1987—. Pres. Dells of Bloomfield Home Owners Assn., Bloomfield Hills, Mich., 1987-88; trustee Kirk in Hills, Bloomfield Hills, 1990-93, elder, 1995—. Mem. Soc. Auto. Engrs., Am. Soc. Quality Control, Engring. Soc. Detroit, Detroit Athletic Club, Stonycroft Hills Golf Club, Pelican Nest Golf Club, Beta Gamma Sigma. Avocations: tennis, golf, photography, travel, gardening. Home: 5286 Kellen Ln Bloomfield Hills MI 48302-2738 Office: Engring Analysis Assocs Inc 30700 Telegraph Rd Ste 4566 Bingham Farms MI 48025-4528

MC KEEN, CHESTER M., JR., business executive; b. Shelby, Ohio, Mar. 18, 1923; s. Chester Mancil and Nettie Augusta (Fox) McK.; m. Alma Virginia Pierce, Mar. 1946; children: David Richard, Karin, Thomas Kevin. BS in Mil. Sci., U. Md., 1962; MBA, Babson Coll., Wellesley, Mass., 1962. Advanced through grades to maj. gen. U.S. Army, 1942-77; dir. logistics Bell Helicopter Internat., Tehran, Iran, 1977-79; v.p. procurement Bell Helicopter Textron, Ft. Worth, 1979-82; v.p. materiel Bell Helicopter Textron, 1982-89; pres. Logistics Svcs. Internat., Arlington, Tex.; chmn. bd. dirs. ISES Inc.; bd. dirs. Exec. Svc. Corps Tarrant County, chmn. Adv. bd. Salvation Army, Cancer Care Svcs. Decorated D.S.M., Legion of Merit (3), Commendation medal (3). Mem. Am. Mgmt. Assn., Am. Def. Preparedness Assn. (v.p. S.W. region), Assn. U.S. Army, Ridglea Country Club, Rotary, Masons (33 degree), Shriners, Sigma Pi. Home: 2310 Woodsong Trl Arlington TX 76016-1037 Office: ISES Inc 328 Pipeline Rd Hurst TX 76053 *To live for oneself is to pursue emptiness. To live for others is to insure fulfillment.*

MCKEEVER, BRIAN EDWARD, general contractor; b. Hartford, Conn., Feb. 24, 1957; s. John Edward and Mary Elizabeth (Quish) McK.; m. Lise Evan Engelbrecht, Apr. 4, 1992; 1 child, Madison Coreigh. Student, Manchester C.C., 1975-77, U. Hartford, 1990—. Cert. emergency med. technician. Pres. BMK Corp./The MAK Co., Manchester, Conn.; mem.-at-large Steel Structures Painting Coun. Northern New Eng. chpt. Mem. Manchester 8th Dist. Vol. Fire Dept., 1973; mem. Emergency Accident-Illness Simulation Team, Conn. Dept. Health, 1975; active Big Bros. Am. Mem. Constrn. Inst. U. Hartford (chairship of mem. com.), Painting and Decorating Contractors Am., Remodeling Contractors Assn., Water Jet Tech. Assn., Internat. Assn. Concrete Repair Specialists, Hartford Indsl. Mgmt. Clu, Better Bus. Bur., Manchester C. of C., Conn. Assn. Real Estate Investors, Civitan, Lions, Elks, Irish Am. Home, NRA, Rockville Fish and Game Club, K.C. Roman Catholic. Office: The MAK Co PO Box 882 Vernon Rockville CT 06066

MCKEEVER, JEFFREY D., computer company executive; b. Marion, Ind., 1942. Grad., U. Ariz., Tucson, 1965; MBA, U. Ariz., 1973. Chmn., CEO, dir. MicroAge Inc., Tempe. Office: MicroAge Inc 2400 S Microage Way Tempe AZ 85282-1824*

MCKEEVER, JOHN EUGENE, lawyer; b. Phila., Oct. 24, 1947; s. John James and Marie Julia (Supper) McK.; m. Kathleen Marie Wynne, Dec. 9, 1995; children: John Joseph, Jeannine Marie. BA magna cum laude with distinction, U. Pa., 1969, JD magna cum laude, 1972. Bar: Pa. 1972, U.S. Dist. Ct. (ea. dist.) Pa. 1972, U.S. Dist. Ct. (mid. dist.) Pa. 1977, U.S. Ct. Appeals (3rd cir.) 1979, U.S. Ct. Appeals (D.C. cir.) 1981, U.S. Supreme Ct. 1981. Assoc. Schnader, Harrison, Segal & Lewis, Phila., 1972-80, ptnr., 1980—. Mem. Pres. Coun. Allentown Coll. St. Francis De Sales, Center Valley, Pa., 1980—, Bus. Leadership Organized for Cath. Schs., Phila., 1984—, adv. com. De Sales Sch. Theology, Washington, trustee, 1988-91; capt. spl. gifts com. Cath. Charities Appeal, Phila., 1986-91; bd. dirs. Jr. Achievement, Phila., 1986—. Mem. Pa. Bar Assn., Phila. Bar Assn., Pro-Life Lawyers' Guild (bd. dirs. 1983-84, chancellor 1984-86), St. Thomas More Soc. (gov. 1979-91, pres. 1981-82), Order of Coif, Phi Beta Kappa, Pi Gamma Mu. Republican. Roman Catholic. Office: Schnader Harrison Segal & Lewis 1600 Market St Ste 3600 Philadelphia PA 19103-7286

MCKEITHEN, WALTER FOX, secretary of state; b. Columbia, La., Sept. 8, 1946; s. John Jesse and Marjorie (Funderburk) McK.; m. Yvonne May; children: Marjorie, Marianne, Rebecca, John Jesse. B in History and Social Studies, La. Tech. U., 1972. Owner, operator Apparel Mart Dept. Store, Columbia, 1974-83, McKeithen Chem. & Cementing, Columbia, 1979-88; mem. appropriation, natural resources and joint budged coms. La. Ho. of Reps., Baton Rouge, 1983-87; sec. of state State of La., Baton Rouge, 1987—; tchr., coach Caldwell Parish High Sch., Grayson, La., 1975-78; past mem. La. Assn. Educators. Past v.p. Caldwell Parish Jaycees; trustee La. Sch. Employees' Retirement System; mem. La. Tourist Devel. Commn.; second injury bd. La. Workmen's Compensation; mem. State Bd. Election Supervisors and State Bond Commn., La. Farm Bur., Am. Petroleum Inst.; administrv. bd. Broadmoor Meth. Ch. Recipient Outstanding Legislator award La. Assn. Educators, 1985, Golden Apple award La. Fedn. Tchrs., 1986. Republican. Methodist. Office: Dept of State State Capitol 20th Fl PO Box 94125 Baton Rouge LA 70804-9125*

MCKELDIN, WILLIAM EVANS, management consultant; b. Richmond, Va., Aug. 14, 1927; s. Robert A.W. and Mary E. (Burke) McK.; BS in Bus. Adminstrn., Temple U., 1951, postgrad., 1951-53; postgrad. U. Pitts., 1953-54; m. Phyllis Shellhase, Jan. 23, 1982; children by previous marriage: William Evans, Roberts Evans. Various employee relations and mgmt. positions with Westinghouse Corp., Pitts., 1950-62, Farrel Corp., Rochester, N.Y., 1963-66, Gen. Signal Corp., Norwalk, Conn. and Watertown, N.Y., 1966-71, Copperweld Steel Co., Warren, Ohio, 1971-75, Tenn. Forging Steel, Knoxville, 1975-77, Val Bradley Assocs., West Chester, Pa., 1977-79; pres. and owner McKeldin Assocs., West Chester, 1979-95; founder and partial owner McKeldin Group, Bala Cynwyd, Pa., 1995—. Bd. dirs. United Fund, YMCA, ARC, Rochester Inst. Tech., Jefferson Community Coll., Kent State U. Served with USAAF, 1945-47. Mem. Inst. Mgmt. Cons., Am. Soc. Safety Engrs., Am. Soc. Personnel Adminstrn., C. of C. (dir.). Republican. Presbyterian. Clubs: Masons, Rotary. Contbr. articles to trade jours. Office: The McKeldin Group 24 Timber Ln Hilton Head Island SC 29926-1002

MCKELL, CYRUS M., college dean, plant physiologist, consultant; b. Payson, Utah, Mar. 19, 1926; s. Robert D. and Mary C. (Ellsworth) McK.; m. Betty Johnson; children: Meredith Sue, Brian Marcus, John Cyrus. BS, U. Utah, 1949, MS, 1950; PhD, Oreg. State U., 1956; postgrad., U. Calif., Davis, 1957. Instr. botany Oreg. State U., Corvallis, 1955-56; range rsch. plant physiologist U. Calif. USDA-Agrl. Research Service, Davis, 1956-60; prof., dept. chmn. U. Calif., Riverside, 1960-69; prof. dept. head., dir. Utah State U., Logan, 1969-80; v.p. research NPI, Salt Lake City, 1980-88; dean Coll. of Sci. Weber State U., Ogden, Utah, 1988-94; pres., prin. Applied Ecol. Svcs. Inc., Salt Lake City, 1995—; cons. Ford Found. 1968-72, Rockefeller Found., 1964-70, 89, UN, 1978, 90, NAS, 1980, 89, 91, 92, 93, USAID, 1972, UN Devel. Program, 1989. Editor: Grass Biology and Utilization, 1971, Useful Wildland Shrubs, 1972, Rehabilitation of Western Wildlife Habitat, 1978, Paradoxes of Western Energy Development, 1984, Resource Inventory and Baseline Study Methods for Developing Countries, 1983, Shrub Biology and Utilization, 1989, Wilderness Issues, Arid Lands of the Western United States, 1992; contbr. over 230 articles to profl. jours. Chmn. Cache County Planning Commn., Logan, 1974-79; mem. Utah Energy Conservation and Devel. Coun., 1976-79, Gov.'s Sci. Adv. Coun., 1988—, chmn., 1990-91, 97-97; mem. Commn. of the Californians, Riverside, 1965-68. Recipient Utah Gov.'s Sci. and Tech. medal, 1990; Fulbright scholar Spain, 1967-68; World Travel grantee Rockefeller Found., 1964. Fellow AAAS (com. chmn. 1979-89, sci. exchange to China grantee 1984-85, 89, sci. panel U.S.-Chile 1987); mem. Am. Soc. Agronomy, Soc. Range Mgmt. (pres. Calif. sect. 1965, pres. Utah sect. 1982). Mem. LDS Ch. Avocations: travel, photography. Home: 2248 E 4000 S Salt Lake City UT 84124-1864 Office: 550 N Main St Ste 222 Logan UT 84321-3957

MCKELLEN, IAN, actor; b. Burnley, Eng., May 25, 1939; s. Denis Murray and Margery (Sutcliffe) McK.; ed. St. Catharine's Coll., Cambridge, Eng. Prof. Oxford U., 1990-91. First stage appearance as Roper in A Man for All Seasons, Belgrade Theatre, Coventry, Eng., 1961; numerous other parts include title roles in Henry V, Luther, Ipswich, 1962-63, Aufidius in Coriolanus, Arthur Seaton in Saturday Night and Sunday Morning, title role in Sir Thomas More, Nottingham Playhouse, 1963-64; London debut as Godfrey in A Scent of Flowers, 1964, Claudio in Much Ado About Nothing, Andrew Cobham in Their Very Own and Golden City, 1966; title part in O'Flaherty, V.C. and Bonapart in The Man of Destiny, 1966, (Broadway debut) Leonidik in The Promise, London, 1966-67, Richard II, Edward II, Hamlet, Prospect Theatre Co., 1968-71; Capt. Plume in The Recruiting Officer; founder-mem. Actors' Co., Edinburgh Festival, 1972 and touring as Giovanni in Tis Pity She's A Whore, Page-Boy in Ruling the Roost, title role Wood Demon; debut with R.S.C. as Dr. Faustus, Edinburgh Festival, 1974; title role in The Marquis of Keith, Philip the Bastard in King John, 1974-75, Young Vic Colin in Ashes, 1975; Royal Shakespeare Co.: Burglar in Too True to be Good, Romeo, Macbeth, Leontes in The Winter's Tale, Face in The Alchemist, Bernick in Pillars of the Community, Langevin in Days of the Commune, 1976-78, Ivanov in Every Good Boy Deserves Favour, Toby Belch in Twelfth Night, Andrei in The Three Sisters, Max in Bent, 1979, Amadeus, N.Y.C., 1980, Iago in Othello, The Other Place, Stratford, 1989; European tour of one-man show Acting Shakespeare, 1983, also Los Angeles, N.Y.C., 1984, one-man show A Knight Out at the Lyceum (devised especially for Gay Games IV U.K. and South African tour), 1994; assoc. dir. Nat. Theatre, London, 1984-86, plays include: Venice Preserved, Wild Honey, Coriolanus, Duchess of Malfi, The Cherry Orchard, King Lear, Richard m. Napoli Milionaria, Uncle Vanya, others; dir. first prodn. The Prime of Miss Jean Brodie, Liverpool Playhouse, 1969, A Private Matter, 1973, The Clandestine Marriage, 1975; films include: Alfred the Great, 1969, The Promise, 1969, A Touch of Love, 1969, The Keep, 1982, Plenty, Zina, 1985, Scandal, 1988, The Ballad of Little Jo, 1992, I'll Do Anything, 1992, Last Action Hero, 1993, Six Degrees of Separation, 1993, The Shadow, 1994, Jack and Sarah, 1994, Restoration, 1994, Richard III, 1995, Amy Foster, 1996, Apt Pupil, 1997; TV appearances include: David Copperfield, 1965, Ross, 1969, Richard II, Edward II and Hamlet, 1970, Hedda Gabler, 1974, Macbeth, Every Good Boy Deserves Favour, Dying Day, 1979, Acting Shakespeare, 1981, The Scarlet Pimpernel, 1982, And the Band Played On, 1993 (Emmy nomination, Supporting Actor - Special, 1994), Cold Comfort Farm, 1995, Rasputin, 1995 (Emmy nomination Supporting Actor, 1996). Recipient Clarence Derwent award, 1964; Variety and Plays and Players awards, 1966; Actor of Year, Plays and Players, 1976; award Soc. of West End Theatres for Best Actor in Revival, 1977, for Best Comedy Performance, 1978, for Best Actor in a New Play, 1979, Tony Award for Best Actor, Drama Desk Award, Outer Critics' Circle Award, N.Y. Drama League Award, 1981; Performer of Yr. award Royal TV soc., 1983. Decorated comdr. Order Brit. Empire, knight Bachelor. Mem. Brit. Actors' Equity (coun. 1970-71). Office: ICM, Oxford House, 76 Oxford St, London W1N 0AX, England

MCKELVEY, ANDREW J., advertising executive. Chmn. bd., pres. TMP Worldwide, Inc., N.Y.C. Office: TMP Worldwide Inc 1633 Broadway Fl 33 New York NY 10019-6708

MCKELVEY, JACK M., bishop; b. Wilmington, Del., Dec. 8, 1941; m. Linda Boardman; children: Heather, Glen, Drew, Marissa. B in Psychology, U. del.; MDiv, Va. Theol. Seminary. ordained to deaconate Episc. Ch., 1966, to priesthood, 1967. Vicar St. John the Baptist Ch., Milton, Del., 1965-70, Holy Trinity Ch., Wilmington, 1970-79; rector St. Paul's Ch., Englewood, N.J., 1979—; elected Suffragan Bishop Diocese of Newark, 1990—; mem. faculty Inter-Met Seminary, Washington, 1976; former mem. diocesan coun. Del., commns. on ministry and standing coms.; pres. standing com. diocese of Newark; co-founder Van Ost Family Inst. Co-author: Inter-Met Seminary: Bold Experiment in Theological Education. Office: 24 Rector St Newark NJ 07102-4512*

MCKELVEY, JAMES MORGAN, chemical engineering educator; b. St. Louis, Aug. 22, 1925; s. James Grey and Muriel (Morgan) McK.; m. Edith Rothbauer, Dec. 28, 1957; children: James, Robert; m. Judith Hood Forgotson, Sept. 4, 1992. B.S., U. Mo.-Rolla, 1945; M.S., Washington U., St. Louis, 1947, Ph.D., 1950. Research engr. E.I. DuPont de Nemours & Co., Inc., 1950-54; asst. prof. chem. engring. Johns Hopkins U., Balt., 1954-57; mem. faculty Washington U., St. Louis, 1957—, dean Sch. Engring. and Applied Sci., 1964-91, prof. chem. engring., 1991—. Recipient Disting. Educator award Soc. Plastics Engrs., 1979. Home: 9861 Copper Hill Rd Saint Louis MO 63124-9999

MC KELVEY, JEAN TREPP, industrial relations educator; b. St. Louis, Feb. 9, 1908; d. Samuel and Blanche (Goodman) Trepp; m. Blake McKelvey, June 29, 1934. AB, Wellesley Coll., 1929; MA, Radcliffe Coll., 1931, PhD, 1933. Mem. faculty Sarah Lawrence Coll., 1932-45, N.Y. State Sch. Indsl. and Labor Rels., Cornell U., Ithaca, N.Y., 1946—; from asst. prof. to assoc. prof. indsl. rels. N.Y. State Sch. Indsl. and Labor Rels., Cornell U., 1946-49, prof., 1949—; vis. prof. Sch. Law Cornell U., 1977-78; mem. pub. panel, hearing officer, arbitrator Nat. War Labor Bd., 1944-45; mem. inquiry into Rochester Transit dispute N.Y. State Bd., 1952; mem. pub. adv. com. to sec. of labor, 1953; mem. N.Y. State Bd. Mediation, 1956-66; mem. presdl. emergency bd. on ry. shopcrafts dispute, 1964, ry. signalmen dispute, 1971; mem. Fed. Svc. Impasses Panel, 1970-90. Author: The Uses of Field Work in Teaching Economics, 1939, AFL Attitudes Toward Production, 1952, Dock Labor Disputes in Great Britain, 1953, Fact Finding in Public Employment Disputes, 1969, Sex and the Single Arbitrator, 1971. Editor: The Duty of Fair Representation, 1977; The Changing Law of Fair Representation, 1985, Cleared For Takeoff: Airline Labor Relations Under Deregulation, 1988; also several vols. on arbitration. Alumnae trustee Wellesley Coll., 1946-53. Mem. Nat. Acad. Arbitrators (past pres.), Am. Fedn. Tchrs. (mem. pub. rev. bd. 1969-73), UAW (pub. rev. bd. 1957—), Indsl. Rels. Rsch. Assn., Phi Beta Kappa. Home: 1570 East Ave Apt 501 Rochester NY 14610-1638 Office: Cornell U NYSSILR 16 Main St W Rochester NY 14614-1601

MC KELVEY, JOHN CLIFFORD, research institute executive; b. Decatur, Ill., Jan. 25, 1934; s. Clifford Venice and Pauline Lytton (Runkel) McK.; m. Carolyn Tenney, May 23, 1980; children: Sean, Kerry, Tara, Evelyn, Aaron. B.A., Stanford U., 1956, M.B.A., 1958. Research analyst Stanford Research Inst., Palo Alto, Calif., 1959-60; indsl. economist Stanford Research Inst., 1960-64; with Midwest Research Inst., Kansas City, Mo., 1964—; v.p. econs. and mgmt. sci. Midwest Research Inst., 1970-73, exec. v.p., 1973-75, pres., chief exec. officer, 1975—; chmn. Menninger Found. Bd., 1994. Trustee Rockhurst Coll., 1993; mem. Civic Coun. of Greater Kansas City; bd. regents Rockhurst Coll., Kansas City, Mo., 1977; bd. dirs. Yellow Corp., North Star Found., 1981, Mid-Am. Mfg. Tech. Ctr., 1991; trustee The Menninger Found., 1975. Clubs: Carriage, Mission Hills, Hallbrook Country. Home: 1156 W 103rd St # 232 Kansas City MO 64114-4511 Office: Midwest Rsch Inst 425 Volker Blvd Kansas City MO 64110-2241

MC KELVEY, JOHN JAY, JR., retired foundation executive; b. Albany, N.Y., July 16, 1917; s. John Jay and Louise E. (Brunning) McK.; m. Josephine G. Faulkner, June 28, 1941; children: John Jay III, Richard Drummond, Edward Faulkner, Laurence Brunning. A.B., Oberlin Coll., 1939; M.S., Va. Poly. Inst., 1941; Ph.D., Cornell U., 1945. Investigator N.Y. State Agrl. Expt. Sta., 1942-45; with Rockefeller Found., 1945-83, dep. dir. agrl. sci., 1966-68, assoc. dir. agrl. scis., 1968-83; cons. in field, 1959—; Mem. survey team natural resources No. Region Nigeria FAO-ICA, 1960; cons. UN spl. fund project agrl. research, Thailand, 1964; study com. manpower needs and ednl. capabilities in Africa Edn. and World Affairs, 1964-65; rev. commn. higher edn. Botswana, Lesotho and Swaziland Overseas Devel. Ministry U.K., 1966; overseas liaison com. study team higher edn., Sierra Leone, 1968; mem. agrl. edn. mission to U.S. Pacific, Overseas Devel. Ministry of U.K., 1970; mem. Africa sci. bd. Nat. Acad. Scis., 1961-68, vice chmn., 1964-68, mem. sci. orgn. devel. bd., 1966-68, mem. bd. sci. and tech. internat. devel., also chmn. Africa sci. panel, 1968—, chmn. adv. panel on arid lands of, sub-Saharan Africa, 1974; chmn. com. African agrl. research capabilities Nat. Acad. Scis./Agrl. Bd., 1971-74; mem. vis. com. for biology and related research facilities Harvard Coll., 1975-81; mem. area adv. com. for Africa Council for Internat. Exchange of Scholars, 1976-80; mem. Chappaqua Internat. Exchange, 1976-78; chmn. USAID/IBAR Task Force, 1978-79. Author: Man Against Tse-tse, 1973; editor: (with R.L. Metcalf) The Future for Insecticides, 1976, (with H.H. Shorey) Chemical Control of Insect Behavior, 1977, (with Louis H. Miller and John A. Pino), Immunity to Blood Parasites of Animals and Man, 1977, (with Bruce F. Eldridge and Karl Maramorosch) Vectors of Disease Agents, 1980, (with K. Maramarosch) Subviral Pathogens of Plants and Animals, 1985; contbr. articles to profl. jours., chpts. to books. Trustee Internat. Inst. Tropical Agr., Ibadan, Nigeria, 1971-87, chmn., 1983-87; vice chmn. governing coun. Internat. Trypanotolerance Ctr., The Gambia, 1981-89, chmn., 1988-89; pres. Internat. Fund for Agrl. Rsch., 1985-87, bd. dirs. 1988, chmn., 1989-93; bd. govs. Inst. for Agrl. Rsch., Ahmadu Bello U., Zaria, Nigeria, 1971-74; moderator Federated Ch. West Winfield, 1995—. Mem. AAAS, Entomol. Soc. Am., Assn. for Advancement Agrl. Sci. in Africa (founding).

MCKELVEY, JUDITH GRANT, lawyer, educator, university dean; b. Milw., July 19, 1935; d. Lionel Alexander and Bernadine R. (Verdun) Grant. B.S. in Philosophy, U. Wis., 1957, J.D., 1959. Bar: Wis. 1959, Calif. 1968. Atty. FCC, Washington, 1959-62; adj. prof. U. Md., Europe, 1965; prof. law Golden Gate U. Sch. Law, San Francisco, 1968—; dean Golden Gate U. Sch. Law (Sch. Law), 1974-81; mem. State Jud. Nominees Evaluation Commn., 1981-82. Contbr. to: Damages Book, 1975, 76. Bd. dirs. San Francisco Neighborhood Legal Assistance Found. Fellow Am. Bar Found.; mem. ABA, Wis. Bar Assn., Calif. Bar Assn., San Francisco Bar Assn. (dir. 1975-77, chmn. legis. com., sec.-treas., pres.-elect 1980-83, pres. 1984), Calif. Women Lawyers (1st pres.), Law in a Free Soc. (exec. com.), Continuing Edn. of Bar (chmn. real estate subcom., mem. joint adv. com.), Legal Svcs. to Children Inc. (pres. 1987-89), San Francisco Neighborhood Legal Assistance Found. (dir. and exec. com. 1985-87), Lawyers Com. for Urban Affairs (dir. and exec. com. 1985-87, co-chairperson 1988-90). Office: Golden Gate U Sch Law 536 Mission St San Francisco CA 94105-2921

MCKELVIE, RODERICK R., federal judge; b. 1946. BA, Harvard U., 1968; ME, Roosevelt U., 1970; JD, U. Pa., 1973. Law clk. to Hon. Caleb Layton U.S. Dist. Ct., Wilmington, Del., 1973-74; assoc. Richards, Layton & Finger, Wilmington, 1974-79; ptnr. Ashby, McKelvie & Geddes, Wilmington, 1979-92; fed. judge U.S. Dist. Ct. (Del. dist.), Wilmington, 1992—. Active World Affairs Coun., 1988—, United Way Govt. Rels. Commn. Mem. ABA, Del. State Bar, Richard S. Rodney Inn of Ct. (mem. exec. com., pres. 1992-93). Office: US Dist Ct Ste Box 10 844 N King St Rm 3124 Wilmington DE 19801-3519*

MCKELVY, NIKKI KAY, nurse; b. Honolulu, May 16, 1956; d. Donald and Virginia Katherine (Davis) McK.; m. David Stuart Murry, Dec. 9, 1978 (dec. 1992); children: Ryan Cobb, Caleb Murry. AA, Saddleback Coll., 1989; BSN, Dominican Coll., 1994. RN. Customer svc. clk. United Parcel Svc., Little Rock, 1974-78; resident/extern Vets. Hosp., Montrose, N.Y., 1993-94; staff nurse Harrison (Ark.) Nursing Ctr., 1995-96. Recipient Student Leadership award Dominican Coll., Orangeberg, N.Y., 1994. Fellow Sigma Theta Tau; mem. Nursing Assn. Dominican Coll. (v.p. 1994—). Democrat. Roman Catholic. Avocations: reading, swimming, travel. Home: Rt 7 Box 243-2C Harrison AR 72601

MCKELWAY, ALEXANDER JEFFREY, religion studies educator; b. Durham, N.C., Dec. 8, 1932; s. Alexander Jeffrey and Alice (Gibbon) McK.; m. Adelaide Bullard, Sept. 17, 1960; children: Alexander J., Daniel, Matthew Phillip. AB, Davidson Coll., 1954; BD, Princeton Theol. Sem., 1954-57;

ThD, U. Basil, 1963. Min. Vienna (Austria) Cmty. Ch., 1958-60; asst. prof. Dartmouth Coll., Hanover, N.H., 1963-65; Paul B. Freeland prof. religion Davidson (N.C.) Coll., 1965—, faculty chair, 1991-94; vis. prof. Princeton (N.J.) Theol. Sem., 1973, 86, 87; active Fulbright Commn., Vienna, 1958-60. Author: The Systematic Theology of Paul Tillich, 1964, The Freedom of God and Human Liberation, 1991; editor: The Context of Contemporary Theology, 1974. Chair jud. com. Synod of N.C., 1975; moderator Charlotte (N.C.) Presbytery, 1985, active, 1972—; active Kincaid for Congress Com., Charlotte, 1980, Exec. Com. Dem. Party, Davidson, 1975-77. Grad. fellow in theology Princeton Sem., 1957, Younger Scholars fellow NEH, 1969, Ctr. for Theol. Inquiry fellow, 1997. Mem. Am. Acad. Religion, Calvin Studies Soc., Duodecim Theol. Soc. (sec.), Am. Theol. Soc. Office: Davidson Coll Dept Religion Davidson NC 28036

MCKENDRY, JOHN H., JR., lawyer, educator; b. Grand Rapids, Mich., Mar. 24, 1950; s. John H. and Lois R. (Brandel) McK.; m. Linda A. Schmalzer, Aug. 11, 1973; children: Heather Lynn, Shannon Dawn, Sean William. BA cum laude, Albion Coll., 1972; JD cum laude, U. Mich., 1975. Bar: Mich. 1975. Assoc., then ptnr. Landman, Latimer, Clink & Robb, Muskegon, Mich., 1976-85; ptnr. Warner, Norcross & Judd, Muskegon, 1985—; dir. debate Mona Shores High Sch., Muskegon, 1979-90; adj. prof. of taxation (employee benefits), Grand Valley State U. Pres. local chpt. Am. Cancer Soc., 1979; bd. dirs. West Shore Symphony, 1993—, v.p. 1995-97, pres., 1997—. Recipient Disting. Service award Muskegon Jaycees, 1981; named 1 of 5 Outstanding Young Men in Mich., Mich. Jaycees. 1982; named to Hall of Fame, Mich. Speech Coaches, 1986, Diamond Key Coach Nat. Forensic League, 1987. Mem. ABA, Mich. Bar Assn., Muskegon County Bar Assn. (trustee 1992-93, sec. 1993-94, treas. 1994-95, v.p. 1995-96, pres. 1996—), Muskegon C. of C. (bd. dirs. 1982-88), Mich. Interscholastic Forensic Assn. (treas. 1979-86). Republican. Roman Catholic. Lodge: Optimists. Home: 1575 Brookwood Dr Muskegon MI 49441-5276 Office: Warner Norcross & Judd LLP 400 Terrace Pla PO Box 900 Muskegon MI 49443-0900

MCKENNA, ALVIN JAMES, lawyer; b. New Orleans, Aug. 17, 1943; s. Dixon N. Sr. and Mabel (Duplantier) McK.; m. Carol Jean Windheim, 1963; children: Sara, Alvin James Jr., Martha, Andrea, Erin, Rebecca. AB, Canisius Coll., 1963; JD, Notre Dame U., 1966. Bar: N.Y. 1966, Ohio 1967, U.S. Dist. Ct. (so. dist.) Ohio 1968, U.S. Dist. Ct. (no. dist.) Ohio 1978, U.S. Ct. Appeals (6th cir.) 1969, U.S. Supreme Ct. 1977. Law clk. to presiding justice U.S. Dist. Ct. (so. dist.), Columbus, Ohio, 1966-68; asst. U.S. atty., 1968-70; ptnr. Porter, Wright, Morris & Arthur, 1970—. Mem. Gahanna (Ohio) City Council, 1972-80, 82-84; chmn. Gahanna Charter Rev. Commn., 1981; v.p. Community Urban Redevel. Corp., Gahanna, 1984—. Named one of Ten Outstanding Young Persons in Columbus, Jaycees, 1974. Mem. ABA, Ohio Bar Assn., Fed. Bar Assn. (pres. Columbus chpt. 1973-74), Columbus Bar Assn. (chair fed. cts. com. 1972-74). Home: 202 Academy Ct Columbus OH 43230-2104 Office: Porter Wright Morris & Arthur 41 S High St Columbus OH 43215-6101

MCKENNA, ANDREW JAMES, paper distribution and printing company executive, baseball club executive; b. Chgo., Sept. 17, 1929; s. Andrew James and Anita (Fruin) McK.; m. Mary Joan Pickett, June 20, 1953; children: Suzanne, Karen, Andrew, William, Joan, Kathleen, Margaret. B.S., U. Notre Dame, 1951; J.D., DePaul U., 1954. Bar: Ill. Chmn., CEO Schwarz Paper Co. (name now Schwarz), Morton Grove, Ill., 1964—; dir. Chgo. Nat. League Ball Club Inc., Chgo. Bears.; bd. dirs. Dean Foods Co., 1st Nat. Bank Chgo., Skyline Corp., Tribune Co., AON Corp., McDonald's Corp., First Chgo. NBD Corp. Chmn. bd. trustees U. Notre Dame, Mus. Sci. & Industry, Chgo.; bd. dirs. Cath. Charities of Chgo., Children's Meml. Med. Ctr. Chgo. Mem. Chgo. Athletic Assn., Econ. Club, Lyric Opera (bd. dirs.), Chgo. Club, Comml. Club, Econs. Club., Execs. Club Chgo., Glenview Golf Club, Old Elm Club, Merit Club, Casino Club, The Island Club. Home: 60 Locust Rd Winnetka IL 60093-3751 Office: Schwarz 8338 Austin Ave Morton Grove IL 60053-3209

MCKENNA, DAVID LOREN, academic administrator, clergyman, consultant, author; b. Detroit, May 5, 1929; s. William Loren and Ilmi E. (Matson) McK.; m. Janet Voorheis, June 9, 1950; children: David Douglas, Debra Lynn, Suzanne Marie, Robert Bruce. AA, Spring Arbor Jr. Coll., 1949; BA magna cum laude in History, Western Mich. U., 1951; MDiv, Asbury Theol. Sem., 1953; MA, U. Mich., 1955, PhD (Clifford Woody scholar), 1958; LLD, Houghton Coll., 1974, Spring Arbor Coll., 1976, Lewis and Clark Coll., 1978, Seattle U., 1982, Marion Coll., 1983; LHD, Roberts Wesleyan Coll., 1986; DD, Asbury Coll., 1994. Ordained to ministry Free Methodist Ch. N.Am., 1950; dean of men Spring Arbor Jr. Coll., 1953-55, instr. psychology, 1955-60, acad. dean, 1955-57, v.p., 1958-60, pres., 1961-68; lectr. higher edn. U. Mich., 1958-60; asst. prof., coord. Ctr. for the Study of Higher Edn., Ohio State U., Columbus, 1960-61; pres. Seattle Pacific U., 1968-82, Asbury Theol. Sem., 1982-94, pres. emeritus, 1994—; del. World Meth. Coun., London, 1966, Nairobi, Kenya, 1987, Singapore, 1991, v.p. N.Am. sect., 1987—; chmn. Mich. Commn. Coll. Accrediting, 1966-68; bd. dirs. Council Advancement Small Colls., 1964-67; pres. Assn. Free Meth. Colls., 1968-70; chmn. Christian Coll. Consortium, 1970-74; participant Internat. Congress World Evangelization, 1974, Consultation on World Evangelization, Pattaya, Thailand, 1980, Lausanne II, Manila, 1989; mem. bd. adminstrn., exec. com. Nat. Assn. Evangelicals, 2d v.p., 1975-81; bd. reference Black Evangelistic Enterprise, Evangelicals for Social Action, Ugandan Relief, Youth for Christ Internat. Author: The Jesus Model, 1976, Awake, My Conscience!, 1977, The Communicator's Commentary: Mark, 1982, The Communicator's Commentary: Job, 1986, Renewing Our Ministry, 1986, Mega Truth, 1986, The Whisper of His Grace, 1987, Discovering Job, 1988, Power to Follow, Grace to Lead, 1989, Love Your Work, 1990, The Coming Great Awakening, 1990, Communicator's Commentary on Isaiah, vol. I, 1993, vol. II, 1994, When Our Parents Need Us Most, 1994, A Future With A History: The Wesleyan Witness of the Free Methodist Church, vols. I and II, 1995; exec. editor: The Urban Crisis, 1969, Minister's Personal Library, 1987-89, Religious Book Club, 1989—; nat. radio commentator: This Is Our World, 1983—; contbr. articles to profl. jours. Pres. United Community Services, Jackson, Mich., 1968, Wash. Coll. Assn., 1970, 76; trustee United Way, Pacific Sci. Ctr., Seattle Found., Spring Arbor Coll., 1983—; bd. dirs. Bread for the World, 1980-86, Jr. Achievement, 1966-68, Land O'Lakes council Boy Scouts Am., 1965-68; mem. Wash. State Council Postsecondary Edn., 1969-74, Pacific Sci. Ctr., 1969-82, Seattle Found., 1975-82; v.p. Bluegrass Tomorrow, 1989-93; chmn. R & D com. United Way Bluegrass, 1984-89, bd. dirs., 1987-93; sec. Nat. Religious Partnership Environment, 1993-95. Named One of Outstanding Young Men of Yr., Jr. C. of C., Seattle and Puget Sound, 1965, Outstanding Citizen of Yr., 1976, Outstanding Educator, Religious Heritage of Am., 1993; recipient Others award Salvation Army, 1994; Named in his honor McKenna Hall, Seattle Pacific U., 1983, David L. and Janet McKenna Chapel, Ashbury Theol. Sem., 1994. Mem. Assn. Am. Colls. (dir. 1974-77), Ind. Colls. Wash. (pres. 1969-71, co-chmn. 1968-70, 79-80), Wash. State Council Econ. Edn. (dir. 1980), Am. Council Edn. (interassn. pres.'s com. on accreditation 1979-80), N.W. Assn. Schs. and Colls. (commr. 1975-79), N. Central Assn. Colls. and Schs. (chmn., dir. 1966-68), Nat. Assn. Ind. Colls. and Univs. (dir. 1976-80, sec. 1978), Council Postsecondary Accreditation (dir. 1979—), Seattle C. of C., Wash. Friends of Higher Edn., Wash. Athletic Club (bd. govs.), Rainier Club (Seattle), The Diet Club, Lafayette (Ky.) Club, Lexington Tennis Club, Rotary (pres. Jackson chpt. 1966-67, Paul Harris fellow 1982), Phi Kappa Phi. *

MCKENNA, FRANK JOSEPH, Canadian government official, lawyer; b. Apohaqui, N.B., Can., Jan. 19, 1948; s. Durward and Olive (Moody) McK.; m. Julie Friel; children: Tobias John, Christine Alice, James Durward. BA with honors, St. Francis Xavier U., 1970; postgrad., Queen's U., 1970-71; LLB, U. N.B., 1974; DSc (hon.), Université de Moncton, Can., 1988; LLD (hon.), University of N.B., Can., 1988, Mt. Allison U., Can., 1991. Spl. asst. to pres. Privy Council, 1971; rsch. asst. Constl. Law Unit, 1973-74; v.p. U. N.B. Faculty of Law Liberal Assn., Fredericton, 1974; ptnr. Martin, Lordon, McKenna & Bowes, Chatham, 1974-87; mem. N.B. Liberal Party, 1982, leader, 1985; premier Province of N.B., Fredericton, 1987—. Recipient Vanier award, 1988, Distinction award Can. Advanced Tech. Assn., 1994; named Econ. Developer of Yr., Econ. Developers' Assn. Can., 1993, Chair, Can. Quality Month, 1994. Mem. Can. Bar Assn., N.B. Bar Assn. Liberal. Avocations: jogging, baseball, hockey. Office: PO Box 6000, Fredericton, NB Canada E3B 5H1

MCKENNA, GEORGE LAVERNE, art museum curator; b. Detroit, Dec. 7, 1924; s. John LaVerne and Carolyn Georgia (Schwab) McK.; m. Janice Ballinger, July 22, 1966. Student, U. Oreg., 1943-44, U. Calif., Berkeley, 1948-49, U. Chgo., 1950; AB, Wayne State U., 1948, MA, 1951. Curator prints, drawings and photographs Nelson-Atkins Mus. Art, Kansas City, Mo., 1952-96; cons, Nelson-Atkins Mus. Art, Kansas City, 1997—; cons. Hallmark Cards, Inc., Kansas City, 1974-76. Curator, author exhbn. and coll. catalogues. With U.S. Army, 1943-46. Mem. Am. Assn. Mus., Print Coun. Am. Office: Nelson-Atkins Mus Art 4525 Oak St Kansas City MO 64111-1818

MCKENNA, J. FRANK, III, lawyer; b. Pitts., Nov. 9, 1948; s. J. Frank Jr. and Antoinette (Schlafly) McK.; m. Colleen Shaughnessy, Mar. 25, 1972; children: Collette M., J. Frank IV, Laura J., Stephen J. BA, Williams Coll., 1970; JD, U. Pitts., 1973. Bar: Pa. 1973. Assoc. Thorp, Reed & Armstrong, Pitts., 1973-82, ptnr., 1982-88; ptnr. Babst, Calland, Clements & Zomnir, Pitts., 1988—. Served to lt. USAFR, 1973-74. Named one of Outstanding Young Men In Am., 1982. Mem. ABA, Pa. Bar Assn., Allegheny County Bar Assn. (chmn. young lawyers sect. 1980, v.p. 1987, bd. govs. 1988-90, pres.-elect 1991, pres. 1992), Am. Law Inst., Acad. Trial Lawyers Allegheny County, Am. Judicature Soc., Pitts. Field Club, Pitts. Athletic Assn. Home: 101 Fox Ridge Farms Dr Pittsburgh PA 15215-1142 Office: Babst Calland Clements & Zomnir 2 Gateway Ctr Pittsburgh PA 15222-1402

MC KENNA, JAMES ALOYSIUS, broadcasting executive, former lawyer; b. Poughkeepsie, N.Y., July 1, 1918; s. James Aloysius and Eleanor Frances (Mahoney) McK.; m. Rebekah Ann Rial, Sept. 1, 1941; children: Michelle M., James A., Dennis M., Matthew M., Marc W., Aileen M. Student, Manhattan Coll., 1934-35; B.S., Cath. U., 1938; LL.B., Georgetown U., 1942. Bar: D.C. 1941, U.S. Supreme Ct. 1947. Counsel Civil Aeronautics Bd., 1941-42; asst. to gen. counsel Office Alien Property Custodian, 1942-44; practicing lawyer Washington, 1946-87; ptnr. McKenna, Wilkinson & Kittner, 1952-87. Lt. (j.g.) USNR; active duty 1944-46. Named Outstanding Alumni Cath. U. Am., 1978; recipient DuBois medal Mt. St. Mary's Coll., 1966. Mem. FCC Bar Assn., Inst. Radio Engrs., Georgetown U. Alumni Assn., Delta Theta Phi. Home: 5219 Oakland Rd Bethesda MD 20815-6640

MCKENNA, JEANETTE ANN, archaeologist; b. N.Y.C., Aug. 6, 1953; d. Edward Patrick and Ann Jeanette (O'Brien) McKenna; children: Stephanie Jane, Daniel Glen Edward. AA in Phys. Edn., Mount San Antonio Jr. Coll., 1974; BA in Anthropology, Calif. State U., Fullerton, 1977, MA in Anthropology, 1982; postgrad., Ariz. State U., 1981-84, U. Calif., Riverside, 1991-92. Field archaeologist Archaeol. Rsch., Inc., Costa Mesa, Calif., 1976-79; rsch. asst. Calif. State U., 1979; lab. dir. Environ. Rsch. Archaeologists, L.A., 1978-79; staff archaeologist Ariz. State U., Tempe, 1979-82; rsch. archaeologist Soil Systems, Inc., Phoenix, 1982-84, Sci. Resource Surveys, Huntington Beach, Calif., 1984-87; co-owner, prin. Hatheway & McKenna, Mission Viejo, Calif., 1987-89; owner, prin. McKenna et al., Whittier, Calif., 1989—; dir. Divsn. Cultural Resource Mgmt. Svcs. EIP Assocs., Chino, Calif., 1996—. Contbr. numerous articles to profl. jours. and reports. Bd. dirs. Whittier Conservancy, 1987—, interim treas., 1994, pres., 1994-95. Recipient Gov.'s award for Hist. Preservation/Calif., The Whittier Conservancy, 1995. Mem. Soc. Profl. Archaeologists (bd. dirs. 1993—), Archaeol. Inst. Am., Am. Soc. Conservation Archaeology, Am. Mus. Natural History, Soc. Am. Anthropology, Ariz. Archaeol. Coun., Ariz. Hist. Found., Calif. Hist. Soc., Nat. Arbor Day Found., Nat. Parks and Conservation Assn., Nat. Trust for Historic Preservation, Soc. Calif. Archaeology, Soc. Hist. Archaeology, S.W. Mus. Assn., Wilderness Soc., Whittier Conservancy, Southwestern Anthrop. Assn., Gene Autry Western Heritage Mus. Assn., Nature Conservancy, Smithsonian Assocs., Sierra Club, otehrs. Democrat. Roman Catholic. Avocations: treaveling, reading, hiking, camping, gardening. Office: McKenna et al 6008 Friends Ave Whittier CA 90601-3724

MCKENNA, JOHN, computer company executive; b. 1955. BA, Trinity Coll. With IBM, Armonk, N.Y., 1976-86, Fisher MacLeod Assocs., N.Y.C., 1986-88, JWP Info. Svcs. Inc., Purchase, N.Y., 1988-93; pres. Entex Info. Svcs., Port Chester, N.Y., 1993—; mem. sales staff IBM, 1977-86; v.p. bus. devel. JWP, 1989, sr. v.p., gen. mgr. info. sys., 1990; pres., CEO ENTEX Info. Svcs., 1993—. Office: ENTEX Info Svcs 6 Internat Dr Port Chester NY 10573

MCKENNA, JOHN DENNIS, environmental testing engineer; b. N.Y.C., Apr. 1, 1940; s. Hubert Guy and Elizabeth Ann (Record) McK.; BSChemE, Manhattan Coll., 1961; MSChemE, Newark Coll. Engring., 1968; MBA, Rider Coll., 1974, PhD, Walden U., 1991; m. Christel Klages, Dec. 26, 1964; children: Marc, Michelle. Tech. asst. to pres. Eldib Engring. & Rsch. Co., Newark, 1964-67; project mgr. Princeton Chem. Rsch., Inc (N.J.), 1967-68; projects dir. Rsch. Cottrell Environ. Systems, Bound Brook, N.J., 1968-72; v.p., then pres. Enviro-Systems & Rsch., Inc., Roanoke, Va., 1973-79; pres. ETS, Inc., Roanoke, 1979-91; chmn. bd., pres. ETS Internat. Inc., 1991—; chmn. air pollution adv. bd. State of Va., 1993; workshop lectr. and sci reviewer publs. EPA, 1978-79. Author chpts. to books; contbr. articles to profl. jours. Recipient Outstanding Engring. Grad. Manhattan Coll. Centennial award, 1992. Mem. AIChE (treas. Ctrl. Va. chpt.), Air Pollution Control Assn., Air and Waste Mgmt. Assn. (divsn. chmn. tech. coun., Pitts.), Tau Beta Pi (N.Y. Xi chpt., Eminent engr.). Roman Catholic. Home: RR 1 Box 1925 Rocky Mount VA 24151-9607 Office: ETS Inc 1401 Municipal Rd NW Roanoke VA 24012-1309

MCKENNA, KATHLEEN KWASNIK, artist; b. Detroit, Nov. 6, 1946; d. John J. and Eleanor H. (Ciosek) K.; m. Frank J. McKenna, Jr., Mar. 16, 1968. Cert., Cooper Sch. Art, Cleve., 1973; student, Art Students' League, N.Y.C., 1972, 74. Instr. portrait painting Baycrafters, Bay Village, Ohio, 1976-79; self-employed painter, 1972—; part-time mem. faculty fine arts dept. Lakeland C.C., Kirtland, Ohio, 1996—. One-person shows include Ctrl. Nat. Bank, Cleve., 1975, Women's City Club Gallery, Cleve., 1979, Kennedy Ctr. Art Gallery, Hiram, Ohio, 1980, Chime Art Gallery, Summit, N.J., 1985, Bolton Art Gallery, Cleve., 1986, 91, Lakeland C.C. Gallery, Kirtland, Ohio, 1996; group shows include Butler Inst. Am. Art, 1981, 89, 91, 93, Mansfield (Ohio) Art Ctr., 1990, Circle Gallery, N.Y.C., 1978, Canton (Ohio) Art Inst., 1990, others. Recipient Pres.'s award Am. Artists Profl. League, 1993, other awards. Mem. New Orgn. for the Visual Arts, Catharine Lorillard Wolfe Art Club (Pastel Soc. plaque 1989, Mae Berlind Bach award 1983, Cert. of Merit 1981), Allied Artists Am. (assoc.; Gold medal of Honor 1989). Roman Catholic. Avocations: art-related travel, tennis, skiing. Studio: 15914 Chadbourne Rd Shaker Heights OH 44120

MCKENNA, LAWRENCE M., federal judge; b. 1933. AB, Fordham Coll., 1956; LLB, Columbia U., 1959. With Simpson Thacher & Bartlett, N.Y.C., 1959-69, Wormser, Kiely, Alessandroni, Hyde & McCann, N.Y.C., 1969-90; judge U.S. Dist. Ct. (so. dist.), N.Y., 1990—. Mem. N.Y. State Bar Assn., Copyright Soc. USA. Office: US Dist Ct 500 Pearl St New York NY 10007-1316*

MC KENNA, MALCOLM CARNEGIE, vertebrate paleontologist, curator, educator; b. Pomona, Calif., July 21, 1930; s. Donald Carnegie and Bernice Caroline (Waller) McK.; m. Priscilla Coffey, June 17, 1952; children: Douglas M., Katharine L., Andrew M., Bruce C. B.A., U. Calif., Berkeley, 1954, Ph.D., 1958. Instr. dept. paleontology U. Calif., Berkeley, 1958-59; asst. curator dept. vertebrate paleontology Am. Mus. Natural History, N.Y.C., 1960-64; assoc. curator Am. Mus. Natural History, 1964-65; Frick assoc. curator, chmn. Frick Lab., 1965-68, Frick curator, 1968—; asst. prof. geology Columbia U., N.Y.C., 1960-64, assoc. prof., 1964-72, prof. geol. scis., 1972—; research assoc. U. Colo. Mus., Boulder, 1962—. Contbr. articles on fossil mammals and their evolution, the dating of Mesozoic and Tertiary sedimentary rocks, and paleogeography and plate tectonics to profl. jours. Bd. dirs. Bergen Community (N.J.) Mus., 1964-67, pres., 1965-66; trustee Flat Rock Brook Nature Assn., N.J., 1979-93, Raymond Alf Mus., Webb Sch. of Calif., 1980—, Dwight-Englewood Sch., Englewood, N.J., 1968-80; bd. dirs. Flat Rock Brook Nature Assn., N.J., 1979-84; trustee Claremont McKenna Coll., Calif., 1983-91; Planned Parenthood Bergen County, N.J., 1979-88, Mus. No. Ariz., 1978-85, 87-93. Nat. Acad. Scis. exchange fellow USSR, 1965. Fellow AAAS, Explorers Club, Geol. Soc. Am.; mem. Grand Canyon Natural History Assn. (bd. dirs. 1972-76), Soc. Systematic Zoology (coun. 1974-77), Soc. Vertebrate Paleontology (v.p. 1975, pres. 1976), Am. Geophys. Union, Am. Soc. Mammalogists, Paleontol. Soc. (award 1992), Soc. for Study Evolution, Polish Acad. Scis. (fgn.), Sigma Xi. Office: Am Mus Nat History Vertebrate Paleontology Central Park St W New York NY 10026-4355

MCKENNA, MARGARET ANNE, college president; b. R.I., June 3, 1945; d. Joseph John and Mary (Burns) McK.; children: Michael Aaron McKenna Miller, David Christopher McKenna Miller. BA in Sociology, Emmanuel Coll., 1967; postgrad., Boston Coll. Law Sch., 1968; JD, So. Meth. U., 1971; LLD (hon.), U. Upsala, N.J., 1978, Fitchburg (Mass.) State Coll., 1979, Regis Coll., 1982; D Community Affairs, U. R.I., 1979. Bar: Tex. 1971, D.C. 1973. Atty. Dept. Justice, Washington, 1971-73; exec. dir. Internat. Assn. Ofcl. Human Rights Agys., Washington, 1973-74; mgmt. cons. Dept. Treasury, Washington, 1975-76; dep. council to Pres. White House, Washington, 1976-79; dep. undersec. Dept. Edn., Washington, 1979-81; dir. Mary Ingraham Bunting Inst., Radcliffe Coll., Cambridge, Mass., 1981-85; v.p. program planning Radcliffe Coll., Cambridge, 1982-85; pres. Lesley Coll., Cambridge, 1985—; bd. dirs. Stride Rite Corp., Cambridge, Best Products Co., Inc., Richmond, Va., Consolidated Natural Gas Co., Pitts., Coun. of Ind. Colls., Washington. Chair higher edn. task force Clinton Transition, 1992-93; chair edn. task force Mayor Thomas Menino Transition Com., 1994. Recipient Outstanding Contribution award Civil Rights Leadership Conf., 1978; named Woman of Yr. Women's Equity Action League, 1979, Outstanding Woman of Yr. Big Sister Assn., 1986. Democrat. Office: Lesley Coll Office of the President 29 Everett St Cambridge MA 02138-2702

MCKENNA, MARIANNE, architect; b. Montreal, Que., Can., Sept. 25, 1950; d. Richard D. and Anna M. (Lohr) McK.; m. Ian C.; children: Cameron Lohr, Portia McKinley. Attended, The Study Montreal, 1969; BA, Swarthmore Coll., 1972; MArch, Yale U., 1976. Asst. architect Bobrow & Fieldman, Montreal, Can., 1976-78; architect Denys Lasdun, Redhouse & Softley, London, 1978-79; architect Barton Myers Assocs., 1980-87, assoc., 1981—; founding ptnr. Kuwabara Payne McKenna Blumberg Archs., Toronto, 1987—; assoc. prof. architecture U. Toronto, 1994—; guest critic, U. Toronto, U. Waterloo, McGill U., Yale U., 1975-87; exec. dir. Ont. Coll. of Art. Selected projects include Union Libr., Toronto, Hasbro Toy Co., N.Y.C.; selected projects present firm York U. Ctr. Fine Arts 3, Tudhope Assocs. Design Studios Toronto, 35 E. Wacker Addition Corp., Kitchener City Hall, Royal Conservatory of Music Master Plan, Grand Valley Instn. for Women, Kitchener, Home for the Aged Providence Ctr. Recipient Gov. Gen.'s award for Architecture, 1997, Royal Archtl. Inst. Can., 1994. Mem. Ont. Assn. Architects, Ordre des architectes de Québec, Royal Architecture Inst. Can., Grand Valley Instn. for Women. Office: Kuwabara Payne McKenna Blumberg Archs, 322 King St W 3rd Fl, Toronto, ON Canada M5V 1J2

MCKENNA, MICHAEL JOSEPH, manufacturing company executive; b. Phila., Feb. 18, 1935; s. Michael J. and Stella Marie (Gramigna) McK.; B.S., LaSalle Coll., 1962; m. Letitia Ward, Feb. 9, 1957; children—Letitia, Carol, Suzanne, Kathleen Jane, Margaret. With Crown Cork & Seal Co., Phila., 1957—, sales rep., 1969, dist. sales mgr., Phila., 1970, regional sales mgr., 1974, v.p. sales and mktg., 1979-86, former sr. v.p., also bd. dirs., exec. v.p., pres. N.Am. Divsn., Crown Cork & Seal Co., Inc., now pres. and COO. Founding bd. dirs. Northampton Twp. Library, 1967-71; pres. Churchville PTA, 1969-70; trustee Nazareth Hosp./St. Agnes Med. Ctr., Phila., La Salle U. Served with U.S. Army, 1955-57. Mem. Can. Mfrs. Inst. (standing com. 1980—), Old Guard Soc. Club. Republican. Roman Catholic. Home: 247 Magnolia Dr Southampton PA 18966-1456 Office: Crown Cork & Seal Co Inc 9300 Ashton Rd Philadelphia PA 19114-3464

MCKENNA, PETER DENNIS, lawyer; b. Amityville, N.Y., Aug. 15, 1937; s. John Paul and Margaret (Foley) McK.; m. Enid Soifer, Nov. 22, 1976; children: Michael A., Suzanne E. AB, Coll. of the Holy Cross, Worchester, Mass., 1959; JD, N.Y.U., 1968. Bar: N.Y. 1968, U.S. Dist. Ct. (so. dist.) N.Y. 1970, U.S. Supreme Ct. 1973, U.S. Ct. Appeals (4th cir.) 1977, U.S. Ct. Appeals (7th cir.) 1979, U.S. Ct. Appeals (2nd cir.) 1983. Assoc. Wachtell, Lipton, Rosen & Katz, N.Y.C., 1968-71, ptnr., 1972-91, of counsel, 1992—; mem. pres.'s coun. NYU, Weinfeld assoc. NYU Law Sch.; regent mem. pres.'s coun. Coll. Holy Cross. Editor-in-chief N.Y.U. Law Review, 1967-68; contbr. articles to profl. jours. Adv. bd. St. Aloyisius Sch. for Cen. Harlem Inner-City Children, 1992—, mem. exec. com., 1994—; mem. Community Sch. Bd. Dist. 26, Queens, N.Y., 1973-77; founding dir. Ctrl. Harlem Initiative for Learning and Devel., 1994—, Mt. St. Michael Acad., 1994—, mem. exec. com., 1994—. Lt. USN 1959-65. MEM. ABA, Fed. Bar Coun., N.Y. State Bar Assn., Assn. of Bar of City of N.Y., Order of Coif. Democrat. Roman Catholic. Avocations: travel, history, public affairs, swimming, golf. Home: 417 E 37th St New York NY 10016 Office: Wachtell Lipton Rosen & Katz 51 W 52nd St New York NY 10019-6150

MCKENNA, RICHARD HENRY, hospital consultant; b. Covington, Ky., Dec. 19, 1927; s. Charles Joseph and Mary Florence (Wieck) McK.; m. Patricia M. Macdonald, Jan. 6, 1979; children: Linda Ann, Theresa K., Joan Marie; stepchildren: Stuart J Goodman, Ann Elizabeth Goodman. BS in Commerce, U. Cin., 1959; MBA, Xavier U., 1963. CPA. Acct., Andrew Jergens Co., Cin., 1947-55; treas., dir. Ramsey Bus. Equipment, Inc., Cin., 1955-59; asst. to pres. Oakley Die and Mfg. Co., Cin.,1959-60, Electro-Jet Tool Co., Inc., Cin., 1959-60; pvt. practice acctg., No. Ky. and Cin., 1960-62; bus. mgr. St. Joseph Hosp., Lexington, Ky., 1962-66; asst. adminstr. fin. U. Ky. Hosp., Lexington, 1966-70; v.p., CFO St. Lawrence Hosp., Lansing, Mich., 1970-87; adj. faculty Aquinas Coll., Grand Rapids, Mich., 1980-89, asst. prof.; chmn. bd. McKenna & McKenna Assocs., Inc., 1983—; chmn. bd. North Grand River Coop. Laundry, 1986-87; v.p., CFO, asst. sec. and treas. St. Joseph's Hosp., Inc., Savannah, Ga., 1987-95, St. Joseph's Health Ctr., Inc., 1987-90, v.p. Midland Enterprises, Richmond Hill, Ga. Former mem. adv. com. to commr. of fin. State of Ky.; chmn. cath. divsn. Oak Hills Bus. Com.; mem. speakers com. Oak Hill Sch. Dist.; bd. dirs. Savannah YMCA, 1992-94, exec. com., 1994-96, YMCA Habersham Branch, 1992-96, chmn. bd. 1994-96. Served with U.S. Mcht. Marine, 1945-47, U.S. Army, 1948-51. Mem. Healthcare Fin. Mgmt. Assn. (Follmer award, past dir. Ky. chpt.), Am. Mgmt. Assn., Am. Inst. CPAs, Ky. Soc. CPAs, Mich. Hosp. Assn. (former mem. com. on reimbursement), Ga. Hosp. Assn. (com. on fin. and mgmt.), Delta Mu Delta, Alpha Sigma Lambda.

MCKENNA, SIDNEY F., technical company executive; b. Detroit, Nov. 27, 1922; s. Michael James and Elizabeth Josephine McK.; m. Helen Mary Spiroff, Sept. 20, 1944; children—Lynne Marie McKenna Hoss, Dennis Michael, Patrick Conlon, Mary Elizabeth McKenna Raimondi, Maureen T. McKenna Anderson, Christopher John. A.B., U. Mich., Ann Arbor, 1947; M.A., Wayne State U., 1948. With Ward Baking Co., Detroit, 1939-41; prodn. worker Cadillac Motor Co. (div. Gen. Motors Corp.), Detroit, 1941-42; mem. indsl. relations staff Ford Motor Co., Dearborn, Mich., 1942-79, v.p., 1974-79; sr. v.p. human resources United Techs. Corp., Hartford, Conn., 1980-86, sr. v.p. employee and external relations, 1986-87, sr. v.p. pub. affairs, 1987-90; ret., 1990; bd. dirs. Schwartz Value Fund. Adv. bd. Providence Hosp., Detroit, 1972-80; bd. dirs. Brighton (Mich.) Hosp., 1976-80, Mercy Coll., Detroit, 1976-80, United Found., 1976-80, St. Francis Hosp., Hartford, Conn., 1983-89, St. Joseph's Coll., 1988-89. Served with USN, 1942-46. Decorated knight St. Gregory. Mem. Labor Policy Assn. (chmn.), Bus. Roundtable, Orgn. Resources Counselors, Nat. Assn. Mfrs. (bd. dirs. 1988-89), Bloomfield Hills Country Club, Birmingham Athletic Club, Mariner Sands Golf Club, K.C. Roman Catholic. Home: 5680 SE Winged Foot Dr Stuart FL 34997-8642

MCKENNA, STEPHEN JAMES, lawyer, corporate executive; b. Islip, N.Y., Sept. 4, 1940; s. John Paul and Margaret (Foley) McK.; m. Lolita Andrea deLeon, Aug. 24, 1963; children: Stephen Jr., Christopher, Matthew, Andrew. BA magna cum laude, Boston Coll., Chestnut Hill, Mass., 1962; JD, Fordham U., 1965. Bar: N.Y. 1966. D.C. 1970, U.S. Supreme Ct. 1990. Atty. Pan Am. World Airlines, N.Y.C., 1965-67, Ea. Airlines, Washington, 1967-69, Lockheed Aircraft Corp., Washington, 1969-72; pvt. practice law Washington, 1972-73; v.p., assoc. gen. counsel Marriott Corp., Bethesda, Md., 1973-93; v.p., gen. counsel Host Marriott Corp., Bethesda, Md., 1993-95, exec. v.p., gen. counsel, 1995-97, of counsel, 1997—; continuing legal edn. panelist Georgetown U. Law Ctr. Founder, pres. Civic Assn. River Falls, Potomac, Md., 1976; committeeman troop 1427 Boy Scouts Am.,

Potomac, 1977-93; mem. fin. com. St. Bartholomew's Ch., Bethesda, 1979—, chmn. sch. bd., 1979; bd. trustees Marymount U., Arlington, Va., 1992—. Mem. ABA (panelist), Am. Coll. Real Estate Lawyers (panelist), D.C. Bar Assn., Assn. Bar City N.Y., N.Y. State Bar Assn. Democrat. Office: Host Marriott Corp 10400 Fernwood Rd Bethesda MD 20817-1109

MCKENNA, TERENCE PATRICK, insurance company executive; b. Oldham, Lancashire, Eng., Sept. 3, 1928; came to U.S., 1929, naturalized, 1939; s. Patrick A. and Mary F. McK.; m. Patricia Buckley, Sept. 22, 1973. Student, St. Thomas Coll., Bloomfield, Conn., 1946-48. With John Hancock Mut. Life Ins. Co., 1951-87; gen. agt. John Hancock Mut. Life Ins. Co., Cherry Hill, N.J., 1963-67; field v.p. gen. agy. dept. John Hancock Mut. Life Ins. Co., Atlanta, 1967-69; field v.p. dist. agy. dept. John Hancock Mut. Life Ins. Co., Boston, 1969-73, 2d v.p. mktg. ops. dept., 1973-74, v.p. dept., 1974-76, sr. v.p. dept., 1976-83, sr. v.p. gen. agy. sales dept., 1983-87; ret. 1987; v.p., also bd. dirs. John Hancock Variable Life Ins. Co.; chmn. bd. mgrs. I.V.A.; bd. dirs. John Hancock Distbrs. Inc., John Hancock Property and Casualty Ins. Co. Served with USMC, 1952-54. Mem. Am. Coll. Life Underwriters, Am. Soc. CLU's, Palm Beach Gardens, Ballen Isles C. C., Univ. Club (Boston), Woods Hole Golf Club (Falmouth, Mass.). Clubs: Univ. (Boston).

MCKENNA, THOMAS MORRISON, JR., social services organization executive; b. Chgo., July 19, 1937; s. Thomas Morrison and Martha (Stanley) McK.; m. Kay Mary O'Connor, Sept. 10, 1960; children: Mark, Lisa. BA, De Pauw U., 1959; MSW, Columbia U., 1961. Group worker Hamilton-Madison House, N.Y.C., 1961-63, exec. dir., 1967-71; assoc. exec. dir. Bronx (N.Y.) River Neighborhood House, 1963-67; exec. dir. United Neighborhood Houses, N.Y.C., 1971-76, State Communities Aid Assn., N.Y.C. and Albany, N.Y., 1976-85; nat. exec. dir. Big Bros./Big Sisters Am., Phila., 1985—; asst. prof. NYU Sch. Social Work, 1974-82; mem. bd. overseers U. Pa. Sch. Social Work, 1991—. Mem. bd. local sch. dist. 8, Bronx, 1964-67; coun. against poverty N.Y.C. Antipoverty Bd., 1971-76; adv. bd. Columbia U. Sch. Social Work, 1980-84; chmn. adv. bd. N.Y.C. Dept. Social Svcs., 1977-85. Mem. NASW (pres. N.Y.C. chpt. 1983-85), One to One Found. Avocations: sailing, tennis. Home: 1307 E Susquehanna Ave Philadelphia PA 19125-2823 Office: Big Bros/Big Sisters Am 230 N 13th St Philadelphia PA 19107-1538

MC KENNA, WILLIAM EDWARD, business executive; b. Boston, Aug. 9, 1919; s. Alfred W. and Mary E.C. (Quigley) McK.; children: William P., Kathleen M., Daniel J., Eileen F., Paul V., Mary Ellen; m. Mary N. Smith, Oct. 3, 1968. A.B., Holy Cross Coll., 1947; M.B.A., Harvard, 1949. Diplomate: C.P.A., N.Y., Calif. Staff accountant Touche, Niven, Bailey & Smart, N.Y.C., 1949-52; v.p., controller Monroe Calculating Machine Co., Orange, N.J., 1952-60; also dir.; v.p., treas., controller Litton Industries, Beverly Hills, Calif., 1960-63; sr. v.p. Litton Industries Bus. Equipment Group, Beverly Hills, 1964-67; also dir.; chmn., chief exec., dir. Hunt Foods & Industries, Inc., Fullerton, Calif., 1967-68; chmn., chief exec., dir. Norton Simon, Inc., Fullerton, 1968-69; bus. cons., 1969-70; chmn., dir. Technicolor, Inc., Hollywood, Calif., 1970-76; chmn. bd. Sambo's Restaurants, Inc., Santa Barbara, Calif., 1979-81, Vencap, Inc., Irvine, Calif., 1977-79; now gen. ptnr. MCK Investment Co., Beverly Hills, Calif.; bd. dirs. Calif. Amplifier, Inc., Safeguard Health Enterprises, Inc., Midway Games, Inc., WMS Industries, Inc., Drexler Tech., Inc.. Mem. pres.'s council, regent, assoc. trustee Coll. Holy Cross; trustee St. John's Hosp. Found.; regent St. Mary's Coll., Calif. Mem. Am. Inst. C.P.A.s, Nat. Assn. Accts., Fin. Execs. Inst., Calif. Soc. C.P.A.s, N.Y. Soc. C.P.A.s, N.J. Soc. C.P.A.s, Tailhook Assn., Delta Epsilon, Alpha Sigma Nu. Home and Office: 912 Oxford Way Beverly Hills CA 90210-2841

MCKENNA, WILLIAM JOHN, textile products executive; b. N.Y.C., Oct. 11, 1926; s. William T. and Florence (Valis) McK.; m. Jean T. McNulty, Aug. 27, 1949 (dec. Nov. 1984); children: Kevin, Marybeth, Peter, Dawn; m. Karen Lynne Hilgert, Aug. 6, 1988; children: Katherine Lynne, William John IV. BBA, Iona Coll., 1949; M.S. (Univ. Store Service scholar), NYU, 1950. V.p. Hat Corp. Am., N.Y.C., 1961-63, v.p. mktg., 1961-63, exec. v.p., 1963-67; pres. Manhattan Shirt Co., N.Y.C., 1967-74, Lee Co., Inc., Shawnee Mission, Kans., 1974-82, also dir.; pres., dir. Kellwood Co., St. Louis, 1982—, chief exec. officer, 1984—, also bd. dirs., chmn., CEO, 1991—; dir. Genovese Drug Stores, Melville, N.Y., United Mo. Bancshares, Kansas City, Mo., United Mo. Bank of St. Louis, Cardinal Ritter Inst. Trustee St. Louis U., Boys Hope; permanent deacon Archdiocese St. Louis. With USN, 1944-46, PTO. Mem. Sovereign Mil. Order Malta, St. Louis Club, Bellerive Country Club. Roman Catholic. Office: Kellwood Co PO Box 14374 Saint Louis MO 63178-4374

MCKENNA, WILLIAM MICHAEL, advertising executive; b. Washington, Apr. 4, 1951; s. William H. and Betty Ann (Cashin) McK.; m. Lynn Stevenson, Dec. 18, 1976; children: James Langdon, Lee Stevenson. BA, Wesleyan U., 1973; MS in Journalism, Boston U., 1978. V.p., creative dir. Ingalls Quinn & Johnson, Boston, 1981-88; sr. v.p., creative dir. Young & Rubicam, N.Y.C., 1988-94; chief creative officer, exec. v.p. AF GL Internat., 1994-95; mng. dir., chief creative officer Citigate Albert Frank, N.Y.C., 1996—. Recipient Clio, Hatch, N.Y. Film Soc. creative advt. awards, 1982-95. Home: 16 Salt Box Ln Darien CT 06820-5231 Office: Citigate Albert Frank 850 3rd Ave New York NY 10022-6222

MCKENNEE, ARDEN NORMA, art educator, retired, consultant; b. N.Y.C.; d. Archibald McKennee and Norma (Bischof) Kirkley. BA, U. Minn., 1953. Exec. sec. John & Mable Ringling Mus. of Art, Sarasota, Fla., 1964-79, mus. edn. programmer, 1980-94; ret., 1994. Mem. Very Spl. Arts Adv. Bd. for Sarasota County, 1988-94. Mem. Nat. Art Edn. Assn., Delta Gamma Alumni Assn.

MC KENNEY, WALTER GIBBS, JR., lawyer, publishing company executive; b. Jacobsville, Md., Apr. 22, 1913; s. Walter Gibbs and Mary (Starkey) McK.; m. Florence Roberta Rea, July 17, 1939. Student, Dickinson Sem., 1935-37; Ph.B. Dickinson Coll., 1939; J.D., U. Va., 1942; LL.D., Dickinson Sch. Law, 1964; LHD, Lycoming Coll., 1984. Bar: Md. 1942. Practiced in Balt., 1942—; partner McKenney, Thomsen & Burke; partner, gen. mgr., editor Taxes & Estates Pub. Co., Balt., 1946—; chmn. trust com. Equitable Bank, N.A., Balt., 1970-84; dir. Equitable Bancorp., 1960-84; lectr. Southwestern Grad. Sch. Banking, 1966-76. Editor Taxes and Estates, 1946—, Minimizing Taxes, 1946-84, The Educator, 1965—, The Patron, 1968-84. Pres. Kelso Home for Girls; mem. bd. child care Balt. Conf. Meth. Ch., pres., 1961-64; pres. Balt. Estate Planning Council, 1963-64; trustee Goucher Coll., 1968-84, Dickinson Coll., Lycoming Coll., Wesley Theol. Sem., Loyola Coll. at Balt., 1975-83, Franklin Sq. Hosp., Franklin Square Found., Franklin Square Health System, Helix Health System. Served to lt. USNR, 1942-45. Mem. ABA, Md., Balt. bar assns. Republican. Methodist. Home: 105 Brightwood Club Dr Lutherville MD 21093

MCKENNON, KEITH ROBERT, chemical company executive; b. Condon, Oreg., Dec. 25, 1933; s. Russel M. and Lois E. (Edgerton) McK.; m. Patricia Dragon, Sept. 30, 1961; children: Brian, Marc, Kevin. B.S., Oreg. State U., 1955. Rsch. chemist Dow Chem. Co., Pittsburg, Calif., 1955-67; sales mgr. Dow Chem. Co., Houston, 1967; research mgr. Dow Chem. Co., Midland, Mich., 1968-69, bus. mgr., 1969-80, v.p., 1980-83, group v.p., 1983-87, exec. v.p., 1987-92, also bd. dirs.; pres. Dow USA, 1987-90; chmn., chief exec. officer Dow Corning Corp., 1992-94, also bd. dirs.; chmn. PacifiCorp, Portland, Oreg., 1994—; bd. dirs. PacifiCorp, Tektronix. Patentee. Recipient Chemical Industry medal Soc. of Chemical Industry, 1994. Republican. Presbyterian. Home: 6079 N Paradise View Dr Paradise Valley AZ 85253 Office: Pacific Corp 700 NE Multnomah St Ste 1600 Portland OR 97232-4194

MCKENNON, RICHARD OTEY, lawyer; b. Wichita Falls, Tex., Apr. 30, 1964; s. Richard Ernest and Linda Sue (Wallace) McK.; m. Kayla L. McKennon; children: Matthew Richard, Meagan Kelley. BA, North Tex. State U., 1985; JD, Tex. Tech U., 1987. Bar: Tex. 1988, U.S. Dist. Ct. (no. dist.) Tex. 1988, U.S. Dist. Ct. (ea. dist.) Tex. 1990, U.S. Supreme Ct. 1994; cert. in personal injury trial law Tex. Bd. Legal Specialization. Assoc. McGuire & Levy, Irving, Tex., 1987-89, Stradley, Schmidt & Wright, Dallas, 1989-92; ptnr. Royse & McKennon, Dallas, 1992-95, Richard O. McKennon, P.C., Dallas, 1995—; instr. civil litigation paralegal program Tex. Wesleyan U. Sch. Law, 1993; presenter in field. Mem. ATLA, Tex. Trial Lawyers Assn., Dallas Bar Assn. Avocations: martial arts, writing fiction and nonfiction. Office: Ste 1030 Abrams Ctr 9330 LBJ Fwy Dallas TX 75243

MCKENNY, COLLIN GRAD, banker; b. Seattle, July 29, 1944; d. Edward Paul and Betty B. (Collins) Grad; m. Jon W. McKenny, June 15, 1975 (div. June 1982); m. Spencer Frank Ison, Dec. 31, 1985. BA, U. Wash., Seattle, 1966; MBA, Seattle U., 1969; grad., Pacific Coast Banking Sch., 1979. From mgmt. trainee to v.p. Peoples Nat. Bank, Seattle, 1966-85; sr. v.p. Barclays Bank of Calif., San Francisco, 1985-88, Star Banc Corp., Cin., 1988-97; mng. dir. Romalazi Resort (Fiji) Ltd., 1997—. Treas. Salvation Army, Federal Way, Wash., 1981-83; bd. dirs. Boys and Girls Clubs, Seattle, 1982-85; mem. risk adv. bds. Visa USA and Visa Internat. Mem. Am. Bankers Assn. (bd. dirs. bancard exec. com., chmn. ann. conf. 1989—, chmn. bankcard schools 1990-94), Cin. Bus. Incubator (chmn.), Bankers Club, Chi Omega. Office: Star Banc Corp 311 Elm St PO Box 956 Cincinnati OH 45201-0956

MCKENZIE, ANDRÉ, academic administrator, educator; b. Chgo., May 4, 1955; s. Alberta Chisholm. BS, Ill. State U., 1977, MS, 1979; MEd, Columbia U., 1985, EdD, 1986. Assoc. residence hall dir. No. Ill. U., DeKalb, 1979-82; asst. dir. student activities Northeastern Ill. U., Chgo., 1982-84; assoc. dean of students St. John's U., Jamaica, N.Y., 1986-89, dir. opportunity programs, 1989-91, asst. v.p., 1991-93; acting dean St. Vincent's Coll., 1993-94, assoc. v.p., 1994—, adj. asst. prof. Sch. Edn.; tng. specialist Anti-Defamation League, N.Y.C., 1989—; cons. coll. Greek letter orgns., 1988—; mem. N.Y State policy bd. Higher Edn. Opportunity Program, 1990-92, v.p., 1992—; facilitator leadership skills workshops, 1986—. Contbr. articles to profl. jours. Mem. N.Y. Urban League, N.Y.C., 1994—, 100 Black Men, N.Y.C. Edn. Policy fellow Inst. for Ednl. Leadership, 1990-91. Mem. Assn. for Humanistic Edn. and Devel. (pres. area II 1992—), Nat. Assn. Student Pers. Adminstrs. (mem. adv. bd. region II 1988-91), Am. Coll. Pers. Assn., Nat. Coun. African-Am. Men, Alpha Phi Alpha (Bro. of Yr. Eta Tau chpt. 1976). Avocations: racquetball, drawing, reading. Office: St Johns U Newman Hall 149 Jamaica NY 11439

MCKENZIE, CLIF ALLEN, Indian tribe official, accountant; b. Lawton, Okla., Sept. 29, 1942; s. Robert Allen and Rubie (Paukei) Williams; m. Michele Ann Martin, Aug. 4, 1972; children: Kasey Roberta, Kristen Marti. BS in Acctg., U. Okla., 1965; MBA, Pa. State U., 1976. Fin. analyst United Tribes of Okla., Shawnee, 1973-75; credit officer Bur. Indian Affairs, Dept. Interior, Horton, Kans., 1975-77, liaison officer, Syracuse, N.Y., 1977-80, program analyst, Denver, 1980-81; tribal adminstr. Kiowa Tribe of Okla., Carnegie, 1981-82; CEO tribal bus. mgr. Cheyenne and Arapaho Tribe of Okla., Concho, 1982-84; pres. Indian Devel. Corp., Oklahoma City, 1973—; contracting officer Bur. Indian Affairs, Anadarko, Okla., 1984-89, agy. ops. officer, Concho, Okla.; contract specialist, Gen. Svc. Adminstr., Ft. Worth, 1989-92, Dept. Health Human Svc., Pub. Health Svc., supervisory contract specialist, Oklahoma City, 1992-94; asset mgr. HUD Loan Mgmt. Br., Oklahoma City, 1994—. police commr. City of Horton, 1976-77, city commr., 1976-77; dir. LECO, Inc., Tulsa. Recipient H.M. Hefner First Amendment award Playboy Found., 1985, Nat. Notary Pub. of the Yr. award Nat. Notary Assn., 1996. Life mem. DAV, U. Okla. Alumni Assn.; mem. Kiowa Black Legging Soc., Nat. Assn. Accts., Am. Soc. Notaries (dir. govt. affairs 1975-80), Nat. Taxpayers Investigative Fund (Whistleblower award 1982). Republican. Served to capt. U.S. Army, 1959-68. Lodges: Elks, Moose. Home: 3708 Epperly Dr Del City OK 73115-3610 Office: Indian Devel Corp PO Box 15613 Oklahoma City OK 73155-5613 also: HUD 500 W Main Oklahoma City OK 73102

MC KENZIE, HAROLD CANTRELL, JR., retired manufacturing executive; b. Carrollton, Ga., Dec. 25, 1931; s. Harold Cantrell and Sue (Tanner) McK.; m. Katherine Branch, Apr. 11, 1958; children—Ansley, Katherine, Harold Cantrell, III. B.Indsl. Engring., Ga. Inst. Tech., 1953; J.D., Emory U., 1955; A.M.P., Harvard Bus. Sch. Bar: Ga. 1955. Law clk. to judge U.S. Dist. Ct., Atlanta, 1956; ptnr. firm Troutman, Sams, Schroder & Lockerman, Atlanta, 1957-67; with Ga. Power Co., 1967-81; dir. Intermet Corp., 1971—; pres. So. Electric Internat., Inc., 1981-85; chmn., chief exec. officer Machine Techs., Inc. (doing bus. as MacTech Inc.), Martinsville, Va., 1986-89; sr. advc. facilities Atlanta Project of Carter Presdl. Ctr., 1992-96. Mem. State Bar Ga., Capital City (Atlanta), Piedmont Driving Club. Episcopalian. Office: 172 Huntington Rd NE Atlanta GA 30309-1504

MCKENZIE, HARRY JAMES, surgeon, surgical researcher; b. Meyersdale, Pa., Aug. 7, 1960; s. Henry Sadrus and Betty Elaine (Reiber) McK.; m. Judith Palmieri, July 6, 1985; 1 child, Henry James. BS, Duquesne U., 1984; postgraduate, U. Pitts., 1986-87; MD, Hahnemann U., 1992. Surg. intern Temple U., Conemaugh Med. Ctr., Johnstown, Pa., 1992-93, surg. resident, 1993-97; mem. problem task force Conemaugh Med. Ctr., 1992-93. Contbr. articles to profl. jours.; presenter in field. Hosp. vol. Ctrl. Med. Pavilion, Pitts., 1981-84, Presbyn. Hosp., Pitts., 1986-87; med. exam. officer, Phila. Special Olympics, 1989-90; grad. banquet spkr. Salisbury (Pa.) H.S., 1993.. Recipient 3d place rsch. competition award, ACS Region III com. on trauma, Norfolk, Va., 1993; recipient 1st place rsch. competition award ACS-Pa. com. on trauma, Hershey, 1993. Mem. ACS, AMA, Am. Soc. Gen. Surgeons, Pa. Med. Soc., Cambria County Med. Soc. Avocations: skiing, golfing, jogging, fishing, hiking. Home: 111 Curtis Dr Johnstown PA 15904

MCKENZIE, HERBERT A(LONZA), pharmaceutical company executive; b. Savannah, Ga., Dec. 23, 1934; s. Herbert A. and Marie L. (Lytjen) McK.; m. Joan B. Baggs, Dec. 17, 1959; children: Catherine B. McKenzie Bowman, Gregory M., Susan M. McKenzie Carson. BS, Clemson U., 1956; grad. exec. program, Stanford U., 1986. Sales mgmt. positions Am. Cyanamid, Wayne, N.J., 1956-71, mktg. mgr., 1971-73, gen. mgr., 1973-80; pres. Hilton Davis Chem. Co. div. Sterling Drug, Inc.; corp. v.p. Sterling Drug, Inc., 1980-81; pres. Sterling Chem. Group, 1982-85, Sterling Japan, Can., Australasia and Pacific Rim Group, Sterling Chem. Group, 1985-88, Sterling Internat.; corp. v.p. Sterling Drug, Inc. subs. Eastman Kodak, 1988-90, corp. exec. v.p.; pres. Sterling Consumer Health Group, N.Y.C., 1991-92; ret., 1992; advisor Synthetic Organic Chem. Mfrs. Assn., 1976-78, Industry Sector. Adv. Com., 1977-80, Office Spl. Trade Negotiations, Dept. Commerce, 1977-80, Romanoff Internat., Inc., Charlotte, N.C., 1990-91. Patentee in field. Bd. dirs. Coop. Ireland, 1988-92, Coun. Better Bus. Bur., 1991-92. With USN, 1959. Mem. Dry Colors Mfg. (pres. 1976-78).

MC KENZIE, JOHN MAXWELL, physician; b. Glasgow, Scotland, Nov. 13, 1927; came to U.S., 1980; s. Thomas Wilson and Isabell Connor (Spencer) McK.; m. Vieno Laine Kangas, June 29, 1957; children—Ann, Ian, Lesley, Gordon. M.B., Ch.B., U. St. Andrews, Scotland, 1950, M.D., 1958. Intern U. St. Andrews, 1950-51, resident, 1953-55, fellow, 1955-56, 57-58; research trainee, fellow Tufts U., 1956-57, 58-59; clin. asst. medicine McGill U., Montreal, Que., Can., 1959-61; asst., then assoc. prof. McGill U., 1961-68, prof., 1968-80; prof. U. Miami, 1980—, chmn. dept. medicine, 1980-94. Contbr. numerous articles to profl. jours. Served with Royal Army Med. Corps, 1951-53. Recipient Killam award Can. Coun., 1980. Mem. Am. Thyroid Assn. (Parke-Davis disting. lectr. 1981, pres. 1983-84), Am. Soc. Clin. Investigation, Endocrine Soc. (Ayerst award 1961, Rorer Pharm. Clin. Investigator award 1990), Am. Physiol. Soc., Assn. Am. Physicians, Am. Fedn. Clin. Rsch., AAAS, Internat. Soc. Neuroendocrinology, European Thyroid Assn. (corr.). Home: 12505 SW 63rd Ave Miami FL 33156-5531 Office: U Miami Jackson Meml Med Ctr 1611 NW 12th Ave Miami FL 33136-1005

MCKENZIE, KAY BRANCH, public relations executive; b. Atlanta, Feb. 12, 1936; d. William Harllee and Katherine (Hunter) Branch; m. Harold Cantrell McKenzie, Jr., Apr. 11, 1958; children: Ansley, Katherine, Harold Cantrell III. Student, Sweet Briar Coll., 1955, Emory U., 1956-57. Account exec. Hill and Knowlton Inc., Atlanta, 1979-80, account supr./dir. S.E. govt. rels., 1981-83; ptnr. McKenzie, Gordon & Potter, Atlanta, 1983-85; pres. McKenzie & Assocs. Inc., Atlanta, 1986-89; sr. v.p. Manning Selvage & Lee, Atlanta, 1989-93; v.p. comm. and creative svcs. 1996 Atlanta Paralympic Games, 1993-96. Mem. Commn. on Future of South, 1974; co-chmn. John Lewis for Congress, Atlanta, 1986; bd. dirs. Bedford Pines Day Care Ctrs., Atlanta, 1987-92, Ga. Clean and Beautiful, 1987-88, Ga. Fund for Edn., 1987-92; regional bd. dirs. Inst. Internat. Edn., 1987-93. Fellow Internat. Bus. Fellows (bd. dirs. 1983-85, 92-93, v.p. 1986-88); mem. Pub. Rels. Soc. Am., Ga. C. of C. (bd. dirs. 1983-97), Leadership Atlanta, Ga. Internat. Horse Park Found. (bd. dirs. 1993-97). Democrat. Episcopalian. Home: 172 Huntington Rd NE Atlanta GA 30309-1504

MCKENZIE, KEVIN PATRICK, artistic director; b. Burlington, Vt., Apr. 29, 1954; s. Raymond James and Ruth (Davison) McK. Grad. high sch., Washington. Mem. corps de ballet Nat. Ballet of Washington, 1972-74; prin. Joffrey Ballet, N.Y.C., 1974-78, Am. Ballet Theatre, N.Y.C., 1979-91; artistic assoc. Washington Ballet, 1991-92; artistic dir. Am. Ballet Theatre, N.Y.C., 1992—; pres. bd. dirs. Am. Ballet Theatre Dancers Fund, Inc., 1982-89; assoc. dir. New Amsterdam Ballet, N.Y.C., 1984—. Appeared in film Unicorn, Gorgon and Monticore, Sta. WETA-TV, Washington, 1971; guest dancer Houston Ballet, 1978, Spoleto Festival, 1980, 84, Theatre des Champs Elysees, Paris, 1981, Sadler's Wells Theatre, London, 1981, Asami Maki Ballet Co., Tokyo, 1983, Aspen Festival, 1982; producer, dir. The Party of the Year, 1982; choreographer Groupo Zambaria Ballet, 1984, Liszt Etudes, 1991, Lucy and the Count, 1992, The Nutcracker, 1993; created roles in Adrienne Dellos' The Blind Man's Daughter, Seoul, Korea, 1986, Amnon V'Tamar, S.P.E.B.S.Q.S.A.; appeared with Martine Van Hamel in Swan Lake, Nat. Ballet of Cuba, Havanna, 1986, Merrill Ashley in Tchaikowsky Pas de Deux, Bolshoi Theater, Moscow, 1986; repertoire as dancer includes La Bayadere, Carmen, Cinderella, Coppelia, Dim Lustre, Don Quixote, Giselle, The Garden of Villandry, Jardin aux lilas, The Leaves Are Fading, Pillar of Fire, Raymonda, Requiem, Rodeo, Romeo and Juliet, The Sleeping Beauty, Swan Lake, La Sylphide; other dances include Paquita, Sylvia Pas de Deux, Theme and Variations. Recipient Silver medal Varna (Bulgaria) Internat. Ballet Competitions, 1972, Artistic Achievement medal Dept. State, U.S. Govt., 1972, Artistic Achievement medal Mayor of Burlington, Vt., 1984, Performing Arts award, Am. Ireland Fund, 1994; Kevin McKenzie Day proclaimed by City of Burlington, 1985. Office: Am Ballet Theatre 890 Broadway New York NY 10003-1211*

MC KENZIE, LIONEL WILFRED, economist, educator; b. Montezuma, Ga., Jan. 26, 1919; s. Lionel Wilfred and Lida (Rushin) McK.; m. Blanche Veron, Jan. 2, 1943; children—Lionel Wilfred (dec.), Gwendolyn Veron, David Rushin. AB, Duke U., 1939; MA, Princeton U., 1946, PhD, 1956; BLitt, Oxford (Eng.) U., 1949; postgrad., U. Chgo., 1950-51, LLD (hon.), 1991. Asst. economist WPB, 1942; instr. Mass. Inst. Tech., 1946; asst. prof., then asso. prof. Duke, 1948-57; prof. econs. U. Rochester, 1957-64, John Munro prof. econs., 1964-67, Wilson prof. econs., 1967-89, Wilson prof. emeritus, 1989—, chmn. dept., 1957-66; Taussig research prof. Harvard U., 1980-81; Mem. math. div. NRC, 1960-63, mem. behavioral scis. div., 1964-70; mem. math., social scis. bd. Center Advanced Study in Behavioral Scis., Palo Alto, Calif., 1964-70, chmn., 1969-70. Assoc. editor Internat. Econs. Rev., 1964-96, Jour. Econ. Theory, 1970-73, Jour. Internat. Econs., 1970-84, Econ. Theory, 1991-95; contbr. articles to profl. jours. Served to lt. (s.g.) USNR, 1943-45. Recipient Rising Sun award Japan, 1995; Rhodes scholar Oriel Coll. Oxford U., 1939; Guggenheim fellow, 1973-74; fellow Center for Advanced Study in Behavioral Scis., 1973-74. Fellow Econometric Soc. (coun. 1973-78, pres. 1977), Am. Acad. Arts and Scis., Am. Econ. Assn.; mem. NAS, Royal Econ. Soc., Am. Math. Soc., Am. Econ. Assn. (Disting. Fellow 1993), Phi Beta Kappa (chpt. v.p. 1968-70, chpt. pres. 1972-73). Home: 225 Dorchester Rd Rochester NY 14610-1322

MCKENZIE, MARY BETH, artist; b. Cleve.; d. William Jennings and Mary Elizabeth (McCray) McK.; m. Tony Mysak, May 8, 1974; children: Zsuzsa McKenzie Mysak, Maria McKenzie Mysak. Student, Mus. Fine Arts, Boston, 1964-65, Cooper Sch. Art, Cleve., 1965-67; diploma, Nat. Acad. Design, N.Y.C., 1974. Painting instr. Nat. Acad. Design, N.Y.C., 1981—, Art Students League, 1995—; represented by Ice Collection Gallery. Author: A Painterly Approach, 1987; contbr. articles to profl. jours.; one-women shows include Nat. Arts Club, N.Y.C., 1976, FAR Gallery, N.Y.C., 1980, Perin and Sharpe Gallery, New Canaan, Conn., 1981, Frank Caro Gallery, N.Y.C., 1988-89, Joseph Keiffer Gallery, N.Y.C., 1991; exhibited in group shows at Sindin Gallery, N.Y.C., 1985-86, Ice Collection, N.Y.C., 1995-96; permanent collections include Met. Mus. Art., N.Y.C., The Butler Mus. Am. Art, Mus. City of N.Y., NAD, Art Student's League of N.Y. Recipient Nat. Scholastic award Mus. Fine Arts, Boston, numerous awards including Thomas B. Clark prize and the Isaac N. Maynard prize Nat. Acad. Design, Greenshields Found. grantee, Stacey Found. grantee. Mem. Nat. Acad. Design, Pastel Soc. Am. (Best In Show, Award of Exceptional Merit, Exhbn. Com. award), Allied Artists Am. (Gold medal, The Jane Peterson award, Grumbacher Cash award, Silver medal), Audubon Artists (Pastel Soc. Am. award). Home: 525 W 45th St New York NY 10036-3405

MCKENZIE, MICHAEL K., wholesale executive. Past pres., CEO G.S.C. Enterprises, Inc., Sulphur Springs, Tex., now chmn. bd., CEO, also bd. dirs. Office: GSC Enterprises Inc 130 Hillcrest Dr Sulphur Springs TX 75482*

MC KENZIE, RAY, anesthesiologist, educator; b. Turua, N.Z., July 9, 1927; s. Robert Keith and Edith Harfield (Collingwood) McK.; m. Barbara Mavis Snelling, Dec. 11, 1954; children: Robyn Kay, William Brett, Melvern Craig, Glenn Carrick. Student, Hauraki Plains Coll., 1939-45; M.B. Ch.B., U. Otago, 1952. Intern Auckland (N.Z.) Hosp., 1953, resident, 1954-56, cons. anesthetist, 1961-66; dir. anesthesia Mowasat Hosp., Kuwait, 1967-69; asst. prof. U. Pitts., 1969-71, assoc. prof., 1971-77, prof., 1977—; dir. surg. anesthesia Magee-Women's Hosp., Pitts., 1971-73, chief anesthesia, 1973-92, prof. rsch., 1992—. Mem. Bro.'s Bro. Found., 1971—. Served with Royal N.Z. Air Force, 1957-59. Fellow Faculty Anesthetists Royal Coll. Surgeons (Eng.); mem. Internat. Rsch. Soc., Am., Pa., Western Pa. socs. anesthesiologists. Home: 325 Richland Ln Pittsburgh PA 15208-2730 Office: Magee Women's Hosp Halket and Forbes St Pittsburgh PA 15213 *There is no electric elevator to success. Step up the stairs. Don't stare up the steps.*

MCKENZIE, ROBERT E., lawyer; b. Cheboygan, Mich., Dec. 7, 1947; s. Alexander Orlando and Edna Jean (Burt) McK.; m. Theresia Wolf, Apr. 26, 1975; 1 child, Robert A. BA in Personnel Adminstrn., Mich. State U., 1970; JD with high honors, Ill. Inst. Tech., 1979. Bar: Ill. 1979, U.S. Dist. Ct. (no. dist.) Ill. 1979, U.S. Tax Ct. 1979, U.S. Ct. Appeals (7th cir.) 1979, U.S. Supreme Ct. 1984; lic. pvt. pilot. Revenue officer IRS, Chgo., 1972-78; ptnr. McKenzie & McKenzie, Chgo., 1979—; lectr. Tax Seminars Inst., Chgo., 1984—. Author: Representation Before the Collection Divison of the IRS, 1989; co-author: Representing the Audited Taxpayer Before the IRS, 1990; contbr. articles to profl. jours. Mem. vocat. adv. bd. Ridgewood High, Norridge, Ill., 1981-86; Lake Briarwood Bd. dirs., Arlington Heights, 1985-86; coordinator John Anderson for Pres., 1980; del. Rep. Nat. Conv., Detroit, 1980, Ill. State Rep. Conv., Peoria, 1980. Served with U.S. Army, 1970. Recipient scholarship Mich. State U., 1966-70, State of Mich., 1966-70, Silas Strawn scholarship ITT, 1977. Mem. ABA (tax sect., co-chmn. bankruptcy task force, chmn. employment tax com. 1992-94), Chgo. Bar Assn. (chmn. com. devel. tax com. 1996-97), N.W. Suburban Bar Assn. (chmn. econs. of law com. 1986-87), Fed. Bar Assn. (tax com.), Rotary (pres. Norridge club 1985-86). Avocation: flying, genealogy. Office: 5450 N Cumberland Ave Chicago IL 60656-1484

MCKENZIE, THOMAS JAMES, lawyer, insurance consultant; b. Hastings, Nebr., May 7, 1930; s. Martin O. and Mary Ella (Graves) McK.; m. Harriet J. Beck, Nov. 10, 1951; children: Bruce, Craig, Scot, Mark. BA, State U. Iowa, 1955, JD, 1958. Bar: Iowa 1958, Ind. 1967, Pa. 1972, U.S. Dist. Ct. (we. dist.) Pa. 1993; CPCU. Atty. Benke & McKenzie, Parkersburg, Iowa, 1958; adjuster State Farm Ins., Dubuque, Iowa, 1958-64; claim and litig. mgr. State Auto Ins., Indpls., 1964-71; ins., claim and litig. mgr. Motor Freight Express, York, Pa., 1971-83; v.p. claims-litig. Mut. Benefit Ins., Huntingdon, Pa., 1983-92; ins. litigator Murphy, Taylor, P.C., Pitts., 1992—; seminar speaker in field. Served to staff sgt. USAF, 1951-53. Mem. ABA, Pa. Bar Assn., Masons, Shriners, Phi Alpha Delta. Home: 2802 Glenmore Ave Pittsburgh PA 15216-2124 Office: Murphy Taylor PC 326 3rd Ave Pittsburgh PA 15222-1911

MCKEON, HOWARD P. (BUCK MCKEON), congressman, former mayor; b. Los Angeles; m. Patricia; 6 children. BS, Brigham Young U. Mem. Coun. City of Santa Clarita, Calif., 1987-92, mayor, 1987-88; mem. 103rd-105th Congresses from 25th Calif. dist., 1993—; founding dir., chmn. Valencia Nat. Bank; co-owner Howard & Phil's Western Wear, Inc. Hon. chmn. Leukemia Soc. Celebrity program, 1990, Red Cross Community Support Campaign, 1992; active Dist. Com. Boy Scouts Am.; chmn., trustee

William S. Hart Sch. dist., 1979-87; chmn., dir. Henry Mayo Newhall Meml. Hosp., 1983-88; mem. Calif. Rep. State Ctrl. Com., 1988-92; bd. dirs. Santa Clarita Valley Sml. Bus. Devel. Ctr., 1990-92, Canyon Country C. of C., 1988-92. Office: US Ho of Reps 307 Cannon Ho Ofc Bldg Washington DC 20515

MCKEOUGH, WILLIAM DARCY, investment company executive; b. Chatham, Ont., Can., Jan. 31, 1933; s. George Grant and Florence Sewell (Woodward) McK.; m. Margaret Joyce Walker, June 18, 1965; children: Walker Stewart, James Grant. BA, U. Western Ont., 1954; LLD (hon.), Wilfred Laurier U., 1980, LL.D. (hon.), 1980. Chmn. McKeough Sons Co., Ltd., McKeough Investments Ltd. C.P.L.; bd. dirs. Beatrice Foods Inc., Can. Imperial Bank Commerce, Can. Gen. Tower Ltd., Global Stone Corp., Intertan Inc., Numac Energy Ltd., Noranda Mines Ltds., St. Mary's Cement Ltd., Zalev Metals Inc. Former mem. exec. com. Anglican Diocese of Huron; former mem. Gen. Synod, Anglican Ch., Can.; mem. Chatham City Council, 1960-63; also mem. Planning Bd. and Lower Thames Valley Conservation Authority; former mem. Chatham-Kent adv. bd. Can. Nat. Inst. of the Blind; former bd. dirs. Chatham YMCA, Chatham Little Theatre; former chmn. and pres. bd. govs. pres. Ridley Coll.; former bd. govs. Stratford Shakespearian Festival, Wilfrid Laurier U.; former mem. Can. group Trilateral Commn.; mem. Ont. Legislature, 1963-78, minister without portfolio, 1966, minister mcpl. affairs, 1967; treas. and minister of econs., also chmn. Treasury Bd., 1971-72, minister mcpl. affairs, 1972, treas. and minister of econs. and intergovtl. affairs, 1972, parliamentary asst. to premier Ont., 1973, minister of energy, 1973-75, treas. and minister econs. and intergovtl. affairs, 1975-78. Decorated officer of Order of Can. Home and Office: PO Box 940, Chatham, ON Canada N7M 5L3

MCKEOWN, JAMES CHARLES, accounting educator, consultant; b. Cleve., Nov. 3, 1945; s. Charles Joseph and Dara Ferrol (Prew) McK.; m. Mary Alinda Park, Jan. 2, 1965 (div. May 1980); children—Jeffrey Charles, Pamela Lynn; m. 2d, Nancy Ann Stratton, Jan. 3, 1981. B.S. in Math. with high honors, Mich. State U., 1966, Ph.D. in Bus. Adminstrn., 1969. Asst. prof. accountancy U. Ill., Urbana-Champaign, 1968-73, assoc. prof., 1973-76, prof., 1976-80, Weldon Powell prof. accountancy, 1980-83, A.C. Littleton prof. accountancy, 1983-89; disting. prof. acctg. Pa. State U., University Park, 1989-92, Ernst & Young prof. acctg., 1992—; cons. research, computers; expert witness. Editor: Inflation and Current Value Accounting, 1979; author computer-delivered acctg. course PLATO for Elementary Accounting, 1978; contbr. numerous articles to acad. jours. Recipient Instructional award U. Ill., Urbana-Champaign, 1970, Weldon Powell award, 1973; Fred Roedgers Research award U. Ill., 1978; Ford Found. fellow, 1967-68. Mem. Am. Acctg. Assn. (Manuscript award 1970), Am. Statis. Assn., Decision Scis. Inst., Inst. Mgmt. Accts. Republican. Office: Pa State U 210 Beam Bus Adminstrn Bldg University Park PA 16802

MCKEOWN, REBECCA J., principal; b. Wayne, Okla., Apr. 4, 1937; d. William S. and Ila Rebekah (Mitchell) Lackey; m. Loren Ferris, Apr. 5, 1958; children: Michael, Thomas, Nancy, David. BS, Okla. State U., 1966; MEd, U. Okla., 1976. Cert. elem. tchr., elem. prin. 6th grade tchr. Ponca City (Okla.) Pub. Schs., 1966-67; 1st and 6th grade tchr. Peru Elem. Sch., Auburn, Nebr., 1967-69; 4th grade tchr. Woodland Hills Sch., Lawton, Okla., 1971-76; asst. prin. Douglass Learning Ctr., Lawton, Okla., 1976-78; prin. Lincoln Elem. Sch., Lawton, Okla., 1978-84, Hugh Bish Elem., Lawton, Okla., 1984—. Recipient Disting. Achievement award Lawton Bd. Edn., 1992, Adminstr. of Yr. award Lawton Area Reading Coun., 1993, Arts Adminstr. of Yr. award Okla. Alliance for Arts, 1993, Nat. Blue Ribbon Sch. Recognition award 1993-94, D.A.R.E. Adminstrn. award Lawton Police Dept., 1993. Mem. ASCD, Okla. Reading Coun., Okla. ASCD, Lawton Area Reading Coun., Elem. Prins. Assn. (pres. 1986-87). Democrat. Methodist. Avocations: reading, walking, music, cooking. Home: 6 SW 71st St Lawton OK 73505-6615 Office: Lawton Pub Schs 751 NW Fort Sill Blvd Lawton OK 73507-5421

MCKEOWN, WILLIAM PHILIP, judge; b. Quebec City, Que., Can., Oct. 3, 1936; s. William and Doris McKeown; m. Elizabeth McKeown; 4 children. B Comm., McGill U., Montreal, Que., 1956; LLB, U. Toronto, 1959. Queen's counsel Ont. 1983. Counsel Dept. Health, Province Ont., Toronto, 1962-63, McMillan Binch, Toronto, 1963-64, Can. GE, Toronto, 1965-74; dep. dir. investigation and rsch. Bur. Competition Policy, Ottawa, Ont., 1974-77; ptnr. Stephens French McKeown, Toronto, 1977-86; judge Supreme Ct. Ont., Toronto, 1986-90, Gen. Divsn., Ont. Ct. Justice, Toronto, 1990-93, Trial Divsn., Fed. Ct. Can., Ottawa, 1993—; judge, chmn. Competition Tribunal, Ottawa. Mem. Can. Bar Assn., Toronto Lawyers' Club. Office: Fed Ct Can, Trial Divsn, Ottawa, ON Canada K1A 0H9

MC KEOWN, WILLIAM TAYLOR, magazine editor, author; b. Ft. Collins, Colo., July 4, 1921; s. Stuart Ellison and Eunice Harris (Akin) Mc K.; m. Lorraine Laredo; children: Elizabeth Ellison, Katherine, Suzanne. AB, Bowdoin Coll., 1942; student, Columbia U. Grad. Sch., 1948. Editor Fawcett Library Series, 1953-56; founding editor True's Boating Yearbook, 1955-56; founding editor Popular Boating mag., 1956, editor-in-chief, 1956-62; CEO The Mc Keown Co., N.Y.C., 1993—; editl. dir. Computer Travel Info., 1994—; travel editor Davis Publs.; outdoor/boating/travel editor Popular Mechanics, 1971-82; sr. editor Outdoor Life, 1983-93. Author weekly NEA syndicated newspaper column American Afloat, 1959-65; contbr. fiction, non-fiction to nat. mags., 1947—; author: Boating Handbook, 1956, Boating in America, 1960. Pilot USAAF, WW II, ETO. Mem. Am. Power Boat Assn., U.S. Power Squadrons, 357 FIghter Group Assn., N.Y. Yacht Club, Overseas Press Club, Royal Danish Yacht Club (Copenhagen), Turtles Internat. Avocation: international competitor in power and sail racing events. Office: The Mc Keown Co 420 Lexington Ave New York NY 10170-0002

MCKERNS, CHARLES JOSEPH, lawyer; b. Shenandoah, Pa., July 17, 1935; s. Charles Francis and Bridgett Ann (Barrett) McK.; m. Helen Patricia Nott, Feb. 13, 1960; children: Charles J. Jr., Michael H., Patricia B. BS, Georgetown U., 1957, JD, 1960. Bar: D.C. 1960, U.S. Ct. Appeals (D.C. cir.) 1961, U.S. Supreme Ct. 1971, Va. 1992. Law clk. to assoc. judge U.S. Ct. Appeals (D.C. cir), Washington, 1960-61; assoc. Dow, Lohnes & Albertson, Washington, 1961-65, ptnr., 1965-91, of counsel, 1991-95; ptnr. McKerns and McKerns, Heathsville, Va., 1991-96; of counsel McKerns and McKerns, Heathsville, 1996—; bd. dirs. Palmer Communications Inc. 1st lt. U.S. Army, 1957-59. Mem. ABA, University Club (Washington), Belle Haven Country Club (Alexandria, Va.), Indian Creek Yacht and Country Club (Kilmarnock, Va.). Republican. Roman Catholic. Avocations: reading, swimming. Home: Windy Blue PO Box 248 Ophelia VA 22530 Office: McKerns & McKerns PO Box 188 McKerns Bldg Heathsville VA 22473-0188 also: Dow Lohnes & Albertson 1255 23rd St NW Washington DC 20037-1125

MCKERROW, AMANDA, ballet dancer; b. Albuquerque; d. Alan and Constance McKerrow; m. John Gardner. Student, Met. Acad. Ballet, Bethesda, Md., Washington Sch. Ballet. With Washington Ballet Co., 1980-82; with Am. Ballet Theatre, N.Y.C., 1982—, soloist, from 1983, prin. dancer, 1987—. Toured Europe with Washington Ballet; danced in Margot Fonteyn Gala at Metropolitan Opera House; featured in Pavlova Tribute film, also many guest appearances; leading roles in Ballet Imperial, La Bayadere, Manon, Birthday Offering, Dim Lustre, Donizetti Variations, Giselle, Graduation Ball, The Leaves Are Fading, Nine Sinatra Songs, The Nutcracker, Pillar of Fire, Requiem, Romeo and Juliet, The Sleeping Beauty, Les Sylphides, Push Comes to Shove, Symphony Concertante, Symphonic Variations, Theme and Variations, Stravinsky Violin Concerto, Swan Lake, Triad, Duets, Etudes, Coppelia, Voluntaries and Rodeo; created leading role in Bruch Violin Concerto No. 1, Some Assembly Required and Agnus De Mille's The Other. Recipient N.Y. Woman award for dance, 1991; co-winner gold prize for women Moscow Internat. Ballet Competition, 1981. Office: Am Ballet Theatre 890 Broadway New York NY 10003-1211*

MCKESSON, JOHN ALEXANDER, III, international relations educator; b. N.Y.C., Mar. 29, 1922; s. John Alexander and Mildred Fleming (Warner) McK.; m. Erna Jensson, Jan. 4, 1950 (dec. May 1971); 1 child, John A. IV. AB, Columbia U., 1941, MA in Internat. Rels., 1942, MA in Art History, 1982; LLD (hon.), Ea. Mich. U., 1972. Fgn. svc. officer Dept. of State, Washington and abroad, 1947-75; Am. amb. Libreville, Gabon, 1971-75; v.p. Etudes Travaux et Gestion, Paris, 1975-78; editor-in-chief UN Plaza Mag., N.Y.C., 1980-81; prof. NYU, N.Y.C., 1983—. Contbr. articles to profl. jours. Lt. USN, 1942-46. Decorated Commdr. Order of Equatorial Star of Gabon, 1975, Nat. Order of Senegal, 1967. Mem. Fgn. Svc. Assn., Regency Club. Episcopalian. Avocation: bridge. Home: 880 Fifth Ave New York NY 10021-4951

MC KETTA, JOHN J., JR., chemical engineering educator; b. Wyano, Pa., Oct. 17, 1915; s. John J. and Mary (Gelet) McK.; m. Helen Elisabeth Smith, Oct. 17, 1943; children: Charles William, John J. III, Robert Andrew, Mary Anne. B.S., Tri-State Coll., Angola, Ind., 1937; B.S.E., U. Mich., 1943, M.S., 1944, Ph.D., 1946; D.Eng. (hon.), Tri-State Coll., 1965, Drexel U., 1977; Sc.D., U. Toledo, 1973. Diplomate: registered profl. engr., Tex., Mich. Group leader tech. dept. Wyandotte Chem. Corp., Mich., 1937-40; asst. supt. caustic soda div. Wyandotte Chem. Corp., 1940-41; teaching fellow U. Mich., 1942-44, instr. chem. engring., 1944-45; faculty U. Tex., Austin, 1946—; successively asst. prof. chem. engring., assoc. prof., then prof. chem. engring. U. Tex., 1951-52, 54—, E.P. Schoch prof. chem. engring., 1970-81, Joe C. Walter chair, 1981—; asst. dir. Tex. petroleum research com., 1951-52, 54-56, chmn. chem. engring. dept., 1950-52, 55-63, dean Coll. Engring., 1963-69; exec. vice chancellor acad. affairs U. Tex. System, 1969-70; J.C. Walter in Chem. Engring. U. Tex., 1970—; editorial dir. Petroleum Refiner, 1952-54; pres. Chemoil Cons., Inc., 1957-73; dir. Gulf Pub. Co., Howell Corp., Houston, Tesoro Petroleum Co., San Antonio; Chmn. Tex. AEC, So. Interstate Nuclear Bd., 1963-70; mem. Tex. Radiation Adv. Bd., 1978-84; chmn. Nat. Energy Policy Com., 1970-72, Nat. Air Quality Control Com., 1972-85; mem. adv. bd. Carnegie-Mellon Inst. Research, 1978-84; pres. Reagans's rep. on U.S. Acid Precipitation Task Force, 1982-88; apptd. mem. Nuclear Waste Tech. Rev. Bd., 1992-97. Author: series Advances in Petroleum Chemistry and Refining; Chmn. editorial com.: series Petroleum Refiner; mem. adv. bd.: series Internat. Chem. Engring. mag; editorial bd.: series Ency. of Chem. Tech; exec. editor: series Ency. of Chem. Processing and Design (65 vols.). Bd. regents Tri-State U., 1957—. Recipient Bronze plaque Am. Inst. Chem. Engrs., 1952, Charles Schwab award Am. Steel Inst., 1973, Lamme award as outstanding U.S. educator, 1976, Joe J. King Profl. Engring. Achievement award U. Tex., 1976, Gen. Dynamics Teaching Excellence award, 1979, Triple E award for contbns. to nat. issues on energy, environment and econs. Nat. Environ. Devel. Assn., 1976, Boris Pregal Sci. and Tech. award NAS, 1978, Internat. Chem. Engring. award, Italy, 1984, Pres. Herbert Hoover award for advancing well-being of humanity and developing richer and more enduring civilization Joint Engring. Socs., 1989, Centennial award exceptional contbn. Am. Soc. Engring. Edn., 1993; named Disting. Alumnus U. Mich Coll. Engring., 1953, Tri-State Coll., 1956; fellow Allied Chem. & Dye, 1945-46; named Disting. fellow Carnegie-Mellon U., 1978. Mem. Am. Chem. Soc. (chmn. Central Tex. sect. 1950), Am. Inst. Chem. Engrs. (chmn. nat. membership com. 1955, regional exec. com., nat. dir., nat. v.p. 1961, pres. 1962, service to soc. award 1975), Am. Soc. Engring. Edn., Chem. Markets Research Assn., Am. Gas Assn. (adv. bd. chems. from gas 1954), Houston C. of C. (chmn. refining div. 1954, vice chmn. research and statistics com. 1954), Engrs. Joint Council (dir.), Engrs. Joint Countil Profl. Devel. (dir. 1963-85), Nat. Acad. Engring., Sigma Xi, Chi Epsilon, Alpha Psi Omega, Tau Omega, Phi Lambda Upsilon, Phi Kappa Phi, Iota Alpha, Omega Chi Epsilon, Tau Beta Pi, Omicron Delta Kappa. Home: 5227 Tortuga Trl Austin TX 78731-4501

MCKEY, THOMAS J., lawyer; b. Detroit, Jan. 9, 1934; s. Thomas J. and Pauline H. (Feys) McK.; m. Lila W. Webber, Sept. 3, 1960; children: Tim, Christopher, Heather, Brenda. BS, USCG Acad., 1955; JD, U. Mich., 1962; MA in Psychology, Antioch U., 1995. Bar: Wash. 1962. Mediator, arbitrator Bogle & Gates, Seattle, 1962-94, ptnr., 1970-94; pres., bd. dirs. North Pacific Dispute Resolution Svc.; former chmn. N.W. Admiralty Law Inst., Seattle; mem. permanent adv. bd. Tulane Admiralty Law Inst., New Orleans, 1981—. Former bd. dirs. Bellvue (Wash.) Area Self-Improvement Coun., N.W. Seaport, Seattle, Coast Guard Mus. N.W., Seattle, Friends of Youth, Seattle; bd. dirs. Resource Inst., Seattle. Comdr. USCGR. Mem. Maritime Law Assn. U.S. (exec. com. 1979-82), Seattle C. of C. (former chmn. maritime steering com.). Office: 4207-43 Ave NE Seattle WA 98105

MCKHANN, GUY MEAD, physician, educator; b. Boston, Mar. 20, 1932; s. Charles Fremont and Emily (Priest) McK.; m. Katherine E. Henderson, Nov. 30, 1957 (div. 1983); children: Ian, James, Emily, Guy, Charles. Student, Harvard U., 1948-51; M.D., Yale U., 1955. Intern New York Hosp., 1955-56; asst. resident pediatrics Johns Hopkins Hosp., Balt., 1956-57; clin. asso. NIH, Bethesda, Md., 1957-60; resident neurology Mass. Gen. Hosp., Boston, 1960-63; asst. and asso. prof. pediatrics and neurology Stanford (Calif.) U., 1963-69; prof. neurology Johns Hopkins, Balt., 1969—, Kennedy prof. neurology, head neurology dept., 1969-88, prof. neurology, dir. Zanuyl Krieger Mind Brain Inst., 1988—. Served with USPHS, 1957-60. Markle scholar, 1964-69; Joseph P. Kennedy Jr. scholar, 1963-69. Fellow AAAS; mem. Am. Acad. Neurology, Am. Neurol. Assn., Am. Neurochem. Soc., Soc. Neuroscis., Inst. Medicine, Alpha Omega Alpha. Research on normal and abnormal human nervous system. Home: 6526 Montrose Ave Baltimore MD 21212-1023 Office: Zanvyl Krieger Mind Inst Johns Hopkins U 338 Krieger Hall Baltimore MD 21218

MCKIBBEN, HOWARD D., federal judge; b. Apr. 1, 1940; s. James D. and Bernice McKibben; m. Mary Ann McKibben, July 2, 1966; children: Mark, Susan. B.S., Bradley U., 1962; M.P.A., U. Pitts., 1964; J.D., U. Mich., 1967. Assoc. George W. Abbott Law Office, 1967-71; dep. dist. atty. Douglas County, Nev., 1969-71, dist. atty., 1971-77; dist. ct. judge State of Nev., 1977-84; judge U.S. Dist. Ct. Nev., Reno, 1984—. Mem. ABA, Nev. Bar Assn., Am. Inns of Ct. (pres. Nev. chpt. 1986-88). Methodist. Avocations: tennis, golf, racquetball. Home: PO Box 588 Verdi NV 89439-0588 Office: US Dist Ct 400 S Virginia St Ste 804 Reno NV 89501-2197

MCKIBBEN, RYAN TIMOTHY, newspaper executive; b. Watertown, S.D., June 25, 1958; s. Bernard Dean and Patricia Martha (Loehr) McK.; m. Mary Elizabeth O'Donnell, Oct. 3, 1981; children: Sean Robert, Michael Patrick. Grad. high sch., Janesville, Wis. Classified advt. exec. Green Bay (Wis.) Press Gazette, 1977-79; display advt. exec. Racine (Wis.) Jour. Times, 1979-80; advt. dir. Oshkosh (Wis.) Northwestern, 1980-82, dir. sales/mktg., 1982-84; advt. dir. Reno Gazette-Jour., 1984-85, Madison (Wis.) Newspapers Inc., 1985-88; v.p., advt. dir., sr. v.p. advt. and mktg. Denver Post, 1988-90, exec. v.p., gen. mgr., 1990-93, pub., 1993—; bd. dirs. Newspapers First, N.Y.C. Mem. mktg. com. Metro Area Boys Clubs, Denver, 1988—; bd. dirs. Nat. Jewish Ctr. for Immunology and Respiratory Medicine, Denver, Denver Metro Conv. Bur., Denver Ctr. for Performing Arts, Colo. Symphony, Colo. Forum, Colo. Concer, Castle Pines Golf Club. Mem. Am. Press Inst., Newspaper Advt. Coop. Network (bd. dirs. 1989—), Internat. Newspaper Advt./Mktg. Execs., (com. mem. 1989—), Denver Advt. Fedn., Boys and Girls Club, Columbine Country Club. Republican. Roman Catholic. Home: 5350 S Race Ct Littleton CO 80121-1430 Office: Denver Post 1560 Broadway Denver CO 80202-6000

MCKIE, FRANCIS PAUL, journalist; b. Jarrow-upon-Tyne, England, Dec. 18, 1958; arrived in Can., 1963; s. Francis David and Sonia (Marley) McK.; m. Ellen Frances Robinson, May 26, 1984; 1 child, Sean David. BA, U. Toronto, 1982. Free-lance film critic Winnipeg (Man., Can.) Free Press, 1985-87, staff film critic, 1988-92, features writer, 1992-94; news reporter, features writer, columnist Winnipeg (Man., Can.) Free Press, $, 1994-95; bus. reporter Winnipeg (Man., Can.) Free Press, 1996—. Mem. Winnipeg Press Club (pres. 1990, house chair/treas. 1989), Media Union Manitoba (bd. dirs., pres. 1997—). Avocations: movies, Trekkies, Blue Jays. Office: Winnipeg Free Press, 1355 Mountain Ave, Winnipeg, MB Canada R2X 3B6

MC KIE, TODD STODDARD, artist; b. Boston, Apr. 25, 1944; s. Roy Albert and Lois E. (Barwood) McK.; m. Judy Anne Kensley, Apr. 10, 1967; 1 son, Jesse Simon. BFA, RISD, 1966. Vis. artist RISD, 1977, Mass. Coll. Art, 1977-78, Sch. Mus. Fine Arts, Boston, 1979; lectr. schs. and museums. Exhibited in one-man shows Harcus Krakow Gallery, Boston, 1977, 79, 83, Aquavella Gallery, N.Y.C., 1978, 79, 81, Hokin-Kaufman Gallery, Chgo., 1983, Helander Gallery, N.Y.C., 1990, 92, Toale Gallery, Boston, 1994, Barbara Singer Gallery, Boston, 1996; exhibited in group shows including, Whitney Museum Am. Art, N.Y.C., 1975, Harcus Krakow Gallery, 1975, 78, Mus. Fine Arts, Boston, 1975, 77, 81, Acquavella Gallery, 1976, 78, 79, 81, Inst. Contemporary Art, Boston, 1979, Addison Gallery Am. Art, 1981; represented in permanent collections including Fogg Art Mus., Cambridge, Mass., M.I.T., Cambridge, Brockton (Mass.) Mus., Mus. Fine Arts, Boston, DeCordova Mus., Lincoln, Mass., Rose Art Mus. Brandeis U.; also numerous pvt. collections. Recipient Blanch E. Colman award Colman Found., 1974; Artists fellowship Villa Montalvo, 1995; Artists Found. fellow Boston, 1975, 89. Home and Office: 82 Holworthy St Cambridge MA 02138

MCKIE, W. GILMORE, human resources executive; b. Marquette, Mich., Aug. 25, 1927; s. Walter G. and Amy Gertrude (Larson) McK.; m. Elenore R. MacNally, Sept. 9, 1950 (div. Nov. 1962); 1 child, Janet; m. Mary Simmons, Mar. 21, 1964 (dec. Aug. 1970) 1 child, Gwen DeBuck; m. Eunice Winifred Curtis, July 10, 1971; children: Ellen Sheive, Norrine Halvorsen. BS in Econs., U. Rochester, 1951. Employment interviewer Taylor Instruments Cos', Rochester, N.Y., 1951-60; employment mgr. Graflex, Inc., Rochester, 1960-62, Gen. Railway Signal Co., Rochester, 1962-67; dir. human resources The Singer Co., Rochester, Binghamton,, N.Y.C., 1967-77, Norwich-Eaton Pharms., Norwich, N.Y., 1977-80; personnel mgr. Ness Automatic Machine Products, Rochester, 1980-84; v.p. human resources Marine Midland Bank, N.A., Rochester, 1984-89; pres. HRM Cons., Inc., Rochester, 1989-93; founder, pres. adr Support Svcs., Rochester, N.Y., 1993—; mgmt. adv. bd. Cornell U. Extension div., Rochester, 1984-90; mem. job svc. employer com. N.Y. State Dept. Labor, 1993—. Co-author: The Contingent Worker - A Human Resource Perspective, 1995. Adv. bd. Salvation Army, Rochester, 1986—; vice chair N.Y. State divsn. Human Rights, Rochester, 1987—; bd. dirs. Ralph Bunche Scholarship Fund, Rochester, 1990-93, Youth at Risk, Rochester, 1988-92; bd. govs. N.Y. State Fingerlakes Regional Edn. Ctr. for Econ. Devel., Rochester, 1984—; exec. com. United Negro Coll. Fund, Rochester, 1986—; adv. bd. chair Coll. Continuing Edn. Rochester Inst. Tech., 1985-90; chair Loftus C. Carson Human Rights Awards Luncheon, Rochester, 1991. Mem. Soc. for Human Resource Mgmt. (dist. dir. N.Y. state 1985-89, pers. rsch. com. 1989—, pres. Genesee Valley chpt. 1982-84, chmn. bd. 1984-87, founder 1982), Industrial Mgmt. Coun. Rochester (mem. human resource adv. com. 1988-90, chmn. industrial pers. group 1983-84, vice chmn. bank pers. group 1985-90), Rochester Assn. Automatic Machining (pres. 1982-83), Rochester Profl. Cons. Network, Pers. Testing Coun. Upstate N.Y., Broome County C. of C. (pres. Industrial Rels. Com. 1977), Chenango C. of C. (dir. 1978), Chenango-Deleware Bus. Edn. Ctr. (past v.p. 1977-78). Republican. Lutheran. Avocations: golf, trap and skeet shooting, woodworking. Office: HRM Support Svcs 2854 Saint Paul Blvd Rochester NY 14617-3740 *I have always endeavored to enhance the growth and achievements of my staff and coworkers. In that same vein guide the youth in our society, so that they might make use of their potential.*

MCKIERNAN, JOHN WILLIAM, mechanical engineer; b. Hannibal, Mo., Jan. 12, 1923; s. Charles and Anna Laura (Turner) McK.; m. Jeannette Dorothy Hagen, Aug. 26, 1945; children—Kathleen J., Linda J., John E. B.S., U. Mo., 1947; M.S., Iowa State Coll., 1950. With E.I. duPont de Nemours & Co., Inc., Richmond, Va., 1947-48; faculty Iowa State Coll., 1948-51; mech. engr. Sandia Nat. Lab., Albuquerque, 1951-85. Served with USAAF, 1943-45. Decorated D.F.C., Air medal. Fellow ASME (v.p., bd. govs.). Mem. Christian Ch. Home: 1709 Cardenas Dr NE Albuquerque NM 87110-6629

MCKIM, PAUL ARTHUR, management consultant, retired petroleum executive; b. Milford, Conn., Feb. 1, 1923; s. Arthur Wheatley and Helen Agnes (Brennan) McK.; m. Daisy Flora Brown, June 18, 1945; 1 dau., Meredith Ann. Student, Lamar Inst. Tech., 1940-42; BS in Chem. Engring., La. State U., 1943, MS, 1947, PhD, 1949; grad. Advanced Mgmt. Program, Harvard, 1959; grad. Aspen Inst. Humanistic Studies Exec. Program, 1970. With Ethyl Corp., 1949-62, asst. gen. mgr. research and devel. operations, 1958-62; v.p., gen. mgr. rsch. and devel. Atlantic Refining Co., Phila., 1962-66; v.p. Atlantic Richfield Co., 1966-78; v.p. comml. devel. Arco Chem. Co., 1966-69, v.p. nuclear operations and comml. devel., 1969-73; exec. v.p. Sinclair Koppers Co., 1973; pres. Arco Polymers, Inc., 1974-78; asst. to pres. Tex. Eastern Corp., 1978-80, v.p., 1980-84, sr. v.p., 1985-88; Chmn. US Organizing com. for 12th World Petroleum Congress, Houston, 1987. Past bd. mgrs. Franklin Inst. Research Labs; past vice chmn. bd. mgrs. Spring Garden Coll., Phila. Coll. Art.; past vice chmn. World Affairs Council of Phila. Served to lt. (j.g.) USNR, 1944-46. Mem. AIChE, Am. Petroleum Inst., Union League, Merion (Pa.) Cricket Club, Merion Golf Club, Houston Club, Shreveport (La.) Country Club, Alpha Chi Sigma, Omicron Delta Kappa, Tau Beta Pi, Phi Lambda Upsilon, Phi Kappa Phi, Delta Kappa Epsilon. Home: 5405 Holly Springs Dr Houston TX 77056-2021

MCKIM, SAMUEL JOHN, III, lawyer; b. Pitts., Dec. 31, 1938; s. Samuel John and Harriet Frieda (Roehl) McK.; children: David Hunt, Andrew John; m. Eugenia A. Leverich. AA cum laude, Port Huron Jr. Coll., 1959; BA cum laude, U. Mich., 1961, JD cum laude, U. Mich., 1964. Bar: Mich. 1965, U.S. Dist. Ct. (so. dist.) Mich. 1965, U.S. Ct. Appeals (6th cir.) 1969, U.S. Supreme Ct., 1994. Assoc. Miller, Canfield, Paddock and Stone, P.L.C., Detroit, Bloomfield Hills, Howell, Kalamazoo, Lansing, Monroe, Traverse City and Grand Rapids, Mich., Washington, N.Y.C., Pensacola, St. Petersburg, Fla., Gdansk, Warsaw, Poland, 1964-71, sr. mem., 1971—, head state and local tax sect., 1985—, chmn. tax dept., 1989-94, mng. ptnr., 1979-85, chmn., mng. ptnr., 1984-85; mem. tax coun. State Bar Mich., 1981-94, chmn. state and local tax com. real property sect., 1982-90; adj. prof. law sch. Wayne State U., 1993—. Bd. dirs., past chmn. Goodwill Industries of Greater Detroit, 1970—; dir. Goodwill Industries Found., 1982-95; elder Presbyn. ch., Stevens min.; coun. mem. at large Detroit area coun. Boy Scouts Am., 1987—. Fellow Am. Coll. Tax Counselors; mem. ABA, Mich. Bar Assn., Detroit Bar Assn., Detroit Club, Barrister's Soc., Ostego Ski Club, Port Huron Golf Club, Order of Coif, Phi Delta Phi. Assoc. editor Mich. Law Rev. Home: 32778 Friar Tuck Ln Beverly Hills MI 48025-2500 Office: Miller Canfield Paddock & Stone 150 W Jefferson Ave Ste 2500 Detroit MI 48226-4432

MCKIMMEY, MARTHA ANNE, elementary education educator; b. Uvalde, Tex., Apr. 9, 1943; d. Aubrey Allan and Nellie Grey (Roberts) Stovall; m. Vernon Hobart McKimmey Jr., July 3, 1965; children: Annette Gay, Patrick Allan. BS, Howard Payne Coll., Brownwood, Tex., 1964; MEd, Tex. Christian U., 1969; PhD, Tex. Women's U., 1995. Cert. elem. tchr., Tex. Tchr. Ft. Worth Ind. Sch. Dist., 1964-66, White Lake Sch., Ft. Worth, 1979-80, Meadowbrook Christian Sch., Ft. Worth, 1983-87. Contbr. articles to mags. Mem. ASCD, Am. Christian Writers. Home: 7104 Jewell Ave Fort Worth TX 76112-5712

MCKINLEY, BRUNSON, diplomat; b. Miami, Fla., Feb. 8, 1943; s. Kenneth William and Louis Rebecca (Hiestand) McK.; m. Nancy Padlon, Sept. 11, 1971; children: Harley Joseph, Sarah Elizabeth. BA, U. Chgo., 1962; MA, Harvard U., 1964. Third sec. U.S. Embassy, Rome, 1971-72; spl. asst. U.S. Liaison Office, Peking, China, 1973-74; dep. prin. officer U.S. Consulate Gen., Danang, Republic of Vietnam, 1975; staff officer Dept. State, Washington, 1975-76, officer-in-charge Italian affairs, 1976-78; first sec. Am. Embassy, London, 1978-81; dep. polit. advisor U.S. Mission, Berlin, 1981-83; dep. exec. sec. Dept. State, Washington, 1983-86; U.S. ambassador Am. Embassy, Port-Au-Prince, Haiti, 1986-89; deputy for policy bur. european affairs U.S. Dept. State, Washington, 1990-91, dep. asst. sec. state for refugee programs, 1991-93, sr. dep. asst. sec. state for population, refugees and migration, 1993-95; Bosnia humanitarian coord. U.S. Dept. of State, Washington, 1995—. Contbr. various publs. in field of migration. Served to capt. U.S. Army, 1965-71, Vietnam. Decorated Air medal, Bronze star, Award for Valor, Superior Hon. award; recipient Haitian Order of Merit. Mem. Army and Navy Club, Bath Club (London), Washington Figure Skating Club, Phi Beta Kappa. Avocations: walking, running, riding, ice skating, languages. Home: 7064 31st St NW Washington DC 20015-1402 Office: Dept of State Washington DC 20520

MCKINLEY, DONALD ROBERT, former school system administrator, education advisor; b. Cottonwood, Idaho, Nov. 17, 1924; s. Howard R. and Elsie May (Wortman) McK.; m. Margaret Faye Burson, March 27, 1948; children: Constance, Kathryn, Philip. BS, U. Idaho, 1948, MS, 1953; EdD, Wash. State U., 1958. Tchr. music and govt. Grangeville (Idaho) Sch. Dist., Idaho, 1948-50; tchr. music and math. Cajon Valley Sch. Dist., El Cajon, Calif., 1952-56; supt.-prin. Ferndale (Calif.) H.S. Dist., 1957-59; prin. Davis

(Calif.) Sr. H.S., 1959-67; asst. supt. Davis Unified Sch. Dist., 1967-70; supt. Placer Union H.S. Dist., Auburn, Calif., 1970-72, San Ramon Valley Sch. Dist., Danville, Calif., 1972-73; chief dep. state supt. Calif. State Dept. Edn., Sacramento, 1973-83; sales and regional mgr. WICAT Edn. Sys., Provo, Utah, 1983-86; mktg. advisor Edn. Sys. Corp., San Diego, 1986-89; edn. advisor Photo & Sound Co., San Francisco, 1989-92, Edunetics Corp., Arlington, Va., 1992-94; search cons. Wilson Riles & Assocs., Sacramento, Calif., 1990—; chmn. Coun. of Chief State Sch. Officers-Study Commn., Washington, 1975-76; mem. Sec. of Edn. Adv. Com., Washington, 1981-86; cons. Optical Data Corp., 1995—, Ameri Data Corp., 1995—. Lt. USN, 1943-46, World War II, 1950-52, Korea. Mem. Am. Assn. Sch. Adminstrs., Calif. Assn. Secondary Sch. Adminstrs. (pres. 1969-70), Assn. Calif. Sch. Adminstrs. (pres. 1971-72). Avocations: golf, fishing, travel. Home: 5332 Adelaide Way Sacramento CA 95841-4304

MCKINLEY, ELLEN BACON, priest; b. Milw., June 9, 1929; d. Edward Alsted and Lorraine Goodrich (Graham) Bacon; m. Richard Smallbrook McKinley, III, June 16, 1951 (div. Oct. 1977); children: Richard IV, Ellen Graham, David Todd, Edward Bacon. BA cum laude, Bryn Mawr Coll., 1951; MDiv Yale U., 1976; STM, Gen. Theol. Sem., N.Y.C., 1979; PhD, Union Theol. Sem., N.Y.C., 1988. Ordained to ministry Episcopal Ch. as deacon, 1980, as priest, 1981. Intern St. Francis Ch., Stamford, Conn., 1976-77; pastoral asst. St. Paul's Ch., Riverside, Conn., 1979-80, curate, 1980-81; asst. St. Saviour's Ch., Old Greenwich, Conn., 1982-90; priest assoc. St. Christopher's Ch., Chatham, Mass., 1987-88, 97—; interim asst. Trinity Ch., Princeton, N.J., 1990-91; priest assoc. All Saints Ch., Princeton, 1992-97, interim rector, 1993; mem. major chpt. Trinity Cathedral, Trenton, 1992-96. Mem. Episcopal Election Com., Diocese of Conn., 1986-87, Com. on Human Sexuality, 1987-90; Com. on Donations and Bequests Diocese of Conn., 1987-90; sec., Greewich Com. on Drugs, 1970-71; bd. dirs. Greenwich YWCA, 1971-72. Mem. Episcopal Women's Caucus, Colonial Dames Am., Jr. League. Clubs: Sulgrave.

MC KINLEY, JOHN KEY, retired oil company executive; b. Tuscaloosa, Ala., Mar. 24, 1920; s. Virgil Parks and Mary Emma (Key) McK.; m. Helen Grace Heare, July 19, 1946; children: John Key Jr., Mark Charles. B.S. in Chem. Engring. U. Ala., 1940, M.S. in Organic Chemistry, 1941, LL.D. (hon.), 1972; grad., Advanced Mgmt. Program, Harvard U., 1962; LL.D. (hon.), Troy State U., 1974. Registered profl. engr., Tex. With Texaco Inc., 1941-86; asst. dir. research Texaco Inc., Beacon, N.Y., 1957-59; asst. to v.p. Texaco Inc., 1959-60, mgr. comml. devel., 1960; gen. mgr. petrochem. dept. Texaco Inc., N.Y.C., 1960-67; v.p. petrochem. dept., v.p. in charge supply and distbn. Texaco Inc., 1967-71, sr. v.p. worldwide refining, petrochems., also supply and distbn., 1971, pres., dir., 1971-80, pres., chief operating officer, chmn. exec. com., 1980, chmn. bd., pres., chief exec. officer, 1980-83, chmn. bd., chief exec. officer, 1983-86, ret., 1986; bd. dirs. emeritus Federated Dept. Stores, Inc. Patentee for chem. processing. Hon. bd. dirs. Met. Opera Assocs.; nat. chmn. Met. Opera Centennial Fund, 1980; bd. dirs. The Ams. Soc.; mem. Bus. Coun. Maj. AUS, 1941-45, ETO. Decorated Bronze Star; recipient George Washington Honor medal Freedoms Found., 1972; Andrew Wellington Cordier fellow Columbia U.; named to Ala. Bus. Hall of Fame, 1982, Ala. Acad. Honor, 1983, State of Ala. Engring. Hall of Fame, 1992. Fellow Am. Inst. Chem. Engrs.; mem. Am. Petroleum Inst. (hon. dir.), Wee Burn Country Club, Links Club, Brook Club, Augusta Nat. Golf Club, Blind Brook Country Club, North River Yacht, Sigma Xi, Tau Beta Pi, Gamma Sigma Epsilon, Kappa Sigma. Office: 1 Canterbury Green Stamford CT 06901

MCKINLEY, LOREN DHUE, museum director; b. Tillamook, Oreg., Feb. 1, 1920; s. Henry Raymond and Flora (Phillips) McK.; m. Mary Eileen Sessions, May 22, 1942; children: Candace Eileen, Scott Dhu, Kevin Loren, Laurie Lee, Maris Colleen. Student, Oreg. State U., U. Oreg.; D.Sc., U. Portland, 1973. Advt. mgr. Headlight Herald, Tillamook, 1946; partner Kenwood Press, Tillamook, 1949; dir. Oreg. Mus. Sci. and Industry, Portland, 1960-78; chief exec. officer Oreg. Mus. Sci. and Industry, 1978—; bd. dirs. Fred Hutchinson Cancer Rsch. Ctr. Found., Oreg. Mus. Sci. and Industry; Portland ops. mgr. Office of Devel. Oreg. State U. Mayor of Tillamook, 1954-60; pres. Leukemia Assn. Oreg. Inc., 1983—; bd. dirs. St. Mary's Acad., 1993—; bd. trustees Oreg. Mus. Sci. and Industry; mem. Oreg. State U Found. Served with AUS, World War II, ETO, MTO. Decorated Bronze Star with oak leaf cluster; named 1st Citizen of Oreg., 1951; recipient award Oreg. Mus. Sci. and Industry, 1965, Elsie M.B. Naumberg award as outstanding sci. mus. dir., 1968, citation for outstanding svc. Oreg. Acad. Sci., 1971, Aubrey Watzek award Lewis and Clark Coll., 1973. Mem. Assn. Sci. and Tech. Ctrs. Am. (pres. 1973—), League Oreg. Cities (past pres.), Kappa Sigma. Republican. Home and Office: 11925 SW Belvidere Pl Portland OR 97225-5805

MCKINLEY, SARAH ELIZABETH, journalist; b. Bucyrus, Ohio, Jan. 4, 1952; d. Harold Kemp and Velma Elizabeth (Vollmer) McK.; m. Paul Robert Serrano, Aug. 17, 1993; 1 child, James Ernest Serrano. BA, Ohio State U., 1974. Co-investigator, researcher Women's Action Collective, Columbus, Ohio, 1976-80; editor, cons. The Nisonger Ctr., Columbus, 1981; freelance editor Columbus, 1982-84; journalist Gas Daily, Washington, 1985, Energy Daily, Washington, 1985-86; sr. editor Natural Gas Intelligence (Intelligence Press), Washington, 1986—; conf. dir. Gas Mart: The Nat. Trade Fair Nat. Gas Mktg., 1986—. Creator Simplified Map North American Pipelines, 1990-97, Storage Map of the United States and Canada, 1991, 93, 95, 97, Simplified Map of Electric Transmission in North America, 1996-97; editor: The Life's Work of a Minor Poet: Collected Fiction, Journalism and Poetry of Edmund McGranaghan, 1982. Pres., bd. dirs. The Commons of Arlington, Va., 1993-95; pres. Columbia Heights Civic Assn., Arlington, 1990-92. Mem. Soc. Profl. Journalists. Home: # 2 2714 Shawn Leigh Dr Vienna VA 22181-6136

MCKINLEY, VICKY LYNN, biology educator; b. Dayton, Ohio, Feb. 13, 1957; d. Dale and Kathryn (Andrick) McK. BS, Wright State U., 1979; MS, U. Cin., 1981, PhD, 1985. Teaching asst. Wright State U., Dayton, 1978-79; chemist Nat. Distillers & Chem. Co., Cin., 1979-80; grad. asst. U. Cin., 1980-83, pre-doctoral rsch. fellow, 1984-85; postdoctoral rsch. fellow U. Calgary, Alta., Can., 1985-86; asst. prof. biology Roosevelt U., Chgo., 1987-92, assoc. prof., 1992—, assoc. dean Coll. of Arts and Scis., 1994—; exam writer Am. Coll. Testing; cons. John Wiley & Sons, Inc., MCAT. Contbr. articles to profl. jours. Recipient Acad. Scholarship award Wright State U., 1975-76, Summer fellowship U. Cin. Rsch. Coun., 1983, Univ. Dean's Disting. Dissertation fellowship, 1984-85, Postdoctoral fellowship Alta. Oil Sands Tech. and Rsch. Authority, 1985—; named All-Star Prof., Chgo. Tribune, 1993. Mem. AAAS, Nat. Assn. Biology Tchrs., Am. Soc. Microbiology (N. Paul Hudson commendation Ohio branch 1981), Ill. Soc. Microbiology, Chgo. Herpetological Soc., Soc. Coll. Sci. Tchrs., Sigma Xi. Avocations: photography, backpacking, antique restoration. Office: Roosevelt U Dept Biology 430 S Michigan Ave Chicago IL 60605-1301

MCKINLEY, WILLIAM THOMAS, composer, performer, educator; b. New Kensington, Pa., Dec. 9, 1938; s. Daniel Edward and Ellen Lee (Henson) M.; m. Marlene Marie Mildner, Apr. 11, 1956; children: Thomas Jr., Derrick, Jory, Sean, Elliott. BFA, Carnegie-Mellon U., 1960; MM, Yale U., 1966, DMA, 1969. Mem. music faculty SUNY-Albany, 1968-69; prof. music U. Chgo., 1969-73; prof. composition and jazz studies New Eng. Conservatory Music, Boston, 1973—. Composer numerous works for orch., chamber ensembles, choral works, oratorio, also solo works; commns. include works for Koussevitsky Music Found., 1982, Lincoln Ctr. Chamber Music Soc., 1985, Boston Symphony Pops, 1986, Concert Artist Guild, 1988, Stan Getz, 1988, Am. Symphony, 1988, (2) Fromm Found., John Williams, 1989, NEA Consortium, Rheinische Philharmonie, Fed. Republic Germany, 1990, Queensland Youth Orch., Australia, 1990, Bolshoi Ballet Theatre Orch. USSR, 1990, Pitts. New Music Ensemble, 1991, Quintet Ams., 1992, Md. Bach Aria Group, 1992, Berlin Saxophone Quartet, 1992, 93, Richard Stolzman, 1993, Seattle Symphony, 1993, Absolut Vodka, 1994; performance recs. with Berlin Radio Symphony and Richard Stolzman, Rheinische Philharm., Warsaw Philharm., St. Petersburg Philharm., Slovak Radio Symphony, Seattle Symphony, Krakow Philharm., Silesian Philharm., Prague Radio Symphony, Solati Trio, Manhattan Sinfonia, Cleve. Quartet. Recipient Naumberg prize Naumberg Found., 1975; Nat. Endowment Arts composer fellow, 1975-83; Am. Acad. Music award, Am. Acad. and Inst. Arts and Letters, 1983; Guggenheim fellow, 1985; 3 Mass Council fellowships. Mem. Am. Composers Alliance, Am. Music Ctr. Home: 240 West St Reading MA 01867-2847 Office: New England Conservatory Music 290 Huntington Ave Boston MA 02115-5018*

MCKINLEY BALFOUR, STEPHANIE ANN, learning resources director, librarian; b. Galesburg, Ill., Mar. 27, 1948; d. William Chester and Virginia Ann (Clugsten) McKinley; m. James Robert Miller, Mar. 2, 1968 (div. Mar. 1978); 1 child, Christopher Antonin Miller; m. David Alan Balfour, Nov. 23, 1991. BA in Speech, Drama, Western Ill. U., 1970; MLS, Drexel U., 1974. Cert. tchr., Ill., media specialist, Ill. Libr. William McKinley Elem. Sch., Phila., 1971-76, Regional Jr. H.S., Amherst, Mass., 1976-77, Garfield Elem. Sch., Monmouth, Ill., 1977-79; dir. learning resources Spoon River Valley Sch. Dist., London Mills, Ill., 1979-95; dir. librs. Spoon River Valley Sch. Dist./Avon Sch. Dist., Ill., 1995—; dir. summer reading program Avon (Ill.) Pub. Libr., 1980-95. Leader 4-H, Avon, 1983-92; vol. EMT Galesburg Hosp. Ambulance Svc., Galesburg/Avon, 1978—; dir. religious edn. Avon Federated Ch., 1984—. Named Outstanding Young Educator by Monmouth Jaycees, 1979. Mem. Am. Found. Vision Awareness Ill. Affiliate (pres.), Nat. Edn. Assn., Ill. Edn. Assn., Ill. Sch. Libr. Media Assn., Phi Delta Kappa, Gamma Lambda-Delta Kappa Gamma Soc. Internat. (pres. 1992-94, 1st v.p. 1990-92, recording sec. 1988-92). Republican. Mem. United Ch. of Christ. Avocations: reading, knitting, crocheting, gardening. Home: 274 Funcheon Ct Avon IL 61415-8853 Office: Spoon River Valley Sch Dist RR 1 London Mills IL 61544-9801

MCKINNELL, ROBERT GILMORE, zoology, genetics and cell biology educator; b. Springfield, Mo., Aug. 9, 1926; s. William Parks and Mary Catherine (Gilmore) McK.; m. Beverly Walton Kerr, Jan. 24, 1964; children: Nancy Elizabeth, Robert Gilmore, Susan Kerr. AB, U. Mo., 1948; BS, Drury Coll., 1949, DSc (hon.), 1993; PhD, U. Minn., 1959. Research assoc. Inst. Cancer Research, Phila., 1958-61; asst. prof. biology Tulane U., New Orleans, 1961-65; assoc. prof. Tulane U., 1965-69, prof., 1969-70; prof. zoology U. Minn., Mpls., 1970—; prof. genetics and cell biology U. Minn., St. Paul, 1976—; vis. scientist Dow Chem. Co., Freeport, Tex., 1976; guest dept. zoology U. Calif., Berkeley, 1979; Royal Soc. guest rsch. fellow Nuffield dept. pathology John Radcliffe Hosp., Oxford U., 1981-82; NATO vis. scientist Akademisch Ziekenhuis, Ghent, Belgium, 1984; faculty rsch. assoc. Naval Med. Rsch. Inst., Bethesda, Md., 1988; secretariat Third Internat. Conf. Differentiation, 1978; mem. amphibian com. Inst. Lab. Animal Resources, NRC, 1970-73, mem. adv. coun., 1974; mem. panel genetic and cellular resources program NIH, 1981-82, spl. study sect., Bethesda, 1990. Author: Cloning: Amphibian Nuclear Transplantation, 1978, Cloning, A Biologist Reports, 1979; sr. editor: Differentiation and Neoplasia, 1980, Cloning: Leben aus der Retorte, 1981, Cloning of Frogs, Mice, and other Animals, 1985; mem. editorial bd. Differentiation, 1973—; assoc. editor: Gamete Research, 1980-86; contbr. articles to profl. jours. Served to lt. USNR, 1944-47, 51-53. Recipient Outstanding Teaching award Newcomb Coll., Tulane U., 1970; Disting. Alumni award Drury Coll., 1979, Morse Alumni Teaching award U. Minn., 1992; Research fellow Nat. Cancer Inst., 1957-58; Sr. Sci. fellow NATO, 1974. Fellow AAAS, Linnean Soc. (London); mem. Am. Assn. Cancer Rsch. (emeritus), Am. Assn. Cancer Edn. (sr.), Metastasis Soc., Am. Inst. Biol. Scis., Soc. for Devel. Biology, Indian Soc. Devel. Biology (lifetime emeritus mem.), Internat. Soc. Study of Comparative Oncology, Inc., Internat. Soc. Differentiation (exec. com., sec.-treas. 1975-92, pres. elect 1992-94, pres. 1994-96), Gown-in-Town Club, Sigma Xi. Home: 2124 Hoyt Ave W Saint Paul MN 55108-1315 Office: U Minn Dept Genetics Cell Bio Saint Paul MN 55108-1095

MCKINNEY, ALEXANDER STUART, neurologist, retired; b. N.Y.C., Feb. 3, 1933; s. John McDowell and Katherine Elizabeth (Morse) McK.; m. Carolyn Clifton Braman, Aug. 15, 1958 (div. July 1985); children: James, David, Mark; m. Susan Lowe Childress, July 30, 1985; children: Josephine, Mary, Jennifer. AB, Princeton U., 1955; MD, Columbia U., 1959. Diplomate Am. Bd. Neurology. Intern St. Luke's Hosp., N.Y.C., 1959-60; resident N.Y. Neurological Inst., 1960-63; prof. neurology Emory U., Atlanta, 1965-85; pvt. practice Mountain Med. Assocs., Clyde, N.C., 1985-95; chief of staff Haywood County Hosp., Clyde, N.C., 1989-90. Contbr. articles to profl. jours. Served to lt. comdr. USNR, 1963-65. Fellow Am. Acad. Neurology, Royal Soc. Medicine; mem. N.C. Med. Soc. (vice councillor 1991-94), N.C. Neurol. Soc. (pres. 1992). Avocations: travel, gardening. Home: 9 Charles Wesley Dr Waynesville NC 28786-2643

MC KINNEY, ALEXIS, public relations consultant; b. Cin., Mar. 13, 1907; s. John Austin and Gertrude (Kofler) McK.; m. Esther Ryker Simmons, Aug. 27, 1930 (dec. 1985); 1 dau., Eunice Christine; m. Margaret Jane Miles, Sept. 14, 1986 (dec. 1990); m. Irene Vogel Stevenson, Apr. 6, 1991. Ed. pub. schs., Colo., and Tex. Enlisted in U.S. Navy, 1923, served aboard U.S.S. New Mexico, 1923-27; circulation agt. Pueblo (Colo.) Star-Jour., 1928; reporter Pueblo Chieftain, 1929, state editor, 1930, city editor, 1931-32; co-pub. and editor Rocky Ford Tribune, 1933-34; news editor Alamosa (Colo.) Daily Courier, 1934-42; statehouse reporter Denver Post, 1942-45; information officer U.S. Bur. Reclamation, Denver, 1945-46; asst. city editor Denver Post, 1946, city editor, 1946-47, mng. editor, 1947-49, asst. pub., 1949-63; project dir. Rio Grande-land, Durango, Colo., 1963-65; dir. pub. relations Denver & Rio Grande Western R.R. Co., 1965-73; pub. relations cons. Rio Grande Industries, Inc., 1973—. Trustee Colo. R.R. Hist. Found. and Mus. Mem. all-Navy championship rifle team, 1927. Mem. Pub. Relations Soc. Am., R.R. Pub. Relations Assn., Soc. Profl. Journalists. Conglist. Address: 3131 E Alameda Ave #505 Denver CO 80209-3411

MCKINNEY, CHARLES CECIL, investment company executive; b. Newdale, N.C., Nov. 30, 1931; s. Sherbert Day and Florence Van (Hall) McK.; children—Emry Lynn, Robin Ashley, Marc Jason; m. Suzanne Reeves, Apr. 3, 1988. B.S.B.A., U. N.C.-Chapel Hill, 1957; student, U. Tenn., 1950-52. V.p., creative dir. J.T. Howard Advt., 1957-68; chmn. bd., chief exec. officer McKinney & Silver, Raleigh, N.C., 1968-90; chmn., pres., chief exec. officer Onyx Corp., 1991—. Trustee N.C. Symphony, Raleigh, 1983-87; bd. visitors U. N.C., Chapel Hill, 1989-91; bd. vis. Kenan Flagler Sch. Bus., 1985-94. Recipient profl. awards. Mem. N.C. Mus. Art, Sphinx Club, Carolina Country Club, Figure Eight Yacht Club. Republican. Home: 1021 Cowper Dr Raleigh NC 27608-2228

MCKINNEY, CYNTHIA ANN, congresswoman; b. Mar. 17, 1955; d. Billy and Leola McKinney; 1 child, Coy Grandison, Jr. B, U. So. Calif.; postgrad., Ga. State U., U. Wis.; Tufts U. Former instr. Clark Atlanta U., Atlanta Met. Coll.; former mem. Ga. Ho. of Reps.; mem. 103rd Congress from 11th Ga. dist., 1993—, mem. banking and fin. svcs. com. housing and cmty. devel., mem. internat. rels. com. internat. ops. and human rights; instr. Agnes Scott Coll. Diplomatic fellow Spellman Coll. Home: 765 Shorter Ter NW Atlanta GA 30318-7140 Office: US Ho of Reps 124 Cannon Bldg Washington DC 20515-1011*

MCKINNEY, DENNIS KEITH, lawyer; b. Ottawa, Ill., May 12, 1952; s. Robert Keith and Delroy Louise (Clayton) McK.; m. Patricia Jean Boyle, Oct. 4, 1986; 1 child, Geoffrey Edward. BS, Ball State U., 1973; JD, Ill. Inst. Tech., 1976. Bar: Ind. 1977, U.S. Dist. Ct. (so. dist.) Ind. 1977, U.S. Supreme Ct. 1993. Appellate dep. Ind. Atty. Gen, Indpls., 1977-78, trial dep., 1978-79, sr. trial dep., 1979-81, chief real estate litigation sect., 1981-94; clk. to Hon. James S. Kirsch Ind. Ct. Appeals, Indpls., 1994-95; staff atty. Ind. Supreme Ct. Disciplinary Commn., Indpls., 1995—. Author: Eminent Domain, Practice and Procedure in Indiana, 1991, A Guide to Indiana Easement Law, 1995, A Railroad Ran Through It, 1996; contbg. author: Indiana Real Estate Transactions, 1996; contbr. articles to profl. jours. Active Indpls.-Scarborough Peace Games, 1983-84. Avocations: reading, volleyball, wargaming. Office: Ind Supreme Ct Disciplinary 115 W Washington St Indianapolis IN 46204-3407

MCKINNEY, DONALD, art gallery director, art dealer; b. N.Y.C., May 2, 1931. Student, Columbia U., 1954-57, London U., 1960-62. Pres. Marlborough Gallery, N.Y.C., 1974-78; dir. Hirschl & Adler Modern Galleries, N.Y.C., 1981-93; sr. dir. Andre Emmerich Gallery, N.Y.C., 1993—. Co-author: Mark Rothko, 1978; contbr. Jackson Pollack Catalogue Raisonne, 1978. Mem. The Century Club.

MCKINNEY, DONALD LEE, magazine editor; b. Evanston, Ill., July 12, 1923; s. Guy Doane and Cora Redfield (Brenton) McK.; m. Mary Frances Joyce, Dec. 14, 1958; children—Jennifer Joyce, Douglas Guy. A.B., U. N.C., 1948. Salesman textbooks John Wiley & Sons, N.Y.C., 1949-52; freelance writer mostly comic books with some short articles and fiction, 1952-54; asst. mng. editor True mag., N.Y.C., 1955-62; editor articles Saturday Evening Post, 1962-69; spl. features editor N.Y. Daily News, 1969-70; mng. editor McCalls mag., N.Y.C., 1969-86; Gonzales prof. journalism U. S.C., Beaufort, 1986-90, prof. emeritus, 1990—. Author: Magazine Writing That Sells, 1994; reporter, book reviewer. Served with USNR, 1943-46. Democrat. Home: 9 Spanish Moss Rd Hilton Head Island SC 29928-4412 *I learned early that it is important to speak up if you think you are being treated unfairly; sometimes it's true, and nobody else will complain if you don't. I also learned that in my business, and probably in most others, it is best to always say what you think. Truth is usually more helpful than any assortment of euphemisms, and it also saves a lot of worry over who you have lied to and just what you've said. Truth is not only the best policy—by all odds it's the easiest to keep track of.*

MCKINNEY, E. KIRK, JR., retired insurance company executive; b. Indpls., Mar. 27, 1923; s. E. Kirk and Irene M. (Hurley) McK.; m. Alice Hollenbeck Greene, June 18, 1949; children: Kirk Ashley, Alan Brooks, Nora Claire McKinney Hiatt, Margot Knight. A.B., U. Mich., 1948. Asst. treas. Jefferson Nat. Life Ins. Co., Indpls., 1949-52, asst. to pres., asst. treas., 1952-53, treas., asst. to pres., 1953-55, v.p., treas., 1955-59, pres., 1959-90, chmn. bd., 1970-90, ret., 1990; vice chmn. bd. Somerset Group Inc., 1986-89, ret., 1990; bd. dirs. Zimmer Paper Products, Inc. Corp. relations com. U. Mich.; former pres., former chief exec. officer, bd. govs. Indpls. Mus. Art, now treas.; bd. dirs., mem. exec. com., past bd. dirs. (hon.) Greater Indpls. Progress Com.; former vice chmn. Indpls.-Marion County Bd. Ethics; former dir. Park Tudor Sch., Community Svc. Coun. Indpls., Hosp. Devel. Corp., Ind. Repertory Theater; past adv. com. Indpls. Retirement Home; former bd. dirs., and pres. Episcopal Community Services, Inc.; former vice chmn., life trustee Nature Conservancy; mem. adv. bd. Ind. U., Purdue U.; active Indpls. Symphony Orch.; former bd. dirs. Ind. Pub. Broadcasting Soc. Capt. Q.M.C., AUS, 1942-46. Mem. Life Office Mgmt. Assn. (bd. dirs. 1981-83), Am. Council Life Ins. (state v.p. 1973-75, dir., exec. com. 1976-79), Assn. Ind. Life Ins. Cos. (pres. 1969-71), Indpls. C. of C., Sigma Chi. Democrat. Club: Economic of Indpls. (bd. dirs.). Home: 250 W 77th St Indianapolis IN 46260-3608 Office: 1330 W 38th St Indianapolis IN 46208-4103

MCKINNEY, ELIZABETH ANNE, government purchasing professional; b. Austin, Tex., Mar. 28, 1962; d. Richard Raymond Sr. and Frances Hester (Coleman) Blair; m. Richard Allen McKinney Jr., Sept. 25, 1993. Student, Averett Coll., 1994—. Clk. typist Fairfax County Govt. Purchasing, Fairfax, Va., 1986-87, jr./asst. buyer, 1987-89, buyer I-contract adminstr., 1989-93, buyer II-contract adminstr., 1993—; adv. mem. regional coop. svc. team Dept. Fire and Rescue, Washington, 1995—; mem Met. Washington Coun. Govts. Purchasing Officers Com., 1994—. Mem. Nat. Inst. Govtl. Purchasing (cert. profl. pub. buyer, sec. Met. Washington chpt. 1993-94, treas. 1994-95, v.p. 1995-96), Internat. Coalition for Procurement Stds. Episcopal. Avocations: horsemanship (5-time world champion ladies' sidesaddle), golf, camping, gardening.

MCKINNEY, GEORGE HARRIS, JR., training systems analyst; b. Birmingham, Ala., Nov. 23, 1943; s. George Harris and Elizabeth Dickey (Fikes) McK.; m. Lynda Jeanne Ponder, June 26, 1965 (div. Aug. 18, 1992; children: Michael Thomas, Carol Elizabeth; m. Tambri Sue Hillis, Aug. 19, 1992. BS in Polit. Sci., U.S. Air Force Acad., 1965; MS in Psychology, Troy State U., 1977. Commd. 2d lt. U.S. Air Force, 1965, advanced through grades to lt. col., 1981; fighter pilot U.S. Air Force, worldwide, 1965-85; ret. U.S. Air Force, 1985; tng. sys. cons. in pvt. practice, Milton, Fla., 1985—. Author tech. reports. Decorated D.F.C. (5), Air medal (26), Purple Heart, Meritorious Svc. medal (3). Mem. Order of Daedalians, USAFA Assn. Grads., Air Force, Assn., Am. Def. Preparedness Assn. Avocations: whitetail deer hunting, fishing. Home: 3101 Chippewa Dr Milton FL 32571-9603

MC KINNEY, GEORGE WESLEY, JR., banking educator; b. Amigo, W.Va., May 27, 1922; s. George W. and Charlotte (Ashworth) McK.; m. Lucille Christian, Sept. 5, 1941; children: George Wesley III, Mary, Ruth. A.B., Berea Coll., 1942; M.A., U. Va., 1947, Ph.D., 1949; postgrad., Stonier Grad. Sch. Banking, 1958. With Fed. Res. Bank Richmond, Va., 1948-60; asst. v.p. Fed. Res. Bank Richmond, 1958-60; with Irving Trust Co., N.Y.C., 1960-82; sr. v.p. Irving Trust Co., 1968-82, head econ. research and planning div., 1968-78, chmn. econ. adv. com., 1978-82; Va. Bankers prof. bank mgmt. McIntire Sch. Commerce U. Va., 1982-88, prof. emeritus, 1988—. Author: Federal Taxing and Spending in Virginia, 1949, Federal Reserve Discount Window, 1960, Management of Commercial Bank Funds, 1974, rev. edit., 1980; Contbr. to books. Bd. visitors Nat. Def. U., 1979-82. Served to capt. AUS, 1942-45. Fellow Nat. Assn. Bus. Economists (pres. 1965-66); mem. Phi Kappa Phi. Office: University of Virginia McIntire School of Commerce Charlottesville VA 22903

MCKINNEY, JAMES CARROLL, baritone, educator; b. Minden, La., Jan. 11, 1921; s. William C. and Carolyn (Hilman) McK.; m. Elizabeth Richmond, Aug. 28, 1949; children: James Carroll, Timothy Richmond, John Kevin. Student, La. Poly. Inst., 1938-41; student, Stanford U., 1943-44; MusB, La. State U., 1949, MusM, 1950; D.Mus. Arts, U. So. Calif., 1969; student in, London, 1979-80, 86. Grad. asst. La. State U., 1949-50; asst. prof. music theory Southwestern Baptist Theol. Sem., Ft. Worth, 1950-54; chmn. dept. music theory, composition Southwestern Baptist Theol. Sem., 1954-56, dean Sch. Ch. Music, disting. prof. of voice, 1956-94, emeritus dean and disting. prof., 1994—; baritone soloist First Presbyn. Ch., Hollywood, Calif., 1957-58, First Methodist Ch., Ft. Worth, 1963-67; guest tchr. U. So. Calif., 1958; vis. evaluator Nat. Assn. Schs. Music; vis. lectr. Hong Kong Bapt. Coll., Hong Kong Bapt. Theol. Sem., 1971-72; participant Internat. Congress Voice Tchrs., Strasbourg, France, 1987; faculty mem. Symposium on Care of the Profl. Voice, N.Y.C., 1988, Phila., 1989-97; master tchr. in NATS intern program, in Singapore, Hong Kong, Indonesia, The Philippines, and Romania, 1995, 96, 97; spkr. in field. Presented solo recitals; appeared TV and choral prodns., Bangkok, Thailand, Hong Kong, Israel, Jordan, 1971-72; Author: The Beginning Music Reader, 1958, The Progressing Music Reader, 1959, You Can Read Music, 1960, The Advanced Music Reader, 1961, Mastering Music Reading, 1964, Study Guide for Fundamentals of Music, 1964, Vocal Fundamentals Kit, 1976, Vocal Development Kit, 1977, The Diagnosis and Correction of Vocal Faults, 1982, 2nd edit., 1994, Five Practical Lessons in Singing, 1982 (trans. into Indonesian, Korean, Portuguese, and Spanish), also articles. Bd. dirs. Ft. Worth Symphony Orch. Assn., Ft. Worth Civic Music Assn., Van Cliburn Internat. Piano Competition, Ft. Worth Opera, 1987-94. Mem. Music Tchrs. Nat. Assn. (pres. Ft. Worth chpt.), Music Educators Nat. Conf., Nat. Assn. Tchrs. Singing (lt. gov., editor jour. 1987—, pres. elect 1996, pres. 1997—), Am. Acad. Tchrs. Singing, Am. Choral Dirs. Assn., Tex. Assn. Music Schs. (pres.), Ft. Worth Voice Tchrs. Forum (pres.), Phi Mu Alpha Sinfonia, Omicron Delta Kappa, Phi Kappa Phi, Pi Kappa Lambda. Baptist. Office: Southwestern Bapt Theol Sem PO Box 22000 1809 W Broadus Ave Fort Worth TX 76115-2137 *The longer I live, the more certain I become that the basic value systems passed on to me by my parents are valid. Inherent in all their systems were personal integrity and abiding respect for the rights of others. My chief hope is that I may be as effective as they in transmitting these values to my own children and to the students with whom I come in contact.*

MCKINNEY, JAMES CLAYTON, electronics executive, electrical engineer; b. Charleston, W.Va., June 3, 1940; s. George Clayton and Leona (Adams) McK. B.S.E.E., W.Va. Inst. Tech., 1963. Mem. staff Sta. WMON, Montgomery, W.Va., 1961-63; stringer AP, Charleston, W.Va., 1961-63; with FCC, Washington, 1963-87, chief ops. br., 1969-73, chief monitoring div., 1973, chief enforcement div., 1974, dep. chief Field Ops. Bur., 1974-80, chief Field Ops. Bur., 1980-81, chief Pvt. Radio Bur., 1981-83; chief Mass Media Bur. FCC, 1983-87; dep. asst. to Pres., dir. White House Mil. Office Washington, 1987-89; chmn. Advanced TV Systems Com., Washington, 1989-96; CEO Model HDTV Sta. Project, Inc., 1996—; chmn. U.S. del. UN Conf. on Radio, Geneva, 1986.; mem. U.S. Dels., Geneva, 1978-79, Can., 1984, Italy, 1985, Mexico, 1986, S.Am., 1986, Fed. Republic Germany, 1990; mem. presdl. dels., NATO, UN, Mexico, USSR, Can., Eng., Finland, Econ. Summit, 1987-88; U.S. Spokesman High Definition TV Conf., Geneva, 1989.

Author: (with Eliot Maxwell) Future of Electronic Information Handling at the FCC—Blue Print for the 80's, 1980; (with G.A. Fehlner) Direct Broadcast Satellites in the United States, 1985; New Look at AM Radio, 1986, HDTV Approaches the End Game, 1991. Vice chmn. Montreux Medal Award Com., 1990-95; chmn. High Definition TV World Conf., 1990-93; chmn. strategic planning roup for Internat. Consultative Com. for Radio, Dept. State, 1990-91; bd. dirs. Bowler Found., 1990-95, PICA Found., Inc., 1996—. Recipient Outstanding Fed. Exec. award FCC, 1979, 80, 82, 83, 85, 86; Presdl. Rank award for disting. exec. svc., 1985, Gold medal for disting. fed. svc., 1987, TV Engring. Achievement award, 1992, NAB award of honor, 1996, Broadcast Pioneers' Disting. Svc. award, 1996. Fellow Radio Club Am., Soc. Broadcast Engrs. (sr.), Broadcast Pioneers, Soc. Motion Picture and TV Engrs. (presdl. proclamation 1991); mem. Fed. Exec. Assn., Cosmos Club of Washington. Episcopalian. Home: 6514 Gretna Green Way Alexandria VA 22312-3114

MCKINNEY, JANE-ALLEN, artist and educator; b. Owensboro, Ky., Jan. 8, 1952; d. William Holland and Jane Wilhoit (Moore) McK. BA, Scarritt Coll., Nashville, 1974; MA, Vanderbilt U., 1977; MFA, Memphis Coll. of Art, 1993. Grad. asst. dept. art Peabody Coll. for Tchrs., Vanderbilt U., Nashville, 1975-76; tchr. Smyrna (Tenn.) Comprehensive Vocat. Ctr., 1977-78; pres., bd. dirs. Jane Allen Flighton Artworks Inc., Nashville, 1978—; jeweler Wright's Jewelry Store, Clarksville, Tenn., 1982; tchr. art Belmont U., Nashville, 1984-88, Met. Centennial Park Art Ctr., Nashville, 1988-91, Cheekwood Mus. of Art, Nashville, 1990-94, Nossi Coll. of Art, Nashville, 1991-94, Western Ky. U., Bowling Green, 1991-94; ednl. cons. fine art Nossi Coll. Art, Nashville, 1993—; artist for Women of Achievement awards, sculptures and jewelry YWCA, Nashville, 1992—; artist for Bus. Award Sculpture, C. of C., Nashville, 1990. One and two person shows include Cheekwood Mus. Art, 1981, 93, Owensboro Mus. Fine Art, 1992, Western Ky. U., 1992-94, Belmont U., 1984, others; exhibited in group shows, including Watkins Art Inst., Nashville, 1991, Western Ky. U., 1992, Parthenon, Nashville, 1992, Owensboro Mus. Art, 1993, Tenn. Performing Arts Ctr., 1995; invitational and juried exhibits include Sculptors of Mid. Tenn. Arts in the Airport, Nashville, 1996, Nat. Coun. on the Edn. of Ceramics Arts, Rochester, N.Y., 1996, Ceramic Exhibn. Tenn. State U., 1996, and numerous others; represented in permanent collections including Chattanooga's Visitors Ctr., IBM, Bapt. Hosp., Nations Bank of Tenn., Mass. Pub. Libr., First Am. Bank Corp., Andrew Jackson Hermitage Mus., Tenn. State U., also numerous pvt. collections. Adv. bd. Belmont U., Nashville, 1984—, Nossi Coll. Art, 1993—; mem edn. com. Nat. Mus. of Women in the Arts, Tenn., 1992—; artist for fundraising sculpture Arthritis Found., Nashville, 1989-90; vol. singer VA Hosp., Nashville, 1989—; bd. dirs. Visual Arts Alliance Nashville, 1996; vol. soloist Vet.'s Hosp., 1991-96; artist for ann. fundraiser YWCA, 1993-96; mem. So. Regional Honors Coun. Recipient Best Tchr. award Nossi Coll. Art, 1992-93; grantee City of Chattanooga Welcome Ctr., 1993, Memphis Arts Festival Spl. Projects, 1994, 96. Mem. AAUW, Assn. of Visual Artists, Soc. of N.Am. Goldsmiths, Visual Artists Alliance of Nashville, Nat. Art Edn. Assn., Internat. Sculpture Ctr., Nat. Coun. on Edn. of the Ceramic Arts, Tenn. Assn. of Craft Artists, Coll. Art Assn. Avocations: boating, running, singing, dancing, hiking. Home: PO Box 120454 Nashville TN 37212-0454

MCKINNEY, JOHN ADAMS, JR., lawyer; b. Washington, Mar. 10, 1948; s. John A. and Cleo G. (Turner) McK.; m. Carol A. Cowen, Dec. 22, 1970; children: John III, Thomas. BA, Principia Coll., 1970; JD, Coll. William and Mary, 1973. Bar: N.J. 1973. Assoc. Mason, Griffin & Pierson, Princeton, N.J., 1973-77; gen. atty. Nabisco, Inc., East Hanover, N.J., 1977-79; asst. counsel Republic Steel Corp., Cleve., 1979-84; atty. and sr. atty. AT&T, Berkeley Heights, N.J., 1984-90; ptnr. McCarter & English, 1990—; adj. prof. Sch. of Law, Seton Hall U., 1997. Co-editor: Cercla Enforcement, 1996. Mem. ABA (vice-chair sect. natural resources energy and environ. law solid and hazardous waste com. 1990—, chair, teleconf. programs 1994-97), N.J. Bar Assn. (dir. environ. law sect. 1992-96, chair 1996-97). Office: McCarter & English 4 Gateway Ctr 100 Mulberry St Newark NJ 07102-4004

MCKINNEY, JUDSON THAD, broadcast executive; b. Sacramento, Aug. 21, 1941; s. Judson Bartlet and Mildred Eoline (Taylor) McK. Student, Sacramento State U., 1959-61, Western Bapt. Bible Coll., 1961-62, Am. River Coll., 1962-63. Prodn. dir. Sta. KEBR, Sacramento, 1962-65; sta. mgr. Sta. KAMB, Merced, Calif., 1965-68, Sta. KEAR, San Francisco, 1975-78, 79-88, WFME, Newark, 1978; western regional mgr. Family Stas. Inc., 1988—. Chmn. bd. 1st Bapt. Ch. of San Francisco, 1985-91. Mem. Nat. Religious Broadcasters., Nat. Assn. Evangelicals. Republican. Lodge: Gideons. Office: Family Stations Inc 290 Hegenberger Rd Oakland CA 94621-1436

MCKINNEY, LARRY, religious organization administrator; m. Debra Ann Dillworth; 2 children. BS in Bible, Phila. Coll. Bible, Langhorne, Pa., 1972; MA in Ednl. Ministries, Wheaton (Ill.) Coll., 1974; EdD in Ednl. Adminstrn., Temple U., 1986. Ordained to ministry Evang. Free Ch., 1974. Former pastor local chs., N.J., Pa.; exec. dir. Fay-West Youth for Christ, Uniontown, Pa., 1972-73, 74-80; dean students, v.p. for student devel. Phila. Coll. Bible, 1980-93; pres. Providence Coll. and Sem., 1993—. Assn. Can. Bible Colls., 1994—; former instr. numerous grad. and postgrad. ednl.-related fields; frequent spkr. for chs., confs., seminars; former mem. or chmn. 6 evaluation teams Accrediting Assn. Bible Colls.; mem. coun. Evang. Fellowship Can. Contbr. numerous articles to mags. and ednl. jours. Avocations: reading, history, running, weightlifting, watching sports. Office: Providence Coll & Sem, Otterburne, MB Canada R0D 1G0

MCKINNEY, LARRY J., federal judge; b. South Bend, Ind., July 4, 1944; s. Lawrence E. and Helen (Byers) McK.; m. Carole Jean Marie Lyon, Aug. 19, 1966; children: Joshua E., Andrew G. BA, MacMurray Coll., Jacksonville, Ill., 1966; JD, Ind. U., 1969. Bar: Ind. 1970, U.S. Dist. Ct. (so. dist.) Ind. 1970. Law clk. to atty. gen. State of Ind., Indpls., 1969-70, dep. atty. gen., 1970-71; ptnr. Rodgers and McKinney, Edinburgh, Ind., 1971-75, James F.T. Sargent, Greenwood, Ind., 1975-79; judge Johnson County Cir. Ct., Franklin, Ind., 1979-87, U.S. Dist. Ct. (so. dist.) Ind., Indpls., 1987—. Presbyterian. Avocations: reading, jogging. Office: US Dist Ct 330 US Courthouse 46 E Ohio St Indianapolis IN 46204-1903

MC KINNEY, MICHAEL WHITNEY, trade association executive; b. San Angelo, Tex., Aug. 23, 1946; s. Wallace Luster and Mitzi Randolph (Broome) McK.; m. Martha LaNan Hooker, Feb. 24, 1973; children: Wallace Blake, Lauren Brooke. BA in Govt., U. Tex., Austin, 1973. Adminstrv. asst. to lt. gov. State of Tex., Austin, 1968-69, adminstrv. asst. to gov., 1969-73, asst. to dir. Tex. Water Quality Bd., Austin, 1973-76; chief of staff Tex. Alcoholic Beverage Commn., 1976-83; v.p. for industry affairs Wholesale Beer Distbrs. Tex., 1984-88, exec. v.p., chief exec. officer, 1989—. Bd. dirs. Tex. Alpha Endl. Found., Inc., Austin, 1969—; mem. Travis County Zoo Task Force, 1986; mem. Senate Com. on Fees and Grants, 1982-83; bd. dirs. Friends of Gov.'s Mansion, 1993-97, Keep Tex. Beautiful, 1997—. Recipient Bert Ford award Tex. Alcoholic Beverage Commn., 1996. Mem. Sam Houston Soc., Knights of the Symphony, Austin Assembly, Phi Kappa Psi. Democrat. Presbyterian. Club: Masons (32 deg., K.T.), Austin Country Club, Austin Club (bd. dirs. 1989—, exec. com. 1994—, Mem. of Yr. 1994). Home: 1708 Intervail Dr Austin TX 78746-7630 Office: 823 Congress Ave Ste 1313 Austin TX 78701-2429

MCKINNEY, OWEN MICHAEL, special education educator, training and security consultant; b. Jeffersonville, Ind., Mar. 9, 1950; s. Owen Howard and Frances Marie (Hall) McK.; m. Janice Elaine Wilson, Sept. 2, 1972; 1 child, Sean Michael. BS in Police Adminstrn., U. Louisville, 1976, postgrad., 1988—; AA, SUNY, Albany, 1978; MS in Adminstrn. of Justice, U. Louisville, 1978; diploma in pastoral ministries, So. Bapt. Conv., 1980; MAT in Secondary Edn., U. Louisville, 1987; cert., Ctr. Ednl. Leadership, Leadership Ky. Cert. 5-12 tchr., learning disabilities, behavior disorders, physically handicapped, community-based edn., learning strategies, social skills, history, geography, polit. sci., sociology, Ky. Probation and parole officer Commonwealth of Ky., Louisville, 1978; security mgr. First Nat. Tower John W. Galbreath & Co., Louisville, 1981-82; v.p. Safety Arms Security & Police Equipment Co., Portsmouth, Va., 1980; area mgr. CPP Security Svc., Norfolk, Va., 1979-80, Louisville, 1982-83; tchr. Jefferson County Pub. Schs., Louisville, 1985-88, spl. edn. tchr., 1988—; pres. Cambridge Cons Inc, Louisville, 1995—; owner Owen McKinney Security Cons., Louisville, 1973—; commr. City of Richlawn, Ky., 1990-92; presenter in field. Editor, writer, publisher The Renaissance Magazine, 1979-81; editor, publisher: Security Gazette, 1982, The Private Investigator, 1983-84, Private Security Report, 1983; editor, writer: (newspaper) Richlawn Gazette, 1990, 91; contbr. articles to profl. jours. Mem. George Bush for Pres., Jefferson County, 1988, Rebecca Jackson for Jefferson County Clerk, 1989, Owen M. McKinney for City Comsnr., Richlawn, 1989, Al Brown for U.S. Congress, 3d congl. dist., Louisville, 1990, Vote for the Library Tax campaign, Jefferson County, 1992; Rep. del. 3d congl. dist. meeting 32d Legis. Dist., 1990, del. Rep. State Conv. 32nd legis. dist. chmn. 1993-94; hon. amb. labor Sec. Labor, Ky. Staff sgt. U.S. Army, 1969-73, Vietnam, mem. USAR, 1977-85, hon. air assault soldier. Recipient Commendation medal U.S. Army, 1971, cert. of appreciation Pres. of U.S., 1973, Outstanding Staff award JCPS, 1919, 92, 93, 94, 95, 96, 97, Minerva award U. Louisville, 1993, Disting. Citizen award Mayor City Louisville; named to Hon. Order Ky. Cols., sr. fellow U. Louisville Soc., numerous others; named Duke of Paducah Mayor City of Paducah, Ky.; named hon. citizen and given key to City of Mayfield, Ky. Mem. ASCD, VFW (life), Assn. U.S. Army, Am. Soc. Indsl. Security (cert. protection profl., chmn. seminar com. Louisville chpt. 1983-84, cert. appreciation Louisville chpt. 1984), Coun. Exceptional Children (chpt. gen. bd. 1988-89, v.p. 1989-90, pres. elect 1990-91, chpt. pres. 1991-92, state gen. bd. 1991-92, chpt. past pres. 1992-93, state v.p. 1993-94, state pres.-elect 1994-95, state pres. 1995-96, 96-97, Svc. award 1990, cert. merit Ky. Fedn. 1990, cert. Outstanding Svc. 1991-92, outstanding mem. of yr. award 1993), Nat. Crime Prevention Alumni Assn., Ky. Ctr. Pub. Issues (charter), Commonwealth Atty.'s Citizen Adv. Coun., DeMolay Alumni Assn. (life, Rep. DeMolay award 1976, 25 Yr. mem.award 1991), U. Louisville Alumni Assn. (program vol. 1990—), Am. Mensa Soc., Am. Legion, Ky. Mid. Sch. Assn., Jesse Stuart Found., York Rite, Scottish Rite, USCG Aux., The Wild Geese (hon.), Masons (past master, grand lodge com.), Order of Eastern Star, Grotto, KP (chancellor comdr. 1994, Internat. Svc. award 1993), Rosicrucian Order, Philalethes Soc., Royal Order Scotland (life), Societas Rosicruciana in Civitatibus Foederatis (life), Shrine, Golden Key Hon. Soc. (life), Internat. High 12 (Internat. Svc. award 1994, chpt. 1st v.p. 1996, chpt. pres. 1997), Alpha Phi Sigma (nat. criminal justice hon. soc. 19750, Phi Delta Kappa (chpt. sec. 1992-93, v.p. 1993-94, Mem. Recognition Cert. 1995). Republican. Baptist. Avocations: reading, tennis, weight lifting, photography, master scuba diver. Home: 212 N Hubbards Ln Louisville KY 40207-2251 Office: Eastern HS 12400 Old Shelbyville Rd Louisville KY 40243-1506 also: Cambridge Cons Inc 212 N Hubbards Ln Louisville KY 40207

MCKINNEY, RICHARD ISHMAEL, philosophy educator; b. Live Oak, Fla., Aug. 20, 1906; s. George Patterson and Sallie Richard (Ellis) McK.; m. Phyllis Vivian Kimbrough, June 27, 1933 (dec. May 1965); children: George Kimbrough, Phyllis Zanaida McKinney Bynum; m. Lena Roberta Martin, Aug. 5, 1967. BA, Morehouse Coll., 1931; BD, Andover Newton Theol. Sch., 1934, STM, 1937; PhD, Yale U., 1942; DD, St. Paul's Coll., Lawrenceville, Va., 1978. Pastor Pond St. Bapt. Ch., Providence, 1933-35; asst. prof. philosophy and religion Va. Union U., Richmond, Va., 1935-42, dean Sch. of Religion, 1942-44, acting v.p., 1978-79; pres. Storer Coll., Harpers Ferry, W.Va., 1944-50; chmn. dept. philosophy Morgan State U., Balt., 1951-76, acting dean Coll. Arts and Scis., 1977-78; disting. scholar in philos. theology Coppin State Coll., Balt., 1983; vis. prof. U. Pa., Phila., spring 1972, U. Ife, Ife-Ife, Nigeria, spring 1974. Author: Religion in Higher Education Among Negroes, 1945, History of First Baptist Church of Charlottesville, Va., 1863-1980, 1981, History of the Black Baptists of Florida, 1850-1985, 1987, Mordecai-The Man and His Message: The Story of Mordecai Wyatt Johnson, 1997; contbr. articles to profl. jours. Bd. dirs. Balt. Urban League, 1958-59, Luth. Hosp., Balt., 1963-65, Am. Cancer Soc., Balt., 1965-70, Enoch Pratt Libr., Balt., 1991—. Mem. AAUP, NEA, Am. Philos. Assn., Soc. for Values in Higher Edn., Soc. for Existential Philosophy and Phenomenology, Phi Beta Kappa, Omega Psi Phi, Sigma Pi Phi (nat. pres. 1986-88), Phi Sigma Tau (nat. pres. 1959-62). Democrat. Avocation: cabinet maker. Home: 2408 Overland Ave Baltimore MD 21214-2440

MC KINNEY, ROBERT MOODY, newspaper editor and publisher; b. Shattuck, Okla., Aug. 28, 1910; s. Edwin S. and Eva (Moody) McK.; married, 1943; 1 child, Mrs. Meade Martin; m. Marie-Louise de Montmollin, May 7, 1970. AB, U. Okla., 1932; LLD, U. N.Mex., 1964. Investment analyst Standard Stats. Co., Inc. (now Standard and Poor's Co.), 1932-34; ptnr. Young-Kolbe & Co., 1934-38, Robert R. Young & Co., 1938-42; exec. v.p., treas. Pathe Film Co., 1934-39, Allegheny Corp., 1936-42, Pittston Corp. and subs., 1936-42; v.p. Fremkir Corp., 1937-50, Allan Corp., 1937-50; exec. v.p., treas. Mo. Pacific R.R., 1938-42; ptnr. Scheffmeyer, McKinney & Co., 1945-50; editor, pub. Santa Fe New Mexican, 1949—; chmn. bd. The New Mexican, Inc., 1949—; profl. corp. dir. 10 N.Y.S.E. cos., 1934-86; chmn. Robert Moody Found.; chmn. N.Mex. Econ. Devel. Commn. and Water Resources Devel. Bd., 1949-51; asst. sec. U.S. Dept. Interior, 1951-52; chmn. panel to report to Congress on impact of Peaceful Uses of Atomic Energy, 1955-56; permanent U.S. rep. to Internat. Atomic Energy Agy., Vienna, 1957-58; U.S. rep. Internat. Conf. Peaceful Uses Atomic Energy, Geneva, 1958; U.S. ambassador to, Switzerland, 1961-63; exec. officer Presdl. Task Force on Internat. Investments, 1963-64; chmn. Presdl. Commn. on Travel, 1968; chmn. bd. visitors U. Okla., 1968-72; U.S. rep. Internat. Centre Settlement Investment Disputes, Washington, 1967-74. Author: Hymn to Wreckage: A Picaresque Interpretation of History, 1947, The Scientific Foundation for European Integration, 1959, On Increasing Effectiveness of Western Science and Technology, 1959, The Red Challenge to Technological Renewal, 1960, Review of the International Atomic Policies and Programs of the United States, 1960, The Toad and the Water Witch, 1985, Variations on a Marxist Interpretation of Culture, 1986. Served from lt. (j.g.) to lt. USNR, 1942-45. Recipient Disting. Service medal U.S. Dept. Treasury, 1968, Disting. Service medal U. Okla., 1972. Mem. Am. Soc. Newspaper Editors, Coun. Fgn. Rels., Coun. of Am. Ambs., Newspaper Assn. of Am., Phi Beta Kappa, Phi Gamma Delta. Democrat. Episcopalian. Clubs: Chevy Chase (Md.); Metropolitan (Washington); University, Brook, Century, Links, Knickerbocker, River (N.Y.C.). Home: Wind Fields 39850 Snickersville Tpke Middleburg VA 20117-3002 Office: PO Box 1705 Santa Fe NM 87504-1705

MC KINNEY, ROSS ERWIN, civil engineering educator; b. San Antonio, Aug. 2, 1926; s. Roy Earl and Beatrice (Saylor) McK.; m. Margaret McKinney Curtis, June 21, 1952; children: Ross Erwin, Margaret E., William S., Susanne C. B.A., So. Meth. U., 1948, B.S. in Civil Engring, 1948; S.M., MIT, 1949, Sc.D., 1951. San. scientist S.W. Found. for Research and Edn., San Antonio, 1951-53; asst. prof. MIT, 1953-58, assoc. prof., 1958-60; prof. U. Kans., 1960-63, chmn. dept. civil engring., 1963-66, Parker prof. civil engring., 1966-76, N.T. Veatch prof. environ. engring., 1976-93, prof. emeritus, 1993—; adv. prof. Tongji U., Shanghai, Peoples Rep. China, 1985; v.p. Rolf Eliassen Assocs., Winchester, Mass., 1954-60; pres. Environ. Pollution Control Services, Lawrence, Kans., 1969-73. Author: Microbiology for Sanitary Engineers, 1962; Editor: Nat. Conf. on Solid Waste Research, 1964, 2d Internat. Symposium for Waste Treatment Lagoons, 1970. Mem. Cambridge (Mass.) Water Bd., 1953-59, Lawrence-Douglas County Health Bd., 1969-76, Kans. Water Quality Adv. Council, 1965-76, Kans. Solid Waste Adv. Council, 1970-76, Kans. Environ. Adv. Bd., 1976-85. Served with USNR, 1943-46. Recipient Harrison P. Eddy award, 1962, Water Pollution Control Fedn. Rudolph Hering award, 1964, U.S. Presdl. Commendation, 1971, Environ. Quality award EPA Region VII, 1979, Chancellors Teaching award, U. Kans., 1986. Mem. ASCE (hon.), Am. Water Works Assn., Water Pollution Control Fedn. (Thomas R. Camp medal 1982), Am. Chem. Soc., Am. Soc. Microbiologists, AAAS, Internat. Assn. Water Pollution Rsch., Am. Acad. Environ. Engrs., Kans. Water Pollution Control Assn. (hon., Gordon M. Fair medal 1991), NAE, Sigma Xi, Sigma Tau, Kappa Mu Epsilon, Chi Epsilon, Tau Beta Pi. Achievements include patent for water treatment process. Home: 3100 Annandale Rd Durham NC 27705-5466

MCKINNEY, SALLY VITKUS, state official; b. Muncie, Ind., Aug. 6, 1944; d. Robert Brookins and Mary (Mann) Gooden; m. Alan George Vitkus (div. Jan. 1979); m. James Larry McKinney, Feb. 1, 1986. AA, William Woods Coll., 1964; BSBA, U. Ariz., 1966; postgrad., U. Nev., Las Vegas, 1966-68. Tchr. Las Vegas Day Sch., 1972-76; salesperson Globe Realty, Las Vegas, 1976-79; owner, pres. Realty West, Las Vegas, 1979-96; chief investigator State of Nev. Real Estate Divsn., 1996—. Rec. sec. Clark County Rep. Cen. Com., Las Vegas, 1982, 1st vice chmn., 1985; vice chmn. Nev. Rep. com., 1986, chmn., 1987-88; mem. Assistance League Las Vegas. Recipient award Nat. Assn. Home Builders, 1981, 82, 83. Mem. Nat. Assn. Realtors, Las Vegas Bd. Realtors, Greater Las Vegas C. of C., Gen. Fedn. Womens Clubs (nominee Outstanding Young Woman Am. 1979, exec. bd. 1980-82), Jr. League Las Vegas, Mesquite Club (chmn. pub. affairs com. 1986-87, past pres., secret witness exec. bd. 1994—). Presbyterian. Avocations: tennis, bridge. Home: 132 Ultra Dr Henderson NV 89014-8306

MCKINNEY, VENORA WARE, librarian; b. Meridian, Okla., June 16, 1937. BA, Langston U., 1959; MLS, U. Ill., 1965. Librarian Milw. Pub. Library, 1962-68, br. librarian, 1979-83, dep. city librarian, 1983—; librarian Peoria Pub. Schs., Ill., 1969, Milw. Pub. Schs., 1972-79; adj. faculty U. Wis., Milw.; mem. Wis. Govs. Coun. on Libr. Devel., 1983-93; bd. dirs. V.E. Carter Child Devel. Group, 1992-96. Bd. dirs. Milw. Repertory Theatre; coun. adv. Sch. Libr. and Info. Sci., U. Wis., Madison, 1992-96. Nat. Forum for Black Pub. Adminstrs. fellow Exec. Leadership Inst., George Mason U. Mem. ALA Black Caucus, Wis. Libr. Assn. (v.p. 1994, pres. 1995—, bd. dirs. 1996), Wis. Black Librs. Network, ALA Pub. Libr. Assn., Links, Delta Sigma Theta. Baptist. Office: Milw Pub Libr 814 W Wisconsin Ave Milwaukee WI 53233-2309

MCKINNEY, WILLIAM T., psychiatrist, educator; b. Rome, Ga., Sept. 20, 1937. BA cum laude, Baylor U., 1959; MD, Vanderbilt U., 1963. Diplomate Nat. Bd. Med. Examiners (mem. psychiatry test com. 1982-87, chmn. 1984-87); cert. Am. Bd. Psychiatry and Neurology (sr. examiner 1979-90, bd. dirs. 1991—, mem. rsch. com., co-chair part I test com., chair added qualifications in geriatric psychiatry test com., mem. part II audio visual com., mem. disability accomodations com., rep. to residency rev. com.). Intern in medicine Bowman Gray Sch. Medicine, Wake Forest U., Winston-Salem, N.C., 1963-64; resident dept. psychiatry Sch. Medicine, U. N.C., Chapel Hill., 1964-66, Sch. Medicine, Stanford (Calif.) U., 1966-67; clin. assoc. psychosomatic sect. adult psychiatry br., tng. specialist, asst. br. chief NIMH, Bethesda, Md., 1967-69; asst. prof. psychiatry dept. psychiatry Sch. Medicine, U. Wis., Madison, 1969-72, assoc. prof. psychiatry, 1972-74, prof. psychiatry, 1974-93; Asher prof. of psychiatry dept. psychiatry and behavioral scis., dir. Asher Ctr. for Study and Treatment of Depressive Disorders Med. Sch., Northwestern U., Chgo., 1993—; part-time clin. pvt. practice, Bethesda, 1967-69; NIMH rsch. career investigator Sch. Medicine, U. Wis., Madison, 1970-75, rsch. psychiatrist Primate Lab., 1974-93, affiliate sci. Wis. Regional Primate Rsch. Ctr., 1974-93, affiliate prof. psychology dept. psychology, 1974-93, chmn. dept. psychiatry, 1975-80, dir. Wis. Psychiat. Rsch. Inst. Ctr. Health Scis., 1975-80; sr. staff psychiatrist William S. Middleton Meml. VA Hosp., Madison, Wis., 1974-93; rschr. sub dept. animal behaviour U. Cambridge, Eng., 1974; mem. rsch. rev. com. VA Behavioral Scis., 1976-79; Abbott Sigma XI Club lectr., 1976; Milw. Psychiat. Hosp. lectr., 1977; mem. program adv. com. and workshop chmn. Dahlem Found. Internat. Conf. on Depression, Berlin, 1982; U. Minn. lectr. at Festshrift, 1982; cons. grad. sch. U. Minn., 1982; fellow Ctr. Advanced Study in Behavioral Scis., Stanford, Calif., 1983-84; mem. external adv. bd. Clin. Rsch. Ctr. Dept. Psychiatry U. N.C., Chapel Hill, 1984—, cons., bd. advisors clin. rsch. fellow tng. program dept. psychology, 1988—; William F. Orr lectr. Vanderbilt U., 1985; vis. prof. dept. psychiatry U. Tex. Health Scis. Ctr., Dallas, 1986, U. Utah Sch. Medicine, Salt Lake City, 1987, U. Minn. Sch. Medicine, Mpls., 1988; cons. biol. scis. tng. br. divsn. manpower and tng. programs NIMH, 1975-76, mem. psychiatry spl. tng. com. 1983, plenary lectr., Clearwater, Fla., 1987, co-chairperson Workshop on Non-Human Primate Models of Psychopathology, 1987, mem. biol. psychopathology spl. rev. com., 1992—; mem. sci. core group MacArthur Found. Mental Health Rsch. Network I: The Psychobiology of Depression and Other Affective Disorders, 1988-93; vis. spkr. So. Calif. Psychiat. Soc., L.A., 1988; plenary lectr. Soc. Biol. Psychiatry ann. meeting, Montreal, 1988; vis. prof. Dalhousie U. Sch. Medicine, N.S., 1989, HCA Riveredge Hosp., Chgo., 1989, U. Pa., Phila., 1991, U. N.Mex., Albuquerque, 1992, Northwestern U., Chgo., 1992; invited spkr. Animal Models in Psychopharmacology Symposium, Duphar, Amsterdam, 1990; vis. spkr., cons. CIBA-GEIGY, Basel, Switzerland, 1990; mem. minority instns. rsch. devel. rev. com. Alcohol, Drug Abuse and Mental Health Adminstrn., 1990; guest spkr. Inst. Pa. Hosp., Phila., 1991; reviewer Human Frontier Sci. Program, 1992—; external cons. dept. psychiatry Mental Health Clin. Rsch. Ctr. U. Tex. Southwestern Med. Ctr., Dallas, 1992—; presenter in field. Author: Animal Models of Mental Disorders: A New Comparative Psychiatry, 1988; co-author: Mood Disorders: Towards a New Psychobiology, 1984; mem. editl. bd. Archives of Psychiatry and Neurol. Scis., Contemporary Psychiatry, 1981-82, Ethology and Sociobiology, Experientia, 1982-89, Trends in Neurosciences, 1982-86, Neuropsychopharmacology, 1987-90; manuscript and book reviewer numerous sci. jours.; contbr. articles to profl. jours. USHPS fellow in biostats. Vanderbilt U., 1962; recipient Beauchamp award Vanderbilt U. Med. Sch., 1963, Rsch. Career Devel. award NIMH, 1975, Rsch. Leave award U. Wis., 1983-84, Am. Acad. Pediats. award, 1991. Fellow Am. Psychiat. Assn. (cons. psychiat. edn. consultation svc. 1983—), Am. Coll. Psychiatrists, Am. Coll. Neuropsychopharmacology (mem. constn. and rules com. 1985-87, mem. ethics com. 1987-89, mem. fin. com. 1990-92, panel chair San Juan, P.R. 1992, panel presenter 1992); mem. Am. Soc. Primatologists, Am. Psychosomatic Soc. (mem. program com. 1975-76), Internat. Primatology Soc., Internat. Coll. Neurobiology, Biol. Psychiatry and Psychopharmacology (lectr. Zurich 1985), Internat. Soc. Devel. Psychobiology, Internat. Soc. Ethological and Behavioral Pharmacology (bd. advisors 1983—), Collegium Internat. Neuro-Psychopharmacologicum, Psychiat. Rsch. Soc., Soc. Neuroscience, Wis. Psychiat. Assn. (chmn. program com. 1972, co-chairperson task force on sexual misconduct and membership edn. 1986-88, pres.-elect 1989-91, pres. 1991-93). Office: Northwestern U Med Sch Dept Psychiatry and Behavioral Scis 303 E Chicago Ave Bldg 9-176 Chicago IL 60611-3008

MCKINNEY-KELLER, MARGARET FRANCES, retired special education educator; b. Houston, Mo., Nov. 25, 1929; d. George Weimer and Thelma May (Davis) Van Pelt; m. Roy Calvin McKinney Sr., Nov. 11, 1947 (dec. Feb. 1990); children: Deanna Kay Little, Roy Calvin Jr.; m. Clarence Elmore Keller, June 8, 1991; 1 child, Dennis Lee Keller. BS with honors, Bradley U., 1963, MA in Counselor Edn., 1968, postgrad., 1992; postgrad., U. Ill., 1993—, Aurora Coll., Ill. Ctrl. Coll. In real estate Peoria, Ill., 1951-57; tchr. Oak Ridge Sch., Willow Springs, Mo., 1947-48, pvt. kindergarten, Washington, Ill., 1957-59, Dist. 50 Schs., Washington, Ill., 1959-67; tchr. socially maladjusted Washington Twp. Spl. Edn. Coop., 1967-70; tchr. behavior disordered Tazewell-Mason Counties Spl. Edn., Washington, Ill., 1970-78; resource tchr. Dist. 50 Schs., Washington, 1978-94; ret., 1994. Cons. moderator Active Parenting Group, Washington, 1972—; adv. bd. to establish Tazewell County Health Dept., 1960s; pres. gov. bd. Faith Luth. Day Care Ctr., Washington, 1970—, Washington Sr. Citizens, 1982-91; coach Spl. Olympics, Washington, 1979—; pres. Faith Luth. Ch. Coun., Washington, 1985-86; laity v.p. No. Conf. Evang. Luth. Ch. Am., Ctrl. Ill., 1986-92; vol. Proctor Hosp., 1994—. Mem. AAUW, Washington Bus. and Profl. Women (pres. 1979-80, 88-89, dist. 9 dir. 1995-96), Am. Legion Aux., German-Am. Soc., Alpha Delta Kappa (state office, ctrl. region). Avocations: travel, cooking, oil painting, crocheting. Home: 603 Sherwood Park Rd Washington IL 61571-1828

MCKINNEY-LUDD, SARAH LYDELLE, middle school education, librarian; b. Feb. 29, 1948. BA, U. Md., 1973; MA, Cen. Mich. U., 1975; MA in Legal Studies, Antioch Sch. Law, Washington, 1982; postgrad., Sch. Edn. George Washington U., 1989—. Cert. advanced profl. tchr. grades 5 through 12, Md., cert. adminstr. Tchr. of learning disabled Azores (Portugal) Elem. Sch., 1974-76; tchr. English Spaulding Jr. High Sch., Forestville, Md., 1976-82, Prince George's Cmty. Coll., 1982-84, Benjamin Tasker Sch., Bowie, Md., 1982-85, Crossland Night Sch., Temple Hills, Md., 1984-85, Thomas Pullen Mid. Sch., Landover, Md., 1985-87, Kettering (Md.) Mid. Sch., 1985-88, Kenmoor Mid. Sch., Landover, 1988-91; tchr. English, libr. Drew Freeman Mid. Sch.(formerly Francis Scott Key Mid. Sch.), District Heights, Md., 1991—; chair multicultural com., chair sch. based mgmt. Francis Scott Key Mid. Sch., 1992—; reader Jarvis Grants, U.S. Dept. Edn., 1990—; acad. coord. Prince George's County Steel Band-Positive Vibrations. Contbr. articles to various publs. Mem. Md. State Tchr.'s Legis. Com., 1987-90; chairperson Profl. Rights and Responsibility, 1978-81; active Prince George's Com. on Acad. Achievement, Prince George's Com. Women's Fair Steering Com., Md. State Hosp. Bd., Prince George's County affiliate United Black Fund, area speakers bur.; programs chairperson, sec. Project Safe Sts.-2000, 1989; pres. Bowie Therapeutic Nursery; judge ACT-SO NAACP,

Washington, 1989—; mem. exec. bd. Prince George's County chpt., 1984-89; active polit. campaigns; bd. dirs. Landover Ednl. Athletic Recreational Non-Profit Found. of Washington Redskins. Mem. Md. State Tchrs. Assn. (editor Women's Caucus), Sigma Gamma Rho (Community Activist award 1992). Home: 4411 Cape Cod Cir Bowie MD 20720-3582 Office: Drew Freeman Mid Sch 5100 Silver Hill Rd Suitland MD 20746-5214

MCKINNIS, MICHAEL B., lawyer; b. St. Louis, May 31, 1945; s. Bayard O. and Doris (Lammert) McK.; m. Patricia Butow, Aug. 24, 1968; children: Scott, Christopher, Elizabeth. BS, Drake U., 1967; JD, U. Mo., 1970. Bar: Mo. 1970, U.S. Dist. Ct. (ea. dist.) Mo. Ptnr., exec. com. Bryan Cave, St. Louis. Editor U. Mo. Law Rev., 1969-70. Mem. ABA, Mo. Bar Assn., Order of Coif, Phi Delta Phi. Office: Bryan Cave 1 Met Sq 211 N Broadway Saint Louis MO 63102-2733

MCKINNON, ARNOLD BORDEN, transportation company executive; b. Goldsboro, N.C., Aug. 13, 1927; s. Henry Alexander and Margaret (Borden) McK.; m. Oriana McArthur, July 19, 1950; children: Arnold Borden Jr., Colin McArthur, Henry Alexander. AB, Duke U., 1950, LLB, 1951; grad. Advanced Mgmt. Program, Harvard U., 1972. Bar: D.C. 1951, N.C. 1966. With Norfolk So. Corp. (formerly So. Ry. System), Norfolk, Va., 1951-71, from v.p. law to chmn., 1971-91; chmn. exec. com., 1992—, also bd. dirs. Bd. dirs. Nat. Maritime Ctr. Found., Norfolk Forum, Inc., CADRE Found.; active Mil. Civilian Liaison Group; mem. bus. adv. com. Northwestern U. Transp. Ctr.; trustee Med. Coll. Hampton Roads Found., Va. Union Theol. Sem.; vice chmn. Va. Gov.'s Econ. Adv. Coun.; commr. Norfolk Redevel. and Housing Authority. With U.S. Army, 1946-47. Mem. ABA, N.C. Bar Assn., D.C. Bar Assn., Am. Soc. Corp. Execs., Norfolk Yacht and Country Club, Harbor Club, Chevy Chase Club, Met. Club, Laurel Valley Golf Club, India House, Cedar Point Club, Bonita Bay Club, Rotary. Presbyterian. Home: 552 Mowbray Arch Norfolk VA 23507-2130 Office: Norfolk So Corp 3 Commercial Pl Norfolk VA 23510-2108

MC KINNON, CLINTON DAN, aerospace transportation executive; b. San Bernardino, Calif., Jan. 27, 1934; s. Clinton Dotson and Lucille V. (McVey) McK.; m. Janice Bernard; children: Holly Jean, Sherri Lynn, Clinton Scott, Lisa Caroline. B.A., U. Mo., 1956; honorary doctorate, Nat. U., 1987. Page U.S. Ho. of Reps., 1950-52; reporter, photographer, advt. salesman Sentinel Newspaper, San Diego, 1960-62; owner, pres. KSON Radio, San Diego, 1962-85, KSON-FM, San Diego, 1964-85; pub. La Jolla (Calif.) Light Jour., 1969-73; owner House of Hits (book and music pub.), San Diego, 1972—; co-owner KIII-TV, Corpus Christi, Tex., 1964—, KBMT-TV, Beaumont, Tex., 1976—, KUSI-TV, San Diego, 1992—; chmn. CAB, Washington, 1981-84; with spl. projects CIA, 1985-86; chmn., pres. North Am. Airlines, Jamaica, N.Y., 1989—. Author: The Good Life, 1974, Bullseye--One Reactor (aka Bullseye Iraq), 1986, Everything You Need to Know Before You're Hijacked, 1986, The Ten Second Message, 1994, Rescue Pilot, 1994, Words of Honor, 1995. Chmn. exec. com. Greater San Diego Billy Graham Crusade. Served as aviator USNR, 1956-60. Recipient Advt. Man of Year award San Diego Advt. and Sales Club, 1971; Radio Sta. Mgr. of Year award Billboard Mag., 1973; Internat. Pres.'s award Youth for Christ, 1975; Man of Distinction award Mexican-Am. Found., 1976; George Washington Honor medal Freedoms Found., 1976; Headliner of Yr. (govt.), San Diego Press Club, 1985. Mem. Country Music Assn. (pres. 1977, recipient pres. award 1980), C. of C. (dir.), Nat. Assn. Broadcasters (bd. dirs. 1970-74), Calif. Broadcasters Assn. (dir.), Navy League (Media Man of Yr. 1980), Wings Club (bd. govs.). Club: Rotary (San Diego). Set Navy helicopter peacetime rescue record of 62 air/sea rescues, 1958; 1st person to close down fed. govt. regulatory agy., CAB, 1984. Office: JFK International N Am Air Ste 250 Jamaica NY 11430

MCKINNON, DANIEL WAYNE, JR., naval officer; b. St. Joseph, Mo., Apr. 26, 1934; s. Daniel Wayne and Amber Ruth (McClanahan) McK.; m. Rae Lynne Hopper, Apr. 21, 1957; 1 child, Daniel W. III. BSBA, U. Mo., 1956; MBA with distinction, U. Mich., 1966; grad. (disting.), Indsl. Coll. Armed Forces, Washington, 1975. Commd. ensign USN, 1956, advanced through grades to rear adm., 1983; exec. asst. to comdr. Naval Supply Systems Command, Washington, 1970-74, dir. supply corps pers., 1982-83, dep. comdr. for inventory and systems integrity, 1983-84, vice comdr., 1984-86, comdr., 1988-91; ship supply readiness officer, supply systems ops. officer Naval Logistic Command, Pacific Fleet, Pearl Harbor, Hawaii, 1975-78; dir. shipbuilding contracts div. Naval Sea Systems Command, Washington, 1978-80; comdg. officer Naval Supply Depot, Subic Bay, The Philippines, 1980-82; dep. dir. for acquisition mgmt. Def. Logistics Agy., Cameron Station, Va., 1986-88; chief Navy supply corps, comdr. Naval Supply Systems, 1988-91; ret. USN, 1991—; pres., CEO NISH (formerly Nat. Industries for Severly Handicapped), Vienna, Va., 1992—. Chmn. Annandale (Va.) Ctrl. Bus. Dist. Planning Com., 1986-91, Pres.'s Com. for Purchase from the Blind and Other Severely Handicapped, Washington, 1986-91; mem. strategic devel. bd. U. Mo.; bd. dirs. Va. Industries for Blind, 1991—, Project Handclasp, 1994—. Decorated D.S.M., Legion of Merit. Recipient Disting. Svc. award Nat. Industries for Severely Handicapped, 1991; Capstone fellow Nat. Def. U., 1986. Mem. Navy Supply Corps Assn. (pres. 1988-91), Nat. Contract Mgmt. Assn. (bd. advisors 1986—), Navy Fed. Credit Union (vice chmn. 1986-92), Navy Mut. Aid Assn. (bd. dirs. 1982-91), Comprehensive Tech. Internat. (bd. dirs. 1992—), Army and Navy Club, Beta Theta Pi, Beta Gamma Sigma, Phi Kappa Phi.

MCKINNON, FLOYD WINGFIELD, textile executive; b. Columbus, Ga., Dec. 1, 1942; s. Malcolm Angus and Sarah C. (Bullock) McK.; m. Barbara Evans Roles, June 18, 1966; children: James Wingfield, Sarah Elizabeth, Robert Kent. AB, Washington and Lee U., 1964. Lic. airplane pilot. V.p. Cotswold Industries, Inc., N.Y.C., 1966—, also bd. dirs.; v.p., corp. sec. Cen. Textiles, Inc., S.C., 1984—, also bd. dirs.; arbitrator Am. Arbitration Assn., 1983—. Pres. Berkley-in-Scarsdale Assn., 1980, Scarsdale Leasing Corp., 1996; admissions rep. Washington and Lee U., 1979-89, 93—. Mem. Aircraft Owner's and Pilot's Assn., St. Andrews Soc. N.Y. Republican. Episcopalian. Clubs: Union League (bd. govs. 1974-77, 88-91, 97—, sec. 1981-83, chmn. admissions com. 1996) (N.Y.C.); Scarsdale Golf (bd. govs. 1983-91, pres. 1990-91) (Hartsdale, N.Y.); Bras Coupe (exec. com. 1980—) (Maniwaki, Can.). Home: 26 Taunton Rd Scarsdale NY 10583-5610 Office: Cotswold Industries 10 E 40th St New York NY 10016-0200

MC KINNON, F(RANCIS) A(RTHUR) RICHARD, utility executive; b. Delburne, Alta., Can., Mar. 5, 1933; s. John Donald and Ruth Rebecca (Sundberg) McK.; m. Elma Lorraine Lebsack, June 1, 1957; children: Kenneth Richard, Stephen David, Karen Diane. B. Commerce, U. Alta., 1954; postgrad., Stanford Exec. Program, Stanford U., 1982. With Alta. Gas Trunk Line Co. Ltd., Calgary, 1960-75, treas., 1971-75; dir. fin. TransAlta Utilities Corp. (formerly Calgary Power Ltd.), 1975—, treas., 1976-81, v.p. fin., 1981—; v.p. fin. Trans Alta Energy Corp., Trans Alta Corp.; pres. Elm Farm Cons., Inc., Calgary, 1996—; bd. dirs. AEC Power Ltd. Past bd. dirs. Foothills Gen. Hosp., Calgary. Fellow Inst. Chartered Accts. of Alta.; mem. Can. Inst. Chartered Accts., Fin. Execs. Inst. Can. (past chmn., past pres., bd. dirs. Calgary chpt., v.p.), Fin. Execs. Inst. (bd. dirs.). Clubs: Calgary Petroleum, Canyon Meadows Golf and Country. Home: 1412 Windsor St NW, Calgary, AB Canada T2N 3X3 Office: TransAlta Utilities Corp, 110 12th Ave SW, Calgary, AB Canada T2P 2M1

MCKINNON, ISAIAH, police chief; b. Montgomery, Ala., June 21, 1943; s. Cota and Lula (Jones) McK.; m. Patrice Anne McKinnon; children: Jeffrey Christopher, Jason Patrick. BA in History/Law Enforcement, Mercy Coll. of Detroit, 1975; MA in Criminal Justice, U. Detroit, 1978; PhD in Adminstrn. and Higher Edn., Mich. State U., 1981; grad., FBI Nat. Acad., 1977. Police officer Detroit Police Dept., 1965-71, sgt., 1971-74, lt., 1974-77, inspector, 1977-84, chief of police, 1994—; dir. pub. safety U. Detroit, 1984-89; dir. security Renaissance Ctr., Detroit, 1989-93; lectr. Detroit Met. Police Acad., Mich. State Police Acad., Mich. Assn. Police; trainer in field; presenter Nat. Bapt. Ministers Conv., Ala. State U.; mem. Leadership and Mgmt. Adv. Bd.; adj. prof. criminal justice U. Detroit, 1984, Wayne State U., 1985-86, Wayne County C.C., 1988—; asst. prof. criminal justice Mercy Coll. of Detroit, 1978-86; security cons. Limbach Co., Detroit, Marathon Petroleum Co., Detroit, State of Mich. Workers Disability Compensation Bldg., Detroit, Rubloff Mgmt. Co., Chgo. Author: Police and the Nurse, 1984, Police and Child Abuse, 1992; contbr. articles to newspapers; guest columnist Mich. Chronicle. Trustee Grosse Point Acad.; past mem., bd. dirs. Ronald McDonald House, Children's Ctr. Wayne County; past mem. youth devel. com. Detroit Urban League; mem. Dad's Club U. Detroit Jesuit H.S.; bd. dirs. U. Detroit, 1974—, Wayne County C.C., Detroit, 1975—. With USAF, 1961-65. Recipient Spirit of Detroit award, numerous citations, commendations. Mem. F.B.I. Nat. Acad. Grads. Office: Police Dept 1300 Beaubien St Detroit MI 48226-2308*

MCKINNON, JAMES BUCKNER, real estate sales executive, writer, researcher; b. Tacoma, Dec. 5, 1916; s. James Mitchell and Rochelle Lenore (Buckner) McK.; m. Mary C. Corbitt, Dec. 1961 (div. June 1963); 1 child, James H.C.; m. Marylyn Adelle Coote, Mar. 12, 1967 (div. May 1977); 1 child, Michelyn; m. Martha Sackmann, June 12, 1977. BA in Internat. Studies, U. Wash., 1983, H.M. Jackson Sch. Police detective Los Angeles Police Dept., 1946-50; bn. security officer 1st med. bn. 1st Marine div. Fleet Marine Force, 1950-53; owner, operator, mgr., dir. promotional sales The Saucy Dog Drive-In, Venice, Calif., 1953-63; salesman new car sales and leasing Burien Mercury, Seattle, 1963-66; real estate salesman and appraiser various firms Seattle, 1966—; instr., lectr. U.S. Naval Support Activity, Sandpoint, Wash., 1964-74; mem., lectr. NRC 11-8, Naval Postgrad. Sch., Monterey, Calif., 1975-76; Burien Mercury announcer KOMO TV. Author: (poetry) On the Threshold of a Dream, Vol. III, 1992, Best Poems of the 90's, 1992; contbr. to anthologies: Where Words Haven't Spoken, 1993, Fire From Within, 1994; contbr. articles to various newspapers and mil. jours. Mem. br. adv. com. Wash. State YMCA, Seattle, 1994—, treas., 1986-94, 95, mem. so. dist. fin. bd., 1989-93, 94, 95-96. With USN, 1939-53, PTO, Korea. Recipient Wilmer Culver Meml. award Culver Alumni Fictioneers, Seattle, 1979, Silver Poet award World of Poetry Press, 1986, Golden Poet award, 1987-92, Best Poet of the 90's Nat. Libr. of Poetry, 1992, First Place with Editor's Preference award Creative Arts and Scis. Enterprises, 1996; Occidental Coll. scholar, 1935; named to Honorable Order Ky. Cols., 1976; named One of Best New Poets, Am. Poetry Assn. Anthology, 1988; inducted into the Internat. Poetry Hall of Fame, 1996. Mem. Internat. Soc. Authors and Artists (1st place award for 1997 poem), Internat. Platform Assn., U.S. Naval Inst. (life), Internat. Soc. Poets (life), N.W. Writers Conf., Ret. Officers Assn. (life), Mensa, Acad. Am. Poets, KP, Masons. Republican. Home: 2312 41st Ave SW Seattle WA 98116-2060 *Personal philosophy: To realize one's greatest potential pursue goals that hold the greatest potential meaning in life.*

MCKINNON, KATHLEEN ANN, software engineer; b. Berwyn, Ill., July 27, 1960; d. James Walter and Linda Lee (Belford) Turek; m. Donald Lee McKinnon, Jr., July 27, 1980; 1 child, Donald Lee III. AA in Computer Sci., Pensacola Jr. Coll., 1980; BS in Computer Sci. and Info. Systems, U. Md., 1986. SIGINT Morse interceptor U.S. Army, Ft. Meade, Md., 1982-86; computer scientist Dept. Def., Ft. Meade, 1986-90; software engr. Harris Corp., Melbourne, Fla., 1990—, group leader, 1994—. Mem. missions com. Pineda Presbyn. Ch., Melbourne, 1991—; moderator Pineda Presbyn. Women, 1995-96. Recipient achievement medal U.S. Army, 1983, spl. achievement award Dept. Def., 1989. Republican. Avocations: painting and drawing, jazzercise.

MCKINNON, ROBERT HAROLD, retired insurance company executive; b. Holtville, Calif., Apr. 4, 1927; s. Harold Arthur and Gladys Irene (Blanchar) McK.; m. Marian Lois Hayes, Dec. 18, 1948; children: Steven Robert, Laurie Ellen, David Martin. BS, Armstrong Coll., 1950, MBA, 1952. Regional sales mgr. Farmers Ins. Group, Austin, Tex., 1961-66, Aurora, Ill., 1966-68; dir. life sales Farmers New World Life, L.A., 1968-75; v.p. mktg. Warner Ins. Group, Chgo., 1975-82; mem. Canners Exchange Dairy Adv. Com., 1977-82; sr. v.p. mktg. The Rural Ins. Cos., Madison, Wis., 1982-89; mktg. cons. ins. and fin. svcs. Nat. Guardian Life Fin. Svcs., Madison, 1989-90, exec. recruiter Sales Cons. Madison, 1990-; ret.. Scoutmaster Boy Scouts Am., 1971-72; vestry mem. St. Dunstan's Episcopal Ch., chair redevel. of Ch. With U.S. Army, 1944-45. Fellow Life Underwriters Tng. Coun.; mem. Madison Life Underwriters Assn., Soc. CPCUs, Rotary (bd. dirs., pres., Paul Harris fellow 1994), Elks. Home: 5 Connecticut Ct Madison WI 53719-2202

MCKINSEY, ELIZABETH, college dean; b. Columbia, Mo., Aug. 10, 1947; d. J. Wendell and A. Ruhamah (Peret) McK.; m. Thomas N. Clough, June 18, 1977; children: Emily, Peter. BA, Radcliffe Coll., 1970; PhD, Harvard U., 1976. From instr. to asst. prof. English Bryn Mawr (Pa.) Coll., 1975-77; from asst. to assoc. prof. English Harvard U., Cambridge, Mass., 1977-85; dir. Bunting Inst. Radcliffe Coll., Cambridge, 1985-89; dean Carleton Coll., Northfield, Minn., 1989—. Author: Niagara Falls: Icon of the American Sublime, 1985; contbr. articles and revs. to profl. jours. and lit. mags. NEH fellow, 1980. Mem. MLA, Am. Conf. Acad. Deans (bd. dirs.), Nat. Coun. for Rsch. on Women (assoc.), Am. Studies Assn., Nat. Assn. Women in Edn., Phi Beta Kappa (pres. Iota of Mass. chpt. 1986-89). Home: 815 2nd St E Northfield MN 55057-2308 Office: Carleton Coll 1 N College St Northfield MN 55057-4001

MCKINZIE, CARL WAYNE, lawyer; b. Lubbock, Tex., Dec. 3, 1939; s. J. Clyde and Flora (Cates) McK.; m. Rowena Ann Williams; children: Wayne, Clinton, Morgan (dec.). BBA, Tex. Tech U., 1962, MBA, 1963; JD, So. Meth. U., 1966. From assoc. to ptnr. Nossaman, Guthner & Knox, L.A., 1966-80; prin. Riordan & McKinzie, L.A., 1980—; bd. dirs. IXC Comm., Inc. Contbr. articles to law jours. Mem. bd. visitors Sch. Law So. Meth. U., Dallas, 1979-82, 90—, bd. dirs., 1970-73, 84-89, chmn. exec. com., 1996—; mem. bd. visitors Coll. Law Ariz. State U., 1990—; bd. dirs. Riordan Found., Rx for Reading; bd. dirs., pub. counsel Calif. Cmty. Found.; mem. bd. govs. Nat. Assn. Real Estate Investment Trusts, 1986-89. Capt. USAF, 1967-70. Recipient disting. alumni award So. Meth. U., Dallas, 1994. Mem. ABA (chmn. current devel. subcom., com. tax problems 1978-80), Calif. Bar Assn., Los Angeles County Bar Assn., Jonathan Club, City Club on Bunker Hill, L.A. Country Club. Republican. Home: 527 21st Pl Santa Monica CA 90402 Office: Riordan & McKinzie 29th Fl 300 S Grand Ave Ste 29 Los Angeles CA 90071-3110

MCKIRAHAN, RICHARD DUNCAN, JR., classics and philosophy educator; b. Berkeley, Calif., July 27, 1945; s. Richard Duncan and Helen Marion (Hixson) McK.; m. Voula Tsouna, June 3, 1961; 1 child, Helen Hamilton. AB, U. Calif., Berkeley, 1966; BA, U. Oxford, Eng., 1969; MA, Oxford U., Eng., 1979; PhD, Harvard U., 1973. Teaching fellow, tutor Harvard U., Cambridge, Mass., 1971-73; asst. prof. classics and philosophy Pomona Coll., Claremont, Calif., 1973-79, assoc. prof., 1979-87, E.C. Norton prof. classics and philosophy, 1987—, chair dept. classics, 1992—. Author: Socrates and Plato, A Comprehensive Bibliography, 1958-73, 78, Plato's Meno, 1986, Principles and Proofs: Aristotle's Theory of Demonstrative Science, 1992, Philosophy Before Socrates, 1994, A Presocratics Reader, 1996; also articles on Greek philosophy, math. and scis. Marshall Aid Commemoration Commn. scholar, U. Oxford, 1966-69; Woodrow Wilson Found. fellow, 1966-67; NEH grantee, 1975, 85, 90. Mem. Am. Philol. Assn., Soc. Ancient Greek Philosophy, Phi Beta Kappa. Office: Pomona Coll Dept Classics 140 W 6th St Claremont CA 91711-4301

MCKISSACK, PATRICIA CARWELL, children's book author; b. Nashville, Sept. 9, 1944; d. Robert and Erma Carwell; m. Fredrick L. McKissack, Dec. 12, 1965; children: Fredrick L. Jr., Robert, John. BA, Tenn. State U., 1964; MA, Webster U., 1975. Jr. high sch. tchr. Kirkland, Mo., 1968-75; children's book editor Concordia Pub. House, 1976-81, Inst. Children's Lit., 1984—; part-time English instr. Forest Park Coll., St. Louis, 1975—; instr. U. Mo., St. Louis, 1978—. Author: Good Shepard Prayer, 1978, God Gives New Life, 1979, Ask the Kids, 1979, Who is Who?, 1983, Martin Luther King, Jr.: A Man to Remember, 1984, Paul Laurence Dunbar: A Poet to Remember, 1984, Michael Jackson, Superstar, 1984, Lights Out, Christopher, 1984, It's the Truth, Christopher, 1984 (C.S. Lewis Silver Medal award Christian Sch. Mag. 1984), The Apache, 1984, Mary McLeod Bethune: A Great American Educator, 1985, Aztec Indians, 1985, The Inca, 1985, The Maya, 1985, Flossie and the Fox, 1986, Our Martin Luther King Book, 1986, Who is Coming?, 1986, Give It with Love, Christopher: Christopher Learns about Gifts and Giving, 1988, Speak Up, Christopher: Christopher Learns the Difference Between Right and Wrong, 1988, A Troll in a Hole, 1988, Nettie Jo's Friends, 1988 (Parent's Choice award 1990), Mirandy and Brother Wind, 1988, Monkey-Monkey's Trick: Based on an African Folk-Tale, 1989, Jesse Jackson: A Biography, 1989, (with Ruthilde Kronberg) A Piece of Wind and Other Stories to Tell, 1990, No Need for Alarm, 1990, A Million Fish-More or Less, 1992, The Dark Thirty: Southern Tales of the Supernatural, 1992, Christmas in the Big House-Christmas in the Quarters, 1992, Sojourner Truth: "Ain't I a Woman?", 1992 (Boston Globe/Horn Book award 1993, NAACP Image award for children's literature 1994); (with Frederick L. McKissack) (with Frederick L. McKissack) Look What You've Done Now, Moses, 1984, Abram, Abram, Where Are We Going?, 1984 (C.S. Lewis Silver Medal award Christian Sch. Mag. 1984), Cinderella, 1985, Country Mouse and City Mouse, 1985, The Little Red Hen, 1985, The Three Bears, 1985, The Ugly Little Duck, 1986, When Do You Talk to God? Prayers for Small Children, 1986, King Midas and His Gold, 1986, Frederick Douglass: The Black Lion, 1987, A Real Winner, 1987, The King's New Clothes, 1987, Tall Phil and Small Bill, 1987, Three Billy Goats Gruff, 1987, My Bible ABC Book, 1987, The Civil Rights Movement in America from 1865 to the Present, 1987, All Paths Lead to Bethlehem, 1987, Messy Bessey, 1987, The Big Bug Book of Counting, 1987, The Big Bug Book of Opposites, 1987, The Big Bug Book of Places to Go, 1987, The Big Bug Book of the Alphabet, 1987, The Big Bug Book of Things to Do, 1987, Bugs!, 1988, The Children's ABC Christmas, 1988, Constance Stumbles, 1988, Oh, Happy, Happy Day! A Child's Easter in Story, Song and Prayer, 1989, God Made Something Wonderful, 1989, Messy Bessey's Closet, 1989, James Weldon Johnson: "Lift Every Voice and Sing", 1990, A Long Hard Journey: The Story of the Pullman Porter, 1990 (Coretta Scott King award 1990, Jane Addams Peace award 1990), Taking a Stand Against Racism and Racial Discrimination, 1990, W.E.B. DuBois, 1990, The Story of Booker T. Washington, 1991, Messy Bessey's Garden, 1991, African Americans, 1991, From Heaven Above: The Story of Christmas Proclaimed by the Angels, 1992, Tennessee Trailblazers, 1993, Black Diamond: The Story of the Negro Baseball League, 1994, African-American Scientists, 1994, African American Inventors, 1994, The Royal Kingdoms of Ghana, Mali, and Songhay: Life in Medieval Africa, 1994; (Great African American series with Frederick McKissack) Carter G. Woodson: The Father of Black History, 1991, Frederick Douglass: Leader Against Slavery, 1991, George Washington Carver: The Peanut Scientist, 1991, Ida B. Wells-Barnett: A Voice Against Violence, 1991, Louis Armstrong: Jazz Musician, 1991, Marian Anderson: A Great Singer, 1991, Martin Luther King, Jr.: Man of Peace, 1991, Mary Church Terrell: Leader for Equality, 1991, Mary McLeod Bethune: A Great Teacher, 1991, Ralph J. Bunche: Peacemaker, 1991, Jesse Owens: Olympic Star, 1992, Langston Hughes: Great American Poet, 1992, Soujourner Truth: A Voice for Freedom, 1992, Zora Neale Hurston: Writer and Storyteller, 1992, Satchel Page: The Best Arm in Baseball, 1992, Paul Robeson: A Voice to Remember, 1992, Madam C.J. Walker: Self-Made Millionare, 1992, Booker T. Washington: Leader and Educator, 1992, Lorraine Hansberry: Dramatist and Activist, 1994; (with others) The World in 1492, 1992; (with Ron Berry and Bartholomew) Scrappy the Squabbler, 1993, Moogie the Messy Beastie, 1993, Hogger the Hoarding Beastie, 1993, Glumby the Grumbler, 1993, Fritter the Wasteful Beastie, 1993, Crassy the Crude Beastie, 1993. Recipient Helen Keating Ott award Nat. Ch. and Synagogue Librs. Assn., 1980. Office: 5900 Pershing Ave Saint Louis MO 63112-1514

MCKISSICK-MELTON, S. CHARMAINE, mass communications educator; b. Durham, N.C., July 31, 1955; d. Floyd Bixler Sr. and Evelyn C. (Williams) McKissick; div. 1990; children: Maceo Christopher Kemp Jr., Daniel Ernest Kemp. BA, U. N.C., 1977; MA, No. Ill. U., 1978; postgrad., U. Ky., 1993-96. Sales mgr. WDUR-AM Radio, Durham, 1979-83; account exec. WTVD-TV 11, Durham, 1983, WKFT-TV 40, Fayetteville, N.D., 1984-85; office mgr. Atty. M. Christopher Kemp, Sr., Lumberton, N.D., 1985-88; learning disabled/extremely mentally handicapped tchr. Lumberton Jr. High Sch., 1988; account exec. WQOK-FM Radio, Raleigh, N.C., 1989; instr. Fayetteville State U., 1989, A&T State U., Greensboro, N.C., 1988-93; assoc. prof. Bennett Coll., Greensboro, 1989—; vis. prof. U. Notre Dame, Ind., 1992. Bd. dirs. N.C. Ctr. for Study of Black History, Durham, 1989-93, Durham Bus. and Profl. Chain, 1990-91, Women's Shelter for hope, Durham, 1989-91, Southeastern Family Violence Ctr., Lumberton, 1985-89. Coca Cola Faculty fellow U. Notre Dame, 1992, Lyman T. Johnson Rsch./Tchg. fellow, 1993-96. Mem. AAUW, AAUP (Bennett Coll. chpt. founding mem.), Speech Comm. Assn., Bennett Coll. Faculty Senate (exec. com. 1991-93), Women in Comm. (faculty advisor 1989-93), Am. Women in Radio and TV (N.C. chpt. pres. 1985-86). Avocations: swimming, aerobics, reading, public speaking. Home: 705 Reynolds Ave Durham NC 27707-4641 Office: Bennett Coll Shell Hall C#3 Box 25 Greensboro NC 27401

MCKISSOCK, DAVID LEE, retired manufacturing company executive; b. Boston, Mar. 27, 1933; s. Allan and Elizabeth (Lee) McK.; m. Diana Parish, Sept. 1, 1956; children: David Lee Jr., Christopher Lee. BA, Middlebury Coll., 1955. Salesman Am. Flange and Mfg. Co., N.Y.C., 1957-62; asst. to v.p. sales Am. Flange and Mfg. Co., Linden, N.J., 1962-64, salesman rip cap closures, 1964-73, v.p. rip cap closures, 1973-89, also bd. dirs. With USNR, 1955-57. Mem. Rumson Country Club, Seabright Lawn Tennis and Cricket Club. Republican. Unitarian. Avocations: tennis, golf, platform tennis. Home: 20 Hance Rd Fair Haven NJ 07704-3210

MCKISSOCK, GARY S., non-commissioned officer; b. Pitts., Feb. 24, 1943; s. Samuel and Evelyn (Virgin) McK.; m. Holly, Oct. 1966 (div.); children: Scott, Heather; m. Betty Pennel, Dec. 31, 1990; children: Kenneth, Natalie. BS in Edn., Edinboro U., 1964; postgrad., Marine Corps Commd. Coll., 1980, Indsl. Coll. Armed Forces, 1984. Commd. 2d lt. USMC, advanced through grades to brigadier gen.; mem. Naval Doctrine Rev. Bd., Washington, 1996. Capstone fellow Nat. Defense U., 1995; decorated Legion Merit with Gold Star, Bronze Star, Meritorious Svc. medal with Gold Star (2). Mem. Marine Corps Assn., Coun. Logistics Mgmt., Masons. Republican. Baptist. Home: 17153 Nicholas St Oceanside CA 92054 Office: 1st FSSG Box 555606 Camp Pendleton CA 92055

MCKISSOCK, PAUL KENDRICK, plastic surgeon; b. Lakeland, Fla., Oct. 27, 1925; s. Percival Kendrick and Helen Williams (Morse) McK.; m. Joan McShane, 1951; children—Ellen, John, Scott. B.A. in Zoology, UCLA, 1950; M.D. (James A. Gibson Anat. award 1953), U. Buffalo, 1956. Diplomate: Am. Bd. Plastic Surgery. Intern Los Angeles County Gen. Hosp., 1956-57; resident VA Hosp., Los Angeles, UCLA, 1957-63; fellow in plastic surgery Queen Victoria Hosp., East Grinstead, Eng., 1963; practice medicine specializing in plastic and reconstructive surgery Torrance, Calif., 1963—; pres. Paul K. McKissock M.D. Inc., 1968—; mem. staff Torrance Meml. Hosp., Little Company of Mary Hosp.; clin. prof. UCLA Med. Sch. Contbr. articles med. publs. Served with USNR, 1943-46. Mem. Am. Soc. Plastic and Reconstructive Surgeons, Am. Soc. Aesthetic Plastic Surgeons, Am. Assn. Plastic Surgeons, Calif. Soc. Plastic Surgeons. Republican. Presbyterian. Home: 75-280 Inverness Dr Indian Wells CA 92210-7636 Office: D-513 44489 Town Center Way Palm Desert CA 92260-2729

MC KITRICK, ERIC LOUIS, historian, educator; b. Battle Creek, Mich., July 5, 1919; s. Fred Louis and Colleen (Hodges) McK.; m. Edyth Carol Stevenson, Dec. 26, 1946; children—Frederick Louis II, Enid Lael, Charles Keith, Mary Caroline. B.S., Columbia U., 1949, M.A., 1951, Ph.D., 1959. Asst. prof. history U. Chgo., 1955-59, Douglass Coll., Rutgers U., 1959-60; asso. prof. history Columbia, 1960-65; prof. Columbia U., N.Y.C., 1965-89, prof. emeritus, 1989—; Pitt prof. Am. history and instns. Cambridge (Eng.) U., 1973-74; Harmsworth prof. Am. history Oxford (Eng.) U., 1979-80. Author: Andrew Johnson and Reconstruction, 1960, Slavery Defended: Views of the Old South, 1963, Andrew Johnson: A Profile, 1969, The Hofstadter Aegis: A Memorial, 1974, (with Stanley Elkins) The Age of Federalism, 1993. Served with AUS, 1941-45. Recipient Dunning prize Am. Hist. Assn., 1960, Bancroft prize, 1994, prize Soc. of the Cincinnati, 1995; fellow Ford Found., 1957-58, Rockefeller Found., 1962-63, Nat. Endowment for Humanities, 1967-68, Guggenheim Found., 1970-71, 76-77. Fellow Am. Philos. Soc., Am. Council Learned Socs. Club: Century (N.Y.C.). Office: Dept of History 875 W End Ave New York NY 10025-4919

MCKITTRICK, WILLIAM DAVID PARRISH, lawyer; b. Phila., June 10, 1942; s. Robert William and Marianna Virginia (Jones) McK.; m. Maureen Elaine Kerr, Jan. 20, 1964 (div. June 1980); children: Terrance, Allison; m. Teresa Jane Hopkins, Mar. 20, 1982; children: Parrish, Tyler. BA, Marshall U., Huntington, W.Va., 1965; JD, W.Va. U., 1968. Bar: W.Va. 1968, U.S. Dist. Ct. (so. dist.) W.Va. 1968. Asst. prosecutor Kanawha County, Charleston, W.Va., 1968-70; ptnr. McKittrick & Vaughn, St. Albans, W.Va., 1970-85, McKittrick & Murray, St. Albans, 1968-89, McKittrick & Assocs., St. Albans, 1990-93, McKittrick & Tantlinger, St. Albans, 1993—; lectr.

numerous seminars. Mem. Am. Trial Lawyers Assn., W.Va. Trial Lawyers Assn. Office: Law Offices of Parrish McKittrick 450 2nd St Saint Albans WV 25177-2857

MCKITTRICK, WILLIAM WOOD, lawyer; b. Mt. Carmel, Ill., July 11, 1915; s. Lafe E. and Mary Lynn (Wood) McK.; m. Carolyn Lenne Davis, Dec. 19, 1942; children—Lynn McKittrick Pond, Bruce W. A.B., DePauw U., 1936; J.D., Northwestern U., 1939. Bar: Ill. Assoc. Pope & Ballard, Chgo., 1939-48, ptnr., 1948-52; atty. Office Gen. Counsel, Panama C.Z., 1942; ptnr. Vedder, Price, Kaufman & Kammholz, Chgo., 1952-95; lectr. on labor law Northwestern U. Sch. Law, Chgo., 1961-62. Case note editor, mem. editorial bd. Ill. Law Rev., 1938-39. Life trustee Orchestral Assn. of Chgo. Symphony Orch., 1980—, Chgo. Symphony Musicians Pension Trust, 1987—; bd. dirs. Am. Symphony Orch. League, 1986-93, mem. exec. com., 1988-91; trustee Newberry Libr., Chgo., 1984—, mem. exec. com., 1989—; vice chmn. exec. bd. Libr. Coun., Northwestern U., 1984-96; chmn. Friends of Ryerson & Burnham Librs., Art Inst. Chgo., 1988-90, mem. com. on librs., 1982-96. Served to lt. USNR, 1943-45, PTO. Recipient Service award Northwestern U., 1968. Mem. ABA, Ill. Bar Assn., Chgo. Bar Assn. (lectr. various programs 1940-70, bd. mgrs. 1961-63), Legal Club of Chgo., Univ. Club (Chgo.), Michigan Shores Club, Skokie Country Club, Caxton Club of Chgo. (v.p. 1982-83, pres. 1983-85). Home: 232 Essex Rd Kenilworth IL 60043-1122

MCKNIGHT, EDGAR VERNON, religion educator; b. Wilson, S.C., Nov. 21, 1931; s. William G. and Carrie B. (DeMars) McK.; m. Shirley Robinson, June 4, 1955; children: Deborah Lynn, Edgar Vernon Jr. BS, Coll. Charleston, 1953; MDiv, So. Bapt. Theol. Sem., 1956, PhD, 1960. From asst. prof. to assoc. dean for academic affairs Furman U., Greenville, S.C., 1963-73; prof. Furman U., Greenville, 1974—. Author: Opening the Bible, 1967, What is Form Criticism, 1969, Meaning in Texts, 1978, The Bible and the Reader, 1985, Postmodern Use of the Bible, 1988. Pres. Torch Club, Greenville, 1992. Fulbright prof. U. Tuebingen, 1981-82, U. Muenster, 1995-96, William R. Kenan Jr. prof. Furman U., 1982—; bye fellow Robinson Coll. Cambridge U., Eng., 1988-89. Mem. AAUP, Am. Acad. Religion, Soc. Bibl. Lit. (coun. mem. 1976-81), Soc. N.T. Studies, Phi Beta Kappa. Home: 201 Alpine Way Greenville SC 29609-5058 Office: Furman U Greenville SC 29613

MCKNIGHT, FREDERICK L., lawyer; b. Kansas City, Mo., Nov. 28, 1947; s. Harry A. and Donna Ruth (Breining) McK.; m. Linda Jean McKnight, June 20, 1970; children: Justin Teague, Cristin Ruth. AB honors, Princeton U., 1969; JD, U. Calif., Berkeley, 1972. Bar: Calif. 1973, N.Y. 1973. adv. com. Jones, Day, Reavis & Pogue, Cleve., 1991—, Calif. regional mng. ptnr., 1997—. Bd. dirs. Econ. Devel. Corp., L.A., 1992—, St. Vincent Med. Ctr. Found., L.A., 1994—. Mem. Assn. Bus. Trial Lawyers. Office: Jones Day Reavis & Pogue 555 W 5th St Ste 4600 Los Angeles CA 90013-3002

MC KNIGHT, JOHN LACY, physics educator; b. Monroe, Mich., Sept. 13, 1931; s. Joseph Daniel and Esther (Lacy) McK.; m. Joyce Nunn, May 30, 1964; 1 son, Andrew. A.B., U. Mich., 1953; M.S., Yale, 1954, Ph.D., 1957. Mem. Faculty Coll. William and Mary, 1957—, prof. physics, 1968—; cons. to Colonial Williamsburg Found. on 17th and 18th century sci. instruments. Mem. editorial bd. Eighteenth Century Life. Pres. Va. Wilderness Com., 1969-70; bd. dirs. Conservation Coun. Va., 1969-71; trustee Va. chpt. Nature Conservancy, 1971-78, chmn. bd., 1975-77. Mem. AAAS, Am. Phys. Soc., Philosophy of Sci. Assn., History of Sci. Soc., Soc. History of Tech., Sci. Instrument Soc., Internat. Sci. Instruments Commn., Phi Beta Kappa, Sigma Xi, Phi Kappa Phi. Home: 701 College Ter Williamsburg VA 23185-3532

MCKNIGHT, JOSEPH WEBB, law educator, historian; b. San Angelo, Tex., Feb. 17, 1925; s. John Banning and Helen Katherine (Webb) McK.; m. Julia Ann Dyer, July 19, 1957; children—John Banton, Joseph Adair; m. Mildred Katherine Virginia Payne, Aug. 9, 1975. B.A., U. Tex., 1947, Oxford U., Eng., 1949; B.C.L., Oxford U., Eng., 1950, M.A., 1954; LL.M., Columbia U., 1959. Bar: Tex. 1951, U.S. Ct. Appeals (5th cir.) 1982. Assoc. Cravath, Swaine & Moore, N.Y.C., 1951-55; asst. prof. So. Meth. U., Dallas, 1955-57, assoc. prof., 1957-63, prof. law, 1963—, acad. dean, 1977-80, Larry and Jane Harlan faculty fellow, 1991—; vis. prof. various univs. Gen. editor Creditors' Rights in Texas, 1963; author: (with William A. Reppy, Jr.) Texas Matrimonial Property Law, 1983; contbr. articles to profl. jours. Pres., Tex. Old Missions and Forts Restoration Assn., 1977-79; bd. dirs. San Jacinto Mus. History Assn., 1976—; mem. exec. coun. Tex. State Hist. Assn., 1988-91. Served to lt. USNR, 1942-47. Rhodes scholar, 1947-50; James Kent fellow, 1958-59; Academico, Acad. Mexicana de Derecho Internat., 1988. Mem. ABA, State Bar Tex., Dallas Bar Assn., Tex. Bar Found. (v.p. 1959), Nat. Legal Aid and Defenders Assn. (bd. dirs. 1963-66), Selden Soc., Am. Soc. Legal History (v.p. 1967-68, bd. dirs. 1967-75), Inst. Texan Cultures (exec. bd. 1990-95), Sigma Chi. Democrat. Episcopalian. Office: So Meth U Law School Dallas TX 75275-0116

MCKNIGHT, JOYCE SHELDON, adult educator, community organizer; b. Meadville, Pa., Oct. 12, 1949; d. Seth Carlyle and Juanita Bessie (Sheets) Sheldon; m. Hugh Frank McKnight, Aug. 22, 1970; children: Frank Nathan, Joanna Michelle. BA in Psychology and Sociology, Allegheny Coll., 1971; MEd in Counseling, Gannon Coll., 1977; EdD, Pa. State U., 1995. Cert. nat. counselor. Asst. met. dir. Ecumenical Inst., Chgo. and Tulsa, 1970-73; health planner East Okla. Devel. Dist., Muskogee, 1973; juvenile counselor Tulsa County Aftercare Program, 1973; program specialist psycho-social rehab. Counseling Svcs. Ctr., Corry, Pa., 1975-77; counselor Adult Diploma Program, Corry, Pa., 1974-79; dir. Anchor House Agy., Corry, Pa., 1977-78; community programs dir. Warren-Forest Counties Econ. Opportunity Coun., Warren, Pa., 1979-80; dir. Corry Ctr. Mercyhurst Coll., Corry, Pa., 1981-87; cons. Pulaski, Pa., 1987-89; adj. faculty Mercyhurst, 1981-87, program devel. cons., 1987-89, program devel. cons. for new ch. Heritage Hills Ch., 1988-89; adj. faculty Allegheny Coll., 1984, Jamestown C.C., 1991—; planner Pa. State U., Shenango Valley, 1989; mentor Empire Coll. SUNY, 1989-93; coord. adult svcs. Alfred State Coll., 1992-95, adj. faculty mem., 1994-95, distance edn. team, 1994-95; dir. Inst. for Support of Cmty. Initiative, 1995—; cons. higher edn., cmty. svc., ch. growth. Contbr. rsch., papers in field. Pres., Corry Concerned for Youth, Inc., 1975-77; pres. Community Care Coun. of Agys., Corry, 1976-79, sec., 1975; mem. steering com. Vol. Action Ctr., Corry, 1977; bd. dirs. Erie County Citizens Coalition for Human Svcs., Erie, 1979-80. Horizon House for Women, 1981-87; mem. coordinating bd. Corry Reindustrialization Coun., 1983-87; mem. Allegany County N.Y. Gateway Project. Mem. AACD, Pa. Assn. Pub. Continuing Adult Edn. (dir. 1977-78), Pa. Assn. for Adult Continuing Edn. (bd. dirs. 1985-90), W. Pa. Conf. United Meth. Ch. Health and Welfare Coun., Moxham Children's Min., Cambria County Ptnr. For A Health Cmty. Methodist. Home and Office: 763 Linden Ave Johnstown PA 15902

MCKNIGHT, LENORE RAVIN, child psychiatrist; b. Denver, May 15, 1943; d. Abe and Rose (Steed) Ravin; m. Robert Lee McKnight, July 22, 1967; children: Richard Rex, Janet Rose. Student, Occidental Coll., 1961-63; BA, U. Colo., 1965, postgrad. in medicine, 1965-67; MD, U. Calif., San Francisco, 1969. Diplomate Am. Bd. Psychiatry and Neurology. Cert. adult and child psychiatrist Am. Bd. Psychiatry. Intern pediatrics Children's Hosp., San Francisco, 1969-70; resident in gen. psychiatry Langley Porter Neuropsychiat. Inst., 1970-73, fellow child psychiatry, 1972-74; child psychiatrist Youth Guidance Center, San Francisco, 1974-74; pvt. practice medicine specializing in child psychiatry, Walnut Creek, Calif., 1974-93; asst. clin. prof. Langley Porter Neuropsychiat. Inst., 1974—; asst. clin. prof. psychiatry U. Calif. San Francisco Med. Ctr. Internat.; med. dir. CPC Walnut Creek (Calif.) Hosp., 1990-93. Insts. Edn. fellow U. Edinburgh, 1964; NIH grantee to study childhood nutrition, 1966. Fellow Am. Acad. Child and Adolescent Psychiatry; mem. Am. Coll. Physician Execs., Internat. Arabian Horse Assn., Diablo Arabian Horse Assn. Avocation: breeding Arabian Horses. Office: Kaiser Martinez Inpat Psych 200 Muir Rd Martinez CA 94553-4614

MCKNIGHT, STEVEN LANIER, molecular biologist; b. El Paso, Tex., Aug. 27, 1949; s. Frank Gillespie and Sara Elise (Stevens) McK.; m. Jacquelynn Ann Zimmer, Sept. 16, 1978; children: Nell, Grace, Frances, John Stevens. BA, U. Tex., 1974; PhD, U.Va., 1977. Postdoctoral fellow Carnegie Instn. Washington, Balt., 1977-79, staff assoc., 1979-81, mem. staff, 1984-92; co-founder, dir., dir. rsch. Tularik Inc., 1991—; prof., chmn. dept. biochemistry U. Tex. Southwestern Med. Ctr., 1995—; hon. prof. Johns Hopkins U. Contbr. articles to jours. in field. With U.S. Army, 1969-71, Vietnam. Decorated ARCOM medal; recipient Eli Lilly prize Am. Soc. Microbiology, 1987, Newcomb-Cleveland prize Sci. mag., 1989, NAS Molecular Biology award Nat. Acad. Sci., 1991. Fellow Carnegie Inst. Washington (hon.), Am. Soc. Microbiology (hon.); mem. NAS, Am. Acad. Arts and Scis., Am. Soc. for Biochemistry and Molecular Biology, Am. Soc. for Clel Biology, Japanese Biochem. Soc. (hon.). Home: 3717 Euclid Ave Dallas TX 75205 Office: U Tex Southwestern Med Ctr Dept Biochemistry 5323 Harry Hines Blvd Dallas TX 75235-7208 Office: Tularik Inc Two Corp Dr South San Francisco CA 94080

MCKNIGHT, THOMAS FREDERICK, artist; b. Lawrence, Kans., Jan. 13, 1941; m. Renate Hödl. BA cum laude, Wesleyan U., Middletown, Conn., 1963; postgrad., Columbia U., 1963-64. One-man shows Basel (Switzerland) Art Fair, 1975-77, Tomic Galerie, Dusseldorf, Germany, 1976, Hartmann Gallery, Munich, 1977, Newport (R.I.) Art Assn., 1981, Kobe (Japan) Mcpl. Art Mus., 1993; exhibited in group shows Llubljana, Yugoslavia, 1981, Tokyo, 1989, Davison Art Ctr., Wesleyan U., 1988, numerous others; represented in permanent collections Davison Art Ctr., N.Y. State Mus., Albany, Smithsonian Instn., Washington, Met. Mus. Art, N.Y.C.; commns. include poster and print U.S. Constn. Bicentennial, 1989, prints Am.'s Cup, 1992, paintings and prints Urban Fair, Kobe, Japan, 1991, White House Christmas card, 1994, 95, 96; author: Thomas McKnight: Voyage to Paradise, 1993.

MCKNIGHT, WILLIAM BALDWIN, physics educator; b. Macon, Ga., July 4, 1923; s. Gilbert Franklin and Exie (Baldwin) McK.; m. Helen Mabel Bowling, Oct. 1, 1955; children: Tandy Ringoringo, Linda McKnight Way. BS, Purdue U., 1950; PhD, Oxford U., 1968. Physicist Underwater Sound Reference Lab., Orlando, Fla., 1952-53; physicist U.S. Army Missile Command, Redstone Arsenal, Ala., 1953-61, supervisory rsch. physicist, 1961-74; cons. Ballistic Missile Def. Advanced Tech. Ctr., 1975; rsch. prof. physics U. Ala., Huntsville, 1974—; pres. Tech. Rsch. Assocs. Inc., 1984—. Contbr. articles to profl. jours. Vice pres. Cotaco Cmtys. League, Somerville, Ala., 1964-65; mem. Madison County Rep. Exec. Com.; mgr. Gordo Area C. of C., 1993—; chmn. transp./infrastructure com. Pickens County Strategic Planning, 1994—; mem. North-South Hwy. Corridor, West Ala. Coalition Task Force, 1995-96. With USAAF, 1943-45. Decorated D.F.C., Air medal with three oak leaf clusters; recipient Research and Devel. award U.S. Army, 1961, 64; Sec. of Army fellow, 1966-67. Fellow Optical Soc. Am.; mem. IEEE (sr.), Am. Phys. Soc., Gordo Area C. of C. (mgr. 1993—), Rotary (v.p. Gordo club 1996-97), Sigma Xi, Sigma Pi Sigma. Mem. Ch. of Christ. Clubs: United Oxford, Cambridge Univ. Home: RR 1 Box 141A Gordo AL 35466-9801 Office: PO Box 1247 Huntsville AL 35807-0247

MCKNIGHT, WILLIAM EDWIN, minister; b. Grenada, Miss., Mar. 21, 1938; s. Leslie Spurgeon and Lucy Jennings (Sistrunk) McK.; m Sue Belle Roberts, Aug. 5, 1960; children: Susan Michele, William Roberts. BA, Millsaps Coll., 1960; BD, Lexington (Ky.) Theol. Sem., 1963. Ordained to ministry, 1964. Chaplain intern Grady Hosp., Atlanta, 1963-64; pastor First Christian Ch., Cleveland, Miss., 1964-67, Inverness, Miss., 1964-67; assoc. pastor First Christian Ch., Jackson, Miss., 1967-70; regional minister Christian Ch. (Disciples of Christ) in Miss., Jackson, 1971—; bd. dirs. Nat. City Christian Ch., Washington, Christian Brotherhood Homes, Jackson, So. Christian Svcs., Macon, Ga.; mem. Gen. Bd. the Christian Ch., Indpls., 1969—, bd. dirs. fin. coun., 1979-82; mem. bd. higher edn., St. Louis, 1979-80. Named one of Outstanding Young Men Am. U.S. Jaycees, 1976. Mem. Miss. Religious Leadership Conf. (pres. 1984-85), Conf. Regional Ministers and Moderators (pres. 1985-86). Office: Christian Ch in Miss 1619 N West St Jackson MS 39202-1418*

MC KNIGHT, WILLIAM WARREN, JR., publisher; b. Normal, Ill., June 9, 1913; s. William Warren and Isabel Alida (Travis) McK.; m. Alice McGuire, Oct. 30, 1937; children: William Warren, III, Michael Joe, John James. B.S. in Bus. Adminstrn., Northwestern U., 1938. With McKnight Pub. Co., Bloomington, Ill., 1938-83; sec.-treas. McKnight Pub. Co., 1949-56, pres., 1956-67, chmn. bd., 1968-79; bd. dirs. Gen. Telephone Co. Ill., Champion Fed. Savs. & Loan Assn., chmn. bd. Pres. Bloomington Rotary Club, 1952, Bloomington C. of C., 1954; mem. Ill. Commn. Higher Edn., 1956-60; chmn. Bloomington-Normal Airport Authority, 1965-70, CETA Pvt. Industry Council Ill. Balance of State, 1979-81. Served with USNR, 1942-46. Recipient Disting. Service award Bloomington Kiwanis Club, 1963, Disting. Service award Normal C. of C., 1973; Good Govt. award Bloomington Jaycees, 1970; Edn. Constrn. award Edn. Council Graphic Arts Industry, 1974; Disting. Alumni award Ill. State U., 1978; Disting. Service award Spirit of McLean County, 1982; Disting. Service citation Epsilon Pi Tau, 1983; award of Merit Am. Vocat. Assn., 1990; disting. assoc. award Coun. on Tech. Tchr. Edn., 1995. Mem. Graphic Arts Edn. Assn., Internat. Tech. Edn. Assn., Nat. Assn. Indsl. and Tech. Tchrs. Educators, Ill. C. of C. (dir. 1964-69), Ill. Mfrs. Assn. (dir. 1954-62). Republican. Presbyterian. Clubs: Coll. Alumni, Bloomington Country. Home: 401 W Vernon Ave Normal IL 61761-3542 Home (winter): 7788 E Stallion Rd Scottsdale AZ 85258-3485

MCKOWN, CHARLES H., dean. Dean Marshall U. Sch. Medicine, Huntington, W.Va. Office: Marshall U Sch Medicine 1801 6th Ave Huntington WV 25703-1585*

MC KOY, BASIL VINCENT CHARLES, theoretical chemist, educator; b. Trinidad, W.I., Mar. 25, 1938; came to U.S., 1960, naturalized, 1973; s. Allan Cecil and Doris Augusta McK.; m. Anne Ellen Shannon, Mar. 18, 1967; 1 son, Christopher Allan. B.Chem. Eng., N.S. Tech. U., 1960; Ph.D. in Chemistry (Univ. fellow), Yale U., 1964. Instr. chemistry Calif. Inst. Tech., 1964-66, asst. prof. chemistry, 1966-69, asso. prof., 1969-75, prof. theoretical chemistry, 1975—, chmn. of faculty, 1985-87; cons. Lawrence Livermore Lab., U. Calif., Livermore, 1974—, Inst. Def. Analysis, 1984—; vis. prof. Max Planck Inst., Munich, Ger., 1976—, U. Paris, 1968—, U. Campinas, Brazil, 1976—; lectr. Nobel Symposium, Goteborg, Sweden, 1979. Contbr. articles to Jour. Physics, London, chem. Physics Lettters, Phys. Rev., Jour. Chem. Physics; bd. editors; Chem. Physics Jour., 1977-79, mem. adv. editoral bd., 1992—; co-editor: Electron-Molecule and Photon-Molecule Collisions, 1979, 83, Swarm Studies and Inelastic Electron-Molecuale Collisions, 1986; co-author: Electron-Molecule Collisions and Photoionization Processes, 1982. Recipient medal Gov.-Gen. Can., 1960; Alfred P. Sloan Found. fellow, 1969-73; Guggenheim fellow, 1973-74. Fellow Am. Phys. Soc. Home: 3855 Keswick Rd La Canada Flintridge CA 91011-3945 Office: Calif Inst Tech Div Chemistry Pasadena CA 91125

MCKUSICK, MARSHALL KIRK, computer scientist; b. Wilmington, Del., Jan. 19, 1954; s. Blaine Chase and Marjorie Jane (Kirk) McK.; domestic ptnr. Eric P. Allman. BSEE with distinction, Cornell U., 1976; MS in Bus. Adminstrn., U. Calif., Berkeley, 1979, MS in Computer Sci., 1980, PhD in Computer Sci., 1984. System designer Hughes Aircraft Co., 1977-79; software cons., 1982—; rsch. computer scientist U. Calif., Berkeley, 1984-93. Author: The Design and Implementation of the 4.4BSD Operating System, 1996 (trans. into German, 1997, Japanese, 1997, French, 1997); contbr. articles to profl. publs. Mem. IEEE, Usenix Assn. (Lifetime Achievement award 1992, pres. 1990-92, bd. dirs. 1986-92), Assn. Computing Machinery. Democrat. Avocations: swimming, scuba diving, hiking. Office: 1614 Oxford St Berkeley CA 94709-1608

MCKUSICK, VICTOR ALMON, geneticist, educator, physician; b. Parkman, Maine, Oct. 21, 1921; s. Carroll L. and Ethel M. (Buzzell) Mc K.; m. Anne Bishop, June 11, 1949; children: Carol Anne, Kenneth Andrew, Victor Wayne. Student, Tufts Coll., 1940-43; MD, Johns Hopkins U., 1946; DSc (hon.), N.Y. Med. Coll., 1974; MD (hon.), Liverpool U., 1976; DSc (hon.), U. Maine, 1978, Tufts U., 1978, U. Rochester, 1979, Meml. U., Nfld., 1979; DMCh (hon.), U. Helsinki, 1981; D Med. Sci. (hon.), Med. U. S.C., 1979; MD (hon.), Edinburgh U., 1984; DSc (hon.), Aberdeen U., 1988, Med. Coll. Ohio, 1988, Bates Coll., 1989; PhD (hon.), Tel Aviv U., 1989; MD (hon.), Zurich (Switzerland) U., 1990; DSc (hon.), Colby Coll., 1991, U. Chgo., 1991, Mt. Sinai Sch. Medicine, 1992. Diplomate Am. Bd. Internal Medicine. Tng. in clin. medicine, lab. rsch. Johns Hopkins U./USPHS, 1946-52; instr. medicine Johns Hopkins Sch. Medicine, 1952-54, asst. prof., 1954-57, assoc. prof., 1957-60, chief divsn. med. genetics, dept. medicine, 1957-73, prof. medicine, 1960-85, prof. epidemiology, biology, 1969-78, William Osler prof. medicine, 1978-85, chmn. dept. medicine, 1973-85; physician-in-chief Johns Hopkins Hosp., 1973-85, Univ. prof. medical genetics, 1985—, chief div. med. genetics, 1957-73, 85-89; mem. rsch. adv. com. Nat. Found., 1959-78, med. adv. bd. Howard Hughes Med. Inst., 1967-83, com. mapping and sequencing of human genome Nat. Acad. Sci., 1986-88; pres. Internat. Med. Congress, Ltd., 1972-78; mem. Nat. Adv. Rsch. Resources Coun., 1970-74; mem. bd. sci. advisers Roche Inst. Molecular Biology, 1967-71; trustee Jackson Lab., 1979—; founding mem. Am. Bd. Med. Genetics, 1979-82; pres. 8th Internat. Congress of Human Genetics, 1991; mem. human genome adv. com. NIH, 1988-92, NIH/DOE work group on ethical, legal and societal implications of human genome project, 1990-95; co-chmn. Centennial of Johns Hopkins Hosp., 1989-90; co-founder, co-dir. ann. short course in med. and exptl. mammalian genetics, Bar Harbor, Maine, 1960—; co-founder, co-dir. European Sch. Med. Genetics Sestri Levante, 1988—; chmn. com. on DNA tech. in forensic sci. NRC/NAS, 1989-92, adv. update com., 1993-96; founder Am. Bd. Med. Genetics. Author: Heritable Disorders of Connective Tissue, 1956, 60, 66, 72, 93, Cardiovascular Sound in Health and Disease, 1958, Medical Genetics 1958-60, 1961, Human Genetics, 1964, 69, On the X Chromosome of Man, 1964, Mendelian Inheritance in Man, 1966, 68, 71, 75, 78, 83, 86, 88, 90, 92, 94, (with others) Osler's Textbook Revisited, 1967, Genetics of Hand Malformations, 1978, Medical Genetic Studies of the Amish, 1978, A Model of its Kind, 1989, Osler's Legacy, 1990, A Century of Biomedical Science at Johns Hopkins, 1993; author, editor: Online Mendelian Inheritance in Man, 1985—; editor-in-chief Medicine jour., 1985—; founding co-editor-in-chief Genomics jour. 1987—; editor med. textbook. Recipient Disting. Achievement award Modern Medicine, 1965, John Phillips award ACP, 1972, Silver medal U. Helsinki, 1974, Gairdner Internat. award, 1977, Premio Internazionale Sanremo per le Ricerche Genetiche, 1983, Col. Saunders award March of Dimes, 1988, Disting. Alumnus award Johns Hopkins U., 1983, Alumnus Svc. award Johns Hopkins Med. Sch., 1989, Passano award, 1989, Disting. Svc. award Miami Biotech. Winter Symposium, 1991, Frank Bradway Rogers Info. Advancement award Med. Libr. Assn., 1991, Silver Columbus medal Comune di Genova, 1992, Maine prize (with twin), 1993, Mendel medal Villanova U., 1995, Big "M" award Maine State Soc. Washington, D.C., 1995; named to Internat. Pediatrics Hall of Fame, 1987; hon. citizen Commune di Genova, 1997, Coriell medal, 1997. Fellow AAAS (chair med. scis. sect. 1991), Am. Acad. Orthopedic Surgeons (hon.), Royal Coll. Physicians (London), Hastings Ctr., Am. Coll. Med. Genetics (hon.); mem. Nat. Acad. Sci. (James Murray Luck award 1982), Am. Philos. Soc. (v.p. 1996—, Benjamin Franklin medal for disting. achievement in scis. 1996), Am. Soc. Human Genetics (pres. 1975, Wm. A. Allan award 1977), Assn. Am. Physicians (Kober medal 1990), Am. Soc. Clin. Investigation (v.p. 1967), The Human Genome Orgn. (founder pres. 1988-89), Am. Acad. Arts and Sci., Little People of Am. (hon. life), Acad. Nat. Médecine (France; corr.), Phi Beta Kappa, Alpha Omega Alpha, Johns Hopkins Club, West Hamilton St. Club, St. Andrew's Soc. Balt. Presbyterian (elder). Home: 221 Northway Baltimore MD 21218-1141 Office: Johns Hopkins Hosp Ctr Med Genetics-Blalock 1007 600 N Wolfe St Baltimore MD 21205-2110

MCKUSICK, VINCENT LEE, former state supreme judicial court chief justice, lawyer; b. Parkman, Maine, Oct. 21, 1921; s. Carroll Lee and Ethel (Buzzell) McK.; m. Nancy Elizabeth Green, June 23, 1951; children: Barbara Jane McKusick Liscord, James Emory, Katherine McKusick Ralston, Anne Elizabeth. A.B., Bates Coll., 1943; S.B., S.M., MIT, 1947; LL.B., Harvard U., 1950; LL.D., Colby Coll., 1976, Nasson Coll., 1978, Bates Coll., 1979, Bowdoin Coll., 1979, Suffolk U., 1983; L.H.D., U. So. Maine, 1978, Thomas Coll., 1981. Bar: Maine 1952. Law clk. to Chief Judge Learned Hand, 1950-51; to Justice Felix Frankfurter, 1951-52; partner Pierce, Atwood, Scribner, Allen & McKusick and predecessors, Portland, Maine, 1953-77; chief justice Maine Supreme Jud. Ct., 1977-92; of counsel to Pierce Atwood (formerly Pierce, Atwood, Scribner, Allen, Smith, & Lancaster), Portland, Maine, 1992—; mem. adv. com. rules civil procedure Maine Supreme Jud. Ct., 1957-59, chmn., 1966-75, commr. uniform state laws, 1968-76, sec. nat. conf., 1975-77; mem. Conf. Chief Justices, 1977-92, bd. dirs., 1980-82, 91-92, pres.-elect, 1989-90, pres., 1990-91; dir. Nat. Ctr. for State Ctrs., 1988-89, chmn.-elect, 1989-90, chmn., 1990-91; spl. master U.S. Supreme Ct. Conn. v. N.H., 1992-93, La. v. Miss., 1994-96; master Mass. S.J.C. Liquidation Am. Mutual Liability Ins. Co., 1995-96; leader Am. Judges Del. to China, 1983, USSR, 1988, U.S. State Dept. Rule of Law Del. to Republic of Ga., 1992; mem. permanent com. Oliver Wendell Holmes Devise, 1993—. Author: Patent Policy of Educational Institutions, 1947, (with Richard H. Field) Maine Civil Practice, 1959, supplements, 1962, 67, (with Richard H. Field and L. Kinvin Wroth) 2d edit., 1970, supplements, 1972, 74, 77; also articles in legal publs. Trustee emeritus Bates Coll.; mem. adv. com. on pvt. internat. law U.S. State Dept., 1980-85, Fed.-State Jurisdiction com., Jud. Conf. of U.S., 1987-89. With AUS, 1943-46. Recipient The Maine prize U. Maine Sys., 1993, Benjamin E. Mays award Bates Coll., 1994, Big M award Maine State Soc. Washington, 1995. Fellow Am. Bar Found. (bd. dirs. 1977-87), Am. Philos. Soc. (coun. 1990-96); mem,. ABA (chmn. fed. rules com. 1966-71, bd. editors jour. 1971-80, chmn. 1976-77, mem. study group to China 1978, ho. dels. 1983-87), Maine Bar Assn., Cumberland County Bar Assn., Am. Arbitration Assn. (bd. dirs. 1994—), Am. Judicature Soc. (dir. 1976-78, 92—), Am. Law Inst. (coun. 1968—), Maine Jud. Coun. (chmn. 1977-92), Inst. Jud. Adminstrn., Supreme Ct. Hist. Soc. (trustee 1994—), Rotary Club (hon., past pres.), Portland Yacht Club, Phi Beta Kappa, Sigma Xi, Tau Beta Pi. Republican. Unitarian. Home: 1152 Shore Rd Cape Elizabeth ME 04107-2115 Office: 1 Monument Sq Portland ME 04101-4033

MCLACHLIN, BEVERLEY, supreme court judge; b. Pincher Creek, Alta., Can., Sept. 7, 1943; m. Roderick McLachlin (dec. 1988); 1 child, Angus; m. Frank E. McArdle, 1992. B.A., U. Alta., MA in Philosophy, LLB, LLD (hon.), 1990; LLD (hon.), U. B.C., 1990, U. Toronto, 1995. Bar: Alta. 1969, B.C. 1971. Assoc. Wood, Moir, Hyde and Ross, Edmonton, Alta., Can., 1969-71, Thomas, Herdy, Mitchell & Co., Fort St. John, B.C., Can., 1971-72, Bull, Housser and Tupper, Vancouver, B.C., 1972-75; lectr., assoc. prof., prof. with tenure U. B.C., 1974-81; appointed to County Ct., Vancouver, 1981; justice Supreme Ct. of B.C., 1981-85, B.C. Ct. of Appeal, 1985-88; chief justice Supreme Ct. of B.C., 1988; justice Supreme Ct. Can., Ottawa, Ont., 1989—. Co-author: B.C. Supreme Court Practice, B.C. Court Forums, Canadian Law of Arch. and Engring.; mem. editorial adv. bd. Family Law Restatement Project, 1987-88, Civil Jury Instruction, 1988; contbr. numerous articles to profl. jours. Office: Supreme Ct Bldg, Wellington St, Ottawa, ON Canada K1A 0J1

MCLAFFERTY, FRED WARREN, chemist, educator; b. Evanston, Ill., May 11, 1923; s. Joel E. and Margaret E. (Keifer) McL.; m. Elizabeth E. Curley, Feb. 5, 1948; children: Sara L., Joel E., Martha A., Samuel A., Ann E. B.S., U. Nebr., 1943, D.Sc. (hon.), 1983, M.S., 1947; Ph.D., Cornell U., 1950; D.Sc. (hon.), U. Liege, Belgium, 1987; DSc (hon.), Purdue U., 1995. Postdoctoral fellow U. Iowa, 1949-50; research chemist, div. leader Dow Chem. Co., 1950-56; dir. Eastern Research Lab., 1956-64; prof. chemistry Purdue U., 1964-68; prof. chemistry Cornell U., 1968-92, Peter J.W. Debye prof. chemistry emeritus, 1992—; mem. chem. sci. and tech. bd., numerical data adv. bd., bd. Army sci. tech., bd. radioactive waste mgmt. NRC; chem. co-chmn. World Bank's Chinese Univ. Devel. Project. Author: Mass Spectrometry of Organic Ions, 1963, Mass Spectral Correlations, 2d edit., 1981, Interpretation of Mass Spectra, 4th edit., 1993, Tandem Mass Spectrometry, 1983, Advances in Analytical Chemistry and Instrumentation, (with C.N. Reilley), Vols. 4-7, 1967-70, Index and Bibliography of Mass Spectrometry, (with J. Pinzelik), 1967, Atlas of Mass Spectral Data; (with E. Stenhagen and S. Abrahamsson), 1969, Registry of Mass Spectral Data, 1974; (with D.B. Stauffer) Wiley/NBS Registry of Mass Spectral Data, 1989, Important Peak Index of Mass Spectral Data, 1991; editor: Accounts of Chemical Research, 1986-94; co-editor: (with E. Stenhagen and S. Abrahamsson) Archives of Mass Spectral Data, 1969-72. Served with AUS, 1942-45, ETO. Decorated Purple Heart, Combat Inf. badge, Bronze Star with 4 oak leaf clusters; recipient Pitts. Spectroscopy award Spectroscopy Soc. Pitts., 1975, Gold medal U. Naples, 1989, Bijvoet medal U. Utrecht, 1997, W.L. Evans award Ohio State U., 1987; John Simon Guggenheim fellow, 1972, Overseas fellow Churchill Coll., Cambridge (Eng.) U., 1979. Fellow NAS, AAAS, N.Y. Acad. Scis., Am. Acad. Arts and Scis.; mem. Soc. Analytical Chemists (Pitts. Analytical Chemist award 1987, Pioneer Analytical Instrumentation award 1994), Am. Chem. Soc. (chmn. analytical chem. divsn. 1969, chmn. Midland sect. 1956, Northeastern sect. 1964, award chem. instrumentation 1971, award analytical chemistry 1981, Nichols medal N.Y. sect. 1984, Oesper award Cin. sect. 1986, award mass spectrometry 1989), Internat. Spectrometry Orgn. (Sir J. J. Thomson medal 1985), Assn. Analytical Chemists (Anachem award 1985), Am. Soc. Mass Spectrometry (founder, sec. 1957-58), Am. Inst. Chemists (Chem. Pioneer award 1996), Sigma Xi, Phi Lambda Upsilon, Alpha Chi Sigma. Home: 103 Needham Pl Ithaca NY 14850-2120

MCLAIN, CHRISTOPHER M., lawyer; b. San Luis Obispo, Calif., July 21, 1943; s. James Latane and Marjorie Patricia (McNalley) McL.; m. Barbara McFarland, Nov. 23, 1968; children—Beth, Brian, Amy. BS in Bus. Adminstrn., U. Calif.-Berkeley, 1965, JD, 1968. Assoc. Knox, Goforth & Ricksen, Oakland, Calif., 1968-69; assoc. Donahue, Gallagher, Thomas & Woods, Oakland, 1969-73, ptnr., 1973-83; sec., counsel Lucky Stores, Inc., Dublin, Calif., 1984-89, v.p., 1985-89; ptnr. Sonnenschein, Nath & Rosenthal, San Francisco, 1989-90; sr. v.p., gen. counsel, sec. Transam. Corp., San Francisco, 1990-94; of counsel Sonnenschein Nath & Rosenthal, San Francisco, 1994-95; sr. v.p., gen. counsel, sec. Crown Vantage Inc., Oakland, Calif., 1995—. Mem. ABA, State Bar Calif., Alameda County Bar Assn., San Francisco Bar Assn., Am. Soc. Corps. Secs. Avocation: skiing. Office: Crown Vantage 300 Lakeside Dr Oakland CA 94612-3524

MCLAIN, DAVID ANDREW, internist, rheumatologist, health facility administrator; b. Chgo., Aug. 16, 1948; s. William Rex and Wilma Lucille (Raschka) McL.; m. Pamela Rose Fullmer, June 15, 1974; children: Edward, Richard. BA, Northwestern U., 1970; MD with Honors, Tulane U., 1974. Diplomate Am. Bd. Internal Medicine, Am. Bd. Rheumatology. Intern Ochsner Clinic, New Orleans, 1974-75; resident Barnes Hosp., St. Louis, 1975-77; fellow in rheumatology Washington U., St. Louis, 1977-79, instr. dept. medicine, 1979-81; with VA Hosp., St. Louis, 1979-81; pvt. practice Birmingham, Ala., 1981—; chief rheumatology sect. dept. internal medicine Brookwood Med. Ctr., Birmingham, 1983-87, 89-90, 1997—, med. dir. phys. therapy, 1986-96, mem. exec. com., chmn. med. edn. com., 1997—; mem. staff St. Vincent's Hosp., Birmingham, 1981—, Shelby Med. Ctr., Alabaster, Ala., 1982—, Lakeshore Rehab. Hosp., Birmingham, 1983—, HealthSouth Hosp., 1989—; dir. courses continuing med. edn., 1983—. Editor: (jour. series) Internal Medicine; contbr. articles, abstracts to profl. jours. Mem. med. adv. com. Birmingham chpt. Lupus Found. Am., 1982—, co-originator Lupus Day, Brookwood Med. Ctr., 1983—; bd. dirs. north ctrl. br. Arthritis Found., 1982—, organizer, originator Benefit Horse Show and Art Fair, Birmingham, 1985, del. nat. coun., 1987, chmn. med. and sci. com. Ala. chpt., 1988-89; active Nat. Arthritis Found.; med. advisor Sjogren's Syndrome Found., 1988—. Recipient award of Appreciation Ala. Podiatry Assn., 1984, Ala. Chpt. Arthritis Found., 1986, award for Decade of Leadership in Rheumatology, 1992, Excellence in Tchg. award Med. Assn. State of Ala., 1995. Fellow ACP, Am. Coll. Rheumatology (founding mem., com. on rheumatol. care network 1997—); mem. AMA (Physicians Recognition award 1979, 82, 85, 88, 91, 94, 97), Am. Soc. Internal Medicine, Am. Med. Equestrian Assn. (bd. dirs. 1995—, coord. ann. meeting 1997), Ala. Soc. Rheumatic Diseases (founding mem., sec.-treas. 1996-97), Ala. Soc. Internal Medicine, Med. Assn. State Ala. (Excellence in Tchg. award 1995), Jefferson County Med. Soc., Brookwood Splty. Physicians Assn. (founding incorporator, bd. dirs., pres. 1990-97), U.S. Combined Tng. Assn. (area coun., editor newsletter, adult riders com., bd. govs. 1992-94, chmn. safety com. 1992—, chmn. ad hoc coalition to promote equestrian helmet safety 1993-95, ann. meeting com. 1997), U.S. Dressage Fedn. (founder aux. U.S. Test Callers Assn.), Alpha Omega Alpha. Avocation: equestrian combined training or eventing. Office: Birmingham Rheumatology McLain Med Assocs 2022 Brookwood Med Ctr Dr Ste 509 Birmingham AL 35209-6807

MCLAIN, JOHN LOWELL, resource specialist, consultant; b. Havre, Mont., Jan. 23, 1942; s. Woodrow B. and Ann Teresa (Bolta) McL.; m. Carolyn Louise Peterson, June 27, 1964; children: Nicole Rachelle, Tanya Lynn. BS in Range Mgmt., Mont. State U., 1969. Cert. range mgmt. cons.; cert. soil erosion & sediment control specialist. Soil conservationist USDA Soil Conservation Svc., Miles City, Mont., 1969-71; range conservationist USDA Soil Conservation Svc., Glendive, Mont., 1971-74; area range conservationist USDA Soil Conservation Svc., Minden, Nev., 1974-76, dist. conservationist, 1976-78; prin. resource specialist Resource Concepts Inc., Carson City, Nev., 1978-90; bd. dirs. Range Mag., Carson City. Mem. citizens adv. bd. U. Nev.-Reno, 1981—; Nev. del. Coun. for Agrl. Rsch. Ext. and Tchg., Washington, 1983-96. Recipient Outstanding Achievement award Carson Valley Conservation Dist., 1978; named Man of 1980s Nevada City Appeal newspaper, 1980. Fellow Soc. for Range Mgmt. (pres. Nev. sect. 1980, Rangeman of Yr. Nev. sect. 1981); mem. Soil Conservation Soc. (pres. Nev. sect. 1980), Soc. Range Mgmt (dir. 1993-96), Resource Restoration Internat. (mem. adv. com. 1992), Range Edn. Inst. (dir. 1995—). Roman Catholic. Avocations: fishing, guitar/singing, horseback riding, skiing, hunting. Home: 2424 Manhattan Dr Carson City NV 89703-5416 Office: Resource Concepts Inc 340 N Minnesota St Carson City NV 89703-4152

MCLAIN, ROGER SETTE, electronics company executive; b. Marinette, Wis., Oct. 6, 1928; s. Addison Theodore and Mabel (Sette) McL.; m. Jean Alice McLain, June 29, 1957; children: Patrick J., Susan E., Katherine A. McLain-Arellano, Anne M. BA, U. Wis., 1954. Sales engr. Semiconductor div. RCA Corp., Somerville, N.J., 1958-62; regional sales mgr. Semiconductor div. Tex. Instruments, Inc., Dallas, 1962-68; mktg. dir. Electronics div. Allen-Bradley Co., Milw., 1968-73, Wecom div. Rockwell Internat., Downers Grove, Ill., 1973-82; v.p. Circuit Systems, Inc., Elk Grove Village, Ill., 1982—. Alderman City of Park Ridge, Ill., 1966-67; troop leader Boy Scouts Am., Bayside, Ill., 1969-72. With U.S. Army, 1951-53. Recipient Christian Svc. award Hinsdale Hosp., 1990. Mem. IEEE, Art Inst. Chgo., Chgo. Hist. Soc., Shedd Aquarium Soc., Chgo. Mus. Sci. and Industry. Republican. Roman Catholic. Avocations: piano and organ, tennis, golf, biking. Office: Circuit Systems Inc 2350 Lunt Ave Elk Grove Village IL 60007-5610

MCLAIN, WILLIAM ALLEN, lawyer; b. Chgo., Oct. 19, 1942; s. William Rex and Wilma L. (Raschka) McL.; divorced; children: William A., David M., Heather A.; m. Kristine R. Zierk. BS, So. Ill. U., 1966; JD, Loyola U., Chgo., 1971. Bar: Ill. 1971, U.S. Dist. Ct. (no. dist.) Ill. 1971, U.S. Ct. Appeals (7th cir.) 1971, Colo. 1975, U.S. Dist. Ct. Colo. 1975, U.S. Ct. Appeals (10th cir.) 1975. Law clk. U.S. Dist. Ct. (no. dist.) Ill., Chgo., 1971-72; assoc. Sidley & Austin, Chgo., 1972-75; ptnr. Welborn, Dufford, Brown & Tooley, Denver, 1975-86; pres. William A. McLain PC, 1986—; ptnr. McLain & Singer, 1990—. Mem. Dist. 10 Legis. Vacancy Commn., Denver, 1984-86. Served with U.S. Army, 1966-68. Recipient Leadership and Scholastic Achievement award Loyola U. Alumni Assn., 1971. Mem. ABA, Colo. Bar Assn. (lobbyist 1983-85), Denver Bar Assn., Colo. Assn. Commerce and Industry (legis. policy coun. 1983-88), Colo. Mining Assn. (state and local affairs com. 1978-88), Inst. Property Taxation. Republican. Clubs: Mount Vernon Country Club, Roundup Riders of the Rockies. Lodges: Masons, Shriners, Scottish Rite, York Rite. Home and Office: 3962 S Olive St Denver CO 80237-2038

MCLAIN, WILLIAM TOME, principal; b. Washington, July 10, 1935; s. Ronald Alpha and Dorothy Smithson (Tome) McL.; m. Meurial Claire Webb, Nov. 20, 1977; 1 child, Laura Louisa McLain. BA, U. Del., 1957, MEd, 1966. Secondary Prin. Cert., Del. Math. tchr. Newark Sch. Dist., 1957-69, high sch. adminstrv. asst., 1969-78; high sch. assoc. prin. New Castle County Sch. Dist., Newark, 1978-81; high sch. asst. prin. Christina Sch. Dist., Newark, 1981-84, middle sch. asst. prin., 1984-87, prin. adult edn. program, 1987—. chmn. Del. Coalition for Literacy. Recipient Tchrs. medal Freedom's Found., 1968, Silver Beaver award Boy Scouts Am., 1967, Walace Johnson Community Svc. award New Castle County C. of C., 1979, Adult, dFamily Lit. Outstanding Svc. award State of Del., 1992. Mem. Del Assn. for Adult and Community Edn., Interagency Coun. on Adult Lit. United Methodist. Avocations: travel, history. Home: 95 Dallas Ave Newark DE 19711-5123 Office: Christina School District 83 E Main St Newark DE 19711-4645

MCLANAHAN, CHARLES SCOTT, neurosurgeon; b. Chgo., Sept. 23, 1946; s. Charles Jackson and Anna Martin (Findley) McL.; m. Mary Ivey, Aug. 23, 1975; children: George, Ward, Matt. BA, Yale U., 1969; MD, Columbia U., 1973. Diplomate Am. Bd. Neurol. Surgery. Resident in neurosurgery Emory U., Atlanta, 1973-78, instr. neurosurgery, 1979; asst. prof. neurosurgery La. State U. Med. Sch., New Orleans, 1979-80; neurosurgeon Charlotte (N.C.) Neurosurg. Assocs., PA, 1980—. Republican. Avocation: golf. Office: Charlotte Neurosurg Assocs 1010 Edgehill Rd N Charlotte NC 28207-1885

MC LANATHAN, RICHARD (BARTON KENNEDY), author, consultant; b. Methuen, Mass., Mar. 12, 1916; s. Frank Watson and Helen (Kennedy) McL.; m. Jane Fuller, Jan. 2, 1942. Grad., Choate Sch., 1934; A.B., Harvard U., 1938, Ph.D., 1951. Instr. English and history Allen-Stevenson Sch., N.Y.C., 1938-43; asst. curator paintings Mus. Fine Arts, Boston, 1946-48; asst. curator decorative arts Mus. Fine Arts, 1949-54, sec. of museum, 1949-56, editor museum publs., 1952-57, asso. curator decorative arts, 1954, curator decorative arts, 1954-57; dir. Mus. Art, Munson-Williams-Proctor Inst., Utica, N.Y., 1957-61; exec. dir. Am. Assn. Museums, Washington, 1976-78; trustee, mem. exec. com. Boston Arts Festival, 1954-59; curator Am. Nat. art exhbn., Moscow, 1959, Am. specialist to, W. Ger., Poland and Denmark, 1959, Yugoslavia, 1961; mem. U.S. Nat. Commn. for UNESCO, 1976-79, Corcoran Biennial Jury, 1960, N.Y. State Council Arts, 1960-64; bd. advisers Albany (N.Y.) Inst. History and Art, 1958-70; cons. in field, 1961-75, 79—. Author: Images of the Universe: Leonardo da Vinci, The Artist as Scientist, 1966, The Pageant of Medieval Art, 1966, The American Tradition in the Arts, 1968, A Guide to Civilisation: The Kenneth Clark Films on the Cultural Life of Western Man, 1970, The Brandywine Heritage, 1971, Art in America, 1973, The Art of Marguerite Stix, 1977, National Gallery of Art, East Building: A Profile, 1978, Romantic America; catalogue of the inaugural exhbn. of Tampa Museum, 1979, World Art in American Museums, A Personal Guide, 1983, Gilbert Stuart, 1986, Leonardo da Vinci, 1990, fgn. lang. edits., 1991, Michelangelo, 1993, Rubens, 1995; co-author: M. and M. Karolik Collection of American Paintings, 1815-1855, 1949; editor: Catalogue of Classical Coins, 1955; cons. editor: Art and Man, Nat. Gallery Art, 1969-76; adv. editor: The Great Contemporary Issues: The Arts, 1978; decorative arts editor: Webster's Unabridged Dictionary, 1955; contbr.: Am. Foundation Philanthropy, 1967. Bd. advisers Boys Clubs Boston, 1950-57; trustee Boys' Club Utica, 1959-61, Brandywine River Mus., 1970-75, Maine Maritime Mus., 1984-89; bd. dirs. St. Luke's Meml. Hosp. Center, Utica, 1957-61. Sr. fellow Am. Acad. Rome, 1948-49; recipient Distinguished Service award USIA, 1959; Prix de Rome, 1948; Rockefeller sr. fellow Met. Mus., 1975-76. Mem. Am. Assn. Museums, Harvard Soc. Fellows. Home: The Stone Schoolhouse Phippsburg ME 04562

MCLANE, DAVID GLENN, lawyer; b. Dallas, Jan. 17, 1943; s. Alfred Ervin and Dixie Marie (Martin) McL.; m. Sally Ruth Payne, Apr. 5, 1963; children: Cynthia Lynn, Kathleen Michelle, Michael Scott; m. Beverly Anne Bledsoe, Feb. 5, 1983; children: Morgan Elizabeth, Nicholas Martin, Elizabeth Clark. BA, So. Meth. U., 1963, LLB, 1966. Bar: Tex. 1966, U.S. Supreme Ct. 1971. Briefing atty. Supreme Ct. Tex., 1966-67; assoc., then ptnr. Gardere & Wynne and predecessors, Dallas, 1967—; mem. faculty So. Meth. U.; lectr. in field. Bd. dirs. Urban Services br. Dallas YMCA, 1977-84, Dallas Symphony Assn., 1980-93; mem. Dallas County AIDS Planning Commn. Task Force, 1988; pres. coun. Dallas Theol. Sem., 1994—. Mem. ABA, Tex. Bar Assn., Dallas Bar Assn., S.W. Benefits Assn. (bd. dirs. 1975-80, pres. 1978-79), So. Meth. U. Law Alumni Assn. (sec., bd. dirs. 1981-85, Vol. of Yr. award 1984), So. Meth. U. Alumni Assn. (bd. dirs. 1972-77). Presbyterian. Contbg. author: Texas Corporations—Law and Practice, 1984; editor: Incorporation Planning in Texas, 1977. Office: 3000 Thanksgiving Tower Dallas TX 75201

MCLANE, DRAYTON, JR., professional baseball team executive. Owner, chmn. Houston Astros, 1993—. Office: Houston Astros PO Box 288 Houston TX 77001-0288 Office: McLane Co Inc PO Box 6115 Temple TX 76503-6115*

MCLANE, FREDERICK BERG, lawyer; b. Long Beach, Calif., July 24, 1941; s. Adrian B. and Arlie K. (Burrell) McL.; m. Lois C. Roberts, Jan. 28, 1967; children: Willard, Anita. BA, Stanford U., 1963; LLB, Yale U., 1966. Bar: Calif. 1967, U.S. Dist. Ct. (cen. dist.) Calif. 1967. Assoc. prof. law U. Miss., Oxford, 1966-68; assoc. O'Melveny & Myers, L.A., 1968-74, ptnr., 1975—; com. of counsel HUD, Los Angeles, 1979-84; lectr. in field. Pres., bd. dirs. Legal Aid Found., L.A., 1974-83; deacon Congl. Ch., Sherman Oaks, Calif., 1979-83; vice-chair L.A. Music Ctr., Unified Fund, 1992-94; bd. dirs. Calif. Mus. Found., 1991—. Mem. ABA (banking com.), Calif. Bar Assn. (fin. insts. com., uniform comml. codes), L.A. Bar Assn., Order of Coif, Calif. Club (L.A.), L.A. Country Club, Lakeside Golf Club (L.A.). Democrat. Avocations: golf, walking, reading. Office: O'Melveny & Myers 400 S Hope St Los Angeles CA 90071-2801

MCLANE, HENRY EARL, JR., philosophy educator; b. Statesboro, Ga., Aug. 18, 1932; s. Henry Earl and Lillie Ora (Beasley) McL.; m. Barbara Helen Gardner, Nov. 7, 1934; children—Debra Lynn, Shawn Creg. B.A., George Washington U., 1955; postgrad., Johns Hopkins U., 1955-56; M.A., Yale U., 1958, Ph.D., 1961. Instr. philosophy Washburn U. of Topeka, Kans., 1960-61; asst. prof. Washburn U. of Topeka, 1961-64, assoc. prof., 1964-65; vis. assoc. prof. philosophy Coll. of William and Mary, Williamsburg, Va., 1965-66, assoc. prof., 1967-77, prof., 1978-96, prof. emeritus, 1996—; diving coach Coll. of William and Mary, 1976-87. Contbr. articles to profl. publs. Danforth Found. fellow, 1955-60. Mem. Am. Philos. Assn. Democrat. Baptist. Avocations: playing violin; music. Home: 116 Dogwood Dr Williamsburg VA 23185-3743

MCLANE, JAMES WOODS, healthcare executive; b. New Canaan, Conn., Jan. 27, 1939; s. William Lawrence and Elizabeth Fish (Benjamin) McL.; m. Fay Sargent, Apr. 27, 1963 (div. 1980); children—James Woods, Benjamin Sargent; m. Nancy Coe, May 5, 1984; 1 child, Joshua Coe. B.A., Yale U., 1961; M.B.A., Harvard U., 1967. Cons. Booz, Allen & Hamilton, N.Y.C., 1967-69; exec. asst. to sec. HEW, Washington, 1969-70; staff asst. to Pres. U.S., White House, 1971-72; dep. dir. Cost of Living Council, Washington, 1972-74; v.p. mcht. banking group Citibank N.A., N.Y.C., 1974-79; sr. v.p. and head corp. fin. div. Citibank N.A., 1980-83; sr. v.p., mng. dir. Citicorp Internat. Bank Ltd., 1983-84; head Europe, Middle East, Africa div (Global Investment Bank), London, 1983-84; pres., chief exec. officer Citicorp Ins. Group Inc., 1985-91; div. exec. Citibank Global Ins. Div., 1985-91, Capital Investments Div., 1988-90; chief exec. officer Aetna Health Plans, Hartford, Conn., 1991-96; group exec. Aetna Life & Casualty, 1992-93, exec. v.p., 1993-96; pres. NovaCare Inc., King of Prussia, Pa., 1997—; chmn. AMBAC, Inc., AMBAC Indemnity, Capital Markets Assurance Corp., Citicorp Ins. (U.S.A.) Inc., Citicorp Ins. (Bermuda) Ltd.; bd. dirs. Citicorp Ins. Brokers Ltd., 1986-91. Chmn. Outward Bound U.S.A., 1993-96; trustee Old State House Assn., Jackson Hole Group, 1992-96, St. George's Sch., 1981-85; mem. exec. com. Health Leadership Coun., 1996; campaign mgr. Mass. Gov. Sargent's Reelection Campaign, 1970; mem. hon. degrees com. Yale U., 1973-74; bd. dirs., 1st v.p., campaign chmn. Greenwich (Conn.) Health Assn., 1981-83; elder Brick Ch., N.Y.C., 1988-91. With USN, 1961-65, Vietnam. Mem. Yale Club of N.Y., Twin Lakes Beach Club, Hartford Golf Club. Republican. Office: NovaCare Inc 1016 W 9th Ave Kng Of Prussa PA 19406-1221

MC LANE, JOHN ROY, JR., lawyer; b. Manchester, N.H., Feb. 19, 1916; s. John R. and Elisabeth (Bancroft) Mc L.; m. Blanche Marshall, Feb. 15, 1935; children: John Roy III, Andrew M. (dec.), Lyn, Blanche M., Angus; m. 2d, Elisabeth Deane, Dec. 30, 1960; children: Towner D., Virginia W., Kathryn E., Duncan C. Bar: N.H. 1941. Practiced in Manchester, since 1941; dir. firm McLane, Graf, Raulerson & Middleton, P.A., 1941-42, 45-93, of counsel, 1997—. Alderman, Manchester, 1952-53; trustee Spaulding-Potter Charitable Trusts, 1958-72, N.H. State Hosp., 1949-62, Hurricane Island Outward Bound Sch., 1972-79; chmn. N.H. Adv. Commn. on Health and Welfare, 1965-68; trustee, sec. Norwin S. and Elizabeth N. Bean Found., 1967-94; trustee, clk. St. Paul's Sch., 1952-83; distbg. dir. N.H. Charitable Fund, 1962-69; bd. dirs. Coun. on Founds, 1968-74, chmn., 1970-72; bd. dirs. Child and Family Svcs. N.H., 1946-71, pres., 1963-71; bd. dirs. Palace Theatre Trust, 1974—. Lt. USNR, 1942-45. Mem. ABA, N.H. Bar Assn., Manchester Bar Assn. Republican. Episcopalian (vestry 1963, 68). Home: 106 Mclane Ln Manchester NH 03104-1641 Office: 900 Elm St PO Box 326 Manchester NH 03105-0326

MCLANE, PETER, broadcast executive; b. New Kensington, Pa., May 21, 1940. BS, U. Nebr., 1961. With Swanco Broadcasting, Dallas, 1964-77; sta. mgr. Sta. WLTE, Mpls., 1977-81; v.p. programming Stoner Broadcasting, Annapolis, Md., 1981-88; gen. mgr. Sta. KGGO AM-FM, Des Moines, 1988—; nat. program advisor Am. Radio Systems. Avocation: railroad history. Office: KGGO Radio Sta 3900 NE Broadway Ave Des Moines IA 50317-8942

MCLANE, WILLIAM DELANO, mechanical engineer; b. Ralls, Tex., Aug. 22, 1936; s. Clyde and Lillian Helen (Earp) McL.; m. Mary Ann Clark, Feb. 17, 1962; children: William Devin, Keri, Kristi, Mandy. BSME, Tex. Tech. U., 1961. Profl. engr. Tex. Engr. Texaco Inc., Tulsa, 1961-63; plant engring. mgr. Owens-Corning Fiberglas Corp., Toledo, 1963-72; pres., CEO Tucker-McLane Tire Corp., Waxahachie, Tex., 1972-89; commr. County of Ellis, Waxahachie, 1989-93; engr. Morrison Knudsen Corp., Dallas, 1993-94; MK-Ferguson, Albuquerque, 1994-95, Parsons Brinckerhoff, Dallas, 1995-96; quality control mgr. Sedalco, Inc., Ft. Worth, Tex., 1996-971996—; maintenance mgr. Temple Re-Con Inc., Waxahachie, Tex., 1997—; mem. adv. bd. Guaranty Fed. Bank, Waxahachie, 1993—, Citizens Nat. Bank, Waxahachie, 1991-92, City of Waxahachie, 1990-91. Sec. bd. Waxahachie Sch. Dist., 1979-88; vice chmn. Ctrl. Tex. Econ. Devel. Dist., Waco, 1989-93. Mem. ASME, ASCE, NSPE, Tex. Soc. Profl. Engrs., Waxahachie C. of C. (pres. 1977), Internat. Conf. Bldg. Officials. Republican. Presbyterian. Avocations: civic and political volunteer work, varmint hunting, photography, cooking. Home: 1612 Alexander Dr Waxahachie TX 75165 Office: Temple Re-Con Inc 2425 N Hwy 77 Fort Worth TX 76137

MCLAREN, DIGBY JOHNS, geologist, educator; b. Carrickfergus, Northern Ireland, Dec. 11, 1919; m. Phyllis Mary Matkin, Mar. 25, 1942; children: Ian, Patrick, Alison. Student, Queen's Coll., Cambridge U., 1938-40; BA, Cambridge U., 1941, MA (Harkness scholar), 1948; PhD, Mich. U., 1951; DSc (hon.), U. Ottawa, 1980, Carleton U., 1993, U. Waterloo, 1996. Geologist Geol. Survey Can., Ottawa, Ont., 1948-80; dir. gen. Geol. Survey Can., 1973-80; sr. sci. advisor Can. Dept. Energy, Mines and Resources, Ottawa, 1981-84; vis. prof. U. Ottawa, 1981-90; 1st dir. Inst. Sedimentary and Petroleum Geology, Calgary, Alta., Can., 1967-73; pres. Commn. on Stratigraphy, Internat. Union Geol. Scis., 1972-76; apptd. 14th dir. Geol. Survey Can., 1973; chmn. bd. Internat. Geol. Correlation Program, UNESCO, 1976-80. Contbr. memoirs, bulls., papers, geol. maps, sci. articles in field of Devonian geology and paleontology of Western and Arctic Canada, internat. correlation and boundary definition, global extinctions and asteroid impacts, and global change. Served to capt. Royal Arty. Brit. Army, 1940-46. Decorated officer Order of Can.; recipient Gold medal (sci.) Profl. Inst. Pub. Service of Can., 1979, Hollis D. Hedberg Energy award So. Meth. U., 1994. Fellow Royal Soc. Can. (pres. 1987-90), Royal Soc. London, European Union of Geoscis. (hon.), U.S. Nat. Acad. Scis. (fgn. assoc.), Geol. Soc. France (hon.), Geol. Soc. London (hon., Coke medal 1986), Am. Philos. Soc. (fgn. mem.); mem. Geol. Soc. Germany (hon., Leopold von Buch medal 1983), Geol. Soc. Am. (pres. 1982), Paleontol. Soc. (pres. 1969), Geol. Assn. Can. (Logan medal 1987), Can. Soc. Petroleum Geologists (pres. 1971, hon.). Home: 248 Marilyn Ave, Ottawa, ON Canada K1V 7E5

MCLAREN, JAMES CLARK, French educator; b. Halifax, N.S., Can., June 19, 1925; came to U.S., 1947, naturalized, 1960; s. Philip Doane and Margaret (MacGregor/Clark) McL.; m. Helen Elizabeth Oestreich, Jan. 25, 1957; children: Susan Atwell, James Philip. B.A., Dalhousie U., 1945, M.A., 1946; diplôme d'études, Sorbonne, Paris, 1947; Ph.D., Columbia U., 1951. Lectr. French Columbia U., N.Y.C., 1947-48; instr. Johns Hopkins U., Balt., 1948-52, asst. prof., 1952-56; assoc. prof., then prof. Chatham Coll., Pitts., 1956-65, chmn. dept. modern langs., 1957-65; prof. French U. Del., Newark, 1965-85, prof. emeritus, 1985—, chmn. grad. program French, 1966-81; vis. lectr. French lit. U. Pitts., 1957-63. Author: The Theatre of André Gide, 1953; essayist in field, reviewer; writer poetry. Recipient Buhl Humanities award Chatham Coll., 1964; French Govt. scholar, Sorbonne, 1946-47; Grad. residence scholar Columbia U., 1948-49; Todd scholar Columbia U., 1948-49. Mem. MLA, Am. Assn. Tchrs. of French. Home: 802 S Chapel St Newark DE 19713-3718 Office: U Del Dept French Newark DE 19716 *My goal as a teacher and writer has been to try to view the relativity and interrelationship of ideas and themes: to attempt a critical synthesis out of any specific analysis of a text or author. However specialized the topic, it loses its relevance if isolated from the broader contexts within which it evolves or contrasts. This, I think, is the real meaning of the Humanities.*

MC LAREN, JOHN ALEXANDER, retired physician; b. Vancouver, B.C., Can., Mar. 21, 1919; came to U.S., 1948, naturalized, 1952; s. Henry Moncrieff and Elizabeth Jean (Dingwall) McL.; m. Valerie Jean Adams, June 24, 1944; children: John Alexander, Jeannie McLaren Martz, Duncan R., Laurie McLaren Gates. B.A., U. B.C., 1939; M.D., C.M., McGill U., Montreal, 1943. Diplomate: Am. Bd. Internal Medicine. Intern and resident Montreal Gen. Hosp.; resident Toronto Gen. Hosp., 1946-48; gen. practice internal medicine Wilmette and Evanston, Ill., 1948-68; v.p. patient care services Evanston (Ill.) Hosp., 1968-74, v.p. mktg., 1976-80; v.p. orgn., planning and staffing Glenbrook Hosp., Glenview, Ill., 1974-76; physician Northcare Med. Group, 1980-84; asst. prof. medicine Northwestern U. Med. Sch.; mem. Nat. Bd. Med. Examiners, 1975-78; long-term care council Joint Commn. Accreditation Hosps., 1971-78. Served with M.C. Can. Army, 1943-46. Mem. Chgo. Med. Soc., AMA. Club: Mission Hills Country (Northbrook). Home: 3741 Mission Hills Rd #201 Northbrook IL 60062-5747

MCLAREN, SUSAN SMITH, therapist, healing touch practitioner, instructor; b. Plymouth Meeting, Pa., Jan. 21, 1941; d. Robertson Fobes and Jane (Leiper) Smith; m. Michael Eric McLaren (div. 1993). BA, Mount Holyoke Coll., 1962; cert. orthoptic technician, Bellevue Hosp., N.Y.C., 1963; MS, Villanova U., 1994. Cert. counselor Nat. Bd. Cert. Counselors, Inc. Orthoptist Bascom Palmer Eye Inst., Miami, Fla., 1963-69; lab. technician Pvt. Pathology Practice, Sydney, N.S.W., Australia, 1970-78, Nambour, Queensland, 1981-87; asst. renal medicine Mater Hosp., Sydney, 1978-81; hospice vol. Hospice of Watauga County, Boone, N.C., 1988-91; cert. practitioner, instr. Healing Touch Internat., Inc., 1991—; Reiki therapist Spirit Releasement Therapy, Kimberton, Pa., 1995—; adv. Camphill Village, Kimberton, 1993—, Cmty. Supported Agr., Kimberton, 1994—. Editl. bd. mem. Aspen Publ., Inc., Gaithersburg, Md., 1994—; contbr. articles to profl. jours. Mem. ACA, Am. Holistic Nurses' Assn., Nat. Hospice Orgn., Nat. Fedn. Spiritual Healers, Australian Spiritual Healers Assn., Inst. Noetic Scis. Avocations: swimming, cross-stitching, cooking, pottery.

MCLARNAN, DONALD EDWARD, banker, corporation executive; b. Nashua, Iowa, Dec. 19, 1906; s. Samuel and Grace (Prudhon) McL.; m. Virginia Rickard, May 5, 1939; children: Marilyn, Marcia, Roxane. A.B., U. So. Calif., 1930; grad., Southwestern U. Law Sch., 1933; postgrad., Cambridge U. Trust appraiser, property mgr. Security-Pacific Nat. Bank, Los Angeles, 1935-54; regional dir. SBA for, So. Calif., Ariz., Nev., 1954-61; area adminstr. SBA for, Alaska, Western U.S., Hawaii, Guam, Samoa, U.S. Trust Terr., 1969-73; pres. Am. MARC, Inc. (offshore oil drillers and mfr. diesel engines), 1961-63, Terminal Drilling & Prodn. Co., Haney & Williams Drilling Co., Western Offshore, 1961-63; v.p., dir. Edgemar Dairy, Santa Monica Dairy Co., 1954-70; founder, pres., chmn. bd. Mission Nat. Bank, 1963-67; pres. Demco Trading Co., Mut. Trading Co.; dir. Coast Fed. Savs. & Loan; cons. numerous corps.; guest lectr. various univs. Contbr. articles on mgmt. and fin. to profl. jours. Chmn. fed. agys. div. Community Chest, 1956; nat. pres. Teachers Day, 1956; bd. councillors U. So. Calif.; founder, chmn., pres. Soc. Care and Protection Injured Innocent; adv. bd. Los Angeles City Coll.; bd. dirs. Calif. Easter Seal Soc.; nat. chmn. U. So. Calif. Drug Abuse Program. Recipient Los Angeles City and County Civic Leadership award, 1959. Mem. Nat. Assn. People with Disabilities (pres.); Mem. Skull and Dagger, Delta Chi. Clubs: Mason (Los Angeles) (K.T., Shriner), Los Angeles (Los Angeles), Jonathan (Los Angeles). Home: 135 S Norton Ave Los Angeles CA 90004-3916 Office: 1111 Crenshaw Blvd Los Angeles CA 90019-3112

MCLARNON, MARY FRANCES, neurologist; b. Montreal, Que., Canada, May 13, 1944; came to U.S., 1969; d. John Francis and Patricia Jessica (Dore) McL.; m. Malcolm Weiner, Dec. 21, 1975; m. Lawrence Zingesser, Oct. 12, 1982; children: Andrea, Eliza. BS, McGill U., 1965, MD, 1969.

Intern St. Vincent's Hosp., N.Y.C., 1969-70; fellow seizure unit Boston Children's Hosp., 1970-71; resident in neurology Albert Einstein Coll. Medicine, Bronx, N.Y., 1971-73; resident in radiology N.Y. Hosp.-Cornell Med. Ctr., N.Y.C., 1973-76; pvt. practice.

MCLARTY, THOMAS F., III (MACK MCLARTY), federal official; b. Hope, Ark., June 14, 1946; s. Thomas Franklin and Helen (Hesterly) McL.; m. Donna Kay Cochran, June 14, 1969; children: Mark Cochran, Franklin Hesterly. BA, U. Arkansas, Fayetteville, 1968. Founder, pres. McLarty Leasing System Inc., Little Rock, 1969-79; pres. McLarty Cos., 1979-83; with Arkla Inc., Shreveport, from 1983, pres., CEO Arkla Gas divsn., 1983; pres., COO Arkla Gas divsn. Arkla, Inc., Shreveport, 1984, chmn. bd., pres., CEO, from 1985; chief of staff The White House, Washington, 1993-94, sr. adviser to President Clinton, 1994—; chmn. Arkla Energy Mktg. Co., Shreveport, La., Arkla Chem. Corp., Shreveport, AER-Ark. Gas Transit Co., Shreveport; chmn., chief exec. officer, Miss. River Transmission Corp., St. Louis, MRT Energy Mktg. Co., St. Louis, Ark. La. Fin. Corp., Shreveport. Mem. Ark. Ho. of Reps., 1970-72; chmn. Ark. Dem. Com.; mem. Dem. Nat. Com., 1974-76; treas. David Pryor Gubernatorial Campaign, 1974, Gov. Bill Clinton campaign, 1978; bd. dirs. Hendrix Coll., Conway, Ark.; bd. visitors U. Ark., Little Rock; former chmn. United Negro Coll. Fund Campaign, fund-raising campaign Ark. Symphony. Mem. Greater Little Rock C. of C. (pres. 1983). Office: The White House 1600 Pennsylvania Ave NW Washington DC 20500-0005*

MCLAUGHLIN, ANN, public policy, communications executive; b. Newark, Nov. 16, 1941; d. Edward Joseph and Marie (Koellhoffer) Lauenstein; m. John McLaughlin, 1975 (div. 1992). Student, U. London, 1961-62; BA, Marymount Coll., 1963; postgrad., Wharton Sch., 1987. Supr. network comml. schedule ABC, N.Y.C., 1963-66; dir. alumnae relations Marymount Coll., Tarrytown, N.Y., 1966-69; account exec. Myers-Infoplan Internat. Inc., N.Y.C., 1969-71; dir. comm. Presdl. Election Com., Washington, 1971-72; asst. to chmn. and press sec. Presdl. Inaugural Com., Washington, 1972-73; dir. Office of Pub. Affairs, EPA, Washington, 1973-74; govt. rels. and comm. exec. Union Carbide Corp., N.Y.C. and Washington, 1974-77; pub. affairs, issues mgmt. counseling McLaughlin & Co., 1977-81; asst. sec. for pub. affairs Dept. Treasury, Washington, 1981-84; under sec. Dept. of Interior, Washington, 1984-87; cons. Ctr. Strategic and Internat. Studies, Washington, 1987; sec. of labor Dept. of Labor, Washington, 1987-89; vis. fellow The Urban Inst., 1989-92; pres., CEO New Am. Schs. Devel. Corp., 1992-93; chmn. Pres.'s Commn. Aviation Security and Terrorism, 1989-90; mem. Am. Coun. on Capital Formation, 1976-78; mem. environ. edn. task force HEW, 1976-77; mem. Def. Adv. Com. of Women in the Svcs., 1973-74; bd. dirs. GM, Fannie Mae, Kellogg Co., Nordstrom Co., Host Marriott Corp., Vulcan Materials Co., Donna Karan Internat., AMR Corp.; chmn. Aspen Inst., 1996—. vice chmn., 1996; pres. Fed. City Coun., 1990-95. Mem. bd. overseers Wharton Sch. U. Pa.; bd. dirs. Charles A. Dana Found., The Conservation Fund, The Shakespeare Theatre, 1994—, Pub. Agenda Found.; trustee Urban Inst., 1989-96. Mem. Cosmos Club, Met. Club, Econ. Club, F St. Club. Republican. Roman Catholic.

MCLAUGHLIN, ANNE ELIZABETH, secondary education educator; b. Springfield, Mass., Sept. 16, 1942; d. Terrence John and Sara Anne (Hartford) McTiernan. BA, Elms Coll., 1966; MEd, U. Lowell, 1976; M in Edn. Administrn., Salem State U., 1988; postgrad., Harvard U., 1995. Cert. reading specialist Mass., N.H.; cert. adminstr. Mass., N.H. Tchr. reading John Duggan Middle Sch., Springfield, Mass., 1967-72, Andover (Mass.) High Sch., 1972-74; with Middlesex Ho. Corrections, Bellrica, Mass., 1974-76; clinician, cons. Northeastern U., Boston, 1976-77; reading specialist Exeter Area Jr. High, N.H., 1977—; evaluator New England Assn. Schs. and Colls., 1987; instr. Elms Coll., Chicopee, Mass., 1991—; chairperson Sch. Adminstr. Unit # 16 staff devel. com., Exeter Area Jr. High. Sch. improvement com.; co-pres. Seacoast Reading Coun.; founder Libr. Card Program for Am. Libr. Week. Fellow Nat. Endowment for Arts, 1979; recipient commendation Internat. Reading Assn., 1992. Mem. NEA (legis. com.), Exeter Edn. Assn. (rep. to Congress), Peace and Justice for Children Caucus, Granite State Reading Coun., Assn. for Supervision and Curriculum Devel., Nat. Coun. Tchrs of English. Avocations: skiing, boating, world traveling. Home: 2 Elbow Ln # B Newburyport MA 01950-2725 Office: Sch Adminstr Unit # 16 Front St Exeter NH 03833

MCLAUGHLIN, CALVIN STURGIS, biochemistry educator; b. St. Joseph, Mo., May 29, 1936; s. Calvin Sturgis and Agnes Jane McLaughlin; m. Chin Helen Moy, Sept. 7, 1960; children—Heather Chin Chu, Christine Leng Oy, Andrew Calvin Moy. BS, King Coll., 1958; postgrad., Yale U., 1958-59; PhD, MIT, 1964. Postdoctoral fellow Institut de Biologie Physico-Chimique, Paris, 1964-66; prof. biochemistry U. Calif., Irvine, 1966—, dir. Cancer Research Inst., 1981-83; vis. prof. Sch. Botany Oxford U., Eng., 1976, 80; mem. peer rev. panels Am. Cancer Soc., NSF, NIH, VA. Contbr. numerous articles to profl. jours.; mem. editorial bds. Jour. Bacteriology, 1975-80, Exptl. Mycology, 1980-86; reviewer profl. jours. Bd. dirs. Am. Cancer Soc., Orange County, 1980-89; mem. Traffic Affairs Com., Newport Beach, Calif., 1972-78. Named Outstanding Tchr. U. Calif.-Irvine, 1978, Gabriel Lester Meml. Lectr. Reed Coll., 1979; fellow Rockefeller Found., 1958-59, Upjohn Found., 1959-60, Nutrition Found., 1960-61, NIH, 1961-64, Am. Cancer Soc., 1964-66. Mem. Genetics Soc. Am., Am. Soc. Biochemistry and Molecular Biology, Am. Soc. Microbiology, Am. Soc. Mycology, Am. Soc. for Cell Biology, Yeast Genetics and Molecular Biology Soc. Am. (co-chair 1986-88), Electrophoresis Soc. Presbyterian. Office: U Calif-Irvine Dept Biol Chemistry Irvine CA 92697-1700

MC LAUGHLIN, DAVID THOMAS, academic administrator, business executive; b. Grand Rapids, Mich., Mar. 16, 1932; s. Wilfred P. and Arlene (Sunderlin) McL.; m. Judith Ann Landauer, Mar. 26, 1955; children: William, Wendy, Susan, C. Jay. B.A., Dartmouth Coll., 1954, M.B.A., 1955. With Champion Internat. Co., 1957-70; v.p., gen. mgr. Champion Internat. Co. (Champion packages div.), 1957-70; pres., chief exec. officer Toro Co., Bloomington, Minn., 1970-77; chmn., chief exec. officer Toro Co., Mpls., 1977-81; pres. Dartmouth Coll., Hanover, N.H., 1981-87; chmn. The Aspen Inst., Aspen, Colo., 1987-88, Queenstown, Md., 1987—; pres., CEO The Aspen Inst., Aspen, Colo., Queenstown, Md.; bd. dirs. Westinghouse Elec. Corp., Pitts., Atlas Air, Denver, Arco, L.A.; chmn. bd. dirs. PartnerRe, Bermuda, Std. Fusee Corp., Easton, Md. Served with USAF, 1955-57. Office: The Aspen Inst PO Box 222 Carmichael Rd Queenstown MD 21658-0222

MCLAUGHLIN, EDWARD DAVID, surgeon, medical educator; b. Ridley Park, Pa., Jan. 8, 1931; s. Edward D. and Catherine J. (Hilbert) McL.; m. Mary Louise Hanlon, June 20, 1959; children: Catherine, Louise, Edward, Patricia. BS magna cum laude Georgetown U., 1952; MD, Jefferson Med. Coll., 1956. Intern, Jefferson Med. Coll., Phila., 1956-57, resident in surgery, 1957-59; resident in surgery Jefferson Med. Coll. Hosp., Phila., 1962-64; practice medicine specializing in surgery; surg. asso. Nat. Cancer Inst., NIH, 1959-61, surgeon, 1961-62; teaching fellow Harvard Med. Sch., Boston and clin. research fellow Mass. Gen. Hosp., Boston, 1964-66; sr. surg. registrar Hawkmoor Chest Hosp., Devon, Eng., 1966-67; sr. surgeon Chestnut Hill Hosp., 1967-71; asst. prof. surgery Jefferson Med. Coll., 1968-72, assoc. prof., 1972—, lectr. Jefferson continuing med. edn. program, 1976-77; assoc. chmn. of surgery Mercy Cath. Med. Center, Phila., 1972-88; pres., treas. Cedar Mgmt. Corp., 1981-86; pres., treas. Garnet Moor Ltd., 1981-91, Garnetmoor Pub. Svc. Ltd., 1986-91, Garnet Valley Acad. Alliance, 1991—, Garnet Valley Academic Assn., 1995—; treas. Physicians and Surgeons Ltd., 1983-86. Chmn., Bethel Twp. Planning Study Group, 1971-72, Bethel Twp. Sewer Authority, 1972-78, Bethel Twp. Planning Commn., 1989-91; mem. bd. of sch. dirs. Garnet Vally Sch. Dist., 1990-97; mem. resources com., Garnet Valley Sch. Bd., 1991-95, chmn. curriculum com., 1992-95, chmn. edn. com., 1995-96, alt. mem. fin. com., 1995-96, mem. policy com., 1995-97, mem. bldg. com., 1995-97, Cmty. Laison Garnet Valley Sch. bd. dirs., 1995-97; mem. facility com., 1995-97. With USPHS, 1959-62. Recipient Mead Johnson award for research, 1962, Americus award KC, 1963, Lindback award Jefferson Med. Coll., 1974; named Outstanding Prof. of 1976-77, Phi Alpha Sigma Jefferson Med. Coll. Diplomate Am. Bd. Surgery. Fellow ACS; mem. Phila. Acad. Surgery, N.Y. Acad. Scis., Med. Soc. State Pa., AAAS, Am. Soc. Artificial Internal Organs, AMA, Pa. Thoracic Soc., Georgetown U. Alumni (bd. govs. 1970-72, senator 1972—), Alpha Sigma Nu, Alpha Kappa Kappa. Contbr. articles on research in cancer to med. jours. and articles on edn. to ednl. jours. Home and Office: 3112 Garnet Mine Rd Boothwyn PA 19061-1718

MCLAUGHLIN, GARLAND EUTREÉ, librarian; b. Asheville, N.C., Nov. 1, 1948; s. Alice Elizabeth (McLauglin) Johnson; m. Gloria D. Hicks, June 26, 1973 (div. May, 1990); 1 child, Garland Laiotis; m. Imani Sheila Newsome, Sept. 26, 1992. BA, Livingstone Coll., 1971; MLS, Simmons Coll., 1976. Young adult libr. Mattapan (Mass.) Br.-Boston Pub. Libr., 1972-76, Boston Pub. Libr., 1978, Dudley Br.-Boston Pub. Libr., Roxbury, Mass., 1978-82; generalist Egleston Br.-Boston Pub. Libr., Roxbury, Mass., 1976-78; br. libr. South End (Mass.) Br.-Boston Pub. Libr., 1982-90, Parker Hill Br.-Boston Pub. Libr., Roxbury, 1990—; pres. hist. materials Cultural Concepts, 1994. Author: African Americans on Postage Stamps, 1992. Historian New Eng. chpt. Tuskegee Airman, 1991—; adv. bd. mem. Harvard Sch. Pub. Health, Boston, 1995. Daniel Sharp Ford scholar Boston Pub. Libr., 1974, Alumni scholar Simmons Coll., 1975. Mem. ALA (black caucus 1990—, pub. librs. 1994—), Mass. Black Libr. Network (recording sec. 1994—), Mass. Livingstone Coll. Alumni Assn. (pres.). Methodist. Avocations: photography, stamp collecting, writing, rose gardening. Home: 147 Hamilton St Cambridge MA 02139-4526 Office: Parker Hill Br Libr 1497 Tremont St Roxbury MA 02120-2909

MC LAUGHLIN, HARRY ROLL, architect; b. Indpls., Nov. 29, 1922; s. William T. and Ruth E. (Roll) McL.; m. Linda Hamilton, Oct. 23, 1954; 1 child Harry Roll Jr. Grad., Wabash Coll., 1983. Registered architect, Ind., Ohio Ill., Nat. Coun. Archtl. Registration Bds.; lic. real estate broker, Ind. Past pres. James Assocs. Inc., Indpls.; specializing in restoration of historic bldgs. and domestic architecture. Restorations include Old State Bank State Meml, Vincennes, Andrew Wylie House, Bloomington, Old Opera House State Meml, New Harmony, Old Morris-Butler House, Indpls. (Merit award 1972), Market St. Restoration and Maria Creek Baptist Ch., Vincennes, Ind., Benjamin Harrison House, Old James Ball Residence, Lafayette, Ind. (1st Design award 1972), Lockerbie Sq. Master Plan Park Sch., Indpls., Knox County Ct. House, Vincennes, 1972, J.K. Lilly House, Indpls., 1972, Waiting Station and Chapel, Crown Hill Cemetery, Indpls., 1972, Blackford-Condit House Ind. State U., Terre Haute, Ind. several Indian houses Angel Mounds Archaeol. Site and Interpretative Center, nr. Evansville, Ind.; architect: Glenn A. Black Mus. Archaeology, Ind. U., Bloomington; Restoration Morgan County Ct. House, Indpls. City Market, Hist. Schofield House, Madison, Ind., Ernie Pyle Birthplace, Dana, Ind., Phi Kappa Psi Nat. Hdqrs, Indpls., 1980 (Design award), East Coll. Bldg, DePauw U., Greencastle, Ind., Pres.'s House Restoration, DePauw U., 1992; contbr. articles to profl. jours.; Illustrator: Harmonist Construction. Past chmn. bd., past pres., now chmn. emeritus Historic Landmarks Found., Ind.; bd. dirs., archtl. adviser, bd. advisers Historic Madison, Inc.; mem. adv. coun. Historic Am. Bldgs. Survey, Nat. Park Svc., 1967-73; past mem. Ind. profl. rev. com. for Nat. Register nominations, 1967-81; past adv. bd. Conner Prarie Mus., Patrick Henry Sullivan Found.; past adviser Indpls. Historic Preservation Commn.; past mem. preservation com. Ind. U.; architect mem. Meridian St. Preservation Commn., Indpls.; hon. mem. Ind. Bicentennial Commn.; bd. dirs. Park-Tudor Sch., 1972-85; past nat. bd. dirs. Preservation Action; bd. dirs. Historic New Harmony; trustee Masonic Heritage Found.; bd. dirs. Masonic Home, 1984-91, Inpls. Pub. Libr. Found., 1986—, treas. 1988, 95—, v.p., 1989, pres. 1990; trustee Eiteljorg Mus. Western Art; past mem. Hamilton County Tourism Commn., 1989-91. Recipient numerous award including gov.'s citation State of Ind., 1967, Sagamore of Wabash award, 1967, 80, 82; Mayor's citation for svcs. in preservation archtl. heritage City of Indpls., sec.'s citation U.S. Dept. Interior, design and environ. citation for work in preservation, 1975. Fellow AIA (mem. nat. com. historic bldgs., chmn. historic resources com. 1970); mem. Ind. Soc. Architects (state preservation coord. 1960—, Biennial award 1972, Design award 1978), Nat. Trust Historic Preservation (past trustee, bd. advisers), Soc. Archtl. Historians (Wilbur D. Peat award Ctrl. Ind. chpt. outstanding contbns. to understanding and appreciation of archtl. heritage 1993, past bd. dirs.), Ind. Com. for Preservation of Archtl. Records, Indpls. Mus. Art. (trustee, chmn. bldgs. com., bd. govs. 1986-95), Assn. Preservation Tech., Zionsville C. of C. (hon. bd. dirs.), U.S. Capitol (hon. trustee), Ind. Hist. Soc. (trustee, bldg. com.), Marion County Hist. Soc. (past v.p., bd. dirs.), Zionsville Hist. Soc. (hon. life), Navy League U.S. (life), Ind. State Mus. Soc. (charter), English Speaking Union (bd. dirs. Indpls.), Newcomen Soc. of U.S., Hamilton County Hist. Soc. (life), Woodstock Club (bd. dirs. 1982-86, pres. 1985, ex-officio 1986), Literary Club Found. (trustee), Amateur Movie Club, Skyline Club (life), Packard Club, Masons (33 deg.). Home and Office: 950 W 116th St Carmel IN 46032-8864

MC LAUGHLIN, JEROME MICHAEL, lawyer, shipping company executive; b. St. Louis, Jan. 11, 1929; s. John Thomas and Mary Adelaide (White) McL.; m. Delphine M. McClellan, June 15, 1957; children—Margaret D., Mary Martha, Elizabeth O., Jerome Michael, John T. A.B., St. Louis U., 1950, J.D., 1954. Bar: Mo. 1954, U.S. Supreme Ct. 1972. V.p. Internat. Indemnity, St. Louis, 1955-56; asst. circuit atty. City of St. Louis, 1957-58; partner firm Willson, Cunningham & McClellan, St. Louis, 1958-78; v.p., gen. counsel Alexander & Baldwin, Inc., Honolulu, 1978-79; sr. v.p. Philippines, Micronesia & Orient Navigation Co., San Francisco, 1979-87, exec. v.p., 1987—, chmn. bd. dirs., 1996—; instr. philosophy St. Louis U., 1955-60. Served to capt. USMC, 1951-53, Korea. Mem. Mo. Bar Assn., Maritime Law Assn. U.S., Soc. Maritime Arbitrators San Francisco (past pres.). Republican. Roman Catholic. Home: 1225 Hillview Dr Menlo Park CA 94025-5510 Office: 353 Sacramento St San Francisco CA 94111

MCLAUGHLIN, JOHN, broadcast executive, television producer, political commentator, journalist; b. Providence, Mar. 29, 1927; s. Augustus Hugh and Eva Philomena (Turcotte) McL.; m. Ann Lauenstein, Aug. 23, 1975 (div. 1992). AB, Boston Coll., 1951, MA in Philosophy, 1952, BDiv, 1959, MA in English, 1961; PhD, Columbia U., 1967. Ordained priest Roman Catholic Ch., 1960. Mem. Jesuit Order, N.E., N.Y. and Washington; resigned order and priesthood, 1975; tchr., dir. communications Fairfield (Conn.) Univ. and Preparatory Sch., 1960-64; assoc. editor America Mag., N.Y.C., 1967-70; dep. spl. asst. to Pres. Richard Nixon and Gerald Ford, Washington, 1971-74; pres. McLaughlin and Co. Pub. Policy Cons., Washington, 1975-79; radio talk-show host Sta. WRC-AM, Washington, 1979-82; pres., chmn. bd. dirs. Oliver Prodns., Inc., Washington, 1983—; lectr. numerous univs., corps. and orgns. nationwide, 1963—; host various TV series, Sta. WJAR-TV, Providence, 1962-63, Sta. WNHC-TV, New Haven, 1963, Sta. WTIC-TV, Hartford, 1963, Sta. WOR-TV, N.Y.C., 1964; host, exec. producer Biafra Today report ABC-TV Network, 1969; radio commentator Sta. WSTC, Stamford, Conn., 1964, CBS Network Radio, N.Y.C., 1964, Nat. Pub. Radio All Things Considered, Washington, 1981-85; dir. film insts. Yale U., Holy Cross Coll., Manhattanville Coll.; juror Am. Film Festival, 1969; congressional testimony pub. broadcasting and TV license renewal, Washington, 1967, 69. Author: Love Before Marriage, 1970; editor National Review, Washington, 1981-89, columnist From Washington Straight, 1982-89; TV host and exec. producer The McLaughlin Group NBC and PBS TV stas., 1982—, John McLaughlin's One on One, 1984—, McLaughlin CNBC cable system, 1989-94; TV appearances (host spl. episode) Cheers, 1990, (cameo) Murphy Brown, 1995; Motion picture appearances: Dave, 1993, Mission Impossible, 1996, Independence Day, 1996, Murder at 1600, 1997. Rep. candidate U.S. Senate, R.I., 1970. Recipient Excellence in Journalism award Cath. Press Assn., 1969, News Media award VFW, 1984; nominee Nat. Acad. Cable Programming ACE award, 1989, 90, 91, 94; The McLaughlin Group named Best Polit. Talk Show, Washingtonian mag., 1987-93. Mem. NATAS (Emmy award 1984), Am. Fedn. TV and Radio Artists, Screen Actors Guild. Office: Oliver Prodns Inc 1211 Connecticut Ave NW Ste 810 Washington DC 20036-2703

MC LAUGHLIN, JOHN FRANCIS, civil engineer, educator; b. N.Y.C., Sept. 21, 1927; s. William Francis and Anna (Goodwin) McL.; m. Eleanor Thomas Trethewey, Nov. 22, 1950; children: Susan, Donald, Cynthia, Kevin. B.C.E., Syracuse U., 1950; M.S. in Civil Engring., Purdue U., 1953, Ph.D., 1957. Mem. faculty Purdue U., 1950—, prof. civil engring., 1963—, head Sch. Civil Engring., 1968-78, asst. dean engring. Sch. Civil Engring., 1977-80, assoc. dean engring., 1980-94, interim dean engring., 1994-95; ret. Sch. Civil Engring., 1995; cons. in field. Served with USAAF, 1945-47. Fellow ASCE, Hwy. Rsch. Bd.; mem. ASTM (bd. dirs. 1984-86), Am. Concrete Inst. (hon. mem., bd. dirs., v.p. 1977-79, pres. 1979), Am. Nat. Stds. Inst. (bd. dirs. 1992-94), Sigma Xi, Tau Beta Pi, Chi Epsilon, Theta Tau. Home: 112 Sumac Dr West Lafayette IN 47906-2157

MCLAUGHLIN, JOHN SHERMAN, lawyer; b. Pitts., Apr. 1, 1932; s. John H. and Dorothy I. (Schrecongost) McL.; m. Suzanne Shaver, June 5, 1971; children—Dorothy, Sarah, Martha. A.B., Harvard U., 1954, LL.B., 1957. Bar: Pa. 1958, U.S. Supreme Ct. 1967. Assoc. Reed, Smith, Shaw & McClay, Pitts., 1957-71; ptnr. Reed, Smith, Shaw & McClay, 1971—. Trustee Harmarville Rehab. Ctr., Inc., 1980-87; pres., trustee Western Pa. Sch. for the Deaf, 1985—; pres. Pa. NG Assn., 1976-78; justice of peace Borough of Edgewood, 1963-73; dir. Pitts. Symphony soc., 1987-94, Winchester Thurston Sch., 1985-94, emeritus trustee, 1994—; life trustee Carnegie Libr. of Pitts. and Carnegie Inst., 1994—; adv. Pitts. Symphony, 1996—. Lt. col. Air NG, 1957-79. Mem. Am. Law Inst., Am. Coll. Trust and Estate Counsel, Allegheny County Bar Assn., Duquesne Club, Rolling Rock Club (Ligonier, Pa.). Office: Reed Smith Shaw & McClay 435 6th Ave Pittsburgh PA 15219-1809

MCLAUGHLIN, JOSEPH, lawyer; b. Newark, Aug. 1, 1941; s. Joseph Nicholas and Genevieve Veronica (Lardiere) McL.; m. Elisabeth Lippold, July 31, 1965; children: Elisabeth, Jessica, Emilie. AB, Columbia U., 1962, LLB, 1965. With Sullivan & Cromwell, N.Y.C., 1968-76; v.p., gen. counsel Goldman, Sachs & Co., 1976-88, cons., 1988-90; ptnr. Brown & Wood, N.Y.C., 1993—; adj. prof. law NYU Sch. Law, 1988-92; spkr., presenter in field. Author: (with C.J. Johnson Jr.) Corporate Finance and the Securities Laws, 2d edit., 1997; contbr. articles to profl. jours. Trustee Greenwich (Conn.) Acad., 1988—; treas. Presbyn. Ch. Old Greenwich, 1988-91; bd. dirs. United Way, Greenwich, 1993-97; mem. Rep. Town com., Greenwich, 1993-96. Jervey fellow Parker Sch. Fgn. Comparative Law, Columbia Law Sch., U. Munich, 1966-68. Mem. ABA (sect. bus. law, fed. regulation securities com., subcom. broker-dealer matters 1985—, subcom. civil litigation and SEC enforcement matters 1989—, chair task force rule 10b-6 1995—, co-chair task force sellers' due diligence and similar defenses under fed. securities laws 1989-92), Am. Law Inst., Assn. of Bar of City of N.Y. (internat. law com. 1979-84, chair 1981-84, civil rights com. 1984-87, internat. arms control and security affairs com. 1988-90), N.Y. Stock Exch. (legal adv. com. to bd. govs. 1985-88, subcom. corp. governance, subcom. internat. issues 1988—), Securities Industry Assn. (fed. regulations com. 1978-88, chair 1982-84), Nat. Assn. Securities Dealers, Inc. (corp. financing com. 1983-86), Am. Arbitration Assn. (dir. 1986-90). Republican. Congregationalist. Office: Brown & Wood 1 World Trade Ctr New York NY 10048-0202

MCLAUGHLIN, JOSEPH MAILEY, lawyer; b. L.A., July 10, 1928; s. James Aloysius and Cecilia Ann (Mailey) McL.; m. Beverly Jane Walker, July 24, 1949; children: Stephen Joseph, Lawrence James, Suzanne Carol, Eileen Louise. JD, Loyola U., L.A., 1955. Bar: Calif. 1955, U.S. Supreme Ct. 1959. Mem. firm McLaughlin and Irvin, L.A., 1955—, San Francisco, 1969—; lectr. labor relations Loyola U., L.A., 1958-60, mem. bd. visitors law sch., 1987—; pres. Food Employers Coun., Inc., 1984-89; pres. L.A. Stock Exch., 1972. Contbg. author: Labor Law for General Practitioners, 1960. Served to 1st lt. USAF, 1951-53. Mem. San Francisco, Long Beach, Los Angeles County, Fed., Am., Internat., Inter-Am. bar assns., State Bar Calif., Am. Judicature Soc., Assn. Bus. Trial Lawyers, Am. Soc. Internat. Law, Calif. Club. Office: 818 W 7th St Ste 920 Los Angeles CA 90017-3432

MCLAUGHLIN, JOSEPH MICHAEL, federal judge, law educator; b. Brooklyn, N.Y., Mar. 20, 1933; s. Joseph Michael and Mary Catherine (Flanagan) McL.; m. Frances Elizabeth Lynch, Oct. 10, 1959; children: Joseph, Mary Jo, Matthew, Andrew. A.B., Fordham Coll., 1954, LL.B., 1959; LL.M., NYU, 1964; LL.D., Mercy Coll., White Plains, N.Y., 1981. Bar: N.Y. 1959. Assoc. Cahill, Gordon, N.Y.C., 1959-61; prof. law Fordham U., N.Y.C., 1961-71, dean Sch. of Law, 1971-81, adj. prof., 1981—; judge U.S. Dist. Ct. Eastern Dist. N.Y., Bklyn., 1981-90, U.S. Ct. Appeals (2nd Cir.), N.Y.C., 1990—; adj. prof. St. John's Law Sch., N.Y.C., 1982—; chmn. N.Y. Law Revision Commn., Albany, 1975-82. Author: (with Peterfreund) New York Practice, 1964, Evidence, 1979; also articles. Served to capt. U.S. Army, 1955-57, Korea. Mem. ABA, Assn. of Bar of City of N.Y., N.Y. State Bar Assn. Roman Catholic. Club: Lotos. Office: US Courthouse US Ct Appeals 40 Foley Sq Rm 2402 New York NY 10007-1502*

MC LAUGHLIN, LEIGHTON BATES, II, journalism educator, former newspaperman; b. Evanston, Ill., Apr. 10, 1930; s. Leighton Bates and Gwendolyn I. (Markle) McL.; m. Beverly Jean Jeske, May 5, 1962; children: Leighton Bates III, Jeffrey, Steven, Patrick. Student English lit., Kenyon Coll., Gambier, Ohio, 1948-50, Northwestern U., 1951; BA in English lit., UCLA, 1983; MA in communications, Calif. State U., Fullerton, 1990. Copyboy, reporter, rewriteman City News Bur., Chgo., 1957-58; reporter, rewriteman Chgo. Sun-Times, 1958-62; rewriteman, asst. city editor Ariz. Jour., Phoenix, 1962; reporter Miami (Fla.) Herald, 1962-64; successively rewriteman, night city editor, 1st asst. city editor, telegraph editor Chgo. Sun-Times, 1964-74; dir. Chgo. Daily News/Sun-Times News Service, 1974-79; editorial coord. electronics newspaper div. Field Enterprises, 1975-79; adminstr. reference libr. and communications ctr. Field Newspapers, 1976-79; editor News Am. Syndicate, Irvine, Calif., 1979-85; mng. editor San Gabriel Valley Daily Tribune, 1986; assoc. prof. journalism Riverside (Calif.) C.C., 1987-96, chmn. performing arts and media dept., 1993-96, coll. publs. editor, 1996—; lectr. in journalism Calif. State U.-Fullerton, 1984-96; fill-in editor The Press-Enterprise, Riverside, Calif., 1988-95; lectr., condr. seminars in field. Author articles in field. Served to 1st lt. USMC, 1951-54. Recipient Stick-o-Type award for best feature story Chgo. Newspaper Guild, 1961, Best News story award Ill. AP and UPI, 1967. Mem. Soc. Profl. Journalists, Verban Soc., Psi Upsilon. Office: Riverside Community Coll 4800 Magnolia Ave Riverside CA 92506-1242 *Reporting the news is like any other intellectual activity in that it involves research, verification, organization, and clarity of presentation. But news reporting is unique in that all this is done on a dead run, in time for the day's editions.*

MCLAUGHLIN, LINDA LEE HODGE, federal judge; b. 1942. BA, Stanford U., 1963; LLB, U. Calif., Berkeley, 1966. With Keatinge & Sterling, L.A., 1966-70, Richards, Martin & McLaughlin, Beverly Hills and Newport Beach, Calif., 1970-73, Bergland, Martin & McLaughlin, Newport Beach, 1973-76, Bergland & McLaughlin, Costa Mesa, Calif., 1976-80; judge North Orange County Mcpl. Ct., Fullerton, Calif., 1980-82, Orange County Superior Ct., Santa Ana, Calif., 1982-92, U.S. Dist. Ct. (ctrl. dist.) Calif., Santa Ana, 1992—; mem. adv. com. jud. forms Jud. Coun., 1978—, mem. adv. com. gender bias in cts., 1987-90. Active Edgewood Sch. Parents Assn., Cate Sch. Parents Aux.; mem. governing bd. Victim-Witness Assistance Program Orange County. Mem. Nat. Assn. Women Judges, Calif. State Bar Assn. (mem. com. profl. ethics 1976-80, disciplinary referee dist. 8 1978-80), Calif. Women Lawyers (gov. dist. 8 1978-80), Calif. Judges Assn. (chair civil law and procedure com. 1985-86), Orange County Bar Assn. (mem. com. adminstrn. justice 1975-78, client rels. com. 1978-80, com. jud. appointments 1979-80), Orange County Women Lawyers, Boalt Hall Alumni Assn., Stanford U. Alumni Assn., Cap and Gown Hon. Soc. Office: US District Court 751 W Santa Ana Blvd Rm 713 Santa Ana CA 92701-4509*

MCLAUGHLIN, LISA MARIE, educational administrator; b. Sioux City, Iowa, Dec. 27, 1957; d. Donald James and Shirley Jean (Bartlett) Warden; m. Steven A. McLaughlin, Apr. 22, 1978; children: Mark Alan, Catherine Lynn. BS, Ctrl. State U., Edmond, Okla., 1978, MEd, 1982. Cert. tchr., Okla. Tchr. learning disabilities Putnam City Schs., Oklahoma City, 1979-80, tchr. visually impaired, 1980-81; devel. therapist Child Study Ctr., Okla. Teaching Hosps., Oklahoma City, 1981-83; ednl. cons. Oklahoma City, 1983-85; regional program specialist Okla. State Dept. Edn., Oklahoma City, 1985-87, spl. edn. data cons., 1987-90, tech. assistance officer, 1990-91, asst. state dir. spl. edn., 1991-92; ednl. cons., vision specialist, special edn. adminstr. Edmond, 1992-95, asst. elem. prin., 1995-96, elem. prin., 1996—. Contbr. chpt. to book. Mem. coun. on adminstrn. Ione br. YWCA, Oklahoma City, 1985-88, 92-94; mem.-at-large bd. dirs. Met. br. YWCA, Oklahoma City, 1989-91; mem. adv. com. Okla. Sch. for Blind, 1992—; chmn. Parkview Sch. for Blind Ednl. Found., 1994-96; bd. dirs. Prevent Blindness Okla., 1993—. Mem. Coun. Exceptional Children (v.p. Oklahoma City chpt. 1988-89, Spl. Educator of Yr. 1991), Learning Disabilities Assn., Assn. for Edn. and Rehab. of Blind and Visually Impaired (state pres. Okla. chpt. 1989-90), Advocates and Parents of Okla. Sight Impaired (treas. 1984-87), Okla. Women in Edn. Adminstrn., Delta Kappa Gamma (2d v.p. 1990-

92), Kappa Delta Pi. Avocations: handmade bobbin lacemaking, reading, piano, walking. Office: 22522 N Pennsylvania Ave Edmond OK 73003-9100

MCLAUGHLIN, MARY RITTLING, magazine editor; b. Buffalo; d. Joseph and Irene (Meyer) Rittling; m. Charles Edward McLaughlin, June 21, 1962 (div. June 1981) children—Daniel (dec.), Maud Rosie. BA, Manhattanville Coll., 1956. Reporter Buffalo Evening News, 1956-58; copywriter Harper's Bazaar, N.Y.C., 1959-61; editor McCall's Mag., N.Y.C., 1973-79; mng. editor Working Mother Mag., N.Y.C., 1979-85; exec. editor Working Mother Mag., 1985—. Mem. Am. Soc. Mag. Editors, Women's Media Group. Office: Working Mother Mag 135 W 50th St New York NY 10020-1201

MCLAUGHLIN, MAUREEN A., federal agency administrator. BA in Econs., Boston Coll., 1977; MA in Pub. Policy, U. Pa., 1979. Asst. assoc. and prin. analyst U.S. Congressional Budget Office, 1979-88; dir. post secondary edn. divsn., Planning and Evaluation Svc. U.S. Dept. Edn., 1988—, acting asst. sec. for postsecondary edn., 1993, acting dep. asst. sec. for higher edn. programs, student fin. assistance programs, 1993-94, sr. policy advisor to the asst. sec. for post secondary edn., 1994-95, dep. asst. sec. for policy, planning & innovation, 1995—. Chair adv. com. mem. Fiscal Affairs 1990-92; mem. bd. dirs. Arlington Symphony, 1990-93, sec. 1992-93, v. chair Arlington Adv. Com. on Arts and Humanities, 1987-88, mem. Commn. on Arlington's Future, 1986, chair task force on housing and neighborhoods. Office: Post Secondary Edn Office US Dept Edn 7th & D St SW Washington DC 20202

MCLAUGHLIN, MICHAEL JOHN, insurance company executive; b. Cambridge, Mass., Feb. 14, 1944; s. Michael John and Evelyn Katherine (Quinn) McL. A.B., Boston Coll., 1965; J.D., N.Y. U., 1968. Bar: N.Y., Mass. With N.Y. Life Ins. Co., 1968—, sr. v.p. info. systems and services dept., 1982-88, sr. v.p., 1988-91, sr. v.p., dep. gen. counsel, 1991-95, sr. v.p., gen. counsel, 1995—. Mem. ABA, N.Y. State Bar Assn. Office: NY Life Ins Co 51 Madison Ave New York NY 10010-1603

MCLAUGHLIN, MICHAEL JOHN, financial executive; b. Bklyn., Apr. 13, 1951; s. Michael John and Dorothy May (Reposky) McL.; m. Patricia Ann Concannon, June 24, 1978; children: Michael, Matthew, Brian. BS, Manhattan Coll., 1972; MBA, St. John's U., Queens, N.Y., 1978; JD, Pace U., 1984. Bar: N.Y. 1985; CPA, N.Y. Auditor Arthur Young & Co., N.Y.C., 1972-75; asst. controller Montrex Corp., N.Y.C., 1975-78; mgr. corp. acctg. Gen. Housewares Corp., Stamford, Conn., 1977-79, asst. controller, 1979-81, controller, 1981-86; v.p.-controller Preway Inc., Stamford and Wisconsin Rapids, Wis., 1986-87, v.p.-controller, sec., treas., 1987-88, v.p. fin., treas., sec., 1988-89; v.p. fin. and adminstrn. Hayden Roofing Co., Inc., West Nyack, N.Y., 1989-91; v.p. fin., chief fin. officer Celadon Group, Inc., 1991-93; v.p. fin. and adminstrn. A.T. Clayton & Co. Inc., Greenwich, Conn., 1993—. Mem. ABA, N.Y. State Bar Assn., Am. Inst. CPA's, N.Y. State Soc. CPA's. Republican. Roman Catholic. Office: A T Clayton & Co Inc 600 Steamboat Rd Greenwich CT 06830-7149

MCLAUGHLIN, PATRICK MICHAEL, lawyer; b. Monahans, Tex., July 23, 1946; s. Patrick John and Ann (Donnelly) M.; m. Christine Manos, Aug. 21, 1970; children—Brian Patrick, Christopher Michael, Conor Andrew. B.Gen. Studies, Ohio U., 1972; J.D., Case Western Res. U., 1976. Bar: Ohio 1976, U.S. Dist. Ct. (no. dist.) Ohio 1978, U.S. Ct. Appeals (6th cir.) 1979, U.S. Supreme Ct. 1980; U.S. Dist. Ct. (so. dist.) Ohio 1989, U.S. Ct. Appeals (5th cir.). Dir. vets. edn. project. Am. Assn. Community and Jr. Colls., Washington, 1972-73; law clk. Common Pleas Ct., Cleve., 1976-77; law clk. to judge 8th Jud. Dist. Ct. of Appeals, Cleve., 1977-78; asst. U.S. atty. No. Dist. Ohio, Cleve., 1978-82; chief civil div. No. Dist. Ohio, 1982-84; U.S. atty. No. Dist. Ohio, Cleve., 1984-88; ptnr. Janik & McLaughlin, Cleve., 1988-89, Mansour, Gavin, Gerlack & Manos Co., L.P.A., Cleve., 1989—; appt. and ind. spl. prosecutor Ohio Attorneys General, 1993-96; cons. Nat. League of Cities, U.S. Conf. Mayors, 1971-72; co-creator Opportunity Fair for Veterans Concept, 1971. Editor-in-chief Case Western Res. Jour. Internat. Law, 1975-76. Chmn. North Ohio Drug Abuse Task Force, 1986-88; chmn. Law Enforcement Coordinating Commn., North Ohio, 1985-88; chmn. civil issues subcom. Atty. Gen.'s Adv. Com., 1986-88; exec. v.p. Greater Cleve. Vets. Meml., Inc., 1993, pres., 1994-97. Decorated Silver Star, Bronze Star, Purple Heart, Army Commendation medal, Vietnamese Cross of Gallantry with Silver and Bronze Stars. Mem. ABA, FBA, Ohio Bar Assn., Cleve. Bar Assn., Nat. Assn. Former U.S. Attys., Soc. 1st Divsn., Order of Ahepa, Vietnam Vets. Am., Nat. Vietnam Vets. Network (Disting. Vietnam Vet. award 1985), Nat. Assn. Concerned Vets. (nat. v.p. external affairs 1971-72, exec. dir. 1972-73), Cuyahoga County Vets. (award 1985), Nat. Soc. SAR (law enforcement commendation medal 1989). Republican. Roman Catholic. Office: Mansour Gavin Gerlack & Manos 2150 Illuminating Bldg 55 Public Sq Cleveland OH 44113-1901

MCLAUGHLIN, PHILIP VANDOREN, JR., mechanical engineering educator, researcher, consultant; b. Elizabeth, N.J., Nov. 10, 1939; s. Philip VanDoren and Ruth Evans (Landis) McL.; m. Phoebe Ann Feeney, Aug. 19, 1961; children: Philip VanDoren III, Patrick Evans, Christi Duff. BSCE, U. Pa., 1961, MS in Engring. Mechanics, 1964, PhD in Engring. Mechanics, 1969. Assoc. engr. Boeing-Vertol, Morton, Pa., 1962-63, engr. II, 1963; rsch. engr. Scott Paper Co., Phila., 1963-65, rsch. project engr., 1965-69, sr. rsch. project engr., 1969; asst. prof. theoretical and applied mechanics U. Ill., Urbana, 1969-73, asst. dean engring., 1971-72; project mgr. Materials Scis. Corp., Blue Bell, Pa., 1973-76; assoc. prof. mech. engring. Villanova (Pa.) U., 1976-81, prof., 1981—; judge Cons. Engrs. Coun. Ill. 1st Ann. Engring. Excellence Awards Competition, 1972; cons. Naval Air Engring. Ctr., Lakehurst, N.J., 1977-79, U.S. Steel Corp., Trenton, 1980-82, RCA Corp., Moorestown, N.J., 1986, Coal Tech Corp, Merion Station, Pa., Air Products and Chems., Inc., Allentown, Pa., 1986, Aircraft divsn. Naval Air Warfare Ctr., Patuxent River, Md., 1995—; vis. prof. dept. engring. U. Cambridge, Eng., 1990-91. Reviewer Prentice Hall, 1980—, Jour. Engring. Mechanics, 1973-83, AIAA Jour., 1970-87, Materials Evaluation, 1988, Jour. Composite Materials, 1988—, Composites Sci. and Tech., 1990—, others; contbr. articles to Jour. Applied Mechanics, Internat. Jour. Solids and Structures, Jour. Engring. Materials and Tech., NDT Internat., others. Rsch. grantee NSF, 1970-72, Naval Air Engring. Ctr., 1978-84, Lawrence Livermore Nat. Lab., 1979-81, Naval Air Devel. Ctr., 1985-86, RCA Corp., 1986-87; sr. rsch. assoc. NRC, Washington, 1983-84; USN-Am. Soc. for Engring. Edn. sr. faculty fellow, 1995. Mem. ASCE (chmn. engring. mechanics divsn. com. on inelastic behavior 1977-79, assoc. editor Jour. Engring. Mechanics Divsn. 1977-79, mem. aerospace divsn. com. on structures and materials 1986—), ASME (chmn. applied mechanics divsn. Phila. sect. 1981-83, mem. materials divsn. com. on composites 1992—), Am. Acad. Mechanics, Am. Soc. for Engring. Edn., Am. Soc. Composites, Sigma Xi. Achievements include research and consulting on composite materials and structures, structural analysis and design and inelastic behavior. Office: Villanova U Dept Mech Engring 800 E Lancaster Ave Villanova PA 19085-1603

MCLAUGHLIN, RICHARD WARREN, retired insurance company executive; b. Boston, Nov. 25, 1930; m. Marilyn Slye, 1956; children: Kathleen, Richard Warren Jr., Thomas, Judy. B.S., Boston Coll., 1952; grad. Advanced Mgmt. Program, Harvard U., 1979. Trainee Travelers Ins. Co., Hartford, Conn., 1956, asst. sec., 1966-69, sec., 1969-70, 2d. v.p., 1970-73, v.p., 1973-81, sr. v.p., 1981-85; exec. v.p. Travelers Corp., Hartford, Conn., 1985-91; pres. Travelers Ins. Co., Hartford, Conn., 1991—; chmn. Travelers Indemnity Co., Hartford, 1991—. Corporator St. Francis Hosp. Capt. USAF, 1952-56, Korea. Mem. Eastward Ho Club (Chatham, Mass.), Hawks Nest Club (Vero Beach, Fla.). Home: PO Box 947 Eastham MA 02642-0947

MCLAUGHLIN, STEPHEN, sound recording engineer. Drummer Small Town No Airport, 1989-93, Jeremy Lodeon Quintet, 1995-96, Ed Jones Quintet, 1997—. Recipient Grammy award for Best Engineered Album, Non Classical ("Wildflowers" by Tom Petty), 1996. Office: c/o Robert Urband 300 S Clark Dr Ph 10 West Hollywood CA 90048-3233

MCLAUGHLIN, T. MARK, lawyer; b. Salem, Mass., Apr. 20, 1953; s. Terrence E. and Mary E. (Donlon) McL.; m. Sandra L. Roman, Oct. 16, 1982; children: Daniel, Kathleen. BA in Econs., U. Notre Dame, 1975, JD, 1978. Bar: Ill. 1978, U.S. Dist. Ct. (no. dist.) Ill. 1978, U.S. Dist. Ct. (cen. dist.) Ill. 1992, U.S. Dist. Ct. (ea. dist.) Wis. 1992, U.S. Ct. Appeals (7th cir.) 1982, U.S. Ct. Appeals (11th cir.) 1982. Assoc. Mayer, Brown & Platt, Chgo., 1978-84, ptnr., 1985—; adj. faculty law Loyola U., Chgo., 1983, 86-90. Bd. dirs. no. Ill. affiliate Am. Diabetes Assn., Chgo., 1985-94. Mem. ABA (franchising forum com. antitrust law sect.), Phi Beta Kappa. Office: Mayer Brown & Platt 190 S La Salle St Chicago IL 60603-3410

MCLAUGHLIN, WILLIAM F., paper company executive; b. 1948. Student, West Point Acad.; MBA, Syracuse Univ. Pres. L.J. Minor Co.; exec. v.p. Nestle Brands Foodservice Co.; CEO Sweetheart Holdings, Chgo. Office: 7575 S Kostner Ave Chicago IL 60652-1141*

MCLAUGHLIN, WILLIAM GAYLORD, health care services company executive; b. Marietta, Ohio, Sept. 28, 1936; s. William Russell and Edna Martha (Hiatt) McL.; children: Debora, Cynthia, Leslie, Teresa, Kristin, Jennifer (dec.). BS in Mech. Engring., U. Cin., 1959; MBA, Ball State U., 1967. Plant engr. Kroger Co., Marion, Ind., 1959-62; with Honeywell, Inc., Wabash, Ind., 1962-75, mgr. metal products ops., 1971-72, gen. mgr. ops., 1972-75; pres. MarkHon Industries Inc., Wabash, 1975-90, pres. Healthy Industries Inc., 1991—; mem. N. Cen. Ind. Pvt. Industry Coun., 1983-84; mem. bus. adv. bd. Manchester Coll. Patentee design electronic relay rack cabinet. Pres. Wabash Assn. for Retarded Children, 1974-75; gen. chmn. United Fund Drive, 1971; mem. Wabash County Arts Coun.; pres. Wabash Valley Dance Theater; treas., Young Reps., Wabash, 1968-70; bd. dirs. Youth Svc. Bur., Sr. Citizens, Jr. Achievement; mem. ofcl. bd. Meth. ch., 1966-71; pres. Meth. men, 1975-77; area comm. chmn. Am. Heart Assn. Recipient Ind. Jefferson award for public service, 1981, Disting. Citizen award Wabash, 1981; named Outstanding Young Man of Year, Wabash Jr. C. of C., 1972. Mem. Indsl. C. of C. (pres. 1973-74), Wabash Area C. of C. (pres. 1976), Precision Metal Forming Assn. (chmn. Ind. dist. 1978, chmn. metal fabrication div.), Ind. Mfg. Assn. (bd. dirs.), Young Pres.'s Orgn. Club: Wabash Country (v.p. 1972-76). Lodges: Rotary (pres. 1970-71, dist. youth exchange officer 1974-77, dist. gov. 1979-80), Masons. Home: 141 W Maple St Wabash IN 46992-2729 Office: 141 W Maple St Wabash IN 46992-2729

MCLAUGHLIN, WILLIAM IRVING, space technical manager; b. Oak Park, Ill., Mar. 6, 1935; s. William Lahey and Eileen (Irving) McL.; student Calif. Inst. Tech., 1953-57; BS, U. Calif.-Berkeley, 1963, MA, 1966, PhD, 1968; m. Karen Bjorneby, Aug. 20, 1960; children: William, Margot, Walter, Eileen. Mem. tech. staff Bellcomm, Inc., 1968-71; mem. tech. staff Jet Propulsion Lab., Pasadena, Calif., 1971—; supr. terrestrial planets mission design group, 1981-83, mission design mgr. for Infrared Astron. Satellite, 1977-83, mgr. flight engring. office for Voyager/Uranus project, 1983-86; mgr. mission profile and sequencing sect., 1986-92; dep. mgr. astrophysics and fundamental physics program office, 1992-96, mgr. mission and syss. architecture sect., 1996—. Served with USMC, 1957-60. Recipient Apollo Achievement award, 1969, Exceptional Svc. medal NASA, 1984, Outstanding Leadership medal NASA, 1986. Fellow Brit. Interplanetary Soc. (Space Achievement Bronze medal 1993); mem. Internat. Acad. Astros., Phi Beta Kappa, Sigma Xi. Columnist Spaceflight mag., 1982—. Office: Jet Propulsion Lab 4800 Oak Grove Dr Pasadena CA 91109-8001

MCLAUGLIN, ROBERT BRUCE, software designer; b. Camden, N.J., Aug. 30, 1959; s. Robert Bruce and Patricia Ann (Renner) McL. Programmer/analyst Computron, N.Y.C., 1979-81; systems analyst Wincester Computer, N.Y.C., 1982-83, Geometric Solutions, N.Y.C., 1983-85; instrument maker Fusion Energy Found., N.Y.C., 1985-87; rsch. engr. Community Computer, Arlington, Va., 1987-89; prin. engr. Pilot Rsch., Vienna, Va., 1989-91; systems architect Unitel Comm., Toronto, Ont., Can., 1991-93; chief scientist Image Telecom, Reston, Va., 1993—; design authority Energis Comm., London, 1993-94; chief scientist Winstar Comm., Vienna, Va., 1994—. Author: Fix Your LAN, 1994, Troubleshooting Your Own LAN, 1992, Fix Your PC, 1989-93; contbr. numerous articles to profl. jours. Mem. IEEE, Assn. Computing Machinery, Soc. of Old Crows, Am. Soc. for Quality Control. Achievements include 4 patents in the areas of video on-demand interactive and multimedia services.

MCLAURIN, HUGH MCFADDIN, III, military officer, historian consultant; b. Sumter, S.C., Jan. 30, 1936; s. Hugh McFaddin and Louise Mellette (Nettles) McL.; m. Virginia Anne Harvin, Aug. 22, 1958; children: Mary Louise, Virginia Harvin, Hugh IV. BS, Clemson U., 1959; hon. grad., Command & Gen. Staff Coll., Ft. Leavenworth, Kans., 1978. Ptnr. McLaurin Farms, Wedgefield, S.C., 1959—; commd. 2d lt. U.S. Army, 1958, advanced through grades to col., 1985; exec. officer 151st Field Artillery Brigade, Sumter, 1975-85; dir. pers. S.C. NG, Columbia, 1986-91, dir. logistics, 1991-95; ret. S.C. NG, 1996; cons. S.C. Ednl. TV, Columbia, 1992-93; moderator Nat. Def. Seminar, Washington, 1978. Author: History of South Carolina National Guard and Militia, 1989. Elder, Presbyn. Ch., Wedgefield, 1961; v.p. Com. for Progress, Sumter, 1963; chmn. bd. dirs. S.C. NG Mus., Columbia, 1982—. Fellow Co. Mil. Historians; mem. Field Artillery Soc. S.C. (pres. 1987), SAR (historian), Sumter County Hist. Soc. (dir. 1996—), The Sumter Assembly (pres. 1991), Hon. Order St. Barbara, Fortnightly Club. Avocation: American Revolution research. Home: 6380 McLaurin Rd Wedgefield SC 29168

MC LEAN, DON, singer, instrumentalist, composer; b. New Rochelle, N.Y., Oct. 2, 1945; s. Donald and Elizabeth (Bucci) McL.; m. Patrisha Shnier, Mar., 1987. Student, Villanova U., 1964; BBA, Iona Coll., 1968. Pres., owner The Benny Bird Co., Inc., Fairfield, Conn.; recorded for United Artists, Artista Records, EMI Records; star BBC-TV spls., 1973, 78. Albums include Tapestry, 1972, American Pie, 1972, Don McLean, 1972, Playin' Favourites, 1973, Homeless Brother, 1974, Solo, 1976, Prime Time, 1987, Chain Lightning, 1979, Very Best of, 1980, Believers, 1982, Dominion, 1983, The Best of Don McLean, 1987, Don McLean's Greatest Hits Then & Now, 1987, Love Tracks, 1988, For the Memories, 1989, Don McLean's Greatest Hits Live, 1990, Headroom, 1991, Classics, 1992, The River of Love, 1995; singles include American Pie, 1971, Vincent, 1971, Crying, 1980; wrote Perry Como hit And I Love You So, 1973. Mem. bd. Hudson River Sloop Restoration, World Hunger Yr., Advs. for Arts; fund raiser Scenic Hudson, Hudson River Fisherman's Assn. Recipient more than 30 gold and platinum records worldwide, 5 grammy award nominations and others; Israel Cultural award, 1981. Mem. Coffee House Club. Office: Atlantic Records 75 Rockefeller Plz New York NY 10019-2302 Office: Benny Bird Co 1838 Black Rock Tpke Fairfield CT 06432-3500*

MC LEAN, DONALD MILLIS, microbiology, pathology educator, physician; b. Melbourne, Australia, July 26, 1926; s. Donald and Nellie (Millis) McL.; married. B.Sc., U. Melbourne, 1947, M.B., 1950, M.D., 1954. Fellow Rockefeller Found., N.Y.C. and Hamilton, Mont., 1955; vis. instr. bacteriology U. Minn., Mpls., 1957; med. officer Commonwealth Serum Labs., Melbourne, 1957; virologist Research Inst., Hosp. for Sick Children, Toronto, Ont., Can., 1958-67; assoc. prof. microbiology, assoc. in pediatrics U. Toronto Med. Sch., 1962-67; prof. med. microbiology U. B.C. Med. Sch., Vancouver, Can., 1967-91, prof. emeritus Pathology, 1991—. Author: Virology in Health Care, 1980, Immunological Investigation of Human Virus Disease, 1982, Same-Day Virus Diagnosis, 1984, Virological Infections, 1988, Medical Microbiology Synopsis, 1991, Acute Viral Infections, 1991; contbr. articles to profl. jours. Fellow Royal Coll. Physicians (Can.), Royal Coll. Pathologists; mem. Am. Epidemiological Soc., Am. Soc. Tropical Medicine, Can. Med. Assn., Am. Soc. Microbiology, Am. Soc. Virology. Home: 6-5885 Yew St, Vancouver, BC Canada V6M 3Y5

MCLEAN, EDGAR ALEXANDER, physicist; b. Gastonia, N.C., July 25, 1927; s. Alexander Milton and Nell Blythe (Miller) McL.; m. Anna Jane Hess, Dec. 29, 1951; children: Susan, Sandra, William, Frederick, Mary Anne. BS Physics, U.N.C., 1949; MS Physics, U. Del., 1951. Rsch. physicist Naval Rsch. Lab., Washington, 1951—; rsch. cons. Rep. Aviation Corp., Farmingdale, N.Y., 1963-65, Vitro Labs., West Orange, N.J., 1964-69, Cath. U. of Am., Washington, 1964-69, U. Western Ont., London, 1972-76. Contbr. over 100 articles to profl. jours., books. Troop com. mem. Boy Scouts of Am., Oxon Hill, Md., 1970-80; sci. fair judge Prince George's County Schs., Md., 1952—. With USN, 1945-46. Mem. Am. Phys. Soc., Optical Soc. Am., IEEE (exec. com. 1976-82), Sigma Xi (local exec. com. 1989-94). Achievements include optical diagnostics in the field of plasma physics, including spectroscopic, laser scattering, interferometric and ultra high-speed photographic measurements on shock waves, laser-matter interactions, and various controlled fusion devices. Discovered high-order harmonic generation produced in 1-micron laser-plasma interactions; discovered x-ray lasing in Cu, Zn, Ga, Ge, and As; demonstrated a new technique for optical imaging in turbid water using range gating. Home: 19 Mel Mara Dr Oxon Hill MD 20745

MCLEAN, EPHRAIM RANKIN, information systems educator; b. Jan. 7, 1936; married; 3 children. BME, Cornell U., 1958; SM in Mgmt., MIT, 1967, PhD in Mgmt., 1970. Mfg. mgmt., then sys. analyst positions Procter & Gamble Co., 1958-65; instr. tracked vehicle sect. automotive br. U.S. Army Ordnance Sch., Aberdeen Proving Ground, Md., 1959; sys. analyst Cambridge (Mass.) Thermionic Corp., 1966-67; rsch. asst. Sloan Sch. Mgmt. MIT, Cambridge, 1966-69, instr. info. sys., 1969; asst. prof. Grad. Sch. Mgmt. UCLA, 1969-75, assoc. prof., 1975-87; prof., George E. Smith eminent scholar's chair Ga. State U., Atlanta, 1987—; dir. computing svcs. Grad. Sch. Mgmt., UCLA, 1970-74, chmn. computers and info. systems, 1972-73, 77-80, 83-84, 86-87, founder/dir. computers and info. systems rsch. program, 1978-87; mem. adv. bd. Info. Inst., Internat. Acad. Santa Barbara, Calif., 1983-87; mem. adv. com. Info. Systems Faculty Devel. Inst., Am. Assembly Collegiate Sch. Bus. and U. Minn., Mpls., 1982, 84; cons. numerous bus. and ednl. orgns., 1967—; vis. prof. U. South Australia, Adelaide, 1993. Author: (with J.V. Soden) Strategic Planning for MIS, 1977; (with E. Turban and J. Wetherbe) Information Technology for Management, 1996; co-editor: Management Applications in APL, 1981, Decision Support Systems: A Decade in Perspective, 1986, The Management of Information Systems, 1989, 2nd edit., 1994, prof. conf. procs.; assoc. editor Data Base, 1990-94, co-editor, 1994—; mem. editl. bd./adv. bd., referee many profl. publs. and pub. cos.; contbr. numerous articles and revs. to profl. jours., mags., other publs. 2nd lt. ordnance corps USAR, 1958-59; 1st lt. ordnance corps N.J. Army N.G., 1959-65; capt. ordnance corps Mass. Army N.G., 1965-68. NDEA doctoral fellow MIT, 1967-69; recipient 1st prize nat. engring. design contest Lincoln Arc Welding Found., 1958; rsch. grantee IBM Corp., 1985, McCormick & Co., Hunt Valley, Md., 1989, InformationWEEK mag., Manhasset, N.Y., 1989, Sellinger Sch. Bus. and Mgmt. Loyola Coll. Md., Balt., 1992. Mem. Internat. Acad. Info. Mgmt. (bd. dirs. 1992—), EDUCOM (affiliate) Decision Scis. Inst., Internat. Fedn. Info. Processing (founding mem. working group on decision support sys. 1981—), Internat. Conf. on Info. Sys. (founding mem. adv. bd. 1980—, chmn. exec. com. 1986-87), Soc. for Info. Mgmt. (Atlanta chpt., mem. nat. pres.'s coun. 1985—, mem. nat. exec. com. 1976-79, 85-87, 3d pl. juried paper award competition 1987), Inst. Mgmt. Scis., ACM, Assn. for Info. Sys. (founding mem., v.p. affiliated orgns.), Mensa, Sigma Xi. Home: 2257 Old Brooke Point Dunwoody GA 30338 Office: Ga State U Computer Info Sys Dept Box 4015 Atlanta GA 30302-4015

MC LEAN, GEORGE FRANCIS, philosophy of religion educator, clergyman; b. Lowell, Mass., June 29, 1929; s. Arthur and Agnes (McHugh) McL. Ph.L., Gregorian U., Rome, 1952, S.T.L., 1956; Ph.D., Cath. U. Am., 1958. Joined Order Oblates of Mary Immaculate, 1949; ordained priest Roman Catholic Ch., 1955; prof. metaphysics, philosophy of religion Cath U. Am., Washington, 1958-94, prof. emeritus, 1994—; rsch. scholar U. Madras, 1969, 77-78, 85, U. Paris, 1970, Ctr. for Oriental Rsch., Cairo, 1991-94; adv. prof. Fudan U., Shanghai, 1994—. Author: Man's Knowledge of God According to Paul Tillich, 1958, Perspectives on Reality, 1966, An Annotated Bibliography of Philosophy in Catholic Thought, 1966, A Bibliography of Christian Philosophy and Contemporary Issues, 1966, Readings in Ancient Western Philosophy, 1970, 2d edit., 1997, Ancient Western Philosophy, 1971, Plenitude and Participation, 1978, Tradition and Contemporary Life: Hermeneutics of Perennial Wisdom and Social Change, 1986, Tradition, Harmond and Transcendence, 1994; editor: numerous books including Philosophy and the Integration of Contemporary Catholic Education, 1962, Philosophy in a Technological Culture, 1964, Christian Philosophy and Religions Renewal, 1966, Philosophy and Contemporary Man, 1968, Religion in Contemporary Thought, 1973, Traces of God in a Secular Culture, 1973, The Impact of Belief, 1974, The Role of Reason in Belief, 1974, New Dynamics in Ethical Thinking, 1974, Philosophy and Civil Law, 1975, Freedom, 1976, Ethical Wisdom East and/or West, 1977, Act and Agent: Philosophical Foundations of Moral Education and Character Development, 1986, 92, Psychological Foundations of Moral Education and Character Development, 1986, 92, Character Development in Schools and Beyond, 1987, 92, Person and Nature, 1988, Person and Society, 1988, Person and God, 1988, The Nature of Metaphysical Knowledge, 1988, The Social Context and Values: Perspectives of the Americas, 1989, Culture Human Rights and Peace in Central America, 1989, On Reading the Philosophers for the 21st Century, 1989, Research on Culture and Values, 1989, Man and Nature: The Chinese Tradition and The Future, 1989, Relations Between Cultures, 1991, Urbanization and Values, 1991, Place of the Person in Social Life, 1991, Chinese Foundations for Moral Education and Character Development, 1991, Morality, Metaphysics and Chinese Culture, 1992, The Foundations of Social Life, 1992, Person and Community, 1992, Tradition, Harmony and Trancendence, 1993, Islam and the Political Order, 1993, Psychology, Phenomenology and Chinese Philosophy, 1994, Values in Philippine Culture and Education, 1994, The Filipino Mind, 1994, The Philosophy of Person: Solidarity and Cultural Creativity, 1994, Private and Public Social Inventions in Modern Societies, 1994, Traditions and Present Problems of Czech Political Culture, 1994, Czech Philosophy in the XXth Century, 1994, Language, Values and the Slovak Nation, 1994, Morality and Public Life in a Time of Change, 1994, National Identity as an Issue of Knowledge and Morality, 1994, Personal Freedom and National Resurgence, 1994, Philosophy of Science and Education, 1995, Normative Ethics and Objective Reason, 1996, Personalist Ethics and Human Subjectivity, 1996, Civil Society in Chinese Context, 1997, Civil Society and Social Reconstruction, 1997, Abrahamic Faiths, Ethnicity and Ethnic Conflicts, 1997, chpts. Chinese Philosophical Studies vols. VIIA, X, XII, XIII, XIV, 1997; area editor: New Cath. Ency. Mem. Am. Cath. Philos. Assn. (nat. sec. 1965-80), World Union Cath. Philos. Socs. (sec. gen. 1973—), InterUniv. Com. Research and Policy Studies (sec. 1975-77), Internat. Soc. Metaphysics (gen. sec. 1974—), Council Research in Values and Philosophy (sec. 1980—), Internat. Fedn. Philos. Socs. (dir. 1978-88), Cath. Learned Socs. and Scholars (sec. 1975-77). Home: 391 Michigan Ave NE Washington DC 20017-1586 Office: Cath U Am Dept Philosophy Washington DC 20064

MCLEAN, IAN SMALL, astronomer, physics educator; b. Johnstone, Scotland, Aug. 21, 1949; s. Ian and Mary (Small) McL.; (div.); 1 child, Jennifer Ann; m. Janet Wheelans Yourston, Mar. 4, 1983; children: Joanna, David Richard, Graham Robert. BS with hons., U. Glasgow, Scotland, 1971, PhD, 1974. Rsch. fellow dept. astronomy U. Glasgow, 1974-78; rsch. assoc. Steward Obs. U. Ariz., Tucson, 1978-80; sr. rsch. fellow Royal Obs. U. Edinburgh, Scotland, 1980-81, sr. sci. officer Royal Obs., 1981-86; prin. sci. officer Joint Astronomy Ctr., Hilo, Hawaii, 1986-89; prof. dept. physics and astronomy UCLA, 1989—, dir. Infrared Imaging Detector Lab., 1989—. Author: Electronic and Computer-Aided Astronomy: From Eyes To Electronic Sensors, 1989, Infrared Astronomy with Arrays: The Next Generation, 1994, Electronic Imaging in Astronomy: Detectors and Instrumentation, 1997; contbr. articles to profl. jours. Recipient Exceptional Merit award U.K. Serc, Edinburgh, 1989; NSF grantee, 1991, 93. Fellow Royal Astron. Soc.; mem. Internat. Astron. Union (pres. com. Paris chpt. 1988-91, v.p. 1985-88), Inst. Physics, Am. Astron. Soc. Achievements include discovery of relationship between polarization of light and orbital inclination of close binary stars; development of first CCD spectropolarimeter, first fully automated infrared camera for astronomy used to achieve images of faintest high redshift galaxies, first twin-channel infrared camera; research in polarization measurements of radiation from astronomical sources, use of CCDs and infrared array detectors. Office: UCLA Dept Physics & Astronomy 405 Hilgard Ave Los Angeles CA 90095-9000

MC LEAN, JACKIE, jazz saxophonist, educator, composer, community activist; b. N.Y.C., May 17, 1932. Bandmaster, counselor N.Y. State Correction Dept.; chmn., prof. Hartt Sch. Music, Hartford, Conn., from 1968; founder Artist Collective, Inc., Hartford, 1970; founder African Am. music program (jazz degree) Hartt sch. music U. Hartford. With Art Blakey's Jazz Messengers, performed with, Charles Mingus; actor: film The Connection; albums include Monuments, New York Calling, Antiquity, Live at Montmarte, Ode To Super, A Ghetto Lullaby, Lights Out, Dr. Jackle, The Meeting, Jack Knife, New and Old Gospel, Let Freedom Ring, Destination Out, One Step Beyond, Grachan Moncur III, (with Jackie McLean Quintet) Dynasty, 1990, Rites of Passage, 1991, Triloka: Rhythm of the Earth, 1992,

Jackie MacAttack, 1993, Rhythm of the Earth, 1993, Jackie's Hat Trick, 1995; guest artist album by Jazz Messengers Midnight Session, 1993; led McLean Jazz Dynasty tour with son Rene in 6 countries in Southern Africa, 1993. Decorated officer of the Arts (France); recipient Bent award U. Hartford, State of Conn. Blue Book, Registration Manual award, 1996; named # 1 in Downbeat Mag. Critics Poll, 1993, 94, 95, # 1 in Jazz Times Mag. Readers' Poll, 1993, 94, 95. Office: care Artists Collective Inc 35 Clark St Hartford CT 06120-2010

MCLEAN, JAMES ALBERT, artist, educator; b. Gibsland, La., Nov. 25, 1928; s. Charles Edward and Lucille (Bowdon) McL.; m. Ocelia Jo Perkins, Nov. 27, 1954; 1 child: Gregory Scott. BA, Southwestern La. Inst., 1950; BD, So. Meth. U., 1953; MFA, Tulane U., 1961. Meth. student dir. Centenary Coll., Shreveport, La., 1957-59; head art dept. LaGrange (Ga.) Coll., 1964-66; assoc. prof. art Ga. State U., Atlanta, 1967-68, prof. art, 1968-95; ret., 1995. Exhibited in numerous group shows including Brooklyn Mus., 1976-77, Positive/Negative Exhbn., 1988, Siggraph Exhbn. 1988, 89, Clemson U. Nat. Print and Drawing Exhbn., 1989, Purdue U. Small Print Exhbn., 1990. Mem. Siggraph. Avocations: animation, puppetry. Home: 1256 Dunwoody Knolls Dr Atlanta GA 30338-3219

MCLEAN, KIRK, professional hockey player; b. Willowdale, Ont., Can., June 26, 1966. Goalie Vancouver (Can.) Canucks. Named to NHL All-Star 2nd Team, 1991-92. Office: Vancouver Canucks, 800 Griffiths Way, Vancouver, BC Canada V6B 6G1*

MCLEAN, R. BRUCE, lawyer; b. N.Y.C., Nov. 15, 1946. BS with honors, Ind. U., 1968, JD cum laude, 1971. Bar: Ind. 1971, D.C. 1974. Atty. appellate ct. branch Nat. Labor Rels. Bd., 1971-73; chmn. Akin, Gump, Strauss, Hauer & Feld L.L.P., Washington; bd. visitors Ind. U. Sch. Law, 1989—. Mem. ABA, Fed. Bar Assn., D.C. Bar, Order Coif, Phi Alpha Delta. Office: Akin Gump Strauss Hauer & Feld LLP Ste 400 1333 New Hampshire Ave NW Washington DC 20036-1532

MCLEAN, ROBERT, III, real estate company executive; b. Balt., May 23, 1928; s. Robert Jr. and Mary Somerville (Iglehart) McL.; m. Elizabeth Madison Lewis, May 21, 1960; children: Elizabeth, Alexander, Mary, John. BA, Yale U., 1950; MA, U. Pa., 1965. Mktg. exec. Owens-Ill., Toledo, Ohio, 1957-65; mktg. cons. Old Phila. Devel. Corp., Phila., 1966-70; exec. dir., mem. bd. Cushman & Wakefield, N.Y.C., 1970—; mem. real estate investment com. Yale U., New Haven, Conn., 1982-90; mem. bd. Cushman & Wakefield/Healey & Baker joint venture, N.Y.C., 1990-94; bd. adv. Windsor/Bermuda Corp., N.Y.C., 1995—. Author: Countdown to Renaissance II, The New Way Corporate America Builds, 1984. Chmn. Nat. Bldg. Mus., Washington, 1992-95; mem. bd. Washington Nat. Cathedral, 1981-87. S/Sgt. USMC, 1953-56. Mem. Rolling Rock Club, Allegheny Country Club, Metropolitan Club, Center Club, Gibson Island Club, Tower Club. Republican. Episcopalian. Avocations: tennis, golf, skiing. Home: 631 Stillwater Rd Gibson Island MD 21056 Office: Cushman & Wakefield 1650 Tysons Blvd Ste 450 McLean VA 22102

MCLEAN, ROBERT DAVID, lawyer; b. Mar. 1, 1945; s. Edward D. McLean; children by previous marriage: Ann P., Robert P.; m. Leslie Taft Breed; children: Edward B., Katherine T. BA, Northwestern U.; JD, Yale U. Law clk. to Justice Thurgood Marshall U.S. Supreme Ct.; ptnr. Sidley & Austin, Chgo., 1975—, also exec. com. chrmn., 1993—. Note and comment editor Yale U. Law Rev. Office: Sidley & Austin 1 First Natl Plz Chicago IL 60603-2003

MCLEAN, (ANDREW) STUART, educator, journalist; b. Montreal, Que., Can., Apr. 19, 1948; s. Andrew Thompson and Margret Patricia (Godkin) McL.; m. Linda Read, July 10, 1982; children: Andrew, Robert, Christopher Trowbridge. Adminstr. Dawson Coll., Montreal, 1971-74; exec. prodr. Sunday Morning CBC Radio, 1981-83; dir. broadcast journalism Ryerson Poly U., Toronto, Ont., Can., 1984—; prof. Ryerson Poly. Inst., Toronto, Ont., Can., 1987—. Co-writer (film) Looking for Miracles; author: The Morningside World of Stuart McLean, 1989, Welcome Home: Travels in Small Town Canada, 1992 (Best Non-fiction award Can. Authors Assn. 1993), Stories from the Vinyl Cafe, 1995; editor: When We Were Young, 1996; contbr.: The New Morningside Papers, 1987, The Latest Morningside Papers, 1989. Recipient Best Documentary award ACTRA, 1979, Human Rights Broadcast Journalism award B'nai Brith, 1985; Rooke fellow for tchg. and writing Trent U., 1994. Office: care Ryerson Polytechnic U, 350 Victoria St, Toronto, ON Canada M5B 2K3

MCLEAN, SUSAN RALSTON, lawyer, federal government; b. Fayetteville, Tenn., Feb. 28, 1948; d. Joseph Frederick and Clara (Robertson) Ralston; m. Arthur Edward McLean, Apr. 16, 1983. AB, Randolph-Macon Woman's Coll., 1970; MAT in English, Vanderbilt U., 1971; JD, U. Tenn., 1979; LLM in Taxation, So. Meth. U., 1984. Bar: Tenn. 1979, Tex. 1981, Ark. 1984. Assoc. Rose Law Firm, Little Rock, 1984-85, Brice & Mankoff, Dallas, 1986-87; counsel tax divsn. Dept. Justice, Dallas, 1987-96. Mem. ABA (tax litigation, bus. law sects., exempt orgn. com. tax sect.), Tex. Bar Assn. (tax and litigation sects.), Dallas Bar Assn., Randolph-Macon Woman's Coll. Alumnae (pres. 1992-94). Republican. Presbyterian. Avocations: swimming, golf, art, music, hiking. Home: 4025 McFarlin Blvd Dallas TX 75205-1723

MCLEAN, VINCENT RONALD, former manufacturing company financial executive; b. Detroit, June 1, 1931; s. Frederick Ronald and Bernice Mary (Vincent) McL.; m. Joyce Adrienne Koch, July 23, 1960; children—Judith Adrienne, Bruce Ronald. B.B.A., U. Mich., 1954, M.B.A., 1955. Fin. analyst Ford Motor Co., Detroit, 1954-55, Mobil Oil Corp., N.Y.C., 1958-69; treas. Mobil Chem. Co., N.Y.C., 1966-69; v.p. fin., treas. NL Industries, N.Y.C., 1969-76, exec. v.p. fin. and planning, dir., 1976-82; exec. v.p., chief fin. officer, dir. Sperry Corp., N.Y.C., 1982-86; sr. advisor Wertheim Schroder & Co., N.Y.C., 1988-89; bd. dirs. Legal and Gen. Am., Inc., William Penn Life Ins. Co. N.Y., Banner Life Ins. Co., Md., MAS Funds. Served with U.S. Army, 1955-57. Mem. N.Y. Soc. Security Analysts, Econ. Club N.Y. Home: 702 Shackamaxon Dr Westfield NJ 07090-3408

MCLEAN, WALTER FRANKLIN, international consultant, pastor, former Canadian government official; b. Leamington, Ont., Can., Apr. 26, 1936; s. J.L.W. McL.; m. Barbara Muriel Scott, Aug. 19, 1961; children: Scott, Chima, Ian, Duncan. BA, Victoria Coll., U. B.C., 1957; M.Div., Knox Coll., U. Toronto, 1960; LLD (hon.), Wilfrid Laurier U., 1995. Ordained to ministry, Presbyterian Ch. Minister Knox Presby. Ch., Waterloo, 1971-79; mem. House of Commons, Ottawa, Ont., Can., 1979-93, Sec. of State of Can., 1984-85, min. of immigration, 1985-86; min. resp. for status of women Govt. of Can., 1984-86; CUSO, Nigeria coord., 1962-67; chaplain U. Nigeria, 1962-67; dep. dir. Internat. Program Can. Centennial, 1967; exec. dir. Man. Assn. for World Devel., 1970; past chmn. World Concerns Commn. Canadian Coun. Chs.; Can. del. Gen. Assemblies UN, 1986-93; apptd. spl. rep. Commonwealth and South African affairs, 1989-93; Can. rep. So. Africa Devel. Coordination Conf., 1987-93; del. Commonwealth Fgn. Mins. Against Apartheid, 1987-93, African Devel. Bank, 1990-91, Assn. West European Parliamentarians Against Apartheid, 1988-89; leader fact finding mission to Mozambique, 1987, Can. delegation UN Conf. on Women, Nairobi, 1985; led Parliamentary del. to observe the pre-election process and attended Namibian Indpedence, Mar. 21, 1990; chmn. paliamentary Com. on Devel. and Human Rights; Commonwealth observer South African and Sri Lanka elections 1994; pres. Franklin Cons. LTD Assoc. KPMG-Can. Alderman City of Waterloo, Ont., 1976-79; co-founder UN based Parliamentarians Global Action; hon. consul of the Rep. of Namibia. Chaplain 404 wing RCAF. Recipient Can. U. Svcs. Overseas award, 1990, Can. Bur. Internat. Edn. award, 1994; Paul Harris fellow, 1984. Mem. UN Assn. Can. (chair human rights com.). Progressive Conservative.

MCLEAN, WILLIAM RONALD, electrical engineer, consultant; b. Bklyn., Mar. 26, 1921; s. Harold W. and Helena Winifred (Farrell) McL.; m. Cecile L. Mills, Aug. 17, 1946 (div.); m. 2d, Evelyn Hupfer, Nov. 29, 1968. BA, Bklyn. Coll., 1980, BS, 1981. Chief electrician U.S. Mcht. Marine, 1942-64; elect. designer, engr., 65-76; sr. elect. engr. M. Rosenblatt & Son, Inc., N.Y.C., 1976-86; cons., 1986—. Mem. Soc. Naval Architects and Marine Engineers, IEEE, Am. Soc. Naval Engrs. Home and Office: 57 Montague St Brooklyn NY 11201-3374

MCLELLAN, A. ANNE, Canadian government official; b. Hants County, N.S., Can., Aug. 31, 1950; d. Howard Gilmore and Joan Mary (Pullan) McL. BA, Dalhousie U., LLB, 1974; LLM, King's Coll., U. London, 1975. Bar: N.S., 1976. Asst. prof. law U. N.B., Can., 1976-80; assoc. prof. law U. Alta., Edmonton, Can., 1980-89, assoc. dean faculty of law, 1985-87, prof. law, 1989-93, acting dean, 1991-92; M.P. for Edmonton Northwest Ho. of Commons, Can., 1993—; min. Natural Resources Can., Ottawa, Ont., Can., 1993—; commentator on Can. Charter of Rights and Freedoms and on human rights issues. Contbr. articles to profl. publs. Past bd. dirs. Can. Civil Liberties Assn., Alta. Legal Aid; past v.p. U. Alta. Faculty Assn. Office: House of Commons, Rm 323 West Block, Ottawa, ON Canada K1A 0A6

MCLELLAN, JOSEPH DUNCAN, critic, journalist; b. Quincy, Mass., Mar. 27, 1929; s. Malcolm and Elsie May (Turner) McL.; m. Estelle Marie Cajolet, Feb. 3, 1951; children—Joseph, Laura, Andree, Sandra. BA, Boston Coll., 1951, MA, 1953. Reporter, columnist The Pilot, Boston, 1953-67; editor fgn. news Religious News Service, N.Y.C., 1967-70; editor mag. AD 1970, South Bend, Ind., 1970; dir. spl. projects N.C. News Svc., D.C., 1970-72; from writer, editor to music critic The Washington Post, D.C., 1972-95; music critic emeritus, 1995—; artistic cons. Alexandria (Va.) Symphony Orch., 1996—. Mem. Music Critics Assn., Book Critics Circle, Assn. U.S. Chess Journalists. Club: Mensa (D.C.). Avocations: chess; computers; video equipment and software; poetry translation. Home: 1224 Fairmont St NW Washington DC 20009-5322

MCLELLAND, JOSEPH CUMMING, philosophy educator, former university dean; b. Scotland, Sept. 10, 1925; s. David and Jessie (Cumming) McL.; m. Audrey Brunton, Aug. 23, 1947; children—Jonathan, Peter, Andrew, Margaret. B.A., McMaster U., Hamilton, Ont., Can., 1946; M.A., U. Toronto, 1949; B.D., Knox Coll., Toronto, 1951; Ph.D., New Coll. U. Edinburgh, Scotland, 1953; D.D., Montreal Diocesan Theol. Coll., 1973, Knox Coll., Toronto, 1976. Ordained to ministry Presbyn. Ch., 1949; minister in Val D'Or, Que., 1949-51, Bolton, Ont., 1953-57; Robert prof. philosophy of religion and ethics Presbyn. Coll., Montreal, 1957-64; McConnell prof. philosophy religion McGill U., 1964-91, prof. emeritus, 1992—, dean faculty religious studies, 1975-85. Author: Visible Words of God, 1957, The Clown and the Crocodile, 1970, God the Anonymous, 1976, Prometheus Rebound: Irony of Atheism, 1988; assoc. editor: Studies in Religion, 1970-73, editor, 1973-75; mem. editl. bd. Theology Today, 1960-80; gen. editor: Peter Martyr Library, 1993—. Co-chmn. Orthodox and Reformed Chs. Consulation N. Am., 1968-72. Can. Council grantee, 1968, 80-81, 85-86, 92—. Mem. Canadian Theol. Soc. (past pres.), Canadian Soc. Study Religion. Office: 3520 University St, Montreal, PQ Canada H3A 2A7

MCLELLON, RICHARD STEVEN, aerospace engineer, consultant; b. Lawton, Okla., May 28, 1952; s. Robert Nelson and Jane (Warriner) McL. BSME, Old Dominion U., 1979. Aerospace engr. Naval Engring. Support Office, Norfolk, Va., 1979-82, U.S. Army Aviation Systems Commd., Ft. Eustis, Va., 1982-86; lead dynamicist Astronautics Space Launch Sys. Lockheed Martin Corp., Denver, 1986—; cons. Aircraft Devel., Inc., Englewood, Colo., 1991—. Mem. Soc. Naval Architects and Marine Engrs. Office: Aircraft Devel Inc PO Box 4292 Highlands Ranch CO 80123

MCLENDON, DOROTHY, school psychologist; b. Crawfordsville, Ind., Feb. 20, 1918; d. Joseph Newton and Dora (Ryall) Fullenwider; m. Hiram James McLendon, May 23, 1942; 1 child, Hiram James McLendon, Jr. AB, Olivet Coll., Kankakee, Ill., 1942; MA, Boston U., 1945, EdD, 1970. Diplomate Am. Bd. of Profl. Psychology. Spl. edn. tchr. Kingsley Schs., Belmont Jr. High, Boston, 1943-46, 56-57; tchr. Homerton Coll., Cambridge, Eng., 1946-47; sch. psychologist Alameda County Schs., Oakland, Calif., 1949-52, Paris Am. Army Dependent Sch., France, 1957-58, Brookline (Mass.) Pub. Schs., 1958-81; pvt. cons. Cambridge, Mass., 1981—; cons. Cocoa, Fla., 1981—.

MCLENDON, GEORGE LELAND, chemistry educator, researcher; b. Ft. Worth, June 6, 1952; s. George and Beata (Shaw) McL.; m. Donna Turner, Aug. 20, 1973; children: Heather, Audrey. BS, U. Tex., El Paso, 1972; PhD, Tex. A&M U., 1976. Asst. prof. chemistry U. Rochester (N.Y.), 1976-80, assoc. prof., 1980-84, prof., 1984—, Tracy Harris prof., 1990-94; R.W. Moore prof. Princeton (N.J.) U., 1994—, chair chemistry dept., 1996—; cons., mem. vis. bd. Solar Energy Rsch. Inst., 1986-89; adv. com. NSF, 1988-91. Contbr. 200 articles and revs. to profl. jours. Recipient Dreyfus Tchr. Scholar award, 1979-84, Gold Nugget Outstanding Alumnus award U. Tex., El Paso, 1996; A.P. Sloan fellow, 1980-85; Guggenheim Found. and Worcester Coll. fellow, Oxford, Eng., 1989. Mem. Am. Chem. Soc. (Pure Chemistry award 1987, Eli Lilly award 1990, Akron sect. award 1992), Am. Phys. Soc., Materials Rsch. Soc. Episcopalian.

MC LENDON, HEATH BRIAN, securities investment company executive; b. San Francisco, May 24, 1933; s. Jesse Heath and Clara Martha (Nelson) McL.; m. Judith Nelson Locke, May 30, 1959; children: Laurie, Eric, Brian and Michael (twins). BA, Stanford U., 1955; MBA, Harvard U., 1959. With Shearson Lehman Brothers, N.Y.C., 1960-93; mng. dir. Smith Barney, 1993—; chmn. Strategy Advisors, N.Y.C., 1971—; chmn. The Italy Fund, Inc., 1986—, Zenix Income Fund; adv. dir. First Empire State Corp. Pres. bd. trustees N.J. Shakespeare Festival, 1975-76; trustee Drew U., 1975—, chmn. bd., 1992-97. Served to 1st lt. AUS, 1955-57. Mem. N.Y. Soc. Security Analysts, N.Y. Assn. Bus. Economists, Money Marketeers. Presbyterian. Clubs: Baltusrol, Bay Head Yacht. Home: 70 Hillcrest Ave Summit NJ 07901-2023 Office: Smith Barney 388 Greenwich St New York NY 10013-2375

MCLENNAN, BARBARA NANCY, management consultant; b. N.Y.C., Mar. 25, 1940; d. Sol and Gertrude (Rochkind) Miller; m. Kenneth McLennan, Aug. 14, 1962; children: Gordon, Laura. BA magna cum laude, CCNY, 1961; MS, U. Wis., 1962, PhD, 1965; JD, Georgetown U., 1983. Bar: D.C. 1983, Va. 1991, U.S. Ct. Internat. Trade 1988, U.S. Ct. Appeals (D.C. cir.) 1988, U.S. Supreme Ct. 1988. From asst. prof. to assoc. prof. Temple U., Phila., 1965-78; budget analyst Com. on Budget, U.S. Ho. of Reps., Washington, 1978-81; legis. asst. fin. and budget Sen. Dan Quayle, Washington, 1981-84; internat. tax specialist IRS, U.S. Dept. Treasury, Washington, 1984-89; dep. asst. sec. trade, info. and analysis U.S. Dept. Commerce, Washington, 1989-91; prin., atty.-at-law Bitonti and Wilhelm, PC., McLean, Va., 1991-93; staff v.p. govt.-legal affairs consumer electronics group Electronic Industries Assn., Washington, 1993-94, staff v.p. tech. policy, consumer electronics group, 1994-95; v.p. Van Scoyoc Assocs., Washington, 1995—; sr. polit. scientist SRI-Internat., Arlington, Va., 1971-74; vis. prof. Am. Coll., Paris, 1975-76; cons. UNESCO, Paris, 1977-78. Author: Comparative Political Systems, 1975; contbr. numerous articles to profl. jours. Mem. parents adv. coun. Randolph-Macon Coll., Ashland, Va., 1989-92. NDEA fellow, 1962-65. Mem. ABA, Am. Soc. Assn. Execs., D.C. Bar Assn., Fed. Bar Assn., Phi Beta Kappa. Home: 6950 Duncraig Ct Mc Lean VA 22101-1568 Office: Van Scoyoc Assocs 1420 New York Ave NW Ste 1050 Washington DC 20005-2122

MCLENNAN, BERNICE CLAIRE, human resources professional; b. Malden, Mass., Dec. 26, 1936; d. Ralph Cyril Worth and Alice Seaman (Hunter) Worth Barrett; m. Hubert Earle McLennan, Oct. 28, 1961; 1 child, Cynthia Alice. Student, Moody Bible Inst., 1958, Salem State Coll., 1988, Bentley Coll., 1989. Youth dir. Faith Evangelical Ch., Melrose, Mass., 1971-77; adminstrv. asst. Boston Redevel. Authority, 1977-85, adminstr. coord., 1985-87, asst. sec. to the authority, 1981—, dir. human resources, 1988-95, asst. dir., 1995—; moderator Faith Evangelical Ch., Melrose, 1985-88, Christian edn. chair, 1973-76. Sec. Melrose (Mass.) Sch. Com., 1983-85; vol. Boston (Mass.) Youth Campaign, 1989, 90. Mem. Internat. Pers. Mgmt. Assn., Assn. Affirmative Action Profls. Avocations: Christian edn., women's issues, drug/alcohol edn. Home: 31 Botolph St Melrose MA 02176-1126 Office: Boston Redevel Authority City Hall One City Hall Sq Boston MA 02201

MCLEOD, E. DOUGLAS, real estate developer, lawyer; b. Galveston, Tex., Aug. 6, 1941; s. Vaughn Watkins McL. and Dorothy (Milroy) Burton; m. Sarah Jackson Helms, Mar. 20, 1965 (div. 1979); children: Chanse, Alexandra, Lindsey; m. Joan Margaret Williams, Dec. 26, 1979; 1 child, Joanie; stepchildren: Meg, Libbie. BBA, U. North Tex., 1965; postgrad., So. Meth. U., 1965-66; JD, South Tex. Coll. Law, 1990; LLM, U. Houston, 1993. Lic. real estate broker. Pres., owner McLeod Properties & co., Galveston, Tex., 1967—; tchr. Galveston Ind. Sch. Dist., 1967-69; banker W.L. Moody & Co., Galveston, 1969-72; developer, broker McLeod Properties/Builders, Galveston, 1972-82; developer Moody Found., Galveston, 1982—; bd. dirs. Am. Nat. Ins. Co., Galveston, Nat. Western Life Ins. Co., Austin, Anrem Corp., Galveston, Moody Gardens Inc., Galveston, , chmn., 1984—; bd. dirs. Colonel Inc., Galveston, v.p., 1985—; bd. dirs. Ctr. Transp. & Commerce, Glaveston. Pres., trustee Galveston Ind. Sch. Dist., 1969-73; mayor pro-tem, mem. city coun. City of Galveston, 1973-76; state legislator Tex. Ho. of Reps., Austin, 1976-83; bd. visitors So. Tex. Coll. Law, 1990-96; mem. adv. bd. U. Houston, 1986-95; bd. dirs. Ronald McDonald House, 1986-93, Trinity Episcopal Sch., 1990-96. With USMC, 1961-67. South Tex. Coll. Law fellow, 1990-95. Mem. Granaderos De Galvez, Marine Corps League. Episcopalian. Avocations: physical fitness advocate, legal history collector, family archivist. Home: 53 Cedar Lawn Cir Galveston TX 77551-4631 Office: The Moody Found 2302 Post Office St Ste 704 Galveston TX 77550-1936

MCLEOD, JOHN WISHART, architect; b. Edinburgh, Scotland, Mar. 24, 1908; s. Thomas and Catherine (Wishart) McL.; m. Helen G. Rath, July 11, 1936; children: Ian Wishart, Cathie Ann. Student, Columbia U., NYU, Beaux-Arts Inst. Design, Columbia Tchrs. Coll. Archtl. tng. in N.Y., N.J. area, 1930-36; ptnr. McLeod, Ferrara & Ensign and predecessor firms, Elizabeth, N.J., 1936-41, Washington, 1946-80; with WPB, 1941-46; mem. Bd. Examiners and Registrars Architects of D.C., 1959-66; mem. U.S. del. UNESCO-IBE Conf. Sch. Bldg., Geneva, 1957; mem., vice chmn. U.S. del. UNESCO-U.K. Conf. Sch. Bldg., London, 1962; mem., co-chmn. constrn. adv. com. fallout shelters Dept. Def., 1962-76; planning cons. Found. Barre De La Maja, La Corunna, Spain, 1976. Prin. works include ednl. facilities; author: Urban Schools in Europe, 1968; co-author: Planning America's School Buildings, 1960. Fellow AIA (chmn. nat. com. ednl. facilities 1950-63, pres. Washington-Met. chpt. 1961); mem. Coun. Ednl. Facility Planners Internat. (Planner of Yr. award 1975), Palm Beach Watercolor Soc. (spl. award 8th ann. exhbn. 1991). Home: 404 NW 72nd St Boca Raton FL 33487-2361

MCLEOD, PHILIP ROBERT, publishing executive; b. Winnipeg, Man., Can., May 4, 1943; s. Donald G. and Phyllis (Brown) McL.; m. Cheryl Amy Stewart, Sept. 25, 1965 (div. 1992); children: Shawn Robert, Erin Dawn; m. Virginia Mary Corner, Nov. 6, 1992. Journalist Bowes Pub., Grande Prairie, Alta Truro, N.S., 1962-76; journalist, dep. mng. editor Toronto (Ont., Can.) Star, 1976-87; editor-in-chief London (Ont.) Free Press, 1987—. Southam fellow Southam Newspapers, 1970. Mem. The London Club. Avocations: canoeing, skiing. Office: The London Free Press, 369 York St, London, ON Canada N6A 4G1

MCLEOD, ROBERT MACFARLAN, lawyer, arbitrator; b. Toronto, Ont., Can., Oct. 13, 1925; s. William Green and Eliza Vest (Macfarlan) McL.; m. Siddney Anne Mercer, June 21, 1950; children—Ann Payne, William Mercer, Elizabeth Macfarlan. B.S., U. Wis.-Madison, 1950; J.D., U. Va., 1952. Bar: Calif. 1953, Va. 1952. Assoc. faculty U. Calif. Law Sch., Berkeley, 1952-53; assoc., then ptnr. Thelen Marrin Johnson & Bridges, San Francisco, 1953-86, of counsel, 1986—; real estate broker Hill & Co., San Francisco, 1986-92; vis. lectr. U. Calif. Law Sch., Berkeley, 1965-86; arbitrator Calif. State Constrn. Arbitration Panel, 1978-90; arbitrator constrn. industry panel Am. Arbitration Assn., 1982—; judge pro tem San Francisco Mcpl. Ct., 1980-81; mem. Calif. Pub. Contract Code Com., 1980-85. Contbr. chpts. to books, articles to profl. jours.; bd. editors Va. Law Rev., 1951-52. Sustaining mem. Mus. Soc., San Francisco, 1974—; mem. Nat. Trust, London, 1982—, Forum for Architecture, N.Y.C., 1984-86, Found. for San Francisco's Archtl. Heritage, 1987-93, Nat. Trust for Hist. Preservation, 1987—. With inf. U.S. Army, 1943-46, ETO. Decorated Bronze Star medal. Mem. Bar Assn. San Francisco, State Bar Calif., The Guardsmen, San Francisco Golf Club, Order of Coif, Phi Alpha Delta, Delta Kappa Epsilon. Republican. Avocations: travel; golf. Office: Thelen Marrin Johnson & Bridges 2 Embarcadero Ctr San Francisco CA 94111-3823

MCLEOD, STEPHEN GLENN, education educator, language educator; b. Pensacola, Fla., Mar. 30, 1949. AA, Pensacola Jr. Coll., 1969; BA, U. West Fla., 1971; MA, Vanderbilt U., 1973; EdD, Nova Southeastern U., 1992. Commd. 2d lt. U.S. Army, 1978, advanced through grades to capt., 1981, resigned, 1984; sr. assoc. prof. mil. edn. program St. Leo Coll., Hurlburt Field, Fla., 1984-92; adj. instr. Pensacola Jr. Coll., 1984-86, 91—; West Fla. cluster coord. programs for higher edn. Nova Southeastern U., Pensacola/Ft. Lauderdale, Fla., 1994—. Contbr. articles to profl. publs. Capt. U.S. Army, 1975-84. Recipient Rsch. award Phi Delta Kappa, 1989. Mem. Two-Year Coll. English Assn. Southeast, Nat. Coun. Tchrs. English, Conf. on Coll. Composition and Comm. Avocations: golf, writing, travel. Home: 1313 Wisteria Ave Pensacola FL 32507

MCLEOD, WILLIAM LASATER, JR., judge, former state legislator; b. Marks, Miss., Feb. 27, 1931; s. William Lasater and Sara Louise (Macaulay) McL.; m. Marilyn Qualls, June 16, 1962; children: Sara Nelson Judson, Martha Ellen, Ruth Elizabeth. AB, Princeton U., 1953; JD, La. State U., 1958. Bar: La. 1958, U.S. Supreme Ct. 1980. Pvt. practice, Lake Charles, La., 1958-62; ptnr. McLeod & Little, Lake Charles, 1976-90; dist. judge Calcasieu Parish, 1991-96, of counsel Judson Law Firm, 1997—; mem. La. Ho. of Reps., 1968-76; mem. La. Senate, 1976-9 0. Chmn. adv. bd. Lake Charles Salvation Army, 1965-66; pres. Calcasieu Area Coun. Boy Scouts Am., 1978; elder Presbyn. Ch. With U.S. Army, 1953-55. Recipient Disting. Svc. award Lake Charles Jaycees, 1963, Civic Svc. award S.W. La. C. of C., 1986. Mem. La. Bar Assn., S.W. La. Bar Assn. (pres. 1980), Masons. Democrat. Office: 130 W Broad St Lake Charles LA 70601-4259

MCLESKEY, CHARLES HAMILTON, anesthesiology educator; b. Phila., Nov. 8, 1946; s. W. Hamilton and Marion A. (Butts) McL.; m. Nanci S. Simmons, June 3, 1972; children: Travis, Heather. BA, Susquehanna U., 1968; MD, Wake Forest U., 1972. Diplomate Am. Bd. Anesthesiology. Intern Maine Med. Ctr., Portland, 1972-73; resident in anesthesiology U. Wash. Sch. Medicine, Seattle, 1973-76, NIH rsch. trainee, 1974-75; clin. teaching assoc. dept. anesthesiology U. Calif., San Francisco, 1976-78; asst. prof. anesthesiology Wake Forest U. Bowman Gray Sch. Medicine, Winston-Salem, N.C., 1978-83, assoc. prof., 1983-84; assoc. prof. U. Tex. Med. Br., Galveston, 1985-87; assoc. prof. anesthesiology U. Colo. Health Sci. Ctr., Denver, 1987-91, prof., 1991-93, dir. acad. affairs, 1987-93; prof., chmn. dept. anesthesiology Tex. A&M U., 1993—; chmn. dept. anesthesiology, med. dir. perioperative svcs. Scott and White Clin. and Meml. Hosp., Temple, Tex., 1993—; assoc. med. dir. Scott and White Health Plan, 1995—; cons., lectr. Janssen Pharmaceutica, Piscataway, N.J., 1980—, Alza Corp., Palo Alto, Calif., 1986—; cons. Glaxo-Wellcome Co., Research Triangle Park, N.C., Abbott Labs., Chgo., Marion Merrill Dow, Kansas City, Kans., Aspect Med., Natick, Mass.; lectr. to over 500 nat. and state med. orgns., 1982—; examiner Am. Bd. Anesthesiology; lectr. Ohmeda, Liberty Corner, N.J. Assoc. editor Anesthesiology Rev.; editor Geriatric Anesthesiology, 1997; contbr. numerous articles to med. jours. Mem. choir Friendswood (Tex.) Meth. Ch., 1985-87; mem. Friendswood Fine Arts Commn., 1985-87; mem. Temple Chamber Arts Adv. Coun., 1997—. Lt. comdr. M.C., USN, 1976-78. Woodruff-Fisher scholar, 1964-68. Mem. Internat. Platform Assn., Nat. Spkrs. Assn., Assn. U. Anesthetists, Am. Soc. Anesthesiologists (del. 1983-85, 88—), Soc. for Edn. in Anesthesiology (past v.p., past pres.), Colo. Soc. Anesthesiologists (past pres.), Internat. Anesthesia Rsch. Soc., Soc. for Ambulatory Anesthesia, Evergreen Newcomers, Temple C. of C. (dir. adv. com. 1997—), Alpha Omega Alpha. Republican. Presbyterian. Avocations: running, fishing, racquetball, squash.

MCLIN, HATTIE ROGERS, school system administrator; b. Prentiss, Miss., Dec. 8, 1946; d. Javan Wilson Sr. and Alberta (Davis) Rogers; m. Prentiss McLin, June 29, 1968; children: Albert Marie, Prentiss II, Javan Wilson. BS, Jackson State U., 1968, MA, 1972, EdS, 1981, EdD, 1987. Tchr. Hinds County Pub. Schs., Clinton, Miss.; assoc. prof. edn. Paul Quinn

Coll., Waco, Tex.; asst. prin. Jackson (Miss.) Mcpl. Separate Sch. Dist., 1992; prin. Johnson Elem. Sch., Jackson, Miss.; adj. prof. Jackson State U., Hinds Community Coll., Jackson. Sec. Jackson City Planning Bd.; bd. dirs. Nurture for Bapt. Chs., Greater Fairview Bapt. Ch.; mem. PTA., Youth Leadership Jackson C. of C., C. of C. Youth Devel. Name Outstanding Elem. Prin., Miss. Educator or the Yr.; Levi Strauss grantee, 1985, 86. Mem. ASCD, Miss. ASCD, NEA, Miss. Assn. Educators, Nat. Assn. Young Children, Bus. Profl. Women Orgn., Kappan Honors Orgn., Kappa Pi Honor Soc., Zeta Phi Beta. Office: Johnson Elem Sch 3319 Oak Park Dr Jackson MS 39212-4124

MCLIN, RHINE LANA, state legislator, funeral service executive, educator; b. Dayton, Ohio, Oct. 3, 1948; d. C. Josef, Jr., and Bernice (Cottman) McL. B.A. in Sociology, Parsons Coll., 1969; M.Ed., Xavier U., Cin., 1972; postgrad. in law U. Dayton, 1974-76, AA in Mortuary Sci., Cin. Coll., 1988. Lic. funeral dir.; cert. tchr., Ohio. Tchr. Dayton Bd. Edn., 1970-72; divorce counselor Domestic Relations Ct., Dayton, 1972-73; law clk. Montgomery Common Pleas Ct., Dayton, 1973-74; v.p., dir., embalmer McLin Funeral Homes, Dayton, 1972—; instr. Central State U., Wilberforce, Ohio, 1982—; mem. Ohio Ho. of Reps., 1988-94; state senator Ohio State Senate, 1994—. com. mem. Human Svcs. and Aging Com., Agrl. Com., Ways and Means Com., Energy, Natural Resources and Environ. Com., Correctional Instl. Inspection Com. Mem. Dem. Nat. Com.; mem. inspection com. V.C. Correctional Instn.; chair Children's Def. Fund. Toll fellow Paul Harris, Femming fellow, BLLD fellow. Mem. Nat. Funeral Dirs. Assn., Ohio Funeral Dirs. Assn., Montgomery County Hist. Soc., NAACP (life), Nat. Council Negro Women (life), Delta Sigma Theta. Home: 1130 Germantown St Dayton OH 45408-1465 Office: Ohio State Senate State House Columbus OH 43215

MCLINDEN, JAMES HUGH, molecular biologist; b. Marion, Kans., July 29, 1949; s. James Edward and Lenora Ann (Waner) McL. BA with honors, Emporia State U., 1971; PhD, U. Kans., 1983. Postdoctoral rsch. asst. biology Ohio State U., Columbus, 1983-87; sr. scientist Am. Biogentic Scis., Inc., Notre Dame, Ind., 1987-89, dir. molecular biology, 1989-91, v.p. molecular biology, 1991—. Author: (with others) Viral Hepatitis, 1990; contbr. articles to Jour. Virology, CRC Critical Revs. in Biotech., Biochem.-Biophysica ACTA, Applied and Environ. Microbiology. Mem. AAAS, Am. Soc. Microbiology, Am. Soc. Virology, N.Y. Acad. Sci., Soc. Indsl. Microbiology, Beta Beta Beta. Achievements include research in methods and material for expression of human plasminogen in eukaryodic cell system lacking a site spectic plasminogen activator; research in cardiovascular disease; patent for Recombinant Hepatitis A Virus Vaccine; development diagnostics for cardiovascular disease. Home: 493 Central Ave Milton MA 02186 Office: Am Biogenetic Scis Inc 801 Albany St Boston MA 02119-2511

MCLOONE, EUGENE P., education educator; b. Phila., Nov. 11, 1929; married. BA, LaSalle Coll., 1951; MS, U. Denver, 1952; PhD, U. Ill., 1961. Rsch. dir. Nat. Ctr. for Edn. Stats./U.S. Dept. Edn., Washington, 1979-81; assoc. prof. U. Md. Coll. Edn., College Park, 1967-75, prof. edn. dept. edn. policy, planning and adminstrn., 1975-95, assoc. prof. dept. econs., 1967-94; assoc. dir. Rsch. Divsn. NEA, Washington, 1968-69, staff contact, 1968-70; atty. gen. State of N.J., 1981-83, State of W.Va., 1981; prof. emeritus U. Md. College Park, 1995—; cons. Addison-Wesleyan Pubs., 1992-93, Bur. of Spl. Edn., Dept. Edn., 1992, Jour. Econs. and Edn., 1989-90, Jour. Edn. Fin., 1989-95, Nat. Tax Assn., 1989, Office Edn. Rsch. and Improvement, 1989, others; lectr. in field; mem. various rsch. couns.; panel mem. Statis. for Supply and Demand of Pre-Collegiate Sci. and Math. Tchrs., Nat. Rsch. Coun., NAS, 1986-90, others. Author: Pre-College Science and Mathematics Teachers: Monitoring Supply, Demand, and Quality, 1990, Report of Panel, Toward Understanding Teacher Supply and Demand: Priorities for Research and Development Interim Report, Profiles in School Support, 1969-70; others; co-author: Public School Finance: Profiles of the State, 1979, Documentation and Analysis of Maryland Special Services Information System, 1977, others; contbr. articles to profl. jours.; editor books in field. Grantee Bur. of the Handicapped, U.S.O.E., 1977, Nat. Ctr. for Edn. Stats., 1971, 73, others; recipient numerous awards in field. Mem. NEA, Am. Econ. Assn., Am. Assn. Sch. Adminstrs., Am. Edn. Fin. Assn. (pres. 1996-97), Phi Delta Kappa.

MCLOUGHLIN, MERRILL, publishing executive. Co-editor U.S. News & World Report, Washington. Office: US News & World Report 2400 N St NW Washington DC 20037-1153*

MC LUCAS, JOHN LUTHER, aerospace company executive; b. Fayetteville, N.C., Aug. 22, 1920; s. John Luther and Viola (Conley) McL.; m. Patricia Knapp, July 27, 1946 (div. 1981); children: Pamela McLucas Byers, Susan, John C., Roderick K.; m. Harriet D. Black, Sept. 25, 1981. B.S., Davidson Coll., 1941; M.S., Tulane U., 1943; Ph.D., Pa. State U., 1950, D.Sc., 1974. V.p., tech. dir. Haller, Raymond & Brown, Inc., State College, Pa., 1950-57; pres. HRB-Singer, Inc., State College, 1958-62; dep. dir. rsch. and engring. Dept. Def., 1962-64; pres., chief exec. officer Mitre Corp., Bedford, Mass., 1966-69; undersec. of Air Force, 1969-73, sec. of Air Force, 1973-75; adminstr. FAA, 1975-77; pres. Comsat Gen. Corp., Washington, 1977-79; exec. v.p. COMSAT, 1979-80, pres. world systems div., 1980-83, exec. v.p., chief strategic officer, 1983-85; chmn. bd. dirs. External Tanks Inc.; bd. dirs. Dulles Access Rapid Transit, Inc., Orbital Scis. Corp., Space Destination Svcs., Inc.; mem. USAF Sci. Adv. Bd., 1967-69, 77-84, Def. Sci. Bd., 1968-69; chmn. USAF SDAG, 1979-83; chmn. bd. dirs. Internat. Space U., 1987-93, active, 1987—. Author: Space Commerce, 1991; contbr. articles to tech. lit. Chmn. bd. Wolf Trap Found., 1986-88; chmn. bd. Arthur C. Clarke Found. of U.S.; chmn. bd. dirs. ISY Internat. Space Yr. Assn. U.S., 1987-93; chmn. NASA adv. council, 1988-91. Served with USNR, 1943-46. Recipient Disting. Service award Dept. Def., 1964, 1st bronze palm, 1973, silver palm, 1975. Fellow IEEE, AAAS, AIAA (hon., pres.); mem. NAE (coun. 1988-93), Nat. Rsch. Coun. (chmn. Air Force studies bd. 1987-91), Belle Haven Club, Sigma Xi, Sigma Pi Sigma. Patentee and author in field. Home and Office: 1213 Villamay Blvd Alexandria VA 22307-2051

MC LURE, CHARLES E., JR., economist; b. Sierra Blanca, Tex., Apr. 14, 1940; s. Charles E. and Dessie (Evans) McL.; m. Patsy Nell Carroll, Sept. 17, 1962. B.A., U. Kans., 1962; M.A., Princeton U., 1964, Ph.D., 1966. Asst. prof. econs. Rice U., Houston, 1965-69, assoc. prof., 1969-72, prof., 1972-79, Allyn R. and Gladys M. Cline prof. econs., 1973-79; exec. dir. for research Nat. Bur. Econ. Research, Cambridge, Mass., 1977-78, v.p., 1978-81; sr. fellow Hoover Instn., Stanford U., 1981—; dep. asst. sec. Dept. Treasury, 1983-85; sec. Dept. Treasury, 1983-85; sr. staff economist Coun. Econ. Advisers, Washington, 1969-70; vis. lectr. U. Wyo., 1972; vis. prof. Stanford U., 1973; cons. U.S. Treasury Dept., Labor Dept., World Bank, UN, OAS, Interam. Devel. Bank, Tax Found., Com. Econ. Devel., IMF, govts. Can., Colombia, Malaysia, Panama, Jamaica, Bolivia, Indonesia, New Zealand, Brazil, Trinidad and Tobago, Venezuela, Guatemala, Peoples Republic China, Egypt, Malawi, Mex., Bulgaria, Brazil, Russia, Ukraine, Romania, Kazakhstan, South Africa, Vietnam. Author: Fiscal Failure: Lessons of the Sixties, 1972, (with N. Ture) Value Added Tax: Two Views, 1972, (with M. Gillis) La Reforma Tributaria Colombiana de 1974, 1977, Must Corporate Income Be Taxed Twice?, 1979, Economic Perperspectives on State Taxation of Multijurisdictional Corporations, 1986, The Value Added Tax: Key to Deficit Reduction, 1987; co-author: Taxation of Income from Business and Capital in Colombia, 1989; also numerous articles on econs. and public finance. Ford Found. faculty research fellow, 1967-68. Mem. Am. Econ. Assn., Nat. Tax Assn., Beta Theta Pi. Home: 250 Yerba Santa Ave Los Altos CA 94022-1609 Office: Stanford U Hoover Instn Stanford CA 94305-6010

MCLURE, JOHN DOUGLAS, government official; b. Melita, Man., Can., July 10, 1942; s. Malcolm Alexander and Rachel (Simpson) McL.; m. Nicole Lafrance, Aug. 26, 1967. BSc, U. Man., Winnipeg, 1963; Ammunition Tech. Officer, Royal Mil. Coll. Sci., Wiltshire, Eng., 1964. Program analyst Treasury Bd. Secretariat, Ottawa, Ont., Can., 1975-79, group chief industry and natural resources divsn., 1979-80, dir. industry and natural resources divsn., 1980-82, asst. sec. econ. devel., 1982-84; asst. dep. min. small bus. and spl. projects Dept. Regional Indsl. Expansion, Ottawa, 1984-85, asst. dep. min. crown investments and spl. projects, 1985-86, asst. dep. min. native econ. devel., 1986-87; asst. dep. min. fin., pers., adminstrn. Dept Industry, Sci. & Tech., Ottawa, 1987-89; asst. dep. min. fin. Dept. Nat. Def., Ottawa, 1989-95, assoc. dep. min., 1995-96; dep. min. Dept. Western Econ. Diversification, Ottawa, 1996—. Maj. Can. Land Forces, 1960-75. Recipient N.Am. Best Practice Recognition, Ctr. Creative Leadership, Greensboro, N.C., 1994. Mem. Assn. Profl. Execs. (Leadership award 1995), Hylands Golf Club. Avocations: golf, alpin skiing. Home: 29 Leroy St, Gloucester, ON Canada K1J 6W8 Office: Dept Western Econ Diversification, 200 Kent St 8th Fl, Ottawa, ON Canada K1P 5W3

MCLURKIN, THOMAS CORNELIUS, JR., lawyer; b. L.A., July 28, 1954; s. Thomas Cornelius and Willie Mae (O'Connor) McL.; m. Charmaine Bobo. BA, U. So. Calif., 1976, MPA, 1980, PhD in Pub. Adminstrn., 1997; JD, U. LaVerne, 1982. Bar: Calif. 1984, U.S. Dist. Ct. (ctrl. dist.) Calif. 1984, U.S. Dist. Ct. Hawaii 1984, U.S. Ct. Appeals (9th cir.) 1984, U.S. Dist. Ct. (ea., no. and so. dists.) Calif. 1985, U.S. Tax Ct. 1988, U.S. Ct. Mil. Appeals 1989, U.S. Army Ct. Mil. Rev. 1993, U.S. Supreme Ct., 1995. Law clk. Dept. Water and Power City of L.A., 1979-82; jud. clk. U.S. Dist. Ct. (cen. dist.) Calif., L.A., 1982-83; law clk. Office City Atty., L.A., 1983-84, Dep. City Atty., 1984—. Author (with others): Facts in American History, 1968, 2nd edit. 1989, Eagle Scout, 1970. Mem. L.A. World Affairs Coun., 1980—, Smithsonian Assocs.; bd. dirs. L.A. Area coun. Boy Scouts Am., Hillsides Homes for Children; provisional patron Tournament of Roses Assn., Pasadena, 1994—; mem. Verdugo Hills Area coun. Boy Scouts Am. Mem. ABA, ALA, L.A. County Bar Assn., Assn. Trial Lawyers Am., Langston Law Assn. L.A., Am. Soc. Pub. Adminstrs., U. So. Calif. Gen. Alumni Assn. (bd. govs. exec. bd. 1986-90), U. So. Calif. Black Alumni Assn.-Ebonics (pres. 1988-89), U. So. Calif. Pres.'s Cir., Elks, Am. Legion, Phi Alpha Delta, Kappa Alpha Psi. Republican. United Methodist. Avocations: sailing, tennis, volunteer work, American and world history. Office: LA City Atty Office 111 N Hope St 340 Los Angeles CA 90012-2607

MCLURKIN-HARRIS, KIMBERLY ELANA, secondary education educator; b. Washington, Mar. 9; d. Samuel Louis and Wheatley McLurkin; m. David Harris, Oct. 11, 1986; 1 child, David Jr. BA, Clark Atlanta U., 1982; MA, U. Ky., 1985. Tchr. U.S. history Montgomery County Pub. Schs., Rockville, Md., 1985—; mem. editorial bd. Montgomery Times, Silver Spring, Md., 1992-93. Bd. dirs. Friends of Olney Theatre. Recipient Outstanding Alumni award Clark Atlanta U., 1997. Mem. Theta Omega Omega (v.p. 1990-92, pres. 1993-95), Alpha Kappa Alpha (Pres. of Yr. for North Atlantic Region 1994). Office: 1901 Randolph Rd Silver Spring MD 20902-1447

MCMAHAN, GALE ANN SCIVALLY, school system administrator; b. Anna, Ill., Oct. 19, 1946; d. George Oliver and Jessie Lee (Johnson) Scivally; m. Joe Henry McMahan, Dec. 14, 1963; children: Randy Scott, Joseph Paul. BS, So. Ill. U., 1971, MS, 1974, PhD, 1994. Cert. tchr., supr., adminstr., Ill. Resource tchr. Jonesboro (Ill.) Sch. Dist. 43, 1971-73, dir. early intervention, 1991-94; resource tchr. Anna Sch. Dist. 37, 1973-94; supt. Lick Creek Sch. Dist. 16, Buncombe, Ill., 1994-95, Vienna (Ill.) Pub. Sch. Dist. 55, 1995—; lectr. Shawnee C.C., Ullin, Ill., 1986-88, So. Ill. U., Carbondale, 1990, 92, 93; reader U. Ill. Bd. Edn., Springfield, 1989, 92; mem. adv. bd. for early intervention Anna Interagy. Coun., 1991—, Ill. Interagy. Coun., Springfield, 1991—; mem. peer monitor spl. edn. dept. Ill. Bd. Edn., 1993—, mem. monitoring team for tchr. preparation programs; mem. content adv. com. Ill. Cert. Testing Sys., 1994—. Co-author: (video) Jenny...Our Child of Today!, 1991; editor: Churches in Clear Creek Association, 1988. Recipient Those Who Excel in Edn. award of recognition Ill. Bd. Edn., 1992, grantee, 1990—. Mem. Coun. Exceptional Children (presenter 1991), Ill. Supt. Assn., Ill. Prin. Assn., Ill. Women Adminstrs., Anna Elem. Edn. Assn. (pres. 1992-94), DAR, Delta Kappa Gamma (scholar 1989-90, co-contbr. article to Bull. 1993), Phi Kappa Phi, Kappa Delta Phi, Phi Delta Kappa. Baptist. Avocations: genealogy, reading, painting, walking, swimming. Home: 4890 State Route 146 E Anna IL 62906-3530

MCMAHAN, GARY LYNN, medical foundation executive; b. Kansas City, Mo., Mar. 2, 1948; s. Stanley Owen and Edith Evelena (Shannon) McM.; m. Kathy Sue Brockman, Mar. 28, 1970 (div. 1974); m. 2d, Mary Garold Hearn, Aug. 20, 1976; 1 dau., Terri Lee. B.A., U. Mo., 1970, M.P.A., 1973. Sr. program planner Bendix Corp., Kansas City, Mo., 1971-73; project adminstr. U. Mo., Kansas City, 1973-79; exec. v.p. Acad. Health Profls., 1979-80; exec. dir. Am. Acad. of Family Physicians Found., 1980-95. Bd. sec. AAFP-MDIS Inc., 1981-95; nat. dir. Organ Transplant Fund, Inc., 1995—. Author: An Evaluation Profile: Summary of the Evaluation Activities of the Individual Area Health Education Centers, 1977. Mem. task force Mo. Govs. Task Force on Rural Health, Jefferson City, 1978; bd. dirs., treas. Jackson County Bd. Services for the Developmentally Disabled, Kansas City, 1981-89, pres., 1985-88. Mem. Nat. Soc. Fund Raising Execs (cert. fund raising exec., bd. dirs. mid. Am. chpt., 1993-95, v.p., 1995—). Home: 5822 Ridgevale Rd Memphis TN 38119-7315 Office: Organ Transplant Fund Inc 1102 Brookfield Rd Ste 202 Memphis TN 38119-3810

MCMAHON, BRIAN, publishing executive. Pub. Car and Driver Machette Filipacchi Mags., Inc., Ann Arbor, Mich. Office: Filipacchi Mags Inc 2002 Hogback Rd Ann Arbor MI 48105 also: 1633 Broadway New York NY 10019*

MCMAHON, CATHERINE DRISCOLL, lawyer; b. Mineola, N.Y., Apr. 28, 1950; d. Matthew Joseph and Elizabeth (Driscoll) McM.; m. Gregory Arthur McGrath, Sept. 10, 1977 (div. 1991); children: Elizabeth Driscoll, Kerry Margaret, Michael Riley. BA, Simmons Coll., 1972; JD, Boston Coll., 1975; postgrad., Suffolk U., 1972-73; LL.M., NYU, 1980. Bar: N.Y. 1976, D.C. 1979, U.S. Supreme Ct. 1980, U.S. Tax Ct., 1991. Tax atty. asst. Exxon Corp., N.Y.C., 1975-76, asst. tax atty., 1976-77, sr. tax atty., 1979-81; tax atty. Exxon Internat. Co., N.Y.C., 1977-79, sr. tax counsel, Florham Park, N.J., 1990-92; sr. tax counsel Exxon Co., U.S.A., Houston, 1992—; tax mgr. Exxon Rsch. & Engring. Co., Florham Park, 1981-90. Bd. dirs. S.E. Morris chpt. ARC, Madison, N.J., 1983. Recipient TWIN award YMCA, Plainfield/Westfield, N.J., 1983. Mem. ABA, N.Y. State Bar Assn., D.C. Bar Assn. Roman Catholic. Office: Exxon Co USA 800 Bell St Houston TX 77002-7426

MC MAHON, CHARLES JOSEPH, JR., materials science educator; b. Phila., July 10, 1933; s. Charles Joseph and Alice (Schu) McM.; m. Helen June O'Brien, Jan. 31, 1959; children: Christine, Charles, Elise, Robert, David. B.S., U. Pa., 1955; Sc.D., MIT, 1963. Instr. metallurgy MIT, 1958-62, research asst., 1962-63; postdoctoral fellow U. Pa., 1963-64; asst. prof. dept. materials sci. and engring., 1964-68, assoc. prof., 1968-74, prof., 1974—; cons. in field. Editor: Microplasticity, 1968; contbr. articles to profl. jours. Served with USN, 1955-58. Churchill Overseas fellow Churchill Coll., Cambridge U., Eng., 1973-74; recipient Alexander von Humboldt Sr. U.S. Scientist award, U. Göttingen, 1983-84. Fellow AIME, Am. Soc. Metals, Nat. Acad. Engring., Inst. Metals U.K.; mem. AAAS, U.S. Rowing Assn., Vesper Boat Club (Phila.). Democrat. Roman Catholic. Home: 7103 Sherman St Philadelphia PA 19119-3306 Office: U Pa Dept Materials Sci & Engring Philadelphia PA 19104

MCMAHON, COLLEEN, judge; b. Columbus, Ohio, July 18, 1951; d. John Patrick and Patricia Paterson (McDanel) McM.; m. Frank V. Sica, May 16, 1981; children: Moira Catherine, Patrick McMahon, Brian Vincent. BA summa cum laude, Ohio State U., 1973; JD cum laude, Harvard U., 1976. Bar: N.Y. 1977, U.S. Dist. Ct. (so. and ea. dists.) N.Y. 1977, U.S. Ct. Appeals (2d cir.) 1978, U.S. Supreme Ct. 1980, U.S. Ct. Appeals (5th cir.) 1985, D.C. 1985. Spl. asst. U.S. mission to the UN, N.Y.C., 1979-80; assoc. Paul, Weiss, Rifkind, Wharton & Garrison, N.Y.C., 1976-79, 80-84, ptnr., 1984-95; judge N.Y. Ct. Claims, N.Y.C., 1995—; acting justice N.Y. Supreme Ct., 1995—; bd. dirs., gen. counsel Danceworks, Inc., N.Y.C., 1977-81; mem. Coun. N.Y. Law Assocs., 1977-81; chair The Jury Project, N.Y. Office Ct. Adminstrn., 1993-94. Bd. dirs. Vol. Lawyers for the Arts, N.Y.C., 1979-83, Dance Theater Workshop, 1978-83; vice chancellor Episcopal Diocese of N.Y., 1992-95. Mem. ABA, Assn. of Bar of City of N.Y. (mem. coun. on jud. adminstrn. 1983-89, chmn. com. on state cts. of superior jurisdiction 1983-86, com. on women profession 1989-95, chmn. 1992-95), Am. Law Inst., Am. Judicature Soc., Westchester County Bar Assn., N.Y. State Bar Assn. (mem. ho. of dels. 1986-89), Fed. Bar Coun. Republican. Episcopalian. Office: Chamber 1146 111 Centre St New York NY 10013-4390

MCMAHON, DEBRA BRYLAWSKI, management consultant; b. Washington, Jan. 1, 1956; d. E. Fulton Brylawski and Laura (Carizzoni) Brylawski Miller; m. Neil M. McMahon, Oct. 2, 1982; children: Alexa Lauren, Brendan Patrick, Morgan Lane. BA, Northwestern U., 1976; MBA, Kellogg Grad. Sch. Mgmt., 1977. Asst. brand mgr. Gen. Mills Inc., Mpls., 1977-80; mgr. new products and corp. devel. William Wrigley Jr. Co., Chgo., 1980-84; v.p., C.I.E. practice, head of Washington office Mercer Mgmt. Cons., Washington, 1984—. Contbr. articles to profl. jours. Mem. Beta Gamma Sigma. Republican. Roman Catholic. Avocations: recreational sports, travel, art. Office: Mercer Mgmt Cons 2300 N St NW Washington DC 20037-1122

MCMAHON, DONALD AYLWARD, investor, corporate director; b. N.Y.C., Feb. 20, 1931; s. William F. and Anne (Aylward) McM.; m. Nancy Lantz, Apr. 12, 1953; children: Gail, Brian, Lisa, Glenn, Ann, Carol, William, Douglas. M.B.A., Emory U., 1982. With Dime Savs. Bank, Bklyn., 1952; salesman Monroe Calculating Machine Co., Bklyn., 1952-55; asst. br. mgr. Monroe Calculating Machine Co., Pitts., 1955-56; br. mgr. Monroe Calculating Machine Co., Phila., 1956-63; asst. gen. sales mgr. Monroe Calculating Machine Co., Orange, N.J., 1963-64; Eastern regional gen. sales mgr. Monroe Calculating Machine Co., 1964-65, v.p. mktg., 1965-66; pres. Monroe Calculator Co. div. Litton Industries, Inc., Orange, 1966-70; v.p. Litton Industries, 1967-70; pres., chief operating officer, dir. Baker Industries, Inc., Parsippany, N.J., 1970-74; pres., chief exec. officer, dir. Royal Crown Cos., Inc., Atlanta, 1975-85; bd. dirs. Intelligent Systems Corp., Atlanta, Norrell Corp., Atlanta. Bd. dirs. Boys Clubs Metro Atlanta. Mem. Sovereign Order of Knights of Malta. Home: 1665 Winterthur Close NW Atlanta GA 30328-4688

MC MAHON, ED, television personality; b. Detroit, Mar. 6, 1923; m. Pam Hurn; children: Claudia, Michael, Linda, Jeffrey, Katherine Mary; 1 stepson, Alexis. Ed., Boston Coll.; B.A., Cath. U. Am. TV announcer: Tonight Show, 1962-92; appeared in films The Incident, 1967, Fun with Dick and Jane, 1975, Butterfly; host TV series The Kraft Music Hall, 1968, Whodunnit?, 1979, TV's Bloopers and Practical Jokes, Ed McMahon's Star Search; host TV specials: Thanksgiving Day Parade, (co-host) Jerry Lewis Labor Day Telethon; numerous other TV appearances; appeared on Broadway in The Impossible Years. Active Muscular Dystrophy Assn. With USMC, PTO; col. res., ret. Address: McMahon Communications 12000 Crest Ct Beverly Hills CA 90210-1328

MCMAHON, EDWARD PETER, systems engineer, consultant; b. Jersey City, May 30, 1940; s. Edward Patrick and Blanche Elizabeth (Verbout) McM.; m. Barbara Ann Reedy, May 7, 1966; children: Joseph, James. AB, BEE, Cath. U. Am., 1963; SMEE, MIT, 1964; PhD, Poly. Inst. Bklyn., 1969. Engr. GE, King of Prussia, Pa., 1964-70; systems engr. GE, Washington, 1970-71; dir. optics system dept. Gen. Rsch. Corp., Arlington, Va., 1971-74; mem. staff CIA, Washington, 1974-81; mem. tech. staff MRJ, Inc., Oakton, Va., 1981-86, v.p., 1986-87, pres., 1987—. Dir. Perkin-Elmer Advanced Devel. Ctr., 1986; cubmaster, asst. scoutmaster Nat. Capitol Area coun. Boy Scouts Am., 1977-86; chmn. edn. com N.Va.Tech. Coun., 1992—; mem. supts. bus. and industry adv. com. Fairfax Pub. Schs., 1992—. Mem. IEEE, Ops. Rsch. Soc. Am., Phi Beta Kappa, Sigma Xi (assoc.), Tau Beta Pi. Republican. Roman Catholic. Avocations: fine art photography, woodworking, hiking, cross-country skiing, model making. Home: 8224 Inverness Hollow Ter Rockville MD 20854-2726

MCMAHON, ELEANOR MARIE, education educator; b. Pawtucket, R.I., Oct. 25, 1929; d. William Frank and Anne Angela (Cunningham) Hess; m. Richard P. McMahon, Feb. 14, 1927. B.S. summa cum laude, Coll. of St. Elizabeth, Convent Station, N.J., 1950, H.H.D. (hon.), 1975; M.A., Brown U., 1954; Ed.D., Harvard U., 1967; D.Pedagogy (hon.), Mt. St. Joseph Coll., Wakefield, R.I., 1974; Sem. of Our Lady of Providence, 1975; Hum.D. (hon.), Providence Coll., 1976; LLD, Regis Coll., 1985, EdD (hon.) Roger Williams Coll., 1986; D in Pub. Svc. (hon.) R.I. Coll., 1988; D in Pub. Policy (hon.) Seton Hall U., 1996. Dir. lab. experiences R.I. Coll., Providence, 1968-70, assoc. dean ednl. studies, 1970-71, dean ednl. studies, 1971-77, acting exec. dir. coll. advancement and support, 1977-78, provost, v.p. acad. affairs, 1978-82; commr. higher edn. State of R.I., Providence, 1982-89; fellow Brown U., 1988—; regent Seton Hall U., S. Orange, N.J., 1992—; Disting. vis. prof. Alfred Taubman Ctr., Brown U., 1989—; vis. prof. dept. govt. Georgetown U., 1990-94; sec.-treas., exec. com. New Eng. Assn. Schs. and Colls., 1982, pres., 1988-89; vice chmn. coun. on acad. affairs, mem. coll. bd., 1984-87; mem. Edn. Commn. of States, Denver, 1983-89, New Eng. Bd. Higher Edn., Boston, 1984—, chair-elect, 1996—; vice-chair Cath. Sch. Bd. Diocese of Providence; active Nat. Com. on Higher Edn. Governance, 1995—. Contbr. articles to profl. publs. Mem. R.I. Strategic Devel. Commn., 1982-84; mem. gov.'s vis. com. to U. Maine, 1984-86; mem. R.I. Commn. EC 1992, 1989-92, Gov. Econ. Strategy Task Force, 1991-92; mem. Rockefeller Brothers Fund Minority Fellowship Program, 1990-94; mem. steering com. R.I. Project on Rethinking Govt., 1992-96; mem. Providence Blueprint for Edn. Commn., 1991-93; mem. corp., mem. exec. com. Providence Coll., 1974-82, Pres. Coun., 1982—; trustee Coll. of St. Elizabeth, 1967-72, Providence Country Day Sch., East Providence, R.I., 1975-81, 90-92; alumnae trustee Brown U., 1985-88. Named to R.I. Hall of Fame, 1986; recipient Outstanding Community Service award Blackstone Valley Jr. Women's Club, 1976, Outstanding Woman award R.I. chpt. Internat. Fedn. Catholic Alumnae, 1977, Disting. Svc. award R.I. Bd. Govs., 1989, Disting. Pub. Svc. award R.I. ASPA, 1989, Disting. Svc. award, R.I. Pub. Expenditure Coun., 1987, Brotherhood award NCCJ, 1992. Roman Catholic. Avocations: travel, reading. Office: Alfred Taubman Ctr Pub Policy & Am Instns Brown U Providence RI 02912

MC MAHON, GEORGE JOSEPH, academic administrator; b. N.Y.C., June 20, 1923; s. Martin Joseph and Mary (O'Connor) McM. AB, Woodstock Coll., 1946, Philosophy licentiate, 1947, MA, 1948, STL, 1954; M.A., Fordham U., 1951; Ph.D., Laval U., 1959. Joined S.J., 1940, ordained priest Roman Cath. Ch., 1953. Instr. physics and Latin Regis H.S., N.Y.C., 1947-49; instr. philosophy St. Peter's Coll., Jersey City, 1958-60, asst. dean, dir. Sch. Bus. Adminstrn., 1961-62; instr. philosophy Loyola Sem., Shrub Oak, N.Y., 1960-61; dean Fordham Coll., Fordham U., Bronx, N.Y., 1962-74; v.p. adminstrn. Fordham U., 1974-87; v.p. Lincoln Ctr. campus Fordham U., N.Y.C., 1987-94, chaplain, 1994—. Author: The Order of Procedure in the Philosophy of Nature, 1958, The Proemium to the Physics of Aristotle, 1957. V.p. Friends of U. Laval, Que., Can.; trustee Marymount Sch. N.Y., Wheeling (W.Va.) Coll.

MCMAHON, JOHN ALEXANDER, law educator; b. Monongahela, Pa., July 31, 1921; s. John Hamilton and Jean (Alexander) McM.; m. Betty Wagner, Sept. 14, 1947 (div. Mar. 1977); children: Alexander Talpey, Sarah Francis, Elizabeth Wagner, Ann Wallace; m. Anne Fountain Willets, May 1, 1977 (dec. June 1996). A.B. magna cum laude, Duke U., 1942; student, Harvard U. Bus. Sch., 1942-43; J.D., Law Sch., 1948; LL.D., Wake Forest U., 1978; D.Sc. (hon.), Georgetown U. Sch. Medicine, 1985. Bar: N.C. 1950. Prof. pub. law and govt., asst. dir. Inst. Govt. U. N.C., 1948-59; gen. counsel, sec.-treas. N.C. Assn. County Commrs., Chapel Hill, 1959-65; v.p. spl. devel. Hosp. Saving Assn., Chapel Hill, N.C., 1965-67; pres. N.C. Blue Cross and Blue Shield, Inc., Chapel Hill, 1968-72, Am. Hosp. Assn., Chgo., 1972-86; chmn. dept. health adminstrn. Duke U., Durham, N.C., 1986-92, exec.-in-residence Fuqua Sch. Bus., 1992—; mem. Chapel Hill bd. N.C. Nat. Bank, 1967-72; bd. govs. Blue Cross Assn., 1969-72; mem. Orange County Welfare Bd., 1956-63; chmn. N.C. Comprehensive Health Planning Coun., 1968-72, Health Planning Coun. of Ctrl. N.C., 1963-69; mem. Pres.' Com. on Health Edn., 1971-72; mem. health svcs. industry and health industry adv. com. Econ. Stablzn. Program, 1971-74; mem. adv. coun. Kate Bitting Reynolds Health Care Trust, 1971-95; mem. adv. coun. Northwestern U., 1973-86; mem. med. adv. com. VA, 1975-85; bd. dirs. The Forest at Duke, Durham, N.C. Author: North Carolina County Government, 1959, The North Carolina Local Government Commission, 1960; editor: N.C. County Yearbook, 1959-64, Proceedings of the Annual National Forum on Hospital and Health Affairs, 1993—. Mem. Orange County Dem. Exec. Com., also chmn. Kings Mill Precinct, 1964-68; chmn. bd. trustees Duke U., 1971-83, chmn. emeritus, 1983—; bd. dirs. Rsch. Triangle Found., 1971-83, 92—, Nat. Ctr. for Health Edn., 1974-86; bd. mgrs., mem. exec. com. Internat. Hosp. Fedn., London, 1975-85, pres., 1981-83. With USAAF, 1942-46, col. Res., ret. Mem. N.C. State Bar, Inst. Medicine of NAS, Duke Alumni Assn. (pres. 1968-70), Hope Valley Country Club (Durham), Dunes Golf and

Beach Club (Myrtle Beach). Presbyterian. Home: 181 Montrose Dr Durham NC 27707-3929 Office: Duke U Fuqua Sch Bus Durham NC 27708-0120

MCMAHON, JOHN J., JR., metal processing company executive. Pres., sec., treas. McWane, Inc., Birmingham, Ala., also chmn. bd. dirs.; now also chief exec. officer Clow Corp., Birmingham. Office: McWane Inc PO Box 43327 Birmingham AL 35243*

MCMAHON, JOHN PATRICK, lawyer; b. Monroeville, Ohio, Feb. 8, 1919; s. George James and Eleanor Helene (Ruffing) McM.; m. Patricia Patterson McDanel, May 6, 1950 (dec. July 1983); children: Colleen, Kevin, Patricia, Brian, Barry, Michael; m. Mary Echard, Mar. 7, 1987. B.A. cum laude, Ohio State U., 1940, J.D. summa cum laude, 1942. Bar: Ohio 1942, U.S. Supreme Ct. 1949, U.S. Dist. Ct. Ohio 1949, U.S. Ct. Appeals (6th cir.) 1959, U.S. Ct. Appeals (D.C. cir.) 1975. Ptnr. George, Greek, King, McMahon, Columbus, Ohio, 1954-79, Baker & Hostetler, Columbus, 1979-85; with nat. coun. Ohio State U. Coll. Law, 1980—. Capt. USAAF, 1943-46, PTO. Mem. ABA, Ohio Bar Assn., Columbus Bar Assn., Transp. Lawyers Assn., Maennerchor (Columbus), Pres.' Club of Ohio State U. (Columbus), Athletic Club (Columbus). Clubs: University (Columbus), Faculty (Columbus), Pres.' of Ohio State U. (Columbus). Home: 2880 Halstead Rd Columbus OH 43221-2916 Office: Baker & Hostetler 65 E State St Columbus OH 43215-4213

MCMAHON, JOSEPH EINAR, lawyer, consultant; b. Chgo., Aug. 26, 1940; s. Reynold Bernard and Dorothy Marie (Oftedahl) McM. B.A. cum laude, Denison U., 1962; J.D., U. Mich., 1965. Bar: Mass. 1968, D.C. 1980. Asst. to Atty. Gen. and Senator Edward Brooke, Boston and Washington, 1965-67; exec. asst. Lt. Gov. Sargent of Mass., Boston, 1967-69; v.p. BedStuy D&S Corp. Restoration, Bklyn., 1969-74; dir. govt. regulations Westinghouse Electric Corp., Washington, 1974-78; v.p. corp. affairs Federated Dept. Stores, Cin., 1978-80; atty., cons. McMahon and Assocs., Washington, 1980—; exec. dir. (part time), bd. dirs. The Get Ahead Found./USA, 1991—. Trustee Denison U.; visitor U. Mich. Law Sch.; 1st v.p. Boston Rep. Com., 1968-69; presdl. appointee Nat. Coun. Econ. Opportunity, 1975-76; exec. dir. Nat. Bus. for Reagan-Bush Com., 1980; dir. Luther Inst., Washington, Fgn. Students Svc. Coun., Rodale Inst., Emmaus, Pa.; trustee Gettysburg Luth. Sem.; co-pres., dir. Luth. Lesbian and Gay Min., San Francisco; mem. outreach bd. Evang. Luth. Ch. in Am., 1995—. Mem. Phi Delta Phi, Pi Sigma Alpha, Omicron Delta Kappa. Lutheran. Clubs: Nat. Press, University, Capitol Hill (Washington). Office: McMahon & Assocs 1924 N St NW Washington DC 20036-1604

MCMAHON, MAEVE, middle school administrator. Pres. Marian Ctrl. Mid. Sch., New Orleans, 1996—. Recipient DOE Elem. Sch. Recognition Program award, 1989-90. Office: Marian Ctrl Mid Sch 2221 Mendez Dr New Orleans LA 70122-5276

MCMAHON, MARIA DRISCOLL, artist; b. Sayre, Pa., Jan. 8, 1959; d. Thomas James and Betty Jane (Taylor) Driscoll; m. Hugh Michael McMahon, May 27, 1978; children: Ian Thomas, Lea Shea. BS in Art Edn. summa cum laude, U. Pa. Kutztown, 1988; MA in Studio Art, Marywood Coll., 1993. Cert. art tchr., N.Y. Tchr. art Horseheads (N.Y.) Ctrl. Sch. Dist., 1989-94; artist Ithaca, N.Y., 1993—; lectr. Allentown (Pa.) Art Mus., 1987; artist, speaker Victims rights Week Ceremony, Dryden, N.Y., 1997; artist Carantouan Greenway Restoration Project, Athens, Pa., 1997. One-person shows include Three River Reading Series, Corning, N.Y., 1996, Arcadian Winery, Watkins Glen, N.Y., 1997; exhibited in group shows at Contemporary Gallery at Marywood Coll., Scranton, Pa., 1997, Bradford County Regional Exhbn., 1995, State of Art Gallery, Ithaca, 1993—, Susquehanna Regional Art Exhbn., 1994, Merit award, 1994, N.Y. State Fair, 1993, State of the Art Gallery, 1996, George Waters Gallery, Elmira Coll., N.Y., 1996; author: (poem) Steele Meml. Libr. Poetry Festival, Elmira, N.Y., 1980, Merit award, 1980. Vol. Schrader Creek Assn., Bradford County, Pa., 1993—. Mem. NYSUT, Cmty. Arts Partnership of Tompkins County. Democrat. Avocations: sailing, theatre, cross country skiing, making children's toys, poetry. Home and Office: 4 Main St Lockwood NY 14859

MCMAHON, MARIBETH LOVETTE, physicist; b. Bradford, Pa., June 8, 1949; d. James Harry and Josephine Rose (Sylvester) Lovette; m. Frank Joseph MaMahon, Nov. 19, 1976. B.S. in Math., Pa. State U., 1971, B.S. in Physics, 1971, M.S. in Physics, 1974; Ph.D. in Physics, 1976. Research asst. Pa. State U., 1971-76; advanced research and devel. engr. GTE Sylvania, Danvers, Mass., 1976-78; sr. physicist 3M Co., St. Paul, 1978-79, market devel. supr., 1979-83; market devel. mgr. Galileo Electro-Optics Corp., Sturbridge, Mass., 1983-84; product mgr. Varian Assocs., Lexington, Mass., 1984-85; mktg. dir. Bowmar, Acton, Mass., 1985-86; pres. Kilduff Inc., Sturbridge, Mass., 1986—. Recipient Cert. in Appreciation of Service Pa. State U., 1971. Mem. Optical Soc. Am., Assn. Women in Sci., Assn. Physicists in Medicine, Sigma Pi Sigma, Sigma Chi. Home: 140 Brookfield Rd Fiskdale MA 01518-1136 Office: Kilduff Inc Sturbridge MA 01566

MCMAHON, NEIL MICHAEL, real estate executive; b. N.Y.C., Oct. 12, 1953; s. Thomas Joseph and Catherine Margaret (Lane) M.; m. Debra Brylawski, Oct. 2, 1982; children: Alexa Lauren, Brendan Patrick, Morgan Lane. BA, Loyola Coll., Balt., 1975; MBA, U. Notre Dame, 1980. Sr. acct. Coopers & Lybrand, Balt., 1975-77; sr. assoc. Korn/Ferry Internat., Chgo., 1980-84; mgr. real estate fin. Prudential Ins. Co., Washington, 1984-87, gen. mgr. real estate devel., 1987-88; mng. dir. Capital Ptnrs. Inc., Washington, 1988—; pres. Madison Investment Assocs., Inc., Washington, 1993—, also bd. dirs. Bd. dirs. Lawrence Hall Sch. for Boys, Chgo., 1981-84. Named Senatorial Scholar State of Md., 1971-75. Mem. Nat. Assn. Indsl. and Office Parks, Real Estate Group Washington, Mortgage Bankers Assn., Notre Dame Club. Republican. Catholic. Avocation: triathalons. Office: Capital Ptnrs Inc 224 E Capitol St NE Washington DC 20003-1036

MCMAHON, PAUL FRANCIS, international management consultant; b. Malone, N.Y., Apr. 28, 1945; s. Philip Francis and Shirley (Roy) M.; m. Sheila Ann Lester, Nov. 30, 1963; children—Michael, Marsha. B.S., Syracuse U., 1968. CPA, N.Y.; cert. mgmt. acct., cert. mgmt. cons. Various staff positions Ernst & Young, Syracuse, N.Y., 1968-73, mgr., 1975-79; ptnr. in charge of mgmt. cons. in Europe Ernst & Young, Brussels, 1979-84; vice chmn. Ernst & Young, Cleve., 1984-87; exec. ptnr. Ernst & Young Internat., N.Y., 1987-93; chmn. Ernst & Young Ea. Europe, 1990-93; regional dir. Asia/Pacific Ernst & Young Internat., Singapore, 1994-96; controller Coop. Mktg. Agy., Syracuse, 1973-75. Treas. Bus. Coun. for Internat. Understanding. Mem. AICPA, N.Y. Soc. CPA's, Inst. Mgmt. Acctg., Assn. Mgmt. Cons. Firms (bd. dirs.), Coun. Cons. Orgns. (past chmn.). Republican. Roman Catholic. Avocations: photography, sculpture, travel, gardening, biographies. Home: PO Box 4070 Wilsonville OR 97070

MCMAHON, ROBERT LEE, JR. (BOB MCMAHON), information systems executive; b. Weatherford, Tex., Feb. 19, 1944; s. Robert Lee Sr. and Gusta Rosann (Collins) McM. AA, Weatherford Coll., 1964; BA, U. Tex., Arlington, 1970; postgrad. in mgmt., Tex. Christian U., 1970-73. Announcer Sta. KZEE, Weatherford, Tex., 1963-65; asst. gen. mgr. Sta. KZEE, Weatherford, 1972-75; programmer Gen. Dynamics, Ft. Worth, 1967-68, sr. programmer, 1968-72, sr. engr., 1975-78, project engr., 1978-79, group supr., 1979-80, sect. chief, 1980-83, dept. mgr., 1983-93; staff specialist Lockheed Ft. Worth Co., 1994-95, retired, 1995; mem. adv. bd. Mfg. Tech. Directorate, USAF, Dayton, Ohio, 1981-91, Automation and Robotics Rsch. Inst., Ft. Worth, 1986-91. Editor: Manufacturing Engineer's Handbook, 1988; mem. editorial bd. Mfg. Engring. mag., 1989-91. Dir. adult edn. program Parker County, Tex., 1972-75; chmn. Weatherford City Charter Revision Commn., 1974-75; mem. Weatherford Planning and Zoning Bd., 1984-88; chmn. 4th precinct Parker County Dem. Com., 1982-92, 27th precinct, 1992—; foreman Grand Jury, 1993. Mem. Soc. Mfg. Engrs., (cert., sr.), Robotic Industries Assn. (sr., bd. dirs. 1984-88), Computer and Automated Sys. Assn. (sr.), Robotics Inst. (sr.), Am. Inst. Indsl. Engrs., Nat. Mgmt. Assn., Masons (33d degree, past master), Phi Theta Kappa (v.p. Weatherford chpt.), Ego Omega, Beta Alpha Psi. Mem. Ch. of Christ. Avocations: photography, pocket billiards, reading, model railroading. Home: 1418 E Bankhead Dr Weatherford TX 76086-4607

MCMAHON, TERRENCE JOHN, retired foriegn service officer; b. Rockford, Ill., Aug. 7, 1936; s. Hugh Raymond McMahon and Lucile Isabelle (Hayes) Driscoll; m. Phyllis Ruth Anderson, Dec. 2, 1967; children: Kevin, Michael, Kathleen, Marianne. BS in Accountancy, U. Ill., 1958; M Internat. Pub. Policy, Johns Hopkins U., 1983. CPA, Ill. Audit supr. Coopers and Lybrand, Rockford, Ill., 1958-68; fin. analyst U.S. AID, Washington, 1968-70; dep. contr. U.S. AID, Rio de Janeiro, 1970-73; contr. U.S. AID, Kabul, Afghanistan, 1973-77, Amman, Jordan, 1977-79; dep. contr. U.S. AID, Washington, 1979-83; contr. U.S. AID, Cairo, 1983-86; dir. Office of Procurement U.S. AID, Washington, 1986-92; dir. U.S. AID, Kiev, Ukraine, 1993-95. Recipient Presdl. Meritorious Svc. award for fgn. svc. Pres. of U.S., 1985, 92. Roman Catholic. Avocations: fishing, boating, travel. Home: 430 Marine Dr Sequim WA 98382

MCMAHON, THOMAS ARTHUR, biology and applied mechanics educator; b. Dayton, Ohio, Apr. 21, 1943; s. Howard Oldford and Lucille (Nelson) McM.; m. Carol Ehlers, June 20, 1965; children: James Robert, Elizabeth Kirsten. B.S., Cornell U., 1965; S.M., MIT, 1967, Ph.D., 1970. Postdoctoral fellow Harvard U., Cambridge, Mass., 1969-70, lectr. bioengring., 1970-71, asst. prof., 1971-74, assoc. prof., 1974-77, prof. applied mechanics and biology, 1977—; cons. numerous industries, legal firms. Author: (novels), Principles of American Nuclear Chemistry, 1970, McKay's Bees, 1979, Loving Little Egypt, 1987; (non-fiction) Muscles, Reflexes and Locomotion, 1984; (with others) On Size and Life, 1983. Grantee NIH; System Devel. Found., Sloan Found.; recipient Richard and Hinde Rosenthal award Am. Acad. and Inst. Arts and Letters, 1988. Mem. Biomed. Engring. Soc., Am. Physiol. Soc., N.Y. Acad. Scis., PEN. Home: 65 Crest Rd Wellesley MA 02181-4620 Office: Harvard U Pierce Hall Dept Applied Scis Cambridge MA 02138

MCMAINS, MELVIN L(EE), controller; b. Oskaloosa, Iowa, Aug. 1, 1941; m. Kathryn Elaine Murphy; children: Kimberly, Lindsay. BA, U. Northern Iowa, 1966, MA, 1968. CPA, Iowa; CMA. Corp. contr., chief acctg. officer HON Industries, Inc., Muscatine, Iowa, 1979—. Mem. AICPA, Fin. Execs. Inst., Iowa Soc. CPA's, Inst. Mgmt. Accts., Geneva Golf and Country Club. Office: HON Industries PO Box 1109 Muscatine IA 52761-7109

MCMANAMAN, KENNETH CHARLES, lawyer; b. Fairfield, Calif., Jan. 25, 1950; s. Charles James and Frances J. (Holys) McM.; m. Carol Ann Wilson, Apr. 15, 1972; children: Evan John, Kinsey Bridget, Kierin Rose. BA cum laude, S.E. Mo. State U., 1972; JD, U. Mo., Kansas City, 1974; grad. Naval Justice Sch., Newport, RI., 1975; MS in Bus. Mgmt. summa cum laude, Troy State U., Montgomery, Ala., 1978. Bar: Mo. 1975, Fla. 1976, U.S. Dist. Ct. (we. dist.) Mo. 1975, U.S. Dist. Ct. (ea. Dist.) Mo. 1978, Fla. 1976, U.S. Dist. Ct. (no., mid. dists.) Fla. 1976, U.S. Ct. Mil. Appeals 1977, U.S. Ct. Appeals (5th, 8th cirs.) 1977, U.S. Supreme Ct. 1978, D.C. 1991; cert. mil. judge. Ptnr. firm O'Loughlin, O'Loughlin & McManaman, Cape Girardeau, Mo., 1978—; prof. bus. law Troy State U., Ala., 1976-78; prof. bus. law S.E. Mo. State U., Cape Girardeau, 1978-84; instr. Mo. Dept. Pub. Safety, S.E. Mo. Regional Law Enforcement Tng. Acad., 1979—, Cape Girardeau Police Res., 1983-93, Naval Justice Sch., 1996; mcpl. judge City of Jackson, Mo., 1980-89, 94—; spl. mcpl. judge City of Cape Girardeau, 1981-89; atty. Ct. Apptd. Spl. Advs./Guardians in Ct. for Children, 1994—; spl. mcpl. judge City of Fredricktown, Mo., 1995. Mem. Cape Girardeau County Coun. on Child Abuse, 1980-89; membership dir. S.E. Mo. Scouting coun. Boy Scouts Am., 1980-82; mem. Cape Girardeau County Mental Health Assn., 1982-92; active local and state Dem. Party, del. Nat. Dem. Conv., San Francisco, 1984, chmn. County Dem. Com., 1984-86; mem. 8th Congl. Dist. Dem. Com., 1984-86, 27th State Dem. Senatorial Com., 1984-86, ward committeeman, 1984-94; bd. dirs. Area wide Task Force on Drug and Alcohol Abuse, 1984-87; sponsor drug edn./prevention program in schs.; bd. dirs. Cape County chpt. Nat. Kidney Found, 1988-93; pres. Jackson Area Soccer Assn., 1987-93. Capt. JAGC, USNR, 1994—. Recipient Robert Chilton award City of Jackson for leadership, integrity, and responsibility, 1995—; named One of Outstanding Young Men of Am. 1981, 82, 84, 85, Outstanding Pub. Svc. award Cape Girardian Police Dept. Mem. ABA (Mo. del. for young lawyers div. 1982-83)., Mo. Bar Assn. (chmn. trial advocacy task force 1982, psychology and the law task force 1983), Mo. Bar (young lawyers sect. council, rep. dist. 13, 1980-85), Fla. Bar Assn., Kansas City Bar Assn., Assn. Trial Lawyers Am., Fed. Bar Assn., Nat. Coll. Dist. Attys., Cape Girardeau County Bar Assn. (founder, pres. young lawyers sect. 1981-82), Naval Res. Assn. (v.p. Southeast Mo.-So. Ill. chpt. 1980-85), S.E. Mo. State U. Alumni Coun., Sigma Chi (numerous awards), Sigma Tau Delta, Pi Delta Epsilon. Roman Catholic. Home: 400 Oak Forest Dr Jackson MO 63755-3504 Office: O'Loughlin O'Loughlin McManaman 1736 N Kingshighway St Cape Girardeau MO 63701-2122

MCMANIGAL, SHIRLEY ANN, university dean; b. Deering, Mo., May 4, 1938; d. Jadie C. and Willie B. (Groves) Naile. BS, Ark. State U., 1971; MS, U. Okla., 1976, PhD, 1979. Lic. med. technologist, clin. lab. dir. Med. technologist, 1958-75; chair dept. med. tech. U. So. Miss., Hattiesburg, 1979-83; chair dept. med. tech. Tex. Tech U. Health Scis. Ctr., Lubbock, 1983-87, dean Sch. Allied Health, 1987—; gov.'s appointee to statewide health coord. coun., 1994—. Leadership Tex., 1992; Lt. Alumnae Regl. dir., 1994-97. Recipient Citation, State of Tex., 1988; named Woman of Yr., AAUW, Tex. div., 1990, Woman of Excellence in Edn. YWCA, Lubbock, 1990. Mem. AAUW (bd. dirs. Tex. 1990-94), Am. Coun. on Edn./Nat. Identification Program (steering com. for Tex.), Clin. Lab. Mgmt. Assn. (chair edn. com. 1989, 91), Am. Soc. Med. Tech., Nat. Assn. Women in Edn., So. Assn. Allied Health Deans at Acad. Health Ctrs., Tex. Soc. Allied Health Professions (pres. 1990-91), Tex. Soc. Med. Tech. (Educator of Yr. 1990), Alpha Eta, Phi Beta Delta. Home: 5003 94th St Lubbock TX 79424-4839 Office: Tex Tech U Sch Allied Health Dept Scis Ctr Lubbock TX 79430

MCMANUS, CLARENCE ELBURN, judge; b. New Orleans, June 3, 1934; s. Otis Clarence and Odell (Hawsey) McM.; m. Barbara Isabella Edmundson, Apr. 3, 1976; children—Elizabeth Ann, Bryan Stephen. B.B.A., Tulane U., 1958; J.D., 1961. Bar: La. 1961, U.S. Ct. Appeals (5th cir.) 1961, U.S. Dist. Ct. (ea. dist.) La. 1961, U.S. Supreme Ct. 1987. Sole practice, Metairie, La., 1961-69; asst. dist. atty. Jefferson Parish, La., 1969-82; state dist. judge 24th Jud. Dist. Ct., Gretna, La., 1982—. Republican. Home: 824 Bonnabel Blvd Metairie LA 70005-2059 Office: Gretna Courthouse Annex Gretna LA 70053

MCMANUS, DECLAN PATRICK See COSTELLO, ELVIS

MC MANUS, EDWARD JOSEPH, federal judge; b. Keokuk, Iowa, Feb. 9, 1920; s. Edward W. and Kathleen (O'Connor) McM.; m. Sally A. Hassett, June 30, 1948 (dec.); children: David P., Edward W., John N., Thomas J., Dennis Q.; m. Esther Y. Kanealy, Sept. 15, 1987. Student, St. Ambrose Coll., 1936-38; B.A., U. Iowa, 1940, J.D., 1942. Bar: Iowa 1942. Gen. practice of law Keokuk, 1946-62, city atty., 1946-55; mem. Iowa Senate, 1955-59; lt. gov. Iowa, 1959-61; chief U.S. judge No. Dist. Iowa, 1962-85, sr. U.S. judge, 1985—. Del Democratic Nat. Conv., 1956, 60. Served as lt. AC USNR, 1942-46. Office: US Dist Ct 329 US Courthouse 101 1st St SE Cedar Rapids IA 52401-1202

MCMANUS, GEORGE ALVIN, JR., state senator, cherry farmer; b. Traverse City, Mich., Dec. 12, 1930; s. George Alvin and Frieda Anna (Fromholz) McM.; m. Clara Belle Kratochvil, Aug. 16, 1949; children: Eliza J. Saints, Molly S. Agostinelli, Margaret L. Egelus, Kathleen E. Nurohammed, Kerry E. Canellos, George A., John K., Bridgett E. Popp, Matthew R. BS, Mich. State U., 1952, MS, 1953. Fruit grower pvt. practice, Traverse City, Mich., 1953—; coop. extension agt. Mich. State U., 1956-82; senator Mich. State Senate, Lansing, Mich., 1991—. Trustee Northwestern Mich. Coll., Traverse City, 1970-90; pres. Traverse City C.of C., 1982, Traverse City Rotary, 1993. Named Citizen of Yr. Traverse City C. of C., 1984. Mem. KC, Elks Club, Rotary Club. Republican. Roman Catholic. Avocation: golf. Office: Mich State Senate 605 Farnum Bldg Lansing MI 48913

MCMANUS, HUGH F., principal. Prin. John T. Hoggard High Sch., Wilmington, N.C. Recipient Blue Ribbon Sch. award, 1990-91. Office: John T Hoggard High Sch 4305 Shipyard Blvd Wilmington NC 28403-6160*

MCMANUS, JAMES WILLIAM, chemist, researcher; b. Atlanta, Oct. 7, 1944; s. Claude William and Sara Louise (Cook) McM.; m. Ruth Krieger, Apr. 10, 1971; children: Angela Ruth, Meagan Joy. BS in Chemistry, Auburn U., 1971. Mgr. Cook's Grocery Co., Atlanta, 1970-73; analytical chemist North Chem. Co., Atlanta, 1973-74; analytical chemist Merck & Co., Inc., Albany, Ga., 1974-75, staff chemist, 1975-76, sr. staff chemist, 1976-78, sr. chemist, 1978-89, rsch. fellow, 1989-94; bd. dirs. M. Taylor, Inc., Albany, 1988—, chmn. chemistry sect., 1994—. Mem. editorial bd. Process Control and Quality, 1990-95; inventor, patentee in field. Mem. Am. Chem. Soc. (cert.). Republican. Baptist. Office: Merck and Co Inc 3517 Radium Springs Rd Albany GA 31705-9596

MCMANUS, JAMES WILLIAM, lawyer; b. Kansas City, Mo., Aug. 1, 1945; s. Gerald B. and Mary M. (Hagan) McM.; m. Julie C. Waters, Feb. 17, 1973. BA, Rockhurst Coll., 1967; JD, St. Louis U., 1971. Bar: Mo. 1971, U.S. Dist. Ct. (we. dist.) Mo. 1972, U.S. Ct. Appeals (8th cir.) 1974, U.S. Supreme Ct. 1979, U.S. Ct. Appeals (10th cir.) 1984. Law clk. to presiding justice U.S. Dist. Ct. (we. dist.) Mo., 1971-73; assoc. Shughart, Thomson & Kilroy, P.C., Kansas City, 1973-76, dir., 1977-94; counsel Dysart, Taylor, Lay, Cotter & McMonigle, P.C., Kansas City, 1994—; course lectr. med. jurisprudence U. Health Scis., Coll. Osteo. Medicine, Kansas City, 1994. Mem. adv. coun. St. Joseph Health Ctr., 1989—. Mem. ABA, Mo. Bar Assn., Kansas City Lawyers Assn., Kansas City Met. Bar Assn. (chmn. alternate dispute resolution com. 1996—, vice chmn. 1994-95, chmn. med. malpractice com. 1989), Mo. Orgn. Def. Lawyers, St. Louis Alumni Assn. (pres. 1984-92), St. Louis U. Law Sch. Alumni Assn. Home: 6824 Valley Rd Kansas City MO 64113-1929 Office: Dysart Taylor Lay Cotter & McMonigle PC 4420 Madison Ave Kansas City MO 64111-3407

MCMANUS, JASON DONALD, editor, retired; b. Mission, Kans., Mar. 3, 1934; s. John Alan and Stella Frances (Gosney) McM.; m. Patricia Ann Paulson, Oct. 18, 1958 (div. Feb. 1966); 1 child, John Alan; m. Deborah Hall Murphy, Dec. 2, 1973; children: Sophie Eleanor, Mage Caroline. B.A., Davidson Coll., 1956, Litt.D. (hon.), 1979; M.P.A., Princeton U., 1958; postgrad., Oxford U., 1958-59; LittD (hon.), Monmouth Coll., 1988, U. N.C., 1991, Loyola U., Balt., 1992. Common Market bur. chief Time Mag., Paris, 1962-64; assoc. editor Time Mag., N.Y.C., 1964-68, sr. editor, 1968-75, asst. mng. editor, 1975-78, exec. editor, 1978-83, mng. editor, 1985-87; corp. editor Time Inc., N.Y.C., 1983-85; editor-in-chief Time Warner Inc., N.Y.C., 1987-95; ret. Author: short stories Introduction, 1960. Mem. presdl. adv. commn. Internat. Edn. Exchange, 1982-83. Rhodes scholar, 1958-59. Club: Century Assn. (N.Y.C.).

MCMANUS, JOHN FRANCIS, association executive, writer; b. Bklyn., Jan. 24, 1935; s. V. Paul and Dorothy F. (Devenport) McM.; m. Mary Helen O'Reilly, Oct. 19, 1957; children: John G., Margaret A. Strauss, Paul J., Mary Anne Power. BS in Physics, Holy Cross Coll., 1957. Elec. engr. Transitron Corp., Wakefield, Mass., 1960-66; field coord. The John Birch Soc., Belmont, Mass., 1966-68, projects mgr., 1968-73, dir. pub. rels., 1973-91; pres. The John Birch Soc., Appleton, Wis., 1991—. Author: An Overview of Our World, 1971, The Insiders: Architects of the New World Order, 1992, 4th edit., 1995, Financial Terrorism: Hijacking America Under the Threat of Bankruptcy, 1993, Changing Commands: The Betrayal of America's Military, 1995; author weekly column, 1973-96. Lt. USMC, 1957-60, capt., USMCR, 1960-68. Avocations: reading, outdoor sports, family. Home: PO Box 3076 Wakefield MA 01880-0772 Office: John Birch Society PO Box 8040 Appleton WI 54913-8040

MCMANUS, JOHN FRANCIS, III, advertising executive; b. Bklyn., Mar. 8, 1919; s. John Francis and Helen Jane (Cleary) McM.; m. Regina Delores Smith, Feb. 12, 1942 (div. June 1950); m. Sara Grace Scerra, Mar. 8, 1951 (dec. Aug. 1970); children: John Francis IV, Jane Frances, Stephan George, Kathleen Elizabeth; m. Jane Caroline Lewis, Apr. 25, 1974. BFA, Cooper Union Inst. Art, N.Y.C., 1941; student, Silvermine Guild Art Ctr., Norwalk, Conn., 1987, 88, 89; BA, NYU, 1947. Advt. dir. Thayer, Inc., Gardner, Mass., 1948-52; account supr. and copy chief Zimmer, Keller, Calvert, Detroit, 1952-57; account mgmt. McCann-Erickson, Inc., N.Y.C., 1957-58; v.p., mgmt. supr. Doyle Dane Bernbach Inc., N.Y.C., 1958-69; sr. v.p., mgmt. Super-Smith/Greenland, Inc., N.Y.C., 1969-70; pres., creative dir. The McManusCo., Westport, Conn., 1970—; bd. dirs. Stamford Art Assn., Homes Conn., Holiday Cruise Lines; official artist USCG, 1988—. Writer series on Am. Way of Life, mag., 1949 (Freedom Found. gold medals 1949, 50); mgmt. supr. Avis, We Try Harder campaign, 1964, Mobil Detergent Campaign, 1968, Rheingold Would You Have the Guts? campaign, 1971 (Clio, Effie awards 1971). Capt. USAAF, 1942-46. Recipient Le Premier Prix Festival Internat., DU Film Publicitaire, Venice, France, 1960, Freedoms Found. Gold medals, Freedoms Found. Inc., Valley Forge, Pa., 1969-70, Effie, Am. Mktg. Assn., N.Y.C., 1972, Archie award, Nat. Assn. Indsl. Advts., N.Y.C., 1984. Mem. Am. Watercolor Soc., Am. Soc. Marine Artists, Westport Arts Council, Fairfield County Bus. Execs. Republican. Roman Catholic. Avocations: painting marine and seascapes, writing, photography, travel. Office: The McManus Co PO Box 446 Greens Farms CT 06436-0446

MCMANUS, MARY HAIRSTON, English language educator; b. Danville, Va., Nov. 23; d. Benjamin and Essie (Walton) Hairston; m. Booker Taliaferro McManus, June 27; children: Philip, Kenneth. BA, Va. State U., Petersburg, MA; PhD, U. Md. Cert. in English lang. and lit. edn. Instr. English Va. State U., Petersburg, 1965-70; lectr. English European div. U. Md., Berlin, 1972-73; instr. English Fayetteville (N.C.) State U., 1975-78; instr. ESOL Venice (Ill.)-Lincoln Tech. Ctr., 1978-83; lectr. English Anne Arundel C.C., Arnold, Md., 1983-84; asst. prof. English Bowie (Md.) State U., 1984—, dir. honors program, 1993—; cons. Anne Arundel County Govt., Glen Burnie, Md., 1983-84, Prince George's County Govt., Upper Marlboro, Md., 1985-86; mem. adv. bd. Collegiate Press, Alta Loma, Calif., 1992—. Recipient Outstanding Educator award Prince George's County Fire Dept., 1988; NEH fellow, 1991. Mem. MLA, Nat. Coun. Tchrs. English, Coll. Lang. Assn., CHUMS Inc. (pres. 1995—), Middle Atlantic Writers Assn., Kiwanis, Alpha Kappa Alpha, Sigma Tau Delta. Democrat. Avocations: reading, travel. Home: 432 Lakeland Rd N Severna Park MD 21146-2420 Office: Bowie State U 14000 Jericho Park Rd Bowie MD 20715-3319

MCMANUS, PATRICK FRANCIS, educator, writer; b. Sandpoint, Idaho, Aug. 25, 1933; s. Francis Edward McManus and Mabel Delana (Klaus) DeMers; m. Darlene Madge Keough, Feb. 3, 1954; children: Kelly C., Shannon M., Peggy F., Erin B. BA in English, Wash. State U., 1956, MA in English, 1962, postgrad., 1965-67. News reporter Daily Olympian, Olympia, Wash., 1956; editor Wash. State U., Pullman, 1956-59; with Ea. Wash. U., Cheney, 1959—; ret., 1983; news reporter Sta. KREM-TV, 1960-62; assoc. prof. Ea. Wash. U., Cheney, 1971-74, prof., 1974-83, prof. emeritus, 1983—. Author: A Fine and Pleasant Misery, 1978, Kid Camping form Aaaaiii! to Zip, 1979, They Shoot Canoes, Don't They?, 1981, Never Sniff a Gift Fish, 1983, The Grasshopper Trap, 1985, Rubber Legs & White Tail-Hairs, 1987, The Night The Bear Ate Gombaw, 1989, Whatchagot Stew, 1989, Real Ponies Don't Go Oink!, 1991, The Good Samaritan Strikes Again, 1992, How I Got This Way, 1994, Never Cry "Arp!" and Other Great Adventures, 1996, (stage play) A Fine and Pleasant: The Humor of Patrick F. McManus, 1994, Misery II: McManus In Love, 1995; assoc. editor Field & Stream mag., 1977-81; editor-at-large Outdoor Life, 1981—. Recipient Booksellers award P.N.W. Booksellers, 1983, Trustees medal EWU, 1984, Gov.'s award Wash. State Libr., 1985, Excellence in Craft award OWAA, 1986, Disting. Achievement award WSU, 1994, Founder's Day award EWU, 1994; named to Idaho's Hall of Fame, 1995. Mem. Authors Guild, Outdoor Writers Am. (bd. dirs. 1981-84, Excellence award 1986). Roman Catholic. Avocations: outdoor sports, woodworking, traveling. Office: PO Box 28216 Spokane WA 99228-8216

MCMANUS, PATRICK J., mayor, lawyer, accountant; b. Lynn, Mass., July 20, 1954; s. Robert A. and Kathryn M. (Gainey) McM. BA in Govt., Bowdoin Coll., 1976; MBA, Suffolk U., 1981; JD, Boston Coll., 1985. CPA, Mass.; cert. managerial acct., Mass. Tchr. Lynn Pub. H.S.; assoc. prof. bus. and fin. Salem (Mass.) State Coll.; lawyer pvt. practice Lynn; councillor at large City of Lynn, 1986-91, mayor, 1992—; mem. adv. bd. U.S. Conf. of Mayors, Washington, Brownsfield Task Force, Washington, Urban and Econ. Policy, Washington, Arts, Culture and Recreation, Washington.

Mem. KC, Ancient Order of Hibernians. Democrat. Roman Catholic. Office: Mayor's Office 3 City Hall Sq Lynn MA 01901-1019*

MCMANUS, RICHARD PHILIP, lawyer, agricultural products company executive; b. Keokuk, Iowa, Oct. 20, 1929; s. Edward William and Kathleen (O'Connor) M.; m. Marjorie Theresa Mullaney, Nov. 5, 1955; children: Michael L., Mark J., Matthew A. BA, St. Ambrose U., Davenport, Iowa, 1949; JD, U. Mich., 1952; MBA, Roosevelt U., Chgo., 1965. Bar: Calif. 1982, Ill. 1958, Iowa 1952. Ptnr. McManus & McManus, Keokuk, 1953-63; div. counsel USN Facility Engring. Command, Great Lakes, Ill., 1963-66; v.p., dir. law Household Fin. Corp., Chgo., 1966-81; exec. v.p., sec. Security Pacific Fin. Svcs., Inc., San Diego, 1981-92; pres., bd. dirs. Mosamac Co., Inc., 1992—; mem. gen. com. Conf. Consumer Fin. Law, Chgo., 1975-92. Contbr. articles to profl. jours. Bd. dirs., treas., atty. Tijuana/San Diego Habitat for Humanity, Inc., 1992-95; trustee Village of Lake Bluff, Ill., 1974-78. Recipient of the Pres. Calif. Bar Pro Bono Svs., award, 1996. Mem. ABA, Calif. Bar Assn., Ill. Bar Assn., San Diego Bar Assn., Calif. Fin. Svcs. Assn. (chmn. law com. 1981-92), Am. Fin. Svcs. Assn. (chmn. law forum 1980-81, Disting. Svc. award 1990), Lions, Elks, KC, Beta Gamma Sigma. Democrat. Roman Catholic. Avocations: golf, flying, sailing, woodworking. Home: 17305 Campillo Dr San Diego CA 92128-2149

MC MANUS, SAMUEL PLYLER, chemist, academic administrator; b. Edgemoor, S.C., Oct. 29, 1938; s. Henry Plyler and Louise (Sanders) McM.; m. Nancy Fincher, Mar. 26, 1959; children: Samuel Plyler, Robert Adair. B.S. in Chemistry, The Citadel, 1960; M.S., Clemson U., 1962, Ph.D. in Chemistry, 1964. Research chemist Du Pont, Phila., 1964; asst. prof. chemistry U. Ala., Huntsville, 1966-68; asso. prof. U. Ala., 1968-73, prof., 1973—, chmn. dept. chemistry, 1970-72, 77-78, dir. materials sci. program, 1988-89, grad. dean, 1989-94, assoc. v.p. acad. affairs, 1990-91, assoc. provost, 1991-93, interim provost, 1993-94, provost, v.p. acad. affairs, 1994—; vis. faculty mem. U. S.C., 1974-75; mem. Ala. Coun. Grad. Deans, 1989-94, (chmn. 1992-93), Conf. So. Grad. Schs. (com. Issues and Planning, 1993-94), Cons. to govt. and industry. Author: Neighboring Group Participation; Editor: Organic Reactive Intermediates, Nucleophilicity; Contbr. articles on chemistry to sci. jours. Committeeman Tenn Valley council Boy Scouts Am., 1973-75. Served to capt. U.S. Army, 1964-66. Named Outstanding Educator U. Ala., Huntsville, 1971, 74; Sigma Xi Researcher of Yr., 1978; Alumni fellow Clemson U., 1961; Petroleum Research Fund grantee, 1968-87 ; NASA-Am. Soc. Engring. Edn. fellow, 1981, 82. Mem. Am. Chem. Soc. (councillor 1970-74, 78-80, 83-93, bd. dirs. 1966-74, 78-80, 83-93, nat. awards com. 1987-89), Ala. Acad. Sci. (v.p. 1973-74, exec. com. 1967, 73-74), AAAS, Am. Assn. State Colls. and Univs. (com. sci. and tech. 1978), Ala. Coun. Chief Acad. Officers (chmn. 1994-96), Sigma Xi (chpt. sect. 1967-69, pres. 1970-71, exec. com. 1967-72), Phi Kappa Phi (chpt. v.p. 1988-89, pres. 1989-90). Clubs: Rotary Internat., Lake Guntersville Yacht (treas. 1975, gov. 1974-83, 88-90, 93-95, commodore 1977, chmn. bd. govs. 1978, chmn. exec. com. 1978-79, 93-94), Yacht Club Assn. Ala. (pres., chmn. bd. commodores 1977). Office: Office of the Provost U Ala Huntsville AL 35899
At the beginning of my academic career I was fortunate to have realized that opportunity always exists. Success requires that one seize even the fleeting opportunity and to be creative with the available resources.

MCMANUS, WALTER LEONARD, investment executive; b. N.Y.C., Apr. 27, 1918; s. Charles E. and Eva M. (Olt) McM.; m. Lillian Ziegler, June 6, 1941; children: Walter Leonard, Peter David, Susan. Student, Harvard Bus. Sch.; BS in Fin. Sci., Georgetown U., 1940. With Crown Cork & Seal Co., Inc., Balt., 1940-60; became sec. Crown Cork & Seal Co., Inc., 1945, v.p., 1949, sec.-treas., 1958-60; pres., dir. Cem Securities Corp.; assoc. Castlewood Realty Co.; dir. Hospice of Martin County, Fla. Mem. Halifax River Yacht Club, Lighthouse Point Yacht Club, Cocoanut Point Yacht Club, Internat. Order of Blue Gavel. Home: 1766 NW Harbor Pl North River Shores Stuart FL 34994 Office: E Joppa Rd Ste 204 Baltimore MD 21286

MCMARTIN, JOHN, actor; b. Warsaw, Ind.; children: Kathleen Alice, Susan Helen. Actor Broadway prodns. including Artist Descending a Staircase, 1989, The Conquering Hero, 1961, Blood, Sweat and Stanley Poole, 1961, Children From Their Games, 1963, A Rainy Day in Newark, 1963, Sweet Charity, 1966-67, Follies, 1971-72, The Great God Brown, 1972-73, Don Juan, 1972-73, The Visit, 1973-74, Chemin de Fer, 1973-74, Love For Love, 1974, Rules of the Game, 1974, Happy New Year, 1980, A Little Family Business, 1982, Show Boat, 1994-95 (Tony nominee - Lead Actor in a Musical, 1995); Off-Broadway prodns. Little Mary Sunshine, 1959-60, The Misanthrope, 1977, Too Much Johnson, 1985, Henry IV, 1985, Julius Caesar, 1988; films: Sweet Charity, 1969, All The President's Men, 1976, Pennies From Heaven, 1981, Brubaker, 1980, Legal Eagles, 1986. Recipient Theatre World award, 1959; nominee 2 Tony awards, 1967, 74; recipient 2 Drama Desk awards, 1974. Club: The Players (N.Y.C.). Office: The Artists Agy 1000 Santa Monica Blvd North Hollywood CA 91601

MCMASTER, BELLE MILLER, religious organization administrator; b. Atlanta, May 24, 1932; d. Patrick Dwight and Lila (Bonner) Miller; m. George R. McMaster, June 19, 1953; children: Lisa McMaster Stork, George Neel, Patrick Miller. BA, Agnes Scott Coll., 1953; MA, U. Louisville, 1970, PhD, 1974. Assoc. corp. witness Presbyn. Ch. USA, Atlanta, 1974-77, dir. corp. witness, 1977-81, dir. div. corp. and social mission, 1981-87; dir. social justice and peacemaking unit Presbyn. Ch. USA, Louisville, Ky., 1987-93; acting dir. program women in theology and ministry Candler Sch. Theology Emory U., 1993-96; dir. advanced studies Candler Sch. Theology Emory U., 1995—; 1993-96; vice moderator chs. commn. internat. affairs World Coun. Chs., 1984-91; chair commn. internat. affairs Nat. Coun. Chs., N.Y.C., 1986-89, v.p., 1990-95, chair ch. world svc. and witness unit com., 1990-95; bd. dirs. Ecumenical Devel. Corp. U.S.A., 1992—, Prison Ministries with Women, 1995—, Christians Assoc. for Rels. with Eastern Europe, 1997—. Author: Witnessing to the Kingdom, 1982, book columnist "What I Have Been Reading" in Church and Society Magazine, 1993—; contbr. articles to profl. jours. Pres. League of Women Voters, Greenville, S.C., 1963-64; bd. dirs. Interfaith Housing, Atlanta, 1975-81. Danforth fellow, 1969-74. Mem. MLA, Acad. Am. Religion, Soc. for Values in Higher Edn., Phi Beta Kappa. Office: Emory U Candler Sch Theology Atlanta GA 30322

MCMASTER, BRIAN JOHN, artistic director; With internat. artists dept. EMI, 1968-73; controller opera planning English Nat. Opera, 1973-76; mng. dir. Welsh Nat. Opera, Cardiff, 1976-91; dir. Edinburgh (Scotland) Internat. Festival, 1991—; artistic dir. Vancouver Opera (B.C., Can.), 1983-89. Office: Edinburgh Internat Festival, 21 Market St, Edinburgh EH1 1BW, Scotland

MCMASTER, JULIET SYLVIA, English language educator; b. Kisumu, Kenya, Aug. 2, 1937; emigrated to Can., 1961, naturalized, 1976; d. Sydney Herbert and Sylvia (Hook) Fazan; m. Rowland McMaster, May 10, 1968; children: Rawdon, Lindsey. B.A. with honors, Oxford U., 1959; M.A., U. Alta., 1963, Ph.D., 1965. Asst. prof. English U. Alta., Edmonton, Can., 1965-70; assoc. prof. U. Alta., 1970-76, prof. English, 1976-86, Univ. prof., 1986—; gen. editor Juvenilia Press, 1993—. Author: Thackeray: The Major Novels, 1971; co-editor: Jane Austen's Business, 1996, Cambridge Companion to Jane Austen, 1997, Jane Austen on Love, 1978, Trollope's Palliser Novels, 1978, (with R.D. McMaster), The Novel from Sterne to James, 1981, Dickens the Designer, 1987, Jane Austen the Novelist, 1995; gen. editor Juvenilia Press, 1993—; illustrator/editor children's picture book: (by Jane Austen) The Beautifull Cassandra, 1993; contbr. articles to profl. jours. Fellow Can. Coun., 1969-70, Guggenheim Found., 1976-77, Killam Found., 1987-89; recipient Molson prize in Humanities for Outstanding Contbn. to Canadian Culture, 1994. Fellow Royal Soc. Can.; mem. Victorian Studies Assn. Western Can. (founding pres. 1972), Assn. Can. Univ. Tchrs. English (pres. 1976-78), MLA, Jane Austen Soc. N.Am. (dir. 1980-91). Office: U Alta, Dept English, Edmonton, AB Canada T6G 2E5

MCMASTER, ROBERT RAYMOND, accountant; b. Cleve., June 14, 1948; s. William G. and Elizabeth (Smith) McM.; m. Jane M. Pepple, June 27, 1970; children: William R., Sarah J. BS in Acctg., Miami U., Oxford, Ohio, 1970. CPA, Ohio, N.Y. Mem. audit staff Sta. KPMG, Columbus, Ohio, 1970-75; mgr. Sta. KPMG, N.Y.C., 1975-76; sr. mgr. Peat Marwick Main & Co., Columbus, 1977-81, ptnr., 1981, mng. ptnr., 1988—, area mng. ptnr., 1992. Pres. Planned Parenthood Ctrl. Ohio, Columbus, 1988, 89; bd. dirs. Riverside Meth. Hosp. Found., Columbus, 1988-91, Unverferth House, 1990-92, Children's Hosp. Found., 1990—, Children's Hosp., chmn., 1993-96; mem. fin. com. Columbus Found.; chmn. Blue Ribbon Commn. on Columbus Pub. Sch. Fins., 1995. Mem. AICPA, Ohio Soc. CPAs (pres. Columbus chpt. 1983-84), Columbus Bar Assn. (ethics com. 1989-91), Scioto Country Club, Muirfield Village Golf Club, Columbus Club. Avocations: golf, tennis, skiing, basketball. Office: KPMG Peat Marwick 2 Nationwide Plz Columbus OH 43215-2422

MCMASTER, SAM, professional sports team official; married. Diploma, U. B.C., U. Toronto. Gen. mgr. Ont. Hockey League's Sault Ste. Marie Greyhounds, 1980-85; scout various profl. teams, 1985-88; past asst dir. of player recruitment Washington Capitals; past dir. ops., gen. mgr. Sudbury Wolves/Ont. Hokey League; gen. mgr. L.A. Kings, 1994—.

MCMASTERS, PAUL KENNETH, foundation executive; b. Dade County, Mo., Jan. 18, 1942; s. James Harvey and Evelyn Gail McMasters; m. Priscilla Jean Thomas, Feb. 19, 1967; 1 child, Amy Elaine. BA, SW Mo. State U., 1965, MA, 1973. From gen. assignment reporter to asst. mng. editor The Daily News, Springfield, Mo., 1970-79; mng. editor Coffeyville (Kans.) Jour., 1979-82; states editor USA Today, Arlington, Va., 1982-83, ops. dir. editorial dept., 1983-87, dep. editorial dir., 1987-91, assoc. editor editorial page, 1991-92; v.p. The Freedom Forum, Arlington, 1992-95; exec. dir. The Freedom Forum 1st Amendment Ctr., Nashville, 1992-95; 1st amendment ombudsman The Freedom Forum, Arlington, Va., 1995—; speaker in field. Mem. editorial bd.: Newspaper Rsch. Jour.; contbr. articles to profl. jours. Bd. dirs. Student Law Press Ctr., The Media Inst., SDX Found. Recipient Inglehart First Amendment award Coll. Media Advisors, 1992, Human Rights Leadership award Freedom Mag., 1993. Mem. Soc. Profl. Journalists (pres. 1993-94, past chmn. freedom of info., past sec.-treas., Wells Meml. Key award 1990), Am. Soc. Newspaper Editors (freedom of info. com.), Assn. Educators in Journalism and Mass Comm. (newspaper divsn. exec. com.). Home: 11871 Troika Ct Woodbridge VA 22192 Office: The Freedom Forum 1st Amendment Ombudsman 1101 Wilson Blvd Arlington VA 22209-2248

MCMEEKIN, DOROTHY, botany, plant pathology educator; b. Boston, Feb. 24, 1932; d. Thomas LeRoy and Vera (Crockatt) McM. BA, Wilson Coll., 1953; MA, Wellesley Coll., 1955; PhD, Cornell U., 1959. Asst. prof. Upsala Coll., East Orange, N.J., 1959-64, Bowling Green State U., Ohio, 1964-66; prof. natural sci. Mich. State U., East Lansing, 1966-89, prof. botany, plant pathology, 1989—. Author: Diego Rivera: Science and Creativity, 1985; contbr. articles to profl. jours. Mem. Am. Phytopath. Soc., Mycol. Soc. Am., Soc. Econ. Bot., Mich. Bot. Soc. (former bd. dirs.), Mich. Women's Studies Assn., Sigma Xi, Phi Kappa Phi. Avocations: gardening, sewing, travel, drawing. Home: 1055 Marigold Ave East Lansing MI 48823-5128 Office: Mich State U Dept Botany-Plant Pathology 335 N Kedzie Hall East Lansing MI 48824-1031

MCMEEKIN, THOMAS OWEN, dermatologist; b. Shelby, Nebr., Apr. 17, 1945; s. Wallace Walton and Evajame (Taber) McM.; m. Susan Jo, Sept. 17, 1966; children: Michele, Sean. BA with distinction, Stanford U., 1967; MD with honors, U. Rochester, 1971. Intern Beth Israel Hosp., Boston, 1971-72; resident U. Rochester (N.Y.), 1974-76, Mass. Gen. Hosp., Boston, 1976-78; clin. assoc. prof. depts. medicine, pediatrics, dermatology U. Rochester Sch. Medicine, 1978—; dermatologist pvt. practice, Rochester, 1978—; clin. asst. prof. SUNY, Buffalo, 1997—; pres. Geneese Valley Laser Ctr., Rochester, 1990—. Capt. USPHS, 1972-74. Kohn fellow U. Rochester, 1980-81; recipient Doren J. Stephens Alumni award U. Rochester, 1971, Brian Flanagan Teaching Svc. award, 1995. Fellow Am. Acad. Dermatology (Svc. award 1993), Am. Bd. Internal Medicine, Am. Soc. LAser MEdicine (co-chmn. 1993-94), Am. Soc. Dermatologic Surgery (edn. com. 1983—); mem. N.Y. State Dermatological Soc. (v.p. 1993, treas. 1992), Buffalo Rochester Dermatological Soc. (pres. 1990), Rochester Dermatological Soc. (pres. 1980-89), Alpha Omega Alpha. Avocations: golf, tennis, computers. Office: 300 White Spruce Blvd Rochester NY 14623-1606

MC MEEL, JOHN PAUL, newspaper syndicate and publishing executive; b. South Bend, Ind., Jan. 26, 1936; s. James E. and Naomi R. (Reilly) McM.; m. Susan S. Sykes, Apr. 16, 1966; children: Maureen, Suzanne, Bridget. BS, U. Notre Dame, 1957. Sales dir. Hall Syndicate, 1960-67; asst. gen. mgr., sales dir. Publishers-Hall Syndicate, 1968-70; co-founder Universal Press Syndicate, Kansas City, Mo., 1970; pres. Andrews McNeel Universal, 1970—; bd. dirs. Newspaper Features Coun., Universal/Belo Prodns.; chmn. bd. Andrews McMeel Pub., 1973—; mem. adv. coun. Inst. for Ch. Life, U. Notre Dame. Co-founder Christmas in October, Kansas City, 1984—, James F. Andrews fellowship program U. Notre Dame, 1981. Mem. Fed. Assn. USA, Sovereign Mil. Order Malta, Internat. Press Inst. (chmn. Am. com.). Home: Three Sunset Pl 5300 Sunset Dr Kansas City MO 64112-2358 Office: Andrews McNeel Universal 4520 Main St Kansas City MO 64111-1816

MCMEEN, ALBERT RALPH, JR., investment advisor; b. Mifflintown, Pa., May 11, 1916; s. Albert Ralph and Elizabeth Smith (Lineweaver) McM.; m. Margaret Parker, June 12, 1940 (dec. Nov. 1960); children: Albert R. III, Marcia Parker McMeen Deignan; m.Janet Haines Wilson, June 12, 1971; children: Frederick, Malcolm. BA, Lafayatte Coll., Easton, Pa., 1939. Retail mgr. E.E. McMeen & Co., Lewistown, Pa., 1939-57; investment salesman Pa. Funds Corp., Phila., 1958-72; divsn. mgr., v.p. Am. Capital-Advantage Capital, Houston, 1973—. Author: PFC Product Knowledge Training Course, 1962. Democrat. Presbyterian. Avocation: promotions training. Home: 536 Franklin Way West Chester PA 19380-5709 Office: Advantage Capital Corp 536 Franklin Way West Chester PA 19380-5709

MCMEEN, ALBERT RALPH, III, writer, lecturer; b. Lewistown, Pa., Oct. 4, 1942; s. Albert Ralph and Margaret McDowell (Parker) McM.; BA in Econs., Williams Coll., 1964; MBA in Fin. (Columbia Internat. Fellows scholar 1964), Columbia U., 1966; m. A. Mary Kelley, June 6, 1965 (div.); children: Albert Ralph, Christopher Benjamin; life ptnr., Hamza Yaldiz. Asst. v.p. Chem. Bank, N.Y.C., 1966-75; v.p. mktg. Irving Leasing Co. subs. Irving Trust Co., N.Y.C., 1975-80; v.p. regional ops. USI Capital and Leasing affiliate U.S. Industries, Inc., N.Y.C., 1980-83; pres. Tng. Assocs., Inc., 1983—; assoc. adj. prof. NYU, 1979-93; asst. prof. L.I. U., 1986-93; tng. cons. Citibank, 1986-87, Barclay's Bank, 1986-89; lectr. Am. Mgmt. Assn., 1986—, cons. N.Y. Life Ins., 1989-91, Am. Bankers Assn., 1992-94, Kocbank, Istanbul, 1993, Fund Democracy and Devel., Moscow, 1995—. Mem. legis. com. Citizens' Union, 1968-75; bd. dirs. Columbia U. Alumni Assn., 1970-75; sec. Gay Fathers Inc. Recipient Columbia Bus. Sch. service award, 1966. Mem. ASTD, Fin. Ind. Tng. Assn. (exec. dir. 1994—). Democrat. Author: Treasurers and Controllers New Equipment Leasing Guide, 1984, Equipment Leasing Guide for Lessees, 1990, Debt Repayment Capacity, 1992, Financial Statement Analysis, 1993, Statement Analysis Series, 1994, Guide to Consumer Lending Computer Based Training, 1995. Home: 333 W 88th St New York NY 10024-2219

MCMEEN, ELMER ELLSWORTH, III, lawyer, guitarist; b. Lewistown, Pa., June 3, 1947; s. Elmer Ellsworth II and Frances Josephine McM.; m. Sheila Ann Taenzler, July 31, 1971; children—Jonathan Ellsworth, Daniel Biddle, James Cunningham and Mary Josephine (twins). A.B. cum laude, Harvard U., 1969; J.D. cum laude, U. Pa., 1972. Bar: 1973, U.S. Ct. Appeals (2d cir.) 1973, U.S. Dist. Ct. (so. and ea. dists.) N.Y. 1975. Assoc. Cravath, Swaine & Moore, N.Y.C., 1972-75; assoc. LeBoeuf, Lamb, Greene & MacRae L.L.P., N.Y.C., 1975-78, ptnr., 1979—; lectr. Editor U. Pa. Law Rev., 1970-72. Author numerous guitar books; contbr. articles to profl. jours; solo guitar recs. Of Soul and Spirit, Irish Guitar Encores by Shanachie Records, Solo Guitar Serenade and Playing Favorites by Piney Ridge Music, solo guitar instructional audio and video lessons Stefan Grossman's Guitar Workshop. Chmn. N.Y.C. regional com. for U. Pa. Law Sch., 1984-86; class sec. Mt. Hermon Sch. Class of 1965, Mass., 1984-91. Fellow Am. Coll. Investment Counsel; mem. ABA, N.Y. State Bar Assn. (mem. corp. law com.), Rockaway River Country Club, Harvard Club (N.Y.C.). Office: LeBoeuf Lamb Greene & MacRae LLP 125 W 55th St New York NY 10019-5369

MCMENAMIN, HELEN MARIE FORAN, home health care, pediatric, maternal nurse; b. Buffalo, May 21, 1943; d. John Michael and Helen Marie (McCarty) Foran; m. John Patrick McMenamin, Aug. 21, 1965; children: Maureen Regina, Kathleen Noelle, Terence Michael, Amy Colleen, Shannon Rosemary, Barry Patrick. BSN, Niagara U., 1965; cert. instr. natural family planning, St. Margaret's Hosp., Boston, 1983. RN N.Y., N.H., Maine, D.C., Va., Md., Pa. Instr. perinatal, neonatal nursing Mercy Hosp. Sch. of Nursing, Portland, Maine, 1981-83; staff/charge nurse neonatal intensive care unit Georgetown Univ. Hosp., Washington, D.C., 1984-93; staff nurse neonatal ICU, renal unit, home care case mgr. Children's Hosp. Nat. Med. Ctr., Washington, 1986-93; educator infant APNEA/CPR, Fairfax Hosp. Infant APNEA Program, Fairfax, Va., 1988-89; pediatric and maternal-child case mgr. Vis. Nurse Assn. No. Va., Arlington, 1992; staff nurse pediatric emergency room Mercy Hosp., Balt., 1992-93; case mgr. maternal-child pediatrics, high-risk neonatal home care Bay Area Health Care, Balt., 1993-95; mgr. maternal-child/neonatal and pediatric program 1st Am. Home Care, Hanover, Pa., 1994-95; pvt. duty pediatric home care Mount Washington Pediatric Hosp., Balt., 1995; coord. high risk maternal-child & pediatric program Future Health Corp., Timonium, Md., 1995—; organizer, co-dir. health clinics Cathedral Elem. Sch., Portland, Maine, 1981-83. Block capt. Am. Cancer Assn., Springfield, Va., 1986-90; mem. Healthy Mothers/Health Babies and Teen Pregnancy Coalition York County. Mem. Nat. Assn. Neonatal Nurses, Nat. Assn. Pro-Life Nurses (bd. dirs. of Pa.), Nat. Assn. Pediatric Nurses. Roman Catholic. Avocations: art, gardening, knitting, piano, baking. Home: RR 1 Box 1456 Brodbecks PA 17329-9603

MCMENAMIN, JOAN STITT, headmistress; b. N.Y.C., May 7, 1925; d. William Britton and Josephene Lloyd (White) Stitt; m. Edward B. McMenamin, Jan. 24, 1953. BA in Econs., Smith Coll., 1946. With Econ. Cooperation Adminstrn., Paris, 1949-50; office mgr. Ford Found., N.Y.C., 1951-52; history tchr. Nightingale-Bamford Sch., N.Y.C., 1962-63, asst. to headmistress, 1963-65, asst. headmistress, 1965-71, headmistress, 1971-92, headmistress emerita, 1992, interim head San Francisco U. H.S., 1996-97; mem. adv. council for nonpub. schs. N.Y. State Commr. of Edn., 1985-87; pres. Guild Ind. Schs. N.Y., 1983-85; mem. admissions com. Nat. Assn. Ind. Schs., 1977-79. Vice chmn. English-Speaking Union Exchange Scholarship Program, 1977-79; spl. advisor Parents League N.Y.; bd. dirs. Council for Religion in Ind. Schs., 1976-79, Ind. Sch. Orchs., Inc., 1980-84; trustee A Better Chance, Inc., 1977-83, The Town Sch., 1975-77, Ind. Ednl. Svcs., 1985-89, The Lawrenceville School, 1989—, Buckley Sch., 1977-92, Coun. for Basic Edn., Washington, 1978-96, Clark Found., 1979—, Robert Coll. of Istanbul, Turkey, 1979—, WICAT Founds., 1976—, Axe-Hought Found., 1985—. Mem. Nat. Assn. Prins. of Girls' Schs. (pres. 1983-85), N.Y. State Assn. Ind. Schs. (chmn. 1985-87), Headmasters Assn., Country Day Sch. Headmasters Assn. (vice pres. 1987-90, exec. com. 1987-90), Headmistresses Assn. of East. Democrat. Episcopalian. Club: Cosmopolitan (N.Y.C.); Bridgehampton (N.Y.). Avocation: reading. Home: PO Box 768 172 Church Ln Bridgehampton NY 11932

MCMENAMIN, JOHN ROBERT, lawyer; b. Evanston, Ill., Sept. 30, 1946. BA, U. Notre Dame, 1968, JD, 1971. Bar: Ill. 1971. Law clk. to presiding judge U.S. Ct. Appeals (7th cir.), 1971-72; ptnr. Mayer, Brown & Platt, Chgo., 1978-89, McDermott, Will & Emery, Chgo., 1989—. Chmn. adv. bd. Holy Trinity High Sch., Chgo., 1986-88. Mem. ABA, Mid-Am. Com. Roman Catholic. Clubs: Law, Legal, University (Chgo.), Econ. (Chgo.). Office: McDermott Will & Emery 227 W Monroe St Chicago IL 60606-5016

MCMENAMY, KRISTEN, model; b. Easton, Pa.; d. Charles and Eileen McM. Modelling contracts with Gianni Versace, Calvin Klein, Karl Lagerfeld. Named Harper's Bazaar Model of Yr., 1993. *

MC MENNAMIN, GEORGE BARRY, advertising agency executive; b. N.Y.C., May 23, 1922; s. Harold G. and Hazel F. (Stanbridge) McM.; m. Marilynn L. Simon, Sept. 9, 1946; children: Marilynn Breeze, Karen Foster. BS, Harvard U., 1945. With Doremus & Co., N.Y.C., 1946-88, exec. v.p., 1967-73, pres., 1973-84, vice chmn., 1984-88, also mem. exec. com.; pub. Worldpaper, Boston, 1988. Served to lt. (j.g.) USNR, 1944-46. Mem. Fin. Advt. and Mktg. Assn. Met. N.Y. (pres. 1967), Down Town Assn., Hasty Pudding Inst. 1770, Harvard Coll. Speakers Club, Harvard Club, New Canaan Country Club, Pilgrims Club of U.S. Republican. Episcopalian. Home: 28 Cross Ridge Rd New Canaan CT 06840-2311

MCMENNAMY, ROGER NEAL, community development company executive; b. Amarillo, Tex., Oct. 9, 1942; s. Wilson Foch and Mildred Evelyn (Freudiger) McM.; m. Marilyn Kay Gibbons, Jan. 1, 1967; children: Timothy Neal, Traci Nicole. Student, Abilene Christian U., 1961-62; BBA in Mgmt. cum laude, U. Tex., Arlington, 1970; MBA in Fin., U. Tex., Austin, 1971. CPA, Tex. Contr., treas. E.N. Wolcott Corp., Houston, 1971-73; mem. corp. staff ELPAC, Inc., Houston, 1973-74; gen. mgr. BS&B Mfg., Houston, 1974-75; gen. mgr. adminstrn. Gulf Interstate Co., Houston, 1975-77; exec. v.p., chief fin. officer NWS Supply Group, Houston, 1977-83; v.p., chief fin. officer Newpark Resources, Inc., Metairie, La., 1983-86; sr. v.p., chief fin. officer Gemcraft, Inc., 1986-88; exec. v.p., chief fin. officer Cooper Communities, Inc., Bella Vista, Ark., 1988-90, pres., chief exec. officer, 1990—, also bd. dirs.; bd. dirs. Boatmen's Bank of N.W. Ark., Fayetteville. Mem. N.W. Ark. Coun., Fayetteville; bd. dirs. Walton Arts Ctr., Fayetteville, 1994—. With USMC, 1962-66, Viet Nam. Mem. AICPA, Am. Resort Devel. Assn., Ark. State C. of C. (bd. dirs.). Avocations: skiing, travel, golf, waterfowl hunting. Office: Cooper Communities Inc 1801 Forest Hills Blvd Bella Vista AR 72715-2395

MCMICHAEL, FRANCIS CLAY, civil engineering educator, environmental engineering consultant; b. Phila., Aug. 8, 1937; s. Francis and Estella Marie (Walker) McM.; m. Catherine Patricia Barati, Aug. 16, 1969; children: Jessica Elizabeth, Laureen Marie. B.S., Lehigh U., 1958; M.S., Calif. Inst. Tech., 1959, Ph.D., 1963. Asst. prof. Princeton U., 1965-67; sr. fellow Mellon Inst., Pitts., 1967-72; assoc. prof. Carnegie-Mellon U., Pitts., 1972-75, prof., 1975—; The Walter J. Blenko Sr. prof. environ. engring. Carnegie-Mellon U., 1981—, dept. head civil engring., 1975-80; sr. tech. advisor ERT Inc., Pitts., 1979-81. Mem. editorial bd. Waste Mgmt. and Rsch. Jour. Served with USPHS, 1962-65. AT&T Found. Indsl. Ecology faculty fellow, 1994-95, 95-96. Mem. ASCE, Water Pollution Control Fedn., Am. Inst. Chem. Engrs., Am. Geophys. Union, Soc. for Risk Analysis, Internat. Solid Wastes Assn. Presbyterian. Home: 7001 Penn Ave Pittsburgh PA 15208-2407 Office: Carnegie-Mellon U Pittsburgh PA 15213

MCMICHAEL, GUY H., III, federal official; b. South Bend, Ind., Dec. 26, 1939; m. Nancy Moore. AB, Harvard U., 1962; JD, U. Mich., 1967. Pvt. practice, 1967-71; dept. prosecuting atty. State of Ind., 1967-71; gen. counsel com. vet. affairs U.S. Senate, Washington, 1971-77; gen. coun. Dept. Vet. Affairs (formerly VA), Washington, 1977-81; adminstrv. judge bd. contract appeals Dept. Vet. Affairs, Washington, 1981-90, chmn., chief adminstrv. judge, 1990—. With U.S. Army, 1962-64. Mem. ABA, Bds. Contract Appeals Judges Assn. (pres. 1989-90), Ind. Bar Assn., D.C. Bar Assn. Office: Dept Vet Affairs Bd Contract Appeals 810 Vermont Ave NW # 09 Washington DC 20420-0001*

MCMICHAEL, JEANE CASEY, real estate corporation executive; b. Clarksville, Ind., May 7, 1938; d. Emmett Ward and Carrie Evelyn (Leonard) Casey; m. Norman Kenneth Wenzler, Sept. 12, 1956 (div. 1968); m. Wilburn Arnold McMichael, June 20, 1978. Student Ind. U. Extension Ctr., Bellermine Coll., 1972-73, Ind. U. S.E., 1973—, Kentuckiana Metroversity, 1981—; Grad. Realtors Inst., Ind. U., 1982; grad. Leadership Tng., Clark County, Ind.; lic. real estate broker, Ind., Ky.; master Grad. Realtors Inst., Cert. Residential Specialist, Cert. Real Estate Broker, Leadership Tng. Grad. Owner, pres. McMichael Real Estate, Inc., Jeffersonville, 1979-88, 90-96; mgr., owner Buzz Bauer Realtors, Clark County, 1989-91; mng. broker Parks & Weisberg Realtors, Jeffersonville, Ind., 1989-91; instr. pre-license real estate Ivy Tech. State Coll., 1995-96, ISTR real estate Tng. Concepts, Inc. Pres. of congregation St. Mark's United Ch. of Christ, 1996, pres., Mr. and Mrs. Class, chmn., fin. trustee and bus. adv., chmn. devel. com., 1993, 94, chmn. com. long range planning, 1997; chmn. bd. trustees, Brooklawn Youth Svcs., 1988-94, chmn. 1994-95; chmn. social com. Rep. party Clark County (Ind.); v.p. Floyd County Habitat for Humanity, 1991, 94/95. Recipient cert. of appreciation Nat. Ctr. Citizen Involvement, 1983; award Contact Kentuckiana Teleminnistries, 1978. Mem. Nat. Assn. Realtors (nat. dir. 1989—), Ind. Assn. Realtors (state dir. 1987—, quick start speaker 1989-91), Nat. Women's Council Realtors (state pres., chmn. coms., state rec. sec., 1984, state pres. 1985-86, Nat. Achievement award 1982, 83, 84, 85, 86, 87, 88, 89, 90, nat. gov. Ind. 1987, v.p. region III 1988, Ind. Honor Realtor award

1982—), Women's Council of Realtors (speaker 1990-94, Mem. of Yr. 1988), Ky. Real Estate Exchange, So. Ind. Bd. Realtors (program chmn. 1986-87, bd. dirs., pres., 1988—, Realtor of Yr. 1985, instr. success series, 1989-92, Snyder Svc. award 1987, Omega Tau Rho award 1988, Excellence in Edn. award 1989), Ind. Assn. Realtors (state dir. 1985—, bd. govs., instr./trainer, speaker 1989-94, chair bd. govs. 1991), Toastmasters (pres. Steamboat chpt.), Psi Iota Xi. Office: McMichael Real Estate Inc 1402 Blackiston Mill Rd Jeffersonville IN 47129-2279 Address: 23 Arctic Spgs Jeffersonville IN 47130-4701 *Personal philosophy: The constant pursuit of excellence brings quality service and respect for every individual.*

MCMICHAEL, LAWRENCE GROVER, lawyer; b. West Orange, N.J., Aug. 18, 1953; s. Robert Gerard McMichael and Mary C. (Bragg) Lewis; children: Elizabeth Joan, David Stern; m. Virginia Lee Hinrichs, Nov. 12, 1994; 1 child John Lawrence. AB, Duke U., 1975, JD, 1978. Bar: Pa. 1978, U.S. Ct. Appeals (3d cir.) 1979, U.S. Dist. Ct. (ea. dist.) Pa. 1980, U.S. Supreme Ct. 1985. Ptnr. Dilworth, Paxson, Kalish & Kauffman, Phila., 1978—. Bd. Dir. Wynnewood Civic. Assn., 1986—. Mem. ABA, Pa. Bar Assn., Phila. Bar Assn., Pa. Bar Inst. (mem. faculty, 1984—). Office: Dilworth Paxson Kalish & Kauffman 3200 The Mellon Bank Ctr 1735 Market St Philadelphia PA 19103-7501

MC MILLAN, BROCKWAY, former communications executive; b. Mpls., Mar. 30, 1915; s. Franklin and Luvena (Brockway) McM.; m. Audrey Wishard, Sept. 2, 1942; children—Sarah Linn McMillan Taylor, Douglas Wishard, Gordon Brockway. Student, Armour Inst. Tech., 1932-34; B.S., Mass. Inst. Tech., 1936, Ph.D., 1939. Procter fellow Princeton, 1939-40, H.B. Fine instr., 1940-41; with Bell Telephone Labs., 1946-61, dir. mil. research, 1959-61; asst. sec. research and devel. U.S. Air Force, 1961-63, under-sec., 1963-65; exec. dir. mil. research Bell Telephone Labs., Whippany, N.J., 1965-69; v.p. mil. devel. Bell Telephone Labs., 1969-79. Mem. Bd. Edn. Summit, N.J., 1958-61. Served with USNR, 1942-45. Fellow AAAS, IEEE; mem. NAE, Soc. Indsl. and Applied Math. (pres. 1959-60), Am. Math. Soc., Math. Assn. Am., Inst. Math. Stats. Home: Carter Point Rd Sedgwick ME 04676

MCMILLAN, CAMPBELL WHITE, pediatric hematologist; b. Soochow, China, Jan. 10, 1927; s. Henry Hudson and Leila McNeill (Memory) McM.; m. Florence Jean MacKenzie, June 11, 1955; children: Ian Johnson, Sally Hudson, Donna Jean, Andrew Duncan, Bridget White, Wendy McNeill. B.S. summa cum laude, Wake Forest Coll., 1948; M.D., Bowman Gray Sch. Medicine, 1952. Diplomate Am. Bd. Pediatrics, Pediatric Hematology-Oncology. Intern Harvard Med. Service, Boston City Hosp., 1952-53; resident in pediatrics Children's Hosp. Med. Center, Boston, 1953-55; registrar in pediatrics St. Mary's Hosp., London, 1955; pediatrician Nemazee Hosp., Shiraz, Iran, 1956-58; fellow in pediatric hematology Harvard U., 1958-60; instr. pediatrics, 1960-61; gen. practice pediatrics Laurinburg, N.C., 1961-63; asst. prof. pediatrics U. N.C., Chapel Hill, 1963-68; asso. prof. U. N.C., 1968-72, prof., 1972-92, chief div. pediatric hematology, 1963-83, prof. emeritus, 1992—; Asso. dir. Clin. Research Center, U. N.C., 1966-78. Assoc. editor: Blood Diseases of Infancy and Childhood, 1978, 84; contbr. articles profl. jours., chpts. in books. Served with USNR, 1945-46. Recipient Lederle Med. Faculty award, 1964, Disting. Alumnus award Bowman Gray Sch. Medicine, 1972. Fellow Am. Acad. Pediatrics; mem. Soc. Pediatric Rsch., Am. Pediatric Soc., Phi Beta Kappa, Alpha Omega Alpha. Democrat. Episcopalian. Home: 408 Ridgecrest Dr Chapel Hill NC 27514-2103 *It was my extremely good fortune to live and to work in a time of the most explosive growth medical knowledge had ever undergone.*

MCMILLAN, CHARLES WILLIAM, consulting company executive; b. Ft. Collins, Colo., Feb. 9, 1926; s. Charles and Margaret (Jennings) McM.; m. Jardell Hollier, Feb. 12, 1951; children: Brett W., Kurt C., Scott P. B.S., Colo. State U., 1948. Asst. 4-H agt. Denver, 1948; county agrl. agt. LaJara, Colo., 1949-50, Julesburg, 1950-53; faculty Colo. State U., 1954; div. head, agrl. research dept. Swift & Co., Chgo., 1954-59; exec. v.p. Am. Nat. Cattlemen's Assn., 1959-77; v.p. Nat. Cattlemen's Assn., 1977-81; asst. sec. for mktg. and inspection services USDA, Washington, 1981-85; pres. McMillan and Farrell Assocs., Inc., Washington, 1985-94, C.W. McMillan Co., Alexandria, Va., 1994—; bd. dirs. RTI Inc.; vice chmn. Western Assocs. Inc. Served to lt. (j.g.) USNR, World War II. Mem. Inst. for Sci. in Soc. (bd. dirs.), Newcomen Soc. N.Am., Sigma Alpha Epsilon. Club: Capitol Hill. Home: 4003 Pine Brook Rd Alexandria VA 22310-2144 Office: PO Box 10009 Alexandria VA 22310-0009

MCMILLAN, DONALD EDGAR, pharmacologist; b. Butler, Pa., Sept. 23, 1937; s. Chandler Burdell and Ruth Elizabeth (Beach) McM.; m. Marjorie Ann Leavitt, Feb. 4, 1963; children: David Craig, Pamela Jean. B.S., Grove City Coll., 1959; M.S., U. Pitts., 1962, Ph.D., 1965. Postdoctoral fellow Harvard U. Med. Sch., 1965-66; instr. in pharmacology SUNY Downstate Med. Ctr., N.Y.C., 1967-68, asst. prof., 1968-69; asst. prof. pharmacology U. N.C., 1969-72, asso. prof., 1972-76, prof., 1976-78; prof., chmn. dept. pharmacology U. Ark. for Med. Scis., 1978-80, prof., chmn. dept. pharmacology and toxicology, 1980—, prof. psychiatry, 1985—, Wilbur D. Mills prof. alcoholism and drug abuse prevention, 1991—; dir. Substance Abuse Treatment Ctr.; vis. lectr. U. Ctrl. Caracas, Venezuela, 1974; IRG mem. neurobiology rev. panel NSF, 1979-80; IRG mem. Nat. Inst. Drug Abuse, 1982-88, 92-95, chair 1994-95, SRC mem., 1988-95; bd. dirs. Chapel Hill (N.C.) Drug Action Com., 1977-78; cons. Health Effects Inst., 1985-87; cons. sci. adv. bd. EPA, 1985-89; spl. merit rev. bd. Armed Forces Radiobiology Rsch. Inst., 1982; mem. com. toxicity data elements NRC, 1980-83. Author: Central Nervous System Pharmacology— A Self Instruction Text, 1974, 2d, rev. edit., 1979; research, numerous publs. in behavioral pharmacology and drug abuse; bd. editors Jour. Pharmacology and Exptl. Therapeutics, 1972—, Psychopharmacology, 1973-81, Neurotoxicology, 1979-82, Toxicology and Applied Pharmacology, 1982-89, Neurobehavioral/Toxicology and Teratology, 1982-90, Behavioral Pharmacology, 1989—. Grantee NIMH, 971-74, Nat. Inst. Environ. Health Scis., 1976-80, N.C. Alcoholism Rsch. Authority, 1975-77, EPA, 1982-85, Kellogg Found., 1987-92, U.S. Dept. Edn., 1989-91, Nat. Inst. Drug Abuse, 1976-96. Mem. AAAS, Behavioral Pharmacology Soc. (pres. 1982-84), Behavioral Toxicology Soc. (pres. 1988-90), Am. Soc. Pharmacology and Exptl. Therapeutics, Am. Psychol. Soc., European Behavioral Pharmacology Soc., Soc. Toxicologists (pres. So. Cen. chpt. 1985-86), Com. on Problems of Drug Dependence. Home: 100 Longway Dr Little Rock AR 72211-9531 Office: U Ark Med Scis Sch Medicine Dept Pharmacology & Toxicol 4301 W Markham St Little Rock AR 72205-7101

MC MILLAN, GEORGE DUNCAN HASTIE, JR., lawyer, former state official; b. Greenville, Ala., Oct. 11, 1943; s. George Duncan Hastie and Jean (Autrey) McM.; m. Ann Louise Dial, Nov. 20, 1971; children: George Duncan Hastie, III, Ann Dial. B.A. magna cum laude, Auburn U., 1966; LL.B. (Southeastern Regional scholar), U. Va., 1969. Bar: Ala. bar 1969. Research asst. dept. agronomy Auburn U., summers 1963-65; law clk. firm Lange, Simpson, Robinson & Somerville, Birmingham, Ala., summers 1967-68; law clk. to judge U.S. Dist. Ct. No. Dist. Ala., 1969-70; instr. U. Ala. Law Sch., 1969-70; individual practice law Birmingham, 1970-71; ptnr. firm McMillan & Spratling, Birmingham, 1971-86; of counsel Haskell, Slaughter, Young and Lewis, 1986; ptnr. McMillan, Jones and Assocs., 1987-90; pres. McMillan Assocs., 1990—; mem. Ala. Ho. of Reps., 1973, Ala. Senate, 1974-78; lt. gov. Ala., 1979-83; vice-chmn. Nat. Conf. Lt. Govs., 1980-82; mem. Permanent Study Comm. on Ala.'s Jud. System, 1975-79. Chmn. Ala. Film Commn., 1976-83; mem. Arts Task Force, Nat. Conf. State Legislatures, 1978-80, Multi-State Transp. Adv. Bd., 1974-79; mem. exec. com. So. Growth Policies Bd., 1974-83, vice chmn., 1981-83; bd. dirs. Campfire, Inc., 1975-82, Met. YMCA, Birmingham, Boys and Girls Ranches, Ala., Positive Maturity, 1987—; chmn. bd., pres. Birmingham Cultural and Heritage Found., 1988—; pres., bd. dirs. Birmingham Repertory Theatre, 1989—; exec. producer City Stages; Served to lt. USAR, 1969. Recipient award Ala. Nurses Assn., 1975; named Legislator of Yr. Ala. Forestry Assn., 1978; Hardest Working Senator Capitol Press Corps, 1976; 1 of 4 Outstanding Young Men Ala. Jaycees, 1977; 1 of 10 Most Outstanding State Legislators Assn. Govtl. Employees, 1978; award Birmingham Emancipation Assn., 1977; award Ala. Hist. Commn., 1978; James Tingle award, 1979, Citizen of Yr. award City of Birmingham, 1990. Mem. Birmingham Bar Assn., Ala. Bar Assn., Am. Bar Assn., Birmingham Jaycees, Ala. Jaycees (dir. 1970-72), Birmingham Urban League, United Negro Coll. Fund. Democrat. Mem. Ch. of Christ. Club: Rotary (Birmingham). Office: Mc Millan & Associates PO Box 11311 Birmingham AL 35202-1311

MC MILLAN, JAMES, manufacturing executive; b. Grosse Pointe Farms, Mich.; s. James Thayer and Anne Davenport (Russel) McM.; m. Virginia Cutting, Jan. 4, 1935; children: Francis Wetmore (Sandy), Virginia. A.B., Yale, 1934. With Detroit & Cleve. Nav. Co., supt., asst. gen. mgr., gen. mgr., pres., chmn. bd., 1934-48; pres. McMillan Packard, Inc.; pres., dir. Great Lakes-Oceanic Line, Inc.; security-ins. broker Multivest Financial Corp., Inc.; dir. Detroit Bank & Trust Co., Packard Motor Car Co., Studebaker Corp., Detroit Bank, Detroit Trust Co., Ferry-Morse Seed Co., Detroit & Cleve. Nav. Co., Am. Presidents Life Ins. Co., Grand Rapids, Mich.; v.p., dir., treas. Boyer-Campbell Co.; adminstrv. exec. asst. Am. Nat. Gas Service Co.; cons. Glover Assos., Inc., N.Y.C., Ordnance Tank Automotive Center, U.S. Army; mgmt. cons. Glover Assos. (Can.) Ltd. Exec. asst. United Found., 1964—; Bd. dirs. ARC; trustee Grosse Pointe War Meml. Assn., Detroit Hist. Assn., Mich. State Appellate Defender Commn., Grace Hosp., Grosse Pointe Country Day Sch., Detroit U., Sch. Corp., Estate James T. McMillan, Katherine K. Brookfield Trust.; Village commr., police commr. Grosse Pointe Park. Mem. Nat. Assn. Security Dealers, Detroit Bd. Commerce (dir. 1938-43), Mich. Hort. Soc. (trustee, treas.), Newcomen Soc. N.Am., Mason Club, St. Clair Flats Shooting Club, Yondotega Club, Detroit Country Club, Grosse Pointe Club (pres. 1953), Detroit Club (pres. 1962), Sakonnet Golf Club (Little Compton, R.I.). Republican. Presbyn. (elder, trustee). Home: 46 Sunningdale Dr Grosse Pointe MI 48236-1664 Office: Free Press Detroit MI 48226-2721

MCMILLAN, JOHN A., retail executive; b. 1931. BA, U. Wash., 1957. With Nordstrom Inc., Seattle, 1957—, exec. v.p., 1975—, pres., 1989—, co-chmn., 1991—, dir., 1995—. Office: Nordstrom Inc 1501 5th Ave Seattle WA 98101-1603*

MCMILLAN, LEE RICHARDS, II, lawyer; b. New Orleans, Aug. 26, 1947; s. John H. and Phoebe (Skillman) McM.; m. Lynne Clark Pottharst, June 27, 1970; children: Leslie Clark, Hillary Anne, Lee Richards III. BS in Commerce, Washington and Lee U., 1969; JD, Tulane U., 1972; LLM in Taxation, NYU, 1976. Bar: La. 1972. Assoc. Jones, Walker, Waechter, Poitevent, Carrere & Denegre, New Orleans, 1976-79, ptnr., 1979—, sect. head, corp. and securities sect., 1987-90, 94—, exec. com., 1990-94, 96—, chmn. exec. com., 1991-94, 96—; vice-chmn. Mech. Equipment Co., Inc., New Orleans, 1980-86, chmn. bd., 1986—, pres. 1989—; bd. dirs. The Chamber/New Orleans and the River Region, 1996—; bd. trustees Alton Ochsner Med. Found., 1995—. Trustee New Orleans Mus. Art, 1989-95; bd. dirs. bur. Govt. Rsch. New Orleans, 1987-93, Louise S. McGehee Sch., New Orleans, 1982-88, co-chmn. capital fund dr., 1984-86, pres. bd. dirs., 1986-88; bd. govs. Isidore Newman Sch., New Orleans, 1991-95. Lt. JAGC USNR, 1972-75. Mem. ABA (com. on negotiated acquisitions 1986-94), La. State Bar Assn. (chmn. corp. and bus. law sect. 1985-86, mem. com. on bar admissions 1986-87), Young Pres. Orgn., Washington and Lee U. Alumni Assn. (bd. dirs. 1995—). Republican. Episcopalian. Avocation: sailing. Office: Jones Walker Waechter Poitevent Carrere & Denegre 201 Saint Charles Ave New Orleans LA 70170-1000

MCMILLAN, LEONARD DAVID, family life specialist, consultant, lecturer; b. Harvard, Ill., Dec. 7, 1938; s. Pearly and Jean (Carter) McM.; m. Karen R. Meyer, Dec. 8, 1956; 1 child, Mitchel D. BA, Andrews U., Berrien Springs, Mich., 1972, MDiv, 1975; PhD, Ephraim-Moore U.-Theol. Sem., Holden, Mo., 1984. Dir. family life and youth Wis. Conf., 7th-day Adventist Ch., Madison, 1974-76; mem. Wash. Conf. 7th-day Adventist Ch., Bothell, 1976-83; mem. South African Union 7th-day Adventist Ch., Bloemfontein, 1983-84; pastor Upper Columbia Conf. 7th-day Adventist Ch., Spokane, Wash., 1984-86; dir. family life Potomac Conf. 7th-day Adventist Ch., Staunton, Va., 1986-95; dir. family life Pacific Health Edn. Ctr. Author: Why Can't My Mate Be More Like Me?, 1986, An Owner's Guide to Male Midlife Crisis, 1986, Person to Person, 1987, The Family of God and How to Live with Them, 1988, Slaying Your Dragons, 1989, Parentwise, 1993, ParentTeen, 1993, First Class Male, 1994, Putting Up with Mr. Right, 1996. With USAF, 1956-60. Mem. Am. Assn. Pastoral Counselors, Nat. Coun. on Family Rels. (cert. family life educator), Assn. Adventist Family Life Profls. (pres. 1991-95), Am. Assn. Christian Counselors. Avocations: restoring classic automobiles, writing, remodeling, landscaping. Office: Pacific Health Edn Ctr 5300 California Ave Ste 200 Bakersfield CA 93309-1642 *In my opinion, all of life now and hereafter can be summed up in a single word: Relationships!.*

MCMILLAN, M. SEAN, lawyer. Diploma U. Munich, 1963; cert. Internat. Sch., Copenhagen, Denmark, 1962; SB, U. So. Calif., 1967; JD, Harvard U., 1970. Bar: Calif. 1971. Spl. projects dir. Mass. Gen. Hosp., Boston, 1967-70; ptnr. Keatinge, Libbott, Bates & Loo, Los Angeles, 1970-74, Loo, Merideth & McMillan, Los Angeles, 1974-85, Bryan Cave LLP, Los Angeles/Santa Monica, 1986—. Mem. Assn. Computing Machinery, ABA, Am. Soc. Internat. Law, Phi Beta Kappa, Phi Kappa Phi. Editor: Harvard Internat. Law Jour., 1968-70. Office: Bryan Cave LLP 120 Broadway Ste 500 Santa Monica CA 90401-2386

MCMILLAN, MARY BIGELOW, retired minister, volunteer; b. St. Paul, July 30, 1919; d. Charles Henry and Allison (McKibbin) Bigelow; m. Richard McMillan, June 26, 1943; children: Richard Jr., Charles B., Douglas D., M. Allison, Anne E. BA, Vassar Coll., 1941; MDiv, United Theol. Sem. Twin Cities, 1978, DDiv (hon.), 1989. Ordained to ministry Presbyn. Ch., 1978. Asst. min. House of Hope Presbyn. Ch., St. Paul, 1978-82; interim pres. United Theol. Sem. Twin Cities, New Brighton, Minn., 1982-83, ret., 1987. Contbr. author: The Good Steward, 1983. Trustee Minn. Ch. Found., Mpls., 1984—, United Theol. Sem. Twin Cities, 1977-89, also chmn. bd. trustees; bd. dirs. Inst. for Ecumenical and Cultural Rsch., Collegeville, Minn., 1982—; regional dir. Assn. Jr. Leagues, N.Y.C., 1959-61, pres. St. Paul chpt., 1957-59; vice chair Ramsey County Welfare Bd., St. Paul, 1962-66, St. Paul Health and Welfare Planning Coun., 1964-70, F.R. Bigelow Found., St. Paul, 1988-95, also 1st vice chair; trustee Wilder Found., 1973-89, 1st vice chair Presbyn. Homes Found., 1996—. Recipient award for community planning United Way, 1965, also for yr. round leadership, 1973, Leadership in Community Svc. award YWCA, 1980, Sisterhood award NCCJ, Mpls., 1989; named Disting Alumna award St. Paul Acad. and Summit Sch., 1988. Mem. New Century Club, Univ. Club., Minnesota Club. Avocations: golf, knitting, reading. Home: 2532 Manitou Is Saint Paul MN 55110-3901

MCMILLAN, NATHANIEL, professional basketball player; b. Raleigh, N.C., Aug. 3, 1964; m. Michelle McMillan; children: Jamelle, Brittany Michelle. Student, Chowan Coll., 1982-84, N.C. State U., 1984-86. Guard Seattle SuperSonics, 1986—. Dir. summer basketball camp. Holder NBA single-game rookie record assists; Seattle SuperSonics all-time leader steals, assists, single-game record assists, single-game playoff record assists; named Jr. Coll. All-Am., top 10 N.C. State list assists, 2d team All-NBA def., 1993-94, 94-95. Avocation: football. Office: Seattle SuperSonics 190 Queen Anne Ave N Ste 200 Seattle WA 98109-4926*

MC MILLAN, R(OBERT) BRUCE, museum executive, anthropologist; b. Springfield, Mo., Dec. 3, 1937; s. George Glassey and Winnie Mae (Booth) McM.; m. Virginia Kay Moore, Sept. 30, 1961; children: Robert Gregory, Michael David, Lynn Kathryn. B.S. in Edn, S.W. Mo. State U., 1960; M.A. in Anthropology, U. Mo., Columbia, 1963; Ph.D. in Anthropology (NSF fellow), U. Colo., Boulder, 1971. Rsch. assoc. in archaeology U. Mo., 1963-65, 68-69; assoc. curator anthropology Ill. State Mus., Springfield, 1969-72; curator anthropology Ill. State Mus., 1972-73, asst. mus. dir., 1973-76, mus. dir., 1977—; exec. sec. Ill. State Mus. Soc., 1977—; lectr. in anthropology Northwestern U., 1973; bd. dirs. Found. Ill. Archaeology, 1978-83. Editor: (with W. Raymond Wood) Prehistoric Man and His Environments, 1976. Mem. Ill. Spl. Events Commn., 1977-79, program chmn., 1977-78; commr. Ill. and Mich. Canal Nat. Heritage Corridor Commn., 1988—. NSF grantee, 1971, 72, 80; Nat. Endowment for Humanities grantee, 1978. Fellow AAAS, Am. Anthrop. Assn.; mem. Am. Assn. Mus. (council 1982-86), Midwest Mus. Conf. (pres.), Soc. Am. Archaeology, Current Anthropology (asso.), Am. Quaternary Assn., Sigma Xi. Office: Ill State Mus Spring and Edwards Sts Springfield IL 62706 also: Dickson Mounds Museum Lewistown IL 61542

MCMILLAN, ROBERT RALPH, lawyer; b. N.Y.C., May 21, 1932; s. Harry and Vivian (Beatty) McM.; m. Jane Gail Arbo, June 7, 1958; children: Robin, Karen, Kenneth. Student, Adelphi U., 1951-52, 55-56; JD, Bklyn. Law Sch., 1960. Bar: N.Y. 1960. Spl. asst. staff of Richard M. Nixon, N.Y., Washington, 1960, 64-65; counsel Senator Kenneth B. Keating, Washington, 1960-62; govt. rels. advisor Mobil Oil Co., N.Y.C., 1962-63, 65-68; v.p. Avon Products, N.Y.C., 1973-78, 79-85; sr. v.p. A&S Dept. Stores, N.Y.C., 1978-79; counsel Rivkin, Radler, Bayh, Hart & Kremer, Uniondale, N.Y., 1986-91; ptnr. McMillan, Rather, Bennett & Rigano, P.C., Melville, N.Y., 1991—; bd. dirs. Cybex Internat., Inc., Bayshore, N.Y., Key Bank N.Y., Empire Blue Cross Blue Shield, Panama Canal Commn., 1989-94, chmn., 1993-94. News commentator Sta. WLIW-TV, 1993—. Trustee Adelphi U., 1984-89; bd. dirs. L.I. (N.Y.) Assn.; chmn. L.I. Housing Parntership, 1988—. 1st lt. U.S. Army, 1952-54. Decorated Bronze Star. Mem. Nassau County Bar Assn., Suffolk County Bar Assn. Republican. Avocations: golf, fishing. Office: McMillan Rather Bennett & Rigano 48 S Service Rd Melville NY 11747-2335

MCMILLAN, TERRY L., writer, educator; b. Port Huron, Mich., Oct. 18, 1951; d. Edward McMillan and Madeline Washington Tillman; 1 child, Solomon Welch. BA in Journalism, U. Calif., Berkeley, 1979; MFA, Columbia Univ., N.Y.C., 1979. Instr. U. Wyoming, Laramie, 1987-90; prof. U. Ariz., Tucson, 1990-92. Author: Mama, 1987, Disappearing Acts, 1989, Waiting to Exhale, 1992, How Stella Got Her Groove Back, 1996; editor: Breaking Ice: An Anthology of Contemporary African-American Fiction, 1990; screenwriter (with Ron Bass) (movie) Waiting to Exhale, 1995. Recipient National Endowment for the Arts fellowship, 1988.

MCMILLAN, WENDELL MARLIN, agricultural economist; b. Dallastown, Pa., June 14, 1923; s. John Walter and Alice Mary (McCormick) McM.; m. Eleanor Unser, July 14, 1946; children: Susan, Barbara, Douglas. Grad., York (Pa.) Jr. Coll., 1943; BS, Juniata Coll., 1948; MS, Pa. State U., 1950, PhD, 1954. Agrl. economist, asst. dir. U.S. Dept. Agriculture, Washington, 1955-64; project mgr., mktg. advisor Food and Agriculture Orgn. of UN, Jordan, Saudi Arabia and Afghanistan, 1964-72; agrl. economist The World Bank, Caribbean, Sudan, 1972-76; agrl. and policy economist U.S. Dept. Agr./USAID, Syria, Indonesia, Lesotho, Liberia, 1977-80; agrl. economist Africa Bur. USAID, Washington, 1980-89; mem. mktg. subcom. Nat. Commn. on Cooperative Devel., Washington, 1964; adj. prof. York (Pa.) Coll., 1990. Author tech./policy publs. on agr. Dist. chmn. Campfire Girls, No. Va., 1959-61; chmn. bd. dirs. Am. Cmty. Sch., Amman, Jordan, 1966-67, UN Staff Assn., Kabul, Afghanistan, 1969-70; bd. dirs. Hist. York, Inc., 1987—, pres., 1995—; mem. Hist. Soc. York County, 1987—, mem. libr. com., 1990—; trustee York County Acad., 1991—. Recipient Fulbright award U.S. Dept. State, Denmark, 1954-55, Merit certificates USDA, 1960, 84. Mem. Am. Agrl. Econs. Assn., Soc. for Internat. Devel., Alumni Assn. York Coll. (bd. dirs. 1986-91, Svc. award 1991, Disting. Alumnus 1982), Alumni Assn. Juniata Coll. (Nat. Alumni Achievement award 1984), Pi Gamma Mu. Democrat. Avocations: stamp collecting, nature study, opera. Home and Office: 101 E Springettsbury Ave York PA 17403-3126

MCMILLEN, ELIZABETH CASHIN, artist; b. Chgo.; d. James Blaine and Hortense (Fears) Cashin; m. John Stephen Jerabek; 1 child, Michael N. Student, Western Coll. for Women, 1961-63; BA, Bard Coll., 1965. coord. com. and juror Spectra I, sponsor state exhbn. women artists Westbrook Coll., Portland, Maine, 1979; dir. Hancock County Auditorium Art Gallery, Ellsworth, Maine, 1984, 85. rin. works include sculpture Ahimsa Gallery, Maine, 1976; exhibited at Frick Gallery, Belfast, Maine, 1993, 94, Maine Coast Artists Juried Show, Rockport, 1994, Portland Children's Mus., 1995, Lakes Gallery, Sebago, Maine, 1995—; one-person shows include Area Gallery, Portland, 1994, Frick Gallery, Belfast, Maine, 1995, Lakes Gallery, Sebago, Maine, 1997; two persons show Maine Coast Artists, Rockport, 1996. Dem. chair Town of Lamoine, Maine, 1984-85, 86-87, 88-89; legislative coord. Amnesty Internat., Ellsworth, 1991-97. Democrat. Episcopalian. Avocations: writing, politics, teaching, African-Am. history.

MCMILLEN, LOUIS ALBERT, architect; b. St. Louis, Oct. 24, 1916; s. Drury A. and Eleanor (Stockstrom) McM.; m. Persis White, Aug. 26, 1949 (dec. 1995); children: Michael Albert, Louis Stockstrom, Leander A.C.; m. Carole Godsborough, Dec. 4, 1996. Grad., St. George's Sch., Newport, R.I., 1935; B.F.A., Yale U., 1940; M.Arch., Harvard U., 1947. Vice pres., dir. Architects Collaborative Inc., Cambridge, Mass., 1947-70; pres. Architects Collaborative Inc., 1970-80; pres. Architects Collaborative Internat. Ltd., Vaduz, 1959—; Architect in residence Am. Acad. Rome, 1968, 69; Mem. planning bd., Concord, Mass., 1958-60. Prin. works include master planning air bases in U.S., ednl. facilities in, New Eng.; commd. to do: U. Bagdad, Iraq, 1959, U. Mosul, Iraq, 1965, W.Va. State Parks, Hawks Nest, Canaan Valley, Pipestem/Bluestone and Twin Falls; office bldg., Kuwait Fund for Arab Econ. Devel., 1968, total tourist facilities, Porto Carras, Sithonia, Greece, 1969. Served to lt. USNR, 1942-46. Fellow AIA; mem. Boston Soc. Architects, Soc. Fellows Am. Acad. in Rome, Zeta Psi. Clubs: Naval and Military (London); Old North Bridge Hounds (joint master retired); Somerset (Boston). Home: PO Box 490 Essex MA 01929-0009

MCMILLEN, ROBERT STEWART, lawyer; b. Yonkers, N.Y., Feb. 25, 1943; s. David Harry and Blodwyn Elizabeth (Evans) McM; m. Dorothea Anne Murray, July 2, 1966; children: Elissa London, Tara Evans. BS, U. Rochester, 1964; JD cum laude, Albany Law Sch. Union U., 1969. Bar: N.Y. 1969, U.S. Dist. Ct. (no. dist.) N.Y. 1969. Assoc. Clark, Bartlett & Caffry, Glens Falls, N.Y., 1969-73; ptnr. Caffry, Pontiff, Stewart, Rhodes & Judge, Glens Falls, 1974-80; prin. Bartlett, Pontiff, Stewart & Rhodes, P.C., Glens Falls, 1981—; sr. law examiner N.Y. State Bd. Law Examiners, Albany, 1986—; pres., bd. dirs. Community Title Agy., Inc., Glens Falls, 1984—. Editor-in-chief Albany Law Rev., 1968-69. Bd. dirs. Adirondack Regional C. of C., 1997—; bd. dirs., officer Voluntary Action Ctr. of Glens Falls Area, Inc., 1970-97; bd. dirs., treas. Arts and Crafts Ctr. of Warren County, Inc., Glens Falls, 1984-94; mem. Warren County Rep. Com., Queensbury, N.Y., 1979—; alt. or del. Rep. Jud. Nomination Com. 4th Jud. Dist. N.Y., 1977—. Recipient Disting. Svc. award Voluntary Action Ctr. of Glens Falls Area, Inc., 1990. Mem. ABA, N.Y. State Bar Assn. (mem. com. profl. ethics 1990—), Warren County Bar Assn. (bd. dirs. 1979-82). Avocations: family activities, downhill skiing, boating, hockey. Home: 27 Moorwood Dr Queensbury NY 12804-1010 Office: 1 Washington St Glens Falls NY 12801-2963

MC MILLEN, THOMAS ROBERTS, lawyer, arbitrator, mediator, retired judge; b. Decatur, Ill., June 8, 1916; s. Rolla C. and Ruth (Roberts) Mc M.; m. Anne Ford, Aug. 16, 1946; children: Margot F., Patricia R., Anne C. Scheyer. AB, Princeton U., 1938; LLB, Harvard U., 1941. Bar: Ill. 1941, U.S. Supreme Ct. 1948. Mem. firm Bell, Boyd, Lloyd, Haddad & Burns, Chgo., 1946-66; judge Cook County Cir. Ct., Cook County, Ill., 1966-71, U.S. Dist. Ct. (no. dist.) Ill., Chgo., 1971-85, ret.; pvt. practice Chgo., 1985—. Mem. arbitration panels Fed. Med. and Conciliation Svc., Chgo. Bd. Options Exch., Ill. State Bd. Edn., Judicate. Maj. CIC, AUS, 1941-45. Decorated Bronze Star medal, European Battle Stars (4), Croix de Guerre. Mem. Chgo. Bar Assn. (mem. bd. mgrs. 1964-66), 7th Cir. Bar Assn., Counter Intelligence Corps Assn., Chgo. Farmers (bd. dirs. 1989), Assn. Am. Rhodes Scholars, Indian Hill Country Club, Univ. Club Chgo., Phi Beta Kappa. Home and Office: 231 Forest St Winnetka IL 60093-3856

MCMILLER, ANITA WILLIAMS, army officer, transportation professional, educator; b. Chgo., Dec. 23, 1946; d. Chester Leon and Marion Claudette (Martin) Williams; m. Robert Melvin McMiller, July 29, 1967 (div. 1980). BS in Edn., No. Ill. U., 1968; MBA, Fla. Inst. Tech., 1979; M of Mil. Arts and Sci., U.S. Army Command & Gen. Staff Coll., 1990; postgrad., U.S. Army War Coll., Carlisle, Pa., 1993-94. Social worker Cook County, Chgo., 1968-69; recruiter analyst, dir. pers. State of Ill., Chgo., 1969-75; commd. 1st lt. U.S. Army, 1975, advanced through grades to col., 1996; platoon leader, motor officer, exec. officer 155th Transp. Co., Ft. Eustis, Va. and Okinawa, Japan, 1976-78; S-1 pers. and adminstrn. officer 38th Transp. Bn., Ft. Eustis, 1978-79; installation transp. officer, fin. mgr. 3d Armor Div., Hanau, Germany, 1979-82, transp. co. comdr., 1982-83; transp.

plans officer Mil. Traffic Mgmt. Command, Falls Church, Va., 1983-85; tour with Sea Land Corp., Menlo Park, N.J., 1985-86; dep. comdr., ops. officer Bremerhaven (Germany) Terminal, 1986-89; logistics staff officer The Pentagon, Washington, 1990-91; comdr. 1320th Port Battalion U.K. Terminal, Felixstowe, Great Britain, 1991-93; dep. legis. asst. to Chmn. Joint Chiefs of Staff, The Pentagon, Washington, 1994—; instr. Ctrl. Tex. Coll., Hanau, Germany, 1981-83, Phillips Bus. Coll., Alexandria, Va., 1983-84, City Colls. Chgo., 1987-89. Editor: Rocks, Inc. Pictoral Album, 1996, Alpha Kappa Alpha 75th Commemorative Album; contbr. articles to profl. jours. Child adv., foster mother Army Cmty. Svc., Hanau, 1980-83; tutor Parent-Tchr. Club Hanau Schs., 1981-83; vol. Vis. Nurses Assn. No. Va., 1983-85; coord., English tutor Adopt-a-Sch. Project, Washington, 1983-85; treas. Bremerhaven Girl Scouts Coun., 1987-89, mem. ARC, Big Sisters. Mem. Nat. Def. Transp. Assn., World Affairs Coun., Assn. U.S. Army, Fedn. Bus. Profl. Women, Rocks, Inc., Am. Legion, British Legion, Am. Hist. Assn., Internat. Platform Assn., Army Women's Profl. Assn., Army-Navy Club (Washington), Alpha Kappa Alpha. Avocations: skiing, golf, running, hist. rsch. Home: 1300 Army Navy Dr Arlington VA 22202 Office: Office of Chmn Joint Chiefs of Staff The Pentagon Washington DC 20318

MCMILLIAN, MARILYN LINDSEY, elementary educator, health, home economics; b. San Antonio, Feb. 23, 1952; d. Jesse Monroe Jr. and Louise (Ottenhouse) Lindsey; m. Joe Curtis McMillian, Dec. 16, 1978; children: Thomas Lindsey, Tyler Remington. BS in Edn. with Kindergarten Edn., Southwest Tex. State U., 1975. Kindergarten tchr. North Forrest Indep. Sch. Dist., Houston, 1976-78, Pearsall (Tex.) Indep. Sch. Dist., 1978-79, Dilley (Tex.) Indep. Sch. Dist., 1979—; mem. Greater Houston Area Reading Coun., Houston, 1977-78, Gifted and Talented Com., Dilley, 1988-92. Mem. Delta Kappa Gamma (vice pres. 1990-92). Methodist. Avocations: interior decorating, antique collecting, travel. Home and Office: PO Box 192 Dilley TX 78017-0192

MCMILLIAN, THEODORE, federal judge; b. St. Louis, Jan. 28, 1919; m. Minnie E. Foster, Dec. 8, 1941. BS, Lincoln U., 1941, HHD (hon.), 1981; LLD, St. Louis U., 1949; HHD (hon.), U. Mo., St. Louis, 1978. Mem. firm Lynch & McMillian, St. Louis, 1949-53; asst. circuit atty. City of St. Louis, 1953-56; judge U.S. Ct. Appeals (8th cir.), 1978—; judge Circuit Ct. for City St. Louis, 1956-72, Mo. Ct. Appeals eastern div., 1972-78; asso. prof. adminstrn. justice U. Mo., St. Louis, 1970—; asso. prof. Webster Coll. Grad. Program, 1977; mem. faculty Nat. Coll. Juvenile Justice, U. Nev., 1972—. Served to 1st lt. Signal Corps U.S. Army, 1942-46. Recipient Alumni Merit award St. Louis U., 1965, ACLU Civil Liberties award, 1995, Disting. Lawyer award Bar Assn. Met. St. Louis, 1996. Mem. Am. Judicature Soc., Am. Bd. Trial Advs. (hon. diplomate), Lawyers Assn. Mo., Mound City Bar Assn., Phi Beta Kappa, Alpha Sigma Nu. Office: US Ct Appeals 8th Circuit 526 US Ct & Custom House 1114 Market St Saint Louis MO 63101-2043

MCMILLIN, DAVID ROBERT, chemistry educator; b. East St. Louis, Ill., Jan. 1, 1948; s. Robert Cecil and Clara Rose (Thereon) McM.; m. Nicole Wilson, Nov. 3, 1974; children: Robert Stephen, Andrew Wilson. BA, Knox Coll., 1969; PhD, U. Ill., 1973. Postdoctoral fellow Calif. Inst. Tech., Pasadena, 1974; asst. prof. chemistry Purdue U., West Lafayette, Ind., 1975-80, assoc. prof., 1980-85, prof., 1985—. Contbr. articles to profl. jours. Recipient F.D. Martin Teaching award Purdue U., 1975. Mem. Am. Chem. Soc., Inter-Am. Photochem. Soc. (sec. 1986-90, v.p. 1994-96, pres. 1996—), Phi Beta Kappa, Sigma Xi. Presbyterian. Avocations: sports, reading. Office: Purdue U Dept Chemistry West Lafayette IN 47907-1393

MC MILLION, JOHN MACON, retired newspaper publisher; b. Coffeyville, Kans., Dec. 25, 1929; s. John Dibrell and Mattie Anna (Macon) McM.; m. Melanie Ann McMillion; children: John Thomas, Johanna, Jennifer, Amanda. Student, Vanderbilt U., 1947-49; B.S. in Journalism, U. Kans., 1956. Police reporter Amarillo (Tex.) Globe-News, 1956; sports editor, telegraph editor Grand Junction (Colo.) Daily Sentinel, 1956-58; mng. editor Alliance (Nebr.) Times-Herald, 1958-59, Clovis (N.Mex.) Jour., 1959-62; gen. mgr. Pasadena (Tex.) Citizen, 1962; bur. mgr. UPI, 1962-66; exec. editor Albuquerque Jour., 1966-69; bus. mgr. Albuquerque Pub. Co., 1971-75; pub. Herald and News-Tribune, Duluth, Minn., 1975-86, Akron (Ohio) Beacon Jour., 1986-90, ret.; campaign mgr. gubernatorial campaign, 1969-71. Served with USN, 1950-54. Address: 12404 Royal Oak Ct NE Albuquerque NM 87111-6237

MCMINDES, ROY JAMES, aggregate company executive; b. Essex, Md., July 12, 1923; s. Roy Preston and Edith S. (Sh) McM.; m. Prudence Atsinger, June 8, 1946; children: Gail Karen, Joan Susan, James Lee. B.S., U. Md., 1948. Pres., Sheridan Corp., Lebanon, Pa., 1951—, Grays Ferry Brick Co., Lebanon, 1971—; pres., Waylite Co., Lebanon, 1976-88; pres. Sheridan Co., Lebanon, PA; chmn. bd. Peoples Nat. Bank, Lebanon, 1984-92, dir., 1965-92. Bd. dirs. Lebanon YMCA, 1968-86, Good Samaritan Hosp., Lebanon, 1970-93. With A.C., USN, 1943-46, mem. USNR, 1946-52. Recipient Founders Day award Lebanon Valley Coll., 1987. Mem. Lebanon Valley C. of C. (pres. 1973), Lebanon Country Club, Shriners, Jesters. Republican. Presbyterian. Office: 1212 W Maple St Lebanon PA 17046-2701

MCMINN, VIRGINIA ANN, human resources consulting company executive; b. Champaign, Ill., Apr. 7, 1948; d. Richard Henry and Esther Lucille (Ellis) Taylor; m. Michael Lee McMinn, Dec. 29, 1973. BA in Teaching of English, U. Ill., 1969; MS in Indsl. Rels., Loyola U., Chgo., 1985. Pers. sec. Solo Cup Co., Urbana, Ill., 1972-74; pers. asst. Rust-Oleum Corp., Evanston, Ill., 1974-75, asst. pers. mgr., 1974-80; mgr. employee rels. Rust-Oleum Corp., Vernon Hills, Ill., 1980-81, mgr. human resources, 1981-84; dir. human resources Field Container Corp., Elk Grove Village, Ill., 1984-87; regional mgr. human resources Hartford Ins. Corp., Chgo., 1987-90; owner, pres. McMinn & Assocs., Ltd., Palatine, Ill., 1988—; founder S.W. Human Resources Group, Chandler, Ariz., 1995; instr. bus. and mgmt. divsn. Trinity Coll., Deerfield, Ill., 1984-85; instr. bus. and social scis. Harper Coll., Palatine, Ill., 1990-93; bd. dirs. Nierman's Hard-To-Find Sizes Shoes, Chgo.; spkr. on legal issues, terminations, employment at will, career planning, job search, and human resources function to area colls., industry and profl. and women's groups. Bd. dirs. Ill. Crossroads coun. Girls Scouts USA, Elk Grove, 1988-92; mem. Ill. Com. to Implement Clean Indoor Air Act, Chgo., 1990-91; past mem. adv. bd. Coll. of Lake County, 1982-84. Mem. Soc. for Human Resource Mgmt., Nat. Network Sales Profls. (program chmn. 1990-93), Women in Mgmt. (chpt. Leadership award corp. category, past pres.), Palatine C. of C., Rotary Club Palatine. Avocations: reading, golf, crafts. Office: 1423 Michele Dr Palatine IL 60067-5656 Office: 1423 E Michelle Dr Palatine IL 60067-5656

MCMORRIS, JERRY, transportation company executive. CEO NW Transport Svc, Denver. Office: NW Transport Svc 717 17th St Ste 500 Denver CO 80202-3304*

MCMORROW, EILEEN, editor periodical. Editor Facilities Design & Mgmt., N.Y.C. Office: Facilities Design & Mgmt 1 Pennsylvania Plz 10th Fl New York NY 10119-1198

MCMORROW, MARY ANN G., judge; b. Chgo., Jan. 16, 1930; m. Emmett J. McMorrow, May 5, 1962; 1 dau., Mary Ann. Student Rosary Coll., 1948-50; J.D., Loyola U., 1953. Bar: Ill. 1953, U.S. Dist. Ct. (no. dist.) Ill. 1960, U.S. Supreme Ct. 1976. Atty. Riordan & Linklater Law Offices, Chgo., 1954-56; asst. state's atty. Cook County, Chgo., 1956-63; sole practice, Chgo., 1963-76; judge of Cir. Ct. Cook County, 1976-85, Ill. Appellate Ct., 1985-92, Supreme Ct. Ill., 1992—. Contbr. articles to profl. jours. Faculty adv. Nat. Jud. Coll., U. Nev., 1984. Mem. Chgo. Bar Assn., Ill. State Bar Assn., Women's Bar Assn. of Ill. (pres. 1975-76, bd. dirs. 1970-78), Am. Judicature Soc., Northwestern U. Assocs., Ill. Judges Assn., Nat. Assn. Women Judges, Advocates Soc., Cath. Lawyers Guild (bd. dirs. 1980—), Northwest Suburban Bar Assn., West Suburban Bar Assn., Loyola Law Alumni Assn. (bd. govs. 1985—), Ill. Judges Assn. (bd. dirs.), Cath. Lawyers Guild (v.p.), The Law Club of the City of Chgo., Inns of Ct. Office: Supreme Ct of Ill 160 N La Salle St Chicago IL 60601-3103

MCMULKIN, FRANCIS JOHN, steel company executive; b. Sault Ste. Marie, Ont., Can., Dec. 7, 1915; s. George Alexander and Leanor Augusta (Zryd) McM.; m. Margaret Lilian Winch, Sept. 21, 1946; children: John Bruce, Mary Diane. B.S. in Metallurgy, Mich. Coll. Mining and Tech., 1937; M.E., Mich. Tech. U., 1945, D.Engring. (hon.), 1972. Formerly metallurgist Algoma Steel Corp., Sault Ste. Marie; then research fellow Ont. Research Found., Mississauga, 1942-47; research and devel. engr. Dominion Foundries & Steel Ltd., Hamilton, Ont., Can., from 1947; then dir. research Dominion Foundries & Steel Ltd., until 1964, v.p. research, 1964-85. Contbr. articles to profl. publs. Recipient Disting. Alumnus award Mich. Tech. U., 1976. Fellow Am. Soc. Metals (life mem., William Hunt Eisenman award 1968), Engring. Inst. Can. (life mem., John Galbraith prize 1945, elected fellow 1981); mem. Can. Inst. Mining and Metallurgy (H.T. Airey Meml. Ann. Conf. lectr. award), AIME (Basic Oxygen Steel award 1963; charter disting. mem. Iron and Steel Soc. 1976, Metall. Soc. Howe meml. lectr. 1973), Acad. Metall. & Materials Engring. (charter), Iron and Steel Inst. (U.K.), Royal Over-Seas League (London), Hamilton Club, Hamilton Golf and Country Club, Mid Ocean Club (Bermuda). Mem. United Ch. of Canada. Home: 270 Roseland Crescent, Burlington, ON Canada L7N 1S3

MC MULLAN, DOROTHY, nurse educator; b. Bloomfield, N.J., June 19, 1911; d. Samuel H. and Anne (Gardiner) McM.; m. Bernard J. Pisani, July 10, 1982. Diploma, Cornell U.-N.Y. Hosp. Sch. Nursing, 1935; B.S., N.Y. U., 1948, M.A., 1950, Ed.D., 1962. Pub. health nurse Henry St. Vis. Nurse Service, N.Y.C., 1935-39; pvt. duty nurse N.Y.C., 1939-41; instr. N.Y. Hosp.-Cornell U. Sch. Nursing, 1947-55; supr. N.Y. Hosp.-Cornell Med. Center, 1947-50, asst. dept. head, 1950-53, adminstrv. asst. nursing services for methods improvements, 1953-55; instr. N.Y. Hosp.-Cornell Med. Center (Sch. Nursing); dir., prof. nursing Russell Sage Coll., 1955-61; dean, prof. Ind. State U. Sch. Nursing, Terre Haute, 1962-71; dir. div. nursing Nat. League for Nursing, N.Y.C., 1971-77; chmn. dept. baccalaureate and higher edn. N.Y. League, 1960-62; mem. Nat. Commn. on Allied Health Edn., 1977-80; cons. on nurse edn., 1977-80; cons. Council on Postsecondary Accreditation, 1977-78; v.p. N.Y. Nurses Assn., 1960-61; pres. Vigo County Coordinating Council, 1966-69; mem. adv. bd. Ind. Regional Med. Planning, 1966-71; sec. exec. com. Ind. Comprehensive Health Council, 1967-71; mem. adv. com. on women in services U.S. Dept. Def., 1971-73; mem. nursing adv. com. Am. Cancer Soc., 1975-77; mem. com. on health manpower Nat. Health Council, 1975-79. Author: (with Hayt, Groeschel) Law of Hospital and Nurse, 1958, The Role of the Nurse as Employee: A Case of Mutual Responsibilities, 1976, Preparation of the Nurse Specialist, 1977. Bd. dirs. Vigo County cancer Soc., Vigo County cerebral Palsy Assn., Goodwill Industries Terre Haute, Cmty. Found. Wabash Valley, 1964-71; mem. Heritage Found.; mem. coun. Citizens Against Govt. Waste. Recipient Ann. award of Vigo County Ind. Bus. and Profl. Women's Orgn., 1967, Army Nurse Corps Spl. award, 1973, Dept. of Def. cert., NYU Founders Day cert., 1963, Pres.'s award Ind. State U., 1988, Disting. Alumnus award Cornell U./N.Y. Hosp. Sch. Nursing Alumni Assn., 1990; recognized for disting. and devoted svc. as pres. Ind. League for Nursing, 1966-71; named in People of Progress in Terre Haute, 1967. Mem. APHA, Cornell U.-N.Y. Hosp. Sch. Nursing Alumnae Assn. (pres. 1950-52), Ind. League for Nursing (pres. 1966-71), So. N.Y. League for Nursing (pres. 1980-82, exec. sec. 1982-88, award 1987, Dorothy McMullan Pisani ann. award 1987), League Nursing (mem. exec. com., chmn. Gt. Lakes Regional Assembly 1969-71), Nat. League Nursing (bd. dirs. 1981-83), Assn. Higher Edn., Inst. Biomed. Edn. (bd. dirs. 1984-89), Am. Assn. for World Health (exec. com. 1980-90, exec. 1984-89), N.Y. County Med. Soc. Auxiliary (v.p. 1984-90), Kappa Delta Pi. Republican. Episcopalian. Home: 209 Sunset Ave Englewood NJ 07631-4413 *The important ingredients to success include self reliance, identifying goals and how to reach them through perseverance, willingness t work hard and to enjoy every step of the way.*

MCMULLAN, WILLIAM PATRICK, III, investment banker; b. Newton, Miss., Dec. 29, 1952; s. William Patrick Jr. and Rosemary (Lyons) McM.; m. Rachel Smiley McPherson, Oct. 16, 1982. BA, Vanderbilt U., 1974; MBA, U. Pa., 1976. V.p. Lehman Bros. Kuhn Loeb, N.Y.C., 1976-82; assoc. dir. Prudential-Bache Securities, N.Y.C., 1982-85; mng. dir. Donaldson, Lufkin & Jenrette Securities Corp., N.Y.C., 1985—. Bd. dirs. Lar Lubovitch Dance Co. Mem. Met. Club, Mashomack Fish and Game Club. Home: 607 6th St Brooklyn NY 11215-3701 Office: Donaldson Lufkin & Jenrette Securities Corp 277 Park Ave New York NY 10072

MCMULLEN, DAVID WAYNE, education educator; b. Canton, Ill., Apr. 6, 1957; s. Earl Eugene and Juanita Elaine (Estep) McM.; m. Faye Anne Whitaker, Mar. 28, 1981; 1 child, James Earl. BS, Bradley U., 1980, MS, 1984; PhD, U. Ill., 1989. Cert. sec. tchr., Ill. Tchr. 7th and 8th grade sci. Bartonville (Ill.) Grade Sch., 1980-83; grad. asst./instr. U. Ill., Urbana, 1985-89; instr. Bradley U., Peoria, Ill., 1987-89, assoc. prof. tchr. edn., 1989-95; dir. Ctr. Rsch. and Svc. Coll. Edn. and Health Scis. Bradley U., Peoria, 1995—; instr. gifted program Bradley U. Inst. for Gifted and Talented Youth, Peoria, summers 1984, 85, 88—; computer cons. MicroComputer Cons., Morton, Ill., 1984-85; instr. Computer Terminal, Peoria, 1984; system operator Free Ednl. Electronic Mail, Peoria, 1991—. Author computer software: Science Fair Success, 1984. Sec. bd. Common Place, Peoria, 1992. Mem. ASCD, Assn. Computing Machinery, Assn. Advancement Computing Edn., Internat. Soc. for Tech. in Edn., Phi Delta Kappa, Phi Kappa Phi, Phi Alpha Theta. Mem. Christian Ch. (Disciples of Christ). Avocations: computers, golf, woodworking. Office: Bradley Univ 208 Westlake Hall Peoria IL 61625

MC MULLEN, EDWIN WALLACE, JR., English language educator; b. Quincy, Fla., Dec. 8, 1915; s. Edwin Wallace and Sara Della (Moore) McM.; m. Marian Elizabeth Hoper, June 9, 1946; children: William Wallace, Charles Edwin. B.A., U. Fla., 1936; M.A., Columbia U., 1939, Ph.D., 1950. Instr. English Pa. State U., 1946-48, State U. Iowa, 1950-52; spl. instr. in report writing U.S. Dept. Def., Washington, 1953; sr. reporter U.S. Dept. Def., 1952-57; asst. editor Merriam Webster Dictionary Co., 1957; asst. prof. English Lehigh U., 1957-61, Fairleigh Dickinson U., Madison, N.J., 1961-62; assoc. prof. Fairleigh Dickinson U., 1962-72, prof., 1973-82, chmn. dept. lang. and lit., 1962-65, emeritus, 1982; founder, dir. Names Inst., 1962-86; chmn. publs. subcom. Morris County Tercentenary Com., N.J., 1962-63. Author: English Topographic Terms in Florida, 1563-1874, 1953; contbr. articles to profl. publs.; editor: Names, 1962-65; editor, contbr.: Pubs, Place-Names and Patronymics: Selected Papers of the Names Institute, 1980; editor, contbr. Names New and Old: Papers of the Names Inst., 1993. Served with Signal Corps, U.S. Army, 1942-46. Mem. MLA, Am. Name Soc. (pres. 1976), Internat. Congress on Onomastic Scis., Internat. Linguistic Assn., Am. Dialect Soc., English Place-Name Soc., Morris County Hist. Soc., Old Guard of Summit (N.J.), Nat. Coun. Tchrs. English, Meth. Friendship Club (past co-pres.). Democrat. Methodist. Home: 15 Rosewood Dr Madison NJ 07940-1120 Office: Fairleigh Dickinson U Dept English Madison NJ 07940 *Chaucer sums up my philosophy in his description of the Clerk: "And gladly wolde he lerne and gladly teche".*

MCMULLEN, JOHN J., professional hockey team executive; m. Jacqueline McMullen; children: Peter, Catharine, John Jr. BSEE, U.S. Naval Acad., 1940; DMechE, Swiss Fed. Tech. Inst.; M in Naval Architecture and Marine Engring., MIT. Commd. ensign USN, 1940, advanced through grades to comdr., resigned, 1954; chief ship constrn. and repair U.S. Maritime Adminstrn. Office, Washington, 1954-57; chmn. John J. McMullen Assocs., Inc., 1957—; ltd. ptnr. N.Y. Yankees Baseball Team, 1974; chmn. Houston Astros Baseball Team, 1979-92, N.J. Devils Hockey Team, East Rutherford, N.J., 1981—. Office: NJ Devils PO Box 504 East Rutherford NJ 07073-0504*

MC MULLEN, THOMAS HENRY, retired air force officer; b. Dayton, Ohio, July 4, 1929; s. Clements and Adelaide Palmer (Lewis) McM.; m. Clara Faye Kirkwood, Mar. 28, 1956; children—Susan Marie, Thomas Clements, John Kirkwood. Student, St. Mary's U. Tex., 1945-47; B.S. in Mil. Engring, U.S. Mil. Acad., 1951; M.S. in Astronautics, Air Force Inst. Tech., 1964; M.S. in Adminstrn, George Washington U., 1971; student, Indsl. Coll. Armed Forces, Ft. McNair, Washington, 1970-71. Commd. 2d lt. U.S. Air Force, 1951, advanced through grades to lt. gen., 1980; flight trainee Hondo AB, Tex., Bryan AFB, Tex. and Nellis AFB, Nev., 1951-52; fighter pilot/flight comdr. (K-13 AB), Suwon, Korea, 1952-53; flight test maintenance officer Kelly AFB, Tex., 1953-59; Air Force flight acceptance test pilot at (Gen. Dynamics Inc.), Ft. Worth, 1959-62; project officer, Gemini Launch Vehicle Program, officer (Space Systems Div.), Los Angeles, 1964-66; air liaison officer 25th Inf. Div. Cu Chi, South Vietnam, 1967-68; asst. mission dir. Apollo Program Hdqrs. NASA Washington, 1968-70; B-1 dep. system program dir. Wright Patterson AFB, Ohio, 1971-73; A-10 System program dir., 1973-74; vice comdr. Tactical Air Warfare Center Eglin AFB, Fla., 1974-75; comdr. (Tactical Air Warfare Center), 1975-76; dep. chief of staff/requirements Hdqrs. Tactical Air Command Langley AFB, Va., 1976-79; dep. chief of staff/systems Hdqrs. Air Force Systems Command Andrews AFB, Md., 1979-80; vice comdr. Tactical Air Command, 1980-82; comdr. Aero. Systems Div. Wright-Patterson AFB, Ohio, 1982-86; ret. USAF, 1986; cons. in aerospace Washington, 1986—. Decorated D.S.M. with two oak leaf clusters, Silver Star, Legion of Merit, D.F.C. with oak leaf cluster, Bronze Star, Meritorious Service medal with oak leaf cluster, Air Force Commendation medal with oak leaf cluster, Air medal with 18 oak leaf clusters, Purple Heart; Cross of Gallantry with palm Vietnam; recipient Exceptional Service medal NASA, 1969, Group Achievement award, 1969, 71. Fellow AIAA (asso.); mem. Air Force Assn., Order Daedalians, Tau Beta Pi. Presbyterian. Home and Office: 6301 Chaucer View Cir Alexandria VA 22304-3548 *The key to success is a combination of fortunate circumstance, hard work, and a willingness to accept responsibility. Few people get ahead without some combination of all three.*

MC MULLIAN, AMOS RYALS, food company executive; b. Jackson County, Fla., Aug. 28, 1937; s. Andrew Jackson and Willie Ross (Ryals) McM.; m. Jackie Williams, Aug. 27, 1960; children: Amos Ryals, Britton Jackelyn. BS, Fla. State U., 1962. Successively asst. controller, data processing coordinator, adminstrv. asst. to gen. mgr., asst. plant mgr., plant mgr. Flowers Baking Co., Thomasville, Ga., 1963-70, pres. Atlanta Baking Co. div., 1970-72, regional v.p. parent co., 1972-74, pres., chief operating officer bakery div., 1974-76, chief operating officer industry, 1976-81, pres., 1976-83, dir., 1981—, chief exec. officer, 1983—, co-chmn. exec. com., 1983—, vice chmn. industry and chmn. exec. com., 1984-85, chmn. bd., CEO, 1985—; bd. dirs. Ga. Rsch. Reliance. Mem. adv. bd. President's Club, Fla. State U.; trustee Southeastern Legal Found.; vestryman, sr. warden Episcopal Ch.; bd. govs. Ga. Pub. Policy Found. With USMC, 1958-61. Named Outstanding Bus. Alumnus, Fla. State U. Mem. NAM (bd. dirs.), Thomasville Landmarks Soc., Atlanta Bakers Club (past pres.), Atlanta Commerce Club, Gridiron Soc. (U. Ga.). Office: Flowers Industries Inc PO Box 1338 Thomasville GA 31799

MCMULLIN, CARLETON EUGENE, automotive business executive; b. Hutchinson, Kans., Feb. 17, 1932; s. Cloys E. and Beatrice (Jennings) McM.; m. Beth Becker; children: Lucinda Lou, Charis Ann. B.A., U. Okla., 1954; M.P.A., U. Kans., 1958. Asst. city mgr. City of Corpus Christi, Tex., 1957-58; city mgr. City of McAlester, Okla., 1958-62, City of Oak Ridge, Tenn., 1962-73, City of Little Rock, 1973-80; pres. NPT, Inc., 1994, PET, Inc., 1997; chmn. Keystone Enterprises Inc., Cemac Corp., Exceltune Corp.; v.p., treas. Devonian Corp.; sec. Precision Tune Franchise Adv. Coun., 1979-80; chmn. Assn. Precision Tune Area Sub-Franchisors, 1979-80, sec., 1991; mem. intergovtl. sci. engring. tech. adv. panel U.S. Office Sci. and Tech. Policy, 1977-79; mem. NSF Adv. Coun., 1977-79; chmn. Urban Tech. Sys. Adv. Bd., 1979; cons. in field. Commr. Little Rock Housing Authority, 1987-92. Served with Signal Corps U.S. Army, 1954-56. Mem. Internat. City Mgmt. Assn., Rotary. Episcopalian. Home: 12821 Ridgehaven Rd Little Rock AR 72211-2207

MC MULLIN, ERNAN VINCENT, philosophy educator; b. Donegal, Ireland, Oct. 13, 1924; came to U.S., 1954; s. Vincent Paul and Carmel (Farrell) McM. BSc, Maynooth (Ireland) Coll., 1945, BD, 1948; postgrad. theoretical physics, Dublin Inst. Advanced Studies, 1949-50; BPh, U. Louvain, Belgium, 1951, LPh, 1953, PhD, 1954; DLitt (hon.), Loyola U., Chgo., 1969, Nat. U. Ireland, 1990; PhD (hon.), Maynooth Coll., Ireland, 1995. Ordained priest Roman Catholic Ch., 1949; faculty U. Notre Dame, 1954-57, 59—, assoc. prof. philosophy, 1964, prof. philosophy, 1966-94, prof. emeritus, 1994—, chmn. dept., 1965-72, O'Hara prof. philosophy, 1984-94; postdoctoral fellow Yale U., 1957-59; vis. prof. U. Minn., 1964-65, U. Cape Town, summers 1972-73, UCLA, 1977, Princeton U., 1991, Yale U., 1992; Cardinal Mercier lectr. U. Louvain, Belgium, 1995, U. Oslo, 1997; mem. exec. bd. Coun. Philos. Studies, 1970-75; chmn. philosophy of sci. div. Internat. Congress Philosophy, 1968, 73; chmn. U.S. Nat. Com. for History and Philosophy of Sci., 1982-84, 86-87. Author: Newton on Matter and Activity, 1978, The Inference That Makes Science, 1992; editor: The Concept of Matter, 1963, Galileo, Man of Science, 1967, The Concept of Matter in Modern Philosophy, 1978, Death and Decision, 1978, Issues in Computer Diagnosis, 1983, Evolution and Creation, 1985, Construction and Constraint: The Shaping of Scientific Rationality; co-editor: (with J.T. Cushing) The Philosophical Consequences of Quantum Theory, 1989, The Social Dimensions of Science, 1992; cons. editor Jour. Medicine and Philosophy, 1977-93, Studies History and Philosophy of Science, 1970-75, 1983—, Brit. Jour. Philos. Sci., 1988—, Perspectives on Science, 1992—. Romanell-Phi Beta Kappa Prof. of Philosophy, 1993-94; NSF rsch. grantee Yale U., 1957-59, Cambridge U., 1968-69; vis. rsch. fellow Cambridge U., 1973-74, 83, 87, U. Pitts., 1979. Fellow AAAS (chmn. sect. L 1977-78), Am. Acad. Arts and Scis., Internat. Acad. History Sci.; mem. Am. Cath. Philos. Assn. (pres. 1966-67, Aquinas medal 1981), Philosophy of Sci. Assn. (governing bd. 1969-73, pres. 1980-82), Metaphys. Assn. Am. (exec. coun. 1968-72, pres. 1973-74, Founder's medal 1997), Am. Philos. Assn. (exec. coun. 1977-81, pres. western divsn. 1983-84), History of Sci. Soc. (exec. coun. 1988-92), Sigma Xi. Address: PO Box 1066 Notre Dame IN 46556-1066

MCMULLIN, KIMBALL RAY, lawyer; b. Boston, Oct. 18, 1945; s. Kimball A. and Anne McM.; m. Lisa M. McMullin, Sept. 19, 1970; children: Birch, Katherine, Christopher, Anne, Alexander. BA, Amherst (Mass.) Coll., 1967; JD, U. Maine, 1974; LLM in Taxation, Boston U., 1978. Bar: Maine 1974, Mass. 1974, U.S. Dist. Ct. Maine 1974, U.S. Dist. Ct. Mass. 1974, U.S. Ct. Claims 1975, U.S. Tax Ct. 1975, Mo. 1981, U.S. Dist. Ct. (ea. dist.) Mo. 1981. Law clk. to judge Randolph Weatherbee, Bangor, Maine, 1974-75; tax assoc. Coopers & Lybrand, Boston, 1975-78; assoc. Burt & Taylor, Marblehead, Mass., 1978-81; from assoc. to ptnr. Lewis, Rice & Fingersh, St. Louis, 1981—. Mem. devel. bd. St. Louis Children's Hosp., 1984-90; bd. dirs. Mary Inst., St. Louis, 1985-86, Camp O-At-Ka, Inc., 1985—, Forest Park Forever, Inc., St. Louis, 1986-88, St. Louis Youth and Family Ctr., 1984—. Mem. ABA, Ill. Bar Assn., Nat. Assn. Health Lawyers, Mo. Health Lawyers Assn., St. Louis Health Lawyers Assn., Healthcare Fin. Mgmt. Assn. Office: Lewis Rice & Fingersh 500 N Broadway Ste 2000 Saint Louis MO 63102-2130

MCMULLIN, RUTH RONEY, publishing company executive, management fellow; b. N.Y.C., Feb. 9, 1942; d. Richard Thomas and Virginia (Goodwin) Roney; m. Thomas Ryan McMullin, Apr. 27, 1968; 1 child, David Patrick. BA, Conn. Coll., 1963; M Pub. and Pvt. Mgmt., Yale U., 1979. Market rschr. Aviation Week Mag., McGraw-Hill Co., N.Y.C., 1962-64; assoc. editor, bus. mgr. Doubleday & Co., N.Y.C., 1964-66; mgr. Natural History Press, 1967-70; v.p., treas. Weston (Conn.) Woods, Inc., 1970-71; staff assoc. GE, Fairfield, Conn., 1979-82; mng. fin. analyst GECC Transp., Stamford, Conn., 1982-84; credit analyst corp. fin. dept. GECC, Stamford, Conn., 1984-85; sr. v.p. GECC Capital Markets Group, Inc., N.Y.C., 1985-87; exec. v.p., COO John Wiley & Sons, N.Y.C., 1987-89, pres., CEO, 1989-90; pres., CEO Harvard Bus. Sch. Pub. Corp., Boston, 1991-94; mem. chmn.'s com., acting CEO UNR Industries Inc., Chgo., 1991-92, also bd. dirs.; mgmt. fellow, vis. prof. Sch. Mgmt. Yale U., New Haven, 1994-95; chairperson trustees, exec. dir. Eagle-Picher Personal Injury Settlement Trust, 1996—; chairperson of trustees Eagle-Pitcher Industries, 1996—; bd. dirs. Bausch & Lomb, Rochester, N.Y., UNR Industries Inc., Chgo., Middlesex (Conn.) Mut. Assurance, Fleet Financial, Secure Techs., Inc.; vis. prof. Sch. Mgmt., Yale U., New Haven, 1994-95; chair bd. trustees Eagle Picher Personal Injury Settlement Trust, 1996—. Mem. dean's adv. bd. Sch. Mgmt. Yale U., 1985-96; bd. dirs. Yale U. Alumni fund, 1986-92, Yale U. Press, Math. Scis. Edn. Bd., 1990-93. Mem. N.Y. Yacht Club, Stamford Yacht Club. Avocations: sailing, skiing. Home: 274 Beacon St Boston MA 02116-1230

MCMURPHY, MICHAEL ALLEN, energy company executive, lawyer; b. Dothan, Ala., Oct. 1, 1947; s. Allen L. and Mary Emily (Jacobs) McM.; m. Maureen Daly, Aug. 8, 1970; children: Matthew, Kevin, Patrick. BS, USAF Acad., 1969; MA, St. Mary's U., San Antonio, 1972; JD, U. Tex., 1975. Bar: Tex. 1975, U.S. Supreme Ct. 1977, U.S. Ct. Appeals (fed. cir.), D.C. 1978.

Commd. 2d lt. USAF, 1969, advanced through grades to capt.; instr. Air U., Ala., 1975-79; resigned USAF, 1979; atty., advisor Oak Ridge (Tenn.) ops. U.S. Dept. Energy, 1979-83; gen. counsel COGEMA, Inc., Washington, 1983-87, v.p., 1987-88; pres., chief exec. officer COGEMA, Inc., Bethesda, Md., 1988—; pres., CEO Va. Fuels, Inc., Lynchburg, 1987-92; bd. dirs. Nuclear Energy Inst., Washington, U.G./USA, Atlanta, Transnuclear, Inc., Hawthorne, N.Y., Cogema Resources, Inc, Casper, Wyo., SGN-Eurisys Svcs. Co., Richland, Wash.; chmn. Numatec Inc., Bethesda, 1989—; pres. Uranium Producers Am., 1991-92. Mem. editorial bd. Air Force Law Rev., 1977-79. Decorated chevalier Nat. Order of Merit (France). Mem. ABA, Fed. Bar Assn. (pres. E. Tenn. chpt. 1982-83). Avocation: skiing. Office: COGEMA Inc 7401 Wisconsin Ave Bethesda MD 20814-3407

MCMURRAY, CAROL DOLBER, human services administrator; b. Marilla, N.Y., July 31, 1948; d. Clinton Charles and Frances Ann (Gilmore) Dolber; m. James Michael McMurray, Oct. 21, 1972; children: Christian, Stefan. BA, SUNY, Binghamton, 1970; MSW, Va. Commonwealth U., 1977. Caseworker Warren County Children Svcs., Lake George, N.Y., 1973-75; social worker Chesterfield (Va.) County Mental Health/MR Svcs., 1977-79; dir. Vol. Emergency Foster Care of Va., 1979-80; regional tng. coord. Va. Bapt. Children's Home and Family Svcs., 1980-82; Va. area program coord. Welcome House Adoption Svcs., Inc., Richmond, Va., 1982-90; child and family trainer, cons., 1988—; adj. faculty Divsn. of Continuing Edn., U. Va., 1992—; trainer Prevent Child Abuse, Va.; pres. Va. Assn. Lic. Child Placing Agys., 1988-90, v.p., 1986-88; mem. trainer Conflict Resolution Team Tng., Richmond Peace Edn. Ctr., Va. Contbr. articles to profl. jours. and mags. Organizer, past pres. Richmond Domestic Violence Project, Richmond, Va., 1977-79; chairperson Bd. of Child Care Ctr., Richmond, 1985-88, Job Study Review Com. of Chs. Profl. Ministerial Staff, Richmond, 1989-90. Mem. Acad. Cert. Social Workers, Nat. Assn. Social Workers, Adoption Devel. Outreach Planning Team, Adoption Therapy Coalition. Avocations: singing, live theatre, craft shows, traveling, gardening. Home and Office: 1915 Floyd Ave Richmond VA 23220-4515

MCMURRAY, JOSEPH PATRICK BRENDAN, financial consultant; b. Bronx, N.Y., Mar. 1912; s. Bartholemew A. and Katherine A. (O'Connell) McM.; m. Isabelle C. Kenny, Nov. 21, 1940 (dec. 1960); children: Gerald, Joseph Patrick Brendan, Kathleen (Mrs. Jeffrey Nelson), Isabelle (Mrs. George M. Pullis), Kevin, Brien; m. Rose-Marie Mooney Barker, Aug. 26, 1961 (dec. 1996); stepchildren: Walter Barker, Diane (Mrs. Patrick Crehan), Robert Barker (dec.). A.B., Bklyn. Coll., 1936; postgrad., New Sch. Social Research, 1937-40; LL.D., Iona Coll., 1959, Holy Cross Coll., 1962, Loyola U., 1969; Litt.D., U. Tampa, 1961; L.H.D., Am. Internat. Coll., 1964. Dir. U.S. Senate Edn. Labor Com., 1944-47; adminstvr. asst. Senator Wagner, 1947-48; cons. staff dir. banking and currency com. U.S. Senate, 1948-54; exec. dir. N.Y.C. Housing Authority, 1954; commr. housing N.Y. State, 1955-59; founding pres. Queensborough Community Coll., Bayside, N.Y., 1959-61; chmn. bd. FHLB, 1961-65; pres. Queens Coll., Flushing, N.Y., 1965-71, Coll. New Rochelle, N.Y., 1971-73; spl. asst. to speaker U.S. Ho. of Reps., Washington, 1974-76; cons. 1st Pennco Securities Inc., N.Y.C., 1977-80, Ameribond Securities Assocs., N.Y.C., 1980-83; adj. prof. L.I. U., 1957-58; trustee Bowery Savs. Bank, 1966-85. Author: Ways and Means of Providing Housing for Families Unable to Afford Rentals or Mortgage Payments Necessary to Adequate Private Housing, 1960; contbr. numerous studies and surveys of housing throughout the world, articles in sociology, econs., bus. jours. Mem. Mayor's Rent Guidelines Bd., N.Y.C., 1969-75; chmn. Pres.-Elect Kennedy Task Force on Housing and Urban Devel., 1960; cons. to Gov. Mario Cuomo Enriched Housing and Care for Elderly, N.Y., 1994. Decorated Knight of Holy Sepulchre N.Y. Roman Cath. Archdiocese; decorated knight officer Order of Merit Italian Republic; recipient award of merit Bklyn. Coll., 1952, Alumnus of Yr., 1959, Presdl. medal 50th Ann. Commencement, 1986, Lifetime Achievment award, 1996. Mem. Am. Econs. Assn., Nat. Housing Ofcls. Assn., Internat. Catholic Peace Assn., Nat. Council Catholic Men, Am. Acad. of Sr. Profls. at Eckerd Coll., Phi Beta Kappa, Pi Gamma Mu, Kappa Delta Pi, Alpha Phi Omega. Roman Catholic. Clubs: Lotus (N.Y.C.), University (N.Y.C.); Congl. County (Md.). Lodge: KC. Home: College Harbor 4650 54th Ave S Saint Petersburg FL 33711-4665

MCMURRY, IDANELLE SAM, educational consultant; b. Morganfield, Ky., Dec. 6, 1924; d. Sam Anderson and Aurelia Marie (Robertson) McM. B.A., Vanderbilt U., 1945, M.A., 1946. Tchr. English Abbot Acad., Andover, Mass., 1946-50, Hockaday Sch., Dallas, 1951-54, San Jacinto High Sch., Houston, 1954-55; dean of girls Kinkaid Sch., Houston, 1955-63; headmistress Harpeth Hall Sch., Nashville, 1963-79, Hockaday Sch., Dallas, 1979-89, ret.; now pvt. sch. cons. The Edn. Group, Dallas; Bd. dirs. Ednl. Records Bur., 1979-85, trustee, 1980-85. Bd. dirs. Tex. council Girl Scouts U.S., 1980-82, Town North YMCA; trustee Winston Sch., 1979-85, Spl. Care Sch., 1979-81, Asheville Sch., Manzano Day Sch. Mem. Nat. Study Sch. Evaluation (bd. dirs. 1979-83), Headmasters Assn., Nat. Assn. Ind. Schs. (bd. dirs. 1974-84, acad. com. 1974-79, sec. 1978-80, chmn. 1980-84), So. Assn. Ind. Schs. (pres. 1974-75), Tenn. Assn. Ind. Schs. (pres. 1967-68), Mid-South Assn. Ind. Schs. (pres. 1972-73), Ind. Schs. Assn. S.W. (v.p. 1967—), Nat. Assn. Prins. Schs. for Girls (sec. 1970-72, pres. 1975-77, coun. 1970-79), Nat. Assn. Secondary Sch. Prins., Country Day Sch. Headmasters Assn. (exe. com. 1984-87, v.p. 1988-89), So. Assn. Colls. and Schs. (adminstrv. coun. 1974-77, ctrl. reviewing com. 1972-77, vice chmn. secondary commn. 1975-76, chmn. 1976-77, bd. dirs. 1976-81), Ladies Hermitage Assn., Vanderilt Aid Soc. (sec. 1971-73, pres. 1994-96), Ind. Edn. Svcs. (trustee 1980-88, chmn. 1986-88), Susan Komen Found. (adv. bd.), Belle Meade Club, Centennial Club, Phi Beta Kappa, Pi Beta Phi. Republican. Presbyterian. Office: 5 Strawberry Hl Nashville TN 37215-4118

MCMURRY, JOHN EDWARD, chemistry educator; b. N.Y.C., July 27, 1942; s. Edward and Marguerite Ann (Hotchkiss) McM.; m. Susan Elizabeth Sobuta, Sept. 4, 1964; children—Peter Michael, David Andrew, Paul Matthew. B.A., Harvard U., 1964; M.A., Columbia U., 1965, Ph.D., 1967. Prof. chemistry U. Calif., Santa Cruz, 1967-80, Cornell U., Ithaca, N.Y., 1980—. Author: Organic Chemistry, 1984, Chemistry, 1995 and other textbooks. Assoc. editor Accounts of Chem. Research, 1975-95. Recipient Humboldt Sr. Sci. award, 1987; Sloan Found. fellow, 1969-71; Career awardee NIH, 1975-80. Fellow AAAS; mem. Am. Chem. Soc. Home: 625 Highland Rd Ithaca NY 14850-1411 Office: Cornell Univ Dept Chemistry Baker Lab Ithaca NY 14853

MC MURTRY, JAMES GILMER, III, neurosurgeon; b. Houston, June 11, 1932; s. James Gilmer and Alberta Elizabeth (Matteson) McM.; student Rice U., Houston, 1950-53; M.D. cum laude, Baylor U., Houston, 1957. Intern, Hosp. U. Pa., Phila., 1957-58; resident gen. surgery Baylor U. Affiliated Hosps., Houston, 1958-59; asst. neurol. surgery Coll. Physicians and Surgeons, Columbia U., N.Y.C., 1959-60; asst. resident neurol. surgery and neurology Neurol. Inst. N.Y., Columbia Presbyn. Med. Center, N.Y.C., 1960-62, chief resident neurol. surgery, 1962-63; Nat. Inst. Neurol. Disease and Blindness spl. fellow neurol. surgery Coll. Physicians and Surgeons, Columbia U., N.Y.C., 1963-64, instr. neurol. surgery, 1963-65, assoc., 1965-68, asst. prof. clin. neurol. surgery, 1968-73, assoc. prof., 1973-89, prof., 1989—; asst. attending neurol. surgeon Neurol. Inst. N.Y., N.Y.C., 1964-73, assoc. attending neurol. surgeon, 1973-89, attending neurol. surgeon, 1989—; chief neurol. surgery clinic Vanderbilt Clinic, Columbia Presbyn. Med. Center, N.Y.C., 1964-68; attending-in-charge neurosurgery Lenox Hill Hosp., N.Y.C., 1970-91; assoc. cons. neurol. surgery Englewood (N.J.) Hosp., 1964—; asst. cons. neurol. surgery Harlem Hosp., N.Y.C., 1964—; cons. neurol. surgery Bronx (N.Y.) VA Hosp., 1964-65; mem. NIH Parkinson Research Group, Columbia U., 1965—; mem. med. adv. bd. N.Y. State Athletic Commn. Jesse H. Jones scholar Baylor U. Coll. Medicine, 1953-57, Allen fellow dept. neurol. surgery Columbia U., 1964-65. Diplomate Am. Bd. Neurol. Surgery. Fellow ACS, Linnean Soc. (London); trustee Glimmerglass Opera, Morris-Jumel, Opera Manhattan. Mem. AAUP, AAAS, AMA, Am. Assn. Neurol. Surgeons, European Congress Pediatric Neurosurgery, Am. Soc. Stereotaxic Surgeons, Pan Am. Med. Assn., N.Y. State Soc. Surgeons, N.Y. State Neurosurgery Soc., N.Y. Acad. Sci., N.Y. Neurosurg. Soc., Med. Soc. State N.Y., N.Y. County Med. Soc., Osler Soc., Baylor U. Coll. Medicine Alumni Assn., Med. Strollers, The Med. Soc. of London, The Harveian Soc., Alpha Omega Alpha. Presbyn. Clubs: The Union (N.Y.C.), The Garrick (London), The Atheneum (London), The Met. Opera (N.Y.C.), The Norfolk Yacht and Country. Author: Medical Examination Review Book-Neurological Surgery, 1970, rev. edit., 1975; Neurological Surgery Case Histories, 1975; contbr. articles to profl. jours. Home: 1 Cobb Ln Tarrytown NY 10591-3003 Office: 710 W 168th St New York NY 10032-2603

MCMURTRY, LARRY JEFF, author; b. Wichita Falls, Tex., June 3, 1936; s. William Jefferson and Hazel Ruth (McIver) McM.; m. Josephine Ballard, July 15, 1959 (div. 1966); 1 child, James. BA, N.Tex. State Coll., 1958; MA, Rice U., 1960. Instr. Tex. Christian U., Ft. Worth, 1961-62; lectr. in English and creative writing Rice U., Houston, 1963-69; co-owner Booked Up Book Store, Washington, from 1970; vis. prof. George Mason Coll., 1970, Am. Univ., 1970-71. Author: (novels) Horseman, Pass By, 1961 (Jesse H. Jones award Texas Inst. of Letters 1962), Leaving Cheyenne, 1963, The Last Picture Show, 1966, Moving On, 1970, All My Friends Are Going to be Strangers, 1972, Terms of Endearment, 1975, Somebody's Darling, 1978, Cadillac Jack, 1982, The Desert Rose, 1983, Lonesome Dove, 1985 (Pulitzer prize for fiction 1986), Texasville, 1987, Anything for Billy, 1988, Some Can Whistle, 1989, Buffalo Girls, 1990, The Evening Star, 1992, Streets of Laredo, 1993, (with Diana Ossana) Pretty Boy Floyd, 1994, The Late Child, 1995, Dead Man's Walk, 1995 (with Diana Ossana) Zeke and Ned, 1997, Commanche Moon, 1997; (essays) In a Narrow Grave: Essays on Texas, 1968, It's Always We Rambled: An Essay on Rodeo, 1974, Film Flam: Essays on Hollywood, 1987; screenwriter: (with Peter Bogdanovich) The Last Picture Show, 1971 (Academy award nomination best adapted screenplay 1971), Texasville, 1990, Montana, 1990, Falling From Grace, 1992, (with Cybill Shepard) Memphis, 1992; also articles, essays, book revs. in N.Y. Times, Saturday Rev., Washington Post, Am. Film, others. Wallace Stegner fellow, 1960, Guggenheim fellow, 1964; recipient Barbara McCombs/Lon Tinkle award Texas Inst. of Letters, 1986. Mem. Tex. Inst. Letters (Jesse H. Jones award 1962). Office: Simon & Schuster 1230 6th Ave New York NY 10020-1513 also: care Saria Co Inc 2509 N Campbell # 95 Tucson AZ 85719*

MCMURTRY, R. ROY, chief justice; b. Toronto, Ont., Can., May 31, 1932; s. Roland Roy and Doris Elizabeth (Belcher) McM.; m. Ria Jean Macrae, Apr. 18, 1957; children: Janet, James, Harry, Jeannie, Erin, Michael. BA with honors, U. Toronto, 1954; LLB, Osgoode Hall Law Sch., 1958; LLD (hon.), U. Ottawa, 1983, Leeds U., U.K., 1988, York U., 1991. Bar: Called to bar 1958, created Queen's counsel 1970. Partner firm Benson, McMurtry, Percival and Brown; mem. Provincial Parliament for Eglinton, 1975-85; atty. gen. for Ont., 1975-85, solicitor gen. for Ont., 1978-82, high commnr. for Can. to Gt. Brit. and No. Ireland, 1985-88; ptnr. Blaney, McMurtry Stapells, Toronto, 1988-91; chmn. Can. Football League, 1989-91; assoc. chief justice Ont. Ct. Justice, Toronto, 1991-94, chief justice, 1994-96; chief justice of Ont. Ont. Ct. of Appeal, Toronto, 1996—; freeman of City of London, 1986. Mem. United Ch. of Can. Office: Ont Ct of Appeal, 130 Queen St W, Toronto, ON Canada M5H 2N5

MCMURTY, ROBERT Y., academic dean; b. Toronto, Mar. 6, 1941; s. Roland Roy and Elizabeth McMurty; m. Jane MacDougall, May 6, 1979; children: Angus, Abbey, Sean, Meaghan. MD, U. Toronto, 1965, degree in Orthopaedic Surgery, 1972. Fellow Hosp. Sick Children, Toronto, Can., 1972-74; orthopedic surgeon, head dept. emergency svcs., founder and dir. regional trauma unit Sunnybrook Med. Ctr., Toronto, 1975-87; asst. to assoc. prof. U. Toronto, 1976-87; head surgery Foothills Hosp., Calgary, Can., 1988-92; dean faculty medicine U. Western (Can.) Ontario, 1992-97; chmn. dept. surgery, prof. surgery U. Calgary, 1988-92; vis. prof., Can. and internationally; presenter in field; chmn. provincial com. on role, function and financing acad. health ctrs., 1994-95; reviewer Provincial Cancer Network, 1994-95. Editor: Management of Blunt Trauma; contbr. articles to profl. jours. and chpts. to books. Am., Brit. Can. Travelling fellow, 1981. Fellow Am. Coll. Surgeons (Can.), Royal Coll. Surgeons; mem. Royal Coll. Physicians Surgeons, Med. Rsch. Coun. Can. Office: U Western Ont, Health Sci Addition Rm 112, London, ON Canada N6A 5CI

MCNABB, DARCY LAFOUNTAIN, medical management company executive; b. Middletown, N.J., Aug. 27, 1955; d. Donald Mark LaFountain and Suzanne (Gilman) LaFountain Westergard; m. Leland Monte McNabb, July 4, 1981 (div. Feb. 1989); 1 child, Leland Monte Jr. BBA in Internat. Fin. cum laude, U. Miami, 1977. Real estate agent, Grad. Realtor's Inst. Market rsch. asst. Burger King Corp., Miami, Fla., 1975-77; regional mktg. supr. Burger King Corp., Huntington Beach, Calif., 1977-78; mgr., restaurant planning Holiday Inns, Inc., Memphis, 1978-79, mgr., nat. promotions, 1979-83; dir., lodging and travel planning Holiday Corp., Memphis, 1983-86; affiliate broker The Hobson Co., Realtors, Memphis, 1986-88, Crye Leike, Memphis, 1988-92; v.p. comm. and planning Medshares Mgmt. Group, Inc., Memphis, 1991—. Active Friends Pink Palace Mus., Memphis, 1987-91, Family Link/Runaway, Memphis, 1980-88; chmn. Foster Care Rev. Bd., Memphis, 1988—; bd. dirs. Bethany House, Memphis, 1989—, pres., 1995; pres., bd. dirs. Am. Cancer Soc., 1994—; mktg. com. Health Industry Coun., 1994-95. Named Profl. Vol. of Yr., Friends of Pink Palace Mus., Memphis, 1989, 93, U.S. Masters Swimming All-Am., 1993, 94; grad. Leadership Memphis, 1995; named Cmty. Hero for Olympic Torch Relay, 1996. Mem. Le Bonheur Club, Memphis Runners Track Club. Republican. Episcopalian. Avocations: competitive long distance running, tennis, swimming. Home: 1948 Harbert Ave Memphis TN 38104-5216 Office: Medshares Mgmt Group Inc 2714 Union Avenue Ext Memphis TN 38112-4402

MCNABB, DIANNE LEIGH, investment banker, accountant; b. Huntsville, Ala., Sept. 7, 1956; d. Walter David and Mary Josephine (Hawkins) McN.; m. William Roland Lantz, July 1, 1983; 1 child, Sarah Elizabeth. BS in Acctg., U. Ala., Tuscaloosa, 1976. CPA, Ga., Ala. Acct. Lilly Flagg Assocs. & Subsidiaries, Huntsville, 1977-78; mgr. Johnston, Joyce & Wigginton, CPA's, Huntsville, 1978-84; sr. mgr. KPMG Peat Marwick, CPA's, Atlanta, 1984-91; v.p. A.G. Edwards & Sons, Inc., Atlanta, 1991—. Mem. ways and means com. Atlanta Jr. League, 1991—; instr., advisor Jr. Achievement, Atlanta, 1985-88; mem. hospitality com. Dem. Nat. Conv., Atlanta, 1988; vol. Ga. Spl. Olympics, Atlanta, 1989-91. Mem. AICPA, Govt. Fin. Officers Assn. (spl. rev. com. 1991-95), Ga. Soc. CPA (govtl. acctg. and auditing com. 1992), Assn. of Govt. Accts. (bd. dirs. Atlanta chpt. 1990-92), Ala. Soc. CPA (sec.-treas. 1984), Am. Soc. Women Accts. (pres. Huntsville chpt. 1983-84), U. Ala. Alumni Assn. (treas. 1983-84), Zeta Tau Alpha (advisor 1988-93, v.p. 1983, treas. 1987-89, pres. 1984, 89-91, panhellenic del. 1988-91, dist. pres. 1993-95, Cert. of Merit 1992, Zeta Lady award 1991, Alum Chum award 1991). Avocations: tennis, scuba. Home: 2530 Alpine Way Duluth GA 30136-4440 Office: A G Edwards 3399 Peachtree Rd NE Ste 1270 Atlanta GA 30326-1150

MCNABB, TALMADGE FORD, religious organization administrator, retired military chaplain; b. Johnson City, Tenn., Mar. 22, 1924; s. Robert Pierce and Dora Isabelle (Bailey) McN.; m. Nesbia Orlene Boswell, Dec. 3, 1950 (dec.); children: Darlene Roberta, Marla Dawn; m. Pirkko Marjotta Pelttari, Nov. 11, 1962; children: Valerie Anne, Lisa Rhea, Marcus Duane. Student, East Tenn. State U., 1941-43, 46; BA, Southwestern U. Assemblies of God, Waxahachie, Tex., 1947, BTh, 1949; BS, Birmingham Southern Coll., 1952; MA, U. Ala., 1957; HHD (hon.), S.E. Univ., Greenville, S.C., 1978. Ordained to ministry Assemblies of God, 1950. Evangelist Assemblies of God, 1948-49; pastor 1st Assembly of God, Warrior, Ala., 1949-53, Tuscaloosa, Ala., 1955-56; commd. 1st lt. U.S. Army, 1955, advanced through grades to lt. col., 1966; chaplain U.S. Army, Ft. Rucker, Ala., 1953-54, Korea, 1954-55, Ft. Benning, Ga., 1957-59, France, 1959-61, Ft. Knox, Ky., 1961-66, Ft. Dix, N.J., 1967-69; chaplain William Beaumont Hosp. U.S. Army, El Paso, Tex., 1971-72; ret. U.S. Army, 1972; writer, evangelist, speaker, 1973—; founder, pres. Worldwide Christian Ministries, Browns Mills, N.J., 1981—; ministered in Ecuador, India, Russia, China, France, Belgium, The Netherlands. Contbr. articles on religious and ethnic topics to newspapers and mags. Mem. DAV (life), Mil. Ret. Officers Assn. (life), Mil. Chaplains Assn. (life, del.). Republican. Home and Office: Worldwide Christian Ministries 1 Springfield Rd Browns Mills NJ 08015-6709 *I believe every person born into this world is gifted by God the Creator with special talents and gifts, and has a niche to fill no other person can fill; to fulfill God's purpose for us is our greatest accomplishment.*

MCNAIR, CARL HERBERT, JR., army officer, aeronautical engineer; b. Pensacola, Fla., Sept. 22, 1933; s. Carl Herbert and Hallie Rebecca (Edwards) McN.; m. Jo Ann Wilson, Oct. 26, 1957; children: Cynthia Leigh, Carl Herbert III, Courtney Ann. B.S., U.S. Mil. Acad., 1955; B.Aero. Engring., Ga. Inst. Tech., 1963, M.S. in Aero. Engring., 1963; M.S. in Pub. Adminstrn., Shippensburg State Coll., 1971. Commd. 2d lt. U.S. Army, 1955, advanced through grades to maj. gen., 1987; comdr. troop brigade U.S. Army Aviation Ctr., Fort Rucker, Ala., 1974-75; dep. for aviation to asst. sec. of Army Office Sec. of Army, U.S. Army, Washington, 1975-77, exec. to dep. chief of staff for research, devel. and acquisition, 1977-78; dep. dir. requirements and aviation officer Office of Dep. Chief of Staff for Ops. and Plans, 1978-79; dep. comdg. gen. U.S. Army Aviation Ctr., Fort Rucker, Ala., 1979-80, comdg. gen., 1980-83; dep. chief staff combat devels. U.S. Army Tng. and Doctrine Command, Fort Monroe, Va., 1983-84, chief of staff, 1985-87; ret. U.S. Army, 1987; v.p. Burdeshaw Assocs., Ltd., Bethesda, Md., 1988-90; pres. Dyncorp Support Svcs. Div., Reston, Va., 1990-94, Dyncorp Enterprise Mgmt., Reston, 1994—; corp. v.p. Dyncorp, Reston, 1994—. Contbr. articles to profl. jours. Pres. Uniformed Svcs. Benefit Assn., Kansas City, Mo., 1980-82, Assn. of U.S. Army, Washington, 1988-92 (Washington chpt., exec. v.p. 2 region 1992-96, pres. 2 region 1996—); v.p. Ala.-Fla. coun. Boy Scouts Am., Dothan, Ala., 1979-83; mem. nat. bd. dirs. Mil. Cmty. Youth Ministries, 1988-93; pres. West Point Soc., Washington, 1992-95; mem. bd. dirs. Army Aviation Mus. Found.; mem. West Poinst Fund Com.; trustee U.S. Mil. Acad., 1992—. Decorated D.S.M. with oak leaf cluster, Legion of Merit with two leaf clusters, D.F.C. with three oak leaf clusters, Bronze Star medal with V devices with oak leaf cluster, Air medal with V devices and 51 oak leaf clusters, Disting. Service medal State of Ala.; named Disting. Grad. Sch. Aerospace Engring. Ga. Inst. Tech., Sigma Gamma Tau, 1963; recipient Silver Beaver Achievement Boy Scouts Am., 1981; recipient Crosses of Military Svc., Korean Conflict, Vietnam, Jeff Davis award United Daus. of the Confederacy, 1987, 88; numerous fgn. awards Korea, Vietnam, France, Republic of China. Mem. Assn. U.S. Army (mil. adviser 1979-87), Army Aviation Assn. Am. (life, v.p. 1979-83, 85-87, 90-93, sec.-treas. 1993-97, sr. v.p. 1997—), Am. Def. Preparedness Assn. (bd. dirs. Washington chpt. 1993—, sec. 1994-95, 2nd v.p. 1995-97, 1st v.p. 1997—), Order of Daedalians (life), Am. Helicopter Soc., Air Force Assn., Navy League, Ret. Officers Assn. (life), Masons, Fairfax County C. of C. (bd. dirs. 1996—), Easter Seal Soc. (child devel. ctr. of No. Va. adv. bd. 1996—). Methodist. Home: 7821 Friars Ct Alexandria VA 22306-2717 *The military service, perhaps more than any other profession, provides us with a unique opportunity to serve both our fellow man and our God -in preserving the Peace and the Freedom cherished by mankind. It is within such a framework that I have charted the course of my life, remembering always Duty-Honor-Country.*

MCNAIR, JOHN FRANKLIN, III, banker; b. Laurinburg, N.C., Apr. 12, 1927; s. John Franklin and Martha (Fairley) McN.; m. Martha Fowler, June 16, 1951; children: John Franklin IV, Elizabeth Fowler. BS, Davidson Coll., 1949; postgrad., U. N.C., 1954-56. Pres. McNair Automotive Co., Inc., Laurinburg, 1949-66, The State Bank, Laurinburg, 1966-68; sr. v.p. Wachovia Bank & Trust, Laurinburg, 1968-70, Raleigh, N.C., 1970-72; exec. v.p. Wachovia Bank & Trust, Winston-Salem, N.C., 1972-77, vice chmn., 1977-85; vice chmn. The Wachovia Corp., Winston-Salem, N.C., 1977-87, pres., chief exec. officer, 1987-90; pres., chief exec. officer Wachovia Bank & Trust Co, 1987-90, also dir.; exec. v.p. First Wachovia Corp., 1986-90; bd. dirs. Piedmont Natural Gas Co.; bd. dirs., pres. N.C. R.R. Co., 1993-97. Mem. N.C. State Hwy. Commn., Raleigh, 1965-69, Commn. on future N.C., raleigh, 1981-83; chmn. N.C. Bd. Econ. Devel., 1979-85, N.C. Coun. Econ. Edn., Greensboro, 1980-82, Ind. Coll. Fund N.C., 1989-91, N.C. Citizens for Bus. and Industry, 1988-89; trustee Peace Coll., Raleigh, 1980-89, Davidson Coll., 1985-93; trustee Old Salem, Inc., 1985—, treas., 1990-97, chmn., 1997—; trustee Winston-Salem Found., 1983-91, chmn., 1989-91; co-chmn. gov.'s adv. com. Superconducting Supercollider Project, 1988; trustee, mem. exec. com. Rsch. Triangle Found., 1986—, vice chmn., 1990-93, chmn., 1992—; trustee exec. com. Winston-Salem Bus., Inc., 1986—, chmn., 1990-95; mem. govt. performance com. State of N.C., 1991-93; bd. dirs. N.C. Enterprise Corp., 1988-93; chmn. Qual Choice of N.C., Inc., 1994—. With USN, 1945-46. Recipient Young Man of Yr. award Laurinburg Jaycees, 1962, Silver Beaver award Boy Scouts Am., 1967, Disting. Alumni award Davidson Coll., 1994. Mem. Am. Bankers Assn. (state v.p. 1980-81), Res. City Bankers Assn., N.C. Bankers Assn. (pres. 1976-77), Cape Fear County Club (Wilmington, N.C.), Old Town Club, Piedmont Club, St. Andrews Soc., Rotary. Democrat. Presbyterian. Home: 234 NW Pine Valley Rd Winston Salem NC 27104-1808 Office: Wachovia Bank NC PO Box 3099 Winston Salem NC 27150

MCNAIR, JOHN WILLIAM, JR., civil engineer; b. Asheville, N.C., June 17, 1926; s. John William and Annie (Woody) McN.; m. June Clemens Kratz; children—Jeffry, Marsha, Cathy. B.S. in Forestry, Pa. State U., 1950; B.S.C.E., Va. Poly. Inst. State U., 1955; postgrad. in engring. U. Va., 1957-58. Registered profl. engr., Va. and other states. Forester U.S. Forest Service, Flagstaff, Ariz., 1950, U.S. Gypsum Co., Altavista, VA., 1951; mem. engring. faculty U. Va., Charlottesville, 1955-58; prin. John McNair & Assocs., Waynesboro, VA., 1958—; owner Brucheum Group, Waynesboro, 1983—; with Va. Bd. Architects, Profl. Engrs. and Land Surveyors, 1969-79, v.p., 1977-78, pres., 1978-79. Author numerous engring. and land mgmt. study reports. Mem. Waynesboro City Council, 1968-72, vice mayor, 1970-72; chmn. Waynesboro INdsl. devel. Authority, 1984—. Served to capt. AUS, 1944-46, 51-53; France, Okinawa. Recipient Disting. Service cert. Va. Soc. Profl. Engrs., 1971. Fellow ASCE; mem. Acad. Environ. Engrs. (diplomate). Republican. Presbyterian. Lodge: Rotary. Office: John McNair and Assocs Wayne Ave LB & B Bldg Waynesboro VA 22980

MCNAIR, ROBERT C., communications executive. BS, U. S.C., 1958. Chmn. Cypress Telecom. Corp., U.S. Telesys, Inc.; founder, CEO Cogen Techs. Energy Group, Houston; chmn. bd. trustees McNair Found., Free Enterprise Inst.; bd. govs. Rice U.; bd. trustees Baylor Coll. Medicine, Houston; bd. dirs. Fed. Res. Bank Dallas; dir. Mosher, Inc.; spkr. in field. Pres. Houston Grand Opera Assn.; trustee Sigma Chi Found.; elder Meml. Drive Presbyn. Ch., Houston. Office: Cogen Techs 1600 Smith St Ste 4300 Houston TX 77002-7348

MCNAIR, RUSSELL ARTHUR, JR., lawyer; b. Detroit, Dec. 2, 1934; s. Russell Arthur and Virla (Standish) McN.; m. Rosemary M. Chesbrough, Apr. 6, 1957; children: Julie McNair Schwerin, Russell Arthur III, Douglas S. AB in Econs. cum laude, Princeton U., 1956; JD with distinction, U. Mich., 1960. Bar: Mich. 1960. Assoc. Dickinson, Wright, Moon, Van Dusen & Freeman, Detroit, 1960-67, ptnr., 1968—, chmn., 1994—; adj. prof. U. Detroit Sch. Law, 1968-72; mem. adv. bd. Fin. Transactions Inst., 1984-94; adj. prof. Wayne State U. Law Sch., 1994-96; spkr. in field. Trustee Children's Home, Detroit, 1975-95, pres. 1986-87, hon. trustee 1995—; mem. community leaders coun., United Way, 1994—; dir. Mich. Jobs Commn., 1995—. Mem. ABA, Mich. Bar Assn., Detroit Bar Assn., Am. Law Inst., Am. Coll. Real Estate Lawyers. Republican. Presbyterian. Avocations: golf, tennis, platform tennis. Home: 308 Touraine Rd Grosse Pointe MI 48236-3311 Office: Dickinson Wright Moon et al 1 Detroit Ctr 500 Woodward Ave Ste 4000 Detroit MI 48226-3423

MCNAIRN, PEGGI JEAN, speech pathologist, educator; b. Dallas, Sept. 22, 1954; d. Glenn Alton Harmon and Anna Eugenia (McVay) Hicks; m. Kerry Glen McNairn, Jan. 27, 1979; children: Micah Jay, Nathan Corey. BS in Speech Pathology, Tex. Christian U., 1977, MS in Communications Pathology, 1978; PhD in Ednl. Adminstrn., Kennedy Western U., 1991. Cert. speech pathologist, mid mgmt. Staff speech pathologist, asst. dir. infant program Easter Seal Soc. for Crippled Children and Adults Tarrant County, Ft. Worth, 1978-80; staff speech pathologist, spl. edn. lead tchr. Sherrod Elem. Sch. Arlington (Tex.) Ind. Sch. Dist., 1981-84, secondary speech/lang. specialist, early childhood assessment staff Spl. Services dept., 1984-89; owner, dir. Speech Assocs., 1989-92; mem. state forms com. Arlington (Tex.) Ind. Sch. Dist., 1985-86, chairperson assessment com., 1986-87; cons. augmentative communication Prentke Romich Co., 1992-97; dir. comms. & tech. Easter Seal Soc. for Children & Adults, 1997—; adj. prof., clin. supr. Tex. Christian U., Ft. Worth, 1978-79; clin. speech pathologist North Tex. Home Health Assn., Ft. Worth, 1980-92; adj. prof. Tex. Women's Univ., 1997—. Author: Quick Tech Activities for Literacy, 1993, Readable, Repeatable Stories and Activities, 1994, Quick Tech Magic: Music-Based Literacy Activities, 1996. Chairperson United Cerebral Palsy Toy Lending Libr., 1989-90; sunday sch. tchr. 1st United Meth. Ch., Arlington, 1982-87; mem. South Arlington Homeowners Assn., Arlington, 1985-87; 3rd v.p. Bebensee Elem. PTA. Recipient Outstanding Svc. to

Handicapped Am. Biog. Inst., 1989; Cert. of Achievement John Hopkins U. for computing to assist persons with disabilities, 1991. Mem. Internat. U.S. Tex. Socs. for Augmentative and Alternate Comm. (sec. Tex. branch, exec. bd. mem. 1996—), Neurodevelopmental Assn., Assn. for Curriculum and Supervision, Am. Speech and Hearing Assn., Tex. Speech-Lang.-Hearing Assn., Tex. Speech and Hearing Assn. (task force mem for augmentative comm.) Teaching Tex. Tots Consortium, Tex. Christian U. Speech and Hearing Alumni Assn., Kappa Delta Pi, Alpha Lambda Delta. Democrat. Avocations: doll making, sewing. Home: 215 Spanish Moss Dr Arlington TX 76018-1540

MCNALLY, ALEXANDER CAMPBELL, wine authority, consultant; b. Indpls., June 29, 1934; s. Edwin Mongan and Dorothea Lauretta (Campbell) McN.; m. Tina Mahar, Apr. 28, 1962; children: Daniel, Alexander. BA, Princeton U., 1956; MBA, Harvard U., 1958, PhD, 1958. Mng. dir. Alexis Lichine & Cie., Bordeaux, France, 1959-62; internat. wine dir. Heublein, Inc., Hartford, Conn., 1962-87; chmn. bd., chief exec. officer McNally Found., 1988—. Author: Wines and Spirits of the World, 1972, What Every Man and Woman Should Know about Wine, 1979. Mem. Rep. Nat. Com., Washington, 1986—; trustee Hartt Sch. Music. Recipient Tilden Fine Arts award Princeton U., 1956. Mem. Princeton Assn. Cen. Conn. (bd. dirs.), Harvard-Radcliffe Assn. of Conn., Conf. des Chevaliers du Tastevin (grand chef du protocole 1975—), Phi Beta Kappa. Methodist. Avocations: boating, music, wine tasting. Home: 31 Woodland St Hartford CT 06105 Office: Woodland House Hartford CT 06105-4339

MCNALLY, ANDREW, IV, publishing executive; b. Chgo., Nov. 11, 1939; s. Andrew and Margaret C. (MacMillin) McN.; m. Jeanine Sanchez, July 3, 1966; children: Andrew, Carrie, Ward. BA, U. N.C., 1963; MBA, U. Chgo., 1969. Bus. mgr. edn. divsn. Rand McNally & Co., Chgo., 1967-70, exec. v.p., sec., 1970-74, pres., 1974—, CEO, 1978—, also chmn. bd. dirs., 1993—; bd. dirs. Mercury Fin. Inc., Hubbell Inc., Morgan Stanley Funds, Zenith Electronics Corp., Allendale Ins., Borg Warner Securities Corp. Trustee Newberry Libr.; bd. dirs. Children's Meml. Hosp.; active vis. com. of libr. U. Chgo. With Air Force N.G., 1963-69. Mem. Chgo. Club, Saddle and Cycle Club, Commonwealth Club, Glen View Golf Club, Links (N.Y.C.). Office: Rand McNally & Co 8255 Central Park Ave Skokie IL 60076-2908

MCNALLY, JAMES HENRY, physicist, defense consultant; b. Orange, N.J., Dec. 18, 1936; s. James Osborne and Edith Maude (Jones) McN.; m. Nancy Lee Eudaley, July 4, 1976. B. in Engring. Physics, Cornell U., 1959; PhD in Physics, Calif. Inst. Tech., 1966. Staff mem. program mgr. Los Alamos (N.Mex.) Nat. Lab., 1965-74; asst. dir for laser and isotope separation tech. AEC/ERDA, Washington, 1974-75; assoc. div. leader, dep. for inertial fusion, asst. for nat. sec. issues Los Alamos Nat. Lab., 1975-86; dep. asst. dir. Arms Control and Disarmament Agy., Washington, 1986-88; dir. office staff Los Alamos Nat. Lab., 1988-90, Washington Inst., 1990-94; cons., 1990—; U.S. del. Geneva Conf. on Disarmament, 1969, 73, 74, Threshold Test Ban Treaty, Moscow, 1974, Nuclear Testing Talks, Geneva, 1986-88. Bd. dirs. Wilson Mesa Met. Water Dist., 1976-88; mem., v.p., pres. Mountain Canine Corps, 1994—. Recipient Meritorious Honor award Arms Control and Disarmament Agy., 1988. Mem. AAAS, Am. Phys. Soc., Internat. Inst. Strategic Studies. Home and Office: 550 Rim Rd Los Alamos NM 87544-2931

MCNALLY, JOHN JOSEPH, lawyer; b. N.Y.C., July 1, 1927; s. Edward E. and Virginia L. (O'Brien) McN.; m. Sally Vose Greeley, Jan. 25, 1958; children: Martha, Sarah, Elizabeth, Julie, Thomas. AB, Coll. Holy Cross, 1950; LLB, Harvard U., 1953. Bar: N.Y. 1953. Assoc. White & Case, N.Y.C., 1953-63, ptnr., 1964-94, ret., 1994; bd. dirs. Mohawk Paper Mills, Inc., Cohoes, N.Y.; panelist in field. Trustee Caedmon Sch., N.Y.C., 1968—; bd. dirs. Cmty. Fund of Bronxville-Eastchester-Tuckahoe, Inc., 1986—, All Hallows H.S., N.Y.C., 1991—; mem. bd. gov's. Lawrence Hosp., Bronxville, N.Y., 1990-95. Fellow Am. Bar Found.; mem. N.Y. State Bar Assn., N.Y. County Lawyers Assn., Assn. of Bar of City of N.Y. Home: 58 Avon Rd Bronxville NY 10708-1723 Office: White & Case 1155 Ave Of The Americas New York NY 10036-2711

MCNALLY, JOSEPH LAWRENCE, space agency executive; b. Calumet Island, Que., Can., July 28, 1930; s. Lawrence and Mary (Ryan) M.; m. Carmen Petticlerc, Apr. 19, 1954; children: Marguerite, Michael, Stephen, Christopher, George, Lawrence, Lisa. BS, U. Ottawa, 1953. With RCA Ltd., Montreal, 1955-63; payload engr. Alouette II Spacecraft, 1963-68; project mgr. ISIS Project, 1968-73; project mgr. dept. comm. CTS Hermes Comm. Satellite, 1973-90; v.p. engring. Can. Space Agy., 1990—; project mgr. Satellite Gound Stas., China, 1971, Mobile Satellite Program Dept. Comm., 1981. Co-author: The ISIS Scanning Auroral Photometer, 1984, A Mobile Satellite System, 1986; contbr. articles to profl. jours. Recipient Merit award Pub. Svc. Can., 1990, award Excellence Treasury Bd. Can., 1991, Commemorative medal 125th Ann. Can. Confedn. Mem. Can. Astronautic & Space Inst. Avocations: violin, flying. Home: 1048 William Mooney Rd RR 3, Ontario, ON Canada K0A 1L0 Office: 6767 rte de l'Aeroport, Saint Hubert, PQ Canada J3Y 8Y9

MCNALLY, TERRENCE, playwright; b. St. Petersburg, Fla., Nov. 3, 1939; s. Hubert Arthur and Dorothy Katharine (Rapp) McN. B.A., Columbia U., 1960. Stage mgr. Actors Studio, N.Y.C., 1961, tutor, 1961-62; film critic The Seventh Art,, 1963-65; asst. editor Columbia Coll. Today, N.Y.C., 1965-66. Author: (plays) The Lady of the Camellias, 1963, And Things That Go Bump in the Night, 1964, Apple Pie and Last Gasps, 1966, Sweet Eros, 1968, Witness, 1968, Tour, 1968, Cuba Si!, 1968, Noon, 1968, Next, 1969, Where Has Tommy Flowers Gone?, 1971, Bad Habits, 1971 (Obie award 1971), Botticelli, 1971, Bringing It All Back Home, 1971, Whiskey, 1973, The Tubs, 1974, The Ritz, 1975 (Obie award best play 1974), The Golden Age, 1975, Broadway, Broadway, 1979, The Five Forty-Eight, 1974, The Lisbon Traviata, 1979, It's Only a Play, 1982, The Rink, 1984, Frankie and Johnny in the Clair de Lune, 1988, The Lisbon Traviata, 1989, Up in Saratoga, 1990, Kiss of the Spider Woman, 1990 (Tony award best book of a musical 1993), Andre's Mother, 1990 (Emmy award), Preludes, Fuges & Rifts, 1991, Lips Together, Teeth Apart, 1991, (screenplay) Frankie and Johnny, 1991, A Perfect Ganesh, 1993 (Pulitzer prize for drama nomination 1994), Love! Valour! Compassion!, 1994 (Outer Critics' Circle award best Broadway play 1995), Master Class, 1994. Recipient Dramatists Guild Hull-Warriner award, 1973, 88, 90; Guggenheim fellow, 1966, 69. Mem. Am. Acad. Arts and Letters, Dramatists Guild (v.p. 1981—). Office: care Gilbert Parker William Morris Agy 1325 Avenue Of The Americas New York NY 10019-6026*

MCNALLY, THOMAS CHARLES, III, lawyer; b. San Francisco, Dec. 5, 1938; s. Thomas Charles and Claire Marie (Egan) McN.; m. Paula Ann Berger, Sept. 3, 1960; children: Megan, Martin, J. Tevis. B.S., U. San Francisco, 1960; J.D., Hastings Coll. Law, U. Cal. at San Francisco, 1963. Bar: Calif. bar 1964. Dep. atty. gen. State Calif., 1964; assoc. firm Bohnert, Flowers & McCarthy, San Francisco, 1965-68; asst. sec., counsel DiGiorgio Corp., San Francisco, 1968-73; sec., counsel DiGiorgio Corp., 1974-75; sec., gen. counsel Consol. Fibres, Inc., San Francisco, 1975-88, v.p., 1981-88; also dir. Consol. Fibres, Inc.; of counsel McInerney & Dillon, P.C., Oakland, Calif., 1989-91; pvt. practice San Francisco, 1991—; lectr. McGeorge Bar Rev., 1964-65, Continuing Edn. of Bar, U. Calif., 1975-76; judge moot ct. U. San Francisco, 1974-84; arbitrator Am. Arbitration Assn., NASD, 1988—. Co-chmn. Mill Valley Citizens Adv. Com., 1974-76; mem. pub. affairs com. San Francisco Assn. Mental Health, 1965-69; commr. Mill Valley Park and Recreation Commn., 1988-93, chmn., 1990. Mem. ABA, State Bar Calif., San Francisco Bar Assn. Republican. Roman Catholic (lector). Clubs: Olympic, Scott Valley Tennis (founder, dir. 1971-76, pres., dir. 1980-82), World Trade. Home: 3 Midhill Dr Mill Valley CA 94941-1490 Office: 455 Market St Fl 19 San Francisco CA 94105-2420

MCNAMARA, A. J., federal judge; b. 1936. BS, La. State U., 1959; JD, Loyola U., New Orleans, 1968. Bailiff, law clk. U.S. Dist. Ct., New Orleans, 1966-68, sole practice, 1968-72; ptnr. Monton, Roy, Carmouche, Hailey, Bivens & McNamara, New Orleans, 1972-78, Hailey, McNamara, McNamara & Hall, 1978-82; judge U.S. Dist. Ct. (ea. dist.) La., New Orleans, 1982—. Mem. La. Ho. of Reps., 1976-80. Office: US Dist Ct C-367 US Courthouse 500 Camp St New Orleans LA 70130-3313*

MCNAMARA, ANN DOWD, medical technologist; b. Detroit, Oct. 17, 1924; d. Frank Raymond and Frances Mae (Ayling) Sullivan; m. Thomas Stephen Dowd, Apr. 23, 1949 (dec. 1980); children—Cynthia Dowd Restuccia, Kevin Thomas Dowd; m. Robert A. McNamara, June 15, 1985. BS Wayne State Univ., 1947. Med. technologist Woman's Hosp. (now Hutzel Hosp.), Detroit, 1946-52, St. James Clin. Lab., Detroit, 1960-62; supr. histopathology lab. Hutzel Hosp., Detroit, 1962-72, Mt. Carmel Mercy Hosp., 1972-87, ret. 1987. docent Domino's Ctr. Architecture & Design, Ann Arbor, Mich. 1988. Mem. Am. Soc. Clin. Pathologists, Am. Soc. Med. Technology, Mich. Soc. Med. Technology, Nat. Soc. Histotechnology, Mich. Soc. Histotechnologists, Wayne State U. Alumni Assn., Smithsonian Assos., Detroit Inst. Arts Founders Soc. Home: 29231 Oak Point Dr Farmington Hills MI 48331

MCNAMARA, ANNE H., lawyer, corporate executive; b. Shanghai, Republic of China, Oct. 18, 1947; came to U.S. 1949; d. John M. and Marion P. (Murphy) H.; m. Martin B. McNamara, Jan. 15, 1977. AB, Vassar Coll., 1969; JD, Cornell U., 1973. Bar: N.Y. 1973, Tex. 1981. Assoc. Shea, Gould, Climenko & Casey, N.Y.C., 1972-76; from asst. corp. sec. to corp. sec. Am. Airlines, Inc., Dallas, 1976-88, v.p. pers. resources, 1988; sr. v.p., gen. counsel Am. Airlines (AMR Corp.), Dallas, 1988—; bd. dirs. Louisville Gas & Electric Co., LG&E Energy Corp., Sabre Group Holdings, Inc. Office: Am Airlines Inc Mail Drop 5618 PO Box 619616 Dallas TX 75261-9616

MCNAMARA, BRENDA NORMA, secondary education educator; b. Blackpool, Lancashire, Eng., Aug. 8, 1945; came to U.S., 1946; d. Milford Hampson and Nola (Welsby) Jones; m. Michael James McNamara, July 19, 1969. BA in History, Calif. State U., Long Beach, 1967; postgrad., Calif. State U., various campuses, 1967—. Cert. secondary tchr. and lang. devel. specialist, Calif. Tchr. history West High Sch., Torrance, Calif., 1968—, dept. chair, 1989—; cons. in field. Co-author: World History, 1988. Western Internat. Studies Consortium grantee, 1988. Mem. Calif. Tchrs. Assn., Calif. Coun. for Social Studies, Torrance Tchrs. Assn. (bd. dirs. 1992—), South Bay Coun. for Social Studies, Nat. Tchrs. Assn., Nat. Coun. for Social Studies. Avocations: travel, theater, mystery reading, gourmet cooking. Office: West High Sch 20401 Victor St Torrance CA 90503-2255

MCNAMARA, EDWARD HOWARD, county official, former mayor; b. Detroit, Sept. 21, 1926; s. Andrew Kursina and Ellen Gertrude (Bennett) McN.; m. Lucille Yvonne Martin, June 26, 1948; children—Colleen, Michael, Nancy, Kevin, Terence. Ph.B., U. Detroit, 1959; Ph.D. (hon.), Madonna Coll., 1982. Mgr. Mich. Bell Telephone Co., Detroit, 1948-70; mayor City of Livonia, Mich., 1970-86; county exec. Wayne County, Detroit, 1987—. Served with USN, 1944-46. Democrat. Roman Catholic. Home: 16501 Park St Livonia MI 48154-2203 Office: Office of the County Exec 600 Randolph St Detroit MI 48226-2831*

MCNAMARA, FRANCIS JOHN, writer; b. Bklyn., Nov. 19, 1915; s. Sylvester John and Adelia Ferris (French) McN.; m. Katherine Elizabeth Foley, Nov. 20, 1945; children: Jane Marie, Ellen Elizabeth. BA, St. John's U., 1938; MA, Niagara U., 1939. Assoc. reg. sales mgr. UN Relief & Rehab. Adminstrn., Jehol & Hupeh Provinces, China, 1946-47; editor Counterattack, N.Y.C., 1950-54; dir. nat. security program VFW, Washington, 1954-58; research analyst and cons. House Com. on Un-Am. Activities, Washington, 1958-61; dir research House Com. on Un-Am. Activities, 1961-62, staff dir., 1962-69; exec. sec. Subversive Activities Control Bd., Washington, 1970-73; exec. dir. The Hale Found., Washington, 1981; vice chmn. Security and Intelligence Found., Arlington, Va., 1987-90; sr. fellow Ctr. for Intelligence Studies, Arlington, 1990-93; bd. dirs. Coun. for Def. of Freedom, Washington, 1952-94; bd. advisors Nathan Hale Inst., Washington, 1983—; sr. cons. Defense Systemns, Inc., McLean, Va., 1987. Author: U.S. Counterintelligence Today, 1985, Patterns of Communist Espionage, 1959; contbr. articles to profl. jours. Served to maj. U.S. Army, 1941-46. Mem. Assn. Former Intelligence Officers. Republican. Roman Catholic. Avocations: gardening, photography. Address: Apt 1417 8100 Connecticut Ave Chevy Chase MD 20815

MCNAMARA, FRANCIS JOSEPH, JR., foundation executive, lawyer; b. Boston, Nov. 30, 1927; s. Francis Joseph and Louise (English) McN.; m. Noreen E. O'Connor, June 18, 1953 (dec. Feb. 1984); children: Francis Joseph III, Moira Patricia (Mrs. Lance F. James), John Allen, Kathleen Louise (Mrs. Robert J. Hugin), Martha Jeanne (Mrs. James R. Bordewick), Mark Jeffrey; m. Louis L. Magner, Jan. 17, 1986. A.B., Georgetown U., 1949, LL.B., 1951; LL.D. (hon.), Fairfield U., 1983. Bar: Conn. 1952. Assoc. firm Pullman, Comley, Bradley & Reeves, 1953; asst. U.S. Atty., dist. Conn., 1953-57; assoc. firm Cummings & Lockwood, Stamford, Conn., 1957-59; ptnr. Cummings & Lockwood, 1959-91; guest lectr. Salzburg (Austria) Seminar, 1981; chmn. grievance com. U.S. Dist. Ct. Conn., 1983-89. Trustee Fairfield (Conn.) U., 1968-80, trustee emeritus, 1980—; trustee Charles E. Culpeper Trust; chmn. bd. Charles E. Culpeper Found., 1968—, pres., 1991—. With USNR, 1946, 51-53. Fellow Am. Bar Found., Am. Coll. Trial Lawyers (state com. 1985-91, state chmn. 1989-90); mem. U.S. Supreme Ct. Hist. Soc. (Conn. state chmn. 1989-91, trustee 1992—), Navy League U.S., Knight of Holy Sepulchre, Knight of Malta, Knight of St. Gregory the Great, Wee Burn Country Club (Darien, Conn.), Bent Pine Golf Club (Vero Beach, Fla.), Turf and Field Club (N.Y.). Republican. Roman Catholic. Home: 75 Bank St New Canaan CT 06840-6203 also: 10 Lost Beach Ln Vero Beach FL 32963 Office: Charles E Culpeper Found 695 Main St Stamford CT 06901-2141

MCNAMARA, FRANCIS T., ambassador; b. Troy, N.Y., Nov. 2, 1927; married; 7 children. BA, Russell Sage Coll., 1953; MS, George Washington U., 1972; grad., Armed Forces Staff Coll., 1967, Naval War Coll., 1971-72. Vice-consul, econ. officer Am. Consulate Gen., Salisbury, Rhodesia, 1957-59; consul-polit. officer Am. Consulate Gen., Lubumbashi, Zaire, 1961-63; polit. and econ. officer Am. Consulate Gen., Dar-Es Salaam, Tanzania, 1964-66; dep. chief mission Am. Embassy, Lusaka, Zambia, 1967; provincial advisor Vinh Long and Quang Tri provinces Viet Nam, 1967-69; consul gen. Am. Consulate Gen., Danang, Vietnam, 1969-71; chargé d'affaires, dep. chief mission Am. Embassy, Cotonou, Benin, 1972-74; consul gen. Am. Consulate Gen., Can Tho, Vietnam, 1974-75, Quebec City, Que., Can., 1975-79; dep. asst. sec. of state for pub. affairs Dept. of State, Washington, 1979-81; amb. to Republic of Gabon and Republic of Sao Tome and Principe Am. Embassy, 1981-84; chargé d'affaires, dep. chief of mission Am. Embassy, Beirut, 1985-87; amb. to Republic of Cape Verde Am. Embassy, 1989—; fgn. affairs fellow Hoover Instn. Stanford (Calif.) U., 1984-85; sr. rsch. fellow Nat. Def. U., 1987-89. Author: France in Black Africa, 1989. With USN, 1944-46, 50-51. Home: 102 Gresham Pl Falls Church VA 22046-3440 Office: Am Embassy, Rua Hojl Ya Yenna 81, Praia Cape Verde

MC NAMARA, J(OHN) DONALD, retired lawyer, business executive; b. Bridgeport, Conn., Feb. 28, 1924; s. John T. and Agnes (Keating) McN.; m. Shirley Addison Holdridge, Nov. 5, 1960. BA, Dartmouth Coll., 1945; MA in Govt., Harvard U., 1947, LLB, 1950. Bar: N.Y. 1951, Conn. 1951. Assoc. Hall, Haywood, Patterson & Taylor, N.Y.C., 1951-53, 55-56; asst. U.S. Atty. U.S. Dist. Ct. (so. dist.) N.Y., 1953-55; assoc. Wickes, Riddell, Bloomer, Jacobi & McGuire, N.Y.C., 1956-57; assoc., then ptnr. Nottingham & McEniry (and successor), N.Y.C., 1957-59; sec., gen. counsel Interpub. Group of Cos., Inc., N.Y.C., 1960-79, dir., 1965-85, sr. v.p., 1966-73, exec. v.p., 1973-79, pres., 1980-85, mem. exec. com., 1967-85, mem. fin. com., 1980-85. Chmn. U.S. Nat. Tennis Championships, 1965. Served to lt. (j.g.) USNR, 1943-46. Mem. River Club, Univ. Club, Met. Opera Club, Ekwanok Country Club (mem. bd. govs. Manchester, Vt. 1991-95), Dorset (Vt.) Field Club (mem. bd. govs. 1996—), West Side Tennis Club (pres. Forest Hills, N.Y. 1964-66, 79-80). Home: 350 E 57th St New York NY 10022-2953 also: River Rd Manchester VT 05254

MCNAMARA, JOHN JEFFREY, advertising executive; b. N.Y., Jan. 31, 1937; s. John Joseph and Alexandra (Salem) M. BA, N.Y. Law Sch., 1963. Asst. v.p. Albert Frank Guenther Law Inc., N.Y., 1959-66; acct. supr., v.p. Doremus and Co., N.Y., 1966-74; v.p., exec. v.p. Wiley Kiernan Inc Charles Barker Ayer, N.Y., 1974-76; v.p. acct. supr. Tinker Campbell Ewald, N.Y., 1976-78; pres., chmn. John McNamara Advt. Inc., N.Y., 1978—; corr. cons. Hamilton College Alumni, Clinton, N.Y., 1978-88. Republican. Presbyterian. Avocations: boating, golf, restoring old cars, houses. Home: 420 Majors Path Southampton NY 11968-2423 Office: 27 Whitehall St New York NY 10004-2117

MCNAMARA, JOHN J(OSEPH), advertising executive, writer; b. Yonkers, N.Y., Mar. 7, 1934; m. Patricia A. Widmann, Sept. 14, 1963; children: Mary, John. B.S., Yale U., 1956; M.B.A., NYU, 1963. Exec. v.p., eastern regional dir. Young & Rubicam, N.Y.C., 1979; pres. Young & Rubicam U.S.A., from 1982; later pres. McCann Erickson Worldwide, ret., 1988; writer, cons., bd. dirs. in field. Author: Advertising Agency Management, 1989. Pres. Pelham United Way, N.Y.; mem. Pelham Manor Zoning Bd.; chmn. Pelham Manor Planning Bd.; trustee City of Pelham Manor, mayor, 1989-90. Served to 1st lt. USMC, 1956-58. Clubs: Pelham Country (pres.), Winged Foot. Office: PO Box 8204 Vero Beach FL 32963-8204

MCNAMARA, JOHN STEPHEN, artist, educator; b. Cambridge, Mass., Feb. 16, 1950; s. John Stephen and Mary (Adams) McN. BFA in Painting, Mass. Coll. Art, Boston, 1971, MFA in Painting, 1977. Tchr. Mus. Fine Arts Sch., Boston, 1983, 90-92; undergrad. and grad. painting tchr. Mass. Coll. Art, Boston, 1988; undergrad. painting tchr. Boston Archtl. Ctr., Boston, 1977; color fundamentals tchr. Mass. Coll. Art, Boston, 1987, undergrad. drawing, 1975-88; vis. lectr. San Francisco Art Inst., 1992, 93, U. Calif., Berkeley, 1993-98. One-man shows include The Exhbn. Space at 112 Greene St., N.Y.C., 1982, Stavaridis Gallery, Boston, 1983-85, 86-89, Bess Cutler Gallery, N.Y.C., 1984, 85, 86, 88, Mass. Coll. Art, 1986, Honolulu Acad. Fine Art, 1987, Nielson Gallery, 1990, 92, Miller Block Gallery, Boston, 1995, others; exhibited in group shows at Boston Collects, Mus. Fine Arts, Stavaridis Gallery, 1986, Bess Cutler Gallery, N.Y.C., 1987, Am. Painters and Sculptors, Met. Mus. Art, N.Y.C., 1988, Resonant Abstraciton, Fuller Mus. Art, Brockton, Mass., 1989-90. Mass. Art and Humanities grantee, 1980, 83, 86, 89, Award in the Visual Arts grantee, 1982, Nat. Endowment Arts grantee, 1981, Outstanding Alumnus award Mass. Coll. Art, 1986; McDowell Colony fellow, 1985. Home: 2127 California St Berkeley CA 94703

MC NAMARA, JOSEPH DONALD, researcher, retired police chief, novelist; b. N.Y.C., Dec. 16, 1934; s. Michael and Eleanor (Shepherd) McN.; divorced; children: Donald, Laura, Karen. BS, John Jay Coll., 1968; fellow, Harvard Law Sch., 1970; DPA (Littauer fellow), Harvard U., 1973. Served to dep. insp. Police Dept., N.Y.C., 1956-73; police chief Kansas City, Mo., 1973-76, San Jose, Calif., 1976-91; rsch. fellow Hoover Instn., Stanford U., 1991—; adj. instr. Northeastern U., 1972, John Jay Coll., 1973, Rockhurst Coll., 1975-76, San Jose State U., 1980; cons. U.S. Civil Rights Commn., 1978; lectr., appearances on nat. TV; apptd. nat. adv. bd. U.S. Bur. Justice Stats., 1980, U.S. Drug Control Policy Office, 1993; commentator Pub. Broadcasting Radio. Author: (non-fiction) Safe and Sane, 1984, (novel) The First Directive Crown, 1985, Fatal Command, 1987, The Blue Mirage, 1990, Code 211 Blue, 1996; contbr. articles to profl. publs. Bd. dirs. Drug Policy Found., Washington; active NCCJ. Served with U.S. Army, 1958-60. Named one of 200 Young Am. Leaders Time mag., 1975; recipient disting. alumni award John Jay Coll., 1979, Pres.'s award Western Soc. Criminology1979, Morrison Gitchoff award Western Soc. Criminology, 1992, H.B. Spear award Drug Policy Found., 1992; Kansas City police named Best in Country by Nat. Newspaper Enterprises, 1974, San Jose Police Dept. named Nat. Model U.S. Civil Rights Commn., 1980; named Law Enforcement Officer of Yr., Calif. Trial Lawyers Assn., 1991. Mem. Internat. Assn. Chiefs of Police, Calif. Police Chiefs Assn., Calif. Peace Officers Assn., Major Cities Police Chiefs Assn., Police Exec. Research Forum (dir.). Office: Hoover Instn Stanford CA 94305 *In our country, social mobility is possible for people from even the most humble backgrounds. Despite problems, our nation has provided more liberty and dignity for the common individual than any other civilization in history. Continuation of our free society depends upon how successful we are in teaching each new generation an appreciation of our precious freedoms and the patience to achieve progress within our democratic process.*

MC NAMARA, LAWRENCE J., bishop; b. Chgo., Aug. 5, 1928; s. Lawrence and Margaret (Knusman) McN. B.A., St. Paul Sem., 1949; S.T.L., Catholic U. Am., 1953. Ordained priest Roman Catholic Ch., 1953; parish priest, tchr. Kansas City-St. Joseph Diocese, 1953-57; dir. diocesan Refugee Resettlement, 1957-60; chaplain Jackson County Jail, 1957-64; exec. dir. Campaign for Human Devel., 1973-77; bishop of Grand Island Nebr., 1978—. Recipient award Cath. Relief Services. Office: Chancery Office PO Box 996 311 W 17th St Grand Island NE 68801-3521*

MCNAMARA, LAWRENCE JOHN, lawyer; b. Evergreen Park, Ill., Aug. 10, 1950; s. William Francis and Florence M. (Nicholson) McN.; m. Martha Ann Sanchez, Jan. 7, 1992. BA, Ill. Coll.; JD, Vanderbilt U. Bar: Tex. 1976, D.C. 1988, U.S. Dist. Ct. (so. dist.) Tex. 1977, U.S. Dist. Ct. (ea. dist.) Tex. 1978, U.S. Dist. Ct. (no. dist.) Tex. 1985, U.S. Dist. Ct. (we. dist.) Tex. 1991, U.S. Ct. Appeals (5th cir.) 1976, U.S. Ct. Appeals (11th cir.) 1981, U.S. Ct. Appeals (7th cir.) 1989, U.S. Ct. Appeals (9th cir.) 1991, U.S. Ct. Appeals (8th cir.) 1994, U.S. Supreme Ct. 1979. Assoc. Baker & Botts, Houston, 1976-85; ptnr. Baker, Smith & Mills, Dallas, 1985-87; ptnr., shareholder Johnson & Gibbs, Dallas, 1987-95; ptnr. Liddell, Sapp, Dallas, 1995—. Mem. ABA, Tex. Bd. Legal Specialization (cert.), Phi Beta Kappa. Roman Catholic. Avocations: golf, running. Office: Liddell Sapp 2200 Ross Ave Ste 900 Dallas TX 75201-6700

MCNAMARA, MARTIN BURR, lawyer, oil and gas company executive; b. Danbury, Conn., Sept. 10, 1947; s. William Joseph and Geraldine Margaret (Young) McN.; m. Anne Rose Hogan, Jan. 15, 1977. BA in English, Providence Coll., 1969; JD, Yale U., 1972. Bar: N.Y. 1973, U.S. Dist. Ct. (so. and ea. dists.) N.Y. 1973, (no. dist.) Tex. 1993, U.S. Ct. Appeals (2d cir.) 1973, Tex. 1980, U.S. Ct. Appeals (5th and 11th cirs.) 1980. Assoc. Shea & Gould, N.Y.C., 1972-76; asst. U.S. atty. (so. dist.) N.Y., N.Y.C., 1976-79; v.p., gen. counsel, sec. Tex. Oil & Gas Corp., Dallas, 1979-91; gen. counsel, sr. v.p. adminstrn. Delhi Gas Pipeline Corp., Dallas, 1979-91; exec. com. ptnr. Gibson, Dunn & Crutcher LLP, Dallas, 1991—; bd. dirs. Transocean Offshore Drilling, Inc.; lectr. State Bar Tex., Dallas Bar Assn., U. Tex. Corp. Counsel Inst., Okla. Bar Assn. Mem. exec. com. Yale Law Sch. Assn., 1983-86. Mem. State Bar of Tex. (vice chmn. corp. counsel sect. 1984-86, chmn.-elect 1987-88, chmn. 1988-89), Bar Assn. Fifth Fed. Cir., Assn. Bar. City of N.Y., N.Y. State Bar Assn., Fed. Energy Bar Assn. Republican. Roman Catholic. Club: Petroleum. Office: Gibson Dunn & Crutcher 5500 Bank One Ctr 1717 Main St Dallas TX 75201-4605

MCNAMARA, MARY E., non-profit executive, asset manager, minister; b. Mpls., Dec. 18, 1943; d. Edward Emmanuel and Gladys Theresa (Mattson) Bjorklund; m. Peter Alexander McNamara II; children: Peter Alexander III, Nathaniel Paul. BA, Carleton Coll., 1965; MDiv, Harvard U., 1968. Program dir. St. Peter's Ch., N.Y.C., 1968-72, program dir., dep. exec., 1977-80; program dir. Ctr. Ch. on-the-Green, N.Y.C., 1972-74; program developer Westminster Presbyn. Ch., Springfield, Ill., 1974-77; assoc. Gen. Assembly Coun. Presbyn. Ch., N.Y.C., 1980-87; dir. not-for-profit sector City of N.Y., 1987-90; pres., exec. dir. Interchurch Ctr., N.Y.C., 1990—; v.p. Pathways for Youth, Bronx, N.Y., 1987-96; pres. Morningside Area Alliance, N.Y.C., 1991—. Moderator Presbyn. N.Y.C., 1995-96, chair com. on ministry, 1992-95, chair implementation task force, 1996-97; bd. dirs., exec. com. mem. Polish Conf. Ctr., Stony Point, 1996—. Mem. N.Y. C. of C., Bldg. Owners and Mgrs. Assn. Home: 5411 Palisade Ave Riverdale NY 10471 Office: The Interchurch Ctr 475 Riverside Dr Ste 253 New York NY 10115-0299

MCNAMARA, MICHAEL JOHN, lawyer; b. Hutchinson, Minn., July 1, 1948; s. John Oliver and Lucille Violet (Wedell) M.; m. Kathleen Elizabeth Dahl; children: Jennifer, Kelly. BA, U. Utah, 1976; JD, U. Minn., 1980. Bar: Minn. 1981, U.S. Dist. Ct. Minn. 1981, U.S. Ct. Appeals (8th cir.) 1982, U.S. Supreme Ct. 1988, Wis. 1992. Pvt. practice Mpls., 1981—; panel arbitrator Am. Arbitration Assn., Hennepin County Dist. Ct.; panelist No-Fault Arbitrators Minn. Supreme Ct. Contbr. articles to profl. jours. Sgt. U.S. Army, 1968-71, Vietnam. Nat. Merit scholar. Mem. FBA, ATLA, The Federalist Soc., Internat. Platform Assn., Minn. State Bar Assn., Wis. State Bar Assn., Minn. Trial Lawyers Assn., Hennepin County Bar Assn. (mem. spkrs. bur.). Avocations: jogging, biking, hiking. Office: Henderson Howard Pawluk & McNamara PA 6200 Shingle Creek Pky Ste 385 Minneapolis MN 55430-2168

MC NAMARA, ROBERT STRANGE, former banking executive, cabinet member; b. San Francisco, June 9, 1916; s. Robert James and Clara Nell (Strange) McN.; m. Margaret Craig, Aug. 13, 1940 (dec.); children: Margaret Elizabeth, Kathleen, Robert Craig. AB, U. Calif., 1937; MBA, Harvard U., 1939; LLD (hon.), U. Calif., U. Mich., Columbia U., Harvard U., George Washington U., Princeton U., Amherst Coll., Williams Coll., U. Ala., Ohio State U., NYU, U. Notre Dame, U. Pa., U. St. Andrews, U. Philippines, Aberdeen U., Oxford U., U. S.C. Asst. prof. bus. adminstrn. Harvard U., 1940-43; exec. Ford Motor Co., 1946-61, pres. co., 1960-61, co. dir., 1957-61; sec. U.S. Dept. Def., 1961-68; pres. World Bank, 1968-81; mem. , trustee pub. and pvt. instns. including Overseas Devel. Coun., Urban Inst., Enterprise Fund., Brookings Inst.; spl. cons. War Dept., 1942. Author: The Essence of Security, 1968, One Hundred Countries-Two Billion People, 1973, The McNamara Years at the World Bank, 1981, Blundering Into Disaster, 1986, Out of the Cold, 1989, In Retrospect, 1995. Served as lt. col. USAAF, 1943-46. Decorated Legion of Merit, D.S.M.; recipient Presdl. Medal of Freedom with distinction, Christian A. Herter Meml. award, Albert Pick Jr. award U. Chgo., 1979, Franklin D. Roosevelt Freedom from Want medal, 1983, Onassis Athinai prize, 1988. Mem. Phi Beta Kappa. Office: 1350 I St NW Washington DC 20005-3305

MCNAMARA, STEPHEN, newspaper executive; b. Chgo., July 9, 1934; s. Robert Charles McNamara Jr. and Susan (Deuel) Shattuck; m. Hanne Morgensen Petterson, Feb. 21, 1960 (div. Aug. 1968); children: Lise, Natalie, Kevin; m. Kay Copeland, June 10, 1978; children: Christopher, Morgan. AB in Am. History, Princeton U., 1955. Reporter Winston-Salem (N.C.) Jour., 1955-57; sports writer Miami Herald, 1957-59; contbg. European editor Car & Driver, N.Y.C., 1960; asst. news editor, exec. sports editor, Sunday editor San Francisco Examiner, 1961-67; CEO, editor, pub. Pacific Sun, Mill Valley, Calif., 1967—; co-pub. The Ark, Tiburon, Calif., 1987—; pres. Marin Sun Printing Co., Mill Valley, 1967-93; mng. gen. ptnr. Sunrise Investment Co., Mill Valley, 1980—; vis. lectr. San Francisco State U., 1967; mem. innovation and planning commn. Calif. Dept. Edn., Sacramento, 1980; co-founder, pres. Marin Solar Village Corp., Mill Valley, 1976—, Marin Cmty. Video, Mill Valley, 1973-78. Mem. Soc. Profl. Journalists, Nat. Assn. Alternative Newsweeklies (pres. 1978-81), Calif. Assn. Alternative Newsweeklies (pres. 1990-92), Calif. Soc. Newspaper Editors (pres. 1985-86, bd. dirs. 1983-93), Calif. Newspaper Pubs. Assn. (bd. dirs. 1989-93), San Francisco Press Club (1st place newspaper writing award 1967, 3-2d place awards), Cap and Gown Club (Princeton U.). Democrat. Home: 2 Bradford Way Mill Valley CA 94941 Office: Pacific Sun Pub 21 Corte Madera Ave Mill Valley CA 94941-1800

MCNAMARA, THOMAS EDMUND, diplomat; b. New Haven, Sept. 16, 1940; s. Joseph Michael and Anne Marie (Meehan) McN.; m. Emma Julia Fonseca, June 11, 1966; children: David Fonseca, Michelle Anne. BA, Manhattan Coll., 1962; MA, Notre Dame U., 1964. Joined fgn. svc. State Dept., 1965; 2nd sec. Am. Embassy, Paris, 1967-69; BENELUX desk officer european bur. State Dept, 1969-71; consul Am. Consulate, Lubumbashi, Zaire, 1971-72, Bukavu, Zaire, 1972-73; with Armed Forces Staff Coll., Norfolk, Va., 1973-74; internat. affairs officer Arms Control & Disarmament Agy., 1974-75; chief external divsn., polit. sect. Am. Embassy, Moscow, 1976-78; office dir., polit.-mil. bur. State Dept., Washington, 1978-80; dep. chief of mission Am. Embassy, Kinshasa, Zaire, 1980-83; dept. asst. sec., bur. polit.-mil. affairs State Dept., Washington, 1983-86; sr. seminar Fgn. Svc. Inst., Washington, 1986-87; dir. counterterrorism and narcotics Nat. Security Coun., 1987-88; amb. to Colombia, 1988-91; special asst. to the pres. White House, Washington, 1991-92; coord. for counterterrorism State Dept., Washington, 1992-93, prin. dep. asst. sec., bur. polit.-mil. affairs, 1993-94, asst. sec., bur. polit.-mil. affairs, 1994—. Contbr. articles to profl. jours. Recipient Superior Honor award Dept. State, 1980, 84, 86. Mem. Am. Fgn. Service Assn., Army-Navy Club. Office: Polit Mil Affairs Bur 2201 C St NW Washington DC 20520-0001

MCNAMARA, THOMAS NEAL, lawyer; b. Washington, Dec. 1, 1930; s. Philip Joseph and Louise Loretta (Ryan) McN.; children: John Michael, George Denison, Mary Louise Higgins; m. Deana Hollingsworth, Dec. 21, 1986; stepchildren: John W. Hollingsworth, Christopher M. Hollingsworth, Kim R. Hollingsworth. B.A., Duke U., 1952; J.D. with honors, George Washington U., 1959. Bar: Va. 1959, Calif. 1960. Assoc. Pillsbury, Madison & Sutro, San Francisco, 1959-66, ptnr., 1967-86; mng. ptnr. L.A., 1986-89, chmn., 1990-95, retired ptnr., 1996—; sr. cons. Hildebrandt, San Francisco, 1996—. Contbr. articles to profl. jours. Trustee Dixie Sch. Dist., San Rafael, Calif., 1964-76; dir. San Francisco Home Health Svc., 1975-82, Hospice of Marin (Calif.), 1988-91, Bay Area Coun., 1990-95, Calif. Sun Dry Foods, 1996—; mem. bd. advisors Nat. Law Ctr., George Washington U. Law Sch., 1991—. Served to lt. comdr. USNR, 1952-56, Korea. Fellow Am. Bar Found. (life), Am. Coll. Tax Counsel; mem. ABA, Calif. Bar Assn., San Francisco Bar Assn., Va. Bar Assn., Internat. Game Fish Assn. (Calif. rep. 1983—), Order of Coif, Pacific-Union Club, Presidio Golf Club. Republican. Roman Catholic. Office: Hildebrandt 44 Montgomery St Ste 2520 San Francisco CA 94104-4712

MCNAMARA, TIMOTHY JAMES, secondary education educator; b. Buffalo, June 24, 1952; s. Vincent Michael and Peggy Jo (Matthews) McN.; m. Julie Ann McCready, Aug. 25, 1979; children: James Vincent, Lucille Ann. BA in Math., Niagara U., 1975; EdM, SUNY, Buffalo, 1979; MBA, SUNY, 1984; cert., Sch. Adminstrv. & Supr., 1997. Tchr. Williamsville East High Sch., East Amherst, N.Y., 1975-84, Maryvale Sr. High Sch., Cheektowaga, N.Y., 1984-86; tchr. gifted math. program SUNY, 1987-90; coord. math. The Nichols Sch ., Buffalo, 1991-93; K-12 math. supr. West Irondequoit Schs., Rochester, 1993—; lectr. in field. Faculty editor student math. jour. The Nth Degree; contbr. articles to profl. jours. Recipient N.Y. State Presdl. award for Excellence in Secondary Math. Teaching, 1993, finalist, 1990, 91. Mem. Nat. Coun. Tchrs. Math., Assn. Math. Tchrs. N.Y. State (exec. bd. dirs. 1992-94), N.Y. State Assn. Math. Suprs., Phi Delta Kappa. Avocations: gardening, travel, bicycling. Home: 1093 Marigold Dr Webster NY 14580-8765 Office: Irondequoit High Sch 260 Cooper Rd Rochester NY 14617-3049

MCNAMARA, TOM, newspaper editor. Managing editor-news USA Today, Arlington, Va. Office: USA Today 1000 Wilson Blvd Arlington VA 22209-3901*

MCNAMARA, TOM, scientific consulting corporation executive; b. Battle Creek, Mich., May 23, 1944; s. George P. (stepfather) and Mildred E. Lunt. Grad. in Chemistry, Boston U., 1966; M.B.A., Northeastern U., 1970; m. Ellen K. LaRue, Sept. 24, 1977; 1 child, George Lunt. With corp. planning dept. Reynolds Aluminum, Richmond, Va., 1970-72; sr. cons. Technomic Cons., Chgo., 1972-74; founder, pres. NUVENTURES Cons., Inc., Chgo. and San Diego, 1975—; speaker trade convs. and confs. worldwide; frequent guest TV and radio talk shows; on water advisor Am.'s Cup, 1988, 91, 94. Author: Henry Lunt and The Ranger, 1991, Henry Lunt and The Spymaster, 1994, Skull and Crossbones, 1997; co-author: America's Changing Workforce, 1990; editor: George and The Pitching Machine, 1994; contbr. articles to profl. publs. Rep. nominee Ill. Gen. Assembly, 1974, 76; mem. various coms. United Fund and Chgo. Assn. Commerce and Industry, 1975-79; Spokesman 200th Anniversary U.S. Bill of Rights tour, 1991. 1st lt. Ordnance Corps, U.S. Army, 1966-69. Recipient Presdl. Commendation for heroism, 1974, Commendation award Chgo. Police Dept., 1974, Pulitzer Prize nominee, 1991. Mem. Acacia, Bahia Corinthian Yacht Club, San Diego Tennis and Racquet Club. Contbr. articles to profl. publs. Office: PO Box 2489 La Jolla CA 92038-2489

MCNAMARA, WILLIAM, priest; b. Providence, Feb. 14, 1926; s. John and Margaret (Gannon) McN. BA in Theology and Philosophy, Cath. U. Am.; MA in Edn. and Psychology, Boston Coll. Became a Discalced Carmelite monk, 1944, ordained Roman Cath. priest, 1951. founder Spiritual Life Inst. Am., 1960. Founder Spiritual Life Mag., 1955, editor, 1955-62; author: The Art of Being Human, 1962, The Human Adventure: Contemplation for Everyman, 1974, Mystical Passion, 1977, Christian Mysticism, 1981, Earthy Mysticism, 1987. Home: Box 219 Crestone CO 81131

MCNAMEE, SISTER CATHERINE, educational association executive; b. Troy, N.Y., Nov. 13, 1931; d. Thomas Ignatius McNamee and Kathryn McNamee Marois. B.A., Coll. of St. Rose, 1953, D.H.L. (hon.), 1975; M.Ed., Boston Coll., 1955, M.A., 1958; Ph.D., U. Madrid, 1967. Grad. asst. Boston Coll., 1954-55; asst. registrar Boston Coll. (Grad. Sch.), 1955-57; acad. v.p. Coll. St. Rose, Albany, N.Y., 1968-75; dir. liberal arts Thomas Edison Coll., Trenton, 1975-76; pres. Trinity Coll., Burlington, Vt., 1976-79, Coll. St. Catherine, St. Paul, 1979-84; dean Dexter Hanley Coll., U. Scranton, Pa., 1984-86; pres. Nat. Cath. Ednl. Assn., Washington, 1986-96; now sr. scholar Inst. Christian Social Thought and Mgmt., U. St. Thomas, St. Paul, Minn., 1996—; bd. dirs. St. mary's Press, De La Salle H.S. Bd. dirs. Am. Forum, Boston Coll., Coll. St. Rose, U.S. Cath. China Bur. Spanish Govt. grantee, 1965-67; OAS grantee, 1967-68; Fulbright grantee, 1972-73. Mem. Inter-Am. Confedn. Cath. Edn., Internat. Orgn. Cath. Edn., Nat. Cath. Ednl. Assn., Internat. Fedn. Cath. Univs., Delta Epsilon Sigma. Roman Catholic. Office: Inst Christian Social Thought and Mgmt U St Thomas Mail #4231 5324 Summit Ave Ste 100 Saint Paul MN 55105

MCNAMEE, EVELYN HAYNES, civilian military employee; b. Monticello, Miss., Dec. 10, 1947; d. Leroy and Leslie (Hammond) Haynes; m. George Allen McNamee Jr., Aug. 23, 1970; children: Leonard, George Allen, Paula Elizabeth, Candace Renee. BS, Alcorn State U., Lorman, Miss., 1969; MS, Tuskegee Inst., 1971. Indsl. hygienist U.S. Army, White Sands Missile Range, N.Mex., 1985-88; sr. indsl. hygienist USN Naval Hosp., San Diego, 1988-90; indsl. hygienist, command staff Naval Aviation Depot Naval Air Sta. North Island, San Diego, 1990-91; sr. indsl. hygienist David Taylor Model Basin Carderock Divsn. Naval Surface Warfare Ctr., Bethesda, Md., 1991—. Mem. Sidwell Friends' Resource Bank, Sidwell Friends' Diversity Group, 1996. Mem. NAFE, Am. Conf. Govt. Indsl. Hygienists, Am. Indsl. Hygiene Assn., Navy Indsl. Hygiene Assn., Internat. Platform Assn., Md. Profl. Spkrs. Assn., Women's Fedn. World Peace, Toastmasters (past pres. local chpt.). Democrat. Roman Catholic. Avocations: reading, rose gardening, walking. Home: 13009 Flack St Silver Spring MD 20906-4068 Office: Nat Navy Med Ctr Bldg 22 Br Med Clinic Carderock DTMB NSWCCD Code 0026IH Bethesda MD 20084

MCNAMEE, LOUISE, advertising agency executive; m. Peter McHugh. Student, Mary Baldwin Coll., Va. With rsch. dept. Kelly Nason, 1973-79; exec. v.p., dir. mktg. and rsch. Della Femina Travisano & Ptnrs. (later Della Femina McNamee), N.Y.C., 1979-92, exec. v.p., ptnr., 1982—, acting pres., from 1984, past pres., chief operating officer, chief exec. officer, 1992-93; now ptnr., pres. Messner, Vetere, Berger, McNamee, Schmetterer, Euro RSCG, N.Y.C., 1993—. Named Advt. Woman of Yr., Advt. Women of N.Y., Adweek, 1988. Office: Messner, Vetere, Berger, McNamee, Schmetterer, Euro RSCG 350 Hudson St New York NY 10014-4504

MCNAMEE, STEPHEN M., federal judge; b. 1942. B.A., U. Cinn., 1964; M.A., J.D., U. Ariz., 1969. U.S. atty. Dist. of Ariz., Phoenix, 1985-90; judge U.S. Dist. Ct. Ariz., Phoenix, 1990—. Office: City of Phoenix US Court Hse & Fed Bldg 230 N 1st Ave Phoenix AZ 85025-0230*

MCNANEY, ROBERT TRAINOR, lawyer; b. Chgo., Nov. 16, 1934; s. Leo F. and Lauretta M. (Scully) McN.; m. Janice M. Haertel, June 21, 1958; children: Susan, Mary, Robert, James. Student, John Carroll U., 1952-54; BS in Humanities, Loyola U., 1956, JD, 1958; postdoctoral, Harvard U., 1984. Bar: Ill. 1959. Jr. atty. Brunswick Corp., Skokie, Ill., 1960-63, atty., 1963-68, sr. atty., 1968-85, gen. counsel, 1985-96; v.p., gen. counsel, 1996—. Served with U.S. Army, 1958-60. Mem. Am. Corp. Counsel Assn., North Shore Gen. Counsels Assn., Chgo. Bar Assn. Avocation: golf. Home: 912 N East Ave Oak Park IL 60302-1330 Office: Brunswick Corp 1 N Field Ct Lake Forest IL 60045-4810

MCNAUGHTON, ROBERT FORBES, JR., computer science educator; b. Bklyn., Mar. 13, 1924; s. Robert Forbes and Helen (Brown) McN.; m. Ann Gerardo, Dec. 20, 1948 (div. 1957); children: Nicholas F., Sarah E. McNaughton Deppa; m. Vivien Leonard, June 23, 1974. Student, Bklyn. Coll., 1942-43, 46; BA, Columbia U., 1948; PhD, Harvard U., 1951. Tchr. philosophy Ohio State U., 1951-52, U. Mich., 1953-54, Stanford U., 1954-57; tchr. computer sci. Moore Sch. Elec. Engring., U. Pa., 1957-64; tchr. computer sci. and elec. engring. MIT, 1964-66; prof. computer sci., math. Rensselaer Poly. Inst., Troy, N.Y., 1966-89, prof. emeritus, 1989—; vis. prof. dept. computer sci. SUNY at Albany, 1989-90; researcher Office Naval Rsch., 1952-53, RCA, Moorestown, summer 1960, Princeton, summer 1963. Served with AUS, 1943-46. Recipient Levy medal Franklin Inst., 1956. Mem. Assn. Symbolic Logic, Assn. Computing Machinery, Am. Math. Soc., Math. Assn. Am., Phi Beta Kappa. Home: 2511 15th St Troy NY 12180-1704

MCNAUGHTON, WILLIAM FRANK, translator, educator; b. Westboro, Mo., May 21, 1933; s. Frank McNaughton and Ruth Ellen (Flanders) Francis; m. Margaret Orminski, Apr. 4, 1956 (div. 1971); children: John Ferenc, Dorothy Ellen; m. Li Ying, Apr. 8, 1990. Student, U. Mo., 1951-53; studied poetry and translation with, Ezra Pound, 1953-56; student, Georgetown U., 1953-54; BA, Bklyn. Coll., 1961; PhD, Yale U., 1965. Asst. prof. Oberlin (Ohio) Coll., 1965-70; lectr. Exptl. Coll., Oberlin, 1970-71; vis. lectr. Bowling Green (Ohio) State U., 1972-74, Denison U., Granville, Ohio, 1972-78; prof. Program for Afloat Coll. Edn. (PACE) USN, Norfolk, Va., 1978-84; vis. prof. King Saud U., Abha, Saudi Arabia, 1984-85; sr. lectr. English, translation City Poly. Hong Kong, 1986-89, prin. lectr. translation, 1989-94; univ. sr. lectr. City U., Hong Kong, 1994-95, assoc. prof., 1995—; guest lectr., U. degli Studii, Venice, Italy, 1975; coord. Tri-Coll. Chinese program, Gt. Lakes Colls. Assn., Ann Arbor, 1965-68; cons., Asian Lit. program, Asia Soc., N.Y.C., 1967-80, Nat. Translation Ctr., Austin, Tex., 1965-68, Ballantine Books, N.Y.C., 1985, Princeton U. Press, 1965; presenter papers at lit. confs. Author: Reading and Writing Chinese, 1979; co-translator: Poem Without a Hero and Selected Poems of Anna Akhmatova, 1989, As Through Dreaming: The Tz'u...of Li Ch'ing-chao, 1977; editor, translator: Light from the East, 1978, The Confucian Vision, 1974, The Book of Songs, 1971, The Taoist Vision, 1971, Guerilla War, 1971; contbr. articles to profl. publs., translations to various lit. mags.; editor-in-chief: City Univ. Bull., 1995—; mem. editl. bd. City Univ. Press, 1996—. Woodrow Wilson Found. fellow, 1961-62; modern fgn. lang. fellow, NDEA, 1962-65; grantee, Nat. Translation Ctr., Austin, 1967, Gt. Lakes Colls. Assn., Ann Arbor, 1965, 67-68, Asia Soc., N.Y.C., 1971-72, 74; Fulbright fellow, 1968-69. Avocations: sailing, music, Venetian culture and history. Home: Flat 5C Block 12, 88 Tat Chee Ave, Kowloon Hong Kong Office: City Univ Hong Kong, 83 Tat Chee Ave, Kowloon Hong Kong

MCNEAL, DALE WILLIAM, JR., biological sciences educator; b. Kansas City, Kans., Nov. 23, 1939; s. Dale William and Geraldine Estelle (Reed) McN.; m. Arlene Joyce Purvis, Feb. 26, 1966. B.A., Colo. Coll., 1962; M.S., SUNY Coll. Environ. Sci. and Forestry, Syracuse, 1964; Ph.D., Wash. State U., 1969. Asst. prof. dept. biol. scis. U. Pacific, Stockton, Calif., 1969-74, assoc. prof., 1974-79, prof., 1979—, chmn. dept., 1978-84. Contbr. articles to profl. jours. Served with U.S. Army, 1964-66. Mem. Am. Bot. Soc., Calif. Bot. Soc. (pres. 1987-88), Am. Soc. Plant Taxonomists, Internat. Soc. Plant Taxonomy, Calif. Acad. Scis., Sigma Xi. Republican. Episcopalian. Office: U Pacific Dept Biol Scis Stockton CA 95211

MCNEALEY, J. JEFFREY, lawyer, corporate executive; b. Cin., Feb. 8, 1944; s. J. Lawrence and Louise McNealey; m. Sara Wilson, Sept. 24, 1988; children: Anne Elizabeth, John Alexander. BA, Cornell U., 1966; JD, Ohio State U., 1969. Ptnr. Porter, Wright, Morris & Arthur, Columbus, Ohio, 1969—; bd. dirs. TRC Cos., Windsor, Conn., 1985—; sec., bd. dirs. The Smoot Corp., Columbus, 1972—. Trustee Columbus Cancer Clinic, 1972—, past pres.; trustee German Village Soc., Columbus, 1986—, past pres.; bd. dirs. Columbus chpt. ARC, 1983-86, Columbus Urban League, 1984-90; active Union League Chgo., 1982—. Mem. ABA, Ohio State Bar Assn. (past chmn. environ. com. 1978-84), Columbus Bar Assn., Columbus Country Club, Capital Club of Columbus, Cornell Club of Ctrl. Ohio (trustee 1978—, past pres.). Episcopalian. Avocations: flying, racquet sports, wood working, flyfishing. Office: Porter Wright Morris & Arthur 41 S High St Ste 30 Columbus OH 43215-6113

MC NEALY, SCOTT, computer company executive; b. 1954. BA, Harvard U., 1976; MBA, Stanford U., 1980. Chmn., pres., chief exec. officer Sun Microsystems Inc., Mountain View, Calif.; with Rockwell Internat. Corp., Troy, Mich., 1976-78, sales engr.; staff engr. FMC Corp., Chgo., 1980-81; dir. ops. Onyx Systems, San Jose, Calif., 1981-82; chmn. bd., pres., CEO Sun Microsystems Inc., Mountain View, Calif., 1982—, now chmn. bd., pres., chief exec. officer, 1982, also dir., 1985. Office: Sun Microsystems Inc 2550 Garcia Ave Mountain View CA 94043-1109*

MCNEAR, BARBARA BAXTER, financial communications executive, consultant; b. Chgo., Oct. 9, 1939; d. Carl Henden and Alice Gertrude (Parrish) Baxter; m. Robert Erskine McNear, Apr. 13, 1968 (div. 1981); 1 child, Amanda Baxter; m. Glenn Philip Eisen, June 7, 1987. B.S. in Journalism, Northwestern U., 1961. Editorial asst. Scott Foresman & Co., Chgo., 1961; pub. rels. dir. Market Facts Inc., Chgo., 1961-63; account supr. Philip Lesly Co., Chgo., 1963-68, 69; account exec. Burson-Marsteller, Chgo., 1968; dir. communications CNA Fin. Corp., Chgo., 1969-74; dir. pub. rels. Gould Inc., Chgo., 1974; v.p. Harris Bank, Chgo., 1974-80, Fireman's Fund Ins. Co., San Francisco, 1980-83; sr. v.p. First Chgo. Corp., 1983-86; v.p. communications Xerox Fin. Svcs., Inc., Stamford, Conn., 1987-93; mgr. shareholder comm. Xerox Corp., Stamford, 1993—. Mem. Pub. Rels. Soc. Am., Fairfield County Pub. Rels. Assn., Nat. Investor Rels. Inst. (pres. Chgo. chpt. 1974-75, bd. dirs. Chgo. chpt.), Cliffdwellers, Princeton Club. Episcopalian. Home: 23 Telva Rd Wilton CT 06897-3733 Office: Xerox Corp 800 Long Ridge Rd Stamford CT 06902-1227

MCNEEL, VAN LOUIS, chemical company executive; b. Laurel, Miss., July 4, 1925; s. George Louis and Pauline (Webb) McN.; m. Betty Tarwater, July 6, 1959 (div. 1966); 1 child, Clayton Webb; m. Diane Kidd, Dec. 30, 1971 (div. 1994); 1 child, Ian Edward. Student, Sanford U. (formerly Howard Coll.); LLB, U. Ala., 1949. Project mgr. Reynolds Metals, N.Y.C. and Jacksonville, Fla., 1949-51; div. mgr. Olin Mathieson Chem. Corp., Atlanta, 1951-60, dir. internat. ops., 1960-63; pres. Polymer Internat. Corp., Tampa, 1964-89; chmn., chief exec. officer McNeel Internat Corp, Tampa, Fla., 1989—. Bd. dirs. Tampa chpt ARC; mem. Golden Triangle Civic Assn., Tampa Bay Area Trade Coun. Fgn. Rels. Mem. Am. Mgmt. Assn., Soc. Plastic Engrs. Clubs: Palma Ceia Golf and Country, Tampa Yacht and Country, Ctr. Club, University (Tampa). Office: McNeel Internat Corp 5401 W Kennedy Blvd Tampa FL 33609-2428

MCNEELEY, DONALD ROBERT, steel company executive; b. Chgo., July 31, 1954; s. Donald Robert and Alma Theresa (Gray) McN.; m. Elizabeth Dianne Smith, Aug. 23, 1975; children: Kelly Dianne, Meghan Maureen. BA, U. Wis., 1979; MBA summa cum laude, George Williams Coll., 1985; PhD cum laude, Columbia Pacific U., 1986; MS in Mgmt. and Organiztional Behavior, Ill. Benedictine Coll., 1991. With Chgo. Tube and Iron Co., 1972-77, ops. mgr., 1977-79, corp. mgr. employee relations, 1979-82, v.p. ops., 1982-84, exec. v.p., 1984-91, pres., chief oper. officer, 1991—, also bd. dirs.; trustee Plumbing and Heating Wholesalers Retirement Income Plan, Chgo., 1987—, negotiator labor com., 1982—; adj. prof. mgmt. De Paul U., Chgo., 1992, mem. bus. adv. coun., mem. Inst. for Bus. and Profl. Ethics, De Paul U. Editor: Employment in Illinois, 1983; contbr. articles to profl. jours. Dir. Com. for Monetary Rsch. and Edn., Charlotte, N.C., 1988-95. Mem. Steel Svc. Ctr. Inst. (trustee, 1st v.p. Found. for Continuing Edn. 1981—, chmn. tubular products coun. 1994—), La Grange Country Club (Ill.). Republican. Roman Catholic. Avocations: golf, reading, investing.

MCNEELY, JOHN J., lawyer; b. Mpls., Oct. 8, 1931; s. John J. Sr. and Mae (Carlin) McN.; children: Mary Ann, John J. Jr., Michael F., Patricia C., David C. BS, Georgetown U., 1955, JD, 1958. Bar: Minn. 1958. Law clk. Minn. Supreme Ct., St. Paul, 1958-59; ptnr. Briggs & Morgan, St. Paul, 1959—. Sgt. USMC, 1950-52. Fellow Am. Coll. Trust and Estate Counsel; mem. ABA, Minn. State Bar Assn., Ramsey County Bar Assn., Prestrwick Country Club. Home: 1183 Ivy Hill Dr Saint Paul MN 55118-1827 Office: Briggs & Morgan 2200 First National Bank Bldg Saint Paul MN 55101-1319

MCNEELY, PATRICIA GANTT, journalism educator; b. Winnsboro, S.C., Dec. 2, 1939; d. William Adolphus and Alice (Woodson) Gantt; m. Alfred Raymond McNeely, Apr. 8, 1960; children: Allison Patricia, Alan David. BA, Furman U., 1960; MA, U. S.C., 1975. Reporter Greenville (S.C.) News, 1958-60; reporter Columbia (S.C.) Record, 1960-66, 66-72, news editor, 1979-80; reporter The State, Columbia, 1965-66; prof. journalism U. S.C., Columbia, 1972—; state mgr. Voter News Svc., N.Y., 1972—; workshop dir. Reader's Digest, Pleasantville, N.Y., 1985—. Mem. Assn. for Edn. in Journalism and Mass Comm. (sec. mag. divsn. 1995-96, head newspaper divsn. 1988-89, standing profl. freedom and responsibility com. 1995—). Office: Univ SC Coll Journalism Mass Comm Blossom at Assembly Sts Columbia SC 29208

MCNEELY, PATRICIA MORSE, middle school educator, poet, writer; b. Galveston, Tex., Apr. 2, 1923; d. Bleecker Lansing Sr. and Annie Maud (Pillow) Morse; m. Chalmers Rankin McNeely, Mar. 22, 1949 (div. Aug. 1959); children: David Lansing, Timothy Ann McNeely Caldwell, Patricia Grace McNeely Dragon, Abigail Rankin McNeely. BS in Edn., U. Tex., 1972; MA in Ednl. Psychology, U. Tex., San Antonio, 1978, MA in Ednl. Psychology-Counseling, 1981. Cert. tchr., Tex.; cert. profl. counselor. Sec./adminstrv. sec. various cos., Galveston & Austin, Tex., 1945-49, 60-70; police stenographer Austin Police Dept., 1970-74; spl. edn. tchr. N.E. Ind. Sch. Dist., San Antonio, 1974-76, S.W. Ind. Sch. Dist., San Antonio, 1978-81; vocat. adjustment coord. East Ctrl. Ind. Sch. Dist., San Antonio, 1981-82; counselor, tchr. Stockdale (Tex.) Ind. Sch. Dist., 1982-84; clinic sec. Humana Hosp., Dallas, 1985-87; tchr. history and spl. edn. Dallas Ind. Sch. Dist., Dallas, 1987—; CTD/TSTA/NEA assn. rep. Hill Mid. Sch., Dallas, 1988-89, E.B. Comstock Mid. Sch., Dallas, 1991—. Author: (poetry) Texas City, 1947, A Gift of Love, 1978, The Key, 1991 (The House 1st prize), Between the Raindrops, 1995 (3d prize 1995); contbr. articles to newsletters and co. publs. V.p. zone, sec., libr., various coms. Parents Without Ptnrs., Inc., Austin, 1965-72, internat. ad hoc com. for writing leadership tng. program, 1968, newsletter editor, 1967-72. Recipient 1st Bernice Milburn Moore scholarship award U. Tex. Austin Alumni Assn., 1972. Mem. AAUW, NEA, Assn. Am. Poets, Internat. Lib. Poetry (Hall of Fame 1997), Internat. Soc. Poets, Tex. State Tchrs., Classroom Tchrs. of Dallas (del. to Tex. State Tchrs. Assn. Conf. 1978-81, 91-97), U. Tex. Austin Alumni Assn., U. Tex. San Antonio Alumni Assn. Episcopalian. Avocations: writing, reading, music, sewing/handicrafts, book collector. Office: Dallas Ind Sch Dist EB Comstock Mid Sch 7044 Hodde St Dallas TX 75217-4830

MC NEICE, JOHN AMBROSE, JR., retired investment company executive; b. Quincy, Mass., Sept. 28, 1932; s. John Ambrose and Gladys Lydia (Starratt) McN.; m. Margarete Emma Aust, Apr. 2, 1956; children: Gabriele S., Margarete Anne. BA magna cum laude, Boston Coll., 1954; MBA, Northeastern U., Boston, 1960. Chartered fin. analyst. With Colonial Mgmt. Assos., Inc. (subsidiary of TCG, Inc.), Boston, 1956—, v.p., 1968-73, dir. investment rsch., 1973, exec. v.p., 1974, pres., chief exec. officer, 1975-83, chmn., 1983-96; chmn. The Colonial Group, Inc., Boston, 1985-96, CEO, 1985-95; bd. dirs., Am. Ireland Fund. Trustee Boston Coll., St. John's Sem., Western Jesuit Sch. Theology, Cath. Charities of Archdiocese of Boston; chmn. bd. trustees Nativity Prep. Sch.; mem. Carney Hosp. Found., Corp. Westworth Inst. Tech.; bd. visitors Peter F. Drucker Ctr., Claremont U.; bd. dirs., treas., exec. com. Peter F. Drucker Found.; bd. dirs., exec. com. United Way Mass. Bay; bd. overseers Northeastern U.; trustee, pres. Boston Cath. Found., Archdiocese of Boston, mem. fin. coun.; dir. Pope John XXIII Med.-Moral Rsch. and Edn. Ctr.; bd. overseers Facing Hist. and Ourselves Nat. Found., Inc.; pres., trustee Better Opportunities Scholarship Found., Inc.; mem. exec. com. CEOs for Fundamental Change in Edn. With U.S. Army, 1954-56. Mem. Knights of Malta, The Milton-Hoosic Club, Wollaston Golf Club. Roman Catholic. Home: 47 Green St Canton MA 02021-1023 Office: The Colonial Group Inc 1 Financial Ctr Boston MA 02111-2621

MCNEIL, BARBARA JOYCE, radiologist, educator; b. Cambridge, Mass., Feb. 11, 1941; d. Archibald Pius and Katherine (Joyce) McN. AB, Emmanuel Coll., 1962; MD, Harvard U., 1966, PhD, 1972. Diplomate Am. Bd. Nuclear Medicine. Intern Mass. Gen. Hosp., Boston, 1966-67, resident in nuclear medicine, 1971-73; prof. radiology and clin. epidemiology Harvard Med. Sch. and Brigham & Women's Hosp., Boston, 1983—, dir. ctr. for cost effective care, 1980-93; chmn. dept. Ridley Watts prof. health care policy Harvard Med. Sch., 1988—; chmn. Blue Cross-Mass. Hosp. Assn. Fund for Coop. Innovation, 1981-87; mem. Prospective Payment Assessment Commn., 1983-91; mem. nat. adv. coun. Agy. for Health Care Policy, Rsch. and Evaluation, 1991—. Editor: Critical Issues in Medical Technology, 1982; contbr. articles to profl. jours. Fellow AAAS, Am. Coll. Nuclear Physicians

(Presdl. award 1995); mem. Am. Acad. Arts and Scis., Inst. Medicine (coun. 1991—), Fleischner Soc., Nat. Coun. on Radiation Protection, Am. Coll. Radiology, Soc. Nuclear Medicine. Office: Harvard Med Sch Dept Health Care Policy 180 Longwood Ave Boston MA 02115-5821

MCNEIL, DAVID JAMES, communications executive, marketing consultant; b. Torrance, Calif., Jan. 20, 1958; s. James Eugene and Nancy Anne (Williams) McN.; m. Sheryl Lillian Stark, Aug. 31, 1980. BA in Bus. Adminstrn. and Mktg., Calif. State U., Northridge, 1982. Pres. McNeil Glass Co., Westlake, Calif., 1978-81; coordinator mktg., pay-per-view devel. Group W Cable, Torrance, 1982-86; mgr. mktg., programming Daniels Cablevision, Arcadia, Calif., 1986, bus. mgr. pay-per-view, 1986; mgr. prodn. and devel. pay-per-view United Artists Entertainment, Inc., Glendora, Calif., 1986-89; asst. v.p. Calif. Casualty Mgmt. Co., Orange, Calif., 1989—; mktg. cons. Cornucopia Mktg. Co., Torrance, 1986-88, Golden Rule Mktg. Co., Torrance, 1986-88. Mem. Am. Mktg. Assn. (life), So. Calif. Mktg. Coun., Mensa, Torrance C. of C., Simi Valley Jaycees, Torrance Sister City Assn., Delta Sigma Pi (life). Avocations: collecting classic automobiles, motorcycle racing, video production. Home: 28879 Modjeska Canyon Rd Silverado CA 92676-9748 Office: Calif Casualty Mgmt Co 600 City Pkwy W Ste 500 Orange CA 92868-2946

MCNEIL, HEIDI LORETTA, lawyer; b. Preston, Iowa, Apr. 7, 1959; d. Archie Hugo and Heidi (Waltert) McN.; m. L. William Staudenmaier III; 1 child Kathleen Louise McNeil Staudenmaien. BA in Journalism and Broadcasting with distinction, U. Iowa, 1981, JD with distinction, 1985. Bar: Ariz. 1985, U.S. Dist. Ct. Ariz. 1985, U.S. Ct. Appeals (9th cir.) 1985, U.S. Ct. Appeals (10th cir.) 1990. Sports journalist The Daily Iowan, Iowa City, 1977-81, Quad City Times, Davenport, Iowa, 1981-82; ptnr. Snell & Wilmer, Phoenix, 1985—; judge pro tem, Maricopa County, Phoenix, 1992—. Mem. ABA (mem. domestic violence commn. 1995, House of Dels. 1995—, chair young lawyers career issues com. 1992-93, mem. affiliate assistance program com. 1992-93, dir. 1993-94, spl. projects coord. 1994-95), Internat. Assn. Gaming Attys., Ariz. Bar Assn. (Indian law sect. exec. coun. and officer 1995—, young lawyers exec. coun. 1991-94, chmn. Indian law sect. 1997—), Maricopa County Bar Assn. (bd. dirs. 1991—, young lawyers divsn. 1987-93, pres. 1991-92, officer 1996—), Ariz. Women Lawyers, Phoenix Assn. Def. Counsel, Native Am. Bar Assocs., Phi Beta Kappa, Phi Eta Sigma. Lutheran. Avocations: running, golf, skiing, hiking, bicycling.

MCNEIL, JOHN W., lawyer; b. Detroit, July 18, 1942. BA, Mich. State U., 1964; JD, U. Mich., 1967. Bar: Mich. 1968. Assoc. Miller, Johnson, Snell & Cummiskey, PLC, Grand Rapids, Mich. Bd. dirs. Goodwill Inds. Am., Inc., 1988—, chmn., 1992—. Mem. ABA, State Bar Mich. (coun. of taxation sect. 1975-82, chmn. taxation sect. 1980-81), Grand Rapids Bar Assn. Office: Miller Johnson Snell & Cummiskey 800 Calder Plz Bldg Grand Rapids MI 49503

MCNEIL, LORI MICHELLE, professional tennis player; b. Dec. 18, 1963; d. Charlie Mc. Student, Okla. State U., 1981-83. 8th ranked woman USTA; winner mixed doubles (with Jorge Lozano) French Open, 1988. Pro Tour Singles Titles include, Colorado Classic, 1992, Japan Open, 1992. Office: US Tennis Assn 70 West Red Oak Ln White Plains NY 10604*

MCNEIL, STEVEN ARTHUR, food company executive; b. Ft. Thomas, Ky., May 6, 1942; s. Arthur James and Ruby Marie (Lindell) McN.; m. Kathryn Louise Knapp, Aug. 27, 1966; children: Andrew James, Kathryn Marie. BA, Ohio Wesleyan U., 1964; MBA, Dartmouth U., 1966. Mgr. mktg. and devel. Gen. Foods Corp., 1966-80; mgr. mktg. and devel. Campbell Soup Co., Camden, N.J., 1980-81, mgr. Swanson bus. unit, 1981-83, gen. mgr., 1983-84, group gen. mgr., 1984-85, corp. v.p., 1985—; pres. Mrs. Paul's, 1988-90; sr. v.p., gen. mgr. N.Am., The Haagen-Dazs Co., Inc., Teaneck, N.J., 1990-91; pres., chief oper. officer Bumble Bee SeaFoods, Inc., San Diego, 1992-93; dean Rowan Coll. of Bus. Rowan U. N.J., 1994—; bd. dirs. South Jersey Industries Inc., Folsom, N.J.; chmn., mem. exec. com. Frozen Food Inst., McLean, Va. Trustee West Jersey Health and Hosp. Found., Camden, sec., 1989-91; co-founder The Friends of the Nyacks, Nyack, N.Y., 1972; bd. dirs. Gloucester County United Way, 1995—; bd. dirs. South Jersey Boy Scouts Am. Mem. South Jersey C. of C. (bd. dirs. 1994—, chmn. Camden Fin. Controls com. 1996—), La Costa Country Club.

MC NEILL, CHARLES JAMES, publishing executive; b. Newton, Kans., Dec. 1, 1912; s. Hugh Andrew and Elizabeth (Sheehan) McN.; m. Mary Elizabeth O'Neill, Nov. 6, 1935; 1 dau., Mary Sharon McGlynn. A.B., St. Benedict's Coll., 1933, L.H.D., 1956; postgrad., U. Denver, 1934-36; B.J., Register Coll. Journalism, Denver, 1935, M.J., 1937, D.Journalism, 1939. Librarian Sacred Heart Jr. Coll., 1933; exec. sec. Cath. Action Com. of Men, Wichita, Kans., 1933-34; staff Cath. Advance, Wichita, 1934; asso. editor Register System of Cath. Newspapers, 1934-43; staff Geo. A. Pflaum, Pub., Inc., Dayton, Ohio, 1946-49, asst. to pres., 1949-51, gen. mgr., 1951-57; asst. European dir. Radio Free Europe, Munich, Germany, 1957-61; treas. Internat. Television Devel. Corp., N.Y.C., 1961-63, Inter Tel N.V., Amsterdam, 1961-63; v.p. Kane, McNeill, Inc., N.Y.C., 1963-72, Cath. Lists, Inc., Mt. Vernon, N.Y., 1965-72; pres. Cath. Lists, Inc., 1972-86; dir. Intertel (Prodns.) S.A., Brussels, 1961-63; Ofcl. del. Internat. Union Cath. Press ECOSOC, 1952-56; nat. council USO, 1956; bd. advisers Nat. Fund Raising Conf., 1968-69; bd. dirs. Our Sunday Visitor, Inc., 1968-86. Author: The Sacramentals, 1938, Prayers, 1939, Catholic Church in Colorado, 1943, (with Gregory Smith) Divine Love Story, 1941. Served with AUS, 1943-46. Recipient Disting. Service award Nat. Cath. Devel. Conf., 1984. Mem. Classroom Periodical Pubs. Assn. (chmn. 1950-57), Cath. Press Assn. (pres. 1954-56, St. Francis de Sales award 1987), Cath. Assn. Internat. Peace (v.p. 1953-59), Nat. Cath. Edn. Assn., C. of C. Democrat. Home: 860 Grand Concourse Bronx NY 10451-2814 Office: 22 W 1st St Ste 511 Mount Vernon NY 10550-3000

MCNEILL, CORBIN ASAHEL, JR., utility executive; b. Santa Fe, July 6, 1939; s. Corbin Asahel and Madeline (Thielen) McN.; m. Dorice Schiller, June 16, 1962; children: Michele, Corbin IV, Kevin, Alicia, Timothy. BS in Marine Engring., U.S. Naval Acad., 1962; postgrad., Naval Nuclear Power Sch., Mare Island, Md., 1962-63, U. Calif., Berkeley, 1975-76, Syracuse U., 1983-84. Commd. ensign USN, 1962, advanced through grades to comdr., 1981, ret., 1981; sr. v.p. nuclear generation N.Y. Power Authority, White Plains, 1981-85, Pub. Service Electric & Gas Co., Hancocks Bridge, N.J., 1985-88; exec. v.p. nuclear div. PECO Energy Co., 1988-90; pres., COO Phila. Electric Co., 1990-95, pres., CEO, 1995—, also chmn., 1997—; pres. Adwin Equipment Co., Phila., 1990—. Trustee The Meml. Hosp. of Salem County (N.J.) Inc., 1986; chmn. TeamWalk March of Dimes, Salem, 1986; bd. dirs. Oswego (N.Y.) C. of C., 1982-83. Mem. Am. Nuclear Soc., Nuclear Utility Mgmt. and Resources Com. Avocation: skiing, reading. Office: PECO Energy Co PO Box 8699 2301 Market St Philadelphia PA 19103*

MCNEILL, DANIEL RICHARD, writer; b. San Francisco, June 1, 1947; s. Daniel Harry and Maureen Evangeline (Sherriff) McN.; m. Rosalind Deborah Gold, Dec. 20, 1984. AB, U. Calif., Berkeley, 1975; JD, Harvard U., 1982. Author: Fuzzy Logic, 1993 (L.A. Times Book prize 1993). Mem. Authors Guild. Avocations: hiking, swimming. Home and Office: 9905 Farragut Dr Apt 2 Culver City CA 90232-3244

MCNEILL, FREDERICK WALLACE, lawyer, educator, writer, U.S. government consultant, former military and commercial pilot; b. Chgo., Jan. 4, 1932; s. James Joseph and Irene Gertrude (Stevenson) McN.; m. Judith Carol Austin, Feb. 9, 1957; children: Marjorie, Tamelyn, Kenneth, Patricia, Darcy, Sean, Meghan. BBA, U. Ariz., 1974, JD, 1977. Bar: Ariz. 1977, U.S. Dist. Ct. Ariz., 1977. Served to maj. USAF, 1949-73; ret., 1973; bus. mgr. Engring. & Research Assocs., Inc., Tucson, 1973-74; mng. ptnr. ERA Shopping Ctr., Tucson, 1973-75; chief pilot, spl. agt. Narcotics Strike Force, Ariz., 1975-77; dep. county atty. Pima County, Ariz., 1977-79; atty. Ariz. Drug Control Dist., 1977-79; ptnr. Rees & McNeill, Tucson, 1979-84; writer, 1984—; coord. legal asst. studies program and adj. prof. Nova U.-Panama Ctr., Republic of Panama, 1987-90; adj. prof. Ctrl. Tex. Coll., Germany, 1990-92, Univ. Phoenix and Pima County Coll., Tucson, 1992—; pvt. practice U.S. law, U.S. mil. and PCC installations, 1987-90; of counsel Carreira-Pitti P.C. Abogados, Panama, 1987-90; cons. Booz, Allen & Hamilton, Inc., Panama, 1989-90; pvt. practice Wurzburg, Fed. Republic of Germany, 1990-92; pvt. practice, Tucson, 1992—, adj. prof. Ctrl. Tex. Coll., Germany, 1990-92, U. Phoenix, Pima C.C., Tucson, 1992—; lectr. air smuggling seminars, organized crime seminars, Ariz., 1977-79. V.p. Indian Ridge Homeowners Assn., 1980-82; bd. dirs. Tucson Boys Chorus Bldg. Fund Com., 1972-74; lt. Ariz. Rangers. Decorated DFC, Air medal (5), Air Force Commendation medal (2). Mem. ABA, ATLA, Ariz. Bar Assn., Pima County Bar Assn., Ariz. Trial Lawyers Assn., Lawyer Pilots Bar Assn., Internat. Platform Assn., Ret. Officers Assn., Air Force Assn., DAV, Vietnam Vets. Am., Order of Daedelians, Quiet Birdmen. Home: 9957 E Stella Rd Tucson AZ 85730

MCNEILL, G. DAVID, psychology educator; b. Santa Rosa, Calif., Dec. 21, 1931; s. Glenn H. and Ethel G. (Little) McN.; m. Nobuko Baba, Dec. 17, 1957; children: Cheryl, Randall Baba. A.B., U. Calif. at Berkeley, 1953, Ph.D., 1962. Research fellow Harvard U., 1962-65; asst. prof. psychology U. Mich., 1965-66, assoc. prof., 1966-68; prof. psychology and linguistics U. Chgo., 1969—, chmn. dept. psychology, 1991—; mem. Inst. Advanced Study, Princeton, 1973-75; fellow Netherlands Inst. for Advanced Studies, 1983-84. Author: The Acquisition of Language, 1970, The Conceptual Basis of Language, 1979, Psycholinguistics: A New Approach, 1987, Gengo Shinrigaku, 1991, Hand and Mind: What Gestures Reveal about Thought, 1992. Recipient Faculty Achievement award Burlington No., 1991, Ann. Excellence in Pub. award Assn. Am. Pubs., Gordon G. Laing award U. Chgo. Press, 1995; Guggenheim fellow, 1973-74; grantee NSF, 1983-89, 97—, Spencer Found., 1979-82, 89-92, 95—, NIDCD, 1992-96. Fellow AAAS, Am. Psychol. Soc.; mem. Cognitive Sci. Soc., Linguistic Soc. Am., Violoncello Soc., Phi Beta Kappa, Sigma Xi. Office: U Chgo Dept Psychology 5848 S University Ave Chicago IL 60637-1515

MCNEILL, JOHN, botanist; b. Edinburgh, Scotland, U.K., Sept. 15, 1933; s. Thomas and Helen Lawrie (Eagle) McN.; m. Bridget Mariel Winterton, July 29, 1961 (div. 1990); children: Andrew Thomas, Douglas Paul; m. Marilyn Lois James, Apr. 6, 1990. BSc with honors, U. Edinburgh, 1955, PhD, 1960. Asst. lectr. dept. agrl. botany U. Reading, Eng., 1957-60, lectr. agrl. botany, 1960-61; lectr. dept. botany U. Liverpool, Eng., 1961-69; rsch. scientist Plant Rsch. Inst. Agriculture, Ottawa, Can., 1969-77; sr. rsch. scientist Biosystematics Rsch. Inst. Agr., Ottawa, Can., 1977-81; prof. dept. biology U. Ottawa, Can., 1981-87; regius keeper Royal Botanic Garden, Edinburgh, Scotland, 1987-89; assoc. dir. Royal Ont. Mus., Toronto, Can., 1989-90, acting dir., 1990-91, dir., 1991—; prof. dept. botany U. Toronto, 1991-97, dir. emeritus, 1997—; curator herbarium U. Liverpool, 1964-69, dep. sr. tutor faculty sci., 1967-69; vis. assoc. prof. dept botany U. Wash., Seattle, 1969; acting assoc. prof. dept. population and environ. biology U. Calif., Irvine, 1969; chief taxonomy and econ. botany sect. Plant Rsch. Inst. Agriculture, Ottawa, Can., 1969-73; sessional lectr. dept. biology U. Ottawa, 1977, chmn. dept. biology, 1981-87, mem. faculty sci. teaching com., 1981, mem. univ. rsch. com., 1986-87, mem. univ. adv. com. on computing, 1984-87, mem. sch. grad. studies, adj. prof., 1987-91; vis. prof. dept. botany U. Toronto, 1978; adj. prof. dept. biology Carleton U., 1973-79; hon. prof. dept. botany U. Edinburgh, 1989, hon. fellow faculty sci., 1988-89; dir. George R. Gardiner Mus. Ceramic Art, Toronto, 1991-96; pres. Royal Ont. Mus. Found., 1992-97; contbr. to numerous sci. meetings throughout U.S., Can. Europe. Author: (with others) Grasses of Ontario, 1980, The Genus Atriplex (Chenopodiaceae) in Canada, 1983, Preliminary Inventory of Canadian Weeds, 1988, also book chpts.; editor: (with others) Phenetic and Phylogenetic Classification, 1964, International Code of Botanical Nomenclature, 1983, 88, 94, French edit., 1988, 95, German edit., 1989, 95, Japanese edit., 1992, Flora of North America, Vols. 1 and 2, 1993, Slovakian edit. 1996, International Code of Nomenclature for Cultivated Plants, 1995; mem. editl. com. Flora of N.Am., 1985—, nomenclature advisor, 1987—; contbr. articles to profl. jours.; mem. internat. bd. editors Edinburgh Jour. Botany, 1996—. NSERC Operating grantee, 1982-85, 1985-88, 1989-92. Fellow Linnean Soc. London; mem. Am. Soc. Naturalists, Am. Soc. Plant Taxonomists, Biol. Coun. Can. (v.p. 1984-85, v.p. and pres.-elect 1985-86, pres. 1986-87), Can. Coun. Univ. Biology Chmn. (v.p. 1982-84, pres. 1984-85, past pres. 1985-86), Bot. Soc. Brit. Isles, Bot. Soc. Edinburgh (v.p. 1987-89), Can. Bot. Assn. (chmn. systematics and phytogeography sect. 1981-83), Natural Scis. and Engring. Rsch. Coun. Can. (mem. population biology grant selection com. 1981-84), Classification Soc., Hennig Soc., Hunt Inst. Bot. Documentation, Internat. Union Biol. Scis. (voting mem. exec. 1985-88, alt. mem. exec. 1991-94), Internat. Assn. Bot. and Mycological Socs. (sec. 1986-93, chmn. 1993—), Internat. Union Biol. Scis., Internat. Union Microbiol. Socs. (internat. com. for bionomenclature 1994—), Internat. Assn. Plant Taxonomy (mem. coun. 1981-87, 93—, adminstr. fin. 1987-93), Internat. Congress Systematic and Evolutionary Biology (mem. internat. com. 1980-90), Internat. Orgn. Plant Biosystematists (mem. coun. 1989-92), Internat. Orgn. for Systematics and Evolutionary Biology (treas. 1996—), Annales Botanici Fennici (mem. adv. bd. 1987-92), Acta Botanica Fennica (mem. adv. bd. 1987-92), Internat. Assn. Bot. Gardens, Internat. Weed Sci. Soc., Orgn. for Phyto-Taxonomic Investigation of Mediterranean Area (bd. dirs. 1989—), Royal Caledonian Hort. Soc., Royal Hort. Soc., Soc. Systematic Biology, Systematics Assn. (mem. coun. 1959-62, 64-66, gen. sec. 1966-69), Ottawa Field Naturalists Club, Scottish Rock Garden Club, Internat. Orgn. for Plant Info. (vice-chmn. 1993-96, chmn. 1996—). Office: Royal Ontario Museum, 100 Queen's Park, Toronto, ON Canada M5S 2C6

MCNEILL, JOHN HUGH, pharmaceutical sciences educator; b. Chgo., July 5, 1938; s. John and Agnes Margaret (McLean) McN.; m. Sharon Keneffly, July 27, 1963; children: Sandra, Laurie. BS, U. Alta., Can., 1960, MS, 1962; PhD, U. Mich., 1967. Lectr. pharmacy Dalhousie U., 1962-63, U. Alta., 1963; research assoc. U. Mich., Ann Arbor, 1963-65, teaching fellow, 1965-66; asst. instr. Mich. State U., East Lansing, 1966-67, asst. prof., 1967-71; assoc. prof. U. B.C., 1971-72, assoc. prof., chmn. div. pharmacology and toxicology, 1972-75, dir. research and grad. studies Faculty Pharm. Scis., 1977-78; prof. Faculty Pharm. Scis., 1975—; asst. dean U. B.C., 1978-81, research prof. Med. Research Council, 1981-82, prof., assoc. dean research and grad. studies, 1982-84, dean Faculty Pharm. Scis., 1985-96. Contbr. over 400 tech. articles to profl. jours. Mem. Pharm. Soc. Can. (various coms. 1974-88, coun. 1977-83, v.p. 1979, pres. 1980-81), Am. Soc. for Pharm. and Therapeutics (J.J. Abel award com. 1981, Upjohn award com., 1978-80, chmn. mem. com. 1983-86), Western Pharm. Soc. (coun. 1977-81, pres. 1979-80, past pres. 1980-81), N.Y. Acad. Scis., Internat. Soc. for Heart Rsch. (coun. 1986-95), AAAS, B.C. Coll. Pharms. (coun. 1985-96), Internat. Union Pharmacologists (Can. rep. 1982-88), Am. Pharm. Assn. Office: The Univ of BC, The Faculty of Pharm Scis, 2146 East Mall, Vancouver, BC Canada V6T IZ3

MCNEILL, K(ENNETH) G(ORDON), medical physicist; b. Cheshire, Eng., Dec. 21, 1926; s. Ferguson and Elizabeth (Stevenson) McN.; m. J. Ruth S. Robertson, Nov. 6, 1959; 1 dau., Diane E.S. B.A., Oxford (Eng.) U., 1947, M.A., 1950, D.Phil. (Harmsworth Sr. scholar), 1950; DSL, U Trinity Coll., Toronto, Ont., Can., 1997. Sir John Dill Meml. fellow Yale U., 1950-51; Nuffield research fellow Glasgow (Scotland) U., 1951-52, lectr., 1952-57; mem. faculty U. Toronto, Ont., Can., 1957-92; prof. physics U. Toronto, Ont., Can., 1963-92, prof. medicine, 1969-92; spl. staff mem. Toronto Gen. Hosp., 1974-92; fellow Trinity Coll., Toronto, 1963-92, prof. emeritus, 1992—; mem. adv. com. radiation protection to Ministry Nat. Health and Welfare, 1964-68; mem. nuclear accident contingency planning bd. Govt. of Ont., 1974—; hon. prof. Monash U., Melbourne, 1988; pres. Kishmul Resources Inc.; dir. Can. Ednl. Stds. Inst.; trustee, mem. exec. com. Toronto Sch. Theology. Author: (with J. Maclachlan, P.T. Spencer, J. Bell) Matter and Energy, 1963, 3d edit., 1987, French edit., 1981; contbr. numerous articles to profl. jours. Mem. governing coun. U. Toronto, 1980-86, 89-92. Fellow Instn. Nuclear Engrs. (U.K.); mem. Can. Assn. Physicists, Can. Radiation Protection Assn. Research on low energy nuclear physics and med. physics. Home: 70 Rathnelly Ave, Toronto, ON Canada M4V 2M6

MCNEILL, MARY KATHRYN MORGAN, librarian; b. Greenville, S.C., Feb. 22, 1958; d. Harvey Eugene and Mary Anna (Walser) Morgan; m. George Terrence McNeill, May 17, 1980; 1 child, Terrence Morgan. BS, Winthrop Coll., 1980; MLS, Emory U., 1985. Media specialist Thurston Elem. Sch., Thomaston, Ga., 1980-85; asst. libr. Oxford (Ga.) Coll. Libr. Emory U., 1985-88, dir., 1988—. Sunday Sch. tchr. Thomaston United Methodist Ch., 1981. Mem. ALA, Assn. Coll. and Rsch. Librs., Libr. Adminstrn. and Mgmt. Assn., Southeastern Libr. Assn., Ga. Libr. Assn., Delta Kappa Gamma (sec. chpt. 1992-96, pres. chpt. 1996—). Home: 3303 Sams Way Conyers GA 30208-2250 Office: Emory U Oxford Coll Libr PO Box 1448 Oxford GA 30267-1448

MCNEILL, ROBERT PATRICK, investment counselor; b. Chgo., Mar. 17, 1941; s. Donald Thomas and Katherine (Bennett) McN.; m. Martha Stephan, Sept. 12, 1964; children—Jennifer, Donald, Victoria, Stephan, Elizabeth. B.A. summa cum laude (valedictorian), U. Notre Dame, 1963; M.Letters, Oxford U., 1967. Chartered investment counselor. Assoc. Stein Roe & Farnham, Chgo., 1967-72, gen. ptnr., 1972-77, sr. ptnr., 1977-86, exec. v.p., 1986-89; pres., mng. dir. Stein Roe Internat., Chgo., 1989—; underwriting mem. Lloyds of London, 1980—; dir. Comml. Chgo. Corp.; vice chmn. bd. Hill Internat. Prodn. Co., Houston, 1982—; dir., adv. bd. Touche Remnant Investment Counselors, London, 1983—; dir. TR Worldwide Strategy Fund, Luxembourg, Konrad Adenauer Fund for European Policy Studies, Fed. Republic Germany. Voting mem., sec Ill. Rhodes Scholarship Selection Com.; voting mem. Ill. rep. Great Lakes Dist. Rhodes Scholarship Selection Com.; bd. dirs. Kennedy Sch. for Retarded Children, Palos Park, Ill., 1972—, Winnetka United Way, Ill., 1984—, Division St. YMCA, Chgo., 1972—; assoc. Rush-Presbyterian-St. Lukes Med. Ctr., Chgo., 1975—; mem. leadership com. Rush Alzheimer's Disease Ctr. Rhodes scholar, 1963. Fellow Fin. Analysts Fedn.; mem. Chgo. Council on Fgn. Relations (bd. dirs., treas. 1975—), Inst. European Studies (bd. govs., vice-chmn. 1981—), Investment Analysts Soc. Chgo. (chgo. com., com. on fgn. affairs, com. on internat. and domestic issues), Assn. for Investment Mgmt. and Rsch., Chgo. Soc. Clubs, Econ. Club of Chgo, Sunset Ridge Country (bd. dirs. Northfield, Ill., 1983—). Avocations: coin collecting; bridge; golf; skiing; art.

MCNEILL, THOMAS B., lawyer; b. Chgo., Oct. 28, 1934; s. Donald T. and Katherine M. (Bennett) McN.; m. Ingrid Sieder, May 11, 1963; children: Christine, Thomas, Stephanie. B.A., U. Notre Dame, 1956, J.D., 1958. Ptnr. Mayer, Brown & Platt, Chgo., 1962—; dir. Deltona Corp., Miami, Fla. Served to capt. JAGC USAF, 1959-62. Mem. Chgo. Bar Assn., Chgo. Council Lawyers, Law Club Chgo., Legal Club Chgo. Club: Indian Hill (Winnetka, Ill.). Home: 930 Fisher Ln Winnetka IL 60093-1563 Office: Mayer Brown & Platt 190 S La Salle St Chicago IL 60603-3410

MCNEILL, THOMAS RAY, lawyer; b. Pitts., June 2, 1952; s. Thomas William McNeill and Mary (Shiveley) Hiss; m. Patsy Lynch, June 25, 1977; children: Elizabeth, Kathleen, Thomas. BSBA, U. Fla., 1974; JD, Emory U., 1977. Bar: Ga. 1977, U.S. Dist. Ct. (no. dist.) Ga. 1977. Assoc. Powell, Goldstein, Frazer & Murphy, Atlanta, 1977-84, ptnr., 1984—, mgr. corp. dept., 1993-95. Mem. Ga. Bar Assn., Emory U. Alumni Assn. (pres. exec. com. Atlanta chpt. 1988-89, Law Sch. coun. 1990—), Beta Gamma Sigma. Office: Powell Goldstein Frazer & Murphy Ste 1600 191 Peachtree St Atlanta GA 30303-1741

MCNEILL, WILLIAM, environmental scientist; b. Evanston, Ill., Jan. 1, 1930; s. John and Ebba Katrina (Hansen) McN.; m. Caryl Mook, June 15, 1951 (dec. 1969); children: Elizabeth Marie, Charles Craig, Margaret Ruth; m. Caecilia Cinquanto, Oct. 10, 1970. BA, Colgate U., 1951; MA, Temple U., 1955, PhD, 1961. Chief phys. chemistry br. Frankford Arsenal U.S. Army, Phila., 1955-70, dir. applied sci., 1970-75; chief scientist, environ. mgr. Rocky Mountain Arsenal U.S. Army, Denver, 1975-80, dir. tech. ops., 1980-85; gen. mgr. Battelle Denver Ops., 1985-88; sr. tech. adviser Sci. Applications Internat. Corp., Golden, Colo., 1989-92; dir. tech. devel. Sci. Applications Internat. Corp., Oak Ridge, Tenn., 1992-93; mem. materials adv. bd. ceramics Nat. Acad. Sci./Nat. Rsch. Coun., Washington, 1966; mem. Gov.'s Task Group on Rocky Mountain Arsenal, 1976, Colo. Pollution Prevention Adv. Bd., Denver, 1991—. Contbr. articles to Jour. Che. Physics, Applied Physics Letters, other profl. publs. Mem. Am. Chem. Soc.,Hazardous Material Control Rsch. Inst., Air and Waste Mgmt. Assn. Achievements include 10 patents for electrochemical processes, inorganic materials sythesis, electro-optical devices; demonstration and use of narrow-band optical absorbers for laser protection; leader in development of Army environmental programs. Home: 319 Cliffrose Ct Lafayette CO 80026

MC NEILL, WILLIAM HARDY, retired history educator, writer; b. Vancouver, B.C., Can., Oct. 31, 1917; s. John Thomas and Netta (Hardy) McN.; m. Elizabeth Darbishire, Sept. 7, 1946; children: Ruth Netta, Deborah Joan, John Robert, Andrew Duncan. B.A., U. Chgo., 1938, M.A., 1939; Ph.D., Cornell U., 1947; 19 hon. degrees. Faculty U. Chgo., 1947-87, prof. history, 1957-87, Robert A. Millikan Disting. Svc. prof., 1969-87, prof. emeritus, 1987—, chmn. dept., 1961-67; pres. Demos Found., 1968-80, chmn. bd., 1980-86; George Eastman vis. prof. Oxford (Eng.) U., 1980-81. Author: Greek Dilemma, War and Aftermath, 1947, Report on the Greeks, 1948, History Handbook of Western Civilization, 1948, rev. and enlarged 6th edit., 1986, America, Britain and Russia, Their Cooperation and Conflict, 1941-46, 1953, Past and Future, 1954, Greece: American Aid in Action, 1947-56, 1957, Rise of the West: A History of the Human Community, 1963, 9th edit., 1991 (Nat. Book award, Gordon J. Laing prize), Europe's Steppe Frontier, 1500-1800, 1964, A World History, 1967, 3d edit., 1979, The Contemporary World, 1967, 2d edit., 1975, The Ecumene: Story of Humanity, 1973, Venice, the Hinge of Europe, 1081-1797, 1974, The Shape of European History, 1974, Plagues and Peoples, 1976, Metamorphosis of Greece since World War II, 1978, The Human Condition, An Ecological and Historical View, 1980, Pursuit of Power, 1982, The Great Frontier, 1983, Mythistory and other Essays, 1986, A History of the Human Community, 1986, 5th edit., 1996, Polyethnicity and National Unity in World History, 1987, Arnold J. Toynbee: A Life, 1989, Population and Politics Since 1750, 1990, Hutchins' University: A Memoir of the University of Chicago 1929-50, 1991, The Global Tradition: Conquerors, Catastrophes and Community, 1992, Keeping Together in Time: Dance & Drill in Human History, 1995, Colebrook: An Historical Sketch, 1996; editor: Lord Acton, Essays in the Liberal Interpretation of History, 1967, (with others) Readings in World History, Vols. I-X, 1968-73, Human Migration, 1978, Jour. Modern History, 1971-79, Jour. Modern Greek Studies, 1983-85; bd. editors Ency. Brit., 1981—; contbr. numerous articles and reviews to profl. jours., chpts. to books. Trustee Athens Coll., 1970-88; vice chmn. Christopher Columbus Quincentenary Jubilee Commn., 1985-93; co-chair curriculum task force Nat. Commn. on Social Studies, 1987-89; mem. Bradley Commn. on the Teaching of History, 1986-89; vice chmn. Nat. Coun. for History Edn., 1990-94, Nat. Coun. for History Standards, 1992-94. Recipient Erasmus prize, 1996; Fulbright Research scholar Royal Inst. Internat. Affairs, Eng., 1950-51; Rockefeller grantee, 1951-52; Ford Faculty fellow, 1954-55; Carnegie grantee, 1957-62, 63-64; Guggenheim fellow, 1971-72, 86-87; Josiah H. Macy grantee, 1973-74; Rockefeller grantee, 1976. Fellow Am. Philos. Soc., Am. Acad. Arts and Scis., Brit. Acad. Arts and Scis. (corr.), Royal Hist. Soc. (corr.); mem. Am. Hist. Assn. (council, del. Am. Council Learned Socs., pres. 1985). Office: PO Box 45 Colebrook CT 06021-0045

MCNELLY, JOHN TAYLOR, journalist, educator; b. Lancaster, Wis., Oct. 2, 1923; s. Stephen Sumner and Caroline Hurd (Taylor) McN.; m. Pamela Edith Thompson, Dec. 20, 1952; children: Barbara, Duncan. B.A., U. Wis., 1946, M.A., 1957; Ph.D., Mich. State U., 1961. Reporter AP, Milw., 1948-52, Reuters, London, 1952-53; news editor U. Wis. News Service, Madison, 1957; instr., then assoc. prof. Mich. State U., East Lansing, 1957-66; assoc. prof., then prof. U. Wis., Madison, 1966-82, Evjue-Bascom prof., 1982-88, prof. emeritus, 1988—; asst. dir. Inter-Am. Mass Communications Program, San Jose, Costa Rica, 1961-62; vis. prof. Berlin Inst. Mass. Communication in Developing Nations, W.Ger., 1965, Agrarian U., Lima, Peru, 1968-69; communication cons. UNESCO, Latin Am., 1970-75; lectr. USIA, Latin Am., 1968, 74, 80. Co-author: Communication and Social Change in Latin America, 1968; assoc. editor: Journalism Quar., 1975-77; contbr. monographs and articles to communication publs. Served with USAF, 1942-43. Fulbright-Hays Faculty fellow Lima, Peru, 1968-69. Home: 134 Larkin St Madison WI 53705-5116

MCNEMAR, DONALD WILLIAM, academic administrator; b. Wilmington, Ohio, June 1, 1943; s. Robert Arthur and Kathryn (Hunt) McN.; m. Britta Schein, Aug. 18, 1968; children—Heather Osborn, Galen Rebecca. B.A., Earlham Coll., Richmond, Ind., 1965; Ph.D., Princeton U., 1971. Asst. prof., then assoc. prof. govt. Dartmouth Coll., 1970-81, assoc. dean faculty social scis., 1978-81; headmaster Phillips Acad., Andover, Mass., 1981-94; cons. Conflict Mgmt. Group, Cambridge, Mass., 1994-96; pres. Guilford Coll., Greensboro, N.C., 1996—; regional adv. bd. BayBank, 1981-

94. Mem. exec. com. N.H. Coun. World Affairs, 1975-81; com. mem. Quaker office UN, 1978-82; trustee Sch. Yr. Abroad, 1981-94, Prep for Prep, 1988-94, Earlham Coll., 1989-95, Northfield Mount Hermon Sch., 1994—. Danforth fellow, 1965-69. Office: Guilford Coll 5800 W Friendly Ave Greensboro NC 27410-4108

MC NEW, BENNIE BANKS, economics and finance educator; b. Greenbrier, Ark., Nov. 12, 1931; s. Roland H. and Stella (Avery) McN.; m. Bonnie Lou Stone, Mar. 31, 1956; children—Bonnie Banks, Mary Kathleen, William Michael. B.S., Ark. State Tchrs. Coll., 1953; M.B.A., U. Ark., 1954; Ph.D., U. Tex., 1961. Asst. nat. bank examiner, 1954-56; indsl. specialist U. Ark. Indsl. Research and Extension Center, 1956-59; lectr. finance U. Tex., 1959-61; prof. banking U. Miss., University, 1961-65; dean U. Miss. (Sch. Bus. Adminstrn.), 1965-79, Sch. Bus., Middle Tenn. State U., Murfreesboro, 1980-88; prof. econs. and fin. U. Cen. Ark., Conway, 1988—; asst. dir., v.p. Grad. Sch. Banking of South, La. State U., 1966-97. Author: (with Charles L. Prather) Fraud Control for Commercial Banks, 1962; contbg. author: Money and Banking Casebook, 1966, The Bankers Handbook, 1966, A History of Mississippi, 1973. Served with AUS, 1950-51. Mem. Southwestern Fin. Assn., So. Fin. Assn., Fin. Execs. Inst., Beta Gamma Sigma, Delta Pi Epsilon, Delta Sigma Pi, Omicron Delta Kappa, Phi Kappa Phi, Lions (pres. Oxford, Miss. 1964-65). Home: 12 Bainbridge Dr Conway AR 72032-7217 Office: Univ Central Arkansas PO Box 5025 Conway AR 72035

MCNICHOLAS, DAVID PAUL, automobile rental company executive; b. Youngstown, Ohio, Mar. 1, 1941; s. Paul James and Mary Frances (Dignan) McN.; m. Patricia Marie McAtee; children: Paula, John, Catherine, Tim, Dan. BBA, Youngstown State U., 1962. With Youngstown Sheet and Tube Co. (now subs. LTV), 1964-78, from trainee to dir. data processing; with Avis Inc., N.Y.C., 1978—, sr. v.p., 1985-90, exec. v.p., 1990-97, also bd. dirs.; exec. v.p., chief info. officer HFS Inc., Parsippany, N.J., 1996—; bd. dirs. Avis Europe Ltd. Office: HFS Inc 6 Sylvan Way Parsippany NJ 07054-3826

MCNICHOLS, GERALD ROBERT, consulting company executive; b. Cleve., Nov. 21, 1943; s. Charles Wellington and June Beatrice (Kalal) McN.; m. Paula Kay Austin, Dec. 26, 1964; children: G. Robert Jr., Kay Lynn Ryan, Melissa Sue Carden. BS with honors, Case-Western Res. U., 1965; MS, U. Pa., 1966; ScD, George Washington U., 1976. Cert. cost estimator/analyst. Sr. ops. analyst Office of Sec., Dept. of Def., Washington, 1970-76; v.p. GenTech, Inc., Bethesda, Md., 1976-77, J. Watson Noah, Inc., Falls Church, Va., 1977-78; pres., chief exec. officer Mgmt. Cons. and Rsch., Inc., McLean, Va., 1978—. Co-author: Operations Research for Decision Making, 1975; editor Cost Analysis, 1984; contbr. articles to profl. jours. Pres. Rondelay Civic Assn., Fairfax Sta., Va., 1985-87. Capt. USAF, 1966-70. Mem. Inst. Cost Analysis (pres. 1985-88), Internat. Soc. Parametric Analysts (bd. dirs. 1982-84), Ops. Rsch. Soc. Am. (chmn. mil. applications sect.), Mil. Ops. Rsch. Soc. (sec., treas. 1986-87, v.p. adminstrn. 1987-88, bd. dirs. 1985-88, 92-96), Soc. Cost Estimating and Analysis (bd. dirs. 1990-93). Home: 23349 Parsons Rd Middleburg VA 20117 Office: Mgmt Cons & Rsch Inc 2000 Corporate Rdg Ste 400 Mc Lean VA 22102-7805

MCNICOL, DAVID LEON, federal official; b. South Gate, Calif., May 18, 1944; s. Charles D. and Mary W. (Heisel) McN.; m. Lore Anne Long, Mar. 25, 1967; children: Katharine Anne, Elizabeth Mary. BA magna cum laude, Harvard U., 1966; MS, MIT, 1968, PhD, 1973. Asst. prof. econs. U. Pa., Phila., 1971-75; sr. staff economist Pres.'s Coun. of Econ. Advisors, Washington, 1976; vis. assoc. prof. econs. Calif. Inst. Tech., Pasadena, 1976-77; sr. economist Office of the Sec., U.S. Dept. of Treasury, Washington, 1977-79; dir. Office of Econ. Analysis U.S. Dept. Energy, Washington, 1980-81, dep. asst. adminstr. Office of Applied Analysis, 1981-82; dir. Econ. Analysis and Resource Planning Divsn. Office of Sec. of Def., Office of Program Analysis and Evaluation, Washington, 1982-88, dep. asst. sec., dep. dir., 1988—, chmn. cost analysis improvement group, 1988—. Author over 20 publs. on commodity markets, regulatory econs., energy issues and econ. aspects of the U.S. def. program. Recipient Spl. Svc. award Dept. Energy, 1981, Presdl. Rank award U.S. Govt., 1988, 93, 96, Disting./Meritorious Civilian Svc. medal Dept. Def., 1988, 91, 93, 96. Mem. Am. Econ. Assn. Home: 6901 Pineway Univ Park MD 20782-1163 Office: Dept Def OSD: PA&E The Pentagon Washington DC 20301

MC NICOL, DONALD EDWARD, lawyer; b. Kew Gardens, N.Y., Aug. 11, 1921; s. William J. and Margaret (McGirr) McN.; m. Carmen Gallego, July 10, 1988; children: Elaine McNicol Postley, Janet McNicol Barton, Donald Edward, Paul Mansfield, Andrea Gallego. AB, Harvard U., 1942, LLB, 1948. Bar: N.Y. 1949. Asso. Davis, Polk, Wardwell, Sunderland & Kiendl, N.Y.C., 1948-54; assoc. Hall, Haywood, Patterson & Taylor, N.Y.C., 1954-56; ptnr. Hall, McNicol, Hamilton & Clark, 1956-92; of counsel Keck, Mahin & Cate, N.Y.C., 1992-96, Schnader, Harrison, Segal & Lewis, N.Y.C., 1996—; bd. dirs. Thomas Pub. Co., Swisher Internat. Group, Inc. Trustee Boys and Girls Club Am. Served with AUS, 1942-46. Mem. Assn. Bar City N.Y., Harvard Club (bd. mgrs. N.Y.C. 1967-69). Home: 461 Berry Hill Rd Syosset NY 11791-1117 Office: Schnader Harrison Segal & Lewis 330 Madison Ave New York NY 10017-5001

MCNIESH, LAWRENCE MELVIN, radiologist; b. Appleton, Wis., Oct. 30, 1949; s. Vaughn Arley and Gladys Marie (Junion) McN.; m. Susan Irene White, July 14, 1972; children: Michael, Matthew, Carrie, Casey, Nicholas. BS, U. Calif., Davis, 1971; MD, Georgetown U., 1975. Diplomate Am. Bd. Med. Examiners, Am. Bd. Radiology. Intern and resident in radiology Letterman Army Med. Ctr., San Francsico, 1975-79; chief skeletal radiology Walter Reed Army Med. Ctr., Washington, 1979-82, 84-87; asst. prof. Uniformed Svcs. U. Health Scis., Bethesda, Md., 1981-82, 84-87, clin. assoc. prof., 1988—; asst. prof. Health Sci. Ctr. U. Tex., San Antonio, 1982-84; chief radiology Audie Murphy VA Hosp., San Antonio, 1983-84; pvt. practice Olney, Md., 1987-91, Johnstown, Pa., 1991—; chief of radiology Windber (Pa.) Hosp., 1992—; pres. med. staff Windber (Pa.) Hosp., 1996; bd. dirs. Conemaugh Health Sys.; cons. in field. Contbr. articles to profl. jours. Vol. Girl Scouts U.S., 1979-95, Montgomery County Coalition for Homeless, 1987-88, Little League Baseball, 1992—. Lt. col. U.S. Army, 1975-82. Mem. AMA, Calif. Scholastic Fedn. (life), Radiol. Soc. N.Am., Am. Coll. Radiology. Republican. Lutheran. Avocations: golf, running, alpine skiing. Home: 252 Tall Timber Dr Johnstown PA 15904-3211 Office: Cambria-Somerset Radiology 1086 Franklin St Johnstown PA 15905-4305

MCNISH, SUSAN KIRK, lawyer; b. San Jose, Calif., Nov. 4, 1940; d. Wallace Garland and Dorothy (Kirk) Shaw; m. Thomas A. McNish, May 12, 1989; children: Jenifer, Michael. BA, U. Calif., 1962; JD, U. Santa Clara, Calif., 1981; postgrad., Stanford U., 1979, U. Mich., 1981. Bar: Mich. 1981, U.S. Dist. Ct. (ea. dist.) Mich. 1981. Various positions Stanford (Calif.) U., 1968-79; law clk. U.S. Dist. Ct. (no. dist.) Calif., San Francisco, 1979; atty. Consumers Power Co., Jackson, Mich., 1981-88; v.p., gen. counsel, corp. sec. Mich. Consol. Gas Co., Detroit, 1988—; mem. clin. svcs. adv. bd. Detroit Med. Ctr., Wayne State U. Mem. Am. Arbitration Assn. (arbitrator, Mich. adv. panel), Am. Gas Assn. (chair state regulatory com., legal sect. mng. com.). Home: 9130 Woodberry Rd Plymouth MI 48170-3441 Office: Mich Consol Gas Co 500 Griswold St Detroit MI 48226-3700

MC NITT, WILLARD CHARLES, business executive; b. Chgo., June 6, 1920; s. Willard C. and Louise (Richardson) McN.; m. Charlotte D. Boyd, Sept. 14, 1946; children: Willard Charles, James D., Peter B. McNitt. B.A., Amherst Coll., 1942; A.M., Harvard Grad. Sch. Bus. Adminstrn., 1942; student, Northwestern Grad. Sch. Bus. Adminstrn., U. Chgo. Sch. Bus. Adminstrn., 1947. Asst. market planning and research Foote, Cone & Belding Co., Chgo., 1946-47; asst. sales promotion and advt. Bell & Gosset Co., Morton Grove, Ill., 1947-48; v.p. sales and mktg. Bowes Industries, Inc., Chgo., 1948-54; gen. mgr. sales and mktg. Clayton Mark & Co., Evanston, Ill., 1954-58; pres., dir. Bowey's, Inc., Chgo., 1958-62; pres., dir., mem. exec. com. H.M. Byllesby Co., Chgo., 1962-63; group v.p., dir. Consol. Foods Corp., Chgo., 1963-67; exec. v.p. consumer products group W.R. Grace & Co., N.Y.C., 1967-72; exec. v.p., dir., mem. exec. com. Ward Foods, Inc., Wilmette, Ill., 1972-73; chief operating officer, pres., dir., mem. exec. com. Ward Foods, Inc., 1973-76; pres., chief exec. officer, dir. Westgate-Calif. Corp., and Sun Harbor Industries, San Diego, 1977-80; pres., chief exec. officer Nalley's Fine Foods, Tacoma, 1980-83; chmn., dir. Joseph Magnin Inc., 1982-85; chmn. Blue Moon Cheese Co., Thorpe, Wis., 1983—; operating ptnr. Wallner & Co., La Jolla, Calif.; vice chmn., pres., chief exec. officer, dir., mem. exec. com. Foremost Dairies, Inc., San Francisco, 1983-85; chmn. Epcom; bd. dirs. ATI, NCIC, Blue Moon Cheese, Del. Lightweight. Troop head local Boy Scouts Am., 1957-67. Served to lt. (s.g.) USNR, 1942-46. Mem. Executives Club (Chgo.), Amherst Club, Harvard Bus. Sch. Club (Chgo., N.Y.C.), Indian Hill Country Club (Winnetka), Dairymen's Club (Boulder Junction, Wis.), Rancho Santa Fe Country Club, Fairbanks Ranch Country Club (Rancho Santa Fe), Rio Mar Country Club (Vero Beach, Fla.), Chi Psi. Republican. Congregationalist. Address: 1630 Sheridan Rd Apt 2C Wilmette IL 60091-1888

MCNULLY, LYNNETTE LARKIN, elementary education educator; b. Iowa City, Iowa, Jan. 22, 1966; d. Ernest F. and Karen (Schaeferle) Larkin; m. William S. McNully, May 14, 1988; 1 child, Bronwyn. BA in English, U. Okla., 1987; MEd in Early Childhood Edn., East Tex. State U., 1994. Cert. tchr., Tex. Pre-kindergarten, kindergarten and 1st grade tchr. Dallas Pub. Schs., 1989—; founding mem. site-based mgmt. coun. Arlington Park Sch., 1994-96. Vol. North Texas Irish Festival, Dallas, 1992, On the Wing Again, Ferris, Tex., 1993—. Named Tchr. of Yr., Arlington Park Sch., Dallas, 1992; Write, Right! grantee Dallas Jr. League, 1993. Mem. Nat. Assn. for Edn. of Young Children, Assn. for Childhood Edn. Internat., Dallas Quilters Guild, Lone Star State Dulcimer Soc., PTA (exec. bd. 1993-96), Phi Beta Kappa. Avocations: quilting, hiking, genealogy, hammered dulcimer.

MCNULTY, CARRELL STEWART, JR., manufacturing company executive, architect; b. Newark, Dec. 4, 1924; s. Carrell Stewart and Marjorie (Yaegerlehner) McN.; m. Barbara Brokaw, June 21, 1952; children: Peter Carrell, Susan Abigail. Student, Emory U., 1941-43, U. N.C., 1943-44; BArch, Columbia U., 1950, MS in Urban Planning, 1963. Registered architect, Pa. Assoc. SMS Architects, Stamford, Conn., 1950-58, gen. ptnr., 1958-73; pvt. practice architecture Weston, Conn., 1973-76; pres. CMW Co., Weston, 1975-77, NB Products, Inc., Horsham, Pa., 1976-94, NB Instruments, Inc., Horsham, 1979-93, Environ. Svcs. and Products, Inc., Horsham, 1994-96; mem. Conn. Soc. Architects, 1963-73, sec., 1964-67, pres., 1969-70. Chair S.W. Regional Planning Agy., Norwalk, Conn., 1967-71; mem. Gov.'s Com. on Environment, New Haven, 1970, chair Gov.'s Task Force on Housing, Norwalk, 1972; bd. dirs., sec. Habitat for Humanity of Greater Bucks, Doylestown, Pa., 1990—; pres. Ctrl. Bucks Crossroads, 1995-96. Lt. (j.g.) USNR, 1943-46; PTO. Recipient citation Am. Assn. Sch. Adminstrs., 1960, 6th Biennial Design award HUD, 1973; grantee HUD, Housing Rsch., 1970. Fellow AIA (mem. urban design com. 1963-73, chmn. 1971); mem. Bucks County Choral Soc., Sigma Nu. Democrat. Mem. United Ch. of Christ (deacon 1965-71, elder 1989-92). Avocations: computers, model building, choral music. Home: Century House # 234 303 W State St Doylestown PA 18901-3559

MCNULTY, DERMOT, public relations executive; b. Dublin, Ireland, Mar. 11, 1949; s. William J. and Margaret M. (Reigh) McN.; m. Paula Ann Gaber, 1977. BA in Journalism, Marquette U., 1971. Sr. v.p. Burson Marsteller, Hong Kong, 1985-87, Cohn & Wolfe, N.Y.C., 1987-88; exec. v.p. Burson Marsteller, N.Y.C., 1988-89, Shandwick N.Am., N.Y.C., 1989-90; dir. internat. mktg. Shandwick plc, London, 1990-91, COO, 1991-94, CEO, 1994—, also bd. dirs. Avocations: arts, golf, tennis. Office: 61 Grosvenor St, London W1X 9DA, England

MCNULTY, JAMES ERGLER, finance educator; b. Pitts., Aug. 2, 1944; s. James E. and Mary Jane (Wilson) McN.; m. Kathleen Ann Colquhoun, June 18, 1966; children: Christine Ann, James Kevin. AB, Coll. William and Mary, 1966; MA, Northwestern U., 1967; PhD, U. N.C., 1975. Economist Fed. Home Loan Bank of Atlanta, 1971-77, asst. sec., economist, 1977-79, asst. v.p., economist, 1979-81, v.p., economist, 1982-89; asst. prof. Fla. Atlantic U., Boca Raton, Fla., 1989-91, assoc. prof., 1991-97, prof., 1997—; cons., expert witness in field, 1989—. Contbr. articles to profl. jours.; reviewer acad. jours. Mem. Fin. Mgmt. Assn., Am. Fin. Assn., So. Fin. Assn., Ea. Fin. Assn. Avocations: wine collecting and tasting, classical music. Home: 10714 Sea Cliff Cir Boca Raton FL 33498 Office: Fla Atlantic Univ College of Bus Boca Raton FL 33431

MCNULTY, JOHN KENT, lawyer, educator; b. Buffalo, Oct. 13, 1934; s. Robert William and Margaret Ellen (Duthie) McN.; m. Linda Conner, Aug. 20, 1955 (div. Feb. 1977); children: Martha Jane, Jennifer, John K. Jr.; m. Babette B. Barton, Mar. 23, 1978 (div. May 1988). A.B. with high honors, Swarthmore Coll., 1956; LL.B., Yale U., 1959. Bar: Ohio 1961, U.S. Supreme Ct. 1964. Law clk. Justice Hugo L. Black, U.S. Supreme Ct., Washington, 1959-60; vis. prof. Sch. Law U. Tex., summer 1960, Yale U., fall 1990; assoc. Jones, Day, Cockley & Reavis, Cleve., 1960-64; prof. law U. Calif., Berkeley, 1964-91, Roger J. Traynor prof. law, 1991—; of counsel Baker and McKenzie, San Francisco, 1974-75; acad. visitor London Sch. Econs., 1985, Cambridge U., 1994, U. Edinburgh, 1994; vis. fellow Wolfson Coll., Cambridge, 1994; vis. prof. Yale U., U. Tex., U. Leiden, U. Tilburg, U. Tokyo, others; lectr. univs. Cologne, Hamburg, Kansei, Kyoto, London, Munich, Seoul, Tokyo, Tilburg, Amsterdam, Rotterdam, Vienna, Tohoku, Tübingen, others; mem. adv. bd. Tax Mgmt. Author: Federal Income Taxation of Individuals, 5th edit., 1995, Federal Estate and Gift Taxation, 5th edit., 1994, Federal Income Taxation of S Corporations, 1992; (with Westin & Beck) Federal Income Taxation of Business Enterprises, 1995; mem. bd. overseers Berkeley Jour. Internat. Law. Guggenheim fellow, 1977. Mem. ABA, Am. Law Inst., Internat. Fiscal Assn. (coun. U.S. br.), Order of Coif, Phi Beta Kappa. Home: 1176 Grizzly Peak Blvd Berkeley CA 94708-1741 Office: U Calif Sch Law 893 Boalt Hall Berkeley CA 94720

MCNULTY, JOHN WILLIAM, retired public relations executive, automobile company executive; b. N.Y.C., June 29, 1927; s. Christopher and Margaret (Kennedy) McN.; m. Margaret Rose Cooney, Nov. 11, 1950 (dec. Aug. 1978); children: Suellen McNulty Kinna, Jean McNulty Crocker, John, Peter, Jodi Wyatt Phelan, Russell Wyatt; m. Jean Fayette Winslow, Sept. 6, 1980. BS, Fordham U., 1949. Dir. pub. relations Lincoln Ctr., N.Y.C., 1958-63; assoc. John D. Rockefeller 3rd, N.Y.C., 1963-66; asst. to Pres. Lyndon B. Johnson, Washington, 1966-68; exec. asst. to exec. v.p. fin., pub./industry-govt. rels. GM, Detroit, 1968-74, exec. asst. to vice chmn., 1974-76, pub. affairs coord., 1976-77, dir. corp. comm., 1977-79, v.p. pub. rels., 1979-90, ret., 1990. Trustee Nat. Racing Mus., Saratoga. Served with USN, 1945-46, PTO. Recipient Communications Achievement award Fordham U., 1977. Mem. Kenwood Club. Democrat. Home: 1071 Celestial St Cincinnati OH 45202-1661

MCNULTY, MATTHEW FRANCIS, JR., health sciences and health services administrator, educator, university administrator, consultant, horse and cattle breeder; b. Elizabeth, N.J., Nov. 26, 1914; s. Matthew Francis and Abby Helen (Dwyer) McN.; m. Mary Nell Johnson, May 4, 1946; children: Matthew Francis III, Mary Lauren. BS, St. Peter's Coll., 1938, DHL (hon.), 1978; postgrad., Rutgers U. Law Sch., 1939-41; grad., Officer Candidate Sch., U.S. Army, 1941, U.S. Army Staff and Command Sch., Ft. Leavenworth, 1945; MHA, Northwestern U., 1949; MPH, U. N.C., 1952; ScD (hon.), U. Ala., 1969, Georgetown U., 1986. Contract writer, mgmt. trainee acturial divsn. Prudential Life Ins. Co., Newark, N.J., 1938-46; dir. med. adminstrn. VA, Chgo. and Washington, 1946-49; project officer to take over and operate new VA Teaching Hosps. VA, Little Rock, Birmingham, Ala. and Chgo., 1949-54; adminstr. U. Ala. Jefferson-Hillman Hosp., Birmingham, 1954-60; founding gen. dir. U. Ala. Hosps. and Clinics, 1960-66; founding prof. hosp. adminstrn. U. Ala. Grad. Sch., 1954-69, vis. prof., 1969—, founding dir. grad. program health adminstrn., 1964-69; prof. epidemiology and preventive medicine U. Ala. Sch. Medicine, 1960-69; founding dean Sch. Health Adminstrn. (now Sch. Health Related Profls.), 1965-69; pres. Matthew F. McNulty, Jr. & Assocs., Inc., 1954-91; founding dir. Coun. Teaching Hosps. and assoc. dir. Assn. Am. Med. Colls., 1966-69; prof. community medicine and internat. health Georgetown U., 1969-89, prof. emeritus 1989—, v.p. med. ctr. affairs, 1969-72, exec. v.p., med. ctr. affairs, 1972-74; chancellor, dir. Georgetown U. Med. Ctr., 1974-86; chancellor emeritus Georgetown U., 1986—; chmn. acad. affairs com., trustee Hahnemann U., Phila, 1987—; trustee Fla. Found. for Active Aging, 1989—; cons. VA Adv. Com. on Geriatrics & Gerontology, 1991—; founding chmn. bd. Univ. D.C. Affiliated Health Plan, Inc., 1974-78; founding chmn. bd. trustees Georgetown U. Community Health Plan, Inc., 1972-80; vis. prof. Cen. U., Caracas, Venezuela, 1957-61; hosp. cons., 1953—; bd. dirs. Kaiser-Georgetown Community Health Plan, Inc., Washington, 1980-85, bd. dirs. Kaiser Health Plans and Hosps., Oakland, Calif., 1980-85, emeritus, 1985—; mem. Statuatory VA Spl. Med. Adv. Group, 1978-89, Higher Edn. Com. on Dental Schs. Curriculum, 1978-79; preceptor hosp. adminstrn. Northwestern U., Washington U., U. Iowa, U. Minn., 1953-69; mem. nat. adv. com. health research projects Ga. Inst. Tech., 1959-65, 73-85; nat. adv. com. health rsch. projects U. Pitts., 1956-60; adv. com. W.K. Kellogg Found., 1960-65; vis. cons., lectr. Venezuelan Ministry Health and Social Welfare, 1967-69; dir. Blue Cross-Blue Shield Ala., 1960-61, 65-68; trustee, mem. exec. com. Blue Cross and Blue Shield Nat. Capital Area, 1973-89, Washington Bd. Trade, 1972-86; mem. feasability study P.R. VA Med. Care, 1949, feasability study Ariz. Med. Edn., 1956. Bd. dirs. Greater Birmingham United Appeal, 1960-66; trustee, chmn. Jefferson County (Ala.) Tb Sanatorium, 1958-64; mem. health services research study sect. NIH, 1963-67; cons. USPHS, 1959-63; mem. White House Conf. on Health, 1965, on Medicare Implementation, 1966, NIH, USPHS and DHEW Commns., 1967-86, others; trustee Nat. Council Internat. Health, 1975-86; pres. Nat. League Nursing, 1979-81. Served to maj. USAAF, 1942-46, lt. col. USAFR, 1946-55. Recipient Disting. Alumnus award Northwestern U., 1973, Disting. Alumnus award U. N.C., John Benjamin Nichol award Med. Soc. D.C., Mayor and D.C. Coun., Matthew F. McNulty, Jr. Unanimous Recognition Resolution of 1986, Centennial award Georgetown U. Alumni Assn. award, 1982, Patrick Healy Disting. Svc. award, 1985, Alumni Life Senator Election award, 1986; named to Hon. Order Ky Cols., 1984. Fellow Am. Pub. Health Assn., Am. Coll. Healthcare Execs. (life, bd. regents and council of regents 1961-67, Disting. Health Sci. Exec. award 1976); mem AAAS, Am. Hosp. Assn. (life, Disting. Service award 1984), Ala. Hosp. Assn. (past pres.), Nat. League for Nursing (past pres.), D.C. League Nursing (past dir.), Nat. Forum Health Planning (past pres., Disting. award, 1987), Council Med. Adminstrn., Internat. Hosp. Fedn., Jefferson County Ala. Vis. Nursing Assn. (past pres., Disting. Service award), Ala. Pub. Health Assn. (past chmn. med. care sect.), Southeastern Hosp. Conf. (past dir.), Birmingham Hosp. Council (past pres.), Hosp. Council Nat. Capital Area (pres. 1985-89, exec. com. 1989—, past pres. 1989-93, treas. 1993—), Assn. Univ. Programs in Hosp. Adminstrn. (Disting. award 1971), Greater Birmingham Area C. of C. (Merit award), Washington Acad. of Medicine, Am. Assn. Med. Colls. (founding chmn. teaching hosp. council 1964-69, Disting. Service Mem.), Royal Soc. Health, Am. Systems Mgmt. Soc. (Disting. award), Orgn. Univ. Health Ctr. Adminstrs., Santa Gertrudis Breeders Internat., Bashkir Curley Horse Breeders Assn., Med. Soc. of D.C. (John Benjamin Nichols award 1982), Univ. Club Ala., Cosmos Club, City Tavern Club, KC (3d degree, coun. 10499 Ocean Springs, 4th degree Francis Deignan Assembly), Knights of Malta, Omicron Kappa Upsilon. Home and Office: Teoc Pentref 3100 Phil Davis Dr Ocean Springs MS 39564-9076

MCNULTY, MICHAEL ROBERT, congressman; b. Troy, N.Y., Sept. 16, 1947; s. John J. and Madelon McN; m. Nancy Ann Lazzaro; children: Michele, Angela, Nancy, Maria. Grad., St. Joseph's Inst., Barrytown, N.Y., 1965, Loyola U. Rome Ctr., 1968, Hill Sch. Ins., N.Y.C., 1970; B.A. in Polit. Sci., Coll. Holy Cross, 1969; LHD honoris causa, Coll. St. Rose, 1991; LLD honoris causa, Siena Coll., 1993. Town supr. Town of Green Island, N.Y., 1969-77, mayor, 1977-82; mem. N.Y. State Assembly, 1982-88, chmn. sub-com. on town and village elections, mem. legis. commn. on rural resources, 1983-88, asst. dir. adminstrv. regulations rev. commn., 1977-82, mem. adminstrv. regulations rev. com., 1983-88; past chmn. planning com. Capital Dist. Transp. Com.; mem. 101st-105th Congresses from 23rd N.Y. dist., 1989-92, 103d-104th Congresses from 21st N.Y. dist., 1993—; mem. internat. rels. com, ways and means com.; past chmn. task force for constrn. Troy-Green Island Bridge; chmn. United Way campaign, 1982. Mem. staff com. on edn. N.Y. State Constl. Conv., 1967; del. Dem. Nat. Conv., 1972, 92; campaign mgr. John J. McNulty Jr. for Sheriff of Albany County, N.Y., 1973; participant 1974 polit. campaign mgmt. inst. Kent State U., Ohio; past mem. Albany County Dem. Com.; past chmn. Green Island Dem. Com.; past mem. N.Y. State Dem. Com. Office: US Ho of Reps 2161 Rayburn HOB Washington DC 20510-3221*

MCNULTY, ROBERT HOLMES, non-profit executive; b. Oakland, Calif., June 20, 1940; s. Frederick James and Ruth (Holmes) McN.; m. Penelope Cuff, Dec. 27, 1964; children: Maria, Abigail. BS in Bus. Adminstrn., U. Calif., Berkeley, 1962, JD, 1965. Property acquisition planner Safeway Stores, Internat., Oakland, 1962; archeol. asst. Colonial Williamsburg, Va., 1968; rsch. asst. Nat. Mus. of History and Tech. The Smithsonian Instn., Washington, 1968-69, asst. to the dir., 1969-70; environ. advisor GSA, Washington, 1970-71; asst. dir. architecture and environ. arts program NEA, Washington, 1971-78; acting dir. grad. program in hist. preservation Sch. Architecture Columbia U., N.Y.C., 1978-79; pres. Ptnrs. for Livable Communities, Washington, 1979—; cons. Task Force on Land Use and Urban Growth, 1972, German Marshall Fund, Washington, 1978; bd. visitors U. Ind. Sch. Pub. Adminstrn., 1991—. Author: Neighborhood Conservation: A Handbook of Methods and Techniques, 1976, Economics of Amenity, 1985, Entrepreneurial American City, 1985, Return of the Livable City, 1986; editor: (report) State of the American Community, 1994. Served to capt. U.S. Army, 1966-68. Smithsonian Inst. grantee, 1972, 73, Graham Found. grantee 1978; Loeb fellow Harvard U., 1973-74, Pierson Coll. guest fellow, Yale U., 1985, adj. sr. fellow Hudson Inst., 1989—. Mem. Calif. Bar Assn., Nat. Press Club. Office: Ptnrs for Livable Community 1429 21st St NW Washington DC 20036-5902

MCNULTY, ROBERTA JO, educational administrator; b. Cin., July 17, 1945; d. Edward Norman and Ruth Marcella (Glass) Stuebing; children: Meredith Corinne, Brian Edward, Stephen Barrett. BS in Edn., U. Cin., 1967; MA in Edn., Coll. of Mount St. Joseph, 1989; PhD in Ednl. Adminstrn. and Supervision, Bowling Green State U., 1993. Elem. tchr. St. Mary Sch., Urbana, Ohio, 1968; elem. tchr. Urbana (Ohio) City Schs., 1968-70, middle sch. tchr., 1970-71; off-campus liaison Mt. St. Joseph Coll., 1987-89; adj. faculty Bowling Green State U., 1990—; gen. edn. supr., testing 540 coord. curriculum devel. and implementation Fulton County (now Northwest Ohio) Ednl. Svc. Ctr., Wauseon, Ohio, 1992—; Lamaze instr. Scioto Meml. Illustrated Lamaze Edn., Portsmouth, Ohio, 1983-84, Tiffin (Ohio) Childbirth Edn. Assn., 1984-87; edn. symposium com. chair Project Discovery, 1995-96; proficiency test rev. com. Ohio Dept. Edn., 1993—. Grad. editor Am. Secondary Edn., 1989-92. Mem. sch. bd. St. Mary Sch., Urbana, 1971-75; mem. parent adv. com. Wheelersburg (Ohio) Local Schs., 1978-84; mem. parents coun. U. Evansville, 1990-93; exec. dir. Am. Cancer Soc., Tiffin, Ohio, 1985; treas. Parents' Boosters Club, Portsmouth YMCA, 1979-84; chmn. Y-Wives com. Tiffin-Cmty. YMCA, 1984-87; mem. Archbold (Ohio) Teen Issues Adv. Com., 1995-96. Recipient Doctoral fellowship Bowling Green State U., 1989-92, Svc. Appreciation award Cub Scouts, 1990-92. Mem. ASCD, Ednl. Leadership Assn., N.W. Ohio Assn. for Supervision and Curriculum Devel., Ohio Sch. Suprs. Assn., Ohio Coun. Tchrs. English Language Arts, Assn. Tchr. Educators, Ohio Assn. Tchr. Educators (nat. del.), Phi Delta Kappa. Office: Northwest Ohio Ednl Svc Ctr 602 S Shoop Ave Wauseon OH 43567-1712

MCNULTY-MAJORS, SUSAN ROSE, special education administrator; b. Fargo, N.D., Oct. 5, 1944; d. Leo G. McNulty and Jane Lyon (McDonald) McNulty-Schmallen; d. Herbert G. Schmallen (stepfather); m. B. Joseph Majors II, Aug. 23, 1975. BS, N.D. State U., 1966; MA, U. Mich., 1969. Lic. tchr., Mass., Minn.; lic. ind. clin. social worker; cert. chem. dependency practitioner. Tchr. sci. Incarnation Sch., Mpls., 1966-67; tchr. English George Daly Jr. High Sch., Flint, Mich., 1967-68; tchr. New Boston (Mich.) Elem. Sch., 1969-70; tchr. home econs. Newton (Mass.) Jr. High Sch., 1970-73; program adminstr. Bell Hill Recovery Ctr., Wadena, Minn., 1973-80, exec. dir., 1980-85; coord. emotionally and behavior disordered edn. Wadena Pub. Schs. TOW Spl. Edn. Coop., 1985-94; dir. spl. edn. PAWN Spl. Edn. Coop., Park Rapids, Minn., 1994-95; educator, cons. emotional/behavioral disorders Northland High, Remer, Minn., 1995—; therapist Neighborhood Counseling, Wadena, Minn., 1995—; emotional/behavioral disorders educator, dir. spl. edn. Remer-Longville Dist. 118, Remer, Minn., 1996—; mem. Wadena Tech. Adv. Bd., 1978—. Mem. adv. bd. Todd-Wadena Community Corrections, Long Prairie, Minn., 1975—, chairperson 1997); mem. Woodview adv. bd., 1990—; mem. fund adminstrn. bd. Ctrl. Minn. Initiative, 1996—. Fresh Air Camp fellow U. Mich., 1968; recipient Ashland Oil Golden Apple Achievement award. Roman Catholic. Avocations: sailing, biking, reading. Home: 843 7th St SW Wadena MN 56482-1934 Office: Northland High Remer MN 56672

MCNUTT, CHARLIE FULLER, JR., bishop; b. Charleston, W.Va., Feb. 27, 1931; s. Charlie Fuller and Mary (Ford) McN.; m. Alice Turnbull, Mar. 3, 1962; children: Thomas Ford, Charlie Fuller III, Alison Turnbull. AB, Washington and Lee U., 1953; MDiv, Va. Theol. Sem., 1956, DD (hon.), 1981; MS, Fla. State U., 1970; DD (hon.) Lebanon Valley Coll. Pa., 1996. Ordained to ministry Episcopal Ch., 1956; bishop, 1980. Vicar, Christ Ch., Williamston, W.Va., 1956-60; asst. rector St. John's Episc. Ch., Tallahassee, Fla., 1960-62; rector St. Luke's Episc. Ch., Jacksonville, Fla., 1962-68; planning dir. Diocese of Fla., 1968-74; archdeacon of Jacksonville Diocese of Fla., 1970-74; rector Trinity Episc. Ch., Martinsburg, W.Va., 1974-80; bishop coadjutor Diocese Ctrl. Pa., 1980-82, diocesan bishop, 1982-95; COO, exec. dir. presiding bishop's fund The Episcopal Ch., 1995—; bd. dirs. Pa. Coun. Chs., Harrisburg, chmn. dept. social ministry, 1982-86, pres., 1991-94. Bd. dirs. Appalachian People's Svc. Orgn., pres., 1985-87; bd. dirs. Boy Scouts Am., Harrisburg, 1981-86; mem. exec. coun. Nat. Ch., 1988-94; mem. standing com. on program, budget and fin. Nat. Episcopal Ch., 1983-90; co-chmn. Pa. Conf. Interch. Cooperation. Mem. Phi Beta Kappa. Democrat. Home: 2428 Lincoln St Camp Hill PA 17011-3637 Office: Episcopal Ch Ctr 815 2nd Ave New York NY 10017-4503

MCNUTT, JACK WRAY, oil company executive; b. Norphlet, Ark., Sept. 7, 1934; s. Fay D. and Mattie E. (Garner) McN.; m. Jordine Chesshir, Aug. 19, 1955; 1 child, Marsha. BS, Harding Coll., 1956; MS, Columbia U., 1957. Acct. Murphy Oil Corp., El Dorado, Ark., 1957-68, exec. mgmt. asst., 1968-69, exec. v.p., 1981-88, chief operating officer, 1986-88, pres., chief exec. officer, 1988-94; ret., 1994; v.p. planning Murphy Ea. Oil Co., London, 1969-72, pres., 1972-81; bd. dirs. First Nat. Bank El Dorado, Ark. Mem. Am. Petroleum Inst. (dir.), 25 Yr. Club. of Petroleum Industry. Home: 1705 W Cedar St El Dorado AR 71730-5309 Office: 101 W Main St Ste 509 El Dorado AR 71730-5641

MCNUTT, KRISTEN WALLWORK, consumer affairs executive; b. Nashville, Nov. 17, 1941; d. Gerald M. and Lee Wallwork; m. David McNutt, Sept. 13, 1969. BA in Chemistry, Duke U., 1963; MS in Nutrition, Columbia U., 1965; PhD in Biochemistry, Vanderbilt U., 1970; JD, DePaul U., 1984. Bar: N.Y. 1984, D.C. 1984. Exec. dir. Nat. Nutrition Consortium, Washington, 1979-81; asst. prof. pub. health U. Ill., Chgo., 1981-83; assoc. dir. Good Housekeeping Inst., N.Y.C., 1982-85; v.p. consumer affairs Kraft Inc., Glenview, Ill., 1985-87; pres. Consumer Choices Inc., Winfield, Ill., 1988—. Author: Nutrition and Food Choices, 1979; editor: Sugars in Nutrition, 1975, Consumer Mags. Digest, 1989—. Bd. dirs. Better Bus. Bur., Chgo. and No. Ill., 1986-88; FDA Food Adv. Com., 1992-94. Mem. N.Y. Bar Assn., D.C. Bar Assn., Fedn. Am. Socs. Exptl. Biology (Congl. Sci. fellow), Soc. for Nutrition Edn. (pres. 1983-84), Am. Inst. Nutrition, Am. Dietetics Assn. Home and Office: Consumer Choices Inc 28w176 Belleau Dr Winfield IL 60190-1722

MCNUTT, RICHARD HUNT, manufacturing company executive; b. Princeton, N.J., Mar. 11, 1943; s. John and Dorothy Elizabeth (Hunt) McN. Student Delaware Valley Coll. Sci and Agr., 1965-68; vocat. edn. cert. Temple U., 1978-81. Cert. mfg. engr. Diemaker, Custom Tool Co., 1964-67; toolmaker Penn Engring., 1967-69; machine shop mgr., research and devel. engr. Inertial Motors Corp., 1969-73; machinery design engr. Phila. Rivet Co., Doylestown, Pa.; 1973-76; rsch. and devel. mgr. PHL, Inc., Doylestown, 1976-82; asst. chief engr. PHL Inc., Levv/Air Inc., Prefco Products Inc., Prefco Products Internat., 1982-85, chief engr., 1985-86, v.p. ops., 1986-89, dir. engring., 1993—; owner Sunrise Solar Heat Co.; cons., Pipersville, Pa., 1976—; ptnr. Mediation Assocs., 1990—. Exec. v.p. Del. Water Study Citizens Group for Sound Resource Mgmt.; councillor Probational Vol. Svcs.; founding bd. dirs. Del-Aware Unltd., Inc., Del-Art Inc., Ctr. for Performing Arts, Bucks County, Pa.; mem. Environ. Polit. Action Com.; founder AWARE, Montgomery County, 1985—, STAND, Bucks County, 1986—, Holicong CSA; mem. exec. bd. Earth Day, 1990, Earth Days Alliance, Bucks County, 1991-93; mem. edn. com. Bucks County Conservation Dist., 1993—, Del. River Greenway, 1994-96, vice chmn., 1995-96, chmn., 1996—, econ. devel. com. Del. River Wild & Scenic Study Commn. Dept. Interior Nat. Park Svc., 1994-96; founder Solebury Forum, Bucks County, Environ. Party Com. Served with USMC, 1960-64. Mem. NRA (life), VFW (life), Soc. Mfg. Engrs., Bucks County Assn. Corrections and Rehab., Am. Legion, Vietnam Vets. Am. (life), Cen. Bucks County C. of C. (environ. and govt. com. 1986—), Plumstead Twp. Parks and Recreation Commn. (sec. 1992-97, vice chmn., 1997—, Plumstead Twp. shade tree commn., vice chmn., 1992—). Republican. Buddhist. Home: 5556 Stump Rd Pipersville PA 18947-1002 Office: Prefco Products Inc 3853 Old Easton Rd Doylestown PA 18901-1195

MCPARTLAND, JAMES MICHAEL, university official; b. N.Y.C., Sept. 26, 1939; s. James J. and Helen M. (Leddy) McP. BS, Cornell U., 1961, MS, 1963; PhD, Johns Hopkins U., 1968. Rschr. U.S. Office Edn., Washington, 1965-67, U.S. Commn. Civil Rights, Washington, 1967-68; asst. dir. Ctr. Social Orgn. Schs., Johns Hopkins U., Balt., 1968-75, co-dir., 1976-94; dir., 1994—. Co-author: Equality of Educational Opportunity, 1966; author: (with others) Encyclopedia of Educational Research, 1992, Review of Research in Education, 1993; co-editor: Violence in Schools, 1977. Mem. Am. Ednl. Rsch. Assn., Am. Sociol. Assn., Am. Statis. Assn. Democrat. Roman Catholic. Avocation: music. Home: 1102 S Streeper St Baltimore MD 21224-4873 Office: Johns Hopkins U CSOS 3505 N Charles St Baltimore MD 21218-2404

MCPARTLAND, PATRICIA ANN, health educator; b. Passaic, N.J.; d. Daniel and Josephine McP. BA, U. Mo., 1971; MCRP, Ohio State U., 1975, MS in Preventive Medicine, 1975; EdD in Higher and Adult Edn., Columbia U., 1988. Cert. holistic, aromatherapy and hypnotherapy. Sr. health planner Merrimack Valley HSA, Lawrence, Mass., 1977-79; planning cons./adminstr. Children's Hosp., Boston, 1979-80; exec. dir. Southeastern Mass. Area Health Edn. Ctr., Marion, Mass., 1980—; v.p. New Bedford (Mass.) Cmty. Health Ctr., 1993-94; chmn. edn. and tng. com. Health and Human Svc. Coalition, 1988-89; vis. lectr. Bridgewater State Coll.; lectr. in field. Editorial bd. Jour. Healthcare Edn. and Tng., 1989-93; author: Promoting Health in the Workplace, 1991; contbr. articles to profl. jours. Vol. speaker March of Dimes Found., Wareham, Mass., 1992-93; coll.-wide vocat. Cape Cod C.C., Hyannis, Mass., 1989—; planning adv. 2nd Internat. Symposium, Pasco, Wash., 1992; v.p. New Bedford chpt. Am. Cancer Soc., 1985-90. Recipient award Excellence in Continuing Edn. Nat. AHEC Ctr. Dirs. Assn., 1994, 95, 96, Sec.'s awards for Outstanding Progam in Community Health, Nat. Cancer Inst., Washington, 1990. Mem. Am. Pub. Health Assn., Inst. for Disease Prevention (steering com. 1982—), Southeastern Mass Health Planning (bd. dirs., sec., 1982-87), Nat. Planning Conf. (mem. com. 1984-85, 86-87). Avocations: writing, dance, theatre, travel, hiking. Home: PO Box 1116 Marion MA 02738-0491 Office: Southeastern Mass AHEC PO Box 69 2 Spring St Marion MA 02738

MCPEAK, MERRILL ANTHONY, business executive, consultant, retired officer; b. Santa Rosa, Calif., Jan. 9, 1936; s. Merrill Addison McPeak and Winifred Alice (Stewart) McPeak Bendall; m. Elynor Fay Moskowitz, Nov. 10, 1956; children—Mark Allen, Brian David. A.B., San Diego State Coll., Calif., 1957; M.S., George Washington U., Washington, 1974. Commd. 2d lt. USAF, 1957, advanced through grades to gen., 1988; pilot USAF Thunderbirds, Nellis AFB, Nev., 1966-68; comdr. Misty Forward Air Controllers, Phu Cat, Republic of Vietnam, 1969, 20th Tactical Fighter Wing, RAF, Upper Heyford, Eng., 1980-81, 12th Air Force, Bergstrom AFB, Tex., 1987-88; comdr.-in-chief Pacific Air Forces, Hickam AFB, Hawaii, 1988-90; chief of staff USAF, Washington, 1990-94; co. dir., cons., 1994—. Officer USAF, retired. Decorated DSM, Silver Star, Legion of Merit, DFC. Mem. Air Force Assn., Coun. Fgn. Rels., Daedalians, Sigma Chi. Home: 17360 Grandview Ct Lake Oswego OR 97034-6362

MCPHAIL, JOANN WINSTEAD, writer, publisher, art dealer; b. Trenton, Fla., Feb. 17, 1941; d. William Emerson and Donna Mae (Crawford) Winstead; m. James Michael McPhail, June 15, 1963; children: Angela C. McPhail Morris, Dana Denise McPhail Gaizutis, Whitney Gold McPhail Casso. Student, Fla. So. Coll., 1959-60, St. John's River Jr. Coll., Palatka, Fla., 1960-61, Houston (Tex.) C.C. With Jim Walter Corp., Houston, 1961-62; receptionist, land lease sec. Oil and Gas Property Mgmt. Inc., Houston, 1962-63; sec. to mng. atty. State Farm Ins. Co., Houston, 1963-64; saleswoman, decorator Oneil-Anderson, Houston, 1973; sec. Law Offices of Ed Christensen, Houston, 1980-82; advt. mgr. Egalitarian Houston (Tex.) C.C. Systems, 1981; fashion display artist, 1985-86; entrepreneur, writer, art agt., playwright Golden Galleries, Houston, 1990—; owner, property mgr. APT Investments, 1994—; lyricist, publisher Anna Gold Classics, 1995—, writer, publisher of song lyrics and music, 1996—; screen playwright, 1996. Freelance writer, photographer: Elegance of Needlepoint, 1970, S.W. Art Mag., A Touch of Greatness, 1973, Sweet 70's Anthology, The Budding of Tomorrow, 1974; columnist, photographer: Egalitarian: The Name Game, Design Your Wall Covering, Student Profile, 1981, National Library of Poetry, Fireworks, 1995; contbr. poetry various publs.; playwright, 1993—; screenwriter, 1996—; writer, pub. religious drama The Missing crown, KYND-AM, World Wide Christian Radio, KCBI-FM, and other radio stations, 1995—. Vol. PTO bd. Sharptown Middle Sch.; active ch. leadership activities. Mem. NAFE, ASCAP, Scriptwriters/Houston. Methodist. Home: 2608 Stanford St Houston TX 77006-2928

MC PHEE, HENRY ROEMER, lawyer; b. Ames, Iowa, Jan. 11, 1925; s. Harry Roemer and Mary (Ziegler) McP.; m. Joanne Lambert, May 19, 1956 (div. Dec. 1991); children: Henry Roemer III, Joanne, Larkin, Charles. AB cum laude, Princeton U., 1947; LLB, Harvard U., 1950. Bar: N.J. 1951, Ill. 1961, D.C. 1966. Exec. asst. to gov. State of N.J., Trenton, 1950-52; assoc. R.E. & A.D. Watson, New Brunswick, N.J., 1952-54; asst. to gen. counsel FTC, Washington, 1954; exec. asst. White House, Washington, 1954-57; asst. spl. counsel Pres. U.S., Washington, 1957-58, assoc. spl. counsel, pres., 1958-61; ptnr. Hamel & Park, Washington, 1961-88; mem. mgmt. com. Hamel & Park, 1975-85, mng. ptnr., 1980-83; ptnr. Hopkins & Sutter, 1988-93, of counsel, 1994—; sec. N.J. Commn. on Interstate Cooperation, 1952-54; gen. counsel Rep. Nat. Fin. Com., 1968-73, Rep. Nat. Com., Washington, 1968. Chmn. bldg. com. Potomac (Md.) Presbyn. Ch., 1965-67; v.p. Rep. Club, Princeton, 1952-54; bd. dirs. Eisenhower World Affairs Inst., 1983—, treas., 1991-93. Mem. ABA, D.C. Bar Assn., N.J. Bar Assn., Lincoln's Inn Soc. Harvard Law Sch. Republican. Presbyterian. Clubs: Tower (Princeton U.); Princeton (Washington) (pres. 1970-72), Metropolitan (Washington), Capitol Hill (Washington). Avocation: tennis. Home: 11615 Partridge Run Ln Potomac MD 20854-1218 Office: Hopkins & Sutter 888 16th St NW Washington DC 20006-4103

MC PHEE, JOHN ANGUS, writer; b. Princeton, N.J., Mar. 8, 1931; s. Harry Roemer and Mary (Ziegler) McP.; m. Pryde Brown, Mar. 16, 1957; children: Laura, Sarah, Jenny, Martha; m. Yolanda Whitman, Mar. 8, 1972; stepchildren: Cole Harrop, Andrew Harrop, Katherine Ryan, Vanessa Speir. AB, Princeton U., 1953; postgrad., Magdalene Coll., Cambridge (Eng.) U., 1953-54; LittD (hon.), Bates Coll., 1978, Colby Coll., 1978, Williams Coll., 1979, U. Alaska, 1980, Coll. William and Mary, 1988, Rutgers U., 1988; ScD, Maine Maritime Acad., 1992. TV playwright for Robert Montgomery Presents, N.Y.C., 1955-56; contbg. editor, assoc. editor Time mag., 1957-64; staff writer The New Yorker mag., 1965—; Ferris prof. journalism Princeton U., 1975—. Author: A Sense of Where You Are, 1965, The Headmaster, 1966, Oranges, 1967, The Pine Barrens, 1968, A Roomful of Hovings, 1968, Levels of the Game, 1969, The Crofter and the Laird, 1970, Encounters with the Archdruid, 1971, The Deltoid Pumpkin Seed, 1973, The Curve of Binding Energy, 1974, Pieces of the Frame, 1975, The Survival of the Bark Canoe, 1975, The John McPhee Reader, 1976, Coming into the Country, 1977, Giving Good Weight, 1979, Basin and Range, 1981, In Suspect Terrain, 1983, La Place de la Concorde Suisse, 1984, Table of Contents, 1985, Rising from the Plains, 1986, The Control of Nature, 1989, Looking for a Ship, 1990, Assembling California, 1993, The Ransom of Russian Art, 1994, The Second JOhn PcPhee Reader, 1996, Irons in the Fire, 1997. Recipient award in lit. Am. Acad. and Inst. Arts and Letters, 1977, Woodrow Wilson award Princeton U., 1982, John Wesley Powell award U.S. Geol. Survey, 1988, John Burroughs medal, 1990, Walter Sullivan award Am. Geophys. Union, 1993. Fellow Geol. Soc. Am.; mem. Am. Acad. Arts and Letters.

MCPHEE, JONATHAN, music director, conductor, composer, arranger. LRAM, Royal Acad. Music; BM, MM, Juilliard Sch. Music dir., prin. condr. Boston Ballet, 1988—. Condr. dance cos. including The Joffrey Ballet, The Martha Graham Dance Co., The Dance Theatre of Harlem, Am. Ballet Theatre, N.Y.C. Ballet, The Royal Ballet, Covent Garden, Nat. Ballet of Can., orchs. including Buffalo Philharm., Joffrey Ballet Orch., Rochester Philharm., N.Y.C. Opera Orch., BBC Scottish Symphony, Hague Philharm., Boston Pops, Syracuse Symphony, San Diego Symphony, San Francisco Symphony, Orchestre Colonne, Paris, The Nat. Philharm. Orch., London, Danish Radio Symphony Orch.; recs. for filming of Martha Graham works, Cave of the Heart, Errand Into the Maze, El Penintent, Michael Gandolfi's Caution to the Wind: author rev. version Stravinsky's Rite of Spring; arrangements pub. by Boosey & Hawkes. Office: Boston Ballet 19 Clarendon St Boston MA 02116-6107

MCPHEE, MARK STEVEN, medical educator, physician, gastroenterologist; b. Kansas City, Mo., Nov. 8, 1951; s. William Robert and Mary Kay (Paige) McP.; m. Christina Marie Luebke, July 14, 1974; children: Molly Amanda, Ian Andrew. BA magna cum laude, Pomona Coll., Claremont, Calif., 1973; MD summa cum laude, U. Kans., Kansas City, 1976. Diplomate Nat. Bd. Med. Examiners; diplomate in internal medicine and gastroenterology Am. Bd. Internal Medicine. Intern, resident, fellow Harvard U. Med. Sch., Boston, 1976-80; dir. gastrointestinal endoscopy unit Kans. U. Med. Ctr., Kansas City, 1980-85; chief sect. gastroenterology St. Luke's Hosp., Kansas City, Mo., 1988-93, chair dept. medicine, 1992-97, assoc. dir. med. edn., 1995-97, dir. med. edn., 1997—; assoc. dean U. Mo.-Kansas City Med. Sch., 1997—; asst. prof. medicine U. Kans., KansasCity, 1980-85, assoc. prof., 1985; clin. prof. medicine U. Mo., Kansas City, 1970-97, prof. medicine, 1997—. Author: Annotated Key References in Gastroenterology, 1982; contbr. chpts. to textbook, articles to profl. jours. Bd. dirs. St. Luke's Hosp., Kansas City,Mo., 1993—, Am. Digestive Health Found., Bethesda, Md., 1996—. Fellow ACP, Am. Coll. Gastroenterology; mem. Am. Gastroent. Assn. (mem. governing bd., treas.), St. Lukes Hosp. Physicians Assn. (bd. dirs.), HealthNet Physician Ptnrs. (bd. dirs.), Alpha Omega Alpha. Episcopalian. Avocations: poetry, hiking/camping, golf, tennis, sporting clay target shooting. Office: St Lukes Hosp Dept Med Edn 44th and Wornall Rd Kansas City MO 64111

MC PHEETERS, EDWIN KEITH, architect, educator; b. Stillwater, Okla., Mar. 26, 1924; s. William Henry and Eva Winona (Mitchell) McP.; m. Patricia Ann Foster, Jan. 29, 1950 (div. 1981); children: Marc Foster, Kevin Mitchell, Michael Hunter; m. Mary Louise Marvin, July 21, 1984. B.Arch., Okla. State U., 1949; M.F.A., Princeton U., 1956. Instr. architecture U. Fla., 1949-51; asst. prof. Ala. Poly. Inst., Auburn U., 1951-54; fellow Princeton U., 1955, 81; from asst. prof. to prof. U. Ark., 1956-66; prof. Rensselaer Poly. Inst., 1966-69, dean, 1966-69; prof. Auburn (Ala.) U., 1969-89, dean Sch. Architecture and Fine Arts,, 1969-88, dean, prof. emeritus, 1989—; adj. prof. Frank Lloyd Wright Sch. of Architecture, 1992—; mem. Ala. Bd. Registration for Architects, 1978-87; profl. adviser South Ctrl. Bell Telephone Co., 1977-79, So. Co., 1979-81, Ala. Power Co., 1979-81, Okla. State U., 1983, Ala. Sch. Fine Arts, 1985-86; cons. Taliesin Architects, 1988-92. Served to 2d lt. USAAC, 1943-45; capt. USAFR 1945-57. Fellow AIA (pres. Ala. coun. 1978, Merit award 1976, East Ala. Design awards 1986, 87, 90, 92); mem. Assn. Collegiate Schs. Arch. (bd. dirs. 1970-77, Disting. Prof. 1989), Blue Key, Kappa Sigma, Omicron Delta Kappa, Kappa Kappa Psi, Tau Sigma Delta, Rotary. Episcopalian.

MC PHERSON, ALICE RUTH, ophthalmologist; b. Regina, Sask., Can., June 30, 1926; came to U.S., 1938, naturalized, 1958; d. Gordon and Viola (Hoover) McP. BS, U. Wis., 1948, MD, 1951. Diplomate Am. Bd. Ophthalmology. Intern Santa Barbara (Calif.) Cottage Hosp., 1951-52; resident anesthesiology Hartford (Conn.) Hosp., 1952; resident ophthalmology Chgo. Eye, Ear, Nose and Throat Hosp., 1953, U. Wis. Hosps., 1953-55; ophthalmologist Davis and Duehr Eye Clinic, Madison, Wis., 1956-57; clin. instr. U. Wis., 1956-57; fellow retina service Mass. Eye and Ear Infirmary, 1957-58; ophthalmologist Scott and White Clinic, Temple, Tex., 1958-60; practice medicine specializing in ophthalmology and retinal diseases Houston, 1960—; mem. staff Meth., St. Luke's, Tex. Children's Hosps., Houston; clin. asst. prof. Baylor Coll. Medicine, Houston, 1959-61, asst. prof. ophthalmology, 1961-69, clin. asst. prof., 1969-75, clin. prof., 1975—, mem. search com. dept. otorhinolaryngology and communicative scis., 1996, search com. dept. medicine, 1997—; cons. retinal diseases VA Hosp., Houston, 1960—, Ben Taub Hosp., Houston, 1960—; mem. adv. com. for active staff appt. sect. ophthalmology Meth. Hosp., 1986-91, mem equipment com., 1993-95, mem. grievance panel, 1997; vol. clin. faculty appts. and promotions com., 1993—; bd. dirs. Highlights of Ophthalmology. Editor: New and Controversial Aspects of Retinal Detachment, 1968, New and Controversial Aspects of Vitreoretinal Surgery, 1977, Retinopathy of Prematurity: Current Concepts and Controversies, 1986. Ambassador Houston Ballet, mem. Houston Ballet Found.; mem. pres.'s council Houston Grand Opera, mem.; mem. conductors circle Houston Symphony, mem. Houston Symphony Soc.; mem. campaign for 80s Baylor Coll. Medicine; mem. Assn. for Community TV, Better Bus. Bur., Physicians' Benevolent Fund, South Tex. Diabetes Assn. Inc., Jr. League Houston. Recipient Honor award Am. Acad. Ophthalmology, 1956, Award of Appreciation, Knights Templar Eye Found., 1978, Woodlands Medal for Outstanding Contbn. to the Econ. Devel. of Community, 1988; Alice R. Mc Pherson Lab for Retina Rsch. dedicated Baylor Ctr. for Biotech., 1988,; Alice R. Mc Pherson Day proclaimed in her honor Mayor of City of Houston, Mar. 12, 1988. Fellow Am. Acad. Ophthalmology (2d v.p. 1979, com. for pub. and profl. rels., vice chmn. program devel. found. bd. trustees 1993—, bd. dirs. opthalmology ednl. trust fund found., sr. honor award 1986), ACS (credentials and Tex. credentials com., com. on applications); mem. Vitreous Soc., AMA, Tex. Med. Assn., Pan-Am. Med. Assn., Internat. Coll. Surgeons (vice regent 1991—), Am. Med. Women's Assn., Retina Soc. (v.p. 1976-77, pres. 1978-79, credentials com.), Internat. Coll. Ocular Surgeons (vice regent 1991), Am. Soc. Contemporary Ophthalmology (Charles Schepens Hon. award), Am. Bd. Laser Surgery, Internat. Assn. Ocular Surgeons, Harris County Med. Soc., Houston Acad. Medicine, Houston Ophthalmol. Soc. (credentials com., pres. 1990-91), Internat. Soc. Eye Research (cred. com. 1992—), Macula Soc. (credentialling com. 1992—), 9th Dist. Med. Soc., Pan Am. Assn. Ophthalmology (bd. dirs., membership com., bd. dirs. Pan Am. ednl. fund, v.p. 1991-92, AJO lectr. 1993, pres.-elect 1992-95, pres. 1995-97), Research to Prevent Blindness, So. Med. Soc., Tex. Med. Assn., Vitreous Soc., Tex. Ophthal. Assn., Soc. Eye Surgeons, Pan Am Assn. of Ophthal. Found. (pres. 1997—), Harris County Med. Soc., Assn. Research Surgeons, U. Wis. Ophthal. Alumni Assn. (founding pres. 1990-93, founded Alice R. McPherson lectureship 1994), French Ophthal. Soc., Internat. Med. Assembly S.W. Tex., Schepens Internat. Soc. (sec. 1986-93, v.p. 1993-95, pres. 1995-97), Jules Gonin Club. Research in vision and ophthalmology. Office: Tex Med Ctr 6560 Fannin St Ste 2200 Houston TX 77030-2715

MCPHERSON, DONALD J., metallurgist; married; children: Marjorie, Linda. B.S., M.S., Ph.D., Ohio State U., D.Sc. (hon.), 1975. Assoc. metallurgist Argonne Nat. Lab., to 1950; research metallurgist, asst. div. mgr., div. mgr., v.p. IIT Research Inst., 1950-69; v.p., dir. tech. Kaiser Aluminum and Chem. Corp., Oakland, Calif., 1969-82; Mem. numerous govt. coms. on devel. titanium for def. applications.; chmn. nat. materials adv. bd. NRC, 1982-84. Contbr. numerous articles on titanium and its alloys to profl. jours. Bd. dirs. Research Found. Ohio State U., Jr. Achievement of Bay Area, 1980-82. Recipient Outstanding Young Men award Chgo. Jr. Assn. Commerce and Industry, 1956; Distinguished Alumnus and Centennial Achievement awards Ohio State U. Fellow Am. Soc. Metals (trustee, Campbell Meml. lectr. 1974), hon. mem.; mem. AIME (chmn. titanium com.; chmn. Inst. of Metals div.; bd. dirs. Metall. Soc.), Am. Ceramic Soc. Home: 9369 E Via Montoya Scottsdale AZ 85255-5013

MCPHERSON, DONALD PAXTON, III, lawyer; b. Balt., Aug. 9, 1941; s. Donald Paxton Jr. and Janet Lewis Russell McPherson; m. Anna Mary Teaff; children: David Russell, Cynthia Quandt. AB, Princeton U., 1963; LLB, Columbia U., 1966. Bar: Md. 1966, U.S. Dist. Ct. Md. 1967, U.S. Ct. Appeals (4th cir.) 1967. Assoc. Piper & Marbury, Balt., 1966-74, ptnr., 1974—, head real estate dept., 1980-94. Mem. ABA, Md. Bar Assn. Democrat. Presbyterian. Avocations: swimming, bicycling, hiking. Office: Piper & Marbury 36 S Charles St Baltimore MD 21201-3020

MC PHERSON, FRANK ALFRED, manufacturing corporate executive; b. Stilwell, Okla., Apr. 29, 1933; s. Younce B. and Maurine Francis (Strauss) McP.; m. Nadine Wall, Sept. 10, 1955; 4 children. B.S., Okla. State U., 1957. With Kerr-McGeeCorp., 1957—; gen. mgr. Gulf Coast Oil and gas ops., Morgan City, La., 1969-73; pres. Kerr-McGee Coal, 1973-76, Kerr-McGee Nuclear, 1976-77; vice chmn. Kerr-McGee Corp., 1977-80, pres., 1980—, chmn., CEO, 1983—; bd. dirs. Kimberly-Clark Corp. Patentee in field. Bd. dirs. Okla. chpt. Nature Conservancy, U.S. Olympic Com. for Okla., Bapt Med. Ctr. Okla., Okla. Med. Rsch. Found., Okla. State U. Found., Okla. State Fair, Bank of Okla., Boys and Girls Clubs of Am., J.&W., Seligman & Co., Inc.; pres. Okla. Found. Excellence; active Bus. Roundtable; adv. com. U. Okla. Coll. Medicine, Oklahoma City Pub. Schs.; mem. bd. visitors U. Okla. Coll. Engring. Mem. Conf. Bd., Soc. Mining Engrs. Am., Am. Petroleum Inst. (dir.), Nat. Petroleum Council, 25-Yr. Club of Petroleum Industry Oklahoma City C. of C. (dir.), Okla. State C. of C. Republican. Baptist. Office: Kerr-McGee Corp PO Box 25861 Oklahoma City OK 73125-0861

MCPHERSON, GARY LEE, lawyer, state representative; b. Auburn, Wash., Dec. 4, 1962; s. Percy Ivan and Vicki Mae (Voyles) McP.; children: Christina, Elizabeth, Ashley. BS in Bus. Adminstrn., Union Coll., 1985; JD, U. Nebr., 1988. Bar: Colo. 1989, Nebr. 1989, U.S. Dist. Ct. Colo. 1989, U.S. Ct. Appeals (10th cir.) 1989. Legal/legis. aide Knudsen, Berkheimer & Richardson, Lincoln, Nebr., 1981-85; law clk. Crosby, Guenzel & Davis, Lincoln, 1986; law clk. ethics com. Nebr. State Bar Assn., Lincoln, 1987; assoc. Hall & Evans, Denver, 1987-89, Elrod, Katz, Preeo & Look, P.C., Denver, 1989-90, Fortune & Lawritson, P.C., Denver, 1990-93; ptnr. McPherson & Hull, P.C., Aurora, Colo., 1993—; state rep. State of Colo., Denver, 1994—. Author: Handbook on Professional Malpractice, 1987, rev. edit., 1988; contbr. articles to profl. jours. Bd. dirs. Arapahoe Park and Recreation Bd., Aurora, 1991-95; dist. capt. Arapahoe County Rep. Dist. 8, Aurora, 1992-95; vice chmn. Ho. Dist. 40, Aurora, 1993-95, state rep.; chmn. Senate Dist. 28, Aurora, 1993-95. Recipient Internat. Acad. Trial Lawyers award, 1987, 88, Aurora Pub. Schs. Supts. award, 1992. Mem. ABA (bd. dirs., litigations com. 1992-93, chmn. young lawyers divsn. prelaw counseling com. 1992-94), Colo. Bar Assn. (sec., treas. young lawyers divsn. 1991-93, chair-elect 1993-94, chmn. 1994-95), Arapahoe County Bar Assn., Aurora Rep. Forum, Arapahoe County Rep. Mens Club. Avocations: aviation, scuba, politics, backpacking, snow skiing. Office: 3300 S Parker Rd Ste 101 Aurora CO 80014-3520

MC PHERSON, HARRY CUMMINGS, JR., lawyer; b. Tyler, Tex., Aug. 22, 1929; s. Harry Cummings and Nan (Hight) McP.; m. Clayton Read, Aug. 30, 1952 (div.); children: Courtenay, Peter B.; m. Mary Patricia DeGroot, Oct. 17, 1981; 1 child, Sam B. B.A., U. South, 1949, D.C.L. (hon.), 1965; student, Columbia U., 1949-50; LL.B., U. Tex., 1956. Bar: Tex. 1955. Asst. gen. counsel Democratic policy com. U.S. Senate, 1956-59, asso. counsel, 1959-61, gen. counsel, 1961-63; dep. under sec. internat. affairs Dept. Army, 1963-64; asst. sec. ednl. and cultural affairs Dept. State, 1964-65; spl. asst. and counsel to Pres. Johnson, 1965-66, spl. counsel, 1966-69; pvt. practice law Washington, 1969—; chmn. task force on domestic policy Dem. Adv. Coun. Elected Ofcls., 1974-76; mem. Pres.'s Commn. on Accident at Three Mile Island, 1979; vice chmn. John F. Kennedy Ctr. for Performing Arts, 1969-76, gen. counsel, 1977-91; bd. dirs. Woodrow Wilson Internat. Ctr. for Scholars, 1969-74; pres. Fed. City Coun., 1983-88; apptd. vice chmn. U.S. Internat. Cultural and Trade Ctr. Commn., 1988-93. Author: A Political Education, 1972, 88, 95. Mem. U.S. Base Closure and Realignment Commn., 1993. 2d lt. USAF, 1950-53. Recipient Disting. Civilian Svc. award Dept. Army, 1964, Arthur S. Flemming award, 1968, Judge Learned Hand Human Rels. award Am. Jewish Com., 1994. Mem. D.C. Bar Assn., N.Y. Council on Fgn. Relations (dir. 1974-77), Econ. Club. of Washington (pres. 1992—). Democrat. Episcopalian. Home: 10213 Montgomery Ave Kensington MD 20895-3325 Office: 901 15th St NW Washington DC 20005-2327

MCPHERSON, JAMES ALAN, writer, educator; b. Savannah, Ga., Sept. 16, 1943; s. James and Mable (Smalls) McP.; 1 dau., Rachel Alice. BA, Morris Brown Coll., 1965; LLB, Harvard, 1968; MFA, U. Iowa, 1971. Asst. prof. lit. U. Calif., Santa Cruz, 1969-71, Morgan State U., 1975-76; assoc. prof. English U. Va., Charlottesville, 1976-81; prof. English U. Iowa, 1981—; mem. lit. panel Nat. Endowment for Arts, 1977-80; lectr., Japan, 1989-90; vis. scholar Yale Law Sch., 1978-79. Author: Hue and Cry, 1969, Railroad,

1976, Elbow Room, 1977 (Pultizer prize 1978), A World Unsuspected, 1987, The Prevailing South, 1988, Confronting Racial Differences, 1990, Lure and Loathing, 1993, Crossings, 1993, Crab Cakes, 1997; editor Double Take Mag., 1995—; contbr. editor Atlantic Monthly, Boston, 1969. Atlantic grantee, 1968; Guggenheim fellow, 1972-73, Ctr. Behavioral Studies fellow, Stanford, Calif., 1997—; Recipient award in lit. Nat. Inst. Arts and Letters, 1970, MacArthur Found. award, 1981, Excellence in Tchg. award U. Iowa, 1991, Green Eyeshades award Soc. So. Journalists, 1994; stories selected for O'Henry Collection and Best American Short Stories, 1969, 73, best Am. Essays, 1990, 93, 94, 95, Pushcart prize, 1995. Mem. ACLU, NAACP, P.E.N., Am. Acad. Arts and Scis. (elected mem. 1995), Authors League.

MC PHERSON, JAMES MUNRO, history educator; b. Valley City, N.D., Oct. 11, 1936; s. James Munro and Miriam (Osborn) McP.; m. Patricia Rasche, Dec. 28, 1957; 1 dau., Joanna Erika. B.A., Gustavus Adolphus Coll., 1958; Ph.D., Johns Hopkins U., 1963. Mem. faculty Princeton U., 1962—, prof. history, 1972—, Edwards prof. Am. history, 1982, George Henry Davis '86 prof. Am. history, 1991. Author: Struggle for Equality, 1964 (Ainsfield-Wolf award race rels. 1965), The Negro's Civil War, 1965, Marching Toward Freedom: The Negro in the Civil War, 1968, Blacks in America: Bibliographical Essays, 1971, The Abolitionist LEgacy: From Reconstruction to the NAACP, 1975, Ordeal by Dire: The Civil War and Reconstruction, 1981, 2d edit., 1992, Battle Cry of Freedom: The Civil War Era, 1988 (Pulitzer prize for history 1989), Abraham Lincoln and the Second American Revolution, 1991, Images of the Civil War, 1992, Gettysburg, 1993, What They Fought For, 1861-1865, 1994, The Atlas of the Civil War, 1994, Drawn With the Sword: Reflections on the American Civil War, 1996, For Ciase and Comrades: Why Men Fought in the Civil War, 1997. Danforth fellow, 1958-62, Guggenheim fellow, 1967-68, Huntington-Nat. Endowment for Humanities fellow, 1977-78, fellow Behavioral Scis. Ctr., Stanford U., 1982-83, Huntington-Seaver Inst. fellow, 1987-88. Mem. Am. Philos. Soc., Am., So. hist. assns., Orgn. Am. Historians, Phi Beta Kappa. Home: 15 Randall Rd Princeton NJ 08540-3609

MCPHERSON, JOHN BARKLEY, aerospace consultant, retired military officer; b. Virginia, Minn., Oct. 4, 1917; s. Barkley John and Anna (Holmgren) McP.; m. Leota Irene Wilson, July 16, 1940; children—Kenneth, Sue McPherson Cain, Shirley McPherson Curs, Robin McPherson Rohrback. B.C.E., U. Ariz., 1940. Commd. 2d lt., cav. U.S. Army, 1940; advanced through grades to lt. gen. USAF, 1968; assigned (B-29s, World War II, PTO); comdr. Walker AFB, Roswell, N.Mex., 1950-52; dir. faculty (Air War Coll.), 1955-56; dep. comdr. (5th Air Div. Morocco), 1956-58; comdr. (379th Bomb Wing), Homestead AFB, Fla., 1958-59, (823d Air Div.), Homestead AFB, 1959-62, (810th Air Div.), Minot AFB, N.D., 1962-64; vice dir. ops., joint staff (Joint Chiefs Staff), 1964-67, vice dir. joint staff, 1967-68, asst. to chmn., 1968-70; comdt. (Nat. War Coll.), 1970-73; ret., 1973; cons. Martin Marietta Aerospace, 1973-85; mem. Sr. Govt. Rev. Panel, 1985-91. Decorated D.S.M. with two oak leaf clusters, Legion of Merit, Bronze Star; recipient Gen. H.S. Vandenberg Aerospace Edn. award, 1984; Centennial medallion award U. Ariz., 1989, Disting. Citizen award, 1995; named Outstanding Young Man of Yr., Roswell, 1951. Mem. Air Force Hist. Found. (pres. 1974-83), Air Force Assn., Nat. Space Club, Order of Daedalians, Theta Tau, Kappa Sigma. Home: Apt 3510 20530 Falcons Landing Cir Sterling VA 20165

MCPHERSON, LARRY E(UGENE), photographer, educator; b. Newark, Ohio, May 1, 1943; s. Eugene Edward and Ethel Grace (Lehman) McP. BA, MA; B.A., Columbia Coll., Chgo., 1976; M.A., No. Ill. U., 1978. Instr. Columbia Coll., 1971-76; assoc. prof. photography U. Memphis, 1978—; instr. Sch. of Art Inst. Chgo., spring 1972; workshop instr. Ohio State U., Columbus, summer 1980, VSW Summer Inst., Rochester, N.Y., summer 1988. One-man shows include Art Inst. Chgo., 1969, 78, 81, Dayton Art Inst., 1992; exhibited in group shows at Mus. Modern Art, N.Y.C., 1978, Corcoran Gallery Art, Washington, 1982, George Eastman House, Rochester, N.Y., 1982, New Orleans Mus. Art, 1992; represented in permanent collections Mus. Modern Art, Art Inst. Chgo., George Eastman House, New Orleans Mus. Art, Mus. Fine Arts, Houston, Memphis Brooks Mus. Art. Faculty Devel. grantee U. Memphis, 1983, 92; grantee-fellow Nat. Endowment for Arts, 1975, 79; Guggenheim fellow, 1980. Mem. Soc. Photog. Edn. Home: 7725 Shadow Bend Ln Arlington TN 38002-8321 Office: U Memphis Dept Art Memphis TN 38152

MCPHERSON, MARY PATTERSON, academic administrator; b. Abington, Pa., May 14, 1935; d. John B. and Marjorie Hoffman (Higgins) McP. A.B., Smith Coll., 1957, LL.D., 1981; M.A., U. Del., 1960; Ph.D., Bryn Mawr Coll., 1969; LL.D. (hon.), Juniata Coll., 1975, Smith Coll., 1981, Princeton U., 1984, U. Rochester, 1984, U. Pa., 1985; Litt.D. (hon.), Haverford Coll., 1980; L.H.D. (hon.), Lafayette Coll., 1982, U. Pa., 1985; LHD (hon.), Med. Coll. Pa., 1985. Instr. philosophy U. Del., 1959-61; asst., fellow and lectr. dept. philosophy Bryn Mawr Coll., 1961-63, asst. dean, 1964-69, assoc. dean, 1969-70; dean Bryn Mawr Coll. (Undergrad. Coll.), 1970-78, assoc. prof., from 1970; acting pres. Bryn Mawr Coll., 1976-77, pres., 1978—; bd. dirs. Provident Nat. Bank of Phila., Bell Telephone Co. Pa., Dayton Hudson Corp.; mem. commn. on women in higher edn. Am. Council on Edn., bd. dirs., 1979-82. Bd. dirs. Agnes Irwin Sch., 1971—; bd. dirs. Shipley Sch., 1972—, Phillips Exeter Acad., 1973-76, Wilson Coll., 1976-79, Greater Phila. Movement, 1973-77, Internat. House of Phila., 1974-76, Josiah Macy, Jr. Found., 1977—, Carnegie Found. for Advancement Teaching, 1978-86, Univ. Mus., Phila., 1977-79, University City Sci. Center, 1979-85, Brookings Inst., 1984—, Phila. Contributionship, 1985—, Carnegie Corp. N.Y., 1985—, Nat. Humanities Ctr., 1986—, Amherst Coll., 1986—. Mem. Soc. for Ancient Greek Philosophy, Am. Philos. Soc. Clubs: Fullerton, Cosmopolitan. Office: Bryn Mawr Coll Office of the President 101 N Merion Ave Bryn Mawr PA 19010-2859*

MCPHERSON, MELVILLE PETER, academic administrator, former government official; b. Grand Rapids, Mich., Oct. 27, 1940; s. Donald and Ellura E. (Frost) McP.; m. Joanne McPherson; 4 children. JD, Am. U., 1969; MBA, Western Mich. U., 1967; BA, Mich. State U., 1963. Peace Corps vol. Peru, 1965-66; with IRS, Washington, 1969-75; spl. asst. to pres. and dep. dir. Presdl. Pers. White Ho., Washington, 1975-77; mng. ptnr. Washington office Vorys, Sater, Seymour & Pease, 1977-81; adminstr. AID, Washington, 1981-87; dep. sec. Dept. Treasury, Washington, 1987-89; group exec. v.p. Bank of Am., San Francisco, 1989-93; pres. Mich. State U., East Lansing, 1993—. Mem. D.C. Bar Assn., Mich. Bar Assn. Republican. Methodist. Office: Office of the Pres Mich State U 450 Administration East Lansing MI 48824-1046

MC PHERSON, PAUL FRANCIS, publishing and investment banking executive; b. Boston, Apr. 30, 1931; s. William Andrew and Margaret Frances (Rice) McP.; m. Mary Loretta Sanders, June 10, 1953; children: Paul, Kevin, Gary, Scott. BSBA, Boston Coll., 1952; MBA, Babson Coll., 1955. With McGraw Hill, Inc., N.Y.C., 1955-89; advt. sales mgr. McGraw-Hill Pub. Co., 1963-66, group v.p., 1973-76, exec. v.p., 1976-79; pres. McGraw-Hill Info. Systems Co., 1979-80; pres. McGraw-Hill Pub. Co., 1980-83, exec. v.p., 1983-89; pres., chief exec. officer FM Bus. Publs. Inc., N.Y.C., 1988-92; sr. advisor AdMedia Corp. Advisors, N.Y.C., 1992-93, mng. dir., 1993—. Served with U.S. Army, 1952-54. Mem. Am. Bus. Press (bd. dirs., past chmn.), Mag. Pubs. Am. (bd. dirs., past chmn.), Advt. Coun. (dir., past vice chmn.), Audit Bur. Circulations (dir., past vice chmn.), Woodway Country Club. Home: 10 Drum Hill Ln Stamford CT 06902-1406 Office: AdMedia Corp Advisors Inc 866 3rd Ave New York NY 10022-6221

MC PHERSON, PETER, academic administrator. BA in Polit. Sci., Mich. State U., 1963; MBA, Western Mich. U., 1967; JD, Am. U., 1969; LHD (hon.), Va. State U., 1984, Mt. St. Mary;s Coll., 1986; LLD (hon.), Mich. State U., 1984. Tax law specialist IRS, 1969-75; spl. asst. to Pres. Ford, deputy dir. presdl. personnel The White House, Washington, 1975-77; ptnr. Vorys, Sater, Swymour & Pease, Washington, 1977-80; adminstr. Agy. for Internat. Devel., 1981-87; deputy sec. Treasury Dept., Washington, 1987-89; group exec. v.p. Bank Am., 1989-93; pres. Mich. State U., East Lansing, 1993—; chmn. bd. Overseas Pvt. Investment Corp., 1981-87. Gen. counsel Reagan-Bush Transition, 1980-81; vol. Peace Corps, Peru, 1964-65. Recipient Humanitarian of Yr. award Am. Lebanese League, 1983, UNICEF award.

MC PHERSON, ROBERT DONALD, retired lawyer; b. Madison, Wis., Dec. 21, 1936; s. Clifford James and Alice Irene (Peterson) McP.; m. Nancy Joann Buenzli, Aug. 17, 1957; children—Sean Kelly, Eileen Patricia, Maureen Teresa, Cathleen Marie. B.A., U. Tex., El Paso, 1960; J.D., South Tex. Coll. Law, Houston, 1969. Bar: Tex. 1969. Tchr. English various schs., El Paso, Tex. and Menomonie, Wis., 1960-62; claims rep. Employers Casualty Co. Tex., 1962-66, staff claims rep., 1966-68; ptnr. Bousquet & McPherson, Houston, 1969-76; pvt. practice Houston, 1976-80; ptnr. McPherson & McPherson, Houston, 1980-87, McPherson & Ruman, Houston, 1987-89; pvt. practice Houston, 1989-90; ptnr. Mc Pherson & Mahar, Houston, 1990-91; instr. history and govt. South Tex. Jr. Coll., 1969-71; adj. prof. law South Tex. Coll. Law, 1972-78. Served with AUS, 1953-56. Mem. State Bar Tex., Order of Lytae.

MC PHERSON, ROLF KENNEDY, clergyman, church official; b. Providence, Mar. 23, 1913; s. Harold S. and Aimee (Semple) McP.; m. Lorna De Smith, July 21, 1931 (dec.); children—Marlene (dec.), Kay; m. Evangeline Carmichael, Jan. 31, 1997. Grad., So. Cal. Radio Inst., 1933; D.D. (hon.), L.I.F.E. Bible Coll., 1944; LLD (hon.), L.I.F.E. Bible Coll., Los Angeles, 1988. Ordained to ministry Internat. Ch. Foursquare Gospel, 1940. Pres. Internat. Ch. Foursquare Gospel, L.A., 1944-88, dir., 1944-92; pres. emeritus, 1988—; pres., dir. L.I.F.E. Bible Coll., Inc., L.A., 1944-88. Mem. Echo Park Evangelistic Assn. (pres. 1944—). Office: Internat Ch Foursquare Gospel 1910 W Sunset Blvd Ste 200 Los Angeles CA 90026-3247

MCPHERSON, RONALD P., federal agency administrator. BS in Meteorology, U. Tex., MS in Environ. Engring., PhD in Atmospheric Scis. Trainee U.S. Weather Bur., 1959; observer/briefer, asst. aviation forecaster, rsch. meteorologist Dept. Commerce, Nat. Weather Svcs, 1968-80, branch chief devel. divsn., 1980-87, chief meteorol. ops. divsn., 1987-88, dep. asst. adminstr., 1988-90; dir. Nat. Ctrs. Environ. Pred., Nat. Weather Svc., 1990—. Contbr. to profl jours. Fellow Am. Meteorological Soc. (pres. 1997). Office: Dept of Commerce-Nat Weather Svc National Meteorological Center 5200 Auth Rd Washington DC 20233-0003

MCPHERSON, SAMUEL DACE, III, computer scientist, instructor, consultant; b. Durham, N.C., May 22, 1957; s. Samuel Dace Jr. and Margaret Courtauld (Finney) McP.; m. Grace Carroll Gilliam, Oct. 11, 1986; children: Stuart Dace, Katherine Finney, Rebecca Banks. BA in Edn., U. N.C., 1979; MEd, U. S.C., 1981. Data entry operator Olsten svcs. No. Telecom, Durham, 1985; computer operator GTE Data Svcs., Durham, 1985-86, sr. computer operator, 1986-87, svc. technician, 1987-88; systems tng. analyst GTE Data Svcs., Tampa, Fla., 1988-90, sr. systems tng. analyst, 1990-92; sr. sales tng. specialist Ascom Timeplex, 1992-93; tech. tng. specialist Fujitsu Network Switching, Raleigh, N.C., 1994-95; founder, pres. Technology Tng. Solutions, Inc., 1995—; presenter pub. and ednl. workshops Wake Tech.; instr./lectr. Am. Rsch. Group. Vol. U.S. Olympic Festival, Durham, 1987, GTE Suncoast Classic, Tampa, 1989-91; instr. Jr. Achievement Tampa, 1989; active Village Presbyn. Ch., Tampa, 1990. Recipient Personal Best Group award GTE, 1992, Quest for Quality award, 1992, Outstanding Achievement award Ascom Timeplex, 1993; Cameron scholar U. N.C., 1978-79. Mem. ASTD (spl. projects com. Suncoast chpt. 1989-90, appreciation award 1989), Data Processing Mgmt. Assn. (dir. mem. edn. 1989-91, presenter local workshop 1991). Republican. Avocations: racquetball, golf, tennis, music, working with others. Home: 5201 Lovell Ct Raleigh NC 27613-5618 Office: Tech Tng Solutions Inc 5201 Lovell Ct Raleigh NC 27613-5618

MCPHERSON, SANDRA JEAN, poet, educator; b. San Jose, Calif., Aug. 2, 1943; d. John Emmet and Joyce (Turney) Todd; adopted d. Walter James and Frances K. (Gibson) McP.; m. Henry D. Carlile, 1966 (div. 1985); 1 child, Phoebe; m. Walter D. Pavlich, 1995. BA in English, San Jose (Calif.) State U., 1965; postgrad., U. Wash., 1965-66. Vis. lectr. U. Iowa Writers Workshop, 1974-76, 78-80; Holloway lectr. U. Calif., Berkeley, 1981; tchr. poetry workshop Oreg. Writers Workshop, Portland, 1981-85; prof. English U. Calif., Davis, 1985—. Author: (poetry) Elegies for the Hot Season, 1970, Radiation, 1973, The Year of Our Birth, 1978, Patron Happiness, 1983, Streamers, 1988, The God of Indeterminacy, 1993, The Spaces Between Birds: Mother/Daughter Poems, 1996, Edge Effect: Trails and portrayals, 1996. Recipient Nat. Endowment for the Arts awards; award in lit. Am. Acad. and Inst. Arts and Letters, 1987; Ingram Merrill Found. fellow; grantee Guggenheim Found., 1976, Oreg. Arts Commn., 1984-85. Democrat. Avocation: collector and exhibitor of African-American quilts. Office: U Calif Dept English Davis CA 95616

MCPHERSON, VANZETTA PENN, federal judge; b. Montgomery, Ala., May 26, 1947; d. Luther Lincoln and Sadie Lee (Gardner) P.; m. Winston D. Durant, Aug. 17, 1968 (div. Apr. 1979); 1 child, Raegan Winston; m. Thomas McPherson Jr., Nov. 16, 1985. BS in Speech Pathology, Howard U., Washington, 1969; MA in Speech Pathology, Columbia U., 1971, JD, 1974. Bar: N.Y. 1975, Ala. 1976, U.S. Dist. Ct. (so. dist.) N.Y. 1975, U.S. Dist. Ct. (mid. dist.) Ala. 1980, U.S. Ct. Appeals (2d cir.) 1975, U.S. Ct. Appeals (11th cir.) 1981, U.S. Supreme Ct. Assoc. Hughes, Hubbard & Reed, N.Y.C., 1974-75; asst. atty. gen. Ala. Atty. Gen. Office, Montgomery, 1975-78; pvt. practice Montgomery, 1978-92; magistrate judge U.S. Dist. Ct. (mid. dist.) Ala., Montgomery, 1992—; co-owner Roots & Wings, A Cultural Bookplace, Montgomery, 1989—. Dir. Ala. Shakespeare Festival, Montgomery, 1987—, Montgomery Symphony Orch., 1995—; chmn. trustees Dexter Ave. King Meml. Bapt. Ch., Montgomery, 1988; chmn. Leadership Montgomery; bd. mem. Lighthouse Counseling Ctr., Montgomery, 1981-84, Montgomery County Pub. Libr., 1989-90; v.p. Lanier High Sch. Parent Tchr. Student Assn., Montgomery, 1990-91. Recipient cert. Ala. Jud. Coll.; named Woman of Achievement Montgomery Advertiser, 1989, Boss of Yr. Montgomery Assn. Legal Secs., 1992. Mem. ABA (law office design award 1985), FBA (pres.-elect Montgomery chpt.), Nat. Bar Assn., Ala. State Bar Assn. (chmn. family law sect. 1989-90), N.Y. State Bar Assn., Montgomery Inn of Cts. (master bencher 1992—), Ala. Black Lawyers Assn. (pres. 1979-80). Office: US Dist Ct Mid Dist Ala PO Box 1629 15 Lee St Montgomery AL 36102

MC QUADE, HENRY FORD, state justice; b. Pocatello, Idaho, Oct. 11, 1915; s. M. Joseph and Mary E. (Farnan) McQ.; m. Mary E. Downing, Apr. 11, 1942; children—Sharon McQuade Grisham, Michael, Frances McQuade Munning, Robert, Joseph, Peter, William. A.B., U. Idaho, 1940, LL.B., 1943. Bar: Idaho 1946. Practice in Pocatello, 1946-51; pros. atty. Bannock County, Idaho, 1946-50; judge 5th Jud. Dist., Idaho, 1951-56; justice Idaho Supreme Ct., 1957-76, chief justice, 1972-75; dep. adminstr. Law Enforcement Assistance Adminstrn., U.S. Dept. Justice, Washington, 1976; adminstrv. law judge Occupational Safety and Health Rev. Commn., Washington, 1976-81; mem. Nat. Commn. on Criminal Justice Standards and Goals, 1971-73, Nat. Commn. Hwy. Traffic Safety, 1971-74. Chmn. Idaho Gov.'s Com. Traffic Safety, 1958-59, Idaho YMCA Youth Legislature, 1958-69, Boise chpt. ARC, 1970-71. Mem. Am. Bar Assn., Am. Judicature Soc., Idaho State Bar. Home: 1002 Ranch Rd Boise ID 83702-1440

MC QUADE, LAWRENCE CARROLL, lawyer, corporate executive; b. Yonkers, N.Y., Aug. 12, 1927; s. Edward A. and Thelma (Keefe) McQ.; m. de Rosset Parker Morrissey, Aug. 3, 1968 (dec. Oct. 1978); 1 child, Andrew Parker; m. Margaret Osmer, Mar. 15, 1980. BA with distinction, Yale U., 1950; BA, Oxford (Eng.) U., 1952, MA, 1956; LLB cum laude, Harvard U., 1954; MA (hon.), Colby Coll., 1981. Bar: N.Y. 1955, D.C. 1968. Assoc. Sullivan & Cromwell, N.Y.C., 1954-60; spl. asst. to asst. sec. for internat. security affairs U.S. Dept. Def., Washington, 1961-63; dep. asst. sec. U.S. Dept. Commerce, Washington, 1963-64, asst. to sec., 1965-67, asst. sec., 1967-69; pres. Procon Inc., Des Plaines, Ill., 1969-75; CEO, dir. Procon Inc., 1969-75; v.p. Universal Oil Products Co., 1972-75; v.p. W.R. Grace & Co., N.Y.C., 1975-78, sr. v.p., 1978-83, exec. v.p., 1983-87, also bd. dirs.; vice chmn. Prudential Mut. Fund Mgmt., N.Y.C., 1988-95; mng. dir. Prudential Securities Inc., 1988-92; chmn. Qualitas Internat., 1994—; chmn., CEO Universal Money Ctrs., 1987-88; co-chmn. River Capital Internat., 1997—; expert advisor commn. on transnat. corps. UN, 1989-93; bd. dirs. Bunzl, Quixote Corp., Oxford Analytica, Applied Biosci. Internat.; dir. Country Baskets Index Fund, Inc. Author: (with others) The Ghana Report, 1959; contbr. (with others) articles to profl. jours. Bd. dirs. Fgn. Bondholders Protective Coun., N.Y.C., 1978—, The Am. Forum, 1985-96, Am. Coun. on Germany, 1985-94; trustee Colby Coll., 1981-89, trustee emeritus, 1989—; chmn., dir. Czech and Slovak Am. Enterprise Funds, 1994-96; chmn. Czech and Slovak AE Fund, 1995-96; mem. Bretton Woods Com. Rhodes scholar Oxford U., 1952. Mem. Coun. Fgn. Rels. N.Y., Chgo. Coun. Fgn. Rels. (bd. dirs. 1969-75), Nat. Fgn. Trade Coun. (bd. dirs. 1979-87), Atlantic Coun. U.S. (bd. dirs. 1969—), Mgmt. and Devel. Inst. (bd. dirs. 1970—), Overseas Devel. Coun. (bd. dirs. 1974-87), Pres.'s Cir. of NAS, Harvard Club, Century Club, Pilgrims Club, Met. Club (Washington), Phi Beta Kappa.

MCQUAID, JOHN GAFFNEY, lawyer; b. N.Y.C., Jan. 4, 1918; s. Paul Augustine and Louise (Gaffney) McQ.; m. Betty Frances Seay, May 27, 1989; children from previous marriage: John G. Jr., Catherine M., Elizabeth L. BA, Yale Coll., 1940, LLB, 1947. Bar: N.Y. 1948, U.S. Supreme Ct. 1954. Assoc. Townley Updike Carter & Rodgers, N.Y.C., 1947-52; with Nat. Prodn. Auth., Washington, 1952-54; pvt. practice White Plains, N.Y., 1954-60; ptnr. Fingar & McQuaid, White Plains, 1960-65; ptnr. McCarthy, Fingar, Donovan, Drazen & Smith, White Plains, 1965-94, counsel, 1995—; dir., asst. sec. Dewey Electronics Corp., Oakland, N.J., 1955—. Co-author, editor: New York Wills and Trusts, 2d edit., 1961, 3d edit., 1990; nat., N.Y. co-editor: Will Manual Svc. 2d lt. U.S. Army, 1942-46. Fellow Am. Coll. Trusts and Estate Counsel, Am. Bar Found., N.Y. Bar Found.; mem. N.Y. State Bar Assn. (chmn. trusts and estates law sect. 1981), White Plains Bar Assn. (pres. 1961), Ardsley Country Club, Westchester Bar Assn. Home: Hudson House PO Box 11 Ardsley-On-Hudson NY 10503-7011 Office: McCarthy Fingar Donovan Drazen & Smith 11 Martine Ave White Plains NY 10606-1934

MCQUAID, JOSEPH WOODBURY, newspaper executive; b. Manchester, N.H., Feb. 12, 1949; s. Bernard John and Margaret (Griffin) McQ.; m. Signe Karin Anderson, Nov. 2, 1975; children—Katharine, Brendan. Student, U. N.H., 1967-69. Reporter Union Leader, Manchester, N.H., 1969-71; Sunday editor N.H. Sunday News, Manchester, N.H., 1971-76; mng. editor Union Leader-Sunday News, Manchester, N.H., 1976-82, editor-in-chief, 1982—, v.p., 1986—; gen. mgr., 1992—; dir. Union Leader Corp., Manchester. Sec. Manchester Indsl. Council, 1974-84. Mem. Greater Manchester C. of C. (dir.). Roman Catholic. Home: 256 N Bay St Manchester NH 03104-2324 Office: Union Leader Corp 100 William Loeb Dr Manchester NH 03109-5309

MCQUARRIE, BRUCE CALE, mathematics educator; b. Easton, Pa., Jan. 6, 1929; s. William Caven Hunter and Florence Mabel (Cale) McQ.; m. Betty Ann Palmer, Dec. 25, 1948 (div. 1983) children—Nancy, Laura, Amy. A.B., Lafayette Coll., 1951; M.A., U. N.H., 1956; Ph.D., Boston U., 1971. Instr. Tucson Indian Sch., Ariz., 1951-52; instr. Wasatch Acad., Mt. Pleasant, Utah, 1956-60; instr. math., asst. prof., assoc. prof. Worcester Poly. Inst., Mass., 1960—, prof. math., dept. head math. scis., 1983-86, prof. emeritus, 1990—. Mem. Democratic Town Com., Auburn, Mass., 1970-90. With U.S. Army, 1952-54. Home: 10 Eames Dr Auburn MA 01501-1308

MCQUARRIE, DONALD GRAY, surgeon, educator; b. Richfield, Utah, Apr. 17, 1931; s. John Gray and LoRetta (Smith) McQ.; m. Dolores Jean Dietrich, July 16, 1956; children—William Gray, Michelle Dolores Colton. B.S., U. Utah, 1952, M.D., 1956; Ph.D., U. Minn., 1964. Diplomate Am. Bd. Surgery, Am. Bd. Thoracic and Cardiovascular Surgery. Intern U. Minn. Hosps., 1956-57; resident in surgery U. Minn., Mpls., 1957-59, resident, 1961-65, asst. prof. surgery, 1964-68, assoc. prof. surgery, 1968-72, prof. surgery, 1972—, vice chmn. dept. surgery, 1993—; mem. surg. staff Mpls. VA Hosp., 1964—, chief surgical svc., 1993—, resident in thoracic surgery, 1965-66, dir. surg. research lab., 1964-78; vis. prof. U. Tex.-San Antonio, 1974, U. Ind. and Indpls. VA, 1977, affiliated program U. Ariz., Phoenix, 1982, Case Western Res. U., 1986. Editor, contbg. author: Head and Neck Cancer, 1986, Reoperations in General Surgery, 1991, 2d edit., 1996; contbr. articles on surg. and basic med. scis. to profl. publs., 1955—. Served to lt. M.C., USN, 1959-61. USPHS postdoctoral fellow, 1962-65. Fellow ACS (commn. on cancer 1980-89, exec. council commn. on operating room environ. 1985-91, pres. Minn. chpt. 1983-84, liaison to Assn. Oper. Rm. Nurses 1985—, gov. 1990—); mem. Minn. Surg. Soc. (pres. 1980-81), Assn. Acad. Surgery, Mpls. Surg. Soc. (pres. 1978-79), Soc. Head and Neck Surgeons, Central Surg. Assn., Soc. Univ. Surgeons, Société Internationale de Chirurgie, Am. Surg. Assn., Assn. VA Surgeons (pres. 1987), Soc. Surg. Oncology, Hennepin County Med. Soc., Minn. Med. Assn., Am. Soc. Clin. Oncology, Phi Beta Kappa, Phi Kappa Phi. Clubs: Minneapolis, Interlachen Country (Mpls.). Avocations: computer applications to medicine; jewelry design; lapidary work. Home: 6625 Mohawk Trl Minneapolis MN 55439-1029 Office: Mpls VA Med Ctr Dept Surgery 1 Veterans Dr Minneapolis MN 55417-2300

MCQUEEN, JEFFERY THOMAS, meteorologist; b. Bklyn., June 1, 1961; s. Roy and Domenica (Sommese) McQ.; m. Jacqueline Theresa Favilla, Feb. 16, 1991. BA, U. Va., 1982; MS, Colo. State U., 1985. Rsch. asst. Colo. State U., Ft. Collins, 1982-85; rsch. meteorologist NASA/Goddard Space Flt. Ctr., Greenbelt, Md., 1985-91, NOAA/Air Resources Lab., Silver Spring, Md., 1991—; mem. WMO Kuwait Oil Fires, Washington, 1991-92, Air Evaluation Team/WMO, Dhahran, Saudi Arabia, 1991; MARRS evaluation com., NASA/NOAA, Cape Kennedy, Fla., 1992, chair mesoscule modeler worksheet, 1996; Inter-Am. Inst. Global Change mem., Montevideo, Uraguay, 1993; organizer working group NOAA Mesoscale Modelers, 1996—; mem. exec. com. on chem. agt. release modeling CIA, 1996—; mem. Dept. of Def./CIA Gulf War Illness Rev. Panel, 1996. Contbr. articles to profl. jours. Vol. Georgetown Ministry Ctr., Washington, 1993—; bd. dirs. 16th St. Civic Assn., Washington, 1992—. DuPont scholarship, 1980; recipient State of Colo. scholarship, 1983, Spl. Achievement award NOAA, 1991. Mem. Am. Meteorology Soc., D.C. Local Am. Meterol. Soc. Roman Catholic. Avocations: woodworking, bicycling. Home: 1429 Longfellow St NW Washington DC 20011-6819 Office: NOAA/Air Resources Lab 1315 E West Hwy Silver Spring MD 20910-3285

MCQUEEN, JUSTICE ELLIS (L. Q. JONES), actor, director; b. Beaumont, Tex., Aug. 19, 1927; s. Justice Ellis and Pat (Stephens) McQ.; m. Sue Helen Lewis, Oct. 10, 1950 (dec.); children: Marlin Randolph, Marilyn Helen, Steven Lewis. Student, Lamar Jr. Coll., 1944, Lon Morris Coll., 1949, U. Tex., 1950-51. Actor numerous motion picture films, TV shows; dir.: motion picture films including A Boy and His Dog, 1975 (recipient Hugo award, Sci. Fiction achievement award for dramatic presentation); producer The Big Thickett, Come In, Children, The Witchmaker; author: The Brotherhood of Satan, 1971. Served with USNR, 1945-46. Nominee 4 Emmy awards. Mem. Screen Actors Guild. Republican. Methodist. Home and Office: 2144 1/2 N Cahuenga Blvd Los Angeles CA 90068-2708 *Contribute to a space that no one can or will fill.*

MC QUEEN, ROBERT CHARLES, retired insurance executive; b. Santiago, Chile, Jan. 23, 1921; s. Charles Alfred and Grace Juanita (Abrecht) McQ.; m. Donna Marie Ikeler, Oct. 6, 1945; children: Scott, Jerry, Monte, Donald. A.B., Dartmouth Coll., 1942. Mathematician, Equitable Life Assurance Soc., N.Y.C., 1945-49; group actuary Union Central Life Ins. Co., Cin., 1949-57; with Mut. Benefit Life Ins. Co., Newark, 1957-85; exec. v.p. Mut. Benefit Life Ins. Co., 1969-71, sr. exec. v.p., chief adminstrv. officer, 1971-85, dir., 1978-85; bd. dirs. St. Barnabas Corp. (formerly Trimark Corp.). Pres. Millburn Twp. (N.J.) Bd. Edn., 1969-71, Naples (Fla.) Bridge Ctr., 1994-96; chmn. BBB Met. N.Y., 1978-80; chmn. bd. trustees St. Barnabas Hosp., Livingston, N.J., 1983-91, trustee, 1991—. With OSS, 1943-45. Fellow Soc. Actuaries; mem. Am. Acad. Actuaries, Internat. Actuarial Assn., Canoe Brook Country Club, Quail Creek Club. Republican. Episcopalian. Home: 12988 Bald Cypress Ln Naples FL 34119-8526

MCQUEEN, SCOTT ROBERT, broadcasting company executive; b. Peekskill, N.Y., June 30, 1946; s. Robert Charles and Donna Marie (Ikeler) McQ.; m. Loretta A. Dybala, May 17, 1980; children: Geoffrey Scott, Mallory Morgan, Brian Daniel; 1 child, by previous marriage, Tasha Lea. B.A., Dartmouth Coll., 1968. Founder Sconnix Radio Ent., Inc., Laconia, N.H., 1968; Founder Sconnix Radio Ent., Inc. (became Sconnix Group Broadcasting, Inc.), 1971, pres., 1971—; pres. Charisma Ventures, Ltd., 1995—. Chmn. Magic Childrens Fund, 1991—; bd. advisors Pincrest Sch., Boca Raton, Fla. With N.H.N.G., 1968-69. Mem. Nat. Assn. Broadcasters, Nat. Radio Broadcsters Assn., Lakes Region C. of C. (dir. 1977-81), Rotary, Royal Palm Yacht and Country Club, Ocean Reef Club (Key Largo, Fla.). Home: 431 Coconut Palm Rd Boca Raton FL 33432-7915 also: Village West Gilford NH 03246

MCQUEENEY, HENRY MARTIN, SR., publisher; b. N.Y.C., Oct. 29, 1938; s. John Henry and Catherine Mary (Quigg) McQ.; m. Elizabeth Bernino, May 14, 1960; children: Mary E., Henry M. Jr., John P., Matthew S. B.B.A., St. Johns U., 1960; postgrad., U. Rochester, 1965-67. City sales rep. Curtis Circulation div. Curtis Pub. Co., 1960-62; asst. mgr. Curtis Circulation div. Curtis Pub. Co., N.Y.C., 1962-63; field mgr. Curtis Circulation div. Curtis Pub. Co., Rochester, N.Y., 1964-67; dept. mgr., account exec. Curtis Circulation div. Curtis Pub. Co., Phila., 1968-74; v.p. sales, exec. v.p. mktg. Manor Books, Inc., N.Y.C., 1974-76, pres., 1976-79; pres. Wood Hill Press, Inc., 1979-89, Scott Mag. Dist. Corp., N.Y.C., 1989-93, Kearny Pub., Inc., N.Y.C., 1993-96, Princeton Pub., Inc., N.Y.C., 1996—; chmn. bd. Oui mag., 1981-82; pres., CEO, J.Q., Adams Prodns., Inc., 1983-94; rep. Western N.Y. Pubs.; cons. Bipad Ednl. Program. Pres. parish bd. Roman Catholic Ch., 1965, editor newspaper, Spencerport, N.Y., 1965, diocesan leader, mem. lay bd., Rochester, 1964-67; certified as tchr. Confraternity Christian Doctrine, Diocese of Rochester, 1964. Served with USAFR, 1956-64. Mem. Am. Legion. Home: 12 Blenheim Ln Centerport NY 11721-1704 Office: Princeton Pub Inc 12 W 27th St New York NY 10001-6903

MCQUEENEY, THOMAS A., publisher; b. N.Y.C., Aug. 21, 1937; s. Henry J. and Jeannette A. (Beaton) McQ.; m. Ellyn M. Carney, Oct. 11, 1970; children: Kicha Lee, Miya Lyn, Jana Mai. BBA, Northeastern U., 1964. Market analyst Gillette Co., Boston, 1964-65; research analyst Chase Manhattan Bank, N.Y.C., 1965-68; portfolio mgr. Portfolio Planning, Inc., N.Y.C., 1968-71; pub., pres. Money Market Directories, Inc., Charlottesville, Va., 1971—. Editor: Real Estate Investing by Pension Fund Adminstrs., 1975. Mem. Indsl. Devel. Bd. Authority, Albemarle County, 1980—. Served to 1st lt., U.S. Army, 1956-58. Mem. Assn. Investment Mgmt. Sales Execs. Republican. Presbyterian. Lodge: Rotary. Avocations: sailing, skiing. Home: 121 Indian Spring Rd Charlottesville VA 22901-1019 Office: Money Market Directories Inc Charlottesville VA 22901

MCQUERN, MARCIA ALICE, newspaper publishing executive; b. Riverside, Calif., Sept. 3, 1942; d. Arthur Carlyle and Dorothy Louise (Krupke) Knopf; m. Lynn Morris McQuern, June 7, 1969. BA in Polit. Sci., U. Calif., Santa Barbara, 1964; MS in Journalism, Northwestern U., 1966. Reporter The Press-Enterprise, Riverside, 1966-72, city editor, 1972-74, capitol corrs., 1975-78, dep. mng. editor news, 1984-85, mng. editor news, 1985-87, exec. editor, 1988-94, pres., 1992—; editor, publisher, 1994—; asst. metro editor The Sacramento Bee, 1974-75; editor state and polit. news The San Diego Union, 1978-79, city editor, 1979-84; juror Pulitzer Prize in Journalism, 1982, 83, 92, 93. Mem. editorial bd. Calif. Lawyer mag., San Francisco, 1983-88. Bd. advisors U. Calif.-Berkeley Grad. Sch. Journalism, 1991-96, U. Calif.-Riverside Grad. Sch. Mgmt., 1994—; pres. Riverside Cmty. Coll. Found., 1996; bd. trustees U. Calif. Riverside, 1996—. Recipient Journalism award Calif. State Bar Assn., 1967, Sweepstakes award Twin Counties Press Club, Riverside and San Bernardino, 1972, Athena award YWCA, 1994. Mem. Am. Soc. Newspaper Editors (bd. dirs. 1992—), Calif. Soc. Newspaper Editors (bd. 1988-95), Calif. Newspaper Pubs. Assn. (bd. dirs. 1992—), Calif. Press Assn. (bd. dirs. 1996—), Soc. Profl. Journalists, U. Calif.-Santa Barbara Alumni Assn. (bd. dirs. 1983-89). Home: 5717 Bedford Dr Riverside CA 92506-3404 Office: Press-Enterprise Co 3512 14th St Riverside CA 92501-3814

MCQUIGGAN, MARK CORBEILLE, urologist; b. Detroit, May 15, 1933; s. Mark Ronald and Catherine Charlotte (Corbeille) McQ.; m. Carolyn Ann Brunk, Mar. 25, 1961. BS, U. Mich., 1954, MD, 1958. Diplomate Am. Bd. Urology. Resident in surgery and urology U. Mich., 1959-64; group practice Urology Assocs., Detroit, 1964-67; dir. med. edn. Providence Hosp., Southfield, Mich., 1967-69; clin. instr. urology U. Mich., 1969-70; pvt. practice Southfield, 1969—; pres. med. staff North Detroit Gen. Hosp., 1983-84, pres. Providence med. staff, 1995, 96; chmn. credentialling com. Providence Hosp., 1997. Fellow ACS; mem. AMA, Am. Urological Assn., Mich. Urological Assn. (exec. com. 1987-94, pres. 1992-93). Republican. Methodist. Home: 29653 Club House Ln Farmington Hills MI 48334-2015 Office: 22250 Providence Dr Ste 203 Southfield MI 48075-6210

MCQUILKIN, JOHN ROBERTSON, religion educator, academic administrator, writer; b. Columbia, S.C., Sept. 7, 1927; s. Robert C. and Marguerite (Lambie) McQ.; m. Muriel Elaine Webendorfer, Aug. 24, 1948; children: Helen Marguerite, Robert Paul (dec.), David John, Virginia Anne, Amy Lambie, Douglas Kent. BA, Columbia Internat. U., 1947; M.Div., Fuller Theol. Sem., 1950; postgrad., No. Bapt. Theol. Sem., 1947-48. Prof. Greek, religious edn. and theology Columbia (S.C.) Internat. U., 1950-52; pres. Internat. U., 1968-90; headmaster Ben Lippen Sch., Asheville, N.C., 1952-55; missionary The Evang. Alliance Mission, Japan, 1956-68; acting pres. Tokyo Christian U., 1963-65. Author: Measuring the Church Growth Movement, 1974, Understanding and Applying the Bible, 1992, The Great Omission, 1984, An Introduction to Biblical Ethics, 1995, Life in the Spirit, 1997; contbr. articles to religious jours. Mem. Evangel. Missiological Soc. (gen. dir. 1994—).

MC QUILLEN, MICHAEL PAUL, physician; b. N.Y.C., Sept. 9, 1932; s. Paul and Dorothy Marian (Moore) McQ.; m. Louise Devlin; children: Daniel, Thomas, Patrick, Kathleen. B.A. cum laude, Georgetown U., 1953, M.D., 1957; MA, U. Va., 1994. Diplomate Am. Bd. Psychiatry and Neurology (bd. dirs. 1991-95, exec. com. 1995). Rotating intern Royal Victoria Hosp., Montreal, Que., Can., 1957-58; resident in neurology Georgetown U. Med. Center, 1958-60; fellow in physiology Johns Hopkins U. Med. Sch. and Hosp., 1960-62, instr. medicine, 1962-65; mem. faculty U. Ky. Med. Center, 1965-74, prof. neurology, 1972-74, prof., chmn. neurology, 1987-93; prof. neurology, chmn. dept. Med. Coll. Wis., Milw., 1974-87; clin. faculty mem. dept. neurology U. Va. Health Sci. Ctr., Charlottesville, 1993-94; prof. neurology U. Rochester St. Mary's Hosp., N.Y., 1995—; vis. sci. Inst. Neurophysiology U. Copenhagen, 1971-72; vis. prof. U. Ky. Med. Ctr., 1978, Royal Coll. Surgeons, Ireland, 1983. Author articles, papers in field. Mem. Cath. Commn. on Intellectual Affairs. Recipient Neurology medal Georgetown U. Med. Sch., 1957; Clin. Teaching award Med. Coll. Wis., 1976; Disting. Service award N.Y. Med. Coll., 1983; named to Johns Hopkins Soc. Scholars, 1981. Fellow Am. Acad. Neurology; mem. Royal Acad. Medicine Ireland, Nat. Myasthenia Gravis Found. (chmn. 1981-83), Am. Neurol. Assn., N.Y. Acad. Scis., Assn. U. Profs. Neurology, Am. Assn. Electromyography and Electrodiagnosis, AMA, Wis. Neurol. Assn. (pres. 81-82), Milw. Acad. Medicine, Alpha Omega Alpha. Home: 4 Bragdon Dr Rochester NY 14618 Office: St Mary's Hosp Dept Neurology Rochester NY 14611

MC QUINN, WILLIAM P., corporation executive; b. Waterbury, Conn., May 2, 1936; s. William and Bridget (Flynn) McQ.; m. Lorese Hucks, Apr. 17, 1964; children: Kathryn, Norah, Linda, Jennifer. B.S., Bryant Coll., 1956. C.P.A., Conn. Mgmt. auditor NASA, Washington, 1962-64; asst. controller Scovill Mfg. Co., Waterbury, 1964-67; controller C F & I Steel Co., Pueblo, Colo., 1967-71; v.p. financial services Loews Corp., N.Y.C., 1971-73; chief exec. officer Williams Hudson Am. subs. Williams Hudson Group Ltd., Eng., 1973-75; pres. Pegasus Design Group (formerly Williams Hudson Am.), 1975-78; v.p. M.W. Houck, Inc., Rye, N.Y., 1979-82; chief operating officer Cusinarts Inc, Greenwich, CT, 1982-88; exec. v.p. CHC of Conn., Inc., 1988-94; chmn., CEO Fin. Svcs. Inc., Old Greenwich, Conn., 1994—. Served with U.S. Army, 1959. Mem. Am. Inst. C.P.A.s, Fin. Execs. Inst. Home: 8 Vista Ave Old Greenwich CT 06870-2135

MCQUISTON, ROBERT EARL, lawyer; b. Pitts., Feb. 4, 1936; s. Theodore O. and Bertha L. (Kegley) McQ.; m. Mary Hope Missimer, June 30, 1962; children: Mary Hope, Elizabeth Ann. BA magna cum laude, Yale U., 1958; JD cum laude, Harvard U., 1961. Bar: Pa. 1962. Assoc. Ballard, Spahr, Andrews & Ingersoll, Phila., Balt., Denver, Washington, Salt Lake City, 1962-69, ptnr., 1969—; mem. nat. adv. group to Commr. IRS, Washington, 1985-87; lectr. in law Temple U., 1968-69, also various tax insts.; bd. dirs. Macromedia Inc., Hackensack, N.J., Gateway Communications, Inc., Binghamton, N.Y. Contbr. articles to profl. jours. Mem. Rep. Fin. Com., Harrisburg, Pa., 1983-86; trustee Am. Soc. Hypertension, 1992—. Mem. ABA (active numerous coms. sect. taxation 1969—, including coun. mem. 1979-85, vice chmn., sec. 1982-85), Phila. Bar Assn. (bd. govs. 1978-80, mem. coun. 1969—, sec. treas sect. on taxation 1973-75, vice chmn. 1976-78, chmn. 1978-80), Am. Coll. Tax Counsel (charter, regent 1990—, vice chmn. 1993-94, chmn. 1994-96), trustee Am. Tax Policy Inst, 1996—, Nat. Conf. Lawyers and CPAs, Pyramid Club. Episcopalian. Home: 111 Ridgewood Rd Wayne PA 19087-2810 Office: Ballard Spahr Andrews et al 1735 Market St 51st Fl Philadelphia PA 19103-7501

MCQUOWN, JUDITH HERSHKOWITZ, author, financial advisor; b. N.Y.C., Apr. 8, 1941; d. Frederick Ephraim and Pearl (Rosenberg) H.; m. Michael L. McQuown, Jan. 13, 1969 (div. 1980); m. Harrison Roth, Dec. 8, 1985 (div. 1997). AB, Hunter Coll., 1963; postgrad., N.Y. Inst. Fin., N.Y.C., 1965-67. Chief underwriting div. mcpl. securities City of N.Y., 1972-73; CEO Judith H. McQuown & Co., Inc., N.Y.C., 1973—. Author: Inc. Yourself: How to Profit by Setting Up Your Own Corporation, 8th edit., 1995, Tax Shelters That Work for Everyone, 1979, The Fashion Survival Manual, 1981, Playing the Takeover Market, 1982, How to Profit After You Inc. Yourself, 1985, Keep One Suitcase Empty: The Bargain Shopper's Guide to the Finest Factory Outlets in the British Isles, 1987, Keep One Suitcase Empty: The Bargain Shopper's Guide to the Finest Factory Outlets in Europe, 1988, Use Your Own Corporation to Get Rich, 1991; contbg. editor Boardroom Reports, Physician's Fin. News, Physician's Guide to Money Mgmt.; seminars The Learning Annex, The Discovery Ctr., Boston Ctr. for Adult Edn. Mem. Am. Soc. Journalists and Authors. Home and Office: 315 E 72nd St New York NY 10021-4625

MCRAE, HAL (HAROLD ABRAHAM MCRAE), former major league baseball team manager; b. Avon Park, Fla., June 10, 1945; m. Johncyna Williams; children: Brian, Cullen, Leah. Student, Fla. A & M U. Player various minor league teams, 1965-69; player Cin. Reds, 1968, 70-72; player Kansas City Royals, 1973-87, hitting coach, 1987, mgr., 1991-94; minor league hitting instr. Pitts. Pirates, 1988-89; hitting instr. Montreal Expos, 1990-91; batting coach Cincinnati Reds, 1995-96, Phila. Phillies, 1997. Named to All-Star team, 1975, 76, 82; recipient Silver Slugger award, 1982. Address: Phila Phillies PO Box 7575 Philadelphia PA 19101

MCRAE, HAMILTON EUGENE, III, lawyer; b. Midland, Tex., Oct. 29, 1937; s. Hamilton Eugene and Adrian (Hagaman) McR.; m. Betty Hawkins, Aug. 27, 1960; children: Elizabeth Ann, Stephanie Adrian, Scott Hawkins. BSEE, U. Ariz., 1961; student, USAF Electronics Sch., 1961-62; postgrad., U. Redlands, Calif., 1962-63; JD with honors and distinction, U. Ariz., 1967; LHD (hon.), Sterling Coll., 1992; vis. fellow, Darwin Coll. and Martin Ctr., Cambridge (Eng.) U. Bar: Ariz. 1967, U.S. Supreme Ct. 1979; cert. real estate specialist, Ariz. Elec. engr. Salt River Project, Phoenix, 1961; assoc. Jennings, Strouss & Salmon, Phoenix, 1967-71, ptnr., 1971-85, chmn. real estate dept., 1980-85, mem. policy com., 1982-85, mem. fin. com., 1981-85, chmn. bus. devel. com., 1982-85; ptnr. and co-founder Stuckey & McRae, Phoenix, 1985—; co-founder, chmn. bd. Republic Cos., Phoenix, 1985—; magistrate Paradise Valley, Ariz., 1983-85; juvenile referee Superior Ct., 1983-85; pres., dir. Phoenix Realty & Trust Co., 1970—; officer Indsl. Devel. Corp. Maricopa County, 1972-86; instr. and lectr. in real estate; officer, bd. dirs. other corps.; adj. prof. Frank Lloyd Wright Sch. Architecture, Scottsdale, Ariz., 1989—; instr. Ariz. State U. Coll. Architecture and Environ. Design; lead instr. ten-state-bar seminar on Advanced Real Estate Transactions, 1992; evaluation com. for cert. real estate specialist Ariz. Bar, 1994-96; mem. real estate adv. commn. Ariz. Bar, 1996—. Exec. prodr. film documentary on relief and devel. in Africa, 1990; contbr. articles to profl. jours. Elder Valley Presbyn. Ch., Scottsdale, Ariz., 1973-75, 82-85, 96—, chair evangelism com. 1973-74, corp. pres., 1974-75, 84-85, trustee, 1973-75, 82-85, chmn. exec. com., 1984, mem. mission com. 1993—; trustee Upward Found., Phoenix, 1977-80, Valley Presbyn. Found., 1982-83, Ariz. Acad., 1971—; trustee, mem. exec. com. Phi Gamma Delta Ednl. Found., Washington, 1974-84; trustee Phi Gamma Delta Internat., 1984-86; bd. dirs. Archon, 1986-87; founder, trustee, pres. McRae Found., 1980—; bd. dirs. Food for Hungry Inc. (Internat. Relief), 1985-95, exec. com., 1986—, chmn. bd. dirs., 1987-92; chmn. bd. dirs. Food for Hungry Internat., 1993-95, pres. adv. coun., 1995—; trustee, mem. exec. com. Ariz. Mus. Sci. and Tech., 1984—, 1st v.p., 1985-86, pres., 1986-88, chmn. bd. dirs., 1988-90; Lambda Alpha Internat. Hon. Land Econs. Soc, 1988—; sec.-treas. Ariz. State U. Coun. for Design Excellence, 1989-90, bd. dirs. 1988—, pres. 1990-91; mem. Crisis Nursery Office of the Chair, 1988-89, Maricopa Community Colls. Found., 1988—, sec. 1990-91, 2d v.p. 1993-94, 1st v.p. and pres. elect 1994-95, pres. 1995—, capital campaign cabinet, 1995-96, mem. nominating com., 1997, Phoenix Cmty. Alliance, 1988-90, Interchurch Ctr. Corp., 1987-90, Western Art Assocs., bd. dirs., 1989-91, Phoenix Com. on Fgn. Rels., 1988—, U. Ariz. Pres.'s Club, 1984—, chmn., 1991-92; bd. dirs. Econ. Club of Phoenix, 1987— , sec.-treas., 1991-92, v.p., 1992-93, pres. 1993-94; bd. dirs. Ctrl. Ariz. Shelter Svcs., 1995—, Ariz. Community Found., 1996—, investing com., 1996—; founding mem. Alliance to Abolish Homelessness, 1996—, bd. dirs., 1996—, mem. exec. com., 1996—; mem. adv. bd. Help Wanted USA, 1990-92; vol. fund raiser YMCA, Salvation Army, others; bd. dirs. Frank Lloyd Wright Found., 1992—; mem. Taliesin Coun., 1985—; bd. dirs. Taliesin Arch., 1992—, Taliesin Conservation Com. (Wis.); founding mem. Frank Lloyd Wright Soc., 1993—; mem. fin. com. Kyl for Congress, 1985-92, bd. dir. campaign bd. Kyl for U.S. Senate, 1993-94; Senator Kyl Coun., 1995—; campaign com. Symington for Gov. '90, 1989—, mem. gubernatorial adv. bd., 1990-91; mem. Gov.'s Selection Com. for State Revenue Dir., 1993; mem. bond com. City of Phoenix, 1987-88; mem. Ariz. State U. Coun. of 100, 1985-89, investment com., 1985-89; bd. govs. Twelve Who Care Hon Kachina, 1991; mem. adv. coun. Maricopa County Sports Authority, 1989-93; mem. Ariz. Coalition for Tomorrow, 1990-92; founding mem., bd. dite Not Inc., 1992-96 pres., 1990-92, chmn., 1992-94, adv. bd. 1996—; bd. dirs. Garden Homes at Teton Pines Home Owners Assn., 1996—; selected as bearer for the Olympic Torch Relay Team, 1996. 1st lt. USAF, 1961-64,. Recipient various mil. award. Mem. ABA, AIEE, AIME, Ariz. Bar Assn., Maricopa County Bar Assn., U. Ariz. Alumni Assn., Nat. Soc. Fund Raising Execs., Clan McRae Soc. N.Am. Phoenix Exec. Club, Internat. Platform Assn., Am. Friends of the U. Cambridge (Eng.), Jackson Hole Racquet Club, Teton Pines Country Club, Tau Beta Pi. Republican. Home: 8101 N 47th St Paradise Valley AZ 85253-2907 Office: Republic Cos 2425 E Camelback Rd Ste 900 Phoenix AZ 85016-4215

MCRAE, JOHN HENRY, educational administrator; b. N.Y.C., Jan. 3, 1948; s. Elliott Hampton and Grace (Williams) McR.; m. Marcia Owens, Dec. 19, 1990; 1 child, John Ashton. AA, Mid. Ga. Coll., 1968; MS, Valdosta State Coll., 1971, MEd, 1975, EdS, 1983. Cert. adminstr., supr., Ga. Tchr. Sallas Mahone Sch., 1970-79; prin. S.L. Mason Sch., Valdosta, Ga., 1979-86; headmaster Valwood Sch., Valdosta, 1986-88; prin. Bullock County Sch., Statesboro, Ga., 1988-90; asst. prof. Ga. So. U., Statesboro, Ga., 1990-92; dir. student asst. program Mental Health for South Ga. Dist., Valdosta, 1994-95; dir., edn. adminstr. Larier Counties, Ga., 1995—. Recipient Disting. Alumni award Valdosta State Coll., 1978, Hayes-Fulbright scholarship, 1977; named Tchr. of Yr., State of Ga., 1978, one of Outstanding Young Men of Am., 1978, 79, 81. Mem. Ga. Tchrs. of Yr. (founder, charter, pres. 1992—), Nat./State Tchrs. of Yr. Assn., Kappa Delta Pi, Phi Delta Kappa, Omicron Delta Kappa, Sigma Phi Epsilon. Republican. Episcopalian. Home: PO Box 3575 Valdosta GA 31604-3575

MC RAE, KENNETH DOUGLAS, political scientist, educator; b. Toronto, Ont., Can., Jan. 20, 1925; s. Douglas Archibald and Margaret Constance McR.; m. Dorothea Annette Simon, Aug. 4, 1950; children: Patricia, Sandra, Karen, Susan. BA, U. Toronto, 1946; AM, Harvard U., 1947, PhD, 1954; postgrad., Oxford (Eng.) U., 1948-50; postdoctoral research, Nuffield Coll., Oxford, 1953-55. Lectr. in polit. sci. U. Toronto, 1950-52; asst. prof. polit. sci. Carleton U., Ottawa, Ont., 1955-57, assoc. prof., 1957-64, prof., 1964-95, prof. emeritus, 1996—; rsch. supervisor Royal Commn. on Bilingualism and Biculturalism, 1964-69. Author: (with Louis Hartz and others) The Founding of New Societies: Studies in the History of the United States, Latin America, South Africa, Canada and Australia, 1964, Switzerland: Example of Cultural Coexistence, 1964, Conflict and Compromise in Multilingual Societies, Vol. 1, Switzerland, 1983, Vol. 2, Belgium, 1986; editor: The Six Bookes of a Commonweale (Jean Bodin), 1962; editor and project dir.: The Federal Capital: Governmental Institutions, 1969; editor, contbg. author: Consociational Democracy: Political Accommodation in Segmented Societies, 1974; contbg. author: Conflict and Peacemaking in Multiethnic Societies, 1990. Fellow Royal Soc. Can. (hon. sec. 1980-83); mem. Can. Polit. Sci. Assn. (pres. 1978-79), Soc. Scientiarum Fennica (fgn. mem.), Renaissance Soc. Am. Office: Carleton U, Dept Polit Sci, Ottawa, ON Canada K1S 5B6

MCRAE, MARION ELEANOR, critical care nurse; b. Kingston, Ont., Can., Sept. 19, 1960; d. James Malcolm and Madeline Eleanor (MacNamara) McR. BSN, Queen's U., Kingston, 1982; MSN, U. Toronto, 1989. RN, Calif., CCRN; cert. BCLS, ACLS, PALS. Staff nurse thoracic surgery Toronto (Can.) Gen. Hosp., 1982-83, staff nurse cardiovascular ICU, 1983-85; nurse clinician critical care St. Michael's Hosp., Toronto, 1985-87; external critical care clin. tchr. Ryerson Poly. Inst., Toronto, 1986-87; staff nurse cardiovascular ICU The Toronto Hosp.-Toronto Gen. Divsn., 1987-89; clin. nurse specialist cardiac surgery The Toronto Hosp., 1989-90; clin. nurse II cardiothoracic ICU UCLA Med. Ctr., 1990-92, clin. nurse III cardiothoracic ICU, 1992—; mem. critical care nursing adv. bd. George Brown Coll., Toronto, 1987-88. Contbr. articles to profl. nursing jours. Recipient Open Master's fellowship U. Toronto, 1987-88, M. Keyes bursary Toronto Gen. Hosp., 1988-89, Nursing fellowship Heart and Stroke Found. Ont., 1988-89, Outstanding Svc. award UCLA Med. Ctr., 1994, Cardiothoracic ICU Nurse of Yr. award UCLA, 1995. Mem. AACN, Am. Heart Assn. Coun. on Cardiovascular Nursing. Home: 1400 Midvale Ave Apt 210 Los Angeles CA 90024-5498 Office: UCLA Med Ctr Cardiothoracic ICU 10833 Le Conte Ave Los Angeles CA 90095-3075

MCRAE, ROBERT MALCOLM, JR., federal judge; b. Memphis, Dec. 31, 1921; s. Robert Malcolm and Irene (Pontius) McR.; m. Louise Howry, July 31, 1943; children: Susan Campbell, Robert Malcolm III, Duncan Farquhar, Thomas Alexander Todd. BA, Vanderbilt U., 1943; LLB, U. Va., 1948. Bar: Tenn. 1948. Practice in Memphis, 1948-64; judge Tenn. Circuit Ct., 1964-66; judge U.S. Dist. Ct. (we. dist.) Tenn., Memphis, 1966-94, chief judge, 1979-86, sr. judge, 1987-94, inactive sr. judge, 1995—; mem. Jud. Council 6th Cir., 1982-85, Jud. Conf. Commn. Adminstrn. Criminal Law, 1979-86, Jud. Conf. U.S., 1984-87. Pres. Episcopal Ch. men of Tenn., 1964-65. Mem. Dist. Judges Assn. 6th Circuit (pres.). Home: 220 Baronne Pl Memphis TN 38117-2906

MCRAE, THOMAS KENNETH, retired investment company executive; b. Richmond, Va., July 7, 1906; s. Christopher Duncan and Sarah Alice (Lawrence) McR.; m. Marion Lanier White, Sept. 11, 1937; children: Thomas Kenneth Jr., John Daniel. B.A., U. Richmond, 1927; postgrad. Sch. Banking, Rutgers U., 1936-38. Asst. cashier First Mchts. Nat. Bank, Richmond, 1940-46, asst. v.p., 1946-49, v.p., 1949-63, sr. v.p., 1963-71; v.p. Davenport and Co., Richmond, 1971-85, sr. investment officer, 1985-90. Trustee Va. Supplemental Retirement System, 1964-71; active Va. Mus. Fine Arts. Mem. Richmond Soc. Fin. Analysts. Republican. Baptist. Clubs: Country of Va. Lodges: Masons, Rotary. Avocations: golf; stamp collecting.

MCRAITH, JOHN JEREMIAH, bishop; b. Hutchinson, Minn., Dec. 6, 1934; s. Arthur Luke and Marie (Hanley) McR. B.A., Loras Coll., Dubuque, Iowa, 1956. Ordained priest, Roman Cath. Ch., 1960. Assoc. pastor St. Mary's Ch., Sleepy Eye, Minn., 1960-64, assoc. pastor, 1968-71; pastor St. Michael's Ch., Mickoy, Minn., 1964-67, St. Leo's Ch., St. Leo, Minn., 1967-68; dir. Nat. Cath. Rural Life, Des Moines, 1971-78; vicar gen. Diocese of New Ulm, Minn., 1978-82; bishop Owensboro, Ky., 1982—. Home: 501 W 5th St Owensboro KY 42301-0765 Office: 600 Locust St Owensboro KY 42301-2130

MCREYNOLDS, LARRY AUSTIN, molecular biologist; b. Eugene, Oreg., May 27, 1946; s. Austin D. and Ellen Gwenn (Ellis) McR.; m. Sara Murphy, Nov. 27, 1977; children: Elizabeth, Andrew. BS in Chemistry with honors, Oreg. State U., 1968; PhD in Cell Biology, Mass. Inst. Tech., 1974. Postdoct. fellow Baylor Coll. Medicine, Houston, 1974-78; asst. prof. biochemistry U. Ariz. Coll. Medicine, Tuscon, 1978-82; sr. scientist New England Biolabs, Beverly, Mass., 1983—; vis. scientist Med. Rsch. Coun. Lab. Molecular Biology, Cambridge, Eng., 1977-78; grant reviewer Rsch. Strenghtening Grants for TDR Fillariasis at WHO, NSF; spl. rev. com. Tropical Med. Rsch. Ctrs., NIH, 1990, 94; WHO steering com. Sci. Group on Filariasis, Geneva, 1987-93. Editorial bd. mem. Molecular and Biochemical Parasitology, 1990-93; reviewer: Am. Jour. Tropical Medicine and Hygiene, Nucleic Acid Rsch.; contbr. articles to profl. jours. Grantee NIH, 1979-82, 85-87, Instnl. Cancer Rsch., 1978-79, WHO, 1987-88, 95-97, Edna McConnell Clark Found. grantee, 1992-94. Mem. AAAS, Am. Soc. Tropical Medicine and Hygiene, Am. Heartworm Soc., Phi Lambda Upsilon. Office: New Eng Biolabs 32 Tozer Rd Beverly MA 01915-5510

MCREYNOLDS, NEIL LAWRENCE, public affairs consultant; b. Seattle, July 27, 1934; s. Dorr E. and Margaret (Gillies) McR.; m. Nancy Joyce Drew, June 21, 1957; children: Christopher, Bonnie. BA in Journalism, U. Wash., 1956, postgrad., 1973-76. Assoc. editor Bellevue (Wash.) Am., 1956-60, editor, 1960-67; press sec. to Gov. Dan Evans State of Wash., Olympia, 1967-73; N.W. regional mgr. for pub. rels. and pub. affairs ITT Corp., Seattle, 1973-80; v.p. corp. rels. Puget Sound Power & Light, Bellevue, 1980-87, sr. v.p., 1987-95; prin. McReynolds & Assocs., Seattle, 1995—; pub. affairs counsel to CEO Group Health Coop. of Puget Sound, 1996—; bd. dirs. Continental Savs. Bank, Seattle, Wash. Dental Svcs., Seattle; chmn. exec. adv. com. Edison Electric Inst., 1984-85; mem. rsch. adv. coun. Electric Power Rsch. Inst., 1989-90. Bd. dirs. Seattle Symphony, 1980-89, Ind. Colls. of Wash., 1984-95, Mus. of History and Industry, 1995—, Corp. Coun. for Arts, 1985-94, Mt. Rainier, North Cascades & Olympic Fund, 1995—, Seattle Repertroy Theatre, 1996—; chmn. bd. dirs. Fred Hutchinson Cancer Rsch. Ctr., 1993-95, Leadership Tomorrow, Seattle, 1987, Seattle-King County Econ. Devel. Coun., 1994; pres. Seattle Ctr. Found., 1979-80; nat. pres. Electric Info. Coun., 1988; chmn. bd. trustees Bellevue C.C., 1976-77; state chmn. Nature Conservancy, 1988-90; mem. Wash. State Commn. on Trial Cts., 1990; chmn. King County 2000, 1988-90. Named Citizen of Yr., Bellevue, One of Wash. State's Three Outstanding Young Men; recipient Pres. medal Pacific Luth. U. Mem. Pub. Rels. Soc. Am. (accredited), N.W. Elec. Light and Power Assn. (pres. 1982-83), Greater Seattle C. of C. (officer 1979-81), Soc. Profl. Journalists, Rainier Club (trustee 1995—), Overlake Golf and Country Club (trustee 1993-96), Rotary (pres. Downtown Seattle Club 1991-92). Republican. Episcopalian. Avocations: golf, hiking, skiing, photography. Home: 14315 SE 45th St Bellevue WA 98006 Office: 2000 Two Union Sq 601 Union St Seattle WA 98101-2327

MCRORIE, WILLIAM EDWARD, life insurance company executive; b. Rutherfordton, N.C., Apr. 8, 1940; s. Cyrus Brown and Rosalie (Thompson) McR.; m. Hope Evangeline Foster, Sept. 9, 1962; children: Mark Edward, Jennifer Lynn. LLB, U. N.C., 1964. CLU; Bar: N.C., Va. State mgr. Sturdivant Life Ins. Co., Lynchburg, Va., 1965-68; sr. v.p. First Colony, Lynchburg, 1969—; sec. Jamestown Life Ins. Co., Lynchburg, 1981—. Councilman City of Lynchburg. Mem. ABA, N.C. Bar Assn., Va. Bar Assn., Assn. Life Ins. Counsel, Christian Legal Soc., John Lynch Soc. (sec. 1970—). Home: 2600 Link Rd Lynchburg VA 24503-3012 Office: First Colony Life Ins Co PO Box 1280 Lynchburg VA 24505-1280

MC ROSTIE, CLAIR NEIL, economics educator; b. Owatonna, Minn., Dec. 16, 1930; s. Neil Hale and Myrtle Julia (Peterson) McR.; m. Ursula Anne Schwieger, Aug. 29, 1968. BSBA cum laude, Gustavus Adolphus Coll., 1952; MA in Mktg., Mich. State U., 1953; Ph.D. in Fin., U. Wis., 1963; postgrad., U. Minn., 1971-72, Am. Grad. Sch. Internat. Mgmt., 1980-81; cert., Coll. for Fin. Planning, 1990. Cert. fin. planner. Faculty Gustavus Adolphus Coll., St. Peter, Minn., 1958—; chmn. dept. econs. and bus. Gustavus Adolphus Coll., 1967-83, chmn., mem. various coms., 1971—; teaching asst. Sch. Commerce, U. Wis., 1960-62; lectr. European div. U. Md., 1966-67; vis. prof. Am. Grad. Sch. Internat. Mgmt., 1980-81; pres. World Trade Week, Inc., 1987. Editor: Global Resources: Perspectives and Alternatives, 1978, The Future of the Market Ecomomy, 1979. Congregation pres. First Luth. Ch., St. Peter, Minn., 1972-73, 93, chmn. pastoral call com., 1968-69, chmn. staffing com., 1975, mem. ch. council, 1968-74, 89-93; chmn. social ministry com. Minn. Synod, Luth. Ch. Am., 1975; chmn. Rep. council arts professions, scis., Minn., 1968-70, co-chmn. state task force on Vietnam, 1968; mem. adv. commn. Minn. Dept. Manpower Services, 1967-71; mem. North Central Regional Manpower Adv. Com.; Bd. dirs. Midwest China Resource Study Center; del. White House Conf. Aging, 1971. Served with U.S. Army, 1954-56. Recipient Leavey Found. award Freedoms Found., Valley Forge, Pa.; Research fellow Fed. Res. Bank of Chgo., 1962-63. Mem. Fin. Execs. Inst., Inst. Cert. Fin. Planners, Fin. Profls. Assn., Soc. Coll. and Univ. Planning, Minn. Econs. Assn. (bd. dirs. 1974-75, 79-80), Sierra Club (exec. com. North Star chpt., Midwest regional conservation com.; 4th officer nat. coun. 1972-78), Alpha Kappa Psi, Iota Delta Gamma, Sigma Epsilon. Republican. Lutheran. Avocations: bird watching, backpacking, fitness and health. Home: Rural Rt 1 RR 1 Box 198 Saint Peter MN 56082-9745 Office: Gustavus Adolphus Coll Dept Econ Saint Peter MN 56082

MCRUER, DUANE TORRANCE, aerospace engineering executive; b. Bakersfield, Calif., Oct. 25, 1925; s. John Torrance and Ruth Inez (Bartlett) McR.; m. Betty June Mechura, Oct. 5, 1955; 1 child, Lara McRuer; 1 stepson, Stephen Harsey. BS in Engring., Calif. Inst. Tech., 1945, MEE, 1948. Registered profl. engr., Calif. Tech. chief, flight controls Northrop Aircraft Inc., Hawthorne, Calif., 1948-54; pres. Controls Specialists Inc., Inglewood, Calif., 1954-57; pres., tech. dir. Sys. Tech. Inc., Hawthorne, Calif., 1957-92, chmn., 1992—; Regents lectr. U. Calif., Santa Barbara, 1976; Hunsaker prof. MIT, 1992-93; mem. NRC Aero. and Space Engring. Bd., Washington, 1987-95, NASA Adv. Coun., 1990—, NASA Aero. Adv. Com., Washington, 1978-88, Am. Automatic Control Coun. (pres. 1969-73). Author: Analysis of Nonlinear Control Systems, 1961, Aircraft Dynamics and Automatic Control, 1974; author more than 150 tech. papers, 1948—; patentee in field. Lt. (j.g.) USNR, 1943-53. Recipient Louis Levy medal Franklin Inst., Phila., 1960, Disting. Alumnus award Calif. Inst. Tech., 1983. Fellow AIAA (Mechanics and Control of Flight award 1970), IEEE, AAAS, NAE, Soc. Automotive Engrs., Human Factors and Ergonomics Soc. (A.W. Williams award 1976), Caltech Assocs., Am. Alpine Club (N.Y.C.), Sierra Club. Episcopalian. Avocation: mountaineering. Office: Systems Tech Inc 13766 Hawthorne Blvd Hawthorne CA 90250-7010

MCSHAN, CLYDE GRIFFIN, II, financial executive; b. New Orleans, Feb. 8, 1945; s. Clyde G. and Ursula C. (Mumme) McS.; m. Deborah A. Lark, Oct. 16, 1971; children: Madylin, Kristy, Suzanne. BA, Southeastern La. U., 1966. Cert. internal auditor, cert. govt. fin. mgr., cert. office automation profl. Auditor Office of the Inspector Gen., New Orleans, 1965-72; audit br. chief Cen. Voucher Payment Ctr., New Orleans, 1972-73; evaluation staff chief Nat. Fin. Ctr., New Orleans, 1973-74, processing br. chief, 1974, ops. div. chief, 1974-78, acctg. div. chief, 1978-79, ops. div. chief, 1979-80, dep. dir., 1980-81, dir., 1981-93; dep. chief fin. officer, dir. fin. mgmt. U.S. Dept. Commerce, 1993-97; v.p. Computer Data Sys., Inc., Rockville, Md., 1997—. Contbr. articles to profl. jours. Chmn. CASU Tenant Bd. Dirs., New Orleans, 1989-93, policy com. Fed. Exec. Bd., New Orleans, 1990-93, chmn., 1989-90, 92-93; chmn. unit I United Way of Greater New Orleans, 1991, vice chmn. community resources divsn. 1991, chair 1992-93, bd. trustees, 1990-94, chmn. unit VII, 1990, chmn. CFC, 1989; mem. Tulane U. pub. adv. com. for computer info. sys., 1987-93; acctg. dept. advt. bd. U. New Orleans, 1991; pres. acctg. bd. U. New Orleans, 1992-93. With U.S. Army, 1965-71. Named Outstanding 1990 Campaign Vol. of Yr. United Way, 1991, Leadership award, 1989; recipient Communication and Leadership award Toastmasters, 1991, award New Orleans chpt. Federally Employed Women, 1990, 91, Presdl. Meritorious Rank award, 1988, 95, New Orleans Fed. Exec. Bd. award for outstanding leadership, 1989, Spl. award Office of the Comptroller Gen., 1989, Disting. Exec. Svc. award Sr. Exec. Assn. USDA, 1989; named as Fed. 100 info. systems mgr. by Fed. Computer Wk., 1990, Elmer Staats Disting. Leadership award, 1993, Donald L. Scantlebury Meml. award for Disting. Leadership in Fin. Mgmt., 1995. Mem. Assn. Govt. Accts. (New Orleans chpt. pres. 1972-73, dir. 1970-71, 73-74, 74-75, 76-77, S.W. region v.p. 1975-76, South Ctrl. region v.p. 1981-82, mem. nat. exec. com. 1983-84, 93—, chmn. fin. mgmt. enhancement bd. 1988-89, chmn. emerging issues 1990-91, chmn. tech. progrm com. 1991—, nat. pres.-elect 1993-94, nat. pres. 1994-95), Inst. Internal Auditors, Sr. Exec. Asn., Fed. Exec. Inst. Alumni Assn. Republican. Roman Catholic. Avocation: gardening. Home: 5624 Camphor St Metairie LA 70003-2210

MCSHANE, FRANKLIN JOHN, III, nurse anesthetist, army officer; b. Columbia, S.C., July 25, 1962; s. Franklin John Jr. and Helga Rita (Fischer) McS.; m. Leesa Ann West, Sept. 24, 1988; children: Amanda Nicole, Hannah Ryan. BSN, U. Mass., 1985; MSN, U. Tex., Houston, 1995. RN, Tex.; cert. RN anesthetist ANCC.; cert. ACLS instr., CPR, PALS, provider Am. Heart Assn. Commd. 2d lt. U.S. Army, 1985, advanced through grades to maj., 1997; clin. staff nurse oncology unit Letterman Army Med. Ctr., San Francisco, 1985-86, clin. staff nurse surg. ICU and post anesthesia care unit, 1987-90; head nurse emergency room 67th Evacuation Hosp., Würzburg, Germany, 1990-92, infection control nurse, 1992-93; staff nurse anesthetist Walter Reed Army Med. Ctr., Washington, 1996—; adj. lectr. emergency med. svcs. tract City Colls. Chgo. Europe, 1991-93; adj. clin. faculty U. Tex. Grad. Program in Anesthesia Nursing, Walter Reed Army Med. Ctr., 1996—; presenter in field. Contbr. articles to nursing jours. Mem. ANA, Am. Assn. Nurse Anesthetists, Sigma Theta Tau. Avocations: reading, cooking, golf. Office: Walter Reed Army Med Ctr Dept Anesthesia Washington DC 20307

MCSHANE, JOSEPH MICHAEL, priest, dean, theology educator; b. N.Y.C., June 19, 1949; s. Owen Patrick and Catherine Veronica (Shelley) McS. AB, Boston Coll., 1972, AM, 1972; MDiv, STM, Jesuit Sch. Theology, Berkeley, Calif., 1977; PhD, U. Chgo., 1981. Ordained priest Roman Cath. Ch., 1977. English tchr. Canisius H.S., Buffalo, 1972-74; asst. prof. religious studies LeMoyne Coll., Syracuse, N.Y., 1982-87, assoc. prof. religious studies, 1987-91, prof., 1991-92, chairperson, 1991-92; dean Fordham Coll., Bronx, N.Y., 1992—, prof. theology, 1992—; vis. prof. history Loyola House, Berkley, Mich., 1986-87; bd. dirs. U. Scranton, Pa., Fordham Prep. Sch., Bronx, N.Y., Regis H.S., N.Y.C., Canisius Coll., Buffalo, St. Joseph's Prep. Sch., Phila. Author: Sufficiently Radical: Catholicism, Progressivism and the Bishops' Program of 1919, 1986; author chpt. to book; creator video: The Pilgrimage of the People of God: An Introduction to the Study of Church History, 1991; contbr. articles to profl. jours. Recipient First prize Cath. Press Assn., 1992. Mem. Am. Cath. Hist. Assn., Am. Soc. Ch. History, Phi Beta Kappa. Democrat. Home: 441 E Fordham Rd Bronx NY 10458 Office: Fordham U Dept Theology Bronx NY 10458

MCSHEFFERTY, JOHN, retired research company executive, consultant; b. Akron, Ohio, Mar. 14, 1929; s. John and Jean (Conway) McS.; m. Glenna Gloria Childs, Apr. 18, 1959; children: John III, Amy Childs. BSc, U. Glasgow, 1953, PhD, 1957. Various rsch. positions Sterling Winthrop Rsch. Inst., Rensselaer, N.Y., 1957-62; dir. pharm. devel. Ortho Pharm. Corp. div. Johnson and Johnson, Raritan, N.J., 1962-75; dir. rsch. Janssen R & D, Inc., Piscataway, N.J., 1975-77; v.p. R & D family products Internat. Playtex, Paramus, N.J., 1977-79; pres. Gillette Rsch. Inst., Gaithersburg, Md., 1979-97; retired, 1997; cons. Germantown, Md., 1997—. Fellow Royal Pharm. Soc. of Gt. Britain; mem. Indsl. Rsch. Inst. (bd. dirs. 1988-92), Am. Acad. Dermatology, Am. Mgmt. Assn. (bd. dirs. 1994—), Am. Chem. Soc., Am. Pharm. Assn., N.Y. Acad. Scis., Soc. Cosmetic Chemists, Dirs. Indsl. Rsch., Assn. Rsch. Dirs., Sigma Xi.

MC SHEFFREY, GERALD RAINEY, architect, educator, city planner; b. Belfast, Ireland, Aug. 13, 1931; s. Hugh and Jane (Piggot) McS.; m. Norma Isabella Lowry, June 4, 1956; children: Laurence, Niall, Aidan. Student, Belfast Coll. Tech., 1950-56; Diploma in Architecture, Univ. Coll., U. London, 1959; Diploma in Civic Design, U. Edinburgh, Scotland, 1963. Archtl. asst. various archtl. firms Belfast, 1950-57; design architect Munce and Kennedy, Belfast, 1957-62; architect/planner Liverpool (Eng.) City Planning Dept. and Livingston New Town, 1963-65; asso. partner James Munce Partnership, Belfast, 1965-68; prin. planning officer (design) Belfast City Planning Dept., 1968-71; prof. architecture U. Kans., 1971-73, dir. archtl. studies, 1976-79; Belfast regional architect, dir. devel. No. Ireland Housing, 1973-76; prof. architecture, dean Coll. Architecture, Planning and Design, Ill. Inst. Tech., 1979-82; dean Coll. Architecture and Environ. Design Ariz. State U., Tempe, 1982-86, prof. architecture, 1988—; v.p. Ariz. State U., West Campus, Phoenix, 1985-88; vis. fellow Princeton (N.J.) U., 1989; external examiner in urban design and landscape studies U. Edinburgh, 1973-76. Author: (with James Munce Partnership) Londonderry Area Plan, 1968. Fulbright award, 1965. Fellow Royal Inst. Brit. Architects; mem. AIA. Episcopalian. Office: Ariz State U Coll Architecture & Environ Design Tempe AZ 85287-1605

MCSHERRY, WILLIAM JOHN, JR., lawyer, consultant; b. N.Y.C., Oct. 28, 1947; s. William John Sr. and Mary Elizabeth (Dunphy) McS.; m. Elizabeth Ann Crosby, June 8, 1974; children: Brendan, Sean, Rory. AB cum laude, Fordham U., 1969; JD cum laude, Harvard U., 1973. Bar: N.Y. 1974, U.S. Dist. Ct. (so. dist.) N.Y. 1975, U.S. Ct. Appeals (2d cir.) 1977. Assoc. Spengler, Carlson, Gubar, Brodsky & Frischling, N.Y.C., 1973-78, ptnr., 1979-88; ptnr. Bryan, Cave, McPheeters & McRoberts, N.Y.C., 1989-91, Battle Fowler LLP, N.Y.C., 1991—; exec. dir. U.S. Football League, N.Y.C., 1985-86; chmn. litigation dept. Battle Fowler, 1992-96; pres., bd. dirs. Playtex Mktg. Corp.; bd. dirs. Questron Tech., Inc. Author: (with others) Tender Offer Regulation: The Federal SEC's Challenge and New York State's Response, Derivatives Risk and Responsibility, 1996. Mem. Zoning Bd. Appeals, Village of Larchmont, N.Y., 1988-92, dep. mayor, 1992—, bd. trustees, 1991—. Served with USAR, 1980-85. Mem. ABA (litigation, antitrust, entertainment and sports, corp. banking and bus. law sects., subcom. litigation 1940 Act; vice-chair commn. alt. dispute resolution), Assn. of Bar of City of N.Y. (mem. 1979-82 com. state cts. superior jurisdiction, 1987-90, com. arbitration and alternative dispute resolution), Fed. Bar Council, Council N.Y. Law Assocs. (bd. dirs., treas. 1975), Phi Beta Kappa. Roman Catholic. Avocations: community involvement, sports, writing. Home: 2 Summit Ave Larchmont NY 10538-2930 Address: 75 E 55th St New York NY 10022-3205

MCSHIRLEY, MARJORIE STONE, art director. Art dir.: (films) Pee-Wee's Big Adventure, 1985, Back to School, 1986, Back to the Future II, 1989, Three Fugitives, 1989, Back to the Future III, 1990, The Addams Family, 1991. Office: care Art Directors Guild 794 Hot Springs Rd Montecito CA 93108-1107*

MCSORLEY, CISCO, lawyer; b. Albuquerque, July 8, 1950; s. Frank N. and Virginia E. (Norton) McS. BA, U. N.Mex., 1974, JD, 1979; postdoctoral sch. govt., Harvard U., 1986. Bar: N.Mex. 1980, U.S. Dist. Ct. N.Mex. 1980. Tchr. Academia Cotopaxi, Quito, Ecuador, S. Am., 1973-76; sole practice Albuquerque, 1980—; mem. N.Mex. State Ho. of Reps., 1984-96, N.Mex. State Senate, 1996—. Mem. ABA, N. Mex. Bar. Assn., N. Mex. Trial Lawyers Assn., Assn. Trial Lawyers Am. Democrat. Mem. Soc. of Friends.

MCSPADDEN, LETTIE, political science educator; b. Battle Creek, Mich., Apr. 9, 1937; d. John Dean and Isma Doolie (Sullivan) McSpadden; m. Manfred Wilhelm Wenner, Apr. 3, 1962; children: Eric Alexis, Adrian Edward. AB, U. Chgo., 1959; MA, U. Calif., Berkeley, 1962; PhD, U. Wis., 1972. Fgn. svc. officer Dept. State, Washington, 1961-63; rsch. assoc. Dept. HEW, Washington, 1965-67; asst. prof. polit. sci. U. Ill., Chgo., 1972-79, assoc. prof. polit. sci., 1979-88; prof. and chair dept. polit. sci. No. Ill. U., De Kalb, 1988-94, prof. dept. polit. sci., 1994—. Author: One Environment Under Law, 1976, The Environmental Decade in Court, 1982, United States Energy and Environmental Interest Groups, 1990. Mem. Am. Polit. Sci. Assn., Midwest Polit. Sci. Assn., Law and Society Assn., Pub. Policy Assn., Audubon Soc., Sierra Club. Democrat. Home: 3112 Fairway Oaks Dr De Kalb IL 60115-4925 Office: No Ill U Dept Polit Sci De Kalb IL 60115

MCSPADDEN, PETER FORD, retired advertising agency executive; b. Montclair, N.J., Oct. 2, 1930; s. Chester F. and Janet (Chase) McS.; m. Barbara Dodds, June 30, 1956; children—Douglas Dodds, David Ford, Peter Chase. A.B., Dartmouth, 1952. Account exec. McCann-Erickson, Inc., N.Y.C., 1956-59; with Dancer-Fitzgerald-Sample, Inc., N.Y.C., from 1959, v.p., account supr., 1965-68, sr. v.p., mgmt. supr., 1968-72, exec. v.p., 1972-74, pres., chief operating officer, from 1974; chmn. bd., chief operating officer Saatchi & Saatchi DFS Inc., N.Y.C., 1986-88, also bd. dirs., ret., 1988; pres., bd. dirs. DFS/Dorland Worldwide; bd. dirs. Am. Advt. Fedn., Am. Assn. Advt. Agys., TriState U.; mem. Nat. Advt. Rev. Bd.; bd. trustees Bradford Coll; vice chmn. Broadstreet TV Inc. 1989—. Chmn. bd. visitors Rockefeller Ctr., Dartmouth Coll.; pres. Greenwich (Conn.) Young Republican Club, 1966-67; bd. dirs. United Way of Tri-State, 1995 Spl. Olympic Games; campaign mgr. Congressman Lowell P. Weicker, 1968, Senator Weicker, 1970, 76, 82, 88; mem. Rep. Town Com., Greenwich, 1965-68; trustee Greenwich Hosp. Served to lt. (j.g.) USNR, 1952-55. Mem. Am. Assn. Advt. Agys. (dir.). Clubs: Riverside (Conn.) Yacht, Greenwich Country, Meguntic ook Golf. Home: 46 Carriglea Dr Riverside CT 06878-2402

MCSTEEN, MARTHA ABERNATHY, organization executive; b. Iowa Park, Tex., May 25, 1923; d. King Peyton and Iva Mae (Dawson) Abernathy; m. George Steven McSteen, Oct. 13, 1943 (dec. Jan. 1945); m. Marshall Parks, Apr. 6, 1991. BA, Rice U., 1944; MA, U. Okla., 1972; JD (hon.), Austin Coll., 1985. Claims rep., supr. and dist. mgr. Social Security Adminstrn., Dallas, 1947-65, regional commr., 1976-83; acting commr. Social Security Adminstrn., Washington, 1983-86; regional adminstr. Medicare, Denver and Dallas, 1965-76; cons. Nat. Com. To Preserve Social Security and Medicare, Washington, 1987-89, pres., 1989—; U.S. rep. to Internat. Social Security Assn., 1985, 86. Bd. dirs. Alliance Rsch. in Aging, Nat. Children's Eye Found., Internat. Fedn. Aging; bd. advisors Internat. Ctr. Rsch. and Tng. for Programs on Aging, Setting Priorities for Retirement Yrs. Found., Washington, 1991—, Claude and Mildred Pepper Found. Recipient Commr.'s citation Social Security Adminstrn., 1961, 66, 71, Disting. Svc. award HEW, 1979, Presdl. Meritorious Exec. award, 1980, Nat. Pub. Svc. award Am. Soc. for Pub. Adminstrn., 1986, Presdl. Disting. Exec. award, 1987; fellow Social Security Adminstrn., 1968-69. Office: Nat Com Preserve Soc Sec & Medicare 2000 K St NW Ste 800 Washington DC 20006-1809

MCSWAIN, RICHARD HORACE, materials engineer, consultant; b. Greenville, Ala., Sept. 27, 1949; s. Howard Horace and La Belle (Henderson) McS.; m. Wanda Lynn Hare, June 9, 1972; children: Rachel Lynn, John Angus, Daniel Richard. BS in Materials Engring., Auburn U., 1972, MS in Materials Engring., 1974; PhD in Materials Engring., U. Fla., 1985. Teaching and rsch. asst. Auburn (Ala.) U., 1972-73; metallurgist So. Rsch. Inst., Birmingham, Ala., 1973-76; materials engr. Naval Aviation Depot, Pensacola, Fla., 1977-88, head metallic materials engring., 1988-90; pres. McSwain Engring., Inc., 1991—; cons. materials engr., Pensacola, 1982-90; presenter in field. Contbr. articles to tech. jours. Mem. ASTM, SAE Internat., ASM Internat. (chpt. edn. chmn. 1975-76), Am. Welding Soc., Nat. Assn. Corrosion Engrs., Electron Microscopy Soc., Internat. Soc. Air Safety Investigators. Presbyterian. Avocations: boating, fishing, running. Home: 1405 Kings Rd Cantonment FL 32533-8951 Office: McSwain Engring Inc PO Box 10847 Pensacola FL 32524-0847

MCSWEENEY, FRANCES KAYE, psychology educator; b. Rochester, N.Y., Feb. 6, 1948; d. Edward William and Elsie Winifred (Kingston) McS. BA, Smith Coll., 1969; MA, Harvard U., 1972, PhD, 1974. Lectr. McMaster U., Hamilton, Ont., Can., 1973-74; asst. prof. Wash. State U., Pullman, 1974-79, assoc. prof., 1979-83, prof. psychology, 1983—, chmn. dept. psychology, 1986-94; cons. in field. Contbr. articles to profl. jours. Woodrow Wilson fellow, Sloan Fellow, 1968-69; NSF fellow, 1970-72; NIMH fellow, 1973. Fellow Am. Psychol. Assn., Am. Psychol. Soc.; mem. Western Psychol. Assn., Psychonomic Soc., Assn. Behavior Analysis, Phi Kappa Phi, Phi Beta Kappa, Sigma Xi. Home: SW 860 Alcora Pullman WA 99163 Office: Wash State U Dept Psychology Pullman WA 99164-4820

MCSWEENEY, MAURICE J. (MARC), lawyer; b. Chgo., July 3, 1938; s. Thomas J. and Margaret F. (Ahern) McS.; m. Sandra A. Panosh, Sept. 30, 1967; children: Erin, Sean. BS, DePaul U., 1960; JD, U. Chgo., 1963. Ptnr. Foley and Lardner, Milw., 1963—. Bd. dirs. Milw. Pub. Schs., 1973-79, Milw. chpt. ARC, 1979-85, Alverno Coll., Milw., 1984—, Health Edn. Ctr. of Wis., 1987-96. Fellow Am. Coll. Trial Lawyers; mem. ABA, Wis. Bar Assn., Milw. Bar Assn., Am. Judicature Soc. (bd. dirs. 1988-93), Rotary (bd. dirs. Milw. 1986-88). Avocations: skiing, tennis, karate. Office: Foley & Lardner 777 E Wisconsin Ave Milwaukee WI 53202-5302

MCSWEENEY, MICHAEL TERRENCE, manufacturing executive; b. Rockford, Ill., Jan. 28, 1937; s. John Carpenter and Julia Elizabeth (McCann) McS.; m. Louise Antionette Walters, Aug. 20, 1960; children—David, Mark. B.S.E., No. Ill. U., 1961. Indsl. engr. MicroSwitch div. Honeywell Inc., Freeport, Ill., 1960-63; sr. v.p. Metromail div. Metromedia, Inc., N.Y.C., 1963-80; v.p., gen. mgr. Harlequin Reader Service, Toronto, Ont., Can., 1980-82; exec. v.p. Harlequin Enterprises, Ltd., Toronto, Ont., Can., 1982-85; pres., chief exec. officer Bear Creek Corp., Medford, Oreg., 1985-88; chmn., CEO, dir. DIMAC Corp., St. Louis, 1988-97, also chmn. bd. dirs.; mem. mktg./direct mktg. adv bd. U. Mo., Kansas City, 1992—; instr. Am. Mgmt. Assn., N.Y.C., 1976-77, Dale Carnegie Mgmt. Instrn., Iowa, Ill., 1968-71; mem., past chmn. mailers tech. adv. com. to postmaster gen., Washington, 1978—; bd. dirs. So. Oreg. State Coll. Regional Adv. Bd., 1986-88; trustee Peter Britt Music & Arts Assn., Medford, 1986-88, Rogue Valley Community Health Ctr., 1987-88. Contbr. articles to profl. jours. County campaign chmn. U.S. senatorial candidate Henry County, Iowa, 1966, 68; trustee St. Elizabeth Hosp., Lincoln, Nebr., 1973-75; bd. dirs. Regional Airport Authority, Burlington, Iowa, 1976-79; trustee Direct Mktg. Edn. Found., 1995—. Served to sgt. USAF, 1954-58. Recipient Leadership award Boy Scouts Am., 1968, Career Counseling commendation Iowa Wesleyan Coll., 1976, Leadership commendation U.S. Post Office, 1982. Mem. Direct Mktg. Assn. (ethics com. 1970-72, bd. dirs. 1987-94, chmn. govt. affairs com. 1987-94, fin. com. 1987-88), Mail Advt. Svc. Assn. (bd. dirs. 1979-80, Commendation award 1980), Can. Direct Mktg. Assn., Direct Mktg. Assn. Toronto, VFW, Phi Kappa Theta (trustee 1979-83, 90—, nat. treas. 1995—). Republican. Roman Catholic. Lodges: Kiwanis, K.C. Avocations: flying; swimming; golf. Home: 12818 Topping Manor Dr Town & Country MO 63131-1815 Office: DIMAC Corp 1 Corporate Woods Dr Bridgeton MO 63044-3807

MCSWEENEY, WILLIAM LINCOLN, JR., publishing executive; b. Boston, Nov. 9, 1930; s. William Lincoln and Ruth Patricia (Desmond) McS.; B.S., Boston Coll., 1953; M.L.A., So. Meth. U., 1980, L.H.D. Rockhurst Coll., 1997; m. Anne Cornelia Bulman, Aug. 18, 1956; children: Anne C., William L., Siobhan White, Arthur J., Sean B. Tchr. English, Killingly (Conn.) High Sch., 1956-57; with Hallmark Cards, Inc., Kansas City, Mo., 1957-86, area pers. mgr., 1968, sales tng. mgr., 1969-86, dir. corp. tng. and devel., 1970-86; pub. Nat. Catholic Reporter Co., 1986-96. Bd. dirs. Cath. Social Svcs., Kansas City Archdiocese, 1975-88, pres., 1980-84; bd. dirs. United Cmty. Svcs. Kansas City, 1978-84, mem. exec. com., 1978-84; bd. dirs. Kansas City Amigos De Las Americas, 1977-80, pres., 1979; bd. dirs. Johnson County YMCA, 1978-79, Jesuit Vol. Corps, Midwest, 1989-95, Mexican Am. Cultural Ctr., San Antonio, 1990—, Minority Mus., 1994—; bd. dirs. Pan Ednl. Inst., 1979-83, pres., 1980-81; mem. Boston Coll. Alumni Admissions Council, 1976—; mem. chancellor's adv. bd. Met. Cmty. Colls., 1979-80; mem. Dem. Com., Johnson County, Kans., 1980-86; bd. advisors Sch. Social Welfare, U. Kans., 1983—, chair 1983-91, 93-94, Avila Coll., 1991—, Ctrl. City Parochial Sch. Bd., chair 1996—, chair Mayor's UN Day Dinner, Kansas City, Mo., 1990, Mayor's Prayer Breakfast, 1994—; trustee NCCJ, 1991-95, co-chmn., 1995—. Served with U.S. Army, 1953-56. Mem. Internat. Rels. Coun. of Kansas City (bd. dirs. 1989—), Cath. Press Assn., Assoc. Ch. Press, Internat. Press Inst., UN Assn., Inter-Am. Press Inst., Kans. City Press Inst., Boston Coll. Alumni Assn. (past bd. dirs.), Boston Coll. Club (Kansas City), Bus. Execs. Nat. Security. Recipient Kansas City World Citizen of the Yr. award, 1995. Roman Catholic. Office: 115 E Armour Blvd PO Box 419281 Kansas City MO 64141

MCSWEENY, WILLIAM FRANCIS, petroleum company executive, author; b. Haverhill, Mass., Mar. 31, 1929; s. William Francis and Mary Florence (Doyle) McS.; m. Dorothy Pierce, Jan. 20, 1969; children: William Francis III, Cathy Ann, Ethan Madden Maverick, Terrell Pierce. Reporter, columnist, fgn. corr. Hearst Newspapers, 1943-67; dep. chmn., dir. pub. affairs Democratic Nat. Com., 1967-68; spl. asst. to White House Chief of Staff, 1968-69; sr. exec. v.p., bd. dirs. Occidental Internat. Corp., Washington, 1969—, pres., 1976-91; exec. v.p. Occidental Petroleum Corp., 1984-91; cons. to chmn. Occidental Petroleum Corp., Washington, 1991—; dir. Fin. Gen. Bankshares Co., Washington, 1978-82, Chevy Chase Savs. and Loan, 1985—; mem. Lloyd's of London; pres.'s rep. to USSR, 1979; mem. Pres.'s Inaugural Com., 1980, 84, 92; Presdl. spl. rep. to Oman, 1980, Bolivia, 1982; Pres.'s com. Korean War Meml., 1987; Pres.'s commr. Exec. Exch., 1976-81; Pres.'s trustee The Kennedy Ctr., 1995—; mem. N.E. White Ho. Fellows Bd.; mem. U.S. Com. UNESCO; spl. counsel speaker of Ho. of Reps., 1971-72. Author: Go Up for Glory, 1965, Violence Every Sunday, 1966, The Impossible Dream, 1967; also articles. Bd. visitors Fletcher Sch. Law and Diplomacy, Tufts U.; bd. advisors Karl F. Landegger Program Internat. Bus. Diplomacy, Sch. Fgn. Svc., Georgetown U.; trustee, pres. Holton Arms; chmn. Washington Episc. Sch.; chmn. Meridian House Internat., life trustee; mem. World Affairs Coun.; bd. dirs. The Atlantic Coun., Overseer Exec. Coun. Fgn. Diplomates, Dept. of State, The Brookings Instn. Coun., 1991—; vice chmn. Sec. of State Fine Arts Commn.; chmn. Ford's Theatre, 1988—; bd. dirs. Very Spl. Arts, Arena State, Corcoran Gallery Art, Africare, Fed. City Coun., Washington Opera, Folger Shakespeare Theater, Cities in Schs. Nat. Learning Ctr., USO, Arms Control Assn., Nat. Assn. So. Poor, Duke Ellington Sch., Washington Ednl. TV, 1989—; v.p. Ct. of Mary Rose, Portsmouth, Eng.; pres. Commn. to Preserve U.S. Cultural Heritage Abroad; co-chair State Dept. diplomatic rooms endowment; chmn. Lombardi Cancer Ctr. Coun., Georgetown U. Med. Ctr.; pres. Ams. Internat. Insts. for Advanced Studies; vice chmn. Kennedy Ctr. Cmty. Bd., 1991-92; trustee V.P. Residence Found.; juror The Heinz Found., 1995—; chmn. Chevy Chase for Cmty. Com., Coun. Ct. Excellence, 1996—. Maj. U.S. Army, 1950-53. Recipient Outstanding Young Man award Boston Jaycees, 1961, U.S. Disting. Svc. award, 1968, Outstanding Svc. spl. award, 1969, D.C. Disting. Citizen award, 1981, Paul Hill award Kennedy Ctr., 1983, D.C. Cultural award, 1983, Armenian Earthquake Hero medal, 1989, Lincoln medal, 1991, Helen Hayes award, 1991, Washingtonian of Yr. award, 1995, also numerous awards for domestic reports and reporting from Vietnam and Mid. East, including Best U.S. Reporting award, 1964. Mem. Smithsonian Inst. (mem. nat. adv. com. Kellogg Project), Alfalfa Club, Cosmos Club, 1925 F St. Club (trustee, Washington), Internat. Club (trustee).

MCSWINEY, CHARLES RONALD, lawyer; b. Nashville, Apr. 23, 1943; s. James W. and Jewell (Bellar) Mc.; m. Jane Detrick McSwiney, Jan. 2, 1970. BA, Kenyon Coll., Gambier, Ohio, 1965; JD, U. Cin., 1968. Assoc. Smith & Schnacke, Dayton, Ohio, 1968-72, ptnr., 1972-89, pres. and mng. ptnr., 1984-89; sr. v.p., gen. counsel The Danis Cos., Dayton, 1989-92; vice chmn. Carillon Capital, Inc., Dayton, 1992—; chmn., CEO Crysteco, Inc., Wilmington, Ohio, 1995—; pres. interchange exec. Presdl. Commn. on Personnel Interchange, Washington, 1972-73. Chmn., pres. bd. trustees Dayton Ballet Assn., 1985-88; trustee Columbus (Ohio) Symphony Orch., 1981-84; chmn. Dayton Performing Arts Fund, 1989-92, Dayton Devel. Coun., 1987-90, Wright State U. Found., Dayton, 1988-94, Miami Valley Sch., Dayton, 1988-94, Arts Ctr. Found., 1986—; mem. bd. advisors Wright State U. Coll. Bus. Adminstrn., 1988—; bd. vis. U. Cin. Coll. Law, 1987-89. Recipient Bronze Medal for Performance U.S. EPA, 1973. Mem. ABA, Ohio Bar Assn., Dayton Bar Assn., Dayton Area C. of C. (trustee 1987-90). Republican. Presbyterian. Home: 3780 Ridgeleigh Rd Dayton OH 45429-1253 Office: Carillon Capital Inc Kettering Tower Ste 1480 Dayton OH 45423-1480

MC SWINEY, JAMES WILMER, retired pulp and paper manufacturing company executive; b. McEwen, Tenn., Nov. 13, 1915; s. James S. and Delia (Conroy) McS.; m. Jewel Bellar, 1940; children: Charles Ronald, Margaret Ann. Grad., Harvard Advanced Mgmt. Program, 1954. Lab. technician, shipping clk. Nashville div. The Mead Corp., 1934-39; asst. office mgr. Harriman div., 1939; plant mgr. Rockport, Ind., 1940; asst. office mgr. Kingsport (Tenn.) div.), 1941-44; exec. asst. to pres. Dayton, Ohio, 1954-57; v.p. devel., 1957-59; adminstrv v.p. Harriman div. (Kingsport (Tenn.) div.), 1959; group v.p., gen. mgr. Mead Bd. div., 1961-63, exec. v.p. corp., 1963-67, pres., chief exec. officer, 1968-71, chmn. bd., chief exec. officer, 1971-78, chmn. bd., 1978-82, also dir.; acct., office mgr., asst. sec.-treas. Brunswick Pulp & Paper Co., Ga., 1944-45; bd. dirs. Ultra-Met, Crysteco, Inc., Energy Innovations Inc., Gosinger, Inc., Sea Island Co.; chmn. bd. Interstate Resources Inc., Riceboro, Ga. Trustee Com. for Econ. Devel.; chmn. bd. dirs. Air Force Found. Inst. of Tech. Aviation cadet USAAF, 1942-44. Home: PO Box 30604 Sea Island GA 31561-0604 Office: Mead World HQs Dayton OH 45463

MCTAGGART, PATRICK WILLIAM, principal; b. East Chicago, Ind., Dec. 3, 1950; s. Frederick M. and Dolores R. (Gourley) McT. BS, Ball State U., 1972; MS, Purdue U., 1977, EdS, 1985. Cert. secondary adminstrn. and supervision. Tchr. Griffith (Ind.) Jr. H.S., 1973-82, asst. prin., 1982-88; prin. Roosevelt Mid. Sch., Monticello, Ind., 1988—. Elder First Presbyn. Ch. Monticello, Ind., 1997—. Mem. ASCD, Nat. Mid. Sch. Assn., Ind. Prin. Leadership Acad. (grad. 1992-93), Ind. Assn. Sch Prins., Sportsmen Acting for the Environ, Ducks Unltd. Avocations: fishing, hunting, golf, tennis, wildlife art collecting. Home: 3608 E Bailey Rd Monticello IN 47960-7041 Office: Roosevelt Mid Sch 721 W Broadway St Monticello IN 47960-2010

MCTAGGART, TIMOTHY THOMAS, secondary education educator; b. Danville, Pa., Dec. 8, 1949; s. Thomas Francis and Mary Elizabeth (Russial) McT. BS, Bloomsburg (Pa.) U., 1971; MDiv, St. Vincent Coll., Latrobe, Pa., 1974; MEd, Millersville (Pa.) U., 1980; EdD, Pacific Western U., Honolulu, 1991. Cert. in secondary edn., Pa. Math. tchr. Lancaster (Pa.) Cath. High Sch., 1978-85; math. and computer sci. tchr. Columbia (Pa.) Sr. High Sch., 1985—; head track coach Columbia High Sch., 1986—. Mem. Pa. Athletic Assn. (football ofcl.), K.C. (knight 4th deg.). Home: 728 Sharon Dr Mount Joy PA 17552-9711 Office: Columbia H S 901 Ironville Pike Columbia PA 17512-9513

MCTAGUE, JOHN PAUL, automobile manufacturing company executive, chemist; b. Jersey City, Nov. 28, 1938; s. James Aloysius and Teresa Eugenia (Hanley) McT.; m. Carole Frances Reilly, Dec. 30, 1961; children: Kevin W., Catherine E., Margaret A., Maureen E. BS in Chemistry, Georgetown U., 1960; PhD, Brown U., 1965. Mem. tech. staff N.Am. Rockwell Sci. Ctr., Thousand Oaks, Calif., 1964-70; prof. chemistry, mem. Inst. Geophysics and Planetary Physics UCLA, 1970-82; chmn. nat. synchrotron light source dept. Brookhaven Nat. Lab., Upton, N.Y., 1982-83; dep. dir. Office Sci. and Tech. Policy, Exec. Office of Pres., Washington, 1983-86, acting sci. advisor to Pres. Reagan, 1986; v.p. rsch. Ford Motor Co., Dearborn, Mich., 1986-90; v.p. tech. affairs Ford Motor Co., 1990—; bd. dirs. Raychem Corp.; adj. prof. chemistry Columbia, U., 1982-83. Mem. Pres.'s Coun. Advisors on Sci. and Tech., 1990-93; mem. adv. bd. Sec. Energy, 1990—. Alfred P. Sloan Research fellow, 1971-73; NATO sr. fellow, 1973; John Simon Guggenheim Meml. fellow, 1975-76. Fellow AAAS, Am. Phys. Soc.; mem. Am. Chem. Soc. (Calif. sect. award 1975), Soc. Automotive Engrs., Engring. Soc. Detroit, Barton Hills Country Club, Sigma Xi. Office: Ford Motor Co The American Rd Dearborn MI 48121

MCTEER, ROBERT D., JR., banker. Pres., CEO, Fed. Res. Bank Dallas, Tex. Office: Fed Res Bank Dallas 2200 N Pearl St Dallas TX 75201-2216

MCTIER, CHARLES HARVEY, foundation administrator; b. Columbus, Ga., Jan. 28, 1939; s. Roy and Julia (Harvey) McT.; m. Margaret Lucy Ruyl, Aug. 23, 1962; children: Margaret Marie, Charles Harvey Jr. BBA, Emory U., 1961. Administrv. asst. hosp. Emory U., Atlanta, 1961-63, bus. mgr. dept. psychiat. Sch. Med., 1963-66, assoc. dir. personnel, 1966-69, asst. to pres., bd. trustees, 1969-71; sec. Robert W. Woodruff Found., Joseph B. Whitehead Found., Lettie Pate Evans Found., Inc., Lettie Pate Whitehead Found., Inc., Atlanta, 1971-77, sec., treas., 1977-87, v.p., sec., treas., 1987-88, pres., 1988—; chmn. Atlanta Founds. Forum, 1985-86; trustee Southeastern Coun. Founds., Atlanta, 1985-92, chmn. membership com., 1986-89, chmn. program com., 1989, chmn. bd. trustees, 1989-90; vice chmn. Coun. on Founds., Washington, program com., 1985-87, mgmt. com., 1987—, nominating com., 1987-88, chmn. audit and fin. com., 1990-95, chmn. mgmt. com., 1996—; chmn. bd. trustees Found. Ctr. N.Y.C., 1994—, fin. and audit com., 1991—, exec. com., 1992—, chmn. nominating com., 1992, chmn. program and fund devel. adv. com., 1993—; pub. mem. Joint Commn. on Accreditation of Health Care Orgns., 1994—; dir. SunTrust Bank of Ga., SunTrust Bank Atlanta. Trustee, North Ga. United Meth. Found., 1985-92; trustee, treas. Meth. Found. Ret. Mins., 1980; chmn. new ch. devel. com. North Ga. United Meth. Conf., 1980-85; trustee North Ga. United Meth. Found., 1985-92; mem. bd. vis. Emory U., 1985-87. Mem. Mgmt. Execs. Soc., Assn. Emory Alumni (bd. govs. 1987-91), Pres.'s Cir. of NAS/Inst. of Medicine, Commerce Club (bd. dirs.), Druid Hills Golf Club. Avocations: golf, travel. Office: Joseph B Whitehead Found 50 Hurt Plz SE Ste 1200 Atlanta GA 30303-2916

MC TIERNAN, JOHN, film director; b. Albany, N.Y., Jan. 8, 1951. Dir., screewriter Nomads, 1985; dir. Predator, 1987, Die Hard, 1988, The Hunt For Red October, 1990, Medicine Man, 1992, The Last Action Hero, 1993, Die Hard With a Vengeance, 1995. Office: CAA 9830 Wilshire Blvd Beverly Hills CA 90212-1804*

MCTIGUE, TERESA ANN, biologist; b. Washington, July 9, 1962; d. William Edward and Bernice Ann (Bakajza) McT. BS in Zoology, U. Md., 1984; MS in Marine Sci., U. S.C., 1986; PhD in Wildlife and Fisheries Scis., Tex. A&M U., 1993. Lab. asst. U. Md., College Park, 1981-83; rsch. asst. U. S.C., Columbia, 1984-86; staff biologist Sea Camp, Galveston, Tex., 1988-93; fisheries biologist Nat. Marine Fisheries Svc., Galveston, 1987-93, Lafayette, La., 1993—. Contbr. articles to profl. jours. Recipient Grad. Rsch. award Sea Grant, 1986. Mem. Estuarine Rsch. Fedn., Gulf Estuarine Rsch. Soc. (pres.-elect), Am. Fisheries Soc., Sigma Xi. Democrat. Roman Catholic. Achievements include rsch. on the dietary habits of juvenile penaeid shrimp in salt marshes, role of infauna in shrimps' diets, regulatory effects of predators on the prey's abundances, settlement patters of brachyuran larvae in Gulf of Mexico; monitoring of impacts of wetland restoration projects, including freshwater diversions, sediment delivery, hydrologic restorations, and marsh management; participation in restoration and monitoring of marshes following oil spills. Office: NMFS Lafayette Office PO Box 42451 Lafayette LA 70504-2451

MCTURNAN, LEE BOWES, lawyer; b. N.Y.C., Sept. 13, 1937; s. Lee M. and Alice (Light) McT.; m. Susan Cassady, Aug. 2, 1969; children: John M., Sarah D. AB magna cum laude, Harvard U., 1959; Diploma in Law, Oxford (Eng.) U., 1961; JD, U. Chgo., 1963. Bar: Ill. 1965, U.S. Dist. Ct. (no. dist.) Ill. 1965, U.S. Ct. Appeals (7th cir.) 1966, U.S. Supreme Ct. 1969, Ind. 1978, U.S. Dist. Ct. (so. dist.) Ind. 1978, U.S. Dist. Ct. (no. dist.) Ind. 1987. Law clk. to hon. justice U.S. Supreme Ct., Washington, 1963-64; assoc. Sidley & Austin, Chgo., 1964-69, ptnr., 1970-78; ptnr. Hackman, McClarnon & McTurnan, Indpls., 1978-88, McTurnan & Turner, Indpls., 1989—; assoc. spl. counsel procs. on chief justice R.I. Commn. Jud. Tenure and Discipline, Providence, 1985; mem. Civil Justice Reform Adv. Com. for So. Dist. Ind. Adminstrv. bd. Meridian St. United Meth. Ch., 1987-90. Mem. ABA, Ind. Bar Assn., Ill. Bar Assn., Indpls. Bar Assn., 7th Cir. Bar Assn., Law Club of Indpls. (pres. 1988-90), Legal Club of Chgo., Columbia Club, Woodstock Club, Lit. Club, Rotary. Republican. Avocations: running, reading, gardening. Home: 115 Bennington Dr Zionsville IN 46077-1134 Office: McTurnan & Turner 2400 Market Tower 10 W Market St Indianapolis IN 46204-2954

MCVAY, JOHN EDWARD, professional football club executive; b. Bellaire, Ohio, Jan. 5, 1931; s. John A. and Helen (Andrews) McV.; m. Eva Lee; children: John R., James P., Timothy G. B.S. in Edn., Miami U., Oxford, Ohio, 1953; M.A. in Sch. Adminstrn., Kent (Ohio) State U., 1963. Asst. football coach, instr. phys. edn. Mich. State U., 1962-65; head coach, dir. athletics U. Dayton, Ohio, 1965-74; head coach, gen. mgr. Memphis in World Football League, 1974-76; head football coach N.Y. Giants, NFL, 1976-78; dir. player pers. San Francisco 49ers, NFL, 1979-80, dir. football ops., 1980-81, v.p. adminstrn., 1981-83, gen. mgr., v.p., 1983-89, v.p. football ops., 1990-96; prin. McVay Sports Cons. Inc., Sanibel, Fla., 1996—. Exec. dir. Catholic Youth Council, Canton, Ohio, 1959-62. Recipient Disting. Citizen award Massillon H.S., 1996; named to Miami U. Athletic Hall of Fame; named NFL Exec. of Yr., 1989. Mem. Sigma Chi (Significant Sig award), Phi Epsilon Kappa, Phi Delta Kappa. Won five Super Bowl Championships 1981, 1984, 88, 89, 94. *

MCVAY, MARY FRANCES, portfolio manager; b. Washington, Sept. 17, 1955; d. Joseph J. and Stella F. (Walejko) McVay; m. Theodore R. Rosenberg, Sept. 21, 1991. BS in Acctg., Va. Tech., 1978, MBA, 1981. CPA; CFA. Auditor CIA, Washington, 1975-83; sr. cons. Booz, Allen & Hamilton, Arlington, Va., 1983-85; portfolio mgr. Burney Mgmt. Co., Falls Church, Va., 1985—. Mem. Inst. Mgmt. Accts. (dir. newsletter 1992—, v.p. adminstrn. 1993—, dir. program roster 1994—), Assn. Investment, Mgmt. and Rsch. Office: Burney Mgmt Co 123 Rowell Ct Falls Church VA 22046-3126

MCVEIGH-PETTIGREW, SHARON CHRISTINE, communications consultant; b. San Francisco, Feb. 6, 1949; d. Martin Allen and Frances (Roddy) McVeigh; m. John Wallace Pettigrew, Mar. 27, 1971; children: Benjamin Thomas, Margaret Mary. B.A. with honors, U. Calif.-Berkeley, 1971; diploma of edn. Monash U., Australia, 1975; M.B.A., Golden Gate U., 1985. Tchr., adminstr. Victorian Edn. Dept., Victoria, Australia, 1972-79; supr. Network Control Ctr., GTE Sprint Communications, Burlingame, Calif., 1979-81, mgr. customer assistance, 1981-84, mgr. state legis. ops., 1984-85, dir. revenue programs, 1986-87; communications cons. Flores, Pettigrew & Co., San Mateo, Calif., 1987-89; mgr. telemarketing Apple Computer, Inc., Cupertino, Calif., 1989-94; prin. The Call Ctr. Group, San Mateo, Calif., 1995—; telecomm. cons. PPG Svcs., 1994—; telecomm. spkr. Dept. Consumer Affairs, Sacramento, 1984. Panelist Wash. Gov.'s Citizens Council, 1984; founding mem. Maroondah Women's Shelter, Victoria, 1978; organizer nat. conf. Bus. Women and the Polit. Process, New Orleans, 1986; mem. sch. bd. Boronia Tech. Sch., Victoria, 1979. Recipient Tchr. Spl. Responsibilities award Victoria Edn. Dept., 1979. Mem. Women in Telecommunications (panel moderator San Francisco 1984), Am. Mgmt. Assn., Peninsula Profl. Women's Network, Am. Telemktg. Assn. (bd. dirs. 1992), Women's Econ. Action League. Democrat. Roman Catholic.

MCVERRY, THOMAS LEO, manufacturing company executive; b. Pitts., Aug. 2, 1938; m. Jean L. Smith, Apr. 29, 1961; children: Thomas, Michael, Amy. BA, U. Pitts., 1961, MBA, 1962. CPA, N.Y., CFP. Sr. acct. Deloitte & Touche, N.Y.C., 1962-66; contr., treas. Church & Dwight Co., Inc., N.Y.C., 1966-73; v.p. fin., resources Rexham Corp., Charlotte, N.C., 1973-90, also bd. dirs.; pres. McVerry & Assocs., Charlotte, 1990—; trustee Keystone Funds; trustee, chmn. audit com. Evergreen Funds; vice chmn. bd. Carolina Coop. Fed. Credit Union. Chmn. bd. edn. Charlotte Cath. High Sch., 1977-84, fin. com. St. Gabriel's Parish, Charlotte, 1976-82; v.p. Waldwick (N.J.) Bd. Edn., 1970-73. Mem. Am. Mgmt. Assn. (fin. coun.), Fin. Execs. Inst. (bd. mem. S.C. chpt.). Home and Office: 4419 N Parview Dr Charlotte NC 28226-3433

MCVEY, DIANE ELAINE, accountant; b. Wilmington, Del., Apr. 20, 1953; d. C. Granville and Margaret M. (Lindell) McV. AA in Acctg., Goldey Beacom Coll. (Del.), 1973, BS in Acctg., 1980; MBA in Mgmt., Fairleigh Dickinson U., 1985. Acct. Audio Visual Arts, Wilmington, 1973; cost acct. FMC Corp., Kennett Sq., Pa., 1973-75; asst. acct. NVF Corp., Kennett Sq., 1978-80; staff analyst GPU Nuclear, Parsippany, N.J., 1980-93; staff acct., 1993-95, GPU Energy, Parsippany, 1995—; owner, Demac Cons., Dover, N.J., 1988—. Elder First Presbyn. Ch., Rockaway, N.J., 1986—, session mem., 1988-91; commr. to bd. adjustment, Dover, N.J., 1994—. With U.S. Army, 1975-78. Mem. Assn. MBA Execs. Republican. Presbyterian. Avocations: reading mystery books, writing and performing music, needlework.

MCVEY, HENRY HANNA, III, lawyer; b. Richmond, Va., Aug. 12, 1935; s. Henry Hanna Jr. and Eva Lawson (Jennings) McV.; m. Reba Jean Robinson, Dec. 12, 1964; children: Margaret Anne McVey Singleton, Lewis Lawson, Ian Douglas. BS, BA magna cum laude, Hampden-Sydney Coll., 1957; LLB, U. Va., 1960. Bar: Va., 1960, U.S. Dist. Ct. (ea. dist.) Va. 1960, U.S. Ct. Appeals (4th cir.) 1965, U.S. Supreme Ct. 1970. Assoc. Battle, Neal, Harris, Minor & Williams, Richmond, 1960-66; ptnr. McGuire, Woods, Battle & Boothe (and predecessor firm), Richmond, 1966—; mem. adv. group under Civil Justice Reform Act of 1990, U.S. Dist. Ct. (ea. dist.) Va. Bd. dirs. Richmond Symphony, 1977-78, 87—, v.p., 1979-81, exec. v.p., 1981-83, pres., 1983-85, chmn. bd. dirs., 1985-87; bd. dirs. Carpenter Ctr. for Performing Arts, 1982-89; trustee Hampden-Sydney Coll., 1989-94, 95—; mem. Commn. on Archtl. Rev., City of Richmond, 1985-95. Fellow Am. Coll. Trial Lawyers; mem. ABA, Va. Assn. Def. Attys. (v.p. 1981-83, treas. 1983-84, pres.-elect 1984-85, pres. 1985-86), Def. Research and Trial Lawyers Assn. (past state chmn., regional v.p. 1985-87, bd. dirs. 1987-90), Am. Bd. Trial Advocacy (adv.), Fedn. Ins. and Corp. Counsel, Bar Assn. City of Richmond, Va. Bar Assn., Country Club of Va., Bull and Bear Club, Capital Club, Ware River Yacht Club. Presbyterian. Home: PO Box 43 Schley VA 23154 Office: McGuire Woods Battle & Boothe One James Ctr Richmond VA 23219

MC VICKER, CHARLES TAGGART, artist; b. Canonsburg, Pa., Aug. 31, 1930; s. Carl Walter and Mary Ruth (Washabaugh) McV.; m. Lucy Claire Graves, Mar. 20, 1954; children—Lauri, Bonnie, Heather. B.A., Principia Coll., Elsah, Ill., 1952; B.F.A., Art Center Coll. Design, Los Angeles, 1957. Staff artist Alexander Chaite Studios, 1957-58; freelance illustrator and painter, 1958—; asst. prof. Pratt Phoenix Sch. Art, N.Y.C., 1979-84, Trenton State Coll., 1985—. One-man shows include Thompson Gallery, N.Y.C., 1967, Capitol Hill Club, Washington, 1988; represented in permanent collections U.S. Capitol, Am. Hist. Assn., Soc. Illustrators, USAF, Princeton U., DuPont Corp., Zimmerli Art Mus. at Rutgers U., Home Life Ins. Co., Wang Corp. Served with AUS, 1952-54. Recipient Ralph Fabri award Nat. Audubon Artists Ann. Juried Show, 1986, Ralph Fabri medal Nat. Soc. Painters in Casein and Acrylic, 1991, Michael Engel Meml. award Nat. Audubon Artists, 1992. Mem. Soc. Illustrators (exec. com. 1972-74, pres. 1976-78), Am. Watercolor Soc., Graphic Artists Guild (v.p. nat. exec. com. 1978-79), Audubon Artists, Princeton Artists Alliance (pres. 1989—), Am. Artists Profl. League. Home and Office: 2344 Perrysville Ave Pittsburgh PA 15214-3560

MCVICKER, JESSE JAY, artist, educator; b. Vici, Okla., Oct. 18, 1911; s. Jesse Allen and Clara Mae (Hendrick) McV.; m. Laura Beth Paul, Aug. 20, 1938. B.A., Okla. State U., 1940, M.A., 1941. Faculty Okla. State U., Stillwater, 1941—; prof. art Okla. State U., 1959-77, prof. emeritus, 1977—, head dept., 1959-77. Exhbns. include Med. Mus. Art, Mus. Non-Objective Painting, Chgo. Art Inst., N.A.D., Library of Congress, San Francisco Mus. Art, Denver Art Mus., Pa. Acad. Fine Arts, Carnegie Inst., Print Club Phila., Salon Des Realities Nouvelles, Paris, France, Dallas, Mus. Fine Arts, Galleria Origine, Rome, Italy, Whitney Mus. Am. Art; represented in permanent collections Library of Congress, Seattle Art Mus., Dallas Mus. Fine Arts, Met. Mus. Art, Joslyn Meml. Art Mus.; bibliography Graphic Works by J. Jay McVicker, 1986. Served with USNR, 1943-46. Mem. Soc. Am. Graphic Artists, Audubon Artists (John Taylor Arms award 1990), Print Club Phila., Pi Kappa Alpha.

MC VIE, CHRISTINE PERFECT, musician; b. Eng., July 12, 1943; m. John McVie (div.); m. Eddy Quintela. Student art sch., pvt. student sculpture. Singer, keyboardist, Fleetwood Mac, from 1970; albums with Fleetwood Mac include: Fleetwood Mac, 1968, Fleetwood Mac in Chicago, 1969, Then Play On, 1969, English Rose, 1969, Kiln House, 1970, Future Games, 1971, Bare Trees, 1972, Penguin, Mystery To Me, 1973, Heroes Are Hard to Find, 1974, Fleetwood Mac, 1975, Rumours, 1977, Tusk, 1979, Fleetwood Mac Live, 1980, Mirage, 1982, Jumping at Shadows, 1985, Tango in the Night, 1987, Greatest Hits, 1988, Behind the Mask, 1990; solo albums include Christine Perfect, 1969, Christine McVie, 1984; composer: songs including Spare Me a Little of Your Love, Don't Stop, You Make Loving Fun, Over and Over, Hold Me, Songbird, Got a Hold on Me, Heroes Are Hard to Find, Little Lies, As Long as You Follow, Save Me, Skies the Limit. Office: care Warner Bros Records 3300 Warner Blvd Burbank CA 91505-4632

MCVISK, WILLIAM KILBURN, lawyer; b. Chgo., Oct. 8, 1953; s. Felix Kilburn and June (DePear) Visk; m. Marlaine Joyce McDonough, June 20, 1975. BA, U. Ill, 1974; JD, Northwestern U., 1977. Bar: Ill. 1977, U.S. Dist. Ct. (no. dist.) Ill. 1977, U.S. Ct. Appeals (7th cir.) 1978. Assoc. Jerome H. Torshen, Ltd., Chgo., 1977-80, Silets & Martin, Chgo., 1980-81; assoc. Peterson & Ross, Chgo., 1981-85, ptnr., 1985-95; ptnr. Johnson & Bell, Chgo., 1995—. Contbr. articles to profl. jours. Mem. ABA, Chgo. Bar Assn., Def. Research Inst., Am. Assn. Hosp. Attys., Ill. Assn. Hosp. Attys., Ill. Assn. Def. Trial Lawyers. Office: Johnson & Bell 222 N La Salle St Chicago IL 60601-1002

MCWALTERS, PETER, state agency administrator; b. Oct. 8, 1946; m. Alice Bond McWalters; children: Jennifer, Molly, Katherine. BA in History and Philosophy, Boston Coll., 1968; MS in Pub. Adminstrn., SUNY Brockport, 1979, cert. advanced study ednl. adminstrn., 1981. Permanent N.Y. State Teaching Cert social studies 7-12, Sch. Adminstrn., Sch. Dist. Adminstrn. Tchr.-trainer Eng. for speakers other langs. U.S. Peace Corps., Rep. Philippines; tchr. Eng. for speakers other langs. City Sch. Dist., Rochester, N.Y., 1970-71; tchr. social studies Interim Jr. High Sch., Rochester, 1971-78; Magnet Sch. planning specialist City Sch. Dist., Rochester, 1978-81; coord. Mgmt. Inst., 1980-81, supervising dir. planning and budgeting, 1981-85, supt. schs., 1985-91; commr. elem. and secondary edn. State of R.I., 1992—; bd. dirs. Nat. Ctr. Edn. and Economy, mem. new standards project; bd. dirs. Ctr. Ednl. Devel., Rochester; mem. Edn. Commn. of States, Coun. Chief State Schs. Officers, Coun. Great Cities Schs., 21st Century Edn. Commn. Bd. dirs. Urban League, Rochester; mem. United Way Task Force, Rochester; gov. bd., exec. com. Rochester New Futures Initiative, Inc.; mem. Goals for Greater Rochester, Inc. Mem. Am. Assn. Sch. Adminstrs., Assn. Supervision and Curriculum Devel., Phi Delta Kappa. Home: 26 Diman Pl Providence RI 02906-2104 Office: Elem and Sec Office Shepard Bldg 255 Westminster St Providence RI 02903-3414*

MCWETHY, JOHN FLEETWOOD, journalist; b. Aurora, Ill., Feb. 28, 1947; s. John Adams and Mary Helen (Bell) McW.; m. Laurie Duncan, June 25, 1971; children: Adam Duncan, James Ian. B.A., DePauw U., 1969; M.S., Columbia U., 1970. Def. writer Congl. Quar., Washington, 1970-72; sci. editor U.S. News & World Report, Washington, 1972-77, chief White House corr., 1977-79; chief Pentagon corr. ABC News, Washington, 1979-84; chief corr. ABC News Nat. Security and Sr. State Dept., Washington, 1984—. Contbg. author: Power of the Pentagon, 1972. Recipient DuPont award Columbia U. Sch. Journalism, 1984; 3 Emmy awards, 1984, 91, 92, Overseas Press Club award for Inside the Other Side, 1987. Home: 5028 30th St N Arlington VA 22207-2717

MCWETHY, PATRICIA JOAN, educational association administrator; b. Chgo., Feb. 27, 1946; d. Frank E. and Emma (Kuehne) McW.; m. H. Frank Eden; children: Kristin Beth, Justin Nicholas. BA, Northwestern U., 1968; MA, U. Minn., 1970; MBA, George Washington U., 1981. Geog. analyst CIA, McLean, Va., 1970-71; research asst. NSF, Washington, 1972-74, spl. asst. to dir., 1975; assoc. program dir. human geography and regional sci. program NSF, 1976-79; exec. dir. Assn. Am. Geographers, Washington., 1979-84, Nat. Assn. Biology Tchrs., Reston, Va., 1984-95, Nat. Sci. Edn. Leadership Assn., Arlington, Va., 1995—; prin. investigator NSF grant on biotech. equipment ednl. resource partnership, 1989-93, NSF funded internat. symposium on "Basic Biol. Concepts: What Should the World's Children Know?", 1992-94; co-prin. investigator NSF grant, 1995—; mem. chmn.'s adv. com. Nat. Com. Sci. Stds. & Assessment, 1992—; mem. Commn. for Biology Edn., Internat. Union Biol. Sci., 1988—; mem. exec. com. Alliance for Environ. Edn., 1987-90, chmn. program com., 1990; condr. seminars in field; lectr. in field. Author monograph and papers in field; editor handbook. NSF grantee, 1989-93, 95—; NSF fellow, 1968-69; recipient Outstanding Performance award, NSF, 1973. Mem. Am. Soc. Assn. Execs., Nat. Sci. Tchrs. Assn., Phi Beta Kappa. Office: PO Box 5556 Arlington VA 22205-0056

MCWHAN, DENIS BAYMAN, physicist; b. N.Y.C., Dec. 10, 1935; s. Bayman and Evelyn (Inch) McW.; m. Carolyn Quick, June 20, 1959; children: Susan, Jeanette, David. BS, Yale U., 1957; PhD, U. Calif., Berkeley, 1961. Disting. mem. tech. staff AT&T Bell Labs., Murray Hill, N.J., 1962-1990; chmn. Nat. Synchrotron Light Source, Brookhaven Nat. Lab., Upton, N.Y., 1990-95; assoc. dir. basic energy scis. programs Brookhaven Nat. Lab., Upton, N.Y., 1995—. Fellow AAAS, Am. Phys. Soc. Achievements include rsch. in condensed matter physics. Office: Brookhaven Nat Lab Bldg 460 Upton NY 11973

MCWHINEY, GRADY, history educator; b. Sherveport, La., July 15, 1928; s. Henry Grady and Mayme (Holland) McW.; m. Sue B. Baca, Nov. 20, 1947. B.S., Centenary Coll. of La., 1950; M.A., La. State U., 1951; Ph.D., Columbia U., 1960. Asst. prof. Troy State U., Ala., 1952-54, Millsaps Coll., Jackson, Miss., 1956-59, Northwestern U., Evanston, Ill., 1960-65; assoc. prof. to prof. U.B. C., Vancouver, Can., 1965-70; vis. prof. U. Calif. - Berkeley, 1959-60, 67-68; prof. Wayne State U., Detroit, 1970-75; vis. prof. Tulane U., New Orleans, summer 1970, U. Mich., Ann Arbor, 1972-73; prof. history, dir. and disting. sr. fellow ctr. for study of so. history and culture U. Ala. University, 1975-83; Lyndon Baines Johnson prof. Am. history Tex. Christian U., Ft. Worth, 1983-96, emeritus, 1996—; disting. historian in residence U. So. Miss., Hattiesburg, 1996-97; mem. NEH Selection Com., 1973, Jefferson Davis Award Com., 1970-72, 75-77; James Murfin Meml. lectr., 1990, Marian Alexander Blake lectr., 1991; Conf. Meml. speaker, 1991; vis. disting. prof. McMurry U., Abilene, Tex., 1997—. Author: Braxton Bragg and Confederate Defeat, Vol. 1, 1969, 2d edit., 1991, Southerners and Other Americans, 1973, (with Perry D. Jamieson) Attack and Die: Civil War Military Tactics and the Southern Heritage, 1982, Cracker Culture: Celtic Ways in the Old South, 1988, (with J.L. Hallock) Braxton Bragg, 2 vols., 1991, An American Civil War Primer, 1992, Battle in the Wilderness: Grant Meets Lee, 1994; editor: (with Sue McWhiney) To Mexico with Taylor and Scott, 1845-1847, 1969, Grant, Lee, Lincoln and the Radicals, 1964, (with Robert Weibe) Historical Vistas, 2 vols., 1963-64, Reconstruction and the Freedmen, 1963, (with Douglas Southall Freeman) Robert E. Lee's Dispatches to Jefferson Davis, 1957, 94. Served with USMC, 1945-47. Recipient Earl A. Davis award, 1996, Frank E. Vandiver award Houston Civil War Round Table, 1993, Charles L. "Pie" Dufour award New Orleans Civil War Round Table, 1994, Outstanding Scholar award U. Ala., 1980, Gallant Service award Chgo. Civil War Round Table, 1979, Harry S. Truman award, 1970, Pacific Br. award Am. Hist. Assn., 1969; Huntington Library fellow, 1984; recipient Jefferson Davis medal United Daughters of the Confederacy, 1992, Honor award Sons Confederate Vets Tex. Divsn., 1993; rsch. fellow Mosher Inst. Defense Studies, 1988—. Fellow St. George Tucker Soc.; mem. Ala. Hist. Assn. (pres. 1978-79), So. Hist. Assn. (exec. council 1976-79), Phila. Soc., St. Louis Civil War Round Table (hon.), Civil War Round Table U.K. (hon.), Main St. Com., Phi Beta Kappa. Office: Dept History McMurry Univ Abilene TX 79697

MCWHINNEY, EDWARD WATSON, Canadian government legislator; b. Sydney, Australia, May 19, 1924; s. Matthew and Evelyn Annie (Watson) McW.; m. Emily Ingalore Sabatzky, June 27, 1951. LLB, U. Sydney, 1949; LLM, Yale U., 1951, D Juridical Sci., 1953; diploma, Acad. de Droit Internat., The Hague, 1950. Bar: Called to Australian bar 1949, apptd. Queen's counsel, Can 1967. Crown prosecutor Sydney, 1949-50; lectr., then asst. prof. Law Sch. and Grad. Sch., Yale U., 1951-55; prof. law, mem. Centre Russian Studies, U. Toronto, Ont., Can., 1955-66; prof. law, dir. Inst. Air and Space Law, McGill U., Montreal, Que., Can., 1966-71; prof. law, dir. internat. and comparative legal studies U. Ind., Indpls., 1971-74; disting. prof. Simon Fraser U., Burnaby, B.C., 1974-93; mem. Permanent Ct. Arbitration, The Hague, 1985-91; Paul Martin prof. U. Windsor, Can., 1986; prof. emeritus, 1992; M.P. Ho. of Commons, Ottawa, Ont., Can., 1993—; co-chmn. joint standing com. Senate and Ho. of Commons, Ottawa, Ont., Can., 1993-95, parliamentary sec. (fisheries and oceans), 1996—; vis. prof. Ecole Libre des Hautes Etudes, 1952, Heidelberg and Max-Planck-Inst., 1960-61, 90, NYU, 1954, Faculté Internat. de Droit Comparé, Luxembourg, 1959-60, U. San Antonio, 1963, U. Laval, Que., 1967, U. Paris, 1968, U. Madrid, 1968, U. Aix-Marseille, 1969, U. Nacional Autónoma de México, 1965, Inst. Univ. Luxembourg, 1972, 74, 76, Acad. Internat. Law, The Hague, 1973, 90, Aristotelian U., Thessaloniki, Greece, 1974, 78, 85, 96, U. Nice, 1976-77, Jagellonian U., Cracow, Poland, 1976, U. Paris I (Sorbonne), 1982, 85, Coll. de France, Paris, 1983, Meiji U., Tokyo, 1987, Inst. Internat. Relations, Bejing, 1987, 92; legal cons. UN, 1953-54; cons. Japanese Commn. Constn., mem. prime minister Ont. Adv. Com. Confedn., 1964-71; cons. U.S. Naval War Coll., 1961-68; legal cons. Ministère de la Justice, Que., 1969-70; 74-75; constl. adviser to prime minister of Que., 1974-75; royal commr. Commn. Lang. Rights. Que., 1968-72; cons. U.S. Senate select com. presdl. campaign activities, 1973; spl. commr. inquiry Legislature B.C., 1974-75; chief adv. Fed. Govt.'s Task Force on Nat. Unity, 1978; commr. of enquiry, City of Vancouver, 1979; constl. adv. Fedn. Can. Municipalities, 1978-82; spl. advisor Can. del. UN Gen. Assembly, ann. sessions, 1981, 82, 83, 96; constl. adviser Indian Nations (Treaties 6-9), Can., 1980-82; mem. Assoc. de l'Inst. de Droit Internat., 1967, membre titulaire, 1975; mem. Assoc. de l'Acad. Internat. de Droit Comparé, Paris, 1986, mem. Deutsche Gesellschaft für Völkerrecht, 1992. Author: Judical Review, 4th edit, 1969, Canadian Jurisprudence, 1958, Föderalismus und Bundesverfassungsrecht, 1961, Constitutionalism in Germany, 1962, Comparative Federalism, 2d edit, 1965, Peaceful Coexistence and Soviet-Western International Law, 1964, Law Foreign Policy and the East-West Détente, 1964, Federal Constitution- Making for a Multi-National World, 1966, International Law and World Revolution, 1967, Conflit idéologique et ordre public mondial, 1970, (with M.A. Bradley) The Freedom of the Air, 1968, New Frontiers in Space Law, 1969, The International Law of Communications, 1970, Aerial Piracy and International Law, 1971, (with Pierre Pescatore) Federalism and Supreme Courts and the Integration of Legal Systems, 1973, Parliament and Parliamentary Power Today, 1976, The Executive and Executive Power Today, 1977, (with J-D Gendron and others) La situation de la lanque française au Québec (3 vols.), 1973, The Illegal Diversion of Aircraft and International Law, 1974, Parliamentary Privilege and the Broadcasting of Parliamentary Debates, 1975, The International Law of Detente, 1978, The World Court and the Contemporary International Law-making Process, 1979, Quebec and the Constitution, 1979, Municipal Government in a New Canadian Federal System, 1980, Conflict and Compromise: International Law and World Order in a Revolutionary Age, 1981, Constitution-Making: Principles, Process, Practice, 1981, Canada and the Constitution, 1982, United Nations Law Making, 1984, Supreme Courts and Judicial Law-Making, 1986, Les Nations-Unies et la Formation du Droit, 1986, Aerial Piracy and International Terorism, 1987, The International Court of Justice and the Western Tradition of International Law, 1987, (with Nagendra Singh) Nuclear Weapons and Contemporary International Law, 1988, Judicial Settlement of International Disputes, 1990, (with G.I. Tunkin and V.S. Vereshchetin) From Coexistence to Cooperation: International Law and Organisation in the Post-Cold War Era, 1991, (with J. Zaslove and W. Wolf) Federalism-in-the-Making, Contemporary Canadian and German Constitutionalism, National and Transnational, 1992, Judge Shigeru Oda and the Progressive Development of International Law, 1992, Judge Manfred Lachs and Judicial Law-Making, 1994; bd. editors Australian Quar., 1949-50, Can. Yearbook of Internat. Law, 1963—, Jour. Media Law and Practice, 1980-85, Annuaire International de Justice Constitutionnelle, 1987—; editorial adv. com. Ency. Britannica, 1985—; contbr. to Ency. Brit. Served as officer Australian Air Force, 1943-45. Fellow Carnegie Endowment, 1951; Fulbright fellow, 1950-51; Sterling fellow Yale, 1950-51; Rockefeller fellow, 1960-61, 66-68; Can. Council fellow, 1960-61; fellow Am. Soc. Internat. Law, 1962-63. Mem. Australian Inst. Polit. Sci. (dir.), Internat. Law Assn. (pres. Toronto br. 1964-66, pres. Montreal br. 1970-71, chmn. exec. com. Canadian br. 1972-75), Canadian Bar Assn. (council Ont. 1956-58), Yale Law Sch. Assn. (pres. Can. 1964-69), Canadian Civil Liberties Assn. (v.p. 1965-67), Am. Soc. Internat. Law (council 1965-68), Am. Fgn. Law Assn., Inst. interamericano de Estudios Juridicos Internacionales (dir. 1965—), Inst. Grand-Ducal de Luxembourg, Internat. Commn. Jurists (mem. coun. Can. br. 1988—), Knights of Mark Twain (U.S.) (hon.). Home: 1949 Beach Ave Ste 402, Vancouver, BC Canada V6G 1Z2

MCWHINNEY, IAN RENWICK, physician, medical educator; b. Burnley, Eng., Oct. 11, 1926; emigrated to Can., 1968, naturalized, 1981; s. Archibald Renwick and Mary (Freeland) McW.; m. Betty Heap, Apr. 30; children: Heather, Julie. MB, BCh, Cambridge (Eng.) U., 1949; MD, Cambridge (Eng.) U., Eng.; MD (hon.), U. Oslo, 1991. Intern St. Bartholomews Hosp., London, 1949-50; resident (Warwick), Eng., 1953-54; pvt. practice medicine Stratford-on-Avon, Eng., 1954-68; prof. family medicine U. Western Ont., London, Can., 1968-92; prof. emeritus U. Western Ont., London, 1992—; med. dir. palliative care unit Parkwood Hosp., 1986-91. Author: The Early Signs of Illness, 1964, Introduction to Family Medicine, 1981, A Textbook of Family Medicine, 1989. Capt. Royal Army M.C., 1951-53. Recipient Excellence cert. Soc. Tchrs. Family Medicine, 1979, Curtis G. Hames Rsch. award, 1989. Fellow Coll. Family Physicians (Victor Johnston orator 1980), Royal Coll. Gen. Practitioners, Royal Coll. Physicians; mem. Inst. Medicine-Nat. Acad. Scis. (fgn. assoc.). Office: U Western Ont, Dept Family Medicine, London, ON Canada N6A 5C1

MCWHINNEY, MADELINE H. (MRS. JOHN DENNY DALE), economist; b. Denver, Mar. 11, 1922; d. Leroy and Alice (Houston) McW.; BA, Smith Coll., 1943; MBA, NYU, 1947; m. John D. Dale, June 23, 1961; 1 child, Thomas Denny. Economist, Fed. Res. Bank N.Y., 1943-73, chief fin. and trade statis. div., 1955-59, mgr. market stats. dept., 1960-65, asst. v.p., 1965-73; pres. First Women's Bank, N.Y.C., 1974-76; trustee Retirement System Fed. Res. Bank, 1955-58; vis. lectr. N.Y.U. Grad. Sch. Bus., 1976-77; pres. Dale, Elliott & Co., Inc., Red Bank, N.J., 1977—; mem. N.J. Casino Control Commn., 1980-82, Women's Econ. Round Table, 1978-89, chmn. 1987-88; bd. govs. Am. Stock Exch., 1977-81. Trustee Monmouth Mus., 1995—, Vis. Nurse Assn. Ctrl. Jersey, 1995—, Planned Parenthood Ctrl. Jersey, 1995—; Carnegie Corp. N.Y., 1974-82, Central Savs. Bank of N.Y., 1980-82, Charles F. Kettering Found., 1975-93, chmn. 1987-91, Inst. Internat. Edn., 1975—, Investor Responsibility Rsch. Ctr., Inc., 1974-81; asst. dir. Whitney Mus. Am. Art, 1983-86; dir. Atlantic Energy Co., 1983-93; trustee The Mgrs. Funds, 1983—; mem. adv. com. prof. ethics N.J. Supreme Ct., 1983—. Recipient Smith Coll. medal, 1971, Alumni Achievement award NYU Grad. Sch. Bus. Adminstrn. Alumni Assn., 1971; NYU Crystal award, 1982. Mem. Am. Fin. Assn. (past dir.), Money Marketeers (v.p. 1960, pres. 1961-62), Alumni Assn. Grad. Sch. Bus. Adminstrn. NYU (dir. 1951-63, pres. 1957-59), Soc. Meml. Ctr., N.J. Com. for Humanities, Phi Beta Kappa Assocs. (v.p. 1979-87). Home: 24 Blossom Cove Rd Red Bank NJ 07701-6302 Office: PO Box 458 Red Bank NJ 07701-0458

MCWHIRTER, BRUCE J., lawyer; b. Chgo., Sept. 11, 1931; s. Sydney and Martha McW.; m. Judith Hallett, Apr. 14, 1960; children: Cameron, Andrew. BS, Northwestern U., 1952; LLB, Harvard U., 1955. Bar: D.C. 1955, Ill. 1955, U.S. Ct. Appeals (7th cir.) 1963, U.S. Supreme Ct. Assoc. Lord, Bissell & Brook, Chgo., 1958-62; from assoc. to sr. ptnr. Ross & Hardies, Chgo., 1962-95, of counsel, 1996—. Editor: Donnelley SEC Handbook, 1972-87; contbr. articles to profl. publs. Served with U.S. Army, 1955-57, Japan. Mem. ABA, Chgo. Bar Assn., Law Club Chgo., Harvard Law Soc. Ill. (bd. dirs. 1984), Harvard Club (N.Y.C.), Phi Beta Kappa. Democrat. Home: 111 Sheridan Rd Winnetka IL 60093-4223 Office: Ross & Hardies 150 N Michigan Ave Ste 2500 Chicago IL 60601-7524

MCWHIRTER, GLENNA SUZANNE (NICKIE MCWHIRTER), retired newspaper columnist; b. Peoria, Ill., June 28, 1929; d. Alfred Leon and Garnet Lorene (Short) Sotier; m. Edward Ford McWhirter (div.); children: Suzanne McWhirter Orlicki, Charles Edward, James Richard. BS in English Lang. and Lit., U. Mich., postgrad., 1960-63. Editl. asst. McGraw-Hill Pub. Co., Detroit, 1951-54; staff writer Detroit Free Press, Inc., Detroit, 1963-88; columnist Detroit News Inc., Detroit, 1988-97; advt. copy writer Campbell-Ewald Co., Detroit, 1967-68; ret., 1997. Author: Pea Soup, 1984. Winner 1st Place Commentary award UPI, Mich., 1979; 1st Place Columns AP, Mich., 1978, 81; 1st Place Columns Detroit Press Club Found., Mich., 1978; Disting. Service award State of Mich., 1985. Mem. Women in Comm. (Headliner award 1978), Alpha Gamma Delta. Avocations: flower gardening; tennis. Home: 88 Meadow Ln Grosse Pointe MI 48236-3803

MCWHIRTER, JAMES HERMAN, consulting engineering business executive, financial planner; b. Mercer, Pa., July 4, 1924; s. John Herman and Blanche Rebecca (Anderson) McW.; m. Suzanne Kibler, July 5, 1952; children: Kathleen, Meg Allyn, John Richard, Thomas Charles, Robert Brian. BS, Columbia U., 1945; MS, Carnegie Inst. Tech., 1947. Registered profl. engr., Pa; cert. fin. planner. Devel. engr. Westinghouse Electric Corp., Sharon, Pa., 1948-65; rsch. engr. Westinghouse Rsch. Labs., Pitts., 1965-89; registered rep. Allegheny Investments, Ltd., Pitts., 1987—; pres. Optimization, Ltd., Murrysville, Pa., 1989—. Contbr. articles on engring. and fin. planning to profl. jours.; spkr. on fin. planning. Lt. (j.g.) USNR, 1945-58. Fellow IEEE. Republican. Presbyterian. Avocation: "Big Band" musician. Home and Office: 3660 Forbes Trail Dr Murrysville PA 15668-1054

MCWHIRTER, JOHN RUBEN, chemical engineering educator; b. East St. Louis, Ill., Dec. 29, 1937; s. Walter and Mildred (Johnson) McW.; m. Gail Balthrope, June 28, 1958 (div. Aug. 1978); children: John Winfield, Andrew James, Mark Steven, Brian Michael; m. Anne Burlingham, Mar. 31, 1979 (div. Dec. 1990); m. Jeanette D. Heiser, Mar. 21, 1992. BS in Chem. Engring., U. Ill., 1959; MS in Chem. Engring., Pa. State U., 1961, PhD in Chem. Engring., 1962; postgrad. exec. program, Stanford U., 1971. Research engr. E.I. Du Pont de Nemours & Co., Wilmington, Del., 1962-63; mgr. research and devel. Mixing Equipment Co., Rochester, N.Y., 1963-66; section engr. engring. devel. lab. Linde div. Union Carbide Corp., Tonawanda, N.Y., 1966-67, div. engr. engring. devel. lab., 1967-68, mgr. chem. engring. div. and special projects, 1968-69, product mgr., 1969-70; mgr. wastewater treatment systems Linde div. Union Carbide Corp., N.Y.C., 1970-72, gen. mgr. environ. systems dept., 1973-76, v.p., gen. mgr. environ. systems dept., 1977-78; v.p., gen. mgr. insecticides and intermediates agrl. products div. Union Carbide, N.Y.C., 1978-83, v.p., gen. mgr. agrl. chems., 1983-86; prof. chem. engring. Pa. State U., State College, Pa., 1986—; pres., CEO McWhirter Property Mgmt., Inc, 1996—, Phosphazene Custom Synthesis, Inc., 1997—. Author: The Use of High Purity Oxygen in the Activated Sludge Process, 1978; contbr. articles to profl. jours.; presented numerous papers at profl. confs.; patentee in field. Recipient Best Paper Presentation award Nat. Am. Inst. Chem. Engrs., 1963, Outstanding Personal Achievement award Chem. Engring. Mag., 1970, Kirkpatrick award, 1971, Outstanding Engring. Alumnus award Pa. State U., 1984, Arthur Dehan Little award Am. Inst. Chem. Engrs., 1991. Mem. AICE, AAAS, Am. Mgmt. Assn., Am. Chem. Soc. (Jacob F. Schoellkopf medal 1976), N.Y. Acad. Scis., Water Pollution Control Fedn., Tau Beta Pi, Phi Lambda Upsilon, Sigma Tau, Alpha Chi Sigma, Delta Tau Delta. Republican. Home: 101 Aspen Dr Boalsburg PA 16827 Office: Pa State U 122 Fenske Lab University Park PA 16802-4400

MCWHORTER, HOBART AMORY, JR., lawyer; b. Birmingham, Ala., Dec. 24, 1931; s. Hobart Amory and Marjorie (Westgate) McW.; remarried Feb. 1, 1997; children: Margaret G., Marjorie W. BA, Yale U., 1953; LLB, U. Va., 1958. Bar: Ala. 1958. Ptnr. Bradley Arant Rose & White, Birmingham, 1958—. 1st lt. U.S. Army, 1953-55. Fellow Am. Coll. Trial Lawyers; mem. Internat. Assn. Ins. Counsel, Nat. Assn. r.R. Counsel. Republican. Presbyterian. Office: Bradley Arant Rose & White 1400 Park Pl Tower 2001 Park Pl Birmingham AL 35203-2735

MCWHORTER, KATHLEEN, orthodontist; b. Houston, May 29, 1953; d. Archer and Lucile (Taft) McW. BA summa cum laude, U. Houston, 1986; DDS with honors, Baylor Coll., 1990. Mgr. Am. Internat. Rent-A-Car, Houston, 1974-79; mktg. researcher Concoco Oil Co., Houston, 1979-83; orthodontist Baylor Coll. Dentistry, Dallas, 1990—; presenter Am. Assn. Dental Rsch., Montreal, Que., Can., 1988, Cin., 1990; rsch. fellow Baylor Coll. Dentistry, Dallas, 1987, 88, 89. Contbr. articles to profl. jours. Mem. ADA, Am. Assn. Orthodontists, Am. Assn. Women Dentists, Am. Assn. Dentistry for Children, Internat. Assn. Dental Rsch., Am. Assn. Dental Rsch., Tex. Dental Assn., Dallas County Dental Soc., The Crescent Club. Avocations: tennis, walking, music, water skiing. Office: Baylor U Coll Dentistry Dept Orthodontics 3302 Gaston Ave Dallas TX 75246-2013

MCWHORTER, RUTH ALICE, counselor, marriage and family therapist; b. Norfolk, Va., May 14, 1946; d. Lester Arthur and Mabel Winifred (Hopwood) Gorman; m. Dean Gundersen, Dec. 27, 1967 (div. Oct. 1971); m. R. Dale Lawhorn, Jan. 6, 1972 (div. Nov. 1979); m. Brent Wilson McWhorter, Aug. 16, 1986; stepchildren: Daniel Chastin, Kenley Reid, Scott Jason. BA in Edn., Ariz. State U., 1970, M of Counseling Psychology, 1979. Cert. profl. counselor, Ariz., cert. marriage and family therapist, Ariz. Tchr. lang. arts Globe (Ariz.) Mid. Sch., 1969-72; tchr. English Isaac Jr. High Sch., Phoenix, Ariz., 1973-74; real estate salesperson Ben Brooks & Assocs., Phoenix, 1975-76, Century 21 Metro, Phoenix, 1976-77; overnight counselor The New Found., Phoenix, 1978-80; family therapist Youth Svc. Bur., Phoenix, 1980-81; owner, corp. officer, profl. counselor/marriage & family Family Devel. Resources (now Family Psychology Assocs.), Phoenix, 1981—; cons., vol. counselor Deseret Industries, Phoenix, 1992-96. Bd. dirs. Westside Mental Health Svcs., Phoenix, 1982-87; vol. facilitator Ariz. Multiple Sclerosis Soc., Phoenix, 1988. Mem. ACA, Internat. Assn. Marriage and Family Therapists, Am. Assn. Marriage and Family Therapists, Am. Mental Health Counselors Assn., Ariz. Counselors Assn., Ariz. Mental Health Counselors Assn. (sec.-treas. ctrl. chpt. 1982, sec. ctrl. chpt. 1995), Am. Assn. Christian Counselors, Assn. Mormon Counselors and Psychotherapists (sec.-treas. 1990—). Avocations: genealogy, movies, reading, golf, logic puzzles. Office: Family Devel Resources PC PO Box 55291 Phoenix AZ 85078-5291

MCWHORTER, SHARON LOUISE, business executive, inventor, consultant; b. Detroit, Feb. 22, 1951; d. Leroy Byron Harris Jr. and Josiebell (Richards) Harris Aaron; m. Abner McWhorter II, Mar. 15, 1969 (div. Aug. 1974); 1 child, Abner III. BA, Wayne State U., 1988; cert., SBA, Detroit, 1978; cert. in sound engring. Detroit Rec. Inst., Warren, Mich., 1982. Directory asst. Mich. Bell Telephone Co., Detroit, 1969; quality control clk. Chevrolet Gear & Axle, Detroit, 1971-74; circulation clk. Wayne County Community Coll., Detroit, 1977-85, mem. library standing com. and open house com., 1983-84; pres. Galactic Concepts & Designs, Detroit, 1977-88, cons., 1983—; gen. ptnr., mgr. S.M.J. Corridor Devel., Detroit, 1982—, hist. researcher, 1982; del. Small Bus. Conf., 1981; ad-hoc mem. Minority Tech. Council, 1981-82; elected alt. Mich. del. White House Conf. on Small Bus., Washington, 1985-86. Author, editor Creative Dilemma newsletter, 1985—. Co-patentee cup holding apparatus. Vol. counselor Barat House/March of Dimes, Detroit, 1977; active Concerned Citizens Cass Corridor, Detroit, 1982-87, Cass Corridor Citizen's Patrol, Detroit, 1983-84, Empowerment Zone Devel. Corp., Detroit, 1996—, bd. dirs., corp. sec. 1997—; pres. Wayne County chpt. MADD, Mich., 1987-88; apptd. citizen review com., 1988—; mem. adv. bd. Neighborhood Family Initiative, Southeastern Community Found.; pres. Am. Res. Tng. Sys., Inc., 1990—; lectr., cons. Recipient Hist. Landmark award Dept. Interior, 1983, cert. appreciation Tri-County Substance Abuse Awareness Com., 1984. Mem. Inventors Council Mich. (bd. dirs. 1985-88), Black Women in Bus. (sec. 1984-85), Greater Detroit C. of C., South Cass Bus. Assn. (v.p. 1987-88, pres. 1988-89), Detroit Econ. Club. Democrat. Methodist. Avocations: inventing; writing, re-adaptive furniture design, photography, video production. Office: SMJ Corridor Devel Co 453 Myrtle St Ste 102 Detroit MI 48201-2311

MCWILLIAM, JOANNE ELIZABETH, religion educator; b. Toronto, Ont., Can., Dec. 10, 1928; d. Cecil Edward and Edna Viola (Archer) McW.; children, Leslie Mary Giroday, Elizabeth McEwen, Sean Dewart, Colin Dewart; m. C. Peter Slater, June 6, 1987. BA, U. Toronto, 1951, MA, 1953; MA, U. St. Michael's, Toronto, 1966, PhD, 1968. Asst. prof. religious studies U. Toronto, 1968-74, assoc. prof., 1974-87, prof., 1987, chairperson dept. religious studies, 1990-92, 93-94; Mary Crooke Hoffman prof. of Dogmatic Theology The Gen. Theol. Sem., N.Y.C, 1994—. Author: The Theology of Grace of Theodore of Mopsuestia, 1971, Death and Resurrection in the Fathers, 1986; editor: Augustine: Rhetor to Theologian, 1991, Toronto Jour. Theology. Mem. Can. Soc. for Patristic Studies (pres. 1987-90), Conf. Anglican Theologians (pres. 1990-91), Can. Soc. for the Study of Religion, Can. Theol. Soc., Am. Theol. Soc., Am. Acad. Religion. Anglican. Home: 59 Duggan Ave, Toronto, ON Canada M4V 1Y1 Office: The Gen Theol Sem 175 9th Ave New York NY 10011-4924

MCWILLIAMS, BETTY JANE, science administrator, communication disorders educator, researcher; d. Harry J. and Martha (McClure) McW. B.S., Ohio State U., 1949; M.S., U. Pitts., 1950, Ph.D., 1953. Speech pathologist Ohio County Easter Seal Soc., Wheeling, W.Va., 1950-51; instr. U. Pitts., 1951-54, asst. prof., 1954-59, assoc. prof. 1959-67, prof., 1967-91, prof. emeritus, 1991—, dir. cleft palate craniofacial ctr., 1969-91, dir. emeritus, 1993—; vis. prof. U. N.C., Chapel Hill, 1962, Howard U., Washington, 1977-78; cons. Western Pa. Hosp., Pitts., 1972-91, Montefiore Hosp., N.Y.C., 1975-87, Walter Reed Army Hosp., Washington, 1984-87; mem. Pa. Acad. Com. on Tech. Devel., Harrisburg, 1984-87; mem. standards and peer rev. com. Pa. Fedn. of Cleft Palate Clinics, 1985-87. Sr. author: Cleft Palate Speech, 1984, revised edit., 1990; contbr. articles to profl. jours. Recipient Herbert Cooper Meml. award Cooper Clinic, 1979, award of recognition Pa. Acad. Dentistry for Children, 1989, award of recognition Pa. Dental Soc., 1991. Fellow Am. Speech, Lang. and Hearing Assn. (cert. clin. competence, Frank R. Kleffner Career award 1995), Am. Coll. Dentists; mem. APA, Am. Cleft Palate Craniofacial Assn. (pres. 1965, asst. sec. gen. 1st internat. congress 1969, editor 1975-81, pres. Found. 1982-83, svc. award 1975, Honors of Assn. 1987), Pa. Fedn. Cleft Palate Clinics (pres. 1980-82, 89-90, legis. con. 1991-94). Avocations: antiques; needlework; cooking; reading. Home and Office: 512 Bigham Rd Pittsburgh PA 15211-1412

MCWILLIAMS, BRUCE WAYNE, marketing professional; b. Vancouver, B.C., Can., Sept. 23, 1932; came to U.S., 1975; s. Lloyd and Mamie (Bateman) McW.; m. Heather Oxland, Nov. 15, 1957 (div.); children: Sandra, Roderick, Anna; m. Sheila Albin, June 23, 1990. Student, U. B.C., Vancouver, 1950-54. Advt. asst. Brit. Petroleum Co., London, 1957-62; asst. dir. B.C. Govt. Travel Bur., 1962-64; mng. dir. HCF-Ergon Advt., Athens, Greece, 1964-67; dir. HCF-Internat., London, 1967-70; dir. pub. relations Occidental Internat. Oil Inc., Paris and London, 1970-75; dir. pub. affairs Occidental Petroleum Corp., Los Angeles, 1975-80; dir. pub. relations and advt. Comark, Newport Beach, Calif., 1980-81; ptnr. Chester Burger & Co. Inc., N.Y.C., 1981-83; sr. v.p. Ogilvy & Mather PR, Chgo., 1983-85; sr. corp. relations officer Internat. Fin. Corp., 1985-88; pres. The McWilliams Co., 1988-90; mktg. dir. Nixon, Hargrave, Devans & Doyle, Rochester, N.Y., 1990-92, Powell, Goldstein, Frazer & Murphy, Washington, 1993—. Mem. Pub. Relations Soc. Am. Club: Naval and Mil. (London).

MCWILLIAMS, C. PAUL, JR., engineering executive; b. Louisville, June 4, 1931; s. Cleo Paul and Audrey Dora (Hale) McW.; m. Barbara Ann Sparks, Feb. 22, 1950 (div. 1962); children: Bruce Kevin, Craig Tinsley; m. Barbara Ann Heintz, Apr. 25, 1980; 1 stepchild, Kimberly Jean Moorhouse Swigert. B Chem. Engring., U. Louisville, 1954, M Engring., 1972. Lic. profl. engr., N.Y., N.C. Sr. process devel. engr. Olin Mathieson Chem. Corp., Brandenburg, Ky., 1958-66, Rochester, N.Y., 1958-66; sr. chem. engr. GTE Sylvania, Seneca Falls, N.Y., 1966-74, Eastman Kodak Co., Rochester, 1974-81; prin., treas. Flint & Sherburne Assocs., P.C., Rochester, 1981-89; project engr. Roy F. Weston, Inc., Rochester, 1989-92; engring. mgr. ECCO, Inc. (Environ. Cons. Co., Inc.), Buffalo, 1992-94; pres. ECCO Engring., Buffalo, 1993-94; staff engr. Environ. Products & Svcs., Inc., Rochester, N.Y., 1994-96; pvt. cons. engr. Webster, N.Y., 1996—; cons. water tech. Water Tech. Corp., Tonawanda, N.Y., 1973-76; product rsch. panel Chem. Engring. Mag., 1982-83. Author: Waste Disposal Manual, 1976. Life mem. Rep. Presdl. Task Force, Webster, N.Y., 1986—; mem. Rep. Nat. Com., Webster, 1991-92. 1st lt. USAF, 1954-58, ret. lt. col. USAF Res., 1982. Decorated Meritorious Svc. medal. Mem. NSPE, AIChE, Soc. Am. Mil. Engrs., Res. Officers Assn. (life), Monroe Profl. Engrs. Soc. (environ. com. 1972-75, chmn. 1973-75, bd. dirs. 1982-84, program chmn. 1984), Cons. Engrs. Coun. N.Y. State (program chmn. Rochester chpt. 1986-87, sec. 1987-88, treas. 1989). Episcopalian. Achievements include replacing boiler feedwater regulators, related instrumentation and control systems and blowdown at a N.Y. State U. facility; system design for dry fabric dust collectors to remove fly ash from coal-fired boilers' flue gas. Home: 1132 Woodbridge Ln Webster NY 14580-8709 Office: C Paul McWilliams PE Cons Engr 1132 Woodbridge Ln Webster NY 14580-8709

MCWILLIAMS, CHRIS PATER ELISSA, elementary school educator; b. Cin., Oct. 23, 1937; d. Ray C. and Mary Loretta (Collins) Pater; m. Nabeel David Elissa, Aug. 15, 1964 (dec. Aug. 1975); children: Sue Renee Caplan, Ramsey Nabeel; m. Jim Bill McWilliams, Apr. 14, 1977 (dec. Sept. 1993). BA, Our Lady of Cin. Coll., 1959; MEd, Xavier U., 1965. Cert. tchr. elem., social studies, environ. edn., Tex. Elem. tchr. Cin. Parochial Schs., 1960-64, Champaign County Schs., Urbana, Ohio, 1968; tchr. social studies St. Mary's Elem. Sch., Urbana, 1968-73; tchr. Granbury (Tex.) Ind. Sch. Dist., 1981—; instr. Tarleton State U., Stephenville, Tex., 1989-90. Contbr. (text) Texas: Yesterday, Today and Tomorrow, 1988; music editor (newspaper) Jerusalem Star, 1966. Me. Hood Gen. Hosp. Aux., 1978—; chmn. Hood County Blood Drive, Granbury, 1978-82. Recipient scholarship Our Lady of Cin. Coll., 1955, Betty Crocker Homemaker award, Gen. Mills, 1955. Mem. Nat. Coun. Social Studies, Tex. Alliance for Geog. Edn., Phi Delta Kappa, Delta Kappa Gamma (pres. Lambda Pi chpt. 1988-90, 96—). Roman Catholic. Avocations: piano, reading, needlework, cooking, walking. Home: 204 Northwood Ct Granbury TX 76049-5709

MCWILLIAMS, DENNIS MICHAEL, lawyer; b. Chgo., Jan. 15, 1941; s. Thomas F. and Dorothy A. (Dorney) McW.; divorced; children: Colleen P., Sean D. BA, U. Notre Dame, 1962, BSME, 1969; JD, Loyola U., Chgo., 1968. Bar: Ill. 1968, U.S. Dist. Ct. (no. dist.) Ill. 1968, U.S. Ct. Appeals (7th cir.) 1968, U.S. Ct. Appeals (fed. cir.) 1985. Patent atty. Borg-Warner Corp., Chgo., 1966-72; assoc. Mann Brown & McWilliams, Chgo., 1972-76; ptnr. Mann, McWilliams, Zummer & Sweeney, Chgo., 1976-89, Lee, Mann, Smith, McWilliams, Sweeney & Ohlson, Chgo., 1989—; instr. John Marshall Law Sch., Chgo., 1986—. Mem. ABA (chmn. com. 1980--), Patent Law Assn. Chgo., Union League Club. Avocations: owning race horses, tennis. Office: Lee Mann Smith McWilliams Sweeney & Ohlson 209 S La Salle St Ste 410 Chicago IL 60604-1203

MCWILLIAMS, EDWIN JOSEPH, banker; b. Spokane, Washington, Aug. 11, 1919; s. Frank S. and Alice (Conlan) McW.; m. Betty J. Galbreath, Aug. 15, 1944; children: Laurence, Barbara Anne, Marijoan, Peter. Student, U. Notre Dame, 1937-38, Marquette U., 1938-40; B.S. in Bus. Adminstrn, Gonzaga U., 1943. With Fidelity Mutual Savings Bank, Spokane, 1940-82; exec. v.p. Fidelity Mutual Savings Bank, 1955-58, pres., 1958-82; pres. Fidelity Service Corp., 1983-87; mem. adv. council Wash. State Dept. Commerce and Econ. Devel., 1977-80; U.S. del. Internat. Savs. Bank Inst., 1975, 76, 79; vice chair, dir. NW Edn. Loan Assn; pres., dir. Heritage Funeral Home. Pres. United Crusade Spokane County, 1966; past pres., mem. exec. bd. Inland Empire coun., region 11 exec. com. Boy Scouts Am.; past pres. Spokane Unltd.; mem. adv. coun. Sch. Bus., Gonzaga U.; bd. dirs., mem. exec. com. Expo '74 World's Fair; past mem. bd. regents Ft. Wright Coll., Spokane; past bd. dirs. Sacred Heart Med. Ctr.; past bd. regents Wash. State U.; bd. dirs. Fairmont Meml. Assn. Served to lt. (j.g.) USNR, 1943-45. Mem. Nat. Assn. Mut. Savs. Banks (chmn. 1976-77), Mut. Savs. Banks Assn. State of Wash. (pres. 1980), Am. Savs. and Loan Inst. (past gov. dist. XI), Spokane C. of C. (pres. 1974-75). Roman Catholic. Clubs: Rotary of Spokane, K.C. Home: 1717 S Upper Terrace Rd Spokane WA 99203-3558

MCWILLIAMS, JOHN LAWRENCE, III, lawyer; b. Phila., Dec. 21, 1943; s. John Lawrence Jr. and Elizabeth Dolores (Chevalier) McW.; m. Paula Ann Root, July 19, 1969 (dec.); children: John Lawrence, IV, Robert Root, Anne Elizabeth, David Stanford, Peter Farrell; m. Kathleen Nolan Pradella, Apr. 3, 1993. BS, St. Joseph's U., 1965; JD, Seton Hall U., 1969. Bar: N.J. 1969, N.Y. 1975, U.S. Supreme Ct. 1975, Fla. 1977. Trial atty. regional office SEC, N.Y.C., 1969-72; assoc. Mudge Rose Guthrie & Alexander, N.Y.C., 1972-77; mem. Freeman, Richardson, Watson & Kelly, P.A., Jacksonville, Fla., 1977-89, chmn., pres., 1984-89, ptnr. Squire, Sanders & Dempsey, 1989—; apptd. spl. asst. to U.S. atty. Dist. of N.J., 1971. Trustee Mcpl. Service Dist. Ponte Vedra Beach, 1981-85, chmn. bd. trustees, 1984-85; treas. Ponte Vedra Cmty. Assn., 1980-82; mem. Leadership Jacksonville, 1981, mem. steering com., 1982; dir. Jacksonville County Day Sch., 1985-87; pres. Jacksonville Beaches Ponte Vedra Unit Am. Cancer Soc., 1988-90. Mem. Nat. Assn. Bond Lawyers, The Fla. Bar, Jacksonville C. of C. Republican. Roman Catholic. Clubs: Ponte Vedra, Sawgrass, River. Home: 3040 Timberlake Pt Ponte Vedra Beach FL 32082-3726 Office: Squire Sanders & Dempsey One Enterprise Ctr 225 Water St Ste 2100 Jacksonville FL 32202-5154

MCWILLIAMS, JOHN MICHAEL, lawyer; b. Annapolis, Md., Aug. 17, 1939; s. William J. and Helen (Disharon) McW.; m. Frances Edelen McCabe, May 30, 1970; children: M. Edelen, J. Michael, James McC. B.S., Georgetown U., 1964; LL.B., U. Md., 1967; LLD (hon.), U. Balt., 1993. Bar: Md. 1967, U.S. Supreme Ct. 1970, U.S. Ct. Internat. Trade 1991, U.S. Ct. Mil. Appeals 1992; cert. mediator NASD. Law clk. Chief Judge Roszel C. Thomsen, U.S. Dist. Ct. Md., 1967-68; assoc. Piper and Marbury, Balt., 1968-69; asst. atty. gen. State of Md., 1969-76; gen. counsel Md. Dept. Transp., 1971-76; sr. ptnr. Tydings and Rosenberg, Balt., 1977-97; permanent mem. 4th Cir. Jud. Conf.; mem. panel of disting. neutrals CPR Inst. for Dispute Resolution, 1994—; pres. McWilliams Dispute Resolution, 1997—. Asst. editor Law Rev., U. Md., 1967. Chmn. Md. adv. coun. to Nat. Legal Svcs. Corp., 1975-78; mem. Gov.'s Commn. to Revise Annotated Code of Md., 1973-78; transition dir. Md. Gov.-Elect Harry Hughes, 1978-79; mem. Md. Indsl. Devel. Financing Authority, 1980; mem. Greater Balt. Com., 1979-94; mem. exec. com. Econ. Devel. Coun. Greater Balt., 1979-83; vice chmn. bd. Washington/Balt. Regional Assn., 1980-83; mem. Md. Econ. and Cmty. Devel. Adv. Commn., 1983-87; chmn. bd. Md. Econ. Devel. Corp., 1984-89. Served to 1st lt. U.S. Army, 1958-60. Fellow Am. Bar Found. (bd. dirs. 1986-88, 91-93), Md. Bar Found. (dir. 1980-82); mem. ABA (pres. 1992-93, mem. ho. of dels. 1976—, chmn. 1986-88, chmn. Md. del. 1976-86, bd. editors jour. 1986-88, 91-93), Internat. Acad. Mediators (cert.), Md. Bar Assn. (pres. 1981-82), Nat. Conf. Bar Pres. (exec. council 1982-85), Bar Assn. Balt. City, Am. Law Inst., Am. Judicature Soc. (dir. 1974-81, exec. com. 1975-77), Am. Acad. Jud. Edn. (dir. 1977), Am. Arbitration Assn. (various panels), Md. Law Rev. (trustee 1980-83), Md. Inst. Continuing Edn. Lawyers (trustee 1980-83), Inst. Internat. Bus. Law and Practice (corr.), Md. Club, Rule Day Club. Democrat. Roman Catholic. Home: 3 Merryman Ct Baltimore MD 21210-2815 Office: 6 South St Fl 26 Baltimore MD 21202-3202

MCWILLIAMS, MARGARET ANN, home economics educator, author; b. Osage, Iowa, May 26, 1929; d. Alvin Randall and Mildred Irene (Lane) Edgar; children: Roger, Kathleen. BS, Iowa State U., 1951, MS, 1953; PhD, Oreg. State U., 1968. Registered dietitian. Asst. prof. home econs. Calif.

State U., L.A., 1961-66, assoc. prof., 1966-68, prof., 1968-92, prof. emeritus, 1992—, chmn. dept., 1968-76; pres. Plycon Press, 1978—. Author: Food Fundamentals, 1966, 6th edit., 1995, Nutrition for the Growing Years, 1967, 5th edit., 1993, Experimental Foods Laboratory Manual, 1977, 4th edit., 1994, (with L. Kotschevar) Understanding Food, 1969, Illustrated Guide to Food Preparation, 1970, 7th edit., 1995, (with L. Davis) Food for You, 1971, 2d edit., 1976, The Meatless Cookbook, 1973, (with F. Stare) Living Nutrition, 1973, 4th edit., 1984, Nutrition for Good Health, 1974, 2d edit., 1982, (with H. Paine) Modern Food Preservation, Fundamentals of Meal Management, 1978, 2d edit., 1993, 3d edit., 1997, (with H. Heller) World of Nutrition, 1984, Foods: Experimental Perspectives, 1989, 3d edit., 1997. Chmn. bd. Beach Cities Symphony, 1991-94. Recipient Alumni Centennial award Iowa State U., 1971, Profl. Achievement award, 1977; Phi Upsilon Omicron Nat. Founders fellow, 1964; Home Economist in Bus. Nat. Found. fellow, 1967; Outstanding Prof. award Calif. State U., 1976. Mem. Am. Dietetic Assn., Inst. Food Technologists, Phi Kappa Phi, Phi Upsilon Omicron, Omicron Nu, Iota Sigma Pi, Sigma Delta Epsilon, Sigma Alpha Iota. Home: PO Box 220 Redondo Beach CA 90277-0220

MCWILLIAMS, MICHAEL G., writer, television critic; b. Detroit, Aug. 28, 1952; s. Henry and Mary (Toarmina) McW. BA, Wayne State U., 1975; MFA, Columbia U., 1978. Free-lance writer Detroit News, Monthly Detroit mag., 1979-82, Village Voice, Rolling Stone, TV Guide, Advt. Age, N.Y. Daily News, L.A. Herald Examiner, N.Y.C., 1982-87; TV critic The Detroit News, 1988—. Author: TV Sirens, 1987, (with others) The Premiere Guide to Movies on Video, 1991. Recipient Assn. of Sunday and Feature Editors award, 1st pl. Arts Criticism, 1992. Mem. Phi Beta Kappa. Avocations: TV, movies, theater, music. Office: Detroit News 615 W Lafayette Blvd Detroit MI 48226-3124

MCWILLIAMS, MIKE C., lawyer; b. Dallas, Nov. 10, 1948; s. Earl Dewitt and Mary Louise (Campbell) McW.; m. Sally Swatzell, Sept. 1, 1973; children: Michael, Matthew. BBA in Fin., U. Tex., 1969, JD, 1973. Bar: Tex. 1973. Assoc. Elliott, Meer, Vetter, Denton & Bates, Dallas, 1973-78; ptnr. Denton & Generis, Dallas, 1978-80, Moore & Peterson, P.C., Dallas, 1980-89, Winstead, Sechrest & Minick, Dallas, 1989—. Editor: Texas International Law Journal, 1972-73. Mem. ABA, Tex. State Bar Assn., Dallas Bar Assn., Phi Delta Phi, Beta Gamma Sigma. Office: Winstead Sechrest & Minick 5400 Renaissance Tower 1201 Elm St Dallas TX 75270-2102

MCWILLIAMS, ROBERT HUGH, federal judge; b. Salina, Kans., Apr. 27, 1916; s. Robert Hugh and Laura (Nicholson) McW.; m. Catherine Ann Cooper, Nov. 4, 1942 (dec.); 1 son, Edward Cooper; m. Joan Harcourt, Mar. 8, 1986. A.B., U. Denver, 1938, LL.B., 1941. Bar: Colo. bar 1941. Colo. dist. judge Denver, 1952-60; justice Colo. Supreme Ct., 1961-68, chief justice, 1969-70; judge U.S. Ct. Appeals (10th cir.), Denver, 1970—. Served with AUS, World War II. Mem. Phi Beta Kappa, Omicron Delta Kappa, Phi Delta Phi, Kappa Sigma. Republican. Episcopalian. Home: 137 Jersey St Denver CO 80220-5918 Office: Byron White US Courthouse 1823 Stout St Rm 216 Denver CO 80257-1823

MEACHAM, BRIAN JAY, professional society administrator; b. Westfield, Mass., Oct. 1, 1962; s. Edward L. and Nancy A. (Gyukery) M.; m. Sharon M. Weber, Oct. 22, 1994. BSEE, Worcester Poly. Inst., 1984, MS in Fire Protection Engring., 1991. Registered profl. engr., Conn. Mgr. sys. engring. Gamewell Corp., Medway, Mass., 1984-89; assoc. mgr. detection and alarm group FirePro Inc., Wellesley, Mass., 1989; sr. assoc. FP&C Cons., Inc., Newton, Mass., 1989-92; founder, prin. Meacham Assocs., Westboro, Mass., 1992; prin. fire protection engr. Cerberus AG, Maennedorf, Switzerland, 1993; co-founder, prin. fire protection engr. FireTech, Meilen, Switzerland, 1993-95; tech. dir. Soc. Fire Protection Engrs., Boston, 1995—. Author: The Evolution of Performance-based Codes and Fire Safety Design Methods, 1996; co-author: Introduction to Performance-Based Fire Safety, 1997. Mem. IEEE, Am. Soc. Safety Engrs., Nat. Fire Protection Assn. (mem. several tech. coms. 1990—), Soc. Fire Protection Engrs. (mem. rsch. and engring. edn. coms. 1993—, mem. organizing com. internat. conf. on performance design), Internat. Assn. Fire Safety Sci., Inst. Fire Safety (U.K.). Avocations: music, sports, cooking, outdoor activities. Office: Soc Fire Protection Engrs One Liberty Sq Boston MA 02109

MEACHAM, CHARLES HARDING, government official; b. Newman, Calif., Sept. 21, 1925; s. Vernon A. and Sara (Paulsen) M.; m. June Lorraine Yunker, June 22, 1946; children—Charles Paulsen, Bruce Herbert. B.S., Utah State U., 1950. Biologist Calif. Dept. Fish and Game, 1950-56, Alaska Dept. Fisheries, 1956-59; regional supr. regions II and III Alaska Dept. Fish and Game, 1959-68; dir. internat. fisheries Office Gov. Alaska, 1968-69; commr. U.S. Fish and Wildlife Service, Dept. Interior, 1969-70, dep. asst. sec. for fish and wildlife, pks. and marine resources, commr. Internat. North Pacific Fisheries Commn. and Gt. Lakes Fishery Commn., 1969-70, commr. Internat. Pacific Salmon Fisheries Commn., 1969-70, commr. Great Lakes Fishery Commn., 1969-70; spl. asst. to area dir. U.S. Fish and Wildlife Service, Dept. Interior, Alaska, 1971-74; dir. internat. affairs Office of Gov., Juneau, Alaska, 1975-80; pres. Meacham & Assocs., Anchorage, 1980—; dep. commr. U.S. North Pacific Fur Seal Commn.; mem. Pacific and North Pacific Fisheries Mgmt. Councils, 1976-81; chmn. nat. park system adv. bd. U.S. Dept. Interior. Bd. dir. Resource Devel. Coun. for Alaska. With USMCR, 1943-46. Mem. Am. Fisheries Soc., Wildlife Soc., Pacific Fisheries Biologists, Internat. Assn. Game, Fish and Conservation Commrs., Ducks Unlimited, Alaska Miners Assn., Am. Legion. Club: Elks. Address: PO Box 428 Sequim WA 98382-0428

MEACHAM, CHARLES P., president, capital consulting; b. Susanville, Calif., Apr. 29, 1947; m. Charlene D. Heriot, 1969; 3 children. BS, Humboldt State U., 1969, MS in Fisheries, 1971. Comml. fisherman Bristol Bay, Alaska, 1963-66; with Bumble Bee Seafoods, Bristol Bay, S.E. Alaska, 1967-69; fisheries cons. Winzler & Kelly Engring., Eureka, Calif., 1970; seafood insp. U.S. Army, Ft. Richardson, Alaska, 1971-74; staff biologist Alaska Dept. of Fish and Game, Juneau, Alaska, 1974-75; rsch. biologist Artic Char investigations Alaska Dept. of Fish and Game, Dillingham, Alaska, 1975-77; Bristol Bay rsch. project leader Alaska Dept. of Fish and Game, Anchorage, 1978-81, regional rsch. supr., 1981-89, mgr. fisher program Exxon Valdez oil spill impact assessment, 1990-91; dep. commr. Alaska Dept. of Fish and Game, Juneau, 1991-95; pres. Capital Consulting, 1995—; affiliate faculty U. Alaska, 1983-87; mem. Bering Sea/Aleutians plan team N. Pacific Fisheries Mgmt. Coun., 1989, Alaska Regional Marine Rsch. Bd., 1992—, Pacific Fisheries Mgmt. Coun., 1991-95; commr. Pacific States Marine Fisheries Commn., 1991-95; presdl. appt. as commr. Pacific Salmon Commn., 1991-95. Mem. Mayor's Task Force on Fisheries, Anchorage, 1988-89, Alaska Tourism Coordinating Commn., 1992-95; mem. rev. team Alaska Sci. & Tech. Found., 1989; alt. mem. Exxon Valdez Oil Spill Trustee Coun., 1992-95; mem. adv. bd. Exxon Valdez Trustee Coun., 1997—. Mem. NAS, OSB (fisheries com., 1992-95), Am. Fisheries Soc. (life, v.p. Alaska chpt. 1975, pres. elect 1977, pres. 1978, chair past pres. com. 1995—), Am. Inst. of Fishery Rsch. Biologists. Home: 533 Main St Juneau AK 99801-1153

MEACHAM, STANDISH, historian, educator; b. Cin., Mar. 12, 1932; s. Standish and Eleanor (Rapp) M.; m. Sarah Shartle, Aug. 24, 1957 (div. 1993); children: Edith, Louisa, Samuel. B.A., Yale U., 1954; Ph.D., Harvard U., 1961. Asst. prof. history Harvard U., 1962-67; mem. faculty U. Tex., Austin, 1967—; prof. history U. Tex., 1970—, chmn. dept. history, 1969-72, 84-89, dean Coll. Liberal Arts, 1989-92. Author: Henry Thornton of Clapham, 1964, Lord Bishop: The Life of Samuel Wilberforce, 1970, A Life Apart, 1977, (with R. Fluckiger and Larry Schaaf) Paul Martin, Victorian Photographer, 1977, (with E. M. Burns and Robert Lerner) Western Civilizations, 12th edit., 1993, Toynbee Hall and Social Reform, 1987; editor: (Edward Bulwer) England and the English, 1970. Trustee Brooks Sch., North Andover, Mass., 1983—; dir. Live Oak Fund for Change, 1992, Planned Parenthood of Austin, 1993—, Tex. Low Income Housing Info. Svc., 1996—. Am. Council Learned Socs. fellow, 1965-66, 79-80; Guggenheim Found. fellow, 1972-73. Office: U Tex Garrison Hall 101 Austin TX 78712-1163

MEACHIN, DAVID JAMES PERCY, investment banker; b. Teignmouth, Devon, Eng., Jan. 1, 1941; came to U.S., 1969; s. James Alfred and Ena Annie Meachin; m. Barbara Marshall Maxwell, Sept. 25, 1971; children: Jonathan J.M., Philip D.M. BS in Phys. Sci., U. Natal, Republic of South Africa, 1960; BSChemE, U. Cape Town, Republic of South Africa, 1963; MS in Petroleum Engring., French Petroleum Inst., Paris, 1965; diploma in Indsl. Mgmt., Cambridge (Eng.) U., 1966; MBA with distinction, Harvard U., 1971. Project engr. Humphreys and Glasgow Ltd., London, 1966-69; 2d v.p. investment banking Smith Barney and Co. Inc., N.Y.C. and Tokyo, 1971-75; v.p., gen. mgr. internat. corp. fin. Salomon Bros., N.Y.C. and London, 1975-81; mng. dir. investment banking Merrill Lynch Capital Markets, N.Y.C., 1981-91; chmn., CEO, Cross Border Enterprises L.L.C., 1991—; dir. Millennium Chemicals Inc. Dir. Spartek Emerging Opportunities of India Fund; dir., past chmn. British Am. Ednl. Found.; elder Brick Presbyn. Ch., N.Y.C., 1988—; bd. dirs., vice-chmn. U. Cape Town Found., N.Y.C., 1985—. Mem. Misquamicut Club (bd. govs.), Watch Hill Yacht Club, Hurlingham Club (U.K.), United Oxford and Cambridge Club (U.K.), Harvard Club, Union Club, Sky Club, Kelvin Grove Club (South Africa). Avocations: sailing, golf, tennis, squash. Home: 40 East 94th St New York NY 10128-0740 Office: Cross Border Enterprises LLC 441 Lexington Ave New York NY 10017-3910

MEAD, BEVERLEY TUPPER, physician, educator; b. New Orleans, Jan. 22, 1923; s. Harold Tupper and Helen Edith (Hunt) M.; m. Thelma Ruth Cottingham, June 8, 1947. B.S., U. S.C., 1943; M.D., Med. Coll. S.C., 1947; M.S., U. Utah, 1958. Intern Detroit Receiving Hosp., 1947-48, resident, 1948-51; asst. prof. U. Utah, 1954-61; assoc. prof. U. Ky., 1961-65; prof. psychiatry and behavioral sci. Creighton U. Sch. Medicine, Omaha, 1965—; chmn. dept. Creighton U. Sch. Medicine, 1965-77, assoc. dean for acad. and faculty affairs, 1980-88. *The approval of others does not concern me as much as my approval of myself.*

MEAD, CARL DAVID, educator; b. Cadiz, Ohio, May 4, 1913; s. Carl David and Neva Eloine (Walker) M.; m. Lillian Martha Felton, Apr. 15, 1938; children: Susan, Nancy. Student, Washington and Jefferson Coll., 1932-34; B.S., Ohio State U., 1936, M.A., 1938, Ph.D., 1947. Instr. English Denison U., 1938-39, Ohio State U., 1946-47; faculty Mich. State U., 1948-81, prof. English, 1957-81, head dept., 1959-66; Fulbright lectr. Philippines, 1964; cons., chief univ. adv. group to U. Ryukyus, Okinawa, 1955-57. Author: Yankee Eloquence in the Middle West, 1951, (with others) Prentice-Hall Handbook for Writers, 1951, The American Scholar Today, 1970; Adv. editor: Dodd, Mead & Co, 1963-75; editor: Centennial Review, 1966-82. Served with AUS, 1943-46. Decorated Legion of Merit. Mem. MLA, Am. Studies Assn. Home: 1229 Glenmeadow Ln East Lansing MI 48823-2223

MEAD, DANA GEORGE, diversified industrial manufacturing company executive; b. Cresco, Iowa, Feb. 22, 1936; s. George Francis and Evelyn Grace (Derr) M.; m. Nancy L. Cooper, Apr. 12, 1958; children: Dana George Jr., Mark Cooper. B.S. (Disting. Cadet), U.S. Mil. Acad., 1957; Ph.D., M.I.T., 1967. Commd. 2d lt. U.S. Army, 1957, advanced through grades to col., 1974; service in W. Ger. and Vietnam; White House fellow, 1970-71; staff asst. to Pres. Nixon, 1970-72; assoc. dir., then dep. dir. Domestic Council, White House, 1972-74; permanent prof. social sci. dept., dep. head U.S. Mil. Acad., 1974-78; ret., 1978; v.p. human resources Internat. Paper Co., N.Y.C., 1978-81, v.p., group exec., 1981-87; sr. v.p. Internat. Paper Co., Purchase, 1987-89, exec. v.p., dir. 1989-92; pres., COO Tenneco, Inc., Houston, 1992-93, chmn., CEO, 1994—, also bd. dirs.; CEO, chmn. J.I. Case, Racine, Wis., 1992-94, chmn., 1994-96; bd. dirs. Unicource Worldwide, Inc., Baker Hughes Corp., Logistics Mgmt. Inst., Washington, Textron, Inc., Newport News Shipbuilding Inc. Author articles on nat. security and domestic policy, business and manufacturing planning. Mem. Pres.'s Commn. on White House Fellowships, West Point Soc., N.Y., 1980—, pres., 1981-83; mem. White House Fellows Assn. and Found., 1981-82; bd. dirs. White House Fellows Found., 1978-83, pres., 1978; mem. MIT Vis. Com. Polit. Scis.; mem. bus. coun., mem. bus. roundtable MIT Corp.; trustee George C. Marshall Found. Decorated Legion of Merit with oak leaf cluster, Bronze Star with oak leaf cluster, Meritorious Service medal, Air medal with 3 oak leaf clusters, Army Commendation medal, Presdl. Service badge, Combat Inf. badge; Vietnam Cross Gallantry with palm, silver and bronze stars. Mem. Am. Soc. Corp. Execs., Nat. Assn. Mfg. (chmn. 1995-96), Coun. Fgn. Rels., Assn. Grads. West Point (trustee), Univ. Club, Met. Club (N.Y.). Republican. Home: 14 Fairway Ln Greenwich CT 06830-4011 Office: Tenneco Inc 1275 King St Greenwich CT 06831-2936

MEAD, FRANK WALDRETH, taxonomic entomologist; b. Columbus, Ohio, June 11, 1922; s. Arlington Alfred and Edith May (Harrison) M.; widowed; children: David Harrison, Gregory Scott. BS, Ohio State U., 1947, MS, 1949; PhD, N.C. State U., 1968. Rsch. asst. dept. physiology Ohio State U., Woods Hole, Mass., summer 1941; rsch. asst. dept. entomology Ohio State U., Columbus, 1948-50; Japanese beetle scout bur. entomology and plant quar. USDA, Columbus, summer 1948, biol. aid bur. entomology and plant quar., 1950-53; entomologist div. plant industry Fla. Dept. Agr., Gainesville, 1953-58, 60, biologist IV, 1983-95, emeritus, 1995—; rsch. asst. N.C. State U., Raleigh, 1958-60; state survey entomologist Fed.-State Coop. Survey, Gainesville, 1969-80; courtesy assoc. prof. dept. entomology U. Fla., Gainesville, 1973-95, emeritus, 1995—, Fla. A&M U., Tallahassee, 1977-95, emeritus, 1995—. Co-editor Tri-ology Technical Report; contbr. articles to profl. jours. Bd. dirs., treas. Alachua Audubon Soc., Gainesville, 1968-75, 77-82; bd. dirs. Alachua County Hist. Soc., Gainesville, 1980-82; mem. steering com. Civitan Regional Blood Bank, Gainesville, 1977-79; vol. photographer P.K. Yonge Devel. Rsch. Sch. U. Fla., Gainesville, 1978—. With U.S. Army, 1943-46, PTO. Ohio Acad. Sci. fellow, 1966. Mem. Entomol. Soc. Am. (bd. dirs. S.E. br. 1978-79), Ga. Entomol. Soc., Fla. Entomol. Soc. (hon., sec. 1968-82, Cert. of Appreciation 1975, 82, 91, Cert. of Merit 1986), Fla. Mosquito Control Assn., Entomol. Soc. Washington, Soc. Systematic Biologists, SAR (Benjamin Franklin chpt. Columbus, Ohio), Fla. Track Club. Avocations: photography, jogging, birding. Home: 2035 NE 6th Ter Gainesville FL 32609-3758 Office: Fla Dept Agr and Cons Svcs Divsn Plant Industry PO Box 147100 Gainesville FL 32614-7100

MEAD, GARY L., hotel executive. Pres. LaQuinta Inns, Inc., San Antonio. Office: LaQuinta Inns Inc PO Box 2636 112 E Pecan St San Antonio TX 78299-2636

MEAD, GEORGE WILSON, II, paper company executive; b. Milw., Oct. 11, 1927; s. Stanton W. and Dorothy (Williams) M.; m. Helen Patricia Anderson, Sept. 3, 1949 (div. Feb. 1990); children: Deborah, David, Leslie; m. Susan A. Feith, Aug. 25, 1990. B.S., Yale U., 1950; M.S., Inst. Paper Chemistry, Wis., 1952. With Consol. Papers, Inc., Wisconsin Rapids, Wis., 1952—, v.p. ops., 1962-66, pres., chief exec. officer, 1966-71, chmn. bd., CEO, 1971-93; chmn. bd., 1993—; also bd. dirs. Consol. Papers, Inc., Wisconsin Rapids, Wis.; chmn., dir. Consol. Water Power Co.; bd. dirs. Snap-On Tools Corp., Firstar Corp. Co-chmn. bldg. fund drive Riverview Hosp., Wisconsin Rapids, 1963-64, mem. bd., 1961-77; pres., dir. Consol.'s Civic Found.; bd. dirs. Nat. Coun. for Air and Stream Improvement; chmn. bd. trustees Inst. Paper Sci. and Tech., 1988-90. Mem. TAPPI (bd. dirs. 1969-72), Am. Paper Inst. (bd. dirs. 1967-69, 80—), Chgo. Club, Elks (exalted ruler 1958), Rotary. Office: Consol Papers Inc PO Box 8050 Wisconsin Rapids WI 54495-8050

MEAD, GILBERT D(UNBAR), geophysicist, lawyer; b. Madison, Wis., May 31, 1930; s. Stanton Witter and Dorothy Elizabeth (Williams) M.; m. Jaylee Montague, Nov. 18, 1968; children: Elizabeth, Diana, Stanton, Robert. BS, Yale U., 1952; PhD in Physics, U. Calif., Berkeley, 1962; JD, U. Md., 1991. Physicist theoretical div. NASA Goddard Space Flight Ctr., Greenbelt, Md., 1962-74, head geophysics br., 1974-79; geophysicist crustal dynamics project NASA Goddard Space Flight Ctr., 1979-87; bd. dirs., mem. nominating com. Consolidated Papers, Inc., Wisconsin Rapids, Wis., 1974—. Editor: (with W. Hess) Introduction to Space Science, 1968; contbr. numerous articles to profl. jours. Trustee Beloit Coll., 1976-87, Mead Family Found., 1989—, Arena Stage, Washington, 1991—, Levine Sch. Music, Washington, 1996—. Recipient Outstanding Svc. award Goddard Space Flight Ctr., 1978, Washington Post award for disting. cmty. svc., 1996. Mem. Md. Bar, D.C. Bar. Home: 2700 Virginia Ave NW Apt 701 Washington DC 20037-1908

MEAD, JAMES MATTHEW, insurance company executive; b. Erie, Pa., June 10, 1945; s. James Leonard and Olga (Richter) M.; m. Rhoda Ginsburg, Sept. 2, 1967 (div. 1971); m. Elaine Margaret Lytle, Mar. 8, 1975. BS, Pa. State U., 1967, MA, 1970. Instr. bus. Pa. State U., Middletown, 1968-71; asst. to ins. commr. Commonwealth of Pa., Harrisburg, 1971-74; asst. to pres. Capital Blue Cross, Harrisburg, 1974-78, sr. v.p., 1978-84, pres., CEO, 1984—; bd. dirs. Blue Cross & Blue Shield Assn., Chgo., BCS Fin., Chgo., Fed. Res. Bank Phila., chmn. 1994-95. Contbr. articles on health care to profl. publs. Mem. bd. advisors Pa. State U., 1985-93; chmn. savs. bond campaign for Ctrl. Pa., U.S. Treasury Dept., Harrisburg, 1986-87; bd. dirs. United Way Capital Region, pres. 1994. Paul Harris fellow Rotary Internat., 1988. Mem. Capital Region C. of C. (bd. dirs., treas. 1987-90), Country Club of Harrisburg, Blue Ridge Country Club. Home: 201 Hearth Rd Camp Hill PA 17011-8455

MEAD, JOHN MILTON, banker; b. Schenectady, Oct. 26, 1924; s. Milton Samuel and Jane (Drake) M.; m. Marguerite Ann Stone, Jan. 3, 1948; children: Ann Elizabeth, Jane Stone, Mary Ames. B.S., U. Mo., 1950; postgrad., U. Wis., 1963-65. Auditor Schenectady Trust Co., 1950-51; v.p., auditor First Trust & Deposit Co., Syracuse, N.Y., 1955-77; v.p., compliance officer Key Corp., Albany, N.Y., 1977-86, ret., 1986. Served with USAAF, 1943-46; Served with USAF, 1951-55. Mem. Inst. Internal Auditors (past pres. Central N.Y. chpt.), Am. Legion (past post comdr.). Republican. Presbyterian. Clubs: Marcellus Optimist (past pres.), Glens Falls Country. Home: 27 Yorkshire Dr Queensbury NY 12804-8620

MEAD, JOHN STANLEY, university administrator; b. Indpls., Dec. 9, 1953; s. Judson and Jane (Stanley) M.; m. Virginia Potter, Aug. 11, 1979; children: Christopher, Carolyn. BA, Ind. U., 1976; JD, U. Ill., 1979. Bar: Ill. Staff atty. Ill. Energy Resources Commn., Springfield, 1979-82, staff dir., 1982-85; mgr. coal rsch. Ill. Dept. Energy Natural Resources, Springfield, 1985-87, dir. office of coal devel. and mktg., 1987-89; dir. coal rsch. ctr. So. Ill. U., Carbondale, 1989—; b. dirs. Mid-West Univ. Energy Consortium Inc., Chgo.; mem., past chair Ill. Clean Coal Inst., 1986—. adv. com. Carbondale Bus. Devel. Corp., 1994. Recipient gold medal Tech. Univ. Ostrava, Czech Republic, 1992. Mem. Am. Radio Relay League, Ill. State Bar Assn., Mil. Vehicle Preservation Assn., Carbondale Rotary. Lutheran. Home: RR 4 Box 340 Carbondale IL 62901-9241 Office: So Ill U Coal Rsch Ctr Mail Code 4623 Carbondale IL 62901*

MEAD, LAWRENCE MYERS, JR., retired aerospace executive; b. Plainfield, N.J., May 11, 1918; s. Lawrence Myers and Eleanor Whitman (Machado) M.; m. Janet Chase, Feb. 21, 1942; children—Lawrence Myers, Kirtland Chase, Jonathan Taylor, Bradford Machado. B.S.E., Princeton U., 1940, C.E., 1941; postgrad. mgmt., Harvard Bus. Sch., 1964. With Grumman Corp., Bethpage, N.Y., 1941-93; v.p. tech. ops. Grumman Aerospace Corp., Bethpage, N.Y., 1972-75, sr. v.p. dept. ops., 1975-81, sr. v.p. tech. ops., 1981-83; sr. mgmt. cons., 1983-93. Trustee, police commr., dep. mayor Village of Huntington Bay, N.Y., 1975-80; trustee N.Y.C. Hall of Sci. Fellow Poly. U., 1981. Fellow AIAA; mem. NAE, L.I. Forum on Tech. (bd. dirs., past chmn. bd.), Soc. Logistic Engrs., Soc. Advancement Materials and Process Engring., Princeton U. Alumni Assn. Democrat. Patentee in field; designer A6A Intruder Navy All Weather Bomber, Gulfstream III Exec. Jet Transport. Home: 88 Notch Hill Rd Apt 253 North Branford CT 06471-1850

MEAD, LOREN BENJAMIN, writer, consultant; b. Florence, S.C., Feb. 17, 1930; s. Walter Russell and Dorothy (Nauss) M.; m. Polly A. Mellette, Aug. 25, 1951; children: Walter Russell, Christopher Allen, Barbara Holladay Mead Wise, Philip Sidney. BA, U. of the South, 1951, DD (hon.), 1982; MA, U. S.C., 1951; MDiv, Va. Sem., Alexandria, 1955, DD (hon.), 1984; DD (hon.), Berkeley Div. Sch., New Haven, 1986. Ordained priest Episcopal Ch., 1956. Rector Trinity Episcopal Ch., Pinopolis, S.C., 1955-57, Ch. of the Holy Family, Chapel Hill, N.C., 1957-69; exec. dir. Project Test Pattern, Washington, 1969-74; founder, pres. Alban Inst., Washington, 1974-94. Author: New Hope for Congregations, 1972, Critical Moment, 1988, The Once and Future Church, 1991, More Than Numbers, 1993, Transforming Congregations For The Future, 1994, Five Challenges for the Once and Future Church, 1996. Recipient Spl. Achievement award Interim Pastor Network, 1990. Mem. Acad. Parish Clergy (bd. dirs. 1973-75), Soc. for Advancement of Continuing Edn. for Ministry. Democrat.

MEAD, PHILIP BARTLETT, healthcare administrator, physician; b. Poughkeepsie, N.Y., June 23, 1937; s. Ralph Allen and Altina (Gervin) M.; m. Ann Elaine Smith, June 27, 1964; children: Ralph Allen II, David Smith. BA, Hamilton Coll., 1959; MD, Cornell U., 1963. Diplomate Nat. Bd. Med. Examiners, Am. Bd. Ob-Gyn. Intern in medicine Bellevue Hosp., N.Y.C., 1963-64; resident in ob-gyn. N.Y. Hosp./Cornell Med. Ctr., N.Y.C., 1964-69; asst. prof. U. Vt. Coll. Medicine, Burlington, 1971-76, assoc. prof., 1976-81, prof., 1981—; hosp. epidemiologist Med. Ctr. Hosp. of Vt., Burlington, 1984-93; dir. clin. sys. Vt. Acad. Med. Ctr., Burlington, 1993-95; sr. v.p., med. dir. Fletcher Allen Health Care, Burlington, 1995—. Lt. comdr. M.C., USN, 1969-71. Fellow ACOG, Infectious Disease Soc. Am.; mem. Infectious Disease Soc. Ob-Gyn. (pres. 1987-88), Soc. Hosp. Epidemiologists, Phi Beta Kappa, Alpha Omega Alpha. Republican. Methodist. Home: 10 Pinehurst Dr Shelburne VT 05482-7240 Office: Fletcher Allen Health Care 111 Colchester Ave Burlington VT 05401-1473 also: 1 S Prospect St Burlington VT 05401-3444

MEAD, PHILOMENA, mental health nurse; b. Yonkers, N.Y., June 23, 1934; d. Alfonso F. and Jennie (Saltarelli) D'Amato; m. Kenneth Mead, Nov. 10, 1956; children: Scott Kenneth, Jeanne Bette. RN, St. Vincents Hosp., Bridgeport, Conn., 1955; BS in Psychology, Sacred Heart U., 1980; cert. in nursing mgmt., Fairfield U., 1988. Cert. psychiat. mental health nurse, nursing specialist, nat. chem. dependency nurse, CPR. Day supr.-relief, night supr. Hall Brooke Hosp., Westport, Conn., 1956-58, day supr., asst. dir. nurses, 1958-66, evening supr.-relief, 1967-68, team nurse, 1974-83, coord. nursing care, 1983-86, adminstrv. coord., 1986-87, nursing care coord. substance abuse treatment unit, 1987-91; charge evening nurse Carolton Hosp., Fairfield, Conn., 1971-73; nurse psychiat. emergency rm. and brief treatment unit West Haven (Conn.) VA, 1991—, mem. staff psychiat. emergency rm., 1995-97, ret., 1997. Roman Catholic. Avocation: genealogy. Home: 67 Adams Rd Fairfield CT 06430-3018

MEAD, PRISCILLA, state legislator; m. John L. Mead; children: John, Willian, Neel, Sarah. Student, Ohio State U. Councilwoman Upper Arlington, Ohio, 1982-90, mayor, 1986-90; mem. Ohio Ho. of Reps. Mem. Franklin County Child Abuse and Neglect Found., Coun. for Ethics and Econs. Recipient Svc. award Northwest Kiwanis, Woman of Yr. award Upper Arlington Rotary, Citizen of Yr. award U.S. C. of C. Mem. LWV, Upper Arlington Edn. Found., Jr. League Columbus, Upper Arlington C. of C., Delta Gamma. Republican. Home: 2281 Brixton Rd Columbus OH 43221-3117 Office: Ohio Ho of Reps State House Columbus OH 43215*

MEAD, TERRY EILEEN, clinic administrator, consultant; b. Portland, Oreg., Mar. 14, 1950; d. Everett L. and Jean (Nonken) Richardson; divorced; 1 child, Sean Knute Wade Adcock. AA summa cum laude, Seattle U., 1972; postgrad., U. Wash., 1971. Project mgr. Assoc. Univ. Physician, Seattle, 1971-74; pathology supr. Swedish Hosp., Seattle, 1974-77; svcs. supr. Transamerica, Seattle, 1977-78; various mgmt. positions Providence Hosp., Seattle, 1978-83; CEO Mead's Med. Mgmt. Cons. Firm, Chiloquin, Oreg., 1980—; adminstr. Evergreen Surg. Ctr., Kirkland, Wash., 1983-86; bus. mgr. Ketchikan (Alaska) Gen. Hosp., 1986—; instr. U. Alaska, Ketchikan, 1990; adminstr. Bethel (Alaska) Family Clinic, 1994—; CEO Southeast Oreg. Rural Health Network, 1996—, Mead's Med. Mgmt. Inc., 1980—; sec. S.E. adv. bd. U. Alaska, Ketchikan, 1987-94; cons. to hosps. and physicians, Wash., Alaska, 1980—; mgr. Practice Mgmt. Cons., Seattle, 1982-83. Mem. City Charter Rev. Com., Ketchikan, 1990-94; High Sch. Facilities Com. Ketchikan, 1990; S.E. dir. search com. U. Alaska, Ketchikan, 1990; treas. Calvary Bible Ch., Ketchikan, 1989-91; bd. dirs. S.E. Alaska Symphony, 1992-94, Jr. Achievement, 1992-93; chmn. fin. com. City of Bethel, 1994-96. Mem. Rotary Internat. Avocations: computers, politics, fishing, music, writing. Home: PO Box 1287 Chiloquin OR 97624-1287 Office: PO Box 379 Chiloquin OR 97624-0379

MEADE, ANGELA KAYE, special education educator; b. Bryon, Ohio, Mar. 14, 1969; d. Douglas MacAuther and Thelma Judy (Williams) Smith; m. Steven Andrew Meade, June 1, 1991; 1 child, Alexander Jefferson. AA in Edn. summa cum laude, S.W. Va. C.C., 1989, AA in Gen. Studies, 1989; BA in English with distinction, U. Va., 1992, M Tchg. in Spl. Edn., 1992. Cert. K-12 tchr. learning disabilities and mental retardation, Va. Tchr. spl. edn. Newport News (Va.) Pub. Schs., 1992—; yearbook sponsor Newport News (Va.) Pub. Schs., 1992-95, implemented collaborative tchg. program, 1994-95; counselor Summer Yough Program, Lebanon and Richmond, Va., 1993-94. Organizer Spl. Olympics Va., Newport News, 1993-94. Mem. ASCD, Internat. Reading Coun., Newport News Reading Coun. (co-chmn. banquet 1993-95).. Avocations: reading, writing. Office: Reservoir Mid Sch 301 Heacox Ln Newport News VA 23608-1809

MEADE, DALE MICHAEL, laboratory director; b. Lodi, Wis., Aug. 7, 1939; s. Merlin Jones and Valborg (Olson) M.; m. Helen Eva Flentje, Oct. 26, 1959 (div. Dec. 1979); children: Loretta, Carla Fleming. BS with high honors in Elec. Engring., U. Wis., 1961, MS in Physics, 1962, PhD in Physics, 1965. Asst. prof. physics U. Wis., Madison, 1967-69, assoc. prof., 1969-72, prof., 1972-74; head FM-1 Princeton (N.J.) Plasma Physics Lab., 1973, head PDX Ops., 1975-80, head exptl. divsn. rsch. dept., head TFTR rsch. program, 1980-82, head exptl. divsn., head TFTR rsch. ops. divsn., 1982-86, head exptl. physics rsch. dept., head TFTR project, 1986-91, dep. dir., 1991—. Recipient Disting. Svc. Citation U. Wis. Coll. Engring., Madison, 1990, Disting. Assoc. award U.S. Dept. Energy, Washington, 1994. Fellow Am. Phys. Soc.; mem. AAAS. Office: Princeton Plasma Physics Lab PO Box 451 US Rt 1 N Princeton NJ 08543

MEADE, EVERARD KIDDER, JR., retired broadcasting and publishing executive; b. Tappahannock, Va., Oct. 3, 1919; s. Everard Kidder and Della (Wright) M.; m. Alice Amory Winslow, Sept. 1944 (div. 1971); children: Mary Devereux, Everard Kidder III, Susanna Fitzhugh. B.S., U.S. Mil. Acad., 1943. Mem. Hoover Commn., U.S. Depts. Def. and State, 1946-53; v.p. Colonial Williamsburg, Inc., 1953-55; assoc. Earl Newsom & Co., 1955-57; v.p. CBS Inc., 1957-82. Served from 2d lt. to lt. col. U.S. Army, 1939-46. Mem. SAR, VFW, Fgn. Policy Assn., Century Assn. (N.Y.C.), Army and Navy Club, Sailfish Club of Fla., Soc. Colonial Wars, Bar Harbor (Maine) Yacht Club, Bath and Tennis Club (Fla.), Rockaway (N.Y.) Hunting Club. Episcopalian.

MEADE, KENNETH ALBERT, minister; b. Sweet Valley, Pa., June 14, 1935; s. Delbert H. and Dorothea I. (Myers) M.; m. Jeanette H. Quigley, Dec. 18, 1954 ; children: Jane M. Meade Ulm, Mark K. Ministerial cert., Ea. Christian Inst., East Orange, N.J., 1955; DD (hon.), Milligan Coll., Tenn., 1986, Ea. Christian Coll., Bel Air, Md., 1986. Ordained to ministry Ch. of Christ, 1955. Student min. Ch. of Christ, Bklyn. and Greenpoint, N.Y., 1952-53; mem. Meade-Bennett Evangelistic Team, East Orange, 1953-55; sr. min. Ch. of Christ at Manor Woods, Rockville, Md., 1956—; pres. N.Am. Christian Conv., Cin., 1986, Ea. Christian Conv., Rockville, 1969, 74, 82. Contbr. numerous articles to religion mags. Trustee Milligan Coll. Recipient Award of Honor, Am. Legion, 1952, Highest Comml. award Lehman High Sch. Alumni Assn., 1952. Office: Ch of Christ at Manor Woods 5300 Norbeck Rd Rockville MD 20853-2303

MEADE, ROBIN MICHELE, news anchor, reporter; b. New London, Ohio, Apr. 29, 1969; d. Linro and Sharon Faye (Shepherd) M.; m. Timothy Harold Keager, Nov. 6, 1993. Student, Malone Coll., 1987, 88, 89, Ashland U., 1989, 90, 91. Reporter, anchor, prodr. WMFD-TV and WVNO Radio, Mansfield, Ohio, 1989-92; anchor, reporter WJW TV8, Cleve., 1993; anchor WCMH TV4, Columbus, Ohio, 1993-94; morning news anchor, health reporter WSVN 7-News, Miami, Fla., 1994-95; morning news anchor, reporter WMAQ Ch. 5, Chgo., 1995—. Office: WMAQ-NBC 5 454 N Columbus Dr Chicago IL 60611-5501

MEADER, JOHN DANIEL, state agency administrator, judge; b. Ballston Spa, N.Y., Oct. 22, 1931; s. Jerome Clement and Doris Luella (Conner) M.; m. Joyce Margaret Cowin, Mar. 2, 1963; children: John Daniel Jr., Julia Rae, Keith Alan. BA, Yale U., 1954; JD, Cornell U., 1962. Bar: N.Y. 1963, U.S. Dist. Ct. (no. dist.) N.Y. 1963, U.S. Ct. Appeals (2d cir.) 1966, U.S. Supreme Ct. 1967, U.S. Ct. Mil. Appeals 1973, Ohio 1978, U.S. Dist. Ct. (no. dist.) Ohio 1979, Fla. 1983, U.S. Ct. Appeals (4th cir.) 1992, U.S. Ct. Appeals (fed. cir.) 1993. Sales engr. Albany (N.Y.) Internat. Corp., 1954-59; asst. track coach Cornell U., 1959-62; asst. sec., asst. to pres. Albany Internat. Corp., 1962-65; asst. atty. gen. State of N.Y., Albany, 1965-68; ops. counsel, attesting sec. GE, Schenectady, 1968-77; gen. counsel, asst. sec. Glidden div. SCM Corp., Cleve., 1977-81; chmn. bd., pres. Applied Power Tech. Co., Fernandina Beach, Fla., 1981-84; pres. Applied Energy, Inc., Ballston Spa, 1984-88; judge N.Y. State Workers Compensation Bd., Albany, 1988—; dir. Saratoga Mut. Fire Ins. Co. Author: Labor Law Manual, 1972, Contract Law Manual, 1974, Patent Law Manual, 1978. Candidate U.S. Ho. of Reps., 29th Dist. N.Y., 1964, N.Y. Supreme Ct., 1975, 87, 93. Col. JAGC, USAR, 1968—, dep. staff judge adv. 3d U.S. Army & Cen. Command, 1984. Nat. AAU High Sch. 1000 Yard Indoor Track Champion, 1949, Nat. AAU Prep. Sch. 440 and 880 Yard Indoor Track Champion, 1950, Nat. AAU Outstanding Performer award, Melrose Games Assn., 1950, Heptagonal Track 880-Yard Champion 1954. Mem. ABA, N.Y. State Bar Assn., Fla. Bar, Amelia Island Plantation Club, Cyprus Temple Club, Yale Club Jacksonville (pres.), Masons. Republican. Presbyterian. Home: 271 Round Lake Rd Ballston Lake NY 12019-1714 Office: NY State Workers Compensation Bd 100 Broadway Albany NY 12241-0001

MEADOR, CHARLES LAWRENCE, management and systems consultant, educator; b. Dallas, Oct. 7, 1946; s. Charles Leon and Dorothy Margaret (Brown), m. Diane E. Collins, May 18, 1985. BSME with honors, U. Tex., 1970; MSME, MS in Mgmt., MIT, 1972. Mem. engring. staff Union Carbide Corp., Houston, 1967-68; instr. Alfred P. Sloan Sch. Mgmt. MIT, Cambridge, 1972-75, asst. dir. Ctr. Info. Systems Rsch., 1976-78, lectr. Sch. Engring., co-dir. Macro-Enging. Rsch. Group, 1978—; founder, pres. Decision Support Tech., Inc., 1974-92; co-founder, vice-chmn., dir. Software Productivity Rsch., Inc., 1985-87; pres., dir. The Softbridge Group, 1989-92; founder, pres. Mgmt. Support Tech. Corp., 1992—; bd. dirs. Coordinated Svcs. Network, Inc., 1993-96; sr. v.p., chief info. officer CIGNA Property and Casualty, 1995—. Editor: How Big and Still Beautiful? Macro-Engineering Revisited, 1980, Macro-Engineering: The Rich Potential, 1981, Macro-Engineering and the Future: A Management Perspective, 1982, Macro-Engineering: Global Infrastructure Solutions, 1992; mem. editorial adv. bd. Computer Comm., 1979-91; mem. editorial bd. Comunicacion e Informatica, 1980—; author papers in field. NSF trainee, 1970; MIT Wilfred Lewis fellow, 1971; Draper Lab. fellow, 1974. Mem. Computer Soc. IEEE (vice-chmn. Ea. Hemisphere and Latin Am. area com. 1977-83), Am. Soc. for Macro-Engring. (bd. dirs. 1992—), Cosmos Club, St. Botolph's Club, Sigma Xi, Tau Beta Pi, Pi Tau Sigma. Home: 3 Windy Hill Ln Wayland MA 01778-2612 Office: Mgmt Support Tech Corp 3 Speen St Framingham MA 01701-4658

MEADOR, DANIEL JOHN, law educator; b. Selma, Ala., Dec. 7, 1926; s. Daniel John and Mabel (Kirkpatrick) M.; m. Janet Caroline Heilmann, Nov. 19, 1955; children: Janet Barrie, Anna Kirkpatrick, Daniel John. B.S., Auburn U., 1949; J.D., U. Ala., 1951; LL.M., Harvard U., 1954. Bar: Ala. 1951, Va. 1961. Law clk. to U.S. Supreme Ct. Justice Hugo L. Black, 1954-55; assoc. firm Lange, Simpson, Robinson & Somerville, Birmingham, 1955-57; faculty U. Va. Law Sch., 1957-66, prof. law, 1961-66; prof., dean U. Ala. Law Sch., 1966-70; James Monroe prof. law U. Va., Charlottesville, 1970-94, prof. emeritus, 1994—; asst. atty. gen. U.S., 1977-79, dir. grad. program for judges, 1979-95; Fulbright lectr., U.K., 1965-66; vis. prof. U.S. Mil. Acad., 1984; Chmn. Southeastern Conf. Assn. Am. Law Schs., 1964-65; chmn. Cts. Task Force Nat. Adv. Commn. on Criminal Justice, 1971-72; dir. appellate justice project Nat. Center for State Cts., 1972-74; mem. Adv. Council on Appellate Justice, 1971-75, Council on Role of Cts., 1978-84; bd. dirs. State Justice Inst., 1986-92. Author: Preludes to Gideon, 1967, Criminal Appeals-English Practices and American Reforms, 1973, Mr. Justice Black and His Books, 1974, Appellate Courts: Staff and Process in the Crisis of Volume, 1974, (with Carrington and Rosenberg) Justice on Appeal, 1976, Impressions of Law in East Germany, 1986, American Courts, 1991, (with J. Bernstein) Appellate Courts in the United States, 1994, His Father's House, 1994, (with Rosenberg and Carrington) Appellate Courts: Structures, Functions, Processes, and Personnel, 1994; editor: Hardy Cross Dillard: Writings and Speeches, 1995; editor Va. Bar News, 1962-65; contbr. articles to profl. jours. Served to 1st lt. AUS, 1951-53. Decorated Bronze Star.; IREX fellow German Dem. Republic, 1983. Mem. ABA (chmn. standing com. on fed. jud. improvements 1987-90), Ala. Bar Assn., Va. Bar Assn. (exec. com. 1983-86), Am. Law Inst., Am. Judicature Soc. (bd. dirs. 1975-77, 80-83), Soc. Pub. Tchrs. Law, Am. Soc. Legal History (bd. dirs. 1968-71), Order of Coif, Raven Soc., Phi Delta Phi, Omicron Delta Kappa, Kappa Alpha. Presbyn. Office: U Va Sch Law 580 Massie Rd Charlottesville VA 22903-1738

MEADOR, JOHN MILWARD, JR., university dean; b. Louisville, Nov. 4, 1946; s. John Milward and Ruth Inez (Miller) M.; m. Judith Ann Hay, Dec. 22, 1969; children: John Milward III, Elise Kathleen. BA, U. Louisville, 1968; MA, U. Tex., 1972, MLS, 1973; cert. in pub. adminstrn., U. Utah, 1982. Cert. tchr., Ky., Tex. Stacks supr. U. Louisville Librs., 1965-68; English bibliographer M.D. Anderson Libr. U. Houston, 1973-74, head reference dept. social scis. and humanities, 1974-77, head gen. reference dept., 1977-80; asst. dir. pub. svcs. Marriott Libr. U. Utah, Salt Lake City, 1980-84; dean libr. svcs. S.W. Mo. State U., Springfield, 1984-93; dean librs. U. Miss., Univeristy, 1993—; bd. dirs. Mo. Libr. Network Corp., 1984-90, St. Louis, S.W. Mo. Libr. Network, Springfield; cons. Dayco Corp., Springfield, 1984-86; chmn. Mo. Northwestern Online Total Integrated Systems (NOTIS) Users Group, 1988-89. Co-author: The Robinson Jeffers Collection at the University of Houston, 1975; contbr. articles to profl. jours. Sponsor Community Alternative Svc. Program, Springfield and St. Louis, 1985-93; mem. governing bd. Mo. Rsch. and Edn. Network, MOREnet, 1991-93; With U.S. Army, 1969-71, Vietnam. Recipient Nat. Essay award Propeller Club of U.S., 1964; named to Honorable Order of Ky. Colonels, Gov. Ky., 1978; summer scholar English-Speaking Union, Edinburgh, Scotland, 1968; Apple Computer's Higher Edn. Acad. Devel. Donation Program grantee, 1990. Mem. ALA, Am. Assn. for Higher Edn., Assn. Coll. Rsch. Librs., Bibliog. Soc. Am., Libr. Adminstrn. and Mgmt. Assn., other profl. orgns., English-Speaking Union Club, Rotary (chmn. students guests com. Springfield chpt. 1986-89, chmn. scholarships com. 1989-90, bd. dirs. 1990-91, bd. dirs. Oxford chpt. 1995-96). Avocations: raising pure bred airedale terriers, fishing, book collecting. Home: PO Box 787 University MS 38677-0787 Office: U Miss J D Williams Libr University MS 38677

MEADOR, RON, newspaper editor, writer; b. Buffalo, N.Y., Nov. 24, 1952; s. Meril E. and Evelyn (Lyons) M.; divorced; 1 child, Benjamin Brian. BA, Ind. U., 1975. Copy editor The Courier-Journal, Louisville, 1975-78, The New York Times, 1978-80; reporter, state editor, city editor, asst. mng. editor Star Tribune, Mpls., Minn., 1980—; mem. editl. bd. Star Tribune, Mpls. Mem. Investigative Reporters and Editors, Inc., Nat. Conf. Editl. Writers. Office: Star Tribune 425 Portland Ave Minneapolis MN 55415-1511

MEADORS, ALLEN COATS, health administrator, educator; b. Van Buren, Ark., May 17, 1947; s. Hal Barron and Allene Coats (Means) M. AA, Saddleback Coll., 1981; BBA, U. Cen. Ark., 1969; MBA, U. No. Colo., 1974; M. in Pub. Adminstrn., U. Kans., 1975; MA in Psychology, Webster U., 1979; MA in Health Svcs. Mgmt., 1980, PhD in Adminstrn, So. Ill. U., 1981. Assoc. adminstr. Forbes Hosp., Topeka, 1971-73; asst. dir. health svcs. devel. Blue Cross Blue Shield of Kans., Topeka, 1973-76; asst. dir. Kansas City Health Dept. (Mo.), 1976-77; program dir., asst. prof. So. Ill. U., Carbondale, and Webster U., St. Louis, 1978-82; assoc. prof., dir. div. health adminstrn. U. Tex., Galveston, 1982-84; exec. dir. N.W. Ark. Radiation Therapy Inst., Springdale, Ark., 1984-87; prof., chmn. dept. health adminstrn. U. Okla., Oklahoma City, dean Coll. Pub. Health, 1989-90; mem. faculty Calif. State U., Long Beach, 1977-81; grad. faculty U. Ark. Sch. Bus. Adminstrn., Fayetteville, 1984-87; prof., chmn. dept. health adminstrn. U. Okla., 1987-90, dean Coll. of Pub. Health, 1989-90; dean Coll. Health, Social and Pub. Svcs. Ea. Wash. U., Cheney, 1990-94; CEO Pa. State U., Altoona, 1994—; cons. Surgeon Gen. Office and Air Force System Command. Bd. dirs. Martin Luther King Hosp., Health Care Svcs. Adv. Bd.; bd. dirs., mem. exec. com. Altoona Symphony Orch.; bd. dirs. Altoona Hosp., 1994—, Home Health Agy., 1995—, Altoona Enterprises, Inc., 1994—. Served with Med. Service Corps, USAF, 1969-73. Fellow Am. Coll. Healthcare Execs., Ark. Hosp. Assn.; mem. Am. Hosp. Assn. Contbr. articles to profl. jours. Home: PO Box 9 Altoona PA 16603-0009 Office: Pa State U 3000 Ivyside Park Altoona PA 16601-3760

MEADORS, HOWARD CLARENCE, JR., electrical engineer; b. Chgo., July 31, 1938; s. Howard Clarence and Eileen May (Baker) M.; m. Phyllis Anne Rennebaum, July 18, 1964; children: Henry Charles, William Howard, Laura Phyllis, Pamela Susan. SB, MIT, 1960, SM, 1962, Profl. Degree in Elec. Engring., 1964; PhD, Poly. Inst. NY., 1976. Mem. tech. staff Bell Tel. Labs., Inc., Holmdel, N.J., 1966-82; disting. mem. tech. staff AT&T Info. Systems Labs., Holmdel, 1983-85, supr. product devel., 1985-86; supr. adv. data communications AT&T Bell Labs., Middletown, N.J., 1986-91; Disting. mem. tech. staff AT&T Bus. Communications Systems, Holmdel, N.J., 1991-94; disting. mem. tech. staff AT&T Network Systems, Holmdel, N.J., 1994-96, Lucent Technologies, Holmdel, N.J., 1996—; ednl. counselor MIT, 1973—, regional vice chmn., 1983-96, ctrl. N.J. chmn., 1996—. Inventor in field. With Signal Corps, U.S. Army, 1964-66. Mem. IEEE (sr. mem. 1987), Sigma Xi, Eta Kappa Nu. Office: Lucent Techs Crawfords Corner Rd Holmdel NJ 07733

MEADOW, LYNNE (CAROLYN MEADOW), theatrical producer and director; b. New Haven, Nov. 12, 1946; d. Frank and Virginia R. Meadow. BA cum laude, Bryn Mawr Coll., 1968; postgrad., Yale U., 1968-70. Dir. Theatre Communications Group, 1978-80; adj. prof. SUNY, Stony Brook, 1975-76, Yale U., Circle in the Sq., 1977-78, 89-91, NYU, 1977-80; theatre and music/theatre panelist Nat. Endowment for Arts, 1977-88; artistic advisor Fund for New Am. Plays, 1988-90. Artistic dir. Manhattan Theatre Club, N.Y.C., 1972—; guest dir. Nat. Playwrights Conf., Eugene O'Neill Theatre Ctr., 1975-77, Phoenix Theatre, 1976; dir. Ashes for Manhattan Theatre Club and N.Y. Shakespeare Festival, 1977; prodr. off-Broadway shows Ain't Misbehavin', 1978, Crimes of the Heart, 1981, Miss Firecracker Contest, 1984, Frankie and Johnny, 1987, Eastern Standard, 1988, Lisbon Traviata, 1989, Lips Together, Teeth Apart, 1991, Four Dogs and a Bone, 1993, Love! Valour! Compassion!, 1994; dir. Principia Scritoriae, 1986, Woman in Mind, 1988 (Drama Desk award), Eleemosynary, 1989, Absent Friends, 1991; dir. Broadway prodn. A Small Family Business, 1992, The Loman Family Picnic, 1993, Nine Armenians, 1996; co-prodr. off-Broadway and Broadway show Mass Appeal, 1981. Recipient Citation of Merit Nat. Coun. Women, 1976, Outer Circle Critics award 1977, Drama Desk award, 1977, Obie award for Ashes, 1977, Margo Jones award for Continued Encouragement New Playwrights, 1981, Critics Circle award Outstanding Revival on or off Broadway for Loot, 1986, Lucille Lortel award for Outstanding Achievement, 1987, Spl. Drama Desk award, 1989, N.Y. Drama Critics Circle award Best Fgn. Play for Aristocrats, 1989, Torch of Hope award, 1989, Manhattan Mag. award, 1994, Lee Reynolds award League Profl. Theatre Women, 1994; named Northwood Inst. Disting. Woman of Yr., 1990, Person of Yr., Nat. Theatre Conf., 1992. Office: Manhattan Theatre Club 453 W 16th St Fl 2 New York NY 10011-5813

MEADOW, SUSAN ELLEN, magazine editor and publisher; b. N.Y.C., Dec. 17, 1936; d. Sol and Betty (Greene) Raunheim; m. Alvin Harvey Meadow, Aug. 17, 1958 (dec. 1994); children—Eric, Douglas, Peter. B.A. in English, U. Mich., 1958; M.S. in Edn., Iona Coll., 1967. Asst. editor N.Y. State Pharmacist, N.Y.C., 1958-60; mng. editor Westchester mag., White Plains, N.Y., 1969-70; editor, pub. Spotlight, Mamaroneck, N.Y., 1977-96. Bd. dirs. ARC, Rye, 1981—; Westchester-Putnam div. Diabetes Assn. Am.; mem. adv. council Westchester Community Coll. Found., 1984-85. Recipient plaque Leukemia Soc., 1983, Am. Cancer Soc., 1984. Mem. Westchester Women in Communications (excellence in periodicals award 1982), Advt. Club Westchester. Democrat. Jewish. Office: Meadow Pub 126 Library Ln Mamaroneck NY 10543-3608*

MEADOWS, DONALD FREDERICK, librarian; b. Regina, Sask., Can., Jan. 13, 1937; s. Frederick John and Doris Eileen (Willock) M.; m. Ruth Susan Cochran, June 10, 1960; children—Scott Frederick, George Edward. B.A., U. Sask., 1962; B.L.S., U. B.C., 1968. Library cons. Sask. Provincial Library, Regina, 1968-69; asst. provincial librarian Sask. Provincial Library, 1969-70, provincial librarian, province of Sask., 1970-81; dir. Met. Toronto Library, 1981-86; dir. Vancouver Island Regional Library, Nanaimo, B.C., Can., 1986—, also bd. dirs. Mem. Canadian Library Assn., ALA, B.C. Library Assn. Mem. United. Ch. Can. Office: Vancouver Island Regional Library, PO Box 3333, Nanaimo, BC Canada V9R 5N3

MEADOWS, GEORGE LEE, communications company executive; b. Toronto, Ont., Can., Nov. 17, 1938; m. Donna McKay, Sept. 26, 1964; children: Lee Ann, Shelly. BA, U. Toronto, 1963. Chartered acct. Acct. Clarkson Gordon, Toronto, 1963-73; v.p. fin. Project Group Can. Ltd., Toronto, 1973-74; sec.-treas. Southam Communications Ltd., Toronto, 1974-77, v.p., 1976-77; asst. to pres. Southam Inc., Toronto, 1977-78, v.p. corp. devel., 1978-84, sr. v.p. communications group, 1984-87; mng. dir., chief exec. officer Selkirk Communications Ltd., Toronto, 1987-88, pres., chief exec. officer, 1988—; chmn. Niagara TV Ltd., Selkirk Broadcasting Ltd., Selkirk Communications Inc., Selkirk Communications (Hallandale) Inc.; pres. Selkirk Communications Corp., Selkirk Films Ltd., Selkirk Holdings; bd. dirs. B.C. Broadcasting Co. Ltd., Calgary TV Ltd., Can. Satellite Communications Inc., Lethbridge TV Ltd., Okanagan Valley TV Co. Ltd., Branksome Hall, U. Toronto Press. Mem. Can. Inst. Chartered Accountants. Clubs: Royal Can. Yacht. Avocations: sailing, skiing, squash, badminton, tennis. Office: Univ of Toronto Press Inc, 10 St Mary St Ste 700, Toronto, ON Canada M4Y 2W8

MEADOWS, JUDITH ADAMS, law librarian, educator; b. Spartanburg, S.C., June 5, 1945; d. Thomas Taylor and Virginia (Dayton) Adams; m. Bruce R. Meadows; children: Beth Ann Blackwood, Ted Adams Meadows. BA, Am. U., 1967; MLS, U. Md., 1979. Law libr. Aspen Sys. Corp., Gaithersburg, Md., 1979-81; dir. Fairfax (Va.) Law Libr., 1981-84, State Law Libr., Helena, Mont., 1984—; vis. prof. U. Wash., Seattle, 1994; adj. prof. U. Great Falls, Mont., 1989-96; presiding ofcl. Gov.'s Conf. on Libr. Info. Svc., Helena, Mont., 1991. Author: (book chpts.) From Yellow Pads to Computers, 1991, Law Librarianship, 1994; contbr. articles to profl. jours. Bd. dirs. Helena Presents, 1986-92, Holter Mus. Art, 1995—. Recipient Disting. Svc. award State Bar of Mont., 1991. Mem. Am. Assn. Law Librs. (treas. 1992-95, v.p., v.p. 1996—, pres. 1997—), N.W. Consortium of Law Librs. (pres.), Mont. Libr. Assn. (sec. 1986-88). Avocations: gourmet cooking, cross-country skiing, reading, gardening. Office: State Law Libr Mont Justice Bldg 215 N Sanders St Helena MT 59601-4522

MEADOWS, LOIS ANNETTE, elementary education educator; b. Harrisville, W.Va., Jan. 12, 1948; d. Orvle Adam and Una Pauline (Slocum) Ingram; m. David Alan Meadows, June 15, 1969; children: Lynecia Ann, Eric Justin. BA, Glenville State Coll., 1969; MA, W.Va. U., 1980. Cert. music, elem. edn., reading, W.Va. Tchr. grade six Acad. Park-Portsmouth (Va.) City Schs., 1969-73; elem. substitute Wood County Schs., Parkersburg, W.Va., 1973-77; real estate agt. Nestor Realty, Parkersburg, 1974-77; tchr. grade five/music Emerson Elem. Wood County Schs., Parkersburg, W.Va., 1977-78, tchr. grade three, 1978—; edn. cons. World Book, Parkersburg, 1986—; mentor tchr.-trainer Wood County Schs., parkersburg, 1990—; W.Va. S.T.E.P. Test com./trainer W.Va. Dept. Edn., Charleston, 1994—, mem. writing assessment com., 1994—; grant writer and speaker in field; mem. W.Va. Dept. Edn. State Writing Manual Com., 1996—. Author: (reading projects) Operation Blackout, 1986-94 (grant 1994), The Reading Room, 1988 (grant 1990), Storytime at the Mall, 1986— (grant 1994, 95). Life mem. Emerson PTA, Parkersburg, 1977—; Sunday Sch. tchr. North Parkersburg Bapt. Ch., 1976—, children's choir dir., 1976-88; fund raiser local charities, Parkersburg. Women of Excellence and Leadership Timely Honored award, W. Va. State Reading Tchr. of Yr., 1988, Finalist W. Va. State Tchr. of Yr., W.Va. Dept. Edn., 1993, Wood County Tchr. of Yr., 1993, Ashland Oil Golden Apple Achiever award, 1995, Wood Co. PTA Outstanding Educator of Yr. award, 1995-96, award for ann. contbrs. and project work Emerson PTA. Mem. W.Va. Reading Assn. (pres. 1993-94, mem. chmn. 1994—), Internat. Reading Assn., Wood County Reading Coun. (past pres. 1986-88, 90-92), Am. Fedn. Tchrs., Delta Kappa Gamma. Republican. Avocations: children's Lit., collecting autographed books, bridge, family times. Home: 102 Jo Mar Dr Parkersburg WV 26101 Office: Wood County Schs Emerson Elem 1605 36th St Parkersburg WV 26104-1939

MEADOWS, PATRICIA BLACHLY, art curator, civic worker; b. Amarillo, Tex., Nov. 12, 1938; d. William Douglas and Irene Bond Blachly; m. Curtis Washington Meadows, Jr., June 10, 1961; children: Michael Lee, John Morgan. BA in English and History, U. Tex., 1960. Program dir. Ex-Students Assn., Austin, Tex., 1960-61; co-founder, dir. Dallas Visual Art Ctr., 1981-86, curator, 1987—, founder The Collectors, 1988—; exhbn. dir. Tex. bd. Nat. Mus. Women in Arts, Washington, 1986-91; mem. acquisition com. Dallas Mus. Art, 1988-92; chmn. adv. bd. Oaks Bank and Trust, 1993-96; juror numerous exhibits, Dallas and Tex.; spkr. on arts subjects; cons. city, state and nat. project concerning arts; bd. dirs., mem. exec. com. Uptown Pub. Improvement Dist., 1993-96; chmn. bd. dirs. State-Thomas TIF Zone #1, 1994—. Author: (art catalogues) Critic's Choice, 1983—, Texas Women, 1989-90, Texas: reflections, rituals, 1991; organizer exhbns. Presenting Nine, D-Art Visual Art Ctr., 1984, Mosaics, 1991—, Senses Beyond Sight, 1992-93. Bd. dirs. Mid-Am. Arts Alliance, Kansas City, Mo., 1989-93, Tex. Bd. Commerce, Austin, 1991-93, Women's Issues Network, Dallas, 1994-96; bd. dirs. Dallas Summit, 1989-95—, pres., 1993-94, mem. 1988—; mem. Charter 100, 1993—, Dallas Assembly, 1993—, Leadership Tex., 1987; co-founder, mem. steering com. Emergency Artists Support League, Dallas, 1992—; mem. originating task force Dallas Coalition for Arts, 1984; also others. Recipient Dedication to Arts award Tex. Fine Arts Assn., 1984, Assn. Artists and Craftsmen, 1984, Southwestern Watercolor Soc., 1985, Flora award Dallas Civic Garden Ctr., 1987, James K. Wilson award TACA, 1988, Maura award Women's Ctr. Dallas, 1991, Disting. Woman award Northwood U., 1993, Excellence in the Arts award Dallas Hist. Soc., 1993, Legend award Dallas Visual Art Ctr., 1996. Mem. Tex. Assn. Mus., Tex. Sculpture Assn. (originating task force), Arts Dist. Mgmt. Assn. (bd. dirs., exec. com. 1984-92, Artists Square design com. 1988-90), Artists and Craftsmen Assn. (pres. bd. dirs. 1982-83), Dallas Women's Club. Presbyterian. Office: 2707 State St Dallas TX 75204-2634

MEADS, DONALD EDWARD, management services company executive; b. Salem, Mass., Sept. 23, 1920; s. Laurence G. and Gertrude F. M.; m. Jane Lightner, June 15, 1943; children: Edward G., Robert C., Laurence G., Judith C. Antrim, Suzanne M. O'Neil, Clifford L., Nancy Chapin. A.B. in Pre-Law, Dartmouth Coll., 1942; M.B.A. in Fin., Harvard U., 1947. Vice-pres., vice-chmn. investment com. N.Y. Life Ins. Co., N.Y.C., 1947-61; v.p. fin., chmn. investment com. Investors Diversified Services Inc., Mpls., 1961-65; pres., chief exec. officer Internat. Basic Economy Corp., N.Y.C., 1965-67, chmn., chief exec. officer, 1967-71; exec. v.p., dir., chief fin. officer, chmn. investment com. INA Corp., Phila., 1971-74; chmn. bd., chief exec. officer CertainTeed Corp., Valley Forge, Pa., 1974-78, dir., 1973-78; chmn. Mateer-Burt Co., Inc., Plymouth Meeting, Pa., 1984-87; chmn. Phila. First Group Inc., 1982-90; chmn. Carver Assocs., Inc., West Conshohocken, Pa., 1978—; hon. life trustee Valley Forge Mil. Acad. & Coll., Wayne Pa., trustee emeritus Thomas Jefferson U., Phila.; bd. dirs. Independence Hall Assn., Phila.; hon. dir. Marine Corps Scholarship Found., Princeton, N.J.; mem. Phila. Com. on Fgn. Relations; bd. dirs. World Affairs Council Phila. Served to capt. USMC, 1942-45. Decorated D.F.C., Air medals (6). Mem. Harvard Club of N.Y.C., Sunday Breakfast Club, Union League (Phila.), Rockefeller Ctr. Club (N.Y.C.).

MEADS, WALTER FREDERICK, executive recruitment consultant; b. Ft. Wayne, Ind., Mar. 11, 1923; s. Frederick C. and Minnie E. (Stephenson) M.; m. Mary E. Smith, Mar. 21, 1975; children by previous marriage: Kenneth W., Catherine L. B.S., Kent State U., 1948; M.A., Fairfield U. With Norman Malone & Assocs., Akron, Ohio, 1946-48, Griswold-Eshleman Co., Cleve., 1949-53, Fuller, Smith & Ross, Cleve., 1953-55; sr. v.p., head of creative svc., mem. mgmt. com., vice chmn. plans and rev. bds. J. Walter Thompson Co., N.Y.C., 1955-72; pres. Meads & Assocs., 1972—. With USAAF, 1943-45. Recipient numerous nat. and local advt. industry awards. Home: 4420 Orangewood Loop E Lakeland FL 33813-1844 Office: 6700 S Florida Ave Ste 4 Lakeland FL 33813-3310 *Creative freedom is probably the core concept at the heart of my life—not only for myself but for others. Life is never static; it either deteriorates or grows. All growth, to me, springs from the creative doers of the world. The rest of humanity goes along for the ride. And creative growth, in any field or endeavor, demands an attitude of freedom to shake off the shackles of habit and find new and better ways of doing things.*

MEAGHER, GEORGE VINCENT, mechanical engineer; b. Halifax, N.S., Can., Apr. 23, 1919; s. John Nicholas and Blanche Margaret (Seals) M.; m.

Evelyn Margaret Hamm, June 2, 1945; children: Maureen, Lindsey, Lise, Shelagh. BSc, Dalhousie U., Halifax, 1940; B of Engring., McGill U., 1942. Engring. and mgmt. positions in industry, 1942-56; with Dilworth, Secord, Meagher & Assocs. Ltd., Toronto, 1957-92; chmn. Dilworth, Secord, Meagher & Assocs. Ltd., 1988-92; pres. Tatacan Ltd., 1985—; vice chmn. Tata-DSMA, Bombay, India; dir. State Bank India, Can. Ltd., Toronto, 1984-94; founding dir., past chmn. Can.-India Bus. Coun.; pres. George V. Meagher Inc. Fellow Engring. Inst. Can.; mem. Designated Cons. Engr., Profl. Engrs. Ont., Nat. Club (Toronto). Home: # 1402, 500 Avenue Rd, Toronto, ON Canada M4V 2J6

MEAGHER, JAMES FRANCIS, atmospheric research executive; b. Sydney, Can., Oct. 23, 1946; came to U.S., 1967; s. James Marcellus and Margaret Evelyn (MacDougall) M.; m. Elizabeth Strapp; children: Jeffrey James, Elizabeth Kathleen. BSc, St. Francis Xavier, 1967; PhD, Cath. U. of Am., 1971. Rsch. fellow U. Wash., Seattle, 1971-73, Pa. State U., 1973-76; dir. atmospheric rsch. Tenn. Valley Authority, Muscle Shoals, Ala., 1976—; mem. sci. adv. com. Nat. Acid Precipitation Assessment Program, Washington, 1987-93; mgr. Atmospheric Scis. TVA, Eviron. Rsch Ctr., 1993—. Contbr. chpt. to book, articles to profl. jours. Mem. Am. Chem. Soc., Am. Geophys. Union, Sigma Xi. Avocations: sailing, youth soccer. Home: 204 Seminole Ct Florence AL 35630 Office: USG TVA 212 Ceb Sheffield AL 35660

MEAGHER, JAMES PROCTOR, editor; b. Rock Island, Ill., June 2, 1935; s. Edmund Joseph and Pauline Marie (Proctor) M.; m. Marie Therese Lyman, Sept. 12, 1959; children: Kathleen Ann, Christopher James. BA, U. Notre Dame, 1957. Copy editor Chgo. Tribune Co., 1959-61; staff writer Nat. Observer, Washington, 1961-62; news editor Nat. Observer, Silver Spring, Md., 1962-65, sr. editor, 1965-76, asst. mng. editor, 1976-77; assoc. editor Barron's Bus. and Fin. Weekly, N.Y.C., 1977-78, news editor, 1978-82, asst. mng. editor, 1982-86, dep. editor, 1986-92, mng. editor, 1992-93, editor, 1993-95; exec. editor Dow Jones Mag. Group, N.Y.C., 1995—. Served to 1st lt. U.S. Army, 1957-59. Mem. Soc. Profl. Journalists, Sigma Delta Chi. Roman Catholic. Home: 25 Hedges Ave Chatham NJ 07928-2503 Office: Barron's Fin Weekly 200 Liberty St New York NY 10281-1003

MEAGHER, MARK JOSEPH, publishing company executive; b. Balt., July 9, 1932; s. Harry Royce and Maria Paula (Demarco) M.; m. Gabriela Sierra, Dec. 24, 1983. Student, U. Notre Dame, 1950-51; B.S., U. Md., 1954. C.P.A. Accountant, auditor Price Waterhouse & Co., Balt., 1954-57; systems analyst IBM, Balt., 1957-58; mgmt. cons. McKinsey Co., Washington, 1958-61; exec. v.p. McGraw Hill Book Co., N.Y.C., 1961-70; v.p. fin. and adminstrn. Washington Post Co., N.Y.C., 1970-74; exec. v.p., gen. mgr. Washington Post Co., 1974-76, pres. newspaper div., 1976-77, pres., chief operating officer co., 1977-80, dir., 1970-81; pres., chief operating officer, dir. Penthouse Internat. Ltd., 1981; ptnr. Holding Capital Group, N.Y.C., 1982—; mem., chmn. Fin. World Ptnrs., N.Y.C., 1983-95; dir., chmn. fin. com., CEO, CFO BKB Pharm., L.L.C., 1995—; dir. Maple Press. V.p. Urban League New Brunswick, N.J., 1967-69; chmn. housing com. Metuchen/Edison (N.J.) unit NAACP, 1968; bd. dirs. World Affairs Coun.; vice chmn., trustee U. Md. Found., 1978-88. Mem. Hon. Accounting Soc., Am. Inst. CPA's (Eisenhower fellow 1980). Republican. Roman Catholic.

MEAGHER, MICHAEL, radiologist; b. New Rochelle, N.Y., Oct. 24, 1942; s. Joseph Aloysius and Elizabeth (Ahern) M.; m. Martha Batten Mitchell, 1968; children: Kelly, Courtney. Student, Rensselaer Poly. Inst., 1960-62; AB with distinction, U. Rochester, 1964; MD, Stanford U., 1969. Diplomate Am. Bd. Radiology, Nat. Bd. Med. Examiners. Intern in medicine Cornell U., N.Y. Hosp., 1969-70; jr. asst. resident in diagnostic radiology U. Wash., Seattle, 1970-71, sr. asst. resident diagnostic radiology, 1973-74, resident diagnostic radiology, 1974-75; active staff mem. dept. radiology Queen's Med. Ctr., Honolulu, 1975—, Leahi Hosp., Honolulu, 1981—, Kahuku (Hawaii) Hosp., 1988—; pres. Radiology Assocs., Inc., 1978, 81-84, 90; chmn. dept. radiology Queen's Med. Ctr., 1979-80, 82-86, 88-90, dir. dept. radiology, 1985-91, dir. magnetic resonance imaging, 1991—, chmn. cancer com., 1980-82; mem. med. staff Hawaii Health Tech. Magnetic Resonance Imaging Facility, Honolulu, 1986—, chief of staff, 1978; clin. instr. dept. radiology U. Hawaii Sch. Medicine, 1983-89, clin. assoc. prof., 1989-93, clin. prof., 1993—, asst. rsch. prof. Cancer Rsch. Ctr. Hawaii, 1989—; clin. asst. prof. dept. radiology U. Wash. Sch. Medicine, 1980-88; presenter in fld. Contbr. articles to profl. publs. Chmn. high tech. adv. com. State Health Planning and Devel. Agy., 1983—; bd. dirs. Friends of Hawaii Pub. TV, 1979-81; pres., CEO Queen's Health Care Plan, Honolulu, 1985-89, chmn. bd. dirs., 1989-91; bd. dirs. Managed Care Mgmt., Inc., Honolulu, 1990; v.p. bd. dirs. Hawaii Opera Theatre, 1990-91, treas., 1991—. Lt. comdr. USN, 1971-73. NIH fellow, 1966; Kaiser Found. grantee, 1967. Fellow Am. Coll. Radiology; mem. AMA, Hawaii State Radiol. Soc. (sec.-treas. 1978-79, v.p. 1979-80, pres. 1980-81), Radiol. Soc. N.Am., Soc. Computer Applications in Radiology (charter), Am. Roentgen Ray Soc. Home: 1234 Maunawili Rd Kailua HI 96734-4642 Office: Queen's Med Ctr Dept Radiology Honolulu HI 96813

MEAHL, BARBARA, occupational health nurse; b. N.Y.C., Aug. 15, 1938; d. Raymond G. and Alice (Duncan) Reynolds; m. Robert P. Meahl, Oct. 29, 1988; children: Susan, Mark, Ruth. Diploma in Nursing, Presbyn. Hosp., Phila., 1959; BS, St. Joseph's Coll., Windham, Maine, 1986. Cert. occupl. health nurse, CCM. Staff nurse various hosps. N.J./Pa., 1959-74; staff nurse AMP Inc., Harrisburg, Pa., 1974-75; mgr. safety and health Carlisle (Pa.) Corp., 1975-86; chief nurse Naval Shipyard, Phila., 1986-89; DON Concorde Inc., Phila., 1990-95; cons. Barbara Meahl & Assoc., Springfield, Pa., 1995—; dir., vice chmn. Am. Bd. Occupational Health Nurses, Inc., Palos Hills, Ill., 1988-92; lectr. in field. Mem./chair Cumberland County Drug and Alcohol Commn., Carlisle, Pa., 1986-88; ordained elder Presbyn. Ch., Springfield, Pa., 1987. Mem. Am. Assn. Occupl. Health Nurses, Pa. Assn. Occupl. Health Nurses (v.p. 1985-86, Outstanding Occupl. Health Nurse 1984), Delaware Valley Assn. Occupl. Health Nurses (v.p. 1987-88, sec. 1994—). Avocations: sewing, gardening.

MEAKER, MARIJANE AGNES, author; b. Auburn, N.Y., May 27, 1927; d. Ellis R. and Ida T. M. B.A., U. Mo., 1949; PhD (hon.), Southampton Coll., 1996. Author: novels (under own name) Sudden Endings, 1965, Hometown, 1967, Game of Survival, 1969, Don't Rely on Gemini, 1971, Shockproof Sydney Skate, 1972, 2d edit., 1990; (under pseudonym M.E. Kerr), Dinky Hocker Shoots Smack, 1972, Gentlehands, 1978, If I Love You, Am I Trapped Forever, 1973, I'll Love You When You're More Like Me, 1977, Is That You, Miss Blue?, 1975, Love is a Missing Person, 1975, The Son of Someone Famous, 1975, Little Little, 1981 (Soc. Children's Books Writers award 1982), What I Really Think of You, 1982, Me Me Me Me Me: Not a Novel (Best Books for Young Adults ALA), 1983, Him She Loves?, 1984, I Stay Near You (Best Books for Young Adults ALA), 1985, Night Kites, 1986, Fell, 1987, Fell Back, 1989, Fell Down, 1990; (under pseudonym Mary James) Shoebag, 1990, The Shuteyes, 1993, Frankenlouse, 1994, Shoebag Returns, 1996, (M.E. Kerr) Linger, 1993, Deliver Us from Evie, 1994, Hello, I Lied, 1997. Recipient Notable Children's Book award ALA, 1972, Book of Yr. award Sch. Library Jour., 1972, 77, 78, Christopher award, 1978, Night Kites award ALA, 1986, Margaret A. Edwards award ALA, 1993.

MEAL, LARIE, chemistry educator, researcher, consultant; b. Cin., June 15, 1939; d. George Lawrence Meal and Dorothy Louise (Heileman) Fitzpatrick. BS in Chemistry, U. Cin., 1961, PhD in Chemistry, 1966. Rsch. chemist U.S. Indsl. Chems., Cin., 1966-67; instr. chemistry U. Cin., 1968-69, asst. prof., 1969-75, assoc. prof., 1975-90, prof., 1990—, researcher, 1980—; cons. in field. Contbr. articles to sci. jours. Mem. AAAS, N.Y. Acad. Scis., Am. Chem. Soc., Internat. Assn. Arson Investigators, NOW, Planned Parenthood, Iota Sigma Pi. Democrat. Avocations: gardening, yard work. Home: 2231 Slane Ave Norwood OH 45212-3615 Office: U Cin 2220 Victory Pky Cincinnati OH 45206-2822

MEALIE, CARL A., physician, educator; b. Astoria, N.Y., Jan. 26, 1948; s. Patrick and Natalie (Previti) M.; m. Maureen Frances Maybury, Apr. 24, 1993. RN, MSN, CCRN, NYU, 1969; MD, N.Y. Med. Coll., 1974. Chmn. Dept. Emergency Medicine St. Mary's Hosp., Roswell, N.Mex., 1975-83; emergency dept. attending physician Guadalupe Med. Ctr., Carlsbad, N.Mex., 1979-83; emergency dept. attending physician L.I. Jewish Med. Ctr., New Hyde Park, N.Y., 1993—, chmn. disaster preparation com., 1991—, asst. chief emergency dept., 1989-95, chief clin. ops., 1995; asst. prof. emergency medicine Albert Einstein Coll. Medicine, N.Y.C., 1995; mem. ambulance adv. bd. Chavez County Med. Soc., Roswell, 1980-83, ambulance bd., 1981-87. Mem. City Roswell EMS Bd., 1981-93. Grantee Min. Health Guatemala Pediat. Inst., 1993. Fellow Am. Coll. Emergency Physicians (key contact 1987—), N.Y. Acad. Medicine; me,. AMA, Am. Acad. Emergency Medicine, N.Y. State Med. Soc., Soc. Acad. Emergency Medicine. Roman Catholic. Avocations: skiing, sailing, hunting, golf. Home: 7 Plume Ct Bay Shore NY 11706 Office: LI Jewish Med Ctr Lakeville New Hyde Park NY 11040

MEALMAN, GLENN, corporate marketing executive; b. Prescott, Kans., June 10, 1934; s. Edgar R. and Mary E. (Holstein) M.; m. Gloria Gail Proch, June 12, 1955; children: Michael Edward, Cathy Gail. BS in Bus., Kans. State Coll., Emporia, 1957; postgrad., Harvard U., 1970. With Fleming Cos., Topeka, 1957—, sr. v.p. mktg., 1981-82, exec. v.p. mktg., 1982-86, exec. v.p. Mid-Am. region, 1986-93, exec. v.p. nat. accts., 1994—; dir. PBI-Gordon Co., KCCI. Pres. bd. Topeka YMCA, 1981; trustee Ottawa U., Kans., 1980. Served with USNR, 1954-56. Mem. Kans. State C. of C. and Industry (bd. dirs. 1991—), Blue Hills Country Club, Rotary. Baptist. Office: Fleming Cos Inc 7101 College Blvd Ste 850 Overland Park KS 66210-1891 also: Fleming Cos Inc 6301 Waterford Blvd Oklahoma City OK 73118-1103

MEALOR, WILLIAM THEODORE, JR., geography educator, university administrator, consultant; b. Atlanta, Apr. 20, 1940; s. William Theodore and Doris (Pittman) M.; m. Jennifer Joyce Hancock, Dec. 28, 1968; children—Stephen Theodore, Augustus Everett, William Griggs. B.A., U. Fla., 1962; M.A., U. Ga., 1964, Ph.D., 1972. Instr. dept. geography U. Ga., Athens, 1970-71; asst. prof. dept. geography and area devel. U. So. Miss., Hattiesburg, 1971-75, assoc. prof., 1975-78; asst. dean Coll. Liberal Arts, 1977-78; prof., chmn. dept. geography U. Memphis, 1978-83, prof., chmn. dept. geography and planning, 1983-86, interim dean Coll. Arts and Scis., 1987-88, assoc. v.p. for acad. affairs, 1988-92, chmn. dept. geography and planning, 1989-90, dir. instnl. self study, 1992-94, interim vice provost Acad. Affairs, 1992-94, prof. geography and planning, 1994—; cons. real estate devel. and land use analysis. Contbr. articles to profl. jours. Active Chickasaw Area Coun. Boy Scouts Am.; mem. coun. Presbytery of Memphis. Served to 1st lt. U.S. Army, 1964-66; Vietnam. Recipient Miss. Marine Resources Coun. award, 1974-75, U.S. Dept. Transp. award, 1974-76, 79-80, Miss. R&D Ctr. award, 1976-77, Carnegie Corp. award, 1988-89, NSF award, 1981, 89-91, 94-97, Nat. Ctr. Acad. Achievement and Transfer award, 1991-94; NASA Remote Sensing grantee, 1972-75. Mem. Assn. Am. Geographers, Am. Geog. Soc., Nat. Council Geog. Edn., Tenn. Geog. Soc. (pres. 1984-86), Sigma Xi, Phi Kappa Phi, Pi Gamma Mu, Gamma Theta Upsilon, Pi Tau Chi, Sigma Chi, Omicron Delta Kappa. Presbyterian. Office: U Memphis Dept Geography Memphis TN 38152

MEALY, J. BURKE (), psychological services administrator. MA in Guidance and Psychology, Assumption Coll., 1966, CAS in Counseling Psychology, 1967; PhD in Clin. Psychology, Duquesne U., 1972. Lic. psychologist, D.C., Md; diplomate Profl. Acad. Custody Evaluators. Clin. psychologist Woodville State Hosp., Carnegie, Pa., 1969-70; dir./psychologist Western State Sch. and Hosp., Canonsburg, Pa., 1970-72; asst. prof. human devel. Calif. State U., Hayward, 1972-73; pvt. practice Md., 1973—; clin. community psychologist Montgomery County Health Dept., Rockville, 1974-78; forensic psychologist Montgomery County Ct., 1978-84; cons. dist., cir. cts. Montgomery County, 1984-88. Mem. Am. Psychol. Assn., Am. Orthopsychiat. Assn., Md. Psychol. Assn. Office: 15817 Crabbs Branch Way Rockville MD 20855-2635

MEANS, ELIZABETH ROSE THAYER, financial consultant, lawyer; b. N.Y.C., Aug. 29, 1960; d. Cyril Chesnut and Rosaline (Limtiuco) M. Student, Harvard Coll., 1980, Tufts U., 1981; Fletcher Sch. Law/Diplomacy, 1983, 84; BS, Chatham Coll., 1983; Cert. in Comparative Law, Heidelberg U., 1988; JD, Samford U., 1989; LLM in Internat. Banking Law, Boston U., 1990. Bar: Mass. 1991, Pa. 1991; cert. for piloting, seamanship and small boat handling USCG Aux. Dancer The N.Y.C. Ballet Co., 1971, Balanchine Cast for PBS "The Nutcracker Suite", N.Y.C., 1971; docent The Hammond Castle Mus., Gloucester, Mass., 1982-85; asst. mgr. The Gallery, Rockport, Mass., 1977-83; cons. The Galleries, Ltd., Wellesley, Mass., 1988; legal intern U. Ala. Health Svcs. Found., Birmingham, 1988-89; loan officer UN/UNFCU, N.Y.C., 1984-86; contracts mgr. for Eastern Region Unisys Corp., Berkeley Heights, N.J., 1990-92; fin. cons. Innovatech, Lexington, Mass., 1992-93, 94-95; contract analyst Guy Carpenter & Co., Inc., N.Y.C., 1994; gen. counsel Mojo Working Prodns., N.Y.C., 1996; chair Cordell Hull Speakers' Forum, Birmingham, 1988-89; alumnae class sec. Chatham Coll. Class of 1980s, Pitts., 1983-87, 97—. Clk. of vestry The Ch. of the Resurrection, N.Y.C., 1993-95, mem. vestry, 1995-97. Recipient Cert. of Appreciation 1990 Alumni award Cumberland Sch. Law, 1990; named to Nat. Dean's List, 1989-90. Mem. DAR (Cape Ann chpt. const. week chair 1993-95, Mass. const. week chair 1995, N.Y.C. chpt. jr. com. mem. Sons and Daus. Gala Ball 1995), The Federalist Soc. (Cumberland chpt. treas. 1988-89, adv. bd. 1983, sec. 1987-88), The Clan Menzies Soc. NA, The Clan Menzies Soc. Scotland, Princeton Club, Thayer Families Assn., Daus. Union Vets. of Civil War 1861-65, Soc. Mayflower Descendants (N.Y.), Baronial Order Magna Charta, Dames of Ct. of Honor, Nat. Soc. Magna Charta Dames and Barons. Republican. Episcopalian. Avocations: lobstering, sailing (cert. in piloting, seamanship and small boat handling), fishing, swimming, bicycling. Address: 13 Salt Island Rd Gloucester MA 01930

MEANS, GEORGE ROBERT, organization executive; b. Bloomington, Ill., July 5, 1907; s. Arthur John and Alice (Johnson) M.; m. Martha Cowart, Aug. 5, 1950. B.Ed., Ill. State U., 1930; A.M., Clark U., 1932; HHD (hon.), Rikkyo U., Tokyo; H.H.D. (hon.), Ill. State U.; HHD (hon.), Ill. Wesleyan U., Ky. Wesleyan Coll. Cartographer, map editor, 1932-35; with Rotary Internat., 1935—; beginning as conv. mgr., successively head Middle Asia office Rotary Internat., Bombay, India; asst. gen. sec. Rotary Internat., 1948-52, gen. sec., 1953-72; sec. Rotary Found., 1953-72; dir. Washington Nat. Corp., 1972-80, 4 Way Test Assn., Hertzberg-New Method, Inc., Ind State Retirement Home Guaranty Fund, 1982-95. Author: Rotary's Return to Japan, also numerous articles. Mem.-at-large nat. council Boy Scouts Am. Served as comdr. USNR, 1942-46. Decorated Legion of Honor France; Chilean Order of Merit; Japanese Order of Rising Sun; Italian Order of Merit; recipient Disting. Service award Geog. Soc. Chgo., 1972; Paul Harris fellow The Rotary Found. Fellow Am. Geog. Soc.; mem. Rotary Club (Evanston, Bloomington, Ill., Sydney, Australia, Kyoto, Osaka and Tokyo, Japan, Seoul, Korea, Cape Town, South Africa, Ituzaingo, Saavedra, Argentina, Greenwood, Ind.), Gamma Theta Upsilon. Home: 1067 Smock Dr Greenwood IN 46143-2426

MEANS, JOHN BARKLEY, foreign language educator, association executive; b. Cin., Jan. 2, 1939; s. Walker Wilson and Rosetta Miller (Barkley) M. BA, U. Ill., 1960, MA, 1963; PhD, U. Ill. at Urbana, 1968. U.S. govt. rsch. analyst on Brazil CIA, Washington, 1962-64; assoc. prof. Spanish and Portugese Temple U., Phila., 1972-82, prof. critical langs., 1982—, co-chmn. dept. Spanish and Portuguese, 1971-75, dir. Center for Critical Langs., 1975—, dir. Inst. for Langs. and Internat. Studies, 1987—, chmn. dept. Germanic and Slavic Langs. and lit., 1992-94, chair univ. core programs, 1995-97; cons. on Brazilian-Portuguese and second lang. acquisition and self-instrnl. programs for less commonly taught langs., 1968—; cons. to founds., pubs., univs. and govt. agys. Editor: Essays on Brazilian Literature, 1971; author: (with others) Language in Education: Theory and Practice, 1988—; contbr. numerous articles to profl. jours. Trustee Bristol (Pa.) Riverside Theatre, 1990—; mng. trustee Means Charitable Trust, 1993—. 1st lt. U.S. Army, 1960-62. NDEA fellow, 1962, 64; grantee U.S. Dept. Edn., 1979-81, Japan Found., 1980, 82, 89-91, ARCO Chem. Found., 1991, 93. Mem. MLA, S.E., S.R., Nat. Coun. on Langs. and Internat. Studies (bd. dirs.), Joint Nat. Com. for Langs. (bd. dirs.), Nat. Assn. Self-Instrnl. Lang. Programs (exec. dir. 1977—, editor jour. 1978-94), Am. Coun. on Teaching Fgn. Lang., Nat. Coun. Orgns. Less Commonly Taught Langs. (exec. sec.-treas.), Nat. Assn. State Univs. and Land Grant Colls., Pi Kappa Phi, Phi Lambda Beta, Sigma Delta Pi. Home: PO Box 565 Yardley PA 19067-8565 Office: Temple U Ctr for Critical Langs Anderson Hall 1114 W Berks St Philadelphia PA 19122-6007

MEANS, MARIANNE, political columnist; b. Sioux City, Iowa, June 13, 1934; d. Ernest Maynard and Else Marie Johanne (Andersen) Hansen; m. Warren Weaver, Jr. B.A., U. Nebr., 1956; J.D., George Washington U., 1977. Copy editor Lincoln (Nebr.) Jour., 1955-57; woman's editor No. Va. Sun, Arlington, 1957-59; Washington bur. corr. Hearst Newspapers, 1959-61, White House corr., 1961-65; polit. columnist King Features Syndicate, 1965—, N.Y. Times News, 1994—; commentator Spectrum CBS radio, Mut. Broadcasting Network, Voice of Am., U.S.I.A. World Network, Post Newsweek Stas., Nat. Pub. Radio. Author: The Woman in the White House, 1963. Recipient Front Page award N.Y. Newspaper Women, 1962; Tex. Headliners award, 1976, Hall of Fame-Sigma Delta Chi, 1988. Mem. White House Corrs. Assn., Nat. Press Found. (chmn.), Internat. Women's Media Found. (bd. dirs.), Gridiron Club, Cosmos Club, Nat. Press Club, Phi Beta Kappa, Delta Delta Delta, Sigma Delta Chi (Hall of Fame). Home: 1521 31st St NW Washington DC 20007-3075 Office: 1701 Pennsylvania Ave NW Washington DC 20006-5805

MEANS, TERRY ROBERT, federal judge; b. Roswell, N.Mex., July 3, 1948; s. Lewis Prude and Doris Emaree (Hightower) M.; m. JoAnn Huffman Harris, June 2, 1973; children: Robert, MaryAnn, Emily. BA, So. Meth. U., Dallas, 1971; JD, So. Meth. U., 1974. Bar: Tex. 1974, U.S. Dist. Ct. (no. dist.) Tex. 1976, U.S. Ct. Appeals (5th cir.) 1978, U.S. Dist. Ct. (we. dist., ea. dist.) Tex. 1991. Ptnr. Means & Means, Corsicana, Tex., 1974-88; presdl. elector, 1980; justice 10th Ct. Appeals, Waco, Tex., 1989-90; judge U.S. Dist. Ct. for Northern Dist. Tex., Ft. Worth, 1991—. Chmn. Navarro County Rep. Party, Corsicana, 1976-88; pres. YMCA, Corsicana, 1984, Ft. Worth Youth Soccer Assn., 1996-97. Mem. State Bar Tex., Tarrant County Bar Assn., McLennan County Bar Assn. Baptist. Avocations: coaching soccer, racquetball. Office: 201 US Courthouse 501 W 10th St Fort Worth TX 76102-3637

MEANS, THOMAS CORNELL, lawyer; b. Charleston, S.C., Oct. 3, 1947; s. Thomas Lucas and Dean (Cornell) M.; m. Judith Faye Perlmutter, Sept. 10, 1977; children: Benjamin, Samuel. AB, Dartmouth Coll., 1969; postgrad., Princeton Theol. Sem., 1970-71; M of Pub. Adminstrn., U. Colo., 1975; JD, George Washington U., 1978. Bar: D.C. 1978, U.S. dist. Ct. (D.C. dist.), U.S. Ct. Appeals (4th and D.C. cirs.) 1979, U.S. Ct. Appeals (10th cir.) 1983, U.S. Ct. Appeals (6th and 11th cirs.) 1989, U.S. Ct. Appeals (9th cir.) 1992, U.S. Ct. Appeals (8th cir.) 1993, U.S. Ct. Appeals (5th cir.) 1996. Social worker Vinyard Childcare, Ann Arbor, Mich., 1969-70; rsch. analyst, registered lobbyist Colo. Counties, Inc., Denver, 1972-75; assoc. Jones, Day, Reavis and Pogue, Washington, 1978-79; assoc. then ptnr. Crowell & Moring, Washington, 1979—; mem. state adv. coun. on pub. Pers. Mgmt., Colo. State Govt., Denver, 1974-75; lectr. mining law; chmn. coal com. Ea. Mineral Law Found., 1988-89, chmn. spl. insts., ass. sec., 1989-91, sec., 1991-92, v.p., 1992-93, pres., 1993-94, exec. com., 1989-96, trustee, 1989—, mem. adv. bd. editors, 1994—; bd. advisors Nat. Law Ctr., 1993-94. Contbr. articles to profl. jours. Mem. George Washington Law Alumni Assn. (bd. dirs. 1986-96, exec. com. 1987-96, treas. 1987-88, sec. 1988-90, pres. 1992-94), Order of Coif, Cosmos Club (Washington), Phi Beta Kappa. Home: 6411 Dahlonega Rd Bethesda MD 20816-2101 Office: Crowell & Moring 1001 Pennsylvania Ave NW Washington DC 20004-2505

MEARA, ANNE, actress, playwright, writer; b. Bklyn., Sept. 20; d. Edward Joseph and Mary (Dempsey) M.; m. Gerald Stiller, Sept. 14, 1954; children: Amy, Benjamin. Student, Herbert Berghoff Studio, 1953-54. Apprentice in summer stock, Southold, L.I. and Woodstock, N.Y., 1950-53; off-Broadway appearances include A Month in the Country, 1954, Maedchen in Uniform, 1955 (Show Bus. off-Broadway award), Ulysses in Nightown, 1958, The House of Blue Leaves, 1970; Broadway plays: Spookhouse, 1983, Bosoms and Neglect, 1986, Shakespeare Co., Two Gentlemen of Verona, Cen. Park, N.Y.C., 1957, Romeo and Juliet, 1988, Eastern Standard, 1989, Anna Christie, 1993 (Tony nomination Best Supporting Actress); film appearances include The Out-of-Towners, 1968, Lovers and Other Strangers, 1969, The Boys From Brazil, 1978, Fame, 1979, Nasty Habits (with husband Jerry Stiller), 1976, An Open Window, 1990, Mia, 1990, Awakenings, 1991, Reality Bites, 1994, Daytrippers, 1997; comedy act, 1963—; appearances Happy Medium and Medium Rare, Chgo., 1960-61, Village Gate, Phase Two and Blue Angel, N.Y.C., 1963, The Establishment, London, 1963; syndicated TV series Take Five With Stiller and Meara, 1977-78; numerous appearances on TV game and talk shows, also spls. and variety shows; rec. numerous commls. for TV and radio (co-recipient Vocie of Imagery award Advt. Bur. N.Y.); star TV series Kate McShane, 1975; other TV appearances Archie Bunker's Place, 1979, The Sunset Gang, The Detective, 1990, Avenue Z Afternoon, 1991, Alf, 1986, Murphy Brown, 1994, (TV movie) Jitters, 1997, All My Children, 1997—; writer, actress TV movie The Other Woman, 1983 (co-recipient Writer's Guild Outstanding Achievement award 1983), Alf, To Make Up to Break Up, The Stiller and Meara Pilot; author, actor (play) After-Play, 1996; video host (with Jerry Stiller) So You Want to Be an Actor?. Recipient Outer Critic's Cir. Playwriting award for "After-Play", 1995.

MEARS, PATRICK EDWARD, lawyer; b. Flint, Mich., Oct. 3, 1951; s. Edward Patrick and Estelle Veronica (Mislik) M.; m. Geraldine O'Connor, July 18, 1981. BA, U. Mich., 1973, JD, 1976. Bar: N.Y. 1977, U.S. Dist. Ct. (so. and ea. dists.) N.Y. 1977, Mich. 1980, U.S. Dist. Ct. (we. and ea. dists.) Mich. 1980, U.S. Ct. Appeals (6th cir.) 1983. Assoc. firm Milbank, Tweed, Hadley & McCloy, N.Y.C., 1976-79, ptnr. Warner, Norcross & Judd, Grand Rapids, Mich., 1980-91; sr. mem. Dykema Gossett PLLC, Grand Rapids, 1991—; adj. prof. Grand Valley State U., Allendale, Mich., 1981-84. Author: Michigan Collection Law, 1981, 2d edit., 1983, Basic Bankruptcy Law, 1986, Bankruptcy Law and Practice in Michigan, 1987; contbr. articles to profl jours. Chairperson legis. com. East Grand Rapids Parent-Tchr. Assn., 1992-94; dir. Children's Law Ctr., 1994, Grand Rapids Ballet, 1994—, East Grand Rapids Pub. Sch. Found., 1994—. Fellow Am. Coll. Bankruptcy; mem. ABA (vice chmn. workouts, enforcement of creditors rights, and bankruptcy com. ABA real property sect. 1995—), Mich. State Bar Assn. (mem., sec. coun. real property sect. 1993—), Am. Bankruptcy Inst., Fed. Bar Assn. (chairperson bankruptcy sect. We. Mich. chpt. 1992-94), Am. C. of C. in France, Grand Rapids Sister Cities Internat. (dir.), Grand Rapids Rotary, World Affairs Coun. of West Mich., West Mich. World Trade Assn., Peninsular Club (Grand Rapids), East Hills Athletic Club. Office: Dykema Gossett 300 Ottawa Ave NW Ste 700 Grand Rapids MI 49503-2308

MEARS, RONA ROBBINS, lawyer; b. Stillwater, Minn., Oct. 3, 1938; d. Glaydon Donaldson and Lois Lorane (Hoehne) Robbins; m. John Ashley Mears, Aug. 20, 1960; children: John LaMonte, Matthew Von. BS, U. Minn., 1960; MBA, JD, So. Meth. U., 1982. Bar: Tex. 1992. Bus. adminstr. 1st Unitarian Ch., Dallas, 1973-77; assoc. atty. Haynes and Boone, Dallas, 1982-89, ptnr., internat. sect., 1989—. Co-editor: International Loan Workouts and Bankruptcies, 1989; contbr. articles to profl. jours. Mem. U.S. Delegation, NAFTA Adv. Com. on Pvt. Comml. Disputes, 1994—. Rsch. fellow Southwestern Legal Found., Dallas, 1986—; recipient 1st prize INSOL Internat. Article Competition, 1989. Mem. ABA (sec. internat. sect. 1994-96), State Bar Tex. (chmn. internat. sect. 1993-94, divorce chmn. 1996—), Tex. -Mex. Bar Assn. (co-chair 1994-95, co-chair 1995—), Dallas Bar Assn. (chmn. internat. sect. 1984-86), Internat. Bar Assn. (mem. com. on creditors rights, coord. internat. insolvency coop. project 1988-91), U.S. - Mex. C. of C. (bd. dirs. S.W. chpt. 1987—). Democrat. Office: Haynes and Boone LLP 3100 Nations Bank Plz 901 Main St Dallas TX 75202-3714

MEARS, WALTER ROBERT, journalist; b. Lynn, Mass., Jan. 11, 1935; s. Edward Lewis and Edythe Emily (Campbell) M.; m. Sally Danton, Dec. 28, 1956 (dec. Dec. 1962); children: Pamela (dec.), Walter Robert Jr. (dec.); m. Joyce Marie Lund, Aug. 4, 1963 (div. 1983); children: Stephanie Joy, Susan Marie; m. Carroll Ann Rambo, Mar. 1, 1986 (div. 1995). B.A., Middlebury Coll., 1956, Litt.D. (hon.), 1977. Newsman AP, Boston, 1956; corr. AP, Montpelier, Vt., 1956-60; state house corr. AP, Boston, 1960-61; newsman AP, Washington, 1961-69; chief polit. writer AP, 1969-72, asst. chief Washington bur., 1973-74, spl. corr., 1975, chief, 1977-83, v.p., 1978—, exec. editor, 1984-88, v.p., columnist, 1989—. Author: (with John Chancellor) The News Business, 1983, The New News Business, 1995. Trustee Middlebury Coll., 1980-84. Recipient ann. award AP Mng. Editors Assn., 1973; Pulitzer prize for Nat. Reporting, 1977. Mem. Phi Beta Kappa, Delta Kappa Epsilon. Clubs: Gridiron, Burning Tree. Home: 1556N 21st Court Arlington VA 22209 Office: Associated Press 2021 K St NW Ste 600 Washington DC 20006-1003

MEAT LOAF (MARVIN LEE ADAY), popular musician, actor; b. Dallas, Sept. 27, 1951; m. Leslie Aday (Edmonds), 1975; children: Pearl, Amanda. Albums include Featuring Stoney and Meat Loaf, 1970, Free For All, 1976, Bat OutOf Hell, 1977, DeadRinger, 1982, Midnight at The Lost and Found, 1983, Bad Attitude, 1984, Hits Out Of Hell, 1985, Blind Before I Stop, 1986, Meat Loaf Live, 1987, Bat Out Of Hell II: Back Into Hell, 1993, Welcome to the Neighborhood, 1995; appeared in plays Hair, The RockyHorror Show, National Lampoon Show, More Than You Deserve, Rockabye Hamlet, BillyThe Kid & Jean Harlow, As You Like It, Othello; appeared in films The Rocky Horror Picture Show, 1975, Americathon, 1979, Scavenger Hunt, 1979, Roadie, 1980,Dead Ringer, 1981, The Squeeze, 1986, Out of Bounds, 1986, Motorama, 1990, Gun & Betty Lou's Handbag, 1991, Wayne's World, 1992, Leap of Faith, 1992; (TV movie) To Catch a Yeti, 1995. Received Grammy for Best Rock Vocal Solo Performance, 1993. Office: c/o MCA Records 70 Universal Terrace Pkwy Universal Cty CA 91608-1001*

MEBANE, WILLIAM BLACK, controller, financial consultant; b. Vernon, Tex., Dec. 15, 1927; s. David Mitchell and Ida Virginia (Black) M.; m. Joan Hebbard Dumper, Nov. 24, 1956; children—David Alexander, Virginia Ann. B.B.A., Tex. A&M U., 1952; M.B.A., Harvard U., 1954. Mem. treas.'s office staff Gen. Motors Corp., N.Y.C., 1954-70; sec.-treas. Alfred P. Sloan Found., N.Y.C., 1971-78; dir. fin. and adminstrn. Am. Diabetes Assn., N.Y.C., 1979-80; dir. planning Am. Diabetes Assn., 1981; v.p., comptroller NCCJ, Inc., N.Y.C., 1981-86, v.p. for fiscal affairs, 1987-88; fin. cons. Internat. House, N.Y.C., 1989-90; ind. fin. cons., 1990-91; contr. Better Bus. Bur., N.Y.C., 1991—. Vol. Essex Council Boy Scouts Am., 1967—. Served with USAAF, 1946-49. Recipient Silver Beaver award Boy Scouts Am., 1982. Republican. Episcopalian. Clubs: Harvard Bus. Sch. (N.Y.C.); Short Hills (N.J.). Home: 36 Haddonfield Rd Short Hills NJ 07078-3402

MEBUS, ROBERT GWYNNE, lawyer; b. Ft. Worth, Aug. 28, 1940; s. Robert Lee and Lucille (Cooke) M.; children: Elizabeth, Mary Ellen. BBA, So. Meth. U., 1962, LLB, 1965. Bar: Tex. 1965, U.S. Dist. Ct. (no. and ea. dists.) 1966, U.S. Ct. Appeals (5th cir.) 1965, U.S. Supreme Ct. 1969. Assoc. Malone, Seay & Gwinn, Dallas, 1965-67; ptnr. Seay, Gwinn, Crawford, Dallas, 1967-69, Seay, Gwinn, Crawford, Mebus, Dallas, 1969-82, Haynes and Boone, Dallas, 1982—; Mem. Tex. State Bar (chmn. labor law sect. 1982-83, chmn. labor law adv. commn. 1982-83), Tex. Bd. Legal Specialization. Contbg. editor: (book) Developing Labor Law, 1967, 2d edit., 1987. Mem. ABA (labor law sect.), Tex. Bar Found. Avocations: tennis, photography, gardening. Office: Haynes and Boone 3100 NationsBank Plz 901 Main St Dallas TX 75202-3714

MEBUST, WINSTON KEITH, surgeon, educator; b. Malta, Mont., July 2, 1933; s. Hans G. and Anna C. (Leiseth) M.; m. Lora June Peterson, Sept. 15, 1955; children—Leanne, Kevin, Kreg, Kari. Student, U. Wash., 1951-54, M.D., 1958. Diplomate: Am. Bd. Urology (trustee 1983-89, pres. 1988-89). Intern King County Hosp., Seattle, 1958-59; resident Virginia Mason Hosp., Seattle, 1959-63, Kans. U. Med. Center, 1963-66; practice medicine, specializing in urology, 1966—; instr. surgery and urology U. Kans. Med. Center, Kansas City, 1966-69; asst. prof. U. Kans. Med. Center, 1969-72, asso. prof., 1972-76, chmn. urology sect., 1974—, prof., 1977—; chief urology service VA Hosp., Kansas City, Mo., 1966-75. Contbr. articles, chpts. to med. jours. and texts. Served with U.S. Army, 1961-63. Mem. ACS, Am. Cancer Soc., Am. Bd. Surgery, Kansas City Urol. Assn., Assn. for Acad. Surgery, Am. Urol. Assn. (pres. S. Ctrl. sect. 1983, exec. com. 1992—, treas. 1996—), Wyandotte Med. Soc., Kans. Med. Assn., Soc. Univ. Urologists, Am. Assn. Genitourinary Surgeons, Sigma Xi, Alpha Omega Alpha. Republican. Home: 292 Seneca Trl W Kansas City KS 66106-9689 Office: 39th and Rainbow Blvd Kansas City MO 66103

MECH, TERRENCE FRANCIS, library director; b. Birdorup Park, Wiltshire, Eng., Feb. 24, 1953; s. Emil Paul and Madelyn (Tremmel) M. BS, U. Wis., Stevens Point, 1975; MS, Ill. State U., 1978; MLS, Clarion U., 1979; EdD, Pa. State U., 1994. Pub. svcs. libr. Tusculum Coll., Greensville, Tenn., 1979-80; libr. dir. Coll. of the Ozarks, Clarksville, Ark., 1980-82; libr. dir. King's Coll., Wilkes-Barre, Pa., 1982-94, v.p. for info. and instrnl. techs., dir. libr., 1994—; bd. dirs. Northeastern Pa. Bibliographic Ctr., 1982—; mem., officer Coun. Pa. Libr. Networks, 1984-89, chair, 1987-89. Contbr. chpts. to books and articles to profl. jours. Mem. ALA, Pa. Libr. Assn. (bd. dirs. 1986-87, various coms. 1985—). Office: Kings Coll 14 W Jackson St Wilkes Barre PA 18701-2010

MECHAM, GLENN JEFFERSON, lawyer, mayor; b. Logan, Utah, Dec. 11, 1935; s. Everett H. and Lillie (Dunford) M.; m. Mae Parson, June 5, 1957; children: Jeff B., Scott R., Marcia, Suzanne. BS, Utah State U., 1957; JD, U. Utah, 1961; grad. Air Command and Staff Coll., Air War Coll., 1984. Bar: Utah 1961, Supreme Ct. U.S., U.S. Ct. Appeals (10th Cir.), U.S. Dist. Ct. Utah, U.S. Ct. Claims. Gen. practice law, 1961-65; atty. Duchesne County, Utah, 1962, City of Duchesne, 1962; city judge Roy City, Utah, 1963-66; judge City of Ogden, Utah, 1966-69, mayor, 1992—; lectr. law and govt. Stevens-Henager Coll., Ogden, 1963-75; asst. U.S. atty., 1969-72; ptnr. Mecham & Richards, Ogden, Utah, 1972-82; pres. Penn Mountain Mining Co., South Pacific Internat. Bank, Ltd.; mem. Bur. Justice Stats. Adv. Bd., U.S. Dept. Justice, U.S. Conf. Mayors. Chmn. Ogden City Housing Authority; chmn. bd. trustees Utah State U., Space Dynamics Lab. Utah State U.; mem. adv. coun. Fed. Home Loan Bank; pres. Utah League Cities and Towns, 1981-82. Col. USAF, 1957. Mem. ABA, Weber County Bar Assn. (pres. 1966-68), Utah Bar Assn., Am. Judicature Soc., Weber County Bar Legal Svcs. (chmn. bd. trustees 1966-69), Utah Assn. Mcpl. Judges (sec.), Sigma Chi, Phi Alpha Delta. Home: 1715 Darling St Ogden UT 84403-0556 Office: City of Ogden 2484 Washington Blvd Ste 300 Ogden UT 84401-2319

MECHAM, STEVEN RAY, school system administrator; b. Salt Lake City, Oct. 10, 1938; s. Milton Claudius and Marjorie (White) M.; m. Donna Jean Johnson, Jan. 22, 1943; children: Brian Paul, Allan LeRoy. AS, Weber State Coll., 1958; BS, U. Utah, 1963; MA, Tchrs. Coll., Columbia U., 1965; postgrad. McGill U.; PhD U. Santa Barbara, Calif., 1981. Prin., Montreal (Que.) Oral Sch., 1966-70; state dir. hearing impaired Conn. Dept. Edn., 1970-71; dir. guidance Lexington Sch. for the Deaf, N.Y.C., 1971-72; supt. Exton Elem., Ana Frank Jr. & Sr. High Sch., Mexico City, 1972-77; coord. spl. edn. Weber Sch. Dist., Ogden, Utah, 1977-78; prin. Roosevelt Elem. Sch., Ogden, 1978-82; asst. supt. Weber County Schs., Ogden, 1982-87, Utah Schs., 1990—, assoc. supt. 1990-93; supt. Weber Sch. Dist., 1993—; instr. U. Utah, 1965-66, St. Joseph Coll., Hartford, Conn., 1970-71; pres. Finnish Mission-LDS Russia and Baltic States, 1987-90; adj. prof. McGill U.; instr. Tchrs. Coll., Columbia U., 1968-70; acting chmn. dept. edn. U. Americas, Mexico City, 1976-77; cons. Far West Labs., San Francisco. Bd. dirs. Instituto Mexicano Norte Americano de Relaciones Culturales, Mexico City, 1975-76; bishop Ch. Jesus Christ of Latter-day Saints, chmn. Cancer Crusade; pres. Finnish Mission Ch. Jesus Christ of Latter-day Saints; bd. dirs. Am. Cancer Soc. Weber County. Mem. Am. Orgn. Educators of Hearing Impaired (pres.), Can. Hearing Soc. (dir.), Utah Assn. Elem. Sch. Prins., Nat. Assn. Elem. Sch. Prins., Internat. Reading Assn., Am. Assn. Sch. Adminstrs., Alexander Graham Bell Assn. Club: Rotary. Contbr. articles to profl. jours. Home: 2163 Jennifer Dr Ogden UT 84403-4965 Office: 5320 Adams Ave Ogden UT 84405-6913

MECHANIC, DAVID, social sciences educator; b. N.Y.C., Feb. 21, 1936; s. Louis and Tillie (Penn) M.; m. Kathleen Mars Wiltshire; children: Robert Edmund, Michael Alexander. B.A., CCNY, 1956; M.A., Stanford U., 1957, Ph.D., 1959. Faculty U. Wis., Madison, 1960-79; prof. sociology U. Wis., 1965-73, John Bascom prof., 1973-79; dir. U. Wis. (Center for Med. Sociology and Health Services Research), 1971-79, chmn. dept. sociology, 1968-70; prof. social work and sociology Rutgers U., New Brunswick, N.J., 1979—; acting dean faculty arts and scis. Rutgers U., 1980-81, Univ. prof., dean faculty arts and scis., 1981-84, Univ. prof. and Rene Dubos prof. behavioral scis., 1984—, dir. Inst. for Health, Health Care Policy and Aging Research, 1985—; mem. panel on health svcs. rsch. Pres.'s Sci. Adv. Com., 1971-72; mem. treatment com. on reduction of cancer mortality Nat. Cancer Inst., 1984; vice-chmn. com. pain, disability and chronic illness behavior Inst. Medicine-NAS, 1985-86, mem. panel on prevention of disability, 1989-90; mem. Com. on Prevention of Mental Disorder, 1992-94; coord. panel Pres.'s Commn. Mental Health, 1977-78; mem. Nat. Adv. Coun. Aging, NIH, 1982-86; expert adv. panel on mental health WHO, 1984-89; mem. health adv. bd. GAO, 1987-95; mem. panel on tech., ins. and health care sys. Office of Tech. U.S. Congress, 1992-95; mem. nat. com. on vital and health stats. HHS, 1988-92; mem. commn. on behavioral and social scis. and edn. NRC, 1992-95, commn. on med. edn. Robert Wood Johnson Found., 1990-92; mem. adv. com. Picker/Commonwealth Scholar's Program, 1992—; nat. adv. com. Robert Wood Johnson Scholars in Health Policy Rsch. Program, 1992—; mem. panel on Rethinking Disability Policy, Nat. Acad. Social Ins., 1993-96; vis. scholar Kings Fund Inst., london, 1994-95. Author: Students Under Stress, 1962, 2d edit., 1978, Medical Sociology, 1968, rev. edit., 1978, Mental Health and Social Policy, 1969, rev. edit., 1980, 89, Public Expectations and Health Care, 1972, Politics, Medicine and Social Science, 1974, (with Charles E. Lewis and Rashi Fein) A Right to Health, 1976, Growth of Bureaucratic Medicine, 1976, Future Problems in Health Care, 1979, From Advocacy to Allocation: The Evolving American Health Care System, 1986, Painful Choices: Research and Essays on Health Care, 1989, Inescapable Decisions: The Imperatives of Health Reform, 1994; author, editor: Symptoms, Illness Behavior and Help-Seeking; editor: Handbook of Health, Health Care and the Health Professions, 1983, Improving Mental Health Services: What the Social Sciences Can Tell Us, 1987; Co-editor: (with Robert Houser, Archibald Haller and Tess Hauser) Social Structure and Personality, 1982, (with Linda Aiken) Applications of Social Science to Clinical Medicine and Social Policy, 1986; Paying for Services: Promises and Pitfalls of Capitation, 1989; (with Marian Osterweis and Arthur Kleinman) Pain and Disability: Clinical Behavior and Public Policy Perspectives, 1987, (with Carl Taube and Ann Hohmann) The Future of Mental Health Services Research, 1989. Fellow Ctr. for Advanced Study in Behavioral Scis., 1974-75, NIMH rsch. fellow, 1965-66, Ford Behavioral Sci. fellow, 1956-57, Guggenheim fellow, 1977-78; recipient Ward medal CCNY, 1956, Med. Sociologists award Am. Sociol. Assn., 1983, Carl Taube award APHA, 1990, Disting. Investigator award Assn. for Health Svcs. Rsch., 1991, Disting. Contbn. award mental health sect. Soc. for Study of Social Problems, 1991, Emily Mumford medal Columbia U., 1991, Investigator award in health policy rsch. Robert Wood Johnson Found., 1995—, Baxter prize, 1997. Fellow AAAS (chmn. sect. social, econ. and polit. scis. 1985); mem. Am. Sociol. Assn. (governing coun. 1977-78, chmn. med. sociol. sect. 1969-70, chmn. publs. com. 1989-91, chmn. mental health sect. 1992-93), Sociol. Rsch. Assn. (pres. 1991-92), Inst. Medicine-Nat. Acad. Scis. (governing coun. 1972-74), Nat. Acad. Scis., Am. Acad. Arts and Scis., Hogg Found. Mental Health (nat. adv. coun. 1987), Phi Beta Kappa. Office: Rutgers U Inst Health Policy Aging Rsch 30 College Ave New Brunswick NJ 08901-1245 Home: 5 Overlook Dr Princeton NJ 08540-3924

MECHANIC, WILLIAM M., television and motion picture industry executive; b. Detroit. BA in English, Mich. State U.; PhD in Film, U. So. Calif. Dir. programming SelecTV, 1978-80, v.p. programming, 1980-82; v.p. pay TV Paramount Pictures Corp., 1982-84; v.p. pay TV sales Walt Disney Pictures and TV, 1984-85, sr. v.p. video, 1985-87, pres. internat. theatrical distbn. and worldwide video, 1987-93; pres., COO 20th Century Fox Film Entertainment, 1993—; now pres. Fox Inc., Beverly Hills, Calif. Office: Fox Inc PO Box 900 Beverly Hills CA 90213-0900*

MECHEM, CHARLES STANLEY, JR., former broadcasting executive, former golf association executive; b. Nelsonville, Ohio, Sept. 12, 1930; s. Charles Stanley and Helen (Hall) M.; m. Marilyn Brown, Aug. 31, 1952; children: Melissa, Daniel, Allison. A.B., Miami U., Oxford, Ohio, 1952; LL.B., Yale U., 1955. Bar: Ohio 1955. Practice in Cin., 1955-67; partner Taft, Stettinius & Hollister, 1965-67; chmn. bd. Taft Broadcasting Co., Cin., 1967-90; commr. LPGA, Daytona Beach, Fla., 1990-95, commr. emeritus, 1995—; chmn. U.S. Shoe, 1993-95; chmn. Cin. Bell, Inc., 1996—; bd. dirs. Star Bank N.A., Cin., AGCO Corp., Myers Y. Cooper Co., Mead Corp., Ohio Nat. Life Ins. Co., Cin. Bell, J.M. Smucker Co. Capt. JAGC, U.S. Army, 1956-59. Mem. Cin. C. of C. (pres. 1977). Club: Commercial (Cin.). Office: Cin Bell Inc 120 E 4th St Ste 7 Cincinnati OH 45202-4010*

MECHLEM, DAPHNE JO, vocational school educator; b. Cin., Oct. 20, 1946; d. Louis Edward Griffith and Esther Eileen (Calvert) Griffith-Schultz; m. James T. Mechlem, Nov. 18, 1967 (div. June 1983); 1 chld, Louis Henry. BS summa cum laude, U. Cin., 1982, MS, 1983, MEd, 1984. Cert. vocat. and adult dir., supr., cosmetology instr., real estate agt. Stylist, mgr. Fashion Flair Styling, Cin., 1965-70, Ann Wolfe Coiffures, Cin., 1970-71; salon owner Curls by Daphne, Cin., 1971-77; tchr. Great Oaks Joint Vocat. Sch. Dist., Cin., 1976-83, adminstrv. intern, 1983; probation officer Hamilton County Juvenile Ct., Cin., 1983—; tchr. Great Oaks Joint Vocat. Sch. Dist., Cin., 1983—; spkr., presenter workshops in field. Author: Critical Issues in Campus Policing, 1983; lectr: workshops, seminars and classes. Sec.-treas. Cin. Fashion Guild. Mem. ASCD, Nat. Cosmetology Assn., Criminal Justice Assn., Am. Vocat. Assn., Ohio Vocat. Assn., Ohio Vocat. Cosmetology Tchrs. Assn. (2d v.p., continuing edn. adminstr.). Avocations: flying, travel, counseling. Home: 5776 Pleasant Hill Rd Milford OH 45150-2301

MECHLIN, GEORGE FRANCIS, electrical manufacturing company executive; b. Pitts., July 23, 1923; s. George Francis and Ruth (Butler) M.; m. Mary Louise Megaffin, June 25, 1949; children—Thomas Walker, Ann Louise. B.S. in Physics, U. Pitts., 1944, M.S. in Physics, 1949, Ph.D. in Physics, 1951. With Westinghouse Electric Corp., 1949-87; gen. mgr. astronuclear/oceanic div. Westinghouse Electric Corp., Balt., 1971-72, v.p. astronuclear lab., oceanic and marine divs., 1972-73; v.p. R & D Westinghouse Electric Corp., Pitts., 1973-87; pub. svc. cons., 1990—. Past bd. dirs. Buhl Planatarium. Recipient Meritorious Public Service award U.S. Navy, 1961, John J. Montgomery award Nat. Soc. Aerospace Profls. and San Diego Aerospace Mus., 1961; Order of Merit award Westinghouse Electric Corp., 1961. Mem. Am. Phys. Soc., AIAA, Nat. Acad. Engring., Sigma Xi. Home: 960 Via Malibu Aptos CA 95003-5617

MECIMORE, CHARLES DOUGLAS, accounting educator; b. Belmont, N.C., Aug. 20, 1934; s. John Edgar and Hattie (Bolick) M.; m. Barbara Jean Chiddie, June 7, 1959; children: Laura Jean, Charles D. Jr., John Amos. BS, Pfeiffer Coll., 1958; MS, U. N.C., 1962; PhD, U. Ala., 1966. CPA, N.C.; CMA. Asst. prof. U. Ala., Tuscaloosa, 1966-67; assoc. prof. U. Ga., Athens, 1967-71; prof. U. Cin., 1971-79; prof. acctg. Sch. Bus. and Econs., U. N.C., Greensboro, 1980—; head dept. U. N.C. Sch. Bus. and Econs., 1980-89, 96—. Served with USAF, 1951-55. Univ. scholar, 1963-66; Haskins and Sells fellow, 1962-64; Beyer bronze medal, 1974. Mem. AICPAs, N.C. Assn. CPAs (Outstanding Educator 1985), Am. Acctg. Assn., Inst. Mgmt. Acctg. Home: 1312 Westridge Rd Greensboro NC 27410-2940 Office: U NC Sch Bus and Econs Greensboro NC 27412

MECKE, THEODORE HART MCCALLA, JR., management consultant; b. Phila., Mar. 6, 1923; s. Theodore Hart McCalla and Genevieve (Loughney) M.; m. Mary E. Flaherty, July 14, 1956; children: William Moyn, Theodore Hart III, John Chetwood, Stephen Campbell. Student, LaSalle U., Phila., 1941, LL.D. (hon.), 1964; D Mgmt. (hon.), Lawrence Technol. U., 1983. Mng. editor Germantown (Pa.) Courier, 1942-43, 46-49; with Ford Motor Co., Dearborn, Mich., 1949-80; gen. pub. rels. mgr. Ford Motor Co., 1957-63, v.p. pub. rels., 1963-69, v.p. pub. affairs group, 1969-80; pres. Econ. Club Detroit, 1980-84, Hartwood Assocs., Detroit, 1984-93; trustee Henry Ford Health Sys., Detroit. Served with AUS, 1943-45. Mem. Mil. Order Loyal Legion, Am. Legion. Roman Catholic. Clubs: Country of Detroit, Cardinal, Yondotega. Home: 400 Chalfonte Ave Grosse Pointe MI 48236-2943

MECKEL, PETER TIMOTHY, arts administrator, educator; b. Yankton, S.D., Nov. 28, 1941; s. Myron Eugene and Cynthia Ann (Turnblom) M.; m. Louise Gloria Mudge, Sept. 8, 1962; children: Christina Louise, Christopher Mark; m. Adrienne Dawn Maravich, Dec. 30, 1972; children: Moya Anne, Jon-Peter. Ed. Rockford Coll., Occidental Coll. Founder, gen. dir. Hidden Valley Music Seminars, Carmel Valley, Calif., 1963—, dir. Hidden Valley Opera Ensemble, Masters Festival of Chamber Music, Master Class Series; cons. in field. Mem. Music Educators Nat. Conf. Congregationalist. Office: Hidden Valley Opera Ensemble PO Box 116 Carmel Valley CA 93924-0116

MECKLENBURG, GARY ALAN, hospital executive; m. Lynn Kraemer; children: John, Sarah. BA, Northwestern U., 1968; MBA, U. Chgo., 1970. Adminstrv. resident Presbyn.-St. Luke's Hosp., Chgo., 1969-70, adminstrv. asst., 1970-71, asst. supt., 1971-76, assoc. supt., 1976-77; assoc. supt. U. Wis. Hosps., Madison, 1977-80; adminstr. Stanford U. Hosp. Clinics, Calif.; pres., CEO St. Joseph's Hosp., Milw., 1980-85; pres., dir. Franciscan Health Care Inc., Milw., 1985; pres., CEO Northwestern Meml. Hosp., Northwestern Meml. Corp., Chgo., 1985—; preceptor, guest lectr., mem. adv. bd. Kellogg Sch. Mgmt., chgo., 1986—; pres., chief exec. officer, dir. Northwestern Healthcare Network, 1990-92. Recipient Harold M. Coon, M.D. Merit award Wis. Hosp. Assn., 1974. Mem. Am. Hosp. Assn. (sect. met. hosps., mem. bd. trustees 1996—, exec. com. 1996—, chmn. sect. 1991, mem. regional policy bd., #5 1984-85, 87-94, 95—, mem. ho. dels. 1984, 87, mem. com. on med. edn. 1987-90), Ill. Hosp. Assn. (bd. dirs. 1988—, chmn. 1994, mem. steering com. coun. tchg. hosps. 1985—), U. Chgo. Hosp. Adminstrn. Alumni Assn. (pres. 1985-86), Econ. Club Chgo., Comml. Club Chgo. Office: Northwestern Meml Hosp 250 E Superior St Ste 290 Chicago IL 60611-2914

MECKLER, ALAN MARSHALL, publisher, author; b. N.Y.C., July 25, 1945; s. Herman Louis and Lillian (Brodsky) M.; m. Ellen Laurie Finkelstein, Sept. 10, 1969; children—Naomi, Kate, Caroline, John. B.A., Columbia Coll., 1967; M.A., Columbia U., 1968, Ph.D., 1980. Pres., chmn., CEO Mecklermedia Corp., Westport, Conn., 1970—; bd. dirs. Princeton Univ. Press. Author: The Draft and Its Enemies, 1973; Micropublishing: A History of Scholarly Micropublishing in America, 1938-80, 1982; Complete Guide to Winning Lotteries by Mail, 1985. Served with USAR, 1969-75. Office: 20 Ketchum St Westport CT 06880-5908

MECREDY, JAMES R., management consultant; b. Roanoke, Va., Sept. 24, 1918; s. James Roderick and Rosalie Digges (Miller) M.; m. Alice Chatfield, April 8, 1944; children: Robert Clark, Thomas Randolph, Russell Edwards. BSME, Purdue U., 1941; attended, Case Inst. Tech., 1946-48, Alexander Hamilton Inst., 1941-43. Student engr. Gen. Motors Corp., Anderson, Ind., 1941-43; foundry foreman Delco-Remy-G.M., Bedford, Ind., 1943-45; foundry engr., trouble shooter Nat. Bronze and Aluminum Foundry Co., Cleve., 1945-46; machine designer Motch & Merryweather Machinery Co., Cleve., 1946-47; engr. Cleve. Range Co., 1947-54, chief engr., 1954-71, v.p. ops., 1971-74; mgmt. cons., 1974-75; tchr. shop, math. Delco-Remy Foundry, Bedford, Ind., 1943-44, blue print reading, 1943-44. Author: (manual) Instrn. and Maintenance Manual, 1973, District Boy Scouts, 1959; patentee. Dir., coach swimming Anderson YMCA, 1941-42; coach Little League Baseball, Lakewood, Ohio, 1950; precinct committeeman Rep. Com., 1945-46; chmn. dist. fund raising Boy Scouts Am., 1975, scoutmaster, 1955-77, chmn. protestant com., 1974-94. Recipient Scouting Wood badge, 1964, Silver Beaver award Boy Scouts Am., 1968, Nat. Hornaday award N.Y. Zool. Body, 1977, St. Georges award Cleve. Cath. Diocese, 1982, God and Svc. award Presbyn. Western Res., 1991, Nat. Eagle Scout Scoutmaster award, 1990. Mem. Nat. Assn. Presbyn. Scouters (trustee, deacon 1957-66, regional v.p. 1992-95), Kiwanis (pres. 1982-83). Avocations: photography, travel, camping, canoeing, wood carving. Home: 13425 Cliff Dr Cleveland OH 44107-1401

MEDAK, PETER, film director; b. Budapest, Hungary; arrived in Eng., 1963; came to U.S., 1979; s. Gyula and Elisabeth (Diamonstein) M.; m. Julia Migenes, July 31, 1989; children: Christopher, Karen, Joshua, Cornelia, Martina, Jessica. Dir. (films) Negatives, 1968, A Day in the Death of Joe Egg, 1970, The Ruling Class, 1971, Ghost in a Nonnday's Sun, 1973, The Odd Job, 1977, The Changling, 1979, Zorro the Gay Blade, 1980, The Men's Club, 1986, The Krays, 1989, La Voix Humane, 1990, Let Him Have It, 1991, Romeo is Bleeding, 1992, Pontiac Moon, 1994, Hunchback of Notre Dame, 1996, Species 2, 1997, (stage) Miss Julie, 1977 (opera) Salome, 1988, La Voix Humane, and others. Mem. Dir.'s Guild of Am., Dir.'s Guild of U.K., Assn. of Cinematographers, Allied Technicians, Dir.'s Guild of Can. Jewish. Office: Fred Actman & Co 9255 W Sunset Blvd Ste 901 Los Angeles CA 90069-3306

MEDAK, WALTER HANS, lawyer; b. Vienna, Austria, May 10, 1915; came to U.S., 1938; s. Hugo and Grete (Figdor) M.; m. Edith Rhodes, 1944 (div. 1957); 1 child, Ronald Harvard; m. Renée Rasens, 1996. Grad., Acad. of Commerce, Vienna, 1934, U. Vienna, 1938; postgrad., U. Ga., 1939-40; MA in Econs., U. Calif., Berkeley, 1949; JD, Harvard U., 1948. Prodn. mgr. Mabs, Inc., L.A., 1942-43; prodn. engr. Kaiser Co., Richmond, Calif., 1943-45; atty. Belli & Medak, Walnut Creek, Calif., 1957-59; pvt. practice law Walnut Creek and Moraga, Calif., 1950—; bd. dirs. Snyder/Newell, Inc., San Francisco; bd. dirs. Carnelian Woods, Carnelian Bay, Calif., pres., 1974-90. Mem. ABA, Calif. County Bar Assn., Assn. Trial Lawyers Am., Calif. Trial Lawyers Assn., Harvard Club (chmn. admissions and scholarship com. San Francisco chpt. 1973-74). Avocations: skiing, swimming, music, travel. Home and Office: 173 Ardith Dr Orinda CA 94563

MEDALIE, JACK HARVEY, physician; b. Buhl, Minn., Jan. 8, 1922; m.; 3 children. BSc, Witwatersrand U., Johannesburg, 1941; MD, BChir, Witwatersrand U., 1945; MPH (hon.), Harvard U., 1958. Instr. dept. anatomy U. Witwatersrand, Johannesburg, 1942-43; sr. lectr. dept. social medicine Hebrew U., Hadassah, Jerusalem, 1962-66; from assoc. prof. to prof., chmn. dept. family medicine Tel-Aviv U., 1966-74; chmn. dept. family medicine Case Western Res. U., 1975-87, prof. cmty. health, 1976-87, prof. family medicine, 1976—, prof. med. and pediat., 1978—, prof. emeritus, 1992—; resident Johannesburg, 1945-47; rural family physician, 1948-53; med. dir. Family and Cmty. Health Ctr., Jerusalem, 1953-62; prin. investigator Israel Ischemic Heart Disease Study, 1962-75; co-prin. investigator congenital abnormality study NIH, 1972-74, Robert Wood Johnson Found. fellowship program C.W.R.U., 1978-88; vis. prof., family medicine and epidemiology U. N.C., Chapel Hill, 1973-74; vis. sr. rsch. scientist, Nat. Heart, Blood and Lung Inst., Bethesda, Md., 1974, 90-91; med. coun. U. Hosps. Cleve., 1975-87, com. impaired physicians, 1980-87; med. edn. com. Case Western Res. U., 1980-85, chmn. ambulatory and primary care clerkship com., 1981-83; task force health consequences bereavement Nat. Acad. Sci., 1982-85, membership com., 1984-88; dir. dept. family practice U. Hosps., Cleve., 1982-87; rsch. coms. Mt. Sinai Med. Ctr., Cleve., 1991—. Contbr. articles to profl. jours. Active IDF, 1948-49. Recipient Lifetime Achievement award in medicine Golden Age Ctrs. Fellow Am. Acad. Family Physicians, Am. Heart Assn., Royal Soc. Med. Found.; mem. Inst. Med.-Nat. Acad. Sci., Soc. Tchrs. Family Medicine (chmn. at. task force 1985-87, Curtis Hames Career Rsch. award 1988, Cert. Excellence 1988, Maurice Saltzman award 1988), Soc. Behavioral Medicine. Office: Case Western Res Univ Dept of Family Medicine 10900 Euclid Ave Cleveland OH 44106-1712

MEDALIE, MARJORIE LYNN, educational administrator, consultant; b. Bklyn., June 25, 1947; d. Charles and Bette P. (Feldman) Drucker; m. Randolph Medalie, Mar. 26, 1970; children: Jeremy Chad, Daniel Bradley. BA, Ithaca Coll., 1969; MA, Adelphi U., 1973, spl. edn. cert., 1985; profl. diploma, C. W. Post Coll., 1991. Cert. spl. educator, sch. dist. adminstr. Tchr. English, Island Trees (N.Y.) Sch. Dist., 1970-73, West Hempstead (N.Y.) Sch. Dist., 1973-76; tchr. spl. edn. Summit Sch., Forrest Hills, N.Y., 1976-77; coord. alternative class program Huntington (N.Y.) U.F.S.D. # 3, 1982-86; tchr. spl. edn. self-contained classroom Center Moriches (N.Y.) Sch. Dist., Riverhead, N.Y., 1986-88; lead tchr. for alternative high schs. Bd. Coop. Scnl. Svcs. 1, Riverhead, N.Y., 1988—; presenter in field. v.p. Am. Cancer Soc., Melville, N.Y., 1974-81; mgr. Tri-Village Little League, Greenlawn, N.Y., 1986-90; active edn. com. Temple Chaverim. Mem. ASCD, Nat. Coun. Tchrs. English, United Fedn. Tchrs., East End Counselors Assn., Western Suffolk Counselors, Kappa Delta Pi, Epsilon Nu Gamma. Jewish. Avocations: skiing, reading, travel, boating, cooking.

MEDALIE, RICHARD JAMES, lawyer; b. Duluth, Minn., July 21, 1929; s. William Louis and Mona (Kolad) M.; m. Susan Diane Abrams, June 5, 1960; children: Samuel David, Daniel Alexander. B.A. summa cum laude, U. Minn., 1952; cert., U. London, 1953; A.M., Harvard U., 1955, J.D. cum laude, 1958. Bar: D.C. 1958, N.Y. 1963. Law clk. to Hon. George T. Washington U.S. Ct. Appeals, Washington, 1958-59; asst. solicitor gen. U.S.,

1960-62; assoc. Kaye, Scholer, Fierman, Hays & Handler, N.Y.C., 1962-65; dep. dir. Ford Found. Inst. Criminal Law and Procedure, Georgetown U. Law Ctr., 1965-68; ptnr. Friedman & Medalie and predecessors, Washington, 1968—; pres. Pegasus Internat., Washington, 1970—; exec. dir. The Appleseed Found., Washington, 1993-94, chmn. bd., 1993—; of counsel Brock, Fensterstock, Silverstein, McAuliffe & Wade, LLC, 1995—; adj. prof. adminstrv. and criminal law Georgetown U. Law Center, 1967-70; Mem. D.C. Law Revision Commn., 1975-87, chmn. Criminal Law Task Force, mem. exec. com., 1978-82; panel comml. arbitrators Am. Arbitration Assn., 1964—; vice chmn. Harvard Law Sch. Fund, 1981-84, chmn. nat. maj. gifts, 1984-86, dep. chmn., 1986-87, chmn. 1987-89. Author: From Escobedo to Miranda: The Anatomy of a Supreme Court Decision, 1966; co-author: Federal Consumer Safety Legislation, 1970; co-author, editor: Commercial Arbitration for the 1990s, 1991; co-editor: Crime: A Community Responds, 1967; staff: Harvard Law Rev., 1956-58; case editor, 1957-58; contbr. articles to legal jours. Bd. dirs. alumni assn. Expt. in Internat. Living, Brattleboro, Vt., 1961-64, pres., 1962-63. Fulbright scholar, 1952-53; Ford fellow, 1954-55. Mem. ABA (program chair 1984, 90, chair legis. subcom. 1986-89, ADR/arbitration com., rep. on adv. com. nat. conf. Emerging ADR Issues in State and Fed. Cts. 1991, vice chair 1991-94, arbitration com. litigation sect., co-chair nat. conf. Critical Issues in Arbitration 1993), D.C. Unified Bar, Assn. Bar City of N.Y., Am. Law Inst., Harvard Law Sch. Assn. D.C. (pres. 1976-77, nat. v.p. 1977-78), Harvard Alumni Assn. (law sch. dir. 1991-95), Cosmos Club, Harvard Club of Washington, Phi Beta Kappa, Phi Alpha Theta. Home: 3113 Macomb St NW Washington DC 20008-3325 Office: 1901 Pennsylvania Ave NW Washington DC 20006-3405

MEDALIE, SUSAN DIANE, management consultant; b. Boston, Oct. 7, 1941; d. Samuel and Matilda (Bortman) Abrams; m. Richard James Medalie, June 5, 1960; children: Samuel David, Daniel Alexander. BA, Sarah Lawrence Coll., 1960; MA, George Washington U., 1962, Cert. Pubs. Spec., 1977; JD, Am. U., 1986. Bar: Pa., 1987, D.C., 1987. Pres. Medalie Cons., Washington, 1980—; dep. dir. U.S. Holocaust Meml. Coun., Washington, 1980-82; assoc. pub. Campaigns & Elections, Washington, 1983-84; legis. analyst Subcom./House Energy and Commerce, Washington, 1985; ea. regional dir. Josephson Found. for Adv. Ethics, L.A., 1986-88; asst. dean for external affairs George Washington U. Nat. Law Ctr., Washington, 1988-90; exec. dir. Internat. Soc. Global Health Policy, Washington and Paris, 1990-93; pvt. practice law Washington, 1993—; corp. liaison First Hosp. Corp., Norfolk, Va., 1986-88; assoc. producer and cons. Prof. Arthur Miller's "Headlines on Trial" (NBC), N.Y.C., 1987-91. Editor/pub.: Getting There mag., 1977-80; sr. editor: Am. Univ. Law Rev., Washington, 1984-86. Nat. dep. fin. dir. Edward M. Kennedy for Pres. com., Washington, 1979-80; co-chair Patricia Roberts harris for Mayor, Washington, 1982. Mem. Florence Crittenton Home (bd. dirs. exec. com. 1980-83), ABA, DC Bar. Office: Medalie Cons 1901 Pennsylvania Ave NW Washington DC 20006-3405

MEDAVOY, MIKE, motion picture company executive; b. Shanghai, China, Jan. 21, 1941; came to U.S., 1957, naturalized, 1962; s. Michael and Dora Medavoy; m. Irena Medavoy; 1 child, Brian. B.A., UCLA, 1963. With Casting dept. Universal Studios, 1963; agt. Bill Robinson Assos., Los Angeles, 1963-64; v.p. motion picture dept. GAC/CMA Co., 1965-71, IFA Co., 1971-74; sr. v.p. United Artists Corp., 1974-78; one of founders, exec. v.p. Orion Pictures Co., Burbank, Calif., 1978-82; exec. v.p. Orion Pictures Corp. (formerly Orion Pictures Co.), Burbank, 1982-90; chmn. Tri-Star Pictures, Inc., Burbank, 1990—, Phoenix Picture Corp., 1995—; bd. dirs. Sony Pictures Corp., co-chmn. Am. Cinematech.; jury chmn. Tokyo Film Festival 1994; hon. co-chair St. Petersburg Film Festival, 1992; adv. bd. Shanghai Film Conf.; co-chmn. Am. Cinematheque, 1997—. Mem. vis. com. Boston Museum Fine Arts.; chmn. Ctr. Internat. Strategic Affairs, UCLA, Com. to Cure Cancer through Immunization UCLA; co-chmn. Olympic Sports Fedn. Com., Music Ctr. Unified Fund Campaign; co-founder Sundance Film Inst.; bd. govs. Sundance Inst., 1980-86; bd. dirs. Calif. Mus. Sci. and Industry, 1984-87. Recipient Academy award for One Flew Over the Cuckoo's Nest, Rocky, Annie Hall, Amadeus, Platoon, Dances With Wolves, Silence of the Lambs, Motion Picture Pioneer award, 1992, Career Achievement award UCLA, 1997. Mem. Acad. Motion Picture Arts and Scis. (gov. 1977-81), UCLA Found., UCLA Chancellors Assocs.

MEDDING, WALTER SHERMAN, environmental engineer; b. St. Louis, Mar. 4, 1922; s. Walter Lyman and Elizabeth Steele (Sherman) M.; m. Mary Agnes Patty Johnson, Apr. 22, 1944; children: Jean, Walter, Mauri. BSCE, Va. Poly. Inst., 1947, MS in Sanitary Engring., 1970. Registered profl. engr., Va., N.C., Kans. Various positions U.S. Army, 1942-64; student officer advanced course The Engr. Sch., Ft. Belvoir, Va., 1952-53, head fixed bridges sect., 1953-55; asst. engr. Asmara Eritrea, chief design br. Mediterranean Divsn., Gulf Dist., Tehran, Iran, 1955-57; asst. divsn. engr. 9th Infantry Divsn., Ft. Carson, Colo., 1957-59; resident engr. USACAG, chief constrn. ops. U.S. Army Engring. Command Europe, Frankfurt, Germany, 1959-72; chief contract adminstrn. U.S. Army Engring. Divsn. Europe, Frankfurt, Germany, 1972-75; chief environ. engring. Office, Chief of Engrs., U.S. Army, Washington, 1975-86; sr. engr. Romem Aqua Sys. Co., Woodbridge, Va., 1986—. Co-author: (textbook) Non-standard Military Fixed Bridges, 1954; contbr. articles to profl. jours. Mem. ASCE, Am. Waterworks Assn., Water Environment Fedn., Conf. of Fed. Environ. Engrs. Republican. Episcopalian. Achievements include development of mil. bridge classification procedures for load carrying and rapid field design. Home: 204 Brooke Dr Fredericksburg VA 22408

MEDDLES, SHARON DIANE GUNSTREAM, school counselor; b. Pasadena, Calif., Feb. 9, 1947; d. Jarrell William and Vivian Irene (Heffner) Gunstream; m. Larry Wayne Meddles, June 16, 1973; children: Brittany Dawn, Brooke Reneé. BA in English, Pasadena Coll., 1968; MEd in Counseling, U. Phoenix, 1996. Cert. tchr., Ariz. Jr. high tchr. Adams County Dist. 12, Northglenn, Colo., 1969-72; jr. high tchr. Washington Elem. Sch. Dist. 6, Phoenix, 1972-76, homebound tchr., 1985-86, 88-90; sr. high tchr. N.W. Christian Acad., Glendale, Ariz., 1986-87; jr. high tchr. Washington Sch. Dist., Phoenix, 1990-96, elem. sch. counselor, 1996—. Core group leader Cmty. Bible Study, Phoenix, 1988-90; bd. dirs. Orangewood Ch. of the Nazarene, Phoenix, 1982-84, 93; local pres. Nazarene World Missionary Soc., 1982-84; dist. dir. Point Loma Alumni Bd., San Diego, 1990-93, sec., 1993-96; mem. Valley Cathedral. Republican. Avocations: singing, cooking. Home: 1115 W Le Marche Ave Phoenix AZ 85023-4429

MEDDLETON, DANIEL JOSEPH, health facility administrator; b. July 11, 1936. AA in Bus. Adminstrn., Broome Tech. Community Coll., Binghamton, N.Y., 1959; BSBA, Mich. Technol. U., 1964; M in Health Care Adminstrn., Univ. Minn., 1966. Asst. adminstr. Clifton Springs Hosp. and Clinic, 1966-68, Univ. Cin. Med. Ctr., 1968-70; assoc. adminstr. Providence Hosp., Anchorage, Alaska, 1970-76; exec. v.p. Benedictine Hosp., Kingston, N.Y., 1976-82; dir. Div. Planning, Policy and Prog. Evaluation State of Alaska/Dept. Health and Social Svcs., 1983-84; owner Kits Cameras, Juneau, Alaska, 1984-90; adminstr. Juneau Pioneers' Home, 1988-93, Alaska Psychiat. Hosp., 1993-95; dir. Dept. Health and Social Svcs. North Slope Borough, Barrow, Alaska, 1995-96; CEO Healthcare Project Mgmt. Group, 1997—. Bd. dirs. Alaska Econ. Devel. Adv. Coun., Benedictine Hosp, Kingston, N.Y., Bartlett Meml. Hosp., Juneau, Barrow Hosp., Samuel Diamonds Meml. Hosp., Barrow, Big Bros./Big Sisters, others; mem. steering com. S.E. Alaska Regional Econ. Devel. Inst., 1987. Fellow Am. Coll. Health Care Execs. (regent 1995—); mem. No. N.Y. Met. Hosp. Assn. (past bd. dirs.), Mid Hudson Health Systems Agy. (past bd. dirs.), Rotary, others. Avocations: outdoor sports, photography, camping, backpacking, sailing, flying. Home: 3220 Evergreen St Anchorage AK 99504

MEDDLETON, FRANCIS CHARLES, elementary and secondary school educator; b. Johnson City, N.Y., Nov. 17, 1942; s. Willett J. and Julia (Curley) M.; m. Linda I. Albright, July 10, 1965; children: Dennis K., Laura D. AA, Cayuga County C.C., Auburn, N.Y., 1964; BS, Old Dominion U., 1969; MEd, U. Va., 1972; MA, U. South Fla., 1978, EdS, 1979; BA, SUNY, Albany, 1986; postgrad., Brigham Young U., 1991, U. Houston, 1991, U. St. Thomas, Houston, 1992-93. Tchr. Pub. Sch. Systems, Va., 1969-72, Fla., 1972-82, Tex., 1982-96; instr. Lee Coll., Baytown, Tex., 1989-94; tchr. specialist Harris County Children Protective Svcs. Houston Ind. Sch. Dist., 1994—; cons. insvc. tng. Galena Park Ind. Sch. Dist., Houston, 1982-83, North Forest Ind. Sch. Dist., Houston, 1983-89, Lee Coll., Baytown, 1989-94, Houston Ind. Sch. Dist., 1994—, San Jacinto Coll., Houston, 1995—. Mem. Rep. Nat. Com., Houston, 1989, Am. Legion, Houston, 1989. With USNR, 1961-67. Decorated Nat. Def. Svc. medal. Mem. NRA, NEA, Tex. Coll. Tchrs. Assn., Tex. Faculty Assn., Tex. State Tchrs. Assn. Roman Catholic. Home: 12811 Woodlite Ln Houston TX 77015-2053

MEDEARIS, DONALD NORMAN, JR., physician, educator; b. Kansas City, Kans., Aug. 22, 1927; s. Donald Norman and Gladys (Sandford) M.; m. Mary Ellen Marble, Aug. 25, 1956; children: Donald Harrison, Ellen Sandford, John Norman, Jennifer Marble. AB, U. Kans., 1950; MD, Harvard U., 1953. Diplomate: Am. Bd. Pediatrics. Intern internal medicine Barnes Hosp., St. Louis, 1953-54; resident pediatrics Children's Hosp., Cin., 1954-56; rsch. fellow pediatrics Harvard U. rsch. div. infectious diseases Children's Med. Ctr., Boston, 1956-58; from asst. to assoc. prof. pediatrics and microbiology Johns Hopkins Sch. Medicine, Balt., 1959-65; Joseph P. Kennedy Jr. Meml. Found. Sr. Rsch. Scholar in Mental Retardation, 1960-65; prof. pediatrics U. Pitts. Sch. Medicine, 1965-74, chmn. dept., 1965-69, dean, 1969-74; med. dir. Children's Hosp., Pitts., 1965-69; prof. pediatrics Case Western Res. U., Cleve., 1974-77; dir. pediatrics Cleve. Met. Gen. Hosp., 1974-77; Charles Wilder prof. pediatrics Harvard U. Med. Sch., 1977-95, Charles Wilder disting. prof. pediatrics, 1995—; chief Children's Svc. Mass. Gen. Hosp., Boston, 1977-95; mem. Pres.'s Commn. on Study Ethical Problems in Medicine and Biomed. and Behavioral Rsch., 1979-82. Contbr. articles to profl. jours., texts. Vestry Trinity Ch., Boston, 1983-87. Served with USNR, 1945-46. Mem. Am. Acad. Pediatrics, Am. Pediatric Soc., Infectious Disease Soc. Am., Inst. Medicine/Nat. Acad. Sci., Alpha Omega Alpha. Office: Massachusetts Gen Hosp Fruit St Boston MA 02114

MEDEARIS, KENNETH GORDON, research consultant, educator; b. Peoria, Ill., Aug. 5, 1930; s. Harold Oscar and Ferol Mae (Rowlett) M.; m. Mary Genevieve Barlow, June 28, 1953; children—Mark Allen, Mary Lynne, Terry Gordon. B.S., U. Ill., 1952, M.S., 1953; Ph.D., Stanford U., 1962. Registered profl. engr., Calif., Colo., N.Mex., Pa. Stress analyst Sandia Corp., Albuquerque, 1957-58; asst. prof. civil engring., U. N.Mex., 1958-62; assoc. prof. engring. Ariz. State U., 1962-63; engr., computer cons., Sunnyvale, Calif., 1963-66; dir. Computer Ctr., prof. civil engring. Colo. State U., Ft. Collins, 1966-69, adj. prof. civil and mech. engring., 1969—; lectr. N.Mex. State U., 1982—; cons. Kenneth Medearis Assoc., Ft. Collins, 1969—; structural dynamics and vibration engring. cons., Ft. Collins., 1969—; evaluation cons. UN. Author: Numerical-Computer Methods for Engineers and Physical Scientists, 1974. Contbr. articles to profl. jours. Mem. Stanford Regional Cabinet. Served to 1st lt. USAF, 1953-56. Recipient Outstanding Engring. Achievement award No. Colo. Profl. Engrs., 1974, Outstanding Engring. Achievement award Profl. Engrs. Colo., 1974, Disting. Engring. Alumnus award U. Ill., 1988, Recipient of The Maurice Simpson Outstanding Tech. Paper award, Inst. of Environ. Scis., 1996. Mem. Colo. Earthquake Research Soc. (v.p.), Univs. Council for Earthquake Engring., Internat. Orgn. for Standardization, UN Tech. Evaluation Team, ASCE, Seismol. Soc. Am., Larimer County Computer Soc. (chmn. 1974—), Aircraft Owners and Pilots Assn., Sigma Xi, Phi Sigma Kappa, Chi Epsilon, Sigma Tau, Tau Beta Pi. Methodist. Lodge: Rotary. Home: 1901 Seminole Dr Fort Collins CO 80525-1537 Office: 1413 S College Ave Fort Collins CO 80524-4115

MEDEARIS, MILLER, lawyer; b. Liberty, Mo., Jan. 19, 1921; s. Thomas Whittier and Mara (Miller) M.; children: Christy Crochet, Kellee Reed. LLB, Cumberland U., 1948; JD, Stamford U., 1969. Bar: Okla. 1948, Calif. 1957. Claims adjustor Transit Casualty Co., L.A., 1950-56, atty., trial counsel, 1956-58; ptnr. Hagenbaugh, Murphy & Medearis, L.A., 1958-69, Medearis and Grimm, L.A., 1969—. Sec., Bd. Med. Quality Assurance, Sacramento, 1979-84, v.p., 1984-86; bd. dirs. Pico Rivera Cmty. Hosp., 1975-85; mem. Dem. Bus. Council, L.A., 1980; commr. L.A. Bd. Transp., 1986-92. With USN, 1945-46. Mem. ABA, State Bar Calif., Calif. Trial Lawyers Assn., Okla. Bar Assn., Lawyers Club L.A. Democrat. Baptist. Avocations: boating, water skiing, downhill skiing. Home: 2175 Ridge Dr Los Angeles CA 90049-1153 Office: Medearis and Grimm 1331 W Sunset Blvd Los Angeles CA 90026-4424

MEDEARIS, ROGER NORMAN, artist; b. Fayette, Mo., Mar. 6, 1920; s. Thomas Whittier and Mara (Miller) M.; m. Elizabeth Burrall Sterling, Jan. 16, 1976; 1 son, Thomas Whittier, III. Pupil of, Thomas Hart Benton, 1938-41. One-man exhbns. include Kende Galleries, N.Y.C., 1949, 50, Capricorn Galleries, Bethesda, Md., 1971, 78, 81, 84, 94; group exhbns. include AAA Galleries, Met. Mus. Art, NAD, N.Y.C., Carnegie Mellon U., Pitts., Butler Inst. Am. Art, Youngstown, Ohio, Albrecht-Kemper Mus. Art, St. Joseph, Mo., Spencer Mus. Art, Lawrence, Kans., many others; represented in numerous pvt. and public collections, including D.C. McJ. Ct., Nat. Mus. Am. Art, Washington, Nelson-Atkins Mus. Art, Kansas City, Butler Inst. Am. Art., Hunt Inst., Pitts., Albrecht-Kemper Art Mus., St. Joseph, Mo., Beach Mus., Kans. State U., Manhattan; commd. by Nat. Recreation & Park Assn., 1982, Print Club Albany, 1994; work reviewed in various articles, monographs; subject of various art books. With USN Dept., 1942-45, AUS, 1945-46. Address: 2270 Melville Dr San Marino CA 91108-2612

MEDENICA, GORDON, publisher; b. Darmstadt, Fed. Republic Germany, Oct. 26, 1951; came to U.S., 1952; s. Walter Vojislav and Heidi Hedwig (Knoerzer) M.; m. Ann Margaret Connolly, Jan. 2, 1982; children: Madeline, Candice. AB, Harvard U., 1973, MBA, 1979. Staff acct. Meahl, McNamara & Co., Boston, 1973-74; exec. dir. BMW Car Club Am., Cambridge, Mass., 1974-77; analyst corp. planning Marriott Corp., Washington, 1979-80, sr. analyst hotel planning, 1981-82; sr. analyst strategic planning N.Y. Times Co., N.Y.C., 1982-83, project mgr. strategic planning, 1984, mgr. strategic planning and corp. devel., 1984-86, dir. planning, 1986-90; v.p. corp. planning, 1990-93, v.p. ops. and planning, 1993-96; sr. v.p., group pub. NYT Mag. Group, N.Y.C., 1996—. Office: NY Times Co Mag Group 1120 Avenue Of The Americas Fl 8 New York NY 10036-6700

MEDEROS, CAROLINA LUISA, transportation policy consultant; b. Rochester, Minn., July 1, 1947; d. Luis O. and Carolina (del Valle) M. BA, Vanderbilt U., 1969; MA, U. Chgo., 1971. Adminstrv. asst. Lt. Gov. of Ill., Chgo., 1972; sr. research assoc. U. Chgo., 1972; project mgr., cons. Urban Dynamics, Inner City Fund and Community Programs Inc., Chgo., 1972-73; legis. asst. to Senate pres. Ill. State Senate, Chgo. and Springfield, 1973-76; program analyst Dept. Transp., Washington, 1976-79, chief, trans. assistance programs div., 1979-81, dir. programs and evaluation, 1981-88, chairwoman, sec.'s safety rev. task force, 1985-88; deputy asst. sec. for safety Dept. Transp., 1988-89; cons. Patton Boggs LLP, Washington, 1990—. Recipient award for Meritorious Achievement, Sec. Transp. 1980, Superior Achievement award U.S. Dept. Transp., 1981, Sec.'s Gold Medal Award for Outstanding Achievement, 1986, Presdl. Rank award, 1987. Mem. Womens Transp. Seminar, Coun. for Excellence in Govt. Home: 2723 O St NW Washington DC 20007-3128 Office: Patton Boggs LLP 2550 M St NW Washington DC 20037-1301

MEDH, JHEEM D., medical educator, biochemistry researcher. BS in Chemistry and Biochemistry, U. Bombay, India, 1982; MS in Biochemistry, U. Bombay, 1984; PhD in Biochemistry, U. Tex. Med. Br., Galveston, 1990. Jr. rsch. fellow, dept. physiology L.T.M. Med. Coll., Bombay, 1984-86; rsch. asst., dept. human biol. chemistry and genetics U. Tex. Med. Br., 1986-90; postgrad. rsch. biochemist, dept. medicine U. Calif., San Diego, 1991-93; asst. rsch. scientist, adj. asst. prof., dept. medicine U. Iowa Coll. Medicine, Iowa City, 1993—. Presenter in field of role of LDL receptor-related protein, receptor-associated protein and lipoprotein lipase on the regulation of lipoprotein metabolism. Juvenile Diabetes Internat. Found. fellow 1992-93; recipient nat. grand-in-aid award Am. Heart Assn., 1995-98; recipient Gip Hudson award Nat. Student Rsch. Forum, 1989, Stephen C. Silverthorne award Grad. Sch. Biomed. Scis., U. Tex. Med. Br. Mem. Am. Heart Assn. (coun. for basic science), Am. Soc. Cell Biology, Juvenile Diabetes Found. Internat. Home: 905 W Benton St Apt 30 Iowa City IA 52246-5937

MEDICUS, HEINRICH ADOLF, physicist, educator; b. Zurich, Switzerland, Dec. 24, 1918; came to U.S., 1950; naturalized, 1995; s. Friedrich Georg and Clara Anna (Frey) M.; m. Hildegard Julie Schmelz, June 15, 1961. Dipl. Naturwiss., Swiss Fed. Inst. Tech., Zurich, 1943, Dr.sc.nat., 1949. Research assoc. Swiss Fed. Inst. Tech., 1943-50; visitor Lawrence Berkeley Lab., Calif., 1950-51, MIT, Cambridge, 1951-52; instr., then vis. asst. prof. MIT, 1952-55; assoc. prof. Rensselaer Poly. Inst., Troy, N.Y., 1955-72, prof., 1972-86, prof. emeritus, 1987—; vis. scientist Atomic Energy Research Establishment Harwell, Eng., 1967-68, Swiss Inst. Nuclear Research, Villigen, 1974-75. Co-author: Fields and Particles, 1973; contbr. articles on physics, history of physics and enology. Pres. Hudson-Mohawk Swiss Soc., Albany, N.Y., 1974—. Served to lt. arty. Swiss Army, 1937-50. Fellow, Swiss Found., 1950-52. Mem. Am. Phys. Soc., Swiss Phys. Soc., Hist. of Sci. Soc., Swiss Am. Hist.Soc., Soc. Wine Educators, Sociètè des Vignerons, Delta Tau Delta (pres. house corp. of Upsilon chpt. 1984-91, faculty advisor 1991-95). Presbyterian. Club: Swiss Alpine (Zurich). Avocations: wine education, internat. student exchange programs. Home: 1 The Knoll East Acres Troy NY 12180 Office: Rensselaer Poly Inst Dept Physics Troy NY 12180

MEDIN, A. LOUIS, computer company executive; b. Balt., Oct. 2, 1925; s. Nathan and Bessie (Zell) M.; B.E. in Chem. Engring., Johns Hopkins U., 1948; Ph.D. in Chem. Engring., Ohio State U., 1951; m. Julia A. Levin, Dec. 24, 1950; children—Douglas, David, Thomas, Linda. Registered profl. engr., Md. Chem. engr. AEC, Wilmington, Del., 1951-53; research engr. Ford Motor Co., Dearborn, Mich., 1953-55; chief chem. nuclear reactor tech. ALCO Products, Schenectady, 1955-58; head nuclear research engr. U.S. Steel, Monroeville, Pa., 1958-63; project mgr. missile design AVCO Corp., Wilmington, Mass., 1963-65; mgr. sci. applications IBM, Manassas, Va., 1965-72, mgr. advanced applications, 1975-87; exec. dir. Inst. for Simulation and Tng., Orlando, Fla., 1987—; chmn. symposia on def. research and devel.; asst. dir. environment and life scis. Dept. Def., 1972-74; lectr. in field. Contbr. articles to profl. and tech. jours. Mem. Monroeville Parks and Recreation Commn., 1960; chmn. Monroeville Mental Health Assn., 1961; mem. Monroeville Zoning and Planning Commn., 1961; dep. precinct chmn. Montgomery County Rep. Com., 1982. Served with USN, 1944-46, PTO. Recipient award Am. Chem. Soc., 1957. Fellow Am. Inst. Chemists; mem. Nat. Security Indsl. Assn., Am. Inst. Chem. Engrs., Am. Def. Preparedness Assn. (chmn. sci. and engring. tech. div. 1981-90, editorial advisor Def. Jour., Am. Def. award 1984, Gold medal 1990), Am. Metall. Soc., Johns Hopkin's U. Alumni Assn., Ohio State U. Alumni Assn. Home: 714 Bear Creek Cir Casselberry FL 32708-3857

MEDIN, JULIA ADELE, mathematics educator, researcher; b. Dayton, Ohio, Jan. 16, 1929; d. Caroline (Feinberg) Levitt; m. A. Louis Medin, Dec. 24, 1950; children: Douglas, David, Thomas, Linda. BS in Maths. Edn., Ohio State U., 1951; MA in Higher Edn., George Washington U., 1977; PhD in Counseling and Edn., Am. U., 1985. Cert. tchr., Fla., Md. Rsch. engr. Sun Oil Co., Marcus Hook, Pa., 1951-53; tchr. maths. Montgomery County Pub. Schs., Rockville, Md., 1973-88; asst. prof. maths. U. Ctrl. Fla., Orlando, 1988-90, sr. ednl. technologist Inst. for Simulation and Tng., 1990—; mem. adv. steering com. U.S. Dept. Edn. Title II, Washington, 1985-89; sr. math educator, rschr. Inst. for Simulation and Tng., Orlando, 1988—; judge NII Nar. Awards. Author: Loc. of Cont. and Test Anxiety of Mar. Math. Studies, 1985; contbg. author: Math for 14 & 17 Yr. Olds, 1987; editor: Simulation and Computer-Based Technology for Education; contbr. articles to profl. jours. Dem. committeewoman Town of Monroeville, Pa., 1962; religious sch. dir. Beth Tikva Religious Sch., Rockville, 1971; cons. Monroeville Mental Health, 1960. Mem. Nat. Coun. Tchrs. Math., Math. Assn. Am. (task force on minorities in math.), Women in Math. in Edn., Nat. Coalition for Tech. in Edn. and Tng., Phi Delta Kappa, Kappa Delta Pi. Home: 714 Bear Creek Cir Winter Springs FL 32708-3857 Office: U Ctrl Fla Inst for Simulation and Tng 3280 Progress Dr Orlando FL 32826-3229

MEDIN, LOWELL ANSGARD, management executive; b. Shafer Twp., Minn., Aug. 28, 1932; s. Ansgaard Phillip Magnus and Adelaide Marie Christine (Grandstrand) M.; m. Frances Irene Knutson, Sept. 13, 1958; children: Kimberly June, James Lowell. *Grandfather Axel Grandstrand came to America as a young lad in 1884 with his parents Johannes and Sara Grandstrand. He was unable to receive a good education as he had to help his family break open the land for farming. He was determined that his children and grandchildren would have a higher education so they could escape the hard farm life. Mother Adelaide Grandstrand Medin became a teacher, and I, with four other of Axel's eight grandchildren, completed their higher education. Grandfather August Medin left Sweden on his 14th birthday in 1880, as his brothers in America sent him passage money to come to America. He became a plasterer, and when he was no longer able to do plastering, he became a successful farmer. From him I learned a career change can be rewarding. Great Grandfather Peter Shoquist left Sweden in 1871 on his 25th birthday. He was a carpenter in Sweden; however, in America he became a Minnesota farmer, where he kept bees and grew tobacco which he smoked in his home-made pipes. His son, Arthur, was a successful flower-grower and from him I learned how to be a gardener and the love of gardening .* AS in Liberal Arts, U. Minn., 1957, BBA, 1959. Dairy farmer Medin Farm, Franconia Twp., 1951-53; silo builder Lindstrom Silo, 1956-58; employment mgr. John Wood Co., St. Paul, 1959; salesperson Diversey Co., LaCrosse, Wis., 1959-60; rebuyer, inventory mgr. Montgomery Ward, St. Paul, 1960-67; rebuyer, rebuyer mgr. Montgomery Ward, Chgo., 1967-85; with sales dept. J.T. Gen. Store, Palatine, Ill., 1986; rebuying mgr. Sportsmen's Guide, Golden Valley, Minn., 1987; inventory mgr. Donald Bruce and Co., Chgo., 1988-91; supr. Pinkerton Security Ops., 1992-96; pics coord. Hickory Farms, Itasca, Ill., 1995-96. Author: (with others) Shafer Swamp to Village, 1978, The Pioneers of Chicago County 1838-1870, 1992, The Knutson/Stavenau Family Roots, 1994. Candidate for polit. office, Mpls., 1967; del. Minn. State Dem.-Farm Labor Conv., 1956, 58; chmn. cancer drive Village of Palatine, 1968, mem. dist. 6 adv. coun., 1989—; mem. Homeowners Coun., Palatine, 1976-77; mem. coun. Christ Luth. Ch., Palatine, 1981-86; officer Chicago County DFL Party, 1956-60; del. Chicago County DFL Conv., 1956, 58; pres. Palonis Park Homeowners Assn., Palatine, 1976-82. Cpl. U.S. Army, 1953-55, ETO. Mem. No. Ill. Civil War Roundtable (chartered officer 1983-86, trustee, sec., 2d v.p.), VFW (life, post 981, Arlington Hts.), Am. Legion (life, post 690, Palatine), Alpha Phi Omega. Republican. Lutheran. Avocations: genealogy, gardening, Am. history, Civil War period. Home: 121 S Linden Ave Palatine IL 60067-6342

MEDIN, MYRON JAMES, JR., city manager; b. Ladysmith, Wis., July 8, 1931; s. Myron James and Mildred Clara (Johnson) M.; m. Alice Louise Moholt, May 14, 1955; children: John, Karen, Anne. BA, St. Olaf Coll., 1954; MPA, U. Mich., 1959. Adminstrv. asst. to city mgr. City of Fond du Lac, Wis., 1959-64, city mgr., 1967-83; city mgr. City of New Ulm, Minn., 1964-67; city adminstr. City of Kansas City, Kans., 1983-85; pres., gen. mgr. Bella Vista Village Property Owners Assn., Ark., 1986-92; mem. com. human devel. Nat. League of Cities, Washington, 1974-80, com. on govtl. relations, 1971-73; chmn. City Plan Commn., Fond du Lac, Wis., 1967-83. Bd. dirs. United Way, Kansas City, Kans., 1984-85, YMCA, 1984-85, Kansas City C.C. Found., 1984-85; mem. Gov.'s Regionalism Task Force Adv. Com., Madison, Wis., 1968-70; trustee Phillips Pro-Celebrity Golf Tennis Charity Classic, 1991-92; vol. historic house mus. and gardens. Lt. USAF, 1955-57. Recipient Community Service award Fond du Lac Assn. of Commerce, 1978. Mem. Internat. City Mgmt. Assn., Wis. City Mgmt. Assn. (pres. 1975-76), Wis. League of Municipalities (bd. dirs. 1978-80), Wis. Alliance of Cities (v.p. 1972-73), Am. Soc. Pub. Adminstrn. (bd. dirs. 1984-85, Pub. Adminstr. of Yr. award 1985), Bella Vista-Bentonville C. of C. (bd. dirs. 1987-91), Nat. Trust for Hist. Preservation, Benton County Hist. Soc., Ret. Officers Assn. Lutheran. Avocations: swimming, reading, tennis, gardening, genealogy. Home: 1 Audley Cir Bella Vista AR 72714-5645

MEDINA, JOSE ENRIQUE, dentist, educator; b. Santurce, P.R., May 1, 1926; s. Jose Wilfredo and Genoveva (de la Baume) M.; m. Betty Lee Mansfield, June 5, 1948 (dec. Feb. 1975); children—Elizabeth Lee, Jose Enrique, Virginia Genoveva; m. Patricia Fay Pachler, Dec. 26, 1975. Student, Johns Hopkins, 1942-44; D.D.S., U. Md., 1948. Instr. Berlitz Sch. Langs., 1944-48; instr. operative dentistry dept. U. Md. Sch. Dentistry, 1948-50, asst. prof., 1950-52, assoc. prof., 1952-57, prof., head, 1957-66, asst. dean, 1964-67; prof. clin. dentistry, assoc. dean Coll. Dentistry, U. Fla., Gainesville, 1967-69; prof. clin. dentistry Coll. Dentistry, U. Fla., 1969—, dean, 1969-74, dir. health center planning and utilization, 1974-76; v.p. for facilities planning and ops. J. Hillis Miller Health Center, 1976-86; Cons. USPHS, U.S. Naval Dental Sch., Bethesda, VA Hosp., Gainesville, Miami.; Pres. So. Conf. Dental Deans and Examiners, 1973; mem. nat. adv. dental research council Nat. Inst. Dental Research, NIH, 1973-76; charter mem. Am. Bd. Operative Dentistry, pres., 1980-87; mentor George M. Hollenback Operative Dentistry Sem. Group, 1961—, N.H. Gold Foil Study Group, 1987—. Pres. Sunnybrook (Md.) Community Assn., 1963-65. Served with

USNR, 1944-46. Decorated Knight Comdr., Order of Bernardo O'Higgins (Chile), 1991; recipient Disting. Alumnus award R.I. Alumni Assn. U. Md., 1965, U. Md. Sch. Dentistry Alumni Assn., 1985, Disting. Faculty award U. Fla. Blue Key, 1986, Tchr. of Yr. award U. Fla., 1987, Outstanding Clinician of Yr. award, 1987, 92, Andres Cendan Dentist of Yr. award Dade Dental Study Group, 1990; named to Hall of Fame, U. Md. Alumni Assn. , 1990; hon. prof. U. De San Carlos, Guatemala, 1960—. Fellow Internat. Coll. Dentists (trustee found. 1993—, dep. regent Fla. sect. 1988-91, regent dist 5 USA sect. 1992—), AADS, Acad. Gen. Dentistry (hon.), Acad. Dentistry Internat.; mem. ADA, Fla. Dental Assn. (Disting. Svc. award 1978), Am. Acad. Gold Foil Operators (editor 1958-63, pres. 1965, Disting. Mem. award 1986), Am. Coll. Dentists (Disting. Faculty award 1989, chmn. Fla. sect. 1992-93, William J. Gies award 1990), Internat. Assn. Dental Rsch., Acad. Operative Dentistry (charter, George Hollenback meml. prize 1985, trustee Acad. Found., 1986—, v.p. 1989, pres. elect 1990, pres. 1991), Am. Acad. Restorative Dentistry, Health Edn. Media Assn. (dir.), Royal Soc. Health, N.Y. Acad. Sci., Am. Acad. Oral Medicine (hon.), Fla. Acad. Dental Practice Adminstrn. (hon.), Guatemala Dental Soc. (hon.), Chile Dental Assn. (hon.), Optimists Club (Md.), Masons, Kiwanis, Omicron Kappa Upsilon. Home: 5002 NW 18th Pl Gainesville FL 32605-3430

MEDINA, KATHRYN BACH, book editor; b. Plainfield, N.J.; d. F. Earl and Elizabeth E. Bach; m. Standish F. Medina Jr.; 1 child, Nathaniel Forde. BA, Smith Coll.; MA, NYU. With Doubleday Pub. Co., Inc., N.Y.C., 1965-85; exec. editor, v.p. Random House, N.Y.C., 1985—; assoc. fellow Jonathan Edwards Coll., Yale U., New Haven, 1982—; fellow Bunting Inst., 1994-95; cons., 1995-96. Editor books by James Atlas, Peter Benchley, Amy Bloom, Tom Brokaw, Anita Brookner, Ethan Canin, Robert Coles, Agnes deMille, Henry Louis Gates, Jr., Mary Gordon, David Halberstam, Kathryn Harrison, Tracy Kidder, Bobbie Ann Mason, James A. Michener, Anna Quindlen, Nancy Reagan, James Reston, William Safire, Maggie Scarf, Christopher Tilghman, Alice Walker, Daniel Yergin, others. Bunting Inst. fellow, 1994-95.

MEDINA, STANDISH FORDE, JR., lawyer; b. Orange, N.J., June 16, 1940; s. Standish F. and Hope Tyler (Kiesewetter) M.; m. Kathryn L. Bach, Apr. 20, 1968; 1 child, Nathaniel Forde. A.B. cum laude, Princeton U., 1962; LL.B. magna cum laude, Columbia U., 1965, LL.M., 1966. Bar: N.Y. 1965, U.S. Supreme Ct. 1970, U.S. Dist. Ct. (so. dist., ea. dist.) N.Y., U.S. Ct. Appeals (2d, 3d, 4th, 5th, 7th, 11th, D.C. cirs.). Assoc. in law Columbia Law Sch., 1965-66; lectr. Columbia Law Sch., N.Y.C., 1992; instr. law orientation program in Am. law Princeton U., summer 1966; assoc. Debevoise & Plimpton, N.Y.C., 1966-72, ptnr., 1973—. Author: Settlement Practices in the Second Circuit, 1988, Reflections Below, 1991. Trustee The Hill Sch., Pottstown, Pa., 1976-91, St. Bernard's Sch., N.Y.C., 1992—, Episc. Sch., N.Y.C., 1988-93. Fellow Am. Coll. of Trial Lawyers; mem. ABA (vice-chmn. com. on fed. cts., litigation sect. 1981-82, co-chmn. com. pleadings motions and pretrial 1986-87), Fed. Bar Coun., N.Y. State Bar Assn., Assn. of Bar of City of N.Y. (mem. exec. com. 1982-86, chmn. membership com. 1986-90, chmn. com. fed. cts. 1978-81, 96—, mem. judiciary com. 1978-81, mem. nominating com. 1986-87, mem. com. on ct. requirements 1978-81, mem. fed. legis. com. 1971-75), Am. Law Inst., 2d Cir. Com. on Improvement Civil Litigation (chmn. 1986-90), Legal Aid Soc. (chmn. assoc. and young lawyers com. 1972). Office: Debevoise & Plimpton 875 3rd Ave New York NY 10022-6225

MEDINA-DIAZ, MARIA DEL ROSARIO, education educator; b. N.Y.C.. BA in Edn., U. P.R., Rio Piedras, 1980, MS in Edn., 1986; PhD in Ednl. Psychology, U. Wis., 1991. Lic. secondary sch. math. tchr. Math. tchr. Dept. Pub. Instrn., San Juan, P.R., 1981-86; project asst. U. Wis., Madison, 1989-91; asst. prof. U. P.R., Rio Piedras, 1992—. Advance opportunity fellow U. Wis., Madison, 1986-89; Nat. Hispanis Scholarship Fund scholar, 1988. Mem. APA, Assn. Math. Tchrs. P.R. (v.p. 1993-94, 96-97, pres. 1997-98), Psychometric Soc., Am. Ednl. Rsch. Assn., Nat. Coun. Ednl. Measurement, Nat. Coun. Tchrs. Math., Am. Evaluation Assn. Office: U PR Faculty Edn Rio Piedras PR 00931

MEDINA-PUERTA, ANTONIO, scientist; b. Almeria, Spain, Jan. 20, 1956; s. Antonio and Maria Mar (Puerta) Medina; m. Mary Medina-Puerta, Sept. 20, 1986. MS, U. Politecnica, Madrid, 1979, MIT, 1982; OD, U. Complutense, Madrid, 1979; diploma in elec. engring., MIT, 1981; PhD, U. Politecnica, Madrid, 1983. Optometrist Centro de Vision Luz, Almeria, 1978-79; engr. Philips, Eindhoven, The Netherlands, 1979-80; rsch. asst. MIT, Cambridge, 1981-83; sci. assoc. Eye Rsch. Inst., Boston, 1983-88; task mgr. Calif. Inst. Tech., Pasadena, 1988-91; adviser NASA, Washington, 1988—, USN, 1989—; dir. rsch. Delta Optics, Covina, 1992—. Contbr. articles to profl. publs.; patentee in field. Fellow Christ's Coll., Cambridge Univ., Eng. Fellow Acad. Applied Sci.; mem. IEEE, Optical Soc. Am., Soc. Photo-optical Instrumentation Engrs., Biomed. Soc. Roman Catholic. Avocations: scuba diving, sailing. Home and Office: 281 E Colorado Blvd # 1002 Pasadena CA 91101-1903

MEDITCH, JAMES STEPHEN, electrical engineering educator; b. Indpls., July 30, 1934; s. Vladimir Stephen and Alexandra (Gogeff) M.; m. Theresa Claire Scott, Apr. 4, 1964; children: James Stephen Jr., Sandra Anne. BSEE, Purdue U., 1956, PhD, 1961; SM, MIT, 1957. Staff engr. Aerospace Corp., Los Angeles, 1961-65; assoc. prof. elec. engring. Northwestern U., 1965-67; mem. tech. staff Boeing Sci. Research Labs., Seattle, 1967-70; prof. U. Calif., Irvine, 1970-77; prof. U. Wash., Seattle, 1977—, chmn. dept. elec. engring., 1977-85, assoc. dean engring., 1987-90. Author: Stochastic Optimal Linear Estimation and Control, 1969; co-editor: Computer Communication Networks, 1984. Fellow IEEE (Disting. mem. control systems soc., 1983, editor Proceedings 1983-85, Centennial medal 1984). Office: U Wash Dept Elect Engring FT-10 Seattle WA 98195

MEDITZ, WALTER JOSEPH, engineering consultant; b. Bklyn., June 4, 1917; s. Joseph and Marie (Gaspar) M.; m. Elizabeth M. Cagney, Jan. 9, 1944; children—Jeannette Jordan, Mary Beth Banks. B.C.E., Bklyn Poly. Inst., 1939, M.M.E., 1941; M.Indsl. Engring., Ga. Inst. Tech., 1951. Research engr., lab. instr. Bklyn. Poly. Inst., 1939-40; civil engr., supt. Spencer, White & Prentice, 1940-41; asst. to design and prodn. mgr. Frederick R. Harris, 1941-43; chief indsl. engr. Naval Aircraft, Norfolk, Va., 1943-46; asst. chief engr. Boyle-Midway, N.Y.C., 1946-47; plant mgr. Boyle-Midway, Atlanta, 1947-51; asst. to pres. Boyle-Midway, N.Y.C., 1951-55, Standard Packaging Corp., N.Y.C., 1955-57; v.p. for mfg. Standard Packaging Corp., 1957-67; mgr. facilities to divisional v.p. Doubleday & Co., Inc., Garden City, N.Y., 1967-83; pres. Meditz Enging. Assocs., 1984—. Served from ensign to lt. (s.g.) USNR, 1943-46. J. Waldo Smith fellow ASCE, 1939; Bklyn. Poly. Inst. fellow, 1939. Mem. Soc. for Adcancement Mgmt., Alpha Pi Mu. Home: 1639 NE 26th St Fort Lauderdale FL 33305

MEDLAND, WILLIAM JAMES, college president; b. Logansport, Ind., Jan. 1, 1944; s. Thomas Gallagher and Mary Elizabeth (Hassett) M.; m. Donna Lee Bahnaman, Mar. 12, 1977; 1 child, Mark David. BA, U. Notre Dame, 1966; student, St. Louis U., 1972-74; MA in History, Ball State U., 1967, MA in Edn., 1979, PhD in History, 1980; postgrad., Inst. for Mgmt. Lifelong Edn., Harvard U., 1985, Ctr. Internat. Cooperation and Security Studies, U. Wis., 1988, Ctr. Internat. Studies, MIT, 1989, Freie Universitat, Berlin, 1991. Instr. history and philosophy Donnelly coll., Kansas City, Kans., 1967-70; curricular advisor Ball State U., Muncie, Ind., 1970-71, teaching fellow, 1977-80; asst. dean St. Louis (Mo.) U., 1971-75; employee supr. Wilson, Inc., Logansport, 1975-76; ops. mgr. Watson-Jenkins, Inc., Indpls., 1976-77; dean of coll., asst. prof. history Springfield (Ill.) Coll., 1980-81; acad. dean, assoc. prof. history and edn. Marymount Coll., Salina, Kans., 1981-86; exec. v.p., provost, prof. history St. Mary's Coll., Winona, Minn., 1986-91; pres., prof. history Viterbo Coll., LaCrosse, Wis., 1991—; edn. cons. Am. Inst. Banking, Springfield, 1980-81; advisor Adv. Com. to Sch. Bd., Salina, 1984, Salina Diocesan Bd. Edn., 1981-83; evaluator North Ctrl. Assn., Chgo., 1987—. Author: Cuban Missile Crisis of 1962-Needless or Necessary?, 1988, reprint, 1990, A Guide to Writing College Research Papers, 1989, The Catholic School: A Bibliographical Resource Guide, 1990; editor: Ind. Acad. Social Scis. jour., 1979, Perspectives: A Liberal Arts Exchange (faculty jour.), 1988. Coll. solicitor United Way, St. Louis, 1973; coord. Coll./Cmty. Artist Series, Salina, 1981-84; bd. dirs. Immaculate Heart of Mary Sem., Winona, 1987-91, La Crosse Med. Health Sci. Consortium; bd. dirs., treas. Wis. Found. for Ind. Colls.; chair La Crosse Diocesan Edn. Commn. Fellow Ctr. Internat. Studies, MIT/Harvard U., 1989. Mem. am. Assn. Higher Edn., Am. Assn. Coll. Pres., Am. Assn. Ind. Coll. Pres., Wis. Assn. Ind. Colls. and Univs. (bd. dirs.), KC, Rotary, Phi Alpha Theta (rsch. award Ball State U. 1979), Phi Delta Kappa. Democrat. Roman Catholic. Avocations: reading, research, hiking, cross-country skiing. Home: 414 29th St S La Crosse WI 54601-6013 Office: Viterbo Coll Office of Pres 815 9th St S La Crosse WI 54601-4777

MEDLEY, ALEX ROY, executive minister; b. Columbus, Ga., Aug. 4, 1948; s. Howard and Clois Mildred (Chumney) M.; m. Patricia Stauffer, May 10, 1975; children: James Ethan, Christopher Jordan. BA magna cum laude, U. Chattanooga, 1970; cert., Grad. Sch. Ecumenical Studies, Celigny, Switzerland, 1973; MDiv, Princeton Sem., 1974. Ordained to ministry Bapt. Ch., 1975. Assoc. pastor First Bapt. Ch. Trenton, N.J., 1974-77; adminstrv. intern Nat. Ministries Am. Bapt. Chs. U.S.A., Valley Forge, Pa., 1977, nat. dir. Christian ctr., 1978-85; min. of world mission support, area min. Am. Bapt. Chs. N.J., East Orange, 1986-92, exec. min., 1992—; intern World Coun. Chs., Geneva, Switzerland, 1973; rep. N.Am. Bapt. Fellowship, Washington, 1975-77; mem. domestic hunger/poverty working group Nat. Coun. Chs. of Christ, 1978-85, mem. gen. assembly; conf. speaker Am. Bapt. Chs., 1979; Am. Bapt. Ch. U.S.A. del. to Nat. Coun. Chs. of Christ. Editor (newsletter) Social Edn. for Action Newsletter, 1978-79. Bd. dirs. Ch. World Svc./CROP, N.J., 1975-77, Occupational Tng. Ctr., Burlington, N.J., 1992; sec. Key Inmate Edn. Project, Trenton, 1986. Mem. Am. Bapt. Regional Exec. Mins. Coun. Avocations: reading, fishing, hiking. Home: 12 Courtland Ln Willingboro NJ 08046-3406 Office: Am Bapt Chs NJ 3752 Nottingham Way Ste 101 Trenton NJ 08690-3802

MEDLEY, DONALD MATTHIAS, education educator, consultant; b. Faulkton, S.D., Feb. 18, 1917; s. Thomas Arnot and Cecilia Agnes (Kellen) M.; m. Betty Ann Robertsen, Aug. 23, 1948; 1 child, Timothy Laurence. B.S., Coll. St. Thomas, St. Paul, 1938; M.A., U. Minn., 1950, Ph.D., 1954. Tchr., Am. Sch. Guadalajara, Mex., 1941-42, Floodwood Pub. Schs., Minn., 1946-48; instr. English, Coll. St. Thomas, 1948-50; asst. prof. CUNY, 1954-59, assoc. prof., 1959-64, prof., 1964-65; sr. research psychologist Ednl. Testing Service, Princeton, N.J., 1965-70; disting. prof. U. Va., Charlottesville, 1970-87, prof. emeritus, 1987—; mem. exec. bd. Consortium for the Improvement of Tchr. Evaluation, Atlanta, 1985-87. Author: Measurement-Based Evaluation of Teacher Performance, 1984; author: (with others) Handbook of Research on Teaching, 1963, The Teacher's Handbook, 1971, Research on Teaching: Concepts, Findings, and Implications, 1979, Encyclopedia of Educational Research, 5th edit., 1982, 6th edit., 1992, Developing Skills for Instructional Supervision, 1984, Advances in Teacher Education, 1984, International Encyclopedia of Education: Research and Studies, 1984, 2d edit., 1994, Assessment of Teaching: Purposes, Practices, and Implications for the Profession, 1990; contbr. articles to profl. jours. Served as staff sgt. U.S. Army, 1942-46. Fellow Am. Psychol. Assn.; mem. Am. Ednl. Research Assn. (div. sec. 1962), Nat. Council on Measurement in Edn., Assn. Tchr. Educators. Democrat. Roman Catholic. Avocations: conjuring, travel.

MEDLIN, CHARLES MCCALL, lawyer; b. Florence, S.C., Dec. 29, 1960. BA magna cum laude, Duke U., 1982; JD with honors, U. N.C., 1990. Bar: Ga. 1990, U.D. Dist. Ct. (no. dist.) Ga. 1990, U.S. Ct. Appeals (11th cir.) 1990. Teaching asst., property contracts U. N.C. Sch. Law, Chapel Hill, 1988-90; ptnr. Bovis Kyle & Burch, LLC, Atlanta, 1990—; coach Mock Trial Team, Holderness Moot Ct., 1991—. Van Hecke scholar, 1987-90; recipient Am. Jurisprudence award civil procedure. Mem. Ga. Bar Assn., Toastmasters Internat., Lawyers Club of Am. Home: 8975 Martin Rd Roswell GA 30076-3260 Office: Bovis Kyle & Burch 53 Perimeter Ctr E Fl 3 Atlanta GA 30346-2206

MEDLIN, JOHN GRIMES, JR., banker; b. Benson, N.C., Nov. 23, 1933; s. John Grimes and Mabel (Stephenson) M. BS in Bus. Adminstrn., U. N.C., 1956; grad., The Exec. Program, U. Va., 1965. With Wachovia Bank & Trust Co., Winston-Salem, N.C., 1959-93, pres., 1974; pres., CEO Wachovia Bank and Wachovia Corp., Winston-Salem, N.C., 1977-93; chmn. bd. Wachovia Corp., Winston-Salem, N.C., 1987—; bd. dirs. US Air Group, Inc., RJR Nabisco, Inc., Wachovia Corp., BellSouth Corp., Nat. Svc. Industries, Inc., Burlington Industries Inc., Media Gen. Inc., Nabisco Holdings, Inc. Trustee Nat. Humanities Ctr., Wake Forest U., Kenan Inst. Pvt. Enterprise, Kenan Inst. Arts, The Duke Endowment; active numerous civic and svc. orgns. With USNR, 1956-59. Mem. Phi Delta Theta. Office: Wachovia Corp PO Box 3099 100 N Main St Winston Salem NC 27150

MEDLOCK, DONALD LARSON, lawyer; b. Port Chester, N.Y., Mar. 8, 1927; s. J. Harold and Emma Adelaide (MacLennan) M.; m. Katharine Smedes Nicholson, May 21, 1955; children: Katharine Baird, Margaret MacLennan, William Nicholson. BA with honors, Yale U., 1947, LLB, 1950. Bar: N.Y. 1950, U.S. Dist. Ct. (so. dist.) N.Y. 1951, U.S. Dist. Ct. (ea. dist.) N.Y. 1952, U.S. Tax Ct. 1952, U.S. Ct. Custom and Patent Appeals, U.S. Ct. Appeals (2d cir.) 1951. Assoc. Putnam & Roberts, N.Y.C., 1950-56, ptnr., 1957-94, sr. counsel, 1995—; bd. dirs. Bancard Sys. of N.Y. Inc., Port Washington. Editor Yale Law Jour., New Haven, 1948-50. Sec., bd. dirs. Port Washington Community Chest, 1959-61; bd. dirs. Port Washington Estates Assn., 1958-61; mem. ann. fund parents com. Taft Sch., 1979-81; bd. mgrs., exec. com. William Sloane Ho. YMCA of Greater N.Y., 1979-84; chmn. univ. coun. com. on Law Sch. Yale U., 1979-86; chmn. Yale Alumni Fund, 1984-86, bd. dirs., 1955—, exec. com., 1980-88; chmn. Yale Law Sch. Fund, 1974-76; mem. devel. bd. Yale U., 1984-88, exec. com., 1984-86; exec. com. Yale Law Sch., 1975-79, hon., 1979—; bd. dirs. Assn. Yale Alumni, 1984-86, rep.-at-large, 1979-82, com. on undergrad. admisssions, 1979-82, com. on Yale medal, 1981; exec. com. Assn. Families U. Denver, 1982-84. Recipient citation Yale Law Sch., 1977, Yale Alumni Fund Chmn.'s award, 1979, 87, Yale medal, 1994. Mem. ABA, Fed. Power Bar Assn., Assn. of Bar of City of N.Y. (com. on profl. ethics 1958-61), Corbey Ct. Yale Law Sch., Tuscarora Club (Margaretville, N.Y., bd. dirs. 1963-95, sec. 1970-86, v.p. 1984-86), Landfall Club, Manhasset Bay Yacht Club, Surf Club, Mory's Assn., India House, Scroll and Key Soc., Yale Club N.Y.C., Phi Beta Kappa, Phi Delta Phi. Avocations: trout fishing, tennis, reading, crossword puzzles. Home: Landfall 800 Oyster Landing Wilmington NC 28405-5292

MEDNICK, MURRAY, playwright; b. Bklyn., Aug. 24, 1939; s. Sol Joseph and Betty (Greenstein) M. Student, CUNY., 1957-62. V.p. N.Y. Theatre Strategy, 1972; artistic dir. Padua Hills Playwrights Workshop, 1978-94. Author: The Hawk, 1968, The Hunter, 1969, The Deer Kill, 1971, Are You Lookin'?, 1973, Black Hole in Space, 1975, Taxes, 1975, The Coyote Cycle, 1978-84, Iowa and Blessings for Public Broadcasting System, 1977, 78, Scar, 1985, Heads, 1987, Shatter 'n Wade, 1990, Fedunn, 1992, Joe & Betty, 1994, Dictator, Kesler's Defiance, Skinwalkers, Sixteen Routines, 1997; also pub. in West Coast Plays; poems in Transatlantic Rev; others.; 1st prodn. at Theatre Genesis, N.Y.C., 1966. Grantee Rockefeller Found., 1968, 72, Guggenheim Found., 1973; recipient Poetry award Nat. Coun. Arts, 1968, Creative Artists Pub. Svc. award, 1973, Obie award for The Deer Kill, 1970, Ovation lifetime achievement award L.A. Theater League, 1992. Mem. Writers Guild, New Dramatists.

MEDNICK, ROBERT, accountant; b. Chgo., Apr. 1, 1940; s. Harry and Nettie (Brenner) M.; m. Susan Lee Levinson, Oct. 28, 1962; children: Michael Jon, Julie Eden, Adam Charles. BSBA, Roosevelt U., Chgo., 1962. CPA, Ill. Staff asst. Arthur Andersen, Chgo., 1962-63, sr. acct., 1963-66, mgr., 1966-71, ptnr., 1971—, mng. dir. SEC policies, 1973-76, mng. dir. auditing procedures, 1976-79, mng. ptnr. profl. and regulatory matters, 1993—; vice chmn. com. on profl. stds. Andersen Worldwide, 1979-82, chmn. com., 1982—. Contbr. articles to profl. jours. Bd. dirs. Roosevelt U., Chgo., 1980—, vice chmn., 1986—, sr. vice chmn., 1994—; bd. dirs. Auditorium Theatre Coun., 1990-96, Lake Shore Drive Synagogue, 1992—; co-chmn. adv. coun. Chgo. Action for Soviet Jewry, Highland Park, Ill., 1983-87; bd. dirs., mem. exec. com. Am. Judicature Soc., 1990-95, vice chmn., 1993-95; bd. overseers Rand Corp. Inst. Civil Justice, 1994—. Sgt. USAFR, 1965-69. Recipient Silver medal Ill. CPA Soc., 1962; named One of Ten Outstanding Young Men in Chgo., Chgo. Jr. C. of C., 1973-74; recipient Rolf A. Weil Disting. Service award, Roosevelt U., Chgo., 1983; Max Block award N.Y. State C.P.A. Soc., 1984; Ann. Literary award Jour. Accountancy, 1986, 88, Andrew D. Bradin award for distinctive contbns. to discipline of accountancy Case Western Res. U., Cleve., 1996; recipient disting. alumni award Roosevelt U. Walter E. Heller Coll. Bus. Adminstrn., 1997. Mem. AICPA (bd. dirs. 1986-87, 92-94, 95—, vice chmn. 1995-96, chmn. 1996-97, numerous coms., Elijah Watt Sells award 1962), Am. Acctg. Assn., Ill. CPA Soc. (acctg. prins. com. 1973, legal liability com. 1986-89, mgmt. of acctg. practice com. 1991-94), Mid-Day Club, Standard Club. Jewish. Avocations: tennis, collecting art.

MEDOFF, MARK HOWARD, playwright, screenwriter, novelist; b. Mt. Carmel, Ill., Mar. 18, 1940; s. Lawrence Ray and Thelma Irene (Butt) M.; m. Stephanie Thorne, June 24, 1972; children: Debra, Rachel, Jessica. B.A., U. Miami, Fla., 1962; M.A., Stanford U., 1966; D.H.L., Gallaudet Coll., 1981. Instr. English and drama N.Mex. State U., 1966-79, dramatist in residence, 1974—, head dept. drama, 1978-87, prof. drama, 1979-93, artistic dir., 1982-87; artistic dir. Am. S.W. Theatre Co., 1984-87. Author: (plays) When You Comin' Back, Red Ryder?, 1974, The Wager, 1975, The Kramer, 1975, The Halloween Bandit, 1978, The Conversion of Aaron Weiss, 1978, Firekeeper, 1978, The Last Chance Saloon, 1979, Children of a Lesser God, 1980 (Soc. West Theatres best play award 1982), The Majestic Kid, 1981, The Hands of Its Enemy, 1984, Kringle's Window, 1985, The Heart Outright, 1986 (novel) Dreams of Long Lasting: (films) When You Comin' Back, Red Ryder?, 1979, Off Beat, 1986, Apology, 1986, Children of a Lesser God, 1986, Good Guys Wear Black, 1978, Clara's Heart, 1988, The Majestic Kid, 1988, City of Joy, 1992, Homage, 1995, Santa Fe, 1997; works appear in Best Plays, 1973-74, 75-75, 79-80, Best Short Plays, 1975, The Homage that Follows, 1987; plays Stumps, 1989, Stefanie Hero, 1990, Showdown On Rio Road, 1995, Gila, 1995, A Christmas Carousel, 1996. Guggenheim fellow, 1974-75; recipient Obie award, Drama Desk award, Outer Critics Circle award, Media award Pres.'s Com. Employment Handicapped, Tony award; Oscar award nominee for Best Screenplay for Children of A Lesser God, 1987. Mem. Dramatists Guild, Writers Guild Am., Actors Equity Assn., Screen Actors Guild Pen. Office: PO Box 3072 Las Cruces NM 88003-3072

MEDVECKY, ROBERT STEPHEN, lawyer; b. Bridgeport, Conn., Feb. 12, 1931; s. Stephen and Elizabeth (Petro) M.; m. Ellen R. Munt, Nov. 11, 1966; children—Allison L., Beth A., Craig R. A.B., Dartmouth, 1952; J.D., Harvard, 1955. Bar: Ill. bar 1955, Conn. bar 1958, D.C. bar 1972, Fla. bar 1989. Asso. firm Lord, Bissell & Brook, Chgo., 1955-57; gen. atty. So. New Eng. Telephone Co., New Haven, 1957-71; v.p., gen. counsel, sec. Amtrak, Washington, 1971-75; partner firm Lord, Bissell & Brook, Washington, 1975-78, Reid & Priest, N.Y.C., 1978-87. Clubs: Harvard (N.Y.C.), Fiddlesticks Country (Ft. Meyers, Fla.), Saphire Valley Country (Cashlers, N.C.). Home: 15491 Kilbirnie Dr Fort Myers FL 33912 Home (summer): 29 Pine Ridge Trl Sapphire NC 28774

MEDVED, MICHAEL, film critic, author; b. Phila., Oct. 3, 1948; s. David Bernard and Renate Rosa (Hirsch) M.; m. Nancy Harris Herman, Aug. 5, 1972 (div. 1983); m. Diane Elvenstar, Jan. 27, 1985; children: Sarah Julia, Shayna Elana, Daniel Joshua. BA, Yale U., 1969; MFA, Calif. State U., San Francisco, 1974. Speech writer, polit. cons. various campaigns and politicians, Conn., Calif., D.C., 1970-73; advt. creative dir. Anrick Inc., Oakland, Calif., 1973-74; freelance writer L.A., 1974—; on-air film critic People Now, Cable News Network, L.A., 1980-83; on-air film critic, co-host Sneak Previews PBS, 1985-96; chief film critic N.Y. Post, 1993—; Hollywood corr. The Sunday Times of London; radio talk show host Sta. KVI, Seattle, 1996—. Author: What Really Happened to the Class of '65?, 1976, The Shadow Presidents, 1979, Hospital, 1983, Hollywood vs. America, 1992; co-author: (with Harry Medved) The 50 Worst Films of All Time, 1978, The Golden Turkey Awards, 1980, The Hollywood Hall of Shame, 1984, Son of Golden Turkey Awards, 1986. Co-founder, pres. Pacific Jewish Ctr., Venice, Calif., 1977-94; pres. Emanuel Streisand Sch., Venice, 1980-85. Mem. Writers Guild Am., AFTRA. Avocation: classical music. Office: 1809 7th Ave Ste 200 Seattle WA 98101-1360 also: NY Post 1211 6th Ave New York NY 10036

MEDVED, PAUL STANLEY, lawyer; b. Milw., May 6, 1956; s. Frank F. and Evelyn F. (Poplawski) M.; m. Danita C. Cole, Aug. 27, 1988. BA with Honors, Marquette U., 1978; JD, Columbia U., 1981. Bar: Wis. 1981, U.S. Dist. Ct. (ea. dist.) Wis. 1981, U.S. Dist. Ct. (we. dist.) Wis. 1984, U.S. Ct. Appeals (7th cir.) 1984. Assoc. Michael, Best & Friedrich, Milw., 1981-88, ptnr., 1988—. Office: Michael Best & Friedrich 100 E Wisconsin Ave Milwaukee WI 53202-4107

MEDVED, SANDRA LOUISE, elementary education educator; b. Moscow, Idaho, May 26, 1953; d. Donald James and Pearl Helen (Brown) Jensen; m. Jeffrey Alan Medved, Aug. 6, 1977. BS in Edn., U. Idaho, 1975; postgrad., Boise State U., 1976, U. Idaho, 1977—. Tchr. St. Mary's Elem. Sch., Boise, Idaho, 1975-78, Coeur d'Alene (Idaho) Sch. Dist., 1978—; puppeteer Coeur d'Alene Sch. Dist., 1985-91, tchr. edn. instr., 1986-88, 92-94, lang. arts com., 1988—, dist. coord. handicap awareness program, 1989-91, staff devel. curriculum adv. com., 1990-95, mentor tchr., 1990-93, mem. phonics spelling com., 1996—, mem. Educator of the Yr. com., 1997—, mem. staff devel. com., 1997—; tchr. edn. U. Idaho, 1987-88; instr. Lewis & Clark State Coll., 1994—; active Idaho State Sch. Reform Com., 1994-95; rep. Goals 2000 Tchr. Forum, 1995. Vol. Kootenai County Diversion Program, Coeur d'Alene, 1980's. Recipient grants EXCEL, Coeur d'Alene, 1991, 92. Mem. ASCD, NEA, Idaho Edn. Assn., Coeur d'Alene Edn. Assn., Internat. Reading Assn., Panhandle Reading Assn., Phi Delta Kappa. Avocations: reading, swimming, walking. Office: Sorensen Elem Coeur d'Alene Sch Dist 9th and Coeur d Alene Ave Coeur D Alene ID 83814

MEE, CHARLES L., playwright, historian, editor; b. Evanston, Ill., Sept. 15, 1938; s. Charles L. and Sarah (Lowe) M.; m. Suzi Baker (div.); children: Erin, Charles; m. Kathleen Tolan; children: Sarah, Alice. BA, Harvard U., 1960. Editor-in chief Horizon mag., 1971-75. Author: Meeting at Potsdam, 1976, A Visit to Haldeman, 1978, The End of Order, 1980, The Marshall Plan, 1982, The Ohio Gang, 1983, Vienna: Lusthaus, 1986, The Investigation of the Murder in El Salvador, 1986, The Genius of the People, 1987, The Constitutional Convention, The Sequel, 1988, Rembrant's Portrait, 1988, The Imperialists at the Club Cave Canem, 1988, Another Person Is A Foreign Country, 1991, Orestes, 1992, The Bacchae, 1993, Playing God, 1993, Agamemnon, 1994, The Trojan Women A Love Story, 1995, My House Was Collapsing Toward One Side, 1996, Time to Burn, 1997. Mem. Urban Inst. (bd. dirs.), En Garde Arts (bd. dirs.). Office: care Lois Wallace 177 E 70th St New York NY 10021-5109

MEECH, KAREN JEAN, astronomer; b. Denver, July 9, 1959; d. Lloyd Augustus and Patricia Ann (Marshall) M. BA cum laude in Physics, Rice U., 1981; PhD in Planetary Astronomy, MIT, 1987. Rsch. asst. Maria Mitchell Obs., Nantucket, Mass., 1978, Am. Assn. Variable Star Observation, Cambridge, Mass., 1979, 81-82; rsch. asst. archaeoastronomy EARTHWATCH, Cusco, Peru, 1980; univ. lab. asst. molecular physics Rice U., Houston, 1980-81, quantum physics grader, 1980-81; rsch. asst. Am. Assn. Variable Star Observers, 1981-82; rsch. specialist MIT, Cambridge, 1981-82, grad. teaching asst., 1982-86, grad. rsch. asst., 1986-87; asst. astronomer Inst. for Astronomy, Honolulu, 1987-91, assoc. astronomer, 1992—; mem. IFA Computer Adv. Com., 1991-93, IFA Endowment Com., 1991, U. Rsch. Coun., 1990-93, NASA Planetary Astronomy Com. II, 1993-94, NASA Planetary Sci. Data Steering Group, 1993-96, IFA Admissions Com., 1992-97, NASA Planetary Astronomy Rev. Panel, 1990-91, Cerro Tololo Interamerican Obs. user's Com., 1991-94, USIA Internat. Teleconf., 1991, NASA Keck Planetary Mgmt. Ops. Working Group, 1996—, Annie Jump Cannon Award Com., 1995-97, U. Hawaii Faculty Senate, 1995—; chair IFA Scholarship Com., 1991; interviewer Rice U. Alumni, 1989—; telescope allocation com. referee Kitt Peak Nat. Obs., 1995—; reviewer. Contbr. articles to Astron. Jour., Astrophys. Jour., Sci., Icarus, Nature, Bull. Am. Astronomy Soc., Info. Bull. Variable Stars, Minor Planet Circular, IAU Circular. Safety diver U. Hawaii Scuba class, 1988-90; vol. Honolulu Zool. Soc. Zoo Fun Run, 1991-92; active dept. edn. H.S. Student Career Program, Honolulu, 1988; organizer H.S. Tchr.-Student Asst. Workshops, 1993-95; local organizing chair divsn. Planetary Astronomy meeting, Kona, Hawaii, 1995; judge Hawaii State Sci. Fair, 1992—; bd. dirs. Kilolokahi, 1995—. Scholar Bd. of Govs., 1980, Grad. Student Rschrs. fellow NASA, 1986-87; recipient Annie Jump Cannon award in Astronomy, 1988, Harold C. Urey prize in Astronomy Am. Astron. Soc., 1994, Heaps prize in Physics, 1981. Mem. Am. Astron. Soc. (divsn. planetary scis., 1995, Asteroid 4367 named

Meech in her honor), Internat. Astron. Union-Commn. 15, Am. Assn. Variable Star Observers. Achievements include co-discovery of the outburst of Halley's comet at the longest distance from the sun for a recorded outburst; discovery of cometary activity on object 2060 Chiron; investigator Hubble space telescope. Office: Inst for Astronomy 2680 Woodlawn Dr Honolulu HI 96822-1839

MEECHAM, WILLIAM CORYELL, engineering educator; b. Detroit; s. William Edward and Mabel Catherine (Wilcox) M.; m. Barbara Jane Brown, Sept. 4, 1948 (dec.); children: Janice Lynn, William James; m. Della Fern Carson,. BS, U. Mich., 1948, MS, 1948, PhD in Physics, 1954. Head acoustics lab. Willow Run Labs., Ann Arbor, Mich., 1959-60; asst. prof. U. Mich., Ann Arbor, 1958-60; prof. U. Minn., Mpls., 1960-67; prof. fluid mechanics and acoustics UCLA, 1967—, chmn. dept. mechanics and structures, 1972-73; cons. Aerospace Corp., El Segundo, Calif., 1975-80, Rand Corp., Santa Monica, Calif., 1964-74, Bolt, Beranek and Newman, Cambridge, Mass., 1968-73, Arete Assocs., Encino, Calif., 1976—, CRT Corp., Chatsworth, Calif., 1985—. Author: (with R. Lutomirski) Lasar Systems, 1973; author 140 papers on fluid mechanics and acoustics. Treas. Unitarian Ch., Ann Arbor, Mich., 1958-60; advisor U.S. Congress Com. on Pub. Works, Congl. Record Report N.J., 1972; mem. Calif. Space and Def. Council, U.S. Congress, 1982—. Served with U.S. Army, 1944-46. Mich. Alumni scholar 1942-44, Donovan scholar U. Mich., 1944-45; UCLA senate rsch. grantee, 1968—, NASA rsch. grantee, 1971—, Office Naval Rsch. grantee, 1977-85; recipient Disting. Svc. award U.S. Army. Fellow Acoustical Soc. Am. (gen. chmn. meeting 1973), AIAA (assoc. fellow); mem. Internat. Inst. Acoustics and Vibration, Am. Phys. Soc. (fluid dynamics div.), Inst. Noise Control Engring., Sigma Xi, Tau Beta Pi. Home: 927 Glenhaven Dr Pacific Palisades CA 90272-2202 Office: UCLA Sch Engring & Applied Sci Los Angeles CA 90024

MEECHAM, WILLIAM JAMES, ophthalmologist; b. Ann Arbor, Mich., Nov. 30, 1958; s. William Coryell and Barbara (Brown) M.; m. Amanda Roberts. AB in Zoology, U. Calif., Berkeley, 1980, MA in Biophysics, 1983; MD, U. Calif., San Francisco, 1987. Diplomate Nat. Bd. Med. Examiners, Am. Bd. Ophthalmology. Med. intern Cabrini Med. Ctr., N.Y.C., 1987-88; resident in ophthalmology U. Calif., San Francisco, 1988-91, ocular oncology fellow, 1991-92, clin. asst. prof., 1991—, ocular plastics fellow, 1992-93; sr. physician depts. ophthalmology and mohs surgery Kaiser Permanente, San Rafael, 1993—. Contbr. articles to profl. publs.; editor-in-chief U. Calif.-San Francisco Synapse, 1984-85. Mem. Am. Acad. Ophthalmology, Am. Soc. Ophthalmic Plastic and Reconstructive Surgeons. Avocations: sailing, astronomy, entomology, hiking. Office: 99 Montecillo Rd San Rafael CA 94903-3308

MEEGAN, BROTHER GARY VINCENT, school administrator, music educator; b. Syracuse, N.Y., Oct. 29, 1952; s. Vincent John and Kathryn Joan (Gettino) M. AAS in Music, Onondaga C.C., 1975; B Music Edn., Syracuse U., 1978; MS in Ednl. Leadership, Calif. State U., Hayward, 1990; postgrad., U. So. Calif., 1991-92, Washington Theol. Union, 1993, U. Tex., 1997. Cert. music educator, adminstr., Calif. Tchr. music West Genesee Cen. Schs., Camillus, N.Y., 1979-80, Modesto (Calif.) City Sch. Dist., 1983-87, Shiloh Sch. Dist., Modesto, 1987-90; asst. prin. Sylvan Union Sch. Dist., Modesto, 1990-93; mem. faculty, dir. studies Holy Cross H.S., San Antonio, Tex., 1995-97; prin. Five Wounds Cath. Sch., San Jose, Calif., 1997—; bd. dirs. Modesto Performing Arts, 1984-89; prin. conductor Stanislaus Youth Symphony, Modesto, 1985-89. Bd. dirs. Townsend Opera Players, Modesto, 1985-87, Modesto Arts Coun., 1986. Mem. ASCD, Nat. Acad. Tel. Arts and Scis., Am. Ednl. Rsch. Assn., Music Educators Nat. Conf., Calif. Music Educators Assn. (task force 1989-90), Stanislaus County Music Educators Assn. (pres. 1989-90), Phi Delta Kappa. Roman Catholic. Avocations: writing, performing, marching band, Santa Clara Vanguard Drum and Bugle Corps. Office: Five Wounds Sch 1390 Five Wounds Ln San Jose CA 95116-1127

MEEHAN, JEAN MARIE ROSS, occupational health and safety management consultant; b. Chgo., Mar. 16, 1954; d. A. Ronald Gonzalez and Barbara Marx Shipley; m. John J. Meehan, 1993; 1 child, Jenna A.; 1 child from previous marriage, Justin L. Ross. Diploma in Nursing, St. Mary of Nazareth Hosp., Chgo., 1974; BS in Health Arts with high honors, Coll. St. Francis, 1988. Cert. occupl. health nurse specialist Am. Bd. for Occupl. Health Nursing. Staff nurse St. Mary of Nazareth Hosp., Chgo., 1973-75; head nurse ambulatory care Edgebrook Med. Diagnostic Ctr., Chgo., 1975-76; occupl. health nurse Williams Electronics, Inc., Chgo., 1976-84; adminstr. safety and benefits Reliable Power Products, Franklin Park, Ill., 1984-90; corp. dir. human resources and risk MacLean-Fogg Co., Mundelein, Ill., 1990—; pres., cons. Auriel Mgmt. Sys., Island Lake, Ill., 1992—; gov., apptd. mem. Ill. Pollution Prevention Adv. Coun., Springfield, Ill., 1993—, mem. coun., 1993—; adv. bd. dirs. Gt. Lakes Health Care Alliance, 1996—; spkr. in workshops. Guest speaker local schs. and environ. groups, also I.E.P.A. and U.S. E.P.A. workshops; corp. campaign chmn. Charitable Preference Drives, Mundelein, Ill., 1991-94. Recipient Leadership Civic citation United Way Charities of Lake County, 1993, 94. Mem. Am. Assn. Occupl. Health Nurses, Ill. Assn. Occupl. Health Nurses, Suburban Chgo. Occupl. Health Nurses, Soc. for Human Resources Mgmt. (also State Line chpt.), Lake County Violence Intervention and Prevention. Avocations: parenting, interior design, reading, entertaining, writing poetry. Office: MacLean-Fogg Co 1000 Allanson Rd Mundelein IL 60060-3804

MEEHAN, JOHN, artistic director; b. Brisbane, Australia. Studied with, Patricia MacDonald; student, Australian Ballet Sch., Melbourne. Mem. Australian Ballet, 1970-72, soloist, 1972-74, prin. dancer, 1974; artistic dir. Royal Winnipeg Ballet, 1990-93; guest artist, prin. dancer Am. Ballet Theatre, 1977. Leading roles include The Sleeping Beauty, Romeo and Juliet, Giselle, Onegin, Fokine's Firebird, Les Sylphides, George Balanchine's Theme and Variations, Teltley's Sphinx, Pierrot Lunaire and Voluntaries, Anthony Tudor's The Leaves are Fading, Lilac Garden, Baryshnikov's Don Quixote; created leading role in Gemini; Can. debut The Merry Widow with the Nat. Ballet of Can., 1986; danced at Kennedy Centre, Washington; co-starred with Karen Kain TV prodn. The Merry Widow, 1987; created two original pas de deux for ABT, Le ReTour, Adagio for Stings; choreographer Echoes for the Washington Ballet; singer, dancer feature role mus. rev. Noel; mus. debut in Song and Dance; dance premiere Dim Lustre, ABT, 1985; dancer Jacob's Pillow Dance Festival, 1985; guest appearances with the N.Y.C. Ballet; with Merrill Ashley in The Nutcracker, Divertimento No. 15, Swan Lake, Gounod Symphony, Piano Concerto No. 2. Scholar Australian Ballet Sch. Address: Box 12 Russell Ave Rhinecliff NY 12574-0019*

MEEHAN, JOHN JOSEPH, JR., hospital administrator; b. Boston, Jan. 29, 1946; s. John Joseph and Marjorie Louise (Hill) M.; m. Pamela Marshall, Mar. 25, 1973; children—Seth, Andrew, Sean. B.A., Dartmouth Coll., Hanover, N.H., 1968; M.H.A., U. Minn., Mpls., 1974. Unit mgr. Boston Hosp. Women, 1971-72; adminstrv. resident Hennepin County Gen. Hosp., Mpls., 1973-74; v.p. Putnam Meml. Hosp., Bennington, Vt., 1974-79; asst. dir. Hartford Hosp., Conn., 1979-81, assoc. exec. dir., 1981-85, exec. v.p., 1985-87, pres., chief operating officer, 1987-89; pres., chief exec. officer, 1989—; faculty Hartford Grad. Ctr., 1979-81; preceptor U. Minn., 1981—, Yale U., New Haven, 1981—; mem. New Eng. Health Care Assembly, 1975—, officer, 1982-92; pres., CEO Hartford Health Care Corp., 1989—, Conn. Health Sys., Inc., 1996—. Active Bennington Lion's Club, 1975-79, Conn. Hosp. Assn., Urban League Greater Hartford, 1979—, Greater Hartford C. of C., 1979—, also bd. dirs., 1994-97, Hartford Downtown Coun., 1997—; chmn. ARC, Bennington, 1978-79; bd. dirs. St. Joseph Coll., ConnectiCare IPA/HMO, 1990-95, Mech. Savs. Bank, 1993—; corporator St. Francis Hosp., 1988—, Inst. Living, 1993—; fellow Am. Leadership Forum, 1993—. Served to lt. (j.g.) USNR, 1968-70. Decorated Naval medals and ribbons, 1968-70; recipient Disting. Naval Grad. award, 1968, Stuart Thompson M.D. award U. Minn., 1974. Mem. Am. Hosp. Assn., Conn. Hosp. Assn. (bd. dirs. chmn. 1996—), Capital Area Health Consortium.

MEEHAN, MARTIN THOMAS, congressman, lawyer; b. Dec. 30, 1956; s. Martin T. and Alice (Britton) M.; m. Ellen T. Murphy. BA in Polit. Sci., Edn. cum laude, U. Mass., Lowell, 1978; MPA, Suffolk U., 1981, JD, 1986; student, Harvard U., 1987-88. Adminstrv. asst. to mayor City of Lowell, Mass., 1978-79; press asst. Congressman James M. Shannon, Mass., 1979-81; del. Dem. Nat. Conv., 1980, 84, 88; head rsch. analyst Joint Com. on Elec. Laws Mass. State Senate, 1981-84; dir. pub. affairs Govt. of Mass., 1985-86, dep. sec. state, 1986-90; 1st asst. dist. atty. Middlesex County, Mass., 1991-92; mem. 103rd-105th Congresses from 5th Mass. dist., 1993—; mem. nat. security com., judiciary com. 103rd-104th Congresses from 5th Mass. dist.; former teacher, adj. instr. U. Lowell, Mass.; lawyer 1986—. Named Student of Yr. Lowell Exchange Club, 1975. Mem. ABA, Mass. Bar Assn., U. Lowell Alumni Assn., The Newspaper Guild, Internat. Fedn. Journalists. Democrat. Roman Catholic. Office: US Ho of Reps 2434 Rayburn Bldg Ofc Bldg Washington DC 20515-2105

MEEHAN, MICHAEL JOSEPH, lawyer; b. St. Louis, Aug. 28, 1942; s. Joseph Michael and Frances (Taylor) M.; m. Sharon Kay McHenry (div. 1988); m. Patricia Ann Shive, July 8, 1989. BS in Engring., U.S. Coast Guard Acad., 1964; JD with high distinction, U. Ariz., 1971. Bar: Ariz. 1971, U.S. Ct. Appeals (6th, 8th, 9th and 10th cirs.), U.S. Supreme Ct. 1975. Law clk. Assoc. Justice William H. Rehnquist, U.S. Supreme Ct., 1972; assoc. Molloy, Jones & Donahue, P.C., Tucson, 1971-75, shareholder, 1975-93; chmn. exec. com., head trial dept., 1986-93; founder Meehan & Assocs., Tucson, 1993—; mem. fed. appellate rules adv. com. Jud. Conf. U.S., 1994—. Author chpt. on appellate advocacy: State Bar of Arizona Appellate Practice Handbook. Fellow Am. Acad. Appellate Lawyers; mem. ABA (sect. on litigation), Ariz. Bar Assn. (mem. exec. coun. appellate advocacy sect. 1995—). Republican. Lutheran. Avocation: golf. Office: Meehan & Assocs PO Box 1671 Tucson AZ 85702-1671

MEEHAN, PATRICK JOHN, public health officer; b. Tulsa, Dec. 30, 1956; married; 2 children. BA in Chemistry, U. Calif., Santa Cruz, 1978; MD, Washington U., St. Louis, 1982. Diplomate Am. Bd. Family Practice; lic. physician, Ga. Resident in family practice Navidad Med. Ctr./U. Calif., Salinas, 1982-85; with Epidemic Intelligence Svc. CDC and Prevention, Ctr. Environ. Health and Injury Control, Atlanta, 1988-89, preventive medicine resident, 1989-91; family practice physician Su Clinica Familiar, Harlingen, Tex., 1985-87; med. dir. prenatal and family planning Region 8 Tex. Dept. Pub. Health, Harlingen, 1986-87; acting health officer, cons. in communicable disease Santa Cruz (Calif.) County Health Dept., 1987-88; dir. N.H. divsn. Pub. Health Svc., 1991-94; dir. Ga. divs. pub. health Dept. Human Resources, Atlanta, 1994—; family practice physician Locum Tenens, Raymondville, Tex., 1987, Salud Para La Gente, Watsonville, Calif., 1987-88; adj. asst. prof. Emory U., Atlanta; clin. assoc. prof. Morehouse Sch. Medicine; lectr. in field. Contbr. numerous articles to profl. jours. Mem. APHA, Med. Assn. Ga., Am. Acad. Family Physicians, Ga. Pub. Health Assn., Assn. of State and Territorial Health Ofcls. (chair com. on injury control, com. on tobacco or health). Office: 2 Peachtree St NW Ste 7-300 Atlanta GA 30303-3142

MEEHAN, RICHARD ANDREW, investment banker; b. Rockville Centre, N.Y., Apr. 22, 1964; s. William Campbell and Therese Marie (Copin); m. Linda Dmytriw, July 27, 1996. BS in Computer Sci., St. John's U., Jamaica, N.Y., 1988. Computer operator asst. Nassau County Dept. Gen. Svcs., Mineola, N.Y., 1988-89; jr. govt. specialist Morgan Stanley & Co., Inc., N.Y.C., 1989-90, sr. govt. specialist, 1990-96; computer lab. asst. St. John's U., 1985-88. Vol. coord. Mary Brennan Inn, Hempstead, N.Y., 1992-93. L.I. Academic Caddie scholar, 1982; named one of Outstanding Young Men of Am., 1987. Avocations: camping, bicycling, boating, swimming. Home: 1919 Palmetto St Ridgewood NY 11385

MEEHL, PAUL EVERETT, psychologist, educator; b. Mpls., Jan. 3, 1920; s. Otto John and Blanche Edna (Duncan) Swedal; m. Alyce M. Roworth, Sept. 6, 1941 (dec. 1972); children: Karen, Erik; m. Leslie Jane Yonce, Nov. 17, 1973. A.B., U. Minn., 1941, Ph.D., 1945; Sc.D., Adelphi U., 1984. Diplomate Am. Bd. Profl. Psychology (clin. psychology, bd. dirs.1957-62, Disting. Svc. and Outstanding Contbns. award 1989). Instr., asst., assoc. prof., chmn. dept. psychology U. Minn., 1951-57, prof., 1952—, prof. dept. psychiatry Med. Sch., 1952-90, regents' prof. psychology, 1968-89, Hathaway-Meehl prof. psychology, 1990-93, regent's prof. psychology emeritus, 1993—; prof. Minn. Ctr. for Philosophy of Sci., 1953-56, 69—, prof. philosophy, 1971—; acting chief clin. psychology VA Hosp., Mpls., 1947-49; participant Dartmouth Conf. on Behavior Theory, 1950; mem. panel on criminal deterrence Nat. Acad. Sci., 1975-77; practice psychotherapy, 1951-94; staff Nicollet Clinic, 1970-80. Author: (with S.R. Hathaway) Atlas for Clinical Use of MMPI, 1951, (with others) Modern Learning Theory, 1954, Clinical Versus Statistical Prediction, 1954, What, Then, Is Man?, 1958, Psychodiagnosis, 1973, Selected Philosophical and Methodological Papers, 1991; contbr. articles to profl., legal and philos. jours. Recipient Ednl. Testing Svc. award for contbns. to measurement, 1994, Clin. Psychology Centennial prize for lifetime achievement APA, Bruno Klopfer disting. contbn. award, 1979, Gold medal for life achievement application of psychology Am. Psychol. Found., 1989, Disting. Svc. award Am. Bd. Profl. Psychologists, 1989, Joseph Zubin prize lifetime contbns. to psychopathology, 1993; William James fellow Am. Psychol. Soc., 1989. Felow Inst. for Advanced Study in Rational Psychotherapy; mem. APA (pres. 1961-62, Disting. Contbr. award clin. divsn. 1967, Disting. Sci. Contr. award 1958, Disting. Scientist award 1976, Disting. Contbn. to Knowledge award 1993, award for Outstanding Lifetime Contbn. to Psychology 1996), Am. Acad. Arts and Scis., Nat. Acad. Sci., Philosophy of Sci. Assn., Phi Beta Kappa, Sigma Xi, Psi Chi. Home: 1544 E River Ter Minneapolis MN 55414-3646 Office: U Minn N218 Elliott Hall 75 E River Rd Minneapolis MN 55455-0280

MEEK, CARRIE P., congresswoman; 3 children. BS, Fla. A&M U., 1946, MS, U. Mich., 1948. Mem. Fla. House, 1979-82, Fla. Senate, 1982-1992. Mem. 103rd-105th Congress from 17th Fla. dist., 1993—; mem. treasury, postal svc. & gen. govt., vets., HUD & ind. agys. postal svc. coms. Democrat. Office: US Ho of Reps 401 Cannon Bldg Ofc Washington DC 20515-0917

MEEK, FORREST BURNS, oil industry executive, trading company executive; b. Tustin, Mich., June 11, 1928; s. Robert B. and Electa I. (Gallup) M.; m. Jean R. Grimes, June 26, 1953; children: Sally, Thomas, Nancy, Charles. AA, Spring Arbor Coll., 1950; AB, Mich. State U., 1953; postgrad., U. Ga., 1965; MA, Cen. Mich. U., 1967. Asst. supt. Tranter Mfg. Co., Lansing, Mich., 1951-53; pres. Pioneer Mortgage Co., Clare, Mich., 1966-74; exec. sec., chmn. bd. Edgewood Press, Clare, 1971—; gen. mgr. Blue Water Imports, 1985; dir. Hanover Ednl. Ctr., Clare, 1986—, Ctr. for Chinese-Am. Scholarly Exchs., Inc., 1989—; gen. mgr. Blue-Water Internat. Trading Co., Inc.; vis. prof. Wuhan U., China, 1986, 87; dist. officer mgr. Fed. Decennial Census, 1990; CFO Am. Petroleum Corp., 1996; pres. MGF Drilling USA, Inc., 1996—; CFO Am. Petroleum, Del. Author: Michigan Timber Battleground, 1976, Michigan Heartland, 1979, One Year in China, 1988, Michigan Logging Railroad Era, 1850-1963, 1989, Railways and Tramways, 1990, Lumbering in Eastern Canada, 1991, Pearl Harbor Remembered, 1991, Heroes of The Twentieth Century, 1996. Coordinator Clare County Bicentennial Com., 1975-76; Rep. fin. chmn., Clare County, 1966-71, asst. treas. 10th dist. Mich, 1967-69; trustee local sch. bd.; chmn. local county jury bd. Mem. Am. Entrepreneur Assn., Mich. Sci. Tchrs. Assn., Mich. Hist. Soc., Heartland Mich. Geneal. Soc., White Pine Hist. Soc. (exec. sec.), Ctr. for Chinese-Am. Scholarly Exchs. Republican. Avocations: astronomy, silviculture, beekeeping.

MEEK, PAUL DERALD, oil and chemical company executive; b. McAllen, Tex., Aug. 15, 1930; s. William Van and Martha Mary (Sharp) M.; m. Betty Catherine Robertson, Apr. 18, 1954; children: Paula Marie Meek Burford, Kathy Diane Meek Hasemann, Carol Ann Meek Miller, Linda Rae Meek. B.S. in Chem. Engring, U. Tex., Austin, 1953. Mem. tech. dept. Humble Oil & Refining Co., Baytown, Tex., 1953-55; with Cosden Oil & Chem. Co., 1955-76, pres., 1968-76; dir. Fina, Inc. (formerly Am. Petrofina, Inc.), Dallas, 1968—, v.p. parent co., 1968-76, pres., chief operating officer, 1976-83, pres., chief exec. officer, 1983-86, chmn. bd., pres., chief exec. officer, 1984-86, chmn. bd., 1986—; apptd. by Gov. Wm. P. Clements, Jr. chmn. Pub. Uitilites Commn. of Tex., 1989-92. Contbg. author: Advances in Petroleum Chemistry and Refining, 1957. Chmn. chem. engring. vis. com. U. Tex., 1975-76; mem. adv. coun. Coll. Engring. Found., U. Tex., Austin, 1979—, U. Tex. Longhorn Found., 1989—, Coll. of NaturalScis. Found., 1989—; life mem.-at-large, bd. visitors McDonald Observatory dept. astonomy U. Tex.; co-chmn. indsl. divsn. United Way of Met. Dallas, 1981-82. Named Disting. Engring. Grad. U. Tex., Austin, 1969. Mem. Am. Petroleum Inst. (bd. dirs.), 25 Yr. Club of the Petroleum Industry, Founders Club of the Petrochem. Industry, Dallas Wildcat Com. (chmn. exec. com. 1987-88). Office: Fina Inc PO Box 2159 8350 N Central Expwy Dallas TX 75221

MEEK, PHILLIP JOSEPH, communications executive; b. Los Angeles, Nov. 17, 1937; s. Joseph Alcinus and Clara Amy (Phillips) M.; m. Nancy Jean LaPorte, June 25, 1960; children: Katherine Amy, Brian Joseph, Laurie Noel. B.A. cum laude, Ohio Wesleyan U., 1959; M.B.A., Harvard U., 1961. Fin. analyst Ford Motor Co., 1961-63, supr. capacity planning, 1963-66, supr. domestic scheduling, 1966, controller mktg. services, 1966-68; on loan as pres. Econ. Devel. Corp. Greater Detroit, 1968-70; pres., pub. Oakland Press Co., Pontiac, Mich., 1970-77; exec. v.p., gen. mgr. Ft. Worth Star-Telegram, 1977-79, pres., editorial chmn., 1980-82, pres., pub., 1982-86; sr. v.p., pres. pub. group Capital Cities/ABC Inc., N.Y.C., 1986—; dir. Calyx & Corolla, 1995—, Roadway Express, 1996—. Past mem. Pontiac Stadium Bldg. Authority; pres. United Way Pontiac-North Oakland, 1977; dir. United Way of N.Y.C., 1994—; pres. Tarrant County United Way, 1982-83, chmn., 1983-84; chmn. North Tex. Commn., 1983-84; trustee Ohio Wesleyan U. Mem. Newspaper Assn. of Am., Tex. Daily Newspaper Assn. (pres. 1984), Phi Beta Kappa, Omicron Delta Kappa, Sigma Delta Chi, Pi Delta Epsilon, Phi Gamma Delta. Methodist. Clubs: Stanwich (Conn.); Crystal Downs (Mich.). Office: ABC Inc 77 W 66th St New York NY 10023-6201

MEEK, VIOLET IMHOF, dean; b. Geneva, Ill., June 12, 1939; d. John and Violet (Krepel) Imhof; m. Devon W. Meek, Aug. 21, 1965 (dec. 1988); children: Brian, Karen; m. Don M. Dell, Jan. 4, 1992. BA summa cum laude, St. Olaf Coll., 1960; MS, U. Ill., 1962, PhD in Chemistry, 1964. Instr. chemistry Mount Holyoke Coll., South Hadley, Mass., 1964-65; asst. prof. to prof. Ohio Wesleyan U., Delaware, Ohio, 1965-84, dean for ednl. svcs., 1980-84; dir. annual programs Coun. Ind. Colls., Washington, 1984-86; assoc. dir. sponsored programs devel. Rsch. Found. Ohio State U., Columbus, 1986-91; dean, dir. Ohio State U., Lima, 1992—; vis. dean U. Calif., Berkeley, 1982, Stanford U., Palo Alto, Calif., 1982, reviewer GTE Sci. and Tech. Program, Princeton, N.J., 1986-92, Goldwater Nat. Fellowships, Princeton, 1990-97. Co-author: Experimental General Chemistry, 1984; contbr. articles to profl. jours. Bd. dirs. Luth. Campus Ministries, Columbia, 1988-91, Luth. Social Svcs., 1988-91, Americom Bank, Lima, 1992—, Lima Symphony Orch., 1993—, Art Space, Lima, 1993—, Allen Lima Leadership, 1993—, Am. House, 1992—, Lima Vets. Meml. Civic Ctr. Found., 1992—; chmn. synodical coms. Evang. Luth. Ch. Am., Columbus, 1982; bd. trustees Trinity Luth. Sem., Columbus, 1996—; chmn. Allen County C. of C., 1995—. Recipient Woodrow Wilson Fellowship, 1960. Mem. Nat. Coun. Rsch. Adminstrs. (named Outstanding New Profl. midwest region 1990), Am. Assn. Higher Edn., Phi Beta Kappa. Avocations: music, skiing, woodworking, Civil War history, travel. Home: 209 W Beechwold Blvd Columbus OH 43214-2012 Office: Ohio State U 4240 Campus Dr Lima OH 45804-3576

MEEKER, GUY BENTLEY, banker; b. Calcutta, India, Nov. 4, 1945; (parents Am. citizens); s. Lincoln Voght and Fortune Helen (Bentley) M.; m. Lavenia Yale Nelson, Apr. 27, 1967 (div. 1979); children: G. Bentley Jr., Melissa Anne ; m. Marcia Lee Zink, Nov. 4, 1984. BSBA, Georgetown U., 1967; MBA, George Washington U., 1970. Cons. OAS, Washington, 1971-73; v.p. The Deltec Banking Corp., Nassau, Bahamas & N.Y.C., 1973-78, Comml. Credit Internat. Banking Corp., Balt., 1978-82; sr. v.p., gen. mgr. Union Planters Internat. Bank, N.Y.C., 1982-84; exec. v.p., gen. mgr. Worthen Bank Internat., N.Y.C., 1984-86; exec. v.p. and chief exec. officer N.Am. Bank Cen. Asia, N.Y.C., 1984-95; supervisory dir. BCA Bank Europe N.V., Amsterdam, The Netherlands, 1993-95; pres. G.B. Meeker & Co., N.Y.C., 1996—. Author articles and monographs in field. Mem. Bankers Assn. Fgn. Trade (internat. adv. coun. 1992-95, vice chmn. IAC 1994-95), Inst. Internat. Bankers (legis. and regulatory com. 1992-94, bd. trustees 1994-95), Asia Soc. (corp. coun. 1987-95), River Club, Dutch Treat Club, Doubles Club. Roman Catholic.

MEEKER, ROBERT ELDON, retired manufacturing company executive; b. Moline, Ill., Sept. 6, 1930; s. Paul Edwin and Esther (Carlson) M.; m. Dorothy Elaine Nelson, Dec. 23, 1951; children: Julie Lynn Meeker Gratton, Laurie Allison Meeker Gamel, Bradford Nelson. B.S. in Chemistry, Ill. Wesleyan U., 1952; Ph.D in Phys. Chemistry, Northwestern U., 1955. Chemist, supr. Shell Devel. Co., Emeryville, Calif., 1955-64; mgr.-dir. synthetic rubber tech. ctr. Shell Chem. Co., Torrance, Calif., 1964-66; mgr. new projects Shell Chem. Co., N.Y.C., 1966-69; dir. exploratory sci., exploration and prodn. rsch. ctr. Shell Devel. Co., Houston, 1969-71; gen. mgr., head new enterprises div. Royal Dutch-Shell Co., London, 1971-72; v.p. comml., gen. mgr. Billiton aluminum B.V. Billiton Internat. Metals subs. Shell Co., The Hague, The Netherlands, 1972-74; pres. Roxana Shale Oil Co. subs. Shell Co., Houston, 1974-76; v.p., gen. mgr. energy systems mgmt. div. TRW, Inc., Redondo Beach, Calif., 1976-80; v.p., gen. mgr. maj. programs TRW, Inc., 1980-86; pvt. practice cons., real estate developer Tucson, 1986-94. Patentee in field. Trustee Ill. Wesleyan U., Bloomington, 1982-94, trustee emeritus, 1994—; v.p., bd. dirs. Cobblestone Homeowners Assn., 1991-92, pres., bd. dirs., 1992-94, sec., security chmn., 1994-97. Recipient Disting. Alumnus award Ill. Wesleyan U., 1981. Mem. Am. Parkinson Disease Assn. Inc. (pres. Ariz. chpt. 1996—, nat. bd. dirs. 1996—), Mercedes Benz Club Am. (pres. Chaparral sect. 1992-94). Republican. Lutheran. Avocations: photography; swimming; travel. Home and Office: 7240 N Star Fury Pl Tucson AZ 85718-1345

MEEKER, ROBERT GARDNER, English language educator; b. Lackawanna, N.Y., Mar. 22, 1927; s. David Magie and Helen Amelia (Kilburn) M.; m. Kathryn Mary Bryan, Sept. 30, 1950 (dec. Apr. 1981); children: David John, Robert Bryan, John Townley; m. Beverly Jane Smith, Mar. 17, 1984. BA in English, Lafayette Coll., 1950; MA in English, U. Scranton, 1962; PhD in English, Lehigh U., 1989. Editl. asst., house organ United Fruit Co., N.Y.C., 1950-52; analyst, report writer Dun and Bradstreet, Newark, 1952-55, Scranton, Pa., 1955-58; English instr. Wyoming Seminary Preparatory Sch., Kingston, Pa., 1958-59; English tchr. Dallas (Pa.) Area H.S., 1959-60; prof. English Bloomsburg (Pa.) State Coll. (now Bloomsburg Univ.), 1962-91; adj. prof. English Wilkes U., Wilkes-Barre, Pa., 1994—; cons. textbooks McGraw Hill Book Co., N.Y.C., 1987. Author: A Descriptive Analysis of the Kinds of Essays in Johnson's Rambler, 1990. Seaman 2d class USN, 1945-46. Mem. AAUP, Am. Soc. for Eighteenth Century Studies, Assn. Pa. State Coll. and Univ. Ret. Faculties. Avocations: classic jazz, bird watching, shelling. Home: 128 Yeager Ave Forty Fort PA 18704

MEEKS, CAROL JEAN, educator; b. Columbus, Ohio, Mar. 9, 1946; d. Clarence Eugene and Clara Johanna (Schwartz) B.; m. Joseph Meeks, Aug. 17, 1968 (div. 1981); 1 child, Catherine Rachael. BS, Ohio State U., Mex., 1968; MS, Ohio State U., 1969, PhD, 1972. Rsch. asst., assoc. Ohio State U., Columbus, 1968-71; internship Columbus Area C. of C., Ohio, 1970; lectr. Ohio State U., Columbus, 1970, 72; asst. prof. U. Mass., Amherst, 1972-74; asst. prof. Cornell U., Ithaca, N.Y., 1974-78, assoc. prof., 1978-80; legis. fellow Senate Com. Banking, 1984; supr. economist, head housing section USDA, Washington, 1980-85; assoc. prof. housing and consumer econs. U. Ga., Athens, 1985-90, prof., 1990—, head housing and consumer econs., 1992—; rsch. fellow Nat. Inst. for Consumer Rsch., Oslo, Norway, 1992; cons. Yale U., 1976-77, HUD, Cambridge, Mass., 1978, MIT Ctr. for Real Estate Devel. Ford Found. Project on Housing Policy; del. N.E. Ctr. for Rural Devel. Housing Policy Conf. Reviewer Home Econ. Rsch. Jour., 1987—, ACCI conf., 1987—; contbr. articles to profl. mags. Mem. panel town of Amherst Landlord Tenant Bd.; bd. dirs. Am. Coun. Consumer Interests; mem. adv. coun. HUD Nat. Mfg. Housing, 1978-80, 91-93; chair Housing Mfg. Inst. Consensus Commn. on Fed. Standards. Recipient Young Profl. award Ohio State U., 1979, Lender award AAFCS, 1996; named one of Outstanding Young Women of Am., 1979; Columbus Womens Chpt. Nat. Assn. Real Estate Bds. scholar, Gen. Foods fellow, 1971-72, HEW grantee, 1978, travel grantee NSF bldg. rsch. bd., AID grantee, USDA Challenge grant, 1995—. Mem. Am. Assn. Housing Educators (newsletter editor 1976-79, pres. 1983-84), Nat. Inst. Bldg. Sci. (bd. sec. 1984, 85, 89—, bd. dirs. 1981-83, 85, 87-93, features commn.), Am. Real Estate and Sci. and Urban Econs. Assn., Internat. Assn. Housing Sci., Com. on Status on Women in Econs., Nat. Assn. Home Builders (Smart House contract 1989), Epsilon Sigma Phi, Phi Upsilon Omicron, Gamma Sigma Delta, Phi Beta

Delta, Kappa Omicron Nu (v.p. of programs 1995-96), others. Office: U Ga 215 Dawson Hall Athens GA 30602-3622

MEEKS, HERBERT LESSIG, III, pastor, former school system administrator; b. National City, Calif., May 12, 1946; s. Herbert Lessig Jr. and Hazel Evelyn (Howard) M.; m. Ardena Lorraine Bice, June 30, 1971; children: Herbert Lessig IV, Laura Dawn, Misty Danae. Grad. in Theology, Bapt. Bible Coll., 1972; BS in Interdisciplinary Studies, Liberty U., Lynchburg, Va., 1989; MS in Edn., Tenn. Temple U., 1989; MA in Religion, Liberty U., 1990. Tchr. Mt. Vernon Christian Sch., Stockbridge, Ga., 1975-82; prin. Mt. Zion Christian Acad., Jonesboro, Ga., 1982-90; elem. prin. Des Moines Christian Sch., 1990-93; prin. N.W. Acad., Houston, 1993-94; sr. pastor 1st Bapt. Ch. Genoa, Houston, 1994—. Instr. ARC, Atlanta; candidate Ga. Ho. of Reps., Atlanta, 1980; bd. dirs. Concerned Christian for Good Govt., Atlanta, 1980-82; notary pub., Clayton County, Ga., 1983-90. Served to sgt. USAF, 1966-69. Mem. Assn. Christian Schs. Internat. (conv. planning com. 1985-90, accreditation/cons. chmn., Behind the Scenes award 1986), Nat. Rifle Assn. (life), Am. Pistol and Rifle Assn. Republican. Avocations: flying, hunting, politics, econs. Home: 12102 Palmcroft St Houston TX 77034-3721 Office: 1st Bapt Ch Genoa 12717 Almeda Genoa Rd Houston TX 77034-4639

MEEKS, KENNETH, magazine editor; b. Louisville, Oct. 26, 1963; m. Feb. 6, 1996. Grad. high sch., Louisville, 1981. Asst. to feature editor Guideposts mag., N.Y.C., 1986-90; reporter, copy editor Amsterdam News, N.Y.C., 1991-94; mng. editor Black Elegance mag., N.Y.C., 1994—. Contbg. author: (anthology) Brotherman, 1995 (award 1995). Rastafarian. Office: Black Elegance 475 Park Ave S New York NY 10016-6901

MEEKS, PATRICIA LOWE, secondary school educator; b. Enid, Okla., Oct. 21, 1928; d. Henry Preston and Veda Gay (Combs) Lowe; m. James Donald Meeks, Feb. 28, 1953 (div. Aug. 1975); children: Mary Gay, Ann Lowe, James Robert David. BA, Phillips U., 1951; MA in English, U. Colo., 1973. Cert. tchr., Colo., Okla. Tchr. English Garber (Okla.) High Sch., 1952-53; tchr. English and journalism Hillcrest High Sch., Dallas, 1955-57; teaching asst. U. Colo., Boulder, 1965-66; tchr. English Cherry Creek High Sch., Englewood, Colo., 1966-91; supr. grades K-12 reading and lang. arts Oklahoma City Pub. Schs., 1991—; cons. Coll. Bd. Rocky Mt. Region, Denver, 1973-91; advanced placement reader, table leader Coll. Bd. and Ednl. Testing Svc., Princeton, N.J., 1970-80, SAT reader, 1989-94, table leader, 1994—. Mem. alumni bd. Phillips U. Fulbright exch. tchr. U.S. Dept. Edn., 1980-81; grantee NEH, 1986, English-Speaking Union, 1987. Mem. ASCD, NEA, AAUW, Nat. Fulbright Assn., Okla. Coun. Tchrs. English, Nat. Coun. Tchrs. English, English-Speaking Union (v.p. Okla. City chpt.), Nature Conservancy, Audubon Soc. Republican. Episcopalian. Avocations: art history, bird watching, jazz, reading. Home: 2700 NW 68th St Oklahoma City OK 73116 Office: Oklahoma City Pub Schs 900 N Klein Ave Oklahoma City OK 73106-7036

MEEKS, WAYNE A., religious studies educator; b. Aliceville, Ala., Jan. 8, 1932; s. Benjamin L. and Winnie (Gavin) M.; m. Martha Evelina Fowler, June 10, 1954; children—Suzanne, Edith, Ellen. BS, U. Ala.-Tuscaloosa, 1953; BD, Austin Presbyn. Theol. Sem., 1956; MA, Yale U., 1964, PhD, 1965; Doctor Theologiae honoris causa, U. Uppsala, Sweden, 1990. Instr. religion Dartmouth Coll., Hanover, N.H., 1964-65; asst. prof. religious studies Ind. U., Bloomington, 1966-68, assoc. prof., 1968-69; assoc. prof. religious studies Yale U., New Haven, 1969-73, prof. religious studies, 1973-84, Woolsey prof. Bibl. studies, 1984—; dir. divsn. of Humanities, 1988-91. Author: Go From Your Father's House, 1964; The Prophet-King, 1967; First Urban Christians, 1983; Moral World of the First Christians, 1986, Origins of Christian Morality, 1993. Contbr. articles to profl. jours. Fulbright fellow, 1956-57; Kent fellow, 1962-64; NEH fellow, 1975-76; Guggenheim fellow, 1979-80. Fellow British Acad.; mem. Soc. Bibl. Lit. (pres. 1985), Am. Acad. Religion (bd. dirs. 1974-77), Studiorum Novi Testamenti Societas (editorial bd. 1979-82). Democrat. Presbyterian. Avocations: cabinet-making; hiking. Office: Yale U Dept Religious Studies PO Box 208287 Yale Station New Haven CT 06520-8287

MEEKS, WILLIAM HERMAN, III, lawyer; b. Ft. Lauderdale, Fla., Dec. 30, 1939; s. Walter Herman, Jr. and Elise Walker (McGuire) M.; m. Patricia Ann Rayburn, July 30, 1965; 1 son, William Herman IV; m. 2d, Miriam Andrea Bedsole, Dec. 28, 1971; 1 dau., Julie Marie. A.B., Princeton U., 1961; LL.B., U. Fla., 1964; LL.M. (tax), NYU, 1965. Bar: Fla. 1964, U.S. Dist. Ct. (so. dist.) Fla. 1965, U.S. Tax Ct. 1966, U.S. Ct. Appeals (11th cir.) 1981, U.S. Supreme Ct. 1985. Ptnr. McCune, Hiaasen, Crum, Ferris & Gardner, Ft. Lauderdale, 1964-89, Fleming, O'Bryan & Fleming, Ft. Lauderdale, 1990-95; ptnr. Niles, Dobbins and Meeks, Ft. Lauderdale, 1995—; dir. Attys. Title Services, Inc., 1978-79, Attys. Title Services of Broward County, Inc., 1971—, chmn. 1976-77; mem. Attys. Real Estate Coun. Broward County. Mem. ABA, Fla. Bar Assn., Broward County Bar Assn., Attys. Title Ins. Fund, Ft. Lauderdale Hist. Soc., Ft. Lauderdale Mus., Phi Delta Phi. Democrat. Presbyterian. Clubs: Kiwanis, Lauderdale Yacht, Tower (Ft. Lauderdale). Office: Niles Dobbins and Meeks 4th Fl 2601 E Oakland Pk Blvd POB 11799 Fort Lauderdale FL 33339-1799

MEEM, JAMES LAWRENCE, JR., nuclear scientist; b. N.Y., Dec. 24, 1915; s. James Lawrence and Phyllis (Deaderick) M.; m. Buena Vista Speake, Sept. 5, 1940; children: James, John. B.S., Va. Mil. Inst., 1939; M.S., Ind. U., 1947, Ph.D., 1949. Aero. research sci. NACA, 1940-46; dir. bulk shielding reactor Oak Ridge Nat. Lab., 1950-53, in charge nuclear operation aircraft reactor expt., 1954-55; chief reactor sci. Alco Products, Inc., 1955-57; in charge startup and initial testing Army Package Power Reactor, 1957; prof. nuclear engring. U. Va., Charlottesville, 1957-81; dept. chmn., dir. reactor facility U. Va., 1957-77, prof. emeritus, 1981—; cons. U.S. Army Fgn. Sci. and Tech. Ctr., 1981-90; vis. cons. nuclear fuel cycle programs Sandia Labs., Albuquerque, 1977-78; vis. staff mem. Los Alamos Sci. Lab., 1967-68; mem. U.S.-Japan Seminar Optimization of Nuclear Engring. Edn., Tokai-mura, 1973. Author: Two Group Reactor Theory, 1964. Fellow Am. Nuclear Soc. (sec. reactor ops. div. 1966-68, vice chmn. 1968-70, chmn. 1970-71, Exceptional Service award 1980); mem. Am. Phys. Soc., Am. Soc. Engring. Edn., SAR. Home: University Village # 1201 2401 Old Ivy Rd Charlottesville VA 22903-4853

MEENAN, PATRICK HENRY, state legislator; b. Casper, Wyo., Sept. 24, 1927; s. Hugh Martin and Margaret (Kelly) M.; BS cum laude, U. Notre Dame, 1949; m. Shirley Louise Byron, Dec. 30, 1950; children: Maurya Ann, Kevin Patrick, Michael James, Patricia Kelly. CPA Raab, Roush & Gaymon, Casper, 1949-53, ptnr. 1960-68; asst. treas. Williston Oil & Gas Co., 1953-55; ptnr. Meenan & Higgins, Casper, 1955-60; pres. KATI-AM & FM, Casper, 1963-81, KAWY Stero Radio, 1967-81; ptnr. Meenan, Miracle & Sherrill, CPAs, 1975-76; sec. dir. Bank of Casper, 1980-87; pres. PM Enterprises, Inc., 1981—; Erin Corp. Councilman City of Casper, 1956-65, v.p., 1961, mayor, 1962, 65; mem. Wyo. Ho. of Reps., 1969-89, majority floor leader, 1983-85, Speaker Pro Tem, 1985-87, Speaker of the House, 1987-89, chmn. house-rules com., chmn. mgmt. council, 1987-89; mem. exec. com. Western Legis. Conf. Coun. of State Govts., 1983-89; chmn. Nat. Conf. State Legis. Energy and Environ. Com., 1985. Named Young Man of Year, Jr. C. of C., Casper, 1962; Boss of Year, 1965; Distinguished Pub. Servant award City of Casper. Mem. AICPA, Casper Country Club, Notre Dame Alumni (nat. dir. 1972-75), Wyo. So. CPAs, Nat., Wyo. assns. broadcasters. Elk, K.C. Republican. Roman Catholic. Home: 3070 E 4th St Casper WY 82609-2104 Office: PM Enterprises Inc 300 Country Club Rd Ste 211 PO Box 50727 Casper WY 80605-0727

MEENAN, ROBERT FRANCIS, academician, rheumatologist, researcher; b. Cambridge, Mass., Apr. 5, 1947; s. Paul Leo and Anna Bernadine (Curtin) M.; m. Lynda Jane Fortman, Apr. 29, 1972; children: Molly, Mark. BA, Harvard U., 1968; MD, Boston U., 1972; MPH, U. Calif., Berkeley, 1977; MBA, Boston U., 1989. Diplomate Am. Bd. Internal Medicine and Rheumatology. Asst. prof. Sch. of Medicine Boston U., 1977-82, assoc. prof. Sch. of Medicine, 1982-88, prof. Sch. of Medicine, 1988—, assoc. dir. Arthritis Ctr., 1977-88, chief arthritis sect. Sch. of Medicine, 1988-92, dir. Arthritis Ctr., 1988-92, dean and prof. Sch. Pub. Health, 1992—; mem. nat. arthritis adv. bd. NIH, Washington, 1988-92; Svartz Meml. lectr. Swedish Med. Soc., 1989. Contbr. Jour. Arthritis Impact Measurement Scales, Jour. Social Security Disability, Jour. Dictionary of Rheumatic Disease, Outcome Assessmentation Clin. Moles; contbr. over 75 articles to profl. jours. Trustee Arthritis Found., 1989—. Internat. League Against Rheumatism fellow, 1981; recipient Nat. Svc. award Arthritis Found., 1989. Fellow ACP, Am. Coll. Rheumatology (pres. 1990-91); mem. Am. Soc. for Clin. Investigation. Achievements include development of arthritis impact measurement scales. Office: Boston U Sch Pub Health 80 E Concord St Roxbury MA 02118-2307

MEENDSEN, FRED CHARLES, retired food company executive; b. Garden City, N.Y., Oct. 28, 1933; s. Frederick Herman and Charlotte Mabel (Reiss) M.; B.A., Colgate U., 1954; M.B.A., Harvard U., 1956; m. Nancy Lou Gross, Nov. 16, 1957; children: Fred Charles, Martha Anne. Mem. mktg. and sales mgmt. dept. Velsicol Chem. Corp., Chgo., 1957-63; with CPC Internat., Inc., Englewood Cliffs, N.J., 1963-96, pres. subs. Peterson/Puritan, Inc., Danville, Ill., 1977-83, pres. subs. Can. Starch Co., 1983-84, v.p. parent co., 1983-96, pres. N.Am. region Corn Wet Milling div., 1984-88, v.p. corp. affairs, 1988-93, v.p. govt. affairs, 1994-96; dir. Can. Starch Co., 1983-88; chmn. Casco Co.; mem. U.S. C. of C. Can. Rels. Com., 1986-96, Food and Agr. Com., 1988-96; sec. Agr. Adv. Comm. on Trade, 1987-92; pres., Colgate U. Alumni Corp., 1991-93, bd. dirs. 1988—; trustee Colgate U., 1993—; gen. chmn. ann. fun drive Chesapeake Bay Maritime Mus. Served to 1st lt. U.S. Army, 1956-59. Author: Atomic Energy and Business Strategy, 1956. Home: 24472 Trice Field Ct Saint Michaels MD 21663-2618

MEERS, HENRY W., investment banker; b. Joliet, Ill., July 12, 1908; s. Robert and Mary (Cullen) M.; m. Evelyn Huckins; children: Henry Weber, Albert Huckins, Robert. A.B., U. Ill., 1930. With Halsey, Stuart & Co., Chgo., 1930-35, Harriman, Ripley & Co., 1936-42; resident partner White, Weld & Co., 1946-72, vice chmn., 1972-78; mng. dir. Merrill Lynch & Co. Investment Banking Group, Chgo., 1978—; dir. Merrill Lynch Trust Co., Chgo., 1992—; dir. DuKane Corp., 1962—; chmn. bd. govs. Assn. Stock Exchange Firms, 1968-69; bd. govs. Midwest Stock Exchange, 1957-60, N.Y. Stock Exchange, 1970-71. Del. Nat. Rep. Conv., 1984, alt. del., 1988; bd. dirs. Nat. Recreation Park Assn. Found.; mem. Chgo. Crime Commn.; chmn. Modern Cts. Ill., 1970, Met. Cursade Mercy, 1967; life trustee U. Cgho., Ch. Internat. House; life trustee, chair Chgo. Ednl. TV Sta.-WTTW, PBS, 1978-89; life trustee Lake Forest Acad.; trustee Lake Forest Coll., 1968-76; bd. dirs. Children's Meml. Hosp., chmn., 1970-75; chair bd. trustees Latin Sch. Chgo., 195-658; bd. dirs. U. Ill. Found.; mem. citizens bd. Loyola U.; chmn. Chgo. coun. Boy Scouts Am., 1952-56; mem. Ill. Compensation Rev. Bd., 1985-96; chair Internat. House, U. Chgo. Commdr. USNR, 1942-46. Recipient Man of Yr. award NCCJ, 1969, Founders award, 1992. Mem. Investment Analysts Soc., Ducks Unltd. (nat. trustee 1980-90), Chgo. Club, Comml. Club Chgo., Links Club, Onwentsia Club, Old Elm Club, Seminole Golf Club, Shore Acres Club, Bohemian Club, The Island Club, Phi Beta Kappa. Home: 550 N Green Bay Rd Lake Forest IL 60045-2146 Office: Merrill Lynch 5500 Sears Tower Chicago IL 60606-6325

MEEUSE, BASTIAAN JACOB DIRK, biologist, educator, researcher; b. Sukabumi, Indonesia, May 9, 1916; came to U.S., 1947; s. Adrianus Dirkszoon and Jannigje (Kruithof) M.; m. Johanne Roberta ten Have, Aug. 28, 1942; children: Karen Barbara, Peter Nicholas. BSc in Biology, U. Leiden, The Netherlands, 1936, M, 1939; D in Tech. Sci., U. Delft, The Netherlands, 1943. Tchr. Hort. Inst., Boskoop, The Netherlands, 1939-42; asst. lectr. U. Delft, 1942-46, chief asst. lectr., 1946-49, lectr., 1949-52; asst. prof. U. Wash., Seattle, 1952-55, assoc. prof., 1955-60, prof. botany, 1960-86, prof. emeritus, 1986—; corr. Royal Dutch Acad. Scis., Amsterdam, The Netherlands, 1965—; vis. prof. U. Nijmegen, The Netherlands, 1985; cons. Shell Devel. Co., Modesto, Calif., 1986-87. Author: The Story of Pollination, 1961, The Sex Life of Flowers, 1984, Old Wine in New Glasses, 1997; contbr. articles to profl. jours. Fellow NSF, 1962-63, Rockefeller Found., 1947-49. Mem. Royal Dutch Bot. Soc., Am. Soc. Plant Physiologists, Am. Bot. Soc., Native Plant Soc., Sigma Xi. Club: Holland-America (Seattle). Avocations: photography, hiking, showing films, lecturing. Office: U Wash Botany Dept KB-15 Seattle WA 98195

MEEZAN, ELIAS, pharmacologist, educator; b. N.Y.C., Mar. 5, 1942; s. Maurice and Rachel (Epstein) M.; m. Elisabeth Gascard, May 14, 1967; children: David, Nathan, Joshua. BS in Chemistry, CCNY, 1962; PhD in Biochemistry, Duke U., 1966. Asst. prof. physiology and pharmacology Duke U., Durham, N.C., 1969-70; asst. prof. pharmacology U. Ariz., Tucson, 1970-75; assoc. prof. U. Ariz., 1975-79; prof., chmn. dept. pharmacology U. Ala., Birmingham, 1979-89, prof., dir. Metabolic Diseases Rsch. Lab., 1989-93, prof. dept. pharmacology, 1993—. Asso. editor: Life Sci, 1973-79. Helen Hay Whitney postdoctoral fellow, 1966-69; recipient NIH Research Career Devel. award, 1977-79. Mem. Am. Soc. Pharmacology and Exptl. Therapeutics, Am. Soc. Biol. Chemistry, AAUP, AAAS, N.Y. Acad. Sci., Assn. Med. Sch.Pharmacology. Democrat. Jewish. Isolated retinal microvasculature; developer method for isolating ultrastructurally and chemically intact basement membranes. Home: 1202 Cheval Ln Birmingham AL 35216-2037 Office: U Ala Dept Pharmacology Birmingham AL 35294

MEGAHY, DIANE ALAIRE, physician; b. Des Moines, Iowa, Oct. 12, 1943; d. Edwin Dare and Georgiana Lee (Butcher) Raygor; m. Mohamed H. Saleh Megahy, Sept. 20, 1969; children: Hassan, Hamed, Hala, Heba. MD, U. Alexandria, Egypt, 1981. Diplomate Am. Bd. Family Practice. Intern Univ. Hosps., Alexandria, Egypt, 1982-83; resident Siu Family Practice, Belleville, Ill., 1987-90; physician St. Joseph's Hosp., Highland, Ill., 1988—. Fellow Am. Assn. Family Practice; mem. AMA, AAUW, Am. Coll. Forensic Examiners, So. Ill. Med. Assn., Ill. Med. Assn., Assn. Emergency Room Physicians. Avocations: student education in local schools. Home: 812 S Virginia Ave Belleville IL 62220-3689 Office: 415 S Main St Columbia IL 62236-2460

MEGAN, THOMAS IGNATIUS, retired judge; b. Chgo., Dec. 24, 1913; s. Charles P. and May M. (Magan) M.; m. Lucyanne Flaherty, Apr. 17, 1948; children: Anne, Thomas, Jane, Sarah, William, Molly. A.B., U. Ill., 1935; J.D., U. Chgo., 1938. Bar: Ill. 1939, N.Y. 1941. Mem. firm Pruitt & Grealis, Chgo., 1939-40, Pruitt, Hale & MacIntyre, N.Y.C., 1941; atty. U.S. Ordnance Dept., Chgo., 1941-42, Chgo., Rock Island and Pacific R.R. Co., Chgo., 1945-70; v.p., gen. counsel Chgo., Rock Island and Pacific R.R. Co., 1970-74, v.p. law, 1974-75; adminstrv. law judge ICC, Washington, 1975-81, HHS, Washington, 1981, FERC, Washington, 1981-96; ret., 1996. Served to maj. AUS, 1942-45. Mem. ABA, Soc. Trial Lawyers Chgo., Chgo. Law Club, Phi Kappa Tau, Phi Delta Phi. Club: Union League (Chgo.). Home: 11108 Waycroft Way Rockville MD 20852-3217

MEGARGEE, KATHLEEN ANNE, state public information officer, producer; b. Somers Point, N.J., Oct. 12, 1954; d. Irwin Ferdinand and Althea Myrtle (Evans) M. BA in English, Montclair State Coll., 1976. News anchor, reporter Radio Sta. WMID, Atlantic City, 1977-78, Radio Sta. WIIN, Atlantic City, 1979-81, Sta. WHAG-TV, Hagerstown, Md., 1982-84, Sta. WHP-TV, Harrisburg, Pa., 1984-86; news writer The Sun newspaper, Atlantic City, 1978; news reporter, anchor Sta. WRBV-TV, Vineland, N.J., 1981; news anchor Radio Sta. WCAU, Phila., 1981-82; news anchor, reporter, prodr. Sta. WQED-TV, Pitts., 1986-89, Sta. WITF-TV, Harrisburg, 1989-91; anchor Radio Sta. KYW, Phila., 1989; press sec. Pa. Dept. Aging, Harrisburg, 1991-96; freelance video and TV prodr., media cons. Vol., fund raiser Mothers Against Drunk Driving, 1985, Alzheimer's Assn., Harrisburg, 1994; vol., reader Harrisburg Area Radio Reading Svc. for the Blind, Harrisburg, 1991—. Recipient N.J. AP Broadcasters Assn. award, 1979, N.J. State Bar Assn. award, 1979, Golden Microphone award Atlantic City Press Club, 1980, Reporter/Prodr. award Chesapeake AP Broadcasters Assn., 1982, Nat. Mature Media Market award, 1993, 94, Corp. Pub. Broadcasting award, 1994. Roman Catholic. Avocations: canoeing, reading, hiking, cross country skiing. Home: 1405D Skyview Cir Harrisburg PA 17110 Office: Pa Dept Aging 400 Market St Harrisburg PA 17101-2301

MEGAW, ROBERT NEILL ELLISON, English educator; b. Ottawa, Ont., Can., Oct. 7, 1920; came to U.S., 1925, naturalized, 1936; s. John Wesley and Eileen (Ellison) M.; m. Ann Barber, Dec. 20, 1947; children—Peter Kenneth McNeill, Margaret McNeill, Laura McNeill. Student, Duke U., 1937-40; M.A., U. Chgo., 1947, Ph.D., 1950. Mem. faculty Williams Colls., 1950-69, prof. English, 1965; Carnegie intern Harvard U., 1955-56; prof. English U. Tex., Austin, 1969-85; chmn. dept. U. Tex., 1969-72, prof. emeritus, 1985—; cons. acad. planning, 1962—; mem. nat. bd. cons. NEH, 1974—. Contbr. poetry to Hellas, Sequoia, Negative Capability, The Spectator, The Formalist, Nimrod, The Lyric, others. Served to 1st lt. USAAF, 1942-45. Nat. Humanities Faculty, 1969—. Mem. MLA, Am. Ednl. Theatre Assn., AAUP (chmn. com. coll. and univ. teaching research and publ. 1965-71, pres. Tex. conf. 1976-78, chmn. assembly state confs. 1979-81), Tex. Assn. Coll. Tchrs., Tex. Faculty Assn., Nat., Fed., State poetry socs., Poetry Soc. Am., Acad. Am. Poets, Common Cause, ACLU, NAACP, Phi Beta Kappa (speaker, panelist 1980—). Democrat. Home: 2805 Bowman Ave Austin TX 78703-1608 Office: U Tex Dept English Parlin Hall Austin TX 78712

MEGEE, GERALDINE HESS, social worker; b. Newark, Ohio, June 9, 1924; d. A.P. Hess and Ethel Stoyle Luther; children: John Megee, Sarah Martens, Thomas Megee. BS, Northwestern U., 1944; MSEd, Ind. U., 1976, MSW, 1978; PhD candidate, Fielding Inst. Cert. social worker, Ill., Fla.; cert. addictions profl., Fla., criminal justice specialist; diplomate social work. Dir. Foster Care Prog., Webster-Cantrel Hall, Decatur, Ill., 1978-81; owner, dir. Family Systems Ctr., Decatur, 1981—; pvt. practice clinic and employee assistance Decatur, 1981—; dir. Charter Counseling Ctr., Charter Glade Hosp., Naples, Fla., 1985-87; owner FamilyWorks, Naples, 1991—. Mem. NASW, Am. Assn. Marriage and Family Therapists, Am. Acad. Sexologists, Sigma Pi Lambda. Home: 9856 Tonya Ct Bonita Springs FL 34135-4717 Office: 5051 Castello Dr Ste 205 Naples FL 34103-8985

MEGGERS, BETTY J(ANE), anthropologist; b. Washington, Dec. 5, 1921; d. William Frederick and Edith (Raddant) M.; m. Clifford Evans, Sept. 13, 1946. AB, U. Pa., 1943; MA, U. Mich., 1944; PhD, Columbia U., 1952; D (hon.), U. de Guayaquil, Ecuador, 1987, U. Fed. Rio de Janeiro, Brazil, 1994. Instr. anthropology Am. U., Washington, 1950-51; rsch. assoc. Smithsonian Instn., 1954—, expert, 1981—; founder, pres. Taraxacum Inc., 1977—; hon. prof. U. de Azuay, Ecuador, 1991. Author: Environmental Limitation on the Development of Culture, 1954, Ecuador, 1966, Amazonia, 1971, 2d edit., 1996, Prehistoric America, 1972, (with Clifford Evans) Archeological Investigations at the Mouth of the Amazon, 1957, Archeological Investigations in British Guiana, 1960, (with Clifford Evans and Emilio Estrada) Early Formative Period of Coastal Ecuador, 1965, (with Clifford Evans) Archeological Investigations on the Rio Napo, Eastern Ecuador, 1968; editor: Prehistoria Sudamericana, 1992. Recipient award for sci. achievement Washington Acad. Sci., 1956; gold medal 37th Internat. Congress of Americanists, 1966; Order Al Merito Govt. Ecuador, 1966; Order Bernardo O'Higgins Govt. Chile, 1985; Sec.'s Gold medal for exceptional service Smithsonian Instn., 1986; Order Andres Bello Govt. Venezuela, 1988; Order Al Mérito por Servicios Distinguidos Govt. Peru, 1989. Hon. fellow Assn. Tropical Biology (councilor 1976-78, pres.-elect 1982, pres. 1983); fellow AAAS; mem. Soc. Am. Archeology (exec. bd. 1962-64), Am. Anthrop. Assn. (exec. sec. 1959-61), Am. Ethnol. Soc., Anthrop. Soc. Wash. (treas. 1955-60, v.p. 1965-66, pres. 1966-68), Academia Nacional Historia, Ecuador (corr.), Phi Beta Kappa, Sigma Xi. Home: 1227 30th St NW Washington DC 20007-3410 Office: Smithsonian Instn Washington DC 20560

MEGGETT, LINDA LINETTE, reporter; b. Charleston, S.C.; d. James Lee and Arabell (Cohen) M. BA in Journalism, Marshall U., 1985. Reporter Herald Dispatch, Huntington, W.Va., 1985-88, Desert Sun, Palm Springs, Calif., 1988-90; reporter govt. Santa Barbara (Calif.) News-Press, 1990-92; reporter gen. assignment Post and Courier, Charleston, S.C., 1992—. Author: Black Issues in Higher Education, 1994. Planning com. mem. YWCA, Charleston, 1994—. Mem. Nat. Assn. Black Journalists, S.C. Coastal Assn. Black Journalists (treas. 1993-95), Sigma Gamma Rho (rec. v.p. Delta Iota Sigma chpt.). Methodist. Avocations: travel, reading, exercise. Home: 7121 Highway 162 Hollywood SC 29449-5603 Office: Post and Courier 134 Columbus St Charleston SC 29403-4809

MEGGS, WILLIAM JOEL, internist, emergency physician, educator; b. Newberry, S.C., May 30, 1942; s. Wallace Nat and Elizabeth (Pruitt) M.; m. Susan Nancy Spring, June 11, 1966; children: Jason Nathaniel, Benjamin Maffey, Thomas Clute. BS, Clemson U., 1964; PhD, Syracuse U., 1969; MD, U. Miami, 1979. Diplomate Am. Bd. Internal Medicine; diplomate Am. Bd. Allergy and Immunology; diplomate Am. Bd. Emergency Medicine, Am. Bd. Med. Toxicology. Resident in internal medicine Rochester (N.Y.) Gen. Hosp., 1979-82; staff fellow in allergy and clin. immunology Nat. Inst. Allergy and Infectious Diseases, Bethesda, Md., 1982-85; asst. dir. med. edn. emergency dept. Washington Hosp. Ctr., 1985-88; asst. prof. allergy, immunology E. Carolina U. Sch. of Medicine, Greenville, N.C., 1988-91, asst. prof. clin. toxicology dept. emergency medicine, 1991-95; assoc. prof. clin. toxicology E. Carolina U. Sch. Medicine, Greenville, 1995—; chmn., dir. emergency dept. Lenoir Meml. Hosp., Kinston, N.C., 1990-91; mem. Emergency Svcs. Com., Lenoir Meml. Hosp., Kinston, N.C., 1988-92; mem workshop on immune testing, Agy. for Toxic Substances and Diseases Registry, 1992, workshop on equity in environ. health, U.S. EPA, 1992, workshop on multiple chem. sensitivity syndrome, Nat. Rsch. Coun., 1991. Contbr. numerous articles and abstracts to profl. jours. Vol. physician Indigent Clinic E. Carolina U., Pitt County Med.Soc., 1988—, Pitt County Shelter, 1989—; advanced cardiac life support instr., E. Carolina U. Sch. of Medicine, 1988—, advanced trauma life support instr., 1991—; mem. Pitt County Traffic Injury Prevention Program, 1989—; bd. dirs. Rachael Carson Coun., 1988—; adv. bd. Pamplico Tar River Found., 1990—. Named Woodrow Wilson Hon. Fellow, 1964, NSF post-doctoral fellow, 1969; grantee:N.C. United Way, 1988-89, Greer Labs., 1989-90, Am. Lung Assn. N.C., 1992-93. Fellow Am. Coll. Emergency Physicians; mem. AMA, Am. Acad. Allergy and Immuniology, The Clin. Immunology Soc., Am. Acad. Clin. Toxicology, Pitt County Med. Soc., N.C. State Med. Soc., Soc. for Acad. Emergency Medicine, N.C. Thoracic Soc. (physicians' sect.). Office: E Carolina U Sch Medicine Dept Emergency Medicin Greenville NC 27858

MEGHERBI, DALILA, electrical and computer engineer, researcher; b. Algiers, Algeria, May 29, 1957; came to U.S., 1983; d. Mohamed and Salima (Astite) M. Diploma in Elec. Engring. with distinction, Ecole Nationale Polytechnique, Algeria, 1983; MSc in Elec. Engring., Brown U., 1986, MSc in Applied Math., 1987, PhD in Elec. Engring., 1993. Rschr. Nat. Ctr. New Energies, Algiers, 1982-83; sr. rsch. engr. Nat. Railway Co., Algiers, 1983; rschr. LEMS lab. divsn. engring. Brown U., Providence, 1986-92, postdoctoral rsch. assoc. LEMS lab. divsn. engring., 1993-94; sr. engr. Loral Aerospace LADS, Cambridge, Mass., 1994—; tech. cons. IDS Co., East Arlington, Mass., 1993; guest lectr. Northeastern U., 1988-91. Reviewer tech. articles; contbr. articles to profl. jours. Mem. AAAS, IEEE, IEEE Computer Graphics, IEEE Computer Soc., IEEE Robotics Soc., Sigma Xi. Achievements include patent for Method and Apparatus for Robot Motion Near Singularities and for Robot Mechanical Design; research in computer-controlled and sensor-based robotics and automation, expert task planning and machine intelligence, robotics applications in space, computer languages and graphics, data processing and pattern recognition, mathematical modeling and system analysis. Home: 1427 Commonwealth Ave Apt 401 Brighton MA 02135-6251

MEGHREBLIAN, ROBERT VARTAN, manufacturing executive, physicist; b. Cairo, Sept. 6, 1922; came to U.S., 1923, naturalized, 1946; s. Vahan V. and Mary (Kurkjian) M.; m. Margaret M. Gordon, 1987; children: David V., Susan L. B.Engring. (Gotshall-Powell scholar), Rensselaer Poly. Inst., 1943; M.S. (Guggenheim fellow), Calif. Inst. Tech., 1950, Ph.D. (Guggenheim fellow), 1953. Lectr. Oak Ridge Nat. Lab., 1952-55, asso. project mgr., 1955-58; chief sect. Physics Jet Propulsion Lab., Calif. Inst. Tech., 1958-60, mgr. space scis. div., 1960-68, dep. asst. lab dir., 1968-71, assoc. prof. applied mechanics, 1960-61; v.p. research and engring. Cabot Corp., Boston, 1971-79, v.p., 1971-87; pres. Distrigas Corp., 1979-85; gen. mgr. Cabot Crystals Bus. Unit, 1985-86, dir. corp. planning and devel., 1986-87. Author: Reactor Analysis, 1960. Served to lt. (j.g.) USN, 1941-46, PTO, ATO. Fellow AIAA (assoc.), Am. Nuclear Soc.; mem. Tennis Club Santa Barbara, Santa Barbara Club, Montecito Assn. (bd. dirs., v.p. 1994, pres. 1995, 96, chair archtl. rev. com. 1993-95), Sigma Xi. Home: 440 Woodley Rd Montecito CA 93108-2006

MEGILL, ALLAN D., historian, educator; b. Regina, Sask., Can., Apr. 20, 1947; came to U.S., 1980; s. Ralph Peter and Jean Tudhope (Dickson) M.; divorced; children: Jason Robert, Jessica Susan, Jonathan David; life ptnr.

Rita Felski; 1 child, Maria Megill Felski. BA, U. Sask., 1969; MA, U. Toronto, 1970; PhD, Columbia U., 1975. From instr. to prof. history U. Iowa, Iowa City, 1974-90; prof. history U. Va., Charlottesville, 1990—; rsch. fellow in history of ideas Australian Nat. U., Canberra, ACT, 1977-79, temp. lectr. modern European studies, 1979. Author: Prophets of Extremity, 1985; editor: Rethinking Objectivity, 1994; co-editor: The Rhetoric of the Human Sciences, 1987; cons. editor Jour. of History of Ideas, 1986-89, mem. editl. bd., 1990—; mem. editl. bd. Social Epistemology, 1986—, Rethinking History, 1996—, U. Press of Va., 1991-94; contbr. articles to profl. jours. Chmn. Page-Barbour and Richard Lectures com. U. Va., 1994-96. Mem. Am. Hist. Assn. Office: University of Virginia Corcoran Dept of History Randall Hall # 221 Charlottesville VA 22903-3284

MEGIVERN, KATHLEEN, association director, lawyer; b. Apalachin, N.Y., Apr. 16, 1950; d. John David and Katherine Augusta (Gibbons) M.; m. James Albert Mecklenburger, Jan. 5, 1986. BA, SUNY, Oneonta, 1972; JD, Cath. U., 1979. Bar: D.C. 1979. Adminstrv. asst. Am. Coun. of the Blind, Washington, 1973-79, staff lawyer, 1979-81; exec. dir. Assn. for Edn. and Rehab. of the Blind, Alexandria, Va., 1981—. Contbg. editor Braille Forum, 1987-90. Bd. dirs. Nat. Accreditation Coun., N.Y.C., 1982-86; treas. Affiliated Leadership League of and for the Blind, L.A., 1986—; mem. Human Rights Commn., Alexandria, 1990-93; chair Commn. on Disabled, Alexandria, 1989-96. Recipient Outstanding Article of Yr. award Am. Coun. Blind, 1979, spl. award Task Force on Rights and Empowerment Ams. with Disabilities, 1991. Mem. Am. Blind Lawyers Assn. (hon.), D.C. Bar Assn. Avocations: movies, folk music, good books. Office: Assn for Edn & Rehab of the Blind 4600 Duke St Alexandria VA 22304-2552

MEGNA, JEROME FRANCIS, university dean; b. Bklyn., Mar. 11, 1939; s. James G. and Irene (Bodkin) M.; m. Doreen Ann Filippi, Dec. 23, 1973; 1 child, Donna Marie. BA, St. Francis Coll., 1966; MA, NYU, 1968; PhD, Ball State U., 1972. Tchr. English Franciscan Bros., Bklyn., 1959-69; instr. English Ball State U., Muncie, Ind., 1969-71; prof. edn. CUNY, Bklyn., 1971-88; dean edn. Rider U., Lawrenceville, N.J., 1988—. Author: Study Guide on Italian Americans, 1978; contbr. articles to profl. jours. Democrat. Roman Catholic. Avocations: reading, music, swimming. Office: Rider U 2083 Lawrenceville Rd Lawrenceville NJ 08648-3001

MEHAFFY, THOMAS N., retired tire company executive; b. Rushden, Northamptonshire, Eng., Sept. 23, 1932; came to U.S., 1977; s. James Edward and Sarah (Moloney) M.; m. Catherine Mary Ryle, Mar. 23, 1963; children: Catherine A., Siobhan M., Deirdre E., Brendan R. BSc in Econs., London Sch. Econs., U. London, 1956. Mgr. econ. studies Dunlop Rubber Co., London, 1959-66; mgr. econs. Ford of Britain, Warley, Essex, Eng., 1966-67; mgr. bus. studies Ford of Europe, Warley, 1967-73; dir. profit analysis Brit. Steel Corp., London, 1973-77; dir. corp. planning and market research Dunlop Tire Corp., Buffalo, 1977-91; bus. advisor Dunlop Tire Corp., 1991-93, Trico Products Corp., Buffalo, N.Y., 1993-94. Served with Brit. Arty., 1951-53. Home and Office: 5129 Willowbrook Dr Clarence NY 14031-1476

MEHALCHIN, JOHN JOSEPH, entrepreneur, financial executive; b. Hazleton, Pa., Aug. 8, 1937; s. Charles and Susan (Korba) M.; divorced; 1 child, Martin. BS with honors (1st in class), Temple U., 1964; MBA, U. Calif., Berkeley, 1965; postgrad., U. Chgo., 1964; Supr. costs Winchester-Western, New Haven, Conn., 1965-67; mgmt. cons. Booz-Allen & Hamilton, N.Y.C., 1967-68; mgr. planning TWA, N.Y.C., 1968-69; officer Smith, Barney, N.Y.C. and Paris, 1970-74; chief fin. officer, pres. leasing co. Storage Tech. Corp., Louisville, 1974-79; sr. v.p. Heizer Corp., 1979; pres., founder Highline Fin. Svcs., Inc. and fgn. subs. Boulder, Colo., London, Paris, and Frankfurt, 1979—. Bd. dirs. Univ. Colo. Denver Ctr. Entrepreneurship; bd. advisors Wolf Ventures. With AUS, 1958-61. U. Calif. fellow, Berkeley, 1964, 65; U. Chgo. scholar, 1964. Mem. Fin. Execs. Inst., Equipment Leasing Assn., Beta Gamma Sigma, Omicron Delta Epsilon. Home and Office: Highline Fin Svcs Inc # 200 2930 Center Green Ct Boulder CO 80301-5419

MEHLE, ROGER W., federal agency administrator; b. Long Beach, Calif., Dec. 28, 1941. BS, U.S. Naval Acad., 1963; MBA, NYU, 1972; JD, Fordham U., 1976. Mng. dir. The First Boston Corp., N.Y.C., 1969-79; sr. v.p., dir. Dean Witter Reynolds, Inc., N.Y.C., 1979-81; asst. sec. for domestic fin. Dept. Treasury, Washington, 1981-83; exec. v.p., mng. dir. PaineWebber, Inc., N.Y.C., 1983-84; banking and securities atty. Washington, 1985-94; chmn. Fed. Ret. Thrift Investment Bd., Washington, 1985-94; exec. dir. Fed. Retirement Thrift Investment Bd., Washington, 1994—. Office: Fed Ret Thrift Investment Bd Office of the Exec Dir 1250 H St NW Washington DC 20005-3952

MEHLENBACHER, DOHN HARLOW, civil engineer; b. Huntington Park, Calif., Nov. 18, 1931; s. Virgil Claude and Helga (Sigfridson) M.; m. Nancy Mehlenbacher; children: Dohn Scott, Kimberly Ruth, Mark James, Matthew Lincoln. BS in Civil Enging., U. Ill., 1953; MS in City and Regional Planning, Ill. Inst. Tech., 1961; MBA, U. Chgo., 1972. Office: 436 Leitch Ave La Grange IL 60525-6126

MEHLER, BARRY ALAN, humanities educator, journalist, consultant; b. Bklyn., Mar. 18, 1947; s. Harry and Esther Mehler; m. Jennifer Sue Leghorn, June 2, 1982; 1 child, Isaac Alan. BA, Yeshiva U., 1970; MA, CCNY, 1972; PhD, U. Ill., 1988. Rsch. assoc. Washington U., St. Louis, 1976-80, instr. history, 1977; NIMH trainee racism program U. Ill., Champaign, 1981-85, rsch. asst. IBM EXCEL project, 1986-88; asst. prof. humanities Ferris State U., Big Rapids, Mich., 1988-93, assoc. prof., 1993—; media cons. Scientist's Inst. for Pub. Info., N.Y.C., 1980—; cons. Calif. Humanities Coun., 1995, ZDF/arte (Zweite Deutsches Fernshen--German pub. TV), 1995, House Subcom. on Consumer Protection, 1994, McIntosh Commn. for Fair Play in Student-Athlete Admissions, 1994, Can. Broadcast Svc., Toronto, Ont., 1985-92; judge Women's Caucus Awards for Excellence, St. Louis, 1989-91, 93; dir. Inst. for Study of Acad. Racism, 1993—. Assoc. editor: Encyclopedia of Genocide, 1997; contbr. more than 100 articles and revs. to profl. jours. Mem. vol. com. parents A Different Look at DARE, 1995. Rsch. fellow NSF, 1976-80, Babcock fellow U. Ill., 1985-86; grantee Rockefeller Found., 1977; Ferris State Bd. of Control cert. of Recognition, 1994; structure learning assistance program grantee Office of Minority Affairs, Lansing, Mich., 1994—. Mem. Am. Hist. Soc., Behavior-Genetics Assn., NAACP, Soc. for Study Social Biology, Ctr. for Dem. Renewal, History of Sci. Soc., B'nai B'rith (Anti-Defamation League), Coalition for Human Dignity, Facing History. Jewish. Avocations: hiking, camping. Home: 216 Rust Ave Big Rapids MI 49307-1726 Office: Ferris State U 901 S State St Big Rapids MI 49307-2251

MEHLINGER, HOWARD DEAN, education educator; b. Hillsboro, Kans., Aug. 22, 1931; s. Alex and Alice Hilda (Skibbee) M.; m. Carolee Ann Case, Dec. 28, 1952; children: Bradley Case, Barbara Ann, Susan Kay. BA, McPherson (Kans.) Coll., 1953; MS in Edn, U. Kans., 1959, PhD, 1964. Co-dir. social studies project Pitts. pub. schs., 1963-64; asst. dir. fgn. relations project North Central Assn. Schs. and Colls., Chgo., 1964-65; mem. faculty Ind. U., Bloomington, 1965—, prof. history and edn., 1974—, dean Sch. Edn., 1981-90, dir. Ctr. for Excellence in Edn., 1990—; social studies adviser Houghton Mifflin Pub. Co.; cons. U.S. Office Edn. Co-author: American Political Behavior, 2d edit., 1977, Count Witte and the Tsarist Government in the 1905 Revolution, 1972, Toward Effective Instruction in the Social Studies, 1974, School Reform in the Information Age, 1995; editl. bd. Education and Society, history tchr.; editor: UNESCO Handbook on the Teaching of Social Studies, 1981; co-editor: Yearbook on the Social Studies, 1981. STAG grantee Dept. State, 1975. Mem. NEA, Nat. Council Social Studies, Am. Edn. Research Assn., Am. Hist. Assn., Am. Assn. for Advancement Slavic Studies, Phi Beta Kappa, Phi Alpha Theta, Pi Sigma Alpha, Phi Delta Kappa. Home: 3271 Ramble Rd E Bloomington IN 47408-1094 Office: Ind Univ Ctr Excellence Edn 230 N Rose St Bloomington IN 47405-1004

MEHLMAN, EDWIN STEPHEN, endodontist; b. Hartford, Conn., Nov. 30, 1935; s. Sol Abraham and Rose (Slitt) M.; m. Lesley Judith Lunin, June 13, 1959; children: Jeffrey Cole, Brian Scott, Erik Van. BA, Wesleyan U., 1957; DDS, U. Pa., 1961; cert. endodontics, Boston U., 1965. Diplomate Am. Bd. Endodontists. Instr. oral medicine Sch. Dental Medicine Harvard U., Boston, 1965-67; clin. instr. endodontics Sch. Dental Medicine Tufts U., Boston, 1968-70; lectr. endodontics Sch. Dental Medicine, Harvard U., Boston, 1970-72, asst. clin. prof. endodontics, 1972—; staff assoc. Forsyth Dental Ctr., Boston, 1965—; asst. prof. endodontics Boston U. Sch. Dental Medicine, 1995—; pvt. practice Providence, 1965—; vis. lectr. dental hygiene U. R.I., Kingston, 1965-71, Community Coll. R.I., Lincoln, 1990—; cons. com. on accreditation of Dentists and Dental Aux. Edn. Programs, 1974-78. Contbr. articles to profl. jours. Pres. Temple Habonim, Barrington, R.I., 1968-70, Bur. Jewish Edn. of R.I., 1980-84; area v.p. Jewish Fedn. R.I., 1975-78; mem. R.I. Legis. Commn. to Study Malpractice Crisis, 1985-86; chmn. R.I. Dental Polit. Action Com., 1987-90. Capt. USAF, 1961-63. Recipient Etherington award Six N.E. Dental Assns. for Outstanding Contbns. to Dentistry. Fellow Am. Coll. Dentists, Internat. Coll. Dentists, Pierre Fauchard Acad. (Award of Merit); mem. ADA (coun. on govt. affairs and fed. dental svcs. 1988-92, vice chmn. 1991-92, 1st v.p. 1994-95), Am. Assn. Endodontists (dir. 1988-91), R.I. Dental Assn. (pres. 1986-87), N.E. Dental Assns. (Outstanding N.E. Dentist 1995). Jewish. Avocations: tennis, reading, civic activities. Home: 6 Ridgeland Rd Barrington RI 02806-4028 Office: 130 Waterman St Providence RI 02906-2010 also: 1090 New London Ave Cranston RI 02920-3035

MEHLMAN, LON DOUGLAS, information systems specialist; b. Los Angeles, Apr. 29, 1959; s. Anton and Diane Mehlman. BA, UCLA, 1981; MBA, Pepperdine U., 1983. Systems programmer Ticom Systems Inc., Century City, Calif., 1978-81; systems analyst NCR Corp., Century City, 1981-83; sr. systems analyst Tandem Computers Inc., L.A., 1983-91; sr. computer scientist Computer Scis. Corp., El Segundo, Calif., 1991—. Author: Establishing an Enterprise Information Systems Infrastructure, 1995, Implimenting TQM, 1995, Lessons Learned from the Navstar GPS Engineering Management System Project, 1997. Mem. Am. Mgmt. Assn., Assn. for Info. and Image Mgmt., Armed Forces Communications and Electronics Assn., Sierra Club, Phi Delta Theta. Avocations: golf, sailing, skiing, world travel. Office: Computer Scis Corp 2100 E Grand Ave El Segundo CA 90245-5024

MEHLMAN, MARK FRANKLIN, lawyer; b. L.A., Dec. 18, 1947; s. Jack and Elaine Pearl (Lopater) M.; m. Barbara Ann Novak, Aug. 20, 1972; children: David, Jennifer, Ilyse. BA, U. Ill., 1969; LLB, U. Mich., 1973. Bar: Ill. 1973; U.S. Dist. Ct. (no. dist.) Ill. 1973. Assoc. Sonnenschein, Nath & Rosenthal, Chgo., 1973-80, mem. exec. com., 1989—. Trustee Groveland Health Svcs., Highland Park (Ill.) Hosp., 1991—; trustee, treas., mem. exec. com. Spertus Inst. Jewish Studies, Chgo., 1992—; vice chmn. regional bd. Anti-Defamation League, 1987-89, hon. life mem. nat. commn., 1993—. Mem. ABA (chmn. mortgages and other debt financing subcom. 1991-95, group chmn. Group I subcom. 1995-97—, supervisory coun. mem. 1997—, mem. com. on coms. 1997—, mem. nominations com. 1997—, mem. goal IX com. 1997—, mem. leadership devel. initiative com. 1997—), Legal Club of Chgo., Lake Shore Country Club, Standard Club. Office: Sonnenschein Nath & Rosenthal 233 S Wacker Dr Ste 8000 Chicago IL 60606-6342

MEHLMAN, MAXWELL JONATHAN, law educator; b. Washington, Nov. 4, 1948; s. Jacob and Betty (Hoffman) M.; m. Cheryl A. Stone, Sept. 15, 1979; children: Aurora, Gabriel. BA, Reed Coll., 1970, Oxford U., England, 1972; JD, Yale U., 1975. Bar: D.C. 1976, Ohio 1988. Assoc. Arnold & Porter, Washington, 1975-84; asst. prof. Case Western Res. U., Cleve., 1984-87, assoc. prof., 1987-90, prof. law, 1990-96, Arthur E. Petersilge prof., 1996—; spl. counsel N.Y. State Bar, N.Y.C., 1988-94, Nat. Kidney Found., 1991; cons. Am. Assn. Ret. Persons, Washington, 1992. Editor: High Tech Home Care, 1991; contbr. articles to profl. jours. Active steering com. AIDS Commn. Greater Cleve., 1986-90. Rhodes scholar, 1970; Rsch. grantee NIH, 1992-94, 97—. Mem. Am. Assn. Law Schs. (chmn. sect. on law, medicine and health care 1990), Phi Beta Kappa. Avocations: skiing, choral music. Office: Case Western Reserve U Sch Law-Law Medicine Ctr Gund Hall 11075 E Blvd Cleveland OH 44106

MEHLMAN, MYRON A., environmental and occupational medicine educator, environmental toxicologist; b. Poland, Dec. 21, 1934; m. Sept. 4, 1960; children: Mara Appel, Hope, Alison, Constance Lloyd. BS, CCNY, 1957; PhD, MIT, 1964. Prof. biochemistry Rutgers U., Newark, 1965-69; prof. biochemistry Coll. of Medicine U. Nebr., Omaha, 1967-71; chief biochem. toxicology FDA, Washington, 1972-73; spl. asst. toxicology dept. HEW, Washington, 1973-75; interagy. liaison officer NIH, Bethesda, Md., 1975-77; dir. toxicology Mobil Oil, Princeton, N.J., 1977-89; prof. U. Medicine and Dentistry of N.J., Piscataway, 1990—. Editor Jour. Environ. Pathology & Toxicology, 1977-81, Jour. Toxicology and Indsl. Health, 1975-78, Jour. Clean Tech. and Environ. Sci., 1989—; contbr. over 100 articles to profl. jours.; edited over 60 books. 1st lt. U.S. Army, 1958-60. Fellow Acad. Toxol. Soc., Am. Coll. Toxicology, Collequim Ramazzinic (bd. dirs.). Achievements include research in toxicology, environmental health, and nutritional and biomedical science. Home: 7 Bouvant Dr Princeton NJ 08540-1208 Office: U Medicine and Dentistry NJ 675 Hoes Ln Piscataway NJ 08854-5627

MEHNE, PAUL RANDOLPH, associate dean, medical educator; b. Wilmington, Del., May 27, 1948; s. Paul Herbert and Doris Ruth (Longfritz) M.; m. Carol Ann Starner, June 12, 1971; children: Meredith Lynn, Amy Elizabeth. BS in Environ. Sci., SUNY, Syracuse, 1970; PhD, SUNY, 1976, Syracuse U., 1976. Asst. prof. Sch. Allied Health East Carolina U., Greenville, N.C., 1975-76, assoc. dir. Ctr. Edn. Devel. and Evaluation Sch. Medicine, 1976-79, coord. of curriculum Sch. Medicine, 1979-81, asst. dean, 1981-85, assoc. dean, 1985-89, assoc. prof., 1988-89, dir. Ctr. Health Scis. Edn. and Info., 1988-89; assoc. dean U. Pa., Phila., 1990-91; assoc. dean acad. and student affairs, assoc. prof. environ. and community medicine, family medicine Robert Wood Johnson Med. Sch., Piscataway, N.J., 1992—; chair univ.-wide telemedicine videocom distance com. U. Medicine and Dentistry N.J., 1995—, chmn. acad. info. tech. adv. com., 1996—; chmn. exec. bd. dirs. MEDCOMP Supercomputer Consortium, Athens, Ga., 1986-89; vis. prof. U. N.C., Chapel Hill, 1986, Tulane U., New Orleans, 1988. Contbr. articles to profl. jours. Chmn. Community Appearance Commn., Greenville, 1980-85. Recipient Interactive Video Instrn. award Digital Equipment Corp., 1985, Med. Edn. Cost Containment award Kate B. Reynolds Health Care Trust, 1985-88, Telemedicine and Med. Informatics award, 1994-96, U.S. Dept. Commerce NTIA/TIIAP award for telemedicine, 1996-98. Mem. IEEE, Am. Pub. Health Assn., Am. Med. Informatics Assn., Am. Edn. Rsch. Assn., Assn. Am. Med. Colls. (chair consortium on student and profl. well-being 1993-94), Soc. for Med. Decision Making, ACM, Soc. of Tchrs. of Family Medicine.

MEHRA, JAGDISH, physicist; b. Meerut, India, Apr. 8, 1937; came to U.S., 1957; s. Bhagwan Das and Shanti Devi (Kakkar) M.; m. Marlis Helene Lehn, Apr. 27, 1959; 1 child Anil. MS, UCLA, 1960; PhD, U. Neuchatel, 1963. Sr. lectr. U. Neuchatel (Switzerland), 1963-64; asst. prof. physics Purdue U., Hammond, Ind., 1964-65; assoc. prof. U. Mass., North Dartmouth, 1965-67; program dir. Sci. Rsch. Assocs. (IBM), Chgo., 1967-69; spl. rsch. assoc. U. Tex., Austin, Tex., 1969-73; inst. prof. Solvay Inst., Brussels, 1973-88; Sir Julian Huxley prof. UNESCO, Paris, 1989-93; disting. prof. physics The Citadel, Charleston, S.C., 1993-96; prof. sci. and humanities U. Houston, 1996—; mem. editl. bd. Founds. of Physics, Denver, 1988—. Author: The Quantum Principle, 1974, Einstein, Hilbert and Theory of Gravitation, 1974, The Solvay Conferences on Physics, 1975, The Historical Development of Quantum Theory, 1982, 87, The Beat of a Different Drum: The Life and Science of Richard Feynman, 1994; editor: The Physicist's Conception of Nature, 1973. Rsch. grantee Krupp Found., 1978-80, J.D. and C.T. MacArthur Found., 1982-85, Minna-James-Heineman Found., 1985-87; recipient Humboldt prize, 1976. Mem. Am. Phys. Soc., Swiss Phys. Soc., History Sci. Soc., Sherlock Holmes Soc. London. Home: 7830 Candle Ln Houston TX 77071-2114

MEHRA, RAJNISH, finance educator; b. New Delhi, Jan. 15, 1950; came to U.S., 1972; s. Mohan Dev and Raj-Mohini (Vadera) M.; m. Neeru Narula, Jan. 4, 1977; 1 child, Chaitanya. BS in Math. honors, St. Stephen's Coll., U. Delhi, 1966-67; BTech in Elec. Enging., Indian Inst. Tech., Kanpur, 1972; MS in Computer Sci., Rice U., 1974; MS in Indsl. Adminstrn., Carnegie-Mellon U., 1975, PhD, 1978. Instr. adminstrn. and mgmt. sci. Carnegie-Mellon U., Pitts., 1974-76; asst. prof. Queens U., Kingston, Ont., Can., 1976-77; asst. prof., then assoc. prof. fin. Columbia U. Grad. Sch. Bus., 1977-85; assoc. prof., then prof. fin. U. Calif., Santa Barbara, 1985—, dir. Masters of Bus. Econs. program, 1992-96; dir. joint econ.-engring. program, 1994-96; vis. asst. prof. UCLA, 1980; vis. prof. fin. U. Lausanne, Switzerland, 1981, U. Chgo. Sch. Bus., 1995—, Sloan Sch. Mgmt. MIT, 1987-89; vis. scholar U. Chgo., 1979, Norwegian Sch. Econs. and Bus. Adminstrn., 1982, Stockholm Sch. Econs., 1988, Wharton Sch. U. Pa., 1980; vis. assoc. Oxford U., 1986; cons. Internat. Monetary Fund, 1989—. Assoc. editor Jour. Econ. Dynamics and Control; contbr. Growth Theory, VOl. 10, Internat. Library of Critical Writings in Economics, 1991, Encyclopedia of Business Cycles, Panics and Depressions, 1997; contbr. articles to profl. jours.; referee maj. jours. in field. William Larimer Mellon fellow, 1974-76; NSF grantee, 1980—. Mem. IEEE (sr.), Am. Econ. Assn., Am. Fin. Assn., Econometric Soc., Tau Beta Pi. Home: 938 W Campus Ln Santa Barbara CA 93117-4344 Office: U Calif Dept Bus Econ Santa Barbara CA 93106

MEHRA, RAMAN KUMAR, data processing executive, automation and control engineering researcher; b. Lahore, Punjab, India, Feb. 10, 1943; came to U.S., 1964; s. Madan Mohan and Vidya Vati (Khanna) M.; m. Anjoo Talwar; children: Archana, Mandira, Kunal. BEE, Punjab Enging. Coll., 1964; MS in Enging., Harvard U., 1965, PhD, 1968. Assoc. prof. Harvard U., Cambridge, Mass., 1972-76; pres., chief exec. officer Sci. Systems, Co., Inc., Woburn, Mass., 1976—. Author: System Identification, 1976; also tech. papers on model algorithmic control (Best Paper award Internat. Fedn. Automatic Control, 1983). Recipient Eckman award Am. Automatic Control Coun., St. Louis, 1971. Fellow IEEE. Avocations: hiking, skiing, tennis. Home: 5 Angier Rd Lexington MA 02173-1608 Office: Sci Systems Co Inc 500 W Cummings Park Woburn MA 01801-6503

MEHRABIAN, ROBERT, academic administrator; b. Tehran, Iran. Former prof. MIT, U. Ill., Urbana; dean Coll. of Engring. U. Calif., Santa Barbara, until 1990; past dir. Ctr. Materials Sci. Nat. Bur. of Standards; pres. Carnegie-Mellon U., Pitts., 1990—. Office: Carnegie-Mellon U 5000 Forbes Ave Ofc Of Pres Pittsburgh PA 15213-3815*

MEHRING, CLINTON WARREN, engineering executive; b. New Haven, Ind., Feb. 14, 1924; s. Fred Emmett and Florence Edith (Hutson) M.; m. Carol Jane Adams, Mar. 9, 1946; children—James Warren, Charles David, John Steven (dec.), Martha Jane. B.S., Case Inst. Tech., 1950; M.S., U. Colo., 1956. Registered profl. engr., Wyo., Colo., Nev. Design engr. U. S. Bur Reclamation, Denver, 1950-56; design engr. Tipton & Kalmbach, Denver, 1956-58; asst. resident engr. Tipton & Kalmbach, Quito, Equador, 1959-61; asst. chief design engr. Tipton & Kalmbach, Lahore, Pakistan, 1962-65; v.p. Tipton & Kalmbach, Denver, 1966-73, exec. v.p., 1973-79, pres., 1979—, also bd. dirs. Served with AUS, 1943-45. Recipient Theta Tau award as outstanding grad. Case Inst. Tech., 1950. Fellow ASCE (life); mem. Am. Cons. Engrs. Coun., U.S. Com. on Large Dams, Am. Concrete Inst., U.S. Com. Irrigation and Drainage (life), Sigma Xi, Tau Beta Pi, Theta Tau, Sigma Chi, Blue Key. Methodist. Club: Denver Athletic. Home: 1821 Mount Zion Dr Golden CO 80401-1733 Office: 1331 17th St Denver CO 80202-1566

MEHRING, MARGARET, filmmaker, retired educator; b. Millbank, S.D., Sept. 3, 1925; d. Robert Dunbrack and Bernice (Case) Jones; m. William Samuel Mehring, June 21, 1947 (dec. June 1958); 1 child, William Dunbrack. BA, Lawrence Coll., 1947; MS in Edn., U. So. Calif., 1972, PhD in Cinema, 1978. Writer, dir., prodr. Mehring Prodns., L.A., 1953—; mem. faculty U. So. Calif. Sch. Cinema and TV, L.A., 1959-91, dir. filmic writing program, 1978-91, dir. emerita, 1991—. Author: The Screenplay, 1989; writer, dir., prodr. numerous ednl., documentary and indsl. tng. films for Employers Ins. Wausau, 1955, 57, 59-62, Golden State Ins. Co., 1964, Techno Electric Mfg. Co., 1965, Calif. Dept. Social Welfare, 1967, Andersen Windowall Corp., 1969, Golden State Mut. Life Ins. Co., 1983; writer, dir. ednl. films for MLA, U. So. Calif., 1959-60, John Tracy Clinic, 1961-62, Calif. Dept. Social Welfare, 1963-64, Am. Assn. Ret. Persons and Nat. Ret. Tchrs. Assn., 1965-67, Profl. Rsch., Inc., 1968, Acad. Comm. Facility, UCLA, 1969, ednl. sound film strips dept. daytime programs ans spl. projects UCLA Ext., 1971, San Diego County Dept. Edn., 1972, Iran film series Instrnl. Media Ctr., Mich. State U., 1975-77; writer films Who's Behind the Wheel, Part 1, 1966, Part II, 1967, Mayday, Mayday, 1970, The Man, Part I, 1972, Part II, 1973, How To Manage Your resources-Safety, Part I, 1973, Part II, 1974 (all for USAF), Immunity-The Power To Resist a Disease, 1970. Pres. El Moro Dem. Club, Los Osos, Calif., 1994-95; bd. dirs. Ctrl. Coast Women's Polit. Com., San Luis Obispo, Calif., 1995-96; vol. Global Vols.-Poland, 1995, Oglala Lakota Coll., Pine Ridge Indian Reservation, Kyle, S.D., 1995. Mem. Univ. Film and Video Assn., Script Coalition for Industry, Profls. and Tchrs., Delta Kappa Alpha (assoc.). Home and Office: PO Box 6171 Los Osos CA 93412-6171

MEHRINGER, CHARLES MARK, medical educator; b. Dickinson, N.D., Nov. 21, 1945; m. Ruth Herrman; 1 child, Sydney.; BS in Biology, Lamar U., 1966; MD, U. Tex., 1970. Diplomate Am. Bd. Radiology, Am. Bd. Neuroradiology. Intern UCLA Hosp., 1970-71; resident in diagnostic radiology Harbor-UCLA Med. Ctr., Torrance, Calif., 1971-74, fellow in neuroradiology, 1976-77; asst. prof. dept. radiology UCLA Sch. Medicine, 1977-80, dir. spl. procedures, 1980-94, assoc. prof. dept. radiology, 1986—; vice-chmn. dept. radiological scis. UCLA Sch. Medicine, Torrance, 1992—, acting chmn. dept. radiology, 1992—, chief diagnostic radiology, 1983-92; chief radiological svcs., cons. U.S. Air Force for Japan and Korea, 1974-76; cons. U. Calif./Irvine (Calif.) Med. Ctr., 1988—, St. Marys Med. Ctr., Long Beach, Calif., 1986—, Long Beach VA Hosp., 1979—, L.A. County Dept. Chief Med. Examiner-Coroner, 1977—; bd. dirs. Rsch. and Ednl. Inst.; presenter in field. Co-author: (with others) Neurological Surgery of the Ear and Skull Base, 1982, Vascular Surgery, 1984, 2d edit., 1994, Youman's Neurological Surgery, 1990, Common Problems in Infertility and Impotence, 1990, Intraluminal Imaging of Vascular and Tubular Organs: Diagnostic and Therapeutic Applications, 1993, Neuroradiology, A Study Guide, 1995; contbr. articles to profl. jours. Bd. dirs., exec. com. Med. Found. Harbor-UCLA Med. Ctr., 1992—. Recipient numerous grants for rsch., 1977—. Mem. Am. Coll. Radiology, Am. Soc. Neuroradiology (sr. mem.), Western Neuroradiologic Soc., L.A. Radiologic Soc., L.A. County Med. Assn. Home: 834 Rome Dr Los Angeles CA 90065-3215 Office: UCLA Med Ctr Box 27 1000 W Carson St Torrance CA 90509

MEHROTRA, SUDHIR C., engineering company executive; b. 1945. BS, India Inst. Tech., Kanpur, India, 1968; PhD (hon.), U. Kan., 1979. Instr., prof. U. Kan., 1968-79; pres., treas. Vigyan, Inc., Hampton, Va., 1979—. Office: Vigyan Inc 30 Research Dr Hampton VA 23666-1325

MEHTA, A. SONNY, publishing company executive; b. India, 1943. Student, Cambridge U. Worked in paperback publishing U.K.; formerly with Pan and Picador pubs., U.K.; pub., pres. Alfred A. Knopf div. of Random House, N.Y.C., 1987—, now pres., editor-in-chief; pres. Knopf Pub. Group, N.Y.C. Office: Alfred A Knopf Inc 201 E 50th St New York NY 10022-7703*

MEHTA, EILEEN ROSE, lawyer; b. Colver, Pa., Apr. 1, 1953; d. Richard Glenn and Helen (Wahna) Ball; m. Abdul Rashid Mehta, Aug. 31, 1973. Student, Miami U., 1971-73; BA with distinction, Fla. Internat. U., 1974; JD cum laude, U. Miami, 1977. Bar: Fla. 1977, U.S. Dist. Ct. (so. dist.) Fla. 1977, U.S. Ct. Appeals (11th cir.) 1981. Law clk. to presiding judge U.S. Dist. Ct. (so. dist.) Fla., Miami, 1977-79; asst. atty. County of Dade, Miami, 1979-89; shareholder Fine Jacobson Schwartz Nash Block & England, Miami, Fla., 1989-94; partner Eckert Seamans Cherin & Mellott, Miami, 1994; lectr. in field; v.p., bd. dirs. Mehtatron Enterprises, Inc., Miami, Shalimar Homes Inc., Anderson, S.C. Miami U. scholar, 1971-73. Mem. ABA, Fla. Bar Assn. Office: Eckert Seamans Cherin & Mellott 701 Brickell Ave Ste 1850 Miami FL 33131-2834

MEHTA, JAY, financial executive; b. Varanasi, India, Aug. 16, 1943; came to U.S., 1970; m. Vineeta Mehta, Feb. 20, 1969; children: Nina, Vineet. MBA in Fin., Rutgers U., 1974; MBA in Taxation, Fairleigh Dickenson U., 1983. CPA, N.J.; cert. mgmt. acct. Contract estimator NE region Otis Elevator Co. Subs. United Techs. Inc., Newark, N.J., 1970-73, sr. contract estimator NE region, 1974-75; corp. staff acct. Otis Elevator Co. Subs. United Techs. Inc., N.Y.C., 1976-77, sr. corp. acct., 1978; div. contr. OKI Electric Overseas Corp., Hackensack, N.J., 1979-84; corp. contr. OKI

Am. Inc., Hackensack, 1984—, sr. dir. fin., treas., 1990, v.p. fin., treas., 1994—; trustee OKI Am. Savs. Plan, 1981—; ofcl. grader Inst. Mgmt. Acctg., Montvale, N.J., 1986—. Mem. Am. Mgmt. Assn., N.J. Soc. CPA's. Republican. Avocations: reading, golf, computers. Office: OKI Am Inc 3 University Plz Hackensack NJ 07601

MEHTA, NARINDER KUMAR, marketing executive; b. Lahore, Punjab, India, Feb. 18, 1938; came to U.S., 1959; s. Puran Chand and Raj Rani Mehta; m. Narayanaswamy Sampath; children: Kiren, Ravi. B of Commerce, U. Delhi, India, 1958; MA, U. Minn., 1961. Program dir. All India Mgmt. Assn., New Delhi, India, 1963-67; with Am. Express Co., Chgo., 1968-82; nat. sales dir. Am. Express Co., N.Y.C., 1975-80, v.p. sales, 1980-82; sr. v.p. Shearson Lehman/Am. Express, Boston, 1982-85, Capital Credit Corp., Fairfield, N.J., 1985—; sr. v.p. Temporary Investment Funds, 1982-85, Trust for Short Term Fed. Securities, 1982-85, Mcpl. Fund for Calif. Investors, 1983-85; conducted seminars for profl. assns., colls. and univs. Contbr. articles to profl. jours. Nat. v.p. Muscular Dystrophy Assn., N.Y.C., 1984-86; student body pres. U. Delhi, India, 1958-59. Recipient 1st prize inter-coll. debate, 1958. Mem. Am. Mgmt. Assn., Tau Kappa Epsilon. Avocations: running, swimming, traveling, reading. Office: Capital Credit Corp 492 Route 46 Fairfield NJ 07004-1906

MEHTA, PESHOTAN RUSTOM, magnetobiologist; b. Bombay, Mar. 4, 1956; s. Rustom Nowroji and Aimai (Mahaluxmivala) M.; m. Amanda Gordon-Smith, Apr. 8, 1991. BS with honors, U. Bombay, 1976; PhD in Biophysics, DSc in Holistic Sci., MD in Oncology, Open Internat. U., 1988, MD in Acupuncture, 1991, MD in Magnetotherapy, MD in Oriental Medicine, 1994, degree in natural therapies, 1995, PhD in Magnetobiology, 1996; diploma honor, Inst. Internat. Affairs, Paris, 1996. Pvt. practice in magnetomedicine, holistic, Tibetan, Ayurved, Unani and Chinese medicine; prof. U. Peace, Brussels, 1996; hon. prof. Open Internat. U., Colombo, Sri Lanka, 1994—, U. St. Petersberg, 1995, U. Moscow, 1995, U. Rio de Janeiro, 1995; prof. U. of Peace, UN, Brussels, 1996; hon. dir. med. rsch., mem. adv. com. Indo Japanese Med. Trust, Osaka, Japan, 1979; sci. advisor Madras (India) Inst. Magnetobiology, 1989; internat. advisor for magnetomedicine Soc. Natural Therapists and Rschrs., Inc., Australia, 1995—, Australian Charter of Natural Medicine Practitioners, 1995; adv. bd. Found. for Jacobson Resonance, 1995, Perspectivism Found., 1995, Inst. Theoretical Physics and Advanced Studies for Biophys. Rsch., 1995; sci. cons. Inserm 2000 U. Paris, 1995; lectr. in field. Editl. advisor the New Physician, 1992; author 17 books, 65 papers and monographs. Recipient Dhanvantri award Ayuved Shikshan Mandal, 1988, Yellow Emperor's award Chinese Acad. Scis., 1990, Dag Hammarsjöld Award for Medicine, UN, 1994, Pax Mundi award, 1994, Silver Medallion, brit. Inst. Homoeopathy, 1994, Fellowship Award for Profl. Excellence, Acad. Diplomatique de la Paix, UN, 1994, Albert Schweitzer prize for medicine Albert Schweitzer Found., 1994, Knight Comdr. The Ecumenical Royal Med. Humanitarian Order of St. John of Jerusalem, 1994, Serge Jurasancus Accolade and gold medal, 1996. Fellow Royal Astron. Soc., Internat. Magnetotherapy Assn., World Found. Integrated Medicine, Indian Found. Devel. of Integrated Medicine, Internat. Inst. Fine Mechanics and Optics, Found. of Oriental Medicine, Internat. Soc. of ECIWO Biology, Royal Soc. Medicine, Brit. Inst. Homoeopathy, Medicina Alternativa, Homoeopathic Found., Commonwealth Inst. Acupuncture and Natural Therapies, Chinese Acad. Sci., Theosophical Soc., Acupuncture Found. Sri Lanka and Register; mem. Internat. Assn. Educators for World Peace (internat. diploma honor and recognition 1996), Whole Health Inst., Australian Inst. Holistic Medicine, Acupuncture Assn. Australia, New Zealand and Asia, Australasian Coll. Phys. Scientists and Engrs. in Medicine, Acad. Peace, Royal Soc. Health, Brit. Homoeopathic Assn., Australian Fedn. Homoeopaths, U.K. Homoeopathic Med. Assn., Soc. Homoeopaths, Inst. Complementary Medicine, Scandinavian Acupuncture Found., Brit. Holistic Med. Assn., Australian Charter for Natural Med. Practitioners, Meteoritical Soc., Internat. Soc. for Bioelectricity, Internat. Soc. for Preventive Oncology, Internat. Assn. Biologically Close Electric Circuits in Biology and Medicine, Internat. Acupuncture Sci. Inst., Acupuncture Assn., Inst. Agrl. and Rural Devel., All India Magnetotherapy Assn., Asian Homoeopathic Med. League, Indian Homoeopathic Orgn., Internat. Homoeopathic Med. Orgn., Indian Assn. Surg. Oncology, AAAS, K.R. Cama Oriental Inst., Cardiol. Soc. India, Soc. for Detection and Prevention of Cancer, Bombay Assn. for Sci. Edn., Universal Assn. Peace Through Coop., Inst. Internat. Affairs, numerous others. Avocations: cosmology, meteoritics, paranormal phenomena, conducting, comparative religion.

MEHTA, VED (PARKASH), writer, literature and history educator; b. Lahore, Punjab, India, Mar. 21, 1934; came to U.S., 1949; s. Amolak Ram and Shanti Devi (Mehra) M.; m. Linn Fenimore Cooper Cary, Dec. 17, 1983; children: Alexandra Sage, Natasha Cary. BA, Pomona Coll., 1956, DLitt (hon.), 1972; BA, Oxford U., Eng., 1959; MA, Harvard U., 1961, Oxford U., Eng., 1962; DLitt (hon.), Bard Coll., 1982, Williams Coll., 1986, Bowdoin Coll., 1995; DUniv. (hon.), Stirling U., Scotland, 1988. Staff writer New Yorker mag., 1961-94; Rosenkranz chair in writing Yale U., New Haven, 1990-93, fellow, 1988—, residential fellow Berkeley Coll., 1990-93, lectr. in English, 1991-93, lectr. in History, 1990-92; Randolph vis. disting. prof. English and history Vassar Coll., N.Y., 1994-96; Arnold Bernhard vis. prof. English and History Williams Coll., Mass., 1994; vis. fellow lit. Balliol Coll., Oxford U., 1988-89; vis. scholar Case Western Res. U., 1974; vis. prof. lit. Bard Coll., 1985, 86; Noble Found. vis. prof. art and cultural history Sarah Lawrence Coll., 1988; vis. prof. English NYU, 1989-90; sr. fellow Freedom Forum, Media Studies Ctr., vis. scholar Columbia U., N.Y.C., 1996-97; fellow Ctr. Advanced Studies Behavioral Scis., Palo Alto, Calif., 1997-98. Author: Face to Face, 1957 (Secondary Edn. Ann. Book award 1958), Walking the Indian Streets, 1960, rev. edit., 1971, Fly and the Fly-Bottle, 1963, 2d edit., 1983, The New Theologian, 1966, Delinquent Chacha, 1967, Portrait of India, 1970, 2d edit., 1993, John is Easy to Please, 1971, Mahatma Gandhi and His Apostles, 1977, 2d edit., 1993, The New India, 1978, The Photographs of Chachaji, 1980, A Family Affair: India Under Three Prime Ministers, 1982, Three Stories of the Raj, 1986, Rajiv Gandhi and Rama's Kingdom, 1995; (autobiography) Continents of Exile: Daddyji, 1972, Mamaji, 1978, Vedi, 1982, The Ledge Between the Streams, 1984, Sound-Shadows of the New World, 1986, The Stolen Light, 1989, Up at Oxford, 1993, also articles; writer, narrator TV film Chachaji, My Poor Relation, 1978 (DuPont Columbia award); mem. usage panel Am. Heritage Dictionary, 1982. Recipient award Assn. Indians in Am., 1978, Signet Silver medal (Harvard), 1983, Disting. Svc. award Asian/Pacific ALA, 1986, Liberty medal Mayor of N.Y.C., 1986, Centenary Barrows award Pomona Coll., 1987, Literary Lion medal N.Y. Pub. Libr., 1990, Asian-Am. Heritage Month award N.Y. State, 1991, Literary Lion Centennial Medal, 1996; Hazen fellow, 1956-59, Harvard Prize fellow, 1959-60, Residential fellow Eliot House (Harvard), 1959-61, Guggenheim fellow, 1971-72, 77-78, MacArthur Prize fellow, 1982-87, N.Y. Inst. for Humanities fellow, 1988-92; Ford Found. grantee, 1971-76, grantee Pub. Policy, 1979-82. Mem. Coun. on Fgn. Rels., Century Assn. (trustee 1972-75). Avocations: Indian and Western music, cycling. Home: 139 E 79th St New York NY 10021-0324

MEHTA, ZARIN, music festival administrator; b. Bombay, India, Oct. 28, 1938; came to Can., 1962, naturalized, 1969; s. Mehli and Tehmina Mehta; m. Carmen Lasky, July 1, 1966; children—Rohanna, Rustom. Chartered acct., London, 1957. Acct. Frederic B. Smart & Co., London, 1957-62, Coopers & Lybrand, Montreal, Que., Can., 1962-81; mng. dir. Orchestre Symphonique de Montreal, 1981-90, dir., 1973-81; exec. dir., chief oper. officer Ravinia Festival, 1990—. Fellow Inst. Chartered Accts. in Eng. and Wales; mem. Ordre des Comptables Agrees du Que. Office: Ravinia Festival 400 Iris Ln Highland Park IL 60035-5208

MEHTA, ZUBIN, conductor, musician; b. Bombay, India, Apr. 29, 1936; came to U.S., 1961; s. Mehli Nowrowji and Tehmina (Daruvala) M.; m. Nancy Diane Kovack; children: Zarina, Merwan. Student, St. Xavier's Coll., Bombay, 1951-53, State Acad. Music, Vienna, Austria, 1954-60; LL.D., Sir George Williams U., Montreal, 1965; D.Mus. (hon.), Occidental Coll.; hon. doctorate, Colgate U., Brooklyn Coll., Westminster Choir Coll., Juilliard Sch., Weizmann Inst. Sci. (Israel). Music dir., Montreal (Can.) Symphony Orch., 1961-67, Los Angeles Philharmonic Orch., 1962-78; mus. dir.: Israel Philharmonic, from 1969, appointed dir. for life, 1981; music dir., N.Y. Philharmonic, 1978-91, guest condr., Met. Opera, Salzburg (Austria) Festival, Vienna Philharmonic, Berlin Philharmonic, La Scala, Milan, Italy, mus. dir., Maggio Musicale Florence, Italy, rec. artist for, Decca, CBS, RCA, New World Records, (recipient 1st prize Liverpool (Eng.) Condrs. Competition 1958). Decorated Padma Bhushan India, 1967, commendatore of Italy. Office: Israel Philharm Orch, 1 Huberman St Box 11292, 61112 Tel Aviv Israel also: Orch Maggio Musicale, Teatro, Comunale Via Solferino 15, I-50123 Florence Italy

MEHTABDIN, KHALID RAUF, economist, educator; b. Sialkot, Pakistan, Nov. 6, 1944; s. Haji and Atiiya Mehtabdin; m. Durdana Ansarie, Jan. 26, 1951; children: Mehvish, Khurram. MA, U. Punjab, 1968; MPA, U. Pitts., 1974, M in Pub. and Internat. Affairs, 1977, PhD, 1979. Asst. prof. econs. Niagara U., Niagara Falls, N.Y., 1980-84, assoc. prof., 1985-86; assoc. prof. St. Rose Coll., Albany, N.Y., 1986—; mem. bus. adv. coun. Niagara U., 1980-86; cons. M.H. Bros., Karachi, Pakistan, 1980-82. Author: Comparative Management, 1986, Reagonomics, 1986, Macro Eco, 1987. Recipient Outstanding Cmty. award Pakistani Cmty. Albany, N.Y., 1995. Mem. Am. Econs. Assn., Ea. Econs. Assn. (bd. dirs. 1986-90), Islamic Ctr. of Capital Dist. Home: 312 Torquay Blvd Albany NY 12203-4927

MEHURON, WILLIAM OTTO, electronics company executive; b. Hammond, Ind., Nov. 20, 1937; s. Arthur and Margaret Irene (Soroka) M.; m. Charlotte Anne Nyheim, Aug. 26, 1982; children: Kimberly Anne, Kristine Lynn. BSEE, Purdue U., 1959; MSEE, U. Pa., 1962, PhD, 1966. Tech. staff RCA, Moorestown, N.J., 1959-64, GE, Phila., 1964-68; group leader Mitre Corp., McLean, Va., 1969-74; tech. dir. naval intelligence Dept. Navy, Washington, 1974-81; dir. rsch. and engring. Nat. Security Agy., Ft. Meade, Md., 1981-85; v.p., gen. mgr. data systems div. Ampex Corp. subs. Allied-Signal Co., Redwood City, Calif., 1985-86; sr. v.p. product ops. Daisy Systems Corp., Mountain View, Calif., 1986-88; v.p., gen. mgr. Networks and Info. Security div. Security div. Unisys Def. Systems, McLean, Va., 1988-91; pres. Mehuron Assocs. Inc., 1991-95; dir. sys. acquisition office NOAA, USG, Washington, 1995—. Avocations: amateur radio (W4XM), running, tennis, cooking, antiques. Home: 8107 Birnam Wood Dr Mc Lean VA 22102-2712

MEIBURG, CHARLES OWEN, business administration educator; b. Seneca, S.C., Dec. 17, 1931; s. Albert and Gladys Katherine (Burley) M.; m. Elizabeth Rhodes Glenn, June 11, 1955; children: Charles O. Jr., Howard Glenn, Elizabeth Rhodes. BS in Arts and Scis., Clemson U., 1953; MA in Econs., U. Va., 1958, PhD in Econs., 1960. Assoc. prof. U. Va., Charlottesville, 1964-69, prof., 1969-82, J. Harvie Wilkinson, Jr. prof. bus. adminstrn., 1982—; dir. Taylor Murphy Inst. U. Va., 1967-83; assoc. dean Darden Sch. U. Va., 1983-89. Co-author: Cases on Financial Institutions, 1979, Cases in Bank Management, 1986; editor (with others) Loan Officers Handbook, 1986. 1st lt. U.S. Army, 1953-55. Mem. Am. Econ. Assn., Fin. Mgmt. Assn., Assn. for U. Bus. and Econ. Rsch. (pres. 1971). Home: 3345 Kirkwood Ct Keswick VA 22947 Office: U Va Darden Sch PO Box 6550 Charlottesville VA 22906-6550

MEIER, AUGUST, historian, educator; b. N.Y.C., Apr. 30, 1923; s. Frank A. and Clara (Cohen) M. AB, Oberlin Coll., 1945; AM, Columbia U., 1949, PhD, 1957; LittD, Rutgers U., 1994. Asst. prof. history Tougaloo (Miss.) Coll., 1945-49; rsch. asst. to Charles S. Johnson, 1953; asst. prof. history Fisk U., 1953-56; asst., assoc. prof. history Morgan State Coll., Balt., 1957-64; prof. history Roosevelt U., Chgo., 1964-67; prof. history Kent (Ohio) State U., 1967-69, univ. prof., 1969-93; univ. prof. emeritus, 1993—. Author: Negro Thought in America, 1880-1915, 1963, (with Elliott Rudwick) From Plantation to Ghetto, 1966, 3d edit., 1976, (with Elliott Rudwick) Black Detroit and the Rise of the UAW, 1979, (with Elliott Rudwick) CORE: A Study In The Civil Rights Movement, 1942-68, 1973, (with Elliott Rudwick) Along the Color Line: Explorations in the Black Experience, 1976, (with Elliott Rudwick) Black History and the Historical Profession, 1986, A White Scholar and the Black Community, 1945-1965, 1993; editor: (with Francis Broderick) Negro Protest Thought in the Twentieth Century, 1966, (with Francis Broderick and Elliott Rudwick) rev. edit. renamed Black Protest Thought in The Twentieth Century, 1971, (with Elliott Rudwick) The Making of Black America, 1969, (with Elliott Rudwick and John H. Bracey, Jr.), Black Nationalism in America, 1970, (with John Hope Franklin) Black Leaders of the Twentieth Century, 1982, (with Leon Litwack) Black Leaders of the Nineteenth Century, 1988; gen. editor: Atheneum Negro in Am. Life Series, 1966-74, University of Illinois Press Blacks in the New World Series, 1972—, (with John H. Bragy), 1994—, (with Elliott Rudwick and John Bracey) University Publications of America Black Studies Research Sources on Microfilm, 1980—; mem. editorial adv. bd.: Booker T. Washington Papers, 1967-85, Civil War History, 1970—, Jour. Am. History, 1974-77. Sec. Newark br. NAACP, 1951-52, 56-57; chmn. Balt. chpt. Ams. for Democratic Action, 1960-61, mem. nat. bd., exec. com., 1960-61; active Newark chpt. CORE, 1963-64, Balt. chpt. SNCC, 1960-63. Advanced grad. fellow Am. Council Learned Socs., 1952; Guggenheim fellow, 1971-72; Nat. Endowment for Humanities fellow, 1975-77; Center for Advanced Study in Behavioral Scis. fellow, 1976-77. Mem. Am. Hist. Assn., So. Hist. Assn. (pres. 1992), Assn. Study Negro Life and History, Orgn. Am. Historians (del. to Am. Coun. Learned Socs. 1979-83, chmn. program com. 1990). Unitarian. Home: 305 W End Ave # 901 New York NY 10023

MEIER, GEORGE KARL, III, pastor, lawyer; b. Glen Ridge, N.J., Jan. 13, 1944; s. George Karl and Mary Claire (Myers) M.; children: G.K., Leslie; m. Therese DesCamp, Oct. 10, 1992. BS, Washington and Lee U., 1966; JD, Dickinson Sch. Law, 1969; MDiv, Pacific Sch. of Religion, 1992. Bar: N.J. 1969, Oreg. 1970, U.S. Dist. Ct. N.J. 1969, U.S. Dist. Ct. Oreg. 1970, U.S. Ct. Appeals (9th cir.) 1971, U.S. Ct. Appeals (fed. cir.) 1987, U.S. Supreme Ct. 1973. Law clk. N.J Superior Court Appellate Div., 1969-70; assoc. Stoel, Rives, Boley, Jones & Grey, Portland, Oreg., 1970-75, ptnr., 1976-89; spl. dep. atty. gen. State of Idaho, 1988-89; spl. asst. to pres. Pacific Sch. Religion, Berkeley, Calif., 1992; pastor Pioneer Congl. Ch., Sacramento, Calif., 1992—. Co-founder Ctrl. City Concern, 1978, SW Youth Svc. Ctr., Portland; chmn. ctrl. adv. bd. Dept. Human Resources; pres. consistory Hillside Cmty. Ch., Portland, 1984-85; acad. com. Pacific Sch. Religion, 1989-91; interim dir. youth programs Epworth Meth. Ch., 1992; bd. dirs. No. Calif. Nev. Conf. the United Ch. Christ, 1993-97, v.p., 1995-96, pres., 1996-97, Francis House, 1992—, chmn., 1995-96, Cathedral Pioneer Ch. Homes, Inc., 1992—. Recipient Outstanding Svc. award Cen. City Concern 1976-89. Mem. Oreg. State Bar Assn. Mem. United Ch. of Christ. Office: Pioneer Congregational Ch 2700 L St Sacramento CA 95816-5614

MEIER, GERALD MARVIN, economics educator; b. Tacoma, Wash., Feb. 9, 1923; s. Max and Bessie (Nagel) M.; m. Gretl Slote, Oct. 23, 1954; children: David, Daniel, Jeremy, Andrew. BA in Econs., Reed Coll., 1947; BLitt in Econs., Oxford (Eng.) U., 1952; PhD, Harvard U., 1953; MA (hon.), Wesleyan U., Middletown, Conn., 1959. Instr. Williams Coll., Williamstown, Pa., 1952-54; asst. prof. Wesleyan U., 1954-59, prof. econs., 1959-63; prof. econs. Stanford (Calif.) U., 1963—; research assoc. Oxford U., 1957-58; vis. lectr. Yale U., New Haven, 1955-56, vis. assoc. prof., 1956-59, vis. prof., 1959-61; vis. prof. Stanford U., 1962; cons. Asia Soc., Bank Am., East-West Ctr., Food and Agrl. Orgn., Goodyear Internat., NSF, others; internat. lectr. in field. Author: International Trade anbd Development, 1963, Leading Issues in Development Economics, 1964, The International Economics of Development, 1968, 2d edit., 1978, Leading Issues in Economic Development: Studies in International Poverty, 6th edit., 1995; (with R.E. Baldwin) Economic Development, 1957; gen. editor: Econ. Devel. Series, Econ. Theory and the Underdevel. Countries, Human Resources as the Wealth of Nations, 1973, Fin. Deepening in Econ. Devel., 1975, Agrl. and Structural Transformation, 1975, Gen. X-Efficiency Theory of Econ. Devel., 1978; editor: International Economic Reform: Collected Papers of Emile Despres, 1973, Problems of Trade Policy, 1973, Problems of a World Monetary Order, 1982, Problemsod Cooperation for Development, 1977, Toward a New International Development, 1982, La Nueva Era de Desarollo, 1978, Internat. Econs. of Development, International Economics: Theory of Policy, 1982, New International Development Policy, 1982, Pricing Policy for Development Management, 1983, Pioneers in Development, 1985, Emerging from Poverty: The Economics that Really Matters, 1984, Financing Asian Development, 1986, Pioneers in Development, 1987, Asian Development: Economic Success and Policy Lessons, World Beyond the Firm, 1997; author numerous chpts. to books and articles to profl. jours. Rhodes scholar, 1948-52, Rockefeller Found. Study Ctr. resident scholar, 1981; Guggenheim fellow, 1957-58, Brookings Nat. Research fellow, 1961-62, Russel Sage Found. resident fellow, 1976-77; Social Sci. Research Council Faculty research grantee, 1968, Internat. Legal Ctr. research grantee, 1970, Rockefeller Found. research grantee, 1974-75. Mem. Am. Assn. Rhodes Scholars, Am. Econ. Assn., Royal Econ. Soc., Am. Soc. Internat. Law, Phi Beta Kappa. Home: 774 Santa Ynez St Palo Alto CA 94305-8441 Office: Stanford U Grad Sch Bus Stanford CA 94305-5015

MEIER, GUSTAV, symphony conductor. Conductor Lansing (Mich.) Symphony. *

MEIER, HENRY GEORGE, architect; b. Indpls., July 14, 1929; s. Virgil and Elizabeth (Whiteside) M.; m. Peggy Nelson, June 28, 1953; children: Scott J., Bruce W., Paul T., Thomas A. BArch, U. Cin., 1953. Lic. architect Ind.; lic. landscape architect Ind. Pvt. practice architecture Indpls., 1964-90; sr. architect Ball State U., Muncie, Ind., 1990-97; ret., 1997. Contbr. Indiana Architect mag. Bd. dirs. Am. Bapt. Chs./U.S.A., Valley Forge, Pa., 1970-77, Bd. Bldg. Appeals, Indpls., 1979-85. Served to 1st lt. USMC, 1953-55. Fellow AIA (bd. dirs. 1981-85); mem. Ind. Soc. Architects (pres. 1975, Edward D. Pierre award 1979), Constrn. Specifications Inst., Interfaith Forum on Religion Art and Architecture (v.p. 1981), Masons, Scottish Rite. Republican.

MEIER, KENNETH J., political science journal editor; b. Aberdeen, S.D., Mar. 3, 1950; s. John and Elizabeth (Malsam) M.; m. Diane Jones Meier, Dec. 31, 1972. BA, U. S.D., 1972; PhD, Syracuse U., 1975. Prof. polit. sci. Rice U., Houston, 1975-78, U. Okla., 1978-85; prof. polit. sci. U. Wis., Madison, 1985-89, Milw., 1989—; fellow com. for hispanic pub. policy issues Inter Univ. Program Social Sci. Rsch. Coun., 1991-92. Author: Race, Class and Education, 1989, The Politics of Hispanic Education, 1991, Politics and the Bureaucracy, 1993, The Politics of Sin, 1994, The Case Against School Choice, 1995, Regulation and Consumer Protection, 1995, Applied Statistics for Public Administration, 1997; editor Am. Jour. Polit. Sci., 1994—. Recipient Clarence A. Kulp award, 1990, Gustavus Myers award, 1991, 93, Herbert Kaufman award, 1992. Mem. APHA, ASPA, Am. Polit. Sci. Assn. Office: Univ Wisconsin Dept Polit Sci PO Box 413 Milwaukee WI 53201

MEIER, LOUIS LEONARD, JR., lawyer; b. Hawthorne, Calif., Oct. 12, 1918; s. Louis Leonard and Celestine Helen (Gabriel) M.; m. Donna Eleonora Tomacelli-Filomarino, June 5, 1954; children: Renée, Sharon Clark, Catherine, Marina. B.S., U.S. Naval Acad., 1942; LL.B., Georgetown U., 1951; grad., U.S. Naval War Coll., 1963. Bar: Va. 1951, U.S. Supreme Ct. 1970, D.C. 1973. Legal and legis. asst. to Chmn. Joint Chiefs of Staff, Washington, 1965-67; comdr. Guided Missile Destroyer Squadron 18, Atlantic Fleet, U.S. Navy, 1967-69; mem policy planning staff Office Sec. State, Washington, 1969-72; Washington counsel ASCE, 1972-82, exec. dir., 1982-83; sole practice Washington, 1983—. Served to capt. USN, 1941-72. Decorated Legion Merit; recipient U.S.S. Gherardi Battle Efficiency award, 1951, U.S.S. John S. McCain Battle Efficiency award, 1954, Pres. award for svc. to country ASCE, 1996. Mem. ABA, Nat. Inst. Bldg. Scis., Conf. Fedn. Environ. Engrs., Met. Club, Chevy Chase Country Club, N.Y. Yacht Club, Spouting Rock Beach Assn. Republican. Roman Catholic. Home and Office: 5132 Baltan Rd Bethesda MD 20816-2350

MEIER, MARK F., research scientist, glaciologist, educator; b. Iowa City, Dec. 19, 1925; s. Norman C. and Clea (Grimes) M.; m. Barbara McKinley, Sept. 16, 1955; children: Lauren G., Mark S., Gretchen A. BSEE, U. Iowa, 1949, MS in Geology, 1951; PhD in Geology and Applied Mechanics, Calif. Inst. Tech., 1957. Instr. Occidental Coll., L.A., 1952-55; chief glaciology project office U.S. Geol. Survey, Tacoma, 1956-85; dir. Inst. Arctic & Alpine Rsch. U. Colo., Boulder, 1985-94; vis. prof. Dartmouth Coll., Hanover, N.H., 1964; rsch. prof. U. Wash., Seattle, 1964-86; profl. geol. scis. U. Colo., 1985—; pres. Internat. Comn. on Snow and Ice, 1967-71; pres. Internat. Assn. Hydrol. Scis., 1979-83; Mendenhall lectr. U.S. Geol. Survey, 1982, Walter Orr Roberts Disting. lectr. Aspen Global Change Inst., 1992. Contbr. articles to profl. jours. With USN, 1945-46. Recipient 3 medals Acad. Scis., Moscow, USSR, 1970-85, Disting. Svc. award (Gold medal) U.S. Dept. of the Interior, 1968; Meier Valley, Antarctica named in his honor U.S. and U.K. Bd. Geographic Names. Fellow AAAS (John Wesley Powell Meml. lectr. 1994), Am. Geophys. Union (com. chmn., Robert E. Horton medal 1996), Geol. Soc. Am., (com. mem.), Internat. Glaciological Soc. (v.p., coun., Seligman Crystal 1985), Arctic Inst. N.Am. (gov. 1987-93). Office: U Colo Inst Inst Arctic and Alpine Rsch 1560 30th St Boulder CO 80303-1012

MEIER, MATTHIAS S(EBASTIAN), historian; b. Covington, Ky., June 4, 1917; s. Matthias J. and Mary (Berberich) M.; married; 5 children. B.A., U. Miami, 1948; M.A., Mexico City Coll., 1949; Ph.D. in Latin Am. History, U. Calif.-Berkeley, 1954. Lectr. U.S. history San Francisco State Coll., summers 1953-55; lectr. U.S. And Latin Am. history Bakersfield Coll., 1955-63; asst. prof. Fresno State Coll., summer 1956, fall 1962; asst. prof. Latin Am. history Santa Clara U., 1963-66, assoc. prof., 1966-72, prof., 1972-89, Patrick A. Donohoe prof. history, 1983-89, emeritus; Fulbright lectr. Nat. U. Tucuman and Inst. Nacional de Profesorado Secundario, Buenos Aires, Argentina, 1958-59; lect. U. Ibero-Am., summer 1965; vis. prof. San Jose State Coll., spring 1968. Author: (with Feliciano Rivera) The Chicanos: A History of Mexican Americans, 1972, A Bibliography for Chicano History, 1972; editor: (with Feliciano Rivera) Readings on La Raza: Twentieth Century, 1973, Dictionary of Mexican American History, 1981, Bibliography of Mexican American History, 1984, Mexican American Biographies, 1988, update of Carey McWilliams's North From Mexico (publ. 1949), 1990, revision, update The Chicanos (new title Mexiacn Americans/American Mexicans), 1993, Notable Latino Americans, 1997. Served with Signal Corps U.S. Army, 1942-46. Mem. Pacific Coast Council Latin Am. Studies (pres. 1964-65, 76-77), Latin Am. Studies Assn., Conf. Latin Am. Historians, Assn. Borderlands Scholars, Nat. Assn. for Chicano Studies. Office: Santa Clara U Dept History Santa Clara CA 95053

MEIER, RICHARD ALAN, architect; b. Newark, Oct. 12, 1934; s. Jerome and Carolyn (Kaltenbacher) M.; m. Katherine Gormley, Jan. 21, 1978 (div.); children: Joseph Max, Ana Moss. BArch, Cornell U., 1957; D (hon.), U. Naples, Italy, 1991, The New Sch., N.Y.C., 1995. Registered profl. arch., N.Y., N.J., Conn., Mich., Va., Fla., Ind., Ga., Calif., Ill., Iowa, Tex., Oreg. Architect Frank Grad & Sons, N.J., 1957, Davis, Brody & Wisniewski, N.Y.C., 1958-59, Skidmore, Owings & Merrill, 1959-60, Marcel Breuer & Assocs., 1960-63; architect, prin. Richard Meier & Assocs., N.Y.C., 1963-80, Richard Meier & Ptnrs., 1980—; resident architect Am. Acad. in Rome, 1973-74; vis. critic Pratt Inst., 1960-62, 65, Princeton, 1963, Syracuse U., 1964; William Henry Bishop vis. prof. architecture Yale U., 1975, 77, vis. critic, 1967, 72, 73, 77; vis. prof. Harvard U., 1977, UCLA, 1988, Eliot Noyes vis. critic in architecture, 1980-81; Harvey S. Perloff vis. prof. architecture UCLA, 1987; adj. prof. architecture Cooper Union, N.Y.C., 1963-73; mem. adv. coun. Cornell U. Coll. Art, Architecture and Planning; mem. Jerusalem Com. Exhbns., XV Triennale, Milan, 1973, Mus. Modern Art, N.Y.C., 1975, 81, Princeton U., Biennale, Venice, Italy, 1976, Cooper-Hewitt Mus., N.Y.C., 1976-77, Leo Castelli Gallery, N.Y.C., 1977, 94, Rosa Esman Gallery, N.Y.C., 1978, 80, N.J. State Mus., 1978, Modernism Gallery, San Francisco, Wadsworth Atheneum, Hartford, Conn., High Mus. Art, Atlanta Harvard U., Max Protech Gallery, 1980, Syracuse U., Whitney Mus. Art, N.Y.C., 1982, Knoll Internat., Tokyo, Japan, 1988, October Gallery, London, 1990, Royal Palace, Naples, Italy, 1991, Palazzo delle Esposizione, Rome, 1993, Aichi Prefectural Mus. Art, Nagoya, Japan, 1996. Prin. works include Westbeth Artists Housing, N.Y.C., Bronx (N.Y.) Devel. Ctr., Smith House, Darien, Conn., Douglas House, Harbor Springs, Mich., Shamberg House, Mt. Kisco, N.Y., Hoffman and Saltzman Houses, East Hampton, N.Y.; houses in Old Westbury, N.Y., Pound Ridge, N.Y., Palm Beach, Fla., Pitts.; Twin Parks NE Housing, N.Y.C., Atheneum, New Harmony, Ind., N.Y., Hartford (Conn.) Sem., Mus. für Kunsthandwerk, Frankfurt, Germany, Des Moines Art Ctr., High Mus. Art, Atlanta, Bridgeport (Conn.) Ctr., Daimler-Benz Office and Lab. Complex, Ulm, Germany, Weishaupt Forum, Schwendi, Germany, City Hall and Cen. Libr., The Hague, The Netherlands, Corp. Hdqs., Royal Dutch Paper Mills, Hilversum, The Netherlands, Cornell U. Alumni and Admissions Ctr., Ithaca, N.Y., Canal Hdqs., Paris, Espace Pitot, Montpellier, France, Maybury Office Park, Edinburgh, Scotland, Hypolux Bank Bldg., Luxembourg, Mus. Contemporary Art, Barcelona, Spain, Arp Mus., Rolandswerth, Germany, Swiss Volksbank, Basel Office Bldg., Singapore, The Getty Ctr., L.A., SwissAir Hdqs., Melville, N.Y., Fed. Courthouse, Islip, N.Y., Phoenix, Mus. TV & Radio, L.A., Gagosian Gallery, L.A., Rachofsky

House, Dallas, Ch. of the Yr. 2000, Rome, others; author: Richard Meier Architect: Buildings & Projects 1966-1976, 1976, On Architecture, 1982, Richard Meier Collages, 1990, The Getty Ctr. Design Process, J. Paul Getty Trust, 1991, Richard Meier Sculpture, 1994; contbr. articles to profl. jours. Decorated officer de l'Ordre des Arts et des Lettres (France), 1984; recipient Arnold Brunner Meml. prize Am. Acad. Arts and Letters, 1972, Albert S. Bard Civic award City Club N.Y., 1973, 1st honor award for excellence in architecture and urban design, 1977, R.S. Reynolds Meml. award, 1977, Archtl. Record award of excellence for design, 1964, 68, 69, 70, 77, Am. Inst. Steel Constrn. award, 1978, 79, design award 1st prize Kunsthandwerk Competition, Frankfurt am Main, Fed. Republic Germany, 1980, Pritzker Prize for Architecture, 1984. Fellow AIA (medal of honor N.Y. chpt. 1980, nat. design com. 1972-74, 12 AIA nat. awards 1968-93, 32 chpt. awards N.Y. 1965-94, Chgo. Arch. award, 1995, 5 Progressive Architecture awards 1979, 89, 90, 91, 95, Gold medal 1997); mem. NAD, Internat. Inst. Archs., Royal Inst. Brit. Archs. (Royal Gold medal 1988), Belgian Royal Acad. Art (Lifetime Achievement award Guild Hall 1991, commdr. de l'Ordre des Arts et Lettres, France, 1992). Address: 475 10th Ave New York NY 10018-1120

MEIER, RICHARD LOUIS, futurist, planner, behavioral scientist; b. Kendallville, Ind., May 16, 1920; s. Walter A. and Mary (Lottman) M.; m. Gitta Unger, May 20, 1944 (dec.); children: Karen Reeds, Andrea Meier Whitmore, Alan; m. Robin Standish, Apr. 21, 1992. Student, No. Ill. State Tchrs. Coll., 1936-39; BS, U. Ill., 1940; MA, UCLA, 1942, PhD, 1944. With Calif. Research Corp., 1943-47; exec. sec. Fedn. Am. Scis., 1947-48; with Petrocarbon, Ltd., 1949-50; Fulbright scholar Manchester U., Eng., 1949-50; asst. prof. program of edn. and research in planning U. Chgo., 1950-56; research social scientist Mental Health Research Inst., U. Mich., Ann Arbor, 1957—; asso. prof. conservation Mental Health Research Inst., U. Mich., 1960-65, prof., 1965-67; prof. environ. design U. Calif., Berkeley, 1967-90; prof. emeritus U. Calif., 1990—; vis. lectr. Harvard U., 1959-60; vis. prof. Grad. Sch. Ekistics, Athens, 1962, U. Calif., Berkeley, 1966; cons. on social planning and resources planning Joint Ctr. for Urban Studies, MIT and Harvard U., in Venezuela, 1963-65; developer program for using inter-active media for edn. of illiterates for econ. devel. and population planning in Africa and Asia. Author: Science and Economic Development, 1956, Modern Science and the Human Fertility Problem, 1959, A Communications Theory of Urban Growth, 1962, Developmental Planning, 1965, Resource-Conserving Urbanism for South Asia, 1968, Planning for an Urban World, 1974, Urban Futures Observed: In the Asian Third World, 1980; contbr. numerous articles to profl. jours. Mem. AAAS, Am. Planning Assn., Am. Chem. Soc., Am. Sociol. Assn., Soc. for Gen. Sys. Rsch., Fedn. Am. Scis., Holis-Soc. for Sustainable Future, Internat. Solar Energy Soc. Home: 636 Colusa Ave Berkeley CA 94707-1518

MEIER, ROBERT JOSEPH, JR., software engineer; b. St. Marys, Pa., Aug. 7, 1959; s. Robert Joseph and Joan (Kerner) M. BS in Physics, Villanova U., 1981, BEE, 1981; MEE, Stanford Coll., 1982, PhD in Elec. Engring., 1988. Registered profl. engr., Ind. Physics rschr. Villanova (Pa.) U., 1979; software engr. Radio Corp. Am., Somerville, N.J., 1980; cons. NSF, Villanova, 1981; sci. group leader Project Pleides Space Sta., Stanford, 1982; software engr. Harris Corp., Melbourne, Fla., 1983; rsch. physicist NASA, Moffett Field, Calif., 1984-88; sr. software engr. proCASE, Inc., Santa Clara, Calif., 1988-89; sr. software engr., cons. Bell Labs. AT&T, Naperville, Ill., 1989-91; sr. software engr. Graphics Software Lab. AT&T, Indpls., 1992-93; cons. Custom Tools, Indpls., 1993—; webmaster FANUC Robotics, 1995—; comml. pilot, 1993. Author: Spaceborne Flotilla Servicing, 1986; inventor in field. Instr. water safety ARC, Santa Clara, 1979-84; capt. Emergency Mgmt. Agy. Radio Unit, Naperville, Ill., 1989-91. Recipient Cert. of Recognition, Ill. Ho. of Reps., 1991; fellow Charles LeGeyt Fortescue, 1981, NSF, 1982-84. Mem. IEEE (pub. referee 1984-89), Usenix Assn., White River Aviation Club, KC (treas. 1986-91), Phi Kappa Phi, Tau Beta Pi, Sigma Pi Sigma. Libertarian. Roman Catholic. Avocations: hang gliding, science fiction, mathematical physics, poetry, writing. Home: 740 Ironwood Dr Apt 307 Rochester MI 48307-1322 also: 2536 Greenwich Rd Winston Salem NC 27104-4143 Office: Fanuc Robotics NAm Inc 2000 S Adams Rd Auburn Hills MI 48326-2800

MEIER, THOMAS KEITH, college president, English educator; b. Houston, Apr. 12, 1940; s. Herbert H. and Madeleine (Keith) M.; m. Mila Hillard, June 30, 1962; children: John Hillard, Keith Reilly. BA, U. Tex., 1962; AM, Columbia U., 1963; MBA, Harvard U., 1967; PhD, Columbia U., 1969. Fin. mgr., employee rels. mgr. Exxon Co., U.S.A. and Exxon Rsch. Engring. Co., Houston, Florham Park, N.J., 1969-79; pres. Castleton (Vt.) State Coll., 1979-87, Elmira (N.Y.) Coll., 1987—; regent Lee Coll., Baytown, Tex., 1972-73; pres. Vt. Higher Edn. Coun., 1981-82; mem. Johnson Found. (Troutbeck) Leadership Seminar, 1991—; mem. adv. coun. The Pres.'s Found. for Support of Higher Edn.; bd. dirs. Chemung Canal Trust Co., Coll. Consortium Finger Lakes, N.Y., Ind. Coll. Fund of N.Y. Author: Defoe and the Defense of Commerce, 1987; contbr. articles to profl. jours. Bd. dirs. Union County Urban League, Elizabeth, N.J., 1973-76, Rutland Region C. of C., 1982-86, Arnot Art Mus., 1987—, So. Tier Econ. Growth, 1987—, N.E.-Midwest Congl. Leadership Coun., 1988—; bd. dirs. Chemung County United Way, 1990-93, chmn. 1992-93; corp. bd. dirs. Rutland Hosp., 1980-87; bd. dirs. Ind. Coll. Fund, 1995—. Lt. U.S. Army, 1963-65. Recipient Outstanding Periodical Essay award Tex. Books Rev., 1979, medal of merit Elmira Coll. Alumni Assn., 1991; Weaver fellow, 1968. Mem. Pico Ski Club, Elmira Country Club, Elmira City Club, Harvard Club of N.Y.C., Phi Beta Kappa, Phi Eta Sigma, Phi Alpha Theta, Omciron Delta Kappa, Theta Xi. Episcopalian. Home: The President's Home 855 College Ave Elmira NY 14901-2001 Office: Elmira Coll Office of Pres Elmira NY 14901

MEIER, WILBUR LEROY, JR., industrial engineer, educator, former university chancellor; b. Elgin, Tex., Jan. 3, 1939; s. Wilbur Leroy and Ruby (Hall) M.; m. Judy Lee Longbotham, Aug. 30, 1958; children: Melynn, Marla, Melissa. BS, U. Tex., 1962, MS, 1964, PhD, 1967. Planning engr. Tex. Water Devel. Bd., Austin, 1962-66, cons., 1967-72; research engr. U. Tex., Austin, 1966; asst. prof. indsl. engring. Tex. A&M U., College Station, 1967-68; assoc prof. Tex. A&M U., 1968-70, prof., 1970-73, asst. head dept. indsl. engring., 1972-73; prof., chmn. dept. indsl. engring. Iowa State U., Ames, 1973-74; prof., head sch. of indsl. engring. Purdue U., West Lafayette, Ind., 1974-81; dean Coll. Engring., Pa. State U., University Park, 1981-87; chancellor U. Houston System, 1987-89; prof. indsl. engring. Pa. State U., University Park, 1989-91; dir. div. engring. infrastructure devel. NSF, Washington, 1989-91; dean Coll. Engring. N.C. State U., 1991-93, prof. indsl. engring., 1991—; mem. bd. visitors Air Force Inst. Technology; cons. Ohio Bd. Regents, 1990, U. Arizona, 1989, Indsl. Rsch. Inst., St. Louis, 1979, Environments for Tomorrow, Inc., Washington, 1970-81, Water Resources Engrs., Inc., Walnut Creek, Calif., 1969-70, Computer Graphics, Inc., Bryan, Tex., 1969-70, Kaiser Engrs., Oakland, Calif., 1971, Tracor, Inc., Austin, 1966-68, div. planning coordination Tex. Gov.'s Office, 1969, Office of Tech. Assessment, 1982-86, Southeast Ctr. for Elec. Engring. Edn., 1978—; mem. rev. team Naval Rsch. Adv. Com. Editor: Marcel Dekker Pub. Co., 1978—; Contbr. articles to profl. jours. Recipient Bliss medal Soc. Am. Mil. Engrs., 1986, Am. Spirit award USAF, 1984; named Outstanding Young Engr. of Yr. Tex. Soc. Profl. Engrs., 1966, Disting. Grad. Coll. Engring., U. Tex. at Austin, 1987; USPHS fellow, 1966. Fellow AAAS, Am. Soc. Engring. Edn. (chmn. indsl. engring. divsn. 1978-83), Inst. Indsl. Engrs. (dir. ops. rsch. div. 1975, pres. Ind. chpt. 1976, program chmn. 1973-75, editorial bd. Trans., publ. chmn., newsletter editor engring. economy div. 1972-73, v.p. region VIII 1977-79, exec. v.p. chpt. ops. 1981-83, pres. 1985-86); mem. Ops. Rsch. Soc. Am., Inst. Mgmt. Scis. (v.p. S.W. chpt. 1971-72), ASCE (sec.-treas. Austin br. 1965-66, chmn. rsch. com., tech. coun. water resources planning and mgmt. 1972-74), Am. Assn. Engring. Socs. (bd. govs. 1984-86), Nat. Assn. State Univ. and Land Grant Colls. (mem. engring. legis. task force 1983-87), Assn. Engring. Colls. Pa. (pres. 1985-86, treas. 1981-87), Air Force Assn. (advisor sci. and tech. com. 1984-87), Nat. Soc. Profl. Engrs., Profl. Engrs. in Edn. (vice chmn. N.E. region 1985-87, bd. govs. 1983-85), Sigma Xi, Tau Beta Pi, Alpha Pi Mu (asso. editor Cogwheel 1970-75, regional dir. 1976-77, exec. v.p. 1977-80, pres. 1980-82), Phi Kappa Phi, Chi Epsilon. Lodge: Rotary. Home: 7504 Grist Mill Rd Raleigh NC 27615-5411*

MEIERING, MARK C., lawyer; b. Roswell, N.Mex., Sept. 28, 1944; m. Gail Marino. BBA, U. Notre Dame, 1966; JD, NYU, 1969. Bar: N.Mex. 1970, U.S. Dist. Ct. N.Mex. 1970, U.S. Ct. Appeals (10th cir.) 1971, U.S. Supreme Ct. 1977; bd. cert. in civil litigation Nat. Bd. Trial Advocacy. Law clk. Hon. D.C. Hill, U.S. Ct. Appeals, Wichita, Kans., 1969-71; asst. U.S. atty. Dist. of N.Mex., Albuquerque, 1971-76; assoc. Rodey Law Firm, Albuquerque, 1976—; asst. staff judge advocate USAR, Albuquerque, 1971-76. Chmn. bd. dirs. Sandia Prep. Sch., Albuquerque, 1991-92. Mem. Am. Bd. Trial Advocates (assoc.). Office: Rodey Law Firm PO Box 1888 Albuquerque NM 87103-1888

MEIGEL, DAVID WALTER, military officer, retired musician; b. Chgo., Feb. 27, 1957; s. Thomas Arent and Annie Elizabeth (Thomas) M. Diploma, USAF NCO Leadership Sch., Chanute AFB, Ill., 1981, USAF/CAP SQD Officer Sch., 1987, USAF NCO Acad., Norton AFB, Calif., 1991. Enlisted USAF, 1976; commd. staff sgt. to 2d lt. CAP, Travis AFB, Calif., 1986; advanced through grades to tech. sgt. USAF, 1989; percussionist 724th USAF Band, McChord AFB, Wash., 1976-78, 752d USAF Band, Elmendorf AFB, Alaska, 1978-80, 505th USAF Band, Chanute AFB, Ill., 1980-84, 504th USAF Band, Travis AFB, 1984-90; prin. percussionist, chief of adminstrn. Am.'s Band in Blue, USAF, Travis AFB, 1990-92. Prin. percussionist San Diego (Calif.) Civic Orch., 1973-76, Poway (Calif.) High Sch. Band, 1974-75; percussionist Anchorage (Alaska) Civic Opera, 1979-80, Anchorage (Alaska) Scottish Soc., 1979-80, Fairfield Civic Theatre, Fairfield, Calif., 1984—; communications officer USAF Civil Air Patrol, Travis AFB, 1986—. Recipient Gov.'s medal Youkon Internat. Invitational Scottish Games, Whitehorse City Coun., B.C., 1980; decorated USAF Achievement medal 1989, 93, USAF Commendation medal 1986, Comdrs. Commendation medal; named one of Outstanding Young Men Am., 1988, 92. Mem. CAP, USAF Aux. Avocations: amateur radio, golf, bowling, computer ops. Home: 3600 Data Dr # 544 Rancho Cordova CA 95670 Office: Intel Corp 1900 Prairie City Rd Folsom CA 95630-9501

MEIGHAN, STUART SPENCE, hospital consultant, internist, writer; b. Glasgow, Scotland, Jan. 30, 1923; came to U.S., 1962; s. Stuart Spence and Annie Louise (Brown) M; m. Anne Stewart Henderson, Nov. 4, 1952 (div. 1968); children: Jane Spence, Stuart Spence; m. Louise Rhys McGregor, July 7, 1985. MB, U. Glasgow, 1945. Registrar, sr. registrar Nat. Health Svc., U.K., 1948-57; sr. staff mem. Allan Blair Meml. Clinic, Regina, Sask., Can., 1957-62; internist Cleland Clinic, Oregon City, Oreg., 1962-64; dir. med. affairs Good Samaritan Hosp., Portland, Oreg., 1964-78; pres. Spence Meighan and Assocs., Portland, 1978—; cons. several hosps. and orgns. Contbr. over 100 articles to profl. jours. Lt. Royal Navy, 1946-48. Recipient Disting. Svc. award Am. Soc. Internal Medicine. Fellow Am. Coll. Physicians, Royal Coll. Physicians. Avocations: sailing, tennis, theater, rugby football, music. Home and Office: 408 NW Rainier Ter Portland OR 97210-3347

MEIGHER, S. CHRISTOPHER, III, communications and media investor; b. N.Y.C., Sept. 23, 1946; s. Stephen Christopher and Denise (Connor) Todd; m. Grace Tebbutt, Aug. 8, 1970; children: Elizabeth, Amanda. A.B., Dartmouth Coll., 1968; P.M.D., Harvard U., 1974. Dir. circulation Fortune mag., N.Y.C., 1972-74, Sports Illustrated mag., N.Y.C., 1974-76, Time mag., N.Y.C., 1976-79; v.p. circulation Time, Inc., N.Y.C., 1981-83; pres. Time Distbn. Services, N.Y.C., 1979-81; pub. People mag., N.Y.C., 1983-85, exec. v.p., group pub., 1985-90; pres. Time Inc. Mags. N.Y., N.Y.C., 1990-92; bd. dirs. Book of the Month Club, N.Y.C., Asiaweek Ltd., Hong Kong, Sunset Pub. Co., Southern Progress (Birmingham), Advt. Council, Inc., Mag. Publishers Assn., America Online, Washington. Trustee Boys Club, N.Y.C., South St. Seaport, N.Y.; bd. dirs. Meml. Sloan Kettering Dream Team, Am. Ballet Theatre, N.Y. Recipient Disting. Service award Brandeis U., 1983. Mem. River Club, Bath & Tennis Club (Palm Beach), Brook Club, Racquet & Tennis Club (N.Y.), N.Y. Yacht Club (trustee), Lake George Club, Clove Valley Rod and Gun Club. Home: 164 E 72nd St New York NY 10021-4363 Office: Meigher Comm LP 100 Avenue Of The Americas New York NY 10013-1689

MEIGS, JOHN FORSYTH, lawyer; b. Boston, Dec. 4, 1941; s. Charles H. and Florence S. (Truitt) M.; m. Faith C. Watson; children: Amy, Perry, John. BA, Yale U., 1964; LLB, U. Pa., 1969. Bar: Pa. 1969, U.S. Supreme Ct. 1977. Assoc. Saul, Ewing, Remick & Saul, Phila., 1969-76, ptnr., 1976—. Trustee Independence Seaport Mus., 1978—; mem. Com. of 70, 1976—; trustee Woodmere Art Mus., 1987—. Contbr. articles to profl. jours. Mem. ABA, Pa. Bar Assn., Phila. Bar Assn. Episcopalian. Home: 6 Norman Ln Philadelphia PA 19118-3617 Office: Saul Ewing Remick & Saul 3800 Centre Sq W Philadelphia PA 19102

MEIGS, JOSEPH CARL, JR., retired English language educator; b. New London, N.C., Aug. 29, 1930; s. Joseph Carl and Lola Vann (Eddins) M.; m. Elizabeth Eleanor Stevenson, Sept. 12, 1953; children: Geoffrey Montgomery, Jonathan Hervey, Edward Stevenson. BA, Wake Forest U., 1952; MA, Tulane U., 1957. English and French tchr. Aquadale (N.C.) High Sch., 1952-53; tchr. Metairie (La.) Park Country Day Sch., 1954-55; instr. in English Salem Coll., Winston-Salem, N.C., 1957-62, Tulane U., New Orleans, 1962-64, Marquette U., Milw., 1964-67; asst. prof., then assoc. prof. English Ea. Conn. State U., Willimantic, 1967-93, chmn. dept. English, 1972-74, 87-88, 1990-93; ret., 1993; vis. prof. U. Hawaii, Hilo, 1988-89, 94-95. Grantee Carnegie Inst., 1953, Danforth Found., 1960. Mem. Linguistic Soc. Am., Soc. for Pidgin and Creole Studies, Phi Beta Kappa, Omicron Delta Kappa. Democrat. Avocations: photography, gardening, cooking, hiking, ceramic arts. Home: PO Box 852 Brooklyn CT 06234-0852

MEIGS, MONTGOMERY CUNNINGHAM, JR., military officer; b. Annapolis, Md., Jan. 11, 1945; s. Montgomery Cunningham and Elizabeth Shoemaker (Griggs) M.; m. Mary Ann Mellenbruch, July 6, 1968; children: William Bradford, Matthew Montgomery. BS, U.S. Mil. Acad., West Point, N.Y., 1967; MA in History, U. Wis., 1977, PhD in History, 1982. Commd. 2d lt. U.S. Army, 1967, advanced through grades to maj. gen.; internat. affairs fellow Coun. Fgn. Rels., N.Y.C., 1981-82; exec. officer 2d Armored Cavalry Regiment, Nurnberg, Germany, 1982-84; comdr. 1st Squadron, 1st Cavalry, 1st AD, Schwabach, Germany, 1984-86; rsch. fellow Nat. Def. U., Washington, 1986-87; chief strategic applications br. J-5 Joint Staff, Washington, 1987-90; comdr. 2d Bde 2d Bn., 1st Armored Divsn., Erlangen, Germany, 1990-91; comdg. gen. 7th Army Tng. Command, Grafenwoehr, Germany, 1991-93; chief of staff V U.S. Corps, Frankfurt, Germany, 1993-94; dep. chief of staff ops. HQ USAREUR & 7th Army, Heidelberg, Germany, 1994-95; commanding gen. 3d Infantry Divsn., 1995—; Comeagle Bosnia-Nurzegovina, 1996—. Author: Slide Rules and Submarines, 1990; contbr. articles to profl. jours. Decorated Disting. Svc. medal, Def. Superior Svc. medal, Legion of Merit with oak leaf cluster, Bronze Star medal with V device and 1 oak leaf cluster, Purple Heart. Avocations: history, hunting. Home: 140 Marne Ln, Wurzburg Germany Office: HQ 1ID Unit 26222 # 1id APO AE 09036-6222

MEIJER, DOUGLAS, retail company executive; b. 1954. With Meijer Inc., 1967—, co-chmn., dir., 1990—, also CEO. Office: Meijer Inc 2929 Walker Ave NW Grand Rapids MI 49544-9424*

MEIJER, FREDERIK, retail company executive; b. 1919. married. Former pres. Meijer, Inc., then chmn. bd., chief exec. officer, 1975-90, chmn. exec. com., chief exec. officer, 1990-97, chmn. exec. com., 1997—, also bd. dirs. Office: Meijer Inc 2929 Walker Ave NW Grand Rapids MI 49544-9424*

MEIJER, HENDRIK, retail company executive; b. 1952. With Meijer Inc., Grand Rapids, Mich., 1963—, co-chmn., 1990—. Office: Meijer Inc 2929 Walker Ave NW Grand Rapids MI 49544-9424*

MEIJER, PAUL HERMAN ERNST, educator, physicist; b. The Hague, Netherlands, Nov. 14, 1921; came to U.S., 1953, naturalized, 1959; s. Herman Willem and Elisabet (Kossmann) M.; m. Marianne Schwarz, Feb. 17, 1949; children: Onko Frans (dec.), Miriam, Daniel, Mark, Corinne. Ph.D., U. Leiden, Netherlands, 1951. Research assoc. U. Leiden, 1952-53, Duke U., 1954-55; vis. lectr. Case Inst. Tech., 1953-54; asst. prof. U. Del., 1955-56; asso. prof. Cath. U., Washington, 1956-60; prof. physics Cath. U., 1960-92, prof. emeritus, 1992—, chmn. dept., 1980-83; vis. prof. U. Paris, 1964-65, 72, 78, U. Nancy, 1984, 88; part-time appointment Nat. Bur. Standards; short time appointments at Naval Ordnance Lab., Livermore Radiation Lab., Naval Research Lab., Night Vision Lab., Ft. Belvoir. Author: (with E. Bauer) Group Theory, 1962; editor: Group Theory and Solid State Physics, 1964. Fulbright grantee, 1953-55, 77-78; Guggenheim grantee, 1964-65; Fulbright sr. fellow, 1978. Fellow Am. Phys. Socs.; mem. European Phys. Soc., Phys. Soc. Netherlands, Fedn. Am. Scientists, Fulbright Alumni Assn., Sigma Xi. Research, publs. statis. mechanics solids and liquids, group theory and other fields. Home: 1438 Geranium St NW Washington DC 20012-1518 Office: Cath U Am Dept Physics Hannan Hall Washington DC 20064 also: Phys and Chem Properties Div Nat Inst Stds and Tech Gaithersburg MD 20899

MEIKLE, PHILIP G., retired government agency executive; b. Glendale, W.Va., Dec. 5, 1937; s. Philip and Caroline Elizabeth (Stephens) M.; m. Linda Kay Price, July 14, 1961 (div. Aug. 1976); children—Philip Kevin, Melissa Kay. B.S. in Mining Engring., W.Va. U., 1961, M.S. in Mining Engring., 1965; M.Engring. Adminstrn., George Washington U., 1980. Registered profl. engr. Mining engr. Duquesne Light Co., Pitts., 1961-63; research engr. W.Va. U., Morgantown, 1963-66; materials engr. Mobay Chem. Co., New Martinsville, W.Va., 1966-68; asst. dir. Nat. Ash Assn., Washington, 1968-72; staff mining engr. U.S. Bur. Mines, Washington, 1972-82, divsn. chief, 1982-95; ret., 1995; mem. U.S. Nat. Com. for Tunneling Tech., Nat. Acad. Scis., Washington, 1985-90, chmn., 1988-89; adj. prof. George Washington U., 1985—. Contbr. articles to profl. jours., chpts. to books. Recipient Superior Svc. award Dept. Interior, 1980, Meritorious Svc. award, 1986, Disting. Svc. award, 1991, Presdl. Rank award, 1991. Mem. Fed. Exec. Inst. Alumni Assn., Sr. Execs. Assn. (life), Sigma Xi (life), Tau Beta Pi (life), Masons, Shriners. Republican. Baptist. Avocations: racquetball; tennis; golf. Home: 6819 Brian Michael Ct Springfield VA 22153-1004

MEIKLE, THOMAS HARRY, JR., retired neuroscientist, foundation administrator, educator; b. Troy, Pa., Mar. 24, 1929; s. Thomas H. and Elizabeth (MacMorran) M.; m. Jane T. Germer, Aug. 26, 1966 (div. 1983); children: David Andrew, Sarah Elizabeth; m. Jacqueline Winterkorn, Sept. 27, 1986. A.B., Cornell U., 1951, M.D., 1954. Intern Jefferson Hosp., Phila., 1954-55; clin. fellow Inst. Neurology, London, Eng., 1957-58; research fellow Inst. Neurol. Scis., U. Pa., Phila., 1958-61; instr., asst. prof., assoc. prof., prof. anatomy Cornell U. Med. Coll., N.Y.C., 1961-87, acting dean medicine, 1976-77, dep. dean, 1977-79, dean, provost, 1980-87; dean Cornell U. Grad. Sch. Med. Scis., 1969-76; v.p. Josiah Macy, Jr. Found., N.Y.C., 1980, pres., 1987—; career scientist Health Research Council, N.Y.C., 1969-71. Served to capt. M.C. AUS, 1955-57, Korea. Markle Found. scholar in acad. medicine, 1963-68. Home and Office: Josiah Macy Jr Found 44 E 64th St New York NY 10021-7306

MEIKLEJOHN, ALVIN J., JR., state senator, lawyer, accountant.; b. Omaha, June 18, 1923; B.S., J.D., U. Denver, 1951; m. Lorraine J. Meiklejohn; children: Pamela Ann, Shelley Lou, Bruce Ian, Scott Alvin. Mem. Colo. Senate from 19th dist., 1976-96, chmn. com. edn.; mem. Edn. Commn. of States, 1981-96, chmn. Colo. Commn. on Ach. in Edn., 1995; chmn., 1993-96. Mem. Jefferson Sch. Dist. No. R-1 Bd. Edn., 1971-77, pres., 1973-77; commr. Commn. on Uniform State Laws, 1988-96. Served to capt. U.S. Army, 1940-46; to maj. USAF, 1947-51. Mem. Colo. Soc. CPA's, Arvada C. of C. Republican. Clubs: Masons, Shriners. Home: 7540 Kline Dr Arvada CO 80005-3732 Office: Jones & Keller PC 1625 Broadway Ste 1600 Denver CO 80202-4725

MEIKLEJOHN, DONALD, philosophy educator; b. Providence, June 1, 1909; s. Alexander and Nannine (LaVilla) M.; m. Betty Moore, Aug. 25, 1941; children: Alexander M., Douglas, Elizabeth, Donald Stuart. AB, U. Wis., 1930; PhD, Harvard, 1936. Instr. philosophy Dartmouth, 1936-38; assoc. prof. philosophy Coll. William and Mary, 1938-46; assoc. prof. U. Chgo., 1946-59, prof., 1959-63; chmn. Coll. Social Sci. Group, 1958-61; prof. philosophy and social sci. Syracuse U., 1963—, dir. pub. affairs and citizenship Maxwell Sch., 1963-75, emeritus, 1975—, adj. prof. pub. affairs, 1989-94; vis. prof. Coll. of the Atlantic, Bar Harbor, Maine, 1979-83, faculty, 1983—. Author: Freedom and the Public, 1965; co-author: Participation in Government, 1988; articles in field. Served from pvt. to 1st lt. AUS, 1942-46. Mem. ACLU (dir. Ill.), AAUP, Phi Beta Kappa. Club: Hyde Park Neighborhood (dir.). Home: 822 Maryland Ave Syracuse NY 13210-2501 *A life-long career as a teacher in American colleges has been tremendously rewarding in terms both of intellectual stimulus and personal association. The chance such a career offers to follow, however inadequately, the example of Socrates in questioning the fundamental values and concepts effective in American public life is as much, I believe, as any teacher may fairly expect. For this I am deeply grateful.*

MEIKLEJOHN, DONALD STUART, lawyer; b. Chgo., Oct. 27, 1950; s. Donald and Elizabeth (Moore) M.; m. Rebecca Schneider, Aug. 9, 1975; children: David Alexander, Sarah. AB, Harvard U., 1971, JD, 1975. Bar: N.Y. 1976, U.S. Dist. Ct. (so. and ea. dists.) N.Y. 1976, U.S. Ct. Appeals (2d cir.) 1981, U.S. Ct. Appeals (5th cir.) 1982, U.S. Ct. Appeals (1st and 8th cirs.) 1990, U.S. Supreme Ct. 1986. Assoc. Sullivan & Cromwell, N.Y.C., 1975-83, ptnr., 1983—. Bd. dirs. Union Settlement, N.Y.C., Lawyer's Com. Civil Rights Under Law, Legal Aid Soc. Mem. ABA, N.Y. State Bar Assn., Assn. of Bar of City of N.Y. Office: Sullivan & Cromwell 125 Broad St New York NY 10004-2400

MEIKSIN, ZVI H., electrical engineering educator; b. 1926. BSEE, Israel Inst. Tech., Haifa, 1950, Dipl. Ing., 1951; MSEE, Carnegie Mellon U., 1953; PhDEE, U. Pitts., 1959. Registered profl. engr., Pa. Design engr. McGraw Edison, Cannonsburg, Pa., 1953-54; sr. project engr. Westinghouse Electric Corp., Pitts., 1956-59; prof. dept. elec. engring. U. Pitts., 1959-91; prof. emeritus, 1991—; pres. Transtek, Inc. (formerly Transcom. Co.), Pitts., 1989-95, Transtek, Inc., Pitts., 1995—; cons. entr. 33 orgns. in U.S., Europe, 1959—. Author: Thin & Thick Films, 1976, Active Filter Design, 1990; co-author: Electronic Design, 1980, 84, Microprocessor Based Design, 1986; jour. referee profl. publs., 1970—; contbr. articles to profl. jours.; inventor, holder 6 patents in field. Fellow IEEE (award coms.); mem. Eta Kappa Nu, Sigma Xi. Office: Transtek Inc PO Box 8113 Pittsburgh PA 15217-0113

MEILAN, CELIA, food products executive; b. Bklyn., Jan. 21, 1920; d. Ventura Lorenzo and Susana (Prego) M. Student, CCNY, 1943-46. Codes and ciphers translator security divsn. U.S. Censorship Office, N.Y.C., 1942-46; sec., treas. Albumina Supply Co., N.Y.C., 1946-55; co-founder, co-owner, sec., treas., fin. officer Internat. Proteins Corp., Fairfield, N.J., 1955-86, exec. v.p., 1986-92, pres., 1992-94, chair emeritus, bd. dirs., 1994—; bd. dirs. Pesquera Taboquilla, Panama City, Republic of Panama, 1969—, Inversiones Pesqueras S.A., Brit. V.I.; v.p., bd. dirs. Atlantic Shippers of Tex. Inc., Port Arthur, 1989, Atlantic Shippers Inc., Morehead City, N.C., Empacadora Nacional S.A., Panama City, Republic of Panama; exec. v.p., bd. dirs. Fairfield Fishing Co., Liberia, Internat. Proteins Chile S.A., Santiago. Named One of Top 50 Women Bus. Owners, Working Woman mag. and Nat. Found. Women Bus. Owners, 1994, 95. Mem. Nat. Found. Women Bus. Owners, Spanish Benevolent Soc. (bd. dirs. 1955-62). Avocations: travel, hand crafts, backgammon, puzzles. Office: 204 Passaic Ave Fairfield NJ 07004-3503

MEILGAARD, MORTEN CHRISTIAN, food products specialist, international educator; b. Vigerslev, Denmark, Nov. 11, 1928; s. Anton Christian Meilgaard and Ane Maria Elisa Larsen; m. Manon Meadows, Oct. 29, 1962; children: Stephen Paul, Justin Christian. MSChemE, Tech. U. Denmark, 1952, DS in Food Sci., 1982. Rsch. chemist Carlsberg Breweries, Copenhagen, Denmark, 1947-57; dir. and co-owner Alfred Jorgensen Lab. for Fermentation, Copenhagen, 1957-67; dir. rsch. and devel. Cerveceria Cuauhtemoc, Monterrey, Mex., 1967-73; v.p. rsch. Stroh Brewery Co., Detroit, 1973-89, pres. Strohtech Inc. div., 1986-91; cons., 1991—; vis. prof. Agrl. U. Denmark, 1994—. Author: Sensory Evaluation Techniques, 1987, 2d edit., 1991; contbr. articles to profl. jours. Recipient Schwarz award, 1974. Fellow Inst. Brewing; mem. Internat. Med. Advisory Group, European Chemoreception Rsch. Orgn., Assn. Chemoreception Scis., Inst. Food Technologists, Am. Chem. Soc., Dansk Ingeniorforening, Am. Wine Soc., Air Pollution Control Assn., Master Brewers Assn. Am. (chmn. various coms., award of merit 1990), Am. Soc. Brewing Chemists (chmn. various coms.), ASTM (chmn. various coms., award of merit 1992), U.S. Hop Rsch. Coun. (pres. 1978-80, 1982-84, founder). Avocations: theatre, music, sailing, skiing. Home: 2938 Moon Lake Dr West Bloomfield MI 48323-1841 Office: Stroh Brewery Co 100 River Place Dr Detroit MI 48207-4295

MEILING, GERALD STEWART, materials scientist; b. Provo, Utah, Sept. 12, 1936; s. Harry Louis and Iona (Falker) M.; m. Jane Olive Sprunt, July 20, 1962; children—John Scott, William David, Marcine Elizabeth. B.S., U. Utah, 1958; M.S., MIT, 1959, Sc.D., 1966. Sr. scientist Corning, Inc., N.Y., 1966-69, devel. assoc., 1971-76, devel. mgr., 1976-82, dir. devel., 1982-86, dir. rsch., 1986—, v.p., 1988-94, sr. v.p. 1994-97; cons., 1997—; sr. rsch. scientist Signetics, Sunnyvale, Calif., 1969-71; bd. dirs. Samsung Corning, Seoul, Korea; mem. earth scis. adv. bd. Stanford U., 1985—; mem. materials sci. adv. bd. U. Calif. Santa Barbara, Cornell U., Los Alamos (N.Mex.) Nat. Lab. Patentee in photochromics and crystal growth. Fellow Am. Ceramic Soc.; mem. IEEE, N.Y. Acad. Scis., Indsl. Rsch. Inst., Sigma Xi. Republican. Mem. LDS Ch.

MEILMAN, EDWARD, physician; b. Boston, Apr. 6, 1915; s. Harry and Jennie (Sholofsky) M.; m. Rhoeda Berman, Mar. 6, 1946. A.B., Harvard U., 1936, M.D., 1940. Intern Mt. Sinai Hosp., N.Y.C., 1940-42; resident Beth Israel Hosp., Boston, 1946-48; assoc. in med. and med. research Beth Israel Hosp., 1948-53; chmn. dept. medicine L.I. Jewish-Hillside Med. Center, New Hyde Park, N.Y., 1953-82, chmn. emeritus dept. medicine, 1982—; prof. medicine SUNY, Stony Brook, 1971—. Contbr. articles to profl. jours. Served with USAAF, 1942-46. Fellow N.Y. Acad. Medicine, N.Y. Acad. Scis.; mem. Am. Heart Assn. (fellow council clin. cardiology, council arteriosclerosis), Am. Fedn. Clin. Research, Harvey Soc., Am. Rheumatism Assn., Phi Beta Kappa, Alpha Omega Alpha. Democrat. Jewish. Club: Harvard (N.Y.C.); Harvard (L.I.).

MEIMA, RALPH CHESTER, JR., corporate executive, former foreign service officer; b. Chgo., Mar. 29, 1927; s. Ralph Chester and Grace Georgine (Larson) M.; children: Ralph Chester III, Stephen H.; m. Elizabeth B. Frazier, 1994. B.A., U. Americas, Mexico City, 1952; M.B.A., Am. U., 1964. With Carborundum Co., Perth Amboy, N.J., 1952-53, Johns-Manville Corp., N.Y.C., 1953-58, Security Storage Co., Washington, 1958-61, Dept. Commerce, 1961-68; joined U.S. Fgn. Service, 1968; consul gen. Marseille, France, 1977-80; on loan as export devel. cons. State of Md., 1980-82; pres. Atlantic Eastern Corp., 1982-87, Phoenix Internat. Mktg. Corp., 1987-89; pres., chief exec. officer FTI Inc., Annapolis, Md., 1989-95; pres. DERCO, Inc., Balt., 1995-96; v.p. IMCO Inc., Columbia, Md., 1997—. Served with USN, 1945-46. Office: PO Box 2815 Columbia MD 21045-0815

MEINDL, MAX J., III, environmental consultant, professional inspector; b. Buffalo, N.Y., June 21, 1951; s. Max John Jr. and Doris Elisabeth (Wessel) M.; m. Rachel Pratt, Apr. 23, 1983; 1 child, Elisabeth Bancroft Wessel Meindl. Student, U. St. Thomas, 1973-75, U. Houston, 1983-84, Tex. A & M U., 1989-91. Lic. profl. insp. Tex. Real Estate Commn.; lic. asbestos cons.; lic. underground storage tank contractor Tex. Natural Resources and Conservation Commn. Prin. E. Daughter & Co., Houston, 1976-91, Texan Inspection & Environ. Svcs., Houston, 1980-89; program mgr. real estate svcs. TSP Inc., Houston, 1989-91; prin. MJM Cons., Houston, 1991—; catastrophe adjuster Crawford & Co., 1995—; cons. Resolution Trust Corp., Houston, 1991, Bridas Oil Co., Argentina; Compaq Computer Corp. facility engr.; coord. Spartan Internat. Project, 1993-95; project mgr., estimator Evans Am. Corp., Disaster Restoration; constrn. insp. Ft. Bend Ind. Sch. Dist., Tex., 1996—. Mem. disaster relief ARC, Houston; disaster insp. Fed. Emergency Mgmt. Agy., Pa., N.C., P.R., Calif., Grand Forks, N.D.; tech. specialist Bechtel/Sonatrach Algerian Pipeline Project, Algeria, 1995; disaster restoration project mgr. Evans Am. Corp., 1996; constrn. insp. Ft. Bend (Tex.) Ind. Sch. Dist., 1996—. Mem. Nat. Assn. Environ. Profls., Am. Assn. Energy and Environ. Engrs., Nat. Asbestos Coun., Nat. Environ. Health Assn., Mensa. Office: MJM Cons PO Box 1464 Houston TX 77251-1464

MEINDL, ROBERT JAMES, English language educator; b. Wausau, Wis., Sept. 17, 1936; s. George Martin and Adeline Emilie (Goetsch) M.; m. Victoria Lynn Chavez; children: Karin Rose, George Andrew, Damian Kurt, Erika Wittmer, Christopher Smith, Gabrielle Remelia. BS, U. Wis., 1958; MA, U. Conn., 1960; PhD, Tulane U., 1965; postdoctoral studies, U. Calif., Berkeley, 1967-68, Goethe Inst., Liblar, Germany, 1879, U. Cologne, Germany, 1970. Teaching asst. U. Conn., Storrs, 1958-60; teaching fellow Tulane U., 1960-62; lectr. U. Wis., Green Bay, 1963-65; from asst. to full prof. English Calif. State U., Sacramento, 1965—. Translator: Studies in John Gower, 1981; book rev. editor Studia Mystica Jour., 1984-89; contbr. numerous articles to profl. jours. With USNR, 1953-61, 79-96. Nat. Endowment for the Humanities fellow Stanford U., 1982. Mem. MLA, Medieval Acad. Am., Medieval Assn. of Pacific, Early English Text Soc., John Gower Soc., New Chaucer Soc. Home: 2301 Pennland Dr Sacramento CA 95825-0329 Office: Calif State U 6000 J St Sacramento CA 95819-2605

MEINEL, ADEN BAKER, optics scientist; b. Pasadena, Calif., Nov. 25, 1922; s. John G. and Gertrude (Baker) M.; m. Marjorie Steele Pettit, Sept. 5, 1944; children: Carolyn, Walter, Barbara, Elaine, Edward, Mary, David. AB, U. Calif., Berkeley, 1947, PhD, 1949; DSc (hon.), U. Ariz., 1990, U. Ariz., 1990. Assoc. prof. Yerkes Obs., U. Chgo., Williams Bay, Wis., 1950-57; dir. Kitt Peak Nat. Obs., Tucson, 1958-60; prof. U. Ariz., Tucson, 1961-85; dir. Steward Obs., Tucson, 1962-67, Optical Scis. Ctr., Tucson, 1966-73; Disting. scientist Jet Propulsion Lab., Pasadena, 1985-93; ret., 1993; regent Calif. Luth. Coll., 1961-71; cons. USAF Spl. Projects Office, 1965-80. Co-author: Applied Solar Energy, 1976, Sunsets, Twilights and Evening Skies, 1983. Recipient Warner prize Am. Astron. Soc., 1954, Van Blesbroeck award Astron. Soc. Pacific, 1990, NASA Exceptional Scientific Achievement medal, 1993; Aden B. Meinel bldg. U. Ariz., dedicated 1993. Fellow Am. Acad Arts and Scis., Optical Soc. Am. (pres. 1972-73, Adolph Lomb medal 1952, Ives medal 1980), Internat. Optical Engring. Soc. (Goddard award 1984, Kingslake medal and prize, 1993, Gold medal 1997). Home: 1600 Shoreline Dr Santa Barbara CA 93109-2024

MEINER, HOWARD, advertising executive; married; two children. CPA, N.Y. Controller Hodes-Daniel, 1968-70; divsnl. controller Cordura Corp., 1970-74, Ogilvy & Mather, 1974-76; various positions including v.p., treas. Ogilvy & Mather Direct, 1976-85, sr. v.p., 1985—; mem. operating com. Ogilvy & Mather Direct, 1984—, exec. com., 1989—. Mem. AICPA, N.Y. State Soc. CPAs, Advt. Agt. Fin. Mgmt. Group. Avocations: theater, movies, golf, basketball, football. Office: Ogilvy & Mather Direct 309 W 49th St New York NY 10019-7316

MEINER, SUE ELLEN THOMPSON, gerontologist, nursing educator and researcher; b. Ironton, Mo., Oct. 24, 1943; d. Louis Raymond and Verna Mae (Goggin) Thompson; m. Robert Edward Meiner, Mar. 5, 1971; children: Diane Thompson Bubb, Suzanne Elaine. AAS, Meramec C.C., 1970; BSN, St. Louis U., 1978, MSN, 1983; EdD, So. Ill. U., Edwardsville, 1991. RN, Mo.; cert. gerontol. nurse practitioner; cert. clin. specialist in gerontol. nursing. Staff RN St. Joseph's Hosp., St. Charles, Mo., 1976-78; nursing supr. Bethesda Gen. Hosp., St. Louis, 1975-76, 71-74; adult med. dir. Family Care Ctr.-Carondelet, St. Louis, 1978-79; program dir., lectr. Webster Coll./Bethesda Hosp., Webster Groves, Mo., 1979-82; diabetes clin. specialist Washington U. Sch. Medicine, St. Louis, 1982; chmn. dept. nursing, asst. prof. St. Louis C.C., 1983-88, Barnes Hosp. Sch. Nursing, 1988-89; instr. U. Mo., St. Louis, 1989; assoc. prof. St. Charles County C.C., St. Peters, Mo., 1990-92, Deaconess Coll. of Nursing, 1991-93; patient care mgr. Deaconess Hosp., St. Louis, 1993-94; assoc. prof. Jewish Hosp. Coll. of Nursing and Allied Health, 1994—; gerontol. nurse, rschr. Wash. U. Sch. Med., St. Louis, 1996—; nat. dir. edn. Nat. Assn. Practical Nurse Edn. and Svc., Inc., St. Louis, 1984-86; mem. task force St. Louis Met. Hosp. Assn., 1987-88; mem. adv. com. Bd. Edn. Sch. Nursing, St. Louis, 1986-90; grant coord. Kellogg Found. Gerontology and Nursing, 1991-92; project dir. NIH Grant Washington U., St. Louis, 1996—. Contbr. articles to profl. jours. and books. Chmn. bd. dirs. Creve Coeur Fire Protection Dist. Mo., 1984-89; vice chmn. Bd. Cen. St. Louis County Emergency Dispatch Svc., 1985-87; asst. leader Girl Scouts U.S., St. Louis, 1975; treas. Older Women's League, St. Louis, 1992-93. Recipient Woman of Worth award Gateway chpt. Older Women's League, 1993. Mem. ANA, Am. Nurses Found., Nat. League for Nursing, Am. Soc. of Aging, Mid-Am. Congress on Aging, Creve Coeur C. of C., Order Ea. Star (chaplain 1970), Jobs Daus. (guardian 1979-80), Sigma Theta Tau (fin. chmn. 1984, archivist 1985-87), Sigma Phi Omega (pres. 1990-91), Kappa Delta Pi. Avocations: travel, reading. Home and Office: 700 Wren Path Ct Ballwin MO 63021-4794 *Personal philosophy: From my earliest memories, I have established goals that were obtainable only through very hard work and perseverance. I always sought support and assistance from significant others as each goal was reached before setting another one. My life has been enriched by family and very dear friends. An important belief and practice has been to return the benefits of my education to my community and to individuals needing its special knowledge. I hold a special place for support of all older adults.*

MEINERS, GINNY, clinical psychologist, nurse consultant; b. St. Louis; d. Robert and Mary Meiners. BA in Psychology, U. Mo., 1977; RN, St. Louis C.C., 1988; MEd in Counseling, U. Mo., 1994; PhD in Clin. Psychology, Washington U., St. Louis, 1997. RN, Mo. Dir. Weight Loss Clinics, St. Louis, 1981-87; sr. adminstr. Mid-East Area Agy., St. Louis, 1987-88; owner Profl. Weight Counseling, Inc., St. Louis, 1988-93; nurse instr., counselor Gen. Protestant Children's Home, St. Louis, 1993—; clin. psychologist Insights Psychol. Svcs., St. Louis, 1994—; spkr. in field. Active Volvo Nat. Tennis Team. Mem. ACA, APA, Am. Assn. Christian Counselors, Mo. Nurses Assn., Assn. for Spiritual, Ethical and Religious Values, St. Louis Track Club, Phi Kappa Phi, Chi Sigma Iota. Avocations: tennis, track. Office: Insights Psychol Svcs 777 S New Ballas Rd Ste 320 W Saint Louis MO 63141-8705

MEINERT, JOHN RAYMOND, clothing manufacturing and retailing executive, investment banker; b. White Cloud, Mich., Aug. 11, 1927; m. Joyce Macdonell, Nov. 5, 1955; children: Elizabeth Tinsman, Pamela Martin. Student, U. Mich., 1944-45; B.S., Northwestern U., 1949. C.P.A., Ill., 1952. With Hart Schaffner & Marx/Hartmarx Corp., Chgo., 1950-90, exec. v.p., 1975-80, vice chmn., 1981-85, sr. vice chmn., 1985-86, chmn., 1987-90, chmn. emeritus, 1990—, also bd. dirs.; prin. investment banking J.H. Chapman Group, Ltd., Rosemont, Ill., 1990—; chmn. J.H. Chapman Group, Ltd., Rosemont, 1995—; bd. dirs. The John Evans Club; trustee Amalgamated Ins. Fund, 1980-90; dir. Evanston Hosp., 1988-94; instr. acctg. Northwestern U., 1949; faculty Lake Forest Grad. Sch. Mgmt., 1994-95; arbitrator Am. Arbitration Assn., 1993—. Bd. dirs. Better Bus. Bur.; chmn. bus. adv. coun. U. Ill., 1989-90; mem. Fin. Acctg. Stds. Adv. Coun., 1989-92, Chgo. Coun. Fgn. Rels., Sisters City Com.; mem. adv. coun. Northwestern U. Kellogg Grad. Sch. Recipient Alumni Merit award Northwestern U. Kellogg Grad. Sch., 1989; named Humanitarian of Yr., Five Hosp. Found., 1995. Mem. AICPA (v.p. 1985-86, bd. dirs. 1975-78, coun. 1971-93, trustee benevolent fund 1992-95, gold medal 1987), Ill. CPA Soc. (pub. svc. award 1996, pres. 1982-83, bd. dirs. 1966-68, 81-84, hon. award), Clothing Mfrs. Assn. (bd. dirs. 1980-90, pres. 1982-87, chmn. 1987-90), Chgo. C. of C. (bd. dirs.), Rotary (pres. Chgo. 1989-90, trustee found. 1991-95), Univ. Club, Execs. Club, Rolling Green Country Club. Presbyterian (elder). Home: 634 N Ironwood Dr Arlington Heights IL 60004-5818 Office: J H Chapman Group Ltd 9700 W Higgins Rd Des Plaines IL 60018-4796

MEINHOLD, CHARLES BOYD, health physicist; b. Boston, Nov. 1, 1934; s. Russell and Jane (Boyd) M.; m. Anne Elizabeth DuVally, Oct. 20, 1956; children: Anne Frances, Patricia Marie, Michael John, Peter Russell, Catherine Louise. BS in Physics, Providence Coll., 1956; postgrad., U. Rochester, 1956-57. Staff scientist health physics div. Brookhaven Nat. Lab., Upton, N.Y., 1957-72, head, sr. health physicist safety and environ. div., 1972-88, sr.scientist, div. head, 1988-91; sr. scientist radiol. sci. divsn. Dept. Advanced Tech., Upton, 1991—; pres. Nat. Coun. on Radiation Protection and Measurement, Bethesda, Md., 1991—; mem. Internat. Commn. on Radiol. Protection, 1978—; mem. Nat. Commn. on Radiol. Protection, 1977—; cons. Consol. Edison Co., 1984—. pres. South Haven Bd. Edn., Brookhaven, N.Y., 1965-87. Named Hon. Prof., China Inst. Atomic Energy, 1995, China Inst. Radiation Protection, 1997. Fellow Health Physics Soc.; mem. Internat. Radiation Protection Assn. (v.p. 1988-92, pres. 1992-96). Roman Catholic. Avocations: woodworking, sailing. Home: 41 Old South Country Rd Brookhaven NY 11719-9526 Office: Dept Nuclear Energy Radiol Sci Div Bldg 703m B Dept Advanced Technology Upton NY 11973

MEINIG, DONALD WILLIAM, geography educator; b. Palouse, Wash., Nov. 1, 1924; s William August and Annie (Malsed) M.; m. Lee McAuliffe, June 29, 1946; children: Laurel, Kristin, Lee. B.S., Georgetown U., 1948; M.A., U. Wash., 1950, Ph.D., 1953; DHL (hon.), Syracuse U., 1994. From asst. prof. to assoc. prof. U. Utah, Salt Lake City, 1950-59; assoc. prof. geography Syracuse U., N.Y., 1959-73, Maxwell prof. geography, 1973-89; Maxwell rsch. prof. Syracuse U., 1990—; lectr. St. Andrews U., Scotland, 1973, Charles Homer Haskins lectr. ACLS, 1992; vis. prof. Hebrew U., Jerusalem, 1974; adv. editor Wadsworth Pub. Co., 1957-61, Harper & Row, N.Y.C., 1965-83; chief editl. cons. Nat. Geog. Soc., Washington, 1982-88, councilor, 1993-96. Author: On the Margins of the Good Earth, 1962, The Great Columbia Plain, 1968, Imperial Texas, 1969, Southwest, 1971, The Shaping of America, Vol. 1: Atlantic America 1492-1800, 1986, Vol. 2: Continental America 1800-1867, 1993; editor: The Interpretation of Ordinary Landscapes, 1979. Mem. N.Y. Council for Humanities, 1979-86. Served to 2d lt. U.S. Army, 1943-46. Recipient Emil and Kathleen Sick award in Western History, 1968, award of Merit Seattle Hist. Soc., 1968, award of Merit Am. Assn. State and Local History, 1969, Summerfield G. Roberts award Sons Republic of Tex., 1969, Faculty Enrichment award Can Embassy, 1980, Master Tchr. award Nat. Coun. for Geog. Edn., 1986, Charles P. Daly medal Am. Geog. Soc., 1986; Fulbright rsch. scholar U. Adelaide, 1958; Guggenheim fellow, 1966-67, NEH fellow, 1987-88. Fellow Brit. Acad. (corr.); mem. Assn. Am. Geographers (councilor 1965-67, Meritorious Contbn. award), Am. Antiquarian Soc. Office: Syracuse U Dept Geography Syracuse NY 13244-1090

MEINKE, ALAN KURT, surgeon; b. Eaton Rapids, Mich., May 25, 1952; s. Richard Keydel and Kaarina Elli (Ranta) M.; m. Lori Anne Alley, Sept., 1985; children: Christopher Richard, Mary Elizabeth, William Alan. BA, Albion (Mich.) Coll., 1974; MD, Wayne State U., 1978. Intern Mayo Clinic, Rochester, Minn., 1978, resident gen. surgery, 1978-82, chief resident, 1982-83; sr. attending physician, dir. surg. edn. Norwalk (Conn.) Hosp., 1983—; ptnr. Surg. Assocs., Westport, Conn., 1985—; med. dir. Wilton Vol. Ambulance Corp., 1983-93; mem. med. adv. com. Fairfield-Westchester Crohn's and Colitis Found., 1992—. Contbr. articles to profl. jours. Active med. sect. United Way of Westport and Weston, 1989-94; bd. dirs. Interfaith Housing Assn., Westport, 1994—. Fellow ACS (credentials com. Conn. chpt. 1991—), Priestly Soc.; mem. AMA, Internat. Microsurg. Soc., Soc. Am. Gastrointestinal Endoscopic Surgeons, Soc. Surgery of Alementry Tract, Am. Coll. Sports Medicine, Conn. Med. Soc., Norwalk Med. Soc., Fairfield County Med. Soc., Phi Beta Kappa. Office: Surg Assocs PC Willow Rd # 125 Weston CT 06883-2534

MEINKE, PETER, writer, retired educator; b. Bklyn., Dec. 29, 1932; s. Harry Frederick Meinke and Kathleen Dorothy (McDonald) Lewis; m. Jeanne Clark, Dec. 14, 1957; children: Perrie Sue, Peter Thomas, Gretchen, Timothy Clark. AB, Hamilton Coll., 1955; MA, U. Mich., 1961; PhD, U. Minn., 1965. Tchr. Mountain Lakes (N.J.) High Sch., 1958-60; instr. Hamline U., St. Paul, 1961-66; prof. literature, dir. writing Eckerd Coll., St. Petersburg, Fla., 1966-93; writer-in-residence Hamline U., St. Paul, 1974, George Washington U., Washington, 1981-82, Thurber House, Columbus, Ohio, 1987, Davidson (N.C.) Coll., 1989, Austin Peay State U., Clarksville, Tenn., 1995; writer-in-residence, vis. disting. writer U. Hawaii, 1993; vis. disting. writer U. N.C., Greensboro, 1996, Nat. Writer's Voice Project, Tampa, Fla., 1996. Author: Night Watch on the Chesapeake, 1987, The Piano Tuner, 1986 (Flannery O'Connor award for short fiction 1986), Trying to Surprise God, 1981, The Rat Poems, 1978, The Night Train and the Golden Bird, 1977, Underneath the Lantern, 1986, Liquid Paper: New and Selected Poems, 1991, Far From Home, 1987, Scars, 1996, Campocorto, 1996. With U.S. Army, 1955-57. Recipient Gustav Davidson award, 1976, Lucille Medwick award, 1984, Robert A. Staub Outstanding Tchr. award Eckerd Coll., 1990, Emily Dickinson award, 1992, Paumanok Poetry award, 1993; creative writing fellow Nat. Endowment for Arts, 1974, 89; named Fulbright Sr. Lectr., U. Warsaw, 1978-79; Master Artists's fellowship, 1995. Mem. PEN, Poetry Soc. Am., Nat. Book Critics Circle. Avocations: sports, music. Home: 147 Wildwood Ln SE Saint Petersburg FL 33705-3222

MEINKE, ROY WALTER, electrical engineer, consultant; b. Cleve., Aug. 7, 1929; s. George F. and Marie (Reyer) M. BS, Miami U., Oxford, Ohio, 1952; postgrad. Ohio State U., 1952-53, 67-68; postgrad. in engring. Columbia Pacific U., 1985—. Asst. instr. dept. math. Ohio State U., Columbus, 1953; tchr. high sch., Edgerton, Ohio, 1953-54, Kingman, Ariz., 1954-56; aerodynamics engr. N.Am. Aviation, Los Angeles, 1956-57; instr. physics dept. Central State Coll., Edmond, Okla., 1957-58; elec. engr. Boeing Co., Seattle, 1958-62, Huntsville, Ala., 1962-74; mem. staff engring. mgmt. Lockheed Corp., Houston, 1974-88; ind. lectr., cons. on aerospace dynamic system, 1988—. Co-pilot Mercy Flight Systems, 1973-74; treas. Houston United Campus Christian Life Com., 1983; dir. S.E. Conf. Chs., 1969-73; rep. Tex. Conf. Chs., 1989-93; judge Harris County Optimists Club Youth Scholarship Fund, 1983-85. Recipient Apollo Achievement award NASA, 1970, Group Achievement awards, 1979, 82, 83; recipient Phase III Pilot Proficiency Wings Dept. Transp., 1982, Awareness Cert. of Appreciation, NASA, 1987. Mem. IEEE (sr.), AIAA (assoc. fellow 1991), AAAS. Mem. United Ch. of Christ. Home: 10212 Longmont Houston TX 77042

MEINWALD, JERROLD, chemist, educator; b. Bklyn., Jan. 16, 1927; s. Herman and Sophie (Baskind) M.; m. Yvonne Chu, June 25, 1955 (div. 1979); children: Constance Chu, Pamela Joan; m. Charlotte Greenspan, Sept. 7, 1980; 1 child, Julia Eve. PhB, U. Chgo., 1947, BS, 1948; MA, Harvard, 1950, PhD, 1952; Ph.D., U. Göteborg, 1989. Mem. faculty Cornell U., 1952-72, 73—, Goldwin Smith prof. chemistry, 1980—, mem. sci. directing group Cornell Inst. Rsch. chem. ecology, 1992—; research dir. Internat. Centre Insect Physiology and Ecology, Nairobi, 1970-77; A. Mellon Term prof., 1992-95; prof. chemistry U. Calif. at San Diego, 1972-73; chem. cons. Schering-Plough Rsch. Inst., 1957—, Procter & Gamble Pharms., 1958-95, Cambridge Neurosci. Rsch., 1988-92; vis. prof. Rockefeller U., 1970, Harvard Med. Sch., 1997; Camille and Henry Dreyfus Disting. scholar Mt. Holyoke Coll., 1981, Bryn Mawr Coll., 1983; Kolthoff lectr. U. Minn., 1985; Beckman lectr. Calif. Inst. Tech., 1986; Swiss "Troisième Cycle" Lectr., 1986; Russell Marker lectr. Pa. State U., 1987; mem. vis. com. chemistry Brookhaven Nat. Lab., 1969-72, chmn., 1972; mem. med. A chemistry study sect. NIH, 1963-67, chmn., 1965-67; mem. adv. bd. Petroleum Rsch. Found., 1971-73; mem. adv. coun. chemistry dept. Princeton U., 1978-83 ; mem. adv. bd. Rsch. Corp., 1978-83; mem. adv. bd. chemistry div. NSF, 1979-83; organizing chmn. Sino-Am. Symposium on Chemistry of Natural Products, Shanghai, 1980; mem. adv. bd. A.P. Sloan Found., 1985-91; Frontiers of Rsch. lectr. Coun. Chem. Rsch., 1987; mem. sci. adv. bd. Agridyne Corp., 1989-93; adv. com. chem. ecology Max-Planck Soc., 1994-96; Carlton Coll. Convocation, 1993; Mary Aldrige lectr., American U., 1993; K. Pfister lectr. MIT, 1992, Hilldale lectr. U. Wis., 1991, Nat. Undergrad. Rsch. Symposium, Plenary lectr., Mpls., 1992; UNOCAL lectr. Calif. State U., Long Beach, 1992; Max T. Rogers lectr. Mich. State U., 1994; Jean Day lectr. Rutgers U., 1994, Max T. Rogers lectr., Mich. State U., 1994, Disting. Grad. Sch. lectr. U. Md., 1994. Merck lectr. Lafayette Coll.; plenary lectr. 3rd Pan Am. Chem. Congress; Inaugural Paul G. Gassman lectr. Canisius Coll., 1996, Disting. Sci. Lectr. Bard Coll., 1996, others. Mem. bd. editors Jour. Organic Chemistry, 1962-66, Organic Reactions, 1968-78, Organic Synthesis, 1968-72, Jour. Chem. Ecology, 1974—, Insect Sci., 1979-90; contbr. articles to profl. jours. Recipient Tyler Environ. Achievement prize U. So. Calif., 1990, Gustavus J. Esselen award for Chemistry in the Pub. Interest, 1991, Heyrovsky medal Acad. Scis. of the Czech Rep., 1996, Pioneer's award Am. Inst. Chemistry, 1997; Sloan fellow, 1958-62, Guggenheim fellow,, 1960-61, 76-77, spl. postdoctoral fellow NIH, 1967-68, fellow Japan Soc. Promotion of Sci., 1983, Ctr. for Advanced Study in Behavioral Sci., 1990-91; Fogarty internat. scholar NIH, 1983-85; Bert L. and Natalie K. Vallee Found., Inc. fellow, 1997. Mem. NAS (exch. scholar 1987), AAAS, Am. Acad. Arts and Scis., Am. Philos. Soc., Am. Chem. Soc. (chmn. organic divsn. 1969, E Guenther award 1985, Disting. Scientist award Kalamazoo sect. 1985, A.C. Cope Scholar award 1989), Internat. Soc. Chem. Ecology (pres. 1988, Silver medal 1991), Phi Beta Kappa, Sigma Xi (nat. lectr. 1965, 75, 92-94). Office: Cornell U Dept Chemistry Baker Lab Ithaca NY 14853-1301

MEIROVITCH, LEONARD, engineering educator; b. Maxut, Romania, Nov. 28, 1928; came to U.S., 1956, naturalized, 1964; s. Carol and Adelle (Schoenfeld) M.; m. Jo Anne Reifer, Oct. 15, 1960. BSc summa cum laude, Technion-Israel Inst. Tech., 1953; MS in Engring., UCLA, 1957, PhD, 1960. Structural engr. Water Planning for Israel, Tel Aviv, 1953-55; asst. sect. head Water Planning for Israel, 1955-56; asst. research engr., asso. in engring. UCLA, 1956-60; staff engr. IBM, Endicott, N.Y., 1960-62; asso. prof. Ariz. State U., 1962-66; prof. U. Cin., 1967-71, Va. Poly. Inst. and State U., Blacksburg, 1971-79; Reynolds Metals prof. Va. Poly. Inst. and State U., 1979-83, Univ. disting. prof., 1983—; cons. Goodyear Aerospace, Phoenix, 1962-63; cons. C.S. Draper Labs., Cambridge, Mass., 1976-78, Naval Research Lab., Washington, 1977-79, Intelsat, Washington, 1980-82. Author: Analytical Methods in Vibrations, 1967, Methods of Analytical Dynamics, 1970, Elements of Vibration Analysis, 1975, 2d edit., 1986, Computational Methods in Structural Dynamics, 1980, Introduction to Dynamics and Control, 1985, Dynamics and Control of Structures, 1990, Principles and Techniques of Vibrations, 1997, also articles; assoc. editor Jour. Spacecraft and Rockets, 1971-76, Jour. Optimization Theory and Applications, 1984—; mem. internat. editorial bd. Jour. European Mechanics, 1977-93. Served with Israeli Army, 1948-49. Recipient Alumni award for rsch. excellence Va. Poly. Inst. and State U., 1981, Japan Soc. Mech. Engrs. medal, 1989, Alexander von Humboldt Sr. Rsch. award Germany, 1991; Am. Soc. Engring. Edn.-NASA fellow, 1964; NAS sr. rsch. assoc. Langley Rsch. Ctr., Hampton, Va., 1966-67. Fellow AIAA (Structures, Structural Dynamics and Materials award 1983, Pendray Aerospace Lit. award 1984, Mechanics and Control of Flight award 1987); mem. Sigma Xi, Tau Beta Pi. Home: 303 Neil St Blacksburg VA 24060-2542

MEIROWITZ, CLAIRE CECILE, public relations executive; b. Frankfurt, Fed. Republic Germany, Jan. 14, 1934; came to U.S., 1939; d. Karl and Margot (Herrmann) Bier; m. Richard Meirowitz, Sept. 12, 1954 (div., July, 1969); children: Diane, Laura, Linda; m. Joseph Spiegel, Apr. 20, 1975. AA, Nassau Community Coll., 1971; BA magna cum laude, Hofstra U., 1976; postgrad., N.Y. Inst. Tech., 1987-90. Pres., owner, editor, writer Profl. Editing Svcs., Babylon, N.Y., 1972-76, 92—; editorial asst. United Technical Publs., Garden City, N.Y., 1976-77; publs. assoc. N.Y. Inst. Tech., Old Westbury, N.Y., 1977-79; asst. dir. coll. rels., dir. publs. SUNY, Old Westbury, 1979-87, dir. of community rels. and publs., 1987-92; pres. SUNY Coun. for Univ. Affairs and Devel., 1987-89; cons. Guarino Graphics, Greenville, N.Y., 1985-92, editor, copywriter, 1986-92. Manuscript editor Jour. of Collective Negotiations in Pub. Sector, 1972-91, editr., 1991—, Jour. of Individual Employment Rights, 1992—; editor art catalog South Afgca/South Bronx, 1981 (art excellence award 1982); author: New Student Prospectus, The College at Old Westbury, 1979, Labor-Management Relations Among Government Workers, 1983; co-editor: Strategies for Impasse Resolution, 1992; editor Alzheimer's Assn. L.I. chpt. newsletter; contbr. articles to profl. jours. v.p., treas., sec., Taxpayers Edn. Assn., Hicksville, N.Y., 1962-68; mem. The Nature Conservancy, Cold Spring Harbor, N.Y., 1980—; tutor Lit. Vols. Am. Suffolk County Chpt., 1996—; newsletter editor Babylon Breast Cancer Coalition, 1997—. Recipient Excellence in Profl. Svc. award SUNY at Albany, 1987, Disting. Svc. award SUNY Coun. Univ. Affairs, 1989, award for excellence in communications SUNY Westbury Alumni Assn., 1992, award for disting. leadership L.I. Women's Coun. for Equal Edn., Employment and Tng., 1992. Mem. L.I. Communicators Assn., Internat. Assn. of Bus. Communicators (steering com. L.I. womens coun. 1990—), Babylon Village Womens Club. Democrat. Jewish. Avocation: computers. Home: 167 Cadman Ave Babylon NY 11702-1607

MEIS, PAUL JEAN, obstetrics and gynecology educator; b. Sioux City, Iowa, Oct. 29, 1934; s. Lee Francis and Dorothy (Trexlar) M.; m. Marcia Rose Donsker, June 28, 1958; children: Steven James, Douglas John. BS, U. Iowa, 1956, MD, 1959. Diplomate Am. Bd. Ob-Gyn., Am. Bd. Maternal-Fetal Medicine. Intern Martin Army Hosp., Ft. Benning, Ga., 1959-60; resident ob/gyn. SUNY Upstate Med. Ctr., Syracuse, 1962-65; pvt. practice, La Crosse, Wis., 1965-75; fellow Harbor Gen. Hosp., Torrance, Calif., 1975-77; asst. prof. dept. ob-gyn. Bowman Gray Sch. Medicine Wake Forest U., Winston-Salem, N.C., 1977-80, assoc. prof., 1980-85, prof., 1985—. Capt. M.C., U.S. Army, 1959-62. Office: Bowman Gray Sch Medicine Dept Ob-Gyn Medical Center Blvd Winston Salem NC 27157*

MEISEL, ALAN, law educator; b. Newark, Dec. 24, 1946; s. Stanley and Beatrice (Katz) M.; m. Linda S. Serody, Mar. 6, 1982; children: Matthew, Julia. BA, Yale U., 1968, JD, 1972. Bar: Conn. 1972, Pa. 1973, U.S. Dist. Ct. Conn. 1972, U.S. Dist. Ct. (we. dist.) Pa. 1973, U.S. Ct. Appeals (3d cir.) 1985. Assoc. Goldstein & Peck, P.C., Bridgeport, Conn., 1972-73; prof. psychiatry U. Pitts., 1973—, prof. law, 1976—, Dickie, McCamey Chilcote prof. bioethics/law and psychiatry, 1995—, co-dir. Ctr. Med. Ethics, 1986-

91, dir., 1991—; asst. dir. for legal studies Pres.'s Commn. for Study of Ethical Problems in Medicine and Biomed. and Behavioral Rsch., Washington, 1982; mem. ethics working group Presdl. Task Force on Healthcare Reform, 1993. Author: The Right to Die, 1989, 2d edit., 1995; co-author: Informed Consent: A Study of Decision Making in Psychiatry, 1984, Informed Consent: Legal Theory and Clinical Practice, 1987; contbr. articles to legal and med. jours. Grantee NIMH, grantee Pres.'s Commn. for Study of Ethical Problems in Medicine and Biomed. and Behavioral Research, 1981-82, Founds. Fund for Research in Psychiatry grantee, 1979-82, Legal Services Corp. grantee, 1985-87; fellow Hastings Ctr.; award for The Right to Die Am. Assn. Publs., 1989. Office: U Pitts Sch Law Pittsburgh PA 15260

MEISEL, GEORGE VINCENT, lawyer; b. St. Louis, Sept. 24, 1933; s. Leo Otto and Margaret (Duggan) M.; m. Joy C. Cassin, May 18, 1963. B.S. summa cum laude, St. Louis U., 1956, J.D. cum laude, 1958. Bar: Mo. 1958. Assoc. Grand Peper & Martin, St. Louis, 1961-64; ptnr. Grand Peper & Martin, 1965; jr. ptnr. Bryan Cave McPheeters & McRoberts, St. Louis, 1966-69; ptnr. Bryan Cave, St. Louis, 1970—. Served to 1st lt. USAF, 1958-61. Mem. ABA, Bar Assn. Met. St. Louis, Mo. Bar Assn. Roman Catholic. Clubs: Saint Louis, Mo. Athletic (St. Louis). Home: 2029 S Warson Rd Saint Louis MO 63124-1151

MEISEL, JEROME, electrical engineer; b. Cleve., Aug. 9, 1934; s. David and Anne Irene (Meisel) Marmorstein; children: Denise Lauren, David Marc. B.S. in Elec. Engring. (Union Carbide scholar), Case Inst. Tech., 1956, Ph.D., 1961; M.S. (Mpls. Honeywell fellow), MIT, 1957. Asst. prof. elec. engring. Case Inst. Tech., 1960-65; mem. tech. staff Bell Telephone Labs., Holmdel, N.J., 1965-66; mem. faculty Wayne State U., Detroit, 1966—; prof. elec. engring. Wayne State U., 1970—, acting chmn. dept., 1985-87; cons. in field. Author: Principles of Electromechanical Energy Conversion, 1966; also articles. Sr. mem. IEEE. Home: 156 Linden Rd Birmingham MI 48009-1609 Office: Wayne State U Dept Elect Engring Detroit MI 48202

MEISEL, JOHN, political scientist; b. Vienna, Austria, Oct. 23, 1923; s. Fryda and Ann M. BA, U. Toronto, 1948, MA, 1950; PhD in Polit. Sci., London Sch. Econs., 1959; LLD (hon.), Brock U., 1983, U. Guelph, 1985, Carleton U., 1990, U. Toronto, 1993, Queen's U., 1996; DU (hon.), U. Ottawa, 1983; D of Social Scis., Laval U., 1988. Head dept. polit. studies Queen's U., Kingston, Ont., Can., 1963-67, Hardy prof. polit. sci., 1963-80; Sir Edward Peacock prof. polit. sci. emeritus Queen's U.; former chmn. Can. Radio-TV and Telecomms. Commn.; moderator symposia on finding common grounds for polit. issues confronting Yugoslavia, UN, Vienna, 1995. Author: The Canadian General Election of 1957, 1962, Papers on the 1962 Election, 1964, Ethnic Relations in Canadian Voluntary Associations, 1972, Working Papers on Canadian Politics, 1975; editor: Internat. Polit. Sci. Rev., 1979-95, (with Jean Laponce) Debating the Constitution/Débat sur la constitution, 1994. Decorated officer Order of Can.; recipient Killam award Can Coun., 1968-73. Fellow Royal Soc. Can. (pres. 1992-95). Home: Colimaison, Tichborne, ON Canada K0H 2V0 Office: Queen's U, Kingston, ON Canada K7L 3N6

MEISEL, LOUIS KOENIG, art dealer, art historian, writer; b. N.Y.C., Sept. 4, 1942; s. Sidney and Grace Elizabeth (Moak) M.; m. Susan Helene Pear, Mar. 26, 1966; 1 child, Ari Ron. Student, Columbia U., 1963, New Sch. for social Rsch., N.Y.C., 1964; BA, Tulane U., 1964. Pres. Eminent Publs., N.Y.C., 1964-78; owner Meisel Gallery, N.Y.C., 1967-72; pres. Louis K. Meisel Gallery, N.Y.C., 1973—; ptnr. Susan P. Meisel Gallery, N.Y.C., 1983—, Meisel Real Estate, N.Y.C., 1988—. Author: Photorealism, 1980, Richard Estes, 1988, Clarice Cliff, 1988, Charles Bell, 1991, Photorealism Since 1980, 1993, The Great American Pin-up, 1996. 2d lt. USAR, 1964-70. Mem. Internat. Soc. Appraisers, Appraiser Assn. Am., Maidstone Club (Easthampton). Jewish. Office: Gallery 141 Prince St New York NY 10012-5315

MEISEL, MARTIN, English and comparative literature educator; b. N.Y.C., Mar. 22, 1931; s. Joseph and Sally (Rössler) Mörsel; m. Martha Sarah Winkley, Dec. 22, 1957; children—Maude Frances, Andrew Avram, Joseph Stoddard. A.B., Queens Coll., 1952; M.A., Princeton U., 1957, Ph.D., 1960; postgrad., U. Rome, 1959. Instr. English Rutgers U., New Brunswick, N.J., 1957-58; instr., asst. prof., assoc. prof. Dartmouth Coll., Hanover, N.H., 1959-65; prof. English U. Wis., Madison, 1965-68; prof. English and comparative lit. Columbia U., N.Y.C., 1968—, Brander Matthews prof. dramatic lit., 1987—, chmn. dept., 1980-83, acting v.p. arts and scis., 1986-87, v.p. arts and scis., 1989-93; trustee Columbia U. Press, 1990-94. Author: Shaw and the 19th Century Theater, 1963, Realizations: Narrative, Pictorial, and Theatrical Arts in 19th Century England (George Freedley Meml. award Theater Libr. Assn. 1984, Barnard Hewitt award Am. Theatre Assn. 1984), 1983; mem. editorial and adv. bds. Jour. Victorian Studies, PMLA, Jour. Contemporary Lit., Bull. Rsch. in the Humanities, 19th Century Contexts. Served with U.S. Army, 1954-56. Fellow Guggenheim Found., 1963-64, 1987-88, Am. Council of Learned Socs., 1970-71, Inst. for Advanced Studies in the Humanities, Edinburgh, 1977, Huntington Library and Art Gallery, 1978, 80, 83, Nat. Humanities Ctr., 1983-84, Wilson Ctr., Smithsonian Instn., 1987-88. Mem. MLA, Acad. Lit. Studies, Am. Soc. Theatre Rsch. Home: 18 Bacon Hill Rd Pleasantville NY 10570-3502 Office: Columbia U 611 Philosophy Hall New York NY 10027

MEISEL, PERRY, English educator; b. Shreveport, La., Jan. 26, 1949; s. I.S. and Rebecca (Abramson) M. BA, Yale U., 1970, MPhil, 1973, PhD, 1975. Asst. prof. English NYU, N.Y.C., 1975-81, assoc. prof. English, 1981-87, prof. English, 1987—. Author: Thomas Hardy, 1972, The Absent Father, 1980, The Myth of the Modern, 1987, The Cowboy and the Dandy, 1997; co-editor: Bloomsbury/Freud, 1985; editor: Freud, 1981. Mem. MLA, AAUP, PEN. Office: NYU Dept English 19 University Pl New York NY 10003-4556

MEISEL, STEVEN, advertising photographer; b. 1954; s. Lenny and Sally. Student, Parsons Sch. Design. Illustrator Women's Wear Daily; advt. photographer The Gap, Revlon, Valentino, Anne Klein, Calvin Klein, Gianfranco Ferré, Prada, Dolce and Gabbana, Lancome, Barney's, Donna Karan, Versace, Alberta Ferretti, Anna Sui, Max Mara, Clinique; photographer Madonna's Sex, 1992; free-lance photographer Vogue, Harper's Bazaar. Recipient Spl. award Photography Coun. Fashion Designers Am., 1992, Internat. Fashion Photography award Festival Internat. de la Photo de Mode, 1994. Office: Steven Meisel Studio 64 Wooster St Fl 4 New York NY 10012-4350

MEISELAS, SUSAN CLAY, photographer; b. Balt., June 21, 1948; d. Leonard and Murrayl (Groh) M. BA, Sarah Lawrence Coll., 1970; EdM, Harvard U., 1971; DFA (hon.), Parsons Sch./New Sch., N.Y.C., 1988, Art Inst. of Boston, 1996. Photographic cons. Community Resources Inst., N.Y.C., 1972-74; artist-in-residence S.C. Arts Commn., 1974-75; photography tchr. New Sch., N.Y.C., 1975; free-lance photographer Magnum Photos, N.Y.C., 1976—, v.p., 1986-91. Author: Carnival Strippers, 1976, Nicaragua, 1981; co-editor: El Salvador, 1983; editor: Chile from Within, 1991; editor Learn to See, 1974; co-dir.: (film) Living at Risk, 1985, Pictures from a Revolution, 1991, Kurdistan: In the Shadow of History, 1997. Recipient Robert Capa gold medal Overseas Press Club, 1979, Leica award of excellence New Sch., 1981, Photojournalist of Yr. award Am. Soc. Mag. Photographers, 1981, award Nat Endowment for Arts, 1987, Hasselblad Found., 1994, Maria Moors Cabot prize Columbia U., 1994; MacArthur fellow, 1992. Office: Magnum Photos Inc 151 W 25th St New York NY 10001-7204

MEISELS, GERHARD GEORGE, academic administrator, chemist, educator; b. Vienna, May 11, 1931; came to U.S., 1951, naturalized, 1961; s. Leo and Adele Josefa Maria (Seehofer) M.; m. Sylvia Claire Knopsnider, June 28, 1958; 1 dau., Laura Germaine. Student, U. Vienna, 1949-51, 52-53; MA, U. Notre Dame, Ind., 1952, PhD, 1956. Postdoctoral rsch. assoc. U. Notre Dame, 1955-56; chemist Gulf Oil Corp., Pitts., 1956-59; part-time instr. Carnegie Inst. Tech., Pitts., 1956-58; chemist nuclear divsn. Union Carbide Corp., Tuxedo, N.Y., 1959-63; asst. group leader Union Carbide Corp., 1964-65; assoc. prof. U. Houston, 1965-70, prof., 1970-75, dept. chmn., 1973-75; prof., chmn. dept. chemistry U. Nebr., Lincoln, 1975-81, dean Coll. Arts and Scis., 1981-88; provost, COO U. South Fla., Tampa, 1988-94; dir. Coalition Sci. Literacy, 1994—, Suncoast Area Ctr. for Ednl. Enhancement (SACEE), 1996—; cons. Union Carbide Corp., Gearhart-Owen Industries. Editor (spl. issue) Jour. Radiation Physics and Chemistry, 1980; contbr. writings in field to profl. publs. Sec., pres. Ramsey (N.J.) Jr. C. of C., 1959-64; active All Children's Hosp. Rsch. Bd. Fulbright fellow, Smith-Mundt fellow, 1951-52; sr. fellow Sci. Rsch. Coun., Eng., 1976. Mem. Am. Chem. Soc. (com. chmn.), Am. Soc. for Mass Spectrometry (charter, com. chmn., v.p. 1984-86, pres. 1986-88, bd. dirs. 1988-90), Nebr. Acad. Scis., AAAS, Am. Phys. Soc., Coun. Sci. Soc. Pres. (exec. bd. 1989-92, chmn. elect 1990, chmn. 1991, chmn. com. on sci. priorities), Coun. for Chem. Rsch. (bd. dirs. 1982-85), Confirmation Judges Assn. Fla. (pres. 1996—), Houston Kennel Club (bd. dirs. 1968-70), Cornhusker Kennel Club (pres., bd. dirs., del. to Am. Kennel Club 1976-81), St. Petersburg Dog Fanciers Assn. (sec. 1996—), Sigma Xi. Home: 870 3rd Ave S Tierra Verde FL 33715-2223 Office: U South Fla 100 5th Ave S Saint Petersburg FL 33701-5010

MEISEN, AXEL, chemical engineering educator, university dean; b. Hamburg, Germany, Oct. 17, 1943; came to Can., 1966; s. Paul and Emmi (Schaaf) M.; children: Nadine Ramona, Kai Noel. B.Sc., Imperial Coll., 1965; M.Sc., Calif. Inst. Tech., 1966; Ph.D., McGill U., 1970. Registered profl. engr., B.C. Asst. prof. chem. engring. U. B.C., Vancouver, 1969-74, assoc. prof., 1975-79, assoc. dean, 1976-85, prof., 1979—, dean, 1985—; environ. engr. Imperial Oil Enterprise Ltd., Sarnia, Ont., 1974-75. Contbr. articles to profl. jours. Chmn. Can. Engring. Accreditation Bd., 1989-90. Fellow Chem. Inst. Can., Instn. Engrs. Ireland, Can. Acad. Engring.; mem. Can. Soc. Chem. Engrs. (pres. 1994), Assn. Profl. Engrs. B.C., Vancouver Club. Office: U BC Office of Dean, 2006-2324 Main Mall, Vancouver, BC Canada V6T 1Z4

MEISINGER, HENRY PETER, electronics engineer; b. N.Y., Mar. 24, 1921; s. Henry Paul and Sophie (Denenberg) M.; m. Jeanne Alma Van Horn, June 1940 (dec. Aug. 1961); children: Shannon Peter, Daniel Claude, Mark Colin; m. Catherine C. Stephenson, Oct. 1962; 1 child, Mary Cover; m. Susan Barney Cushing, June 25, 1969. Registered profl. engr., D.C. Chief engr. U.S. Recording Co., Washington, 1940-41; engr. radio station WINX, Washington, 1940-42; engr. Recording Lab. Libr. Congress, Washington, 1941-42; engr. in charge Radio Sect. Dept. Interior, Washington, 1942-47; chief engr. U.S. Recording Co., Washington, 1947-54; dir. engr. Lab. Elec. Engring., Washington, 1954-58; pres. Versitron Inc., Washington, 1958-85; pres. elec. group Keene Corp., N.Y.C., 1982-85; cons. engr. Vienna, Va., 1985—; dir. NationsBank D.C., 1984-94; adv. Nat. Security Agy., Ft. Meade. Contbr articles to profl. jours. Pres. Cen. H.S. Alumni Assn., 1976-77. Capt. USMC, 1943-46, PTO, 1950-52, Korea. Fellow Audio Engring. Soc. (chmn. 1974-76); mem. IEEE (sr.), Inst. Radio Engrs. (sr.; chmn. 1952-54, Disting. Svc. award 1962), Wash. Audio Soc. (pres. 1949-50), Ind. Telephone Pioneers (pres. 1973-74). Achievements include pioneer work in fiber optics, loudspeaker system design, and microgroove disk recording. Home and Office: 8618 Wolftrap Rd Vienna VA 22182-5025

MEISLICH, HERBERT, chemistry educator emeritus; b. Bklyn., Mar. 26, 1920; s. Isidore and Bessie (Rose) M.; m. Estelle Kalechstein, July 1, 1951; children—Mindy, Debrah, Susan. A.B., Bklyn. Coll., 1940; A.M., Columbia U., 1947, Ph.D., 1950. With Edgewood Arsenal, Md., 1942-44; asst. prof. chemistry CCNY, 1946-62, assoc. prof., 1963-68, prof., 1969-86, prof. emeritus, 1986—. Author: Introduction to Organic Chemistry, 1960, Fundamentals of Chemistry, 1966, 5th edit., 1980, Introduction to Chemistry, 1968, Schaum's Organic Chemistry, 1977, 2d edit., 1991, Schaum's 3000 Solved Problems in Organic Chemistry, 1993. Mem. New Milford (N.J.) Bd. Edn., 1967-81. Served to lt. (j.g.) USN, 1944-46. Sloan Kettering fellow, 1956. Mem. Am. Chem. Soc. (past chmn. N.Y. sect., councilor). Home: 338 Lacey Dr New Milford NJ 07646-1128 Office: CUNY Dept Chemistry Convent Ave and 138th St New York NY 10027

MEISNER, GARY WAYNE, landscape architect; b. Terre Haute, Ind., Oct. 19, 1949; s. Ervin Gustav and Mary Lou (Maret) M.; children: Christopher Wayne, Kira Valora. BS in Landscape Architecture, Mich. State U., 1972. Lic. landscape architect, Ohio, Mich., Ind., Ill., Ky., W.Va. Designer Huron Clinton Metro Parks, Detroit, 1969, City of East Lansing, Mich., 1970, Fairfax County Park Authority, Annandale, Va., 1971; city design adminstr. Akron (Ohio) Dept. Planning and Urban Devel., 1972-79; prin. Bentley Meisner Assocs., Inc, Cin., 1979-94, Myers, Schmalenberger, Meisner Inc., Cin. and Columbus, Ohio, 1994—. Designer Akron Downtown Plan, 1978, King Sch. Plan, 1980 (honor award 1982), master plan Toyota Regional Office, 1983 (honor award 1987), Falls at Cumberland Hill, 1987 (honor award 1989), Cin. Mus. Ctr., 1990 (honor award 1990), Walk Across Am. Garden, 1990 (honor award 1991), Dayton Nat. Cemetery, 1993 (honor award 1994), Piatt Park on Garfield Place, 1990 (honor award OPWA grand award 1992), Dayton Plaza of Flight (honor award 1995), Taylor Park Historic Riverwalk, 1995 (gov.'s award 1996). Trustee Cin. Hillside Trust, 1987—, Capitol Square Renovation Found., Columbus, Ohio, 1987-93, Cin. Sculpture Coun., 1989-94, Hubbard Ednl. Trust, 1988—. Recipient gov.'s commendation State of Ohio, 1985, Ohio Arts Coun. fellow, 1992-93, Apple award Architecture Found. of Cin., 1995. Fellow Am. Soc. Landscape Architects (nat. trustee 1982-89, chmn. nat. cmty. assistance team program 1983-86, chmn. editorial bd. Garden Design mag. 1986-90, mem. nat. publs. bd. 1988-92, 96—, Nat. Com. Assistance Team commendation 1986, Trustee commendation 1989); mem. Am. Soc. Botanic Garden and Arboretum, Urban Land Inst., Am. Underground Space Assn (treas. Scenic Ohio 1985—). Mem. Unity Ch. Home: 4137 Jora Ln Cincinnati OH 45209-1406 Office: Myers Schmalenberger Meisner Inc 2043 Madison Rd Cincinnati OH 45208-3218

MEISNER, JUDITH ANNE, clinical social worker, marital and sex therapist, psychotherapist; b. Dayton, Ohio, Mar. 20, 1931; d. Lowell DeWight and Mary Elizabeth (Anderson) Richardson; m. S. Clair Varner, 1953 (div. 1964); m. Carl E. Meisner, Dec. 31, 1970; children: Christopher, Cynthia, Deborah, Catherine; stepchildren: Janet, Elizabeth, Barbara. BA, Oberlin Coll., 1952; MSW, Fla. State U., 1970; PhD, Inst. Advanced Study Human Sexuality, 1987. Cert. Acad. Cert. Social Workers; bd. cert. diplomate; lic. clin. social worker; lic. marriage and family therapist; diplomate Am. Bd. Sexology, Am. Coll. Sexologists, clin. supr. Am. Bd. Sexology. Psychiat. aide Inst. Living, Hartford, Conn., 1952-53; caseworker, supr. Div. Family Svcs., Dept. Health and Rehabilitative Svcs., St. Petersburg, Fla., 1964-66, 66-68; dir. standing com. on health and rehabilitative svcs. Fla. Ho. Reps., Fla. State Legis., Tallahassee, 1970-72; adj. prof. grad. sch. social work Fla. State U., Tallahassee, 1972-73; family life cons. Family Counseling Ctr., St. Petersburg, 1973-75; coord. Teenage Info. Program for Students Pinellas County Sch. Bd., St. Petersburg, 1975-78, coord. Citizen's Task Force on Edn. for Family Living, 1978-80; psychotherapist Counseling & Cons. Svcs., St. Petersburg, 1975—; profl. adv. bd. Nat. Found. March of Dimes Pinellas chpt., Clearwater, Fla., 1976-85, Parents Without Ptnrs. chpt. 186, St. Petersburg, 1973—; mem. Family Life Edn. Coun. Pinellas County Sch. Bd., Clearwater, 1980-85. Bd. dirs. Neighborly Sr. Svcs., Clearwater, 1974-85, pres., bd. dirs., 1982, 83; bd. dirs. Marriage and Family Counseling of Pinellas County, Inc., 1993—. Fellow Am. Acad. Clin. Sexologists (life); mem. NASW, Am. Assn. for Marriage and Family Therapists (clin.), Pinellas Assn. for Marriage and Family Therapists (clin.), Am. Assn. Sex. Educators, Counselors and Therapists (life, cert. sex educator, sex therapist), Soc. for the Sci. Study of Sex, Fla. Soc. Clin. Social Workers, Soc. of Neuro-Linguistic Programming (cert. master practitioner), Harry Benjamin Internat. Gender Dysphoria Assn., Fla. Soc. of Clin. Hypnosis. Avocations: tennis, travel, jazz, singing, reading. Home: 7 Marina Ter Treasure Is FL 33706-1203

MEISSNER, DORIS, federal commissioner; b. Nov. 3, 1941; d. Fred and Hertha H. (Tromp) Borst; m. Charles F. Meissner, June 8, 1963 (dec.); children: Christine M., Andrew D. BA, U. Wis., 1963, MA, 1969. Asst. dir. student fin. aid U. Wis., 1964-68; exec. dir. Nat. Women's Polit. Caucus, 1971-73; asst. dir. office policy and planning U.S. Dept. Justice, 1975, exec. dir. cabinet com. illegal aliens, 1976, dep. assoc. atty. gen., 1977-80, acting commr. immigration and naturalization svc., 1981, exec. assoc. commr. immigration and naturalization svc., 1982-86; sr. assoc., dir. immigration policy project The Carnegie Endowment for Internat. Peace, 1986-93; commr. immigration and naturalization svc., 1993; adv. coun. U.S./Mex. project Overseas Devel. Coun., 1981-86; trustee Refugee Policy Group, 1987-93; adv. bd. Program for Rsch. on Immigration Policy Rand Corp./Urban inst., 1988-92; cons. panel to comptroller gen. GAO, 1989-93; with Coun. Fgn. Rels., 1990—, Washington Office Latin Am., 1989-93. White Ho. fellow, 1973-74. Mem. Nat. Women's Polit. Caucus (nat. adv. bd. 1976—), White House Fellows Alumni Assn. and Found. (sec., exec. com. 1979-82, Assn. Governing Bds. Colls. and Univs. (panel higher edn. issues 1990-92), Phi Kappa Phi, Mortar Board, Alpha Chi Omega. Office: US Dept Justice Immigration & Naturalization Svc 425 I St NW Rm 7100 Washington DC 20536-0001

MEISSNER, DOROTHY THERESA, reading specialist; b. Jersey City, N.J., Apr. 20, 1932; d. John and Mary (Garofalo) Biondo; m. Carl Frederick Meissner; children: Kathleen Ann, Mary Gretl. BA summa cum laude, Jersey City State Coll., 1970, MA summa cum laude, 1974. Cert. tchr. of reading, reading specialist, supr. and adminstr. Metallographer Engelhard Industries, Newark, N.J., 1953-61; 2nd grade tchr. Rutherford (N.J.) Bd. Edn., 1970-74, 4th grade tchr., 1974, reading specialist, 1974-94, 94—; instr. Fairleigh Dickinson U., Rutherford, 1977; spl. edn. steering com. Kearny (N.J.) Pub. Schs., 1968-69; G&T adv. coun. Rutherford Pub. Schs., 1978-79; v.p. Union Fin. Chain, Rutherford, 1985-89, pres., 1989-92; adj. prof. reading dept. Jersey City State Coll. Contbr. articles to profl. jours.; designer sculpture; artist charcoal drawing (hon. mention 1987). Lector Roman Cath. Ch., Kearny, 1988—; coord. William Carlos Williams Project, Rutherford, 1984. Recipient Gov.'s Tchr.'s Recognition State of N.J., 1987, Mary G. Filosa reading tchr. of yr. award N.J. Reading Tchrs. Assn., 1996-97; seminar grantee N.J. Coun. for Humanities, 1995. Mem. Internat. Reading Assn. (program chair 1992-93, v.p. 1994-95, pres. 1995—, rec. sec. North Jersey coun. 1996—), N.J. Reading Assn. (tchr. of yr. 1996-97, hospitality chair for conf.), Women's Coll. Club, Phi Delta Kappa, Kappa Delta Pi. Avocations: reading, tennis, gardening, art, theater. Home: PO Box 355 Kearny NJ 07032-0355

MEISSNER, EDWIN BENJAMIN, JR., real estate broker; b. St. Louis, Dec. 27, 1918; s. Edwin B. and Edna R. (Rice) M.; m. Nina Renard, Dec. 17, 1946; children: Edwin Benjamin III, Wallace, Robert, Donald. B.S., U. Pa., 1940. Joined St. Louis Car Co., 1934, asst. to pres., v.p., exec. v.p., 1950-56, pres., gen. mgr., 1956-61; pres. St. Louis Car div. Gen. Steel Industries, Inc., 1961-67; sr. v.p., dir. Gen. Steel Industries, Inc., 1968-74; v.p. Bakewell Corp., 1974-85; real estate broker, v.p. Hilliker Corp., St. Louis, 1985-96; dir. First Ill. Bank. Mem. pres.' coun. St. Louis U.; bd. dirs. Washington U. Med. Ctr. Redevel. Corp., Barnard Free Skin and Cancer Hosp.; past bd. dirs. James S. McDonnell USO; trustee, bd. dirs. Washington U. Task Force; com., bd. dirs. St. Louis Symphony Youth Orch.; outreach com. St. Louis Symphony Soc.; hon. dir. Humane Soc. Mo.; v.p. Gateway Ctr. Met. St. Louis; chmn. Ladue (Mo.) Police and Fire Commn.; mem. Jefferson Nat. Expansion Meml. Commn.; mil. affairs com. Regional Commerce. Mem. St. Louis Flood Assn. (dir.), Am. Ordnance Assn. (life), Internat. Assn. Chiefs of Police (assoc.), Mo. Assn. Chiefs of Police, Mo. Athletics Club, Westwood Country Club, Bridlespur Hunt Club, St. Louis Club, Beta Gamma Sigma. Home: 40 Roan Ln Saint Louis MO 63124-1480 Office: 509 Olive St Ste 608 Saint Louis MO 63101-1855

MEISSNER, SUZANNE BANKS, pastoral associate; b. Flint, Mich., July 12, 1943; d. Leon J. and Eunice Alberta (Conners) Banks; m. Edward J. Meissner, Aug. 20, 1966 (div. Sept. 1975). BA, North Park Coll., 1965; MA, Ea. Mich. U., 1979; M in Pastoral Studies, Loyola U., New Orleans, 1991. Cert. secondary educator, spiritual dir., Hypnotist, Mich. Tchr. Flint (Mich.) Cmty. Schs., 1965-94; pastoral assoc. St. Michael Ch., Flint, 1985—; listening ministries adv. bd. Diocese of Lansing, Mich., 1994—, co-chair Profl. Pastoral Mins. Assn., 1994—, chair diocesan pastoral coun., 1986-88. Mem. Internat. Assn. Counselors & Therapists, Phi Kappa Phi, Phi Delta Kappa. Democrat. Avocations: theatre, opera, travel. Home: 7217 N Mckinley Rd Flushing MI 48433-9046 Office: Saint Michael Church 609 E 5th Ave Flint MI 48503-1503

MEISSNER, WILLIAM WALTER, psychiatrist, clergyman; b. Buffalo, Feb. 13, 1931; s. William Walter and Mary Emma (Glauber) M. BA, St. Louis U., 1956, PhL, 1957, MA, 1957; STL, Woodstock Coll., 1962; MD, Harvard U., 1967. Diplomate Am. Bd. Psychiatry and Neurology, Bd. Psychoanalysis. Entered S.J., 1951; intern Mt. Auburn Hosp., Cambridge, Mass., 1967-68; resident Mass. Mental Health Ctr., Boston, 1968-71; mem., instr. Boston Psychoanalytic Inst., 1971—, tng. and supervising analyst, 1980—; staff psychiatrist Mass. Mental Health Ctr., 1971-87, Cambridge (Mass.) Hosp., 1971-78; asst. clin. prof. psychiatry Harvard U. Med. Sch., 1973-76, assoc. clin. prof., 1976-81, clin. prof. psychiatry, 1981-87; prof. psychoanalysis Boston Coll., 1987—. Author: Annotated Bibliography in Religion and Psychology, 1961, Group Dynamics in the Religious Life, 1965, Foundations for a Psychology of Grace, 1966, The Assault on Authority-Dialogue or Dilemma, 1971, Basic Concepts in Psychoanalytic Psychiatry, 1973, The Paranoid Process, 1978, Internationalization in Psychoanalysis, 1981, The Borderline Spectrum, 1984, Psychoanalysis and Religious Experience, 1984, Psychotherapy and the Paranoid Process, 1986, Life and Faith: Psychoanalytic Perspectives on Religious Experience, 1987, Treatment of Patients in the Borderline Spectrum, 1988, What is Effective in Psychoanalytic Therapy, 1991, Ignatius of Loyola: The Psychology of a Saint, 1992, Thy Kingdom Come: Psychoanalytic Perspectives on the Messiah and the Millenium, 1995, The Therapeutic Alliance, 1996; mem. editl. bd. Psychoanalytic Inquiry, 1983—, Jour. Geriatric Psychiatry, 1980—, Rev. of Psychoanalytic Books, 1980-84, Psychoanalytic Study of Society, 1981—, Theol. Studies, 1981-91, Dynamic Psychotherapy, 1982-89, Internat. Forum for Psychoanalysis, 1983—, Internat. Jour. Psychoanalytic Psychotherapy, 1984—, Psychoanalytic Edn., 1990—, Bull. of Menninger Clinic, 1985—, Jour. Am. Psychoanalytic Assn., 1995—, Psychoanalysis and Psychotherapy, 1989—, Internat. Series in Psychology of Religion, 1990—, Am. Jour. Psychotherapy, 1993—. Recipient Deutsch prize Boston Psychoanalytic Inst., 1969. Fellow Am. Psychiat. Assn. (task force on treatments of psychiat. disorders 1989, Oskar Pfister award 1989), Mass. Psychiat. Soc., Ctr. for Advancement Psychoanalytic Studies; mem. Am. Psychoanalytic Assn. (councilor-at-large 1980-84), Internat. Psycho-Analytical Assn., Boston Psychoanalytic Inst., Am. Psychotherapy Seminar Ctr. (mem. prof. adv. com. 1991—), Sigma Chi, Psi Chi. Office: Boston College Carney Hall 420 D Chestnut Hill MA 02167-3806

MEISTAS, MARY THERESE, endocrinologist, diabetes researcher; b. Grand Rapids, Mich., July 22, 1949; d. Frank Peter and Anne Therese (Karsokas) M. MD, U. Mich., 1975. Diplomate Am. Bd. Internal Medicine, Am. Bd. Endocrinology. Intern, then resident in internal medicine Cleve. Clinic Hosp., 1975-78, endocrinology fellow, 1978-79; fellow in pediatric endocrinology Johns Hopkins Hosp., Balt., 1979-81; diabetes researcher Joslin Diabetes Ctr., Boston, 1981-86; assoc. in medicine Brigham and Women's Hosp., Boston, 1981-86; asst. in medicine, diabetes researcher Mass. Gen. Hosp., Boston, 1986-92; staff endocrinologist Emerson Hosp., Concord, Mass., 1989—. Mem. ACP, Am. Diabetes Assn., Am. Fedn. Clin. Research, Endocrine Soc. Office: Emerson Hosp 747 Main St Ste 111 Concord MA 01742-3302

MEISTER, BERNARD JOHN, chemical engineer; b. Maynard, Mass., Feb. 27, 1941; s. Benjamin C. M. and Gertrude M. (Meister); m. Janet M. White, Dec. 31, 1971; children: Mark, Martin, Kay Ellen. B.S. in Chem. Engring., Worcester Poly. Inst., 1962; Ph.D. in Chem. Engring., Cornell U., 1966. Engring. researcher Dow Chem. Co., Midland, Mich., 1966—, sr. rsch. specialist, 1978-81, assoc. scientist, 1981-85, sr. assoc. scientist, 1985-92, rsch. scientist, 1992—. Contbr. articles to profl. jours. Mem. Am. Inst. Chem. Engrs., Am. Chem. Soc., Soc. Plastics Engrs., Soc. Rheology, Sigma Xi. Mem. Ch. of Nazarene. Home: 2925 Chippewa Ln Midland MI 48640-4181 Office: Dow Chem Co 438 Bldg Midland MI 48667 *Free the mind of things you can't change, and let it focus on things you can accomplish.*

MEISTER, DORIS POWERS, investment management executive; b. Ames, Iowa, Sept. 12, 1954; d. James Phillip and Doris (Goess) P.; m. Gilbert Meister Jr., Oct. 18, 1980. AB, Smith Coll., 1976; MBA, U. Chgo., 1979. Mgr. currency Harris Trust & Savs. Bank, Chgo., 1976-78; sr. engagement mgr. McKinsey & Co. Inc., N.Y.C., London, 1979-84; dir., dept. head portfolio strategies dept., adminstrv. mgr. fixed income rsch. group C S First Boston, N.Y.C., 1984-90; exec. v.p., COO Christie, Manson & Woods Internat. Inc., N.Y.C., 1990-94; mng. dir. Copley Real Estate Advisors,

Boston, 1994—. Bd. dirs. Arts Connection, 1990, Am. Women's Econ. Devel. Corp., 1994. Named one of "Top 40 under 40" Execs., Crain's N.Y., 1992. Mem. Fin. Women's Assn., Com. of 200, Women's Forum. Episcopalian. Office: Copley Real Estate Advisors 399 Boylston St Boston MA 02116-3305

MEISTER, MARK JAY, museum director, professional society administrator; b. Balt., June 26, 1953; s. Michael Aaron and Yetta (Haransky) M.; m. Carla Steiger, Aug. 7, 1977; children: Rachel, Kaitlin. AB, Washington U., St. Louis, 1974; MA, U. Minn., 1976; cert. mus. mgmt., U. Calif., Berkeley, 1983. Asst. lectr. St. Louis Art Mus., 1974; asst. coord. young people's program Mpls. Inst. Arts, 1975-76, coord. mobile program, 1976, coord. tchrs. resource svcs., 1976-77; dir. Mus. Art and History, Port Huron, Mich., 1978-79, Midwest Mus. Am. Art, Elkhart, Ind., 1979-81; exec. dir. Children's Mus., St. Paul, 1981-86; dir. Mus. Art, Sci. and Industry, Bridgeport, Conn., 1986-89; exec. dir. Archaeol. Inst. of Am., Boston, 1989—; adj. lectr. museology Kenyon Coll., Gambier, Ohio, 1977; adj. lectr. art history Ind. U., South Bend, 1980-81; regional reviewer Inst. Mus. Svcs., Washington, 1985-86, 89; treas., vice chmn. Minn. Assn. Mus., St. Paul, 1983-86; ex-officio trustee U.S. com. Internat. Coun. on Monuments and Sites, 1995—. Bd. dirs. Seaway Arts Coun., St. Clair County, Mich., 1978-79; mem. Mayor's Arts Adv. Com., Elkhart, 1981; mem. projects with industry bus. adv. coun. Goodwill Industries of Southwestern Conn., 1988-89; mem. exec. com., Conf. Adminstrv. Officers, Am. Coun. Learned Socs., 1994-97. NEH museology fellow, Mpls. Inst. Arts, 1976-77, Kress fellow U. Minn. 1977-78, Bush leadership summer fellow, Bush Found., St. Paul, 1983; named One of Outstanding Young Men Am., 1981. Mem. Am. Assn. Mus., Am. Coun. Learned Socs., Conf. Adminstrv. Officers, Am. Soc. Assn. Execs., Soc. for Am. Archaeology, Archeol. Inst. of Am. Office: Archaeol Inst of Am 656 Beacon St Boston MA 02215-2006

MEISTER, STEVEN GERARD, cardiologist, educator; b. Boston, Sept. 13, 1937; s. Harry and Edith (Segal) M.; m. Carol Anne Ross, Jan. 28, 1966; children: Laura Ilise, Elizabeth Lee. BA, Bowdoin Coll., 1958; MD, Tufts U., 1962. Diplomate: Am. Bd. Internal Medicine. Intern in medicine Ind. U. Med. Center, Indpls., 1962-63; asst. resident in medicine Boston VA Hosp., 1965-66, resident in medicine, 1966-67; research fellow in medicine Boston City Hosp., 1967-68, Peter Bent Brigham Hosp., Boston, 1968-70; research fellow in cardiology Tufts U., 1967-68, Harvard U., 1968-70; practice medicine specializing in cardiology Phila., 1970—; dir. cardiac catheterization lab. Med. Coll. Pa. and Hosp., 1973-79, acting dir. div. cardiology, 1978-79, dir. div. cardiology, 1979—; asst. prof. medicine U. Pa., Phila., 1970-73; asso. prof. medicine Med. Coll. Pa. and Hosp., 1973-78, prof., 1978—; cons. cardiology VA hosps. Contbr. numerous articles on cardiology to profl. jours. Mem. Oversight Com. for Cardiac Catheterization. Capt. U.S. Army, 1963-65. Fellow ACP, Am. Coll. Cardiology; mem. Am. Fedn. Clin. Rsch., Am. Heart Assn. (Upper Atlantic rsch. com. 1977-79), Phila. Acad. Cardiology (v.p. 1988-89, pres. 1989-90).

MEITES, SAMUEL, clinical chemist, educator; b. St. Joseph, Mo., Jan. 3, 1921; s. Benjamin and Frieda (Kaminsky) M.; m. Lois Pauline Maranville, Mar. 11, 1945; 1 child, David Russell. AS, St. Joseph Jr. Coll., 1940; AB, U. Mo., 1942; PhD, Ohio State U., 1950. Diplomate Am. Bd. Clin. Chemistry. Clin. biochemist VA Hosp., Poplar Bluff, Mo., 1950-52, Toledo Hosp., 1953-54, Children's Hosp., Columbus, Ohio, 1954-91; prof. dept. pediatrics Ohio State U. Coll. Medicine, Columbus, 1972-91, prof. emeritus, 1991—, prof. dept. pathology, 1974-91; cons. Brown Labs., Columbus, 1968-83, VA, Chillicothe, Ohio, 1980-84. Co-author: Manual of Practical Micro and General Procedures in Clinical Chemistry, 1962. Editor: Standard Methods of Clinical Chemistry, Vol. 5, 1965; Pediatric Clinical Chemistry, 1st edit., 1977, 2d edit., 1981, 3rd edit., 1989; co-editor: Selected Methods for the Small Clinical Chemistry Laboratory, 1982, Biography of Otto Folin, 1989; assoc. editor Geriatric Clin. Chemistry, 1994. Contbr. articles to profl. jours. Recipient Manitoba Soc. Clin. Chemists award, 1992, Johnson & Johnson award Nat. Acad. Clin. Biochemistry, 1996. Served to 1st lt. U.S. Army, 1942-46. Fellow AAAS; mem. Am. Chem. Soc., Am. Assn. Clin. Chemistry (sec. 1975-77, Bernard Katchman award Ohio Valley sect. 1971, Fisher award 1981, Miles-Ames award, 1990. chmn. com. on archives, 1982-86, history divsn., 1992—). Democrat. Jewish. Avocations: gardening, history of clinical chemistry. Office: Childrens Hosp 700 Childrens Dr Columbus OH 43205-2664

MEITNER, PAMELA, lawyer, educator; b. Phila., Aug. 23, 1950; d. Alfred Victor Meitner and Claire Jane (Carroll) Harmer; m. William Bruce Larson, Sept. 13, 1980; 1 child, William Bruce, Jr. BS in chem. engring., Drexel U., 1973; JD, Del. Law Sch., 1977. Bar: Del. 1977, U.S. Dist. Ct. Del. 1977, U.S. Patent and Trademark Office 1977. Engr. DuPont Co., Deepwater, N.J., 1973-77; lawyer DuPont Co., Wilmington, Del., 1977; prof. Del. Law Sch., Wilmington, 1985—. Commr. State Emergency Response Com., Dover, Del., 1986-90. Mem. Del. Bar Assn. Club: DuPont Country (Wilmington) (bd. govs. 1984-85). Home: 211 Welwyn Rd Wilmington DE 19803-2951 Office: DuPont Co Legal Dept 1007 Market St Wilmington DE 19801-1227

MEITZEN, MANFRED OTTO, religious studies educator; b. Houston, Dec. 12, 1930; s. Otto Hugo and Laura Emma (Munsch) M.; m. Fredrica Haden Kilmer, May 16, 1970. BA, Rice U., 1952; MDiv, Wartburg Sem., 1956; PhD, Harvard U., 1961. Assoc. prof. religious studies Rocky Mountain Coll., Billings, Mont., 1961-65; assoc. prof. religious studies, chmn. dept. W.Va. U., Morgantown, 1965-70, prof., chmn. religious studies, 1970—, prof. clin. psychiatry Med. Sch., 1991—, chmn. program humanities Coll. Arts and Scis., 1972-77, mem. senate, 1968-82, 84—; vis. scholar Christ Ch. Coll., Oxford (Eng.) U., 1973; columnist Morgantown Dominion-Post, 1975-76, 80-89. Contbr. articles to profl. jours. and chpts. to books. Harvard Div. Sch. scholar, 1957, fellow, 1958; Rockefeller fellow, 1959-60; Sheldon Traveling fellow, 1961; W.Va. U. Study grantee, 1970; recipient Outstanding Tchr. award W.Va. U., 1971-72, Coll. Arts & Scis., 1979-80, 87-88, Outstanding Educator Am. award, 1974-75, W.Va. Assocs. award, 1974-75, Golden Apple Tchg. award, 1995. Mem. Am. Guild Organists, Am. Acad. Religion, W.Va. Assn. for Humanities (pres. 1976-77), Harvard Alumni Assn., Univ. Profs. for Acad. Order (nat. 1st v.p. 1977-79, nat. pres. 1979, dir. 1974—, nat. sec.-treas. 1986-91), assoc. mem. Second Marine Divsn. Assn., Nat. Assn. Scholars, Am. Rifle Assn., Rice U. Alumni Assn., Harvard Found. for Advanced Study and Rsch., Delta Phi Alpha. Lutheran. Home: 119 Forest Dr Morgantown WV 26505-2323 *It is very important, particularly in our times, not to sell one's own ideas and convictions short in face of the increasing pressure in academe and throughout society to comply with standardized opinion on moral, political and social issues.*

MEITZLER, ALLEN HENRY, electrical engineering educator, automotive scientist; b. Allentown, Pa., Dec. 16, 1928; s. Herbert Henry and Estella Irene (Wagner) M.; m. Joan Catherine Egan, June 13, 1953; children: Thomas Joseph, Peter Michael, David Christopher. B.S., Muhlenberg Coll., Allentown, Pa., 1951; M.S., Lehigh U., 1953, Ph.D., 1955. Mem. tech. staff Bell Labs., Whippany and Murray Hill, N.J., 1955-72; prin. research scientist, research staff Ford Motor Co., Dearborn, Mich., 1972-96, elec. engring. educator, 1996—; adj. prof. U. Mich.-Dearborn. Patentee ultrasonic and ferroelectric devices, automotive electronic devices and systems. Prof. Wackernagel scholar, 1947-51; Hood grad. fellow, 1954-55. Fellow IEEE, Acoustical Soc. Am.; mem. Am. Phys. Soc., Soc. Automotive Engrs., Am. Ceramic Soc. Republican. Home: 3055 Foxcroft St Ann Arbor MI 48104-2827

MEIXSELL, BERRAE NEVIN (MIKE MEIXSELL), distribution executive; b. Palmerton, Pa., June 28, 1936; s. Earl Henry and Beatrice Ellen (Walk) M.; m. Hilda Elizabeth Landis, July 5, 1980; children: Berrae Jr., Tracy Young, Pamela Thomas, Gail Machella, Craig Horner, Michele Utterbach, Michael Meixsell. Diploma, Lehighton High Sch., 1954. Asst. mgr., then mgr. G.C. Murphy Co., 1952-64, W.T. Grant Co., 1964-67; mgr., buyer Norman Purchasing Corp., Silver Spring, Md., 1967-83; dir. purchasing Oscar Robbins Corp., Pitts., 1983-86; dist. sales mgr. Shakespeare Fishing Tackle Corp., Pitts., 1986-88; pres., CEO Nisito-Meixsell & Assocs., Ltd., Parker, Pa., 1988-96; pres., owner Mike Meixsell & Assocs., Parker, 1994—. Elected ofcl. Butler County, Butler, Pa., 1992-93. Recipient Eagle Scout award Boy Scouts Am., 1952, Silver award Boy Scouts Am., 1954, award of merit Am. Legion, 1950. Republican. Lutheran. Avocations: hunting, fishing. Home: RR 2 Box 311A Parker PA 16049-7908 Office: Mike Meixsell & Assoc RR #2 Box 311A Parker PA 16049

MEKEEL, ROBERT K., lawyer; b. Ossining, N.Y., Mar. 21, 1950; s. Ira III and Carmen E. (Munson) M.; m. Martha J. Keller, Sept. 29, 1979; 1 child, Meryl Fox. BA, Wesleyan U., Middletown, Conn., 1972; JD, U. Puget Sound, 1978. Bar: N.H. 1978, N.Y. 1979, U.S. Dist. Ct. (so. dist.) N.Y. 1980, U.S. Ct. Appeals (2d cir.) 1981, U.S. Dist. Ct. N.H. 1983, U.S. Ct. Appeals (1st cir.) 1983. Asst. dist. atty. Westchester County N.Y. Dist. Atty., White Plains, N.Y., 1979-82; assoc. Craig Wenners & McDowell, Manchester, N.H., 1983-84; clk. ct. Coos County Superior Ct., Lancaster, N.H., 1985; ptnr. McKible & Mekeel, P.A., Concord, N.H., 1986-89, Cullity Kelley & McDowell, Manchester, 1989-93, McDowell & Mekeel P.A., Manchester, 1994-96; pvt. practice, Concord, 1996—; mem. mentor program Franklin Pierce Law Sch., Concord, 1992; lectr. Nat. Bus. Inst., Eau Claire, Wis., 1993-95; mem. Million Dollar Advocates forum; mediator N.H. Superior Cts.; pvt. mediator, arbitrator disputes involving personal injury claims. Fellow N.H. Bar Found.; mem. ATLA, N.H. Trial Lawyers Assn. (amicus com. 1994-96), N.H. Bar Assn. (com. on cooperation with cts., lectr. evidence seminar 1994). Democrat. Avocations: running, biking, swimming, drawing, wood working. Home: 73 Main St Hopkinton NH 03229-2628 Office: Century Bldg 185 N Main St Concord NH 03301-5039

MEKENNEY, C. ROBERT, management analyst, tax accountant; b. Chester, Pa., Nov. 30, 1944; s. William Hatred and Alfreda Frances (Laskoski) M.; m. Susan Mary Szollosi, Sept. 2, 1977; children: Jonathan, Christopher. BS in Bus. Mgmt., Pa. State U., 1966. Cert. tax specialist. Pers. mgmt. specialist Drug Enforcement Adminstrn., Phila., 1972-74; regional pers. officer Drug Enforcement Adminstrn., Kansas City, Mo., 1974-76; pers. mgmt. specialist Drug Enforcement Adminstrn., Washington, 1976-78; employee benefits specialist U.S. Customs Svc., Washington, 1978-80, employee benefits officer, 1980-90, mgmt. analyst, 1990—, inst. orgnl. mgmt., 1978—; participant Citizen Amb. Program teaching acctg. to Russian businessmen. Exec. treas. Boy Scouts Am., Falls Church, Va., 1993—. Served with USN, 1967-71. Mem. Nat. Assn. Tax Practitioners, Nat. Soc. Pub. Accts., Internat. Assn. for Fin. Planning, Nat. Soc. Tax Profls. Roman Catholic. Avocations: cooking.

MEKLER, ARLEN B., lawyer, chemist; b. N.Y.C., May 4, 1943; s. Lev A. and Ethel (Fox) M.; children from previous marriage: Jeffrey Arlen, Rebecca Ann, Ann-Marie Laura, Victoria Arlene, Lamar Adam, Lars Arlen; m. Molly L. Malone, Feb. 3, 1995. B.S. in Chemistry, Reed Coll.-San Jose State U., 1953; M.S. in Organic Chemistry, Iowa State U., 1955; Ph.D., Ohio State U., 1958; J.D., Temple U., 1972. Bar: Del. 1972, Pa. 1972, U.S. Supreme Ct. 1976. Sr. rsch. chemist E.I. du Pont de Nemours & Co., Wilmington, Del., 1958-69; ptnr. Mekler and Maurer, Wilmington, 1972—; chief appellate div. Office Pub. Defender, State of Del., 1973-77; pres. Del. Law Ctr., Wilmington, 1973—; instr. constl. law Wilmington Coll., 1976-80; dir. Bar Rev. Del., 1972—; mem. 3d Circuit Ct. Appeal Jud. Nominating Commn., 1977-81, 3d Circuit Ct. Appeals Jud. Conf. Contbr. monographs to legal pubs. Pres. Mental Health Aux. for Gov. Bacon Health Ctr., 1964-66; mem. Citizens Conf. for Modernization of State Legislatures, 1964-68; state chmn., Reform Commn. for Modernization Polit. Party Rules, 1965-68; pres. Del. Citizens for Fair Housing, 1965-69; state commr. Nat. Conf. on Uniform State Laws, 1972—; pres. Democratic Forum Del., 1966-70; mem. Del. Dem. Platform Com., 1966, 68, 72, 76; research dir. Del. Citizens for Humphrey-Muskie, 1968, Citizens for Biden, 1972, 78, 84, Citizens for McDowell, 1986—, Biden for Pres., 1986—; del. Dem. Nat. Conv., 1980; mem. social action com. Unitarian Ch., Wilmington, 1962-68. Recipient Keyman award, 1964, 65; State Govtl. Affairs award, 1964, 65. Mem. ABA, Del. Bar Assn. (com. on rules of criminal procedure 1973-74, supreme ct. com. on revision of criminal law 1973—, supreme ct. com. on rules of evidence 1976—, com. on revised rules of evidence 1976—, com. on revised rules of Del. Supreme Ct. 1974—, family law com. 1979—, continuing legal edn. com. 1981—), Pa. Bar Assn., Am. Chem. Soc., N.Y. Acad. Scis., Chem. Soc. (London), AAAS, Catalyst Club Phila., Wilmington Organic Chemists Club, ACLU (bd. dirs.), Sigma Xi, Phi Alpha Delta. Home: Brandywine Hills 714 W Matson Run Pky Wilmington DE 19802-1912 Office: PO Box 2285 Wilmington DE 19899-2285

MELADY, THOMAS PATRICK, academic administrator, ambassador, author, public policy expert, educator; b. Norwich, Conn., Mar. 4, 1927; m. Margaret Judith Badum; children: Christina, Monica. BA, Duquesne U., 1950; MA, Cath. U. Am., 1952, PhD, 1954; hon. doctorates from 26 univs. Former mem. faculties Fordham and St. John's Univs.; founder Inst. African Affairs Duquesne U., 1957; cons. to founds., govts., corps., 1959-67; hon. doctorates from 27 univs. Africa Service Inst.; prof. Afro-Asian affairs, chmn. dept. Asian studies and NonWestern civilization Seton Hall U., South Orange, N.J., 1967-69, regent, 1987-90; prof. Afro-Asian affairs, dir. Office of Internat. Studies, 1973-74; exec. v.p., prof. politics St. Joseph's U., Phila., 1974-76; pres. Sacred Heart U., Fairfield, Conn., 1976-86, prof. polit. sci., 1976-86, pres. emeritus, 1986—; asst. sec. for postsecondary edn. U.S. Dept. Edn., Washington, 1981-82; amb. to Burundi, 1969-72, amb. to Uganda, 1972-73; sr. adviser to U.S. del. to 25 UN Gen. Assembly, 1970; chmn. Conn. Conf. Ind. Colls., 1979-81; pres., chief exec. officer Conn. Pub. Expenditures Coun., 1986-89; U.S. amb. to The Holy See, Vatican City, 1989-93, 94-95; exec. dir. Cath. Network of Vol. Svc., 1993-94; disting. vis. prof. George Washington U. and St. John's U., 1993-94; chmn. nat. com. Cath. Campaign for Am., 1994—; counsel Hayward Internat., 1994—. Author: Ambassadors Story: The United States and The Vatican in World Affairs, 1994, and 14 other books. Knighted by Pope Paul VI, 1968 and by Pope John Paul II, 1983, 91; honored by 5 countries; recipient Native Son award, Grand Cross, Order of Malta, 1993. Mem. Order of Malta, The Sacred Mil. Constantinian Order of St. George.

MELAMED, ARTHUR DOUGLAS, lawyer; b. Mpls., Dec. 3, 1945; s. Arthur Charles and Helen Beatrix (Rosenberg) M.: m. Carol Drescher Weisman, May 26, 1983; children: Kathryn Henrie, Elizabeth Allyn. B.A., Yale U., 1967; J.D., Harvard U., 1970. Bar: D.C. 1970, U.S. Ct. Internat. Trade 1985, U.S. Ct. Appeals (9th cir.) 1971, U.S. Ct. Appeals (2d cir.) 1975, U.S. Ct. Appeals (D.C. cir.) 1978, U.S. Ct. Appeals (8th cir.) 1981, U.S. Ct. Appeals (fed. cir.) 1985, U.S. Ct. Appeals (4th cir.) 1989, U.S. Ct. Appeals (10th cir.) 1993, U.S. Supreme Ct. 1981. Law clk. U.S. Ct. Appeals for 9th Circuit, 1970-71; assoc. Wilmer, Cutler & Pickering, Washington, 1971-77, ptnr., 1978-96; prin. dep. asst. atty. gen. antitrust divsn. U.S. Dept. Justice, 1996—; vis. prof. Georgetown U. Law Ctr., 1992-93, adj. prof., 1993-94. Contbr. articles to profl. jours. Class agt. Alumni Fund Yale U.; D.C. area chair Yale campaign, 1993—; mem. social scis. coun. com. Yale U., 1989-94; trustee Nat. Child Rsch. Ctr., 1990-93. Mem. ABA, D.C. Bar Assn., Am. Law Inst., Yale Club (N.Y.C.), Kenwood Country Club. Office: 2445 M St NW Washington DC 20037-1435

MELAMED, CAROL DRESCHER, lawyer; b. N.Y.C., July 12, 1946; d. Raymond A. and Ruth W. (Schwartz) Drescher; children: Stephanie Weisman, Deborah Weisman; m. Arthur Douglas Melamed, May 26, 1983; children: Kathryn, Elizabeth. AB, Brown U., 1967; MAT, Harvard U., 1969; JD, Catholic U. Am., 1974. Bar: Md. 1974, D.C. 1975, U.S. Ct. Appeals, (D.C. cir.) 1975, U.S. Dist. Ct. D.C. 1981, U.S. Supreme Ct. 1982. Tchr. English, Wellesley High Sch., Mass., 1968-69; law clk. U.S. Ct. Appeals, (D.C. cir.), Washington, 1974-75; assoc. Wilmer, Cutler & Pickering, Washington, 1975-79; dir. govt. affairs, assoc. counsel, The Washington Post, 1979-95, v.p. govt. affairs, 1995— . Mem. Phi Beta Kappa. Office: The Washington Post 1150 15th St NW Washington DC 20071-0001

MELAMED, LEO, investment company executive; b. Bialystok, Poland, Mar. 20, 1932; came to U.S., 1941, naturalized, 1950.; s. Isaac M. and Fayga (Barakin) M.; m. Betty Sattler, Dec. 26, 1953; children: Idelle Sharon, Jordan Norman, David Jeffrey. Student, U. Ill., 1950-52; JD, John Marshall Law Sch., Chgo., 1955. Bar: Ill. 1955. Sr. ptnr. Melamed, Kravitz & Verson, Chgo., 1956-66; chmn., CEO Sakura Dellsher, Inc., Chgo., 1965—; mem. Chgo. Merc. Exch., 1953—, mem. bd. govs., 1967-91, chmn. emeritus, 1991—, chmn. bd., 1969-71, 75-77, chmn. exec. com. 1985-91, also spl. counsel, apptd. sr. policy advisor, 1997; chmn. bd. Internat. Monetary Market, 1972-75, spl. counsel, 1976-91; mem. Chgo. Bd. Trade, 1969—; mem. corp. adv. bd. U. Ill., Chgo., 1991; mayor Chgo. Coun. Manpower and Econ. Advisors, 1972. Author: (sci. fiction novel) The Tenth Planet, 1987, Leo Melamed on the Markets, 1993, Escape to the Futures, 1996; editor: The Merits of Flexible Exchange Rates, 1989. Trustee John Marshall Law Sch., 1991; coun. mem. U.S. Holocaust Meml. Mus., dir. Named Man of Yr., Israel Bonds, 1975; recipient Am. Jewish Com. Human Rights medallion, 1991. Fellow Internat. Assn. Fin. Engrs. (sr.); mem. ABA, Am. Judicature Soc., Ill. Bar Assn., Chgo. Bar Assn., Nat. Bur. Econ. Rsch. (bd. dirs.), Econs. Club Chgo., Nat. Futures Assn. (chmn. 1982-89), Am. Contract Bridge League (life master), Union League Club, Chgo. Club, Standard Club. Avocations: writing, jogging. Office: Sakura Dellsher Inc 10 S Wacker Dr Chicago IL 60606-7407

MELAMID, ALEXANDER, artist; b. Moscow, July 14, 1945. Student, Stroganov Inst. Art and Design, Moscow, 1967. Ptnr. Komar & Melamid Studio, N.Y.C., 1965—; instr. visual art Moscow Regional Art Sch., 1968-76. Exhibitions include Wadsworth Atheneum, Hartford, Conn., 1978, Mus. Modern Art, Oxford, Eng., Mus. Decorative Art, Paris, 1985, Neuen Gesellschaft für Gildende Kunst, Berlin, 1988, Bklyn. Mus., 1990, Alternative Mus., N.Y.C., 1994, Storefrong for Art and Arch., N.Y.C., 1995, Ukraine State Mus., Kiev, 1995, Mus. Modern Art, Cologne, Germany, 1997; exhibited in group shows Met. Mus. Art, N.Y.C., 1982, 84, Chrysler Mus., Norfolk, Va., 1983, Sydney, 1986, Kassel, Germany, 1987, Solomon R. Guggenheim Found., 1987, FIAC, Paris, 1989, Bklyn. Mus., 1990; represented in permanent collections Whitney Mus. Am. Art, N.Y.C., Stedeliyk Mus., Amsterdam, The Netherlands, Guggenheim Mus., Mus. Modern Art, Met. Mus. Art; commns. include mural Unity, 1st Interstate Bank Bldg., L.A., 1993, murals Liberty as Justice, N.Y. Percent for Art Program, 1994. Grantee Nat. Endowment Arts, 1982.

MELANÇON, TUCKER LEE, judge; b. 1946. BS, La. State U., 1968; JD, Tulane U., 1973. Atty. Knoll & Knoll, 1973-75; pvt. practice Marksville, La., 1975-83; prin. Melancon & Rabalais, Marksville, 1984-94; judge U.S. Dist. Ct. (we. dist.) La., Monroe, 1994—; mem. adv. bd. Catalyst Old River Hydroelectric Partnership, Vidalia, La., 1989-92, La. Workers Compensation, 1990-91; mem. com. Study Backlog in Cts. of Appeal, 1st and 3d Cirs., 1991; bd. dirs. Catalyst Vidalia Corp., N.Y.C., 1993-94. Active La. Pub. Broadcasting. Mem. Am. Judicature Soc., Am. Inns of Ct., La. State Bar Assn., Bar Assn. 5th Fed. Cir., New Orleans Track Club. Office: US Dist Ct 705 Jefferson St Ste 303 Lafayette LA 70501-6936

MELANSON, SUSAN C., property manager; b. Boston, May 6, 1946; d. Arthur Wood and Marion (Saunders) Chapman; m. Arthur S. Melanson. AA, Colby-Sawyer Coll., 1966; BA, Hiram Coll., 1970. Founder, pres. Gem Island Software, Reading, Mass., 1985-90; dir. Gem Island Software, Carlisle, Mass., 1990-93; property mgr. Finard & Co., Burlington, Mass., 1993—; co-owner Washington Kennel; breeder, trainer, racer Siberian and Alaskan huskies. Class historian Wellesley High Class, 1964; leader, bd. dirs. Camp Fire, Reading, Antiquarian Soc., Reading, 1990-93; mem. steering com., officer Reading 350th Celebration, 1989-94. Mem. Soc. Property Mgmt. Profls., Omicron Beta. Avocations: genealogy, gardening, collecting Inuit art, running a sawmill, producing maple syrup. Office: Finard & Co 1 Monument Sq Ste 200 Portland ME 04101-4033

MELBINGER, MICHAEL S., lawyer; b. Chgo., Sept. 5, 1958; s. Donald G. and Joyce A. (Haynes) M.; m. Karen Mary Melbinger, June 16, 1984; children: Peter Donald, Charlotte Anna, Lucy Grace. BA, U. Notre Dame, 1980; JD, U. Ill., 1983. Bar: Ill. Assoc. McDermott, Will & Emery, Chgo., 1983-88, ptnr., 1989-93; ptnr., head employee benefits dept. Schiff, Hardin & Waite, Chgo., 1993—; author, speaker Coll. for Fin. Planning, Denver, 1990—. Mem. editorial bd. Taxation for Lawyers, N.Y.C., 1989—, Employee Benefits Counselor, 1993—, Pension Management, 1995—; contbr. articles to profl. jours.; author: Employee Benefit Trust Compliance Manual. Precinct capt. Regular Rep. Orgn., Cook County, Ill., 1985—. Mem. Union League Club. Home: 623 W Campbell St Arlington Heights IL 60005-1419 Office: Schiff Hardin & Waite 7200 Sears Tower Chicago IL 60606-6327

MELBY, EDWARD CARLOS, JR., veterinarian; b. Burlington, Vt., Aug. 10, 1929; s. Edward C. and Dorothy H. (Folsom) M.; m. Jean Day File, Aug. 15, 1953; children: Scott E., Susan J., Jeffrey T., Richard A. Student, U. Pa., 1948-50; D.V.M., Cornell U., 1954. Diplomate: Am. Coll. Lab. Animal Medicine. Practice veterinary medicine Middlebury, Vt., 1954-62; instr. lab. animal medicine Johns Hopkins U. Sch. Medicine, Balt., 1962-64; asst. prof. Johns Hopkins U. Sch. Medicine, 1964-66, assoc. prof., 1966-71, prof., dir. div. comparative medicine, 1971-74; prof. medicine, dean Coll. Vet. Medicine, Cornell U., Ithaca, N.Y., 1974-84; v.p. R & D SmithKline Beecham Animal Health, 1985-90, v.p. sci. and tech. assessment, 1990-91; ind. cons., 1992—; cons. VA, Nat. Research Council, NIH. Author: Handbook of Laboratory Animal Science, Vols. I, II, III, 1974-76. Served with USMC, 1946-48. Mem. Am., N.Y. State, Md., Pa. Veterinary Med. Assns., Am. Assn. Lab. Animal Sci., Am. Coll. Lab. Animal Medicine, AAAS, Phi Zeta. Home: PO Box 248 Charlotte VT 05445-0248 Office: 736 Lime Kiln Rd Charlotte VT 05445-9141

MELBY, JOHN B., composer, educator; b. Whitehall, Wis., Oct. 3, 1941; s. John B. Sr. and Margaret (Edmundson) M.; m. Carol A. Wurtz, July 7, 1961 (div. 1977); 1 child, John; m. Jane H. Thompson, June 15, 1978; children: Kirsten, Charles. MusB, Curtis Inst., 1966; MA, U. Pa., 1967; MFA, Princeton U., 1971, PhD, 1972. Assoc. prof. West Chester (Pa.) U., 1971-73; prof. music U. Ill., Urbana, 1973—; assoc. U. Ill. Ctr. for Advanced Studies, 1989-90. Composer numerous mus. works for live performers, computer-synthesized tape, vocal, chamber and orchestral music, works pub. by Am. Composers Edit., Merion Music Co., Margun Music, Inc.; recs. on Composers Recs., Inc., New World Records, Advance Records, Centaur Records, Zuma Records. Recipient 1st prize 7th Internat. Electroacoustic Music Awards, Bourges, France, 1979, Am. Acad./Inst. Arts and Letters award, 1984; Guggenheim fellow, 1983. Mem. BMI, Am. Composers Alliance. Democrat. Avocations: railroading, cooking, herpetology. Office: U Ill Sch Music 2136 Music Bldg 1114 W Nevada St Urbana IL 61801

MELBY, ORVILLE ERLING, retired banker; b. Butte, Mont., Oct. 9, 1921; s. Ole and Esther (Jacobsen) M.; m. Arvilla L. Underland, Nov. 24, 1956; children—Steve E., James E., Ann-Margaret. B.A. magna cum laude, U. Wash., 1949. C.P.A., Wash., Oreg. Treas. Boeing Co., 1956-66; sr. v.p. fin. Continental Airlines, Los Angeles, 1966; v.p. Bank of Am., San Francisco, 1967; treas. Bendix Corp., Detroit, 1968; v.p., treas. Vought Aeronautics, Dallas, 1969-70, Bonanza Internat., Dallas, 1971-74; vice chmn. Rainier Nat. Bank, Seattle, 1974-87; bd. dirs. Health Care Property Investors, Los Angeles. Served with USAAF, 1942-46. Mem. Fin. Execs. Inst., Phi Beta Kappa. Presbyterian. Club: Mason. Home: 9439 Lake Washington Blvd NE Bellevue WA 98004-5410

MELCHER, JERRY WILLIAM COOPER, clinical psychologist, army officer; b. Bloomington, Ill., Oct. 17, 1948; m. Margaret Frances Orban; children: Heather, Shawna, Jay. BS, Lincoln U., Jefferson City, Mo., 1975; MS, Tex. A&I U., 1976; PhD, Tex. A&M U., 1980. Psychometrist Lamar U., Beaumont, Tex., 1978-79, psychologist, 1979-81; commd. 1st lt. U.S. Army, 1981, advanced through grades to lt. col., 1987; clin. intern William Beaumont Army Med. Ctr., 1981-82; psychologist 1st Cav. Divsn., Fort Hood, Tex., 1982-84; chief psychology svc. Darnall Army Community Hosp., Fort Hood, 1984-85, Blanchfield Army Community Hosp., Fort Campbell, Ky., 1986-87; clin. psychologist, owner Area Counseling Assocs., Millington, Tenn., 1987—; clin. psychologist U.S. Army Res., Memphis, 1988-93; comdr. 1451st Combat Stress Detachment, Jackson, Miss., 1997—; clin. dir. Genesis Treatment Ctr., Memphis, 1990-94; v.p., psychol. dir. Life Time Resources, 1994-97; tng. coord. CETA, Beaumont, 1980-81; rsch. psychologist Operation Desert Storm, Fort Gordon, Ga., 1991. Bd. dirs. Family Aid Network, Killeen, Tex., 1984-85; vol. Rape Crisis Ctr., Beaumont, 1979. Decorated Bronze Star with valor device, Meritorious Svc. medal; Cross of Gallantry with palm (Vietnam). Mem. APA. Avocations: physical wellness, travel, gardening, computer games. Office: Area Counseling Assocs 8222 US Highway 51 N Millington TN 38053-1708

MELCHERT, JAMES FREDERICK, artist; b. New Bremen, Ohio, Dec. 2, 1930; s. John Charles and Hulda Lydia (Egli) M.; m. Mary Ann Hostetler, June 18, 1954; children: Christopher, David, Renee. A.B., Princeton U., 1952; M.F.A., U. Chgo., 1957; M.A., U. Calif., Berkeley, 1961. Prof. art U. Calif., Berkeley, 1965-76, 81-84, 88-92, prof. emeritus, 1992—; dir. Am.

Acad. in Rome, 1984-88; dir. Visual Arts Program, Nat. Endowment for Arts, Washington, 1977-81. Exhibited in one man shows at San Francisco Art Inst., 1970, San Francisco Mus. Modern Art, 1975, Holly Solomon Gallery, N.Y.C., 1991; group shows at Biennale de Paris, 1963, Whitney Mus., N.Y.C., 1966, 68, 70, Documenta 5, Kassel, Germany, 1972, Sydney (Australia) Biennal, 1976; commd. for Artwork (new Biology Bldg.) at MIT, 1993-94, Biomed. Rsch. Bldg. at Case Western Res. U., 1994. Recipient Adaline Kent award San Francisco Art Inst., 1970; Nat. Endowment for Arts artist fellow, 1973; hon. DFA, San Francisco Art Inst., 1984, Md. Inst. Coll. Arts, 1993. Home: 6077 Ocean View Dr Oakland CA 94618-1844

MELCONIAN, LINDA JEAN, state senator, lawyer; b. Springfield, Mass.; d. George and Virginia Elaine (Noble) Melconian. B.A., Mt. Holyoke Coll., 1970; M.A., George Washington U., 1976, J.D., 1978. Bar: Mass. Chief legis. asst. to Ho. of Reps. Speaker Thomas P. O'Neill, Jr., U.S. Congress, Washington, 1971-80; pros. atty. Hampden County Dist. Atty., Springfield, Mass., 1981-82; state senator Mass. Gen. Ct., Boston, 1983—; instr. Western New Eng. Coll., Springfield, 1978-82; Our Lady of the Elms Coll., Springfield, 1982-83. Chmn., Heart Fund Ball, Western Mass., 1983; incorporator Springfield Coll., 1982—; ex officio trustee Ella T. Grasso Found., Conn., 1982—; active Democratic State Com., Mass., 1983, Hampden County Dems. Recipient Appreciation award Vietnam Vets. of Greater Springfield, 1983; Equal Edn. for All Children award Bilingual Parents of Springfield, 1983; Appreciation award Vets.-Hampden County Council, 1984. Mem. Hampden County Bar Assn. Home: 257 Fort Pleasant Ave Springfield MA 01108-1521 Office: Mass State Senate Rm 213-B Boston MA 02133

MELCZEK, DALE J., bishop; b. Nov. 9, 1938. A.B., St. Mary Coll., Orchard Lake, Mich.; M.Div., St. John Sem., Plymouth, Mich.; M.A. in Edn., U. Detroit; postgrad., U. Notre Dame. Ordained priest Roman Cath. Ch., 1964, appointed aux. bishop, 1982. Assoc. pastor St. Sylvester Ch., Warren, Mich., 1964-70, co-pastor, 1970-72; pastor St. Christine Ch., Detroit, 1972-75; vicar West Detroit Vicariate, 1973-75; asst. vicar for parishes Archdiocese of Detroit, 1975-77, sec. to archbishop and vicar gen., 1977-82, archdiocesan consultor, 1972-83, aux. bishop, titular bishop of Trau, 1982-95; regional bishop Detroit N.W. Region, 1983-92; apostolic adminstr. Diocese of Gary, Ind., 1992-95; coadjutor Bishop of Gary Diocese of Gary, Ind., 1995-96; bishop of Gary Diocese of Gary, Ind., 1996—.

MELDMAN, CLIFFORD KAY, lawyer; b. Milw., July 27, 1931; s. Edward H. and Rose (Bortin) M.; children: Mindy, David, Linda, James, Noah. JD, Marquette U., 1956. Bar: Wis. 1956. Ptnr. Meldman & Meldman, Milw., 1956-73; pres. Meldman & Meldman S.C., Milw., 1973—. Contbr. articles to profl. jours., also editor. Fellow Am. Acad. Matrimonial Lawyers (pres. 1982); mem. Milw. Bar Assn. (bd. dirs. 1984-86, pres. 1986-87, chmn. family law sect.), Wis. Bar Assn. (chmn. family law sect.). Home: 170 W Cherokee Cir Milwaukee WI 53217-2716 Office: Meldman & Meldman SC PO Box 17397 Milwaukee WI 53217-0397

MELDMAN, ROBERT EDWARD, lawyer; b. Milw., Aug. 5; s. Louis Leo and Lillian (Gollusch) M.; m. Sandra Jane Setlick, July 24, 1960; children—Saree Beth, Richard Samuel. B.S., U. Wis., 1959; LL.B., Marquette U., 1962; LL.M. in Taxation, NYU, 1963. Bar: Wis. 1962, fla. 1987, colo. 1990, U.S. Ct. Fed. Claims, U.S. Tax Ct. 1963, U.S. Supreme Ct. 1970. Practice tax law Milw., 1963—; pres. Meldman, Case & Weine, Ltd., Milw., 1975-85; dir. tax div. Mulcahy & Wherry, S.C., Milw., 1985-90; shareholder Reinhart, Boerner, Van Deuren, Norris & Rieselbach, S.C., 1991—; adj. prof. taxation U. Wis., Milw., 1970—, mem. tax adv. coun., 1978—; sec. Profl. Inst. Tax Study, Inc., 1978—; bd. dirs. Wis. Bar Found., 1988-94; exec. in residence Deloitte & Touche Ctr. for Multistate Taxation, U. Wis., Milw., 1996—. Co-author: Federal Taxation Practice and Procedure, 1983, 86, 88, 92, Practical Tactics for Dealing with the IRS, 1994, A Practical Guide to U.S. Taxation of International Transactions, 1996; editor Jour. Property Taxation; mem. editorial bd. Tax Litigation Alert, 1995—; contbr. articles to legal jours. Recipient Adj. Taxation Faculty award UWM Tax Assn., 1987; named Outstanding Tax Profl. 1992 Corp. Reports Wis. Mag. and UWM Tax Assn. Fellow Am. Coll. Tax Coun.; mem. ABA, Fed. Bar Assn. (pres. Milw. chpt. 1966-67), Milw. Bar Assn. (chmn. tax sect. 1970-71), Wis. Bar Assn. (bd. dirs. tax sect. 1964-78, chmn. 1973-74), Internat. Bar Assn., The Law Assn. for Asia and the Pacific, Marquette U. Law Alumni Assn. (bd. dirs. 1972-77), Milw. Athletic Club, Wis. Club, Country Club of Wis., B'nai B'rith (trustee, Ralph Harris Meml. award Century Lodge 1969-70), Phi Delta Phi, Tau Epsilon Rho (chancellor Milw. chpt. 1969-71, supreme nat. chancellor 1975-76, v.p. Wis. chpt., tech. 1992—). Jewish (trustee congregation 1972-77). Home: 7455 N Skyline Ln Milwaukee WI 53217-3327 Office: 1000 N Water St Ste 2100 Milwaukee WI 53202-3197

MELDONIAN, SUSAN LUCY, elementary education educator; b. N.Y.C., Apr. 21, 1955; d. John Sarkis and Margaret (Avdoyan) M. BA in Elem. Edn., William Paterson Coll., Wayne, N.J., 1977, MEd in Reading, 1993. Cert. tchr. K-8, reading specialist, K-12, N.J. Basic skills tchr. K-4 Walter O. Krumbiegel Sch., Hillside, N.J., 1979; tchr. 1st grade Margaret L. Vetter Sch., Eatontown, N.J., 1979-88; tchr. 1st grade Cherry Hill Sch., River Edge, N.J., 1988-94, tchr. 3d grade, 1994—. Contbg. author: Moving Forward with Literature: Basals, Books and Beyond, 1993; contbr. articles to profl. jours. Mem. NEA, N.J. Edn. Assn., Internat. Reading Assn., Pi Lambda Theta. Mem. Armenian Apostolic Ch. Avocations: piano, singing, travel, bowling. Office: Cherry Hill Sch 410 Bogert Rd River Edge NJ 07661-1813

MELDRUM, DANIEL RICHARD, general surgeon, physician; b. Flint, Mich., Sept. 27, 1965; s. Richard Terrance and Patricia Ellen (Klug) M. BS, U. Mich., 1987; MD, Mich. State U., 1992. Teaching asst. dept. biochemistry U. Mich., Ann Arbor, 1986, rsch. asst., 1987-88; rsch. student fellow Mich. State U., East Lansing, 1989-92; resident surgery U. Colo., 1992—; capt. USAR, 1993—; advisor Mich. State U. Adv. Com., 1990-92; supr., adv. Biochemistry Teaching Assts., Ann Arbor, 1986; guest speaker 30 internat. and nat. confs. Contbr. more than 60 articles to profl. jours. Del. Am. Med. Student Assn.; coord. Mich. State U. Red Cross Med. Sch. Blood Drives, 1989-90. Recipient Young Investigator award The Shock Soc., 1992, Student Rsch. award Assn. Acad. Surgery, 1992, Moorhead Rsch. award Gramec Found., 1991, NIH Biomed. Rsch. grant 1989, 90, Excellence award Mich. State U., 1992, Nat. Rsch. Svc. award NIH, 1994-97, Ben Eiseman award, 1993, 95, Ack A. Barney award, 1995, Shock Young Investigator award, 1997. Mem. AMA, AAAS, N.Y. Acad. Scis., Shock Soc., Assn. Acad. Surgery, Am. Med. Student Assn. (pres. 1989-90), Am. Assn. Med. Colls. (rep.), Internat. Soc. for Heart Rsch., Alpha Omega Alpha. Achievements include work in ATP-MgCl2 restores macrophage and lymphocyte energetics and functions after shock; immunoprotective effects of calcium channel blockers after hemorrhage; the energetics of defective macrophage antigen presentation after hemorrhage; mechanisms of endogenous adaptation; cardial reconditioning; endotoxin tolerance; endogenous adaptation. Home: 870 Dexter St Apt 301 Denver CO 80220-4141 Office: U Colo Dept Surgery 4200 E 9th Ave Denver CO 80220-3706

MELDRUM, PETER DURKEE, venture capital/biotechnology company executive; b. Salt Lake City, June 26, 1947; s. Benjamin Nibley and Grace Natalie (Durkee) M.; m. Catherine Roper, June 16, 1970; children: Christopher Shawn. BS in Chem. Engring., U. Utah, 1970, MBA, 1974. Asst. to pres. Terra Tek, Inc., Salt Lake City, 1974-78; pres., chief exec. officer Resource Enterprises, Inc., Salt Lake City, 1978-81; pres., CEO, AgriDyne Techs., Salt Lake City, 1981-91, bd. dirs., 1979-93; pres., CEO, Founder's Fund Inc., 1991-95; pres., CEO Myriad Genetics Inc., Salt Lake City, 1992—; bd. dirs. Dairy Equipment Co. Utah, Salt Lake City, Paradigm Bioscis. Inc., Cognetix Inc., Vaxsys Corp., Alaxis, Inc. Vice chmn. fundraising Salt Lake Boy's Club, 1978-79; bd. dirs., vice chmn. ARC Golden Spike, Salt Lake City, 1980-90; mem. State of Utah Council Sci. and Tech., 1984-89; adv. bd. High Tech Mktg. Rev., Austin, Tex., 1986-88; mem. Gov.'s Task Force on Entrepreneurship; mem. rev. panel Utah Tech. Fin. Corp., Gov.'s Com. on Biomed. Industry, 1988-91; mem. bioengring. adv. bd. U. Utah, bus. adv. bd. Coll. Bus. Weber State U.; bd. arbitrators NASD, 1991—. Served to 1st lt. USAR, 1970-72. Mem. Utah Life Scis. Assn. (bd. dirs. 1995—), Tau Beta Pi, Phi Kappa Phi, Beta Gamma Sigma. Republican. Presbyterian. Avocations: skiing, backpacking, basketball, racquetball. Home: 1808 Mohawk Way Salt Lake City UT 84108-3363 Office: Myriad Genetics 320 Wakara Way Salt Lake City UT 84108-1214

MELE, ALFRED R., philosophy educator; b. Detroit, May 22, 1951; s. Alfred Emil and Rosemary (Pardo) M.; m. Constance, July 18, 1970; children: Al, Nick, Angela. BA, Wayne State U., 1973; PhD, U. Mich., 1979. Asst. prof. Philosophy Davidson (N.C.) Coll., 1979-85, assoc. prof., 1985-91, prof., 1991-95, Vail prof., 1995—. Author: Irrationality, 1987, Springs of Action, 1992, Autonomous Agents, 1995; contbr. articles to profl. jours. Fellow NEH, 1985-86, 92-93, Nat. Humanities Ctr., Rsch. Triangle Park, N.C., 1992-93. Mem. Am. Philos. Assn., So. Assn. Philosophy and Psychology, N.C. Philos. Soc. (pres. 1987-89). Avocations: racquetball, tennis. Office: Davidson Coll PO Box 1719 Davidson NC 28036-1719

MELEIS, AFAF IBRAHIM, nurse sociologist, educator, clinician, researcher; b. Alexandria, Egypt, Mar. 19, 1942; d. Abdel Baki Ibrahim and Soad Hussein Hassan; m. Mahmoud Meleis, Aug. 21, 1964; children: Waleed, Sherief. BS magna cum laude, U. Alexandria, 1961; MS, UCLA, 1964, MA, 1966, PhD, 1968; D of Pub. Svc. (hon.), U. Portland, 1989. Instr. U. Alexandria, 1961-62; acting instr. UCLA, 1966-68, asst. prof. nursing, then assoc. prof., 1968-75; assoc. prof., dean Health Inst., Kuwait, 1975-77; prof. nursing U. Calif., San Francisco, 1977—, also dir. Study Immigrant Health and Adjustment; vis. prof. colls. in Sweden, Brazil, Japan, Saudi Arabia, Kuwait, Egypt; 1st Centennial prof. Columbia U., N.Y.C., 1992-94; cons., speaker in field. author: theoretical Nursing: Development & Progress, 1985 (Book of Yr., am. Jour. Nursing, 1985), 2d edit., 1991; contbr. articles to rsch. and profl. jours. Recipient Helen Hahm award U. Calif. Sch. Nursing, San Francisco, 1981, Teaching awards U. Calif., San Francisco, 1981, 85, Pres. Hosni Mubarak medal of Excellence, 1990; Kellogg Internat. fellow, 1986-89. Fellow Am. Acad. Nursing; mem. Coun. Nurse Researchers, Western Soc. Research in Nursing, Am. Nurses Assn. Avocations: jogging, symphony, reading, international affairs, women's issues. Home: 39 Corte Ramon Greenbrae CA 94904-1228 Office: U Calif San Francisco Sch Nursing N511Y San Francisco CA 94143-0608

MELENDEZ, EDWIN MANUEL, orthopaedic hand surgeon; b. Rio Piedras, P.R., Jan. 2, 1958; s. Manuel and Olga (Martinez) M.; m. Mari Lopez, Feb. 23, 1985; children: Andre G., Gian-Franco, Stephan A. BS in Chemistry magna cum laude, U. P.R., 1978, MD, 1982, grad. in Orthop. Surgery, 1987. Diplomate Am. Bd. Orthopaedic Surgery, sub.-bd. Surgery of the Hand, also Nat. Bd. Med. Examiners. Gen. surgery intern U. P.R. Sch. Medicine, resident in orthopaedic and fracture surgery; fellowship in hand surgery Hosp. for Joint Diseases, Orthop. Inst., N.Y.C., 1988; pvt. practice hand and orthop. surgeon Tampa, Fla., 1991—; chmn. emergency/trauma liaison St. Joseph's Hosp., Tampa, 1996—. Contbr. articles to profl. jours. Maj. USAF, 1988-91. Fellow Am. Acad. Orthop. Surgeons; mem. Am. Assn. for Hand Surgery, Fla. Med. Assn., Fla. Hand Soc., Hillsborough County Med. Assn. Roman Catholic. Avocations: tennis, piano. Office: 4602 N Armenia Ave Ste D-3 Tampa FL 33603-2626

MELENDEZ, JOAQUIN, orthopedic assistant; b. San Gabriel, Calif., Aug. 16, 1929; s. Guadalupe and Gudelia (Maldonado) M.; m. Lola Hester Harris, Sept. 3, 1954. BS, Instituto del Estado, Chihuahua, Mex., 1949; AA, Foothill Coll., Los Altos Hill, Calif., 1973. Enlisted U.S. Army, 1950, advanced through grades to sgt. 1st class, ret., 1971; orthopedic asst. St. Vrain Valley Orthopedics (name now Longmont Orthopedics and Sports Medicine Clinic), Longmont, Colo., 1973—; tchr. pub. spkg. and Spanish for med. office use. Author: (poems) Saturday Night, 1990, Reflections, 1991, Freedom, 1992. With U.S. Army, 1950-71. Decorated Bronze Star with V, Meritorious Svc. medal with V; recipient marathon awards. Mem. Nat. Assn. Orthopedic Technologist, Colo. Acad. Physician Assts., Nat. Assn. Parlimentarians, Toastmasters Internat. (named Outstanding Divsn. Gov. 1988-89, Divsn. Gov. of Yr. 1995-96, Silver Level of Recognition 1995, recipient speech awards), Internat. Soc. Poets. Republican. Roman Catholic. Avocations: pub. speaking, writing, photography, running, hist. rsch. Home: 3331 Mountain View Ave Longmont CO 80503-2155 Office: Front Range Orthopedics 2030 Mountain View Ave Ste 200 Longmont CO 80501-3180

MELENDEZ, SARA E., non-profit organization executive; b. San Juan, P.R., Jan. 20, 1941; d. Pablo and Lucia (Espinosa) M.; 1 child, Adam. BA, Bklyn. Coll., 1967; MS, L.I. U., 1974; EdD, Harvard U., 1981. Tchr. N.Y.C. Bd. of Edn., Bklyn.; asst. prof. U. Hartford (Conn.), 1980-83; dir. Spl. Minority Initiatives Am. Coun. on Edn., Washington, 1983-89; vice provost, dean arts and humanities U. Bridgeport (Conn.), 1989-91; pres. Ctr. for Applied Linguistics, 1991-94, Independent Sector, Washington, 1994—. Author (book) Bilingual Education: A Sourcebook, 1987. Danforth fellow, Ford fellow. Mem. Soc. for Values in Higher Edn. (dir.). Office: Independent Sector 1828 L St NW Washington DC 20036-5104

MELENDY, DAVID RUSSELL, broadcast journalist; b. Corpus Christi, Tex., Oct. 19, 1948; s. Harold Orville and Marguerite Doris (Waller) M.; m. Lorna Sandra Katz, Mar. 19, 1972; children: Seth Howard, Andrew Scott. Student, George Washington U., 1966-70; BA magna cum laude, U. Hartford, 1972. News dir. Sta. WINY, Putnam, Conn., 1971-77; news anchor, reporter Sta. WPOP, Hartford, Conn., 1977-80; news dir. Sta. WNVR, Waterbury, Conn., 1980-81; news anchor Sta. WCBS-FM, N.Y.C., 1981; prodr., assignment editor, anchor, reporter AP Broadcast Svcs., Washington, 1981—; instr. journalism Briarwood Coll., Southington, Conn., 1977-81; mem. broadcast adv. com. Briarwood Coll., Southington, 1978-81. Prodr., writer, reporter (audio spl. report series) Star Wars: Strategic Defense Initiative, 1985, (daily audio feature) Flashback, 1986—. Publicity chmn. Woodstock (Conn.) Players Cmty. Theater, 1972-77; publicity chmn. Quinebaug Valley C.C. Found., Danielson, Conn., 1973-75, fundraising chmn., 1976; neighborhood coord. Am. Heart Assn., Washington, 1994; mem. Barker Found., Washington, 1983—. Mem. House and Senate Radio-TV Corr. Assn. Avocations: personal computers, photography, hiking, swimming. Office: AP Broadcast Svcs 1825 K St NW Washington DC 20006-1202

MELHORN, WILTON NEWTON, geosciences educator; b. Sistersville, W.Va., July 8, 1921; s. Ralph Wilton and Pauline (Jones) M.; m. Agnes Leigh Beck, Aug. 25, 1961; children—Kristina L., Kimberly M. B.S., Mich. State U., 1942, M.S., 1951; M.S., N.Y. U., 1943; Ph.D., U. Mich., 1955. Hydrogeologist Mich. Geol. Survey, Lansing, 1946-49; hydrologist U.S. Weather Bur., Indpls., 1949-50; asst., then asso. prof. engring. geology Purdue U., Lafayette, Ind., 1954-70; head dept. geoscis. Purdue U., 1967-70, prof., 1970-91, prof. emeritus, 1991—; vis. prof. U. Ill. at Urbana, 1960-61, U. Nev., Reno, 1971-72, adj. prof., 1973-82; geol. cons. Cook County Hwy Commn., Chgo., 1955-56, Martin-Marietta Corp., Balt., 1964-66, Calif. Nuclear, Inc., Lafayette, 1966-68. Editor 3 books; contbr. articles to tech. jours. Served to maj. USAAF, 1942-46. Fellow Geol. Soc. Am., AAAS, Ind. Acad. Scis. (pres. 1988, exec. officer 1992-94), Explorers Club; mem. Am. Assn. Petroleum Geologists, Soc. Econ. Geologists and Paleontologists, Speleological Soc., Mich. Acad. Arts, Sci. and Letters, Am. Meteorol. Soc., Sigma Xi, Sigma Gamma Epsilon. Home: 2065 S 9th St Lafayette IN 47905-2168

MELICAN, JAMES PATRICK, JR., lawyer; b. Worcester, Mass., Sept. 8, 1940; s. James Patrick and Abigail Helen (Donahue) M.; m. Debra A. Burns, Dec. 2, 1978; children: Marlane, James P., David, Molly, Megan. BA, Fordham U., 1962; JD, Harvard U., 1965; MBA, Mich. State U., 1971. Bar: Mich 1966, Calif. 1983. Supervising atty. product liability sect. Gen. Motors Corp., Detroit, 1971-73; atty.-in-charge trade regulation Gen. Motors Corp., 1973-77, atty.-in-charge mktg. and purchasing, 1977-80, asst. gen. counsel, 1980-81; gen. counsel Toyota Motor Sales, U.S.A., Inc., Torrance, Calif., 1981-82, v.p., gen. counsel, 1982-84; v.p., gen. counsel Internat. Paper Co., N.Y.C., 1984-87, sr. v.p., gen. counsel, 1987-91; exec. v.p. legal and external affairs Internat. Paper Co., Purchase, N.Y., 1991—; bd. dirs. Nat. Assn. Mfrs., Scitex Corp., Ltd.; bd. trustees Fordham Prep. Sch. Mem. ABA, NAM (bd. dirs.), Am. Law Inst., Assn. Bar City of N.Y., Assn. Gen. Counsel, Industry Sector Adv. Com. on Paper and Paper Products for Trade Policy Matters. Roman Catholic. Home: 39 Willowmere Cir Riverside CT 06878 Office: Internat Paper Co 2 Manhattanville Rd Purchase NY 10577-2118

MELICH, MITCHELL, retired lawyer; b. Bingham Canyon, Utah, Feb. 1, 1912; s. Joseph and Mary (Kalembar) M.; m. Doris M. Snyder, June 3, 1935; children: Tanya (Mrs. Noel L. Silverman), Michael, Nancy, Robert A. LL.B., U. Utah, 1934. Bar: Utah 1934. Pvt. practice Moab, 1934-63, city atty., 1934-55; county atty. Grand County, 1940-42; sec., dir. Utex Exploration Co., Moab, 1953-62; pres., dir. Uranium Reduction Co., Moab, 1954-62; cons. to pres. Atlas Minerals, div. Atlas Corp., 1962-67; dir., treas. New Park Mining Co., 1962-65; assoc. Ray, Quinney & Nebeker, 1973-96; ret., 1996; solicitor Dept. Interior, Washington, 1969-73;. Mem. of Colorado River Com. of Utah, 1945-47; mem. Utah Water and Power Bd., 1947; chmn. Citizens Adv. Com. on Higher Edn., 1968; mem. nat. adv. council U. Utah, 1976—; Mem. Utah Senate, 1942-50, minority leader, 1949-50; mem. Utah Legislative Council, 1949-54; del. Republican Nat. Conv., 1952-72; mem. Rep. Nat. Com. for Utah, 1961-64; Rep. candidate for gov., 1964; cons. on staff Congressman Sherman P. Lloyd, Utah, 1967-68; bd. dirs. St. Marks Hosp., 1973-87; bd. regents U. Utah, 1961-65, also mem. devel. fund com., mem. nat. adv. council, 1968-73, 76—; mem. Utah Statewide Health Coordinating Coun., 1985; mem. Utah Fusion Energy Coun., 1989—. Recipient Disting. Alumni award U. Utah, 1969, Man of Yr. award, Arthritis Found., 1991. Mem. Am. Bar Assn., Utah State Bar, Utah Mining Assn. (pres. 1962-63), Kappa Sigma. Republican. Club: Alta Salt Lake Country (Salt Lake City). Lodges: Masons; Shriners. Home: 1236 Roosevelt Ave Salt Lake City UT 84105

MELICHAR, BARBARA EHRLICH, educational administrator; b. Butte, Mont., Oct. 12, 1949; d. Louis Earl and Jennie Muriel (Friberg) Ehrlich; m. Kenneth Edward Melichar, Mar. 21, 1972; 1 child, Leah Jane. BA, U. Mont., 1972; MEd, U. Ga., 1988, EdD, 1993. Adminstr. North Ga. Tech. Inst., Clarkesville, Ga., 1986—. Editorial assoc.: Adult Basic Edn. jour. Mem. Am. Assn. Adult and Continuing Edn., Phi Kappa Phi, Kappa Delta Phi. Avocations: knitting, walking, hockey fan. Office: North Ga Tech Inst PO Box 65 Clarkesville GA 30523-0065

MELICHER, RONALD WILLIAM, finance educator; b. St. Louis, July 4, 1941; s. William and Lorraine Norma (Mohart) M.; m. Sharon Ann Schlarmann, Aug. 19, 1967; children: Michelle Joy, Thor William, Sean Richard. BSBA, Washington U., St. Louis, 1963; MBA, Washington U., 1965, DBA, 1968. Asst. prof. fin. U. Colo., Boulder, 1969-71, assoc. prof., 1971-76, prof. fin., 1976—, chmn. fin. div., 1978-86, 90; chmn. fin. and econ. div., 1993—; MBA/MS programs dir. U. Colo., Boulder, 1990-93; assoc. dir. space law bus. and policy ctr. U. Colo., 1986-87; rsch. cons. FPC, Washington, 1975-76, GAO, Washington, 1981, RCG/Hagler, Bailly, Inc., 1985—, Ariz. Corp. Commn., 1986-87, Conn. Dept. Pub. Utility Control, 1989, U.S. SEC, 1992-95; cons. tech. edn. IBM Corp., 1985-91; dir. ann. Exch. Program for Gas Industry, 1975-94; instr. ann. program Nat. Assn. Regulatory Utility Commrs., Mich. State U., 1981-94. Co-author: Real Estate Finance, 1978, 2d edit. 1984, 3d edit, 1989, 5th edit., 1982; Finance: Introduction to Markets, Institutions and Management, 1980, 84, 88, 92, Finance: Introduction to Institutions, Investments, and Management, 9th edit., 1997; assoc. editor Fin. Mgmt. Jour., 1975-80, The Fin. Rev., 1988-91. Recipient News Ctr. 4 TV Teaching award, 1987, MBA/MS Assn. Teaching award, 1988, Boulder Faculty Assembly Teaching award, 1988, Grad. Bus. Students Teaching award, 1995; grantee NSF, 1974, NASA, 1986, 87; scholar W.H. Baughn Disting., 1989—, U. Colo. Pres.'s Teaching, 1989—. Mem. Fin. Mgmt. Assn. (mem. com. 1974-76, regional dir. 1975-77, v.p. ann. mtg. 1985, v.p. program 1987, pres. 1991-92, exec. com. 1991-93, bd. trustees 1992—, chmn. 25th Anniversary com. 1994-95, mem. search. comm. for editor of Financial Mgmt. Jour., 1995-96, chmn. search com. editor of Fin. Practice and Edn. Jour. 1996), Am. Fin. Assn. Western Fin. Assn. (bd. dirs. 1974-76), Fin. Execs. Inst. (acad. mem. 1975—), Ea. Fin. Assn., Southwestern Fin. Assn., Midwest Fin. Assn. (bd. dirs. 1978-80), Alpha Kappa Psi, Beta Gamma Sigma. Presbyterian. Home: 6348 Swallow Ln Boulder CO 80303-1456 Office: U Colo Coll Bus PO Box 419 Boulder CO 80303

MELICK, GEORGE FLEURY, mechanical engineer, educator; b. Morristown, N.J., Sept. 7, 1924; s. George Fleury and Esther Purdy (Udall) M.; m. Florence Miriam Bevins, Dec. 28, 1946; children: Robert A., Linda S., Judith E., Karen L. BSE, Princeton U., 1944; MS, Stevens Inst. Tech., 1955; ME, Columbia U., 1963; MA, NYU, 1970. Registered profl. engr., N.J. Asst. chief engr. Worthington Corp., Harrison, N.J., 1946-55; asst. prof. Stevens Inst. Tech., Hoboken, N.J., 1955-58; assoc. in mech. engring. Columbia U., N.Y.C., 1958-61; assoc. prof. mech. engring., dean Rutgers U., New Brunswick, N.J., 1961-77; cons. engr. Stone & Webster Engring. Corp., Cherry Hill, N.J., 1977-87; dir. engring. mgmt. program Drexel U., Phila., 1987-91; chmn. bd. Anastasio & Melick Assocs., Cherry Hill, N.J., 1987—; cons. Worthington Corp., Harrison, 1956-65, Pub. Svc. Elec. & Gas, Newark, 1966-76. Author: John Mark and the Origin of the Gospels, 1979. Mem. countycom. Dem. Party, Franklin Twp., N.J., 1976. 1st lt. U.S. Army, 1945-52. Decorated Bronze Star medal. Mem. ASME (life), Am. Soc. Engring. Mgmt. (life), Am. Soc. Engring. Edn. (life), Soc. Bibl. Lit., Am. Acad. Religion (charter), Sigma Xi, Pi Tau Sigma, Tau Beta Pi. Presbyterian. Home: 6 Raven Ct Mount Laurel NJ 08054-3043 Office: Anastasio & Melick Assocs 1892 Greentree Rd Cherry Hill NJ 08003-2000

MELICKIAN, GARY EDWARD, trade association executive; b. L.A., Apr. 2, 1935; s. Ara Harry Melickian and Virginia Anne (Gargan) Jardine; m. Greta Gail Rasbury, Aug. 20, 1955 (div. 1972); children: Mark Stanley, Lynn Anne; m. Sharon Anne McDaniel, July 28, 1989. Student, UCLA, 1953-55; EM, Colo. Sch. Mines, 1959; postgrad., U. So. Calif., 1961-67, Calif. Poly. Inst., 1969-71. Lic. geologist, Calif., Alaska, engring. geologist, Calif.; cert. profl. geologist. Geologist Humble Oil & Refining Co., L.A., 1959; civil engr. L.A. County Flood Control Dist., L.A., 1960; geophysicist Dames & Moore, L.A., 1961, project geologist, 1962-64, mgr. pers., 1965-66, mgr. pub. rels., 1967-69, ptnr., 1970-84; dir. mining Dames & Moore, Denver, 1970-80; dir. tech. svcs. Dames & Moore, Bethesda, Md., 1980-84; pres., bd. dirs. Consultation Networks, Inc., Washington, 1985-90, Expert Witness Network, Washington, 1985-90; dir. indsl. mktg. Am. Gas Assn., Arlington, Va., 1990—; tech. project advisor Gas Rsch. Inst., Indsl. Gas Tech. Commercialization Ctr., Gas Tech. Can., Can. Gas Assn.; presenter in field. Contbr. articles to profl. jours. Fellow Geol. Soc. Am. (editor Engring. Geology newsletter 1966-67); mem. NSPE, ASME, Am. Inst. Profl. Geologists (pres. Calif. sect. 1971, bd. dirs. 1972-73, sec.-treas. 1982, Cert. of Merit 1982, 83), Soc. Mining Engrs. (bd. dirs. 1972-74, chmn. Peele award com., publs. com., program com.), Assn. Engring. Geologists (del. Internat. Geol. Congress, Prague), Hist. Earth Sci. Soc., Am. Soc. Metals, Tech. Assn. Pulp and Paper Industry, Assn. Iron and Steel Engrs., Assn. Energy Engrs. Avocations: art history, mineral collecting, stamps, western U.S. history, collecting rare books. Office: Am Gas Assn 1515 Wilson Blvd Arlington VA 22209-2402

MELILLO, JOSEPH VINCENT, producer, performing arts; b. New Haven, Conn., Nov. 15, 1946; s. Vincent and Viola (Fucci) M. BA, Sacred Heart U., 1968; MFA, Cath. U. Am., 1972. Adminstr. City Ctr. Music and Drama, N.Y.C., 1972-75; mktg. dir. The Walnut St. Theatre, Phila., 1975-76; dir. FEDAPT, N.Y.C., 1976-80; gen. mgr. New World Festival of Arts, Miami, Fla., 1982; dir. Next Wave Festival, N.Y.C., 1983-89; artistic dir. N.Y. Internat. Festival, N.Y.C., 1990-91; producing dir. Bklyn. Acad. Music, 1991—; trustee EnGarde Arts, N.Y.C., 1991-96; v.p., bd. dirs. Assn. Performing Arts Presenters, Washington, 1991-93; cons.-specialist Opera Am. Washington, 1991-93; cons. The Japan Found. "Performing Arts Japan", The Bush Found., St. Paul, Arts Internat., N.Y.C.; adj. prof. Theater Dept. Bklyn. Coll. Editor: Market the Arts, 1980. Mem. adv. bd. materials for the arts program com. N.J. Performing Arts Ctr., Newark, 1997—; mem. New Haven Festival of the Arts and Ideas. Democrat. Avocations: reading, travel.

MELIN, ROBERT ARTHUR, lawyer; b. Milw., Sept. 13, 1940; s. Arthur John and Frances Magdalena (Lanser) M.; m. Mary Magdalen Melin, July 8, 1967; children: Arthur Walden, Robert Dismas, Nicholas O'Brien, Madalyn Mary. B.A. summa cum laude, Marquette U., 1962, J.D., 1967. Bar: Wis. 1966, U.S. Dist. Ct. (ea. dist.) Wis. 1966, U.S. Ct. Appeals (7th cir.) 1966, U.S. Ct. Mil. Appeals 1967, U.S. Supreme Ct. 1975. Law clk. U.S. Dist. Ct. Eastern Dist. Wis., 1966; instr. bus. law U. Ga., Hinesville, 1968, also lectr. bus. law U. Md., Asmara, 1970; lectr. law Haile Selassie I U. Law Faculty, Addis Ababa, Ethiopia, 1971-72; mem. firm Walther & Halling, Milw., 1973-74, Schroeder, Gedlen, Riester & Moerke, Milw., 1974-82; ptnr. Schroeder, Gedlen, Riester & Melin, Milw., 1982-84, Schroeder, Riester, Melin & Smith, 1984—; rep. Class of 2000, West Point Parent Assn. of Wis., 1996-97. Lectr. charitable solicitations and contracts Philanthropy Monthly 9th Ann. Policy

Conf., N.Y.C., 1985. Chmn. Milw. Young Democrats, 1963-64; Class of 2000 rep. West Point Parent Assn. of Wis., 1996-97. Served to capt. JAGC, AUS, 1967-70. Mem. Wis. Acad. Trial Lawyers, ABA, Wis. Bar Assn., Milw. Bar Assn., Am. Legion, Friends of Ethiopia, Delta Theta Phi, Phi Alpha Theta, Pi Gamma Mu. Roman Catholic. Author: Evidence in Ethiopia, 1972; contbg. author to Annual Survey of African Law, 1974; contbr. numerous articles to legal jours. Home: 8108 N Whitney Rd Milwaukee WI 53217-2752 Office: 135 W Wells St Milwaukee WI 53203-1807 *Notable cases include: Anderson vs. Continental Ins. Co. 85 Wis. 2d 675, 271 NW 2d 368, 1978, new tort cause of action for insurer's bad-faith refusal to honor claim of 1st party insured; Allstate Ins. Co. vs. Met. Sewerage Commn. 80 wis. 2d 10, 258 N.W. 2d 148, 1977, broad application of remaining vestiges of mcpl. immunity doctrine in Wis. applied in favor of mcpl. client; Met. Sewerage Commn. vs. R.W. Constrn., Inc. 78 Wis 2d 451, 255 NW 2d 293, 1977, breach of sewer constrn. contract case.*

MELKONIAN, HARRY G., insurance executive, rancher; b. Bridgeport, Conn., June 18, 1949; s. Harry Artin and Hermina (Barsumian) M. BA, U. Rochester, 1971; JD cum laude, NYU, 1974. Bar: N.Y. 1975, Calif. 1977, U.S. Supreme Ct. 1984. Atty. Breed Abbott & Morgan, N.Y.C., 1974-76, Rifkind Sterling & Lockwood, Beverly Hills, Calif., 1976-78; atty. Buchalter Nemer Fields & Younger, L.A., 1978-81, ptnr., 1981-87; ptnr. White & Case, L.A., 1987-96; mng. dir. First Am. Title Ins. Co. Australia Pty. Ltd., Sydney, First Australian Title Co. Editor NYU Law Review, 1973-74. Trustee Project Literacy L.A., 1990-92; bd. govs. The Pilgrim Sch., L.A., 1992-95; bd. dirs. HopeNet, L.A., 1990-91; chmn. bd. deacons 1st Congl. Ch. L.A., 1992-93, trustee, 1994-96. Mem. Calif. Club, Phi Alpha Delta. Republican. Avocations: fishing, boating. Office: First Am Title Ins of Australia, 4 Martin Pl Level 11, Sydney NSW 2000, Australia

MELLA, ARTHUR JOHN, insurance company executive; b. New York, N.Y., Sept. 25, 1937; s. Anthony Arthur and Angela Helen (Morrongiello) M.; m. Louise Vetere, May 5, 1962; children: Douglas James, Gregory Arthur. BS, Fordham U., 1959. CPCU. Supr. Liberty Mut. Ins. Co., N.Y.C., 1960-70; v.p. The Home Ins. Co., N.Y.C., 1970-80, Skandia Am. Reinsurance Co., N.Y.C., 1980-85; sr. v.p. Reliance Reinsurance Corp., Phila., 1985—. With USNG, 1960-63. Mem. Fedn. Ins. and Corp. Counsel, Excess Surplus Lines Claims (pres. 1988-89, v.p. 1987-88, bd. dirs. 1986-87), Broker and Reins. Underwriting, Soc. CPCU. Republican. Roman Catholic. Avocations: gardening, book collecting, golf. Office: Reliance Reinsurance Co 1 Penn Center Plz Philadelphia PA 19103-1821

MELLA, GORDON WEED, physician; b. Menlo Park, Calif., Aug. 22, 1931; s. Hugo and Pearl (Weed) M.; m. Dorothee Lusson, June 23, 1953 (div. May 1970); children: Richard, Glen, Gordon; m. Lynne Daniels Mella, Aug. 11, 1973; children: William, Cynthia, Heidi, Amanda. BS, Ursinus Coll., Collegeville, Pa., 1952; MD, Thomas Jefferson U., Phila., 1956. Fellow Am. Acad. Pediatrics, 1961. Med. officer, pediatrician USN, 1956-68, USNR, 1982-92; pvt. practice gen. pediatrics Gaithersburg, Md., 1968—. Team physician Winston Churchill H.S., Potomac, Md., 1985—. Fellow Am. Acad. Pediatrics (chmn. sch. health com. 1995—); mem. AMA, Montgomery County Med. Soc., Montgomery-Prince George's Pediatric Soc., Med. and Chirurgical Faculty of Med. Mem. Ch. of Latter Day Saints. Avocations: running, cycling, tennis. Office: Pediatric Medicine 19251 Montgomery Village Ave Gaithersburg MD 20879-2026

MELLANBY, SCOTT EDGAR, professional hockey player; b. Montreal, June 11, 1966. Hockey player Fla. Panthers, 1993—.

MELLBERG, JAMES RICHARD, dental research chemist; b. Manitowac, Wis., June 3, 1932; s. Millard Filmore Mellberg and Marion Eleanor (Elmer) Zimmerman; m. Gail Maureen Loehning, Sept. 26, 1956; children: Eric, Diane, Laura. BS, Wis. State U., Oshkosh, 1955; MS, Loyola U., Chgo., 1960. Head dental rsch. dept. Kendall Co., Barrington, Ill., 1958-75; assoc. dir. dental rsch. Colgate-Palmolive Co., Piscataway, N.J., 1975-94; cons. Naval Dental Rsch. Inst., Great Lakes, Ill., 1972—. Author: Fluoride in Preventive Dentistry, 1983; patentee in field; contbr. over 150 articles in field to sci. publs. Recipient 20 sci. exhibit awards ADA, 1964-87. Mem. Internat. Assn. Dental Rsch. (Disting. Scientist award). Avocations: cycling, woodworking. Home: PO Box 227 Pottersville NJ 07979-0227

MELLBERG, LEONARD EVERT, physicist; b. Springfield, Mass., Dec. 18, 1935; s. Evert and Dorothy (Baker) M. BS in Physics, U. Mass., 1961; MS in Physics, Trinity Coll., Hartford, Conn., 1968. Rsch. physicist Navy Underwater Sound Lab., New London, Conn., 1961-68, SACLANT Undersea Rsch. Ctr., LaSpezia, Italy, 1968-72, Office of Naval Rsch., London, 1968-72, Naval Underwater Systems Ctr., Newport, R.I., 1972-91; sr. scientist Marine Acoustics Inc., Newport, 1991-94; rsch. physicist sci. applications Internat. Corp., Newport, R.I., 1994-97; physicist Harvard U., Cambridge, Mass., 1997—; mem. numerous govt. and profl. tech. adv. bds. and coms. Contbr. over 70 articles to profl. jours. Pres. Verdandi Swedish Cultural Found., Providence, 1992-97; bd. dirs. Verdandi Chorus Am. Union Swedish Singers, Providence, 1992-97. Recipient Naval Underwater Sys. Ctr. Excellence in Sci. award, 1977, 84, Civilian Navy Meritorious Svc. medal Dept. of Navy, 1991. Fellow Acoustical Soc. Am.; mem. IEEE (sr.), AIAA (svc. award 1977), Am. Geophys. Union, Oceanic Soc. of IEEE. Achievements include research in ocean physics, ocean acoustic propagation, anti-submarine warfare acoustics, Arctic sea-ice ridges and lighter than air vehicles. Home and Office: 20 Willow Ave Middletown RI 02842-4948

MELLEMA, DONALD EUGENE, retired radio news reporter and anchor; b. Chgo., Mar. 30, 1937; s. Raymond Cornelius and Dorothy Sofia (Miller) M.; m. Freda Dieterlen Mellema, Sept. 23, 1961; children: Darryl Emerson, Duane Edward. BA in Speech, Beloit (Wis.) Coll., 1959. News dir. WGEZ Radio, Beloit, 1959; evening host, newsman WOSH Radio, Oshkosh, Wis., 1959-63; morning host, newsman WANE Radio, Ft. Wayne, Ind., 1963-65; news dir. WATI Radio, Indpls., 1965-67; news writer WGN Radio, Chgo., 1967-69; news reporter, anchor WBBM Radio, Chgo., 1969-96; ret., 1996; mem. publs. adv. bd., pres's adv. coun., cons. Beloit Coll., 1996—, also profl.-in-residence. Speaker, motivator Chgo. Pub. Sch. Youth Motivation Program, 1993-96; advisor, cons. media rels. to various police and civic orgns.; commr., unit leader Boy Scouts Am., 1971-81; ch. deacon Park Ridge (Ill.) Presbyn. Ch., 1980-83. Recipient regional award Radio TV News Dirs. Assn., 1994, Newsfinder award AP, 1995, career recognition award Chgo. Police Dept., 1997, Mark Twain award Ill. AP, 1997; named to Taft H.S. Hall of Fame, 1995. Mem. Ill. News Broadcasters Assn. (Silver Dome 1st Place award 1994), Soc. Profl. Journalists (Peter Lisagor award 1991, 96), Am. Legion. Republican. Avocations: woodworking, reading, photography, birding, travel.

MELLEN, FRANCIS JOSEPH, JR., lawyer; b. Williamsport, Pa., Dec. 19, 1945; s. Francis Joseph and Mary Emma (Oberst) M.; m. Mary Wilder Davison, Aug. 2, 1975 (div. 1987); children: Elizabeth, Catherine, Robert, Christine. BA, U. Ky., 1967, MA, 1971; JD, Harvard U., 1973. Bar: N.Y. 1974, Ky. 1975, U.S. Dist. Ct. (so. dist.) N.Y. 1974, U.S. Dist. Ct. (ea. dist.) Ky. 1977, U.S. Dist. Ct. (we. dist.) Ky. 1978, U.S. Ct. Appeals (2d cir.) 1975, U.S. Ct. Appeals (6th cir.) 1982. Assoc. atty. Rogers & Wells, N.Y.C., 1973-75, Wyatt, Grafton & Sloss, Louisville, 1975-80; ptnr. Wyatt, Tarrant & Combs, Louisville, 1980—. Co-author: Kentucky Mineral Law, 1986, Kentucky Forms and Transactions, 1991. Contbr. articles to profl. jours. Mem. spl. study com. for Uniform Commercial Code, Ky. Legis. Rsch. Comsn., Frankfort, 1984-91. Lt. USNR, 1967-69, Vietnam. Bd. Dirs. Leadership Louisville Found. (counsel 1996-97), Stage One: The Louisville Children's Theatre, Louisville-Jefferson County A.W.A.R.E. Coalition; Mem. ABA, Am. Arbitration Assn. (panel), Ky. Bar Assn. (ho. dels. 1986-92), Louisville Bar Assn. (chmn. Com. profl. responsibility 1992-94), Jefferson Club, Filson Club, American Mensa. Republican. Home: 429 Trinity Hills Ln Louisville KY 40207-2132 Office: Wyatt Tarrant & Combs 2800 Citizens Plz Louisville KY 40202

MELLENCAMP, JOHN (JOHN COUGAR), singer, songwriter; b. Seymour, Ind., Oct. 7, 1951; m. Vicky C. (div.); children: Michelle, Teddy Joe, Justice; m. Elaine Irwin, Sept. 5, 1992. Student, Vincennes U., Ind. Albums include Chestnut Street Incident, 1977, Biography, 1978, Johnny Cougar, 1979, Nothing Matters and What If It Did, 1980, Night Dancin, 1980, American Fool, 1982, Uh-huh, 1983, Scarecrow, 1985, The Lonesome Jubilee, 1988, Big Daddy, 1989, Whenever We Wanted, 1991, Human Wheels, 1993, Dance Naked, 1994, Mr. Happy Go Lucky, 1996; performed one song for Folkways: A Vision Shared (A Tribute to Woody Guthrie and Leadbelly), 1988; film actor, dir., soundtrack performer: Falling From Grace, 1992; TV appearance Bob Dylan: The 30th Anniversary Concert Celebration, 1993. Office: Mercury Records 825 8th Ave New York NY 10019*

MELLETTE, M. SUSAN JACKSON, physician, educator, researcher; b. Raleigh, N.C., June 4, 1922; d. Donald Rudolph and Bessie Lou (Mull) Jackson; m. Peter A. Mellette, June 16, 1943; children: Susan E. Mellette Lederhouse, Peter Mason. AB, Meredith Coll., 1942; postgrad., U. N.C., 1942-43, U. Pa. Med. Sch., 1944; MD, U. Cin., 1947. Fels rsch. asst. U. N.C., Chapel Hill, 1942-43; intern Cleve. City Hosp., 1947-48; resident in internal medicine St. Barnabas Hosp., N.Y.C., 1949-51, Koch Hosp., St. Louis, 1952-54; rsch. assoc. U. Louisville, 1952; NIH rsch. fellow Med. Coll. Va., 1955-57, Damon Runyon cancer rsch. fellow, 1957-58; rsch. assoc. Med. Coll. Va., Richmond, 1958-60, asst. prof. internal medicine, 1960-69, assoc. prof., 1969-79, prof. internal and rehab. medicine, 1979-93, prof. emerita, 1993—, cancer coord., 1961-66, dir. Cancer Rehab. Program, 1974-93; mem. behavioral medicine study sect. NIH, Bethesda, Md., 1986-91; mem. cancer edn. com. Nat. Cancer Inst., NIH, 1974-78, mem. task force on rehab. rsch., 1990, mem. expert panel on advances in cancer treatment Nat Cancer Inst., 1992. Contbr. numerous articles and book chpts. on cancer treatment and rehab. to profl. publs. Mem. Commn. on Terminal Care Legislature Va., Richmond, 1982-83; adv. bd. Women's Bank, Richmond, 1979-81. Recipient Hoover award Va. Rehab. Assn., 1979, Nat. Brotherhood award NCCJ, 1987, Profl. of Yr. award Va. Assn. Professions, 1989. Fellow Am. Assn. Cancer Edn. (pres. 1975); mem. N.Y. Acad. Sci., Am. Congress Rehab. Medicine (chmn. cancer rehab. com. 1984-87), Am. Cancer Soc. (nat. svc. and rehab. com. 1982-92, nat. patient svcs. com. 1992-94, Profl. Edn. award Va. divsn. 1982, Nat. Humanitarian award 1996), Am. Assn. Med. Colls., Med. Coll. Va. Alumni Assn. (named disting. prof. 1995), Alpha Omega Alpha. Home: 1502 Wilmington Ave Richmond VA 23227-4430 Office: Med Coll Va Richmond VA 23298

MELLI, MARYGOLD SHIRE, law educator; b. Rhinelander, Wis., Feb. 8, 1926; d. Osborne and May (Bonnie) Shire; m. Joseph Alexander Melli, Apr. 8, 1950; children: Joseph, Sarah Bonnie, Sylvia Anne, James Alexander. BA, U. Wis., 1947, LLB, 1950. Bar: Wis. 1950. Dir. children's code revision Wis. Legis. Coun., Madison, 1950-53; exec. dir. Wis. Jud. Coun., Madison, 1955-59; asst. prof. law U. Wis., Madison, 1961-66, assoc. prof., 1966-67, prof., 1967-84; Voss-Bascom prof. U. Wis., 1985-93, emerita, 1993—; assoc. dean U. Wis., 1970-72, rsch. affiliate Inst. for Rsch. on Poverty, 1980—; mem. spl. rev. bd. Dept. Health and Social Svcs., State of Wis., Madison, 1973—. Author: (pamphlet) The Legal Status of Women in Wisconsin, 1977, (book) Wisconsin Juvenile Court Practice, 1978, rev. edit., 1983, (with others) Child Support & Alimony, 1988, The Case for Transracial Adoption, 1994; contbr. articles to profl. jours. Bd. dirs. Am. Humane Assn., 1985-95. Named one of five Outstanding Young Women in Wis., Jaycees, 1961; rsch. grantee NSF, 1983; recipient award for Outstanding Contbn. to Advancement of Women in State Bar of Wis., award for Lifelong Contbn. to Advancement of Women in the Legal Prof., 1994. Fellow Am. Acad. Matrimonial Lawyers (exec. editor jour. 1985-90); mem. Am. Law Inst. (reporter, cons. project on law of family dissolution), Internat. Soc. Family Law (v.p.), Wis. State Bar Assn. (reporter family law sect.), Nat. Conf. Bar Examiners (chmn. bd. mgrs. 1989). Democrat. Roman Catholic. Avocations: jogging, swimming, collecting art. Home: 2904 Waunona Way Madison WI 53713-2238 Office: U Wis Law Sch Madison WI 53706

MELLING, JACK, biotechnologist; b. Aspull, Lancashire, Eng., Feb. 8, 1940; s. John and Mary (Marsden) M.; m. Susan Melling, May 27, 1967. BSc, Manchester U., Eng., 1963, MSc, 1965; PhD, Bath U., Eng., 1968. Rsch. asst. Bath U., Eng., 1965-68; lectr. Heriot-Watt U., Scotland, 1968-69; sr. sci. officer Ministry of Def., Eng., 1969-73, prin. sci. officer, 1973-79; dir. vaccine rsch. and product lab. Pub. Health Lab. Svc., Eng., 1979-87; head biologics div. and dep. dir. Ctr. for Applied Microbiology & Rsch., Porton Down, Salisbury, England, 1987-92; dir. Ctr. for Applied Microbiology & Rsch., Porton Down, Salisbury, Eng., 1992-96, Salk Inst., Swiftwater, Pa., 1996—; mem. MRC Vaccine Com., 1979-96; sec. Brit. Coord. Com. for Biotech., London, 1981-85; mem. Com. Safety of Medicines, Biologic, London, 1982—, Ministry of Agr. Toxicants in Foods com., London, 1982-94; counsellor, tutor Open U., Salisbury, 1971-74. Editor: Microbial Adhesion, 1980; editor Chem. Tech. and Biotech. Jour., 1985—; contbr. more than 100 articles to profl. jours. Mem. Swiss Diasaster Relief Orgn. Fellow Royal Pharm. Soc. G.B., Inst. of Biology. Fellow Royal Soc. Medicine; mem. Soc. Chem. Industry (coun. mem. 1975-83, sec. 1975-81, chmn. biotech. group 1981-83). Avocations: skiing, walking. Office: Salk Inst Biol Studies PO Box 250 Rt 611 N Swiftwater PA 18370

MELLINK, MACHTELD JOHANNA, archaeologist, educator; b. Amsterdam, Holland, Oct. 26, 1917; came to U.S., 1949; d. Johan and Machteld (Kruyff) M. B.A., U. Amsterdam, 1938, M.A., 1941; Ph.D., Utrecht (Netherlands) U., 1943; LLD (hon.), U. Pa., 1987, Anatolian U., Turkey, 1990. Faculty Bryn Mawr Coll., 1949-88, prof. classical and Near Eastern archaeology, 1962-88, chmn. dept., 1955-83; staff mem. excavations Tarsus, Turkey, 1947-49, Gordion, Turkey, 1950-74; field dir. excavations Karatas-Semayuk, Lycia, Turkey, 1963—; Troy, 1988—; research asso. U. Mus., U. Pa., 1955-82, con. scholar, 1982—. Author: A Hittite Cemetery at Gordion, 1956; author: (with Jan Filip) Frühe Stufen der Kunst-Propyläen Kunstgeschichte XIII, 1974; editor: Dark Ages and Nomads c. 1000 B.C., 1964, Troy and the Trojan War, 1986, Elmali-Karatas I, 1992, II, 1994; contbr. articles to profl. jours. Recipient Lucy Wharton Drexel medal U. Pa. Mus., 1994—. Fellow Am. Acad. Arts and Scis.; mem. Archaeol. Inst. Am. (pres. 1981-84, gold medal 1991), German Archaeol. Inst., Am. Oriental Soc., Am. Philos. Soc.; corr. mem. Royal Netherlands Acad. Scis., Austrian Archaeol. Inst. (corr.), Türk Tarih Kurumu (hon.), Am. Research Inst. Turkey (v.p. 1977-87, pres. 1988-92). Home: 264 Montgomery Ave Haverford PA 19041-1531

MELLINKOFF, DAVID, lawyer, educator; b. 1914. AB, Stanford U., 1935; LLB, Harvard U., 1939. Bar: Calif. 1939. Sole practice Calif., 1939-41, 46-64; lectr. UCLA Law Sch., 1964-65, prof., 1965-85, prof. emeritus, 1985—. Author: The Language of the Law, 1963, 12th printing, 1994, The Conscience of a Lawyer, 1973, 4th printing, 1978, Lawyers and the System of Justice, 1976, Legal Writing: Sense of Nonsense, 1982, 4th reprint, 1995, Mellinkoff's Dictionary of American Legal Usage, 1992, 2d printing, 1993; also articles. Served to capt. U.S. Army, 1941-46. Home: 744 Holmby Ave Los Angeles CA 90024-3320 Office: UCLA Law Sch 405 Hilgard Ave Los Angeles CA 90095-9000

MELLINKOFF, SHERMAN MUSSOFF, medical educator; b. McKeesport, Pa., Mar. 23, 1920; s. Albert and Helen (Mussoff) M.; m. June Bernice O'Connell, Nov. 18, 1944; children: Sherrill, Albert. BA, Stanford U., 1941, MD, 1944; LHD (hon.), Wake Forest U., 1984, Hebrew Union Coll., L.A., 1988. Diplomate Am. Bd. Internal Medicine, Am. Bd. Gastroenterology, Am. Bd. Nutrition. Intern asst. resident Stanford U. Hosp., San Francisco, 1944-45; asst. resident Johns Hopkins Hosp., Balt., 1947-49, chief resident, 1950-51, instr. in medicine, 1951-53; fellow in gastroenterology Hosp. of U. Pa., Phila., 1949-50; from asst. prof. to prof. medicine UCLA Sch. of Medicine, L.A., 1962-86; dean UCLA Sch. Medicine, L.A., 1962-86, emeritus prof. of medicine, 1990—; disting. physician of VA Wadsworth VA Medical Ctr., L.A., 1990-93; mem. sci. adv. panel Rsch. to Prevent Blindness, Inc., N.Y.C., 1975-93; mem. program devel. com. Nat. Med. Fellowships, Inc., N.Y.C., 1984—. Editorial bd. The Pharos, 1986; contbr. articles to profl. jours. Apptd. by Gov. of Calif. to McCone Com., 1965. Capt. U.S. Army, 1945-47. Recipient Abraham Flexner award Assn. Am. Med. Colls., 1981, J.E. Wallace Sterling Disting. Alumnus award Stanford U. Sch. of Medicine, 1987. Master ACP; fellow Royal Coll. of Physicians; mem. Am. Gastroenterol. Assn. Assn., of Am. Physicians, Inst. of Medicine of NAS, Am. Acad. of Arts and Scis., The Johns Hopkins Soc. of Scholars. Avocations: reading, hiking. Office: UCLA Sch of Medicine Dept of Medicine 44-143 CHS Los Angeles CA 90024

MELLINS, HARRY ZACHARY, radiologist, educator; b. N.Y.C., May 23, 1921; s. David J. and Ray (Hoffman) M.; m. Judith Alice Weiss, Dec. 26, 1950; children—Elizabeth, William, Thomas. A.B., Columbia Coll., 1941; M.D., L.I. Coll. Medicine, 1944; M.S. in Radiology, U. Minn., 1951; A.M. (hon.), Harvard U., 1970. Intern Jewish Hosp., Bklyn., 1944-45, asst. resident in radiology, 1945-46; resident in radiology U. Minn., 1948-50, instr. radiology, 1950-52, asst. prof., 1952-53; clin. asst. prof. radiology Wayne State U., Detroit, 1953-56; dir. radiology Sinai Hosp., Detroit, 1953-56; prof., chmn. dept. radiology SUNY, Coll. Medicine, N.Y.C., 1956-69; chief radiology Kings County Hosp. Center, Bklyn., 1956-69; radiologist-in-chief State Univ. Hosp., Bklyn., 1966-69; prof. radiology Harvard Med. Sch., Boston, 1969-91, prof. radiology emeritus, 1991—; dir. diagnostic radiology Peter Bent Brigham Hosp., 1969-79; dir. diagnostic radiology Brigham and Women's Hosp., 1980-87, dir. edn. and tng., dept. radiology, 1987-94; co-dir. edn. and tng. dept. radiology, 1994—; chief of radiology Harvard U. Health Svc., 1988—; nat. cons. in radiology to surgeon gen. U.S. Air Force, 1968-79; mem. radiation study sect. NIH, 1967-71; mem. subcom. for written exam. in diagnostic radiology Am. Bd. Radiology, 1970-75; mem. radiology tng. com. research tng. grants br. Nat. Inst. Gen. Med. Scis.; mem. diagnostic research adv. group div. cancer biology and diagnosis Nat. Cancer Inst., 1975-79; guest examiner Am. Bd. Radiology. Served to capt. M.C. USAAF, 1946-48. Mem. Bklyn. Radiol. Soc. (pres. 1965-66), N.Y. Roentgen Soc. (pres 1966-67), Assn. Univ. Radiologists (pres. 1969-70, Gold medal 1986), Soc. Uroradiology (pres. 1975-76), Am. Roentgen Ray Soc. (pres. 1977-79, Gold medal 1989), Radiol. Soc. N.Am., New Eng. Roentgen Ray Soc. (pres. 1986-87), Soc. Gastrointestinal Radiology, Alpha Omega Alpha. Office: Brigham and Women's Hosp 75 Francis St Boston MA 02115-6110

MELLINS, JUDITH WEISS, retired archivist; b. St. Paul, Nov. 25, 1924; d. Louis Robert and Gertrude (Simon) Weiss; m. Harry Zachary Mellins, Dec. 26, 1950; children: Elizabeth Deborah, William Weiss, Thomas Harrison. BA, U. Minn., 1945; MA, Harvard U., 1947. Rsch. economist Ninth Dist. Fed. Res. Bank, Mpls., 1947-50; project researcher Law Sch. Harvard U., Cambridge, Mass., 1980-83, manuscripts assoc. Law Sch., 1983-93, manuscripts rsch. svcs. supr. Law Sch., 1993-95; ret., 1995. Mem. New Eng. Archivists, Soc. Am. Archivists, U.S. Supreme Ct. Hist. Soc., Law Librarians New Eng., Harvard-Radcliffe Archivists Group. Avocations: reading, fitness excercise, drama, music. Home: 385 Heath St Chestnut Hill MA 02167-2328

MELLINS, ROBERT B., pediatrician, educator; b. N.Y.C., Mar. 6, 1928; s. David J. and Ray H. (Hoffman) M.; m. Sue Mendelsohn, Apr. 19, 1959; children: Claude Ann, David Rustin. A.B., Columbia U., 1948; M.D., Johns Hopkins U., 1952. Intern Johns Hopkins Hosp., 1952-53; mem. epidemic intelligence svc, founder poison control ctr. Ctr. Disease Control, Chgo., 1953-55; resident in pediatrics N.Y. Hosp., 1955-56; resident in pediatrics Presbyn. Hosp., N.Y.C., 1956-57, dir. pediatric ICU, 1970-75; assoc. prof. pediatrics Columbia U., 1970-75, prof. pediatrics, 1975—, dir. Cystic Fibrosis Ctr., 1978-91, dir. pediatric pulmonary div., 1972—; founding mem. sect. on pulmonology Am. Bd. Pediatrics, 1985—; Christmas Seal prof. Can. Lung Assn., 1979-80; 1st Deans Disting. lectr. in clin. scis. Columbia U. Coll. P&S, 1982. Mem. editl. bd. Am. Rev. Respiratory Diseases, 1974-81, assoc. editor, 1984-90; contbr. articles to med. jours. Bd. dirs. Am. Lung Assn., 1981-93, nat. v.p., 1987-89, bd. dirs. N.Y. chpt., 1984—, v.p., 1994-96, pres., 1996-98; bd. dirs. L.A. Jonas Found., 1970-78, 90—, Syphony of UN, 1990—; chmn. steeering com. Multictr. Study of Heart and Lung Complications of HIV Infection in Children, NIH, 1989—. Recipient Career Devel. award NIH, 1966-71, Career Scientist award Health Rsch. Coun. N.Y.C. Health Rsch. Coun., 1975, Stevens Triennial award for rsch. Columbia U., 1980, Health Edn. Rsch. award Nat. Asthma Edn. Program, 1992, Will Ross medal Am. Lung Assn., 1996. Mem. Am. Pediatric Soc., Soc. Pediatric Rsch., Am. Physiol. Soc., Am. Soc. Pharmacology and Exptl. Therapautics, Am. Acad. Pediat. (Med. Edn. Lay Edn. award 1995, Med. Edn. award 1995), Am. Thoracic Soc. (bd. dirs. 1975-75, 81-84, nat. pres. 1982-83, v.p., Disting. Achievement award 1996), Soc. Critical Care Medicine, Fleischner Soc. (pres. 1995—), Am. Acad. Allergy and Immunology, Alpha Omega Alpha. Home: 2 W 67th St New York NY 10023-6241 Office: Columbia U 630 W 168th St New York NY 10032-3702

MELLMAN, LEONARD, real estate investor and advisor; b. Phila., Mar. 23, 1924; s. Morris and Luba (Levin) M. BA, Temple U., 1949. Owner, mgr. L. Mellman Co., Phila., 1949-84; ret., 1984; owner, mgr. Mellman Investments, 1960—; ptnr. Mellman, Blume Co., 1979—, Cunniff, Mellman Co., 1982—; gen. ptnr. Diamond Acres, Phila., 1981-86, Van Pelt Ct. Ltd. pres., 1985-91; pres. MLC Bd. Settlement Music Sch., Phila., 1985-91, sec. ctrl. bd., 1985-91, v.p. ctrl. bd., 1997—. Served with Signal Corps, U.S. Army, 1943-46, ETO, PTO. Pres. arts and sci. alumni bd. Temple U., 1976-78. Mem. Credit Mchts. Assn. (pres. 1970-72, Man of Yr. award 1970), Phila. Bd. Realtors, Temple U. Gen. Alumni Assn. (pres. 1992-94, Disting. Alumni award 1985), Singing City Choir Bd. (pres. 1988-90), Phila. Opera Guild (bd. mem. 1995—, pres. 1997—). Democrat. Jewish. Club: Union League. Home and Office: 2530 Panama St Philadelphia PA 19103-6412

MELLON, JOHN, publishing executive; b. 1940. Chmn. IPC mags., Reed Bus. Pub., Reed Regional Newspapers; CEO Reed Pub. Europe; dir. Reed Internat., 1990—, exec. dir., 1992—; mem. exec. com. Reed Elsevier, 1994—; mem. adv. com. on advt. for the Ctrl. Office of Info. Office: Reed Elsevier plc, 25 Victoria St, London SWIH OEX, England

MELLON, PAUL, retired art gallery executive; b. Pitts., June 11, 1907; s. Andrew W. and Nora (McMullen) M.; m. Mary Conover, Feb. 2, 1935 (dec. Oct. 1946); children: Catherine Conover, Timothy; m. Rachel Lambert Lloyd, May 1, 1948. AB, Yale U., 1929, LHD (hon.), 1967; AB, Cambridge (Eng.) U., 1931, MA, 1938, LLD (hon.), 1983; Litt.D. (hon.), Oxford U., 1961; LL.D. (hon.), Carnegie Inst. Tech., 1967; DVM (hon.), Royal Vet. Coll., U. London, 1991. Pres. Nat. Gallery Art, Washington, to 1979; chmn. bd. trustees Nat. Gallery Art, 1979-85, hon. trustee, 1985—; trustee Andrew W. Mellon Found., N.Y.; assoc. fellow Berkeley Coll., Yale U.; hon. fellow Clare Coll., Cambridge, Eng., St. John's Coll., Annapolis; Benjamin Franklin fellow Royal Soc. Arts, London, 1969. Served from pvt. to 1st lt. Cav. AUS, 1941-43; 1st lt. to maj. overseas service with OSS, 1943-45. Recipient Yale medal award, 1953; Horace Marden Albright Scenic Preservation medal, 1957; award for distinguished service to arts Nat. Inst. Arts and Letters, 1962; Benjamin Franklin medal Royal Soc. Arts, London, 1965; Skowhegan Gertrude Vanderbilt Whitney award, 1972, Nat. Medal of Arts, 1985, Thomas Jefferson Meml. Found. medal in architecture, 1989, Hadrian award World Monuments Fund, 1989, medal disting. philanthropy Am. Assn. Mus., 1993; decorated hon. knight comdr. Order Brit. Empire, 1974; decorated Knight Grand Officer of the Order of Orange Nassau, 1982. Fellow AAAS; mem. Scroll and Key Soc., Am. Philos. Soc. (Benjamin Franklin award 1989); hon. mem. AIA. Clubs: Metropolitan (Washington); Racquet and Tennis (N.Y.C.), Grolier (N.Y.C.), Links (N.Y.C.), Knickerbocker (N.Y.C.), Jockey (N.Y.C.), Nat. Steeplechase and Hunt Assn. (N.Y.C.); Society of the Dilettanti (London), Roxburghe (London), Buck's (London), English Jockey (hon.). Office: 1140 Connecticut Ave NW Washington DC 20036-4003

MELLON, RICHARD PROSSER, charitable foundation executive; b. Chgo., May 19, 1939; s. Richard King and Constance Mary (Prosser) M.; m. Gertrude Alice Adams, Apr. 28, 1962 (div. 1976); children: Richard Adams, Armour Negley; m. 2d Katherine Woodward Hooker, Dec. 2, 1976. Student, U. Pitts, 1958-60; A.A. (hon.), Valley Forge Mil. Jr. Coll., 1970. Chmn. Richard King Mellon Found., Pitts., 1980—. Bd. dirs. Ducks Unltd. Found.; nat. trustee, mem. nat. exec. com. life mem. Ducks Unltd., Inc.; corporator Western Pa. Sch. for Blind. Served to 1st lt. USAR, 1958-67. Episcopalian. Clubs: Duquesne (Pitts.); Laurel Valley Golf (Ligonier), Rolling Rock (Ligonier), Rolling Rock-Westmoreland Hunt (Ligonier); Links (N.Y.C.); Nat. Steeplechase and Hunt Assn. (Ligonier). Office: Mellon Found One Mellon Bank Center 500 Grant St Ste 4106 Pittsburgh PA 15219-2502*

MELLON, SEWARD PROSSER, investment executive; b. Chgo., July 28, 1942; s. Richard King and Constance Mary (Prosser) Mellon Burrell; m. Karen Leigh Boyd, Sept. 10, 1966 (div. 1974); children—Catharine Leigh, Constance Elizabeth; m. Sandra Springer Stout, 1975. Grad., Choate Sch., 1960; B.A., Susquehanna U., 1965, DH, 1993. With Mellon Nat. Corp., Pitts., 1965-69; with T. Mellon & Sons, Pitts., 1969-71; pres. Richard K. Mellon & Sons, Ligonier, 1971—; bd. dirs. Mellon Bank N.A., Mellon Nat. Corp. Trustee Richard King Mellon Family Found.; trustee, pres. Richard King Mellon Found.; chmn. real estate com., chmn. bd. mem. fin. and exec. com. Valley Sch. Ligonier. Mem. Western Pa. Conservancy (life),

LoyalHanna Assn. (pres.), Vintage Club (Palm Springs, Calif.), Duquesne Club (Pitts.), Laurel Valley Golf Club (Ligonier), Rolling Rock Club, Rolling Rock Hunt, Phi Mu Delta. Republican. Home: Huntland Downs Box K Ligonier PA 15658 Office: PO Box RKM Ligonier PA 15658-0780

MELLON, THOMAS S., lawyer; b. Phila., Nov. 18, 1956. BA, Ohio Wesleyan U., 1978; JD cum laude, Vt. Law Sch., 1989. Bar: Pa. 1989, N.J. 1991, U.S. Dist. Ct. N.J., U.S. Dist. Ct. Pa. (ea. and mid. dists.), U.S. Ct. Appeals (3d Cir.). Atty. DeSantis DeSantis & Essig, Reading, Pa., 1989-90, Krusen Evans and Byrne, Phila., 1990-94, Murphy & O'Connor, Phila., 1994—; alumni dir. William Penn Charter Sch. Avocations: golf, squash, racketball, softball. Office: Murphy & O'Connor 2 Penn Center Plz Ste 1100 Philadelphia PA 19102-1721 Also: 65 Haddon Ave Haddonfield NJ 08033

MELLON, TIMOTHY, transportation executive. CEO Guilford Transp. Industries, North Billerica, Mass. Office: Guilford Transp Industries High St Iron Horse Pk North Billerica MA 01862*

MELLOR, JAMES ROBB, electronics executive; b. Detroit, May 3, 1930; s. Clifford and Gladys (Robb) M.; m. Suzanne Stykos, June 8, 1953; children: James Robb, Diane Elyse, Deborah Lynn. BS in Elec. Engring. and Math., U. Mich., 1952, MS, 1953. Mem. tech. staff Hughes Aircraft Co., Fullerton, Calif., 1955-58; pres. Data Systems divsn. Litton Industries, Van Nuys, Calif., after 1958; exec. v.p. Litton Industries, Inc., Beverly Hills, Calif.; pres., COO AM Internat., Inc., L.A., to 1981; exec. v.p., dir. Gen. Dynamics Corp., Falls Church, Va., 1981-90, pres., 1990—, COO, 1990-93, CEO, 1993-94, chmn., CEO, 1994—; bd. dirs. Bergen Brunswig Corp., Kerr, Computer Scis. Corp., Pinkerton, U.S. Surg. Inc. Patentee in fields of storage tubes and display systems; contbr. articles to profl. publs. 1st lt., Signal Corps, AUS, 1953-55. Mem. IEEE, Am. Mgmt. Assn., Armed Forces Comm. and Electronics Assn. (bd. dirs.), Computer and Bus. Equipment Mfrs. Assn. (former chmn.), L.A. Country Club, Calif. Club, Eldorado Club, Congl. Country Club, Burning Tree Club, Sigma Xi, Tau Beta Pi, Eta Kappa Nu. Home: 7901 Sandalfoot Dr Potomac MD 20854-5449 Office: Gen Dynamics Corp 3190 Fairview Park Dr Falls Church VA 22042-4510

MELLOR, JOHN WILLIAMS, economist, policy consultant firm executive; b. Paris, Dec. 28, 1928; came to U.S., 1929; s. Desmond W. and Katherine (Beardsley) M.; m. Arlene Patton, June 15, 1950 (div. Sept. 1972); children: Michael, Brian, Mark (dec.); m. Uma Lele, Feb. 17, 1973 (div. Apr. 1992). BS, Cornell U., 1950, MS, 1951, PhD, 1954; Diploma, Oxford (Eng.) U., 1952. Prof. Cornell U., Ithaca, N.Y., 1953-75; chief economist USAID, Washington, 1975-77; dir. Internat. Food Policy Rsch. Inst., Washington, 1977-91; pres. John W. Mellor Assocs., Inc., Washington, 1991—; mem. bd. on agrl. NAS, 1989-92; mem. Agrl. Credit Commn., Res. Bank India, 1986-88. Author: Economics of Agricultural Development, 1966 (Am. Agrl. Econs. Assn. award 1978), Accelerating Food Production Growth in Sub-Saharan Africa, 1987, Agricultural Price Policy for Developing Countries, 1988 (hon. mention Am. Agrl. Econs. Assn. 1989). Mem. Internat. Commn. on Food and Peace, 1988—. Recipient Wihuri Internat. prize Wihuri Found., Helsinki, 1985, Presdl. End Hunger award The White House, 1987, Outstanding Alumni award Cornell U., 1987. Fellow AAAS, Am. Acad. Arts and Scis., Am. Agrl. Econs. Assn. (Best Pub. Rsch. award 1967). Avocations: sailing, skiing. Office: John Mellor Assocs Inc Ste PH18 801 Pennsylvania Ave NW Washington DC 20004-2615

MELLOR, MICHAEL LAWTON, lawyer; b. Yorkshire, Eng., July 20, 1922; came to U.S., 1922; s. Bethel and Carmen (Lawton) M.; m. Mary Gordon, May 17, 1952 (dec.); children—Wendy, Jane, Christie. A.B., U. Calif.-Berkeley, 1943, LL.B., 1950. Bar: Calif. 1951. Assoc., Thelen, Marrin, Johnson & Bridges, San Francisco, 1950-62, ptnr., 1962-90, of counsel, 1990-93, retired ptnr., 1993—; dir. various bus. cos. Bd. dirs. San Francisco Attic Theatre, 1979-83, Robinson Jeffers Tor House Found., Carmel, Calif., 1980-96, Pacific Vision Found., San Francisco, 1982—, Friends of San Francisco Pub. Libr., 1984-92, Dance Through Time, Kentfield, Calif., 1986-92, Internat. Visitors Ctr., 1990-96. 1st lt. U.S. Army, 1943-45, Philippines, Japan. Mem. ABA, Calif. State Bar, San Francisco Bar Assn. Democrat. Club: The Family (dir., sec.) (San Francisco). Home: 81 5th Ave San Francisco CA 94118-1307 Office: Thelen Marrin Johnson & Bridges 2 Embarcadero Ctr San Francisco CA 94111

MELLOR, RONALD JOHN, history educator; b. Bklyn., Sept. 30, 1940; s. Ronald Green and Eleanor Teresa (Walsh) M.; m. Anne Tidaback Kostelanetz, June 7, 1969; 1 child, Ronald Blake. AB, Fordham Coll., 1962; cert., U. Louvain, Belgium, 1961; AM, Princeton U., 1964, PhD in Classics, 1968. From acting asst. prof. to asst. prof. Classics Stanford (Calif.) U., 1965-75; assoc. prof. history UCLA, 1976-82, prof. history, 1982—; vice-chmn. history UCLA, 1991-92, chmn. history, 1992-97; visitor Princeton Inst. Advanced Studies, 1997—. Author: Thea Rhome, 1975, From Augustus to Nero: The First Dynasty of Imperial Rome, 1990, Tacitus, 1993, Tacitus and the Classical Tradition, 1995, The Historians of Ancient Rome, 1997. Fellow NEH, 1969, Am. Coun. Learned Socs., 1972, Humanities Rsch. Ctr. Australian Nat. U., Canberra, Australia, 1990; hon. fellow U. Coll. London, Eng., 1969, 72, 83-85. Mem. Am. Hist. Assn., Am. Philol. Assn., Am. Inst. Archaeology, Assn. Ancient Historians, Soc. for the Promotion of Roman Studies. Democrat. Avocations: opera, travel, theater, tennis. Home: 2620 Mandeville Canyon Rd Los Angeles CA 90049-1004 Office: UCLA Dept History 405 Hilgard Ave Los Angeles CA 90095-9000

MELLORS, ROBERT CHARLES, physician, scientist; b. Dayton, Ohio, 1916; s. Bert S. and Clementine (Steinmetz) M.; m. Jane K. Winternitz, Mar. 25, 1944; children: Alice J., Robert C., William K., John W. Ph.D., Western Res. U., 1940; M.D., Johns Hopkins, 1944. Diplomate Am. Bd. Pathology. Intern Nat. Naval Med. Ctr., Bethesda, Md., 1944-45; rsch. fellow medicine Meml. Center Cancer and Allied Diseases, N.Y.C., 1946-50; rsch. fellow pathology Meml. Ctr. Cancer and Allied Diseases, 1950-53, asst. attending pathologist, 1953-57, assoc. attending pathologist, 1957-58; sr. fellow Am. Cancer Soc., 1947-50; sr. clin. rsch. fellow Damon Runyon Meml. Fund, 1950-53; asst. attending pathologist Meml. Hosp., N.Y.C., 1953-57, assoc. attending pathologist, 1957-58; asst. attending pathologist Ewing Hosp., N.Y.C., 1953-57, assoc. attending pathologist, 1957-58; instr. biochemistry Western Res. U., 1940-42; rsch. assoc. Poliomyelitis Rsch. Ctr. and Dept. Epidemiology Johns Hopkins U. Sch. Hygiene, 1942-44; asst. prof. biology Meml. Ctr. Cancer and Allied Diseases, N.Y.C., 1952-53; asst. prof. pathology Sloan Kettering div. Cornell U., 1953-57, assoc. prof., 1957-58; prof. pathology Cornell U. Med. Coll., 1961-90, prof. emeritus, 1990—; assoc. attending pathologist N.Y. Hosp., 1961-72, attending pathologist, 1972-86; pathologist-in-chief, dir. labs., 1958-84, emeritus, 1984-85, hon. staff, 1986—; assoc. dir. rsch. Hosp. for Spl. Surgery, N.Y.C., 1958-69, dir. rsch., 1969-84, emeritus, 1984-85, scientist emeritus, 1986—; mem. rsch. adv. com. NIH, 1962-66; adv. com. Nat. Inst. Environ. Health Sci., 1966-69; com. nomenclature and classification of disease Coll. Am. Pathologists, 1960-64. Author: Analytical Cytology, 1955, 2d edit., 1959, Analytical Pathology, 1957. Served as lt. (j.g.), M.C. USNR, 1944-46. Recipient Kappa Delta award Am. Acad. of Orthopedic Surgeons, 1962. Fellow Royal Coll. Pathologists, Molecular Medicine Soc., Am. Soc. Clin. Pathology; mem. Am. Assn. Pathologists, Am. Assn. Immunologists, Am. Soc. Biochemistry and Molecular Biology, Am. Coll. Rheumatology, Am. Orthopedic Assn. (hon.). Home: 3 Hardscrabble Cir Armonk NY 10504-2222

MELLOTT, ROBERT VERNON, advertising executive; b. Dixon, Ill., Jan. 1, 1928; s. Edwin Vernon and Frances Rhoda (Miller) M.; m. Sarah Carolyn Frink, June 11, 1960; children: Lynn Mellott Finzer, Susan Mellott Dodge, David Robert. BA, DePauw U., 1950; postgrad. Grad. Sch., Ind. U., 1950-51, Law Sch., 1959-61, MA, 1983. TV producer, dir. Jefferson Standard Broadcasting Co., Charlotte, N.C., 1951-59; asst. dist. mgr. GM., Flint, Mich., Chgo., 1961-62; TV and radio comml. supr. NW Ayer & Son, Chgo., 1962-65; TV and radio producer Foote, Cone & Belding Advt. Inc., Chgo., 1965-67, mgr. midwest prodn., 1967-69, mgr. comml. coordination, 1969-74, v.p., mgr. comml. svcs., Chgo., 1974-93 (ret.); cons. speech and broadcasting comm. Mem. media adv. com. Coll. of Dupage, Glen Ellyn, Ill., 1971-82; chmn. Cub Scout Com., Wheaton, Ill., 1978-79; bd. dirs. Chgo. Unltd., 1969-71. Mem. Am. Assn. Advt. Agys. (broadcast adminstrn. policy com., broadcast talent union rels. ANA-AAAA joint policy com. 1984-93), World Communication Assn., Phi Delta Phi, Alpha Tau Omega. Republican. Mem. Evang. Christian Ch. Clubs: DePauw U. Alumni Assn., Ind. U. Alumni Assn. Home: 26w130 Tomahawk Dr Wheaton IL 60187-7823

MELLOY, MICHAEL J., federal judge; b. 1948; m. Jane Anne Melloy; children: Jennifer, Katherine, Bridget. BA, Loras Coll., 1970; JD, U. Iowa, 1974. With O'Conner & Thomas P.C. (formerly O'Conner, Thomas, Wright, Hammer, Bertsch & Norby, Dubuque, Iowa, 1974-86; judge U.S. Bankruptcy Ct. (no. dist.) Iowa, 1986-92; apptd. chief judge U.S. Dist. Ct. (no. dist.) Iowa, Cedar Rapids, 1992—. With U.S. Army, 1970-72, USAR, 1972-76. Mem. ABA, Comml. Law League Am., Nat. Conf. Bankruptcy Judges, Eighth Cir. Judicial Coun. (bankruptcy judge rep., bankruptcy com.), Iowa State Bar Assn. (coun. mem. bankruptcy and comml. law sect.), Ill. State Bar Assn., Dubuque County Bar Assn., Linn County Bar Assn., Mason L. Ladd Inn of Ct., Rotary. Office: US Dist Ct 101 1st St SE Ste 304 Cedar Rapids IA 52401-1202*

MELLUM, GALE ROBERT, lawyer; b. Duluth, Minn., July 5, 1942; s. Lester Andrew and Doris Esther (Smith) M.; m. Julie Murdoch Swanstrom, July 23, 1966; children: Eric Scott, Wendy Jane. BA summa cum laude, U. Minn., 1964, JD magna cum laude, 1968. Bar: Minn. 1968. Assoc. Faegre & Benson, Mpls., 1968-75, ptnr., 1976—; mem. mgmt. com. Faegre & Benson, 1986—; mem. adv. bd. Quali Tech Inc., Chaska, Minn., 1985—; bd. dirs. Edn. Alts. Inc., Mpls.; adv. bd. Excelsior-Henderson Motorcycle Mfg. Co., 1996—. Hockey chmn. LARC Bd., Mpls., 1980-85. Mem. ABA (fed. securities regulation com.), Minn. Bar Assn., Hennepin County Bar Assn. (securities regulation com.). Republican. Lutheran. Avocations: tennis, golf, snow and water skiing, handball, boating. Home: 4889 E Lake Harriet Pky Minneapolis MN 55409-2222 Office: Faegre & Benson 2200 Norwest Ctr 90 S 7th St Minneapolis MN 55402-3903

MELMON, KENNETH LLOYD, physician, biologist, pharmacologist, consultant; b. San Francisco, July 20, 1934; s. Abe Irving and Jean (Kahn) M.; m. Elyce Edelman, June 9, 1957; children: Bradley S., Debra W. AB in Biology with honors, Stanford U., 1956; MD, U. Calif. at San Francisco, 1959. Intern, then resident in internal medicine U. Calif. Med. Ctr., San Francisco, 1959-61; clin. assoc., surgeon USPHS, Nat. Heart, Lung and Kidney Inst., NIH, 1961-64; chief resident in medicine U. Wash. Med. Ctr., Seattle, 1964-65; chief div. clin. pharmacology U. Calif. Med. Ctr., 1965-78; chief dept. medicine Stanford U. Med. Ctr., 1978-84, Arthur Bloomfield prof. medicine, prof. pharmacology, 1978-86, prof. medicine and molecular pharmacology, 1978—; assoc. dean postgrad. med. edn., 1994—; dir. tech. transfer program Stanford U. Hosp., 1986-93; mem. sr. staff Cardiovasc. Rsch. Inst.; chmn. joint commn. prescription drug use Senate Subcom. on Health, Inst. Medicine and HEW-Pharm. Mfrs. Assn.; mem. Nat. Bd. Med. Examiners, 1987-97; pres. Bio 2000, Woodside, Calif., 1983-85; co-founder Immulogic, Waltham, Mass., 1988; sci. advisor Hoffman LaRoche, Epoch, Vysis, others; cons. FDA, 1965-82, Office Tech. Assessment, 1974-75, Senate Subcom. on Health, 1975—; bd. dirs. Vysis, Chgo., Immologic, Boston, Epoch, Seattle; cons. to govt.; founder Inst. Biol. and Clin. Investigation, Ctr. for Molecular and Genetic Medicine, Stanford Cmty. of Internists Stanford Med. Group, Intergrate Ctr. Clin. Immunology; chmn. acad. senate Sch. Medicine, Stanford U., 1996—, mem. steering com. acad. senate, 1996—. Author articles, chpts. in books, sects. encys.; Editor: Clinical Pharmacology: Basic Principles in Therapeutics, 3d edit., 1992, Cardiovascular Therapeutics, 1974; assoc. editor: The Pharmacological Basis of Therapeutics (Goodman and Gilman), 1984; mem. editorial bd. numerous profl. jours. Surgeon USPHS, 1961-64. Burroughs Wellcome clin. pharmacology scholar, 1966-71; John Simon Guggenheim fellow Weizman Inst., Israel, 1971, NIH spl. fellow, Bethesda, 1971. Fellow AAAS (nat. coun. 1985-89); mem. Am. Fedn. Clin. Rsch. (pres. 1973-74), Am. Soc. Clin. Investigation (pres. 1978-79), Assn. Am. Physicians, Western Assn. Physicians (pres. 1983-84), Am. Soc. Pharmacology and Exptl. Therapeutics, Am. Soc. Clin. Pharmacology and Therapeutics (Oscar Hunter award in therapeutics 1994), Inst. Medicine of NAS, Am. Physiol. Soc., Calif. Acad. Medicine, Med. Friends of Wine, Phi Beta Kappa. Democrat. Jewish. Achievements include initiation of founding of Ctr. of Molecular and Genetic Medicine, The Integrated Ctr. for Clin. Immunology, Stanford, Stanford Health Info. Network for Edn., others. Home: 51 Cragmont Way Woodside CA 94062-2307 Office: Stanford U Med Ctr Dept Medicine # S025 Stanford CA 94305

MELNER, SINCLAIR LEWIS, insurance company executive, retired; b. Reno, Apr. 6, 1928; s. Abraham H. and Carol Rachel (Myers) M.; m. Roma F. Garner, Dec. 26, 1949; children: Catherine, Michael, Joan. B.S., U. Nev., 1949; M.S. in Internat. Affairs, George Washington U., 1969. Commd. 2d lt. U.S. Army, 1949; advanced through grades to lt. gen. U.S. Army, Ft. Benjamin Harrison, Ind., formerly comdg. gen.; later dep. chmn. NATO Mil. Command, Brussels; ret., 1984; v.p., corp. sec. Hudson Inst., 1984-88; sr. advisor Am. Amicable Life Ins. Co. Tex., 1989-95; ret., 1995. Decorated Silver Star with oak leaf cluster, Def. Superior Service medal, Def. D.S.M., Army D.S.M., Legion of Merit with oak leaf cluster. Home: 301 E Braeburn Dr Phoenix AZ 85022-3621

MELNGAILIS, IVARS, solid state research executive; b. Riga, Latvia, Nov. 13, 1933; came to U.S., 1949; s. Janis and Jakobine (Zile) M.; m. Valda Dreimanis, June 6, 1964; children: Nils, Zinta. BS, Carnegie-Mellon U., 1956, MS, 1957, PhD, 1961. Mem. staff. Lincoln Lab., MIT, Lexington, 1961-67, asst. group leader, 1967-71, group leader, 1971-75, assoc. div. head, 1975-96; cons., 1996—. Fellow IEEE; mem. Am. Phys. Soc., Am. Optical Soc. Office: MIT Lincoln Lab Solid State Div 244 Wood St Lexington MA 02173-6426

MELNICK, DANIEL, film producer; b. N.Y.C., Apr. 21, 1932; 1 son, Peter. Partner Talent Assos.; v.p., then sr. v.p. charge worldwide prodn. M.G.M., 1972-76; ind. film producer, 1976-77, 79—; in charge worldwide prodn. Columbia Pictures Industries Inc., 1977-78, pres. motion picture div., 1978; now independent prodr. Indie Prodn. Co. Prodr. films: Straw Dogs, First Family, 1981, Making Love, 1982, Footloose, 1985, Quicksilver, 1986, Roxanne, 1987, Punchline, 1988, Mountains of the Moon, 1990, Air America, 1990, L.A. Story, 1991, The Quick and the Dead, 1994; exec. prodr. films: That's Entertainment, That's Entertainment II, All That Jazz, Altered States, Footloose. Recipient Nat. Acad. TV Arts and Scis. Emmy award for Death of a Salesman and The Ages of Man. Office: Tristar Bldg 10202 Washington Blvd # 211 Culver City CA 90232-3119*

MELNICK, JOSEPH L., virologist, educator; b. Boston, Oct. 9, 1914; s. Samuel and Esther (Melny) M.; m. Matilda Benyesh, 1958; 1 child, Nancy. AB, Wesleyan U., 1936; PhD, Yale U., 1939; DSc, Wesleyan U., 1971; MD (hon.), Charles U., Prague, Czech Republic, 1993. Asst. in physiol. chemistry Sch. Medicine Yale U., New Haven, 1937-39; Asst. in physiol. chemistry, Finney-Howell Research Found. fellow Sch. Medicine Yale U., 1939-41, NRC fellow in med. scis., 1941-42, rsch. asst. in preventive medicine with rank of instr., 1942-44, asst. prof., 1944-48, rsch. assoc., 1948-49, assoc. prof. microbiology, 1949-54, prof. epidemiology, 1954-57; chief virus labs. divsn. biologics stds. NIH, USPHS, 1957-58; prof., chmn. virology and epidemiology Coll. Medicine Baylor, Houston, 1958-68; Disting. Svc. prof. Coll. Medicine Baylor, 1974—, dean grad. scis., 1968-91, dean emeritus, 1992—; mem. com. on viral diseases WHO, 1957—, mem. internat. task force on hepatitis B immunization, 1992—, dir. Internat. Ctr. Enteroviruses, 1963-93, mem. cons. group on poliomyelitis vaccine, 1973—, dir. Collaborating Ctr. for Virus Reference and Rsch., 1970—; mem. com. on live poliovirus vaccines USPHS, 1958-61; mem. virus reference bd. NIH, 1962-70, mem. dir. adv. com. on DNA recombinants, 1976, mem. evaluation com. divsn. rsch. resources, 1975-76, mem. nat. adv. cancer coun., 1965-69; mem. human cancer virus task force Nat. Cancer Inst., NIH, USPHS, 1962-67; sec.-gen. Internat. Congresses Virology, Helsinki and Budapest, 1968-71; chmn. Internat. Conf. on Viruses in Water, Mexico City, 1974; mem. rsch. coun. Am. Cancer Soc., 1971-75; mem. com. on hepatitis NAS/NRC, 1972-77; lectr., cons. Chinese Acad. Med. Scis., 1978, 79, 93; mem. adv. com. Comparative Virology Orgn., 1978-86; chmn. adv. com. on viral hepatitis Ctr. fo Disease Control, 1989, 95, mem. adv. com. on respiratory and enteric viruses, 1991, mem. adv. com. on evaluation of U.S. polio cases, 1963-75, 76-84; cons. devel. program for health manpower and svcs. of Palestinian people UN, 1981-83. Author: Textbook of Medical Microbiology; editor: Progress in Medical Virology and Monographs in Virology, also over 1000 rsch. papers in virology; editor-in-chief ofcl. jour. virology Intervirology, Internat. Union Microbiol. Socs., 1972-85. Bd. dirs. Houston Acad. Medicine-Tex. Med. Ctr. Libr., 1967-90, chmn., 1988-89; trustee Albert B. Sabin Vaccine Found., 1994—; chmn. U.S. Commn. on Polio Eradication, 1994—. Univ. scholar Yale U., 1939; co-recipient Internat. medal for rsch. in immunity to poliolyelitis Argentinian Found. Against Infantile Paralysis, 1949, Indsl. Rsch.-100 award, 1971, 74; recipient Humanitarian award Jewish Inst. Med. Rsch., 1964, Modern Medicine Disting. Achievement award, 1965, Eleanor Roosevelt Humanities award, 1965, Inventor of Yr. award Houston Patent Law Assn., 1972, Gold medal South African Poliomyelitis Rsch. Found., 1979, Maimonides award State of Israel, 1980, Raymond E. Baldwin medal for Disting. Svc., Wesleyan U., 1986; named to Nat. Found.'s Polio Hall of Fame, 1958. Fellow AAAS, APHA, N.Y. Acad. Scis. (Freedom Found. award for rsch. in virology 1973), Am. Acad. Microbiology; mem. Am. Soc. Microbiology, Am. Soc. Virology, Soc. Exptl. Biology and Medicine (mem. coun. 1965-69), Am. Assn. Immunologists, Am. Epidemiol. soc., Am. Assn. Cancer Rsch. (pres. S.W. sect. 1968), Internat. Assn. Microbiol. Socs. (life, chmn. sect. on virology 1970-75, mem. exec. com. 1976-79, mem. internat. commn. on microbiol. ecology 1972-87, mem. internat. com. on taxonomy of viruses 1966—, Albert Sabin medal for work in polio vaccines 1996), Microbiol. Soc. Israel (hon.), Microbiol. Soc. Argentina (hon.), USSR Soc. Microbiologists and Epidemiologists (hon.), Chinese Soc. Med. Virology (hon.), Med. Soc. Bulgaria (hon.), Phi Beta Kappa, Sigma Xi.

MELNICK, VIJAYA LAKSHMI, biology educator, research center director; b. Kerala, India; came to U.S., 1959; m. Daniel Melnick, June 28, 1963; 1 child, Anil D. BS, Madras Agriculture Coll., India, 1959; MS, U. Wis., 1961, PhD, 1964, postgrad., 1964-66. Asst. prof. dept. biology Fed. City Coll., Washington, 1970-74; assoc. prof. dept. biology U. D.C., Washington, 1974-77, prof. biology, 1977—; dir. Ctr. for Applied Rsch. and Urban Policy, Washington, 1992—; sr. staff assoc. Internat. Ctr. Inter-Disciplinary Studies in Immunology Georgetown U. Med. Sch., 1978-85, assoc. dir. tech. transfer, edn. and community outreach Ctr. Inter-Disciplinary Studies in Immunology, 1985—; sr. rsch. scholar Ctr. for Applied Rsch. and Urban Policy, Washington, 1984-85; spl. asst. policy and bioethics Nat. Inst. Aging/NIH, Bethesda, Md., 1980-82; vis. prof., rsch. participant Carnegie program Oak Ridge Grad. Sch. Biomed. Sci., U. Tenn., 1974-78; vis. scientist Biology and Medicine Inst., Lawrence Livermore Labs., U. Calif., 1972-73; invited del. cell biologist to People's Republic of China, 1990, to Initiave on Edn. Sci. & Tech. to Republic South Africa, 1995; mem. health edn. adv. com. Internat. Med. Svc. for Health, Washington; mem. Nestle Infant Formula Audit Commn., 1981-91; mem. Mayor's Adv. Bd. on Infant and Maternal Health, 1987—; del. 1st Asian-Pacific Orgn. for Cell Biology Congress, Shanghai, 1990; mem. nat. coun. on rsch. in child welfare Child Welfare League Am., Inc., 1992—; mem. adv. coun. D.C. family policy seminar Georgetown U. Grad. Pub. Policy Program, 1993—; mem. adv. com. tng. program for postdoctoral program in devel. immunology Internat. Ctr. Interdisciplinary Studies in Immunology, Georgetown U. Med. Ctr., 1993—; mem. steering com. Nat. Consortium for African Am. Children, Nat. Commn. to Prevent Infant Mortality, 1993—; host scientist Science in American Life exhibition Nat. Mus. Am. Hist. The Smithsonian Inst., 1994—. Invited del. initiative on edn., sci., and tech. to Republic of South Africa, 1995. Recipient Outstanding Svc. award March of Dimes, 1987; postdoctoral fellow U. Wis. Med. Sch., 1964-66. Mem. APHA, AAAS, Am. Soc. Cell Biology, Assn. for Women in Sci., Am. Polit. Sci. Assn., Nat. Assn. Minority Med. Educators (legis. com. 1977—), Nat. Assn. for Equal Opportunities in Higher Edn. (sci. and tech. adv. com. 1982), N.Y. Acad. Sci., Sigma Xi, Sigma Delta Epsilon. Office: U DC Ctr Applied Rsch 4200 Connecticut Ave NW Washington DC 20008-1122

MELNIK, ROBERT EDWARD, aeronautical engineer; b. N.Y.C., Nov. 19, 1933; s. Adam Edward and Anna Elizabeth (Petroccia) M.; m. Carol Joan Ceparano, Sept. 24, 1960; children: Joann, Christine. B.Aero.Engring., Poly. Inst. Bklyn., 1956, M.Aero. Engring., 1961, Ph.D., 1965. Research scientist Grumman Aerospace Corp., Bethpage, N.Y., 1956-66; head aerodynamics research group Grumman Aerospace Corp., 1966-73, dir. fluid mechanics, 1973-89; tech. mgr. Northrop Grumman Corp., Bethpage, 1994-97; prof. computational engr. Miss. State U., 1997—. Assoc. editor: AIAA Jour, 1978-80; mem. editorial com.: Ann. Rev. Fluid Mechanics, 1982-87; contbr. articles to profl. jours. Bd. dirs. Family Service League of Suffolk, 1975—. Rsch. fellow, 1989-94. Fellow AIAA; mem. Am. Phys. Soc. Office: Northrop Grumman Corp Bethpage NY 11714

MELNYK, STEVEN ALEXANDER, business management educator; b. Hamilton, Ont., Can., Apr. 12, 1953; came to U.S., 1980; s. Stephen and Mary (Sahan) M.; m. Christine Ann Halstead, July 10, 1976; children: Charles Edward Phillip, Elizabeth Victoria Michaela. BA in Econs., U. Windsor, Ont., 1975; MA in Econs., U. We. Ont., London, 1976, PhD in Ops. Mgmt., 1981. Asst. prof. ops. mgmt. Mich. State U., East Lansing, 1980-85, assoc. prof., 1985-90, prof., 1990—. Author: Shop Floor Control, 1985, 87, Production Activity Control, 1987, Computer Integrated Manual, 1992-96, Operations Management A Valve Driven Approach, others. Recipient Tchr.-Scholar award Mich. State U., 1985, other awards. Mem. Am. Prodn. and Inventory Control Soc. (software editor 1991—, cons. 1980—, Paul Berkobile award 1992), Nat. Assn. Purchasing Mgrs., Decision Sci. Inst. (editor procs. 1991, Outstanding Theoretical Paper award 1982), Soc. Mfg. Engrs., Inst. Mgmt. Sci. Episcopalian. Avocations: Civil War history, baseball history, bicycling. Office: Mich State U N431 NBC East Lansing MI 48824-1122

MELNYKOVYCH, ANDREW O., journalist; b. Mpls., Aug. 23, 1952; s. George and Oksana (Demianchuk) M.; m. Debra Denise Mamigonian, May 24, 1986; children: Alexander Vartan, Anna Emilia. BS in Biology, Yale U., 1975, M in Forest Sci., 1977; postgrad., U. Wyo., 1978-82. Lab. instr. dept. biochemistry U. Wyo., Laramie, 1982-83; corr. Casper (Wyo.) Star-Tribune, 1982-83, environ. writer, 1983-86, Washington reporter, 1986-90; environ. writer Louisville Courier-Jour., 1990—; contbg. writer High Country News, Paonia, Colo., 1987-90, The Post-Register, Idaho Falls, Idaho, 1989-90. Recipient George S. Polk award L.I. U., N.Y., 1989, 2d pl. Barnet Nover award Standing Com. of Corrs., Washington, 1989. Mem. Soc. Environ. Journalists. Avocations: birding, photography. Office: Louisville Courier-Jour 525 W Broadway Louisville KY 40202-2206*

MELOAN, TAYLOR WELLS, marketing educator; b. St. Louis, July 31, 1919; s. Taylor Wells and Edith (Graham) M.; m. Anna Geraldine Leukering, Dec. 17, 1944 (div. 1974); children: Michael David, Steven Lee; m. Jane Innes Bierlich, Jan. 30, 1975. B.S. cum laude, St. Louis U., 1949; M.B.A., Washington U., St. Louis, 1950; D of Bus. Admin., Ind. U., 1953. Advt. mgr. Herz Corp., St. Louis, 1941-42; sales promotion supr. Liggett & Myers Tobacco Co., St. Louis, 1942-43; asst. prof. mktg. U. Okla., Norman, 1953; asst., then assoc. prof. mktg. Ind. U., Bloomington, 1953-59; prof., chmn. dept. mktg. U. So. Calif., Los Angeles, 1959-69, prof. mktg., 1969-92, Robert E. Brooker prof. mktg., 1970-79, Robert E. Brooker disting. prof. mktg. emeritus, 1991—; disting. emeritus prof. U. So. Calif., L.A., 1997—, dean Sch. Bus. Adminstrn., 1969-71, assoc. v.p. acad. adminstrn. and research, 1971-81; prof. bus. adminstrn. U. Karachi, Pakistan, 1962; vis. prof. mktg. Istituto Post U. Per Lo Studio Dell Organizzazione Aziendale, Turin, Italy, 1964, U. Hawaii, 1993, Madrid Bus. Sch., 1993; disting. vis. prof. U. Witwatersrand, Johannesburg, 1978, U. Hawaii, 1993; editl. advisor bus. adminstrn. Houghton Mifflin Co., Boston, 1959-73; cons. to industry and govt., 1953; bd. dirs Inst. Shipboard Edn. Author: New Career Opportunities, 1978, Innovation Strategy and Management, 1979, Direct Marketing: Vehicle for Department Store Expansion, 1984, Preparing the Exporting Entrepreneur, 1986, The New Competition: Dilemma of Department Stores in the 1980's, 1987, Franchise Marketing: A Retrospective and Prospective View of a Contractual Vertical Marketing System, 1988; co-author: Managerial Marketing, 1970, Internationalizing the Business Curriculum, 1968, Handbook of Modern Marketing, contbg. author, 1986; co-author, co-editor: International and Global Marketing: Concepts and Cases, 1994, International and Global Marketing Concepts and Cases, Vol. 2, 1997; bd. editors Jour. Mktg., 1965-72. Trustee World Affairs Coun. Orange County, 1994—. Lt. (j.g.) U.S. Maritime Svc., 1943-46. Mem. Am. Mktg. Assn. (pres. L.A. chpt. 1963-64), Order of Artus, Beta Gamma Sigma, Delta Pi Epsilon, Calif. Yacht Club, Univ. Club, Rotary. Home: 59 Lakefront Irvine CA 92604-4683 Office: U So Calif Dept Mktg Los Angeles CA 90089-1421

MELODY, MICHAEL EDWARD, publishing company executive; b. Streator, Ill., Dec. 22, 1943; s. Giles Lambert and Rose Mary (Moreschi) M.;

m. Carol Ann Weir, June 8, 1968 (div.); 1 dau., Alison Anne; m. Bonnie Kaye Binkert, Mar. 26, 1983. BA, Ala. Coll., 1966. Exec. editor, asst. v.p. Prentice-Hall, Inc., Englewood Cliff, N.J., 1974-79; v.p., editor-in-chief coll. div. Macmillan Pub. Co., N.Y.C., 1979-80, sr. v.p., pres. coll. div., 1980-87, pres. sch. div., 1987-88; v.p. higher edn. group Simon & Schuster, N.Y.C., 1988-90; sr. v.p. Houghton Mifflin Co., Boston, 1990-91, exec. v.p., 1991-95; prin. Michael E. Melody Cons., Boston, 1995-96; v.p., gen. mgr. info. prod. Inso Corp., Boston, 1996—; chmn. bd. dirs. Appleton & Lange, N.Y.C., 1989-90. Bd. overseers Huntington Theatre Co., Boston, 1993—; bd. advisors Boston U. Sch. for the Arts, 1997—; bd. dirs. Judge Baker Ctr. for Children, Harvard U. Med Sch., 1997—; mem. corp. Judge Baker Children's Ctr., 1997—. Served with USAR, 1967. Mem. Assn. Am. Pubs. (vice chmn. coll. divsn. 1981-83, chmn. coll. divsn. 1983-86, exec. com. sch. divsn. 1987-88, exec. com. higher edn. divsn. 1990—), Nat. Assn. Coll. Stores (trustee 1986-87, 94-95).

MELONAKOS, CHRISTINE MARIE, educational administrator; b. Shelby, Mich., Apr. 29, 1960; d. L.V. Charles and Dorothy June (Arman) Besemer; m. Paul W. Melonakos, May 31, 1983; children: Christian, Timothy, Kandice, Emerson. BS in Psychology, Brigham Young U., 1989. Presch. tchr. Minnieland, Manassas, Va., 1989-90; kindergarten tchr. Manassas Christian Sch., 1990-91; presch. owner Appleseed Presch., Manassas, 1991-92; pres., founder Applebrook Family Enrichment Network, Fremont, Mich., 1992-95, Applebrook Inst., Newaygo, Mich., 1994—; pub. spkr. various orgns., 1990-95; parent educator various orgns., Va. and Mich., 1989-95; creator (tchg. method) Interactive Assistance, 1992. Author: Starting Right, 1993, Cooperation Kit, 1993, Parenting Success Program, 1995; editor Motivated Mother Newsletter, 1990-91. Sec. PTA, Manassas, 1991-92; children's program dir. Parents Anonymous, Manassas, 1991. Recipient Va. Mother of Yr. award Am. Mothers Assn., 1992. Mem. ASCD, Interactive Parents Assn. (founder, pres. 1993—). Republican. Avocations: sewing, antiques, country line dancing, Victorian postcards. Office: Applebrook Inst PO Box 40 Fremont MI 49412

MELONE, JOSEPH JAMES, insurance company executive; b. Pittston, Pa., July 27, 1931; s. Dominick William and Beatrice Marie (Pignone) M.; m. Marie Jane DeGeorge, Jan. 23, 1960; children—Lisa, Carol. B.S., U. Pa., 1953, M.B.A., 1954, Ph.D. in Econs, 1961. C.P.C.U., 1964, ChFC, 1984. Assoc. prof. ins. U. Pa., 1959-66, mem. pension research council, 1961-66; research dir. Am. Coll. Life Underwriters, 1966-68; v.p. Prudential Ins. Co., Boston, 1969-76; sr. v.p. Prudential Ins. Co., Newark, 1976-81, exec. v.p., 1981-84, pres., 1984-90; pres., COO, bd. dirs. The Equitable Life Assurance Soc. U.S., 1990-94; pres., COO The Equitable Life Assurance Soc. of U.S., 1990-94, also bd. dirs.; pres., COO The Equitable Cos., Inc., 1992-96, also bd. dirs.; pres., CEO The Equitable Cos., Inc., N.Y.C., 1996—; chmn. The Equitable Life Assurance Soc. U.S., N.Y.C., 1994—; chmn., CEO Equitable Variable Life Ins. Co.; bd. dirs. Foster Wheeler Corp., Alliance Capital Mgmt., Donaldson, Lufkin & Jenrette, Equity and Law, AT&T Capital Corp.; chmn. LICONY, ACLI. Author: Collectively Bargained Multi-Employer Pension Plans, 1961; co-author: Risk and Insurance, 1963, Pension Planning, 1966. Trustee Newark Mus.; chmn. ins. divsn. Cardinal's Commn. Laity N.Y. Archdiocese; ptnr. N.Y.C. Partnership; bd. overseers Wharton Sch. U. Pa.; bd. dirs. Am. Coll., Huebner Found.-U. Pa.; bd. dirs. Greater N.Y. couns. Boy Scouts Am. Mem. Am. Risk and Ins. Assn., Am. Soc. CLUs, Am. Coll. (trustee), Am. Inst. Property and Liability Underwriters (trustee), Pa. State U. Internat. Ins. Soc., Internat. Acad. Mgmt., Health Ins. Assn. Am. (bd. dirs., past chmn.), Health Ins. Assn. Am. (bd. dirs., past chmn.), U.S.-Korea Bus. Coun., Morris County Country Club, Baltusrol Golf Club, Alpha Tau Omega. Home: 281 Hartshorn Dr Short Hills NJ 07078-1916 Office: Equitable Cos Inc 1290 Avenue Of The Americas New York NY 10104-0199

MELONI, ANDREW P., protective services official; b. Rochester, N.Y., Apr. 10, 1931; s. Andrew and Carrie (DeMaria) M.; m. Laura Ann Tiebe, June 28, 1952; children: Andrew, Michael, Philene Cromwell, Mary Therese Damiano, Stephen. BS, Empire State Coll., 1975. Desk dep. Monroe County Sheriff, Rochester, 1955-60, records sgt., 1960-63, records lt., 1963-65, asst. chief dep., 1965-68, undersheriff, 1968-73; pub. safety commr. Monroe County, Rochester, 1974-77; dir. security U. Rochester, 1977-79; sheriff Monroe County, Rochester, 1980—; commr. accreditation Commn. Accreditation Law Enforcement, Washington, 1993-94. Author: National Code of Ethics, 1991, National Standards for Sheriff & Deputy Sheriff, 1992. Mem. exec. com. Italian Charities, Rochester, 1981—, Rochester Fights Back Drug Com., 1990—. Staff sgt. U.S. Army, 1951-53. Recipient Hall of Fame award Aquinas Inst., 1993. Mem. Nat. Sheriffs Assn. (chmn. stds. and ethics com. 1983—), N.Y. State Sheriffs Ann. (mem. exec. com. 1981—). Republican. Roman Catholic. Avocations: coin collecting, jazz, golf. Office: Monroe County Sheriff's Office 130 Plymouth Ave S Rochester NY 14614-2209

MELOY, SYBIL PISKUR, lawyer; b. Chgo., Dec. 1, 1939; d. Michael M. and Laura (Stevenson) Piskur; children: William S., Bradley M. BS with honors, U. Ill., 1961; JD, Chgo. Kent Coll. Law, 1965. Bar: Ill. 1965, Fla. 1985, D.C. 1995, U.S. Dist. Ct. (no. dist.) Ill. 1965, U.S. Supreme Ct. 1972, U.S. Ct. Appeals (fed. cir.) 1983, U.S. Dist. Ct. (so. dist.) Fla. 1985, D.C. 1995. Patent chemist, patent atty., sr. atty., internat. counsel G.D. Searle & Co., Skokie, Ill., 1961-72; regional counsel Abbott Labs., North Chicago, Ill., 1972-78; pvt.practice, Arlington Heights, Ill., 1978-79; asst. gen. counsel Alberto Culver Co., Melrose Park, Ill., 1979-83; corp. counsel Key Pharms., Inc., Miami, Fla., 1983-86; assoc. Ruden, Barnett McCloskey, Smith, Schuster and Russell, Pa., 1987-89, ptnr., 1990-91; ptnr. Foley & Lardner, Miami, Washington 1991—; adj. prof. Univ. of Miami Sch. of Law, 1986-92. Recipient Abbott Presdl. award, 1977; Bur. Nat. Affairs prize, 1965; Law Rev. prize for best article. Mem. ABA, Chgo. Bar Assn. (chmn.-elect and vice chmn. internat. and fgn. law com.), Am. Patent Law Assn., Am. Chem. Soc., Licencing Execs. Soc., Phi Beta Kappa, Phi Kappa Phi. Patentee oral contraceptive, 1965; contbr. article on fertility control and abortion laws, book rev. on arbitration to law revs. Home: 1915 Brickell Ave Apt 1108C Miami FL 33129-1736 also: 1676 32nd St NW Washington DC 20007-2960 Office: Foley & Lardner 3000 K St NW Washington DC 20007-5109

MELROSE, BARRY JAMES, sportscaster, former professional hockey team coach; b. Kelvington, Sask., Can., July 15, 1956. Player various minor league teams, 1973-77, 82-83, 83-86, 86-87; player Cin. Stingers, 1976-79, Winnipeg Jets, 1979-81, Toronto Maple Leafs, 1981-82, 82-83, Detroit Red Wings, 1983-84, 85-86; former gen. mgr., head coach Adirondack Red Wings; now head coach L.A. Kings, 1992-94; sportscaster ESPN, 1995—. Office: care ESPN Inc 935 Middle St Bristol CT 06010-1000*

MELSHEIMER, MEL P(OWELL), consumer products business executive; b. Los Angeles, July 9, 1939; s. Oscar Merrill M.; m. Sara Sturdevant, Sept. 1, 1962; children: Heidi, Erich, Douglas. A.B. in Econs., Occidental Coll., 1961; M.B.A., U. So. Calif., 1965. With United Calif. Bank, Los Angeles, 1962-66; sr. fin. analyst Ford Motor Co., Newport Beach, Calif., 1966-67; v.p., chief fin. officer Pepsi Cola Co. Pepsico, Inc., Purchase, N.Y., 1968-75; exec. v.p., chief operating officer AZL Resources, Inc., 1975-84; chmn. bd., chief exec. officer PHX Pacific, Inc., 1984-89; pres., chief exec. officer MPM Capital Corp., 1987-89; exec. v.p. Finevest Foods, Inc., Greenwich, Conn., 1989-92; pres., CEO Land-O-Sun Dairies Inc., 1991-92, Atlanta Dairies, Inc., 1991-92; exec. v.p., sec., chief oper. officer Dairy Holdings, Inc., Johnson City, Tenn., 1992-94; exec. v.p., COO, CFO Sonex Internat. Corp., Brewster, N.Y., 1994; pres., CEO M.P. Melsheimer & Co., Ridgefield, Conn., 1994-97, NFX, 1995-96; pres., COO, CFO Harris & Harris Group, Inc., N.Y.C., 1997—; pres. NFX Corp., 1995—. Served with U.S. Army, 1961-62.

MELSHER, GARY W., lawyer; b. Cleve., Mar. 8, 1939. BS, Ohio State U., 1961; JD, Case Western Reserve U., 1964. Bar: Ohio 1964. Ptnr. Jones, Day, Reavis & Pogue, Cleve. Mem. Order of Coif. Office: Jones Day Reavis & Pogue North Point 901 Lakeside Ave E Cleveland OH 44114-1116

MELSOP, JAMES WILLIAM, architect; b. Columbus, Ohio, June 2, 1939; s. James Brendan and Juanita Kathryn (Van Scoy) M.; m. Sandra Lee Minnich, Sept. 21, 1957; children: Deborah Lee, Susan Elizabeth, Kathryn Anne. BArch, Ohio State U., 1964; MArch, Harvard U., 1965; MBA, U. Chgo., 1975. Reg. architect, profl. engr. Architect The Austin Co., Chgo., 1967-69, mgr. bus. devel., 1969-74, asst. dist. mgr., 1974-75; pres., mng. dir. Austin Brasil, Sao Paulo, 1975-78; asst. dist. mgr. The Austin Co., Roselle, N.J., 1978-80; dist. mgr. The Austin Co., 1980-81; v.p., dist. mgr. The Austin Co., Cleve., 1986, group v.p., dir., 1986—, exec. v.p. chief oper. officer, 1992, pres., CEO, 1992—, also bd. dirs. Mem. Am. Inst. Architects., Harvard Club, Presidents' Club, Ohio State U. Pres. Club (Disting. Alumnus award 1989). Home: 3165 Trillium Trail Cleveland OH 44124-5205 Office: Austin Co 3650 Mayfield Rd Cleveland OH 44121-1734*

MELSTED, MARCELLA H., retired administrative assistant, civic worker; b. Mayville, N.D., Mar. 3, 1922; d. Hans Morris and Betsy (Stenerson) Hanson; m. Alvin K. Melsted, June 6, 1965 (dec. June 1994). BS in Commerce, U. N.D., 1946, postgrad. Sec. Off. Sci. R&D, Washington, 1943-45; adminstrv. asst. Am. Embassy (Marshall Plan), Oslo, 1948-50, Paris, 1950-52; adminstrv. asst. N.D. Geol. Soc., Grand Forks, 1953-65. Co-editor: Memories of Homemakers, 1988. Pres. Borg Home Auxiliary, 1984—; apptd. cons. rep. State Plumbing Bd.; chmn. needlepointing dining room chairs N.D. Gov.'s mansion; parliamentarian N.D. Extension Homemakers, Women of Evang. Luth. Ch. Am., v.p., bd. dirs., 1985-91; mem. N.D. Humanities Coun., 1985-91; bd. dirs. Friends of N.D. Mus.; mem. Quad County Cmty. Action Bd., 1995—. Mem. AAUW (parliamentarian N.D. State divsn., 2 fellowships, author branch history, state pres. 1962-64, nat. membership com. 1964-66), N.D. State Fedn. Garden Clubs (state pres., life, tree chmn. nat. bd., state treas. 1991—), Four Seasons Garden Club (sec.-treas. 1987—), Homemakers Clubs (various coms.), China Painters Guild (various coms.). Democrat. Avocations: antiques, china painting, stamp collecting. Home: 7862 127th Ave NE Edinburg ND 58227-9604

MELTEBEKE, RENETTE, career counselor; b. Portland, Oreg., Apr. 20, 1948; d. Rene and Gretchen (Hartwig) M. BS in Sociology, Portland State U., 1970; MA in Counseling Psychology, Lewis and Clark Coll., 1985. Lic. profl. counselor, Oreg.; nat. cert. counselor. Secondary tchr. Portland Pub. Schs., 1970-80; project coord. Multi-Wash CETA, Hillsboro, Oreg., 1980-81; coop. edn. specialist Portland C.C., 1981-91; pvt. practice career counseling, owner Career Guidance Specialists, Lake Oswego, Oreg., 1988—; mem. adj. faculty Marylhurst (Oreg.) Coll., 1989-93, Portland State U., 1994—; assoc. Drake Beam Morin Inc., Portland, 1993-96; career cons. Occupl. Health Svcs. Corp., 1994—, Career Devel. Svcs., 1990—, Life Dimensions, Inc., 1994; presenter Internat. Conf., St. Petersburg, Russia, 1995. Rotating columnist Lake Oswego Rev., 1995—. Pres. Citizens for Quality Living, Sherwood, Oreg., 1989; mem. Leadership Roundtable on Sustainability for Sherwood, 1994-95. Mem. ASTD, Assn. for Psychol. Type, Nat. Career Devel. Assn., Oreg. Career Devel. Assn. (pres. 1990), Assn. for Quality Participation, Assn. for Humanistic Psychology, Willamette Writers. Avocations: walking, swimming, bicycling, cross-country skiing, photography. Home: 890 SE Merryman St Sherwood OR 97140-9746 Office: Career Guidance Specialists 15800 Boones Ferry Rd Ste C104 Lake Oswego OR 97035-3437

MELTON, AUGUSTUS ALLEN, JR., airport executive; b. New Bern, N.C., Feb. 18, 1942; s. Augustus Allen and Margaret (Tucker) M.; m. E. LaRhett Fagan, Oct. 27, 1995; children from previous marriage: Augustus Allen III, Harold David. B.S., Howard U., 1965. Ops. safety officer FAA, Washington, 1971-72; airport cert. and safety insp. FAA, Atlanta, 1972-75; airport cert. safety specialist FAA, Washington, 1976-79, airport mgr., 1980—. Office: Office of Airport Mgr Washington Nat Airport Washington DC 20001

MELTON, CAROL A., publishing executive; b. 1654; m. Joseph M. Hassett; children: Matthew, Meredith. BA with honors, Wake Forest U.; MA in Journalism and Comms., U. Fla.; JD with honors, Am. U. Assoc. in comms. group Hogan and Hartson, Washington, 1981-82; asst. gen. counsel Nat. Cable TV Assn., 1983-86; legal advisor Fed. Comms. Commn. Chmn. Mark Fowler, 1986-87; Washington counsel Warner Comms., 1987-91; v.p. law and pub. policy Time Warner Inc. (merged with Warner Comms.), Washington, 1992—. Vol. St. Patrick's Episcopal Day Sch., The Potomac Sch. Mem. Fed. Comms. Bar Assn. Found. (bd. trustees). Office: Time Warner Inc 800 Connecticut Ave NW Ste 800 Washington DC 20006-2718

MELTON, CHARLES ESTEL, retired physicist, educator; b. Fancy Gap, Va., May 18, 1924; s. Charlie Glenn and Ella (Ayers) M.; m. Una Faye Hull, Dec. 7, 1946; children—Sharon (Mrs. Lawrence Husch), Wayne, Sandra (Mrs. Glenn Allen). B.A., Emory and Henry Coll., 1952, D.Sc., 1967; M.S., Vanderbilt U., 1954; Ph.D., U. Notre Dame, 1964. Physicist Oak Ridge Nat. Lab., 1954-67; prof. chemistry U. Ga., Athens, 1967-97; head dept. U. Ga., 1972-77; now ret. Author: Principles of Mass Spectrometry and Negative Ions, 1970, Ancient Diamond Time Capsules, Secrets of Life and the World, 1985, Primordial Petroleum, 1989; contbr. articles to profl. jours. Served with USNR, 1943-46. Recipient DeFriece medal Emory and Henry Coll., 1959, numerous research grants. Fellow AAAS; mem. Am. Phys. Soc., Am. Chem. Soc., Ga. Acad. Sci. Presbyterian. Home: 34 Glen Carrie Rd Hull GA 30646-9778 Office: Univ Georgia Dept Chemistry Athens GA 30602

MELTON, DAVID REUBEN, lawyer; b. Milw., Apr. 4, 1952; s. Howard and Evelyn Frances (Cohen) M.; m. Nancy Hillary Segal, May 22, 1981; children: Michelle, Hannah. BA, U. Wis., 1974; JD, U. Chgo., 1977. Bar: Ill. 1977, U.S. Dist. Ct. (no. dist.) Ill. 1977, U.S. Ct. Appeals (7th cir.) 1981, U.S. Supreme Ct. 1982, U.S. Fed. Ct. (6th cir.), 1991. Assoc. Karon, Morrison & Savikas, Ltd., Chgo., 1977-83; ptnr. Karon, Morrison & Saviskas, Ltd., Chgo., 1983-87, Karon, Savikas & Horn, Ltd., Chgo., 1987-88, Keck, Mahin & Cate, Chgo., 1988-96; counsel Mayer, Brown & Platt, Chgo., 1996—. Office: Mayer Brown & Platt 190 S Lasalle St Ste 3900 Chicago IL 60603-3410

MELTON, EMORY LEON, lawyer, publisher, state legislator; b. McDowell, Mo. June 20, 1923; s. Columbus Right and Pearly Susan (Wise) M.; student Monett Jr. Coll., 1940-41, S.W. Mo. State U., 1941-42; LLB, U. Mo., 1945; m. Jean Sanders, June 19, 1949; children: Stanley Emory, John Russell. Bar: Mo. 1944; pvt. practice, Cassville, Mo., 1947—; pres. Melton Publs., Inc., 1959—; pros. atty. Barry County (Mo.), 1947-51; mem. Mo. Senate, 1973-97. Chmn., Barry County Republican Com., 1964-68. Served with AUS, 1945-46. Recipient Meritorious Pub. Svc. award St. Louis Globe-Democrat, 1976. Mem. Mo. Bar Assn., Lions, Masons. Baptist. Office: PO Box 488 Cassville MO 65625-0488

MELTON, G. KEMP, mayor; b. Charleston, W.Va., Nov. 19, 1929; m. Corena Mae Melton; 4 children. BS in Bus., W.Va. U. Sheriff, treas. Kanawha County, W.Va., 1965-68, 73-80, assessor, 1981-95; mayor City of Charleston, W.Va., 1995—. 1st lt. U.S. Army, 1953-55, Korea. Presbyterian. Office: Office of Mayor PO Box 2749 Charleston WV 25330

MELTON, GARY BENTLEY, psychology and law educator; b. Salisbury, N.C., June 4, 1952; s. Harold Sumner Jr. and Marion Adair (Reeves) M.; m. Julia Ann Young, Aug. 25, 1973; children: Jennifer Lynn, Stephany Beth. BA, U. Va., 1973; MA, Boston U., 1975, PhD, 1978. Lic. psychologist, Nebr. Asst. prof. psychology Morehead (Ky.) State U., 1978-79, U. Va., Charlottesville, 1979-81; from asst. prof. to full prof. psychology and law U. Nebr., Lincoln, 1981-87, Carl A. Happold prof. psychology and law, 1987-94; prof. neuropsychiatry U. S.C., Columbia, 1994—, adj. prof. law, pediat. and psychology, 1994—, dir. Inst. Families in Soc., 1994—; dir. Consortium on Children, Families and the Law. Author: Child Advocacy: Psychological Issues and Interventions, 1993; co-author: Community Mental Health Centers and the Courts: An Evaluation of Community-Based Forensic Services, 1985, Psychological Evaluations for the Courts: A Handbook for Mental Health Professionals and Lawyers, 1987, 2d edit., 1997, Pediatric and Adolescent AIDS: Research Findings from the Social Sciences, 1992, Ethical and Legal Issues in AIDS Research, 1995; editor numerous books. Mem. U.S. Adv. Bd. on Child Abuse and Neglect, 1989-93, vice-chair, 1991-93. Recipient Frederick Howell Lewis award Psi Chi, 1993. Fellow APA (chmn. various coms., Disting. Contbn. to Psychology in Pub. Interest award 1985, Cert. of Recognition for Psychology in Pub. Interest 1981, Nicholas Hobbs award 1992, Harold Hildreth award 1992); mem. Am. Psychology-Law Soc. (pres. 1990-91), Nat. Com. to Prevent Child Abuse (Donna Stone award 1992). Democrat. Mem. Unitarian Ch. Office: Inst for Families in Soc Univ of SC Columbia SC 29208

MELTON, HOWELL WEBSTER, SR., federal judge; b. Atlanta, Dec. 15, 1923; s. Holmes and Alma (Combee) M.; m. Margaret Catherine Wolfe, Mar. 4, 1950; children—Howell Webster, Carol Anne. JD, U. Fla., 1948. Bar: Fla. 1948. With Upchurch, Melton & Upchurch, St. Augustine, 1948-61; judge 7th Jud. Circuit of Fla., St. Augustine, 1961-77, U.S. Dist. Ct. (mid. dist.) Fla., Jacksonville, 1977—; past chmn. Fla. Conf. Cir. Judges, 1974; past chmn. coun. bar pres.'s Fla. Bar. Trustee Flagler Coll., St. Augustine. Served with U.S. Army, 1943-46. Recipient Disting. Service award St. Augustine Jaycees, 1953. Mem. ABA, St. Johns County Bar Assn., Jacksonville Bar Assn., Fed. Bar Assn., Fla. Blue Key, Ponce de Leon Country Club, Marsh Creek Country Club, St. Augustine Fla. Officers Club, Masons, Phi Delta Theta, Phi Delta Phi. Methodist. Office: US Dist Ct PO Box 52957 Jacksonville FL 32201-2957

MELTON, LYNDA GAYLE, reading specialist, educational diagnostician; b. Gatesville, Tex., Mar. 11, 1943; d. Dee and Myrtle (Dunlap) White; divorced; children: Melanie Gayle, William Matthew. BS, U. Tex., 1964; MA, U. North Tex., 1979, PhD, 1983, postgrad., 1993, 94; postgrad., Tex. Womans U., 1983. Cert. elem. tchr., spl. edn. tchr., supervision, spl. edn. supr., learning disabilities tchr., orthpedically handicapped tchr., reading specialist, Tex., adminstrs., ednl. diagnostician. Tchr. 2d and 4th grades, spl. edn. tchr. Irving (Tex.) Ind. Sch. Dist., 1964-79, tchr., 1982-83; 4th grade tchr. Northwest Ind. Sch. Dist., Justin, Tex., 1980-81; asst. prin. Grapevine-Colleyville Ind. Sch. Dist., Tex., 1983-87; tchr. reading improvement Carrollton (Tex.)-Farmers Branch Ind. Sch. Dist., 1988-89; cons. lang. arts Edn. Svc. Ctr. Region 10, Richardson, Tex., 1989-91; pvt. practice diagnostic reading and ednl. diagnostician Trophy Club, Tex., 1991—; reading clinician N.Tex. State U., Denton, 1980; instr. spl. edn. U. Tex., Dallas, 1983, U Tex., Arlington, 1988; vis. prof. Tex. Women's U., Denton, 1983, 84, 87-88. Contbr. Reading Rsch. Revisited, also revs. to Case Mgmt. Monthly Confs., Scottish Rite Hosp. and profl. jours. Mem. ASCD, Internat. Reading Assn. (North Tex. coun.), Learning Disabilities of Tex., Orton Disability Soc., Coun. for Exceptional Children, Phi Delta Kappa. Home and Office: 30 Sonora Dr Trophy Club TX 76262

MELTON, MARIE FRANCES, retired university dean; b. Bayshore, N.Y.; d. Edward Kilgallon and Anne (Mohan) M. BS in Edn., St. John's U., Jamaica, N.Y., 1960, MS in Edn., 1975; MLS, Pratt Inst., Bklyn., 1961; EDD, St. John's U., Jamaica, N.Y., 1981. Dir. media ctr. Mater Christi High Sch., Astoria, N.Y., 1961-72; libr. sci. libr. St. John's U., Jamaica, N.Y., 1972-76, asst. dir., 1976-83, dir. Univ. Libr., 1983-89, dean Univ. Libr., 1989—. Mem., officer St. John's Prep Bd. of Trustees, Astoria, N.Y., 1980—, Holy Cross High Sch., Flushing, N.Y., 1979-89; chair Sunnyside Hist. Com., Sunnyside, N.Y., 1988-91. Mem. Am. Libr. Assn., Cath. Libr. Assn., N.Y. Libr. Assn., Council Nat. Libr. & Info. Assns. Roman Catholic.

MELTON, MELINDA WALLACE, archaeologist, laboratory director; b. Wisconsin Rapids, Wis., Mar. 27, 1966; d. Mike Wallace and Peggy Kay (O'Brien) Maley; m. Japhy Arlo Melton, Feb. 20, 1993; children: Anna J'Nevelyn, Kathryn Allison. BA in Anthropology, U. Tex., El Paso, 1991. Archaeologist, lab. dir. Human Systems Rsch., Ft. Bliss, El Paso, Tex., 1991-94; lab dir. Archaeol. Rsch., Inc., El Paso, 1995, Ctr. de Investigationes Arqueologicas, El Paso, 1996—. Contbg. author: Along the River's Edge, 1996. Mem. NOW, ACLU. Avocation: stained glass. Home: 415 W Redd Rd 6A El Paso TX 79932 Office: Ctr Investigaciones Arqeol 140 N Stevens St Ste 202 El Paso TX 79905-1222

MELTZER, ALLAN H., economist, educator; b. Boston, Feb. 6, 1928; s. George B. and Minerva I. (Simons) M.; m. Marilyn Ginsburg, Aug. 27, 1950; children: Bruce Michael, Eric Charles, Beth Denise. A.B., Duke U., 1948; M.A., UCLA, 1955, Ph.D., 1958. Univ. prof. polit. economy and pub. policy, 1991—; Lectr. econs. U. Pa., Phila., 1956-57; mem. faculty Carnegie Mellon U. Grad. Sch. Indsl. Adminstrn., Pitts., 1957—; prof. econs. Carnegie Mellon U. Grad. Sch. Indsl. Adminstrn., 1964—, Maurice Falk prof. econs. and social sci., 1970-80, John M. Olin univ. prof. polit. economy and pub. policy, 1980-91; Univ. prof. polit. economy and pub. policy Carnegie Mellon U. Grad. Sch. Indsl. Adminstrn., 1991—; vis. prof. U. Chgo., 1964-65, Fundacao Getulio Vargas, Rio de Janeiro, 1976-79, City U., London, 1979-86; vis. fellow Hoover Instn., 1977-78; vis. scholar Am. Enterprise Inst., Washington, 1989—; co-chmn. Shadow Open Market Com., 1974-89, chmn., 1989—; cons. U.S. Treasury, joint econ. com. U.S. Congress, 1960; com. on banking and currency U.S. Ho. of Reps., 1963-64; mem. Pres.'s Econ. Policy Adv. Bd., 1988-90; acting mem. Coun. Econ. Advisors, 1988-89; panel econ. advisors Congl. Budget Office, 1995—; cons., bd. govs. FRS, FDIC; dir. Cooper Tire & Rubber Co., chmn. audit and compensation com., 1996—; hon. advisor Inst. Monetary and Econ. Studies Bank of Japan, 1987—; bd. dirs. Sarah Scaife Found., Commonwealth Foun.; dir. Stillhalter Vision AG, Zurich, 1994—, Advanced Materials Group, 1994—. Author: Monetary Economics, 1989, Keynes's Monetary Theory: A Different Interpretation, 1988, (with Karl Brunner) Money and the Economy: Issues in Monetary Analysis, 1993, (with Alex Cukierman and Scott Richard) Political Economy, 1991; editor: (with Karl Brunner) Carnegie-Rochester Conf. Series, 1976-89, (with Charles Plosser), 1989-97; contbr. articles to profl. jours. Recipient award for Outstanding Achievement UCLA, 1983, Money Marketeers, 1997, Social Sci. Rsch. Coun. fellow, 1955-56; Ford Found. fellow, 1962-63; Man of Yr in Fin., Pitts., 1995-96. Fellow Nat. Assn. Bus. Economists; mem. Am. Econ. Assn. (v.p. 1990), Western Econ. Assn. (pres. 1985-86), Am. Fin. Assn., Phila. Soc. (v.p. 1981-83), Cosmos Club. Avocations: research in macroeconomics, money, political economy. Office: Carnegie Mellon U Dept Econs Pittsburgh PA 15213

MELTZER, BERNARD DAVID, legal educator; b. Phila., Nov. 21, 1914; s. Julius and Rose (Welkov) M.; m. Jean Sulzberger, Jan. 17, 1947; children: Joan, Daniel, Susan. A.B., U. Chgo., 1935, J.D., 1937; LL.M., Harvard U., 1938. Bar: Ill. 1938. Atty., spl. asst. to chmn. SEC, 1938-40; assoc. firm Mayer, Meyer, Austrian & Platt, Chgo., 1940; spl. asst. to asst. sec. state, also acting chief fgn. funds control div. div. State 1941-43; asst. trial counsel U.S. stafff Internat. Nuremberg War Trials, 1945-46; from professorial lectr. to disting. svc. prof. law emeritus U. Chgo. Law Sch., 1946—; counsel Vedder, Price, Kaufman & Kamnholz, Chgo., 1954-55, Sidley and Austin, Chgo., 1987-89; hearing commr. NPA, 1952-53; labor arbitrator; spl. master U.S. Ct. Appeals for D.C., 1963-64; bd. publs. U. Chgo., 1965-67, chmn., 1967-68; mem. Gov. Ill. Adv. Commn. Labor-Mgmt. Policy for Pub. Employees in Ill., 1966-67, Ill. Civil Service Commn., 1968-69; cons. U.S. Dept. Labor, 1969-70. Author: Supplementary Materials on International Organizations, 1948, (with W.G. Katz) Cases and Materials on Business Corporations, 1949, Labor Law Cases, Materials and Problems, 1970, supplement, 1972, 75, 2d edit., 1977, supplements, 1980, 82 (with S. Henderson), 3d edit. (with S. Henderson), 1985, supplement, 1988; also articles. Bd. dirs. Hyde Park Community Conf., 1954-56, S.E. Chgo. Commn., 1956-57. Served to lt. (j.g.) USNR, 1943-46. Mem. ABA (co-chmn. com. devel. law under NLRA 1959-60, mem. spl. com. transp. strikes), Ill. Bar Assn., Chgo. Bar Assn. (bd. mgrs. 1972-73), Nat. Acad. Arbitrators, Am. Law Inst., Coll. Labor and Employment Lawyers, Am. Acad. Arts and Scis., Order of Coif, Phi Beta Kappa. Home: 1219 E 50th St Chicago IL 60615-2908 Office: U Chgo Law Sch 1111 E 60th St Chicago IL 60637-2702

MELTZER, BERNARD N(ATHAN), sociologist, educator; b. N.Y.C., Oct. 17, 1916; s. Philip and Anna (Kemper) M.; m. Ida Wasserman, June 11, 1944; children: Iris Jean, William Jay. B.A., Wayne State U., 1943, M.A., 1944; Ph.D., U. Chgo., 1948. Research assoc. U. Chgo., 1948-49; asst. prof. sociology McGill U., 1949-51; mem. faculty Central Mich. U., Mt. Pleasant, 1951-87; prof. sociology Central Mich. U., 1955-87, chmn. dept., 1959-87, prof. emeritus, 1987—. Author: Education in Society: Readings, 1958, The Social Psychology of George Herbert Mead, 1959, Symbolic Interaction: A Reader in Social Psychology, 3d edit., 1978, Symbolic Interactionism: Genesis, Varieties and Criticism, 1975; contbr. articles to profl. periodicals and books. Chmn. Isabella County Civil Rights Com., 1959. Recipient citation Mich. Acad. Sci., Arts and Letters, 1969; Ascher fellow social sci. U. Chgo., 1944; Univ. fellow sociology, 1945; Marshall Field fellow sociology, 1946; grantee Can. Social Sci. Research Council, 1950. Fellow Am. Sociol. Assn.; mem. Mich. Sociol. Assn. (pres. 1961-62), North Central Sociol. Assn. (v.p. 1971-72), Soc. Study Symbolic Interaction. Home: 318 E Cherry St Mount Pleasant MI 48858-2606

MELTZER, BRIAN, lawyer; b. Chgo., Apr. 15, 1944; s. Maurice and Ethel (Goldstein) M.; m. Rosemary Labriola, Sept. 11, 1982; children: Stuart Joseph, Alan Phillip, Martin Angelo. BA in Math., Cornell U., 1966; JD, Harvard U., 1969. Bar: Ill. 1969. Assoc. atty. D'ancona & Pflaum, Chgo., 1969-72; assoc. then ptnr. Schwartz & Freeman, Chgo., 1972-88; ptnr. Keck, Mahin & Cate, Chgo., 1988-95, Meltzer, Purtill & Stelle, Schaumburg, Ill., 1996—. Office: 1515 E Woodfield Rd Schaumburg IL 60173-6046

MELTZER, DANIEL J., law educator; b. 1951. AB, Harvard U., 1972, JD, 1975. Bar: Ill. 1975, D.C. 1978, Mass. 1983. Law clk. to Hon. Carl McGowan, 1975-76, law clk. to Hon. Potter Stewart, 1976-77; spl. asst., sec. Dept. Health, Edn. and Welfare, 1977-78; assoc. Williams & Connolly, 1979-81; asst. prof. Harvard U., Cambridge, Mass., 1982-87, prof., 1987—, assoc. dean, 1989-93. Office: Law Sch Harvard U Cambridge MA 02138

MELTZER, DAVID, author, musician; b. Rochester, N.Y., Feb. 17, 1937; s. Louis and Roseamunde (Lovelace) M.; m. Christina Meyer, Apr. 1, 1958; children—Jennifer, Margaret, Amanda, Adam Benjamin ben David. Student, Los Angeles City Coll., 1955-56, U. Calif. at Los Angeles, 1956-57. Mem. cons. bd. Coordinating Coun. of Lit. Mags.; instr. M.A. program in poetics New Coll., San Francisco, 1980—, coord. writing and lit. program in undergrad. humanites program, 1987—. Author: numerous books of poetry, including Tens, Selected Poems, 1973, Six, 1976, Two-Way Mirror: Notebook on Poetry, 1977, The Art, The Veil, 1981, The Name: Selected oetry, 1973-83, 1983; editor: The San Francisco Poets, 1971, Birth, 1973, The Secret Garden: Anthology of the Classic Kabbalah, 1977, Birth: An Anthology of Ancient Texts, Songs, Prayers, and Stories, 1981, Death: An Anthology of Ancient Texts, Songs, Prayers and Stories, 1983, The Book Within the Book: Approaching the Kabbalah, 1990, Arrows: Selected Poetry: 1952-92, 1994, Reading Jazz, 1993, Writing Jazz, 1997, Tree; editor, pub. The Agency, 1968, The Agency Trilogy, 1994, Under, 1995, also Tree Books; song-writer, musician, vocalist: Serpent Power, 1968, Poet Song, 1970; soundtrack for Chance, 1978. Bd. dirs. Before Columbus Found., 1977—. Coordinating Coun. of Lit. Mags. grantee, 1973-74, 81, Nat. Endowment of Arts grantee for creative writing, 1974, for pub., 1975, Calif. Arts Coun. grantee, 1979; recipient Tombstone award for poetry John Ryan Morris Meml. Found., 1992. Office: PO Box 9005 Berkeley CA 94709-0005

MELTZER, DONALD RICHARD, treasurer; b. Boston, Sept. 1, 1932; s. Leo N. and Betty (Flesher) M.; m. Mary Douglas Seelye, Dec. 7, 1963; children: Kimberly, Christopher. AB, Dartmouth Coll., 1954, MBA, 1955. Mgr. Peat, Marwick, Mitchell & Co., Boston, 1955-67; asst. controller United Fruit Corp., Boston, 1968-69, controller, 1969-70, v.p., controller, 1970-73; v.p., chief acctg. office United Brands Co., N.Y.C., 1973-74, v.p. fin. and adminstrn., 1974-76; v.p. fin., treas. Instron Corp., Canton, Mass., 1976-88; v.p. fin. and adminstrn., treas., chief fin. officer Dialogue, Inc., Braintree, Mass., 1988-90; corp. fin. cons., Sudbury, Mass., 1988—. Overseer Children's Hosp. Med. Ctr., Boston, 1980-94; fin. com. Town of Sudbury, Mass., 1967; chmn. bd. trustees First Parish Ch., Sudbury, 1970-71, treas., 1991-93; pres. Mass. Parents Assn. for Deaf and Hard of Hearing, Boston, 1976-77, bd. dirs., 1973-86. Mem. AICPA, Mass. Soc. CPAs, Fin. Execs. Inst., Am. Assn. Indsl. Mgmt. (bd. dirs. 1980-85), Walk 'N Mass Volkssport Club (co-pres. 1993-95). Avocation: postal history, stamp collecting. Home: 341 Old Lancaster Rd Sudbury MA 01776-2035

MELTZER, HERBERT YALE, psychiatry educator; b. Bklyn., July 29, 1937; s. David and Estelle (Gross) M.; m. Sharon Rae Bittenson, June 12, 1960; children—David, Danielle. A.B., Cornell U., 1958; M.A., Harvard U., 1959; M.D., Yale U., 1963. Diplomate Am. Bd. Neurology and Psychiatry. Prof. U. Chgo., 1968-85; dir. biol. psychiatry lab. Ill. State Psychiat. Inst., Chgo., 1975-84; Bond prof. psychiatry Case Western Res. U., Cleve., 1985-96; dir. psychiat. research Univ. Hosp., Cleve., 1985-96; prof. psychiatry Vanderbilt U., Nashville, 1996—; dir., divsn. psychopharmacology, 1996—. Editor: Neuropsychopharmacology; contbr. articles to profl. jours. Recipient Efron prize Am. Coll. Neuropsychopharmacology, 1981, Noyes prize for schizophrenia rsch. Commonwealth of Pa., 1990, Sachar award Columbia U., gold medal Soc. Biol. Psychiatry, 1993, Dean prize Am. Coll. Psychiatry, 1996. Mem. NIMH, Am. Coll. Neuropsychopharmacology (pres. 1984-85), Am. Psychiat. Assn., Soc. Biol. Psychiatry (editorial bd.), Nat. Alliance Rsch. Schizophrenia Affective Disorders (Lieber prize 1992). Avocation: music. Office: Psych Hosp at Vanderbilt 1601 23rd Ave S Nashville TN 37212-3133

MELTZER, JACK, consultant, retired college dean; b. Bayonne, N.J., Aug. 21, 1921; s. Louis and Debbie (Gold) M.; m. Rae Libin, June 26, 1944; children: Richard, Marc, Ellen. B.A., Wayne State U., 1941; M.A., U. Chgo., 1947. Dir. planning Michael Reese Hosp., Chgo., 1953-54; S.E. Chgo. Commn. and U. Chgo., 1954-58; propr. Jack Meltzer Assos. (planners), 1958-63; acting dir. Am. Soc. Planning Ofcls., 1967-68; prof., dir. Center Urban Studies, U. Chgo., 1963-71; prof. div. social scis., prof. Sch. Social Service Adminstrn., 1965-83; prof., dean Sch. Social Scis. U. Tex.-Dallas, 1983-86; pvt. practice cons., 1986—; cons. to govt. and industry, 1945—. Author book revs., articles, books. Village trustee, Park Forest, Ill., 1950-52, mem. plan commn., 1949; Served to capt. USAAF, World War II. Mem. AAUP, Am. Soc. Planning Ofcls. (past treas.), Am. Inst. Planners (past v.p. pvt. practice dept.), Nat. Assn. Housing and Renewal Ofcls., Am. Soc. Pub. Adminstrn. Home: Apt 803 4550 N Park Ave Chevy Chase MD 20815-7237

MELTZER, JAY H., lawyer, retail company executive; b. Bklyn., Mar. 30, 1944; s. Solomon G. and Ethel L. (Kraft) M.; m. Bonnie R. Rosenberg, June 27, 1965; children: Wendy, Elizabeth, Jonathan. A.B., Dartmouth Coll., 1964; JD, Harvard U., 1967. Bar: N.Y. 1968, Mass. 1978, U.S. Dist. Ct. Mass. 1979. Law clk. to U.S. dist. judge, 1967-68; assoc. firm Shearman & Sterling, N.Y.C., 1968-72; with Damon Corp., Needham Heights, Mass., 1972-84; gen. counsel, sec. Damon Corp., 1973-84, v.p., 1979-84; v.p., corp. counsel The TJX Cos., Inc., Framingham, Mass., 1984-87, v.p., gen. counsel, sec., 1987-89, sr. v.p., gen. counsel, sec., 1989—. Dir. coun. Better Bus. Bur., 1990-93. Mem. ABA, Am. Soc. Corp. Secs., Am. Corp. Counsel Assn. (bd. dirs. N.E. chpt.), Retailers Assn. Mass. (bd. dirs., exec. com., sec.), New Eng. Corp. Counsel Assn. (bd. dirs.). Office: TJX Cos Inc 770 Cochituate Rd Framingham MA 01701-4672

MELTZER, MILTON, author; b. Worcester, Mass., May 8, 1915; s. Benjamin and Mary (Richter) M.; m. Hilda Balinky, June 22, 1941; children: Jane, Amy. Student, Columbia, 1932-36. adj. prof. history U. Mass., Amherst, 1977-80. Author: Mark Twain Himself, 1960; (with Walter Harding) A Thoreau Profile, 1962, Langston Hughes: A Biography, 1968, Bread and Roses, 1967, Brother, Can You Spare a Dime, 1968, Never to Forget: The Jews of the Holocaust, 1976, Dorothea Lange: A Photographer's Life, 1978; co-editor: Lydia Maria Child: Selected Letters, 1817-1880, 1982, The Terrorists, 1983, A Book About Names, 1984, The Black Americans, 1984, Ain't Gonna Study War No More, 1985, Mark Twain: A Writer's Life, 1985, Poverty in America, 1986, George Washington and the Birth of Our Nation, 1986, The Landscape of Memory, 1987, The American Revolutionaries, 1987, Benjamin Franklin: The New American, 1988, Rescue: The Story of How Gentiles Saved Jews in the Holocaust, 1988, Starting From Home: A Writer's Beginnings, 1988, Voices From the Civil War, 1989, Columbus and the World Around Him, 1990, The Bill of Rights: How We Got It and What It Means, 1990, Crime in America, 1990, Thomas Jefferson: Revolutionary Aristocrat, 1991, The Amazing Potato, 1992, Slavery: A World History, 1993, Lincoln: In His Own Words, 1993, Andrew Jackson and His America, 1993, Gold, 1993; (with Langston Hughes, C. Eric Lincoln, and Jon Michael Spencer) A Pictorial History of African-Americans, 1994, Cheap Raw Material: How Our Youngest Workers Are Exploited and Abused, 1994, Theodore Roosevelt, 1994, Who Cares? Millions Do: A Book About Altruism, 1994, Frederick Douglass: In His Own Words, 1995, Weapons and Warfare, 1996, Tom Paine, 1996. Served with USAAF, 1942-46. Mem. Orgn. Am. Historians, Authors Guild, P.E.N. Address: 263 W End Ave New York NY 10023-2612

MELTZER, YALE LEON, economist, educator; b. N.Y.C., Nov. 3, 1931; s. Benjamin and Ada (Luria) M.; BA, Columbia U., 1954, postgrad. Sch. Law, 1954-55; MBA, NYU, 1966; m. Annette Schoenberg, Aug. 7, 1960; children: Benjamin Robert, Philippe David. Asst. to chief patent atty. Beaunit Mills, Inc., Elizabethton, Tenn., 1955-56, prodn. mgr., 1956-58, rsch. chemist N.Y. Med. Coll., N.Y.C., 1958-59; rsch. chemist H. Kohnstamm & Co., Inc., mfg. chemists, N.Y.C., 1959-66, mgr. comml. devel., market rsch., patents and trademarks, 1966-68; sr. security analyst Harris, Upham & Co., Inc., 1968-70; instr. dept. econs. N.Y. U., 1972-79; adj. asst. prof. dept. acctg., fin. and mgmt. Pace U., N.Y.C., 1974-80, adj. assoc. prof., 1980-84; lectr. dept. polit. sci., econs. and philosophy Coll. S.I., CUNY, 1977-82, asst. prof. dept. polit. sci., econs. and philosophy, 1983—; lectr. bus., fin., econs., sci. and tech.; presenter papers confs. Mem. AAAS, Am. Econ. Assn. Author: Soviet Chemical Industry, 1966; Chemical Trade with the Soviet Union and Eastern European Countries, 1967; Chemical Guide to GATT, The Kennedy Round and International Trade, 1968; Phthalocyanine Technology, 1970; Hormonal and Attractant Pesticide Technology, 1971; Urethane Foams: Technology and Applications, 1971; Water-Soluble Polymers: Technology and Applications, 1972; Encyclopedia of Enzyme Technology, 1973; Economics, 1974; Foamed Plastics; Recent Developments, 1976; Water-Soluble Resins and Polymers: Technology and Applications, 1976; Putting Money to Work: An Investment Primer, 1976; (with W.C.F. Hartley) Cash Management: Planning, Forecasting, and Control, 1979; Water-Soluble Polymers: Recent Developments, 1979; Putting Money to Work: An Investment Primer for the '80s, 1981, updated edit., 1984; Water-Soluble Polymers: Developments since 1978, 1981; Expanded Plastics and Related Products: Developments Since 1978, 1983. Contbr. articles to profl. publs. Translator, Russian, French and German tech. lit. Home: 14110 82nd Dr Jamaica NY 11435-1134 Office: 2800 Victory Blvd Staten Island NY 10314-6609

MELVILLE, RICHARD ALLEN, investment company executive; b. Springfield, Mass., Sept. 15, 1932; s. Charles Raymond and Vera Alice (Brooks) M.; m. Maria-Angela Garcia-Martinez, June 15, 1963; children: Thomas Alexander, Andrew Michael, Charles Peter. BA, Bates Coll., Lewiston, Maine, 1954; MA, Johns Hopkins U., 1959. Counsel U.S. State Dept., Phnom Penh, Cambodia, 1959-63; v.p. Irving Trust Co., N.Y.C., 1963-70; pres., CEO Allied Bank Group, N.Y.C., 1970-83; dir. Fiduciary Trust Internat., N.Y.C., 1984-87; chmn. bd. Alexander, Andrews & Peters, Hong Kong, 1988—; chief internat. advisor State Commn. for Reform of the Economy, Govt. of People's Republic of China, Beijing, 1993—; cons. Govt. of State of Cambodia, 1991-93. Editor: Second Chance, 1989; author: Cambodia: HRAF, 1963; contbr. articles to profl. jours. Trustee Johns Hopkins U., Balt., 1979-85, Bates Coll., 1976-90; adv. coun. Hopkins-Nanjing Ctr., China, 1981-90, Nitze Sch. of Advanced Internat. Studies, Washington, 1978-90. With Mil. Dist. of Washington, 1955-56. Mem. Coun. on Fgn. Rels. Republican. Episcopalian. Avocations: cycling, tennis, writing. Home: Box 125 Bristol Rd Bristol ME 04539 Office: China Internat Centre, 18 Bei San Huan, Beijing 100011, China

MELVILLE, ROBERT SEAMAN, chemist; b. Worcester, Mass., Nov. 20, 1913; s. Carey Eyster and Maud Tesmer (Seaman) M.; m. Eleanor Elisabeth Vogel, Mar. 6, 1942; children: Robert Andrew, John Frederick, Margaret Ellen, Emily Jean, Martin Carroll. AB in Chemistry, Clark U., 1937; PhD in Biochemistry, State U. Iowa, 1950. Chief chemist St. Luke's Hosp., Chgo., 1950-54; chief biochemist VA Hosp., Iowa City, 1954-63; chief biochemist, lab. requirement specialist VA Cen. Office, Washington, 1963-65; health sci. adminstr. Nat. Inst. Gen. Med. Scis., NIH, Bethesda, Md., 1965-67, chief automated clin. lab. program, 1967-77, spl. asst. to dir. of biomed. engring., 1977-81; dir. In Vitro Diagnostic Device Standards div. Bur. Med. Devices, FDA, Silver Spring, Md., 1981-82; cons. in clin. scis., 1983—; clin. prof. pathology George Washington U. Med. Ctr., Washington, 1977—; pres. Trans-Tech. Biomed., 1983—. Contbr. articles on clin. lab. automation to profl. publs. With U.S. Army, 1942-46. Fellow AAAS, Am. Chem. Soc., Am.. Assn. Clin. Chemistry (Joseph H. Rowe award 1972, Nat. Fisher award 1976, pres. 1969-70), Instrument Soc. Am., Assn. for Advancement of Med. Instrumentation; mem. Am. Bd. Clin. Chemists (pres. bd. dirs. 1978-81), Am. Inst. Chemists (chmn. cert. commn. in chem. engring. and chemistry 1981-84, 87-91, cert. chemist 1989—), Alpha Chi Sigma (Profl. Chemist award 1990), Lambda Chi Alpha. Unitarian. Club: Cosmos. Lodge: Masons. Home and Office: 11112 Kenilworth Ave PO Box 56 Garrett Park MD 20896-0056

MELVILL-JONES, GEOFFREY, physician, educator; b. Cambridge, Eng., Jan. 14, 1923; emigrated to Can., 1961, naturalized, 1974; s. Benett and Dorothy Laxton (Jotham) Melvill J.; m. Jenny Marigold Burnaby, June 21, 1953; children—Katharine F., Francis H., Andrew J., Dorothy H. B.A., Cambridge U., 1944, M.A., 1947, M.B.,B.Ch., 1949. House surgeon Middlesex (Eng.) Hosp., 1950; sr. house surgeon in otolaryngology Addenbrooke's Hosp., Cambridge, 1950-51; sci. officer Med. Research Council Gt. Britain, 1955-61; assoc. prof. physiology McGill U., Montreal, Que., Can., 1961-68; prof. McGill U., 1968-92, prof. emeritus, 1992—, Hosmer research prof., 1978-92, dir. aerospace med. research unit, 1961-89; adj. prof. dept. clin. neurosci., faculty medicine U. Calgary, 1992—; vis. prof. Stanford U., 1971-72, College de France, 1979, 95; Ashton Graybiel lectr. U.S. Naval Aerospace Lab., Fla. Author: Mammalian Vestibular Physiology, 1979, Adaptive Mechanisms in Gaze Control, 1985; contbr. numerous articles to profl. publs. Flying pers. med. officer RAF, 1951-55. Recipient SkyLab Achievement award NASA, 1974, Dohlman medal Toronto U., 1986, Wilbur Franks award Can. Soc. Aerospace Medicine, 1988. Fellow Can. Aero. and Space Inst., Aerospace Med. Assn. (Harry G. Armstrong Lectureship award 1968, Arnold D. Tuttle award 1971), Royal Soc. (London), Royal Soc. Can. (McLaughlin medal 1991), Royal Aero. Soc. (London) (Stewart Meml. award 1989, Buchanan Barbour award 1990); mem. U.K. Physiol. Soc., Can. Physiol. Soc., Can. Soc. Aviation Medicine, Internat. Collegium Otolaryngology, Soc. Neurosci., Bárány Soc. (Gold medal 1988). Office: U Calgary Dept Clin. Neuroscis, 3330 Hospital Dr NW, Calgary, AB Canada T2N 4N1

MELVIN, BEN WATSON, JR., petroleum and chemical manufacturing executive; b. Nashville, Mar. 27, 1926; s. Ben Watson and Virginia (Darden) M.; m. Elizabeth Cooper Hershey, May 10, 1952; children—Ben W., Landis Anne, Thomas C., Mark C. B.Chem. Engring., U. Del., 1950. With E. I. duPont de Nemours & Co., Inc., Wilmington, Del., 1950-91, ret., 1991. Served with USAAF, 1944-46. Mem. AICE, Soc. Plastics Engrs., So. Chem. Industry, Wilmington Country Club.

MELVIN, BILLY ALFRED, clergyman; b. Macon, Ga., Nov. 25, 1929; s. Daniel Henry and Leola Dale (Seidell) M.; m. Marcia Darlene Eby, Oct. 26, 1952; children: Deborah Ruth, Daniel Henry II. Student, Free Will Baptist Bible Coll., Nashville, 1947-49; B.A., Taylor U., Upland, Ind., 1951; postgrad., Asbury Theol. Sem., Wilmore, Ky., 1951-53; B.D., Union Theol. Sem., Richmond, Va., 1956; D.D., Azusa (Calif.) Coll., 1968; LL.D. (hon.), Taylor U., 1984; DD, Huntington Coll., 1995. Ordained to ministry Free Will Baptist Ch., 1951; pastor First Free Will Baptist Chs., Newport, Tenn., 1951-53, Richmond, 1953-57; pastor Bethany Ch., Norfolk, Va., 1957-59; exec. sec. Nat. Assn. Free Will Baptists, 1959-67; exec. dir. Nat. Assn. Evangelicals, 1967-95.

MELVIN, CHARLES ALFRED, III, superintendent of schools; b. Milw., May 19, 1950; s. Charles A. Jr. and Audry M. (Dart) M.; m. Almira M. Tiedke, Aug. 1985; children: Sean Charles, Katherin Almira. Ba, U. Wis., 1972, MA, 1975, PhD, 1979. Supr. U. Wis., Madison, 1975; prin. Sch. Dist. Beloit (Wis.) Turner, 1980, dir. instr., 1982, supt., 1986—. Recipient sch. improvement grant, Carnegie Found., Beloit Found.; named one of Top 100 Exec. Educators, NSBA. Mem. ASCD, Am. Assn. Sch. Adminstrs., Nat. Assn. Secondary Sch. Prins. Home: 1911 Vail Ter Beloit WI 53511-3148

MELVIN, CHARLES EDWARD, JR., lawyer; b. Greensboro, N.C., July 13, 1929; s. Charles Edward and Mary Ruth (Plunkett) M.; m. Jacklyn McDaniel, Mar. 1, 1958; 1 child, Dana W. BS, U. N.C., 1951, JD with honors, 1956. Bar: N.C. 1956. Ptnr. Smith, Helms, Mulliss & Moore, L.L.P., Greensboro, 1958—. Capt. U.S. Army, 1952-54. Mem. N.C. Bar Assn. (chmn. real property sect. 1981), Am. Coll. Real Estate Lawyers, Greensboro C. of C. (pres. 1978). Office: Smith Helms Mulliss & Moore Ste 1400 PO Box 21927 300 N Greene St Greensboro NC 27420

MELVIN, DOROTHY MAE, retired microbiologist; b. Fayetteville, N.C., Jan. 27, 1923; d. Willie James and Lillie Mae (Bain) Melvin. AB, U. N.C.-Greensboro, 1942; MS, U. N.C.-Chapel Hill, 1945; PhD, Rice U., 1951. Cert. Am. Acad. Microbiology. Microbiologist parasitology trng., Ctrs. for Disease Control, Atlanta, 1945-49, 1951-61, chief parasitology tng. sect., Atlanta, 1962-85. Mem. Am. Soc. Tropical Medicine and Hygiene, Am. Soc. Parasitologists, Sigma Xi. Author manuals; contbr. articles to sci. jours. Home: 2418 Kingscliff Dr NE Atlanta GA 30345-2124

MELVIN, NORMAN CECIL, lawyer; b. Balt., Aug. 21, 1916; s. Norman Cecil and Anna H. (Holzworth) M.; m. Louise A. Gillen, Feb. 10, 1945 (dec. Oct. 1958); children: Leigh G., Norman Cecil III; m. Virginia Brown Lester, Nov. 2, 1959; 1 dau., Susan A. A.B., Johns Hopkins U., 1939; LL.B., Harvard U., 1942. Bar: Md. 1942. Practice law Balt., 1946—; mem. firm Brown & Brune, 1946-52; gen. atty. Western Md. Ry. Co., Balt., 1952-66; gen. solicitor Western Md. Ry. Co., 1966-68, v.p., gen. counsel, 1968-75, dir., 1970-75; asst. peoples counsel Pub. Service Commn. Md., 1951-52; instr. U. Balt., 1957-66. Served to capt. AUS, 1942-46. Recipient Erskine M. Ross essay award ABA, 1950. Mem. ABA, Md. Bar Assn., Balt. Bar Assn., Soc. Colonial Wars (coun. 1966-69), SAR, Johns Hopkins Alumni Assn. (pres. 1968-70, Disting. Alumni award 1970, Heritage award 1980), Harvard Club, Johns Hopkins Club. Home: 4202 Wickford Rd Baltimore MD 21210-2930

MELVIN, ROBERT DOUGLAS, professional sports team executive; b. Aug. 8, 1952; m. Ellen Schultz; children: Ashley, Cory. Pitcher Pirates and Yankees Orgns., 1972-78; with N.Y. Yankess, 1979-85; spl. asst. Balt. Orioles Orgn., 1986-87, dir. player personnel, 1987-94, asst. gen. mgr., 1988-94; v.p., gen. mgr. Tex. Rangers, 1994—. Office: Tex Rangers 100 Ballpark Way Arlington TX 76011

MELVIN, RONALD MCKNIGHT, retired museum director; b. Regina, Sask., Can., Oct. 25, 1927; came to U.S., 1953; s. M. Gordon and Mary Gillespie (McKnight) M.; m. Gwen Ellis, Apr. 30, 1955; children: Mary Fleming, Catharine Hastings. Student, U. B.C., 1945-49. Various positions Powell River Co. Ltd., Vancouver, B.C., Can., 1947-56; asst. to pres. Trans Union Corp., Chgo., 1956-58; mng. dir. Procor Ltd. subs. Trans Union Corp., Toronto, Ont., Can., 1958-64; ptnr. Blunt Ellis & Simmons, Chgo., 1964-71, pres., 1971-78; vice chmn. Blunt Ellis & Loew, Chgo., 1978-80; founding dir. Terra Mus. Am. Art, Evanston, Ill., 1980-84; dir. Chef Pierre, Traverse City, Mich., 1972-77, Lawter Internat., Chgo., 1977-84. Author, organizer: (art exhbns.) Important Western Art from Chicago Collections, 1980 Five American Masters of Watercolor, 1981, American Naive Paintings From National Gallery of Art, 1982, Solitude--Inner Visions in American Art, 1982, Woman, 1984. Republican. Avocation: collecting Worcester porcelain. Home: PO Box 278 Norfolk Rd Southfield MA 01259

MELVIN, RUSSELL JOHNSTON, magazine publishing consultant; b. New Castle, Pa., Nov. 16, 1925; s. Russell Conwell and Anna Katharine (Johnston) M.; m. Helen Margaret Connery, Aug. 6, 1949; children: Thomas Kirk, Meredith. B.A., U. Pa., 1949. Reporter Phila. Inquirer, 1949; copywriter, then asst. to circulation mgr. Time mag., 1949-53; with Newsweek mag., 1953-86, dir. Pacific edits., 1960-64, mng. dir. internat. edits., 1964-68, mng. editor internat. editorial service, 1969-86; cons. internat. affairs and profl. edn. Mag. Pubs. Am. (formerly Mag. Pubs. Assn.), N.Y.C., 1986—; v.p. Newsweek, Inc., 1965-85; founding editor The Journal, Tokyo, 1963; founding dir. Newsweek Feature Service, 1968; mem. UN Communications Adv. Coun. Served with USNR, 1942-46. Mem. Internat. Advt. Assn. (chmn., CEO 1980-85, exec. dir. Chgps. Corp. 1985-86, bd. dirs. 1988-91, mem. world coun. 1990), Internat. Fedn. Periodical Press (mem. exec. and mgmt. bd.), Univ. Club, Chappaqua Tennis Club, The Century Assn. Episcopalian. Home: 153 Douglas Rd Chappaqua NY 10514-3104 Office: Mag Pubs Am 919 3rd Ave New York NY 10022

MELVIN C., HIGH, protective services official. Police chief Norfolk, Va. Office: 100 Brooke Ave Norfolk VA 23510-1826

MELZACK, RONALD, psychology educator; b. Montreal, Que., Can., July 19, 1929; s. Joseph and Annie (Mandel) M.; m. Lucy Birch, Aug. 7, 1960; children: Lauren, Joel. BSc, McGill U., Montreal, 1950, MSc, 1951, PhD, 1954; DLitt (hon.), U. Waterloo, 1992. Lectr. Univ. Coll., London, 1957-58; assoc. prof. MIT, 1959-63; lectr. psychology McGill U., 1953-54, prof., 1963—; E.P. Taylor prof. McGill U., $D, $D, $D, 1986. Author: The Day Tuk Became a Hunter, and Other Eskimo Stories, 1967, Raven, Creator of the World, 1970, The Puzzle of Pain, 1973, Why the Man in the Moon is Happy, and Other Eskimo Creation Stories, 1977, (with P.D. Wall) The Challenge of Pain, 1982, 2nd edit., 1988, Pain Measurement and Assessment, 1983, (with P.D. Wall) Textbook of Pain, 1984, 3rd edit., 1994, (with D.C. Turk) Handbook of Pain Assessment, 1992. Decorated Officer, Order of Can., 1995; recipient Molson prize Can. Coun., 1985, Gaston Labat award Am. Soc. Regional Anesthesia, 1989, J.J. Bonica award VI World Congress on Pain, 1990, Prix du Qu. Marie-Victorin, 1994; recipient Disting. Contbn. award Can. Pain Soc., 1995. Fellow APA, AAAS, Royal Soc. Can., Can. Psychol. Assn. (Disting. Contbns. to Psychol. Sci. award 1986, hon. pres. 1988-89); mem. Internat. Assn. Study of Pain (hon., past pres.). Home: 51 Banstead Rd, Montreal, PQ Canada H4X 1P1

MEMORY, JASPER DURHAM, academic administrator, physics educator; b. Raleigh, N.C., Dec. 10, 1936; s. Jasper Livingston and Margaret Moore (Durham) M.; m. Carolyn Hofler, June 4, 1961; children—Margaret Carolyn, Jasper William. B.S. summa cum laude, Wake Forest U., 1956; Ph.D., U. N.C., 1960. Successively asst. prof., assoc. prof. physics U. S.C., Columbia, 1960-64; assoc. prof. N.C. State U., Raleigh, 1964-67, assoc. dean, physics and math. scis., 1973-82, prof., 1967—, vice-provost, grad. dean, 1982-86; v.p. for research U. N.C. System, Chapel Hill, 1986—; bd. govs. Research Triangle Inst., Research Triangle Park, N.C., 1983-84, Triangle Area rsch. dir., 1981—; cons. NASA Langley, Hampton, Va., 1970-74, Ohio Bd. Regents, 1993-95, Ark. Bd. Regents, 1987; N.C. State U. rep. Oak Ridge Associated Univs., 1982-85, Grad. Record Exam. Bd., 1985-90, chair, 1989, Policy Coun., Test of English as a Fgn. Lang., 1987-88, chair, 1988. Author: Quantum Theory of Magnetic Resonance Parameters, 1968; (with others) NMR of Aromatic Compounds, 1982, High Resolution NMR in the Solid State: Fundamentals of CP/MAS, 1994. Recipient Outstanding Tchr. award N.C. State U., 1967, Disting. Alumni Service award Wake Forest U., 1981. Fellow Am. Phys. Soc.; mem. Am. Assn. Physics Tchrs., Phi Beta Kappa, Sigma Xi. Democrat. Presbyterian. Home: 124 Talon Dr Cary NC 27511-8604 Office: Univ NC Gen Adminstrn Chapel Hill NC 27515-2688

MENACK, STEVEN BOYD, lawyer, mediator; b. Phoenix, Ariz., Nov. 13, 1959; s. Max Joseph and Clara (Fischer) M.; m. Stefanie Menack. BA in Psychology, U. Ariz., 1982; MPA, Harvard U., 1984; JD, Columbia U., 1987; postgrad., Seton Hall U., 1991-92. Bar: N.J. 1987, U.S. Dist. Ct. N.J. 1987, N.Y. 1988, U.S. Dist. Ct. (so. dist.) N.Y. 1989, U.S. Dist. Ct. (ea. dist.) N.Y. 1989. Assoc. Phillips, Nizer, Benjamin, Krim & Ballon, N.Y.C., 1987-90, Herrick, Feinstein, N.Y.C., 1990-91; atty., mediator Porzio, Bromberg & Newman, P.C., Morristown, N.J., 1991-93; pres., CEO A Better Solution-Quality Mediation and Arbitration Svcs., locations throughout U.S., 1993—; CEO Law Offices of Steven Boyd Menack, Esquire, N.Y.C. and Somerville, N.J., 1993—; intern to Gov. Bruce Babbit, Tucson, Ariz., 1979-82, Senator Dennis DeConcini, U.S. Senate, Washington, 1980, 1983; fair housing tech. cons. Town of Arlington, Mass., 1984; divorce mediator Inst. Dispute Resolution Seton Hall U., Montclair, N.J., 1991-92; civil comml. mediator N.J. Superior Ct. Morris County, Morristown, N.J., 1992; contract and comml. mediator, gen. equity chancery mediator N.J. Superior Ct. Bergen County, Hackensack, N.J., 1992—; mediator and arbitrator Am. Arbitration Assn., 1993—, panelist Panel of Arbitrators, 1993—; arbitration cons.; lectr., spkr. in field. Contbr. articles to profl. jours. Precinct committeeman Pima County, Ariz., Tucson, 1981. Mem. ABA (cert. civil litigation, alternative dispute resolution com. family law sect., divorce laws and procedural com., pretrial practice and discovery com.), N.J. Bar Assn. (dispute resoltion com., mediation subcom.), N.J. Assn. Profl. Mediators (founder and cert. divorce mediator, 1991, pres. elect 1992-93, cert. bus. and commercial mediator 1992, cert. advanced divorce and bus. mediator 1992, statewide pres. 1993-94), Nat. Assn. of Profl. Mediators (founder, pres. 1997). Avocations: alternative dispute resolution counseling, mediation, travel, politics/government, arbitration. Address: 280 Park Ave S Apt 8M New York NY 10010-6129

MENAKER, RONALD HERBERT, bank executive; b. N.Y.C., Dec. 17, 1944; s. Harold L. Menaker and Gladys (Bleiberg) Ross; m. Kathleen Sager Thomas, Sept. 11, 1966; children: Meredith E., Kyri D. Student, Queen's Coll., 1965-66. Mng. dir., head of corp. svcs. J.P. Morgan & Co., Inc.,

N.Y.C., 1966—; dir. J.P. Morgan Svcs., Wilmington, Del. Trustee, chmn. N.Y. Downtown Hosp., N.Y.C., 1991—; trustee NYU Med. Ctr., St. Huberts Giralda Animal Welfare and Edn. Ctr., Madison, N.J., The Dog Mus., St. Louis, 1989—; bd. dirs. Am. Kennel Club, N.Y.C. Mem. Westminster Kennel Club (gov., show chmn. 1990—), Am. Kennel Club (bd. dirs.). Avocations: sporting art, judging dogs. Office: JP Morgan & Co Inc 60 Wall St New York NY 10005-2836

MENAKER, SHIRLEY ANN LASCH, psychology educator, academic administrator; b. Jersey City, July 22, 1935; d. Frederick Carl and Mary Elizabeth (Thrall) Lasch; m. Michael Menaker, June 4, 1955; children: Ellen Margaret, Nicholas. BA in English Lit., Swarthmore Coll., 1956; MA, Boston U., 1961, PhD in Clin. Psychology, 1965. Adminstrv. asst. N.J. State Fedn. Dist. Bds. Edn., Trenton, 1956-59; trainee clin. psychology Mass. Mental Health Ctr., Boston, 1960-61; intern clin. psychology Thom Guidance Clinic for Children, Boston, 1961-62; research assoc. ednl. psychology U. Tex.-Austin, 1964-67, asst. prof. ednl. psychology, 1967-70. assoc. prof., 1970-79, assoc. dean grad. sch., 1975-77, psychology cons. Research and Devel. Ctr. for Tchr. Edn., 1965-67, faculty investigator, 1967-74; assoc. prof. counseling psychology U. Oreg., Eugene, 1979-85, prof., 1985-87 , assoc. dean grad. sch., 1979-84, acting dean grad. sch., 1980-81, 82-83, dean grad sch., 1984-87; assoc. provost for acad. support, prof. gen. faculty, U. Va., Charlottesville, 1987—. Bd. dirs. Nat. Grad. Record Exam. Bd. and Policy Council-Test of English as Fgn. Lang., Ednl. Testing Services, 1984-88. Contbr. articles to profl. jours. NIMH fellow, 1963-64. Office: U Va Madison Hall Charlottesville VA 22906-9014

MENARD, EDITH, English language educator, artist, poet, actress; b. Washington, Dec. 5, 1919; d. Willis Monroe and Edith Berncenia (Gill) M. BS summa cum laude, Miner Tchrs. Coll., Washington, 1940; MA in English, Howard U., 1942; postgrad., NYU, 1944-46; MA in Tchg. English, Columbia U., 1952; postgrad. in edn., George Washington U., 1966-79, 89-92, doctoral candidate, 1992—. Instr. English and speech Howard U., Washington, 1946-53; high sch. tchr. English D.C. Pub. Schs., Washington, 1953-73; chmn. dept. English Woodrow Wilson H.S., Washington, 1972-73; adj. asst. prof. English fundamentals U. D.C., 1988-90; founder, dir. Miss Menard's Exclusive English Tutorial Svc., 1991—; substitute tchr. D.C. and Montgomery County (Md.) pub. schs., Prince George's County (Md.) Pub. Sr. H.S., 1996-97. Contbr. articles and poetry to various publs., including At Day's End, 1994. Reader poetry to civic orgns.; vol. Washington Nat. Cathedral Assn., 1993—. Recipient Golden Poet award World of Poetry, 1988, Silver Poet award, 1989, Editor's Choice award The Nat. Libr. of Poetry, 1994; Julius Rosenwald fellow Yale U., 1943-44. Mem. Internat. Soc. Poets (Disting. mem. 1995, Merit award 1995), Smithsonian Assocs. Episcopalian. Avocations: interior decorating and restoration, pub. speaking and politics, painting, writing. Home: Ste 916 6101 16th St NW Washington DC 20011-1766

MENARD, JOHN R., lumber company executive; b. 1940. Pres., ceo Menard Inc., Eau Claire, Wis., 1960—. Office: Menard Inc 4777 Menard Dr Eau Claire WI 54703-9604*

MENARD, LOUIS JACQUES, professional sports team executive; b. Chicoutimi, Que., Can., Jan. 29, 1946; m. Marie-José Ratelle; children: Louis-Simon, Anne-Valérie. B.Comm., Loyola Coll.; MBA, U. Western Ont. With Nesbitt Burns, Montreal, 1972—, vice chmn., mng. dir.; chmn. bd. partnership com. Montreal Expos, 1991—; past chmn. Montreal Stock Exch., Greater Montreal Bd. of trade; dir. Alliance Forest Products, Inc. Dir. Tennis Canada, Can. Policy Rsch. Network; gov. Concordia U.; dir. various cmty. orgns. Office: Montreal Expos, 4549 Pierre-de-Coubertin, Montreal, PQ Canada H1V 3N7

MENASCO, WILLIAM WYATT, mathematics educator; b. Lancaster, Calif., Sept. 7, 1954; s. Lawrence Clifton and Dixie Lorene (Smith) M.; m. Melissa Ahn, Aug. 14, 1976; children: Timothy William, Ryan Wyatt. BA, UCLA, 1975; PhD, U. Calif., Berkeley, 1981. Hill asst. prof. Rutgers U., New Brunswick, N.J., 1981-84; asst. prof. math. U. Buffalo, 1984-91, assoc. prof., 1991-94, prof. math., 1994—; prof. des universités Institut non Lineaire de Nice-Universite de Nice, Sophia Antipolis, France, 1994—; vis. prof. Institut Des Hautes Études Scientifiques, Bores-sur-Yvette, France, 1992. Contbr. articles to profl. jours. Am. Math. Soc. rsch. fellow, 1992-94; NSF rsch. grantee, 1983-87, 90-92, 92—. Mem. Am. Math. Soc. Avocations: fly fishing, clarinet playing. Office: U Buffalo Dept Math Diefendorf Hall Buffalo NY 14214

MENCER, GLENN EVERELL, federal judge; b. Smethport, Pa., May 18, 1925; s. Glenn Hezekiah and Ruth Leona (Rice) M.; m. Hannah Jane Freyer, June 24, 1950; children—Ruth Ann, Cora Jane, Glenn John. B.B.A., U. Mich., 1949, J.D., 1952. Bar: Pa. 1953, U.S. Dist. Ct. (we. dist.) Pa. 1953, U.S. Supreme Ct. 1958. Sole practice Eldred, Pa., 1953-64; dist. atty. McKean County, Pa., 1956-64; judge 48th Jud. Dist. Ct., Smethport, 1964-70, Commonwealth Ct. of Pa., Harrisburg, 1970-82, U.S. Dist. Ct., Erie, Pa., 1982—. Served with U.S. Army, 1943-45, ETO. Mem. Fed. Judges Assn., Pa. Bar Assn., McKean County Bar Assn. Republican. Methodist. Lodge: Masons (33 degree). Home: 30 W Willow St Smethport PA 16749-1524 Office: US Dist Ct Fed Courthouse PO Box 1820 Erie PA 16507-0820

MENCH, JOHN WILLIAM, retail store executive, electrical engineer; b. N.Y.C., Feb. 27, 1943; s. John William and Edna (Ilgen) M.; m. Rose Irene Miller, Aug. 12, 1962 (dec. 1997); 1 child, William Ilgen. BSEE, U. S.C., 1969; MBA, Ohio U., 1983; PhD, Calif. Coast U., 1994. Elec. engr. Uniroyal, Shelbyville, Tenn., 1969-74; facility engr. Kroger, Nashville, 1974-77; asst. mgr. facility engring. Kroger, Atlanta, 1977-79; Kroger mktg. area mgr. facility engring. Kroger, Columbus, Ohio, 1979-85; div. mgr. facility engring., v.p. Safeway Stores, Inc., Oakland, Calif., 1985-86; v.p. constrn., engring. Big V Supermarkets, Inc., Florida, N.Y., 1986-95; pres. Mench & Assocs. Inc., 1994—; mem. faculty Pa. Coll. Tech., 1996—. Author tech. manuals in field. Trustee Meth. Ch., 1987-93; bd. dirs. Goshen Day Care Ctr., 1988-95; past v.p. Tri State V.W. Assn.; mem. exec. adv. bd. Ohio U. Coll. Bus. Adminstrn., 1992—; mem. bd. dirs. Elec. Distbn. Systems, 1993-94. Mem. IEEE (sr.), Assn. Energy Engrs. (sr.). Republican. Methodist. Avocation: Volkswagens.

MENCHER, BRUCE STEPHAN, judge; b. Washington, May 21, 1935; s. Emanuel and Bertha Miriam (Robbin) M.; m. Janet Patricia Whitfield, Nov. 24, 1974; children by previous marriage: Sean Robbin, Marc Nadzo. B.A., George Washington U., 1957, J.D. with honors, 1960. Bar: D.C. 1960, U.S. Supreme Ct. 1964. Gen. atty. Office Gen. Counsel, Dept. Agr., 1960-61; asst. corp. counsel for D.C., 1961-67; atty.-adviser Office Gen. Counsel, Bur. for Africa, AID, 1967-69; ptnr. Wilkes & Artis, Washington, 1969-75; assoc. judge Superior Ct. D.C., 1975-91; sr. judge, 1991—; presiding judge Family div. Superior Ct. D.C., 1988-90; professorial lectr. law George Washington U. Nat. Law Ctr., 1982-83; lectr. criminal justice Nat. Cathedral Sch./St. Albans Sch., 1985; faculty advisor Nat. Jud. Coll., 1995. Asst. rsch. editor George Washington Law Rev., 1959-60; contbr. articles to law revs. Mem. gen. alumni gov. bd. George Washington U., 1972-80; bd. dirs. Nat. Child Support Enforcement Assn., 1994—, The Washington Savoyards Ltd., 1991-96. Recipient Alumni Svc. award, 1975, Judge of Yr. award Assn. Plaintiffs Trial Attys., 1983, Samuel Green award for disting. svc. to Washington legal comty. and Phi Delta Phi, 1985, Disting. Alumni Achievement award George Washington U., 1987, also various appreciation and recognition awards local bar assns., D.C. and fed. govts. for work in area of family law and child support enforcement. Mem. Am., D.C. bar assns., George Washington Law Assn. (exec. com. 1972-77), The Barristers (exec. com. 1981), Phi Delta Phi (pres. Barrister Inn 1974-75). Office: Superior Ct DC 500 Indiana Ave NW Rm 5520 Washington DC 20001-2131 *While it may sound old-fashioned, I attribute my appointment to the bench, in large part, to hard work, dedication, a love of the law and respect for my fellow man. One should maintain his sense of balance, always try to understand the other person's position and, at all costs, maintain a sense of humor throughout.*

MENCHER, MELVIN, journalist, retired educator; b. Bklyn., Jan. 25, 1927; s. Peter and Theresa (Sherman) M.; m. Helen Chamberlain, Aug. 27, 1947; children: Thomas, Marianne, Nicholas. Student, U. N.Mex., 1943-44; B.A., U. Colo., 1947; postgrad. (Nieman fellow), Harvard, 1952-53. Reporter UP, 1947-50; state polit. corr. Albuquerque Jour., 1951-54; reporter Fresno (Calif.) Bee, 1954-58; asst. prof. journalism U. Kans., Lawrence, 1958-62; asst. prof. Columbia U., N.Y.C., 1962-65, assoc. prof., 1965-75, prof., 1975-90, assoc. dir. summer program for journalism edn. of minorities, 1971, prof. emeritus, 1990—. Contbg. author: Evaluating the Press, 1973; author: News Reporting and Writing, 1977, Basic Media Writing, 1983; editor: The FNMA Guide to Buying, Financing and Selling Your Home, 1973; contbr. articles to profl. jours. Mem. Soc. Profl. Journalists, Nat. Council Coll. Pubs. Advisers, Kappa Tau Alpha. Home: 450 Riverside Dr New York NY 10027-6821 Office: Grad Sch Journalism Columbia U New York NY 10027

MENCHER, STUART ALAN, sales and marketing executive; b. N.Y.C., Apr. 25, 1939; s. Meyer H. and Mildred B. (Finger) M.; m. Judith Leslie Schneider; children: Jane Lizabeth, Tracy Ellen. B in Mgmt. Engring., Rensselaer Poly. Inst., 1960; MBA, NYU, 1965. Sales rep. Sperry Rand Univac, Albany, N.Y., 1960-62; various sales and mktg. mgmt. positions IBM Corp., White Plains, N.Y., 1965-78; br. mgr. data processing div. IBM Corp., Harrison, N.Y., 1978-81; dr. mktg. ops. planning, bus. mktg. dept. AT&T, Basking Ridge, N.J., 1981-83; dir. market planning, sales and mktg. div. AT&T Info. Systems, Morristown, N.J., 1983; dir. data systems mktg. AT&T Info. Systems, Morristown, 1983-84, v.p. mktg., large bus. systems div., 1985-87; sr. v.p. sales and mktg. MCI Communications Corp., Washington, 1987-90; sr. v.p., gen. mgr. U.S. distbn. div. Motorola/Codex Corp., Mansfield, Mass., 1990-91; sr. v.p., gen. mgr. Teleport Communications, N.Y.C., 1992-93; sr. v.p. nat. sales and mktg., 1994—. Pres. Westfield Men's Coll. Scholarship Club, N.J., 1977; coach Westfield Young Soccer Assn., 1976-81; mem. budget rev. com. United Fund, Westfield, 1983-85; mem. adv. bd. N.Y.C. Tech. Coll., 1993; mem. Mayor's Telecomms. Mutual Aid and Restoration Com. N.Y.C., 1992-93. Lt. USCGR, 1962-65. Avocations: golf, soccer coaching, sailing. Office: Teleport Comm Group 429 Ridge Rd Dayton NJ 08810-1323

MENCHIK, PAUL LEONARD, economist, educator; b. N.Y.C., Sept. 16, 1947; s. Irving and Eleanor (Swedlow) M.; m. Bettie Ann Landauer, May 28, 1972; children: Daniel Aron, Jeremy Matthew. BA, SUNY, Binghamton, 1969; AM, U. Pa., 1971, PhD, 1976. Lectr. Rutgers Coll., New Brunswick, N.J., 1974-76; rsch. assoc. Inst. for Rsch. on Poverty, U. Wis., Madison, 1976-79; prof., chairperson dept. econs. Mich. State U., East Lansing, 1979—; sr. economist, econ. policy Office Mgmt. & Budget, Washington, 1990-91; acad. visitor Stanford (Calif.) U., 1980, London Sch. Econs., 1987-88; vis. assoc. prof. U. Pa., Phila., 1982-83; cons., advisor in field. Mem. editl. bd. Jour. Income Distbn., Amsterdam, 1992—; contbr. articles to profl. jours. Grantee NSF, Social Security Adminstrn., U.S. Dept. Health and Human Svcs.; recipient Best Article of Yr. award Econ. Inquiry, 1987. Mem. Am. Econ. Assn., Nat. Tax Assn., Nat. Bur. Econ. Rsch. Conf. on Income & Wealth. Avocations: bowling, racquetball, golf, travel, camping. Office: Mich State U 101 Marshall Hall E Circle Dr East Lansing MI 48824

MENCHIN, ROBERT STANLEY, marketing executive; b. Kingston, N.Y., Oct. 31, 1923; s. Abraham H. and Gertrude (Gorlin) M.; m. Marylin Barsky, Dec. 26, 1949; children: Jonathan, Scott. BA, NYU, 1948. Account exec. DKG Advt., N.Y.C., 1949-51; dir. spl. projects Am. Visuals Corp., N.Y.C., 1952-59; dir. advt. and pub. rels. Arthur Wiesenberger & Co., N.Y.C., 1959-65; pres. Wall St. Mktg. Communications, Inc., N.Y.C., 1967-77; dir. mktg. communications Chgo. Bd. Trade, 1977-83, v.p. communication and member rels., 1983-87; pres. Wall Street Mktg., Chgo., 1987—. With AUS, 1942-45. Mem. Am. Mktg. Assn., Pub. Rels. Soc. Am., Fin. Planners Assn. Author: The Last Caprice, 1964, Where There's a Will, 1977, The Mature Market: A Strategic Marketing Guide to America's Fastest-Growing Population Segment, 1989, New Work Opportunities for Older Americans, 1993. Home: Lake Point Tower 505 N Lake Shore Dr Ste 1407-08 Chicago IL 60611-3427

MENDE, HOWARD SHIGEHARU, mechanical engineer; b. Hilo, Hawaii, Nov. 19, 1947; s. Tsutomu and Harue (Kubomitsu) M. BSME, U. Hawaii, 1969; MSME, U. So. Calif., 1975. Registered profl. engr., Calif. Mem. tech. staff I Rockwell Internat., Anaheim, Calif., 1970-71; mem. tech. staff I Rockwell Internat., L.A., 1971-73, mem. tech. staff II, 1973-77, mem. tech. staff IV, 1984-86; devel. engr. AiRsch. Mfg. Co., Torrance, Calif., 1977-83; mech. engr. Def. Contracts Mgmt. Dist. West, Santa Ana, Calif., 1987-94, electronics engr., 1994—; lectr. Pacific States U., L.A., 1974-75. Mem. ASME (assoc.). Democrat. Buddhist. Home: 1946 W 180th Pl Torrance CA 90504-4417 Office: Def Contracts Mgmt 2525 W 190th St Torrance CA 90504-6002

MENDE, ROBERT GRAHAM, retired engineering association executive; b. Newark, Dec. 4, 1926; s. Herman Ernest and Etta (Hillenbrand) M.; m. Joan B. Tamlyn, Apr. 12, 1958; children: Lisa Anne, Robert Graham Jr. Student, Mass. Inst. Tech., 1944-45; degree, N.Y. State Maritime Acad., 1947; B.S., Webb Inst. Naval Architecture, 1951. Project engr. Foster Wheeler Corp., N.Y.C., 1953-56; dist. mgr., naval architect Bird-Johnson Co., N.Y.C., 1956-62; sr. naval architect J.J. Henry Co., Inc., N.Y.C., 1962-69; exec. dir. Soc. Naval Architects and Marine Engrs., 1969-91; mem. marine engring. coun. Underwriters Labs., Inc., 1969-91; ad hoc vis. com. Engrs. Coun. for Profl. Devel., 1970-72. Bd. dirs. Friends of World Maritime U., 1987-91; trustee Webb Inst. Naval Architecture, 1987-91. Lt. USNR, 1951-53. Fellow Royal Inst. Naval Architects, Soc. Naval Architect and Marine Engrs. (hon. life v.p., chmn. N.Y. sect. 1968-69, Vice Admiral E.S. Jerry Land medal 1991, Robert G. Mende Bldg. hdqrs. bldg. named in his honor); mem. ASME, Am. Soc. Naval Engrs., Am. Soc. Assn. Execs., Coun. Engring. and Sci. Soc. Execs. (bd. dirs. 1988-91), Maritime Coll. Assn., N.E. Coast Inst. Engrs. and Shipbuilders, Webb Alumni Assn. (pres. 1970-72). *Hard work, perseverance, humility and a dash of deprivation almost always insure success. It also doesn't hurt to be in the right place at the right time.*

MENDEL, JERRY MARC, electrical engineering educator; b. N.Y.C., May 14, 1938; s. Alfred and Eleanor (Deutch) M.; m. Letty Susan Grossman, June 26, 1960; children: Jonathan, Aileen. BMechE cum laude, Poly. U., 1959, MEE, 1960, PhD in Elec. Engring., 1963. Registered profl. engr., Calif. Instr. elec. engring. Poly. Inst. Bklyn., 1960-63; engring. scientist and sect. chief McDonnell-Douglas Astronautics Co., Huntington Beach, Calif., 1963-74; prof. dept. elec. engring. systems U. So. Calif., L.A., 1974—, chmn. dept., 1984-91, dir. Signal and Image Processing Inst., 1991-94, assoc. dir. edn. Integrated Media Sys. Ctr., 1996—; pres., founder MENTECH, Culver City, Calif., 1983—; pres. United Signals and Systems, Inc., 1989—. Author: Discrete Techniques of Parameter Estimation: The Equation Error Formulation, 1973, Optimal Seismic Deconvolution: An Estimation Based Approach, 1983 (Phi Kappa Phi award 1984), Lessons in Digital Estimation Theory, 1987, Maximum-Likelihood Deconvolution, 1990, Lessons in Estimation Theory for Signal Processing, Communications and Control, 1995; editor: Prelude to Neural Networks: Adaptive and Learning Systems, 1994; co-editor: Adaptive Learning and Pattern Recognition Systems, 1970. Fellow IEEE (centennial medal 1984); Disting. mem. IEEE Control Systems Soc. (pres. 1986). Office: U So Calif Dept Elec Engring Systems EEB 438 Los Angeles CA 90089-2564

MENDEL, MAURICE, audiologist, educator; b. Colorado Springs, Colo., Oct. 6, 1942; married; 3 children. BA, U. Colo., 1965; MS, Washington U., 1967; PhD in Audiology, U. Wis., 1970. Asst. prof. audiology U. Iowa Hosp., 1970-74, assoc. rsch. scientist, 1975-76; assoc. prof. U. Calif., Santa Barbara, 1976-84, prof. audiology, 1984-88; chmn. dept. audiology and speech pathology Memphis State U., 1988-92; dean Sch. Audiology and Speech-Lang. Pathology U. Memphis, 1993—; program dir. speech and hearing sci. U. Calif., Santa Barbara, 1980-82. Fellow Am. Speech-Lang.-Hearing Assn., Soc. Ear Nose and Throat Advance in Children; mem. Am. Acad. Audiology, Internat. Elec. Response Audiology Study Group, Internat. Soc. Audiology, Tenn. Assn. Audiology and Speech-Lang. Pathologists, Sigma Xi. Achievements include research in middle components of the auditory evoked potentials and their subsequent clinical applications to hearing testing. Office: U Memphis CRISCI 807 Jefferson Ave Memphis TN 38105-5042

MENDELEJIS, LEONARDO NIERMAN, artist; b. Mexico City, Nov. 1, 1932; s. Chanel and Clara (Mendelejis) N.; m. Esther Ptak, Feb. 16, 1957; children: Monica, Daniel, Claudia. BS in Physics and Math, U. Mexico; degree in bus. adminstrn., U. Mex., 1959, degree in music, hon. degree, 1960; D (honoris causa), Concordia U., 1994. One-man shows, Proteo Gallery, 1958, 60, C.D.I. Gallery, 1956, Misrachi Gallery, 1964, Galeria Merkup, 1969, Mus. Modern Art, 1972, all Mexico City, Galeria Sudamericana, N.Y.C., 1958, Hammer Galleries, N.Y.C., 1960, I.F.A. Galleries, Washington, 1952, 62, 65, 68, 71, Edgardo Acosta Gallery, Beverly Hills, Calif., 1961, Art Collectors Gallery, Beverly Hills, 1966, Main St. Gallery, Chgo., 1961, Doll & Richard Gallery, Boston, 1963, Pucker Safrai Gallery, Boston, 1969, El Paso (Tex.) Mus Art, 1964, 71, Wolfard's Gallery, Rochester, N.Y., 1964, Pub. Library Rockville Centre, N.Y., 1964, Little Gallery, Phila., 1964, Neusteters Gallery Fine Arts, Denver, 1965, Judah L. Magnes Meml. Mus., Berkeley, Calif., 1967, Galerie Katia Granoff, Paris, 1969, Little Gallery, Phila., 1970, Aalwin Gallery, London, 1970, Gallery Modern Art, Scottsdale, Ariz., 1971, Mus. Contemporary Arts, Bogota, Colombia, 1973, 74, Galerie Dresdnere, Ont., Can., Casa de la Cultura, Cucuta, Colombia, 1974, also mus., galleries, Haifa, Israel, Rome, Italy, Toronto, Ont., Can., Paris, France, 1962—; exhibited group shows mus., Caracas, Venezuela, 1958, Mexico City, 1958—, Havana, Cuba, 1959, Tokyo, Japan, 1963, Paris, France, 1961, Nagoya, Japan, 1963, Kyoto, Japan, 1963, Osaka, Japan, 1963, Bogota, 1963, Santiago, Chile, 1963, Buenos Aires, Argentina, 1963, Rio de Janeiro, Brazil, 1963, Costa Rica, 1963, Panama, 1963, Oslo, Norway, 1965, Warsaw, Poland, 1965, Madrid, Spain, 1965, Stockholm, Sweden, 1966, Brussels, Belgium, 1966; also exhibitions at the Mus. Contemporary Art, Bogota, Colombia (diploma d'honneur of fine arts in Monaco), 1976, B. Lewin Galleries, Los Angeles, 1977, I.F. A. Galleries, Washington, 1977, Merrill Chase Galleries, Chgo., 1977, Am. Mus., Hayden Planetarium, N.Y.C., 1978, Cumberland Mus. of Sci. Ctr., Nashville, 1978, Fernback Sci. Ctr., Atlanta, 1978, Nahan Galleries, New Orleans, 1980, Broward Galleries, Pompano Beach, Fla., 1980, Mus. Sci. and Industry, Chgo., 1980, Galeria de Arte Misrachi, Mexico City, 1982, Calif. Mus. Sci. and Industry, 1982, Museo de Arte e Historia, Ciudad Juarez, Mexico, 1984, Centro de Artes Visuales e Investigaciones Esteticas, Mexico, 1984, Barbara Gillman Gallery, Miami, 1984, MIT Mus., Boston, 1984, Merrill Chase Galleries, Chgo., 1987, Museo de Arte Costarricense, Art Ctr. Galleries Hawaii Inc., 1988, Maison de L'Amerique Latine de Monaco, Monte Carlo, 1990, Centro Cultural San Angel, Mex.; also exhibited Expo, 1958, also numerous mus., univs., Eastern and Western U.S., Can., 1958—; executed murals, Sch. Commerce University City, Mexico, 1956, Bank San Francisco, 1965, physics bldg., Princeton, 1969; also executed stained glass windows, Mexican synagogues, 1968-69; executed tapestries Concert & Opera House, Salzburg, 1989, Majestic Theatre, San Antonio 1989, Theatre An Der Wein, Austria; prin. sculptures in including at Birmingham (Ala.) Mus. Art, Mexican Nat. U., Yeshiva U., N.Y., Hebrew U. Jerusalem, Sherman Bldg. Mount Scopus, City of Monterrey, Mex., Eleanor Roosevelt Inst., Denver, Wichita (Kans.) Airport; represented in permanent collections, Mus. Modern Art in Mexico, Atlanta Mus., Mus. Modern Art Haifa, Gallery Modern Art, N.Y.C., Phoenix Art Mus., Pan Am. Union, Washington, Detroit Inst. Arts, Bogota Mus. Contemporary Arts, Mus. Contemporary Arts, Madrid, Acad. Fine Arts, Honolulu, Tucson Art Center, Tel-Aviv Mus., Israel Mus., Jerusalem, Kennedy Art Center, Washington, Boston Mus. Fine Arts, U. Va., No. Ill. Univ., Chgo. Art Inst., New Orleans Mus. Art, other mus. and galleries. (Recipient 1st prize Mexican Contemporary Art, Art Inst. Mexico 1964, Palme d'or Beaux Arts, Monaco 1969, gold medal Tomasso Campanella Found. 1972). Patron Acad. St. Martin in the Fields, 1993—. Recipient Gold medal Internat. Parliament for Safety and Peace-U.S.A.-Italy, 1983; named Accademico D'Europe, Centro Studi di Ricerchi L'Accademia D'Europa, Italy; European Banner of Arts Prize, Italy, 1984, Oscar D'Italia, 1984; winner of world-wide competition to do a sculpture for U. Cen. Fla., Orlando, 1986. Life fellow Royal Soc. Arts (London, Eng.). Office: Reforma 16B San Angel, 01000 Mexico City 20, Mexico also: Lublin Graphics 95 E Putnam Ave Greenwich CT 06830-5611*

MENDELL, OLIVER M., banking executive; b. N.Y.C., Apr. 4, 1925; s. M. Lester and Malvina Mendell; grad. Washington and Lee U., 1950; postgrad. Columbia U. Exec. Course, 1969; m. Shelley R. Disick, Sept. 24, 1962; children—Steven, David. Asst. treas. Bankers Trust Co., N.Y.C., 1950-56; v.p., dir. Queens Nat. Bank, N.Y.C., 1956-58; sr. v.p. Chem. Bank (now Chase Manhattan Bank), N.Y.C., 1958—; dir. Cartier, Inc., 1967-69. Pres., Fifth Ave. Assn., 1978-82, chmn., 1982-87; trustee Washington and Lee U. Alumni, vice chmn. alumni fund campaign; bd. dirs. Citizens Budget Commn. N.Y., SSS, 1962-76, JFK Internat. Synagogue, Park 86th Apt. Corp., 1966-71, Joint Distbn. Com.; bd. govs. Sch. Banking and Money Mgmt., Adelphi U., 1975-82; gov. USO World Bd. Govs.; chmn. USO of Met. N.Y.; co-treas., bd. dirs. United Jewish Appeal Greater N.Y., Inc.; mem. adv. bd. Regional Emergency Med. Services Council of N.Y.C.; bd. dirs., mem. exec. com. Am. Jewish Com.; trustee Bernard J. Moncharsh Found., Inc., Temple Shaaray Tefila, 1971-74, Fedn. Jewish Philanthropies, B'nai Brith Banking Lodge; mem. com. legacies and bequests ARC; trustee NYU Real Estate Inst.; vice-chmn. steering com., treas. N.Y. Bus. Council for Clean Air, 1966-71; fellow Brandeis U. Served as navigator USAF, 1943-46. Recipient numerous civic awards. Mem. Assn. for Better N.Y. (mem. exec. com.), Phi Epsilon Pi (nat. budget com.), Omicron Delta Kappa. Clubs: Harmonie (N.Y.C.); Rockrimmon Country (Stamford, Conn.). Home: 1040 Park Ave New York NY 10028-1032 Office: Chase Manhattan Bank 270 Park Ave New York NY 10017-2014

MENDELOVICI, EFRAIM ELIAHU, materials chemistry and earth sciences researcher; b. Botosani, Rumania, May 15, 1936; arrived in Venezuela, 1948; s. Heinic and Brana (Mates) Mendelovici; married; 3 children. Licenciado in chemistry, Ctrl. U. Venezuela, Caracas, 1961; D in Agronomic Scis. with gran distinction, U. Louvain, Belgium, 1967. Prof. U. Los Andes, Merida, Venezuela, 1961-75; sr. investigator, lectr. Inst. Venezolano de Investigaciones Cientificas, 1975—, chief materials physico-chemistry lab., 1976—, head dept. materials sci., 1989—; vis. rschr., conferee, Sidney and Beatrice Wolberg chair Israel Inst. Tech., Technion, Haifa, 1982-83; councillor at large Internat. Confedn. Thermal Analysis, Hatfield, Eng., 1992; plenary lectr. ICTAC, Phila., 1996. Contbr. articles to sci. jours. Jewish. Avocations: music, bible study, jogging, swimming, chess. Office: IVIC, Apdo 21827, Caracas 1020A, Venezuela also: Bamco CCS 199-00 PO Box 025322 Miami FL 33102-5322

MENDELOW, GARY N., physician, emergency consultant; b. Buffalo, N.Y., Sept. 4, 1940; s. Martin and Katherine (Rosenthal) M.; m. Elaine Susan Barron, Mar. 31, 1973; children: Ronald, Raquel. Attended, U. Buffalo, 1958-60; natural science cert., U. Basel, Switzerland, 1962, MD, 1970. Diplomate Am. Bd. Emergency Medicine, 1991. Intern Charity Hosp., New Orleans, La., 1970-71; resident Erie County Med. Ctr., Buffalo, 1972-74; emergency physician Am. Coll. Emergency Physicians, Dallas, 1974—. Fellow Am. Coll. Emergency Physicians; mem. AMA, N.Y. Med. Soc. Jewish. Avocations: jogging, tennis, swimming. Home: 134 Brandywine Dr Buffalo NY 14221 Office: Twin Cities Physician PE 64 Cleveland Ave Buffalo NY 14222-1610

MENDELS, JOSEPH, psychiatrist, educator; b. Cape Town, South Africa, Oct. 29, 1937; came to U.S., 1964; s. Max and Lily (Turecki) M.; m. Ora Kark, Jan. 22, 1960; children: Gilla Avril, Charles Alan, David Ralph. MB, BChir, U. Cape Town, 1960; MD, U. Witwatersrand, Johannesburg, South Africa, 1965. Asst. prof., assoc. prof. psychiatry and pharmacology U. Pa., Phila., 1967-73; prof. U. Pa. and VA Hosp., Phila., 1973-80; med. dir. Fairmount Inst., Phila., 1980-81; prof. psychiatry and human behavior Thomas Jefferson Med. Ctr., 1985—; med. dir. Med. Inst., Phila., 1981-95, Therapeutics PC, Phila., 1981—; cons. NIMH, NIH, numerous pharm. cos., 1968—; lectr. to univs. and hosps. worldwide, 1968—. Author, editor: Concepts of Depression, 1971, Biological Psychiatry, 1973, Psychobiology of Affective Disorders, 1981; contbr. over 200 articles to med. jours. Fellow Internat. Coll. Neuropsychopharmacology, Am. Coll. Neuropsychopharmacology, Am. Coll. Clin. Pharmacology; mem. Am. Psychiat. Assn. (Lester N. Hofheimer prize 1976). Office: 9 Laurel Rd E Stratford NJ 08084-1322

MENDELSOHN, HAROLD, sociologist, educator; b. Jersey City, Oct. 30, 1923; s. Louis and Bessie (Yulinsky) M.; m. Irene Sylvia Gordon, Apr. 10, 1949; 1 dau., Susan Lynn. B.S., CCNY, 1945; M.A., Columbia U., 1946; Ph.D., New Sch. Social Research, 1956. Sr. survey analyst U.S. Dept. State, Washington, 1951-52; research assoc. Bur. Social Sci. Research, Am. U., Washington, 1952-56; assoc. mgr. mktg. communications McCann-Erickson Advt., N.Y.C., 1956-58; assoc. dir. Psychol. Corp., N.Y.C., 1958-62; prof. dept. mass communications U. Denver, 1962-89, prof. emeritus, 1989—, chmn., 1970-78, dean faculty social scis., 1984-86, spl. asst. to chancellor,

1986-88; Morton vis. disting. prof. Ohio U., spring 1981; cons. FTC, Denver Rsch. Inst., U.S. Consumer Product Safety Commn., The Gallup Orgn., Ford Found., Fedn. Rocky Mountain States, CBS, ABC, Children's TV Workshop. (Emmy award Nat. Acad. TV Arts Scis. 1968, Gold Camera award U.S. Indsl. Film Festival 1972); Author: Mass Entertainment, 1966, (with David H. Bayley) Minorities and the Police: Confrontation in America, 1969, (with Irving Crespi) Polls, Television and the New Politics, 1970, (with others) Television and Growing Up: The Impact of Televised Violence, 1972, (with Garrett O'Keefe) The People Choose a President, 1976; editor: Mass Communications series, 1967-69; contbr. articles to profl. jours. Mem. Denver Coun. Pub. TV, 1970-78; mem. U.S. Surgeon Gen.'s Sci. Adv. Com. on TV and Social Behavior, 1969-71; bd. dirs. Nat. Safety Coun., 1963-69; mem. pub. affairs adv. bd. Air Force Acad. Found., 1972-76; mem. cancer control and rehab. adv. com. Nat. Cancer Inst., 1976-81; mem. adv. coun., prevention div. Nat. Inst. Alcoholism and Alcohol Abuse, 1977-82; trustee Colo. Med. Svc., Inc., 1973-78. Recipient award TV Bur. Advt., 1962, Met. Life award Nat. Safety Council, 1967; Gold Eagle award, 1973; Silver award Internat. Festival Film and TV, 1974. Fellow Am. Psychol. Assn., Am. Sociol. Assn.; mem. Am. Assn. Pub. Opinion Research (pres. 1973-74), AAAS, N.Y. Acad. Scis., Sigma Delta Chi, Omicron Delta Kappa. Club: Chicago Press. Home: 1451 E Cornell Pl Englewood CO 80110-3013 Office: U Denver Dept Mass Communications Denver CO 80208

MENDELSOHN, JOHN, oncologist, hematologist, educator; b. Cin., Aug. 31, 1936; s. Joe and Sarah (Feibel) M.; m. Anne Charles, June 23, 1962; children: John Andrew, Jeffrey Charles, Eric Robert. BA, Harvard U., 1958, MD, 1963. Diplomate Am. Bd. Internal Medicine, Am. Bd. Hematology, Am. Bd. Med. Oncology. Intern, resident Peter Bent Brigham Hosp., Boston, 1963-65, 67-68; fellow in hematology Washington U. Sch. Medicine, St. Louis, 1968-70; asst. prof. to prof. medicine U. Calif., San Diego, 1970-85; Am. Cancer Soc. prof. clin. oncology U. Calif., La Jolla, 1982-85, dir. Cancer Ctr., 1977-85; prof. medicine Cornell U. Med. Coll., N.Y.C., 1985-96; chmn. dept. medicine Meml. Sloan Kettering Cancer Ctr., N.Y.C., 1985-96; pres., prof. medicine U. Tex. M.D. Anderson Cancer Ctr., Houston, 1996—; mem. bd. sci. counselors divsn. cancer treatment Nat. Cancer Inst., 1986-90; bd. dirs. Am. Assn. Cancer Rsch.; cons. Hybritech, Genentech, Immunex, Im Clone, Merck, Prism, Bristol-Myers; founder, 1st dir. U. Calif. San Diego Cancer Ctr. Editor-in-chief: (textbook) The Molecular Basis of Cancer; mem. editl. bd. Jour. Immunology, Blood, Cancer Rsch., Jour. Clin. Oncology, Growth Factors; editor-in-chief Clin. Cancer Rsch.; contbr. numerous articles in field of oncology to profl. jours. Mem. Gov.'s Cancer Adv. Coun., Calif., 1982-85; bd. dirs. Am. Cancer Soc., San Diego, 1981-85. Officer USPHS, 1965-67. Fulbright scholar U. Glasgow, Scotland, 1958-59; named Headliner of Yr. in Medicine, San Diego, 1985. Mem. Assn. Am. Physicians, Am. Soc. Clin. Investigation, Am. Soc. Clin. Oncology, Am. Assn. Cancer Rsch., Am. Soc. Hematology, Century Assn., Harvard Club N.Y., Phi Beta Kappa, Alpha Omega Alpha. Achievements include laboratory research establishing inhibition of tumor growth by antibodies against growth factor receptors. Avocations: tennis, music, history, hiking. Office: U Tex MD Anderson Cancer Ctr 1515 Holcombe Blvd Houston TX 77030-4009

MENDELSOHN, LOUIS BENJAMIN, financial analyst; b. Providence, R.I., Mar. 26, 1948; s. Alvin Harold and Frances (Leitner) M.; m. Illyce Deborah Greenspan, Aug. 29, 1976; children: Lane Jeffrey, Ean Graham, Forrest Lee. BS, Carnegie Mellon U., 1969; MSW, SUNY, Buffalo, 1973; MBA with hons., Boston U., 1977. Rsch. asst. Mass. Gen. Hosp., Boston, 1969-71; regional health planner Comprehensive Health Planning Coun., Buffalo, 1973-74; adminstv. resident New Eng. Hosp., Boston, 1976; mgmt. specialist Humana Hosp. Bennett, Ft. Lauderdale, Fla., 1977-78; asst. exec. dir. Humana Women's Hosp., Tampa, Fla., 1978-80; pres., CEO Market Technologies Corp., Wesley Chapel, Fla., 1979—; pres. Mendelsohn Trading Corp., Wesley Chapel, 1980—. Contbg. rschr.: The Encyclopedia of Technical Market Indicators, 1988; contbg. author: High Performance Futures Trading, 1990, Virtual Trading, 1995, Artificial Intelligence in the Capital Markets, 1995; contbg. writer Tech. Analysis of Stocks and Commodities Mag.; editor newsletter Neural-Financial News, 1991; developer investment software ProfitTaker, 1980—, VantagePoint, 1988—. USPHS fellow, 1975-77. Mem. Market Technicians Assn., Colleague Internat. Fedn. of Tech. Analysts, Beta Gamma Sigma. Achievements include development of system testing and optimization in technical analysis software for microcomputers; introduction of first commercial system testing trading software in financial industry for microcomputers. Avocations: raising horses, antique collecting. Office: Mkt Techs Corp 25941 Apple Blossom Ln Wesley Chapel FL 33544-5108

MENDELSOHN, ROBERT VICTOR, insurance company executive; b. N.Y.C., July 18, 1946; s. Harold Victor and Mary Ellen (Muldoon) M.; A.B., Georgetown U., 1968; J.D., Harvard U., 1971; Bar: N.Y. 1971. Atty. firm Willkie Farr & Gallagher, N.Y.C., 1971-74; pres., dir. W.R. Berkley Corp., Greenwich, Conn., 1974-93; CEO Royal & Sun Alliance USA, Inc., Charlotte, N.C.; dir. Royal Ins., plc, London. Trustee Jose Limon Dance Found., 1979—. Mem. Am. Ins. Assn. (vice chmn.), Inst. CPCU/Ins. Info. Inst. (bd. trustees); Clubs: Innis Arden Golf , N.Y. Athletic, Riverside (Conn.) Yacht, TPC-Piper Glen. Office: PO Box 1000 9300 Arrowpoint Blvd Charlotte NC 28201-1000

MENDELSON, ALAN CHARLES, lawyer; b. San Francisco, Mar. 27, 1948; s. Samuel Mendelson and Rita Rosalie (Spindel) Brown; children: Jonathan Daniel, David Gary; m. Agnès Marie Barbariol. BA with great distinction, U. Calif., Berkeley, 1969; JD cum laude, Harvard U., 1973. Bar: Calif. 1973. Assoc. Cooley, Godward LLP, San Francisco, 1973-80; mng. ptnr. Cooley, Godward, Castro, Huddleson & Tatum, Palo Alto, 1990-95, 96—; sec., acting gen. counsel Amgen Inc., Thousand Oaks, Calif., 1990-91; acting gen. counsel Cadence Design Sys., Inc., San Jose, Calif., 1995-96; bd. dirs. Isis Pharms. Inc., CoCensys, Inc., Elexsys Internat., Inc., Acuson Corp.; sec. Walker Interactive Sys., 1982—, PetsMart, 1986—, Arris Pharm. Corp., 1993—, Aviron, 1992—, CV Therapeutics, Inc., 1992—; mem. mgmt. com. Cooley Godward, LLP; chmn. Cos. Practice Group, 1990—. Chmn. Piedmont (Calif.) Civil Svc. Commn., 1978-80; den leader Boy Scouts Am., Menlo Park, Calif.; fundraiser Crystal Springs Upland Sch., Hillsborough, Calif., 1981—; coach Menlo Park Little League, 1982-86; pres., mem. exec. com., bd. dirs. No. Calif. chpt. Nat. Kidney Found., 1986—. With USAR, 1969-75. Recipient Disting. Svc. award Nat. Kidney Found., 1992; named U. Calif. Berkeley Alumni scholar, 1966, Scaife Found. scholar, 1966. Mem. Harvard U. Law Sch. Alumni Assn., Bohemian Club, Phi Beta Kappa. Jewish. Avocations: golf, tennis, softball, basketball, photography. Home: 76 De Bell Dr Atherton CA 94027-2253 Office: Cooley Godward LLP 5 Palo Alto Sq 3000 El Camino Real Palo Alto CA 94306-2120

MENDELSON, ELLIOTT, mathematician, educator; b. N.Y.C., May 24, 1931; s. Joseph and Helen (Bienstock) M.; m. Arlene Zimmerman, Jan. 25, 1959; children—Julia, Hilary, Peter. A.B., Columbia U., 1952; M.A., Cornell U., 1954, Ph.D., 1955. Instr. U. Chgo., 1955-56; jr. fellow Soc. Fellows, Harvard U., 1956-58; Ritt instr. Columbia U., 1958-61; mem. faculty Queens Coll., CUNY, 1961—, prof. math., 1965—; dir., instr. NSF math. program for high sch. students, 1964-71; researcher axiomatic set theory and math. logic, especially ind. various important propositions of axiomatic set theory, axiom of choice, axiom of restriction. Author: Introduction to Mathematical Logic, 1964, Boolean Algebra and Switching Circuits, 1970, Number Systems, 1973, Beginning Calculus, 1985, 3000 Solved Problems in Calculus, 1988, Differential and Integral Calculus, 1990; contbr. articles to profl. jours. Mem. Am. Math. Soc., Math. Assn. Am., Assn. for Symbolic Logic, Phi Beta Kappa. Home: 10 Pinewood Rd Roslyn NY 11576-2420 Office: Queens Coll Dept Math Flushing NY 11367

MENDELSON, HAIM, artist, educator, art gallery director; b. Siemiatycze, Bielsk, Poland, Oct. 15, 1923; s. David Cemach and Frieda (Konopiati) M.; m. Lita Joan Gordon, Mar. 30, 1955 (div. June 1966); children: Paul, Jan. Student, Am. Artists Sch., 1938-41, Saul Baizerman Sch. Art, 1940-43, Ednl. Alliance Art Sch., 1946. Tchr. Ednl. Alliance, N.Y.C., 1956-61; instr. CCNY, 1961-64; tchr. Columbia Grammar Sch., 1963-64, City and Country Sch., N.Y.C., 1964-91; dir. Hudson Guild Art Gallery, N.Y.C., 1971-94. One-man shows include Creative Galleries, N.Y.C., 1954, Caravan Gallery, N.Y.C., 1957, Chase Gallery, N.Y.C., 1960, Hudson Guild Art Gallery, N.Y.C., 1961, 76, 79, 82, 94, Yellow Poui Art Gallery, Grenada, W.I., 1973, 76, 79, 82, Ednl. Alliance, N.Y.C., 1976, Berkshire Artisans Gallery, Pittsfield, Mass., 1987, Hudson Guild, 1994; group shows include Mus. Modern Art, N.Y.C., 1940-41, Pa. Acad. Fine Arts, 1965, Butler Inst. Am. Art, Ohio, 1965, 67, St. Paul Art Ctr., 1961, 66, NAD, N.Y.C., 1965, 68, 75, 77, 90, Bronx Mus. Arts, 1976, Prints U.S.A., 1982, Gallery Assn. N.Y. State, 1975-78, Internat. Art Biennale, Malta, 1995, Glass Gallery, N.Y.C., 1995, 96; represented in permanent collections N.Y. Pub. Libr., Minn. Mus. Art, Edward Ulrich Mus., Wichita, Kans., St. Vincent Coll., Latrobe, Pa., Griffiths Art Ctr., Canton, N.Y., Manhattan Coll., Riverdale, N.Y., Flint (Mich.) Inst. Fine Arts; portfolio drypoint engravings Grass, 1963, The Artist and His Dead, 1975. Recipient numerous awards including Spl. Distinction award Graphics Internat. Art Biennial Malta, 1995, N.Y. Ctrl. graphics award Audubon Artists, 1996. Mem. Fedn. Modern Painters and Sculptors, Audubon Artists, Print Consortium, Am. Soc. Contemporary Artists. Home: 234 W 21st St # 63 New York NY 10011-3451 *Art is the avenue in which I express the significant experiences of my life. Out of feelings of expressive need, new forms and techniques spontaneously arise. The forms of the future are in life itself.*

MENDELSON, LEE M., film company executive, writer, producer, director; b. San Francisco, Mar. 24, 1933; s. Palmer C. and Jeanette D. (Wise) M.; m. Desiree Mendelson; children: Glenn, Linda, Jason, Sean. BA, Stanford U., 1954. With Sta. KPIX-TV, 1961-63; chmn. bd., pres. Lee Mendelson Film Prodns. Inc., Los Angeles and Burlingame, Calif., 1963—; guest instr. in communications Stanford U. Exec. producer, co-writer (miniseries) This Is America, Charlie Brown; producer: Charlie Brown, Cathy, Betty Boop, (TV spls.) John Steinbeck's Travels with Charley, American and Americans, The Fantastic Funnies, You Asked for It, Here Comes Garfield, (animated films) A Boy Named Charlie Brown, Snoopy Come Home, Race for Your Life Charlie Brown, Peanuts, Bon Voyage Charlie Brown (And Don't Come Back), Garfield and Friends, Mother Goose and Grim. Served to 1st lt. USAF, 1954-57. Recipient 7 Emmy awards, 3 Peabody awards. Mem. Writers Guild Am., Dirs. Guild Am. Office: 1440 Chapin Ave Ste 350 Burlingame CA 94010-4011*

MENDELSON, LEONARD M., lawyer; b. Pitts., May 20, 1923; s. Jacob I. and Anna R. M.; m. Emily Solomon, Dec. 2, 1956; children: Ann, James R., Kathy S. AB, U. Mich., 1947; JD, Yale U., 1950. Bar: Pa. 1951, U.S. Supreme Ct. 1955. Mem. Hollinshead, Mendelson, Bresnahan & Nixon, P.C., Pitts., chmn. bd., 1974-95, of counsel, 1995—; chmn. Lawyer-Realty Joint Com., Pitts., 1971-72. Mem. Pitts. Bd. Pub. Edn., 1975-76. Mem. ABA, Pa. Bar Assn., Allegheny County Bar Assn. Office: 820 Grant Bldg Pittsburgh PA 15219-2257

MENDELSON, RALPH RICHARD, water heater manufacturing executive; b. Cleve., July 11, 1917; s. Louis Ralph and Ruth Margaret (Cohen) M.; m. Mary Adlaide Jones, Feb. 22, 1941 (div. 1982); children: Walton, Philip. BS in Mech. Engring., U. Mich., 1939; MA in Psychology, Cleve. State U., 1993. Staff Hotstream Heater Co., Cleve., 1941-48, v.p., 1948-59, pres., 1959-61; pres. Glass-Lined Water Heater Co., Lakewood, Ohio, 1961-82; cons. heating equipment design pvt. practice, Lakewood, 1982-87; lectr. psychology Cleve. State U., 1994—; instr. Cuyahoga C.C., 1986-93; leader-tchr. Case Western Reseve U., 1984-93—. Author: Solar Energy, 1978, Where Did I Put My Glasses? How You Can Improve Your Memory As You Grow Older, 1993; patentee water heater, infra-red heater. Bd. dirs. Urban League of Cleve., 1957-61, Merrick House, Cleve., 1972-86. pres. 1980-82; vis. com. Case Western Reserve U., 1972-80. Lt. USAAF, 1942-46. Mem. Assn. Energy Engrs., Oil Heat Inst. No. Ohio (bd. dirs. 1966-67, pres. 1969-70), Heights C. of C. (bd. dirs. 1953-60), Cleve. Play House. Democrat. Jewish. Home: 536 E 140th St Cleveland OH 44110-1977

MENDELSON, RICHARD DONALD, former communications company executive; b. N.Y.C., Dec. 2, 1933; s. George and Martha (Goodman) M.; m. Marilyn Miller, July 28, 1956; children: Sandra, Kenneth. BS, Wharton Sch. U. Pa., 1955; JD, NYU, 1959. Bar: N.Y., 1960; CPA, N.Y. Asst. atty. gen. N.Y. State Dept. Law, N.Y.C., 1959-70; v.p., treas. Petry TV, N.Y.C., 1971-75; v.p., dir. corp. devel. Katz Communications, Inc., N.Y.C., 1975-77, sr. v.p. ops., 1977-79, sr. v.p., chief fin. officer, 1979-81, exec. v.p., chief operating officer, 1981-82, pres., chief oper. officer, 1982-89; free-lance writer, 1989—. Mem. Employee Stock Ownership Assn. Am. (pres. 1987-88, bd. dirs.). Home and Office: 71 Saint George Pl Palm Beach Gardens FL 33418-4024

MENDELSON, ROBERT ALLEN, polymer scientist, rheologist; b. Cleve., 1930; s. Julius and Theodora Anne (Bloch) M.; m. Lura Lauzon, 1971; children: John A. Blackstone, Marie L. Taylor. BS in Indsl. Chemistry, Case Inst. Tech., 1952, PhD in Phys. Chemistry, 1956. From sr. rsch. chemist to sci. fellow rsch. dept. Monsanto Co., Texas City, Tex., 1956-71; sci. fellow Monsanto Co., Springfield, Mass., 1972-89, sr. sci. fellow, 1989-91; rheology focus area leader Baytown (Tex.) Polymers Ctr. Exxon Chem., 1991-94; rheology principal investigator, 1995—; mem. com. for pub. policy Am. Inst. Physics, 1985-89; collaborator Univ. Rsch. Programs, Cornell U., 1989-91. Mem. editorial bd. Journal of Rheology, 1986—; contbr. articles to profl. jours.; patentee in field. Mem. Soc. Rheology (pres. 1989-91, v.p. 1987-89, sec. 1974-78), Am. Chem. Soc. (Arthur Doolittle award div. organic coatings and plastics 1982), Soc. Plastics Engrs., AAAS. Home: 16503 Scenic Peaks Ct Houston TX 77059-5554 Office: Exxon Chem Co 5200 Bayway Dr Baytown Polymers Ctr Baytown TX 77522

MENDELSON, SOL, physical science educator, consultant; b. Checonovska, Poland, Oct. 10, 1926; came to U.S., 1927; s. David C. and Frieda (Cohen) M. BME, CCNY, 1955; MS, Columbia U., 1957, PhD, 1961. Prof. engring. CCNY, 1955-58; sr. scientist Sprague Electric Co., North Adams, Mass., 1962-64, Airborne Instruments Lab., Melville, N.Y., 1964-65; phys. metallurgist Bendix Rsch. Lab., Southfield, Mich., 1966-67; cons., rschr., writer, N.Y.C. and Troy, Mich., 1968-72; adj. prof. phys. sci. CUNY, 1972-87. Contbr. numerous articles to sci. jours. Mem. Am. Phys. Soc., Fedn. Am. Scientists, Sigma Xi, Tau Beta Pi, Pi Tau Sigma. Achievements include research on theory and mechanisms of Martensitic transformations. *We have to keep reminding ourselves that data proclaims theory, but theory does not proclaim anything if it does not address crucial data. Many a scientist has gained prominence for a theory by exaggerating ambiguous data or unrealistic models, but those who succeed in solving a problem are able to develop a theory which accounts for crucial experimental data.*

MENDENHALL, JOHN RYAN, retired lawyer, transportation executive; b. Des Moines, Jan. 17, 1928; s. Merritt Blake and Elizabeth M. (Ryan) M.; m. Joan Lois Schafer, June 20, 1953; children: Thomas, James, Jane, Julie, Robert, Jennifer. BS, U. Notre Dame, 1950; JD, Harvard U., 1953. Bar: Iowa 1953, U.S. Tax Ct. 1954, D.C. 1975, U.S. Ct. Claims 1975. Mem. tax staff Arthur Andersen & Co., Cleve., 1953-63, ptnr., 1963-66; dir. taxes Arthur Andersen & Co., Chgo., 1966-70; ptnr. Arthur Andersen & Co., Washington, 1970-74, Williams, Connolly & Califano, Washington, 1974-76; gen. tax counsel Union Pacific Corp., N.Y.C., 1977-80, v.p. taxes, 1980-93; bd. dirs. Empire Steel Castings, Reading, Pa. Co-author: Reforming the Tax Structure, 1973; contbr. articles on taxes to various jours. Bd. dirs. Cook County Hosp., Chgo., 1968-71, Inst. Rsch. on Econs. of Taxation, Washington, 1977-93, Burnside Plantation Inc., Bethlehem, Pa., 1989-93; trustee Convent of Sacred Heart, Greenwich, Conn., 1976-80; bd. govs. Bethlehem Area Found., 1989-93, chmn. 1991-92; pres. Greenwich Br. of English Spkg. Union. With U.S. Army, 1946-47, Japan. Mem. ABA (tax sect., chmn. indexing com. 1985-86), Am. Coun. Capital Formation (bd. dirs. 1972-88), Bus. Roundtable (tax adv. group 1977-92), C. of C. U.S. (mem. tax com. 1972-92), Am. Law Inst. (tax adv. group 1974-88), Nat. Tax Assn. (pres. 1981-82), Nat. Chamber Found. (chmn. tax com. 1984-93), Chevy Chase (Md.) Club, Harvard Club (N.Y.C.), Met. Club (Washington), Belle Haven Club. Republican. Roman Catholic. Home: 47 Lafayette Pl Apt 6H Greenwich CT 06830-5401

MENDENHALL, ROBERT VERNON, mathematics educator; b. Geneva, Ind., Dec. 27, 1920; s. Carl and Lulu (Niswander) M.; m. Gay Dalrymple, Dec. 15, 1944; children—Lisa, Robin, Valerie. B.A. summa cum laude, Ohio State U., 1947, M.A., 1949, Ph.D., 1952. Instr. Ohio State U., 1951-53; sr. engr. N.Am. Aviation Corp., 1953-55; mathematician Vitro Labs., Inc., 1955; asst. prof. U. Miami, 1955-62; assoc. prof. Ohio Wesleyan U., 1962-66, prof. math., 1966-89, prof. emeritus, 1989—; cons. math Benares Hindu U., 1965, Andhra (India) U., 1966, U. Roorkee, India, 1970. Author: (with Herman Meyer) Techniques of Differentiation and Integration, 1966. Served with AUS, 1942-46, ETO. Mem. Am., Indian math. socs., Math. Assn. Am., Phi Beta Kappa, Sigma Xi. Home: 129 Oak Hill Ave Delaware OH 43015-2519

MENDEZ, ALBERT ORLANDO, industrialist, financier; b. Bogota, Colombia, Sept. 7, 1935; came to U.S., 1960; naturalized, 1968; s. Angelino Benjamin and Ana Isabel (Gutierre de Cetina) M.; children: Nicole C., Eric A. BS in Nuclear Physics, N.C. State U., 1961, MS in Nuclear Engring., 1963; MBA, U. Hartford, 1970. Physicist, mgr. mfg. Combustion Engring. Co., Windsor, Conn., 1963-67; mgr. corp. devel. and planning Gulf Oil Corp., Pitts., 1967-71; v.p. mktg., controller for Latin Am. Xerox Corp., Stamford, Conn., 1971-76; exec. v.p., COO, chmn. ops. com., bd. dirs. Ogden Corp., N.Y.C., 1976-84; chmn., chief exec. officer, prin. shareholder Am. Indstl. Corp., Stamford, 1984—, Argo-Tech Corp., Aerospace, Cleve., 1986-89; bd. dirs. Catalyst Energy Co., N.Y.C., 1st Prin. Corp., N.Y.C., Demag, AG, Hamburg, Germany; gen. ptnr. Agnem Holdings Ltd. Partnership, New Canaan, Conn., 1984—; pres., CEO, bd. dirs., prin. shareholder Agnem Investment Co., New Canaan, 1983—; pres., CEO, prin. shareholder AM World Trade Corp., West Palm Beach, Fla.; mem. Pres.'s Adv. Com. on Def. Preparedness and Intelligence, 1986-92. Contbr. articles to profl. jours. Mem. Internat. Platform Assn., Am. mgmt. Assn., Assn. of Corp. Dirs., The Conf. Bd., Am. Nuclear Soc., Palm Beach (Fla.) Polo Club.

MENDEZ, CELESTINO GALO, mathematics educator; b. Havana, Cuba, Oct. 16, 1944; s. Celestino Andres and Georgina (Fernandez) M.; came to U.S., 1962, naturalized, 1970; BA, Benedictine Coll., 1965; MA, U. Colo., 1968, PhD, 1974, MBA, 1979; m. Mary Ann Koplau, Aug. 21, 1971; children: Mark Michael, Matthew Maximilian. Asst. prof. maths. scis. Met. State Coll., Denver, 1971-77, assoc. prof., 1977-82, prof., 1982—, chmn. dept. math. scis., 1980-82; adminstrv. intern office v.p. for acad. affairs Met. State Coll., 1989-90. Mem. advt. rev. bd. Met. Denver, 1973-79; parish outreach rep. S.E. deanery, Denver Cath. Cmty. Svcs., 1976-78; mem. social ministries com. St. Thomas More Cath. Ch., Denver, 1976-78, vice-chmn., 1977-78, mem. parish council, 1977-78; del. Adams County Rep. Conv., 1972, 74, 1994, Colo. 4th Congl. Dist. Conv., 1974, Colo. Rep. Conv., 1982, 88, 90, 92, 96, Douglas County Rep. Conv., 1980, 82, 84, 88, 90, 92, 94, 96; alt. del. Colo. Rep. Conv., 1974, 76, 84, 5th Congl. dist. conv., 1976, mem. rules com., 1978, 80, precinct committeeman Douglas County Rep. Com., 1976-78, 89-92, mem. cen. com., 1976-78, 89-92; dist. 29 Rep. party candidate Colo. State Senate, 1990; mem. Colo. Rep. Leadership program, 1989-90, bd. dirs., 1990—; Douglas county chmn. Rep. Nat. Hispanic Assembly, 1989—; bd. dirs. Rocky Mountain Better Bus. Bur., 1975-79, Rowley Downs Homeowners Assn., 1976-78; trustee Hispanic U. Am., 1975-78; councilman Town of Parker (Colo.), 1981-84, chmn. budget and fin. com. 1981-84; chmn. joint budget com. Town of Parker-Parker Water and Sanitation Dist. Bds., 1982-84; commr. Douglas County Planning Commn., 1993—; dir. Mile High Young Scholars Program, 1995—. Recipient U. Colo. Grad. Sch. excellence in teaching award, 1965-67; grantee Benedictine Coll., 1964-65, Math. Assn. Am. SUMMA grantee Carnegie Found. N.Y., 1994, NSF, 1995—. Mem. Math. Assn. Am. (referee rsch. notes sect. Am. Math. Monthly 1981-82, gov. Rocky Mountain section 1993—, investment com. 1995—, devel. com. 1995—, task force on reps. 1994—), Am. Math. Soc., Nat. Coun. Tchrs. of Math., Colo. Coun. Tchrs. of Maths. (bd. dirs. 1994—), Colo. Internat. Edn. Assn., Assoc. Faculties of State Insts. Higher Edn. in Colo. (v.p. 1971-73). Republican. Roman Catholic. Assoc. editor Denver Metro. Jour. Math. and Computer Sci., 1993—; contbr. articles to profl. jours. including Am. Math. Monthly, Procs. Am. Math. Soc., Am. Math. Monthly, Jour. Personalized Instruction, Denver Met. Jour. Math. and Computer Sci., and newspapers. Home: 39 Hummingbird Dr Castle Rock CO 80104 Office: PO Box 173362 Denver CO 80217-3362

MENDEZ, HERMANN ARMANDO, pediatrician, educator; b. Guatemala, Apr. 26, 1949; came to U.S., 1980; citizen of El Salvador; s. Hermann and Martha (Abularach) Mendez Fortun; m. Maria Elena Ortiz, Feb. 23, 1971; children: Natalia, Amalia. MD, U. El Salvador, 1977. Diplomate Am. Bd. Pediatrics, Am. Bd. Pediatric Infectious Diseases. Asst. prof. pediatrics Health Sci. Ctr. SUNY, Bklyn., 1988-91, assoc. prof., 1991—. Recipient Asst. Sec. for Health award USPHS, 1990, United U. Professions Excellence awardHealth Sci. Ctr., Bklyn., 1991. Fellow Am. Acad. Pediatrics, Infectious Disease Soc. Am. Achievements include clinical research in perinatal transmission of HIV, AIDS in children, adolescents and their families; development of systems of care for these populations. Office: SUNY HSCB Dept Pediatrics Box 49 450 Clarkson Ave Brooklyn NY 11203-2012

MENDEZ, JESUS, history educator, education administrator; b. Havana, Cuba, Oct. 3, 1951; came to U.S., 1960; s. Jesus Mendez and Maria (del Carmen) Gonzalez. BS, U. Miami, 1972, MA, 1974; PhD, U. Tex., 1980. Teaching asst. U. Tex., Austin, 1974-80; lectr. SUNY, Binghamton, 1981; asst. prof. history Barry U., Miami Shores, Fla., 1981-87, assoc. prof. history, 1987—, dept. chmn., 1989-93, asst. dean, 1993—; textbook cons. Glencoe Pub., Westerville, Ohio, 1991-92, 95-96. Contbr. articles to profl. jours. Advisor Dade Heritage Trust, Dade County, Miami, 1995—; bd. dirs. Fulbright Assn., Washington, 1995—. Recipient Travel Rsch. grant NEH, 1988, Rsch. grant Rockefeller Archive Ctr., 1984, Fulbright Rsch. grant USIA, 1983, Dissertation Rsch. grant Orgn. Am. States, 1977-78. Mem. Am. Hist. Assn., Am. Cath. Hist. Assn., Southeastern Coun. Latin Am. Studies, Fla. Hist. Assn., Nat. Collegiate Honors Coun., Fulbright Assn. (pres. south Fla. chpt.). Avocation: literature on classic ocean liners. Home: 720 Minorca Ave Coral Gables FL 33134-3759 Office: Barry Univ 11300 NE 2nd Ave Miami FL 33161-6628

MENDIUS, PATRICIA DODD WINTER, editor, educator, writer; b. Davenport, Iowa, July 9, 1924; d. Otho Edward and Helen Rose (Dodd) Winter; m. John Richard Mendius, June 19, 1947; children: Richard, Catherine M. Graber, Louise, Karen M. Chooljian. BA cum laude, UCLA, 1946; MA cum laude, U. N.Mex., 1966. Cert. secondary edn. tchr., Calif., N.Mex. English teaching asst. UCLA, 1946-47; English tchr. Marlborough Sch. for Girls, L.A., 1947-50, Aztec (N.Mex.) High Sch., 1953-55, Farmington (N.Mex.) High Sch., 1955-63; chair English dept. Los Alamos (N.Mex.) High Sch., 1963-86; sr. technical writer, editor Los Alamos Nat. Lab., 1987—; adj. prof. English, U. N.Mex., Los Alamos, 1970-72, Albuquerque, 1982-85; English cons. S.W. Regional Coll. Bd., Austin, Tex., 1975—; writer, editor, cons. advanced placement English test devel. com. Nat. Coll. Bd., 1982-86, reader, 1982-86, project equality cons., 1985-88; book selection cons. Scholastic mag., 1980-82. Author: Preparing for the Advanced Placement English Exams, 1975; editor Los Alamos Arts Coun. bull., 1986-91. Chair Los Alamos Art in Pub. Places Bd., 1987-92; chair adv. bd. trustees U. N.Mex., Los Alamos, 1987-93; pres. Los Alamos Concert Assn., 1972-73, 95—; chair Los Alamos Mesa Pub. Libr. Bd., 1990-94, chair endowment com., 1995—. Mem. Soc. Tech. Communicators, AAUW (pres. 1961-63, state bd. dirs. 1959-63, Los Alamos coordinating coun. 1992-93, pres. 1993-94), DAR, Order Ea. Star, Mortar Bd., Phi Beta Kappa (pres. Los Alamos chpt. 1969-72, v.p. 1996-97), Phi Kappa Phi, Delta Kappa Gamma, Gamma Phi Beta. Avocations: swimming, reading, hiking, astronomy, singing. Home: 124 Rover Blvd Los Alamos NM 87544-3634 Office: Los Alamos Nat Lab Diamond Dr Los Alamos NM 87544

MENDONSA, ARTHUR ADONEL, retired city official; b. Wauchula, Fla., Apr. 5, 1928; s. Arthur Abner and Mamie (Swafford) M.; m. Beverly Glover, Sept. 6, 1951; children—Arthur Adonel, George Andrew; m. Suzanne Danzig, Sept. 7, 1980. B.A., Emory U., 1952; M City Planning, Ga. Inst. Tech., 1954. Planning dir. Gainesville-Hall County (Ga.) Planning Commn., 1954-56, 57-60; sr. planner Charleston (S.C.) County Planning Commn., 1956-57; exec. dir. Savannah-Chatham (Ga.) County Met. Planning Commn., 1960-62; city mgr. Savannah, 1962-67, 71-95; dir. field svcs., asst. prof. Inst. Govt., U. Ga., Athens, 1967-69; exec. asst. to chmn. DeKalb County Bd. Commrs., Decatur, Ga., 1969-71; mem. Coastal Area Planning and Devel. Commn., 1972-90, chmn., 1983-85; mem. Ga. Gov.'s Adv. Council on Coastal Zone Mgmt., 1976-78, Ga. Coastal Mgmt. Bd., 1978-82. Author: Simplified Financial Management in Local Government, 1969. Recipient All-Pro City Mgmt. Team City and State mags., 1986, 87, 88. Mem. Am. Inst. Planners (bd. examiners), Am. Soc. Pub. Adminstrn., Internat. City

Mgrs. Assn. (Outstanding Mgmt. Innovator award 1979), Ga. City-County Mgrs. Assn. (pres. 1974-75), Kiwanis.

MENDOZA, GEORGE, poet, author; b. N.Y.C., June 2, 1934; s. George and Elizabeth Mendoza; m. Ruth Sekora, 1967; children: Ashley, Ryan. BA, State Maritime Coll., 1953; postgrad., Columbia U., 1954-56. Author over 100 books for children and adults published worldwide; many included in Boston U.'s George Mendoza Collection, established 1984; children's books on display at the Centre Nat. d'Art et de Culture Georges Pompidou. Works include: And Amedeo Asked, How Does One Become a Man?, (illustrated by Ati Forberg), 1959, The Puma and the Pearl, 1962, The Hawk Is Humming: A Novel, 1964, A Piece of String, Astor-Honor, 1965, Gwot! Horribly Funny Hairticklers (illustrated by Steven Kellog), 1967, The Crack in the Wall and Other Terribly Weird Tales (illustrated by Mercer Mayer), 1968, Flowers and Grasses and Weeds (illustrated by Joseph Low), 1968, The Practical Man (illustrated by Imero Gobbato), 1968, Hunting Sketches (illustrated by Ronald Stein), 1968, A Beastly Alphabet (illustrated by J. Low), 1969, The Digger Wasp (illustrated by Jean Zallinger), 1969, Herman's Hat (illustrated by Frank Bozzo), 1969, The Starfish Trilogy (illustrated by Ati Forberg), 1969, (compiler) The World From My Window: Poems and Drawings (children's writings), 1969, Are You My Friend? (illustrated by F. Bozzo), 1970, The Marcel Marceau Alphabet Book, 1970, The Thumbtown Toad (illustrated by Monika Beisner), 1970, The Inspector, 1970, The Good Luck Spider & other bad luck stories, 1970, The Fearsome Brat (illustrated by F. Bozzo), 1971, Fish in the Sky (illustrated by Milton Glaser), 1971, Moonfish and owl scratchings, 1971, Moonstring, 1971, The Hunter, the Tick and the Gumberoo, 1971, The Marcel Marceau Counting Book, 1971, The Scarecrow Clock (illustrated by Eric Carle), 1971, Big Frog, Little Pond, 1971, The Scribbler, 1971, The Christmas Tree Alphabet Book, 1971, Shadowplay, 1974, Lord, Suffer me to Catch a Fish, 1974, Fishing the Morning Lonely, 1974, (with Carol Burnett) What I Want to Be When I Grow Up, 1975, (with Zero Mostel) The Sesame Street Book of Opposites, 1975, Norman Rockwell's Americana ABC (illustrated by N. Rockwell), 1975, Doug Henning's Magic Book, 1975, Lost Pony, 1976, Norman Rockwell's Boys and Girls at Play, 1976, Secret Places of a Trout Fisherman, 1977, Norman Rockwell's Diary for a Young Girl (illustrated by N. Rockwell), 1978, Magic Tricks, 1978, Mon livre de magie (French edit. of My Book of Magic), Norman Rockwell's Scrapbook for a Young Boy (illustrated by N. Rockwell), 1979, (with Andres Segovia) Segovia, My Book of the Guitar, 1979, Need a House? Call Ms. Mouse! (illustrated by Doris Susan Smith), 1981, Alphabet Sheep (illustrated by K. Reidy), 1982, The Sheepish Book of Opposites, 1982, Silly Sheep and other sheepish rhymes, 1982, Norman Rockwell's Four Seasons, 1982, Norman Rockwell's Happy Holidays, 1983, Henri Mouse (illustrated by Joelle Boucher), 1985, Henri La Souris, 1987, Norman Rockwell's Patriotic Times, 1986, (with Ivan Lendl) Hitting Hot, 1986, (with Sam Snead) Slammin' Sam, 1986, Norman Rockwell's Love and Remembrance, 1986, Top Tennis, 1987, L'Album des Noeuds, 1988, Norman Rockwell's Old Fashioned American Cookbook, 1988, Hairticklers (illustrated by Gahan Wilson), 1989, The Hunter I Might Have Been, reprint 1989, Were You a Wild Duck, Where Would You Go? (illustrated by Jane Osborn-Smith), 1990, Traffic Jam (illustrated by David Stoltz), 1990; also author screenplays for Petals from a Poem Flower, You Show Me Yours and I'll Show You Mine and scripts for Sesame Street; numerous others; over 15 books of poetry including The Hunter I Might Have Been (Lewis Carroll Shelf award 1968), The Mist Men, Goodbye, River, Goodbye; also dozens of articles in The N.Y. Times, Herald Tribune, Stern, Vogue, Harper's Bazaar, Ms., Esquire, Town & Country, Sports Afield, Men's Journal, Philadelphia Inquirer; special travel corr. Toronto Globe & Mail, 1991-94. Cited by Pres. Reagan for Norman Rockwell's Patriotic Times. Avocation: trout and salmon fishing. Worldwide fishing expeditions recorded for TV spls. *I believe we are living in a world where people no longer see each other as individuals. We have become invisible. It is necessary to save our souls. Go out to a field and pick up a fallen leaf. Look at the veins that river the leaf. Follow them until nothing else matters except for the leaf in your hand. Then you will become visible. You will see others and others will see you.*

MENDOZA, STANLEY ATRAN, pediatric nephrologist, educator; b. Pitts., May 7, 1940; s. Joseph William and Marian Ruth (Atran) M.; m. Carole Ann Klein, June 23, 1963; children: Daniel, Joseph. Student, Harvard U., 1957-59; B.A., Johns Hopkins U., 1961, M.D., 1964. Diplomate: Am. Bd. Pediatrics. Intern Johns Hopkins Hosp., Balt., 1964-65; jr. asst. resident dept. medicine Children's Hosp. Med. Ctr., Boston, 1965-66; asst. attending physician, dir. renal rsch. labs Children's Meml. Hosp., Chgo., 1969-71; asst. prof. pediatrics Sch. Medicine U. Calif., San Diego, 1971-73; assoc. prof. Sch. Medicine U. Calif., 1973-79, prof. pediatrics, dept. pediatrics, div. pediatric nephrology, 1979—, vice chmn. dept. pediatrics, 1986-87, chmn. dept. pediatrics, 1992—. Contbr. article in field to profl. publ. Served With USPHS, 1966-69. Fogarty Sr. Internat. fellow, 1978-79; Alan J. Wurtzburger research scholar, 1964; recipient Johns Hopkins Med. Soc. award, 1964, hon. mention Borden Undergrad. research award in medicine, 1964; Eleanor Roosevelt internat. fellow Internat. Union Against Cancer, 1984-85. Mem. Am. Fedn. Clin. Research, Am. Pediatric Soc., Am. Physiol. Soc., Am. Soc. Nephrology, Am. Soc. Pediatric Nephrology, Internat. Soc. Nephrology. Office: U Calif San Diego Dept Pediatrics 200 W Arbor Dr San Diego CA 92103-1911

MENEELEY, EDWARD STERLING, artist; b. Wilkes-Barre, Pa., Dec. 18, 1927; s. Edward Sterling and Louina Halter M. Student, Murray Art Sch., Wilkes-Barre, 1947-50, Sch. Visual Arts, N.Y.C., 1952-53. vis. lectr. Belleville Coll., St. Louis, Art Students League, N.Y.C.; lectr. Lehigh Valley Sch. System, 1987, Rogers College, Istanbul, Turkey, 1991; pres. ESM Documentations, N.Y.C.; fine arts cons. Arts Initiatives, Inc., N.Y.C.; founder Portable Gallery Press, 1957-67. One-man exhbs. include, Donovan Gallery, Phila., 1952, Parma Gallery, N.Y.C., 1962, Teuscher Gallery, N.Y.C., 1966, 68, Inst. Contemporary Arts, London, 1971, Victoria and Albert Mus., London, 1972, U. Sussex, Eng., 1972, Whitechapel Art Gallery, London, 1973, Demos Gallery, Athens, Greece, 1976, Frank Marino Gallery, N.Y.C., 1978, 79, 80, 81, 82, Sordoni Gallery, Wilkes (Pa.) Coll., 1981, Ericson Gallery, N.Y.C., 1980, Portfolio Gallery, Atlanta, 1983, Angela Flowers Gallery, London, 1985, J.T. Gallery, Jim Thorpe, Pa, 1987, 55 Mercer St., N.Y.C., 1987, Anita Shapolsky Gallery, N.Y.C., 1988, Bucknell U. Gallery Art, Lewisburg, 1988, Recent Painting & Sculptute, Coll. Misericordia, Dallas, Pa., 1989, Mixed Media, Craft Alliance Gallery, St. Louis, 1990, Provincetown (Mass.) Art Mus., 1993. Served with USNR, 1945-47, 50-52. Nat. Endowment Arts grantee; Pollock-Krasner Found. grantee, 1986, 90. Mem. Artist Club N.Y.C., Inst. Contemporary Arts London, Josiah White Soc., Weissport, Pa.

MENEFEE, SAMUEL PYEATT, lawyer, anthropologist; b. Denver, June 8, 1950; s. George Hardiman and Martha Elizabeth (Pyeatt) M. BA in Anthropology and Scholar of Ho. summa cum laude, Yale U., 1972; diploma in Social Anthropology, Oxford (Eng.) U., 1973, BLitt, 1975; JD, Harvard U., 1981; LLM in Oceans, U. Va., 1982, SJD, 1993; MPhil in Internat. Rels., U. Cambridge, Eng., 1995. Bar: Ga. 1981, U.S. Ct. Appeals (11th cir.) 1982, Va. 1983, La. 1983, U.S. Ct. Mil. Appeals 1983, U.S. Ct. Internat. Trade 1983, U.S. Ct. Claims 1983, U.S. Ct. Appeals (10th cir.) 1983, (fed., 1st, 3d, 4th, 5th, 6th, 7th, 8th and 9th cirs.) 1984, D.C. 1985, Nebr. 1985, Fla. 1985, U.S. Supreme Ct. 1985, U.S. Ct. Appeals (D.C. cir.) 1986, Maine 1986, Pa. 1986. Assoc. Phelps, Dunbar, Marks, Claverie & Sims, New Orleans, 1983-85; of counsel Barham & Churchill PC, New Orleans, 1985-88; sr. assoc. Ctr. for Nat. Security Law U. Va. Sch. Law, 1985—; lectr. U. Cape Town, 1987; vis. asst. prof. U. Mo.-Kansas City, 1990; law clk. Hon. Pasco M. Bowman, U.S. Ct. Appeals (8th cir.), 1994-95; vis. prof. Regent U., 1996-97; adv. The Mariners' Mus. and The Am. Maritime Forum, 1997, lectr. various nat. and internat. orgns.; mem. ICC Consultative Task Force on Comml. Crime, 1996—. Author: Wives for Sale: An Ethnographic Study of British Popular Divorce, 1981, Contemporary Piracy and International Law, 1995, Trends in Maritime Violence, 1996; co-editor: Materials on Ocean Law, 1982, Trends in Maritime Violence, 1996; contbr. numerous articles to profl. jours. Recipient Katharine Briggs prize Folklore Soc., 1992; Bates traveling fellow Yale U., 1971, Ctr. for Oceans Law and Policy fellow Law Sch. U. Va., 1982-83, sr. fellow, 1985-89, Maury fellow, 1989—, Cosmos fellow Sch. Scottish Studies U. Edinburgh, 1991-92, IMB fellow, ICC Internat. Maritime Bur., 1991—, Regional Piracy Ctr. fellow, Kuala Lumpur, 1993—; Rhodes scholar, 1972. Fellow Royal Anthrop. Inst., Am. Anthrop. Assn., Royal Asiatic Soc., Royal Soc. Antiquaries of Ireland, Soc. Antiquaries (Scotland), Royal Geog. Soc., Soc. Antiquaries; mem. ABA (vice-chmn. marine resources com. 1987-90, chmn. law of the sea com. subcom. naval warfare, maritime terrorism and piracy 1989—, mem. law of the sea com. steering com. 1996—, mem. working group on terrorism), Southeastern Admiralty Law Inst. (com. mem.), Maritime Law Assn. (proctor, com. mem., chmn. subcom. law of the sea 1988-91, vice chmn. com. internat. law of the sea 1991—, chair working group piracy 1992—), Marine Tech. Soc. (co-chmn. marine security com. 1991-95, chmn. 1995—), Selden Soc., Am. Soc. Internat. Law Internat. Law Assn. (com. mem., rapporteur Am. br. com. EEZ 1988-90, rapporteur Am. br. com. Maritime Neutrality 1992, observer UN conv. on Law of the Sea meeting of States Parties 1996, chmn. Am. br. com. on Law of the Sea 1996—), Am. Soc. Indsl. Security (com. mem.), U.S. Naval Inst., USN League, Folklore Soc., Royal Celtic Soc., Internat. Studies Assn., Royal Scottish Geog. Soc., Royal African Soc., Egypt Exploration Soc., Arctic Inst. N.Am., Internat. Studies Assn., Am. Hist. Soc., Internat. Assn. Rsch. on Peasant Diaries (nat. editor 1996—), Nat. Eagle Scout Assn., Raven Soc., Jefferson Soc., Fence Club, Mory's Assn., Elizabethan Club, Yale Polit. Union, Leander Club, Cambridge Union, United Oxford and Cambridge Univ. Club, Yale Club (N.Y.C.), Paul Morphy Chess Club, Pendennis Club, Round Table Club (New Orleans), Phi Beta Kappa, Omicron Delta Kappa. Republican. Episcopalian. Avocations: anthropology, archaeology, social history, crew, hill walking. Office: U Va Ctr Nat Sec Law 580 Massie Rd Charlottesville VA 22903-1738

MENENDEZ, ADOLFO, engineering company executive; m. Silvia Perez; children: José Adolfo, Mercedes Silvia. BSME, Manhattan Coll.; postgrad., Golden Gate U. Registered profl. engr. D.C., Va., Miss. Project mgr. internat. ops. Bechtel Power Corp.; pres., COO K & M Engrng. & Cons. Corp., Washington; bd. dirs. KMR Power Corp.; cons. Wold Bank, Internat. Fin. Corp., European Bank for Reconstruction and Devel., USAID, others. Mem. Georgetown Club, U. Club, Lakewood Country Club. Office: K & M Engring & Consulting Corp 2001 L St NW Ste 500 Washington DC 20036-4944*

MENENDEZ, MANUEL, JR., judge; b. Tampa, Fla., Aug. 2, 1947; s. Manuel and Clara (Marin) M.; m. Linda Lee Stewart, Aug. 31, 1969; children: Jennifer Kay, Christine Marie. AA, U. Fla., 1967, BA, 1969, JD with Honors, 1972. Bar: Fla. 1972, U.S. Dist. Ct. (mid. dist.) Fla. 1973, U.S. Ct. Appeals (5th cir.) 1973, U.S. Ct. Claims 1974, U.S. Tax Ct. 1974, U.S. Ct. Customs and Patent Appeals 1974, U.S. Supreme Ct. 1976, U.S. Ct. Appeals (11th cir.) 1983, U.S. Ct. Appeals (D.C. cir.) 1984. Asst. U.S. atty. Dept. Justice, Jacksonville, Fla., 1973-77; chief asst. U.S. atty. Dept. Justice, Tampa, 1978-83; assoc. Law Office Jack Culp, Jacksonville, 1977-78; ptnr. Culp & Menendez, P.A., Jacksonville, 1978; county judge jud. br. State of Fla., Tampa, 1983-84, cir. judge jud. br., 1984—; dept. head, faculty mem. Fla. Coll. of Advanced Jud. Studies; faculty mem. pre-bench program Fla. New Judges Coll., 1993; faculty mem. Fla. Bar Prosecutor-Pub. Defender Advocacy Tng. Program, 1989-91, 94—; mentor judge coord. 13th Cir. Ct., 1995—; co-chair edn. steering com. Fla. Cir. Judge's Conf., 1996. Exec. editor U. Fla. Law Rev., 1971-72. Mem. adv. bd. Salvation Army, 1988-91. Recipient Pub. Service Meritorious Achievement award West Tampa Civic Clubs Assn., 1983. Mem. ABA, Fla. Bar Assn. (mem. criminal procedure rules com. 1988-94, chmn. 1991-92, chmn. rules and jud. adminstrn. com. 1995-96), Fed. Bar Assn. (v.p. Jacksonville chpt. 1974-75, pres. Tampa Bay chpt. 1980-85), Hillsborough County Bar Assn. (media law com. 1984—, trial lawyers sect. 1985—, Liberty Bell award selection com. 1991-93, jud. evaluation com. 1993), Am. Judicature Soc., Am. Judges Assn., Am. Inns of Ct. (master of bench, pres. 1991—), U. Fla. Alumni Assn., U. Fla. Law Ctr. Assn., First U.S. Calvary Regiment Rough Riders Inc., Propellor Club, Tampa Gator Club. Avocations: fishing, golf, Univ. Fla. athletics, coaching little league sr. girls softball. Office: Hillsborough County Courthouse 419 N Pierce St Ste 375 Tampa FL 33602-4025

MENENDEZ, ROBERT, congressman, lawyer; b. N.Y.C., Jan. 1, 1954; s. Mario and Evangelina (Lopez) M.; m. Jane Jacobsen, June 5; children: Alicia, Robert. BA, St. Peter's Coll., 1976; JD, Rutgers U., 1979. Bar: N.J. 1980. Sole practice Union City, N.J., 1980-92; mem. 103d-105th Cngresses from 13th Dist. N.J.; Dem. whip at large 103d-104th Cngresses from 13th Dist. N.J.; mem. Congl. Arts Caucus; mem. western hemisphere, aviation, water resources & environment coms. Mayor of Union City, 1986-92; sec. Union City Bd. Edn., 1978-82, trustee, 1974-78; pres. Alliance civic Orgn., 1982-92; mem. Gov.'s Hispanic Adv. Com., Trenton, N.J., 1984—; mem. Gov.'s Ethnic Adv. Com., Washignton, 1985—. Recipient Cmty. Svc. award Gran Logia del Norte, 1981, Outstanding Svc. award Hispanic Law Enforcement, 1981, Outstanding Cmty. Svc. Revista Actualidades, 1982, Disting. Citizen award U. Medicine and Dentistry N.J., 1994, Man of Yr. award Kiwanis, 1994. Mem. N.J. Hispanic Elected and Apptd Ofcls. (chair), Hoboken Elks Club. Democrat. Roman Catholic. Avocations: chess, racquetball. Office: 405 Cannon Bldg Washington DC 20515-3013 also: 911 Bergen Ave Jersey City NJ 07306-4301*

MENES, PAULINE H., state legislator; b. N.Y.C., July 16, 1924; d. Arthur B. and Hannah H. Herskowitz; m. Melvin Menes, Sept. 1, 1946; children: Sandra Jill Menes Ashe, Robin Joy Menes Elvord, Bambi Lynn Menes Gavin. BA in Bus. Econs. and Geography, Hunter Coll., N.Y.C., 1945. Economist Quartermaster Gen. Office, Washington, 1945-47; geographer Army Map Service, Washington, 1949-50; chief clk. Prince George's County Election Bd., Upper Marlboro, Md., 1963; substitute tchr. Prince George's County H.S.s, Md., 1965-66; mem. Md. Ho. of Dels., Annapolis, 1966—, mem. judiciary com., 1979—, mem. com. on rules and exec. nominations, 1979-94, 95—, chmn. spl. com. on drug and alcohol abuse, 1986—, chmn. Prince George's County del., 1993-95, parliamentarian, 1995—. Mem. Md. Arts Coun., Balt., 1968-95, Md. Commn. on Aging, Balt., 1975-95; bd. dirs. Prisoner's Aid Assn., Balt., 1971-94. Recipient Internat. Task Force award Women's Yr., 1977; named to Hall of Fame Hunter Coll. Alumni Assn., 1986, Women's Hall of Fame Prince George County, 1989. Mem. NOW, Nat. Conf. State Legislators (com. on drugs and alcohol 1987), Md. NOW (Ann London Scott Meml. award for legis. excellence 1976), Nat. Order Women Legislators (pres. 1979-80), Women's Polit. Caucus, Bus. and Profl. Women. Avocations: theater, music, dance show attending, stamp collector. Home: 3517 Marlbrough Way College Park MD 20740-3925 Office: Md Ho of Reps Rm 210 Lowe State Office Bldg Annapolis MD 21401

MENG, JACK, food products executive. CEO Schreiber Foods. Office: Schreiber Foods PO Box 19010 Green Bay WI 54307-9010 Office: PO Box 19010 Green Bay WI 54307-9010*

MENGDEN, JOSEPH MICHAEL, investment banker; b. Houston, Sept. 28, 1924; s. Hippolyt Frederick and Amalia (Dittlinger) M.; m. Suzanne Miner, Sept. 30, 1950 (dec. July 1990); children: Anne Elise Mengden Giliberto, Amanda Mary, Michael Joseph, Charles Louis, Melissa Mary Mengden Bunker, Mary Miner Mengden Fitch; m. Dorothy Duggan, July 27, 1991. Ph.B., U. Notre Dame, 1949. V.p. Nat. Bank of Detroit, 1950-67; exec. v.p. First of Mich. Capital Corp., Detroit, 1967-90, sr. cons., 1990-95, chmn. bd., 1994-95; bd. dirs. First of Mich. Captial Corp., Detroit, 1969-96; retired; bd. dirs. Saginaw (Mich.) Bay Broadcasting Corp. Served to 1st lt. USAAF, World War II. Decorated Air medal with 2 oak leaf clusters. Home: 321 Rivard Blvd Grosse Pointe MI 48230-1625

MENGEL, CHARLES EDMUND, physician, medical educator; b. Balt., Nov. 29, 1931; s. Charles LeRoy and Anna (Apgar) M.; m. Paula Padgett, June 5, 1978; children: Cheryl Lynn, Charles Edmund, Gregory John, Scott Alan, Carol Ann, Michael Daniel. A.B. in Chemistry, Lafayette Coll., 1953; M.D., Johns Hopkins U., 1957. Intern Johns Hopkins Hosp., 1957-58; resident Duke Hosp., 1958-59, 61-62; clin. assoc. NIH, 1959-61; mem. faculty Duke U. Med. Sch., 1961-65; Doan prof., dir. hematology and oncology Ohio State U., 1965-69; prof. medicine U. Mo., Columbia, 1969-82; chmn. dept. U. Mo., 1969-81; pvt. practive gen. medicine Moberly, Mo., 1982-88; prof. medicine Kans. U. Med. Ctr., Kansas City, 1988—. Author textbook; contbr. articles to med. publs. Served with USPHS, 1959-61. Markle scholar acad. medicine, 1963. Mem. ACP, Am. Fedn. Clin. Research, Am. Soc. Hematology, Am. Soc. Clin. Investigation. Home: 3221 Meadow Rd Leavenworth KS 66048-4764 Office: Va Med Ctr Leavenworth KS 66048

MENGEL, CHRISTOPHER EMILE, lawyer, educator; b. Holyoke, Mass., Sept. 11, 1952; s. Emile Oscar and Rose Ann (O'Donnell) M.; m. Ellen Christine Creager, Dec. 6, 1991; children: Meredith Anne, Celia Claire; stepchildren: Cara Elizabeth Creager, Kristen Michele Creager. Student, U. Notre Dame, 1970-71; BA, Holy Cross Coll., 1974; JD, Detroit Coll. Law, 1979. Bar: Mich. 1979, U.S. Dist. Ct. (ea. dist.) Mich. 1989, U.S. Ct. Appeals (6th cir.) 1990. Tchr. Holyoke Pub. Schs., 1974-76; assoc. Fried & Sniokaitis P.C., Detroit, 1980-82; prof. law Detroit Coll. Law, 1982-85; pvt. practice law Detroit, 1982-91; mng. ptnr. Berkley, Mengel & Vining, PC, 1992—. Mem. coun. St. Ambrose Parish, Grosse Pointe Park, Mich., 1985-88, pres. 1986-87. Matthew J. Ryan scholar, 1970. Mem. ABA, Mich. Bar Assn., Detroit Bar Assn. Democrat. Roman Catholic. Avocations: baseball, sailing, photography. Home: 1281 N Oxford Rd Grosse Pointe MI 48236-1857 Office: Berkley Mengel & Vining PC 3100 Penobscot Bldg Detroit MI 48226

MENGEL, DAVID BRUCE, agronomy and soil science educator; b. East Chicago, Ind., May 1, 1948; s. Bill M. and Thelma Lee (Miller) M.; m. Susan Kay Haverstock, Aug. 30, 1968; children: David, Erin. BS in Agricultural Edn., Purdue U., 1970, MS in Agronomy, 1972; PhD in Soil Sci., N.C. State U., 1975. Cert. prof. agronomist, soil scientist. Asst. prof. agronomy La. State U., Crowley, 1975-79; asst. prof. agronomy Purdue U., West Lafayette, Ind., 1979-82, assoc. prof., 1982-86; prof. agronomy Purdue U., West Lafayette, 1986—;. Mem. Am Soc. Agronomy, Soil Sci. Soc. Am., Internat. Soil Sci. Soc., Sigma Xi, Gamma Sigma Delta, Epsilon Sigma Phi, Delta Tau Delta. Avocations: fishing, woodworking. Office: Purdue U Dept Agronomy 1150 Lilly Hall West Lafayette IN 47907-1150

MENGEL, PHILIP R(ICHARD), investment banker; b. Memphis, Oct. 30, 1944; s. John P. and Marjorie Ann M.; m. Jayne E. Frutig, Dec. 20, 1980; 1 child, Jill Kathryn. AB, Princeton U., 1968; cert., Woodrow Wilson Sch. Pub. & Internat. Affairs, 1968. With Fiduciary Trust Co. N.Y., N.Y.C., 1968-79, v.p., 1970-79, exec. com., 1973-79; pres., dir. Fiduciary Investment Corp., N.Y.C., 1973-79; founder, pres., dir. Mengel & Co., Inc. (formerly Mengel, McCabe & Co., Inc.), N.Y.C., 1979-90; chmn., pres. Mengel & Co., Inc., N.Y.C., 1979-90; pres., CEO Glen-Gery Corp., Wyomissing, Pa., 1990—, also bd. dirs.; CEO Ibstock PLC, 1996—, also bd. dirs.; bd. dirs. Brick Inst. Am., Compagnia de Celulose do Caima, S.A., Portugal. Trustee St. Stephen's Sch., Rome, 1976-88, chmn. bd. 1978-82; co-chmn. Graham Windham Childcare Benefit, 1986-88. Mem. Racquet and Tennis Club, U.S. Ct. Tennis Assn. (bd. dirs. 1993—), The Brook, Racquet Club of Phila., Tuxedo Club (gov. 1988—), The Queens Club. Episcopalian. Office: 1166 Spring St Reading PA 19610-1721 also: 40 Montpelier Sq, London England

MENGELING, WILLIAM LLOYD, veterinarian, virologist, researcher; b. Elgin, Ill., Apr. 1, 1933; s. William Paul and Blanche Joyce (Wormwood) M.; m. Barbara Ann Kethcart, Aug. 23, 1958; children: Michelle, Michael. BS, Kans. State U., 1958, DVM, 1960; MS, Iowa State U., 1966, PhD, 1969. Diplomate M. Coll. Vet. Microbiologists (chmn. 1977-78, bd. dirs. 1975-77). Vet. clinician St. Francis Animal Hosp., Albuquerque, 1960-61; vet. medical officer Nat. Animal Disease Ctr., Ames, Iowa, 1961-69, rsch. leader, 1969—; rsch. leader U.S. Sr. Exec. Svc., 1991—; cons. numerous state, fed., pvt. U.S. and fgn. agys.; collaborative prof., mem. grad. faculty Iowa State U. Co-editor: Diseases of Swine, 5th, 6th, 7th editions; contbr. articles to jours., chpts. to books. With U.S. Army, 1953-55. Recipient cert. appreciation USDA, 1978, George Fleming award Brit. Vet. Jour., 1978, Disting. Svc. award USDA, 1984, Gov.'s medal sci. State of Iowa, 1985, Vet. Med. Rsch. award Am. Feed Industry Assn., 1989, Leadership Merit awards USDA, 1989, 90, 91, 93. Mem. AVMA (Vet. Med. Rsch. award 1989), U.S. Animal Health Assn., Conf. Rsch. Workers in Animal Disease (pres. 1987-88, coun. 1981-86), Kiwanis (pres. 1975-76). Methodist. Avocations: wilderness survival, canoeing, camping, fishing. Address: 4220 Phoenix St Ames IA 50014-3922

MENGES, CARL BRAUN, investment banker; b. N.Y.C., Sept. 17, 1930; s. Hermann and Alice (Braun) M.; m. Cordelia Sykes, Apr. 24, 1965; children: James C., Benjamin W., Samuel G. B.A., Hamilton Coll., 1951; M.B.A., Harvard U., 1953. Salesman Owens Corning Fiberglas Corp., 1954-59, mktg. mgr., 1959-63; with instl. sales dept. Model Roland Co., N.Y.C., 1963-65; with instnl. sales dept., syndicate mgr., dir. internat. Donaldson, Lufkin & Jenrette Inc., 1965-77, mng. dir., 1972—, chmn. fin. services group, 1984-87, vice chmn. of bd., 1987—; chmn. bd. dirs. Winthrop Focus Funds, 1986—; bd. dirs. Med. Indemnity Assurance Corp., The Greenwall Found., G-Tech Corp. Trustee Hosp. for Spl. Surgery, 1977—, Hamilton Coll., Clinton, N.Y., trustee 1985—; v.p., treas., trustee The Allen-Stevenson Sch., N.Y.C., 1979-86, bd. dirs. Boys Club of N.Y. Mem. Union Club (gov.), Maidstone Club (gov. 1969-86, pres. 1982-86), Nat. Golf Links Am., Regency Whist Links, Colony Club, Leash Club, L.I. Wyandanch Club (gov.). Office: Donaldson Lufkin & Jenrette Securities Corp 277 Park Ave New York NY 10172

MENGES, CHRIS, cinematographer, film director; b. Kington, Eng., Sept. 15, 1940. Began career as cameraman with British TV, 1963. Cinematographer: Poor Cow, 1967, Gumshoe, 1970, Kes, 1970, Blackjack, 1979, Warlords of the 21st Century, 1982, Danny Boy Angel, 1983, Local Hero, 1983, Comfort and Joy, 1984, The Killing Fields, 1984 (Acad. award 1984), Marie, 1985, A Sense of Freedom, 1985, The Mission, 1986 (Acad. award 1986), Walter and June, 1986, Shy People, 1987, High Season, 1988, Singing the Blues in Red, 1988; film dir.: A World Apart, 1988 (Grand prize Cannes Internat. Film Festival), Second Best, 1994. Office: Casarotto Co Ltd, Nat House, 60-66 Wardour St, London W1V 3HP, England also: The Fron, Duthlas Nr Knighton, Powys LD7 1RH, Wales Also: 7 Wesleyan Pl, London NW5, England

MENGLE, TOBI DARA, mechanical engineer, consultant; b. Pottsville, Pa., Dec. 17, 1960; s. Richard H. and Joyce Pauline (Shuey) M.; m. Barbara A. Brickey, 1992; children: Chase Tucker, Tanner Richard. BS, Pa. State U., 1982. Registered profl. engr., Pa. Assoc. engr. IBM Corp., East Fishkill, N.Y., 1982-84; devel. engr. AT&T Microelectronics, Reading, Pa., 1984-90; sr. mfg. engr. Lutron Electronics, Coopersburg, Pa., 1990-91; cons. AT&T Microelectronics, Reading, 1991-92, AT&T Bell Labs., Breinigsville, Pa., 1991-93, Associated Bio-Engrs. and Cons., 1993-95, Dana Spicer Systems Div., 1995-96; prin. engr., ptnr. Bio-Process Cons., 1996, pvt. practice, Birdsboro, Pa., 1997—. Mem. Union of Concerned Scientists, Cambridge, Mass., 1991. Named Lehigh Valley Young Engr. of Yr., 1993. Mem. ASME (sec. chmn. 1991-93), Internat. Soc. Pharm. Engring. Avocations: flying (instrument rated pilot), scuba diving, bicycling. Home and Office: 931 Lincoln Rd Birdsboro PA 19508-8831

MENGUY, RENE, surgeon, educator; b. Prague, Czechoslovakia, Feb. 4, 1926; came to U.S., 1951, naturalized, 1957; s. Auguste and Beatrice (Adam) M.; m. Emilie Rigacci, Aug. 10, 1950; children—John, Ghislaine. B.A., U. Hanoi, Indochina, 1944; M.D., U. Paris, France, 1951; Ph.D., U. Minn., 1957. Fellow gen. surgery Mayo Clinic, 1952-57; mem. faculty U. Okla. Med. Sch., 1957-61, U. Ky. Med. Center, 1961-65; prof. surgery, chmn. dept. U. Chgo. Med. Sch., 1965-71; prof. surgery U. Rochester Med. Sch., 1971—; surgeon Genesee Hosp., 1971-96, Highland Hosp., Rochester, 1996—; Mem. clin. research tng. com. NIH, 1965-69; cons. VA, 1964—. Author: Peptic Ulcer, 1975; Mem. editorials bd. jours. in field.; Contbr. articles to profl. jours. Recipient citation French Expeditionary Corps, Hanoi, 1946; Fulbright travel grantee, 1951-52; recipient Alumni award meritorious research Mayo Found., 1956; John and Mary R. Markle scholar med. scis., 1958-63. Mem. A.C.S., Am. Fedn. Clin. Research, N.Y. Acad. Scis., Soc. Exptl. Biology and Medicine, Am. Assn. Cancer Research, Am. Gastroenterol. Assn., Soc. Univ. Surgeons, Soc. Surgery Alimentary Tract, Am. Physiol. Soc., Internat. Soc. Surgery, Surg. Biology Club, Soc. Clin. Surgery, Am. Surg. Assn., Acad. Chir. (Paris), Surg. Research Soc. So. Africa (corr.), Congrès Francais de Chirurgie (hon.), Sigma Xi. Home: 8 Highland Hts Rochester NY 14618-1116 Office: Highland Hosp 990 South Ave Ste 20 Rochester NY 14620-2740

MENHALL, DALTON WINN, lawyer, insurance executive, professional association administrator; b. Edgerton, Wis., Aug. 1, 1939; s. Joseph Laurence and Mary Winn (Dalton) M.; m. Lilian Marilyn Christie, Oct. 19, 1968; children: Dalton Winn II, Rebecca Lynn, Katherine Elizabeth. B.A., Ill. Coll., 1962; J.D., Vanderbilt U., 1965. Bar: Wis. 1965; cert. assn. exec.

Staff asst. State Bar of Wis., Madison, 1965-72, dir., 1972-76, legis. counsel, dir. continuing legal edn., 1972-76; exec. dir. N.J. State Bar Assn., Trenton, 1976-86; nat. programs dir. Herbert L. Jamison & Co., 1987-91; v.p. Edward Poll & Assocs., 1995; exec. dir. San Diego County Bar Assn., 1996—; trustee St. Patricks' Day Sch., 1994-96. Exec. v.p. Phi Alpha Delta Pub. Svc. Ctr., Washington, 1991-94; exec. dir. Phi Alpha Delta Law Frat. Internat., Granada Hills, Calif., 1992-94; bd. dirs. Am. Cancer Soc., 1996-97. Fellow Am. Bar Found.; mem. ABA (cons., youth edn. and citizenship com 1993—), Nat. Assn. Bar Execs. (pres. 1985-86), N.J. State Bar Assn., State Bar Wis., Am. Soc. Assn. Execs., Am. Judicature Soc., Nat. Assn. Bar Execs. (hon.), So. Calif. Soc. Assn. Execs., San Diego Soc. Assn. Execs. (bd. dirs. 1997).

MENINO, THOMAS M., mayor; b. Dec. 27, 1942; m. Angela Faletra; children: Susan, Thomas Michael, Jr. Degree in Community Planning, U. Mass., 1988; cert. in State and Local Govt. Program, Harvard U. Mem. City Coun., Boston, 1985—, pres., 1993; acting mayor Boston, 1993—; sr. rsch. asst. Joint Com. Urban Affairs, 1978-83. Contbr. articles to historic preservation jours. Regional chmn. Nat. Trust Historic Preservation; bd. dirs. Nat. League Cities, 1985—, mem. various coms. Office: Office of Mayor 1 City Hall Plz Fl 5 Boston MA 02201-1001*

MENIUS, ESPIE FLYNN, JR., electrical engineer; b. New Bern, N.C., Mar. 5, 1923; s. Espie Flynn and Sudie Grey (Lyerly) M.; BEE, N.C. State U., 1947; MBA, U. S.C., 1973; adopted children: James Benfield, Ruben Hughes, James Sechler, Steve Walden. With Carolina Power & Light Co., 1947-63, asst. to dist. mgr., Raleigh, Henderson, N.C., Sumter, S.C., 1947-50, elec. engr., Asheville, Southern Pines, Dunn, N.C., 1950-52, dist. engr. Hartsville, S.C., 1952-63; sr. elec. engr. Sonoco Products Co., Hartsville, 1963-74, engring. group leader, 1974-89, sr. profl. engr., 1989-91; profl. con., electrical engr., 1991—; instr. Florence-Darlington Tech. Ednl. Center. Mem. Hartsville Vol. Fire Dept., 1958—; Eagle Scout, Boy Scouts Am., 1938, scout troop leader New Bern, N.C., 1940-41, Raleigh, 1941-47, Henderson, 1948-49, Asheville, N.C., 1950, Southern Pines, N.C., 1951-52, Sumter, 1949-50, Hartsville, 1952-64; bd. mgrs. Nazareth Children's Home, Rockville, N.C., 1980—; chmn. bd. examiners City of Hartsville, 1980—; advocate Thornwell Children's Home, Clinton, S.C., 1990—; bd. dirs. Darlington (S.C.) County Youth Home, 1992—; active Hartsville Leadership Coun., 1993—. Served with AUS, 1943-46. Recipient Silver Beaver award Boy Scouts Am., 1959, Citizenship award S.C. State Firemen's Assn., 1993; named Hartsville's Citizen of Yr., Rotary, 1960; named to S.C. Fire Fighters Hall of Fame, 1995. Registered profl. engr., N.C., S.C., Tenn., Ga., Fla. Mem. IEEE, AAAS, VFW, Nat. Assn. Engrs., Am. Legion, Knight of St. Patrick, Scabbard and Blade, Eta Kappa Nu, Pine Burr, Phi Eta Sigma, Theta Tau, Beta Gamma Sigma. Presbyn. (elder, trustee, tchr. men's Bible class). Club: Civitan (past dir.). Author articles in field. Home and Office: 423 W Richardson Cir Hartsville SC 29550-5437

MENK, CARL WILLIAM, executive search company executive; b. Newark, Oct. 19, 1921; s. Carl William and Catherine Regina (Murray) M.; m. Elizabeth Cullum, May 31, 1947; children: Carl, Elizabeth (dec.), Mary, Paul. BSBA, Seton Hall U., 1943; MA, Columbia U., 1950. Sr. v.p. P. Ballantine & Sons, Newark, 1946-69; pres. Boyden Assocs., Inc., N.Y.C., 1969-84; chmn. Canny, Bowen, Inc., N.Y.C., 1984—; dir. Howard Savs. Bank, 1980-91. 2d Lt., pilot USAAF, 1943-46. Mem. Union League N.Y., Spring Lake Golf Club, Bent Pine Golf Club, John's Island Club, Knights of Malta, Internat. Exec. Svc. Corps. Republican. Roman Catholic. Home: 950 Beach Rd Johns Island Vero Beach FL 32963 Office: Canny Bowen Inc 200 Park Ave New York NY 10166-0005

MENK, LOUIS WILSON, retired manufacturing company executive; b. Englewood, Colo., Apr. 8, 1918; s. Louis Albert and Daisy Deane (Frantz) M.; m. Mary Louise Menk; children: David Louis, Barbara Ann. Student, Denver U., 1937-38; grad., Advanced Mgmt. Program, Harvard U., 1953, Transp. Sch., Northwestern U., 1959; LL.D., Drury Coll., 1965, Denver U., 1966, Monmouth Coll., 1967. With U.P. R.R., 1936-40; with St. L.-S.F. R.R., 1940-65, telegrapher, 1940, chmn., pres., 1964-65; pres., dir. Burlington Lines, Chgo., 1965-66, No. Pacific R.R., St. Paul, 1966-70; pres. Burlington No. Inc., 1970-71, chmn., chief exec. officer, 1971-78, chmn. bd., 1978-81, also dir.; chmn., chief exec. officer Internat. Harvester, 1982, chmn., 1982-83; bd. dirs. Beverly Enterprises; chmn. bd. Black Mountain Gas Co. Presbyterian. Clubs: Desert Forest Golf (Carefree, Ariz.). Lodge: Masons. Home: 34815 N Arroyo Carefree AZ 85377 also: PO Box 1353 Carefree AZ 85377-1353

MENKE, ALLEN CARL, industrial corporation executive; b. Huntingburg, Ind., Feb. 16, 1922; s. William Ernest and Clara (Moenkhaus) M.; m. Virginia Lee MacDonald, Apr. 14, 1944; children: Janet, William, Sarah. B.S. in Mech. Engring, Purdue U., 1943, M.S., 1948. Instr. Purdue U., 1946-48; with Trane Co., 1948-68, v.p. sales, 1963-64, exec. v.p. sales, mfg. and engring., 1964-68; v.p. Borg-Warner Corp., Chgo., 1969-76; chmn., pres., chief exec. officer Artesian Industries, Northbrook, Ill., 1976-88; bd. dirs. Trane Co., SPS Techs., Hoover Co., Consolidated Papers Corp., York Corp. Pres. Met. Housing Devel. Corp.; founder, pres. Winnetka Interch. Coun.; bd. dirs., chmn. Presbyn. Home; past chmn. dean's adv. coun. Krannert Sch. Mgmt. Purdue U.; bd. dirs. McCormick Sem., U. Chgo.; trustee Kenilworth Union Ch. Served to 1st lt. AUS, 1944-46. Named Disting. Alumnus, Purdue U., 1965, Outstanding Engr. Grad., 1991, mem. Purdue Hall of Fame. Mem. Sigma Chi (Significant award). Presbyterian (elder). Lodge: Mason. Home: 1420 Tower Rd Winnetka IL 60093-1629

MENKELLO, FREDERICK VINCENT, computer scientist; b. Boston, Mar. 22, 1942; s. Albert Frederick and Angelina Marie (Tecci) M. BS, Boston U., 1964, MEd, 1965; PhD, Tex. A&M U., 1975. Commd. 2d lt. USAF, 1966, advanced through grades to lt. col.; scientist Environ. Tech. Applications Ctr., Washington, 1967-69; rsch. scientist NASA, Greenbelt, Md., 1969-70; sect. chief Global Weather Cen., Offutt AFB, Nebr., 1973-77; div. chief Mil. Airlift command, Scott AFB, Ill., 1978-82; br. chief Office Sec. Def., Washington, 1982-85; dir. Computer Acquisition Ctr., Hanscom AFB, Mass., 1985-86; ret., 1986; prin. engr. for R & D, Vitro Corp., Silver Spring, Md., 1986-96; mgr. sys. integration Tracor Info. Sys. Co., Rockville, Md., 1997—. Mem. Assn. for Computing Machinery, Soc. for Indsl. and Applied Math., Phi Kappa Phi, Upsilon Pi Epsilon. Avocations: weightlifting, jogging, theater, reading. Office: Tracor Info Sys Co 1601 Research Blvd Rockville MD 20850-3173

MENKEL-MEADOW, CARRIE JOAN, law educator; b. N.Y.C., Dec. 24, 1949; d. Gary G. and Margot (Sinn) Menkel; m. Robert Gary Meadow, Aug. 22, 1971. AB magna cum laude, Columbia U., 1971; JD cum laude, U. Pa., 1974; LLD (hon.), Quinnipiac Coll. Law, 1995. Bar: Pa. 1974, U.S. Ct. Appeals (3d cir.) 1975, Calif. 1979, D.C., 1997. Dir. legal writing U. Pa. Law Sch., Phila., 1974-75; clin. supt., lectr. U. Pa. Law Sch., 1976-79; staff atty. Cmty. Legal Svcs., Phila., 1975-77; prof. UCLA, 1979—, prof. law, 1979—; prof. law Georgetown Law Ctr., Washington, 1996—; panel mem. NAS, Washington, 1986-87, NSF, Washington, 1987—; cons. ABA, Chgo., 1979-84; dir. UCLA Ctr. for Conflict Resolution, 1994—. Contbr. articles to profl. jours. Chairperson Ctr. for Study of Women, UCLA; bd. dirs. Western Ctr. on Law and Poverty, L.A., 1980-86; chair CPR Commn. on Ethics and ADR. Recipient Rutter award, 1992, 1st prize for Acad. Scholarship on Alternative Dispute Resolution Ctr. for Pub. Resources, 1983, 91. Mem. Soc. Am. Law Tchrs. (trustee), Assn. Am. Law Schs. (alt. dispute resolution sect., law and social sci. sect., women in law sect., mem. accreditation com. 1987—), Ctr. for Law and Human Values (bd. dirs.), Law and Soc. Assn. (trustee), Am. Bar Found. (bd. dirs., exec. com. 1994—), Phi Beta Kappa. Democrat. Office: Georgetown Law Ctr 600 New Jersey Ave NW Washington DC 20001-2075

MENKEN, ALAN, composer; b. 1949. Student, NYU. Composer, lyricist, performer Lehman Engel Mus. Theatre Workshop at BMI; ptnr. with Howard Ashman. Works include: (theatre) Off-Broadway debut God Bless You, Mr. Rosewater, (with Howard Ashman) Little Shop of Horrors, Kicks, The Apprenticeship of Duddy Kravitz, Diamonds, Personals, Let Freedom Sing, Weird Romance, Beauty and the Beast, A Christmas Carol; (films) Little Shop of Horrors, 1986 (Acad. award nominee for best original score 1986), The Little Mermaid, 1988 (Acad. award for best original score 1989, Acad. award for best original song 1989), Beauty and the Beast, 1990 (Acad. award for best original score 1991, Acad. award for best original song 1991), Newsies, 1992, Aladdin, 1992, (Acad. award for best original score 1993, Acad. award best original song 1993, 3 Grammy awards 1994), Lincoln, 1992, Life With Mikey, 1993; (with Stephen Schwartz) Pocahontas, 1995 (Golden Globe award 1996, Acad. award for best original score 1996, Acad. award for best original song 1996). Office: The Shukat Co 340 W 55th St Ste 1A New York NY 10019-3744

MENKEN, JANE AVA, demographer, educator; b. Phila., Nov. 29, 1939; d. Isaac Nathan and Rose Ida (Sarvetnick) Golubitsky; m. Matthew Menken, 1960 (div. 1985); children: Kenneth Lloyd, Kathryn Lee; m. Richard Jessor, Nov. 13, 1992. A.B., U. Pa., 1960; M.S., Harvard U., 1962; Ph.D., Princeton U., 1975. Asst. in biostats. Harvard U. Sch. Pub. Health, Boston, 1962-64; math. statistician NIMH, Bethesda, Md., 1964-66; research assoc. dept. biostats., Columbia U., N.Y.C., 1966-69; mem. research staff Office of Population Research Princeton U., N.J., 1969-71, 75-87, asst. dir., 1978-86, assoc. dir., 1986-87, prof. sociology, 1980-82, prof. sociology and pub. affairs, 1982-87; prof. sociology and demography U. Pa., Phila., 1987—, UPS Found. prof. social scis., 1987—, dir. Population Studies Ctr., 1989-95; mem. social scis. and population study sect., NIH, Bethesda, Md., 1978-82, chmn., 1980-82, population adv. com. Rockefeller Found., N.Y.C., 1981-93, com. on population and demography, NAS, Washington, 1978-83, com. on population, 1983-85, com. nat. stats., 1983-89, com. on AIDS research, 1987-94, co-chair panel data and rsch. priorities for arresting AIDS in sub-Saharan Africa, 1994—, Commn. on Behavioral and Social Scis. and Edn., 1991—, sci. adv. com., Demographic and Health Surveys, Columbia, Md., 1985-90, Nat. Adv. Child Health and Human Devel. Council, 1988-91; cons. Internat. Centre for Diarrhoeal Disease Research, Bangladesh, Dhaka, 1984—. Author: (with Mindel C. Sheps) Mathematical Models of Conception and Birth, 1973; editor: (with Henri Leridon) Natural Fertility, 1979, (with Frank Furstenberg, Jr. and Richard Lincoln) Teenage Sexuality, Pregnancy and Childbearing, 1981, World Population and U.S. Policy: The Choices Ahead, 1986; contbr. articles to profl. jours. Bd. dirs. Alan Guttmacher Inst., N.Y.C., 1981-90, 93—. Nat. Merit scholar, 1957; John Simon Guggenheim Found. fellow, 1992-93, Ctr. for Advanced Study in Behavioral Scis. fellow, 1995-96. Fellow AAAS, Am. Statis. Assn.; mem. NAS, Am. Acad. Arts and Scis., Population Assn. Am. (Mindel Sheps award 1982, pres. 1985), Am. Pub. Health Assn. (Mortimer Spiegelman award 1975, program devel. bd. 1984-87), Am. Sociol. Assn., Soc. for Study of Social Biology, Internat. Union for Sci. Study of Population (coun. 1989—), Sociol. Research Assn. (exec. com. 1991—). Office: U Pa Population Studies Ctr 3718 Locust Walk Philadelphia PA 19104-6209

MENKES, JOHN HANS, pediatric neurologist; b. Vienna, Austria, Dec. 20, 1928; came to U.S., 1940; s. Karl and Valerie (Tupler) M.; m. Miriam Trief, Apr. 14, 1957 (div. Feb. 1978); m. Joan Simon Feld, Sept. 28, 1980; children: Simon, Tamara, Rafael C. AB, U. So. Calif., 1947, MS, 1951; MD, Johns Hopkins U., 1952. Diplomate Am. Bd. Pediatrics, Am. Bd. Psychiatry and Neurology. Intern, jr. asst. resident Children's Med. Ctr., Boston, 1952-54; asst. resident pediatrics Bellevue Hosp., N.Y.C., 1956-57; resident neurology, trainee pediatric neurology Columbia-Presbyn. Med. Ctr., Neurological Inst. N.Y., N.Y.C., 1957-60; asst. prof. pediatrics Johns Hopkins U., Balt., 1960-63, assoc. prof., 1963-66, asst. prof. neurology, 1964-66, chief pediatric neurology div., 1964-66; prof. pediatrics and neurology UCLA, 1966-74, chief pediatric neurology div., 1966-70, prof. psychiatry, 1970-74; chief Neurology-Neurochem. Lab. Brentwood (Calif.) VA Hosp., 1970-74; clin. prof. psychiatry, neurology and pediatrics UCLA, 1974-77, clin. prof. pediatrics and neurology, 1977-84, prof. pediatrics and neurology, 1985-89, prof. emeritus pediatrics and neurology, 1989—; dir. pediatric neurology Cedars-Sinai Med. Ctr., 1997—; mem. metabolism study sect. NIH, 1968-70, project com., 1969-70; mem. adv. com. Nat. Inst. Child Health and Human Devel., 1985-87; mem. Dept. Health Svcs., Calif., 1980-87; mem. vaccine safety commn. Nat. Inst. Medicine, 1995—; mem. Coun. Child Neurology Soc., Dysautonomia Found., med. adv. bd. Nat. Orgn. Rare Diseases, Nat. Wilson's Disease Found.; trustee Dystonia Med. Rsch. Found., Vancouver, Can., 1985—. Author: Textbook of Child Neurology, 5th edit., 1995, (plays) The Last Inquisitor, 1985 (Drama-Logue Critics award 1985), The Salvation of Miguel Toruna, 1987, (screen plays) Miguel, Open Ward, 1989, The Countess of Silgo, 1992, The White Darkness, 1996; contbr. numerous articles to pediatric and neurol. jours. Served with USAF, 1954-56. Mem. Am. Acad. Neurology, Am. Acad. Pediatrics, Am. Chem. Soc., Soc. for Pediatric Rsch., Sociedad Peruana de Neuro-Psychiatra (hon.), Am. Neurochem. Soc., Am. Neurol. Assn., Am. Pediatric Soc., Child Neurology Soc. (Hower award 1980), Dramatist Guild, PEN. Jewish. Home: 1201 Park Way Beverly Hills CA 90210-3334 Office: 9320 Wilshire Blvd Beverly Hills CA 90212-3216

MENN, JULIUS JOEL, scientist; b. Danzig, Free City (now Poland), Feb. 20, 1929; came to U.S., 1950, naturalized, 1959; s. David Gregory and Regina (Ajzenstadt) M.; m. Alma R. Zito, Aug. 31, 1952 (div. 1981); children: Leslie, David (dec.), Diana (dec.); m. Dianne R. Sagner, Apr. 17, 1992. BS, U. Calif., Berkeley, 1953, MS, 1954, PhD, 1958. Dir. biochem. and insecticide rsch. Stauffer Chem. Co., Mountain View, Calif., 1957-79; dir. agrichem. research Zoecon Corp., Palo Alto, Calif., 1979-85; nat. program leader crop protection Agrl. Rsch. Svc., USDA, Beltsville, Md., 1985-88, assoc. dep. area dir. Beltsville Agrl. Rsch. Ctr., 1988-94, ret. 1994; internat. cons. crop protection & agr. biotechnology, 1994—; chmn. Gordon Rsch. Conf., 1989; adj. prof. environ. toxicology San Jose State U., Calif., 1979-84; adj. prof. entomology U. Md., College Park, 1986—, internat.cons. Crop Protection and Agrl. Biotech., 1994—; mem. U.S./USSR Team on Environ. Pollution, 1974-85; tech. expert UNIDO, 1995—. Editor: Insect Juvenile Hormones, 1972, Insect Neuropeptides, 1991, 10 other tech. books; contbr. over 125 articles to profl. jours.; pioneered pesticide metabolism studies and research on selective insect control agents including juvenile hormones and neuropeptides; patentee in field. Recipient Bussart Meml. award Eastern Br. Entomol. Soc. Am., 1990, Ciba-Geigy Recognition award, Eastern Br. Entomol. Soc. Am. 1991, 92. Mem. Am. Chem. Soc. (fellow pesticide chem. div. 1973, chmn. 1976, councilor 1981-89, adv. bd. books dept. 1991-94, Burdick & Jackson Internat. award for rsch. in pesticide chem. 1979, Internat. Soc. Study Xenobiotics (councilor 1983-86), Cosmos Club (Washington).

MENNINGER, EDWARD JOSEPH, public relations executive; b. N.Y.C., 1931; s. Edward Joseph and Pauline Loretta (Sessa) M.; m. Catherine Ann Giordano, Nov. 1, 1952 (div. 1978); children: Christopher, Catherine, Carl, Carolyn, Lisa; m. Ann Clementine Hunt, Jan. 5, 1979. B Social Sci. magna cum laude, Fordham U., 1952. Retail adv. sales promotion Sears, Roebuck and Co., N.Y.C., 1958-62; pub. rels. exec. Sears, Roebuck and Co., Chgo., N.Y.C., 1962-72; sr. buyer, buyer Sears, Roebuck and Co., N.Y.C., 1972-73; nat. mdse. mgr. Sears, Roebuck and Co., Chgo., N.Y.C., 1974-81; v.p., group mgr. Burson-Marsteller, N.Y.C., 1981-87, sr. v.p. consumer retail mktg., 1987-92, mng. dir., 1992-93, exec. v.p., 1993—, dir. employee devel. and tng. for U.S. and Americas region, 1996; mem. comm. mgmt. adv. com., Syracuse U. Sch. Pub. Comm., 1996, 97; mem. bus. adv. bd. Am. Sch. Counselors Assn., 1995-96; mem. exec. bd. N.Y. Yeats Soc., 1996, 97; lectr. in field. Contbr. articles to profl. jours. With M.I., U.S. Army, 1953-55. Mem. PRSA (accredited, edn. affairs commr. 1982-85, 87-88, v.p. Chgo. chpt. 1971-72, Chmn.'s Cert. of Recognition 1969, 73, 76, 84, 91, 92, Toth award Washington chpt. 1983, Silver Anvil award 1983, 89, 92, Big Apple award N.Y. chpt. 1991, 93, 94), Pub. Rels. Student Soc. Am. (profl. advisor 1983-84, Recognition award 1992). Office: Burson-Marsteller 230 Park Ave S New York NY 10003-1513

MENNINGER, ROSEMARY JEANETTA, art educator, writer; b. N.Y.C., Feb. 2, 1948; d. Karl Augustus and Jeanetta (Lyle) M. BA, Washburn U., 1983, BFA, 1984. Cert. tchr., Kans. Rsch. specialist, grant writer Navajo Tribe Navajo Community Coll., Many Farms, Ariz., 1969, 71; adminstrv. asst., counselor San Francisco Drug Treatment Program, 1972-73; exec. dir. Inst. Applied Ecology, San Francisco, 1973-80; coord. Calif. Community Gardening program Gov.'s Office State of Calif., Sacramento, 1976-80; editor Whole Earth Catalogs and CoEvolution Quar., Sausilito, Calif., 1973-80; editor, rsch. specialist Dept. Agr. Scis. Colo. State U., Ft. Collins, 1981-82; instr. Mulvane Art Ctr., Topeka, 1982-86, 90—; art tchr. Topeka Pub. Schs., 1985—. Author: Community Gardening in California, 1977; editor: (newspaper) California Green, 1977-80; contbr. articles to profl. jours. Mem. San Francisco Parks and Recreation Open Space Commn., 1975-78; mem. master plan task force Calif. State Fair, Sacramento, 1978-80; commr. Gov.'s Commn. on Children and Families, Topeka, 1988-89; bd. dirs. The Villages, Inc., 1989—. Democrat. Presbyterian. Avocations: painting, gardening, swimming. Home: 1819 SW Westwood Cir Topeka KS 66604-3269

MENNINGER, ROY WRIGHT, medical foundation executive, psychiatrist; b. Topeka, Oct. 27, 1926; s. William Claire and Catharine (Wright) M.; m. Beverly Joan Miller, Mar. 4, 1973; children: Heather, Ariel, Bonar, Eric, Brent, Frederick, Elizabeth. AB, Swarthmore (Pa.) Coll., 1947; MD, Cornell U., 1951; DHL, Ottawa (Kans.) U., 1977; LittD, William Jewell Coll., Liberty Mo., 1985. Diplomate Am. Bd. Psychiatry and Neurology, 1959. Intern N.Y. Hosp., 1951-52; resident in psychiatry Boston State Hosp., 1952-53, Boston Psychopathic Hosp., 1953-56; from resident psychiatrist to assoc. med. psychiatrist Peter Bent Brigham Hosp., Boston, 1956-61; teaching and rsch. fellow Harvard U. Med. Sch., Boston, 1956-61; staff psychiatrist Menninger Found., Topeka, 1961-63, dir. dept. preventative psychiatry, 1963-67, pres., CEO, 1967-93; chmn., 1991—; bd. dirs. Bank IV Topeka N.A., CML Corp., The New Eng., U.S. Behavioral Health; mem. Karl Menninger Sch. Psychiatry, Topeka, 1972—, Ind. Sector, 1990—; clin. prof. psychiatry U. Kans. Med. Ctr., Wichita, 1977—; cons. Colmery-O'Neil VA Med. Ctr., Topeka, 1979—. Author: Trends in American Psychiatry: Implication for Psychiatry in Japan; co-author: The Medical Marriage, 1988, The Psychology of Postponement in the Medical Marriage; cons. editor Jour. Medical Aspects Human Sexuality, 1967-90; editor adv. bd. Parents mag., 1966-80, Clin. Psychiatry News, 1973—; reviewer Am. Jour. Psychiatry, 1980—. Mem. sponsoring com. Inst. Am. Democracy, 1967-70; mem. adv. group Horizons '76 Am. Revolution Bicentennial Commn.; adv. bd., steering com. Topeka Inst. Urban Affairs, 1967-70; adv. bd. Highland Park-Pierce Neighborhood House, Topeka, 1967-70; bd. dirs. Shawnee council Campfire Girls, Topeka, 1962-69, A.K. Rice Inst., Washington, Sex Info. and Edn. Council U.S., 1972-73, mem. edn. com., long range planning com., 1972-73; bd. dirs. Goals for Topeka, Topeka Inst. Urban Affairs, 1969-74, v.p., 1973; med. adv. com. VA Hosp., 1972-78; mem. Gov.'s Com. on Criminal Adminstrn., 1971-74; trustee People-to-People, Kansas City, Mo., 1967-69, Baker U., 1968-72, Midwest Research Inst., 1967-1986, 86—, mem. exec. com., 1970-86; vis. lectr. Fgn. Service Inst., State Dept., 1963-66; chmn. social issues com. Group Advancement Psychiatry, 1972-82; community adv. bd. Kans. Health Workers Union, 1968-70; adv. com. to bd. dirs. New Eng. Mut. Life Ins. Co., 1968-70. With U.S. Army, 1953-55. Recipient Disting. Svs. citation U. Kans., 1985; Pacific Rim Coll. Psychiatry fellow. Fellow Am. Psychiat. Assn. (life), Joint Info. Svc. (exec. com.), Am. Coll. Psychiatry, Am. Orthopsychiat. Assn., Am. Coll. Mental Health Adminstrs.; mem. AAAS, Northeastern Group Psychotherapy (hon.), Physicians Social Responsibility, Kans. Psychiat. Soc., Greater Topeka C. of C. (dir.). Episcopalian. Avocations: stamp collecting, chamber music, microcomputers. Office: Menninger Found PO Box 829 Topeka KS 66601-0829*

MENNINGER, WILLIAM WALTER, psychiatrist; b. Topeka, Oct. 23, 1931; s. William Claire and Catharine Louisa (Wright) M.; m. Constance Arnold Libbey, June 15, 1953; children: Frederick Prince, John Alexander, Eliza Wright, Marian Stuart, William Libbey, David Henry. A.B., Stanford U., 1953; M.D., Cornell U., 1957; LittD (hon.), Middlebury Coll., 1982; DSc (hon.), Washburn U., 1982; LHD (hon.), Ottawa U., 1986; LLD (hon.), Heidelberg Coll., 1993. Diplomate: Am. Bd. Psychiatry and Neurology, Am. Bd. Forensic Psychiatry. Intern Harvard Med. Service, Boston City Hosp., 1957-58; resident in psychiatry Menninger Sch. Psychiatry, 1958-61; chief med. officer, psychiatrist Fed. Reformatory, El Reno, Okla., 1961-63; assoc. psychiatrist Peace Corps, 1963-64; staff psychiatrist Menninger Found., Topeka, 1965—, coordinator for devel., 1967-69, dir. law and psychiatry, 1981-85, dir. dept. edn., dean Karl Menninger Sch. Psychiatry and Mental Health Scis., 1984-90, exec. v.p., chief of staff, 1984-93; CEO Menninger Found., 1993—, pres., 1993-96; clin. supr. Topeka State Hosp., 1969-70, sect. dir., 1970-72, asst. supt., clin., dir. residency tng., 1972-81; pres. Menninger Clinic, Topeka, 1991-96; staff Stormont-Vail Hosp., Topeka, 1984-94, assoc., 1994—; clin. prof. Kans. U. Med. Coll.; adj. prof. Washburn U., Wichita State U.; instr. Topeka Inst. for Psychoanalysis; mem. adv. bd. Nat. Inst. Corrections, 1975-88 , chmn., 1980-84; cons. U.S. Bur. Prisons; mem. Fed. Prison Facilities Planning Council, 1970-73; bd. dirs. Mercantile Bank Topeka (formerly Mchts. Nat. Bank, Topeka); pres. Menninger Found.. 1993-96. Syndicated columnist: In-Sights, 1975-83; author: Happiness Without Sex and Other Things Too Good to Miss, 1976, Caution: Living May Be Hazardous, 1978, Behavioral Science and the Secret Service, 1981, Chronic Mental Patient II, 1987; editor: Psychiatry Digest, 1971-74; mem. editorial bd. Bull. Menninger Clinic, 1985—; contbr. chpts. to books, articles to profl. jours. Mem. nat. health and safety com. Boy Scouts Am., 1970-92, chmn., 1980-85, mem. nat. exec. bd., 1980-90, mem. nat. adv. coun., 1990—; mem. Kans. Gov.'s Adv. Commn. on Mental Health, Mental Retardation and Community Mental Health Svcs., 1983-90; bd. dirs. Nat. Com. for Prevention Child Abuse, 1975-83; mem. nat. adv. health coun. HEW, 1967-71; mem. Nat. Commn. Causes and Prevention Violence 1968-69, Kans. Gov.'s Penal Planning Coun., 1970; chmn. Kans. Gov.'s Criminal Justice Adv. Commn., 1991-94, rsch. adv. com. U.S. Secret Svc., 1990—; trustee Kenworthy-Swift Found., 1980—; ruling elder 1st Presbyn. Ch., Topeka, 1992-95; active Ks. Gov.'s Commn. on Crime Reduction and Prevention/Koch Commn. 1994—; dir. Police Found., Washington, 1996—; trustee Midwest Rsch. Inst., Kansas City, Mo., 1996—. With USPHS, 1959-64. Fellow ACP, Am. Psychiat. Assn. (chmn. com. on chronically mentally ill 1984-86, chmn. Guttmacher award bd. 1990-96), Am. Coll. Psychiatrists; mem. AAAS, AMA, Group for Advancement of Psychiatry (chmn. com. mental health svcs. 1974-77, 91—), Inst. Medicine NAS, Am. Psychoanalytic Assn. (chmn. com. on psychoanalysis, community and society 1984-93), Am. Acad. Psychiatry and Law, Stanford (Univ.) Assocs. Office: Menninger Found PO Box 829 Topeka KS 66601-0829

MENNIS, EDMUND ADDI, investment management consultant; b. Allentown, Pa., Aug. 12, 1919; s. William Henry and Grace (Addi) M.; m. Selma Adinoff, Sept. 25, 1945; children: Ardith Grace, Daniel Liam. BA, CCNY, 1941; MA, Columbia U., 1946; PhD, NYU, 1961. Security analyst Eastman, Dillon & Co., N.Y.C., 1945-46; sr. rsch. asst. Am. Inst. Econ. Rsch., Great Barrington, Mass., 1946-50; security analyst Wellington Mgmt. Co., Phila., 1950-61; dir. rsch. Wellington Mgmt. Co., 1958-61, v.p., mem. investment com., 1958-66, economist, 1953-66; sr. v.p., chmn. trust investment com. Republic Nat. Bank, Dallas, 1966-72; sr. v.p., chmn. investment policy com. Security Pacific Nat. Bank, L.A., 1973-81; pres., dir. Bunker Hill Income Securities, Inc., 1973-81; chmn. bd. Security Pacific Investment Mgrs., Inc., 1977-81; ind. cons. to investment mgmt. orgns., 1982—; tech. cons. Bus. Coun., Washington, 1962-66, 72-77, 79-81; econ. adviser sec. commerce, 1967-68; mem. investment adv. panel Pension Benefit Guaranty Corp., 1981-83. Assoc. editor Fin. Analysts Jour., 1960-88; editor: C.F.A. Digest, 1971-86, Bus. Econs., 1985—, Bank Funds Mgmt. Report, 1993—; author or editor books, chpts., numerous articles in field of econs. and investments. Trustee Fin. Analysts Rsch. Found., 1981-86. 1st lt. USAAF, 1942-45; capt. USAF, 1951-53. Fellow Nat. Assn. Bus. Economists (coun. 1967-69, David L. Williams Lifetime Achievement award 1996); mem. Fin. Analysts Fedn. (dir. 1970-72, Graham and Dodd award 1972, Molodovsky award 1972), Am. Econ. Assn., Am. Fin. Assn., L.A. Soc. Fin. Analysts, Conf. Bus. Economists (vice chmn. 1977, chmn. 1978), Inst. CFAs (pres. 1970-72, trustee 1968-74, C. Stewart Sheppard award 1978). Home: 721 Paseo Del Mar Palos Verdes Estates CA 90274 Office: PO Box 1146 Pls Vrds Est CA 90274-7946

MENO, JOHN PETER, chorepiscopus; b. Carlinville, Ill., Aug. 22, 1942; s. John Victor and Margaret Mary (Cena) M.; m. Rolanda A. Abyad, Sept. 14, 1968; 1 child, Peter James. MA, Am. U. Beirut, 1969; STM, Union Theol. Sem., 1972. Ordained priest Syrian Orthodox Ch. of Antioch, 1972, elevated to chorepiscopus, 1983. Gen. sec. Archdiocese of Syrian Orthodox Ch. for Eastern U.S., Lodi, N.J., 1972—; cathedral rector St. Mark's Syrian Orthodox Cathedral, Teaneck, N.J., 1975—; co-sec. Standing Conf. of Oriental Orthodox Chs. in Am., N.Y.C., 1973—; co-chmn. U.S. Roman Cath.-Oriental Orthodox Cons., 1989—. Editor: Hymns of the Syrian Orthodox Church of Antioch, 1976. Recipient Golden Cross of the Archdiocese of the Syrian Orthodox Ch. in U.S., and Can., 1992. Home: 263 Elm Ave Teaneck NJ 07666-2323 Office: St Marks Syrian Orth Cathedral 260 Elm Ave Teaneck NJ 07666-2318

MENO, LIONEL R., state agency administrator. Commr. edn. Tex. Edn Agy., Austin; dist. supt. Board of Coop. Education Services, Angola, NY. Office: Board of Coop Education Svcs 8685 Erie Rd Angola NY 14006-9620

MENON, MANI, urological surgeon, educator; b Trichur, Kerala, India, July 9, 1948; came to U.S., 1972, naturalized, 1977; s. Balakrishna and Sumathie Menon; m. Shameem Ara Begum, Oct. 17, 1972; children: Nisha, Roshen. MBBS, Madras U., India, 1971. Diplomate Am. Bd. Urology. Intern Bryn Mawr (Pa.) Hosp., 1973-74; resident Brady Urol. Inst., The Johns Hopkins Hosp., Balt., 1974-80; asst. prof. urology Washington U. Med. Ctr., St. Louis, 1980-83, assoc. prof., 1983; prof. urology, chmn. div. urology and transplant surgery U. Mass. Med. Ctr., Worcester, 1983—; prof. physiology, U. Mass. Med. Ctr., Worcester, 1986—. Mem. AAAS, Am. Assn. Genito Urinary Surgeons, Am. Urol. Assn. (Gold Cytoscope award 1990), Am. Fedn. Clin. Rsch., Am. Soc. Transplantation and Vascular Surgery, Rschrs. on Calculus Kinetics, Johns Hopkins Med. and Surg. Assn., Mass. Med. Soc., Mass. Soc. Med. Rsch. Avocations: tennis, puzzles, mystery fiction. Office: U Mass Med Ctr Div Urology Worcester MA 01655

MENOTTI, GIAN CARLO, composer; b. Cadegliano, Italy, July 7, 1911; came to U.S., 1928; s. Alfonso and Ines (Pellini) M. Grad. in composition, Curtis Inst. Music, 1933, Mus.B. (hon.), 1945. Tchr. Curtis Inst. Music, 1941-45. Writer chamber music, songs and operas; composer: (operas) Amelia al ballo, 1936, The Old Maid and the Thief, 1939, The Island God, 1942, The Medium, 1945 (Pulitzer Prize for music 1950), The Telephone, 1947, The Consul, 1949; Amahl and the Night Visitors, 1951, The Saint of Bleecker Street, 1954 (Pulitzer Prize for music 1955, Drama Critics' Circle Award 1955, New York Music Critics' Award 1955), Maria Golovin, 1958, The Last Savage, 1963, Labyrinth, 1963, Martin's Lie, 1964, Help, Help, the Globolinks, 1968, The Most Important Man, 1971, Arrival, 1973, Tamu-Tamu, 1973, The Egg, 1976, The Hero, 1976, The Trial of the Gypsy, 1978, Chip and His Dog, 1979, La loca, 1979, The Mad Woman, 1979, St. Teresa, 1982, A Bride from Pluto, 1982, The Boy Who Grew Too Fast, 1982, Goya, 1986, Giorino di Nozze, 1988; (symphonies/orchestral) Pastorale and Dance, 1934, (from Amelia al ballo) Prelude, 1937, (from The Old Maid and the Thief) Prelude, 1939, (from The Island God) Two Interludes, 1942, Piano Concert in F, 1945, Sebastian, 1945, Apocalypse, 1951, Introduction, March Shepherds' Dance, 1951, Violin Concerto, 1952, Triple Concerto a tre, 1970, Fantasia, 1975, Symphony No. 1: The Halcyon, 1976, Double Bass Concerto, 1983; (chamber/instrumental) Variations on a Theme of Schumann, 1931, Six Compositions, 1934, Four Pieces, 1936, Trio for a House-Warming Party, 1936, Poemetti per Maria Rosa, 1937, Ricercare e toccata, 1949, Suite, 1973, Cantilena scherzo, 1977; (vocal/choral) Baba's Aria, 1946, The Black Swan, 1946, Monica's Waltz, 1946, Lucy's Aria, 1947, Magda's Aria, 1950, Shepherd's Chorus, 1951, The Hero, 1952, The Death of the Bishop of Brindisi, 1963, Canti della lontananza, 1967, Landscapes and Remembrances, 1976, Missa o pulchritudo, 1979, Four Songs, 1981, Notturno, 1982, Muero porque no muero, 1982; (ballets) Sebastian, 1944, Errand in the Maze, 1947, The Unicorn, the Gorgon and the Manticore, or The Three Sundays of a Poet, 1956; writer own libretti.; Founder: Festival of Two Worlds, Spoleto, Italy, 1958; composer, artistic dir. Spoleto Festival USA, Charleston, S.C., 1988—. Recipient Guggenheim award, 1946, 47; Honary associate, Nat'l Inst. for Arts and Letters, 1953, Kennedy Ctr. award, 1984, N.Y.C. Mayor's Liberty award, 1986; George Peabody Medal, Johns Hopkins Univ., 1987; named Musician of Yr., Musical Am., 1991. Mem. ASCAP. Address: 27 E 62nd St New York NY 10021

MENSCHEL, RICHARD LEE, investment banker; b. N.Y.C., Jan. 6, 1934; s. Benjamin and Helen (Goldsmith) M.; m. Ronay Arlt, Aug. 21, 1974; children: Charis, Sabina, Celene. B.S., Syracuse U., 1955; M.B.A., Harvard U., 1959. Assoc. securities sales adminstr. Goldman, Sachs & Co., N.Y.C., 1959-67; v.p. Goldman, Sachs & Co., N.Y.C., 1967-69; ptnr. securities sales Goldman, Sachs & Co., N.Y.C., 1969-88, mgmt. com., 1980-88, ltd. ptnr., 1988—; bd. dirs. T. Rowe Price. Co-chmn. City of N.Y. Transitional Gov. Search Panel, 1977; pres., bd. dirs. Joffrey Ballet Found., 1977-79; bd. dirs. Nat. Corp. Fund for Dance, 1977-79; trustee Fed. Protestant Welfare Agys., 1978-81, The Hastings Ctr., Nightingale Bamford Sch., The Jewish Mus., Nantucket Conservation Found., Storm King Art Ctr.; mng. dir. Horace W. Goldsmith Found., 1980—; bd. dirs. Mcpl. Art Soc., 1980-92; trustee, mem. exec. com. George Eastman House, Rochester, N.Y., 1980-94, Vera Inst. Justice, 1989—, Pierpont Morgan Libr.; trustee, treas., mem. exec. com. N.Y. Acad. Medicine; mem. vis. com. Harvard Grad. Sch. Bus. Adminstrn., 1985-91; dean's coun. Harvard Sch. Pub. Health; mem. exec. com. on univ. resources, co-chair Harvard U. campaign; mem. adv. bd. Mus. Modern Art, Oxford, 1987—; co-chmn., trustee Hosp. for Spl. Surgery. 2d lt. USAF, 1955-56. Clubs: India House, Harvard. Home: 660 Park Ave New York NY 10021-5963 Office: Goldman Sachs & Co 85 Broad St New York NY 10004-2434

MENSCHEL, ROBERT BENJAMIN, investment banker; b. N.Y.C., July 2, 1929; s. Benjamin and Helen (Goldsmith) M.; m. Joyce Virginia Frank, Dec. 5, 1968; children: David F., Lauren E. BS, Syracuse U., 1951, LLD (hon.), 1991; postgrad., NYU, 1951-53. Mem. N.Y. Stock Exchange, N.Y.C., 1950-51; specialist HW Goldsmith and Co., N.Y.C., 1951-54; with Goldman, Sachs & Co., N.Y.C., 1954-66, gen. ptnr. instl. sales, 1966-78, ltd. ptnr., 1979—. V.p. bd. trustees, mem. fin. and exec. com. Temple Emanu-El, N.Y.; trustee Mus. Modern Art, mem. investment com., co-chmn. photography com.; trustee Inst. Advanced Study Princeton, Chess in the Schs., N.Y.C. ; trustee, exec. com. Syracuse U., Montefiore Hosp., N.Y., Guild Hall, East Hampton, past chmn. bd.; pres. bd. trustees, exec. com. Dalton Sch., N.Y.C.; past bd. advs. Grad. Sch. Inst. Internat. Bus. Pace U.; mem. exec. bd. N.Y. chpt. Am. Jewish Com.; bd. dirs., mem. fin. and budget com. N.Y. Pub. Library, N.Y.C.; bd. dirs. Parks Council; bd. dirs., v.p. Emanu-El Midtown YMHA; mng. dir. Horace W. Goldsmith Found.; bd. dirs. associated YM-YWHA; mem. Pres. Clinton's com. on the arts and the humanities. Recipient George Arents medal Syracuse U., 1984. Mem. Investment Assn. N.Y. Clubs: India House, City Athletic (N.Y.C.); Dunes Racquet (East Hampton, N.Y.). Home: 920 5th Ave New York NY 10021-4160 also: Further East Ln Amagansett NY 11930 Office: Goldman Sachs & Co 85 Broad St New York NY 10004-2434

MENSCHER, BARNET GARY, steel company executive; b. Laurelton, N.Y., Sept. 5, 1940; s. Samuel and Louise (Zaimont) M.; student Centenary Coll., 1958-59; B.B.A., U. Tex., 1963; m. Diane Elaine Gachman, June 12, 1966; children—Melissa Denise, Corey Lane, Scott Jay. Vice pres. mktg. Ella Gant Mfg., Shreveport, La., 1964-66; warehouse mgr., dir. material control Gachman Steel Co., Fort Worth, 1966-68, gen. mgr., Houston, 1968-70, v.p., sales mgr. Gulf Coast, 1971-76; pres. Menko Steel Service, Inc., Houston, 1979—; v.p., treas. Gachman Metal Co.; investment cons. D & L Enterprises, 1966—. Mem. solicitation com. United Fund, 1969-76; mem. Nat. Alliance of Businessmen Jobs Program, 1969—. Served with AUS, 1963-65. Mem. Tex. Assn. Steel Importers, Purchasing Agts. Assn. Houston, Credit Assn. Houston, Am. Mgmt. Assn., Assn. Steel Distbrs., Nat. Assn. Elevator Contractors, Phi Sigma Delta, Alpha Phi Omega. Home: 314 Tealwood Dr Houston TX 77024-6113 Office: PO Box 40296 Houston TX 77240-0296

MENSE, ALLAN TATE, research and development engineering executive; b. Kansas City, Mo., Nov. 29, 1945; s. Martin Conrad Mense and Nancy (Tate) Johnson; children from previous marriage: Melanie Georgia, Eileen Madelaine. BS, U. Ariz., 1968, MS, 1970; PhD, U. Wis., 1976. Scientist Oak Ridge (Tenn.) Nat. Lab, 1976-79; sr. staff sci. and tech. comm. U.S. Ho. Reps., Washington, 1979-81; sr. scientist McDonnell Douglas Astro. Co., St. Louis, 1981-85; from dep. chief scientist to chief scientist Dept. Def. Strategic Def. Initiative Orgn., Washington, 1985-88; v.p. rsch. Fla. Inst. Tech., Melbourne, 1988-92; pres. Advanced Tech. Mgmt., Inc., Tempe, Ariz., 1992—; vis. scholar Sloan Sch., MIT, 1995-96. Contbr. over 60 articles to profl. jours. Ariz. State U. scholar, 1996-97. Mem. AIAA (sr. mem.), IEEE (chmn. energy com. 1985—, sr. mem.), Am. Def. Preparedness Assn., Am. Phys. Soc., Am. Nuclear Soc., Inst. Indsl. Engrs., Fla. Com. Nat. Space Club (charter), Navy League, Sigma Xi, Theta Tau, Pi Mu Alpha. Episcopalian. Home and Office: MSC-280 PO Box 22555 Tempe AZ 85282

MENSES, JAN, artist, draftsman, etcher, lithographer, muralist; b. Rotterdam, Netherlands, Apr. 28, 1933; emigrated to Can., 1960, naturalized, 1965; s. Jan and Elisabeth Wilhelmina (Schwarz) M.; m. Rachel Régine Kadoch, Dec. 7, 1958; children: Salomon, Hnina Sarah, Nechamah Elisabeth Halo. Student, Acad. Fine Arts, Rotterdam, Officers Acad. Royal Dutch Air Force, 1953-55. lectr. in fine arts Concordia U., Montreal, 1973-76, others. One-man shows include Montreal Mus. Fine Arts, 1961, 65, 76, Isaacs Gallery, Toronto, Ont., Can., 1964, Delta Gallery, Rotterdam, 1965, Galerie Godard Lefort, Montreal, 1966, Gallery Moos, Toronto, 1967, Rotterdam Art Found., 1974, Galerie Mira Godard, Toronto, 1977, Montreal, 1978, Seasons Galleries, The Hague, 1980, U. B.C. Fine Arts Gallery, Vancouver, 1981, Galerie Don Stewart, Montreal, 1981, Mead Art Mus., Amherst, Mass., 1983, Agnes Etherington Art Mus., 1984, Blom and Dorn Gallery, N.Y.C., 1985, 86-93, Marywood Coll. Mus., Scranton, Pa., 1985, Saraya-Wolfson Ctr., Safed, Israel, 1987, Mayanot Gallery, Jerusalem, 1987-88, Esperanza Gallery, Montreal, 1988, 89, Gallery Hamaayan Haradum, Safed, Israel, 1989-93, 94, 95, Blom and Dorn Gallery, Hartford, Conn., 1995, Nora Gallery, Jerusalem, 1995, 96, 97, Artist's Colony, Safed, Isreal; over 300 group shows include Montreal World Exhbn., 1967, Salon Internat. Art, Basel, Switzerland, 1972, 74, Can. Nat. Exhbn., 1972, Centennial Exhbn., Royal Can. Acad., Toronto, 1980, Que. Biennale I, II, III, Montreal, 1977, 79, 81, Foire Internat. D'Art Contemporain Paris and Internat. Fair Koln Germany, 1986, Migdal Ha-Emek, Israel, 1988, Group of 8 Israel, Toronto, 1990, Royal Can. Acad. Show, Toronto, 1991; represented in permanent exhbn. Gallery Hamaayan Haradum, Safed, Profl. Artists' Assn., Artists Colony, Safed; represented in permanent collections Museo Ciani di Villa Caccia, Lugano, Switzerland, The Art Gallery of Hamilton, Ont.,Can., David Giles Carter Collection, New Haven, Gallery of Nova Scotia-Halifax, Can, Jewish Public Libr. Collection, Montreal, Can., Cadillac Fairview Collection, Toronto, Can, Museum Modern Art, N.Y.C., Phila. Mus. Art, Solomon R. Guggenheim Mus., N.Y.C., Yivo Inst., N.Y.C., Bklyn. Mus., Art Inst. Chgo., Cleve. Mus. Art, Detroit Inst. Arts, Yale U., U. Montreal, Queens U., Kingston, Mead Art Mus., Amherst Coll., Jonathan Edwards Coll., New Haven, Victoria & Albert Mus., London, Vatican Mus., Rome, Quebec Art Bank, Concordia U., Montreal, Haifa Mus. Modern Art, Hebrew U., Jerusalem, Govt. of Que., Yad Vashem Holocaust Meml., Jerusalem, Mus. Boymans-van Beuningen, Rotterdam, Stedelijk Mus., Amsterdam, Rijksmuseum, Amsterdam, Nat. Gallery Can., Ottawa, Gallery Stratford, Montreal Mus. Fine Arts, Musée d'Art Contemporain, Montreal, Que. Provincial Mus., Que. Art Bank, Art Bank of the Can. Coun., Ottawa, Ariz. State Mus., Tucson, Hebrew U., Jerusalem, City of Safed-Israel, Holocaust Meml. Ctr., Toronto, Lavalin Mus. Coll, Montreal, Oshawa Mus., Ont., Dept. External Affairs Govt. Can., Ottawa, Can. Jewish Congress Mus., Montreal, Israel Mus., Jerusalem, McGill U., Montreal, Olympia & York Collection, Toronto, CBC Collection, Montreal, Kingston (Ont.) U. Mus. Collection, N.Y. Pub. Libr., Worcester (Mass.) Art Mus., Currier Gallery Art, Manchester, N.H., Art Gallery of U. N.H., Durham, Mus. Art. RISD, Providence, Olympia & York Collection, Toronto, Collection Rishon Le'Zion, Jerusalem, Rose Art Mus., Brandeis U., Waltham, Mass., C.I.L. Collection Montreal, Tel Aviv U., McGill U. Coll., Montreal, Can. Jewish Congress Mus., Montreal, Young Israel of Montreal (Coll.), Can., Confedn. Art Ctr., Charlottetown-Prince Edward Island, Can., Thomas More Inst., Montreal; paintings include Klippoth Series, 1963-78, Kaddish Series, 1964-80, Hechaloth Series, 1973—, Tikkun Series, 1978—; mural for, Montreal Holocaust Meml. Center. Mem. Pres.'s Coun. of U. N.H. Served with Royal Dutch Air Force Res., 1953-55. Recipient 5 1st prizes Nat. Art Exhbn., Quebec, Que., 1960-65; Grand prize Concours Artistiques de la Province de Que., 1965; prize X and XI Winnipeg (Man., Can.) Shows, 1966, 68; prize IX Internat. Exhbn. Drawings and Prints, Lugano, 1966; prize Ofcl. Centennial Art Competition, Toronto; 1st prize Hadassah, 1969, 71, 82; Recipient Imago award U. Montreal, 1971; award Reeves of Can., 1969; Tigert award Ont. Soc. Arts, 1970; Loomis and Toles award, 1972; J. I. Segal award J. I. Segal Fund Jewish Culture, 1975; Gold medal Accademia Italia Delle Arte, Italy, 1980; Gold medal Internat. Parliament U.S.A., 1982; Gran Premio delle Nazioni, Italy, 1983, European Banner of Arts with Gold medal, 1984, Oscar d' Italia, 1985, 1st prize III Que. Biennale, 1981, OSA award of merit, Toronto, 1981, 82; World Culture prize Italy, 1984; Golden Flame of World Parliament (U.S.A.) award, 1986; Ish Shalom award Jerusalem, 1993; numerous others; Can. Council sr. arts fellow, 1969-70, 71-72, 81-82; grantee, 1966-67, 67-68; travel grantee, 1968, 73. Mem. Royal Can. Acad. Arts, Acad. Italia Arte e del Lavoro, Acad. Nazioni, Maestro Accademico-Accademia Bedriacense (Italy), Jewish Am. Acad. Arts and Scis., Israeli Art Assn. (Telaviv), Israel Assn. Profl. Artists Safed, Acad. Europa, Academician Italy, Israel Assn. Visual Art (Jerusalem). Jewish. Office: care Blom & Dorn Gallery 140 Huyshope Ave Ste 613 Hartford CT 06106-2892 *My works have dealt with death, the eclipse of faith, exile, the Galut. They are shaped by my childhood experiences, real and imagined, in Nazi-occupied Europe; influenced by and rooted in my principles and standards of conduct as an Orthodox Jew in the post-holocaust/pre-Messianic era. They are an attempt to translate these experiences into visual contemporary terms (imagery conflicts and reconciliations of conflicts) in order to ascend from the personal/specific to the universal/general. They are a lament, an elegy, a denial and confirmation, an expression of the attitude of the soul in its debasement and dignity towards its Creator; a striving towards serenity in anticipation of the Redemption: a form of prayer.*

MENTZ, HENRY ALVAN, JR., federal judge; b. New Orleans, Nov. 10, 1920; s. Henry Alvan and Lulla (Bridewell) M.; m. Ann Lamantia, June 23, 1956; children: Ann, Carli, Hal, Frederick, George. BA, Tulane U., 1941; JD, La. State U., 1943. Bar: La. 1943, U.S. Dist. Ct. (ea. dist.) La. 1944. With legal dept. Shell Oil, New Orleans, 1947-48; pvt. practice Hammond, 1948-82; judge U.S. Dist. Ct. (ea. dist.) La., New Orleans, 1982—, sr. judge, 1992—. Editor: Combined Gospels, 1976. Pres. La. Soc. Music and Performing Arts, 1994—, L.A. Civil Svc. League, 1979-81; bd. dirs. Southea. La. U. Found., Salvation Army; chmn. Tulane U. 50th Anniversary Reunion for 1991. Decorated 2 Battle Stars, Bronze Star; recipient Disting. Svc. award AMVETS, 1950. Mem. SAR, Royal Soc. St. George (pres.), Boston Club New Orleans, Delta Tau Delta. Republican. Episcopalian. Home: 2105 State St New Orleans LA 70118-6255 Office: US Dist Ct C-114 US Courthouse 500 Camp St New Orleans LA 70130-3313

MENTZER, JOHN RAYMOND, electrical engineer, educator; b. Arch Spring, Pa., June 16, 1916; s. Walter Ray and Katheryn Henderson (Barr) M.; m. Bernice Roslyn Simon, Feb. 17, 1945; children—Jacqueline Ferne, Richard Alan. B.S., Pa. State U., 1942, M.S., 1948; Ph.D., Ohio State U., 1952. Engr. Westinghouse Electric Corp., Balt., 1942-46, Ordnance Research Lab., 1946-48; research asso. Ohio State U., 1948-52; mem. staff Lincoln Lab., M.I.T., 1952-54; mem. faculty Pa. State U., 1954—, prof. engring. scis., 1956—, head dept. engring. sci. and mechanics, 1974-81, prof. emeritus engring. scis., 1981—. Author: Scattering and Diffraction of Radio Waves, 1955. Recipient Service award Pa. State U., 1979. Sr. mem. IEEE; mem. Am. Soc. Engring. Edn., AAAS, Sigma Xi. Home: 557 Clarence Ave State College PA 16803-3456 Office: 227 Hammond Bldg University Park PA 16802-1401

MENUHIN, YEHUDI, violinist; b. N.Y.C., Apr. 22, 1916; s. Moshe and Marutha M.; m. Nola Ruby Nicholas, May 26, 1938; children: Zamira, Krov; m. Diana Gould, Oct. 19, 1947; children: Gerard, Jeremy. Educated by pvt. tutors; studied music under, Sigmund Anker, Louis Persinger, San Francisco, Georges Enesco, Rumania and Paris, Adolph Busch, Switzerland; MusD (hon.), U. Oxford, 1962, Queen's U., Belfast, 1965, U. Leicester, 1965; LLD (hon.), U. St. Andrews, 1963, U. Liverpool, 1963, U. Sussex, 1966, U. Bath, 1969; LittD (hon.), U. Warwick, 1968; MusD (hon.), U. London, 1969, U. Cambridge, 1970. Pres. Halle Orch., 1992; Established Yehudi Menuhin Sch. at Stoke D'Abernon, Eng.; pres. Internat. Music Council of UNESCO, Folkestone Menuhin Internat. Violin Competition, Royal Philharmonic Orch., 1982—. Completed his first round-the-world concert tour, 1935; appearing in 110 concert engagements; has toured in Latin Am., S.Am., Australia, South Africa and Pacific Islands; played 22 concerts during 12 day tour in Israel; filmed series of complete concert programs; opened Japan to world concert artists, 1951, concert tours in India, 1952, 54, also charity concerts various instns.; has own yearly summer festival in Gstaad, Switzerland, 1957—; debut as condr. symphony orch. in Am. with Am. Symphony Orch., Carnegie Hall, 1966, dir., Bath Festival, Eng., 1958-68, Bath Festival Orch.; presented his first festival at Windsor, 1969; held over 500 concerts for armed forces, Red Cross, others; followed U.S. Army into, France and Belgium, first artist to play in liberated Paris, Brussels, Bucharest, Budapest and Antwerp, also first in Moscow after cessation of hostilities; prin. guest condr. English Sting Orch., 1988—; author: The Violin: Six Lessons by Yehudi Menuhin, 1971, Theme and Variations, 1972, The Violin and Viola, 1976, The King, the Cut, and the Fiddle, 1983, Life Class, 1986, The Compleat Violinist: Thoughts, Exercises and Reflections of a Humanist Violinist, 1986; autobiography Unfinished Journey, 1977; co-author: The Music of Man, 1979. Goodwill Amb. UNESCO, 1992. Decorated officer Legion of Honor; chevalier de L'Ordre des Arts et des Lettres (France); Order of Leopold (Belgium); Ordre de la Couronne (Belgium); Order of Merit (West German Republic); knight comdr. Order Brit. Empire (Gt. Britain); Royal Order Phoenix (Greece), Order of Merit (Gt. Britain); Gran Cruz de la Order del Gerito Civil (Spain); recipient Jawaharlal Nehru award for Internat. Understanding India, 1968, Mendelssohn prize, 1986, 10 Grammy awards, Golden Viotti prize, 1987, Glenn Gould prize Glenn Gould Found., 1990, Wolf prize in Arts, 1991. Fellow World Acad. Art and Sci.; mem. and/or officer numerous U.S., fgn. orgns. Research in expansion violin concert repertoire; introduced many rare and important works both classical and modern. Office: care Columbia Artists Mgmt 165 W 57th St New York NY 10019-2201 also: Menuhin Festival, Gstaad-Saanen/Alpengala, CH-3780 Gstaad Switzerland also: SYM Music Co, PO Box 6160, London SW1W OXJ, England*

MENY, ROBERT, medical research administrator; b. Hackensack, N.J., Jan. 7, 1945; m. Janet McHugh, Apr. 28, 1990; children: Danielle, Ellen. BS, Tulane U., 1966; MD, Columbia U., 1971. Intern and resident in pediat. N.Y. Hosp., N.Y.C., 1971-73; fellow in neonatology U. Md. Hosp., Balt., 1975-77; mem. staff neonatal ctr. Rutgers Med. Sch., New Brunswick, N.J., 1977-80; dir. Hurley Neonatal Ctr., Flint, Mich., 1980-83; dir. Sudden Infant Death Syndrome Inst. U. Md., Balt., 1983—. Capt. USAFR. Mem. Am. Assn. Sudden Infant Death Prevention Physicians (pres.-elect 1995). Office: U Md SIDS Inst 22 S Greene St Rm N5w67 Baltimore MD 21201-1544

MENYHERT, STEPHAN, retired chemist; b. Nagyatad, Hungary, Sept. 18, 1937; came to U.S., 1952; s. Steven and Elfriede A. (Brockmann) M.; m. Roberta Powers, May 27, 1962 (div. Feb. 1978); children: Oleg A., Piroska L., Steven R., George M. BSChemE, U. Cin., 1962; MBA, Xavier U., 1981. Process rsch. chemist Emery Industries, Inc., Cin., 1962-74, mgr. pilot plant, 1974-82; quality assurance chemist II Henkel, Emery Group (formerly Emery Industries, Inc.), Cin., 1982-93; ret., 1994. Tech. advisor Colerain Twp. Vol. Fire Dept., Cin., 1964-76. Mem. AIChE, Am. Chem. Soc., Am. Soc. for Quality Control, Germania Soc. (chmn. bldg. com. Cin. chpt. 1974-77, pres. 1985-87, 94-95). Presbyterian. Avocations: photography, video, music, reading, translating. Office: 3435 Statewood Dr Cincinnati OH 45251-2383

MENYUK, PAULA, developmental psycholinguistics educator; b. N.Y.C., Oct. 2, 1929; d. Louis and Helen (Weissman) Nichols; m. Norman Menyuk, Mar. 5, 1950; children—Curtis R., Diane E., Eric D. B.S., NYU, 1951; Ed.M., Boston U., 1955, Ed.D., 1961. Chief lang. therapist Mass. Gen. Hosp., Boston, 1952-54; teaching fellow Boston U., 1957-60; NIMH post-doctoral fellow MIT, Cambridge, 1961-64, mem. research staff, 1964-72; prof. edn. Boston U., 1972, dir. div., vice chmn. faculty coun., 1981-87, chmn. faculty coun., 1990-91; cons. Children's Hosp., Boston, 1964-92, Kennedy Hosp., Boston, 1981-89, NIH, Bethesda, Md., 1972-80, 89-94, Nat. Found. March of Dimes, White Plains, N.Y., 1977-93; rsch. assoc. MIT, 1972-90. Author: Sentences Children Use, 1969, Acquisition and Development of Language, 1971, Language and Maturation, 1977, Language Development: Knowledge and Use, 1988, Early Language Development in Full-Term and Premature Infants, 1995. NIH fellow, 1958-64; Fulbright fellow, 1971, 88. Fellow Am. Speech, Lang. and Hearing Assn. (Disting. Svc. award 1976, highest honors 1992); mem. AAAS, Soc. Rsch. in Child Devel., Linguistic Soc. Am., Internat. Soc. Study Behavioral Devel., Am. Assn. Phonetic Scis. Home: 162 Mason Ter Brookline MA 02146-2772 Office: Boston U 605 Commonwealth Ave Boston MA 02215-1605

MENZER, ROBERT EVERETT, toxicologist, educator; b. Washington, Dec. 21, 1938; s. Russell Ernest and Ora Taylor (Oates) M.; m. Sara Lee Gribbon, Dec. 29, 1962; children: R. Eric, Paul D., Joan Coleraine. B.S. in Chemistry, U. Pa., 1960; M.S., U. Md., 1962; Ph.D., U. Wis., 1964. Instr. U. Wis., Madison, 1964; mem. faculty U. Md., 1964-89, asst. prof. entomology, 1964-69, assoc. prof., 1969-73, prof., 1973-89, assoc. dean grad. studies and research, 1974-77, acting dean, 1977-80, chmn. grad. program marine-estuarine-environ. scis., 1978-89, dir. Water Resources Research Ctr., 1981-89; dir. environ. rsch. lab. EPA, Gulf Breeze, Fla., 1989-95; sr. sci. advisor EPA, Washington, 1995—; prof. emeritus U. Md., 1990—; chmn. hazardous substances data bank rev. panel Nat. Library Medicine, 1973-97. Contbr. articles to profl. jours. Recipient U. Md. Alumni award, 1974. Fellow Washington Acad. Scis.; mem. AAAS, Am. Chem. Soc., Soc. Toxicology, Soc. for Environ. Toxicology and Chemistry, Estuarine Rsch. Fedn., Sigma Xi, Phi Kappa Phi. Republican. Episcopalian. Club: Cosmos (Washington). Home: 1611 Alliston St NW Washington DC 20011-4213 Office: USEPA (8701) 401 M St SW Washington DC 20460-0001

MENZIE, DONALD E., petroleum engineer, educator; b. DuBois, Pa., Apr. 4, 1922; s. James Freeman and Helga Josephine (Johnson) M.; m. Jane Cameron Redsecker, Nov. 6, 1946; children: Donald, William Lee, John Peter, Thomas Freeman. B.S in Petroleum and Natural Gas Engring., Pa. State U., 1942, M.S, 1948, Ph.D., 1962. Marine engr. Phila. Navy Yard, 1943-46; rsch. asst. air-gas dr. recovery Pa. State U., 1946-48, instr. petroleum and natural gas engring., 1948-51; asst. prof. petroleum engring. U. Okla., Norman, 1951-55, assoc. prof., 1955-64, prof., 1964-91, Kerr-McGee Centennial prof. Petroleum and Geol. Engring., 1991—, Halliburton Disting lectr., 1982-84; disting. lectr. Okla. U., 1986-87; dir. Sch. Petroleum and Geol. Engring U. Okla., Norman, 1963-72, petroleum engr. rsch. info. systems program, 1979-88, assoc. exec. dir. Energy Resources Ctr., 1988; assoc. exec. dir. Microbial Enhanced Oil Recovery Rsch. Project, Norman, 1982-; microbial enhanced oil recovery rsch. project U. Okla., 1982—; pres., owner Petroleum Engring. Educators, Norman, 1971—; cons. in field. Author: Reservoir Mechanics, 1954, Waterflooding for Engineers, 1968, Applied Reservoir Engineering for Geologists, 1971, New Recovery Techniques, 1975, Microbial Enhanced Oil Recovery, 1987, Dispersivity As An Oil Reservoir Rock Characteristic, 1989; contbr. articles to profl. jours. Mem. enhanced oil com. Interstate Oil and Gas Compact Commn., 1982-; commr., scoutmaster Last Frontier Coun. Boy Scouts Am., 1951-81; mem. adminstrv. bd. McFarlin United Meth. Ch., Norman, also sunday sch. tchr., pres. fellowship class, treas.; pres. Jackson PTA, Norman, 1962-68; treas. Cleveland County Rep. Com.; mem. Norman Park Commn., 1974-80; co-chmn., dir. Norman Parks Found., 1983-; mem. Cen. Com. U. Okla., 1987-. Mem. AIME, Am. Assn. Petroleum Geologists, Okla. Soc. Profl. Engrs., Nat. Soc. Profl. Engrs., Am. Soc. Engring. Edn., Soc. Petroleum Engrs., Am. Petroleum Inst., AAAS, Okla. Engring. and Tech. Guidance Coun., Okla. Anthopol. Soc., Soc. Petroleum Engrs. (recipient Nat. Disting. Achievement award for petroleum engring. faculty 1989), Sigma Xi, Pi Epsilon Tau, Alpha Chi Sigma, Phi Lamda Upsilon, Phi Kappa Phi. Clubs: Sportsmen of Cleve. County, Sooner Swim (dir. 1966-78). Lodge: Masons. Home: 1503 Melrose Dr Norman OK 73069-5366 Office: U Okla F314 The Energy Ctr Norman OK 73019

MENZIES, HENRY HARDINGE, .rchitect; b. Hickory, N.C., Apr. 20, 1928; s. Henry Hardinge and Hallie (Lloyd) M.; AB in Lit., U. N.C., 1948; postgrad. U. So. Calif., 1948-49; BArch, N.C. State U., 1958. Founder, ptnr. The Architects Group, Boston, 1962-63; individu l practice architecture, Boston, 1964-78; ptnr. Menzies and LeMieux, N.Y.C., 1978-82; pvt. practice architecture, New Rochelle, N.Y., 1983—; lectr. in field; works include coll. and seminary, Natick, Mass., 1964, Heights Sch., Washington, 1965, St. Marie's Ch., Lowell, Mass., 1966, Central Cath. High Sch., Lawrence, Mass., 1971, Walker Sch., Needham, Mass., 1972, Baird Residence, Sherborn, Mass., 1972, Layton Cultural Center, Brookfield, Wis., 1974, Shellbourne Conf. Center, Valparaiso, Ind., 1974, Wespine Study Center, St. Louis, 1981, Arnold Hall Conf. Center, Pembroke, Mass., 1982, alterations to residences in Greenwich, Conn., 1984, Garwood Bldg. at Arnold Hall, 1986, Midtown Ctr. Chgo., 1986, Student Ctr. Houston, 1986, Windmoor Ctr. South Bend, Ind., 1986., alterations to student residences in Milw. and Providence, 1989-91, renovation of interior St. Aloysius Ch., New Canaan, Conn., 1993-96, chapel at Warwick House, Pitts., 1993, chapel at Westfield Residence, L.A., 1994, chapel at Allview Ctr., Columbia, Md., 1994, chapel at St. John Fisher Residence, Stamford, Conn., 1994, master plan, crypt chapel St. Mary of the Angels Church, 1996-97, shrine at Conf. Ctr., Schulenberg, Tex., 1996—, shrine at New Caney, Tex., 1996-97, chapel Lincoln Green student residence, 1997—, new facade of St Bloysios Ch., 1997—; contbr. articles to profl. jours. Served to 1st lt. USNR, 1951-55. Mem. AIA (chmn. profl. services com. Boston chpt. 1976-77, N.Y. chpt. 1978-84, Westchester/Mid-Hudson chpt. 1985—). Roman Catholic. Office: 99 Overlook Cir New Rochelle NY 10804-4501

MENZIES, IAN STUART, newspaper editor; b. Glasgow, Scotland, Mar. 11, 1920; came to U.S., 1944, naturalized, 1948; s. John S. and Gertrude (Mephius) M.; m. Barbara Edith Newton, June 16, 1945; children: Marla Ann, Gillian Jean, Alexa Stuart, Deborah Newton. Student, Royal Tech. Coll., 1937-39; Nieman fellow, Harvard U., 1961-62; L.H.D., Salem State Coll., 1978. Reporter Boston Globe, 1948-57, sci. editor, 1957-63, fin. editor, 1963-65, mng. editor, 1965-70, assoc. editor, 1970-85; sr. fellow John McCormack Inst. Pub. Affairs, U. Mass., Boston, 1985—; vis. assoc. Joint Ctr. for Urban Studies, Mass. Inst. Tech.-Harvard, 1970-71. Mem. Hingham (Mass.) Sch. Com., 1962-68. Served to lt. Royal Naval Vol. Res., 1939-46. Decorated D.S.C.; recipient Pub. Service award Nat. Edn. Writers, 1961, Pub. Service award AAAS, 1963, Heywood Broun award, 1961, Sevellon Brown award, 1959, Rudolph Elie award, 1959, A.P. Big City award, 1958, U.P.I. award, 1959. Mem. Harvard Club, Hingham Yacht Club, Brit. Officers Club New Eng. Home: 479 Main St Hingham MA 02043-4705 Office: U Mass McCormack Inst Boston MA 02125

MENZIES, JOHN ALEXANDER, mechanical and chemical engineer; b. London, June 11, 1947; s. James and Rose (Howlett) M.; m. Jean Frances Kindell, Sept. 27, 1969; children: Cheryl Joanne, Heather Jean, Claire. Degree mech. engring., Harrow Coll., London, 1968; degree chem. engring., Southbank U., London, 1970. Piping designer M.W. Kellogg Co., London, 1963-68, mech. engr., 1968-70, project engr., 1970-71, process engr., 1971-73; project mgr. M.W. Kellogg Co., London and Houston, Tex., 1973-84; dir. proposals M.W. Kellogg Co., Houston, 1984-87, dir. ops., 1987-91, v.p. project mgmt., 1991—. Contbr. articles to profl. jours. Gov. Richmond Coll., London, 1990-91. Mem. AIChe, ASME, PMI. Avocations: tennis, golf, squash, fishing, bowling. Office: The MW Kellogg Co 601 Jefferson St Houston TX 77002-7900

MEO, ROXANNE MARIE, critical care nurse; b. Saginaw, Mich., Oct. 10, 1959; d. Joseph S. and Margaret V. (Gillam) M. BSN, Saginaw Valley State U., University Center, Mich., 1982; student, Delta Coll., 1987-90; overseas studies, Mich. State U., 1983, postgrad., 1995. Nurse extern St. Luke's Hosp., Saginaw, 1982, staff nurse, 1983-88; Nurse in Washington intern Nat. Fedn. Specialty Nursing Orngs., 1987; resource nurse Ask-A-Nurse, Saginaw, 1988-91, Seton Health Care Corp. East Cen. Mich.; staff nurse St. Mary's Med. Ctr., Saginaw, 1983, 91—. Mem. ANA, Am. Assn. Neurosci. Nurses, Mich. Nurses Assn., Saginaw Nurses Assn., Soc. Gastrointestinal Assts., Emergency Nurses Cancel Alcohol Related Emergencies, Sigma Theta Tau.

MEOLA, TONY, professional soccer player, actor; b. Belleville, N.J., Feb. 21, 1969; s. Vincent and Maria Meola; m. Colleen Meola; 1 child, Jonathan. Student, U. Virginia, 1986-89. Goalkeeper CONCACAF World Cup Qualifying Games, 1989, U.S. World Cup Team, 1990, Brighton Football Club, England, 1990, Fort Lauderdale Strikers, Amer. Prof. Soccer League, 1991, U.S. Nat. Team, 1992-94, Long Island Roughriders, 1994-95, U.S. World Cup Team, 1994, NY-NJ MetroStars, Secaucus, 1996—; drafted ctr. fielder N.Y. Yankees; tried out as placekicker for N.Y. Jets, 1994. Appeared in play Tony N' Tina's Wedding, 1995. Named Hermann Trophy winner, Mo. Athletic Club Player of Yr., 1989, MVP U.S. Cup, 1993. mem., N.J. State H.S. Soccer Champions, 1986, NCAA Division I Co-Champions, 1989. Office: care NY-NJ MetroStars One Harmon Plaza Secaucus NJ 07094*

MERACHNIK, DONALD, superintendent of schools. AB, Upsala Coll., 1951; MS, City Coll. of N.Y., 1952; PhD, N.Y. U., 1961. Supt. Union County Regional H.S., Springfield, N.J., 1971—. Named Nat. Supt. of Yr. for N.J., Am. Assn. Sch. Adminstrs., 1993. Office: Union Co Regional HSD Jonathan Dayton Regional HS Mountain Ave Springfield NJ 07081

MERANUS, ARTHUR RICHARD, advertising agency executive; b. Bklyn., May 27, 1934; s. Herbert and Dorothy (Newman) M.; m. Phyllis Ochitell, Sept. 21, 1958; children—Lisa, Leonard, Steven. Grad., Cooper Union, 1956. With Gaynor & Ducas, N.Y.C., 1961-63; with Norman, Craig & Kummel, Inc., N.Y.C., 1963-65; with Cunningham & Walsh Advt. Inc., N.Y.C., 1965-87, sr. v.p., 1978-87, creative dir., 1979-81, dir. creative svcs., 1981-87; mng. dir. creative svcs. N.W. Ayer, N.Y.C., 1987-88, exec. v.p., mng. dir. creative svcs., 1988—, also bd. dirs., 1988-96; exec. creative dir. N.W. Ayer & Ptnrs., N.Y.C., 1996—. Served with USAR, 1956-57, 60-61. Recipient Clio award, Art Dirs. Club N.Y. award, One Show awards, Andy award, Effie award. Mem. Garden State Yacht Club. Office: NW Ayer & Ptnrs Inc Worldwide Plz 825 8th Ave Fl 35 New York NY 10019-7416

MERANUS, LEONARD STANLEY, lawyer; b. Newark, Jan. 7, 1928; s. Norman and Ada (Binstock) M.; m. Jane B. Holzman, Sept. 20, 1989; children: Norman, James M., David. LittB, Rutgers U., 1948; LLB, Harvard U., 1954. Bar: Ohio 1954. Assoc. Paxton & Seasongood, Cin., 1954-59, ptnr., 1959-85, pres., 1985-89; ptnr. Thompson, Hine and Flory, 1989—, ptnr.-in-charge Cin. office, 1989-91, mem. firm mgmt. com., 1991-93. Co-editor: Law and the Writer, 1978, 81, 85. Chmn. bd. dirs. Jewish Hosp., 1982-86; trustee Andrew Jergens Found., 1962—. Mem. ABA, Ohio Bar Assn., Internat. Bar Assn., Cin. Bar Assn., Am. Arbitration Assn. (Ohio, Ind., Ky. regional adv. com., chmn. comml. arbitration com., Ohio panel large, complex arbitration cases), Union Internationale des Avocats. Office: Thompson Hine & Flory 312 Walnut St Ste 14 Cincinnati OH 45202-4024

MÉRAS, PHYLLIS LESLIE, journalist; b. Bklyn., May 10, 1931; d. Edmond Albert and Leslie Trousdale (Ross) M.; BA, Wellesley Coll., 1955; MS in Journalism, Columbia U., 1954; Swiss Govt. Exchange fellow, Inst. Higher Internat. Studies, Geneva, 1957; m. Thomas H. Cocroft, Nov. 3, 1968. Reporter, copy editor Providence Jour., 1954-57, 59-61; feature writer Ladies Home Jour. mag., 1957-58; editor Weekly Tribune, Geneva, Switzerland, 1961-62; copyeditor, travel sect. N.Y. Times, 1962-68; mng. editor Vineyard Gazette, Edgartown, Mass., 1970-74, contbg. editor, 1974—; assoc. editor Rhode Islander, Providence, 1970-76; travel editor Providence Jour., 1976-95; editor Wellesley Alumnae mag., 1979-96; assoc. in journalism U. R.I., 1974-75; adj. instr. Columbia U. Sch. Journalism, 1975-76. Author: First Spring: A Martha's Vineyard Journal, 1972, A Yankee Way With Wood, 1975, Miniatures: How to Make Them, Use Them, Sell Them, 1976, Vacation Crafts, 1978, The Mermaids of Chenonceaux and 828 Other Tales: An Anecdotal Guide to Europe, 1982, Exploring Rhode Island, 1984, Castles, Keeps and Leprechauns: Tales, Myths and Legends of Historic Sites in Great Britain and Ireland, 1988, Eastern Europe: A Traveler's Companion, 1991; co-author: Christmas Angels, 1979, Carry-out Cuisine, 1982, New Carry Out Cuisine, 1986, Rhode Island Explorer's Guide, 1995. Pulitzer fellow in critical writing, 1967. Mem. Soc. Am. Travel Writers. Home: Music St PO Box 215 West Tisbury MA 02575-9999

MERAT, FRANCIS LAWRENCE, engineering educator; b. Frenchville, Pa., Aug. 22, 1949; s. Lawrence Clarence and Lucille Magdalen (DeMange) M. BSEE, Case Western Res. U., 1972, MSEE, 1975, PhDEE, 1978. Rsch. engr. Case Western Res. U., Cleve., 1978-79; assoc. prof. engring. Case Western Res. U., Cleve., N.Y., 1979-85; assoc. prof. Case Western Res. U., Cleve., 1985—, exec. officer dept. elec. engring. and applied physics, 1994—; co-founder, sec./treas. PGM Diversified Industries, Inc., Parma Heights, Ohio, 1986—; fellow summer faculty program USAF, Griffiss AFB, N.Y., 1980, U.S. Army, Ft. Belvoir, Va., 1987; cons. various law firms (expert forensic engr.) ,NASA Lewis Rsch. Ctr. Contbr. articles to tech. jours. Named Disting. Advisor, Nat. Assn. Acad. Counseling and Advising, 1985. Mem. IEEE (sect. chmn. 1983-84, reviewer IEEE Robotics and Automation), Soc. Mfg. Engrs., Assn. Computing Machinery, Soc. Photo-optical Instrumentation Engrs., Sigma Xi. Roman Catholic. Avocations: photography, science fiction, movies. Home: 4398 Groveland Rd University Ht OH 44118-3958 Office: Case Western Res Univ 10900 Euclid Ave Cleveland OH 44106-1712

MERBAUM, MICHAEL, psychology educator, clinical psychologist; b. N.Y.C., Nov. 6, 1933; s. Max J. and Molly (Rubin) M.; m. Marta Ettinger, Nov. 18, 1962; children: Tal, Marc. BA, Drake U., 1954; MA, U. Mo., Kansas City, 1956; PhD, U. N.C., 1961. Diplomate Am. Bd. Clin. Psychology. Staff psychologist U. Chgo., 1961-64; asst. prof. Bowling Green (Ohio) State U., 1964-66; assoc. prof. Adelphi U., N.Y.C., 1966-72; prof. U. Haifa, Israel, 1972-78; prof., dir. clin. tng. Washington U., St. Louis, 1978—; corp. psychologist Wetterau, Inc., St. Louis, 1988-94, psychologist Right Career Mgmt. Cons., 1996—. Editor: Personality: Readings in Theory and Research, 1964, 3d edit., 1978, Behavior Change Through Self-control, 1973. Mem. Am. Psychol. Assn., Assn. for Advancement Behavior Therapy. Democrat. Jewish. Avocations: tennis, reading, music. Home: 825 Fairfield Lake Dr Chesterfield MO 63017-5926 Office: Washington U Dept Psychology Saint Louis MO 63130

MERCADANTE, ANTHONY JOSEPH, special education educator; b. Newark, N.J., Mar. 10, 1951; s. Anthony Joseph Jr. and Anna Rose (Cocuzzo) M.; m. Barbara Ferrari, May 27, 1979; children: Anthony, Lisa, David. BS in Edn., Seton Hall U., 1973; MA in Audiology and Communication Sci., Kean Coll., 1978; cert. in adminstrn. and supervision, U. S. Fla., 1987. Cert. audiologist, adminstr./supr., tchr. bus. edn., tchr. hearing impaired. Acctg. clerk supply div. U.S. Steel Corp., Newark, 1973-75; acctg. and bookkeeping instr. Sch. Data Programming, Union, N.J., 1976-78; bus. adminstrn. instr., curriculum coord. Roberts-Walsh Bus. Sch., Union, 1978-83; clin. audiologist Ea. Speech, Lang. and Hearing Ctr., Woodbridge, N.J., 1980-83; ednl. audiologist exceptional student edn. dept. Polk County Pub. Schs., Bartow, Fla., 1983—; advisor Fla. Audiologists in Edn., Orlando, 1987—; mem. multidisciplinary team Polk County Pub. Schs., 1983—; mem. planning com. Project Healthy Start, Polk County Pub. Schs., Bartow, 1994—. Baseball coach S. Lakeland Babe Ruth Baseball League, Lakeland, Fla., 1993, baseball mgr., 1994. Mem. Am. Speech, Lang. and Hearing Assn., Nat. Youth Sports Coaches Assn., Fla. Speech, Lang. and Hearing Assn., Scott Lake Elem. PTA. Avocations: tennis, golf, bowling, swimming, coaching. Home: 6122 Donegal E Lakeland FL 33813-3713 Office: Polk Life and Learning Ctr 1310 S Floral Ave Bartow FL 33830-6309

MERCER, CHET ATOM, retired elementary educator; b. Missoula, Mont., June 3, 1946; s. J. William and Genevieve E. (Gruly) M.; m. Linda K. Adams, Sept. 8, 1973; children: Chet W., Daniel T., Rheanna M. BA in Edn., U. Mont., 1971, MEd, 1976. Tchr. Lolo (Mont.) Sch. Dist. 7, 1971-74; tchr. Browning (Mont.) Sch. Dist. 9, 1974-78; prin. elem. sch. Heart Butte (Mont.) Sch. Dist. 1, 1978-79, supt., 1979-80; tchr. Frenchtown (Mont.) Sch. Dist. 40, 1980-96; ret., 1996. Medic fire fighter Frenchtown Vol. Fire Dept., 1982—. With USMC, 1965-71, Vietnam. Mem. Am. Fedn. Tchrs., Mont. Fedn. Tchrs. Avocations: hunting, fishing, sports, reading. Home: 6050 Mercer Ln Missoula MT 59802-8941

MERCER, DAVID ROBINSON, cultural organization administrator; b. Van Nuys, Calif., Aug. 14, 1938; s. Samuel Robinson and Dorothy (Lenox) M.; m. Joyce Elaine Dahl, Aug. 23, 1958; children: Steven, Michael, Kimberly. BA, Calif. State U., L.A., 1961. Exec. dir. YMCA of L.A., 1963-69, sr. v.p., 1969-80; reg. mgr. Am. City Bur., Hoffman Estates, Ill., 1980-82; pres. YMCA of San Francisco, 1982-90; nat. exec. dir. YMCA of USA, Chgo., 1990—; cons. fin. devel. YMCAs throughout U.S., 1975—. Mem. The Family, Rotary (bd. dirs. 1987-89). Republican. Methodist. Avocations: golf, bridge, flying, back packing. Office: YMCA of USA 101 N Wacker Dr Chicago IL 60606-1718

MERCER, DOUGLAS, lawyer; b. Sharon, Mass., Feb. 16, 1918; m. Pauline Loring Tobey, 4 children. AB, Harvard U., 1940, LLB, 1947. Bar: Mass. 1947. Ptnr. Ropes & Gray, Boston, 1957-90, of counsel, 1991—; moderator, panelist various Am. Law Inst.-ABA and other investment co. seminars. Former mem. and chmn. Planning Bd., Town of Weston, Mass., also former selectman, former mem. fin. com.; former trustee, treas. Social Law Library; chmn. Harvard Coll. Fund, 1975-77; chmn. Boston area Harvard Campaign for $350 Million; former mem. overseers resources com. Harvard U.; former trustee Groton Sch.; mem. corp. Belmont Hill Sch. Served to lt. comdr. USN, 1942-46, PTO. Mem. ABA, Boston Bar Assn. Clubs: The Country. Office: Ropes & Gray 1 Internat Pl Boston MA 02110-2624

MERCER, EDWIN WAYNE, lawyer; b. Kingsport, Tenn., July 19, 1940; s. Ernest LaFayette and Geneva (Frye) M. BBA, Tex. Tech U., 1963; JD, S. Tex. Coll. Law, 1971. Bar: Tex. 1971, U.S. Dist. Ct. (no. dist.) Tex 1975, U.S. Supreme Ct. 1976, U.S. Ct. Appeals (5th Cir.) 1979. Pvt. practice law Houston, 1971-73; gen. counsel, corp. sec. Alcon Labs., Inc., Ft. Worth, 1973-81; ptnr. Gandy Michener Swindle Whitaker Pratt & Mercer, Ft. Worth, 1981-84; v.p., gen. counsel, corp. sec. Pengo Industries, Inc., Ft. Worth, 1984-90, also bd. dirs. Bd. dirs. Soc. for Prevention Blindness, 1979—. Mem. ABA, State Bar Tex., Houston Bar Assn., Ft. Worth-Tarrant County Bar Assn., Coll. State Bar Tex., South Tex. Coll. Law Alumni Assn., Tex. Tech U. Ex-Assn., Ft. Worth Club, Delta Theta Phi, Phi Delta Theta. Methodist.

MERCER, LEE WILLIAM, lawyer, corporate executive, former government agency administrator; b. East Orange, N.J., July 16, 1943; m. Deborah Clare Robottom, Sept. 11, 1965 (div. Mar. 1980); children: James W., Charles A.; m. Deborah Anne O'Brien, Sept. 20, 1986; 1 child, Garrett W. BA, Dartmouth Coll., 1965; JD, Boston U., 1971, LLM in Tax, 1974. Ptnr. Sheehan, Phinney, Bass & Green, Manchester, N.H., 1971-80; counsel, legis. dir. U.S. Sen. Warren Rudman, Washington, 1981-84; v.p. The 1st Phillips Corp., Acton, Mass., 1985; dep. under sec. U.S. Dept. Commerce, Washington, 1986-90; export mgr. Digital Equipment Corp., Washington, 1990-94; pres. U.S. Fiber Optics & Telecomms. Corp., 1994-95, Baraka Art & Frame Co., 1995-96, Nat. Assn. Small Bus. Investment Cos., 1996—. Served to cpl. USMC, 1966-68. Mem. N.H. Bar Assn. Republican. Office: NASBIC 666 11th St NW Washington DC 20001-4542

MERCER, LEONARD PRESTON, II, biochemistry educator; b. Ft. Worth, 1941; s. Leonard Preston and Margie (Miller) M.; m. Diane Cottingham, 1963; children: Cindy Louise, Timothy Clayton, Megan Hope. BS in Chemistry, U. Tex., 1968; PhD in Biochemistry, La. State U., 1971. NIH postdoctoral fellow U. Ala., Birmingham, 1971-73; instr. U. South Ala., Mobile, 1973-74, asst. prof., 1974-77; asst. prof. Oral Roberts U. Sch. Medicine, Tulsa, 1977-80, assoc. prof., 1980-84, prof., chmn. dept., 1984-90, assoc. dean biomed. scis., 1989-90; prof., chmn. dept. nutrition and food sci. U. Ky., Lexington, 1990—; cons. in math. modeling phys. responses and neurochemistry of appetite control; prof. sci. and sustainable devel. UN/Third World Acad. Scis. Contbr. articles to profl. jours., chapters in books. Fellow Am. Coll. Nutrition; mem. Am. Inst. Nutrition, Am. Chem. Soc., Am. Soc. for Biochemistry, Soc. Math. Biology. Avocations: reading, computer programming. Home: 4633 Spring Creek Dr Lexington KY 40515-1506 Office: U Ky 204 Funkhouser Bldg Lexington KY 40506-0054

MERCER, MARGARET TEELE, medical and film industry marketing executive; b. Bronxville, N.Y., Sept. 10, 1962; d. William Earl Jr. and Judith (Forster) M.; m. Robert Mitchell Fromcheck, May 23, 1993. BS, U. Colo., 1985. Assoc. product mgr. Prescription Products divsn. Fisons Pharms., Denver, 1988-92; mktg. mgr. HealthScan Products, Cedar Grove, N.J., 1992-93; account exec. Sandler Comm., N.Y.C., 1993-94; mktg. dir. Proctor Cos., Littleton, Colo., 1995—. Youth leader Calvary Ch., Denver, 1988-91. Mem. NAFE, Healthcare Bus. Assn. Avocations: athletics, travel, reading. Home: 2 Rose Clover Littleton CO 80127-2220

MERCER, RICHARD JOSEPH, retired advertising executive, freelance writer; b. Elizabeth, N.J., Mar. 29, 1924; s. George Washington and Margaret Elizabeth (Walsh) M.; m. Muriel Davis, June 24, 1945; children: Richard George, Karen, James Davis, Lesley Ann. L.B. in Journalism, Rutgers U., 1949. Announcer, copywriter, news reporter Sta. WCTC, New Brunswick, N.J., 1946-49; asso. creative dir., then v.p., dir. BBDO, Inc., N.Y.C., 1949-76; sr. v.p., creative exec. SSC&B, Inc., N.Y.C., 1977-83, exec. v.p. creative, 1983-85; sr. v.p., assoc. creative dir. McCann-Erickson, Inc., N.Y.C., 1985-87; part-time lectr. Rutgers U. Sch. Bus., New Brunswick, N.J., 1988-89; speaker in field. Chmn. Roselle (N.J.) Police Raise Referendum Com., 1958; promotion chmn. Cranford (N.J.) United Fund, 1960; publicity dir. Friends of Mendham (N.J.) Libr., 1974-75; bd. dirs. Friends of Nantucket Atheneum, 1991—; trustee Atheneum, 1993—, pres. 1996—. With A.C. USNR, 1943-45. Decorated Air medal.; Recipient 10 Clio awards, 2 Effie awards, also Silver Key award Advt. Writers Assn. N.Y.C. Mem. NATAS, Air Force Assn. (life), Col. Henry Rutgers Soc. Roman Catholic. Home: 24 Pleasant St Nantucket MA 02554-3374

MERCEREAU, JAMES EDGAR, physicist, educator; b. Sharon, Pa., Apr. 3, 1930; s. James T. and S. Francis (Festermaker) M.; m. Gabriella Lengyel, Dec. 23, 1967; children: James A., Michael D., Steven F. B.A., Pomona Coll., 1953, Sc.D. (hon.), 1968; M.S., U. Ill., 1954; Ph.D., Calif. Inst. Tech., 1959. Research physicist Hughes Research Lab., 1954-59; asst. prof. physics Calif. Inst. Tech., 1959-62, prof., 1969—; prin. scientist Ford Sci. Lab., 1962-65; mgr. Ford Cryogenic Labs., 1965-69; Dir. R.A.I. Corp.; Mem. adv. com. NASA; mem. Nat. Acad. Com. Adv. to Nat. Bur. Standards. Contbr. articles profl. jours. Named one of America's 10 Outstanding Young Men U.S. Jr. C. of C., 1965; recipient achievement award in physics Am. Acad. Achievement, 1966. Fellow Am. Phys. Soc. Patentee in field. Home: 24652 El Camino Capistrano Dana Point CA 92629-3012 Office: 1201 E California Blvd Pasadena CA 91125-0001

MERCHANT, DONALD JOSEPH, microbiologist; b. Biltmore, N.C., Sept. 7, 1921; s. Oscar Lowell and Bess Lee (Clark) M.; m. Marian Adelaide Yeager, May 31, 1943; children—Nancy Adele, Barry Scott, Karen Ruth. A.B., Berea Coll., 1942; M.S., U. Mich., 1947, Ph.D., 1950. Instr. U. Mich., 1948-51, asst. prof., 1951-58, asso. prof., 1958-64, prof., 1964-69; dir., scientist W. Alton Jones Cell Sci. Center, Tissue Culture Assn., Lake Placid, N.Y., 1969-72; prof. U. Vt., 1969-72; prof., chmn. dept. microbiology and immunology Eastern Va. Med. Sch., Norfolk, 1973-86, prof. emeritus, 1986—; dir. Tidewater Regional Cancer Network, 1974-88; cons. U.S. Army Biol. Lab., 1966-68; mem. sci. adv. bd. Found. for Research on the Nervous System, Boston, 1965-69, Masonic Med. Research Lab., Utica, N.Y., 1970-75; mem. Nat. Prostatic Cancer Task Force, Nat. Cancer Inst., 1972-79, 83-86. Author: (with others) Handbook of Cell and Organ Culture, 1960, 2d edit., 1964; Editor: (with J.V. Neel) Approaches to the Genetic Analysis of Mammalian Cells, 1962, Cell Cultures for Virus Vaccine Production, 1968, (with others) Biology of Connective Tissues Cells, 1962; Contbr. (with others) chpts. to books, articles to profl. jours. Served with U.S. Army, 1944-46. Mem. Am. Acad. Microbiology, Am. Soc. Microbiology (past pres. Mich. br.), Soc. Exptl. Biology and Medicine, Am. Soc. Cell Biology, Tissue Culture Assn. (pres. 1964-68), Va. Acad. Sci., N.Y. Acad. Sci., Assn. Community Cancer Centers, Brit. Soc. Cell Biology, Royal Soc. Medicine. Presbyterian. Home: Apt 622 3100 Shore Dr Virginia Beach VA 23451

MERCHANT, ISMAIL NOORMOHAMED, film producer and director; b. Bombay, Dec. 25, 1936; arrived in U.S., 1958; s. Noormohamed and Hazrabi (Memon) Rehman. BA, St. Xavier's Coll., Bombay, 1958; MBA, NYU, 1960. V.p. Merchant Ivory Prodns. Inc., N.Y.C., 1962—. Prodr.: (films) Creation of Woman, 1960, The Householder, 1963, Shakespeare Wallah, 1965, The Guru, 1969, Bombay Talkie, 1970, Adventures of a Brown Man in Search of Civilization, 1971, Savages, 1972, Mahtma and the Mad Boy, 1973, Autobiolgraphy of a Princess, 1975, The Wild Party, 1975, Sweet Sounds, 1976, Roseland, 1977, Hullabaloo Over Georgie and Bonnie's Pictures, 1978, The Europeans, 1979, The Five-Forty-Eight, 1979, Jane Austen in Manhattan, 1980, Quartet 1981, Heat and Dust, 1983, The Bostonians, 1984, A Room With A View, 1986, The Deceivers, 1988, Slaves of New York, 1988, Mr. and Mrs. Bridge, 1990, Howards End, 1992, The Remains of the Day, 1993, Jefferson in Paris, 1995; director: Helen, Queen of the Nautch Girls, 1973, The Courtesans of Bombay, 1982, In Custody, 1993, The Proprietor, 1996; author: Ismail Merchant's Indian Cuisine, 1986, The Making of the Deceivers, 1988, Ismail Merchant's Vegetarian Cuisine, 1991, Ismail Merchant's Florence, 1993, Ismail Merchant's Passionate Meals: The New Indian Cuisine for Fearless Cooks and Adventurous Eaters, 1994, Once Upon A Time...The Proprietor, 1996, Commandeur des Arts et Lettres, 1996. Home: 400 E 52nd St New York NY 10022-6404 Office: 250 W 57th St Ste 1913A New York NY 10107-1999

MERCHANT, MYLON EUGENE, physicist, engineer; b. Springfield, Mass., May 6, 1913; s. Mylon Dickson and Rebecca Chase (Currier) M.; m. Helen Silver Bennett, Aug. 4, 1937; children: Mylon David (dec.), Leslie Ann Merchant Alexander, Frances Sue Merchant Jacobson. B.S. magna cum laude, U. Vt., 1936, D.Sc. (hon.), 1973; D.Sc., U. Cinn., 1941; D.Sc. (hon.), U. Salford, Eng., 1980; D of Engring (hon.), GMI Engring. and Mgmt. Inst., 1994. Research physicist Cinn. Milacron, Inc., 1940-48, sr. research physicist, 1948-51, asst. dir. research, 1951-57, dir. phys. research, 1957-63, dir. sci. research, 1963-69, dir. research planning, 1969-81, prin. scientist, mfg. research, 1981-83; dir. advanced mfg. research Metcut Research Assocs., Inc., 1983-90; sr. cons. Inst. Advanced Mfg. Scis., Cinn., 1990—; adj. prof. mech. engring. U. Cin., 1964-69; vis. prof. mech. engring. U. Salford, Eng., 1973—; hon. prof. U. Hong Kong, 1995—. Bd. dirs. Dan Beard council Boy Scouts Am., 1967-80, pres.'s council, 1980—. Recipient Georg Schlesinger prize City of Berlin, 1980; Otto Benedikt prize Hungarian Acad. Scis., 1981; ; named to Automation Hall of Fame, 1995. Fellow Soc. Tribologists and Lubrication Engrs. (pres. 1952-53), Am. Soc. Metals Internat., Ohio Acad. Sci., Soc. Mfg. Engrs. (hon. mem., pres. 1976-77); mem. NAE, ASME (hon.), Internat. Instn. Prodn. Engring. Rsch. (hon., pres. 1968-69), Engrs. and Scientists of Cin. (pres. 1961-62), Fedn. Materials Socs. (pres. 1974), Phi Beta Kappa, Sigma Xi, Tau Beta Pi. Achievements include research on systems approach to manufacturing. Home: 3939 Erie Ave Apt 105 Cincinnati OH 45208-1913 Office: Inst of Advanced Mfg Scis 1111 Edison Dr Cincinnati OH 45216-2265

MERCHANT, ROLAND SAMUEL, SR., hospital administrator, educator; b. N.Y.C., Apr. 18, 1929; s. Samuel and Eleta (McLymont) M.; m. Audrey Bartley, June 6, 1970; children: Orelia Eleta, Roland Samuel, Huey Bartley. BA, NYU, 1957, MA, 1960; MS, Columbia U., 1963, MSHA, 1974. Asst. statistician N.Y.C. Dept. Health, 1957-60, statistician, 1960-63; statistician N.Y. Tb and Health Assn., N.Y.C., 1963-65; biostatistician, adminstrv. coord. Inst. Surg. Studies, Montefiore Hosp., Bronx, N.Y., 1965-72; resident in adminstrn. Roosevelt Hosp., N.Y.C., 1973-74; dir. health and hosp. mgmt. Dept. Health, City of N.Y., 1974-76; from asst. adminstr. to adminstr. West Adams Cmty. Hosp., L.A., 1976; spl. asst. to assoc. v.p. for med. affairs Stanford U. Hosp., Calif., 1977-82, dir. office mgmt. and strategic planning, 1982-85, dir. mgmt. planning, 1986-90; v.p. strategic planning Cedars-Sinai Med. Ctr., L.A., 1990-94; cons. Roland Merchant & Assocs., L.A., 1994—; clin. assoc. prof. dept. family, community and preventive medicine Stanford U., 1986-88, dept. health rsch. and policy Stanford U. Med. Sch., 1988-90. With U.S. Army. 1951-53. USPHS fellow. Fellow Am. Coll. Healthcare Execs., APHA; mem. Am. Hosp. Assn., Nat. Assn. Health Svcs. Execs., N.Y. Acad. Scis. Home: 27335 Park Vista Rd Agoura Hills CA 91301-3639 Office: Roland Merchant & Assocs 27335 Park Vista Rd Agoura Hills CA 91301-3639

MERCIECA, CHARLES, history, philosophy and political science educator; b. Hamrun, Malta, Feb. 3, 1933; came to U.S. 1961; s. Carmelo and Julia (Brincat) M.; m. Sherry Jean Watson, May 15, 1950; children: Juliette, Alexander. BA in English, Loyola U., Malta, 1955; BA Philosophy, Aloisianum Coll., Varese, Italy, 1958; MS in Mgmt., Kans. State U., 1964; PhD in Philosophy and Hist. Founds., U. Kans., 1966. Prof. history, philosophy and polit. sci. Ala. A&M U., Normal, 1967—; supr. Ala. A&M U., 1969-75, asst. to pres., 1987-91, dir. Inst. for Internat. Rels., 1988—; exec. v.p. Internat. Assn. of Educators for World Peace, Huntsville, Ala.; cons. UN, N.Y.C., 1973—, UNESCO, Paris, 1973—, Drug Rehab. prog., Montgomery, Ala., 1988—; Assoc. in Edn. prof. Harvard U., 1984-85; vis. prof. Tver State U., Russia, 1992-93, U. Santa Ana, El Salvador, spring 1990. Author: Mismanagement in Higher Education, 1986 (citation 1987), Iscariots of Killversity, 1987 (citation 1988), Teaching Methods: On Making Classroom Instruction More Effective and Relevant, 1990, Education for Peace: What It Entails, 1991, Administrative Skills and the Development of the Human Potential, 1992, Buddhist Spirituality: An Asset to Christianity, 1993, Perspective of Yeltsin's Russia: Problems and Challenges, 1994, A Malignant Tumor Develops on the United States Constitution, 1995, World Peace and Spirituality of the Third Millennium, 1996, Crucial Political Issues Facing the World: Is the U.S. Capable of Providing Political Leadership to Bring about a Permanent World Peace in the 21st Century?, 1997. Recipient Ky. Col., 1983; Grand Cross of Honor & Merit, Federal Republic Germany, 1990; Albert Schweitzer Peace award, 1992. Mem. AAUP, NEA, Internat. Parliament for Safety and Peace (fed. magistrate 1987—), Internat. Assn. Educators for World Peace (sec.-gen. 1970-78, exec. v.p. 1978—), World Constn. and Parliament Assn. (trustee mem.). Office: Internat Assn Educators World Peace PO Box 3282 Huntsville AL 35810-0282

MERCIER, EILEEN ANN, management consultant; b. Toronto, Ont., Can., July 7, 1947; d. Thomas Sidley and Frances Katherine (Boone) Falconer; m. Ernest Cochrane Mercier, Jan. 29, 1980; children: Jenny, Sheelagh, Peter, Michael, Stuart. BA with honors, Waterloo Luth. U., 1968; MA, U. Alta., Can., 1969; fellow, Instn. Can. Bankers, 1975; MBA, York U., 1977. Mgr. corp. fin. Toronto-Dominion Bank, 1972-78, portfolio mgr. TD capital; dir., U.S. comm. ops. Canwest Capital Corp., Toronto, 1978-81; mgr. fin. strategy & planning Gulf Can. Ltd., Toronto, 1981-86, mgr. corp. fin.; v.p. The Pagurian Corp., Toronto, 1986-87; v.p., treas. Abitibi-Price, Inc., Toronto, 1987-88, v.p. corp. devel., 1989-90, sr. v.p., CFO, 1990-95; bd. dirs. C.I. Covington Fund, Inc., Reko Internat. Group Inc., Journey's End Corp., The CGI Group Inc., Winpak Ltd., Ing Trust Co. Can., Jannock Ltd. Bd. dirs. Workers' Compensation Bd. Ont., Toronto Hosp. Found.; past chmn., mem. bd. govs. Wilfrid Laurier U., Waterloo, Ont. Recipient Outstanding Bus. Leader award Sch. Bus. and Econs., Wilfrid Laurier U., 1991, Award for Outstanding Contbn. Schulich Sch. of Bus. York U., 1997. Office: Finvoy Mgmt Inc, 77 Strathallan Blvd, Toronto, ON Canada M5N 1S8

MERCIER, FRANCOIS, lawyer; b. Paris, France, Apr. 13, 1923; s. Oscar and Jeanne (Bruneau) M.; m. Lucile Rouleau, May 25, 1946; children—Genevieve, Madeleine, Jean Francois, Helene. B.A., Loyola Coll., Montreal, Que., Can., 1942; LL.B., U. Montreal, 1945. Bar: Called to bar Que 1945. Since practiced in Montreal; sr. partner Stikeman, Elliott and predecessors, 1964—; lectr. ins. law U. Montreal, 1945-58. Pres. La Librairie Fernand Nathan Can. Ltée.; vice chmn. Société des Hôtels Méridien Can., Ltée. Decorated officer Order of Can. Fellow Am. Coll. Trial Lawyers; mem. Can. bar assns., Montreal bar assns. Home: One Spring Grove Crescent, Outremont, PQ Canada H2V 3H8 Office: Stikeman Elliott, 1155 Dorchester St, Montreal, PQ Canada

MERCORELLA, ANTHONY J., lawyer, former state supreme court justice; b. N.Y.C., Mar. 6, 1927; s. Sante and Josephine (Bozzuti) M.; m. Maria G. Delucia, June 16, 1956; children: Anne Mercorella Flynn, Susan Mercorella Creavin, Robert, Carole. B.A., L.I. U., 1949; LL.D., Fordham U., 1952. Bar: N.Y. Law asst. City Ct., City of N.Y., 1955-62; chief law asst. Civil Ct. City of N.Y., 1962-65; mem. N.Y. State Assembly, 1965-72; councilman City N.Y., 1973-75; judge Civil Ct. City of N.Y., 1975-79; justice Supreme Ct., N.Y.C., 1980-84; ptnr. Wilson, Elser, Moskowitz, Edelman & Dicker, N.Y.C., 1984—; currently arbitrator and mediator in various dispute resolution systems. Served with USN, 1945-46, Europe, Pacific. Mem. ABA (del. N.Y. State Bar Assn.), N.Y. State Bar Assn., Assn. of Bar of City of N.Y., Bronx County Bar Assn. (pres. 1971), Columbian Lawyers Westchester County (pres. 1984). Office: Wilson Elser Moskowitz Edelman & Dicker 150 E 42nd St New York NY 10017-5612

MERCOUN, DAWN DENISE, human resources executive; b. Passaic, N.J., June 1, 1950; d. William S. and Irene F. (Micci) M. BS in Bus. Mgmt., Fairleigh Dickinson U., 1978. Personnel payroll coordinator Bentex Mills, Inc., East Rutherford, N.J., 1969-72; employment mgr. Inwood Knitting Mills, Clifton, N.J., 1972-75; gen. mgr. Consol. Advance, Inc., Passaic, 1975-76; v.p. human resources Gemini Industries, Inc., Clifton, 1976-96; CEO, sr. human resource cons. DDM Cons. L.L.C., Bloomingdale, N.J., 1996—; v.p., bd. dirs. Contact Morris-Passaic. Mem. Soc. for Human Resource Mgmt., Am. Compensation Assn., Internat. Found. Employee Benefits, Earthwatch Rsch. Team, IMA Mgmt. Assn. (bd. dirs., trustee 1996-97), Daus. of the Nile (Maalas Temple No. 20, elective officer 1993-96, queen 1996-97). Republican.

MERCURIO, RENARD MICHAEL, real estate corporation executive; b. N.Y.C., June 22, 1947; s. Pasquale J. and Ann F. Mercurio; m. Abbie Gonzalez, June 29, 1968; children—Kristin, Allison. B.A., Queens Coll., N.Y.C., 1968; M.B.A., U. Rochester, 1969. CPA, N.Y.; lic. real estate broker, Calif. Sr. accountant Peat, Marwick & Mitchell, N.Y.C., 1969-73; mgr. Gulf & Western Industries, Inc., N.Y.C., 1973-78; v.p., treas. Famous Players Ltd., Toronto, Ont., Can., 1978-81; exec. v.p. Famous Players Realty Ltd., Toronto, 1981-84; v.p. Design Twenty-Seven Ltd., Toronto, 1984-87; pres. Renric Holdings, Ltd., 1987—; craniosacral therapist Upledger Inst., 1995—. Mem. AICPA, N.Y. State Soc. CPAs, Calif. Assn. Mortgage Brokers, Calif. Assn. Realtors.

MERDEK, ANDREW AUSTIN, publishing/media executive, lawyer; b. Portland, Maine, Oct. 11, 1950; s. Philip and Eleanor (Weiss) M.; m. Jeanne Mullen, July 22, 1983; children: David, Jonathan. AB, Middlebury Coll., 1972; JD, U. Va., 1978. Bar: D.C. 1978, U.S. Dist. Ct. D.C. 1979, U.S. Ct. Appeals (D.C. cir.) 1979, U.S. Supreme Ct. 1982. Reporter, editor Portland Press Herald, 1973-75; assoc. Dow, Lohnes & Albertson, Washington, 1978-86, ptnr., 1986-87; v.p., gen. mgr. Atlanta Constitution and Journal, 1987-92; v.p. legal affairs, corp. sec. Cox Enterprises, Inc., Atlanta, 1993—. Mem. Order of Coif, Phi Beta Kappa. Home: 445 Mount Vernon Hwy NW Atlanta GA 30327-4313 Office: Cox Enterprises Inc 1400 Lake Hearn Dr NE Atlanta GA 30319-1464

MERDINGER, CHARLES JOHN, civil engineer, naval officer, academic administrator; b. Chgo., Apr. 20, 1918; s. Walter F. and Catherine (Phelan) M.; m. Mary McKelleget, Oct. 21, 1944; children: Anne, Joan, Susan, Jane. Student, Marquette U., 1935-37; BS, U.S. Naval Acad., 1941; BCE, Rensselaer Poly. Inst., 1945, MCE, 1946; DPhil (Rhodes scholar), Brasenose Coll., Oxford U., Eng., 1949; LHD (hon.), Sierra Nev. Coll., 1987; DLitt (hon.), U. Nev., Reno, 1994. Registered profl. engr., Wis. Commd. ensign U.S. Navy, 1941, advanced through grades to capt. Civil Engr. Corps, 1959; served aboard USS Nevada, USS Alabama Atlantic and Pacific, 1941-44; design, constrn. pub. works Panama, 1946-47, Washington, Bremerton, Wash., Adak, Alaska and Miramar, Calif., 1949-56; comdg. officer, dir. U.S. Naval Civil Engring. Lab., Port Hueneme, Calif., 1956-59; pub. works officer U.S. Fleet activities, Yokosuka, Japan, 1959-62; head English, history and govt. dept. U.S. Naval Acad., Annapolis, Md., 1962-65; asst. comdr. ops. & maintenance Naval Facilities Engring. Command, Navy Dept., 1965-67; pub. works officer Seabees (NSA), DaNang, Vietnam, 1967-68; comdg. officer Western div. Naval Facilities Engring. Command, San Bruno, Calif., 1968-70; pres. Washington Coll., Chestertown, Md., 1970-73; v.p. Aspen (Colo.) Inst. Humanistic Studies, 1973-74; dep. dir. Scripps Instn. Oceanography, La Jolla, Calif., 1974-80; dir. Avco, 1978—. Author: Civil Engineering Through the Ages, 1963; contbr.: articles to Ency. Britannica; others. Mem. Md., Calif., Oreg. and Nev. Selection Coms. for Rhodes Scholars, sec. Nev. Com., 1980-89; exec. vol. Boy Scouts Am.; sec., mem. exec. com. Md. Ind. Coll. and Univ. Assn., 1971-72; mem. So. Regional Edn. Bd, 1971-73, Nat. Com. History and Heritage of Am. Civil Engring., 1965-72; Alumni trustee U.S. Naval Acad., 1971-74; mem. coun. Rensselaer Poly. Inst., 1972—; trustee Found. for Ocean Rsch., 1976-80, Desert Rsch. Inst. Found., Nev., 1983-92, U. Nev. Reno Found., 1986-93; chmn. bd. trustees Sierra Nev. Coll., 1980-87, chmn. bd. emeritus, 1987; commr. N.W. Assn. Commn. on Colls., 1988-93. With Wis. Nat. Guard, 1935-37. Decorated Legion of Merit with combat V; named All-Am. in lacrosse, 1945, Papal Knight Grand Cross Equestrian Order of Holy Sepulchre of Jerusalem, 1992; inducted into Rensselaer Athletic Hall of Fame, 1983; recipient Disting. Eagle Scout award, 1984. Fellow ASCE (Nat. History and Heritage award 1972), Explorers Club, Soc. Am. Mil. Engrs. (Toulmin medal 1952, 57, 61); mem. NSPE, Soc. History Tech., Am. Soc. Engring. Edn., Brasenose Soc., Pearl Harbor Survivors Assn., Nat. Eagle Scout Assn. (regent), Phalanx, Sigma Xi, Tau Beta Pi, Chi Epsilon. Roman Catholic. Clubs: Vincent's, Oxford. Home: 726 Tyner Way PO Box 7249 Incline Village NV 89452 also: 5538 Caminito Consuelo La Jolla CA 92037-7217

MERDINGER, EMANUEL, retired chemistry educator; b. Suczawa, Austria, Mar. 29, 1906; came to U.S., 1947; s. Josef and Rosa (Stanger) M.; m. Raidie Poole, Mar 23, 1953. M of Pharmacology and Pharmacy, German U., Prague, 1931; D of Pharmacy, Ferrara (Italy) State U., 1934, D of Chemistry, 1935, D of Natural Scis., 1939. Assoc. prof. Ferrara State U., 1936-38, 45-47; prof. Roosevelt U., Chgo., 1947-72; rsch. assoc. U. Chgo., 1954-56; Disting. Lectr. Loyola U. Med. Sch., Maywood, Ill., 1972-76; sr. chemist rsch. Chem. & Bacteriological Lab., Gainesville, Fla., 1976-77; researcher U.S. Agrl. Lab., Gainesville, 1977-82; disting. prof. Dept. Entomol. Biochem. and Lang. Dept. U. Fla., Gainesville, 1978-91, U. Fla., 1980—; NAS exch. scientist to Romania, Bulgaria and Germany, 1971, 74, personal amb. to Romania; pres. Ill. State Acad. Sci., 1972-73, hon. mem.; head biochemistry sect. Roosevelt U. Mem. Am. Chem. Soc. (emeritus), Soc. Med. Balkanique (hon.), Union de Socs. (hon.), Med. Rumania (hon.). Avocations: playing the violin, composing little songs. Home: 4908 NW 16th Pl Gainesville FL 32605-3412

MEREDITH, ALICE FOLEY, publisher, consultant; b. Roslindale, Mass., Jan. 1, 1941; d. Francis Gerard and Alice Elizabeth (Hayes) Foley; m. Ellis Edson Meredith; children: Candace Rodal, Scott Corcoran; stepchildren: Shane Meredith Snowdon, Scott Emery, Kent Williamson. Grad., Boston Sch. Bus. Edn., 1960. Exec. sec., adminstrv. asst. various firms, 1960-68; asst. to pres. Am. Apparel Mfrs. Assn., Arlington, Va., 1968-77; pres. ACS Assocs., Bethesda, Md., 1972—; pres., treas. Newsletters, Inc., Bethesda, 1986—, also bd. dirs.; pres., treas. Food Execs. Internat. Found., Bethesda, 1988—, also bd. dirs.; asst. treas. Am. Apparel Polit. Action Com., Fairfax, Va., 1973-78; dir. adminstrn., treas. Orgn. Mgmt., Inc., Washington, 1973—, also bd. dirs.; pres. Polit. Action, Inc., Fairfax, 1976-89; treas. Allied Realty Corp., Bethesda, 1978-85. Gen. mgr., treas. Apparel Polit. Edn. Com., Fairfax, 1976-78. Roman Catholic.

MEREDITH, DALE DEAN, civil engineering educator, consultant; b. Centralia, Ill., Mar. 24, 1940; s. Leslie Edward Meredith and Beulah Marie (McClelland) Nattier; m. Linda Jean Hutson, July 3, 1965; children: Sarah Elizabeth, Laura Jane. AA, Centralia Twp. Jr. Coll., 1961; BS, U. Ill., 1963, MS, 1964, PhD, 1968. Registered profl. engr., N.Y., Ill. Asst. prof. U. Ill., Urbana, 1968-73; assoc. prof. civil engring. SUNY, Buffalo, 1973-79, prof., 1979—; chmn. dept. civil engring., 1987-96. Co-author: Design and Planning Engineering Systems, 1973, 2d edit., 1985; also over 50 articles. Vice pres. Baptist Conv. N.Y., Syracuse, 1982-84, 94-95, chmn. exec. bd., 1987. Grantee U.S. Office Water Research and Tech., 1966-73, 75-78, U.S. Dept. Interior, 1968-79, U.S. Dept. Commerce, 1976-79, various pvt. cos., 1979—, N.Y. State Agys., 1980—. Fellow ASCE (chmn. exec. com. Water Resources Planning and Mgmt. div., 1988, editor jour. Water Resources Planning and Mgmt. 1982-84); mem. Am. Geophys. Union, Am. Soc. Engring. Edn., Am. Water Resources Assn. (editor Water Resources Bull. 1990-91), Internat. Assn. Water Resources. Office: SUNY Dept Civil Engring Buffalo NY 14260-4300

MEREDITH, DONALD LLOYD, librarian; b. Batesville, Miss., Sept. 11, 1941; s. Duward Lee and Julia Mae (Ferguson) M.; m. Evelyn Charlene Rickett, Aug. 15, 1964; Christopher Todd, Tracey Hope. BA, Harding U., 1964; MTh, Harding Grad. Sch., 1967; MS in Libr. Sci., U. N.C., 1968. Asst. libr. Harding Grad. Sch. Religion, Memphis, 1968-70, assoc. libr., 1970-83, libr., 1983—. Mem. Am. Theol. Libr. Assn., Tenn. Theol. Libr. Assn. (pres. 1981-82), Memphis Libr. Coun. (chmn. 1982-83, treas. 1994—). Home: 4897 Welchshire Ave Memphis TN 38117-5646 Office: Harding Grad Sch Libr 1000 Cherry Rd Memphis TN 38117-5424

MEREDITH, ELLIS EDSON, association and business executive; b. Mobile, Ala., Sept. 5, 1927; s. Charles Elmer and Eleanor Emery (Ellis) M.; m. Alice Foley; children: Shane Snowdon, Kent Williamson, Scott Emery; stepchildren: Scott Corcoran, Candace Rodal. AB, U. Chgo., 1948, George Washington U., 1950. Exec. dir. Allied Florists Assn. of Greater Washington, 1952-55; legis. dir. Am. Assn. Nurserymen, 1955-58; asst. mgr. assn. dept. C. of C. U.S., 1958-60; pres. Am. Apparel Mfrs. Assn., Arlington, Va., 1960-84; pres. Nat. Ctr. for Missing and Exploited Children, 1986-89, emeritus nat. dir., 1989—; chmn. bd. dirs., CEO Allied Realty Corp.; chmn. Newsletters Inc., Food Execs. Internat. Found., 1989—; chmn. Orgn. Mgmt., Inc.; bd. dirs. Phillips Van Heusen Corp., Internat. Apparel Fedn.; mem. adv. bd. Prodn. Group Internat. Fin. chmn. Md. Rep. Party, 1977-78; mem. bd. visitors Sch. Pub. Affairs, U. Md.; bd. dirs., chmn. U. Md. Found. Mem. Am. Soc. Assn. Execs. (chmn. 1980), Greater Washington Soc. Assn. Execs. (pres. 1965-66), Met. Club, Bethesda Country Club, Capitol Hill Club. Episcopalian.

MEREDITH, GEORGE (MARLOR), association executive, writer; b. Somerville, N.J., Apr. 21, 1923; s. Gilbert Judson and Dorothea (Pope) M.; m. Mary Elizabeth Heilker, June 9, 1945 (div. 1955); 1 child, Gilbert Judson III; m. Elizabeth Jean Moore, Nov. 15, 1955; 1 child, Scott Arthur. Student, Columbia U., 1940-41. Indsl. engring. writer Johns-Manville Corp., 1942-44; mng. editor Mast, 1944-47; editor Premium Practice, 1947-55; ptnr., editorial dir. Meredith Assocs., 1956-67, pres., 1967-88, chmn., 1989-91; pres. Meredith Rsch. Corp., 1962-74; mng. dir. Meredith & Henry, 1977-92, chmn., 1992—; exec. sec. Assn. Incentive Mktg., 1957-67, exec. dir., 1967-74, pub. rels. dir., 1972—; mng. dir. Eastman Editorial Rsch., 1979-87; exec. sec. Nat. Assn. Food Equipment Mfrs., 1957-59; exec. dir. Nat. Premium Mfrs. Reps., 1963-66; dir. Mktg. New Bur., Red Bank, N.J., 1973-92; exec. dir. Trading Stamp Inst. Am., Assn. Retail Mktg. Svcs., 1979-91, editorial dir., 1991—, pub. rels. dir., 1993-95; mng. dir., Mktg. Comms. Execs. Internat., 1981-85, exec. dir. N.Y. chpt. 1981-82. Author: Effective Merchandising with Premiums, 1962, Creative Application of Sales Incentive Plans, 1972, (film) The Caine Coil, 1973, Incentives in Marketing, 1977, Incentives in Marketing & Motivation, 1997; editor: Premiums in Marketing, 1971; exec. editor, rsch. dir. Incentive Marketing Facts, 1968-87; rsch. dir. Incentive Mag., 1988-92; editor, pub. Sales Motivation Letter, 1973-74; editor The Register, 1979-97, The Communicator, 1982-85, Creative Mktg. newsletter, 1989—; contbr. articles to profl. publs. Coord., moderator Premiums and Incentives Conf. NYU, 1972; pub. rels. dir. Soc. Incentive Travel Execs., 1974-79. Recipient Premium Man of Yr. award Nat. Premium Mfrs. Reps., 1973, Nat. Premium Sales Execs. Past Pres.'s award, 1966, Disting. Achievement award Premium Advt. Assn. Am., 1963. Mem. Overseas Press Club, Am. Soc. Assn. Execs., Incentive Fedn. (vice chmn. 1984-88, 89-95, chmn. 1988-89), Assn. Incentive Mktg., Premium Mktg. Club N.Y., Am. Humanist Assn., Lions. Home: 3 Caro Ct Red Bank NJ 07701-2315

MEREDITH, MERI HILL, reference librarian, educator; b. Riverside, Calif., May 30, 1943; d. William Beans and Marie Louise (Zantzinger) Hill; m. William Rinehardt Meredith, Mar. 17, 1970 (div.); children William Rinehardt III, Sarah Daingerfield Meredith. AB in French, George Washington U., Washington, 1967; MLS, Ind. U., 1980. Cataloger Ind. U., Bloomington, 1980-81; bus. libr. Cummins Engine Co., Columbus, Ind., 1981-88; pres. Info. and Comm. Rsch., Inc., Columbus, 1989-92; reference libr. Ohio State U. Bus. Libr., 1992—; bd. dirs. Sch. of Libr. and Info. Sci., Ind. U., Bloomington; pres., co-founder Ind. On-Line Users Group, Indpls. Mem. AAUP, Spl. Librs. Assn., Acad. Libr. Assn. of Ohio. Republican. Roman Catholic. Home: 1800 Lafayette Pl Apt A1 Columbus OH 43212-1609 Office: Ohio State U Bus Libr 110 Page Hall 1810 College Columbus OH 43210

MEREDITH, MICHAEL, science educator, researcher; b. London, Jan. 15, 1942; came to U.S., 1967; s. Philip George and Dorothy Mary M.; married. BSc with honors, U. Birmingham, England, 1963; PhD, U. Pa., 1974. Rsch. assoc. Rockefeller U., N.Y.C., 1975-77, Worcester Found. Exptl. Biology, Shrewsbury, Mass., 1977-81; rsch. assoc. Fla. State U., Tallahassee, 1981-84, asst. prof., 1984-88, co-dir. program in neurosci., 1986—, assoc. prof., 1988-93, prof., 1993—; cons. site visits, grant revs. NIH, Washington, grant proposals, peer revs. NSF, Washington. Contbr. articles to profl. jours., chpts. to books. Pre-Doctoral Rsch. fellow NIH, 1970-73, Post-Doctoral Rsch. fellow, 1978-80, Rsch. grantee NIH, 1982-85, 88-91, 90-94, 94—, NSF, 1984-87, 87-90. Mem. Soc. Neurosci. (pres. local chpt. 1991-92, 94-95, 97-98), Assn. Chemoreception Scis. (councillor 1981-83, chair membership 1986-88, program com. 1990-91, exec. chair 1996-97), N.Y. Acad. Scis. Office: Fla State U Dept Biol Sci Tallahassee FL 32306-4075

MEREDITH, OWEN NICHOLS, public relations executive, genealogist; b. Etowah, Tenn., Mar. 27, 1924; s. Owen Habner and Ora (Nichols) M.; m. Mary Virginia Wright, July 19, 1980. BA, U. Va., 1946; MA, Syracuse U., 1952. Sub-features editor Together mag.-Meth. Pub. House, Nashville and Chgo., 1953-57; pub. info. dir. Nashville-Davidson County ARC, 1957-70; exec. dir. Tenn. State Mus., Nashville, 1970-72; owner, mgr. Gazetteer Typesetters, Nashville, 1973-74; pub. relations dir. Tenn. ARC, Nashville, 1974-89; pvt. practice Nashville, 1989—. Author: The Parish Activities Handbook, 1996, (with R. McBride) The Hedden Family of North Georgia, 1957, The Nichols Family of North Georgia, 1960, (with Lee Seitz) A History of the American Red Cross in Nashville, Tennessee, 1982; editor: (with McBride and M. Rothrock) Eastin Morris' 1834 Tennessee Gazetteer, 2d edit., 1971; contbr. articles, photographs and book revs. to hist. jours. Mem. ARC Disaster Res., 1989—; vol. archivist Diocese of Nashville, 1992—. Mem. Pub. Rels. Soc. Am. (cert.), Tenn. Soc. Health Care Pub. Rels., Internat. Assn. Bus. Communicators, Confederate Meml. Lit. Soc. (Tenn regent 1972-80), Tenn. Exec. Residence Preservation Found., 1971—), Conf. for Pastoral Planning and Coun. Devel. Office: 410 Lancaster Ave Nashville TN 37212-4013

MEREDITH, THOMAS C., academic administrator. Vice chancellor exec. affairs U. Miss., until 1988; pres. Western Ky. U., Bowling Green, 1988-97; chancellor U. Ala. Sys., Tuscaloosa, 1997—. Office: Univ Ala Sys 401 Queen City Ave Tuscaloosa AL 35401-1551

MERENBLOOM, ROBERT BARRY, hospital and medical school administrator; b. Balt., July 13, 1947; Philip William and Florence Ruth (Surosky) M.;. B.A., U. Md., 1969; M.S., Morgan State U., 1973; M.B.A., U. Balt., 1980. Mem. staff Mayor Balt. Office Manpower Resources, 1972-73; assoc. staff mem. Office Dean, U. Md. Med. Sch., 1976-80; adminstrv. officer rsch. and devel. Balt. VA Med. Ctr., 1974-80; assoc. adminstr. dept. medicine Sch. Medicine Johns Hopkins U., Balt., 1980-84, adminstr. dept. medicine Johns Hopkins Hosp., 1984-88, assoc. Sch. Hygiene and Pub. Health, 1984-88; lectr. dept. medicine Bowman Gray Sch. Medicine Wake Forest U., 1988-93, asst. chmn. dept. medicine, 1988-91, assoc. chmn. dept. medicine, 1991-93; vice chmn., asst. prof. medicine, clin. asst. prof. health adminstrn. & policy, asst. dean clin. ops. Med. U. S.C., Charleston, 1993—, asst. dean for clin. ops., 1993—; instr. sociology U. Balt., 1973-76; adj. faculty Weekend Coll., Coll. Notre Dame, Balt., 1980—; assoc. mgmt. Babcock Grad. Sch. Bus. Wake Forest U. Exec. dir. J. Paul Sticht Ctr. on Aging. Recipient Hon. Corpsmen Leader award Office Mayor Balt., 1973; Outstanding Performance award Balt. VA Med. Ctr., 1975, Superior Performance award, 1980. Mem. Am. Gerontology Soc., So. Gerontology Soc., Soc. Rsch. Adminstrs., Nat. Coun. Univ. Rsch. Adminstrs., Adminstrs. Internal Medicine, Assn. Am. Med. Colls. (group on bus. affairs), Am. Hosp. Assn., Am. Pub. Health Assn., Am. Coll. Healthcare Adminstrs., Soc. Gen. Internal Medicine, Johns Hopkins Club, Piedmont Club, Harbour Club.

MERENDINO, K. ALVIN, surgical educator; b. Clarksburg, W.Va., Dec. 3, 1914; s. Biagio and Cira (Bivona) M.; m. Shirley Emojane Hill, July 6, 1943; children: Cira Anne Watts, Nancy Jane Napuunoa, Susan Hill Mitchell, Nina Merendino-Sarich, Maria King Merendino-Stillwell. BA, Ohio U., 1936, LLD (hon.), 1967; MD, Yale U., 1940; PhD, U. Minn., 1946. Diplomate Am. Bd. Surgery, Am. Bd. Thoracic Surgery. Intern Cin. Gen. Hosp., 1940-41; resident U. Minn. Hosp., Mpls., 1941-45; rsch. asst. Dr. Owen H. Wangensteen, 1942-43; trainee Nat. Cancer Inst., 1943-45; dir. program in postgrad. med. edn. in surgery Ancker Hosp., St. Paul, 1946-48; instr. dept. surgery U. Minn., Mpls., 1944-45, asst. prof. dept. surgery, 1945-48; assoc. prof. dept. surgery U. Wash., Seattle, 1949-55, dir. exptl. surgery labs., dept. surgery, 1950-72, prof. dept. surgery, 1955-81, prof. emeritus, 1981—, prof. and adminstrv. officer dept. surgery, 1957-64, prof., chmn., 1965-72; chmn. dept. surgery King Faisal Specialist and Rsch. Ctgr., Riyadh, Saudi Arabia, 1976, dir. med. affairs, 1976-79, dir. Cancer Therapy Inst., spl. cons. to Coun., supr. for exec. mgmt., assoc. dir. med. affairs, 1981-82; dir. ops. King Faisal Med. City, Riyadh, 1981-85; mem. adv. com. for med. rsch., Boeing Airplane Co., 1959-67, chmn., 1962l cons. Children's Orthopedic Hosp., Seattle, 1972-82; mem. adv. com. on heart disease and surgery for crippled children's svc., Wash. State Dept. Health and Div. Vocational Rehab., 1961; mem. surgery study sect. NIH, 1958-62, subcom. on prosthetic valves for cardiac surgery, chm. 1st Nat. Conf., 1960, mem. adv. com. 2d Nat. Conf. on Prosthetic Heart Valves, 1969, Surgery A study sect. chmn., 1970-72, Nat. Heart and Lung Inst. Tng. Com., 1965-69; cons. VA, Seattle, 1949-59, 65-81; mem. adv. com. on hosps. and clinics, USPHS, 1963-66; mem. surgery test com. Nat. Bd. Med. Examiners, 1963-67; mem. surgery resident rev. com., Conf. Com. on Grad. Edn. in Surgery, 1963-73, vice-chmn., 1972-73; chmn. 2d Saudi Arabian Med. Conf., Riyadh, 1978; mem. com. on postgrad. med. edn., Kingdom of Saudi Arabia Ministry of Health, 1978-79. Editor in chief: Prosthetic Valves for Cardiac Surgery, 1961; assoc. editor: Prosthetic Heart Valves, 1969; mem. editorial bd. Am. Jour. Surgery,. 1958-83, Jour. Surg. Rsch., 1961-69, Pacific Medicine and Surgery, 1964-68, King Faisal Hosp. Medicine Jour. (renamed Annals of Saudi Medicine), 1981-85; contbr. articles to profl. jours., chpts. to books; producer movies on surgery. Recipient cert. of merit Ohio U. Alumni Assn., 1957, Outstanding W.Va. Italian-Am. award W.Va. Italian Heritage Festival Inc., Clarksburg, W.Va., 1984, Spirit of Freedom award A. James Mancin, Sec. State W.Va., 1984, Disting. W. Virginian award State of W.Va., 1984, John Baird Thomas Meml. award Ohio U.; named Surgery Alumnus of Yr., U. Minn., 1981, Disting. Citizen Wash. State, Lt. Gov. John Cherberg, 1981; NIH grantee, 1951-76. Fellow ACS (numerous coms., bds.), Soc. of Univ. Surgeons (councilman at large 3 yrs.), Internat. Soc. Surgery; mem. Am. Surg. Assn. (adv. mem. com. 1959-64, v.p. 1972-73), Am. Assn. for Thoracic Surgery, Halsted Soc., Henry N. Harkins Surg. Soc., N. Pacific Coast Surg. Assn., Seattle Surg. Soc. (honored special tribute annual meeting 1997), So. Surg. Soc. (Arthur H. Shipley award 1972), Am. Bd. Surgery 1958-64 (vice chmn. 1962-63, chmn. 1963-64, emeritus 1964—); University Club, Seattle Golf Club, Phi Beta Kappa, Sigma Xi, Beta Theta Pi (sec., pres.), Phi Beta Pi (hon.). Republican. Episcopalian. Avocations: golf, fly fishing, bird hunting, gardening. Home: The Highlands Seattle WA 98177 Office: U Wash Sch Med Dept Surgery Seattle WA 98195

MERGLER, H. KENT, investment counselor; b. Cin., July 1, 1940; s. Wilton Henry and Mildred Amelia (Pulliam) M.; m. Judith Anne Metzger, Aug. 17, 1963; children: Stephen Kent, Timothy Alan, Kristin Lee. BBA with honors, U. Cin., 1963, MBA, 1964. Chartered fin. analyst, chartered investment counselor. Portfolio mgr. Scudder, Stevens & Clark, Cin., 1964-68, exec. v.p., Chgo., 1970-73; v.p. Gibraltar Rsch. and Mgmt., Ft. Lauderdale, Fla., 1968-70; ptnr., pres., dir. and prin. Stein Roe & Farnham, Inc., Ft. Lauderdale, 1973-84, Chgo., 1984-91, also exec. com.; pres. Stein Roe Investment Trust; mng. ptnr. Loomis, Sayles & Co., L.P., Palm Beach Gardens, Fla., 1992—; bd. dirs. Gold Coast Mag., Inc., 1994—; arbitrator Nat. Assn. Security Dealers, Inc., 1976-82. Chmn. adminstrv. bd. Christ United Meth. Ch., Ft. Lauderdale, 1981-83; mem. fin. com. Kenilworth Union Ch., 1989-92, Broward Community Found. (Investment Com.), 1992—, chmn., 1994—, bd. dirs., 1995—, Martin County Econ. Coun., 1992—; bd. dirs. Pine Crest Prep. Sch., 1982-84, bd. advisors, 1984-87; mem. corp. adv. bd. U. Cin. Coll. Bus. Adminstrn., 1991-94; bd. dirs. Hibiscus House Children's Found., 1993—, chmn. inv. com. 1994—; bd. dirs. Coral Ridge Little League, 1976-84, pres., 1980-81. Mem. Fin. Analysts Soc. So. Fla. (bd. dirs. 1974-78, pres. 1975), Bond Club Ft. Lauderdale (dir. 1978-82), Highlands Country Club (N.C.), Cullasaja Club (Highlands, N.C.), Sailfish Point Yacht and Country Club (Stuart, Fla.), City Club of Palm Beach, Beta Theta Pi, Beta Gamma Sigma. Republican. Home: 7036 SE Harbor Cir Stuart FL 34996-1922 Office: 4400 PGA Blvd Ste 600 Palm Beach Gardens FL 33410

MERGLER, HARRY WINSTON, engineering educator; b. Chillicothe, Ohio, June 1, 1924; s. Harry Franklin and Letitia (Walburn) M.; m. Irmgard Erna Steudel, June 22, 1948; children—Myra A. L., Marcia B. E., Harry F. B.S., MIT, 1948; M.S., Case Inst. Tech., 1950, Ph.D., 1956. Aero. research scientist NACA, 1948-56; mem. faculty Case Inst. Tech., 1957—, prof. engring., 1962—, Leonard Case prof. elec. engring. emeritus, 1988—; dir. Digital Systems Lab., 1959—; vis. scientist, USSR, 1958; vis. prof. Norwegian Tech. U., 1962; cons. to industry, 1957—; editor Control Engring. mag., 1956—; pres. Digital/Gen. Corp., 1968-72; cons. Exploratory Research div. NSF. Author: Digital Systems Engineering, 1961, also articles, chpts. in books. Served with AUS, 1942-45. Recipient Case gold medal for sci. achievement Case Inst. Tech., 1980. Fellow IEEE (bd. dirs. 1987-89, v.p. 1989, Lamme medal 1978, Centennial medal 1984); mem. NAE, Indsl. Electronic Soc. (pres. 1977-79), Cleve. Engring. Soc., N.Y. Acad. Scis., Blue Key, Sigma Xi, Tau Beta Pi, Theta Tau, Pi Delta Epsilon, Zeta Psi. Home: 9658 Halyards Ct Fort Myers FL 33919-4455

MERHIGE, ROBERT REYNOLD, JR., federal judge; b. N.Y.C., Feb. 5, 1919; s. Robert Reynold and Eleanor (Donovan) M.; m. Shirley Galleher, Apr. 24, 1957; children: Robert Reynold III, Mark Reynold. LLB, U. Richmond, 1942, LLD (hon.), 1976; LLM, U. Va., 1982; LLD (hon.), Washington and Lee U., 1990, Wake Forest U., 1994. Bar: Va. 1942. Ptnr. Bremner Merhige Montgomery & Baber, Richmond, 1945-67; judge U.S. Dist. Ct., Richmond, 1967—; guest lectr. trial tactics Law Sch. U. Va., Ewald disting. prof. law, 1987-88; adj. prof. Law Sch. U. Richmond, 1973-

87; appeal agt. Henrico County Draft Bd., 1954-67; mem. NCAA spl. com. on discipline rules; profl.-in-residence, Zambia, Africa, 1994. Co-author: Virginia Jury Instructions. Mem. Richmond Citizens Assn. Served with USAAF, World War II. Decorated Air medal with four oak leaf clusters; recipient Amara Civic Club award, 1968, Spl. award City of Richmond, 1967; named Citizen of the Yr., 3d Dist. Omega Psi Phi, 1972, Citizen of the Yr., Richmond Urban League, 1977, Richmonder of Yr. Style mag., 1984, 87, Citizen of Yr., 1986; recipient Disting. Alumni award U. Richmond, 1979, Disting. Svc. award Nat. Alumni Coun., U. Richmond, 1979, Herbert T. Harley award Am. Judicature Soc., 1982, Athenian Citizen medal, 1979, Torch of Liberty award Anti-Defamation League of B'nai Brith, 1982, T.C. Williams Sch. of Law Disting. Svc. award, 1983, Pres.'s award Old Dominion Bar Assn., 1986, William J. Brennan award, 1986, Merit Citation award NCCJ, 1987, William B. Green award for professionalism U. Richmond, 1989, Marshall-Wythe medallion (William & Mary Faculty award), 1989. Fellow Va. Law Found.; mem. Va. Bar Assn., Richmond Bar Assn. (pres. 1963-64, multi-dist. litigation panel 1990—, Hill-Tucker award 1991), Am. Law Inst. (faculty), Va. Trial Lawyers Assn. (chmn. membership com. 1964-65, Disting. Svc. award 1977), Jud. Conf. U.S., John Marshall Inns of Ct. (founding mem.), Omicron Delta Kappa. Office: Lewis F Powell Jr 1000 E Main St Richmond VA 23219-3525

MERIANOS, JOHN JAMES, medicinal chemist; b. Krokeai Sparta Laconia, Greece, Feb. 12, 1937; came to the U.S., 1957; s. Demetrios Nicholaos and Eleni (Patrianakos) M.; m. Stavroula P. Doumas, Apr. 21, 1974; children: Laura, Helen, Demetri. BS in Pharmacy magna cum laude, New Eng. Coll. Pharmacy, 1961; MS in Pharm. Chemistry, U. Wis., 1963, PhD in Medicinal Chemistry, 1966. Registered pharmacist, N.J. Rsch. chemist FMC Corp., Princeton, N.J., 1966-68; rsch. scientist, sr. rsch. scientist Millmaster Onyx Corp., Jersey City, N.J., 1968-87; sr. rsch. scientist GAF Corp., Wayne, N.J., 1987-92; rsch. fellow ISP Corp., Wayne, 1992-95; dir. R & D Sutton Labs., Chatham, N.J., 1992—; sr. rsch. fellow ISP Internat. Specialty Products, Chatham, N.J., 1992—; exec. dir. MerPan Chem. Cons. Diagnostic Reagents, Pharmaceutics, Middletown, N.J., 1974—. Contbr. chpt. to book: Disinfection, Sterilization and Preservation, 4th edit., 1991. Pres. Krokeai Soc., U.S. and Can., 1990-95. Recipient Kappa Psi gold key Kappa Psi Fraternity, Boston, 1961. Mem. Am. Chem. Soc., Am. Assn. Pharm. Scientist, Soc. Cosmetic Chemists, Soc. Indsl. Microbiology, N.J. Pharm. Assn. Greek Orthodox. Achievements include 95 patents in indsl. biocides and synergisms in cosmetic preservatives; inventor of Onamer M, Polyquaternium-1 Polyquad TM a preservative system for contact lens cleaners. Avocations: volleyball, soccer, bowling. Home: 32 Doherty Dr Middletown NJ 07748-3303 Office: Sutton Labs/ISP Group Mem 116 Summit Ave Chatham NJ 07928-2727

MERICLE, SALLY DIANE, graphic artist; b. Balt., Nov. 11, 1952; d. Mervin William and Virginia Lee (Cruse) Mericle; m. Jonathan Steven Bor, June 3, 1984; 1 child, Benjamin Andrew. BFA summa cum laude, Bradley U., Peoria, Ill., 1978. Broadcast designer WMBD-TV, Peoria, 1978-80; promotion dir. Poughkeepsie (N.Y.) Jour., 1980-84; broadcast designer WSTM-TV, Syracuse, N.Y., 1984-85; freelance designer Balt., 1986-91; instr. graphic design Coll. of Notre Dame of Md., Balt., 1991—; owner/designer Mars Tokyo Rubber Stamps, Balt., 1991—; mem. panel presentation at UN's 4th World Conf. on Women, Women's Caucus for Art, Beijing, China, 1995. Author/designer (catalogs): Mars Tokyo Catalog #1, 1991, #2, 1994; artist of prints; solo shows include Chapman Art Ctr., Cazenovia (N.Y.) Coll., 1985; group exhbns. include Internat. Mail Art Exhibit on Theme of Justice, 1986, Everson Mus., Syracuse, N.Y., 1984, New Orleans World's Fair, 1984, AAO Gallery, Buffalo, 1983, The Print Club, Phila., 1983, Port of History Mus., Phila., 1983, CVAA Nat. Print and Drawing Show, LaGrange, Ga., 1981, Monmouth (Ill.) Coll., 1980, Lakeview Mus., Peoria, 1980, U. Wis., Platteville, 1980, 57th Shreveport (La.) Art Guild Nat., 1980, U. Kans., 1979, Ky. Watercolor Soc./Owensboro Art Mus., 1979, Evanston (Ill.) Art Ctr., 1979, West Hubbard St. Gallery, Chgo., 1978, 79, Springfield (Mo.) Art Mus., 1978, 79, Harry Nohr Gallery, Platteville, 1979, Bradley U., Peoria, 1979, Duryea Gallery, Peoria, 1978, Ill. Ctrl. Coll., 1977, Ill. State U., Normal, 1972. Corp. sponsor The House of Ruth, Balt., 1993—; participant Women-on-Line project, Global Internet, 1995; mem. Pyramid Atlantic Ctr. for Arts, 1992-95, Women's Caucus for Art, 1978-94. Recipient Purchase award 9th Nat. Print and dRawing Show, Minot, N.D., 1979, Best in Show, 7 State Art Invitational, Harry Nohr Gallery, Platteville, 1979, Purchase award Permanent Collection, U. Wis., Platteville, 1980, Patron Purchase award Watercolor U.S.A., Springfield, Mo., 1978, Patricia Lambert Harris award 57th Shreveport Art Guild Nat., 1980. Office: Mars Tokyo Rubber Stamp Co PO Box 65006 Baltimore MD 21209

MERIDEN, TERRY, physician; b. Damascus, Syria, Oct. 12, 1946; came to U.S., 1975; s. Izzat and Omayma (Aidi) M.; m. Lena Kahal, Nov. 17, 1975; children: Zina, Lana. BS, Sch. Sci., Damascus, 1968; MD, Sch. Medicine, Damascus, 1972, doctorate cum laude, 1973. Diplomate Am. Bd. Internal Medicine. Resident in infectious diseases Rush Green Hosp., Romford, Eng., 1973; house officer in internal medicine and cardiology Ashford (Eng.) Group Univ. Hosps., 1973-74; sr. house officer in internal medicine and neurology Grimsby (Eng.) Group Univ. Hosps., 1974; registrar in internal medicine and rheumatology St. Annes Hosp., London, 1974-75; jr. resident in internal medicine Shadyside Hosp., Pitts., 1975-76, sr. resident in internal medicine, 1976-77; fellow in endocrinology and metabolism Shadyside Hosp. and Grad. Inst., Pitts., 1976-77; clin. asst. prof. U. Ill., Peoria, 1979; pres. Am. Diabetes Assn., Peoria, 1982-84; dir. Proctor Diabetes Unit, Peoria, 1984—, 1984—; adviser to the Gov. of Ill. on Diabetes. Mem. editorial bd. Diabetes Forecast mag., Clin. Diabetes, 1990; contbr. articles to profl. jours. Fellow ACP, FACE, Am. Coll. Endocrinology; mem. AMA (Recognition award 1985, ADA (chmn. profl. edn. and rsch. 1980—, mem. editl. bd. and Spanish lit. bd. nat. bd. dirs. 1986—, vice chmn. nat. com. on diabetes edn. and affiliate svcs. 1986—, Outstanding Svc. award 1984, Outstanding Diabetes Educator award 1986), Am. Cancer Soc. (Life Line award 1983), Am. Assn. Clin. Endocrinology (founding), Am. Coll. Endocrinology, The Obesity Found. (Century award 1984, Recognition award 1985). Home: 115 E Coventry Ln Peoria IL 61614-2103 Office: 900 Main St Ste 300 Peoria IL 61602-1005

MERIGAN, THOMAS CHARLES, JR., physician, medical researcher, educator; b. San Francisco, Jan. 18, 1934; s. Thomas C. and Helen M. (Greeley) M.; m. Joan Mary Freeborn, Oct. 3, 1959; 1 son, Thomas Charles III. BA with honors, U. Calif., Berkeley, 1955; MD, U. Calif., San Francisco, 1958. Diplomate: Am. Bd. Internal Medicine. Intern in medicine 2d and 4th Harvard med. services Boston City Hosp., 1958-59, asst. resident medicine, 1959-60; clin. assoc. Nat. Heart Inst., NIH, Bethesda, Md., 1960-62; asso. Lab. Molecular Biology, Nat. Inst. Arthritis and Metabolic Diseases, NIH, 1962-63; practice medicine specializing in internal medicine and infectious diseases Stanford, Calif., 1963—; asst. prof. medicine Stanford U. Sch. Medicine, 1963-67, assoc. prof. medicine, 1967-72, head div. infectious diseases, 1966-92, prof. medicine, 1972—, George E. and Lucy Becker prof. medicine, 1980—; dir. Diagnostic Microbiology Lab., Univ. Hosp., 1966-72, Diagnostic Virology Lab., 1969—, Ctr. AIDS Rsch. Stanford U., 1988—; hosp. epidemiologist, 1966-88; mem. microbiology rsch. tng. grants com. NIH, 1969-73, virology study sect., 1974-78; cons. antiviral substances program Nat. Inst. Allergy and Infectious Diseases, 1970-94, mem. AIDS clin. drug devel. commn., 1986-94; mem. Virology Task Force, 1976-78, bd. sci. counselors, 1980-85; mem. U.S. Hepatitis panel U.S. and Japan Coop. Med. Sci. Program, 1979-90, AIDS subcom. Nat. Adv. Allergy and Infectious Diseases Coun., 1988-89; co-chmn. interferon evaluation Group Am. Cancer Soc., 1978-81; mem. vaccines and related biol. products adv. com. Ctr. for Drugs and Biols., FDA, 1984-88; mem. internat. adv. com. on biol. sci. Sci. Council, Singapore, 1985-88; mem. adv. com. J.A. Hartford Found., 1979-84; mem. Albert Lasker awards jury, 1981-84; mem. peer review panel U.S. Army Med. Rsch. and Devel. Com., 1986-88; nat. com. to rev. current procedures for approval New Drugs for Cancer and AIDS, 1989-90; mem. Com. to Study Use of Coms. within FDA, 1991-92. Contbr. numerous articles on infectious diseases, virology and immunology to sci. jours.; editor: Antivirals with Clinical Potential, 1976, Antivirals and Virus Diseases of Man, 1979, 2d edit., 1984, 3d edit., 1990, 4th edit., 1997, Regulatory Functions of Interferon, 1980, Interferons, 1982, Interferons as Cell Growth Inhibitors, 1986; assoc. editor: Virology, 1975-78, Cancer Research, 1987-91; co-editor: monograph series Current Topics in Infectious Diseases, 1975—, Cytomegloviras Infect and Ganciclovir, 1988, Focus on Didanosine (ddI), 1990, Practical Diagnosis of Viral Infection, Textbook of AIDS Medicine, 1994, Surrogate Markers for HIV Infection, 1995; editl. bd.: Archives Internal Medicine, 1971-81, Jour. Gen. Virology, 1972-77, Infection and Immunity, 1973-81, Intervirology, 1973-85, Proc. Soc. Expt. Biology and Medicine, 1978-87, Reviews of Infectious Diseases, 1979-89, Jour. Interferon Research, 1980-89, Antiviral Research, 1980-86, Jour. Antimicrobial Chemotherapy, 1981-91, Molecular and Cellular Biochemistry, 1982-89, AIDS Research and Human Retroviruses, 1983—, Jour. Virology, 1984-89, Biotechnology Therapeutics, 1988—, Jour. Infectious Diseases, 1989-94, Clinical Drug Investigation, 1989—, HIV: Advances in Research and Therapy, 1990—, Internat. Jour. Antimicrobial Agts. 1990—, The AIDS Reader, 1991—, AIDS, 1993, Clinical Immunotherapeutics, 1994—, Antiviral Therapy, 1996—. Recipient Borden award for Outstanding Rsch., Am. Assn. Med. Colls., 1973, Merit award, Nat. Inst. Allergy and Infectious Diseases, 1988, Maxwell Finland award Infectious Diseases Soc. Am., 1988; Guggenheim Meml. fellow, 1972. Fellow AAAS; mem. AMA, Assn. Am. Physicians, Western Assn. Physicians, Am. Soc. Microbiology, Am. Soc. Clin. Investigation (coun. 1977-80), Am. Assn. Immunologists, Am. Fedn. Clin. Rsch., Western Soc. Clin. Rsch., Soc. Exptl. Biology and Medicine (publ. com. 1985-89), Infectious Diseases Soc. Am., Am. Soc. Virology, inst. Medicine, Pan Am. Group for Rapid Viral Diagnosis, Internat. Soc. Interferon Rsch. (coun. 1983-89), Calif. Med. Assn., Santa Clara County Med. Soc., Calif. Acad. Medicine, Royal Soc. Medicine, Alpha Omega Alpha. Home: 148 Goya Rd Portola Valley CA 94028-7307 Office: Stanford U Sch Medicine Div Infectious Diseases Stanford CA 94305

MERILAN, JEAN ELIZABETH, statistics educator; b. Columbia, Mo., Sept. 18, 1962; d. Charles Preston and Phyllis Pauline (Laughlin) M. PhD in Statistics, U. Ariz., 1996; AB summa cum laude, U. Mo., 1985, MA in Math., MA in Stats., 1987; PhD in Stats., U. Ariz., 1996. Grad. teaching asst. U. Mo., Columbia, 1985-87; grad. rsch. asst. U. Ariz., Tucson, 1988-89, grad. tchg. asst., 1989-93. Nat. Merit scholar, Univ. Curators scholar U. Mo., 1981-85, Grad. Acad. scholar U. Ariz., 1990-91, Arts and Sci. Grad. scholar U. Mo., 1985-87; Gregory fellow U. Mo., 1985-87, Faculty of Sci. fellow U. Ariz., 1987-88. Mem. Am. Statis. Assn., Inst. Math. Stats., Soc. for Indsl. and Applied Math., Biometric Soc., Am. Math. Soc., Math. Assn. Am., Golden Key Nat. Honor Soc., Sigma Xi, Phi Beta Kappa, Phi Kappa Phi, Phi Eta Sigma, Pi Mu Epsilon.

MERILAN, MICHAEL PRESTON, astrophysicist, dean, educator; b. Columbia, Mo., Jan. 5, 1956; s. Charles Preston and Phyllis Pauline (Laughlin) M.; m. Karene Anne Yanuklis, Sept. 2, 1995. BS summa cum laude in Physics, U. Mo., Columbia, 1978, MS, 1980; PhD in Astronomy, Ohio State U., 1985. Grad. tchg. asst. U. Mo., Columbia, 1978-80; grad. tchg. assoc., instr. dept. astronomy Ohio State U., Columbus, 1980-85; asst. prof. dept. physics and astronomy SUNY, Oneonta, 1985-91, assoc. prof., 1991—, chmn. dept. physics and astronomy, 1990-93, acting dean divsn. sci. and social sci., 1993-96, dean, 1996—; astron. cons. Ohio Dept. Natural Resources, 1982-83; Oneonta smart node advisor Cornell Nat. Supercomputer Facility, Oneonta, 1987-92. Contbr. articles to profl. jours. O.M. Stewart fellow U. Mo., 1979; U. Mo. Curators scholar, 1974-78; Mahan Writing award U. Mo., 1975. Mem. AAAS, IAPPP, Am. Astron. Soc., Astron. Soc. Pacific, Sigma Xi, Phi Eta Sigma, Phi Kappa Phi, Phi Beta Kappa, Pi Mu Epsilon, Sigma Pi Sigma, Omicron Delta Kappa. Achievements include analytic and numeric investigation of protostellar hydrodynamics; determination of the properties of static and slowly rotating partially degenerate semirelativistic stellar structures. Office: Dean Sci and Social Sci SUNY-Oneonta 336 Netzer Bldg Oneonta NY 13820

MERIN, ROBERT GILLESPIE, anesthesiology educator; b. Glens Falls, N.Y., June 16, 1933; s. Joseph Harold and Jessie Louisa (Gillespie) M.; m. Barbara R. Rothe, Mar. 1, 1958; children: Michael, Jan, Sarah. BA, Swarthmore Coll., 1954; MD, Cornell U., 1958. Diplomate Nat. Bd. Med. Examiners, Am. Bd. Anesthesiology. From asst. prof. to prof. anesthesiology U. Rochester (N.Y.) Med. Ctr., 1966-81; prof. anesthesiology U. Tex. Health Sci. Ctr., Houston, 1981-92; prof anesthesiology Med. Coll. Ga., Augusta, 1992—; mem. anesthetic life support drug com. FDA, Washington, 1982-87, spl. cons., 1987—; Murray Mendolsohn Meml. lectr. U. Toronto Sch. Medicine, 1976, Harry M. Shields Meml. lectr., 1988; Litchfield lectr. Oxford U., 1977, William and Austin Friend Meml. vis. prof. Queens U., 1981, Joseph F. Artusio endowed lectr. Cornell U. Med. Coll., N.Y.C., 1991, and others. Editorial bd. Anesthesiology, 1977-86; contbr. articles to Anesthesiology, Jour. Pharmacology and Exptl. Therapeutics. Capt. U.S. Army, 1961-63. Recipient Rsch. Career Devel. award NIH, 1972-77. Mem. Assn. Univ. Anesthesiologists (pres. 1987-88), Am. Soc. Pharmacology and Exptl. Therapeutics. Achievements include pioneering work in demonstrating effects of anesthetics on myocardial perfusion and metabolism; cardioactive drug interactions with anesthetic drugs. Office: Med Coll Ga Dept Anesthesiology 1120 15th St Augusta GA 30912-0004

MERINI, RAFIKA, foreign language and literature and women's studies educator; b. Fès, Morocco; came to U.S., 1972; d. Mohamed and Fatima (Chraibi) M. BA in English cum laude, U. Utah, 1978, MA in Romance Langs. and Lits., 1981; postgrad., U. Wash., 1980-82; cert. in translation, SUNY, Binghamton, 1988, PhD in Comparative Lit., 1992. Tchg. asst. U. Utah, Salt Lake City, 1978-80, U. Wash., Seattle, 1980-82; adminstrv. asst., tchr. French, interpreter The Lang. Sch., Seattle, 1982-83; lectr. Pacific Luth. U., Tacoma, Wash., 1983; instr. Ft. Steilacoom C.C. (now Pierce C.C.), 1983-85; tchg. asst. dept. romance langs. SUNY, Binghamton, 1985-87, tchg. asst. women's studies dept., 1988, tchg. asst. comparative lit. dept., 1986-88; vis. instr. Union Coll., Schenectady, N.Y., 1988-89; vis. instr. dept. fgn. langs. and lits. Skidmore Coll., Saratoga Springs, N.Y., 1989-90; assoc. prof. dept. fgn. langs. State U. Coll., Buffalo, 1990—; coord. women's studies interdisciplinary unit SUNY, Buffalo, 1993—, adviser French Club, 1990-93; mem. French Circle, Buffalo, 1990—, also mem. women's studies coun. Contbr. articles to profl. pubs.; presenter at seminars, workshops, confs. Grantee Nat. Defense Student Award. Mem. MLA, Nat. Women's Studies Assn., Am. Assn. Tchrs. French, Women in French, Conseil Internat. d'Etudes Francophones, Pi Delta Phi, Soc. Hon. Française, Kappa Theta (hon.). Home: PO Box 1063 Buffalo NY 14213-7063 Office: State Univ Coll-Buffalo Dept Fgn Langs 1300 Elmwood Ave Buffalo NY 14222-1004

MERIWETHER, HEATH J., newspaper publisher; b. Columbia, Mo., Jan. 20, 1944; s. Nelson Heath and Mary Agnes (Immele) M.; m. Patricia Hughes, May 4, 1979; children: Graham, Elizabeth. BA in History, BJ, U. Mo., 1966; MA in Teaching, Harvard U., 1967. Reporter Miami (Fla.) Herald, 1970-72, editor Broward and Palm Beach burs., 1972-77, exec. city editor, 1977-79, asst. mgr. editor news, 1979-80, mng. editor, 1981-83, exec. editor, 1983-87; exec. editor Detroit Free Press, 1987-95, publisher, 1996—. Trustee Greenhills Sch., 1995—; bd. dirs. Detroit Symphony Orch., 1996—. Served to lt. USNR, 1967-70. Journalism fellow Stanford U., 1980. Roman Catholic. Avocation: tennis. Office: Detroit Free Press 321 W Lafayette Blvd Detroit MI 48226

MERIWETHER, JAMES BABCOCK, retired English language educator; b. Columbia, S.C., May 8, 1928; s. Robert Lee and Margaret (Babcock) M.; m. Nancy Anderson Callcott, July 29, 1955 (div. May 1992); children: Rebecca, Robert, George, Nicholas, Margaret; m. Anne M. Blythe, Nov. 14, 1992. BA, U. S.C., 1949; MA, Princeton U., 1952, PhD, 1958. Asst. prof. English U. Tex., Austin, 1958-59; asst. prof. English U. N.C., Chapel Hill, 1959-62, assoc. prof., 1962-64; prof. U. S.C., Columbia, 1964-70, McClintock prof. So. letters, 1970-90, dir. So. studies program, 1974-80, disting. prof. emeritus, 1990—; appointed Bd. Fgn. Scholarships, Washington, 1982, 86, vice chmn., 1984, chmn. 1984-87; Fulbright prof. U. Paris, 1970-71, U. Bonn, 1980, Chinese U. Hong Kong, 1993. Author: The Literary Career of William Faulkner, 1961, others; editor: Essays, Speeches and Public Letters of William Faulkner, others; contbr. articles to profl. jours. Served with U.S. Army, 1953-56. Fellow Am. Coun. Learned Socs., 1960-61, Guggenheim Found., 1963-64, Earhart Found., 1989-90. Mem. MLA, Bibliographical Soc. Am., Am. Studies Assn., South Atlantic Modern Lang. Assn., Phi Beta Kappa. Home: 2526 Monroe St Columbia SC 29205

MERK, ELIZABETH THOLE, sales representative; b. Salt Lake City, July 29, 1950; d. John Bernard and Emily Josephine Knotek; 1 child, William Lance Ulich; m. J. Eliot Merk, July 26, 1996. BA, U. Hawaii, Hilo, 1984, paralegal cert. cum laude, 1989; postgrad.in bus. administrn., U. Hawaii, Manoa, 1985-86. Lic. ins. agt. Hawaii, Calif., Fla., N.C., Tex., W.Va. Regional rep. Lightolier, Inc., Salt Lake City, 1978-80; group sales rep. FHP/Utah, Salt Lake City, 1980-81; health net rep. Blue Cross Corp., L.A., 1981-82; v.p. fin. Bus. Support Systems, Hilo, 1983-89; rep. Prudential Ins. and Fin. Svcs., Honolulu, 1989—; registered rep. Pruco Securities Corp. subs. Ins. & Fin. Svcs., 1989—. Docent Lyman House, 1984-85, L.A. County Mus. of Art, 1980-81, S.L.C. Art Mus., 1970-80; bd. dirs. YWCA, Hawaii Island, 1980-91, 1st v.p., 1988. Named YWCA Vol. of Yr., 1991; recipient Nat. Quality award 1991, 92, 93, 94, Nat. Sales Achievement award 1992, 93; Paul Harris fellow Rotary Internat., 1997. Fellow Life Underwriters Tng. Coun.; mem. AAUW (fundraiser chair Kona chpt. 1992, bd. dirs. Hilo chpt. 1987-89, comty. area rep. 1989), Am. Bus. Women's Assn. (past pres. Nani O Hilo chpt. 1995-96, cmty. svc. chair 1993-95, membership chair 1996—, audit com. chair Kanoelani chpt. 1992, program chair Hilo chpt. 1985, expansion com. Hilo Lehua chpt. 1985, Steven Bufton grantee 1985, ways and means com. 1984, memberships chair Lehua chpt. 1983), Nat. Assn. Life Underwriters (legis. rep. West Hawaii 1989—), Million Dollar Round Table (qualifying mem. 1992, 93, 94, 95). Roman Catholic.

MERK, FREDERICK BANNISTER, biomedical educator, medical researcher; b. Cambridge, Mass., Feb. 21, 1936; s. Frederick and Lois Alberta (Bannister) M.; m. Linda Jean Poole, Oct. 22, 1966 (dec. Dec. 1994); children: John F., R. Daniel. AB, Harvard Coll., 1958; PhD, Boston U., 1971. Asst. prof. pathology Boston U. Sch. Medicine, 1972-73; assoc. prof. pathology and anatomy Tufts U. Sch. Medicine, Boston, 1973—; also dir. electron microscopy facility, 1975-85; cons. electron microscopy Mass. Gen. Hosp., Boston, 1964-85; cons. toxicol. testing Transgenic Scis., Worcester, Mass., 1988-91. Contbr. articles to profl. jours. Trustee Broadway United Meth. Ch., Lynn, Mass., chmn. 1994—. Named Outstanding Tchr. in Basic Scis., Tufts U. Sch. Medicine, 1989, 91, 92, 93; NIH grantee, 1994—. Mem. Am. Soc. Cell Biology, Fedn. Am. Soc. Exptl. Biology, Am. Assn. Anatomists, Microscopy Soc. Am., Sigma Xi. Achievements include research on biology of cells in target organs responding to hormones with emphasis on benign prostatic hypertrophy (enlargement) and prostate cancer. Avocations: photography, indoor gardening, swimming. Home: 17 Jefferson Rd Winchester MA 01890-3116 Office: Tufts Univ Sch Medicine Dept Pathology 136 Harrison Ave Boston MA 02111-1817

MERKER, STEVEN JOSEPH, lawyer; b. Cleve., Feb. 21, 1947; s. Steven Joseph and Laverne (Zamenik) M.; m. Janet L. Whyatt; children: Steven, Rena, Ashley, Matthew. BS, Case Inst. Tech., 1968; MS, U. Fla., 1973. Bar: Ohio 1976, U.S. Dist. Ct. (no. dist.) Ohio, 1976, U.S. Dist. Ct. Colo. 1979, U.S. Ct. Appeals (10th cir.) 1979, U.S. Supreme Ct. 1989. Assoc. Jones, Day, Reavis & Pogue, Cleve., 1976-78; assoc. Davis, Graham & Stubbs, Denver, 1978-82, ptnr., 1983-96, chmn. labor and employment group, 1989-96; mem., chmn. litigation and labor and employment groups Merrick, Calvin & Merker, L.L.P., 1996—. Legal counsel Coloradans for Lamm-Dick campaign, Denver, 1982, Nancy Dick for U.S. Senate Com., Denver, 1984, Cantrell for Dist. Atty., Jefferson County, Colo., 1984; bd. dirs. Very Spl. Arts, Colo., 1994—. Served as capt. USAF, 1969-72. Mem. ABA, Colo. Bar Assn., Denver Bar Assn. Office: Merrick Calvin and Merker 600 17th St Ste 950S Denver CO 80202-5439

MERKIN, ALBERT CHARLES, pediatrician, allergist; b. Chgo., Sept. 4, 1924; s. Harry A. and Goldie (Lamasky) M.; m. Eunice Aprill, Aug. 22, 1948; children: Audrey, Ellen, Joseph. Student, U. Ill., 1942-44; MD, U. Ill., Chgo., 1949. Diplomate Am. Bd. Allergy and Immunology, Am. Bd. Pediatrics. Intern, resident Cook County Hosp., Chgo.; resident Children's Meml. Hosp., Chgo.; with Valley Pediatric and Allergy Clinic, Las Vegas, Nev. Capt. USAF, 1950-53. Fellow Am. Acad. Pediatrics (state chmn. Nev. 1961-64, sect. allergy and immunology), Am. Coll. Allergy; mem. Am. Acad. Allergy, Allergy Subsplty. Group of Acad. Pediatrics. Avocations: reading, travel. Office: Valley Pediat & Allergy Clinic 222 S Rainbow Blvd Ste 119 Las Vegas NV 89128-5343

MERKIN, WILLIAM LESLIE, lawyer; b. N.Y.C., Apr. 30, 1929; s. Jules Leo Merkin and Rae (Levine) Lesser; children—Monica Jo, Lance Jeffrey, Tiffany Dawn. B.A., U. Tex., Austin, 1950; J.D., St. Mary's U., San Antonio, Tex., 1953. Bar: Tex. 1953, U.S. Ct. Mil. Appeals 1954, U.S. Dist. Ct. (we. dist.) Tex. 1957, U.S. Ct. Appeals (5th cir.) 1969, U.S. Supreme Ct. 1970. Pvt. practice, El Paso, Tex., 1956-71; sr. ptnr. firm Merkin & Gibson, El Paso, 1972-78, Merkin, Hines & Pasqualone, 1978-90, ret.; lectr. U. Tex.-El Paso, 1978—; cons. in field. Served to capt. JAGC, U.S. Army, 1953-56. Mem. Tex. State Bar Assn., El Paso County Bar Assn., San Diego County Bar Assn., Soc. of Profls. in Dispute Resolution, Am. Trial Lawyers Assn., Tex. Trial Lawyers Assn., Common Cause, Internat. Wine and Food Soc. (pres. 1979-80), Am. Arbitration Assn. (part-time arbitrator), Nat. Assn. Securities Dealers (part-time arbitrator), Del Norte Club (El Paso), B'nai B'rith (pres. 1961-62), Phi Delta Phi. Home: 1442 Seacoast Dr Apt 2 Imperial Beach CA 91932-3179

MERLINO, ANTHONY FRANK, orthopedic surgeon; b. Providence, Jan. 21, 1930; s. Anthony Frank and C. Mildred (Campagna) M.; m. Dolores Mary Aucello, Nov. 22, 1956; children: Christa Marianne, Paula Nicole. BS, Providence Coll., 1951; MS, U. Conn., 1952; MD, Jefferson Med. Coll., 1956. Diplomate Am. Bd. Orthopedic Surgery. Intern St. Joseph Hosp., Providence, 1956-57; resident orthopedic surgery VA Hosp., Phila., 1959-63; pvt. practice medicine specializing in orthopedic surgery, Phila., 1963-68, Providence, 1968—; attending orthopedic surgeon St. Joseph Hosp., Providence, pres. med. staff, 1974-75, trustee, 1973-76, med. staff/trustee joint conf. com. 1982; attending orthopedic surgeon Our Lady of Fatima Hosp., North Providence, R.I.; vis. orthopedic surgeon R.I. State Hosp., Howard, 1968-75; asst. orthopedic surgery Hahnemann Med. Coll., Phila., 1965-69; pediatric orthopedic surg. cons. Crippled Children's Program of R.I., 1968-86; cons. orthopedic surgeon Roger Williams Gen. Hosp., Providence, 1969-89; v.p. R.I. Orthopedic Group, Inc., Providence, 1969-83; pres., 1983—; team physician hockey and basketball teams Providence Coll., 1968-87; mem. R.I. Gov.'s Med. Malpractice Commn., 1975-77, R.I. Bd. Examiners in Chiropractic, 1977-80; mem. study commn. R.I. Med. Rev. Bd., 1977-85; mem. corp. Blue Cross/Shield R.I., 1976-87; physician-adv. R.I. Assn. Med. Assts., 1979-84; mem. R.I. Workers' Compensation Adv. Panel, 1978-88; mem. adv. bd. Cath. Social Svcs., 1981-84; police surgeon Am. Law Enforcement Officers' Assn., 1980; cons. orthopedic surgery Am. Assn. Medicolegal Cons., 1980-90; pres. Hindle Bldg. Assocs., 1983—. Contbr. articles to profl. jours. Mem. med. splty. adv. bd. Medical Malpractice Prevention, 1985-90. Capt., M.C., USAF, 1957-59. Recipient Dr. William McDonnell award Providence Coll. Alumni Assn., 1981. Fellow Am. Acad. Orthopedic Surgeons, ACS, (pres. R.I. chpt. 1982-84), Internat. Coll. Surgeons, Latin Am. Soc. Orthopedics and Traumatology; mem. AMA, Orthopaedic Rsch. and Edn. Found. (life), Am. Coll. Legal Medicine, Am. Fracture Assn., Pan-Pacific Surg. Assn., New Eng., R.I. (sec.-treas. 1978-80, v.p. 1980-82, pres. 1982-84), Ea. Orthopedic Socs., Jefferson Orthopaedic Soc., R.I. Med. Soc. (commr. profl. rels. 1976, ho. of dels. 1976-82, commr. internal affairs 1982), Providence Med. Assn., Am. Profl. Practice Assn., Am. Acad. Compensation Medicine, Am. Coll. Sports Medicine, Am. Orthopedic Soc. for Sports Medicine, Am. Med. Photography Assn., Internat. Soc. Orthopedics and Traumatology, Internat. Soc. Rsch. in Orthopedics and Trauma, Am. Soc. Law and Medicine, Thomistic Inst. Drs. Guild, R.I. Hist. Soc., Boston Orthopedic Club, Mal Brown Club, The 100 of R.I. Club. Roman Catholic. Home: 2 Countryside Dr N Providence RI 02904-3419 Office: 655 Broad St Providence RI 02907-1444

MERLIS, GEORGE, television producer; b. Bklyn., Feb. 7, 1940; s. Martin Richard and Ethel (Pollack) M.; m. Susan Haviland Crane, Nov. 21, 1963; children: James Duncan, Andrew Richard. B.A., U. Pa., 1960; M.S., Columbia U. Grad. Sch. Journalism, 1961. Sports editor Rome (Italy) Daily Am., 1961; reporter N.Y. World-Telegram and Sun, N.Y.C., 1962-65; asst. city editor N.Y. World-Telegram and Sun, 1965-67; day city editor World Jour. Tribune, N.Y.C., 1967; supr. editorial tng. program N.Y. News, N.Y.C., 1967-68; dir. pub. relations ABC News, N.Y.C., 1967-72; field producer Reasoner Report, 1972-75; exec. producer Good Morning America, 1975-81, CBS Morning News, 1981-83, Entertainment Tonight, 1983-84, Dick Cavett, USA, 1985, Great Weekend, 1987-88; supervising producer ABC-TV's Home Show, 1988-91; exec. producer Willard Scott's Home and Garden Almanac, 1994—, Kitty Bartholomew You're Home, 1994—, The Urban Gardener with Mesach Taylor, 1996; exec. producer, writer, dir. Harlem Hellfighters, 1997; pres. Jaand Prodns., Inc.; founder, chmn. J-Nex

TV News Services, Inc.; chmn. Sunrise News Co. Author: V.P. a Novel of Vice Presidential Politics, 1971, (with Al Ubell) Al Ubell's Energy-Saving Guide for Homeowners, 1980; contbr. articles to TV Guide. Mem. Nat. TV Acad. Arts and Scis., Home Video Acad. Arts and Scis., Internat. Assn. Bus. Communicators, N.Y. Newspaper Guild. Office: Fisher Merlis Television 5455 Wilshire Blvd Ste 2007 Los Angeles CA 90036-4242

MERMANN, ALAN CAMERON, pediatrics educator, chaplain; b. Bklyn., June 23, 1923; s. William Joseph and Ada Fischer (McCree) M.; m. Constance Barnes, Sept. 4, 1948 (div. Mar. 1988); children: Edith, Constance, Sarah, Elizabeth; m. Cecily Allen Reynolds, Apr. 15, 1989. BA, Lehigh U., 1943; MD, Johns Hopkins U., 1947; MDiv, Yale U., 1979, MST, 1988. Diplomate Am. Bd. Pediatrics; med. license, Conn.; ordained to Christian ministry, United Ch. of Christ, 1979. Intern pediatrics Bellevue Hosp., N.Y.C., 1947-48, Johns Hopkins Hosp., Balt., 1948-49; sr. asst. resident pediatrician N.Y. Hosp., N.Y.C., 1949-50; resident pediatrician Meml. Hosp., N.Y.C., 1950-51; rsch. fellow Sloane-Kettering Inst., N.Y.C., 1953-54; pvt. practice pediatrics Guilford, Conn., 1954-82; clin. instr. pediatrics Yale Sch. Medicine, 1954-59, asst. clin. prof. pediatrics, 1959-71, assoc. clin. prof. pediatrics, 1971-79, clin. prof. pediatrics, 1979—; trustee New Eng. Coll., Henniker, N.H., 1969-91; fellow Branford Coll., Yale U., 1979—; mem. instnl. rev. bd. Union Carbide Corp., Danbury, Conn., 1991—; lectr. pastoral theology Yale Divinity Sch., 1979-82; asst. pastor First Congregational Ch., Guilford, 1979-82; assoc. pastor Ch. of Christ Congl., United Ch. of Christ, Norfolk, Conn., 1995—; chaplain Yale Sch. Medicine, 1982—, human investigation com., 1983-91, med. ctr. bioethics com., chair pediatrics ethics com., sch. medicine admissions com., com. on well-being of students. Contbr. articles to profl. jours. Lt. USNR, 1951-53. Fellow Am. Acad. Pediatrics. Democrat. Avocations: Dixieland, jazz, dancing, gardening. Home: 36 Eld St New Haven CT 06511-3816

MERMELSTEIN, ISABEL MAE ROSENBERG, financial consultant; b. Houston, Aug. 20, 1934; d. Joe Hyman and Sylvia (Lincove) Rosenberg; m. Robert Jay Mermelstein, Sept. 6, 1953 (div. July 1975); children: William, Linda, Jody. Student U. Ariz., 1952, Mich. State U., 1974, Lansing (Mich.) C.C., 1975. Exec. dir. Shiawassee County YWCA, Owosso, Mich., 1975-78; real estate developer F&S Devel. Corp., Lansing, Mich., 1978-79, Corum Devel. Corp., Houston, 1979-81; adminstrv. fin. planner, sr. citizen cons. Investec Asset Mgmt. Group, Inc.; owner Ins. Filing Svcs. Sr. Citizens, 1985—; guardian VA, 1990—. Author: For You! I Killed the Chicken, 1972. Mem. Older Women's League, Houston, 1st Ecumenical Council of Lansing, Nat. Mus. Women in Arts, Judaica Mus., Houston, Mus. Fine Arts, Houston, Mus. Natural Sci., Houston; docent Holocaust Mus., Houston; mem. African-Jewish Dialogue Group, Houston. Recipient State of Mich. Flag, 1972, Key to City, City of Lansing, 1972-73. Mem. Nat. Assn. Claims Assistance Profls., Afro-Am. Jewish Dialogue Group, Internat. Women's Pilot Orgn. (The 99's), Jewish Geneal. Soc., Internat. Directorate Disting. Leadership. Republican. Jewish. Lodges: Zonta, Licoma, B'nai B'rith, Hadassah, Nat. Fedn. Temple Sisterhoods. Flew All Women's Transcontinental Air Race (Powder Puff Derby), 1972, 73. Avocations: flying, gourmet cooking, needlepoint, knitting, skiing. Home: 4030 Newshire Dr Houston TX 77025-3921

MEROLLA, MICHELE EDWARD, chiropractor, broadcaster; b. Providence, Feb. 20, 1940; s. Joseph and Viola (Horne) M.; m. Ednamarie H.; children: Michele Edward II, Matthew Joseph, Samantha Joan, Alexandra Marie. BSc, Bryant Coll., 1961; DC, Chiropractic Inst. N.Y., 1965; LHD, Logan Chiropractic Coll., St. Louis, 1973. Owner chiropractic clinics, New Bedford, Taunton, Somerset, Seekonk, Attleboro, North Attleboro and Westport, Mass., 1965—. Daily Network radio talk show host Holistic Hotline; owner radio sta. WARA-AM, Attleboro, Mass. Mem. New Bedford City Coun., 1969-73, Airport Commn., 1972-75, Sch. Com., 1978-83, Recreation Commn., 1983-89; pres. New Bedford Aid Ctr., 1977; bd. dirs. Your Theatre Inc. Recipient Svc. award New England Chiropractic Coun., 1973. Mem. Nat. Assn. Broadcasters, Mass. Assn. Broadcasters, Southeastern Mass. Chiropractic Soc. (bd. dirs.), Mass. Chiropractic Soc., Am. Chiropractic Assn., N.Y. Acad. Sci., Fla. Chiropractic Soc., New Bedford Preservation Soc. (bd. dirs.). Editor: New England Jour. Chiropractic, 1965-75. Home: 62 Rear Manhattan Ave Fairhaven MA 02719 also: 3300 NE 23d Ave Lighthouse Point FL 33064 Office: 100 Bedford St New Bedford MA 02740-4839

MERON, THEODOR, law educator, researcher; b. Kalisz, Poland, Apr. 28, 1930; came to U.S., 1978, naturalized, 1984; s. Yhiel and Bluma (Lipschitz) Znamirowski; m. Monique Jonquet, Mar. 13, 1981; children: Daniel, Amos. M.J., Hebrew U., 1954; LL.M., Harvard U., 1955, S.J.D., 1957; diploma in Pub. Internat. Law, Cambridge U., Eng., 1957. Bar: Israel 1971, N.Y. 1984. Legal advisor to Fgn. Ministry of Israel, 1967-71; Israeli ambassador to Can., 1971-75; permanent rep. Geneva, 1977; prof. law Sch. Law, NYU, N.Y.C., 1978—; Carnegie lectr. Hague Acad. Internat. Law, 1980; Sir Hersch Lauterpacht Meml. lectr.; vis. fellow All Souls Coll., Oxford U., Eng., Max-Planck Inst., Heidelberg, Germany; vis. prof. Grad. Inst. Internat. Studies, Geneva, prof. law, 1991-95; pub. mem. U.S. Del. Conf. on Human Dimension Conf. on Security and Cooperation in Europe, Copenhagen, 1990. Author: Investment Insurance in International Law, 1976, The United Nations Secretariat, 1977, Human Rights Law-Making in the United Nations, 1986, Human Rights in Internal Strife: Their International Protection, 1987, Human Rights and Humanitarian Norms as Customary Law, 1989, Henry's Wars and Shakespeare's Laws, 1993; editor: Human Rights in International Law, 1984; editor in chief: Am. Jour. Internat. Law; contbr. articles to profl. publs. Bd. dirs. Helsinki Watch, Americas Watch, Internat. League of Human Rights. Rockefeller Found. fellow, 1975-76; Humanitarian Trust student Cambridge U., 1956-57. Mem. Am. Soc. Internat. Law (Cert. Merit 1987), French Soc. Internat. Law, Internat. Law Assn., Can. Coun. on Internat. Law, Coun. on Fgn. Rels., UN Assn. of the U.S. (hon.). Office: NYU Law Sch 40 Washington Sq S New York NY 10012-1005

MEROW, JAMES F., federal judge; b. Salamanca, N.Y., Mar. 16, 1932; s. Walter and Helen (Smith) M. AB, George Washington U., 1953, JD, 1956. Bar: Va. Trial atty. U.S. Dept. Justice, Washington, 1959-78; trial judge U.S. Ct. Claims, Washington, 1978-82, judge, 1982—. With JAGC, U.S. Army, 1956-59. Mem. ABA, Va. State Bar. Office: US Ct Fed Claims 717 Madison Pl NW Washington DC 20005-1011*

MEROW, JOHN EDWARD, lawyer; b. Little Valley, N.Y., Dec. 20, 1929; s. Luin George and Mildred Elizabeth (Stoll) M.; m. Mary Alyce Smith, June 19, 1957; 1 child, Alison. Student, UCLA, 1947-48; BS in Engring., U. Mich., 1952; JD, Harvard U., 1958. Bar: N.Y. 1958, U.S. Supreme Ct. 1971. Assoc. Sullivan & Cromwell, N.Y.C., 1958-64, ptnr., 1965-96, vice chmn., 1986-87, chmn., sr. ptnr., 1987-94, sr. counsel, 1997—; bd. dirs. Seligman Group Investment Cos., Commonwealth Aluminum Corp., Alflex Corp.; chmn. bd. dirs. N.Y. and Presbyn. Hosps. Care Network, Inc.; bd. govs. N.Y. Hosp.; mem. joint bd. N.Y. Hosp.-Cornell Med. Ctr.; bd. govs. N.Y. and Presbyn. Hosps. Healthcare Sys., Inc., vice chmn. for network affairs. Chmn. bd. dirs. Am.-Australian Assn.; bd. dirs. The U.S.-New Zealand Coun., Mcpl. Art Soc. N.Y.; chmn. Mcpl. Art Soc. Coun.; trustee, v.p. Am. Friends of Australian Nat. Gallery, Inc.; trustee, mem. exec. com. U.S. Coun. Internat. Bus.; bd. dirs., sec. Met. Opera Club, 1986-94. Mem. Assn. of Bar of City of N.Y. (chmn. com. on securities regulation 1974-77), Am. Law Inst. (advisor corp. governance project 1978-92), Coun. on Fgn. Rels., Fgn. Policy Assn. (bd. govs.), Links Club, Pilgrims, Piping Rock Club, Down Town Assn., The Calif. Club, Union Club, Griffis Faculty Club. Home: 350 E 69th St New York NY 10021-5706 also: 51 Fruitledge Rd Brookville NY 11545-3316 Office: Sullivan & Cromwell 125 Broad St New York NY 10004-2400

MERRELL, JAMES LEE, religious editor, clergyman; b. Indpls., Oct. 24, 1930; s. Mark W. and Pauline F. (Tucker) M.; m. Barbara Jean Burch, Dec. 23, 1951; children: Deborah Lea Merrell Griffin, Cynthia Lynn Merrell Archer, Stuart Allen. A.B., Ind. U., 1952; M.Div., Christian Theol. Sem., 1956; Litt.D., Culver-Stockton Coll., 1972. Ordained to ministry Christian Ch., 1955; assoc. editor World Call, Indpls., 1956-66; editor World Call, 1971-73; pastor Crestview Christian Ch., Indpls., 1966-71; editor The Disciple, St. Louis, 1974-89; sr. v.p. Christian Bd. Publ., 1976-89; sr. minister Affton Christian Ch., St. Louis, 1989-94; interim chaplain Culver-Stockton Coll., Canton, Mo., 1995; interim sr. pastor Friedens United Ch. of Christ, Warrenton, Mo., 1995—; bd. dirs. Horizons mag., 1995—. Author: They Live Their Faith, 1965, The Power of One, 1976, Discover the Word in Print, 1979, Finding Faith in the Headlines, 1985, We Claim Our Heritage, 1992. Chmn. bd. Kennedy Meml. Christian Home, Martinsville, Ind., 1971-73; trustee Christian Theol. Sem., 1978-81. Recipient Faith and Freedom award Religious Heritage of Am., 1983. Mem. Associated Ch. Press (award 1973, 79, 80, 81, 82, dir. 1974-75, 78-81, 1st v.p. 1983-85), Christian Theol. Sem. Alumni Assn. (pres. 1966-68), Religious Pub. Rels. Coun. (awards 1979, 80, 84, 87, 90, pres. St. Louis chpt. 1985-86), Sigma Delta Chi (award 1952), Theta Phi. Home: 5347 Warmwinds Ct Saint Louis MO 63129-3013 *As a religious communicator and as a pastor, I have always believed in applying the same standards in the sacred realm as in the secular. I have tried to pursue the truth, to keep my constituency informed, to celebrate the noble in life, to fight against those who would lie, distort and hide God's truth in the name of some supposed good.*

MERRELL, JESSE HOWARD, writer; b. Shelby, Ala., Dec. 9, 1938; s. James Walton and Emma Thelma (Davis) M.; m. Betsy Lee Davis, Jan. 11, 1964 (div. 1979); children: Sandra, Mark, Brad, Carolyn, Gwen. Grad., Shelby High Sch., Columbiana, Ala., 1957. Pitcher Cin. Redlegs, 1958-62; reporter, news dir. WHAP Radio, Hopewell, Va., 1963; writer/editor Hopewell News, 1963-65; state editor Daily Progress, Charlottesville, Va., 1965-68; assoc. editor Transport Topics, Washington, 1968-75; spl. asst. to pres. Am. Trucking Assn., Washington, 1975-76; editor Transport Topics, Washington, 1976-77; pres. Merrell Ent., Washington, 1977—; pub. rels. com. Am. Movers Conf., Washington, 1969-72; instr. Dale Carnegie courses, Washington, 1974-81, 1st pres., 1980-81; cons. Mid. Atlantic Conf., Riverdale, Md., 1981-82, Contract Carrier Conf., 1977-82; speechwriter ICC, Washington, 1982. Author: (novel) A Christmas Gift, 1979; syndicated columnist Religion and the Times, Washington Welter, (genealogy) The Merrells of Alabama, 1995. Mem. Nat. Trust for Hist. Preservation. With U.S. Army, 1960-62. Recipient Liberty award Congress of Freedom, Jackson, Miss., 1970, 71, Honor Cert., Freedoms Found., 1972, 1st place editorial writing Va. Press Assn., 1965, 1st place news writing, 1966. Mem. Nat. Press Club, Colonial Williamsburg Capitol Soc. (charter mem.). Avocation: photography. Office: Merrell Ent 2610 Garfield St NW Washington DC 20008-4104

MERRELL, RONALD CLIFTON, surgeon, educator; b. Birmingham, Ala., June 18, 1946; s. Greene Lawrence and Florence (Jones) M.; m. Marsha Karen Cox, Dec. 24, 1966; children: Alexandria, Alison, R. Clifton. BS in Chemistry, U. Ala., 1967, MD, 1970. Diplomate Am. Bd. Surgery. Resident and fellow in surgery Wash. U., St. Louis, 1970-77; asst. prof. surgery Stanford (Calif.) U., 1979-84; assoc. prof. surgery U. Tex. Med. Sch., Houston, 1984-88, prof. surgery, 1988-94; prof. surgery M.D. Anderson Cancer Ctr., Houston, 1988-94; assoc. dean clin. affairs U. Tex. Med. Sch., Houston, 1988-92, vice dean, 1992-94; prof. surgery, chmn. dept. surgery Yale U., 1994—. Author 2 books; contbr. 61 articles to profl jours., 18 chpts. to books. Maj. U.S. Army, 1977-79. Recipient Basil O'Connor award March of Dimes, 1979, Rsch. Career Devel. award NIH, 1979-84, Henry J. Kaiser award Stanford U., 1982, 83, John P. McGovern Outstanding Tchr. award U. Tex. Med. Sch., 1988, Dean's Teaching Excellence award, 1983-89. Fellow ACS, Soc. Univ. Surgeons; mem. Am. Assn. Endocrine Surgery, Soc. Internat. de Chirurgie, Alpha Omega Alpha. Democrat. Episcopalian. Achievements include research in the transplantation of islets of Langerhans. Office: Yale U PO Box 208062 New Haven CT 06520-8062*

MERRELL, THERESE ELIZABETH, trade show production executive; b. Anaheim, Calif., July 16, 1964; d. Darrell Eugene Merrell and Linda Karen (Petersen) Walker. Student, Fullerton Coll., 1982-85. Asst. mgr. ITT Fin. Corp., Santa Ana, Calif., 1985-87; convention svc. mgr. Hilton Hotels Corp., Anaheim, 1987-90; asst. show mgr. IDG World Expo, Framingham, Mass., 1990-91, show dir., 1992-94, v.p., gen. mgr., 1994-96, group v.p., 1996—; mem. E3 Operating Com., Framingham, 1996—. Mem. IAEM (bd. dirs. New Eng. chpt. 1994-95). Republican. Roman Catholic. Avocations: jogging, golf, tennis, hiking. Office: IDG World Expo Corp 3 Speen St Ste 360 Framingham MA 01701-4658

MERRELL, WILLIAM JOHN, JR., oceanography educator; b. Grand Island, Nebr., Feb. 16, 1943; s. William John and Dorothy Belle (Dye) M.; m. June Bearden, Oct. 12, 1970; children: Bethany Susan, Meredith Megan. BS, Sam Houston State U., 1965, MA, 1967; PhD, Tex. A&M U., 1971. Rsch. assoc. Dept. Oceanography, Tex. A&M U., 1970-71, 73-74, postdoctoral rsch. assoc., 1971-72, lectr., dep. dept. head, 1977-79, dep. dept. head, 1981-83, assoc. prof., 1981-85, prof., 1985—; co-investigator oceanography remote sensing project Tex. A&M U., 1969-70, dep. sea grant dir., 1977-78, asst. to dean geoscis., 1978-79, assoc. dir. Earth Resources Inst., 1978-79; dir. Earth Resources Inst. Coll. Geoscis., Tex. A&M U., 1983-84, assoc. dean, 1983-85, dir. div. atmospheric and marine scis., 1985; rsch. program mgmt. system officer Office Internat. Decade Ocean Exploration, NSF, 1972-73, exec. officer, 1974-77, asst. dir., 1985-87; oceanographer, mgr. Climate and Coastal Zone Br. Sci. Applications Inc., 1979-80; pres. Tex. A&M U., Galveston, 1987-91; v.p. rsch. policy Tex. A&M U., 1992-93; vice chancellor for strategic programs Tex. A&M U. System, Galveston, 1993-96; pres. Tex. Inst. Oceanography, 1989-91; program mgr. Gulf of Mex. Topographic Features Synthesis, 1981-83, prin. investigator ocean drilling program, 1983-85; mem. human exploration of space-space studies bd., chmn. ocean studies bd., mem. bd. on sustainable devel., mem. global change com., chmn. internat. spce programs com. NRC; pres. H. John Heinz Ctr. for Sci. Econs. and the Environment, Washington, 1995—; adv. com. on rsch. programs State of Tex.; adv. com. for Geosci. NSF. Contbr. articles to profl. jours. Bd. dirs. Galveston Hist. Fedn.; bd. govs. Galveston Econ. Devel. Corp.; bd. trustees Galveston Wharves. Recipient Disting. Svc. award NSF, 1987, Disting. Alumnus award Sam Houston State U., 1988, Disting. Achievement award Coun. for Geosciences and Earth Resources, 1990. Mem. The Oceanography Soc., Vanda Club (Antarctica), Sigma Xi (Disting. Mem. award 1987), Sigma Phi Sigma, Alpha Chi, Phi Kappa Phi. Office: Tex A&M U PO Box 1675 Galveston TX 77553-1675

MERRIAM, DWIGHT HAINES, lawyer, land use planner; b. Norwood, Mass., Apr. 20, 1946; s. Austin Luther and Lillian Diana (Olsen) M.; m. Cynthia Ann Hayes, May 21, 1966 (div. June 1992); children: Sarah Ann Leilani, Jonathan Hayes; m. Susan Manning Standish, May 6, 1995; 1 child, Alexander Harlan. BA cum laude, U. Mass., 1968; M in Regional Planning, U. N.C., 1974; JD, Yale U., 1978. Bar: Conn. 1978, Mass. 1980, U.S. Dist. Ct. Conn. 1981, U.S. Dist. Ct. Hawaii 1984, U.S. Supreme Ct. 1990, U.S. Ct. Appeals (4th cir.) 1993. Land use planner Charles E. Downe, Newton, Mass., 1968; assoc. Byrne, Buck & Steiner, Farmington, Conn., 1978, Robinson, Robinson & Cole, Hartford, Conn., 1979-83; ptnr. Robinson & Cole, Hartford, 1984—; adj. prof. law Western New Eng. Coll., 1978-86, U. Conn., 1982, 84-87, Vt. Law Sch., 1994—; instr. planning U. Bridgeport, 1981-83, U. Conn., 1986-92; mem. faculty Nat. Coll. Dist. Attys., 1983-87, Nat. Jud. Coll., 1994; mem. faculty Am. Law Inst.-ABA Land Use Inst., 1988—; instr. city and regional planning Memphis State U., 1989, 94; speaker in field. Co-editor: Inclusionary Zoning Moves Downtown, 1985; contbr. more than 50 articles and book revs. to profl. jours. Bd. dirs. Growth Mgmt. Inst., Washington, 1992—, Housing Edn. Resource Ctr., 1984-88, Housing Coalition for Capitol Region, Inc., 1984-86; bd. dirs. Conn. Fund for Environment, 1981-85, legal adv. com., 1985-88, legal adv. bd., 1978-81; mem. Environment 2000 environ. plan adv. bd. Conn. Dept. Environ. Protection, 1987-91; assoc. Environ. Law Inst., 1987—; mem. housing task force Conn. Dept. on Aging, 1981; mem. Gov.'s Housing Task Force, Conn., 1980-81. With USN, 1968-75, Vietnam; capt. USNR; with USNR Res., 1975—. Mem. ABA, Conn. Bar Assn. (exec. com. zoning & planning sect. 1985-87, 91—), Am. Planning Assn. (bd. dirs. 1988-90, chmn. planning & law divsn. 1984-86, exec. com. planning & law divsn. 1978-88, chmn. legis. com. Conn. chpt. 1978-80, editorial adv. bd. 1984-92), Nat. Inst. Mcpl. Law Officers (chmn. sect. on zoning, planning & land devel. 1988-89, sect. vice-chmn. 1987), Assn. State Floodplain Mgrs., Am. Inst. Cert. Planners (pres. 1988-90), Am. Coll. Real Estate Lawyers, U. N.C. Alumni Assn. Democrat. Unitarian. Avocations: sailing, skiing. Home: 1 Linden Pl Apt 410 Hartford CT 06106-1745 Office: Robinson & Cole 1 Commercial Plz Hartford CT 06103-3599

MERRIAM, JANET PAMELA, special education educator; b. L.A., Jan. 11, 1958; d. Allen Hugo and Linda (Teagle) Warren; m. Marshal Lockhart Merriam, Aug. 4, 1984 (div. June 1991); 1 child, Jennifer Elizabeth. BA, San Jose State U., 1981. Cert. tchr. learning handicapped, lang. devel. specialist, Calif. Asst. youth edn. dir. Christ Ch. Unity, San Jose, 1988-90; substitute tchr. Santa Clara (Calif.) Unified Sch. Dist., 1990; spl. day class tchr. Oak Grove Sch. Dist., San Jose, 1990—. Sunday sch. tchr. Christ Ch. Unity, San Jose, 1980-92. Mem. Coun. for Exceptional Children, Learning Disabilities Assn. Calif. Republican. Avocations: reading, Star Trek, old movies. Home: 1657 Glenville Dr San Jose CA 95124-3808 Office: 530 Gettysburg Dr San Jose CA 95123-3234

MERRIAM, ROBERT W., engineering executive, educator; b. Providence, July 18, 1923; s. Paul Adams and Marian Lewis M.; m. Nancy Ann Allen, Dec. 21, 1954; children: Susan Allen Jones, Paul Adams, II. BS, Harvard Coll., 1949, MS, 1950. Reg. profl. engr., R.I. Instr. elec. engring. Swarthmore (Pa.) Coll., 1950-52; engr. Metals & Controls Corp., Attleboro, Mass., 1953-55; pres. Merriam Instruments, East Greenwich, R.I., 1955—; assoc. prof. U. R.I., Kingston, 1969-79. Editor: History of Wireless Communication in the U.S., 1989; patentee in field; contbr. articles to popular publications. Pres., dir. N.E. Wireless and Steam Mus., East Greenwich, 1964—; chmn. Planning Bd., East Greenwich, 1970s. With U.S. Army Signal Corp., 1942-46, ETO. Fellow Radio Club Am. (Batcher award 1979); mem. IEEE (life), Am. Radio RElay League, Nat. Marine Electronic Assn. (hon., dir. 1957), Nat. Assn. Power Engrs. (hon.), Vet. Wireless Assn. (Marconi Gold medal 1995), 20:00 Club (Meritorious Amateur Seamanship award 1955), Hope Club, Harvard Club (Boston).

MERRICK, BEVERLY CHILDERS, journalism, communications educator; b. Troy, Kans., Nov. 20, 1944; d. Horace Buchanan Merrick and Vola Yolantha (Clausen) Maul; m. John Douglas Childers, July 10, 1963; children: John Kevin, Pamela Christine, Jessica Faye. BA in Journalism with honors, Marshall U., 1980, BA in English with honors, 1980, M Journalism, 1982; M Creative Writing, Ohio U., 1986, cert. in Women's Studies, 1984, PhD in Comm. with honors, 1989. Reporter, photographer Ashland (Ky.) Daily Ind., 1981; tchr., instr. Albuquerque Pub. Schs., 1986-89; gen. assignment reporter, photographer Rio Rancho (N.Mex.) Observer, 1986; editor, rsch. cons. Ins. Pub. Law, Sch. of Law U. N.Mex., Albuquerque, 1990; asst. prof. Ga. So. U., Statesboro, 1991-94; assoc. prof. dept. mass comm. U. S.D., Vermillion, 1994-95; asst. prof. dept. journalism and mass comm. N. Mex. State U., Las Cruces, 1995—; part-time tchr., tchg. assoc. Ohio U., Athens, 1981-84; part-time copy editor Albuquerque Tribune, 1991; vis. prof. East Carolina U., Greenville, N.C., 1989-90; adj. prof. Embry-Riddle U., Kirtland AFB, N.Mex., 1989, 91; organizer diversity conf., 1st amendment conf. Ga. So. U.; mem. session MIT, 1989; chair campus com. N.Mex. State U. Author: (poetry) Navigating the Platte, 1986, Pearls for the Casting, 1987, Closing the Gate, 1993; contbr. poems to profl. publs., jours. and chpts. to books. Pub. rels. liaison Nat. Convention Bus. and Profl. Women, Albuquerque, 1988; pres. Albuquerque Bus. and Profl. Women, 1986-87, Rio Rancho Civic Assn., 1987-89, So. Ohio Improvement League, 1973-76; pres. bd. dirs. Pine Creek Conservancy Dist., 1976-83. Named Outstanding Citizen, N.Mex. Legislature, Truly Fine Citizen of Ohio, Ohio Gen. Assembly, 1973, Outstanding Homemaker of Ohio, Gov. of Ohio, 1974; grantee Reader's Digest, 1980, 83; John Houk Meml. grantee W.Va. Women's Conf., 1982; fellow Nat. Women's Studies Inst., Lilly Found., 1983, Freedom Forum Ethics, 1995, Am. Newspaper Inst., 1996; E.W. Scripps scholar, 1984; recipient Silver Clover award 4-H, Writing award Aviation/Space Writers Assn., 1981, 1st place open rsch competition Nat. Assn. Women's Dean's, Adminstrs. and Counselors, 1990; rsch. grantee N.Mex. State U. 1996. Mem. Soc. Profl. Journalists, Assn. for Edn. in Journalism and Mass Comm. (mem. nat. conv. com. 1993-94, vice head mag. divsn. 1995-96, head mag. divsn., 1996-97,), N.Mex. State Poetry Soc. (pres. 1987-89), Sigma Tau Delta. Home: 985 Ivydale Las Cruces NM 88005

MERRICK, DOROTHY SUSAN, interior designer; b. N.Y.C.. BA, Skidmore Coll.; MA, Adelphi U. Owner, pres. Dorothy Merrick Interiors Ltd., Sands Point, N.Y., 1968—. Project published in Newsday, N.Y. Times, House Mag. Recipient Gold Archi award Nassau/Suffolk AIA, 1986. Mem. Internat. Interior Designers Assn., Am. Soc. Interior Designers, Allied Bd. of Trade, Knickerbocker Yacht Club. Avocations: sailing, reading, opera.

MERRICK, GEORGE BOESCH, aerospace company executive; b. Burlington, Iowa, Mar. 9, 1928; s. Dale McKeen and Marjorie May (Boesch) M.; m. Eleanor Gamble Moore, Sept. 1, 1951; children: Charles, Ellen, Elizabeth. B.S., U. Minn., 1949. With N.Am. Aviation (name changed to Rockwell Internat.), 1949; dir. Apollo Command and Service Module, Space div., 1966-72; v.p., program mgr. Apollo Program, 1972-74, v.p., program mgr. Space Shuttle Orbiter Program, 1974-76; pres. space div. Rockwell Internat., Downey, Calif., 1976-78; pres. space systems group Rockwell Internat., 1978-80, corp. v.p., 1980—. Recipient Pub. Service award NASA. Fellow Am. Astron. Soc., AIAA. Office: 2201 Seal Beach Blvd Seal Beach CA 90740-5603

MERRICK, ROSWELL DAVENPORT, educational association administrator; b. Kings County, N.Y., July 20, 1922; s. George Roswell and Marguerite Regina M.; m. Gladys K. Kinley, June 26, 1948; children—Gregory, Susan, Peter. B.S., Springfield Coll., 1944; M.A., N.Y. U., 1947; Ed.D., Boston U., 1953. Assoc. prof., head basketball coach Central Conn. Coll., New Britain, 1946-53; asst. dean (Coll. Edn.); dir. div. health, phys. edn., recreation and athletics So. Ill. U., Carbondale, 1953-58; exec. dir. Nat. Assn. Sport and Phys. Edn., Reston, Va., 1958-91, U.S. Fitness and Sport Coun., 1991—. Contbr. articles to profl. jours. U.S. Olympic Com. Served with USAAF, 1944-46. Mem. AAHPERD, Mt. Vernon Yacht Club. Methodist. Address: 4739 Neptune Dr Alexandria VA 22309-3132

MERRICK, WILLIAM ANDREW, neuropsychologist; b. Champaign, Ill., July 3, 1953; s. John Wendell and Carol Kay (Hough) M.; m. Marianne Lombardo, Dec. 27, 1981; children: Alena Kay, Kristina Lee, David Andrew. BA, Northeastern Ill. U., 1976; MA, U. Chgo., 1982, PhD, 1989. Pre-doctoral fellow Yale U., New Haven, 1987-88; post-doctoral fellow Whiting Forensic Inst., Middletown, Conn., 1988-90; lectr. sch. nursing Yale U., New Haven, 1987, clin. interviewer dept. Epidemiology, 1989-90; neuropsychologist The Psychology Ctr., Madison, Wis., 1991—, Aandrus Med. Clinic, 1995—; vis. scholar Northwestern U., 1985, 86. Contbr. articles to profl. jours. U. Chgo. Adult Devel./Aging Tng. grantee, 1983, 84, 85, recipient Nat. Rsch. Svc. award, 1985, 86. Mem. APA, Okla. Neuropsychol. Soc. (founder), Internat. Neuropsychol. Soc., Nat. Acad. of Neuropsychol. Soc. Avocations: fishing, skiing, reading. Office: Aandrus Med Clinic 6510 Grand Teton Plz Madison WI 53719-1029

MERRIER, HELEN, actress, writer; b. Chgo., Mar. 10, 1932; d. Miner Thompson and Helen (Hembree) Coburn; m. Tim Meier, Dec. 23, 1954; 1 child, William Frank. BA, Mills Coll., 1954; BS, Northwestern U., 1955. Actress (radio) Ma Perkins, One Man's Family, Standard School House of the Air, 1934-52, (stage) Lady Lucinda's Scrapbook, Weston Park, Shropshire; French House, London, 1997, Edinburgh Fringe Festival, Scotland, 1996, New Am. Conservatory Theater, San Francisco, 1996, Time and the Conways, Remains Theater, 1991, Cinderella, Milw., 1991, Chgo. theatres including Second City ETC, Organic Theatre, Center Theatre, Court, Drury Lane Oakbrook, Hull House, Kingston Mines, other theatres, including Cleveland Play House, Coconut Grove Playhouse, Fla., Evergreen Stage Co., L.A., M & W Prodns., Milw., Guthrie Theatre, Mpls., (musicals) Woman of Year, Drury Lane, Evergreen Park, Ill., 1989, Sweeney Todd, Calo Theater, Chgo., 1991, Dreams of Defiance, N.Y.C., Chgo. and Ohio, Aristophanes' The Birds, Wisdom Bridge Theatre, Chgo., 1993, Dreams of Defiance, Theatre Bldg., Chgo., 1994, (film) Women in Treatment, 1990; dir. (stage) Center, Chgo., 1993. Women's bd. dirs. No. Ill. divsn. Salvation Army, 1965—; bd. dirs. Chgo. chpt. Prin. Found., 1972—, Women's Coll. Bd., 1956-66, Scottish Cultural Soc., 1976-89; mem. Gaelic League, 1981-86, Celtic League, 1985-96, Clan Irvine Assn., 1992—, Am. Anthrop. Soc., 1955-70, Am. Folklore Soc., 1955-70, Primitive Art Soc., 1975-85; mem. Apollo Chorus of Chgo., 1982-87, bd. mgmt., 1984-85. Mem. AFTRA, Actors Equity Assn. (Midwest adv. bd. 1983-84), Screen Actors Guild, Mills Coll. Club Chgo. (bd. dirs. 1962-81), Brit. Club Chgo., The Arts Club Chgo. Home: 915 Linden Ave Wilmette IL 60091-2712

MERRIFIELD, DONALD PAUL, university chancellor; b. Los Angeles, Nov. 14, 1928; s. Arthur S. and Elizabeth (Baker) M. B.S. in Physics, Calif. Inst. Tech., 1950; M.S., U. Notre Dame, 1951; A.M., Ph.L. in Philosophy, St. Louis U., 1957; Ph.D., MIT, 1962; S.T.M., U. Santa Clara, Calif., 1966; S.T.D. (hon.), U. So. Calif., 1969; D.H.L. (hon.), U. Judaism, 1984, Hebrew Union Coll.-Jewish Inst. Religion, 1986. Joined Soc. of Jesus, 1951; ordained priest Roman Cath. Ch., 1965; instr. physics Loyola U., Los Angeles, 1961-62; lectr. Engring. Sch., Santa Clara, 1965; cons. theoretical chemistry Jet Propulsion Lab., Calif. Inst. Tech., 1962-69; asst. prof. physics U. San Francisco, 1967-69; pres. Loyola Marymount U., Los Angeles, 1969-84, chancellor, 1984—. Mem. Sigma Xi. Home: Loyola Marymount U Xavier Hall Los Angeles CA 90045 *In today's world, we all stand in need of that pragmatic hope which allows us to see the possibilities for building a more just society and meeting the challenges before us. Without such hope we are paralyzed before our difficulties. With a less realistic hope, too idealistic, we are continually overwhelmed by failures. But with an openness to possibilities, we can move ahead with determination.*

MERRIFIELD, DUDLEY BRUCE, business educator, former government official; b. Chgo., June 13, 1921; s. Fred and Anna (Marshall) M.; m. Paula Sorensen, June 8, 1949; children: Bruce, Robert, Marshall. AB in Chemistry, Princeton U., 1942; MS in Chemistry, U. Chgo., 1948, PhD in Chemistry, 1950. Sr. rsch. chemist Monsanto, St. Louis, 1950-56; mgr. polymer rsch. Tex.-U.S. Chem. Co., Parsippany, N.J., 1956-63; dir. rsch. and devel. Petrolite Corp., St. Louis, 1963-68; v.p. tech. and ventures Occidental Petroleum Co., Houston, 1968-77; v.p. tech. and venture mgmt. Continental Group, Stamford, Conn., 1977-82; asst. sec. for productivity, tech. and innovation Dept. Commerce, Washington, 1982-89; undersec. econ. affairs, 1986-87; Walter Bladstrom prof. emeritus U Pa., Phila., 1989-94; pres., CEO Pinnacle Rsch. Inst. Devel. Co., 1991—; mem. adv. bd. Binat Research and Devel. Found., U.S., Israel, France, India, 1979—. Contbr. articles to profl. jours.; patentee in field. Mem. exec. com. Episcopal Ch., 1973-79; chmn. Princeton Alumni Coun., 1968-72. With USMC, 1943-46. Fellow AAAS, Inst. for Chemists; mem. Am. Chem. Soc., Indsl. Rsch. Inst. (dir., pres.-elect 1977-82 M. Holland Best Article award), Am. Mgmt. Assn. (trustee, chmn. rsch. coun.), Dirs. Rsch., Sigma Xi. Republican. Episcopalian. Office: Pridco Mgmt Corp 1655 Fort Myer Dr Ste 700 Arlington VA 22209-3108

MERRIFIELD, ROBERT BRUCE, biochemist, educator; b. Ft. Worth, Tex., July 15, 1921; s. George E. and Lorene (Lucas) M.; m. Elizabeth Furlong, June 20, 1949; children: Nancy, James, Betsy, Cathy, Laurie, Sally. B.A., UCLA, 1943, Ph.D., 1949. Chemist Park Research Found., 1943-44; research asst. Med. Sch., UCLA, 1948-49; asst. Rockefeller Inst. for Med. Research, 1949-53, assoc., 1953-57; asst. prof. Rockefeller U., 1957-58, assoc. prof., 1958-66, prof., 1966-92, John D. Rockefeller prof., 1984-92, emeritus prof., 1992—; Developed solid phase peptide synthesis; completed (with B. Gutte) 1st total synthesis of an enzyme, 1969. Assoc. editor: Internat. Jour. Peptide and Protein Research; contbr. articles to sci. jours. Recipient Lasker award biomed. rsch., 1969, Gairdner award 1970, Intra-Sci. award, 1970, Nichols medal, 1973, Alan E. Pierce award Am. Peptide Symposium, 1979, Nobel prize in chemistry, 1984, Rudinger award European Peptide Soc., 1990, Chem. Pioneer award Am. Inst. Chemists, 1993. Mem. Am. Chem. Soc. (award creative work synthetic organic chemistry 1972, Hirschmann award in peptide chemistry 1990, Glenn T. Seaborg award 1993), NAS USA, Am. Soc. Biol. Chemists, Sigma Xi, Phi Lambda Upsilon, Alpha Chi Sigma. Office: Rockefeller Univ Dept Chemistry 1230 York Ave New York NY 10021-6307

MERRILL, ARTHUR ALEXANDER, financial analyst; b. Honolulu, June 17, 1906; s. Arthur Merton and Grace Graydon (Dickey) M.; m. Elsie Louise Breed, Aug. 17, 1929; 1 child, Anne Louise Merrill Breiling. B.S. in Elec. Engring, U. Calif., 1927; M.B.A., Harvard U., 1929. Mem. engring., statistics, and mgmt. depts. Gen. Electric Co., Schenectady, also N.Y.C., 1927-61; fin. writer and analyst, pres. Merrill Analysis Inc., Haverford, Pa., 1961—. Author: How Do You Use a Slide Rule, 1961, Behavior of Prices on Wall Street, 1985, Battle of White Plains, 1975, Seasonal Tendencies in Stock Prices, 1975, Filtered Waves, Basic Theory, 1977, Bias in Hourly, Daily and Weekly Wave Patterns, 1979, Remembering Names, 1985; editor: Tech. Trends, 1961-88. Mem. Market Technicians Assn. (chartered, Ann. award 1977), Fin. Analysts Fedn., N.Y. Soc. Security Analysts, Mensa, Intertel, Soc. Preservation and Encouragement Barber Shop Quartet Singing Am., Sigma Xi, Theta Chi, Tau Beta Pi, Eta Kappa Nu. Republican. Congregationalist. Home and Office: 3300 Darby Rd Apt 3325 Haverford PA 19041-1071

MERRILL, ARTHUR LEWIS, retired theology educator; b. Tura, Assam, India, Sept. 14, 1930; s. Alfred Francis and Ida (Walker) M.; m. Barbara Jean Mayer, Aug. 18, 1951 (dec. June 1978); children: Margaret Jean, Katherine Merrill Nelson, Robert L.; m. Margaret Z. Morris, Sept. 11, 1985. BA, Coll. of Wooster, 1951; BD with distinction, Berkeley Bapt. Div. Sch., 1954; PhD, U. Chgo., 1962. Ordained to ministry United Ch. of Christ, 1954. Asst. prof. Bapt. Missionary Tng. Sch., Chgo., 1957-58; assoc. prof. Mission House Theol. Sem., Plymouth, Wis., 1958-62; assoc. prof. United Theol. Sem. Twin Cities, New Brighton, Minn., 1962-67, prof., 1967-95, prof. emeritus, 1995—. Author: United Theological Seminary of the Twin Cities: An Ecumenical Venture, 1993; co-author: Biblical Witness and the World, 1967; co-editor: Scripture in History and Theology, 1977; contbr. articles to profl. publs. ATS-Lilly postdoctoral fellow, 1966-67. Mem. Soc. Bibl. Lit., Am. Schs. Oriental Rsch., Israel Exploration Soc., Minn. Theol. Libr. Assn. (pres. 1994-95). Home: 1601 Bessmore Park Rd Rochester IN 46975-9095

MERRILL, CHARLES EUGENE, lawyer; b. San Antonio, Aug. 26, 1952; s. Charles Perry and Florence Elizabeth (Kupper) M.; m. Carol Ann Rutter, Apr. 28, 1984; children: Elizabeth C., Charles C. AB, Stanford U., 1974; JD, U. Calif., Berkeley, 1977. Bar: Mo. 1977, Calif. 1983, Ill. 1993. Ptnr. Husch & Eppenberger, St. Louis, 1977—. Mem. ABA, Bar Assn. of Met. St. Louis. Office: Husch & Eppenberger 100 N Broadway Ste 1300 Saint Louis MO 63102-2706

MERRILL, COOK, congressman; b. Phila., May 6, 1946; m. Camille Sanders; 5 children. BA in Econs. with high honors, U. Utah, 1969; MBA in Internat. Fin., Harvard U., 1971. Mmgt. cons., profl. budget analyst Arthur D. Little, Inc., Cambridge, Mass., 1971-73; founder, pres. Cook Slurry Co., Utah, 1973-96; mem. 105th Congress from 2nd Utah dist., 1996—; Mem. Transp. and Infrastructure Com., Banking and Fin. Svcs. Com. mem. transp. and infrastructure com., banking and fin. svcs. com., sci. com. Missionary LDS Ch., Eng., 1965-67; del. Nat. Rep. Conv., 1976-96. Office: 1431 Longworth HOB Washington DC 20515

MERRILL, DAVID NATHAN, ambassador; b. Balt.; s. Maurice B. and Ann (Nathanson) M.; m. Darlene J. Luke, 1976; four children. BA cum laude, Brandeis U., 1964; MA, Tufts U., 1965; MPA, Harvard U., 1974. Congl. liaison officer AID, 1976-79, rep. to Burma, 1979-83, deputy dir. legis. affairs, 1983-84, dir. East Asia affairs, 1984-87, mission dir. to Indonesia, 1987-90, dep. asst. adminstr., Europe Bur., 1990-94; U.S. amb. to Bangladesh, 1994—. Recipient Disting. Honor award AID, 1987, President's Meritorious Svc. award Dept. State, 1989. Mem. Am. Fgn. Svc. Assn. Office: US Embassy Dhaka Dept of State Washington DC 20521-6120

MERRILL, EDWARD WILSON, chemical engineering educator; b. New Bedford, Mass., Aug. 31, 1923; s. Edward Clifton and Gertrude (Wilson) M.; m. Genevieve de Bidart, Aug. 19, 1948; children—Anne de Bidart, Francis de Bidart. AB, Harvard U., 1945; DSc, MIT, 1947. Research engr. Dewey & Almy div. W.R. Grace & Co., 1947-50; mem. faculty MIT, 1950—, prof. chem. engring., 1964—, Carbon P. Dubbs prof., 1973-96, emeritus, 1996—; cons. in field, 1950—; cons. in biochem. engring. Harvard U. Health Services, 1982-94. Author articles on polymers, rheology, med. engring. Pres. bd. trustees Buckingham Sch., Cambridge, 1969-74; trustee Browne and Nichols Sch., Cambridge, 1972-74, hon. trustee, 1974—. Fellow Am. Inst. for Med. and Biol. Engring., Am. Acad. Arts and Scis.; mem. AIChE (Alpha Chi Sigma award 1984, Charles M.A. Stine award 1993), Am. Chem. Soc., Soc. for Biomaterials. Patentee chem. and rheological instruments. Home: 90 Somerset St Belmont MA 02178-2010

MERRILL, GEORGE VANDERNETH, lawyer, investment executive; b. N.Y.C., July 2, 1947; s. James Edward and Claire (Leness) M.; m. Janice Anne Humes, May 11, 1985; children: Claire Georgina, Anne Stewart. AB magna cum laude, Harvard U., 1968, JD, 1972; MBA, Columbia U., 1973. Bar: N.Y. 1973, U.S. Dist. Ct. (so. and ea. dists.) N.Y. 1974, U.S. Ct. Appeals (2d cir.) 1974. Assoc. Cleary, Gottlieb, Steen & Hamilton, N.Y.C., 1974-77, Hawkins, Delafield & Wood, N.Y.C., 1977-79; v.p. Irving Trust Co., N.Y.C., 1980-82; v.p., gen. counsel Listowel Inc., N.Y.C., 1982-84, bd. dirs., exec. v.p., gen. counsel, 1984-93, also bd. dirs. Pres. Arell Found., N.Y.C., 1985-93, also bd. dirs.; pres. Northfield Charitable Corp., N.Y.C., 1986-93; v.p., sec. Brougham Prodn. Co., N.Y.C., 1986-89, bd. dirs., sr. v.p., sec., 1990-93; v.p., sec. Marinetics Inc., N.Y.C., 1988-90, sr. v.p., sec., 1991-93, also bd. dirs., 1989-93; v.p. Sci. Design and Engring. Co., Inc., N.Y.C., 1987-88, bd. dirs., exec. v.p., 1989-93; v.p. Instl. Portfolio Mgmt., Shawmut Investment Advisors, 1993-95; co-mgr. Shawmut Growth & Income Equity Mut. Fund, Galaxy Growth and Income Equity Mut. Fund; v.p. Instl. Portfolio Mgmt., Fleet Investment Advisors, 1995-96; v.p. Trust and Instl. Portfolio Mgmt., No. Trust Corp., Chgo., 1996—. Recipient Detur award Harvard U., 1968, John Harvard scholar. Mem. ABA, Am. Mgmt. Assn., Assn. of Bar of City of N.Y., The Brook, Union Club (N.Y.C.), Down Town Assn., Racquet and Tennis Club, Somerset Club (Boston), Pilgrims of U.S., Riviera Country Club (Coral Gables, Fla.). Home: 4011 Granada Blvd Coral Gables FL 33146 Office: Northern Trust Bank 700 Brickell Ave Miami FL 33131-2802

MERRILL, HARVIE MARTIN, manufacturing executive; b. Detroit, Apr. 26, 1921; s. Harvie and Helen (Nelson) M.; m. Mardelle Merrill; children—Susan, Linda. B.S. in Chem. Engring, Purdue U., 1942. Devel. engr. Sinclair Refining Co., 1946-47; research and gen. mgr. 3M Co., St. Paul, 1947-65; v.p. fabricated products Plastics div. Stauffer Chem. Co., N.Y.C., 1965-69; with Hexcel Corp., San Francisco, 1969-86, pres., chief exec. officer, 1969-86, chmn. bd., 1976-88; adv. dir. Arrow Venture Ptnrs., N.Y.C. With USAF, 1942-46. Mem. Pacific-Union Club, Bohemian Club San Francisco, Villa Taverna (San Francisco), Burlingame Country Club. Home: 1170 Sacramento St San Francisco CA 94108-1943

MERRILL, JEAN FAIRBANKS, writer; b. Rochester, N.Y., Jan. 27, 1923; d. Earl Dwight and Elsie (Fairbanks) M. B.A., Allegheny Coll., 1944; M.A., Wellesley Coll., 1945. Feature editor Scholastic Mags., 1947-50; editor Lit. Cavalcade, 1956-57; publs. div. Bank St. Coll. Edn., 1964-65. Children's books include Henry, the Hand-Painted Mouse, 1951, The Woover, 1952, Boxes, 1953, The Tree House of Jimmy Domino, 1955, The Travels of Marco, 1956, A Song for Gar, 1957, The Very Nice Things, 1959, Blue's Broken Heart, 1960, Shan's Lucky Knife (Jr. Lit. Guild selection), Emily Emerson's Moon, 1960 (Jr. Lit. Guild selection), The Superlative Horse (Jr. Lit. Guild selection), 1961 (Lewis Carroll Shelf award 1963), Tell About the Cowbarn, Daddy, 1963, The Pushcart War (Lewis Carroll Shelf award), 1964 (Boys Club Am. Jr. Book award), High, Wide & Handsome, 1964 (Jr. Lit. Guild selection), The Elephant Who Liked to Smash Small Cars, 1967, Red Riding, 1968, The Black Sheep, 1969, Here I Come—Ready or Not!, 1970, Mary, Come Running, 1970, How Many Kids are Hiding on My Block?, 1970, Please, Don't Eat My Cabin, 1971, The Toothpaste Millionaire (Dorothy Canfield Fisher Meml. award 1975-76), 1972 (Sequoyah award 1977), The Second Greatest Clown in the World, 1972, The Jackpot, 1972, The Bumper Sticker Book, 1973, Maria's House, 1974, The Girl Who Loved Caterpillars, 1992; poetry books edited include A Few Flies and I, 1969; libretto for chamber opera Mary Come Running, 1983. Fulbright fellow India, 1952-53. Mem. N. Am. Mycol. Assn., Authors League, Vt. Arts. Coun., War Resisters League, Vt. Inst. Natural Sci., Dramatists Guild, Vt. Nat. Resources Coun., Vt. League Writers, Soc. Children's Book Writers, Fulbright Assn., Sierra Club, Audobon Soc., Phi Beta Kappa. *My interest in writing children's books may have derived from the impact certain books had on me as a child, and a wish to recreate the quality of that experience. As to my general motivation as a writer, I would say that it is to celebrate those aspects of the human experience that affirm the creative and life-reverencing instinct in man. I always hope that my stories may be essentially liberating, opening the reader to emotional, as well as intellectual experience, and that they may be entertaining, encouraging the capacity for joy by evoking the free play of a reader's curiosity, humor and inventiveness.*

MERRILL, JOSEPH HARTWELL, religious association executive; b. Norway, Maine, Jan. 16, 1903; s. Wiggin L. and Ella M. (Porter) M. Grad. high sch. Head retouching dept. Bachrach, Inc. (photographers), Newton, Mass., 1937-61; sec. Mass. Assn. Spiritualists, 1953-61; exec. sec. Nat. Spiritualist Assn. Chs., Milw., 1961-71; v.p. Nat. Spiritualist Assn. Chs., 1971-73, pres., 1973-94; v.p. Internat. Spiritualist Fedn. Spiritualists, London, 1975-81; lectr. social legislation for oldsters Townsend Orgn. Served with AUS, 1942-43. Address: 13 Cleveland Ave Lily Dale NY 14752

MERRILL, KENNETH COLEMAN, retired automobile company executive; b. South Bend, Ind., Feb. 20, 1930; s. Kenneth Griggs and Helen Shapley (Coleman) M.; m. Helen Jean Tagtmeyer, June 10, 1956; children: Barry, Diane, John. B.A., Cornell U., 1953; M.B.A., Ind. U., 1956. With Ford Motor Co., Dearborn, Mich., 1956-91; asst. controller Ford Motor Co., Dearborn, 1967-71, gen. asst. controller, 1971-73, controller N.Am. automotive ops., 1973-79, exec. dir. parts ops., 1979-80, exec. dir. bus. planning and trust mgmt., 1980-87; pres. Ford Motor Credit Co., Dearborn, 1987-91, ret., 1991; bd. dirs. Am. Dental Techs., 1990-96; v.p. Wadsworth (Ohio) Ford, 1992—. Pres. Plymouth (Mich.) Symphony Soc., 1969-70; vice chmn. bd. dirs. Detroit Inner City Bus. Improvement Forum, 1977-79; bd. dirs. Schoolcraft Coll. Found., 1982-94, pres., 1984-86; bd. dirs. Crossroads, 1992-94, 96—, treas., 1994. Mem. Fin. Execs. Inst., Greater Detroit C. of C. (bd. dirs. 1988-91, exec. com. 1990-91), Detroit Econ. Club, Barton Hills Country Club, Oaks Club (Sarasota, Fla.), Beta Gamma Sigma, Psi Upsilon. Episcopalian (treas. 1973-74, 79—). Home: 1450 Maple St Plymouth MI 48170-1516 also: 8779 Midnight Pass Rd Sarasota FL 34242

MERRILL, LELAND GILBERT, JR., retired environmental science educator; b. Danville, Ill., Oct. 4, 1920; s. Leland Gilbert and May (Babcock) M.; m. Virginia Gilhooley, Sept. 14, 1949; children: Susan Jane, Alison Lee. B.S., Mich. State U., 1942; M.S., Rutgers U., 1948, Ph.D., 1949. Research asst. entomology Rutgers U., 1946-49; asst. prof. entomology Mich. State U., 1949-53; mem. faculty Rutgers U., 1953-82, research specialist entomology, 1960-61, dean agr., 1961-71, dir. Inst. Environ. Studies, 1971-76, prof. center coastal and environ. studies, 1976-82; exec. sec. N.J. Acad. Sci., 1984-92. Served to maj. AUS, 1942-46. Medallist, Wrestling XIV Olympiad, 1948. Mem. AAAS, Entomol. Soc. Am., Coastal Soc., Sigma Xi, Alpha Gamma Rho, Phi Kappa Phi, Alpha Zeta, Epsilon Sigma Phi. Home: 49 Gulick Rd Princeton NJ 08540-4111

MERRILL, MARTHA, instructional media educator; b. Anniston, Ala., Apr. 21, 1946; d. Walter James and Polly (McCarty) M. BA, Birmingham-So. Coll., 1968; MS, Jacksonville (Ala.) State U., 1974; PhD, U. Pitts., 1979. Social worker Tuscaloosa (Ala.) County Dept. Human Resources, 1968-71, Calhoun County Dept. Human Resources, Anniston, Ala., 1971-73; social scis./bus. libr. Jacksonville State U., 1974-86, prof. instrnl. media, 1987—. Mem. Friends of Libr. bd. Anniston-Calhoun County Pub. Libr., 1984—. Recipient Ala./SIRS Intellectual Freedom award, Intellectual Freedom Com., Ala. Libr. Assn., 1992, Ala. Beta Phi Mu chpt. Libr. of Yr. award, 1997. Mem. ALA (exec. bd., Intellectual Freedom Round Table 1987-93), Ala. Libr. Assn. (pres. 1990-91, Disting. Svc. award 1995), Ala. Assn. Coll. and Rsch. Librs. (pres. 1989-90), Southeastern Libr. Assn. (chair intellectual freedom com. 1986-88, chair resolutions com. 1990-92). Office: Jacksonville State U Dept Ednl Resources Coll Edn Jacksonville AL 36265

MERRILL, MARY LEE, professional society administrator; b. Wilmington, Del., Dec. 6, 1925; d. Claude William and Sue Athelia (Savage) Sutton; m. Alan Douglas Merrill, Sept. 1, 1962; 1 child, Stephen Andrew. Grad. high sch., Wilmington, 1944. Exec. sec. E.I. du Pont de Nemours, Wilmington, 1950-65; founder, gov. Pilgrim Edward Doty, Wilmington, 1982-87, The Fuller Soc., Friendship, Maine, 1992—. Pres. United Meth. Women, Waldoboro, Maine, 1992-95; vol. Farnsworth Mus., Rockland, Maine, 1995; docent Olson House, Cushing, Maine, 1995. Mem. Nat. Mayflower Soc. (historic sites com. 1995), Del. Mayflower Soc. (councillor 1986-88), Daus., Founders, Patriots (treas. 1992—), Daus. of 1812 (registrar 1991-92), Maine Mayflower Soc. (chmn. pub. rels. 1992-95), Waldoboro Woman's Club (chmn. pub. rels. 1993—). Republican. Avocations: genealogy, travel, reading, civic work. Home: Martins Point Rd Friendship ME 04547

MERRILL, RICHARD JAMES, educational director; b. Milw., Apr. 15, 1931; s. Henry Baldwin and Doris (Lucas) M.; m. Kathleen Emden Keely, June 14, 1953 (dec. Jan. 1974); children—Wendy Ann, Vicki Louise, Robin Kay, Christina Suzanne; m. Terry Bradley Alt, Aug. 10, 1974 (div. 1976); m. Shannon Ann Lynch, June 19, 1977. B.S., U. Mich., 1953; M.A., Columbia U., 1957, Ed.D., 1960. Tchr. sci. Ramona High Sch., Riverside, Calif., 1958-62; secondary sci. coordinator Riverside city schs., 1960-62; exec. dir. chem. edn. material study Harvey Mudd Coll. and U. Calif. at Berkeley, 1962-65; curriculum specialist Mt. Diablo Unified Sch. Dist., Concord, Calif., 1965-91, dir. curriculum, 1980-81; assoc. dir. Inst. for Chem. Edn. and Project Phys. Sci., U. Calif., Berkeley, 1990-94; bd. dirs. San Francisco Bay Area Sci. Fair; mem. sci. adv. com. Calif. Assessment Program, 1983-89, also mem. assessment adv. com. to state supt., pub. instrn., 1984-86; dir. N. Calif. W. Nev. Jr. Sci. and Humanities Symposium, 1993—; lectr. Calif. State U., Hayward, 1996—. Author: (with David W. Ridgway) The CHEM Study Story, 1969; co-author: National Science Teachers Association Guidelines for Self-Assessment of Secondary Science Programs, 1975, Science Framework for California Public Schools, 1978, 84; co-author, editor: The Physical Science of Living in California, 1993. Bd. dirs. Ctr. for New Ams., Concord, Calif., 1984-91. Served from ensign to lt. (j.g.) USN, 1953-56. Mem. Nat. Sci. Tchrs. Assn. (past pres., past mem. exec. com.), Nat. Sci. Suprs. Assn., Elem. Sch. Sci. Assn. (coun. 1975-82, pres. 1983), Calif. Sci. Tchrs. Assn. (Disting. Svc. award 1990), Assn. Calif. Sch. Adminstrs., Acacia, Phi Delta Kappa. Home: 1862 2nd Ave Walnut Creek CA 94596-2553 Office: U Calif Lawrence Hall of Sci Berkeley CA 94720

MERRILL, ROBERT, baritone; b. Bklyn., June 4, 1919; s. Abraham and Lillian (Balaban) Miller; m. Marion Machno, May 30, 1954; children—David Robert, Lizanne. MusD (hon.), Gustavus Adolphus Coll., 1970, CUNY, 1996. Ind. baritone N.Y.C. and on tour, 1945—. Baritone in concert, opera and on radio and TV; winner, Met. Auditions of the Air, 1945, debut in opera, 1945; operatic roles include Escamillo in Carmen, Germont in La Traviata, Valentine in Faust, Amonasro in Alda, Marcello in La Boheme, Don Carlo in La Forza del Destino, Sir Henry Ashton in Lucia de Lammermoor; sang in La Traviata condr. Arturo Toscanini over NBC network; singer with NBC, 1946—; opened Met. Opera season Rodrigo in Don Carlo, 1950; appeared in Toscanini's final opera performance and rec. as Renato in Un Ballo in Maschera; opened Met. season as Valentine in Faust, 1953, as Figaro in Barber of Seville, 1954, Rigoletto in Rigoletto; Barnaba in Giocanda, Scarpia in Tosca, Renato in Un Ballo in Maschera, Iago in Otello, Count di Luna in Il Trovatore, Tonio in Pagliacci, Gerard in Andrea Chenier, 1962, Sir Henry in Lucia, 1964, Valentine in Faust, 1965, Germont in La Traviata, 1966, Amonasro in Aida, 1969; also opened Met. Opera season, 1971; opened Royal Opera House-Covent Garden season as Germont in La Traviata, 1967, Met. Opera visit to Japan, Tokyo, 1975; appeared in concerts, London, Bournemouth, Geneva, Israel, 1975; rec. artist: RCA-Victor, Angel, London, Columbia labels; stage debut as Tevye in Fiddler on the Roof, 1970; author: (novel) The Divas, 1978, (autobiography) Once More From the Beginning, 1965, Between Acts, 1976. Mem. Nat. Council of the Arts, 1968-74. Recipient Music Ann. award for rec. Ah, Dite Alla Giovine, 1946, best opera rec. award NARAS, 1962, 64, Harriet Cohen Internat. Music award, 1961, Handel medal City of N.Y., 1970, medal Westchester C.C. Found., 1981, Nat. Medal of Arts, 1993, Internat. Dor L'Dor award B'nai B'rith, 1994, Lawrence Tibbett award Am. Guild Mus. Artists Relief Fund, 1996; named Father of Yr. in Music, 1980. Mem. Opera Guild, AFTRA, AGVA, Actors Equity Assn., Screen Actors Guild, Am. Guild Mus. Artists. Club: Friars (monk 1968—). Avocations: golf, baseball, fine art. Achievements: 1st Am. opera singer to give 500 performances at Met. Opera, N.Y.C., 1973; ofcl. singer New York Yankees, 1969—; performer for Pres. Roosevelt, Truman, Eisenhower, Kennedy, Johnson, Nixon, Ford, Carter, Reagan; only singer to perform before both houses of Congress at Roosevelt Meml. Office: Robert Merrill Assocs Inc 79 Oxford Rd New Rochelle NY 10804-3712 *If you honestly feel that you are doing your best, it makes good criticism even sweeter and bad criticism less painful.*

MERRILL, STEPHEN, former governor. Student, U. N.H., Georgetown U. Former personal counsel to Sec. Air Force, Pentagon; atty. gen. State of N.H., Concord, 1985-89; gov. State of N.H., 1993-96; mem. N.H. task force on Child Abuse and Neglect, former pres., legal counsel; cons. Choate, Hall & Steward Assocs., Boston, 1996—. Served to capt., USAF. Fellow ABA; mem. Ea. Assn. Attys. Gen. (chmn.), Phi Beta Kappa. Office: Choate Hall & Steward Assocs Exchange Pl 53 State St Boston MA 02109*

MERRILL, THOMAS ST. JOHN, medical photographer; b. Jersey City, N.J., Feb. 21, 1946; s. Willard St. John and Frances Minnie (Havlieck) M.; m. Marie Knoetig, Mar. 19, 1967; children: Monica Marie-Rose, Michelle St. John. Student, Fairleigh Dickenson U., 1963-64, Germain Sch. Photography, 1967-68; AA, Saddleback Coll., 1990; student, Mt. San Antonio Coll., 1990-92; BS in Bus. Adminstrn., U. Phoenix, 1995. Cert. retinal angiographer. Photography asst. VA Hosp., N.Y.C., 1968; dept. head, photography Manhatten Eye, Ear and Throat Hosp., N.Y.C., 1968-69; med. photographer Don Allen Studio, N.Y.C., 1969-71; sr. ophthalmic photographer Mt. Sinai Sch. Medicine, N.Y.C., 1971-76; ophthalmic photographer U. Calif., Irvine, 1976-86; photographer Allergan Inc., Irvine, 1986-89; owner, pres. The Med. Image, Chino, Calif., 1983—; sr. med. photographer Providence St. Joseph Med. Ctr., Burbank, Calif., 1991—. Mem. Luth. Hour Rose Float Com., Pasadena, Calif. With U.S. Army, 1964-67, Vietnam. Mem. Biol. Photographic Assn. (fellow 1991, chmn. so. Calif. chpt. 1990-92), Ophthalmic Photographers' Soc., VFW (life), AMVETS. Avocations: Rose parade float operator. Home: 4395 Goldenrod Ct Chino CA 91710-1618 Office: Saint Joseph Med Ctr 501 S Buena Vista St Burbank CA 91505-4809

MERRILL, THOMAS WENDELL, lawyer, law educator; b. Bartlesville, Okla., May 3, 1949; s. William McGill and Dorothy (Glasener) M.; m. Kimberly Ann Evans, Sept. 8, 1973; children: Jessica, Margaret, Elizabeth. BA, Grinnell Coll., 1971, Oxford U., 1973; JD, U. Chgo., 1977. Bar: Ill. 1980, U.S. Dist Ct. (no. dist.) Ill. 1980, U.S. Ct. Appeals (5th cir.) 1982, U.S. Ct. Appeals (7th cir.) 1983, U.S. Ct. Appeals (9th and D.C. cirs.) 1984, U.S. Supreme Ct. 1985. Clk. U.S. Ct. Appeals (D.C. cir.), Washington, 1977-78, U.S. Supreme Ct., Washington, 1978-79; assoc. Sidley & Austin, Chgo., 1979-81, counsel, 1981-87, 90—; dep. solicitor gen. U.S. Dept. Justice, 1987-90; prof. law Northwestern U., Chgo., 1981—, John Paul Stevens prof., 1993—. Contbr. articles to profl. jours. Rhodes scholar Oxford U., 1971; Danforth fellow, 1971. Home: 939 Maple Ave Evanston IL 60202-1717 Office: Northwestern U Sch Law 357 E Chicago Ave Chicago IL 60611-3008

MERRILL, VINCENT NICHOLS, landscape architect; b. Reading, Mass., Apr. 28, 1912; s. Charles Clarkson and Bessie Louise (Nichols) M.; m. Anna Victoria Swanson, Jan. 20, 1943. AB, Dartmouth Coll., 1933; M in Landscape Architecture, Harvard U., 1937. Registered landscape architect, Mass. Office asst. Shurcliff & Shurcliff, Boston, 1937-42, 47-54, ptnr., 1954-58; ptnr. Shurcliff & Merrill and predecessors Shurcliff, Shurcliff & Merrill, Boston, Mass., 1958-81; prin. Shurcliff & Merrill, Cambridge, Mass., 1981-89. Founder, bd. dirs., pres. Charles River Watershed Assn., Auburndale, Mass., 1963-75; bd. dirs. Charles Basin Adv. Com., Boston, 1979-82; pres. Hubbard Ednl. Trust, Cambridge, 1981-89, bd. dirs., 1989-95. Capt. U.S. Army, 1942-46, ETO. Recipient Gold medal Mass. Hort. Soc., 1988. Fellow Am. Soc. Landscape Architects; mem. Boston Soc. Landscape Architects (pres. 1961-63), Hort. Club of Boston (pres. 1992-94). Avocation: home landscaping. Home and Office: 141 Old County Rd Lincoln MA 01773-3506

MERRILL, WILLIAM DEAN, retired architect, medical facility planning consultant; b. Portland, Oreg., June 1, 1915; s. Charles O. and Grace (Ruhl) M.; m. Bernice E. Wickham, Apr. 19, 1943 (dec. Sept. 1996); 1 child, Sue Ann Merrill Boardman. Student in Fine Arts and Forestry, Oreg. State U., 1936-38; student in Architecture, U. Oreg., 1939-42. Registered architect, Oreg., Calif. Prin. W.D. Merrill, Architect, Portland, 1956-64; architect, ptnr. Bissell & Merrill, Architects, Stockton, Calif., 1964-68; architect Kaiser Found. Hosps. design and constrn., 1968-81; pvt. practice hosp. design and constrn., residential design and constrn., Bay Area, 1981-91; hosp. and sch.

constrn. insp. Office of State Health Planning and Devel., State of Calif., 1984-93; ret. 1996. Served as lt. (j.g.) USNR, 1942-44, PTO. Mem. AIA (emeritus). Republican. Address: 14349 SE Sieben Pky Clackamas OR 97015-6319

MERRILL, WILLIAM DICKEY, architect; b. Honolulu, Mar. 21, 1909; s. Arthur Merton and Grace (Dickey) M.; m. Evelyn Gregory Selfridge, Oct. 23, 1936; children: Elizabeth, Thomas Selfridge. BA, U. Calif., Berkeley, 1930; MArch, Harvard U., 1932; PhD, Edinburgh U., 1974. Staff achitect Am. Schs. Oriental Rsch., Jerusalem, 1933-35; assoc. C.W. Dickey, architect, Honolulu, 1936-42; ptnr. Merrill, Simms and Roehrig, architects, Honolulu, 1942-60; pres. Merrill, Roehrig, Onodera and Kinder, Inc., Honolulu, 1960-65; cons. architect Honolulu, 1965-81; mem. affiliate grad. faculty U. Hawaii, 1971. Prin. works include Neill Blaisdell Concert Hall, campus Mid-Pacific Inst., campus Kamehameha Elem. Sch., class rm. bldg. Kamehameha Girls Sch., Foremost Dairies, TH-3 Hawaii Housing Authority, other comml., indsl., ednl. and mil. structures, hosps. in Hawaii. Mem. com. mgmt. Armed Svcs. YMCA, 1952-69; bd. dirs. Hawaiian Humane Soc., 1954-65, Hawaiian Mission Children's Soc., 1945-64. Fellow AIA (past pres. Hawaii, mem. emeritus). Home: 8545 Carmel Valley Rd Carmel CA 93923-9556

MERRIM, LOUISE MEYEROWITZ, artist, actress; b. N.Y.C.; d. Leo and Jeanette (Harris) Meyerowitz; m. Lewis Jay Merrim, June 27, 1948; children: Stephanie, Andrea Merrim Goff (dec.). BFA, Pratt Inst., 1947; MFA, Columbia U., 1951; postgrad., Post Coll., 1971-72, New Sch., 1977-78. Art tchr. pub. schs., N.Y.C., 1947-51, Port Washington, N.Y., 1970-83. One-woman shows include Plandome Gallery, L.I., Isis Gallery, N.Y., San Diego art Inst., Pan Pacific Hotel, San Diego; exhibited in group shows at Nassau County Fine Arts Mus. (Bronze award), Heckscher Mus. (Nora Mirmont award), Nat. Acad., Nat. Assn. Women Artists (Medal of Honor, Charlotte Whinston award), Audubon Artists (Stephen Hirsch Meml. award), Cork Gallery, Warner Comm. Gallery, L.I. Art Tchrs. (two awards of excellence), L.I. Art Tchrs. Award Winners Show, Pt. Washington Libr. Invitational, Glen Cove (2d prize), Manhasset Art Assn. (best in show, five 1st prizes), San Diego Art Inst., San Diego Mus. Art (Gold award), La Jolla Art Assn. (hon. mention), Hank Baum Gallery, San Francisco, Tarbox Gallery, Clark Gallery, Knowles Gallery, San Diego, Henry Chastain Gallery, Scottsdale; appeared in numerous theatrical prodns. including Fiddler on the Roof, Barefoot in the Park, N.Y., Anything Goes, The Musical Comedy Murders of 1940, Anastasia (Drama award), Fiddler on the Roof, The Music Man, What's Wrong With this Picture?, Marvin's Room, San Diego, The Foreigner; dir. Under Milkwood; dir., appeared in Spoon River Anthology. Mem. Nat. Assn. Women Artists, N.Y. Soc. of Women Artists, Contemporary Artists Guild of N.Y., Audubon Artist (N.Y.), San Diego Art Inst., Artists Guild of San Diego Art Mus. (pres. 1993), Artists Equity, Actors Alliance. Avocations: tennis, poetry, travel. Home: 3330 Caminito Vasto La Jolla CA 92037-2929

MERRIN, SEYMOUR, computer marketing company executive; b. Bklyn., Aug. 13, 1931; s. Joseph and Esther Bella (Manelis) M.; m. Elaine Cohen, Sept. 4, 1960 (dec. May 1962); m. Elizabeth Jenifer Slack, Oct. 12, 1963 (dec. Mar. 1995); children: Charles Seymour, Marianne Jenifer Weights. BS, Tufts Coll., 1952; MS, U. Ariz., 1954; PhD, Pa. State U., 1962. Geologist Magma Copper Co., Superior, Ariz., 1954; geologist U.S. Geol. Survey, 1956-58; chemist IBM, Poughkeepsie, N.Y., 1962-64; mgr. package devel., mgr. reliability and failure analysis Sperry Semicondr. div. Sperry Rand, Norwalk, Conn., 1965-68; cons. materials tech. Fairfield, Conn., 1967-69; v.p., dir. Innotech Corp., Norwalk, 1969-74; div. mgr. Emdex div. Exxon Enterprises, Milford, Conn., 1974-78; chmn., dir. Computerworks, Westport, Conn., 1978-85; v.p., dir. personal computing service Gartner Group, Inc., Stamford, Conn., 1984-87; pres. Merrin Resources, Southport, Conn., 1987-89, Merrin Info. Svcs., Inc., Palo Alto, Calif., 1987—; bd. dirs. Micrografx Corp., Richardson, Tex.; mem. adv. panel Apple Computer Co., Cupertino, Calif., 1982-83; mem. adv. bd. Compaq Computer Corp., Houston, 1984-85, Computer and Software News, N.Y.C., 1984-89; mem. program adv. bd. Comdex, Boston, 1985—; lectr. in field. Contbr. numerous articles to profl. publs.; patentee in field. Served with U.S. Army, 1954-56. Fellow Geol. Soc. Am., Am. Inst. Chemists; Computing Tech. Industry Assn. (founder, pres. 1981-83, bd. dirs. 1981-84). Home: 143 Buckthorn Way Menlo Park CA 94025-3027 Office: 2275 E Bayshore Rd Palo Alto CA 94303-3222

MERRION, ARTHUR BENJAMIN, mathematics educator, tree farmer; b. Williamstown, N.J., Oct. 25, 1938; s. Anthony Robert and Eva May Merrion; m. Martha Jane Banse, Dec. 26, 1965 (div. May 1977); children: Benjamin Thomas, Elizabeth Jane. AB in Math., Pfeiffer Coll. (now Univ.), 1965; MS in Numerical Sci., Johns Hopkins U., 1976. Navigations scientist Def. Mapping Agy. Hydrographic Ctr., Suitland, Md., 1966-78; fellow ops. rsch. analysis Sec. Army Pentagon, Washington, 1978-80; ops. rsch. analyst Asst. Sec. Army, Washington, 1980-86; tree farmer Huntingtown, Md., 1986—; instr. math. and stats. Embry-Riddle Aeronautical U., 1993-94; math. instr. Charles County C.C., 1990-91; tutor Literary Coun.; recruiter for cadets at West Point. Author: A Short Story By Edgar Allen Pooh. With U.S. Army, 1957-58. Mem. Md. Soc. SAR. Avocations: chess, violin, judo, wrestling, ice skating. Home: PO Box 395 Huntingtown MD 20639-0395 *The Bible says many different things to many different people. To Thomas Alva Edison it was a "Chemist's Handbook". To me it is the source of all man's creativity, directly from the greatest Creator of all. It is a source of inspiration, a solace for periods of depression, and a prescription when I'm in error.*

MERRISS, PHILIP RAMSAY, JR., banker; b. N.Y.C., June 7, 1948; s. Philip Ramsay and Elisabeth (Paine) M.; m. Janet Henry Hylan, Oct. 27, 1973. AB in Econs. magna cum laude, Lafayette Coll., 1970, MBA with high distinction, Dartmouth Coll., 1972. Assoc. corp. fin. dept. A.G. Becker and Co. Inc., N.Y.C., 1972-73; fin. analyst corp. banking dept. Chase Manhattan Bank, 1973, asst. treas. N.Y.C. dist., 1974-75, 2d v.p. mining and metals div., 1976-78, 2d v.p. petroleum div., 1978-79, v.p. global petroleum div., 1979-86, client exec., v.p. pub. utilities component, 1986-87, client exec., v.p. global energy component, 1987-89, credit supervising officer, div. exec., v.p. U.S. pvt. banking, 1989-94; credit exec. Chase Manhattan Pvt. Bank, N.Y.C., 1994-97, mng. dir. and credit exec., 1997—. Served to capt. U.S. Army, 1978. Tuck scholar Dartmouth Coll., 1972. Mem. Am. Econ. Assn., Fin Mgmt. Assn., Aircraft Owners and Pilots Assn., N.Y. Road Runners Club, Weston Gun Club, Yale Club, Fairfield County Fish and Game Club, Phi Beta Kappa. Republican. Episcopalian. Home: 100 Hillspoint Rd Westport CT 06880-5111 Office: Chase Manhattan Bank 1211 Avenue Of The Americas New York NY 10036-8701

MERRITT, BRUCE GORDON, lawyer; b. Iowa City, Iowa, Oct 4, 1946; s. William Olney and Gretchen Louise (Kuever) M.; m. Valerie Sue Jorgensen, Dec. 28, 1969; children: Benjamin Carlyle, Alicia Marie. AB magna cum laude, Occidental Coll., 1968; JD magna cum laude, Harvard U., 1972. Bar: Calif. 1973, D.C. 1996, N.Y. 1996. Assoc. Markbys, London, 1972-73; assoc. Nossaman, Krueger & Marsh, L.A., 1973-79, ptnr., 1979-81; asst. U.S. atty., L.A., 1981-85; ptnr. Hennigan & Mercer, L.A., 1986-88; ptnr. Debevoise & Plimpton, L.A., 1989-95, N.Y., 1996—. Bd. dirs. Inner City Law Ctr., 1991-96. Fellow Am. Coll. Trial Lawyers; mem. Calif. State Bar Assn. (exec. com. litigation sect. 1992-95), L.A. County Bar Assn. (del. state bar conf. 1984-86), Phi Beta Kappa. Office: Debevoise & Plimpton 875 3rd Ave New York NY 10022-6225

MERRITT, DEBORAH FOOTE, state legislator, vocational coordinator; b. Peterborough, N.H., June 19, 1961; d. William Lewis and Mary Elizabeth (Moore) Foote. BA in Sociology, Bowdoin Coll., 1983; MPA, U. N.H., 1994. Tchr. math. Buckley Sch., Sherman Oaks, Calif., 1983-84, Chaminade Coll. Prep. Sch., Canoga Park, Calif., 1984-85; saleswoman Smith Barney, L.A., 1985-87, B.R. Stickle & Co., Chgo., 1987; trader Harris Trust, Chgo., 1988-90; bus. mgr. Merritt Chiropractic, Durham, N.H., 1990-94; state rep. N.H. Gen. Ct., Concord, 1993—; marketer Devel. Svcs. of Stafford County, Dover, 1994; residential counselor Our House, Dover, 1994; vocat. coord. Riverbend Cmty. Mental Health, Concord, N.H., 1995—. Bd. dirs. Our House, 1993-94, counselor, 1994-95; adv. bd. health & human svcs. dist. coun. Inst. Disability. Mem. NOW, N.H. Women's Lobby, Gt. Concord C. of C., Planned Parenthood No. New Eng., Women's Legis. Lobby (vice chair Strafford County del. 1994-95, chmn. 1996—), N.H. Assn. for the Blind (bd. dirs.). Democrat. Home: 20 Cedar Point Rd Durham NH 03824-3305 Office: Riverbend Cmty Mental Health PO Box 2032 Concord NH 03302

MERRITT, DORIS HONIG, pediatrics educator; b. N.Y.C., July 16, 1923; d. Aaron and Lillian (Kunstlich) Honig; children: Kenneth Arthur, Christopher Ralph. BA, CUNY, 1944; MD, George Washington U., 1952; DS (hon.), Purdue U., 1997. Diplomate Am. Bd. Pediatrics, Nat. Bd. Med. Examiners. Pediatric intern Duke Hosp., 1952-53; teaching and rsch. fellow pediatrics George Washington U., 1953-54; pediatric asst. resident Duke U. Hosp., 1954-55, cardiovascular fellow pediatrics, 1955-56, instr. pediatrics, dir. pediatric cardiorenal clinic, 1956-57; exec. sec. cardiovascular study sect., gen. medicine study sect. div. rsch. grants NIH, 1957-60; dir. med. rsch. grants and contracts Sch. Medicine Ind. U., 1961-62, asst. prof. pediatrics Sch. Medicine, 1961-68, asst. dean med. rsch. Sch. Medicine, 1962-65, asst. dir. med. rsch., aerospace rsch. application ctr. Sch. Medicine, 1963-65, assoc. dir. med. rsch. Sch. Medicine, 1965-68, asst. dean for rsch., office v.p. rsch. and dean advanced studies Sch. Medicine, 1965-67, dir. sponsored programs, asst. to provost Sch. Medicine, 1965-68, assoc. dean for rsch. and advanced studies, office v.p. and dean for rsch. and advanced studies Sch. Medicine, 1967-71, assoc. prof. pediatrics Sch. Medicine, 1968-73, prof. Sch. Medicine, 1973-80, assoc. dean Sch. Medicine, 1987-96, prof. emeritus, 1996—, acting assoc. v.p. rsch., 1997—; rsch. tng. and rsch. resource officer NIH, 1980-87, acting dir. Nat. Ctr. Nursing Rsch., 1986-87; acting dean Sch. Engring. and Tech. to acting assoc. rsch. Purdue U., 1995-96, 97—; prof. emeritus Ind. U., 1996—; bd. dirs. Ind. Health Industry Reform; cons. USPHS, NIH div. rsch. grants Div. Health Rsch. Facilities and Resources, Nat. Heart Inst., 1963-78, Am. Heart Assn., 1963-67, Ind. Med. Assn. Commn. Vol. Health Orgns., 1964-67, Bur. Health Manpower, Health Profession's Constrn. Program, 1965-71, Nat. Library Medicine, Health Ctr. Libr. Constrn. Program, 1966-72; dir. office sponsored programs Ind. U.-Purdue U. Indpls. Office Chancellor, 1968-71, dean rsch. and sponsored programs, 1971-79; mem. Nat. Library Medicine biomed. communications rev. com., 1970-74; mem. com. to study rsch. capabilities acad. depts. ob-gyn Inst. Medicine, 1990-91. Contbr. articles to profl. jours. Chmn. Indpls. Consortium for Urban Edn., 1971-75; v.p. Greater Indpls. Progress Com., 1974-79; mem. Community Svc. Council, 1969-75; bd. dirs. Bd. for Fundamental Edn., 1973-77, Ind. Sci. Edn. Found., 1977-78, Community Addiction Svc. Agy., Inc., 1972-74; trustee Marian Coll., 1977-78; exec. com. Nat. Council U. Rsch. Adminstrs., 1977-78; bd. regents Nat. Library Medicine, 1976-80; chmn. adv. screening com. for life scis. Council Internat. Exchange of Scholars, 1978-81; bd. dirs. Community Svc. Coun. Cen. Ind., 1989-94, Univ. Hosp. Consortium, Tech. Assessment Ctr., 1990-93; mem. Ind. Health Industry Forum, 1993-96; chmn. scientific and tech. review bd. on biomedical and behavioral rsch. facilities NIH Ctr. for Rsch. Resources, 1994-97. Served to lt. (j.g.) USNR. Fellow Am. Acad. Pediatrics; mem. AAAS, George Washigton U., Duke U. Med. Alumni Assns., Phi Beta Kappa, Alpha Omega Alpha., NIHNCRR (chair scientific and tech. rev. bd. on biomed. and biobehavioral rsch. facilities 1994-97). Office: Deans Office Ind U Sch of Medicine 1102 South Dr Indianapolis IN 46202-5135 *The era in which I have lived and worked has been one of transition for women entering traditional male fields. What recognition and advancement I have achieved, have been due to maintaining high standards of performance on equal terms with my professional peers. I consider the three essential ingredients of success to be competence, optimistic tenacity of purpose and an enduring sense of humor.*

MERRITT, GILBERT STROUD, federal judge; b. Nashville, Tenn., Jan. 17, 1936; s. Gilbert Stroud and Angie Fields (Cantrell) M.; m. Louise Clark Fort, July 10, 1964 (dec.); children: Stroud, Louise Clark, Eli. BA, Yale U., 1957; LLB, Vanderbilt U., 1960; LLM, Harvard U., 1962. Bar: Tenn. 1960. Asst. dean Vanderbilt U. Law Sch., 1960-61, lectr., 1963-69, 71-75, assoc. prof. law, 1969-70; assoc. Boult Hunt Cummings & Conners, Nashville, 1962-63; city atty. City of Nashville, 1963-66; U.S. Dist. atty. for (mid. dist.) Tenn., 1966-69; ptnr. Gullett, Steele, Sanford, Robinson & Merritt, Nashville, 1970-77; judge U.S. Ct. Appeals (6th cir.), Nashville, 1977—; chief judge U.S. Ct. Appeals (6th cir.), 1989—; exec. sec. Tenn. Code Commn., 1977. Mng. editor: Vanderbilt Law Rev, 1959-60; contbr. articles to law jours. Del. Tenn. Constl. Conv., 1965; chmn. bd. trustees Vanderbilt Inst. Pub. Policy Studies. Mem. ABA, Fed. Bar Assn., Tenn. Bar Assn., Nashville Bar Assn., Vanderbilt Law Alumni Assn. (pres. 1979-80), Am. Law Inst., Order of Coif. Episcopalian. Office: US Ct Appeals Custom Hse 701 Broadway Nashville TN 37203-3944*

MERRITT, HOWARD SUTERMEISTER, retired art educator; b. Ithaca, N.Y., June 12, 1915; s. Ernest and Bertha (Sutermeister) M.; m. Florence Sederquest Hill, June 27, 1941; children—Jessica, Stephen, Jonathan, James. B.A., Oberlin Coll., 1936; M.F.A., Princeton U., 1942, Ph.D., 1958. Mem. faculty U. Rochester, N.Y., 1946-80; prof. emeritus U. Rochester, 1980—; cons. 19th Century Am. Painting, 1960—. Contbr. articles to various publs. Served with AUS, 1942-45. Decorated Bronze Star; Nat. Endowment for Humanities summer grantee, 1966-68. Mem. Coll. Art Assn. Home: 85 Bellevue Dr Rochester NY 14620-2703 Office: Dept of Fine Arts University Rochester Rochester NY 14627

MERRITT, JACK NEIL, retired army officer; b. Lawton, Okla., Oct. 23, 1930; s. Theodore and Lovell Wood; m. Rosemary Ralston, Oct. 31, 1953; children—Stephen Cahill, Grover Wood, Roger William. B.S., U. Nebr., Omaha, 1959; M.B.A., George Washington U., 1965; grad., F.A. Officer Advance Course, 1961, Air Command and Staff Coll., 1965, Indsl. Coll. Armed Forces, 1970; PhD (hon.), The Citadel. Commd. 2d lt. U.S. Army, 1953, advanced through grades to gen., 1985; served in various command and staff assignments U.S., Korea, Germany, 1953-65; served with (Army Gen. Staff, Pentagon), 1965-66; mem. staff (Asst. Sec. Def. for Systems Analysis), Washington, 1966-68; bn. comdr. (Riverine Arty.), Vietnam, 1968-69; staff (Asst. to Pres. for Nat. Security Affairs, White House), 1970-73; div. arty. comdr. 1st Cavalry Divsn., Ft. Hood, Tex., 1973-74, chief of staff, 1974-75, asst. div. comdr., 1975-77; comdg. gen. U.S. Army F.A. Center and comdt. U.S. Army F.A. Sch., Ft. Sill, Okla., 1977-80; comdt. U.S. Army War Coll., Carlisle, Pa., 1980-82; comdg. gen. Ft. Leavenworth, Kans., 1982-83; dir. joint staff Joint Chiefs of Staff, 1983-85; U.S. Rep. NATO Mil. Com., 1985-87; ret., 1987; pres. Assn. U.S. Army, Arlington, Va., 1988—; chmn. mil. profl. devel. com. West Point Study, 1977; adj. fellow Ctr. Strategic and Internat. Studies; mem. Commn. on West Point Honor Code, 1988-89. Bd. dirs. Atlantic Coun. Marshall Found., Brassey's, Inc.; chmn. adv. com. The Citadel. Decorated D.S.M., Silver Star, Legion of Merit, D.F.C., Soldiers medal, Bronze Star, Air medal, Joint Commendation medal, Navy Commendation medal, Army Commendation medal; named to Okla. Hall of Fame. Mem. Internat. Inst. Strategic Studies, Assn. U.S. Army, F.A. Assn., 1st Cavalry Div. Assn., 9th Inf. Div. Assn., Kappa Alpha. Office: Assn US Army 2425 Wilson Blvd Arlington VA 22201-3326

MERRITT, JOE FRANK, industrial supply executive; b. Paris, Tex., Dec. 9, 1947; s. Henry Grady and Margaret Leon (Murrell) M.; m. Barbara Jean Sands (div. May 1973); 1 child, Daniel Joe; m. Bonnie Louise McLure, Feb. 1, 1975; 1 stepchild, David Wright Dwyer. BA in Govt., U. Tex., Arlington, 1970. Cert. contractor Dept. Def. USA and Can. With purchasing A.F. Holman Boiler Works Inc., Dallas, 1970-77; supply salesman Stanco Indsl. Supply, Dallas, 1977-79, Tool Specialty Indsl. Supply, Dallas, 1979-80, Briggs-Weaver Indsl. Supply, Dallas, 1980-81; owner, pres. Joe F. Merritt & Co., Inc., Carrollton, Tex., 1981; v.p., gen. mgr. Abrasives & Buffs Co., Dallas, 1981-83; owner, pres. Buff, Polish & Grind Indsl. Supply Co., Inc., Argyle, Tex., 1984—; cons. The Broadway Collection, OLathe Kans., 1990, Ofenhauser Co., Houston, 1993, 94; Innovation Industries, Russellville, Ark., 1994; instr. buff, polish and grind methods quality control dept. Rsch. Facility, Peterbilt Motors Co., 1994; trainer Peterbilt Madison-Tenn. plant, 1997. Creator State of the Art Rsch. and Tchg. Facility, 1984, 100% Virgin Lambswool Buffing Belt, 1987, spl. extra wide spindle buffers to be manufactured by Baldor Electric, Ft. Smith, Ark., 1995; contbr. article to profl. jour. Recipient Cert. of Appreciation, City of Carrollton, Tex., 1981. Mem. Soc. Mfg. Engrs. Republican. Methodist. Avocations: sailing, coin collecting, travel, animals, sports cars. Office: Buff Polish & Grind Indsl Supply 1907 Fm 407 E Argyle TX 76226-9447

MERRITT, JOHN AUGUSTUS, geriatrician, educator; b. Greenwich, Conn., Nov. 1, 1931. AB, Dartmouth Coll., 1954; MD, Yale U., 1958. Diplomate Am. Bd. Internal Medicine, Am. Bd. Hematology, Am. Bd. Geriatric Medicine. Intern Upstate Med. Ctr., Syracuse, N.Y., 1958-59; resident in internal medicine Boston City Hosp., 1959-61, clin. fellow in hematology, 1961-62, rsch. fellow in hematology, 1962-63, assoc. vis. physician I and II med. svcs., 1966-70; asst. prof. medicine U. Md. Sch. Medicine, Balt., 1970-72; asst. prof., assoc. prof., prof. medicine U. Mass. Med. Sch., Worcester, 1972-88; chief geriatric medicine Hosp. of St. Raphael, New Haven, 1988—; asst. prof. dept. medicine Tufts U. Sch. Medicine, Boston, 1967-70; lectr. medicine Harvard U. Sch. Medicine, Boston, 1969-70; attending physician Boston VA Hosp., 1966-70; chief div. hematology York (Pa.) Hosp., 1970-72; chief div. medicine and geriatric medicine Worcester City Hosp., 1985-88; tng. Geriatric Edn. Ctr., Harvard U., 1986-87; asst. clin. prof. medicine Yale U. Sch. Medicine, New Haven, 1989—. Author textbooks; contbr. articles to med. jours. Fellow ACP; mem. Am. Geriatric Soc. (co-founder, bd. dirs. Mass. com.), Gerontol. Soc. Am., Nat. Coun. on Aging, Conn. Med. Soc. (ho. of dels., bd. govs.), New Haven County Med. Assn. Office: Hosp of St Raphael 1450 Chapel St New Haven CT 06511-4405

MERRITT, JOSHUA LEVERING, JR., retired engineering executive, consultant; b. Balt., July 28, 1931; s. Joshua Levering Sr. and Sarah Ethel (Sparks) M.; m. Eleanor Grace Williams , June 26, 1954; children: Nancy Lynn Mann, Debra Sue Stevens, Steven Edward. BSCE, Lehigh U., 1952; MSCE, U. Ill., 1955, PhD in Engring., 1958. Registered civil, structural, geotech. engr., Calif.; registered civil and structural engr., Nev.; registered structural engr., Ill.; registered profl. engr., N.M. Rsch. asst., civil engr. U. Ill., Urbana, 1952-54, rsch. assoc., civil engr., 1954-58, asst. prof. civil engring., 1958-60, assoc. prof., 1960-66, prof., 1966-68; vis. prof. U. Ill., Urbana, Ill., 1968-69; mgr. hard rock silo devel. program TRW, 1968-70, mgr. facilities engring., 1970-71; pres. Merritt Cases, Inc., Yucaipa, Calif., 1971—; dir. Redlands ops. BDM Internat., Inc., 1986-91; mem. U.S. nat. com. on rock mechanics NRC, 1989-90; expert mem. panel on underground tech. devel. NRC, 1990; chmn. bd. appeal Dept. Bldg. and Safety, San Bernardino County, Calif.; cons. in field, Urbana, 1958-68, Yucaipa, 1991—. Author more than 70 articles and rsch. reports. Fellow ASCE (local and nat. com.); mem. Am. Underground Constrn. Assn., Structural Engrs. Assn. So. Calif., Inst. for Shaft Drilling Tech. (charter mem.), Internat. Soc. for Rock Mechanics, Internat. Soc. for Soil Mechanics and Found. Engrs., Internat. Tunnelling Assn., Seismol. Soc. Am., Am. Concrete Inst., Earthquake Engring. Rsch. Inst., Sigma Xi, Phi Kappa Phi, Chi Epsilon. Presbyterian. Achievements include research in fields of structural dynamics, earthquake engineering and behavior of materials.

MERRITT, KENNI BARRETT, lawyer; b. Houston, Feb. 4, 1950; d. Walter Kenneth and Lydia (Jackson) M.; m. Thomas J. Barrett, Mar. 17, 1978. BA in Psychology, U. Okla., 1972, MEd, 1973, JD, 1979. Bar: Okla. 1980, U.S. Dist. Ct. (we. dist.) Okla. 1980. Dir. internat. office, fgn. student advisor U. Okla., Norman, 1973-77; assoc. Crowe & Dunlevy, Oklahoma City, 1980-85; dir. Crowe & Dunlevy, 1985—; mem. Select Com. to Advise the Okla. Securities Commn., Oklahoma City, 1986—; mem. Legis. Com. on Securities Ind. Reform, Okla., 1988-89. Contbr. articles to profl. jours. Recipient Outstanding Trial Advocacy award, Internat. Trial Lawyers Assn., 1979. Mem. ABA (forum com. on franchising), Okla. Bar Assn. (chmn. bus. assns. sect. 1993—), Oklahoma County Bar Assn., Phi Delta Phi. Office: Crowe & Dunlevy 1800 Mid America Towers Oklahoma City OK 73102

MERRITT, LAVERE BARRUS, engineering educator, civil engineer; b. Afton, Wyo., Mar. 11, 1936; s. Joseph M. and Lera (Barrus) M.; m. Jackie Call, Jan. 5, 1956; children: Teri F., Lynn T., Rachel R., Shaun S. BSCE, U. Utah, 1963, MSCE, 1966; PhD, U. Wash., 1970. Registered profl. engr., Utah. Prof. civil and environ. engring. Brigham Young U., Provo, Utah, 1970—, co-chmn. dept. civil engring., 1986-92; co-chmn. faculty senate, 191996-97; spl. cons. Utah Div. Health, Salt Lake City, 1973-74; cons. engring. firms, 1970—. Chmn. Provo Met. Water Bd., Utah, 1978-87. Named Utah Engring. Educator of the Yr. Utah Joint Enring. Coun., 1987. Mem. ASCE (nat. dir. 1982-85), Am. Acad. Environ. Engrs., Water Environment Fedn. (nat. dir. 1981-84, Bedell award), Am. Water Works Assn., Am. Soc. Engring. Edn., No. Am. Lake Mgmt. Soc., Sigma Xi. Republican. Mormon. Home: 562 E 3050 N Provo UT 84604-4264 Office: Brigham Young U 368 Cb Provo UT 84602-1021

MERRITT, NANCY-JO, lawyer; b. Phoenix, Sept. 24, 1942; d. Robert Nelson Meeker and Violet Adele Gibson; children: Sidney Kathryn, Kurt, Douglas. BA, Ariz. State U., 1964, MA, 1974, JD, 1978. Bar: Ariz. 1978, U.S. Dist. Ct. Ariz. 1978, U.S. Ct. Appeals (9th cir.) 1984. Assoc. Erlichman, Fagerberg & Margrave, Phoenix, 1978-79, Pearlstein & Margrave, Phoenix, 1979-81, Corwin & Merritt, P.C., Phoenix, 1982-87; with Nancy-Jo Merritt & Assocs., P.C., Phoenix, 1987-88; shareholder Bryan Cave, Phoenix, 1988-97; ptnr. Bacon and Merritt, Phoenix, 1997—. Author: Understanding Immigration Law, 1993; assoc. editor: Immigration and National Bylaws Handbook, 1993—; contbr. articles to profl. jours. Active Ariz. Coalition for Immigration Representation, Phoenix, 1988—; chair bd. dirs. TERROS, 1995—. Fellow Ariz. Bar Found.; mem. ABA, Am. Immigration Lawyers Assn. (chairperson Ariz. chpt. 1985-87, several coms., Pro Bono award), Am. Immigration Law Found. (trustee), Ariz. Bar Assn. (immigration sect.), Nucleus Club. Democrat. Avocations: modern literature, South American literature, hiking, scuba diving, gardening. Office: Bacon and Merritt 340 E Palm Ln Ste 240 Phoenix AZ 85004

MERRITT, ROBERT EDWARD, lawyer, educator; b. San Francisco, Jan. 31, 1941; s. Robert Edward and June Adele (Reynolds) M.; m. Robin Susan Kragen, July 2, 1966; children: Kim, Kevin, Kristin, Kate. BA, Sacramento State U., 1963; JD, U. Calif., Berkeley, 1966. Bar: Calif. 1967. Ptnr. Steinhart & Falconer, San Francisco, 1968-82, McCutchen, Doyle, Brown & Enersen, San Francisco, 1982—; lectr. U. Calif. Extension, Berkeley, 1976—, U. Calif. Extension, Davis, 1980—, U. Calif. Boalt Hall, 1989; mem. subdiv. adv. com. Calif. Dept. Real Estate, 1984-96; cons. real property law subcom. U. Calif. Continuing Edn. of Bar, 1983—; mem. planning com. Real Property Inst., 1984—; mem. editorial bd. Land Use and Environment Forum, U. Calif. Continuing Edn. of Bar, 1991-96. Author: Guide to Subdivision Sales Law, 1974, California Real Estate Forms and Commentaries Law and Business, Inc., 1985, California Subdivision Map Act Practice, 1987, Understanding Development Regulations, 1994; contbr. articles to profl. publs. Trustee Moraga (Calif.) Sch. Dist., 1977-89/. Named Citizen of Yr., Lesher Publs.-Morage Kiwanis Club, 1983. Mem. ABA, State Bar Calif., Am. Coll. Real Estate Lawyers. Home: 227 Paseo Del Rio Moraga CA 94556-1628 Office: McCutchen Doyle Brown & Enersen 1331 N California Blvd Walnut Creek CA 94596-4537

MERRITT, SUSAN MARY, computer science educator, university dean; b. New London, Conn., July 28, 1946; d. Nelson Alfred and Mary (Cory) M. BA summa cum laude, Cath. U. Am., 1968; MS, NYU, 1969, PhD, 1982; Cert., Inst. for Edn. Mgmt., Harvard U., 1985. Joined Sisters of Divine Compassion, 1975; permanent cert. tchr., N.Y. Systems programmer Digital Equipment Corp., Maynard, Mass., 1969-70; tchr. Good Counsel Acad. High Sch., White Plains, N.Y., 1970-75; adj. instr. computer sci. Pace U., 1972-78; asst. prof. Pace U., White Plains, 1978-82, assoc. prof., 1982-85, prof., 1985—, chmn. dept., 1981-83, dean Sch. Computer Sci., 1983—; mem. gen. coun. Sisters Divine Compassion, 1988-92. Contbr. articles to profl. jours. Recipient Cert. of Appreciation IEEE, 1990. Mem. Assn. for Computing Machinery (edn. bd. 1988—), Phi Beta Kappa, Sigma Xi. Roman Catholic. Office: Pace U 1 Martine Ave White Plains NY 10606

MERRITT, THOMAS BUTLER, lawyer; b. Toledo, Apr. 3, 1939; s. George Robert and Bernice (Gerwin) M.; m. Mary Jane Bothfeld, July 23, 1966; children—Thomas Butler, Haidee Soule, Theodore Bothfeld. A.B. magna cum laude, Harvard U., 1961, LL.B. cum laude, 1966. Bar: Mass. 1966, U.S. Supreme Ct. 1974, N.H. 1994. Law clk. to assoc. justice Arthur E. Whittemore Supreme Jud. Ct. Mass., Boston, 1966-67; assoc. Nutter, McClennen & Fish, Boston, 1967-69, Palmer & Dodge, Boston, 1969-73; asst. counsel to Gov. Mass., 1973; reporter of decisions Supreme Jud. Ct. Mass., Boston, 1974-94; pvt. practice Hollis, N.H., 1994—. Mem. Conservation Commn. Town of Sherborn, Mass., 1969-74, chmn., 1972-74; mem. corp. Tenacre Country Day Sch., Wellesley, Mass., 1972-84, trustee, 1973-78. Served to 1st lt. U.S. Army, 1962-63, capt. USAR, 1963-69. Mem. Mass. Bar Assn., N.H. Bar Assn., Fed. Bar Assn., Am. Law Inst., Am. Soc. Internat. Law, Internat. Law Assn. (Am. br.), Nat. Assn. Reporters of Jud. Decisions (pres. 1983-84).

Episcopalian. Clubs: Union, Harvard (Boston). Office: PO Box 344 Hollis NH 03049-0344

MERRITT, WILLIAM ALFRED, JR., lawyer, telecommunications company executive; b. N.Y.C., Aug. 7, 1936; s. William Alfred and Florence Anne (O'Connor) M.; m. Christine Marie Cartnick, Sept. 27, 1969; children—William Tyler, Brian Edward, Elizabeth Cody. BA in Econs., Holy Cross Coll., Worcester, Mass., 1958; LLB, Harvard U., 1964. Bar: N.Y. 1965. Assoc. Olwine, Connelly, Chase, O'Donnell & Weyher, N.Y.C., 1964-68; atty., v.p. ops. and controls Bunge Corp., N.Y.C., 1968-81; exec. v.p. TIE/Communications Inc., Seymour, Conn., 1981-90; pres. Wiltel Communications Systems Inc, Rolling Meadows, Ill., 1991-92; gen. counsel Carolina Barnes Capital Inc., N.Y.C., 1992—; ptnr. Seaboard Equities Inc., Stamford, Conn., 1992—, KM Group, Stamford, Conn., 1994—, Navigator Comms., LLC, Mt. Laurel, N.J., 1995—. Served to capt. USNR, 1958-80. Mem. Wee Burn Club. Avocations: skiing, boating, tennis. Home: 83 Brookside Rd Darien CT 06820-3505 Office: Ste 602 One Dock St Stamford CT 06902

MERRY, ROBERT WILLIAM, publishing executive; b. Tacoma, Wash., Mar. 5, 1946; s. Robert Ellsworth and Carol Beatrice (Rasmussen) M.; m. Susan Diane Pennington, Sept. 20, 1969; children: Robert Ellsworth II, Johanna Lynn, Stephanie Ann. BA in Comms., U. Wash., 1968; MS in Journalism, Columbia U., 1972. Legis. reporter, gen. assignment reporter, copy editor Denver Post, 1972-74; reporter Nat. Observer Dow Jones & Co., Inc., 1974-77, reporter Wall St. Jour., 1977-86; exec. editor Roll Call, Newspaper of Capitol Hill, 1986-87; mng. editor Congl. Quar., Inc., Washington, 1987-89, exec. editor, 1990-97, also bd. dirs., pres., publisher, 1997—; appeared on CBS Face the Nation, NBC Meet the Press, ABC Good Morning Am., CNN Newsmakers, and Take Two, C-SPAN, numerous other local and Can. programs. Author: Taking On the World: Joseph and Stewart Alsop—Guardians of the American Century, 1996; contbr. chpt. to book. With U.S. Army, 1968-71. Avocations: jogging, biking, hiking, biography, movies. Office: Congl Quarterly Inc 1414 22nd St NW Washington DC 20037-1003

MERRYDAY, STEVEN D., federal judge; b. 1950. BA, U. Fla., 1972, JD, 1975. With Holland & Knight, Tampa, 1975-83; ptnr. Glenn, Rasmussen, Fogarty, Merryday & Russo, Tampa, 1983-91; federal judge U.S. Dist. Ct. (mid. dist.), Fla., 1992—. Mem. Fed. Bar Assn., The Fla. Bar, Hillsborough County Bar Assn. Office: US Courthouse 611 N Florida Ave Ste 310 Tampa FL 33602-4500*

MERSER, FRANCIS GERARD, manufacturing company executive, consultant; b. Boston, Jan. 23, 1930; s. Herbert Bartlett and Irene (Bonier) M.; m. Mary Elizabeth Snedeker, Aug. 8, 1936; children: Pamela Bartlett, Alison Gerrish. BS, Babson Coll., 1957; grad. Stanford exec. program, Stanford U., 1982. Product mgr. Dennison Mfg. Co., Framingham, Mass., 1960-70, mktg. mgr., 1970-75, div. gen. mgr., 1975-80, v.p., 1980-85, group v.p., 1985-90, ret., 1990; cons. Avery-Dennison Corp., Framingham, 1990—; overseer Myles Meml. Hosp., Damariscotta, Maine, 1979—. Approx. 35 patents in fastening methods. Served with USAF, 1951-55. Clubs: Cabadetis Boat, Cruising of Am., Manchester Yacht. Avocations: squash, racquetball, ocean racing. Office: Dennison Mfg Co Avery-Dennison Mfg Co 1 Clarks Hl Framingham MA 01702-8163

MERSEREAU, HIRAM STIPE, wood products company consultant; b. Portland, Oreg., Aug. 4, 1917; s. E.W. and Ruth (Stipe) M.; m. Margaret Daggett, Dec. 25, 1937; children: Hiram Stipe, John Bradford, Timothy Daggett. Student, George Washington U., 1936-37, Harvard U., 1959. With Weyerhauser Timber Co., Klamath Falls, Oreg., 1937-38, Alexander-Yawkey Lumber Co., Prineville, Oreg., 1938-52; gen. mgr. lumber div. Crossett Co., Ark., 1954-62; corp. sr. v.p., gen. mgr. So. div. Ga.-Pacific Corp., 1963-82, cons., 1982—; past dir. Citizens & So. Nat. Bank, Augusta, Appalachian Hardwood Mfrs. Inc., Merry Cos., Inc., Augusta. Past bd. dirs. Young Life, Ga. Conservancy, Jr. Achievement Augusta; bd. dirs. Augusta br. Boys Clubs Am., Augusta Cancer Fund; trustee Paine Coll., Augusta. Mem. Nat. Forest Products Assn. (exec. com., dir.). Republican. Presbyterian (elder). Home: 6 Turnberry Ln Sea Pines Plantation Hilton Head Island SC 29928

MERSEREAU, JOHN, JR., Slavic languages and literatures educator; b. San Jose, Calif., Apr. 16, 1925; s. John Joshua and Winona Beth (Roberts) M.; m. Nanine Landell, July 11, 1953; children: Daryl Landell, John Coates. AB, U. Calif., 1945, MA, 1950, PhD, 1957. Teaching fellow, Slavic dept. U. Calif., Berkeley, 1950-52, research asst., 1953-54; instr. Slavic dept. U. Mich., Ann Arbor, 1956-59, asst. prof., 1959-61, assoc. prof., 1961-63, prof., 1963—, chmn. dept., 1961-71, 85-89, prof. emeritus, 1990—, dir. Residential Coll., 1977-85; mem. Joint Com. Eastern Europe of Am. Council Learned Socs./Social Sci. Research Council, 1971-74, chmn., 1973-74. Author: Mikhail Lermontov, 1962, Baron Delvig's Literary Almanac: Northern Flowers, 1967, Translating Russian, 1968, Russian Romantic Fiction, 1983, Orest Somov, 1989; assoc. editor Mich. Slavic Publs., 1962—; contbr. articles to profl. jours. Served to lt. (j.g.) USNR, 1943-46, PTO. Calmerton Slavic scholar U. Calif., Berkeley, 1954-55; Ford Found. fellow, London and Paris, 1955-56, Guggenheim fellow, 1972-73; recipient Disting. Service award U. Mich., Ann Arbor, 1961. Mem. Am. Assn. Advancement Slavic Studies, U. Mich. Research Club. Club: Waterloo Hunt (Grass Lake, Mich., sec. 1970-80); Commanderie de Bordeaux (Detroit). Avocations: flying, gourmet cuisine, raising horses. Office: U of Mich Slavic Dept Ann Arbor MI 48109

MERSEREAU, SUSAN S., clinical psychologist; b. Atlanta, Apr. 9, 1947; d. John Andy Jr. and Dorothy Grace (Smith) Smith; m. Peter Roland Mersereau, May 30, 1970; children: Barrett, Travis, Courtney. AB, Vassar Coll., 1969; MSEd, Elmira Coll., 1973; D in Psychology, Pacific U., 1989. Lic. psychologist, Oreg.; diplomate Am. Coll. Forensic Medicine, Nat. Registry of Cert. Group Psychotherapists. Psychology intern Pacific Gateway Hosp., Portland, Oreg., 1987-88, Psychol. Svcs. Ctr., Hillsboro, Oreg., 1988-89; psychology resident Lee Doppelt, Beaverton, Oreg., 1990-91; staff Pac. Gateway Hosp., 1990—; pvt. practice psychologist Beaverton, 1991-93; dir. Pacific Ctr. for Attention and Learning, Beaverton, 1993—; mem. Neuropsychology Delegation to South Africa, 1996. Tchr. Incentive grantee Guam Dept. Edn., 1979. Mem. APA, Oreg. Psychol. Assn., Nat. Register Health Svc. Providers, Am. Coll. Forensic Examiners (diplomate Citizen Amb. program), Nat. Registry Group Psychotherapist (cert. group psychotherapist), Vassar Club Oreg. (admissions com. 1984—, pres. 1984-88). Avocations: gardening, orchid growing. Office: Pacific Ctr Attention & Learning 3800 SW Cedar Hills Blvd Beaverton OR 97005-2035

MERSKY, ROY MARTIN, law educator, librarian; b. N.Y.C., Sept. 1, 1925; s. Irving and Rose (Mendelson) Mirsky; m. Deena Hersh, Feb. 3, 1951; children—Deborah, Lisa, Ruth. BS, U. Wis., 1948, JD, 1952, MALS, 1953. Bar: Wis. 1952, U.S. Supreme Ct. 1970, Tex. 1972, U.S. Ct. Appeals (5th cir.) 1981, N.Y. 1983. U.S. govt. documents cataloger U. Wis. Law Libr., 1951-52; reference asst. Madison (Wis.) Free Libr., 1952; pvt. practice law Wis., 1952-54; readers adv., reference and catalog libr., mcpl. reference libr. at City Hall, Milw. Pub. Libr., 1953-54; chief readers and reference svc. Yale Law Libr., 1954-59; dir. Wash. State Law Libr., 1959-63; exec. sec. Jud. Coun. Commn. Wash. Court Report, State of Wash., 1959-63; prof. law, law libr. U. Colo., Boulder, 1963-65; prof. law, dir. rsch. U. Tex., Austin, 1965-84, William Stamps Farish Centennial prof. law, 1984—, adj. prof. Grad. Sch. Libr. and Info. Sci., 1976—; vis. prof. law, dir. law libr. N.Y. Law Sch., N.Y.C., 1982-84; M.D. Anderson Found. vis. prof. law Queen Mary and Westfield Coll., U. London, 1994; interim dir. Jewish Nat. and Univ. Libr., Hebrew U., 1972-73; cons. to legal pubs. and law schs.; panelist various confs.; lectr. in field. Author: A Treasure in Jerusalem, 1974, (with J. Myron Jacobstein Dunn) Fundamentals of Legal Research, 1977, 6th edit., 1994, (with Jacobstein Dunn) Legal Research Illustrated, An Abridgement of Fundamentals of Legal Research, 6th edit., 1994, (with Albert P. Blaustein) The First One Hundred Justices: Statistical Studies on the Supreme Court of the United States, 1978, (with Gary R. Hartman and Suzanne F. Young) A Documentary History of the Legal Aspects of Abortion in the United States, 1990, 96 (with Jacobstein Dunn and Bonnie Koneski-White) Reports on Successful and Unsuccessful Nominations, 1992, 94, 96; contbr. articles to profl. jours., chpts. to books; editor numerous books in field. Bd. dirs. ACLU Cen. Tex. chpt., pres. Austin chpt., 1969; bd. advisors Anti-Defamation League Austin lodge, 1974-78; bd. dirs. Hillel Found., 1980-83; bd. dirs. Tex. Com. for Humanities, 1978-80, chair, 1980-82, conf. facilitator, 1982. With U.S. Army, 1944-46, ETO. Decorated Bronze Star. Fellow Am. Bar Found., Coll. Law Practice Mgmt., Tex. Bar Found.; mem. ABA (com. sect. econs. of law practice, gavel com., various other coms.), AAUP (chmn. nominating com. 1979-80), ATLA (chair law libr. com. 1984—), Am. Law Inst., Assn. Am. Law Schs. (various coms.), Internat. Assn. Lawyers and Jurists (bd. govs. Am. sect. 1980-95), Nat. Bar Assn., Am. Assn. Law Librs. (chair various coms.), Am. Soc. Info. Sci. (pres. Tex./Okla. chpt. 1992-93), Scribes (bd. dirs. 1974-95, book awards com. 1978-95, pres. 1991-93, chair Scribes Law Review Competition award com. 1993—), Soc. Am. Law Tchrs. (bd. govs. 1979-88, nominations com. 1984), ALA (rsch. librs. group 1987, libr. edn. divsn.), Am. Soc. Indexers, Internat. Assn. Law Librs. (U.S. adv. coun.), Internat. Fedn. Libr. Assns., Nat. Librs. Assn. (pres. 1980-81), Spl. Libr. Assn., State Bar Tex. (com. Tex. Bar Jour. 1983-90), State Bar Wis. (bd. mem. nonresident lawyers divsn. 1992—), Nat. Assn. Coll. and Univ. Attys., Tex. Assn. Coll. Tchrs., Tex. Humanities Alliance (bd. dirs. 1986—), Tex. Supreme Ct. Hist. Soc. (bd. trustees 1988—), Order of Coif (mem. triennial book award com.). Home: 6412 Cascada Dr Austin TX 78750-8157 Office: U Tex Sch Law Tarlton Law Libr 727 E 26th St Austin TX 78705-3224

MERTEN, ALAN GILBERT, academic administrator; b. Milw., Dec. 27, 1941; s. Gilbert Ervin and Ruth Anna (Ristow) M.; m. Sally Louise Otto; children: Eric, Melissa. BS, U. Wis., 1963; MS, Stanford U., 1964; PhD, U. Wis., 1970. Asst. prof. U. Mich., Ann Arbor, 1970-74, assoc. prof., 1974-81, prof., 1981-86, assoc. dean, 1983-86; dean U. Fla., Gainesville, 1986-89; dean Johnson Grad. Sch. of Mgmt. Cornell U., Ithaca, N.Y., 1989-96; pres. George Mason U., Fairfax, Va., 1996—; bd. dirs. Comshare, Inc., Ann Arbor; mem. inf. sys. adv. coun. Whirlpool Corp., Benton Harbor, Mich., 1987—; mem. Fla. Gov.'s Select Com. on Workforce 2000, 1988-89. Author: Internal Control in U.S. Corporations, 1980, Senior Management Control of Computer-Based Information Systems, 1983. Bd. dirs. Univ. Musical Soc., Ann Arbor, 1985-86, Common Sense Trust, Houston, 1990—, BTG, Inc., Vienna, Va., 1996—, INDUS Group, Inc., San Francisco, 1995—, Washington Campus, 1993-96; mem. Airport Authority, Gainesville, Fla., 1986-89; mem. Speakers Adv. Com. on the Future, Tallahassee, Fla., 1987-88. Served to capt. USAF, 1963-67. Lutheran. Home: 11020 Popes Head Rd Fairfax VA 22030 Office: George Mason U Office of Pres Fairfax VA 22030-4444

MERTENS, JOAN R., museum curator, art historian; b. N.Y.C., Oct. 10, 1946; d. Otto R. and Helen H. M. B.A., Radcliffe Coll., 1967; Ph.D., Harvard U., 1972. Curatorial asst. Met. Mus. Art, N.Y.C., 1972-73, asst. curator, 1973-76, assoc. curator, 1976-81, curator Greek and Roman dept., 1981—; curator, adminstr. Met. Mus. Art, 1983-90, mem. editorial bd. Mus. Jour., 1976—; adj. prof. NYU, Inst. Fine Arts, 1992—. Author: Attic White-Ground—Its Development, 1977, Greek Bronzes in the Metropolitan Museum of Art, 1985. Mem. Archaeol. Inst. Am., German Archael. Inst. (corr. mem.). Home: 124 E 84th St New York NY 10028-0915 Office: Met Mus Art Fifth Ave at 82nd St New York NY 10028

MERTENS, THOMAS ROBERT, biology educator; b. Fort Wayne, Ind., May 22, 1930; s. Herbert F. and Hulda (Burg) M.; m. Beatrice Janet Abair, Apr. 1, 1953; children—Julia Ann, David Gerhard. B.S., Ball State U., 1952; M.S., Purdue U., 1954, Ph.D., 1956. Research assoc. dept. genetics U. Wis.-Madison, 1956-57; asst. prof. biology Ball State U., Muncie, Ind., 1957-62, assoc. prof., 1962-66, prof., 1966-93, dir. doctoral programs in biology, 1974-93, disting. prof. biology edn., 1988-93; prof. emeritus Ball State U., 1993—. Author: (with A. M. Winchester) Human Genetics, 1983 (with R.L. Hammersmith) Genetics Laboratory Investigations, 9th edit., 1991, 10th edit., 1995; contbr. numerous articles to profl. jours. Fellow NSF, 1963-64, Ind. Acad. Sci., 1969; co-recipient Gustav Ohaus award for Innovative Coll. Sci. Teaching, Nat. Sci. Tchrs. Assn., 1986; recipient Dist. Service to Sci. Edn. citation Nat. Sci. Tchrs. Assn., 1987. Fellow AAAS; mem. Nat. Assn. Biology Tchrs. (pres. 1985, hon. mem. 1988), Am. Genetic Assn., Genetics Soc. Am. Episcopalian. Home: 2506 W Johnson Rd Muncie IN 47304-3066 Office: Ball State U Dept Biology Muncie IN 47306

MERTINS, JAMES WALTER, entomologist; b. Milw., Feb. 18, 1943; s. Walter Edwin and Harriet Ellen (Sockett) M.; m. Marilee Eloise Joeckel, Dec. 8, 1979. BS in Zoology, U. Wis., Milw., 1965; MS in Entomology, U. Wis., 1967, PhD in Entomology, 1971. Project assoc. dept. entomology U. Wis., Madison, 1971-75, rsch. assoc. dept. entomology, 1975-77; asst. prof. dept. entomology Iowa State U., Ames, 1977-84; entomol. cons. Ames, 1984-89; entomologist Nat. Vet. Svcs. Labs. USDA Animal and Plant Health Inspection Svc., Ames, 1989—. Co-author: (textbook) Biological Insect Pest Suppression, 1977, Russian edit., 1980, Chinese edit., 1988; contbr. articles to profl. jours. NSF Grad. fellow, 1970. Mem. Entomol. Soc. Am. (Insect Photography award 1984, 86), Entomol. Soc. Can., Mich. Entomol. Soc., Wis. Entomol. Soc. (pres., sec., treas., bd. dirs.), Cyclone Corvettes, Inc. (co-founder, pres. 1978, 79, sec., treas., bd. dirs., Mem. of Yr. 1982), Am. Mensa. Avocations: insect photography, Corvette automobile activities, gardening, movies, insect collecting. Office: Animal & Plant Health Inspection Svc USDA PO Box 844 Ames IA 50010-0844

MERTON, ROBERT C., economist, educator; b. N.Y.C., July 31, 1944; s. Robert K. and Suzanne (Carhart) M. BS in Engrng. Math., Columbia U., 1966; MS in Applied Math., Calif. Inst. Tech., 1967; PhD in Econs., MIT, 1970; MA (hon.), Harvard U., 1989; LLD (hon.), U. Chgo., 1991; Prof. honoris causa degree, HEC Sch. Mgmt., Paris, 1995; D (hon.), U. Lausanne, Switzerland, 1996; Dr honoris causa, U. Paris Dauphine, 1997. Instr. econs. MIT, Cambridge, 1969-70; asst. prof. fin. Alfred P. Sloan Sch. Mgmt., 1970-73, assoc. prof., 1973-74, prof., 1974-80, J.C. Penney prof. mgmt., 1980-88; vis. prof. fin. Harvard U., Boston, 1987-88, George Fisher Baker prof. bus. adminstrn., 1988—; rsch. assoc. Nat. Bur. Econ. Rsch., 1979—; prin., co-founder Long-Term Capital Mgmt., L.P., Greenwich Conn.; mem. internat. bd. sci. advisors Tinbergen Inst.; adv. bd. Ctr. for Global Mgmt. and Rsch., George Washington U. Author: Continuous-Time Finance, 1990, rev. edit., 1992; co-author: Casebook in Financial Engineering: Applied Studies of Financial Innovation, 1995, The Global Financial System: A Functional Perspective, 1995; editor: The Collected Scientific Papers of Paul A. Samuelson, vol. III, 1972, Finance Series, Basil Blackwell, 1987—; mem. editl. bd. Internat. Econ. Rev., 1972-77, Jour. Fin., 1973-77, Jour. Money, Credit and Banking, 1974-79, Jour. Fin. Econs., 1974-83, Jour. Banking and Fin., 1977-79, 92—, Fin. India, 1988—, Geneva Papers on Risk and Ins., 1989—, Jour. Fixed Income, 1991—, Fin. Rev., 1992—, Jour. Fin. Edn., European Fin. Rev.; mem. adv. bd. The New Palgrave Dictionary of Money and Finance, Math. Fin., Rev. Derivatives Rsch., Nihon Finance Gakkai, The Brookings-Wharton Papers on Financial Policy; contbr. articles to profl. jours. Recipient Leo Melamed prize U. Chgo. Sch. Bus., 1983, Roger Murray prize Inst. for Quantitative Rsch. in Fin., 1985, 86, Disting. Scholar award Ea. Fin. Assn., 1989, Internat. INA-Nat. Acad. Lincei prize Nat. Acad. Lincei, Rome, 1993, FORCE award for fin. innovation Fuqua Sch. Bus., Duke U., 1993, Fin. Engr. of Yr. award Internat. Assn. Fin. Engrs., 1993. Fellow Internat. Assn. Fin. Engrs. (sr.), Econometric Soc., Am. Acad. Arts and Scis.; mem. NAS, Am. Fin. Assn. (dir. 1982-84, pres. 1986), Soc. for Fin. Studies (v.p. 1993), Tau Beta Pi, Sigma Xi. Office: Harvard U Grad Sch Bus Adminstrn Morgan 397 Soldiers Field Rd Boston MA 02163

MERTON, ROBERT K., sociologist, educator; b. Phila., July 4, 1910; s. Harry David and Ida (Rosoff) Schkolnick; m. Suzanne Carhart, 1934 (sep. 1968, dec. 1992); children: Stephanie, Robert C., Vanessa; companion Harriet Zuckerman, 1968-92, m. June, 1993. AB, Temple U., 1931, LLD (hon.), 1956; MA, Harvard U., 1932, PhD, 1936, LLD (hon.), 1980; LHD (hon.), Emory U., 1965, Loyola U., Chgo., 1970, Kalamazoo Coll., 1970, Cleve. State U., 1977, U. Pa., 1979, Brandeis U., 1983, SUNY-Albany, 1986, New Sch. Social Rsch., 1995, Long Island U., 1996; Dr. honoris causa, U. Leyden, 1965, Jagiellonian U., Cracow, Poland, 1989; LLD (hon.), Western Res. U., 1966, U. Chgo., 1968, Tulane U., 1971, U. Md., 1982; LittD (hon.), Colgate U., 1967, SUNY, 1984, Columbia U., 1985, SUNY, Albany, 1986, Oxford U., 1986; Dr. Social Sci. (hon.), Yale, 1968; DSC in Econ. (hon.), U. Wales, 1968; PhD (hon.), Hebrew U. of Jerusalem, 1980, U. Oslo, Norway, 1991; D of Polit. Sci. (hon.), U. Bologna, 1996. Tutor, instr. sociology Harvard U., 1936-39; prof., chmn. dept. Tulane U., 1939-41; from asst. prof. to prof. Columbia U., 1941-63, Giddings prof., 1963-74, univ. prof., 1974-79, spl. svc. prof., 1979-84, Univ. prof. emeritus, 1979—; assoc. dir. Bur. Applied Social Rsch., 1942-71; adj. faculty Rockefeller U., 1979—; George Sarton prof. hist. sci. U. Ghent, Belgium, 1986-88; adv. editor sociology Harcourt Brace 1947—; ednl. adv. bd. Guggenheim Found., 1963-79, chmn., 1971-79. Author: Science Technology and Society in 17th Century England, 2d edit., 1970, Mass Persuasion, 2d edit., 1971, Social Theory and Social Structure, rev. edit., 1968, On the Shoulders of Giants, 1965, vicennial edit., 1985, post-Italianate edit., 1993, On Theoretical Sociology, 1967, The Sociology of Science, 1973, Sociological Ambivalence, 1976, Sociology of Science: An Episodic Memoir, 1979, Social Research and the Practicing Professions, 1982, Opportunity Structure, 1995, On Social Structure and Science, 1996; co-author: the Focused Interview, rev. edit., 1956, 3d edit., 1990, Freedom to Read, 1957, I Viaggi e le Avventura della "Serendipity", 1997; co-editor, co-author: Continuities in Social Research, 1950, Social Policy and Social Research in Housing, 1951, Reader in Bureaucracy, 1952, The Student-Physician, 1957, Sociology Today, 1959, Contemporary Social Problems, 4th edit., 1976, The Sociology of Science in Europe, 1977, Toward a Metric of Science, 1978, Qualitative and Quantitative Social Research: Papers in Honor of Paul F. Lazarsfeld, 1979, Sociological Traditions from Generation to Generation, 1980, Continuities in Structural Inquiry, 1981; co-editor Internat. Ency. of Social Scis., vol. 19, 1991, Social Sci. Quotations, 1992. Trustee Ctr. Advanced Study Behavioral Scis., 1952-75, Temple U., 1964-68, Inst. Sci. Info., 1968—; mem. bd. guarantors Italian Acad. for Advanced Studies in Am., 1992—. Recipient Commonwealth award for Disting. Svc. to Sociology, 1979, award Meml. Sloan-Kettering Cancer Ctr., 1981, Nat. Medal of Sci., 1994, Derek Price award Scientometrics, 1995, Sutherland award Am. Soc. Criminology, 1996; Disting. scholar in humanities Am. Coun. Learned Socs., 1962, Russell Sage Found. scholar, 1979—, Haskins lectr., 1994; NIH lectr. in recognition of outstanding sci. achievement, 1964; Guggenheim fellow, 1962, MacArthur Prize fellow, 1983-88. Fellow Am. Acad. Arts and Scis. (Talcott Parsons prize 1979), Brit. Acad. (fgn., corr.); mem. NAS, Am. Philos. Soc., Sociol. Rsch. Assn. (pres. 1968), Nat. Acad. Edn., Nat. Inst. Medicine, Am. Sociol. Assn. (pres. 1957, Disting. Scholarship award 1980), Ea. Sociol. Soc. (pres. 1969), History of Sci. Soc., World Acad. Arts and Scis., Soc. Social Studies of Sci. (pres. 1975, Bernal prize), Royal Swedish Acad. Scis. (fgn.), Academia Europaea (fgn.), Polish Acad. Scis. (fgn.). Home: 450 Riverside Dr New York NY 10027-6821

MERTZ, EDWIN THEODORE, biochemist, emeritus educator; b. Missoula, Mont., Dec. 6, 1909; s. Gustav Henry and Louise (Sain) M.; m. Mary Ellen Ruskamp, Oct. 5, 1936; children: Martha Ellen, Edwin T.; m. Virginia T. Henry, Aug. 1, 1987. B.A., U. Mont., 1931, D.Sc. (hon.), 1979; M.S. in Biochemistry, U. Ill., 1933, Ph.D. in Biochemistry, 1935; D.Agr. (hon.), Purdue U., 1977. Research biochemist Armour & Co., Chgo., 1935-37; instr. biochemistry U. Ill., 1937-38; research assoc. pathology U. Iowa, 1938-40; instr. agrl. chemistry U. Mo., 1940-43; research chemist Hercules Powder Co., 1943-46; prof. biochemistry Purdue U., West Lafayette, Ind., 1946-76; emeritus Purdue U., 1976—; vis. prof. U. Notre Dame, South Bend, Ind., 1976-77; cons. in agronomy Purdue U., 1977-94; affiliate prof. crops and soils Mont. State U., Bozeman, 1995—. Author: Elementary Biochemistry, 1969; author, editor: Quality Protein Maize, 1992. Recipient McCoy award Purdue U., 1967; John Scott award City of Phila., 1967; Hoblitzelle Nat. award Tex. Research Found., 1968; Congressional medal Fed. Land Banks, 1968; Disting. Service award U. Mont., 1973; Browning award Am. Soc. Agronomy, 1974; Pioneer Chemist award Am. Inst. Chemists, 1976. Mem. AAAS, AAUP, Nat. Acad. Scis., Am. Soc. Biol. Chemists, Am. Inst. Nutrition (Osborne-Mendel award 1972), Am. Chem. Soc. (Spencer award 1970), Am. Assn. Cereal Chemists. Lutheran. Co-discoverer high lysine corn, 1963. Office: Montana State Univ Dept Plant and Soils Bozeman MT 59717

MERTZ, FRANCIS JAMES, academic administrator; b. Newark, Sept. 24, 1937; s. Frank E. and Marian E. (Brady) M.; m. Gail Williams, Apr. 11, 1964; children: Lynn, Christopher, Suzanne, David, Amy, Jonathan. BA, St. Peter's Coll., 1958; JD, NYU, 1961; LLD (hon.), Felician Coll., 1984, Stevens Inst. Tech., Hoboken, N.J., 1988. Bar: N.J. 1967. Exec. v.p. St. Peter's Coll., Jersey City, 1972-78; v.p., CFO N.Y. Med. Coll., Valhalla, 1978-79; dir. adminstrn. Sage Gray Todd and Sims, N.Y.C., 1979-81; pres. Ind. Coll. Fund N.J., Summit, 1981-90, Assn. Ind. Colls. and Univs. N.J., Summit, 1982-90, Fairleigh Dickinson U., Teaneck, N.J., 1990—; bd. dirs. Summit Bancorp (formerly UJB Fin.), Princeton, N.J., Summit Bank. Trustee, sec. St. James Found., Westfield, N.J., 1987—; bd. dirs. Ready Found., Tri County Scholarship Fund, Paterson, N.J., 1992—, New Cmty. Found., Libr. Sci. Ctr. Mem. N.J. State Bar Assn., University Club. Home: 167 Stanie Brae Dr Watchung NJ 07060-6233 Office: Fairleigh Dickinson U 1000 River Rd Teaneck NJ 07666-1914

MERTZ, STUART MOULTON, landscape architect; b. Wayne, Pa., Dec. 4, 1915; s. Walter Smith and Elizabeth Armenia (Day) M.; m. Constance Coulter Buck, June 27, 1942 (dec. Mar. 17, 1978); children: Stuart Moulton, Maurice Walter; m. Theodora Lucks Hager, Oct. 13, 1979 (div. Dec. 1987); married, Sept. 13, 1988. B.S. in Landscape Architecture, Pa. State U., 1937; B.Landscape Architecture, Cornell U., 1938; travelling fellow, Am. Acad. Rome, 1938-40, fellow, 1940. With John Noyes, St. Louis, 1940-41; chief designer Harland Bartholomew & Assocs., St. Louis, 1941-49; pvt. practice landscape architecture St. Louis, 1949-83; sr. assoc. Austin Tao & Assocs., Inc., 1984-92; lectr. nurserymen's short course Tex. A & M Coll.; lectr. landscape architecture Iowa State U., also S.W. Park Tng. Inst., U. Kans., U. Ga., Mich. State U., others. Work includes 26 parks and playgrounds for City and County of St. Louis, St. John's Hosp., St. Lukes Hosp. West, Visitation Acad., Florissant Valley C.C., Bettendorf Stores, Meramec C.C., Barnwell Art and Garden Ctr., Shreveport, La. golf course and facilities design St. Andrew's Golf Club, St. Charles, Mo., site planning and recreational facilities design for Bellevive Country Club, Meadowbrook Country Club, Bogey Golf Club. Pres., People's Art Center Assn., 1960-62, bd. dirs., 1959-63; bd. dirs. Spirit of St. Louis Fund, 1960-62; mem. adv. council U. Mo. Sch. Forestry, Fisheries and Wildlife, 1974-83. Served to 2d lt. USAAF, 1943-45. Recipient Centennial medal for disting. achievement in landscape architecture Am. Acad. in Rome, 1994. Fellow Am. Soc. Landscape Architects (chmn. St. Louis 1960-63, trustee Missouri Valley chpt. 1954-60, nat. sec.-treas. 1963-67, nat. 2d v.p. 1967-69, chmn. Coun. of Fellows 1977-79, bd. soc. found. 1965-69, 71-75, sec.-treas. 1967-69); mem. Mo. Assn. Landscape Architects (pres. 1966-86), Sovestor's Investment Club (sec. 1988-92, pres. 1992-94), Cornell Club St. Louis (pres. 1955-56), Penn State Club, Chi Phi. Presbyterian. Home: 9009 Sedgwick Place Dr Saint Louis MO 63124-1890

MERTZ, WALTER, retired government research executive; b. Mainz, Germany, May 4, 1923; s. Oskar and Anne (Gabelmann) M.; m. Marianne C. Maret, Aug. 8, 1953. M.D., U. Mainz, 1951. Intern County Hosp., Hersfeld, Germany, 1952-53; resident Univ. Hosp., Frankfurt, Germany, 1953; vis. scientist NIH, Bethesda, Md., 1953-61; chief dept. biol. chemistry Walter Reed Army Inst. Research, Washington, 1961-69; mem. staff Nutrition Inst., Agrl. Research Service, Dept. Agrl., Beltsville, Md., 1969-72, chmn. inst., 1972-92; ret.; dir. Human Nutrition Research Ctr.; lectr. George Washington U. Med. Sch., 1963-73. Served with German Army, 1941-46. Recipient Osborne and Mendel award Am. Inst. Nutrition, 1971, Superior Performance award Dept. Agr., 1972, Lederle award in Human Nutrition, 1982, Internat. prize for Modern Nutrition, 1987, award for Disting. Svc., Dept. Agr., 1988. Mem. Am. Inst. Nutrition, Am. Soc. Biol. Chemists, Am. Soc. Clin. Nutrition. Home: 12401 Saint James Rd Rockville MD 20850-3744

MERWIN, DAVIS UNDERWOOD, newspaper executive; b. Chgo., June 22, 1928; s. Davis and Josephine (Underwood) M.; m. Nancy Snowden Smith Tailer, Nov. 14, 1958 (dec. Feb. 1995); children: Davis Fell, Laura Howell, James B. Tailer. AB, Harvard U., 1950; LLD (hon.), Ill. Wesleyan U., 1991. Pres. Evergreen Comm., Inc., Bloomington, Ill., 1969-80; pub. Daily Pantagraph, 1968-80; pres. Wood Canyon Corp., Tucson, 1989-93; vice-chmn. Bloomington Broadcasting Corp., 1994—; bd. dirs. Crown C Cattle Co. Bd. dirs., mem. exec. com. Adlai E. Stevenson Lectures; trustee emeritus Ill. Wesleyan U., Inland Daily Press Found., chmn. investment com., 1983-91; trustee Ill. Nature Conservancy. Recipient Disting. Svc. award U.S. Jaycees, 1959. Mem. Am. Newspaper Pubs. Assn., Inland Daily Press Assn. (pres. 1977, chmn. bd. dirs. 1978), Harvard Club (Chgo.), Phoenix-SK Club, Hasty Pudding Club, Bloomington Country Club, Ristigouche Salmon Club. Republican. Unitarian. Office: 236 Greenwood Ave

Bloomington IL 61704-7243 Mailing Address: PO Box 8 Bloomington IL 61702-0008

MERWIN, EDWIN PRESTON, health care consultant, educator; b. Revere, Mass., Oct. 13, 1927; s. George Preston and Edith Charlotte (Miller) M.; m. Marylynn Joy Bicknell, Nov. 3, 1979; 1 son by previous marriage, Ralph Edwin; stepchildren: Charles John Burns, Patrick Edward Burns, Stephen Allen Burns, John David Light, Robert Allen Light, Frederick John Light. BS, U. So.Calif., 1955, postgrad. Law Sch., 1955-57; postgrad., San Fernando Valley State Coll., 1965-66; M in Pub. Health (USPHS fellow), U. Calif. at Berkeley, 1970; PhD, Brantridge Forest (Eng.), 1971. Tng. officer Camarillo (Calif.) State Hosp., 1961-66; asst. coord. Mental Retardation Programs, State of Cal., Sacramento, 1966-67; project dir. Calif. Council Retarded Children, Sacramento, 1967-69; asst. dir. Golden Empire Comprehensive Health Coun., Sacramento, 1970-76, health care cons., 1976-77; gen. ptnr. EDRA Assocs., 1976—; cons. Calif. Dept. Health, 1977-78; cons. Calif. Office Statewide Health Planning and Devel., 1978-79; chief Health Professions Career Opportunity Program State of Calif., Sacramento, 1979-81; chief Health Personnel Info. and Analysis Sect., Office of Statewide Health Planning and Devel., 1981-82, asst. div. chief div. Health Professions Devel., 1982-84, asst. dep. dir., 1984-86; project dir. Alzheimers Disease Insts., Calif., 1986-87; chief Demonstration Project Sect. div. Health Projects and Analysis, 1987-89, chief Policy Analysis and Professsions Devel. Sect., 1989-93; tchr. Ventura (Calif.) Coll., 1962-66, Merritt Coll., Oakland, Calif., 1969; sr. adj. prof. Golden Gate U., 1976—; lectr. continuing edn. program U. Calif. at Berkeley; instr. Los Rios C.C. Dist., 1982—; mem. Task Force for New Health Care Sys. in Macedonia; mem. adv. com. Health Faculty, Golden Gate U., 1995—; cons.. NIMH, HEW, Calif. Assn. Health Facilities. Mem. Health Adv. Council San Juan Sch. Dist., 1972-73; treas. Calif. Camping and Recreation Council, 1972-73. Bd. dirs. Sacramento Rehab. Facility, 1970-86, v.p., 1973-76, bd dirs. Sacramento Vocational Svcs., 1986-93. Recipient Pres.'s award Golden Gate U., 1982. Mem. Am. Assn. Mental Deficiency, Calif. Pub. Health Assn., Sacramento Mental Health Assn., Sacramento Assn. Retarded (life mem., dir., svc. award 1984), Nat. Assn. for Retarded Children, DAV (life), Am. Legion, Marines Meml. Assn. (life), AAAS, SCAPA Praetors U. So. Calif., Miles Merwin Assn. Founder, editor: T. Patrick Heck Meml. Case Series, 1982; co-author textbook: (with Dr. Fred Heck) Written Case Analysis, 1982; founder, cons. Internat. U. Am., 1995—; contbr. articles to profl. lit. Home: 8008 Archer Ave Fair Oaks CA 95628-5907 Office: Golden Gate U 3620 Northgate Blvd Ste 100 Sacramento CA 95834-1619

MERWIN, HARMON TURNER, retired regional planner; b. Middlefield, Ohio, July 10, 1920; s. Harry Elverton and Ora (Turner) M.; m. Eldred Louise Merwin, Apr. 10, 1954; children: Elaine, Brian, Kathryn (dec.). B in Landcape Architecture, Ohio State U., 1950. Planner, then dir. Franklin County Regional Planning Commn., Columbus, Ohio, 1951-69; dep. dir. Mid-Ohio Regional Planning Commn., Columbus, 1970-74; program mgr. Mid-Ohio Regional Planning Commn., 1975-80, spl. projects sr. cons., 1975-80, sr. cons., 1981-91; retired, 1991; cons. in field. Bd. dirs., Columbus Met. Area Community Action Orgn., 1963-65; mem. facilities com., environ. health subcom., Mid-Ohio Health Planning Fedn., Columbus; pres. Ohio Planning Conf., 1963-65. Sgt. USAAF, 1942-46, ETO. Mem. Am. Inst. Cert. Planners (past pres. Ohio chpt.). Republican. Methodist. Avocations: photography, table tennis, travel. Home: 2325 Lytham Rd Columbus OH 43220-4637

MERWIN, JOHN DAVID, lawyer, former governor; b. Frederiksted, St. Croix, V.I., Sept. 26, 1921; s. Miles and Marguerite Louise (Fleming) M.; m. Marjorie Davis Spaulding, Feb. 18, 1993. Student, U. Lausanne, Switzerland, 1938-39, U. P.R., 1939-40; BSc, Yale U., 1943; LLB, George Washington U., 1948. Bar: Conn., V.I. 1949. Practice law St. Croix, V.I., 1949-50, 1953-57, 67-85; gen. counsel, v.p. Rob't L. Merwin & Co., Inc., 1953-57; senator-at-large V.I. Legislature, 1955-57; govt. sec. for V.I., 1957-58, gov. V.I., 1958-61; rep. Chase Manhattan Bank, Nassau, Bahamas, 1961-65; exec. v.p. Equity Pub. Corp. Orford, N.H., 1965-67. Chmn. V.I. Port Authority, 1972-75; Rep. candidate for Pres. N.H. Primary Election, 1992; pres. The Nason Found., Cleve., 1981—. Served from 2d lt. to capt. F.A. AUS, 1942-46, 50-53. Decorated Bronze Star; Croix de Guerre with silver star. Mem. Conn., N.H., V.I. bar assns., Phi Delta Phi. Episcopalian. Clubs: Tennis of St. Croix (V.I.), Yale (N.Y.C.), Cosmos (Washington). Home and Office: PO Box 778 Franconia NH 03580-0778

MERZ, MICHAEL, federal judge; b. Dayton, Ohio, Mar. 29, 1945; s. Robert Louis and Hazel (Appleton) M.; m. Marguerite Logan LeBreton, Sept. 7, 1968; children: Peter Henry, Nicholas George. AB cum laude, Harvard U., 1967, JD, 1970. Bar: Ohio 1970, U.S. Dist. Ct. (so. dist.) Ohio 1971, U.S Supreme Ct. 1974, U.S. Ct. Appeals (6th cir.) 1975. Assoc. Smith & Schnacke, Dayton, Ohio, 1970-75, ptnr., 1976-77; judge Dayton Mcpl. Ct., 1977-84; magistrate U.S. Dist. Ct. (so. dist.) Ohio, 1984—; adj. prof. U. Dayton Law Sch., 1979—; mem. rules adv. com. Ohio Supreme Ct., 1989-96. Bd. dirs. United Way, Dayton, 1981-95; trustee Dayton and Montgomery County Pub. Libr., 1991—, Montgomery County Hist. Soc., 1995—, Ohio Libr. Coun., 1997—. Mem. ABA, Fed. Bar Assn., Am. Judicature Soc., Fed. Magistrate Judges Assn., Ohio State Bar Assn., Dayton Bar Assn. Republican. Roman Catholic. Office: US Dist Ct 902 Federal Bldg 200 W 2nd St Dayton OH 45402-1430

MERZBACHER, EUGEN, physicist, educator; b. Berlin, Germany, Apr. 9, 1921; came to U.S., 1947, naturalized, 1953; s. Siegfried and Lilli (Wilmersdoerffer) M.; m. Ann Townsend Reid, July 11, 1952; children: Celia, Charles, Matthew, Mary. Licentiate, U. Istanbul, 1943; A.M., Harvard U., 1948, Ph.D., 1950; DSc (hon.), U. N.C., Chapel Hill, 1993. High sch. tchr. Ankara, Turkey, 1943-47; mem. Inst. Advanced Study, Princeton, N.J., 1950-51; vis. asst. prof. Duke U., 1951-52; mem. faculty U. N.C., Chapel Hill, 1952—; prof. U. N.C., 1961—, acting chmn. physics dept., 1965-67, 71-72, Kenan prof. physics, 1969-91, Kenan prof. physics emeritus, 1991—, chmn. dept., 1977-82; vis. prof. U. Wash., 1967-68, U. Edinburgh, Scotland, 1986; Arnold Bernhard vis. prof. physics Williams Coll., 1993; vis. rsch. fellow Sci. and Engring. Rsch. Coun., U. Stirling, 1986; chair Internat. Conf. on Physics of Electronic and Atomic Collisions, 1987-89, chair APS task force on jour. growth, 1994-95. Author: Quantum Mechanics, 2d edit, 1970; also articles. NSF Sci. Faculty fellow U. Copenhagen, Denmark, 1959-60; recipient Thomas Jefferson award U. N.C., 1972; Humboldt sr. scientist award U. Frankfurt, Germany, 1976-77. Fellow AAAS, Am. Phys. Soc. (pres. 1990); mem. Am. Assn. Physics Tchrs. (Oersted medal 1992), Sigma Xi. Achievements include research on applications of quantum mechanics to study atoms and nuclei. Home: 1396 Halifax Rd Chapel Hill NC 27514-2724

MESA, JOSE RAMON, professional baseball player; b. Azua, Dominican Republic, May 22, 1966. Grad., high sch., Dominican Republic. With Balt. Orioles, 1990-92; pitcher Cleve. Indians, 1992—. Selected to All-Star Team, 1995-96; named Sporting News Am. League Fireman of the Yr., 1995. Achievements include most saves (46) in American League, 1995, most consecutive saves (38) in American League history, 1995. Office: Cleve Indians 2401 Ontario St Cleveland OH 44115-4003*

MESA-LAGO, CARMELO, economist, educator; b. Havana, Cuba, Aug. 11, 1934; s. Rogelio M. and Ana Maria (Lago); m. Elena Mesa-Gross, Sept. 3, 1966; children: Elizabeth, Ingrid, Helena. LLB, U. Havana, 1956; LLD, U. Madrid, 1958; MA in Econs., U. Miami, 1965; PhD, Cornell U., 1968. Asst. prof. Cath U. Villanueva, Havana, Cuba, 1956-57, 59-61; research assoc. U. Miami, Fla., 1962-65; asst. prof. U. Pitts., 1968-71, assoc. prof., 1971-76, prof., 1976-81, disting. prof. econs. and Latin Am. affairs, 1981—; dir. Ctr. Latin Am. Studies, 1974-86; vis. prof. Oxford U., 1977, Mellon vis. prof. Fla. Internat. U., 1995, vis. prof. Inst. Univ. Ortega y Gasset, 1990-91; Bacardi chair U. Miami, 1994; regional advisor Econ. Commn. Latin Am., Santiago, Chile, 1983-84; rsch. assoc. Max-Planck-Inst., Munich, 1991-92, Free U. Berlin, 1997; cons. in field. Author: Cuba in the 1970's, 1974, 2d edit. 1978, Social Security in Latin America, 1978, The Economy of Socialist Cuba, 1981 (A.P. Whitaker 1982), The Crisis of Social Security and Health Care: Latin American Experiences and Lessons, 1985, Ascent to Bankruptcy: Financing Social Security in Latin America, 1989, Health Care for the Poor in Latin America and the Caribbean, 1992, Cuba After the Cold War, 1993, Changing Social Security in Latin America, 1994 (Outstanding Book Choice award 1995), Are Economic Reforms Propelling Cuba To the Market?, 1994; former editor: Yearbook Cuban Studies. Recipient numerous rsch. grants, 1986—, Alexander von Humboldt sr. rsch. prize, 1990-91, 96-97. Mem. Latin Am. Studies Assn. (pres. 1980), Caribbean Studies Assn. (eec. coun. 1973-74), Am. Econ. Assn., Assn. Comparative Econs., Internat. Assn. Labor Law and Social Security, Coun. on Fgn. Rels. and the Nat. Acad. of Social Ins., Spanish Club (Pitts., v.p.). Democrat. Roman Catholic. Office: U Pittsburgh Dept Econ 4M38 Forbes Quadrangle Pittsburgh PA 15260

MESCHAN, ISADORE, radiologist, educator; b. Cleve., May 30, 1914; s. Julius and Anna (Gordon) M.; m. Rachel Farrer, Sept. 3, 1943; children: David Farrer, Eleanor Jane Meschan Foy, Rosalind Weir, Joyce Meschan Lawrence. BA, Western Res. U., 1935, MA, 1937, MD, 1939; ScD (hon.), U. Ark., 1983. Instr. Western Res. U., 1946-47; prof., head dept. radiology U. Ark., Little Rock, 1947-55; prof., dir. dept. radiology Bowman Gray Sch. Medicine, Wake Forest U., Winston-Salem, N.C., 1955-77; now prof. emeritus Bowman Gray Sch. Medicine, Wake Forest U. Author: Atlas of Normal Radiographic Anatomy, 1951, Roentgen Signs in Clinical Diagnosis, 1956, (with R. Meschan) Synopsis of Roentgen Signs, 1962, Roentgen Signs in Clinical Practice, 1966, Radiographic Positioning Related Anatomy, 1969, 2d edit., 1978, Analysis of Roentgen Signs, 3 vols, 1972, Atlas of Anatomy Basic to Radiology, 1975, Synopsis of Analysis of Roentgen Signs, 1976, Synopsis of Radiographic Anatomy, 1978, 2d rev. edit., 1980, (with B.W. Wolfman) Basic Atlas of Sectional Anatomy, 2d edit.; co-author: Atlas of Cross-Sectional Anatomy, 1980, Roentgen Signs in Diagnostic Imaging, vol. 1, 1984, vol. 2, 1985, vol. 3, 1986, vol. 4, 1987; editor: The Radiologic Clinics of North America, 1965; contbr. articles to profl. jours. Recipient Disting. Alumnus award Case-Western Res. U. Sch. Medicine, 1984, Disting. Faculty Svc. Alumni award Wake Forest U. Bowman Gray Sch. Medicine, 1989. Fellow Am. Coll. Radiology (com. chmn., Gold medal 1978, Living Legends of Radiology 1986); mem. Am. Roentgen Ray Soc., AMA, Radiology Soc. N.Am., N.C. Radiol. Soc., So. Med. Assn., Soc. Nuclear Medicine, Assn. U. Radiologists, Phi Beta Kappa, Sigma Xi, Alpha Omega Alpha. Home: 5221 Bermuda Village Advance NC 27006

MESCHAN, RACHEL FARRER (MRS. ISADORE MESCHAN), obstetrics and gynecology educator; b. Sydney, Australia, May 21, 1915; came to U.S., 1946, naturalized, 1950; d. John H. and Gertrude (Powell) Farrer; m. Isadore Meschan, Sept. 3, 1943; children: David Farrer-Meschan, Jane Meschan Foy, Rosalind Meschan Weir, Joyce Meschan Lawrence. MB, BS, U. Melbourne (Australia), 1940; MD, Wake Forest U., 1957. Intern Royal Melbourne Hosp., 1942; resident Women's Hosp., Melbourne, 1942-43, Bowman-Gray Sch. Medicine, Wake Forest U., Winston-Salem, N.C., 1957-73, asst. clin. prof. dept. ob-gyn, 1973—; also marriage counselor. Co-author (with I. Meschan): Atlas of Radiographic Anatomy, 1951, rev., 1959; Roentgen Signs in Clinical Diagnosis, 1956; Synopsis of Roentgen Signs, 1962; Roentgen Signs in Clinical Practice, 1966; Radiographic Positioning and Related Anatomy, 1968; Analysis of Roentgen Signs in General Radiology, 1973; Roentgen Signs in Diagnostic Imaging, Vol. III, 1986, Vol. IV, 1987. Home: 5221 Bermuda Village Advance NC 27006

MESCHES, ARNOLD, artist; b. Bronx, N.Y., Aug. 11, 1923; s. Benjamin and Anna (Grosse) M.; m. Sylvia Snetsky, Apr. 8, 1945 (div. 1972); children: Paul Elliot, Susan Jean; m. Jill Karen Ciment, Mar. 19, 1983. Student, Art Ctr. Sch., 1943-45, Jepson's Art Inst., 1945, Chouinard's Art Inst., 1945. Instr. painting U. So. Calif., L.A., 1950; instr. painting and drawing Kann Inst. Art, L.A., 1950-55, New Sch. of Art, L.A., 1955-58, Otis Art Inst., L.A., 1963-67, U. Calif., L.A., 1972-77, Otis/Parsons Art Inst., L.A., 1975-84; instr. advanced painting and drawing Parsons Sch. Design, N.Y.C., 1986; guest prof. grad painting Rutgers U., New Brunswick, N.J., 1985; instr. grad. painting NYU, N.Y.C., 1988—; art dir. Frontier mag., L.A., 1954-60; ct. rm. artist Walter Cronkite Program, CBS, L.A., 1968-70. One-man shows include L.A. Mcpl. Art Gallery, 1983, Civilian Warfare Gallery, N.Y.C., 1984, 85, Hallwalls, Buffalo, 1985, Haines Gallery, San Francisco, 1988, 91, 93, 96, Jack Shainman Gallery, Washington and N.Y.C., 1985, 86, 89, Castellani Art Mus. and Burchfield Art Ctr., Buffalo, 1988, Carlo Lamagna Gallery, N.Y.C., 1989, East Hampton Ctr. for Contemporary Art, 1990, Robert Berman Gallery, Santa Monica, 1990, Donahue Sosinski Gallery, N.Y.C., 1991, 93, 94, 97, Inst. Contemporary Art, Phila., 1994, numerous others. Grantee John F. and Anna Lee Stacey Sch. Fund, 1954, 56, NEA, 1982, N.Y. Found. for Arts, 1991; Ford Found. Faculty grantee, 1979-80; Altos de Chavon fellow Dominican Republic, 1994, 97. Home: 254 E 7th St # 15-16 New York NY 10009-6053

MESCHKE, HERBERT LEONARD, state supreme court justice; b. Belfield, N.D., Mar. 18, 1928; s. G.E. and Dorothy E. Meschke; m. Shirley Ruth McNeil; children: Marie, Jean, Michael, Jill. B.A., Jamestown Coll., 1950; J.D., U. Mich., 1953. Bar: N.D. Law clk. U.S. Dist. Ct. N.D., 1953-54; practice law Minot, N.D., 1954-85; justice N.D. State Supreme Ct., 1985—; mem. N.D. Ho. of Reps., 1965-66, N.D. Senate, 1967-70. Mem. ABA, Am. Law Inst., Am. Judicature Soc., N.D. Bar Assn. Office: ND State Supreme Ct State Capitol 600 E Boulevard Ave Bismarck ND 58505-0660

MESCHUTT, DAVID RANDOLPH, historian, curator; b. N.Y.C., May 29, 1955; s. Philip Frederick and Mary Evelyn (Mahanes) M.; m. Sarah Caroline Bevan, July 14, 1990. BA in Journalism, Washington and Lee U., 1977; MA in History Mus. Studies, SUNY, Cooperstown, 1988; postgrad., Attingham Summer Sch., Gt. Britain, 1988. Rschr. Thomas Jefferson Meml. Found., Charlottesville, Va., 1977-78, Frick Art Reference Libr., N.Y.C., 1980-86; curator art West Point (N.Y.) Mus./U.S. Mil. Acad., 1988—; guest curator N.Y. State Hist. Assn., Cooperstown, 1986-87, Brandywine River Mus., Chadds Ford, Pa., 1992; cons. Curatorial Office, U.S. Dept. Treasury, Washington, 1988, Albany (N.Y.) Inst. History and Art, 1988. Author: A Bold Experiment: John Henri Isaac Browere's Life Masks of Prominent Americans, 1988; co-author: The Portraits and History Paintings of Alonzo Chappel, 1992; assoc. editor and contbr. Am. Nat. Biography, Oxford U. Press, 1994—; contbr. articles to profl. jours. Nourse Found. fellow, 1986-87, Nat. Endowment for Arts fellow, 1987, Soc. Colonial Wars fellow, 1988, Andrew W. Mellon fellow Va. Hist. Soc., 1992, Anne S.K. Brown fellow Brown U., 1993. Mem. Assn. Historians Am. Art, Historians Brit. Art, Herbert Howells Soc., Va. Hist. Soc., N.Y. State Hist. Assn., Walpole Soc. Methodist. Avocation: music. Office: West Point Mus US Mil Acad West Point NY 10996

MESELSON, MATTHEW STANLEY, biochemist, educator; b. Denver, Col., May 24, 1930; s. Hymen Avram and Ann (Swedlow) M.; m. Jeanne Guillemin, 1986; children: Zoe, Amy Valor. Ph.B., U. Chgo., 1951, D.Sc. (hon.), 1975; Ph.D., Calif. Inst. Tech., 1957; Sc.D. (hon.), Oakland Coll., 1964, Columbia, 1971, Yale U., 1987, Princeton U., 1988. From research fellow to sr. research fellow Calif. Inst. Tech., 1957-60; asso. prof. biology Harvard U., 1960—, prof. biology, 1964-76, Thomas Dudley Cabot prof. natural scis., 1976—. Recipient Eli Lilly award microbiology and immunology, 1964, Alumni medal U. Chgo., 1971; Lehman award 1975, Presidential award 1983, N.Y. Acad. Scis., 1975; Alumni Disting. Svc. award Calif. Inst. Tech., 1975; Leo Szilard award Am. Phys. Soc., 1978; MacArthur fellow, 1984-89. Fellow AAAS (Sci. Freedom and Responsibility award, 1990); mem. NAS (Molecular Biology prize 1963), Inst. Medicine, Am. Acad. Arts and Scis., Fedn. Am. Scientists (chmn. 1986-88, Pub. Svc. award 1972), Coun. Fgn. Rels., Accademia Santa Chiara, Am. Philos. Soc., Royal Society (London), Académie des Sciences (Paris), Genetics Soc. Am. (Thomas Hunt Morgan medal 1995). Office: Harvard U Fairchild Biochem Bldg 7 Divinity Ave Cambridge MA 02138-2019

MESERVE, MOLLIE ANN, publisher; b. Dallas, Dec. 9, 1944; d. Ralph and Emly (Stewart) Lacey; m. Walter Joseph Meserve, June 18, 1981. BA, U. Tex., Dallas, 1976; MFA, Ind. U., 1981. Pres. Feedback Theatrebooks, Brooklin, Maine, 1983—, Prospero Press, N.Y.C., 1992—; play reader Bonderman award Ind. U./Purdue U. Indpls., 1984-94. Co-author: A Chronological Outline of World Theatre, 1992, The Theatre Lover's Cookbook, 1992, The Musical Theatre Cookbook, 1993; editor, compiler The Playwright's Companion, 1985-98; co-editor: Prospero's Almanac, Vol. I, 1997. Recipient Open Cir. Playwright award Goucher Coll., 1977, Biennial Promising Playwright award Colonial Players, 1977, Playwright Contest award Country Playhouse, 1984, Winning Work-in-Progress award Nat. Playwrights Showcase, 1988. Avocations: reading, gourmet cooking, travel, gardening. Office: Feedback Theatrebooks 305 Madison Ave Ste 1146 New York NY 10165

MESERVE, RICHARD ANDREW, lawyer; b. Medford, Mass., Nov. 20, 1944; s. Robert William and Gladys Evangeline (Swenson) M.; m. Martha Ann Richards, Sept. 20, 1966; children: Amy, Lauren. BA, Tufts U., 1966; JD, Harvard U., 1975; PhD in Applied Physics, Stanford U., 1976. Bar: Mass. 1975, D.C. 1980, U.S. Supreme Ct. 1982. Law clk. Mass. Supreme Jud. Ct., Boston, 1975-76; law clk. to presiding justice U.S. Supreme Ct., Washington, 1976-77; legal counsel Pres. Sci. Adviser, Washington, 1977-81; ptnr. Covington & Burling, Washington, 1981—; chmn. com. to assess safety and tech. issues at Dept. Energy reactors, NAS, 1987-88, chmn. com. on fuel economy of automobiles and light trucks, 1991-92, chmn. com. on declassification of info. for Dept. Energy's environ. programs, 1994-95; co-chmn. AAAS-ABA Nat. Conf. Lawyers and Scientists, 1988-94; mem. adv. bd. Sec. Energy, 1996—; bd. dirs. Carnegie Instn., Washington. Fellow AAAS, Am. Phys. Soc., Am. Acad. Arts and Scis.; mem. Phi Beta Kappa, Sigma Xi. Democrat. Home: 708 Berry St Falls Church VA 22042-2402 Office: Covington & Burling PO Box 7566 1201 Pennsylvania Ave NW Washington DC 20004-2401

MESERVE, WALTER JOSEPH, drama studies educator, publisher; b. Portland, Maine, Mar. 10, 1923; s. Walter Joseph and Bessie Adelia (Bailey) M.; m. Mollie Ann Lacey, June 18, 1981; children by previous marriage—Gayle Ellen, Peter Haynes, Jo Alison, David Bryan. Student, Portland Jr. Coll., 1941-42; AB, Bates Coll., Lewiston, Maine, 1947; MA, Boston U., 1948; PhD, U. Wash., 1952. From instr. to prof. U. Kans., Lawrence, 1951-68; prof. dramatic lit. and theory Ind. U., Bloomington, 1968-88, assoc. dean rsch. and grad. devel., 1980-83, dir. Inst. for Am. Theatre Studies, 1983-88; disting. prof. grad. ctr. CUNY, N.Y.C., 1988-93, disting. prof. emeritus, 1993—; v.p. Feedback Svcs., N.Y.C., 1983—. Author: History of American Drama, 1965, rev. edit., 1994, Robert Sherwood, 1970, An Emerging Entertainment, 1977, Heralds of Promise, 1986, A Chronological Outline of World Theatre, 1992; editor: Plays of WD Howells, 1960, On Stage, America! A Selection of Distinctly American Plays, 1996; editor-in-chief Feedback Theatrebooks, 1985—; co-editor Jour. Am. Drama and Theatre, 1989-93; co-compiler: Who's Where in the American Theatre, 1990, 3d edit., 1992, Musical Theatre Cookbook, 1993, Playhouse America!, 1991, The Theatre Lover's Cookbook, 1992; adv. bd. College Literature, 1990-95. Reader Guggenheim Found., 1988—. With AC, U.S. Army, 1943-46. Fellow NEH, 1974-75, 83-84, 88-89, Rockefeller Found., 1979, Guggenheim Found., 1984-85. Mem. Cosmos Club.

MESERVE, WILLIAM GEORGE, lawyer; b. Medford, Mass., June 14, 1940; s. Robert William and Gladys Evangeline (Swenson) M.; m. Susan Mary Rycroft, Oct. 21, 1967; children: Daniel Scott, Susan Elizabeth, Jonathan Robert. BA, Tufts U., 1962; LLB, Harvard U., 1965; MSc, London Sch. Econs., 1966. Bar: Mass. 1966, U.S. Dist Ct. Mass. 1970, U.S. Ct. Appeals (1st cir.) 1973. Legal asst. to commr. FTC, Washington, 1966-67; staff counsel com. on commerce U.S. Senate, Washington, 1967-69; assoc. Ropes & Gray, Boston, 1970-76, ptnr., 1976—; geology field asst. McMurdo Sound, Antarctica, 1959-60, Inglefield Land, Greenland, summer 1965. Bd. visitors Fletcher Sch. Law and Diplomacy, Tufts U., Medford, 1971—; trustee Tufts U., 1979—, AFS Intercultural Programs Inc., N.Y.C., 1979-92, 93-96, New Eng. Med. Ctr., Inc., Boston, 1988—; bd. dirs. United South End Settlements, Boston, 1979—, Earthwatch Expdns., Inc., The Ctr. for Field Rsch., Watertown, 1996—; bd. govs. New Eng. Med. Ctr. Hosps., Boston, 1982-94, 95—. Fellow Am. Coll. Trial Lawyers; mem. ABA, Boston Bar Assn., Phi Beta Kappa. Democrat. Club: Appalachian Mountain (Boston) (rec. sec. 1977-78). Office: Ropes & Gray One International Pl Boston MA 02110

MESHBESHER, RONALD I., lawyer; b. Mpls., May 18, 1933; s. Nathan J. and Esther J. (Balman) M.; m. Sandra F. Siegel, June 17, 1956 (div. 1978); children: Betsy F., Wendy S., Stacy J.; m. Kimberly L. Garnaas, May 23, 1988; 1 child, Jolie M. BS in Law, U. Minn., 1955, JD, 1957. Bar: Minn. 1957, U.S. Supreme Ct. 1966. Prosecuting atty. Hennepin County, Mpls., 1958-61; pres. Meshbesher and Spence Ltd., Mpls., 1961—; lectr. numerous legal and profl. orgns.; mem. adv. com. on rules of criminal procedure Minn. Supreme Ct., 1971-91; cons. on recodification of criminal procedure code Czech Republic Ministry of Justice, 1994. Author: Trial Handbook for Minnesota Lawyers, 1992; mem. bd. editors Criminal Law Advocacy Reporter; mem. adv. bd. Bur. Nat. Affairs Criminal Practice Manual; contbr. numerous articles to profl. jours. Mem. ATLA (bd. govs. 1968-71), ABA, Minn. Bar Assn., Internat. Acad. Trial Lawyers, Am. Coll. Trial Lawyers, Am. Bd. Trial Advs., Am. Bd. Criminal Lawyers (v.p. 1983), Am. Acad. Forensic Scis., Nat. Assn. Criminal Def. Lawyers (pres. 1984-85), Minn. Trial Lawyers Assn. (pres. 1973-74), Minn. Assn. Criminal Def. Lawyers (pres. 1991-92), Trial Lawyers for Pub. Justice, Calif. Attys. for Criminal Justice. Avocations: biking, photography, travel, flying. Home: 2010 Sugarwood Dr Orono MN 55356-9339 Office: Meshbesher & Spence 1616 Park Ave Minneapolis MN 55404-1631

MESHEL, HARRY, state senator, political party official; b. Youngstown, Ohio, June 13, 1924; s. Angelo and Rubena (Markakis) Michelakis; children: Barry, Melanie. BSBA, Youngstown Coll., 1949; MS, Columbia U., 1950; LLD (hon.), Ohio U.; Youngstown State U.; LLD (hon.), Ohio Coll. Podiatric Medicine; LHD (hon.), Youngstown State U. Exec. asst. to mayor City of Youngstown, Ohio, 1964-68; urban renewal dir. City of Youngstown, Ohio, 1969; mem. 33d district Ohio Senate, Columbus, 1971-93; Dem. minority leader Ohio Senate, 1981-82, 85-90, pres. and majority leader, 1983-84, com. mem. econ. develop., sci. & tech., state & local govt., ways & means, commerce & labor, controlling bd., state employment compensation bd., fin. chmn., 1974-81, rules chmn., 1983-84, com. mem. rules, reference & oversight, 1985-90; state chair Ohio Dem. Party, 1993-95; real estate broker; adj. prof. polit. sci. Ohio U.; faculty mem. (limited svc.) Youngstown State U.; div. mgr. investment firm; Ohio Senate special com. mem. Task Force on Drug Strategies, Ohio Acad. Sci. Centennial Celebration Commn., Motor Vehicle Inspection & Maintenance Program, Legis. Oversight Com., Ohio Boxing Commn., Correctional Inst. Inspection Com., Ohio Small Bus. & Entrepreneurship Coun., Gov.'s Adv. Coun. Travel & Tourism, Legis. Svc. Commn., Capital Sq. Rev. & Adv. Bd., others. Past pres., past lt. gov. Am. Hellenic Ednl. Prog. Assn. (AHEPA); precinct committeeman Mahoning County Dem. Party, ward captain, mem. exec. com.; campaign mgr. local candidates, county campaign mgr. presdl. candidates; del. Dem. Mid-Term Conv., 1981; founder Great Lakes/N.E. Legis. Coalition; chmn., founder Nat. Dem. State Legis. Leaders Assn.; dir. State Legis. Leaders Found.; state/fed. assembly, mem. communications com. Nat. Conf. State Legis., legis. mgmt. com., govt. opers. com.; chair fiscal affairs com. Midwest Conf. Coun. State Govts., task force on econs. & fiscal affairs; del., exec. com. Dem. Nat. Com.; mem. Dem. Leadership Coun., State Dem. Exec. Com.; exec. com. Assn. State Dem. Chairs; bd. trustees Nat. Hall of Fame for Persons with Disabilities; mem. St. Nicholas Greek Orthodox Ch. With USN, 1943-46. Decorated two Bronze Battle Stars; recipient Dist. Svc. award Office of Pres., Top Legislator award Ohio Union Patrolmen Assn., Dist. Citizen award Med. Coll. Ohio, City of Hope Leadership award, 1993, Legis. Leadership award Ohio Coalition for Edn. of Handicapped Children, Phillips Medal of Pub. Svc., Ohio U., John E. Fogarty award Gov.'s Com. of Employment of Handicapped, Gov.'s award, 1992, U. Cin. Award for Excellence, Lamp of Learning award Ohio Edn. Assn., Black Cultural Soc. award East Liverpool, Mahoning Valley Man of Yr. award, Mahoning Valley Econ. Devel. Corp., Office Holder of Yr. award Truman-Johnson Dem. Women, Best Interest of Children award Fathers of Equal Rights, Founders Day award Circle of Friends Found., Helping Hand award Easter Seal Soc., Honorary Riverboat Captain award Mahoning County Dem. Party, Community Svc. and Special Svcs. awards Eastern Orthodox Men's Soc., Periclean award AHEPA, Academy of Achievement award Nat. AHEPA Ednl. Found., Nat. Svc. Dem. award AHEPA, 1994, Disting. Citizen award Youngstown State U. Alumni Assn., numerous appreciation and recognition awards; recipient Outstanding Legislator awards Ohio Acad. Trial Lawyers, Ohio Assn. Pub. Sch. Employes, Ohio Rehab. Assn., League Ohio Sportsmen; recipient Dist. Svc. awards Youngstown State U., Ohio Edn. Assn., Ohio Union Patrolmen Assn., Ohio Disabled Vets., AFL-CIO Ohio Barbers Union, AFL-CIO Nat. Assn. of Theatre Owners of Ohio; named Guardian of the Menorah, Youngstown B'nai B'rith, Outstanding Dem., Fairfield Dem. Club, 1993. Mem. (life) NAACP, ACLU, AMVETS (Legislator of Yr. 1993), VFW, Am. Legion, Cath. War Vets (Dist. Legislator award), Vet. Boxers Assn. Mercer County, Pa., Trumbull County Boxers' Legends of Leather (Man of Yr. award Hall of Fame), William Holmes McGuffey Hist. Soc., Buckeye Elks Lodge (hon.); mem. Kiwanis Internat., Urban League, Alliance C. of C., Southern Community Jaycees (hon.), Soc. for Preservation of Greek Heritage, Greek Am. Progressive Assn., Pan Cretan Assn., Arms Hist. Mus. Soc., Eagles, Moose, The Stambaugh Pillars.

MESHII, MASAHIRO, materials science educator; b. Amagasaki, Japan, Oct. 6, 1931; came to U.S., 1956; s. Masataro and Kazuyo M.; m. Eiko Kumagai, May 21, 1959; children: Alisa, Erica. BS, Osaka (Japan) U., 1954, MS, 1956; PhD, Northwestern U., 1959. Lectr., rsch. assoc. dept. materials sci. and engring. Northwestern U., Evanston, Ill., 1959-60, asst. prof., assoc. prof., then prof., 1960-88, chmn. dept. materials sci. and engring., 1978-82, John Evans prof., 1988—; vis. scientist Nat. Rsch. Inst. Metals, Tokyo, 1970-71; NSF summer faculty rsch. participant Argonne (Ill.) Nat. Lab., 1975; guest prof. Osaka U., 1985; Acta/Scripta Metallurgica lectr., 1993-95. Co-editor: Lattice Defects in Quenched Metals, 1965, Martensitic Transformation, 1978, Science of Advanced Materials, 1990; editor: Fatigue and Microstructures, 1979, Mechanical Properties of BCC Metals, 1982; contbr. over 235 articles to tech. publs. and internat. jours. Recipient Founders award Midwest Soc. Electron Microscopists, 1987. Fellow ASM (Henry Marion Howe medal 1968), Japan Soc. Promotion of Sci.; mem. AIME, Metallurgical Soc., Japan Inst. Metals (Achievement award 1972). Home: 3051 Centennial Ln Highland Park IL 60035-1017 Office: Northwestern U Dept Materials Sci Eng Evanston IL 60208

MESHKE, GEORGE LEWIS, drama and humanities educator; b. Yakima, Wash., Oct. 7, 1930; s. George Joseph and Marye Elizabeth (Lopas) M. BA, U. Wash., 1953, MA, 1959, PhD in Drama, 1972. Cert. tchr., Wash. Tchr. English and drama Zillah High Sch., Wash., 1955-58; tchr. English and drama high sch., Bellevue, Wash., 1958-60, Federal Way, Wash., 1960-70; dir., actor Old Brewery Theatre, Helena, Mont., 1962-66; prof. drama Yakima Valley C.C., Yakima, 1970—; casting dir., dir. summer seminar Laughing Horse Summer Theatre, Ellensburg, Wash., 1989—; lectr. Inquiring Mind series Wash. State Humanities, 1989-91; regional dir. Am. Coll. Theatre Festival, Washington, 1980-86; arts dialogue J.F. Kennedy Ctr., Washington, 1987—; casting dir., actor Hollywood Ind. Prodns.; mem. adv. coun. Kennedy Ctr. Author, producer Towers of Tomorrow, 1985. Regional bd. dirs. Common Cause, Yakima, 1971-73; active Nat. Hist. Soc., Nat. Wilderness Soc., Roosevelt Meml. Found., Wash. State Commn. Humanities. With U.S. Army, 1953-55, Austria. Recipient Gold medallion Kennedy Ctr., 1985, Wash. State Humanities medal, 1983, NISAD medallion, 1989. Mem. ACLU, Wash. Edn. Assn., N.W. Drama Assn., Am. Edn. Theatre Assn., Am. Fedn. Tchrs., Phi Delta Kappa. Democrat. Avocations: travel, mountain climbing, skiing, reading. Home: 5 N 42nd Ave Yakima WA 98908-3214 Office: Yakima Valley CC 16th And Nob Hill Blvd Yakima WA 98907

MESINGER, JOHN FREDERICK, psychologist, special education educator; b. Indpls., July 17, 1929; s. William F. and Thelma E. (Hardin) M.; m. Marguerite E. Rudolf, June 12, 1954; children: Karen Mesinger-Miller, Stuart F., Brian W.L. AB in Psychology, Hamilton Coll., 1951; MA in Psychology, Butler U., 1952; PhD in Experimental Child Psychology, Pudue U., 1955. Lic. psychologist, Va., clin. psychologist, Pa. Clin. psychologist, spl. edn. supr. Allegheny County, Pa. Schs., Pitts., 1958-64; prof. spl. edn. dept. curriculum, instruction and spl. edn. U. Va., Charlottesville, 1964-96, prof. emeritus, 1996; lectr. Sch. Edn., U. Pitts., 1959-63, Pa. State U., 1963-64, Syracuse U., 1966; mem. U. Va. Sch. Edn. Editl. Policy Bd., 1971; cons. Avonworth Union Sch. Dist., 1958-64, Easter Seal Soc., 1958-64; evaluator Allegheny County Juvenile Ct., 1958-64, Thornhill Instn., 1958-64, Oak Hill Sch., 1958-64; mem. staff Consultative Resource Ctr. Sch. Desegregation, U. Va., 1968-69; co-dir. Ctr. Youth and Family Svcs., 1977-80; dir. Va. Educateur Program, 1977-88, Beginning Tchr. Assistance Program, Region III, 1988-91; lectr. Internat. Conf. Children with Learning Disabilities, Washington, 1977, Nat. Adolescent Conf., Pensacola, Fla., 1984, Correctional Edn. Conf., San Francisco, 1987, Tri-State Optometric Conf. Reading, Pitts., 1963, Va. Mental Health Assn., 1965, Va. State Psychiat. Assn., 1972, Va. Assn. Sch. Psychologists, 1974, Va. State CEC Conf., Roanoke, 1977, Va. Optometric Assn., Norfolk, 1977, Va. State Conf. Adminstrs. Spl. Edn., 1991, Va. Assn. Correctional Educators, 1991, Villages Conf. Menninger Found., Topka, Kans., 1991; bd. dirs. Charlottesville-Albemarle Mental Health Assn., 1965-69, mem. adv. bd.; bd. dirs. Charlottesville-Albemarle chpt. ACLU, 1975-80, Adventure Bound Sch., 1980-84; chmn. adv. bd. Va. Rehab. Sch. Authority, 1975-78; cons. Va. State Dept. Spl. Edn., 1965—; mem. rev. teams SEA, 1965—; cons. Peking Med. Union, 1988, Va. Dept. Edn. Task Force, 1989-91. Author: Children and Youth in Need of Care and Supervision, 1978; (with others) Problems and Issues in Education of Exceptional Children, 1971, Contemporary Issues in Educational Psychology, 1987; cons. editor Behavioral Disorders, 1981-93, The Jour. of Correctional Edn., 1984-96; contbr. 35 articles to profl. jours. Chmn. Pres.'s Com. Equal Ednl. and Employment Opportunities, Obligations and Rights, 1967-71; tutor grades K-1, 1996—. With U.S. Army, 1956-58. Grantee Bur. for Edn. of the Handicapped, 1964-65, NIMH, 1969, Law Enforcement Assistance Agy., 1973-75, Edwin Gould Found., 1981, Dept. Edn., 1981-83, Beginning Tchr. Assistance Program, 1989-90, 90-91. Mem. AAUP, Am. Orthopsychiat. Assn., Pa. PTA (life), Correctional Edn. Assn. (lectr. internat. convs. 1990, 91), Coun. for Children with Behavioral Disorders (pres. Va. chpt. 1986-87, editor Jour. 1986-91), Coun. Exceptional Children (lectr. internat. convs. 1968, 70, 72, 79, 88, lectr. Va. state chpt. 1979), Sigma Xi, Alpha Kappa Delta, Phi Delta Kappa. Avocations: photography, fishing, gunsmithing, gardening. Office: U Va Curry Sch Edn 405 Emmet St Charlottesville VA 22903

MESIROV, LEON ISAAC, lawyer; b. Phila., Jan. 19, 1912; s. Isaac and Zippa (Robbins) M.; m. Sylvia W. Portner, June 25, 1935; children: Joan C. Rondell Sparens, Judy Lynn, Jill P. AB, U. Pa., 1931, LLB, 1934. Bar: Pa. 1934, U.S. Dist. Ct. (ea. dist.) Pa. 1934, U.S. Ct. Appeals (3d and Fed. cirs.) 1948, U.S. Ct. Internat. Trade 1948. Pvt. practice law Phila., 1934—; ptnr. Mesirov, Gelman, Jaffe, Cramer & Jamieson, Phila., 1959-88, counsel, 1988—. Commr. Phila. Civil Svc., 1952-70; pres. Jewish Community Rels. Coun., 1952-55, hon. pres., 1955—; commr. Phila. Fellowship Commn., 1952—, counsel, 1959—; sec. Jewish Y's and Ctrs., 1967-71; Trustee Fedn. Jewish Ags., 1960-71, Com. of Seventy, 1972—. Mem. ABA, Pa., Phila. bar assns., Order of Coif, Beta Sigma Rho. Jewish. Home: 2131 Saint James Pl Philadelphia PA 19103-4804 Office: Mesirov Gelman Jaffe Cramer & Jamieson 1735 Market St Philadelphia PA 19103-7501

MESKILL, THOMAS J., federal judge; b. New Britain, Conn., Jan. 30, 1928; s. Thomas J. M.; m. Mary T. Grady; children—Maureen Meskill Heneghan, John, Peter, Eileen, Thomas. B.S., Trinity Coll., Hartford, Conn., 1950, LL.D., 1972; J.D., U. Conn., 1956; postgrad., Sch. Law, NYU; LL.D., U. Bridgeport, 1971, U. New Haven, 1974. Bar: Conn. 1956, Fla. 1957, D.C. 1957, U.S. Ct. Appeals (2d cir.) 1975, U.S. Supreme Ct. 1971. Former mem. firm Meskill, Dorsey, Sledzik and Walsh, New Britain; mem. 90th-91st Congresses 6th Conn. Dist.; gov. Conn., 1971-75; judge U.S. Ct. Appeals (2d cir.), New Britain, Conn., 1975—, chief judge, 1992-93. Pres. New Britain Council Social Agys.; Asst. corp. council City of New Britain, 1960-62, mayor, 1962-64, corp. counsel, 1965-67; mem. Constl. Conv., Hartford, 1965. Served to 1st lt. USAF, 1950-53. Recipient Disting. Svc. award Jr. C. of C., 1964, Jud. Achievement award ATLA, 1983, Learned Hand medal for Excellence in Fed. Jurisprudence, Fed. Bar Coun., 1994. Mem. Fla. Bar Assn., Con. Bar Assn. (Henry J. Naruk Jud. award 1994), Hartford County Bar Assn., New Britain Bar Assn., KC. Republican. Office: US Ct Appeals Old Post Office Plaza Ste 204 114 W Main St New Britain CT 06051-4223

MESKILL, VICTOR PETER, college president, educator; b. Albertson, N.Y., May 9, 1935; s. James Joseph and Ida May (Pfalzer) M.; m. Gail King Heidinger, 1986; children by previous marriage—Susan Ann, Janet Louise, Gary James, Glenn Thomas, Kenneth John, Matthew Adam. B.A., Hofstra U., 1961, M.A. (grad. scholar), 1962; Ph.D., St. John's U., 1967; postgrad. insts., Ohio State U., 1968, Harvard U., 1972; postgrad., NYU, 1973; DSc (hon.), Samara State Aerospace U., Russia, 1993; LHD (hon.), St. John's U., 1995; DCL (hon.), Moscow Internat. U., Russia, 1996; DCL (hon.), D Ecology/Biosphere (hon.), Coll. Puschino State U., Moscow. Lab. asst., instr. biology Hofstra U., 1960-62; N.Y. State teaching fellow St. John's U., 1962-63; instr. biology Nassau (N.Y.) Community Coll., 1963-64; tchr. sci. Central High Sch. Dist. 2, Floral Park, N.Y., 1963-64; lectr. biology C.W. Post Coll., Greenvale, N.Y., 1963-64, instr. biology, 1964-67, asst. prof., 1967-68, assoc. prof., 1968-74, assoc. dir. Inst. for Student Problems, supr. student tchrs., 1967-68, asst. dean Coll., dean summer sch., coordinator Admissions Office, coordinator adult and continuing edn. programs, 1968-69; dean adminstrn. C.W. Post Ctr. of L.I. U., 1969-70, v.p. adminstrn., 1970-77, prof. biology, 1975-77; pres. Dowling Coll., Oakdale, L.I., 1977—; hon. prof. Minjiang U., Fuzhou, Peoples Republic of China, 1994; cons. in edn. and biology; chem. technician, detective Tech. Rsch. Bur., Nassau County Police Dept., 1958-63, mem. sci. adv. com., 1970; mem. adv. coun. Aerospace Edn. Coun. Inc., 1968; trustee, mem. state legis. com. Commn. Ind. Colls. and Univs.; mem. evaluation teams Mid. States Assn., 1971—; mem. higher edn. adv. com. N.Y. State Senate; mem. Nassau-Suffolk Comprehensive Health Planning Coun.; chmn. Internat. and Mediterranean Studies Group Conf. Author book; contbr. articles to profl. jours. Founding mem., vice chmn. bd. trustees Nassau Higher Edn. Consortium; bd. dirs. Suffolk County coun. Boy Scouts Am.; mem. N.Y. State Energy Rsch. and Devel. Authority, Town of Islip Devel. Commn.; chmn. bd. trustees L.I. Regional Adv. Coun. Higher Edn.; chmn. L.I. Mid Suffolk Bus. Action; bd. dirs. Southside Hosp., N.Y.; v.p. L.I. Forum for Tech.; former commr. Suffolk County Vanderbilt Mus.; mem. Bus. Coun. N.Y.; hon. mem. U. Pau and Pays de l'Adour, Pau, France, 1994; active Life Keeping Dept. Justice, Moscow. Decorated commendatore dell'Ordine al Merito (Italy), Knight of Arts and Letters (France); NSF rsch. grantee, 1967-69; Named Tchr. of Year, Aesculapius Med. Arts Soc., C.W. Post Coll. of L.I. U., 1967; Disting. Faculty Mem. of Year, C.W. Post Ctr. L.I. U., 1977, Educator of Yr. WLIW Channel 21, 1996; recipient George M. Estabrook award Hofstra U., 1978, Higher Edn. Leadership award Corning Glass Works, 1987, Disting. Leadership award L.I., 1989, Diploma Merito, Garibaldi Inst., Rome, Diploma of Honor, Rsch. Ctr. for Islamic History, Art and Culture, Istanbul, Turkey. Mem. AAAS, Coun. Advancement and Support of Edn., Am. Assn. Collegiate Registrars and Admissions Officers, Am. Assn. Higher Edn., Am. Inst. Biol. Scis., Am. Soc. Zoologists, Am. Assn. U. Adminstrs., Nat. Assn. Biology Tchrs., Nat. Sci. Tchrs. Assn., Soc. Protozoologists, N.Y. Acad. Scis., Camilo José Cela Found. (hon.), Met. Assn. Coll. and Univ. Biologists (founder, mem. steering com.), Bus. Coun. N.Y., Oakdale C. of C. (founding mem., dir.), Russian Soc. Plant Physiologists (corr.), Universal Life Keeping Problems Acad. Moscow, Tsiolkovski Space Acad. Moscow (fgn.), Univ. Club (N.Y.C.), Wings Club (N.Y.C.), Nat. Arts Club (N.Y.C.), L.I. Assn. Commerce and Industry (v.p. edn., dir.), Alpha Chi, Kappa Delta Pi, Phi Delta Kappa, Sigma Xi, Beta Beta Beta, Alpha Eta Rho, Delta Mu Delta, Kappa Delta Rho. Office: Dowling Coll Office of Pres Oakdale NY 11769

MESLOH, WARREN HENRY, civil and environmental engineer; b. Deshler, Nebr., Mar. 17, 1949; s. Herbert Frederick and Elna Florence (Petersen) M.; m. Barbara Jane Anderson, Sept. 7, 1969; children: Christopher Troy, Courtney James. BS, U. Kans., 1975; postgrad., Kans. State U., 1976-77. Registered profl. engr. Colo., Kans., Nebr.; cert. expert witness ACEC. Project mgr. Wilson & Co. Engrs., Salina, Kans., 1975-80, process design dir., 1980-82; engring. dir. Taranto, Stanton & Tagge, Fort Collins, Colo., 1982-85; pres. The Engring. Co., Fort Collins, Colo., 1985—; mem. civil engring. adv. bd. Kans. U., Lawrence, 1982—. Contbg. author (book) Pumping Station Design, 1989, (water pollution control manual) Manual of Practice No. OM-2, 1991, ACEC Certified Exper Witness, 1996; contbr. articles to profl. jours. Cub master Boy Scouts Am., Salina, 1980-81; active Luth. Ch., 1982—; vol. Paralyzed Vets. Orgn., Fort Collins, 1985—; pres. Foothills Green Pool Assn., Fort Collins, 1987-88. Sgt. U.S. Army, 1971-73, Germany. Named Outstanding Engr.-In-Tng. NSPE, 1978. Mem. Am. Pub. Works Assn., Am. Water Works Assn., Water Pollution Control Fedn., Fort Collins Country Club. Republican. Avocations: golf, boating, snow skiing. Office: The Engring Co 2310 E Prospect Rd Fort Collins CO 80525-9770

MESNIKOFF, ALVIN MURRAY, psychiatry educator; b. Asbury Park, N.J., Dec. 25, 1925; s. Nathan and Rachel (Feinberg) M.; m. Wendy Savin, June 15, 1952; children: Nathaniel, Rachel, Joel, Ann. A.B., Rutgers U., 1948; M.D., U. Chgo., 1954; cert. Psychoanalytic medicine, Columbia U., 1962. Diplomate: Am. Bd. Psychiatry and Neurology. Pvt. practice, 1958—; collaborating psychoanalyst Columbia U. Psychoanalytic Ctr. for Tng. and Rsch., N.Y.C., 1962—; dir. Washington Heights Community, N.Y. State Psychiat. Inst., N.Y.C., 1965-68; assoc. clin. prof. psychiatry Columbia U. Coll. Physicians and Surgeons, 1958-68; prof. psychiatry SUNY, Bklyn., 1968-81; dir. South Beach Psychiat. Ctr., S.I., N.Y., 1968-75; regional dir. N.Y. State Dept. Mental Health, N.Y.C., 1975-78, dep. commr. research, 1978-81; Marion E. Kenworthy prof. Psychiatry Columbia U. Sch. Social Work, 1981-89; lectr. Union Theol. Sem., N.Y.C., 1989-90; cons. St. Vincent's Hosp., S.I., 1970-76; attending psychiatrist S.I. Hosp., 1972-76; sr. attending psychiatrist St. Luke's/Roosevelt Hosp. Ctr., N.Y., 1987—; cons. Ford Found., N.Y.C., 1980-81. Contbr. chpts. to books, articles to profl. jours. Bd. dirs. Reality House, 1967-74; mem. task force med. sch. enrollment and physician manpower N.Y. State Bd. Regents, 1973-75; mem. task force on gen. and splty. hosp. care N.Y. State Health Planning Commn., 1973-74. Served with U.S. Army, 1943-45. Grantee Ford Found., 1982. Fellow Am. Psychiat. Assn. (life); mem. Am. Psychoanalytic Assn., Assn. Psychoanalytic Medicine, Am. Friends Tel Aviv U. (chmn. 1974-75), Phi Beta Kappa. Jewish. Office: 360 Central Park W New York NY 10025-6541

MESROBIAN, ARPENA SACHAKLIAN, publisher, editor, consultant; b. Boston; d. Aaron Harry and Eliza (Der Melkonian) Sachaklian; m. William John Mesrobian, June 22, 1940; children: William Stephen, Marian Elizabeth (Mrs. Bruce MacCurdy). Student, Armenian Coll. of Beirut, Lebanon, 1937-38; A.A., Univ. Coll., Syracuse (N.Y.) U., 1959, B.A. magna cum laude, 1971; MSsc, Syracuse U., 1993. Editor Syracuse U. Press, 1955-58, exec. editor, 1958-61, asst. dir., 1961-65, acting dir., 1965-66, editor, 1968-85, assoc. dir., 1968-75, dir., 1975-85, 87-88, dir. emeritus, 1985; dir. workshop on univ. press. pub. U. Malaysia, Kuala Lumpur, 1985; cons. Empire State Coll. Book rev. editor: Armenian Rev., 1967-75; mem. publs. bd. Courier, 1970-94; mem. adv. bd. Armenian Rev., 1981-83; contbr. numerous articles, revs. to profl. jours. Pres. Syracuse chpt. Armenian Relief Soc., 1972-74; sponsor Armenian Assembly, Washington, 1975; mem. mktg. task force Office of Spl. Edn., Dept. Edn., 1979-84, Adminstrn. of Developmental Disabilities, HHS; mem. publs. panel Nat. Endowment for Humanities, Washington; bd. dirs. Syracuse Girls Club, 1982-87; pres. trustees St. John the Bapt. Armenian Apostolic Ch. and Cmty. Ctr., 1991-95. Named Post-Standard Woman of Achievement, 1980; recipient Chancellor's award for disting. service Syracuse U., 1985; Nat. award U.S. sect. World Edn. Fellowship, 1986; N.Y. State Humanities scholar. Mem. Women in Communications, Soc. Armenian Studies (adminstrv. council 1976-78, 85-87, sec. 1978, 85-87), Syracuse U. Library Assocs. (v.p. 1983-88), Am. Univ. Press Services (dir. 1976-77), Armenian Lit. Soc., Armenian Community Center, Assn. Am. Univ. Presses (v.p. 1976-77), UN Assn. (bd. dirs. 1983-88, v.p. 1985), Phi Kappa Phi, Alpha Sigma Lambda. Mem. Armenian Apostolic Ch. (past trustee). Club: Zonta of Syracuse (pres. 1979-80, 1st v.p. 1985-86, dist. historian Dist. 2 Zonta Internat. 1993-96). Home: 4851 Pembridge Cir Syracuse NY 13215-1023

MESSA, JOSEPH LOUIS, JR., lawyer; b. Phila., Mar. 24, 1962; s. Joseph Louis and Virginia (Ciaffoni) M. BS, Tulane U., 1984; JD, Temple U., 1988. Bar: Pa. 1988, N.J. 1988, U.S. Dist. Ct. (ea. dist.) Pa. 1990, U.S. Dist. Ct. (cen. dist.) N.J. 1988. Assoc. Duane Morris & Heckscher, Phila., 1988-90; ptnr. Ominsky, Messa, & Tanner P.C., Phila., 1990—. Ward leader Rep. Party, Phila. 1985—, city com., 1985—, exec. com., 1985—. Mem. ATLA, ABA, Pa. Trial Lawyers (cons., seminar presenter, liability com.), Phila. Trial Lawyers. Roman Catholic. Avocations: physical fitness, bodybuilding, waterskiing, boating, traveling. Office: Ominsky Messa & Tanner 1760 Market St 10th Fl Philadelphia PA 19103

MESSEMER, GLENN MATTHEW, lawyer; b. Hartford, Conn., Jan. 7, 1947; s. Joseph M. and Mary S. Messemer; BSBA, Georgetown U., 1968; JD, U. Conn., 1971. Bar: Conn. 1972. Staff atty. Kaman Corp., Bloomfield, Conn., 1972-74, asst. sec., 1974-79, asst. v.p., 1979-81, v.p., sec., gen. counsel, 1981—; prof. bus. law Sch. Bus. Adminstrn., U. Hartford (Conn.), 1974-80; legal counsel Am. Helicopter Soc.; arbitrator Am. Arbitration Assn., 1978-82. Bd. dirs., trustee, regent U. Hartford, 1993—. Served with M.I., U.S. Army, 1969-75. Mem. ABA, Conn. Bar Assn. (founding; exec. com., sec.), Hartford County Bar Assn. Clubs: Hartford Golf, Hartford, Masons. Office: Kaman Corp Old Windsor Rd Bloomfield CT 06002

MESSENGER, GEORGE CLEMENT, engineering consultant; b. Bellows Falls, Vt., July 20, 1930; s. Clement George and Ethel Mildred (Farrar) M.; m. Priscilla Betty Norris, June 19, 1954; children: Michael Todd, Steven Barry, Bonnie Lynn. BS in Physics, Worcester Poly. U., 1951; MSEE, U. Pa., 1957; PhD in Engring., Calif. Coast U., 1986. Rsch. scientist Philco Corp., Phila., 1951-59; engring. mgr. Hughes Semicondr., Newport Beach, Calif., 1959-61; div. mgr. Transitron Corp., Wakefield, Mass., 1961-63; staff scientist Northrop Corp., Hawthorne, Calif., 1963-68; cons. engr., Las Vegas, Nev., 1968—; lectr. UCLA, 1969-75; v.p., dir. Am. Inst. Fin., Grafton, Mass., 1970-78; gen. ptnr. Dargon Fund, Anaheim, Calif., 1983—; v.p., tech. dir. Messenger and Assoc., 1987—, registered investment adviser, 1989—. Co-author: The Effects of Radiation on Electronic Systems, 1986; contbg. author: Fundamentals of Nuclear Hardening, 1972; contbr. numerous articles to tech. jours.; patentee microwave diode, hardened semicondrs. Recipient Naval Rsch. Lab. Alan Berman award, 1982; Best Paper award HEART Conf., 1983, Spl. Merit award HEART Conf., 1983, Goddard award for outstanding profl. achievement Worcester Polytechnic Inst., 1996; fellow IEEE, 1976, annual merit award 1986, Pete Haas award. HEART Conf., 1992. Mem. Rsch. Soc. Am., Am. Phys. Soc. Congregationalist. Home and Office: 3111 Bel Air Dr Apt 7F Las Vegas NV 89109-1510

MESSENGER, JAMES LOUIS, lawyer; b. Youngstown, Ohio, Oct. 18, 1942; s. William Robert and Georgette Elizabeth (Capehart) M.; m. Barbara Ann Vasslides, June 21, 1969; children: William, John. BBA, Ohio U., 1964; LLB, Syracuse U., 1967. Bar: Ohio 1967, U.S. Dist. Ct. (no. dist.) Ohio 1968, U.S. Ct. Appeals (6th cir.) 1976, U.S. Supreme Ct. 1982, U.S. Ct. Appeals (3d cir.) 1989. Assoc. Henderson, Covington, Stein & Donchess, Youngstown, 1967-74; ptnr./ Henderson, Covington, Stein, Donchess & Messenger, Youngstown, 1974-94, Henderson, Covington, Messenger, Newman & Thomas, Co., L.P.A., Youngstown, 1995—; bd. dirs. YSD Industries, Inc., Youngstown. Chmn., bd. dirs., founding mem. Ohio Coun. Sch. Bd. Attys., Columbus, Ohio, 1975—; active Civil Svc. Commn., Youngstown, 1991—. Mem. ABA, Ohio State Bar Assn., Mahoning County Bar Assn. (pres., award 1983). Republican. Episcopal. Avocations: thoroughbred horse racing, golf, handball. Home: 1811 Bears Den Rd Youngstown OH 44511-1361 Office: 600 Wick Ave Youngstown OH 44502-1215

MESSENGER, JON CARLETON, government project manager; b. York, Pa., Oct. 20, 1960; s. Charles Henry and Nancy Gross (Hawkins) M.; m. Laura Christine LeGay, Jan. 7, 1984. BS in Pub. Svc., Pa. State U., 1982; MPA, Pa. State U., Middletown, 1985. Mgmt. intern Commonwealth of Pa., Harrisburg, 1984-85; presidential mgmt. intern U.S. Dept. Labor, Washington, 1985-87, project mgr. employment and tng. R&D, 1987—. Co-author: (monographs) Measuring Structural Unemployment, 1987, Self-Employment Programs for Unemployed Workers, 1992; co-editor: Self Employment as a Reemployment Option: Demonstration Results and National Legislation, 1994. Task force mem. Pub. Svc. Acad., Washington, 1992—. Mem. Am. Soc. Pub. Adminstrn. (bd. dirs. nat. capital chpt. 1991-95, 97—, Spl. Recognition award 1991, Presdl. Citation of Merit award 1992), Nat. Young Profls. Forum (nat. chair 1991-92), Presdl. Mgmt. Alumni Group. Presbyterian. Avocations: skiing, skin diving, travel. Home: 630 Concerto Ln Silver Spring MD 20901-5005 Office: US Dept Labor/ETA Office Policy & Rsch 200 Constitution Ave NW Washington DC 20210-0001

MESSENGER, RON J., health facility administrator; b. 1944. MBA, U. So. Calif., 1968. Engr. CASH, L.A., 1968-73; v.p. Nat. Med. Enterprises, Santa Monica, Calif., 1973-84; pres. L.A. Cmty. Hosp., 1984—, Hollywood (Calif.) Cmty. Hosp., 1984—; pres., sec., CEO Paracelsus Healthcare Corp., Pasadena, Calif., 1984—. Office: Paracelsus Healthcare 155 N Lake Ave Ste 1100 Pasadena CA 91101-1857*

MESSENKOPF, EUGENE JOHN, real estate and business consultant; b. N.Y.C., Jan. 26, 1928; s. John Philip and Helen Bessie (Holden) M.; m. Martha Ann Crane, Jan. 29, 1955; children: Diane, Nancy, Eugene John, Susan. BBA, Iona Coll., 1950; MBA, NYU, 1956. CPA, N.Y. Sec.-treas. KLM Process Co., N.Y.C., 1952-54; acct. Am. Tobacco Co., N.Y.C., 1954-56; staff acct. Peat, Marwick & Mitchell, N.Y.C., 1956-60; exec. v.p. Donaldson, Lufkin & Jenrette, Inc., N.Y.C., 1960-84, pres., chief exec. officer real estate div., 1977-84; pres., chief exec. officer Meridian Investing and Devel. Corp., 1977-84; pvt. practice cons., 1984—; mem. adv. bd. NYU Real Estate Inst., 1981-85; mem. exec. coun. small scale devel. Urban Land Inst., 1983-90; chmn. Wall St. Tax Com., N.Y.C., 1965-68; bd. dirs. SIA Acctg. Div., N.Y.C., 1965-79. Trustee, chmn. fin. com. Mt. Vernon Hosp., 1982-87. Served as sgt. AUS, 1950-52, Korea. Recipient Brother Loftus award Iona Coll., 1976. Mem. AICPA, N.Y. State Soc. CPAs, Fin. Execs. Inst. Republican. Roman Catholic. Walked 2000 mile Appalachian Trail, 1987.

MESSER, ALLEN, insurance consultant, trainer, educator; b. Hamilton, Ohio, Apr. 28, 1949; s. Oscar Bishop Messer, Sr. and Alena (Richardson) Lathery. BA, U. Evansville, 1971. Cert. ins. counselor; CPCU. Claims rep. United Farm Bur. Mut. Ins. Co., Indpls., 1971-74, gen. agt., 1974; dist. sales mgr. Meridian Mut. Ins. Co., Indpls., 1974-77; br. mgr. Mich. Mut. Ins. Co., Indpls., 1977-81; v.p. M.J. Schuetz Agy., Indpls., 1981-87; account exec. Waterfield Ins. Agy., Inc., Indpls., 1987-90; v.p. Comprehensive Fin. Svcs., Muncie, Ind., 1990-91, Jackson-McCormick Ins., Lebanon, Ind., 1991-92; exec. dir. Soc. Cert. Ins. Counselors, Austin, Tex., 1992-93; cons., Ins. Concepts & Svcs., Inc., Indpls., 1989—. Editor: PF&M, The Rough Notes Company, 1993-94. Mem. Soc. CPCU, Soc. Cert. Ins. Counselors, Elks, Masons, Highland Golf & Country Club, Valparaiso Country Club. Home and Office: 205 Woodside Ln Valparaiso IN 46383-6035

MESSER, DONALD EDWARD, theological school president; b. Kimball, S.D., Mar. 5, 1941; s. George Marcus and Grace E. (Foltz) M.; m. Bonnie Jeanne Nagel, Aug. 30, 1964; children: Christine Marie, Kent Donald. BA cum laude, Dakota Wesleyan U., 1963; M. Divinity magna cum laude, Boston U., 1966, PhD, 1969; LHD (hon.), Dakota Wesleyan U., 1977. Asst. to commr. Mass. Commn. Against Discrimination, Boston, 1968-69; asst. prof. Augustana Coll., Sioux Falls, S.D., 1969-71; assoc. pastor 1st United Meth. Ch., Sioux Falls, 1969-71; pres. Dakota Wesleyan U., Mitchell, S.D., 1971-81, Iliff Sch. Theology, Denver, 1981—. Author: Christian Ethics and Political Action, 1984, Contemporary Images of Christian Ministry, 1989, Send Me? The Intinerary in Crisis, 1991, The Conspiracy of Goodness, 1992, Caught in the Crossfire: Helping Christians Debate Homosexuality, 1994, Calling Church and Seminary Into the 21st Century, 1995, Unity, Liberty, and Charity: Building Bridges Under Icy Waters, 1996, How Shall We Die? Helping Christians Debate Assisted Suicide, 1997; contbr. articles to Face to Face, The Christian Century, The Christian Ministry. Active Edn. Commn. of U.S., 1973-79; co-chmn. Citizens Commn. Corrections, 1975-76; vice chmn. S.D. Commn. on Humanities, 1979-81. Dempster fellow, 1967-68; Rockefeller fellow, 1968-69. Mem. Soc. Christian Ethics, Am. Acad. Religion, Assn. United Meth. Theol. Schs. (v.p. 1986-91, pres. 1991-92). Democrat. Office: Iliff Sch Theology Office Pres 2201 S University Blvd Denver CO 80210-4707

MESSER, THOMAS MARIA, museum director; b. Bratislava, Czechoslovakia, Feb. 9, 1920; came to U.S., 1939, naturalized, 1944; s. Richard and Agatha (Albrecht) M.; m. Remedios Garcia Villa, Jan. 10, 1948. Exch. student, Inst. Internat. Edn., 1939; student, Thiel Coll., Greenville, Pa., 1939-41; BA, Boston U., 1942; degree, U. Sorbonne, Paris, 1947; MA, Harvard U., 1951; DFA (hon.), U. Mass., 1962, U. of Arts, Phila., 1988. Dir. Roswell (N.Mex.) Mus., 1949-52; asst. dir. Am. Fedn. Arts, N.Y.C., 1952-53, dir. exhbns., 1953-55, dir. fedn., 1955-56, trustee, 1972-75; dir. Inst. Contemporary Art, Boston, 1957-61, Solomon R. Guggenheim Mus., N.Y.C., 1961-88, Peggy Guggenheim Collection, Venice, Italy, 1980-88, Solomon R. Guggenheim Found., N.Y.C., trustee, 1980-90, dir. emeritus, 1990—; chief curator Schirn Kunsthalle, Frankfurt, 1994; adj. prof. Harvard U., 1960, Barnard Coll., 1966, 71; prof. Hochschule für Angewandte Kunst, Vienna, Austria, 1984; prof. Goethe U., Frankfurt, 1991-92, 93-96; pres. Assn. Art Mus. Dirs., 1974-75; founding mem. exec. com. Am. Arts Alliance, Washington, 1978-81; pres. The MacDowell Colony Inc., 1977-78, 93-95; mem. adv. bd. Palazzo Grassi, Venice, 1986—; trustee Fontana Found., N.Y.C., 1996—, The Isamu Noguchi Found., N.Y.C., 1988—; sr. cultural advisor Am.'s Soc., 1988—; sr. advisor visual arts Caixa Found., 1991—; mem. coun. Nat. Gallery, Czech Republic, 1994—. Author: Edvard Munch, 1973; contbr. to mus. catalogues, art jours. Decorated chevalier Legion d'Honneur, France, 1980, Officier Legion d'Honneur, France, 1989; recipient Goethe medal Fed. Republic Germany; spl. fellow for study in Brussels Belgian-Am. Ednl. Found., 1953; sr. fellow Ctr. Advanced Studies, Wesleyan U., 1966. Mem. Internat. com. for Mus. and Collections Modern Art (hon. pres.), Met. Opera (N.Y.C.), Century Assn. (N.Y.C.). Home: 35 Sutton Pl New York NY 10022 Office: Americas Soc 205 E 77th St New York NY 10021-2061

MESSERLE, JUDITH ROSE, medical librarian, public relations director; b. Litchfield, Ill., Jan. 16, 1943; d. Richard Douglas and Nelrose B. Wilcox; m. Darrell Wayne Messerle, Apr. 26, 1968; children: Kurt Norman, Katherine Lynn. BA in Zoology, So. Ill. U., 1966; MLS, U. Ill., 1967. Cert. med. libr. Libr., St. Joseph's Sch. Nursing, Alton, Ill., 1967-71, dir. med. info. ctr., 1971-76, dir. info. services, 1976-79, dir. ednl. resources and community relations, St. Joseph's Hosp., Alton, Ill., 1979-84; dir. Med. Ctr. Libr., St. Louis U., 1985-88; libr. Francis A. Countway Libr. for the Harvard Med. Sch. and Boston Med. Libr., 1989—; instr. Lewis and Clark Coll., 1975; cons. 1973—; instr. Med. Library Assn. Bd. dirs. Family Services and Vis. Nurses Assn., Alton, 1976-79. Mem. Med. Library Assn. (dir. 1981-84, pres. 1986-87, task force for knowledge and skills, 1988-92, Legis. task force 1986-90, nom. com. 1996, search com. for exec. dir. 1979), Ill. State Libr. Adv. Com., Midwest Health Sci. Libr. Network (dir. health sci. council), St. Louis Med. Librs., Hosp. Pub. Relations Soc. of St. Louis, Nat. Libr. Medicine (biomed. libr. rev. com. 1988-92), AMA (com. on allied health edn. and accreditation 1991-94), Assn. Acad. Health Sci. Libr. Dirs. (pres. 1993, joint legis. task force 1992—, editorial bd. for ann. stats. 1989-94, Region 8 Adv. Bd. 1992-93), Am. Med. Informatics Assn. (planning com. 1990, publications com. 1994-96, annual mtg. com. 1996—), OCLC (spl. libr. adv. com. 1994—). Office: Countway Libr of Medicine 10 Shattuck St Boston MA 02115-6011

MESSERSCHMIDT, GERALD LEIGH, pharmaceutical industry executive, physician; b. Vancouver, B.C., Can., Feb. 2, 1950; s. George Gus and Joan May (Chapman) M.; m. Donna Kay Mackinley, Sept. 29, 1990; children: Jacqueline Diane, Victoria Leigh, Jonathan Leigh. BS, Portland State U., 1972; MD, U. Oreg., Portland, 1976. Diplomate Am. Bd. Internal Medicine, Am. Bd. Med. Oncology, Am. Bd. Hematology. Resident in internal medicine Letterman Army Med. Ctr., San Francisco, 1976-79; fellow in oncology and hematology NIH, Bethesda, Md., 1979-82; head exptl. hematology Nat. Cancer Inst., NIH, Bethesda, Md., 1981-82; dir. bone marrow transplants for Dept. of Def. Wilford Hall Med. Ctr., San Antonio, 1982-88; dir. bone marrow transplants U. Mich. Med. Ctr., Ann Arbor, 1988-90; dir. med. affairs Ciba-Geigy Pharm., Summit, N.J., 1990-92, exec. dir. med. affairs, 1992-93; v.p. med. and regulatory affairs DNX Corp., Princeton, N.J., 1993-94; corp. v.p. C.R. Bard Inc., Murray Hill, N.J., 1994-95, sr. v.p., 1995-96; CEO, pres. Kimeragen, Inc., N.Y.C., 1996—. Maj. USAF, 1982-88. Fellow ACP; mem. Am. Soc. Med. Oncology, Am. Soc. Hematology. Office: Kimeragen Inc 300 Pheasant Run Newtown PA 18940-3422

MESSIER, MARK DOUGLAS, professional hockey player; b. Edmonton, Alta., Can., Jan. 18, 1961. With Indpls. Racers, 1978, Cin. Stingers, 1979; with Edmonton Oilers, 1979-91, team capt., 1988-91; with N.Y. Rangers, 1991—; player NHL All-Star Game, 1982-84, 86, 88-92, 94, Stanley Cup Championship Game, 1984, 85, 87, 88, 90, 94. Recipient Conn Smythe trophy, 1984, Lester B. Pearson award, 1989-90, 91-92, Hart trophy, 1990, 92; named NHL Player of Yr., 1989-90, 91-92; named to Sporting News All-Star Team, 1981-82, 82-83, 89-90, 91-92. Office: NY Rangers 4 Pennsylvania Plz New York NY 10001*

MESSIER, PIERRE, lawyer, manufacturing company executive; b. Montreal, Que., Can., Mar. 3, 1945; s. Lionel and Anita (Caron) M.; m. Ginette Piche, July 11, 1970; 1 child, Mathieu. BA, Coll. St. Viateur, Outremont, Que., 1964; LLL, U. Montreal, 1968; DSA, Ecole Hautes Etudes Commerciales, Montreal, 1973. Bar: Que. 1969. Assoc. Lemay & Messier, Montreal, 1969-75; v.p., sec. gen. counsel Can. Cement Lafarge, Ltd., Montreal, 1975-84; v.p., sec. Lafarge Corp., 1983-84; v.p. bus. devel., legal affairs Norsk Hydro Can. Inc., Montreal, 1989—; v.p. Que. Bar Svc. Corp. Pres. Clinique Pedagogique de Montreal; v.p. Coll. Jean de Brebeuf; pres. Greenfield Park Bd. Revision, 1973-74; bd. dirs. Societe Progres Rive Sud, Longueuil, Que., 1974-75. Mem. ABA, Can. Bar Assn. (pres. young lawyers sect. 1976, nat. exec. 1977-78), Montreal Jr. Bar (treas. 1972), Que. Mfrs. and Exporters Alliance (bd. dirs.), St. Denis Club (Montreal). Office: Norsk Hydro Canada Inc, 2000 Peel # 700, Montreal, PQ Canada H3A 2W5

MESSIN, MARLENE ANN, plastics company executive; b. St. Paul, Oct. 6, 1935; d. Edgar Leander and Luella Johanna (Rahn) Johnson; m. Eugene Carlson (div. 1972); Rick, Debora, Ronald, Lori; m. Willard Smith (dec. 1975); m. Frank Messin, Sept. 24, 1982; 5 stepchildren. Bookkeeper Jeans Implement Co., Forest Lake, Minn., 1952-53, part-time bookkeeper, 1953-57; bookkeeper Great Plains Supply, St. Paul, 1960-62; bookkeeper Plastic Products Co., Inc., Lindstrom, Minn., 1962-75, pres., 1975—; co-owner, treas. Gustaf's Fine Gifts, Lindstrom, Minn., 1985—. Bookkeeper Trinity Luth. Ch., Lindstrom, 1976-81. Mem. Nat. Assn. Women Bus. Owners, Soc. Plastic Engrs., Swedish Inst. Home: 28940 Olinda Trl N Lindstrom MN 55045-9429 Office: 30355 Akerson St Lindstrom MN 55045-9456

MESSING, ARNOLD PHILIP, lawyer; b. N.Y.C., Sept. 2, 1941; s. Louis Messing and Ruth Aaron; m. Esther S. Buchman, Oct. 1, 1967; 1 child, Noah. BA magna cum laude, NYU, 1962; JD, Yale U., 1965. Bar: N.Y. 1966, Mass. 1976, Pa. 1985, U.S. Dist. Ct. (so. and ea. dists.) N.Y., U.S. Dist. Ct. Mass. 1976, U.S. Ct. Internat. Trade 1977, U.S. Ct. Appeals (1st, 2d, 6th and D.C. cirs.), U.S. Supreme Ct. 1977, U.S. Tax Ct. 1984. Assoc. Cravath, Swaine & Moore, N.Y.C., 1967-76; ptnr. Gaston & Snow and predecessor firm, Boston, 1976-91, Choate, Hall & Stewart, Boston, 1991—. V.p. Union Am. Hebrew Congregations, N.E. Coun. Served to sgt. USAFR, 1965-71. Mem. ABA, Boston Bar Assn., Mass. Bar Assn. Jewish. Home: 271 Mill St Newton MA 02160-2438

MESSING, KAREN, occupational health researcher; b. Springfield, Mass., Feb. 2, 1943. BA, Harvard U., 1963; MSc, McGill U., 1970, PhD in Biology, 1975. Rsch. asst. biochemistry Jewish Gen. Hosp., Montreal, Can., 1970-71; NIH fellow genetics Boyce Thompson Inst. Plant Rsch., 1975-76; prof. women's occupl. health U. Quebec, Montreal, 1976—, dir. Ctr. Study Biol. Interactions & Environ. Health, 1990-95; disting. fellow Que. Coun. for Social Rsch., 1995-97; invited rschr. Inst. Cancer Montreal, 1983-95; mem. bd. dirs. Quebec Sci. & Tech. Muc., 1984-86, Quebec Coun. Social Affairs, 1984-90. Editor Recherches Feministes. Mem. Am. Pub. Health Assn., Human Factors Assn. Can. Office: Univ Que at Montreal, CP 8888 succursale Centre-ville, Montreal, PQ Canada H3C 3P8

MESSINGER, DONALD HATHAWAY, lawyer; b. Lyons, N.Y., July 1, 1943; s. Donald H. and Thelma (Hubbard) M.; m. Sara L. Stock, June 3, 1967; children—Michael David, Robert Stephen, Daniel Mark. BA, Colgate U., 1965; JD, Duke U., 1968. Bar: Ohio 1968. Assoc. Thompson, Hine & Flory, Cleve., 1968-76, ptnr., 1976—, vice chair corp. practice group, 1989-92, ptnr.-in-charge Cleve. office, 1991-96, mem. mgmt. com., 1996—; sec., bd. dirs. Am. Steel and Wire Corp., 1986-93; bd. dirs. Cedar Fair Mgmt. Co., 1993—. Trustee Community Info.-Vol. Action Ctr., 1981-88, pres. 1981-84; trustee Free Med. Clinic Greater Cleve., 1970—, sec., 1970-82, v.p. 1982-86, 96—; trustee Cleve. Hearing and Speech Ctr., 1980—, v.p. 1984-86, 92-93, pres., 1986-88; trustee U. for Young Ams., 1982-95, sec., 1982-86, pres., 1986-88, chmn. 1991-95; mem. exec. bd. Boy Scouts Am., 1983-88; Leadership Cleve., 1984—; trustee, sec. Bus. Volunteerism Coun., 1992—; sec. Buckeye Area Devel. Corp., 1970-90; mem. adv. bd. Greater Cleve. New Stadium. Recipient Community Svc. award Fedn. for Community Planning, 1981-82; named one of Outstanding Young Citizens of Greater Cleve., 1971-75. Mem. ABA, Ohio Bar Assn., Cleve. Bar Assn. (trustee 1975-79, chmn. securities law inst. 1983), Nat. Assn. Bond Lawyers. Home: 21550 Shelburne Rd Cleveland OH 44122-1951

MESSINGER, SCOTT JAMES, advertising agency executive; b. Bklyn., Feb. 27, 1952; s. Nathaniel Bernard and Joy Black (Artson) M.; m. Michele Barbaro, Sept. 1988; children: Katherine Lydon, Zachary Ryan, Gabriella Lucia, Victoria Joy, Ryan Gregory. BS in Journalism, Northwestern U., 1974, MS in Journalism, 1975. Asst. account exec. Ted Bates/N.Y., N.Y.C., 1975-78, account exec., 1978-79, account supr., 1979-80, v.p., account supr., 1980-84, sr. v.p., mgmt. rep., 1984-90, Scali McCabe Sloves, 1990—, exec. v.p. acct. dir., 1990—, dir. client svcs., 1991—, mng. dir., 1992-94; exec. dir. Lowe & Ptnrs./SMS, N.Y.C., 1994-96; per diem maintenance staff Village of Saltaire, Fire Island, 1996; exec. v.p. Teahan, Burden & Charles, 1997—. Home: PO Box 55 Bright Waters NY 11718-0055 Office: Village of Grottaine TBC 1030 N Charles Baltimore MD 21201

MESSINGER, SHELDON L(EOPOLD), law educator; b. Chgo., Aug. 26, 1925; s. Leopold J. and Cornelia (Eichel) M.; m. Mildred Handler, June 30, 1947; children—Adam J., Eli B. Ph.D. in Sociology, UCLA, 1969. Assoc. rsch. sociologist Ctr. Study Law and Soc. U. Calif., Berkeley, 1961-69, rsch. sociologist, 1969-70, prof. criminology, 1970-77, prof. law jurisprudence and social policy program, 1977-88, Elizabeth J. Boalt prof. law, 1988-91, prof. law emeritus, 1991—, prof. grad. sch., 1995-97, vice chmn., 1961-69, acting dean criminology, 1970-71, dean criminology, 1971-75, chmn. program, 1983-87. Author, co-author numerous books, articles. Home: 860 Indian Rock Ave Berkeley CA 94707-2051 Office: U Calif Sch Law Boalt Hall Berkeley CA 94720

MESSITTE, PETER JO, judge; b. Washington, July 17, 1941; s. Jesse B. and Edith (Wechsler) M.; m. Susan P. Messitte, Sept. 5, 1965; children: Zachariah, Abigail. BA cum laude, Amherst Coll., 1963; JD, U. Chgo., 1966. Bar: Md. 1969, D.C. 1969, U.S. Ct. Appeals (4th cir.) 1977, U.S. Supreme Ct. 1973, U.S. Ct. Appeals (D.C. cir.) 1982, U.S. Ct. Appeals (5th cir.) 1983. Assoc. Zuckert, Scoutt & Rasenberger, Washington, 1968-71; solo practice, Chevy Chase, Md., 1971-75; mem. Messitte & Rosenberg, P.A., Chevy Chase, 1975-81, Peter J. Messitte, P.A., Chevy Chase, 1981-85; assoc. judge Cir. Ct. for Montgomery County, Md., Rockville, 1985-93; judge U.S. Dist. Ct. Md., 1993—. Bd. dirs. Cmty. Psychiat. Clinic, Montgomery County, Md., 1974-85, v.p., 1980-85, Peace Corps vol., Sao Paulo, Brazil, 1966-68; Md. del. Dem. Nat. Conv., N.Y.C., 1980. Recipient teaching citations Fed. Deposit Ins. Corp. Bank Exam. Sch., 1975, 79, Am. Inst. Banking, 1978; Elizabeth Scull award for Outstanding Svc. to Montgomery County, Md., 1993, Spl. citation Div. Roundtable Montgomery County, 1993, Contbr. Mental Health Cmty. Psychiat. Clinic, 1986. Mem. ABA, Fed. Bar Assn., Inter-Am. Bar Assn., D.C. Bar Assn., Md. Bar Assn., Montgomery County Bar Assn., Am. Law Inst., Fed. Judges Assn. (4th jud. cir.), Charles Fahy Inn of Ct. (master 1987-88), Montgomery County Inn of Ct. (pres. 1988-90), Jud. Inst. Md. (bd. dirs. 1989-93). Jewish. Office: US Courthouse 6500 Cherrywood Ln Greenbelt MD 20770-1249

MESSMAN, JACK L., oil executive; b. Clarksburg, W.Va., Mar. 13, 1940; s. Marvin C. and Betty L. (Jones) M.; divorced; children—Valerie Lynne, Kyle Andrew. B.Chem. Engring., U. Del.-Newark, 1962; M.B.A., Harvard U., 1968. Ptnr. Butcher & Singer, Phila., 1971-73; pres. Norcross, Inc., West Chester, Pa., 1973-80; v.p. corp. devel. UGI Corp., Valley Forge, Pa., 1980-81; exec. v.p. Safeguard Scientifics, King of Prussia, Pa., 1981-83; pres., chief exec. officer Novell Data Systems, Inc., Orem, Utah, 1981-83; exec. v.p., chief fin. officer Warner Amex, N.Y.C., 1983-86; chmn., chief exec. officer Somerset House Corp., Houston, 1986-88; chief exec. officer, bd. dirs. USPCI, Inc., Oklahoma City, 1988-91; pres., CEO, Union Pacific Resources, Inc., Ft. Worth, 1991—; bd. dirs. Wawa, Inc. (Pa.), Novell Inc., Utah, Safeguard Scientifics, Inc., Cambridge Technology Ptnrs. Served to 1st lt. U.S. Army, 1963-65. Republican. Episcopalian. Clubs: Aronimink Golf (Newtorn Square, Pa.), River Crest Country (Ft. Worth), Mira Vista (Ft. Worth). Office: Union Pacific Resources Inc 801 Cherry St Fort Worth TX 76102-6803

MESSMER, DONALD JOSEPH, business management educator, marketing consultant; b. St. Louis, July 30, 1936; s. Edgar Louis and Lucille Louise (Straub) M.; m. Charlotte Jean Fox; 1 child, Angeline Charlotte. BSBA with honors, Washington U., St. Louis, 1969, PhD, 1974. Asst. mgr. M.A. Bell Co., St. Louis, 1956-61; dist. sales exec. U. S. Gypsum Co., St. Louis, 1962-65; br. sales exec. Victor Comptometer Corp., St. Louis, 1965-68; asst. prof. Coll. William and Mary, Williamsburg, Va., 1973-76, assoc. prof., 1976-81, prof., 1981—, J.S. Mack prof., 1982—, dir. exec. MBA program, 1988-91; pres. The Wessex Group, Ltd., Williamsburg, 1979—; bd. dirs. Williamsburg Winery, Ltd., Chateau Hotels, Ltd.; chmn. bd. dirs. Community Svcs. Coalition, Inc. Assoc. editor Decision Scis. jour., 1985-88; contbr. articles to profl. jours. Bd. dirs., treas. Community Action Agy., Williamsburg, 1984-91, United Way of Greater Williamsburg, 1985-91, pres., 1989. Mem. Decision Scis. Inst. (mktg. coord. 1985-86), Southeastern Decision Scis. Inst. (pres. 1985-86), Am. Mktg. Assn. (Dissertation award 1974), Rotary (bd. dirs. 1990-92), Alpha Mu Alpha, Beta Gamma Sigma. Republican. Avocations: fishing, golf. Office: Coll William and Mary Grad Sch Bus Williamsburg VA 23185-8795

MESSMORE, DAVID WILLIAM, construction executive, former psychologist; b. Indpls.; s. Max J. and Betty G. (Miller) M.; m. Sondra Renée Bastian, Aug. 22, 1981; children: Kristen Nicole, Eric Christian William David. AB in Social Sci., Calif. State Coll., Long Beach, 1968; PhD in Student Devel., Counseling and Clin. Psychology, Mich. State U., 1972. Lic. class A gen. contractor, Tex., Va.; lic. psychologist, Calif., Mich.; lic. sch. psychologist, Calif. Counselor Okemas (Mich.) Pub. Sch., 1970-72; psychologist Frederick Ctr. Day Hosp., Grand Rapids, Mich., 1972-73, Newport-Mesa Schs., Newport Beach, Calif., 1973-80; commr. Bd. Med. Quality Assurance, State of Calif. Psychol. com., Sacramento, 1980-82; pres. Bridgewater Constrn., Inc., Chesapeake, Va., 1987—; psychol. counselor Camp Highfields Residential Sch., Onondago, Mich., 1971; cons. The Open Door, Lansing, Mich., 1971-72, Juv. and Domestic Rels. Ct. the Family Ct., State of Va., Chesapeake, 1989-91; pres. Bridgewater Consultation Svcs., Chesapeake, 1989-91; intern Counseling Ctr., Calif. State U., Long Beach, asst. prof. ednl. psychology, 1981; instr. Golden West Coll., Huntington Beach, Calif., 1977-78; advisor, counselor dean of students Mich. State U., 1969-71; pres., CEO Hampton Rds. Multimedia, 1996—. Author: (manual) The Impact of Divorce on Families, 1989; designer sch. crest Long Beach City Coll., 1965. Active Gt. Bridge Conf. Com., Chesapeake, 1987-91; treas. Paint Your Heart Out, Chesapeake, 1993, Hampton Rds. Rep. Alliance, 1996—; coach parks and recreation, commr. transp. and safety City of Chesapeake, 1994—, vice-chmn., 1995-96; fin. com. city com. Rep. Party of Chesapeake, vice-chmn., 1996—; treas. Citizens for a Better Chesapeake, 1996-97. Served with USMC, 1959-63. Recipient Cert. of Appreciation Chesapeake Vols. in Youth Svcs., Inc., 1989, Outstanding Svc. award, 1990, Gov.'s award State of Va., 1990. Mem. Rotary Internat. (bd. dirs. Chesapeake club 1990-94, co-chmn. programs 1996—, Disting. Svc. award 1990), Nat. Youth Sports Coaches Assn., Delta Tau Delta. Avocations: tennis, reading, investments.

MESSMORE, THOMAS ELLISON, asset management company executive; b. Monongahela, Pa., June 30, 1945; s. Lindsay Ellison and Margaret (Hoffmann) M.; m. Sharon Weaver, Aug. 19, 1966; children: Lauren, Beth, Benjamin, William. BS in Indsl. Engring., W.Va. U., 1967; MBA, Harvard U., 1969. Chartered fin. analyst. Asst. treas. State Street Bank and Trust Co., Boston, 1969-72; fin. product mgr. Interactive Data Corp., Waltham, Mass., 1972-75; sr. v.p. Keystone Custodian Funds, Inc., Boston, 1975-80; sr. v.p. and chief fin. officer Keystone Mass. Group, Boston, 1981-83; sr. v.p. The Travelers Ins. Co., Hartford, Conn., 1984-94; pvt. cons. Hartford, 1994-95; pres., CEO, UBS Asset Mgmt., N.Y.C., 1995-96; dir. Energy BioSystems Corp. Mem. Assn. for Investment Mgmt. and Rsch. Home: Apt 33A 111 W 67th St New York NY 10023

MESSNER, HOWARD MYRON, professional association executive; b. Newark, June 10, 1937; s. Elias and Freda (Trachtenberg) M.; m. Aletha Bragg, 1960 (div. 1980); children: Jennifer, Linda, David; m. Melba June Meador, June 22, 1986. BA, Antioch Coll., 1960; MA, U. Mass., 1962. Mgmt. analyst Office Gov., Mass., 1960-61; staff asst. to adminstr. NASA, Washington, 1962-65; mgmt. analyst Bur. Budget, Washington, 1965-71; dir. adminstrn. EPA, Washington, 1971-75, asst. adminstr. for adminstrn., 1983-87; asst. dir. Congl. Budget Office, Washington, 1975-77, Office Mgmt. and Budget, Washington, 1977-83; controller Dept. Energy, Washington, 1983; exec. v.p., chief exec. officer Am. Cons. Engrs. Council, 1987—. Recipient William A. Jump Meml. award, 1971, Presdl. Disting. Exec. award, 1986, Outstanding Pub. Service award Nat. Capital chpt. Am. Soc. Pub. Adminstrn., 1986, Chancellor's medal U. Mass., 1988. Mem. Nat. Acad. Pub. Adminstrn. (trustee), Cosmos Club. Democrat. Jewish. Home: 1683 Justin Dr Gambrills MD 21054-2012 Office: Am Cons Engrs Coun 1015 15th St NW Washington DC 20005-2605

MESSNER, ROBERT THOMAS, lawyer, banking executive; b. McKeesport, Pa., Mar. 27, 1938; s. Thomas M. and Cecilia Mary (McElhinny) M.; m. Anne Margaret Lux, Dec. 3, 1966; children: Megan Anne, Michael Thomas. A.B., Dartmouth Coll., 1960; LL.B., U. Pa., 1963. Bar: Pa. 1965. With firm Rose, Schmidt & Dixon, Pitts., 1965-68; with G.C. Murphy Co., McKeesport, 1968-86; corp. sec. G.C. Murphy Co., 1974—, gen. counsel, 1975-86, v.p., 1976-86; v.p., gen. counsel, corp. sec. Dollar Bank, Pitts., 1986—; dir. G.C. Murphy Found. Bd. dirs. McKeesport YMCA, Downtown Pitts. YMCA, Mon-Yough Heritage Found., 1981-83, Braddock's Field Hist. Soc., 1994—; mem. adv. bd. Pa. Human Rels. Commn., 1968, 69; Rep. candidate for Pa. Legis., 1986, fin. adv. bd. Wilkinsburg, Pa., 1988—. 1st lt. U.S. Army, 1963-65. Decorated Commendation medal. Mem. ABA, Pa. Bar Assn. (chmn. corp. law dept. com.), Allegheny County Bar Assn. (coun. on corp., banking and bus. law), Am. Soc. Corp. Secs. (pres. Pitts. regional group, dir.), Am. Mgmt. Assn., Pa. Assn. Savs. Instns. (chmn. legal com. 1989—), Am. Corp. Counsel Assn., Theta Delta Chi. Clubs: Dartmouth Western Pa., Rivers. Home: 1061 Blackridge Rd Pittsburgh PA 15235-2719 Office: Dollar Bank Three Gateway Ctr Pittsburgh PA 15222

MESSNER, THOMAS G., advertising executive, copywriter; b. N.Y.C., Jan. 26, 1944; s. Malcolm V. Messner and Virginia M. Burkard; m. Terry Carol Bonaccolta, Nov. 28, 1971; 1 child, Zachary. Letter carrier U.S. Post Office, N.Y.C., 1965-67; copywriter Occidental Life Calif., L.A., 1967-68; mail boy D'Arcy Advt., N.Y.C., 1968; copywriter BBDO, N.Y.C., 1968-69, Doyle Dane Bernbach, N.Y.C., 1969-72; creative dir. Ally and Gargano, N.Y.C., 1972-86; ptnr. Messner Vetere Berger Carey Schmetterer, N.Y.C., 1986-92, Messner Vetere Berger McNamee Schmetterer Euro RSCG, N.Y.C., 1992—; bd. dirs., US. bd., internat. bd. Eurol RSCG. Copywriter Ronald Reagan, 1984 presdl. campaign, Republican Nat. Com., N.Y., 1984, Andrew O'Rourke for Gov., N.Y., 1986, George Bush 1988 presdl. campaign. Named CLIO Hall of Fame. Roman Catholic. Office: Messner Vetere Berger McNamee Schmetterer Euro RSCG 40 E 84th St New York NY 10028-1115

MESTRALLET, GÉRARD, professional society administrator; b. Paris, Apr. 1, 1949; arrived in Belgium, 1991; s. Georges Julien Marie and Paule Andrée Augustine (Besnard) M.; m. Joëlle Emilienne Renée Arcens, Sept. 7, 1974; children: Stephanie, Caroline, Bastien. Student, Ecole Polytech., Paris, 1968, Ecole Aviation Civile, Paris, 1971, Inst. for Study of Politics, Toulouse, France, 1973, Ecole Nat. d'Adminstrn., Paris, 1978. Counsellor Minister Transp., Econs., Fins., & Budget, Paris, 1973-84; chargé de mission Suez, Paris, 1984-86, dél. adjoint indsl. affairs, 1986-91, dir. gen. adjoint, 1991—; CEO Soc. Gen. de Belgique, Brussels, 1991; chmn., CEO Compagnie de Suez, Paris, 1995—. Office: Compagnie de Suez, 1 rue d'Astorg, 75008 Paris France

MESTRE, OSCAR LUIS, financial consultant; b. Havana, Cuba, Nov. 26, 1959; came to U.S., 1960; s. Oscar Luis and Ana Victoria (Arango) M.; m. Margaret M. Bozak, May 17, 1986; children: Melissa Anne, Victoria Elizabeth, Jessica Margaret. BS and BA, U. Del., 1982; cert. CLU, Am. Coll., Bryn Mawr, Pa., 1988, cert. ChFC, 1988. Account exec. Keystone Fin. Group, Bryn Mawr, 1982-87, New Eng. Fin. Group, Radnor, Pa., 1987—; ptnr. in charge of mktg. internat. ins., liason for Latin Am., internat. banking and securities AG Transnat., Ltd., Radnor and Huntington, N.Y., 1991—. Chmn. U. Del. golf fundraising com., Newark, 1986-92; bd. dirs. Haverford (Pa.) Sch. Alumni Assn., 1988—, chmn. annual giving campaign, 1993-94; mem. profl. adv. coun. Cedars Med. Ctr., Miami, Fla., 1990-93; vol. St. Monica's Ch., Berwyn, Pa., Am. Heart Assn., Pa. chpt. Recipient Hon. Mention All Am. award NCAA Div. I Golf, 1980, 81, Top Club award Penn Mut. Life Ins. Co., Phila., 1982, Ins. Production Recognition award Clerical Med. Internat., 1992. Mem. Am. Soc. CLUs and ChFCs (cert.). Avocations: golf, travel, theater, music, family activities. Office: New Eng Fin Group Two Radnor Corp Ctr Ste 300 Radnor PA 19087

MESTRES, JEAN L. See SULC, JEAN LUENA

MESTRES, RICARDO A., III, motion picture company executive; b. N.Y.C., Jan. 23, 1958; s. Ricardo Angelo Jr. and Ann (Farnsworth) M.; m. Tracy Stewart; children: Alexander Carson, Carrie Ann. AB, Harvard U., 1980. Creative exec. Paramount Pictures, L.A., 1981-82, exec. dir. prodn., 1982-84, v.p. prodn., 1984-85; v.p. prodn. Walt Disney Pictures, Burbank, Calif., 1985-86, sr. v.p. prodn., 1986-88; pres. prodn. Touchstone Pictures, Burbank, Calif., 1988-89; pres. Hollywood Pictures, Burbank, Calif., 1989-94; co-founder Great Oaks Entertainment, Burbank, 1995—. Producer (movies) Jack, 101 Dalmations, Reach the Rock, Flubber, Home Alone 3. Mem. Acad. Motion Picture Arts and Scis. Office: Great Oaks Entertainment 500 S Buena Vista St Burbank CA 91521-0001*

MESTRES, RICARDO ANGELO, JR., lawyer; b. N.Y.C., Aug. 12, 1933; s. Ricardo Angelo and Anita (Gwynne) M.; m. Ann Farnsworth, June 18, 1955; children: Laura, Ricardo III, Lynn, Anthony. AB, Princeton U., 1955; LLB, Harvard U., 1961. Bar: N.Y. 1962, U.S. Supreme Ct. 1970. Assoc. Sullivan & Cromwell, N.Y.C., 1961-67, ptnr., 1968—, chmn., sr. ptnr., 1995—. Trustee Unitarian Ch. All Souls, N.Y.C., 1973-79, 84-87; trustee Phillips Exeter Acad., 1989—, pres. bd. trustees, 1993—. Served to lt. USN, 1955-58. Mem. ABA, N.Y. State Bar Assn., Assn. Bar City N.Y. (corp. law, securities regulation law and state legis. coms.), Am. Law Inst., Phi Beta Kappa. Clubs: Downtown Assn., Links (N.Y.C.); Mill Reef (Antigua). Office: Sullivan & Cromwell 125 Broad St New York NY 10004-2400

MESTRIL, RUBEN, biochemist, researcher; b. N.Y.C., Jan. 21, 1951; s. Fernando and Renee (Casanova) M.; m. Ilona Erika Brelewski, Dec. 16, 1984; 1 child, Sebastian. BA in Chemistry summa cum laude, St. Thomas U., 1981; PhD in Biochemistry, U. Miami, Coral Gables, Fla., 1986. Postdoctoral fellow German Cancer Rsch. Ctr., Heidelberg, 1986-88; asst. rsch. biochemist U. Calif., San Diego, 1988-92, asst. adj. prof., 1992—. Reviewer Circulation jour., San Diego, 1991—; contbr. revs., articles to profl. jours., chpts. to books. Grantee NSF, 1980, Am. Heart Assn., 1991, NIH, 1994. Mem. AAAS, Am. Inst. Chemists, Am. Soc. Biochemistry and Molecular Biology, Am. Heart Assn. (basic sci. coun. 1991—), Internat. Soc. Heart Rsch. Democrat. Achievements include research in heat shock and adaptive response to ischemia, regulation of heat shock genes in Drosophila, steroid hormone regulation. Office: U Calif San Diego 9500 Gilman Dr La Jolla CA 92093-5003

MESZAR, FRANK, publishing executive, former army officer; b. East Chicago, Ind., Sept. 5, 1915; s. Frank Rach and Julia (Labois) M.; m. Carla Ruth Jorgensen, May 21, 1965; children—Frank, Sarah. B.S. in Civil Engring, U.S. Mil. Acad., 1940; grad., Army War Coll., 1955; M.B.A., Ga. So. Coll. Commd. 2d lt. U.S. Army, 1940, advanced through grades to brig. gen., 1965; chief aviation affairs Dept. Army, 1959-62; asst. dep chief staff ops. U.S. Army Europe, 1962-65; asst. dep. chief staff Continental Army Command, Ft. Monroe, Va., 1965-67; comdg. gen. Army Flight Tng. Center, Hunter AFB, Ga., 1967-68; asst. comdg. gen. 1st Cav. Div., 1969-70; ret., 1970; v.p. finance U.S. Medicine, Inc., Washington, 1970—; treas. Profl. Lithography, Inc., Washington. Pres. Savannah Symphony Soc., 1970-79, Savannah West Point Soc., 1972, Savannah Symphony Soc.; trustee Ga. Infirmary; hon. judge Chatham County, Ga.; vestryman, sr. warden St. John's Episc. Ch. Decorated D.S.M. with oak leaf cluster, Legion of Merit, D.F.C., Silver Star with oak leaf cluster, Bronze Star with 3 oak leaf clusters, Purple Heart with oak leaf cluster; Legion of Honor; Croix de Guerre France). Clubs: Oglethorpe, Rotary. Home: 802 E 46th St Savannah GA 31405-2257 Office: US Medicine 1155 21st St NW Washington DC 20036-3302

MÉSZÁROS, PETER ISTVAN, astrophysicist, researcher, astronomy educator; b. Budapest, Hungary, July 15, 1943; came to U.S., 1968; m. Deborah Ann Runde, Nov. 2, 1974; 1 child, Andor Istvan. MS in Physics, U. Buenos

Aires, 1967; PhD, U. Calif., Berkeley, 1972. Rsch. assoc. Princeton (N.J.) U. Obs., 1972-73; rsch. fellow Inst. of Astronomy Cambridge (Eng.) U., 1973-75; staff scientist Max Planck Inst. for Astrophysics, Garching, Fed. Republic of Germany, 1975-83; assoc. prof. Pa. State U., University Park, 1983-87, prof., 1987—, head dept. astronomy and astrophysics, 1993—; vis. scientist NASA-Goddard Space Flight Ctr., Greenbelt, Md., 1980-82, Harvard-Smithsonian Ctr. for Astrophysics, Cambridge, 1982-83, 90; cons. Max Planck Inst. for Astrophysics, Garching, 1983-87, NASA, 1987—, Tokyo Met. U., 1990, Cambridge U., 1991, Inst. Theoretical Physics, U. Calif. Santa Barbara, 1995. Author: (monograph) High Energy Radiation From Magnetized Neutron Stars; contbr. articles to Astrophys. Jour., Phys. Rev., Astron & Astrophysics; contbr. over 130 articles to profl. jours. U. Calif. fellow, 1970-72, Irex fellow NRC, 1986, Smithsonian Inst. fellow, 1982, 83, 90, Royal Soc. Guest Rsch. fellow, 1991; recipient First prize Gravity Rsch. Found., 1976. Fellow Am. Phys. Soc.; mem. Am. Astron. Soc. (exec. com. 1987-89), Internat. Astron. Union. Achievements include discovery of growth rate of cold matter perturbations in radiation dominated cosmological models; development of radiative cross sections for cyclotron radiation in neutron stars; research in spherical accretion on black holes, the development of models of accreting pulsars and neutron stars, and development of models for cosmological gamma-ray burst sources. Office: Pa State U Dept Astron & Astrophysics 525 Davey University Park PA 16802

MESZNIK, JOEL R., investment banker; b. Beirut, Oct. 3, 1945; s. Hans and Eugenie (Bagdadi) M.; m. Lynne Gladstein, Mar. 25, 1979; children: Daniel, Jared, Kara. BS, CCNY, 1967; MBA, Columbia U., 1970. Engr. Ebasco Svcs., N.Y.C., 1967-70; banker Citibank, N.Y.C., 1970-71, Newhouse Capital, N.Y.C., 1971-72, Matthews & Wright, N.Y.C., 1972-76; mng. dir. Drexel Burnham Lambert, N.Y.C., 1976-89; pres. Mesco Ltd., 1990—. Office: 122 E 42nd St Rm 4906 New York NY 10168-4999

METCALF, ARTHUR GEORGE BRADFORD, electronics company executive; b. Boston, Nov. 1, 1908; s. Franklin B. and Emma A. (Maclachlan) M.; m. Mary G. Curtis, Feb. 22, 1935; children: Anne C., Helen C., Mary Lee, Hope S. Student, Mass. Inst. Tech., 1932; S.B., Boston U., 1935, LL.D., 1974; S.M., Harvard U., 1939; S.D., Franklin Pierce Coll., 1966. Engrng. test pilot, 1930—; prof. math., physics Boston U., 1935; pres. Electronics Corp. Am., Cambridge, Mass., 1954—. Mil. editor: Strategic Rev; contbr. articles to profl. jours. Chmn. emeritus, bd. trustees, exec. com. Boston U.; bd. overseers Mus. Fine Arts, Boston; mem. trustee coun. Boston U. Med. Ctr.; chmn. U.S. Strategic Inst., Washington. Served to lt. col. AUS, WWII. Decorated Legion of Merit, Commendation medal.; Benjamin Franklin fellow Royal Soc. Arts London, 1972. Asso. fellow Royal Aero. Soc. (London), Inst. Aero. Scis.; mem. Am. Def. Preparedness Assn. (dir.), Phi Beta Kappa. Clubs: Harvard (Boston, N.Y.C.); Harvard Faculty (Boston), Algonquin (Boston); Edgartown (Mass.) Yacht; Army and Navy (Washington). Home: 45 Arlington St Winchester MA 01890-3732 Office: 125 Bay State Rd Boston MA 02215-1708

METCALF, BRUCE BARBER, visual artist, craft critic; b. Amherst, Mass., Sept. 30, 1949; s. Leroy Alfred and Catharine (Bartlett) M. BFA, Syracuse U., 1972; MFA, Tyler Sch. Art, Phila., 1977. Temporary instr. Colo. State U., Ft. Collins, 1977-78; instr. Mass. Coll. Art, Boston, 1979-80; asst. prof. art Kent (Ohio) State U., 1981-86, assoc. prof., 1986-91; sr. lectr. The Univ. of the Arts, Phila., 1994-95, 97; lectr. in U.S., Can., Korea. Solo exhbns. include Heller Gallery, N.Y.C., 1982, Ind. U. Bloomington, 1985, Contacto Directo Galeria, Lisbon, 1992, Jewelerswerk Galerie, Washington, 1985, 92, Perimeter Gallery, Chgo., 1987, 89, 93, Susan Cummins Gallery, Mill Valley, Calif., 1990, 92, 94, 96, Helen Drutt Gallery, Phila., 1979, 95, 97; exhibited in group shows Renwick Gallery, Washington, 1981, Am. Craft Mus., 1984, V&V Galerie, Vienna, 1988, Galerie Marzee, Nijmegen, Netherlands, 1989, Kunsthal Rotterdam, Netherlands, 1993, others; contbg. editor, mem. editl. adv. com. Metalsmith mag., 1981-97; author numerous articles on craft theory. Mass. Artists Found. fellow, 1980, Ohio Arts Coun. fellow, 1983, 84, 88, Fulbright teaching/rsch. fellow, Korea, 1990, Nat. Endowment for Visual Arts fellow, 1977, 92, Pew fellow in the Arts, 1996. Mem. Soc. N.Am. Goldsmiths (Disting. mem.). Home: 3586 Indian Queen Ln Philadelphia PA 19129

METCALF, JACK, congressman, retired state senator; b. Marysville, Wash., Nov. 30, 1927; s. John Read and Eunice (Grannis) M.; m. Norma Jean Grant, Oct. 3, 1948; children: Marta Jean, Gayle Marie, Lea Lynn, Beverlee Ann. Student U. Wash., 1944-45, 47; BA, BEd, Pacific Luth. U., 1951. Tchr., Elma (Wash.) pub. schs., 1951-52, Everett (Wash.) pub schs., 1952-81; mem. Wash. Ho. of Reps., 1960-64; mem. Wash. Senate, 1966-74, 80-92, U.S. congressman, Wash. 2nd Dist., 1995—; chmn. environment and natural resources com., 1988-92; mem. domestic & internat. monetary policy, fin. instns. & consumer credit, aviation, surface transp. coms. Chmn. Honest Money for Am. Mem. Council State Govts., Wash. Edn. Assn. (dir. 1959-61), Wash. Assn. Profl. Educators (state v.p. 1979-81, state pres. 1977-79). Mem. Nat. Conf. State Legislatures, Western States Recycling Coalition, South Whidbey Kiwanis, Deer Lagoon Grange. Republican. Home: 3273 E Saratoga Rd Langley WA 98260-9694 Office: US House Reps 1510 Longworth Bldg Washington DC 20515-4702*

METCALF, KAREN, foundation executive; b. Reading, Mass., Dec. 12, 1936; d. Albion Edmund and Natalie Viola (Ives) M. AB, Vassar Coll., 1958; MBA, Harvard U., 1968. CFA. Sec. Radio Liberty Com., N.Y.C., 1958-60; rsch. asst. Air Inc., Cambridge, Mass., 1960-64; sys. analyst Keydata Corp., Watertown, Mass., 1964-66; customer edn. cons. Interactive Data Corp., N.Y.C., 1968; portfolio mgr. Scudder, Stevens & Clark, N.Y.C., 1969-81; v.p. fin. and adminstrn. N.Y. Cmty. Trust, N.Y.C., 1981—. Episcopalian. Avocations: travel, opera. Office: NY Cmty Trust 2 Park Ave New York NY 10016-5675

METCALF, ROBERT CLARENCE, architect, educator; b. Nashville, Ohio, Nov. 7, 1923; s. George and Helen May (Drake) M.; m. Bettie Jane Sponseller, Sept. 15, 1943. Student, Johns Hopkins U., 1943; B.Arch., U. Mich., 1950. Draftsman G.B. Brigham, Jr., Architect, Ann Arbor, Mich., 1948-52; pvt. practice architecture Ann Arbor, 1953—; lectr. architecture U. Mich., Ann Arbor, 1955-58; asst. prof. U. Mich., 1958-63, asso. prof., 1963-68, prof., 1968-91, chmn. dept., 1968-74; dean U. Mich. (Coll. Architecture and Urban Planning), 1974-86; Emil Lorch prof. emeritus U. MIch., 1991—, dean emeritus, 1991—; sec. Mich. Bd. Registration for Architects, 1975-79, chmn., 1980-82. Designer 130 bldgs., Ann Arbor, 1953—. Served with U.S. Army, 1943-46, ETO. Decorated Silver Star; recipient Sol King award for excellent teaching in architecture U. Mich., 1974; named Emil Lorch Professor of Architecture, 1989. Fellow AIA; mem. Mich. Soc. Architects, Assn. Collegiate Schs. Architecture, Phi Kappa Phi, Tau Sigma Delta. Home: 1052 Arlington Blvd Ann Arbor MI 48104-2816 Office: U Mich 2150 Art Architecture Bldg Ann Arbor MI 48109 also: 2211 Medford Rd Ann Arbor MI 48104-5004

METCALF, VIRGIL ALONZO, economics educator; b. Branch, Ark., Jan. 4, 1936; s. Wallace Lance and Luella J. (Yancey) M.; m. Janice Ann Maples, July 2, 1958; children: Deborah Ann, Robert Alan. BS in Gen. Agr., U. Ark., 1958, MS in Agrl. Econs., 1960; Diploma in Econs., U. Copenhagen, 1960; PhD in Agrl. Econs., U. Mo., 1964. Asst. prof. U. Mo., Columbia, 1964-65, asst. to chancellor, 1964-69, assoc. prof., 1965-69, prof., exec. asst. to the chancellor, 1969-71; prof. econs., v.p. adminstrn. Ariz. State U., Tempe, 1971-81, prof. Sch. Agribus. and Natural Resources, 1981-88, prof. internat. bus. Coll. of Bus., 1988—; asst. to the chancellor U. Mo., 1964-69, coord. internat. programs and studies, 1965-69, mem. budget com., 1965-71, chmn., co-chmn. several task forces; cons. Ford Found., Bogota, Colombia, 1966-67; mem. negotiating team U.S. Agy. for Internat. Devel., Mauritania, 1982, cons., Cameroon, 1983, agrl. rsch. specialist, India, 1984, agribus. cons., Guatemala, 1987, 88, asst. dir. Reform Coops. Credit Project, El Salvador, 1987-90; co-dir. USIA univ. linkage grant Cath. U., Bolivia, 1984-89; cons. World Vision Internat., Mozambique, 1989. Contbr. numerous articles to profl. jours. Mem. City of Tempe U. Hayden Butte Project Area Com., 1979; bd. commrs. Columbia Redevel. Authority; mem. workable project com. City of Columbia Housing Authority. Econs. officer USAR, 1963, econ. analyst, 1964-66. Fulbright grantee U. Copenhagen, 1959-60, U. Kiril Metodij, Yugoslavia, 1973. Mem. Am. Assn. Agrl. Economists, Soc. for Internat. Devel., Samaritans (chmn. 1976, bd. dirs. 1976, mem. task force of health svc. bd. trustees 1974, health svc. 1974-78, chmn. program subcom. 1975), Kiwanis, Blue Key, Gamma Sigma Delta, Alpha Zeta, Alpha Tau Alpha. Democrat. Home: 1357 W Crystal Spring Dr Gilbert AZ 85233 Office: Ariz State U Coll Bus Tempe AZ 85287

METCALF, WILLIAM EDWARDS, museum curator; b. East Grand Rapids, Mich., Dec. 16, 1947; s. George Ellington and Ruthanne (Schnitzler) M.; m. Margaret Mary Finn, May 21, 1972 (annulled 1984); 1 son, Daniel F.; m. Jane Salinger, Oct. 26, 1991. B.A., U. Mich., 1969, M.A., 1970, Ph.D. in Classical Studies (Horace H. Rackham prize fellow), 1973. Asst. curator Roman and Byzantine coins Am. Numismatic Soc., N.Y.C., 1973-75; assoc. curator Am. Numismatic Soc., 1975-78, curator, dep. chief curator, 1978-79, chief curator, 1979—; adj. prof. art history and archaeology Columbia U., 1978; adj. prof. history, 1993; adj. prof. classics NYU, 1996. Author: The Cistophori of Hadrian, 1980, The Silver Coinage of Cappadocia, Vespasian-Commodus, 1995; editor: Studies in Early Byzantine Gold Coinage, 1988, America's Gold Coinage, 1990, Mnemata: Papers in Memory of Nancy M. Waggoner, 1991; mem. adv. com. Lexicon Iconographicum Mythologiae Classicae, 1979—; mem. adv. bd. Am. Jour. Archaeology, 1980; editor book revs. Am. Jour. Numismatics, 1989; contbr. articles on Roman and Byzantine coinage and revs. to profl. jours. NEA fellow for mus. profls., 1978; mem. Inst. for Advanced Study, 1988-89. Mem. Am. Numismatic Soc., Royal Numismatic Soc., Am. Philol. Assn. (subcom. on classical bibliography 1979-89), Archaeol. Inst. Am. (exec. com. N.Y. 1976-80), Columbia U. Seminar on Classical Civilization, Internat. Numismatic Commn. Office: Am Numismatic Soc Broadway & 155th St New York NY 10032-7598

METCALFE, DARREL SEYMOUR, agronomist, educator; b. Arkansaw, Wis., Aug. 28, 1913; s. Howard Lee and Mabel (De Marce) M.; m. Ellen Lucille Moore, May 16, 1942; children: Dean Darrel, Alan Moore. Tchr. cert., U. Wis. at River Falls, 1931; B.S. in Agronomy, U. Wis., 1941; M.S., Kans. State U., 1942; Ph.D., Iowa State U., 1950. From instr. to prof. agronomy Iowa State U., 1946-56, asst. dir. student affairs, 1956-58; asso. dean, dir. resident instrn., asst. dir. agrl. expt. sta., agronomist U. Ariz., Tucson, 1958—; dean U. Ariz., 1978-82, dean emeritus, 1982—; Chmn. resident instrn. sect., div. agr. Nat. Assn. State Univs. and Land Grant Colls., 1958-59; mem. com. edn. agr. and natural resources Nat. Acad. Sci., 1966-70, mem. rev. panel for Egypt, 1980-83, mem. Inst. Internat. Edn. Com., Somalia and Kenya, 1980-82; U.S. rep. OECD Conf. Higher Edn. in Agr., Paris, 1963-65; trustee Consortium for Internat. Devel., 1978-82; mem. AID missions to Brazil, 1962, 64, 66, 69, 71, 72, 73, Sultan Qaboos U. Com., Oman, 1982-86. Co-author: Forages, 4th edit., 1985, Crop Production, rev. edits, 1957, 72, 80. Served with AUS, 1942-46, PTO. Named Hon. Alumnus U. Ariz., 1985. Fellow Am. Soc. Agronomy (Agronomic edn. award 1958, Agronomic Svc. award 1980, chmn. student activities sect. 1950-53, edn. div. 1956, editorial bd., tech. editor jour. 1961-65), Nat. Assn. Colls. and Tchrs. Agr. (E.B. Knight award 1967, pres. 1970-71, Disting. Educator award 1980, U. Ariz. Lifetime award), Kiwanis, Sigma Xi, Phi Kappa Phi, Phi Eta Sigma, Gamma Sigma Delta, Alpha Tau Alpha, Delta Theta Sigma, Acacia (medallion of merit 1966). Home: 5811 E 9th St Tucson AZ 85711-3221

METCALFE, DEAN DARREL, medical research physician; b. Medford, Oreg., June 27, 1944; s. Darrell S. and Lucille E. (Moore) M.; m. Joan I. Peterson, Dec. 21, 1977; children: Justin, Jonathan, Elisabet. BS, No. Ariz. U., 1966; MS in Microbiology, U. Mich., 1968; MD, U. Tenn., 1972. Medicine residency Univ. Mich. Hosps., Ann Arbor, 1972-74; clin. assoc. NIH, Bethesda, Md., 1974-77; Rheum fellow Harvard Med. Sch. and Hosp., Boston, 1977-79; clin. investigator NIH, Bethesda, 1979-85; head mast cell physiology sect. lab. of clin. investigation Nat. Inst. of Allergy and Infectious Diseases, Bethesda, 1985-93; heal allergic diseases sect., 1994—; co-dir. Allergy-Immunology Tng. Program, NIAID/NIH, Bethesda, 1979—; dir. Am. Bd. Allergy-Immunology, Phila., 1990—; bd. dirs. Am. Acad. Allergy and Immunology. Capt. USPHS, 1979—. Recipient Commendation medal USPHS, 1985, Outstanding Svc. medal, USPHS, 1991. Fellow Am. Acad. Allergy and Immunology, Am. Rheumatism Assn.; mem. Am. Fedn. for Clin. Rsch., Am. Soc. for Clin. Investigators, Assn. Am. Physicians. Office: NIAID NIH Rm 11c205 MSC-1881 Bethesda MD 20892-1881*

METCALFE, ROBERT DAVIS, III, lawyer; b. Bridgeport, Conn., July 2, 1956; s. Robert Davis Jr. and Barbara Ann (Peaslee) M. BA summa cum laude, U. Conn., 1978, JD, 1981; MA, Trinity Coll., 1982. Bar: Conn. 1981, U.S. Supreme Ct. 1986. Judge adv. USN, Norfolk, Va., 1982-85; spl. asst. U.S. atty. U.S. Dept. Justice, Norfolk, 1985; trial atty. U.S. Dept. Justice, Washington, 1985—. Instr. ARC, Hartford, Conn., 1976-80; legis. asst. Conn. Gen. Assembly, Hartford, 1977. Served to lt. USN, 1982-85. Mem. Fed. Bar Assn., Conn. Bar Assn., Judge Adv. Assn., Mensa, Phi Beta Kappa. Republican. Roman Catholic. Avocations: martial arts, reading, sailing, trap and skeet shooting, philately.

METCALFE, TOM BROOKS, chemical engineering educator; b. Smithville, Tex., Feb. 26, 1920; s. Joseph Franklin and Ethel Louise (Taylor) M.; m. Gwendolyn Imogene Soward, July 3, 1944; children: Gwendolyn Jean Metcalfe Ellis, Linda Gail Metcalfe Gallup, Marilyn Louise, Carolyn Marguerite Metcalfe Montiel. BS, U. Tex., 1941, MS, 1947; PhD, Ga. Inst. Tech., 1953. Registered profl. engr., Tex. Chemist Dow Chem. Co., Freeport, Tex., 1941-43; rsch. scientist U. Tex., 1947-50; rsch. engr. Ga. Inst. Tech., 1951-52, Shell Oil Co., Houston, 1952-62; asst. prof. U. Houston, 1953-56, rsch. prof., 1975; head dept. chem. engring. W.Va. Inst. Tech., 1962-63; prof., head dept. chem. engring. U. Southwestern La., 1963-82, Found. prof., 1982-85, adj. prof., 1985—; vis. prof. U. Tex., Austin, 1982; founder, pub. Pinehill Pub. Co.; cons. U.S. Bur. Public Rds.; U.S. Dept. Interior Office of Saline Water. Author: Radiation Spectra of Radionuclides, 1970, Chemical Engineering as a Career, 1966, Safe Handling of Radioactive Materials, 1964; Contbr. articles to profl. jours. Pres. Edgewood Civic Corp., 1954, 57, 59; mem. Houston Mayor's Com. on Zoning, 1958-60; chmn. bd. dirs. U. Southwestern La. Wesley Found., 1966-67; mem. ofcl. bd. area Meth. ch. Lt. USNR, 1943-46, PTO. Fellow AIChE (nat. chmn. acad. dept. heads 1967-69, 80); mem. Am. Soc. Engring. Edn., Masons, Sigma Xi, Phi Eta Sigma, Omega Chi Epsilon, Phi Lambda Upsilon, Tau Beta Pi. Home: 5907 Overlook Dr Austin TX 78731-4221 *Seek good and not evil; bless them who curse you; with God, all things are possible.*

METCALFE, WALTER LEE, JR., lawyer; b. St. Louis, Dec. 19, 1938; s. Walter Lee and Carol (Crowe) M.; Cynthia Williamson, Aug. 26, 1965; children—Carol, Edward. A.B., Washington U., St. Louis, 1960; J.D., U. Va., 1964. Bar: Mo. 1964. Ptnr. Armstrong, Teasdale, Kramer & Vaughan, St. Louis, 1964-81; sr. ptnr. Bryan Cave LLP, St. Louis, 1982—, now chmn. Bd. dirs. Grand Ctr., Inc. chmn., 1994—; bd. dirs. St. Louis Regional Health Care Corp. Mem. ABA, Mo. Bar Assn., St. Louis Bar Assn. Episcopalian. Club: Bogey, Noonday. Home: 26 Upper Ladue Rd Saint Louis MO 63124-1675 Office: Bryan Cave 1 Metropolitan Sq Saint Louis MO 63102-2733

METHENY, PATRICK BRUCE, musician; b. Lee's Summit, Mo., Aug. 12, 1954. Student, U. Miami, Fla. Instr. dept. music U. Miami; mem. faculty Nat. Stage Band Camps, Fla., Berklee Coll. Music, Boston. Guitarist with Gary Burton Quintet, 3 yrs, mus. dir. and guitarist, Pat Metheny Group, 1978—; performing tours in U.S., Europe, Can., Japan, USSR, S.Am.; rec. artist ECM Records, currently Geffen Records; composer for guitar and band: records include Bright Size Life, 1976, Watercolors, 1977, Pat Metheny Group, 1978, New Chautauqua, 1979, American Garage, 1980, 80/81, 1980, As Falls Wichita, So Falls Wichita Falls, 1981, Offramp, 1982, Travels, 1983, Rejoicing, 1983, Works, 1984, First Circle, 1984, Still Life (Talking), 1987, Works II, 1988, Letter From Home, 1989, (with Roy Haynes and Dave Holland, Grammy award Best Jazz Composition 1990) Question and Answer, 1990, Secret Story, 1992, The Road to You, 1993 (Jazz Instrumental Grammy award, 1994); (with Ornette Coleman) Song X, 1986 (Best Jazz Album award Downbeat mag. Readers' Poll, 1986, Downbeat Readers Poll Jazz Album of Yr., Guitarist of Yr., 1989, USA Today, 1986, Best Jazz Colloboration Album award Cashbox mag., 1986, John Pareles Top Albums of 1986 award N.Y. Times); composer film scores: (with David Bowie) The Falcon and the Snowman, 1984, Twice in a Lifetime, 1985. Nominated for Grammy award, 1980, 81; recipient 7 Grammy awards; Outstanding Jazz Album award Boston Music Awards, 1986; named Best Jazz Musician Jazziz Readers' Poll, Best Jazz Guitarist Downbeat mag., 1986, Guitar Player mag., 1986, Guitar Player mag. Gallery of Greats, 1982-86, Outstanding Guitarist Boston Music Awards, 1986, Outstanding Jazz Fusion Group Boston Music Awards, 1986. Office: Geffen Records 9130 Sunset Blvd Los Angeles CA 90404*

METIVIER, ROBERT EMMETT, mayor; b. Panama Canal Zone, Nov. 5, 1934; came to the U.S., 1956; s. William Henry and Loretta Jane (Rooney) M.; m. Carol Ann O'Brien, Aug. 16, 1958; 1 child, Michael E. (dec.). AA, Canal Zone Jr. Coll., 1954; student, U. Md., 1957-58; BS in Bus. Adminstrn., Bryant Coll., 1960. Bd. dirs. Pawtucket (R.I.) Credit Union, 1976-91, treas., mgr., 1977-87, pres., CEO, 1987-91; cons. R.I. Credit Union League, Providence, 1991; mayor City of Pawtucket, R.I., 1992—; past pres. credit Exec. Assn. SNE; bd. mem. Meml. Hosp. Pawtucket, Pawtucket Local Devel. Corp.; rep. of 911 Uniform Emergency Telephone Sys. Adv. Commn. With U.S. Army, 1954-56. Recipient Len Tune awards Nat. Credit Union Mgmt. Assn. Mem. NRI C. of C., To Kalon Club, Panama Canal Soc. Fla., R.I. League of Cities and Towns (pres.). Democrat. Roman Catholic. Home: 59 Woodside Ave Pawtucket RI 02861-2753 Office: City of Pawtucket 137 Roosevelt Ave Pawtucket RI 02860-2129

METREY, GEORGE DAVID, social work educator, academic administrator; b. Milw., July 23, 1939; s. Richard Joseph and Catherine (Evans) M.; m. Cheryl Ann Mosca, June 21, 1969; 1 child, Mary Beth. A.B., Marquette U., 1961; M.S.W., Fordham U., 1963; Ph.D., NYU, 1970. Lic. ind. clin. social worker, R.I., N.J. Social worker N.J. Diagnostic Ctr., Edison, 1963-64, asst. social work supr., 1964-66, dir. psychiat. social work, 1966-70; coordinator undergrad. social work program Kean Coll., N.J., 1970-73, assoc. prof. social work, 1970-74, prof., 1974-79, chmn. dept. sociology, anthropology and social work, 1973-77, dir. social work program, acting assoc. dean Sch. Arts and Sci., 1977-79; dean Sch. Social Work, prof. R.I. Coll., Providence, 1979—; field instr. Fordham U. Sch. Social Service, 1966-70, adj. prof., 1969-77; adj. assoc. prof. Rutgers U. Grad. Sch. Social Work, 1972-73. Mem. program com. R.I. affiliate Am. Heart Assn., 1980—, bd. dirs., 1983-89, chmn. program com., 1985-87, exec. com., 1985-87; sec. bd. dirs. Ocean State Adoption Resource Exch., 1987-89, pres. bd. dirs., 1989-92. Recipient Fordham U. Grad. Sch. Social Svc. Outstanding Alumni, 1984, Spl. award disting. award R.I. Coll. Alumni Assn., 1996. Mem. NASW (N.J. Social Worker of Yr. 1977, pres. 1978-80, parliamentarian R.I. 1981—, treas. R.I. chpt. 1986-87, mem. nat. competence cert. commn. 1989-91, nat. 2d v.p. 1978-80, chair nat. program com. 1981-83), Coun. on Social Work Edn. (bd. dirs. 1979-82, mem. commn. on accreditation 1996—), Acad. Cert. Social Workers, Nat. Assn. Deans and Dirs. Schs. Social Work (nominating com. 1993-96, program com. 1993-96), Alpha Phi Omega, Gamma Pi Mu, Alpha Delta Mu (regional v.p.). Roman Catholic. Home: 540 Waverly Rd Wyckoff NJ 07481-1229 Office: RI Coll Sch Social Work Providence RI 02908

METS, MARILYN BAIRD, pediatric ophthalmologist; b. Providence, R.I., Jan. 1, 1948; d. Russell James and Beatrice (Wentworth) Baird; m. Laurens Jan Mets, June 12, 1971; children: Rebecca Baird, David Gavin, Catherine Wentworth. BA, Wheaton Coll., 1969; MS, Harvard Sch. Pub. Health, 1971; MD, George Washington U., 1976. Instr. Rush-Presbyn. St. Luke's Hosp., Chgo., 1981-83; asst. prof. U. Chgo., 1983-90; assoc. prof. Northwestern Hosp., Chgo., 1990—; assoc. prof. Children's Meml. Hosp., Chgo., 1990—; lectr. Rush Presbyn. St. Lukes, 1993—; staff ophthalmologist Evanston/Glenbrook Hosp., Glenview, Ill., 1993—, Michael Reese Hosp., Chgo., 1994—; bd. dirs. Toxoplasmosis Rsch. Inst., Chgo., 1991—; dir. retinal physiol. lab. Northwestern U. Med. Sch., 1990—. Editor-in-chief Focal Points, 1992—. Sec. bd. dirs. Ill. Soc. for the Prevention of Blindness, Chgo., 1986-94. Fellow Am. Acad. Ophthalmology (honor award 1992); mem. Am. Assn. Pediat. Ophthalmology & Strabismus, Pan Am. Assn. Ophthalmology, Costenbader Soc., Ophthalmic Genetics Study Soc., Sigma Xi. Avocations: biking, skiing, running, sailing, reading, writing. Office: Children's Meml Hosp 2300 N Childrens Plz # 70 Chicago IL 60614-3318

METTE, JOE, museum director. Dir. California State Capitol Mus., Sacramento, Calif. Office: Calif State Capitol Museum State Capitol Rm B-27 Sacramento CA 95814-4906*

METTERS, THOMAS WADDELL, sports writer; b. Columbus, Ohio, Apr. 17, 1939; s. Thomas Hammond and Charlotte Ann (Waddell) M. BS in Journalism, Ohio U., 1965. Sports editor The Traveller, Ft. Lee, Va., 1960-62; sports writer The Athens (Ohio) Messenger, 1965—; asst. to officials Legion Baseball, Athens, 1962—. Contbr.: Ohio Interscholastic Athletic Media Guide, 1985. Bd. dirs. Athens H.S. Booster Club, 1975—; official scorekeeper Am. Legion World Series, Millington, Tenn., 1989. With U.S. Army, 1959-62. Named to Ohio H.S. Basketball Coaches Assn. Hall of Fame, 1993; recipient Contributor award Ohio H.S. Track & Field Coaches Assn., 1995. Mem. Soc. Profl. Journalists (Recognition plaque 1973), Ohio Associated Press Sports Writers Assn. (pres. 1984), Green & White Club (sec. 1983—, Jonesy Sams award 1987), Ohio Prep Sports Writers Assn. (Hall of Fame 1990), Ky. Colonels, Am. Legion. Republican. Avocation: bowling. Home: 71 Sunnyside Dr Athens OH 45701-1921 Office: The Athens Messenger Rt 33 N and Johnson Rd Athens OH 45701

METTINGER, KARL LENNART, neurologist; b. Helsingborg, Sweden, Nov. 1, 1943; came to the U.S., 1989; s. Nils Allan and Anna Katarina (Hallberg) M.; m. Chesne Maree Ryman, Jan. 27, 1979. MD, U. Lund, 1973; PhD, Karolinska Inst., 1982. Intern Stockholm Hosps., 1973-74; resident Karolinska Hosp., Stockholm, 1974-77, clin. neurologist, 1977-85; med. dir. Kabi Hematology, Stockholm, 1985-87; dep. gen. mgr. Kabi Cardiovascular, Stockholm, 1987-89; med. dir. Ivax/Baker Norton Pharms., Miami, Fla., 1989-93, sr. clin. rsch. dir., 1993—; assoc. prof. Karolinska Inst., Stockholm, 1983-91; cons. neurologist Odenplan Med. Ctr., Stockholm, 1984-89. Author: Cerebral Thromboembolism, 1982, Refaat--Myths and Billions in Biotech, 1987; editor: Coronary Thrombolysis: Current Answers to Critical Questions, 1988, Controversies in Coronary Thrombolysis, 1989. Lt. Swedish Army, 1979. Recipient Silver award Spanish Health Ministry, 1989, Classical Langs. award King Gustav V Found., 1963. Mem. Swedish Stroke Soc. (bd. dirs. 1979-89, pres. 1984-86), Swedish Med. Soc., Swedish Christian Med. Soc. (bd. dirs. 1972-88, pres. 1983-88), Am. Heart Assn., N.Y. Acad. Scis., Nat. Found. for Advancement of Arts, Internat. Assn. Christian Physicians (exec. com. 1975-86). Home: 5005 Collins Ave Apt 1411 Miami FL 33140-2535 Office: IVAX 4400 Biscayne Blvd Miami FL 33137-3212

METTLER, GERALD PHILLIP, reliability engineer; b. Ft. Wayne, Ind., Oct. 24, 1936; s. Joseph Lucian and Dorothy Louise (Bixler) M.; m. Patricia Parent Mettler, May 23, 1959; children: James Anthony, Kenneth Joseph, Lisa Catherine, Charles Matthew. BS in Physics, Ill. Benedictine Coll. (now Benedictine U.), 1958; MS in Mgmt. Engring., George Washington U., 1972. Engr. Sperry Gyroscope Co., Great Neck, N.Y., 1958-66; reliability engr. ARINC Rsch. Corp. subs. Aero. Radio INC, Annapolis, Md., 1966-77; founder, pres. Reltem Rsch., Paw Paw, Mich., 1977-80; prin. reliability engr. Gould Ocean Systems, Cleve., 1980-83; staff reliability engr. Tactical Def. Sys. Lockheed Martin, Akron, Ohio, 1983—; presenter in field. Contbr. articles to symposiums. Cath. youth orgn. advisor St. Piux X Ch., Ft. Worth, 1960-62; tchr. Sunday sch. Sacred Heart Ch., Warner Robins, Ga., 1962-65; instnl. rep. Boy Scouts Am., Bowie, Md., 1972-77. Mem. IEEE, Am. Soc. Qualtiy Control, Motivators Square Dance Club (pres. 1992—). Roman Catholic. Achievements include research in predictive technology. Office: Lockheed Martin 1210 Massillon Rd Akron OH 44315-0001

METZ, CHARLES EDGAR, radiology educator; b. Bayshore, N.Y., Sept. 11, 1942; s. Clinton Edgar and Grace Muriel (Schienke) M.; m. Maryanne Theresa Bahr, July, 1967 (div. 1988); children: Rebecca, Molly. BA, Bowdoin Coll., 1964; MS, U. Pa., 1966, PhD, 1969. Instr. radiology U. Chgo., 1969-71, asst. prof., 1971-75, assoc. prof., 1976-80, dir. grad. programs in med. physics, 1979-85, prof., 1980—, prof. structural biology, 1984-86; mem. diagnostic rsch. adv. group Nat. Cancer Inst., 1980-81; mem.

sci. com. Nat. Coun. on Radiation Protection and Measurements, 1982-95, Internat. Commn. on Radiation Units and Measurements, 1988-96, chmn. sci. com., 1992-96; cons. and lectr. in field. Assoc. editor Radiology jour., 1986-91, Med. Physics jour., 1992-95; mem. editl. bd. Med. Decision Making, 1980-84; contbr. over 175 articles to sci. jours. and chpts. to books. Mem. Radiol. Soc. N.Am., Am. Assn. Physicists in Medicine, Soc. Med. Decision Making, Assn. Univ. Radiologists, Soc. for Health Svcs. Rsch. in Radiology, Phi Beta Kappa, Sigma Xi. Office: U Chgo Dept Radiology MC2026 5841 S Maryland Ave Chicago IL 60637-1463

METZ, CRAIG HUSEMAN, legislative administrator; b. Columbia, S.C., Aug. 26, 1955; s. Leonard Huseman and Annette (Worthington) M.; m. Karen Angela McCleary, Aug. 11, 1984; 1 child, Preston Worthington. BA, U. Tenn., 1977; JD, U. Memphis, 1986; cert., U.S. Ho. of Reps. Rep. Leadership Parlimentary Law Sch., 1987. Bar: S.C., D.C., U.S. Ct. Claims, U.S. Supreme Ct., U.S. Ct. Appeals (4th cir.). Canvass coord., liaison Campaign to Re-elect Congressman Floyd Spence, 1978; del., chmn. Shelby County Del. to 1983 Tenn. Young Rep. Fedn. Conv.; vice chmn. Shelby County Young Reps., 1983-84, chmn., 1984-85; Shelby County adminstr., asst. to Tenn. state exec. dir. Reagan-Bush Campaign, 1984; field rep. Campaign to Re-elect Congressman Floyd Spence, 1986; spl. asst. to Congressman Floyd Spence, 1986-88; counsel com. on labor and human resources U.S. Senate, 1988-90; commr.'s counsel U.S. Occupational Safety and Health Rev. Commn., Washington, 1990-91; spl. asst. to asst. sec. for legis. and congl. affairs; dep. asst. sec. for congl. liaison U.S. Dept. Edn., Washington, 1991-93; asst. dir. Divsn. Congl. Affairs AMA, Washington, 1993; chief of staff Congressman Floyd Spence, Washington, 1993—. Judge nat. writing competition U.S. Constn. Bicentennial, S.C. 1987-88; mem. Ch. of the Ascension and Saint Agnes, Washington. Recipient award of merit Rep. Party of Shelby County, 1985, Outstanding Leadership award Shelby County Young Reps., 1985. Mem. ABA, Rep. Nat. Lawyers Assn. (state chmn. S.C. chpt. 1987-90), Federalist Soc., Freedoms Found. Valley Forge, Va. Hist. Soc., Assn. for Preservation Va. Antiquities, Va. Geneal. Soc., U. South Caroliniana Soc., Nat. Trust for Hist. Preservation (assoc. Capital region), SAR, St. David's Soc., St. Andrew's Soc. Washington, Mil. Soc. War of 1812, Vet. Corps Arty. State of N.Y., Gen. Soc. War of 1812, Mil. Order Loyal Legion of U.S., Order of St. John (hospitalier), Confederate Meml. Assn., SCV, Mil. Order Stars and Bars, Nat. Cathedral Assn., U. Tenn. Nat. Alumni Assn., Sigma Alpha Epsilon, Phi Alpha Delta (v.p. McKellar chpt., Outstanding Svc. award 1983). Republican. Episcopalian. Home: 8505 Westown Way Vienna VA 22182-2513 Office: 2405 Rayburn Bldg Washington DC 20515-4002

METZ, DONALD JOSEPH, retired science educator; b. Bklyn., May 18, 1924; s. Emil Arthur and Madeline Margaret (Maas) M.; m. Dorothy Gorman, Aug. 30, 1947. BS, St. Francis Coll., Bklyn., 1947; DSc (hon.), St. Francis Coll., 1984; MS, N.Y. Poly. U., 1949, PhD, 1955. From lectr. to prof. St. Francis Coll., 1947-76; from assoc. to sr. scientist sci. edn. Brookhaven Nat. Lab., Upton, N.Y., 1954-93, ret., 1993; ednl. cons. Brookhaven Nat. Lab., Upton, N.Y., 1993-95. With U.S. Army, 1943-46, ETO. Roman Catholic. Home: 147 Southern Blvd East Patchogue NY 11772-5810

METZ, EMMANUEL MICHAEL, investment company executive, lawyer; b. Pitts., Sept. 19, 1928; s. Solomon and Gertrude (Krieger) M.; m. Janine Spaner, Apr. 3, 1964. BA, Dartmouth Coll., 1949; LLB, Harvard U., 1952; LLM, NYU, 1958. Bar: N.Y. 1952. Atty. ABC, N.Y.C., 1956-58; security analyst Standard & Poor's, N.Y.C., 1958-68; mng. dir. Oppenheimer & Co., Inc., N.Y.C., 1968—. Author: Street Fighting at Wall and Broad, 1982. Lt. USN, 1952-56. Home: 150 E 56th St New York NY 10022-3631 Office: Oppenheimer & Co Inc 200 Liberty St New York NY 10281-1003

METZ, FERDINAND, chef, educator, academic administrator; b. Munich. BBA, U. Pitts., 1973, MBA, 1975. Cert. master chef. European apprentice in cooking and baking; garde manger, entremetier Le Pavillon, N.Y.C., 1962; banquet chef Plaza Hotel, N.Y.C., 1964; former experimental chef, sr. mgr. Heinz, U.S.A., Pitts., 1965-80; pres. Culinary Inst. Am., Hyde Park, N.Y.; capt., team mgr., chmn. U.S. Culinary Team. Co-recipient World Championship, hot foods divsn. Internat. Culinary Competition, 1988, Medal of French Republic, Gold Plate award Internat. Foodservice Mfrs. Assn. Mem. Am. Culinary Fedn. (past pres., chmn.), Internat. Foodsvc. Mfrs. Assn. Office: Culinary Inst Am Roth Hall Hyde Park NY 12538

METZ, FRANK ANDREW, JR., data processing executive; b. Winthrop, Mass., Jan. 28, 1934; s. Frank Andrew and Frances E. (Fallon) M.; married; children: Christopher, Lelia, Amy, Patrick, Joshua, Rebecca; m. Judith Ann Mapes, July 21, 1979. A.B., Bowdoin Coll., 1955. With IBM, 1955—; dir. fin. planning data processing group IBM, Harrison, N.Y., 1969-72; div. v.p. office products IBM, Franklin Lakes, N.J., 1972-75; asst. controller IBM, Armonk, N.Y., 1975-78, controller, 1978-80; v.p., asst. group exec. IBM, White Plains, N.Y., 1980-84, sr. v.p., group exec., 1984-86, sr. v.p., chief fin. officer, bd. dirs., 1986-93, ret., 1993; bd. dirs. Allegheny Power Systems, Monsanto Co., Norrell Corp. Trustee St. Luke's Roosevelt Hosp., N.Y.C., 1979-96, chmn. 1994-96; trustee Am. Mus. Natural History, 1986-96. 1st lt. Transp. Corps U.S. Army, 1956. Roman Catholic.

METZ, MARILYN JOYCE, bank executive; b. Denver, Colo., Nov. 10, 1949; d. James C. and Lois M. (Roach) M.; m. Jack W. Calabrese, Apr. 15, 1977 (div. 1981); m. Frank C. Margowski, Oct. 13, 1986 (div.). Student, Colo. State U., 1968-72; diploma, Colo. Grad. Sch. Banking, 1983. With First Interstate Bank Denver, 1972-83; v.p., mgr. United Banks Colo., Denver, 1983-88; v.p., area mgr. First Interstate Bank Oreg., Portland, 1988-89; v.p., dist. mgr. 5 brs. lst Interstate Bank Wash., Seattle, 1989-91; v.p., dist. mgr. 11 brs. 1st Interstate Bank, Bellevue, Wash., 1991-96; v.p., trust officer Wells Fargo Bank, Bellevue, Wash., 1996—. Bd. dirs., Met. Child Dental Care Assn., 1985-87, Standing Ovation, 1993—; panel chair United Way King County, 1996—. Mem. Nat. Assn. Bank Women (state pres. Colo. 1986-87), Cherry Creek Commerce Assn., Seattle C. of C., Pres. Club Seattle. Republican. Avocations: travel, reading, skiing. Office: Wells Fargo Bank 225 108th Ave NE Bellevue WA 98004-5705

METZ, MARY HAYWOOD, sociologist; b. Zurich, Switzerland, Oct. 2, 1939; came to U.S., 1939; d. Richard Mansfield and Margaret Rider (Mowbray) Haywood; m. Donald Lehman Metz, July 31, 1965; children: David Haywood, Michael Lehman. AB, Radcliffe Coll., 1960; MA, U. Calif., Berkeley, 1966, PhD, 1971; postgrad., U. Freiburg, 1960-61. Author: Classrooms and Corridors, 1978, Different by Design, 1986. German Acad. Exch. Commn. fellow, Bonn, Germany, 1960-61, Woodrow Wilson fellow, Princeton, N.J., 1961-62, Kent fellow Danforth Found., St. Louis, 1965-69. Mem. Am. Edn. Rsch. Assn. (mem. coun. and exec. bd. 1991-94), Am. Sociol. Assn. (chair soc. edn. sect. 1985-86), Soc. Values Higher Edn. (bd. dirs. 1972-74). Mem. United Ch. of Christ. Home: 2952 N Stowell Ave Milwaukee WI 53211-3349 Office: U Wis 1000 Bascom Mall 221 Edn Bldg Madison WI 53706

METZ, MARY SEAWELL, university dean, retired college president; b. Rockhill, S.C., May 7, 1937; d. Columbus Jackson and Mary (Dunlap) Seawell; m. F. Eugene Metz, Dec. 21, 1957; 1 dau., Mary Eugena. BA summa cum laude in French and English, Furman U., 1958; postgrad., Institut Phonetique, Paris, 1962-63, Sorbonne, Paris, 1962-63; PhD magna cum laude in French, La. State U., 1966; HHD (hon.), Furman U., 1984; LLD (hon.), Chapman Coll., 1985; DLT (hon.), Converse Coll., 1988. Instr. French La. State U., 1965-66, asst. prof., 1966-67, 1968-72, assoc. prof., 1972-76, dir. elem. and intermediate French programs, 1966-74, spl. asst. to chancellor, 1974-75, asst. to chancellor, 1975-76; prof. French Hood Coll., Frederick, Md., 1976-81, provost, dean acad. affairs, 1976-81; pres. Mills Coll., Oakland, Calif., 1981-90; dean of extension U. Calif., Berkeley, 1991—; vis. asst. prof. U. Calif.-Berkeley, 1967-68; mem. commn. on leadership devel. Am. Coun. on Edn., 1981-90, adv. coun. Stanford Rsch. Inst., 1985-90, adv. coun. Grad. Sch. Bus., Stanford U.; assoc. Gannett Ctr. for Media Studies, 1985—; bd. dirs. PG&E, Pacific Telesis, PacTel & PacBell, Union Bank, Longs Drug Stores, S.H. Cowell Found. Author: Reflets du monde francais, 1971, 78, Cahier d'exercices: Reflets du monde francais, 1972, 78, (with Helstrom) Le Francais a decouvrir, 1972, 78, Le Francais a vivre, 1972, 78, Cahier d'exercices: Le Francais a vivre, 1972, 78; standardized tests; mem. editorial bd.: Liberal Edn., 1982—. Trustee Am. Conservatory Theater. NDEA fellow, 1960-62,, 1963-64; Fulbright fellow, 1962-63; Am. Council Edn. fellow, 1974-75. Mem. Western Coll. Assn. (v.p. 1982-84, pres. 1984-86), Assn. Ind. Calif. Colls. and Univs. (exec. com. 1982-90), Nat. Assn. Ind. Colls. and Univs. (govt. rels. adv. coun. 1982-85), So. Conf. Lang. Teaching (chmn. 1976-77), World Affairs Coun. No. Calif. (bd. dirs. 1984-93), Bus.-Higher Edn. Forum, Women's Forum West, Women's Coll. Coalition (exec. com. 1984-88), Phi Kappa Phi, Phi Beta Kappa. Address: PO Box 686 Stinson Beach CA 94970-0686

METZ, ROBERT ROY, publisher, editor; b. Richmond Hill, N.Y., Mar. 23, 1929; s. Robert Roy, Sr. and Mary (Kissel) M.; m. Susan Lee Blair, 1984; children: Robert Sumner, Christopher Roy. B.A., Wesleyan U., Middletown Conn., 1950. Copyboy N.Y. Times, 1951, asst. fgn. news desk, 1952; rewriteman cable desk I.N.S., 1953, overnight cable editor, 1954-56, asst. feature editor, 1956-58; asst. news editor Newspaper Enterprise Assn., 1958, news editor, 1959-63, mng. editor, 1963-66, exec. editor, 1966-68, v.p., 1967-71, editorial dir., 1968-71, pres., editor, dir., 1972-94; dir. Berkeley-Small Inc., 1974-77; chmn. Berkley-Small Inc., 1976-77; v.p., dir. United Feature Syndicate, 1976-77, pres., editor, 1978; pres., editor, dir. United Media, 1978-93, chmn., 1993-94; media cons., 1994—. Pres. Peter Pan Children's Fund, 1997—. Lutheran. Club: Union League (N.Y.C.). Home: 170 E 77th St New York NY 10021-1912

METZ, RONALD IRWIN, retired priest, addictions counselor; b. Walthill, Nebr., Aug. 11, 1921; s. Harry Elmer and Emma Rilla (Howe) M.; m. Helen Chapin, July 14, 1951; children: Mary Selden Metz Evans, Helen Winchester Metz Ketchum, Grace Chapin. BA in Chinese and Far Ea. Studies, U. Calif., Berkeley, 1945; MA in Mid. Ea. Studies, Am. U., Beirut, 1954; M Div., Yale U., 1969, STD, 1975. Ordained priest Episcopal Ch., 1969. Intelligence officer various govtl. intelligence agys., Far East and Washington, 1944-52; exec. Arabian/Am. Oil Co., Dhahran and Riyadh, Saudi Arabia, 1954-66; deacon Grace Cathedral, San Francisco; priest St. George's Cathedral, Jerusalem, 1969; exec. asst. to archbishop Jerusalem and Mid. East Archbishopric, 1969-75; rector Ch. of the Holy Spirit, Erie, Pa., 1976-81; chaplain Brent Sch., Baguio, Philippines, 1981-82; counselor of chemically dependent Washington, 1982—; addictionologist, vol. New Beginnings Treatment Ctr., P.I.W. Hosp., Washington, 1989-90, Found. Next Step Outpatient Treatment Ctr., Washington, 1991-92; adj. clergy St. Margaret's Ch., Washington; mem. D.C. Diocesan Commn. on Alcohol and Drug Abuse, Washington, 1982-89. Bd. dirs. Mid. East Inst., Washington, 1959-60, Pub. Broadcasting System, n.w. Pa., 1976-81; mem. adv. bd. Children's Aid Internat., 1988-89. Served to col. U.S. Army, 1942-45, CBI, OSS. Decorated Bronze Star. Mem. Iran Diocesan Assn. U.S.A., Phi Beta Kappa, Sigma Chi (chaplain D.C. alumni assn. 1982—). Democrat. Avocations: home movies, double crostics. Home: 3001 Veazey Ter NW Apt 334 Washington DC 20008-5455

METZ, STEVEN WILLIAM, small business owner; b. Inglewood, Calif., Nov. 30, 1946; s. Glenn Ludwig and Kathleen Martha (Peterson) M.; m. Michelle Marie McArthur, Aug. 11, 1989; 1 child, Glenn Christian. Student, Fullerton Coll., Calif. Supt. Oahu Interiors, Honolulu, 1969-71, Hackel Bros., Miami, Fla., 1971-73; exec. v.p. Tru-Cut Inc., Brea, Calif., 1974-82; gen. mgr. The Louvre', Grass Valley, Calif., 1983-85; mfg. engring. mgr. Rexnord Aerospace, Torrance, Calif., 1986-87; pres., founder Metz/Calcoa Inc., Torrance, Calif., 1987—; mfg. rep. consul Orange County Spring, Anaheim, 1987—, TALSCO, 1994—, Precision Resources, 1994—, GEMTECH, 1994—; mfg. rep. consul Alard Machine Products, Gardena, Calif., 1988—, v.p. spl. projects, 1997—. Charter mem. Rep. Presdl. Task Force, 1991—; mem. L.A. Coun. on World Affairs, 1991-92. With U.S. Army, 1966-68. Recipient Appreciation awards DAV, 1968, Soc. Mfg. Engrs., 1991. Fellow Soc. Carbide Engrs.; mem. Soc. Carbide and Tool Engrs. (chpt. pres. 1980-82, Appreciation award 1981), Rep. Presdl. Legion of Merit. Avocations: golf, swimming, riding, boating.

METZ, T(HEODORE) JOHN, librarian, consultant; b. Erie, Pa., Nov. 5, 1932; s. Theodore John and Dorothy Pearl (Schutte) M.; m. Dorothy Page Neff, June 11, 1955; 1 child, Margaret Elizabeth. Mus.B., Heidelberg Coll., 1954; M.A. in Music, Miami U., Oxford, Ohio, 1955; M.L.S., U. Mich., 1959. Librarian II U. Wis., Madison, 1959-61; asst. librarian Lawrence U., Appleton, Wis., 1961-67; dir. libraries U. Wis.-Green Bay, 1967-75; exec. dir. Midwest Region Library Network, Evanston, Ill., 1975-79; coll. librarian, assoc. prof. Carleton Coll., Northfield, Minn., 1979—; speaker, participant, coord. numerous confs. and insts., 1969—; chmn. several state libr. groups, 1971-76; mem. several nat. libr. adv. coms., 1974-80; bldg. cons. Carleton Coll., others, 1978—; mem. Citizen Amb. Rsch. Librs. del. to Ea. Europe, 1992. Author: MIDLNET Symposium Report, 1976. Chmn. Green Bay Symphony, 1971-76; mem. various bds. coms., relating to mus. activities; performer Green Bay and other orchs., 1955—. Library Service scholar U. Mich., 1957; Library Service fellow U. Mich., 1958. Mem. ALA, Assn. Coll. Rsch. Librs., Internat. Fedn. Libr. Assns. Avocations: musical activities; hunting; fishing; gardening. Home: 1200 Elm St Northfield MN 55057-2906 Office: Carleton Coll Libr Northfield MN 55057-4097

METZENBAUM, HOWARD MORTON, former U.S. senator; b. Cleve., June 4, 1917; s. Charles I. and Anna (Klafter) M.; m. Shirley Turoff, Aug. 8, 1946; children: Barbara Jo, Susan Lynn, Shelley Hope, Amy Beth. B.A., Ohio State U., 1939, LL.D., 1941. Chmn. bd. Airport Parking Co. Am., 1958-66, ITT Consumer Services Corp., 1966-68; chmn. bd. ComCorp, 1969-74; chmn. bd. dirs. Consumer Fedn. Am.; mem. War Labor Panel, 1942-45, Ohio Bur. Code rev., 1949-50, Cleve. Met. Housing Authority, 1968-70, Lake Erie Regional Transit Authority, 1972-73, Ohio Ho. of Reps., 1943-46, Ohio Senate, 1947-50; chmn. anti-trust sub-com., labor sub-com. U.S. Senate; mem. intell com., budget com., environ. and pub. works com., judiciary com., labor and human resources, energy and natural resources, dem. policy com. Trustee Mt. Sinai Hosp., Cleve., 1961-73, treas, 1966-73; bd. dirs. Coun. Human Rels., United Cerebral Palsy Assn., Nat. Coun. Hunger and Malnutrition, Karamu House, St. Vincent Charity Hosp., Cleve., St. Jude Rsch. Hosp., Memphis; nat. co-chmn. Nat. Citizen's Com. Conquest Cancer; vice chmn. fellows Brandeis U.; chmn. Am. Friend Rabin Ctr., Tel Aviv, Israel; mem. Bd. Nat. Peace Garden Found. Mem. ABA, Ohio Bar Assn., Cuyahoga Bar Assn., Cleve. Bar Assn., Am. Assn. Trial Lawyers, Order of Coif, Phi Eta Sigma, Tau Epsilon Rho. Office: Consumer Fedn Am 1424 16th St NW Ste 504 Washington DC 20036-2238*

METZER, PATRICIA ANN, lawyer; b. Phila., Mar. 10, 1941; d. Freeman Weeks and Evelyn (Heap) M.; m. Karl Hormann, June 30, 1980. BA with distinction, U. Pa., 1963, LLB cum laude, 1966. Bar: Mass. 1966, D.C. 1972, U.S. Tax Ct. 1988. Assoc., then ptnr. Mintz, Levin, Cohn, Glovsky and Popeo, Boston, 1966-75; assoc. tax legis. counsel U.S. Treasury Dept., Washington, 1975-78; shareholder, dir. Goulston & Storrs, P.C., Boston, 1978—; lectr. program continuing legal edn. Boston Coll. Law Sch., Chestnut Hill, Mass., spring 1974; mem. adv. com. NYU Inst. Fed. Taxation, N.Y.C., 1981-87; mem. practitioner liaison com. Mass. Dept. Revenue, 1985-90; spkr. in field. Author: Federal Income Taxation of Individuals, 1984; mem. adv. bd. Corp. Tax and Bus. Planning Review, 1996—; mem. editl. bd. Am. Jour. Tax Policy, 1995—; contbr. articles to profl. jours., chpts. to books. Bd. mgrs. Barrington Ct. Condominium, Cambridge, Mass., 1985-86; bd. dirs. University Road Parking Assn., Cambridge, 1988—; trustee Social Law Libr., Boston, 1989-93. Mem. ABA (tax sect., mem. coun. 1996—, chmn. subcom. allocations and distbns. partnership com. 1978-82, vice chmn. legis. 1991-93, chmn. 1993-95, com. govt. submissions, vice liaison 1993-94, liaison 1994-95, North Atlantic regn, co-liaison 1995-96, N.E. region, regional liaison meetings com.), FBA (coun. on taxation, chmn. corp. taxation com. 1977-81, chmn. com. partnership taxation 1981-87), Mass. Bar Assn., Boston Bar Assn. (coun. 1987-89, chmn. tax sect. 1989-91), Am. Coll. Tax Counsel. Avocation: vocal performances (as soloist and with choral groups). Office: Goulston & Storrs PC 400 Atlantic Ave Boston MA 02110-3331

METZGER, BARRY, lawyer; b. Newark, June 11, 1945; s. William and Dorothy (Bagoon) M.; m. Jacqueline Sue Ivers, June 26, 1966; children: Darren Thomas, Rebecca Lynne. AB magna cum laude, Princeton U., 1966; JD cum laude, Harvard U., 1969. Bar: D.C. 1970. Asst. to Prin. Ceylon Law Coll., Colombo, 1969-71; dir. Asian programs Internat. Legal Ctr., N.Y.C., 1971-74; ptnr. Coudert Brothers, N.Y.C., 1974-76, resident in Hong Kong, 1976-84, Sydney, 1984-89, London, 1989-95; gen. counsel Asian Devel. Bank, Manila, 1995—; mem. New South Wales Atty. Gen.'s Commn. on Comml. Dispute Resolution, Com. for Econ. Devel. Australia; arbitrator ICC Ct. Arbitration.; v.p. Internat. Legal Aid Assn., 1972-80; pres. Harvard Legal Aid Bur., 1968-69; trustee Princeton-in-Asia. Editorial advisor: Internat. Fin. Law Rev.; editor: Legal Aid and World Poverty, 1974; contbr. articles to profl. jours. Sheldon Meml. fellow, 1969. Mem. ABA, Assn. Bar City N.Y., Internat. Bar Assn. Democrat. Home: 3 Flame Tree Place, South Forbes Park Manila The Philippines Office: Office Gen Counsel Asian Devel Bank, PO Box 789, 0980 Manila The Philippines

METZGER, BRUCE MANNING, clergyman, educator; b. Middletown, Pa., Feb. 9, 1914; s. Maurice Rutt and Anna Mary (Manning) M.; m. Isobel E. Mackay, July 7, 1944; children—John Mackay, James Bruce. A.B., Lebanon Valley Coll., 1935, D.D., 1951; Th.B., Princeton Theol. Sem., 1938, Th.M., 1939; A.M., Princeton U., 1940, Ph.D., 1942; L.H.D., Findlay U., 1962; D.D., St. Andrews U., Scotland, 1964; D.Theol., Münster U., Fed. Republic Germany, 1970; D.Litt., Potchefstroom U., South Africa, 1985. Ordained to ministry Presbyn. Ch., 1939. Teaching fellow N.T. Princeton Theol. Sem., 1938-40, mem. faculty, 1940—, prof. N.T. lang. and lit., 1954-64, George L. Collord prof. N.T. lang. and lit., 1964-84, emeritus, 1984—; vis. lectr. Presbyn. Theol. Sem. South, Campinas, Brazil, 1952, Presbyn. Theol. Sem. North, Recife, Brazil, 1952; mem. Inst. Advanced Study, Princeton, 1964-65, 73-74; scholar-in-residence Tyndale House, Cambridge, 1969; vis. fellow Clare Hall, Cambridge, 1974, Wolfson Coll., Oxford U., 1979, Macquarie U., Sydney, Australia, 1982, Caribbean Grad. Sch. of Theology, Jamaica, 1990, Seminario Internacional Teológico Bautista, Buenos Aires, 1991, Griffith Thomas Lectrs., Dallas Theol. Sem., 1992; mem. mng. com. Am. Sch. Classical Studies, Athens, Greece; mem. Standard Bible com. Nat. Coun. Chs., 1952—, chmn., 1975—; mem. seminar N.T. studies Columbia U., 1959-80; mem. Kuratorium of Vetus-Latina Inst., Beuron, Germany, 1959—; adv. com. Inst. N.T. Text Rsch., U. Münster, 1961—, Thesaurus Linguae Graecae, 1972-80; Collected Works of Erasmus, 1977—; chmn. Am. com. versions Internat. Greek N.T., 1950-88; participant internat. congresses scholars, Aarhus, Aberdeen, Bangor, Basel, Bonn, Brussels, Budapest, Cairo, Cambridge, Dublin, Exeter, Frankfurt, Heidelberg, London, Louvain, Manchester, Milan, Munich, Münster, Newcastle, Nottingham, Oxford, Praque, Rome, St. Andrews, Stockholm, Strasbourg, Toronto, Trondheim, Tübingen; mem. Presbytery, N.B. Author: The Saturday and Sunday Lessons from Luke in the Greek Gospel Lectionary, 1944, Lexical Aids for Students of New Testament Greek, 1946, enlarged edit., 1955, A Guide to the Preparation of a Thesis, 1950, An Introduction to the Apocrypha, 1957, Chapters in the History of New Testament Textual Criticism, 1963, The Text of the New Testament, Its Transmission, Corruption, and Restoration, 1964, 3d enlarged edit., 1992, (with H.G. May) The Oxford Annotated Bible with the Apocrypha, 1965, The New Testament, Its Background, Growth, and Content, 1965, Index to Periodical Literature on Christ and the Gospels, 1966, Historical and Literary Studies, Pagan, Jewish, and Christian, 1968, Index to Periodical Literature on the Apostle Paul, 1970, 2d edit., A Textual Commentary on the Greek New Testament, 1971, 2d edit., 1994, The Early Versions of the New Testament, 1977, New Testament Studies, 1980, Manuscripts of the Greek Bible, 1981, The Canon of the New Testament, 1987, (with Roland Murphy) The New Oxford Annotated Bible with the Apocrypha, 1991, (with M.D. Coogan) The Oxford Companion to the Bible, 1993, Breaking the Code-Understanding the Book of Revelation, 1993; mem. editorial com.: Critical Greek New Testament, 1956-84; chmn. Am. com., Internat. Greek New Testament Project, 1970-88; sec. com. translators: Apocrypha (rev. standard version); editor: New Testament Tools and Studies, 19 vols, 1960-94, Oxford Annotated Apocrypha, 1965, enlarged edit., 1977; Reader's Digest Condensed Bible, 1982; co-editor: United Bible Societies Greek New Testament, 1966, 4th edit., 1993; compiler: Index of Articles on the New Testament and the Early Church Published in Festschriften, 1951, supplement, 1955, Lists of Words Occurring Frequently in the Coptic New Testament (Sahidic Dialect), 1961, Annotated Bibliography of the Textual Criticism of the New Testament, 1955, (with Isobel M. Metzger) Oxford Concise Concordance to the Holy Bible, 1962 (with R.C. Dentan and W. Harrelson), The Making of the New Revised Standard Version of the Bible, 1991; contbr. articles to jours. Chmn. standard bible com. Nat. Coun. Chs., 1977—. Recipient cert. Disting. Svc. Nat. Coun. Chs., 1957, Disting. Alumnus award Lebanon Valley Coll. Alumni Assn., 1961, citation of appreciation Laymen's Nat. Bible Assn., 1986, Disting. Alumnus award Princeton Theol. Sem., 1989, lit. competition prize Christian Rsch. Found., 1955, 62, 63, E.T. Thompson award, 1991. Mem. Am. Philos. Soc., Soc. Bibl. Lit. (pres. 1970-71, past del. Am. Coun. Learned Socs.), Am. Bible Soc. (bd. mgrs. 1948—, chmn. com. transls. 1964-70), Am. Philol. Assn., Studiorum Novi Testamenti Societas (pres. 1971-72), Cath. Bibl. Assn., N.Am. Patristic Soc. (past pres.), Soc. Textual Scholarship (pres. 1995), Am. Soc. Papyrologists; hon. fellow, corr. mem. Higher Inst. Coptic Studies, Cairo; corr. fellow Brit. Acad. (Burkitt medal in Bibl. studies 1994). Republican. Home: 20 Cleveland Ln Princeton NJ 08540 Office: Princeton Theol Sem Mercer St Princeton NJ 08542

METZGER, ERNEST HUGH, aerospace engineer, scientist; b. Nurnberg, Germany, Oct. 22, 1923; came to U.S., 1939, naturalized, 1943; s. Paul Arthur and Charlotte Babette (Kann) M.; m. Sarah Temple Grinnell, Nov. 19, 1956; children: Lisa Metzger Dunning, Charlotte Bennett, George Grinnell. B.S., CCNY, 1949; M.S., Harvard U., 1950. Automatic control engr. Bell Aerospace Co. div. Textron, Buffalo, 1950-54, tech. dir. inertial nav. systems, 1954-60, chief engr., inertial instruments, 1960-70, chief engr., gravity gradiometer systems, 1970-83, dir. gravity sensor systems, 1983-86, exec. dir. engring., 1986-89, cons., 1989-95; cons. Bell Geospace Inc., Buffalo, 1995—; mem. panel future navigation systems Nat. Acad. Sci., com. on geodesy NRC, 1988-89, accelerator criteria com. NASA, tech. com. navigation guidance and control, AIAA, 1989—; vis. lectr. dept. aernautics and astronautics Stanford U., 1990. Contbr. articles to profl. jours.; patentee in field. Served with AUS, 1943-46. Recipient Aerospace Pioneer award Niagara Frontier sect. AIAA, 1977; named to Niagara Frontier Aviation Hall of Fame, 1992. Mem. IEEE, Inst. Navigation (Thurlow award for outstanding contbn. to sci. navigation 1983), AAAS, Air Force Assn., N.Y. Acad. Scis., Explorers Club, Sigma Xi, Tau Beta Pi, Eta Kappa Nu. Clubs: Harvard, Buffalo Ski. Home: 90 High Park Blvd Buffalo NY 14226-4209

METZGER, FRANK, management consultant; b. Mainz, Fed. Republic Germany, Feb. 27, 1929; came to U.S., 1938; s. Paul Alfred and Anna (Daniel) M.; m. Lore Lichter, Dec. 21, 1952; children: Peter D., Mark S. BS in Indsl. Edn., N.Y. State Tchrs.'s Coll., 1951; MS in Psychology, Carnegie Mellon U., 1953, PhD in Indsl. Psychology, 1954. Lic. psychologist, N.Y., Ill. Supr. tech. adminstrn. Gen. Electric, Lynn, Mass., 1956-58; dir. mgmt. devel. Raytheon, Newton, Mass., 1958-59; asst. dir. personnel ITT, N.Y.C., 1959-69; sr. v.p. adminstrn. Nytronics Inc., Pelham, N.Y., 1969-71; sr. v.p. corp. and orgn. devel. CNA Fin. Corp., Chgo., 1971-75; pres. Metzger and Co. Inc., Chgo., 1975-76; sr. v.p. adminstrn. Bairnco Corp., N.Y.C., 1976-88; prin. Metzger & Co., Rye, N.Y., 1988—; bd. dirs. Genlyte Group Inc., Union, N.J. Contbr. articles to profl. jours. Mem. Pres. Com. on Equal Opportunity, Washington, 1962-65. Served with signal corps. U.S. Army, 1954-56. Office: Metzger & Co 16 Norman Dr Rye NY 10580-2250

METZGER, HENRY, federal research institution administrator; b. Mainz, Germany, Mar. 23, 1932; came to U.S., 1938; naturalized, 1945; s. Paul Alfred and Anne (Daniel) M.; m. Deborah Stashower, June 16, 1957; children: Eran D., Renée V., Carl E. MD, Columbia U., 1957. Chief chem. immunology sect. Nat. Inst. Arthritis & Musculoskeletal & Skin Disease/NIH, Bethesda, Md., 1973—; br. chief USPHS, Bethesda, 1983-94, sci. dir., 1987—, med. officer grade VI, 1975—; Carl Prausnitz Meml. lectr., 1982; Ecker Meml. lectr. Case Western Res. U., Cleve., 1984; Harvey Soc. lectr., 1984; Eli Nadel Meml. lectr. St. Louis U., 1987; Rodney Porter Meml. lectr., 1993; Burroughs-Wellcome lectr., 1994; R.E. Dyer lectr.; mem. health rsch. coun. BMFT, German Govt., 1994—. Editor: Fc Receptors & the Action of Antibodies, 1990; assoc. editor Ann. Rev. Immunology, 1982-96; contbr. numerous articles to profl. jours.; mem. editorial bd. numerous sci. jours. Recipient Meritorious Svc. award USPHS, 1978, Disting. Svc. award, 1985, Joseph Mather Smith prize Columbia U., 1984. Fellow AAAS, Am. Acad. Allergy and Immunology; mem. NAS, Am. Assn. Immunologists (pres. 1991-92), Am. Soc. Biol. Chemists, Am. Soc. Cell Biology, Am. Rheumatism Assn., Internat. Union Immunol. Soc. (pres. 1992-95), Found. for Advanced Edn. in the Scis. (pres. 1990-92), Alpha Omega Alpha. Home: 3410 Taylor St Bethesda MD 20815-4024 Office: NIH 9000 Rockville Pike Rm 9n228 Bethesda MD 20814-1436

METZGER, H(OWELL) PETER, writer; b. N.Y.C., Feb. 22, 1931; s. Julius Radley and Gertrude (Fuller) M.; m. Frances Windham, June 30, 1956 (div. July 1987); children: John, James, Lisa, Suzanne; m. Valerie A. Farnham, Jan. 12, 1990 (div. Sept. 1995). BA, Brandeis U., 1953; PhD, Columbia U., 1965. Host radio talk show KTLN, Denver, 1966-68; mgr. advanced programs Ball Bros. Rsch. Corp., Boulder, 1968-70; rsch. assoc. dept. chemistry U. Colo., Boulder, 1966-68; sr. rsch. scientist N.Y. State Psychiat. Inst., N.Y.C., 1965-66; syndicated columnist N.Y. Times Syndicate, 1972-74, Science Critic, Newspaper Enterprise Assn., 1974-76; sci. editor Rocky Mt. News, Denver, 1973-77; mgr. public affairs planning Public Svc. Co. Colo., Denver, 1977-96; cons. Environ. Instrumentation, 1970-72; dir. Colspan Environ. Sys., Inc., Boulder, Colo., 1969-72. Author: The Atomic Establishment, 1972; contbr. articles in field to profl. jours., nat. mags. Pres. Colo. Com. for Environ. Info., Boulder, 1968-72; mem. Colo. Gov.'s State Health Planning Coun., 1969-72, Colo. Gov.'s Adv. Com. on Underground Nuc. Explosions, 1971-74; mem. spl. project on energy policy mgmt. Heritage Found., 1980; mem. 1981 U.S. Presdl. Rank Rev. Bd., U.S. Office Pers. Mgmt., 1981; bd. dirs. Wildlife-2000, 1970-72, Colo. Def. Coun., 1972-75. USPHS fellow, 1959-65; prin. investigator, 1968; archivee Hoover Instn. Stanford U., 1982. Mem. ACLU (state bd. dirs. 1968-71), Am. Alpine Club, Sigma Xi, Phi Lambda Upsilon. Address: 2595 Stanford Ave Boulder CO 80303-5332

METZGER, ROBERT STREICHER, lawyer; b. St. Louis, Sept. 27, 1950; s. Robert Stanley and Jean Harriet (Streicher) M.; m. Stephanie Joy Morgan, Nov. 16, 1980; children: Michael, Kristen, Marisa. BA, Middlebury Coll., 1974; JD, Georgetown U., 1977. Bar: Calif. 1978, D.C. 1978. Legis. aide U.S. Rep. Robert F. Drinan, Washington, 1972-73; legis. asst. U.S. Rep. Michael J. Harrington, Washington, 1973-75; rsch. fellow Ctr. for Sci. and Internat. Affairs Harvard U., Cambridge, Mass., 1977-78; assoc. Latham & Watkins, L.A., 1978-84, ptnr., 1984-90; ptnr. Kirkland & Ellis, L.A., 1990-93, Troop, Meisinger, Steuber & Pasich and predecessor, L.A., 1993—; cons. Congl. Rsch. Svc., Washington, 1977-78. Contbr. articles to profl. jours. Mem. ABA (litigation pub. contracts sect.), Internat. Inst. for Strategic Studies, Jonathan Club. Office: Troop Meisinger Steuber & Pasich 10940 Wilshire Blvd Los Angeles CA 90024-3915

METZGER, VERNON ARTHUR, management educator, consultant; b. Baldwin Park, Calif., Aug 13, 1918; s. Vernon and Nellie C. (Ross) M.; BS, U. Calif., Berkeley, 1947, MBA, 1948; m. Beth Arlene Metzger, Feb. 19, 1955; children: Susan, Linda, 1 step-son, David. Estimating engr. C. F. Braun & Co., 1949; prof. mgmt. Calif. State U. at Long Beach, 1949-89, prof. emeritus, 1989—, founder Sch. Bus.; mgmt. cons., 1949-89. Mem. Fire Commn. Fountain Valley, Calif., 1959-60; pres. Orange County Dem. League, 1967-68; mem. State Dept. mgmt. task force to promote modern mgmt. in Yugoslavia, 1977; mem. State of Calif. Fair Polit. Practices Commn., Orange County Transit Com. Served with USNR, 1942-45. Recipient Outstanding Citizens award Orange County (Calif.) Bd. Suprs. Fellow Soc. for Advancement of Mgmt. (life; dir.); mem. Acad. Mgmt., Orange County Indsl. Rels. Rsch. Assn. (v.p.), Beta Gamma Sigma, Alpha Kappa Psi, Tau Kappa Upsilon. Home: 1938 Balearic Dr Costa Mesa CA 92626-3513 Office: 1250 N Bellflower Blvd Long Beach CA 90840-0006

METZGER, W. JAMES, JR., physician, researcher, educator; b. Pitts., Oct. 30, 1945; s. Walter James Sr. and Marion Smith (Vine) M.; m. Carol Louise Hughes, Sept. 14, 1968; children: James Andrew, Joel Robert, Anne Elizabeth. BA, Stanford U., 1967; MD, Northwestern U., Chgo., 1971. Intern, resident Northwestern U. Sch. of Medicine, Chgo., 1971-74, rsch. fellow, 1974-76; asst. prof. medicine U. Iowa Coll. of Medicine, Iowa City, 1978-84; assoc. prof., sect. head East Carolina U. Sch. of Medicine, Greenville, N.C., 1984-90, prof., sect. head, 1990—, vice chmn medicine for rsch., 1993—; asst. dean clin. rsch., chmn. med. rsch. East Carolina U. Sch. of Medicine, 1989-96; mem. study sect. merit rev. Nat. VA Rsch. Com., 1991-94. Co-editor: Drugs and the Lung, 1994; mem editl. Allergy Procs., 1989-93; contbr. chpts. to books, papers to med. jours. Forum leader Jarvis Meml. United Meth. Ch., Greenville, 1985-95. NIH grantee, Bethesda, Md., 1988-92. Fellow ACP, Am. Coll. Chest Physicians; mem. Am. Acad. Allergy Rsch. Coun. (vice chair 1988-92, 93-95, chair 1995-97), Am. Acad. Allergy Asthma (chair bronchoalveolar lavage com. 1994-95), Rhinitis, Respiratory Diseases (chair interest sect. 1991-92), Chilean Lung Soc. (hon.). Achievements include 2 patents; research in allergic diseases; Dx and management, principles and practice in allergy, immunology and allergy clinics, immunopharmacology and investigation and classification of drugs. Office: East Carolina U Sch Medicine Brody Bldg Rm 3E-129 Greenville NC 27834

METZINGER, TIMOTHY EDWARD, lawyer; b. L.A., Aug. 21, 1961; s. Robert Cole and Mary Jean (Cusick) M.; m. Cynthia Lee Stanworth, Nov. 16, 1991. BA, UCLA, 1986; JD, U. San Francisco, 1989. Bar: Calif. 1989, U.S. Dist. Ct. (ctrl., so., ea. and no. dists.) Calif. 1989, U.S. Ct. Appeals (9th cir.) 1989, U.S. Supreme Ct. 1994. Assoc. Bronson, Bronson & McKinnon, L.A., 1989-93, Price, Postel & Parma, Santa Barbara, Calif., 1993—. Dir. Santa Barbara County Bar Assn. Mem. Santa Barbara County Bar Assn. (bd. dirs.), Santa Barbara Barristers Club (pres.), Order of Barristers, Am. Inns. Ct. Avocations: diving, moutaineering, sailing. Office: Price Postel & Parma 200 E Carrillo St Santa Barbara CA 93101-2118

METZKER, RAY K., photographer; b. Milw., Sept. 10, 1931; s. William Martin and Marian Helen (Krueger) M. B.A., Beloit Coll., 1953; M.S., Inst. Design, Ill. Inst. Tech., 1959. Mem. faculty photography-film dept. Phila. Coll. Art, 1962-81, prof., chmn. dept., 1978-79; vis. assoc. prof. U. N.Mex., 1970-72; vis. adj. prof. R.I. Sch. Design, spring 1977; adj. Columbia Coll., Chgo., 1980-83; Smith Disting. vis. prof. art George Washington U., 1987-88. Author: Sand Creatures, 1979; one-man exhbns. include, Art Inst. Chgo., 1959, Mus. Modern Art, N.Y.C., 1967, Milw. Art Ctr., 1970, The Picture Gallery, Zurich, Switzerland, 1974, Marion Locks Gallery, Phila., 1978, 83, Internat. Ctr. Photography, N.Y.C., 1978, Light Gallery, N.Y.C., 1979, Shadai Gallery, Tokyo Inst. Polytechnics, 1992, Turner/Krull Gallery, L.A., 1992, Zola Lieberman Gallery, Chgo., 1995, Lawrence Miller Gallery, 1984, 85, 87, 88, 90, 92, 94; represented in permanent collections, Mus. Modern Art, N.Y.C., Art Inst. Chgo., Smithsonian Inst., Washington, Met. Mus. Art, N.Y.C., Phila. Mus. Art, Bibliotheque Nat., Paris: 25 Yr. Retrospective, Mus. Fine Art, Houston and six other U.S. mus.; subject of monograph: Unknown Territory: Ray K. Metzker, 1984. Served with U.S. Army, 1954-56. Guggenheim fellow, 1966, 79; Nat. Endowment Arts fellow, 1974, 88; residency LaNapoule Art Found., France, 1989. Home: 733 S 6th St Philadelphia PA 19147-2109

METZLER, DWIGHT FOX, civil engineer, retired state official; b. Kans., Mar. 25, 1916; s. Ross R. and Grace (Fox) M.; m. Lela Ross, June, 1941; children: Linda Diane, Brenda Lee, Marilyn Anne, Martha Jeanne. BSCE, Kans. U., 1940, CE, 1947; SM, Harvard U., 1948. Registered profl. engr., Kans., N.Y.; diplomate Am. Acad. Environ. Engrs. Asst. engr. Kans. Bd. Health, 1940-42, san. engr., 1946-48; chief engr. Topeka, 1948-62; assoc. prof. dept. civil engring. U. Kans., 1948-59, prof., 1959-66; exec. sec. Kans. Water Resources Bd., Topeka, 1962-66; dep. commr. N.Y. State Dept. Health, Albany, 1966-70, N.Y. State Dept. Environ. Conservation, Albany, 1970-74; sec. Kans. Dept. Health and Environment, Topeka, 1974-79, dir. water supply devel., 1979-84, retired, 1984; cons. san. engring. Fed. Pub. Housing Authority, USPHS, 1943-46; housing cons. Chgo.-Cook County Health Survey, 1946; cons. water supply and water pollution control USPHS, 1957-66; adviser Govt. of India, 1960; mem. ofcl. exchange to USSR on environ.health research and practice, 1962; adviser WHO, 1964-84; cons., expert witness Occidental Chem. Co., Love Canal, 1990-91; mem. Water Pollution Bd., Internat. Joint Commn., 1967-74, Assembly of Engring. NRC, 1977-80. Assoc. editor Internat. Jour. Water Pollution Rsch.; contbr. articles to profl. jours. Chmn. Kans. Bible Chair Bd., 1957-66; chmn. com. for new bldg. U. Kans. Sch. Religion. Recipient Disting. Service award U. Kans., 1970, Disting. Engring. Service award U. Kans., 1984. Fellow Royal Soc. Health Gt. Britain (hon.), Am. Pub. Health Assn. (former mem. governing council, exec. bd., pres., chmn. action bd., Centennial award 1972, Sedgwick medal 1981), ASCE (sec. sanitary engring. div. 1959-61, chmn. 1963); mem. Am. Water Works Assn. (Fuller award 1954, Purification div. award 1958), Water Pollution Control Fedn. (Bedell award 1963, hon. mem. 1983), Kans. Pub. Health Assn. (Crumbine award 1965), Kans. Engring. Soc. (Outstanding Engring. award 1978), Nat. Acad. Engring., Kans. Rural Water Assn. (Conger award 1990), Sigma Xi, Tau Beta Pi. Home: 900 SW 31st St Apt 325 Topeka KS 66611-2196

METZLER, ROBERT J., II, lawyer; b. Allentown, Pa., Feb. 5, 1948; s. Robert J. and Jean (Rockey) M.; m. Deborah Anne Tamoney, Aug. 21, 1976; children: Melissa, Robert III, Margot, Matthew. BA, Princeton U., 1970; JD, U. Conn., 1973. Bar: N.Y. 1974, Conn. 1976, U.S. Dist. Ct. (so. and ea. dists.) N.Y. 1974, U.S. Ct. Appeals (2d cir.) 1976. Atty. N.Y.C. Law Dept., 1973-75; law clk. to Hon. Thomas J. Meskill U.S. Ct. Appeals (2d cir.), N.Y.C. and New Britain, Conn., 1975-76; assoc. atty. Tyler, Cooper & Alcorn, New Haven, Conn., 1976-81; ptnr. Tyler, Cooper & Alcorn, New Haven and Hartford, Conn., 1982—. Dir. Common Ground Youth Leadership Forum, Hartford, 1987—, W. Hartford Youth Hockey Assn., 1988-93, United Way Capital Region, Hartford, 1989—. Fellow Am. Coll. Investment Counsel; mem. Nat. Assn. Stock Plan Profls., Conn. Bar Assn. (chmn. pub. utility law sect. 1982-84). Office: Tyler Cooper & Alcorn City Pl Fl 35 Hartford CT 06103

METZLER, ROGER JAMES, JR., lawyer; b. East Orange, N.J., Feb. 4, 1945; s. Roger James and Dorothy Marie (Clark) M.; m. Marilyn Carol Schick, Apr. 19, 1969; children: Andrea C., Maria N. BS, Brown U., 1967; JD, Santa Clara U., 1975. Bar: Calif. 1975. Ptnr. Farrand, Cooper, Metzler & Bruiniers, San Francisco, 1975-88, McQuaid, Bedford, Clausen & Metzler, San Francisco, 1988-89, Keck, Mahin & Cate, Chgo. and San Francisco, 1990-96, McQuaid, Metzler, McCormick & Van Zandt, San Francisco, 1996—. Avocation: soccer referee. Office: McQuaid Metzler McCormick & Van Zandt 1 Maritime Plz Fl 23 San Francisco CA 94111-3404

METZNER, CHARLES MILLER, federal judge; b. N.Y.C., Mar. 13, 1912; s. Emanuel and Gertrude (Miller) M.; m. Jeanne Gottlieb, Oct. 6, 1966. A.B., Columbia U., 1931, LL.B., 1933. Bar: N.Y. 1933. Pvt. practice, 1934; mem. Jud. Council State N.Y., 1935-41; law clk. to N.Y. supreme ct. justice, 1942-52; exec. asst. to U.S. atty. Gen. Herbert Brownell, Jr., 1953-54; mem. firm Chapman, Walsh & O'Connell, 1954-59; judge U.S. Dist Ct. (so. dist.) N.Y., 1959—; Mem. Law Revision Commn. N.Y. State, 1959; chmn. com. adminstrn. magistrates system U.S. Jud. Conf., 1970-81; chmn. Columbia Coll. Coun., 1965-66. Pres. N.Y. Young Republican Club, 1941; Trustee Columbia U., 1972-84, trustee emeritus, 1984—; bd. dirs. N.Y.C. Ctr. Music and Drama, 1969-74. Recipient Lawyer Div. of Joint Def. Appeal award, 1961, Columbia U. Alumni medal, 1966, Founders award Nat. Coun. U.S. Magistrates, 1989. Mem. ABA, Am. Law Inst., Fed. Bar Coun. (cert. Disting. Jud. Svc. 1989).

METZNER, RICHARD JOEL, psychiatrist, psychopharmacologist, educator; b. L.A., Feb. 15, 1942; s. Robert Gerson and Esther Rebecca (Groper) M.; children: Jeffrey Anthony, David Jonathan; m. Leila Kirkley, June 26, 1993. BA, Stanford U., 1963; MD, Johns Hopkins U., 1967. Intern, Roosevelt Hosp., N.Y.C., 1967-68; resident in psychiatry Stanford U. Med. Center, 1968-71; staff psychiatrist div. manpower and tng. NIMH-St. Elizabeths Hosp., Washington, 1971-73; chief audiovisual edn. system VA Med. Center Brentwood, L.A., 1973-79, chmn. VA Dist. 26 Ednl. Task Force, 1976-78; asst. prof. psychiatry UCLA Neuropsychiat. Inst., 1973-80, assoc. clin. prof., 1980-96, clin. prof., 1996—, lectr. Sch. Social Welfare, 1975-84; pvt. practice medicine specializing in psychiatry, Bethesda, Md., 1972-73, L.A., 1973—; dir. Western Inst. Psychiatry, L.A., 1977—; pres. Psychiat. Resource Network, Inc., 1984—; Served with USPHS, 1968-71. Recipient 6 awards for film and videotape prodns., 1976-80; diplomate Am. Bd. Psychiatry and Neurology (cons. 1974-78, producer audiovisual exam. programs 1975-77). Fellow Am. Psychiat. Assn.; mem. So. Calif. Psychiat. Soc., Mental Health Careerists Assn. (chmn. 1972-73), Phi Beta Kappa. Democrat. Jewish. Contbr. numerous articles to profl. publs., 1963—; producer, writer numerous ednl. films and videotapes, 1970—.

MEUSER, FREDRICK WILLIAM, retired seminary president, church historian; b. Payne, Ohio, Sept. 14, 1923; s. Henry William and Alvina Maria (Bouyack) M.; m. Jeanne Bond Griffiths, July 29, 1951; children: Jill Martha, Douglas Griffiths. AB, Capital U., 1945, BD, 1948, DD (hon.), 1989; STM, Yale U., 1949, MA, 1953, PhD, 1956; DD (hon.), Tex. Luth. Coll., 1980, Capital U., 1989; LHD (hon.), Augustana Coll., 1985. Ordained to ministry Am. Lutheran Ch., 1948; asst. pastor 1st Luth. Ch., Galveston, Tex., 1948, Christ Luth. Ch., North Miami, Fla., 1949-51; campus minister Yale U., 1951-53; prof. ch. history Luth. Theol. Sem., Columbus, Ohio, 1953-78, dean grad. studies, 1963-69, pres., 1971-78; pres. Trinity Luth. Sem., Columbus, 1978-88; exec. sec. div. theol. studies Luth. Council in U.S.A., 1969-71; del. World Council Chs., 1968, Luth. World Fedn., 1970; v.p. Am. Luth. Ch., 1974-80; mem. Commn. for a New Luth. Ch., 1982-86; asst. pastor St. Paul Luth. Ch., Westerville, Ohio, 1995—. Author: The Formation of the American Lutheran Church, 1958, Luther the Preacher, 1983; author: (with others) Church in Fellowship, 1963, Lutherans in North America, 1975; translator: (with others) What Did Luther Understand by Religion, 1977, The Reconstruction of Morality, 1979; editor: (with others) Interpreting Luther's Legacy, 1967. Recipient Disting. Churchman's award Tex. Luth. Coll., 1972, Joseph Sittler award Trinity Luth. Sem., 1990; named Outstanding Alumnus Capital U., 1977; Am. Assn. Theol. Schs. fellow, 1961-62. Mem. Am. Soc. Ch. History. Home: 6392 Claypool Ct Columbus OH 43213-3435 Office: 2199 E Main St Columbus OH 43209-3913

MEUTER, MARIA COOLMAN, lawyer; b. New Albany, Ind., July 17, 1915; d. William Edmund and Hundley Love (Wells) Coolman; m. Walter Frederick Meuter, Jan. 9, 1942; children: Stephen, Craig Frederick. Student, New Albany Bus. Coll., 1933; LLB, Jefferson Sch. Law, 1939; JD, U. Louisville, 1971. Bar: Ky. 1939, U.S. Ct. Internat. Trade, 1980. Clk. Fed. Land Bank of Louisville, 1933-41; exec. dir. Louisville Bar Assn., 1952-70; trial judge County Ct., Jefferson County, Louisville, 1962-70; assoc. dir. Law Alumni Affairs, U. Louisville, 1970—; exec. dir. Continuing Legal Edn., U. Louisville, 1978-83; pvt. practice, Louisville, 1970—; life trustee Law Alumni Found. Vice pres. Beechmont Civic Club, Louisville, 1987-91. Named Disting. Alumnae, U. Louisville Sch. Law, 1976, Ky. col., 1968, Master of Steamboat Flotilla of Jefferson County, 1968. Mem. Ky. Bar Assn. (rec. sec. ho. of dels. 1964-68), Louisville Bar Assn., Jefferson County Women Lawyers (pres.), Nat. Assn. Bar Execs. (rec. sec. 1969-70), DAR (com. chmn. John Marshall chpt. 1991), Daus. Am. Colonists (regent Falls of Ohio chpt. 1997—), Colonial Dames, Law Alumni Assn. U. Louisville (treas., sec. 1970-75), South Park Country Club. Republican. Episcopalian. Avocations: golf, bridge, Polynesian dance. Home: 1313 Marret Pl Louisville KY 40215-2368 also: 2885 Gulf Shore Blvd N Naples FL 34103

MEVERS, FRANK CLEMENT, state archivist, historian; b. New Orleans, Oct. 10, 1942; s. Lloyd F. and Mary Ashley (Collins) M.; m. Kathryn Ann Hayes, Dec. 23, 1967; children: John F., Lauren K. BA in History, La. State U., 1965; PhD in Am. History, U. N.C., 1972; MA, La. State U., 1967. Editor Papers of James Madison, Charlottesville, Va., 1972-74, Papers of Josiah Bartlett, Concord, N.H., 1974-77, Papers of William Plumer, Concord, 1977-79; state archivist State of N.H., Concord, 1979—. Editor, author: New Hampshire: State That Made US a Nation, 1989. Mem. Pub. Libr. Bd. Trustees, Concord, 1979—. With U.S. Army, 1967-69, Korea. Episcopalian. Avocation: stamp collecting. Home: 29 Bradley St Concord NH 03301-6432 Office: NH State Archives 71 S Fruit St Concord NH 03301-2410

MEW, THOMAS JOSEPH, III (TOMMY MEW), artist, educator; b. Miami, Fla., Aug. 15, 1942; s. Thomas Joseph and Maude Edith (Perry) M.; m. Mary Ann Kelley, June 17, 1966; 1 son, Thomas Joseph. B.S., Fla. State U., 1962, M.A., 1964; Ph.D., N.Y. U., 1966. Grad. instr. Fla. State U., 1963; asst. prof. art Troy State U., 1966-68, Jacksonville U., 1968-70; prof., chmn. dept. art Berry Coll., 1970—, Dana prof. art; juror art shows: vis. artist; lectr. in field, cons. art; dir. Fluxus West/Southeast. Exhibited in oneman shows Parkway Gallery, Miami, 1962-63, 319 Gallery, N.Y.C., 1968, Meridian (Miss.) Mus., 1976, C.D.O. Gallery, Parma, Italy, 1978, Calif. State U., Sacramento, 1979, Miss. Mus. Art, Jackson, 1979, Art Inst. for Permian Basin, ITex, Arte Studio, Bergamo, Italy; group shows include High Mus., Atlanta, 1971, 72, 74, New Reform Gallery, Aalst, Belgium, 1975, U. Guelph, Ont., Can., 1975, Neuberger Mus., Purchase, N.Y., 1978, Arte Fiera, Bologna, Italy, 1979; represented in permanent collections, Kansas City Art Inst., Mildura Art Centre, Australia, Wichita Art Mus., Jacksonville (Fla.) Art Mus., Macon Mus. Art, AT&T, Harn Mus., U. Iowa; host: Cable TV show Art: The Mew View, 1978—; Filmmaker, 1966-69; contbr. articles to profl. jours. Bd. dirs. Rome Arts Council, 1984—; bd. dirs. Interface. Recipient Gellhorn award N.Y. U., 1966; Cowperthwaite grantee, 1972; Lilly Found. grantee, 1975; Gulf Life grantee, 1977. Mem. Southeastern Coll. Art Conf., Coll. Art Assn. Am., Am. Fedn. Arts, Nat. Art Edn. Assn., Am. Assn. Art Dealers. Home: Rosewood Cottage PO Box 495028 Mount Berry GA 30149 Office: Berry Coll Art Dept Mount Berry GA 30149 *I've always moved in the direction of my dreams . . . always tried to make the great dream a reality.*

MEWHINNEY, BRUCE HARRISON NICHOLAS, publisher; b. Charlottesville, Va., Apr. 15, 1949; m. Elyse Tager, June 5, 1982. BA, Antioch Coll., 1971. Editorial prodn. mgr. Computer Currents Mag., Emeryville, Calif., 1988-90; assoc. editor MacUser Mag., Foster City, Calif., 1990-93; pres. Diosa Internat. Design, Alameda, Calif., 1993—; tech. mgr. Am. Online forum of Preview Travel, San Francisco, 1995-96; forum mgr. in "eWorld" online svc., Apple Computer, Cupertino, Calif., 1993-94. Author, photographer: Down Below: Aboard the World's Classic Yachts, 1980. Avocations: sailing, boatbuilding, multimedia devel. Office: Diosa Internat Design 3028 Alta Vista Alameda CA 94502-6804

MEYAART, PAUL JAN, distilling company executive; b. Berchem, Belgium, Mar. 6, 1943; came to U.S., 1965; s. Joseph and Leonie (Devreese) M.; m. Mary-Ann Mota, Mar. 18, 1967; children—Peter, Antoine, Danielle. B.Commerce, U. Antwerp, Belgium, 1965; M.B.A. (Ford internat. fellow 1965-67, Fulbright grantee 1965-67), U. Chgo., 1967. Fin. planning mgr. Sinclair Belgium S. A., Brussels, 1967-70; controller-treas. Knoll Internat. Inc., N.Y.C., 1971-74; v.p. fin., treas. Boyle Midway div. Am. Home Products Co., N.Y.C., 1974-78; v.p. fin. and adminstrn., treas. Am. Distilling Co. Inc., N.Y.C., 1978—. Mem. Fin. Execs. Inst. Home: 897 Franklin Lakes Rd Franklin Lakes NJ 07417-2115 Office: 245 Park Ave New York NY 10167-0002

MEYBERG, BERNHARD ULRICH, entrepreneur; b. Norden, Germany, Aug. 29, 1917; s. Peter Bernhard and Katharine (v. Oterendorp) M.; m. Lotte Essig, Apr. 1949; children: Horst Eugen, Ursula Eugenie, Gabriele Christine. Student, U. Greifswald/Pommern, 1943-45. Apprentice Savingsbank, Norden, 1935-37, employee, 1937-38; collaborator Eug Essig, Ludwigsburg, Fed. Republic Germany, 1948-70; pvt. practice Möglingen, Fed. Republic Germany, 1970—. Contbr. essays to newspapers. 1st lt. German Air Force, 1938-45, prisoner of war, 1945-47. Mem. Internat. Furniture-Carpet-Purchase Assn. (mem. exec. com.), Chamber Industry and Trade (mem. com.), Italian Chamber Trade for Germany (mem. com.). Lutheran. Avocations: sports, tennis, sailing. Home: Max-Ostheimerstrasse 6, 87534 Oberstaufen Germany Office: Eugen Essig, Daimlerstrasse 62, Moglingen Germany

MEYBURG, ARNIM HANS, transportation engineer, educator, consultant; b. Bremerhaven, W. Ger., Aug. 25, 1939; came to U.S., 1965; s. Friedel and Auguste (Kleeberg) M.; m. Ruth Meyburg; 1 child, Jennifer Susan. Student, U. Hamburg, 1960-62, Free U. Berlin, 1962-65; M.S. (Fulbright travel grantee), Northwestern U., 1968, Ph.D., 1971. Research assoc. Transp. Center, Northwestern U., 1968-69; asst. prof. transp. engring. Cornell U., 1969-75, assoc. prof., 1975-78, prof., 1978—, acting chmn. dept., 1977-78, chmn. dept., 1980-85, dir. Sch. Civil and Environ. Engring., 1988—, chmn. bd. Univ. Transp. Rsch. Ctr., 1992-95; dir. Transp. Infrastructure Rsch. Consortium, 1995—; vis. mem. faculties U. Calif., Irvine, Tech. U. Munich, Germany, (Fulbright lectr.) U. Sao Paulo, Brazil, 1984, Tech. U. Brunswick, W. Ger., 1985-86; Humboldt Found. research fellow, 1978-79; prin. investigator projects Dept. Transp., NSF, Nat. Coop. Hwy. Research Program, N.Y. State Dept. Transp., U.S. Dept. Transp. Author: (with others) Urban Transportation Modeling and Planning, 1975, Transportation Systems Evaluation, 1976, Survey Sampling and Multivariate Analysis for Social Scientists and Engineers, 1979, Survey Methods for Transport Planning, 1995; co-editor: (with others) Behavioral Travel-Demand Models, 1976, New Horizons in Travel-Behavior Research, 1981, Selected Readings in Transport Survey Methodology, 1992; contbr. articles to profl. jours., chpts. to books. NSF Research Initiation grantee, 1973; recipient Humboldt U.S. Sr. Scientist award, 1984, Fulbright sr. lectr. award, 1984. Mem. ASCE, AAUP, Transp. Rsch. Bd., Transp. Rsch. Forum, Sigma Xi, Chi Epsilon. Office: Cornell U 220 Hollister Hall Ithaca NY 14853-3501

MEYE, ROBERT PAUL, retired seminary administrator, writer; b. Hubbard, Oreg., Apr. 1, 1929; s. Robert and Eva (Pfau) M.; m. Mary Cover, June 18, 1954; children: Marianne Meye Thompson, Douglas, John. BA, Stanford U., 1951; BD, Fuller Theol. Sem., 1957, ThM, 1959; DTheol magna cum laude, U. Basel, Switzerland, 1962; DD Eastern Bapt. Theol. Sem., 1990. Prof. No. Bapt. Theol. Sem., Lombard, Ill., 1962-77, dean, 1971-77; dean Sch. Theology, Fuller Theol. Sem., Pasadena, Calif., 1977-90, dean emeritus, 1992—, assoc. provost for Ch. Rels. and Christian Community, 1990-92, prof. N.T. interpretation, 1977-92, prof. emeritus, 92—. Author: Jesus and The Twelve;1968, co-editor: Studies in Old Testament Theology, 1992; contbr. articles to profl. jours., dictionaries and encys. Served to lt. (j.g.) USN, 1946-47, 51-54, Korea. Am. Assn. Theol. Schs. grantee, 1970-71; 75-76. Mem. Nat. Assn. Bapt. Profs. of Religion, Studiorum Novi Testamenti Societas, Chgo. Soc. Bibl. Res., Soc. Bibl. Lit., Inst. Bibl. Research. Republican. Home: 1170 Rubio St Altadena CA 91001-2027 Office: Fuller Theol Sem 135 N Oakland Ave Pasadena CA 91182-0001

MEYER, ALBERT JAMES, educational researcher; b. Cleve., Sept. 24, 1929; s. Jacob Conrad and Esther Agnes (Steiner) M.; m. Mary Ellen Yoder, Aug. 21, 1954; children: Richard, Anne, Kathryn, Barbara, Elaine. BA, Goshen Coll., 1950; MA, Princeton U., 1952, PhD, 1954. Asst. in teaching and rsch. Princeton (N.J.) U., 1950-53; fellow U. Basel, Switzerland, 1953-54, rsch. assoc., 1956-57; dir. for France, rep. European peace sect. Mennonite Ctrl. Com., 1954-57; asst. prof. physics Goshen (Ind.) Coll., 1958-61, prof., rsch. prof., 1967-89, adj. rsch. prof., 1989—; acad. dean, prof. Bethel Coll., North Newton, Kans., 1961-66, Menno Simons lectr., 1993; exec. sec., pres. Mennonite Bd. Edn., Elkhart, Ind., 1967-95; vis. fellow Princeton (N.J.) U., 1995-96; exec. for secretariat Puidoux Theol. Confs., 1955-57; former mem. staff Mennonite Student Svcs. Com.; former coord. com. on liberal arts edn. North Ctrl. Assn. Colls. and Secondary Schs.; vis. rsch. scientist U. Paris, 1974-75; vis. rschr. New Coll. Berkeley, 1986-87; presenter in field; former cons. Conrad Grebel Coll., U. Waterloo, Ont., Can.; mem. peace and social concerns com. Mennonite Ch., 1959-71; former mem. Continuation Com. of Hist. Peace Chs. Contbr. articles to denominational periodicals and sci. jours. Princeton U. exch. fellow and Charles Foster Kent fellow Nat. Coun. for Religion in Higher Edn., 1935-54. Mem. Denominational Execs. for Ch.-Related Higher Edn. (chmn. 1984-86), Am. Assn. for Higher Edn., Am. Assn. Physics Tchrs. Avocations: tennis, hockey, hiking. Home: 708 Emerson St Goshen IN 46526-3904 Office: Mennonite Bd Edn 500 S Main St Elkhart IN 46516-3207

MEYER, ALDEN MERRILL, environmental association executive; b. Buffalo, Mar. 21, 1952; s. Arthur Merrill Meyer and Susan (Rogers) Meyer Markle. BA, Yale U., 1975; MS, Am. U., 1990. Energy policy analyst Conn. Citizen Action Group, Hartford, 1975-78, Environ. Action Found., Washington, 1979-82; exec. dir. Environ. Action, Inc., 1983-85, League Conservation Voters, Washington, 1985-88; dir. climate change and energy policy Union of Concerned Scientists, Washington, 1989-92, legis. dir., 1992-95, dir. govt. rels., 1995—; bd. dirs. Ams. for Environment, Washington, 1983-87, chmn., 1985-87; bd. dirs. Urban Environment Conf., Washington, 1984-87, Zero Population Growth, 1989—; pres. bd. dirs. Safe Energy Communication Council, Washington, 1980-85; chmn. U.S. Climate Action Network, 1990—; mem. state and local adv. bd. U.S. Dept. Energy, 1994—, mem. elec. syss. reliability task force, 1997—. Mem. Yale Whiffenpoofs, 1975. Democrat. Avocations: hiking; camping; skiing; singing. Home: 15 Montgomery Ave Takoma Park MD 20912-4614 Office: Union of Concerned Scientis 1616 P St NW Washington DC 20036-1434

MEYER, ALICE VIRGINIA, state official; b. N.Y.C., Mar. 15, 1921; d. Martin G. and Marguerite Helene (Houzé) Kliemand; m. Theodore Harry Meyer, June 28, 1947; children: Robert Charles, John Edward. BA, Barnard Coll., 1941; MA, Columbia U., 1942. Tchr. pub. schs. Elmont, N.Y., 1942-43; tchr. Fairlawn (N.J.) High Sch., 1943-47; office mgr., sales rep. N.Y.C., 1948-55; substitute tchr. Pub. Schs., Easton, Conn., 1965-72; state rep., asst.

minority leader Conn. State Legislature, Hartford, 1976-93; mem. Ct. Bd. of Govs. for Higher Edn., 1993—, vice-chair, chair. Mem. bd. trustees Discovery Mus., 1980—, United Way Regional Youth Substance Abuse Project, Bridgeport, 1983-93; bd. dirs. 3030 Park, 1993—, Fairfield County Lit. Coalition, Bridgeport, 1988-94; vice chmn. Easton Rep. Town Com., 1970-78; mem. strategic planning com. Town of Easton, 1993—; vice-chmn. ct. adv. coun. on intergovtl. rels., 1988—; mem. Conn. Commn. on Quality Edn., 1992-93; supporter of Conn. Small Towns, 1988; mem. lt. gov.'s commn. on mandate reduction, 1995; sec. Easton Free Sch. Scholarship Fund, 1980—. Named Legislator of Yr. Conn. Libr. Assn., 1985; Guardian Small Bus. grantee Nat. Fedn. Ind. Bus., 1987; honoree Fairfield YWCA Salute to Women, 1988; named grant to AAUW Fellowship Fund, Bridgeport Br., 1970, Conn. State AAUW, 1974. Mem. AAUW (past local pres. 1976, bd. dirs. 1982), LWV, Bus. and Profl. Women, Nat. Order Women Legislators (regional dir. 1987—, past pres. Conn. chpt.). Congregationalist. Avocations: swimming, sailing, bridge. Home: 18 Lantern Hill Rd Easton CT 06612-2218

MEYER, ANDREW R., manufacturing executive; b. Phila., Feb. 15, 1956; s. Herbert C. and Joan (Freedman) M.; m. Constance B. Goldberg, Dec. 20, 1981; children: Jacob Abraham Meyer, Gabrielle Taryn Meyer. BBA, U. Miami, 1977; degree, Gemological Inst. Am., Santa Monica, Calif., 1978. Cert. gemologist, registered supplier, Am. Gem. Soc., Calif. V.p. Oxford Jewelry, Inc., Wyncote, Pa., 1978-80, Bookend Jewelry Inc., Jenkintown, Pa., 1980-84; pres. Andrew Meyer Jewelry, Inc., Fort Washington, Pa., 1985—. Coach Upper Dublin (Pa.) Soccer Club, 1990—, Upper Dublin Baseball; mem. bd. dirs. Temple Sinai, Debeers Christmas Collection Program, Debeer Diamond Occasions Program. Mem. Am. Gem. Soc. (chmn. suppliers com., bd. dirs. 1990—, pres. 1997), Meadowlands Country Club, Commonwealth Nat. Golf Club. Republican. Jewish. Avocations: golf, tennis, kids, plying. Office: 550 Paretown Rd Ste 234 Fort Washington PA 19034-0100

MEYER, ANDREW W., publishing executive; b. Phila., July 29, 1941; s. John O. and Katherine (Wachter) M.; m. Helen Hope Hogan, Oct. 1963; children: Kelly Ann, Michael, Melissa, Suzanne, Jennifer. BS in Accounting, St. Joseph's U., Phila., 1963; MBA in Finance, U. Conn., 1973. CPA. Sr. accountant Jenkins Fetterolf, Phila., 1963-67; asst. treas. PA & S Small Co., York, 1967-71; v.p. finance Xerox Pub. Group, Greenwich, Conn., 1971-82, R.R. Bowker, N.Y.C., 1982-94; COO Reed Reference Pub., New Providence, N.J., 1995-1996; v.p. admin., pub. Bus. Info. Svcs. Grp. Lexis-Nexis, New Providence, N.J., 1996—. Office: Reed Elsevier New Providence 121 Chanlon Rd New Providence NJ 07974-1541*

MEYER, ARMIN HENRY, retired diplomat, author, educator; b. Ft. Wayne, Ind., Jan. 19, 1914; s. Armin Paul and Leona (Buss) M.; m. Alice James, Apr. 23, 1949; 1 dau., Kathleen Alice. Student, Lincoln (Ill.) Coll., 1931-33; A.B., Capital U., 1935, LL.D., 1957; M.A., Ohio State U., 1941, LL.D., 1972; LL.D., Wartburg Coll., S.D. Sch. Mines and Tech., 1972. Faculty Capital U., Columbus, Ohio, 1935-41; staff OWI, Egypt, Iraq, 1942-46; U.S. pub. affairs officer Baghdad, Iraq, 1946-48; pub. affairs adviser U.S. Dept. State, 1948-52; sec. Am. embassy, Beirut, Lebanon, 1952-55; dep. chief mission Kabul, Afghanistan, 1955-57; dep. dir. Office South Asian Affairs Dept. State, 1957-58, dep. dir. Office Near Eastern Affairs, 1958-59, dir. Office Nr. Ea. Affairs, 1959-61, dep. asst. sec. of state for Nr. Ea. and South Asian Affairs, 1961; US ambassador to Lebanon, 1961-65, Iran, 1965-69, Japan, 1969-72; spl. asst. to sec. state, chmn. Cabinet Com. to Combat Terrorism, 1972-73; vis. prof. Am. U., 1974-75; dir. Ferdowsi project Georgetown U., 1975-79, adj. prof. diplomacy, 1975-86; dir. Internat. Affairs Ecology and Environ. Inc.; Woodrow Wilson vis. fellow, 1974—; cons. internat. bus. and environment, 1975—. Author: Assignment Tokyo: An Ambassador's Journal, 1974; co-author: Education in Diplomacy, 1987. Hon. mem. Lincoln Sesquicentennial Commn., 1959; bd. dirs. Washington Inst. Fgn. Affairs, 1979—, pres., 1988—. Recipient Meritorious Svc. award Dept. State, 1958, Superior Honor award, 1973; decorated Order of Rising Sun, 1st class (Japan), 1982; inducted into Hall of Excellence Ohio Fedn. Ind. Colls., 1989. Mem. Sigma Psi. Lutheran. Home: 4610 Reno Rd NW Washington DC 20008-2941 *Faith in God; where there is a will there is a way; if a job is worth doing it is worth doing well; and the Golden Rule.*

MEYER, AUGUST CHRISTOPHER, JR., broadcasting company executive, lawyer; b. Champaign, Ill., Aug. 14, 1937; s. August C. and Clara (Rocke) M.; m. Karen Haugh Hassett, Dec. 28, 1960; children: August Christopher F., Elisabeth Hassett. BA cum laude, Harvard U., 1959, LLB, 1962. Bar: Ill. 1962. Ptr. Meyer, Capel, Hirschfeld, Muncy, Jahn and Aldeen, Champaign, Ill., 1962-77, of counsel, 1977—; owner, dir., officer Midwest TV, Inc., Sta. KFMB-TV-AM-FM, San Diego, Sta. WCIA-TV, Champaign, Ill. , Sta. WMBD-TV-AM, WMXP, Peoria, Ill., 1968—; pres. Sta. KFMB-TV-AM-FM, San Diego, Sta. WCIA-TV, Champaign, Ill. , Sta. WMBD-TV-AM, WMXP, 1976—; bd. dirs. BankIll.; spl. asst. atty. gen. State of Ill., 1968-76. Chmn. bd. trustees Carle Found. Hosp., Urbana, Ill. Mem. Ill. Bar Assn., Champaign County Bar Assn. Club: Champaign Country. Home: 1408 S Prospect Ave Champaign IL 61820-6837 Office: Midwest TV Inc PO Box 777 509 S Neil St Champaign IL 61820-5219 also: Sta KFMB PO Box 85888 7677 Engineer Rd San Diego CA 92111-1515

MEYER, B. FRED, small business executive, home designer and builder, product designer; b. Long Island, N.Y., Jan. 6, 1918; s. Barthold Fred and Edna May (Clark) M.; m. Mary E. Carman, July 18, 1951; children: Patricia Meyer Sauer, Susan Meyer Sachs. Student, Pratt Inst., 1935-39, Johns Hopkins U., 1946-48, Wayne State U., 1954-55. Registered builder, Fla. Project engr. Lear, Inc., Grand Rapids, Mich., 1948-51; engring. exec. GM Corp., Warren, Mich., 1951-75; pres. BFM Assocs., Inc. (name Fred Meyer, Inc. 1990), Sarasota, Fla., 1975—. Patentee on pendulum type seat belt retractor, power window switch, power window actuator, 6-way seat switch, 6-way seat actuator, rear trunk pull-down mechanism, numerous others. Capt. USAAF, 1942-46, ETO. Mem. Oaks Country Club (Osprey, Fla.). Avocations: golf, computers, travel, tennis. Home and Office: 4131 Boca Pointe Dr Sarasota FL 34238-5573

MEYER, BERNARD STERN, lawyer, former judge; b. Balt., June 7, 1916; s. Benjamin and Josephine Meyer; m. Elaine Strass, June 25, 1939 (div.); children: Patricia, Susan; m. Edythe Birnbaum, Apr. 18, 1975; m. Hortense Fox, Oct. 29, 1991. B.S., Johns Hopkins U., 1936; LL.B., U. Md., 1938; LL.D., Hofstra U., 1980, Western State U. Coll. Law, 1982, Union U., 1984. Bar: Md. 1938, D.C., N.Y. 1947. Assoc. Fisher & Fisher, Balt., 1938-41; with Office Gen. Counsel Treasury Dept., Washington, 1941-43; pvt. practice, N.Y.C., 1948-54; ptnr. Meyer, Fink, Weinberger & Levin, N.Y.C., 1954-58; justice N.Y. State Supreme Ct., 1959-72; of counsel Fink, Weinberger, Fredman & Charney, P.C., N.Y.C., 1973-79; ptnr. Meyer, English & Cianciulli, P.C., Mineola, N.Y., 1975-79; assoc. judge N.Y. Ct. Appeals, Albany, 1979-86; dep. atty. gen. in charge spl. Attica investigation State of N.Y., 1975; ptnr. Meyer, Suozzi, English & Klein P.C., Mineola, 1987—; assoc. spl. counsel Moreland Commn. To Study Workmen's Compensation Adminstrn. and Costs, 1955-57; mem. com. on govt. integrity State of N.Y., 1987-90; mem. com. Madera Cts., 1987—. Contbr. articles to profl. jours. Founder United Fund L.I.; former mem. adv. bd. Commn. Law and Social Action, Am. Jewish Congress; chmn. Task Force on Permanency Planning for Foster Children, 1986-91; past pres., bd. dirs. Health and Welfare Coun. Nassau County; former mem. bd. dirs. Nassau-Suffolk region NCCJ, Nassau County coun. Boy Scouts Am., Nat. Ctr. for State Cts.; mem. Coalition for Effective Govt., 1991—. Lt. USNR, WWII. Recipient Disting. Svc. award L.I. Press, Presdl. medal Hofstra U., Disting. Svc. award Legal Aid Soc. Nassau County, N.Y., Johns Hopkins U. Disting. Alumnus award. Mem. ABA, Am. Bar Found., Am. Coll. Trial Lawyers, Am. Law Inst., N.Y. Bar Assn. (chmn. jud. sect., com. on legis. policy), N.Y. Bar Found., Bar of City of N.Y. (chmn. libr., matrimonial, election law com.), Nassau County Bar Assn. (Disting. Svc. medallion 1982), Nat. Conf. State trial Judges (exec. com., past chmn.), Nat. Coll. State Jud. (bd. dirs.), Assn. Supreme Ct. Judges (past pres., chmn. pattern jury instrn. com. 1962-79), Supreme Ct. Hist. Soc., Com. Modern Cts., Nassau County Lawyers Assn. (award), Scribes, Order of Coif, Omicron Delta Kappa. Office: Meyer Suozzi English & Klein PC 1505 Kellum Pl Mineola NY 11501-4811

MEYER, BILL, newspaper publisher, editor; b. Pratt, Kans., Aug. 6, 1925; s. Otto William and Ruth Clarinda (Jones) M.; m. Joan Aileen Wight, Sept. 11, 1949; 1 child, Eric Kent. BS in Journalism, U. Kans., 1948. News editor Marion County Record, Hoch Pub. Co., Inc., Marion, Kans., 1948-67, editor, pub., 1967—; owner Cottonwood Valley Agy., Marion, 1990—; editor 99th Inf. Divsn. Assn., Marion, 1971—; lectr. media law Wichita (Kans.) State U., 1985; polit. interviewer St. KPTS-TV, Wichita, 1983-91; bd. dirs. Ctrl. Nat. Bank, Junction City, Kans.; mil. cons., travel agt. Battlefield Tours, Slidell, La., 1990—. Past pres. Marion Sch. dist. Bd. Edn., Marion County Hosp. Dist.; bd. dirs. Marion Manor Nursing Home, Kans. Hist. Soc., 1985-94; trustee, past pres. William Allen White Found., Lawrence, Kans.; mem. selection com. for judges, 8th Jud. Dist., 1994—. With U.S. Army, 1943-45, ETO. Recipient commendation Kans. Ho. of Reps., 1982, 99th Inf. Div. Assn., 1986, 89, named Hon. Col. Kans. Calvary, 1987, Hon. Ky. Col., 1990. Mem. Nat. Newspaper Assn., Kans. Press Assn. (pres. 1982-83, Boyd Community Svc. award 1979), Marion C. of C. (past bd. dirs.), Marion Country Club, Masons, Shriners, Kiwanis (pres. Marion 1957), Sigma Delta Chi. Republican. Methodist. Avocation: military history. Home: PO Box 99 Marion KS 66861-0099 Office: Hoch Pub Co Inc 117 S 3rd St Marion KS 66861-1621

MEYER, BILLIE JEAN, special education educator; b. Kansas City, Mo., July 27, 1943; d. Charles William and Dorothy Ellen (Alt) Emerson; m. Kenneth Lee Morris, Aug. 24, 1963 (div. Oct. 1985); 1 child, Darla Michele Morris Stewart; m. Gordon Frederick Meyer, June 1, 1986 (dec. May 1994); stepchildren: Ardith Helmer, Susan Stanford, Gary, Geneace, Patti Draughon, Shari Mohr. BS in Edn., Northeastern State U., 1965, M in Tchg., 1968. Cert. tchr., Okla.; cert. visually impaired, Braille. Substitute tchr. Muskogee (Okla.) Pub. Schs., 1965; elem. tchr. Okla. Sch. for the Blind, Muskogee, 1965-67, elem. tchr., computer tchr., 1969—; adj. lectr. Northeastern State U., Tahlequah, summers 1990-92, 94, 95, 96, 97; on-site team mem. Nat. Accreditation Coun., 1987; mem. com. revision cert. stds., State of Okla., 1982. Author: A Sequential Math Program for Beginning Abacus Students, 1979. Mem. Assn. of Edn. and Rehab. of the Blind and Visually Impaired, Okla. Assn. of Ednl. Rehab. of the Blind and Visually Impaired (pres.-elect 1985-86, pres. 1986-87, sec. 1993-97), Computer Using Educators, Epsilon Sigma Alpha (state pres. 1981-82, Girl of Yr. 1971). Avocations: stained glass, photo preservation, gardening, traveling, bird watching. Office: Okla Sch for the Blind 3300 Gibson St Muskogee OK 74403-2811

MEYER, BRUD RICHARD, pharmaceutical company executive; b. Waukegan, Ill., Feb. 22, 1926; s. Charles Lewis and Mamie Olive (Broom) M.; m. Betty Louise Stine (dec. 1970); children: Linda (Mrs. Gary Stillabower), Louise (Mrs. Donald Knochel), Janet (Mrs. Gerald Cockrell), Jeff, Karen, Blake, Amy; m. Barbara Ann Hamilton, Nov. 26, 1970. B.S., Purdue U., 1949. With Eli Lilly & Co., Indpls., 1949-87, indsl. engr., 1949-56, supr. indsl. engr., 1956-59, sr. personnel rep., 1960-64; personnel mgr. Eli Lilly & Co., Lafayette, Ind., 1964-67; asst. dir. Eli Lilly & Co., Lafayette, 1967-69, dir. adminstrn., 1969-79, dir. personnel and public relations, 1980-87, ret., 1987. Bd. dirs. Lafayette Home Hosp., 1977—, Hanna Community Ctr., 1983—, Tippecanoe Hist. Corp., 1985—; bd. dirs. United Way Tippecanoe County, 1970-76, pres., 1974; bd. dirs. Legal Aid Soc. Tippecanoe County, 1973—, Jr. Achievement, pres., 1979; bd. dirs. Lilly Credit Union, 1969-75, pres., 1973-74; mem. Citizen's Com. on Alcoholism, 1966-72; bd. dirs. Greater Lafayette Community Centers, 1975-79, pres., 1977-78; mem., mng. dir. Battle Tippecanoe Outdoor Drama Bd. Served with USAAF, 1943-45. Mem. Pi Tau Sigma, Lambda Chi Alpha, C. of C. Greater Lafayette (bd. dirs., v.p. 1969-73), Battleground Hist. Soc. Methodist. Home: 4217 Trees Hill Dr Lafayette IN 47905-3451 Office: Eli Lilly & Co PO Box 7685 Lafayette IN 47903-7685

MEYER, CAROL FRANCES, pediatrician, allergist; b. Berea, Ky., June 2, 1936; d. Harvey Kessler and Jessie Irene (Hamm) Meyer; m. Daniel Baker Cox, June 5, 1955 (div. Apr. 1962). AA, U. Fla., 1955; BA, Duke U., 1957; MD, Med. Coll. Ga., 1967. Diplomate Am. Bd. Pediatrics, Am. Bd. Allergy and Immunology. Intern in pediatrics Med. Coll. Ga., Augusta, 1967-68; resident in pediatrics Gorgas Hosp., Canal Zone, 1968-69; fellow in pediatric respiratory disease Med. Coll. Ga., 1969-71, instr. pediat., 1971-72; med. officer pediatrics Canal Zone Govt., 1972-79; med. officer pediatrics Dept. of Army, Panama, 1979-82, med. officer allergy, 1982-89, physician in charge allergy clinic, 1984-89; asst. prof. pediatrics and medicine Med. Coll. Ga., Augusta, 1990—; mem. Bd. of Canal Zone Merit System Examiners, 1976-79. Contbr. articles to profl. jours. Mem. First Bapt. Ch. Orch., 1992—; founding mem., violoncello Curundu Chamber Ensemble, 1979-89. Recipient U.S. Army Exceptional Performance awards, 1985, 86, 89, Merck award Med. Coll. Ga.,, 1967; U. Fla. J. Hillis Miller scholar, 1954. Mem. AAAS, Am. Coll. Rheumatology, Allergy and Immunology Soc. Ga., Hispanic-Am. Allergy and Immunology Assn., Ga. Pediatric Soc., Pan Am. Med. Assn., Soc. Leukocyte Biology, Am. Coll. Allergy, Asthma and Immunology, Am. Acad. Allergy, Asthma and Immunology, Am. Acad. Pediat., Am. Med. Women's Assn., Panama Canal Soc. Fla., Ga. Ornithol. Soc., Ga. Thoracic Soc., Am. Lung Assn. (Ga. East Ctrl. br. exec. bd.), Am. Assn. Ret. Persons, Nature Conservancy, Royal Soc. for Preservation Birds, Nat. Assn. Ret. Fed. Employees, Nat. Audubon Soc., Panama Audubon Soc., Willow Run Homeowner's Soc. (pres.), Alpha Omega Alpha. Office: Med Coll Ga BG 232 1120 15th St # 232 Augusta GA 30912-0004

MEYER, CATHERINE DIEFFENBACH, lawyer; b. Seattle, Mar. 27, 1951; d. Patrick Andrew and Hope Dieffenbach; m. Michael E. Meyer, Nov. 21, 1982; children. AB, Bryn Mawr Coll., 1973; JD, Northwestern U., 1979. Bar: Calif. 1979, U.S. Dist. Ct. (cen. dist.) Calif., 1979, U.S. Ct. Appeals (9th cir.) 1982, U.S. Dist. Ct. (ea., no. and so. dists.) Calif. 1987. Assoc. Lillick, McHose & Charles, L.A., 1979-85, ptnr., 1985-88; ptnr. Lillick & McHose, L.A., 1988-90, Pillsbury Madison & Sutro, L.A., 1990—. Office: Pillsbury Madison & Sutro 725 S Figueroa St Ste 1200 Los Angeles CA 90017-5443

MEYER, CORD, columnist; b. Washington, Nov. 10, 1920; s. Cord and Katharine (Thaw) M.; m. Mary Pinchot, Apr. 19, 1945 (div. July 1958); children: Quentin, Mark; m. Mary Starke Patteson, Jan. 8, 1966. BA summa cum laude, Yale U., 1942; postgrad., Harvard U., 1946-47, 49-51. Spl. asst. to H. Stassen U.S. Del. to Founding Conf. of U.N., San Francisco, 1945; pres. United World Federalists, N.Y.C., 1947-49; with CIA, Washington, 1951-77, asst. dep. dir. for ops., 1967-73; station chief CIA, London, 1973-76; columnist Washington, 1978—. Author: Peace or Anarchy, 1947, Facing Reality, 1980. Pres. United World Federalists, N.Y., 1947-49. Capt. USMC, 1942-45. Decorated Bronze star USMC, Guam, 1945, Purple Heart, USMC, Guam, 1945, Presdl. citation USMC, Guam, 1945, three Disting. Intelligence medals CIA, Washington. Mem. Coun. on Fgn. Rels., Washington Inst. on Fgn. Affairs, Met. Club. Democrat. Avocations: tennis, trout fishing. Home: 1523 34th St NW Washington DC 20007-2727 Office: 1529 18th St NW Washington DC 20036-1358

MEYER, DANIEL JOSEPH, machinery company executive; b. Flint, Mich., May 31, 1936; s. John Michael and Margaret (Meehan) M.; m. Bonnie Harrison, June 22, 1963; children—Daniel P., Jennifer. B.S., Purdue U., 1958; M.B.A., Ind. U., 1963. C.P.A., N.Y. Mgr. Touche, Ross & Co., Detroit, 1964-69; contr. Cin. Milacron, Inc., 1969-77, v.p. fin., treas., 1977-83, exec. v.p. fin. and adminstrn., 1983-86, pres., chief operating officer, 1987-90, pres., chief exec. officer, 1990-91, chmn., chief exec. officer, 1991-92, also bd. dirs.; bd. dirs. E.W. Scripps Inc., Hubbell Inc., Star Bank Corp. Served with U.S. Army, 1959. Mem. Am. Inst. C.P.A.'s. Club: Kenwood Country (Cin.). Home: 8 Grandin Ln Cincinnati OH 45208-3304 Office: Cin Milacron Inc 4701 Marburg Ave Cincinnati OH 45209-1025

MEYER, DANIEL KRAMER, real estate executive; b. Denver, July 15, 1957; s. Milton Edward and Mary (Kramer) M. Student, Met. State Coll., Denver, 1977-78, U. Colo., 1978-80. Ptnr., developer RM & M II (Ltd. Partnership), Englewood, Colo., 1981-87; pres. Centennial Mortgage and Investment, Ltd., Englewood, Colo., 1984-87; prin. Capriole Properties, Greenwood Village, Colo., 1983—. Alumni mem. bd. trustees Kent Denver Country Day Sch., 1981-83; sec. dist. 37 ctrl. and vacancy com. Colo. Ho. of Reps., 1991-92. Recipient Pamela Davis Beardsley devel. award Kent Denver Sch., 1995. Mem. Greenwood Athletic Club. Republican. Avocations: climbing, rollerblading, political economy, 20th century English lit., metaphysics.

MEYER, DENNIS IRWIN, lawyer; b. Dayton, Ohio, Oct. 20, 1935; s. Luther Edward and Mary (McGee) M.; m. Rita Murray, June 23, 1962; children: Matthew, Michael, Rita Catherine, Peter, Denise, Abigail. BS, U. Dayton, 1957; LLB, Georgetown U., 1960, LLM, 1962. Bar: Ohio 1960, D.C. 1962. Atty.-advisor U.S. Tax Ct., Washington, 1960-62; ptnr. Baker & McKenzie, Washington, 1965—; bd. dirs. United Fin. Banking Cos., Vienna, Va., Splty. Retailing, College Park, Md., Oakwood Homes, Greensboro, N.C., Daily Express, Inc., Carlisle, Pa.; gen. ptnr. Potomac Investment Assoc., Md., 1976—. Mem. ABA, Internat. Fiscal Assn., Met. Club, 1925 F Street Club of Washington, Belle Haven Country Club, Avenel Golf Club, Robert Trent Jones Golf Club. Roman Catholic. Office: Baker & McKenzie 815 Connecticut Ave NW Washington DC 20006-4004

MEYER, DIANNE SCOTT WILSON, secondary school educator, librarian; b. Austin, Tex., Nov. 28, 1941; d. Herbert Cook and Velma Estelle (Scott) Wilson; m. George Edward Hopper, Jr., Apr. 11, 1963 (div. Mar., 1983); children: David Scott, Daniel Wilson; m. James Raymond Meyer, June 21, 1984; step children: Karen Ray, Sheila Kay, Jayme Caroline. BA, Baylor U., 1962; postgrad., Sam Houston State U., 1973, 79-81, 94, U. St. Thomas, 1989; MLA, Houston Bapt. U., 1991; postgrad., Sam Houston State U., 1973, 79-81, 94, U. Houston, 1979-83, 84-88. Cert. tchr. secondary schs. (provisional) Tex., cert. libr. Tex. Tchr. 7th and 8th grades history and lang. arts La Marque (Tex.) Jr. H.S., 1962-64; tchr. English II and IV Lincoln H.S., La Marque, 1966-67; 7th and 8th grades history and lang. arts Tom Browne Jr. H.S., Corpus Christi, Tex., 1967-68; tchr. English II Tioga (La.) H.S., 1969; tchr. 8th grade lang. arts Anson Ward Sch., Anson, Tex., 1969-72; tchr. English II and IV Cypress Fairbanks H.S., Houston, 1972-81; journalism tchr. yearbook and newspaper Westchester H.S., Houston, 1981-83; tchr. study skills 9th gr. Cypress Creek H.S., Houston, 1983-87, tchr. English I, II and IV, 1988—, tchr. humanities 10th gr., 1992-93; dir. summer recreation City of La Marque, Tex., 1964; leader Gt. Books Found., 1990-97; presenter in field. Sponsor lit. mag. Equinox of Cy Fair H.S., 1973-76. Grassroots organizer Harris County Dems., Houston, 1978-79; mem. steering com. John Hill Gubernatorial Campaign, Houston, 1978-79; pres. Cy-Fair Edn. Assn., 1978-79; vol. KUHT-TV (PBS sta.), Houston, 1975—; pres. Band Aides Parent-Boosters of Jersey Village H.S. Band, 1981; organizing hostess Marching Bands of Am. Competition, C.F.I.S.D., 1981. Named Cypress Fairbanks H.S. Tchr. of Yr., Houston, 1975, 78, Cypress Fairbanks Ind. Sch. Dist. Tchr. of Yr. 1978; NEH Common Ground grantee: U. Houston, 1992. Mem. AAUW, ALA, NEA (del. 1976), Young Adult Libr. Assn., Tex. Libr. Assn., West Houston Coun. Tchrs. of English, N. Harris County Coun. Tchrs. of English, Tex. Coun. Tchrs. of English (nominating com. 1991), Nat. Coun. Tchrs. of English, Tex. State Tchrs. Assn. (del. state and nat. 1975-79, pres. Houston 1978-79, mem.steering com. 1962-95), Delta Kappa Gamma Internat. (charter mem. Kappa Alpha chpt.), Kappa Alpha Theta (charter mem. Epsilon Epsilon chpt.), Baylor Ex-Students Assn. (life alumnae mem.). Democrat. Baptist. Avocations: antiquing, reading, travel, genealogical research, gardening. Office: Cypress Creek HS 9815 Grant Rd Houston TX 77070-4501

MEYER, DONALD RAY, psychologist, brain researcher; b. Rhineland, Mo., July 31, 1924; s. Julius Caesar and Annie Laurie (Wagner) M.; m. Patricia Lee Morgan, Dec. 31, 1957; 1 child, Julia Catherine. A.B., U. Mo., 1947, M.S., U. Wis., 1948, Ph.D., 1950. Asst. prof. psychology Ohio State U., Columbus, 1950-51, assoc. prof. psychology, 1951-57, prof. psychology, 1957-85, prof. emeritus, 1985—; dir. lab. comparative and physiol. psychology Ohio State U., Columbus, 1958-85. Consulting editor to various jours.; contbr. articles to profl. jours. Served with USAF, 1943-46. Fellow AAAS, APA (pres. div. comparative and physiol. psychology 1975), Midwestern Psychol. Assn. (pres. 1971), Soc. Exptl. Psychologists, Am. Psychol. Soc., Phi Beta Kappa, Sigma Xi. Republican. Calvinist. Achievements include participation in Project Mercury, 1st manned space program. Avocation: arborist. Home: 476 Overbrook Dr Columbus OH 43214-3127 Office: Dept Psychology Ohio State U 1885 Neil Ave Columbus OH 43210-1222

MEYER, DONALD ROBERT, banker, lawyer; b. Phoenix, June 4, 1942; s. Donald Duncan and Eleanor M.; m. Virginia Whitesel, Sept. 3, 1966; 2 children. AB, U. Calif., Berkeley, 1964, JD, 1967; postgrad. Harvard U. Sch. Bus. Adminstrn., 1968. Bar: Calif. 1972. Lectr. Seoul Nat. Univ., Korea, 1969-70; assoc. Graham & James, San Francisco, 1971-76; asst. sec. Calif. First Bank (name now Union Bank), San Francisco, 1973-76, v.p., 1976-78, gen. counsel, 1976-96, sr. v.p., 1978-96; corp. sec., exec. v.p. gen. counsel Union Bank Cal Corp., 1996—. Contbr.: Intro to the Law & Legal System of Korea, 1983. Mem. World Affairs Council, San Francisco, Sierra Club; co-chmn. San Francisco/Seoul Sister City Com., 1980-90; trustee Asian Art Found. of San Francisco, 1985-92; commr. Asian Art Mus., San Francisco, 1985-91. Recipient Key to Seoul, Korea, 1984. Mem. ABA, San Francisco Bar Assn., Am. Bankers Assn. (v.p. Calif. State 1982-83), Calif. Bankers Assn. (chmn. legal affairs com. 1982-84, svc. award 1989), Korean-Am. C. of C. (dir. San Francisco sec., bd. dirs. 1974-93, pres. 1996—), Soc. Calif. Pioneers, Univ. Club of San Francisco, Bohemian Club. Republican. Episcopalian. Office: Union Bank of Calif NA 350 California St # H-800 San Francisco CA 94104

MEYER, EDMOND GERALD, energy and natural resources educator, resources scientist, entrepreneur, former chemistry educator, university administrator; b. Albuquerque, Nov. 2, 1919; s. Leopold and Beatrice (Ilfeld) M.; m. Betty F. Knobloch, July 4, 1941; children: Lee Gordon, Terry Gene, David Gary. B.S. in Chemistry, Carnegie Mellon U., 1940, M.S., 1942; Ph.D., U. N.Mex., 1950. Chemist Harbison Walker Refractories Co., 1940-41; instr. Carnegie Mellon U., 1941-42; asst. phys. chemist Bur. Mines, 1942-44; chemist research div. N.Mex. Inst. Mining and Tech., 1946-48; head dept. sci. U. Albuquerque, 1950-52; head dept. chemistry N.Mex. Highlands U., 1952-59; dir. Inst. Sci. Rsch., 1957-63; dean Grad. Sch., 1961-63; dean Coll. Arts and Sci., U. Wyo., 1963-75, v.p., 1974-80, prof. energy and natural resources, 1981-87, prof. and dean emeritus, 1987—; exec. cons. Diamond Shamrock Corp., 1980; bd. dirs. Carbon Fuels Corp., First Nat. Bank, Laramie; sci. adviser Gov. of Wyo., 1964-90; pres. Coal Tech. Corp., 1981—; cons. Los Alamos Nat. Lab., NFS, HHS, GAO, Wyo. Bancorp; contractor investigator Rsch. Corp., Dept. Interior, AEC, NIH, NSF, Dept. Energy, Dept. Edn.; Fulbright exch. prof. U. Concepcion, Chile, 1959. Co-author: Chemistry-Survey of Principles, 1963, Legal Rights of Chemists and Engineers, 1977, Industrial Research & Development Management, 1982; contbr. articles to profl. jours.; patentee in field. Chair, Laramie Regional Airport Bd., 1989-93, treas., 1994-97; mem. Laramie City Coun., 1997—. Lt. comdr. USNR, 1944-46, ret. Recipient Disting. Svc. award Jaycees; rsch. fellow U. N.Mex., 1948-50. Fellow AAAS, Am. Inst. Chemists (pres. 1992-93, chmn. 1994-95); mem. Assoc. Western Univs. (chmn. 1972-74), Am. Chem. Soc. (councilor 1962-90, chmn. Wyo. sect. 1997), Biophys. Soc., Coun. Coll. Arts and Scis. (pres. 1971, sec.-treas. 1972-75), dir. Washington office 1973), Laramie C. of C. (pres. 1984), Sigma Xi. Home: 1058 Colina Dr Laramie WY 82072-5015 Office: U Wyo Coll Arts and Scis Laramie WY 82071-3825

MEYER, EDWARD HENRY, advertising agency executive; b. N.Y.C., Jan. 8, 1927; s. I.H. and Mildred (Driesen) M.; m. Sandra Raabin, Apr. 26, 1957; children: Margaret Ann, Anthony Edward. B.A. with honors in Econs, Cornell U., 1949. With Bloomingdale's div. Federated Dept Stores, 1949-51, Biow Co. (agy.), 1951-56; with Grey Advt., Inc., N.Y.C., 1956—; exec. v.p. Grey Advt., Inc., 1963-68, pres., chief exec. officer, 1968—, chmn. bd., 1970—; bd. dirs. May Dept. Stores co., Ethan Allan Interiors Inc., Harman Internat. Industries, Inc., Bowne & Co., Inc., 30 mut. funds Merrill Lynch Asset Mgmt., Inc. Trustee Am. Mus. Natural History, Guggenheim Mus., NYU Med. Ctr., Film Soc. of Lincoln Ctr. With USCGR, 1945-47. Mem. Econ. Club (N.Y.C.), Univ. Club (N.Y.C.), Harmonie Club (N.Y.C.), Century Country Club, Atlantic Golf Club. Office: Grey Advt Inc 777 3rd Ave New York NY 10017

MEYER, EDWARD PAUL, advertising executive; b. Chgo., May 23, 1949; s. Edward and Eleanor Kathryn (DeJong) M.; m. Marsha L. Tower, Aug. 10, 1974; children: Paul Edward, Sarah Linnea. BA in Econs. and Bus. Adminstrn., Wheaton (Ill.) Coll., 1971, MA in Comm., 1983. Asst. dir. Wheaton Coll. Alumni Assn., 1972-81; v.p. corp. comm. The Yarmouth Group, Inc. (formerly Richard Ellis Co.), Chgo., 1981-88, sr. v.p., 1988—; cons. mktg. Service Auto Glass, Lombard, Ill., 1979—. Active with Coll.

Ch. Wheaton, 1974—; pres., bd. dirs. Crusader Club Wheaton Coll., 1985-88; bd. dirs. Christian Svc. Brigade, Wheaton, 1985—, chmn., 1991—. Mem. Pub. Rels. Soc. Am., Internat. Assn. Bus. Communicators. Republican. Home: 1303 E Harrison Ave Wheaton IL 60187-4422 Office: The Yarmouth Group Two Prudential Pla Ste 1300 Chicago IL 60601

MEYER, EUGENE CARLTON, retired editor; b. McGregor, Iowa, Dec. 10, 1923; s. Gilbert Nelson and Christine Winnifred (Henkes) M.; m. Maxine Beth Mallory, June 1, 1947; children—Bruce, Mary Lynn, John. B.S., Iowa State U., 1946. Farm news editor Sta. WHO, Des Moines, 1947-48; assoc. editor Hoard's Dairyman, Fort Atkinson, Wis., 1948-72, mng. editor, 1972-88. Trustee Fort Atkinson Meml. Hosp., 1966-81, pres. bd. trustees, 1976-81. Navigator, USAAF. Recipient Disting. Service award Am. Dairy Sci. Assn., 1980, Disting. Grad. award Iowa State Dairy Sci. Club, Iowa State U., 1981, Agrl. Leadership award Alpha Gamma Rho, 1982, Award of Distinction U. Wis.-Madison, 1982, Disting. Citizen of Agr. Nat. Milk Producers, 1988, Henry A. Wallace award Iowa State U., 1989, Richard E. Lyng award, 1989, Econ. Contribution award Ft. Atkinson C. of C., 1982, Nat. Assn. Animal Breeders Disting. Svc. award, 1988, Disting. Svc. award for Cmty. Svc. Ft. Atkinson Lions Club, 1995; named Industry Person of Yr. World Dairy Expo, 1988. Mem. Nat. Dairy Shrine (pres. 1980, Guest of Hon. 1986). Republican. Methodist. Home: 524 Jackson St Fort Atkinson WI 53538-1356

MEYER, F. WELLER, bank executive; b. Washington, Dec. 15, 1942; s. Martin William and Sallie Rita (Weller) M.; m. Brenda Burton, Sept. 27, 1972; children: F. Weller Jr., Brandon Michael. BS, U. Md., 1977. V.p. W.S. Steed Mortgage Co., Wheaton, Md., 1970-73; asst. dir. Mortgage Bankers Assn., Washington, 1973-77; mng. dir. Mortgage Systems Corp., Bethesda, Md., 1977-83; pres., chief executive officer Westmark Mortgage Corp., Rockville, Md., 1983-87, Acacia Fed. Savs. Bank, Falls Church, Va., 1987—; dir. Acacia Federal Svcs. Bank, Acacia Svc. Corp., Falls Church, Calvert Group Ltd., Am.'s Cmty. Bankers, Va. Bankers Assn. Co-author: Residential Mortgage Underwriting, 1981, Consturction Lending—Residential, 1981, Construction Lending—Residential Income Property, 1981, Income Property Underwriting, 1981. Dir. Make-A-Wish Found. of the Mid-Atlantic, No. Va. Comty. Found., Fairfax, Va., 1989; mem. Citizen's Housing Adv. Com., Montgomery County, Md., 1988-90. 1st lt. U.S. Army, 1967-70, Vietnam. Mem. Optimists (pres. Washington 1978-79). Republican. Roman Catholic. Avocations: golf, hunting, jogging. Home: 9809 Kendale Rd Rockville MD 20854-4246

MEYER, FRANCES MARGARET ANTHONY, elementary and secondary school educator, health education specialist; b. Stella, Va., Nov. 15, 1947; d. Arthur Abner Jr. and Emmie Adeline (Murray) Anthony; m. Stephen Leroy Meyer, Aug. 2, 1975. BS, Longwood Coll., 1970; MS, Va. Commonwealth U., 1982, PhD, 1996. Cert. tchr., Va. Health, phys. edn., and dance tchr. Fredericksburg (Va.) City Pub. Schs., 1970-89; AIDS edn. coord. Va. Dept. Edn., Richmond, 1989-90, health edn. specialist, 1990-94, comprehensive sch. health program specialist, 1994—; mem. rev. bd. Nat. Commn. for Health Edn. and Credentialing, Inc. Author: (with others) Elementary Physical Education: Growing through Movement--A Curriculum Guide, 1982; health editor Va. Jour., 1994—; contbr. articles to profl. jours. Mem. pub. edn. coun., comprehensive sch. health edn. team Va. affiliate, Am. Cancer Soc., Richmond, 1990—; dir. Va. Children's Dance Festival, Hist. Fredericksburg Found., Inc., 1981-96; vol. ARC, Fredericksburg, 1976-84; vol. Va. affiliate AHA, 1982-93. Recipient gov.'s medal for substance abuse and prevention edn. State of Va., 1997. Mem. AAUW (com. 1989-90), ASCD, NEA, AAPHERD (past v.p., chmn. divsn. 1970—, mem. Nat. Mid. Sch. Assn., So. Dist. honor award 1995, president's recognition award 1997, svc. award 1997), Nat. Dance Assn. (bd. dirs. 1996—), Va. Edn. Assn., Va. Mid. Sch. Assn., Va. Alliance for Arts Edn., Internat. Coun. for Health, Phys. Edn., Recreation, Sport and Dance (internat. commns. for health edn. and commn. for dance and dance edn.), Va. Health Promotion and Edn. Coun. (bd. dirs. 1990-96), Soc. State Dirs. Health, Phys. Edn. and Recreation (legis. affairs com. 1994—, mem. applied strategic planning com. 1994—, pres.-elect 1997, Presdl. award 1996, Presdl. Recognition award 1997), Longwood Coll. Alumni Coun. (bd. dirs. 1987-90), Nat. Network for Youth Svcs. (rev. panel, adv. bd. 1994—), Am. Coll. Health Assn. (curriculum and tng. rev. panel 1992-94), Va. Alliance for Arts Edn. (adv. bd. 1980-83, 89-90, 95-96), Va. Assn. for Health, Phys. Edn., Recreation and Dance (past pres., various coms. 1970—, Tchr. of Yr. 1983, Va. Honor award 1988, Gov.'s medal for substance abuse prevention edn. 1997), Delta Kappa Gamma (pres. Beta Eta chpt. 1988-90). Baptist. Avocations: traveling, dancing, swimming, reading, attending theatrical performances.

MEYER, FRED JOSEF, advertising executive; b. Zurich, Switzerland, Jan. 1, 1931; came to U.S., 1959; s. Josef and Claire (Lehmann) M.; m. Beverly Ruth Carter, Apr. 9, 1961 (div. Feb. 1975); children: Fred Jay, Marcus Clinton, Michael Josef; m. Marie-Noelle Vigneron, Oct. 30, 1975. MS, Fed. Inst. Tech., Zurich, 1956; MBA, Harvard U., 1961; LLD (hon.), Sacred Heart U., 1981. Vice pres. plannng and adminstrn. Sandoz Inc., Hanover, N.J., 1971-73, exec. v.p., chief fin. officer, 1973-78; pres., chief exec. officer Sandoz U.S., Inc., Greenwich, Conn., 1978-81; mng. dir., chief exec. officer Wander Ltd., Berne, Switzerland, 1981-82; sr. v.p., chief fin. officer CBS Inc., N.Y.C., 1982-88; chief fin. officer, Omnicom Group, Inc., N.Y.C., 1988—; bd. dirs. Zurich-Am. Ins. Cos., Ill., SoGen Internat. Fund, Inc., N.Y.C., SoGen Funds, Inc., N.Y.C., Sandoz Corp., SyStemix, Inc., Palo Alto, Calif. Mem. Fin. Execs. Inst., Econ. Club, Harvard Club (N.Y.C.), Greenwich Country Club. Republican. Presbyterian. Office: Omnicom Group Inc 437 Madison Ave New York NY 10022-7001

MEYER, FRED WILLIAM, JR., memorial parks executive; b. Fair Haven, Mich., Jan. 7, 1924; s. Fred W. and Gladys (Marshall) M.; m. Jean Hope, Aug. 5, 1946; children—Frederick, Thomas, James, Nancy. AB, Mich. State Coll., 1946. Salesman Chapel Hill Meml. Gardens, Lansing, Mich., 1946-47; mgr. Roselawn Meml. Gardens, Saginaw, Mich., 1947-49; dist. mgr. Sunset Meml. Gardens, Evansville, Ind., 1949-53; pres., dir. Memory Gardens Mgmt. Corp., Indpls., Covington Meml. Gardens, Ft. Wayne, Ind., Chapel Hill Meml. Gardens, Grand Rapids, Mich., Forest Lawn Memory Gardens, Indpls., Lincoln Memory Gardens, Indpls., Chapel Hill Meml. Gardens, South Bend, Ind., Mercury Devel. Corp., Indpls., Quality Marble Imports, Indpls., Quality Printers, Indpls., Am. Bronze Craft, Inc., Judsonia, Ark. Mem. C. of C., A.I.M., Am. Cemetery Assn., Sigma Chi, Phi Kappa Delta. Clubs: Columbia, Meridian Hills Country, Woodland Country. Home: 110 E 111th St Indianapolis IN 46280-1051 Office: 3733 N Meridian St Indianapolis IN 46208-4305

MEYER, G. CHRISTOPHER, lawyer; b. Fremont, Nebr., Mar. 27, 1948; s. Gerald William and Mildred Ruth (Clausen) M.; m. Linda Haines, Dec. 27, 1969; children: Katie, Stacy, Jon, Robert. Student, Grinnell (Iowa) Coll., 1966-69; BA, U. Kans., 1970; JD, U. Pa., 1973. Bar: Ohio 1973, U.S. Dist. Ct. (no. dist.) Ohio 1975, U.S. Ct. Appeals (6th cir.) 1982. Assoc. Squire, Sanders & Dempsey, Cleve., 1973-82, ptnr., 1982—. Mem. ABA, Ohio State Bar Assn., Greater Cleve. Bar Assn. Office: Squire Sanders & Dempsey 4900 Key Tower 127 Public Sq Cleveland OH 44114-1216

MEYER, GEORGE HERBERT, lawyer; b. Detroit, Feb. 19, 1928; s. Herbert M. and Agnes F. (Eaton) M.; m. Carol Ann Jones, 1958 (div. 1981) children: Karen Ann, George Herbert Jr.; m. Katherine Palmer White, Nov. 12, 1988. AB, U. Mich., 1949; JD, Harvard U., 1952; cert., Oxford (Eng.) U., 1955; LLM in Taxation, Wayne State U., 1962. Bar: D.C. bar 1952, Mich. bar 1953. Assoc. firm Fischer, Franklin & Ford, Detroit, 1956-63; mem. firm Fischer, Franklin & Ford, 1963-74; established firm George H. Meyer, 1974-78; sr. mem. firm Meyer and Kirk, 1978-85; sr. mem. Meyer, Kirk, Snyder & Safford PLLC, Bloomfield Hills and Detroit, Mich., 1985—; curator Step Lively exhibit Mus. Am. Folk Art, N.Y.C., 1992; lectr. Am. Folk Art. Author: Equalization in Michigan and Its Effect on Local Assessments, 1963, Folk Artists Biographical Index, 1986, American Folk Art Canes: Personal Sculpture, 1992. Chmn. Birmingham (Mich.) Bd. Housing Appeals, 1964-68; vice chmn. Birmingham Bd. Zoning Appeals, 1966-69; mem. Birmingham Planning Bd., 1968-70; trustee, Bloomfield Village, Mich., 1976-80, pres., 1979-80; trustee Mus. Am. Folk Art, N.Y.C., 1987—; mem. exec. bd. Detroit Area coun. Boy Scouts Am., 1976—, counsel, 1986-95,v.p., 1996—; mem. nat. adv. bd. Folk Art Soc. Am., 1994—; trustee Detroit Sci. Ctr., 1985—. 1st lt. JAG, USAF, 1952-55, maj. Res. ret. Recipient Silver Beaver award Detroit Area coun. Boy Scouts Am., 1989. Mem. ABA, Detroit Bar Assn., Oakland County Bar Assn., State Bar Mich., Harvard Law Sch. Assn. Mich. (dir. 1959—, pres. 1970-78), Detroit Sci. Mus. Soc. (pres. 1961-74, chmn. 1974-76), Am. Folk Art Soc., Prismatic Club, Scarab Club, Harvard Club (N.Y.C.), Detroit Club, Detroit Athletic Club, Masons, Rotary, Phi Beta Kappa, Alpha Phi Omega. Republican. Unitarian. Home: 1483 N Cranbrook Rd Bloomfield Village MI 48301 Office: Meyer Kirk Snyder & Stafford 100 W Long Lake Rd Ste 100 Bloomfield Hills MI 48304-2773

MEYER, GEORGE WILBUR, internist, health facility administrator; b. Cleve., Apr. 30, 1941; s. George Wilbur and Emily Fuller (Campbell) M.; m. Carolyn Edwards Garrett, Apr. 8, 1967; children: Robert James, Elizabeth Jackson, Dobro Goodale. BS, MIT, 1962; MD, Tulane Med. Sch., 1966. Intern So. Pacific Hosps. Inc., San Francisco, 1966-67; resident Pacific Presbyn. Med. Ctr., San Francisco, 1969-72; commd. 1st lt. USAF, advanced through grades to col., 1980; fellow in gastroenterology David Grant USAF Med. Ctr., Travis AFB, Calif., 1974-76; asst. chair dept. medicine USAF Med. Ctr., Keesler AFB, Miss., 1976-78; asst. prof. dept. medicine Uniformed Svcs. Univ., Bethesda, Md., 1978-80; chair dept. medicine Wright Patterson AFB, Dayton, Ohio, 1980-82; chief of medicine Wilford Hall USAF Med. Ctr., Lackland AFB, Tex., 1982-86; chief clin. svcs. USAF Acad., Colo., 1986-88; comdr. 1st Med. Groups, Langley AFB, Va., Germany, 1988-89, 86th Med. Group, Ramstein AFB, Germany, 1989-92; program dir. internal medicine Ga. Bapt. Med. Ctr., Atlanta, 1993—; cons. Walter Reed Army Med. Ctr., Washington, 1978-80, Nat. Naval Med. Ctr., Bethesda, 1978-80; assoc. prof. Wright State U. Sch. Medicine, Dayton, 1980-82; cons. Dayton VA Med. Ctr., 1980-82; clin. assoc. prof. medicine U. Tex. Health Sci. Ctr., San Antonio, 1982-86, Med. Coll. Ga., Augusta, 1993—. Mem. editl. bd. Gastrointestinal Endoscopy, 1993—; contbr. articles and revs. to profl. jours. and chpts. to books. Mem. leadership com. Am. Cancer Soc., Ramstein AFB, 1989-93, bd. dirs. Atlanta City Unit, 1995-97, Ga. divsn. 1996-97, El Paso Teller Unit, Colorado Springs, 1986-88, Bexar Metro Unit, San Antonio, 1984-86; adv. com. United Health Svcs., Dayton, 1980-82. Fellow ACP, Am. Coll. Gastroenterology; mem. Am. Soc. for Gastro Endoscopy, Am. Gastrointestinal Assn., Am. Assn. for Study of Liver Diseases. Avocations: squash, tennis, scuba, stamps. Office: Ga Bapt Med Ctr 303 Parkway Dr NE Atlanta GA 30312-1212

MEYER, GOLDYE W., psychologist, educator; b. Wilkes Barre, Pa., Feb. 6, 1927; d. Harry Samuel Weisberger and Jennie Iskowitz; div.; children: Jodie, Howard, Natlee. BS, Wilkes U., Wilkes Barre, 1962; MS, Temple U., Phila., 1964; PhD, U. Conn., Storrs, 1975. Day camp dir. JCC, Wilkes Barre, 1962-64; chemistry instr. Wilkes U., Wilkes Barre, 1962-64, U. Bridgeport, Conn., 1964-65; prof. sec. edn. U. Bridgeport, 1966-74, assoc. prof. counseling and human resources, 1974-78, prof. counseling and human resources, 1978-91; owner pvt. cons. firm, Bridgeport, 1977-90; pvt. psychotherapy practice Fairfield, Conn., 1975—; internat. bioenergetic analysis trainer Switzerland, Israel, 1981—; trainer bioenergetic analysis Conn. Bioenergetic Soc., Conn., 1980-83; adj. prof. Nova U., Ft. Lauderdale, Fla., 1991-93; doctoral adv., acad. supr. Columbia-Pacific U., San Rafael, Calif., 1992—; adj. prof., doctoral adv. The Union Inst., Cin., 1994—; dir. Fairfield (Conn.) Orgnl. Cons., 1977-90, Brooklawn Family Ctr., Fairfield, 1985—; mem. human resources adv. bd. U. Bridgeport, 1986-90; mem. bd. edn. adv. bd. Bridgeport Schs., 1984-87; leader AIDS caregiver support group The Yale New Haven Hosp., 1992—. Contbr. articles to jours, chpts. to books. Co-chair Fairfield Citizens for Edn. Recipient Doctoral Rsch. Grant U. Conn., 1974, Multicultural Rsch. Grant U. Bridgeport, 1980. Mem. ACLU, NOW, APA, Am. Acad. Psychotherapists, Nat. Substance Abuse Counselors, Conn. Coun. for Substance Abuse Counselors, Mass. Soc. for Bioenergetic Analysis (chair ethics com. 1993—), Sierra Club, Appalachian Club. Hebrew. Avocations: photography, tennis, biking, traveling, music. Home: 615 Brooklawn Ave Fairfield CT 06432-1807

MEYER, GREG CHARLES, psychiatrist; b. Bismarck, N.D., Aug. 17, 1935; s. Oscar Clarence and Agnes Josephine (Pearson) M. Degree in profl. engring., Colo. Sch. Mines, 1958, Alexander Hamilton Bus. Inst., 1960; MME, U. So. Calif., 1965; MD, Marquette U., 1970. Diplomate Am. Bd. Psychiatry and Neurology. Engr. Minuteman-Thiokol, Brigham City, Utah, 1958-61; sr. engr. Saturn S-II N.Am. Aviation, Downey, Calif., 1962-65; design specialist Titan-Martin, Denver, 1965-66; rotating intern Weld Country Gen. Hosp., Greenly, Colo., 1970-71; psychiatric resident Ariz. State Hosp., Phoenix, 1971-74, psychiatrist, 1974-76; pvt. practice Mesa-Tempe, Ariz., 1975—; psychiatrist Ariz. Ctrl. Med. Ctr., 1995—; med. dir. Ctrl. Ariz. Med. Ctr., 1997; chmn. psychiatry Desert Samaritan Hosp., Mesa, 1982-86, 90-94, chmn. joint mental health, 1981-83, mem. edn. com., 1979-82, quality assurance com., 1979; exec. com. Desert Vista Hosp., Mesa, 1988-94, chief of staff, 1989; chmn. psychiatry Mesa Luth. Hosp., 1984-85, exec. com., 1984-85; mng. ptnr. Desert Samaritan Med. Bldg. II, Mesa, 1985-86; rsch. edn. com. East Valley Camel Back Hosp., 1989-90, quality assurance com., 1985; med. dir. Ctrl. Ariz. Med. Ctr., 1997. Co-discoverer Larson-Meyer Transform. Coach Pop Warner Football, 1974. With USMCR, 1953-59. Mem. AMA, Am. Psychiatric Assn., Ariz. Med. Assn., Ariz. Psychiatric Assn., Phoenix Psychiatric Coun., Maricopa Country Med. Assn., Christian Med./Dental Assn., Triple Nine Soc., Sons of Confederate Vets. Republican. Lutheran. Avocations: multi engine instrument pilot, sailing, computers, canoeing, photography.

MEYER, HARRY MARTIN, JR., retired health science facility administrator; b. Palestine Tex., Nov. 25, 1928. s. Harry Martin and Marjory Isabel (Griffin) M.; m. Mary Jane Martin, Aug. 19, 1949 (div. 1966); children: Harry, Mary, David; m. Barbara Story Chalfart, Nov. 21, 1966. BS Hendrix Coll., 1949, MD U. Ark., 1953; Diplomate Am. Bd. Pediatics, 1960. instr. biology Little Rock Coll., 1949, intern. Walter Reed Army Hosp., Washington, 1953-54, med. officer dep. virus and rickettsial diseases, Walter Reed Army Inst. Rsch., 1954-57, asst. resident dep. pediatrics, N.C. Meml. Hosp., Chapel Hill, 1957-59, head virology sect. div. biologics standards, NIH, Bethesda, Md., 1959-64, chief lab. of viral immunol., div. biologics standards, NIH, 1964-72, dir. bur. biologics FDA, Bethesda, 1972-82, dir. Ctr. for Drugs & Biologics FDA, Rockville, Md., 1982-86, pres. med. research div. Am. Cyanamid Co., Pearl River, N.Y., 1986-93; retired 1993. Served to rear admiral USPHS, 1959-86, capt. U.S. Army, 1953-57. Mem. AMA, Am. Epidemiol. Soc., Am. Acad. Pediatrics, Am. Pediatric Soc. Protestant. Avocations: sailing, scuba diving, skiing, back packing. Conbr. articles to profl. jours.; patentee in field.

MEYER, HARVEY KESSLER, II, retired academic administrator; b. Carlisle, Pa., Feb. 6, 1914; s. Harvey Kessler and Frances May (Shultz) M.; m. Jessie Irene Hamm, Feb. 22, 1935; children: Carol Frances, Harvey Kessler III, Howard Madison. BA, Berea (Ky.) Coll., 1936; MA, Eastern Ky. U., 1942; D Edn., U. Fla., Gainesville, 1951. Surveyor Wash. State Hwy. Engrs., 1932; furniture designer Berea Woodwork, 1932-36; lic. contractor Bailey Constrn. Co., Seattle, Wash., 1935, Alachua County, Fla., 1948-50.; instr. U. Fla., Ocala, 1936-37; supr. Nat. Youth Adminstrn., Jacksonville, Fla., 1937-38; vocat. tchr. Richmond (Ky.) City Schs., 1938-40; asst. prof. Eastern Ky. U., Richmond, 1940-43; tchr. P.K.Yonge Lab. Sch., Gainesville, Fla., 1946-47, prin., 1947-48; assoc. prof. U. Fla., Gainesville, 1948-51, prof., 1951-65; dean divsn radio & TV Fla. Inst. Continuing U. Studies, 1962-65; assoc. dean acad. affairs Fla. Atlantic U., Boca Raton, 1965-68, grad. prof., 1968-73; dir. Indsl. Arts and Vocat. Edn., Managua, Nicaragua, 1955-57; founder Instituto Nacional Educacion Vocacional, Nicaragua; dir., trustee Moravian Theol. Sem., Bethlehem, Pa., 1976; dean radio and TV Fla. Inst. for Continuing Univ. Studies, 1962-65; adminstrv. cons. Brit.-Am. Investment Fund, Luxembourg City, Europe, 1969-71; owner, design Plantation Glen, Alachua County, 1948-77, Hacienda Ocotlan, Clay County, N.C., 1975-78. Author: Technical Eduction in Nicaragua, 1958, Historical Dictionary Nicaragua, 1972, Historical Dictionary Honduras, 1976, rev. edit., 1994. Pres. Fla. dist. Moravian Ch., 1970-73, Melrose (Fla.) Library Assn., 1983—, pres., 1984-90, 92—; trustee Moravian Coll. and Sem., 1966-78. Comdr. USNR, ret.; naval aviation observer. Named Disting. Alumnus Berea Coll., 1986. Mem. Fla. Assn. Ednl. TV (pres. 1963), Berea Coll. Alumni Assn. (pres. 1990-91), Rotary, Phi Kappa Phi, Phi Delta Kappa, Epsilon Pi Tau (trustee 1950—). Democrat. Avocations: boating, architecture, pistol shooting, furniture design and building, archaeology. Home: Quinta la Maya Atlán 2805 NW 83d St #405C Gainesville FL 32606-6288

MEYER, HELEN (MRS. ABRAHAM J. MEYER), retired editorial consultant; b. Bklyn., Dec. 4, 1907; d. Bertolen and Esther (Greenfield) Honig; m. Abraham J. Meyer, Sept. 1, 1929; children—Adele Meyer Brodkin, Robert L. Grad. pub. schs. With Popular Sci., McCall's mag., 1921-22; pres., dir. Dell Pub. Co., Inc., N.Y.C., 1923-57, Dell Distbg., Inc., from 1957, Dell Internat., Inc., from 1957; pres. Dell Pub. Co., Inc., Montville Warehousing Co., Inc.; chmn. bd. Noble & Noble Pubs., Inc.; v.p. Dellprint, Inc., Dunellen, N.J.; pres. Dial Press.; later editorial cons. Doubleday & Co., N.Y.C.; cons. Fgn. Rights, N.Y.C. Bd. dirs. United Cerebral Palsy. Named to Pub.'s Hall of Fame, 1986. Mem. Assn. Am. Pubs. (dir.). Home: 1 Claridge Dr Apt 608 Verona NJ 07044-3054

MEYER, HENRY LEWIS, III, banker; b. Cleve., Dec. 25, 1949; s. Henry Lewis and Anne (Taylor) M.; m. Jane Kreamer, July 15, 1978; children: Patrick Harrison, Andrew Taylor, Christopher Bicknell. BA, Colgate U., 1972; MBA, Harvard U., Boston, 1978. Asst. v.p. Soc. Nat. Bank, Cleve., 1972-76, v.p., 1978-81, sr. v.p., 1981-83; exec. v.p. Soc. Bank, N.Am., Dayton, Ohio, 1983-85, pres., chief operating officer, 1985-87; sr. exec. v.p. Soc. Bank, N.Am., Cleve., 1987-89, vice chmn. bd., 1989—; exec. v.p. Soc. Corp., 1987—; bd. dirs. Soc. Bank, Columbus, Soc. Investor Svcs. Corp., Nat. Fin. Svcs. Corp., Soc. Mortgage Co. Trustee Am. Cancer Soc. (Cuyahoga County Unit), Fedn. for Neighborhood Progress, Inc., A.M. McGregor Home, Cleve. Mus. Nat. History. Republican. Episcopalian. Clubs: Kirtland Country (Cleve.), The Union (Cleve.).

MEYER, HORST, physics educator; b. Berlin, Germany, Mar. 1, 1926. BS, U. Geneva, 1949; PhD in physics, U. Zurich, 1953. Fellow Swiss Assn. Rsch. Physics and Math. Studies, Oxford, Eng., 1953-55; Nuffield fellow Clarendon Lab. U. Oxford, 1955-57; lectr., rsch. assoc. dept. engring. and applied physics Harvard U., Cambridge, Mass., 1957-59; from asst. prof. to prof. Duke U., Durham, N.C., 1959-84, Fritz London prof. physics, 1984—; vis. prof. Technische Hochschule, Federal Republic of Germany, 1965, Tokyo U., 1980, 81, 83; traveling fellow Japanese Soc. for Promotion Sci., 1971, vis. scientist, 1979; guest scientist Inst. Laue-Langevin, France, 1974, 75; Yamada Found. fellow, Japan, 1986; guest scientist USSR Acad. Sci., 1988; chmn. Gordon Conf. on Solid H2, 1990; western chmn. conf. quantum crystals, Almaty, Kazakhstan, 1995. Editor Jour. Low Temperature Physics, 1992—, mem. editorial bd., 1988-92; contbr. articles to profl. jours. Alfred P. Sloan fellow, 1961-65. Fellow Am. Phys. Soc. (Jesse Beams prize, 1982, Fritz London prize 1993). Exptl. rsch. on the properties of liquid and solid helium, solid hydrogen and deuterium, magnetic insulators, critical phenomena. Office: Duke U Dept Physics PO Box 90305 Durham NC 27708-0305

MEYER, IRWIN STEPHAN, lawyer, accountant; b. Monticello, N.Y., Nov. 14, 1941; s. Ralph and Janice (Cohen) M.; children: Kimberly B., Joshua A. BS, Rider Coll., 1963; JD, Cornell U., 1966. Bar: N.Y. 1966; CPA, N.J. Tax mgr. Lybrand Ross Bros. & Montgomery, N.Y.C., 1966-71; mem. Ehrenkranz, Ehrenkranz & Schultz, N.Y.C., 1971-74; prin. Irwin S. Meyer, 1974-77, 82-96; mem. Levine, Honig, Eisenberg & Meyer, 1977-78, Eisenberg, Honig & Meyer, 1978-81, Eisenberg, Honig, Meyer & Fogler, 1981-82, Jamow & Meyer, LLC., 1997—. With U.S. Army, 1966-71. Mem. ABA, N.Y. Bar Assn., Am. Assn. Atty.-CPA, N.Y. Assn. Atty-CPA, N.J. Soc. CPA. Office: 1 Blue Hill Plz Ste 1006 Pearl River NY 10965-3100

MEYER, J. THEODORE, lawyer; b. Chgo., Apr. 13, 1936; s. Joseph Theodore and Mary Elizabeth (McHugh) M.; m. Marilu Bartholomew, Aug. 16, 1961; children: Jean, Joseph. B.S., John Carroll U., 1958; postgrad. U. Chgo.; J.D., DePaul U., 1962. Bar: Ill. 1962, U.S. Dist. Ct. (no. dist.) Ill. 1962. Ptnr. Bartholomew & Meyer, Chgo., 1963-83; mem. Ill. Gen. Assembly, House of Rep., 28th Legis. Dist., 1966-72, 74-82, chmn. House environ. study com., 1968; chmn. energy environ. com. and natural resources com.; mem. appropriations and exec. com.; chmn. Joint House/Senate com. to review state air and water plans, 1968; mem. Fed. State Task Force on Energy; chmn., founder Midwest Legis. Coun. on Environ., 1971; mem. State of Ill. Pollution Control Bd., Chgo., 1983—; mem. Joint Legis. Com. on Hazardous Waste in Lake Calumet Area, 1987; lectr. in field. Recipient Appreciation award Ill. Wildlife Fedn., 1972, Environ. Quality award Region V, EPA, 1974, Pro Bono Publico award Self-Help Action Ctr., 1975, Merit award Dept. Ill. VFW, 1977, Environ. Legislator of Yr. award Ill. Environ. Coun., 1978-79; Disting. Lawyer Legislator of Yr.; commd. hon. lt. aide-de-camp Ala. State Militia; commd. Hon. Tex. Citizen. Fellow Chgo. Bar Found.; mem. ABA, Ill. Bar Assn., Chgo. Bar Assn., Nat. Rep. Legis. Assn., Nat. Trust Hist. Preservation, Nat. Wildlife Fedn., Ill. Hist. Soc., Beverly Tennis Club, Beverly Hills Univ. Club. Republican. Roman Catholic. Office: State of Ill Ctr 100 W Randolph St Ste 11500 Chicago IL 60601-3220

MEYER, JACKIE MERRI, publishing executive; b. Phila., Oct. 19, 1954; m. W. Scot Carouge, May 23, 1982. BFA, The Cooper Union, N.Y.C., 1977. Art dir. Macmillan Pub. Co., N.Y.C., 1980-85; v.p., creative dir. Warner Books, N.Y.C., 1985—; pub. Warner Treasures, An Imprint of Warner Books, 1995; tchr. Parsons Sch. Design, N.Y.C., 1984-85; lectr. Fashion Inst. Tech., N.Y.C., 1984-85, Am. Illustration, N.Y.C., 1984, Balt. Pub. Assn., NYU Pub. Inst. Co-author: I Loathe New York, 1981. Mem. exec. bd. The Cooper Union Alumni Assn., N.Y.C., 1977—. Recipient numerous profl. awards, orgns. including Advt. Club, Desi awards, Art Direction mag., Print mag., Graphis, Comm. Arts. Mem. ADC, WICI, AFTRA, Am. Inst. Graphic Arts (awards), Art Dirs. Club (awards). Avocations: photography, gardening, painting, travel, writing. Office: Warner Books Inc Rm 1714 1271 Avenue Of The Americas Lbby 9 New York NY 10020-1302

MEYER, JAMES PHILIP, secondary education social studies educator; b. Berwyn, Ill., May 2, 1946; s. Albert Fred and Eleanore Ann (Szydlowski) M.; m. Candice Marie Richter, Dec. 19, 1970; children: Teri Lynn, David Philip. Student, Athenaeum of Ohio, 1964-66, Maryknoll Coll., 1966-67; BA in Classics, Loyola U., Chgo., 1969; postgrad., Roosevelt U., 1972-76, U. Ill., 1990, Bradley U., 1994. Cert. tchr. 6-12, Ill. Tchr. Cass Sch. Dist. # 63, Darien, Ill., 1969—; football coach Cass Sch. Dist. #63, Darien, Ill. 1969-84, basketball and softball coach, 1969-87; official scorekeeper and statistician at Downers Grove N. Girls Basketball, 1988—. Campaign mgr. Citizens for Donohue 13th dist. U.S. Congress, Naperville, Ill., 1984; campaign. coord. County Bd. candidate, Lombard, Ill., 1986, sec. DuPage County Dems., Lombard, 1986-90; bd. dirs., program com. Jr. Achievement, Chgo., 1987—. Recipient Excellence in Teaching award Ill. Math. and Sci. Acad., Aurora, Ill., 1991, Bus.-Edn. Partnership award Ill. State Bd. Edn., 1994. Mem. Ill. Norsk Rosemalers Assn. (computer records com., Swedish days com.). Roman Catholic. Avocation: computers. Home: 4216 Elm St Downers Grove IL 60515-2115 Office: Cass Sch Dist # 63 8502 Bailey Rd Darien IL 60561-5333

MEYER, JEAN-PIERRE GUSTAVE, mathematician, educator; b. Lyon, Rhone, France, Aug. 5, 1929; s. Jules and Germaine (Becker) M.; m. Marily Joan Pettit, 1959; children: David, Susan, Steven, Alison, Nadine, Nicholas; m. Roselyne Fischer-Laverton, 1996. BA, Cornell U., 1950, MS, 1951, PhD, 1954. Asst. prof. math. Syracuse (N.Y.) U., 1956; research assoc. math. Brown U., Providence, R.I., 1956-57; from asst. to assoc. to prof. Johns Hopkins U., Balt., 1957—, chmn. dept. math., 1985-90; dir. Japan-U.S. Math. Inst., 1992—. Co-author: Fundamental Structures of Algebra, 1963; contbr. articles to profl. jours. Served with U.S. Army, 1954-56. Grad. fellow NSF, 1953. Mem. Am. Math. Soc. Avocations: mineral collecting, archaeology. Home: 3601 Greenway Baltimore MD 21218-9999 Office: Johns Hopkins U Dept Math Baltimore MD 21218

MEYER, JEROME J., diversified technology company executive; b. Caledonia, Minn., Feb. 18, 1938; s. Herbert J. and Edna (Staggemeyer) M.; m. Sandra Ann Beaudoin, June 18, 1960; children—Randall Lee, Lisa Ann, Michelle Lynn. Student, Hamline U., 1956-58; B.A., U. Minn., 1960. Devel. engr. Firestone Tire & Rubber Co., Akron, Ohio, 1960-61; v.p., gen. mgr. Sperry Univac, St. Paul, 1961-79; group v.p. Honeywell, Inc., Mpls., 1979-84; pres., chief operating officer Varian Assocs., Palo Alto, Calif., 1984-86, also bd. dirs.; pres., chief exec. officer Honeywell Inc., 1986-90; from pres. to chmn., CEO Tektronix Inc., Beaverton, Oreg., 1990—; bd. dirs. Portland Gen. Corp., Esterline Tech., Oregon Bus. Coun., AMP. Trustee Oreg. Grad. Inst., Willamette U., Oreg. Children's Found. Mem. Oregon

Golf Club. Avocation: golf. Office: Tektronix Inc PO Box 1000 26600 S W Pky Wilsonville OR 97070*

MEYER, JOHN EDWARD, nuclear engineering educator; b. Pitts., Dec. 17, 1931; s. Albert Edward and Thelma Elizabeth (Brethauer) M.; m. Gracyann Lenz, June 13, 1953; children: Susan Meyer Heydon, Karl, Karen Meyer Gleasman, Thomas. B.S., Carnegie Inst. Tech., 1953, M.S., 1953, Ph.D. (ASME Student award 1955), 1955. Engring. and mgmt. positions Westinghouse Bettis Atomic Power Lab., West Mifflin, Pa., 1955-75; vis. lectr. U. Calif., Berkeley, 1968-69; prof. nuclear engring. M.I.T., 1975—; cons. in field. Author papers in field. Recipient Bettis Disting. Service award, 1962, Outstanding Tchr. award nuclear engring. M.I.T., 1979, Alumni Merit award Carnegie Mellon U., 1987. Fellow Am. Nuclear Soc.; mem. ASME, Sigma Xi. Office: Room 24-202 77 Massachusetts Ave Rm 24-202 Cambridge MA 02139-4301

MEYER, JOHN ROBERT, economist, educator; b. Pasco, Wash., Dec. 6, 1927; s. Philip Conrad and Cora (Kempter) M.; m. Lee Stowell, Dec. 17, 1949; children: Leslie Karen, Ann Elizabeth, Robert Conrad. Student, Pacific U., 1945-46; BA, U. Wash., 1950; PhD (David A. Wells prize), Harvard U., 1955. Jr. fellow Harvard U., 1953-55, asst. prof., 1955-58, assoc. prof., 1958-59, prof. econs., 1959-68, prof. transportation and logistics, 1973-83; prof. Yale U., 1968-73; Harpel prof. capital formation and econ. growth Harvard U., 1983-96, prof. emeritus, 1997—; dir. Dun & Bradstreet, Rand McNally, AC Nielsen; vice chmn. Union Pacific Corp., 1982-83, now dir.; trustee Mut. Life. Ins. Co. N.Y., Pacific U. Author: (with others) The Investment Decision—An Empirical Inquiry, 1957, Economics of Competition in the Telecommunications Industry, 1980, Autos, Transit and Cities, 1981, Deregulation and the Future of Intercity Passenger Travel, 1987, Going Private: The International Experience with Transport Privatization, 1993, other books; contbr. articles to profl. jours. Mem. Presdl. Task Forces on Transp., 1964, 80, Presdl. Commn. on Population Growth and Am. Future, 1970-72; pres. Nat. Bur. Econ. Research, 1967-77. Served with USNR, 1946-48. Guggenheim fellow, 1958. Fellow Am. Acad. Arts and Scis., Econometric Soc.; mem. Am. Econ. Assn. (mem. exec. com. 1971-73), Council Fgn. Relations, Econ. History Assn. Home: 9439 Cotten Ct Sanibel FL 33957 Office: Harvard U Ctr Bus & Govt 79 Jfk St Cambridge MA 02138-5801

MEYER, JOHN STIRLING, neurologist, educator; b. London, Feb. 24, 1924; came to U.S., 1940; s. William Charles and Alice Elizabeth (Stirling) M.; m. Wendy Haskell, July 20, 1947 (dec. 1986); children: Jane, Anne, Elizabeth, Helen, Margaret; m. Katharine Sumner, Aug. 2, 1987; m. Cora Bess Parks, Apr. 6, 1996. BSc, Trinity Coll., Hartford, Conn., 1944; MD, CM, McGill U., Montreal, Que., 1948, MSc, 1949. Diplomate Am. Bd. Neurology and Psychiatry. Intern Yale-New Haven Hosp., 1948-49, resident immunology, 1949-50; resident neurology Boston City Hosp., 1950-52, resident neurophysiology, 1952-53, fellow neurophysiology, 1954-55; instr. rsch. assoc. Harvard Med. Sch., Boston, 1955-57; resident neurophysiology Harvard Med. Sch., 1952-53; prof., chair dept. Wayne State U., Detroit, 1957-69; prof., chair dept. Baylor Coll. Medicine, Houston, 1969-75, prof. neurology, 1976—; demonstrator neuropathology and teaching fellow neurology Harvard U. Med. Sch., 1950-52; sr. rsch. fellow USPHS, 1952-54; instr. medicine Harvard U. Med. Sch., 1954-56; assoc. vis. physician neurology Boston City Hosp., 1956-57; cons. and lectr. neurology U.S. Naval Hosp., Chelsea, Mass., 1957; prof. neurology and chmn. dept. sch. medicine Wayne State U., 1957-69, chmn. dept., 1969-76; prof. neurology, dir. stroke lab. Baylor Coll. Medicine, Houston, 1976—; with VA Med. cTr., Houston; chair stroke panel Pres.' Commn. on Heart Disease Cancer & Stroke, Washington, 1964-65; mem. nat. adv. coun. Nat. Inst. Neurol. Diseases & Stroke, Bethesda, Md., 1965-69. Author 28 books; contbr. 768 articles to profl. jours. Mem. jury Albert Lasker Med. Rsch. Awards, N.Y.C., 1965-69. Lt. (s.g.) Med. Corps USN, 1953-55, Korea. Recipient Harold G. Woff award, Am. Assn. for Study of Head Ache, 1977, 79, Baylor Coll. Medicine award, Houston, 1980, 85, 90, Mihara award Mihara Found., Tokyo, 1987, Bertha Lecture award Salzburg Conf., Washington, 1992. Mem. Am. Heart Assn. (bd. dirs. 1968-70, chair coun. on stroke 1968-70). Republican. Episcopalian. Achievements include development of xenon contrast method for measuring cerebral blood flow using computerized toneography. Office: VA Med Ctr Rm 225 2002 Holcombe Blvd Bldg 110 Houston TX 77030-4211

MEYER, JON KEITH, psychiatrist, psychoanalyst, educator; b. Springfield, Ill., May 6, 1938; s. Samuel Barclay and Finela Hermoine (Roehl) M.; m. Eleanor Fumie Yamashita, June 6, 1964; children: David Christopher, Laura Tamiko. AB summa cum laude, Dartmouth Coll., 1960; MD, Johns Hopkins U., 1964; grad., Washington Psychoanalytic Inst, 1980. Intern internal medicine Johns Hopkins Hosp., Balt., 1964-65, resident in psychiatry, 1965-67, 69; resident in psychiatry St. Elizabeth's Hosp., Washington, 1968; spl. asst. to dir. NIMH, Bethesda, Md., 1969-71; asst. prof. psychiatry Johns Hopkins Med. Sch., Balt., 1971-76, assoc. prof., 1976-83; prof. psychiatry Med. Coll. Wis., Milw., 1983—, prof. psychoanalysis, 1996—, prof. family medicine, 1990—; tng. and supervising analyst Chgo. Inst. for Psychoanalysis, 1987—; vice chmn. Dept. of Psychiatry, 1993—; chief psychiatry Froedtert Meml. Luth. Hosp., Milw., 1994-97; med. dir. Wis. Psychoanalytic Found., Milw., 1987-91, sec. bd. dirs., 1988-91; bd. dirs. DePaul Hosp. Author books; contbr. chpts. to books, numerous articles to profl. jours. Comdr. USPHS, 1967-71. Daniel Webster Nat. scholar Dartmouth Coll., 1956-60, sr. fellow, 1959-60, Dennison rsch. fellow Johns Hopkins Med. Sch., 1964; Erik Erikson scholar-in-residence Austen Riggs Ctr., Stockbridge, Mass., 1991-92. Fellow Am. Psychiat. Assn., Am. Coll. Psychoanalysts, Am. Coll. Psychiatrists, Am. Coll. Psychiatrists; mem. Internat. Psychoanalytic Assn., Am. Psychoanalytic Assn. (exec. councilor 1993-97, chmn. com. on exec. coun. structure and function 1995-97, sec. 1997—), Internat. Acad. Sex Rsch., Wis. Psychoanalytic Soc. (pres. 1989-91). Avocations: photography, hiking, kayaking. Office: Med Coll Wis 4th Fl 2025 E Newport Ave Fl 4 Milwaukee WI 53211-2906

MEYER, JOSEPH B., academic administrator, former state attorney general; b. Casper, Wyo., 1941; m. Mary Orr; children: Vincent, Warren. Student, Colo. Sch. Mines; BA, U. Wyo., 1964, JD, 1967; postgrad., Northwestern U., 1968. Dep. county atty. Fremont County, Wyo., 1967-69; assoc. Smith and Meyer, 1968-71; asst. dir. legis. svc. office State of Wyo., Cheyenne, 1971-87, atty. gen., 1987-95; spl. asst. to pres. Univ. Wyo., Laramie, 1995—; conductor numerous govt. studies on state codes including Wyo. probate, criminal, state adminstrn., banking, domestic rels., game and fish, state instn., employment security, worker's compensation, motor vehicle, others; conductor legis. rev. of adminstrv. rules; negotiator with Office of Surface Mining for Wyo. state preemption; instr. Wyo. Coll. Law, fall 1986; lectr. Rocky Mountain Mineral Law Found., 1977; chmn. Conf. Western Atty. Gen., 1992-93; mem. exec. com. Nat. Assn. Attys. Gen. Bd. dirs. Cheyenne Jr. League, 1982-85, Jessup PTO, 1980-81; instr. Boy Scouts Am. Mem. Rotary. Congregationalist. Avocations: golf, tennis, gardening, wood carving, rock hunting. Office: Univ Wyoming External Rels Box 3315 Laramie WY 82071

MEYER, JUDITH CHANDLER PUGH, history educator; b. Detroit, Oct. 22, 1948; d. Howard Chandler and Margaret Elizabeth (Bentley) Pugh; m. Paul Rudolph Meyer Jr., Aug. 17, 1974; children: Matthew Paul, Timothy Chandler. BA, Lawrence U., 1970; MA, U. Iowa, 1972, PhD, 1977. Tchg. asst. U. Iowa, Iowa City, 1974-76; instr. Ind. Cen. U., Indpls., 1977-78; asst. prof. history Smith Coll., Northampton, Mass., 1978-79; lectr. Fairfield (Conn.) U., 1985, 87, 89; lectr. in history U. Conn., Stamford, 1981-89; asst. prof. history U. Conn., Waterbury, 1989-95, assoc. prof. history, 1995—. Author: (monograph) Reformation in La Rochelle: Tradition and Change in Early Modern Europe, 1500-1568, 1996; contbr. articles to profl. jours. NDEA fellow U. Iowa, 1970-73, Fulbright fellow, Paris and La Rochelle, France, 1973-74, jr. faculty summer fellow and rsch. grantee The Rsch. Found., U. Conn., 1991-92. Mem. Am. Hist. Assn., Soc. for Reformation Rsch., 16th Century Studies Conf. Methodist. Avocations: reading, music, travel, hiking. Home: 184 College Park Dr Fairfield CT 06430-6365 Office: U Conn-Waterbury 32 Hillside Ave Waterbury CT 06710-2217

MEYER, KARL ERNEST, journalist; b. Madison, Wis., May 22, 1928; s. Ernest Louis and Dorothy (Narefsky) M.; m. Sarah Nielsen Peck, Aug. 12, 1959 (div. 1972); children—Ernest, Heather, Jonathan; m. Shareen Blair Brysac, Jan. 6, 1989. B.A., U. Wis., 1951; M.P.A., Princeton U., 1953, Ph.D., 1956. Reporter N.Y. Times, N.Y.C., 1952, mem. editorial bd., 1979—; editorial writer Washington Post, 1956-65, chief London Bur., 1965-70, N.Y.C. corr., 1970-71; Washington corr. New Statesman, 1961-65; sr. editor, TV critic Saturday Rev., N.Y.C., 1975-79; corr. in residence Fletcher Sch. Law and Diplomacy, Tufts U., 1979; vis. journalist fellow Duke U., Durham, N.C., 1988; vis. prof. Yale U., 1983, 90, McGraw prof. in writing Princeton (N.J.) U., 1993-94. Author: The New America, 1961, (with Tad Szulc) The Cuban Invasion, 1962, Fulbright of Arkansas, 1963, The Pleasures of Archaeology, 1971, The Plundered Past, 1973, Teotihuacán, 1975, The Art Museum: Power, Money, Ethics, 1979, Pundits, Poets and Wits: An Omnibus of American Newspaper Columns, 1990. Recipient citation for excellence Overseas Press Club, 1961, Bronze medal for edit. writing Sigma Delta; George Foster Peabody Broadcasting award 1983, Disting. Achievement award Sch. Journalism, U. Wis., 1985; Davenport Coll. of Yale U. fellow; Wisenschaftskolleg Inst. Adv. Studies (Berlin) fellow, 1994-95, Reuter fellow Oxford (Eng.) U., 1996-97. Mem. PEN Club Internat., Coun. on Fgn. Rels., NYU Soc. Fellows, Century Assn. Home: 50 W 96th St New York NY 10025 Office: NY Times 229 W 43rd St New York NY 10036-3913

MEYER, KARL WILLIAM, retired university president; b. Ft. Wayne, Ind., May 8, 1925; s. K.W. and L. (Hofacker) M.; m. Margery R. Hamman, Apr. 15, 1950; children—Mary, William, Frederick, Ann, Jean. A.B., Valparaiso U., 1948; M.F.S., U. Md., 1949; Ph.D., U. Wis., 1953; postgrad., U. Basel, Switzerland, 1948-49; postdoctoral fellow, U. Mich., 1958-59. Faculty Valparaiso U., 1952-53, Augustana Coll., 1953-55, Wis. State U., 1955-58; dean instrn., dir. grad. studies Wayne State Coll., 1959-63; asst. dir. bd. regents Wis. State Colls., Madison, 1963-64; pres. U. Wis.-Superior, 1964-87. Author: Karl Liebknecht: Man Without a Country, 1957; Contbr. articles to profl. jours. Served with USAAF, 1943-46, ETO. Home: 7012 S Maple Creek Rd Lake Nebagamon WI 54849-9220

MEYER, KATHLEEN MARIE, English educator; b. St. Louis, Oct. 29, 1944; d. Richard Henry and Leonora (Moser) Bailey; m. Thomas A. Meyer, Dec. 26, 1966; children: Richard, Amy, Mindy, Heidi. BA, Webster Coll., Webster Groves, Mo., 1966; MA, Fla. Atlantic U., 1981; postgrad., No. Ill. U., 1982—. Cert. secondary tchr., Mo., Ill. Tchr. English Notre Dame High Sch., St. Louis, 1966-67; tchr. English, chmn. dept. Rosary High Sch., Aurora, Ill., 1981-91; instr. English DeKalb Coll., Decatur, Ga., 1992—; mem. adv. bd. Univ. High Sch.; mem. joint enrollment coun. DeKalb Coll. Mem. ASCD, Nat. Coun. Tchrs. English.

MEYER, L. DONALD, retired agricultural engineer, researcher, educator; b. Concordia, Mo., Apr. 14, 1933; s. Lawrence Dick and Florence Malinda (Uphaus) M.; m. Loretta Lou Bush, Dec. 26, 1954; children: Dan W., James B., David J. Student, Cen. Coll., Fayette, Mo., 1950-51; BS in Agrl. Engring., U. Mo., 1954, MS in Agrl. Engring., 1955; PhD, Purdue U., 1964. Cert. profl. soil erosion and sediment control specialist; registered profl. engr., Ind. Agrl. engr. Agrl. Rsch. Svc., USDA, West Lafayette, Ind., 1955-73; agrl. engr. Nat. Sedimentation Lab., USDA, Oxford, Miss., 1973-93; asst. prof., assoc. prof. Purdue U., West Lafayette, 1965-73; adj. prof. agr.-biol. engring. Miss. State U., Starkville, 1975—. Contbr. articles to profl. jours. Recipient Outstanding Performance award USDA Agrl. Rsch. Svc., 1959, 88, 89, 90, 91. Fellow Am. Soc. Agrl. Engrs. (dir. publs. 1968-69, chmn. soil and water div. 1972-73, Hancor award 1985), Soil and Water Conservation Soc.; mem. Soil Sci. Soc. Am.

MEYER, LASKER MARCEL, retail executive; b. Houston, Jan. 8, 1926; s. Lasker M. and Lucille (Dannenbaum) M.; m. Beverly Jean Goldberg; children: Lynn Meyer Brown, Susan Meyer Sellinger. Student, Rice U., 1942-43. Pres. Foley's, Houston, 1979, chmn., chief exec. officer, 1982-87; chmn., chief exec. officer Abraham and Straus, Bklyn., 1980-81; vice chmn. bd. Splty. Retailers, Inc., Houston, 1989-93; bd. dirs. BookTronics, Inc., Houston. Past chmn. bd. United Way Tex. Gulf Coast. Mem. Bentwater Yacht and Country Club. Jewish.

MEYER, LAWRENCE GEORGE, lawyer; b. East Grand Rapids, Mich., Oct. 2, 1940; s. George and Evangeline (Boerma) M.; children from previous marriage: David Lawrence, Jenifer Lynne; m. Linda Elizabeth Buck, May 31, 1980; children: Elizabeth Tilden, Travis Henley. BA with honors, Mich. State U., 1961; JD with distinction, U. Mich., 1964. Bar: Wis., 1965, Ill. 1965, U.S. Supreme Ct. 1968, D.C. 1972. Assoc. Whyte, Hirschboeck, Minahan, Hardin & Harland, Milw., 1964-66; atty. antitrust div. U.S. Dept. Justice, Washington, 1966-68; legal counsel U.S. Senator Robert P. Griffin, Mich., 1968-70; dir. policy planning FTC, Mich., 1970-72; ptnr. Patton, Boggs & Blow, Washington, 1972-85, Arent, Fox, Kintner, Plotkin & Kahn, Washington, 1985-96, Gadsby & Hannah, 1996—. Contbr. articles on antitrust and trial practice to law jours.; asst. editor. U. Mich. Law Rev., 1960-61. Bd. dirs. Hockey Hall of Fame, Toronto, 1993—. Recipient Disting. Svc. award FTC, 1972. Mem. ABA, D.C. Bar Assn., Wis. Bar Assn., Ill. Bar Assn., U.S. Senate Ex S.O.B.s Club, City Tavern Club, Congl. Country Club. Home: 8777 Belmart Rd Potomac MD 20854-1610

MEYER, LAWRENCE ROBERT, journalist; b. Chgo., Nov. 27, 1941; s. Fernando Kolomon and Gertrude M.; m. Aviva Sagalovitch, June 15, 1968; children: Ariel David, Evan Asher, Noa Anne. BA, U. Mich., 1963; MA, Columbia U., 1965, MS, 1965. Reporter Times-Herald Record, Middletown, N.Y., 1965-66, Louisville Times, 1968-69; reporter Washington Post, 1969-87, editor Nat. Weekly Edit., 1987—. Author: A Capitol Crime, 1977, False Front, 1979, Israel Now: Portrait of a Troubled Land, 1982. Sgt. USMC, 1966-68. Jewish. Home: 3311 Ross Pl NW Washington DC 20008-3332 Office: Washington Post 1150 15th St NW Washington DC 20071-0001

MEYER, LEONARD B., musician, educator; b. N.Y.C., Jan. 12, 1918; s. Arthur S. and Marion (Wolff) M.; m. Janet M. Levy; children: Marion L., Carlin, Erica Cecile. Student, Bard Coll., 1936-37; BA, Columbia, 1940, MA, 1948; PhD, U. Chgo., 1954; LHD, Grinnell Coll., Loyola U., Chgo., Bard Coll., U. Chgo. Faculty U. Chgo., 1946-75, head humanities sect., 1958-60, prof. music, 1961-75, chmn. music dept., 1961-70, Phyllis Fay Horton disting. svc. prof., 1972-75; Benjamin Franklin prof. music U. Pa., 1975-88, Benjamin Franklin prof. emeritus, 1988—; fellow Ctr. for Advanced Studies, Wesleyan U., Middletown, Conn., 1960-61, Ctr. for Advanced Study in Behavioral Scis., Stanford, Calif., 1994; Ernest Bloch prof. music U. Calif., Berkeley, 1971, sr. fellow Sch. Criticism and Theory, 1975-88; resident scholar Bellagio Study and Conf. Ctr., 1982; Tanner lectr. Stanford U., 1984; Patten lectr. Ind. U., 1985. Author: Emotion and Meaning in Music, 1956, (with G.W. Cooper) The Rhythmic Structure of Music, 1960, Music, the Arts and Ideas, 1967, Explaining Music: Essays and Explorations, 1973, Style and Music: Theory, History and Ideology, 1994; gen. editor: Studies in the Criticism and Theory of Music, 1980-96; mem. editorial bd. Critical Inquiry, 1974-96, Music Perception, 1983; contbr. articles to profl. jours. Guggenheim fellow, 1971-72. Fellow AAAS, Am. Acad. Arts and Scis.; mem. Am. Musicological Soc. (hon.), Soc. Music Theory, Soc. Music Perception and Cognition, Phi Beta Kappa. Home: 165 W End Ave Apt 23M New York NY 10023-5513 Office: U of Pa Dept of Music Philadelphia PA 19104

MEYER, LOUIS B., superior court judge, retired state supreme court justice; b. Marion, N.C., July 15, 1933; s. Louis B. and Beulah (Smith) M.; m. Evelyn Spradlin, Dec. 29, 1956; children: Louis B. III, Patricia Shannon, Adam Burden. B.A., Wake Forest U., 1955, J.D., 1960; LLM, U. Va., 1992. Bar: N.C. 1960, U.S. Dist. (ea. dist.) N.C. 1960, U.S. Ct. Appeals (4th cir.) 1960, U.S. Supreme Ct. 1962. Law clk. Supreme Ct. N.C., Raleigh, 1960; spl. agent FBI, 1961-62; atty. Lucas, Rand, Rose, Meyer, Jones & Orcutt P.A., Wilson, N.C., 1962-81; assoc. justice Supreme Ct. N.C., Raleigh, 1981-95, ret., 1995; spl. judge Superior Ct., 1995—. Former county chmn. Wilson County Dems., N.C.; former mem. N.C. State Exec. Com. Dem. Party. Served to 1st lt. U.S. Army, 1955-57. Mem. Wilson County Bar Assn. (former pres.), 7th Jud. Dist. Bar Assn. (former pres.), N.C. Bar Assn. (former v.p.), Masons. Baptist.

MEYER, MARA ELLICE, special education educator, consultant; b. Chgo., Oct. 28, 1952; d. David and Harriett (Lazar) Einhorn; m. Leonard X. Meyer, July 20, 1986; children: Hayley Rebecca, David Joseph. BS in Speech and Hearing Sci., U. Ill., 1974, MS in Speech Pathology, 1975, ABD in Pub. Policy Analysis, 1990—. Cert. speech and lang. pathologist, spl. edn. tchr., reading tchr. Speech and lang. pathologist Macon-Piatt Spl. Edn. Dist., Decatur, Ill., 1975-76; speech and lang. pathologist, reading specialist, learning disabilities coord. Community Consolidated Sch. Dist. # 59, Arlington Heights, Ill., 1976-87; test cons. Psychol. Corp., San Antonio, 1987-89; adj. prof. Nat.-Lewis U., Evanston, Ill., 1985-87; ednl. cons. Am. Guidance Svc., Circle Pines, Minn., 1989-94; pvt. practice ednl. cons. Deerfield, Ill., 1994—; project dir. Riverside Pub. Co., Chgo., 1993-94; mem. adv. coun. to Headstart, Dept. Human Svsc., City of Chgo., 1990—; cons. Spl. Edn. Dist. of Lake County, 1995—, Waukegan Pub. Schs., 1997. Area coord. Dem. Party, Lake County, Ill., 1978—; pres. Park West Condo Assn., Lake County, 1983-88. Mem. NEA, ASCD, Am. Speech-Lang. and Hearing Assn., Internat. Reading Assn., Coun. on Exceptional Children. Avocations: family, golf, skiing, leisure reading, technical reading. Home: 1540 Central Ave Deerfield IL 60015-3963

MEYER, MARGARET ELEANOR, microbiologist, educator; b. Westwood, Calif., Feb. 8, 1923; d. Herman Henry and Eleanor (Dobson) M. B.S., U. Calif., Berkeley, 1945; Ph.D., U. Calif., Davis, 1961. Pub. health analyst USPHS, Bethesda, Md., 1945-46; swine Brucellosis control agt. Dept. Agr., Davis, 1946-47; bacteriologist U. Calif., Davis, 1947-61; research microbiologist U. Calif. (Sch. Vet. Medicine), 1961-77, prof. vet. pub. health and microbiologist exptl. sta., 1977—; research microbiologist U. Calif. Med. Sch., Los Angeles, 1961-77; supr. Brucella identifications lab. WHO, U. Calif.-Davis, 1964—, prof. vet. pub. health, 1973—; also dir. M.A. program in preventive vet. medicine; cons. subcom. on Brucella Internat. Com. Bacterial Taxonomy, 1962—, mem., 1966—; mem. 5th Pan Am. Congress Veterinary Medicine, Venezuela, 1966; mem. Internat. Congress Microbiology, Moscow, 1966, Mexico City, 1970, Munich, Ger., 1978, mem., officer, Eng., 1986; mem. Internat. Conf. Culture Collections, Tokyo, 1968; mem. adv. com. to Bergey's Manual Determative Bacteriology, 1967; cons. in resident Pan Am. Health Orgn., Zoonoses Lab., Buenos Aires, 1968; mem. brucellosis tech. adv. com. U.S. Animal Health Assn., 1977; FAO cons. on brucellosis control in dairy animals, Tripoli, Libya, 1981, mem. 3d internat. brucellosis symposium, Algiers, 1983; cons. Alaska Dept. Fish and Game, 1976, FAO, Libya, 1981, Bering Straits Reindeer Herders Assn., Nome, Alaska, 1981; invited speaker Internat. Symposium on Advances in Brucellosis Rsch., Tex. A&M U., 1989, Internat. Bison Conf.; resident cons. on brucellosis control in sheep and goats Am. Near East Refugee Aid, East Jerusalem, 1989; cons. on brucellosis in Yellowstone Nat. Pk., Nat. Pk. Svc., 1991—; invited mem. nat. symposium on brucellosis in the Greater Yellowstone Area, Jackson Hole, Wyo., 1994; cons. on brucellosis control in livestock for Armenia, 1994—. Contbr. articles to profl. jours. Bd. dirs. Carmichael Park and Recreation Dist., Calif., 1975. Recipient Research Career Devel. award USPHS-NIH, 1963. Fellow Am. Pub. Health Assn., Am. Acad. Microbiology; mem. Soc. Am. Microbiologists, N.Am. Conf. Animal Disease Research Workers, Am. Coll. Vet. Microbiologists (hon. affiliate), U.S. Animal Health Assn. (chmn. brucellosis tech. advisory com. 1978-79), Internat. Assn. Microbiol. Socs. (mem. 1st intersect. congress 1974), AAUW, No. Calif. Women's Golf Assn., U. Calif. Alumni Assn., Sigma Xi. Clubs: U. Calif. Faculty (Davis); El Dorado Royal Country (Shingle Springs, Calif.); Reno Women's Golf. Home: 5611 Fair Oaks Blvd Carmichael CA 95608-5503 Office: U Calif Sch Vet Medicine Dept Epidemiology & Preventive Medicine Davis CA 95616

MEYER, MARION M., editorial consultant; b. Sheboygan, Wis., July 14, 1923; d. Herman O. and Viola A. (Hoch) M. BA, Lakeland Coll., 1950; MA, NYU, 1957. Payroll clk. Am. Chair Co., Sheboygan, 1941-46; tchr. English and religion, dir. athletics Am. Sch. for Girls, Baghdad, Iraq, 1950-56; mem. edn. and publ. staff United Ch. Bd. for Homeland Ministries, United Ch. Press/Pilgrim Press, 1958-64, sr. editor, 1965-88, ret., 1988; cons. to individuals and orgns. on editorial matters and copyrights. Editor Penney Retirement Cmty. Newsletter, 1990—; contbr. articles to various publs.; writer hymns Look to God, Be Radiant, 1989, Be Still, 1990, Come, God, Creator, 1992, Something New! (extended work), 1993, Our Home is PRC, 1996. Incorporating mem. Contact Phila., Inc., 1972, bd. dirs., 1972-75, v.p., chmn. com. to organize community adv. bd., chmn. auditing com., editor newsletter, 1972-74, pres., 1974-75, assoc. mem., 1977—; mem. ofcl. bd. Old First Reformed Ch., Phila., 1984-89, Penney Meml. Ch., Penney Farms, Fla., 1997—; del. to coun. Nat. Interfaith Coalition on Aging as rep. of United Ch. of Christ, 1997—; deacon United Ch. Christ, 1984—, Mid.-East Conf. of Pa. SE Conf. United Ch. Christ, 1986-88. Honored as role model United Ch. of Christ, 1982, 85. Mem. AAUW, NOW, Nat. Mus. Women in the Arts (charter mem.), Nat. Trust for Hist. Preservation. Home: PO Box 656 Penney Farms FL 32079-0656

MEYER, MARY COELI, management consultant; b. Brighton, Mass.; d. Herbert Walter and Eleanor Louise (Beecher) M. BEd, Nat. Coll. Edn., 1965; MBA, Calif. Western U., 1977; PhD, Calif. Coast U., 1982. Educator pub./pvt. schs., univs., Ohio, Ind., Ill., Ga., 1965-72; pub. rels. Watts, Lamb, Kenyon & Herrick, Chagrin, Ohio, 1973; rsch. asst. Addressograph Multigraph, Cleve., 1973; supr. personnel AMI Brunging Divsn., Schaumber, Ill., 1974, mgr. human resources, 1975, acting dir. strategic manpower planning, tng., devel., 1976; pres. Cheshire Ltd., Chgo., Atlanta, 1977—; speaker in field. Author: Personnel Records Management, 1985, Time, Mind and Achievement, 1993, (with I. Berchtold, J. Oestreich, F. Collins) Sexual Harrassment, 1981, (with I. Berchtold) Getting the Job: How To Interview Successfully, 1982, (ednl. materials) So You Think It's Time To Change Jobs, 1976, Creative Guide to Finding Scholarships, 1977, How to Avoid an Unemployment Crisis, 1982, The Small Business Guide to Marketing, 1984, (videos) Power Pinch, 1981, The Leadership Link, 1985, Sexual Harrassment, 1985; (audio-cassette porgrams) Getting the Job: How to Interview, 1981, Demotivation/Remotivation, 1981. Avocation: mushroom hunting. Office: Cheshire Ltd 1601 Shadowbrook Dr Acworth GA 30102-2447

MEYER, MARY-LOUISE, art gallery executive; b. Boston, Feb. 21, 1922; d. Alonzo Jay and Louise (Whitledge) Shadman; m. Norman Meyer, Aug. 9, 1941; children: Wendy C., Bruce R., Harold Alton, Marilee, Laurel. BA, Wellesley Coll., 1943; MS, Wheelock Coll., 1965. Head tchr. Page Sch., Wellesley Coll., Mass., 1955-60; instr. early childhood edn. Pine Manor Coll., Brookline, Mass., 1960-65; chaplain/counselor Charles St. Jail, Boston, 1974-79; Christian Sci. practitioner, Wellesley, Mass., 1974—; owner Alpha Gallery, Boston, 1972-87; cons. Living & Learning Centers, Boston, 1966-69; 2d reader Christian Sci. Ch., 1979-82. Contbr. articles to profl. jours. Overseer Sturbridge Village, 1981—, trustee, 1986; visitor Am. Decorative Arts dept. Mus. Fine Arts, Boston, 1973—; chmn. Wellesley Voters Rights Com., 1983-84; state organizer Ednl. Channel 2 Group, Boston, 1960; cofounder Boston Assn. for Childbirth Edn., 1950; overseer Strawberry Banke Living Mus., 1987; trustee Maine Coast Artists, Rockport, Maine, 1991, v.p. Friends of Montpelier (Knox Mansion-Thomaston), 1994-96, pres. 1996—; trustee Bay Chamber Concerts, Rockport, 1990; bd. dirs. Down East Singers, 1996. Mem. Mus. Trustees Assn., Farnsworth Mus., Waldoboro Hist. Soc., Soc. for Pres. New Eng. Antiquities (mem. Maine coun.), Wellesley Coll. Club.

MEYER, MAURICE WESLEY, physiologist, dentist, neurologist; b. Long Prairie, Minn., Feb. 13, 1925; s. Ernest William and Augusta (Warnke) M.; m. Martha Helen Davis, Sept. 3, 1946; children—James Irvin, Thomas Orville. B.S., U. Minn., 1953, D.D.S., 1957, M.S., 1959, Ph.D., 1961. Teaching asst. U. Minn. Sch. Dentistry, 1954-55, USPHS fellow, 1955-56, rsch. fellow, 1956-57, mem. faculty, 1960—; prof. physiology, dentistry and neurology U. Minn., 1976-88, prof. emeritus, 1988—; investigator Ctr. Rsch. and Cerebral Vascular Disease, 1969—; dir. lab. Center Research and Cerebral Vascular Disease, 1975—; postdoctoral research fellow Nat. Inst. Dental Research, 1957-60, research fellow, 1958-61, mem. faculty, 1961—, asso. prof. neurology, 1974-80, mem. grad. faculty, 1973—; trainee Inst. Advanced Edn. in Dental Research, 1964—; vis. asso. prof., also vis. research fellow dept. physiology and Sch. Dentistry Cardiovascular Research Inst., U. Calif., San Francisco, 1971. Contbr. articles to profl. jours. Served to col. Dental Corps AUS, 1943-50. Decorated D.F.C., Air medal with 3 oak leaf clusters. Fellow AAAS; mem. ADA, Minn. Dental Soc., Internat. Assn. Dental Research (pres. Minn. sect. 1967-68), Soc. Exptl. Biology and Medicine, Am. Physiol. Soc., Microcirculatory Soc., Am. Assn. Dental Schs. (chmn. 1972-73), Can. Physiol. Soc., Sigma Xi, Omicron Kappa Upsilon. Club: Masons. Home: 560 Rice Creek Ter NE Minneapolis MN 55432-4472 Office: U Minn 6-255 Millard Minneapolis MN 55455

MEYER, MAX EARL, lawyer; b. Hampton, Va., Oct. 31, 1918; s. Earl Luther and Winifred Katherine (Spacht) M.; m. Betty Maxwell Dodds, Sept. 22, 1945; children—Scott Maxwell, Ann Culliford. AB, U. Nebr., 1940, JD, 1942. Bar: Nebr. 1942, Ill. 1946. Assoc. firm Lord, Bissell & Brook, Chgo., 1945-53; ptnr. Lord, Bissell & Brook, 1953-85; chmn. Chgo. Fed. Tax Forum, 1965, U. Chgo. Ann. Fed. Tax Conf., 1972; mem. Adv. Group to Commr. of IRS, 1967; lectr. in field. Bd. dirs. Music Acad. of the West, chmn. 1993-94. Mem. ABA (mem. council tax sec. 1969-72), Ill. Bar Assn. (mem. council tax sect. 1973-76), Nebr. Bar Assn., Chgo. Bar Assn. (chmn. taxation com. 1959-61), Am. Coll. Tax Counsel. Republican. Presbyterian. Clubs: Legal, Law (Chgo.); Valley Club of Montecito, Birnam Wood Golf. Lodge: Masons.

MEYER, MICHAEL EDWIN, lawyer; b. Chgo., Oct. 23, 1942; s. Leon S. and Janet (Gorden) M.; m. Catherine Dieffenbach, Nov. 21, 1982; children: Linda, Mollie, Patrick, Kellie. BS, U. Wis., 1964; JD, U. Chgo., 1967. Bar: Calif. 1968, U.S. Supreme Ct. 1973. Assoc. Lillick & McHose, L.A., 1967-73, ptnr., 1974-90, mng. ptnr., 1986-87; ptnr. Pillsbury Madison Sutro, 1990—, mem. mgmt. com., 1990-92; judge pro tem Beverly Hills Mcpl. Ct., Calif., 1976-79, Los Angeles Mcpl. Ct., 1980-86; lectr. in field. Bd. dirs. Bldg. Owners and Mgrs. Assn. of Greater L.A., L.A. Coun. Boy Scouts Am.; pub. counsel United Way Greater L.A., Los Angeles County Bar Found. Recipient Good Scout award L.A. coun. Boy Scouts Am., 1992, Man of Yr. award United Way, 1996. Mem. ABA, Am. Arbitration Assn. (arbitrator), Calif. Bar Assn., L.A. Bar Assn., U. Chgo. Alumni Assn. So. Calif. (pres. 1980-82), Calif. Club, U. L.A. Club (dir. 1979-85, pres. 1984-85), L.A. Country Club. Jewish. Home: 4407 Roma Ct Marina Del Rey CA 90292-7702 Office: Pillsbury Madison Sutro 725 S Figueroa St Los Angeles CA 90017-5524

MEYER, MICHAEL LOUIS, lawyer; b. Buffalo, Dec. 17, 1940; s. Bernard H. and Florence (Nusbaum) M.; m. Jo Ann Ackerman, Sept. 21, 1990. AB, Princeton U., 1962; LLB, Harvard U., 1965. Bar: Ill. 1965, D.C., 1978. Assoc. Schiff Hardin & Waite, Chgo., 1965-72, ptnr., 1972—. Lt. USN, 1965-68. Mem. ABA (mem. fed. regulation of security com.), Chgo. Bar Assn., Chgo. Coun. Lawyers, Chgo. Yacht Club, Metropolitan Club. Office: Schiff Hardin & Waite 7200 Sears Tower Ste 1200 Chicago IL 60606-6327

MEYER, MILTON EDWARD, JR., lawyer, artist; b. St. Louis, Nov. 26, 1922; s. Milton Edward and Jessie Marie (Hurley) M.; m. Mary C. Kramer, Nov. 5, 1949; children: Milton E. III, Melanie M. Meyer Francis, Daniel K., Gregory N. B.S. in Bus. Adminstrn, Washington U., 1943; LL.B., St. Louis, U., 1950; LL.M., N.Y. U., 1953. Bar: Mo. 1950, Colo. 1956. Trust adminstr. Mississippi Valley Trust Co., St. Louis, 1946-50; asso. firm Burnett, Stern & Liberman, St. Louis, 1953-56; founding partner firm Hindry & Meyer, Denver, 1956-79; chmn. bd. Hindry & Meyer, 1970-79; spl. counsel Schmidt, Elrod & Wills, and predecessors, 1979-83, pres., 1980-82; sec. C.A. Norgren Co., Littleton, Colo., 1960-78; dir. C.A. Norgren Co., 1971-78. Contbr. articles to profl. jours. Bd. dirs. Nat. Club Assn., 1971-91, pres., 1976-78; bd. dirs., pres. Denver Community Concert Assn., 1960-64; bd. dirs. Sewall Rehab. Ctr., Denver, 1965-68, Carl A. Norgren Found., 1960-70, Denver Leadership Found., 1983-93; bd. dirs. Found. Colo. Women's Coll., 1982-86, chmn., 1984-86; bd. dirs. Conf. Pvt. Orgns., 1982-89, chmn., 1984-88; chmn. Denver Rotary's Artists of Am. Exhbn., 1990-92. With airborne inf. U.S. Army, 1943-46, 50-52. Mem. ABA, Colo. Bar Assn., Denver Bar Assn., Greater Denver Tax Counsels Assn. (founder, chmn. 1957, Denver Estate Planning Coun. (founder, pres. 1958), Am. Coll. Probate Counsel, Knickerbocker Artists, Pastel Soc. Am., Pastel Soc. West Coast (Disting. Pastellist award), Internat. Assn. Pastel Socs. (founder, dir. 1994—), Salmagundi Club, Cherry Hills Country Club, Pinehurst Country Club (pres. 1979-80), Denver Execs. Club, Hundred Club Denver, Rotary (bd. dirs. 1991-93), Phi Eta Sigma, Beta Gamma Sigma, Omicron Delta Kappa, Beta Theta Pi. Republican. Roman Catholic. Home and Studio: 5784 E Oxford Ave Cherry Hills Village CO 80111

MEYER, NICHOLAS, screenwriter, director; b. N.Y.C., Dec. 24, 1945; s. Bernard Constant and Elly (Kassman) M. B.A. in Theatre and Film, U. Iowa, 1968. Assoc. publicist Paramount Pictures, N.Y.C., 1968-69; story editor Warner Bros., N.Y.C., 1970-71. Writer, dir.: (films) Time After Time, 1979 (Avoriaz Film Festival grand prize, Academy of Science Fiction, Fantasy, and Horror Films award), Company Business, 1991, Star Trek VI: The Undiscovered Country, 1991; writer: (films) Invasion of the Bee Girls, 1973, The Seven-Per-Cent Solution, 1976 (Academy award nomination best adapted screenplay 1976), Sommersby, 1993, (TV movies) Judge Dee, 1974, Please Stand By, 1975, The Night That Panicked America, 1975; dir.: (films) Startrek II: The Wrath of Khan, 1982, Volunteers, 1985, The Deceivers, 1988, (TV movies) The Day After, 1983; playwright, dir.: Loco Motives; author: (nonfiction) The Love Story, 1971, (novels) Target Practice, 1974 (Mystery Writers Guild award), The Seven-Percent Solution: Being a Reprint from the Reminiscences of John H. Watson, M.D., 1974 (Gold Dagger award British Crime Writers Assn.), The West End Horror: A Posthumous Memoir of John H. Watson, M.D., 1976, (with Barry J. Kaplan) Black Orchid, 1977, Confessions of a Homing Pigeon, 1981, The Canary Trainer, 1993. Recipient Anne Radcliffe award Count Dracula Soc. Mem. Authors Guild, Writers Guild. Democrat. Home: 13785 W Sunset Blvd Pacific Palisades CA 90272-4021 Office: Creative Artists Agy 9830 Wilshire Blvd Beverly Hills CA 90212-1804*

MEYER, PATRICIA MORGAN, neuropsychologist, educator; b. Delaware, Ohio, June 23, 1934; d. Thomas Wendell and Ceola (Drummond) Morgan; m. Donald Ray Meyer, Dec. 31, 1957; 1 dau., Julia Catherine. A.B., Ohio Wesleyan U., 1956; M.A., Ohio State U., 1958, Ph.D., 1960. Research assoc. Ohio State U., Columbus, 1960-76, prof. psychology, 1976-85, prof. psychology emeritus, 1985—. Editor Physiol. Psychology jour., 1980-85. Recipient Career Devel. award NIMH, Ohio State U., 1966-76. Fellow Am. Psychol. Assn. (bd. sci. affairs 1973-76), Midwestern Psychol. Assn., Psychonomic Soc., Soc. for Neuroscis. Republican. Methodist. Avocation: videography. Home: 476 Overbrook Dr Columbus OH 43214-3127 Office: Ohio State U Dept Psychology 1885 Neil Ave Columbus OH 43210-1222

MEYER, PAUL I., lawyer; b. St. Louis, Jan. 5, 1944. AB magna cum laude, Harvard U., 1966, JD cum laude, 1969. Bar: Calif. 1970. Atty. Latham & Watkins, San Diego. Capt. USMCR, 1970-73. Mem. ABA (Profl. Merit award 1970), San Diego County Bar Assn. Office: Latham & Watkins 701 B St Ste 2100 San Diego CA 92101-8116

MEYER, PAUL WILLIAM, arboretum director, horticulturist; b. Cin., Aug. 30, 1952; s. Edward F. and Dorothy (Schroeder) M.; m. Debra L. Rodgers, May 16, 1990. BSc, Ohio State U., 1973; MSc, U. Del., 1976; diploma, U. Edinburgh, 1988. Curator Morris Arboretum U. Pa., Phila., 1976-91, dir., 1991—. Bd. dirs. The Henry Found., 1992-93; chair Springfield Twp. planning com., Montgomery County, Pa., 1993. Mem. Am. Assn. Bot. Gardens and Arboreta (bd. dirs. Montgomery County Land Trust). Avocations: bicycling, swimming, backpacking, gardening. Office: Morris Arboretum of Univ Pa 9414 Meadowbrook Ave Philadelphia PA 19118-2624

MEYER, PEARL, executive compensation consultant; b. N.Y.C.; d. Allen Charles and Rose (Goldberg) Weissman; m. Ira A. Meyer. BA cum laude, NYU, postgrad. Statis. specialist, exec. comp. div. Gen. Foods Corp., White Plains, N.Y.; exec. v.p. and cons. Handy Assocs., Inc., N.Y.C.; founder, pres. Pearl Meyer & Ptnrs., N.Y.C., 1989—; lectr. on exec. compensation at confs. and seminars. Contbr. numerous articles to profl. jours. Recipient Entrepreneurial Woman award Women Bus. Owners N.Y., 1983. mem. Am. Mgmt. Assn., Am. Compensation Assn., Soc. for Human Resources Mgmt. (cert. accredited pers. diplomate), Women's Econ. Roundtable, Pers. Accreditation Inst., Women's Forum, Sedgewood Club, Sky Club, Phi Beta Kappa, Pi Mu Epsilon, Kappa Pi Sigma. Office: Pearl Meyer & Partners Inc 300 Park Ave 21st Fl New York NY 10022-7402

MEYER, PRISCILLA ANN, Russian language and literature educator, writer, translator; b. N.Y.C., Aug. 26, 1942; d. Herbert Edward and Marjorie Rose (Wolff) M.; m. William L. Trousdale, Sept. 15, 1974; 1 dau., Rachel V. B.A., U. Calif.-Berkeley, 1964; M.A., Princeton U., 1966, Ph.D., 1971. Lectr. in Russian lang. and lit. Wesleyan U., Middletown, Conn., 1968-71, asst. prof., 1971-75, assoc. prof., 1975-88, prof., 1988—; vis. asst. prof. Yale U., 1973; tchr. John Lyman Elem. Sch., Middlefield, Conn., 1982, 83. Editor: Dostoevsky and Gogol, 1979; Life in Windy Weather (by Andrei Bitov), 1986; Find What The Sailor Has Hidden: Vladimir Nabokov's Pale Fire, 1988; co-editor: Essays on Gogol: Logos and the Russian Word, 1992; translator stories; contbr. articles to profl. jours. Sr. scholar exchange Internat. Research and Exchange Bd., 1973; Ford Found. grantee, 1964-68, 70. Mem. Am. Council Tchrs. Russian (dir. 1983-86), Am. Assn. Tchrs. Slavic and East European Langs., Am. Assn. for Advancement of Slavic Studies, Vladimir Nabokov Soc., Tolstoi Soc., Dostoevsky Soc., Conn. Acad. Arts and Scis. Office: Russian Dept Wesleyan U Middletown CT 06459

MEYER, PUCCI, newspaper editor; b. N.Y.C., Sept. 1, 1944; d. Charles Albert and Lollo (Offer) M.; m. Thomas M. Arma, Sept. 16, 1979. BA, U. Wis., 1966. Asst. editor Look mag., N.Y.C., 1970-71; editorial asst. Look mag., Paris, 1967-69; reporter Newsday, Garden City, L.I., N.Y., 1971-73; style editor N.Y. Daily News Sunday Mag., N.Y.C., 1974-76, assoc. editor, 1977-82, editor, 1983-86; sr. editor Prodigy, White Plains, N.Y., 1987; spl. projects editor N.Y. Post, N.Y.C., 1988-89, style editor, 1990-92, food editor, 1992-93, assoc. features editor, 1993—, travel editor, 1994—. Contbr. articles to various nat. mags. Recipient Pulitzer prize as mem. Newsday investigative team that wrote articles and book The Heroin Trail, 1973. Office: NY Post 1211 6th Ave New York NY 10036

MEYER, RACHEL ABIJAH, foundation director, artist, theorist, poet; b. Job's Corners, Pa., Aug. 18, 1963; d. Jacob Owen and Velma Ruth (Foreman) M.; children: Andrew Carson, Peter Franklin. Student, Lebanon Valley Coll., 1982-84. Restaurant owner Purcy's Place, Ono, Pa., 1985-87; restaurant mgr. King's Table Buffet, Citrus Heights, Calif., 1987-89; product finalizer TransWorld Enterprises, Blaine, Wash., 1989-91; dir., support svcs. adminstr. Tacticar Found., Sacramento, 1991—; tchr. Tacticar Inst., 1995; chair Conirems, Sacramento, 1996—. Author: Year of the Unicorn, 1994. Avocations: researching, writing, painting. Studio: 3329 1/2 Douglas St Sacramento CA 95838-4649

MEYER, RAYMOND JOSEPH, former college basketball coach; b. Chgo., Dec. 18, 1913; s. Joseph E. and Barbara (Hummel) M.; m. Margaret Mary Delaney, May 27, 1939 (dec. 1985); children—Barbara (Mrs. Gerald Starzyk), Raymond Thomas, Patricia (Mrs. Thomas Butterfield), Merianne (Mrs. James McGowan), Joseph, Robert. A.B., U. Notre Dame, 1938. Asst. coach U. Notre Dame, 1941-42; basketball coach DePaul U., Chgo., 1942—. Author: How To Play Winning Basketball, 1960, Basketball as Coached by Ray Meyer, 1967, Ray Meyer, 1 Coach, 1980, Coach, 1987. Named Coach of Yr. Chgo. Basketball Writers, 1943, 44, 48, 52, Coach of Yr. Nat. Assn. Basketball Coaches, 1978-79, Sportwriters Coach of Yr., 1978, Salvation Man of Yr., 1990; recipient Marine Corps Sportsman of Yr. award, 1979, Bunn award, 1981, Victor award, 1981, Lincoln Acad. award, 1988, Nat. Basketball Coach's Golden Jubilee award; inducted into Basketball Hall of Fame, 1979, Basketball Hall of Fame Chgo., 1981, Basketball Hall of Fame Ill., Golden Anniversay award Nat. Basketball Coaches, 1992. Mem. Nat. Basketball Coaches Assn. Roman Catholic. Home: 2518 W Cedar Glen Dr Arlington Heights IL 60005-4336 Office: 1011 W Belden Ave Chicago IL 60614-3205

MEYER, RICHARD CHARLES, microbiologist; b. Cleve., May 2, 1930; s. Frederick Albert and Tekla Charlotte (Schrade) M.; m. Carolyn Yvonne Patton, Apr. 6, 1963; children: Frederick Gustav, Carl Anselm. B.Sc., Baldwin-Wallace Coll., 1952; M.Sc., Ohio State U., 1957, Ph.D., 1961. Teaching and research asst. Ohio State U., 1956-61, research assoc., 1961-62; microbiologist Nat. Cancer Inst., NIH, Bethesda, Md., 1962-64; asst. prof. vet. pathology and hygiene and microbiology U. Ill., Urbana-Champaign, 1965-68; assoc. prof. U. Ill., 1968-73, prof., 1973-89, prof. emeritus, 1989—. Served with C.E. U.S. Army, 1952-54. Mem. Am. Acad. Microbiology, AAAS, Am. Inst. Biol. Sci., Am. Soc. Microbiology, Gamma Sigma Delta, Phi Zeta. Republican. Lutheran. Home: 1504 Buckthorn Ln Mahomet IL 61853-3632 Office: Dept Vet Pathobiology U Ill at Urbana-Champaign Urbana IL 61801

MEYER, RICHARD JONAH, broadcast executive, consultant; b. Bklyn., Feb. 15, 1933; s. Max and Evelyn (Berman) M.; m. Sylvia R. Marshall, Feb. 21, 1956 (div. 1974); children: Adina, Mahlon, Rachel; m. Susan Diane Harmon, Apr. 9, 1983. BA, Stanford U., 1954, postgrad., 1954, 60, MA, 1960; PhD, NYU, 1967; postgrad., Harvard U., 1978. Prodn. asst. Sta. KQED-TV, San Francisco, 1961; dir. ednl. TV Wichita (Kans.) State U., 1961-64; v.p. Sta. WNET-TV, N.Y.C., 1965-72; gen. mgr. Sta. KCTS-TV, Seattle, 1972-82; pres., gen. mgr., chief exec. officer Stas. KERA-FM-TV, KDTN-TV, Dallas, Ft. Worth, Denton, Tex., 1982-96; cons. SUNY-Albany, 1967-68, UNESCO, Paris, 1970—, Corp. for Pub. Broadcasting, Washington, 1971—, USIA, Washington, 1972—; broadcaster-in-residence, sr. fellow East-West Ctr., 1989; adj. prof. U. North Tex., 1990, U. Tex., Dallas, 1994. Contbr. chpts. to books; exec. producer (TV series) Communications and Edn., 1967. Bd. dirs. NAEB, 1971-73, Henry Art Gallery, Seattle, 1974, PBS, 1979-84, Nat. Mus. Comm.; trustee Va. Mason Rsch. Ctr., 1979, Goals for Dallas, 1988; v.p. bd. dirs. Silent Film Festival, San Francisco, 1995—. Fulbright scholar Nat. Chengchi U., Taipei, Taiwan, China, 1996-97; Russell Sage fellow Columbia U., 1968. Mem. Nat. Assn. Underwater Instrs., Internat. Brecht Soc. Jewish. Club: City (Dallas). Office: NCCU, 64 Chinaw Rd SEC 4, Taipei Taiwan China

MEYER, RICHARD SCHLOMER, food company executive; b. Rapid City, S.D., Dec. 31, 1945; s. Harm Henry Schlomer and Marie Charolette (Hoffman) Meyer; m. Bonnie June Francis, July 15, 1970; children: Jennifer June, Christina Francis, Robert Schlomer. BS, Wash. State U., 1968, MS, 1970; PhD, Cornell U., 1974. Sr. scientist Nestle Co., New Milford, Conn., 1974-76; mgr. research and devel. Armour & Co., Scottsdale, Ariz., 1976-81; v.p. and tech. mgr. research and devel. Griffith Labs., Alsip, Ill., 1981-82; v.p. tech. dir. research and devel. Kitchens of Sara Lee, Deerfield, Ill., 1982-84, Nalley's Curtice-Burns div. Agway, Tacoma, 1984-88; tech. v.p. Western regional lab. Curtice-Burns, Tacoma, 1988-95; v.p. tech. McCain Foods, Inc., Oak Brook, Ill., 1995-96; pres. Wash. Farms, Inc., Tacoma, 1996—; strategic planning com. N.W. Food Processor's Assn., Portland, Oreg., 1985—; pres. agrl. mktg. adv. bd. State of Wash., gov. coun. on agr. and environ., 1994—; pres. adv. bd. Wash. State U. Coll. Agr. and Home Econs., bd. trustees, 1992—; mem. U.S. Trade Mission to Indonesia, 1992; adj. prof. Wash. State U., Oreg. State U.; adv. coun. on food processing Elec. Power Rsch. Inst., 1994—; adv. com. food sci. dept. Cornell U., 1994—. Contbr. articles to profl. jours.; holder 24 patents in field. Mem. exec. com. Cornell U., 1973-74, mem. adv. bd. food sci. dept., 1994; mem. bd. edn. New Milford Pub. Schs., 1975-81; bd. regents Wash. State U., 1969-70, trustee, 1992—, pres. Coll. Agr. and home econs. adv. bd., mem. food svc. and human nutrition adv. bd.; Rep. state committeeman and precinct capt., Phoenix, 1979-81; mem. indsl. food coun., food sci. dept. Oreg. State U., 1990—; mem. food engring. adv. coun. U. Calif., Davis, 1990—; mem. agrl. mktg. adv. bd. Wash. State U., 1991—; food industry rep. WSU-Kellogg Found. Edn. Sys. for U.S. Food Industry, 1994. NIH fellow, 1971, 72. Mem. Inst. Food Technologists, Internat. Rsch. Inst., Nutrition Today Soc., Wash. Agr. and Forestry Found., Can. Inst. Food Sci. and Tech., Am. Meat Sci. Assn., Coll. of Agr. and Home Econs. Alumni Assn. (pres. 1990-92), World Poultry Sci. Assn., Shriner, Masons, Phi Kappa Phi, Alpha Zeta. Mem. Christian Ch. Office: Washington Farms Inc 3813 80th St E Tacoma WA 98443-1054

MEYER, RICHARD TOWNSEND, service company executive; b. Pitts., June 28, 1925; s. Howard Christian and Florence Leonore (Miller) M.; m. Faye Marie Cornell, Nov. 5, 1986; children Cynthia, Scott, Tracy, Richard, Lisa. BS, Allegheny Coll., 1949; postgrad., U. Buffalo, 1950-53; LLB, LaSalle U., Chgo., 1962. Eastern sales mgr. Hoover Co., Canton, Ohio, 1953-55; circulation dir. Time Inc., Chgo., 1955-62; v.p. sales Macmillan, Inc., Chgo., 1962-65; exec. v.p. mktg./sales Macmillan, Inc., N.Y.C., 1965; pres. chief exec. officer MacMillan Inc., N.Y.C., 1965-72; pres. R.T. Meyers Assoc., San Diego, 1972-80; chmn., pres., chief exec. officer Exec. Transitions Internat., Inc., Washington, 1980—. Lt. USN 1942-46, PTO. Mem. Pitts. Athletic Assn., Walden Country Club, Sigma Alpha Epsilon. Republican. Avocations: golf, racquetball, sailing. Home: 1409 Kensington Pl Crofton MD 21114-2615 Office: Exec Transitions Internat Inc 1655 Fort Myer Dr Ste 1150 Arlington VA 22209-3108

MEYER, ROBERT ALAN, insurance company executive; b. N.Y.C., Mar. 20, 1946; s. Leonard and Mildred M.; m. Gail Rein, Oct. 29, 1967; children: Jonathan, Caroline. BA in Econs., Am. Internat. Coll., 1967; MBA, NYU, 1973. 2nd v.p., mgr. mcpl. bond research Smith Barney Harris Upham and Co., Inc., N.Y.C., 1973-76; 1st v.p., dir. mcpl. bond research E.F. Hutton and Co. Inc., N.Y.C., 1976-82; v.p., mgr. mcpl. bond research Merrill Lynch Pierce Fenner and Smith Inc., N.Y.C., 1982-84; pres. Bond Investors Guaranty Ins. Co., N.Y.C., 1984-90; pres., chief exec. officer Greig Fester Fin. Guaranty Brokers, Inc., N.Y.C., 1991-94; prin. Meyer Cons. Group Inc., Holmdel, N.J., 1994-97; chmn., chief exec. officer RAM Reinsurance Co. Ltd., Hamilton, Bermuda, 1997—. Mem. Soc. Mcpl. Analysts, India House, Mcpl. Forum N.Y. Home: 20 Stoney Brook Rd Holmdel NJ 07733-1120

MEYER, ROBERT ALLEN, human resource management educator; b. Wisconsin Rapids, Wis., May 31, 1943; s. Charles Harold and Viola Bertha (Stoeckmann) M.; 1 child, Timothy Charles. BA, Valparaiso (Ind.) U., 1966; MA, Mich. State U., 1967, PhD, 1972, postgrad., 1981. Asst. prof. Muskingum Area Tech. Coll., Zanesville, Ohio, 1972-74; adj. prof. U. Fla., Gainesville, 1974-80; dean acad. affairs Santa Fe Community Coll., Gainesville, 1974-80; asst. prof. Purdue U., W. Lafayette, Ind., 1982-84, Ga. State U., Atlanta, 1985-89; assoc. prof., program coord. U. N. Tex., Denton, 1989-91; Fulbright profl. scholar, Bangkok, 1991-92; coord. travel, tourism, hotel, restaurant mgmt. program U. Hawaii Manoa Campus, Honolulu, 1992—; investor, asst. mgr. LaSiene Restaurant, Ann Arbor, Mich., 1970-72; investor, cons. Cafe Brittany St. Thomas, U.S. V.I., 1974-80, owner, operator, Houston, 1980; pres. RTM Cons., Honolulu, Hawaii, 1989—; educator World Tourism Orgn., 1993—; mem. vis. ind. coun. C. of C., 1993—; club mgr. Assn. Am., 1994—. Contbr. articles to profl. jours. Recipient White House Commendation for Partnerships with Industry and Higher Edn.,1984, George Washington Medal of Honor for innovations in higher edn., Freedoms Found., 1985, 86, Achievement award in hospitality edn. Coun. of Hotel, Restaurant & Instl. Edn., 1987. Mem. Tarrant County Hotel and Motel Assn., Dallas Hotel Assn., Am. Soc. Tng. and Devel., Travel Ind. Assn. Tex., Hotel Sales & Mktg. Assn. (bd. dirs. 1985-89), Coun. of Hotel, Restaurant and Instl. Edn. (grad. com. 1989-90). Home: 2611 Ala Wai Blvd Apt 1608 Honolulu HI 96815-3907 Office: U Hawaii Manoa Campus 2560 Campus Rd Honolulu HI 96822-2217

MEYER, ROBERT LEE, secondary education educator; b. St. Joseph, Mo., July 9, 1952; s. Robert James and Jerry Lee (Patterson) M.; m. Barbara Anita Stickles, Aug. 2, 1986. BS in Edn., Mo. Western State Coll., 1974; MA in Edn., U.S. Internat. U., 1988. Cert. tchr., Calif., Mo.; cert. specialist learning handicapped, resource specialist cert., adminstr., Calif. Spl. edn. tchr., learning handicapped Mann Jr. High Sch., San Diego, 1978-80, Serra High Sch., San Diego, 1980-84, Morse High Sch., San Diego, 1984-85; magnet seminar tchr. Bell Jr. High Sch., San Diego, 1985-91; project resource tchr., dir. student activities Serra High Sch., San Diego, 1991-94, resource specialist, 1994-95; magnet coord. Ctr. for Sci., Math. and Computer Tech. Samuel Gompers Secondary Sch., San Diego, 1995—; chmn. resource com. Western Assn. Schs. & Colls. accreditation Serra High Sch., San Diego, 1995, chmn. process com. Western Assn. Schs. and Colls. accreditation Gompers Secondary Sch., San Diego, 1996-97, sch. site coun., 1992-97, gov. team mem., 1992-95, chair spl. edn. dept., 1983, mem. sch. leadership team, 1992-95, sr. class advisor, 1994-95, liaison Partnerships in Edn., 1996-97; monitor City Schs. Race Human Rels. Monitoring Team, 1991-92, African Am. students pupil advocate program adv. coun., 1995-97; restructuring coord. Senate Bill 1274 Grant, 1993-95, resource specialist, 1994-95; chmn. process com. Western Assn. Schs. and Colls. accreditation Gompers Sec. Sch., adv. com. mem. African Am. students program. Contbr.: (book) History of Andrew Meyer Family, 1989. Alternate del. Dem. Party 6th Dist. and State Conventions, Holt County, Mo., 1976. Mem. Neighborhood House, Delta Chi. Democrat. Roman Catholic. Avocations: collecting political buttons, antiques, travel.

MEYER, ROGER JESS CHRISTIAN, pediatrics educator; b. Olympia, Wash., May 14, 1928; s. Paul Eugene and Martha Bell Rogers Meyer; m. Joyce Langley, Mar. 14, 1959; children: Paul, John, William, Douglas, Nancy, Liz. BS in Chemistry, U. Wash., Seattle, 1951; MD, Washington U., St. Louis, 1955; MPH, Harvard U., 1959. Cert. pediatric bds. eligible rehab., preventive medicine, family practice. Instr. pediatrics Harvard Med. Sch., Boston, 1959-62; asst. prof. U. Vt. Coll. Medicine, Burlington, 1962-65; assoc. prof. U. Va. Sch. Medicine, Charlottesville, 1965-68; assoc. prof. pediatrics Northwestern U., Chgo., 1968-76; asst. dean U. Ill. Sch. Pub. Health, Chgo., 1974-76; prof. pediatrics and pub. health Sch. Medicine U. Wash., Seattle, 1976—; with U.S. Army Res. Med. Corps, 1982; advanced through grades to col. U.S. Army, 1986; chair, bd. dirs. community pediatrics sect. Am. Acad. Pediatrics, Evanston, Ill., 1973-74; pres. Child and Family Health Found., 1976—; bd. dirs. Nat. Com. Prevention Child Abuse, Chgo., 1974-76. Author 140 books and articles. Bd. dirs. N.W. orgn. ARC, Miller Bay Estates and Indianola Land Trust, Unitarian Universalist Ch., Bainbridge; chief pub. health Pacific Rim, U.S. Army Med. Corps 364 Civil Affairs, 1986-93; staff Madigan Army Med. Ctr.; faculty Def. Dept. JMRTC. Decorated Army Achievement medal (2) for disting. svc. 1988-89; recipient NIMH Social Sci. in Medicine award Harvard U., 1961, Children's Hosp. Ann. award, Boston, 1959; Shaller scholar U. Wash., 1950-51, NIMH Health scholar U. Rochester, 1957-58; Oxford fellow, 1992. Mem. APHA, Am. Acad. Pediat. (sect. on child devel., ethics, pediat. mil.), Marine Sci. Soc. Pacific N.W. (N.W. global epidemiology com., pres.), N.W. Pediat. Soc., Res. Officers Assn., Harvard U. Alumni Assn., Washington U. Alumni Assn. Home: 22125 Apollo Dr NE Poulsbo WA 98370-7719

MEYER, RON, agent; b. 1944; m. Kelly Chapman; children, Jennifer, Sarah, Carson. With Paul Kohner Agency, 1965-1970; agent William Morris Agency, Beverly Hills, CA, 1970-1975; co-founder, pres. Creative Artists Agency, Inc., Beverly Hills, CA, 1975-95; pres., ceo Universal City Studios Inc., Universal City, 1995—; now pres., COO MCA Inc., Universal City, Calif. Served with USMC. Office: MCA Inc 100 Universal City Plz Universal Cty CA 91608-1002*

MEYER, RUSSEL WILLIAM, JR., aircraft company executive; b. Davenport, Iowa, July 19, 1932; s. Russell William and Ellen Marie (Matthews) M.; m. Helen Scott Vaughn, Aug. 20, 1960; children: Russell William, III, Elizabeth Ellen, Jeffrey Vaughn, Christopher Matthews, Carolyn Louise. B.A., Yale U., 1954; LL.B., Harvard U., 1961. Bar: Ohio 1961. Mem. firm Arter & Hadden, Cleve., 1961-66; pres., chief exec. officer Grumman Am. Aviation Corp., Cleve., 1966-74; exec. v.p. Cessna Aircraft Co., Wichita, Kans., 1974-75; chmn. bd., chief exec. officer Cessna Aircraft Co., 1975—; bd. dirs. Western Resources, Nations Bank; presdl. appointee Aviation Safety Commn., 1987—; mem. Pres.' Airline Commn., 1993. chmn. bd. trustees 1st Bapt. Ch., Cleve., 1972-74; bd. dirs. United Way, Wichita and Sedgwick County, Wichita State U. Endowment Assn.; trustee Wesley Hosp. Endowment Assn., Wake Forest univ.; bd. govs. United Way Am., 1993—. Served with USAF, 1955-58. Recipient Collier trophy Nat. Aeronautic Assn., 1986, George S. Dively award Harvard U., 1992, Wright Bros. Meml. trophy, 1995. Mem. ABA, Ohio Bar Assn., Kans. Bar Assn., Cleve. Bar Assn., Gen. Aviation Mfrs. Assn. (chmn. bd. dirs. 1973-74, 81-82, 93-94), Wichita C. of C. (chmn. 1988—, bd. dirs.). Clubs: Wichita, Wichita Country, Pine Valley, Castle Pines, Latrobe Country, Flint Hills Nat. Home: 600 N Tara Ct Wichita KS 67206-1830 Office: Cessna Aircraft PO Box 7704 1 Cessna Blvd Wichita KS 67215-1400

MEYER, RUTH KRUEGER, museum administrator, educator, art historian; b. Chicago Heights, Ill., Aug. 20, 1940; d. Harold Rohe and Ruth Halbert (Bateman) Krueger; m. Kenneth R. Meyer, June 15, 1963 (div. 1978); 1 child, Karl Augustus. B.F.A., U. Cin., 1963; M.A., Brown U., 1968; Ph.D., U. Minn., 1980. Lectr. Walker Art Ctr., Mpls., 1970-72; instr. U. Cin., 1973-75; curator Contemporary Arts Ctr., Cin., 1976-80; dir. Ohio Found. Arts, Columbus, 1980-83, Taft Mus., Cin., 1983-93; prof. Miyazaki (Japan) Internat. Coll., 1994—; adj. prof. The Union Inst., Cin., 1994. Pub. Dialogue Mag., Columbus, 1980-83; author: (exhbn. catalogues) Sandy Rosen Vestal Vases, 1986, Oblique Illusion: An Installation by Rick Paul, 1986, David Black an American Sculptor, 1985, Brad Davis: The Pines, 1984, The American Weigh, 1983, New Epiphanies, 1982, (with others) The Tafts Collection: The First Ten Years of Its Development, 1988, The Tafts of Pike St., 1988, (exhbn. catalogue) The History of Travel: Paintings by William Wegman, 1985-90, 1990, The Artist Face to Face: Two Centuries of Self-Portraits from the Paris Collection of Gerald Shurr, 1989, Tributes to the Tafts, 1991, The Taft Museum: Its Collection and Its History, 1995, (with Madeleine Fidell-Beaufort) Collecting in the Gilded Age: art Patronage in Pittsburgh, 1997; contbr. articles to profl. jours. Recipient rsch. award Kress Found., 1967, 76; named Chevalier in the Order of Arts and Letters, Govt. of France, 1989. Mem. Internat. Assn. Art Critics, Coll. Art Assn. Democrat. Office: Miyazaki Internat College, 1405 Kano Kiyotake-Cho, Miyazaki 88916, Japan

MEYER, SANDRA W(ASSERSTEIN), bank executive, management consultant; b. N.J., Aug. 20, 1937; children—Jenifer Anne Schweitzer, Samantha Boughton Schweitzer. Student, U. Mich.; B.A. cum laude, Syracuse U., 1957; postgrad., London Sch. Econs., 1958. Advt. account exec. London Press Exchange, 1959-63; product mgr. Beecham Products Inc., Clifton, N.J., 1963-66; with Gen. Foods Co., White Plains, N.J., 1966-76; mktg. mgr. coffee div. Gen. Foods Co., 1973-74, dir. corp. mktg. planning, 1975-76; with Am. Express Co., N.Y.C., 1976-84; pres. communications div. Am. Express Co., 1980-84; mng. dir. Russell Reynolds Assocs., N.Y.C., 1985-89; sr. corp. officer corp. affairs Citicorp, N.Y.C., 1989-93; sr. partner Clark & Weinstock, N.Y.C., 1993—. Trustee Met. Opera Guild, East Hampton Guild Hall; mng. dir. Met. Opera Assn.; bd. dirs. St. Luke's Orch. Office: Clark & Weinstock 52 Vanderbilt Ave New York NY 10017-3808

MEYER, SHELDON, publisher; b. Chgo., June 8, 1926; s. Arthur Christof and Hester Truslow (Sheldon) M.; m. Margaret Mary Kirk, July 29, 1964; children: Arabella Christina, Andrew Kirk. A.B. summa cum laude, Princeton U., 1949; MA (hon.), U. Oxford, 1993. With Funk & Wagnalls Co., 1951-55; assoc. editor Grosset & Dunlap, 1955-56; with Oxford Univ. Press, N.Y.C., 1956—; editor Oxford Univ. Press, 1956-70; exec. editor Trade Books, 1970-82, v.p., 1974-79, sr. v.p., 1982-96, consulting editor, 1997—. Mem. Am. Assn. Univ. Presses (bd. dirs. 1969-71, 79-82, v.p. 1979-80), Am. Hist. Assn., Orgn. Am. Historians, Inst. Early Am. History and Culture (bd. dirs. 1985-87), So. Hist. Assn., Am. Studies Assn., Am. Musicol. Assn., Century Assn., Phi Beta Kappa. Home: 180 Riverside Dr New York NY 10024-1021 Office: Oxford U Press Inc 198 Madison Ave New York NY 10016-4308

MEYER, STUART LLOYD, cons. in field; dir. bds. SpeedFam Internat., Chandler, Ariz., Televideo Cons., Inc., Peer Mgmt. Cons., Ltd., Evanston, Ill. Office: JL Kellogg Grad Sch Mgmt 2001 Sheridan Rd Evanston IL 60208-0814 *To live and work for the sharing of ideas and feelings while helping to create atmospheres of mutuality and understanding can lead to genuine communication. One hopes such efforts will enhance harmony between people everywhere.*

MEYER, SUSAN MOON, speech language pathologist, educator; b. Hazleton, Pa., Mar. 8, 1949; d. Robert A. and Jane W. (Walters) Moon; m. John C. Meyer Jr., Feb. 16, 1989; children: Chris, Scott. BS, Pa. State U., 1971, MS, 1972; PhD, Temple U., 1983. Cert. tchr., Pa. Speech-lang. pathologist, instr. Elmira (N.Y.) Coll., 1973-74; speech-lang. pathologist Arnot-Ogden Hosp., Elmira, 1973-74; supr. Sacred Heart Hosp. Speech and Hearing Ctr., Allentown, Pa., 1974-75; speech-lang. pathology instr. Kutztown (Pa.) U., 1975-78, asst. prof., 1978-82, assoc. prof., 1982-85, prof., 1985—; owner Speech and Lang. Svcs., Allentown, 1975-87; cons. Vis. Nurses Assn., Allentown, 1975-85, Home Care, Allentown, 1975-85. Mem. Am. Speech-Lang.-Hearing Assn. (cert., councilor 1986-89, Continuing Edn. award 1982, 85, 88, 91, 93, 94, 95, 96, 97), Pa. Speech-Lang.-Hearing Assn. (cert., v.p. profl. preparation 1985-89, Appreciation award 1987, 88, 89), Northeastern Speech and Hearing Assn. Pa. (pres. 1984-86, Outstanding Dedication award 1985), Coun. Suprs. Speech-Lang. Pathology and Audiology. Avocations: family activities, cross-country skiing, British sports cars, reading. Office: Kutztown U Dept Speech-Lang Kutztown PA 19530

MEYER, SYLVAN HUGH, editor, magazine executive, author; b. Atlanta, Oct. 7, 1921; s. David Norman and Ray (Levinsohn) M.; m. Annemie Heineman, Jan. 19, 1947; children: Erica, David, Jason. A.B. in Journalism, U. N.C., 1943; D.H.L. (hon.), Oglethorpe U., 1973; DL (hon.), Fla. Internat. U., 1994. Editor The Times, Gainesville, Ga., 1950-69; editor Miami (Fla.) News, 1969-73; editor, pres. Miami/South Fla. Mag., 1975-87; pub. South Florida Home & Garden Mag., 1984-87; pub. cons., 1988—; disting. vis. prof. Fla. Internat. U., Miami, 1973-75; project dir. Commn. on Future of South, 1974; chmn. 3d Century U.S.A., Bicentennial Commn. Dade County, 1973-76; chmn., Ga. adv. com. U.S. Commn. Civil Rights, 1958-65; mem. nat. adv. coun. ACLU, 1959—; mem. adv. bd. Pulitzer prize, 1968-73, bd. dirs., 1966-73; adv. com. sch. of communications FIU, 1985—; adj. prof. journalism, U. Miami, 1986-87. Author: (with Seymour C. Nash) Prostate Cancer: Making Survival Decisions, 1994. Mem. So. Growth Policy Bd., 1980-88; mem. exec. com. So. Regional Coun., 1980-86, 92—; mem. Speaker Ho. Rep. Com. on Future of Fla., 1985-89; chair Edn. for Info. Age campaign Fla. Internat. U. Lt. USNR, 1943-46. Nieman fellow Harvard U., 1951; recipient Disting. Svc. Editorial Writing award, 1957, award Sidney Hillman Found., 1961, Dept. of Army Patriotic Civilian Svc. award, 1961, Nat. Jour. award Am. Soc. Planning Ofcls., 1961, Civic award Miami Area Jewish Com. Human Rels., 1989. Mem. City/Regional Mag. Assn. (bd. dirs. 1983-88, pres. 1986-87, Lifetime Achievement award 1991), Am. Coun. on Edn. in Journalism, Greater Miami C. of C. (bd. govs. 1970-74), U. N.C. Alumni Assn. (bd. dirs. 1973), Chattahoochee Country Club, La Gorce Country Club, Sigma Delta Chi, Tau Epsilon Phi. Home and Office: 5500 Collins Ave Apt 901 Miami FL 33140 Address: 936 Azalea Ridge Dahlonega GA 30355

MEYER, THOMAS J., chemistry educator; b. Dennison, Ohio, Dec. 3, 1941; s. Harold Arthur and Sybil (Reece) M.; m. Sandra L. Meyer, June 5, 1963; children: Tyler, Justin. BS, Ohio U., 1963; PhD, Stanford U., 1966. NATO postdoctoral research fellow U. Coll. London, 1967; asst. prof. chemistry U. N.C., Chapel Hill, 1968-72; assoc. prof. chemistry U. N.C., 1972-75, prof. chemistry, 1975—, M.A. Smith prof. chemistry, 1982-86, Kenan prof. chemistry, 1986—, chmn. dept. chemistry, 1985-90, dir. Curriculum in Applied Scis., 1991-94, vice chancellor and provost for grad. studies and rsch., 1994—; ednl. cons. Dillard U., New Orleans, 1974; mem. exec. com. Material Research Ctr., U. N.C., 1974-77; mem. NATO ASI com. on mixed valence compounds in chemistry, physics and biology, Oxford U., 1979; mem. chem. dynamics rev. NSF, 1980; adv. com. proram in molecular biology and biotechnology U. N.C., 1986—, faculty indsl. relations com. Sch. Medicine, 1986—; mem. dept. chemistry Haverford Review Com., 1986; mem. chemistry rev. com. Dept. Energy-SERI, 1986-88, chmn., 1987-88; mem. rev. com. for chemistry Argonne Nat. Lab., U. Chgo., 1987; chmn. outside rev. panel U. Rochester Sci. and Tech. Ctr., 1989-94, rev. com. for chemistry Brookhaven Nat. Lab., 1990-94. Bd. editors Inorganic Chemistry Jour., Am. Chem. Soc., 1985, Accounts Chem. Rsch., 1990—. Mem. N.C. Bd. Sci. and Tech., 1995—; bd. dirs. N.C. Biotech. Ctr., 1994—, Triangle Univs. Ctr. for Advanced Study, Inc., 1995—; bd. trustees Assoc. Univs. Inc., 1995—. Woodrow Wilson fellow, 1963-64; NSF grad. fellow, 1965-66, NATO postdoctoral fellow, 1967, Alfred P. Sloan fellow, 1975-77, Guggenheim fellow, 1983, Erskine fellow, 1985; recipient Tanner award for teaching excellence U. N.C., 1972, Dwyer medal U. NSW, Australia, 1989, Centenary medal Royal Soc. Chemistry, 1991, N.C. Disting. Chemist award N.C. Inst. of Chemists divsn. Am. Inst. Chemists, Inc., 1993, Interamerican Photochem. Soc. award, 1997. Fellow AAAS, NAS, Am. Acad. Arts and Scis.; mem. AAUP, Am. Chem. Soc. (exec. com. divsn. inorganic chemistry 1982-84, chair 1994, Charles H. Stone award Piedmont sect. 1982, Monsanto Co. award in inorganic chemistry 1990, So. Chemist of Yr. award Memphis sect. 1992, chair divsn. inorganic chemistry 1994), Royal Australian Chem. Inst. (inorganic divsn. Nyholm award 1996), Interam. Photochem. Soc. (award 1997). Office: U NC Dept Chemistry Cb 3290 Venable Hall Chapel Hill NC 27599

MEYER, THOMAS JAMES, editorial cartoonist; b. Fort Benning, Ga., May 8, 1955; s. Edward Charles and Carol (McCunniff) M. B.A., U. Mich., 1977. Congl. aide U.S. Ho. of Reps., Washington, 1977-79; free lance cartoonist, illustrator Washington Post, Fed. Times, Bus. Rev. of, Washington, 1979-81; editorial cartoonist San Francisco Chronicle, 1981—. Co-illustrator: The Church In A Democracy: Who Governs?, 1981. Mem. Am. Assn. Editorial Cartoonists. Roman Catholic. Office: San Francisco Chronicle 901 Mission St San Francisco CA 94103-2905*

MEYER, TODD KENT, secondary school educator; b. Spencer, Iowa, Sept. 3, 1964; s. Cleber Daniel and Marlys Elaine (Fie) M.; m. Lynette Elizabeth Frohrip, Jan. 1, 1994. BA in Comm./Theater Arts, U. No. Iowa, 1987, BA in Social Sci. Edn., 1990; MA in History, U. S.D., 1995. Tchr. Am. history Waterloo East (Iowa) H.S., 1990; tchr. Am. studies, Am. history Watertown (S.D.) H.S., 1990—; drama dept. dir. Watertown H.S., 1993-95; adv. WHS Travel Club, 1992—; treas. Social Sci. Consortium S.D., 1996—; state contact person Nat. Coun. History Edn., 1996—. Contbr. articles to local newspapers. Vol. ARC, Cedar Falls, Iowa, 1985-90, Spl. Olympics, Cedar Falls, 1985-90; bd. dirs. Watertown Town Players Cmty. Theater, 1992-95. NEH Thomas Jeffer Seminar fellow, 1992, Monticello-Stratford Hall Summer Seminar, Thomas Jefferson Meml. Found., 1993, James Madison Meml. Found. fellow, 1993-95. Mem. S.D. Social Studies Coun. (pres. 1993-94, treas. 1996—). Home: 521 4th St NE Watertown SD 57201-2547 Office: Watertown High Sch 200 9th St NE Watertown SD 57201-2863

MEYER, URSULA, library director; b. Free City of Danzig, Nov. 6, 1927; came to U.S., 1941; d. Herman S. and Gertrud (Rosenfeld) M. BA, UCLA, 1949; M.L.S., U. So. Calif., 1953; postgrad., U. Wis., 1969. Librarian Butte County (Calif.) Library, 1961-68; asst. pub. libraries div. library devel. N.Y. State Library, Albany, 1969-72; coordinator Mountain Valley Coop. System, Sacramento, 1972-73; chmn. 49-99 Coop. Library System, Stockton, Calif., 1974-85; dir. library services Stockton-San Joaquin County Pub. Library, 1974-94. Higher Edn. Title II fellow, 1968-69. Active Freedom to Read Found. Mem. ALA (council 1979-83, chmn. nominating com. 1982-83, legis. com. 1985-87), Calif. Library Assn. (pres. 1978, council 1974-82), Am. Assn. Pub. Adminstrs., Sierra Club. AAUW, LWV, Common Cause. Lodges: Rotary, Soroptimists.

MEYER, WALTER H., retired food safety executive, consultant; b. Cin., Aug. 19, 1922; s. Walter R. and Daisy M. (Spaulding) M.; m. Margaret M. Motz, Sept. 30, 1944; children: Walter H. Jr., Stephen E., Elizabeth A. Meyer Smith. BSChE, Mich. State U., 1948. Assoc. dir. food product devel. Procter & Gamble, Cin., 1948-88; chmn. sci. adv. group Nat. Coffee Assn., 1962-77; chmn. food industry liaison to AMA Food and Nutrition Com., Chgo., 1975-80; chmn. tech. com. Edible Oils Inst., Washington, 1960-88, Grocery Mfrs. Assn., Washington, 1978. Mem. coun. Amberley Village, Ohio, 1963-84. 1st lt. U.S. Army, 1943-46, ETO. Republican. Presbyterian. Avocation: farming. Home: 7651 Sagamore Dr Cincinnati OH 45236-3015

MEYER, WILLIAM DANIELSON, retired department store executive; b. Mpls., May 5, 1923; s. J.A. and Florence (Danielson) M.; m. Betty Ann McBride, May 28, 1950; children—Patricia Ann, Janet Elizabeth, Jean Louise. BS, UCLA, 1947. With actuarial dept. Prudential Ins. Co. Am., L.A., 1948-53; with Carter Hawley Hale Stores, Inc., L.A., 1953-93; ret. L.A., 1993; asst. sec. Carter Hawley Hale Stores, Inc., 1962-64, sec., 1964-73, dir. employee benefits, asst. sec., 1973-93. Bd. dirs. Profit Sharing Coun., chmn., 1984-86; bd. dirs. Travelers Aid Soc., L.A., pres., 1976-77; trustee Profit Sharing Rsch. Found.; v.p. U.S. Diving Found., 1982-84, 90-94, trustee, 1994—. Mem. Am. Soc. Corp. Secs., Personnel and Indsl. Relations Assn., Los Angeles C. of C., Gold Key, Sigma Pi (Founder's award 1992), Alpha Kappa Psi, Phi Phi. Republican. Presbyterian. Home: 1725 Durklyn Ct San Marino CA 91108-2035

MEYER, WILLIAM MICHAEL, mortgage banking executive; b. Fort Wayne, Ind., Oct. 21, 1940; s. Henry and Lola Mae (Leedy) M.; m. Phyllis Ann Ruetschilling, Aug. 12, 1961; children: Michael Dean, Blaine Aaron, Nathan Daniel, Andrea Rene. Degree in Bus., Ind. U., 1970. V.p. Waterfield Mortgage Corp., Fort Wayne, 1963-73, First Nat. Bank, Colorado Springs, Colo., 1973-78, Underwood Mortgage Co., Lawrenceville, N.J., 1978-79, Data Link Systems, South Bend, Ind., 1979-82; sr. v.p. Inland Mortgage Corp., Indpls., 1982—; bd. dirs. Ctrl. Ind. Quality Leadership Forum, Indpls. Bd. dirs. Edyvean Repertory Theatre, 1996—. Mem. Mortgage Bankers Assn. (mem. com. 1979—), Ind. Mortgage Bankers (bd. dirs. 1992—), Rotary (Zionsville bd. dirs. 1990-93). Republican. Roman Catholic. Avocations: skiing, gardening, swimming, golf. Home: 8025 Allisonville Rd Indianapolis IN 46250-1771

MEYER-BAHLBURG, HEINO F. L., psychologist, educator; b. Hamburg, Germany, Feb. 26, 1940; came to U.S., 1969; s. Wilhelm and Marie Luise Meyer-B. Vordiplom in Psychology, U. Hamburg, 1963, Diplom Psychology, 1966; Dr.rer.nat., U. Duesseldorf, 1970. Sci. asst. U. Duesseldorf, 1970; rsch. asst., then rsch. assoc. prof. psychiatry and pediatrics SUNY Med. Sch., Buffalo, 1970-77; rsch. scientist N.Y. State Psychiat. Inst., N.Y.C., 1977—; from assoc. clin. prof. med. psychology to prof. clin. psychology in psychiatry Columbia U. Coll. Physicians and Surgeons, 1978—; pediatric behavioral endocrinologist in psychiat. svc. prof. psychology Presbyn. Hosp., N.Y.C., 1978—. Contbr. numerous articles to profl. pubs. Recipient Disting. Sci. Achievement award Soc. for Sci. Study of Sex, 1993; grantee NIMH. Mem. AAAS, APA, Soc. Pediatric Psychology, Internat. Acad. Sex Rsch., Internat. Soc. Rsch. on Agression, German Sexual Rsch. Soc., Internat. Soc. Psychoneuroendocrinology, Soc. Sci. Study Sex, Soc. Rsch. Child Devel., Soc. Sexual Therapy and Rsch., Lawson Wilkins Pediatric Endocrine Soc., Harry Benjamin Internat. Gender Dysphoria Assn., Internat. AIDS Soc. Office: Columbia U. Dept Psychiatry 722 W 168th St Unit 10 New York NY 10032-2603

MEYERHOFF, ERICH, librarian, administrator; b. Braunschweig, Germany, Nov. 24, 1919; came to U.S., 1935; s. Karl and Irma Meyerhoff; m. Inge Zuber; children—Tina, C. Michael. B.S., CCNY, 1943; M.S., N.Y. Sch. Social Work, 1949; M.S.L.S., Columbia U., 1951, cert. advanced librarianship, 1974. Social worker various orgns., to 1951; reference librarian Columbia U. Med. Library, N.Y.C., 1951-57; librarian, asst. prof. Downstate Med. Ctr., SUNY, Bklyn., 1957-61; dir. Med. Library Ctr. N.Y., 1961-67; librarian Health Scis. Library, SUNY-Buffalo, 1967-70; librarian Cornell U. Med. Coll., N.Y.C., 1970-86, asst. dean, 1977-86; chief library service VA Med. Ctr., N.Y.C., 1986-88; archives librarian NYU Med. Ctr., 1980-91; adj. instr. biomed. communications Columbia U., 1976-81; cons. U. Mich., Ann Arbor, 1968, N.Y. Met. Reference and Research Library Agy., 1968-69, Coll. Physicians of Phila., 1969-70. Fellow Med. Library Assn. (cert., bd. dirs. 1972-76, chmn. various coms. 1968-72, 78-81, Inst. for Sci. Info. award 1981-82, Janet Doe lectr. 1977), N.Y. Acad. Medicine; mem. AAAS, AAUP, Spl. Libraries Assn., Archons of Colophon, am. Assn. for the History of Medicine, Am. Printing History Assn., Met. New York Archivists Roundtable, Soc. of Am. Archivists. Avocations: traveling, hiking. Home: 90 La Salle St New York NY 10027-4720 Office: NYU Med Ctr Archives 550 1st Ave New York NY 10016-6481

MEYERHOFF, JACK FULTON, financial executive; b. Joliet, Ill., May 15, 1926; s. Charles F. and Helen (Ferguson) M.; m. Mary Margaret Williams, Jan. 2, 1949; children—Keith F., Greg H., Deborah S., Todd C. B.S., Miami U., Oxford, Ohio, 1947; postgrad., Ohio Wesleyan U., 1944-45; grad. Advanced Mgmt. Program, Harvard U., 1968. C.P.A., Ohio, Ill. Mgr. Arthur Andersen & Co., Chgo., Cin., Cleve., 1947-59; treas. MacGregor Sports, Cin., 1959-63; v.p., corp. controller Brunswick Corp., Chgo., 1963-77; chief fin. officer Brunswick Corp., 1972-77, v.p. corp. affairs, 1977-80, v.p. human resources, 1980-81; chmn., chief exec. officer MarJac Assocs., Nokomis, Fla., 1981—; pres., dir. Charles Oxford Corp., Nokomis, 1984—; bd. dirs. Sherwood Med. Industries, Inc., Old Orchard Bank & Trust Co., Tech: Time Inc., Nokomis; organizer, vice chmn. bd. trustees Caldwell Trust Co. and Trust Cos. Am., Venice, Fla., 1993—. Treas., bd. dirs. Cove Schs.; bd. dirs., pres. Skokie Valley Cmty. Hosp., No. Ill. Indsl. Assn.; v.p., bd. dirs. Jr. Achievement; bd. dirs. Chgo. Responsibility Growth, Gulf Area Med. Properties; chmn. bd. Bon Secours-Venice Hosp., Venice Hosp. Found.; bd. dirs. J. Clifford MacDonald Handicapped Ctr. of Tampa, Sarasota Com. of 100, Triangle Econ. Devel. Coun., Manatee Cmty. Coll. Found.; mem. adv. coun. Miami U., Georgetown U., U. So. Fla. With USNR, 1944-46. Mem. Am. Inst. C.P.A.s, Ohio Soc. C.P.A.s, Ill. Soc. C.P.A.s, Fin. Execs. Inst., Nat. Assn. Accts., Harvard Bus. Sch. Alumni Assn., Miami U. Exec. Alumni Council (bd. dirs., treas.), Venice Area C. of C. (bd. dirs.), Sigma Alpha Epsilon, Delta Sigma Pi, Beta Alpha Psi, Beta Gamma Sigma. Methodist. Clubs: Venice Yacht, Mid America, Economic, Misty Creek Country, Saddlebrook Country. Lodges: Masons, Rotary. Home: 20 Inlets Blvd Nokomis FL 34275-4108 Office: MSW Assocs PO Box 1326 Nokomis FL 34274-1326

MEYERHOFF, JAMES LESTER, medical researcher; b. Phila., Dec. 12, 1937; s. Lester Bacharach and Natalie Hatch (Rosenberg) M. BA, U. Pa., 1962, MD, 1966. Diplomate Nat. Bd. Med. Examiners, Am. Bd. Psychiatry and Neurology; lic. physician, Md. Intern Misericordia Hosp., Phila., 1966-67; resident U. Chgo. Hosp., 1967-70; postdoctoral fellow Johns Hopkins U., 1970-71; rsch. assoc. Walter Reed Army Inst. Rsch. and Med. Ctr., Washington, 1971-72, head neurochemsitry sect., 1972-74, chief dept. neuroendorcinology, 1974-76, chief neuroendocrinology and neurochemistry bd., 1976—; rsch. prof. psychiatry Uniformed Svcs. U. Health Scis., 1978, 96, rsch. prof. neurology, 1996; clin. assoc. prof. psychiatry Georgetown U., 1977. Contbr. numerous articles to profl. jours.; mem. editl. bd. Psychosomatic Medicine. Maj. M.C., U.S. Army, 1969-72. Fellow APA, Acad. Behavioral Medicine; mem. Am. Psychosomatic Soc., Soc. for Neurosci. Office: Walter Reed Army Inst Rsch & Med Ctr Washington DC 20307-5100

MEYEROWITZ, ELLIOT MARTIN, biologist, educator; b. Washington, May 22, 1951; s. Irving and Freda (Goldberg) M.; m. Joan Agnes Kobori, June 17, 1984; 2 children. AB, Columbia U., 1973; MPhil, Yale U., 1975, PhD, 1977. Rsch. fellow Stanford U., Calif., 1977-79; asst. prof. biology Calif. Inst. Tech., Pasadena, 1980-85, assoc. prof. 1985-89, prof., 1989—, exec. officer, 1995—. Mem. editl. bd. Trends in Genetics, Current Biology, Cell, Devel.; contbr. articles to profl. jours., 1978—. Recipient LVMH Sci. pour l'Art Sci. prize, 1996; Jane Coffin Childs Meml. Fund fellow, 1977-79, Sloan Found. fellow, 1980-82. Fellow AAAS; mem. NAS, Am. Acad. Arts and Scis., Am. Soc. Plant Physiologists (Gibbs medal 1995), Bot. Soc. Am. (Pelton award 1994), Genetics Soc. Am. (medal 1996), Internat. Soc. Devel. Biology (bd. dirs.), Internat. Soc. for Plant Molecular Biology (pres. 1995-97, bd. dirs.). Office: Calif Inst Tech Divsn Biology Pasadena CA 91125

MEYERROSE, SARAH LOUISE, bank holding company executive; b. Jefferson City, Mo., Nov. 26, 1955; d. William J. and Mary L. (Fricke) Wollenburg; m. Michael J. Meyerrose, Aug. 18, 1978. BA, Vanderbilt U., 1978, MBA, 1987. Chartered fin. analyst. Corp. fin. asst. Commerce Union Corp., Nashville, 1978-80, money market sales rep., 1980-82; asst. treas. First Tenn. Nat. Corp., Memphis, 1982-84, v.p., treas., 1984-88, v.p. sr. fin. officer, 1988-90; sr. v.p. fin. & adminstrn. First Tenn. Nat. Corp., 1990-93; exec. v.p. retail, mortgage, trust First Tenn. Bank, N.A., Johnson City, 1993-95; pres. First Tenn. Bank, N.A., Kingsport, 1996—; guest lectr. Vanderbilt U., 1987; instr. Am. Inst. Banking, Memphis, 1985, Tenn. Bankers Assn., Nashville, 1987, 88, 89. Chair Johnson City Symphony Orch., 1994-95; bd. dirs. United Way, Kingsport Tomorrow, Girls, Inc., YMCA, Salvation Army. Mem. Fin. Analysts Fedn., Kingsport C. of C. (bd. dirs.), Econs. Club Memphis. Avocations: ch. organist and pianist, choir dir. Office: First Tenn Bank NA 235 E Center St Kingsport TN 37660-4303

MEYERS, ABBEY S., foundation administrator; b. Bklyn., Apr. 11, 1944; d. Herbert and Blossom (Ruben) Feldman; m. Jerrold B. Meyers, Oct. 23, 1966; children: David, Adam, Laura. AAS, N.Y.C. Community Coll., 1962. Comml. artist various advt. agys., N.Y.C., 1962-65; dir. patient svcs. Tourette Syndrome Assn., Bayside, N.Y., 1980-85; exec. dir., founder Nat. Org. for Rare Disorders, New Fairfield, Conn., 1985-95, pres., 1995—; U.S. commr. Nat. Commn. on Orphan Diseases, Washington, 1986-89; mem. subcom. Human Gene Therapy NIH, Bethesda, Md., 1989-92; mem. recombinant DNA adv. com. NIH, 1992-96; mem. Health Care Payor Adv. Commn. on Conn. Commn. on Hosps. and Health Care, 1992-94. Author: (with others) Orphan Drugs and Orphan Diseases: Clinical Reality and Public Policy, 1983, (with others) Cooperative Approaches to Research and Development of Orphan Drugs, 1985, (with others) Tourette Syndrome: Clinical Understanding and Treatment, 1988, (with others) Physicians Guide to Rare Diseases, 1992. Bd. dirs. Nat. Orphan Drug and Device Found., N.Y.C., 1982-85; leader Coalition to Pass Orphan Drug Act of 1983, 1979-82. Recipient Pub. Health Svc. award HHS, 1985, Commr.'s Spl. citation FDA, 1988. Mem. Nat. Health Coun. (bd. dirs. 1989-94), Alliance of Genetic Support Groups (bd. dirs. 1987-89). Avocations: reading, horseback riding. Office: Nat Org for Rare Disorders PO Box 8923 Fairwood Profl Bldg New Fairfield CT 06812*

MEYERS, ALBERT IRVING, chemistry educator; b. N.Y.C., Nov. 22, 1932; s. Hyman and Sylvia (Greenberg) M.; m. Joan Shepard, Aug. 10, 1957; children—Harold, Jill, Lisa. BS, NYU, 1954, PhD, 1957. Rsch. chemist Cities Svc. Oil Co., Cranbury, N.J., 1957-58; asst., assoc. prof., prof. La. State U., New Orleans, 1958-70, Boyd prof., 1969; prof. Wayne State U., Detroit, 1970-72; prof. Colo. State U., Fort Collins, 1972—, disting. prof., 1986—, John K. Stille prof. chemistry, 1993—; spl. postdoctoral fellow Harvard U., Cambridge, 1965-66; cons. G.D. Searle Co., Skokie, Ill., 1972-84, Mid-West Rsch. Inst., Kansas City, Mo., 1974-77, NIH, Bethesda, Md., 1977-79, 85-89, Bristol-Myers Squibb Co., 1983-95, Roche Bioscience, 1989—, Smith Kline Beecham Co., 1994—. Editor Jour. Am. Chem. Soc., 1979-85; mem. editl. adv. bd. Jour. Organic Chemistry, 1990-95, Tetrahedron, 1990—, Jour. Chem. Soc. Perkin, 1993, Jour. Chem. Soc. Chem. Commn., 1996; contbr. over 400 articles to profl. jours. Recipient Alexander von Humboldt award Fed. Republic of Germany, 1984, Disting. Alumni award NYU, 1990, award in synthetic chemistry Am. Chem. Soc., 1985, A.C. Cope award, 1987, Yamada prize, Japan, 1996, award Internat. Soc. Heterocyclic Chemistry, 1997; named Man of Yr., New Orleans Jaycees, 1968, Boyd Prof. La. State U., 1969. Fellow AAAS, Nat. Acad. Sci.; mem. Royal Soc. Chemistry (silver medalist 1982), Phila. Organic Chemistry Soc. (Allan Day award 1987). Home: 1500 Hepplewhite Ct Fort Collins CO 80526-3822 Office: Colorado State Univ Dept Chemistry Fort Collins CO 80523

MEYERS, ARTHUR SOLOMON, library director; b. N.Y.C., Dec. 14, 1937; s. Nathan and Selma (Leeser) M.; m. Marcia Indianer, June 11, 1961; children: Naomi, Ruth. AB in History, U. Miami, 1959; MS in LS, Columbia U., 1961; MA in English, U. Mo., St. Louis, 1980; MA in History, Ball State U., Muncie, Ind., 1987. Cert. libr. I, Ind. Young adult libr. N.Y. Pub. Libr., N.Y.C., 1959-61; adult and young adult libr. Detroit Pub. Libr., 1963-67; adult and young adult specialist Enoch Pratt Free Libr., Balt., 1967-73; mgr. brs. and cmty. svc. St. Louis Pub. Libr., 1973-80; dir. Muncie Pub. Libr., 1980-86, Hammond (Ind.) Pub. Libr., 1986-97, Russell Libr., Middletown, Conn., 1997—; past pres. Ednl. Referral Ctr., Lake County, Ind.; condr. workshops and insts. in field; presenter in field; past pres. N.W. Ind. Area Libr. Svcs. Authority: mem. Libr. Svcs. to Aging Population Com., Reference and Adult Svcs. Divsn. Contbr. articles to profl. jours. Past sec. Calumet Ethnic Heritage Alliance, Lake County, past panelist Ind. Humanities Coun., Ind. Arts Commn. With U.S. Army, 1961-63. Mem. ACLU, NAACP, ALA (pres. reference and adult svcs. divsn. 1989-90), Ind. Jewish Hist. Soc. (past pres.), Ind. Hist. Soc., Freedom To Read Found., Democrat. Jewish. Avocations: local and family history research, ethnic heritage research, reference book reviewing. Home: 538 Town Colony Dr Middletown CT 06457-5911 Office: Russell Libr 123 Broad St Middletown CT 06457-3327

MEYERS, DOROTHY, education consultant, writer; b. Chgo., Jan. 9, 1927; d. Gilbert and Harriet (Levitt) King; m. William J. Meyers, Oct. 9, 1947; children: Lynn, Jeanne. BA, U. Chgo., 1945, MA, 1961, postgrad.; postgrad. Columbia U., New Sch. Social Rsch., Northwestern U. Instr. sr. adults, Chgo. Bd. and/City Colls. Chgo., 1961-78; coord. pub. affairs forum and health maintenance program City Colls. Chgo.-Jewish Community Ctrs., Chgo., 1975-78; lectr. adult program City Colls. Chgo., 1984; tchr. Dade County Adult Edn. Program, Miami, Fla., 1983-85; discussion leader Brandeis U. Adult Edn., 1985-86; cons., lectr. in field. Contbr. articles to profl. jours. Chmn. legis. PTA; discussion leader Great Decisions, 1984-86; chmn. civic assembly Citizens Sch. Com.; v.p. community rels. Womens Fedn. and Jewish United Fund; discussion leader LWV, Gt. Decisions, Fgn. Policy Assn.; program chmn. Jewish Community Ctrs., 1966-67, mem. sr. adult com.; bd. dirs. coun. Jewish Elderly, Open U.; mem. art and edn. com. Chgo. Mayor's Com. for Sr. Citizens and Handicapped; mem. com. on media Met. Coun. on Aging; active Bon Secour's Villa Maria Hosp.; founder Mt. Sinai Hosp., Miami Beach; sponsor Miami Heart Inst.; active Royal Notable Alzheimer Care Unit-Douglas Home Miami; com. mem. March of Dimes; amb. Project Newborn U. Miami Pre Natal Unit. Recipient Prima Donna award Men's Opera Guild-Fla., 1995, Miami Children's Hosp. honor, 1996. Mem. ASA, Gerontol. Assn., Nat. Coun. Aging, Nat. Coun. Jewish Women, Women's Auxiliary Jewish Community Ctr., Chgo. Met. Sr. Forum (media com.), Coun. Women Chgo. Real Estate Bd., Women in Communications,

Chgo. Real Estate Bd., Nat. Assn. Real Estate Bds., Cultural Ctr. (Miami, Fla.), Mus. Art Ft. Lauderdale, Miami Internat. Press Club, Gastrointestinal Rsch. Found., Brandeis U., Art Inst. Chgo., Mus. Contemporary Art (life), Mus. Art Boca Raton, Brandeis Women's Auxiliary, Circumnavigator Club (Chgo. and Fla. chpts.). Office: 77 W Washington St Chicago IL 60602-2801

MEYERS, EDWARD, photographer, writer, publisher; b. Flushing, N.Y., Nov. 2, 1934; s. Gerson G. and Hester (Noble) M.; m. Marcia Rothman, June 29, 1958; children: Beth, Adam, Rosemarie. BFA, Rochester (N.Y.) Inst. Tech., 1957. Tech. editor Modern Photography mag., N.Y.C., 1957-66; photographer-writer N.Y.C., 1966-70; exec. editor Popular Photography mag., N.Y.C., 1971-86; assoc. pub. Silver Halide Press, N.Y.C., 1986—; lectr. Sch. Visual Arts, 1968—; U.S. corr. FotoPro Reflex mag., Italy, FotoVideo, Spain. Editor: Modern Photography Photo Almanac, 1967, 69; co-editor: The Official Depth of Field Tables, 1962. Served with U.S. Army, 1957-58. Recipient Alumni Achievement award Rochester Inst. Tech., 1972, Art Dir.'s Gold award, 1986. Mem. N.Y. Press Photographers Assn., Am. Soc. Picture Profls., Internat. Assn. Panoramic Photographers, N.Y.C. Audubon Soc., Joint Ethics Com., Nat. Writers Union. Home: 61-68 77th St Middle Village NY 11379

MEYERS, ERIC MARK, religion educator; b. Norwich, Conn., June 5, 1940; s. Karl D. and Shirlee M. (Meyer) M.; m. Carol Lyons, June 25, 1964; children: Julie Kaete, Dina Elisa. AB, Dartmouth Coll., 1962; MA, Brandeis U., 1964; PhD, Harvard U., 1969. Prof. religion, archeology, biblical studies, ancient hist. Duke U., Durham, N.C., 1969—; dir. Annenberg Inst., Phila., 1991-92; pres. Am. Schs. of Oriental Rsch., Balt., 1990-96. Author 10 books; co-author: The Cambridge Companion to the Bible, 1997; editor-in-chief The Oxford Encyclopedia of Archaeology in the Near East, 5 vols., 1997; contbr. more than 300 articles to profl. jours. Jewish. Avocation: singing (baritone). Home: 3202 Waterbury Dr Durham NC 27707-2416 Office: Duke U PO Box 90964 Bldg Durham NC 27708-0964

MEYERS, GEORGE EDWARD, plastics company executive; b. N.Y.C., June 26, 1928; s. Sol and Ethel (Treppel) M. Student, Sampson Coll., 1948-49, Columbia U., 1949-50; m. Marianna Jacobson, June 12, 1955; children: Deborah Lynn, Joanne Alyssa. Technician Manhattan Project, 1944; tech. rep. Mearl Corp., 1952-56; sales mgr. Rona Labs., Bayonne, N.J.1956-59; v.p. Dimensional Pigments Corp., Bayonne, 1959-60; pres. Plastic Cons. Internat., Inc., Dix Hills, N.Y., 1959—, Tech. Machinery Corp., Plainview, N.Y., 1963-69; pres. Extrudyne, Inc., Amityville, N.Y., 1970-77, also bd. dirs.; bd. dirs. rsch. and devel. Homeland Industries, Bohemia, N.Y., 1977-80; bd. dir. ops. Aqua-Sol, Inc., Deer Park, N.Y., 1980-85; tchr., staff cons. N.Y.C. Bd. Higher Edn., Bronx C.C., 1966-70; lectr. NYU, Technion, Haifa, Israel; lectr. in field. Patentee in field; contbr. articles to profl. jours. Served with CIC, AUS, 1946-48. Mem. Soc. Plastics Engrs. (sr. mem., v.p. N.Y. sect. 1967-68), Soc. Plastics Industry (profl. mem.), Am. Ordnance Assn., Aircraft Owners and Pilots Assn, NRA (life mem., cert. instr.), Am. Chem. Soc., Internat. Assn. Housing Sci. (charter mem.), Internat. Assn. Soilless Culture, Army Counter-Intelligence Corps Assn., U.S. Constabulary Assn. Seminar conductor in plastics and hydroponics and seminar leader Modern Plastics Mag. courses. Avocations: flying, numismatics, pistol shooting, antique collector, tech. expert to legal firms and qualified expert witness in state and federal courts. Home and Office: 25 Penn Dr Dix Hills NY 11746-8532

MEYERS, GERALD CARL, management consultant, author, educator, lecturer, former automobile company executive; b. Buffalo, Dec. 5, 1928; s. Meyer and Berenice (Meyers) M.; m. Barbara Jacob, Nov. 2, 1958. BS, Carnegie Inst. Tech., 1950, MS with distinction, 1954. With Ford Motor Co., Detroit, 1950-51, Chrysler Corp., Detroit and Geneva, 1954-62; with Am. Motors Corp., Detroit, 1962—; v.p. Am. Motors Corp., 1967-72, group v.p. product, 1972-75, exec. v.p., 1975-77, pres., 1977—, chief operating officer, 1977, chief exec. officer, 1977—, chmn., 1978-82; pres. Gerald C. Meyers Assocs., Inc., West Bloomfield, Mich.; Ford disting. prof. Carnegie Mellon U. Grad. Sch. Indsl. Adminstrn.; prof. Sch. Bus. U. Mich., Ann Arbor; expert witness. Served as 1st lt. USAF, 1951-53. Decorated French Legion of Honor. Mem. Econ. Club Detroit, Tau Beta Pi, Phi Kappa Phi, Omicron Delta Kappa. Office: 5600 W Maple Rd Ste 216B West Bloomfield MI 48322-3707

MEYERS, HAROLD VERNON, chemist; b. New Orleans, Feb. 21, 1961; s. Albert Irving and Joan (Shepard) M.; m. Jane Allin Bybee, Aug. 9, 1986; 1 child, Kimberly Allin. BS, Colo. State U., 1982; PhD, Yale U., 1988. Postdoctoral fellow Columbia U., N.Y.C., 1988-89; scientist Vertex Pharms., Cambridge, Mass., 1989-93; head Cambridge rsch. Sphinx-Cambridge div. Eli Lilly & Co., 1993—. Editor Dodecahedron Abstracts, Yale U., 1984-85, Chem. Highlights, Columbia U., 1988-89; contbr. articles to profl. jours. Univ. fellow Yale U., 1982-86. Mem. ACS (div. medicinal chemistry, div. organic chemistry). Achievements include patents on chemical methods or composition of matter. Home: 46 Van Ness Rd Belmont MA 02178-3405 Office: Sphinx-Cambridge 840 Memorial Dr Cambridge MA 02139-3771

MEYERS, HOWARD L., lawyer; b. Dec. 22, 1948. BS, U. Del., 1970; JD, U. Va., 1973. Bar: Pa. 1973. Mng. ptnr., sr. ptnr. in bus. and fin. sect. Morgan, Lewis & Bockius, Phila. Mem. ABA, Pa. Bar Assn., Phila. Bar Assn., Greater Phila. C. of C. (mem. exec. com., bd. dirs., gen. counsel). Office: Morgan Lewis & Bockius 2000 One Logan Sq Philadelphia PA 19103

MEYERS, JAMES WILLIAM, judge; b. Natick, Mass., Sept. 16, 1942. BSA with high honors, Bentley Coll., 1964; JD, Harvard U., 1970. Bar: Mass., Calif. Sr. acct. Ernst & Ernst, Boston, 1964-67; trial atty. criminal div. Dept. Justice, Washington, 1970-72; chief appellate sect. Office U.S. Atty., So. Dist. Calif., 1972-76; judge U.S. bankruptcy Ct. (so. dist.) Calif., San Diego, 1976—; mem. bankruptcy appellate panel Ninth Cir. Ct. of Appeals, 1985—; presiding judge, 1996—. Office: US Bankruptcy Ct Jacob Weinberger Courthouse 325 W F St Rm 210 San Diego CA 92101-6017

MEYERS, JAN, former congresswoman; b. Lincoln, Nebr., July 20, 1928; m. Louis Meyers; children: Valerie, Philip. A.A. in Fine Arts, William Woods Coll., 1948; B.A. in Communications (hon.), U. Nebr.-Lincoln, 1951; LittD, William Woods Coll., 1986; LLD (hon.), Baker U., 1993. Mem. Overland Park (Kans.) City Coun., 1967-72; pres. Overland (Kans.) Park City Council; mem. Kans. Senate, 1972-84, chmn. pub. health and welfare com., local govt. com.; mem. 99th-103rd Congresses from 3rd Kans. Dist., 1985-96, mem. com. internat. rels., chmn. sml. bus. com., mem. com. on econ. and ednl. opportunities. 3rd Dist. co-chmn. Bob Dole for U.S. Senate, 1968; chmn. Johnson County Bob Bennett For Gov., 1974; mem. Johnson County Cmty. Coll. Found.; bd. dirs. Johnson County Mental Health Assn. Recipient Outstanding Elected Ofcl. of Yr. award Assn. Cmty. Mental Health Ctrs. Kans., Woman of Achievement Matrix award Women in Communications, Disting. Service award Bus. and Profl. Women Kansas City, William Woods Alumna award of distinction, Cmty. Svc. award Jr. League Kansas City, 1st Disting. Legislator award Kans. Assn. C.C.s, Outstanding Svc. award Kans. Library Assn., United Community Services, Kans. Pub. Health Assn., award Gov.'s Conf. Child Abuse and Neglect, Outstanding Legislator award Kans. Action for Children, Friend award Nat. Assn. County Park and Recreation Ofcls., 1987, Disting. Alumna award, 1991, numerous others. Mem. LWV (past pres. Shawnee Mission). Methodist. Office: US Ho of Reps 2303 Rayburn Bldg Ofc Washington DC 20515-3217

MEYERS, JOHN ALLEN, magazine publisher; b. Winnetka, Ill., Feb. 21, 1929; s. Fred W. and Ruth B. (Burras) M.; m. Jane Bowers, Sept. 18, 1954; children: Jennifer, Katherine, John. B.A., Mich. State U., 1951, Litt.D. (hon.), 1978; postgrad., Columbia U., 1965. Mgr. Cleve. Time mag., 1960-63, mgr. Chgo., 1963-65; mgr. Time mag., N.Y.C., 1965-68, worldwide advt. sales dir., 1968-72; v.p. Time, Inc., publisher Sports Illustrated mag., 1972-78; pub. Time mag., 1978-85; chmn. Time Inc. Mag. Co., 1985-88; chmn. emeritus Time Inc., 1988—; appointed presdl. bd. adv. on Pvt. Sector Initiatives; chmn. J.A.M. Enterprises; bd. dirs. Tambrands. Editor-in-chief Constitution mag. Pres., Found. for the U.S. Constn. Served with USMC, 1951-53. Decorated Purple Heart. Office: Time & Life Bldg 1221 Avenue Of The Americas New York NY 10020-1001

MEYERS, JUDITH ANN, education educator; b. Scranton, Pa., Aug. 5, 1946; d. Paul Meyers and Elaine Jenkins; m. Stuart M. Olinsky, July 10, 1977; children: Seth, Noah. BA with honors, Rutgers U., 1969; MA in Early Childhood Edn., Kean Coll., 1973. Cert. tchr. early childhood K-8, N.J., Pa. Tchr. Tchr.'s Corp., Newark, 1970-71; head tchr. Arlington Ave. Presch., East Orange, N.J., 1972-75, ednl. dir., 1976-78, exec. dir., 1979-81; program developer for early childhood program, instr. early childhood Williamsport (Pa.) Area C.C./Penn Tech., 1987-89; community mem. curriculum rev. com. Penn Tech. C.C., Williamsport, 1990-91; parent mem. West Branch. Sch., tchr. selection com., 1991-93, tchr. evaluation com., 1991-93, curriculum devel. com., 1993. Author, program developer early childhood edn. courses. Chmn. Victorian Williamsport Preservation Com., 1993-94; bd. dirs. Community Theatre, Williamsport, 1993-94. Avocation: painting. Home: 150 Selkirk Rd Williamsport PA 17701-1869

MEYERS, KAREN DIANE, lawyer, educator, corporate officer; b. Cin., July 8, 1950; d. Willard Paul and Camille Jeannette (Schutte) M.; m. William J. Jones, Mar. 27, 1982. BA summa cum laude, Thomas More Coll., 1974; MBA, MEd, Xavier U., 1978; JD, U. Ky., Covington, 1978. Bar: Ohio 1978, Ky. 1978; CLU; CPCU. Clk. to mgr. Baldwin Co., Cin., 1970-78; adj. prof. bus. Thomas More Coll., Crestview Hill, Ky., 1978—; asst. sec., asst. v.p., sr. counsel The Ohio Life Ins. Co., Hamilton, 1978-91; prin. KD Meyers & Assocs., 1991; v.p. Benefit Designs, Inc., 1991—. Bd. dirs. ARC, Hamilton, 1978-83, vol., 1978—; bd. dirs. YWCA, Hamilton, 1985-91; v.p. Benefit Designs Inc., 1991—. Gardner Found. fellow, 1968-71; recipient Ind. Progress award Bus. & Profl. Women, 1990. Fellow Life Mgmt. Inst. Atlanta; mem. ABA, Soc. Chartered Property Casualty Underwriters (instr. 1987—), Cin. Bar Assn., Butler County Bar Assn., Ohio Bar Assn., Ky. Bar Assn. Roman Catholic. Avocations: aerobics, jogging, crafts. Home: 7903 Hickory Hill Dr Cincinnati OH 45241-1363

MEYERS, LAWRENCE EDWARD, judge; m. Barbara; children: Kelli, Clay. BA in History and Chemistry, So. Meth. U., 1970; JD, U. Kans., 1973; postgrad., U. Tex., Arlington, Tex. Wesleyan U. Asst. dist. atty. Montgomery County, Kans., 1973-75; pvt. practice Ft. Worth, 1975-88; assoc. justice U.S. Ct. Appeals (2nd cir.), Ft. Worth, 1988-92; judge Ct. Criminal Appeals, Ft. Worth, 1992—; instr. Tex. Christian U., Ft. Worth. Mem. parish coun. St. Mary's of Assumption, Ft. Worth. Mem. State Bar Tex., State Bar Kans., Tarrant County Bar Assn. Republican. Office: Court of Criminal Appeals PO Box 12308 Austin TX 78711

MEYERS, LOUISA ANN, business and communications consultant; b. Omaha, July 5, 1956; d. V. William and Darinka Stephania (Shuput) M. BA in Liberal Studies magna cum laude, U. Nebr., Omaha, 1983. Wardrobe asst. Royal Shakespeare Theatre, Stratford-upon-Avon, Eng., 1977-78, asst. adminstr., 1978-79; stage/asst. co. mgr. Omaha Cmty. Playhouse, Nebr. Theatre Caravan, 1979-80; stage/prodn. mgr. Firehouse Dinner Theater, Omaha, 1980-81; pers. benefits technician Bergan Mercy Hosp., Omaha, 1981-82, unit sec., 1981-83; planning mgr. Mercy Health Sys. of Midlands, Omaha, 1984-85; staff asst. Omaha City Coun., 1985-86; mayoral aide City of Omaha, 1986-87; cmty. devel. mgr. City of Omaha, 1987-89, mayor's spl. projects mgr., 1989; exec. dir. Neighborhood Housing Svcs., Omaha, 1989-90; dir. Office Comms., legis. liaison Nebr. Dept. Health, Lincoln, 1993-95; co-founder, mng. ptnr. Mercury Bus. Comms., Omaha, 1989—; presenter on pub. policy to various comty. orgns.; flood disaster coord. Nebr. Dept. Health, 1993; state rep. Nat. Pub. Health Info. Coalition, 1993-95; film. commr. City of Omaha, 1986-89, rep. to League of Nebr. Municipalities, 1986-87; festival coord. City of Omaha, 1985-86; adminstr. City of Omaha Cable TV, 1985-86; writer various grants, reports for City of Omaha; mem. efficiency task force City of Omaha. Contbr. articles to profl. jours.; reporter Gateway newspaper, 1982; author, co. mgr., stage mgr. dramatic touring prodn. Nebraska Heritage, 1974-75. Mem. chancellor's adv. com. U. Nebr., Omaha, 1974, bicentennial com., 1975; chair Joslyn Chamber Music Series, 1986-87; coord. fundraiser Queen Elizabeth Hosp., Birmingham, Eng., 1979; exec. dir. Omaha Coalition for Homeless, 1990-91; campaign mgr. Horgan for Legislature, Omaha, 1990; vol. Jesse Rasmussen for Legislature Campaign, Omaha, 1994; mem. City of Omaha Efficiency Commn., 1996—; bd. dirs. Black Student Cath. Scholarship Fund, fin. and scholarship com., 1996. Medill Sch. Journalism scholar, 1973, Margaret Builta scholar, 1983; recipient Admiralty award Nebr. Navy, 1993. Mem. LWV, NOW, Nat. Mus. Women in Arts (charter mem.), Phi Kappa Phi, Alpha Psi Omega. Avocations: dog obedience training competition, property restoration and renovation, design. Home: 4927 Pinkney St Omaha NE 68104-3663 Office: Mercury Bus Comms PO Box 31397 Omaha NE 68131-0397

MEYERS, MARLENE O., hospital administrator; m. Eugene Meyers; children: Lori, Lisa, Dean. BSc, U. Sask., 1962; MSc, U. Calgary, Alta., Can., 1976. Instr., chair Mount Royal Coll. Allied Health, Calgary, 1969-82; asst. exec. dir. Rockyview Hosp., Calgary, 1982-85; v.p. patient svcs. Calgary Gen. Hosp., 1985-91, pres., CEO, 1991-95; pres., CEO Meyers and Assocs. Health Care Mgmt. Cons., Calgary, 1995—; surveyor Can. Coun. on Health Facilities Accreditation, 1986—. Rotary Intl. Named Calgary Woman of Yr. in field of Health, 1982; recipient Heritage of Svc. award, 1992. Mem. Alta. Assn. RNs. (hon. mem., 1996), Can. Coll. Health Svcs. Org., Can. Exec. Svcs. Org. Office: Meyers and Assocs 139 Coleridge Rd NW, Calgary, AB Canada T2K 1X5

MEYERS, MARY ANN, writer, consultant; b. Sodus, N.Y., Sept. 30, 1937; d. Harold Galpin and Clarice Mildred (Daniel) Dye; m. John Matthew Meyers, Aug. 22, 1959; children: Andrew Christopher, Anne Kathryn. BA magna cum laude, Syracuse U., 1959; MA, U. Pa., 1965, PhD, 1976. Editorial asst. Ladies' Home Jour., Phila., 1959-62; editor, asst. dir. news bur. U. Pa., Phila., 1962-65, asst. to pres., 1973-75, univ. sec., lectr. Am. civilization, 1980-90; contbg. writer The Pennsylvania Gazette, Phila., 1965—; dir. coll. rels., editor Haverford Horizons, lectr. in religion Haverford (Pa.) Coll., 1977-80; pres. The Annenberg Found., St. Davids, Pa., 1990-92; v.p. for external affairs Moore Coll. Art and Design, Phila., 1995-97. Author: A New World Jerusalem, 1983; contbg. author: Death in America, 1975, Gladly Learn, Gladly Teach, 1978, Coping with Serious Illness, 1980, Religion in American Life, 1987; contbr. articles to profl. jours. Judge recognition program Coun. for Advancement and Support Edn., Washington, 1977-78, chair creative editing and writing workshop, 1978; mem. Picker Found. Program on Human Qualities in Medicine, N.Y.C. and Phila., 1980-83; del. Phila.-Leningrad Sister Cities Project, 1986; trustee U. Pa. Press, 1985—, vice chmn. U. Pa., 250th Anniversary Commn., 1987-90, mem. steering com. of bd. trustees, U. Pa., Annenberg Sch. for Communications, 1990-92, mem. adv. bd. U. Pa., Annenberg Ctr. for the Performing Arts, 1990—; mem. bd. overseers, U. Pa., Sch. Arts and Scis., 1990-97; mem. steering com. of bd. trustees Annenberg Ctr. for Communication, U. So. Calif., L.A., 1990-92, The Annenberg Washington Program in Communications Policy Studies of Northwestern U., Washington, 1990-92; trustee Am. Acad. Polit. and Social Sci., 1992—, World Affairs Coun. Phila., 1990-95; dir. Diagnostic and Rehab. Ctr., Phila., 1993—; dir. Partnership for Rsch. on Religion and At-Risk Youth, Phila, 1997—. Recipient Excellence award Women in Communications, Inc., 1973-74, award for pub. affairs reporting Newsweek/Coun. for Advancement and Support Edn., 1977, Silver medal Coun. for Advancement and Support Edn., 1986. Mem. Cosmopolitan Club, Sunday Breakfast Club, Phi Beta Kappa (mem. steering com. Delaware Valley chpt. 1995—). Roman Catholic. Avocations: reading, theater, classical music, biking. Home: 217 Gypsy Ln Wynnewood PA 19096-1112

MEYERS, MORTON ALLEN, physician, radiology educator; b. Troy, N.Y., Oct. 1, 1933; s. David and Jeanne Sarah (Dunn) M.; m. Beatrice Applebaum, June 1, 1963; children—Richard, Amy. M.D., SUNY, Upstate Med. Coll., 1959. Diplomate: Am. Bd. Radiology. Intern Bellevue Hosp., N.Y.C., 1959-60; resident in radiology Columbia-Presbyn. Med. Ctr., N.Y.C., 1960-63; fellow Am. Cancer Soc., 1961-63; prof. dept. radiology Cornell U. Med. Center, N.Y.C., 1973-78; prof., chmn. dept. radiology SUNY Sch. Medicine, Stony Brook, 1978-91; prof. dept. radiology SUNY Sch. Medicine, 1991—; vis. investigator St. Mark's Hosp., London, 1976; spkr. Radiol. Soc. N.Am., 1986. Author: Diseases of the Adrenal Glands: Radiologic Diagnosis, 1963, Dynamic Radiology of the Abdomen: Normal and Pathologic Anatomy, 1976, 4th edit., 1994, Iatrogenic Gastrointestinal Complications, 1981; series editor: Radiology of Iatrogenic Disorders, 1981-86; editor: Computed Tomography of the Gastrointestinal Tract: Including the Peritoneal Cavity and Mesentery, 1986; founding editor in chief Abdominal Imaging, 1976—; mem. editorial bd. Iatrogenics, Surg. and Radiol. Anatomy; contbr. chpts. to med. textbooks, articles to med. jours.; speaker in field. Served to capt. M.C. U.S. Army, 1963-65. Fellow Am. Coll. Radiology; mem. AAAS, Am. Coll. Gastroenterology, Radiol. Soc. N.Am., Am. Roentgen Ray Soc., Am. Gastroenterol. Assn., Soc. Uroradiology, Soc. Gastrointestinal Radiologists, Assn. Univ. Radiologists, N.Y. Roentgen Ray Soc., N.Y. Acad. Gastroenterology, Phila. Roentgen Soc., Harvey Soc., N.Y. Acad. Scis., L.I. Radiologic Soc., Alpha Omega Alpha. Home: 14 Wainscott Ln East Setauket NY 11733-3816 Office: SUNY Health Scis Ctr Sch Medicine Dept Radiology Stony Brook NY 11794

MEYERS, NANCY JANE, screenwriter, producer; b. Phila., Dec. 8, 1949; d. Irving H. and Patricia (Lemisch) M. BA, Am. U., Washington, 1971. Co-writer, prodr.: (films) Private Benjamin (Acad. award nominee, Writers Guild award 1980), Irreconcilable Differences, 1984, Baby Boom, 1987, Father of the Bride, 1991, I Love Trouble, 1994, Father of the Bride Part II, 1995. Mem. ASCAP, Acad. Motion Picture Arts and Scis., Writers Guild Am. West. Office: Starr & Co 350 Park Ave Fl 9 New York NY 10022-6022

MEYERS, PETER L., banker; b. Syracuse, N.Y., Mar. 19, 1939; s. Edwin Clark and Phyllis (Schiess) M.; m. Teresa Maley, Mar. 2, 1963; children: Gary, Gregory, Cheryl. BBA, Syracuse U., 1974. With Merchants Nat. Bank & Trust Co., Syracuse, N.Y., 1963-92, v.p., comml. loan officer, 1975-78, v.p., sr. loan officer, 1978-79, sr. v.p., 1979, exec. v.p., 1980-88, exec. v.p., COO, 1988, pres., CEO, 1988-92; vice chmn. OnBank & Trust Co., Syracuse, 1993—; dir. Security Mutual Life Ins. Co.; chmn. bd. dirs. N.Y. Bus. Devel. Corp. Bd. dirs. Met. Devel. Assn.; chmn. United Way Ctrl. N.Y., Mus. Sci. and Tech. Found.; trustee Erie Canal Mus.; bd. regents LeMoyne Coll.; active Syracuse Onondaga County Youth Bd., Onondaga Lake Mgmt. Conf. Mem. Am. Inst. Banking, Syracuse U. Alumni Assn., Onondaga Golf and Country Club. Avocations: golf, fishing. Office: OnBank & Trust Co 101 S Salina St PO Box 4983 Syracuse NY 13221

MEYERS, RICHARD JAMES, landscape architect; b. Columbus, Ohio, Jan. 25, 1940; s. Ralph Joseph and Margaret Mary (Kruse) M.; m. Mary Igoe, Jan. 12, 1963; children: Gregory James, Helen Marie, Andrew James. B.Landscape Arch., Ohio State U., 1961. Registered landscape architect, Ohio, Mich., Fla., Ind.; cert. Council Landscape Archtl. Registration Bds. Jr. planner Columbus Planning Commn. (Ohio), 1960-62; landscape architect Behnke-Nes & Assocs., Cleve., 1962-65, Arthur Hills & Assocs., Toledo, 1965-67; ptnr. Mortensen-Meyers Assocs., Toledo, 1967-69; prin. MMSS Inc., Toledo, 1969-71, The Collaborative, Inc., Toledo, 1973—; bd. dirs., past pres. Council Landscape Archtl. Registration Bd., Syracuse, N.Y., 1978-86, Ohio Bd. Landscape Architect Examiners, 1975-83. Mem. St. Vincent Hosp. and Med. Ctr. Assocs., Toledo, 1978-83; bd. dirs. Family Svcs. Greater Toledo, 1977-82; com. mem. Toledo Met. Area Coun. of Govt., 1972-79, 87-89, Toledo Bot. Gardens Design Rev. Bd., 1988-90, Downtown Toledo Vision, Inc., 1988—; chmn. Toledo Lucas County Plan Commn., 1989—; chmn. Toledo Adminstrv. Bd. Zoning Appeals, 1994—, Met. Parks Com. of 25, 1991; chmn. campaign divsn. United Way, 1991; mem. adv. bd. U. Toledo-Stranahan Arboretum, 1994—, Scenic Ohio, 1996—. Dumbarton Oaks Jr. summer scholar, 1960; recipient First Honor Design award Am. Assn. Nurserymen, 1974; named Disting. Alumnus, Ohio State Univ. Coll. Enging., 1996. Fellow Am. Soc. Landscape Architects (merit design award Ohio chpt. 1975, 81, 83, 85, Outstanding Svc. to Profession award 1983, Ohio Chpt. medal 1984); mem. AIA, Ohio Soc. of Am. Soc. Landscape Architects (v.p. 1974-76), Urban Land Inst., Soc. for Coll. and Univ. Planning, Am. Forestry Assn., Am. Planning Assn., Rails to Trails Conservancy, Ohio Pks. and Recreation Assn., Heatherdowns Country Club (bd. dirs. 1983). *I am fortunate to be part of a profession dedicated to improving and beautifying our physical environment through the preservation and protection of our natural resources and by the sensitive blending of economic and social needs with these natural systems. Landscape architecture provides me with a great deal of personal satisfaction.*

MEYERS, ROBERT ALLEN, physical chemist, publisher; b. L.A., May 15, 1936; s. Jack B. Meyers and Pearl (Cassell) Thorpe; m. Roberta Lee Hart, June 24, 1961 (div. 1976); children: Tamara, Robert Jr.; m. Ilene Braun, Feb. 27, 1977; children: Jenifer, Jacalyn. BA, San Diego State U., 1959; PhD, UCLA, 1963. Postdoctoral fellow, mem. faculty Calif. Inst. Tech., Pasadena, 1963-64; rsch. scientist Bell & Howell Rsch. Ctr., Sierra Madre, Calif., 1965; project mgr. TRW Def. & Space, Redondo Beach, Calif., 1966-81; bus. area mgr. TRW Energy Group, Redondo Beach, 1981-86; mgr. process devel. TRW Def. & Space, Redondo Beach, 1986-88, mgr. new projects devel., 1988-95; pres. Ramtech Ltd., Tarzana, Calif., 1995—; del. U.S.-USSR Working Group, Washington and Moscow, 1973-80; chmn. adv. bd. Guide to Nuclear Power Tech., N.Y.C., 1982-84; mem. adv. coun. chemistry dept. UCLA, 1991—. Author: Coal Desulfurization, 1977; editor: Coal Handbook, 1981, Coal Structure, 1982; editor: Handbook of Petroleum Refining Processes, 1986, 2d edit., 1996, Handbook of Synfuels Technology, 1984, Handbook of Energy Technology and Economics, 1983, Handbook of Chemicals Production Processes, 1986, others; editor-in-chief Ency. of Phys. Sci. and Tech., 1987, 92, Ency. of Modern Physics, 1990, Ency. of Lasers and Optics, 1991, Encyclopedia of Telecommunications, 1989, Molecular Biology and Biotech., 1995, Encyclopedia of Molecular Biology and Molecular Medicine, 1995. Mem. Am. Chem. Soc., Am. Inst. Chem. Engrs. Avocations: swimming, bicycling, running. Home: 3715 Gleneagles Dr Tarzana CA 91356-5622 Office: Ramtech Ltd 3715 Gleneagles Dr Tarzana CA 91356-5622

MEYERS, SHELDON, engineering company executive; b. N.Y.C., Sept. 6, 1929; s. Charles and Charlotte (Farb) M.; m. Anne Catherine Dietzel, Apr. 14, 1962; children—James, John, Catherine, Peter, Paul. B.Engring., SUNY, 1952; M.S.E., U. Mich., 1955; M.B.A., N.Y. U., 1967. Engr. Cities Svc. Oil Co., N.Y.C., 1955-56, Westinghouse Co., Pitts., 1957-58, Argonne (Ill.) Nat. Lab., 1958-69; engr., div. dir. AEC, N.Y.C., 1970-78; dir. Office Air Quality Planning and Standards EPA, 1982-83, dep. asst. adminstr. Office Air and Radiation, 1983-84; dir. Office Radiation EPA, Washington, 1983-87, assoc. adminstr. internat. activities, 1987-88; dep. asst. sec. Office Nuclear Waste Mgmt. Dept. of Energy, Washington, 1978-82; v.p. Jacobs Engring., Arlington, Va., 1988—. Princeton U. fellow, 1964-65. Mem. ASME. Home: 3506 Dundee Dr Chevy Chase MD 20815-4741 Office: Jacobs 1300 17th St N Ste 602 Arlington VA 22209-3801

MEYERS, TEDSON JAY, lawyer; b. Bayonne, N.J., May 6, 1928; s. Irving and Norma Miriam (Anson) M.; m. Patricia Elizabeth Sullivan, Apr. 10, 1965 (div. Apr. 1978); children: Mary, John, Katherine; m. Lynn Scholz, Aug. 6, 1978 (div. Oct. 1992). Student, Ohio State U., 1945-47; BA, NYU, 1949, MA, 1950; JD, Harvard U., 1953. Bar: D.C. 1953, N.Y. 1957, U.S. Supreme Ct. 1971. Asst. counsel Office Gen. Counsel, Dept. Navy, Washington, 1955-56; assoc. Liebman, Eulau & Robinson, N.Y.C., 1956-58; staff counsel for govt. regulations ABC, N.Y.C., 1958-61; adminstrv. asst. to chmn. FCC, Washington, 1961-62; asst. to dir., dir. overseas ednl. TV projects Peace Corps, Washington, 1962-68; pvt. practice Washington, 1968-70; ptnr. Sullivan Beauregard Meyers & Clarkson, Washington, 1970-74, Peabody Lambert & Meyers, Washington, 1974-84, Reid & Priest, Washington, 1984-96, Coudert Brothers, Washington, 1996—; adj. prof. comm. San Diego State U., 1993—; founding pres. Harvard Legis. Rsch. Bur., 1952-53; mem. White House Task Force on Ednl. TV Overseas, 1966-68, adv. panel on internat. telecomm. law U.S. State Dept., 1987—; bd. govs. Internat. Coun. on Computer Comm., 1986—; bd. dirs. Internat. Ctr. for Comms. Contbr. conf. papers and articles to profl. publs. Mem. City Coun. Washington, 1972-75; bd. govs. Met. Washington Coun. Govts., 1973-75; chmn. Bicycle Fedn. of Am., 1977—; bd. dirs. U.S. Coun. for World Comm. Yr. 83, 1982-84; dir. The Arthur C. Clarke Found. of the U.S. Inc., 1987—. Lt. USMC, 1953-55, Korea. Rsch. fellow Carnegie Found., 1949. Mem. ABA (co-founder and chmn. internat. telecomm. com., sect. sci. and tech. 1982-85, coun. mem. sect. sci. and tech. 1983-87), Fed. Comm. Bar Assn., Internat. Inst. Comm., Royal TV Soc., Pacific Telecomm. Coun., Soc. Satellite Profls., Cosmos Club (pres. 1988-90), Cosmos Club Found. (trustee, chmn. 1985-88, 90—), Potomac Boat Club, Alpha Epsilon Pi. Avocations: computers, sculling, bicycling, motorcycling, military music. Office: Coudert Brothers 1627 I St NW Ste 1200 Washington DC 20006-4007

MEYERS, WAYNE MARVIN, microbiologist; b. Huntingdon County, Pa., Aug. 28, 1924; s. John William and Carrie Venca (Weaver) M.; m. Esther

Louise Kleinschmidt, Aug. 26, 1953; children: Amy, George, Daniel, Sara. BS in Chemistry, Juniata Coll., 1947; diploma, Moody Bible Inst., 1950; M.S. in Med. Microbiology, U. Wis., 1953, Ph.D. in Med. Microbiology, 1955; M.D., Baylor Coll. Medicine, 1959; DSc (hon.), Juniata Coll., 1986. Instr. Baylor Coll. Medicine, 1955-59; intern Conemaugh Valley Meml. Hosp., Johnstown, Pa., 1959-60; staff physician Berrien Gen. Hosp., Berrien Ctr., Mich., 1960-61; missionary physician Am. Leprosy Missions, Burundi and Zaire, Africa, 1961-73; prof. pathology Sch. Medicine U. Hawaii, Honolulu, 1973-75; chief microbiology divsn. Armed Forces Inst. Pathology, Washington, 1975-89, chief mycobacteriology, 1989—, registrar leprosy registry, 1975—; mem. leprosy panel U.S.-Japan Coop. Med. Sci. Program, 1976-83; mem. sci. adv. bd. Leonard Wood Meml., 1981-85, sci. cons. dir., 1985-87, sci. dir., 1987-90; cons., 1990—; rsch. affiliate Tulane U., 1981—; corp. bd. dirs. Gorgas Meml. Inst. Tropical and Preventive Medicine, Inc. Bd. dirs. Internat. Jour. Leprosy, 1978—; contbr. numerous chpts. and articles on tropical medicine to textbooks and jours. Adv. bd. Damien-Dutton Soc. for Leprosy Aid, Inc., 1983-96, corp. bd. dirs., 1996—; adv. bd. Am. Leprosy Missions, Inc., 1979-88, chmn. bd., 1985-88, program cons. to bd., mem. bd. reference, 1988—; mem. Hansen's Disease Ctr., Carville, La., 1983-85; chmn., 1985—. With U.S. Army, 1944-46. Allergy Found. Am. fellow, 1957, 58; WHO rsch. grantee, 1978-87. Mem. Internat. Leprosy Assn. (councillor 1978-88, pres. 1988-93), Internat. Acad. Pathology, Internat. Soc. Tropical Dermatology, Am. Soc. Tropical Medicine and Hygiene, Am. Soc. Microbiology, Binford-Dammin Soc. Infectious Disease Pathologists (sec.-treas. 1988-91, pres. 1995-96), Internat. Soc. Travel Medicine, Sigma Xi. Achievements include researching human and experimental leprosy. Office: Armed Forces Inst Pathology Washington DC 20306-6000

MEYERS, WILLIAM HENRY, economics educator; b. Souderton, Pa., Nov. 24, 1941; s. Isaac Claude and Mary (Wismer) M.; m. Dalisay Honorata Cuento, Jan. 1, 1972; children: Naila-Jean, Celina-Beth. BA in Math. and Physics, Goshen (Ind.) Coll., 1963; MS in Agrl. Econs., U. of The Philippines, Los Banos, 1972; PhD in Agrl. Econs., U. Minn., 1977. Team leader Internat. Vol. Svc., Can Tho, Vietnam, 1966-67; VEP coord. United Meth. Ch., Washington, 1968; rsch. fellow Internat. Rice Rsch. Inst., Los Banos, 1971-72; grad. asst. U. Minn., St. Paul, 1972-77; agrl. economist USDA, Washington, 1977-79; prof. econs. Iowa State U., Ames, 1979—; co-dir. Food and Agr. Policy Rsch. Inst., Ames, 1984—; assoc. dir. Ctr. for Agrl. and Rural Devel., Ames, 1985—, interim dir., 1996—; exec. dir. MATRIC, Ames, 1987—; agr. policy cons. World Bank, Washington, 1992—; ad hoc group of experts East/West, OECD, Paris, 1993—; vis. prof. Inst. Agrl. Econs., Christian-Albrechts U., Kiel, Germany, 1991; agrl. economist Forecast Support Group and Food and Agrl. Policy Br., Econ. Rsch. Svc., USDA, Washington, 1977-79; rsch. fellow Internat. Rice Rsch. Inst., 1971-72; lectr. in field; cons. in field. N.Em. editor Agrl. Econs., 1991-94; editor: Iowa Ag Rev., 1995-96; mem. editl. bd. Agrl. Econs., 1989-91; assoc. editor Am. Jour. Agrl. Econs., 1987-90; article referee Agrl. Econs. Rsch., Am. Jour. Agrl. Econs., North Ctrl. Jour. Agrl. Econs., Western Jour. Agrl. Econs., Can. Jour. Agrl. Econs.; contbr. numerous articles to profl. jours., chpts. to books. Mem. coun. of founders Baltic Mgmt. Found., Vilnius, Lithuania, 1991—. Rsch. grantee Mo. Valley Rsch. Assocs., 1982-83, USDA, 1982-83, Iowa Soybean Promotion Bd., 1984-86, Nat. Corn Devel. Found., 1982-86, Coop. State Rsch. Svc./USDA, 1983-95, ERS/USDA, 1986, US AID, 1984-87, 89-90, U.S. Feed Grains Coun., 1986-88, Iowa Lottery Funds, 1987-88, U.S. AID, 1988-90, Nat. Ctr. for Food and Agrl. Policy, Resources for Future, 1990-91, Agrl. Can., 1988-95, Asian Devel. Bank, 1990-92, Farm Credit Svc., 1992-93, Pioneer Hi-Bred Internat., 1994-95, others. Mem. Ames C. of C., Am. Agrl. Econs. Assn. (Disting. Policy Contbn. award 1991, Quality of Comm. award 1991), Assn. for Advancement of Baltic Studies, Am. Econs. Assn., Am. Assn. for Advancement of Slavic Studies, European Assn. Agrl. Economists, Internat. Agrl. Trade Rsch. Consortium, Internat. Assn. Agrl. Economists, Internat. Agribus. Mgmt. Assn., Western Agrl. Econs. Assn. (1994 Published Rsch. award), Gamma Sigma Delta, Phi Kappa Phi, Phi Beta Delta. Office: FAPRI Iowa State Univ 578 Heady Hall Ames IA 50011

MEYERSON, ADAM, magazine editor, foundation executive; b. Phila., Aug. 2, 1953; s. Martin and Margy Ellin (Lazarus) M.; m. Nina Hope Shea, Sept. 13, 1986; children: Thomas Abraham, William Ulysses, Henry Elijah. BA, Yale U., 1974; student, Harvard U., 1977-79. Mng. editor The Am. Spectator, Bloomington, Ind., 1974-77; editorial writer Wall St. Jour., N.Y.C., 1979-83; editor Policy Rev. The Heritage Found., Washington, 1983—, v.p. ednl. affairs, 1993—. Co-editor: The Wall Street Journal on Management, 1985. Mem. bd. selectors Am. Inst. Pub. Svc., Washington, 1989—; mem. Coun. Fgn. Rels., 1980-85; bd. dirs. PERC, Bozeman, Mont., Inst. Children, Cambridge, Mass. Mem. Phila. Soc. Home: 3714 Ingomar St NW Washington DC 20015-1820 Office: Heritage Foundation 214 Massachusetts Ave NE Washington DC 20002-4958

MEYERSON, BARBARA TOBIAS, elementary school educator; b. Rockville Centre, N.Y., May 17, 1928; d. Sol and Hermine (Sternberg) Tobias; m. Daniel Meyerson, Sept. 4, 1962; children: George D., Barbara Meyerson Ayers. BEd, SUNY, New Paltz, 1948; postgrad., NYU, Hofstra U. Tchr. kindergarten Dix Hills (N.Y.) pub. schs., Hicksville (N.Y.) pub. schs., Valley Stream (N.Y.) pub. schs.; tchr. 6th grade Flushing (N.Y.) Bd. Edn. Dist. commr. Boy Scouts Am., mem. tng. staff, organizer new units; founder, sec. Repertory Theatre, Rio Rancho, N.Mex.; sec. Italian Am. Assn., Rio Rancho; vol. Rio Rancho City Hall Pub. Offices. Mem. ACE, VFW (jr. v.p.), United Fedn. Tchrs. Home: 6127 Cottontail Rd NE Rio Rancho NM 87124-1545

MEYERSON, BRUCE ELLIOT, lawyer; b. N.Y.C., Apr. 10, 1947. BS, Ariz. State U., 1968; JD, Georgetown U., 1972. Bar: Ariz. 1972. Exec. dir. Ariz. Ctr. for Law in Pub. Interest, 1974-82; judge Ariz. Ct. Appeals, 1982-86; gen. counsel Ariz. State U., 1986-90; atty. Meyer, Hendricks, Victor, Osborn & Maledon, Phoenix; adj. prof. law Ariz. State U., 1985-88. Mem. nat. governing bd. Common Cause, 1978-81; bd. dirs. Community Legal Svcs., 1979-81; chair ad hoc com. on human rels. City of Phoenix, 1984. Office: Meyer Hendricks Victor Osborn & Maledon PO Box 33449 2929 N Central Ave Ste 2100 Phoenix AZ 85012-2765

MEYERSON, MARTIN, university executive, professor, urban and regional planner; b. N.Y.C., Nov. 14, 1922; s. Samuel and Etta (Berger) M.; m. Margy Ellin Lazarus, Dec. 31, 1945; children: Adam, Laura (dec.), Matthew. BA, Columbia U., 1942; MCP, Harvard U., 1949; LLD, U. Pa., 1970; LLD (hon.), Queen's U., Can., 1968, Shiraz U., Iran, 1973, U. Edinburgh, 1976; PhD (hon.), Hebrew U., 1987; also 17 other hon. doctorates including ScD, LHD, LittD, DFA, 1967-94. Mem. staff Michael Reese Hosp., Chgo., 1945-47; asst. prof. coll. and grad. social scis. U. Chgo., 1948-52; assoc. Com. on Nat. Policy, Yale U., 1948; assoc. prof., city and regional planning U. Pa., 1952-56, prof., 1956-57, pres., 1970-81, pres. emeritus, 1981—, chmn. bd. dirs. U. Pa. Press, Inst. for Rsch. on Higher Edn. Fels Ctr. Govt., bd. dirs. Inst. Contemporary Art, Mahoney Inst. Neuroscis., Lauder Inst. Mgmt. and Internat. Studies, co-chmn. Commn. for U. Pa. 250th Anniversary, 1987-90; Univ. prof. U. Pa. Found., 1977—, chmn., 1981—; exec. dir. Am. Council to Improve Our Neighborhoods, 1955-56, vice chmn., 1956-66; Frank Backus Williams prof. city planning and urban research Harvard U., 1957-63, acting dean Grad. Sch. Design,, 1963; founding dir. Joint Center for Urban Studies, MIT and Harvard U., 1958-63; dean, prof. urban devel. Coll. Environ. Design, U. Calif., Berkeley, 1963-66; interim chancellor U. Calif., Berkeley, 1965; pres., prof. public policy SUNY, Buffalo, 1966-70; dir. visitor Inst. for Advanced Study, Princeton, N.J., 1983-84; pres. Found. for Internat. Exchange of Sci. and Cultural Info. by Telecommunications, Switzerland-U.S., 1986—; dir. Real Estate Research Corp., 1961-67, Marine Midland Bank, 1966-70, 1st Fidelity Bancorp., Scott Paper Co., Penn Mut. Life, Saint Gobain Corp., Certain Teed, Norton, Avatar, Universal Health Services; cons. to govts., pvt. firms U.S. and abroad, UN missions to, Japan, Indonesia, Yugoslavia, 1958-65; sr. advisor Arthur D. Little, Inc., 1958-66; cons. Sears Roebuck Found., 1958-69, Ford Found., various times; chmn. bd. Western N.Y. Nuclear Research Center, 1966-70; mem. adv. com. U.S. Census, 1958-61; adv. com. NASA, 1960-65; White House Office Sci. and Tech., 1962-66, White House task forces, 1960-69; mem. council Electric Power Research Inst., 1973-77; mem. U.S. del. UN Conf. on Sci. and Tech. for Less Developed Areas, 1963. Author: (with E. C. Banfield) Politics, Planning and the Public Interest, 1955, Housing, People and Cities, 1962, Face of the Metropolis, 1963, Boston, 1966, Gladly Learn and Gladly Teach, 1978; editor: Conscience of the City, 1970, McGraw-Hill Series; mem. editorial bd. Ency. Britannica, 1980—, Daedalus, 1972-90. Mem. Air Conservation Commn., 1962-66; mem. Bay Area Conservation and Devel. Commn., 1965-66; chmn. Assembly Univ. Goals and Governance, 1969-74; commr. N.Y. State Commn. on Post-Secondary Sch. Edn., 1976-77; hon. prof. Nat. U. Asuncion, 1969—, Beijing U., 1996—; bd. dirs. Phila. Bicentennial Corp., 1970-76, Greater Phila. Partnership, 1973-81, Afro-Am. Film Found., 1966-70, Niagara U., 1968-70, Center for Community Change, 1968-72, Acad. Religion and Mental Health, 1970-78, Center for Ednl. Devel., 1967-70, Phila. Mus. Art, 1974—, Nat. Urban Coalition, 1969-78; trustee, Niagara U., 1968-70, Am. Coll., 1982-92, Curtis Inst. Music, 1987-94, United World Coll.N. Mex., 1984—, Am. Schs. Oriental Rsch., 1985—, Tel Aviv U., Coll. Bd., 1986-92, Hebrew U., Internat. House Ctr., Monell Chem. Senses Ctr., chmn., 1993—, Fgn. Policy Rsch. Inst., 1981—, Panasonic Found., 1982—, Ctr. for Visual History, U.S. Com. on the Constl. System; founding dir. Internat. Centre for Study East Asian Devel. Japan; Inst. for Internat. Edn., 1971—, chmn., 1981-85; bd. dirs. Internat. Council Ednl. Devel., 1971-94, Am. Council Financial Aid to Edn., 1975-81, Open Univ. Found., U.K., 1979-82; chmn. council pres. Nat. Accelerator Lab., 1972-73; co-chmn. Images (French TV), 1976-79, Salzburg Seminar Bd., 1978—, sr. fellow, 1997—; co-chmn. Marconi Internat. Fellowship Found., chair exec. com., 1978-96, chmn. bd. dirs., 1996—; Internat. gov. Center Environ. Studies, London, 1966-84; mem. sr. exec. council Conf. Bd., 1970-77; trustee Aspen. Inst., 1976-96; chair adv. group for UN Centre for Regional Devel., Nagoya, Japan, 1983-93; chair internat. selection commn. Phila. Liberty Medal, 1988—; bd. overseers Koc Univ., Bosphorus, Turkey, 1994—; bd. dirs. Internat. Literacy Inst., 1995—. Decorated Commendatore Order of Merit (Italy); chevalier de l'Ordre Nat. de Mérite (France); Order of the Rising Sun, Gold and Silver Star Govt. Japan; recipient Einstein medal Am. Technion Soc., 1976, Disting. Achievement award U. Calif. Berkeley, 1984, John Jay award Columbia U., 1982, Disting. Educator award Assn. Collegiate Schs. of Planning, 1996; overseas fellow Churchill Coll., Cambridge U., 1983; hon. fellow Soc. for Tech. Communication, 1988; Meyerson Hall named in his honor U. Pa. Grad. Sch. Fine Arts; Meyerson Professorship named in honor U. Pa. Fellow Am. Acad. Arts and Scis., Royal Soc. Arts (Franklin fellow), Am. Philos. Soc., Nat. Acad. Edn.; mem. Am. Soc. Planning Ofcls. (past dir.), Am. Inst. Planners (past gov., award winner), Internat. Assn. Univs. Paris (Am. dir. 1975—, v.p., interim pres. 1981-85, hon. pres. 1985—), Council Fgn. Relations, European Acad. Arts, Scis. and Letters (academician), Phi Beta Kappa (hon.). Clubs: Philadelphia, Century (N.Y.C.), Cosmos (Washington), U. Pa. (N.Y.C.). Office: Univ Pa 225 Van Pelt Library Philadelphia PA 19104

MEYERSON, SEYMOUR, retired chemist; b. Chgo., Dec. 4, 1916; s. Joseph and Rena (Margulies) M.; m. Lotte Strauss, May 22, 1943; children: Sheella, Elana. SB, U. Chgo., 1938, postgrad., 1938-39, 47-48; postgrad., George Williams Coll., 1939-40; DSc (hon.), Valparaiso Univ., Ind., 1995. Chemist Deavitt Labs., Chgo., 1941-42; inspector powder & explosives Kankakee Ordnance Works, Joliet, Ill., 1942; from chemist to rsch. cons. Standard Oil Co. (Ind.) Rsch. Dept., Whiting, Ind.-Naperville, Ill., 1946-84; mem. indsl. adv. coun. chemistry dept. U. Okla., Norman, 1967-69; Frontiers in Chemistry lectr. Wayne State U., 1965; invited spkr. James L. Waters Symposium, Pitts. Conf., Chgo., 1995. Charter mem. editl. adv. bd. Organic Mass Spectrometry, 1968-87, Mass Spectromony Revs., 1980-87; author, co-author 190 sci. publs. 2d lt. AUS, 1943-46, ETO. Mem. emeritus Am. Chem. Soc. (Frank H. Field and Joe L. Franklin award for outstanding achievement in mass spectrometry 1993), Am. Soc. for Mass Spectrometry. Achievements include many contributions to systematic chemistry of gas-phase organic ions; 2 patents in field. Home: 650 N Tippecanoe St Gary IN 46403-2262

MEYLER, WILLIAM ANTHONY, financial executive; b. Newark, Oct. 29, 1944; s. Raymond Francis and Margaret (Loveless) M.; BS, St. Joseph's Coll., 1966; MBA, Fairleigh Dickinson U., 1974; m. Dana Irene Brennan, May 3, 1975; children: Daniel, Diana. CPA, N.J. Sr. acct. Ernst & Young, Trenton, N.J., 1970; dir. acctg. Baker Industries, Inc., Parsippany, N.J., 1971-72; mgr. corp. acctg. Witco Chem. Corp., N.Y.C., 1973-75, asst. to controller, 1976-79, asst. controller world-wide ops., 1977-82, asst. controller mgmt. info. systems, 1982-84; ptnr. Letters, Meyler & Co., CPAs, 1984-91; cons., exec. v.p. Investment Techs., Inc., Edison, N.J., 1985-91, also bd. dirs.; pvt. practice, Middletown, N.J., 1991—; exec. v.p., CFO Gateways to Space, Inc., 1994-96, also bd. dirs.; adj. prof. Monmouth Coll., 1983-85. Fellow N.J. Soc. CPA's; mem. AICPA, Am. Acctg. Assn., Middletown C. of C., Rotary. Home: 30 Southview Ter S Middletown NJ 07748-2415 Office: One Arin Park 1715 Highway 35 Middletown NJ 07748

MEYR, SHARI LOUISE, webmaster; b. San Diego, Dec. 6, 1951; d. Herchell M. and Etta Louise (Bass) Knight; m. William Earl Groom, Oct. 22, 1977 (div. Sept. 1989), Herbert Carl Meyr Jr., Feb. 23, 1990. AS in Fire Scis., San Diego Mesa Coll., 1976. T.O.S.S. specialist Spectrum Scis. & Software, Mountain Home AFB, 1989-94; Internet webmaster Computer-Land of Boise, 1995—; equestrian instr. Summerwind Ctr., Mountain Home, Idaho, 1979-91; Chow Chow breeder Meyr Kennels, Mountain Home, 1990—; webmaster, CEO Access to Answers, Mountain Home, 1990—; seasonal zoo keeper Soco Gardens Zoo, Maggie Valley, N.C., 1995. Docent Zoo Boise, 1996—. Mem. U.S. Ski Assn. (competition lic., alpine ofcl. profl. coach, master's alpine racer 1991—), Gorilla Found., Summerwind Riding Club (founder, pres. 1981-89), Mountain Home Ski Club (founder, bd. dirs. 1991—), Bogus Basin Ski Club, Sun Valley Ski Club, Amateur Trapshooting Assn. (life), Mountain Home Internet Users Group (founder, dir. 1995—), Idaho Zool. Soc. (edn. com.), Zool Soc. San Diego (Pres.'s Assoc.), Mensa. Home: 570 E 16th N Mountain Home ID 83647-1717

MEYSENBURG, MARY ANN, principal; b. L.A., Sept. 16, 1939; d. Clarence Henry and Mildred Ethel (McGee) Augustine; m. John Harold Meysenburg, June 17, 1967; children: Peter Augustine, Amy Bernadette. BA magna cum laude, U. So. Calif., 1960; MA Pvt. Sch. Adminstrn. magna cum laude, U. San Francisco, 1995. Cert. elem. tchr., Calif. Auditor, escrow officer Union Bank, L.A., 1962-64; v.p., asst. mgr. Bank of Downey, Calif., 1964-66; cons., tchr. Santa Ana (Calif.) Coll. Bus., 1964-66; elem. tchr. St. Bruno's Sch., Whittier, Calif., 1966-70, Pasadena (Calif.) Unified Sch. Dist., 1971-84, Holy Angels Sch., Arcadia, Calif., 1985-89; vice prin., computer coord. Our Mother of Good Counsel, L.A., 1989-93; prin. St. Stephen Martyr, Monterey Park, Calif., 1993—; master catechist religious edn. L.A. Archdiocese, 1988—. Author: History of the Arms Control and Disarmament Organization, 1976; organizer, editor newsletter Cath. Com. for Girl Scouts and Campfire. Eucharistic min. Our Mother of Good Counsel, 1989-95; sec. of senatus Legion of Mary, 1980-85; counselor Boy Scouts Am., 1985—; mem. Cath. com. for Girl Scouts U.S.A. and Campfire, vice chmn. acad. affairs L.A. Archdiocese, 1985-90. Recipient Pius X medal L.A. Archdiocese, 1979, St. Elizabeth Ann Seton award Cath. Com. for Girl Scouts, 1988, St. Anne medal Cath. Com. for Girl Scouts, 1989, Bronze Pelican award Cath. Com. for Boy Scouts, 1989; grantee Milken Family Found., 1989, 92. Mem. Phi Beta Kappa, Phi Delta Kappa (historian 1991-92, founds. rep. 1992-93, treas. 1993-94, 1st v.p. 1994-95, pres. 1995-96), Phi Kappa Phi. Avocations: tennis, walking, swimming, reading. Home: 6725 Brentmead Ave Arcadia CA 91007-7708 Office: 119 S Ramona Ave Monterey Park CA 91754-2802

MEZAINIS, VALDIS E., federal agency administrator; b. Chgo.. BS in Biology, Loyola U.; M in Fisheries and Aquatic Ecology, Auburn U., 1977; PhD in Soil and Water Sci., U. Ariz. Numerous positions Peace Corps; dir. office internat. cooperation and devel. divsn. internat. tng. USDA, 1985-88, dir. divsn. rsch. and sci. exch. Fgn. Agrl. Svc., 1988-95; dep. chief Internat. Forestry, Washington, 1995—. Mem. Am. Fisheries Soc., Am. Soc. Agronomy, Soil Sci. Soc. Am., Crop Sci. Soc. Am., Soc. Am. Foresters. Office: Internat Forestry PO Box 96090 Washington DC 20090-6090*

MEZEY, JUDITH PAUL, social worker; b. N.Y.C., Nov. 14, 1946; d. Chester Eugene and Shirley (Bagley) Paul; m. Robert Joseph Mezey, Apr. 6, 1968; children: Jennifer Robin, Barry Paul. BS, Boston U., 1968; EdM, Columbia U., 1972; MSW, Barry U., 1990. Lic. social worker; RN. Pediatric staff nurse Albert Einstein Coll., N.Y.C., 1967-69; clin. instr. Morrisania-Montefiore Hosp., N.Y.C., 1969-71; grad. student nursing Tchrs. Coll., Columbia U., N.Y.C., 1971-72; clin. instr. Pace U., N.Y.C., 1972-74, U. Miami, 1976-77, Fla. Internat. U., Miami, 1978-79; clin. instr. Barry U., Miami, 1979-86, social work grad. student, 1987-90; psychotherapist A&A Profl. Assocs., South Miami, 1991-93; pvt. practice Miami, Fla., 1993—; facilitator support group Bapt. Hosp., Miami, 1991—. Bd. dirs. Dave and Mary Alper Jewish Cmty. Ctr., Miami, 1986—, chmn. spl. needs com., Miami, 1988—; founding chairperson Spl. Needs Program, 1988. Recipient Fed. Nurse Traineeship grant U.S. Govt., 1970. Mem. NASW. Democrat. Jewish. Avocations: tennis player, orchid grower, duplicate bridge. Home: 6740 SW 99th Ter Miami FL 33156-3240 Office: 9260 Sunset Dr Ste 203 Miami FL 33173-3255

MEZEY, ROBERT, poet, educator; b. Phila., Feb. 28, 1935; s. Ralph and Clara (Mandel) M.; m. Olivia Simpson (div.); children: Naomi, Judah, Eve. Student, Kenyon Coll., 1951-53; BA, U. Iowa, 1959; postgrad., Stanford U., 1960-61. Lectr. Western Res. U., Cleve., 1963-64, Franklin & Marshall Coll., Lancaster, Pa., 1965-66; asst. prof. Fresno (Calif.) State U., 1967-68, U. Utah, Salt Lake City, 1973-76; prof., poet-in-residence Pomona Coll., Claremont, Calif., 1976—. Author: (poems) The Lovemaker, 1960, White Blossoms, 1965 (Lamont award), The Door Standing Open, 1970, Selected Translations, 1981, Evening Wind, 1988 (Bassine citation, PEN prize 1989); editor Naked Poetry, 1968, Poems from the Hebrew, 1973, Collected Poems of Henri Coulette, 1990; translator: Tungsten (César Vallejo), 1987. With U.S. Army, 1953-55. Fellow Ingram Merrill, 1973, 89, Guggenheim Found., 1977, Stanford U., 1960, NEA, 1987; recipient Poetry prize Am. Acad. Arts and Letters, 1982. Avocations: tennis, chess. Home: 1663 Chattanooga Ct Claremont CA 91711-2917 Office: Pomona Coll Dept English 140 W 6th St Claremont CA 91711-4301

MEZVINSKY, EDWARD M., lawyer; b. Ames, Iowa, Jan. 17, 1937; m. Marjorie Margolies; 11 children. BA, U. Iowa, 1960; MA in Polit. Sci., U. Calif., Berkeley, 1963, JD, 1965. State rep. Iowa State Legislature, 1969-70; U.S. congressman 1st Dist., Iowa, 1973-77; U.S. rep. UN Commn. on Human Rights, 1977-79; chmn. Pa. Dem. State Com., 1981-86. Author: A Term to Remember; contbr. articles to law jours. Mem. Pa. Bar Assn., Omicron Delta Kappa. Office: 815 N Woodbine Ave Narberth PA 19072-1430

MEZZULLO, LOUIS ALBERT, lawyer; b. Balt., Sept. 20, 1944; m. Judith Scales, Jan. 2, 1970. BA, U. Md., 1967, MA, 1976; JD, T.C. Williams Law Sch., 1976. Bar: Va. 1976. Sales rep. Humble Oil (name now Exxon), Richmond, Va., 1970-72; acctg. Marcoin, Inc., Richmond, 1972-73; pvt. practice bookkeeping, tax preparation Richmond, 1973-76; assoc. McGuire, Woods, Battle and Boothe, Richmond, 1976-79; dir. Mezzullo & McCandlish, Richmond, 1979—. Contbr. articles to profl. jours. Bd. dirs. Richmond Symphony; former pres. Southampton Citizens Assn., Richmond, 1986. Served with USAR, 1969-75. Mem. ABA (tax sect.), Internat. Acad. Estate and Trust Law, Am. Coll. Trust and Estate Counsel, Am. Coll. Tax Counsel, Va. State Bar (tax sect.), Va. Bar Assn., Am. Bar Found., Va. Law Found., Estate Planning Coun. Richmond, Trust Adminstrs. Coun., Willow Oaks Country Club. Home: 2961 Westchester Rd Richmond VA 23225-1842 Office: Mezzullo & McCandlish PO Box 796 Richmond VA 23218

MFUME, KWEISI, former congressman; b. Balt., Oct. 24, 1948; divorced; children: Donald, Kevin, Keith, Ronald, Michael. BS, Morgan State U.; MA, Johns Hopkins U., 1984. Mem. Balt. City Council, 1979-87, 100th-104th Congresses from 7th Md. dist., 1987—; former chmn. congl. black caucus, ranking minority mem., mem. banking and fin. svcs. subcom. on gen. oversight and investigations, mem. small bus. com., mem. joint econ. com.; head NAACP, 1997—; former adj. prof. polit. sci. Morgan State U., Balt. Baptist. Office: NAACP 4805 Mount Hope Dr Baltimore MD 21215*

MIAH, ABDUL MALEK, electrical engineer, educator; b. Dhaka, Bangladesh, Feb. 14, 1948; came to U.S., 1985; s. Abdur Rahim Miah and Monjuman Begum; m. Meherunnesa Begum, Dec. 11, 1972; children: Tanveer Ahmed, Rudia Begum. BSEE, Bangladesh U. Engring. & Tech., 1969, MSEE, 1981; PhD in Elec. Engring., Wayne State U., 1992. Asst. works mgr. Bangladesh Ordnance Factories, Ghazipur, 1972-76; asst. prof. Bangladesh U. Engring. and Tech., Dhaka, 1976-82; elec. engr. SWS Engring., Inc., Birmingham, Mich., 1989; asst. prof. S.C. State U., Orangeburg, 1990-95, assoc. prof., 1995—. Mem. IEEE. Avocations: reading, watching tv, travel.

MIAN, AHMAD ZIA, economist; b. Panjab, Pakistan, Aug. 8, 1942; came to U.S., 1971; s. Ahmad Hussain and Zohra (Sharif) M.; m. Avil Alcott Newman (div. July 1986); children: Tauneel, Michael. BA with honors, Panjab U., Lahore, Pakistan, 1960; MA, Panjab U., 1962; LLB, Karachi U., Pakistan, 1970; MS, U. W.I., Kingston, Jamaica, 1979; postgrad., U. Pa., 1988. Staff economist Pakistan Inst. Devel. Econ., Karachi, 1962-65; investment analyst Esso Ea. Inc. (Exxon), Karachi, 1965-70; systems specialist Ins. Svc. Office, N.Y.C., 1971-72; sr. indsl. economist Govt. Jamaica, Kingston, 1972-74, energy planner, 1974-78; energy advisor UN, N.Y.C., 1978-80; sr. ops. officer The World Bank, Washington, 1980—; energy advisor Govt. Jamaica, Kingston, 1990-94. Author various energy reports; contbr. articles to profl. jours. Mem. rev. com. task force on energy Trilateral Commn., 1978. Named Ky. col. Commonwealth of Ky., 1989. Mem. Am. Econ. Assn.

MIAN, FAROUK ASLAM, chemical engineer, educator; b. Lahore, Punjab, Pakistan, Aug. 10, 1944; came to U.S., 1969; s. Mohd Aslam and Qureshia Mian; m. Zahida Perveen, July 16, 1970; children: Shoaib F., Sophia F. BS in Chem. Engring., Inst. Chem. Tech., Punjab U., Lahore, 1964, MS in Chem. Engring., 1965; postgrad., Ill. Inst. Tech., Chgo., 1972-74. Registered profl. engr., Tex., Calif., Colo., La., Miss., Wis., Wyo.; registered environ. engr.; diplomate Am. Acad. Environ. Engrs. Chem. engr. Kohinoor/Didier-Werke, 1965-69, Nuclear Data, Inc., Palatine, Ill., 1969-71; prodn. supr. Searle Corp., Arlington Heights, Ill., 1971-74; lead process engr. Austin Co., Des Plaines, Ill., 1974-76, Crawford and Russell, Inc., Houston, 1976-77; supr. process Bechtel, Inc., Houston, 1977-80; process mgr. Litwin Corp., Houston, 1980; mgr. chems., product-chems. line mgr. Brown and Root, Inc., Houston, 1980—; chmn.'s adviser U.S. Congl. Adv. Bd., Am. Security Coun. Found., Washington, 1983-84. Contbr. articles to profl. publs. Mem. AICE, NSPE, Technologists. Achievements include engring. design/rsch. in petrochemicals, petroleum refining, inorganic/organic chemicals, specialty and fine chemicals, polymers, petroleum refining and coal gasification processes, chlor-alkali and electro-chemicals, food/pharmaceuticals; advisor, cons. to fin. instns. and investment banks on the major transactions in the chlor-alkali (chlorine caustic) soda ash, speciality chemicals, vinyl chemicals, petrochemicals, and related finished products. Office: Brown and Root Inc PO Box 4574 Houston TX 77210-4574

MIAN, GUO, electrical engineer; b. Shanghai, Feb. 6, 1957; came to U.S., 1987; s. Wenseng Mian and Guorong Sun; m. Ann Wang, Nov. 1, 1989. BS in Physics, Shanghai U. Sci. & Tech., 1982; MS in Physics, Western Ill. U., 1989; DSc in Elec. Engring., Washington U., 1992. Mgr. Rec. Media Lab. Magnetic Rec. Ctr., Shanghai (China) Ctrl. Chem. Ltd., 1982-85; vis. scientist materials sci. lab. Keio U., Yokohama, Japan, 1985-87; sr. rsch. elec. engring. Quantum Corp., Milpitas, Calif., 1992-93, Conner Peripherals, San Jose, Calif., 1993-95; sr. mgr. HDD R&D Ctr. Samsung Info. Sys. Am., San Jose, Calif., 1995—. Contbr. articles to Jour. Materials Sci., IEEE Trans. Magnetics, Jour. Magnetism & Magnetic Materials, Jour. Applied Physics, Japanese Jour. Applied Physics, Jour. Japanese Magnetic Soc. Recipient C & C Promotion award Found. for C & C Promotion, Tokyo, 1986. Mem. IEEE, IEEE Magnetics Soc., IEEE Computer Soc., Am. Phys. Soc. Achievements include discovery of transverse correlation length in magnetic thin film media, a linear relationship between correlation function of media noise and an off track displacement of a recording head, an algorithm to determine an autocorrelation signal to noise ratio for an arbitraty data sequence in time domain, an algorithm to determine a nonlinear bit shift in high density magnetic storage by a time domain correlation analysis which has been implemented in Lecory 7200 and 9350 digital scopes, an in-situ measurement of exchange coupling of magnetic thin film, mechanism of residual stress forming and releasing in electronic ceramics processing; inventor in field. Home: 105 Serra Way # 362 Milpitas CA 95035-5206

MIANO, LOUIS STEPHEN, advertising executive; b. N.Y.C., July 28, 1934; s. Louis Clyde and Zefira (Palombo) M. BA, Dartmouth Coll., 1955; MA, Columbia U., 1958. Writer Look Mag., N.Y.C., 1960-61; editor Show

Mag., N.Y.C. and L.A., 1961-63; assoc. producer ABC-TV, N.Y.C. and L.A., 1963-66; vice-chmn., dir. creative services AC&R Advt., N.Y.C., 1966-90; sec. EEE Theatrical Ventures, N.Y.C., 1974—; cons. in field. Co-producer plays: Design for Living, Corpse, The Seagull, Legends, Inner Voices, 1974-86. Trustee Marymount Manhattan Coll., N.Y.C., 1980—; cons. Home Box Office, 1991-92; bd. dirs. The Nat. Bd. of Rev. of Motion Pictures, 1995—; bd. dirs., sec. Circle-in-the Square. Mem. N.Y. Athletic Club. Home and Office: 430 E 57th St New York NY 10022-3061

MIASKIEWICZ, THERESA ELIZABETH, secondary education educator; b. Salem, Mass., Aug. 29, 1933; d. Chester and Anastasia (Zmijewski) M. BA, Emmanuel Coll., Boston, 1954. Cert. tchr., Mass.; lic. real estate broker, Mass. Tchr. fgn. lang. dept. Salem Sch. Dept., 1954-94; head tchr. Salem High Sch., 1954-94; ret., 1994; vol. Salem Hosp., 1979-88, Salem Hosp. Aux., 1980—; playground instr. City of Salem summers, 1951-54; mem. vis. com. New Eng. Assn. Secondary Schs. and Colls., Salem Sch. Com., 1996—, Mass. Assn. Sch. Coms., 1996—, chmn. bldgs. and grounds, 1996-97, curriculum health adv., 1996-97, assessment com., 1997; active Salem Sch. Com., 1996—. Vol. Salem Hosp., 1979-88, House of Seven Gables, Salem, summers, 1987-89; active North Shore Med. Ctr. Aux.; mem. com. Salem Sch., 1996. Mem. Am. Assn. Ret. Persons (NRTA divsn.), Ret. State, County and Mcpl. Employees Assn., Nat. Ret. Tchrs. Assn., New Eng. Assn. Secondary Schs. and Colls., Mass. Ret. Tchrs. Assn., Mass. Fedn. Polish Women's Clubs (v.p. 1988-89, regional chmn. scholarship com.), Mass. Assn. Scg. Coms., Polish Bus. and Profl. Women's Club Greater Boston (past corr. sec., chmn. scholarship com.,pres. 1988-89). Avocations: travel, floral design, cooking, reading, arts and crafts.

MICA, JOHN L., congressman; b. Binghamton, N.Y., Jan. 27, 1943; s. John and Adeline Resciniti M.; m. Patricia Szymanek, 1972; children: D'anne, Clark. AA, Miami (Fla.)-Dade C.C., 1965; BA, U. Fla., 1967. Chief of staff U.S. Senate; v.p. Winter Park (Fla.) Antique Mall; pres. M.K. Devel. Corp., Winter Park; mem. Fla. Ho. of Reps., 1976-80; mem. appropriations com., mem. ethics com., mem. elections com., mem. cmty. affairs com.; mem. transp. and infrastructre com., govt. reform and oversight com., chmn. civil svc. com. 103rd Congress from 7th Fla. Dist., 1993—. Author: Factor affecting local government reorganization efforts in Florida, Urban and Environmental Issues. Active Beth Johnson Mental Health Bd., PTA Bd., Zora Neale Hurston Meml. Com. Recipient Outstanding Svc. award Fla. Conservative Union, Outstanding Svc. award Fla. Cancer Soc., Outstanding Svc. award Sertoma, Outstanding Young Men of Am. award; named one of five outstanding Young Men in Fla. Mem. Kiwanis, Winter Park Jaycees (Good Govt. award 1972), Fla. Jaycees Statewide (Good Govt. award 1973), Tiger Bay. Republican. Episcopal. Office: PO Box 756 Winter Park FL 32790-0756 Office: US House of Reps 106 Cannon Bldg Washington DC 20515-0907

MICCICHE, SALVATORE JOSEPH, retired journalist, lawyer; b. Everett, Mass., Jan. 27, 1928; s. Calogero and Marianna M.; m. Theresa Ellen Miraglia, Oct. 11, 1953; children: Charles M., Marlene, Marcia E. B.S. in Journalism, Boston U., 1950; LL.B., Suffolk U., 1968. Bar: Mass. 1968, U.S. Dist. Ct. Mass. 1977. Reporter Portsmouth (N.H.) Herald, 1953-55; with Boston Globe, 1955-90, editorial writer, 1969-70, Washington bur., 1970-75, asst. to editor, 1975-77, mng. editor for adminstrn., 1977-80, ombudsman, 1980-82, assoc. editor for editorial dept. legal matters, 1982-85, asst. exec. editor, 1985, ret., 1990. Served with U.S. Army, 1950-52. Mem. Mass. Bar (bar-press com. 1975-90), Boston Bar Assn., Orgn. Newspaper Ombudsmen (past dir.), Am. Soc. Newspaper Editors. Roman Catholic. Home: PO Box 152 33 Martha's Ln South Harwich MA 02661

MICEK, ERNEST S., food products executive; b. Arcadia, Wis., Feb. 18, 1936; m. Sally; 4 children. BS in Chem. Engring., U. Wis., 1959. Mgr. Cargill, Inc., Mpls., 1959, Spain; asst. v.p., gen. mgr. corn milling dept. Cargill, Inc., Mpls., 1973, v.p. milling divsn., 1978, pres. corn milling divsn., 1981, pres. food sector, 1992, exec. v.p., 1993, pres., 1994—, chmn., CEO, 1995—; bd. dirs. Cargill, Inc., Schneider Nat.; mem. bd. overseers, mem. internat. adv. bd. Carlson Sch. Mgmt.; mem. vis. com. chem. engring. dept. U. Wis., chmn. indsl. liaison coun. Bd. dirs. United Way Exec. Com., Mpls.; trustee U. St. Thomas., U. Wis. Rsch. Found. Recipient Disting. Svc. citation U. Wis. Dept. Engring., 1991. Mem. Nat. Assn. Mfrs. (chmn. trade tech. policy group, bd. dirs., exec. com.). Office: Adminstrv office Cargill Inc PO Box 5724 Minneapolis MN 55440

MICH, CONNIE RITA, mental health nurse, educator; b. Nebr., Feb. 5, 1926; d. Henry B. and Anna (Stratman) Redel; m. Richard Mich. BSN, Alverno Coll.; postgrad., Marquette U.; MSN, Cath. U. Am. Asst. clin. dir. in-patient svcs. Fond du Lac (Wis.) County Health Ctr., 1974-78; head nurse, program coord. acute psychiat. unit St. Agnes Hosp., Fond du Lac, 1979-83; mental health clinician Immanuel Med. Ctr., Omaha, 1984-89; instr., clin. supr., asst. prof. psychiat. mental health Coll. St. Mary, Omaha, 1989-93; med. programs dir. Inst. Computer Sci. Ltd., 1989—; program dir. med. programs Gateway Coll., Omaha, 1995; chairperson Examining Coun. on RNs; writer items State Bd. Test Pool Exam.; pres. Milw. Coun. Cath. Nurses; vice chairperson Wis. Conf. Group Psychiat. Nursing Practice. Mem. Sigma Theta Tau, Pi Gamma Mu.

MICHA, DAVID ALLAN, chemistry and physics educator; b. Argentina, Sept. 12, 1939; came to U.S., 1966, naturalized, 1974; s. Simon David and Catalina (Cohen) M.; m. Rebecca Stefan, 1991; children: Michael F., Anna K. MS, U. Cuyo, Bariloche, Argentina, 1962; DSc, U. Uppsala, Sweden, 1966. Rsch. assoc. Theoretical Chemistry Inst. U. Wis., Madison, 1966-67; asst. rsch. physicist Inst. Pure and Applied Sci. U. Calif., La Jolla, 1967-69; assoc. prof. chemistry and physics U. Fla., Gainesville, 1969-74, prof., 1974—, dir. Ctr. Chem. Physics, 1982-91; vis. prof. U. Gothenburg, Sweden, 1970, Harvard U., 1972, 90, Max-Planck Inst., Göttingen, Germany, 1976, 96, Imperial Coll., London, 1977, U. Calif., Santa Barbara, 1982, U. Colo. and Weizmann Inst., Israel, 1983, U. Buenos Aires, 1988, 95, Supercomputer Inst., Fla. State U., 1991; mem. adv. panel div. advanced sci. computing NSF, 1990-92, Max-Planck Inst. Astrophysik, Munich, Germany, 1996, 97. Mem. editl. bd. Internat. Jour. Quantum Chemistry, 1979-88, Few-Body Systems, 1985—; editor Finite Systems and Multiparticle Dynamics, 1990—, symposium procs.; contbr. several book chpts., numerous articles to sci. jours. Recipient U.S. Sr. Scientist award A. Von Humboldt Found., 1976, Sr. Faculty Rsch. award Sigma Xi, 1985; Alfred P. Sloan Found. fellow, 1971-74; Nat. Bur. Standards JILA fellow, 1983. Fellow Am. Phys. Soc. (vice chmn. topical group on few body sys. and multi-particle dynamics 1986-88, chmn. 1988-89); mem. Am. Chem. Soc., Sigma Xi. Office: U Fla 366 Williamson Hall Gainesville FL 32611-8435

MICHAEL, ALFRED FREDERICK, JR., physician, medical educator; b. Phila.; s. Alfred Frederick and Emma Maude (Peters) M.; children: Mary, Susan, Carol. M.D., Temple U., 1953. Diplomate: Am. Bd. Pediatrics (founding mem. sub-bd. pediatric nephrology, pres. 1977-80). Diagnostic lab. immunology and pediatric nephrology intern Phila. Gen. Hosp., 1953-54; resident Children's Hosp. and U. Cin. Coll. Medicine, 1957-60; postdoctoral fellow dept. pediatrics Med. Sch., U. Minn., Mpls., 1960-63; asso. prof. Med. Sch., U. Minn., 1965-68, prof. pediatrics, lab. medicine and pathology, 1968—, dir. pediatric nephrology, Regents' Prof., head Dept. Pediatrics, 1986—, interim dean, 1996—; established investigator Am. Heart Assn., 1963-68. Mem. editorial bd. Internat. Yr. Book of Nephrology, Kidney Internat., Am. Jour. Nephrology, Kidney Internat., Am. Jour. Nephrology, Clin. Nephrology, Am. Jour. Pathology; contbr. articles to profl. jours. Served with USAF, 1955-57. Recipient Alumni Achievement award in clin. scis. Temple U. Sch. Medicine, 1988; NIH fellow, 1960-63; Guggenheim fellow, 1966-67; AAAS fellow, 1995. Mem. AAAS, AMA, Am. Acad. Pediat., Am. Soc. Clin. Investigation, Assn. Am. Physicians, Am. Pediat. Soc., Soc. for Pediat. Rsch., Am. Assn. Investigative Pathology, Am. Soc. Cell Biology, Ctrl. Soc. for Clin. Rsch., Am. Soc. Nephrology (coun., pres.-elect 1992—, pres. 1993), Internat. Soc. Nephrology, Soc. for Exptl. Biology and Medicine, Am. Fedn. Clin. Rsch., Minn. Med. Assn. Congregationalist. Office: U Minn Hosp Dept Pediatrics PO Box 391 Minneapolis MN 55455

MICHAEL, DONALD NELSON, social scientist, educator; b. Chgo., Jan. 24, 1923; s. Albert Abraham and Jean (Lewis) M.; m. Margot Jean Murphy, Apr. 7, 1956; 1 child, Geoffrey William. S.B., Harvard U., 1946, Ph.D., 1952; M.A., U. Chgo., 1948; D.Sc. (hon.), Marlboro Coll., 1964. Staff social scientist Weapons Systems Evaluation Group U.S., Joint Chiefs Staff, Washington, 1953-54; adviser Office Spl. Studies NSF, Washington, 1954-56; sr. research asso. Dunlap & Assos., Stanford, Conn., 1956-59; sr. staff mem. Brookings Instn., Washington, 1959-61; dir. Peace Research Inst., Washington, 1961-63; resident fellow Inst. Policy Studies, Washington, 1963-66; prof. planning and pub. policy U. Mich., Ann Arbor, 1967-82, prof. psychology, 1966-82, prof. emeritus, 1982—, program dir. Ctr. Rsch. Utilization Sci. Knowledge, 1966-82; rsch. assoc. Inst. Urban and Regional Design, U. Calif., Berkeley, 1980—; mem. Commn. Study Orgn. Peace, 1965-74; sr. mgmt. cons. SRI Internat., 1980-88; spl. rschr. Shanghai Inst. for Sci. of Sci., 1988—; adj. faculty Saybrook Inst., San Francisco, 1983-91. Author: Proposed Studies on the Implications of Peaceful Space Activities for Human Affairs, 1961, Cybernation: The Silent Conquest, 1962, The Next Generation, 1965, The Unprepared Society, 1968, On Learning to Plan —And Planning to Learn, 1973; 2d rev. edit. 1997. Founding mem. nat. bd. U.S. Assn. for Club of Rome, 1978-81; mem. nat. bd. Citizen Involvement Network, 1975; mem. nat. bd. dirs. Girl Scouts U.S.A., 1969-72, Congl. Inst. for Future; mem. exec. bd. Wash. Assn. Scientists, 1961-66, chmn., 1963-64; founding bd. dirs., mem. adv. bd. Rollo May Ctr. for Humanistic Studies, San Francisco, 1988—; bd. dirs. San Francisco chpt. UN Assn., 1989-92; mem. adv. bd. Resource Renewal Inst., Sausalito, Calif., 1991—; adv. bd. Commonweal, Bolinas, Calif., 1993—. named lectr. 10th Ann. John Dewey Soc., 1967; NIMH spl. rsch. fellow, 1968-70, vis. fellow Inst. Internat. Studies U. Calif., Berkeley, 1972-73, fellow Sch. Mgmt. and Strategic Studies We. Behavioral Sci. Inst., La Jolla, Calif., 1981-92; recipient Aurelio Peccei prize L'eta Verde, Rome, 1987; named hon. rsch. prof. Rsch. Ctr. Econ., Tech. and Social Devel. of State Coun., Shanghai, 1988. Fellow AAAS, APA, Inst. Soc. Ethics Life Scis., Soc. for Psychol. Study Social Issues, World Acad. Art and Sci.; mem. Am. Soc. Cybernetics (founding bd. 1964-68), Internat. Soc. for Panetics (founding mem., founding bd. govs. 1991-94), N.Y. Acad. Scis., Fedn. Am. Scientists, Meridian Internat. Inst. (founding bd. 1992—), Club of Rome, Cosmos Club, Sigma Xi.

MICHAEL, ERNEST ARTHUR, mathematics educator; b. Zurich, Switzerland, Aug. 26, 1925; came to U.S., 1939; s. Jakob and Erna (Sondheimer) M.; m. Colette Verger Davis, 1956 (div. 1966); children: Alan, David, Gerard; m. Erika Goodman Joseph, Dec. 4, 1966; children: Hillary, Joshua. B.A., Cornell U., 1947; M.A., Harvard U., 1948; Ph.D., U. Chgo., 1951. Mem. faculty dept. math. U. Wash., Seattle, 1953—; asst. prof. U. Wash., 1953-56, assoc. prof., 1956-60, prof., 1960-93, prof. emeritus, 1993—; mem. Inst. for Advanced Study, Princeton, 1951-52, 56-57, 60-61, 68, Math. Research Inst., E.T.H., Zürich, 1973-74; vis. prof. U. Stuttgart, Ger., 1978-79, U. Munich, Fed. Republic Germany, 1987, 88, 92-93. Editor: Procs. Am. Math. Soc., 1968-71, Topology and Its Applications, 1972-94; contbr. articles to profl. jours. Served with USNR, 1944-46. Grantee AEC; Grantee Office Nav. Research; Grantee NSF; Grantee Guggenheim Found.; Grantee Humboldt Found. Mem. Am. Math. Soc., Math. Assn. Am., ACLU, Amnesty Internat. Jewish. Home: 16751 15th Ave NW Seattle WA 98177-3842 Office: U Washington Dept Math GN 50 Seattle WA 98195

MICHAEL, GARY G., retail supermarket and drug chain executive; b. 1940; married. BS in Bus., U. Idaho, 1962. Staff acct. Ernst & Ernst, CPA's, 1964-66; with Albertson's, Inc., Boise, Idaho, 1966—, acct., 1966-68, asst. controller, 1968-71, controller, 1971-72, v.p., controller, 1972-74, sr. v.p. fin., treas., 1974-76, exec. v.p., 1976-84, vice chmn., CFO, corp. devel. officer, 1984-91, chmn., CEO, 1991—; also dir. Albertson's, Inc. Served to 1st lt. U.S. Army, 1962-64. Office: Albertsons Inc PO Box 20 250 Parkcenter Blvd Boise ID 83726*

MICHAEL, GARY LINN, architect, artist; b. Portland, Oreg., Apr. 27, 1934; s. Donald Glenn and Ida Marie (Luoto) M.; m. Sandra Ann Schori, Sept. 16, 1956 (div. 1982); children: Brian Russell, Laura Joy, Jesse Daniel. B.Arch., U. Oreg., 1957; M.Arch., Yale U., 1965. Partner Campbell, Michael, Yost, Portland, 1965-68; prin. Architects & Planners Gary L. Michael, Portland, 1969-74; pres. Michael & Kuhns, Architects, Portland, 1974—; mem. Oreg. Bd. Architect Examiners, 1978-84; guest archtl. design critic Portland State U., U. Oreg.; guest lectr. pub. schs., colls., tchr. tng. seminars. Works include Mentor Graphics Child Development Center, Wilsonville, Oreg., 1991, Zach Studio and Residence, Elmira, Oreg., 1969, Cowles Bldg, Portland, 1973, Unthank Plaza Pub. Housing, Portland, 1977, Duniway Ctr., Portland, 1982, student housing at Wash. State U., U. Wash., U. Alaska, Portland State U., The Evergreen State Coll., So. Oreg. State Coll., Linfield Coll., Reed Coll.; landscape paintings are included in private and corp. collections. Mem. Portland Sch. Dist. Eco-Aesthetics Bd., 1972-74; mem. citizens coordinating com. Oreg. Hwy. Div., 1973; chmn. Sensible Transp. Options for People, Portland, 1974; mem. Downtown Housing Adv. Com., 1978-81; chair adv. com. Milw. Riverfront Devel., 1987-89. Ion Lewis Traveling fellow, 1957. Fellow AIA (11 local design awards 1960-80, nat. design award 1973, pres. Portland chpt. 1972). Home: 11907 SE 19th Ave Milwaukie OR 97222-7801 Office: Michael & Kuhns Archs PC 421 SW 6th Ave Portland OR 97204

MICHAEL, GAYLE GRANATIR, English language educator, educational consultant; b. Phila., Dec. 6, 1938; d. Michael and Anne (Quittle) Rosenfeld; widowed; children: Matthew, Geoffrey. BA, Temple U., 1960; MA, St. Joseph's U., 1967. Cert. tchr., Pa. Tchr., coach Media (Pa.) Boro Sch. Dist., 1960-63, Camden (N.J.) City Sch. Dist., 1963-66; prodn. mgr. Advt. Agy., Phila., 1966-67; tchr., coach Norristown (Pa.) Area Sch. Dist., 1968-71; instr. Rutgers U., Camden, 1972-73; ednl. cons., acad. tutor Bala Cynwyd, Pa., 1982—; pvt. practice polit. cons. Bala Cynwyd, 1994—; ghost writer, Bala Cynwyd, 1982—; pub. speaking coach, Bala Cynwyd, 1982—, polit. cons. Bala Cynwyd, 1994—; bd. dirs. Main Line Women's Network, Lower Merion, Pa., 1988-90. Alumni bd. govs. St. Joseph's U., Phila., 1992—; committeewoman Montgomery County Rep. Party, Norristown, 1992—; bd. dirs. Rep. Women of Main Line, Lower Merion, Pa., 1989—; weather spotter U.S. Dept. Commerce, Washington, 1989—; charter mem. Nat. Coun. Women Advisors to U.S. Congress, 1995—; bd. dirs. Montgomery County Women's Rep. Leadership Com., 1995—; candidate Rep. Congrl. Primary, 1994. Named to Pa. Honor Roll of Women, 1996. Mem. MLA, Inter Collegiate Studies Inst., Bala Cynwyd Neighborhood Club, World Affairs Coun., Nat. Rifle Assn., Nat. Fedn. Rep. Women. Avocations: travel, research, writing. Office: PO Box 141 Bala Cynwyd PA 19004-0141

MICHAEL, GEORGE (GERGIOS KYRIAKOU PANAYIOTOU), musician, singer, songwriter; b. London, Eng., June 25, 1963; s. Jack and Lesley Panayiotou. Formed group The Executive with Andrew Ridgeley, 1979, band became Wham!, 1980-86. Albums with Wham! Fantastic, 1982, Make it Big, 1984, Music From the Edge of Heaven, 1985; album (with Lisa Stransfield) Five Live, 1993; solo releases Faith, 1987 (best dir. MTV Video award 1988, Best Pop Male Vocalist Am. Music award, 1989, best soul R&B vocalist Am. Music award 1989, best soul R&B album Am. Music award 1989), Listen Without Prejudice, Vol. I, 1990; contbr. albums Two Rooms: Celebrating the Songs of Elton John and Bernie Taupin, 1991, Red, Hot & Dance, 1992, A Very Special Christmas II, 1992; duet (with Aretha Franklin) I Knew You Were Waiting For Me, 1987 (Grammy award best duo R&B 1987); prodr., writer Trojan Souls. Recipient Best New Video Artist award Am. Video Awards, 1985, Grammy nomination Wham! best pop performance by duo, 1985. Office: Elektra 3300 Warner Blvd Burbank CA 91505*

MICHAEL, HAROLD KAYE (BUD MICHAEL), sales and marketing executive; b. Tracy, Calif., Dec. 3, 1955; s. Harold Kaye Sr. and Marjorie (Goodwin) M.; m. Barbara Ann Samuels, Sept. 5, 1981; children: Sean Solomon, Stephen Goodwin. BA in Econs., Stanford U., 1978; Grad. Bus., U. Santa Clara, Calif., 1981. Mktg. engr. Intel Corp., Santa Clara, Calif., 1978-82; sales engr. Intel Corp., El Segundo, Calif., 1982-84; sales exec. Tandem Computers, Culver City, Calif., 1984-85, br. sales mgr., 1985, dist. sales mgr., 1985-86, regional sales mgr., 1986-88; v.p. sales ops. Atalla (a Tandem Co.), San Jose, Calif., 1988-90; dir. field mktg. Sequent Computer Systems, Denver, 1990-92; COO R-Squared Distbg., Denver, 1992-93; pres. Solutions Mktg., Denver, 1993-94; v.p., gen. mgr. RSA, Inc., Denver, 1994-96; v.p. sales & mktg. Client Systems, LLC, Denver, 1996—. Polit. intern U.S. Congress, Washington, 1985. Mem. Am. Mgmt. Assn., Stanford Alumni Assn. (life), Kiwanis Club (v.p. 1986-87, pres. 1987-88). Republican. Avocations: running, golf, sailing, tennis, racquetball.

MICHAEL, HAROLD LOUIS, civil engineering educator, consultant; b. Columbus, Ind., July 24, 1920; s. Louis Edward and Martha (Armuth) M.; m. Elsie Marie Ahlbrand, Aug. 15, 1943 (dec. Sept. 1951); m. Elizabeth Annette Welch, Dec. 12, 1954 (dec. Jan. 30, 1989); stepchildren: Betty, Ellen, Harold, Thomas Williams; 1 child, Edward Michael. BSCE with highest distinction, Purdue U., 1950, MSCE, 1951, DEng (hon.), 1992. Registered profl. engr., Ind. Grad. asst. Purdue U., 1950-51; dir. urban transp. studies Ind. State Hwy. Commn., 1951-54; research asst., instr. Purdue U., West Lafayette, Ind., 1952-54, asst. prof. hwy. engring., asst. dir. joint hwy. research project, 1954-56, assoc. prof. hwy. engring., assoc. dir. joint hwy. research project, 1956-61, prof. hwy. engring., head transp. and urban engring., assoc. dir. joint hwy. research project, 1961-78, head Sch. Civil Engring., prof. hwy. engring., dir. joint hwy. research project, 1978-91, prof. emeritus, 1991—; chmn. exec. com. Transp. Rsch. Bd., NRC, 1976, mem. exec. com., 1973-79, chmn. or mem. adv. panels for Nat. Coop. Hwy. Research Programs, 1971-79; mem. adv. bd. Hwy. Extension and Research Program for Ind. Counties, 1971-91; chmn. Nat. Com. on Uniform Traffic Control Devices, 1971-74, mem., 1969—; chmn. Nat. Com. on Uniform Traffic Laws and Ordinances, 1990-95, vice chmn. com. on ops., 1973-90; mem. adv. panel on nat. accident sampling system Nat. Hwy. Traffic Safety Adminstrn., 1978-80; mem. exec. res. U.S. Dept. Transp., 1967-83; mem. com. on transp. NRC, 1976-80; mem. bd. cons. Eno Found. Transp., 1978-82; chmn. Traffic Commn., West Lafayette, Ind., 1956—, chmn. transp. tech. com., Greater Lafayette, 1965—. Served to capt. U.S. Army, 1942-46, ETO; with USAR, 1946-64, ret. lt. col. Decorated Bronze Star; recipient citation for Disting. Service State Ind., 1967, Service award Ind. Soc. Profl. Engr., 1969, Disting. Service award Transp. Research Bd., 1976, Roy W. Crum award Transp. Research Bd., 1978, award in recognition of disting. service Ind. Soc. Profl. Engrs., 1978, Theodore M. Matson award, 1979, George S. Bartlett award Am. Assn. Hwy. and Transp. Ofcls., Am. Rd. and Transp. Builders Assn. and Transp. Research Bd., 1982; named Engr. of Yr., Ind. Soc. Profl. Engrs., 1972; Sagamore of Wabash, Ind. Fellow Inst. Transp. Engrs. (pres. 1974-75, Marsh award 1984), ASCE (hon., mem. ABET visitors com. 1978-83, G. Brooks Earnest Lecture award Cleve. sect. 1981, Laurie Prize 1981, Wilbur S. Smith award 1991); mem. NAE, NSPE (nat. dir. 1964-78), Am. Rd. and Transp. Builders. Assn. (life, vice chmn. 1978-80, chmn. hwys. adv. council 1981-94, Disting. Svc. award 1994), Ind. Constructors, Inc. (hon. life), Am. R.R. Engring. Assn. (chmn. subcom. hwys. 1970-87), Am. Soc. Engring. Edn., Am. Pub. Works Assn. (trustee Research Found. 1976-79), Inst. Transp. Engrs. (hon., Wilbur S. Smith Disting. Transp. Engring. Career Educator 1994), Rotary (dist. gov.), Theta Xi. Avocations: gardening; golf; stamp collecting; coin collecting. Home: 1227 N Salisbury St West Lafayette IN 47906-2415 Office: Purdue U Civil Engring Bldg West Lafayette IN 47907

MICHAEL, HENRY N., geographer, anthropologist; b. Pitts., July 14, 1913; s. Anthony M. and Albina (Dubska) M.; m. Ida Nemez, June 18, 1943; children: Susan Shelley, Richard Carleton, Andrew Paul. B.A., U. Pa., 1948, M.A., 1951, Ph.D., 1954. Instr. geography U. Pa., 1948-54; faculty Temple U., 1958-80, prof. geography, chmn. dept., 1965-73, prof., 1965-80; research assoc. Univ. Mus., Phila., 1959-82, sr. fellow, 1982—; mem. Bi-Nat. Commn. on Social Scis. and Humanities, Am. Council Learned Socs./Acad. Scis. USSR, 1975—. Editor: Anthropology of the North, 1959-72; editor, author: Dating Techniques for the Archaeologist, 1971, 73, 82; translator, editor various archaeol. and ethnographic works; mem. adv. publs. com. Mus. Applied Sci. Ctr. for Archaeology, U. Pa., Anthropology and Archaeology of Eurasia-A Jour. of Transls., Alaska-Siberia Rsch. Ctr.; mem. editorial bd. Expedition-The Univ. Mus. Mag. Archaeology and Anthropology, U. Pa.; contbr. articles to profl. jours. Served to 1st lt. AUS, 1942-45. Decorated Purple Heart. Fellow Am. Anthrop. Assn., Arctic Inst. N.Am.; mem. Phila. Anthrop. Soc. (coun. 1954-90), Delaware Valley Assn. Geographers, Assn. Am. Geographers, Sigma Xi. Home: 2712 Pine Valley Ln Ardmore PA 19003-1719 Office: Univ Museum U Pa Philadelphia PA 19104

MICHAEL, JAMES HARRY, JR., federal judge; b. Charlottesville, Va., Oct. 17, 1918; s. James Harry and Reuben (Shelton) m. Barbara E. Puryear, Dec. 18, 1946; children: Jarrett Michael Stephens, Victoria von der Au. BS, U. Va., 1940, LLB, 1942. Bar: Va. 1942. Sole practice Charlottesville; ptnr. Michael & Musselman, 1946-54, J.H. Michael, Jr., 1954-59, Michael & Dent, 1959-72, Michael, Dent & Brooks Ltd., 1972-74, Michael & Dent, Ltd., 1974-80; assoc. judge Juvenile and Domestic Rels. Ct., Charlottesville, 1954-68; judge U.S. Dist. Ct., Charlottesville, 1980-95, sr. judge, 1996—; mem. Va. Senate, 1968-80; exec. dir. Inst. Pub. Affairs, U. Va., 1952; chmn. Council State Govts., 1975-76, also mem. exec. com.; chmn. So. Legis. Conf., 1974-75. Mem. Charlottesville Sch. Bd., 1951-62; bd. govs. St. Anne-Belfield Sch., 1952-76. Served with USNR, 1942-46; comdr. Res. ret. Wilton Park fellow Wilton Park Conf., Sussex, Eng., 1971. Fellow Am. Bar Found.; mem. ABA, Va. Bar Assn. (v.p. 1956-57), Charlottesville-Albermarle Bar Assn. (pres. 1966-67), Am. Judicature Soc., 4th Jud. Conf., Va. Trial Lawyers Assn. (Va. disting. svc. award 1993), Assn. Trial Lawyers Am., Raven Soc., Sigma Nu Phi, Omicron Delta Kappa. Episcopalian (lay reader). Office: US Dist Ct 255 W Main St Rm 320 Charlottesville VA 22902-5058

MICHAEL, JERROLD MARK, public health specialist, former university dean, educator; b. Richmond, Va., Aug. 3, 1927; s. Joseph Leon and Esther Leah M.; m. Lynn Y. Simon, Mar. 17, 1951; children: Scott J., Nelson L. B.C.E., George Washington U., 1949; M.S.E., Johns Hopkins U., 1950; M.P.H., U. Calif., Berkeley, 1957; Dr. P.H. (hon.), Mahidol U., 1983; Sc.D. (hon.), Tulane U., 1984. Commd. ensign USPHS, 1950, advanced through grades to rear adm., asst. surgeon gen., 1966; ret., 1970; dean Sch. Pub. Health, U. Hawaii, Honolulu, 1971-92, prof. pub. health, 1971-95; emeritus prof. pub. health U. Hawaii, Honolulu, 1995—; bd. dirs. Nat. Health Coun., 1967-78, Nat. Ctr. for Health Edn., 1977-90; mem. nat. adv. coun. on health professions edn., 1978-81; chmn. bd. dirs. Kuakini Med. Ctr., Honolulu; sec., treas. Asia-Pacific Acad. Consortium Pub. Health; vis. prof. U. Adelaide, 1993, George Washington, 1994; hon. prof. Beijing Med. U., 1994. Contbr. articles to profl. jours.; assoc. editor Jour. Environ. Health, 1958-80, Asia-Pacific Jour. of Pub. Health, 1986-95. Served with USNR, 1945-47. Decorated D.S.M., comdr. Royal Order of Elephant (Thailand); recipient Walter Mangold award, 1961, J.S. Billings award for mil. medicine, 1964, gold medal Hebrew U. Jerusalem, 1982, San Karcil gold medal Govt. of Malaysia, 1989, Disting. Svc. award Gov. of Hawaii, 1989, Assn. Schs. Pub. Health, 1992, recognition of svc. award Pacific Island Health Officers Assn., 1992, USPHS awards, also others. Fellow Am. Public Health Assn.; mem. Am. Acad. Health Adminstrn., Am. Soc. Cert. Sanitarians, Nat. Environ. Health Assn., Am. Acad. Environ. Engrs. Democrat. Jewish. Club: Masons. Home: 16736 Gooseneck Terrace Olney MD 20832

MICHAEL, JONATHAN EDWARD, insurance company executive; b. Columbus, Ohio, Mar. 19, 1954. BA, Ohio Dominican Coll., 1977. CPA, Ohio. Acct. Coopers & Lybrand, Columbus, Ohio, 1977-82; chief acct. RLI Ins. Co., Peoria, Ill., 1982-84, controller, 1984-85, v.p. fin., CFO, 1985—, exec. v.p., 1991-94, pres., 1994—. Roman Catholic. Club: Mt. Hawley Country (Peoria). Avocation: golf. Home: 12706 Georgetowne Rd Dunlap IL 61525-9462 Office: RLI Ins Co 9025 N Lindbergh Dr Peoria IL 61615-1431

MICHAEL, M. BLANE, federal judge; b. Charleston, S.C., Feb. 17, 1943. AB, W.Va. U., 1965; JD, NYU, 1968. Bar: N.Y. 1968, U.S. Dist. Ct. (so. and ea. dists.) N.Y. 1968, W.Va. 1973, U.S. Ct. Appeals (4th cir.) 1974, U.S. Dist. Ct. (no. dist.) W.Va. 1975, U.S. Dist. Ct. (so. dist.) W.Va. 1981. Counsel to Gov. W.Va. John D. Rockefeller IV, 1977-80; atty. Jackson & Kelly, Charleston, W.Va., 1981-93; fed. judge U.S. Ct. Appeals (4th cir.), Charleston, W.Va., 1993—; active 4th Jud. Conf. Mem. ABA, W.Va. Bar Assn., Kanawha County Bar Assn., Phi Beta Kappa. Office: US Ct Appeals Fed Bldg 500 Quarrier St Charleston WV 25301-2130*

MICHAEL, MARY AMELIA FURTADO, retired educator, freelance writer; m. Eugene G. Michael; children: David, Douglas, Gregory. BA, Albertus Magnus Coll.; MS, U. Bridgeport, 1975; CAS, Fairfield U., 1982. Cert. secondary sch. sci. tchr., ednl. adminstr. Housemaster, sci. tchr. Fairfield (Conn.) Pub. Schs., adminstrv. housemaster, sci. tchr., sci. dept. coord., 1992, retired, 1992; freelance fin. rsch. and investment writer and cons., 1994—. Author: The Art and Science of Cooking, 1996; contbr. articles to profl. jours. Mem. Discovery Mus., Conn. Arts & Sci. Mus.

Mem. AAUW, LWV, Conn. Assn. Suprs. and Curriculum, Fairfield Sch. Adminstrs. Assn., Retired Educators of Fairfield, Fairfield Hist. Soc. Avocations: collecting antiques, gourmet cooking, collecting old cookbooks and recipes, photography, writing. Home: 942 Valley Rd Fairfield CT 06432-1671

MICHAEL, SANDRA DALE, reproductive endocrinology educator, researcher; b. Sacramento, Calif., Jan. 23, 1945; d. Gordon G. and Ruby F. (Johnson) M.; m. Dennis P. Murr, Aug. 12, 1967 (div. 1974). BA, Calif. State Coll., Sonoma, 1967; PhD, U. Calif., Davis, 1970. NIH predoctoral fellow U. Calif., Davis, 1967-70, NIH postdoctoral fellow, 1970-73, asst. rsch. geneticist, 1973-74; asst. prof. SUNY, Binghamton, 1974-81, assoc. prof., 1981-88, prof. reproductive endocrinology, 1988—, dept. chair, 1992—; adj. prof. dept. ob-gyn. SUNY Health Scis. Ctr., Syracuse; mem. NIH Reproductive Endocrinology Study Sect., 1991-95; cons., presenter in field; grant reviewer NIH, NSF, USDA and others. Contbr. articles to profl. jours. Vice chair Tri Cities Opera Guild, Binghamton, 1987-90, chair, 1990-92; mem. Harpur Forum, Binghamton, 1987—, SUNY Found., Binghamton, 1990-96. Fulbright Sr. scholar Czech Republic, 1994; grantee NIMH, 1976-79, Nat. Cancer Inst., 1977-80, 83-87, Nat. Inst. Environ. Health Scis., 1979-80, NSF, 1981-83, NIH, 1987—. Mem. Endocrine Soc., Soc. for the Study of Reprodn., Soc. for Study of Fertility, Am. Soc. for Immunology of Reprodn., Women in Endocrinology (sec.-treas. 1992-95), Soc. for Exptl. Biology and Medicine, N.Y. Acad. Sci., Sigma Xi. Avocations: golf, skiing, bridge, opera, literature. Office: State Univ of NY Dept Biol Scis Binghamton NY 13902

MICHAEL, WILLIAM BURTON, psychologist, educator; b. Pasadena, Calif., Mar. 6, 1922; s. William Whipple and Helen Augusta (Schultz) M.; m. Martha Walker Hennessey, Aug. 30, 1947 (dec. 1959); m. Joan Yvonne Johnson, Aug. 26, 1966. A.B., UCLA, 1943; M.S. in Edn., U. So. Calif., Los Angeles, 1945, M.A. in Psychology, 1946, Ph.D., 1947. Lic. psychologist Calif. Lectr. engring. math. Calif. Inst. Tech., Pasadena, 1942-45; asst. prof. psychology Princeton U., N.J., 1947-50; research assoc. Rand Corp., Santa Monica, Calif., 1951-52; dir. testing bur. U. So. Calif., Los Angeles, 1952-62, prof. edn. and psychology, 1957-62, 1967—; prof. edn. and psychology U. Calif., Santa Barbara, 1962-67; cons. in field; lectr. math, psychology and edn. U. So. Calif., 1944-47, others. Author: Teaching for Creative Endeavor, 1967; co-author: Psychological Foundations of Learning and Teaching, 2d edit., 1974, Handbook in Research and Evaluation, 3d edit., 1995 (standardized tests) Study Attitudes and Methods Survey, Dimensions of Self-Concept; editor Ednl. and Psychol. Measurement, 1985-95; cons. editor Jour. Pers. Evaluation in Edn., Ednl. Rsch. Quar.; contbr. chpts. to books and articles to profl. jours. Mem., bd. dirs. Neuro-Psychiat. Clinic, Los Angeles and Pasadena, 1958—; mem. Los Angeles Philharmonic Assn., 1965—; advisor Sch. of Communication, Arcadia, Calif., 1981—. Fellow APA, mem. Am. Ednl. Rsch. Assn. (exec. com., editor Rev. Edn. Rsch. 1962-65), Western Psychol. Assn., Northeastern Ednl. Rsch. Assn., Nat. Coun. on Measurement in Edn., Calif. Ednl. Rsch. Assn. (pres. 1965), Phi Beta Kappa, Sigma Xi, Phi Kappa Phi, Psi Chi, Phi Delta Kappa. Independent. Congregationalist. Avocations: Music; travel; reading; ice cream gourmet. Home: 3470 Truesale Way Los Angeles CA 90089-0031 Office: U So Calif Sch Edn 3470 University Ave Los Angeles CA 90007-3503

MICHAELIDES, CONSTANTINE EVANGELOS, architect, educator; b. Athens, Greece, Jan. 26, 1930; came to U.S., 1955, naturalized, 1964; s. Evangelos George and Kalliopi Constantine (Kefallonitis) M.; m. Maria S. Canellakis, Sept. 3, 1955; children: Evangelos Constantine, Dimitri Canellakis. Diploma in Architecture, Nat. Tech. U., Athens, 1952; M.Arch., Harvard U., 1957. Practice architecture Athens, 1954-55, St. Louis, 1963—; asso. architect Carl Koch, Jose Luis Sert, Hideo Sasaki, Cambridge, Mass., 1957-59, Doxiadis Assos., Athens and Washington, 1959-60, Hellmuth, Obata & Kassabaum, St. Louis, 1962; instr. Grad. Sch. Design Harvard U., 1957-59, Athens Inst. Tech., 1959-60; asst. prof. architecture Washington U., St. Louis, 1960-64, assoc. prof., 1964-69, prof., 1969-94, assoc. dean Sch. Architecture, 1969-73; dean Washington U., Sch. Architecture, 1973-93, dean emeritus, 1993—; Ruth and Norman Moore vis. prof. Washington U., St. Louis, 1995; vis. prof. (Sch. Architecture), Ahmedabad, India, 1970; counselor Landmarks Assn. St. Louis., 1975-79. Author: Hydra: A Greek Island Town: Its Growth and Form, 1967; contbr. articles to profl. jours. Mem. Municipal Commn. on Arts, Letters, University City, Mo., 1975-81. Served to lt. Greek Army Res., 1952-54. Fellow AIA (Rsch. award 1963-64, Presdl. Citation 1992); mem. Tech. Chamber of Greece, Soc. Archtl. Historians, Modern Greek Studies Assn., Hellenic Soc. St. Louis (pres. 1991, 95, 96). Home: 735 Radcliffe Ave Saint Louis MO 63130-3139 Office: Washington U Sch Architecture 1 Brookings Dr Saint Louis MO 63130-4862

MICHAELIS, KAREN LAUREE, law educator; b. Milw., Mar. 30, 1950; d. Donald Lee and Ethel Catherine (Stevens) M.; m. Larry Severtson, Aug. 2, 1980 (div. Aug. 1982); 1 child, Quinn Alexandra Michaelis. BA, U. Wis., 1972, BS, 1974; MA, Calif. State U., L.A., 1979; PhD, U. Wis., 1988, MS, 1985, JD, 1989. Bar: Wis., U.S. Dist. Ct. (we. dist.) Wis. Asst. prof. law Hofstra U., Hempstead, N.Y., 1990-93; assoc. prof. law Ill. State U., Normal, 1993-95; asst. prof. law Wash. State U., Pullman, 1995—. Author: Reporting Child Abuse: A Guide to Mandatory Requirements for School Personnel, 1993, Theories of Liability for Teacher Sexual Misconduct, 1996; editor Ill. Sch. Law Quarterly, 1993-95; mem. editl. bd. Nat. Assn. Profs. of Ednl. Adminstrn., 1994-95, Planning and Changing, 1993-95, Jour. Sch. Leadership, 1991—, People & Education: The Human Side of Edn., 1991-96. Mem. ABA, Nat. Coun. Profs. Ednl. Adminstrn. (program com. 1994-95, morphet fund com. 1993—), Nat. Orgn. Legal Problems in Edn. (publs. com. 1993—, program com. 1995). Office: Wash State U Cleveland Hall 351 Pullman WA 99164-2136

MICHAELIS, MICHAEL, management and technical consultant; b. Berlin, June 8, 1919; s. George and Martha (Bluth) M.; m. Diana Ordway Tead, Sept. 11, 1954; children: Ordway Peter, David Tead; m. Cintra McIlwain Williams, Mar. 19, 1966 (div. Nov. 1975); m. Caroline Crutcher Bishop, Mar. 17, 1984. B.Sc. in Engring., U. London, 1941. Research asst., group leader Research Labs. Gen. Electric Co., Ltd., U.K., 1935-45; staff physicist and cons. Gen. Electric Co., Ltd., 1945-49; dir. physics div. Radiochem. Centre, U.K. Atomic Energy Authority, 1949-51; cons. Arthur D. Little, Inc., Cambridge, Mass., 1951-52; staff cons. Arthur D. Little, Inc., 1952-61, sr. asso., 1957-61, head nuclear mgmt. cons. services, 1956-61, internat. bus. devel. services, 1959-61, policy adviser to several large corps, 1954-61, mgr. Washington ops., 1963-72, sr. cons., 1972-81; pres., chief exec. officer Partners In Enterprise, Inc., 1981—; cons. to Pres.'s Spl. Asst. Sci. and Tech., 1961-63; exec. sec. The White House Panel on Civilian Tech., 1961-63; exec. dir. rsch. mgmt. adv. panel, com. on sci. and tech. U.S. Ho. of Reps., 1963-67; dep. coord. then Pres.-elect Carter's Task Force on Sci. and Tech. Policy, 1976; mem. tech. adv. bd. to U.S. Sec. Commerce, 1978-81; mem. citizens adv. coun. Congl. Caucus for Sci. and Tech., 1983-86; mem. nat. com. Am. Goals and Resources, Nat. Planning Assn., 1964-67, mem. adv. com. sci., tech. and economy, 1966-68; vice chmn. com. internat. affairs Atomic Indsl. Forum, 1958-60; assoc. with Anglo-Am. Radar Rsch. Project, World War II. Editor, project dir.: Federal Funding of Civilian Research and Development, 1976; Contbr. articles to publs., periodicals. Fellow AAAS (chmn. engring. sect. 1980-82, exec. dir. sr. scientists and engrs. program 1989-90); mem. IEEE (sr.), Sci. Film Assn. (founder 1943, sec. 1943-48, v.p. 1948-51), Am. Nuclear Soc., Boston Com. Fgn. Rels., Royal Inst. Physics and Phys. Soc., Soc. Internat. Devel., Royal Instn. Elec. Engrs., Assn. Hosp. Physicists, Nat. Planning Assn., World Future Soc. (dir.), U.S. C. of C. (chmn. com on govt.-industry rels. in sci. and tech. 1963-64), Interdisciplinary Comm. Assocs. Inc. (dir. 1969-79), Am. Econ. Assn., Am. Soc. Cybernetics, Am. Soc. for Pub. Adminstrn., Atlantic Coun. U.S., Cosmos Club (Washington, sec. 1994-97, v.p. 1997—), Harvard Faculty Club. Home and Office: 6812 Meadow Ln Chevy Chase MD 20815-5018 *The Constitution of the U.S. diffuses power so as to better secure liberty. But it also intends that practice will integrate the dispersed powers into a workable government. It confers upon its branches autonomy but also reciprocity, separateness but also interdependence. It is incumbent on each of us to help make this system work, and to make it responsive to the human needs of our country and the world.*

MICHAELIS, PAUL CHARLES, engineering physicist executive; b. Bronx, N.Y., June 18, 1935; s. Paul Fredrick and Rose (Landsbury) M.; m. Geraldine A. DeCuollo, June 29, 1958; 1 son, Paul Charles. B.S. in Elec. Engring, Newark Coll. Engring., 1964, M.S. in Physics, 1967. With AT&T Bell Labs., Murray Hill and Whippany, N.J., 1953-96; assoc. mem. tech. staff Bell Telephone Labs., 1963-67, mem. tech. staff, 1967-82, tech. mgr., 1982-96, ret., 1996; founder P.C. Michaelis Tech. Cons. Inc., Watchung, N.J., 1996—; lectr. USSR Acad. Scis., 1972. Contbr. articles to profl. jours.; patentee in optics, magnetics, mechanics and electronics. Mem. IEEE (Morris N. Liebmann award 1975), Am. Phys. Soc., AAAS, U.S. Naval Inst., Am. Soc. Naval Engrs., Lions (past pres. Watchung club), Raritan Yacht Club (sec.). Home: 103 High Tor Dr Watchung NJ 07060-5408 Office: Bell Labs PO Box 903 67 Whippany Rd Whippany NJ 07981-1406 Office: PC Michaelis Tech Cons Inc 103 High Tor Dr Watchung NJ 07060-5424

MICHAELS, ALAN RICHARD, sports commentator; b. Bklyn., Nov. 12, 1944; s. Jay Leonard and Lila Ruth (Ross) M.; m. Linda Anne Stamaton, Aug. 27, 1966; children—Steven, Jennifer. BA, Ariz. State U., 1966. TV/radio play-by-play announcer Cin. Reds, 1971-73, San Francisco Giants, 1974-76; sports commentator ABC TV Network, N.Y.C., 1976—. Recipient Nat. Sportscaster of Yr. award Nat. Sportscasters and Sportswriters Assn., 1980, 83, 86, Emmy award, 1987. Avocations: reading; tennis. Office: ABC Sports Inc 47 W 66th St New York NY 10023-6201*

MICHAELS, CINDY WHITFILL (CYNTHIA G. MICHAELS), educational consultant, telecommunications representative; b. Plainview, Tex., Aug. 31, 1951; d. Glenn Tierce and Ruby Jewell (Nichols) Whitfill; m. Terre Joe Michaels, July 16, 1977. BS, W. Tex. State U., 1972; MS, U. Tex., Dallas, 1976; postgrad. cert., E. Tex. State U., 1982. Registered profl. ednl. diagnostician, Tex.; cert. supr. (gen. and spl. edn.), elem. edn. tchr., K-8 English tchr., spl. edn. tchr. (generic and mental retardation), Tex. Gen. and spl. edn. tchr. Plano (Tex.) Ind. Sch. Dist., 1972-76; dependents' sch. tchr. U.S. Dept. Def., Office of Overseas Edn., Schweinfurt, West Germany, 1976-77; asst. dir. edn. dept. spl. edn. Univ. Affiliated Ctr., U. Tex., Dallas, 1977-80; asst. to acting dir. edn., dept. pediatrics, Southwestern Med. Sch. Univ. Affiliated Ctr., U. Tex. Health Sci. Ctr., Dallas, 1980-82; dir. Collin County Spl. Edn. Coop., Wylie, Tex., 1982-89; dir. spl. svcs. Terrell (Tex.) Ind. Sch. Dist., 1989-92; cons. for at-risk svcs. instrnl. svcs. dept. Region 10 Edn. Svc. Ctr., Richardson, Tex., 1992-93, cons. for staff devel., 1993-95; cons. Title I Svcs., 1995-96; ind. rep. Am. Communications Network, 1995—; owner Strategic Out-Source Svcs., Garland, Tex., 1996—; self-employed ednl. cons. Strategic Outsource Svcs., 1996—; regional cons. presenter and speaker Region 10 Adminstrs. Spl. Edn., Dallas, 1982-92; state conf. presenter and speaker Tex. Assn. Bus. Sch. Bds., Houston, 1991, Tex. Edn. Agy., Austin, 1992, grant reviewer, 1984; cons. S.W. regional tng. program educators U. So. Miss., 1992-93; regional coord. H.S. mock trial competition State Bar Tex., 1993; regional liaison Tex. Elem. Mentor Network, 1993-96; state presenter Tex. Vocat. Educators Conf., 1994. Active Dance-A-Thon for United Cerebral Palsy, Dallas, 1986; area marcher March of Dimes, Dallas, 1990, Park Cities Walkathon for Multiple Sclerosis, 1994, 95. Grantee Job Tng. & Partnership Act, 1991, Carl Perkins Vocat. Program, 1991, Tex. Edn. Agy., 1990, 91, 92; named Outstanding Young Woman in Am., Outstanding Young Women in Am., 1981. Mem. AAUW, Assn. Compensatory Educators of Tex. (state conf. com. 1996), Tex. Assn. for Improvement of Reading, Tex. Assn. Sect. 504 Coords. and Hearing Officers, Nat. Coun. Adminstrs. Spl. Edn., Coun. Exceptional Children (chpt. pres. 1973-74), Tex. Assn. Supervision & Curriculum Devel. (mem. leadership team Project Pathways 1992-93), Tex. Coun. Adminstrs. Spl. Edn. (region 10 chairperson 1985-87, state conf. presenter 1989, 92), Tex. Ednl. Diagnosticians Assn. (Dal-Metro v.p., state conf. program chair 1982-83, state conf. presenter 1983), Internat. Reading Assn., Nat. Assn. Supervision and Curriculum Devel., Alpha Delta Pi (Richardson alumnae, philanthropy chair 1988, v.p. 1989, 90, 91, v.p./sec. 1993-94, v.p. 1994-95, 95-96, 96-97). Avocations: aerobics, snow skiing, travel, dancing. Home: 2613 Oak Point Dr Garland TX 75044-7809 also: 232 Broadmoor Alto NM 88312

MICHAELS, CRAIG ADAM, psychologist; b. N.Y.C., Mar. 2, 1954; s. Melvin A. and Helen (Courtney) M.; m. Susan Jane Knowles; children: Noah Lynn, Alana Rose, Esther Leor. BFA, San Francisco Art Inst., 1976; MA in Spl. Edn., NYU, 1979, ABD, 1990, PhD, 1993. Cert. rehab. counselor, 1990. Reading specialist Stephen Gaynor Sch., N.Y.C., 1978-80; vocat. program coord. Endeavor Learning Ctr., Silver Springs, Md., 1981-85; sr. learning disability specialist Nat. Ctr. on Employment and Disability, Albertson, N.Y., 1985-86, coordinator learning disability project, 1986-87, sr. coord. learning disability projects, 1987-88, sr. coord. spl. rehab. projects, 1988-94; dir. Rsch. and Tng. Inst., Nat. Ctr. for Disability Scvs., Albertson, N.Y., 1994—. Author, editor: From High School to College, 1988, How to Succeed in College, 1988, Transition Strategies for Persons with Learning Disabilities, 1994; contbr.: Dyslexia: A Neuropsychological and Learning Perspective, 1988; author, editor: Social Skills for the World of Work and Beyond, 1991, Gateways to the Working World, 1991, Transition Strategies for Persons with Learning Disabilities, 1994. Mem. Nat. Rehab. Assn., Am. Ednl. Rsch. Assn., Learning Disabilities Assn. Am., Am. Assn. for Counseling and Devel., Coun. on Exceptional Children. Avocations: swimming, bicycling, painting, cooking. Office: Nat Ctr For Disability Svcs 201 I U Willets Rd Albertson NY 11507-1516

MICHAELS, JAMES WALKER, magazine editor; b. Buffalo, June 17, 1921; s. Dewey and Phyllis (Boasberg) M.; m. Jean A. Briggs, June 1985; children: Robert Matthews, James Walker, Anne Phyllis. B.S. cum laude, Harvard U., 1942. Ambulance driver Am. Field Service, India and Burma, 1943-44; with USIS, New Delhi, Bangkok, 1944-46; fgn. corr. UP; bur. mgr. UP, New Delhi, 1946-50; with Forbes mag., N.Y.C., 1954—; mng. editor Forbes mag., 1956-61, editor, 1961—. Contbr. articles to mags. Office: Forbes Inc 60 Fifth Ave New York NY 10011-8802*

MICHAELS, JENNIFER ALMAN, lawyer; b. N.Y.C., Mar. 1, 1948; d. David I. and Emily (Arnow) Alman; 1 child, Abigail Elizabeth. BA, Douglas Coll., 1969; JD, Cardozo Sch. of Law, 1990. Ptnr. Alman & Michaels, Highland Park, N.J., 1990—. Author, composer: (record) Music for 2's and 3's, 1981; producer, writer: (film) Critical Decisions in Medicine, 1983. Mem. ABA, Middlesex County Bar Assn., N.J. State Bar Assn., Am. Trial Lawyers Assn., Phi Kappa Phi. Avocations: aviculture, sailing. Office: Alman and Michaels 611 S Park Ave Highland Park NJ 08904-2928

MICHAELS, JENNIFER TONKS, foreign language educator; b. Sedgley, England, May 19, 1945; d. Frank Gordon and Dorothy (Compston) Tonks; m. Eric Michaels, 1973; children: Joseph, David, Ellen. MA, U. Edinburgh, 1967, McGill U., 1971; PhD, McGill U., 1974. Teaching asst. German dept. Wesleyan U., 1967-68; instr. German dept. Bucknell (Pa.) U., 1968-69; teaching asst. German dept. McGill U., Can., 1969-72; prodn. asst. Pub. TV News and Polit. program, Schenectady, N.Y., 1974-75; from asst. prof. to assoc. prof. Grinnell (Iowa) Coll., 1975-87, prof., 1987—; vis. cons. German dept. Hamilton Coll., 1981; cons. Modern Lang. dept. Colby Coll.; panelist NEH, 1985; spkr. in field. Author: D.H. Lawrence, The Polarity of North and South, 1976, Anarchy and Eros: Otto Gross' Impact on German Expressionist Writers, 1983, Franz Jung: Expressionist, Dadaist, Revolutionary and Outsider, 1989, Franz Werfel and the Critics, 1994; contbr. numerous articles, revs. to profl. jours. Mem. MLA, Am. Assn. Tchrs. of German, Soc. Exile Studies, German Studies Assn. (sec. treas. 1991-92, v.p. 1992-94, pres. 1995-96, numerous coms.). Democrat. Avocations: music, travel, reading. Office: Grinnell Coll German Dept PO Box 805 Grinnell IA 50112-0805

MICHAELS, KEVIN RICHARD, lawyer; b. Buffalo, Feb. 9, 1960; s. Richard Ronald and Marlene Constance (Mnich) M.; m. Beatrice Mary Szeliga, Jan. 15, 1983; 1 child, Jaena René. BS in Govt., U. Houston, 1987; JD, South Tex. Coll. Law, 1992. Bar: Tex. 1992, U.S. Dist. Ct. (so. dist.) Tex. 1996. Ct. coord. Harris County Dist. Clk., Houston, 1985-88; paralegal O'Quinn, Kerensky, McAninch & Laminack, Houston, 1988-92, atty., 1992—. Recipient Commendation medal U.S. Army, 1984, Oak Leaf Cluster, 1985, Good Conduct medal, 1985. Mem. Assn. Trial Lawyers Am. (Tex. gov. New Lawyers div. 1994—). Avocations: golf, camping. Office: O'Quinn Laminack & Laminack 440 Louisiana St Ste 2300 Houston TX 77002-1636

MICHAELS, LORNE, television writer, producer; b. Toronto, Ont., Can.. Grad., U. Toronto, 1966. Chmn. bd. Broadway Video, N.Y.C. Creator, exec. producer: Saturday Night Live, NBC, 1975-80, 85—, Late Night with Conan O'Brien, 1993—; writer, co-producer: 3 Lily Tomlin spls., Paul Simon spl.; exec. producer: (HBO spl.) Simon and Garfunkel, Concert in the Park, Paul Simon Born at the Right Time in Cen. Park, 1991, (ABC-TV spl) Rolling Stone's 30 Years of Rock 'n' Roll, 1988; exec. producer: (TV series) Night Music, NBC, Kids in the Hall, HBO, (spl.) Stones Retro., HBO; exec. producer and producer: (spl.) Saturday Night 15th Anniversary Spl., 1989; producer: I (spl.), Wayne's World; producer, co-writer: Steve Martin's Best Show Ever 81; writer, producer: (movie) Three Amigos; producer: (movie): Wayne's World II, Coneheads, Tommy Boy, Black Sheep, Kids in the Hall: Brain Candy, Lassie. Recipient 4 awards Writers Guild Am., 8 Emmy awards Nat. Acad. TV Arts and Scis.; named Broadcaster of Yr. Internat. Radio and TV Soc., 1992; recipient George Foster Peabody award for Saturday Night Live, 1991. Office: Broadway Video 1619 Broadway New York NY 10019-7412

MICHAELS, PATRICK FRANCIS, broadcasting company executive; b. Superior, Wis., Nov. 5, 1925; s. Julian and Kathryn Elizabeth (Keating) M.; AA, U. Melbourne, 1943; BA, Golden State U., 1954; PhD, London U., 1964; m. Paula Naomi Bowen, May 1, 1960; children—Stephanie Michelle, Patricia Erin. War corr. CBS; news editor King Broadcasting, 1945-50; war corr. Mid-East Internat. News Service, 1947-49; war corr. MBS, Korea, 1950-53; news dir. Sta. WDSU-AM-FM-TV, 1953-54; fgn. corr. NBC, S. Am., 1954-56; news dir. Sta. KWIZ, 1956-59; commentator ABC, Los Angeles, 1959-62; fgn. corr. Am. News Services, London, 1962-64; news commentator McFadden Bartell Sta. KCBQ, 1964-68; news commentator ABC, San Francisco, 1968-70; news dir. Sta. KWIZ, Santa Ana, Calif., 1970-74, station mgr., 1974-81; pres. Sta. KWRM, Corona, Calif., Sta. KQLH, San Bernardino, Calif., 1981-88; chmn. Michaels Media, Huntington Beach, Calif., 1988—. Bd. dirs. Econ. Devel. Corp. Mem. Nat. Assn. Broadcasters (bd. dirs.), Calif. Broadcasters Assn. (v.p.), Am. Fedn. TV and Radio Artists, Orange County Broadcasters Assn. (pres.), Sigma Delta Chi (ethics com.). Republican. Clubs: Rotary, Balboa Bay (bd. govs.), South Shore Yacht, Internat. Yachting Fellowship of Rotarians (staff commodore). Home: PO Box 832 Corona Del Mar CA 92625-0832

MICHAELS, WILLARD A. (BILL), retired broadcasting executive; b. Omaha, May 13, 1917; s. Gus M. and Bessie (Kerstine) M.; m. Helen Louise Mintel, Nov. 20, 1938; children: Marcella, Lawrence Richard, Betty Michaels Westbrook. BA, Trinity U., 1940. Asst. sports editor San Antonio Express, 1937-40; sports announcer, sales mgr., gen. mgr. KABC, San Antonio, 1940-53; gen. mgr. KGBS-TV, 1954; v.p. WJBK-TV, Detroit, 1955-61; dir. Storer Broadcasting Co., Miami Beach, Fla., 1960-85; TV v.p. Storer Broadcasting Co., 1961-66, exec. v.p., 1966-67, pres., 1967-74, chmn., 1974-82, ret., 1982; chmn. New Boston Garden Corp. (Boston Bruins), 1972-75; dir., mem. exec. com. Northeast Airlines, 1965-72, pres., 1970-72; dir. Delta Airlines, 1972-90, adv. dir., 1990—. Trustee Storer Found. Please spell out your middle name. Home: 100 Tuscarora Trail Shavano Park San Antonio TX 78231

MICHAELSON, ARTHUR M., lawyer; b. N.Y.C., May 16, 1927; s. Samuel H. and Augusta L. M.; m. Arline L. Kahn, June 30, 1957; children: Barbara L., Sarah E., David N. A.B., Columbia U., 1947; LL.B., Yale U., 1950. Bar: N.Y. 1950, U.S. Supreme Ct 1964. Partner Wachtel & Michaelson, N.Y.C., 1957-66; v.p. McCrory Corp., N.Y.C., 1966-68, Glen Alden Corp., N.Y.C., 1968-73; partner Miller, Singer, Michaelson & Raives, N.Y.C., 1973-84; counsel Hofheimer Gartlir & Gross, 1984—. Author: (with J. Blattmachr) Income Taxation of Estates and Trusts, 1980, 85, 89, 95. Bd. dirs., mem. exec. com. Amnesty Internat. of U.S.A., Inc., 1972-81, vice chmn., 1975-76. Served with USN, 1945-46. Mem. ABA, Assn. Bar City N.Y. Office: 633 3rd Ave New York NY 10017-6706

MICHAELSON, BENJAMIN, JR., lawyer; b. Annapolis, Md., May 30, 1936; s. Benjamin and Naomi Madora (Dill) M.; m. Frances Means Blackwell, Apr. 12, 1986; children: Benjamin, Robert Wendell. BA, U. Va., 1957; JD, U. Md., 1962. Bar: Md. 1962, U.S. Dist. Ct. Md. 1976. Assoc. Goodman, Bloom & Michaelson, Annapolis, 1962-63; pvt. practice, Annapolis, 1963-73; sr. ptnr. Michaelson & Christhilf, P.A., Annapolis, 1973-77, Benjamin Michaelson, Jr., P.A., Annapolis, 1977-81, Michaelson & Simmons, P.A., Annapolis, 1982-86, Michaelson & Newell, P.A., 1987-88, Michaelson, Krause & Ferris, P.A., 1988-91; pvt. practice law, 1991—; reg. dir. O'Conor, Piper & Flynn Title Svcs., L.L.C., 1997—; gen. counsel, dir. Annapolis Fed. Savs., 1965-94; bd. dirs. Security Title Guarantee Corp. Balt. Counsel Anne Arundel County (Md.) Bd. Edn., 1966-76; bd. trustees Hammond-Haswood House Mus.; mem. vestry St. Anne's Episcopal Ch., Annapolis, 1997—. Lt. U.S. Army, 1957-59. Named one of Outstanding Young Men Am., Severna Park chpt. U.S. Jaycees, 1965. Fellow Am. Coll. Mortgage Attys.; mem. ABA, Md. Bar Assn. (chmn. real property, planning and zoning sect. council 1982-84, grievance commn. inquiry panel 1976-85, vice-chmn. 1983-85, grievance commn. rev. bd. 1985-88), Anne Arundel County Bar Assn., Jaycees (Md. state legal counsel 1964-65, nat. dir. 1965-66), Sailing Club of Chesapeake (commodore 1982), Rotary (pres. 1975-76, Paul Harris fellow), Delta Theta Phi. Republican. Episcopalian. Home: 3 Southgate Ave Annapolis MD 21401-2709 Office: 275 West St Ste 216 Annapolis MD 21401-3463

MICHAELSON, MARTIN, lawyer; b. Boston, Apr. 12, 1943; s. Eliot D. and Charlotte (Selib) M.; m. Anne Taylor, Aug. 30, 1987; children: Andrew M., Daniel M.; stepchildren: Rachel T., Hannah T. BA, U. Chgo., 1965; JD, Boston Coll., 1968. Bar: N.Y. 1968, D.C. 1973, U.S. Supreme Ct. 1973, Mass. 1983, U.S. Dist. Ct. N.Y. 1969, D.C. 1973, U.S. Ct. Appeals (1st, 2d, 3d, 4th, 9th cirs.). Atty. Cravath, Swaine & Moore, N.Y.C., 1968-71; legis. asst. Congressman Robert F. Drinan, Washington, 1971-73; atty. Hogan & Hartson, Washington, 1973-76, ptnr., 1976-83, 89—; dep. gen. counsel Harvard U., Cambridge, Mass., 1983-88, univ. counsel, 1989. Office: Hogan & Hartson Columbia Square 555 13th St NW Washington DC 20004-1109

MICHAELSON, RICHARD AARON, health science facility administrator; b. Newton, Mass., Feb. 7, 1952; s. Eliot David and Charlotte Natalie (Selib) M.; m. Allyn Joan Shaloff, Apr. 11, 1981; children: David Benjamin, Robyn Leigh. BA in Psychology, U. Rochester, 1973; MS in Mgmt., MIT, 1977. Research asst. MIT Ctr. Info. Systems Research, Cambridge, Mass., 1976-77; analyst IBM Biomed. Systems Group, Mt. Kisco, N.Y., 1977-79; staff fin. analyst IBM Gen. Bus. Group, White Plains, N.Y., 1979-80; dir. fin. planning MetPath, Inc., Teterboro, N.J., 1980-82, dir. fin. services, 1982-84, v.p. fin., chief fin. officer, 1984-86, v.p. corp. devel., 1986-92; v.p., treas. Corning Lab Svcs. Inc., 1990-92; sr. v.p., CFO Unilab Corp., Tarzana, Calif., 1992—. Bd. dirs. United Jewish Assn. Fedn. of North N.J., 1987-96; co-pres. Temple Beth Shalom, Fairlawn, N.J., 1995-97. Club: MIT Sloan (N.Y.C.) (regional gov. 1986-89, mem. sch. alumni adv. bd. 1989-91). Home: 11-18 Fairhaven Pl Fair Lawn NJ 07410-1683 Office: Unilab Corp 18448 Oxnard St Tarzana CA 91356-1504

MICHAK, HELEN BARBARA, educator, nurse; b. Cleve., July 31; d. Andrew and Mary (Patrick) M. Diploma Cleve. City Hosp. Sch. Nursing, 1947; BA, Miami U., Oxford, Ohio, 1951; MA, Case Western Res. U., 1960. Staff nurse Cleve. City Hosp., 1947-48; pub. health nurse Cleve. Div. Health, 1951-52; instr. Cleve. City Hosp. Sch. Nursing, 1952-56; supr. nursing Cuyahoga County Hosp., Cleve., 1956-58; pub. information dir. N.E. Ohio Am. Heart Assn., Cleve., 1960-64; dir. spl. events Higbee Co., Cleve., 1964-66; exec. dir. Cleve. Area League for Nursing, 1966-72; dir. continuing edn. nurses, adj. assoc. prof. Cleve. State U., 1972-86; asst. regional cons. Ohio Bd. Nursing, 1991—. Trustee N.E. Ohio Regional Med. Program, 1970-73; mem. adv. com. Dept. Nursing Cuyahoga C.C., 1967-87; mem. long term care com. Met. Health Planning Corp., 1974-76, plan devel. com. 1977; mem. policy bd. Ctr. Health Data N.E. Ohio, 1972-73; mem. Rep. Assembly and Health Planning and Devel. Commn., Welfare Fedn. Cleve., 1967-72, Cleve. Cmty. Health Network, 1972-73, United Appeal Films and Speakers Bur., 1967-73; mem. adv. com. Ohio Fedn. Lic. Practical Nurses, 1970-73; mem. tech. adv. com. No. Ohio Lung Assn., 1967-74, 90-93; mem. Ohio Commn. on Nursing, 1971-74; mem. citizens com. nursing homes Fedn. Community Planning, 1973-77; mem. com. on home health services Met. Health Planning Corp., 1973-75; mem. profl. adv. com. on home care Fairview Gen. Hosp., 1987-91. Mem. Nat. League Nursing (mem. com. 1970-72), Am. Nurses

Assn. (accreditation visitor 1977-78, 83-88) Ohio Nurses Assn., (com. continuing edn. 1974-79, 82-87, 89-92, chmn. 1984-86), Greater Cleve. (joint practice com. 1973-74, Greater Cleve. Nurses Assn. (trustee 1975-76), Cleve. Area Citizens League for Nursing (trustee 1976-79, v.p. 1988-90), Zeta Tau Alpha, Sigma Theta Tau. Home and Office: 4686 Oakridge Dr North Royalton OH 44133-2070

MICHALAK, EDWARD FRANCIS, lawyer; b. Evanston, Ill., Sept. 6, 1937; s. Leo Francis Michalak and Helen Sophie (Wolinski) Krakowski; m. Margaret Mary Minx, Jan. 2, 1978. BSBA, Northwestern U., 1959; LLB, Harvard U., 1962. Bar: Ill. 1962. Assoc. McDermott, Will & Emery, Chgo., 1963-69, ptnr., 1969—. Served to sgt. USAR, 1962-68. Mem. Ill. Bar Assn., Chgo. Bar Assn., Beta Gamma Sigma, Beta Alpha Psi. Roman Catholic. Club: Mid-Day (Chgo.). Avocations: golf, opera. Home: 3409 Summit Ave Highland Park IL 60035-1111 Office: McDermott Will & Emery 227 W Monroe St Chicago IL 60606-5016

MICHALAK, JANET CAROL, reading education educator; b. Buffalo, Mar. 22, 1949; d. Theodore and Thelma Ruth (Roesch) Vukovic; m. Gerald Paul Michalak, June 19, 1971; children: Nathan, Justin. BS in Edn., SUNY Coll. at Buffalo, Buffalo, 1970; MS in Edn., SUNY, Buffalo, 1971, EdD, 1981. Cert. tchr. nursery, kindergarten, grades 1-6, reading tchr., English tchr. grades 7-12, N.Y. Reading tchr. Tonawanda (N.Y.) Sch. System, 1971-80; instr. Niagara County C.C., Sanborn, N.Y., 1980-82, asst. prof., 1982-85, assoc. prof., 1985-91, prof., 1991—; adj. lectr. SUNY, Buffalo, 1990-91. Recipient Pres.'s award for Excellence in Teaching, Niagara County C.C., 1990, Nat. Inst. for Staff & Orgnl. Devel. Excellence award, 1991, SUNY Chancellor's award for Excellence in Teaching, 1991. Mem. Coll. Reading Assn., Internat. Reading Assn., N.Y. Coll. Learning Skills Assn., Niagara Frontier Reading Coun. (bd. dirs. 1986-88, 97—). Republican. Avocation: reading. Home: 184 Montbleu Dr Getzville NY 14068-1329 Office: Niagara County CC 3111 Saunders Settlement Rd Sanborn NY 14132-9487

MICHALIK, JOHN JAMES, legal educational association executive; b. Bemidji, Minn., Aug. 1, 1945; s. John and Margaret Helen (Pafko) M.; m. Diane Marie Olson, Dec. 21, 1968; children: Matthew John, Nicole, Shane. BA, U. Minn., 1967, JD, 1970. Legal editor Lawyers Coop. Pub. Co., Rochester, N.Y., 1970-75; dir. continuing legal edn. Wash. State Bar Assn., Seattle, 1975-81, exec. dir., 1981-91; asst. dean devel. & cmty. rels. Sch. of Law U. Wash., 1991-95; exec. dir. Assn. Legal Adminstrs., 1995. Mem. Am. Soc. Assn. Execs., Nat. Assn. Bar Execs., Am. Mgmt. Assn., Nat. Trust Hist. Preservation, Coll. Club Seattle. Lutheran. Office: Assn Legal Adminstrs 175 E Hawthorn Pkwy Vernon Hills IL 60061-1463

MICHALKO, JAMES PAUL, library association administrator; b. Cleve., May 13, 1950; s. Paul James and Lillian (Fanta) M.; 1 child, Alexandra. BA, Georgetown U., 1971; MLS, MBA, U. Chgo., 1974. Asst. to v.p., adminstrn. Technicare Inc. (formerly BCC Industries), Cleve., 1971-72; asst dir., adminstrn. U. Pa. Librs., Phila., 1974-80; dir. bus. and fin. Rsch. Librs. Group, Stanford, Calif., 1980-85, v.p. fin. and adminstrn., 1985-87, acting pres., 1988-89; pres. Rsch. Librs. Group, Mountain View, Calif., 1989—. Contbr. to Libr. Quar., Coll. & Rsch. Librs.; reviewer for Libr. Quar., Coll. & Rsch. Librs., Acad. of Mgmt. Rev., Jour. Acad. Librarianship, Jour. Libr. Adminstrn. Office: Rsch Librs Group Inc 1200 Villa St Mountain View CA 94041-1106*

MICHALS, LEE MARIE, retired travel agency executive; b. Chgo., June 6, 1939; d. Harry Joseph and Anna Marie (Monaco) Perzan; children: Debora Ann, Dana Lee, Jami. BA, Wright Coll., 1959. Cert. travel specialist and cons., destination specialist. Internat. travel sec. E.F. MacDonald Travel, Palo Alto, Calif., 1963-69; pres. Travel Experience, Santa Clara, Calif., 1973-88; ptnr. Cruise Connection, Mountain View, Calif., 1983-85; travel specialist Allways Travel, Sunnyvale, Calif., 1992—; former stars rep. Hertz, Ritz Carlton, Marriott Hotels, various airlines and tour cos. Mem. Am. Soc. Travel Agts., Inst. Cert. Travel Agts., Bay Area Travel Assn., Pacific Area Travel Agts., San Jose Women in Travel (organizing pres. 1971, 1st v.p. 1989). Office: Allways Travel 139 S Murphy Ave Sunnyvale CA 94086-6113

MICHALSKI, CAROL ANN, medical, surgical and psychiatric nurse, writer, poet; b. Balt., Feb. 21, 1955; d. John B. Rassa and Genevieve J. Ryncewicz; m. Martin Joseph Michalski, June 21, 1976; children: Matthew, Nathan. RN, Grand View Hosp., Sellersville, Pa., 1976; BS in Health Care Adminstrn., Pacific Western U., 1986, PhD in Religious Studies/Ministry, 1987. RN; ordained to ministry Christian Ch., 1983. Staff nurse Md. Gen. Hosp., Balt., 1974-75, Union Meml. Hosp., Balt., 1975-77; head nurse Levindale Chronic Hosp., Balt., 1977-79; charge staff nurse Franklin Sq. Hosp. Ctr., Balt., 1979—, pain mgmt. liaison, 1993—; head procedure com. Levindale Chronic Hosp., Balt., 1978-79; min. Faith Seed Ministries, Balt., 1983—; Bible Coll. adminstr. L.W. Christian Ctr., Balt., 1987-89. Author: Don't Blame God-Making Sense Out of Tragedy and Suffering, 1995; contbr. articles and poetry to profl. jours. and anthologies. Asst. youth activities Ridgeleigh Cmty. Assn., Balt., 1980; block capt. Woodcroft Civic Assn., Balt.; coord. Churchville Christian Sch., 1993-94; Christian Home Educator's Network group coord. Teen Boys Group, 1995—. Recipient Nursing Achievement award Johnston Sch.-Union Meml. Hosp., 1984, Ministry Recognition Certs. Gospel Tabernacle Balt., 1990, 91, poetry awards. Mem. Md. League Nursing, Nat. Author's Registry, Internat. Soc. Poets. Avocations: art, crafts, writing, hiking, water sports.

MICHALSKI, THOMAS JOSEPH, city planner, developer; b. Waukesha, Wis., Jan. 28, 1933; s. Thomas and Anna (Benca) M. B.Arch., U. Mich., 1956, M.City Planning, 1959; postgrad., Magdalene Coll., U. Cambridge, Eng., 1988—. Urban renewal planner City of Milw., 1956-57; land planner, urban designer Baltimore County, Md., 1959-60; planning cons. City of N.Y., 1961-77; project mgr. Yanbu Indsl. Complex, Royal Comm., Saudi Arabia, 1980-83; cons. UN Ctr. for Human Settlements, Habitat Nairobi, Kenya, 1984—; bd. Community Housing Initiative Trust, 1993—; faculty U. Mich., 1994—; mem. faculty NYU, 1965-66, CUNY, 1970-71, Rollins Coll., 1992—; town planning cons. new town in Iran, 1977; mem. Community Bd. 8, N.Y.C., 1972-76, chmn. landmarks com.; cons. Islamic Devel. Bank, 1989—, Fla. Solar Energy Ctr. Affordable Living Conf., 1991. Author: In Search of Purpose: Essays on Planning the Human Environment, 1961, Human Values and the Emerging City, 1967. Founding mem. Friends of Cen. park; 1000 Friends of Fla., 1987—; pres. Brevard 21 Inc., 1988—; bd. govs. Coll. Architecture and Urban Planning, U. Mich., 1984-88; bd. ACLU, 1993—. Wis. Architects Found. scholar, 1953-56; Vincent Astor Found. grantee, 1971, World Wildlife Fund Successful Communities grantee, 1991. Fellow Am. Hort. Soc.; mem. Am. Planning Assn. (charter), Am. Inst. Cert. Planners, Royal Town Planning Inst., Town and Country Planning Assn., Internat. Fedn. Housing and Planning, Nat. Trust for Historic Preservation, Wis. Soc. Archtl. Historians, Mich. Urban Planning Alumni Soc. (bd. dirs. 1984-88), Audubon Soc. Fla. (chmn. conservation com. 1987-91), Assn. for Asian Studies, Worldwatch Inst., English-Speaking Union (London), Brevard County (Fla.) Democratic exec. com., U. Mich. Club (N.Y.C.), Delta Chi (Morrey Outstanding Alumnus award 1984). Roman Catholic. Address: 3325 Rivercrest Dr Melbourne FL 32935 *The educated person prepares mightily to do something constructive about that which is displeasing, to sustain that which is good, and to discriminate the one from the other.*

MICHALSKI, (ŻUROWSKI) WACŁAW, adult education educator; b. Pierzchnica, Poland, Sept. 14, 1913; came to the U.S., 1951; s. Antoni and Józefa (Skrybuś) M.; m. Urszula Lewandowska, Nov. 12, 1959 (dec. 1986); 1 child, Anthony Richard. MA, Tchr.'s Coll., Poland, 1934; grad., Officer's Mil. Sch., Poland, 1934-35; postgrad., U. Wis. M.A.T.C., 1951-55. Lic. real estate broker, Wis. Tchr. jr. high sch. Poland, 1936-39; mgr. acctg. Amproo Metal Co., Milw., 1951-84; tchr., educator Marquette U., U. Wis. Ext., Milw., 1962-90, Milw. Area Tech. Coll., 1963—; real estate agt. Wauwatosa Realty Co., Milw., 1955—. Contbr. articles to profl. jours. Archivist Holy Cross Brigade and Nat. Armed Forces of Poland, 1991-96. With underground resistance, Poland, 1939-45; officer Holy Cross Brigade, Poland, 1944-55, which joined U.S. 3rd Army, Czechoslovakia, 1945; Polish guard U.S. Army, Germany, 1945-47; officer Internat. Refugee Orgn., Germany, 1947-51. Recipient Polish Heritage award Pulaski Coun. Milw., 1992, Cert. of Appreciation State Hist. Soc. Wis., 1987, Vol. Svc. award Inner Agy. Coun. Volunteerism, 1986, Cert. of Commendation for Exemplary Work as an Older Worker in Our Community Milw. Com. for Nat. Older Work Week, 1995. Mem. Polish Am. Congress, N.Am. Polish Ctr. Study, Polish Western Assn. Am. (Diploma of Merit 1988), Vets. Orgns. WWI, WWII. Roman Catholic. Avocations: chess, bridge. Home: 5505 Bentwood Ln Greendale WI 53129-1314 Office: Wauwatosa Realty Co 5300 S 108th St Hales Corners WI 53130-1368

MICHAUD, GEORGES JOSEPH, astrophysics educator; b. Que., Can., Apr. 30, 1940; s. Marie-Louis and Isabelle (St. Laurent) M.; m. Denise Lemieux, June 25, 1966. BA, U. Laval, Que., 1961, BSc, 1965; PhD, Calif. Tech. Inst., Pasadena, 1970. Prof. Universite de Montreal, Can., 1969—; dir. Centre du Recherche en Calcul Appliqué, 1992-96. Recipient Steacie prize NRC, 1980, Medaille Janssen, Academie des Sciences, Paris, 1982, Prix Vincent, ACFAS, 1979; Killam fellow Conseil des Arts, 1987-89. Office: Universite de Montreal, Dept de Physique, Montreal, PQ Canada H3C 3J7

MICHAUD, HOWARD HENRY, conservation educator; b. Berne, Ind., Oct. 12, 1902; s. Justin Album and Bertha Amelia (Baumgartner) M.; m. Ruth M. Hefner, Aug. 19, 1928; 1 child, Ted C. AB, Bluffton Coll., 1925; MA, Ind. U., 1930. High sch. tchr. Ft. Wayne, Ind., 1925-45; chief naturalist Ind. State Parks, 1934-45; prof. conservation Purdue U., 1945-71, prof. emeritus, 1971—; head program of conservation edn. Pub. Sch. Ind., 1945-71; dir. Conservation Edn. Camp for Tchrs., 1946-59; del. conf. Internat. Union for Conservation of Nature and Natural Resources Conf., N.Y., 1949, Lucerne, Switzerland, 1966. Editor: (pamphlets on conservation) Ind. Dept. Pub. Instrn.; contbr. articles to profl. jours. Past mem. Bd. Pks. and Recreation, West Lafayette. Recipient Purdue Conservation award, 1945-71, Chase S. Osborn Wildlife award Purdue U., 1959, Sagamore of the Wabash award Gov. of Ind., 1991, Theodore Roosevelt award U.S. EPA, 1993; NSF grantee, 1960-61. Mem. Nat. Assn. Biology Tchrs. (pres. 1948), Ind. Audubon Soc. (past pres., Earl Brooks Conservationist of Yr. award 1986), Conservation Edn. Assn. (pres. 1956-57, v.p. 1953-55, Key Man award 1967), Ind. Acad. Sci. (pres. 1963), Soil Conservation Soc. Am. (hon.), Izaak Walton League Am. (div. pres. 1953), Am. Nature Study Soc., Am. Assn. Interpretive Naturalists (founder), Environ. Edn. Assn. Ind. Inc. (pres. 1972-73, editor newsletter 1972-88), Nat. Wildlife Fedn., Ind. Park and Recreation Assn. (Outstanding Svc. award 1984), Nat. Recreation and Park Assn., Pi Kappa Phi, Xi Sigma Pi. Democrat. Presbyterian. Lodge: Lafayette Noon Optimists (Optimist of Yr. award 1986). Avocations: travel, photography, lapidary. Home: 2741 N Salisbury St Lafayette IN 47906-1499

MICHAUD, MICHAEL ALAN GEORGE, diplomat, writer; b. Hollywood, Calif., Aug. 22, 1938; s. George Emile and Nathalie Adele (Neagles) M.; m. Carmen Yvonne Mitchell, Sept. 1960 (div. 1963); m. M. Grace Russo, June 5, 1965 (div. 1996); m. Sandra Arbuthnot, July 31, 1996; children: Jon C., Cassandra M., Jason M., Joshua M. B.A., UCLA, 1960, M.A., 1963; postgrad., Georgetown U., 1978-79. Commd. fgn. service officer Dept. State, 1963; consular officer Dacca, East Pakistan, 1963-65; analyst Bur. Intelligence and Research/Dept. State, Washington, 1965-66; staff asst. Bur. Near Eastern and South Asian Affairs Dept. State, Washington, 1966-67; polit. officer Am. Embassy, Tehran, 1967-68, econ. officer, 1968-70; info. officer USIS, Bombay, India, 1970-72, co-dir., 1971-72; country officer for Iran Dept. State, 1972-74, country officer Australia, Papua New Guinea and Solomon Islands, Bur. East Asian Affairs, 1974-76; dep. dir. Office Internat. Security Policy, Bur. Politico-Mil. Affairs, 1976-78; trainee Georgetown U., Washington, 1978-79; officer-in-charge U.K. and Bermuda Affairs, Bur. European Affairs Dept. State, 1979-80; consul gen. Am. Consulate Gen. Belfast, No. Ireland, 1980-83; Una Chapman Cox fellow Fgn. Service Inst. Dept. State, 1983-84, div. chief fgn. service counseling and assignments, 1984-85, spl. asst. for space policy, 1985-86, dir. Office Advanced Tech., 1986-89; counselor sci., tech. and environ. affairs Am. Embassy, Paris, 1989-93; minister-counselor environ. sci. and tech. Am. Embassy, Tokyo, 1993-95. Author: Reaching for the High Frontier, 1986; editor: Flotsam and Jetsam lit. ann., 1956; founding editor: Open Forum, 1974-76 (Honor award 1976); mem. editorial bd.: Fgn. Service Jour., 1977-79; contbr. numerous articles, papers, book revs., short stories to various publs. Recipient Superior Honor award Dept. State, 1966; recipient Meritorious Honor award Dept. State, 1976; Scott fellow, 1962. Fellow Brit. Interplanetary Soc.; mem. Internat. Inst. Space Law, Internat. Acad. Astronautics, AAAS, AIAA, Royal Soc. Asian Affairs, Planetary Soc., Space Studies Inst., Nat. Space Soc., Space Studies Inst., Am. Astron. Soc., Nature Conservancy. Home and Office: USTR Geneva Dept State Washington DC 20521

MICHAUD, NORMAN PAUL, association administrator, logistics consultant; b. Fall River, Mass., June 28, 1931; s. Amedee and Mary Veronica (Simcoe) M.; m. Helen P. Pettine, Oct. 11, 1952; children: Marianne, Norman, Elizabeth, Robert, Virginia. Cert. in Engring., U. Mass; student, Queens Coll., 1958-61. Joined U.S. Army, 1948, advanced through grades to master sgt., 1958, ret., 1958; field engr. Raytheon Co., 1958-67; dept. mgr. Raytheon Svc. Co., Burlington, Mass., 1968-92; exec. dir. Soc. Logistics Engrs., Hyattsville, Md., 1992-95; pvt. practice logistics cons. Londonderry, N.H., 1995—. Editor (tech. jour.) Logistics Spectrum, 1992-95, (newsletter) Soletter, 1992-95; contbr. articles to profl. jours. Pres. Chelmsford (Mass.) PTA, 1968-71, mem. coun., 1969-70. Fellow Soc. Logistics Engrs. (cert. profl. logistician, bd. dirs. 1985-96, exec. bd. 1986-92, Pres.'s award for merit 1992-93, Tech. Field award 1985). Roman Catholic. Home and Office: 381 Winding Pond Rd Londonderry NH 03053-3391

MICHAUDON, ANDRÉ FRANCISQUE, physicist; b. Cavaillon, Vaucluse, France, May 14, 1929; s. Maurice Louis and Jeanne Francoise (Chatal) M.; children: Claire Hello, Helene Caron. Engring. degree, Ecole Supérieure Ingenieurs Arts et Métiers, Paris, 1951, Ecole Supérieure Electricite, Paris, 1953; DSc, U. Paris, 1964. Rsch. engr. Le Materiel Teléphonique, Boulogne, France, 1954-56; group leader Commissariat à Energie Atomique, Cen Saclay, France, 1956-64, 65-72; theorist MIT, Cambridge, 1964-65; div. head Commissariat à Energie Atomique, Bruyeres le Chalel, France, 1972-79; dept. dept. head Commissariat à l'Energie Atomique, Limeil, France, 1979-83; French co-dir. Inst. Laue Langevin, Grenoble, France, 1983-89; prof. Inst. Nat. des Scis. et Techniques Nucléaires, Saclay, Orsay, France, 1969-84; physicist Los Alamos Nat. Lab., 1989—; mem. exec. coun. European Sci. Found., Strasbourg, France, 1987-90; mem. adv. coun. Cen. Bur. for Nuclear Measurements EU, Geel, Belgium, 1990-95; cons. Orgn. for Econ. Cooperation and Devel., Paris, 1989-92. Author, editor: Nuclear Fission, 1981; co-gen. editor: Neutron Sources, 1983, Neutron Radiative Capture, 1984, Probability & Statistics, 1991; contbr. articles to profl. jours. Lt. French Navy, 1953-54. Recipient written congratulations Minister of the Navy, France, 1954, award Acad. des Sciences, Paris, 1980; named knight Order of Merit, Paris, 1984. Fellow Am. Phys. Soc., Am. Nuclear Soc.; mem. Soc. Francaise de Physique, N.Y. Acad. Scis. Avocations: music, tennis, skiing, golf, hiking. Home: 211 W Water Sante Fe NM 87501 Office: Los Alamos Nat Lab Lansce 3 MS H 855 Los Alamos NM 87545

MICHEL, ANTHONY NIKOLAUS, electrical engineering educator, researcher; b. Rekasch, Romania, Nov. 17, 1935; came to U.S., 1952; s. Anton Michel and Katharina (Metz) Malsam; m. Leone Lucille Flasch, Aug. 17, 1957; children: Mary Leone, Katherine Jean, John Peter, Anthony Joseph, Patrick Thomas. B.S.E.E., Marquette U., 1958, M.S. in Math., 1964, Ph.D. in Elec. Engring., 1968; D.Sc. in Math., Tech. U. Graz (Austria), 1973. Registered profl. engr., Wis. Engr. in tng. U.S. Army C.E., Milw., 1958-59; project engr. AC Electronics div. Gen. Motors Corp., Milw., 1959-62, sr. research engr., 1962-65; asst. prof. elec. engring. Iowa State U., Ames, 1968-69, assoc. prof., 1969-74, prof., 1974-84; prof. and chmn. dept. elec. engring. U. Notre Dame, Ind., 1984-87, Frank M. Freimann prof. engring., chmn. dept. elec. and computer engring., 1987-88, dean coll. engring., 1988—; cons. Houghton Mifflin Co., 1975, Acad. Press, 1983; cons. editor William C. Brown Co. Pubs., Dubuque, Iowa, 1982-83. Author: (with others) Qualitative Analysis of Large Scale Dynamical Systems, 1977, Mathematical Foundations in Engineering and Science, 1981, Ordinary Differential Equations, 1982, Applied Linear Algebra and Functional Analysis, 1993, (with Derong Liu) Dynamical Systems with Saturation Nonlinearities, 1993, (with Kaining Wang) Qualitative Theory of Dynamical Systems, 1994, (with Panos J. Antsaklis) Linear Systems, 1997; contbr. articles to profl. jours., chpts. to books. Research grantee NSF, 1972—; research grantee Dept. Def., 1968-72; Fulbright fellow Tech. U. Vienna, Austria, 1992. Fellow IEEE (mem. editor Trans. on Cirs. and Sys. 1981-83, Best Trans. Paper award 1978, 83, 93, Centennial medal 1984); mem. IEEE Cirs. and Sys. Soc. (pres.s 1989, Myril B. Reed Outstanding Paper award 1993, Tech. Achievement award 1995), Russian Acad. Engring. (hon.), Sigma Xi, Eta Kappa Nu, Pi Mu Epsilon, Phi Kappa Phi. Home: 17001 Stonegate Ct Granger IN 46530-6948 Office: U Notre Dame Coll Engring Notre Dame IN 46556

MICHEL, CLIFFORD LLOYD, lawyer, investment executive; b. N.Y.C., Aug. 9, 1939; s. Clifford William and Barbara Lloyd (Richards) M.; m. Betsy Shirley, June 6, 1964; children: Clifford Fredrick, Jason Lloyd, Katherine Beinecke. AB cum laude, Princeton U., 1961; JD, Yale U., 1964. Bar: N.Y. 1964, U.S. Dist. Ct. (so. dist.) N.Y. 1968, U.S. Ct. Appeals (2d cir.) 1967, U.S. Supreme Ct. 1972. Assoc. Cahill Gordon & Reindel, N.Y.C., 1964-67, Paris, 1967-69, N.Y.C., 1969-71; ptnr. Cahill Gordon & Reindel, Paris, 1972-76, N.Y.C., 1976—; bd. dirs. Alliance Capital Mgmt. Mut. Funds, Placer Dome Inc., Tempo Tech. Corp. Bd. dirs. Jockey Hollow Found., Michel Found., St. Mark's Sch., Morristown Meml. Hosp., Meml. Health Found., Atlantic Health Sys. Mem. ABA, FBA, N.Y. State Bar Assn., New York County Lawyers Assn., Am. Soc. Internat. Law, City Midday Club, Racquet and Tennis Club, River Club, The Links, Shinnecock Hills olf Club, Somerset Hills Country Club, Essex Hunt Club, Sankaty Head Golf Club (Mass.), Golf de Morfontaine Club (France), Travellers Club (Paris), Loch Lomond Club (Scotland), Nantucket Golf Club. Republican. Office: Cahill Gordon & Reindel 80 Pine St New York NY 10005-1702

MICHEL, DONALD CHARLES, editor; b. Ventura, Calif., Nov. 17, 1935; s. Charles J. and Esther Caroline (Heilert) M.; m. Loretta Perron, May 4, 1963; children: Edwin, Robert, Christopher. B.A., UCLA, 1958, M.S., 1959. Editor San Fernando (Calif.) Sun, 1958-60; successively reporter, weekend editor, mng. editor Valley Times Today, North Hollywood, Calif., 1960-63; feature editor Houston Chronicle, 1963-68; asst. mng. editor features Chgo. Daily News, 1968-77; exec. v.p., editor Chgo. Tribune-N.Y. News Syndicate, 1977-84; v.p. adminstrn. and editl. devel. L.A. Times Syndicate, 1984-93, dir. book devel., 1993—. Mem. Am. Assn. Sunday and Feature Editors, Features Coun., Sigma Delta Chi. Home: 3000 Adornos Way Burbank CA 91504-1609 Office: Los Angeles Times Syndicate Times Mirror Sq Los Angeles CA 90012

MICHEL, HENRY LUDWIG, civil engineer; b. Frankfurt, Germany, June 18, 1924; s. Maximilian Frederick and Loschka (Hepner) M.; m. Mary Elizabeth Strolis, June 5, 1954; children—Eve Musette, Ann Elizabeth. B.S.C.E., Columbia U., 1949. Registered profl. engr., Pa., N.Y. Pres., CEO, Parsons Brinckerhoff, Inc., 1975-90, chmn., 1990-94, chmn. emeritus, 1994—; chmn. Parsons Brinckeroff Internat., Inc., 1975-96; guest lectr. NYU, Columbia U., Colo. State U., Cornell U., MIT, U. Ark.; sr. lectr. N.Y. Poly. U.; vice chmn. Bldg. Futures Coun., 1980—; instrumental in devel. and mgmt. of maj. transp. and pub. works project in U.S. and abroad; mem. Nat. Acad. Engrs., 1995—. Contbr. numerous articles on mgmt. and transp. engring. to engring. jours. Fellow ASCE, Soc. Am. Mil. Engrs., Instn. Civil Engrs.; mem. Internat. Rd. Found. (chmn. 1989-92, bd. dirs. 1977—), Constrn. Industry Pres. Forum (chmn. 1990-91), Civil Engring. Rsch. Found. (chmn. 1992-96), Columbia U. Engring. Sch. Alumni Assn. (Egelston medal 1992, Alumni medal 1991), Am. European Cmty. Assn. (bd. dirs. 1983—), Spain-U.S. C. of C. (bd. dirs. 1993—). Home: 35 Sutton Pl New York NY 10022-2464 Office: Parsons Brinckerhoff Interna Inc One Penn Plaza New York NY 10119

MICHEL, JAMES H., ambassador, lawyer; b. St. Louis, Aug. 25, 1939; s. Paul J. and Margaret K. (Scheitlin) M.; m. Conception L. Trejo, Sept. 10, 1960; children—Mark, Kurt, Linda, Paul. J.D., St. Louis U., 1965. Bar: Mo. 1965, D.C. 1973. Atty. Dept. State, Washington, 1965-74, asst. legal adviser, 1974-78, dep. legal adviser, 1978-83, dep. asst. sec. for Inter-Am. affairs, 1983-87; ambassador to Guatemala, 1987-89; asst. adminstr. Latin Am. and Carribbean Bur. AID, Washington, 1990-93; pres. devel. assistance com. OECD, Paris, 1994—. Pres. St. Thomas More Fed. Credit Union, Arlington, Va., 1970-87. Recipient Superior awards Dept. State, 1971, 76, 83, Meritorious Exec. award, 1980, 87, Disting. award, 1981, Disting. Exec. award, 1982, 92. Mem. Fed. Bar Assn. (Tom C. Clark award 1982), D.C. Bar Assn., Mo. Bar Assn., Am. Soc. Internat. Law, Inter-Am. Bar Assn. Roman Catholic. Office: 2 rue Andre Pascal, Paris 75116, France

MICHEL, MARY ANN KEDZUF, nursing educator; b. Evergreen Park, Ill., June 1, 1939; d. John Roman and Mary (Bassar) Kedzuf; m. Jean Paul Michel, 1974. Diploma in nursing, Little Company of Mary Hosp., Evergreen Park, 1960; BS in Nursing, Loyola U., Chgo., 1964; MS, No. Ill. U., 1968, EdD, 1971. Staff nurse Little Co. of Mary Hosp., 1960-64; instr. Little Co. of Mary Hosp. (Sch. Nursing), 1964-67, No. Ill. U., DeKalb, 1968-69; asst. prof. No. Ill. U., 1969-71; chmn. dept. nursing U. Nev., Las Vegas, 1971-73; prof. nursing U. Nev., 1975—, dean Coll. Health Scis., 1973-90; pres. PERC, Inc.; mgmt. cons., 1993—; mgmt. cons. Nev. Donor Network, 1993; mem. So. Nev. Health Manpower Task Force, 1975; mem. manpower com. Plan Devel. Commn., Clark County Health Sys. Agy., 1977-79, mem. governing body, 1981-86; mem. Nev. Health Coordinating Coun., Western Inst. Nursing, 1971-85; mem. coordinating com. assembly instnl. adminstrs. dept. allied health edn. and accreditation AMA, 1985-88; mem. bd. advisors So. Nev. Vocat. Tech. Ctr., 1976-80; sec.-treas. Nev. Donor Network, 1988-89, bd. dirs., 1986-90, chmn. bd., 1988-90. Contbr. articles to profl. jours. Trustee Desert Spring Hosp., Las Vegas, 1976-85; bd. dirs. Nathan Adelson Hospice, 1982-88, Bridge Counseling Assocs., 1982, Everywoman's Ctr., 1984-86; chmn. Nev. Commn. on Nursing Edn., 1972-73, Nursing Articulation Com., 1972-73, Yr. of Nurse Com., 1978; moderator Invitational Conf. Continuing Edn., Am. Soc. Allied Health Professions, 1978; mgmt. cons. Nev. Donor Network, 1994—, Donor Organ Recovery Svc., Transplant Recipient Internat. Orgn., S.W. Eye Bank, S.W. Tissue Bank. Named Outstanding Alumnus, Loyola U., 1983; NIMH fellow, 1967-68. Fellow Am. Soc. Allied Health Professions, 1991, (chmn. nat. resolutions com. 1981-84, treas. 1988-90, sec's. award com. 1982-83, 92-93, nat. by-laws com. 1985, conv. chmn. 1987); mem. AAUP, Am. Nurses Assn., Nev. Nurses Assn. (dir. 1975-77, treas. 1977-79, conv. chmn. 1978), So. Nev. Area Health Edn. Coun., Western Health Deans (co-organizer 1985, chair, 1988-90), Nat. League Nursing, Nev. Heart Assn., So. Nev. Mem. Hosps. (mem. nursing recruitment com. 1981-83, mem. nursing practice com. 1983-85), Las Vegas C. of C. (named Woman of Yr. Edn.) 1988, Slovak Catholic Sokols, Phi Kappa Phi (chpt. sec. 1981-83, pres.-elect 1983, pres. 1984, v.p. Western region 1989-95, editl. bd. jour. Nat. Forum 1989-93), Alpha Beta Gamma (hon.), Sigma Theta Tau, Zeta Kappa. Office: U Nev Las Vegas 4505 S Maryland Pky Las Vegas NV 89154-9900

MICHEL, PAUL REDMOND, federal judge; b. Philadelphia, Pa., Feb. 3, 1941; s. Lincoln M. and Dorothy (Kelley) M.; m. Sally Ann Clark, 1965 (div. 1987); children: Sarah Elizabeth, Margaret Kelley; m. Elizabeth Morgan, 1989. BA, Williams Coll., 1963; JD, U. Va., 1966. Bar: Pa. 1967, U.S. Supreme Ct. 1970. Asst. dist. atty. Dist. Atty's Office, Phila., 1967-71, dep. dist. atty. for investigations, 1972-74; asst. spl. prosecutor Watergate investigation Dept. Justice, Washington, 1974-75, dep. chief pub. integrity sect., Criminal div. and prosecutor "Koreagate" investigation, 1976-78, assoc. dep. atty. gen., 1978-81, acting dep. atty. gen., 1979-80; asst. counsel intelligence com. U.S. Senate, 1975-76, counsel and adminstrv. asst. to Sen. Arlen Specter, 1981-88; judge U.S. Ct. Appeals (Fed. cir.), Washington, 1988—; instr. appellate practice and procedure George Wash. U. Nat. Law Ctr., 1991—, appellate advocacy John Marshall Law Sch., Chgo. 2d lt. USAR, 1966-72. Office: US Ct Appeals Fed Cir 717 Madison Pl NW Ste 808 Washington DC 20439-0002

MICHEL, ROBERT CHARLES, retired engineering company executive; b. N.Y.C., July 14, 1927; s. Charles John and Helen Carolyn (Wagner) M.; m. Alice Virginia Kraissl, June 16, 1951; children: Richard Charles, Ann Florence, Susan Jean. SB in Chem. Engring., MIT, 1950, SM in Chem. Engring., 1951. Registered profl. engr., N.J. Chmn., pres. The Kraissl Co., Inc., Hackensack, N.J., 1986-92. Pres. Bd. Edn., River Edge, N.J., 1968-72. With USNR, 1945-46. Mem. Am. Inst. Chem. Engrs., ASME, ASM, Bergen County Soc. Profl. Engrs. (pres. 1960-61), U.S. Power Squadron, Palisades Power Squadron (comdr. 1982-83), Elks, Tau Beta Pi, Sigma Xi. Home: 470 Prospect St Glen Rock NJ 07452-1909 Office: The Kraissl Co Inc 299 Williams Ave Hackensack NJ 07601-5225

MICHEL, THOMAS MARK, internal medicine educator, scientist, physician; b. Portland, Oreg., July 14, 1955. AB in Biochem. Scis., Harvard

U., 1977; PhD in Biochemistry, Duke U., 1983, MD, 1984. Diplomate Am. Bd. Internal Medicine, Am. Bd. Cardiovasc. Disease. House officer, jr. and sr. resident in medicine Brigham and Women's Hosp., Boston, 1984-87, clin. and rsch. fellow in medicine cardiovasc. div., 1987-88, assoc. physician, staff physician cardiovasc. div., 1988—; clin. fellow in medicine Harvard U. Med. Sch., Boston, 1984-87, rsch. fellow dept. genetics, 1988-90, instr. medicine, 1988-89, asst. prof., 1989-95, assoc. prof., 1995—; tutor in biochem. scis. Harvard Coll., Harvard U., Cambridge, Mass., 1990—; lectr. molecular mechanisms of disease Harvard Med. Sci.-MIT health scis. and tech. program, 1990—; speaker at seminars, confs. and univs.; vis. lectr. U. Alta., U. Calgary, U. Alcala, Madrid, St. Bartholomew's Hosp., London; Cecilie Greig vis. prof. Hammersmith Hosp., Royal Postgrad. Med. Sch., London; plenary lectr., Nitric Oxide Forum, Tokyo. Contbr. articles to med. jours. Recipient John J. Abel award in Pharmacology Am. Soc. for Pharmacology Therapeutics, 1995, young scholar's award Am. Soc. Hypertension, 1991; Harvard nat. scholar Harvard U., 1973-77; fellow NIH, 1977-84. Fellow Am. Coll. Cardiology; mem. ACP, Am. Fedn. for Clin. Rsch., Henry Christian award for excellence in rsch. 1992, 93), Am. Heart Assn. (Established Investigator award 1993—, Clinican-Scientist award 1988-93), Am. Soc. for Biochemistry and Molecular Biology, Mass. Med. Soc. Office: Brigham & Women's Hosp Harvard Med Sch 75 Francis St Boston MA 02115-6110

MICHELI, FRANK JAMES, lawyer; b. Zanesville, Ohio, Mar. 23, 1930; s. John and Theresa (Carlini) M.; m. Doris Joan Clum, Jan. 9, 1954; children: Michael John, James Carl, Lisa Ann, Matthew Charles. Student, John Carroll U., Cleve., 1947-48, Xavier U., Cin., 1949-50; LL.D., Ohio No. U., Ada., 1953. Bar: Ohio 1953. Since practiced in Zanesville; partner Leasure & Micheli, 1953-65, Kincaid, Micheli, Geyer & Ormond, 1965-75, Kincaid, Cultice, Micheli & Geyer (and predecessor), 1982-92; ptnr. Micheli, Baldwin, Bopeley & Northrup, 1992—; Instr. bus. law Meredith Bus. Coll., Zanesville, 1956; lectr. on med. malpractice, hosp. and nurse liability. Dir. Public Service for, City of Zanesville, 1954. Mem. Internat. Assn. Ins. Counsel, Def. Rsch. Inst., Ohio Def. Assn., Am. Ohio bar assns., Am. Judicature Soc., Am. Arbitration Assn. (mem. nat. panel), Am. Bd. Trial Advs. (bd. dirs. Ohio chpt. 1991-95, pres. 1997). Club: Elk. Home: 160 E Willow Dr Zanesville OH 43701-1249 Office: PO Box 2687 2806 Bell St Zanesville OH 43701

MICHELINI, SYLVIA HAMILTON, auditor; b. Decatur, Ala., May 16, 1946; d. George Borum and Dorothy Rose (Swatzell) Hamilton; m. H. Stewart Michelini, June 4, 1964; children: Stewart Anthony, Cynthia Leigh. BSBA summa cum laude, U. Ala., Huntsville, 1987. CPA, Ala.; cert. govt. fin. mgr., cert. fraud examiner. Acct. Ray McCay, CPA, Huntsville, 1987-88; auditor Def. Contract Audit Agy., Huntsville, 1989-92; auditor-office of inspector general George C. Marshall Space Flight, Center, Ala., 1992—. Mem. exec. bd. Decatur City PTA, 1976-78; pres., v.p. Elem. Sch. PTA, Decatur, 1977-79; leader Girl Scouts U.S. and Cub Scouts, Decatur, 1972-77; active local ARC, 1973-77. Mem. AAUW (chpt. treas. 1988-90), Nat. Assn. Accts. (dir. community svc. 1987-88, v.p. adminstrn. and fin. 1988-89, pres. 1989-90, nat. com. on ethics 1990-91), Am. Inst. CPAs, Am. Soc. Women Accts. (chpt. treas. 1989-90, dir. chpt. devel. 1989-90), Assn. Govt. Accts. (sec. 1992-93, chmn. pub. rels. 1993-94), Ala. Soc. CPAs (profl. ethics com. 1993-94), Inst. Internal Auditors (dir. awards and recongnition 1996-97), Inst. Mgmt. Accts. (v.p. communications, dir. program book 1991—, Dixie coun. dir. newsletters 1992-93, dir. ednl. programs 1992-93, 93-94, nat. com. ethics, 1990—), Ala. Soc. CPAs (govtl. acctg. and auditing com. 1994—), Inst. Mgmt. Accts. (nat. bd. dirs. 1994—), Phi Kappa Phi. Baptist. Avocations: reading, walking, sewing, research, music. Home: 2801 Sylvia Dr SE Decatur AL 35603-9381 Office: NASA Office Inspector Gen M-DI Marshall Space Flight Ctr Huntsville AL 35812

MICHELMAN, FRANK I., lawyer, educator; b. 1936. BA, Yale U., 1957; LLB, Harvard U., 1960. Bar: N.Y. 1961, Mass. 1967. Law clk. to assoc. justice William J. Brennan, U.S. Supreme Ct., Washington, 1961-62; asst. to asst. atty. gen., Tax Div., Dept. Justice, 1962-63; asst. prof. Harvard U., Cambridge, Mass., 1963-66, prof., 1966-93, Robert Walmsley Univ. prof., 1993—; cons. HUD, 1966; cons. Boston Model City Program, 1968-69; mem. Boston Home Rule Commn., 1969-71; mem. Gov.'s Task Force on Met. Devel., 1974-75. Mem. Am. Soc. for Polit. and Legal Philosophy, Am. Acad. Arts and Scis. Author: (with Sandalow) Materials on Government in Urban Areas, 1970. Office: Law Sch Harvard U Cambridge MA 02138

MICHELS, ROBERT, psychiatrist, educator; b. Chgo., Jan. 21, 1936; s. Samuel and Ann (Cooper) M.; m. Verena Sterba, Dec. 23, 1962; children—Katherine, James. BA, U. Chgo., 1953; MD, Northwestern U., 1958. Intern Mt. Sinai Hosp., N.Y.C., 1958-59; resident in psychiatry Columbia Presbyn.-N.Y. State Psychiat. Inst., N.Y.C., 1959-62; mem. faculty Coll. Physicians and Surgeons, Columbia U., N.Y.C., 1964-74; assoc. prof. Coll. Physicians and Surgeons, Columbia U., 1971-74; psychiatrist student health service Columbia U., 1966-74; supervising and tng. analyst Columbia U. Center for Psychoanalytic Tng. and Research, 1972—; attending psychiatrist Vanderbilt Clinic, Presbyn. Hosp., N.Y.C., 1964-74; Barklie McKee Henry prof. psychiatry Cornell U. Med. Coll., N.Y.C., 1974-93, prof. psychiatry, 1993-96, chmn. dept. psychiatry, 1974-91; Stephen and Suzanne Weiss dean Cornell U. Med. Coll., 1991-96; provost for med. affairs Cornell U., 1991-96, Walsh McDermott U. prof. of medicine, 1996—; psychiatrist-in-chief N.Y. Hosp., 1974-91, attending psychiatist, 1991—; attending psychiatrist St. Luke's Hosp. Ctr., N.Y.C., 1966—. Co-author: The Psychiatric Interview in Clinical Practice, 1971; contbr. articles to profl. jours. Served with USPHS, 1962-64. Mem. Am. Psychiat. Assn., Am. Coll. Psychiatrists, N.Y. Psychiat. Soc., Royal Medico-Psychol. Assn., Psychiat. Rsch. Soc., Assn. Rsch. in Nervous and Mental Diseases, Assn. Acad. Psychiatry, Am. Psychoanalytic Assn., Internat. Psychoanalytic Assn., Ctr. Advanced Psychoanalytic Studies, N.Y. Acad. Scis., Alpha Omega Alpha. Office: Cornell U Med Coll 525 E 68th St # 170 New York NY 10021-4873

MICHELSEN, CHRISTOPHER BRUCE HERMANN, surgeon; b. Boston, Aug. 18, 1940; s. Jost Joseph and Ingeborg Elizabeth (Dilthey) M.; BA, Bowdoin Coll., 1961; MD, Columbia U., 1969; m. Amy Lee; children: Heidi Elizabeth, Matthew Christopher, Joshua Jost. Intern Columbia Presbyn. Med. Center, N.Y.C., 1969-70, resident, 1970-71; orthopedic resident N.Y. Orthopedic Hosp., N.Y.C., 1971-73, jr. Anne C. Kane fellow, 1973-74, sr. Anne C. Kane fellow and hip fellow, 1974-75, traveling fellow, 1975-76; internat. A-O fellow, postgrad. fellow in biomechanics, instr. biomed. engrng. Case-Western Res. U.; prof. clin. orthopaedic surgery Columbia Coll. Physicians and Surgeons; co-dir. combined orthopaedic neuro surg. spine svc.; chief orthopaedic spine surgery svc., chief orthopaedic svc. Allen Pavillion, Columbia Presbyn. Med. Ctr., 1994, attending orthopedic surgeon; chief orthopaedic svc. Individual Mobilization Designee, Fitzsimmons Army Med. Coll., 1995—. Col. USAR, 1961—. Diplomate Am. Bd. Orthopaedic Surgery. Fellow ACS, N.Y. Acad. Medicine, Am. Assn. for Surgery of Trauma, Am. Orthopaedic Assn., N.Am. Spine Soc., Am. Acad. Orthopaedic Surgeons, Internat. Coll. Surgeons; mem. AMA, Am. Coll. Physician Execs., Orthopaedic Research Soc., Am. Soc. Bone & Mineral Rsch., Royal Soc. Medicine (affiliate). Home: 102 Shearwater Ct E Jersey City NJ 07305-5417 Office: 5141 Broadway New York NY 10034-1159

MICHELSEN, W(OLFGANG) JOST, neurosurgeon, educator; b. Amsterdam, Holland, Aug. 20, 1935; came to U.S., 1936; s. Jost Joseph and Ingeborg Mathilde (Dilthey) M.; m. Constance Richards, Sept. 21, 1963 (div. 1987); children: Kristina, Elizabeth, Ingrid; m. Claude Claire Grenier, Mar. 30, 1988 (div. Oct. 1992); m. Martha Reed, Sept. 21, 1996. AB magna cum laude, Harvard U., 1959; MD, Columbia U., 1963. Diplomate Am. Bd. Neurol. Surgery. Intern in surgery Case Wester Res. U. Hosps., Cleve., 1963-64; asst. resident in neurology Mass. Gen. Hosp., Boston, 1964-65; asst. resident, then chief resident neurol. surgery Columbia-Presbyn. Med. Ctr., N.Y.C., 1965-69; from instr. to assoc. prof. neurosurgery Columbia U. Coll. Physicians and Surgeons, N.Y.C., 1969-89, prof. clin. surgery, 1990—; fellow in neurosurgery Presbyn. Hosp., N.Y.C., 1969-71, dir. neuro vascular surgery, 1989-90; dir. neurosurgery St. Luke's Roosevelt Hosp. Ctr., N.Y.C., 1990—; prof. and chmn. dept. neurological surgery Albert Einstein Coll. Medicine, Bronx, N.Y., 1992—; dir. neurosurgery Montefiore Med Ctr, Bronx, 1992—; asst. attending in neurosurgery, St. Luke's Hosp. Ctr., 1970—; cons. neurosurgeon Nyack (N.Y.) Hosp., 1972—, Englewood (N.J.) Hosp., 1972—; vis. prof. neurosurgery Tufts U., 1975, Emery U., 1977, Presbyn.-St. Luke's Hosp. Ctr., Chgo., 1978, Yale U., 1980; guest faculty Northwestern U., 1977, 78, U. Chgo., 1977, Colby Coll., 1980; mem. numerous panels on neurosurgery. Contbr. articles to profl. publs. 1st lt. U.S. Army, 1954-57. Grantee NIH, USPHS. Fellow ACS, Am. Heart Assn.; Mem. AMA, Am. Assn. Neurol. Surgeons (mem. sect. pediatric neurosurger), Neurosurg. Soc. Am. (v.p. 1984-85, pres. 1987-88), Congress Neurol. Surgeons, N.Y. Neurosurg. Soc., Neurosurg. Soc. State N.Y., N.Y. Acad. Scis., Assn. Rsch. in Nervous and Mental Diseases, Internat. Neurosurg. Soc., Internat. Pediatric Neurosurg. Soc., Explorers Club, N.Y. State Med. Soc., N.Y. County Med. Soc. Office: Montefiore Med Ctr 111 E 210th St Bronx NY 10467-2401

MICHELSON, EDWARD J., journalist; b. Northampton, Mass., Apr. 3, 1915; s. Isadore Henry and Fannie (Avrich) M.; m. Dorothea Adair Pohlman, Feb. 3, 1938; children—Kathleen (Mrs. Howard J. Connolly), Paul, Emily. B.A., Williams Coll., 1937. Reporter St. Louis Post-Dispatch, 1937-38; sci. writer Westinghouse Electric Co., 1939-40; day editor, internat. shortwave news div. CBS, 1941-44; spl. asst. Office Sec. War, 1946; mem. hist. sect. strategic services unit War Dept., 1946; asso. Robert S. Allen (syndicated columnist), 1946-50; Washington corr. N.Am. Newspaper Alliance, 1946—; Washington corr. Boston Herald, 1952-57; Washington editor Forbes mag., 1956-63, Printer's Ink mag., 1958-63; mag. editor Ocean Sci. News, 1958-63, 1968; Washington editor Sci. and Tech. mag., 1969—; Exec. Enterprises Publs.; Research dir. pub. works subcom. on water resources U.S. Ho. of Reps., 1951. Contbr. to gen., financial, spl. bus. periodicals.; Editor: (Wright Patman) Our American Government, 1948. Served with OSS, AUS, 1944-46. Mem. Gargoyle Soc. Club: Cosmos. Home: 2300 Indian Creek Blv W # C-302 Vero Beach FL 32966

MICHELSON, GAIL IDA, lawyer; b. N.Y.C., Sept. 19, 1952; d. Max and Virginia (Seames) M. BA, Columbia U., 1984; JD, W.Va. U., 1993. Bar: W.Va. 1993, U.S. Dist. Ct. (so. dist.) W.Va. Assoc. Kopelman & Assocs., Charleston, W.Va., 1994; asst. atty. gen. consumer protection, profl. licensing bd. Atty. Gen. State of W.Va., Charleston, 1995—; counsel to state licensing boards. Actor: (soap operas) Another World, Guiding Light, All My Children, 1976-79; contbg writer W.Va. Quar. Dir./staff Am. Theatre of Actors, N.Y.C., 1985-90; mem. policy bd. Mental Health Assn. Mem. ABA, ACLU, W.Va. Bar Assn., W.Va. Trial Lawyers Assn., Mental Health Assn. (policy making com.). Home: 300 Park Ave Charleston WV 25302 Office: Atty Gen State of W Va Capitol Complex Charleston WV 25305

MICHELSON, GERTRUDE GERALDINE, retired retail company executive; b. Jamestown, N.Y., June 3, 1925; d. Thomas and Celia Rosen; m. Horace Michelson, Mar. 28, 1947; children: Martha Ann (dec.), Barbara Jane. B.A., Pa. State U., 1945; LL.B., Columbia U., 1947; LLD with honors, Adelphi U., 1981; DHL with honors, New Rochelle Coll., 1983; LLD with honors, Marymount Manhattan Coll., 1988. With Macy's N.Y., N.Y.C., 1947—; mgmt. trainee Macy's N.Y., 1947-48, various mgmt. positions, v.p. employee personnel, 1963-70, sr. v.p. for labor and consumer relations, 1970-72, dir., mem. exec. com., 1970—; sr. v.p. pers. labor and consumer rels. Macy & Co., Inc., 1972-79, sr. v.p. external affairs, 1979-80; sr. v.p. external affairs R.H. Macy & Co., Inc., 1980-92, sr. advisor, 1992-94; retired, 1995; bd. dirs. Chubb Corp., GE Co., Stanley Works, Inc., Goodyear Tire & Rubber Co.; bd. dirs., trustee Rand Corp.; former dep. chmn. N.Y. Fed. Res. Bank; gov. Am. Stock Exch. Chmn. Helena Rubenstein Found.; dir. Markle Found.; chmn. emeritus bd. trustees Columbia U.; life trustee Spelman Coll.; mem. adv. coun. Catalyst; bd. dirs., bd. overseers Tchrs. Ins. and Annuity Assn. of Am.—Coll. Retirement Equities Fund. Recipient Disting. Svc. medal Pa. State U., 1969. Mem. N.Y. City C. of C. (bd. dirs., mem. exec. com., vice chmn.), N.Y.C. Ptnrship. (vice chmn.), Women's Forum, Econ. Club N.Y. Home: 70 E 10th St New York NY 10003-5102 Office: Federated Dept Stores Inc 151 W 34th St New York NY 10001-2101

MICHELSON, HAROLD, production designer; b. N.Y.C., Feb. 15, 1920; s. Max and Gussie (Reichel) M.; m. Lillian Farber, Dec. 14, 1947; children: Alan Bruce, Eric Neil, Dennis Paul. Student, Pratt Inst., 1938, NYU, 1939, Art Students League, N.Y.C., 1945-47, Calif. Sch. Art, L.A., 1947-49. Illustrator Columbia Pictures, L.A., 1949-52; illustrator Paramount Pictures, L.A., 1953-58, art dir., prodn. designer, 1959-95; illustrator Warner Bros., Burbank, Calif., 1959-89; art dir. 20th Century Fox, Beverly Hills, Calif., 1959-89, visual cons., 1990-91; ind. prodn. designer, Hollywood, Calif., 1959-95; visual cons. Metro-Goldwyn-Mayer, Hollywood, 1992—; lectr. U. So. Calif., L.A., 1988-95; instr. UCLA, 1989-90, Maine Photog. Workshop, Rockport, Maine, 1991; mem. faculty Am. Film Inst., L.A., 1992-95. Exhibited in group show Storyboard-Le Cinema Dessiná, 1992. 1st lt. USAAF, 1941-45, ETO. Decorated Air medal with 7 oak leaf clusters. Mem. Soc. Motion Picture Art Dirs. (exec. bd. 1985-95), Acad. Motion Picture Arts and Scis. (membership bd. 1975—, 2 Acad. award nominations 1978, 84).

MICHELSON, LILLIAN, motion picture researcher; b. Manhattan, N.Y., June 21, 1928; d. Louis and Dora (Keller) Farber; m. Harold Michelson, Dec. 14, 1947; children: Alan Bruce, Eric Neil, Dennis Paul. Vol. Goldwyn Libr., Hollywood, Calif., 1961-69; owner Former Goldwyn Rsch. Libr., Hollywood, Calif., 1969—; ind. location scout, 1973—. Bd. dirs Beverlywood After Care Ctr., L.A., 1988—; mem. Friends of L.A. Pub. Libr. Mem. Acad. Motion Picture Arts and Scis. Office: care Dreamworks SKG 100 Universal Plz Lakeside Bldg #601 Universal City CA 91608

MICHENER, CHARLES DUNCAN, entomologist, researcher, educator; b. Pasadena, Calif., Sept. 22, 1918; s. Harold and Josephine (Rigden) M.; m. Mary Hastings, Jan. 1, 1941; children: David, Daniel, Barbara, Walter. B.S., U. Calif., Berkeley, 1939, Ph.D., 1941. Tech. asst. U. Calif., Berkeley, 1939-42; asst. curator Am. Mus. Natural History, N.Y.C., 1942-46; assoc. curator Am. Mus. Natural History, 1946-48, research assoc., 1949—; assoc. prof. U. Kans., 1948-49, prof., 1949-89, prof. emeritus, 1989—, chmn. dept. entomology, 1949-61, 72-75, Watkins Disting. prof. entomology, 1959-89, acting chmn. dept. systematics, ecology, 1968-69, Watkins Disting. prof. systematics and ecology, 1969-89; dir. Snow Entomol. Museum, 1974-83, state entomologist, 1949-61; Guggenheim fellow, vis. research prof. U. Paraná, Curitiba, Brazil, 1955-56; Fulbright fellow U. Queensland, Brisbane, Australia, 1958-59; research scholar U. Costa Rica, 1963; Guggenheim fellow, Africa, 1966-67. Author: (with Mary H. Michener) American Social Insects, 1951, (with S.F. Sakagami) Nest Architecture of the Sweat Bees, 1962, The Social Behavior of the Bees, 1974, (with M.D. Breed and H.E. Evans) The Biology of Social Insects, 1982, (with D. Fletcher) Kin Recognition in Animals, 1987, (with R. McGinley and B. Danforth) The Bee Genera of North and Central America, 1994; contbr. articles to profl. jours.; editor: Evolution, 1962-64; Am. editor: Insectes Sociaux, Paris, 1954-55, 62-90; assoc. editor: Ann Rev. of Ecology and Systematics, 1970-90. Served from 1st lt. to capt. San. Corps AUS, 1943-46. Fellow Am. Entomol. Soc., Entomol. Soc. Am., Am. Acad. Arts and Scis., Royal Entomol. Soc. London, AAAS; mem. NAS, Linnean Soc. London (corr.), Soc. for Study Evolution (pres. 1967), Soc. Systematic Zoologists (pres. 1969), Am. Soc. Naturalists (pres. 1978), Internat. Union for Study Social Insects (pres. 1977-82), Kans. Entomol. Soc. (pres. 1950), Brazilian Acad. Scis. (corr.). Home: 1706 W 2nd St Lawrence KS 66044-1016

MICHENER, JAMES ALBERT, author; b. N.Y.C., Feb. 3, 1907; s. Edwin and Mabel (Haddock) M.; m. Patti Koon, July 27, 1935 (div.); m. Vange Nord, Sept. 2, 1948 (div.); m. Mari Yoriko Sabusawa, Oct. 23, 1955 (dec. 1994). A.B. summa cum laude, Swarthmore Coll., 1929; A.M., U. No. Colo., 1937; research study, U. Pa., U. Va., Ohio State U., Harvard U., U. St. Andrews, Scotland, U. Siena, Italy, Brit. Mus. London; research study (Lippincott Traveling fellow), 1930-33, numerous hon. degrees. Tchr. Hill Sch., 1929-31, George Sch., Pa., 1933-36; prof. Colo. State Coll. Edn., 1936-41; vis. prof. Harvard U., 1939-40; asso. editor Macmillan Co., 1941-49; mem. adv. com. on arts State Dept., 1957; mem. adv. council NASA, 1980-83; mem. U.S. Adv. Commn. on Info., 1971; mem. Citizen's Adv. Stamp Com., 1982-87; mem. bd. for Internat. Broadcasting. Author: Unit in the Social Studies, 1940, Tales of the South Pacific, 1947 (Pulitzer prize), The Fires of Spring, 1949, Return to Paradise, 1951, The Voice of Asia, 1951, The Bridges at Toko Ri, 1953, Sayonara, 1954, Floating World, 1955, The Bridge at Andau, 1957, Rascals in Paradise, (with A. Grove Day), 1957, Selected Writings, 1957, The Hokusai Sketchbook, 1958, Japanese Prints, 1959, Hawaii, 1959, Report of the County Chairman, 1961, Caravans, 1963, The Source, 1965, Iberia, 1968, Presidential Lottery, 1969, The Quality of Life, 1970, Kent State, 1971, The Drifters, 1971, A Michener Miscellany, 1973, Centennial, 1974, Sports in America, 1976, Chesapeake, 1978, The Covenant, 1980, Space, 1982, Poland, 1983, Texas, 1985, Legacy, 1987, Journey, 1988, Alaska, 1988, Caribbean, 1989; (with John Kings) Six Days in Havana, 1989, The Novel, 1991, The World Is My Home, 1991, Writer's Handbook, 1992, Mexico, 1992, My Lost Mexico, 1992, Creatures of the Kingdom: Stories of Animals and Nature, 1993, Literary Reflections: Michener on Michener, Hemingway, Capote, and Others, 1993, Recessional, 1994, Miracle in Seville, 1995, This Noble Land: My Vision for America, 1996; editor: Future of Social Studies for N.E.A, 1940. With USNR, 1944-46. Recipient U.S. Medal of Freedom, Disting. Svc. medal NASA, Golden Badge of Order of Merit, 1988. Mem. Phi Beta Kappa. Democrat. Mem. Soc. of Friends. Office: Tex Ctr for Writers PCL 3.102 Mail Code S5401 Austin TX 78713*

MICHENER, JAMES LLOYD, medical educator; b. Dec. 19, 1952; m. Gwendolyn Curtis Murphy; children: Rebecca Liane, Joshua Kieran. BA, Oberlin (Ohio) Coll., 1974; MD, Harvard Med. Sch., 1978. Diplomate Am. Bd. Family Practice. Resident in family medicine Duke U. Med. Ctr., Durham, N.C., 1978-81, Kellogg fellow, 1981-82, clin. prof. dept. cmty. and family medicine, 1994—, chmn. dept. cmty. and family medicine, 1994—; v.p. Durham Health Care, Inc., 1985-86. Co-author: Nutrition in Practice, 1990, 2d edit., 1992; contbr. numerous articles to med. pubs. including Academic Medicine, The Jour. of Family Practice, Medical Care, others; mem. editl. bd. Rx Nutrition, 1989-91; presenter in field. Bd. dirs. N.C. Med. Soc. Found., 1995—; STFM rep. resource com. on nutrition edn. Am. Acad. Family Practice Found., 1987-91. Grantee The Fullerton Found., Inc., The Josiah Macy, Jr. Found., U.S. Dept. Health and Human Svcs. Mem. AMA, Assn. Tchrs. of Preventive Medicine, Am. Acad. of Family Physicians Found., Am. Heart Assn. (del. Nat. Cholesterol Edn. Program 1987), N.C. Acad. Family Physicians (bd. dirs. 1995—). Home: 4011 Duck Pond Trail Chapel Hill NC 27514 Office: Duke U Med Ctr Box 2914 Durham NC 27710*

MICHENFELDER, JOHN DONAHUE, anesthesiology educator; b. St. Louis, Apr. 13, 1931; s. Albert A. and Ruth J. (Donahue) M.; m. Margaret Grey Nick, Oct. 22, 1955 (dec. Nov. 1971); children: Carol, David, Joseph, Paul, Matthew, Laura; m. Mary Monica Milroy, Aug. 11, 1972; 1 child, Patrick. BS, St. Louis U., 1951, MD, 1955. Diplomate Am. Bd. Anesthesiology. Intern Presbyn. St. Luke's Hosp., Chgo., 1955-56; resident in internal medicine Presbyn. St. Luke's Hosp., 1956; resident in anesthesiology Mayo Clinic, Rochester, Minn., 1958-61, cons. in anesthesiology, 1961-91; prof. anesthesiology Mayo Med. Sch., Rochester, 1976-93, emeritus prof., 1993—. Author: Anesthesia and the Brain, 1988, Clinical Neuroanesthesia, 1990. Lt. USN, 1956-58. NIH grantee, 1966-89, 91-95; Faculty Anaesthetists of Royal Coll. Surgeons Ireland fellow, 1982, Faculty Anaesthetists Royal Coll. Surgeons Eng. fellow, 1988. Mem. Am. Soc. Anesthesiologists (Excellence in Rsch. award 1990, Disting. Svc. award 1990), Inst. Med., Assn. Univ. Anesthetists (councilman 1975-78). Avocations: upland game bird hunting, gardening, reading, writing. Home: 325 1st Ave NW Oronoco MN 55960-1410 Office: Mayo Clinic Emeritus Office 200 1st St SW Rochester MN 55902-3008

MICHENFELDER, JOSEPH FRANCIS, public relations executive; b. Webster Groves, Mo., Mar. 30, 1929; s. Albert Aloysius and Ruth Josephine (Donahue) M.; m. Audrey Laurine Glynn, Aug. 8, 1970. BA, N.Y. State U., N.Y.C., 1951, STB, 1954, MRE, 1955; MS in Journalism, Columbia U., 1958. Projects dir. Maryknoll Headquarters, Ossining, N.Y., 1955-57; communications dir. Maryknoll Headquarters, Ossining, 1958-62; dir., chief exec. officer Noticias Aliadas, S.A., Lima, Peru, 1962-69; pub. rels. dir. Pub. Affairs Analysts, Inc., N.Y.C., 1970-72; exec. v.p. Pub. Affairs Analysts, Inc., 1973-89; sr. v.p. Napolitan Assocs./PAA, Inc., N.Y.C., 1989-95; pres., CEO, 1995—; pres. IDOC/N.Am., Inc., N.Y.C., 1976—. Mng. Editor (polit. quarterly) POLITEIA, 1970-73; co-producer: TV documentary A Quiet Revolution, 1987. Trustee The Fund for Peace, 1994—, Coun. on Hemispheric Affairs, Washington, 1980—; cons. UNESCO WHO, Bogota, Lima, 1964-66; bd. dirs. Jobs for Youth, Inc., N.Y.C., 1978-84. Mem. Internat. Pub. Relations Assn., Internat. Assn. Polit. Cons., Columbia U. Journalism Alumni Fed. (pres. 1971-74), Ovrses Press Club, Columbia Club. Democrat. Avocations: theater arts, film, creative writing, ecology, Third World affairs. Office: Napolitan Assocs PAA Inc 55 5th Ave New York NY 10003-4301

MICHERO, WILLIAM HENDERSON, retired retail trade executive; b. Fort Worth, June 19, 1925; s. William Alvin and Lela Belle (Henderson) M.; m. Nan Elaine Henderson, July 9, 1948; children—Jane Elaine Michero Christie, William Sherman, Thomas Edward. B.S. in Commerce, Tex. Christian U., 1948. Sec. Tandy Corp., Fort Worth, 1960-75; v.p. Tandy Corp., 1970-75; with Tandycrafts, Inc., Fort Worth, 1975-90; sr. v.p., sec., dir. Tandycrafts, Inc., 1979-83, chmn. bd., 1983-90, ret., 1990; Sec. B.F. Johnston Found., Fort Worth, 1962-90. Bd. dirs. David L. Tandy Found., Fort Worth, 1968—, Oakwood Cemetery Assn., 1979-89, Panther Boys Club, 1974-78, Fort Worth Mus. Sci. and History, 1973-75, pres. 1975, United Way; chmn. Distributive Edn. Council, 1970. Served with U.S. Navy, 1943-46. Clubs: Fort Worth, Colonial Country. Home: 4705 Shady Ridge Ct Fort Worth TX 76109-1803 Office: 550 Bailey Ave Fort Worth TX 76107-2155

MICHIE, SARA H., pathologist, educator; b. Tulsa, Okla., Jan. 3, 1955. BS in Biology, Stephen F. Austin U., 1977; MD, U. Tex., Houston, 1981. Diplomate Am. Bd. Pathology. Resident anatomic pathology Stanford (Calif.) U. Med. Ctr., 1981-83, postdoctoral fellow immunology dept. pathology, 1983-84, 86-87, postdoctoral fellow diagnostic immunopathology, 1984-85; resident dept. pathology U. Iowa, Iowa City, 1985-86, postdoctoral fellow, 1986; assoc. investigator lab. svc. VA Hosp., Palo Alto, Calif., 1988-89, staff physician, 1989—, assoc. investigator, 1990-91; clin. instr. pathology dept. Stanford U., 1989-92, asst. prof. pathology, 1992—. Contbr. articles to profl. jours. Recipient Rsch. award Am. Diabetes Assn., 1996. Mem. Am. Soc. Investigative Pathology, Soc. Investigative Pathology, Bay Area Flow Cytometry Group, Sigma Xi, Alpha Omega Alpha. Office: VA Hosp Palo Alto 3801 Miranda Ave Stop 1545 Palo Alto CA 94304-1207

MICHLIN, ARNOLD SIDNEY, finance executive; b. Altoona, Pa., Sept. 2, 1920; s. John Mandel and Zelda (Solomon) M.; m. Florence Karbal, Aug. 17, 1941; children: Leslye Joyce Borden, Kenneth Brian, Steven Bruce, Joan Mindy Ennis. BS in Chemistry, Detroit Inst. Tech., 1944. Salesman Michlin Co., Detroit, 1934-41; chemist Ford Motor Co., Dearborn, 1941-44; chief chemist Continental Aviation and Engrng., Detroit, 1944-45; chemist U.S. Dept. of Chem. Warfare, Edgewood, Md., 1945-46; ptnr. Michlin Surplus Co., Detroit, 1947-83; pres. Michlin Indsl. Finishes, 1954-81; chem. cons. Michlin Chem. Corp., Madison Heights, Mich., 1981-82; fin. planner PA Securities, Southfield, Mich., 1980-83, Korn Womack Stern & Assocs., Southfield, 1983-89; registered rep. Titan Value Equities Group, Southfield, 1989—; cons. Project Equality, Archdiocese Detroit, 1970, Michlin Computer Cons., Ann Arbor, 1986—, LaserLand, Sylvan Lake, Mich., 1991—. Patentee in field. Bd. dirs. Ecumenical Inst. for Jewish and Christian Study, 1983, pres., 1992-93; founder Am. Arabic and Jewish Friends, Detroit, 1981; mem. Detroit Com. for Soviet Jewry, 1970—, co-founder, 1979, Materials for People of Palestine, 1946, co-founder, 1946, Muslim Christian Jewish Trialog, 1986—, co-founder. Recipient Heart of Gold award United Found., 1988. Mem. NCCJ (bd. dirs. Interfaith Roundtable, nat. bd. mem.), Internat. Assn. Fin. Planners, B'nai B'rith (pres. Detroit coun. 1982), Zionist Orgn. Am., Anti Defamation League, Cong. Shaarey Zedek Men's Club (program chmn. 1985—, Man of Yr. award 1994). Avocation: bowling. Home: 31460 Stonewood Ct Farmington Hills MI 48334

MICHNA, ANDREA STEPHANIE, real estate agent and developer; b. Chgo., Nov. 4, 1948; d. Andrew Stephen and Ann Barbara (Ciesla) M. Student, Northwestern U., 1984-86. Travel cons. Internat. Sporting Travel, Chgo., 1975-77; office mgr., legal asst. Law Office of J.A. Rosin, Chgo., 1977-83; asst. to pres. Mt. Sinai Hosp., Chgo., 1983-85; exec. v.p. real estate Continental Fin., Ltd., Northbrook, Ill., 1985—. Avocations: tng. and showing of dressage horses. Office: Continental Financial Ltd 555 Skokie Blvd Ste 350 Northbrook IL 60062-2834

MICK, HOWARD HAROLD, lawyer; b. Newton, Kans., Oct. 21, 1934; s. Marvin Woodrow and Edith (Bergen) M.; m. Susan Siple, Sept. 5, 1957; children: Martha, Julie, Elizabeth. Student, U. Okla., 1952-54; BS, LLB, U. Colo., 1958. Bar: Colo. 1958, Mo. 1959. Assoc. Stinson, Mag & Fizzell, Kansas City, Mo., 1959-62; ptnr. Stinson, Mag & Fizzell, Kansas City, 1962—. Bd. dirs. Ctr. Mgmt. Assistance, Kansas City, Mo., 1984-88; mem. adv. coun. Kansas City Salvation Army, 1987—, Milbank Mfg. Co., Kansas City, Mo., 1996—. Mem. ABA, Lawyers Assn. Kansas City, Kansas City Bar Assn., Rotary, Kansas City Club, Indian Hills Country. Democrat. Presbyterian. Avocations: golf, tennis, boating. Office: Stinson Mag & Fizzell PO Box 419251 Kansas City MO 64141-6251

MICKEL, EMANUEL JOHN, foreign language educator; b. Lemont, Ill., Oct. 11, 1937; s. Emanuel John and Mildred (Newton) M.; m. Kathleen Russell, May 31, 1959; children: Jennifer, Chiara, Heather. BA, La. State U., 1959; MA, U. N.C., 1963, PhD, 1965. Asst. prof. U. Nebr., Lincoln, 1965-67, assoc. prof., 1967-68; assoc. prof. Ind. U., Bloomington, 1968-73, prof., 1973—, dir. Medieval Studies Inst., 1976-91, chmn. French and Italian, 1984-95; cons. NEH; French advisor Soc. Rencesvals, 1995—; adv. bd. mem. Nineteenth Century French Studies, 1995—. Author: Marie de France, 1974, Eugene Fromentin, 1982, Ganelon Treason and the Chanson de Roland, 1989, Jules Vernes Complete Twenty Thousand Leagues Under the Sea, 1992. Capt. U.S. Army, 1963-65. Grantee NEH, Washington, 1978-84; Lilly Open fellow Lilly Found., Indpls., 1981-82; Chevalier dans l'Ordre des Palmes Academiques, 1997. Avocations: music, theater, sports, travel, ancient literature. Office: French & Italian Dept Indiana Univ 642 Ballantine Rd Bloomington IN 47401-5020

MICKEL, JOSEPH THOMAS, lawyer; b. Monroe, La., Nov. 12, 1951; s. Toufick and Ruth Ella (Phelps) M.; m. Carlene Elise Nickens, Dec. 10, 1981 (div.); children: Thomas, Matthew. BA, La. State U., 1975; postgrad., Tulane U., 1977-78; JD, So. U., 1979. Bar: La. 1979, U.S. Dist. Ct. (mid. dist.) La. 1981, U.S. Ct. Appeals (5th cir.) 1981, U.S. Dist. Ct. (we. dist.) La. 1983, U.S. Ct. Mil. Appeals 1985, U.S. Supreme Ct. 1985. Staff atty. Pub. Defenders Office, Baton Rouge, La., 1979-80; assoc. Law Offices of Michael Fugler, Baton Rouge, 1981; asst. dist. atty. La. 4th Jud. Dist. Atty.'s Office, Monroe, 1982-89; ptnr. Bruscato, Loomis & Street, Monroe, 1984-85; asst. U.S. atty. western dist. U.S. Atty.'s Office, Lafayette, 1989—; adj. prof. Northeast La. U., Monroe, 1988; mem. U.S. Dept. Justice Organized Crime Drug Task Force, 1992-93; instr. Acadiana Law Enforcement Tng. Acad., U. Southwestern La., Lafayette, 1995—. Mem. ABA. Republican. Presbyterian. Avocations: trapshooting, skeetshooting, bird hunting, fishing. Home: PO Box 91961 Lafayette LA 70509-1961 Office: US Atty Office 600 Jefferson St Ste 1000 Lafayette LA 70501-6935

MICKELSON, ARNOLD RUST, consultant, religious denominational official; b. Finley, N.D., Jan. 8, 1922; s. Alfred B. and Clara (Rust) M.; m. Marjorie Arveson, June 8, 1944; 1 son, Richard. BA, Concordia Coll., Moorhead, Minn., 1943, LLD (hon.), 1972; LLD (hon.), Calif. Luth. U., 1983, Luther Coll., 1987. Owner, mgr. Luther Book Store, Decorah, Iowa, 1946-48; credit supr. Gen. Motors Acceptance Corp., Fargo, N.D., 1948-53; mgr. Epko Film Service, Fargo, 1953-58; asst. to pres. No. Minn. dist. Evang. Luth. Ch., 1958-61, No. Minn. dist. Am. Luth. Ch., 1961-66; gen. sec. The Am. Luth. Ch., Mpls., 1967-82; coordinator Commn. for a New Luth. Ch., Mpls., 1982-87; pres. A.M. Cons., Amery, Wis., 1987—; councilor Luth. Council in U.S.A., 1966-82, sec., 1969-72, pres., 72-75; mem. U.S.A. Nat. Com. Luth. World Fedn., 1966-82, sec., 1966-69, 72-75, v.p., 1979-81, pres., 1981-82; mem. Consultation on Luth. Unity, 1970-76, sec., 1970-73, chmn., 1974-76; mem. Com. on Luth. Unity, 1976-82; del. 4th Assembly World Coun. Chs., Uppsala, Sweden, 1968, 5th Assembly, Nairobi, Kenya, 1975; chmn. Faith-in-Life Dialogue, Fargo-Moorhead, 1964, observer-trainer, Duluth, 1965; gen. sec. emeritus Am. Luth. Ch., 1982—; pres. Ctrl. Luth. Ch., Mpls., 1992-93. Mem. Mpls.-St. Paul Town Meeting Coun., 1968-76, Conf. on Inflation, 1974; bd. dirs. Midwest League, 1979—; mem. bd. mgrs. Am. Bible Soc., 1979—; trustee Suomi Coll., 1981—; mem. com. on hearing officers Evang. Luth. Ch. in Am., 1993—; pres. Luth. Leadership Inst., 1994-95, Luth. Resources Network, 1995—. With AUS, 1943-46. Recipient Civic Service award Eagles, 1965, Ch. award Suomi Coll., 1987, Judge Graven Lay Leadership award Wartburg Coll., 1990. Mem. Ch. Staff Workers Assn. (past pres.), Concordia Coll. Alumni Assn. (past pres.), Mpls. Athletic Club, Alpha Phi Gamma, Zeta Sigma Pi. Home: 1235 Yale Pl Apt 409 Minneapolis MN 55403-1944 Office: AM Cons 1232 Marina Dr Amery WI 54001-5132

MICKELSON, PHIL, professional golfer; b. San Diego, June 16, 1970. Profl. golfer, 1992—. Recipient Fred Haskins award, 1990, 91, 92, Jack nicklaus award, 1990, 91, 92; won NCAA Championships, 1989, 90, 92, No. Telecom Open, 1991, 95, Buick Invitational Calif., The Internat., 1993, Mercedes Championships, 1994, Nortel Open, 1996, Phoenix Open, 1996, Byron Nelson Classic, 1996; 1st team All-Am. with Sun Devils; one of 4 collegians ever to win NCAA crown as freshman; 1st left-hander to win U.S. Amateur, 1990; 1st player in PGA history to win same tournament as amateur and profl. (No. Telecom Open). Office: care PGA Box 109601 100 Ave of Champions Palm Beach Gardens FL 33410

MICKELSON, SIG, broadcasting executive, educator; b. Clinton, Minn., May 24, 1913; s. Olaf and Harriet (Reinholdson) M.; m. Maybelle Brown, June 8, 1940 (dec. Apr., 1985); children: Karen Ann (Mrs. Christiaan De Brauw), Alan; m. Elena Mier y Teran, June 14, 1986. B.A., Augustana Coll., 1934, LLD, 1987; M.A., U. Minn., 1940. With CBS, N.Y.C., 1943-61; pres. CBS News, 1954-61; v.p., dir. Time-Life Broadcast, Inc., N.Y.C., 1961-70, Ency. Brit. Ednl. Corp., Chgo., 1970-72; prof., chmn. editorial dept. Medill Sch. Journalism, Northwestern U., Evanston, Ill., 1972-75; pres. RFE/RL, Inc., Washington, 1975-78; Disting. vis. prof. San Diego State U., 1978-79, exec. dir. Ctr. for Communications, 1979-82, adj. prof, 1984-90, Van Deerlin prof. communications, 1989-90; pres. San Diego Communications Coun., 1989-90; Manship prof. journalism La. State U., 1991-93, disting. prof. comm., 1994—; rsch. fellow Hoover Instn., 1981—; advisor Nat. News Coun., 1973-80; ex-officio Bd. Internat. Broadcasting, 1975-78; dir. Stauffer Comms. Inc., 1979-95. Author: The Electric Mirror, 1972, America's Other Voice, 1983, The First Amendment: The Challenge of New Technology, 1989, From Whistle Stop to Sound Bite, 1989, The Northern Pacific Railroad and the Selling of the West, 1993. Bd. regents Augustana Coll., 1983-95. Mem. Radio TV News Dirs. Assn. (founder, v.p. 1946-48, pres. 1948-49), Internat. Inst. for Comm. (founder, chmn. 1970-71, chmn. exec. com. 1967-70, 71-73), Coun. on Fgn. Rels. Clubs: Century Assn. (N.Y.C.); Cosmos (Washington). Home: 6443 Pasatiempo Ave San Diego CA 92120-3823

MICKELSON, STACEY, state legislator. BA, Minot State U., 1994. Asst. mgr. Wild Things Gallery; rep. Dist. 38 N.D. Ho. of Reps., 1994—, mem. fin. and taxation and transp. coms.; mem. interim legis. audit & fiscal rev., adminstrv. rules coms. Mem. Minot Symphony Assn. (bd. dirs., 2nd v.p.), Minot Adult Literacy Vols., B.I.L.L.D. Fellow, Flemming Fellows. Home: PO Box 117 Minot ND 58702-0117

MICKEY, BRUCE EDWARD, neurosurgeon; b. New Orleans, Sept. 5, 1952; m. Barbara Ann Schultz, Jan. 23, 1988. AB, Harvard U., 1974; MD, U. Tex. Southwestern Med. Sch., 1978. Diplomate Am. Bd. Neurol. Surgery. Intern U. Tex. Southwestern Med. Sch., Dallas, 1978-79, resident in neurol. surgery, 1979-84, asst. prof., 1984-90, assoc. prof., 1990—. Mem. Am. Assn. Neurol. Surgeons, Congress Neurol. Surgeons, North Am. Skull Base Soc. Office: U Tex Southwestern Med Sch 5323 Harry Hines Blvd Dallas TX 75235-7208

MICKIEWICZ, ELLEN PROPPER, political science educator; b. Hartford, Conn., Nov. 6, 1938; d. George K. and Rebecca (Adler) Propper; m. Denis Mickiewicz, June 2, 1963; 1 son, Cyril. B.A., Wellesley Coll., 1960; M.A., Yale U., 1961, Ph.D., 1965. Lectr. dept. polit. sci. Yale U., 1965-67; asst. prof. dept. polit. sci. Mich. State U., East Lansing, 1967-69; assoc. prof. Mich. State U., 1969-73, prof., 1973-80; prof. dept. polit. sci. Emory U., Atlanta, 1980-88; dean Grad. Sch. Arts and Scis. Emory U., 1980-85, Alben W. Barkley prof. polit. sci., 1988-93; James R. Shepley prof. pub. policy, prof. polit. sci. Duke U., Durham, N.C., 1994—, dir. DeWitt Wallace Ctr. for Comm. and Journalism Terry Sanford Inst. Pub. Policy, 1994—; vis. prof. Kathryn W. David Chair Wellesley Coll., 1978; vis. com. dept. Slavic lang. and lit. Harvard U., 1978-85, vice chmn. vis. com. Russian Rsch. Ctr., Harvard U., 1986-92; mem. subcom. on comms. and society Am. Coun. Learned Socs./Soviet Acad. Scis., 1986-90; mem. com. on internat. security studies, Am. Acad. Arts and Scis., 1988-90; fellow The Carter Ctr., 1985—, dir. Commn. on Radio and TV Policy; mem. area adv. com. for Ea. Europe and USSR, Coun. for Internat. Exch. Of Scholars, 1987-90; mem. acad. adv. coun. The Kennan Inst. for Advanced Russian Studies, 1989-93; mem. bd. overseers Internat. Press Ctr., Moscow, 1995; dir., commr. Commn. Radio and TV Policy, 1990. Author: Soviet Political Schools, 1967, Media and the Russian Public, 1981, Split Signals: Television and Politics in the Soviet Union, 1988 (Electronic Book of Yr. award Nat. Assn. Broadcasters and Broadcast Edn. Assn. 1988); co-author: Television and Elections, 1992, Television/Radio News and Minorities, 1994, Changing Channels: Television and the Struggle for Power in Russia, 1997; editor: Soviet Union Jour., 1980-90; co-editor: International Security and Arms Control, 1986, The Soviet Calculus of Nuclear War, 1986; editor, contbr.: Handbook of Soviet Social Science Data, 1973; mem. editl. bd. Jour. Politics, 1985-88, Harvard Internat. Jour. Press/Politics, 1995—, Polit. Comms., 1996—. Founder, 1st chmn. bd. dirs. Opera Guild of Greater Lansing, Inc., 1972-74. Recipient Outstanding Svc. to Promote Dem. Media in Russia award Journalists Union of Russia, 1994; Ford Found. Fgn. Area Tng. fellow, 1962-65, Guggenheim fellow, 1973-74; Sigma Xi grantee, 1972-74, John and Mary R. Markle Found. grantee, 1984-88, 94-96, 95—, Ford Found. grantee, 1985, 88-91, 92—, Rockefeller Found. grantee, 1985-87, W. Alton Jones Found. grantee, 1987-88, Eurasia Found. grantee, 1993-94, Carnegie Corp. of N.Y. grantee, 1996—. Mem. Am. Assn. for Advancement Slavic Studies (bd. dirs. 1978-81, mem. awards com., mem. endowment com. 1984-86, pres. 1987-88), Am. Polit. Sci. Assn.,Internat. Studies Assn. (v.p. N.Am. 1983-84), Dante Soc. Am., So. Conf. Slavic Studies (exec. com. 1983-84), Counc. Fgn. Rels. Office: Duke U Sanford Inst Pub Policy PO Box 90241 Durham NC 27708-0241

MICKLITSCH, CHRISTINE NOCCHI, health care administrator; b. Hazleton, Pa., Oct. 23, 1949; d. Nicholas Edmund and Matilda Nocchi; m. Wayne D. Micklitsch, May 20, 1972; children: Sarah N., Emily M. BS, Pa. State U., State College, 1971; MBA, Boston U., 1979. Blood bank med. technologist The Deaconess Hosp., Boston, 1971-73; sr. blood bank med. technologist Tufts New Eng. Med. Ctr., Boston, 1973-76, environ. svcs. coord., 1976-78; adminstrv. resident Joslin Diabetes Found., Boston, 1978-79; sr. analyst Analysis, Mgmt. & Planning, Inc., Cambridge, Mass., 1979-80; adminstrv. dir. Hahnemann Family Health Ctr., Worcester, Mass., 1980-84; exec. dir. Swampscott (Mass.) Treatment & Trauma Ctr., 1984-85; dir. practice mgmt., instr. U. Mass. Med. Ctr., Worcester, 1985-91; dir. adminstrv. svcs. The Fallon Clinic, Worcester, 1991-94; mgr. physician network devel. The Fallon healthcare Sys., Worcester, 1994—. Co-author: Physician Performance Management: Tool for Survival and Success, 1996. Incorporator, pres. Newton (Mass.) Highlands Cmty. Devel. Corp., 1981-82; treas. Patriot's Trail coun. Girl Scouts U.S., Newton, 1993—; Christian edn. instr. Newton Highlands Congl. Ch., 1987-94. Kellogg fellow Ctr. for Rsch. in Ambulatory Health Care Adminstrn., Denver, 1979; grantee in grad. tng. in family medicine HHS, U. Mass. Med. Sch., Worcester, 1989. Fellow Am. Coll. Med. Practice Execs. (state coll. forum rep. 1989—, ea. sect. coll. forum rep. 1993—); mem. Am. Coll. Med. Practice Execs. (mem. chair 1995-96), Mass. Med. Group Mgmt. Assn. (pres. 1987-89, newsletter editor 1984—), Boston U. Health Care Mgmt. Program Alumni Assn., Alpha Omicron Pi (parlimentarian Epsilon Alpha chpt. 1969-70). Avocations: classic cars, real estate. Home: 320 Lake Ave Newton MA 02161-1212 Office: Fallon Healthcare Sys Chestnut Pl 10 Chestnut St Worcester MA 01608-2804

MICKO, ALEXANDER S., financial executive; b. Munich, May 8, 1947; came to U.S., 1952, naturalized, 1957; s. Zygmunt and Maria (Huber) M.; m. Sharon E. Judge, June 7, 1969; 1 child, Brian A. BS, LaSalle U., 1969. CPA, N.J., Pa. Audit mgr. Price Waterhouse, Phila., 1970-77; asst. chief fin. investigations div. of Casino Gaming Enforcement, State of N.J., Trenton, 1977-79; v.p. fin. TeleScis., Inc., Mt. Laurel, N.J., 1979-87; v.p. fin., chief fin. officer, asst. sec. Dechert, Price & Rhoads, Phila., 1987-89; v.p. fin., treas., sec. NET Atlantic, Inc., Thorofare, N.J., 1989-92; v.p., contr. AAA Mid-Atlantic, Inc., Phila., 1992—; owner AM Fin. Services, Medford, N.J., 1986—; cons. United Computer Services, Berlin. N.J., 1982—; lectr. in field. Bd. dirs. Forest Hills Civic Assn., Williamstown, N.J., 1976. With USMC, 1969-75. Recipient Michael A. DeAngelis Outstanding Profl. Achievement award, LaSalle U., Phila., 1985. Mem. AICPA, N.J. Soc. CPAs, Pa. Inst. CPAs, Fin. Execs. Inst., Nat. Assn. Accts. Roman Catholic. Avocations: skiing, golf. Home: 5 Huntington Cir Medford NJ 08055-3315 Office: AAA Mid Atlantic Inc 2040 Market St Philadelphia PA 19103-3302

MICKS, DON WILFRED, biologist, educator; b. Mt. Vernon, N.Y., Nov. 23, 1918; s. Wilfred Wallace and Bernice (Barbour) M.; m. Martha Millican, Feb. 15, 1944; children—Donald Frederick, Stephen Alan, Marjorie Ellen, Carol Jeanne. B.S., N. Tex. State U., 1940, M.S., 1942; Sc.D., Johns Hopkins, 1949. Faculty Med. Br. U. Tex., Galveston, 1949-86; prof., chmn. preventive medicine, community health Med. Br. U. Tex., 1966-86; prof. emeritus, 1993—; Scientist-biologist div. Environmental Health, WHO, Geneva, Switzerland, 1958-59; cons. WHO, Pakistan, 1969. Contbr. articles to profl. jours. Chmn. bd. St. Vincent's House, 1969-70; mem. adv. bd. Tex. Air Control Bd. Served to lt. USNR, 1942-45, PTO. Named Disting. Alumnus North Tex. State U., 1970; Fulbright sr. rsch. scholar U. Pavia, Italy, 1953-54; recipient Excellence in Teaching award, 1991; named suite dedication Ewing Hall, Dept. Preventive Medicine and Cmty. Health. Fellow Am. Pub. Health Assn., Royal Soc. Tropical Medicine and Hygiene, AAAS; mem. Assn. Tchrs. Preventive Medicine, Soc. Exptl. Biology and Medicine, Am. Soc. Tropical Medicine and Hygiene, Internat. Soc. Toxinology, Entomol. Soc. Am., Am. Mosquito Control Assn., Sigma Xi. Episcopalian (vestryman 1968-70, 74-76).

MICOZZI, MARC STEPHEN, health executive, physician, educator; b. Norfolk, Va., Oct. 27, 1953; s. Edio Dominic and Huguette (Picon) M.; m. Carole Ann O'Leary, Oct. 8, 1982; 1 child, Alicia Madeleine. Cadet, USAF Acad., 1971-72; BA, Pomona Coll., 1974; MD, U. Pa., 1979, PhD, 1986. Diplomate Am. Bd. Pathology. Rsch. fellow City of Hope Nat. Med. Ctr., Duarte, Calif., 1973; chem. engr. Gould Corp., El Monte, Calif., 1974; Luce Found. scholar Mindanao, The Philippines, 1976-77; clin. applications chemist McDonnell-Douglas Corp., Pasadena, Calif., 1978; postdoctoral fellow Allied Inst. Environ. Health, Princeton, N.J., 1979; resident in pathology Pa. Hosp., Phila., 1980-83; med. examiner Dade County Med. Examiner's Office, Miami, Fla., 1983-84; sr. investigator Nat. Cancer Inst., Bethesda, Md., 1984-86; dir. Nat. Mus. Health and Medicine, Washington, 1986-95; exec. dir. Coll. Physicians' of Phila., 1995—; adj. prof. Uniformed Svcs. U. Health Scis., Bethesda, 1986-95, U. Pa. Sch. Medicine, 1996—; vis. lectr. Georgetown U. Sch. Medicine, Washington, 1986—, Johns Hopkins U. Sch. Medicine, Balt., 1988—; adj. prof. dept. phys. medicine U. Pa., 1996—. Editor: Nutrition and Cancer, 1989; assoc. editor Health Care, Jour. Human Orgn., 1983-89; contbr. chpts. to books and numerous articles to profl. jours. Del. White House Conf. on Youth, Estes Park, Colo., 1971, UN Conf. on Human Environ., Stockholm, 1972, NATO Advanced Study Inst., Brussels, 1982; mem. Calif. Gov.'s Adv. Com., 1972-74. Fellow Human Biology coun., Soc. for Applied Anthropology, Am. Anthrop. Assn.; Am. Acad. Forensic Scis., Am. Pub. Health Assn., N.Y. Acad. Scis. Roman Catholic. Office: Coll Physicians 19 S 22nd St Philadelphia PA 19103-3001*

MICZEK, KLAUS ALEXANDER, psychology educator; b. Burghausen, Bavaria, Germany, Sept. 28, 1944; came to U.S., 1967; s. Erich and Irene (Wirthl) M.; m. Christiane Baerwaldt, Aug. 8, 1970; 1 child, Nikolai A. Tchrs. cert., Paedagogische Hochschule, Berlin, 1966; PhD, U. Chgo., 1972. Asst. prof. Carnegie-Mellon U., Pitts., 1972-74, assoc. prof., 1974-79; assoc. prof. Tufts U., Medford, Mass., 1979-83, prof., 1983-93, Moses Hunt prof. psychiatry, psychology, pharmacology, 1993—; cons. Solray-Duphar v.b., Weesp, The Netherlands, 1984—, Nat. Inst. Drug Abuse, Rockville, Md., 1984—; Boerhaave prof. U. Leiden, The Netherlands, 1987; mem. panel on violence, NAS, 1989-92. Editor: Ethopharmacology, 1983, Ethopharmacological Aggression Research, 1984; field editor, coord. editor Behavioral Pharmacology, Jour. Psychopharmacology; contbr. articles on psychopharmacology, 1973—. Rsch. grantee Nat. Inst. Drug Abuse, 1973—, Nat. Inst. Alcoholism and Alcohol Abuse, 1981—; recipient Solvay-Duphar award APA, 1993, Bundesverdienstkrenz Cross of Merit, Fed. Republic of Germany, 1996. Fellow Am. Psychol. Assn. (program chmn. 1981, pres. div. psychopharmacology 1990-91), Behavioral Pharmacological Soc. (pres. 1992-94), Internat. Soc. for Rsch. on Aggression (councilor 1987); mem. Soc. Neurosci., N.Y. Acad. Scis., Internat. Primatol. Soc. Office: Tufts U Dept Psychology 490 Boston Ave Medford MA 02155-5532

MICZUGA, MARK NORBERT, metal products executive; b. Chgo., Feb. 14, 1962; s. Norbert and Rita (Kamper) M.; m. Maria Del Carmen Caballero, Sept. 19, 1992; children: Angelica Pamela, Henry. BS, DePaul U., 1984, MBA, 1989. Mgr. steel products Mitsubishi Internat. Corp., Chgo., 1985-93; v.p. sales MC Fabrication Industries, Inc., Oak Brook Terrace, Ill., 1993—. Mem. Assn. MBA Execs. Office: MC Fabrication Industries 1 Lincoln Ctr Ste 340 Villa Park IL 60181-4205

MIDANEK, DEBORAH HICKS, portfolio manager, director; b. N.Y.C., Nov. 30, 1954; d. Frederick Stevens and Mary Leavenworth (Barnes) H.; m. James Ira Midanek, Sept. 29, 1985; children: Benjamin Abraham, Thomas Hicks. AB, Bryn Mawr Coll., 1975; MBA, U. Pa., 1980. Asst. dir. admissions Bryn Mawr (Pa.) Coll., 1975-78; asst. v.p. Bankers Trust, N.Y.C., 1980-84; v.p. Drexel Burnham Lambert, N.Y.C., 1984-90; CEO Solon Asset Mgmt. Corp., 1990—; mng. dir. mutual funds Montgomery Asset Mgmt., San Francisco, 1992-93; bd. dirs. Drexel Burnham Lambert Group, 1990-92, Std. Brands Paint Co., chmn. compensation com., 1993—, chmn. of the bd., 1995—, CEO, 1996—. Trustee, treas. New St. Found., 1992-94; bd. dirs. Pelham (N.Y.) Art Ctr., 1989-91, Mgmt. Decision Lab. Stern Sch. Bus., NYU, 1990-93, United Way of Pelham, 1990-93; mem. exec. bd. exploring divsn. Greater N.Y. coun. Boy Scouts Am., 1991-93; trustee Warren Wilson Coll., Asheville, N.C., 1993—; trustee for Economic Dev., 1995—. Mem. N.Y. Soc. Securities Analysts, Bryn Mawr Coll. Club of N.Y. (pres. 1991-93), Econ. Club of N.Y. Republican. Home: 375 La Casa Via Walnut Creek CA 94598-4842 Office: Solon Asst Mgmt LP 1981 N Broadway Ste 325 Walnut Creek CA 94596-3841

MIDDAUGH, ROBERT BURTON, artist; b. Chgo., May 12, 1935; s. John Burton and Mae Knight (Crooks) M. Student, U. Chgo., 1960-64; BFA, Art Inst. Chgo., 1964. curator art collection 1st Nat. Bank Chgo., 1971-83. Designed, executed ednl. display, Prehistoric Project at Oriental Inst. of U. Chgo., 1968; One-man shows include, Kovler Gallery, Chgo., 1965, 67, 69, Martin Schweig Gallery, St. Louis, 1970, 72, 79, 83, U. Wis., 1976, 81, 82, Fairweather Hardin Gallery, Chgo., 1977, 80, 83, 85, Rockford Art Mus., 1987, Zaks Gallery, Chgo., 1992, 93, 97; group shows, including, Art Inst. Chgo., 1964, 66, 78, 79, Evanston (Ill.) Art Center, 1966, Joslyn Art Mus., Omaha, 1968, U. Notre Dame, 1969, Va. Mus. Fine Arts, Richmond, 1966; represented in permanent collections, Art Inst. Chgo., Boston Mus. Fine Arts, Fine Art Mus. of South, Mobile, Ala., Los Angeles County Mus., Phoenix Art Mus., Worcester (Mass.) Art Mus., Ill. State Mus., Springfield. Served with U.S. Army, 1958-60. Mem. Arts Club Chgo.

MIDDELKAMP, JOHN NEAL, pediatrician, educator; b. Kansas City, Mo., Sept. 29, 1925; s. George H. and Clara M. (Ordelheide) M.; m. Roberta Gill, Oct. 3, 1949 (div. 1970); children—Sharon Ann, Steven Neal, Susan Jean, Scott Alan; m. Lois Harper, Mar. 1, 1974. B.S., U. Mo., 1946; M.D., Washington U., St. Louis, 1948. Diplomate Am. Bd. Pediatrics. Intern D.C. Gen. Hosp., Washington, 1948-49; resident St. Louis Children's Hosp., 1949-50, 52-53; instr. pediatrics Washington U., 1953-57, asst. prof. pediatrics, 1957-64, assoc. prof., 1964-70, prof., 1970—; dir. ambulatory pediatrics St. Louis Children's Hosp., 1974-91. Author: Camp Health Manual, 1984; contbr. articles, chpts. to profl. publs. Served to comdr. M.C., USNR, 1943-66. NIH postdoctoral fellow, 1961-62. Mem. Am. Acad. Pediatrics, Am. Soc. Microbiology, Infectious Diseases Soc. Am., Am. Pediatric Soc., Ambulatory Pediatric Assn., Sigma Xi, Alpha Omega Alpha. Home: 8845 Paragon Cir Saint Louis MO 63123-1114 Office: 1 Childrens Pl Saint Louis MO 63110

MIDDENDORF, J. WILLIAM, II, investment banker; b. Balt., Sept. 22, 1924; m. Isabelle Paine, Mar. 7, 1953; children: Frances, Amy, John W. IV, Ralph Henry. B in Naval Sci., Holy Cross Coll., 1945; AB, Harvard U., 1947; MBA, NYU, 1954; LLD (hon.), Troy State U.; LittD (hon.), Sch. of Ozarks, Am. Christian Coll.; D. Social Scis. (hon.), Netherlands-Am. Inst. Commd. ensign USN, 1945, advanced through grades to lt. (j.g.), ret., 1946; with credit dept. Chase Manhattan Bank, 1947-52; ptnr. Wood Struthers and Co., 1958-61; sr. ptnr. Middendorf, Colgate and Co., 1962-69; ambassador to The Netherlands, 1969-73; sec. USN, 1974-77; pres., CEO Fin. Gen. Bankshares, Inc., 1977-81; ambassador to Orgn. Am. States, 1981-85, European Communities, 1985-87; chmn. Middendorf & Assocs., Inc., 1989—; chmn. presdl. task force Project Econ. and Social Justice, 1986-90; mem. U.S. Del. to supervise elections in Suriname, 1988; treas. Internat. Rep. Inst. Composer 8 symphonies, 100 marches, (opera) King Richard, nat. independence march for Belize, other compositions for Latin Am. countries; guest condr. Boston Pops, St. Louis Symphony, Ind. U., others; contbr. articles to profl. jours. Mem. U.S. Olympic com., 1979-89, U.S. Olympic Selection com. for field hockey; judge field hockey Olympics, Rome, 1960; former mem. vis. com. dept. Am. paintings Met. Mus. Art, N.Y.C., vis. com. dept. Am. Art, Mus. Fine Arts, Boston; hon. v.p. Naval Hist. Found.; treas. Goldwater for Pres. com., 1962-64, Presdl. Transition com. 1968, Rep. Nat. Com., 1964-69; alt. del. for Gov. Reagan, 1980; del. State of Conn., 1964, 68, State of Va., 1996; co-chmn. Virginians for Reagan, 1980, fin. com. Va. GOP, 1980-81; coordinator internat. econ. and naval adv. com. Reagan for Pres. campaign, 1980; chmn. Congl. Boosters com., 1978-81; chmn. CIA Transition Team, 1980-81; chmn. fin. com. Pres. Reagan's 1981 Inaugural com.; trustee NavaL War Coll. Found., Heritage Found., Washington; past trustee Hoover Instn. for War Revolution and Peace, Corcoran Gallery, N.Y. Hist. Soc., Balt. Mus. Art, Greenwich Hist. Soc., Boston Symphony, Middlesex Sch., Concord, Mass., Nat. Symphony Orch., Mass. Gen. Hosp., Boys Club N.Y.; bd. electors Ins. Hall of Fame; bd. dirs. Georgetown U., John Philip Sousa Meml. Found.; chmn. bd. dirs. council statesmen Ludwig von Mises Inst.; bd. dirs. Newport Art Mus. and Mariners' Mus., Norfolk, Va.; chmn. Netherlands-Am. Amity Trust; chmn. Com. for Monetary Research and Edn. Inc.; chmn. Def. Forum Found.; former mem. com. Dept. State Fine Arts Com.; chmn. Navy League Awards com., 1977—; founding chmn. U.S. Navy Meml. Found.; past chmn. Netherlands-Am. Inst., Wolf Trap Farm Park, John Carter Brown Library Assocs., Providence, Asian Composers Expo., European Council of Boy Scouts. Recipient Superior Honor award Dept. State, 1974, Disting. Pub. Service award Dept. Def., 1975, 76, Navy Disting. Pub. Service award, 1976, Naval Disting. Service medal Republic Brazil, 1976, Ludwig von Mises Free Market award, 1985, Inter-Am. Music Council award, 1985, Edwin Franko Goldman award Am. Bandmasters Assn., 1987, Assn. Harvard Clubs Am. award, Disting. Service medal Purdue Univ. Bands, Netherlands Soc. Phila. Gold medal, Good Citizenship medal Nat. Soc. SAR, Medal of Honor, Midwest Nat. Band Assn., Invest in Am. Am. Eagle award, 1988, Eugene J. Keogh Disting. Pub. Svc. award NYU, 1989, Nat. Commendation award Pres.' Coun. Phys. Fitness and Sports, 1989, Leadership award Am. Friends of Turkey, 1989; decorated Grand Master Order of Orange Nassau, Netherlands, Order of Arab Republic of Egypt, 1979, Grand Master of Order of Naval Merit, Republic Brazil, 1974; named Alumnus of Yr. NYU, 1978; Nat. Masters Sculling champion, 1979. Mem. Am. Antiquarian Soc., Harvard Alumni Assn. (permanent class com. 1947), Soc. Cin. (hon.), ASCAP, Walpole Soc., Co. Mil. Historians, Mil. Order Loyal Legion, SAR, Soc. of SAR, Field Hockey Assn. Am. (past pres., player/mgr. nat. team 1963), U.S. Naval Inst., Navy League. Clubs: Angler's, Downtown Assn., Union (N.Y.C.); Army-Navy, Capitol Hill, Met., Potomac Boat (Washington); Narragansett Boat (Providence); Sakonnet Golf (Little Compton, R.I.); Somerset (Boston). Office: Middendorf & Assocs Inc 1730 K St NW # 1100 Washington DC 20006-2402

MIDDENDORF, JOHN HARLAN, English literature educator; b. N.Y.C., Mar. 31, 1922; s. George Arlington and Margaret (Hofmann) M.; m. Beverly Bruner, July 14, 1943 (dec. 1983); children: Cathie Jean Middendorf Hamilton, Peggy Ruth Middendorf Brindisi; m. Maureen L. MacGrogan, Jan. 31, 1986. AB, Dartmouth Coll., 1943; AM, Columbia U., 1947, PhD, 1953. Lectr. English CCNY, 1946, Hunter Coll., 1946-49; faculty Columbia, 1947—, prof. English, 1965-89, prof. emeritus, 1990—, dir. grad. studies, 1971-74, vice-chmn., 1976-80; chmn. English test com. Coll. Entrance Exam. Bd., 1967-69. Contbr. articles, revs. to profl. jours.; Editor: English Writers of the Eighteenth Century, 1971; asst. editor: Johnsonian News Letter, 1950-58; co-editor, 1958-78, editor, 1978-90; asso. editor: Yale edit. Works Samuel Johnson, 1962-66; gen. editor, 1966—. Served to lt. (j.g.) USNR, 1943-46.

Faculty fellow Fund Advancement Edn., 1951-52; grantee Coun. Rsch. Humanities, 1958-59, Am. Philos. Soc., 1962, Am. Coun. Learned Socs., 1962, NEH, 1976-88. Mem. Johnsonians (sec.-treas. 1958-68, chmn. 1969, 79), Univ. Seminar on 18th Century European Culture (chmn. 1973-75, 85-87), Oxford Bibliog. Soc., Grolier Club, English Inst. (mem. supervisory com. 1963-66), Modern Lang. Assn., Conf. Brit. Studies, Soc. Textual Scholarship (adv. bd.), Am. Soc. 18th Century Studies, Phi Beta Kappa. Home: 404 Riverside Dr New York NY 10025-1861 Office: Columbia U Dept English New York NY 10027

MIDDENDORF, WILLIAM HENRY, electrical engineering educator; b. Cin., Mar. 23, 1921; s. William J. and Mary J. (Frommeyer) M.; m. Evelyn B. Taylor, Nov. 20, 1946; children—Judith A., Mark E., Jeffrey W., Craig A., Susan A. B. Elec. Engring., U. Va., 1946; M.S., U. Cin., 1948; Ph.D., Ohio State U., 1960. Mem. faculty U. Cin., 1948-91, prof. elec. engring., 1960-91, assoc. head. dept., 1986-91; prof. emeritus, 1991—; with Wadsworth Elec. Mfg. Co., Covington, Ky., 1966-90, dir. engring. and research, 1966-86, sr. cons., 1986-90; dir. research Cin. Devel. and Mfg. Inc., 1960-66. Author: Electric Circuit Analysis, 1956, Introductory Network Analysis, 1966, Engineering Design, 1969; author: Invention, 1981, Design of Devices and Systems, 1986, 2d edit., 1990; co-author: Product Liability, 1979; editor book series: Marcel Dekker, Inc. (85 vols.), Continuing Edn. Series (30 vols.); contbr. to profl. publs.; holder 27 patents. Trustee St. Elizabeth Hosp., Covington, 1967-83, pres. bd., 1977-80. With USNR, 1943-46. Recipient Herman Schneider award Tech. Socs. of Cin., 1978, U. Cin. Public Service award, 1981, Rieveschl award for scholarly and creative works U. Cin., 1989; NSF fellow, 1958-59. Fellow IEEE (life); mem. Am. Soc. Engring. Edn. Home: 1941 Provincial Ln Covington KY 41011-1816

MIDDLEBROOK, DIANE WOOD, English language educator; b. Pocatello, Idaho, Apr. 16, 1939; d. Thomas Isaac and Helen Loretta (Downey) Wood; m. Jonathan Middlebrook, June 15, 1963 (div. 1972); 1 child, Leah Wood Middlebrook; m. Carl Djerassi, June 21, 1985. BA, U. Wash., 1961; MA, Yale U., 1962, PhD, 1968. Asst. prof. Stanford (Calif.) U., 1966-73, assoc. prof., 1973-83, prof., 1983—, D, dir. Ctr. for Rsch. on Women, 1977-79. Author: Walt Whitman and Wallace Stevens, 1974, Worlds into Words: Understanding Modern Poems, 1980, Anne Sexton, A Biography, 1991, (poems) Gin Considered as a Demon, 1983; editor: Coming to Light: American Women Poets in the Twentieth Century, 1985. Founding trustee Djerassi Resident Artists Program, Woodside, Calif., 1980-83, chair, 1994; trustee San Francisco Art Inst., 1993. Ind. study fellow NEH, 1982-83, Bunting Inst. fellow Radcliffe Coll., 1982-83, Guggenheim Found. fellow, 1988-89, Rockefeller Study Ctr. fellow, 1990; recipient Yale Prize for Poetry; finalist Nat. Book award, 1991. Mem. MLA. Avocations: collecting art, theater. Home: 1101 Green St Apt 1501 San Francisco CA 94109-2016 Office: Stanford U Dept English Stanford CA 94305-2087

MIDDLEBROOK, STEPHEN BEACH, lawyer. BA, Yale U., 1958, LLB, 1961. Bar: Conn. 1961. Counsel Aetna Life and Casualty Co., Hartford, Conn., 1969-71, asst. gen. counsel, 1971-78, corp. sec., 1973-83, v.p., gen. counsel, 1981-88, sr. v.p., gen. counsel, 1988-90, sr. v.p., exec. counsel, 1990-94; spl. counsel Day, Berry & Howard, Hartford, 1995—; vis. fellow Rand, Santa Monica, Calif., 1994, cons., 1995—. Office: Day Berry & Howard City Place I Hartford CT 06103-3499

MIDDLEBROOKS, EDDIE JOE, environmental engineer; b. Crawford County, Ga., Oct. 16, 1932; s. Robert Harold and Jewell LaVerne (Dixon) M.; m. Charlotte Linda Hardy, Dec. 6, 1958; 1 child, Linda Tracey. BCE, U. Fla., 1956, MS, 1960; PhD, Miss. State U., 1966. Registered profl. engr., Ariz., Miss., Utah; registered land surveyor, Fla. Asst. san. engr. USPHS, Cin., 1956-58; field engr. T.T. Jones Constrn. Co., Atlanta, 1958-59; grad. teaching asst. U. Fla., 1959-60; research asst. U. Ariz., 1960-61; asst. prof., then assoc. prof. Miss. State U., 1962-67; research engr., asst. dir. San. Engring. Research Lab., U. Calif.-Berkeley, 1968-70; prof. Utah State U., Logan, 1970-82, dean Coll. Engring., 1974-82; Newman chair natural resources engring. Clemson U., 1982-83; provost, v.p. acad. affairs Tenn. Tech. U., 1983-88; provost, v.p. acad. affairs U. Tulsa, 1988-90, prof. chem. engring., 1988-92, Trustees prof. chem. engring., 1990-92, acting pres., 1990; prof. civil engring. U. Nevada, Reno, 1992—; mem. nat. drinking water adv. council EPA, 1981-83; cons. EPA, UN Indsl. Devel. Orgn., Calif. Water Resources Control Bd., also numerous indsl. and engring. firms. Author: Modeling the Eutrophication Process, 1974, Statistical Calculations-How To Solve Statistical Problems, 1976, Biostimulation and Nutrient Assessment, 1976, Water Supply Engineering Design, 1977, Lagoon Information Source Book, 1978, Industrial Pollution Control, Vol. 1: Agro-Industries, 1979, Wastewater Collection and Treatment: Principles and Practices, 1979, Water Reuse, 1982, Wastewater Stabilization Lagoon Design, Performance and Upgrading, 1982, Reverse Osmosis Treatment of Drinking Water, 1986, Pollution Control in the Petrochemicals Industry, 1987, Natural Systems for Waste Management and Treatment, 1988, 2d edit., 1995; mem. editl. adv. bd. Lewis Pubs. Inc., Environment Internat., Environ. Abstracts; contbr. tech. articles to profl. jours. Fellow ASCE; mem. AAAS, Water Environment Fedn. (dir. 1979-81, 91-92), Eddy medal 1969), Assn. Environ. Engring. Profs. (pres. 1974), Utah Water Pollution Control Assn. (pres. 1976), Internat. Assn. on Water Quality, Am. Soc. Engring. Edn., Am. Acad. Environ. Engrs. (diplomate, trustee 1992-95, v.p. 1995, pres. 1997), Sigma Xi, Omicron Delta Kappa, Phi Kappa Phi (Disting. mem.), Tau Beta Pi, Sigma Tau. Home: 3855 Skyline Blvd Reno NV 89509-5661 Office: U Nevada Dept Civil Engring Reno NV 89557

MIDDLEBUSHER, MARK ALAN, computer scientist; b. Springhill, La., Aug. 22, 1966; s. Jerry Almond and Karen Rae (York) M. BS in Computer Sci., U. South Ala., 1989. Sys. analyst Internat. Paper, Vicksburg, Miss., 1989-90, sr. sys. analyst, 1990-91, process sys. analyst, 1991-94, auditor corp. environment, 1994-96; EHS coord. decorative products divsn. Internat. Paper, Hanover, Md., 1996—. Bd. dirs. Vicksburg Chamber Choir, 1992-93; deacon Presbyn. Ch., 1992-96; mem. allocations com. United Way of West Ctrl. Miss., 1993-96. Home: 9392 Ridings Way Laurel MD 20723-6331 Office: Internat Paper Decorative Products Divsn 7240 Parkway Dr Ste 310 Hanover MD 21076

MIDDLEDITCH, LEIGH BENJAMIN, JR., lawyer, educator; b. Detroit, Sept. 30, 1929; s. Leigh Benjamin and Hope Tiffin (Noble) M.; m. Betty Lou Givens, June 27, 1953; children: Leigh III, Katherine Middleditch McDonald, Andrew B. BA, U. Va., 1951, LLB, 1957. Bar: Va. 1957. Assoc. James H. Michael, Jr., Charlottesville, Va., 1957-59; ptnr. Battle, Neal, Harris, Minor & Williams, Charlottesville, 1959-68; legal adviser U. Va., Charlottesville, 1968-72; ptnr. McGuire, Woods, Battle & Boothe, Charlottesville, 1972—; lectr. Grad. Bus. Sch., U. Va., Charlottesville, 1958-94, lectr. Law Sch., 1970-90. Co-author: Virginia Civil Procedure, 1978, 2d edition, 1992; contbr. articles to profl. jours. Chmn. U. Va. Health Svcs. Found., 1988—; bd. mgrs. U. Va. Alumni, 1994—; bd. dirs. Va. Health Care Found., 1992—; trustee Claude Moore Found., 1991—; mem. Va. Health Planning Bd., 1989—; bd. visitors U. Va., 1990-91; trustee Thomas Jefferson Meml. Found., Monticello, 1994—. Fellow Am. Bar Found., Va. Bar Found., Am. Coll. Tax Counsel; mem. ABA, Va. State Bar (coun., chmn. bd. govs. various sects.), Charlottesville-Albemarle Bar Assn. (pres. 1979-80), U. Va. Law Sch. Alumni Assn. (pres. 1979-81), Va. C. of C., Omicron Delta Kappa. Episcopalian. Office: McGuire Woods Battle & Boothe PO Box 1288 Charlottesville VA 22902-1288

MIDDLEKAUFF, ROBERT LAWRENCE, history educator, administrator; b. Yakima, Wash., July 5, 1929; s. Harold and Katherine Ruth (Horne) M.; m. Beverly Jo Martin, July 11, 1952; children: Samuel John, Holly Ruth. B.A., U. Wash., 1952; Ph.D., Yale U., 1961. Instr. history Yale U., New Haven, Conn., 1959-62; asst. prof. history U. Calif.-Berkeley, 1962-66, assoc. prof., 1966-70, prof., 1970-80, Margaret Byrne prof. history, 1980-83; dir. Huntington Library, Art Gallery and Bot. Gardens, San Marino, Calif., 1983-88; prof. history U. Calif., Berkeley, 1988-92, Preston Hotchkiss prof., 1992—; Harmsworth prof. history Oxford (Eng.) U., 1996-97; mem. council Inst. Early Am. History and Culture, Williamsburg, Va., 1974-76, 85-88. Author: Ancients and Axioms, 1963, The Mathers, 1971, The Glorious Cause: The American Revolution, 1763-1789, 1982, Benjamin Franklin and His Enemies, 1996. Served to 1st lt. USMC, 1952-54, Korea. Recipient Bancroft prize, 1972; recipient Commonwealth Club Gold medal, 1983; fellow Am. Council Learned Socs., 1965, NEH, 1973, Huntington Library, 1977. Fellow Am. Acad. Arts and Scis.; mem. Am. Hist. Assn., Orgn. Am. Historians, Soc. Am. Historians, Am. Antiquarian Soc., Assocs. Early Am. History and Culture (mem. exec. com.), Colonial Soc. Mass. (corr.). Home: 5868 Ocean View Dr Oakland CA 94618-1535 Office: Univ Calif Dept History Berkeley CA 94720-2550

MIDDLETON, ANTHONY WAYNE, JR., urologist, educator; b. Salt Lake City, May 6, 1939; s. Anthony Wayne and Dolores Caravena (Lowry) M.; m. Carol Samuelson, Oct. 23, 1970; children: Anthony Wayne, Suzanne, Kathryn, Jane, Michelle. BS, U. Utah, 1963; MD, Cornell U., 1966. Intern, U. Utah Hosps., Salt Lake City, 1966-67; resident in urology Mass. Gen. Hosp., Boston, 1970-74; practice urology Middleton Urol. Assos., Salt Lake City, 1974—; mem. staff Primary Children's Hosp., staff pres., 1981-82; mem. staff Latter-Day Saints Hosp., chmn. divsn. of Urology, Salt Lake Regional Med. Ctr. 1995—; assoc. clin. prof. surgery U. Utah Med. Coll., 1977—; vice chmn. bd. govs. Utah Med. Self-Ins. Assn., 1980-81, 96—, chmn. 1985-87; med. dir. Uroquest Co., 1996—. Bd. dirs. Utah chpt. Am. Cancer Soc., 1978-86; bishop, later stake presidency Ch. Jesus Christ Latter-day Saints; vice chmn. Utah Med. Polit. Action Com., 1978-81, chmn., 1981-83; chmn. Utah Physicians for Reagan, 1983-84; mem. U. Utah Coll. Medicine Dean's Search Com., 1983-84; bd. dirs. Utah Symphony, 1985—, Primary Children's Found., 1989-96. Capt. USAF, 1968-70. Editor (monthly pub.) AACU-FAX, 1992—; assoc. editor Millenial Star Brit. LDS mag. 1960-61. Mem. ACS, Utah Med. Assn. (pres. 87-88, disting. svc. award 1993), Am. Urologic Assn. (socioecons. com. 1987-90, chmn. western sect. socioecons. com. 1989—, western. sect. health policy com. chmn., 1990—), AMA (alt. del. to House of Dels. 1989-92, 94, 96—), Salt Lake County Med. Assn. (sec. 1965-67, pres. liaison com. 1980-81, pres.-elect 1981-83, pres. 1984), Utah Urol. Assn. (pres. 1976-77), Salt Lake Surg. Soc. (treas. 1977-78), Am. Assn. Clin. Urologists (bd. dirs. 1989-90, nat. pres. elect 1990-91, pres. 1991-92, nat. bd. chmn. urologic polit. action com. UROPAC, 1992—), Phi Beta Kappa, Alpha Omega Alpha, Beta Theta Pi (chpt. pres. Gamma Beta 1962). Republican. Contbr. articles to profl. jours. Home: 2798 Chancellor Pl Salt Lake City UT 84108-2835 Office: Hellenic Airforce Com 1060 1st Ave Salt Lake City UT 84103-4147

MIDDLETON, CHARLES RONALD, history educator; b. Hays, Kans., Sept. 16, 1944; s. Charles Buster and Dorothy Bryant (Parsons) M.; m. Sandra Leigh Paulson, Dec. 19, 1964 (dec. 1986); children: Charles Christopher, Kevin Andrew, Kathryn Gillian. AB with honors, Fla. State U., 1965; MA, Duke U., 1967, PhD, 1969. Asst. prof. U. Colo., Boulder, 1969-77, assoc. prof., 1977-85, asst. dean, 1979-80, prof. history, 1985-96, assoc. dean Coll. Arts and Scis., 1980-88, dean Coll. Arts and Scis., 1988-96; prof. history, provost, v.p. acad. affairs Bowling Green (Ohio) State U., 1996—. Contbr. articles to profl. jours. Bd. dirs. Found. for World Health, Denver and Boulder, 1985-87, Boulder County AIDS Project (hon.), 1990—, The Consenting Adults Theatre Co., Washington, 1992—. Recipient Faculty Teaching Excellence award U. Colo., Boulder, 1978; research grantee Am. Philos. Soc., 1977, U. Colo., 1972. Fellow Royal Hist. Soc.; mem. N.Am. Conf. on Brit. Studies, Western Conf. on Brit. Studies (pres.-elect 1985-86, pres. 1986-87), Western Humanities Conf. (bd. dirs. 1990-95), Am. Hist. Assn. (mem. com. gay and lesbian history), Am. Com. for Irish Studies, Brit. Politics Group, So. Conf. on Brit. Studies, Rotary, Coun. of Colls. and Arts and Scis. (bd. dirs. 1993-96), Phi Beta Kappa, Phi Eta Sigma. Democrat. Avocations: fishing, cooking, travel, cycling. Office: Bowling Green State U 230 McFall Ctr Bowling Green OH 43403

MIDDLETON, CHRISTOPHER, Germanic languages and literature educator; b. Truro, Cornwall, Eng., June 10, 1926; came to U.S., 1966; s. Hubert Stanley and Dorothy May (Miller) M. BA, U. of Oxford, Eng., 1951, PhD, 1954. Lectr. King's Coll., London, 1955-65; prof. Germanic langs. and lit. U. Tex., Austin, 1966—. Author: Selected Writings, 1989, Andalusian Poems, 1993, The Balcony Tree, 1992, Intimate Chronicles, 1996. Recipient trans. prize Schlegel-Tieck/Govt. Fed. Republic Germany, 1985, Anglo-Swiss Cultural Rels. prize Max Geilinger Stiftung, Zurich, Switzerland, 1987; Guggenheim Found. poetry fellow, 1974-75, NEA poetry fellow, 1980. Mem. Akademie der Künste Berlin. Office: U Tex Dept Of Germanic Langs Austin TX 78712

MIDDLETON, DAVID, physicist, applied mathematician, educator; b. N.Y.C., Apr. 19, 1920; s. Charles Davies Scudder and Lucile (Davidson) M.; m. Nadea Butler, May 26, 1945 (div. 1971); children: Susan Terry, Leslie Butler, David Scudder Blakeslee, George Davidson Powell; m. Joan Bartlett Reed, 1971; children: Christopher Hope, Andrew Bartlett, Henry H. Reed. Grad., Deerfield Acad., 1938; AB summa cum laude, Harvard U., 1942, AM, 1945, PhD in Physics, 1947. Tchg. fellow electronics Harvard U., Cambridge, Mass., 1942, spl. rsch. assoc., Radio Rsch. Lab., 1942-45, NSF predoctoral fellow physics, 1945-47, rsch. fellow electronics, 1947-49, asst. prof. applied physics, 1949-54; cons. physicist Cambridge, 1954—, Concord, Mass., 1957-71, N.Y.C., 1971—; adj. prof. elec. engring. Columbia U., 1960-61; adj. prof. applied physics and comm. theory Rensselaer Poly. Inst., Hartford Grad. Ctr., 1961-70; adj. prof. communication theory U. R.I., 1966—; adj. prof. math. scis. Rice U., 1979-89; U.S. del. internat. conf. Internat. Radio Union, Lima, Peru, 1975; lectr. NATO Advanced Study Inst., Grenoble, France, 1964, Copenhagen, 1990, Luneburg, Germany, 1984; mem. Naval Rsch. Adv. Com., 1970-77; mem., cons. Inst. Def. Analyses; mem. sci. adv. bd. Supercomputing Rsch. Ctr., 1987-91; cons. physicist since 1946, orgns. including Johns Hopkins U., SRI Internat., Rand Corp., USAF, Cambridge Rsch. Ctr., Comm. Satellite Corp., Lincoln Lab., NASA, Raytheon, Sylvania, Sperry-Rand, Office Naval Rsch., Applied Rsch. Labs., U. Tex., GE, Honeywell Transp. Sys. Ctr. of Dept. Transp., Dept. Commerce Office of Telecom., NOAA, Office Telecom. Policy of Exec. Office Pres., Nat. Telecom. and Info. Adminstrn., Sci. Applications Inc., Naval Undersea Warfare Ctr., Lawrence Livermore Nat. Labs., Planning Rsch. Corp., Applied Physics Labs. U. Wash., 1992—, Kildare Corp., 1995—, others. Author: Introduction to Statistical Communication Theory, 1960, 3d edit., 1996, Russian edit. Soviet Radio Moscow, 2 vols., 1961, 62, Topics in Communication Theory, 1965, 87, Russian edit., 1966; sci. editor English edit. Statistical Methods in Sonar (V.V. Ol'shevskii), 1978; mem. editl. bd. Info. and Control, Advanced Serials in Electronics and Cybernetics, 1972-82; contbr. articles to tech. jours. Recipient award (with W.H. Huggins) Nat. Electronics Conf., 1956; Wisdom award of honor, 1970; First prize 3d Internat. Symposium on Electromagnetic Compatibility Rotterdam, Holland, 1979; awards U.S. Dept. Commerce, 1978. Fellow AAAS., IEEE (life, awards 1977, 79), Am. Phys. Soc., Explorers Club, Acoustical Soc. Am., N.Y. Acad. Scis.; mem. Am. Math. Soc., Author's Guild Am., Electromagnetics Acad. MIT, Harvard Club (N.Y.C.), Cosmos Club (Washington), Dutch Treat (N.Y.C.), Phi Beta Kappa, Sigma Xi. Achievements include research in radar, telecommunications, underwater acoustics, oceanography, seismology, systems analysis, electromagnetic compatibility, communication theory; pioneering research in statistical communication theory. Home and Office: 127 E 91st St New York NY 10128-1601 also: MIND 48 Garden St Cambridge MA 02138-1561 also: 13 Harbor Rd Harwich Port MA 02646-2409

MIDDLETON, DAWN E., education educator; b. Pottstown, Pa.; d. William H. and Sara G. Bowman; m. Stephen R. Mourar, June 1983; children: William Middleton, Shelly Mourar. AA in Early Childhood Edn., Montgomery Community Coll., 1972; BS in Elem. Edn., West Chester State Coll., 1974; MA in Edn. Curriculum and Instrn. Edn., Pa. State U., 1982, DEd, 1984. Instr. Continuing Edn. Pa. State U., University Park; dir. specialized early childhood programs and svcs. Wiley House, Bethlehem, Pa.; dir. Children's Sch. of Cabrini Coll., Radnor, Pa.; dept. chmn., assoc. prof. edn. Cabrini Coll., Radnor. Home: 208 Bethel Rd Spring City PA 19475-3200

MIDDLETON, ELLIOTT, JR., physician; b. Glen Ridge, N.J., Dec. 15, 1925; s. Elliott and Dorothy (Thoman) M.; m. Elizabeth Blackford, Sept. 25, 1948; children: Elliott III, Ellen Alice, Blackford, James Jay. A.B., Princeton U., 1947; M.D., Columbia U., 1950. Diplomate: Am. Bd. Internal Medicine, Am. Bd. Allergy and Immunology. Intern Presbyn. Hosp., N.Y.C., 1950-51; resident in medicine Presbyn. Hosp., 1951-52; asst. in medicine immunochem. lab. Coll. Physicians and Surgeons, Columbia U., 1952-53; clin. assoc. Nat. Heart Inst., 1953-55; fellow in allergy R.A. Cooke Inst. Allergy, Roosevelt Hosp., N.Y.C., 1955-56; practice medicine Montclair, N.J., 1956-69; dir. clin. services and research Children's Asthma Research Inst. and Hosp., Denver, 1969-76; assoc. clin. prof. medicine U. Colo., 1969-76; prof. medicine and pediatrics, dir. allergy div. Sch. Medicine, SUNY, Buffalo, 1976-92; emeritus prof. medicine SUNY, Buffalo, 1995; hon. staff physician Buffalo Gen. Hosp.; prof. medicine emeritus, 1995. Editor-in-chief Allergy: Principles and Practice, 1978, 4th edit., 1993; editor Jour. Allergy and Clin. Immunology, 1983-88; contbr. numerous articles to jours. chpts. to books. Served with M.C. USNR, 1944-50; Served with M.C. USPHS, 1950-55. Fellow Am. Acad. Allergy and Immunology (pres. 1972, Disting. Svc. award 1991), Am. Coll. Physicians; mem. AAAS, Am. Assn. Immunologists. Episcopalian. Home and Office: RR 1 Box 596 Chebeague Island ME 04017-9758

MIDDLETON, GEORGE, JR., clinical child psychologist; b. Houston, Feb. 26, 1923; s. George and Bettie (McCrary) M.; m. Margaret MacLean, Nov. 17, 1953. BA in Psychology, Birmingham-Southern Coll., 1948; MA in Psychology, U. Ala., Tuscaloosa, 1951; PhD in Clin. Psychology, Pa. State U., 1958. Lic. psychologist, La.; diplomate Am. Bd. Examiners, Am. Bd. Forensic Examiners. Asst. clin. psychology Med. Coll. Ala., Birmingham, 1950-52; dir. dept. psychology Bryce Hosp., Tuscaloosa, 1952-54; instr. counseling Coll. Bus. Adminstrn. Pa. State U., 1956-58; asst. prof. spl. edn. McNeese State U., 1962-65, assoc. prof. spl. edn., 1962-65; dir. La. Gov.'s Program for Gifted Children, 1963—; prof. spl. edn. McNeese State U., 1965-73, prof. psychology, 1973-74; pvt. practice clin. psychology and neuropsychology, 1974—; cons. psychologist Calcasieu Parish Sch. Bd., 1975—; cons. Charter Hosp. Adolescent Psychiat. Unit, dir. psychol. svcs., 1990-95. Mem. Am. Psychol. Assn., Nat. Acad. Neuropsychology, Internat. Neuropsychol. Soc., La. Psychol. Assn. (pres. 1973-74), La. Sch. Psychol. Assn., S.W. La. Psychol. Assn. (pres. 1965, 73, 84), La. State Bd. Examiners Psychologists (chmn. 1977-78), Coun. for Exceptional Children, Am. Coll. Forensic Examiners, 1996. Assn. for the Gifted. Episcopalian. Home and Office: 2001 Southwood Dr Ste A Lake Charles LA 70605-4139

MIDDLETON, HARRY JOSEPH, library administrator; b. Centerville, Iowa, Oct. 24, 1921; s. Harry J. and Florence (Beauvais) M.; m. Miriam Miller, Oct. 29, 1949; children—Susan, Deborah, James Miller, Jennifer. Student, Washburn U., 1941-43; B.A., La. State U., 1947. Reporter AP, N.Y.C., 1947-49; news editor Archtl. Forum mag., N.Y.C., 1949-52; writer March of Time, N.Y.C., 1952-54; free lance writer, author, film dir., 1954-66; staff asst. to Pres. Lyndon B. Johnson, Washington, 1966-69; spl. asst. Pres. Lyndon B. Johnson, Austin, Tex., 1969-70; dir. Lyndon Baines Johnson Libr., U. Tex., Austin, 1970—. Author: Compact History of the Korean War, 1965, LBJ: The White House Years, 1990, Lady Bird Johnson: A Life Well-Lived, 1992. Mem. Am. Battle Monuments Commn., 1968—. Served with AUS, 1943-46, 50-52. Mem. Sigma Delta Chi. Home: 2201 Exposition Blvd Austin TX 78703-2209 Office: Lyndon Baines Johnson Libr & Mus 2313 Red River St Austin TX 78705-5702

MIDDLETON, HERBERT HUNTER, JR., tobacco manufacturing company executive; b. Phila., Oct. 19, 1926; s. Herbert Hunter and Anna Klauder (Elston) M.; m. Frances Anne Staubus, Aug. 28, 1949; children—Lucia Middleton Hughes, John S., Anna Middleton Bauer. B.A., Amherst Coll., 1950. Pres. John Middleton, Inc., King of Prussia, Pa., 1965—; chmn. council Dayoh, Inc., Phila., 1982—. Chmn. bd. The Shipley Sch., Bryn Mawr, Pa., 1980—; campaign chmn. Rep. Richard A. McClatchy, Jr., 1978—. Served with U.S. Army, 1944-46. Mem. Assoc. Tobacco Mfrs. Inc. (pres. 1966—), Tobacco Inst. (bd. dirs.). Republican. Presbyterian. Clubs: Phila. Country (Gladwyne, Pa.); Merion Cricket (Haverford, Pa.); Union League (Phila.). Avocations: tennis; swimming. Home: 416 Morris Ave Bryn Mawr PA 19010-2922 Office: John Middleton Inc Church & Hillside Rds King Of Prussia PA 19406

MIDDLETON, HERMAN DAVID, SR., theater educator; b. Sanford, Fla., Mar. 24, 1925; s. Arthur Herman and Ruby Elmerry (Hart) M.; m. Amelia Mary Eggart, Dec. 1, 1945; children—Herman David, Kathleen Hart. B.S., Columbia U., 1948, M.A., 1949; Ph.D., U. Fla., 1964; postgrad., N.Y. U., 1950, Northwestern U., 1951. Instr., dir. drama and speech Maryville (Tenn.) Coll., 1949-50; instr., designer, tech. dir. theatre U. Del., 1951-55; asst. prof., head dept. drama U. N.C., Greensboro, 1956-59; assoc. prof., head dept. drama and speech U. N.C., 1959-65, prof., head dept., 1965-74, prof., 1974-79, Excellence Fund prof. dept. communication and theatre, 1979-90, prof. emeritus, 1990; designer Chucky Jack, Great Smokey Mountains Hist. Soc., Gatlinburg, Tenn., 1956, designer, dir., 1957; communications cons. N.C. Nat. Bank, 1968, Jefferson Standard Life Ins. Co., Greensboro, N.C., 1969, Gilbarco, Inc., Greensboro, 1969-70, 73. Drama critic, columnist: Sunday Star, Wilmington, Del., 1952; theatre editor: Players Mag, 1959-61; theatre columnist: Sunday editions Greensboro Daily News, 1959-62; contbr. articles to profl. jours. Mem. N.C. Arts Council Commn., 1964-66, Guilford County Bi-Centennial Celebration Commn., 1969-70; pres. Shanks Village Players, Orangeburg, N.Y.C., 1947-48, Univ. Drama Group, Newark, Del., 1954-55; bd. dirs. Broadway Theatre League Greensboro, 1958-60, Greensboro Community Arts Council, 1964-67, 69-72, Greensboro Community Theatre, 1983-86, Carolina Theatre Commn., 1990—; organizer-cons. The Market Players, West Market St. United Meth. Ch., 1979-82. Served with USN, 1943-46. Recipient O. Henry award Greensboro C. of C., 1966, Gold medallion Amoco Oil Co., 1973, Suzanne M. Davis award Southeastern Theatre Conf., 1975, Marian A. Smith Disting. Career award N.C. Theatre Conf., 1990. Mem. Am. Nat. Theatre and Acad. (organizer, exec. v.p. Piedmont chpt. 1957-60), Am. Theatre Assn. (chmn. bd. nominations 1971-72), Am. Coll. Theatre Festival (regional festival dir. 1973, 80, regional dir., mem. nat. com. 1978-80), Assn. for Theatre in Higher Edn. (founding mem. 1986-87), Speech Communication Assn. Am., Nat. Collegiate Players, Southeastern Theatre Conf. (bd. dirs. 1963-68, 87-92, pres. 1965, pres. pro-tem 1966), Carolina Dramatic Assn. (bd. dirs. 1958-59), N.C. Drama and Speech Assn. (pres. 1966-67), N.C. Theatre Conf. (co-organizer 1971, bd. dirs. 1984-92, pres. 1987-88), Assn. for Theater in Higher Edn., Phi Delta Kappa, Phi Kappa Phi, Theta Alpha Phi, Alpha Psi Omega. Democrat. Methodist. Home: 203A Village Ln Greensboro NC 27409-2502

MIDDLETON, JACK BAER, lawyer; b. Phila., Jan. 13, 1929; s. Harry C. and Mildred Cornell (Baer) M.; m. Ann Dodge, Aug. 22, 1953; children: Susan D., Jack B. Jr., Peter C. AB, Lafayette Coll., 1950; JD cum laude, Boston U., 1956. Bar: N.H. 1956, U.S. Dist. Ct. Vt. 1988, U.S. Ct. Appeals (1st cir.) 1957, U.S. Supreme Ct. 1972. Assoc. McLane, Graf, Raulerson & Middleton, Manchester, N.H., 1956-62; ptnr., dir. McLane, Graf, Raulerson & Middleton, Manchester, 1962—; spl. justice Merrimack (N.H.) Dist. Ct., 1964-87; bd. dirs. Greater Manchester Devel. Corp., 1983-95; commr. Uniform State Laws, 1971-74; trustee New Eng. Law Inst., 1977-80. Author: (with others) Summary of New Hampshire Law, 1964, Compendium of New Hampshire Law, 1969, Trial of a Wrongful Death Action in New Hampshire, 1977; editor Boston U. Law Rev., 1954-56; contbr. articles to legal jours. Mem. Mt. Washington Commn., 1969—, Bedford (N.H.) Sch. Bd., 1960-66; mem. adv. bd. Merrimack Valley Coll.; trustee, sec. Mt. Washington Obs., 1957—; chmn. bd. trustees White Mountain Sch., 1976-79; campaign chmn. United Way Greater Manchester, 1987, bd. dirs., 1986-92, chmn., 1990-91; bd. dirs. N.H. Pub. Radio, 1988-91; bd. govs. N.H. Pub. TV, 1994—. Sgt. USMCR, 1950-52. Fellow Am. Coll. Trial Lawyers (chmn. N.H. sect. 1988-90), Am. Bar Found. (life); mem. ABA (ho. dels. 1984—, bd. govs. 1996—), New Eng. Bar Assn. (bd. dirs. 1977-88, pres. 1982-83), N.H. Bar Assn. (pres. 1979-80), N.H. Bar Found. (bd. dirs. 1979-92, chair 1983-90), Nat. Conf. Bar Found. (trustee 1985-92, pres. 1989-90), Nat. Conf. Bar Pres. (exec. coun. 1987-95, pres. 1993-94), N.H. Bus. and Industry Assn. (bd. dirs. 1988—, sec. 1990—), Manchester C. of C. (bd. dirs. 1967-89, chmn. 1984-85), New Eng. Coun. (bd. dirs. 1991—). Office: McLane Graf Raulerson & Middleton 900 Elm St Manchester NH 03101-2007

MIDDLETON, JAMES ARTHUR, oil and gas company executive; b. Tulsa, Mar. 15, 1936; s. James Arthur and Inez (Matthews) M.; m. Victoria Middleton; children: Robert Arthur, James Daniel, Angela Lynn; stepson: Andrew Davis Fitzhugh. B.A., Rice U., 1958, B.S. in Mech. Engring., 1959. With Atlantic Richfield Co., 1959-96; design engr. Dallas, 1962-67; tech. planner, 1967-69; mgr. shale devel. Grand Junction, Colo., 1969-72; mgr. engring. dept. Los Angeles, 1972-74; mgr. Prudhoe Bay project Pasadena, Calif., 1974-80; v.p., mgr. corp. planning Los Angeles, 1980-81; pres. ARCO Coal Co., Denver, 1981-82; sr. v.p. ARCO Oil and Gas Co., Dallas, 1982-85, pres., 1985-90, sr. v.p. parent co., 1981-87, exec. v.p. parent co., 1987-94, also bd. dirs.; chmn., CEO Crown Energy Corp., Salt Lake City, 1996—; bd. dirs. Tex. Utilities Co., Dallas., ARCO Chem. Co. Corp. rep. Circle Ten coun. Boy Scouts Am.; bd. dirs. L.A. coun. Boy Scouts Am., United Way Met. Dallas, Dallas Coun. on World Affairs, Jr. Achievement So. Calif. 2d lt. C.E., AUS, 1959-60. Reicpient ASME Petroleum div. Oil Drop award. Mem. Soc. Petroleum Engrs. of AIME, Tex. Mid-Continent Oil and Gas Assn., Am. Petroleum Inst., Rocky Mountain Oil and Gas Assn., We. States Petroleum Assn. (chmn. bd. dirs.), Nat. Gas Suppliers Assn. (chmn.), L.A. C. of C. (bd. dirs.), L.A. Music Ctr. Founders, Ctr. for Strategic and Internat. Studies (CSIS)-Dallas Round Table, Am. Enterprise Forum Chief Execs. Round Table, Dallas Petroelum Club, Tower, Northwood, Calif. Club, Bel-Air Country Club, L.A. Country Club. Office: 574 Chapala Dr Pacific Palisades CA 90272-4429 also: Crown Energy 215 S State Ste 550 Salt Lake City UT 84111

MIDDLETON, JAMES BOLAND, lawyer; b. Columbus, Ga., Aug. 19, 1934; s. Riley Kimbrough and Annie Ruth (Boland) M.; 1 child, Cynthia. BA in Psychology, Ga. State U., 1964; JD, Woodrow Wilson Coll. Law, 1972. Draftsman, paralegal and office mgr. to patent atty., Atlanta, 1955-68, for Jones & Thomas, Atlanta, 1968-72; Bar: Ga. 1972, U.S. Patent Office; assoc. Jones and Thomas, Atlanta, 1972-76; pvt. practice intellectual property, Decatur, Ga., 1976—. Mem. editorial bd. Atlanta Lawyer, 1973-82, assoc. editor, 1978-81, editor-in-chief, 1981-82. Bd. dirs. arts coun. Unitarian-Universalist Congregation Atlanta, 1989-91; Bd. dirs. Unitarian Universalist Endowment Fund, 1993-96, vice chair, 1994-95, sec., 1995-96; bd. dirs., sec. Decatur Arts Alliance, 1990-94. With U.S. Army, 1957-59. Mem. ABA, Am. Intellectual Property Law Assn., Atlanta Bar Assn., DeKalb Bar Assn., State Bar of Ga. (editorial bd. jour. 1985-92, mem. patent trademark and copyright sect. 1972—, chmn. 1982-83, pub. rels. com. 1982-88), Fed. Cir. Bar Assn., Am. Arbitration Assn. (comml. panel 1983-94). Office: 315 W Ponce de Leon Ste 550 PO Box 1968 Decatur GA 30031-1968

MIDDLETON, JOHN ALBERT, retired communications executive; b. Bradford, Yorkshire, Eng., Mar. 20, 1915; came to U.S., 1922; s. Albert Henry and Priscilla (Lambert) Ml; m. Marjorie Frances Crossett, May 29, 1942; children: John Gary, Pamela Mary, Gregory Chester, Susan Jeanne. Diploma, Manchester Ctrl. H.S., 1934. Repair supr. New Eng. Telephone, Claremont, N.H., 1946-77. City councilor, Claremont, 1986-94, asst. mayor, 1987-88, 90, 93-94, mayor, 1991; state rep., Concord, N.H., 1989-92; Justice of the Peace, N.H., 1990—; vice-chair fin. Sullivan County Delegation, N.H., 1989-92; mem. Sullivan County Econ. Devel. Coun., 1986-95; mem. Claremont Indsl. Devel. Authority, 1994; chmn. health com., Claremont, 1993-94; mem. strategic planning com. Claremont Sch. Dist., 1994-95; sr. warden Union Ch., Claremont. With U.S. Army, 1942-46, PTO. Master Hiram Lodge (sec. 1986-89), Masons (Major Gen. John Sullivan medal, Disting. Svc. award 1986); mem. VFW (life), Am. Legion (life), Am. Vets. (life), Shrine Legion of Honor (life), Hist. Soc., Telephone Pioneers Am. (pres. 1985-86, 95), Anniversary Lodge (charter), William Pitt Tavern Lodge (charter), Sullivan Hugh-De Payens (treas. 1979-89). Republican. Episcopalian. Avocation: woodworking. Home: 4 S Park St Claremont NH 03743-2842

MIDDLETON, LESLIE LYLES, journalist; b. Charleston, S.C., Dec. 22, 1964; d. Julian Leslie and Mary Margaret (Willis) Lyles; m. Henry Woodward Middleton, Jr., Dec. 10, 1995; 1 child, Henry Woodward III. Student, Brenau Women's Coll., 1982-83; AB in Journalism, U. Ga., 1987. Anchor/reporter WCBD-TV, Charleston, S.C., 1987-94, KDNL-TV, St. Louis, 1994—. Telethon host United Way, St. Louis, 1995; telethon host, bd. dirs. Carolina Children's Charity, Charleston, 1989-94; celebrity host Charity Dance, St. Louis, 1995; co-host Women's Event for Breast Cancer Rsch., 1995, others. Named Humanitarian of the Yr., United Forresters, 1993, Young St. Louisun of Yr., Jr. C. of C., 1996; recipient Cert. of Commendation USMC, 1996, Best News Anchor award East Cooper Mag., 1991, 92, 93, Alfred I. DuPont/Columbia U. award for excellence in broadcast journalism, 1989-90, AP awards, 1991, 92, Emmy awards, 1990, 94, Green Eyeshade award Atlanta Soc. Profl. Journalists, 1992, 93, RTNDA-Edward R. Murrow award for best newscast in nation, 1994, others. Office: KDNL 1215 Cole St Saint Louis MO 63106-3818

MIDDLETON, LINDA JEAN GREATHOUSE, lawyer; b. Poplar Bluff, Mo., Sept. 22, 1950; d. Casper Scott and Anna Garnelle (Qualls) Greathouse; m. Roy L. Middleton, Sept. 27, 1969. BS cum laude, Ark. State U., 1972; JD, Baylor U., 1974. Bar: Tex., 1974; CPCU, CLU. Asst. v.p., asst. sec., atty. Equitable Gen. Ins. Co., Ft. Worth, 1977-81; gen. counsel, corp. sec. Chilton Corp., Dallas, 1981-83; mgr. pub. affairs Fina Oil and Chem., Dallas, 1983-85, corp. sec., sr. atty., 1983—; sec. Parliamentarian, Dallas, 1985—. Sec. Homeowners Assn., Dallas, 1981—. Mem. Tex. Bar Assn., Dallas Bar Assn. Baptist. Avocations: oil painting, sewing, piano. Office: Fina Inc 8350 N Ctrl Expwy PO Box 2159 Dallas TX 75221

MIDDLETON, NORMAN GRAHAM, social worker, psychotherapist; b. Jacksonville, Fla., Jan. 21, 1935; s. Norman Graham and Betty (Quina) M.; m. Judy Stephens, Aug. 1, 1968; stepchildren: Monty Stokes, Toni Stokes. BA, U. Miami (Fla.), 1960; MSW, Fla. State U., 1962. Casework counselor Family Svc., Miami, 1962-64; psychiat. social worker assoc. firm Drs. Warson, Steele, Wiener, Sarasota, Fla., 1964-66; psychotherapist, Sarasota, 1966—. Instr. Manatee Jr. Coll., Bradenton, Fla., 1973-76. Author: The Caverns of My Mind, 1985, Imaginative Healing, 1993. Pres. Coun. on Epilepsy, Sarasota, 1969-70. Served with USAF, 1954-58. Fellow Fla. Soc. Clin. Social Work (pres. 1978-80); mem. Am. Group Psychotherapy Assn., Am. Assn. Sex Educators and Counselors (cert. sex educator). Democrat. Episcopalian. Home: 16626 Winburn Dr Sarasota FL 34240-9221 Office: 1257 S Tamiami Trl Sarasota FL 34239-2219

MIDDLETON, TIMOTHY GEORGE, writer; b. Alton, Ill.; s. Elbert George and Freda Margaret Middleton; m. Joyce Elaine Rhea; children: Brendan Mansfield, Michael Travis, Margaret Hart. BA, So. Ill. U. Reporter, copy editor Wall St. Jour., 1981-84; dep. mng. editor Crain's N.Y. Bus., 1984-92. Author: Corporate and Foundation Fundraising, 1982, Grass Roots Fundraising, 1982; writer for Reader's Digest, N.Y. Times, Bus. Week, Money Mag., Computer Life, Field and Stream; editl. cons.; radio personality WCBS-AM N.Y. Fellow U. Mo., 1977. Mem. Outdoor Writers Assn. Am., Am. Soc. Journalists and Authors, KC. Roman Catholic. Avocations: fishing, hunting. Home: 34 Pine Ter E Short Hills NJ 07078-2548

MIDDLETON-DOWNING, LAURA, psychiatric social worker, artist, small business owner; b. Edinburg, Ind., Apr. 20, 1935; d. John Thomas Jr. and Rowene Elizabeth (Baker) Middleton; m. George Charles Downing, 1974 (div. 1986). BA in English Lit., U. Colo., 1966, MFA, 1969, BA in Psychology, 1988; MSW, U. Denver, 1992; Doctor of Clin. Hypnotherapy, Am. Inst. Hypnotherapy, 1995. Cert. clin. hypnotherapist, Calif.; cert. past-life therapist, Colo. Profl. artist Silver Plume and Boulder, Colo., 1965—; profl. photographer Silver Plume, 1975-87; art tchr. U. Colo., Boulder and Longmont, 1971-73; mem. survey crew Bur. of Land Mgmt., Empire, Colo., 1984-85; cons. social work and psychotherapy Boulder, 1992—; med. social worker Good Samaritan Health Agy., Boulder, 1993—; pvt. practice clin. hypnotherapy Boulder, 1995—, pvt. practice past-life therapist, 1995—; ind. distbr. Super Blue Green, 1996—. Author, photographer Frontiers, Vol. IV, No. 1, 1979; works exhibited in 10 one-woman shows, 1969-88; numerous group exhbns. Trustee Town of Silver Plume, Colo., 1975-84; co-founder, pres. Alma Holm Rogers Nat. Orgn. Women, Clear Creek County, 1975-82; mem. Ctrl. Mountain Coun., Clear Creek County, 1980; bd. dirs. Clear Creek Day Sch., Idaho Springs, Colo., 1981-82; chairperson Mary Ellen Barnes Cmty. Ctr. Project, Silver Plume, Colo., 1983; vol. Rape Crisis Team, Boulder, 1989-90, Child & Family Advocacy Program, Boulder, 1992-97; adv. bd. mem. Good Samaritan Agy., Boulder, 1993-97; caring minister vol. First Congl. Ch., Boulder, 1995-97. Recipient Juried Exhbn. Merit award Colo. Women in the Arts, 1979; Women's Incentive scholar U. Colo., Boulder, 1989; Grad. Sch. Social Work scholar U. Denver, 1991; Colo. Grad. grantee U. Denver, 1992. Mem. NASW, DAR, Colo. Advs. for Responsible Mental Health Svcs., Eye Movement Desensitization Reprocessing Network, Assn. for Past-Life Rsch. and Therapies, Inc. (Colo. group leader), Habitat for Humanity, Natural Resources Def. Coun., The Nature Conservancy, Bus. Women's Leadership Group, Psi Chi. Avocations: inline skating, scuba diving, photography, travel, volunteerism. Office: PO Box 2312 Boulder CO 80306-2312

MIDELFORT, HANS CHRISTIAN ERIK, history educator; b. Eau Claire, Wis., Apr. 17, 1942; s. Peter Albert and Gerd (Gjems) M.; m. Corelyn Forsyth Senn, June 16, 1965 (div. Dec. 1981); children: Katarina, Kristian; m. Cassandra Clemons Hughes, May 25, 1985 (div. April 1996); 1 child, Lucy; m. Anne L. McKeithen, June 22, 1996. BA, Yale U., 1964, MPhil, 1967, PhD, 1970. Instr. Stanford (Calif.) U., 1968-70; asst. prof. U. Va., Charlottesville, 1970-72, assoc. prof., 1972-87, prof., 1987—, Charles Julian Bishko prof. history, 1996—; vis. prof. Harvard U., Cambridge, Mass., 1985, Univ. Stuttgart, Germany, 1988, Univ. Bern, Switzerland, 1988; prin. Brown Coll., U. Va., 1996—. Author: Witch Hunting in Southwestern Germany, 1972 (Gustave Arlt prize 1972), Mad Princes of Renaissance Germany, 1991 (Roland H. Bainton prize 16th Century Studies Conf. 1995); translator: Revolution of 1525 (Peter Bickle), 1981, Imperial Cities and the Reformation (Bernd Moeller), 1972. Mem. Soc. Reformation Rsch. (pres. 1992-93). Office: U Va Dept History Charlottesville VA 22903

MIDGLEY, A(LVIN) REES, JR., reproductive endocrinology educator, researcher; b. Burlington, Vt., Nov. 9, 1933; s. Alvin Rees and Maxine (Schmidt) M.; m. Carol Crossman, Sept. 4, 1955; children: Thomas, Debra, Christopher. B.S. cum laude, U. Vt., 1955, M.D. cum laude, 1958. Intern U. Pitts., 1958-59, resident dept. pathology, 1959-61; resident dept. pathology U. Mich., Ann Arbor, 1961-63, instr. pathology, 1963-64, asst. prof., 1964-67, assoc. prof., 1967-70, prof., 1970—, dir. Reproductive Scis. Program; chmn. BioQuant of Ann Arbor, Inc., 1985-89. Contbr. articles to med. jours. Recipient Parke-Davis award, 1970; Ayerst award Endocrine Soc., 1977; Smith Kline Bio-Sci. Labs. award, 1985; NIH grantee, 1960—; Mellon Found. grantee, 1979-91. Mem. Soc. Study Reprodn. (pres. 1983-84), Endocrine Soc., Am. Assn. Pathology, Am. Physiol. Soc. Home: 101 W Liberty Apt 340 Ann Arbor MI 48104-1313 Office: U Mich Reproductive Scis Program 300 N Ingalls St Fl 11 Ann Arbor MI 48109-2007

MIDKIFF, DONALD WAYNE, program manager; b. Post, Tex., Sept. 26, 1940; s. Colvert Crockett Midkiff and Judy M. (Poss) Hinckley; m. Olga Maria Androvitch, June 21, 1961 (div. 1968); m. Manbeth Jean Crowell, Apr. 29, 1979. BS in Tech. Mgmt., Denver Tech. Coll., 1988; MS in Mgmt., Colo. Tech. U., 1994. With USAF, 1960, advanced through grades to sgt., 1968; electronics supr. Lockheed Aircraft, Jidda, Saudi Arabia, 1969-71; site mgr. Kentron Hawaii, Ltd., Pleiku, South Vietnam, 1971-73; supr. Kentron, Kwajalein, Marshall Islands, 1973-80, range ops. engr., 1980-84; ops. supr. Kentron PRC, Maui, Hawaii, 1984-87; ops. mgr. Kentron PRC, Colorado Springs, Colo., 1985-87; divsn. security mgr. PRC, Colorado Springs, Colo., 1987-89; program mgr. PRC Inc., Colorado Springs, Colo., 1989—; advisor Denver Tech. Coll., Colorado Springs, 1991—. CPR instr. Am. Red Cross, 1980-86; pres. Kwajalein Dive Club, 1981-83, Kwajalein Tennis Club, 1978-80. Recipient Group Achievement award NASA, 1992. Mem. AFCEA, Mensa, Nat. Contract Mgmt. Assn., Profl. Assn. Diving Instrs. (dive master). Republican. Avocations: golf, tennis, trap shooting, scuba diving, reading. Office: PRC Inc 985 Space Center Dr Ste 260 Colorado Springs CO 80915-3642

MIDKIFF, ROBERT RICHARDS, financial and trust company executive, consultant; b. Honolulu, Sept. 24, 1920; s. Frank Elbert and Ruth (Richards) M.; m. Evanita Sumner, July 24, 1948; children: Mary Lloyd, Robin Starr, Shelley Sumner, Robert Richards Jr., David Wilson. BA, Yale U., 1942; grad. Advanced Mgmt. Program, Harvard U., 1962. Asst. sec. Hawaiian Trust Co., 1951-56, asst. v.p., 1956-57, v.p., 1957-65; dir. Am. Factors, Ltd., 1954-65; v.p. Amfac, Inc., 1965-68; exec. v.p., dir. Am. Security Bank, Honolulu, 1968-69, pres., dir., 1969-71; pres., CEO, dir. Am. Trust Co. Hawaii, Honolulu, 1971-93; chmn. bd. dirs. Bishop Trust Co. Ltd., Honolulu, 1984-93; pres., CEO Am. Fin. Svcs. of Hawaii, 1984-93; bd. dirs. Persis Corp., Honolulu. Co-chmn. Gov.'s Archtl. Adv. Com. on State Capitol, 1960-65; co-chmn. Gov.'s Adv. Com. on Fine Arts for State Capitol, 1965-69; past chmn., bd. dirs. Hawaii Visitors Bur.; past pres., bd. dirs. Downtown Improvement Assn., Lahaina Restoration Found., Hawaii Cmty. Found.; bd. dirs., pres. Atherton Family Found.; past chmn. Profit Sharing Rsch. Found.; bd. dirs. Coun. on Founds.; chmn. bd. dirs. Hawaii Theatre Ctr.; chmn. bd. dirs. Good Beginnings Alliance. Mem. Coun. on Founds., Profit Sharing Coun. Am. (bd. dirs.), Small Bus. Coun. Am. (bd. dirs.), Pacific Club, Waialae Golf Club, Oahu Country Club, Phi Beta Kappa. Democrat. Episcopalian. Office: 4477 Kahala Ave Honolulu HI 96816-4924

MIDLARSKY, MANUS ISSACHAR, political scientist, educator; b. N.Y.C., Jan. 28, 1937; s. Max and Rachel (Potechin) M.; m. Elizabeth Steckel, June 25, 1961; children—Susan, Miriam, Michael. B.S., CUNY, 1959; M.S., Stevens Inst. Tech., 1963; Ph.D. (Ford Found. fellow), Northwestern U., 1969. Instr. polit. sci. U. Colo., Boulder, 1967-68, asst. prof., 1968-71, assoc. prof., 1971-74, prof., 1974-89, dir. Ctr. Internat. Relations, 1983-89; Moses and Annuta Back prof. internat. peace and conflict resolution Rutgers U., New Brunswick, N.J., 1989—; cons. USAF, 1968. Author: On War: Political Violence in the Internationsal System, 1975, The Disintegration of Political Systems: War and Revolution in Comparative Perspective, 1986, The Onset of World War, 1988; editor: Inequality and Contemporary Revolutions, 1986, Handbook of War Studies, 1989, 93, The Internationalization of Communal Strife, 1992, (with J. Vasquez and P. Gladkov) From Rivalry to Cooperation: Russian and American Perspectives on the Post-Cold War Era, 1994, Inequality, Democracy and Economic Development, 1997. Faculty fellow Richardson Inst. Conflict and Peace Research, London, 1977-78; faculty fellow Council Research and Creative Work, U. Colo., 1977-78; NSF grantee, 1973-76, 81-83, 83-85, 86-89; Nat. Endowment Humanities grantee, 1980, 83, U.S. Inst. of Peace grantee, 1997—. Mem. Am. Polit. Sci. Assn. (pres. conflict processes sect. 1985-88) Internat. Studies Assn. (pres. West 1980-81, v.p. 1986-87), Am. Soc. Polit. and Legal Philosophy, Inter-Univ. Seminar in Armed Forces and Soc. Office: Rutgers U Dept Polit Sci Hickman Hall New Brunswick NJ 08903

MIDLER, BETTE, singer, entertainer, actress; b. Honolulu, Dec. 1, 1945; m. Martin von Haselberg, 1984; 1 child, Sophie. Student, U. Hawaii, 1 year. Debut as actress film Hawaii, 1965; mem. cast Fiddler on the Roof, N.Y.C., 1966-69, Salvation, N.Y.C., 1970, Tommy, Seattle Opera Co., 1971; nightclub concert performer on tour, U.S., from 1972; appearance Palace Theatre, N.Y.C., 1973, Radio City Music Hall, 1993; TV appearances include The Tonight Show, Bette Midler: Old Red Hair is Back, 1978, Gypsy, 1993 (Golden Globe award best actress in a mini-series or movie made for television 1994, Emmy nomination, Lead Actress - Special, 1994), Seinfeld, 1995; appeared Clams on The Half-Shell Revue, N.Y.C., 1975; recs. include The Divine Miss M, 1972, Bette Midler, 1973, Broken Blossom, 1977, Live at Last, 1977, The Rose, 1979, Thighs and Whispers, 1979, Songs for the New Depression, 1979, Divine Madness, 1980, No Frills, 1984, Mud Will Be Flung Tonight, 1985, Beaches (soundtrack), 1989, Some People's Lives, 1990; motion picture appearances include Hawaii, 1966, The Rose, 1979 (Academy award nomination best actress 1979), Divine Madness, 1980, Jinxed, 1982, Down and Out in Beverly Hills, 1986, Ruthless People, 1986, Outrageous Fortune, 1987, Oliver and Company (voice), 1988, Big Business, 1988, Beaches, 1988, Stella, 1990, Scenes From a Mall, 1991, For the Boys, 1991 (Academy award nomination best actress 1991), Hocus Pocus, 1993, Get Shorty, 1995, The First Wives Club, 1996, That Old Feeling, 1997; appeared in cable TV (HBO) prodn. Bette Midler's Mondo Beyondo, 1988; author: A View From A Broad, 1980, The Saga of Baby Divine, 1983. Recipient After Dark Ruby award, 1973; Grammy awards, 1973, 1990; spl. Tony award, 1973; Emmy award for NBC Spl., Ol' Red Hair is Back, 1978; 2 Golden Globe awards for The Rose, 1979, Golden Globe award for The Boys, 1991; Emmy award The Tonight Show appearance, 1992. Office: care Atlantic Records 1290 Ave of the Americas New York NY 10104*

MIDORI (MIDORI GOTO), classical violinist; b. Osaka, Japan, Oct. 25, 1971. Attended, Juilliard Sch. Music; grad., Profl. Childrens Sch., 1990. Performer worldwide, 1981—; founder Midori and Friends, 1992. Recordings on Philips, Sony Classical, Columbia Masterworks; performed with N.Y. Philharmonic Orch., Boston Symphony Orch.; worldwide performances include Berlin, Chgo., Cleve., Phila., Montreal, London; recordings include Encore, Live at Carnegie Hall. Named Best Artist of Yr. by Japanese Govt., 1988; recipient Dorothy B. Chandler Performing Arts award, L.A. Music Ctr., 1989, Crystal award Ashani Shimbun Newspaper contbn. arts, Suntory award, 1994. Office: Sony Classical Sony Music Entertainment Inc 550 Madison Ave New York NY 10022-3211 also: Midori and Friends 850 7th Ave Ste 1103 New York NY 10019*

MIEL, GEORGE JOSEPH, computer scientist, mathematician, system engineer; b. Paris, Sept. 7, 1943; s. Joseph and Josephine (Modlinska) M. BS, U. Ill., 1964, MS, 1965; PhD, U. Wyo., 1976. Mem. tech. staff Bellcomm, 1967-69, NASA, 1967-69; cons. Siemens A.G., Munich, 1969-70; computer scientist Applied Rsch. Labs., Ecublens, Switzerland, 1970-73; assoc. prof. U. Nev., Las Vegas, 1978-85; researcher Hughes Aircraft Co., Malibu, Calif., 1985—; prof. U. Nev., Las Vegas, 1991—, chmn. dept. math. scis., 1997—; rsch. on environ. engring. and modeling Las Vegas, 1995—; vis. asst. prof. U. Calgary, Can., 1976-78; vis. assoc. prof. Ariz. State U., Tempe, 1983-84; cons. on computer modeling and parallel processing, Las Vegas, 1994—; rschr. on environ. engring. and modelling, 1995—. Contbr. numerous articles to profl. jours. Recipient numerous rsch. grants, Chauvenet prize Math. Assn. Am., 1986. Mem. IEEE, AIAA (vice chmn. com. on software sys. 1993—), Aerospace Industries Assn. (chmn. computational sci. com. Washington 1989-91), Soc. Indsl. Applied Math. Office: PO Box 72226 Las Vegas NV 89170-2226

MIELE, ALFONSE RALPH, former government official; b. N.Y.C., Jan. 6, 1922; s. Angelo and Alesia (Laudadio) M.; m. Gloria I. Litrento, Nov. 22, 1942 (dec. Dec. 1977); children: Richard Lynn, Barbara Jo, Steven Arnold; m. Ann Carlino Valerio, Mar. 31, 1979 (dec. June 1988); m. Dorothy A. McGowan, July 7, 1990. AB in Litteris Gallicis with honors, Fordham U., 1942; postgrad., U. Nancy, France, 1945; MA, Columbia U., 1947, PhD, 1958. Commd. 2nd lt. U.S. Army, 1942; advanced through grades to col. USAF, 1961; served in 377th Automatic Weapons Bn., 1942-45; ret., brig. gen.; instr. French and pub. speaking Fordham Prep. Sch., N.Y.C., 1946-47; asst. prof. French and Russian U.S. Naval Acad., 1949-52; exec. officer to NATO comdrs., 1953-55; teaching asst. Columbia U., 1955-58; assoc. prof. French USAF Acad., 1958-60, prof., head dept. fgn. langs., 1960-67, assoc. dean, chmn. divsn. humanities, 1967-68; exec. v.p. Loretto Heights Coll., Denver, 1968-70; pres. Coll. St. Rose, Albany, 1970-72; prof. gen. edn. Schenectady County C.C., Schenectady, N.Y., 1972-73; dep. asst. adminstr. internat. aviation affairs FAA, Washington, 1973-75, edn. specialist, 1976—; 1968; asst. dir. pub. affairs U.S. Dept. Interior, Washington, 1975-76; chief negotiator civil aviation tech. agreement with USSR, 1973-75; project dir. Nat. Aviation Edn. Program for Am. Indians, 1978; asst. dir. Union County (N.J.) Coord. Agy. for Higher Edn., 1979-82; rep. Eckhart Assocs., 1983-88; relocation specialist Bradley/Wildman Co., Monument, Colo., 1989-92. Mem. Westfield (N.J.) Bd. Edn., 1985-88; bd. dirs. Pike's Peak chpt. ARC, 1990-93; pres. Colorado Springs World Affairs Coun., 1993-95. Decorated Bronze Star, Legion of Merit; chevalier Palmes Academiques France; recipient Encaenia award Fordham Coll., 1962. Mem. Monument C. of C. (bd. dirs. 1992-94). Home: PO Box 321 Monument CO 80132-0321 *Be ever curious and willing to dare. The sweet becomes even sweeter when the bitter is overcome. Each living moment is a learning experience and adds to the anticipation of better tomorrows. The journey of life is exciting—live with that thought in mind.*

MIELE, ANGELO, engineering educator, researcher, consultant, author; b. Formia, Italy, Aug. 21, 1922; came to U.S., 1952, naturalized, 1985; s. Salvatore and Elena (Marino) M. D.Civil Engring., U. Rome, Italy, 1944, D.Aero. Engring., 1946; DSc (hon.), Inst. Tech., Technion, Israel, 1992. Asst. prof. Poly. Inst. Bklyn., 1952- 55; prof. Purdue U., 1955-59; dir. astrodynamics Boeing Sci. Research Labs., 1959-64; prof. aerospace scis., math. scis. Rice U., Houston, 1964-88, Foyt Family prof. engring., 1988-93, Foyt prof. emeritus engring., aerospace scis., math. scis., 1993—; cons. Douglas Aircraft Co., 1956-58, Allison divsn. GM Corp., 1956-58, U.S. Aviation Underwriters, 1987, Boeing Comml. Airplane Co., 1989; Breakwell Meml. lecturership Internat. Astron. Fedn., 1994. Author: Flight Mechanics, 1962; editor: Theory of Optimum Aerodynamic Shapes, 1965, Applied Mathematics in Aerospace Science and Engineering, 1994; editor-in-chief Jour. Optimization Theory and Applications, 1966—; assoc. editor Jour. Astronautical Scis., 1964-93, Applied Math. and Computation, 1975—; series editor Math. Concepts and Methods in Sci. and Engring., 1975—, Optimal Control Applications and Methods, 1979—; mem. editl. bd. RAIRO-Ops. Rsch., 1990—; mem. adv. bd. AIAA Edn. Series, 1991—; contbr. numerous articles on aerospace engring., windshear problems, hypervelocity flight, math. programming, optimal control theory and computing methods to sci. jours. Pres. Italy in Am. Assn., 1966-68. Decorated knight comdr. Order Merit Italy, 1972; recipient Levy medal Franklin Inst. of Phila., 1974, Brouwer award AAS, 1980, Schuck award Am. Automatic Control Coun., 1988. Fellow AIAA (Pendray award 1982, Mechanics and Control of Flight award 1982), Am. Astronautical Soc., Franklin Inst.; mem. NAE, Russian Acad. Scis. (fgn.), Internat. Acad. Astronautics, Acad. Scis. Turin (corr.). Home: 3106 Kettering Dr Houston TX 77027-5504 Office: Rice Univ MS-322 Aero-Astronautics Group 6100 Main St Houston TX 77005-1827

MIELE, ANTHONY WILLIAM, retired librarian; b. Williamsport, Pa., Feb. 12, 1926; s. Harry John and Louise Casale (Troyano) M.; m. Ruth Cassidy, Jan. 29, 1955; children—Terri Ann, Anthony William, Robert John, Elizabeth Ann. B.S. in Bus. Adminstrn, Marquette U., Milw., 1951; M.L.S., U. Pitts., 1966. Partner, mgr. restaurant Williamsport, 1960-66; dir. Elmwood Park (Ill.) Pub. Libr., 1967-68; asst. dir. Oak Park (Ill.) Pub. Libr., 1968-70; asst. dir. tech. services Ill. State Libr., Springfield, 1970-75; state librn. Ala. Pub. Libr. Service, Montgomery, 1975-86; coord. Libr. Svcs. and Constrn. Act, 1986-87; dir. library extension div. Ariz. Dept. Libr., Archives and Pub. Records, Phoenix, 1987-95; ret.; exec. dir. Ill. Nat. Libr. Week, 1970, ALA Nat. Libr. Week Commn., 1971-74; mem. Pub. Printer's Adv. Coun. Depository Librs., 1975-78, vice chmn., 1977-78; mem. CLSI Nat. Adv. Com., 1983-87; reader NEH, 1987; exhibits chair for confs. Mountain Plains Libr. Assn., Ariz. State Libr. Assn., Ariz. Edn. Media Assn., 1992; co-chair ASLA/AEMA Annual Conf., 1993. Assoc. editor Govt. Publs. Rev., 1974-85; contbr. articles to profl. publs. Mayor Arrowhead Community, 1984; bd. dirs. Amigos Libr. Network, 1990-94. Recipient cert. of appreciation Am. Libr. Trustee Assn., 1986. Mem. ALA (chmn. govt. documents round table 1974-76, chair state libr. agy. sect. 1992-93, mem. coun. 1994-98), Ill. Libr. Assn., Ala. Libr. Assn. (Exceptional Svc. citation 1986), Ariz. State Libr. Assn. (pres. award of recognition 1993, mem-at-large 1995-98, Disting. Svc. award 1996), Nat. Microfilm Assn., Spl. Libr. Assn., Chief Officers State Libr. Agys. (sec. 1978-80). Roman Catholic.

MIELE, JOEL ARTHUR, SR., civil engineer; b. Jersey City, May 28, 1934; s. Jene Gerald Sr., and Eleanor Natale (Bergida) M.; m. Faith Roseann Trombetta, July 21, 1952 (div. 1954); m. 2d Josephine Ann Cottone, Feb. 14, 1959; children: Joel Arthur, Jr., Vita Marie, Janet Ann. B.C.E., Poly. Inst. Bklyn., 1955. Registered profl. engr. N.Y., n.J., Fla.; profl. planner N.J. Civil engr. Yudell & Miele, Queens, N.Y., 1955-57; chief engr. Jene G. Miele Assocs., Queens, 1960-68; prin., CEO Miele Assocs., Queens, 1968-94; commr. City Planning Commn., N.Y., 1990-94; commr. Dept. of Bldgs. City of N.Y., 1994-96; commr. Dept. Environ. Protection, N.Y., 1996—; mem. Cmty. Bd. 10, Queens, 1971-90. Patentee masonry wall constrn. Mem. bd. visitors Creedmoor State Hosp., 1978—, pres., 1979; chair Cmty. Bd. 10, Queens, 1978-90; trustee Queens Borough Pub. Libr., 1979—, pres., 1995-96; bd. mem. Queens County Overall Econ. Devel. Corp., 1989-94, pres., 1991-94; trustee, treas. Queens Pub. Cmty. Corp., 1993—; exec. v.p. Queens County and Nat. County Boy Scouts Am., 1991—, pres., 1990—; dir. Queens Libr. Found., 1997; mem. membership com. Assn. Met. Water Agencies, 1997—. Lt. (j.g.) USN, 1957-60; capt. USNR, 1960-88, ret., 1988. Named Italian-Am. of Yr. Ferrini Welfare League, Queens, 1980, Hon. Mem. of Queens Chpt. AIA, 1994, Prof. Affiliated Mem. (Hon.), N.Y. Soc. Architects, 1994; recipient Outstanding Cmty. Leader award Boy Scouts Am., 1987, Pride of Queens award, 1990, Pub. Servant Extraordinaire award United Cerebral Palsy of Queens, 1994, Good Scout award Greater N.Y. Coun. Boy Scouts Am., 1994. Fellow ASCE; mem. ASTM, NSPE (trustee polit. action com. 1990-96), N.Y. State Soc. Profl. Engrs. (v.p. 1984-86, pres. 1988-89, nat. dir. 1987-90, Engr. of Yr. 1983), Soc. Am. Mil. Engrs., N.Y. State Assn. of Professions (founding), Am. Parkinson Disease Assn. (dir. 1985—, exec. com. 1987—). Democrat. Congregationalist. Office: City of New York Dept Environ Protection 59-17 Junction Blvd Corona NY 11368

MIELKE, CLARENCE HAROLD, JR., hematologist; b. Spokane, Wash., June 18, 1936; s. Clarence Harold and Marie Katherine (Gillespie) M.; m. Marcia Rae, July 5, 1964; children: Elisa, John, Kristina. BS, Wash. State U., 1959; MD, U. Louisville, 1963. Intern, San Francisco Gen. Hosp., 1963-64; resident in medicine Portland VA Hosp., 1964-65, San Francisco Gen. Hosp., 1965-67; fellow in hematology U. So. Calif., 1967-68; teaching fellow, asst. physician, instr. Tufts-New Eng. Med. Ctr. Hosps., Boston, 1968-71; sr. scientist Med. Rsch. Inst., San Francisco, 1971-90; chief hematology Presbyn. Hosp., San Francisco, 1971-82; asst. clin. prof. medicine U. Calif. Sch. Medicine, San Francisco, 1971-80, assoc. clin. prof., 1979-90, bd.92—dirs. Inst. Cancer Rsch.; trustee, bd. dirs. Med. Rsch. Inst. San Francisco, Sacred Heart Hosp. Found., 1994—. NIH grantee, 1973-88; dir. emeritus Inst. Cancer Rsch.; trustee emeritus, bd. dirs. Med. Rsch. Inst., 1988—; dir. Health Rsch. and Edn. Ctr., Wash. State U., 1989—, prof. pharmacology, 1989—, prof. vet. medicine, 1989—, assoc. dean rsch., 1992—. Fellow ACP, Internat. Acad. Clin. & Applied Thrombosis & Hemostasis, Internat. Soc. Hematology, Am. Coll. Angiology; mem. Am. Soc. Internal Medicine, Internat. Soc. Thrombosis and Hemostasis, Am. Heart Assn., N.Y. Acad. Scis., AMA, San Francisco Med. Soc., Am. Thoracic Soc., AAAS, Internat. Soc. Angiology. Editor emeritus, Jour. Clin. Aphersis, 1981; contbr. chpts. to books, articles to med. jours. Office: Wash State U Health Rsch & Edn Ctr West 601 First Ave Spokane WA 99204-0399

MIELKE, JAMES EDWARD, geochemist; b. Toledo, Oct. 6, 1940; s. Herbert Edward and Naomi Hilletje (Raabe) M.; m. Laurie Beth Retter, Dec. 19, 1966; children: Erin Christine, Emily Jane. BS, MIT, 1962; MS, U. Ariz., 1965; PhD, George Washington U., 1974. Mine geologist potash exploration N.S. Rsch. Found., 1962; geologist S.W. field party Universal Engring. Corp., Boston, 1963-64; geochemist C-14 dating lab. Smithsonian Instn., Washington, 1964-73; specialist in marine and earth scis. Congl. Rsch. Svc./Libr. of Congress, Washington, 1973—; liaison to Nat. Materials Adv. Bd., Nat. Rsch. Coun., Washington, 1981-86. Author more than 150 publs. including articles in profl. jours., com. prints, Congl. Rsch. Svc. reports; co-author: Strategic and Critical Materials, 1985, Review of Research in Modern Problems in Geochemistry, 1979. Pres. Home Buyers, Inc., Washington, 1976-83. Smithsonian Instn. Rsch. grantee, 1966-69. Mem. AAAS, Am. Geophys. Union, Marine Tech. Soc., Internat. Marine Minerals Soc. Republican. Lutheran. Avocation: folk dancing. Home: 2803 Washington Ave Chevy Chase MD 20815 Office: Congressional Research Svc Library of Congress Washington DC 20540

MIELKE, JON ALAN, elementary school administrator; b. Racine, Wis., Mar. 29, 1954; s. Paul Gilbert and Gloria Ester (Bronson) M.; m. Judy Mae Pelz, June 16, 1979; children: Jeremy, Justin, Jonathan. BA, Concordia Coll., 1979, MA, 1986. Lic. elementary administrator, Wis. Tchr. Grace Luth. Sch., St. Petersburg, Fla., 1979-84; adminstr. First Immanuel Luth. Sch., Cedarburg, Wis., 1986—. Mem. Ea. Ofcls. Assn., Luth. Educators Assn., Assn. for Supervision and Curriculum Devel. Republican. Avocations: officiating high school and college basketball, golf, softball, water skiing. Home: W67n787 Franklin Ave Cedarburg WI 53012-1180 Office: First Immanuel Lutheran Sch W67n622 Evergreen Blvd Cedarburg WI 53012-1848

MIELKE, PAUL WILLIAM, JR., statistician; b. St. Paul, Feb. 18, 1931; s. Paul William and Elsa (Yungbauer) M.; m. Roberta Roehl Robison, June 25, 1960; children: William, Emily, Lynn. BA, U. Minn., 1953, PhD, 1963; MA, U. Ariz., 1958. Teaching asst. U. Ariz., Tucson, 1957-58; teaching asst. U. Minn., Mpls., 1958-60, statis. cons., 1960-62, lectr., 1962-63; from asst. to assoc. prof. dept. statistics Colo. State U., Fort Collins, 1963-72, prof. dept. statistics, 1972—. Contbr. articles to Am. Jour. Pub. Health, Jour. of Statis. Planning and Inference, Ednl. and Psychol. Measurement, Biometrika, Earth-Sci. Revs. Capt. USAF, 1953-57. Recipient Banner I. Miller award Am. Meteorological Assn., 1994. Fellow Am. Statis. Assn.; mem. Am. Meteorol. Soc. (Banner I. Miller award 1994), Biometric Soc. Achievements include proposal that common statistical methods (t test and analysis of variance) were based on counter intuitive geometric foundations and provided alternative statistical methods which are based on appropriate foundations. Home: 736 Cherokee Dr Fort Collins CO 80525-1517 Office: Colo State U Dept Stats Fort Collins CO 80523-1877

MIELKE, WILLIAM JOHN, civil engineer; b. Waukesha, Wis., May 20, 1947; s. John Horace and Lois Margaret (Trakel) M.; m. Barbra Jean Mahnke, Dec. 28, 1968; 1 child, Anne Marie. BS in Civil Engring., U. Wis., 1971. Registered profl. engr., land surveyor Wis.; diplomate Am. Acad. Environ. Engrs. Field engr. Wis. Dept. Nat. Resources, Madison, 1968-70; civil engr. Ruekert & Mielke, Inc., Waukesha, 1971—, chief exec. officer, 1982—, pres., 1990—; bd. dirs. Mut. Savs. Bank, Excel Pub. Co.; pres. Wis. Underground Related Materials and Systems, 1990; diplomat Am. Acad. Environ. Engrs. Mem. Legis. Study Com. Milw. Sewerage Dist., 1985-86; mem. Southeastern Wis. Regional Planning Commn. Com., Waukesha, 1986; mem. League of Wis. Municipalities Com., Madison, 1986-90; apptd. to Govs. Clean Water Task Force, 1987-88; apptd. to legis. com. on land use policies State of Wis., 1997. Mem. Nat. Soc. Profl. Engrs. (chmn. profl. selection com. 1986-92, del. to com. Fed. procurement archl. engring. services, 1987-92, Profl. Engrs. in Pvt. Practice merit award 1989, nat. award for outstanding engr. in pvt. practice 1993), Am. Cons. Engrs. Coun. (chmn. profl. procurement com. 1991-93), Nat. Profl. Engrs. in Pvt. Practice, Wis. Soc. Profl. Engrs. (pres. Waukesha chapt. 1981-82, Wis. Young Engr. Yr. 1982, Wis. Engr. Yr., 1991), Wis. Profl. Engrs. in Pvt. Practice (chmn. 1986-87, Wis. Engr. of Yr. in Pvt. Practice 1988), Wis. Assn. Cons. Engrs. (pres. 1988, chmn. QBS com. 1988-91, mem. legis. com. 1992—, chmn. 1993), Am. Pub. Works Assn., Am. Waterworks Assn., Coun. Fed. Procurement Archtl./Engring. Svcs. (chmn. elect 1994, chmn. 1995), Joint Architect/Engr. Com. Fed. Constrn. (chmn. 1994). Republican. Episcopalian. Avocations: private pilot, scuba diving, sports. Home: 640 W Glenview Ave Oconomowoc WI 53066-2710 Office: Ruekert & Mielke Inc W239n1812 Rockwood Dr Waukesha WI 53188-1113

MIERZWICKI, ANTHONY JOSEPH, real estate executive; b. Balt., Oct. 7, 1939; s. Anthony W. and Margaret T. (Dregier) M.; m. Ruth R. Pasela, Oct. 29, 1967; children: Karen Spampinato, Stephanie Kelly, Karen Randlett, Debbie Mierzwicki. Student, U. Pa., 1984; Cert. in Property Mgmt., Inst. Real Estate Mgmt.; student, U. Md. Salesman, rental agent Guardian Real Estate, Balt., 1960-62; owner, pres. Tempest Realty, Inc., Balt., 1962—; regional mgr. apt. divsn. Monumental Properties, Inc., Balt., 1969-73, dir. land acquisition apt. divsn., 1972-73, asst. v.p., regional mgr. apt. divsn., 1974-79, dir. credit and collection dept., 1976; sr. v.p., regional mgr. The Town and Country Mgmt. Corp., Balt., 1979-84; exec. v.p., CEO Fairmount Mgmt. Co., Balt., 1985-90; dir. property mgmt. DeChiaro Properties, Balt., 1990—. Pres. The Essex Cmty. Coll. Found., Balt., 1995, Housing Am. Through Tng., Inc., Balt., 1995. With US Army, 1957-60. Mem. Md. Inst. Home Builders, Inc. (bd. dirs. 1982, state pres. 1980, chmn. legis. com. 1976-78, Cert. Disting. Citizenship 1980), Apt. Builders and Owners Coun. (pres. 1975, chmn. membership com. 1974), Home Builders Assn. Md. (pres. 1983, bd. dirs., mem. exec. com., Spl. Projects award, 1972, 75, Outstanding Svc. award 1977, Builder of the Yr. 1984), Nat. Assn. Home Builders (life dir., chmn. bd. govs. registered apt. mgrs., Recognition of Dedicated Svcs. 1988), Gtr. Balt. Bd. Realtors. Roman Catholic. Avocations: racquetball, golf, scuba diving. Office: DeChiaro Properties 920 Providence Rd Ste 400 Baltimore MD 21286-2979

MIFFLIN, FRED J., Canadian government official; b. Bonavista, Nfld., Can., 1938; m. Gwenneth Davies; children: Cathy, Mark, Sarah. Grad., Can. Navy's Venture Tng. Program, U.S. Naval War Coll., Nat. Def. Coll., Kingston, Ont. Enlisted Can. Navy, 1954, advanced through ranks to rear admiral, 1985, head nat. def. secretarian; mem. parliament Canadian Govt., 1988-96, parliamentary sec. to min. nat. def. & vet. affairs, 1993, min. fisheries & oceans, 1996—. Avocations: jogging, country music, gourmet cooking, raising golden retrievers. Office: Fisheries & Oceans, Stn 1570 200 Kent St, Ottawa, ON Canada K1A 0E6*

MIGALA, LUCYNA JOZEFA, broadcast journalist, arts administrator, radio station executive; b. Krakow, Poland, May 22, 1944; d. Joseph and Estelle (Suwala) M.; came to U.S., 1947, naturalized, 1955; student Loyola U., Chgo., 1962-63, Chicago Conservatory of Music, 1963-70; BS in Journalism, Northwestern U., 1966. Radio announcer, producer sta. WOPA, Oak Park, Ill., 1963-66; writer, reporter, producer NBC news, Chgo., 1966-69, 1969-71, producer NBC local news, Washington, 1969; producer, coord. NBC network news, Cleve., 1971-78, field producer, Chgo., 1978-79; v.p. Migala Communications Corp., 1979—; program and news dir., on-air personality Sta. WCEV, Cicero, Ill., 1979—; lectr. City Colls. Chgo., 1981, Morton Coll., 1988. Columnist Free Press, Chgo., 1984-87. Founder, artistic dir., gen. mgr. Lira Ensemble (formerly The Lira Singers), Chgo., 1965—, Artist-in-Residence, Loyola U. Chgo.; mem., chmn. various cultural coms. Polish Am. Congress, 1970-80; bd. dirs. Nationalities Svcs. Ctr., Cleve., 1973-78; bd. dirs., v.p. Cicero-Berwyn Fine Arts Coun., Cicero, Ill.; mem. City Arts I and II panels Chgo. Office of Fine Arts, 1986-89, 94; v.p. Chgo. chpt. Kosciuszko Found., 1983-86; bd. dirs. Polish Women's Alliance Am., 1983-87, Ill. Humanities Coun., 1983-89, mem. exec. com., 1986-87; bd. dirs. Ill. Arts Alliance, 1989-92; founder, gen. chmn. Midwest Chopin Piano Competition (now Chgo. Chopin Competition), 1984-86; founding mem. ethnic and folk arts panel Ill. Arts Coun., 1984-87, 92-94. Recipient AP Broadcasters award, 1973, Emmy award NATAS, 1974, Cultural Achievement award Am. Coun. for Polish Culture, 1990, Award of Merit Advocates Soc. Polish Am. Attys., 1991, Human Rels. Media award City of Chgo., 1992, Outstanding Achievement in Polish Culture award Minister of Fgn. Affairs, Rep. of Poland, 1994; decorated Cavalier's Cross of Merit Govt. of Poland, 1996; Washington Journalism Ctr. fellow, spring 1969. Mem. Soc. Profl. Journalists. Office: Sta WCEV 5356 W Belmont Ave Chicago IL 60641-4103 also: The Lira Ensemble 6525 N Sheridan Rd # Sky 905 Chicago IL 60626

MIGDEN, CHESTER L., professional society administrator; b. N.Y.C., May 21, 1921; s. Albert and Louise (Jawer) M.; m. Dina Vohl, July 22, 1944; children: Barbara, Ann, Amy. B.A., CCNY, 1941; LL.B., Columbia U., 1947. Bar: N.Y. State 1947. Atty. NLRB, N.Y.C., 1947-51; various positions Screen Actors Guild Inc., Hollywood, 1952-81; nat. exec. sec. Screen Actors Guild Inc., 1973-81; v.p. Internat. Fedn. Actors, 1973-81, Calif. Labor Fedn., 1974-81, Associated Actors and Artistes Am., 1973-81; exec. dir. Assn. Talent Agts., 1982-94; ret., 1994; officer, trustee Producers-Screen Actors Guild pension, welfare plans, 1960-81; v.p. Motion Picture and TV Fund, 1975—; instr. extension program UCLA. Contbr. articles to profl. jours. Mem. Acad. Motion Picture Arts and Scis., Am. Arbitration Assn. (arbitrator), Labor Rels. Cons. Democrat.

MIGEON, BARBARA RUBEN, pediatrician, geneticist; b. Rochester, N.Y., July 31, 1931; d. William Saul and Sara (Gitin) Ruben; m. Claude Jean Migeon, Apr. 2, 1960; children: Jacques Claude, Jean-Paul, Nicole. BA, Smith Coll., 1952; MD, SUNY, Buffalo, 1956. Diplomate Am. Bd. Pediatrics; cert. in med. genetics. Pediatric residency The Johns Hopkins U., Balt., 1956-59; fellow in endocrinology Harvard U. Med. Sch., Boston, 1959-60; fellow in genetics The Johns Hopkins Sch. Medicine, Balt., 1960-62, assoc. prof. pediatrics, 1970-79, joint appointment in biology, 1978—, prof. in pediatrics, 1979—, dir. PhD program in human genetics, 1979-89; mem. Genetics Study Sect., NIH, Bethesda, Md., 1975-77, Mammalian Genetics Study Sect., NIH, Bethesda, 1977-79, Human Genome Study Sect., NIH, Bethesda, 1991-93. Contbr. more than 100 rsch. papers to profl. publs. Named Prin. Investigator NIH grant, 1970—; recipient Outstanding Woman Physician award Med. Coll. Pa.; Vis. investigator Carnegie Instn. of Washington, 1975, Exch. prof. Guys Hosp., 1986. Mem. Am. Pediatric Soc., Am. Soc. Human Genetics, Genetics Soc. Am. Office: Ctr for Med Genetics CMSC 10-04 The Johns Hopkins U Baltimore MD 21287-3914

MIGEON, CLAUDE JEAN, pediatricics educator; b. Lievin, Pas-De-Calais, France, Dec. 22, 1923; came to U.S., 1950, naturalized, 1967; s. André and Pauline (Descamps) M.; m. Barbara Lou Ruben, Apr. 2, 1960; children: Jacques, Jean-Paul, Nicole. M.D., Sch. Medicine, U. Paris, 1950. Fellow dept. pediatrics Sch. Medicine, Johns Hopkins U., 1950-52, asst. prof., 1954-60, asso. prof., 1960-71, prof. pediatrics, 1971—; instr. biochemistry U. Utah, 1952-54; pediatrician Johns Hopkins Hosp., 1954—; mem. diabetes and metabolism tng. grants com. NIH, 1963-67, gen. clin. research centers com., 1968-71, mem. endocrinology study sect., 1974-78; cons. Med. Research Council Can., 1969-85, others; vis. prof. Maadi Armed Forces Hosp., Cairo, 1985, Guy's Hosp., London, 1986. Co-editor: (textbook) The Diagnosis and Treatment of Endocrine Disorders in Childhood and Adolescence, 4th edit., 1994; mem. editl. bd.: Johns Hopkins Med. Jour., 1970-72, Jour. Clin. Endocrinology and Metabolism, 1971-77, Hormone Rsch., 1979—; contbr. articles to profl. jours. Fulbright fellow, 1950; Am. Field Service fellow, 1950-51; Andre and Bella Meyer fellow, 1951-52; recipient research career award NIH, 1964-85. Fellow AAAS; mem. Endocrine Soc. (coun. 1971-74, chmn. pub. affairs com. 1974-91, Ayerst award, Williams award), Soc. Pediatric Rsch. (emeritus), Am. Pediatric Soc., Lawson Wilkins Pediatric Endocrine Soc. (founding pres. 1972), Am. Soc. Clin. Investigation (emeritus), Am. Physiol. Soc., Japanese Pediatric Endocrine Soc. (hon.), Found. for Am. Meml. Hosp. (bd. dirs. 1985—), Soc. Francaise d'Endocrinologie (fgn. corr. mem.). Home: 502 Somerset Rd Baltimore MD 21210-2720 Office: Johns Hopkins Hosp CMSC 3-110 Baltimore MD 21205

MIGGINS, MICHAEL DENIS, retired career officer, arms control analyst; b. White Plains, N.Y., Aug. 8, 1944; s. Michael Joseph Miggins and M. Gabrielle (Daly) O'Neill, stepfather: James O'Neill; m. Kathleen Ann Isherwood, Oct. 22, 1966; children: Kristin D., Michael C. BA in Polit. Sci., Providence Coll., 1966; MA in Internat. Rels., St. John's U., 1972. Commd. lt. U.S. Army, 1966, advanced through grades to col., 1989; company comdr. and platoon leader 2d Battalion, 325th Inf., 82nd Airborne Div., Ft. Bragg, N.C., 1966-68; dist. sr. advisor An Xuyen Province, Ca Mau, Vietnam, 1968-69; instr. ROTC St. John's U., Jamaica, N.Y., 1969-72; with joint security area Armistice Affairs div. UN Forces, Pan Mun Jom, Korea, 1973-74; ops. officer, company comdr., intelligence officer 4th Battalion, 6th Inf., Berlin (Germany) Brigade, 1974-77; sec. gen. staff Army Combined Arms Test Activity, Ft. Hood, Tex., 1978-80; staff officer ODCSOPS Army Staff, Washington, 1980-84; br. chief priorities, programs and budget br. Army Staff, 1984-85; exec. officer 1st brigade (armored) 1st Cavalry Divsn. U.S. Army, Ft. Hood, Tex., 1985-86, chief exercise divsn. III Corps., 1986-87; mem. joint staff, internat. negotiations divsn. Washington, 1987-91; U.S. del. mutual and balanced force reduction negotiations mandate talks Conventional Armed Forces in Europe Negotiation, Vienna, Austria, 1987-89; mil. advisor to U.S. rep. High Level Task Force NATO, Brussels, 1988-90; rep. to interagy. conventional arms control Joint Staff, Washington, 1990-91; sr. advisor to chmn. verification coord. com., internat. staff, polit. affairs divsn. NATO, Brussels, 1991-93; mgr. conventional arms ctrl. and open skies projects Ctr. Verification Rsch. Sci. Applications Internat. Corp., Newington, Va., 1994—. Decorated Silver Star, Bronze Star, Legion of Merit, Def. Superior Svc. medal, Meritorious Svc. medal, Army Commendation medal. Mem. Assn. U.S. Army, Army and Navy Club. Republican. Roman Catholic. Avocations: skiing, bicycling, jogging, military history. Home: 9352 Braymore Cir Fairfax Station VA 22039-3124 Office: Ctr for Verification Rsch Cinder Bed Rd Newington VA 22122

MIGHELL, KENNETH JOHN, lawyer; b. Schenectady, N.Y., Mar. 17, 1931; s. Richard Henry and Ruth Aline (Simon) M.; m. Julia Anne Carstarphen, Aug. 24, 1961; children: Thomas Lowry, Elizabeth Anne. BBA, U. Tex., 1952, JD, 1957. Bar: Tex. 1957. Assoc. Scurry, Scurry, Pace & Wood, Dallas, 1957-61; asst. U.S. Atty. Justice Dept., Dallas, 1961-77; 1st asst. No. Dist. Tex., 1972-77; U.S. Atty. No. Dist., Tex., 1977-81; ptnr. Cowles & Thompson, 1981-96, of counsel, 1996—. Chmn. bd. mgmt. Downtown Dallas YMCA, 1974-76; pres. Dallas Area Am. Lung Assn., 1985-87; bd. dirs. YMCA Met. Dallas, 1987—; chmn. adv. bd. Southwestern Law Enforcement Inst., 1994—. With USN, 1952-54; capt. USNR, 1954-78. Mem. ABA, Fed. Bar Assn., Dallas Bar Assn. (bd. dirs. 1984-89, chmn. 1989, v.p. 1990-91, pres. 1993), State Bar Tex. (bd. dirs. 1994-95), Nat. Assn. Former U.S. Attys. (pres. 1995). Democrat. Methodist. Office: 4000 Nations Bank Plz Dallas TX 75202

MIGHT, THOMAS OWEN, newspaper company executive; b. Fort Walton Beach, Fla., Apr. 22, 1951; s. Gerald William and Rosina (Bugner) M.; m. Sept. 22, 1973; children—Matthew, Daniel. B.S. in Indsl. Enging., Ga. Tech. U., 1972; M.B.A., Harvard Bus. Sch., 1978. Asst. to pub. Washington Post, 1978-80, mgr. plant, 1980-81, v.p. prodn., v.p. marketing; now pres., COO, divsn. Post-Newsweek cable The Washington Post Co., Phoenix. Served to capt. U.S. Army, 1972-76. Roman Catholic. Office: Washington Post Co Divsn Post-Newsweek Cable 4742 N 24th St Ste 270 Phoenix AZ 85016-4860*

MIGIELICZ, GERALYN, photojournalist; b. St. Louis, Feb. 15, 1958; d. Edward J. and Mary Ann (McCarthy) M. BJ, U. Mo., 1979. Photographer Emporia (Kans.) Gazette, 1979-80; chief photographer St. Joseph (Mo.) News-Press & Gazette, 1980-83; photo editor, photographer Seattle Times, 1984; picture editor Rocky Mountain News, Denver, 1985-86; graphics editor San Jose (Calif.) Mercury News, 1986-92, dir. photography, 1992—. Recipient Individual Editing awards Soc. Newspaper Designers, 1988-92, Editing awards, 91-92; named for Overall Excellence in Editing, Picture of Yr. Contest, U. Mo., 1993. Office: San Jose Mercury News 750 Ridder Park Dr San Jose CA 95131-2432*

MIGL, DONALD RAYMOND, therapeutic optometrist, pharmacist; b. Houston, Tex., Sept. 18, 1947; s. Ervin Lawrence and Adele Marie (Boenisch) M.; m. Karen S. Coale, Mar. 23, 1974; children: Christopher Brian, Derek Drew, Monica Michelle. BS in Pharmacy, U. Houston, 1970, BS, 1978, OD, 1980, cert., 1992; postgrad., U. Ala. Med. Ctr., Birmingham, 1974-76, Stephen F. Austin State U., Nacogdoches, Tex., 1987-88. Registered pharmacist; cert. Nat. Bds. Examiners Optometry, Treatment & Mgmt. Ocular Disease; cert. therapeutic optometrist. Pharmacist Tex. Med. Ctr., Houston, 1967-69, St. Luke's and Tex. Childrens Hosp., 1967-69, Meml. Hosp., 1969-70, Ben Taub (Harris County) Hosp., 1970-71, Shades Mountain Pharmacy, Birmingham, 1974-76, Westbury Hosp., Houston, 1976-81; instr. pharmacology lab. Coll. Optometry U. Houston, 1980; pvt. practice, Nacogdoches, Tex., 1981—; mem. interdisciplinary health teams, 1977; charter advisor publ. Contact, CIBA Vision Corp., 1988-89. Judge health sci. div. Houston Area Sci. Fair, 1970. Recipient svc. award Houston Community Interdisciplinary Health Screening Programs, 1977, Spl. Academic Achievement award in pharmacy and optometry U. Houston, 1980. Mem. Am. Optometric Assn. (Optometric recognition award 1985-97), Tex. Optometric Assn. (recognition cert. 1979), Piney Woods Optometric Soc. (pres. 1984), Am. Pharm. Assn. (recognition cert. 1970), Tex. Pharm. Assn., Am. Soc. Hosp. Pharmacists, U.S. Jaycees, Gold Key, Omicron Delta Kappa. Methodist. Lodge: Rotary (Paul Harris Fellow 1987, Pres. award Outstanding Svc., 1991-92). Home: 4122 Ridgebrook Dr Nacogdoches TX 75961 Office: Eagle Eye 20/20 Plus Vision 4122 Ridgebrook Dr Nacogdoches TX 75961-2271

MIGLIARO, MARCO WILLIAM, electrical engineer; b. N.Y.C., Mar. 29, 1948; s. Marco Salvatore and Anna (Dalton) M.; children: Kristen Marie, Meredith Anne, Marie Angela, Marco Thomas; m. Jasoda Badlu, Nov. 19, 1988. BEE, Pratt Inst., 1969; postgrad., N.J. Inst. Tech., 1970-72. Registered profl. engr., N.Y., N.J., Pa., Mass., Fla. Engr. Am. Electric Power, N.Y.C., 1969-78; staff engr. Gibbs & Hill, Inc., N.Y.C., 1978-81; sr. cons. engr. Ebasco Svcs., Inc., N.Y.C., 1981-88; tech. mgr. ABB Impell Corp., Melville, N.Y., 1988-90; sr. staff specialist for nuclear engring. Fla. Power & Light, Juno Beach, 1990-96, chief elec./I&C engr., 1996—; developer seminar on stationary batteries, 1987. Contbg. author: Handbook of Power Calculations, 1984; also articles. Recipient Meritorious Svc. award Am. Nat. Standards Inst., 1994. Fellow IEEE (bd. dirs. 1990-92, fin. com. 1990-92, dir. stds. 1990-91, mem. exec. com. 1992, v.p. stds. activities, 1992, Stds. medal 1986, Stds. Bd. Disting. Svc. award 1993, Charles Proteus Steinmetz award 1996); mem. IEEE Power Engring. Soc. (Disting. Svc. award 1988, 92). Avocations: fishing, travel. Home: PO Box 9253 Jupiter FL 33468-9253 Office: Fla Power & Light PO Box 14000 (JPN/JB) Juno Beach FL 33408-0420

MIGNON, PAUL KILLIAN, laboratory executive; b. Manchester, Conn., Nov. 26, 1960; s. Charles William and Mary Anne (Killian) M.; m. Kimberly Anne Ray, Dec. 6, 1956; children: Rudolph, Sophia, Frank. AAS in Environ. Lab. Tech., S.E. C.C., Lincoln, 1983; BS in Chemistry, Doane Coll., 1996. Analytical lab. technician Hoskins-Western-Sonderegger, Inc., Lincoln, 1983-87; mgr. analytical svcs. divsn. HWS Cons. Group, Inc., Lincoln, 1987—; seminar leader Nebr. Wastewater Operators Conf., 1991-92, 95, Govt. Refuse Collection and Disposal Assn., Nebr., 1988; conf. presenter in field. Mem. ASTM, Am. Chem. Soc., Water Environment Fedn. Avocations: golf, hiking, camping. Home: RR 1 Box 95 Martell NE 68404-9750 Office: HWS Cons Group Inc 825 J St Lincoln NE 68508-2958

MIGNONE, MARIO B., Italian studies educator; b. Benevento, Italy, July 26, 1940; came to U.S., 1960; s. Roberto and Palmina (Iannace) M.; m. Lois Dolores Pontillo, June 29, 1968; children: Pamela Anne, Cristina Maria, Elizabeth Maria. BA, CCNY, 1967; MA, Rutgers U., 1969, PhD, 1972. Prof. Italian lang. SUNY, Stony Brook, 1970—, dir. undergrad. studies, 1976-83, dir. grad. studies, 1983-87; founder, exec. dir. Ctr. for Italian Studies, chmn. French and Italian dept., Stony Brook, 1988—. Author: The Theater of Eduardo De Filippo, 1974, Abnormality and Anguish in the Narrative of Dino Buzzati, 1981, Eduardo De Filippo, 1984, Pirandello in America, 1988, Columbus: Meeting of Cultures, 1993, Italy Today: A Country in Transition, 1995; assoc. mng. editor Forum Italicum, 1986-94, editor, 1994—; contbr. articles to profl. jours. Mem. Am. Assn. Tchrs. Italian (pres. 1982-84), Assn. Italian Am. Educators (pres. 1997—). Home: 26 Hopewell Dr Stony Brook NY 11790-2339 Office: SUNY Dept French Italian Stony Brook NY 11794

MIGUE, JEAN LUC, economics educator; b. Montreal, Que., Can., Apr. 13, 1933; s. Joseph Alfred and Marie Laurence (Venne) M.; m. Renee Caron, Sept. 13, 1958; children—Paule, Pascal, Nicolas. B.A. in Econs, U. Montreal, 1953, M.A., 1956; Ph.D. in Econs, Am. U., 1968. Researcher Bank of Can., 1957-58; prof. Laval U., 1962-70; prof. econs. Nat. Sch. Public Adminstrn., Quebec, 1970—; mem. staff Econ. Council Can., 1973-74. Author: The Price of Health, 1974, Le Prix du Transport, 1978, Nationalistic Policies of Canada, 1979, L'Economiste et La chose Publique, 1979, The Public Monopoly of Education, 1989, Federalism and Free Trade, 1993. Massey Found. fellow, 1956. Fellow Royal Soc. Can.; mem. Am. Econ. Assn., Can. Econ. Assn., Public Choice Soc. Roman Catholic. Office: 945 Wolfe, Quebec, PQ Canada G1V 3J9

MIGUEL DESOUSA, LINDA J., critical care nurse, nursing educator; b. Honolulu, Dec. 6, 1946; d. Gregory and Irene N. (Calasa) Furtado; children: Joseph H. Miguel Jr., Brett A. Miguel. ADN, Maui Community Coll., Kahului, Hawaii, 1980; BSN, U. Hawaii, 1987, MS, 1990. RN, Hawaii. Charge nurse ICU-CCU Maui Meml. Hosp., Wailuku, 1980-88; nursing instr. Maui Community Coll., Kahului, 1988; unit supr.-coronary care Straub Clinic and Hosp., Honolulu, 1988-90; nursing instr. Kapiolani Community Coll., Honolulu, 1990-92; edn. dir. Waianae Health Acad., 1992-97; nursing svcs. mgr. Kula Hosp., Maui, 1997—; researcher in field. Contbr. articles to profl. jours. Outer Island Students Spl. Nursing scholar, 1988-90, Rsch. scholarship, 1989. Mem. AACN, Hawaii Nurses Assn., Hawaii Soc. for Cardiovascular and Pulmonary Rehab., Assn. Am. Women in C. C.s, Sigma Theta Tau. Home: 98-402 Koauka Loop #1202 Aiea HI 96701 Office: Kula Hosp 204 Kula Hwy Kula HI 96790-9471

MIHAL, SANDRA POWELL, distance learning specialist; b. Balt., Dec. 15, 1941; d. Sanford William and Mary Louise (Barry) Powell; m. James George Anderson, June 15, 1963; children: Robin Marie, James Brian, Melissa Lee, Derek Claire; m. Charles Turner Barber, Apr. 18, 1978; stepchildren: Gretchen Jayco, Katrina Hope; m. Ladislaw Paul Mihal, May 25, 1991; stepchildren: Alexander Paul, Suzie May, Natasha Elizabeth, Rudy Darius. BA, Mt. St. Agnes Coll., 1963; MA, N.Mex. State U., 1970, Purdue U., 1975; EdD, Vanderbilt U., 1990. Cert. tchr., Md. Tchr. Ridgely-Dulaney Jr. H.S., Towson, Md., 1964; grad. asst. N.Mex. State U., Las Cruces, 1967-69; acad. advisor, instr. polit. sci. Purdue U., West Lafayette, Ind., 1974-78; prof., acad. sys. analyst U. So. Ind., Evansville, 1978-82; assoc. prof., chair dept. computer info. sys. Henderson (Ky.) C.C., 1982-88; prof. computer tech., divsn. chair Anne Arundel C.C., Arnold, Md., 1988-91; computer sys. analyst Immigration & Naturalization Svc., Dept. of Justice, Washington, 1991-92, Glynco, Ga., 1995—; bd. dirs. Ind. Polit. Sci. Assn., Muncie, 1984-88, Internat. Studies Assn.-Midwest, Chgo., 86-88; pres. Ky. Acad. Computer Users' Group, Lexington, 1985-86; mem. telecom. adv. bd. C.C. Sys., Annapolis, Md., 1990-91; computer syst. network analyst CLARC Svcs., Pt. Charlotte, Fla., 92-95; adj. prof. history and polit. sci. Edison C.C., Punta Gorda, Fla., 1993-95. Author: Learning By Doing BASIC, 1983, Computers Learning By Doing, 1984; contbr. to several profl jours. 1980-90;

author, spkr. series Faculty/Staff Edison CC 94, Ednl. Tech. Nova U., 1995. Block coord. several neighborhood assns.; mem. Henderson County Sch. Computer Adv. Bd. 1982-88; chmn. Newburgh (Ind.) Youth Orgn., 78-86; judge Sci. Fair, Annapolis, 1988-90; mem. nomination bd. Ky. Higher Edn. Assn., 1989-91; mem. Charlotte Chorale, Port Charlotte, 1992-94, Peace River Power Squadron, Port Charlotte, 1994-96. Md. State Tchr. Bd. Edn. scholar, 1960-63; fellow Sloan Found., 1973-75, U. Ky., 1984. Mem. Soc. Applied Learning Tech., Am. Legion, Assn. Computing Machinery (v.p. 1985—), Pi Gamma Mu. Democrat. Roman Catholic. Avocations: sailing, singing, swimming, cooking. Home: 112 Oak Ridge Rd Brunswick GA 31525 Office: USINS Distance Learning Staff FLETC Bldg 63 Rm 109 Glynco GA 31523

MIHALAS, DIMITRI MANUEL, astronomer, educator; b. Los Angeles, Mar. 20, 1939; s. Emmanuel Demetrious and Jean (Christo) M.; m. Alice Joelen Covalt, June 15, 1963 (div. Nov. 1974); children: Michael Demetrious, Genevieve Alexandra; m. Barbara Ruth Rickey, May 18, 1975 (div. Dec. 1992). B.A. with highest honors, UCLA, 1959; M.S., Calif. Inst. Tech., 1960, Ph.D., 1964. Asst. prof. astrophys. scis. Princeton U., 1964-67; asst. prof. physics U. Colo., 1967-68; asso. prof. astronomy and astrophysics U. Chgo., 1968-70, prof., 1970-71; adj. prof. astrogeophysics, also physics and astrophysics U. Colo., 1972-80; sr. scientist High Altitude Obs., Nat. Center Atmospheric Research, Boulder, Colo., 1971-79, 82-85; prof. astronomy U. Ill., 1985—; astronomer Sacramento Peak Obs., Sunspot, N.Mex., 1979-82; cons. Los Alamos Nat. Lab, 1981—; vis. prof. dept. astrophysics Oxford (Eng.) U., 1977-78; sr. vis. fellow dept. physics and astronomy Univ. Coll., London, 1978; mem. astronomy adv. panel NSF, 1972-75. Author: Galactic Astronomy, 2d edit, 1981, Stellar Atmospheres, 1970, 2d edit., 1978, Theorie des Atmospheres Stellaires, 1971, Foundations of Radiation Hydrodynamics, 1984; assoc. editor Astrophys. Jour, 1970-79, Jour. Computational Physics, 1981-87, Jour. Quantitative Spectroscopy, 1984—; mem. editorial bd. Solar Physics, 1981-89. NSF fellow, 1959-62; Van Maanen fellow, 1962-63; Eugene Higgins vis. fellow, 1963-64; Alfred P. Sloan Found. Research fellow, 1969-71; Alexander von Humboldt Stiftung sr. U.S. scientist awardee, 1984. Mem. U.S. Nat. Acad. Sci., Internat. Astron. Union (pres. commn. 36 1976-79), Am. Astron. Soc. (Helen B. Warner prize 1974), Astron. Soc. Pacific (dir. 1975-77). Home: 1924 Blackthorn Dr Champaign IL 61821-6300 Office: Dept Astronomy U Ill 1002 W Green St Urbana IL 61801-3074

MIHALY, EUGENE BRAMER, corporate executive, consultant, writer, educator; b. The Hague, The Netherlands, Nov. 11, 1934; s. Eddy and Cecile (Bramer) Kahn; stepson of Eugene Mihaly; m. Stacey Beth Pulner, Apr. 21, 1996; children: Lisa Klee, Jessica; stepchildren: Stephanie Pulner, Andrew Pulner. AB magna cum laude, Harvard U., 1956; PhD, London Sch. Econs. and Polit. Sci., 1964. Aviation/space editor Hartford (Conn.) Courant, 1960-61; internat. economist AID, Washington, 1964-65; dep. dir. Peace Corps, Tanzania, 1966, dir., 1967-68; dep. dir. East Asia/Pacific bur. Peace Corps, Washington, 1969, dir. office program devel., evaluation and rsch., 1969-70; assoc. dir. Inst. Internat. Studies, U. Calif., Berkeley, 1970-72; pres. Mihaly Internat. Corp., 1972—; chmn. bd. Mihaly Internat. Can., Ltd., 1992—; pres., CEO MI Energy Ptnrs., L.P., 1995—; sr. lectr. Haas Sch. Bus. U. Calif., Berkeley, 1991-95; adj. prof. Amos Tuck Sch. Dartmouth Coll., 1997—; bd. dirs. Shaman Power Corp., Can. Author: Foreign Aid and Politics in Nepal: A Case Study, 1965; contbr.: Political Development in Micronesia, 1974, Management of the Multinationals, 1974; also articles to various publs. Vice chmn. bd. dirs. Childreach (Plan Internat. U.S.A.); trustee World Without War Coun.; chmn. emeritus Calif.-S.E. Asia Bus. Coun.; mem. Dist. Export Coun. No. Calif.; mem. adv. bd. World Resources Inst.; mem. U.S. nat. com. Pacific Econ. Coop. Mem. Coun. on Fgn. rels., Signet Soc. Home: 153 Rumstick Rd Barrington RI 02806-4855

MIHAN, RICHARD, retired dermatologist; b. L.A., Dec. 20, 1925; s. Arnold and Virginia Catherine (O'Reilly) M.; student U. So. Calif., 1945; MD, St. Louis U., 1949. Rotating intern Los Angeles County Gen. Hosp., 1949-51, resident in dermatology, 1954-57; practice medicine specializing in dermatology, Los Angeles, 1957-95; emeritus clin. prof. dept. medicine, dermatology and syphilology U. So. Calif., 1989—. Served as lt. (j.g.) M.C., USNR, 1951-53, ret. as lt. comdr. Diplomate Am. Bd. Dermatology. Fellow ACP; mem. Internat. Soc. Dermatology, Soc. Investigative Dermatology, Pacific Dermatologic Assn. (exec. bd. 1971-74), Calif. Med. Assn. (chmn. dermatologic sect. 1973-74), AMA, Los Angeles Dermatol. Soc. (pres. 1975-76), Am. Acad. Dermatology, L.A. Acad. Medicine (pres. 1988-89), Order of St. Lazarus (comdr.); Club: Calif. Roman Catholic. Home: 3278 Wilshire Blvd Apt 503 Los Angeles CA 90010-1431

MIHELICH, EDWARD DAVID, chemist; b. Coeur D'Alene, Idaho, June 24, 1950; s. Joseph Anthony and Alma Josephine (Folden) M.; m. Loren Marie O'Connor, May 20, 1972; children: Christopher Colin, Patrick Joseph. BS, Ill. Inst. Tech., Chgo., 1972; PhD, Colo. State U., 1975. Postdoctoral rsch. assoc. Harvard U., Cambridge, Mass., 1975-77; chemist Procter & Gamble Co., Cin., 1977-83; rsch. scientist Eli Lilly and Co., Indpls., 1983-90, sr. rsch. scientist, 1991—. Contbr. articles to profl. jours. bd. dirs. Sycamore Sch., 1993-96. Mem. Am. Chem. Soc. Office: Lilly Rsch Labs DC 0540 Lilly Corp Ctr Indianapolis IN 46285

MIHICH, ENRICO, medical researcher; b. Fiume, Italy, Jan. 4, 1928; came to U.S., 1957; s. Milan and Rosina (Lenaz) M.; m. Renata Marisa Mustacchi; 1 child, Sylvia. B.S., U, Milan, Italy, 1944, M.D., 1951, docent, 1962; MD (honoris causa), U. Marseille, 1986. Research asst. Inst. Pharmacology U. Milan, Italy, 1951, asst. prof., 1954-56; vis. research fellow Sloan Kettering Inst. Cancer Research, N.Y.C., 1952-54; head pharmacology lab. Valeas Pharm. Industry, Milan, 1954-56; sr. cancer research scientist dept. exptl. therapeutics Roswell Park Cancer Inst., Buffalo, 1957-59, assoc. cancer research scientist, 1959-66, prin. scientist, 1966-71, dir. dept. exptl. therapeutics and Grace Cancer Drug Ctr., 1971—, v.p. for sponsored programs, 1987-97; prof. pharmacology SUNY-Buffalo, 1960—, research asst., 1960-66, research assoc., 1966-68, research prof. pharmacology, 1968-69, chmn. dept. pharmacology, 1969—; assoc. prof. biochem. pharmacology Sch. of Pharmacy, 1963-68, adj. prof. biochem. pharmacology, 1968—; cons., lectr. in field; participant numerous symposia; sci. advisor govt. agys., pvt. industry; mem. Nat. Cancer Adv. Bd., 1984-90. Author more than 261 books, articles, chpts. in books; editor-in-chief for N.Am. and Japan, Cancer Immunology and Immunotherapy; mem. editorial bd. Advances in Cancer Chemotherapy, Internat. Jour. Immunopharmacology, Cancer and Metastasis Revs., others; adv. editor Oncology Rsch., Selective Cancer Therapeutics jours. Recipient numerous grants for med. rsch.; Fulbright travel fellow, 1952-53, Sloan Found. fellow, 1953-54; recipient Lifetimw Sci. award Inst. Advanced Studies in Immunology and Aging, 1994; named Myron Karon Meml. lectr., 1981. Office: Grace Cancer Drug Ctr Roswell Park Cancer Inst Elm And Carlton St Buffalo NY 14263-0001

MIHM, JOHN CLIFFORD, chemical engineer; b. Austin, Tex., July 28, 1942; s. Clifford Henry and Adeline (Cleary) M.; m. Janet Elanor Skales, May 29, 1964; 1 child, Mary Lynn. AA, Frank Phillips Coll., 1962; BSChemE, Tex. Tech. Engring., 1964. Registered profl. engr., Tex. With Phillips Petroleum Co., 1964—; v.p. corp. engring. Phillips Petroleum Co., Bartlesville, Okla., 1987-92, v.p. R & D, 1992-93, sr. v.p. corp. technology, 1993—; engr. mgr. E & P Phillips Petroleum Co., Stavanger, Norway, 1977-82; adv. bd. Tex. Tech. Engring., Lubbock, Tex., 1985—, pres. deans coun., 1996—. Bd. dirs. Boy Scouts Am., Bartlesville, 1986—. Mem. ASME (ind. adv. bd. 1989—), NSPE (mem. adv. bd. 1994—), AIChE (ECC divsn., bd. dirs. 1989-93, chmn. 1992-93), Okla. Soc. Profl. Engrs. (Outstanding Engr. in Mgmt. award 1991), Soc. Profl. Engrs., Okla. Engring. Found. (bd. dirs., pres. 1993—). Republican. Roman Catholic. Office: Phillips Petroleum Co 4th and Keeler Sts Bartlesville OK 74004

MIHM, MICHAEL MARTIN, federal judge; b. Amboy, Ill., May 18, 1943; s. Martin Clarence and Frances Johannah (Morrissey) M.; m. Judith Ann Zosky, May 6, 1967; children—Molly Elizabeth, Sarah Ann, Jacob Michael, Jennifer Leah. B.A., Loras Coll., 1964; J.D., St. Louis U., 1967. Asst. prosecuting atty. St. Louis County, Clayton, Mo., 1967-68; asst. state's atty. Peoria County, Peoria, Ill., 1968-69; asst. city atty. City of Peoria, Ill., 1969-72; state's atty. Peoria County, Peoria, Ill., 1972-80; sole practice Peoria, Ill., 1980-82; U.S. dist. judge U.S. Govt., Peoria, Ill., 1982—; chief U.S. dist. judge U.S. Dist. Ct. (ctrl. dist.) Ill., 1991—; chmn. com. internat. jud. rels. U.S. Jud. Conf., 1994-96, mem. exec. com., 1995—; mem. com. jud. br., 1987-93; adj. prof. law John Marshall Law Sch., 1990—. Past mem. adv. bd. Big Brothers-Big Sisters, Crisis Nursery, Peoria; past bd. dirs. Salvation Army, Peoria, W.D. Boyce council Boy Scouts Am., State of Ill. Treatment Alternatives to Street Crime, Gov.'s Criminal Justice Info. Council; past vice-chmn. Ill. Dangerous Drugs Adv. Council; trustee Proctor Health Care Found., 1991—. Recipient Good Govt. award Peoria Jaycees, 1978. Mem. Peoria County Bar Assn. (former bd. dirs., past chmn. entertainment com.). Roman Catholic. Office: US Dist Ct 204 Federal Bldg 100 NE Monroe St Peoria IL 61602-1003

MIHRAN, THEODORE GREGORY, retired physicist; b. Detroit, June 28, 1924; s. Miro Krikor and Zaroohi (Mesrobian) M.; m. Hermine Misirian, July 26, 1953 (dec. 1980); children: Gregory Charles, Joyce Hermine, Richard Theodore; m. Jean Wilson, Aug. 22, 1981; stepchildren: Mark Whitcomb, Susan Rebecca. A.B., Stanford U., 1944, M.S., 1947, Ph.D. (Fortescue fellow, 1948-49), 1950. Physicist Rsch. and Devel. Ctr., Gen. Electric Co., Schenectady, 1950-92; ret., 1992; vis. prof. elec. engring. dept. Cornell U., Ithaca, N.Y., 1963-64; adj. prof. Union Coll., Schenectady, 1960-61; lectr. Chalmers Inst., Gothenburg, Sweden, 1965; cons. in field. Contbr. articles to profl. publs. Pres., bd. dirs. Schenectady Symphony, 1962-63. Served with USN, 1944-46. Fellow IEEE (editor Trans. on Electron Devices 1970-73); mem. Am. Phys. Soc., Inst. Microwave Power, Sigma Xi, Phi Beta Kappa, Tau Beta Pi. Mem. Niskayuna Reformed Church. Patentee. Home: 898 Ash Tree Ln Niskayuna NY 12309-1723

MIIKE, LAWRENCE HIROSHI, public health officer; m. Kiliwehi Kono, 1993; 3 stepchildren, Kapono, Nainoa, Makana. BS in Chemistry, Amherst Coll., 1962; MD, U. Calif., San Francisco, 1966; JD, UCLA, 1972. Intern Phila. Gen. Hosp., 1966-67; with Nat. Ctr. Health Svcs. Rsch. and Devel., Washington, 1972-73; faculty Health Policy Program Sch. Medicine U. Calif., San Francisco, 1973-75, Med. Sch. Georgetown U., Washington, 1977-89; sr. assoc. Office of Tech. Assessment, U.S. Congress, Washington, 1977-89; founder, exec. dir. Papa Ola Lōkahi, Hawaii, 1989-92; prof. family prace and cmty. health U. Hawaii, Honolulu, 1989-94; med. dir. Hawaii QUEST Program, Honolulu, 1993-95; dir. Dept. Health, State of Hawaii, Honolulu, 1995—. With USAF, 1967-69. Office: 1250 Punchbowl St Honolulu HI 96813-2416

MIILLER, SUSAN DIANE, artist; b. N.Y.C., June 10, 1953; d. Elwood Charles and Alyce Mary (Gebhardt) Knapp; m. Denis Miiller, May 22, 1982. MA, Queens Coll., 1980; BFA, SUNY, 1988; MFA, U. North Tex., 1992. Palynologist Phillips Petroleum Co., Bartleville, Okla., 1980-85; scenic designer Forestburgh (N.Y.) Playhouse, 1989; rsch. asst. Lamont-Doherty Geol. Observatory, Palisades, N.Y., 1990; adj. prof. Tex. Christian U., Ft. Worth, 1992-94; lectr. U. Tex., Dallas, 1995—; lectr. U. Tex., Dallas, 1995-96; treas. mem. 500X Gallery, Dallas, 1991-92. One-woman shows include Western Tex. Coll., 1993, Brazos Gallery, Richland Coll., 1993, Women & Their Work Gallery, 1995 (Gallery Artists Series award 1995), A.I.R. Gallery, 1996, Milagros Contemporary Art, 1996, Pentimenti Gallery, Pa., 1996. Recipient 4th Nat. Biennial Exhbns., Grand Purchase award, 1991, Mus. Abilene award, 1992, Lubbock Art Festival Merit award, 1992, 2d pl. award Matrix Gallery, 1995, Hon. Mention award 3d Biennial Gulf of Mex. Exhbn., 1995, 1st place award Soho Gallery, 1996. Mem. Tex. Fin Arts Assn., Dallas Mus. Art, Coll. Art Assn., Dallas Visual Art Ctr., Art Initiatives. Home: 449 Harris St # J102 Coppell TX 75019-3224 Studio: 3309 Elm St # 3E Dallas TX 75226-1637

MIKA, JOSEPH JOHN, library educator, consultant; b. McKees Rocks, Pa., Mar. 1, 1948; s. George Joseph and Sophie Ann (Stec) M.; children: Jason-Paul Joseph, Matthew Douglas, Meghan Leigh. BA in English, U. Pitts., 1969, M.L.S., 1971, Ph.D. in L.S., 1980. Asst. librarian, instr. Ohio State U., Mansfield, 1971-73; asst. librarian, asst. prof. Johnson State Coll. (Vt.), 1973-75; grad. asst., teaching fellow Sch. Libr. and Info. Sci. U. Pitts., 1975-77; asst. dean, assoc. prof. libr. svc. U. So. Miss., Hattiesburg, 1977-86, dir. libr. and info. sci. program, Wayne State U. Libr. and Info. Sci. program, 1986-94, prof., 1994—; cons. to libraries. Co-editor Jour. of Edn. for Libr. and Info. Sci., 1995—. Served to col. USAR. Decorated D.S.M., Army Res. Components Achievement medal, Meritorius Svc. medal, Army Commendation medal. Mem. ALA (councilor 1983-86, chmn. constn. and bylaws com. 1985-86), Assn. Libr. and Info. Sci. Edn., (chmn. membership com. 1982-83, chmn. nominating com. 1982, exec. bd. 1986), Miss. Libr. Assn. (pres.-elect 1985), Mich. Libr. Assn. (chair libr. edn. com. 1989), Leadership Acad. (oversight com. 1989-95), Assn. Coll. and Rsch. Librs. (chmn. 1982-83, chmn. budget com. 1982-83), Soc. Miss. Archivists (treas., exec. bd. 1981-83), Mich. Ctr. for The Book (chair 1994—), Beta Phi Mu (pres.-elect 1987-89, pres. 1989-91), Phi Delta Kappa. Lodge: Kiwanis (Hattiesburg). Contbr. articles to profl. jours. Home: 11357 Highland Hills Dr Jerome MI 49249 Office: Wayne State U Libr and Info Sci Program 106 Kresge Library Detroit MI 48202

MIKALOW, ALFRED ALEXANDER, II, deep sea diver, marine surveyor, marine diving consultant; b. N.Y.C., Jan. 19, 1921; m. Janice Brenner, Aug. 1, 1960; children: Alfred Alexander, Jon Alfred. Student Rutgers U., 1940; MS, U. Calif., Berkeley, 1948; MA, Rochdale U. (Can.), 1950. Owner Coastal Diving Co., Oakland, Calif., 1950—, Divers Supply, Oakland, 1952—; dir. Coastal Sch. Deep Sea Diving, Oakland, 1950—; capt. and master rsch. vessel Coastal Researcher I; mem. Marine Inspection Bur., Oakland. marine diving contractor, cons. Mem. adv. bd. Medic Alert Found., Turlock, Calif., 1960—. Lt. comdr. USN, 1941-47, 49-50. Decorated Purple Heart, Silver Star. Mem. Divers Assn. Am. (pres. 1970-74), Treasury Recovery, Inc. (pres. 1972-75), Internat. Assn. Profl. Divers, Assn. Diving Contractors, Calif. Assn. Pvt. Edn. (no. v.p. 1971-72), Authors Guild, Internat. Game Fish Assn., U.S. Navy League, U.S. Res. Officers Assn., Tailhook Assn., U.S. Submarine Vets. WWII, Explorer Club (San Francisco), Calif. Assn. Marine Surveyors (pres. 1988—), Soc. Naval Archs. and Marine Engrs. (assoc.), Masons, Lions. Author: Fell's Guide to Sunken Treasure Ships of the World, 1972; (with H. Rieseberg) The Knight from Maine, 1974. Office: 320 29th Ave Oakland CA 94601-2104

MIKALSON, JON DENNIS, classics educator; b. Milw., Aug. 1, 1943; s. John Martin and Evelyn Kathryn (Heuser) M.; m. Mary Helen Villemonte, Aug. 28, 1966; children: Melissa, Jacquelyn. BA, U. Wis., 1965; postgrad., Am. Sch. Classical Studies, Athens, Greece, 1968-69; PhD, Harvard U., 1970. Asst. prof. classics U. Va., Charlottesville, 1970-75, assoc. prof., 1975-84, prof., 1984—, chmn. dept. classics, 1978-90; vis. scholar Corpus Christi Coll., Cambridge, Eng., 1977-78; mem. Inst. for Advanced Study, Princeton, N.J., 1984-85; Whitehead prof. Am. Sch. Classical Studies, 1995-96. Author: The Sacred and Civil Calendar of the Athenian Year, 1975, Athenian Popular Religion, 1983, Honor Thy Gods: Popular Religion in Greek Tragedy, 1991; contbr. articles to profl. and scholarly jours. James Rignall Wheeler fellow Am. Sch. Classical Studies, 1968-69, NEH fellow, 1977-78, Herodotus fellow Inst. for Advanced Study, 1984-85. Mem. Am. Philol. Assn., Am. Sch. Classical Studies, Archeol. Inst. of Am., Classical Assn. of Middle West and South (pres. so. sect. 1988-90), Classical Assn. of Va., Phi Beta Kappa, Phi Eta Sigma, Phi Kappa Phi, Omicron Delta Kappa. Club: Lions. Home: PO Box 664 Crozet VA 22932-0664 Office: University of Virginia Dept of Classics 451 Cabell Hall Charlottesville VA 22903-3196

MIKAN, GEORGE, retired basketball player; b. Joliet, Ill., June 18, 1959. Grad., Depaul U., 1946. Basketball player Chgo. Am. Gears, 1946-47; basketball player Mpls. Lakers, 1947-54, 55-56, coach, 1957-58. Named to Basketball Hall of Fame, 1959, NCAA All-Am., 1944-46; recipient greatest player award AP; selected NBA All-Star Team, 1952-54, named MVP, 1953; mem. Championship Team, 1947, 48, 49, 50, 52-54; led NBA in scoring, 1949-52. Office: care Basketball Hall Fame PO Box 179 Springfield MA 01101-0179

MIKE, DEBORAH DENISE, systems engineering consultant; b. Norfolk, Va., Oct. 19, 1959; d. William A. and Mophecia (Cook) Brickhouse. BA in Math., U. Va., 1981; postgrad., Johns Hopkins U., 1982-83; MS in Computer Systems Mgmt., U. Md., 1994. Primary systems engr. GTE Govt. Systems Corp., Rockville, Md., 1984-85, Vienna, Va., 1985-87; computer analyst Info. Systems and Networks Corp., Arlington, Va., 1987-88; realtor Mount Vernon Realty, Chevy Chase, Md., 1988-89; primary systems engr. Grumman Corp., McLean, Va., 1988-91, J.G. Van Dyke & Assocs., Alexandria, Va., 1991-93; systems engr. Pulse Engring., Inc., Beltsville, Md., 1993-94; sr. systems software quality assurance engr. Unisys at NASA, Greenbelt, Md., 1995-96; owner Quality Solutions Designs by Debbie, Adelphi, Md., 1996—, Enterprise Info. Svcs., Falls Church, Va., 1996—. Active Smithsonian Resident Assoc. Program, 1988; mem. Friends of the Kennedy Ctr. Mem. NAFE (bd. dirs. Reston chpt. 1986), Nat. Assn. Realtors, Md. Assn. Realtors, Montgomery County Bd. Realtors, N.Y. Inst. Photography, U. Va. Alumni Assn., U. Va. Club Washington. Avocations: sewing and fashion planning, photography, sketching, painting, designing jewely.

MIKEL, THOMAS KELLY, JR., laboratory administrator; b. East Chicago, Ind., Aug. 27, 1946; s. Thomas Kelly and Anne Katherine (Vrazo) M.; BA, San Jose State U., 1973; MA, U. Calif.-Santa Barbara, 1975. Asst. dir. Santa Barbara Underseas Found., 1975-76; marine biologist PJB Labs., Ventura, Calif., 1976-81; lab. dir. CRL Environ., Ventura, 1981-88; lab. dir. ABC Labs, Ventura, 1988—; instr. oceanography Ventura Coll., 1980-81. Chair joint task group, section author 20th edit. Std. Methods Examination Water & Wastewater APHA, 1996. With U.S. Army, 1968-70. Mem. Assn. Environ. Profls., Soc. Population Ecologists, ASTME (rsch. contbr. 10th ann. symposium 1986), Soc. Environ. Toxicology and Chemistry. Biol. coord. Anacapa Underwater Natural trail U.S. Nat. Park Svc., 1976; designer ecol. restoration program of upper Newport Bay, Orange County, Calif., 1978; rsch. contbr. 3d Internat. Artificial Reef Conf., Newport Beach, Calif., 1983, Ann. Conf. Am. Petroleum Inst., Houston. Democrat.

MIKELS, J(AMES) RONALD, bank executive; b. Knoxville, Tenn., Nov. 21, 1937; s. Jesse R. and Virginia L. (Walters) M.; m. Norma Jean Weatherly, Jan. 8, 1966; 1 child, J. Richard. M in Graphoanalysis, Internat. Graphoanalysis Soc., Chgo., 1961; BS, U. Tenn., 1980; MRE, Bethany Theol. Sem., 1993. Cert. human resources profl. Electronic data processing auditor Park Nat. Bank, Knoxville, 1956-78; retirement specialist U. Tenn., Knoxville, 1979-80; dir. pers. Home Fed. Bank, Knoxville, 1980—; instr. U. Tenn., Knoxville, 1972-77; mem. adv. com. Pellissippi State Coll., Knoxville, 1986-88; ct. handwriting expert, 1968—; instr. Am. Inst. Banking, 1996, 97. Contbr. articles to mags. and jours. Campaign coord. United Way, Knoxville, 1985-97; cons. Jr. Achievement, Knoxville, 1990, 92, 93, 94. Mem. Full Gospel Businessmen's Fellowship Internat., Tenn. League Savs. Instns. (bd. dirs. 1989). Wesleyan Methodist. Office: Home Fed Bank 515 Market St Knoxville TN 37902-2145

MIKELS, RICHARD ELIOT, lawyer; b. Cambridge, Mass., July 14, 1947; s. Albert Louis and Charlotte Betty (Shapiro) M.; m. Deborah Gwen Katz, Aug. 29, 1970; children: Allison Brooke, Robert Jarrett. BS in Bus. Adminstrn., Boston U., 1969, JD cum laude, 1972. Bar: Mass. 1972, U.S. Dist. Ct. Mass. 1974, U.S. Ct. Appeals (1st cir.) 1978. Legal examiner ICC, Washington, 1972-74; ptnr. Riemer & Braunstein, Boston, 1974-80; ptnr., chmn. comml. law sect. Peabody & Brown, Boston, 1980-88; mem., chmn. comml. law sect. Mintz, Levin, Cohn, Ferris, Glovsky and Popeo, P.C., Boston, 1988—. Contbr. articles to profl. jours. Tng. adv. com. Jewish Vocat. Svc., Boston, 1991, 95, 96, bd. dirs., 1995, 96, 97; vice-chair lawyers com. Combined Jewish Philanthropies, 1994, 95. Fellow Am. Coll. Bankruptcy; mem. ABA, Am. Bankruptcy Inst., Assn. Comml. Ins. Attys., Comml. Law League Am., Mass. Bar Assn., Boston Bar Assn. Home: 4 Barley Ln Wayland MA 01778-1600 Office: Mintz Levin Cohn Ferris Glovsky & Popeo PC Financial Center Boston MA 02111

MIKELSONS, J. GEORGE, air aerospace transportation executive. Chmn., CEO Am. Trans Air, Inc., Indpls. Office: Am Trans Air Inc Indpls Internat Airport Box 51609 Indianapolis IN 46251-0609

MIKESELL, MARVIN WRAY, geography educator; b. Kansas City, Mo., June 16, 1929; s. Loy George and Clara (Wade) M.; m. Reine-Marie de France, Apr. 1, 1957. B.A., UCLA, 1952, M.A., 1953; Ph.D., U. Calif.-Berkeley, 1959. Instr. to prof. geography U. Chgo., 1958—, chmn. dept. geography, 1969-74, 83-86; del. U.S. Nat. Commn. for UNESCO. Author: Northern Morocco, 1961; editor: Readings in Cultural Geography, 1962, Geographers Abroad, 1973, Perspectives on Environment, 1974. Fellow Am. Geog. Soc. (hon.); mem. Assn. Am. Geographers (pres. 1975-76, Disting. Career award 1995). Club: Quadrangle. Home: 1155 E 56th St Chicago IL 60637-1530 Office: Com Geog Studies 5828 S University Ave Chicago IL 60637-1515

MIKESELL, RAYMOND FRECH, economics educator; b. Eaton, Ohio, Feb. 13, 1913; s. Otho Francis and Josephine (Frech) M.; m. Desyl De-Lauder, July 6, 1937 (div.); children: George DeLauder and Norman De-Lauder (twins); m. Grace Schneiders, Apr. 12, 1997. Student, Carnegie Inst. Tech., 1931-33; BA cum laude, Ohio U., 1935, MA, 1935, PhD, 1939. Asst. prof. econ. U. Wash., 1937-41; economist OPA, Washington, 1941-42, U.S. Treasury Dept., 1942-46; rep. U.S. Treasury Dept., Cairo, Egypt, 1943-44; cons. U.S. Treasury Dept., 1946-47; on Middle East affairs FOA, 1953; chief fgn. minerals div. Pres.'s Materials Policy Commn., 1951-52; mem. staff Fgn. Econ. Policy Com. (Randall Com.), 1953-54; mem. U.S. Currency Mission to Saudi Arabia, 1948; spl. U.S. rep. to Israel, summer 1952; mem. U.S. mission to Israel, Ethiopia, summer 1953; prof. econs. U. Va., 1946-57; W.E. Miner prof. econs. U. Oreg., 1957-87, prof. econs., 1987—; dir. Inst. Internat. Studies and Overseas Adminstrn., 1958-60; assoc. dir. Inst. Internat. Studies and Overseas Adminstrn. U. Oreg., 1960-68; vis. prof. Grad. Inst. Internat. Studies, Geneva, 1964; sr. staff mem. Council Econ. Advisers, Exec. Office of Pres., 1955-56, cons. to Council Econ. Advisers, 1956-57; cons. Pan Am. Union, 1954-63, Dept. State, 1947-53, 63-67, 71-83, Ford Found., 1962, Dept. Commerce, 1962-64, ICA, 1952-53, 61-62, OAS, 1963-73, AID, 1964-71; mem. UN Econ. Commn. for Latin Am. working group on regional market, 1958; cons. Senate Fgn. Relations Com., 1962, 67, World Bank, 1968, Inter-Am. Devel. Bank, 1968-75; mem. panel advisers Sec. Treasury, 1965-69; sr. fellow Nat. Bur. Econ. Research, 1972-73. Author: U.S. Economic Policy and International Relations, 1952, Foreign Exchange in the Postwar World, 1954, The Emerging Pattern of International Payments, 1954, Foreign Investments in Latin Am, 1955, Promoting United States Private Investment Abroad, 1957, Agricultural Surpluses and Export Policy, 1958, U.S. Private and Government Investment Abroad, 1962, (with H. Chenery) Arabian Oil, 1949, (with M. Trued) Postwar Bilateral Payments Agreements, 1955, (with J. Behrman) Financing Free World Trade with the Sino-Soviet Bloc, 1958, Public International Lending for Development, 1966, (with R.W. Adler) Public External Financing of Devel. Banks, 1966, Public Fgn. Capital for Private Enterprises in Developing Countries, 1966, The Economics of Foreign Aid, 1968, Financing World Trade, 1969, (with others) Foreign Investment in the Petroleum and Mineral Industries, 1971, (with H. Furth) Foreign Dollar Balances and the International Role of the Dollar, 1974, Foreign Investment in the Copper Industry, 1975, The World Copper Industry, 1979, New Patterns of World Mineral Development, 1979, The Economics of Foreign Aid and Self-Sustaining Development, 1983, Foreign Investment in Mining Projects, 1983, Petroleum Company Operations and Agreements in the Developing Countries, 1984, Stockpiling Strategic Materials, 1986, Nonfuel Minerals: Foreign Dependence and National Security, 1987; (with John W. Whitney) The World Mining Industry: Investment Strategy and Public Policy, 1987, The Global Copper Industry: Problems and Prospects, 1988, (with Lawrence F. Williams) International Banks and the Environment, 1992, Economic Development and the Environment, 1992, The Bretton Woods Debates, 1994; mem. editorial adv. bd. Middle East Jour., 1947-58; mem. bd. editors: Am. Econ. Rev., 1953-55. Home: 2290 Spring Blvd Eugene OR 97403-1860

MIKESELL, RICHARD LYON, lawyer, financial counselor; b. Corning, N.Y., Jan. 29, 1941; s. Walter Ray and Clara Ellen (Lyon) M.; m. Anna May Creese, Mar. 16, 1973; 1 child, Joel. BSChemE, U. Calif., Berkeley, 1962; LLB, Duke U., 1965; BA in Liberal Studies, UCLA, 1977. Bar: U.S. Supreme Ct. 1971, Ohio 1965, Calif. 1967, U.S. Ct. Appeals (9th cir.) 1982, U.S. Ct. Appeals (2d cir.) 1993, U.S. Patent Office 1967. Patent atty. Procter & Gamble, Cin., 1965-66, Rocketdyne divsn. N.Am. Aviation, L.A., 1966-69; pvt. practice law L.A., 1969-81; prin. Law Offices of R.L. Mikesell, L.A., 1981—; fin. counselor L.A. Police Dept., 1986—; arbitrator Am. Arbitration Assn., L.A., 1980—. Pres. San Fernando Valley Fair Housing Coun., L.A., 1969-72, Valley Women's Ctr., L.A., 1990; line res. officer L.A. Police Dept., 1969-72. Named Res. Officer of Yr. L.A. Police Dept., 1990. Avocation: high power rifle shooting. Office: 14540 Hamlin St Ste B Van Nuys CA 91411-1626

MIKI, ARATA, law educator; b. Mifune, Kumamoto, Japan, Jan. 15, 1928; s. Gunji Yamashita and Chiyo M.; m. Michiko Kogure, May 9, 1959. LLB, Nagoya (Japan) Law Sch., 1953; postgrad., Nagoya Grad. Sch. Law, 1956. Prof. faculty law Kyoto (Japan) Sangyo U., 1969-79, leading prof. Grad. Sch. Law, 1972-79, prof., leading prof. faculty law Grad. Sch. Law, 1980—; fellow Japan Found., Tokyo, 1979-80; Japan Found. vis. fellow Rheinische Friedrich Wilhelms U. Bonn, Germany, 1979-80; sr. assoc. mem. governing body St. Anthony's Coll., U. Oxford, Eng., 1980; vicarious exec. dir. Inst. World Affairs, Tokyo, 1974-76; dean faculty law Kyoto Sangyo U., 1982-88, pres. Grad. Sch. Law, 1982-88; trustee Found. Kyoto Sangyo U., 1985-89. Author: Systematic Motivation to the Philosophy of Law, 1974; joint chmn./joint author: What is Law to Japanese?, 1974; proponent/joint editor: Acta Humanistica Scientifica Universitatis Sangio Kyotiensis, 1977, 78, 79; contbr. articles to profl. jours. Mem. Assn. Music, Opera and Culture, Tokyo, 1975—, Tokyo Round Table, 1985-95, Japan Com. for East Asia Econ. Cmty., Tokyo, 1992—, Japan Philanthropic Assn., Tokyo, 1992—. Named Hon. Citizen of Huntsville (Ala.), 1973. Mem. Internat. Assn. Philosophy Law and Social Philosophy, Inst. Nat. Politics, St. Anthony's Soc. U. Oxford. Avocations: walking, Japanese traditional Noh play, classical music, opera, pictures. Office: care Kyoto Sangyo U, 36 Kamigemo Motoyama Kitaku, Kyoto 603, Japan

MIKITA, JOSEPH KARL, broadcasting executive; b. nr. Richmond, Va., Oct. 3, 1918; s. John and Catherine (Wargofcak) M.; m. Mary Therese Benya, Nov. 26, 1942; children: Patty-Jane Mikita Cashman, Michael, M. Noël Mikita Garagiola. BS, Fordham U., 1939; MS, Columbia U., 1940. Treas., controller Capital Cities Broadcasting Co., Albany, N.Y., 1955-58; controller Westinghouse Broadcasting Co., Inc., N.Y.C., 1958-60, v.p. fin., 1960-64, v.p. fin. and adminstrn., 1964-65, sr. v.p., 1965-69, 1975—; also dir., exec. v.p. Westinghouse Electric Corp. for Broadcasting, Learning and Leisure Activities, N.Y.C., 1969-75; dir. Sutro Tower, Inc. Author: (with others) The Business of Broadcasting, 1964. Bd. dirs. Fordham U. Council, Albany County Workshop, Albany County Heart Assn., Citizens For Reasonable Growth, Boca Raton; chmn. bd. Instructional TV. Served to maj. AUS, 1940-45, ETO. Recipient Order of Merit (Silver), Westinghouse Electric Corp., Disting. Service Alumni award Fordham U., 1969. Mem. AICPA, Internat. Radio and TV Soc., N.Y. Soc. CPAs, Fin. Execs. Inst. (dir., past pres. Manhattan chpt.), Inst. Broadcasting Fin. Mgmt. (past dir.), Town Club, Westchester Country Club, Boca Raton Club, M.G.A., JDM Country Club, Royal Palm Yacht and Country Club, Rotary (1st v.p. N.Y.). Home: 3125 NE 7th Dr Boca Raton FL 33431-6906 Office: 90 Park Ave New York NY 10016

MIKITKA, GERALD PETER, investment banker, financial consultant; b. Chgo., July 7, 1943; s. Michael and Helen (Cuprisin) M.; m. Nancy Lee Parker, Mar. 6, 1977; children: Richard, Jeffrey, Jennifer. B.S.B.A. in Fin., Roosevelt U., 1966, postgrad., 1967. Diplomate: registered investment advisor. Sr. investment exec. Shearson Hammill & Co., Chgo., 1967-73; chmn., pres. Capital Directions, Inc., Chgo., 1973—; pres. CDI Fin. Advisors, Chgo., 1974—, CDI Properties, Chgo., 1974—, CDI Communications, Inc., Chgo., 1978—, A.B. Properties Inc., Chgo., 1986—, Am. Eagle Realty Inc., Chgo., 1988—, Grand Caribbean Properties Inc., Chgo., 1988, Cain Estates Inc., Chgo., 1988—, Caribbean Sea Properties Inc., Chgo., 1989—. Served with U.S. Army, 1967-69. Mem. Nat. Assn. Securities Dealers, Securities Investment Protection Assn., Broadcast Fin. Mgmt. Assn., Nat. Radio Broadcast Assn., Internat. Assn. Fin. Planning. Lodge: Rotary.

MIKKELSEN, ARLID VERNER AGERSKOV, retired basketball player; b. Fresno, Calif., Oct. 21, 1928. Grad., Hamline U., 1949. Basketball player Mpls. Lakers, 1949-59; coach Minn. Pipers, 1968-69. Named to Basketball Hall of Fame, 1995; selected All-NBA 2d Team, 1951, 52, 53, 55; record-holder for most disqualifications; mem. NBA Championship Team, 1950, 52, 53, 54. Office: care Basketball Hall Fame PO Box 179 Springfield MA 01101-0179

MIKKELSON, DEAN HAROLD, geological engineer; b. Devils Lake, N.D., July 25, 1922; s. John Harold and Theodora (Eklund) M.; m. Delphene Doss, May 30, 1946; 1 child, Lynn Dee Hoffman. Student, N.D. State Coll., 1940-41; midshipman, U.S. Naval Acad., 1942-45; BS in Geological Engring., U. N.D., 1956. Registered profl. engr., Okla. 2d officer U.S. Lines, Quaker Lines-States Lines, Portland, Oreg., 1945-48; ptnr. J.I. Case Farm Machinery & Packard Automobile Franchises, Devils Lake, N.D., 1948-52; oil and gas lease broker Devils Lake, N.D., 1952-54; geologist Sohio Petroleum Co., Oklahoma City, 1956-58; geol. engr. Petrobras, Belem do Para, Brazil, 1958-60; pvt. practice Oklahoma City, 1961-78; pres., owner Dogwatch Petroleum, Inc., Oklahoma City, 1978—; agrl. pilot, N.D., Mont., Tex., N.Mex., summers, 1952-56. Author: (as Dee Geo) Danny; contbr. articles to profl. jours. Candidate Okla. Rep. State Legislature, Oklahoma City, 1958; del. various county and state conv., N.D. and Okla., 1948-68. With N.D. N.G., 1938-40, U.S. Army Air Corps., 1942. Mem. Oklahoma City Geol. Soc., Masons, Shriners, Jesters, Am. Legion, Sportsmans Country Club. Republican. Avocations: hunting, fishing, golf, oil painting, singing. Office: Dogwatch Petroleum Inc 4430 NW 50 St Ste H Oklahoma City OK 73112-2295

MIKLASZEWSKI, JAMES ALAN, television news correspondent; b. Milw., July 8, 1949; s. Bernard Anthony Miklaszewski and LaVerne Dorothy (Venus) Montagano; m. Cheryl Ann Heyse; children: James Alexander, Jeffrey Alan. Reporter WISM Radio, Madison, Wis., 1970-71; new dir. WIZM Radio, LaCrosse, Wis., 1971-72; reporter WBAP Radio, Ft. Worth, 1972-75; news dir. KRXV Radio, Ft. Worth, 1975-80; corr. CNN, Dallas, N.Y.C., 1980-83; White House corr. CNN, Washington, 1983-84, nat. corr., 1984-85; Pentagon corr. NBC TV News, Washington, 1985-88, White House corr., 1988—. Recipient ACE award Nat. Cable Acad., 1983, Edward R. Murrow award Bnai Brith, 1985, Pres.' award Wesley Coll., 1994. Mem. White House Corrs. Assn. Methodist. Avocations: ornithology, golf. Office: NBC News Washington Bur 4001 Nebraska Ave NW Washington DC 20016-2733*

MIKLOSHAZY, ATTILA, bishop. Ordained priest Roman Cath. Ch., 1961, consecrated bishop, 1989. Titular bishop Castel Minore; bishop Apostolate to Hungarians, Scarborough, Ont., Can., 1989—. Mem. Jesuit Soc. Office: St Augustine's Sem, 2661 Kingston Rd, Scarborough, ON Canada M1M 1M3*

MIKLOVIC, DANIEL THOMAS, research director; b. St. Louis, Oct. 1, 1950; s. John Joseph and Ruby Irene (Cloyd) M.; m. Linda Lois Pinkley, July 12, 1975; 1 child, Aimee Linette. AS in Nuclear Tech., Air Force Community Coll., Randolph AFB, Tex., 1977; BSEE, U. Mo., 1979; MS in Systems Mgmt., U. So. Calif., 1986. Engr. Weyerhaeuser, Raymond, Wash., 1979-82, Scott Paper, Skowhegan, Maine, 1982-83; researcher Weyerhaeuser, Tacoma, 1983-86, mktg. mgr., 1986-88, tech. mgr., 1988-90, mgr. corp. planning, 1990-92; marketing dir. Indsl. Systems, Inc., Bothell, Wash., 1992-95; rsch. dir. Gartner Group, Stamford, Conn., 1995—; owner Mfg. Integration Planning Svcs., Issaquah, Wash., 1992—. Author: Real-Time Control Networks, 1993; contbr. monthly columnm Mfg. Comms., Automation and Control, Jour. Inst. of Measurement and Control publs. Chmn. Pierce Coll. Vocat. Adv. Com., Puyallup, Wash., 1985-91. Staff sgt. USAF, 1973-77. Mem. IEEE, TAPPI, Instrument Soc. Am., Indsl. Computing Soc. (fellow chpt. bd. dirs., pres.), Soc. Mfg. Engrs., Tau Beta Pi, Eta Kappa Nu, Delta Tau Delta. Office: Gartner Group 56 Top Gallant Rd Stamford CT 06902-7747

MIKULAS, JOSEPH FRANK, graphic designer, educator, painter; b. Jacksonville, Fla., Sept. 15, 1926; s. Joseph and Marina (Zeman) M.; m. Joyce Gregory Haddock, Sept. 29, 1946; children—Joyce Marina Mikulas Abney, Juliana Claire Mikulas Catlin. Student Harold Hilton Studios, 1942-50. Art dir. Peeples Displays, Inc., 1945-50, 53-56, Douglas Printing Co. Inc., 1950-53, 56-59; ptnr., graphic design exec. Benton & Mikulas Assocs., Inc., Jacksonville, 1960-67; pres. Mikulas Assocs., Inc., Jacksonville, 1968-92, exec. graphic designer, retired dir. communications, adj. prof. advt. design Jacksonville U.; mem. adv. bd. Pub. TV. Chmn. Youth Resources Bur.; chmn. Mayor's Medal Com. Served with USAAF, 1945. Recipient Gold medal Am. Advt. Fedn., 4th dist., 1971; numerous other awards, 1960-81. Sr. Warden, St. John's Cathedral. Mem. Advt. Fedn. of Jacksonville (past pres. 1970), Jacksonville Watercolor Soc. Republican. Clubs: San Jose Country, River, Art Dirs. of Jacksonville (past pres.). Lodges: Masons, Rotary (past pres. S. Jacksonville 1970, Paul Harris fellow), Torch of Jacksonville (past pres. 1977). Creator over 40 trademarks for local, regional, nat. and internat. use by corps. based in Jacksonville. Home: 2014 River Rd Jacksonville FL 32207-3906 Office: 3886 Atlantic Blvd Jacksonville FL 32207-2035

MIKULSKI, BARBARA ANN, senator; b. Balt., July 20, 1936; d. William and Christine (Kutz) M. BA, Mt. St. Agnes Coll., 1958; MSW, U. Md., 1965; LLD (hon.), Goucher Coll., 1973, Hood Coll., 1978, Bowie State U., 1989, Morgan State U., 1990, U. Mass., 1991; DHL (hon.), Pratt Inst., 1974. Tchr. Vista Tng. Ctr. Mount St. Mary's Sem., Balt.; social worker Balt. Dept. Social Services, 1961-63, 66-70; mem. Balt. City Council, 1971-76, 95th-99th Congresses from 3d Md. Dist., 1977-87; U.S. senator from Md., 1987—, sec. Dem. Conf. 104th Congress; adj. prof. Loyola Coll., 1972-76. Bd. visitors U.S. Naval Acad. Recipient Nat. Citizen of Yr. award Buffalo Am.-Polit. Eagle, 1973, Woman of Yr. Bus. & Profl. Women's Club Assn., 1973, Outstanding Alumnus U. Md. Sch. Social Work, 1973, Govt. Social Responsibility award, 1991. Mem. LWV.

MIKULSKI, PIOTR WITOLD, mathematics educator; b. Warsaw, Poland, July 20, 1925; came to U.S., 1957; s. Julian and Zofia (Zalewska) M.; m. Barbara H. Mikulski, Sept. 2, 1960; 1 son, Antony F. B.S., Sch. Stats., Warsaw, Poland, 1951, M.S., 1952; Ph.D., U. Calif.-Berkeley, 1961. Adj. Sch. Stats., 1950-57, Inst. Math., Warsaw, Poland, 1952-57; teaching and research asst. U. Calif.-Berkeley, 1957-61; asst. prof. math. U. Ill., Urbana, 1961-62; asst. prof. U. Md., College Park, 1962-66, assoc. prof., 1966-70, prof., 1970. Assoc. editor: Am. Jour. Math. and Mgmt. Sci., 1982—; contbr. articles to profl. jours. Mem. Inst. Math. Stats., Polish Inst. Arts and Scis. Am. Home: 2525 Sandy Run Ct Annapolis MD 21401-7371 Office: U Md Dept Math College Park MD 20742

MIKUS, ELEANORE ANN, artist; b. Detroit, July 25, 1927; d. Joseph and Bertha (Englot) M.; m. Richard Burns, July 6, 1949 (div. 1963); children: Richard, Hillary, Gabrielle. Student, Mich. State U., 1946-49, U. Mex., summer 1948; B.F.A., U. Denver, 1957, M.A., 1967; postgrad., Art Students League, 1958, NYU, 1959-60. Asst. prof. Cornell U., Ithaca, N.Y., 1979-80, assoc. prof., 1980-92, prof. art, 1992-94, prof. emerita, 1994—; asst. prof. art Monmouth Coll., West Long Branch, N.J., 1966-70, prof. Cornell, Rome, 1989; vis. lectr. painting Cooper Union, N.Y.C., 1970-72, Central Sch. Art and Design, London, 1973-77, Harrow (Eng.) Coll. Tech. and Art, 1975-76. Exhibited in 14 one-person shows at, Pace Gallery, N.Y.C. and O.K. Harris Gallery, N.Y.C., Baskett Gallery, Cin., 1982, 84, 85; represented in permanent collections including, Mus. Modern Art, N.Y.C., Whitney Mus., N.Y.C., Los Angeles County Mus., Cin. Mus., Birmingham (Ala.) Mus. Art, Indpls. Mus. Art, Nat. Gallery Art, Washington, Victoria and Albert Mus., London, Library of Congress, Washington; subject of book Eleanore Mikus, Shadows of the Real (by Robert Hobbs and Judith Bernstock), 1991. Guggenheim fellow, 1966-67; Tamarind fellow, summer 1968; MacDowell fellow, summer 1969; grantee Cornell U., 1988. Mem. AAUP. Home: PO Box 6586 Ithaca NY 14851-6586 Office: Cornell U Dept Art Tjaden Hall Ithaca NY 14853 *I have always adhered in my paintings to an almost classic simplicity of expression; it is the simplicity of the child as seen through the eyes of the artist—impulsive, dramatic and yet close to the rhythm of childlike expression, born of an innocence which is all the more sophisticated for being so. It doesn't pretend—it just is.*

MIKVA, ABNER JOSEPH, lawyer, retired federal judge; b. Milw., Jan. 21, 1926; s. Henry Abraham and Ida (Fishman) M.; m. Zoe Wise, Sept. 19, 1948; children: Mary, Laurie, Rachel. JD cum laude, U. Chgo., 1951; DL (hon.), U. Ill., Am. U., Northwestern U., Tulane U.; DHL (hon.), Hebrew U.; DHL (Hon.), U. Wis.; DL (hon.), Ill. Inst. Tech. Bar: Ill. 1951, D.C. 1978. Law clk. to U.S. Supreme Ct. Justice Sherman Minton, 1951; ptnr. firm Devoe, Shadur, Mikva & Plotkin, Chgo., 1952-68, D'Ancona, Pflaum, Wyatt & Riskind, 1973-74; lectr. Northwestern U. Law Sch., Chgo., 1973-75, U. Pa. Law Sch., 1983-85, Georgetown Law Sch., 1986-88, Duke U. Law Sch., Durham, N.C., 1990-91, U. Chgo. Law Sch., 1992-93; mem. Ill. Gen. Assembly from 23d Dist., 1956-66, 91st-92d Congresses from 2d Dist. Ill., 94th-96th Congresses from 10th Dist. Ill., ways and means com., judiciary com.; chmn. Dem. Study Group; resigned, 1979; judge U.S. Circuit Ct. Appeals D.C., 1979-91, chief judge, 1991-94; counsel to the President The White House, Washington, 1994-96; vis. prof., Walter Schaefer chair in pub. policy U. Chgo., 1996—. Author: The American Congress: The First Branch, 1983, The Legislative Process, 1995. Served with USAAF, World War II. Recipient Page One award Chgo. Newspaper Guild, 1964; Best Legislator award Ind. Voters Ill., 1956-66, Alumni medal U. Chgo., 1996; named one of ten Outstanding Young Men in Chgo., Jr. Assn. Commerce and Industry, 1961. Mem. ABA, Chgo. Bar Assn. (bd. mgrs. 1962-64), D.C. Bar Assn., Am. Law Inst., U.S. Assn. Former Mems. Congress, Order of Coif, Phi Beta Kappa. Home: 5020 S Lake Shore Dr PH8 Chicago IL 60615

MILAM, JOHN DANIEL, pathologist, educator; b. Kilgore, Tex., May 22, 1933; s. Ott G. and Effie (White) M.; m. Carol Jones Milam, Aug. 1, 1959; children: Kay, Beth, John Jr., Julie. BS, La. State U., 1955, MS, 1957, MD, 1960. Attending pathologist St. Luke's Episcopal Hosp., Houston, 1967-89; cons. in pathology Tex. Children's Hosp., Houston, 1979—; prof. lab. medicine M.D. Anderson Cancer Ctr., U. Tex., Houston, 1990—; prof. pathology and lab. medicine U. Tex. Med. Sch., Houston, 1989—; chief pathology Lyndon B. Johnson Gen. Hosp., Houston, 1995—. Contbr. numerous articles to profl. jours., chpts., abstracts to books. Trustee Am. Bd. Pathology, 1985-96, pres., 1995; bd. dirs. Harris County chpt. ARC, 1978—. Mem. Am. Assn. Blood Banks (pres. 1984, Disting. Svc. award 1988), Tex. Soc. Pathologists (George T. Caldwell award 1981). Republican. Baptist. Home: 11927 Arbordale Ln Houston TX 77024-5001 Office: U Tex Houston Med Sch Dept Pathology 6431 Fannin St Rm 2022 Houston TX 77030-1501

MILAM, WILLAM BRYANT, diplomat, economist; b. Bisbee, Ariz., July 24, 1936; s. Burl Vivian and Alice Vera (Pierce) M.; m. Faith Adele Handley; step-children: Erika, Fred. AB, Stanford U., 1959; MA, U. Mich., 1970; postgrad., Am. U., 1973. Polit. officer Dept. of State, Washington, 1967-69; fin. economist Dept. of State, Washington and, U.S. Embassy, London, 1970-75; energy economist Dept. of State, Washington, 1975-77, dep. office dir., 1977-80, office dir., 1980-83; dep. chief of mission U.S. Embassy, Yaounde, Cameroon, 1983-85; dep. asst. sec. Dept. of State, Washington, 1985-90; U.S. amb. to Bangladesh, 1990-93; spl. negotiator Oceans Environ. Sci. Dept. State, Washington, 1993-95; chief of mission U.S. Embassy, Monrovia, Liberia, 1995—. Calif. State scholar, 1956-59; recipient James Clement Dunn award Dept. of State, 1981, Superior Honor award, 1983, Pres.'s Meritorious Svc. award U.S. Govt., 1990, Pres. Outstanding Svc. award, 1991. Avocations: reading, golf. Home and Office: US Embassy Monrovia Dept of State Washington DC 20521-8800

MILAN, MARJORIE LUCILLE, early childhood education educator; b. Ludlow, Colo., June 24, 1926; d. John B. and Barbara (Zenonian) Pinamont; m. John Francis Milan, June 18, 1949; children: Barbara, J. Mark, Kevin. BA, U. Colo., 1947, MA, 1978; PhD, U. Denver, 1983. Cert. tchr., adminstr., supt., Colo. Tchr. Boulder (Colo.) Pub. Schs., 1947-49, Denver Pub. Schs., 1949-51, 67—; adminstr. T. Tot Kindergarten, Denver, 1951-55; tchr. Colo. Women's Coll., Denver, 1956-57; adminstr. Associated Schs., Denver, 1956-67; adv. bd. George Washington Carver Nursery, Denver, 1960-85. Mem. Assn. Childhood Edn. (state bd. 1960—, Hall of Excellence 1991), Rotary (pres. chpt. 1994-95), Philanthropic Ednl. Orgn., Phi Delta Kappa, Delta Kappa Gamma. Avocations: swimming, music. Home: 1775 Lee St Lakewood CO 80215-2855

MILAN, THOMAS LAWRENCE, accountant; b. Balt., Md., Nov. 23, 1941; s. Lawrence Francis and Mary Elizabeth (Feeley) M.; m. Mary Agnes LaCoste; children: Thomas Brian, Kathrine Mary. BS, U. Balt., 1965; attended Darden Sch. U. Va., 1987. CPA, Md., Va., Washington. With Ernst & Young, Balt., 1965-80, ptnr., 1976-80, Ernst & Young, Richmond, Va., 1980-88, regional dir. acctg. and auditing, Washington, 1988—; nat. dir. SEC practice Ernst & Young, 1989—. Dir. U. Balt. Edn. Found. Mem. AICPA (chmn. SEC regulations com. 1994—), Annapolis Yacht Club, Commonwealth Club, TPC at Avenel, Beta Alpha. Republican. Roman Catholic. Avocations: boating, waterfowling, tennis. Home: 9721 Meyer Point Dr Rockville MD 20854-5420

MILANDER, HENRY MARTIN, educational consultant; b. Northampton, Pa., Apr. 17, 1939; s. Martin Edward and Margaret Catherine (Makovetz) M.; children: Martin Henry, Beth Ann. BS summa cum laude, Lock Haven U., Pa., 1961; MA, Bowling Green (Ohio) State U., 1962; EdS (Future Faculty fellow 1964), U. No. Iowa, 1965; EdD, Ill. State U., Normal, 1967. Instr. Wartburg Coll., Waverly, Iowa, 1962-64; asst. prof. Ill. State U., 1966-67; dean instrn. Belleville (Ill.) Area Coll., 1967-69; v.p. acad. affairs Lorain County Community Coll., Elyria, Ohio, 1969-72; pres. Olympic Coll., Bremerton, Wash., 1972-87, Northeastern Jr. Coll., Sterling, Colo., 1988-95; ednl. cons., 1995—; pres. Bremers, Inc., 1986-87. Contbr. articles to profl. jours. Pres. Kitsap County Comprehensive Health Planning Council, 1975-76; pres. Logan County Colo. United Way, 1992-93. Recipient Faculty Growth award Wartburg Coll., 1963, Community Service award, 1975, Chief Thunderbird award, 1985. Mem. Am. Assn. C.C., Am. Assn. Sch. Adminstrs., N.W. Assn. Cmty. and Jr. Colls., Wash. Assn. C.C. (pres. 1984-85), Wash. C.C. Computing Consortium (chmn. bd. dirs. 1985-87), Puget Sound Naval Bases Assn. (pres. 1982-86), Wash. Assn. C.C. Pres. (pres. 1984-85), Bremerton Area C. of C. (pres. 1977-78), Colo. Assn. C.C. Pres. (pres. 1993-94), Rotary (pres. Sterling Club 1992-93), Kappa Delta Pi, Phi Delta Kappa. Lutheran. Home: 12779 Vista Dr NE Bainbridge Island WA 98110-4314

MILANICH, JERALD THOMAS, archaeologist, museum curator; b. Painesville, Ohio, Oct. 13, 1945; s. John Joseph and Jean Marie (Bales) M.; m. Maxine L. Margolis, Dec. 20, 1970; 1 child, Nara Bales. BA, U. Fla., 1967, MA, 1968, PhD, 1971. Cert. Soc. Profl. Archaeologists, 1975. Post doctoral fellow Smithsonian Inst., Washington, 1971-72; asst. prof. anthropology U. Fla., Gainesville, 1972-75; asst. curator Fla. Mus. Natural History, 1975-77; assoc. curator, 1977-81, chmn. dept. anthropology, 1981-83, 91—, curator, 1981—. Author: (with Samuel Proctor) Tacachale—Essays on the Indians of Florida and Southeastern Georgia during the Historic Period, 1978; (with Charles Fairbanks) Florida Archaeology, 1980; McKeithen Weeden Island, 1984; Early Prehistoric Southeast, 1985; (with Susan Milbrath) First Encounters, Spanish Explorations in the Caribbean and the United States, 1492-1570, 1989; The Hernando de Soto Expedition, 1990; Earliest Hispanic-Native America Interactions in the Greater American Southwest, 1991, (with Charles Hudson) Hernando de Soto and the Indians of Florida, 1993, Archaeology of Precolumbian Florida, 1994, Florida Indians and the Invasion of Europe, 1995, The Timucuas, 1996. Recipient Ripley P. Bullen awards, 1980, Rembert Patrick Book award, 1994, 95; grantee NSF, 1970-71, 73-75, 77-81, 82, Wentworth Found., 1976-77, 81-84, 91, NEH, 1985, 87-89. Mem. Am. Anthrop. Assn., Soc. Am. Archaeology (exec. bd. 1990-93), Soc. Profl. Archeologists (pres. 1981-82), So. Anthrop. Soc., S.E. Archeol. Conf. (pres. 1986-88), Explorers Club. Office: Fla Mus Natural History Gainesville FL 32611

MILANOVICH, NORMA JOANNE, training company executive, occupational educator; b. Littlefork, Minn., June 4, 1945; d. Lyle Albert and Loretta (Leona) Drake; m. Rudolph William Milanovich, Mar. 18, 1943; 1 child, Rudolph William Jr. BS in Home Econs., U. Wis., Stout, 1968; MA in Curriculum and Instrn., U. Houston, 1973, EdD in Curriculum and Program Devel., 1982. Instr. human svcs. dept. U. Houston, 1971-75; dir. videos project U. N.Mex., Albuquerque, 1976-78, dir. vocat. edn. equity ctr., 1978-88, asst. prof. tech. occupational edn., 1982-88, coord. occupational vocat. edn. programs, 1983-88, dir. consortium rsch. and devel. in occupational edn., 1984-88; pres. The Alpha Connecting Tng. Corp., Albuquerque, 1988—; adj. instr. Cen. Tng. Acad., Dept. Energy, Wackenhut; mem. faculty U. Phoenix; mem. adj. faculty So. Ill. U., Lesley Coll., Boston. Author: Model Equitable Behavior in the Classroom, 1983, Handbook for Vocational-Technical Certification in New Mexico, 1985, A Vision for Kansas: Systems of Measures and Standards of Performance, 1992, Workplace Skills: The Employability Factor, 1993; editor: Choosing What's Best for You, 1982, A Handbook for Handling Conflict in the Classroom, 1983, Starting Out. . .A Job Finding Handbook for Teen Parents, Going to Work. . Job Rights for Teens; author: JTPA Strategic Marketing Plan, 1990, We, The Arcturians, 1990, Sacred Journey to Atlantis, 1991, The Light Shall Set You Free, 1996, JTPA Strategic Mktg. Plan, 1990; editor: Majestic Raise newsletter, 1996, Celestial Voices newsletter, 1991-96. Bd. dirs. Albuquerque Single Parent Occupational Scholarship Program, 1984-86; del. Youth for Understanding Internat. Program, 1985-90; mem. adv. bd. Southwestern Indian Poly. Inst., 1984-88; com. mem. Region VI Consumer Exch. Com., 1982-84; ednl. lectures, tng., tour dir. internat. study tours to Japan, Austria, Korea, India, Nepal, Mex., Eng., Greece, Egypt, Australia, New Zealand, Fed. Republic Germany, Israel, Guatemala, Peru, Bolivia, Chile, Easter Island, Tibet, China, Hong Kong, Turkey, Italy, Russia, Ukraine, Sweden, Norway, Kenya, Tanzania, Zimbabwe, North Pole Arctic Region, Antarctica, Argentina, Ireland, Scotland. Grantee N.Mex. Dept. Edn., 1976-78, 78-86, 83-86, HEW, 1979, 80, 81, 83, 84, 85, 86, 87. Mem. ASTD, Am. Vocat. Assn., Vocat. Edn. Equity Coun., Nat. Coalition for Sex Equity Edn., Am. Home Econs. Assn., Inst. Noetic Scis., N.Mex. Home Econs. Assn., N.Mex. Vocat. Edn. Assn., N.Mex. Adv. Coun. on Vocat. Edn., Greater Albuquerque C. of C., NAFE, Phi Delta Kappa, Phi Upsilon Omicron, Phi Theta Kappa. Democrat. Roman Catholic.

MILASKI, JOHN JOSEPH, business transformation industry consultant; b. Johnson City, N.Y., Sept. 16, 1959; s. John Walter and Nellie Joan (Panaro) M.; m. Ann Mildred Caldwell, Jan. 22, 1994. AAS, Broome C.C., 1979; BSEE, Rochester Inst. Tech., 1984; MBA, Syracuse U., 1991. Registered engr., N.Y.; cert. bus. transformation cons. Design engr. IBM, Endicott, N.Y., 1979-84; systems engr. IBM, Endicott, 1984-85, mktg. cons., 1985-91, cons. Cons. & Sys. Integration Svcs. upstate N.Y., 1992-94; cons. Worldwide Document Mgmt. Solutions Group IBM, 1995-96, con. Worldwide Cons. Svcs., 1996—; Ga. state advisor to Nat. Rep. Senatorial Com. Inventor. Vol. IBM Olympic Force Team 1996 Summer Olympics; trust mgr. Nat. Trust for Historical Preservation; charter mem. Statue of Liberty-Ellis Island Found., Inc.; Ga. state advisor Nat. Rep. Senatorial Com. Recipient Utilities Industry Mktg. Excellence award IBM Systems Engring. Symposium, 1989, 91. Mem. IEEE (sr.), ASME (sr.), Am. Mgmt. Assn., Am. Prodn. and Inventory Control Soc. (sr.), Internat. Platform Assn., Computer and Automated Sys. Assn., N.Y. State Sheriff's Assn., Ga. State Sheriff's Assn., Ga. State Troopers Assn., U.S. Holocaust Meml. Mus. (charter mem.), IBM 100 Percent Club, U.S. C. of C., Internat. Directory of Disting. Leadership, Nat. Mus. of the Am. Indian (charter), Nat. WWII Meml. Soc. (charter), Statue of Liberty-Ellis Island Found. (charter), Libr. of Congress (charter), Nat. Trust for Historic Preservation, Centennial Olympic Pk. in Atlanta (constructing donor). Republican. Roman Catholic. Avocations: skiing, skating, tennis, sailing, chopping wood. Home: 6170 Song Breeze Trce Duluth GA 30155

MILAVSKY, HAROLD PHILLIP, real estate executive; b. Limerick, Sask., Can., Jan. 25, 1931; s. Jack and Clara M. B in Commerce, U. Sask., Saskatoon, Can., 1953; LLD (hon.), U. Sask., 1995, U. Calgary, 1995. Chief acct., treas., controller Loram Internat. Ltd. div. Mannix Co. Ltd., Calgary, Alta., Can., 1956-65; v.p., chief fin. officer Power Corp. Devels. Ltd., Calgary, Alta., Can., 1965-69; exec. v.p., bd. dirs. Great West Internat. Equities Ltd. (name now Trizec Corp. Ltd.), Calgary, Alta., Can., 1976-94; pres. Trizec Corp. Ltd., Calgary, Alta., Can., 1976-86, bd. dirs., 1976-94, chmn., 1986-93; chmn. Quantico Capital Corp., Calgary, 1994—; bd. dirs. Brascan Ltd., Toronto, Can., Toronto, London Life Ins. Co., London Ins. Group Ltd., London Reins. Group, Nova Corp. Alberta, Calgary, Telus Corp., Edmonton, Encal Energy, Inc., Calgary, Prime West Energy Inc., Calgary. Past dir. Terry Fox Humanitarian Award Program; past dir. Conf. Bd. Can.; past. gov. Acctg. Edn. Found. Alta.; hon. col. 14th Svc. Battalion, Calgary. Recipient Commemorative medal B'nai Brith, 1992. Fellow Inst. Chartered Accts. Alta.; mem. Inst. Chartered Accts. Sask., Can. Inst. Pub. Real Estate Cos. (past pres., bd. dirs.), Can. C. of C. (past chmn.), Internat. Profl. Hockey Alumni (founding dir.), Petroleum Club, Ranchmen's Club. Avocations: skiing, tennis, horseback riding. Office: Quantico Capital Corp, 1920-855 Second St SW, Calgary, AB Canada T2P 4J7

MILBANK, JEREMIAH, foundation executive; b. N.Y.C., Mar. 24, 1920; s. Jeremiah and Katharine (Schulze) M.; m. Andrea Hunter, July 19, 1947 (dec. Oct. 1982); children: Jeremiah III, Victoria Milbank Whitney, Elizabeth

Milbank Archer, Joseph H.; m. Rose Jackson Sheppard, May 4, 1991. B.A., Yale U., 1942; M.B.A., Harvard U., 1948; L.H.D. (hon.), Ithaca (N.Y.) Coll., 1976, Sacred Heart U., Conn.; LL.D., Manhattan Coll. With J.M. Found., N.Y.C.; pres. J.M. Found., 1971—; pres. Cypress Woods Corp., 1972—. Author: First Century of Flight in America, 1942. Chmn. emeritus Boys and Girls Clubs Am.; hon. pres. Internat. Ctr. for the Disabled, 1991—; fin. chmn. Rep. Nat. Com., 1969-72, 75-77. Lt. USNR, 1943-46. Mem. Brook Club, River Club (N.Y.C.), Round Hill Club (Greenwich), Yale Club. Republican. Home: 535 Lake Ave Greenwich CT 06830-3831 Office: 60 E 42nd St New York NY 10165

MILBOURNE, WALTER ROBERTSON, lawyer; b. Phila., Aug. 27, 1933; s. Charles Gordon and Florie Henderson (Robertson) M.; m. Georgena Sue Dyer, June 19, 1965; children: Gregory Broughton, Karen Elizabeth, Walter Robertson, Margaret Henderson. A.B., Princeton U., 1955; LL.B., Harvard U., 1958. Bar: Pa. 1959. Assoc. firm Pepper, Hamilton & Sheetz, Phila., 1959-65, Obermayer, Rebmann, Maxwell & Hippel, Phila., 1965-67; ptnr. Obermayer, Rebmann, Maxwell & Hippel, 1968-84, Saul, Ewing, Remick & Saul, 1984—; bd. dirs. Pa. Lumbermen's Mut. Ins. Co., Phila. Reins. Corp.; co-chmn. Nat. Conf. Lawyers and Collection Agys., 1979-90; chmn. bus. litigation com. Def. Rsch. Inst., 1986-89, mem. law instsn. com., 1989-95. Chmn. mental health budget sect. Phila. United Fund, 1967-70. Served with Army N.G., 1958-64. Fellow Am. Coll. Trial Lawyers (mem. internat. com. 1992-93); mem. ABA, Pa. Bar Assn., Phila. Bar Assn., Internat. Assn. Def. Counsel (exec. com. 1985-88, pres. IADC Found. 1997—), Assn. Def. Counsel, Union League, Merion Cricket Club, Princeton Club, Idle Hour Tennis Club (pres. 1968-68, Phila. Lawn Tennis Assn. (pres. 1969-70). Republican. Home: 689 Fernfield Cir Wayne PA 19087-2002 Office: Saul Ewing Remick & Saul 3800 Centre Sq W Philadelphia PA 19102

MILBRATH, ROBERT HENRY, retired petroleum executive; b. Apr. 17, 1912; s. Paul and Mabel (Volkman) M.; m. Margaret Ripperger, Jan. 19, 1940; children: Robert S., Constance, Susan. B.S., U.S. Naval Acad., 1934. With Standard Oil Co. N.J., 1934-74; v.p., gen. mgr. Esso Sociedad Anonima Petrolera Argentina, 1938-42, 45-50; area contact East Coast South Am., mktg. coordination, 1950-52; dir. Internat. Petroleum Co., 1954—, v.p., 1956; v.p., dir. Esso Export Corp. N.Y., 1957-59, exec. v.p., dir., 1959-61; pres., dir. chmn. exec. com. Esso Internat., Inc. (formerly Esso Export Corp.), 1961-66; exec. v.p. Esso Europe, 1966-68; logistics coordinator Standard Oil Co. (N.J.) (now Exxon Corp.), 1968-69, dir., v.p., 1969-70, dir., sr. v.p., 1970-73, ret., 1974. Cons. Boys Clubs Am., 1978-84. Served to lt. comdr. USNR; asst. naval attache 1942, Buenos Aires; chief Latin Am. sect. Army-Navy Petroleum Bd. 1943-45, Washington. Mem. U.S. Naval Acad. Alumni Assn. Republican. Clubs: Univeristy (N.Y.C.), Ponte Vedra Club. Home: 214 Pablo Ct Ponte Vedra Beach FL 32082-1802

MILBURN, HERBERT THEODORE, federal judge; b. Cleveland, Tenn., May 26, 1931; s. J.E. and Hazel (Shanks) M.; m. Elaine Dillow, Aug. 23, 1957; children: Blair Douglas, Elizabeth Elaine. Student, U. Chattanooga, 1949-50, Boston U., 1950-51; BS, East Tenn. State U., 1953; JD, U. Tenn., 1959. Bar: Tenn. 1959, U.S. Supreme Ct. 1971. Assoc. Folts, Bishop, Thomas, Leitner & Mann, Chattanooga, 1959-63; ptnr. Bishop, Thomas, Leitner, Mann & Milburn, Chattanooga, 1963-73; judge Hamilton County Cir. Ct., Chattanooga, 1973-83, U.S. Dist. Ct. (ea. dist.) Tenn., Chattanooga, 1983-84; judge U.S. Ct. Appeals (6th cir.), Chattanooga, 1984—, sr. judge, 1996—; mem. faculty Nat. Jud. Coll. U. Nev., Reno, 1980, Tenn. Jud. Acad., Vanderbilt U., Nashville, 1982. Pres. Hamilton County Young Reps., Chattanooga, 1965; mem. Chancellor's Roundtable U. Tenn., Chattanooga, 1983-86; pres. Lakeside Kiwanis, 1964. With U.S. Army Security Agy., 1953-56. Recipient award Chattanooga Bd. Realtors, 1987, Outstanding Alumnus award East Tenn. State U., 1988; named Outstanding Young Rep., Hamilton County Young Reps., 1965. Mem. ABA, Tenn. Bar Assn. (commr. 1971-73, mem. profl. ethics and grienvance com.), Chattanooga Bar Assn. (sec.-treas. 1967), Fed. Bar Assn. (chairperson U.S. jud. conf. com. on adminstrv. office of U.S. cts. 1994—), Am. Legion, East Tenn. State U. Found., Signal Mountain Golf and Country Club, Univ. Club Cin., Kiwanis. Republican. Episcopalian. Office: US Ct Appeals PO Box 750 Chattanooga TN 37401-0750

MILBURN, RICHARD ALLAN, aerospace company executive; b. Washington, May 30, 1933; s. Robert Andrew and Anna Janet (Schmidtman) M.; m. Joan (Frances) Hurst, Oct. 15, 1955; children: Jennifer Leigh, Michele Lynn. BS in Aeronautic and Space Engring. with honors, Okla. U., 1964, MS in Aerospace Engring. with honors, 1965. Commd. 2d lt. USAF, 1954, advanced through grades to col., 1980, interceptor pilot Aerospace Def. Command, 1955-64; designer, supr. constrn. ultra low speed wind tunnel Okla. U. Rsch. Inst., 1964-65, project engr. Aerospace Def. Command, 1965-68, chief weapons system div. Joint Chiefs of Staffs, 1968-71; asst. air attache, chief Fgn. Tech. Office Okla. U. Rsch. Inst., London, 1971-75; deputy chief East Asia divsn., chief east and south Asia Defense Security Agy. Dept. Def., 1975-77; chief Mut. Def. Assistance Office Am. Embassy, Tokyo, 1977-80; chief rsch., devel., and systems acquisition Mgmt. Policy div. Hdqrs. USAF, 1980, ret., 1980; dir. def. programs Grumman Internat., Inc., 1980-82, v.p. def. programs, 1982-85, v.p. Washington ops., 1985-87, sr. v.p., 1987-94; v.p. policy, plan and industrial corp. Northrop Grumman Internat., Arlington, Va., 1994—; chmn. fin. and compensation com., mem. exec. com. US/ROC Econ. Coun.,1991 chmn. NATO Industrial adv. group, Brussels, 1996—; bd. dirs. Robert C. Byrd Nat. Aviation Edn. and Tng. Ctr., 1990—. Fellow AIAA (assoc.); mem. Nat. Security Industries Assn. (bd. dirs. Washington), Am. Def. Preparedness Assn. (bd. dirs. Washington), Am. League Export and Security Assistance (chmn., pres. 1994—), Royal Aero. Soc., Aerospace Industries Assn. (mem. internat. coun.), Order of Daedalians. Methodist. Home: 2200 Hunter Mill Rd Vienna VA 22181-3025 Office: Northrop Grumman Internat 1000 Wilson Blvd Ste 2400 Arlington VA 22209-3901

MILBURN, RICHARD HENRY, physics educator; b. Newark, June 3, 1928; s. Richard Percy and Lucy Elizabeth (Karr) M.; m. Nancy Jeannette Stafford, Aug. 25, 1951; children—Sarah Stafford, Anne Douglas. A.B., Harvard U., 1948, A.M., 1951, Ph.D., 1954. Instr. Harvard U., Cambridge, Mass., 1954, 56-57, asst. prof., 1957-61; assoc. prof. physics Tufts U., Medford, Mass., 1961-65, prof., 1965—, John Wade prof., 1990—; Fulbright lectr., India, 1984. Trustee Cambridge Friends Sch., 1989-95. With U.S. Army, 1954-56. Sheldon travelling fellow, 1948-49; NSF fellow, 1952-53; Guggenheim fellow, 1960. Fellow Am. Phys. Soc. (past chmn. New Eng. sect.); mem. Am. Assn. Physics Tchrs., AAAS, AAUP. Research on high energy and elementary particles physics. Home: 1 Plymouth Rd Winchester MA 01890-3620 Office: Tufts Univ Medford MA 02155

MILBURY, MIKE, professional hockey coach; b. Boston, 1953; married; 1 child, Caitlin. Player Boston Bruins, NHL, 1976-87, coach, gen. mgr. Am. Hockey League affiliate Maine, 1987-89, head coach, asst. gen. mgr., 1989-91, asst. gen. mgr., 1991-96; gen. mgr. N.Y. Islanders, 1996—. Office: New York Islanders Nassau Collisium Uniondale NY 11553*

MILCHAN, ARNON, film producer; b. Dec. 6, 1944. Prodr.: (plays) Tomb, It's So Nice To Be Civilized, Amadeus (Paris prodn.), (TV) MASADA, 1981, (films) The Medusa Touch, 1978, The King of Comedy, 1983, Once Upon a Time in America, 1984, Brazil, 1985, Stripper, 1986, Legend, 1986, Man on Fire, 1987, The Adventures of Baron Munchausen, 1989, Who's Harry Crumb, 1989, The War of the Roses, 1989, Big Man on Campus, 1990, Pretty Woman, 1990, Q&A, 1990, Guilty by Suspicion, 1991, JFK, 1991, The Mambo Kings, 1992, Memoirs of an Invivsible Man, 1992, The Power of One, 1992, Under Siege, 1992, Sommersby, 1993, Falling Down, 1993, Made in America, 1993, Free Willy, 1993, The Nutcracker, 1993, That Night, 1993, Heaven and Earth, 1993, The New Age, 1993, Striking Distance, 1993, Six Degrees of Separation, 1993, Second Best, 1994, Boys on the Side, 1994, The Client, 1994, Bogus, 1995, A Time to Kill, 1996, The Mirror Has Two Faces, 1996, Tin Cup, 1996. Office: Regency Enterprises 4000 Warner Blvd Bldg 66 Burbank CA 91522-0001*

MILDREN, JACK, legal services company executive, former state official; b. Kingsville, Tex., Oct. 10, 1949; s. Larry J. and Mary Glynne (Lamont) M.; m. Janis Susan Butler, Jan. 14, 1972; children: Leigh, Lauren, Drew. BBA, U. Okla., 1972. Cert. petroleum landman. Mem. Balt. Colts Football Club, 1972-73, New England Patriots Football Club, 1974; v.p. Saxon Oil Co., 1972-79; co-founder, pres. Regency Exploration Inc., 1977-88; ind. oil oper., 1988-90; lt. gov. State of Okla., Oklahoma City, 1990-95; pres., CEO Pre-Paid Legal Svcs. Inc., Ada, OK, 1995. Bd. dirs. Children's Med. Rsch. Found., Arts Coun. Oklahoma City, Nat. Football League Players Found. and Hall of Fame, State Ctr. Com., Jim Thorpe Club; mem. Leadership Okla., Leadership Oklahoma City; mem. Com. to Devel. Biotech. Industry in Okla. Named All-Am. Football Player, 1971, Acad. All-Am., 1971, NAt. Football Found. Hall Fame, 1971, Most Valuable Player Sugar Bowl, 1972. numerous other athletic awards. Mem. Beta Gamma Sigma, Phi Delta Theta (past pres., bd. dirs.). Meth. Home: 1701 Guilford Oklahoma City OK 73120 Office: Pre-Paid Legal Svcs Inc 321 E Main St Ada OK 74820-5605

MILDVAN, DONNA, infectious diseases physician; b. Phila., June 20, 1942; d. Carl David and Gertrude M.; m. Rolf Dirk Hamann; 1 child, Gabriella Kay. AB magna cum laude, Bryn Mawr Coll., 1963; MD, Johns Hopkins U., 1967. Diplomate Am. Bd. Internal Medicine and Infectious Diseases. Intern, resident Mt. Sinai Hosp., N.Y.C., 1967-70, fellow, infectious diseases, 1970-72; asst., assoc. prof. clin. medicine Mt. Sinai Sch. Medicine, N.Y.C., 1972-87; prof. clinical medicine Dept. Medicine, Mt. Sinai Sch. Medicine, N.Y.C., 1987-88, prof. medicine, 1988-94; physician-in-charge infectious diseases Beth Israel Med. Ctr., N.Y.C., 1972-79, chief, div. infectious diseases, 1980—; prof. medicine Albert Einstein Coll. of Medicine, N.Y.C., 1994—; mem. AIDS charter rev. com., NIH/Nat. Inst. Allergy and Infectious Diseases, Bethesda, 1987—; cons. FDA, Rockville, 1987—, Ctrs. for Disease Control, Atlanta, 1985-86; among first to describe AIDS, "Pre-AIDS", AIDS Dementia, 1982, among first to study AZT, 1986; Keynote speaker, II Internat. Conf. on AIDS, Paris, 1986 and other achievements in field; Sophie Jones Meml. lectr. in infectious diseases U. Mich. Hosps., 1984. Contbr. numerous articles to profl. jours; co-editor two books, several book chpts. and abstracts on infectious diseases and AIDS. Grantee N.Y. State AIDS Inst., 1986-87; Henry Strong Denison scholar Johns Hopkins U. Sch. Medicine, 1967; recipient Woman of Achievement award AAUW, 1987; contract for antiviral therapy in AIDS, Nat. Cancer Inst./Nat. Inst. Allergy and Infectious Diseases, 1985-86, subcontract Nat. Inst. Allergy and Infectious Diseases, ACTU, 1987—. Fellow Infectious Diseases Soc. Am.; mem. Am. Soc. Microbiology, AAAS, Harvey Soc., Internat. AIDS Soc. Democrat. Jewish. Avocation: old movies. Office: Beth Israel Med Ctr 1st Ave New York NY 10003-7903

MILEDI, RICARDO, neurobiologist; b. Mexico City, Sept. 15, 1927; m. Ana Mela Garces, Dec. 17, 1955; 1 child, Rico. B.Sc., Instituto Cientifico y Literario, Chihuahua, Mex., 1945; M.D., U. Nacional Autónoma de Mex., 1955, Doctor Honoris Causa Universidad del Pais Vasco, 1992. Researcher Instituto Nacional de Cardiologia, Mex., 1954-56; fellow John Curtin Sch. Med. Res., Canberra, Australia, 1956-58; mem. faculty U. Coll., London, 1959-85, Foulerton research prof. of Royal Soc., 1975-85, head dept. biophysics, 1978-85; Disting. prof. dept. psychobiology U. Calif., Irvine, 1984—. Editor Archives of Med. Rsch. Trustee The Grass Found., PEW L.Am. Fellows Program. Fellow Royal Soc. London, Am. Acad. Arts and Scis.; mem. AAAS, NAS, 3d World Acad. Scis., (titular) European Acad. Arts, Scis., Humanities, N.Y. Acad. Scis., Hungarian Acad. Scis. (hon.), Mex. Acad. Scis., Mex. Acad. Medicine. Home: 9 Gibbs Ct Irvine CA 92612-4032 Office: U Calif Dept Psychobiology 2205 Bio Sci Ii Irvine CA 92697-4550

MILES, ARTHUR J., financial planner, consultant; b. N.Y.C., Sept. 2, 1920; s. Levi and Rachel Goldsworthy (Hiscock) M.; m. Pearl Cooper, Nov. 27, 1947; children: Beverly Miles Kerns, Douglas Robert. B.B.A., Pace U., 1958; M.B.A., NYU, 1963; postgrad., Dartmouth Coll., 1966, Brown U., 1970-71. With Dime Savs. Bank, N.Y.C., 1938-81, exec. v.p., treas., 1975-78, sr. exec. v.p., treas., 1978-81; pres. AJM Assocs., Floral Park, N.Y., then Sarasota, Fla., 1981—; newscaster Sta. WUSF-FM, Tampa, Fla.; bd. dirs. Cultural Instns. Retirement System, N.Y.C., 1968—; fin. cons. Bklyn. Inst. Arts and Scis., 1972—. Trustee, nat. treas. Alcoholics Anonymous, N.Y.C., 1970-79; tech. adviser N.Y.C. Fin. Liason Com., 1975-76. Served to sgt., inf. U.S. Army, 1942-45, Philippines. Fellow Fedn. Fin. Analysts; mem. Nat. Assn. Bus. Economists, Internat. Assn. Fin. Planners, Broadcast Pioneers, NYU Club, Marco Polo Club (N.Y.C.), Tournament Players Club. Republican. Office: AJM Assocs 8325 Shadow Pine Way Sarasota FL 34238-5624

MILES, CYNTHIA LYNN, theatrical costume designer, consultant; b. Tucson, June 18, 1954; d. Bob D. Davis and Ella Kathleen (Kay) Clements; m. Ronald E. Anderson, May 1980 (div. July 1981); m. Charles D. Miles, Apr. 25, 1982; children: Wesley Clements, Travis Nichols. BA, U. N.Mex., 1977. Propr. Cindy's Couture et Costume, 1988—; freelance costume designer Honolulu, 1991-93; costume designer Opera House Theatre Co., Wilmington, N.C., 1987-89, Tapestry Theatre Co., Wilmington, 1989-91, Honolulu Theatre for Youth, 1991-92, Diamond Head Theatre, Honolulu, 1992, Manoa Valley Theatre, Honolulu, 1991-93; costume mgr. Opera House Theatre Co., 1987-89, Manoa Valley Theatre, 1992-93; costume asst. Diamond Head Theatre, Honolulu Theatre for Youth, asst. props mgr., 1991, state mgr./tour mgr., 1991, program specialist, 1991-92; stitcher Mo. Repertory Theatre, Kansas City, 1994-96, dresser, 1995. costume designer for plays My Fair Lady, Company, One Flew Over the Cuckoo's Nest, Camelot, South Pacific, Harvey, A Streetcar Named Desire, Mister Roberts, Brigadoon, Last of the Red Hot Lovers, Hello Dolly, Steel Magnolias, Kiss Me Kate, Opera House Theatre Co., Corn is Green, Lion in Winter, Importance of Being Earnest, Tapestry Theatre Co., Wuthering Heights, Hoggard High Sch., N.C., The Garden, James Burke Prodns., N.C., Fool for Love, Triad Prodns., N.C., 1987-90, Murder at Howard Johnson's, Sweeney Todd (Po'Okela award for Costume Excellence, State of Hawaii 1992), Beyond Therapy, Manoa Valley Theatre, Spoon River Anthology (Po'Okela award for Best Overall Prodn. of a Play, State of Hawaii), Revenge of The Space Pandas, Honolulu Theatre for Youth, 1991-93; asst. to designer Into The Woods, Leader of The Pack, Big River, Manoa Valley Theatre, 1991-93; stitcher Dancing at Lughnasa, Christmas Carol, Whispers in The Mind, Mo. Repertory Theatre, 1994, The Deputy, The Dickens Faire, Julius Caesar, Mo. Repertory Theatre, 1994, The Dickens Faire, Christmas Carol, Two Gentlemen of Verona, 1995, Imaginary Invalid, 1995, (film), Kansas City, 1995, (ballet) The Nutcracker, State Ballet of Mo., Kansas City, 1995; key costumer: (TV show) Time Piece; costume supr.: (TV show) Love's Deadly Triangle, The Texas Cadets Murder, 1996. Democrat. Episcopalian. Avocations: sewing, designing, weaving, sailing, reading.

MILES, DAVID MICHAEL, lawyer; b. Jackson, Mich., Aug. 5, 1954; s. Richard George and JoAnn Marie (Stefanoff) M.; m. Noelle Susan McHugh, Sept. 6, 1986. Student, U. Mich., 1972-74; BA cum laude, Clark U., 1976; JD magna cum laude, George Washington U., 1979. Bar: D.C. 1979, U.S. Ct. Appeals (4th cir.) 1980, U.S. Dist. Ct. Md. 1980, U.S. Dist. Ct. D.C. 1983, U.S. Supreme Ct. 1983, U.S. Ct. Appeals (D.C. cir.) 1981, U.S Ct. Appeals (9th cir.) 1984, U.S. Ct. Appeals (2d cir.) 1986. Law clk. to hon. chief judge U.S Dist. Ct. Md., 1979-80; law clk. to hon. judge U.S. Ct. Appeals, Washington, 1980-81; assoc. Fried, Frank, Harris, Shriver & Jacoboson, Washington, 1981-86, ptnr., 1986-92; ptnr. Sidley & Austin, Washington, 1992—. Co-author: The Law of Financial Services, 1988; contbr. articles to profl. jours. Democrat. Roman Catholic. Home: 3434 Porter St NW Washington DC 20016-3126 Office: Sidley & Austin 1722 I St NW Washington DC 20006-3705

MILES, ELLEN GROSS, art historian, museum curator; b. N.Y.C., July 28, 1941; d. Mason Welch and Julia (Kernan) Gross; m. Nathan Reingold. BA, Bryn Mawr Coll., 1964; MPhil, Yale U., 1970, PhD, 1976. Registrar Corcoran Gallery Art, Washington, 1965-66; asst. to dir. Nat. Portrait Gallery, Washington, 1971-77, assoc. curator, 1977-84, curator dept. painting and sculpture, 1984-94, chair dept. painting and sculpture, 1994—; guest curator Iveagh Bequest, Kenwood, London, 1979; vis. lectr. dept. Am. studies George Washington U., 1982. Co-author: American Colonial Portraits: 1700-1776, 1987; editor: The Portrait in 18th Century America, 1993; author: Saint-Mémin and the Neoclassical Profile Portrait in America, 1994, American Paintings of the Eighteenth Century, 1995. Rsch. grantee Smithsonian Instn., 1973-74, 79, 82, 87. Mem. Assn. Historians Am. Art, Am. Soc. for Eighteenth-Century Studies, Coll. Art Assn. Office: Nat Portrait Gallery 8th and F Sts NW Washington DC 20560

MILES, ELSIE E., counselor, educator; b. Washington; d. James O. and Annie (Wint) Miles. BS, U. D.C.; MA, Howard U., Washington; MA, Cath. U., Washington; postgrad., U. Wis., 1977, U. Mich., 1984. Lic. profl. counselor; nat. cert. counselor. Tchr., guidance counselor Washington, D.C. Pub. Schs., 1967-85; program planner, presenter and del. profl. confs.; govt. rels. chair ASGW Govt. Rels. Commn., 1985-92. Editor (newsletter) D.C. Elem. Sch. Counselors Assn., D.C. Sch. Counselors Assn.; editor Assn. for Specialists in Group Work Govt. Rels. Communique; contbr. articles to profl. jours. & bulls. Civic and cmty. activist for civil and human rights. Recipient award Assn. for Multicultural Counseling and Devel. Am. Counseling Assn., C. Harold McCully Recognition award, 1992. Mem. AAUW, Am. Counseling Assn., Am. Psychol. Soc., Am. Mental Health Counselors Assn. (award), D.C. Mental Health Counselor Assn. (pres. 1993-94, exec. bd. dirs., editor newsletter), D.C. Counseling Assn. (pres. 1987-88, pub. policy and legis. chair 1989-96, award), D.C. Sch. Counselors Assn. (exec. bd. dirs., editor newsletter, award), D.C. Assn. for Specialists in Group Work (pres. 1984-85, govt. rels. chair 1985-91, exec. bd. dirs., editor newsletter), Internat. Assn. for Marriage and Family Therapists, Am. Orthopsychiat. Assn., World Future Soc., Nat. Orgn. of Victims Assistance, Am. Bus. Women's Assn. (sec. Adams Morgan Civic Assn., Federal City chpt. program chair 1994-96), Women's Fedn. for World Peace, Habitat for Humanity D.C., Chi Sigma Iota, others.

MILES, FRANK CHARLES, retired newspaper executive; b. Detroit, Jan. 1, 1926; s. Nelson and Ethel Jane (Mennill) M.; m. Catharine Estelle Coleman, Sept. 4, 1948; children: Barbara Ann, Diana Estelle. Student, Westervelt Bus. Coll., 1947-48. With Thomson Newspapers Ltd., Cambridge, Ont., Can., 1950-52, 54-55; bus. mgr. Sarnia (Ont.) Obs., 1952-54; gen. mgr. Pembroke (Ont.) Obs., 1956-58, Moose Jaw (Sask.) Times-Herald, Can., 1958-62; pub. Austin (Minn.) Daily Herald, 1962-66; sr. v.p., gen. mgr. Thomson Newspapers Inc., Des Plaines, Ill., 1966-89, exec. v.p. acquisitions, 1990-91, ret., 1991, also bd. dirs. Vol. assignments Internat. Media Fund, Baltics, Albania, 1992-93; Knight fellowship Moscow 1994, Ctr. for Ind. Journalism, Bucharest, Romania, Spring, 1995, Kocise SLovakia, 1996, IREX, Zagreb, Croatia, 1997. With USNR, 1943-46. Mem. Am. Newspaper Pubs. Assn., Inland Daily Press Assn., Sigma Delta Chi. Republican. Mem. United Ch. of Christ. Home: 4 Duxbury St Rolling Meadows IL 60008-1918

MILES, JACK (JOHN RUSSIANO), journalist, educator; b. Chgo., July 30, 1942; s. John Alvin and Mary Jean (Murphy) M.; m. Jacqueline Russiano, Aug. 23, 1980; 1 child, Kathleen. LittB, Xavier U., Cin., 1964; PhB, Pontifical Gregorian U., Rome, 1966; student, Hebrew U., Jerusalem, 1966-67; PhD, Harvard U., 1971. Asst. prof. Loyola U., Chgo., 1970-74; asst. dir. Scholars Press, Missoula, Mont., 1974-75; postdoctoral fellow U. Chgo., 1975-76; editor Doubleday & Co., N.Y.C., 1976-78; exec. editor U. Calif. Press, Berkeley, 1978-85; book editor L.A. Times, 1985-91, mem. editl. bd., 1991-95; dir. Humanities Ctr. Claremont (Calif.) Grad. Sch., 1995—; contb. editor Atlantic Monthly, 1995—. Author: Retroversion and Text Criticism, 1984, God: A Biography, 1995; contbr. learned and popular articles to various periodicals; book reviewer. Recipient Pulitzer prize for biography, 1996; Guggenheim fellow, 1990-91. Mem. PEN, Nat. Book Critics Circle (pres. 1990-92), Am. Acad. Religion, Amnesty Internat. Episcopalian. Home: 3568 Mountain View Ave Pasadena CA 91107-4616 Office: Grad Humanities Ctr Claremont Grad Sch Claremont CA 91711

MILES, JEANNE PATTERSON, artist; b. Balt.; d. Walter and Edna (Webb) M.; m. Frank Curlee, Dec. 31, 1935 (dec.); m. Johannes Schiefer, Feb. 11, 1939 (div.); 1 child, Joanna. BFA, George Washington U.; postgrad., Philips Meml. Gallery Sch., Atelier Gromaire, Grand Chaumiere, Paris. One-woman shows include Betty Parsons Gallery, N.Y.C., 1945, 52, 55, 56, 59, 77, 82, Grand Central Moderns, N.Y.C., 1968, Wesbeth Galleries, N.Y.C., 1972; group shows include N.Y. Rome Found., 1957, Walker Art Gallery, Mpls., 1954, Corcoran Biennial, Yale U. Mus., 1957, Chateau Gagnes, France, 1938, Whitney Mus., 1963, Nat. Fedn. Am. Art, 1963, Mus. Modern Art, 1966, Riverside Mus., N.Y.C., 1964, Guggeheim Mus., 1965-66, Geodok Am. Women Show, Hamburg and Berlin, 1972, Springfield (Mass.) Art Mus., 1975, Hunterton Art Center, Clinton, N.J., 1975, Betty Parsons Gallery, 1977, 82, Sid Deutch, 1978, 79, Marlyn Pearl Gallery, N.Y.C., 1986, 88, Bronx Mus. Art, 1986, George Washington, 1989, 55 Mercer St, N.Y.C., 1989, Marlyn Pearl Gallery, N.Y.C., 1991, Anita Shapalsky Gallery, N.Y.C., 1994, Shapalsky Gallery, 1993; represented in permanent collections NYU, Santa Barbara (Calif.) Mus., Muson Proctor Mus., Utica, N.Y., Rutgers Coll., U. Ariz., Guggenheim Mus., Cin. and Newark museums, White Art Mus., N.Y. State U. at Purchase, Cornell U., Ecumenical Inst., Garrison, N.Y., Graymoor, Garrison, Springfield Art Mus., Weatherspoon Art Mus., U. N.C., Wichita (Kans.) Mus., Mus. of Wichita, Mus. of St. Mary's (Md.) Coll., L.A. County Mus., Alexander Mus., La., also pvt. collections, N.Y.C. and France; traveling exhibits; poster and cover for catalogues, 1987-92; video tape showing of exhibits on cable TV, N.Y.C., 1989. Charles C. Ladd painting scholar Tahiti, 1938, 56, traveling scholar France, 1937-48; grantee Am. Inst. Arts and Letters, 1968, Mark Rothko Found., 1970-73, Pelham von Stoeffler Art Fund, 1974; invited residency (award) to Yaddo Art Colony, Saratoga Springs, N.Y., 50s and 60s, MacDowell Colony, N.H. Mem. Abstract Artists Am., George Washington U. Alumni Assn. (Disting. Achievement award 1987). *My paintings, I find, come out successfully when I keep a steady grip on an interior focus.*

MILES, JESSE MC LANE, retired accounting company executive; b. De Funiak Springs, Fla., June 17, 1932; s. Percy Webb and Dora (Pippin) M.; m. Catherine Rita Eugenio, July 18, 1959; children—Jesse Jr., Catherine, Teresa, John, Thomas, Robert. B.S.B.A., U. Fla., 1954. C.P.A., N.Y. Mem. staff, mgr., prin. Arthur Young & Co., N.Y.C., 1954-63, ptnr., 1963-89, dep. chmn.-internat., 1985-89; chmn. Arthur Young Internat., 1985-89; ptnr. Ernst & Young, 1989-92; co-chmn. Ernst & Young Internat., 1989-92; ret., 1992. Mem. AICPA, N.Y. Inst. CPAs, Burning Tree Country Club (Greenwich, Conn.), Blind Brook Club (Rye Brook, N.Y.), Boca Pointe Country Club (Boca Raton, Fla.), Adios Golf Club (Coconut Creek, Fla.). Home: 18 Red Coat Ln Greenwich CT 06830-3432

MILES, JIM, state official. Prof. of law Greenville Tech. Coll.; sec. of state S.C. Mem. Soc. Internat. Bus. Office: Sec of State PO Box 11350 Columbia SC 29211-1350

MILES, JOANNA, actress, playwright; b. Nice, France, Mar. 6, 1940; came to U.S., 1941, naturalized, 1941; d. Johannes Schiefer and Jeanne Miles; m. William Burns, May 23, 1970 (div. 1977); m. Michael Brandman, Apr. 29, 1978; 1 child, Miles. Grad., Putney (Vt.) Sch., 1958. Mem. Actors Studio, N.Y.C., 1966; co-founder, mem. L.A. Classic Theatre, 1986; represented by Artist's Agy.; founder, artistic dir. Playwrights Group at St. Ambrose Art Ctr. and L.A. Women's Workshop/The Playwrights Group. Appeared in: (motion pictures) The Way We Live Now, 1969, Bug, 1975, The Ultimate Warrior, 1975, Golden Girl, 1978, Cross Creek, 1983, As Is, 1986, Blackout, 1988, Rosencrants and Guildenstern Are Dead, 1991, The Rhinehart Theory, 1994, Judge Dredd, 1994, Alone, 1996; numerous television films, including In What America, 1965, My Mothers House, 1963, Glass Menagerie, 1974, Born Innocent, 1974, Aloha Means Goodbye, 1974, The Trial of Chaplain Jensen, 1975, Harvest Home, 1977, Fire in the Sky, 1978, Sophisticated Gents, 1979, Promise of Love, 1982, Sound of Murder, 1983, All My Sons, 87, The Right To Die, 1987, The Habitation of Dragons, 1991, Heart of Justice, 1991, Water Engine, 1991, Cooperstown, 1992, Legionnaires, 1992, Life Lessons, 1992, Willing to Kill, 1992, The American Clock, 1993, Dark Reflections, 1993, Outcry, 1994, Everything to Gain, 1995; episodes in numerous (TV series) including: Barney Miller, Dallas, St. Elsewhere, The Hulk, Trapper John, Kaz, Cagney and Lacey, Studio 5B, 1989, Star Trek: The Next Generation, 1990, 91, Life Stories, 1991, HBO Life Stories, 1993; stage plays Walk-Up, 1962, Once in a Life Time, 1963, Cave Dwellers, 1964, Drums in the Night, 1968, Dracula, 1968, Home Free, 1964, One Night Stands of A Noisy Passenger, 1972, Dylan, 1973, Dancing for the Kaiser, 1976, Debutante Ball, 1985, Kramer, 1977, One Flew Over The Cuckoo's Nest, 1989, Growing Gracefully, 1990, Cut Flowers, 1994; performed in radio shows Sta. KCRW Once in a Lifetime, 1987, Babbit, 1987, Sta. KPFK, Grapes of Wrath, 1989, The White Plague, Sta. KCRW, 1991, Chekhov Short Stories, Sta. KCRW, 1992; playwright, v.p. Brandman Productions; author: (plays) Ethanasia, A Woman in Reconstruction, Hostages, Feathers. Pres. Children Giving to Children. Recipient 2 Emmy awards, 1974, Women in Radio and TV award, 1974, Actors Studio Achievement award, 1980.

Mem. Acad. Motion Picture Arts and Scis., Acad. TV Arts and Scis., Dramatists Guild. Office: Brandman Productions 2062 N Vine St Ste 5 Hollywood CA 90068

MILES, JOHN FREDERICK, retired manufacturing company executive; b. Fredericton, N.B., Can., Aug. 13, 1926; s . Ralph Edward and Hazel Jean (Young) M.; m. Frances Power, Oct. 2, 1950; children: John F., Robert D., Dalyce J., Leytha J. Sr. Matric, U. N.B., 1944; B.Sc. in Chem. Engring., Queen's U., Kingston, Ont., Can., 1948. Prodn. mgr. Dominion Steel & Coal Corp. Ltd., 1948-65, jr. engr., 1948-49, battery foreman coke ovens, 1949-51, gen. foreman coke ovens, 1951-56, rsch. engr. coke ovens and blast furnaces, 1956-57, asst. supt. blast furnace dept., 1957-58, asst. to gen. supt., 1958-60, asst. works mgr. Sidney Works, 1960-62, gen. mgr. Etobicoke Works, 1962-65; works mgr. Slater Steels—Hamilton Splty. Bar Div. (div. Slater Industries), Hamilton, Ont., Can., 1965-66, 1966-71, v.p. mfg., 1971-86, div. pres., 1986-91, pres., CEO, 1991-93, bd. dirs., 1991—. Mem. Assn. Profl. Engrs. Ont., Assn. Iron and Steel Engrs.

MILES, JOHN KARL, marketing executive; b. Indpls., June 17, 1937; s. Louis John and Rachel Anna (Robbins) M.; m. Nancy Margaret McCay, Aug. 22, 1959; children—John Karl, Ann McCay, James Vance. B.A., DePauw U., 1959; B.F.A., U. Ill., 1965, M.F.A., 1966. Design mgr. Arvin Industries Inc., Columbus, Ind., 1966-72; dir. design and mktg. Gen. Housewares Corp., Atlanta, 1972-77; exec. v.p. Homecrest Industries Inc., Wadena, Minn., 1977-88; pres. Crestmark Internat., Atlanta, 1988—; pres. bd. advisors Dallas Market Ctr., 1983-86; bd. dirs. Garden Window Network, Summer Casual Furniture Mfrs. Assn., pres. 1990-92, chair bd. 1993—, Atlantic Market Center Accessories Center, 1992; mem. adv. bd. Atlanta Market Ctr. Gift and Home Accents, 1994—. Inventor, designer electric heater, shoe buffer, bowling game table, electric scissors. Del. Wadena County Republican Conv., 1980-84; pres. Wadena Devel. Authority, 1986-87; mem. United Meth. Ch. Dist. Com. on Superintendency, 1985-88; lay leader Wadena United Meth. Ch., 1987; bd. dirs. Wadena Econ. Devel. Council, Community Edn. Adv. Com., Wadena. Served to 1st lt. USAF, 1959-62. Recipient Exec. of Yr. award Nat. Secs. Assn., Wadena, 1980. Mem. Summer and Casual Furniture Mfrs. Assn. (pres. bd. dirs. 1984—), Nat. Home Furnishings Coun. (bd. dirs. 1988—), Nat. Furnishings Coun. (bd. dirs. 1994), Wadena C. of C. (bd. dirs. 1985, pres. 1987, Citizen of Yr. 1988), Elks, Rotary. Methodist. Avocations: antiques, reading, drawing. Home: 601 Old Post Rd Madison GA 30650-1852 Office: Homecrest/ Crestmark Internat 240 Peachtree St NW Atlanta GA 30303-1302

MILES, LAVEDA ANN, advertising executive; b. Greenville, S.C. Nov. 21, 1945; d. Grady Lewis and Edna Sylvia (Mahaffey) Bruce; m. Charles Thomas Miles, Nov. 10, 1974; 1 child, Joshua Bruce. A in Bus. Adminstrn., North Greenville Jr. Coll. Traffic mgr. WFBC-TV, Greenville, S.C., 1968-74; pub. svc. dir., traffic mgr. WTCG-TV, Atlanta, 1974-75; traffic mgr. Henderson Advt. Co., Greenville, 1975-77, broadcast coord., 1977-79, dir. broadcast bus., 1979-82, dir. broadcast bus., v.p., 1982-89, bus. mgr. creative dept., 1989-91, dir. creative svcs., 1991-93, sr. v.p., 1993—. Named one of 100 Best and Brightest Women for 1988 Ad Age and Advt. Women of N.Y. Mem. Advt. Fedn. of Greenville (sec. 1979-81, Leadership S.C. Class 1994-95). Democrat. Baptist.

MILES, LELAND WEBER, university president; b. Balt., Jan. 18, 1924; s. Leland Weber and Marie (Fitzpatrick) M.; m. Mary Virginia Geyer, July 9, 1947; children: Christine Marie, Gregory Lynn. AB cum laude, Juniata Coll., 1946; MA, U. N.C., 1947, PhD, 1949; postgrad., Duke U., 1949; DLitt (hon.), Juniata Coll., 1969; LHD (hon.), Rosary Hill Coll., 1970; LLD (hon.), Far East U., 1979; DHC (hon.), U. Guadalajara (Mex.), 1984; Order of Merit, Alfred U., 1986. Assoc. prof. English Hanover Coll., 1949-50, prof., chmn. English dept., 1950-60; assoc. prof., asst. to head English dept. U. Cin., 1960-63, prof., 1963-64, founder humanities reading program for engrs., 1961; dean Coll. Arts and Scis., U. Bridgeport, Conn., 1964-67; pres. U. Bridgeport, 1974-87, founder Sch. Law, 1977, pres. emeritus, 1987—; pres. Alfred U., 1967-74; bd. dirs. United Illuminating, 1978-94, chmn. audit com., 1992-94, Grolier, 1984-88, Wright Managed Investment Funds, 1988—, Internat. Peace Acad., 1982-90, mem. adv. coun., 1990—; mem. adv. coun. Internat. Exec. Svc. Corps, 1993—; Danforth scholar Union Theol. Sem., 1956; Lilly fellow Sch. Letters Ind. U., 1959; Am. Council Learned Socs. fellow Harvard, 1963-64; Sr. Fulbright Research scholar Kings Coll. U. London, 1964, vis. scholar, 1972; seminar leader, deans and presidents insts. Am. Council on Edn., 1973-79; chmn. bd. Acad. Collective Bargaining Info. Service, Washington, 1977-79; producer, moderator Casing the Classics CBS Sta. WHAS-TV, Louisville, 1958-61; moderator Aspen (Colo.) Inst. for Humanistic Studies, 1969-70; lectr. Keedick Lecture Bur., N.Y.C., 1956-83. Author: John Colet and the Platonic Tradition, 1961; editor: St. Thomas More's Dialogue of Comfort Against Tribulation, 1965, Where Do You Stand On Linquistics?, 1964, revised, 1968; sr. editor: (with Stephen Graubard and later Stephen B. Baxter) Studies in British History and Culture, 1965-79; contbg. editor Nat. Forum, 1983-91, editl. advisor, 1991-94; contbr. articles to learned jours., chpts. in books. Trustee Western N.Y. Nuclear Rsch. Ctr., 1967-73; chmn. bd. Coll. Ctr. Finger Lakes, 1968-71; vice chmn. bd. Empire State Found., 1969-71, chmn., 1971-73; mem. New Eng. Bd. Higher Edn., 1985-87, Ambs. Roundtable, 1986-92, Fuld Found./ Nat. League Nursing Adv. Coun. on Accreditation, 1986-88; chmn. Ettinger scholarship com. ednl. Found. Am., 1987-93; bd. dirs. Conn. Grand Opera, 1978-89, Bridgeport Bus. Coun., 1982-88, Save the Children, 1988-95; chmn. adv. coun. Save the Children, 1990-94, mem. adv. coun., 1995—. 1st lt. USAAF, 1944-45; capt. USAFR. Decorated DFC with oak leaf cluster, Crown Decoration of Honor 3rd Order Iran, 1978; chevalier l'Ordre des Palmes Académique (France), 1984; recipient Rosa and Samuel Sachs prize Cin. Inst. Fine Arts, 1961, Cultural medal Republic of China, 1983, Disting. Svc. award Greater Bridgeport Bar Assn., 1986, Outstanding Civilian Svc. medal Dept. Army, 1988; Miles scholars Alfred U., 1995—. Fellow Royal Soc. Arts, Manufactures and Commerce (life); mem. Renaissance Soc. Am., English Speaking Union, Internat. Assn. Univ. Pres. (pres. 1981-84, pres. emeritus 1984—, chief UN mission 1988-87, World Peace award 1987, chmn. commn. on arms control edn. 1991-96, mem. coun. sr. advisers 1992—), Knights of Malta (order of the Orthodox Knights Hospitaller of St. John of Jerusalem, Russian orthodox br.), Phi Kappa Phi. Episcopalian. Clubs: Univ. (N.Y.C.); Country of Fairfield (Conn.).

MILES, LEON F. (LEE MILES), vocational education educator; b. Pitts., July 18, 1954; m. Nancy E. Dodson, May 14, 1976; 1 child, Brian C. AA, Point Park Coll., 1976, BA in Psychology, 1983; MEd in Instrn. and Learning, U. Pitts., 1988. Cert. mktg. edn. and coop. work experience tchr., Pa.; cert. entrepreneurship instr. Instr. fashion merchandising program Art Inst. Pitts., 1985-87; tchr. diversified occupations North Area Alternative High Sch., Allison Park, Pa., 1987; tchr., coord. mktg. edn. Taylor Allderdice High Sch., Pitts., 1988—; mktg. edn. tchr. cert. exam validator Ednl. Testing Svc., 1990, PSAT essay evaluator, 1994; mem. Blue Ribbon Sch. Self-Evaluation Com., 1995. Author curriculum materials. Adult leader Pitts. area Boy Scouts Am., 1985-96, exploring advisor. Recipient Excellence in Tchg. award U. of Pitts. Sch. of Edn. and Pitts. Post Gazette, 1994. Mem. (DECA) Distbv. Edn. Clubs Am. (chpt. advisor, state officer advisor, state collegiate pres. 1987-88), Nat. Mktg. Edn. Assn., Pa. Mktg. Edn. Assn. (Western region v.p. 1990-91, Tchr. of Yr. 1990). Home: 1521 Beechview Ave Pittsburgh PA 15216-3335 Office: Taylor Allerdice High Sch 2409 Shady Ave Pittsburgh PA 15217-2409

MILES, RANDALL DAVID, investment company executive; b. Junction City, Kans., May 10, 1956; s. Dave Clay and Barbara L. (Hubert) M.; m. Karen A. Fredricks (div. Nov. 1992); m. Karen D. Cahill, Jan. 22, 1994; 1 child, Spencer C.; 1 stepchild, Marc J.. BA, U. Wash., 1979. Mgr. product devel. GE Credit Corp., Stamford, Conn., 1979-85; v.p. The First Boston Corp., N.Y.C., 1985-88; sr. v.p. Greenwich Capital Markets, Inc., Greenwich, Conn., 1988-96; mng. dir. The Stone Pine Cos., N.Y.C., 1996—; pres., CEO Advantage Funding Group, Inc., Boston, 1996—; pres. NAFCO Holding Co., Inc., Dallas, 1996—; bd. dirs. N.W. Securities, Inc., Seattle, Advantage Funding Group, Inc., Boston; NWEI, Inc., Seattle, 1990—, NAFCO Holdings, Inc., Dallas, 1996—, Pacific Consumer Funding, Dallas, 1996—, ADA Capital Corp, Buffalo, N.Y., 1996—. Rep. committeeman, Easton, Conn., 1993—. Mem. Mortgage Bankers Assn. Am., Consumer Bankers Assn., Redding Country Club. Episcopalian. Avocations: golf, stock and real estate investment, running, tennis. Home: 20 Sky Line Dr Easton CT 06612-1056 Office: The Stone Pine Companies 100 Park Ave Fl 28 New York NY 10017-5516

MILES, RAYMOND EDWARD, former university dean, organizational behavior and industrial relations educator; b. Cleburne, Tex., Nov. 2, 1932; s. Willard Francis and Wilma Nell (Owen) M.; m. Lucile Dustin, Dec. 27, 1952; children: Laura, Grant, Kenneth. B.A. with highest honors, N. Tex. State U., 1954, M.B.A., 1958; Ph.D., Stanford U., 1963. Clk. Santa Fe R.R., Gainesville, Tex., 1950-55; instr. mgmt. Sch. Bus. N. Tex. State U., Denton, 1958-60; asst. prof. organizational behavior and indsl. relations Sch. Bus. Adminstrn. U. Calif.-Berkeley, 1963-68, assoc. prof., 1968-71, prof., 1971—, assoc. dean Sch. Bus. Adminstrn., 1978-81, dean, 1983-90; dir. Inst. Indsl. Relations, 1982-83; cons. various pvt., pub. orgns. Author: Theories of Management, 1975, (with Charles C. Snow) Organization Strategy, Structure and Process, 1978, (with Charles C. Snow) Fit, Failure, and the Hall of Fame, 1994; co-author: Organizational Behavior: Research and Issues, 1976; co-editor, contbg. author: Organization by Design: Theory and Practice, 1981. Served to 1st. lt. USAF, 1955-58. Mem. Indsl. Relations Research Assn., Acad. Mgmt. Democrat. Unitarian. Home: 8640 Don Carol Dr El Cerrito CA 94530-2733 Office: U Calif-Berkeley Walter A Haas Sch Bus Berkeley CA 94720

MILES, RICHARD, diplomat; b. Little Rock, Ark., 1937; m. Sharon O'Brien, June 18, 1960; children: Richard, Elizabeth. AA, Bakersfield Coll., 1960; AB, U. Calif., Berkeley, 1962; MA, Ind. U., 1964; grad., U.S. Army Russian Inst., Garmisch-Partenkirchen, Germany. With voter registration, political leadership tng. S.C. Voter Edn. Project, 1964-67; with Fgn. Svc., Oslo, Moscow, Belgrade, 1967-88; consul gen. Leningrad, 1988-91; prin. officer U.S. Embassy Office, Berlin, 1991-92; with Soviet, East European, Yugoslav Affairs, Politico-Military Bureau State Dept., amb. to Azerbaijan, 1992-93; dep. chief mission Am. Embassy, Moscow, 1993-96; chief of mission Am. Embassy, Belgrade, 1996—. With USMC, 1954-57. Am. Polit. Sci. fellow for Sen. Ernest F. Hollings, 1983-84; fellow Harvard U. Ctr. Internat. Affairs, 1987-88. Office: Belgrade Dept of State Washington DC 20521-5070

MILES, RICHARD BRYANT, mechanical and aerospace engineering educator; b. Washington, July 10, 1943; s. Thomas Kirk and Elizabeth (Bryant) M.; m. Susan McCoy, May 14, 1983; children: Thomas, Julia. BSEE, Stanford U., 1966, MSEE, 1967, PhD in Elec. Engring., 1972. Rsch. assoc. elec. engring. dept. Stanford (Calif.) U., summer 1972; asst. prof. mech. and aerospace engring. dept. Princeton (N.J.) U., 1972-78, assoc. prof., 1978-82, prof., 1982—, chmn. engring. physics program, 1980-96; lectr. Northwestern Poly. U., Xian, China, 1987; rsch. scientist CNRS; vis. prof. U. Marseilles, France, spring, 1995. Contbr. articles to profl. publs., chpt. to book Advances in Fluid Mechanics Measurements, 1989; patentee in field. Bd. dirs. Fannie and John Hertz Found., Livermore, Calif., 1989—. Fannie and John Hertz Found. fellow, 1969-72; NSF summer trainee, 1972. Mem. AIAA (assoc. fellow), IEEE (sr.), Am. Phys. Soc., Optical Soc. Am. Office: Princeton U Mech & Aerospace Engring D-414 Eng Quad Olden St Princeton NJ 08544

MILES, RICHARD ROBERT, art historian, writer; b. Tokyo, Apr. 1, 1939; s. Robert Henri and Eleanor Alfrida (Child) Perreau-Saussine. BA, UCLA, 1972. Novelist, screenwriter various, 1965-72; dir. Meilinki Enterprises Ltd., 1980—; pres. Burbank (Calif.) Tchrs. Assn., 1984-85; bd. dirs. Balcom Trading Co., Tokyo, 1979-82. Author: That Cold Day in the Park, 1965 (Dell Book award 1965), Angel Loves Nobody, 1967 (Samuel Goldwyn award UCLA, 1969); (art history) Prints of Paul Jacoulet, 1982, Elizabeth Keith-The Prints, 1989, The Watercolors of Paul Jacoulet, 1992, others. Mem. Internat. Soc. of Fine Art Appraisers, New Eng. Appraisers Assn., Writers Guild of Am. West, Acad. of Am. Poets. Office: Meilinki Enterprises Ltd 214 N Bowling Green Way Los Angeles CA 90049-2816

MILES, ROBERT HENRY, management consultant, educator; b. Norfolk, Va., Mar. 10, 1944; s. Henry Bateman and Mildred Verda (Cuthrell) M.; m. Jane Irving Calfee, Aug. 27, 1966; children: Alexander Bateman, Holen Irving. BS, U. Va., 1967; PhD, U. N.C., 1974. Ops. analyst Ford Motor Co., Norfolk, 1968; project mgr. Advanced Rsch. Projects Agy. Office Sec. Def., Washington, 1970-71; asst. prof., co-founder Mgmt. Inst., U. Ala. Grad. Sch. Bus., Tuscaloosa, 1974-75; asst. prof. Sch. Orgn. and Mgmt. Yale U., New Haven, 1975-78; assoc. prof. Harvard Bus. Sch., Boston, 1978-85; vis. prof. Stanford Exec. Inst., Palo Alto, Calif., 1987-95; Isaac Stiles Hopkins prof. orgn. & mgmt. Goizueta Bus. Sch. Emory U., Atlanta, 1987-89; dept. dean Emory U. Bus. Sch., Atlanta, 1989-90, dean of faculty, 1990-93, Hopkins fellow, 1995—; mem. sec.'s adv. bd. U.S. Dept. Energy, Washington, 1993—; prin. Corp. Transformation Resource, Atlanta and Boston, 1996—; mem. adv. bd. orgn. effectiveness programs The Conf. Bd., N.Y.C., 1994—; mem. adv. bd. McIntire Sch. Commerce, U. Va., Charlottesville, 1987-95. Author: Macro Organizational Behavior, 1980, (with J.R. Kimberly) The Organizational Life Cycle: Issues in the Creation, Transformation, and Decline of Organizations, 1980, Managing the Corporate Social Environment: A Grounded theory, 1987, Corporate Comeback: The Renewal and Transformation of National Semiconductor, 1996, Leading Corporate Transformation: A Blueprint for Business Renewal, 1997; (in collaboration with K.S. Cameron) Coffin Nails and Corporate Strategies, 1982, (with A. Bhambri) The Regulatory Executives, 1983, (with W.A. Randolph) The Organization Game: A Simulation, 1979, 83, 93; mem. edit. bd. Adminstrv. Sci. Quar., 1978-86, Mgmt. Sci., 1979-82. Mem. exec. adv. bd. Ivan Allen Coll., Ga. Inst. Tech., 1997—. 1st lt. U.S. Army, 1969-71. Decorated Army Commendation medal; recipient Disting. Svc. award Emory U., 1993. Mem. Acad. Mgmt. (chmn. orgn. and mgmt. theory divsn. 1984-85), Strategic Mgmt. Soc., Harvard Club (Boston), Commerce Club (Atlanta), Cherokee Town Club (Atlanta), Beta Gamma Sigma. Unitarian Universalist. Avocations: boating, tennis. Home and Office: 3414 Habersham Rd NW Atlanta GA 30305 Home (summer): 177 Fox Hill Rd Chatham MA 02633-1157

MILES, RUBY WILLIAMS, secondary education educator; b. Petersburg, Va., Jan. 19, 1929; d. Richard Allen and Elizabeth (Penny) Williams; m. John Oscar Miles, Jan. 7, 1950 (div. 1966); children: Karen Jonnia Miles George, Steven Ricardo. BA, Va. State Coll., Petersburg, 1971, MA, 1977. Cert. high sch. tchr., Va. Tchr. English Dinwiddie (Va.) Sch., 1971-78, Clarksville (Tenn.) Sch., 1978-80; tchr. English Petersburg Pub. Schs., 1982—, head English dept., 1991-96, ret., 1996; instr. St. Paul's Coll., Lawrenceville, Va., 1981-82; asst. prof. St. Leo Coll., Ft. Lee, Va., 1988; tchr., counselor Upward Bound project Va. State U., summer, 1974; tchr. Hopewell Pub. Schs., Va. summer 1983—; instr. John Tyler C.C., Fort Lee Va., 1992—. Bd. dirs. Playmaker Fellows Ltd., Petersburg, 1983; co-dir. Exclusively Youth Models, 1984-85. Recipient Leadership award Va. Edn. Assn., 1985. Mem. Petersburg Edn. Assn. (past pres.), Am. Bus. Women's Assn., Nat. Orgn. for Women, Nat. Assn. Female Execs., NEA, Nat. Coun. Tchrs. English, Delta Sigma Theta. Avocations. writing, traveling. Home: 2733 Rollingwood Rd Petersburg VA 23805-2317

MILES, SAMUEL ISRAEL, psychiatrist, educator; b. Munich, Mar. 4, 1949; came to U.S., 1949; s. Henry and Renee (Ringel) M.; m. Denise Marie Robey, June 26, 1977; children: Jonathan David, Justin Alexander. BS, CCNY, 1970; MD, N.Y. Med. Coll., 1974; PhD, So. Calif. Psychoanalytic Inst., 1986. Diplomate Am. Bd. Psychiatry and Neurology with added qualifications in forensic psychiatry. Intern D.C. Gen. Hosp., Washington, 1974-75; resident in psychiatry Cedars-Sinai Med. Ctr., Los Angeles, 1975-78; practice medicine specializing in psychiatry Los Angeles, 1978—; ind. med. examiner Calif. Dept. Indsl. Relations, 1984-91, qualified med. examiner, 1991—; asst. clin. prof. psychiatry UCLA Sch. Medicine, 1978—; attending psychiatrist Cedars-Sinai Med. Ctr., 1978—; attending psychiatrist Brotman Med. Ctr., Culver City, Calif., 1978—; mem. faculty So. Calif. Psychoanalytic Inst., 1986—; mem. psychiat. panel Superior Ct. Los Angeles County, 1990—, Fed. Ct., 1990—. Fellow Am. Acad. Psychoanalysis, Am. Orthopsychiat. Assn.; mem. Acad. Psychiatry and the Law, Am. Coll. Legal Medicine, Calif. Psychiat. Assn. (mem. managed care com. 1991-96), So. Calif. Psychiat. Soc. (coun. rep. 1985-88, 92-95, chairperson pvt. practice com. 1988-92, sec. 1991-92, mem. worker's compensation com. 1992—, trea.-elect 1996, treas. 1997), So. Calif. Psychoanalytic Inst. (pres. clin. assocs. orgn. 1981-82, mem. admissions com. 1988-96, mem. ethics stds. com. 1991-92, chairperson ethics stds. com. 1993—, mem. exec. com. 1993—). Jewish. Avocations: aviation, swimming. Office: 8631 W 3rd St Ste 425E Los Angeles CA 90048-5908

MILES, THOMAS CASWELL, aerospace engineer; b. Atlanta, Mar. 21, 1952; s. Franklin Caswell and Eugenia Frances (Newsom) M.; m. Linda Susan Duggleby, Aug. 10, 1980. BMET, So. Poly. State U., 1977; postgrad., Troy State U., 1978-80. Assoc. engr. aircraft design Lockheed Martin Aero. Sys., Marietta, Ga., 1980-82, engr., aircraft design, 1982-85, sr. engr., aircraft design, 1985-89, group engr., 1989-90, specialist engr., 1990—; mem. SAE-A-6 Mil. Aircraft & Helicopter Panel, 1987-91, SAE-A-10 Aircraft Oxygen Equipment Com., 1996—. Mem. AIAA (sr.), ASME, ASTM, Nat. Mgmt. Assn., Lockheed Ga. Mgmt. Assn. (now named Lockheed Martial Mgmt. Assn.-Aero. Sys.; bd. dirs. 1996, 97), Soc. Automotive Engrs. (SAE co. rep., SAE Atlanta sect. vice chmn. aircraft), Oxygen Standardization Coord. Group Assn. Fraternity Advisors (affiliate), Wick's Lake Homeowners Assn. (pres. 1995, v.p. 1996, 97), Tau Kappa Epsilon (dist. pres. 1987-88, dist. v.p. 1984—, chpt. advisor 1980-87, key leader 1985, 90, So. Order of Honor 1989). Avocations: sailing, scuba diving, screen printing. Home: 1926 Wicks Ridge Ln Marietta GA 30062-6777 Office: Lockheed Martin Aero Sys Dept 73-05 cc-34 Marietta GA 30063-0199

MILES, TRAVIS ANTHONY, state senator; b. Eagle City, Okla., Dec. 6, 1937; s. Paul McDill and Stella (McCrary) M.; student Phillips U., 1954-59; 1 dau., Laura Lynne Maxwell. Mem. Ark. Senate, 1981-94; pres. Miles, Beals & Assocs. Advt. Agy., Inc., Ft. Smith, Ark., 1961—. Served with U.S. Army, 1953-64. Pres. council Boy Scouts Am., 1977-78; pres. Ft. Smith Girls' Club, 1979-81, hon. girl, 1979. Named outstanding young man, Jaycees, 1967; recipient Silver Beaver award Boy Scouts, 1968, disting. service award, 1979, outstanding service award St. Edward Med. Center, 1979, Svc. to Mankind award Sertoma Club, 1982, Rep. Pioneer award Ark. Rep. Party, 1986, numerous civic, profl. and govtl. awards. Mem. Fort Smith/ Van Buren Advt. Fedn. (pres. 1972-73), Old Ft. Christian Bus. Men (chmn. com. 1976-78). Mem. Christian Ch. (Disciples of Christ). Club: Kiwanis (past pres.). Office: PO Box 2108 Fort Smith AR 72902-2108

MILES, VIRGINIA (MRS. FRED C. MILES), marketing consultant; b. N.Y.C., Apr. 20, 1916; d. Samuel and Jeanette (Shalet) Goldman; m. Fred C. Miles, Mar. 24, 1940; 1 dau., Erica. B.A., Wellesley Coll., 1936; M.A., Columbia, 1938, Ph.D., 1940. Asso. dir. research R.H. Macy & Co., N.Y.C., 1940-46; instr. dept. psychology Coll. City N.Y., 1946-48; advt. research dir. Alexander Smith & Co., Yonkers, N.Y., 1948-50; v.p., research dir. McCann-Erickson Advt. Agy., N.Y.C., 1950-60; v.p. spl. planning Young & Rubicam, Inc., N.Y.C., 1960-71; sr. v.p. new product devel. Young & Rubicam, Inc., 1971-75; mktg. cons. Englewood, N.J., 1975—. Contbr. articles to profl. jours., trade mags. Active Urban Coalition. Mem. Advt. Women of N.Y., Am. Assn. Pub. Opinion Rsch., Am. Mktg. Assn., Internat. Advt. Assn., Sigma Zi. Democrat. Jewish. Avocations: reading, music, gardening, travel. Home and Office: 91 Glenbrook Pky Englewood NJ 07631-2105

MILES, WENDELL A., federal judge; b. Holland, Mich., Apr. 17, 1916; s. Fred T. and Dena Del (Alverson) M.; m. Mariette Bruckert, June 8, 1946; children: Lorraine Miles, Michelle Miles Kopinski, Thomas Paul. AB, Hope Coll., 1938, LLD (hon.), 1980; MA, U. Wyo., 1939; JD, U. Mich., 1942; LLD (hon.), Detroit Coll. Law, 1979. Bar: Mich. Ptnr. Miles & Miles, Holland, 1948-53; Miles, Mika, Meyers, Beckett & Jones, Grand Rapids, Mich., 1961-70; pros. atty. County of Ottawa, Mich., 1949-53; U.S. dist. atty. Western Dist. Mich., Grand Rapids, 1953-60; U.S. dist. judge Western Dist. Mich., 1974—, chief judge, 1979-86, sr. chief judge, 1986—; cir. judge 20th Jud. Cir. Ct. Mich., 1970-74; instr. Hope Coll., 1948-53, Am. Inst. Banking, 1953-60; adj. prof. Am. constl. history Hope Coll., Holland, Mich., 1979—; mem. Mich. Higher Edn. Commn.; apptd. Fgn. Intelligence Surveillance Count, Washington, 1989—. Pres. Holland Bd. Edn., 1952-63. Served to capt. U.S. Army, 1942-47. Recipient Liberty Bell award, 1986. Fellow Am. Bar Found.; mem. ABA, Mich. Bar Assn., Fed. Bar Assn., Ottawa County Bar Assn., Grand Rapids Bar (Inns of Ct. 1995—), Am. Judicature Soc., Torch Club, Rotary Club, Masons. Office: US Dist Ct 236 Fed Bldg 110 Michigan Ave NW Grand Rapids MI 49503-2313

MILES-LAGRANGE, VICKI LYNN, federal judge; b. Oklahoma City, Sept. 30, 1953; d. Charles and Mary (Greenard) Miles. BA, Vassar Coll., 1974; LLB, Howard U., 1977. Congl. aide Speaker of the Ho., Rep. Carl Albert, 1974-76; law clk. Hon. Woodrow Seals (U.S. Dist. Judge), Tex., 1977-79; formerly grad. fellow, trial atty. U.S. Dept. Justice, 1979-82; mem. Okla. Senate from Dist. 48, 1987-93; U.S. atty. U.S. Dept. of Justice, Oklahoma City, Okla., 1993-94; judge U.S. Dist. Ct. (we. dist.), Oklahoma City, 1994—. Democrat. Baptist.

MILEWSKI, BARBARA ANNE, pediatrics nurse, neonatal intensive care nurse; b. Chgo., Sept. 11, 1934; d. Anthony and LaVerne (Sepp) Witt; m. Leonard A. Milewski, Feb. 23, 1952; children: Pamela, Robert, Diane, Timothy. ADN, Harper Coll., Palatine, Ill, 1982; BS, Northern Ill. U., 1992; postgrad., North Park Coll. RN, Ill.; cert. CPR instr. Staff nurse Northwest Community Hosp., Arlington Heights, Ill., Resurrection Hosp., Chgo.; nurse neonatal ICU Children's Meml. Hosp., Chgo.; day care cons. Cook County Dept. Pub. Health; CPR instr. Stewart Oxygen Svcs., Chgo.; instr., organizer parenting and well baby classes and clinics; vol. Children's Meml. Hosp.; health coord. CEDA Head Start; cons. day care Cook County Dept. Pub. Health. Vol. first aid instr. Boy Scouts Am.; CPR instr. Harper Coll., Children's Meml. Hosp.; dir. Albany Park Cmty. Ctr. Head Start, Chgo.; day care cons. Cook County Dept. Pub. Health. Mem. Am. Mortar Bd., Sigma Theta Tau.

MILEWSKI, STANISLAW ANTONI, ophthalmologist, educator; b. Bagrowo, Poland, June 16, 1930; s. Alfred and Sabina (Sicinska) M.; came to U.S., 1959, naturalized, 1967; BA, Trinity Coll., U. Dublin (Ireland), 1954, MA, 1959, B. Chir., M.B., B.A.O., 1956; m. Anita Dobiecka, July 11, 1959; children: Andrew, Teresa, Mark. House surgeon Hammersmith Hosp. Postgrad. Sch. London, 1958; intern St. Raffael Hosp., New Haven, 1960-61; resident in ophthalmology Gill Meml. Hosp., Roanoke, Va., 1961-64; practice medicine specializing in surgery and diseases of the retina and vitreous; mem. staff Manchester (Conn.) Meml. Hosp., 1964-71, chief of ophthalmology, sr. attending physician St. Francis Hosp., Hartford, Conn., 1971—; asst. clin. prof. ophthalmology U. Conn., 1972—. Clin. fellow Montreal (Que., Can.) Gen Hosp., McGill U., 1971-72, Mass. Eye and Ear Infirmary, Harvard Med. Sch., Boston, 1974; diplomate Am. Bd. Ophthalmology. Fellow ACS; mem. AMA, New England Ophthal. Soc., Conn. Soc. Eye Physicians, Vitreous Soc. Republican. Roman Catholic. Home: 127 Lakewood Cir S Manchester CT 06040-7086 Office: 191 Main St Manchester CT 06040-3556 also: 43 Woodland St Ste 100 Hartford CT 06105-2339

MILEY, GEORGE HUNTER, nuclear engineering educator; b. Shreveport, La., Aug. 6, 1933; s. George Hunter and Norma Angeline (Dowling) M.; m. Elizabeth Burroughs, Nov. 22, 1958; children: Susan Miley Hibbs, Hunter Robert. B.S. in Chem. Engring., Carnegie-Mellon U., 1955; M.S., U. Mich., 1956, Ph.D. in Chem.-Nuclear Engring., 1959. Nuclear engr. Knolls Atomic Power Lab., Gen. Electric Co., Schenectady, 1959-61; mem. faculty U. Ill., Urbana, 1961—; prof. U. Ill., 1967—, chmn. nuclear engring. program, 1975-86, dir. Fusion Studies Lab., 1976—, fellow Ctr. for Advanced Study, 1985-86; dir. rsch. Rockford Tech. Assocs. Inc., 1990-94; vis. prof. U. Colo., 1967, Cornell U., 1969-70, U. New South Wales, 1986, Imperial Coll. of London, 1987; mem. Ill. Radiation Protection Bd., 1988—; mem. Air Force Studies Bd., 1990-94; chmn. tech. adv. com. Ill. Low Level Radioactive Waste Site, 1990—; chmn. com. on indsl. uses of radiation Ill. Dept. Nuclear Safety, 1989—. Author: Direct Conversion of Nuclear Radiation Energy, 1971, Fusion Energy Conversion, 1976; editor Jour. Fusion Tech., 1980—; U.S. assoc. editor Laser and Particle Beams, 1982-86, mng. editor, 1987-91, editor-in-chief, 1991—; U.S. editor Jour. Plasma Physics, 1995—. Served with C.E. AUS, 1960. Recipient Western Electric Tchg.-Rsch. award, 1977, Halliburton Engring. Edn. Leadership award, 1990, Edward Teller medal, 1995, Scientist of Yr. award Jour. New Energy, 1996; Inst. for New Energy 1996 Scientist of the Yr.; NATO sr. sci. fellow, 1975-76, Guggenheim fellow, 1985-86, Japanese Soc. Promotion of Sci. fellow, 1994. Fellow IEEE, Am. Nuclear Soc. (dir. 1980-83, Disting. Svc. award 1980, Outstanding Achievement award Fusion Energy divsn. 1992), Am. Phys. Soc.; mem. Am. Soc. Engring. Edn. (chmn. energy conversion com. 1967-70, pres. U. Ill.

chpt. 1973-74, chmn. nuclear divsn. 1975-76, Outstanding Tchr. award 1973), Sigma Xi, Tau Beta Pi. Presbyterian. Achievements include research on fusion, energy conversion, reactor kinetics. Office: U Ill 214 Nuclear Engring Lab 103 S Goodwin Ave Urbana IL 61801-2901 *My professional goal has been to insure that future generations have a plentiful supply of economical, readily available energy such as offered by fusion. Not only should this insure a continued improvement in the standard of living for persons in all nations, but it should help maintain peace which is threatened by the struggle to obtain and control limited natural sources of energy.*

MILFORD, FREDERICK JOHN, retired research company executive; b. Cleve., July 1, 1926; s. Frederick Charles and Florence M.; m. Jean Irene Olson, Sept. 8, 1951; 1 child, Cheryl Lynn. B.S. in Physics, Case Inst. Tech., 1949; Ph.D. in Physics, M.I.T., 1952. Instr. Case Inst. Tech., Cleve., 1952-56; asst. prof. Case Inst. Tech., 1956-59; div. cons. Battelle Columbus Labs., 1959-62, div. chief, 1962-64, sr. fellow, 1964-66, dir. research in phys. scis., 1966-73, scientist, 1973, dept. mgr., 1973-76, assoc. dir., 1976-85, chief scientist, 1985-87, v.p. spl. programs, 1987-89, ret., 1989; vis. prof. physics U. Wash., 1969. Author: (with J.R. Reitz) Foundations of Electromagnetic Theory, 1960, 4th edit., 1993. Mem. adv. bd. Central Ohio Salvation Army. Served with USNR, 1945-46. George Eastman fellow, 1951-52; Focke scholar, 1948-49. Fellow Am. Phys. Soc.; mem. Masons, Army and Navy Club, Kit Kat Club. Home: 1411 London Dr Columbus OH 43221-1543

MILFORD, MURRAY HUDSON, soil science educator; b. Honey Grove, Tex., Sept. 29, 1934; s. Murray Lane and Vivian Ione (Hudson) M.; m. Marsha Ann Rasmussen, July 21, 1961; children: Rebecca Ione, Murray Daniel. BS in Agronomy, Tex. A&M, 1955, MS in Agronomy, 1959; PhD in Soil Science, U. Wis., 1962. Cert. profl. soil scientist. Rsch. assoc. Cornell U., Ithaca, N.Y., 1962-63; asst. prof. Cornell U., Ithaca, 1963-68, assoc. prof., 1968; assoc. prof. Tex. A&M U., College Station, 1968-74, prof., 1974—. Author: (lab. manual) Soils and Soil Science-Lab. Exercises, 1970. 1st lt. USAR, 1955-57. Recipient so. region award for excellence in coll. and univ. tchg. in food and agrl. scis. Nat. Assn. State Univs. and Land Grant Colls., Higher Edn. Program, USDA, 1995. Fellow AAAS, Am. Soc. Agronomy (pres. Tex. chpt. 1982-83, Resident Edn. award 1978), Soil Sci. Soc. Am. (Edn. award 1988); mem. Soil and Water Conservation Soc. (pres. Tex. coun. of chpts. 1987). Democrat. Presbyterian. Home: 3606 Tanglewood Dr Bryan TX 77802-3320 Office: Tex A&M Univ Soil & Crop Scis Dept College Station TX 77843-2474

MILGRAM, JEROME H., marine and ocean engineer, educator; b. Phila., Sept. 23, 1938; s. Samuel J. and Fannie M. BSEE, MIT, 1961, BS in Naval Architecture and Marine Engring., 1961, MS, 1962, PhD in Hydrodynamics, 1965. Registered profl. engr., Mass. With Scripps Inst. Oceanography, San Diego, summer 1961; project engr. Block Assocs., Cambridge, Mass., 1961-67; asst. prof. MIT, Cambridge, 1967-70, assoc. prof., 1970-77, prof. ocean engring., 1977-89, William I. Koch prof. marine tech., 1989—; rsch. assoc. in biophysics Harvard U. Med. Sch., 1974-76; vis. prof. in naval architecture and marine engring. U. Mich., 1988-89; design dir. Am. 3 Found., 1991-95; guest investigator Woods Hole Oceanog. Instn., 1996—; vis. prof. Johns Hopkins U., 1996-97. Contbr. articles to profl. jours. Recipient Am. Bur. Shipping award, 1961, Alan Berman Outstanding Rsch. Publ. award U.S. Naval Rsch. Lab., 1990, AT&T Design Innovation award, 1992. Mem. Soc. Naval Archs. and Marine Engrs. (life), Nat. Acad. Engring. (life). Patentee in field. Home: 322 Ridge St Arlington MA 02174-1703 Office: MIT 77 Massachusetts Ave Rm 5-318 Cambridge MA 02139-4301

MILGRAM, RICHARD MYRON, music school administrator; b. Moultrie, Ga., Nov. 9, 1943; s. Bernard Byron and Libbie Elaine M.; m. Judith Lee Milgram; children: Rhonda Beth, Gary David. MusB, Berklee Coll. Music, Boston, 1966; MusM, Boston U., 1973. Cert. tchr. Mass., Conn. Tchr. Norwood (Mass.) Pub. Schs., 1969-72; asst. prof. Merrimack Coll., North Andover, Mass., 1972-75; tchr. Guilford (Conn.) Pub. Schs., 1975-77; pres., co-founder Shoreline Sch. Art and Music, Branford, Conn., 1978—; mem. music edn. coun./student tchr. practicum com. Westfield (Mass.) State Coll., 1978-81, New Haven Arts Coun., 1979; judge various music competitions; clarinet performance Carnegie Hall, 1997; guest conductor Conn. Symphonic Band, 1997. Contbr. revs. to music jours. Mem. Phi Mu Alpha Sinfonia. Office: Shoreline Sch Art and Music Inc 482 E Main St Branford CT 06405-2919

MILGRIM, FRANKLIN MARSHALL, merchant; b. N.Y.C., Aug. 24, 1925; s. Charles and Sally (Knobel) M.; m. Carol E. Kleinman, Sept. 2, 1945; children: Nancy Ellen, Catherine. Grad. with honors, Woodmere (N.Y.) Acad., 1943; B.S. in Econs. with honors, Wharton Sch. U. Pa., 1949. Asst. mgr. Milgrim, Cleve., 1949-50; merchandiser, buyer H. Milgrim Bros., Inc., N.Y.C., 1950-52; v.p., gen. merchandiser H. Milgrim Bros., Inc., 1952-57; pres., dir. Milgrim, Inc., Cleve. and Columbus, Ohio, 1957—; v.p., dir. Milgrim, Inc. (Mich.), Detroit, 1962-66, The 9-18 Corp., Cleve., 1969—; pres., treas., dir. Milgrim Suburban, Inc., 1963—, Milo, Inc., Columbus, 1966—, The Milgrim Co., Cleve., 1966—; pres., dir. Frankly Paul Bailey Inc., Cleve., 1965—; Dir., v.p. M and M Receivers Assn., Cleve., 1959-68. Pres. Severance Center Mchts. Assn., Cleveland Heights, 1963-66; Pres., bd. dirs. Greater Cleve. Area chpt. Nat. Council on Alcoholism, 1973—; chmn. bd. Alcoholism Services of Cleve., 1977—; fin. chmn. adv. council Salvation Army Harbor Light Complex, 1976—, chmn. bd. adv. council, 1981—; mem. Greater Cleve. adv. bd. Salvation Army, 1981—; founding bd. dirs. Sister Mary Ignatia Gavin Found.; foreman Cuyahoga County Grand Jury, 1986. Served with USNR, 1943-46. Mem. Oakwood Country Club (Cleve.), Cleve. Mid-Day Club, City Club (Cleve.), Cleve. Playhouse, Turnberry club (North Miami Beach, Fla.). Home: 4000 Towerside Terr #1908 Miami FL 33138 also: 1 Bratenahl Pl Apt 807 Cleveland OH 44108-1154 also: 1 Bratenahl Pl Apt 807 Cleveland OH 44108-1154

MILGRIM, ROGER MICHAEL, lawyer; b. N.Y.C., Mar. 22, 1937; s. Isreal and Iola (Lash) M.; m. Patricia Conway, July 10, 1971; children: Justin, Alex. BA, U. Pa., 1958; LLB, NYU, 1961, LLM, 1962. Bar: N.Y., U.S. Supreme Ct. Assoc. Baker & McKenzie, Paris, 1963-65, Nixon Mudge et al, N.Y.C., 1965-68; mem. Milgrim Thomajan & Lee P.C., N.Y.C., 1968-92; ptnr. Paul, Hastings, Janofsky & Walker, N.Y.C., 1992—; adj. prof. sch. law NYU, N.Y.C., 1974—. Author: Milgrim on Trade Secrets, 1968, supplement, 1997, Milgrim on Licensing, 1990, supplement, 1997. Trustee Coll. Wooster, 1994—, Bklyn. Hosp., 1982-91. Mem. Knickerbocker Club, Phila. Cricket Club. Republican. Home: 14 Sutton Pl S New York NY 10022-3071 Office: Paul Hastings Janofsky & Walker 399 Park Ave New York NY 10022

MILGROM, FELIX, immunologist, educator; b. Rohatyn, Poland, Oct. 12, 1919; came to U.S., 1958; naturalized, 1963; s. Henryk and Ernestina (Cyryl) M.; m. Halina Miszel, Oct. 15, 1941; children: Henry, Martin Louis. Student, U. Lwow, Poland, 1937-41, U. Lublin, Poland, 1945; MD, U. Wroclaw, Poland, 1947; MD (hon.), U. Vienna, Austria, 1976, U. Lund, Sweden, 1979, U. Heidelberg, Fed. Republic Germany, 1979, U. Bergen, Norway, 1980; DSc (hon.), U. Med. Dent., N.J., 1991. Rsch. assoc., prof. dept. microbiology Sch. Medicine U. Wroclaw, 1946-54, chmn. dept., 1954; prof., head dept. microbiology Sch. Medicine, Silesian U., Zabrze, Poland, 1954-57; rsch. assoc. Svc. de Chime Microbienne, Pasteur Inst., Paris, 1957; rsch. assoc. prof. dept. bacteriology and immunology U. Buffalo Sch. Medicine, 1958-62; assoc. prof., then prof. and disting. prof. microbiology Sch. Medicine, SUNY, Buffalo, 1962—, chmn. dept., 1967-85. Author: Studies on the Structure of Antibodies, 1950; co-editor: International Convocations on Immunology, 1969, 75, 79, 85, Principles of Immunology, 1973, 2d edit., 1979, Principles of Immunological Diagnosis in Medicine, 1981, Medical Microbiology, 1982; editor in chief Internat. Archives of Allergy and Applied Immunology, 1965-91; contbg. editor Vox Sanguinis, 1965-76, Transfusion, 1966-73, Cellular Immunology, 1970-83, Transplation, 1975-78; contbr. numerous articles to profl. jours. Recipient Alfred Jurzykowski Found. prize, 1986, Paul Ehrlich and Ludwig Darmstaedter prize, 1987. Mem. Am. Assn. Immunologists, Transplantation Soc. (v.p. 1976-78), Am. Acad. Microbiology, Coll. Internat. Allergologicum (v.p. 1970-78, pres. 1978-82, hon. mem. 1990—), Polish Acad. Arts and Scis., Sigma Xi. Achievements include research on the serology of syphillis, Tb, rheumatoid arthritis, organ and tissue specificity including blood groups, transplantation and autoimmunity. Home: 474 Getzville Rd Buffalo NY 14226-2555

MILHAVEN, JOHN GILES, religious studies educator; b. N.Y.C., Sept. 1, 1927; s. John Michael and Rose (Burns) M.; m. Anne Teresa Lally, May 21, 1970; 1 child, Shelly. B.A., Woodstock Coll., 1949, M.A. in Teaching, Licentiate in Philosophy, 1950; Licentiate in Theology, Facultés Théologiques de la Compagnie de Jésus d'Enghien, Belgium, 1957; Ph.D. in Philosophy, U. Munich, Germany, 1962. Instr. philosophy Canisius Coll., Buffalo, 1951-53; asst. prof. philosophy Fordham U., N.Y.C., 1961-66; assoc. prof. moral theology Woodstock Coll., Md., 1966-70; assoc. prof. religious studies Brown U., Providence, 1970-76; prof. religious studies Brown U., 1976—; lectr. med. ethics Georgetown U. Med. Sch., Washington, 1966-68. Author: Towards a New Catholic Morality, 1970, Good Anger, 1989, Hadewijch and Her Sisters: Other Ways of Loving and Knowing, 1993; contbr. articles to various publs. Mem. Am. Acad. Religion, Soc. Christian Ethics, Cath. Theol. Soc. Am. Roman Catholic. Home: 20 Penrose Ave Providence RI 02906-5620 Office: Brown U Dept Religious Studies Providence RI 02912 *I believe I succeeded when I effectively shared with others something of my evasive but persistent experience of human life as important.*

MILHORAT, THOMAS HERRICK, neurosurgeon; b. N.Y.C., Apr. 5, 1936; s. Ade Thomas and Edith Caulkins (Herrick) M.; m. Edith Milhorat, 1961; children: John Thomas, Robert Herrick. BA, Cornell U., 1957, MD, 1961. Intern, asst. resident in gen. surgery N.Y. Hosp.-Cornell Med. Ctr., 1961-63; clin. assoc., dept. surg. neurology Nat. Inst. Neurol. Diseases and Blindness, Bethesda, 1963-65; asst. resident, chief resident in neurosurgery N.Y. Hosp.-Cornell Med. Ctr., 1965-68, asst. neurosurgeon NIH, 1968-71; assoc. prof. neurol. surgery, assoc. prof. child health and devel. George Washington U. Sch. Medicine, Washington, 1971-74; prof. child health and devel. George Washington U., Washington, 1974-81, prof. neurol. surgery, 1974-81; chmn. dept. neurosurgery Children's Hosp. Nat. Med. Ctr., Washington, 1971-81; prof. neurol. surgery, dept. chmn. SUNY Health Sci. Ctr., Bklyn., 1982—; neurosurgeon-in-chief Kings County Hosp. Ctr.; regional chmn. neurol. surgery L.I. Coll. Hosp., 1986—, Coney Island Hosp., 1986—; program dir. Neurosurgery Rsch. Tng. Program, 1982—; mem. Nat. Coun. Scientists, NIH, 1969-82. Author: Hydrocephalus and Cerebrospinal Fluid, 1972, Pediatric Neurosurgery, 1978, Cerebrospinal Fluid and the Brain Edemas, 1987, (with M.K. Hammock) Cranial Computed Tomography in Infancy and Childhood, 1981; contbr. 265 articles to sci. publs. and chpts. to books. Chmn. bd. Internat. Neurosci. Found., pres. 1986—; chmn. med. adv. bd. Am. Spingomyelia Alliance Project, 1996—. Lt. commdr. USPHS, 1963-65. Recipient 1st prize in pathology, Cornell U. Med. Sch. Dept. Ob-Gyn., 1960, Charles L. Horn prize Cornell Med. Sch., 1961, Best Paper award ann. combined meeting N.Y. Acad. Medicine/N.Y. Neurosurg. Soc., 1965, Pudenz award for Excellence in CSF Physiology, 1994; named one of N.Y.'s Best Doctors, N.Y. Mag., 1992, 96. Mem. AAAS, Internat. Soc. Pediat. Neurosurgery, Am. Assn. Neurol. Surgery (pediat. sect.), Am. Syringomyelia Alliance Project (chmn. med. adv. bd. 1996—), Am. Acad. Pediat. (surg. sect.), Soc. Pediat. Rsch., N.Y. Acad. Medicine, N.Y. Soc. Neurosurgery (pres. 1988-90), Bklyn. Neurologic Soc. (pres. 1988-95), Soc. Neurosci., Internat. Soc. Neurosci., Soc. Neurol. Surgeons, Med. Club Bklyn., Sigma Xi. Avocations: golf, billiards, gardening. Office: SUNY Health Sci Ctr Bklyn 450 Clarkson Ave PO Box 1189 Brooklyn NY 11203

MILHOUSE, PAUL WILLIAM, bishop; b. St. Francisville, Ill., Aug. 31, 1910; s. Willis Cleveland and Carrie (Pence) M.; m. Mary Frances Noblitt, June 29, 1932; children: Mary Catherine Milhouse Hauswald, Pauline Joyce Milhouse Vermillion, Paul David. A.B., U. Indpls. (formerly Ind. Cen. U.), 1932; D.D., U. Ind. (formerly Ind. Cen. U.), 1950; B.D., Am. Theol. Sem., 1937, Th.D., 1946; L.H.D., Westmar Coll., 1965; S.T.D., Oklahoma City U., 1969; D.D., So. Meth. U., 1969. Ordained to ministry United Brethren Ch., 1931; pastor Birds, Ill., 1928-29, Elliott, Ill., 1932-37, Olney, Ill., 1937-41; pastor 1st Ch., Decatur, Ill., 1941-51; asso. editor Telescope-Messenger, 1951-58; exec. sec. gen. council Evang. United Brethren Ch., 1959-60, bishop, 1960-68; bishop United Meth. Ch., 1968—; presiding bishop Southwestern Area, Evang. United Brethren Ch., 1960-68; presiding bishop Okla., 1968-80; pres. Coun. United Meth. Bishops, 1977-78; bishop-in-residence Oklahoma City U., 1980-91, U. Indpls., 1992—; mem. commn. to unite Evang. United Brethren Ch. and Meth. Ch., 1960-68. Author: Enlisting and Developing Church Leaders, 1946, Come Unto Me, 1946, Lift Up Your Eyes, 1955, Doorways to Spritual Living, 1950, Except the Lord Build the House, 1949, Christian Worship in Symbol and Ritual, 1953, Laymen in the Church, 1957, At Life's Crossroads, 1959, Phillip William Otterbein, 1968, Nineteen Bishops of the Evangelical United Brethren Church, 1974, Organizing for Effective Ministry, 1980, Theological and Historical Roots of United Methodists, 1980, Detour Into Yesterday, 1984, Okla. City U., Miracle at 23d and Blackwelder, 1984, Transforming Dollars into Service, A History of Methodist Manor, 1987, St. Lukes of Oklahoma City, 1988; also articles; editor: Facing Frontiers, 1960. Trustee Westmar Coll., 1960-68, Western Home, 1960-68, So. Meth. U., 1968-80, Oklahoma City U., 1968-80, hon. life trustee, 1980—, Francis E. Willard Home, 1968-80, Meth. Manor, 1968-80, Boys Ranch, 1968-80, Last Frontier coun. Boy Scouts Am., 1968-80; hon. life trustee United Theol. Sem. Recipient Disting. Alumnus award Ind. Ctrl. U. (now U. Indpls.), 1978, Disting. Friend award Oklahoma City U., 1979, Disting. Svc. award Oklahoma City U., 1980, Top Hand award Oklahoma City C. of C., 1980, Bishop Paul W. Milhouse award Oklahoma City U., 1990, Disting. Svc. award for contbns. to United Meth. history Gen. Commn. on Archives and History, 1996. Mem. Mark Twain Writers Guild, Epsilon Sigma Alpha, now Alpha Chi. *Life is a gift to be lived in harmony with the purpose of God, who holds us accountable.*

MILIC-EMILI, JOSEPH, physician, educator; b. Sezana, Slovenia, May 27, 1931; arrived in Can., 1963; s. Joseph Milic-Emili and Giovanna Milic-Emili Perlavec; m. Ann Harding, Nov. 2, 1957; children: Claire, Anne-Marie, Alice, Andrew. MD, U. Milan, 1955; Dr. honoris causa, U. Louvain, Belgium, 1987, Kunming Med. Coll., China, 1987, U. Ferrara, Italy, 1996. Asst. prof. physiology and exptl. medicine McGill U., Montreal, Que., Can., 1963-65, assoc. prof., 1965-69, prof., 1970—, dir. Meakins-Christie Labs., 1979-94; vis. prof. Lab. de Physiologie Faculte de Medecine Saint-Antoine, Paris, Svc. de Pneumologie Hosp. Beaujon, Paris, 1978-79, 94-95, chmn. dept. physiology, 1973-78; vis. cons. medicine Royal Postgrad. Med. Sch., London, 1969-70; vis. cons. aeronautics Imperial Coll. Tech., London, 1969-70; asst. prof. physiology U. Liege, Belgium, 1958-60; asst. prof. U. Milan, 1956-58. Mem. editl. bd. Jour. Applied Physiology, 1970-76, Rev. Française des Maladies Respiratories, 1979-96, Rivista de Biologia, 1979-86, Am. Rev. Respiratory Disease, 1982-89, Reanimation, Soins Intensifs, Medicine d'Urgence, 1984—. Mem. applied physiology and bioengring. study sect. NIH, 1975-78. Decorated Order of Can.; recipient Gold medal C. Forlanini U. Pavia, Italy, 1982, Am. Coll. Chest Physicians medal, 1984, Harry Wunderly medal Thoracic Soc. Australia, 1988, medal Italian Sch. Mil. Medicine, 1990, medal Med. Sch. Brest, 1997; author of one of 100-most cited articles in clin. rsch. of 1960s; named one of 1,000 most-cited contemporary scientists, 1965-78. Fellow Royal Soc. Can., Slovenian Acad. Scis. (fgn. corr.); mem. Am. Physiol. Soc., Can. Physiol. Soc., Can. Thoracic Soc., Med. Rsch. Coun. (mem. grants com. 1980), Soc. Pneumologie Belge (hon.), Brazilian Physiol. Soc. (hon.), Hellenic Thoracic Soc. (hon.), Polish Pneumological Soc. (hon.). Home: 4394 Circle Rd, Montreal, PQ Canada H4W 1Y5 Office: McGill U Meakins-Christie Labs, 3626 St Urbain St, Montreal, PQ Canada H2X 2P2

MILIORA, MARIA TERESA, chemist, psychotherapist, psychoanalyst, educator; b. Somerville, Mass., June 29, 1938; d. Andrew and Maria Civita (Gallinaro) Migliorini. BA cum laude, Regis Coll., 1960; PhD, Tufts U., 1965; MSW, Boston U., 1985. Rsch. asst. Tufts U., Medford, Mass., 1960-64; rsch. assoc. Tufts U., 1965-66; assoc. prof. Suffolk U., Boston, 1965-68; asso. prof. Suffolk U., 1968-71, prof., 1971—, chmn. dept. chemistry, 1972-84, mem. presdl. search com., 1980; faculty rep. univ. strategic planning com. Suffolk U., Boston, 1992—; faculty Boston Inst. for Psychotherapy, 1992—; faculty mem. Tng. and Rsch. Inst. for Self Psychology, N.Y.C., 1994—; research asso. Bio-Research Inst., Cambridge, Mass., 1968. Contbr. articles to profl. jours. Faculty rep. to trustees Joint Coun. on Univ. Affairs, Suffolk U., 1973-77, 79-81; convenor Pres.'s Commn. on Status of Women, 1974-78, speaker ednl. policy com., 1972-73; chair cultural diversity CLAS Curriculum, 1991—. Mem. AAUP (chpt. pres. 1970), NASW, Am. Chem. Soc. (alt. councillor 1976-79, 82—, councillor 1979-82, bd. dirs. Northeastern sect. 1976—, chmn. pub. rels. sect. 1977-79), Mass. Acad. Clin. Social Work, Nat. Assn. for Advancement Psychoanalysis, Nat. Membership Com. on Psychoanalysis, Sigma Xi (chpt. pres. 1972-73), Sigma Zeta (chpt. sect. 1970—), Alpha Lambda Delta, Delta Epsilon Sigma. Home: 41 Irving St Newton MA 02159-1611 Office: Suffolk University Beacon Hill Boston MA 02114

MILITELLO, SAMUEL PHILIP, lawyer; b. Buffalo, Dec. 16, 1947; s. Samuel Anthony and Katherine (Pesono) M.; m. Anne Little, May 27, 1972; children: Matthew Samuel, Rebecca Anne, Caitlin Frances. BA, Canisius Coll., 1969; JD, SUNY, Buffalo, 1972. Bar: N.Y. 1972, U.S. Ct. Mil. Appeals 1973, U.S. Army Ct. of Mil. Rev. 1976, U.S. Ct. Claims 1977, U.S. Supreme Ct. 1977, U.S. Dist. Ct. (we. dist.) N.Y. 1986, U.S. Dist. Ct. (no. dist.) N.Y. 1987, U.S. Dist. Ct. (ea. dist.) N.Y. 1994, U.S. Ct. Appeals (2d cir.), 1990. Assoc. Williams & Katzman, Watertown, N.Y., 1978-79; legal counsel, mgr. of litigation Parsons Corp., Pasadena, Calif., 1979-84; gen. counsel, sec. Envirogas, Inc., Hamburg, N.Y., 1984-86; assoc. Bond, Schoeneck & King, Watertown, 1987-88; mng. ptnr. The Militello Law Office, P.C., Watertown, 1989—; counsel Parsons Gilbane, New Orleans, 1979-81; gen. counsel The Stebbins Engring. and Mfg. Co. and subs., 1986—. Capt. JAGC, U.S. Army, 1973-78. Decorated Army Commendation medal with one oak leaf cluster, Meritorious Service medal. Mem. ABA (pub. contracts sect.), N.Y. State Bar Assn., N.Y. Criminal and Civil Cts. Bar Assn., Bar Assn. of Erie County (N.Y.), Bar Assn. of Jefferson County (N.Y.), No. N.Y. Builders Exchange, Assoc. Gen. Contractors Am., Am. Legion, K.C. (adv. 1978-79). Roman Catholic. Office: PO Box 6800 1619 Ohio St Watertown NY 13601

MILIUS, RICHARD A., organic chemist; b. Lawrence, Mass., Nov. 10, 1950; s. Leo and Teresa (Liehr) M.; m. Amy L. Dingley, Sept. 29, 1979; children: James, Elena, Joseph, Jillian. BS, Marquette U., 1972; PhD, Northeastern U., 1981. Rsch. chemist Miles Labs., Inc., Elkhart, Ind., 1972-74; chemist New Eng. Nuclear Corp., Boston, 1974-77; rsch. assoc. Harvard Med. Sch., Boston, 1981-84; tech. dir. Rsch. Biochems. Internat., Natick, Mass., 1984-94; dir. sponsored rsch. Rsch. Biochems. Internat., Natick, 1994-96, dir. mktg. svcs., 1996—; chmn. small bus. rsch. rev. com. NIMH, Washington, 1991-93; instr. Univ. Coll. Northeastern U., Boston, 1988-92. Co-chmn. Norwood/Brockton chpt. Open Door Soc. Mass., 1989-90. Recipient Marie Curie award European Assn. Nuclear Medicine, 1992. Mem. AAAS, Am. Chem. Soc., Soc. Neurosci., Soc. Nuclear Medicine. Achievements include patents for astatinated organic compounds, iodinated neuroprobe for mapping monoamine reuptake sites. Office: Rsch Biochems Internat 1 Strathmore Rd Natick MA 01760-2418

MILKMAN, ROGER DAWSON, genetics educator, molecular evolution researcher; b. N.Y.C., Oct. 15, 1930; s. Louis Arthur and Margaret (Weinstein) M.; m. Marianne Friedenthal, Oct. 18, 1958; children: Ruth Margaret, Louise Friedenthal, Janet Dawson Milkman Lussenhop, Paul David. A.B., Harvard U., 1951, A.M., 1954, Ph.D., 1956. Student, asst., instr., investigator Marine Biol. Lab., Woods Hole, Mass., 1952-72, 88-96; instr., asst. prof. U. Mich., Ann Arbor, 1957-60; assoc. prof., prof. Syracuse U., N.Y., 1960-68; prof. biol. scis. U. Iowa, Iowa City, 1968—, chmn. univ. genetics PhD program, 1992-93; vis. prof. biology Grinnell (Iowa) Coll., 1990; mem. genetics study sect. NIH, 1986-87; NSF panelist, 1996—. Translator: Developmental Physiology, 1970; editor: Perspectives on Evolution, 1982, Experimental Population Genetics, 1983, Evolution jour., 1984-86; mem. editl. bd. Molecular Phylogenetics and Evolution; contbr. articles to profl. jours. Sec. Soc. Gen. Physiologists, 1963-65, Am. Soc. Naturalists, 1980-82; alumni rep. Phillips Acad., Andover, Mass., 1980-94. NSF grantee, 1959—; USPHS grantee, 1984-87. Fellow AAAS; mem. Am. Soc. for Microbiology, Genetics Soc. Am., Corp. Marine Biol. Lab., Soc. for Gen. Microbiology (U.K.), Soc. Study Evolution, Soc. Molecular Biology and Evolution, Internat. Soc. for Molecular Evolution. Jewish. Avocation: mountain hiking. Home: 12 Fairview Knoll NE Iowa City IA 52240-9147 Office: U Iowa Dept Biol Scis 138 Biology Building Bldg Iowa City IA 52242-1324

MILLANE, LYNN, town official; b. Buffalo, N.Y. Oct. 14, 1928; d. Robert P. Schermerhorn and Justine A. (Ross) m. J. Vaughan Millane, Jr.; Aug. 16, 1952 children: Maureen, Michele, John, Mark, Kathleen. EdB, U. Buffalo, 1949, EdM, in Health Education 1951. Mem. Amherst Town Bd., 1982—, dep. town supr., 1990—, supr., 1996—; pres., E. J. Meyer Hosp. Jr. Bd., 1962-64; pres. Aux. to Erie County Bar Assn., 1966-68; pres. Women's Com. of Buffalo Philharm. Orch., 1976-78, v.p. adminstrn., 1975-76, v.p. pub. affairs, 1974-75, chmn. adv. bd., 1979-82; v.p. Buffalo Philharm. Orch. Soc., Inc., 1976-78, mem. coun., trustee, 1979-87, bd. overseers, 1987-92; dir. 8th jud. dist. N.Y. State Assn. of Large Towns, 1989-90, 90-91; bd. dirs. oper. bd. Millard Fillmore Suburban Hosp., 1992-2001; 1st v.p. Fans for 17, 1980-82; 1st. v.p. Friends of Baird Hall, SUNY-Buffalo, 1980-82; exec. bd. mem. Longview Protestant Home for Children, 1979-85, 2d v.p., 1982-85; bd. dirs. ARC, Town of Amherst br., 1982-91, by-laws com., 1981, 84, chmn. sr. concerns com., 1982-91, liaison code of ethics com., 1987-89; bd. dirs. Amherst Symphony Orch. Assn., 1981-87, roster chmn., 1982-84, nominating chmn., 1985-86, vice-chmn. 50th anniversary com., 1994—; nat. music com. Women's Assn. for Symphony Orchs. in Am. and Can., 1977-79; coun. mem. Am. Symphony Orch. League; sec. Amherst Sr. Citizen's Adv. Bd., 1980-81, liaison from Amherst Town Bd., 1982—; founder, liaison 1st adult day svcs. adv. bd. Town of Amherst, 1988; liaison to ad hoc cable TV com., 1992-96, liaison to Amherst C. of C., 1993-96, mem. 1st records mgmt. adv. bd., liaison ethics bd. Town of Amherst, 1994—, dep. supr. 1990-95, supr., 1996—; liaison to the Alternate Fuel and Clean Cities Com., 1994-96; dir.-at-large community adv. coun. SUNY-Buffalo, 1981-91; co-assoc. chmn. maj. gift div. capital campaign Daemen Coll., 1983-84; co-chmn. Women United Against Drugs Campaign, 1970-72; founding mem. Lunch and Issues, Amherst, 1981—; mem. edn. com. Network in Aging of Western N.Y., Inc., 1982-89, bd. dirs., 1982-89, housing com., 1987-89; bd. dirs. Amherst Elderly Transp. Corp., 1982—; committeeman dist. Town of Amherst Republican Com.; treas. Town and Country Rep. Club, 1980-81; mem. nominating com. Fedn. Rep. Women's Clubs Erie County, 1980; exec. bd. mem. Women's Exec. Coun. of Erie County Rep. Com., 1969-71; dir. Amherst Rep. Women's Club, 1963-65; delegate N.Y. State Govs. Conf. on Aging, 1995, White House Conf. on Aging, 1995, named mem. aging svcs. adv. com. N.Y. State Office of the Aging Gov. George Pataki, 1996—; mem. Erie County Indsl. Devel. Agy., Erie County Regional Devel. Corp., 1996—. Named Homemaker of Yr., Family Circle Mag., 1969; Woman of Substance, 20th Century Rep. Women, 1983; Woman of Yr., Buffalo Philharm. Orch. Soc., Inc., 1982; Outstanding Woman in Community Svc., SUNY-Buffalo, 1985; recipient Good Neighbor award Courier Express, 1978; Merit award Buffalo Philharm. Orch., 1978; award Fedn. Rep. Women's Clubs Erie County, 1982; Disting. Svc. award Town of Amherst Sr. Ctr., 1985; Susan B. Anthony award Interclub Coun. of Western N.Y., 1991, Community Svc. award Amherst Rep. Com., 1991, D.A.R.E. award Town of Amherst Police Dept., 1994, Disting. Svc. award Amherst Adult Day Care and Vis. Nurses Assn., 1994, Outstanding Cmty. Svc. award Amherst Sr. Citizen Found., 1997; Rep. honoree Town of Amherst, 1996. Mem. Amherst C. of C. (VIP dinner com. 1984), LWV, SUNY-Buffalo Alumni Assn. (life, presdl. advisor 1977-79), Zonta (pres. Amherst chpt. 1986-88, Zontian of Yr. 1992), Pi Lambda Theta (hon.).

MILLAR, GORDON HALSTEAD, mechanical engineer, agricultural machinery manufacturing executive; b. Newark, Nov. 28, 1923; s. George Halstead and Dill E. (McMullen) M.; m. Virginia M. Jedryczka, Aug. 24, 1957; children—George B., Kathryn M., Juliet S., John G., James H. B.M.E., U. Detroit, 1949, D.Sc. (hon.), 1977; Ph.D., U. Wis., 1952; L.H.D., West Coast U., 1984; D.Sc. (hon.), Western Mich. U., 1986. Registered profl. engr., Fla., Ill., Iowa, Mich., Minn., Ohio. Supr. new powerplants Ford Motor Co., 1952-57; engring. mgr. Meriam Instrument Co., Cleve., 1957-59; dir. new products McCulloch Corp., Los Angeles, 1959-63; with Deere & Co., 1963-84; v.p. engring. Deere & Co., Moline, Ill., 1972-84; exec. assoc. Southwest Research Inst., 1987; mem. Fed. Adv. Com. Indsl. Innovation, 1979; chmn. West Ctrl. Ill. Ednl. Telecom. Corp.; pres. Accreditation Bd. for Engring. and Tech., 1983-85; pres., fellow Accreditation Bd. for Engring. and Tech. Contbr. articles to profl. jours.; patentee in field. Chmn. Quad Cities chpt. United Way, 1976-77; bd. dirs.; adv. council Bradley U. Coll. Engring. and Tech.; mem. exec. com. Illowa council Boy Scouts Am., 1977-79. Served with U.S. Army, World War II. Decorated Purple Heart; recipient Alumnus of Year award U. Detroit, 1976, Comdrs. medal for pub. svc. Dept. Army, 1989. Fellow ASME (hon. life mem.), Soc. Automotive Engrs. (pres. 1984, bd. dirs. 1984-86, mem. nat. nominating com.); mem. NAE, NSPE, Engrs. Joint Coun., Indsl. Rsch. Inst., Engring.

Soc. Detroit, Am. Soc. Agrl. Engrs., Ill. Soc. Profl. Engrs., Moline C. of C., Aviation Coun. Home: 1840 Wiley Post Trl Daytona Beach FL 32124-6756

MILLAR, JAMES ROBERT, economist, educator, university official; b. San Antonio, Tex., July 7, 1936; s. James G. and Virginia M. (Harrison) M.; m. Gera Ascher, July 4, 1965; children: Leo Schaeg (dec.), Mira Gail. B.A., U. Tex., 1958; Ph.D. in Econs, Cornell U., 1965. Asst. prof. dept. econs. U. Ill., Urbana, 1965-70, assoc. prof., 1970-72, prof., 1973-89, assoc. vice chancellor for acad. affairs, 1984-89, dir. internat. programs and studies, 1984-89; prof. econs. and internat. affairs George Washington U., Washington, 1989—, dir. Inst. for European, Russian and Eurasian Studies, 1989—, assoc. dean Elliott Sch. Internat. Affairs, 1989-95, acting dean, 1994; mem. acad. coun. Kennan Inst. Advanced Russian, 1975-84; young faculty exchangee Moscow State U., 1966; cons. to congressmen and various U.S. govt. depts., 1972—; dir. Soviet Interview Project, 1981-88; sec., bd. dirs. Midwest Univs. Consortium for Internat. Activities, 1984-88, chmn. bd., 1988-89. Author: The ABCs of Soviet Socialism, 1981, The Soviet Economic Experiment, 1990; editor, contbr. The Soviet Rural Community, 1971; editor: Slavic Rev., Am. Quar. Soviet and East European Studies, 1975-80, Problems of Post-Communism, 1996—; editor, contbr. Politics, Work and Daily Life, A Survey of Former Soviet Citizens, 1987; editor, contbr. Cracks in the Monolith: Party Power in the Brezhnev Era, 1992, The Social Legacy of Communism, 1994; contbr. articles on studies on Soviet/Russian economy and econ. history to scholarly jours. Served with Q.M.C. U.S. Army, 1960. Ford Found. fgn. area fellow, 1961-64; sr. scholar rsch. travel grantee to USSR, 1972; Am. Coun. Learned Socs./USSR Acad. Scis. travel exchangee, 1979; fellow Woodrow Wilson Internat. Ctr. for Scholars, 1988-89, Guggenheim fellow, 1995-96; IREX advanced rsch. grantee, 1996. Mem. AAAS, Econ. History Assn., Assn. Evolutionary Econs., Am. Assn. Slavic Studies (del. Am. Coun. Learned Soc. 1992—, bd. dirs. 1995—), Am. Coun. Learned Soc. (treas., bd. dirs. 1996—, sec. 1995-96, mem. exec. com. del., chair 1993-95, mem. joint com. with Social Sci. Rsch. Coun. 1990-95), Am. Assn. Pub. Opinion Rsch., N.Y. Acad. Sci. Home: The Westchester 4000 Cathedral Ave NW Apt 143B Washington DC 20016-5249 Office: George Washington U Inst Eur Russ Eurasian Studies 2013 G St NW Ste 401 Washington DC 20006-4205

MILLAR, JEFFERY LYNN, columnist; b. Houston, July 10, 1942; s. Daniel Lynn Millar and Betty Ruth (Shove) Coons; m. Lynne McDonald, Dec. 21, 1964 (div. Aug. 1983); m. Peggy V. Watson, Apr. 1, 1994. BA, U. Tex., 1964. Reporter Houston Chronicle, 1964-65, film critic, 1965—, columnist, 1972—. Writer, co-creator: (comic strip) Tank McNamara, Universal Press Syndicate, Kansas City, 1974—. Office: Houston Chronicle PO Box 4260 Houston TX 77210-4260

MILLAR, JOHN DONALD, occupational and environmental health consultant, educator; b. Newport News, Va., Feb. 27, 1934; s. John and Dorothea Virginia (Smith) M.; m. Joan M. Phillips, Aug. 17, 1957; children: John Stuart, Alison Gordon, Virginia Taylor. B.S., U. Richmond, 1956; M.D., Med. Coll. Va., 1959; D.T.P.H., London Sch. Hygiene and Tropical Medicine, 1966; D of Pub. Svc. (hon.), Greenville (Ill.) Coll., 1994. Cert. specialist in Gen. Preventive Medicine, 1969. Intern U. Utah Affiliated Hosps., Salt Lake City, 1959-60, asst. resident in medicine, 1960-61; chief Epidemic Intelligence Svc., Ctr. for Disease Control, USPHS, HEW, Atlanta, 1961-63, dep. chief surveillance sect. epidemiology br., 1962-63, chief smallpox unit, 1963-65, dir. smallpox eradication program, 1966-70, dir. Bur. State Svcs., 1970-78, asst. dir. Ctr. for Disease Control for Pub. Health Practice, 1979-80; dir. Ctr. for Environ. Health Atlanta, 1980-81; dir. Nat. Inst. for Occupation Safety and Health, Atlanta, 1981-93; pres. Don Millar & Assocs., Inc., Atlanta, 1993—; adj. prof. occupational and environ. health Sch. Pub. Health Emory U., Atlanta; cons. on smallpox, smallpox eradication, immunization programs and occupational and environ. health WHO; mem. WHO expert adv. panel on occupational health; bd. dirs. Farm Safety 4 Just Kids, 1993—; tech. adv. bd. Ctr. Protect Workers' Rights, 1993; adv. group Ctr. Workplace Excellence, 1995—. Mem. editl. bd. Am. Jour. Indsl. Medicine, 1985—, Am. Jour. Occupl. Psychology, 1993—, Am. Jour. Preventive Medicine, 1993—; contbr. articles to profl. jours. Recipient Surgeon Gen's. Commendation medal, 1965, Okeke prize London Sch. Hygiene and Tropical Medicine, 1966, Presdl. award for mgmt. improvement, 1972, W.C. Gorgas medal Assn. Mil. Surgeons U.S., 1987, Lucas lectr. Faculty Occupational Medicine Royal Coll. Physicians, London, 1987, Outstanding Med. Alumnus award Med. Coll. Va., 1988; also recipient Equal Employment Opportunity award, 1975, Medal of Excellence, 1977, Joseph W. Mountin lectr. award, 1986, all from Ctrs. for Disease Control, Disting. Svc. medal USPHS, 1983, 88, Exemplary Svc. medal Surgeon Gen. U.S., 1988, Giants in Occupational Medicine lectr. U. Utah, 1989, William S. Knudsen award Am. Coll. Occupational Medicine, 1991, presdl. citation APA, 1991, William Steiger Meml. award Am. Conf. Govtl. Indsl. Hygienists, 1993, Health Watch award for outstanding contbns. toward improving health of minority popyulations, 1992, Award of Merit Minerva Edn. Inst., 1993, Alumni Disting. Svc. award U. Richmond, 1993; named to Order Bifurcated Needle, World Health Orgn., 1978, Faculty Occupational Medicine, Royal Coll. Physicians, London, 1990. Mem. Am. Indsl. Hygiene Assn. (hon.). Office: Don Millar & Assocs Inc Ste 201 3243 Wake Robin Trail Atlanta GA 30341-5721

MILLAR, RICHARD WILLIAM, JR., lawyer; b. L.A., May 11, 1938. LLB, U. San Francisco, 1966. Bar: Calif. 1967, U.S. Dist. Ct. (cen. dist.) Calif. 1967, U.S. Dist. Ct. (no. dist.) Calif. 1969, U.S. Dist. Ct. (so. dist.) Calif. 1973, U.S. Supreme Ct. Assoc. Iverson & Hogoboom, Los Angeles, 1967-72; ptnr. Eilers, Stewart, Pangman & Millar, Newport Beach, Calif., 1973-75, Millar & Heckman, Newport Beach, 1975-77, Millar, Hodges & Bemis, Newport Beach, 1979—. Fellow Am. Bar Found.; mem. ABA (litigation sect., trial practice com., ho. of dels. 1990—), Calif. Bar Assn. (lectr. CLE), Orange County Bar Assn. (chmn. bus. litigation sect. 1981, chmn. judiciary com. 1988-90), Balboa Bay Club, Bohemian Club (San Francisco). Home: 2546 Crestview Dr Newport Beach CA 92663-5625 Office: Millar Hodges & Bemis One Newport Pl Ste # 900 Newport Beach CA 92660

MILLAR, SALLY GRAY, nurse; b. Madison, Wis., Dec. 8, 1946; d. William Llewellyn and Janet Josephine (Dean) M. Student, U. Iowa, 1964-65; R.N., St. Joseph Hosp. Sch. Nursing, 1968; M.B.A., Simmons Coll. Grad. Sch. Mgmt., 1985. Staff nurse Bryn Mawr (Pa.) Hosp., 1968-69; team leader, cardiac surg. intensive care unit Mass. Gen. Hosp., Boston, 1969-78, head nurse, respiratory/surg. intensive care unit, 1978-81, clin. nurse leader, intensive care nursing service, 1981-85, project dir. patient classification system, 1985-86, dir. nursing info. systems, 1986-97, dir. integrated clin. support svcs., 1997—. Editor: Focus on Critical Care, 1978-80; editor-in-chief: Methods in Critical Care, 1980, Procedure Manual for Critical Care, 1985. Mem. Am. Assn. Critical Care Nurses (pres. 1980-81, dir. 1976-82), Soc. Critical Care Medicine. Republican. Roman Catholic. Home: 849 Boston Post Rd E Apt 3-e Marlborough MA 01752-3727 Office: Mass Gen Hosp 32 Fruit St Boston MA 02114-2620

MILLARD, CHARLES WARREN, III, museum director, writer; b. Elizabeth, N.J., Dec. 20, 1932; s. Charles Warren and Constance Emily (Keppler) M. A.B. magna cum laude, Princeton U., 1954; M.A., Harvard U., 1963, Ph.D., 1971. Asst. to dir. Fogg Art Mus. Harvard U., Cambridge, Mass., 1963-64; asst. to dir. Dumbarton Oaks, Washington, 1965-66; dir. Washington Gallery Modern Art, 1966-67; teaching fellow Harvard U., 1968-69; curator 19th Century European art Los Angeles County Mus. Art, 1971-74; chief curator Hirshhorn Mus. and Sculpture Garden Smithsonian Instn., Washington, 1974-86; adj. prof. Johns Hopkins U., Balt., 1983-86; dir. Ackland Art Mus. U. N.C., Chapel Hill, 1986-93, adj. prof., 1986-93; chmn. vis. com. to fine arts dept. Boston U., 1977-80. Author: The Sculpture of Edgar Degas, 1977, La Vie D'Auguste Preault, Auguste Preault Sculpteur Romantique, 1809-1879, 1997; art editor Hudson Rev., 1972-87; contbr. articles to profl. jours. Served with USN, 1956-59.

MILLARD, NEAL STEVEN, lawyer; b. Dallas, June 6, 1947; s. Bernard and Adele (Marks) M.; m. Janet Keast, Mar. 12, 1994; 1 child, Kendall Layne. BA cum laude, UCLA, 1969; JD, U. Chgo., 1972. Bar: Calif. 1972, U.S. Dist. Ct. (cen. dist.) Calif. 1973, U.S. Tax Ct. 1973, U.S. Ct. Appeals (9th cir.) 1987, N.Y. 1990. Assoc. Willis, Butler & Schiefly, Los Angeles, 1972-75; ptnr. Morrison & Foerster, Los Angeles, 1975-84, Jones, Day, Reavis & Pogue, Los Angeles, 1984-93, White & Case, L.A., 1993—; instr. Calif. State Coll., San Bernardino, 1975-76; lectr. Practising Law Inst., N.Y.C., 1983-90, Calif. Edn. of Bar, 1987-90; adj. prof. USC Law Ctr., 1994—. Citizens adv. com. L.A. Olympics, 1982-84; trustee Altadena (Calif.) Libr. Dist., 1985-86; bd. dirs. Woodcraft Rangers, L.A., 1982-90, pres., 1986-88; bd. dirs. L.A. County Bar Found., 1990—; mem. Energy Commn. of County and Cities of L.A., 1995—; bd. dirs. Inner City Law Ctr., 1996—. Mem. ABA, Calif. Bar Assn., N.Y. State Bar Assn., L.A. County Bar Assn. (trustee 1985-87), Pub. Counsel (bd. dirs. 1984-87, 90-93), U. Chgo. Law Alumni Assn. (bd. dirs. So. Calif. chpt. 1981—), Calif. Club, Phi Beta Kappa, Pi Gamma Mu, Phi Delta Phi. Office: White and Case 633 W 5th St Ste 1900 Los Angeles CA 90071-2027

MILLARD, RICHARD STEVEN, lawyer; b. Pasadena, Calif., Feb. 6, 1952; s. Kenneth A. and Kathryn Mary (Paden) M.; m. Jessica Ann Edwards, May 15, 1977; children: Victoria, Elizabeth, Andrew. AB, Stanford U., 1974; JD magna cum laude, U. Mich., 1977. Bar: Calif. 1977, Ill. 1985. Assoc. Heller, Ehrman, White & McAuliff, San Francisco, 1977-81; assoc. Mayer, Brown & Platt, Chgo., 1982-83, ptnr., 1984—. Mem. ABA, Order of Coif. Office: Mayer Brown & Platt 190 S La Salle St Chicago IL 60603-3410

MILLARD, STEPHENS FILLMORE, electronics company executive; b. Balt., Dec. 5, 1932; s. Lyman Clifford and Frances Louise (Stephens) M.; m. Suzanne Taylor, Nov. 2, 1957 (div. 1990); children: Anne, Stephens, William; m. Linda Dyer, 1995. BS in Econs., U. Pa., 1955; MBA, Northwestern U., 1963. Dist. sales mgr. Olin Mathieson Chem. Corp., Chgo., 1958-63; Western Sales mgr. Champion Papers, Inc., San Francisco, 1963-70; U.S. sales mgr. MacMillan Bloedel, Ltd., Vancouver, B.C., Can., 1970-72; dir. new product devel. Crown Zellerbach Corp., San Francisco, 1972-75; Midwestern sales mgr. paper group Internat. Paper Co., Chgo., 1975-79; v.p. mktg. Mead Corp., Dayton, Ohio, 1979-83; co-founder, sr. v.p. Packet Techs., Inc. (now Stratacom/Cisco, Inc.), Cupertino, Calif., 1983-86; co-founder, Cable Data, Inc., GTE Comm., Cisco, Inc., Metricom, Inc., Com-21; adv. bd. The Snider Entrepreneurial Ctr. Wharton Sch. U. Pa., 1996—, Kellogg Sch. Northwestern U., 1996—. Dir. alumni ann. giving Northwestern U.; trustee Severn Prep. Sch., Severna Park, Md.; chmn. devel. com. Santa Fe Inst., 1993; bd. visitors Nat. Def. U., Ft. McNair, Washington, 1994— (Nat. War Coll., Armed Forces Staff Coll., Industrial Coll. of the Armed Forces); adv. bd. Bionomics Inst., San Rafael, Calif., 1995—. Recipient Rolland Marshall Teel award Severn Sch., 1994. Served to 1st lt., U.S. Army, 1955-57. Mem. Northwestern U. Grad. Sch. Bus. Alumni Assn. (nat. pres. 1967-68), Wharton Sch. Alumni Assn. (v.p.), Active Core Execs., The February Group. Republican. Episcopalian. Home: 5 Fremontia St Portola Vally CA 94028-8032

MILLBERG, JOHN C., lawyer; b. New London, Conn., Jan. 4, 1956; s. Melvin Roy and Dorothy (Van Zandt) M.; m. Lori Bruce Millberg, Oct. 18, 1981; children: Kathryn Faye, Rebecca Ann, Melvin Roy III. BA, Bowling Green State U., 1977; JD, Wake Forest U., 1980. Bar: Tex. 1980, N.C. 1986, U.S. Dist. Ct. (so. dist.) Tex. 1981, U.S. Dist. Ct. (ea., mid. and we. dists.) N.C. 1986, U.S. Ct. Appeals (4th cir.) 1986, U.S. Ct. Appeals (5th and 11th cir.) 1981. Assoc. Crain Caton James & Womble, Houston, 1981-85; assoc., dir. Maupin, Taylor, Ellis & Adams, Raleigh, N.C., 1985-94; mng. ptnr. Millberg & Gordon, Raleigh, N.C., 1994—; mem. bar candidate com. N.C. Bd. Law Examiners, 1988-90. Scholar Wake Forest U. Sch. Law, 1977-80. Mem. N.C. Assn. Def. Attys., Nat. Assn. R.R. Trial Counsel. Office: Millberg & Gordon 1030 Washington St Raleigh NC 27605-1258

MILLENDER-MCDONALD, JUANITA, congresswoman, former school system administrator; b. Birmingham, Ala., Sept. 7, 1938; d. Shelly and Everlina (Dortch) M.; m. James McDonald III, July 26, 1955; children: Valeria, Angela, Sherryll, Michael, Roderick. BS, U. Redlands, Calif., 1980; MS in Edn., Calif. State U., L.A., 1986; postgrad., U. So. Calif. Manuscript editor Calif. State Dept. Edn., Sacramento; dir. gender equity programs L.A. Unified Sch. Dist.; mem. 105th Congress from 37th Calif dist., Washington, 1996—. City councilwoman, Carson; bd. dirs. S.C.L.C. Pvt. Industry Coun. Policy Bd., West Basin Mcpl. Water Dist., Cities Legis. League (vice chmn.; mem. Nat. Women's Polit. Caucus; mem. adv. bd. Comparative Ethnic Tng. U. So. Calif.; founder, exec. dir. Young Advocates So. Calif. Mem. NEA, Nat. Assn. Minority Polit. Women, NAFE, Nat. Fedn. Bus. and Profl. Women, Assn. Calif. Sch. Adminstrs., Am. Mgmt. Assn., Nat. Coun. Jewish Women, Carson C. of C., Phi Delta Kappa. Office: US House of Reps 419 Cannon Bldg Washington DC 20515-0537*

MILLER, AILEEN ETTA MARTHA, medical association administrator, consultant, metabolic nutritionist; b. Sullivan, Ind., Oct. 4, 1924; d. Arthur Henry and Alice Maria (Michael) Dettmer; m. Robert Charles Miller, Sept. 1, 1945; children: Robert Conrad, Debra Carol, Theresa Marie. D of Chiropractic, Palmer Coll. Chiropractic, 1945. Sec. Soroptimist Internat., East Detroit, Mich., 1951-52, Mich. State Chiropractic Assn. Dist. 1, East Detroit, 1957-58, Macomb County Chiropractic Assn., East Detroit, 1982-86; pres. Macomb County Chiropractic Assn., Warren, Mich., 1986-87; cons. Chiropractic Physicians, Warren, 1986—. Recipient Humanitarian and Svc. award Palmer Coll., 1995. Mem. Internat. Chiropractic Assn., Mich. State Chiropractic Assn., Roy Sweat Rsch. and Edn. Found., Found. Chiropractic Edn. and Rsch., Palmer Coll. Alumni Assn., Atlas Orthogonal Chiropractic Assn. (humanitarian and svc. award 1995), Assn. for Rsch. and Enlightenment (assoc. licentiate of United Metaphysical Chs., East Pointe, Mich. divsn.), Order of Ea. Star. Avocations: organ, art appreciation, traveling, bible study. Office: Chiropractic Physicians 30020 Schoenherr Rd Warren MI 48093-3100

MILLER, ALAN, software executive, management specialist; b. Bklyn., Apr. 20, 1954; s. Michael and Lillian Charlotte (Garment) M.; m. Zelda Sara Bochlin, Nov. 16, 1974; children: Michael Glenn, Dara Jennifer. BS in Computer Sci. magna cum laude, SUNY, 1975; MBA in Mgmt. with honors, Adelphi U., 1982. Tech. svcs. mgr. Guardian Life Ins. Co., N.Y.C., 1977-81; project mgr. Mfrs. Hanover Trust Co., N.Y.C., 1981-83; asst. v.p. Bankers Trust Co., N.Y.C., 1983-86; v.p., MIS dir. Bank Am. Trust Co. of N.Y., N.Y.C., 1986-87; assoc. John Diebold and Assocs., N.Y.C., 1987-89; mgr. banking practice AGS Info. Svcs., N.Y.C., 1989-90; v.p. bus. devel., product mgr. global trade fin. BIS Banking Systems, N.Y.C., 1990-93; sr. cons. Computer Scis. Corp. Consulting, 1994-95; mgr. global govt., healthcare, ins., banking, fin. and securities industry IBM Corp., Somers, NY, worldwide, 1995—. Chmn. Sch. Dist. Adv. Com., Plainview, N.Y., 1981-83; exec. producer Oklahoma prodn. Patio Players, Plainview, 1990-91; bd. dirs. men's club Plainview Jewish Ctr., 1986-95. Mem. Delta Mu Delta. Jewish. Avocations: softball, theater, games shows, volleyball. Home: 21 Beaumont Dr Plainview NY 11803-2507 Office: Rte 100 Somers NY 10589

MILLER, ALAN B., hospital management executive; b. N.Y.C., Aug. 17, 1937; s. Daniel and Mary (Blumenthal) M.; m. Jill K. Stein, Oct. 5, 1968; children: Marc Daniel, Marni Elizabeth, Abby Danielle. BA, Coll. William and Mary, 1958; MBA, U. Pa., 1960. V.p. Young & Rubicam, Inc., N.Y.C., 1964-69; sr. v.p. Am. Medicorp., Inc., L.A., 1970; pres., chief exec. officer Am. Medicorp., Inc., Phila., 1973-77, chmn. bd., 1977; chmn. bd. Hosp. Underwriting Group, 1977-78; founder, pres., chmn. bd. Universal Health Svcs., King of Prussia, Pa., 1978—; chmn., founder UHT-Real Estate Trust, King of Prussia, 1986—; formerly health care adviser Fed. Mediation and Conciliation Svc.; bd. mem. Leonard Davis Inst. U. Pa.; past mem. adv. bd. Temple U. Sch. Bus.; chmn., pres. Universal Health Svcs. Real Estate Investment Trust, N.Y. Stock Exch., 1986—; bd. dirs. Genesis Health, GMIS, Inc. Trustee Penn Mut. Life; former trustee Coll. of William and Mary; bd. dirs. Penjerdel Coun., pres. Opera Co. of Phila. Capt. USAR. Mem. Phila. C. of C. (bd. dir.). Home: 57 Crosby Brown Rd Gladwyne PA 19035-1512 Office: Universal Health Svcs Inc 367 S Gulph Rd Kng Of Prussa PA 19406-2832

MILLER, ALAN GERSHON, lawyer; b. Boston, Feb. 24, 1931; s. Harold Louis and Etta (Futransky) M.; m. Maxine Schreiber, July 2, 1951 (div. 1971); m. Natalie Cohen, Oct. 6, 1977; 1 child, Geoffrey Paul. AB, U. Ill., 1952; JD, Harvard U., 1955. Bar: Mass. 1955, U.S. Dist. Ct. Mass. 1956, U.S. Ct. Appeals (1st cir.) 1956, Fla. 1979, R.I. 1996, U.S. Dist. Ct. R.I. 1996. Assoc. Morrison, Mahoney & Pearlman, Boston, 1955-59; ptnr. Morrison, Mahoney & Miller, Boston, 1959—. Co-author: Business Interruption Insurance, 1986. Mem. ABA, Internat. Bar Assn., Boston Bar Assn., Fedn. Ins. Corp. & Counsel, Def. Rsch. Inst., Fla. Bar Assn., Soc. of CPCU's. Office: Morrison Mahoney & Miller 250 Summer St Boston MA 02210-1134

MILLER, ALAN JAY, financial consultant, author; b. Bklyn., July 11, 1936; s. Louis and Claire (Maltz) M.; m. Susan Ruth Morris, Oct. 29, 1961; children—Laurie Ann, Adam Louis. B.A., Cornell U., 1957. Chartered fin. analyst. Pres. Analysis-in-Depth Inc., N.Y.C., 1965-67; mng. editor Value Line Investment Survey, N.Y.C., 1967-68; research dir. Emanuel Deetjen & Co., N.Y.C., 1968-69; exec. v.p., dir. Intersci. Capital Mgmt. Corp., N.Y.C., 1969-71; pres., dir. ICM Equity Fund Inc., N.Y.C., 1970-71, ICM Fin. Fund Inc., N.Y.C., 1970-71; v.p., assoc. research dir. Bache & Co., Inc., N.Y.C., 1972, G.H. Walker & Co., Inc., N.Y.C., 1972-73; 1st v.p., assoc. research dir. Blyth Eastman Dillon & Co. Inc., N.Y.C., 1974-76; dir. research E.F. Hutton & Co., Inc., N.Y.C., 1976-81, sr. v.p., 1976-80, exec. v.p., 1981-88; dir. Hutton Investment Mgmt., 1976-88; mng. dir. SLH Asset Mgmt. Shearson Lehman Hutton, Inc, N.Y.C., 1988-90; sr. v.p. Martin E. Segal Co., N.Y.C., 1990-92; adj. assoc. prof. Columbia U. Grad. Sch. Bus., 1978-79; mem. faculty N.Y. Inst. Fin., 1977—; adj. prof. Adelphi U. Coll., 1993—. Author: Socially Responsible Investing: How to Invest with Your Conscience, 1991, Standard and Poor's 401(k) Planning Guide, 1995. Mem. N.Y. Soc. Security Analysts, Fin. Analysts Fedn.

MILLER, ALAN M., editor, educator, writer; b. N.Y.C., July 24, 1934; s. Philip and Sylvia (Lubash) M.; m. Roberta F. Brody, Sept. 2, 1956 (div. 1977); children: Neil, Peter, Stephanie, Douglas; m. Ferne Mayer Steckler, Jan. 13, 1978 (div. 1985); m. Sharon A. Tanenbaum, Aug. 29, 1996. AB, Syracuse U., 1955, LLB, 1958, JD, 1968. Commr., Village of Woodsburgh, N.Y., 1980; asst. counsel 3 joint legis. coms. N.Y. State Legislature, 1968-70; counsel to minority Nassau County Bd. Suprs., 1974-75; legal assoc. editor West Group, Westbury, N.Y., Eagan, Minn., 1985—; adj. prof. Hofstra U. Sch. Law, 1978-85, Emory U. Sch. Law, 1982, Touro Coll. Law, 1983-85; N.E. regional faculty mem., sect. leader Nat. Inst. Trial Advocacy, 1978-85, mem. nat. teaching team, 1982; adj. faculty N.Y. State Inst. Tech., 1974-75, Nassau C.C., 1978-80; anchor, regular panelist Joe Franklin TV Show, WWOR-TV and cable, 1990-93; mem. adj. faculty screenwriting and writing Hofstra U., 1990—, Discovery Ctr., 1990-94, N.Y. Inst. Tech., Old Westbury, 1987-89. Presenter 2d Internat. Conf. Law and Psychiatry, Israel, 1986. Columnist South Shore Record, Woodmere, N.Y., Another Viewpoint, 1985— (awards N.Y. Press Assn. 1988, 89, 94, Best Column award 1992), Single-Minded, 1991-92, N.Y. Bowler, 1991-93 (Bowling Mag. awards 1990-93, Best Column award 1992), Nostalgia Mag., 1990-91, Never Too Late, Writer's Digest (award winning screenplay 1992), Paradox, (Screenplay awards 1994-95, Maui Writing Conf. Quarter Final, Nicholls Screenwriting fellow), The Sharks (Semi-Finalist Writer's Network 1996); contbr. numerous articles to various publs. including N.Y. Times, Newsday, Newsday Mag., Mpls. Star-Tribune, Nat. Press. Assn. Assembly dist. leader N.Y. State Democratic Com., 1965-76. Recipient awards for coverage of Persian Gulf War from Israel, 1991, Nat. Coun. Jewish Women, 1991, 5 town's Sr. Coun's. Mem. Am. Film Inst. Jewish. Office: 9900 Drew Ave S Apt 210 Bloomington MN 55431-2778

MILLER, ALAN STANLEY, ecology center administrator, law educator; b. Detroit, Dec. 22, 1949; s. Ralph and Ruth (Leeman) M.; m. Susan O'Hara, Aug. 25, 1973; 1 child, Joanna. AB in Goverment, Cornell U., 1971; JD, U. Mich., 1974, M of Pub. Policy, 1974. Bar: Mich. 1974, D.C. 1975. Rsch. atty. Environ. Law Inst., Washington, 1974-77; atty. ABA, Washington, 1978-79, Natural Resources Def. Coun., Washington, 1979-84; assoc. World Resources Inst., Washington, 1984-86; asst. prof. law Widener U., Wilmington, Del., 1988-89; exec. dir. Ctr. Global Change, College Park, Md., 1989-96; prof. Vermont Law School, South Royal, Vt., 1991-93; exec. dir. Renewable Energy Policy Project Univ. Md., 1996-97; sr. environ. specialist GEF Secreariat, Washington, 1997—; head EPA Transition Team for Pres. Clinton Wash. D.C. 1992, Energy Task Force State of Md. Annapolis, Md. 1991-92; bd. dirs. Environmental Exchange; adjunct prof. Maryland Law Sch. 1989—; vis. asst. prof. U. Iowa Coll. of Law 1979, Wash. Coll. of Law Am. U., Wash., D.C. 1986, Duke U. N.C. 1990, Vt. Law Sch 1991, 92; mem. adv. bd. Office Tec. Assessment, Washington, 1989. Co-author: (book) International Regulation Flourocarbons, 1980, Green Gold, 1994; monographs) Growing Power, The Sky is the Limit, 1985, Environmental Regulation, 1992. Bd. dirs. Solar Light Fund, 1988, Renewable Energy Inst., 1995—. Fulbright scholar Macquarie Univ., Australia, 1977-87, Fulbright scholar Tokyo Univ. Law Sch., Japan, 1987-87; Stratospheric Ozone Protection award U.S. EPA Washington, D.C. 1992. Mem. ABA (global climate com. 1992-93, chair 1993-94). Avocations: jogging white-water rafting, writing. Office: GEF Secretariat Rm G6-106 1818 H NW Washington DC 20433*

MILLER, ALBERT JAY, retired librarian, educator; b. Beaver Falls, Pa., Dec. 7, 1927; s. Joseph Jefferson and Alberta Fae (Shaffer) M. B.S., Geneva Coll., 1952; M.L.S., Rutgers U., 1958; postgrad., U. Chgo., 1960-61, U. Pitts., 1963-68, U. Mich., 1969. Librarian West Allegheny Jr. High Sch., Imperial, Pa., 1959-60, Butler (Pa.) Area Sr. High Sch., 1962-67; librarian Pa. State U., New Kensington, 1969-89, tchr.-librarian continuing edn. dept., 1970-89, ret., 1989. Author: A Selective Bibliography of Existentialism in Education and Related Topics, 1969, Confrontation, Conflict and Dissent, 1972, Death: A Bibliographical Guide, 1977; book and media rev. editor: Learning Today, 1978—, mem. editorial bd., 1979—. Instr. water safety ARC, New Kensington, 1969—, Citizens Gen. Hosp., 1971-72; active Boy Scouts Am., 1970—; bd. dirs. Westmoreland County, Butler County mental health assns.; mem. Allegheny-Kiski Human Relations Council, 1976-77; bd. dirs. Allegheny-Kiski Sr. Citizens Center, 1976-77, fund raising chmn., 1989-90; 2nd v.p., 1997—; bd. corporators Geneva Coll., Beaver Falls, Pa., 1987—; Sunday Sch. tchr. Manchester Ref. Presbyn. Ch., 1970—, elder, 1984—, emeritus, clk. of session, 1984—, Sabbath Sch. supt., 1990; mem., pub. rels. dir. Twirling Unltd, Akron, Ohio; baton twirler Kensington Firemens Band; mem. Alle-Kiski Revitalization Corp. Mem. NEA, Pa. Edn. Assn., ALA, Pa. Library Assn. Democratic. Home: 417 Charles Ave New Kensington PA 15068-5335

MILLER, ALLAN JOHN, lawyer; b. Beachwood, Ohio, Oct. 17, 1921; s. Carl Frederick and Rhoda (Warren) M.; m. Marjorie Hewitt Pirtle, Aug. 10, 1946; children: James W., Patricia Anne. B.B.A., Fenn Coll., 1946; LL.B., Western Res. U., 1948; D. (hon.), Dyke Coll., Cleve., 1986. Bar: Ohio 1948. With Standard Oil Co., Ohio, 1948-77; treas. Standard Oil Co., 1967-77; mem. firm Kiefer, Knecht, Rees, Meyer & Miller, Cleve., 1977-81; dir. United Screw & Bolt Corp., 1977-97. Chmn. bd. dirs. Luth. Med. Ctr., Cleve., 1967-82; pres. Luth. Med. Ctr. Med. Staff Found., 1979-85; bd. dirs. Christian Residencies Found., 1972-77, St. Luke's Hosp. Assn., 1973-84; chmn. bd. trustees Dyke Coll., Cleve., 1971-86. With AUS, 1943-46, PTO. Mem. Cleve. Treas.'s Club, Cleve. Soc. Security Analysts. Presbyterian. Club: Capri Isles Golf Club (Venice, Fla.). Home: 1364 Capri Isles Blvd Venice FL 34292-4459

MILLER, ANDREW PICKENS, lawyer; b. Fairfax, Va., Dec. 21, 1932; s. Francis Pickens and Helen (Hill) M.; m. Penelope Farthing, Nov. 18, 1990; children: Julia Lane, Andrew Pickens, Elise Givhan, Winfield Scott, Lucia Holcombe. AB magna cum laude, Princeton U., 1954; postgrad., New Coll., Oxford (Eng.) U., 1954-55; LLB, U. Va., 1960. Bar: Va. 1960, U.S. Supreme Ct. 1967, D.C. 1979. Asso. Penn, Stuart & Stuart, 1960-62; partner Penn, Stuart & Miller, Abingdon, Va., 1963-69; atty. gen. Va., 1970-77; partner Mays, Valentine, Davenport & Moore, Richmond, Va., 1977-78, Dickstein, Shapiro, Morin & Oshinsky, LLP, Washington, 1979—. Pres., Young Democratic Clubs Va., 1966-67; chmn. Washington County Dem. Com., 1967-69; Dem. nominee for U.S. Senate from Va., 1978; bd. dirs. Barter Found., 1962-69; trustee King Coll., 1966-74; mem. adv. bd. Ams. for Effective Law Enforcement, 1973-77, Center for Oceans Law and Policy, 1975-79; vice-chmn. Va. Bd. Corrections, 1983-86. Served to 1st lt. AUS, 1955-57. Fellow Am. Bar Found.; mem. ABA (ho. dels. 1971-76, mem. action commn. to reduce ct. costs and delay 1979-84, commn. on pub. understanding about the law 1992-95,), So. Conf. Attys. Gen. (vice chmn. 1972-73, chmn. 1973-74), Nat. Assn. Attys. Gen. (exec. com. 1973-74, chmn. antitrust com. 1971-76, Wyman Meml. award 1976), Va. Bar Assn. (chmn. young lawyers sect. 1967-68, exec. com. 1985-88), Am. Judicature Soc. (bd. dirs. 1973-76, exec. com. 1974-76), Soc. of Cin. (Va. standing com. 1986-89, 93-96, asst. sec., 1992-95, sec. gen. 1995—), The John Marshall Found. (pres. 1987-89), Phi

Beta Kappa, Omicron Delta Kappa. Presbyn. Home: 1503 35th St NW Washington DC 20007-2729 Office: Dickstein Shapiro Morin & Oshinsky LLP 2101 L St NW Washington DC 20037-1526

MILLER, ANTHONY BERNARD, physician, medical researcher; b. Woodford, Eng., Apr. 17, 1931; married, 1952; 5 children. BA, U. Cambridge, 1952, MB, BChir, 1955. House officer Oldchurch Hosp., Romford, Eng., 1955-57; med. registrar Luton and Dunstable Hosp., Eng., 1959-62; mem. sci. staff Med. Research Council Tb and Chest Disease Unit, London, 1962-71; assoc. prof. preventive medicine and biostats. U. Toronto, 1972-76, prof., 1976—, chmn. dept., 1992-96, dir. grad. program in epidemiology, 1986-91; dir. epidemiology unit Nat. Cancer Inst. Can., Toronto, 1971-86; dir. Nat. Breast Screening Study, 1980—, WHO Collaborating Ctr. on Evaluation of Screening for Cancer, 1991—; Nat. Health scientist, 1988-93; mem. working cadre Bladder Cancer Project, U.S., 1973-75; mem. epidemology com. Breast Cancer Task Force, U.S., 1973-77, chmn., 1975-77; mem. Fed. Task Force Cervical Cytol. Screening, Can., 1974-76, 80-81, Union Internat. Contre le Cancer com., controlled therapeutic trials, 1978-82, Multidisciplinary project breast cancer, 1978-82, chmn. project on screening, 1982-93; mem. sci. council Internat. Agy. Research Cancer, Lyon, 1981-85, chmn., 1985; mem. com. on diet, nutrition and cancer NRC of U.S., 1980-83, mem. oversight com. radioepidemiologic tables, 1983-84, com. on diet and health, 1986-89, com. on dietary guidelines implementation, 1988-91, chmn. com. on environmental epidemiology, 1990-94; chmn. Ont. Task Force on Primary Prevention of Cancer, 1994-95. Served with RAF, 1957-59. Mem. Can. Oncology Soc. (sec.-treas. 1975-79, pres. 1980-81), Soc. Epidemiology Research, Internat. Epidemiology Assn., Am. Soc. Preventive Oncology (pres. 1983-85), Am. Coll. Epidemiology (bd. dirs. 1987-89). Office: U Toronto Dept Preventive Med & Biostats, McMurrich Bldg, Toronto, ON Canada M5S 1A8

MILLER, ARJAY, retired university dean; b. Shelby, Nebr., Mar. 4, 1916; s. Rawley John and Mary Gertrude (Schade) M.; m. Frances Marion Fearing, Aug. 18, 1940; children: Kenneth Fearing, Ann Elizabeth (Mrs. James Olstad). B.S. with highest honors, UCLA, 1937; LL.D. (hon.), 1964; postgrad., U. Calif.-Berkeley, 1938-40; LL.D. (hon.), Washington U., St. Louis; LL.D., Whitman Coll., 1965, U. Nebr., 1965, Ripon Coll., 1980. Teaching asst. U. Calif. at Berkeley, 1938-40; research technician Calif. State Planning Bd., 1941; economist Fed. Res. Bank San Francisco, 1941-43; asst. treas. Ford Motor Co., 1946-53, controller, 1953-57, v.p., controller, 1957-61, v.p. finance, 1961-62, v.p. of staff group, 1962-63, pres., 1963-68, vice chmn., 1968-69; dean Grad. Sch. Bus., Stanford U., 1969-79, emeritus, 1979—; former chmn. Automobile Mfrs. Assn., Econ. Devel. Corp. Greater Detroit; councillor The Conf. Bd.; past chmn., life trustee Urban Inst.; mem. Public Adv. Commn. on U.S. Trade Policy, 1968-69, Pres.'s Nat. Commn. on Productivity, 1970-74. Trustee Internat. Exec. Svc. Coirps.; hon. trustee The Brookings Instn.; dir. emeritus S.R.I. Internat.; chmn. Pub. Policy Inst. Calif.; former pres. Detroit Press Club Found.; former chmn. Boy Area Coun. Capt. USAAF, 1943-46. Recipient Alumnus of Year Achievement award UCLA, 1964; Distinguished Nebraskan award, 1968; Nat. Industry Leader award B'nai B'rith, 1968. Fellow Am. Acad. Arts and Scis. Presbyterian. Clubs: Pacific Union, Bohemian.

MILLER, ARNOLD, electronics executive; b. N.Y.C., May 8, 1928; s. Sam and Mina (Krutalow) M.; m. Beverly Shayne, Feb. 5, 1950; children: Debra Lynn, Marla Jo, Linda Sue. BS in Chemistry, UCLA, 1948, PhD in Phys. Chemistry, 1951. Registered profl. engr., Calif. Rsch. phys. chemist Wrigley Rsch. Co., Chgo., 1951; supr. phys. chemistry Armour Rsch. Found., Chgo., 1951-54, mgr. chemistry and metals, 1954-56; chief materials sci. dept. Borg-Warner Rsch. Ctr., Des Plaines, Ill., 1956-59; dir. rsch. Rockwell Corp., Anaheim, Calif., 1959-66, dir. microelec. ops., 1967-68; group exec. materials ops. Whittaker Corp., L.A., 1968-70; pres. Theta Sensors, Orange, Calif., 1970-72; mgr. xeroradiography Xerox Corp., Pasadena, Calif., 1972-75; corp. dir. rsch. and adv. devel. Xerox Corp., Stamford, Conn., 1975-78; corp. dir. rsch. and adv. devel. Xerox Corp., El Segundo, Calif., 1978-81, v.p. electronics div., 1981-84, pres. electronics div., 1984-87; corp. officer Xerox Corp., Stamford, 1984-87; pres. Tech. Strategy Group, Fullerton, Calif., 1987—; bd. dirs. Spectro Diode Labs, San Jose, Calif., Semicondr. Rsch. Corp., Colorep Inc., Carlsbad, Calif.; bd. dirs., chair audit com. Merisel Computer Products, El Segundo, Calif., lead dir., 1989—; mem. vis. com. on materials sci. U. So. Calif., L.A., 1966-68; mem. State of Calif. Micro Bd., 1984—. Editorial adv. bd. Advances in Solid State Chemistry; co-editor Electronics Industry Development; contbr. numerous articles to profl. jours. and monographs; patentee in field. Mem. civilian adv. group Dept. Commerce, 1959-60; mem. 5th decade com., also adv. com. on engrng. and mgmt. program UCLA, 1984—; mem. com. on scholarly commn. with People's Republic of China, Tech. Transfer Task Force, Nat. Acad. Sci., Washington, 1985; bd. dirs. Orange County Pacific Symphony, Fullerton, Calif., 1982—; mem. univ.'s adv. bd. Calif. State U.-Fullerton, 1986—, chair, 1991—; v.p., bd. dirs. Heritage Pointe Home for the Aging, 1987—; chmn. Indsl. Assocs. sch. engrng. and computer sci. Calif. State U., 1987—, trustee continuing learning ctr., 1993—; mem. Overseas Devel. Coun., 1988—; mem. Nat. Com. U.S.-China Rels., 1990—; trustee So. Calif. Coll. of Optometry, 1996—, sec.-treas. 1997—. Recipient Sci. Merit award Navy Bur. Ordnance/Armour Rsch. Found., 1952, IR-100 award, 1964, 69; named hon. alumnus Calif. State U., Fullerton, 1996. Fellow AAAS; mem. IEEE, AIME, Am. Chem. Soc., So. Calif. Coalition Edn. Mfg. Engrng. (bd. dirs. 1994—), Soc. Photog. and Instrumentation Engrs. and Scientists, Elec. Industry Assn. (past chmn. microelectronics), Phi Beta Kappa, Sigma Xi, Phi Lamda Upsilon. Home: 505 Westchester Pl Fullerton CA 92835-2706 Office: Tech Strategy Group PO Box 5769 Fullerton CA 92838-0769

MILLER, ARTHUR, playwright, author; b. N.Y.C., Oct. 17, 1915; s. Isadore and Augusta (Barnett) M.; m. Mary Grace Slattery, Aug. 5, 1940 (div. 1956); children: Jane Ellen, Robert; m. Marilyn Monroe, June 1956 (div. 1961); m. Ingeborg Morath, Feb. 1962; children: Rebecca Augusta, Daniel. AB, U. Mich., 1938, LHD, 1956; LittD (hon.), Oxford U., 1995, Harvard U., 1997. Assoc. prof. drama U. Mich., 1973-74. Author: (plays) Honors at Dawn, 1936 (Avery Hopwood award for playwriting U. Mich. 1936), No Villain: They Too Arise, 1937 (Avery Hopwood award for playwriting U. Mich. 1937), Man Who Had All the Luck, 1944 (Nat. prize Theatre Guild 1944), That They May Win, 1944, All My Sons, 1947 (N.Y. Drama Critics Circle award 1947, Tony award best play 1947, Donaldson award 1947), Death of a Salesman, 1949 (N.Y. Drama Critics Circle award 1949, Tony award best play 1949, Donaldson award 1949, Pulitzer prize in drama 1949), The Crucible, 1953 (Tony award best play 1953, Donaldson award 1953, Obie award 1958), A View from the Bridge, 1955, A Memory of Two Mondays, 1955, After the Fall, 1964, Incident at Vichy, 1964, The Price, 1968, Fame, 1970, The Reason Why, 1970, The Creation of the World and Other Business, 1972, Up From Paradise, 1974, The Archbishop's Ceiling, 1976, The American Clock, 1980, Some Kind of Love Story, 1983, Elegy for a Lady, 1983, Playing for Time, 1986, Danger: Memory!, 1986, The Last Yankee, 1990 (BBC Best Play award 1992), The Ride Down Mt. Morgan, 1991, Broken Glass, 1994 (Olivier award Best Play London 1995); (play adaptation) Enemy of the People (Ibsen), 1950; (screenplays) The Story of G.I. Joe, 1945, The Misfits, 1961, The Hook, 1975, Everybody Wins, 1990, The Crucible, 1995; (teleplays) Death of a Salesman, 1966, The Price, 1971, Fame, 1978, Playing for Time, 1980 (George Foster Peabody award 1981, Outstanding Writing Emmy award 1981), All My Sons, 1987, An Enemy of the People, 1990, The American Clock, 1994; author: Situation Normal, 1944, Focus, 1945, Jane's Blanket, 1963, I Don't Need You Anymore, 1967, In Russia, 1969, In the Country, 1977, The Theatre Essays of Arthur Miller, 1978, Chinese Encounters, 1979, Salesman in Beijing, 1987, Timebends: A Life, 1987, The Misfits and Other Stories, 1987, (novella) Homely Girl, 1994; exec. prodr. Death of a Salesman, 1985 (Outstanding Drama/Comedy Spl. Emmy award 1985). Recipient Bur. New Plays prize Theatre Guild, 1938, Nat. Assn. Ind. Schs. award, 1954, Gold Medal for drama Nat. Inst. Arts and Letters, 1959, Anglo-Am. award, 1966, Creative Arts award Brandeis U., 1970, Lit. Lion award N.Y. Pub. Libr., 1983, John F. Kennedy Lifetime Achievement award, 1984, Algur Meadows award So. Meth. U., 1991. Home: Tophet Rd Roxbury CT 06783

MILLER, ARTHUR MADDEN, investment banker, lawyer; b. Greenville, S.C., Apr. 10, 1953; s. Charles Frederick and Kathryn Irene (Madden) M.; m. Roberta Beck Connolly, Apr. 17, 1993; children: Isabella McIntyre Madden, Roberta Beck Connolly. AB in History, Princeton U., 1973; MA in History, U. N.C., 1976; JD with distinction, Duke U., 1978; LLM in Taxation, NYU, 1982. Bar: N.Y. 1979, U.S. Dist. Ct. (so. dist.) N.Y. 1979. Assoc. Mudge Rose Guthrie Alexander & Ferdon, N.Y.C., 1978-85; v.p. pub. fin. Goldman, Sachs & Co., N.Y.C., 1985—. mem. adv. bd. Mary Baldwin Coll., Staunton, Va., 1982-86; trustee Princeton U. Rowing Assn., N.J., 1980—, pres., 1986-95; trustee Rebecca Kelly Dance Co., N.Y.C., 1984-86. Mem. ABA (tax sect. com. on tax exempt financing 1985—), Nat. Assn. Bond Lawyers (lectr. 1985—), Pub. Securities Assn. (cons. 1985—), Practising Law Inst. (lectr. 1980, editor/author course materials 1980), Bond Attys. Workshop (editor/author course material 1983—, lectr. 1983—), Princeton Club. Office: Goldman Sachs & Co 85 Broad St New York NY 10004-2434

MILLER, ARTHUR RAPHAEL, legal educator; b. N.Y.C., June 22, 1934; s. Murray and Mary (Schapin) M.; m. Ellen Monica Joachim, June 8, 1958 (div. 1978); 1 child, Matthew Richard.; m. Marilyn Tarmy, 1982 (div. 1988.); m. Sandra L. Young, 1992. AB, U. Rochester, 1955; LLB, Harvard U., 1958; student, Bklyn. Coll., 1952, 55, CCNY, 1955. Bar: N.Y. 1959, U.S. Supreme Ct. 1959, Mass. 1983. With Cleary, Gottlieb, Steen & Hamilton, N.Y.C., 1958-61; assoc. dir. Columbia Law Sch. Project Internat. Procedure, N.Y.C., 1961-62; instr. Columbia U. Law Sch., 1961-62; asso. prof. U. Minn. Law Sch., 1962-65; prof. law U. Mich. Law Sch., 1965-72; vis. prof. Harvard U. Law Sch., 1971-72, prof., 1972-86, Bruce Bromley prof., 1986—; rsch. assoc. Mental Health Research Inst., 1966-68; dir. project computer assisted instn. Am. Assn. Law Schs., 1968-75; spl. rapporteur State Dept. concerning chpt. II of Hague Conv., 1967; del. U.S.-Italian Conf. Internat. Jud. Assistance, 1961, 62; chmn. task force external affairs Interuniv. Communications Council, 1966-70; mem. law panel, com. sci. and tech. info. Fed. Council Sci. and Tech., Pres.'s Office Sci. and Tech., 1969-72; mem. adv. group Nat. Acad. Sci. Project on Computer Data Banks, 1970-78; mem. spl. adv. group to chief justice Supreme Ct. on Fed. Civil Litigation; mem. com. on automated personal data systems HEW, 1972-73; chmn. Mass. Security and Privacy Council, Mass. Commn. on Privacy; mem. U.S. Commn. New Technol. Uses Copyrighted Works, 1975-79; reporter U.S. Supreme Ct.'s Adv. Com. on Civil Rules, 1978-86, mem. 1986-91; faculty Fed. Jud. Ctr.; reporter study on complex litigation Am. Law Inst.; bd. dirs. Research Found. on Complex Litigations, 1975-80. Author: The Assault on Privacy: Computers, Data Banks, and Dossiers, 1971, Miller's Court, 1982; (with others) New York Civil Practice, 8 vols., Civil Procedure Cases and Materials, 6th edit., 1993, Federal Practice and Procedure: Civil, 32 vols., 1969—, CPLR Manual, 1967; host syndicated TV shows in Context, Miller's Law, Miller's Court, Headlines on Trial; legal expert Good Morning America. Served with AUS, 1958-59. Recipient Nat. Emmy award for The Constitution, That Delicate Balance. Mem. Am. Law Inst. Office: Harvard U Law Sch Cambridge MA 02138 also: Good Morning Am 147 Columbus Ave New York NY 10023-5900

MILLER, B. JACK, investment company executive; b. N.Y.C., Mar. 1, 1945; s. Bertram Jackson and Charlotte (Kea) M.; m. Lynsie Schaberg; children: Molly, Andrew. AB, Princeton U., 1966; MBA, U. Mich., 1968. Various positions Eli Lilly and Co., Indpls., 1968-80, dir. benefit plan investments, 1980-88; v.p. benefit investments Philip Morris Cos. Inc., N.Y.C., 1988-89, v.p., corp. contr., 1989-92; v.p. J.P. Morgan Investment Mgmt., N.Y.C., 1992—. Served with M.I., USAR, 1968-74. Mem. Fin. Execs. Inst., Princeton Club N.Y. Avocations: golf, bridge. Office: JP Morgan Investment Mgmt 522 Fifth Ave New York NY 10036-7601

MILLER, BARBARA KAYE, lawyer; b. Omaha, Aug. 21, 1964; d. Carl Reuben and Sandra Jean (Matthews) Wright; m. Julius Anthony Miller, May 4, 1991. BA, U. Iowa, 1987, JD, 1990. Bar: Ohio 1990, U.S. Dist. Ct. (no. dist.) Ohio 1991. Assoc. Fuller & Henry, Toledo, Ohio, 1990-92; law clk. to Hon. John W. Potter U.S. Dist. Ct. (no. dist.) Ohio, Toledo, 1992-93; asst. prosecutor Lucas County Prosecutor's Office, Toledo, 1994-96; ptnr. Wise People Mgmt., Toledo, 1994—, Ryan, Wise, Miller & Dorner, Toledo, 1995—; adj. prof. Lourdes Coll., Sylvania, Ohio, 1994—. Bd. dirs. Toledo Ballet Assn., 1992-94, Hospice, Toledo, 1992-94. Martin Luther King scholar, 1987; named to Profl. Women in Christ, 1992. Mem. ABA, Lucas County Bar Assn., Toledo Bar Assn. (mem. grievance com. 1994—), Thurgood Marshall Law Assn. (v.p. 1993-94), Lawyers Roundtable of Toledo (mem. steering com., recruiting program com. 1994—). Avocations: tennis, biking, swimming. Office: Wise People Mgmt 151 N Michigan St Ste 333 Toledo OH 43624-1941 also: Ryan Wise Miller & Dorner Ste 333 151 N Michigan St Toledo OH 43624

MILLER, BARNEY E., biochemist; b. Chattanooga, Tenn., Apr. 3, 1952; s. Gilbert R. and Marcella (Wear) M.; m. Merry A. Noel, June 11, 1983; Children: Corwin Andrew, Melanie Kay. BA in chemistry, U. Tenn., Chattanooga, 1975; PhD in biochemistry, U. Tenn., Memphis, 1983; post doctoral in biochemistry, Duke U., 1985. Rsch. assoc. Duke U. Hughes Med. Inst., Durham, N.C., 1985-88; project leader Abbott Labs, North Chgo., 1988-90, sr. sci., 1990-92; lab chief Molecular Geriat., Lake Bluff, Ill., 1992-94; sec. Neurosci. Cons. Inc., Libertyville, Ill., 1992—; v.p. rsch. Nymox Labs, Johnson City, Tenn., 1994-95, Med. Toolworks, Inc., Evanston, Ill., 1995—; assoc. prof. psychiatry East Tenn. State U., Johnson City, 1994—; cons. Med. Toolworks, 1994—, Neurosci. Cons., Libertville, 1992—. Contbr. articles to profl. jours. Mem. Am. Assn. for the Advancement of Sci., N.Y. Acad. of Sci., Am. Chem. Soc., Soc. for Neurosci. Republican. Presbyterian. Avocations: rafting, hiking, animation, computer programing. Home: 504 W Maple St Johnson City TN 37604-6604 Office: East Tenn State U W Memorial Ctr Rm 213 University Pkwy Johnson City TN 37604-7339

MILLER, BARRY, research administrator, psychologist; b. N.Y.C., Dec. 25, 1942; s. Jack and Ida (Kaplan) M.; m. Susan Hallermeier; children: Eric, Arianne, Kristina, Barrie. BS in Psychology, Bklyn. Coll., 1965; MS in Psychology, Villanova U., 1967; PhD in Psychiatry, Med. Coll. Pa., 1971. Instr. psychology Villanova (Pa.) U., 1971-73; asst. dir. dept. behavioral sci., med. rsch. scientist Ea. Pa. Psychiatric Inst., Phila., 1971-73, sr. med. rsch. scientist, 1973-80; dir. Pa. Bur. Rsch. and Tng., Harrisburg, 1973-81; asst. prof. psychology U. Pa. Med. Sch., Phila., 1975-78, clin. prof. psychology, 1978—; assoc. prof. psychiatry Med. Coll. Pa., Phila., 1981-90, rsch. assoc. prof. medicine, 1983-90, assoc. dean for rsch., 1981-90; dir. for rsch. devel. Albert Einstein Healthcare Network, Phila., 1990-95; dir. The Permanente Med. Group Rsch. Inst., Oakland, Calif., 1995—; adj. assoc. prof. psychiatry Med. Coll. Pa., Phila., 1990—; rsch. assoc. prof. psychiatry Temple U. Sch. Med., Phila., 1990—; mem. sci. and tech. task force Pa. Econ. Devel. Partnership, Harrisburg, 1987-88, adv. com. Clin. Rsch. Ctr. Psychopathology of Elderly, Phila., 1985-88; mem. cancer control prgram Pa. Dept. Health, 1994; vis. rsch. assoc. prof. Med. Coll. Pa., Phila., 1991—. Contbr. articles to profl. jours.; mem. editorial bd. Jour. Mental Health Adminstrn., 1988—, assoc. editor, 1989—. Bd. dirs. Community Mental Health Ctr. 6A, Phila., 1969-73, Northwest Jewish Youth Ctrs., Phila., 1974-75; mem. Lafayette Hill Civic Assn., 1973-86, Citizens Coun. Whitemarsh (Pa.) Twp., 1975-86; pres., bd. dirs. Golden Eagle Luxury Homeowners Assn., Pleasanton, Calif. Grantee HHS, NIH. Mem. AAAS, Am. Psychol. Assn., Assn. Mental Health Adminstrs., Assn. Univ. Tech. Mgrs., Soc. Rsch. Adminstrs., Calif. Psychol. Assn. Avocation: tennis. Office: The Permanente Med Group 1800 Harrison St Oakland CA 94612-3429

MILLER, BENJAMIN K., state supreme court justice; b. Springfield, Ill., Nov. 5, 1936; s. Clifford and Mary (Luthyens) M. BA, So. Ill. U., 1958; JD, Vanderbilt U., 1961. Bar: Ill. 1961. Ptnr. Olsen, Cantrill & Miller, Springfield, 1964-70; prin. Ben Miller-Law Office, Springfield, 1970-76; judge 7th jud. cir. Ill. Cir. Ct., Springfield, 1976-82, presiding judge Criminal div., 1977-81, chief judge, 1981-82; justice Ill. Appellate Ct., 4th Jud. Dist., 1982-84, Ill. Supreme Ct., Springfield, 1984—; chief justice Ill. Supreme Ct., 1991-93; adj. prof. So. Ill. U., Springfield, 1974—; chmn. Ill. Cts. Commn., 1988-90; mem. Ill. Gov.'s Adv. Coun. on Criminal Justice Legis., 1977-84, Ad Hoc Com. on Tech. in Cts., 1985—. Mem. editorial rev. bd. Illinois Civil Practice Before Trial, Illinois Civil Trial Practice. Pres. Cen. Ill. Mental Health Assn., 1969-71; bd. govs. Aid to Retarded Citizens, 1977-80; mem. Lincoln Legals Adv. Bd., 1988—. Lt. USNR, 1964-67. Mem. ABA (bar admissions com. sect. of legal edn. and admissions to bar 1992—), Ill. State Bar Assn. (bd. govs. 1970-76, treas. 1975-76), Sangamon County Bar Assn., Women's Bar Assn. of Ill., Ctrl. Ill. Women's Bar Assn., Am. Judicature Soc. (bd. dirs. 1990-95), Abraham Lincoln Assn. (bd. dirs. 1988—). Office: Supreme Ct Ill 1st Of America Ste 560 Springfield IL 62701

MILLER, BENNETT, physicist, former government official; b. N.Y.C., Jan. 18, 1938; s. Meyer Leon and Henrietta (Abramowitz) M.; m. Patricia Dawn Schoenhut, June 3, 1961; children: Beth Ann, Jeffrey Martin. A.B. magna cum laude (U.S. Rubber Co. scholar), Columbia U., 1959, M.A. (Eugene Higgins fellow), 1961, Ph.D., 1965. Research assoc. plasma physics lab. Columbia U., 1965-69, adj. asst. prof. physics, 1969; adj. assoc. prof. physics Fairleigh Dickinson U., 1967-69; asst. prof. nuclear engrng. Ohio State U., cons. Battelle Meml. Inst, Columbus, Ohio, 1969-70; physicist div. controlled thermonuclear research U.S. Dept. Energy (formerly AEC and ERDA), Washington, 1970-74; dep. asst. dir. for research, acting chief exptl. plasma research br. U.S. Dept. Energy (formerly AEC and ERDA), 1974-75, asst. dir. research, 1975-76; dir. Office Plans, Budget and Program Implementation Solar, Geothermal and Advanced Energy Systems, U.S. Dept. Energy, 1976-78, program dir. solar, geothermal, electric and storage systems, 1978-80, dep. asst. sec. solar energy, 1980-81; v.p. energy programs McLaren Hart Inc. (formerly Fred C. Hart Assocs., Inc.), 1981-83; pres. Alternate Gas, Inc., Washington, 1983—, Miller Energy Corp., 1987—; v.p. tech. Kira, Inc., 1992—. Assoc. editor Jour. Solar Engrng, 1980-84; contbr. articles to profl. jours. Pres. Columbia Coll. Class of 1959 Alumni, 1965-69, 84-89; v.p. Watkins Mill Elem. Sc. PTA, Gaithersburg, Md., 1970-71, pres., 1972-73. Finalist White House Fellows Program, 1966; recipient Spl. Achievement certificate AEC, 1973; Exceptional Service award Dept. Energy, 1979; Presdl. citation for meritorious service, 1980; hon. Woodrow Wilson fellow, 1960. Mem. Nat. Wood Energy Assn. (v.p., vice chmn. 1983-84, chmn. 1984-85, bd. dirs. 1983-87), Phi Beta Kappa. Home and Office: 7805 Fox Gate Ct Bethesda MD 20817-4100

MILLER, BERNARD JOSEPH, JR., advertising executive; b. Louisville, July 31, 1925; s. Bernard J. Sr. and Myrtle (Herrington) M.; m. Jayne Hughes, Aug. 7, 1948 (div. Oct. 1970); children: Bernard J. III, Jeffrey, Janet Marie.; m. Brita Naujok, Nov. 24, 1970; 1 child, Brian. BS, Ind. U., 1949. Merchandising mgr. Brown-Forman Distillers, Inc., Louisville, 1949-54; v.p. Phelps Mfg. Co., Terre Haute, Ind., 1954-60; pres. Columbian Advt. Inc., Chgo., 1960-87, chmn., 1987—. 2d lt. USAF, 1943-46, PTO. Mem. Point of Purchase Advt. Inst. (dir. 1970-73), Saddle and Cycle Club (bd. dirs. 1987-90). Avocations: tennis, downhill skiing, collecting first edition autographed books. Office: Columbian Advt Inc 201 E Ohio St Chicago IL 60611-3238

MILLER, BETTY BROWN, freelance writer; b. Altus, Ark., Dec. 21, 1926; d. Carlos William and Arlie Gertrude (Sublett) Brown; m. Robert Wiley Miller, Nov. 15, 1953; children: Janet Ruth, Stephen Wiley. BS Okla. State U., 1949; MS, U. Tulsa, 1953; postgrad., Am. U., 1966-68. Tchr. LeFlore (Okla.) High Sch., 1947-48, Osage Indian Reservation High Sch., Hominy, Okla., 1948-50, Jenks (Okla.) High Sch., 1950-51; instr. Sch. Bus., U. Tulsa, 1950-51; tchr. Tulsa public schs., 1951-54; instr. Burdette Coll., Boston, 1954-55; reporter Bethesda-Chevy Chase Tribune, Montgomery County, Md., 1970-73; freelance writer, contbr. newspapers and mags., 1973—. V.p. Kenwood Park (Md.) Citizens Assn., 1960; mem. Ft. Sumner Citizens Assn., editor newsletter, 1969; mem. Md. State PTA, editorial coord. leadership conf., 1973-74; founder and chmn. Montgomery County Forum for Edn., 1970-75; trustee Friends Valley Forge Nat. Hist. Park; bd. dirs. Friends Curtis Inst. Music; mem. The Nat. Mus. Women in the Arts, The Musical Fund Soc. Phila.; bd. trustee, adv. Help the Aged. Mem. Nat. Soc. Arts and Letters (past editor mag., bd. dir. pub. rels., past nat. corr. sec.), Nat. League Am. Pen Women (budget chmn., past nat. treas.) PEO, Montgomery County Press Assn., Internat. Platform Assn., The Nat. Gravel Soc., Melba T. Croft Music Club, Capital Speakers Club of Washington (past pres.), Adventures Unltd. (chmn. Washington chpt.), U.D.C., Soc. Descs. of Washington's Army at Valley Forge (nat. comdr. in chief, past insp. gen.), DAR, Huguenot Soc. Pa. (v.p. 1989—, pres. 1993-95, past bd. dirs.), Washington Club, Sedgeley Club (pres. 1985-88, Phila.), The Acorn Club, Phila. Republican. Address: PO Box 573 Valley Forge PA 19481-0573

MILLER, BEVERLY WHITE, past college president, education consultation; b. Willoughby, Ohio; d. Joseph Martin and Marguerite Sarah (Storer) White; m. Lynn Martin Miller, Oct. 11, 1945 (dec. 1986); children: Michaela Ann, Craig Martin, Todd Daniel, Cass Timothy, Simone Agnes. AB, Western Res. U., 1945; MA, Mich. State U., 1957; PhD, U. Toledo, 1967; LHD (hon.), Coll. St. Benedict, St. Joseph, Minn., 1979; LLD (hon.), U. Toledo, 1988. Chem. and biol. researcher, 1945-57; tchr. schs. in Mich., also Mercy Sch. Nursing, St. Lawrence Hosp., Lansing, Mich., 1957-58; mem. chemistry and biology faculty Mary Manse Coll., Toledo, 1958-71; dean grad. div. Mary Manse Coll., 1968-71, exec. v.p., 1968-71; acad. dean Salve Regina Coll., Newport, R.I., 1971-74; pres. Coll. St. Benedict, St. Joseph, Minn., 1974-79; pres. Western New Eng. Coll., Springfield, Mass., 1980-96, pres. emerita, 1996—; higher edn. cons., 1996—; cons. U.S. Office Edn., 1980; mem. Pvt. Industry Count./Regional Employment Bd., exec. com., 1982-94; mem. Minn. Pvt. Coll. Coun., 1974-79, sec., 1974-75, vice chmn., 1975-76, chmn., 1976-77; cons. in field. Author papers in field. Corporator Mercy Hosp., Springfield, Mass. Recipient President's citation St. John's U., 1979; also various service awards. Mem. AAAS, Am. Assn. Higher Edn., Assn. Cath. Colls. and Univs. (exec. bd.), Internat. Assn. Sci. Edn., Nat. Assn. Ind. Colls. and Univs. (govt. rels. adv. com., bd. dirs. 1990-93, exec. com. 1991-93, treas. 1992-93), Nat. Assn. Biology Tchrs., Assn. Ind. Colls. and Univs. of Mass. (exec. com. 1981-96, vice chmn. 1985-86, chmn. 1986-87), Nat. Assn. Rsch. Sci. Teaching, Springfield C. of C. (bd. dirs.), Am. Assn. Univ. Adminstrs. (bd. dirs. 1989-92), Delta Kappa Gamma, Sigma Delta Epsilon. Office: 6713 County Road M Delta OH 43515-9778

MILLER, BRIAN KEITH, airline executive; b. Cin., Aug. 12, 1958; s. Charles Eugene and Vera Adeline (Garrison) M.; m. Victoria Lee Vaughan, Oct. 20, 1990. BBA, Tex. A&M U., 1980. CPA, Tex. From audit staff to audit mgr. Ernst and Young, Dallas, 1980-86; corp. controller and treas. Metro Airlines, Inc., Dallas, 1986-90, v.p. controller and treas., 1990-91, sr. v.p., chief fin. officer, sec., treas., 1991-92, pres., 1992—; v.p., CFO Lone Star Airlines, Ft. Worth, 1994-95. Mem. steering com. Dallas Bus. Forum, 1989-92; active The 500, Inc., Dallas, 1983-86; bd. dirs. Partnership for Arts, Culture and Edn. Inc., 1996—. Mem. AICPA, Treasury Mgmt. Assn., Fin. Execs. Inst., Tex. Soc. CPAs. Avocation: travel. Office: PO Box 612626 DFW Airport Dallas TX 75261-2626

MILLER, BURTON LEIBSLE, sales executive; b. L.A., July 17, 1944; s. Kenneth Wilbur and Dorothy (Leibsle) M.; m. April Suydam, Dec. 22, 1969 (div. 1983); children: Brandon, Gregory; m. Linda L. Reynolds, Aug. 11, 1990. BSCE, San Jose State U., 1968; MS in Engring., U. So. Calif., 1977. Civil engr. USN, San Bruno, Calif., 1968-74; cost engr. Bechtel Corp., L.A., 1974-79; supr. Bechtel Corp., Saudi Arabia, 1979-81; project mgr. Bechtel Corp., San Francisco, 1981-84, Bay Area Contractors, San Francisco, 1984—; dist. sales mgr. ISC, San Francisco, 1994—; cons. KMD/Kimco Mgmt. Co., San Francisco, 1989-90. Mem. World Affairs Coun., San Francisco, 1991, C. of C., San Francisco, 1986. Recipient Commendation, V.P. Dan Quayle, 1992, Cert. of Appreciation, Pres. George Bush, 1989, Cert. of Appreciation, Congressman Bob Mitchel, 1991. Mem. Commonwealth Club of Calif., Olympic Club, Project Mgmt. Inst. Republican. Avocations: snow skiing, scuba diving, real estate investment. Home: 634 28th Ave San Francisco CA 94121

MILLER, C. ARDEN, physician, educator; b. Shelby, Ohio, Sept. 19, 1924; s. Harley H. and Mary (Thuma) M.; m. Helen Meihack, June 26, 1948; children—John Lewis, Thomas Meihack, Helen Lewis, Benjamin Lewis. Student, Oberlin Coll., 1942-44; M.D. cum laude, Yale, 1948. Intern, then asst. resident pediatrics Grace-New Haven Community Hosp., 1948-51; faculty U. Kans. Med. Center, 1951-66, dir. childrens rehab. unit, 1957-60, dean Med. Sch., dir., 1960-66; prof. pediatrics and maternal and child health U. N.C., Chapel Hill, 1966—, vice chancellor health scis., 1966-71, chmn. dept. maternal and child health, 1977-87; chmn. exec. com. Citizens Bd. Inquiry into Health Services for Am., 1968-71. Mem. editorial bd.: Jour. Med. Edn, 1960-66; Author numerous articles in field. Trustee Appalachian Regional Hosps., 1974-84, Alan Guttmacher Inst., Planned Parenthood Fedn. Am. Markle scholar in med. scis., 1955-60; recipient Robert H. Felix Distinguished Service award St. Louis U., 1977, Martha Mae Eliot award in pub. health, 1984, Sedgwick Meml. medal Am. Pub. Health Assn., 1986, O. Max Gardner award U. N.C., 1987. Fellow Royal Soc. Health (hon.), Clare Hall Cambridge (Eng.) U. (life); mem. Am. Pub. Health Assn. (chmn. action bd. 1972-75, pres. 1974-75), Soc. Pediatric Research, Assn. Am. Med. Colls. (v.p. 1965-66), Inst. of Medicine of Nat.

Acad. Sci., Sigma Xi, Alpha Omega Alpha, Delta Omega. Home: 908 Greenwood Rd Chapel Hill NC 27514-3910

MILLER, CALVIN FRANCIS, geology educator; b. Escondido, Calif., Aug. 6, 1947; s. Wells Wait and Alice Atherton (Bakeman) M.; m. Molly Beth Fritz, Apr. 19, 1971; children: Spring Alice, Zachary Fritz. BA, Pomona Coll., 1969; MS, George Washington U., 1973; PhD, UCLA, 1977. Instr. Pomona Coll., Claremont, Calif., 1976-77; asst. prof. Vanderbilt U., Nashville, 1977-84, assoc. prof., 1984-89, prof., 1989—, chair dept. geology, 1991—; vis. rsch. assoc. prof. Rensselaer Polytechnic Inst., Troy, N.Y., 1984-85. Assoc. editor Jour. Geophys. Rsch., Washington, 1995—. Lt. USCG, 1969-73. Grantee NSF, 1978—. Mem. Am. Geophys. Union, Geol. Soc. Am. (assoc. editor Bull. 1989-94), Mineral. Soc. Am. Achievements include understanding the growth histories and geochemical significance of accessory minerals in the crust, the origins of peraluminous granites, and the history of the crust of Ea. Calif. and So. Nev. Home: 6744 Pennywell Dr Nashville TN 37205-3010 Office: Vanderbilt U Dept Geology Box 117, Sta B Nashville TN 37235

MILLER, CANDICE S., state official; b. May 7, 1954; m. Donald G. Miller; 1 child, Wendy Nicole. Student, Macomb County C.C., Northwood Inst. Sec., treas. D.B. Snider, Inc., 1972-79; trustee Harrison Twp., 1979-80, supr., 1980-92; treas. Macomb County, 1992-95; sec. of state State of Mich., Lansing, 1995—; chair Mich. State Safety Commn., 1995—; mem. M-59 Task Force Strategy Com. Mem. community coun. Selfridge Air Nat. Guard Base. Mem. Boat Town Assn., Ctrl. Macomb C. of C., Harrison Twp. Indsl. Corridor. Avocations: boating, yachting. Office: Treasury Building 430 W Allegan, 1st Fl Lansing MI 48918-9900*

MILLER, CARL CHET, business educator; b. Richmond, Va., June 23, 1961; s. Carl Chester and Nancy Ellis (Peters) M.; m. Laura Bridget Cardinal, Dec. 28, 1982. BA summa cum laude, U. Tex., 1982, PhD, 1990. Shift mgr. Frontier Enterprises, Austin, Tex., 1983; instr. Ind. U., Bloomington, 1983-84; tchg. asst. U. Tex., Austin, 1984-85, instr., 1985, rsch. assoc., 1985-89; asst. prof. bus. Baylor U., Waco, Tex., 1989-95, assoc. prof. bus., 1995—; mem. faculty senate, 1996-99; reviewer Acad. of Mgmt. Jour., Briarcliff Manor, N.Y., 1991—, Mgmt. Sci., Providence, 1987, 88, 93—, Orgn. Sci., Providence, 1990, 94, 95. Contbr. articles to profl. jours., chpts. to books; author numerous conf. papers; liaison Tex. Conf. on Orgns., Austin, 1989—. Bd. dirs. Windridge Home Owners Assn., Dallas, 1993—; pres. Assn. Mgmt., Austin, 1985-87; bd. advs. Cin. Glory Drum and Bugle Corps, 1995—. Grantee Hankamer Sch. Bus., 1990, 91, 92, 94, 95, 96, 97, Grad. Sch. Bus., U. Tex. Bonham Meml. Rsch. Fund, 1985, 89. Mem. Acad. Mgmt. (divsnl. regional liaison 1994-96, reviewer ann. meeting 1987, 88, 93—), Inst. Mgmt. Scis., Phi Beta Kappa (chpt. scholarship chair 1992-94), Phi Kappa Phi. Avocations: sailing, reading, golf. Office: Baylor U Hankamer Sch Bus PO Box 98006 Waco TX 76798

MILLER, CARL FRANK, business appraiser; b. Nurenberg, Germany, Jan. 30, 1964; came to U.S., 1964; s. Carl Dennis and Jill Framar (Muller) M.; m. Dana Marie Spears, Aug. 11, 1990. BA, U. Va., 1985; MBA, Tex. A&M U., 1991. CFA, Md. Rsch. analyst Tex. A&M U., College Station, 1989-91, fin. instr., 1991; valuation cons. Arthur Andersen & Co., Houston, 1991-93; sr. valuation cons. Ellin & Tucker, Chartered, Balt., 1993—. Mem. Dick Bennet for Md. Atty. Gen. Campaign, Balt., 1994; chmn., host Balt. City Mayoral Debate, 1995. 1st lt. U.S. Army, 1985-89. Mem. Am. Soc. Appraisers, Balt. Security Analysts Soc., Assn. for Investment Mgmt. and Rsch., Assn. for Corp. Growth, Balt. Jr. Assn. Commerce (treas. 1994, past bd. dirs., Project of Yr. award 1994, best new project award 1995), Md. Alumni U. Va. (exec. com.). Avocations: reading, hiking, camping. Home: 6516 Maplewood Rd Baltimore MD 21212-2008 Office: Ellin & Tucker Chartered 36 S Charles St Baltimore MD 21201-3020

MILLER, CAROL LYNN, librarian; b. Kingsville, Tex., Mar. 31, 1961; d. Walter Edward Jr. and Emma Lee (Nelson) M. BS in Early Childhood Edn., So. Nazerene U., 1985; M in Early Childhood Edn., Ala. A & M U., 1987; MLS, U. Ala., 1993. Office worker Salvation Army, Huntsville, 1979-83; libr. Madison (Ala.) Branch Library, 1985; sub. tchr. Huntsville (Ala) City and Madison County Sch. System, 1986-87; br. head Madison Br. Libr., 1987-92, Madison Square Mall Br. Libr., Huntsville, 1992—. Mem. Asbury Meth. Ch., Upbeat Vol. Program. Mem. ALA. Office: Huntsville Madison City Library Madison Square M 5901 University Dr NW Huntsville AL 35806

MILLER, CAROLE ANN LYONS, editor, publisher, marketing specialist; b. Newton, Mass., Aug. 1; d. Markham Harold and Ursula Patricia (Foley) Lyons; m. David Thomas Miller, July 4, 1978. BA, Boston U., 1964; bus. cert., Hickox Sch., Boston, 1964; cert. advt. and mktg. profl. UCLA, 1973; cert. retail mgmt. profl. Ind. U., 1976. Editor Triangle Topics, Pacific Telephone, L.A.; programmer L.A. Cen. Area Speakers' Bur., 1964-66; mng. editor/mktg. dir. Teen mag., L.A. and N.Y.C., 1966-76; advt. dir. L.S. Ayres & Co., Indpls., 1976-78; v.p. mktg. The Denver, 1978-79; founder, editor, pub. Clockwise mag., Ventura, Calif., 1979-85; mktg. mgr., mgr. pub. rels. and spl. events Robinson's Dept. Stores, L.A., 1985-87, exec. v.p., dir. mktg. Harrison Svcs., 1987-93; pres. divsn. Miller & Miller Carole Ann Lyons Mktg., Camino, Calif., 1993—; instr. retail advt. Ind. U., 1977-78. Recipient Pres.'s award Advt. Women of N.Y., 1974; Seklemian award 1977; Pub. Svc. Addy award, 1978. Mem. Retail Advt. & Mktg. Assn., Advt. Women N.Y., Calif. Videographers Assn., Retail Advt. & Mktg. Assn., Fashion Group Internat., Bay Area Integrated Mktg., San Francisco Fashion Group, San Francisco Direct Mktg. Assn. UCLA Alumni Assn., Internat. TV Videographer's Assn. (Sacramento chpt.). Editor: Sek Says, 1979. Home: 3709 Carson Rd Camino CA 95709-9593

MILLER, CAROLINE, editor-in-chief. Exec. editor Variety mag., N.Y.C., 1989-92; editor-in-chief Lear's mag., N.Y.C., 1992-94, Seventeen mag., N.Y.C., 1994-96, New York mag., N.Y.C., 1996—. Office: New York Mag 444 Madison Ave Fl 14 New York NY 10022-6903

MILLER, CARROLL GERARD, JR. (GERRY MILLER), lawyer; b. San Antonio, Tex., Dec. 12, 1944; s. Carroll Gerard Sr. and Glyn (Roddy) M.; m. Sylvia Louise Mertins, Mar. 7 1971 (dec. 1982); children: Glyn Marie Bennett, Roddy Gerard, Gina Louise. AS, Del Mar Coll., 1965; BS, U. Houston, 1967; JD, Tex. Tech. U., 1970. Bar: Tex. Ct. Criminal Appeals 1970, U.S. Dist. Ct. (so. dist.) Tex. 1971, U.S. Ct. Appeals (5th cir.) Tex. 1973, U.S. Supreme Ct. 1974, U.S. Ct. Appeals (D.C. 1986), Colo. 1987, D.C. 1989. Assoc. Allison, Madden, White & Brin, Corpus Christi, Tex., 1970-71; asst. city atty. City of Corpus Christi, 1971; asst. dist. atty. Nueces County Dist. Attys. Office, Corpus Christi, 1971-73; asst. city atty. civil div. City of Corpus Christi, 1973-74; atty. Corpus Christi Police Dept.-City of Corpus Christi, 1974-77; pvt. practice Corpus Christi, 1973—; adj. prof. Bee County Coll., Beeville, Tex., 1973-74, Tex. A & I U., Corpus Christi, 1975-76. Past treas. and diaconate First Presbyn. Ch., Corpus Christi; bd. dirs., incorporator Iron Curtain Outreach; 20/20 coun. Open Doors. Mem. SAR, SCV, Assn. Trial Lawyers Am., Tex. Criminal Def. Lawyers Assn., Nat. Criminal Def. Lawyers Assn., Coll. State Bar Tex., Sons of Republic Tex., Crime Stoppers, Inc. (past dir.), Bay Yacht Club (dir.). Republican. Avocations: sailing, scuba diving, photography. Home: 1209 Sandpiper Dr Corpus Christi TX 78412-3821 Office: 1007 Kinney St Corpus Christi TX 78401-3009

MILLER, CARROLL LEE LIVERPOOL, educational researcher; b. Washington, Aug. 20, 1909; s. William and Georgie E. (Liverpool) M. B.A. magna cum laude, Howard U., 1929, M.A., 1930; Ed.D., Columbia U., 1952. Instr. Miles Coll., 1930-31; mem. faculty Howard U., 1931—, prof. edn., 1957-88, chmn. dept., 1961-68, assoc. dean Coll. Liberal Arts, 1961-64, acting dean Grad. Sch., 1964-66, dean Grad. Sch., 1966-74, prof. higher edn., 1974-88, prof. emeritus edn., 1988—, cons. sch. social work, 1987—, adv. bd. sch. continuing edn., 1987—, coord. Grad. Internat. Programs, 1980-88, dir. summer session, 1964-70; chmn. Charles H. Thompson Lecture/Symposium, 1984—; instr. social studies D.C. pub. schs., evenings 1933-40, summer 1934; research asst. Commonwealth Va., 1938-39; Mem. adv. com. Nat. Conf. Problems Rural Youth Okla., 1963; participant conf. Commn. Civil Rights, 1962; mem. exec. council Episcopal Diocese Washington, 1964-66, mem. dept. coll. work, 1957-67, mem. standing com., 1967-68, chmn. Interracial Task Force, 1969-70, mem. Commn. on Ministry, 1971-72, mem. Rev. Bd., 1973-76; mem. Episcopal Council Overseas Students and Visitors, 1960-63; mem. adv. com. Anglican/Episcopal Ministry, Howard U., 1988—; coord. Ch. Bros., St. Augustine's Episcopal Ch., and Riverside Bapt. Ch., 1985-89; steering com. LEAD-Leadership in Ednl. Adminstrn.-D.C. Pub. Schs., 1990-93; bd. dirs. Samaritan Ministry of Greater Washington, 1990-96; coord. The Role Model Forum, Christian Youth Report, Seminarian's Lay Com., Ch. of Holy Communion, 1990-94, lay eucharistic minister, 1995-96; mem. field work adv. com. Va. Theol. Sem., 1991-96, Grad. Record Exams. Bd., 1965-70; exec. com. Council Grad. Schs. U.S., 1968-71; mem. com. grad. deans African-Am. Inst. Author: Role Model Blacks: Known But Little Known, 1982; mem. editorial bd. Jour. Negro Edn; contbg. editor Profiles; contbr. to ednl. jour. Bd. dirs. D.C. Tb Assn., 1953-59, 65-71, D.C. Episcopal Center for Children, 1964-76; bd. dirs. New Ednl. Ways, 1977-87 , pres., 1980-81; trustee Absalom Jones Theol. Inst.; cons. Nigerian Univs. Commn., 1981. Mem. Am. Assn. for Counseling and Devel. (del. assembly 1963-65, 68-69, bd. dirs. 1972), Consortium of Univs. of Washington Met. Area (adminstrv. com. 1964-88), Am. Assn. Colls. Tchr. Edn. (liaison rep. D.C. 1963-65), Am. Coll. Personnel Assn., Nat. Career Devel. Assn., Assn. for Humanistic Edn. and Devel. (pres. 1971-72), Nat. Soc. Study Edn., Assn. for Multicultural Counseling and Devel., Soc. Profs. Edn., AAAS, So. Regional Council, Nat. Guild of Churchmen, Columbia Tchrs. Coll. Alumni Council, Am. Ednl. Studies Assn., Nat. Cath. Assn., Phi Delta Kappa, Kappa Delta Pi. Home: 1301 Delaware Ave SW North 406 Washington DC 20024-3929

MILLER, CECELIA SMITH, chemist; b. Tyron, N.C., Apr. 3, 1965; d. Thad Lewis Jr. and Johnnie Lucille (Staley) Smith; m. Ronnie Edward Miller, Apr. 16, 1988; children: Joshua Edward, Jaylin. BA in Chemistry, Converse Coll., 1987. Lab. technician Groce Labs., Greer, S.C., 1988; quality assurance technician Baxter Pharmaseal, Spartanburg, S.C., 1988-89; lab. dir. CAPSCO, Inc., Greenville, S.C., 1989, quality assurance mgr., 1989—. Mem. Am. Soc. Quality Control, S.C. Lab. Mgmt. Soc. Democrat. Baptist. Avocations: cooking, reading, music. Home: 3017 Southfield St Inman SC 29349-9190 Office: CAPSCO Inc 1101 W Blue Ridge Dr Greenville SC 29609-3350

MILLER, CHARLES, business management research and measurements consultant; b. Crowley, La., Nov. 1, 1959; s. Rufus Paul and Rose (Lacombe) M.; m. Monica Lynn Habetz, Aug. 10, 1985. BS, La. State U., 1981, MS, 1985; PhD, Ohio State U., 1989. Rsch. asst. horticulture dept. La. State U., Baton Rouge, 1977-78, La. State Soil Testing Lab., Baton Rouge, 1978-81; rsch. assoc. La. Rice Rsch. Sta., Crowley, 1982; agriculture tchr. Acadia Parish Sch. Bd., Crowley and Iota, 1982-87; rsch. assoc. Ohio State U., Columbus, 1987-89, asst. prof., 1989-92; sr. cons., mgr. measurements S4 Cons. Inc., Powell, Ohio, 1992—. Minister, lector St. John Neumann Ch., Sunbury, Ohio, 1992—. Recipient project grant for tchr. prep. program U.S. Dept. Edn., 1990, Am. Farmer award Nat. Future Farmers Am., 1979. Mem. Am. Soc. for Quality, Omicron Tau Theta (editor 1991-92, Outstanding Svc. award 1992), Phi Delta Kappa, Gamma Sigma Delta, Alpha Zeta. Democrat. Roman Catholic. Avocation: woodworking. Office: S4 Cons Inc 1480 Manning Pkwy Powell OH 43065

MILLER, CHARLES A., lawyer; b. Oakland, Calif., Feb. 7, 1935; s. Frank and Janice (Greene) M.; m. Jeanette Segal, Sept. 27, 1964; children: Jennifer Fay, Charlotte Irene Marvin, Ira David. AB, U. Calif., Berkeley, 1955, LLB, 1958. Law clk. to assoc. justice U.S. Supreme Ct., Washington, 1958-59; assoc. Covington & Burling, Washington, 1959-67, ptnr., 1967—, chmn. mgmt. com., 1991-95; mem. criminal justice coordinating bd., Washington, 1977-78; chmn. hearing com. Bd. on Profl. Responsibility, Washington, 1980-86. Pres. U. Calif. Alumni Club, Washington, 1962-70; mem. various coms. and adv. bds. Washington Pub. Sch. System, 1972-79; chmn. lawyers com. Washington Performing Arts Soc., 1984-86; bd. dirs. Dumbarton Concert Series, Washington, 1986—, chmn., 1990—; chair D.C. Citizens Welfare Transformation Com., 1996-97; co-chair Task Force on D.C. Governance, 1996—. Fellow Am. Coll. Trial Lawyers; mem. ABA, D.C. Bar Assn., U. Calif. Alumni Assn. (trustee 1989-92). Democrat. Jewish. Club: Burning Tree (Bethesda, Md.). Office: Covington & Burling 1201 Pennsylvania Ave NW PO Box 7566 Washington DC 20044

MILLER, CHARLES DALY, self-adhesive materials company executive; b. Hartford, Conn., 1928; married. Grad., Johns Hopkins U. Sales and mktg. mgr. Yale & Towne Mfg. Co., 1949-59; assoc. Booz, Allen & Hamilton, 1959-64; with Avery Internat. Corp., Pasadena, Calif., 1964—; v.p., mng. dir. Materials Europe, 1965-68; v.p. Fasson Internat. Ops., 1968; group v.p. materials group Avery Internat. Corp., Pasadena, 1969-75, pres., bd. dirs., COO, 1975-77, pres., CEO, 1977-83; chmn., CEO Avery Dennison Corp. (formerly Avery Internat. Corp.), Pasadena, 1983—. Office: Avery Dennison Corp PO Box 7090 Pasadena CA 91109-7090

MILLER, CHARLES EDMOND, library administrator; b. Bridgeport, Conn., Aug. 3, 1938; s. Edmond and Irene Ovelia (Boudreaux) M.; m. Alice Ann Phillips, June 2, 1962; children—Alison, Charles Edmond, Catherine, Susan. Student, U. Hawaii, 1957-58; B.A., McNeese State U., 1964; M.S. in L.S, La. State U., 1966. Tchr. Lake Charles (La.) High Sch., 1964-65; mem. staff La. State U. Library, Baton Rouge, 1966-69; assoc. dir. Tulane U. Library New Orleans, 1969-73; dir. Fla. State U. Library, Tallahassee, 1973—; vis. coms. So. Assn. Colls. and Schs.; bd. dirs. SOLINET, 1979-81, 85-86, corp. v.p., vice chmn., 1980-81; cons. in field; adv. com. State Libr. Fla.; bd. dirs. Ctr. for Rsch. Librs., 1976-77, 91-97, sec., 1993-96; mem. policy bd. Fla. Libr. Network; pres. Assn. Southeastern Rsch. Librs., 1982-84; mem. rsch. libr. adv. com. Online Computer Libr. Ctr., Inc., Dublin, Ohio, 1993—. Asst. editor: La. Library Assn. Bull, 1967; contbr. articles to library sci. jours.; book revs. to Southeastern Librarian. Served with USMCR, 1956-59. Mem. ALA, Fla. Libr. Assn. (dir. 1979-81), Southeastern Libr. Assn., Assn. Coll. and Rsch. Librs., Assn. Rsch. Librs. (bd. dirs. 1985-90, v.p., pres.-elect 1987-88, pres. 1988-89), Fla. Ctr. Libr. Automation (chmn. bd. dirs. 1985-96), Rsch. Librs. Group (exec. com. 1988-90, bd. dirs. 1991-94), Phi Kappa Phi, Beta Phi Mu, Sigma Tau Delta.

MILLER, CHARLES HAMPTON, lawyer; b. Southampton, N.Y., Jan. 25, 1928; s. Abraham E. and Ethel (Simon) M.; m. Mary Fried, Aug. 26, 1956; children—Cathy Lynn, Steven Scott, Jennifer Lee. B.A., Syracuse U., 1949; LL.B., Columbia U., 1952. Bar: N.Y. 1952, Republic Korea 1954, U.S. Ct. Appeals (2d cir.) 1958, U.S. Supreme Ct. 1969, U.S. Ct. Appeals (3d cir.) 1972, U.S. Ct. Appeals (7th cir.) 1973, U.S. Ct. Appeals (9th cir.) 1995; cert. mediator and early neutral evaluator (so. and ea. dists.) N.Y., 1994—, mediator Supreme Ct. N.Y. County, 1996—. Asst. counsel Waterfront Commn. N.Y. Harbor, 1954-56; asst. atty. U.S. Atty. for So. Dist. N.Y., 1956-58; assoc. Cole & Deitz, N.Y.C., 1958-61; assoc. Marshall Bratter Greene Allison & Tucker, N.Y.C., 1961-64, ptnr., 1964-82; ptnr. Hess Segall Guterman Pelz Steiner & Barovick, N.Y.C., 1982-86, Loeb and Loeb, N.Y.C., 1986—; mem. faculty Continuing Legal Edn. Columbia U. Law Sch., 1976-82. Served with U.S. Army, 1952-54. Fellow Am. Bar Found.; mem. ABA, N.Y. State Bar Assn. (chmn. fed. ct. com. 1976-79, vice chmn. com. on specialization 1976-79, mem. fin. com. 1980-81), Assn. Bar City N.Y., Fed. Bar Council. Home: 171 Ralph Ave White Plains NY 10606-3813 Office: Loeb & Loeb LLP 345 Park Ave New York NY 10154-0004

MILLER, CHARLES LESLIE, civil engineer, planner, consultant; b. Tampa, Fla., June 5, 1929; s. Charles H. and Myrle Iona (Walstrom) M.; m. Roberta Jean Pye, Sept. 9, 1949; children—Charles Henry, Stephen, Jonathan, Matthew. BCE, MIT, 1951, MCE, 1958. Registered profl. engr., Mass., Fla., Tenn., N.H., R.I., P.R. Successively field engr., project engr., exec. engr. Michael Baker, Jr., Inc. (cons. engrs.), Rochester, Pa., 1951-55; asst. prof. surveying, dir. photogrammetry lab. Mass. Inst. Tech., 1955-59, asso. prof. civil engring., head data engring. div., 1959-61, prof. civil engring., 1961-77, head dept., 1961-70, dir. urban systems lab., 1968-75, dir. civil engring. systems lab., 1961-65, dir. inter-Am. program civil engring., 1961-65, assoc. dean engring., 1970-71; cons. engr., 1955—; chmn. bd., sr. cons., pres. CLM Systems, Inc., C.L. Miller Co., Inc.; adviser Commonwealth of P.R; dir. Geo-Transport Found.; Chmn. Pres.-elect's Task Force on Transp., 1968-69. Author: The COGO Book, 1990; contbr. articles to tech. jours. Recipient Outstanding Young Man of Greater Boston award. Fellow ASCE, Am. Acad. Arts and Scis.; mem. Am. Inst. Cons. Engrs., Am. Soc. Engring. Edn. (George Westinghouse award), Am. Soc. Photogrammetry, Am. Congress Surveying and Mapping, Am. Rd. Builders Assn., Transp. Rsch. Bd., Assn. Computing Machinery, Sigma Xi, Chi Epsilon, Tau Beta Pi. Originator of DTM, COGO, ICES, CEAL computer systems. Office: CL Miller Co 4315 W Beachway Dr Tampa FL 33609-4202

MILLER, CHARLES MAURICE, lawyer; b. L.A., Sept. 7, 1948; s. Samuel C. and Sylvia Mary Jane (Silver) M.; m. Terri Lee Senesac, Mar. 25, 1979; children: Samuel Mark, Seth Michael. BA cum laude, UCLA, 1970; postgrad., U. So. Calif., L.A., 1970-71; JD, U. Akron, 1975. Bar: Ohio 1975, Calif. 1978, U.S. Dist. Ct. (cen. dist.) Calif. 1978, U.S. Ct. Appeals (9th cir.) 1978, U.S. Supreme Ct. 1981. Gen. atty. U.S. Immigration & Naturalization Svc., U.S. Dept. Justice, L.A., 1976-79; ptnr. Miller Law Offices, L.A., 1979—; adj. prof. law U. West L.A., 1989-90. Co-editor: The Visa Processing Guide: Process and Procedures at U.S. Consulates and Embassies, 4d edit., 1996; articles editor U. Akron Law Rev., 1974-75. Mem. Calif. Bd. Legal Specialization, San Francisco, 1988-89. Mem. Bar of Calif. (chmn. immigration splty. 1988-89, commr. immigration splty. 1987-90), Am. Immigration Law Found. (bd. trustees 1995—), Am. Immigration Lawyers Assn. (chair So. Calif. chpt. 1993-94, co-chair membership 1989-90, co-chair mentor program 1990-91, co-chair visa office liaison 1991-92, vice chair 1994-95, co-chair consular rev. task force 1993-95, Jack Wasserman Meml. award for excellence in immigration litigation 1995). Office: Miller Law Offices 12441 Ventura Blvd Studio City CA 91604-2407

MILLER, CHARLES Q., engineering company executive; b. 1945. BA, Balt. Polytechnic Inst., 1963; BS in Mech. Engrng. and Math., U.S. Naval Acad., Annapolis, 1967; MS in Applied Mechanics, Stanford U., 1970; JD, Rutgers U., 1980. Ensign US Navy, 1967-74; with Raytheon Engineers and Constructors, Phila., 1974—, now CEO. Office: Raytheon Engrs & Constructors 141 Spring St Lexington MA 02173-7860*

MILLER, CHARLES RICKIE, thermal and fluid systems analyst, engineering manager; b. New Albany, Ind., Oct. 4, 1946; s. Marshall Christian and Thelma Virginia (Martin) M.; m. Janel Howell, Nov. 24, 1968; children: Kimberly, Brian, Audrey, Rachel. BA in Physics, DePauw U., 1969; postgrad., Rice U., 1969-70, U. Houston, 1972-76. Tech. editor ITT/Fed. Electric Corp., Houston, 1970-71, LTV/Svc. Tech. Corp., Houston, 1971; sys. safety engr. Boeing Aerospace Corp., Houston, 1971-76; thermal analyst space sys. divsn. Rockwell Internat. Corp., Houston, 1976-89; mgr. thermal and fluid sys. for space shuttle payloads Space Shuttle Program, Office NASA/L.B. Johnson Space Ctr., Houston, 1989—; mem. edtl. team Apollo 14, 15 preliminary sci. reports, 1971-72; mem. sys. integration negotiating team for Space Shuttle to Mir Space Sta. rendezvous and docking missions, 1993—, chmn. negotiating team for Space Shuttle to Mir Space Sta. water preparation and transfer, 1994—, space shuttle program co-chmn. for shuttle/internat. space sta. program joint tech. working groups for thermal control, environ. control and life support sys., 1996—. Bd. dirs. Space City Aquatic Team, Houston, 1990-91. Rector scholar DePauw U., 1964-68; Rice fellow Rice U., 1969-70. Mem. AIAA, ASME, Nat. Space Soc., Air Force Assn., Am. Inst. Physics, Sigma Pi Sigma. Avocations: children's sports, jogging, science fiction, military history. Home: 806 Walbrook Dr Houston TX 77062 Office: NASA Mail Code MS2 LB Johnson Space Ctr Houston TX 77058

MILLER, CHARLES S., clergy member, church administrator. Exec. dir. Division for Church in Society of the Evangelical Lutheran Church in America, Chicago, Ill. Office: Evangelical Lutheran Church Am 8765 W Higgins Rd Chicago IL 60631-4101*

MILLER, CHRISTINE MARIE, marketing executive; b. Williamsport, Pa., Dec. 7, 1950; d. Frederick James and Mary (Wurster) M.; m. Robert M. Ancell, Mar. 30, 1985. BA, U. Kans., 1972; MA, Northwewstern U., 1978, PhD, 1982. Pub. rels. asst. Bedford County Commr., Bedford, Pa., 1972-73; teaching asst. Northwestern U., Evanston, Ill., 1977-80; asst. prof. U. Ala., Tuscaloosa, 1980-82, Loyola U., New Orleans, 1982-85; vis. prof. Ind. U. Sch. Journalism, Bloomington, 1985-86; mktg. dir. Nat. Inst. Fitness & Sport, Indpls., 1986-88; program dir. Nat. Entrepreneurship Acad., Bloomington, 1986-88; mgmt. assoc. community and media rels. Subaru-Isuzu Automotive, Inc., Lafayette, Ind., 1988-91; dir. pub. rels. Giddings & Lewis, Fond Du Lac, Wis., 1991-93; v.p. comm. and enrollment mgmt. Milton Hershey (Pa.) Sch., 1993-94, dir. adminstrn., 1994-95; mktg. comms. mgr. MCI Govt. Markets, McLean, Va., 1995—. Co-author: The Biographical Dictionary of World War II General and Flag Officers, 1996; contbr. articles to profl. jours. Bd. dirs. Indpls. Entrepreneurship Acad., 1988-91, Area IV Agy., Greater Lafayette Mus. Art, 1989-91. With USN, 1973-77, comdr. USNR, 1977—. Mem. Pub. Rels. Soc. Am., Naval Order of the U.S. (nat. pub. affairs com.), Naval Res. Assn. (v.p. pub. affairs), Res. Officers Assn. Presbyterian. Avocations: cooking, swimming, reading, travel, cycling. Home: 7406 Salford Ct Alexandria VA 22315 Office: MCI Govt Markets 6th Fl 8200 Greensboro Dr Fl 6 Mc Lean VA 22102-3803

MILLER, CHRISTINE ODELL COOK, judge; b. Oakland, Calif., Aug. 26, 1944; d. Leo Marshall II and Carolyn Odell Cook; m. Dennis F. Miller. AB in Polit. Sci., Stanford Univ., 1966; JD, Univ. of Utah, 1969. Cert. gemologist. Law clk. to chief judge U.S. Court of Appeals, 10th circuit, Salt Lake City; trial atty. Dept. of Justice Honors Program, Foreign Litigation Unit, Ct. of Claims Sect. of Civil Div., 1970-72; team leader atty. FTC, 1972-74; with Hogan & Hartson, D.C., 1974-76; spl. counsel Pension Benefit Guaranty Corp., 1976-80; dep. gen. counsel U.S. Railway Assn., 1980-82; with Shack & Kimball, D.C., 1980-82; judge U.S. Ct. of Fed. Claims, D.C., 1982—. Mem. D.C. Bar Assn., Calif. State Bar, Univ. Club (bd. govs.). Office: US Court of Federal Claims 717 Madison Pl NW Ste 709 Washington DC 20005-1011*

MILLER, CHRISTINE TALLEY, physical education educator; b. Wilmington, Del., Sept. 11, 1959; d. Willard Radley and Anna Rose (Oddo) Talley; m. Jeffrey Lynch Miller, Nov. 14, 1987; children: Radley Edward, Rebecca Anna. BS in Phys. Edn., U. Del., 1981, MS in Phys. Edn., 1984. Cert. phys. edn. tchr., Del. Phys. edn. tchr. Pilot Sch. Inc., Wilmington, 1981-85; EKG technician Med. Ctr. Del., Newark, 1978—; phys. edn. tchr. Red Clay Consol. Sch. Dist., Wilmington, 1985—; mem. stds. revision com. Del. Dept. Pub. Instrn., 1991; mem. stds. rev. com. Red Clay Consol. Sch. Dist., 1993-94, curriculum revision com., 1988-92; coach spl. olympics, 1985-88. Contbg. author: A Legacy of Delaware Women, 1987. Jump Rope for Heart coord. Am. Heart Assn., Newark, 1994—; mem. Gov.'s Coun. for Lifestyles and Fitness, State of Del., 1991-93. Recipient Gov.'s Cup award for outstanding phys. edn. program Gov. Mike Castle, Del., 1991. Mem. AAHPERD, Del. Assn. for Health, Phys. Edn., Recreation and Dance (sec. 1981-86, v.p. health, Outstanding Phys. Edn. Tchr. of Yr. 1986). Home: 1206 Arundel Dr Wilmington DE 19808-2137

MILLER, CLAIRE ELLEN, periodical editor; b. Milw., July 17, 1936; d. Emil George Benjamin and Phyllis Dorothy (Rahn) Holtzen; m. Gerald Ray Miller, June 21, 1958; children: Karin Miller O'Callaghan, Russell Bruce Miller. BS in Edn., Concordia U., 1961. Catalog clk. U. Ill. Libr., Urbana, 1960-61; tchr. Grace Episcopal Day Sch., Silver Spring, Md., 1971-77, The Norwood Sch., Bethesda, Md., 1977-79; title I tchr. Rock Creek Forest Elem., Silver Spring, 1979-80; writer Media Materials, Balt., 1980; project editor Ednl. Challenges, Alexandria, Va., 1981; asst. mng. editor Ranger Rick Mag., Nat. Wildlife Fedn., Vienna, Va., 1981-87, mng. editor, 1988—. Author numerous activity books for presch. thru jr. high, 1979-80; project editor 6 vocabulary books, 1981; author numerous children's stories to mag. Mem. Ednl. Press. Assn. of Am., Md. Ornithol. Soc. Democrat. Lutheran. Avocation: birding. Home: 17501 Kirk Ln Rockville MD 20853-1033 Office: Nat Wildlife Fedn Ranger Rick Mag 8925 Leesburg Pike Vienna VA 22182-1742

MILLER, CLIFFORD ALBERT, merchant banker, business consultant; b. Salt Lake City, Aug. 6, 1928; s. Clifford Elmer and LaVeryl (Jensen) M.; m. Judith Auten, Sept. 20, 1976; 1 child, Courtney; children by previous marriage, Clifford, Christin, Stephanie. Student, U. Utah, 1945-50, UCLA, 1956. Pres. Braun & Co., L.A., 1955-82, chmn., 1982-87; exec. v.p. Gt. Western Fin. Corp., Beverly Hills, Calif., 1987-91; chmn. Clifford Group, Inc., bus. cons., 1992—; mng. dir. Shamrock Holdings, Inc., 1992—, Shamrock Capital Advisors, L.P., 1992—; bd. dirs. First Am. Corp., First Am. Bankshares, Inc., Washington, The Grand Union Co., Wayne, N.J., Shamrock Broadcasting , Inc., Burbank, Calif., L.A. Gear, Inc., Santa Monica, Calif.; cons to White House, 1969-74. Trustee Harvey Mudd Coll.,

Claremont, Calif., 1974—, chmn. bd. trustees, 1991; chmn. bd. dirs. L.A. Master Chorale, 1989-93, chmn. emeritus, 1993; mem. chmn.'s coun. Music Ctr. Unified Fund Campaign. Mem. UCLA Chancellor's Assocs., Skull and Bones, The Lakes Country Club, Calif. Club, Wilshire Country Club, Jeremy Golf and Country Club, Pi Kappa Alpha. Office: Shamrock Holdings Inc PO Box 7774 4444 W Lakeside Dr Burbank CA 91510-7774

MILLER, CLIFFORD JOEL, lawyer; b. L.A., Oct. 31, 1947; s. Eugene and Marian (Millman) M.; m. Coco Ando, Apr. 9, 1990. BA, U. Calif., Irvine, 1969; JD, Pepperdine U., 1973. Bar: Calif. 1974, Hawaii 1974, U.S. Dist. Ct. Hawaii 1974. Ptnr. Rice, Lee & Wong, Honolulu, 1974-80, Goodsill Anderson Quinn & Stifel, Honolulu, 1980-89, McCorriston, Miho, Miller & Mukai, Honolulu, 1989—. Mem. ABA, Calif. Bar Assn., Hawaii Bar Assn., Am. Coll. Real Estate Lawyers. Avocations: sailing, volleyball, swimming, history. Office: McCorriston Miho Miller & Mukai 5 Waterfront Pla 500 Ala Moana Blvd Honolulu HI 96813-4920

MILLER, CLINT, technology company executive. Pres. Maxim Tech., Inc., Dallas. Office: Maxim Tech Inc 2342 Fabens Rd Dallas TX 75229-3313

MILLER, CORBIN RUSSELL, financial executive; b. Huntington, W.Va., Apr. 6, 1948; s. Corbin Russell and Ernestine (Thorne) M.; m. Kathryn Ann Anderson, Sept. 16, 1978. AB cum laude, Princeton (N.J.) U., 1971. Trainee Morgan Guaranty Trust Co., N.Y.C., 1972-74, asst. treas., 1974-77; assoc. Wm. Sword & Co. Inc., Princeton, 1977-79; v.p. J. Henry Schroder Corp., N.Y.C., 1979-83, J. Henry Schroder Bank & Trust, N.Y.C., 1983-87; sr. v.p. IBJ Schroder Bank & Trust Co., N.Y.C., 1987-90; chmn. Koala Techs. Corp., Pleasanton, Calif., 1990-91; mng. dir. Regent Ptnrs. Inc., N.Y.C. and Denver, 1991-92; exec. v.p. S.N. Phelps & Co., Greenwich, Conn., 1992-95; exec. v.p., CFO Carey Internat., Inc., Washington, 1995-96; pres. Lombard North Am. Inc., San Francisco, 1997—; bd. dirs. Lombard Investments, Inc., San Francisco. Bd. dirs. Met. Opera Guild, N.Y.C., 1994—. Mem. Am. Soc. Order St. John of Jerusalem, Met. Opera Club (pres. 1992-94), Knickerbocker Club, Rockaway Hunting Club, Racquet and Tennis Club, The Brook. Republican. Episcopalian. Avocation: golf. Home: 1165 5th Ave New York NY 10029-6931 Office: Lombard North Am Inc 600 Montgomery St 36th Fl San Francisco CA 94111

MILLER, CURTIS HERMAN, bishop; b. LeMars, Iowa, May 3, 1947; s. Herman Andrew and Verna Marion (Lund) M.; m. Sharyl Susan Vander-Tuig, June 2, 1969; children: Eric, Nathan, Paul. BA, Wartburg Coll., 1969; MDiv., Wartburg Sem., 1973; DD (hon.), Wartburg Coll., 1987. Assoc. pastor Holy Trinity Luth. Ch., Dubuque, Iowa, 1973-75; pastor St. Paul Luth. Ch., Tama, Iowa, 1975-82; coord. for congl. life Am. Luth. Ch. Iowa dist., Storm Lake, 1982-87; bishop Western Iowa Synod Evang. Luth. Ch. in Am., Storm Lake, 1987—. Bd. regents Waldorf Coll., Forest City, Iowa, 1987—; bd. dirs. Luth. Social Svcs. of Iowa, Des Moines, 1987. Office: Evang Luth Ch Am Western Iowa Synod PO Box 1145 Storm Lake IA 50588-1145*

MILLER, DAN, congressman; b. Mich., 1943; m. Glenda Darsey; children: Daniel, Kathryn. Grad., U. Fla., 1964; MBA, Emory U.; PhD, La. State U. Ptnr. Miller Enterprises, Bradenton, Fla.; restaurant owner Memorial Pier, Fla., 1977—; instr. Ga. State U., U. South Fla., Sarasota; mem. 103rd-105th Congresses from 13th Fla. Dist., 1993—; mem. appropriations com., mem. budget com. Active Rep. Leader's Task Force on Health. Mem. Manatee C. of C. Episcopalian. Office: US Ho of Reps 102 Cannon HOB Washington DC 20515-0913*

MILLER, DANIEL NEWTON, JR., geologist, consultant; b. St. Louis, Aug. 22, 1924; s. Daniel Newton and Glapha (Shuhardt) M.; m. Esther Faye Howell, Sept. 9, 1950; children: Jeffrey Scott, Gwendolyn Esther. B.S. in Geology, Mo. Sch. Mines, 1949, M.S., 1951; Ph.D., U. Tex., 1955. Intermediate geologist Stanolind Oil and Gas Co., 1951-52; sr. geologist Pan Am. Petroleum Corp., 1955-60, Monsanto Chem. Co., 1960-61; cons. geologist Barlow and Haun, Inc., Casper, Wyo., 1961-63; prof. geology, chmn. dept. So. Ill. U., 1963-69; state geologist, exec. dir. Wyo. Geol. Survey, 1969-81; adj. prof. geology U. Wyo., 1969-81; asst. sec. energy and minerals Dept. Interior, 1981-83; geol. cons., 1983-89; dir. Anaconda Geol. Documents Collection U. Wyo., 1989-92; mem. Interstate Oil Compact Commn., 1969-81. Co-editor: Overthrust Belt of Southwestern Wyoming, 1960; gen. editor: Geology and Petroleum Production of the Illinois Basin, 1968; Contbr. articles to profl. jours. Served with USAAF, 1942-46. Decorated Air medal; recipient award merit So. Ill. U., 1967. Mem. Assn. Am. State Geologists (pres. 1979-80, chmn. govt. liaison com. 1970-71), Am. Assn. Petroleum Geologists (pres. Rocky Mountain sect. 1987, Pub. Svc. award), Am. Inst. Profl. Geologists (pres. 1992, Ben H. Parker Meml. medal 1993, Martin Van Couvering Meml. award 1994), Assn. Am. State Geologists (pres. 1979-80, hon. mem. 1982), Rocky Mountain Assn. Geologists (Disting. Pub. Svc. award). Achievements include patent for exhausto-port for automobiles. Home: 402 Colony Woods Dr Chapel Hill NC 27514-7908 *Use everything you know, in everything you do, all the time.*

MILLER, DARCY M., publishing executive; b. Glen Ridge, N.J., June 17, 1953; d. Paul Richardson and Susan (Alling) Miller; m. James R. Donaldson III, Feb. 6, 1988 (div.); 1 child, Zoe Alling; m. James R. Moffa, June 30, 1996. Co-founder, assoc. pub. Mus. Mag., N.Y.C., 1979-83; pub. Crop Protection Chemicals Reference, N.Y.C., 1983-85; assoc. pub. Chief Exec. Mag., N.Y.C., 1986-87, pub., 1987-89, exec. v.p., 1989-96; pub. Stagebill, N.Y.C., 1996—. Mem. ASCAP, Advt. Women of N.Y. Democrat. Episcopalian. Office: Stagebill 144 E 44th St New York NY 10017-4008

MILLER, DAVID, lawyer, advertising executive; b. Fort Worth, Dec. 12, 1906; s. Max and Tillie (Hoffman) M.; m. Rosalie Agress, Jan 31, 1929; children—Allan David, Martha Sally. A.B. cum laude, U. Tex., 1926; LL.B. cum laude, Harvard, 1929. Bar: N.Y. State bar 1931. With law firm of Jones, Clark & Higson, N.Y. City, 1929-33; pvt. practice with Harold W. Newman, Jr., 1937-44; mem. law firm of Engel, Judge & Miller, 1944-74; counsel RFC, Washington, 1933-34; asst. gen. counsel Md. Casualty Co., Balt., 1934-36; with Office of Gen. Counsel, Securities & Exchange Commn., 1936-37; v.p. and gen. counsel Young & Rubicam, Inc. (Advt. agy.), 1951-71, sec., dir., sr. v.p., 1971; counsel Squadron, Ellenoff & Plesent, 1974—; v.p., sec., gen. counsel The Music Project for TV, Inc., 1973—; Trustee Motion Picture Players Welfare Fund, Am. Fedn. TV & Radio Artists Pension and Welfare Fund.; Cons. joint policy com. Am. Assn. Advt. Agys.-Assn. Nat. Advertisers. Lecturer on radio and TV law for professional groups.; Editor: Harvard Law Review, 1927-29. Mem. Am. Bar Assn., Assn. Bar City N.Y., N.Y. County Lawyers' Assn., Am. Assn. Advt. Agencies (cons. broadcast business affairs com.), Phi Beta Kappa. Club: Harvard (N.Y.). Home: 30 Arleigh Rd Great Neck NY 11021-1327 Office: 551 Fifth Ave New York NY 10176

MILLER, DAVID ANTHONY, lawyer; b. Linton, Ind., Oct. 6, 1946; s. Edward I. and Jane M. (O'Hern) M.; m. Carol E. Martin, Aug. 9, 1970; 1 child, Jennifer Rose. Student, Murray State U., 1965; BS, Ind. State U., 1969; JD, Ind. U., Indpls., 1973. Bar: Ind. 1973, U.S. Dist. Ct. (so. dist.) Ind. 1973, U.S. Supreme Ct. 1981, U.S. Ct. Appeals (7th cir.) 1982. Dep. atty. gen. State of Ind., Indpls., 1973-76, dir. consumer protection divsn. office atty. gen., 1976-93, asst. atty. gen., 1977-80, chief counsel office atty. gen., 1981-93; prin. Hollingsworth, Meek, Miller and Minglin, Indpls., 1993—. Youth dir. Emmanuel Luth. Ch., Indpls., 1981-85, exec. dir., 1988-90; chmn. bd. Chambers Found., 1994—; mem. bd. Lutheran H.S. Mem. ABA, Ind. State Bar. Assn., Indpls. Bar Assn., Ind. State U. Alumni Assn., Columbia Club, Lambda Chi Alpha. Republican. Avocations: numismatics, golfing. Home: 5320 E Fall Creek Pky North Dr Indianapolis IN 46220-5737 Office: 9202 N Meridian St Ste 100 Indianapolis IN 46260-1810

MILLER, DAVID EDMOND, physician; b. Biscoe, N.C., June 6, 1930; s. James Herbert and Elsie Dale (McGlaughon) M.; m. Marjorie Willard Penton, June 4, 1960; children: Marjorie Dale, David Edmond. AB, Duke U., 1952, MD, 1956. Diplomate Am. Bd. Internal Medicine (subspecialty bd. cardiovasular disease). Internmed. ctr. Duke U., Durham, N.C., 1956-57, resident in internal medicine, 1957-58, 59, 60, research fellow cardiovascular disesase, 1958-59, 61, assoc. internal medicine and cardiology, 1963-79, clin. asst., prof. medicine cardiology, 1979—; practice medicine specialising in internal medicine and cardiology Durham, 1964—; attending physician internal medicine div. cardiology Watts Hosp., Durham, 1964-76, chief medicine, 1975-76; attending physician cardiology divsn. internal medicine Durham Regional Hosp. (formerly Durham County Gen. Hosp.), 1976—, chmn. dept. internal medicine, 1976-82, pres. med. staff, 1980-81; adv. com. Duke Med. Ctr. Contbr. articles to profl. jours. Council clin. cardiology N.C. chpt. Am. Heart Assn., 1963—. Served to lt. comdr. USNR, 1961-63. Fellow ACP, Am. Coll. Cardiology, Royal Soc. Medicine, Royal Soc. Health; mem. AMA, So. Med. Assn., N.C. Med. Soc. (del. ho. of dels. 1981, 82, 83), N.C. Durham-Orange County Med. Soc., Am. Soc. Internal Medicine, N.C. Soc. Internal Medicine (exec. coun. 1984-92), Am. Fedn. Clin. Rsch. Methodist. Clubs: Capitol, Hope Valley Country, Univ., Duke Faculty, Carolina Yacht. Home: 1544 Hermitage Ct Durham NC 27707-1680 Office: 2609 N Duke St Ste 403 Durham NC 27704-3048

MILLER, DAVID EMANUEL, physics educator, researcher; b. Bethel, Vt., Aug. 30, 1943; s. Manuel Southworth and Lucille (Shurtleff) M. BA, U. Vt., 1965; MA, SUNY, Stony Brook, 1967, PhD, 1971; Habilitation in Theoretical Physics, U. Bielefeld, Fed. Republic Germany, 1978. Instr. physics SUNY, Stony Brook, 1970-71; Wissenschaftlicher asst. Freie U., Berlin, 1972-75; scientist U. Bielefeld, 1975-78, Heinrich-Hertz Stipendium, 1977-78; privat dozent U. Bielefeld, 1978-83, univ. prof., 1987—; asst. prof. of physics Pa. State U., Hazelton, 1983-86, assoc. prof., 1986-92, prof., 1992—. Recipient Heinrich-Hertz stipendium, 1977-78, Fulbright award U. Wroclaw, Poland, 1997. Mem. Am. Phys. Soc., Am. Assn. Physics Tchrs., Deutsche Physikalische Gesellschaft, Deutscher Hochschulverband, N.Y. Acad. Sci., Am. Math. Soc., Phi Beta Kappa, Sigma Xi. Home: PO Box 611 Conyngham PA 18219-0611 Office: Pa State U High Acres Hazleton PA 18201

MILLER, DAVID EUGENE, soil scientist, researcher; b. Scipio, Utah, July 31, 1926; s. Henry and Josie (Peterson) M.; m. Jo Ann Peterson, Mar. 17, 1950; children: Ross H., Dale E., Diane. BS, Utah State U., 1950; MS, Colo. State U., 1953; PhD, Wash. State U., 1959. Cert. agronomy, crops and soils profl. Asst. agronomist Colo. State U., Grand Junction, 1950-53; soil scientist USDA Agrl. Rsch. Svc., Grand Junction, 1953-54; rsch. soil scientist USDA Agrl. Rsch. Svc., Prosser, Wash., 1958-89, ret., 1989; acting instr. soils Wash. State U., Pullman, 1954-58. Contbr. numerous articles to profl. jours. Sgt. U.S. Army, 1944-46, ETO. Fellow Am. Soc. Agronomy, Soil Sci. Soc. Am. (chair S-6 1982-83); mem. Western Soc. Soil Sci. (pres. 1979-80), Internat. Soc. Soil Sci., Soil and Water Conservation Soc. Mem. LDS Ch. Avocations: camping, sports, gardening, travel. Home: 809 Orondo Ave Wenatchee WA 98801-2703

MILLER, DAVID HEWITT, environmental scientist, writer; b. 1918; m. Enid Woodson Brown; 1 child. AB cum laude, UCLA, 1939, MA, 1944; PhD, U. Calif., Berkeley, 1953; DLitt (hon.), U. Newcastle, 1979. Meteorologist U.S. Corps Engrs., 1941-43; forecaster TWA, 1943-44; climatologist Quartermaster Gen.'s Office, 1944-46; meteorologist, hydrologist Corp. Engrs. Snow Investigations, San Francisco, 1946-53; geographer U.S. Natick (Mass.) Labs., 1953-59; meteorologist, hydrologist U.S. Forest Svc., 1959-64; prof. geography U. Wis., Milw., 1964-75, prof. atmospheric scis., 1975—; sr. acad. meteorologist NOAA, 1981-82; Fulbright lectr., Australia, 1966, 71, 79; exchange scientist Acad. Scis., Moscow, 1969; mem. adv. com. climatology Nat. Acad. Scis., 1958-64. Author: Snow Cover and Climate, 1955, (with others) Snow Hydrology, 1956, Heat and Water Budget of Earth's Surface, 1965, Energy at the Surface of the Earth, 1981, Water at the Surface of the Earth, 1982; editor: Climate and Life (M.I. Budyko), 1974. NSF fellow, 1952-53. Fellow AAAS (life); mem. Am. Geophys. Union (life, transl. bd. 1972-76), Am. Meteorol. Soc. (profl. life), Ecol. Soc. Am., Assn. Am. Geographers, Inst. Australian Geographers, Internat. Assn. Landscape Ecology, We. Snow Conf., Phi Beta Kappa, Sigma Xi. Office: Univ Wis Dept Geoscis PO Box 413 Milwaukee WI 53201-0413

MILLER, DAVID W., lawyer; b. Indpls., July 1, 1950; s. Charles Warren Miller and Katherine Louise (Beckner) Dearing; m. Mindy Miller, May 20, 1972; children: Adam David, Ashley Kay, Amanda Katherine Kupfer. BA, Ind. U., Bloomington, 1971; JD summa cum laude, Ind. U., Indpls., 1976. Bar: Ind. 1977. Investigator NLRB, Indpls., 1971-76; assoc. Roberts & Ryder, Indpls., 1977-80, ptnr., 1981-86; ptnr. Baker & Daniels, Indpls., 1986—; bd. dirs. Everybody's Oil Corp., Anderson, Ind. Mem. Ind. Bar Assn. (chmn. labor law sect. 1981-82). Republican. Office: 300 N Meridian St Ste 2700 Indianapolis IN 46204-1750

MILLER, DAVID WILLIAM, historian, educator; b. Coudersport, Pa., July 9, 1940; s. Arthur Charles and Kathryn Marie (Long) M.; m. Margaret Vick Richardson, Aug. 22, 1964; 1 child, Roberta Neal. BA, Rice U., 1962; MA, U. Wis., 1963; PhD, U. Chgo., 1968. Instr. history Carnegie Mellon U., Pitts., 1967-68, asst. prof., 1968-73, assoc. prof., 1973-80, prof., 1980—. Author: Church, State and Nation in Ireland, 1898-1921, 1973, Queen's Rebels: Ulster Loyalism in Historical Perspective, 1978; editor: Peep o'Day Boys and Defenders: Selected Documents on the Disturbances in County Armagh, 1784-1796, 1990; assoc. editor: New Dictionary of National Biography, 1994—; mem. editl. bd.: Hist. Methods, 1991-93; prin. developer: (interactive atlas) Great American History Machine, 1994. Sr. research fellow Inst. Irish Studies Queen's U., Belfast, Northern Ireland, 1975-76. Mem. Am. Hist. Assn., Am. Conf. for Irish Studies. Democrat. Presbyterian. Avocations: walking, singing. Office: Carnegie Mellon Univ Dept of History Schenley Park Pittsburgh PA 15213

MILLER, DEANE GUYNES, salon and cosmetic studio owner; b. El Paso, Tex., Jan. 12, 1927; d. James Tillman and Margaret (Brady) Guynes; degree in bus. adminstrn. U. Tex., El Paso, 1949; m. Richard George Miller, Apr. 12, 1947; children: J. Michael, Marcia Deane. Owner four Merle Norman Cosmetic Studios, El Paso, 1967-96; pres. The Velvet Door, Inc., El Paso, 1967-96; dir. Mountain Bell Telephone Co. Pres. bd. dirs. YWCA, 1967; v.p. Sun Bowl Assn., 1970; bd. dirs. El Paso Symphony Assn.; bd. dirs., treas. El Paso Mus. Art, pres., trustee, 1990, pres., 1991—; chmn. bd. El Paso Internat. Airport; bd. dirs., sec. Armed Services YMCA, 1987, 1st v.p., 1990. Named Outstanding Woman field of civic endeavor, El Paso Herald Post. Mem. Women's C. of C. (pres. 1969), Pan Am. Round Table (dir., pres. 1987). Home: 1 Silent Crest Dr El Paso TX 79902-2160 Office: 4141 Pinnacle Ste 103 El Paso TX 79902

MILLER, DEBORAH JEAN, computer training and document consultant; b. Elmhurst, Ill., Oct. 2, 1951; d. Thomas Francis and Ruthe Conn (Johnston) M. BFA, Ill. Wesleyan U., 1973; MA, Northwestern U., 1974. Pres. Miller & Assocs., Evanston, Ill., 1980—. Mem. AAUW, NOW, Internat. Interactive Comm. Soc., Soc. Tech. Comm., Ind. Writers Chgo. (bd. dirs. 1985-86), Chgo. Coun. Fgn. Rels., Internat. Soc. Performance and Instrn. (Chgo. chpt.), Northwestern U. Alumni Assn. Office: 814 Mulford St Evanston IL 60202-3331

MILLER, DECATUR HOWARD, lawyer; b. Balt., June 29, 1932; s. Lawrence Vernon and Katherine Louise (Baum) M.; m. Sally Burnam Smith, Nov. 23, 1963; 1 dau., Clemence Mary Katherine. B.A., Yale U., 1954; LL.B., Harvard U., 1959. Bar: Md. 1959. Assoc. Piper & Marbury, Balt., 1959-62, 1963-66, ptnr., 1967-94, ptnr. emeritus, 1995—, mng. ptnr., 1974-87, chmn., 1987-94; Md. Securities commr., 1962-63. Trustee Enoch Pratt Free Libr., 1975—, v.p., 1977-85, pres., 1985-89; bd. dirs. Balt. Symphony Orch., 1970—, v.p., 1978-86, 88-90, pres., 1990-92; trustee Calvert Sch., 1976-89, pres., 1982-87; trustee Walters Art Gallery, 1987-91; bd. dirs. United Way Ctrl. Md., 1988-91, The Leadership, 1990-93, Empower Balt. Mgmt. Corp., 1995—; bd. dirs. Coll. Bound Found., 1990—, chmn., 1994-96; bd. dirs. Greater Balt. Com., 1988-96, chmn., 1992-94; mem. bd. sponsors Sellinger Sch. Bus. and Mgmt. Loyola Coll., 1990—; mem. Mayor's Bus. Adv. Coun., 1993—; mem. bd. visitors U. Md. Baltimore County, 1994—; mem. bus. sch. adv. coun. Morgan State U., 1994—. With U.S. Army, 1954-56. Mem. ABA, Md. Bar Assn., Balt.Bar Assn., Am. Law Inst., Am. Bar Found., Md. Bar Found., Elkridge Club, 14 W. Hamilton St. Club, Ctr. Club, Elizabethan Club, Lawyers Round Table. Home: 26 Whitfield Rd Baltimore MD 21210-2928 Office: Piper & Marbury 36 S Charles St Baltimore MD 21201-3020

MILLER, DENNIS, comedian; b. Pitts., Nov. 3, 1953; m. Ali Espley, 1988; 2 children, Holden, Marlon. BA, Point Park Coll. Stand-up comic, cast mem. Saturday Night Live, 1985-91; prodr., writer, host Dennis Miller Show, 1992; exec. prod., writer, host Dennis Miller Live, 1994—. HBO spls. include: Mr. Miller Goes to Washington, 1988, host 13th Annual Young Comedians Show, 1989, (also prodr., writer) Black & White, 1990, They Shoot HBO Specials, Don't They?, 1993; host Freedomfest: Nelson Mandela's 70th Birthday Celebration, The America's Choice Awards, 1990, 43d Annual Primetime Emmy Awards Presentation, 1991; albums include The Off-White Album, 1989; film appearances include: Disclosure, 1994, The Net, 1995, Tales From the Crypt Presents: Bordello of Blood, 1996, Murder at 1600, 1997; TV series include NewsRadio, 1995. Recipient Best Writing Emmy award for a Variety/Music Program for Dennis Miller Live, 1994, 1995. Address: Internat Creative Mgmt Inc 8899 Beverly Blvd Los Angeles CA 90048-2412 also: Internat Creative Mgmt Inc 8942 Wilshire Blvd Beverly Hills CA 90211-1934*

MILLER, DENNIS DIXON, economics educator; b. Chillicothe, Ohio, May 1, 1950; s. Kermit Baker and Martha (Ralston) M. BA, Heidelberg Coll., 1972; MA, U. Colo., 1979, PhD, 1985. Instr. in econs. Am. U., Cairo, Egypt, 1982-84; internat. economist USDA, Washington, 1985-86; assoc. prof. Baldwin-Wallace Coll., Berea, Ohio, 1987—; rsch. assoc. Internat. Ctr. Energy and Econ. Devel., Boulder, Colo., 1979-82, 84-85; vis. scholar Hoover Instn., Stanford U., Palo Alto, fall 1986; acad. advisor Heartland Inst., Chgo., 1988—, Buckeye Ctr.; book reviewer Choice mag., 1984—; , manuscript reviewer Dryden Press, 1994—; pub. policy advisor Heritage Found.'s Listing, Washington, 1991—, econ. cons. gen., 1991—; vis. prof. Mithibai Coll., U. Bombay, India, summer and fall 1991; coord. agy. Air Quality Pub. Adv. Task Force, 1993; v.p. Adam Ferguson Inst., 1996—; vis. prof. The U. of the Autonomous Regions of the Caribbean Coast of Nicaragua, Bluefield, fall 1996. Earhart Found. fellow, 1977-78. Mem. AAAS, Am. Econs. Assn., Cleve. Coun. on World Afairs, Assn. Pvt. Enterprise Edn., Intertel, Nat. Assn. Forensic Economists, Assn. for Study of Grants Edn., N.Am. Econ. and Fin. Assn., Middle East Inst., Sierra Club, Nature Conservancy, Mensa. Avocations: running, tennis, reading, travel. Home: 12 Adelbert St Apt 2 Berea OH 44017-1753 Office: Baldwin Wallace Coll Dept Of Econs Berea OH 44017

MILLER, DENNIS EDWARD, health medical executive; b. Detroit, Dec. 21, 1951; m. Deborah Ann Keith, Feb. 12, 1977. BS, Austin Peay State U., 1973; MBA, U. South Fla., 1981. CPA. Chief exec. officer Hosp. Corp. of Am., Bennettsville, S.C., 1976-84; div. v.p. Westworld Community Healthcare, Waco, Tex., 1984-86; group v.p. Nat. Healthcare, Inc., Dothan, Ala., 1986-87; COO Healthcare Connections, Brentwood, Tenn., 1988; cons. VHA Physician Svcs., Inc., Dallas, 1988-90; asst. adminstr., CFO Clarksville (Tenn.) Meml. Hosp., 1990; Franklin, Tenn., 1990; sr. v.p., COO Eastside Ventures, Inc., Birmingham, Ala., 1990-93; sr. v.p. Ea. Health System, Inc., Birmingham, 1993—; chmn. Minority Leadership Task Force, Ea. Health System, Inc., 1994-95. Sec. Ala. Health Svcs. Bd.; mem. Literacy Coun. Ala., Ala. Hosp. Assn. State Legis. Com., future directions com.; chmn. Birmingham Regional Healthcare Exec. Forum; chmn. friends of scouting campaign Boy Scouts Am., 1996. Fellow Am. Coll. Healthcare Execs. (chmn diplomate credentials com., Ala. Regent's award for exec. excellence 1995), Hosp. Fin. Mgmt. Assn. (Follmer Bronze Merit award for outstanding svc.); mem. AICPA, Tenn. Soc. CPAs, Ala. Soc. CPAs (chmn. state legis. com.), Ala. Hosp. Assn. (future directions com.), Birmingham C. of C. (chmn. memberhsip com.), Birmingham East Rotary Club (pres., chmn. membership com.), Mensa, Shriners, Masons, Birmingham Touchdown Club, Sigma Chi. Avocations: hunting, fishing, gardening, antique collecting. Office: Ea Health System Inc 48 Medical Park Dr E Birmingham AL 35235-3400

MILLER, DIANE WILMARTH, human resources director; b. Clarinda, Iowa, Mar. 12, 1940; d. Donald and Floy Pauline (Madden) W.; m. Robert Nolen Miller, Aug. 21, 1965; children: Robert Wilmarth, Anne Elizabeth. AA, Colo. Women's Coll., 1960; BBA, U. Iowa, 1962; MA, U. No. Colo., 1994. Cert. tchr., Colo.; vocat. credential, Colo.; cert. sr. profl. in human resources. Sec.-counselor U. S.C., Myrtle Beach AFB, 1968-69; instr. U. S.C., Conway, 1967-69; tchr. bus. Poudre Sch. Dist. R-1, Ft. Collins, Colo., 1970-71; travel cons. United Bank Travel Svc., Greeley, Colo., 1972-74; dir. human resources Aims Community Coll., Greeley, 1984—; instr. part-time Aims Community Coll., Greeley, 1972—. Active 1st Congl. Ch., Greeley. Mem. Coll. Univ. Pers. Assn., Coll. Univ. Pers. Assn. Colo., No. Colo. Human Resources Assn., Soc. Human Resource Mgmt., Philanthropic Ednl. Orgn. (pres. 1988-89), Women's Panhellenic Assn. (pres. 1983-84), Scroll and Fan Club (pres. 1985-86), WTK Club, Questers. Home: 3530 Wagon Trail Pl Greeley CO 80634-3405 Office: Aims Cmty Coll 5401 W 20th St PO Box 69 Greeley CO 80632-3002

MILLER, DON ROBERT, surgeon; b. Highland, Kans., July 6, 1925; s. Pleasant V. and Lucy Anna (Hammond) M.; m. Geraldine Ellen Nelson, Sept. 6, 1947; children: Don R., Laurie, Todd, Marcia, Kristen, Felicia. A.B., Westminster Coll., 1944; M.D., U. Kans., 1948. Mem. faculty U. Kans., Kansas City, 1957-73; prof. surgery U. Kans., 1970-73; prof. surgery U. Calif. Irvine, 1973-92, prof. emeritus, 1992—, vice chmn., chief dept. surgery, pres. med. staff, 1989-91; dir. surgery Orange County (Calif.) Med. Center, 1973-77. Contbr. articles to profl. jours. Gov. 1988-92. Served with USNR, 1943-45, 50-52. Spl. research fellow Zurich, Switzerland, 1965-66. Fellow A.C.S., Am. Coll. Cardiology; mem. Am. Soc. Univ. Surgeons, Am. Surg. Assn., Soc. Vascular Surgery, Am. Assn. Thoracic Surgery, Am., Central, Western surg. assns., Internat. Cardiovascular Soc., Sigma Xi, Alpha Omega Alpha. Research extracorporeal circulation, myocardial function. Home: 743 Louisiana St Lawrence KS 66044-2339

MILLER, DON WILSON, nuclear engineering educator; b. Westerville, Ohio, Mar. 16, 1942; s. Don Paul and Rachel (Jones) M.; m. Mary Catherine Thompson, June 25, 1966; children: Amy Beth, Stacy Catherine, Paul Wilson Thompson. BS in Physics, Miami U., Oxford, Ohio, 1964, MS in Physics, 1966; MS in Nuclear Engring., Ohio State U., 1970, PhD in Nuclear Engring., 1971. Rsch. assoc. Ohio State U., Columbus, 1966-68, univ. fellow, 1968-69, tchg. assoc., 1969-71, asst. prof. nuclear engring., 1971-74, assoc. prof., 1974-80, chmn. nuclear engring. program, 1977—, prof., 1980—, dir. nuclear reactor lab., 1977—; sec., treas. Cellar Lumber Co., Westerville, Ohio, 1972-84, 85—; cons. Monsanto Rsch. Corp., Miamisburg, Ohio, 1979, NRC, Washington, 1982-84, Scantech. Corp., Santa Fe, 1984-95, Neoprobe Corp., Columbus, 1990, Electric Power Rsch. Inst., Palo Alto, Calif., 1992-94; mem. adv. com. on reactor safeguards Nuclear Regulator Commn., 1995—. Patentee in field; contbr. articles to profl. jours. Mem. Westerville Bd. Edn., 1976-91, pres., 1977-78, 86-88; mem. Ohio Sch. Bd.'s Assn., Columbus, 1976-91; mem. fed. rels. com. Nat. Sch. Bd.'s Assn., Washington, 1984-86. With USAR, 1960-68. Named Tech. Person of Yr. Columbus Tech. Coun., 1979; named to All Region Bd. Ohio Sch. Bd's. Assn., 1981, 86; recipient Coll. of Engring Rsch. award Ohio State U., 1984, Achievement award Mid Ohio Chpt Multiple Sclerosis Soc., 1988. Fellow Am. Nuclear Soc. (chmn. edn. divsn. 1986-87, bd. dirs. 1989-91, chair human factors divsn. 1993-94, v.p./pres. elect 1995, pres. 1996-97, Cert. Ppreciation 1991); mem. IEEE, Am. Soc. Engring. Edn. (chmn. nuclear engring. divsn. 1978-79, Glenn Murphy award 1989), Instrument Soc. Am. (sr. mem.), Nuclear Dept. Heads Orgn. (chmn. 1985-86), Westerville Edn. Assn. (Friend of Edn. award 1992), Rotary (Courtright Cmty. Svc. award 1989), Kiwanis, Hoover Yacht Club, Alpha Nu Sigma (chmn. 1991-93). Avocations: sailing, Am. history, traveling, amateur radio (extra class license). Home: 172 Walnut Ridge Ln Westerville OH 43081-2464 Office: Ohio State U Dept Mech Engring Nuclear Engring Program 206 W 18th Ave Columbus OH 43210-1189

MILLER, DONALD, art critic; b. Pitts., Dec. 21, 1934; s. LeRoy Gatskell and Alyse G. (McFarland) M. BA, U. Pitts., 1956, MA, 1975. Art and architecture critic Pitts. Post-Gazette, 1956—; instr. Carnegie-Mellon U., Pitts., 1979-80; lectr. Community Coll. Allegheny County, 1973, Westmoreland Mus. Art, 1973, U. Pitts., 1978—; art critic Sta. KDKA-TV, 1970-71. Author: (with others) Organic Vision: The Architecture of Peter Berndtson, 1980 (Merit award Pa. Soc. Architects 1981), Malcolm Parcell Wizard of Moon Lorn, 1985. Contbr. articles to profl. jours., also chpts. to various books. Chmn. Art and Antiques auction, Sta. WQED-TV, 1975. Recipient Golden Quill award Pitts. Press Club, 1980, 87, Forbes medal Ft. Pitt Mus., 1986; co-founder Malcolm Parcell Found., 1989—, past pres., 1994-95; co-founder Adhoc Com. for Visual Arts, Pitts., 1997. Assoc. Artists Pitts. (hon.), Friends of Art for the Pitts. Pub. Schs., The Newspaper Guild, Phi

Beta Kappa. Democrat. Office: Pitts Post-Gazette 34 Blvd Of The Allies Pittsburgh PA 15222-1204

MILLER, DONALD EUGENE, minister, educator; b. Dayton, Ohio, Dec. 2, 1929; m. Phyllis Gibbel, Aug. 19, 1956; children: Bryan Daniel, Lisa Kathleen, Bruce David. Student, Manchester Coll., 1947-49; MA, U. Chgo., 1952; postgrad., United Theol. Sem., 1955-56; BD, Bethany Theol. Sem., 1958; PhD, Harvard U., 1962; postgrad., Yale U., 1968-69, Cambridge (Eng.) U., 1975-76. Ordained minister Ch. of the Brethren, 1957. Dir. material aid Brethren Svc. Commn. in Europe, 1952-54; tchr. Madison Twp. High Sch., Trotwood, Ohio, 1954-55; social worker Dayton, 1954-56; tchr. Gregory Sch., Chgo., 1957-58; interim pastor Salem Ch. of the Brethren, Dayton, 1959; assoc. prof. Christian Edn. and Ethics Bethany Theol. Sem., Oak Brook, Ill., 1961-70, prof., 1970-82, dir. grad. studies, 1973-86, Brightbill prof. ministry studies, 1982-86; gen sec. Ch. of the Brethern Gen. Bd., Elgin, Ill., 1986—; lectr. Pastoral Psychotherapy Inst., Park Ridge, Ill., U. Chgo., Princeton Theol. Seminary, Princeton, N.J.; guest tchr. Theol. Coll. No. Nigeria, 1983. Author: A Self Instruction Guide Through Brethren History, 1976, The Wingfooted Wanderer: Conscience and Transcendence, 1977, The Self Study of the Chicago Cluster of Chicago Schools, 1981, Story and Context: An Introduction to Christian Education, 1986, The Gospel and Mother Goose, 1987; (with Warren F. Groff) The Shaping of Modern Christian Thought, 1968; (with Jack L. Seymour) Marking Choices, 1981, Contemporary Approaches to Christian Education, 1982, Theological Approaches to Christian Education, 1990; (with Robert W. Neff and Graydon F. Snyder) Using Biblical Stimulations, vol. 1, 1973, vol. 2, 1975; (with James N. Poling) Foundation for a Practical Theology of Ministry, 1985; designer programs include Edn. for A Shared Ministry, 1976-86, Tng. in a Ministry, 1984; TV host Christianity and the Arts, 1963. Mem. faith and order commn. Nat. Counc. Chs., 1976-81; del. to Russian Orth. Chs., 1967. Fellow Case Study Inst., 1972; rsch. fellow U. Chgo., 1951-52; teaching fellow Harvard U., 1960-61; faculty fellow Am. Assn. Theol. Schs. Faculty, 1968-69. Mem. Assn. for Profl. Edn. for Ministry (editor yearbook 1972, pres. 1976), Assn. Profs. and Researchers in Religious Edn. (pres. 1968), Am. Theol. Soc., Am. Soc. Christian Ethics., Religious Edn. Assn. Office: Ch of the Brethren 1451 Dundee Ave Elgin IL 60120-1674

MILLER, DONALD EUGENE, aerospace electronics executive; b. Providence, Mar. 20, 1947; s. Meyer Samuel and Beatrice (Wattman) M.; m. Deborah Neary Miller, Mar. 14, 1987. BA, Boston U., 1968; JD, U. Pa., 1972. Law clk. Assoc. Justice Alfred H. Joslin Supreme Ct., Providence, 1972-73; prin., lawyer Temkin, Merolla & Zurier, Providence, 1973-81, Temkin & Miller, Ltd., Providence, 1981-91; sr. v.p., gen. counsel, corp. sec. The Fairchild Corp., Chantilly, Va., 1991—. Author: (treatise) Buying and Selling a Small Business, 1987. Mem. R.I. Bar Assn., Mass. Bar Assn. Avocations: dog breeding, table tennis. Home: 10704 Riverwood Dr Potomac MD 20854-1332 Office: Fairchild Corp PO Box 10804 300 W Service Rd Chantilly VA 22094

MILLER, DONALD KEITH, venture capitalist, asset management executive; b. Akron, Ohio, Feb. 2, 1932; s. Clinton Raymond and Hazel Elizabeth (Curl) M.; m. Barbara Dewees Duff, Sept. 25, 1971 (div. 1983); children: Prescott Clinton, Barclay St. John; m. Priscilla Corwith Barker, Sept. 17, 1988. BS, Cornell U., 1954; MBA, Harvard U., 1959. Asst. treas. Chase Manhattan Bank, N.Y.C., 1959-62; asst. to v.p. Electric Bond & Share, N.Y.C., 1962-66; gen. ptnr. G.H. Walker & Co. Inc., N.Y.C., 1966-74; sr. v.p. White Weld & Co., N.Y.C., 1974-77; mng. dir. Blyth Eastman Paine Webber Inc., N.Y.C., 1978-86; chmn. Greylock Fin., N.Y.C., 1987—, Christensen Boyles Corp., Salt Lake City, 1987-95; dir. Layne Christensen, 1995—; chmn., CEO Thomson Adv. Group L.P., Stamford, Conn., 1990-93, vice chmn., 1993-94; pres., CEO TAG Inc., 1994—; bd. dirs. PIMCO Advisors L.P., Newport Beach, Calif.; bd. dirs. Fibreboard Corp., Walnut Creek, Calif.; bd. dirs. chmn. audit com. RPM, Inc., Medina, Ohio, 1972—, Huffy Corp., Dayton, Ohio, 1988—. 1st lt. U.S. Army, 1954-57. Avocation: tennis, squash. Home: 588 Round Hill Rd Greenwich CT 06831-2724

MILLER, DONALD LANE, publishing executive; b. Pitts., May 14, 1918; s. Donald Edwin and Arvilla (Lane) M.; A.B., Kenyon Coll., 1940; Russian interpreter cert. U. Colo., 1946; postgrad. U. Pitts., 1947-48; m. Norma Reno, Feb. 2, 1951. Reporter, Pitts. Sun-Telegraph, 1940-42, Washington Post, 1946; with pub. rels. dept. Westinghouse Electric Corp., Pitts., 1947-51; reporter Billboard and Tide, 1953; pub. rels. dir. Nat. Agrl. Chem. Assn., Washington, 1954-58; sec. Donald Lerch & Co., Washington, 1958-61; pres. Asso. Pub. Rels. Counselors, Washington, 1961-77; chmn. Braddock Comm., Inc.; chmn. emeritus Children's Aid Internat.; exec. dir. All Am. Conf., Washington, 1962-75. Editor GOP Nationalities News, Rep. Nat. Com., 1960; pub. rels. nationalities div. Rep. Nat. Com., 1964; coord. life underwriters sect. Citizens for Nixon-Agnew, 1968; co-pub. Cmty. Forum, 1996—. Served from ensign to lt., USNR, 1942-46; from lt. to lt. comdr., 1951-53. Decorated Knight of Europe. Mem. English Speaking Union, SAR, Phi Beta Kappa, Delta Tau Delta. Clubs: Nat. Press. Author: Strategy for Conquest, 1966, George to George: 200 Years of Presidential Quotations, 1989, Call of the Northern Neck, 1992. Home: 428 Fleets Bay Rd PO Box 1978 Kilmarnock VA 22482-1978 Office: 11501 Sunset Hills Rd Ste 200 Reston VA 20190-4704

MILLER, DONALD LESESSNE, publishing executive; b. N.Y.C., Jan. 10, 1932; s. John H. and Mamie (Johnson) M.; m. Ann Davie, Aug. 12, 1951 (div. 1981); children: Lynn, Mark; m. Gail Aileen Wallace, June 27, 1981. BA, U. Md., 1967; cert., Harvard Grad. Sch. Bus. Adminstrn., 1969. Enlisted U.S. Army, 1948, advanced through grades to maj., 1966, ret., 1968; spl. asst. to pres., mgr. corp. recruitment Inmont Corp., N.Y.C., 1968-70; v.p. indsl. relations Seatrain Shipbldg. Corp., N.Y.C., 1970-71; dep. asst. sec. def. U.S. Dept. Def., Washington, 1971-73; v.p. personnel mgmt. Columbia U., N.Y.C., 1973-78; dir. personnel devel. and adminstrn. Internat. Paper, N.Y.C., 1978-79; v.p. employee relations Consol. Edison N.Y., N.Y.C., 1979-86, Dow Jones & Co., Inc., N.Y.C., 1986-95; CEO, pub. Out World News, LLC; bd. dirs. Bank of N.Y. and Bank of N.Y. Co., N.Y.C. Author: An Album of Black Americans in the Armed Forces, 1969. Chmn. bd. emeritus Associated Black Charities, N.Y.C., 1982-94; trustee Pace U., 1979—. Decorated Legion of Merit; decorated Commendation Medal; recipient Disting. Civilian Service medal Dept. Def., 1973, Disting. Alumnus award U. Md., 1977. Mem. Alpha Sigma Lambda, Pi Sigma Alpha, Phi Kappa Phi, Alpha Phi Alpha, Sigma Pi Phi. Office: Our World News LLC 201 N Charles St Ste 300 Baltimore MD 21201-4114

MILLER, DONALD MORTON, physiology educator; b. Chgo., July 24, 1930; s. Harry Madison and Anna Loraine (Zeller) M.; 1 son, Tad Michael. A.B. in Zoology, U. Ill., Urbana, 1960, M.A. in Physiology, 1962, Ph.D. (NIH fellow), 1965; NIH postgrad. fellow, UCLA, 1965-66. Insp. Buick Jet div. Gen. Motors Corp., Willow Springs, Ill., 1953-55; sci. asst. Organic Chemistry Lab., U. Ill., 1960-62, counselor residence halls, 1960-63, teaching asst. physiology, 1960-64; mem. faculty So. Ill. U., Carbondale, 1966—, prof. physiology, 1976-94, retired, 1995, vis. prof., 1995; adj. prof. McKendree Coll., Lebanon, Ill., 1986-88, Queensland U. of Tech., Brisbane, Australia, 1989; Damon lectr., 1973-74; lectr. trauma edn. Ill. Hwy. Div., So. Ill. Health Manpower Consortium, Critical Care Nurse Program; judge Ill. Jr. Acad. Sci; vis. instr. Nakajo, Japan, 1992. Contbr. articles to profl. jours. Treas. Jackson County chpt. ARC, 1973-79; active CAP, 1968-79. Served with USAF, 1955-59. USPHS summer grantee, 1962, 73, NIH grantee, 1968-80, NASA grantee, 1973-85, Coll. Sea Grant Program grantee, 1983-88, U.S. Army Med. Rsch. Inst. grantee, 1987-92. Mem. Am. Physiol. Soc., Biophys. Soc., Am. Microscopic Soc., Neurosci. Soc., Am. Soc. Zoologists, N.Y. Acad. Scis., Am. Soc. Photobiology (charter), Am. Soc. Parasitologists (ednl. policies com.), Am. Midwest Conf. of Parasitologists (pres. 1980-81 sec.-treas. 1985-93), Am. Trauma Soc., Sigma Xi (past chpt. pres.), Chi Gamma Iota. Clubs: Elks, Lions. Home: 9 New Swan Lake Rd Murphysboro IL 62966-5539

MILLER, DONALD MUXLOW, accountant, administrator; b. Luverne, Minn., Feb. 21, 1924; s. Henry Clay and Mildred Eva (Muxlow) M.; m. Eunice Jean Gibson, Feb. 19, 1944; children: SueRilla M., Donna Jean Eichten, Patsy Ann Pushee. Student, Metro State, St. Paul, Minn., 1973-84. Lic. pub. acct. Mgr. Hines & Paulus, CPA, Worthington, Minn., 1952-65; commandant Minn. Vets. Home, Mpls., 1965-68; prin. D.M. Miller, Acct., 1968-70, 76-78; asst. sec. Minn. State Senate, St. Paul, 1970-72; comptr. Western Oil Co., Mpls., 1972-76; commr. Dept. Vet. Affairs, State of Minn., St. Paul, 1978-81; pres. D.M. Miller & Assoc., Ltd., Mpls., 1981—; chief exec. officer MARD, Inc., Mpls., 1985-95; v.p. Miller, Micketts & Assocs. Ltd., Mpls., 1993-96; pres. D.M. Miller & Assoc. Ltd., Mpls., 1997—. Trustee Heart Professorship Found., 1987-91; pres. Legionville Sch. Patrol Camp, Brainerd, Minn., 1963-64; pres. bd. govs. Big Island Vets. Camp, Mpls., 1986-88. 2nd lt. USAAC, 1942-46; 1st lt. USAF, 1951-52. Recipient Volunteer of the Year award Kidney Found., 1975. Mem. VFW, Nat. Soc. Pub. Accts., Minn. Assn. Pub. Accts., Nat. Assn. State Vets. Homes (hon. life mem., reg. v.p. 1967-68), Nat. Assn. State Dirs. Vets Affairs (reg. v.p. 1978-79), Minn. Gaming Assn. (exec. sec. 1987-92), Am. Legion (hon life mem., comdr. Minn. 1962-63, com. chmn. 1980-84, pres. Minn. Found. Bd. 1990-91). Presbyterian. Avocation: golf.

MILLER, DONALD ROSS, management consultant; b. Huntington, N.Y., Aug. 5, 1927; s. George Everett and Ethel May (Ross) M.; m. Constance Higgins, 1948 (div. 1955); children: Donald Ross Jr., Cynthia Lynn, Candace Lee; m. Janet Heyman Behr, Apr. 15, 1965; children: Jeffrey Lawrence, Wendy Lorraine. BS/BEA, MIT, 1950. Cert. mgmt. cons. Inst. of Mgmt. Cons. Staff engr. Stop & Shop, Inc., Boston, 1950-56; v.p., dir. Cresap, McCormick and Paget, Inc., N.Y.C., 1956-76; mng. dir. Donald R. Miller Mgmt. Cons., Forest Hills, N.Y., 1977—; pres., CEO Carl Fischer Inc., N.Y.C., 1996; bd. dirs. Nash Finch Co., Mpls., chmn. bd. dirs., 1995—; bd. dirs. Michael Anthony Jewelers, Inc., Mt. Vernon, N.Y. Author: Management Practices Manual, 3 vols., 1963, (booklet) Management of Managerial Resources, 1969. Bd. dirs. Queens Mus. Art, Flushing, N.Y., 1982-93, pres., 1988-92; pres. Lexington House, Forest Hills, 1984—. With U.S. Maritime Svc., 1945-46, ETO, U.S. Army, 1946-48. Mem. Nat. Assn. Corp. Dirs., Inst. Mgmt. Cons. (cert. com. 1986—), Sky Club. Episcopal. Avocations: tennis, reading. Home: 68-10 108th St Forest Hills NY 11375-3367 Office: PO Box 649 Forest Hills NY 11375-0649

MILLER, DOROTHY ANNE SMITH, retired cytogenetics educator; b. N.Y.C., Oct. 20, 1931; d. John Philip and Anna Elizabeth (Hellberg) Smith; m. Orlando Jack Miller, July 10, 1954; children: Richard L., Cynthia K., Karen A. BA in Chemistry magna cum laude, Wilson Coll., Chambersburg, Pa., 1952; PhD in Biochemistry, Yale U., 1957. Rsch. assoc. dept. ob-gyn Columbia U., N.Y.C., 1964-72, from rsch. assoc. to asst. prof. dept. human genetics-devel., 1973-85; prof. depts. molecular biology and genetics Wayne State U., Detroit, 1985-94, prof. dept. pathology, 1985-96, prof. Ctr. for Molecular Medicine and Genetics, 1994-96; vis. scientist clin. and population cytogenetics unit Med. Rsch. Coun., Edinburgh, Scotland, 1983-84; vis. prof. dept. genetics and molecular biology U. la Sapienza, Rome, 1988; vis. disting. fellow La Trobe U., Melbourne, Australia, 1992. Contbr. numerous articles to sci. jours. Grantee March of Dimes Birth Defects Found., 1974-93, NSF, 1983-84. Mem. Am. Soc. Human Genetics, Genetics Soc. Am., Genetics Soc. Australia, Phi Beta Kappa. Presbyterian. Home: 1915 Stonycroft Ln Bloomfield Hills MI 48304-2339 Office: Wayne State U 540 E Canfield St Detroit MI 48201-1928

MILLER, DOROTHY ELOISE, education educator; b. Ft. Pierce, Fla., Apr. 13, 1944; d. Robert Foy and Aline (Mahon) Wilkes. BS in Edn., Bloomsburg U., 1966, MEd, 1969; MLA, Johns Hopkins U., 1978; EdD, Columbia U., 1991. Tchr. Cen. Dauphin East High Sch., Harrisburg, Pa., 1966-68, Aberdeen (Md.) High Sch., 1968-69; asst. dean of coll., prof. Harford C. C., Bel Air, Md., 1969—; owner Ideas by Design, 1995—; mem. accreditation team Mid. States Commn., 1995, 96, 97. Editor: Renewing the American Community Colleges, 1984; contbr. articles to profl. jours. Pres. Harlan Sq. Condominium Assn., Bel Air, 1982, 90-96, Md. internat. divsn. St. Petersburg Sister State Com., 1993—; edn. liaison AAUW, Harford County, Md., 1982-92; cen. com. mem. Rep. Party, Harford County, 1974-78; crusade co-chair Am. Cancer Soc., Harford County, 1976-78; mem. faculty adv. com. Md. Higher Edn. Commn., 1993-96; mem. people's adv. coun. Harford County Coun., 1994—. Recipient Nat. Tchg. Excellence award Nat. Inst. for Staff and Orgn. Devel., U. Tex.-Austin, 1992. Charter mem. Nat. Mus. Women in the Arts. Republican. Methodist. Avocations: skiing, swimming, reading, image consulting, interior design, writing, travel. Office: Harford Community Coll 401 Thomas Run Rd Bel Air MD 21015-1627

MILLER, DOUGLAS ANDREW, lawyer; b. Chgo., May 10, 1959; s. Walter William and Jean (Johnson) M.; m. Birgitte Jorgensen, Aug. 4, 1984. BS, Boston Coll., 1981; JD, Ill. Inst. Tech. Chgo., 1986. Bar: Fed. Trial, Ill., U.S. Dist. Ct. (no. dist.) Ill. Legal asst. Lupel & Amari, Chgo., 1984-86; assoc. Bresnahan, Garvey, O'Halloran & Colman, Chgo., 1986-90, Williams & Montgomery, Ltd., Chgo., 1990—. Contbr. articles to profl. jours. Mem. ABA, Ill. State Bar Assn. (civil practice sect., torts sect.), Chgo. Bar Assn. (vice-chmn. bench and bar com., trial techniques sect., ins. law sect.), Ill. Assn. of Def. Trial Counsel. Avocation: distance running. Office: Williams & Montgomery Ltd 20 N Wacker Dr Ste 2100 Chicago IL 60606-3003

MILLER, DOUGLAS L., stockbroker, money manager; b. N.Y.C., July 1, 1952; s. Allan Zander Miller and Joyce Carol (Soman) Berman. BS in Biochemistry and Bus. Mgmt., Cornell U., 1978. Candidate CFA Level III. Asst. buyer Abraham & Strauss, Bklyn., N.Y., 1978-79; mgr. Queensboro Farms Inc., Long Island City, N.Y., 1979-81; salesman Tiffany & Co., N.Y.C., 1981; account exec. Merrill Lynch, N.Y.C., 1982-84; assoc. Papamarkou, Petra & Co., N.Y.C., 1984; account exec. Oppenheimer & Co., N.Y.C., 1984-85; fin. cons., sr. v.p., investment rep. Lehman Bros., N.Y.C., 1985-94; sr. v.p. investments Gruntal & Co., N.Y.C., 1994-96; private client services Bear, Stearns & Co., N.Y.C., 1996—. Mem. N.Y. Soc. Security Analysts, Fin. Analysts Fedn., Assn. Investment Mgmt. and Rsch., Market Technicians Assn. (affiliate). Avocations: running, swimming, windsurfing, reading, music. Office: 245 Park Ave New York NY 10167-0002

MILLER, DUANE KING, health and beauty care company executive; b. N.Y.C., Mar. 1, 1931; s. Henry Charles and Helen Marion (King) M.; A.B. in Econs. and Fin., NYU, 1951; m. Nancy L. Longley, June 6, 1954; children—Cheryl L., Duane L. Vice pres. mktg. Warner-Chilcott div. Warner Lambert Co., Morris Plains, N.J., 1970-72, pres. div., 1973-77, exec. v.p. Am. Optical div. and pres. Am. Optical Internat. div., Southbridge, Mass., 1978; pres. biol. and proprietary products divs., v.p. Revlon Health Care Group, Revlon Corp., Tuckahoe, N.Y., 1978-80, pres. ethical, proprietary and vision care divs., 1981-82, corp. v.p. parent co., 1982, pres. Revlon Health Care Group, 1983-92, corp. exec. v.p. parent co., 1984-92, pres. Revlon Health Beauty Care and Internat. Group, 1988-92, ret., 1992; pres. DKL Properties, health care cons. Promedex Techs., 1992—. Mem. Republican Nat. Com. Mem. Am. Mgmt. Assn., Am. Mktg. Assn. (pres. N.J. chpt. 1967-68), Sales Exec. Club N.Y. Clubs: Princeton N.Y.; Cripple Creek (Del.) Golf; Masons, Shriners. Author: (with others) Marketing Planning for Chief Executives and Planners, 1966. Home: 8 Western Dr Colts Neck NJ 07722-1271 Office: 1 Bethany Rd Ste 44 Hazlet NJ 07730-1662

MILLER, DUANE LEON, insurance company executive; b. Oskaloosa, Iowa, July 31, 1937; s. Marvin L. and Cora Mae (Ver Steeg) M.; m. Suzanne Schoon, May 1, 1958; children—Debra, Jeffrey. Student, Central Coll., Pella, Iowa, 1955-57; B.A. in Math, U. Iowa, 1959; M.B.A., Ill. State U., Normal, 1972. C.P.A., Ill. With Ill. Agrl. Assn. (and its affiliate), 1959-81; asst. v.p. fin., asst. treas. Ill. Agrl. Assn. (and its affiliate), Bloomington, 1971-72; v.p. fin., treas. Ill. Agrl. Assn. (and its affiliate), 1972-74; exec. v.p., chief exec. officer Country Life Ins. Co., Country Mut. Ins. Co., Country Casualty Ins. Co., Country Capital Mgmt. Co., CC Services, Inc. and 3 related, Bloomington, 1974—; pres. Ill. Ins. Info. Service, 1978-79. Bd. dirs. Brokaw Hosp., Normal, 1976-84, pres., 1980-82; pres. United Way of McLean County, Ill., 1977. Mem. Nat. Assn. Ind. Insurers (governing bd.), Conf. Casualty Ins. Cos. (past dir.), Nat. Assn. Ind. Insurers Safety Assn. (gov.), Am. Inst. C.P.A.'s. Presbyterian. Office: 1701 N Towanda Ave Bloomington IL 61701-2090

MILLER, DWIGHT RICHARD, cosmetologist, corporate executive, hair designer; b. Johnstown, Pa., Jan. 24, 1943. Grad., Comer & Doran Sch., San Diego; DSci. (hon.), London Inst. for Applied Rsch., 1973. Cert. aromatherapist; lic. cosmetologist., instr.; Brit. Mastercraftsman. Styles dir. Marinello-Comer, Hollywood, Calif., 1965-67; expert Pivot Point Internat., Chgo., 1967-68; styles dir. Lapins, L.A., 1969; dir. Redken, L.A., 1970, Vidal Sassoon, London, 1971-74; world amb. Pivot Point, New Zealand and Australia, 1974-75; internat. artistic dir. Pivot Point, Chgo., 1975-78; internat. dir., co-founder Hair Artists Inst. & Registry, 1978-81; internat. artistic dir. Zotos Internat., Darien, Conn., 1981-87, Matrix Essentials, Inc., Solon, Ohio, 1987-92; bd. dirs., founder, v.p. creative Anasazi Exclusive Salon Products, Inc., Dubuque, Iowa, 1992-96; pres. Anasazi Salon Sys., Dubuque, 1996—; cons. Anasazi Exclusive Salon Products, Inc., Dubuque, Iowa; judge hairdressing competitions including Norwegian Masters, Australian Nat. Championships; pres. Intercrimpers, London, 1974-75. Author: Sculptic Cutting Pivot Point 75, Prismatics, 1983; prod., dir. 15 documentaries, numerous tech. and industry videos; contbr. articles, photographs to popular mags.; developer several profl. product lines including Vidal Sassoon-London, Design Freedom, Bain de Terre, Ultra Bond, Vavoom!, Systeme Biolage. Cons. American Crew, Anasazi; with USMC, 1960-64. Named Artistic Dir. Yr. Am. Salon mag.; presented with Order of White Elephant, 1976; recipient London Gold Cup for Best Presentation London Beauty Festival, 1982, Dr. Everett G. McDonough award for Excellence in Permanent Waving, World Master award Art and Fashion Group, 1992. Mem. Cercle des Arts et Techniques de la Coiffure, Intercoiffure, Haute Coiffure Franchaise, Soc. Cosmetic Chemists, Hair Artists Great Britain, Internat. Assn. Trichogists, Nat. Cosmetologists Assn. (HairAmerica), Am. Soc. Phytotherapy and Aromatherapy, HairChicago (hon.), Art and Fashion Group (pres. 1993), 'Dressers MC (pres. 1990—), London's Alternative Hair Club (patron), The Salon Assn. Address: 13900 Watt Rd Novelty OH 44072-9741

MILLER, E. WILLARD, geography educator; b. Turkey City, Pa., May 17, 1915; s. Archie Howard and Tessie Bernella (Master) M.; m. Ruby Skinner, June 27, 1941. MA, U. Nebr., 1939; PhD, Ohio State U., 1942, DSc (hon.), 1997. Instr. Ohio State U., 1941-43; asst. prof. geography and geology Western Res. U., 1943-44; asso. prof. geography Pa. State U., University Park, 1945-49; prof. Pa. State U., 1949—, chief div. geography, 1945-53, head dept. geography, 1954-63; asst. dean for resident instrn. Coll. Earth and Mineral Scis., 1964-72, asst. dean, 1972-80, assoc. dean for resident instrn. and continuing edn., 1967-69; dir. Acad. Year Inst., Earth Scis., NSF, 1967-71; geographer OSS, Washington, 1944-45; spl. research on Arctic environ. problems for Q.M. Gen., U.S. Army, 1947-50; permanent councilor Pa. Geog. Soc., 1990; geographic adviser Thomas Y. Crowell Co., hon. chmn. Nat Coun. Geog. Edn. (Disting. Mentor award, 1995) 21st Century Endowment Fund, 1994—. Author: Careers in Geography, 1948 (rev. 1955), (with others) The World's Nations: An Economic and Regional Geography, 1958, A Geography of Manufacturing, 1962, An Economic Atlas of Pennsylvania, 1964, (with G. Langdon) Exploring Earth Environments: A World Geography, 1964, Energy Resources of the United States, 1968, Mineral Resources of the United States, 1968, A Geography of Industrial Location, 1970, A Socio-Economic Atlas of Pennsylvania, 1974, Manufacturing: A Study of Industrial Location, 1977, Industrial Location: A Bibliography, 1978, Physical Geography: Earth Systems and Human Interactions, 1985, Pennsylvania: A Keystone to Progress, 1986, (with Ruby M. Miller) United States Immigration, 1969, During Business In and With Latin America, 1987, (with Ruby M. Miller) Economic, Political and Regional Aspects of the World's Energy Problems, 1979, The Third World: Natural Resources, Economics, Politics and Social Conditions, 1981, Africa: A Bibliography on the Third World, 1981, The American Coal Industry: Economic, Political and Environmental Aspects, 1980, Manufacturing in Nonmetropolitan Pennsylvania, 1980; (with Ruby M. Miller) Latin America: A Bibliography on the Third World, 1982, South America: A Bibliography in the Third World, 1982, Middle America: A Bibliography on the Third World, 1982, Industrial Location and Planning: Theory, Models and Factors of Localization: A Bibliography, 1984, Industrial Location and Planning: Localization, Growth and Organization: A Bibliography, 1984, Industrial Location and Planning: Regions and Countries: A Bibliography, 1984; Pennsylvania: Architecture and Culture: A Bibliography, 1985, United States' Foreign Relation: Western Europe, 1987, United States' Foreign Relations: Soviet Union and Eastern Europe, 1987, United States' Foreign Relations: United States and Canada, 1987, Industrial Parks, Export Processing Zones, and Enterprise Zones: A Bibliography, 1987, The 1976 Presidential Elections: A Bibliography, 1987, The 1980 Presidential Election: A Bibliography, 1987, The 1984 Presidential Election: A Bibliography, 1987, The Third World: Economic Development, 1988, The Third World: Government and Political Relations, Social Conditions, Population, Urbanization, Education, and Communications, 1988, The Third World: Economic Activities, 1988, Natural Resources and Commerical Policy, 1988, others; editl. dir.: Earth and Mineral Scis. Bull, 1967-69; editor: (with S.K. Majumdar) Pennsylvania Coal: Resources, Technology and Utilization, 1983, Hazardous and Toxic Wastes: Management and Health Effects, 1984, Solid and Liquid Wastes: Managment Methods and Socioeconomic Considerations, 1984, Management of Radioactive Materials and Wastes: Issues and Progress, 1985, Environmental Consequences of Energy Production, 1987, Ecology and Restoration of the Delaware River Basin, 1988, A Geography of Pennsylvania, 1995; (with S.K. Majumdar, R.F. Schmalz) Management of Hazardous Materials and Wastes: Treatment, Minimization and Environmental Impacts, 1989, (with Ruby M. Miller) Environmental Hazards: Air Pollution, 1989, (with S.K. Majumdar and R.R. Parizek) Water Resources in Pennsylvania, 1990, (with S.K. Majumdar and R.F. Schmalz) Environmental Radon, 1990; (with Ruby M. Miller) Environmental Hazards: Radioactive Wastes and Materials, 1990, Environmental Hazards: Toxic Materials and Hazardous Wastes, 1991; (with S.K. Majumdar, L.M. Rosenfeld, P.A. Rubba and R.F. Schmalz) Science Education in the United States, Issues, Crises and Priorities, 1991; (with S.K. Majumdar and John Cahir) Air Pollution, 1991, (with G. Forbes, R.F. Schmalz and S.K. Majumdar) Natural and Technological Disasters, 1992, (with S.K. Majumdar, L.S. Kalkstein, B.M. Yarnal, and L.M. Rosenfeld) Global Climatic Change: Implications Challenges and Mitigation Measures, 1992, (with Ruby M. Miller) Water: Quality and Availability, 1993, (with S.K. Majumdar, L.S. Kalkstein, B.M. Yarnal and L.M. Rosenfeld) Global Climatic Change: Implications, Challenges and Mitigation Measures, 1992, (with S.K. Majumdar et al) Conservation and Resource Management, 1993, (with S.K. Majumdar, D.E. Baker, E.K. Brown, J.R. Pratt and R.F. Schmaltz) Conservation and Resource Management, 1993, (with Ruby M. Miller) Energy and American Society, 1993, United States Immigration, 1996, (with others) Biological Diversity: Problems and Challenges, 1994, Environmental Contaminants: Ecosystems and Human Health, 1995, Forests: A Global Perspective, 1996, (with Miller) America's International Trade, 1995, (with S.K. Majumder, Fred J. Brenner) Ecology of Wetlands and Associated Features, 1997; assoc. editor The Pennsylvania Geographer, Jour. of Pa. Acad. Scis.; media materials editor: Jour. Geography, 1981-84; contbg. editor: Producers Monthly Mag; editor Middle States Geographer, 1991-94; contbr. articles to sci. jours. Recipient cert. of merit from OSS, 1995, Whitbeck award Nat. Coun. Geog. Edn., 1950, Pa. Gov.'s citation for Contbn. to Commonwealth, 1975, Pa. Dept. Commerce Sec.'s Meritorious Svcs. award, 1975, Disting. Alumnus Clarion U., 1989; named Hon. Alumnus Pa. State U., 1991. Fellow AAAS, Am. Geog. Soc., Explorers Club, Nat. Coun. Geog. Edn.; mem. Am. Inst. Mining, Metall. and Petroleum Engrs., Am. Soc. Profl. Geographers (sec. 1944-48, pres. 1948), Assn. Am. Geographers (Honors award 1990), Pa. Geog. Soc. (pres. 1962-63, dir. 1965—, Meritorious Service award 1974, 84, 93), Pa. Acad. Sci. (pres. 1966-68, editorial bd. Procs. 1985—, Spl. Services award 1976, 87, Appreciation award 1992, George C. and Kathryn Shoffstal Sci. Leadership award 1996), Obelisk Soc., Mount Nittany Soc. of Pa. State U., Pres.'s Club of Pa. State U., George Atherton Soc. Pa. State U., Sigma Xi, Pi Gamma Mu, Beta Gamma Sigma, Gamma Theta Upsilon. Home: 845 Outer Dr State College PA 16801-8234

MILLER, EDMOND TROWBRIDGE, civil engineer, educator, consultant; b. Pitts., Dec. 9, 1933; s. George Ellsworth and Billie Sue (Watson) M.; m. Nancy Lee Cooper, July 21, 1956; children: Carol Anne, Nancy Ruth, Laura Elizabeth. B.C.E., Ga. Inst. Tech., 1955, M.S.C.E., 1957; C.E., MIT, 1963; Ph.D., Tex. A&M U., 1967. Registered profl. engr., Ala., Fla. Asst. prof. civil engring. U. Ala., Tuscaloosa, 1963-64, assoc. prof., 1967-71, prof., 1971-75; v.p. William S. Pollard Cons., Memphis, 1976-77; chmn. dept. civil engring. U. Louisville, 1977-81; prof. U. Ala., Birmingham, 1981-96, chmn. dept. civil engring., 1981-90, interim dean Sch. Engring., 1984; ret., 1996; instr. civil engring. Tex. A&M U., 1964-67. Served to capt. C.E. AUS, 1956-57. Automotive Safety Found. fellow, 1964-65; recipient Outstanding Achievement in Edn. award Ky. Soc. Profl. Engrs., 1980. Fellow ASCE (dist. 9 council 1978-80), Inst. Transp. Engrs.; mem. Am. Soc. Engring. Edn., Transp. Research Bd., Sigma Xi, Phi Kappa Phi, Tau Beta Pi, Chi

Epsilon. Christian Scientist. Home: 2566 Dalton Dr Pelham AL 35124-1448 Mailing Address: PO Box 158 Pelham AL 35124-0158

MILLER, EDMUND KENNETH, retired electrical engineer, educator; b. Milw., Dec. 24, 1935; s. Edmund William and Viola Louise (Ludwig) M.; m. Patricia Ann Denn, Aug. 23, 1958; children: Kerry Ann, Mark Christopher. BSEE, Mich. Tech. U., 1957; MS in Nuclear Engring., U. Mich., 1958, MSEE, 1961, PhD in Elec. Engring., 1965. Rsch. assoc. U. Mich., Ann Arbor, 1965-68; sr. scientist MB Assocs., San Ramon, Calif., 1968-71; group leader engring. rsch. div. Lawrence Livermore Lab., Livermore, Calif., 1971-78, leader engring. rsch. div., 1978-83, leader nuclear energy systems div., 1983-85; regents prof. elect. and computer engring. U. Kans., 1985-87; mgr. electromagnetics Rockwell Sci. Ctr., Thousand Oaks, Calif., 1987-88; dir. electromagnetics rsch. operation Gen. Rsch. Corp., Santa Barbara, Calif., 1988-89; group leader MEE div. Los Alamos (N.Mex.) Nat. Lab., 1989-93, ret., 1993. Stocker vis. prof. of elec. and computer engring., Ohio U., Athens, 1994-95. Editor: Time Domain Measurements in Electromagnets, 1986; past assoc. editor Radio Sci.; assoc. editor IEEE Potentials, 1985-91, editor, 1992—; assoc. editor IEEE AP-S mag.; co-editor (with L. Medgyesi-Mitschang and E.H. Newman) Computational Electromagnetics, 1991; editorial bd. Internat. Jour. Numerical Modeling, 1990—, Computer Applications in Engring. Edn., 1992—; editor: Jour. Electromagnetic Waves and Applications, 1991—, Jour. of Applied Computational Electromagnetics Soc., IEEE Computer Soc. Mag. Computational Sci. and Engring., 1994—; contbr. 100 articles to profl. jours. Singer Lyra Male Chorus, Ann Arbor, Mich., 1966-68, Livermore Civic Chorus, 1969-71. Fellow IEEE (mem. press. bd. 1991—), mem. Am. Phys. Soc., Optical Soc. Am., Acoustical Soc. Am., Am. Soc. Engring. Edn., Electromagnetics Soc. (past bd. dirs.) Internat. Sci. Radio Union (past chmn. U.S. Commn. A), Applied Computational Electromagnetics Soc. (past pres.). Home: 3225 Calle Celestial Santa Fe NM 87501

MILLER, EDWARD ARCHIE, military physician; b. New Brunswick, N.J., Sept. 27, 1946; s. Archie Edward and Hannah M.; m. Helen Naomi Pitts, Dec. 24, 1966; children: Laura, Andrew, Brooke. BS, Howard U., 1968, MS, 1969; MD, Howard Coll. Medicine, 1976. Diplomate Am. Acad. Family Physicians. Comdr. USAF Clinic, Ankara, Turkey, 1973-84; dir. ambulatory/emergency svcs. Malcolm Grow Med. Ctr., Andrews AFB, Md., 1984-87; comdr. USAF Clinic, Rhein-Main AFB, Germany, 1987-89; med. dir. Malcolm Grow Med. Ctr., 1989-91; dir. profl. affairs Office Asst. Sec. Def., Pentagon, D.C., 1992-95; comdr. 1st med. group USAF Air Combat Command, Langley AFB, Va., 1995—; mem. Presdl. Task Force on Nat. Health Care Reform, Washington, 1993; faculty Catholic U. Sch. Nursing, Washington, 1986; assoc. prof. Uniformed Svcs. U. Health Scis., Bethesda, Md., 1989-91. Col. USAF, 1969—. Fellow Am. Acad. Family Physicians; mem. Nat. Med. Assn. Avocations: distance running, civil war and Bible history. Office: 45 Pine St Langley AFB VA 23665-2025

MILLER, EDWARD BOONE, lawyer; b. Milw., Mar. 26, 1922; s. Edward A. and Myra (Munsert) M.; m. Anne Harmon Chase Phillips, Feb. 14, 1969; children by previous marriage: Barbara Miller Anderson, Ellen Miller Gerkens, Elizabeth Miller Lawhun, Thomas; stepchildren: T. Christopher Phillips, Sarah Phillips Parkhill. B.A., U. Wis., 1942, LL.B., 1947; student, Harvard Bus. Sch., 1942-43. Bar: Wis. 1947, Ill. 1948. With firm Pope, Ballard, Shepard & Fowle, Chgo., 1947-51, 52-70, ptnr., 1953-70, 75-93, mng. partner, 1979-82, chmn. labor and employment law dept., 1975-76, 87-88, 90-91; of counsel Seyfarth, Shaw, Fairweather, and Geraldson, Chgo., 1994—; mem. adv. com. Ctr. for Labor Mgmt. Dispute Resolution, Stetson U., 1984—, Inst. Indsl. Rels., Loyola U., 1987-91, Kent Pub. Employee Labor Rels. Conf., 1988—, Ill. Ednl. Labor Rels. Bd., 1988—; exec. asst. to industry mems. Regional Wage Stblzn. Bd., Chgo., 1951-52, industry mem., 1952; chmn. NLRB, Washington, 1970-74; mem. panel of labor law experts Commerce Clearing House, 1987—; dir. Chgo. Wheel & Mfg. Co., 1965-70, 75-88, Andes Candies, Inc., 1965-68, 75-80. Mem. Gov. Ill. Commn. Labor-Mgmt. Policies for Pub. Employees, 1966-67; chmn. Midwest Pension Conf., 1960-61; mem. labor relations com. Ill. C. of C., 1953-70; bd. dirs. Am. Found. Continuing Edn., 1960-69. Served to lt. USNR, 1943-46. Mem. ABA (NLRB practice and procedures com., internat. labor law com.), Ill. Bar Assn., Wis. Bar Assn., Chgo. Assn. Commerce and Industry (chmn. labor relations com. 1980-86, bd. dirs. 1987—), Am. Employment Law Coun. (mem. adv. bd. 1995—), Coll. Labor and Employment Lawyers (emeritus mem.), Order of Coif. Republican. Congregationalist. Clubs: Legal (Chgo.), Law (Chgo.), Cliff Dwellers (Chgo.); North Shore Country (curling mem.). Home: 632 Chatham Rd Glenview IL 60025-4402 Office: 55 E Monroe St Chicago IL 60603-5701

MILLER, EDWARD DANIEL, banker; b. 1940; married. Grad., Pace U. With Mfrs. Hanover Trust Co., N.Y.C., 1959—, former sr. v.p. consumer credit, sr. v.p., dep. gen. mgr. br. banking group, 1980-82, exec. v.p., head retail banking div., 1982-85, sector exec. v.p. retail banking, 1985-88; vice chmn. Mfrs. Hanover Corp. and Mfrs. Hanover Trust Co., 1988-92; vice chmn. Chem. Banking Corp., N.Y.C., 1992-93, pres., 1994-96, also bd. dirs.; sr. vice chmn., bd. dirs. Chase Manhattan Corp., 1996—. Office: Chase Manhattan Corp 270 Park Ave New York NY 10017-2014

MILLER, EDWARD DAVID, non-profit association administrator; b. Bradenton, Fla., July 5, 1934; s. Louis and Pauline (Goldman) M.; m. Denise Daniel, Dec. 26, 1973. BA, Fla. So. Coll., 1958; MA, Appalachian State U., 1966; EdS, Cath. U., 1976; EdD, U. Ark., 1988. Cert. tchr., D.C., Fla. Assoc. exec. Nat. Bus. Edn. Assn., Washington, 1969-73; pres., chief exec. officer Future Bus Leaders Am., Washington, 1973-97; retired, 1997. Chmn. nat. coordinating coun. Vocational Student Orgn., Washington, 1980—, Nat. Adv. Coun. for Vocat. Edn., Washington, 1983-86; commr. Nat. Commn. for Employment Policy, Washington, 1983-85. With U.S. Army, 1957-59. Named to Hon. Order Ky. Cols., 1970, Hon. Citizen City of Stateboro, Ga., 1975, One of Outstanding Commrs. Nat. Commn. for Employment Policy, 1983. Mem. Am. Vocat. Assn., Am. Soc. Assn. Execs., Nat. Bus. Edn. Assn., Nat. Assn. State Suprs. Vocat. Edn. Republican. Avocations: music, collecting fine art and gems. Office: FBLA PBL Inc 1912 Association Dr Reston VA 20191-1502

MILLER, EDWARD DORING, JR., anesthesiologist; b. Rochester, N.Y., Feb. 1, 1943; s. Edward D. and Natalie (Sidam) M.; m. Leslie Coombs, June 15, 1968 (dec. Apr. 1987); children: Sara Davenport, Katherine Coombs; m. Lynne Perkins, Apr. 30, 1988. AB, Ohio Wesleyan U., 1964; MD, U. Rochester, 1968. Diplomate Am. Bd. Anesthesiology, Am. Coll. Anesthesiology; cert. critical care medicine. Surg. intern University Hosp., Boston, 1968-69; anesthesia resident Peter Bent Brigham Hosp., Boston, 1969-71; fellow in physiology Harvard Med. Sch., Boston, 1971-73; dir. anesthesia research Brooke Army Med. Ctr., Ft. Sam Houston, Tex., 1973-75; asst. prof. anesthesiology U. Va. Med. Ctr., Charlottesville, Va., 1975-79, assoc. prof. anesthesiology, 1979-82, prof. anesthesiology, 1982-83, prof. anesthesiology, surgery, 1983-86; E.M. Papper prof. anesthesiology, chmn. dept. Columbia U. Coll. Physicians and Surgeons, N.Y.C., 1986-94; Mark C. Rogers prof., chmn. dept. anesthesiology Johns Hopkins U., Balt., 1994—, interim dean med. faculty, v.p. medicine Sch. Medicine, 1996-97, dean Sch. of Medicine, 1997—, CEO, 1997—; sr. scientist physiology, pharmacology Hosp. Necker, Paris, 1981-82; examiner Am. Bd. Anesthesiology; v.p. clin. faculty U. Va., 1983-85, pres. 1985-86. Editor Anesthesia and Analgesia, 1982-92; contbr. numerous articles to profl. jours. Pres. Barracks-Rugby-Preston Neighborhoods, Va., 1977-79; vestry Christ Episc. Ch., Va., 1985-86. Served to maj. M.C., U.S. Army, 1973-75. Recipient Research Career Devel. award Nat. Inst. Gen. Med. Scis., 1978-83; NIH grantee, 1977-87, Inst. Nat. de la Sante et de la Recherche Medicale grantee, 1981-82. Mem. Assn. U. Anesthetists (sec. 1984-87), Am. Soc. Anesthesiologists, Am. Physiol. Soc., Internat. Anesthesia Research Soc. (trustee 1988—), Soc. Critical Care Medicine, Soc. Cardiovascular Anesthesiologists, Assn. Univ. Anesthesiologists (pres. 1990-92), Found. for Anesthesia Edn. and Rsch. (bd. dirs. 1986—), Up Med. Bd. Presbyn. Hosp. Home: 15 Meadow Rd Baltimore MD 21212-1022 Office: Johns Hopkins U Sch Med Blalock #1415 600 N Wolfe St Baltimore MD 21205-2110

MILLER, EILEEN RENEE, counselor; b. Flushing, N.Y., Aug. 28, 1951; d. Edward and Alice Miller; m. Gary Martin Russell. BA, Syracuse U., 1972, MS, 1975, MSW, 1997. Cert. employee assistance prof., master addiction counselor, nat. cert. addiction counselor II, substance abuse counselor, cert. alcohol counselor. Dir. residence hall Syracuse (N.Y.) U., 1975-76; counselor Liverpool (N.Y.) Schs., 1976-83, Family Svc. Assocs., Liverpool, 1985—, Confidential Assistance Svcs., Liverpool, 1986—; supr. employee assistance program OCM Bd. Coop. Ednl. Svcs., Syracuse, 1984—; presenter in field; chmn. Upstate N.Y. Student and Employee Assistance Program Edn. Network, Syracuse, 1987—. Bd. dirs. Rape Crisis Ctr., Syracuse, 1982-85; com. mem. City-County Drug Commn., Syracuse, 1991—. Recipient award of appreciation Upstate N.Y. Employee Assistance Program Edn. Network, 1993; grantee OSHA, 1984-86, OASAS, 1985-88. Mem. ACA, NASW, N.Y. State Assn. Counseling and Devel., Employee Assistance Program Assn., NYFAC, Mental Health Assn. Avocations: skiing, racquetball, photography, rollerblading, travel. Office: Confidential Assistance Svc 129 Sun Harbor Dr Liverpool NY 13088-4323

MILLER, ELDON EARL, corporate business publications consultant, retired manufacturing company executive; b. Hutchinson, Kans., Jan. 1, 1919; s. Robert Dewalt and Martha Velva (Stauffer) M.; m. Margaret Borgsdorf, Mar. 26, 1950. B.A., UCLA, 1941. Formerly newspaper editor, mag. editor, pub. relations cons., polit. writer; with Purex Industries, Inc., Lakewood, Calif., 1950-85; asst. sec. Purex Industries, Inc., 1971-72, v.p. corp. relations, 1972-85, cons. bus. publs., corp. relations, 1985—. Republican. Presbyterian. Home and Office: 26685 Westhaven Dr Laguna Hills CA 92653-5767

MILLER, ELLEN S., marketing communications executive; b. Indpls., June 28, 1954; d. Harold Edward and Lilian (Gantner) M. BA, DePauw U., 1976; postgrad., Sch. Visual Arts, N.Y.C., 1981-82. Editorial asst. Daisy mag., N.Y.C., 1976-77; asst. dept. mgr., Christmas hiring mgr. Bloomingdale's, N.Y.C., 1978; sales rep. Rosenthal USA Ltd., N.Y.C., 1979, mktg. asst., 1980-81, dir. mktg. comms., 1982-90; mgr. consumer mktg. Creamer Dickson Basford, Providence, 1990, v.p., 1991-94; prin. E.S. Miller Comm., Providence, 1994—; instr. Learning Connection. Editor Community Prep. Sch. newsletter, 1993. Trustee Cmty. Prep Sch., Providence, 1993—. Recipient Bell Ringer award New Eng. Pub. Club, 1992, 93, Iris award N.J. chpt. Internat. Assn. Bus. Communicators, 1993, Silver Quill award Dist. I, 1993. Mem. Pub. Rels. Soc. Am., Nat. Tabletop Assn. (com. chair 1989), Internat. Tabletop Awards (bd. dirs. 1989). Republican. Presbyterian.

MILLER, ELLIOTT CAIRNS, retired bank executive, lawyer; b. Cambridge, Mass., May 4, 1934; s. James Wilkinson and Mary Elliott (Cairns) M.; m. Mary Killion, July 2, 1960; children: Jonathan Vaill, Stephen Killion. Grad., Matthew Whaley Sch., Williamsburg, Va., 1952; A.B., Harvard Coll., 1956; J.D., U. Mich., 1961; LL.M., Boston U., 1970. Bar: Conn. 1962. Assoc. Robinson & Cole, Hartford, Conn., 1961-66, ptnr., 1967-72; v.p., counsel Soc. for Savs., Hartford, Conn., 1972-73, sr. v.p., 1973-78, exec. v.p., 1978, pres., chief exec. officer, dir., 1979-90; pres., chief exec. officer Soc. for Savs. Bancorp Inc., 1987-90; bd. dirs. nat. council Savs. Inst., Washington, 1984-88. Trustee, chmn. Kingswood-Oxford Sch., West Hartford, 1977-87; trustee Coordinating Coun. on Founds., 1987-90; bd. dirs. Downtown Coun., Hartford, 1975-90; trustee Greater Hartford Arts Coun., 1980-88; trustee Wadsworth Atheneum, 1990—; trustee Hartford Stage Co., 1973-85, hon. trustee, 1985—; corporator Hartford Hosp., Mt. Sinai Hosp., Inst. of Living. With U.S. Army, 1956-58. Mem. Conn. Bar Assn. Home: 9 Champlin Sq Essex CT 06426-1101

MILLER, EMANUEL, retired lawyer, banker; b. N.Y.C., Jan. 22, 1917; s. Mayer and Helen (Stein) M.; m. Ruth Marcus, Jan. 3, 1942; children—Linda Alice, Henry Ward, Marjorie Joan. B.A., Bklyn. Coll., 1937; LL.B., St. Lawrence U., Bklyn., 1941. Bar: N.Y. bar 1942. With Harold W. Zeamans, Flushing, N.Y., 1950-51; firm White & Case, N.Y.C., 1951-53; with Bankers Trust Co., N.Y.C., 1953-89; v.p., counsel Bankers Trust Co., 1976-89, ret., dir. various affiliates; lectr. in field. Contbr. legal publs. Served with U.S. Army, 1942-45. Mem. Am., N.Y. State bar assns., Iota Theta. Club: Indian Spring Golf (Boynton Beach, Fla.). Home: 6370 Evian Pl Boynton Beach FL 33437-4909 *Never let the poetry of evil doctrine or thought, regardless of its literary artistry and excellence, debase our staunch adherence to our principles of righteousness, morality, justice and love of America.*

MILLER, EMILIE F., former state senator, consultant; b. Chgo., Aug. 11, 1936; d. Bruno C. and Etta M. (Senese) Feiza; m. Dean E. Miller; children: Desireé M., Edward C. BS in Bus. Adminstrn., Drake U., 1958. Asst. buyer Jordan Marsh Co., Boston, 1958-60, Carson, Pirie, Scott & Co., Chgo., 1960-62; dept. mgr., asst. buyer Woodward & Lothrop, Washington, 1962-64; state labor coord. Robb Davis Daliles Joint Campaign; legis. aide Senator Adelard Brandt, Va., 1980-83; fin. dir. Saslaw for Congress, 1984; legis. cons. Va. Fedn. Bus. Profl. Women, 1986-87; senator Va. Gen. Assembly, Richmond, 1988-92; cons. apptd. by Gov. Wilder to bd. dirs. Innovative Tech. Authority, 1992-94, Ctr. for Innovative Tech., 1992-94; cons., 1992—; mem. Edn. and Health com., Gen. Laws com., Local Gov. com., Rehab. and Social Scis. com.; bus. tng. seminars Moscow, Nizhny Novgorod, Russia, 1993, Novgorod, St. Petersburg, 1995; cons. in field. Guest editorial writer No. Va. Sun, 1981; host, producer weekly TV program, Channel 61. Mem. State Ctrl. Com. Dem. Party Va., Richmond, 1974-92, Fairfax County Dem. Com., 1968—, Presdl. Inaugural Com., 1977, 1992 Dem. Nat. Platform Com., Va. mem. on temp. coms., Dem. Adv. Com. Robb-Spong Commn., 1978-79; founder, chmn. Va. Assoc. Dem. County and City Chmn., 1976-80, Fairfax County Dem. Com., 1976-80; security supr. 1980 Dem. Nat. Conv.; v.p. Va. Fedn. Dem. Women, 1992-94; bd. dirs. Stop Child Abuse Now, 1988, Ctr. Innovative Tech., 1992-94, Ct. Apptd. Spl. Advs., 1993—; mem. nat. alumni bd. J.A. Achievement, BRAVO adv. com. for the first Gov.'s Awards for Arts in Va., 1979-80; lay tchr. St. Ambrose Cath. Ch., 1963-80; del. to White House Conf. on Children, 1970; chmn. Va. Coalition for Mentally Disturbed, 1992-94; mem. com. of 100, Va. Opera Bd., 1993—; bd. dirs. SALT (Social Action Linking Together). Recipient Disting. Grad. award Jr. Achievement, 1973, Woman of Achievement award Fairfax (Va.) Bd. Suprs. and Fairfax County Commn. for Women, 1982, Cmty. Svc. award Friends of Victims Assistance Network, 1988, Founders award Fairfax County Coun. of Arts, 1989, Mental Health Assn. of Northern Va. Warren Stambaugh award, 1991, Ann. Svc. award Va. Assn. for Marriage and Family Therapy, 1991, Psychology Soc. of Washington Cmty. Svc. award, 1993, pacesetter award So. Women in Pub. Leadership Conf., 1996. Mem. NOW, Nat. Mus. Women in the Arts, Va. Assn. Female Execs. (mem. adv. bd., bd. dirs., v.p. 1992—), Va. Assn. Cmty. Svc. Bds. (chmn. 1980-82), North Va. Assn. Cmty. Bds. (chmn. 1978-79, 95—), Fairfax County Coun. Arts (v.p. 1980—, mem. exec. com. internat. children's festival, Founders award 1989), Fairfax County C. of C. (mem. legis. com.), Greater Merrifield Bus. and Profl. Assn., Mental Health Assn. No.Va. (bd. dirs.), Ctrl. Fairfax C. of C., Falls Church C. of C., Bus. and Profl. Women's Fedn. Va., Mantua Citizen's Assn. (mem. exec. bd.), Tower Club (Fairfax), Bus. and Profl. Women's Club (pres. Falls Church chpt. 1994-96, Woman of Yr. award 1990), Women's Nat. Dem. Club (past v.p., mem. bd. govs.), Downtown Club (Richmond), Va. Assn. Female Execs. (bd. dirs. 1992—), Phi Gamma Nu. Roman Catholic. Avocations: Cubs fan, tennis, art. Home: 8701 Duvall St Fairfax VA 22031-2711

MILLER, ERNEST CHARLES, management consultant; b. Bronx, N.Y., July 14, 1925; s. Ernest Philip and Elizabeth (Hellwig) M.; m. Edith Grosvenor Porterfield, Nov. 11, 1947 (div. Oct. 3, 1963); children: Laura Lee, Marcy Rogers, Ernest Charles; m. Tung-fen Lin, Jan. 8, 1985. A.B., Yale U., 1945; M.A., U. Pa., 1949. Lic. psychologist, N.Y. Instr. U. Pa., 1947-51, cons., 1950-53; br. mgr., bd. dirs. Richardson, Bellows, Henry & Co., Inc., 1953-55; mgr. personnel tech. Am. Standard, Inc., 1955-59; mng. prin. Hellwig, Miller & Assos., Westport, Conn., 1959-61; sr. assoc. Cresap, McCormick & Paget, Inc., N.Y.C., 1961-63; with Am. Mgmt. Assns., N.Y.C., 1964-83; pres. AMACOM div. Am. Mgmt. Assns., 1978-81, group v.p. AMA Publs. Group, 1981-83; pres. Miller, Hellwig Assocs., 1984—. Author works in strategic planning, orgn. devel., human resources, exec. compensation and mgmt. Bd. dirs. La Jolla Inst. for Allergy and Immunology; mem. Columbia U. All-Univ. Seminar, China Internat. Bus. Orgn. and Mgmt. NEH fellow, 1980. Mem. Am. Psychol. Assn., Japan Soc., Soc. Indsl. and Orgnl. Psychology, Inc. Episcopalian. Office: Miller Hellwig Assocs 150 W End Ave New York NY 10023-5702

MILLER, EUGENE, university official, business executive; b. Chgo., Oct. 6, 1925; s. Harry and Fannie (Prosterman) M.; m. Edith Sutker, Sept. 23, 1951 (div. Sept. 1965); children: Ross, Scott, June; m. Thelma Gottlieb, Dec. 22, 1965; stepchildren: Paul Gottlieb, Alan Gottlieb. BS, Ga. Inst. Tech., 1945; AB magna cum laude, Bethany Coll., 1947, LLD, 1969; diploma, Oxford (Eng.) U., 1947; MS in Journalism, Columbia U., 1948; MBA, NYU, 1959; postgrad., Pace U., 1973—. Reporter, then city editor Greensboro (N.C.) Daily News, 1948-52; S.W. bur. chief Bus. Week mag., Houston, 1952-54; assoc. mng. editor Bus. Week mag., N.Y.C., 1954-60; dir. pub. affairs and communications McGraw-Hill, Inc., 1960-63, v.p., 1963-68; sr. v.p. pub. rels. and investor rels., exec. com. N.Y. Stock Exch., N.Y.C., 1968-73; sr. v.p. CNA Fin. Corp., Chgo., 1973-75; chmn. Eugene Miller & Assos., Glencoe, Ill., 1975-77; v.p. USG Corp., Chgo., 1977-82, sr. v.p., 1982-85, mem. mgmt. com., 1982-91, exec. v.p., CFO, 1985-87, elected vice chmn., CFO, 1987-91, mem. exec. com., also bd. dirs.; prof., exec.-in-residence Coll. Bus. Fla. Atlantic U., 1991—; chmn., CEO Ideon Group, Inc., Jacksonville, Fla., 1996; adj. prof. mgmt. NYU, 1963-65; prof. bus. adminstrn. Fordham U., 1969-75; prof. fin., chmn. dept. Northeastern Ill. U., 1975-78; lectr. to bus. and ednl. groups; bd. dirs. MRFI, Inc., Chgo., bd. dirs., mem. adv. bd. dirs. Nationwide Acceptance Corp., Chgo.; cons. to sec. Dept. Commerce, 1961-66; editor-in-residence U. Oreg., 1992; exec.-in-residence U. Ill., 1991, U. Wis., 1991, U. Toronto, 1992; exec.-in-residence, POHL fellow U. Wyo., 1992; mem. adv. bd. CFO mag., 1991—; bd. dirs. IMX Corp., Boca Raton, Fla.; cons. Tutor Time Learning Systems, Inc., Boca Raton, 1997—. Author: Your Future in Securities, 1974, Barron's Guide to Graduate Business Schools, 1977, 10th edit., 1997; contbg. editor: Public Relations Handbook, 1988, Boardroom Reports, 1986—; writer syndicated bus. column., 1964-86; mem. editl. bd. IRQ mag., 1997—. Trustee Bethany Coll.; mem. alumni bd. Columbia U. Sch. Journalism. Comdr. USNR, World War II, ret. Recipient outstanding achievement award Bethany Coll., 1963, 50th anniversary award Sch. Journalism Columbia U., also honors award, 1963, Sch. Journalism Ohio U., 1964, disting. svc. award in investment edn. Nat. Assn. Investment Clubs, 1980, Roalman award Nat. Investor Rels. Inst., 1987. Fellow Pub. Rels. Soc. Am.; mem. Nat. Assn. Bus. Economists, Soc. Am. Bus. Editors and Writers (founder), Fin. Execs. Inst., Arthur Page Soc., Mid-Am. Club, St. Andrew's Country Club, Sigma Delta Chi, Alpha Sigma Phi. Home: 7351 Ballantrae Ct Boca Raton FL 33496-1423 Office: Fla Atlantic U 777 Glades Rd Boca Raton FL 33431-6424

MILLER, EUGENE ALBERT, bank executive; married. B.B.A., Detroit Inst. Tech., 1964; grad., Sch. Bank Adminstrn., Wis., 1968. With Comerica Bank-Detroit (formerly The Detroit Bank, then Detroit Bank & Trust Co.), 1955—, v.p., 1970-74, controller, 1971-74, sr. v.p., 1974-78, exec. v.p., 1978-81, pres., 1981-89, chief exec. officer, 1989—, chmn., 1990—; with parent co. Comerica Inc. (formerly DETROITBANK Corp.), 1973—, treas., 1973-80, pres., 1981—, chief exec. officer, 1989-92, chmn. bd., 1990-92; pres., COO Comerica Inc. (merger with Manufacturers Nat. Corp.), Detroit, 1992—; also bd. dirs. Comerica Inc. (formerly DETROITBANK Corp.); chmn., CEO Comerica Bank (merged with Manufacturers Nat. Corp.), Detroit, 1993—; chmn., CEO Comerica Inc., Detroit, 1993—, also bd. dirs. Office: Comerica Inc 500 Woodward Ave Detroit MI 48226-3423

MILLER, EWING HARRY, architect; b. Toledo, Ohio, Oct. 5, 1923; s. Ewing Harry and Esther Alice (Graves) M.; m. Gladys Jacquelyn Good, Dec. 18, 1948 (dec.); children: Victoria Alice, Paul Ewing. BA, U. Pa., 1947, MA, 1948. Draftsman Harbeson, Hough, Livingston & Larson, Phila., 1948; designer Nolen & Swinburne, Phila., 1950-52; project architect Gilboy & O'Malley, London, 1953-55; partner Miller, Vrydagh & Miller, Terre Haute, Ind., 1955-65; pres. Ewing Miller Partnership, Terre Haute, 1965-70; pres. Archonics Corp., 1970-76, chmn. bd., 1976-79; sr. ptnr. for design Archonics Design Partnership, Indpls., 1979-84; assoc. ptnr. architecture eastern region U.S. Howard Needles, Tammen & Bergendoff, 1985-92; archtl. cons. Design & Bldg. Industry, 1992—; gen. ptnr. Lockerbie Devel. Co., 1978-86, Lockerbie Glove Devel. Co., 1983-86, East St. Devel. Co., 1979-86. Contbr. articles to profl. jours.; archtl. critic Indpls. Monthly Mag.; major archtl. works include: various bldgs. Ind. U., including grad. biology lab., Ind. State U., master plan and edn. bldgs., residence halls and power ctr., Southwestern Ind. U., master plan and edn. bldgs., Ind. and Ohio Laborers Tng. Ctr., Prairie Elem. Sch., Indpls. Westin Conv. Hotel; various office parks, Indpls. Pub. Transp. Corp. facility, addition to Duesenberg Factory; master plan Ind. State Govt. Complex, State of Ind. and design of new state office bldg.; prin. in charge printing facility Ho. of Rep. Architect of the Capitol, prin. in charge of Prospectus Devel. Study for design and restoration of Old Exec. Office Bldg., Washington; master plan for remodeling The Pentagon, Washington; prin. in charge design for remodeling Dept. of State, Washington; client rep. for remodeling Midwest Direct Mktg. Ctr., B.M.G., Inc., N.Y. Mem. Ind. Gov.'s Commn. on Aging, 1959-62; pres. Gov.'s Commn. on Comprehensive Health Planning, Ind., 1970-75, Behavioral Research Found., 1965-85; bd. mgrs. Sheldon Swope Art Gallery, 1965-80, pres., 1965-73; bd. dirs. Center for Exploration of Values and Meaning, 1978-85, Herron Art Gallery, 1980-88; chmn. Indpls. Arts and Cultural Alliance, 1983; v.p. Am. Chestnut Land Trust, Port Republic, Md.; sec. Cove Point Natural Heritage Trust, Solomons Island, Md., 1995—. Recipient design citation, biennial awards program Ind. Soc. Architects; Honor awards, triennial design awards East Central Region AIA; Archtl. award of excellence Am. Inst. Steel Constrn.; 1st Honor award and winner Internat. Competition for Housing, Indpls.; award of excellence for univ. bldgs. Am. Sch. and Univ. Mag., 1985; Ind. Soc. Architects Honor award restoration of Circle Theater, various office bldgs., 1985, 86. Fellow AIA (mem. com. on design, chmn. com. on architecture for edn., mem. Vision 2000 study, architecture in coming decade), Lambda Alpha Hon. Soc. Home and Office: 2230 Birch Rd Port Republic MD 20676-2640 also: The Pennsylvania Apts #1201 601 Pennsylvania Ave NW Washington DC 20004-2601

MILLER, FRANCES SUZANNE, historic site curator; b. Defiance, Ohio, Apr. 17, 1950; d. Francis Bernard Johnson and Nellie Frances (Holder) Culp; m. James A. Batdorf, Aug. 7, 1970 (div. Aug. 1979); 1 child, Jennifer Christine Batdorf; m. Rodney Lyle Miller, Aug. 8, 1982 (div. Apr. 1987). BS in History/Museology, The Defiance Coll., 1990; AS in Bus. Mgmt., N.W. Tech. Coll., 1986. With accts. receivable dept. Ohio Art Co., Bryan, Ohio, 1984-87; leasing agent Williams Met. Housing Authority, Bryan, 1987-91; curator, property mgr. James A. Garfield Nat. Historic Site, Mentor, Ohio, 1991—. Mem. AAUW (pres. 1993-95, treas. 1995-97), Nat. Trust Hist. Preservation, Ohio Mus. Assn., Ohio Assn. Host. Socs. and Mus., Cleve. Restoration Soc., Phi Alpha Theta. Avocations: needlework, reading. Office: James A Garfield Nat Historic Site 8095 Mentor Ave Mentor OH 44060-5753

MILLER, FRANCIE LORADITCH, college counselor; b. Avilton, Md., Apr. 18, 1937; d. John William and Agnes Wilda (Broadwater) Loraditch; m. George Aloys Miller, Feb. 27, 1965; children: Peter Raymond, Sandra Patricia. Student, Kent State U., 1955-57; BA in English, Calif. State U., Dominguez Hills, 1978, Ma in English, 1980. Flight attendent Western Airlines, L.A., 1957-65; lectr. English Calif. State U., Carson, 1980-82, asst. coord. learning assistance ctr., 1979-84, asst. dir. univ. outreach svcs., 1984-96; dir. advisement & transfer svcs. Marymount Coll., Palos Verdes, Calif., 1996—; mem. L.A. Regional Intersegmental Adv. Bd., 1996. Editor Campus Staff Newsletter, 1992-96. Mem. edn. com. Palos Verdes (Calif.) C. of C., 1994—; vol. Olympic Games, L.A., 1984; campus rep. Statewide Alumni Coun., Sacramento, 1982-84; participant Civic Chorale, Torrance, Calif., 1993—; apptd. statewide campus adv. com. Project Assist, 1996. Acad. scholar Kent State U., 1955. Mem. Calif. Intersegmental Articulation Coun. (newsletter editor 1993-96, vice chair 1995-96), Nat. Acad. Advising Assn., Western Assn. Coll. Admission Counselors, South Coast Higher Ednl. Coun., Phi Kappa Phi (chpt. pres. 1992—, mem. nat. comm. com. 1996). Republican. Roman Catholic. Avocations: singing, dancing, golf. Office: Marymount Coll 30800 Palos Verdes Dr E Palos Verdes Peninsula CA 90275-6273

MILLER, FRANK WILLIAM, legal educator; b. Appleton, Wis., May 15, 1921; s. Frank Paul and Ruth Margaret (Arft) M.; m. Lucille Gloria Rinnan, Sept. 8, 1945; children: Deborah Lynn, Patrica Elizabeth. B.A., U. Wis., 1946, LL.B., 1948, S.J.D., 1954. Bar: Wis. 1948. Mem. faculty Washington U., St. Louis, 1948-91, Coles prof. criminal law and adminstrn., 1962-64, James Carr prof. criminal jurisprudence, 1964-91, prof. emeritus, 1991—; Dan Hopson Disting. prof. So. Ill. U., Carbondale, 1992; summer vis. prof. law U. Ark., 1952, 54, 56, Stetson U., 1955, U. Wis., 1957, U. Tex., 1975, 85; vis. prof. law So. Ill. U. at Carbondale, 1973-74, summers 1976-81; chmn. round table council criminal law Assn. Am. Law Schs., 1961; chmn. Pub. Defender Adv. Com. St. Louis County, 1962. Author: (with A.C. Becht)

Factual Causation in Negligence and Strict Liability Cases, 1961, Prosecution: The Decision to Charge a Suspect with a Crime, 1969; editor: (with R.O. Dawson, George E. Dix, Raymond I. Parnas) Criminal Justice Administration, 1976, 4th edit., 1991, (with Dawson, Dix, Parnas) The Police Function, 1982, 5th edit., 1991, Sentencing and The Correctional Process, 1976, The Juvenile Justice Process, 1976, 3d edit., 1985, The Mental Health Process, 1976, Prosecution and Adjudication, 1982, 4th edit., 1991. Served with AUS, 1942-45. Recipient citation for outstanding teaching Washington U. Alumni Fedn., 1965, Washington U. Law Alumni Assn., 1991. Mem. ABA, Am. Law Inst. (Guttmacher award 1977), Order of Coif. Democrat.

MILLER, FREDERICK, pathologist; b. N.Y.C., Apr. 5, 1937; s. Alex and Sarah M.; m. Emilie J. Kronish, June 2, 1962; children: David, Allison. B.S., U. Wis., 1956; M.D., N.Y. U., 1961. Diplomate: Am. Bd. Pathology. Intern Bellevue Hosp., N.Y.C., 1961-62, resident, 1962-63; practice medicine specializing in pathology, 1965—; clin. assoc., attending physician Nat. Inst. Arthritis and Metabolic Diseases, 1963-65; resident chief pathology dept. NYU Med. Ctr., 1965-67; attending pathologist Bellevue and Univ. Hosps., N.Y.C., 1967; asst. prof. pathology NYU, 1967-70, assoc. prof., 1970; assoc. prof. SUNY, Stony Brook, 1970-75, prof., 1975—, chmn. dept. pathology, 1977—, Marvin Kuschner prof. pathology, 1991, dir. lab. for arthritis and related diseases, 1976—; dir. labs. Univ. Hosp., Stony Brook, 1978—, pathologist-in-chief, 1979—; mem. Nat. Bd. Med. Examiners in Pathology, 1996—. Contbr. articles to med. jours. Served with USPHS, 1963-65. Recipient Bausch and Lomb medal for rsch., 1961; Pres.'s award SUNY, Stony brook, 1990, Chancellor's award, 1990, Aesculapius award, 1993; Golden Apple award ASMA, 1995; NIH grantee, 1963-87. Mem. AAAS, Harvey Soc., Soc. Clin. Immunology, Am. Soc. Investigative Pathology, Am. Soc. Clin. Pathologists (award 1961), Internat. Acad. Pathology, N.Y. Acad. Sci., Am. Assn. Immunologists, Assn. Pathology Chairmen, Suffolk Orchid Soc., Sigma Xi, Alpha Omega Alpha. Hort. authority on roses and orchids. Home: 46 Manchester Ln Stony Brook NY 11790-2826 Office: SUNY Stony Brook Dept Pathology Hsc Stony Brook NY 11794

MILLER, FREDERICK ROBESON, banker; b. Oakland, Calif., Oct. 11, 1927; s. Charles Lennon and Juliet Robeson (Chamberlain) M.; m. Nancy McDaniel, July 19, 1952; children: Susan Chase Miller Clark, Stephen Robeson, Elizabeth Rockwell. B.A., Yale U., 1952. With J.P. Morgan & Co., Inc., 1952-54; v.p. Phila. Nat. Bank, 1954-69; pres. Waterbury Nat. Bank, Conn., 1969-71, City Nat. Bank, Bridgeport, Conn., 1971-72, Conn. Nat. Bank, Bridgeport, 1973-83; also chief exec. officer, vice chmn. Conn. Nat. Bank; vice chmn. Hartford Nat. Corp., until 1984. Served with U.S. Army, 1946-47. Mem. Tubac Valley Country Club. Republican. Episcopalian. Home: PO Box 1503 Tubac AZ 85646

MILLER, FREDERICK STATEN, music educator, academic administrator; b. Lima, Ohio, Dec. 12, 1930; s. Donald Frederick and Esther Lillian (Moore) M.; m. Florence Dorothy Mistak, June 20, 1959; children: Jennifer Leigh, John Staten. B of Music Edn., Northwestern U., 1957, M in Music, 1958; D of Music Performance, U. Iowa, 1974. Mem. music faculty U. Ark., Fayetteville, 1958-64; asst. dir. bands Northwestern U., Evanston, Ill., 1964-70, assoc. dean, sch. music, 1970-76; dean, sch. music DePaul U., Chgo., 1976-95, ret.; bd. dirs. Concertante de Chgo., 1985—; accreditation evaluator North Cen. Assn., Boulder, Colo., 1982—, Nat. Assn. Schs. Music, Washington, 1981—. Composer/arranger numerous pub. works for band; editor music publs. Served with USN, 1948-52. Mem. ASCAP, Nat. Assn. Schs. Music (hon. life, regional chmn. 1982-84, instl. rep., treas. 1984-88, v.p. 1988-91, pres. 1991-94), Pi Kappa Lambda (bd. regents 1970-74), Phi Kappa Phi. Roman Catholic. Clubs: University (Chgo.); Sheridan Shore Yacht (Wilmette, Ill.). Avocations: sailing, cooking, jazz performance. Home: 1322 Greenwood Ave Wilmette IL 60091-1624

MILLER, FREDERICK WILLIAM, publisher, lawyer; b. Milw., Mar. 18, 1912; s. Roy W. and Kathryn (Oehlers) M.; m. Violet Jane Bagley, Mar. 31, 1939. B.A., U. Wis., 1934, LLB, 1936. Bar: Wis. 1936. Assoc. Tenney & Davis, Madison, 1935-36; atty. State of Wis., Madison, 1936-77; pub. The Capital Times Co., Madison, 1979—, also dir.; dir. Madison Newspaper, Inc., 1970—, chmn. bd., 1980—; dir. Evjue Found., Inc., Madison, 1957—. Trustee Evjue Charitable Trust, Madison, 1970—. Mem. Wis. Bar Assn. Clubs: Madison Club, Univ. Club. Home: 2810 Arbor Dr Madison WI 53711-1826 Office: Capital Times Co PO Box 8056 1901 Fish Hatchery Rd Madison WI 53713-1248

MILLER, GABRIEL LORIMER, physicist, researcher; b. N.Y.C., Jan. 18, 1928; s. Hugh Lorimer and Olga (Katzin) M.; m. Natalie Coffin, May 20, 1962; children: Matthew, Jonathan, Katharine. BS in Physics, London U., 1949, MS in Math., 1952, PhD in Physics, 1957. Sr. demonstrator Birkbeck Coll. London U., 1953-57; physicist Brookhaven Nat. Lab., Upton, L.I., N.Y., 1957-63; mem. tech. staff AT&T Bell Labs., Murray Hill, N.J., 1963-82, head dept. interactive systems rsch., 1982-96; vis. prof. U. Aarhus, Denmark, 1969-70, Rutgers U., New Brunswick, N.J., 1972-73; mem. vis. coms. Oak Ridge, Lawrence Berkeley and Brookhaven nat. labs. Contbr. numerous publs. on instrumentation, measurement and sensors, holder more than 40 patents; past assoc. editor Rev. Sci. Instruments. Fellow IEEE (mem. nuclear instruments com. 1960—, Centennial medal 1984), Am. Phys. Soc.; mem.IEEE Indsl. Electronics Soc. (assoc. editor Robotics 1985—), Bohmische Phys. Soc. Home: 1000 Samoset Rd Eastham MA 02642

MILLER, GALE TIMOTHY, lawyer; b. Kalamazoo, Sept. 15, 1946; s. Arthur H. and Eleanor (Johnson) M.; m. Janice Lindvall, June 1, 1968; children: Jeremy L., Amanda E., Timothy W. AB, Augustana Coll., 1968; JD, U. Mich., 1971. Bar: Mich. 1971, Colo. 1973, U.S. Dist. Ct. Colo. 1973, U.S. Ct. Appeals (10th cir.) 1979, U.S. Supreme Ct. 1997. Trial atty. FTC, Washington, 1971-73; assoc. Davis, Graham & Stubbs, L.L.P., Denver, 1973-77, ptnr., mem., 1978—. Bd. dirs. Sr. Housing Options, Inc., 1980-93; chair Colo. Lawyers Com., 1989-91, bd. dirs. 1987—, Individual Lawyer of Yr. 1994. Mem. ABA (antitrust sect. task force on model civil antitrust jury instrns. 1984—), Colo. Bar. Assn. (chair antitrust sect. 1996—), Denver Bar Assn. Democrat. Lutheran. Office: Davis Graham & Stubbs LLP PO Box 185 Denver CO 80201-0185

MILLER, GARY, sports network host, sports anchor; b. Oct. 31, 1956. BS in Radio and TV, So. Ill. U., 1978. Sports dir. Sta. WSIU-AM, Carbondale, Ill., 1974-78; stringer AP and UPI Radio; sports dir. Sta. WSAV-TV, Savannah, Ga., 1978-82; sports anchor/reporter World Series, All-Star Game, others CNN, 1982-90; host Baseball Tonight, anchor SportsCenter ESPN, 1990—, host SportsCenter's World Series, 1991, 92, anchor Major League Baseball winter meetings, 1992, anchor Nat. Baseball Hall of Fame Induction Ceremonies show, 1992. Named Sportscaster of Yr. by baseball's So. League.

MILLER, GARY ALLEN, financial planner; b. Redding, Calif., Nov. 28, 1960; s. Orland Lee and Velma Bernice (Hess) M.; m. Sherry Lee Starr, Nov. 2, 1979 (div. Aug., 1981); 1 child Sharon Danielle; m. Teresa Lynn Rice, June 4, 1983 (div. July 1992); children: Justin, Allen, Chelsea. Chartered fin. cons. cert., Am. Coll., Bryn Mawr, Pa., 1989. Owner, mgr. Miller TV and Electronics, Topeka, Kans., 1982-86; fin. planner Tantillo and Miller, Inc., Topeka, 1986—. Mem. Toastmasters, Million Dollar Round Table. Avocations: camping, canoeing, hot air ballooning, karate. Home: 139 SE 46th St Topeka KS 66609-1801 Office: Tantillo & Miller Inc 3706 SW Topeka Blvd Ste 400 Topeka KS 66609-1239

MILLER, GARY EVAN, psychiatrist, mental health services administrator; b. Cleve., Aug. 19, 1935; s. Henry M. and Mollie (Price) M.; m. Karen Ann Marie Barrett, Sept. 16, 1972; children: Anna Charis, Rebecca Elizabeth. MD, U. Tex., Galveston, 1960. Diplomate in psychiatry, addiction psychiatry, and geriatric psychiatry Am. Bd. Psychiatry and Neurology. Intern Montefiore Hosp., N.Y.C., 1960-61; resident in psychiatry Univ. Hosps. Cleve., 1961-62, Austin (Tex.) State Hosp., 1963-65; dep. commr. mental health services Tex. Dept. Mental Health and Mental Retardation, 1967-70; dir. Rio Grande State Center for Mental Health and Mental Retardation, Tex. Dept. Mental Health, Harlingen, 1966-67; asst. commr., dir. Rochester regional office N.Y. State Dept. Mental Hygiene, 1970-72; clin. asst. prof. psychiatry U. Rochester Sch. Medicine and Dentistry, 1970-72; asst. clin. prof. psychiatry SUNY, Buffalo, 1970-72; cons. mental health Ga. Dept. Human Resources, Atlanta, 1972; dir. div. mental health Ga. Dept. Human Resources, 1972-74; clin. prof. psychiatry Emory U. Sch. Medicine, Atlanta, 1972-74; vice chmn. Ga. State Planning and Adv. Council for Devel. Disabilities Services and Constrn., 1972-73; cons. mental health services orgn. and adminstrn., 1974-76; dir. mental health and devel. services State of N.H. Concord, 1976-82; commr. Tex. Dept. Mental Health and Mental Retardation Austin, 1982-88; clin. prof. psychiatry U. Tex. Health Sci. Ctr., Houston; adj. assoc. prof. psychiatry U. Tex. Health Sci. Ctr., San Antonio, 1984-95; dir. profl. svcs. HCA Gulf Pines Hosp., Houston, 1988-94, chief of staff, 1993; clin. dir. adult psychiatry Cypress Creek Hosp., Houston, 1994—, pres. med. staff, 1996; assoc. clin. psychiatry Post Oak Psychiatry Assocs., Houston, 1988-90; pres. Alternative Svcs. Network, Houston, 1990—; clin. dir. adult psychiatry Cypress Creek Hosp., Houston, 1994—, pres.-elect med. staff, 1995, pres., 1996—; dir. state alcoholism program in Ga., 1972-74, also, South Tex. region, 1966-67; mem. faculty U. S.C. Sch. Alcohol and Drug Studies, 1975; bd. dirs. nat. patient rights policy research project NIMH, 1981; Bd. dirs. Genessee Regional Health Planning Council, Rochester, 1970-72. Contbr. articles to profl. jours. Served as capt. M.C., U.S. Army, 1962-63. Recipient Cert. of Recognition, Ga. Psychol. Assn., 1973. Fellow Am. Psychiat. Assn. (cert. in adminstrv. psychiatry 1983); mem. AMA, Am. Soc. Addiction Medicine (cert. alcoholism and other drug dependencies 1993), N.H. Psychiat. Soc. (pres. 1981-82), Nat. Assn. State Mental Health Program Dirs. (bd. dirs. 1984-88, sec. 1986-88), N.H. Med. Soc., Am. Acad. Psychiatry and the Law, Am. Assn. Psychiat. Adminstrs. (pres. Tex. chpt.), Tex. Med. Assn., Tex. Soc. Psychiat. Physicians, Mental Health Assn. Houston and Harris County (bd. dirs. 1989-95, v.p. advocacy 1990-95), Alpha Omega Alpha. Home: 5314 Westminister Ct Houston TX 77069-3338 Office: 530 Wells Fargo Dr Ste 110 Houston TX 77090-4026

MILLER, GARY J., political economist; b. Urbana, Ill., Jan. 2, 1949; s. Gerald J. and Doris Elaine (Miner) M.; m. Anne Colberg, Jan. 29, 1971; children: Neil, Ethan. BA, U. Ill., 1971; PhD, U. Tex., 1976. Asst. prof. Calif. Inst. Tech., Pasadena, 1976-79; assoc. prof. Mich. State U., East Lansing, 1979-86; Taylor prof. of polit. economy Washington U., St. Louis, Mo., 1986—; assoc. dean for acad. affairs Olin Sch. Bus. Washington U., St. Louis, 1995-96. Author: Cities by Contract, 1981, Reforming Bureaucracy, 1987, Managerial Dilemmas, 1992. NSF grantee, 1981, 83, 92. Mem. Phi Beta Kappa, Phi Kappa Phi (Disting. Faculty award 1994). Democrat. Office: Washington U Dept Polit Sci 1 Brookings Dr Saint Louis MO 63130-4862

MILLER, GAY DAVIS, lawyer; b. Florence, Ariz., Dec. 20, 1947; d. Franklin Theodore and Mary (Belshaw) Davis; m. John Donald Miller, May 15, 1971; 1 child, Katherine Alexandra. BA, U. Colo., 1969; JD, Am. U., 1975. Bar: D.C. 1975. Atty., spl. asst. to gen. counsel, sr. counsel corp. affairs Inter Am. Devel. Bank, Washington, 1975-78, 83—; atty. Intelsat, Washington, 1978-80. Articles editor Am. U. Law Rev., 1974-75. Bd. dirs. Hist. Mt. Pleasant, Inc., Washington, 1985-86, Washington Bridle Trails Assn., 1992—. Mem. ABA, Am. Soc. Internat. Law, Inter Am. Bar Assn., Women's Bar Assn. Office: Inter Am Devel Bank 1300 New York Ave NW Washington DC 20577-0001

MILLER, GAYLE D., health facility administrator, nurse, health educator; b. Greenville, Pa., Sept. 19, 1946; d. Edward F. and Frances E. (Banic) Deets; m. John R. Miller, Oct. 12, 1974. Student, Oil City Hosp. Sch. Nursing, 1967, Penn State U., 1972—; BSN, Thiel Coll., 1989; MEd in Health, Pa. State U., 1991. Nurse med. surg. Horizon Hosp. System (formerly Greenville (Pa.) Regional Hosp. div. Horizon Hosp. System until 1992), 1967-71, head nurse orthopedics, 1971-84, coord. patient health edn., 1984-93; regional adminstr. Life Care Cancer Ctr., Stoneboro, Pa., 1994—; EquiMed Inc., State College, Pa., 1994—; speaker in field; presenter, coord. diabetes workshop Greenville Regional Hosp., 1984-91. Contbr. articles to profl. jours. Mem. Nat. Assn. Orthopedic Nurses, Oncology Nursing Soc. Home: 19 Woodview Dr Transfer PA 16154-2231

MILLER, GENE EDWARD, newspaper reporter and editor; b. Evansville, Ind., Sept. 16, 1928; m. Electra Sonia Yphantis, Apr. 13, 1952 (dec. May 1993); children: Janet Irene, Theresa Jean, Thomas Raphael, Roberta Lynn. A.B. in Journalism, Ind. U., 1950, LL.D. (hon.), 1977; Nieman fellow, Harvard U., 1967-68. Reporter Jour.-Gazette, Ft. Wayne, Ind., 1950-51, Washington Bur. Wall St. Jour., 1953-54, Richmond (Va.) News Leader, 1954-57, Miami (Fla.) Herald, 1957—. Author: Invitation To A Lynching, 83 Hours Till Dawn. Served with AUS, 1951-53. Recipient Pulitzer prize for local reporting, 1967, 76. Office: 1 Herald Plz Miami FL 33132-1609

MILLER, GENEVIEVE, retired medical historian; b. Butler, Pa., Oct. 15, 1914; d. Charles Russell and Genevieve (Wolford) M. AB, Goucher Coll., 1935; MA, Johns Hopkins U., 1939; PhD, Cornell U., 1955. Asst. in history of medicine Johns Hopkins Inst. of History of Medicine, Balt., 1943-44, instr., 1945-48, rsch. assoc., 1979-94; asst. prof. history of medicine Sch. Medicine, Case Western Res. U., Cleve., 1953-67, assoc. prof., 1967-79, assoc. prof. emeritus, 1979—; research assoc. in med. history Cleve. Med. Library Assn., 1953-62, curator Howard Dittrick Mus. of Hist. Medicine, 1962-67, dir. Howard Dittrick Mus. Hist. Medicine, 1967-79. Author: William Beaumont's Formative Years: Two Early Notebooks 1811-1821, 1946; The Adoption of Inoculation for Smallpox in England and France (William H. Welch medal Am. Assn. for History of Medicine 1962), 1957; Bibliography of the History of Medicine of the U.S. and Canada, 1939-1960, 1964; Bibliography of the Writings of Henry E. Sigerist, 1966; Letters of Edward Jenner and Other Documents Concerning the Early History of Vaccination, 1983; assoc. editor Bull. of History of Medicine, 1944-48, acting editor, 1948, mem. adv. editorial bd. 1960-92; mem. bd. editors Jour. of History of Medicine and Allied Scis., 1948-65; editor Bull. of Cleve. Med. Library, 1954-72; editor newsletter Am. Assn. for History of Medicine, 1986-96; contbr. articles in field to profl. jours. Am. Council Learned Socs. fellow, 1948-50; Dean Van Meter fellow, 1953-54. Alumna trustee Goucher Coll., Balt., 1966-69; trustee Judson Retirement Cmty., Cleve., 1993—. Hon. fellow Cleve. Med. Library Assn.; mem. Am. Assn. for History of Medicine (pres. 1978-80, mem. council 1960-63), Am. Hist. Assn., Internat. Soc. for History of Medicine, Soc. Archtl. Historians, Phi Beta Kappa; corr. mem. fgn. socs. for history of medicine. Democrat. Home and Office: Judson Manor 1890 E 107th St Apt 816 Cleveland OH 44106-2245 *The desire to see as much of the world as possible and to retrace its past adds enormously to the richness and pleasure of life.*

MILLER, GEORGE, mayor; b. Detroit; m. Roslyn Girard; 4 children. BA, U. Ariz., 1947, MEd, 1952. Tchr. high schs., owner, prin. painting contracting co., until 1989; mayor City of Tucson, 1991—. Active mem. Dem. Party So. Ariz., 1960—, treas. Pima County div., state chmn. Presdl. Del. Selection Reform Commn.; bd. dirs. Tucson Jewish Community Ctr., Anti-Defamation League of B'nai B'rith; councilman Tucson City Coun., 1977-91, also vice mayor. With USMC, WWII. Decorated Purple Heart; recipient Recognition award United Way, Cmty. Svcs. Support award Chicano Por La Causa (2), Met. Edn. Commn. Crystal Apple award, cert. appreciation San Ignacio Yaqui Coun., Old Pasqua, Dr. Martin Luther King Jr. Keep the Dream Alive award, 1995; named Father of Yr. 1995, Man of Yr. So. Ariz. Home Builders Assn., Outstanding Pub. Ofcl. Ariz. Parks and Recreation Assn., 1995. Office: Office of Mayor PO Box 27210 Tucson AZ 85726-7210*

MILLER, GEORGE, film director; b. Brisbane, Australia, Mar. 3, 1945. MD, U. NSW, Australia, 1970. Former physician St. Vincent's Hosp., Sydney, Australia. Films include: dir., writer: Violence in the Cinema, Part I, 1971, Mad Max, 1979, The Road Warrior-Mad Max II, 1982, Mad Max: Beyond the Thunderdome, 1985, Lorenzo's Oil, 1992 (Acad. award nominee for best original screenplay 1992), 40,000 Years of Dreaming, 1996; dir.: Devil in Evening Dress, 1973, Twilight Zone: The Movie, 1983, The Witches of Eastwick, 1987; editor Frieze, an Underground Film, 1973; assoc. prodr.: Chain Reaction, 1980; prodr.: The Year My Voice Broke, 1988, Dead Calm, 1989, Flirting, 1990, Video Fool For Love, 1996; prodr., writer: Babe, 1995 (Acad. award nominee for best film and for best screenplay 1996). Office: Kennedy Miller Prodns, 30 Orwell St Kings Cross, Sydney 2011, Australia

MILLER, GEORGE, congressman; b. Richmond, Calif., May 17, 1945; s. George and Dorothy (Rumsey) M.; m. Cynthia Caccavo, 1964; children: George, Stephen. B.A., San Francisco State Coll., 1968; J.D., U. Calif., Davis, 1972. Legis. counsel Calif. senate majority leader, 1969-73; mem. 94th-104th Congresses from 7th Calif. dist., 1975—; chmn. subcom. on oversight and investigations, 1985—, chmn. subcom. on labor stds., 1981-84, chmn. select com. on children, youth and families, 1983-91, chmn. com. on natural resources, 1991-94; mem. com. on edn. and lab., dep. majority whip, 1989-94; vice chair Dem. Policy Com., 1995—. Mem. Calif. Bar Assn. Office: House of Representatives 2205 Rayburn Bldg Washington DC 20515-0507

MILLER, GEORGE ARMITAGE, psychologist, educator; b. Charleston, W.Va., Feb. 3, 1920; s. George E. and Florence (Armitage) M.; m. Katherine James, Nov. 29, 1939 (dec. Jan. 1996); children: Nancy, Donnally James. BA, U. Ala., 1940, MA, 1941; AM, Harvard U., 1944, PhD, 1946; Doctorat honoris causa, U. Louvain, 1976; D Social Sci. (hon.), Yale U., 1979; DSc honoris causa, Columbia U., 1980; DSc (hon.), U. Sussex, 1984, New Sch. Social Rsch., 1993; LittD (hon.), Charleston U., 1992. Instr. psychology U. Ala., 1941-43; research fellow Harvard Psycho-Acoustic Lab., 1944-48; asst. prof. psychology Harvard U., 1948-51, assoc. prof., 1955-58, prof., 1958-68, chmn. dept psychology, 1964-67, co-dir. Ctr. for Cognitive Studies, 1960-67; prof. Rockefeller U., N.Y.C., 1968-79; adj. prof. Rockefeller U., 1979-82; prof. psychology Princeton U., 1979-90, James S. McDonnell Disting. Univ. prof. psychology, 1982-90, James S. McDonnell Disting. Univ. prof. psychology emeritus, 1990—, program dir. McDonnell-Pew Program in Cognitive Neurosci., 1989-94; assoc. prof. MIT, 1951-55; vis. Inst. for Advanced Study, Princeton, 1972-76, 82-83, mem., 1950, 70-72; vis. prof. Rockefeller U., 1967-68; vis. prof. MIT, 1976-79, group leader Lincoln Lab., 1953-55; fellow Ctr. Advanced Study in Behavioral Scis., Stanford U., 1958-59; Fulbright research prof. Oxford (Eng.) U., 1963-64; Sesquicentennial prof. U. Ala., 1981. Author: Language and Communication, 1951, (with Galanter and Pribram) Plans and the Structure of Behavior, 1960, Psychology, 1962, (with Johnson-Laird) Language and Perception, 1976, Spontaneous Apprentices, 1977, Language and Speech, 1981, The Science of Words, 1991; editor Psychol. Bulletin, 1981-82. Recipient Disting. Service award Am. Speech and Hearing Assn., 1976, award in behavioral scis. N.Y. Acad. Scis., 1982, Hermann von Helmholtz award Cognitive Neurosci. Inst., 1989, Nat. Medal Sci. NSF, 1991, Gold Medal Am. Psychological Found. 1990, Nat. Medal of Sci. 1991, Louis E. Levy medal Franklin Inst., 1991; Guggenheim fellow, 1986, William James fellow Am. Psychological Soc., 1989; Fondation Fyssen Priz Internat. for cognitive sci., 1992. Fellow Brit. Psychol. Assn. (hon.); mem. NAS, AAAS (chmn. sect. J 1981), Am. Psychol. Assn. (pres. 1968-69, Disting. Scientific Contbn. award 1963, William James Book award divsn. gen. psychology 1993), Eastern Psychol. Assn. (pres. 1961-62), Acoustical Soc. Am., Linguistic Soc. Am., Am. Statis. Assn., Am. Philos. Soc., Am. Physiol. Soc., Psychometric Soc., Soc. Exptl. Psychologists (Warren medal 1972), Am. Acad. Arts and Scis., Psychonomic Soc., Royal Netherlands Acad. Arts and Scis. (fgn.), Sigma Xi. Home: 753 Prospect Ave Princeton NJ 08540-4080 Office: Princeton Univ Dept Psychology Green Hall Princeton NJ 08544

MILLER, GEORGE DAVID, retired air force officer, marketing consultant; b. McKeesport, Pa., Apr. 5, 1930; s. George G. and Nellie G. (Cullen) M.; m. Barbara Aex; 1 child from previous marriage: George David Jr. BS, U.S. Naval Acad., 1953; MS in Aerospace Engring, Air Force Inst. Tech., 1966; postgrad., Nat. War Coll., 1970-71. Commd. 2d lt. U.S. Air Force, 1953, advanced through grades to lt. gen., 1981; ops. officer, comdr. 22d Spl. Ops. Squadron, Nakhon Phanom Royal Thai AFB, Thailand, 1970-71; dep. comdr. for ops., vice comdr., comdr. 55th Strategic Reconnaissance Wing, Offutt AFB, Nebr., 1971-74; comdr. 17th Air div., 307th Strategic wing, U-Tapao Airfield, Thailand, 1974-75; comdr. 57th Air Div. Minot AFB, N.D., 1975-76; asst. dep. chief staff ops. hdqrs. SAC, Offutt AFB,, Nebr., 1976-77; dep. dir. single integrated operational plan Joint Strategic Target Planning Staff, Joint Chiefs of Staff, 1977-79; dir. plans, dep. chief of staff ops., plans and readiness Hdqrs. USAF, Washington, 1979-80; asst. dep. chief staff ops., plans and readiness Hdqrs. USAF, 1980-81; vice comdr.-in-chief SAC, Offutt AFB, Nebr., 1981-84; exec. dir., sec.-gen. U.S. Olympic Com., 1984-87. Pres., exec. dir. Morris Animal Found., 1989-92; pres., CEO Nat. Fire Protection Assn., 1992—, chmn. bd. NFPA Rsch. Found.; trustee U.S. Naval Acad. Found. Decorated Def. D.S.M., Air Force DSM, Legion of Merit, D.F.C. with 3 oak leaf clusters Air medal with 18 oak leaf clusters, others. Mem. VFW, Air Force Assn., Am. Legion, Masons, Scottish Rite, Shriners, Daedalians. Lutheran. Home: 20 Phillips Pond Natick MA 01760-5643 Office: NFPA PO Box 9101 1 Batterymarch Pk Quincy MA 02269-9101

MILLER, GEORGE DEWITT, JR., lawyer; b. Detroit, Aug. 20, 1928; s. George DeWitt and Eleanor Mary Miller; m. Prudence Brewster Saunders, Dec. 28, 1951; children: Margaret DeWitt, Joy Saunders. BA magna cum laude, Amherst Coll., 1950; JD with distinction, U. Mich., 1953. Bar: Mich. 1953, U.S. Dist. Ct. (so. dist.) Mich. 1953, U.S. Ct. Appeals (6th cir.) 1960, U.S. Tax Ct. 1960. Assoc. Bodman, Longley & Dahling, Detroit, 1957-61, ptnr., 1962—. Trustee, mem. Matilda R. Wilson Fund, 1993—; trustee Maplegrove Ctr./Kingswood Hosp., Henry Ford Health Sys., 1995—. Capt. USAF, 1953-56. Recipient Commendation medal. Mem. ABA, State Bar Mich., Detroit Bar Assn., Detroit Club, Detroit Athletic Club, Orchard Lake Country Club, Order of Coif, Phi Beta Kappa. Episcopalian. Avocations: yacht racing, shooting. Home: 320 Dunston Rd Bloomfield Hills MI 48304-3415 Office: Bodman Longley & Dahling 100 Renaissance Ctr Ste 34 Detroit MI 48243-1003

MILLER, GEORGE H., historian, educator; b. Evanston, Ill., Aug. 5, 1919; s. Donald Crandon and Janet Gordon (Hall) M. BA, U. Mich., 1941, MA, 1946, PhD in History, 1951; MA, Harvard U., 1949; LHD (hon.), Ripon Coll., 1985. Instr. history U. Mich., Ann Arbor, 1951-54; from asst. prof. to prof. Ripon (Wis.) Coll., 1954-81; ret., 1981; bd. curators State Hist. Soc. Wis., Madison, 1980—, pres., 1989-91; dir. Wis. History Found., Madison, 1989—. Author: Railroads and the Granger Laws, 1971; co-author: Ripon College: A History, 1990; editor: A History of Ripon, Wisconsin, 1964. Mem., pres. Ripon Hist. Soc., 1962—; bd. dirs. Wis. Humanities Commn., Madison, 1973-79. With AUS, 1941-45. Recipient honor medal DAR, 1986; fellow Ford Found., 1951. Mem. Univ Club (Chgo.). Home: 778 Hillside Ter Unit J Ripon WI 54971-1607

MILLER, G(EORGE) WILLIAM, merchant banker, business executive; b. Sapulpa, Okla., Mar. 9, 1925; s. James Dick and Hazle Deane (Orrick) M.; m. Ariadna Rogojarsky, Dec. 22, 1946. BS in Marine Engring., U.S. Coast Guard Acad., 1945; JD, U. Calif., Berkeley, 1952; hon. degree, Babson Coll, Boston U., Brown U., Bryant Coll., Fairfield U., Fla. State U., R.I. U. Bar: Calif. 1952, N.Y. 1953. Asst. sec. Textron Inc., 1956-57, v.p., 1957-60, pres., 1960-74, COO, 1960-67, CEO, 1967-78; chmn. Fed. Res. Bd., Washington, 1978-79; sec. of Treasury Washington, 1979-81; chmn. G. William Miller & Co. Inc., Washington, 1981—; chmn., CEO Federated Dept. Stores, Inc., 1990-92; chmn. bd. Waccamaw Corp., 1995—; bd. dirs. Repligen Corp., GS Industries, Inc., Kleinwort Benson Australian Income Fund, Inc., Simon-DeBartolo Group, Inc.; past chmn. adv. coun. Pres.'s Com. EEO, 1963-65; mem. coun. Nat. Found. Humanities, 1966-67; bd. dirs. USCG Acad. Found., 1969-78, pres., 1973-77, chmn., 1977-78; chmn. U.S. Indsl. Payroll Savs. Bond Com., 1977, Pres.'s Com. HIRE, 1977; co-chmn. Polish-U.S. Econ. Coun., 1977-78, U.S.-USSR Trade and Econ. Coun., 1977-78, Pres.'s Cir. NAS, 1989-92. Bd. dirs. Washington Opera; bd. trustees Marine Biological Laboratory, Woods Hole, Mass. U. Calif. fellow, Berkeley. Mem. State Bar Calif., Nat. Alliance Businessmen (bd. dirs. 1968-78, chmn. 1977-78), Conf. Bd. (trustee 1972-78, chmn. 1977-78), Bus. Coun., Lyford Cay Club (Nassau), Acoaxet Club (Westport, Mass.), Brook Club (N.Y.C.), Burning Tree Club, Chevy Chase Club, Order of Coif, Phi Delta Phi. Office: 1215 19th St NW Washington DC 20036-2401

MILLER, GERALD CECIL, immunologist, laboratory administrator, educator; b. Wichita, Kans., Dec. 20, 1944; s. Cecil William and Mildred Ester (Carlisle) M.; m. Josephine Buller, June 1, 1968; children: Nathan Gerald, Natalie Buller. BA, Emporia (Kans.) State U., 1967, MS, 1969; PhD, Kans. State U., 1972. Diplomate Am. Bd. Med. Lab. Immunology. Rsch. fellow Mayo Med. Sch. and Mayo Found., Rochester, Minn., 1972-75; sr. scientist Health Cen. Rsch. Found., Mpls., 1975-77; grad. teaching and rsch. asst. Emporia State U., 1967-69; grad. teaching and rsch. asst. Kans. State U., Manhattan, 1969-70, NIH predoctoral fellow, 1970-72; ast. prof. microbiology and immunology Oral Roberts U. Sch. Medicine, Tulsa, 1977-82;

owner, dir. Immuno-Diagnostics Lab. Inc., Tulsa, 1982-94; adj. assoc. prof. Oral Roberts U. Sch. Medicine, Tulsa, 1986-90; mem. ancillary med. staff Children's Med. Ctr., Tulsa, 1979—; chief immunology, microbiology and flow cytometry Regional Med. Lab., Tulsa, 1994—; clin. lab. immunologist Pathology Lab. Assocs., Tulsa, 1994—; adj. asst. prof. U. Okla. Med. Coll., Tulsa, 1986—. Mem. editl. bd. Jour. Clin. Lab. Analysis; contbr. articles and abstracts to sci. jours. Trustee 1st United Meth. Ch., 1994-97, mem. adminstrv. bd., 1978—; bd. dirs. Brush Creek Boys Ranch, 1996—; cert. ofcl. USA Track and Field, 1986—. Named Outstanding Faculty Mem., Oral Roberts U. Sch. Medicine, 1982. Mem. AAAS, Am. Soc. Microbiology, Assn. Med. Lab. Immunologists (treas.), Clin. Immunology Soc., N.Y. Acad. Scis., Sigma Xi. Avocations: outdoor art, hunting, hiking, canoeing, backpacking. Office: Regional Med Lab 1923 S Utica Ave Tulsa OK 74104-6520

MILLER, G(ERSON) H(ARRY), research institute director, mathematician, computer scientist, chemist; b. Phila., Mar. 2, 1924; m. Mary Alexa Heath, Jan. 28, 1961; children: Byron, Alexandra. BA, Pomona Coll., 1949; MEd in Counseling and Pers., Temple U., 1951; PhD. in Ednl. Psychology, U. So. Calif., 1957; MS in Math., U. Ill., 1982, postgrad., 1963-65. Jr. high sch. and jr. coll. instr. math. L.A. Sch. Dist., 1953-57; assoc. prof. Western Ill. U., Macomb, 1957-60; prof. Towson State U., Balt., Md., 1960-61; prof. math. and edn. Parsons Coll., Fairfield, Iowa, 1961-65; prof. Tenn. Technol. U., Cookeville, 1966-89; prof. math. and computer sci. Edinboro (Pa.) U., 1968-71, 81-89, asst. dir. Institutional Rsch., 1972-80; dir. Studies On Smoking, Inc. and SOS Stop Smoking Clinic, Edinboro, 1972—; spkr. state, nat. and internat. profl. meetings; condr. seminars on smoking and health London, Fed. Republic Germany, Alaska, New Brunswick, N.J., Chgo., Costa Rica, Nice; dir. Nat. Study Math. Requirements for Scientists and Engrs., 1966-73. Contbr. numerous articles to profl. jours. Pres. Edinboro YMCA, 1972-83; bd. dirs. Common Cause, Harrisburg, Pa., 1975-80; Sgt. USAAF, 1943-46, PTO. Grantee U.S. Office Edn., 1968, 70, No Other World, 1973, NAS, 1980, ITT Life Ins. Corp., 1983, Erie Community Found., 1987. Fellow Am. Inst. Chemists (cert. profl. chemist), AAAS; mem. APHA, Am. Assn. World Health, Am. Chem. Soc., Am. Soc. Engrng. Edn., Internat. Assn. Pure and Applied Chemists, Internat. Soc. for Preventive Oncology, Math. Assn. Am., Am. Diabetes Assn., Nat. Coun. Tchrs. Math., Sch. Sci. and Math. Assn., N.Y. Acad. Scis. (hon.), Acad. Sr. Profls. (hon.). Home and Office: Studies on Smoking Inc 125 High St Edinboro PA 16412-2552 also: 25 Crescent Pl S Saint Petersburg FL 33711-5118

MILLER, GREGORY R., prosecutor. Chief asst. U.S. atty. Dept. Justice, Tallahassee, Fla., U.S. atty., 1993—. Office: US Attys Office 315 S Calhoun St Ste 510 Tallahassee FL 32301-1837

MILLER, H. TODD, lawyer; b. Buffalo, N.Y., Sept. 19, 1947; s. Henry Opel and Irene Teresa (Hauck) M.; m. June Diehl Lancaster, Aug. 1, 1970; children: Catharine Maclay, Todd Lancaster, Peter Hanes. BA, SUNY, Buffalo, 1969; JD, Duke U., 1971. Bar: N.C. 1971, D.C. 1973. Jud. clerk to Hon. Charles R. Simpson U.S. Tax Ct., Washington, 1971-73; assoc. atty. Hogan & Hartson, Washington, 1973-78, ptnr., 1979—. Mem. Phi Beta Kappa, Order of the Coif. Episcopalian. Office: Hogan & Hartson Columbia Sq 555 13th St NW Washington DC 20004-1109

MILLER, HAINON ALFRED, lawyer, investor; b. Kosciusko, Miss., Oct. 9, 1930; s. J. Wesley and Louise (Johnston) M.; m. Lillian Henderson, June 4, 1956; children: Nadalyn, Philip, Kendall, Melissa, Lyon. BA, Miss. Coll., 1951; LLB, Tulane U., 1954. Bar: Miss. 1954, U.S. Dist. Ct. (no. and so. dists.) Miss. 1954, U.S. Ct. Appeals (5th cir.) 1972. Sole practice Greenville, Miss., 1954-92; mem. Miss. Senate, Jackson, 1987-95. Mem. Miss. Ho. of Reps., 1968-84; sec. Washington County Dem. Exec. Com., 1955-60. Recipient Disting. Service award U.S. Jr. C. of C., 1957, Humanized Edn. award Miss. Assn. Educators, Jackson, 1979. Mem. Kiwanis (lt. gov. dist. 1959). Baptist.

MILLER, HARBAUGH, lawyer; b. Wilkinsburg, Pa., July 23, 1902; s. Charles Shively and Ella (Harbaugh) M.; m. Ruth M. Davis, Nov. 8, 1952. B.S., U. Pitts., 1922, J.D., 1925. Bar: Pa. 1925. Ptnr. Miller & Entwisle, Pitts., 1949-95. Pres. Goodwill Industries, 1958-61, YMCA Pitts., 1956-58; trustee U. Pitts., 1945-60, 66-72, trustee emeritus, 1973—; trustee Western Theol. Sem., 1955-58. Fellow Am. Bar Found., Am. Coll. Trust & Estate Counsel; mem. ABA (ho. of dels.), Am. Law Inst., Am. Judicature Soc., Pa. Bar Assn., Allegheny County Bar Assn. (pres. 1955), Pitts. Coun. Chs. (pres. 1951-53), SAR (pres. Pitts. 1940), U. Pitts. Alumni Assn. (pres. 1940), Univ. Club, Duquesne Club, Masons, Shriners, Pitts. Athletic Assn., Phi Delta Theta, Omicron Delta Kappa, Beta Gamma Sigma, Phi Delta Phi. Presbyterian. Home: 154 N Bellefield Ave Pittsburgh PA 15213-2655 Office: 614 Oliver Bldg Pittsburgh PA 15222-2404

MILLER, HAROLD ARTHUR, lawyer; b. St. Marie, Ill., Aug. 18, 1922; s. Arthur E. and Luletta (Noé) M.; m. Michele H. Rogivue, Nov. 21, 1947; children: Maurice H., Jan Leland, Marc Richard. BS in Acctg., U. Ill., 1942, JD, 1950. Bar: Ill. 1950, U.S. Dist. Ct. Ill. 1950, U.S. Tax Ct. 1950. Fgn. svc. officer U.S. State Dept., Paris, France, 1945-48; ptnr. Filson, Williamson & Miller, Champaign, Ill., 1950-60, Williamson & Miller, Champaign, 1960-72, Miller & Hendren, Champaign, 1972—; atty. Christie Clinic Assn., Champaign, 1960—; atty. pub. schs. dists., Champaign & Vermilion Counties, Ill., 1960—; atty. for municipalities in Champaign County, Ill., 1970—. Author: Estate Planning for Doctors, 1961, Intervivos Trusts Alternative to Probate, 1996. Bd. dirs., officer Urbana Ill. Sch. Dist., 1957-69; chmn., trustee Parkland Coll., Champaign, 1971-91; founding bd. mem. CCDC Found., Champaign-Urbana Ednl. Found., Moore Heart Found., Christie Found.; life mem. PTA. With inf. U.S. Army, 1942-45, ETO. Mem. ABA, Am. Judicature Soc., Ill. and Local Bar Assns., Ill. Trial Lawyers Assn., Alpha Kappa Psi. Presbyterian. Office: Miller & Hendren Attys 30 E Main St #200 Champaign IL 61820-3629

MILLER, HAROLD EDWARD, retired manufacturing conglomerate executive, consultant; b. St. Louis, Nov. 23, 1926; s. George Edward and Georgenia Elizabeth (Franklin) M.; m. Lilian Ruth Gantner, Dec. 23, 1949; children—Ellen Susan, Jeffrey Arthur. B.S.B.A., Washington U., St. Louis, 1949. Vice pres. Fulton Iron Works Co., St. Louis, 1968-71; pres. Fulton Iron Works Co., 1971-79, chmn. bd., 1979-90; v.p. Katy Industries Inc., Elgin, Ill., 1976-77; exec. v.p. Katy Industries Inc., 1978-90, also dir., to 1990; pres. HM Consulting, Palatine, Ill., 1990—; internat. cons. Vigel Spa, Italy; v.p. Vigel U.S.A. Inc., 1996—. Served with U.S. Army, 1945-46. Mem. Barrington Tennis Club, Inverness Golf Club. Presbyterian.

MILLER, HARRIET SANDERS, art center director; b. N.Y.C., Apr. 18, 1926; d. Herman and Dorothy (Silbert) S.; m. Milton H. Miller, June 27, 1948; children—Bruce, Jeffrey, Marcie. B.A., Ind. U., 1947; M.A., Columbia U., 1949; M.S., U. Wis., 1962, M.F.A., 1967. Dir. art sch. Madison Art Ctr., Wis., 1963-72; acting dir. Center for Continuing Edn., Vancouver, B.C., 1975-76; mem. fine arts faculty Douglas Coll., Vancouver, 1972-78; exec. dir. Palos Verdes Arts Center, Calif., 1978-84; dir. Junior Arts Center, Los Angeles, 1984—; one woman exhibits at Gallery 7, Vancouver, 1978, Gallery 1, Toronto, Ont., 1977, Linda Farris Gallery, Seattle, 1975, Galerie Allen, Vancouver, 1973. Mem. Calif. Art Edn. Assn., Museum Educators of So. Calif., Arts and Humanities Symposium. Office: Junior Arts Ctr 4814 Hollywood Blvd Los Angeles CA 90027-5302

MILLER, HARRY BRILL, scenic designer, director, acting instructor, lyricist, interior designer; b. Jersey City, Jan. 26, 1924; s. Max Joseph Miller and Lillian (Hirsch) Grodjesk. BA, U. Mich., 1946; MA, Smith Coll., 1948. Set designer, asst. scenic designer various Broadway, Off Broadway and summer shows, N.Y.C., 1948-72; scenic designer NBC-TV, N.Y.C., 1950-63; art dir. MPO-Video Prodns., N.Y.C., 1962; scenic designer CBS-TV, N.Y.C., 1963-91; indsl. show designer Norelco, Thompson CSF, Engelhard, N.Y.C., 1958-75; interior designer Interior Comml. Constrn. Assocs., Hialeah, Fla., 1969-70; dir., writer Miramar Minstrels, N.Y.C., 1979-96; dir. PACT Theaters, N.Y.C., 1995-96; acting tchr. Emmanuel Midtown Young Men and Young Women's Hebrew Assn., N.Y.C., 1989-90. Set designer (TV shows) Princeton '54, '55, '56 (Peabody 1954, 55), The Price is Right, 1962-63, Jackie Gleason Show, 1969-70, CBS News and Special Events, 1986-91, (mus. show) Nashville at the Garden, 1972; art dir. (TV show) Guiding Light, 1978-86 (2 Emmys 1984, 85), The Edge of Night, 1964-69; prodn. designer TV show Captain Kangaroo, 1970-78 (various Peabody awards); set design asst. (Broadway mus.) Funny Girl, 1964, (Broadway play) Sign in Sidney Brustein's Window. Sgt. U.S. Army, 1943-46. Recipient Teaching Assistanship French Govt., Paris, 1948. Mem. United Scenic Artists, Miramar Ski Club (trip chair 1991-93, v.p. 1997—). Avocations: skiing, dancing, swimming, painting, acting. Address: 333 W 56th St Apt 7B New York NY 10019-3770

MILLER, HARRY GEORGE, education educator; b. Waukesha, Wis., Feb. 15, 1941; s. Harry Fricke and Ethel Ruth (D'Amato) M.; m. Mary Frances Shugrue, June 20, 1964; children: Alicia, Michael, Anne, Dierdre, Courtney. B.A., Carroll Coll., 1963; M.Ed., U. Nebr., 1967, Ed.D., 1970. Tchr. Westside Community Schs., Omaha, 1964-67; demonstration tchr. East Edn. Complex, Lincoln (Nebr.) Pub. Schs., 1967-68; instr. curriculum research Tchrs. Coll., U. Nebr., Lincoln, 1968-70; faculty So. Ill. U., Carbondale, 1970—; asso. prof. secondary edn. So. Ill. U., 1972—, chmn. dept. secondary edn., 1973-75, prof., chmn. dept. ednl. leadership, 1975—; dean, prof. Coll. Tech. Careers, 1980-89; assoc. v.p. acad. affairs So. Ill. U., 1989-92; dean, prof. Ctr. Adult and Continuing Edn. The Am. U., Cairo, 1992—; rsch. prof. Ministry Edn., Thailand, 1978; vis. prof. Ministry Edn., Sabah, East Malaysia, 1980, Korea, 1985; vis. prof. Vladimir State U., Russia, 1989; vis. prof. PRC, 1991; cons. to various orgns. and instns., 1969-74. Author: Beyond Facts: Objective Ways to Measure Thinking, 1976, Adults Teaching Adults, 1977, Responsibility Education, 1977, The Adult Educator: A Handbook for Staff Development, 1978, An Introduction to Adult and Continuing Education, 1979, The Education of Adults, 1981, The Life-long Learning Experience, 1986, Grassroots, 1992, Veiled Voices, 1993; also monographs; mem. editorial bd. Traning, 1976. Mem. Ill. Migrant Council, 1974; Adv. bd. Evaluation and Devel. Center, Rehab. Inst., Carbondale, 1974-80; bd. dirs. St. Joseph's Hosp. Fulbright grantee Republic of Togo, 1982. Mem. Pub. Adult and Continuing Edn. Assn., Rural Edn. Assn., Ill. Coun. for Social Studies (hon.), Community Svcs. Assn. Cairo (bd. dirs. 1994—), Greater Cleve. Coun. for Social Studies (hon.), Ednl. Coun. fo 100 Inc., Coll. of Cons. Democrat. Roman Catholic. Club: K.C. Office: The Am U Ctr for Adult and Con Edn, PO Box 2511 113 Sharia Kass Aini, Cairo Egypt

MILLER, HARVEY ALFRED, botanist, educator; b. Sturgis, Mich., Oct. 19, 1928; s. Harry Clifton and Carmen (Sager) M.; m. Donna K. Hall, May 9, 1992; children: Valerie Yvonne, Harry Alfred, Timothy Merk, Tanya Merk, Jasper Adam, Carmen Kristin. B.S., U. Mich., 1950; M.S., U. Hawaii, 1952; Ph.D., Stanford U., 1957. Instr. botany U. Mass., 1955-56; instr. botany Miami U., Oxford, Ohio, 1956-57, asst. prof., 1957-61, assoc. prof., curator herbarium, 1961-67, adj. prof. botany, 1985—, vis. prof., 1994—; prof., chmn. program in biology Wash. State U., 1967-69; vis. prof. botany U. Ill., 1969-70; prof., chmn. dept. biol. scis. U. Cen. Fla., 1970-75, prof., 1975-94; v.p. Marine Research Assocs. Ltd., Nassau, 1962-65; assoc. Lotspeich & Assocs., natural systems analysts, Winter Park, Fla., 1979-94; v.p. D.H. Miller and Assocs., Oxford, 1994—; botanist U. Mich. Expdn. to Aleutian Islands, 1949-50; prin. investigator Systematic and Phytogeographical Studies Bryophytes of Pacific Islands, NSF, 1959, Miami U. Expdn. to Micronesia, 1960; dir. NSF-Miami U. Expdn. to Micronesia and Philippines, 1965; prin. investigator NSF bryophytes of So. Melanesia, 1983-86; research assoc. Orlando Sci. Ctr., Orlando; vis. prof. U. Guam, 1965; cons. tropical botany, foliage plant patents, also designs for sci. bldgs.; field researcher on Alpine meadows in Irian Jaya, 1991, 1992. Author: (with H.O. Whittier and B.A. Whittier) Prodromus Florae Muscorum Polynesiae, 1978, Prodromus Florae Hepaticarum Polynesiae, 1983; Field Guide to Florida Mosses and Liverworts, 1990; editor: Florida Scientist, 1973-78; contbr. articles to sci. jours. Chmn. exec. bd. scholarship and grant selection com. Astronauts Scholarship Found. (formerly Mercury Seven Found.), 1985—. Recipient Acacia Order of Pythagoras; recipient Acacia Nat. award of Merit; Guggenheim fellow, 1958. Fellow AAAS, Linnean Soc. London; mem. Pacific Sci. Assn. (chmn. sci. com. for botany 1975-83), Assn. Tropical Biology, Am. Inst. Biol. Scis., Am. Bryol. Soc. (v.p. 1962-63, pres. 1964-65), Brit. Bryol. Soc., Bot. Soc. Am., Internat. Assn. Plant Taxonomists, Internat. Assn. Bryologists, Mich. Acad. Sci. Arts and Letters, Hawaiian Acad. Sci., Am. Soc. Plant Taxonomists, Fla. Acad. Sci. (exec. sec. 1976-83, pres. 1980), Nordic Bryol. Soc., Acacia, Explorers Club, Sigma Xi, Phi Sigma, Beta Beta Beta. Home: PO Box 6004 Oxford OH 45056-6004 Office: Miami U Dept Botany Oxford OH 45056

MILLER, HARVEY R., lawyer, bankruptcy reorganization specialist; b. Bklyn., Mar. 1, 1933; married;. Grad., Columbia U. Law Sch., 1959. Ptnr. Weil Gotshal and Manges, N.Y.C. Office: Weil Gotshal & Manges 767 Fifth Ave New York NY 10153

MILLER, HARVEY S. SHIPLEY, foundation trustee; b. Phila., Sept. 28, 1948; s. Frank Leroy and Betty Charlotte (Elfont) M. BA, Swarthmore Coll., 1970; JD, Harvard U., 1973. Bar: N.Y. 1973. Assoc. Debevoise & Plimpton, N.Y.C., 1973-75; curator and dir. dept. collections and spl. exhbns. Franklin Inst., Phila., 1975-81; v.p. Energy Solutions, Inc., N.Y.C., 1982-84; pres., chief exec. officer, dir. Daltex Med. Scis., Inc., N.Y.C., 1983-86, dir. exec. com., 1983-94, chief operating officer, vice chmn., 1986-91, pres., chief operating officer, 1991-93; trustee The Judith Rothschild Found., N.Y.C., 1993—. Author: Milton Avery: Drawings and Paintings, 1976, It's About Time, 1979; author, editor: New Spaces: Exploring the Aesthetic Dimensions of Holography, 1979; co-author: Rapid Inactivation of Infectious Pathogens by Chlorhexidine-coated Gloves, 1992; contbr. articles to profl. jours. Mem. vis. com. on photography George Eastman House, Rochester, N.Y., 1976-78; trustee Milton and Sally Avery Arts Found., N.Y.C., 1983—, sec., 1996—; trustee The Franklin Inst., Phila., 1993-95, Phila. Mus. Art, 1985—, exec. com., 1993—; assoc. trustee U. Pa., 1981-95; bd. govs. Print Club, Phila., 1976-87; bd. overseers U. Pa. Sch. Nursing, 1981—, Edith C. Blum Art Inst. Bard Coll., 1984-87; bd. dirs., mem. corp. MacDowell Colony, N.Y.C., 1982-85; exec. bd. dirs. Fabric Workshop, Phila., 1976-86; mem. prints and drawings and photographs trustees adv. com. Phila. Mus. Art, 1974—, trustee, 1985—, investment com., 1989-95, exec., devel. and exhbn. coms., 1993—; bd. assocs. Swarthmore Coll. Librs., Phila., 1978-86; treas., dir. Arcadia Found., Norristown, Pa., 1981—; chmn. adv. bd. Inst. Contemporary Art U. Pa., 1982-84; trustee, vice chmn. coms. on instrn. Pa. Acad. Fine Arts, 1982-91, trustee emeritus, 1991—, chmn. collections and exhbns. com., 1985-87; trustee N.Y. Studio Sch., 1974-80, U. of the Arts, 1979-86; mem. exec. bd. Citizens for Arts in Pa., 1980; bd. dirs. Once Gallery, Inc., 1974-75, Wildlife Preservation Trust Internat., Inc., 1990-95; mem. Mayor's Cultural Adv. Coun., Phila., 1987-91; chair Mayor's Art-in-City Hall Program, Phila., 1992-94; trustees coun. Nat. Gallery Art, Washington, 1995—; mem. collections com. Hist. Soc. Pa., 1991-93, councilor trustee, 1992-93; mem. vis. com. photographs Met. Mus. Art, 1996—; mem. trustees' com. on drawings Mus. Modern Art, 1996—. Mem. ABA, Assn. of Bar of City of N.Y., Athenaeum, Libr. Co. Phila., Am. Philos. Soc., Hist. Soc. Pa., Phila. Art Alliance, Union League of Phila., Harvard Club of N.Y.C., Swarthmore Club Phila., Phi Sigma Kappa. Republican. Home: Moorhope Mathers Ln Fort Washington PA 19034 Office: 1110 Park Ave New York NY 10128-1201

MILLER, HASBROUCK BAILEY, financial and travel services company executive; b. Gloversville, N.Y., Aug. 1, 1923; s. Edward Waite and Lorraine (Taylor) M.; m. Elizabeth J. Wilson, Jan. 5, 1949; children: Kimberly Elizabeth, Stacey Wilson, Hasbrouck Bailey, Sloan Taylor. B.A., Hamilton Coll., 1944; postgrad., U. Lausanne, Switzerland, 1946, Sch. Advanced International. Studies, Washington, 1947, Stanford Grad. Sch. Bus., 1961. With Am. Express Co. (and subsidiaries), 1948—, v.p., sec., 1964-65, sr. v.p., 1965-68, exec. v.p., 1968-83; exec. v.p. Am. Express Internat., Inc., 1960-83; ret., 1983. Served with OSS, AUS, 1942-45. Mem. Morris County Golf Club (Convent Station, N.J.). Home: Fox Hollow Rd Morristown NJ 07960

MILLER, HENRY FORSTER, architect; b. Sept. 16, 1916; s. Rutger Bleecker and Dorothy (Forster) M.; m. Maria Stockton Bullitt, Apr. 6, 1942; children: Maria, Andrew, Dorothy, Steven, Henry Jr. BA, Yale U., 1938, MArch, 1948. Registered architect, Conn., R.I., Mass. Instr. archtl. design Yale Sch. Architecture, New Haven, 1948-49; assoc. dir. facilities planning office Yale U., New Haven, 1974-90; assoc. Harold H. Davis Architect, New Haven, 1949-56; ptnr. Davis, Cochran & Miller, New Haven, 1956-69, Davis, Cochran, Miller, Baerman, Noyes, New Haven, 1969-74; pvt. practice Orange, Conn., 1990—; pres. Conn. Bldg. Congress, 1957-58. Prin. works include Booth Meml. Boys Club Bldg. (Archtl. Design award 1971), Columbus Sch. New Haven (HUD Design Excellence award 1970). Mem. bd. govs. New Haven Boys and Girls Club, 1956-93; v.p. Comty. Coun. Greater New Haven, 1964-66; apptd. mem. State Housing Commn., Conn., 1970-72; mem. Conn. Rev. Bd. for Nat. Register of Hist. Places, 1974-81; founding dir. Conn. Trust for Hist. Preservation, 1975-86, pres., 1975-77; bd. dirs. New Haven Preservation Trust. Maj. F.A. AUS, 1941-46, ETO. Fellow AIA (Conn. state preservation coord. 1965-90, exec. com. 1967-69), Mory's Assn. Democrat. Roman Catholic. Avocations: tennis, hiking, drawing, painting. Home and Office: 30 Derby Ave Orange CT 06477-1403

MILLER, HENRY FRANKLIN, lawyer; b. Phila., May 19, 1938; s. Lester and Bessie (Posner) M.; m. Barbara Ann Gendel, June 20, 1964; children: Andrew, Alexa. AB, Lafayette Coll., 1959; LLB, U. Pa., 1964. Bar: Pa. 1965. Law clk. U.S. Dist. Ct. Del., Wilmington, 1964-65; assoc. Wolf, Block, Schorr & Solis-Cohen, Phila., 1965-71, ptnr., 1971—. Pres. Soc. Hill Synagogue, Phila., 1978-79, Big Brothers/Big Sisters Assn. of Phila., 1980-81, Jewish Family & Children's Agy., Phila., 1986-88. 1st lt. U.S. Army, 1959-60. Mem. Am. Coll. Real Estate Lawyers. Avocations: swimming, hiking, reading. Office: Wolf Block Schorr & Solis-Cohen 12th Fl Packard Bldg 15th and Chestnut St Philadelphia PA 19102-2625

MILLER, HERBERT DELL, petroleum engineer; b. Oklahoma City, Sept. 29, 1919; s. Merrill Dell and Susan (Green) M.; BS in Petroleum Engring., Okla. U., 1941; m. Rosalind Rebecca Moore, Nov. 23, 1947; children: Rebecca Miller Friedman, Robert Rexford. Field engr. Amerada Petroleum Corp., Houston, 1948-49, Hobbs, N.Mex., 1947-48, dist. engr., Longview, Tex., 1949-57, sr. engr., Tulsa, 1957-62; petroleum engr. Moore & Miller Oil Co., Oklahoma City, 1962-78; owner Herbert D. Miller Co., Oklahoma City, 1978—. Maj., F.A., AUS, 1941-47; ETO. Decorated Bronze Star with oak leaf cluster, Purple Heart (U.S.); Croix de Guerre (France). Registered profl. engr., Okla., Tex. Mem. AIME. Republican. Episcopalian (pres. Men's Club 1973). Clubs: Oklahoma City Golf, Country. Home and Office: 6708 NW Grand Blvd Oklahoma City OK 73116-6016

MILLER, HERBERT ELMER, accountant; b. DeWitt, Iowa, Aug. 11, 1914; s. Elmer Joseph and Marian (Briggs) M.; m. Lenore Snitkey, July 1, 1938; 1 dau., Barbara Ruth. A.B., State U. Iowa, 1936, M.A., 1937; Ph.D., U. Minn., 1944; Dr. h.c., Free U. Brussels, 1982; D.H.L. (h.c.), De Paul U., 1983. C.P.A., Iowa. Acctg. prof. U. Minn., U. Mich., Mich. State U., 1938-70; ptnr. Arthur Andersen & Co., Chgo., 1970-78; dir. Sch. Acctg., U. Ga., Athens, 1978-83. Co-author: Finney-Miller accounting series, 1950-70; editor, contbr.: C.P.A. Rev. Manual, 1951-79. Mem. AICPA (bd. dirs. 1968-70), Am. Acctg. Assn. (pres. 1965-66), Federated Schs. Acctg. (pres. 1982), Beta Gamma Sigma, Beta Alpha Psi (nat. pres. 1961-62). Home: 145 S Stratford Dr Athens GA 30605-3025

MILLER, HERBERT JOHN, JR., lawyer; b. Mpls., Jan. 11, 1924; s. Herbert John and Catherine (Johnson) M.; m. Carey Kinsolving, Apr. 3, 1948; children—John Kinsolving William Grady. Student, U. Minn., 1941-43; B.A., George Washington U., 1948, LL.B., 1949. Bar: D.C. 1949. Asso. Kirkland, Fleming, Green, Martin & Ellis, Washington, 1949-58; partner Kirkland, Ellis, Hodson, Chaffetz and Masters, 1958-61; asst. atty. gen., criminal div. Dept. Justice, 1961-65; partner Miller, Cassidy, Larroca & Lewin, Washington, 1965—; chmn. U.S. del. Conferees Attys. Gen. Ams., Mexico City, 1963, Mins. of Govt., Interior and Security of Cen. Am., Panama, and U.S., 1964, 65; chmn. Pres.'s Commn. on D.C. Crime, 1965-67. Capt. AUS, 1943-46. Mem. ABA, Am. Coll. Trial Lawyers, D.C.Bar Assn. (pres. 1970-71), Order of Coif, Phi Delta Phi, Alpha Delta Phi. Club: Congressional (Washington). Home: 17017 Whites Store Rd Boyds MD 20841-9665 Office: Miller Cassidy Larroca & Lewin 2555 M St NW Washington DC 20037-1302

MILLER, HERMAN LUNDEN, retired physicist; b. Detroit, Apr. 23, 1924; s. Josiah Leonidas and Sadie Irene (Lunden) M.; m. Dorothy Grace Sack, Sept. 15, 1951. BS in Engring. Physics, U. Mich., 1948, MS in Physics, 1951. Registered profl. engr., Mich. Physicist Ethyl Corp., Ferndale, Mich., 1948-49, Dow Chem. Co., Denver, 1950-55; mem. project rsch. staff Princeton (N.J.) U., 1955-65; physicist Bendix Aerospace, Ann Arbor, Mich., 1965-72; nuclear engr. Commonwealth Assocs., Jackson, Mich., 1973-80. Author: Lewiston in the Lumbering Era, 1992, Lumbering in Early Twentieth Century Michigan, The Kneeland-Bigelow Company Experience, 1995.; contbr. articles to profl. jours. With USAF, 1943-46, PTO, lt. col. Res. Mem. IEEE, Am. Phys. Soc., Am. Nuclear Soc.

MILLER, HOPE RIDINGS, author; b. Bonham, Tex.; d. Alfred Lafayette and Grace (Dupree) Ridings; m. Clarence Lee Miller, Sept. 26, 1932 (dec. Jan. 1965). B.A., U. Tex.; M.A., Columbia; D.Litt., Austin Coll. Society editor Washington Post, 1938-45; Washington editor Town and Country mag., 1944-46, The Argonaut mag., 1945-49; Washington columnist Promenade mag., 1945-51; syndicated column McNaught, 1945-50; asso. editor Diplomat mag., 1952-55, editor in chief, 1956-66; television prodn. staff Metromedia, Inc., 1966-70; Washington editor Antique Monthly, 1976-89; mem. editorial adv. bd. Horizon mag., 1978-89. Author: Embassy Row: The Life and Times of Diplomatic Washington, 1969, Great Houses of Washington, 1969, Scandals In The Highest Office: Facts and Fictions in the Private Lives of Our Presidents, 1973; script for cassette tape Circling Lafayette Square, 1976. Mem. women's bd. Columbia Hosp., Friends of the Folger Library, Washington Heart Assn. Mem. Nat. Press Club, Hist. Soc. Washington, Friends of LBJ Libr., Am. News women's Club, The Circle of the Nat. Gallery of Art, Stephen F. Austin Soc., Am. Archives of Art, Smithsonian Assocs., Nat. Mus. Women in the Arts, Sulgrave Club. Home: 1868 Columbia Rd NW Washington DC 20009-5183

MILLER, HUGH THOMAS, computer consultant; b. Indpls., Mar. 22, 1951; s. J. Irwin and Xenia S. Miller; m. Linda Anderson, 1975 (div. 1987); 1 child, Jonathan William; m. Katherine McLeod, 1988 (div. 1995). BA, Yale U., 1976; SM in Mgmt., MIT, 1985. Owner Hugh Miller Bookseller, New Haven, 1976-83, Hugh Miller Cons., New Haven; ind. cons. microcomputers, 1981-85; supr. decision techs. divsn. Electronic Data Sys., Inc., Troy, Mich., 1985-86, supr. product and mfg. engring. divsn., 1986-90, product mgr. Indsl. Bus. Devel., supr. Packard Electric Acct., 1990-92, acct. mgr., 1992-93, with mfg. profl. devel. program, 1993, requirements mgr. Consistent Engring. Environ., 1994—. Editor, ptnr. The Common Table, pub. firm. Bd. dirs. Irwin-Sweeney-Miller Found., Columbus, Ind., 1972—; bd. of govs. MIT Sloan Sch. Mgmt., 1989-94; mem. univ. coun. com. info. tech. Yale U., 1997—. Home: 1173 Lake Angelus Rd Lake Angelus MI 48326-1028 Office: EDS 3310 W Big Beaver Rd Ste 200 Troy MI 48084-2807

MILLER, IRVING FRANKLIN, chemical engineering educator, biomedical engineering educator, academic administrator; b. N.Y.C., Sept. 27, 1934; s. Sol and Gertrude (Rochkind) M.; m. Baila Hannah Milner, Jan. 28, 1962; children: Eugenia Lynne, Jonathan Mark. BS in Chem. Engring., NYU, 1955; MS, Purdue U., 1956; PhD, U. Mich., 1960. Rsch. scientist United Aircraft Corp., Hartford, 1959-61; from asst. prof. to prof., head chem. engring. Poly. Inst. Bklyn., 1961-72; prof. bioengring., head bioengring. program U. Ill., Chgo., 1973-79, acting head sys. engring. dept., 1978-79, assoc. vice chancellor rsch., dean Grad. Coll., 1979-85, prof. chem. engring., head chem. engring., 1986-95, dir. Ctr. for Advanced Edn. and Rsch., 1989-90, dir. Office of Spl. Projects, 1990-92, dir. bioengring. program, 1992-95; dean Coll. Engring. U. Akron, Ohio, 1995—; cons. to industry, also NAS, NIH. Editor: Electrochemical Bioscience and Bioengineering, 1973; contbr. articles profl. jours. Mem. AIChE, AAAS, Am. Chem. Soc., Biomed. Engring. Soc., N.Y. Acad Scis. Home: 23299 Shaker Blvd Shaker Heights OH 44122-2659 Office: ASEC 201 Akron OH 44325-3901

MILLER, ISRAEL, rabbi, university administrator; b. Balt., Apr. 6, 1918; s. Tobias and Bluma (Bunchez) M.; m. Ruth Joan Goldman, Oct. 16, 1945; children: David, Michael, Deborah, Judith. B.A. magna cum laude, Yeshiva Coll., 1938, D.D., 1967; M.A., Columbia U., 1949. Ordained rabbi, 1941. Rabbi Kingsbridge Heights Jewish Center, Bronx, 1941-68; rabbi emeritus Kingsbridge Heights Jewish Center, 1968—; asst. to pres. Yeshiva U., N.Y.C., 1968-70; v.p. Yeshiva U., 1970-80, sr. v.p., 1980-94, sr. v.p. emeritus, 1994—; counselor B'nai B'rith Hillel Found., Hunter Coll., Bronx, 1951-60; lectr. homiletics Yeshiva U., 1954-55; prof. applied rabbinics Rabbi Isaac Elchanan Theol. Sem., 1968—. Editor: Sermon Manual, 1951. V.p.

Bronx Coun. Am. Jewish Congress, 1954-60, Bronx Coun. Jewish Edn., 1964-68; pres. Rabbinical Coun. Am., 1964-66, hon. pres., 1966-68; mem. exec. com. World Zionist Orgn., 1971-76; chmn. Am. Jewish Conf. on Soviet Jewry, 1965-67, Am. Zionist Council, 1967-70; pres. Am. Zionist Fedn., 1970-74, hon. pres., 1974—; v.p. Religious Zionists Am., 1966-68; religious cons., retreat master Dept. Def. in, Europe, 1954, 63-64, Alaska, 1958, Japan, 1960; Conf. Pres.'s Am. Jewish Orgns., 1969-74; chmn. Conf. Pres.'s Major Am. Jewish Orgns., 1974-76; vice chmn. N.Y. Jewish Community Rels. Coun., 1976—; exec. com. Bronx coun. Boy Scouts Am., 1951-58; mem. Nat. Citizens Com. Community Rels., 1946—; bd. dirs. Nat. Jewish Welfare Bd., v.p., 1969—; chmn. Commn. Jewish Chaplaincy, 1962-65; bd. dirs. Bd. Jewish Edn. N.Y.C., Nat. Jewish Community Relations, United Israel Appeal, 1968—; bd. dirs., acting pres. Conf. on Jewish Material Claims Against Germany, 1983, pres., 1984—; pres. Conf. on Jewish Material Claims Against Austria, 1984—; sec. Meml. Found. for Jewish Culture, 1973-94, mem. bd. dirs. ad personam, 1994—; bd. govs. Jewish Agy. for Israel, 1971-76; vice chmn. Am. Israel Pub. Affairs Com., 1983-91; mem. Jerusalem Com., 1990—; bd. dirs. The Jerusalem Found., 1985—; hon. chmn. Jewish Nat. Fund. Served as chaplain USAAF, 1945-46. Recipient Bernard Revel award Yeshiva Coll. Alumni Assn., 1961, Nat. Rabbinic Leadership award Union of Orthodox Jewish Congregations, 1966, 81, Shofar award Boy Scouts Am., 1965, Frank L. Weill award Nat. Jewish Welfare Bd., 1972, Louis Lipsky Meml. award Am. Jewish League for Israel, 1993, Dr. Harris J. Levine award B'nai Zion, 1979, Lifetime Achievement award Rabbinical Coun. Am., 1996, Nat. award Inst. Pub. Affairs, 1996, Remembrance award Internat. Soc. Yad Vashem, 1996; named Man of Yr. Nat. Coun. Young Israel, 1976. Mem. Am. Zionist Youth Found. (life), Jewish War Vets. (nat. chaplain 1962-63), Assn. Jewish Chaplains Armed Forces (pres. 1955-56), Rabbinic Alumni Yeshiva U. (pres. 1960-62). Home: 2619 Davidson Ave Bronx NY 10468-4103 Office: Yeshiva U 2540 Amsterdam Ave New York NY 10033-2807 *In life I have found the verbs more important than the nouns and adjectives. We show who we are by how we act, respond, love or hate.*

MILLER, J. PHILIP, television producer, director, educator; b. Barberton, Ohio, July 10, 1937; s. Cloy M. and Mary (Yoder) M.; children—Kimberly Lowell, Marc Cloy. B.A., Haverford Coll., 1959; EdM, Harvard U., 1960. Tchr. public schs. Newton and Lexington, Mass., 1959-63; dir., lead guitarist profl. folksinging trio Boston, 1963-66; prodn. coordinator, prodn. asst. Candid Camera, N.Y.C., 1966-67; unit mgr., assoc. producer NBC-TV, N.Y.C., 1967-73; instr. TV prodn. NYU; freelance producer, dir. N.Y.C., 1973—; exec. producer Miller Greenewood Prodns., N.Y.C., 1982-83; sr. spls. producer WCVB-TV, Boston, 1983-85; asst. prof. broadcasting and film Coll. Communication Boston U., 1985-89, assoc. prof., 1989—; dir., writer, head writer Kids-TV series showtime, N.Y.C., 1989-90. Programs include Go Show, 1973-75, Special Treat, 1975, 77, First Tuesday, 1970-71, Tonight Show, 1969, Christmastime with Mr. Rogers, 1978, 3-2-1 Contact, 1979, The Bloodhound Gang, 1979, Getting the Most Out of Television, 1980. Recipient Emmy awards, 1976, 84, 86; Peabody award, 1975; Ohio State award, 1985, 86; Chgo. Internat. Film Festival Cert., 1975, Silver Circle award Nat. Acad. TV Arts and Scis., 1994. Mem. Dirs. Guild Am., Writers Guild Am., Nat. Acad. TV Arts and Scis., Assn. Ind. Video and Filmmakers, Phi Delta Kappa. Avocations: photography, tennis. Home: 161 W Newton St Boston MA 02118-1204 Office: Boston U Coll of Communication 640 Commonwealth Ave Boston MA 02215-2422

MILLER, JACK CONWAY, landscape artist, art gallery director, owner; b. Collegeville, Pa., Jan. 23, 1924; s. John W. and Marguerite Blanche (Conway) M.; m. Marguerite F. Martin, Feb. 10, 1948 (dec. Feb. 1978); children: Lynne, Craig, Mark (dec.), Susan; m. Carmen Aline Morin, Sept. 9, 1983. BSc, Phila. Coll. Pharmacy & Sci., 1944, MSc, 1948; PhD in Art Therapy (hon.), La. State U., 1988. Mgr. Ampul & Injection dept. McNeil Labs., Phila., 1948-52; sales mgr. Curtiss Breeding Svcs., Gary, Ill., 1952-71; co-founder Indoor Racket Complex Frog Hollow, Inc., Worcester, Pa., 1970-71; owner, operator Equity Semen Svcs., Inc., Trappe, Pa., 1970-76; co-owner, officer, operator Village Market, Inc., Boyertown, Pa., 1971-73; co-owner Equity Art Svcs., Collegeville, 1977—; owner Dans La Forêt Gardens & Nursery, Collegeville, 1981—; co-owner Morin-Miller Galleries, N.Y.C., 1985-90; prin. Japanese Gardens Landscaper, 1981—; lectr., tchr. in field. Created Japanese Zen Garden at Pagoda Bldg. in Bala Cynwyd, 1995, Rosemont sect. Montreal, Que., Can., 1997; editor Pa. Farm-O-Gram Dairy Newsletter, 1965-71;. Bd. dirs. Pa. All Am. Dairy Show, Harrisburg, 1970, 71. Mem. Am. Rhododendron Soc., Pa. Horticultural Soc., Rock Garden Soc. Avocations: music, reading, traveling.

MILLER, JACK DAVID R., radiologist, physician, educator; b. Johannesburg, South Africa, Apr. 15, 1930; s. Harold Lewis and Inez (Behrman) M.; m. Miriam Sheckter, Dec., 1988. B.Sc., M.B., Ch.B., U. Witwatersrand, Johannesburg, 1956. Diplomate: Am. Bd. Radiology. Intern Coronation Hosp., Johannesburg, 1957-58; resident in radiology Passavant Meml. Hosp., Chgo., 1959-62; Wesley Meml. Hosp., Chgo., 1959-62; fellow in radiology Northwestern U. Med. Sch., 1962-63; chmn. dept. radiology U. Hosp., Edmonton, Alta., Can., 1971-83; clin. prof. biology U. Alta., 1971-97, prof. emeritus radiology, 1997—; clin. prof. radiology U. Alta., 1971—. Fellow Royal Coll. Physicians Can., Am. Coll. Radiology. Office: U Alberta Dept Radiology, Edmonton, AB Canada

MILLER, JACQUELINE WINSLOW, library director; b. N.Y.C., Apr. 15, 1935; d. Lynward Roosevelt and Sarah Ellen (Grevious) W.; 1 child, Percy Scott. BA, Morgan State Coll., 1957; MLS, Pratt Inst., 1960; grad. profl. seminar, U. Md., 1973. Cert. profl. librarian. With Bklyn. Pub. Libr., 1957-68; head extension svcs. New Rochelle (N.Y.) Pub. Libr., 1969-70; br. adminstr. Grinton Will Yonkers (N.Y.) Pub. Libr., 1970-75; dir. Yonkers Pub. Libr., 1975-96; mem. adj. faculty grad. libr. studies Queens Coll., CUNY, 1989, 90. Mem. commr.'s com. Statewide Libr. Devel., Albany, N.Y., 1980; mem. N.Y. Gov.'s Commn. on Librs., 190, 91; bd. dirs. Community Planning Coun., Yonkers, N.Y., 1987; mem. Yonkers Black Women's Polit. Caucus, 1987; pres. bd. Literacy Vols. of Westchester County, 1991-92; mem. fair practices com. LWV, 1996—. Recipient Yonkers Citizen award Ch. of Our Saviour, 1980, 2d Ann. Mae Morgan Robinson award Yonkers chpt. Westchester Black Women's Polit. Caucus, 1992, 3d Ann. Equality Day award City of Yonkers, 1992, African-Am. Heritage 1st award YWCA, 1994; named Outstanding Profl. Woman Nat. Assn. Negro Bus. and Profl. Women's Clubs Inc., 1981. Mem. ALA (councilor 1987-91), N.Y. State Libr. Assn., Pub. Libr. Dirs. Assn. (exec. bd.), N.Y. State Pub. Libr. Dirs. Assn., Westchester Libr. Assn., Yonkers C. of C. (bd. dirs. 1992-95), Rotary (Yonkers chpt.).

MILLER, JAMES, construction company executive; b. Scotland, Sept. 1, 1934; s. Sir James and Lady Ella Jane M.; m. Kathleen Dewar, 1959; 3 children; m. 2d, Iris Lloyd Webb, 1969; 1 child. MA in Engring. Sci., Oxford (Eng.) U., 1958; D.Univ., Heriot Watt, 1996. With Miller Group Ltd. (formerly James Miller & Ptnrs.), Edinburgh, Scotland, 1958—; chmn. Miller Group Ltd. (formerly James Miller & Ptnrs.), 1970—; chmn. Fedn. Civil Engring. Contractors, 1985-86, pres., 1990-93; bd. dirs. Brit. Linen Bank Ltd., Bank of Scotland; mem. Scottish adv. bd. Brit. Petroleum, 1990—. Chmn. Ct. Heriot-Watt U., 1990-96. Mem. City Livery Club, Merchants of City of Edinburgh (master 1992-94). Avocation: shooting. Office: Miller Group Ltd Miller Hse, 18 S Groathill Ave, Edinburgh EH4 2LW, Scotland

MILLER, JAMES A., wholesale grocery executive. Pres. Alliant Food Svc. Inc., Deerfield, Ill., now CEO. Office: Alliant Food Svc Inc PO Box 324 Deerfield IL 60015-2532*

MILLER, JAMES ALEXANDER, oncologist, educator; b. Dormont, Pa., May 27, 1915; s. John Herman and Emma Anna (Stenger) M.; m. Elizabeth Cavert, Aug. 30, 1942; children: Linda Ann, Helen Louise; m. Barbara Butler, Dec. 21, 1988. B.S. in Chemistry, U. Pitts., 1939; M.S., U. Wis., 1941, Ph.D. in Biochemistry, 1943; D.Sc. (hon.), Med. Coll. Wis., 1982, U. Chgo., 1991. Finney-Howell fellow in cancer research U. Wis., Madison, 1943-44; instr. oncology U. Wis., 1944-46, asst. prof., 1946-48, asso. prof., 1948-52, prof., 1952-85, Wis. Alumni Research Found. prof. oncology, 1980-82, Van Rensselaer Potter prof. on oncology, 1982-85, prof. emeritus, 1985—; mem. advisory coms. Nat. Cancer Inst., Am. Cancer Soc., 1950—. Contbr. numerous articles on chemical carcinogenesis and microsomal oxidations to profl. jours. Recipient awards (with E.C. Miller); Langer-Teplitz award Ann Langer Cancer Research Found., 1962; Lucy Wortham James award James Ewing Soc., 1965; G.H.A. Clowes award Am. Assn. Cancer Research, 1969; Bertner award M.D. Anderson Hosp. and Tumor Inst., 1971; Papanicolaou award Papanicolaou Inst. Cancer Research, 1975; Rosenstiel award Brandeis U., 1976; award Am. Cancer Soc., 1977; Bristol-Myers award in cancer research, 1978; Gairdner Found. ann. award Toronto, 1978; Founders award Chem. Industry Inst. Toxicology, 1978; 3M Life Sci. award Fedn. Am. Socs. Exptl. Biology, 1979; Freedman award N.Y. Acad. Sci., 1979; Mott award Gen. Motors Cancer Research Found., 1980, Noble Found. Research award, 1986, 1st E. C. Miller and J. A. Miller Disting. Lectureship in Exptl. Oncology award Rutgers U., 1989. Fellow Am. Acad. Arts and Scis., Wis. Acad. Scis., Arts and Letters; mem. Am. Assn. for Cancer Research (hon.), Am. Soc. Biol. Chemists, AAAS, Japanese Cancer Soc. (hon.), Am. Chem. Soc., Soc. Toxicology, Soc. for Exptl. Biology and Medicine, Nat. Acad. Scis. Home: 5517 Hammersley Rd Madison WI 53711-3556 Office: U Wis Mcardle Lab Madison WI 53706

MILLER, JAMES CLIFFORD, III, economist; b. Atlanta, June 25, 1942; s. James Clifford and Annie (Moseley) M.; m. Demaris Humphries, Dec. 22, 1961; children: Katrina Demaris, John Felix, Sabrina Louise. BBA, U. Ga., 1964; PhD in Econs., U. Va., 1969. Asst. prof. Ga. State U., Atlanta, 1968-69; economist U.S. Dept. Transp., Washington, 1969-72; assoc. prof. econs. Tex. A&M U., College Station, 1972-74; economist U.S. Council Econ. Advs., Washington, 1974-75; asst. dir. U.S. Council Wage and Price Stability, Washington, 1975-77; resident scholar Am. Enterprise Inst., 1977-81; adminstr. Office Info. and Regulatory Affairs, Office Mgmt. and Budget and exec. dir. Presdl. Task Force on Regulatory Relief, Washington, 1981; chmn. FTC, Washington, 1981-85; dir. Office Mgmt. and Budget, Washington, 1985-88; disting. fellow, chmn., counsellor Citizens for a Sound Economy, 1988—; disting. fellow Ctr. for Study of Pub. Choice George Mason U., 1988—; pres., chmn. bd. Econ. Impact Analysts, Inc., 1978—. Author: Why the Draft?: The Case for a Volunteer Army, 1968, Economic Regulation of Domestic Air Transport: Theory and Policy, 1974, Perspectives on Federal Transportation Policy, 1975, Benefit-Cost Analyses of Social Regulation: Case Studies from the Council on Wage and Price Stability, 1979, Reforming Regulation, 1980, The Economist as Reformer, 1989, Fix the U.S. Budget: Urgings of an "Abominable No-Man," 1994. Candidate for Rep. nomination for U.S. Senate for Va., 1994, 96. Thomas Jefferson fellow, 1965-66, DuPont fellow, 1966-67, Ford Found. fellow, 1967-68. Mem. Am. Econ. Assn., Pub. Choice Soc., So. Econ. Assn. (exec. com. 1980-81, v.p. 1990-91), Adminstrv. Conf. U.S. (vice chmn. 1987-88). Republican. Presbyterian. Office: Citizens for Sound Economy 1250 H St NW Washington DC 20005-3952

MILLER, JAMES EDWARD, computer scientist, educator; b. Lafayette, La., Mar. 21, 1940; s. Edward Gustave and Orpha Marie (DeVilbis) M.; m. Diane Moon, June 6, 1964; children—Deborah Elaine, Michael Edward. B.S., U. La.-Lafayette, 1961, Ph.D., 1972; M.S., Auburn U., 1964. Systems engr. IBM, Birmingham, Ala., 1965-68; asst. prof. U. West Fla., Pensacola, 1968-70, chmn. systems sci., 1972-86; grad. researcher U. La.-Lafayette, 1970-72; computer systems analyst EPA, Washington, 1979; prof., chmn. computer sci. and stats. U. So. Miss., Hattiesburg, 1986-92; prof. U. So. Miss., 1992—; program evaluator Computer Sci. Accreditation Commn., 1986-92, cons., lectr. in field; co-dir. NASA/Am. Soc. Engring. Edn. Summer Faculty Fellowship Program-Stennis Space Flight Ctr., 1990—. Author numerous articles for tech. publs. Mem. Computer Soc. of IEEE, Assn. Computing Machinery (editor Computer Sci. Edn. spl. interest group bull. 1982—), Data Processing Mgmt. Assn. (dir. edn. spl. interest group 1985-86), Info. Systems Security Assn., Internat. Assn. Math. and Computer Modeling. Democrat. Methodist. Avocations: Research on parallel computing, computer sci. edn. and optimal sensor deployment. Office: U So Miss Computer Sci & Stat PO Box 5106 Hattiesburg MS 39406-5106

MILLER, JAMES EDWIN, JR., English language educator; b. Bartlesville, Okla., Sept. 9, 1920; s. James Edwin and Leona (Halsey) M.; m. Barbara Anderson, July 3, 1944 (dec. 1981); children: James E. III, Charlotte Ann; m. Kathleen Farley, Mar. 15, 1990. B.A., U. Okla., 1942; M.A., U. Chgo., 1947, Ph.D., 1949. Asst. prof. English U. Nebr., Lincoln, 1953-56; prof., chmn. dept. U. Nebr., 1956-62, Charles J. Mach Regents prof. English, 1961-62; prof. English U. Chgo., 1962—, chmn. dept., 1978-84, Helen A. Regenstein prof. lit., 1983-90, prof. emeritus, 1990—; vis. prof. Northwestern U., 1962, U. Hawaii, 1964, The Sorbonne, Paris, 1984-85, 86, Beijing, China, 1994; Fulbright lectr., Italy, 1958-59, Kyoto, Japan, 1968, Australia, 1976; Otto Salgo prof. Am. studies, Budapest, Hungary, 1991-93. Author: A Critical Guide to Leaves of Grass, 1957, (with Bernice Slote and Karl Shapiro) Start with the Sun, 1960, Walt Whitman, 1962, rev. 1990, Reader's Guide to Herman Melville, 1962, F. Scott Fitzgerald: His Art and His Technique, 1964, J.D. Salinger, 1965, Quests Surd and Absurd: Essays in American Literature, 1967, Word Self, Reality: The Rhetoric of Imagination, 1972, T.S. Eliot's Personal Waste Land, 1977, The American Quest for a Supreme Fiction: Whitman's Legacy in the Personal Epic, 1979, Leaves of Grass: America's Lyric-Epic of Self and Democracy, 1992; Editor: Complete Poetry and Selected Prose of Walt Whitman, 1959, Myth and Method: Modern Theories of Fiction, 1960, Dimensions of Poetry, 1962, Dimensions of the Short Story, 1964, Whitman's Song of Myself: Origin, Growth, Meaning, 1964, Dimensions of Literature, 1967, The Arts and The Public, 1967, Theory of Fiction: Henry James, 1972, Heritage of American Literature, 2 Vols., 1991, (with Ed Farrell) The Perceptive I: A Personal Reader and Writer, 1997. Capt. U.S. Army, 1942-46, 50-52. Recipient Walt Whitman award Poetry Soc. Am., 1958, Poetry Chap Book award, 1961; Distinguished Service award Nat. Council Tchrs. English, 1975; Guggenheim fellow, 1969-70; Nat. Endowment for Humanities sr. fellow, 1974-75. Mem. Modern Lang. Assn., Nat. Council Tchrs. of English (editor Coll. English 1960-66, pres. 1970), Am. Studies Assn., Assn. Depts. English (exec. council 1981-84, pres. 1984), AAUP (council 1964-67), Midwest Modern Lang. Assn. (pres. 1961-62), Phi Beta Kappa. Home: 5536 S Blackstone Ave Chicago IL 60637-1834

MILLER, JAMES GEGAN, research scientist, physics educator; b. St. Louis, Nov. 11, 1942; s. Francis John and Elizabeth Ann (Caul) M.; m. Judith Anne Kelvin, Apr. 23, 1966; 1 child, Douglas Ryan. A.B., St. Louis U., 1964; M.A., Washington U., 1966, Ph.D., 1969. Asst. prof. physics Washington U., St. Louis, 1970-72, assoc. prof., 1972-77, prof. physics, 1977—, dir. lab. for ultrasonics, 1987—, research asst. prof. medicine, 1976-81, research assoc. prof. medicine, 1981-88, research prof. medicine, 1988—. Contbr. articles to profl. jours.; patentee in field. Recipient I-R 100 award Indsl. Research Devel. Mag., 1974, 78; NIH, NASA grantee. Fellow Am. Inst. Ultrasound in Medicine, Acoustical Soc. Am.; mem. IEEE (sr., gov. com. Ultrasonics, Ferroelectrics and Frequency Control Soc. 1978-80, 86-88, 92-94), Am. Phys. Soc., Sigma Xi (nat. lectr. 1981-82). Home: 444 Edgewood Dr Saint Louis MO 63105-2016 Office: Washington U Box 1105 Dept Physics Saint Louis MO 63130

MILLER, JAMES (JIM) ALFRED LOCKE, JR., aircraft maintenance technician; b. Freeport, N.Y., June 6, 1943; s. James Alfred Locke and Leila James (Wootten) M. AA in Paralegal Tech., Ctrl. Carolina Tech. Inst., 1976; AA in Aviation Maintenance, Wayne C.C., 1981; BS in Aviation Mgmt., So. Ill. U., Carbondale, 1989. Lic. aircraft mech. FAA. Ramp serviceman Eastern Air Lines, Raleigh-Durham, N.C., 1965-71; U.S. Customs warehouse officer R.J. Reynolds Tobacco Co., Winston-Salem, N.C.; seaman/helmsman USNS Mizar T-AGOR 11, 1972; mech. Naval Air Depot, Cherry Point, N.C., 1981-87, Piedmont Airlines, Winston-Salem, 1987; FAA/FCC tech. US Airways, Winston-Salem, 1987—. Mem. SAR, Assn. Former Intelligence Officers, Profl. Aviation Maintenance Assn., Internat. Assn. Machinist and Aerospace Workers, N.C. A. Philip Randolph Inst., Soc. Indsl. Archaeology, Can. Auction Maintenance Coun., U.S. Horse Cavalry Assn. Republican. Episcopalian. Avocations: genealogy, history. Home: 2810-K Carriage Dr Winston Salem NC 27106-5328 Office: US Airways Smith Reynolds Airport 4001 N Liberty St Winston Salem NC 27105-3811

MILLER, JAMES LYNN, lawyer; b. Fairmont, W.Va., June 1, 1951; s. Robert Ogden Jr. and Dora Alice (Ward) M.; m. Maureen Clancy, Apr. 16, 1983; children: James Clancy, Bailey Ward. BA, Calif. State U., Humboldt, 1973; JD, U. Calif., Berkeley, 1976. Bar: Calif. 1976, Hawaii 1988. From assoc. to ptnr. Brobeck, Phleger & Harrison, San Francisco, 1976-95; with antitrust divsn. U.S. Dept. Justice, San Francisco, 1995—. Republican. Avocation: fishing. Office: Dept of Justice Antitrust Divsn 450 Golden Gate Ave San Francisco CA 94102-3478

MILLER, JAMES MCCALMONT, pediatrician; b. Springfield, Mass., Sept. 25, 1938; s. John Haynes and Josephine (Darrah) M.; m. Jane Rose, July 7, 1975; children: John, Charlotte, Willard. AB, Hamilton Coll., 1960; MD, Cornell U., 1964. Resident U. Colo. Med. Ctr., Denver, 1964-67; staff pediatrician Kaiser Permanente Med. Ctr., Walnut Creek, Calif., 1969-87, chief pediatrician, 1971-82; chief pediatrician Kaiser Permanente Med. Ctr., Pleasanton, Calif., 1982-87; staff pediatrician Appalachian Regional Health, Hazard, Ky., 1987-92, Northwest Pediatric Ctr., Centralia, Wash., 1992—; clin. assoc. U. N.Mex., Albuquerque, 1967-69; instr. U. Calif., San Francisco, 1969-87, U. Ky., Lexington, 1988-92. With U.S. Army, 1967-69. Fellow Am. Acad. Pediatrics; mem. Wash. State Med. Assn. Office: Northwest Pediatric Ctr 908 S Scheuber Rd Centralia WA 98531-9027

MILLER, JAMES ROBERT, lawyer; b. McKeesport, Pa., Aug. 2, 1947; s. Robert Charles and Ethel Margaret (Yahn) M.; m. Kathleen Ann Galka, June 6, 1975; children: Jesse J., Cassidy A. BA, NYU, 1969; JD, Duquesne U., 1972. Bar: Pa. 1972, U.S. Dist. Ct. (we. dist.) Pa. 1974, U.S. Ct. Appeals (3d cir.) 1978, U.S. Ct. Appeals (11th cir.) 1989, U.S. Supreme Ct. 1990. Law clerk to Hon. James C. Crumlish, Jr. Commonwealth Ct. of Pa., Phila., 1972-74; shareholder Dickie, McCamey & Chilcote, Pitts., 1974—. Mem. ABA, Am. Coll. Trial Lawyers, Pa. Bar Assn., Acad. Trial Lawyers. Avocation: sports. Office: Dickie McCamey & Chilcote Two PPG Pl Ste 400 Pittsburgh PA 15222

MILLER, JAMES RUMRILL, III, finance educator; b. Phila., Dec. 21, 1937; s. James Rumrill and Elizabeth Pleasants (King) M.; m. Bettie M. Studer, May 1, 1989; children from previous marriage: Elizabeth, Katharine, Kerry. A.B., Princeton U., 1959; M.B.A. (Woodrow Wilson fellow), Harvard U., 1962; Ph.D., M.I.T., 1966. Systems analyst MITRE Corp., Bedford, Mass., 1962-67; asst. prof. bus. adminstrn. Stanford U., 1967-69, asso. prof., 1970-73, prof., 1973—, Walter and Elise Haas prof. bus. adminstrn., 1977—; asso. dean Stanford U. (Bus. Sch.), 1974-76; cons. in field. Author: Professional Decision Making, 1970; contbr. numerous articles to profl. jours. Mem. Phi Beta Kappa. Republican. Episcopalian. Office: Stanford U Bus Sch Stanford CA 94305

MILLER, JAMES VINCE, university president; b. Waynetown, Ind., July 16, 1920; s. J. Vince and Hazel B. (Spore) M.; m. Mildred Mae Hockersmith, June 13, 1943; children: Marylyn Jean, Rachel Katherine. B.A. in Philosophy and English, U. Indpls., 1942; M.Div. in History and Lit., United Sem., Dayton, Ohio, 1945; postgrad., Earlham Coll., 1945-46; Ph.D. in Philosophy, Boston U., 1955; LL.D. (hon.), Otterbein Coll., 1971, U. Indpls., 1979. Ordained to ministry Evang. United Brethren Ch., 1945; pastor Greensfork, Ind., 1944-46, Stow, Mass., 1946-48; faculty dept. philosophy and religion Bates Coll., Lewiston, Maine, 1950-64; prof. Bates Coll., 1960-64, chmn. dept., 1958-64; acad. dean Otterbein Coll., Westerville, Ohio, 1964-68; v.p. for acad. affairs, acad. dean Otterbein Coll., 1968-71; pres. Pacific U., Forest Grove, Oreg., 1971-83, pres. emeritus, 1983—; pres. Nat. Coll. of Naturopathic Medicine, Portland, Oreg., 1989-93, pres. emeritus, 1993—; adj. prof. Union Grad. Sch., 1970-78, San Francisco Theol. Sem., 1979-86; chmn. N.W. Assn. Pvt. Colls. and Univs., 1974-76; treas. Oreg. Ind. Coll. Assn., 1974-75, 76-78, chmn., 1978-79; adv. com. Oreg. Ednl. Coordinating Commn., 1976-79; chmn. council for higher edn. United Ch. Bd. Homeland Missions, 1975-76; former mem. adv. com. Gov.'s Listening Post; former mem. spl. com. on future of edn. in Oreg., Oreg. Ednl. Coordinating Commn.; mem. Oreg. Bd. Optometry, 1988-92; bd. dirs. Terwilliger Plz., Inc. Methodist. Lodge: Rotary.

MILLER, JAN DEAN, metallurgy educator; b. Dubois, Pa., Apr. 7, 1942; s. Harry Moyer and Mary Virginia (McQuown) M.; m. Patricia Ann Rossman, Sept. 14, 1963; children: Pamela Ann, Jeanette Marie, Virginia Christine. B.S., Pa. State U., 1964; M.S., Colo. Sch. of Mines, 1966, Ph.D., 1969. Research engr. Anaconda Co., Mont., 1966, Lawrence Livermore Lab., Calif., 1972; asst. prof. metallurgy U. Utah, Salt Lake City, 1968-72, assoc. prof., 1972-78, prof., 1978—; cons. on processing of mineral resources to various cos. and govt. agys. Editor: Hydrometallurgy, Research, Development, and Plant Practice, 1983. Contbr. over 200 articles to profl. jours. First commercial plant using air-sparged hydrocyclone tech. for deinking flotation in wastepaper recycling plant, 1992, 24 patents. Bethelehem Steel fellow, 1964-68; recipient Marcus A. Grossman award Am. Soc. Metals, 1974; Van Diest Gold medal Colo. Sch. Mines, 1977; Mellow Met award U. Utah, Salt Lake City, 1978, 82, 94, Stefanko award coal divsn. Soc. Mining Engrs., 1988, Extractive Metallurgy Tech. award, Metall. Soc., 1988, Richards award Am. Inst. Mining, Metall. and Petroleum Engrs., 1991, Extractive and Processing Lectr. award The Minerals, Metals and Materials Soc., 1992, Disting. Achievement medal Colo. Sch. of Mines, 1994, Centennial Fellow, The Coll. of Earth and Mineral Scis., Penn State U., 1996. Mem. Soc. Mining, Metallurgy and Exploration (chmn. mineral processing div. 1980-81, Disting. mem. Antoine M. Gaudin award 1992), Fine Particle Soc., AIME (Henry Krumb lectr. 1987, mineral industry edn. award, 1997), NAE, Am. Chem. Soc., Soc. Mining Engrs. (bd. dirs. 1980-83, program chmn. 1982-83, Taggart award, 1986), Metall. Soc. Baptist. Clubs: Salt Lake Swim and Tennis; U. Utah Faculty. Office: U Utah 412 WBB Dept Metallurgy Salt Lake City UT 84112

MILLER, JANEL HOWELL, psychologist; b. Boone, N.C., May 18, 1947; d. John Estle and Grace Louise (Hemberger) Howell; BA, DePauw U., 1969; postgrad. Rice U., 1969; MA, U. Houston, 1972; PhD, Tex. A&M U., 1979; m. C. Rick Miller, Nov. 24, 1968; children: Kimberly, Brian, Audrey, Rachel. Asso. sch. psychologist Houston Ind. Sch. Dist., 1971-74; research psychologist VA Hosp., Houston, 1972; asso. sch. psychologist Clear Creek Ind. Sch. Dist., Tex., 1974-76; instr. psychology, counseling psychology intern Tex. A. and M. U., 1976-77; clin. psychology intern VA Hosp., Houston, 1977-78; coordinator psychol. services Clear Creek Ind. Sch. Dist., 1978-81, assoc. dir. psychol. services, 1981-82; pvt. practice, Houston, 1982—; faculty U. Houston-Clear Lake, 1984—; adolescent suicide cons., 1984—. DePauw U. Alumni scholar, 1965-69; NIMH fellow U. Houston, 1970-71; lic. clin. psychologist, sch. psychologist, Tex. Mem. APA, Tex. Psychol. Assn., Houston Psychol. Assn. (media rep. 1984-85), Am. Assn. Marriage and Family Therapists, Tex. Assn. Marriage and Family Therapists, Houston Assn. Marriage and Family Therapists, Soc. for Personality Assessment. Home: 806 Walbrook Dr Houston TX 77062-4030 Office: Southpoint Psychol Svcs 11550 Fuqua St Ste 450 Houston TX 77034-4537

MILLER, JANISE LUEVENIA MONICA, lawyer; b. Atlanta, Dec. 25, 1956; d. James Thomas and Vera Luevenia (Brown) M.; 1 child, Brandyn Matthew Cooper. BA, Spalding U., 1976; JD, John Marshall Law Sch., 1979. Bar: Ga. 1982, U.S. Ct. Appeals (11th cir.) 1989. Mental health law specialist Ga. Legal Svcs., Atlanta, 1987-88; atty., paralegal Rogers & Sparks, Atlanta, 1980-82; staff counsel Ga. Dept. Med. Assistance, Atlanta, 1982-83; assoc. atty. Cuffie, Mitchell & Assocs., Atlanta, 1983-84, Cuffie & Assocs., Atlanta, 1984-85; pvt. practice Atlanta, 1985-86; of counsel Albert A. Mitchell & Assocs., Atlanta, 1987-92, A.A. Mitchell & Assocs., Atlanta, 1987-92; pvt. practice, 1993—; judge pro hac vice Atlanta Mcpl. Ct. 1989-91. Assoc. editor Nexus, 1980. Chairperson, pres. United Schleroderma Found., Atlanta, 1991-92. Fellow Ga. Bar Found.; mem. State Bar of Ga., Ga. Assn. of Black Women Attys. (Svc. award 1986), Atlanta Bar Assn. (chairperson, seminar com. 1987-88, sec./treas. criminal law sect. 1988-89), Nat. Bar Assn. (chairperson Gertrude Rush Dinner 1992), Gate City Bar Assn. (pres. 1987, editor newsletter 1992). Democrat. Roman Catholic. Avocations: reading, writing, swimming, cooking. Office: PO Box 11229 Atlanta GA 30310-0229

MILLER, JAY ALAN, civil rights association executive; b. Cleve., Feb. 8, 1928; s. Herbert Phillip Miller and Ruth Weisbach; m. Joyce Dannen, Feb. 1, 1952 (div. Oct. 1964); children: Joshua, Adam, Rebecca; m. Maryanne Carol Dust, Jan. 1, 1989; stepchild, Joshua Kalin. Student, Roosevelt U., 1948; BSc, U. Ill., 1950. Organizer Amalgamated Clothing Workers, Chgo., 1950-52; bus. agt., edn. dir. Amalgamated Clothing Workers, Wilkes-Barre, Pa., 1956-61; organizer United Packing House Workers, Chgo., 1952-53; reporter Cleve. Press, 1954-56; peace edn. dir. Am. Friends Svc. Com.,

Chgo., 1961-65; exec. dir. ACLU of Ill., Chgo., 1965-71, 78—, ACLU of No. Calif., San Francisco, 1971-74; assoc. dir. legis. office ACLU, Washington, 1975-78. Pres. AFL-CIO Labor Coun., Hazelton, Pa., 1959-61, mem. trade union delegation to USSR, 1960; chmn. Turn Toward Peace, Chgo., 1962-64; coord. Com. for a Test Ban Treaty, Ill. and Wis., 1962-63; dep. dir. Ill. Rally for Civil Rights, Chgo., 1964. With U.S. Army, 1946-48, PTO. Home: 2573 N Clark St Chicago IL 60614-1717 Office: ACLU 203 N La Salle St Ste 1405 Chicago IL 60601-1225

MILLER, JAYNE ELLEN, journalist, educator; b. Danville, Pa., Apr. 26, 1954; d. John R. Jr. and Eleanor Irene (McMullen) M. BA in Journalism, Pa. State U., 1976. Anchor, reporter Sta. WHP-TV, Harrisburg, Pa., 1976-78, Sta. WQED-TV, Pitts., 1978-79; reporter Sta. WBAL-TV, Balt., 1979-82, CBS News, Washington, 1982-84; sr. reporter Sta. WBAL-TV, Balt., 1984-89, consumer advocate, 1989-92, investigative reporter, 1992—; instr. U. Md.-Baltimore County, Catonsville. Bd. dirs. Pa. State Coll. of Comms. Alumni Soc., University Park, Pa., 1988—, Women Entrepreneurs of Balt., 1993—, Hearing-and-Speech Agy., Balt., 1994—. Recipient Nat. Headline award Atlantic City Press Club, 1987; Pa. State Alumni fellow, 1993. Mem. AFTRA (Washington chpt., Balt. chpt., local chpt., bd. dirs.), Investigative Reporters/Editors. Office: Sta WBAL-TV 3800 Hooper Ave Baltimore MD 21211-1313

MILLER, JEAN PATRICIA SALMON, art educator; b. Little Falls, Minn., Sept. 28, 1920; d. Albert Michael and Wilma (Kaestner) Salmon; m. George Fricke Miller, Sept. 8, 1951 (dec. Apr. 1991); children: Victoria Jean, George Laurids. BS, St. Cloud State Tchrs. Coll., 1942; MS, U. Wis., Whitewater, 1976. Lic. cert. secondary English, art, Wis. Tchr. elem. and secondary art Pub. Schs. Sauk Center, Minn., 1943; tchr. secondary art Bd. Edn., Idaho, 1945; tchr. elem. and secondary art Elkhorn (Wis.) Area Schs., 1950-78; tchr. art adult edn. Kenosha Tech. Coll., Elkhorn, Wis., 1969; cooperating tchr., supr. art majors in edn. U. Wis., Whitewater, 1970-77; coord. Art Train Project, Madison. Represented in permanent collections Irwin L. Young Auditorium, Fern Young Ter., U. Wis., Whitewater. Sec. Walworth County Needs of Children and Youth, Williams Bay, Wis., 1956-57; co-chair, sponsor Senate Bill 161-art requirement for h.s. grad., 1988-89. Recipient Grand award painting Walworth County Fair, 1970, 3rd award painting Geneva Lake Art Assn., Lake Geneva, Wis., Acrylic Painting First award Badlants Art Assn., 1994. Mem. Nat. Art Edn. Assn., Wis. Women in Arts, Wis. Art Edn. Assn., Wis. Regional Artists Assn. (co-chmn. Wis. regional art program 1992, 93, corr. sec. 1992—), Walworth County Art Assn. (bd. dirs. 1979-94, pres. 1986-87), Kiwanis, Elks, Alpha Delta Kappa (pres. Theta chpt. Wis. 1968-70). Home and Office: 671 24th St W Apt 8 Dickinson ND 58601-2762

MILLER, JEANNE-MARIE ANDERSON (MRS. NATHAN J. MILLER), English language educator, academic administrator; b. Washington, Feb. 18, 1937; d. William and Agnes Catherine (Johns) Anderson m. Nathan John Miller, Oct. 2, 1960. BA, Howard U., 1959, MA, 1963, PhD, 1976. Instr. dept. English Howard U., Washington, 1963-76, asst. prof., 1976-79, assoc. prof., 1979-92, prof., 1992—, also asst. dir. Inst. Arts and Humanities, 1973-75, asst. acad. planning, office v.p. for acad. affairs, 1976-90; cons. Am. Studies Assn., 1972-75, Silver Burdett Pub. Co., Nat. Endowment for Humanities, 1978—; adv. bd. D.C. Libr. for Arts, 1973—, John Oliver Killens Writers Guild, 1975—, Afro-Am. Theatre, Balt., 1975—. Editor, Black Theatre Bull., 1977-86; Realism to Ritual: Form and Style in Black Theatre, 1983; assoc. editor Theatre Jour., 1980-81; contbr. articles to profl. jours. Mem. Washington Performing Arts Soc., 1971—, Friends of Sta. WETA-TV, 1971—, Mus. African Art, 1971—, Arena Stage Assos., 1972—, Washington Opera Guild, 1982—, Wolf Trap Assocs., 1982—, Drama League N.Y., 1995—. Ford Found. fellow, 1970-72, So. Fellowships Fund fellow, 1973-74; Howard U. rsch. grantee, 1975-76, 94-95, 96-97, ACLS grantee, 1978-79, NEH grantee, 1981-84. Mem. AAUP, ACLU, MLA, Nat. Coun. Tchrs. English, Coll. English Assn., Am. Studies Assn., Assn. for Theatre in Higher Edn., D.C. LWV, Common Cause, Am. Acad. Polit. and Social Sci., Coll. Lang. Assn., Am. Assn. Higher Edn., Nat. Assn. Women Deans, Adminstrs. and Counselors, Friends of Kennedy Ctr. for Performing Arts, Pi Lambda Theta. Democrat. Episcopalian. Home: 504 24th St NE Washington DC 20002-4818

MILLER, JEFFREY CLARK, lawyer; b. Boston, Aug. 17, 1943; s. Andrew Otterson and Jeanne (White) M.; m. Susanne Jackson, Oct. 23, 1970; children: Gordon, Andrew, Katharine, Eric. BA, Yale U., 1965; JD, Cornell U., 1968. Bar: N.Y. 1970. Assoc. Miller, Montgomery, Spalding & Sogi, N.Y.C., 1968-69; sec. Jamaica Water & Utilities Inc., Greenwich, Conn., 1969-72; assoc. Reid & Priest, N.Y.C., 1972-86, ptnr., 1986-93; asst. gen. coun. Northeast Utilities Svc. Co., Berlin, Conn., 1993—. Bd. dirs. Wilson Point Property Owners Assn., Norwalk, Conn., 1972-74, pres., 1988-92; trustee St. Luke's Sch., New Canaan, Conn., 1992—, chmn., 1995—; sec. Yale U. Class 1965, 1990—. Mem. ABA, N.Y. State Bar Assn. (sec. pub. utility com. 1983-87). Home: 1 Valley Rd Norwalk CT 06854-5010 Office: Northeast Utilities Svc Co PO Box 270 Hartford CT 06141-0270

MILLER, JEFFREY VEACH, biochemist, researcher; b. Schenectady, N.Y., Apr. 11, 1955; s. Ray H. and Donna L. (Veach) M. BA, U. Calif., Berkeley, 1978; PhD, U. Calif., Santa Cruz, 1995. Biochemist Syva Co., Palo Alto, Calif., 1979-81, Genentech Inc., South San Francisco, 1981-83, Genencor Inc., South San Francisco, 1983-88, U. Calif., Santa Cruz, 1988. Contbr. articles to profl. jours.; patentee in field. Avocation: yacht racing.

MILLER, JERRY ALLAN, JR., pediatrician; b. Abingdon, Va., May 31, 1951. MD, Med. Coll. Ga., Augusta, 1976. Diplomate Am. Bd. Pediat. Intern in family practice U. Tex. Med. Sch., Houston, 1976-77, resident in pediatrics, 1977-80; with Nat. Health Svc. Corps, Thomson, Ga., 1980-82; pvt. practice Augusta (Ga.) Pediatric Assocs., 1982—; chmn. bd. dirs. Summer Med. Inst., Phila., Augusta, 1992—. Fellow Am. Acad. Pediat.; mem. Phi Beta Kappa, Alpha Omega Alpha. Presbyterian. Avocations: tennis, surfing. Office: Augusta Pediatric Assocs PC 1230 Augusta West Pkwy Augusta GA 30909-1854

MILLER, JERRY HUBER, retired university chancellor; b. Salem, Ohio, June 15, 1931; s. Duber Daniel and Ida Claire (Holdereith) M.; m. Margaret A. Setter, 1958; children: Gregory, Joy, Carol, Beth, David. BA, Harvard U., 1953; MDiv., Hamma Sch. Theology, 1957; DD (hon.), Trinity Luth. Sem., 1981. Ordained to ministry Luth. Ch., 1957. Research assoc., intern Cornell U., Ithaca, N.Y., 1955-56; instr. Wittenberg U., Springfield, Ohio, 1956-57; parish pastor Ch. of Good Shepherd, Cin., 1957-62; asst. to pres. Ohio Synod Luth. Ch. Am., 1962-66; sr. campus pastor, dir. campus ministry U. Wis., Madison, 1966-69; regional dir. Nat. Luth. Campus Ministry, Madison, 1969-76; exec. dir. Nat. Luth. Campus Ministry, Chgo., 1977-81; pres. Calif. Luth. U., Thousand Oaks, 1981-92, chancellor, 1992-94, pres. emeritus, 1994—; ret. Ventura County Maritime Mus., Channel Islands Harbor, Calif., 1993-95; chmn. Los Robles Bank, Thousand Oaks; mem. exec. com. Coun. Ind. Colls., Washington, Assn. Ind. Calif. Colls. and Univs., 1981-92, Coun. Luth. Colls., Luth. Ednl. Conf. N.Am., 1977-94; vice chair bd. behavioral sci. State Calif. Editor: The Higher Disciplines, 1956; contbr. articles to profl. jours. Bd. dirs. Wittenberg U., Augustana Coll., Rock Island, Ill., United Way, Thousand oaks, Ventura County chpt. ARC, Thousand Oaks, YMCA; chmn. bd. dirs. Los Robles Hosp. Named Man of Yr., Salem, 1975; Siebert Found. fellow, 1975. Mem. Am. Assn. Higher Edn., Council Advancement and Support Edn., Harvard Alumni Assn., Western Coll. Assn. (bd. dirs.), Conejo Valley C. of C. (bd. dirs.), Conejo Symphony Orch. (bd. dirs.). Club: Harvard (Ill., Ohio, Wis., Calif.), YMCA (regional bd. dirs.), Rotary. Avocations: skiing, golfing, hiking, travelling.

MILLER, JIM, film editor. Editor: (TV pilots) Feel the Heat, 1993, The Wizard, 1986, (TV movies) Two Fathers' Justice, 1985, Alice in Wonderland, 1985, (films) (with Dede Allen) The Breakfast Club, 1985, Blue City, 1986, (with Allen) The Milagro Beanfield War, 1988, (with Allen) Let It Ride, 1990, (with Allen) The Addams Family, 1991, (with Arthur Schmidt) Addams Family Values, 1993, For Love or Money, 1993. Office: 3926 Corte Cancion Thousand Oaks CA 91360-6915 Office: The Gersh Agency 232 N Canon Dr Beverly Hills CA 90210-5302*

MILLER, JOANNE LOUISE, middle school educator; b. Milton, Mass., Apr. 4, 1944; d. Joseph Louis and Marion Theresa (Saulnier) Fasci; m. William Frederick Miller, Dec. 4, 1962; 1 child, Robert Joseph. BS, U. Oreg., 1972, MS in Curriculum and Instrn., 1973; EdD, Brigham Young U., 1980; postgrad., Oreg. State U., 1995. Lic. counselor, tchr., adminstr., Oreg. Tchr. South Lane Sch. Dist., Cottage Grove, Oreg., 1973—, lang. arts div. chairperson, 1975-78, 89-90, reading coord., 1978-79, 7th grade block chairperson, 1982-92, mid. sch. talented and gifted coord., 1992-93, counselor, 1991-93; mem. Oreg. State Assessment Content Panel Reading, Salem, 1987-88; mem. Oreg. Lang Arts Curriculum Devel. Com., Salem, 1985-87; del. to Citizen Amb. Program of People to People Internat. 1st U.S.-Russia Joint Conf. on Edn., Moscow, 1994. Vol. Am. Cancer Soc., Am. Diabetes Assn., 1990—; aux.- charter mem. Assistance League of Eugene. Mem. ACA, NEA, Internat. Reading Assn., Am. Sch. Counselor Assn., Oreg. Counseling Assn., Oreg. Edn. Assn., South Lane Edn. Assn., Oreg. Reading Assn., Oreg. Mid. Level Assn., Delta Kappa Gamma, Alpha Rho State (v.p. 1995-97, pres. 1997—). Democrat. Roman Catholic. Avocations: travel, reading. Home: 85515 Appletree Dr Eugene OR 97405-9738 Office: Lincoln Mid Sch 1565 S 4th St Cottage Grove OR 97424-2955

MILLER, JOEL STEVEN, solid state scientist; b. Detroit, Oct. 14, 1944; s. John and Rose (Schpok) M.; m. Elaine J. Silverstein, Sept. 20, 1970; children: Stephen D., Marc A., Alan D. BS in Chemistry, Wayne State U., 1967; PhD, UCLA, 1971. Mgr. rsch. Occidental Rsch. Corp., Irvine, Calif., 1979-83; supr. rsch. Cen. R & D Lab. E. I. Du Pont Nemours & Co., Wilmington, Del., 1983-93; prof. chemistry U. Utah, 1993—, adj. prof. Materials Sci.; adj. prof. materials sci., 1994—; assoc. Inorganic Synthesis Corp., Chgo.; vis. prof. U. Calif., Irvine, 1980, Weizmann Inst., Rehovot, Israel, 1985, U. Pa., Phila., 1988, U. Paris-Sud, 1991. Editor 9 books; mem. adv. bd. Jour. Chemistry Materials, 1990—, Jour. Materials Chemistry, 1991—, Advanced Materials, 1994—; contbr. over 280 articles to sci. jours. Indsl. fellow in material sci. Northwestern U., 1991-93. Mem. Am. Chem. Soc. (chmn. solid state subdiv. 1989). Achievements include discovery and development of molecular-based conductors and magnets. Office: U Utah Dept Chemistry Salt Lake City UT 84108

MILLER, JOHN, foundation administrator. BA in Psychology, U. Del., 1970. Exec. v.p. Am. Cancer Soc., Jefferson City, Mo., 1979-83, Am. Coll. Sports Medicine, Indpls., 1983-88, Am. Camping Assn., Martinsville, Ind., 1988—; cons. CUBE, Inc., 1988-90. Vol. leadership devel. Am. Cancer Soc.; active numerous civic orgns., including Kingsway Christian Ch., Indpls., Indpls. Conv. and Vis. Assn., 1985-86, XXIII FIMS World Congress on Sports Medicine, Brisbane, Australia/speaker, 1986, others. Mem. Am. Soc. Assn. Execs. Office: Am Camping Assn 5000 State Rd 67N Martinsville IN 46151-7902

MILLER, JOHN ALBERT, university administrator, consultant; b. St. Louis County, Mo., Mar. 22, 1939; s. John Adam and Emma D. (Doering) M.; m. Eunice Ann Timm, Aug. 25, 1968; children: Michael, Kristin. AA, St. Paul's Coll., 1958; BA with high honors, Concordia Sr. Coll., 1960; postgrad., Wash. U., St. Louis, 1960-64; MBA, Ind. U., 1971, D.B.A. in Mktg., 1972. Proofreader, editor Concordia Pub. House, St. Louis, 1960-62, periodical sales mgr., 1964-68; asst. prof. Drake U., Des Moines, 1971-74; cons. FTC, Washington, 1974-75; vis. assoc. prof. Ind. U., Bloomington, 1975-77; assoc. prof. U. Colo., Colorado Springs, 1977-79, prof., 1977-86, prof. mktg., resident dean, 1980-84; v.p. market devel. Peak Health Care Inc., Colorado Springs, 1984-85; dean Valparaiso (Ind.) U., 1986-96, prof. mktg., 1986—; cons. and rschr. govt. and industry; dir. health maintenance orgn.; bd. dirs. Ind. Acad. Social Scis., 1988-90; adv. bd. N.W. Ind. Small Bus. Devel. Ctr., 1989-91; consulting dean USIA project to form Polish Assn. of Bus. Schs., 1995. Author: Labeling Research The State of the Art, 1978; contbr. articles to profl. jours. Mem. Colorado Springs Symphony Orch. Coun., 1980-86; cons. Citizens Goals of Colorado Springs, 1985-86, Jr. League Colorado Springs, 1981-82; bd. dirs. Christmas in April-Valparaiso, 1991-96. With U.S. Army, 1962-64. U.S. Steel fellow, 1970-71. Mem. Assn. Consumer Rsch. (chmn. membership 1978-79), Am. Mktg. Assn. (fed. govt. liaison com. 1975-76), Am. Acad. Advt., Ind. Acad. Social Scis. (bd. dirs. 1988-90), Greater Valparaiso C. of C. (accreditation com. 1991, planning com. 1989-92, chair 1992), Am. Assembly Collegiate Schs. Bus. (internat. affairs com. 1991-93, mem. peer rev. team 1994, 96, com. mem., seminar leader, faculty mem., program chair for New Deans seminar and other workshops 1992—), Beta Gamma Sigma, Alpha Iota Delta. Lutheran. Avocations: racquetball, jogging, walking. Home: 1504 Del Vista Dr Valparaiso IN 46383-3322 Office: Valparaiso U Dept Mktg Valparaiso IN 46383

MILLER, JOHN DAVID, agronomist; b. Todd, N.C., Aug. 9, 1923; s. Reuben Patterson and Chessie (Graham) M.; B.S., N.C. State U., 1948, M.S., 1950; Ph.D., U. Minn., 1953; m. Frances McCollum, June 9, 1946 (dec.); children—John David, Glenn, Mary; m. 2d Jimmie Heard, Mar. 24, 1984. Research fellow U. Minn., 1953; asst. prof. Kans. State Coll., 1953-57; research agronomist Agrl. Research Service, U.S. Dept. Agr., Blacksburg, Va. and Tifton, Ga., 1957-75, research leader, 1972-79, sr. agronomist, 1975-91. Dist. commr. Boy Scouts Am., 1971-74. Served with AUS, 1943-46. Decorated Bronze Star medal. Mem. Am. Soc. Agronomy, Phi Kappa Phi, Gamma Sigma Delta, Sigma Xi. Clubs: Toastmasters, Lions. Home: 801 E 12th St Tifton GA 31794-4115 Office: USDA Coastal Plain Sta Agrl Rsch Svcs Tifton GA 31793

MILLER, JOHN DAVID, manufacturing company executive; b. Utica, N.Y., Mar. 24, 1945; s. David Gordon and Eleanor Katherine (Brant) M., m. Ann Geraldine Johnston, Feb. 25, 1968; children: Shannon, Adra. BSME, Rochester Inst. Tech., 1968. Jr. engr. Pall Corp., Cortland, N.Y., 1968-70; staff engr., 1970-71; group leader Pall Corp., Cortland, N.Y., 1971-76, mgr. filter design, 1976-78, v.p., tech. dir., 1978-86, sr. v.p., 1986—. Patentee filter equipment. Mem. ASME. Democrat. Unitarian. Avocations: song writing, sculpture, rowing, squash. Home: 511 Kline Rd Ithaca NY 14850-2305 Office: Pall Corp 3669 State Route 281 Cortland NY 13045-8857

MILLER, JOHN E., cardiovascular surgeon; b. Cochranville, Pa., Apr. 25, 1918; s. John Wilbur and Esther Elizabeth (Cunningham) M.; m. Nov. 25, 1945; children:Bradford, Toy, Kim, Garth. BA, Pa. State, 1938; MD, Jefferson Med. Coll., 1942. Diplomate Am. Bd. General Surgery, Am. Bd. Thoracic Surgery. Fellow thoracic surgery U. Mich., Ann Arbor, 1948-50; chief thoracic and vascular surgery Md. Gen. Hosp., Balt., 1950-86, St. Joseph's Hosp., Towson, Md., 1974-86; ret., 1986. trustee Bon Secours Hosp., Balt., 1988-96. Capt. USAR, 1943-46. Fellow Am. Coll. Surgeons (Md. chpt. pres. 1966-67), Am. Coll. Chest Physicians; mem. AMA, Am. Thoracic Soc., Am. Heart Assn., Am. Lung Assn. (pres.), So. Assn. Thoracic Surgery, Md. Thoracic Soc. (pres. 1965-67), Md. Lung Assn. (pres. 1977-78), Balt. City Med. Soc., Soc. Thoracic Surgeons. Home: 723 Chapel Ridge Rd Lutherville Timonium MD 21093-1807

MILLER, JOHN EDDIE, lawyer; b. Wayne, Mich., Nov. 14, 1945; s. George Hayden and Georgia Irene (Stevenson) M.; m. Nancy Carol Sanders, Jan. 7, 1968; children: Andrea Christine, Matthew Kit. BA, Baylor U., 1967; JD, U. Memphis, 1973; LLM, U. Mo., 1980. Bar: Mo. 1974, U.S. Dist. Ct. (we. dist.) Mo. 1974, Tex. 1982. Asst. prof. Central Mo. State U., Warrensburg, 1973-74; sole practice, Sedalia, Mo., 1974-79; sr. contract adminstr. Midwest Research Inst., Kansas City, Mo., 1979-81; sr. contract adminstr Tracor Inc., Austin, Tex., 1981-84; contract negotiator Tex. Instruments, Austin, 1984-86; sr. contract adminstr., Tracor Aerospace Inc., Austin, 1986-87, Radian Corp., Austin, 1987-96; asst. co. sec., Radian Internat. LLC, Austin 1996—, Radian Corp., Austin, 1987-96; corp. sec. Radian Southeast Asia (SEA) Ltd., Bangkok, 1995—, dir. Radian Southeast Asia (SEA) Ltd., Bangkok, 1996—, Radian Sys. Corp., Austin, 1995—; corp. sec. Radian Internat. Overseas Mgmt. Co., 1996—; instr. bus. law State Fair Community Coll., Sedalia, 1974-79, Austin Community Coll., 1983-84. Bd. dirs. Legal Aid Western Mo., 1977-79, Boy's Club, Sedalia, 1974-79, Austin Lawyers Care, 1987—. Served with U.S. Army, 1968-71. Mem. Mo. Bar Assn. (mem. internat. law com., mem. computer law com.), Tex. Bar Assn. (intellectual property law sec., internat. law sect., corp. sec.), Coll. of State Bar of Tex., Nat. Contract Mgmt. Assn., Travis County Bar Assn., U.S. Tennis Assn., AM Tennis Club, Phi Alpha Delta. Baptist. Office: Radian International LLC 8501 N Mopac Blvd PO Box 201088 Austin TX 78720-1088

MILLER, JOHN EDWARD, army officer, educational administrator; b. Paragould, Ark., May 8, 1941; s. Wardlow Knox and Anna Mae (Danford) M.; m. Joan Carolyn Capano, Oct. 5, 1968; children: C. Claire, J. Andrew, JoAnna M., Mary Ellen. BS in Math., S.W. Mo. State U., 1963; MS in Ops. Rsch., Ga. Inst. Tech., 1971; postgrad., Yale U., 1991. Commd. 2d lt. U.S. Army, 1963, advanced through grades to lt. gen., 1993; student, then author, instr., grad. studies faculty mem. U.S. Army Command and Gen. Staff Coll., Ft. Leavenworth, Kans., 1974-77; bn. comdr. 4th Brigade, 4th Inf. Div., Wiesbaden, Fed. Republic Germany, 1977-79; ops. officer 8th Inf. Div., Badkreuznach, Fed. Republic Germany, 1979-81; student U.S. Army War Coll., Carlisle, Pa., 1982; div. chief Office Dep. Chief of Staff for Rsch. Devel. and Acquisition, Dept. Army, Washington, 1982-84; brigade comdr., chief of staff 9th Inf. Div., Ft. Lewis, Wash., 1984-87; asst. for combat devels. U.S. Army Tng. and Doctrine Command, Ft. Monroe, Va., 1987-88; asst. div. comdr. 8th Inf. Div., Baumholder, Fed. Republic Germany, 1988-89; dep. comdt. U.S. Army Command and Gen. Staff Coll., Ft. Leavenworth, 1989-91; comdr. 101st Airborne Div., Ft. Campbell, Ky., 1991-93; U.S. army command, gen. staff coll. U.S. Army, Ft. Leavenworth, 1993-95; dep. comdg. gen. U.S. Army Tng. and Doctrine Command, Ft. Monroe, Va., 1995—. Recipient Outstanding Alumni award, S.W. Mo. State U., 1993. Mem. Assn. U.S. Army, Army Aviation Assn. Am., 101st Airborne Divsn.Assn. Republican. Avocations: tennis, skiing, sailing. Office: HQ TRADOC Fort Monroe VA 23651

MILLER, JOHN FRANCIS, association executive, social scientist; b. Canton, Ill., Aug. 3, 1908; s. Frank Lewis and Minnie Grace (Eyerly) M.; m. Ruth Roby, May 29, 1937; children: Joan, Kent R., Dana R. AB, U. Ill., 1929, AM, 1930; postgrad., Columbia U., 1930-31, 34-35; German-Am. student exch. fellow, U. Frankfurt on Main, 1931-33. Staff Commn. Inquiry on Pub. Svc. Pers., 1934-35, Regent's Inquiry Character and Cost Pub. Edn., 1936; cons. Pres.'s Com. on Adminstrv. Mgmt., 1936-37, Com. Civil Svc. Improvement, 1939, Inst. Pub. Adminstrn., 1937-38, Pub. Adminstrn. Clearing House, 1938; chief field svc. Nat. Resources Planning Bd., 1938-43; asst. dir. Nat. Planning Assn., 1943-50, asst. chmn., 1951-77, exec. sec., 1951-71, pres., 1971-79, vice chmn., 1977-89; trustee Nat. Planning Assn., Washington, 1977—; sec. Canadian-Am. Com., 1957-76, N.Am. sec. Brit.-N.Am. Com., 1969-85. Author: Veteran Preference in the Public Service, 1935. Trustee, mem. adv. com. Nat. Conf. on Family, 1946-49; mem. adv. council social security Senate Com. on Finance, 1947-48. Mem. The Planning Forum, Am. Econ. Assn., Am. Polit. Sci. Assn., Am. Hist. Assn., Phi Beta Kappa, Cosmos Club (Washington), Univ. Club (N.Y.). Home: Washington Hill Rd Chocorua NH 03817 Office: Nat Planning Assn 1424 16th St NW Ste 700 Washington DC 20036-2240

MILLER, JOHN GRIDER, magazine editor; b. Annapolis, Md., Aug. 23, 1935; s. John Stanley and Ruby Corinne (Young) M.; m. Susan Bradner Bailey, Oct. 26, 1974; children: Kerry, John, Alison. BA, Yale U., 1957. Commd. 2d lt. USMC, 1957, advanced through grades to col., inf./ops. advisor Vietnamese Marine Corps., 1970-71; prin. speechwriter for Commandant USMC, Washington, 1971-76; commd. officer Battalion Landing Team USMC, 1977-78; asst. chief of staff ops. and plans III Amphibious Force USMC, Okinawa, 1982-83; dep. dir. Marine Corps History USMC, Washington, 1983-85; ret. USMC, 1985; mng. editor Procs. and Naval History U.S. Naval Inst., Annapolis, Md., 1985—. Author: The Battle to Save the Houston, 1985, Pocket Books edit., 1992, the Bridge at Dong Ha, 1989, 90, Punching Out: A Guide to Post-Military Transition, 1994. Decorated Legion of Merit with gold star, Bronze Star with combat V, Cross of Gallantry, Vietnamese Marine Corps.; recipient Author of Yr. award Naval Inst., 1990. Mem. Marine Corps Hist. Found. (bd. dirs., Gen. Wallace M. Greene Jr. Book award 1989), Mil. Order of World Wars (past chpt. comdr., chmn. nat. mag. com.), Civitan Internat. (past chpt. pres.), Washington Naval and Maritime Corrs.' Cir., New Providence Club. Avocations: music, piano, choral singing, boating. Home: 21 Sands Ave Annapolis MD 21403 Office: US Naval Inst 118 Maryland Ave Annapolis MD 21402-1321

MILLER, JOHN HENRY, clergyman; b. Ridgeway, S.C., Dec. 3, 1917; s. Fletcher and Frances Helo (Turner) M.; BA, Livingstone Coll., 1941; M. Div., Hood Theol. Sem., 1945; postgrad. Hartford Theol. Sem. Found., 1954; m. Bernice Frances Dillard, June 27, 1945; children: George Frederick, John Henry. Ordained to ministry, AME Zion Ch., 1939-40; ordained bishop, 1972. Bishop, 10th Dist., 1972-80, 8th Dist., Dallas, 1980-84, 7th Dist., 1984-88, 5th Dist, 1988—, ret.; mem. Gov.'s Advocacy Com. on Children and Youth, 1985—; chmn. bd. AME Zion Ch. Trustee Livingstone Coll.; former chmn. bd. Lomax-Hannon Jr. Coll.; chmn. bd. Black Reps. N.C., 1985—; chmn. hon. degrees com. L.C. Mem. NAACP, World Meth. Council, Alpha Phi Alpha. Republican. Clubs: Masons, Elks. Office: African Meth Episcopal Zion Ch 8605 Caswell Ct Raleigh NC 27613-1101

MILLER, JOHN LAURENCE, professional golfer; b. San Francisco, Apr. 29, 1947; s. Laurence O. and Ida (Meldrum) M.; m. Linda Strouse, Sept. 17, 1969; children: John Strouse, Kelly, Casi, Scott, Brent, Todd. Student, Brigham Young U., 1965-69. Profl. golfer, 1969—; Pres. Johnny Miller Enterprises, Inc.; golf commentator, NBC. Author: Pure Golf, 1976, Johnny Miller's Golf for Juniors, 1987. Named PGA Player of Yr., 1974. Major tournaments won Southern Open, 1971, Heritage Classic, 1972, 74, Ortago Golf Classic, New Zealand, 1972, U.S. Open at Oakmont County Club, 1973, Lancome Trophy Tournament, Paris 1973, 74, Bing Crosby Pro Am, 1974, Phoenix Open, 1974, 75, Dean Martin-Tucson Open, 1974, 75, Tournament of Champions, 1974, Westchester Classic, 1974, World Open, 1974, Dunlop Phoenix, Japan, 1974, Kaiser Internat., 1974, 75, Bob Hope Desert Classic, 1975, 76, British Open Crown, 1976, NBC Tucson Open, 1976, Jackie Gleason Inverarry Classic, 1980, Sun City, 1981, Joe Garagiola Tucson Open, 1981, Glen Campbell L.A. Open, 1981, Wickes Andy Williams San Diego Open, 1982, Honda Inverrary Classic, 1983, AT&T Pebble Beach Nat. Pro-Am, 1987, 94, World Cup individual titles, 1973, 75, Ryder Cup, 1975, 81. Office: PO Box 2260 Napa CA 94558-0060

MILLER, JOHN R., accountant; b. Wilkes-Barre, Pa., Nov. 28, 1946; s. John Turner and Elsie May (Johns) M.; m. Cathy Lynn Redstone, July 27, 1968; children: Stephen, Jo-El. BS in Commerce and Fin., Wilkes U., 1968. CPA, Pa., N.Y.; cert. govt. fin. mgr. Audit exec. Com. of Pa., Harrisburg, 1971-73; sr. acct. KPMG Peat Marwick, Phila., 1968-71; mgr. KPMG Peat Marwick, Harrisburg, 1973-76; sr. mgr. KPMG Peat Marwick, N.Y.C., 1976-79, ptnr., 1979—; ptnr.-in-charge Metro N.Y. govt. practices, N.Y.C., 1993-95; also bd. dirs. KPMG Peat Marwick, N.Y.C.; ptnr.-in-charge of nat. assurance and resource mgmt. practices, 1995-97; northeast regional ptnr.-in-charge KPMG Consulting, N.Y.C., 1997—; nat. mng. ptnr. pub. svcs. mgmt. com. KPMG Peat Marwick, 1997—; mem. U.S. Auditing Standards Adv. Coun., Washington, 1990-93, 97—, Govtl. Acct. Standards Adv. Coun., Norwalk, Conn., 1987-91. Bd. dirs. Rye (N.Y.) YMCA, 1988-97, Osborn Retirement Community; mem. Nat. Civic League, Denver, 1985—; trustee Citizens Budget Commn., N.Y.C., 1985—; Prin. Coun. for Excellence in Govt., Washington, 1987—. Mem. AICPA (chmn. govt. acctg. and auditing com. 1987-90, chmn. audit quality 1991-95), Pa. Inst. CPAs (Leadership award 1968), N.Y. State Soc. CPAs, Masons, Marco Polo Club, Coveleigh Club. Episcopalian. Avocations: travel, reading, sports. Office: KPMG Peat Marwick LLP 345 Park Ave New York NY 10154-0004

MILLER, JOHN RICHARD, interior designer; b. Washington, Feb. 11, 1927; s. John Henry and Helen (Vermillion) M.; m. Audrey Gene Owens, Nov. 6, 1946; children: Pamela Dawn, Felicity Amanda, Timothy John. Diploma in interior design, Colbert Inst., Washington, 1950. Designer Hollidge Interiors, Washington, 1950-51; pres. Miller's Interiors Inc., Temple Hills, Md., 1951—; bd. dirs. St. Barnabas Venture, Temple Hills. Author: Training for Design Related Trades, 1976; columnist Washington Star, 1971-79. Mem. Pres.'s Com. on Employment of Handicapped, 1978-82, White House Design Com., 1969-74, Presdl. Barrier Free Design Com., 1972-80. With USN, 1944-46, PTO. Fellow Am. Soc. Interior Designers (pres. Potomac chpt. 1973-80, nat. dir. 1960-74, chmn. opportunity guidance coun. 1972-74); mem. Nat. Soc. Interior Designers (pres. Potomac chpt. 1974-76), Tantallon Country Club (Oxon Hill, Md.). Democrat. Episcopalian. Avocations: tennis, reading. Home: 13710 Piscataway Dr Fort Washington MD 20744 Office: Millers Interiors Inc PO Box 441711 Fort Washington MD 20749

MILLER, JOHN ROBERT, environmental recycling company executive; b. Lima, Ohio, Dec. 28, 1937; s. John O. and Mary L. (Zickafoose) M.; m. Karen A. Eier, Dec. 30, 1961; children: Robert A., Lisa A., James

E. BSChE with honors, U. Cin., 1960, D.Comml. Sc. hon., 1983. With Standard Oil Co., Cleve., 1960-86, dir. fin., 1974-75, v.p. fin., 1975-78, v.p. transp., 1978-79, sr. v.p. tech. and chems., 1979-80, pres., COO, 1980-86; bd. dirs. Cleve.; pres., CEO TBN Holdings, Pepper Pike, Ohio, 1986—; bd. dirs. Waterlink, Inc., Eaton Corp.; former chmn. Fed. Res. Bank, Cleve. Mem. Pepper Pike Club, Chagrin Valley Hunt Club, Country Club, Nat. Assn. Chem. Recyclers (bd. dirs.), Tau Beta Pi. Office: 3550 Lander Rd Cleveland OH 44124-5727

MILLER, JOHN T., JR., lawyer, educator; b. Waterbury, Conn., Aug. 10, 1922; s. John T. and Anna (Purdy) M.; children: Kent, Lauren, Clare, Miriam, Michael, Sheila, Lisa, Colin, Margaret. AB with high honors, Clark U., 1944; JD, Georgetown U., 1948; Docteur en Droit, U. Geneva, 1951; postgrad., U. Paris, 1951. Bar: Conn. 1949, D.C. 1950, U.S. Ct. Appeals (3d cir.) 1958, U.S. Ct. Appeals (D.C. cir.) 1952, U.S. Ct. Appeals (5th cir.) 1957, U.S. Supreme Ct. 1952. With Econ. Cooperation Adminstn. Am. Embassy, London, 1950-51; assoc. Covington & Burling, 1952-53, Gallagher, Connor & Boland, 1953-62; pvt. practice Washington, 1962—; adj. prof. law Georgetown U. Law Ctr., Washington, 1959—; mem. Panel on Future of Internat. Ct. Justice. Co-author: Regulation of Trade, 1953, Modern American Antitrust Law, 1948, Major American Antitrust Laws, 1965; author: Foreign Trade in Gas and Electricity in North America: A Legal and Historical Study, 1970, Energy Problems and the Federal Government: Cases and Material, 8th edit., 1996; contbr. articles, book revs. to legal publs. Trustee Clark U., 1970-76; bd. trustees De Sales Sch. of Theology, 1993-97; bd. advisors Georgetown Visitation Prep. Sch., 1978-94, bd. trustees, 1994-96, emeritus trustee, 1996—; former fin. chmn. troop 46 Nat. Capital Area coun. Boy Scouts Am.; pres. Thomas More Soc. Am., 1996-97. 1st lt. U.S. Army, 1943-46, 48-49. Recipient 10 yr. teaching award Nat. Jud. Coll., 1983. Mem. ABA (coun., chmn. adminstrv. law sect. 1972-73, ho. dels. 1991-93), AAUP, Am. Arbitration Assn. (panel arbitrators), D.C. Bar Assn., Fed. Energy Bar Assn. (pres. 1990-91), Internat. Bar Assn., Internat. Law Assn., Congl. Country Club, Army and Navy Club, DACOR, Prettyman-Leventhal Am. Inn of Ct. (master, pres. 1995-96), Sovereign Mil. Order of Malta (knight). Republican. Roman Catholic. Home: 4721 Rodman St NW Washington DC 20016-3234 Office: 1001 Connecticut Ave NW Washington DC 20036-5504

MILLER, JOHN ULMAN, minister, author; b. N.Y.C., Dec. 9, 1914; s. Clarence James and Edythe Gladys (Shaffer) M.; m. Marcella E. Hubner, June 12, 1937; children: John U., Mark C. (dec.), Mary Kay (Mrs. Charles Bolin, dec.), Gretchen (Mrs. Ernest Micka). BA cum laude, Taylor U., 1937; MA, Butler U., 1942; DD, Geneva (Wis.) Theol. Coll., 1968. Ordained to ministry Bapt. Ch., 1937; pastor First Bapt. Ch., Bluffton, Ind., 1946-49, Boston, 1949-56; pastor Tabernacle Ch., Utica, N.Y., 1956-63, United Ch. of Christ, Hagerstown, Ind., 1963-66, St. John's Evang. Ch., Louisville, 1967-77; Participant Churchmen Weigh News, WNAC, Boston, 1953-56; preacher Meml. Chapel; instr. religion N.Y. Masonic Home, Utica, 1957-62; broadcast weekly services WKBV, Richmond, Ind., 1965-66; preacher Fellowship Chapel WHAS, Louisville, 1967-77; maintains 24 hour Dial-A-Prayer, Louisville, 1968-77; minister Royal Poinciana Chapel, Palm Beach, Fla., 1978-84; ret., 1984. Author: Only to the Curious, The Voice of St. John, Providence on Pilgrimage, Two Wonders I Confess, Stop! Look! Listen!, He Opened the Book, Christian Ethic in the Sermon on the Mount, Windows on the Agony, Prayers Under Pressure, 1989. Chmn. Campaigns Crippled Children, Tb, U.S.O., 1946-49. Capt. USAAF, 1942-45, PTO. Named Community Leader Am. News Pub. Co., 1969. Mem. Ind.-Ky. Conf. United Ch. of Christ, Bach Soc. Louisville. Home: 4409 Green Pine Dr Louisville KY 40220-1542 *Reverence is my name—the unwritten law of the universe, the invisible order of time, the cardinal virtue of life. Call me sovereign, for so I am, the gift of God to the world of man. Follow me, if you will, and I will disclose to you the life of God in the affairs of man. Charity is my attitude—the most pure of all gifts in the world, the ever redemptive spirit of time, the reconciling power of life. Call me sovereign, for so I am, the gift of God to the world of man. Seek me, if you will, and I will disclose to you the blessings of the eternal in the world of the temporal. Justice is my goal—the incredible design of the universe, the rightness of all things, the inescapable oughtness of life. Call me sovereign, for so I am, the gift of God to the world of man. Pursue me if you will and I will disclose to you the triumph of right amid the shadows of wrong.*

MILLER, J(OHN) WESLEY, III, lawyer, author; b. Springfield, Mass., Oct. 3, 1941; s. John Wesley Jr. and Blanche Ethel (Wilson) M. AB, Colby Coll., 1963; AM, Harvard U., 1964, JD, 1981. Bar: Mass. 1984, U.S. Dist. Ct., 1984, U.S. Supreme Ct. 1993. Instr. English Heidelberg Coll., Tiffin, Ohio, 1964-69, U. Wis., 1969-77; real estate broker, 1977-84; founder Miller-Wilson Family Papers, U. Vt., Madison (Wis.) People's Poster and Propaganda Collection, St. Hist. Soc. Wis. Author: History of Buckingham Junior High School, 1956, The Millers of Roxham, 1958, Giroux Genealogy, 1958, Symphonic Heritage, 1959, Community Guide to Madison Murals, 1977, Aunt Jennie's Poems, 1986; founding editor: Hein's Poetry and the Law Series, 1985—; editor: The Curiosities and Law of Wills, 1989, The Lawyers Alcove, 1990, Famous Divorces, 1991, Legal Laughs, 1993; founding editor: Law Libr. Microform Consortium Arts Law Letters Collection, 1991—; exhibitor A Salute to Street Art, State Hist. Soc. Wis., 1974; represented in permanent collections U. Vermont, Colby Coll. Archives, State Hist. Soc. Wis., Boston Pub. Libr.; contbr. The Poems of Ambrose Philips, 1969, Dictionary of Canadian Biography, 1980, Collection Building Reader, 1992; also numerous articles on Am. street lit., bibliography, ethics, history, edn., law, religion, librarianship, mgmt. of archives. Mem. MLA, Am. Philol. Assn., Milton Soc., New Eng. Historic Geneal. Soc., Vt. Hist. Soc., Wis. Acad. Scis., Arts & Letters, Social Law Library, Pilgrim Soc., Ancient and Hon. Arty. Co., Mayflower Soc., Soc. Colonial Wars, Sons and Daus. of the Victims of Colonial Witch Trials, Mensa, Springfield Renaissance Group. Recipient Cmty. Activism award Bay State Objectivist, 1993, 94, 95. Office: 5 Birchland Ave Springfield MA 01119-2708 *The advancement of learning is my goal. Professionalism is the standard, and nothing else will do.*

MILLER, JOHN WILLIAM, JR., bassoonist; b. Balt., Mar. 11, 1942; s. John William and Alverta Evelyn (Rodemaker) M.; m. Sibylle Weigel, July 12, 1966; children: Christian Desmond, Andrea Jocelyn, Claire Evelyn. BS, M.I.T., 1964; MusM with highest honors, New Eng. Conservatory, 1967, Artist's Diploma, 1969. Instr. bassoon Boston U., 1967-71, U. Minn., 1971—; prin. bassoonist, founding mem. Boston Philharmonia Chamber Orch., 1968-71; prin. bassoonist Minn. Orch., Mpls., 1971—; dir. Boston Baroque Ensemble, 1963-71, John Miller Bassoon Symposium, 1984—; mem. Am. Reed Trio, 1977—; faculty Sarasota Music Festival, 1986—, Affinis Seminar, Japan, 1992; vis. faculty Banff Ctr. for Arts, 1987; faculty Nordic Bassoon Symposium, 1993—. Soloist on recs. for Cambridge, Mus. Heritage Soc., Pro Arte; featured guest artist 1st Internat. Bassoon Festival, Caracas, Venezuela, 1994. Recipient U.S. Govt. Fulbright award, 1964-65, Irwin Bodky award Cambridge Soc. Early Music, 1968. Mem. Internat. Double Reed Soc., Minn. Bassoon Assn. (founder). Home: 706 Lincoln Ave Saint Paul MN 55105-3533 Office: 1111 Nicollet Mall Minneapolis MN 55403-2406

MILLER, JON, sports commentator. Play-by-commentator NHL Calif. Golden Seals, 1972-73, NBA's Golden State Warriors, 1979-82; basketball commentator U. San Francisco, 1975-80, San Jose Earthquakes, 1975-76, Wash. Diplomats of the Am. Soccer League, 1977; broadcaster Boston Red Sox, 1980-82, Tex. Rangers, 1978-79; commentator Major League Baseball ESPN, 1986-89; commentator Balt. Orioles Sta. WBAL Radio Network, 1983—, Sta. WMAR-TV Network, 1991-92; play-by-play commentator Sunday Night Baseball ESPN, 1990—; popular banquet spkr., imitator of such baseball announcers as Harry Caray and Vin Scully; guest appearances include ESPN's Close Up, Late Night with David Letterman, 1991, The Dennis Miller Show, 1992. Named Balt.'s Best Radio Sportscaster, Balt. Mag., 1986, Best Play-by-Play Broadcaster, Washingtonian mag., 1986; recipient Sports Play-by-Play Cable Ace award, 1990. Office: care ESPN ESPN Pla Bristol CT 06010

MILLER, JON PHILIP, research and development organization executive; b. Moline, Ill., Mar. 30, 1944; s. Clyde Sheldon and Alice Mae (Taes) M.; m. Shirley Ann Hymes, Aug. 21, 1965; children: Melissa, Elizabeth. AB, Augustana Coll., 1966; PhD, St. Louis U., 1970; MBA, Pepperdine U., 1983. Rsch. assoc. to sr. biochemist ICN Pharm., Inc., Irvine, Calif., 1970-72, leader molecular pharmacology group, 1972-73, head molecular pharmacology/drug metabolism dept., 1973-76, dir. biology div., 1975-76; dir. SRI-NCI liaison group SRI Internat. (formally Stanford Rsch. Inst.), Menlo Park, Calif., 1976-78, sr. bioorganic chemist, 1978-80, head medicinal biochemistry program, 1980-84, dir. biotech. rsch. dept., 1982-85, dir. biotech. and biomed. rsch. lab., 1985-92, assoc. dir. life scis. div., 1989-92; dir. bus. devel. Panlabs, Inc., Bothell, Wash., 1992—. Office: MDS Panlabs West Coast Office Ste 205 1191 Chess Dr Foster City CA 94404-1110

MILLER, JON WILLIAM, emergency physician; b. Louisville, Aug. 7, 1949; s. John William and Anne Woodroof (Trosper) M.; m. Sandra Leigh Merzweiler; children: John William, Jeremy Brian. BS in Chemistry, U. Louisville, 1971, MD, 1975; degree in risk mgmt., U. South Fla., 1995. Asst. prof. U. Louisville, 1978-80; asst. prof. U. Ky., Lexington, 1978-80, 90-95, assoc. prof., 1996—; instr., paramedic Rowan County Emergency Med. Svc., Morehead, Ky., 1990—; med. dir. Polk County Rescue and Assocs., Lakeland, Fla., 1984-90; paramedic instr. Louisville/Jefferson County Emergency Med. Svc., Louisville, 1976-80; medico-legal reviewer for various contracts, New Port Richy, Fla., 1987-90. Author: (textbook chpt.) Emergency Medicine, 1994; contbr. articles to profl. jours. Fellow Am. Coll. Emergency Physicians, Am. Coll. Emergency Medicine, Am. Assn. Emergency Physicians, Am. Bd. Quality Assurance (utilization rev. physician 1990—). Avocations: master marksman pistol shooting, collecting curios and relics, scuba diving, cert. and lic. in Class B Explosives. Office: St Claire Med Ctr 222 Medical Cir Morehead KY 40351-1179

MILLER, JONATHAN WOLFE, theater and film director, physician; b. London, July 21, 1934; s. Emanuel Miller; m. Helen Rachel Collet, 1956; 3 children. Ed. St. John's Coll., Cambridge U.; MB, BCh, Univ. Coll. Hosp. Med. Sch., London, 1959; DLitt (hon.), U. Leicester, 1981; Dr. (hon.), Open U., 1983. Dir. Nottingham Playhouse, 1963-69; assoc. dir. Nat. Theatre, 1973-75; mem. Arts Council, 1975-76; vis. prof. drama Westfield Coll., U. London, 1977-78; artistic dir., Old Vic, 1988-90; lectr. Nat. Gallery, 1995, Met. Mus., N.Y.C., 1995. Co-author, actor in Beyond the Fringe, 1961-64; dir. Under Plain Cover, Royal Ct. Theatre, 1962, The Old Glory, N.Y.C., 1964, Prometheus Bound, Yale Drama Sch., 1967, Oxford and Cambridge Shakespeare Co. prodn. of Twelfth Night, on tour in U.S., 1969; dir. for Nat. Theatre, London: The Merchant of Venice, 1970, Danton's Death, 1971, The School for Scandal, 1972, The Marriage of Figaro, 1974; other prodns. include: The Tempest, London, 1970, Prometheus Bound, London, 1971, The Taming of the Shrew, Chichester, Eng., 1972, The Seagull, Chichester, 1973, The Malcontent, Nottingham, Eng., 1973, The Family in Love, 1974, The Importance of Being Earnest, 1975, All's Well That Ends Well, Measure For Measure, Greenwich Season, 1975, Three Sisters, 1977; dir. operas Arden Must Die, 1973, Sadler's Well Theatre, 1974, The Cunning Little Vixen, Glyndebourne, 1975, 77, Marriage of Figaro, Vienna State Opera, 1991, Robert Deveureux, Monte Carlo, 1992, Die Gezeichnete, Zurich, 1992, Maria Stuarda, Monte Carlo, 1993, The Secret Marriage, Opera North, 1993; dir. for English Nat. Opera: The Marriage of Figaro, 1978, The Turn of the Screw, 1979, 91, Arabella, 1980, Othello, 1981, Rigoletto, 1982, 85 (also at Met. Opera, N.Y.C.), Fidelio, 1982, 83, Don Giovanni, 1985, The Magic Flute, 1986, Tosca, 1986, The Mikado, 1986, 88, The Barber of Seville, 1987, Cosí fan Tutte, 1995, Carmen, 1995; dir. for Kent Opera: Cosí Fan Tutte, 1975, Rigoletto, 1975, Orfeo, 1976, Eugene Onegin, 1977, La Traviata, 1979, 96, Falstaff, 1980, 81, Fidelio, 1982, 83, 88; dir. for La Scala Milan: La Fanciulla del West, 1991, Manon Lescaut, 1992; dir for Maggio Musicale, Florence: Don Giovanni, 1990, Cosí fan Tutte, 1991, 94, Marriage of Figaro, 1992, La Bohème, 1994, La Bohème, which transfered to La Bastille , 1995, dir., Strass Ariadne auf Naxos, 1997; dir Met. Opera, N.Y.: Katya Kabanova, 1991, Pelléas et Mélisande, 1995; dir. in co-prodn. with L.A. Music Ctr. and Houston Grand Opera House Der Rosenkavalier, 1994 dir. Broadway play Long Day's Journey Into Night, 1986, The Taming of the Shrew at Royal Shakespeare Co., Stratford, 1987, Andromache, One Way Pendulum, Bussy D'Ambois, all at Old Vic, 1988, The Tempest, 1988, Turn of the Screw, 1989, King Lear, 1989, The Liar, 1989; films include: Take a Girl Like You, 1969; TV films include: Whistle and I'll Come to You, 1967, Alice in Wonderland, 1967, The Body in Question series, 1978, Henry the Sixth, part one, 1983, States of Mind series, 1983; exec. producer Shakespeare TV series, 1979-81; author: McLuhan, 1971, The Body in Question, 1978, States of Mind, 1983, The Human Body, The Facts of Life, Subsequent Performances, 1986; editor: Freud: The Man, His World, His Influence, 1972, The Don Giovanni Book, 1990. Decorated Order Brit. Empire; named dir. of Yr., Soc. West End Theatre Awards, 1976; recipient Silver medal Royal TV Soc., 1981; fellow Univ. Coll. London; hon. fellow St. John's Coll., Cambridge U.; research fellow in history of medicine Univ. Coll., London U., 1970-73. Office: care IMG Artists, Media House 3 Burlington Ln, London W4 2TH, England

MILLER, JUDITH, federal official. BS summa cum laude, Beloit Coll., 1972; JD, Yale U., 1975. Bar: U.S. Supreme Ct., U.S. Ct. Appeals (D.C. cir.), U.S. Ct. Appeals (armed forces cir.). Clk. to presiding justice Harold Leventhal U.S. Ct. of Appeals (D.C. cir.); clk. to assoc. justice Potter Stewart Supreme Ct. of U.S.; asst. to sec. and dep. sec. of def. Office of the Spl. Asst., 1977-79; mem. adv. bd. on the investigative capability Dept. of Def., gen. counsel, 1994—; mem. civil justice reform act adv. group U.S. Dist. Ct. D.C.; mem. jud. conf. D.C. Cir. Recipient Vol. Recognition award Nat. Assn. of Attys. Fellow Am. Bar Found.; mem. ABA (litigation sect.), Am. Law Inst. *

MILLER, JUDITH ANN, retired financial executive; b. Chgo., Sept. 8, 1941; d. Frank G. and Kathryn M. (Stocklin) Bell; m. William J. Shrum, Aug. 3, 1958 (div. 1976); children: Steven W., Vickie L. White, Lisa A. Rhodes, Mark A., Brian D.; m. William L. Miller Jr., Nov. 28, 1976. Student, Ind. Cen. Coll., 1959-60, DePaw U., 1964-65. Lic. minister Christian Ch. (Disciples of Christ). Office cashier, mgr. G.C. Murphy Co., Indpls., 1967-70; asst. treas., office mgr. Missions Blvd. Fed. Credit Union, Indpls., 1970-72; treas., office mgr. Bd. Higher Edn., Christian Ch. (Disciples of Christ), Indpls. and St. Louis, 1972-77; dir. fin. Mt. Olive United Meth. Ch., Arlington, Va., 1978-79; exec. dir. Interfaith Forum on Religion, Art and Architecture, Washington, 1979-82; devel. assoc. Nat. Benevolent Assn., Des Moines, Iowa, 1982-85; adminstrv. asst. Davis, Hockenberg, Wine, Brown, Koehn & Shors, Des Moines, 1985-88; fin. officer Episcopal Diocese of Iowa, Des Moines, 1988-93; ret., 1993; owner Cakes by Judy, Manteo, N.C., 1994—. Mem. citizen adv. coun. Parkway Schs., St. Louis, 1976-77; county rep., mem. Fairfax County Sch. Bd. adv. coun., Springfield, Va., 1979-81; treas. congl. campaign Des Moines, 1983-85; mem. exec. St. Louis Children's Home, 1976-78; v.p., treas. Emmaus Fellowship Project on Aging, Washington, 1980-82; bd. dirs. Urban Mission Coun., Des Moines, 1983-86, Pre-Trial Release Prog., Des Moines, 1984-87; mem. steering com. Iowa Interfaith Network on AIDS, Des Moines, 1989-94; chmn. Cancer Awareness Sunday, Am. Cancer Soc., 1990; mem. pub. rels com. Dare County Librs., 1996—; vol. Hotline, Dare County. Named Vol. of Yr., Iowa Victorian Soc., 1985, Our Community Kitchen, 1986. Mem. NAFE, Nat. Soc. Fund Raising Execs. (chpt. sec. 1985-87), Nat. Assn. Ch. Bus. Adminstrs. Dare County Libr. Assn. Democrat. Mem. Christian Ch. (Disciples of Christ). Avocations: camping, sewing, knitting, reading, cooking. Home: PO Box 194 Manteo NC 27954-0194

MILLER, JUDSON FREDERICK, lawyer, former military officer; b. Tulsa, Dec. 5, 1924; s. Herbert Frederick and Martha (Davidson) M.; m. June Hirakis, Aug. 4, 1967; children by previous marriage: Kathleen, Shelley, Douglas, Judson Frederick. BS, U. Md., 1961; postgrad., Army War Coll., 1961-62; MA, George Washington U., 1962; JD, U. Puget Sound, 1980. Bar: Wash. 1981. Commd. 2d lt. U.S. Army, 1943, advanced through grades to maj. gen., 1975; platoon leader, co. comdr. 4th Cav. Group, Europe, 1944-46, 82d Airborne Div., 1947-50; with 187th Airborne RCT and Hdqrs. 8th Army, 1950-52; instr. Armored Sch., 1953-56; bn. comdr. 14th Armored Cav., 1958-60; with Hdqrs. U.S. Strike Command, 1963-65; brigade comdr., chief of staff 4th Inf. Div., Vietnam, 1966-67; mem. gen. staff Dept. Army, 1967-68; dep. comdg. gen. Ft. Ord, Cal., 1968-69; asst. chief of staff Hdqrs. Allied Forces Central Europe, 1969-71; asst. comdr. 3d Inf. Div., Germany, 1971-73; chief of staff I Corps Group, Korea, 1973-75; dep. comdg. gen. VII Corps, Germany, 1975-77; ret., 1977; assoc. F.G. Enslow and Assocs., Tacoma, 1981—. Decorated Silver Star, Legion of Merit, Bronze Star with V device and oak leaf cluster, Joint Service Commendation medal, Air medal with 8 oak leaf clusters, Purple Heart, Vietnamese Gallantry Cross with palm; named to Okla. Mil. Acad. Hall of Fame, 1988. Mem. ABA, Assn. U.S. Army. Club: Tacoma Country, Lakewood Racquet. Home: 8009 75th St SW Tacoma WA 98498-4817 Office: Tacoma Mall Office Bldg 4301 S Pine St Ste 205 Tacoma WA 98409-7205

MILLER, KARL A., management counselor; b. Reading, Pa., Feb. 27, 1931; s. Harvey and Kathleen Schwartz (Bechtel) M.; B.S. Indsl. Engring, Pa. State U., 1953; M.S. Indsl. Mgmt., M.I.T., 1963; m. Carol Joann Mickle, July 28, 1956; children: Dawn Alison, Kevin Bryan. Bus. mgr. GE, Evendale, Ohio, 1953-55, Lynn, Mass., 1956-63; asst. to pres. Burn & Roe, N.Y.C., 1964-65; cons. George Armstrong Co., N.Y.C., 1966-68; sr. cons. H.B. Maynard Co., N.Y.C., 1968-70; mng. partner Kamid Assocs., mgmt. cons. to newspapers, electronic media, agribus., govt., architects, engrs., constrn., mfg. and health care delivery firms, Yonkers, N.Y., 1971—; owner David Goliath Ltd.; developer, owner joint tech. projects serving Pacific Rim Aircraft Maintenace Sta., 1990—; ptnr. Power Jets Unlimited, 1992—, Pegasus Power Prodrs. Ltd., 1994—; arbitrator Better Bus. Bur. of N.Y.C., 1982-84; lectr. fin. profitability and mktg. Bucknell U., Pa., Mercy Coll., N.Y., Dominican Coll., Blauvelt, N.Y., 1981-82; speaker in field. Pres. men's brotherhood Collegiate Ch. of N.Y.C., 1970-72; pres. Westchestertowne Houses Condominium, Yonkers, 1971-76, Coun. of Condominiums of N.Y. State, 1972-76; commr. of deeds City of Yonkers, 1976, chmn. citizens' budget adv. com., 1975-76. Recipient Speak Up award Peabody (Mass.) Jr. C. of C., 1960, Minuteman citation, 1960, Henry B. Kane award MIT, 1990. Mem. Internat. Platform Assn., Yonkers C. of C. (pres.'s club 1975-78), M.I.T. Alumni Center N.Y.C. (gov. 1970-81), Army/Navy Club Washington, Air Force Assn. (Westchester Falcon Chapter Pres 1995—), U.S. Naval Inst. (life mem.), U.S. Naval Meml. Found (nat. adv. coun. 1993—), Nat. Mus. Naval Aviation Found. (Pensacola), Nat. Parks & Conservation Assn., Am. Legion (vice comdr. 1995, post comdr. 1996—, life mem.), Chinese-Am. MIT, Westchester Personal Computer Users Group, Triangle Frat., Sigma Tau. Republican. Mem. Protestant Dutch Reformed Ch. Author: Networking in Jet Engine Retrofitting, 1963, The Farm Machinery Market, 1973; also articles. Editor: Jet Engine Newsletter, 1955-56. Home: 412-21 N Broadway Yonkers NY 10701-1106 Office: PO Box 63 Yonkers NY 10703-0063

MILLER, KEN LEROY, religious studies educator, consultant, writer; b. San Antonio, July 29, 1933; s. Eldridge and Paskel Dovie (Vick) M.; m. Eddie Juanell Crawford, June 14, 1953 (dec. Apr. 1981); children: Kimberly Miller Stern, Kerry, Karen Miller Davis; m. Carolyn Gayle Jackson, May 4, 1982; children: Sheila Stanley, Keith Conatser. BA, Abilene Christian U., 1958; MEd, Trinity U., 1965; EdD, Ariz. State U., 1975. Cert. tchr., Tex. Tchr. SAn Antonio Ind. Sch. Dist., 1957-58; tchr., adminstr. N.E. Ind. Sch. Dist., San Antonio, 1958-69; min. edn. MacArthur Park Ch. of Christ, San Antonio, 1960-69; prin. Ralls (Tex.) Ind. Sch. Dist., 1969-70; minister of edn. S.W. Ch. of Christ, Phoenix, 1970-74; adminstr., tchr. Lubbock (Tex.) Christian Sch./U., 1974-77; minister of edn. Sunset Ch. of Christ, Lubbock, 1977-87; prof. religious edn. Harding U., Searcy, Ark., 1987—; curriculum cons. Sweet Pub. Co., Ft. Worth, 1988-91; leader internat. and nat. religious edn. workshops and seminars. Author: Moral and Religious Stages of Development, 1975, (curriculum) Old Testament Personalities, 1980, Organization, Administration, Supervision of the Bible School, 1993, Recruiting, Training, Retaining Teachers in the Bible School, 1993, Curriculum for the Bible School, 1993; editor: Recipes for Living and Teaching, 1982, (curiculum) Growing in Knowledge, 1977-90, The MINNITH series, 1991-95; guest editor, contbr. Christian Family 1984. With U.S. Army, 1954-56. Mem. Christian Educators, Christian Edn. Assn., Religious Edn. Assn., Assn. Secondary Schs. and Colls., Alpha Psi Omega, Sigma Tau Delta. Republican. Mem. Ch. of Christ. Avocations: fishing, hunting, reading, travel, writing, poetry readings. Home: 111 Water Oak Searcy AR 72143-4551 Office: Harding U 900 E Center Ave Stop 792 Searcy AR 72149-0002

MILLER, KENNETH EDWARD, sociologist, educator; b. N.Y.C., June 17, 1929; s. Joseph F. and Irene (Edersheim) M.; m. Andrée Nora Barthelemy, Feb. 14, 1959 (div. Nov. 1984); children: Jennifer Andrée, Christopher Kenneth; m. Janet Sue Daniels, May 21, 1990. B.A., U. Ala., 1953, M.A., 1956; Ph.D., Duke, 1965; MS, Drake U., 1986. Asst. to pres., dir. devel. Jacksonville (Fla.) U., 1957-60; dir. Health Council, assoc. dir. Community Planning Council, Birmingham, Ala., 1960-62; asst. prof. sociology Emory U., Atlanta, 1966-70; acting chmn. dept. Emory U., 1969-70; prof. sociology Drake U., Des Moines, 1970-96; chmn. dept. Drake U., 1970-79, 82-88, asst. to dean for grad. studies, 1991-92, prof. emeritus, 1996—; research sociologist U. Ala., 1956-57; research asso. U.S. Civil Service Commn., summer 1968. Served with USN, 1946-48. Postdoctoral research fellow Duke, 1965-66. Mem. Midwest Sociol. Soc. Home: 2129 NW 140th St Clive IA 50325-8730

MILLER, KENNETH GREGORY, retired air force officer; b. Bryan, Tex., July 28, 1944; s. Max Richard and Catherine Mae (Sultzman) M.; m. Ann Marguerite Perpich, Nov. 25, 1966; children: Keith G., Deborah J., Craig S. BS in Aero. Engring., Purdue U., 1966; MS in Systems Mgmt., U. So. Calif., 1970; grad., Nat. War Coll., Washington, 1986; postgrad., U. Va., 1988. Commd. 2d lt. USAF, 1966, advanced through grades to brig. gen., 1990; with Office Sec. Def., Washington, 1980-81; various positions to dir. field ops. F-16 System Program Office, Wright-Patterson AFB, Ohio, 1981-86; chief engring. div. Sacramento Air Logistics Ctr., McClellan AFB, Calif., 1986-87; dir. materiel mgmt. Ogden (Utah) Air Logistics Ctr., Ga., 1987-89; vice comdr. Acquisition Logistics Div., Wright-Patterson AFB, 1989-90; comdr. contract mgmt. div. Air Force Systems Command, Kirtland AFB, N.Mex., 1990; comdr. western dist. Def. Contract Mgmt. Command, L.A., 1990-91; dir. C-17 Program Office, Wright-Patterson AFB, 1991-93; dep. asst. sec. of AF for acquistion Washington, 1993-94; dir. supply Hdqs. USAF, Washington, 1994-95; v.p. for gulf ops. BDM Fed., 1995-96; v.p. for aerospace tech. svcs. group RJO Enterprises, Inc., 1997—. Decorated Disting. Svc. medal, Legion of Merit (2), Def. Superior Svc. medal; recipient award of merit Freedom Found. Mem. Nat. Contract Mgmt. Assn. (bd. advisors 1990-92), Soc. Logistics Engrs. Office: RJP 4200 Col Glenn Hwy Dayton OH 45431

MILLER, KENNETH MERRILL, computing services company executive; b. Lowell, Mass., Dec. 13, 1930; s. Harry Dow and Marjorie Louise (Morris) M.; m. Mary Jo Putnam, June 8, 1952 (div. Aug. 1979); children: Debra, Pamela, Carol; m. Eileen Anne Durnin, Feb. 4, 1980; 1 child, Andrew. BS, Am. U., 1964; MBA, Syracuse U., 1966. Commd. 2d lt. U.S. Army, 1953, advanced through grades to col., 1974; assigned to France, Fed. Republic Germany, Korea, Vietnam; ret., 1978; v.p. Robert W. Baird & Co., Inc., Milw., 1978-79; sr. v.p. Automatic Data Processing, Inc., Roseland, N.J., 1979—. Decorated Legion of Merit with three oak leaf clusters, Bronze Star, Purple Heart. Mem. Ont. Club (Toronto). Office: ADP Inc, 4 King St W, Toronto, ON Canada M5H 1B6

MILLER, KENNETH MICHAEL, electronics executive; b. Chgo., Nov. 20, 1921; s. Matthew and Tillie (Otto) M.; student Ill. Inst. Tech., 1940-41, UCLA, 1961; m. Dolores June Miller, Jan. 16, 1943 (dec. Dec. 1968); children: Barbara Anne Reed, Nancy Jeanne Hathaway, Kenneth Michael, Roger Allan; m. Sally J. Ballingham, June 20, 1970. Electronics engr. Rauland Corp., Chgo., 1941-48; gen. mgr. Lear, Inc., Santa Monica, Calif., 1948-59; v.p., gen. mgr. Motorola Aviation Electronics, Inc., Culver City, Calif., 1959-60; v.p., gen. mgr. Instrument div. Daystrom, Inc., Los Angeles, 1961; gen. mgr. Metrics div. Singer Co., Bridgeport, Conn. and Los Angeles, 1962-65; v.p., gen. mgr. Lear Jet Corp., 1965-66; pres., dir. Infonics Inc., 1967-68; v.p., gen. mgr. Computer Industries, Inc., 1968-69; dir. ops., tech. products group Am. Standard Corp., McLean, Va., also v.p., gen. mgr. Wilcox Electric div., Kansas City, Mo., 1969-71; pres. Wilcox Electric, Inc. subs. Northrop Corp., Kansas City, 1971-72, v.p., dir. World Wide Wilcox, Inc. subs., McLean, Va., 1971-72; pres., chief exec. officer Penril Corp., Rockville, Md., 1973-86, dir. 1973-86, pres. K-M Miller and Assocs., Rockville, Md., 1986—; dir., George Mason Bank, NA, Washington, D.C., Palmer Nat. Bank, Washington, D.C. Mem. regional planning coun. Community Mental Health Svcs., Bridgeport, 1964; mem. Bridgeport Capital Fund Com.; trustee Park City Hosp.; vice dir. Montgomery County Arts Council; bd. dirs. U. Bridgeport; mem. Md. State Com. High Tech. Recipient Job Makers award Mfrs. Assn. Bridgeport, 1963. Follow Radio Club Am. (dir., chmn. grants-in-aid com.); mem. AIAA. IEEE, Aircraft Owners and Pilots Assn., Am. Mgmt. Assn., Armed Forces Communications and Electronics Assn. (life), Electronic Industries Assn., Instrument Soc. Am. (life), Nat. Aero. Assn.,

Soc. Non-Destructive Testing, Soc. Automotive Engrs., Air Force Assn., Am. Radio Relay League (life), Amateur Satellite Corp. (life), Am. Def. Preparedness Assn. (life), Aero. Elec. Soc. (life), Nat. Capital DX Assn. (pres. 1987-88), Assn. Old Crows (life), Mfrs. Assn. Bridgeport (dir.), Bridgeport Engring. Inst., Bridgeport C. of C. (pres. 1964), Quarter Century Wireless Assn. (life, Disting. Svc. award 1994), Soc. Wireless Pioneers. Clubs: Rolling Hills Country (Wichita); Algonquin (Bridgeport). Mem. adv. bd. Washington Bus. Jour.; contbr. articles to profl. jours. Home and Office: 16904 George Washington Dr Rockville MD 20853-1128

MILLER, KENNETH RAYMOND, biologist, educator; b. Rahway, N.J., July 14, 1948; s. Claude Ray and Marion Ruth (Hamill) M.; m. Jody Annette Zanot, June 10, 1972; children: Lauren Beth, Tracy Erin. BS in Biology, Brown U., 1970; PhD, U. Colo., 1974. Asst. prof. Harvard U., Cambridge, Mass., 1974-80; asst. prof. Brown U., Providence, 1980-82, assoc. prof., 1982-86, prof., 1986—. Author: Biology: Discovering Life, 1991, 2d edit., 1994, Biology, 1991, 3d edit., 1995; contbr. articles to profl. jours. Grantee NIH, 1977—, NSF, 1982—. Mem. AAAS, Am. Soc. Cell Biology (chmn. edn. com. 1986-90). Office: Brown U PO Box G-b589 Providence RI 02912

MILLER, KENNETH ROY, management consultant; b. Uniontown, Pa., Oct. 22, 1902; s. Franklin Pierce and Annabelle (Darby) M.; m. Mary E. Hunnicutt, June 14, 1930; 1 son, Stephen Goodrich. Student, Emerson Inst., 1922-23, George Washington U., 1923-25; LL.D., Lebanon Valley Coll., 1957, Fla. Atlantic U., 1975. Dir. conservation dept. Acacia Mut. Life Ins. Co., Washington, 1926-28; asst. supt. agencies Occidental Life Ins. Co., Raleigh, N.C., 1928-31; cons. Life Ins. Agy. Mgmt. Assn., Hartford, 1931-38; supt. agencies Atlantic Life Ins. Co., Richmond, Va., 1938-41; mng. dir. Nat. Fed. Sales Execs., N.Y.C., 1941-42; asst. to program vice chmn., dir. ops. analysis WPB, Washington, 1942-43; with NAM, N.Y.C., 1943-64; asst. to exec. v.p., asst. treas., treas., bus. mgr., sr. v.p. NAM, 1943-55, mng. dir., 1955-57, gen. mgr., 1957-62, group v.p., 1962-63, sr. v.p., adviser, 1963-64; prin. Kenneth R. Miller & Assos. (mgmt. and fin. cons.), Boca Raton, Fla., from 1964. Bd. dirs., past pres., dir. emeritus Fla. Atlantic U. Found., Boca Raton; founder, sponsor dept. ocean engring. Fla. Atlantic U.; former mem. Boca Raton Airport Authority; retired chmn. bd. Caldwell Theatre Co.; former chmn. adv. council Music Guild of Boca Raton.; mem. Friends of Caldwell Playhouse; former moderator Congl. Ch. of Boca Raton; citizens adv. com. Boca Raton Downtown Redevel. Agy. Mem. Economic Roundtable (treas., exec. com.), English-Speaking Union (past pres. Boca Raton br.), Phi Sigma Kappa, Pi Delta Epsilon. Club: Bankers (Boca Raton) (past pres.). Address: 699 SW 5th St Boca Raton FL 33486-4615

MILLER, KENNETH WILLIAM, holding company executive, financier; b. Albany, N.Y., Sept. 25, 1947; s. Kenneth Carpenter and Rose May (Chatfield) M.; m. Barbara Ann Tortorici, Aug. 5, 1967 (div. Nov. 1991); children: Justin Carpenter, Jason Chatfield. BBA, SUNY, Albany, 1970. Exec. v.p., chief operating officer Texgas Corp., Houston, 1981-84; chief exec. officer The Edge Group, Inc., Houston, 1984—, Edge Mgmt. Group, Inc., Houston, 1984—, Superior Energy Group, Ltd., Houston, 1985-94, Gulf Butane Co., Houston, 1985-89, Auto-Quip Leasing Co., Houston, 1986—, MetroGas Corp., Mpls., 1986-89, MetroGas Supply Corp., Houston, 1986—, TRICO, Inc., Savannah, Ga., 1986-90, Tri-County Gas & Appliance Co., Tifton, Ga., 1986-90, Delta Storage and Distbn. Co., Hattiesburg, Miss., 1987-94, Edge Fin. Group, Inc., Atlanta, N.Y.C. and Houston, 1989—, Edge Realty Group, Inc., Houston, 1991—, AMC Funding, Inc., Houston, Little Rock, 1992-95, Edge Funding, Inc., 1995—, Edge Ins. Holdings, Houston, 1993—, Edge Transp. Group, Inc., Houston, 1994-95; CEO Harper Energy Group, Atlanta, 1994—, DaVinci Sci. Corp., L.A., 1995-96, Medici Med. Group, Inc., 1996—; mem. adv. commn. N.Y. Cotton Exch., N.Y.C., 1984-87; del. to USSR Am. People Amb. Program, 1989, Western Europe, 1990; bd. dirs. ProLine Golf Corp. Pres. Hidden Dunes Community Assn., Destin, Fla., 1988-90. With USAR, 1968-74. Mem. Nat. Propane Gas Assn. (bd. dirs. 1984-95), Gov.'s Club, Pine Forest Country Club, West Side Tennis Club. Avocations: tennis, water sports, scuba diving, skiing. Office: The Edge Group Inc 16225 Park Ten Pl Ste 380 Houston TX 77084-5150

MILLER, KENNETH WILLIAM, II, business consultant, educator; b. Cleve., May 11, 1951; s. Kenneth William and Margaret Mary (Leonard) M.; m. Joan Ellen Pattillo, Aug. 12, 1972 (div. Oct. 1992); children: Kenneth William III, Victoria Joan, Christopher John. BSEE, MIT, 1974; MS in Mgmt., Ashland Coll., 1983; postgrad., Cornell U., Am. U. of Paris, 1994—, Harvard. Programmer Fed. Res. Bank, Boston, 1972-74; various Corning (N.Y.) Glass Works, 1974-81; mgr. product devel. Duracell, Tarrytown, N.Y., 1983-85; with Lucent Technologies, 1985; v.p. Frey Holdings/Frey Sci., Richland County, Ohio, 1985-89, also bd. dirs.; mgr. AT&T Tech. Systems, 1985; with Idea Disclosure Program AT&T, 1992—; with Intellogistics, 1989; guest lectr. Ohio State U., 1988; co-owner The Sewing Basket, Corning, 1975-77. Mem. Greensboro Ctr. for Leadership, 1987; mem. Rep. Exec. Com., Richland County, Ohio, 1991. Mem. Ohio Acad. Sci. (life), Amnesty Internat., Eagle Scout Assn. (life), Internat. Telecomms. Union (Geneva). Republican. Methodist. Lodge: Rotary.

MILLER, KERRY LEE, lawyer; b. West Palm Beach, Sept. 11, 1955; s. Clyde Howard and Alice (Hummel) M.; m. Myrna Patricia Garza, June 9, 1979; children: Alexander James, Eric Anthony. BA, George Mason U., 1977; JD, Cath. U., 1981. Bar: D.C. 1981, Va. 1982, U.S. Dist. Ct. (D.C. dist.) 1982, U.S. Ct. Appeals (D.C. and 4th cirs.) 1982, U.S. Ct. Appeals (fed. cir.) 1989, U.S. Ct. Claims 1989, U.S. Supreme Ct. 1989, U.S. Dist. Ct. (ea. and we. dists.) Va. 1993. Asst. gen. counsel Office Gen. Counsel U.S. Govt. Printing Office, Washington, 1981-87, assoc. gen. counsel contracts and procurement, 1987—. Mem. Fed. Bar Assn. (Capital Hill chpt.), Bd. Contract Appeals Bar Assn., Computer Law Assn. Office: US Govt Printing Office Office Gen Counsel 732 N Capitol St NW Washington DC 20401-0003

MILLER, KEVIN D., corporate services executive; b. Chgo., Feb. 7, 1949; s. Donald D. and Anna Agnes (Long) M.; m. Patricia D. Hallberg, Sept. 5, 1995; children: Angela Christy, Jenny Lynne Hallberg, Julie Anne Judd, Suzanne Michelle. BSBA cum laude, Upper Iowa U., 1984. Cert. info. sys. security profl., cert. disaster recovery planner. Detective Dolton (Ill.) Police Dept., 1970-78; systems analyst United Airlines, Chgo., 1978-88; dir. corp. svcs. Apollo Travel Svcs., Rolling Meadows, Ill., 1989—. Mem. Am. Soc. Indsl. Security, Internat. Facilities Mgmt. Assn., Info. Sys. Security Assn. (past pres. Chgo. chpt.). Avocations: traveling, reading, comedy writing, acting. Home: 236 Skylark Ct Bartlett IL 60103-2024

MILLER, KIRK EDWARD, lawyer, health foundation executive; b. San Jose, Calif., June 9, 1951; s. Edward R. and Katherine Miller; children: Anja, Jenny. BA in Polit. Sci., U. Calif., Riverside, 1973; JD, Syracuse U., 1976. Bar: Colo. 1976, Calif. 1980, Tex. 1993. Assoc. Hughes & Dorsey, Denver, 1977-78; v.p., assoc. gen. counsel Am. Med. Internat., Inc., Dallas, 1979-88, v.p., sec., gen. counsel, 1988-91; with McGlinchey Stafford Lang, Dallas, 1991-94; sr. v.p., sec., gen. counsel Kaiser Found. Health Plan, Inc., Kaiser Found. Hosps., Inc., Oakland, Calif., 1994—; instr. Syracuse U., 1975-76. Mem. ABA (co-vice chair com. health care fraud and abuse 1994-96). Office: Kaiser Found Health Plan 1 Kaiser Plz Oakland CA 94612-3610

MILLER, L. MARTIN, accountant, financial planning specialist; b. N.Y.C., Sept. 17, 1939; s. Harvey and Julia (Lewis) M.; m. Judith Sklar, Jan. 21, 1962; children: Philip, Marjorie. BS, Wharton Sch., U. Pa., 1960. CPA; CFP; accredited fin. planning specialist. Jr. acct. Deloitte, Haskins & Sells, N.Y.C., 1960-62, sr. acct., Phila., 1962-64; mng. partner Cogen, Sklar LLP, Phila., 1964—; treas. Coronet Container Co., Inc., Phila., Val Mar Realty Corp., N.Y.C.; dir. Penn Internat. Trading Co., Phila.; mng. dir. CPA Tax Forum, 1966-69; underwriting mem. Lloyds of London, 1978-95, chmn. Mid-Atlantic region, 1991-92; mem. faculty Wharton Sch. U. Pa., 1992—; lectr., discussion leader on fin. and taxation; columnist Montgomery and Bucks County Dental News. Mem. Phila. Rep. com., 1963-67; chmn. Lower Merion Twp. scholarship fund, 1975-78; bd. dirs. Penn Valley Civic Assn., 1973-79, Gladwyne Civic Assn., 1992-95; mem. Lower Merion Planning Commn., 1978-82, Gov.'s Tax Study Commn.; pres. Mensa Edn. and Rsch. Found., 1984-86; mem. SEC Forum on Small Bus. Capital Formation, 1983, Pa. Impact, 1995; apptd. to Pa. State Bd. Accountancy, 1985-94, chmn., 1990-91; elected sch. bd. dir. Lower Merion Twp., 1993—, also chmn. fin. com. Served with U.S. Army, 1961-62. Recipient Outstanding Achievement award Germantown Civic Assn., 1965. Mem. Pa. Inst. CPAs (edn. com. 1975-78, bd. dirs. 1979-81, by-laws chmn. 1980-83, mem. non-profit orgns. com. 1995—, Nat. Assn. State Bds. Accountancy (edn. com. 1987, nominating com. 1989, experience com. 1990, continuing edn. com. 1995—), Cert. Fin. Planner (bd. ethics 1995—), AICPAs (nat. tax commn. 1979-82, exec. com. self regulation div. for CPA firms 1984-87, acctg. and rev. svcs. com. 1985-88, ethics div. 1985-88, specialization bd. 1989-90, ethics exec. com. 1990-93, mem. curriculum and acctg. edn. 1993-96, chmn. fin. assistance task force 1995), Little 10 Acctg. Assn. (edn. chmn. 1980-84), Main Line C. of C. (govt. affairs com. 1991—), Mensa (internat. fin. officer 1970-74), Beta Alpha Psi. Clubs: Masons (past master) Plays and Players (treas. 1978-79). Author: Accountants Guide to S.E.C. Filings, 1968; contbr. articles to profl. jours. Home: 204 Dove Ln Haverford PA 19041-1902 Office: Cogen Sklar LLP 150 Monument Rd Bala Cynwyd PA 19004-1725

MILLER, LARRY H., professional sports team executive, automobile dealer; b. Salt Lake City; m. Gail Miller; 5 children. Formerly with auto parts bus., Denver and Salt Lake City; now owner auto dealerships, Salt Lake City, Albuquerque, Denver and Phoenix; part-owner Utah Jazz, NBA, Salt Lake City, 1985-86, owner, 1986—. Office: care Utah Jazz 301 W South Temple Salt Lake City UT 84101-1216 Office: Larry H Miller Group 5650 S State St Murray UT 84107-6131*

MILLER, LELAND BISHOP, JR., food processing and financial consultant; b. Bloomington, Ill., June 17, 1931; s. Leland Bishop and Nellie (Jolly) M.; m. Alice P. Elder; children: Susan Elizabeth, James Bishop, Steven Robert. B.S. in Chem. Engring, U. Ill., 1954, M.S. in Chem. Engring, 1955, M.B.A., 1978. Research engr. Exxon Research & Engring., Linden, N.J., 1955-58; research asst. Purdue U., 1958-59; with A. E. Staley Mfg. Co., Decatur, Ill., 1959-85; dir. corp. planning A. E. Staley Mfg. Co., 1971-73, asst. treas., 1973-77, corp. treas., 1977-81, v.p., treas., 1981-85; v.p., treas. Staley Continental Inc., Rolling Meadows, Ill., 1985-88; exec. v.p., chief fin. officer MultiFresh Systems, Inc., Hoffman Estates, Ill., 1989-90; exec. v.p. MWT Ltd., Inc., Barrington, Ill., 1990-93; fin. cons., 1993—; pres. Indsl. Devel. Research Council, 1973-74. State v.p. United Cerebral Palsy of Ill., 1971-72; pres. United Cerebral Palsy of Macon County, Ill., 1972-73; bd. dirs. Progress Resource, Inc., Decatur. Served to 1st lt. U.S. Army, 1955-57. Mem. Am. Mgmt. Assn. (fin. council), Fin. Mgmt. Assn., Nat. Assn. of Corp. Treas., Alpha Chi Sigma, Phi Lambda Upsilon, Sigma Chi.

MILLER, LENORE, labor union official; b. Union City, N.J., Mar. 10, 1932; d. Louis and Lillian (Bergen) Shapiro; m. Louis Miller, Dec. 25, 1952; 1 child, Jessica. BA, Rutgers U., 1952; postgrad., Purdue U., 1952-56, New Sch. Social Research, 1957. Sec., asst. to pres. Panel of Ams.; sec., asst. to pres. Retail, Wholesale & Dept. Store Union, AFL-CIO, CLC, N.Y.C., 1958-78, v.p., 1978-80, sec.-treas., 1980-86, pres., 1986—; vice chair civil rights com. AFL-CIO, 1990-95, chair occupl. safety and health com., 1996—; exec. bd. AFL-CIO Indsl. Union Dept., Washington, 1980-82, AFL-CIO Food & Beverage Trades Dept., Washington, 1980—, Maritime Trades Dept., 1986; v.p. Transp. Trades Dept. AFL-CIO, 1992—; vice-chmn. Nat. Trade Union Coun. for Human Rights, N.Y.C., 1980—; mem. Nat. Bd. Workers Def. League, N.Y.C., 1980—; pres. Commn. Tariff & Trade, 1994—, Apparel Ind. Coal, 1996—; mem. com. Am. Trade Union Coun. for Histradut & Afro-Asian Inst., N.Y.C., 1980—; chmn. RWDSU Welfare and Pension Plan, 1986—. Bd. dirs. A. Philip Randolph Inst. Fund, 1988; chair Cen. Labor Rehab. Coun. N.Y., Grand Marshall Labor Day Parade; charter trustee Rutgers U., 1988-94; pres. Jewish Labor Com., 1989—; mem. platform com. Dem. Nat. Conv., del. 1992, 96; mem. Dem. Nat. Com., 1993—; mem. Pres. Commn. on Family and Med. Leave, 1993-96. Named to Acad. of Women Achievers YWCA, 1987. Mem. AFL-CIO (v.p. 1987—, mem. exec. coun.), Douglass Soc. Office: Retail Wholesale & Dept Store Union AFL-CIO CLC 30 E 29th St Fl 4 New York NY 10016-7925

MILLER, LEONARD DAVID, surgeon; b. Jersey City, July 8, 1930; s. Louis Abner and Esther (Levy) M.; children—Steven Lawrence, Jason Lloyd. A.B., Yale U., 1951; M.D., U. Pa., 1955. Intern Hosp. of U. Pa., Phila., 1955-56; resident Hosp. of U. Pa., 1956-57, 59-65; practice medicine, specializing in surgery Phila., 1965—; vice chmn. dept. research and surgery U. Pa., 1972-75, acting chmn., 1975-78, John Rhea Barton prof., 1978-83, chmn. dept. surgery, 1978-83; dir. Harrison Dept. Surgery. Mem. editorial bd.: Annals of Surgery, 1973—. Served to capt., M.C. USAF, 1957-59. Recipient Lindback award for disting. teaching, 1969, Student award for clin. teaching, 1965. Mem. Am. Surg. Assn., AAAS, Soc. for Surgery of Alimentary Tract, Nat. Soc. Med. Research (rep.), Soc. Univ. Surgeons, Am. Soc. Surgery of Trauma, Coll. Physicians of Phila., N.Y. Acad. Sci., Sigma Xi, Alpha Omega Alpha. Office: Univ Pa Hosp Dept Surgery 4 Silverstein 3400 Spruce St Philadelphia PA 19104

MILLER, LEROY BENJAMIN, architect; b. Cleve., Dec. 24, 1931; s. Harry Simon and Carol Jane (Goldberg) M.; m. Sue Firestone, July 1, 1956; children: Laurie, Janet, David, Matthew. BArch, U. Mich., 1956. Registered architect, Calif. From assoc. to v.p. Daniel Dworsky & Assocs., L.A., 1958-66; prin., pres. Leroy Miller Assocs., L.A., Santa Monica, Calif., 1966—; tchr. Calif. State Poly. Coll., Pomona, 1971-72. Exhibited in group shows, 1976, 84, 94. Pres. Leo Baeck Temple, L.A., 1991-93. Cpl. U.S. Army, 1956-58. Recipient Design awards City of Ventura, 1982, City of W. L.A., 1988, City of Pasadena, 1997. Fellow AIA (Design awards L.A. chpt. 1966, 69, 72, 89). Democrat. Jewish. Avocations: writing, music, skiing, racquetball. Office: Leroy Miller Assocs 2800 Olympic Blvd Santa Monica CA 90404-4101

MILLER, LEROY PAUL, JR., secondary English educator; b. Holyoke, Mass., Feb. 21, 1949; s. Leroy Paul Sr. and Rose Marie (Danehey) M. AA, Northampton (Mass.) Jr. Coll., 1972; BA, U. New. Eng., Biddeford, Maine, 1974; MEd, Springfield (Mass.) Coll., 1977; postgrad., Am. Internat. Coll., Springfield. Cert. elem. tchr., history/English tchr., guidance counselor, Mass. Sch. adjustment counselor Holyoke Pub. Schs., 1978-79, ednl. programmer, 1979-80, tutor Chpt. I, 1980-81; tutor Amherst (Mass.) Pub. Schs., 1982-84; tchr. West Springfield (Mass.) Pub. Schs., 1985-86; tchr. English Springfield Pub. Schs., 1986—; fund raiser M. Marcus Kiley Mid. Sch.; alumni counselor U. New Eng., 1977—. Alumni counselor U. New Eng., 1990—. Mem. NEA, ASCD, Nat. Coun. Tchrs. English, Mass. Tchrs. Assn., Springfield Edn. Assn. (faculty rep. 1986—), U. New Eng. Alumni Assn. (v.p. 1990—), Elks, Psi Chi. Democrat. Roman Catholic. Avocations: reading, bowling. Home: 2 Gerard Way Holyoke MA 01040-1204 Office: M Marcus Kiley Mid Sch 180 Cooley St Springfield MA 01128-1108

MILLER, LESLIE ANNE, lawyer; b. Franlin, Ind., Nov. 4, 1951; d. G. Thomas and Anne (Gaines) Miller; m. Richard B. Worley, Feb. 14, 1987. AB cum laude, Mt. Holyoke Coll., South Hadley, Pa., 1973; MA in Polit. Sci., Eagle Inst. Politics Rutgers U., New Brunswick, N.J., 1974; JD, Dickinson Sch. of Law, Carlisle, Pa., 1977; LLM with honors, Temple U., 1994. Bar: Pa. 1977, U.S. Dist. Ct. (ea. dist.) Pa. 1977, U.S. Ct. Appeals (3d cir.) 1980, U.S. Dist. Ct. (ea. dist.) Pa. 1987. Assoc. LaBrum & Doak, Phila., 1977-81; ptnr. LaBrum & Doak, 1982-86, Goldfein & Joseph, Phila., 1986-95, McKissock & Hoffman, P.C., Phila., 1995—; bd. dirs. WHYY-TV; del. Third Circuit Jud. Conf., 1981, 82, 85; mem. Jud. Inquiry and Rev. Bd., 1990-94, chair, 1993-94; mem. faculty trial advocacy program Dickinson Sch. Law, 1992, 94; mem. hearing com., disciplinary bd. Supreme Ct. Pa., 1996—; mem. faculty Acad. Advocacy Temple U., 1994—. Chmn. Com. on Jud. Selection and Retention, Phila., 1987-89; mem. acad. ball com. Phila. Orch., 1986-87, 89-91, 95-96; mem. Open Space Task Force Com., Lower Merion Twp., Pa., 1990—, bd. dirs., 1990-94, mem. counsel, 1990—, Lower Merion Conservancy, 1995—, others; bd. dirs. Med. Coll. Pa., 1985—, sec., 1987-92, chair presdl. search com., 1993, chair presdl. inauguration, 1987, chair com. on acad. affairs, 1989—, chair dean's search com., 1994—, chair nomenclature com., 1996; bd. dirs. Allegheny Health Edn. and Rsch. Found., 1993-96, Hahnemann U. Med. Sch., 1994-96, United Hosps., 1991-94, Pa. Ballet, 1994—, St. Christopher's Hosp. for Children, 1991-94, vice chair, 1992—; bd. dirs. Med. Coll. Pa., 1985-96, sec., 1987-92, chair presdl. inauguration, 1987, chair presdl. search com., 1993, chair com. on acad. affairs, 1989-95, hon. mem. Alumnae Assn., 1990, chair nomenclature com., 1996. Recipient Mary Lyon award, Mt. Holyoke Alumni Assn., 1985, Alumnae Medal of Honor, 1988, Hon. Alumnae award, 1989, Pres.'s award Med. Coll. Pa., 1993; named to Pa. Honor Roll of Women, 1996. Fellow Am. Bar Found., Pa. Bar Found.; mem. ABA, Phila. Bar Assn. (mem. exec. com. divsn. young lawyers 1982-85, mem. bicentennial com 1986-87, bd. govs. 1990-93, mem. gender bias task force 1993, chair com. on jud. selection and retention 1987-89, chair Andrew Hamilton Ball 1989, trustee Phila. Bar Found. 1990—, co-chair century three commn. 1995—, others), Pa. Bar Assn. (found. ho. dels. life fellow, bd. govs. 1980-83, 84-87, 91-93, chair young lawyers divsn. 1982-83, mem. long range planning com. 1985-87, mem. com. on professionalism, 1987-91, vice chmn. jud. inquiry and rev. bd. study com. 1989-91, sec. 1984-87, chair ho. dels. 1991-93, chair commn. on status of women in the profession 1993-95, v.p. 1996-97), Pa. Bar Inst. (mem. faculty, course planner), Phila. Assn. Def. Counsel (mem. exec. coun. 1987-90, 94, mem. joint trial demonstration with Phila. Trial Lawyers Assn. 1993), Def. Rsch. Inst. (spkr. toxic torts seminar 1993), Phila. Bar Edn. Advocacy Women Litigators (course planner, mem. faculty), Women's Assn. Women's Alternatives (bd. dirs. 1983-94, vice chair 1985-94), Mt. Holyoke Alumnae Assn. (bd. dirs. 1986-89). Democrat. Lutheran. Avocations: collecting Am. antiques, gardening, running. Office: McKissock & Hoffman PC 1700 Market St Ste 3000 Philadelphia PA 19103-3930

MILLER, LEVI, publishing administrator; b. Millersburg, Ohio, Sept. 15, 1944; s. Andrew A. and Mattie (Schlabach) M.; m. Gloria E.; children: Jakob, Hannah, Elizabeth. Student, Kent State U., 1963-64; BA in English/History, Malone Coll., 1968; MA in English, Bowling Green State U., 1976. Tchr. English pub. schs. Orocovis, P.R., 1968-71; editor Mennonite Pub. House, Scottdale, Pa., 1971-82, dir. congl. lit. divsn., 1990—; tchr., pastor Eastern Mennonite Bd. Missions, Caracas, Venezuela, 1982-84; program dir. Laurelville Mennonite Ch. Ctr., Mt. Pleasant, Pa., 1984-90; sec. Allegheny Mennonite Conf., 1976-79. Contbr. articles to profl. jours.; author: Ben's Wayne, 1989, Our People, 1983, 2d edit. 1992; editor Allegheny Conf. News, 1979-82; editor Found. Series for Youth and Adults, Mennonite Pub. House, 1981-83. Mem. sch. bd. Southmoreland Sch. Dist., Scottdale, 1989—. Home: 903 Arthur Ave Scottdale PA 15683-1543 Office: Mennonite Pub House 1600 Walnut St Scottdale PA 15683

MILLER, LEWIS NELSON, JR., banker; b. 1944. BA, Washington and Lee U., 1966; postgrad., U. Va., 1972. With 1st & Mchts. Nat. Bank, 1969-70; planning mgr. Cen. Fidelity Bank N.A., Richmond, Va., 1972-73, planning officer, then asst. v.p., 1973-75, v.p., 1975-76, sr. v.p., mgr. fin. group, 1976-78, chief fin. officer, 1978-79, exec. v.p., 1979-82, exec. v.p., chief adminstrv. officer, from 1982; with Cen. Fidelity Banks Inc., Richmond, 1972—, sr. v.p., 1980-82, corp. exec. officer, 1982-83; exec. v.p. Cen. Fidelity Banks Inc., Richmond, Va., 1983-84; pres., later also treas., bd. dirs. Cen. Fidelity Banks Inc., Richmond, from 1984; now chmn., pres., chief exec. officer Cen. Fidelity Banks, Richmond. Lt. USN, 1966-69. Office: Cen Fidelity Banks Inc PO Box 27602 1021 E Cary St Richmond VA 23219-4000

MILLER, LILLIE M., nursing educator; b. Atlanta, Nov. 16, 1937; d. George W. and Lillie M. (Reese) McDaniel; m. Harold G. Miller, June 30, 1962; children: Daren K., Lisa K. Diploma in nursing, Jewish Hosp. of Cin., 1959; BSN, U. Cin., 1961; MEd, Temple U., 1970; MSN, Villanova U., 1987. RN, Pa.; cert. sch. nurse, cert. clin. specialist in med.-surg. nursing ANCC. Instr. sch. nursing Jewish Hosp. Cin., 1959-62; instr. Phila. Gen. Hosp. Sch. Nursing, 1962-67; sch. nurse Norristown (Pa.) Area Sch. Dist., 1967-70; nursing instr. Villanova U., Villanova, Pa., 1988; asst. prof. Montgomery County C.C., Blue Bell, Pa., 1983-93, assoc. prof, 1993—; advisor Student Nurses Assn. Pa. Recipient Pi Tau Delta scholarship, Chapel of Four Chaplains. Mem. ANA, Nat. League for Nursing, Pa. League for Nursing, Jewish Hosp. Alumni Assn., Temple U. Alumni Assn., Villanova U. Alumni Assn., Sigma Theta Tau.

MILLER, LINDA B., political scientist; b. Manchester, N.H., Aug. 7, 1937; d. Louis and Helene (Chase) M. A.B. cum laude, Radcliffe Coll., 1959; M.A., Columbia U., 1961, Ph.D., 1965. Asst. prof. Barnard Coll., 1964-67; research asso. Princeton U., 1966-67; research asso. Harvard U., 1967-71, 76-81, lectr. polit. sci., 1968-69; assoc. prof. Wellesley (Mass.) Coll., 1969-75, prof. polit. sci., 1975—, chmn. dept., 1985-89; vis. prof. rsch. Watson Inst., Brown U., 1997. Author: World Order and Local Disorder: The United Nations and Internal Conflicts, 1967, Dynamics of World Politics: Studies in the Resolution of Conflicts, 1968, Cyprus: The Law and Politics of Civil Strife, 1968; co-author, co-editor: Ideas and Ideals: Essays on Politics in Honor of Stanley Hoffmann, 1993; also articles and monographs. Internat. Affairs fellow Coun. Fng. Rels., 1973-74, Rockefeller Found. fellow, 1976-77, Oceanographic Instn. sr. fellow, 1979-80, 82-83, NATO social sci. rsch. fellow, 1982-83. Mem. Inst. Strategic Studies, Internat. Studies Assn., Coun. Fgn. Rels., Phi Beta Kappa. Home: PO Box 415 South Wellfleet MA 02663-0415 Office: Wellesley Coll Dept Polit Sci Wellesley MA 02181

MILLER, LINDA J., healthcare consultant; b. Orange County, Ind., July 12, 1942; d. John E. and Geraldine B. (Turner) M. BA, Anderson U., 1964; MSSW, U. Louisville, 1967; Cert. in Health Adminstrn., U. Calif., 1972. Dir. family care Ind. Dept. Mental Health, Madison, 1964-69; dir. patient svcs. Meml. Med. Ctr., Long Beach, Calif., 1969-74; v.p., corp. svcs. Mem. Med. Ctr., Long Beach, 1979-83; CEO Community Hosp., Anderson, Ind., 1974-79; cons. First Cons. Group, Long Beach, 1983-86, v.p., mgmt. cons., 1986-89; chief op. officer First Cons. Group, Indpls., 1989-93; healthcare cons. Anderson, 1993—; active numerous healthcare bds., task forces and coms.; lectr. and presenter in field. Mem. Am. Coll. Healthcare Execs., Healthcare Fin. Mgmt. Assn., Am. Hosp. Assn. Home: 1015 Layton Rd Anderson IN 46011-1526

MILLER, LLOYD DANIEL, real estate agent; b. Savannah, Mo., May 25, 1916; s. Daniel Edward and Minnie (Wiedmer) M.; m. Mabel Gertrude Kurz, June 9, 1939; children: Sharon Miller Schumacher, Donna Miller Bodinson, Rosemary Rae Miller, Jeffrey Lloyd. B.S. in Agrl. Journalism, U. Mo., 1941. Reporter, feature writer, photographer, market editor Corn Belt Farm Dailies, Chgo., Kansas City, Mo., 1941-43; asst. agrl. editor U. Mo., 1946; dir. pub. relations Am. Angus Assn., Chgo., 1946-67, St. Joseph, Mo., 1967; asst. sec., dir. pub. relations Am. Angus Assn., 1968, exec. sec., 1968-78, sr. cons., 1978-81; realtor The Prudential Summers Realtors, 1978—; mem. U.S. Agrl. Tech. Adv. Com. on Livestock and Livestock Products for Trade Negotiations, 1975-79. Bd. dirs. Mo. Western State Coll. Found., 1976-82, pres., 1978-79; deacon Wyatt Park Bapt. Ch.; chmn. Heartland Ctr., Heartland Hosp. West, 1987-89, bd. dirs. 1987-95. With AUS, 1943-45. Recipient Silver Anvil award Pub. Relations Soc. Am., 1962, Faculty-Alumni award U. Mo.-Columbia, 1975. Mem. Nat. Assn. Realtors, St. Joseph Area C. of C. (pres. 1969, dir., chmn. agri-bus. coun. 1971), St. Joseph Regional Bd. Realtors (pres. 1986), Realtors Land Inst. (v.p. Mo. chpt. 1987-90), Am. Angus Heritage Found., Masons (32 deg.), Shriners, Kiwanis, Sigma Delta Chi. Home: 3208 Miller Rd Saint Joseph MO 64505-1532 Office: 1007 E Saint Maartens Dr Saint Joseph MO 64506-2993

MILLER, LORRAINE, business owner. BA in History, U. Utah. Lab. technician U. Utah Med. Ctr., 1972-75; pres. Cactus & Tropicals, Inc., Salt Lake City, 1975—; mem. adv. bd. Utah Securities Commn., 1994; panelist Am. Arbitration Assn., 1991; pres., bd. dirs. Phoenix Inst., 1986-87. Vol. VISTA, 1966-69; mem. Gov.'s Task Force Entrepreneurism, 1988, Gov.'s Task Force Work Force Devel., 1994; mentor Women's Network Entrepreneurial Tng., Small Bus. Adminstrn., 1990; mem. adv. bd. Utah Dem. Health Care Task Force, 1991, Women's Bus. Devel. Office State of Utah, 1990-92; employer Supportive Employment for the Handicapped, 1990-92. Recipient Pathfinder award Salt Lake C. of C., 1986, Women of Achievement award YWCA, 1992; named Nat. Small Bus. Person of Yr. by U.S. Small Bus. Adminstrn., 1994. Mem. Nat. Assn. Women's Bus. Owners (pres. Salt Lake chpt. 1992), Utah Assn. Women's Bus. Owners (pres. 1992, 1st v.p. 1991, bd. dirs. 1985, 89-90, named Woman Bus. Owner of Yr. 1987), Wasatch Cactus & Succulent Soc. (co-founder). Office: Cactus & Tropicals of Utah 2735 S 20th St E Salt Lake City UT 84109

MILLER, LOUIS H., lawyer; b. Lampeter, U.K., Apr. 22, 1945; m. Diane Matuszewski, Dec. 31, 1973; children: Margaret, Anthony. BA in History, Rutgers Coll., 1967; JD, Temple U., 1970. Bar: N.J. 1970, U.S. Dist. Ct. N.J. 1970, U.S. Supreme Ct. 1996. Law clk. to Judge Thomas Beetel Hunterdon County Ct., Flemington, N.J., 1970-71; law clk. to Judge Baruch Seidman Superior Ct. N.J. Chancery, Trenton, N.J., 1971-72; assoc. Jefferson, Jefferson & Vaida, Flemington, 1972-75; ptnr. Vaida & Miller, Flemington, 1975-78; pvt. practice Flemington, 1978-81, 88—; judge Superior Ct. N.J., Flemington, 1981-88; of counsel Levinson Axelrod Wheaton & Grayzel, Flemington, 1990-97; spl. dep. atty. gen. N.J. Hunterdon County Prosecutor Office, Flemington, 1972-73; condemnation commr. Appt. Superior Ct. N.J., Flemington, 1988—, assembly spkrs. commr.; commr. N.J. State Commn. Investigation, Trenton, 1993—; arbitrator U.S. Fed. Dist. Ct. N.J., 1989—. Twp. committeeman Alexandria Twp. Com., R.D. Milford, N.J., 1978-81. Mem. Am. Judges Assn., Am. Judicature Soc., N.J. State Bar Assn. (mem. dist. ethics com. 1980-81), Hunterdon County Bar Assn., Warren County Bar Assn., Consular Law Soc., Welsh Am. Geneal. Soc. Republican. Avocations: paleontology, traveling, hiking. Office: PO Box 850 40 Main St Flemington NJ 08822

MILLER, LOUIS HOWARD, biologist, researcher; b. Balt., Feb. 4, 1935; s. David and Daisy (Arenson) M.; m. Nancy Jo Harned, Sept. 26, 1959; 1 child, Jennifer. BS, Haverford Coll., 1956; MD, Washington U., St. Louis, 1960; MS in Parasitology, Columbia U., 1964. Asst. prof. then assoc. prof. Coll. of P & S, Columbia U., N.Y.C., 1967-71; head malaria sect. NIAID, NIH, Bethesda, Md., 1971-92, chief lab. parasitic diseases, 1992—. Contbr. articles to profl. jours. Capt. U.S. Army, 1965-67. Recipient Paul Ehrlich/Ludwig Darmstaedter prize, 1989, Bristol-Myers Squibb award for disting. achievement in infectious disease rsch., 1996. Fellow Royal Soc. Tropical Med. Hygiene, Queensland Inst. Med. Rsch., ACP; mem. Am. Soc. Tropical Medicine & Hygiene (pres. 1988), NAS, Inst. of Medicine, Assn. Am. Physicians. Office: NIH Building 4 Rm 126 Bethesda MD 20892

MILLER, LOUIS RICE, lawyer; b. Frankfort, Ind., Feb. 28, 1914; s. Louis A. and Josephine (Rice) M.; m. Jean Preston Russell, Feb. 1, 1941; 1 child, Mary Melissa. A.B., U. Chgo., 1935, J.D., 1937. Bar: Ill. 1938. Assoc. Gardner, Carton & Douglas, Chgo., 1937-40; atty. Armour & Co., Chgo., 1940-71, Phoenix, 1971-79; v.p., chief legal officer Armour & Co., (acquired by Greyhound Corp. 1970), 1967-79; v.p., gen. counsel Greyhound Corp. (now The Viad Corp.), Phoenix, 1972-79. Served with AUS, 1941; Served with USNR, 1942-45. Mem. ABA, Assn. Gen. Counsel. Club: Paradise Valley Country (Phoenix). Home: 7541 N Shadow Mountain Rd Paradise Valley AZ 85253-3311 Office: Dial Corp Phoenix AZ 85077-2212

MILLER, LOWELL DONALD, pharmaceutical company research executive; b. Chgo., Jan. 20, 1933; s. Nick William and Otillie M.; m. Marian N. Couranz, Aug. 22, 1959; children—Lowell Donald, Jeanette L. B.S., U. Mo., 1957, M.S. in Biochemistry, 1958, Ph.D. in Biochemistry, 1960. Dir. biol. sci. Neisler Labs., Decatur, Ill., 1960-69; assoc. dir. biomed. sci. Warren-Teed, Columbus, Ohio, 1969-71; pres. Lab. Exptl. Biology, St. Louis, 1971-73; sci. dir. Marion Labs., Kansas City, Mo., 1973-78, corp. v.p. research and devel., 1978-87, sr. v.p. research and devel., 1987-89; cons., 1989—; bd. dirs. Air Methods. Contbr. numerous articles to profl. jours. Bd. dirs. Kansas City Eye Bank, 1981-90. Served with U.S. Army, 1953-55. Fellow Am. Inst. Chemists; mem. Soc. Toxicology, Am. Soc. Clin. Chemists, Am. Chem. Soc.

MILLER, LOYE WHEAT, JR., journalist, corporate communications specialist; b. Knoxville, Tenn., Mar. 20, 1930; s. Loye Wheat and Sara Vance (Davis) M.; children: Lissa Wethey, Loye Wheat. AB, Dartmouth Coll., 1951; MS in Journalism, Columbia U., 1952. Mem. staff Charlotte (N.C.) observer, 1955-59, asst. city editor, 1959; corr. Washington bur. Time mag., 1959-64, 69-70; chief Midwest news bur. Time-Life mags., 1964-69; corr. Washington bur. Knight-Ridder Newspapers, 1970-77; chief Washington bur. Chgo. Sun-Times, 1977-78; corr. Washington Bur. Gannett Newspapers, 1978-79; chief polit. writer Newhouse Newspapers, 1979-85; dir. pub. affairs U.S. Dept. Edn., Washington, 1985-88, U.S. Dept. Justice, Washington, 1988-89; dir. pub. info. Northrop Corp., Arlington, Va., 1989-94. Lt. (j.g.) USNR, 1952-55. Home: 1672D Beekman Pl NW Washington DC 20009-6542

MILLER, LYNNE MARIE, critical care nurse, administrator; b. Chgo., Apr. 7, 1947; d. Michael John and Helen (Eckardt) Patzek; m. Harry James Miller, Aug. 10, 1968; children: Gretchen Hope, Gary Rutherford. Diploma, Abington (Pa.) Meml. Hosp., 1968; BS, Phila. Coll. Textile and Sci.; MSN, Gwynedd Mercy Coll. Pediatric staff nurse Fitzgerald Mercy Hosp., Darby, Pa., 1968-69; vis. nurse Community Nursing Svc., Lansdowne, Pa., 1969-72; staff critical care nurse ICU Doylestown (Pa.) Hosp., 1972-80, night supr., 1980-86, nurse mgr. med./surg., telemetry, ventilator care and cardiac rehab., 1986-90, clin. system mgr., 1990-93, dir. operating rm., 1993—; dir. Surg. Svcc. ICU course 7 yrs. Contbg. editor Springhouse Corp. Mem. AACN, AAORN, Am. Orgn. Nurse Execs. Pa. Orgn. Nurse Leaders, Southeastern Pa. Orgn. Nurse Leaders, East Pa. Assn. Post-Anesthesiology Nurses, Sigma Theta Tau-Iota Kappa (cert.). Office: Doylestown Hosp 595 W State St Doylestown PA 18901-2554

MILLER, MALCOLM HENRY, manufacturing sales executive, real estate developer; b. Elgin, Ill., Feb. 6, 1934; s. Carl Theodore and Alice Lucy (Garbisch) M. BA, U. Wis., 1957; postgrad., Am. Inst. Fgn. Trade, 1961, U. N.Mex., 1963. Sales engr. Fairbanks Morse Corp., Beloit, Wis., 1962; pvt. practice real estate Albuquerque, 1964-75; supt., v.p. Walworth Foundries, Inc., Darien, Wis., 1959-61, exec. v.p. sales, co-owner, 1975—; v.p. sales, co-owner Waukesha Specialty Co., Inc., Darien, 1975—; treas. Fastcast, Inc., Albuquerque, 1993—. Loan advisor, developer Community Assn. for Sr. Housing, Albuquerque, 1967-70; Rep. candidate for state senator N.Mex., 1970; active fin. com. Bernalillo County Reps., N.Mex., 1970-80, Walworth County Reps., Wis., 1976-77. Served to 1st lt. U.S. Army, 1957-59. Mem. Am. Foundrymen's Assn., Dairy Food Industries Supply Assn., Dairy Food Industries Supply Assn. (bd. dirs. 1992-95), Santa Fe Opera Guild, Big Foot Country Club, Nat. "W" Club, Masons, The Madison Club, Sigma Alpha Epsilon. Republican. Episcopalian. Avocations: health activities, cinema, opera. Home: 223 Fremont St PO Box 37 Walworth WI 53184 Office: Walworth Foundries Inc PO Box 160 Hwy 14 and Hwy 15 Interchange Darien WI 53114

MILLER, MALCOLM LEE, retired lawyer; b. Canton, Ohio, Jan. 4, 1923; s. Thomas Maxwell and Margaret (Unkefer) M.; m. Laura Washburn; children: Stephen Washburn, Ann Mayo. JD, Ohio State U., 1949. Bar: Ohio 1950. Assoc. Law Office of Paul R. Gingher, Columbus, Ohio, 1950-53; assoc. Gingher & Christensen, Columbus, 1953-58, ptnr., 1958-86; of counsel Baker & Hostetler, Columbus, 1986-87; asst. counsel legal dept. Columbus Mut. Life Ins. Co., 1987-89, Columbus Life Ins. Co., 1989-90. Bd. dirs. Columbus Area chpt. ARC, 1972-94. 2d lt. USAAF, 1943-45. Mem. Sigma Chi, Phi Delta Phi. Home: 1427 London Dr Columbus OH 43221-1543

MILLER, MARCIA E., federal government official; married; 1 son. BA, Miami U., Oxford, Ohio, 1977; MA, Johns Hopkins U., 1981. With internat. trade divsn. Am. Textile Mfrs. Inst.; internat. economist Wilmer, Cutler & Pickering, 1985-87; profl. staff mem. Senate Com. on Fin., 1987-93, chief internat. trade counsellor, 1993-95, minority chief internat. trade counsellor, 1995-96; chmn. U.S. Internat. Trade Commn., Washington, 1996—. Office: US Internat Trade Commn USITC Bldg 500 E St SW Washington DC 20024-2760*

MILLER, MARGARET ALISON, education association administrator; b. L.A., Dec. 17, 1944; d. Richard Crump and Virginia Margaret (Dudley) M.; m. Spencer Hall, Aug. 21, 1967 (div. 1977); 1 child, Justin Robinson; m. Alan Blair Howard, Oct. 7, 1990. BA, UCLA, 1966; postgrad., Stanford U., 1966-67; PhD, U. Va., 1971. English instr. U. Va., Charlottesville, 1971-72; prof. English U. Mass., North Dartmouth, 1972-86, co-dir. women's studies program, 1981-83, asst. to dean arts and scis., 1983-85, asst. to pres., 1985-86; acad. affairs coord. State Coun. Higher Edn. for Va., Richmond, 1986-87, assoc. dir. for acad. affairs, 1987-97; pres. Am. Assn. for Higher Edn., Washington, 1997—; cons. Coun. Rectors, Budapest, 1993, Minn. State U. System, Mpls., 1992, U.S. Dept. Edn., Washington, 1990-94, S.C. Higher Edn. Commn., 1989-90, Edn. Commn. States, Denver, 1994. Contbr. articles to profl. jours. Mem. Am. Assn. Higher Edn. (leadership coun.), Am. Coun. on Edn. (exec. com. identification program in Va. 1988—, participant nat. identification program's 41st nat. forum for women leaders in higher edn. 1989). Avocations: reading, gardening, travel. Home: 2176 Lindsay Rd Gordonsville VA 22942-1620 Office: Am Assn Higher Edn Ste 360 One Dupont Cir Washington DC 20036-1110

MILLER, MARGARET HAIGH, librarian; b. Ashton-under-Lyne, Lancashire, Eng., Feb. 26, 1915; came to U.S., 1915, naturalized, 1919; d. Errwood Augustus and Florence (Stockdale) Savage; m. Mervin Homer Miller, June 30, 1940; children: Nancy Elaine Reich, Edward Stockdale, Jane Elizabeth Miller-Dean. B.S. in Edn., Millersville U. (Pa.), 1937; M.S. in L.S., U. So. Calif., 1952; postgrad. in supervision Calif. State U.-Northridge, 1957-59. High sch. librarian Phoenixville Sch. Dist. (Pa.), 1937-40; jr. high sch. librarian Los Angeles Unified Sch. Dist., 1952-55, coordinating librarian, 1955-62, coll. head librarian, 1959-62, supr. library services, 1962-83; lectr. children's lit. U. So. Calif., Los Angeles, 1959-76, advisor Sch. Library and Info. Sci., 1980-83; resource person Nat. Council for Accreditation Tchr. Edn., Washington, 1976-85; cons. Pied Piper Prodns., Glendale, Calif., 1978—, David Sonnenshein Assocs., Los Angeles, 1983-85, Baker & Taylor Co., Inc., N.Y.C., 1979-83, H.W. Wilson Co., N.Y.C., 1975—, Mook & Blanchard, La Puente, Calif., 1985—, Enslow Pub., Inc., Hillside, N.J, 1986—. Mem. Los Angeles area planning com. Library of Congress Yr. of the Young Reader, 1989. Editor: Book List for Elementary School Libraries, 1966; Books for Elementary School Libraries, 1969; Children's Catalog, 13th edit., 1976; Multicultural Experiences in Children's Literature, Grades K-6, 1978; Periodicals for School Libraries, Grades K-12, 1977; Multicultural Experiences in Literature for Young People, Grades 7-12, 1979; Baker & Taylor School Selection Guide, K-12, 1980, 81, 82, 83; Supplement to Multicultural Experiences in Children's Literature, 1982; Special Books for Special People: A Bibliography about the Handicapped, 1982. Bibliographer: Concepts in Science, Levels 1 through 6 students' edits. (P. Brandwein et al), 1972; Concepts in Science Teacher's Education, 1972. Columnist, book reviewer Los Angeles Times, various jours. Recipient Dorothy McKenzie award for disting. contbn. outstanding svc. in field of children's literature. Mem. Los Angeles Sch. Library Assn. (cons. 1952—), Calif. Assn. Sch. Librarians (pres. So. sect. 1971-72, state pres. 1975-76, many coms. 1952-77), Calif. Media and Library Educators Assn. (various coms. 1977-95), ALA (many coms.), Young Adult Svcs., Am. Assn. Sch. Librarians, Assn. Library Service to Children, Friends Children and Lit. (dir. 1979—, pres. 1987-88), So. Calif. Council on Lit. for Children and Young People (dir. 1961—, pres. 1973-74, 1st v.p. 1986, 3d v.p. 1987-88, awards chair 1989, 90, 91), Calif. Sch. Library Assn., Young Adult Reviewers Booklist Com. (sec. 1995), Assn. Adminstrs. Los Angeles Unified Sch. Dist., Women's Nat. Book Assn (Los Angeles chpt.), Beta Phi Mu (dir. 1977-79, 84-86, pres. 1979-80, Calif. Readers bd. dirs. 1996—), Pi Lambda Theta (chpt. pres. 1964-66, 91-92), Delta Kappa Gamma (chpt. sec. 1962-64), Phi Delta Kappa (contest essay judge). Republican. Home: 4321 Matilija Ave Sherman Oaks CA 91423-3659

MILLER, MARGARET JOANNE, pediatrics nurse; b. Rolette, N.D., Apr. 12, 1939; d. William J. and Nora (Slaubaugh) Graber; m. Ervin S. Miller, June 16, 1962; children: Charlene, Angela, Lisa. ASN, Vincennes U., 1960; student, St. Mary's-of-the-Woods Coll., Terre Haute, Ind., 1986-87, Ind. U., South Bend, 1989, Regents Coll., 1995-96. RN, Ind., Tex. Head nurse St. Joseph Mem. Hosp., Kokomo, Ind., 1975-77; asst. dir. Mennonite Mutul Aid, 1982-84; staff nurse Meml. Hosp., South Bend, Ind., 1984-87, asst. head nurse, 1987-89, asst. unit dir., 1989-91; unit dir. for pediatrics, adult medical unit Med. Ctr. Hosp., Odessa, Tex., 1992—. Mem. Soc Pediatric Nurses. Home: 3411 Rocky Lane Rd Odessa TX 79762-5046

MILLER, MARGERY SILBERMAN, psychologist, speech and language pathologist, higher education adminstrator; b. Roslyn, N.Y., May 7, 1951; d. Bernard and Charlotte (Schatzberg) Silberman; m. Donald F. Moores; children—Kip Lee, Tige Justice. Lic. speech pathologist, N.Y., Md.; cert. tchr. nursery-6th grades, spl. edn., N.Y., advanced profl. tchr. speech and hearing, Md.; cert. sch. psychologist, Md. B.A., Elmira Coll., 1971; M.A., NYU, 1972; Ed.S., M.S., SUNY-Albany, 1975; M.A. Towson State U., 1987, Ph.D Georgetown U., 1991. Speech and lang. pathologist Mental Retardation Inst., Flower and Fifth Ave. Hosp., N.Y.C., 1971-72; community speech/lang. pathologist N.Y. State Dept. Mental Hygiene, Troy, dir. speech and hearing services, 1972-74; instr. communication disorders dept. Coll. of St. Rose, Albany, N.Y., 1975-77; clin. supr. U. Md., College Park, 1978; speech/lang. pathologist Md. Sch. for Deaf, Frederick, 1978-84; auditory devel. specialist Montgomery County Pub. Schs., Rockville, Md., 1984-87; coordinator Family Life program Nat. Acad. Gallaudet U., Washington, 1987-88, interim dir., 1988-89, dir. Counseling & Devel. Ctr. N.W. Campus, 1989-93; assoc. prof. psychology Gallaudet U., 1993—; instr. sign lang. program Frederick Community Coll.; dance instr. for deaf adolescents; diagnostic cons. on speech pathology; mem. editorial rev. com. Gov.'s Devel. Disabilities Council of Md., 1984; presenter at confs. Author: It's O.K. To Be Angry, 1976; contbr. chpt. to Cognition, Education, and Deafness: Directions for Research and Instruction, 1985; contbr. articles to profl. jours. Vol., choreographer Miss Deaf Am. Pageant, 1984. Office of Edn. Children's Bur. fellow, 1971. Mem. Am. Speech, Lang. and Hearing Assn. (cert. clin. competence in speech/lang. pathology), Md. Speech, Lang. and Hearing Assn., D.C. Speech, Lang. and Hearing Assn., Nat. Assn. of Deaf, Nat. Assn. Sch. Psychologists, Am. Psychol. Assn. Jewish. Home: 9807 Meriden Rd Potomac MD 20854-4311 Office: Gallaudet U 800 Florida Ave NE Washington DC 20002-3660

MILLER, MARILYN LEA, library science educator. AA, Graceland Coll., 1950; BS in English, U. Kans., 1952; AMLS, U. Mich., 1959, PhD of Librarianship and Higher Edn., 1976. Bldg.-level sch. libr. Wellsville (Kans.) High Sch., 1952-54; tchr.-libr. Arthur Capper Jr. High Sch., Topeka, Kans., 1954-56; head libr. Topeka High Sch., 1956-62; sch. libr. cons. State of Kans. Dept. of Pub. Instrn., 1962-67; from asst. to assoc. prof. Sch. Librarianship Western Mich. U., Kalamazoo, 1967-77; assoc. prof. libr. sci. U. N.C., Chapel Hill, 1977-87; prof., chair dept. libr. and info. studies U. N.C., Greensboro, 1987-95, prof. emeritus, 1996—; vis. faculty Kans. State Tchrs., Emporia, 1960, 63, 64, 66, U. Minn., Mpls., 1971, U. Manitoba, Winnipeg, Can., 1971; vis. prof. Appalachian State U., Boone, N.C., 1987; mem. adv. bd. sch. libr. media program Nat. Ctr. for Ednl. Stats., 1989, mem. user rev. panel, 1990; chair assoc. dean search com. Sch. Edn., 1988, coord. Piedmont young writers conf., 1989-94, chair race and gender com., 1990-93, SACS planning and evaluation com., 1990, 91, learning resources ctr. adv. com., 1991-93; hearing panel for honor code U. N.C. Greensboro, 1988-91, assn. women faculty and administrv. staff, 1987—, faculty coun., 1987—, univ. libr. com., 1987-88, com. faculty devel. in race and gender scholarship, 1990-92; lectr. and cons. numerous confs., seminars in field. Mem. editorial bd. The Emergency Librarian, 1981—, Collection Building: Studies in the Development and Effective Use of Library Resources, 1978—; contbr. numerous chpts. to books, and articles to profl. jours., procs. and revs. Selected as one of four children's libr. specialists to visit Russian sch. and pub. librs., book pubs., Moscow, Leningrad, Tashkent, 1979; hon. del. White House Conf. on Libr. and Info. Svcs., Washington, 1991; head del. Romanian Summer Inst. on Librarianship in U.S., 1991; citizen amb. People to People Internat. Program, People's Republic of China, 1992, Russian and Poland, 1992, Russia, 1994, Barcelona, 1995. Recipient Freedom Found. medal, 1962, Disting. Svc. to Sch. Librs. award Kans. Assn. Sch. Librs., 1982, Disting. Svc. award Graceland Coll., 1992, Disting. Alumnus award Sch. Libr. and Info. Studies, U. Mich., 1988; Delta Kappa Gamma scholar, 1972. Mem. ALA (chair rsch. com., exec. dir. 1994, pres. 1992-93, adv. com. Nat. Ctr. Ednl. Stats. 1984, standing com. libr. edn. 1987-91, chair 1989-90, chair Chgo. conf. resolutions 1972, awards com. 1971-72, chair 1973-75, resolutions com. 1976-78, yearbook adv. com. 1988-90, Disting. Svc. award Am. Assn. Sch. Librs. 1993, other coms.), Am. Assn. Sch. Librs. (nominating com. 1980, pub. com. 1981-82, v.p.-pres.-elect 1985-86, chair search com. exec. dir. 1985, pres. 1986-87, coord. coms. nat. stds. vision and implementation 1995—), Assn. for Ednl. Comms. and Tech., Assn. of Libr. Svc. to Children (bd. dirs. 1976-81, pres. 1979-80, rsch. com. 1982-85, chair 1984-85, chair nominating com. 1984, other coms.), N.C. Libr. Assn. (edn. libr. com. 1978-80, 82-86, exec. bd. status of women roundtable 1989—, chmn.-elect 1995-97), N.C. Assn. Sch. Librs., Southeastern Libr. Assn. (chair libr. educators sect. 1990-92), So. Assn. of Colls. and Schs. (mem. accreditation team 1988).

MILLER, MARK KARL, journalist; b. Meadville, Pa., Aug. 5, 1953; s. Richard Karl and Ellener Louise (Zimber) M. BA in Comms. and Journalism, Shippensburg U. of Pa., 1975. Editl. asst. Broadcasting mag., Washington, 1975, staff writer, 1976-77, asst. editor, 1977-80, sr. news editor, 1980-87, asst. mng. editor, 1987-91; mng. editor Broadcasting & Cable mag., Washington, 1991—; mem. editl. adv. bd. Shippensburg U. of Pa., 1989-94, mem. profl. adv. bd. comm./journalism dept., 1994-96. Recipient Outstanding Alumnus award Shippensburg U., 1992. Mem. Soc. Profl. Journalists, Art Deco Soc. of Washington (bd. dirs., publs. chair 1986—), Nat. Press Club. Home: 2425 Valley Way Cheverly MD 20785 Office: Broadcasting & Cable 1705 Desales St NW Washington DC 20036

MILLER, MARSHALL LEE, lawyer; b. Chattanooga, Tenn., Oct. 18, 1942. BA, Harvard U., 1964; student, Oxford U., Eng., Heidelberg U., Germany; JD, Yale U., 1970. Bar: D.C. 1971, U.S. Supreme Ct. 1979. Spl. asst. to adminstr. U.S. EPA, 1971-73; assoc. dep. atty. gen. U.S. Dept. Justice, 1973-74; asst. sec. labor (acctg.), dep. adminstr. OSHA, 1975-76; ptnr. Baise & Miller, Washington. Bd. editors: Yale Law Jour.; Soviet Mil. editor: Armed Forces Jour., 1983-87; author books internat. and environ. topics. Bd. dirs. Bulgarian-Am. Enterprise Fund, Electronic Warfare Assocs., Am. Coun. of Internat. Living, Am. Assn. Advancement Sci. Office: Baise & Miller 815 Connecticut Ave NW Ste 620 Washington DC 20006-4004

MILLER, MARVIN EDWARD, building materials company executive; b. Far Rockaway, N.Y., Jan. 28, 1929; s. Philip J. and Dorothy B. (Verby) M.; m. Beverly Kolikof, June 7, 1953; children: Lisa, Deborah, James. BS, Ind. U., 1949; MS, Columbia U., 1950. Salesman M. Verby Co., Jamaica, N.Y., 1953-56; pres. Miller Supply Corp., White Plains, N.Y., 1956-74, chmn. bd., 1975—; pres. Grip-Rite Ltd., Hong Kong, 1979—; chmn., co-chief exec. officer PrimeSource, Inc., 1990—. Bd. dirs., v.p. Westchester Jewish Community Svcs., Hartsdale, N.Y., 1985. With AUS, 1951-53. Mem. Masons, Shriners. Republican. Avocation: tennis. Home: 17153 Ericarose Ct Boca Raton FL 33496-5939 Office: PrimeSource Inc 1800 John Connally Dr Carrollton TX 75006-5403

MILLER, MARY HELEN, retired public administrator; b. Smiths Grove, Ky., June 30, 1936; d. Walter Frank and Lottie Belle (Russell) Huddleston; m. George Ward Wilson, Sept. 12, 1958 (div. Sept. 1973); children: Ward Glenn, Amy Elizabeth Huddleston; m. Francis Guion Miller Jr., June 6, 1981. BA, Western Ky. U., 1958. Tchr. Fayette County Schs., Lexington, Ky., 1958-60, Seneca High Sch., Louisville, 1960-63, Shelby County High Sch., Shelbyville, Ky., 1963-69; rsch. analyst Legis. Rsch. Com., Frankfort, Ky., 1973-79, asst. dir., 1979-83, 90-91; chief exec. asst. Office Gov., Frankfort, 1983-87, 93-95, legis. liaison, 1991-93; cabinet sec. Natural Resources and Environ. Protection Cabinet, Frankfort, 1987-88; sales assoc. W. Wagner, Jr. Comml. Real Estate, Louisville, 1989-91; ret., 1996. Author: (constl. revision) Citizens Guide To/Perspective, 1978, (booklet) A Look at Kentucky General Assembly, 1979, A Guide to Education Reform, 1990, (handbook) Gubernatorial Transition in Kentucky, 1991. Active Leadership Ky. Alumni, Frankfort, 1986, Waterfront Devel. Corp. Bd., Louisville, 1986-87, Greater Louis Partnership Econ. Devel., 1988-92, Shelbyville 2000 Found. Bd., 1991-92; mem., sec. Regional Airport Authorty Bd., Louisville, 1986-89; pres. Shelby County Cmty. Theatre Bd., Shelbyville, 1989-90; active Ky. Long Term Policy Bd., 1992—, chair, 1995; active Ky. Hist. Properties Commn., 1995—; chair Shelby County Cmty. Found., 1995; active Ky. Applachian Commn., 1995-96. Mem. Pendennis Club. Democrat. Episcopalian. Avocations: reading, theatre, gardening, antiques. Home: 1116 Main St Shelbyville KY 40065-1420

MILLER, MARY HOTCHKISS, lay worker; b. Washington, Dec. 4, 1936; d. Neil and Esther LeMoyne (Helfer) H.; m. Ronald Homer Miller, May 20, 1961; 1 child, Timothy Ronald. BA, Western Md. Coll., 1958; MRE, Union Theol. Sem, 1960; Cert., Windham House, N.Y.C., 1960. Dir. Christian Edn. Bruton Parish ch., Williamsburg, Va., 1960-61; dir. Christian Edn. (part-time) All Saints Episcopal Ch., Bklyn., 1961-62; adminstrv. and program asst., Christian Social Rels. Dept., Exec. Coun. Episcopal Ch. U.S.A. Episcopal Ch. Ctr., N.Y.C., 1967-72; nat. treas., chmn. Episcopal Peace Fellowship, Washington, N.Y.C., 1972-85; exec. sec. Episcopal Peace Fellowship, Washington, 1989—; bd. dirs., exec. com. Nat. Campaign for Peace Tax Fund, Washington, 1989—; bd. dirs., consultative coun. Nat. Interreligious Svc. Bd. for COs, Washington, 1989—. Contbr. articles to Witness mag. and jours., newsletters in field; editl. bd. ISSUES of Gen. Convs. of the Episcopal Ch., 1973-91; designer ch. vestments and banners. Democrat. Office: PO Box 28156 Washington DC 20038-8156

MILLER, MARY JEANNETTE, office management specialist; b. Washington, Sept. 24, 1912; d. John William and David Evengeline (Hill) Sims; m. Cecil Miller, June 17, 1934 (dec.); children: Sylvenia Delores Doby, Ferdi A., Cecil Jr. (dec.). Student, Howard U., 1929-30, U. Ill., 1940-42, Dept. Agr. Grad. Sch., 1957-59, U. Md., 1975; cert. in Vocat. Photography, Prince George's C.C., 1986. Chief mail processing unit Bur. Reclamation, Washington, 1940-57; records supr. AID, Manila, Korea, Mali, Guyana, Dominican Republic, Indonesia, Laos, 1957-71; office engr. Bechtel Assocs., Washington, 1976-79; real estate assoc; tchr. English as 2d lang. Ministry of Edn., Seoul, Korea, 1960-61, Ministry of Fin., Laos, 1968-70; cons. to Ministry of Fin. Royal Lao Govt., 1971-74; cons. AID missions to Yemen, Sudan, Somalia, 1982; records mgmt. cons. AID, Monrovia, Liberia, 1980-81, Sri Lanka, 1984; docent Mus. African Art Smithsonian Inst., Washington, 1986-89; circulation asst. Prince George County Meml. Libr. System, Hyattsville, Md., 1987-91, ret.; mem. Friends of Internat. Edn. Com., 1985-92; sec./treas., bd. dirs. Miller Transitional, Inc.Author handbooks on office mgmt. Mem. AARP, NAFE, Mayor's Internat. Adv. Coun. Mem. Soc. Am. Archivists, Am. Mgmt. Assn., Montgomery County Bd. Realtors, Am. Fgn. Svc. Assn., Nat. Trust Hist. Preservation, Assn. Am. Fgn. Svc. Women's Writer Group, Consumer Mail Panel, Zeta Phi Beta. Roman Catholic. Home: 14200 Pimberton Dr Hudson FL 34667-8542

MILLER, MARY LOIS, retired nurse midwife; b. Altoona, Pa., Feb. 21, 1933; d. Isaac Emory and Lucinda Jane (Brumbaugh) Miller. Diploma, West Suburban Hosp. Sch., 1953; BSN, Wheaton (Ill.) Coll., 1955; MRE, Grace Theol. Sem., 1957; nurse midwife, Frontier Nursing Svc., 1959. Cert. nurse midwife. Nurse obstetrics Delnor Hosp., St. Charles, Ill., 1953-55; head nurse McDonald Hosp., Warsaw, Ind., 1955-57; med. missionary Fgn. Missionary Soc. Grace Brethren Ch., Winona Lake, Ind., 1959-79; cert. nurse midwife Lewistown (Pa.) Hosp., 1979-97; ret., 1997. Mem. APHA, Am. Coll. Nurse Midwives (sec.), Nat. Perinatal Assn., Pa. Perinatal Assn., Nat. Assn. Childbearing Ctrs. Home: 46 Taylor Dr Reedsville PA 17084

MILLER, MAURICE JAMES, lawyer; b. Barron, Wis., May 14, 1926; s. James Martin and Fern (Harvey) M.; m. Marguerite Joyce Mielke, Nov. 1, 1952; children: Maureen J., Mark J. B.B.A., U. Wis., 1951, J.D., 1955. Bar: Ill., Wis. 1955, .; C.P.A., Wis. Assoc. Sidley & Austin, Chgo., 1955-62, ptnr., 1963-90, counsel, 1991—. Trustee William H. Miner Found., 1994—. With U.S. Army, 1944-46. Mem. ABA, Chgo. Bar Assn., Phi Alpha Delta. Republican. Methodist. Clubs: Chicago, Mid-Day. Home: 925 Brand Ln Deerfield IL 60015-3403 Office: Sidley & Austin 1 First Natl Plz Chicago IL 60603-2003

MILLER, MAVIS MOSS, school administrator, social worker; b. Irwin County, Ga., June 4, 1953; d. Jimmie Lee and Ruthie Mae (Stepherson) Moss; children: Denitra Michell, LaTravia Lemar, Samantha Levette. BS, Albany State Coll., 1975; MEd, Ga. State U., 1980, M in Adminstrn., 1996. Cert. tchr., Ga. Tchr. Irwin County Bd. Edn., Ocilla, Ga., 1975-91, coord. drug edn., 1991—; coord. Youth Alliance Project, Ocilla, 1991—; chair Ocilla Drug Adv. Bd., 1991—, Irwin County Action Team, Ocilla, 1992—; evaluator Ga. Tchr. Evaluation Instrument; implementer Good Touch Bad Touch. Former Adult leader Ocilla area Boy Scouts Am.; mem. Irwin County Arts Coun., Ocilla Civic Club; chair com. Community Svc. Ctr. Named Tchr. of Yr. 1983-84. Mem. NEA, Ga. Edn. Assn., Ga. Assn. Educators (pres.), Irwin County Child Abuse Coun., Irwin County Heart Assn., Troubled Children Com., Delta Sigma Theta. Democrat. Baptist. Avocation: reading. Office: Irwin County Bd Edn 210 Apple St Ocilla GA 31774

MILLER, MAX DUNHAM, JR., lawyer; b. Des Moines, Oct. 17, 1946; s. Max Dunham and Beulah (Head) M.; m. Melissa Ann Dart, Jan. 10, 1969 (div. July 1975); 1 child, Ann Marie Victoria; m. Caroline Jean Armendt, Sept. 19, 1981; children: Alexander Bradshaw, Benjamin Everrett. BS with high honors, Mich. State U., 1968; postgrad., George Washington U., 1970-71; JD, U. Md., 1975. Bar: Md. 1976, U.S. Dist. Ct. Md. 1976, U.S. Ct. Appeals (4th cir.) 1981, U.S. Supreme Ct. 1982. Engr. U.S. Dept. of Def., Aberdeen Proving Ground, Md., 1968-72; law clk. to presiding judge Md.

Cir. Ct., Higinbothom in Bel Air, Md., 1975-76; asst. county atty. Harford County, Bel Air, 1976-79; assoc. Lentz & Hooper P.A., Balt., 1979-81; ptnr. Miller, Olszewski & Moore, P.A., Bel Air, 1981-94; prin. Law Offices of Max D. Miller, P.A., 1994—; county atty. Harford County, Md., 1983-88. Mem. Md. Bar Assn., Assn. Trial Lawyers Am., Md. Trial Lawyers Assn., Harford County Bar Assn., Phi Kappa Phi, Phi Eta Sigma. Avocations: carpentry, sailing, canoeing, bicycling, ice and roller hockey. Home: 308 Whetstone Rd Forest Hill MD 21050-1332 Office: Law Office Max D Miller PA 5 S Hickory Ave Bel Air MD 21014-3732

MILLER, MAYNARD MALCOLM, geologist, educator, research institute director, explorer, state legislator; b. Seattle, Jan. 23, 1921; s. Joseph Anthony and Juanita Queena (Davison) M.; m. Joan Walsh, Sept. 15, 1951; children: Ross McCord, Lance Davison. BS magna cum laude, Harvard U., 1943; MA, Columbia U., 1948; PhD (Fulbright scholar), St. John's Coll., Cambridge U., Eng., 1957; student, Naval War Coll., Air War Coll., Oak Ridge Inst. Nuclear Sci.; D of Sci. (hon.), U. Alaska, 1990. Registered profl. geologist, Idaho. Asst. prof. naval sci. Princeton (N.J.) U., 1946; geologist Gulf Oil Co., Cuba, 1947; rsch. assoc., coordinator, dir. Office Naval Rsch. project Am. Geog. Soc., N.Y.C., 1948-53; staff scientist Swiss Fed. Inst. for Snow and Avalanche Rsch., Davos, 1952-53; instr. dept. geography Cambridge U., 1953-54, 56; assoc. producer, field unit dir. film Seven Wonders of the World for Cinerama Corp., Europe, Asia, Africa, Middle East, 1954-55; rsch. assoc. Lamont Geol. Obs., N.Y.C., 1955-57; sr. scientist dept. geology Columbia U., N.Y.C., 1957-59; asst. prof. geology Mich. State U., East Lansing, 1959-61, assoc. prof., 1961-63; prof. Mich. State U., 1963-75; dean Coll. Mines and Earth Resources U. Idaho, Moscow, 1975-88, prof. geology, dir. Glaciological and Arctic Scis. Inst., 1975—; dir., state geologist Idaho Geol. Survey, 1975-88; elected rep. Legislature of State of Idaho, Boise, 1992—; prin. investigator, geol. cons. sci. contracts and projects for govt. agys., univs., pvt. corps., geographic socs., 1946—; geophys. cons. Nat. Park Svc., NASA, USAF, Nat. Acad. Sci.; organizer leader USAF-Harvard Mt. St. Elias Expdn., 1946; chief geologist Am. Mt. Everest Expdn., Nepal, 1963; dir. Nat. Geographic Soc. Alaskan Glacier Commemorative Project, 1964—; organizer field leader Nat. Geographic Soc. Joint U.S.-Can. Mt. Kennedy Yukon Meml. Mapping Expdn., 1965, Muséo Argentino de Ciencias Naturales, Patagonian expdn. and glacier study for Inst.. Geologico del Peru & Am. Geog. Soc., 1949-50, participant adv. missions People's Republic of China, 1981, 86, 88, geol. expdns. Himalaya, Nepal, 1963, 84, 87, USAF mission to Ellesmere Land and Polar Sea, 1951; organizer, ops. officer USN-LTA blimp geophysics flight to North Pole area for Office Naval Rsch., 58; prin. investigator U.S. Naval Oceanographic Office Rsch. Ice Island T-3 Polar Sea, 1967-68, 70-73; dir. lunar field sta. simulation program USAF-Boeing Co., 1959-60; co-prin. investigator Nat. Geographic Soc. 30 Yr. Remap of Lemon & Taku Glaciers, Juneau Icefield, 1989-92; exec. dir. Found. for Glacier and Environ. Rsch., Pacific Sci. Ctr., Seattle, 1955-95, chmn., 1992—, pres., 1955-85, trustee, 1960—, organizer, dir. Juneau (Alaska) Icefield Rsch. Program (JIRP), 1946—; cons. Dept. Hwys. State of Alaska, 1965; chmn., exec. dir. World Ctr. for Exploration Found., N.Y.C., 1968-71; dir., mem. adv. bd. Idaho Geol. Survey, 1975-88; chmn. nat. coun. JSHS program U.S. Army Rsch. Office and Acad. Applied Sci., 1982-89; sci. dir. U.S. Army Rsch. Office-Nat. Sci. and Humanities Symposia program, 1991—; disting. guest prof. China U. Geoscis., Wuhan, 1981-88, Changchun U. Earth Scis., People's Republic of China, 1988—; adj. prof. U. Alaska, 1986—. Author: Field Manual of Glaciological and Arctic Sciences; co-author books on Alaskan glaciers and Nepal geology; contbr. over 200 reports, sci. papers to profl. jours., ency. articles, chpts. to books, monographs; prodr., nat. lectr. films and videos. Past mem. nat. exploring com., nat. sea exploring com. Boy Scouts Am.; past mem. nat. adv. bd. Embry Riddle Aero. U.; bd. dirs. Idaho Rsch. Found.; pres. state divsn. Mich. UN Assn., 1970-73; mem. Centennial and Health Environ. Commns., Moscow, Idaho, 1987—. With USN, 1943-46, PTO. Decorated 11 campaign and battle stars; named Leader of Tomorrow Seattle C. of C. and Time mag., 1953, one of Ten Outstanding Young Men U.S. Jaycees, 1954; recipient commendation for lunar environ. study USAF, 1960, Hubbard medal (co-recipient with Mt. Everest expdn. team) Nat. Geog. Soc., 1963, Elisha Kent Kane Gold medal Geog. Soc. Phila., 1964, Karo award Soc. Mil. Engrs., 1966, Franklin L. Burr award Nat. Geog. Soc., 1967, Commendation Boy Scouts Am., 1970, Disting. Svc. commendation plaque UN Assn. U.S., Disting. Svc. commendation State of Mich. Legis., 1975, Outstanding Civilian Svc. medal U.S. Army Rsch. Office, 1977, Outstanding Leadership in Minerals Edn. commendations Idaho Mining Assn., 1985, 87, Nat. Disting. Tchg. award Assn. Am. Geographers, 1996; recipient numerous grants NSF, Nat. Geog. Soc., others, 1948—. Fellow Geol. Soc. Am., Arctic Inst. N.Am., Explorers Club; mem. councilor AAAS (Pacific divsn. 1978-88), AIME, Am. Geophys. Union, Internat. Glaciological Soc. (past councilor), ASME (hon. nat. lectr.), Assn. of Am. State Geologists (hon.), Am. Assn. Amateur Oarsmen (life), Am. Alpine Club (past councilor, life mem.), Alpine Club (London), Appalachian Club (hon. corr.), Brit. Mountaineering Assn. (hon., past v.p.), The Mountaineers (hon.), Cambridge U. Mountaineering Club (hon.), Himalyan Club (Calcutta), English Speaking Union (nat. lectr.), Naval Res. Assn. (life), Dutch Treat Club, Circumnavigators Club (life), Adventurers Club N.Y. (medalist), Am. Legion, Harvard Club (N.Y.C. and Seattle), Sigma Xi, Phi Beta Kappa (pres. Epsilon chpt. Mich. State U. 1969-70), Phi Kappa Phi. Republican. Methodist. Avocations: skiing, mountaineering, photography. Home: 514 E 1st St Moscow ID 83843-2814 Office: U Idaho Coll Mines & Earth Resources Mines Bldg Rm 204 Moscow ID 83843 also: House of Reps Idaho State House Boise ID 83720 also: Found for Glacier & Environ Rsch 4470 N Douglas Hwy Juneau AK 99801

MILLER, MICHAEL EVERETT, chemical company executive; b. Indiana, Pa., Sept. 4, 1941; s. Everett Michael and Elizabeth Mary (Becker) M.; m. Eleanor Ann Flyn, June 19, 1965; children: Elizabeth Anne, Christopher. BS in History, St. Louis U., 1963, MS in History, 1965; grad. Advanced Mgmt. Program, Stanford U., 1982. Tchr. Ferguson/Florissant Sch. System, St. Louis, 1965; sales rep. inorganic chems. div. Monsanto Chem. Co., St. Louis, 1965, dir. mktg., cycle-safe, 1976-77, dir. mktg., detergents and phosphates, 1977-80, comml. dir., water treatment chems., 1980-83, gen. mgr., detergent materials, 1983-86, v.p., gen. mgr., detegents div., 1986-88, v.p. rubber chems. and instruments div. and Asia Pacific, 1988-89, corp. v.p. adminstrn., 1989-93; sr. v.p. ops. The Chem. Group, 1993, group v.p. indsl. products, 1993, pres. splty. products, 1995—, sr. v.p. adminstrn., 1997; bd. dirs. Watlow Electric Mfg. Co., St. Louis, Group Health Plan; adv. bd. Emerson Electric Ctr. for Bus. Ethics, St. Louis U. Vice chmn. bd. trustees Fontbonne Coll., St. Louis, 1990. Mem. Algonquin Golf Club. Avocations: golf, skiing, racquetball, restoration of early model Corvettes. Office: Monsanto Company 800 N Lindbergh Blvd Saint Louis MO 63141-7843

MILLER, MICHAEL JEFFREY, publishing executive. BS in Computer Sci., Rensselaer Polytechnic Inst., 1979; MS in Journalism, Northwestern U., 1980. West Coast bur. chief Popular Computing, N.Y.C., 1983-85; exec. editor InfoWorld, N.Y.C., 1985-89, editor, 1989-90, editor-in-chief, 1990-91; v.p., editor-in-chief PC Mag., N.Y.C., 1991—. Office: PC Mag-Ziff Davis Publ Co One Park Ave New York NY 10016

MILLER, MICHAEL JON, survey engineer, local government manager; b. Parkers Prairie, Minn., Mar. 17, 1950; s. Buford Kenneth and Gretchen Cena (Sharp) M.; m. Terry Lynn Peck, May 20, 1972; children: Livia Mica, David Peter. BS, U. Wis., Platteville, 1972; M of Pub. Adminstrn., Ariz. State U., 1988. Cert. profl. land surveyor, Wis., Ariz., soil tester, Wis. Chief of surveys Hovelsrud Cons. Assn., Richland Ctr., Wis., 1972-78; ops. mgr. Tech, Advisors, Inc., Phoenix, 1978-82; profl. surveyor Coe and Van Loo, Inc., Phoenix, 1982-83; survey engr. City of Phoenix, 1983—; land surveyor mem. Ariz. Bd. Tech. Registration, sec., 1990-91, vice chmn., 1991, chmn., 1991-92, vice chmn. 1993-94, chmn. 1994-95. Contbr. articles to profl. jours. Dep. registrar Dem. Party of Ariz., Phoenix, 1983-94; clk. Phoenix Friends Meeting, 1985-86; recording clk. Intermountain Yearly Meeting of Religious Soc. of Friends, 1984-85. Fellow Am. Congress on Surveying and Mapping (membership chmn. 1987-88); mem. Nat. Soc. Profl. Surveyors (gov. for Ariz. 1985-89), Western Fedn. Land Surveyors (state del. 1988-89), Ariz. Profl. Land Surveyors (sec. 1983-84, pres. 1985-86, Outstanding award 1981, life mem. award 1996), Nat. Coun. Examiners for Engrs. and Surveyors, Am. Pub. Works Assn., Am. Soc. for Pub. Adminstrn., World Clown Assn., Internat. Jugglers Assn., Greater Ariz. Bicycle Assn. Democrat. Avocations: hist. research, writing, juggling, bicycling. Home: 4026 E Campbell Ave Phoenix AZ 85018-3709

MILLER, MICKEY LESTER, retired school administrator; b. Albuquerque, July 26, 1920; s. Chester Lester and Myra Easter (Cassidy) M.; m. Louise Dean Miller, Aug. 30, 1946; children: Linda Miller Kelly, Lee Miller Parks, Lynne Miller Carson. BS, U. N.Mex., 1944; MS, Columbia U., 1949. Coach, tchr. math. Jefferson Jr. H.S., Albuquerque, 1946-49; coach, dept. chair, athletic dir. Highland H.S., Albuquerque, 1949-64, asst. prin., 1964-70; dist. program coord. Albuquerque Pub. Schs., 1970-90; ret., 1990. Author: Guide to Administration of Secondary Athletics, 1990; author brochures, handbooks, articles. Pub. mem. N.Mex. Bd. Dentistry, 1992—; recommending scout Pitts. Pirates Baseball, 1985—. With USN, 1942-46. Recipient Honor award S.W. Dist. Am. Alliance Health, Phys. Edn., Recreation and Dance, 1971, N.Mex. Coaches Assn., 1981, Hall of Fame award N.Mex. Activities Assn., 1985; named Retiree of Yr., S.W. Dist. Am. Alliance Health, Phys. Edn., Recreation and Dance, 1994; named to U. N.Mex. Alumni Lettermen Hall of Honor, 1994; named to Albuquerque Sports Hall of Fame, 1995. Mem. AAHPERD (life, budget/nominating rep. 1985), U. N.Mex. Alumni Assn., U. N.Mex. LOBO Lettermen Club (pres., treas. 1972). Democrat. Methodist. Avocations: golf, travel, baseball scouting. Home: 1201 Richmond Dr NE Albuquerque NM 87106

MILLER, MILDRED, opera singer, recitalist; b. Cleve.; d. William and Elsa (Friedhofer) Mueller; m. Wesley W. Posvar, Apr. 30, 1950; children: Wesley, Margot Marina, Lisa Christina. MusB, Cleve. Inst. Music, 1946; hon. doctorate, Cleve. Ins. Music, 1983; artists' diploma, New England Conservatory Music, 1948, hon. doctorate, 1966; MusD (hon.), Bowling Green State U., 1960; hon. doctorate, Washington and Jefferson U., 1988. Founder, artistic dir. Opera Theater of Pitts., 1978—; mem. music faculty Carnegie-Mellon U., 1996. Operatic debut in Peter Grimes, Tanglewood, 1946; appeared N.E. Opera Theater, Stuttgart State Theater, Germany, 1949-50, Glyndebourne Opera, Edinburgh Festival; debut as Cherubino in Figaro, Met. Opera, 1951; 23 consecutive seasons Met. Opera; radio debut Bell Telephone Hour; TV debut Voice of Firestone, 1952; appeared in films including Merry Wives of Windsor (filmed in Vienna), 1964; Vienna State Opera debut, 1963, appearances with San Francisco, Chgo. Lyric, Cin. Zoo, San Antonio, Berlin, Munich, Frankfurt, Pasadena, Ft. Worth, Kansas City, Pitts., Tulsa and St. Paul operas. Bd. dirs. Gateway to Music. Recipient Frank Huntington Beebe award for study abroad, 1949, 50, Grand Prix du Disque, 1965, Outstanding Achievements in Music award Boston C. of C., 1959, Ohioana Career medal, 1985, Outstanding Achievement in Opera award, Slippery Rock U., 1985, YWCA Ann. Tribute to Women award, 1989, Keystone Salute award Pa. Fedn. Music Clubs, 1994; named one of outstanding women of Pitts., Pitts. Press-Pitts. Post-Gazette, 1968, Person of Yr. in Music, Pitts. Jaycees, 1980. Mem. Nat. Soc. Arts and Letters (pres. 1989-90, Gold medal 1984), Disting. Daus. Pa. (pres. 1991-93), Tuesday Mus. Club, Phi Beta Kappa, Phi Delta Gamma, Sigma Alpha Iota. Office: PO Box 110108 Pittsburgh PA 15232-0608

MILLER, MILTON ALLEN, lawyer; b. Los Angeles, Jan. 15, 1954; s. Samuel C. and Sylvia Mary Jane (Silver) M.; m. Mary Ann Toman, Sept. 10, 1988; 1 child, Mary Ann. AB with distinction and honors in Econs., Stanford U., 1976; JD with honors, Harvard U., 1979. Bar: Calif. 1979, U.S. Ct. Appeals (9th cir.) 1979, U.S. Dist. Ct. (cen., no. and so. dists.) Calif., U.S. Supreme Ct. 1989. Law clk. U.S. Ct. Appeals (9th cir.), Sacramento, 1979-80; assoc. Latham & Watkins, L.A., 1979-87, ptnr., 1987—; chmn. ethics com. Latham & Watkins. Author: Attorney Ethics; articles editor Harvard Law Rev., 1978-79. Mem. Am. Cancer Soc., L.A. Mem. ABA, ATLA, Calif. State Bar Assn. (mem. com. on profl. responsibility), Los Angeles County Bar Assn. (chmn. profl. responsibility and ethics com.), Phi Beta Kappa. Office: Latham & Watkins 633 W 5th St Ste 4000 Los Angeles CA 90071-2005 *Notable cases include Raquel Welch vs. MGM Corp.; served as trial and insurance counsel in San Juan Dupont Plaza Hotel Fire litigation.*

MILLER, MORGAN LINCOLN, textile manufacturing company executive; b. New Rochelle, N.Y., Feb. 11, 1924; s. Harry H. and Belle M.; m. Marjorie Leff, June 8, 1952; children—Betsy, Harry Robert, Amy, Cindy. B.A., Lehigh U., Bethlehem, Pa., 1947. With Nat. Spinning Co., Inc., 1959—; exec. v.p. Nat. Spinning Co., Inc., N.Y.C., from 1964; now vice chmn. Nat. Spinning Co., Inc.; pres. Jr. Accent Dress Mfg. Co., 1956—; pres. Nat. Yarn Crafts subs. Coquet Bathing Suit Mfg. Co., 1954—; Bd. dirs. BHC Comm., Inc. V.p. Westchester (N.Y.) Reform Temple, 1971, Westchester Jewish Cmty. Svcs., White Plains, N.Y., 1970; trustee Beth Israel Med. Ctr.; pres. Craft Youth Coun. Am. With USNR, 1942-45. Named Industry Man of Year United Jewish Appeal, 1980. Mem. Craft Yarn Coun. Am., Beach Point Club. Republican. Office: 183 Madison Ave New York NY 10016-5102

MILLER, MORRIS HENRY, lawyer; b. Thomasville, Ga., June 14, 1954; s. Gibbes Ulmer and Marianne (Morris) M.; m. Anita Carol Payne, Mar. 23, 1985; children: Morris Payne, Rose Elizabeth, David Gibbes, Paul Louis Henry, John Henry. BS in Acctg. summa cum laude, Fla. State U., 1976; JD, U. Va., 1979. Bar: Fla. 1979. Assoc. Holland & Knight, Tampa, Fla., 1979-84; ptnr. Holland & Knight, Tallahassee, Fla., 1984-89, ptnr., chmn. health law practice, 1985—, co-chmn. technology and intellectual property task force. Dist. fin. chmn. Gulf Ridge coun. Boy Scouts Am., 1988-89, mem. pack com., cubmaster Pack 23, Suwannee River Area coun., 1995—; mem. Leadership Tampa, 1986, Leadership Tampa Bay, 1989; bd. dirs. Tallahassee YMCA, 1994—; founder, chmn. Tampa Bus. Com. for Arts, Inc., 1988-89; elder Presbyn. Ch. Mem. ABA (health law forum and fed. regulation securities), Fla. Bar (chmn., vice chmn. computer law com. 1983-89, Fla. corp. law revision com. 1986-89, health law sect.), Tallahassee Bar Assn., Tallahassee Area C. of C. (strategic plan implementation com., Tallahassee trustees), Fla. Acad. Hosp. Attys. (chair govtl. hosp. com.). Office: Holland & Knight 315 S Calhoun St Tallahassee FL 32301-1807

MILLER, NAN LOUISE, museum director; b. Atlanta, Aug. 6, 1948; d. William Mitchell and Harriet Irene (Wilkie) Schotanus; B.S., Kans. State U., 1970; postgrad. UCLA, 1979-80, Media Communications, 1981, Weist Barron Sch. TV, 1982, East Tenn. State U., 1982-83; m. Robert W. Miller Jr., Oct. 31, 1981. Buyer, Jones Store Co., Kansas City, Mo., 1971-75, Harzfeld's, Kansas City, 1975-76; exec. sales rep. Monet, Los Angeles, 1976-80; mgr. corp. buying offices Trifari, N.Y.C., 1980-82, field mktg. coordinator and media pub. relations rep., 1981-82; co-owner, v.p. mktg. Devel. Resources Corp., Kingsport, Tenn., 1982-89; exec. dir. Hands On! Regional Mus., Johnson City, Tenn., 1989-93, Richmond (Va.) Children's Mus., 1993—; bd. dirs., v.p. Assn. Youth Museums; bd. dirs. Leadership Metro Richmond, The Women's Club, Commonwealth Girl Scout Coun. Mem. Assn. Youth Mus. (bd. dirs. nat. coun.), Am. Assn. Mus., S.E. Mus. Conf., Va. Assn. Mus., Jr. League of Richmond, Rotary Club Richmond, Chi Omega. Presbyterian. Home: 3600 Noble Ave Richmond VA 23222-1834 Office: Richmond Children's Mus 740 Navy Hill Dr Richmond VA 23219-1418

MILLER, NANCY ELLEN, computer consultant; b. Detroit, Aug. 30, 1956; d. George Jacob and Charlotte Miller. BS in Computer and Comm. Sci., U. Mich., 1978; MS in Computer Sci., U. Wis. Madison, 1981. Product engr. Ford Motor Co., Dearborn, Mich., 1977; computer programmer Unique Bus. Sys., Inc., Southfield, Mich., 1978; tchg. asst. computer sci. dept. U. Wis., Madison, 1978-82; computer scientist Lister Hill Nat. Ctr. for Biomed Comm., Nat. Libr. Medicine NIH, Bethesda, Md., 1984-88; knowledge engr. Carnegie Group, Inc., Dearborn, 1989; computer cons. West Bloomfield, Mich., 1993—. Mem. Nat. Abortion and Reproductive Rights Action League, Washington, 1984—, Nat. Women's Polit. Caucus, Washington, 1984—, Jewish Fedn. Met. Detroit, Bloomfield Hills, 1991—. Recipient Jour. of Am. Soc. for Info. Sci. Best Paper award, 1988. Mem. IEEE Computer Soc., Assn. for Computing Machinery (sec. S.E. Mich. spl. interest group on artificial intelligence 1993-94), Am. Assn. for Artificial Intelligence and Spl. Interest Groups in Mfg. and Bus., Assn. for Logic Programming, U. Wis. Alumni Assn. (life), U. Mich. Alumni Assn. (life). Democrat. Jewish. Home and Office: 6220 Village Park Dr Apt 104 West Bloomfield MI 48322-2146

MILLER, NAOMI, art historian; b. N.Y.C., Feb. 28, 1928; d. Nathan and Hannah M. B.S., CCNY, 1948; M.A., Columbia U., 1950, NYU, 1960; Ph.D., NYU, 1966. Asst. prof. art history R.I. Sch. Design, 1963-64; asst. prof. U. Calif.-Berkeley, 1969-70; asst. to assoc. prof. Boston U., 1964—, prof. art history, 1981—; vis. prof. U. B.C., Vancouver, 1967, Hebrew U., Jerusalem, 1980, U. Padua, 1990; vis. scholar I Tatti, 1984-85. Author: French Renaissance Fountains, 1977, Heavenly Caves, 1982, Renaissance Bologna, 1989; co-author: Fons Sapientiae: Garden Fountains in Illustrated Books, 16th-18th Centuries, 1977, Boston Architecture 1975-90, 1990; book rev. editor: Jour. Soc. Archtl. Historians, 1975-81, editor, 1981-84; articles, catalogues. Jr. fellow NEH, 1972-73; sr. fellow Dumbarton Oaks, 1976-77, 83-89; vis. sr. fellow Ctr. for Advanced Study in Visual Arts, 1988, 95. Mem. Coll. Art Assn., Soc. Archtl. Historians, Renaissance Soc. Office: 725 Commonwealth Ave Boston MA 02215-1401

MILLER, NATE, professional boxer; b. Phila., Aug. 3, 1963. Named WBA Cruiserweight Champion, 1995. Achievements include record of 29 wins and 4 losses, with 25 knock-outs. Office: care Consejo Mundial de Boxeo, Genova 33 Despacho # 503, 06600 Mexico City Mexico

MILLER, NEAL ELGAR, psychologist, emeritus educator; b. Milw., Aug. 3, 1909; s. Irving E. and Lily R. (Fuenfstueck) M.; m. Marion E. Edwards, June 30, 1948; children: York, Sara. B.S., U. Wash., 1931; M.S., Stanford U., 1932; Ph.D., Yale U., 1935; D.Sc., U. Mich., 1965, U. Pa., 1968, St. Lawrence U., 1973, U. Uppsala, Sweden, 1977, LaSalle Coll., 1979, Rutgers U., 1985. Social sci. research fellow Inst. Psychoanalysis, Vienna, Austria, 1935-36; asst. research psychologist Yale U., 1933-35; instr., asst. prof., research asst. psychol. Inst. Human Relations, 1936-41, assoc. prof., research assoc., 1941-42, 46-50, prof. psychology, 1950-52, James Rowland Angell prof. psychology, 1952-66; fellow Berkeley Coll., 1955—; prof. Rockefeller U., N.Y.C., 1966-81; prof. emeritus Rockefeller U., 1981—; research affiliate Yale U., 1985—; expert cons. Am. Inst. Research, 1946-62; spl. cons. com. human resources Research and Devel. Bd., Office Sec. Def., 1951-53; mem. tech. adv. panel Office Asst. Sec. Def., 1954-57; expert cons. Ops. Research Office and Human Resources Research Office, 1951-54; bd. of sci. counsellors Nat. Inst. of Aging, 1987-90; bd. gov.s and mem. of exec. com. N.Y. Acad. of Scis., 1987. Author: (with J. Dollard et al) Frustration and Aggression, 1939, (with Dollard) Social Learning and Imitation, 1941, Personality and Psychotherapy, 1950, Graphic Communication and the Crisis in Education, 1957, N.E. Miller: Selected Papers, 1971; contbr. chpts. to psychol. handbooks; editor: Psychological Research on Pilot Tng., 1947. Chmn. bd. sci. dirs. Roscoe B. Jackson Meml. Lab., Bar Harbor, Maine, 1962-76, hon. trustee, 1980—; bd. sci. counsellors NIMH, 1957-61; fellowship com. Founds. Fund for Research in Psychiatry, 1956-61; mem. central council Internat. Brain Research Orgn., 1964; v.p. bd. dirs. Foote Sch., 1964-65; chmn. NAS/NRC Com. on Brain Scis., 1969-71; bd. sci. counsellors Nat. Inst. Child Health and Human Devel., 1969-72; v.p. Inst. for Advancement of Health, 1982-90. Maj. USAAC, 1942-46; officer in charge research, Psychol. Research Unit 1, Nashville 1942-44; dir. psychol. research project Hdqrs. Flying Tng. Command, Randolph Field, Tex. 1944-46. Recipient Warren medal for exptl. psychology, 1954, Newcomb Cleveland prize, 1956, Nat. medal of sci., 1964, Kenneth Craik Rsch. award U. Cambridge, 1966, Wilbur Cross medal Yale U., 1966, Alumnus Summa Laude Dignitatus U. Wash., 1967, Disting. Alumnus award Western Wash. State Coll., Gold medal award Am. Psychol. Found., 1975, Mental Health Assn. rsch. achievement award, 1978, Inst. for Advancement of Health Sci. and Art of Health award, 1988, Disting. Scholar award Internat. Soc. for Behavioral Medicine, 1990. Fellow Am. Acad. Arts and Scis. (coun. 1979-83), Brit. Psychol. Soc. (hon. fgn.), Internat. Soc. Rsch. on Aggression (life); mem. Am. Philos. Soc., N.Y. Acad. Scis. (hon. life), Spanish Soc. Psychology (hon.), APA (coun. reps. 1954-58, pres. exptl. divsn. 1952-53, pres. 1960-61, pres. divsn. health psychology 1980-81, Disting. Sci. Contbn. award 1959, award for Disting. Contbns. to Knowledge 1983, citation for Outstanding Lifetime Contbn. to Psychology, 1991, establishment of Neal E. Miller Disting. Lectr. in Neurosci. 1995—, Divsn. Health Psychology Centennial award for outstanding achievement 1992), Eastern Psychol. Assn. (pres. 1952-53), NRC (divsn. anthropology and psychology 1950-53, chmn. 1958-60), Nat. Acad. Sci. (chmn. sect. psychology 1965-67, chmn. com. brain sci. 1969-71, sr. fellow Inst. of Medicine 1983—, bd. mental health and behavioral medicine 1980-85), German Soc. Behavioral Medicine and Behavior Modification (hon.), Soc. Exptl. Psychologists, AAAS, Soc. Neurosci. (pres. 1971-72, pres. award for Career of Outstanding Neurosci. Rsch. Teaching and Svc. 1994), Biofeedback Soc. Am. (pres.-elect 1983, pres. 1984, Outstanding Rsch. award 1987, Disting. Rsch. award 1995), Acad. Behavioral Medicine Rsch. (pres. 1978-79, Neal E. Miller New Investigator award established 1989), Mory's Grad. Club (New Haven), Grad. Club Assn., Sigma Xi (pres. Rockefeller U. chpt. 1968-69), Phi Beta Kappa. Office: Yale U Dept Psychology PO Box 208-205 New Haven CT 06520-8205

MILLER, NEIL AUSTIN, biology educator; b. Grand Rapids, Mich., Apr. 9, 1932; s. Kennith C. and Marjorie (Linsenmeyer) M.; m. Sally Bond, June 23, 1961; children: Anne C., Mary Leigh. AS, Grand Rapids Jr. Coll., 1956; BS, Mich. State U., 1958; MS, Memphis State U., 1964; PhD, So. Ill. U., 1968. Asst. prof. Western Ky. Coll., Bowling Green, 1964-65; fellow So. Ill. U., Carbondale, 1965-68; prof. The Univ. Memphis, 1968—; Disting. prof. U. Memphis, 1984; ecologist Hall, Blake and Assocs.; cons. Continental Engrng., Inc., B.F.I., Inc., wetland ecologist cons.; environ. cons. Republic of Estonia. With USCG, 1950-53. Named Tenn. Conservation Educator of Yr., 1983. Baptist. Home: 6898 Trowbridge Cv Memphis TN 38138-1822 Office: The Univ Memphis Biology Dept Life Sci 225 Memphis TN 38152

MILLER, NEIL STUART, financial officer, advertising executive; b. N.Y.C., July 30, 1958; s. Irving Israel Maltz and Lenore (Goldstein) M.; m. Karen Joyce Salomon, Nov. 22, 1987; children: Lindsay Alexandra, Jacqueline Olivia, Sara Allison. BS, SUNY, Buffalo, 1980; MBA, SUNY, Binghamton, 1982. CPA, N.Y. Staff auditor Peat Marwick Mitchell & Co., N.Y.C., 1982-83; ops. auditor Gulf & Western Industries, N.Y.C., 1983-84; spl. projects acct. Mickelberry Comms., N.Y.C., 1984-86; v.p. fin. Ptnrs. & Shevack Inc. (subs. Mickelberry Comms. Inc.), N.Y.C., 1986-87, sr. v.p. fin., 1987-89, exec. v.p., CFO, 1989-96, exec. v.p., COO, 1996—. Mem. AICPA, Am. Mgmt. Assn., N.Y. State Soc. CPA's (past mem. com. CFOs and advt.), Advt. Agy. Fin. Mgmt. Group, Fin. Execs. Inst. Avocations: skiing, motorcycling, golf. Home: 594 W Saddle River Rd U Saddle Riv NJ 07458-1115 Office: Ptnrs & Shevack Inc 1211 Ave of Americas New York NY 10036-8701

MILLER, NEWTON EDD, JR., communications educator; b. Houston, Mar. 13, 1920; s. Newton Edd and Anastasia (Johnston) M.; m. Edwina Whitaker, Aug. 30, 1942; children: Cathy Edwina, Kenneth Edd. B.S., U. Tex., 1939, M.A., 1940; Ph.D., U. Mich., 1952; LL.D., U. Nev., Reno., 1974. Tutor U. Tex., Austin, 1940-41; instr. U. Tex., 1941-45, asst. prof. speech, 1945-47; research asst. Navy Conf. Research, 1947-52; mem. faculty U. Mich., Ann Arbor, 1947-65; successively lectr., instr., asst. prof. speech U. Mich., 1947-55, assoc. prof., 1955-59, prof., 1959-65, asst. dir. summer session, 1953-57, assoc. dir., 1957-63, asst. to v.p. acad. affairs, 1963-65; chancellor U. Nev., Reno, 1965-68; pres. U. Nev., 1968-73, U. Maine, Portland-Gorham, 1973-78; chmn. communications dept. No. Ky. U., 1978-87, emeritus, 1987—, interim gen. mgr. Sta. WNKU, 1985-86; mem. adv. com. to commr. of edn. U.S. Office of Edn., Accreditation and Instl. Eligibility, 1976-79, acting chmn., 1977-78; mem. Judicial Edn. Study Group Am. Univ. Law Inst., 1977-78; mem. Nat. Accreditation Commn. for Agys. Serving Blind and Physically Handicapped, 1988-97, pres., 1991-92. Author: Post War World Organization, Background Studies, 1942, (with J.J. Villareal) First Course in Speech, 1945, (with W.M. Sattler) Discussion and Debate, 1951, Discussion and Conference, 2d edit., 1968, (with Stephen D. Boyd) Public Speaking: A Practical Handbook, 1985, 2d edit., 1989; co-editor: Required Arbitration of Labor Disputes, 1947. Pres. bd. dirs. Perry Nursery Sch., 1956-57, Sierra Cmty. Orch., 1989-94; mem. Ann Arbor Bd. Edn., 1959-65, Washtenaw County Bd. Edn.; sec. bd. dirs. Behringer Crawford Mus.; bd. dirs. Siera Arts Found., 1992—; pres. Reno/Sparks Theater Cmty. Coalition, 1994-96; mem. Nev. Humanities Com., 1994—. Mem. Mich. Assn. Sch. Bds. (dir.), N.W. Assn. Colls. and Secondary Schs. (chmn. higher commn. 1971-73), Am. Forensic Assn. (pres. Midwest sect. 1950-53), Central States Speech Assn. (pres. 1958-59), Mich. Speech Assn. (exec. sec. 1950-55), Speech Communication Assn. (chmn. fin. bd.), Assn. Western Us. (chmn. 1971-72), Delta Sigma Rho (nat. v.p. 1948-52), Phi Kappa Phi. Address: 1480 Ayershire Ct Reno NV 89509-5248

MILLER, NORMAN CHARLES, JR., newspaper editor; b. Pitts., Oct. 2, 1934; s. Norman Charles and Elizabeth (Burns) M.; m. Mollie Rudy, June 15, 1957; children—Norman III, Mary Ellen, Teri, Scott. B.A., Pa. State U., 1956. Reporter Wall Street Jour., San Francisco, 1960-63; reporter Wall Street Jour., N.Y.C., 1963-64; bur. chief Wall Street Jour., Detroit, 1964-66; Washington corr. Wall Street Jour., 1966-72, Washington Bur. chief, 1973-83; nat. editor Los Angeles Times, 1983—. Author: The Great Salad Oil Swindle, 1965. Served to lt. (j.g.) USN, 1956-60. Recipient Disting. Alumnus award Pa. State U., 1978; George Polk Meml. award L.I. U., 1963; Pulitzer Prize, 1964. Roman Catholic. Club: Gridiron (Washington). Avocation: tennis. Office: Los Angeles Times Times Mirror Sq Los Angeles CA 90012

MILLER, NORMAN RICHARD, diversified manufacturing company executive; b. Balt., Mar. 7, 1922; s. Samuel and Tobie Hildreth (Engleman) M.; m. Nancy Lee Rosenthal, 1967; children: Hilary S., Dana A. B.S. in Indsl. Engring., Ga. Inst. Tech., 1947; M.B.A., Harvard U., 1950. Indsl. cons. George S. Armstrong & Co., Inc., N.Y.C., 1950-51; ind. mgmt. cons. Italy, 1952-56; founder Italian Postgrad. Bus. Sch., Turin, 1953-55; dir. analysis and bus. planning RCA, 1957-61, v.p. div. bus. planning, 1962-68, v.p., gen. mgr. Graphic Systems Div., 1968-71; cons. Office Sci. and Tech., 1971-72; pres., chief exec. officer, dir. Lynch Corp., N.Y.C., 1972-73; exec. v.p., dir. Radiation Dynamics, Inc., Westbury, N.Y., 1973-76; v.p. Diebold Group, N.Y.C., 1976-82; pres., dir. Conn. Corridor Cellular Communications Cos., Inc., West Hartford, Conn., 1982-87, Broadcast Enterprises Inc., N.Y.C., 1985-92; pres. Twenver, Inc., Denver, 1986-93, Continental Divide PCS Ltd., 1993—; project mgr. Christo's Over the River, 1996—. Pres. Merce Cunningham Dance Found., 1976-83; trustee Phila. Mus. Art, 1967-89; trustee, mem. exec. com. Am. Fedn. Arts, 1982-90; mem. Boulder County Cultural Com., 1993—, Sci. and Cultural Facilities Dist., Denver, 1993—, Denver Found. Arts and Culture, 1994—. 2d lt. AUS, 1943-46. Mem. Inst. Aero. Scis., Ga. Tech. Alumni Assn., Tau Beta Pi, Omicron Delta Kappa, Phi Delta Epsilon, Phi Epsilon Pi. Home: 5411 Sunshine Canyon Dr Boulder CO 80302-9777

MILLER, ORLANDO JACK, physician, educator; b. Oklahoma City, Okla., May 11, 1927; s. Arthur Leroy and Iduma Dorris (Berry) M.; m. Dorothy Anne Smith, July 10, 1954; children: Richard Lawrence, Cynthia Kathleen, Karen Ann. B.S., Yale U., 1946, M.D., 1950. Intern St. Anthony Hosp., Oklahoma City, 1950-51; asst. resident in obstetrics and gynecology Yale-New Haven Med. Center, 1954-57, resident, instr., 1957-58; vis. fellow dept. obstetrics and gynecology Tulane U. Service, Charity Hosp., New Orleans, 1958; hon. research asst. Galton Lab., Univ. Coll., London, 1958-60; instr. Coll. Physicians and Surgeons Columbia U., N.Y.C., 1960, asso. dept. obstetrics and gynecology, 1960-61, asst. prof., 1961-65, asso. prof., 1965-69, prof. dept. human genetics and devel., dept. obstetrics and gynecology, 1969-85; asst. attending obstetrician, gynecologist Presbyn. Hosp., N.Y.C., 1964-65, assoc., 1965-70, attending obstetrician and gynecologist, 1970-85; prof. molecular biology, genetics and ob-gyn. Wayne State U. Sch. Medicine, Detroit, 1985-94, prof. Ctr. for Molecular Medicine and Genetics, 1994-96, prof. emeritus, 1996—, chmn. dept. molecular biology and genetics, 1985-93, dir. Ctr. for Molecular Biology, 1987-90; bd. dirs.Am. Bd. Med. Genetics, 1983-85, v.p., 1983, pres., 1984, 85. Editor: Cytogenetics, 1970-72; assoc. editor: Birth Defects Compendium, 1971-74, Cytogenetics and Cell Genetics, 1972-97; mem. editl. bd. Cytogenetics, 1961-69, Am. Jour. Human Genetics, 1969-74, 79-83, Gynecologic Investigation, 1970-77, Teratology, 1972-74, Cancer Genetics and Cytogenetics, 1979-84, Jour. Exptl. Zoology, 1989-92, Chromosome Rsch., 1994—; mem. editl. bd. com. Genomics, 1987-93, assoc. editor, 1993-96; mem. adv. bd. Human Genetics, 1978—; cons. Jour. Med. Primatology, 1977-94; consulting editor McGraw-Hill Yearbook of Sci. and Tech., 1995—; contbr. chpts. to textbooks and articles to med. and sci. jours. Mem. sci. adv. com. on rsch. Nat. Found. March of Dimes, 1967-96, mem. sci. com., 1996—; mem. sci. rec. com. Basil O'Connor starter grants, 1973-77, 86-94; mem. human embryology and devel. study sect. NIH, 1970-74, chmn., 1972-74; mem. com. for study of inborn errors of metabolism NRC, 1972-74; mem. sci. adv. com. virology and cell biology Am. Cancer Soc., 1974-78, mem. sci. adv. com. cell and devel. biology, 1986-90; mem. human genome study sect. NIH, 1991-94; U.S. rep. permanent com. Internat. Congress of Human Genetics, 1986-91. With AUS, 1951-53. James Hudson Brown Jr. fellow Yale U., 1947-48; NRC fellow, 1953-54; Population Council fellow, 1958-59; Josiah Macy Jr. fellow, 1960-61; NSF sr. postdoctoral fellow U. Oxford, 1968-69; vis. scientist U. Edinburgh, 1983-84; Disting. vis. fellow, Fogarty Internat. fellow LaTrobe U., Melbourne, Australia, 1992. Fellow AAAS; mem. AAAS, Am. Genetic Assn., Am. Soc. Cell Biology, Am. Soc. Human Genetics (bd. dirs. 1970-73, 86-90), Genetics Soc. Am., Genetics Soc. Australia, Human Genome Orgn., Acad. Scholars, Wayne State U. (life, pres. 1996-97), Sigma Xi. Presbyterian. Home: 1915 Stonycroft Ln Bloomfield Hills MI 48304-2339 Office: 540 E Canfield St Detroit MI 48201-1928

MILLER, PAMELA GUNDERSEN, city official; b. Cambridge, Mass., Sept. 7, 1938; d. Sven M. and Harriet Adams Gundersen; A.B. magna cum laude, Smith Coll., 1960; m. Ralph E. Miller, July 7, 1962; children—Alexander, Erik, Karen. Feature writer Congressional Quar., Washington, 1962-65; dir. cable TV franchizing Storer Broadcasting Co., Louisville, Bowling Green, Lexington, and Covington, Ky., 1978-80, 81-82; mem. 4th Dist. Lexington, Fayette County Urban Council, 1973-77, councilwoman-at-large, 1982-93, vice-mayor, 1984-86, 89-93, mayor, 1993—; dep. commr. Ky. Dept. Local Govt., Frankfort, 1980-81; pres. Pam Miller, Inc., 1984—, Community Ventures Corp., 1985—. Mem. Fayette County Bd. Health, 1975-77, Downtown Devel. Commn., 1975-77; alt. del. Dem. Nat. Conv., 1976; bd. dirs. YMCA, Lexington, 1975-77, 85-90, Fund for the Arts, 1984-93, Council of Arts, 1978-80, Sister Cities, 1978-80; treas. Prichard Com. for Acad. Excellence, 1983—. Named Woman of Achievement YWCA, 1984, Outstanding Woman of Blue Grass, AAUW, 1984. Mem. LWV (dir. 1970-73), Profl. Women's Forum, NOW, Land and Nature Trust of the Bluegrass. Home: 140 Cherokee Park Lexington KY 40503-1304 Office: 200 E Main St Lexington KY 40507-1315

MILLER, PAMELA LYNN, sales director; b. Elmhurst, Ill., Sept. 14, 1958; d. Gilbert Jack and Joan Leona (Friedberg) Mintz; m. Arthur Neal Miller, Mar. 5, 1994. BS, Ariz. State U., 1980. Virologist Automated Pathology, Inc., Phoenix, Ariz., 1980-81; territory mgr. MetPath Lab., Inc. (Corning, Inc.), Phoenix, Ariz., 1981-91; regional sales dir. Lab. Corp. of Am., Phoenix, 1991—; advisor med. home project Acad. Pediat., Phoenix, 1995. Vol. Phoenix Children's Cancer Ctr., 1990—. Avocations: golf, travel.

MILLER, PATRICIA ANNE, speech and language pathologist; b. Lamesa, Tex., Aug. 19, 1957; d. Warren Layton and Evelyn Joyce (Pearson) Oliver; m. John Ernest Roberts, May 25, 1979 (div.); 1 child, Jason Aaron; m. Michael David Miller, Nov. 30, 1984; children: Jennifer Anne, Catherine Denise. BS, Howard Payne Coll., 1979; postgrad., Baylor U., 1983. Cert. tchr., Tex.; lic. speech-lang. pathologist, Tex. Speech therapist Crosbyton (Tex.) Cen. Ind. Sch. Dist., 1980-81; speech therapist Hillsboro (Tex.) Spl. Edn. Coop., 1981, speech therapy cons., 1982-83; speech therapist Cleburne (Tex.) Ind. Sch. Dist., 1987-89, Levelland (Tex.) Ind. Sch. Dist. Coop., 1989; speech therapist Speech, Lang. and Hearing Ctr. Lamesa Ind. Sch. Dist., Lubbock, Tex., 1990-95; speech-lang. pathologist Sundance Rehab. Corp., Lamesa, Tex., 1995-96, Lumesa Ind. Sch. Dist. and Seminole Ind. Sch. Dist., 1997—. Mem. Tex. Speech and Hearing Assn. Baptist. Avocations: flute, tennis, volleyball, reading.

MILLER, PATRICIA ELIZABETH CLEARY, American and British literature educator; b. Kansas City, Mo., May 2, 1939; d. John M. and Helen Elizabeth (Kelton) Cleary; m. James Ludlow Miller, July 8, 1961; children: Jo Zach James, Honour Helena, Marika Elizabeth. AB in French, Harvard/Radcliffe, 1961; MA in English, U. Mo., Kansas City, 1970; M. Philosophy, U. Kans., 1977, PhD in English, 1979. Asst. instr. U. Kans., Lawrence, 1974-75; instr. U. Mo., Kansas City, 1979-83; asst. prof. Rockhurst Coll., Kansas City, 1983-92, dir. creative writing program, 1986—, assoc. prof., 1992—, chair English dept., 1993—; chair English dept., 1993—; corp. sec. Midwest Ctr. for Lit. Arts, Inc.; officer, founding bd. dirs. Helicon Nine, 1979—. Author: Westport: Missouri's Port of Many Returns, 1983, Starting A Swan Dive, 1993; contbr. book revs. to profl. jours. Chmn. Vis. Nurse Assn. Corp., 1985-88; bd. dirs. Harvard Alumni Assn., 1982—; mem. nat. adv. coun. Nat. Conf. Cath. Bishops, 1984-87; mem. bd. mgmt. Radcliffe Coll. Alumnae Assn., 1990-93, mem. leadership coun., 1992-93. Poetry fellow The Bunting Inst. Radcliffe Coll., 1993-94. Mem. DAR, MLA, AAUP, Midwest MLA, Nat. Coun. Tchrs. of English, Mo. Philol. Assn., Mo. Folklore Soc., Westport Hist. Soc., Jackson County Hist. Soc., Soc. Fellow of the Nelson-Atkins Mus., Kansas City Country Club, Rockhill Tennis Club. Home: 708 E 47th St Kansas City MO 64110-1559 Office: Rockhurst Coll Dept English 1100 Rockhurst Rd Kansas City MO 64110-2508

MILLER, PATRICK DWIGHT, JR., religion educator, minister; b. Atlanta, Oct. 24, 1935; s. Patrick Dwight and Lila Morse (Bonner) M.; m. Mary Ann Sudduth, Dec. 27, 1958; children: Jonathan Sudduth, Patrick James. AB, Davidson Coll., 1956; BD, Union Theol. Sem., Va., 1959; PhD, Harvard U., 1964. Ordained to ministry Presbyn. Ch., 1963. Pastor, minister Trinity Presbyn. Ch., Traveler's Rest, S.C., 1963-65; asst. prof. Bibl. studies Union Theol. Sem., Richmond, Va., 1966-68, assoc. prof., 1968-73, prof., 1973-84, dean of faculty, 1979-83; prof. of Old Testament Theology Princeton (N.J.) Theol. Sem., 1984—. Author: The Divine Warrior in Early Israel, 1973, The Hand of the Lord, 1977, Sin and Judgment in the Prophets, 1982, Interpreting the Psalms, 1986, Deuteronomy, 1990, They Cried to the Lord, 1994; editor: Theology Today, 1990—. Mem. Soc. of Bibl. Lit. (sec.-treas. 1987-88, pres.-elect 1997), Rev. Std. Version Translation Com. Democrat. Presbyterian. Home: 58 Mercer St Princeton NJ 08540-6826 Office: Princeton Theol Sem PO Box 821 Princeton NJ 08542-0803

MILLER, PATRICK WILLIAM, research administrator, educator; b. Toledo, Sept. 1, 1947; s. Richard William and Mary Olivia (Rinna) M.; m. Jean Ellen Thomas, Apr. 5, 1974; children: Joy, Tatum, Alex. BS in Indstrl. Edn., Bowling Green State U., 1971, MEd in Career Edn. and Tech., 1973; PhD in Indstrl. Tech. Edn., Ohio State U., 1977; Master's cert. Govt. Contract Adminstrn., George Washington U., 1995. Tchr. Montgomery Hills Jr. High Sch., Silver Spring, Md., 1971-72, Rockville (Md.) High Sch., 1973-74; asst. prof. Wayne State U., Detroit, 1977-79; assoc. prof., grad. coord. indstrl. edn. and tech. Western Carolina U., Cullowhee, N.C., 1979-81; assoc prof. U. No. Iowa, Cedar Falls, 1981-86; dir. grad. studies practical arts and vocat.-tech. edn. U. Mo., Columbia, 1986-89; devel. editor Am. Tech. Pubs., Homewood, Ill., 1989-90; proposal mgr. Nat. Opinion Rsch. Ctr. U. Chgo., 1990-96; dir. grants & contracts City Colls. Chgo., 1996—; pres. Patrick W. Miller and Assocs., Munster, Ind., 1981—; presenter, advisor and cons. in field. Author: Nonverbal Communication: Its Impact on Teaching and Learning, 1983, Teacher Written Tests: A Guide for Planning, Creating, Administering and Assessing, 1985, Nonverbal Communication: What Resarch Says to the Teacher, 1988, How To Write Tests for Students, 1990; mem. editl. bd. Jour. Indsl. Tchr. Edn., 1981-88, Am. Vocat. Edn. Rsch. Jour., 1981-85, 94—, Tech. Tchr., 1982-84, Jour. Indsl. Tech., 1984—, Jour. Vocat. and Tech. Edn., 1987-90, Human Resource Devel. Quar., 1989—; also articles. Sec. U. No. Iowa United Faculty, Cedar Falls, 1983-84, pres., 1984-86. Lance cpl. USMC, 1966-68, Vietnam. Recipient editl. recognition award Jour. Indsl. Tchr. Edn., 1984, 86, 88; named One of Accomplished Grads. of Coll. Tech., Bowling Green State U., 1995. Mem. ASTD, Am. Ednl. Rsch. Assn., Am. Vocat. Assn., Am. Vocat. Edn. Rsch. Assn., Nat. Assn. Indsl. Tech. (chmn. rsch. grants 1982-87, pres. industry div. 1991-92, chmn. exec. bd. 1992-93, past pres. 1993-94, Leadership award 1992, 93), Nat. Assn. Indsl. and Tech. Tchr. Educators (pres. 1988-89, past pres. 1989-90, trustee 1990-93, Outstanding Svc. award 1988, 90), Internat. Tech. Edn. Assn., Coun. Tech. Tchr. Edn., Epsilon Pi Tau, Phi Delta Kappa. Office: City Colls Chgo 226 W Jackson Blvd Rm 1424 Chicago IL 60606-6902

MILLER, PAUL AUSBORN, adult education educator; b. East Liverpool, Ohio, Mar. 22, 1917; s. Harry A. and Elizabeth (Stewart) M.; m. Catherine Spiker, Dec. 9, 1939 (dec. Dec. 1964); children—Paula Kay, Thomas Ausborn; m. Francena Lounsbery Nolan, Jan. 15, 1966. B.S., U. W.Va., 1939; M.A., Mich. State U., 1947, Ph.D., 1953. County agrl. agt. in W.Va., 1939-42; extension specialist sociology and anthropology Mich. State U., East Lansing, 1947-55; asst. prof. Mich. State U., 1947-52, asso. prof., 1953, prof., 1953-61, provost, 1959-61; pres. W.Va. U., Morgantown, 1962-66; asst. sec. for edn. HEW, 1966-68; disting. prof. edn., dir. univ. planning studies U. N.C., Charlotte; prof. adult edn. N.C. State U. at Raleigh, 1968-69; pres. Rochester (N.Y.) Inst. of Tech., 1969-79, pres. emeritus, 1979—, prof., 1979-93; sr. program cons. W.K. Kellogg Found., 1979-83; adj. prof. rural sociology U. Mo.-Columbia, 1994—. Author: Community Health Action, 1953; co-author: Patterns for Lifelong Learning, 1973; contbr. to publs. in field. Mem. Colombian Commn. Higher Edn., 1960-61. Served as 1st lt. USAAF, 1942-46. Fellow Am. Sociol. Assn.; mem. Rural Sociol. Soc., Phi Kappa Phi, Epsilon Sigma Phi. Home: 1909 Walden Ct Columbia MO 65203-5407

MILLER, PAUL DEAN, breeding consultant, geneticist, educator; b. Cedar Falls, Iowa, Apr. 4, 1941; s. Donald Hugh and Mary (Hansen) M.; m. Nancy Pearl Huser, Aug. 23, 1965; children: Michael, Steven. BS, Iowa State U., 1963; MS, Cornell U., 1965, PhD, 1967. Asst. prof. animal breeding Cornell U., Ithaca, N.Y., 1967-72; v.p. Am. Breeders Svc., De Forest, Wis., 1972-95; dir. ops. Nat. Dairy Herd Improvement Assn., 1996—; pres. Windsor (Wis.) Park Inc., 1985—; dir. ops. Nat. Dairy Herd Improvement Assn., Columbus, Ohio, 1996—; adj. prof. U. Wis., Madison, 1980—. Contbr. articles to profl. jours. Mem. Beef Improvement Fedn. (disting. service award 1980), Am. Soc. Animal Sci., Am. Dairy Sci. Assn., Nat. Assn. Animal Breeders (dir. 1983, v.p. 1986). Republican. Home: 3665 Windsor Rd De Forest WI 53532-2727 Office: Nat Dairy Herd Improvement 3021 E Dublin Granville Rd Columbus OH 43231-4031

MILLER, PAUL FETTEROLF, JR., retired investment company executive; b. Phila., 1927; s. Paul Fetterolf and Katharine Mills (Thompson) M.; m. Ella Warren Shafer, June 14, 1952; children: Ella Warren, Katharine Shafer, Paul Fetterolf III. BS, U. Pa., 1950, LLD (hon.), 1982; LLD (hon.), Washington & Lee U., 1988. Chartered fin. analyst. Founding ptnr. Miller, Anderson & Sherrerd, West Conshohocken, Pa.; bd. dirs. Mead Corp., Rohm & Haas Co., Hewlett-Packard. Trustee U. Pa., Ford Found., 1982-94, Colonial Williamsburg; trustee Sci. Ctr. of N.H.; mem. bd. overseers Wharton Sch. Mem. Fin. Analysts Phila., World Wildlife Fund (dir.), Merion Golf Club, Merion Cricket Club, Philadelphia Club, Useppa Island Club, Beta Theta Pi. Home: 115 Maple Hill Rd Gladwyne PA 19035-1305 Office: One Tower Bridge West Conshohocken PA 19428

MILLER, PAUL GEORGE, computer company executive; b. Louisville, Dec. 13, 1922; s. George Moore and Pauline Louise (Koob) M.; m. Doris Kahl Ingram, Feb. 17, 1979; children: George, James, Randolph. B.M.E., Purdue U., 1948; B.S., U.S. Naval Acad., 1946; B.S. in Electronics Engring., Mass. Inst. Tech., 1949, postgrad. in Nuclear Sci., 1949. Gen. mgr. control systems div. Daystrom (later acquired by Control Data Corp.), La Jolla, Calif., 1957-65; v.p., gen. mgr. communications and spl. systems group Control Data Corp., Mpls., 1965-67; v.p., group gen. mgr. computer systems and devel. Control Data Corp., 1967-69, sr. v.p., mktg. group exec., 1970-72, sr. v.p., 1973—; pres. Control Data Mktg. Co.; chmn., chief exec. officer Comml. Credit Co., 1977-83; bd. dirs. Merrill Corp., Bon Secours Health System, LSC, Inc. Served to lt. USN, 1946-57. Recipient Distinguished Alumnus award Purdue U., 1968. Mem. IEEE (sr.), Sigma Xi, Tau Beta Pi, Eta Kappa Nu, Delta Tau Delta. Home: 11203 Falls Rd Lutherville MD 21093 Office: PO Box 725 Brooklandville MD 21022-0725

MILLER, PAUL J., lawyer; b. Boston, Mar. 27, 1929; s. Edward and Esther (Kalis) M.; children—Robin, Jonathan; m. Michal Davis, Sept. 1, 1965; children—Anthony, Douglas. B.A., Yale U., 1950; LL.B., Harvard U., 1953. Bar: Mass. 1953, Ill. 1957. Assoc. Miller & Miller, Boston, 1953-54; assoc. Sonnenschein Nath & Rosenthal, Chgo., 1957-63, ptnr., 1963—; bd. dirs. Oil-Dri Corp. Am., Chgo. Trustee Latin Sch. of Chgo., 1985-91. 1st lt. JAGC, U.S. Army, 1954-57. Fellow Am. Bar Found.; mem. Tavern Club, Saddle and Cycle Club, Law Club, Phi Beta Kappa. Avocations: jogging; sailing. Office: Sonnenschein Nath & Rosenthal 233 S Wacker Dr Ste 8000 Chicago IL 60606-6342

MILLER, PAUL LUKENS, investment banker; b. Phila., Dec. 6, 1919; s. Henry C.L. and Elsie (Groff) M.; m. Adele Olyphant, Nov. 4, 1950; children: Paul L. (dec.), Hilary, Beverly, Leslie. Student, William Penn Charter Sch., Phila., 1937; A.B., Princeton U., 1941. With First Boston Corp., N.Y.C., 1946—; v.p. First Boston Corp., 1955-64, dir., 1959-78, pres., 1964-78, sr. advisor, 1978—. Served to maj., F.A. AUS, 1941-46. Clubs: Ivy (Princeton); Links, River (N.Y.C.). Office: First Boston Corp 11 Madison Ave New York NY 10010-3629

MILLER, PAUL MCGRATH, JR., executive search consulting company executive; b. Bowling Green, Ky., Oct. 31, 1935; s. Paul McGrath and Lena D. (Carr) M.; m. Charlene F. Russnak, Sept. 12, 1970 (div.); children: Andrew McGrath, Christopher Paul; m. C. Sue Whitehouse, Aug. 12, 1989. B. Mech. Engring., Cornell U., 1958; M.B.A., Harvard U., 1966. Foreman, Procter & Gamble, Cin., 1958-60; market analyst United Aircraft Co., Sunnyvale, Calif., 1963-64; asst. to chmn. bd. Boise Cascade Corp. (Idaho), 1966, gen. mktg. mgr. Insulite div., 1966-67, nat. sales mgr. Lumber and Plywood, 1967-68, asst. to exec. v.p. Paper Group, 1968-69; group dir. mktg. Am. Standard, Inc., N.Y.C., 1969-71; dir. corp. communications Indian Head, Inc., N.Y.C., 1971-74; v.p. mktg. Ball & Socket Mfg. Co., Cheshire, Conn., 1975; v.p. mktg. Cory Coffee Service, Chgo., 1976, v.p., gen. mgr., 1977-80; v.p., ptnr. Korn/Ferry Internat., Chgo., 1980-87; ptnr. Lamalie Assocs. Inc., Chgo., 1987—. Mem. Winnetka Caucus (Ill.), 1980. Served to capt. USAF, 1960-63. Mem. Racquet Club (Chgo.), Harvard Club (N.Y.C.), Harvard Bus. Sch. Club (Chgo., dir.), Harvard U. Club (Chgo., dir.). Episcopalian. Office: Lamalie Amrop Internat 225 W Wacker Dr Chicago IL 60606-1224

MILLER, PAUL S(AMUEL), lawyer; b. Paterson, N.J., Apr. 8, 1939; s. Louis and Etta (Wolff) M.; m. Carol Plesser, Mar. 26, 1961; children: Nicole F., Margo H., Jason E. BA, Rutgers U., 1960, JD magna cum laude, 1962. Bar: N.Y. 1963. Assoc. Kaye, Scholer, Fierman, Hayes & Handler, N.Y.C., 1962-63, Rubin, Baum & Levin, N.Y.C., 1964; ptnr. Fishman, Miller & Zimet, N.Y.C., 1964-70; counsel Leasing Cons., Inc., Rosyln, N.Y., 1970-71; with Pfizer Inc., N.Y.C., 1971—, assoc. gen. counsel, v.p., gen. counsel, 1986—, sr. v.p., gen. counsel, 1992—; official corr. Pharm. Mfrs. Assn., mem., chmn. exec. com. law sect., 1989-90. Mem. United Jewish Appeal Com., Essex County, 1981-83, co-chmn. Livingston sect., 1982; mem. bus. adv. coun. Touro Law Sch.; bd. dirs. Mgmt. Decision Lab. NYU Sch. Bus. Adminstrn., 1982—, Citizens Crime Commn. of N.Y.C., Inc., Jewish Conciliation Bd. Am., Inc., Nat. Com. for Futherance of Jewish Edn., Lawyers for Civil Justice; mem. exec. com. Am. Israel Pub. Affairs Com. Mem. ABA (antitrust law sect., corp. banking and bus. law sect., natural resources law sect., sci. and tech. sect., mem. health law forum com.), N.Y. State Bar Assn. (antitrust law sect., food and drug law sect., mem. internat. trade com., mem. long range policy proposals com.), Nat. Inst. Dispute Resolution (bd. dirs.), U.S. C. of C. (mem. govt. and regulatory affairs com.). Avocation: golf. Office: Pfizer Inc 235 E 42nd St New York NY 10017-5703

MILLER, PEGGY MCLAREN, management educator; b. Tomahawk, Wis., Jan. 12, 1931; d. Cecil Glenn and Gladys Lucille (Bame) McLaren; m. Richard Irwin Miller, June 25, 1955; children: Joan Marie, Diane Lee, Janine Louise. BS, Iowa State U., 1953; MA, Am. U., 1959; MBA, Rochester Inst. Tech., 1979; PhD, Ohio U., 1987. Instr. Beirut Coll. for Women, 1953-55, U. Ky., Lexington, 1964-66, S.W. Tex. State U., San Marcos, 1981-84; home economist Borden Co., N.Y.C., 1955-58; cons. Consumer Cons., Chgo., Springfield, Ill., 1972-77; sr. mktg. rep. N.Y. State Dept. Agr., Rochester, 1978-79; asst. prof., coord. bus. and mgmt. Keuka Coll., Keuka Park, N.Y., 1979-81; lectr. mgmt. Ohio U., Athens, 1984—. Co-editor: Fifty States Cookbook, 1977; contbr. articles to profl. jours. Mem. Soc. for Advancement of Mgmt. (advisor campus chpt.), Mortar Bd., Phi Kappa Phi. Home: 17 Briarwood Dr Athens OH 45701-1302 Office: Ohio U Copeland Hall Athens OH 45701

MILLER, PHILIP EFREM, librarian; b. Providence, Feb. 18, 1945; s. Jacob and Natalie (Rouslin) M.; m. Zenia Weiner, Dec. 20, 1969; 1 son, Paul Jeremy. B.S.L., Georgetown U., 1967; M.S., U. Mich., 1968, A.M.L.S., 1973; Ph.D., NYU, 1984. Asst. libr. Hebrew Union Coll., N.Y.C., 1973-76, acting libr., 1976-78, librarian, 1978—. Author: Karaite Separatism in 19th Century Russia, 1993. Mem. Assn. Jewish Libraries (pres. 1982-84), Jewish Book Coun. (exec. bd. 1977—), Am. Soc. for Jewish Music (exec. bd. 1990—), Assn. Jewish Studies. Home: 56 Truman Dr Marlboro NJ 07746-1122 Office: Hebrew Union Coll-Jewish Inst of Religion Klau Libr 1 W 4th St New York NY 10012-1105

MILLER, PHILLIP EDWARD, environmental scientist; b. Waterloo, Iowa, May 29, 1935; s. Joe Monroe and Katherine Elva (Groom) M.; m. Cathy Ann Love, Sept. 15, 1962; children: Eric Anthony, Bryan Edward, Stefan Patrick, Gregory Joseph. BA in Sci. Edn., U. No. Iowa, 1961; MA in Sci. Edn., U. Iowa, 1964; postgrad., U. Wis., 1966-68. Physics and chemistry tchr. Millersburg (Iowa) Community High Sch., 1961-62; supervising tchr. NSF Insvc. Inst. U. Iowa, Iowa City, 1962-64; instr. biology, area coord. Office Equal Opportunity Western Ky. U., Bowling Green, 1964-66; sci. editor, journalism instr.-sci. and tech. Mich. State U., East Lansing, 1968-74; asst. prof. agr., forestry and home econs. U. Minn., St. Paul, 1974-77; sr. editor atomic energy div. E.I. du Pont de Nemours and Co., Aiken, S.C., 1977-89; sr. scientist environ. protection dept. Westinghouse Savannah River Co., Aiken, 1989—; pres. Agy. for Book Authors, Collectors and Understanding of Sci., Aiken, 1994—; panelist 26th Internat. Tech. Comm. Conf., L.A., 1979; participant Dept. Energy/Westinghouse Sch. for Environ. Excellence, Cin., 1991; invited contbr. to proceedings of the 1st Tatarstan Symposium on Energy, Environment and Econs., Kazan, Tatarstan, Russia, 1992. Mem. publs. com. Cen. Assn. Sci. and Math. Tchrs., Iowa City, 1969-72; editor Nat. Task Force on Agrl. Energy R&D, Washington, 1976; editor, contbr. Minn. Sci. Mag., 1974-77; contbr. several hundred med., sci. and engring. articles including to Procs. of Iowa Acad. Sci., Sch. Sci. and Math., Am. Biology Tchrs., Procs. of Internat. Communication Conf., and Procs. of Westinghouse Computer Symposium. Pres. Savannah River Rifle & Pistol Club, Aiken, 1981-82, Aiken Toastmasters, 1984; judge speech contests Optimist and 4-H Club Contests, Aiken, 1985-86. Sgt. U.S. Army, 1955-58. Decorated Disting. Marksman Badge gold medal; recipient 1st place sci. writing Argonne Labs. Assn., 1973, Profl. Achievement Permanent Profl. cert. Iowa State Bd. of Pub. Instrn., 1974, Blue Ribbon, Am. Assn. Agrl. Coll. Editors, Tex. A&M, 1976. Mem. AAAS, N.Y. Acad. Scis., Am. Chem. Soc., Phi Delta Kappa, Sigma Xi. Achievements include research in the causes and timing of pre-adolescent initial interest in science; discovery that low-zinc root environment causes delay of development and acceleration of senescence in tobacco plants; creation of publicity for the MSU discovery of platinum drugs-among the most widely used cancer drugs and models for future drugs to destroy tumors by locking onto cancer DNA. Office: Westinghouse Savannah River Co Environ Protection Dept Aiken SC 29801

MILLER, PHOEBE AMELIA, marketing professional; b. Jan. 13, 1948; d. William Prescott and Elizabeth Helen (Lucker) M.. BA in Math., U. Wis., 1970; postgrad., Stanford U., 1973, Golden Gate U., 1975-76. Engr. Bechtel, San Francisco, 1972-77; asst. mgr. Rand Info. Systems, San Francisco, 1977-79; sr. mktg. rep. Computer Sci. Corp., San Francisco, 1979-81; mgr. distbr. sales COGNOS Corp., Walnut Creek, Calif., 1981-86; owner, mgr. P.A. Miller & Assocs., San Francisco, 1986—. Office: PA Miller & Assocs 1750 Montgomery St San Francisco CA 94111-1003

MILLER, RALPH, coach, retired; b. Chanute, Kans., Mar. 9, 1919. Coach Wichita State U., 1951-64, U. Iowa, 1964-70, Oreg. State U., 1970-89. Named Nat. Coach of Yr., AP, 1981, 82, Basketball Hall of Fame, 1988. Achievements include coach of Big 10 Title Team, 1970; coach PAC 10 Conference Title Team, 1980-82; coach eighth winningest team in Divsn. 1 history. Office: care Basketball Hall of Fame PO Box 179 Springfield MA 01101-0179

MILLER, RALPH BRADLEY, lawyer, state legislator; b. Fayetteville, N.C., May 19, 1953; s. Nathan David and Margaret Virginia (Hale) M.; m. Esther Susan Hall, Dec. 19, 1981. BA, U. N.C., 1975; MSc, London Sch. Econs., 1978; JD, Columbia U., 1979. Bar: N.C. 1979, U.S. Dist. Ct. (ea. dist.) N.C. 1980, U.S. Ct. Appeals (4th cir. 1980), U.S. Dist. Ct. (mid. dist.) N.C. 1983. Law clk. to Hon. J. Dickson Phillips Jr. U.S. Ct. Appeals (4th cir.), 1979-80; assoc. Allen, Steed & Allen, Raleigh, N.C., 1980-82, Barringer, Allen & Pinnix, Raleigh, N.C., 1982-84, LeBoeuf, Lamb, Leiby & MacRae, Raleigh, N.C., 1985-88; prin. Nichols, Miller & Sigmon, Raleigh, N.C., 1988-90; pvt. practice Raleigh, N.C., 1991—; mem. N.C. Ho. of Reps., Raleigh, 1993-94, N.C. Senate, Raleigh, 1997—. Chmn. Wake County Dem. Com., 1985-87; mem. state exec. com. N.C. Dem. Com., 1985-89, 91-97; mem. N.C. Environ. Rev. Commn., 1994-95. Mem. ATLA, N.C. Bar Assn.,

Wake County Bar Assn., N.C. Acad. Trial Lawyers, Am. Judicature Soc., Raleigh Civitan Club. Democrat. Episcopalian. Home: 3211 Coleridge Dr Raleigh NC 27609-7201 Office: 4006 Barrett Dr Raleigh NC 27609-6604

MILLER, RAYMOND EDWARD, computer science educator; b. Bay City, Mich., Oct. 9, 1928; s. Martin Theophil and Elizabeth Charlotte (Zierath) M.; m. Marilyn Lueck, June 18, 1955; children: Patricia Ann, Laura Jean, Donna Lyn, Martha Eileen. BS in Mech. Engring., U. Wis., 1950; BEE, U. Ill., 1954, MS in Math., 1955, PhD in Elect. Engring., 1957. Design engr. IBM, Endicott, Poughkeepsie, N.Y., 1950-51; mem. rsch. staff IBM, Yorktown Heights, N.Y., 1957-81; dir., prof. Ga. Inst. Tech., Atlanta, 1980-89, prof. emeritus, 1989—; dir. Ctr. Excellence in Space Data and Info. Scis. NASA, Greenbelt, Md., 1988-93; prof. U. Md., College Park, 1989—; pres. Computing Scis. Accreditation Bd., N.Y.C., 1985-87. Author: Switching Theory, Vols. I and II, 1965; editor: (with J.W. Thatcher) Complexity of Computer Computation, 1972; patentee in field. Lt. USAF, 1951-53. Fellow AAAS, IEEE; Assn. for Computing Machinery, IEEE Computer Soc. (v.p. edn. acts 1991-92). Lutheran. Avocations: tennis, fishing. Office: U Md Dept of Computer Sci A V Williams Bldg College Park MD 20742

MILLER, RAYMOND JARVIS, agronomy educator; b. Claresholm, Alta., Can., Mar. 19, 1934; came to U.S., 1957, naturalized, 1975; s. Charles Jarvis and Wilma Macy (Anderson) M.; m. Frances Anne Davidson, Apr. 28, 1956; children—Cheryl Rae, Jeffrey John, Jay Robert. B.S. (Fed. Provincial grantee 1954-56, Dan Baker scholar 1954-56), U. Alta., Edmonton, 1957; M.S., Wash. State U., 1960; Ph.D., Purdue U., 1962. Mem. faculty N.C. State U., 1962-65, U. Ill., 1965-69; asst. dir., then asso. dir. Ill. Agrl. Expt. Sta., 1969-73; dir. Idaho Agrl. Expt. Sta., 1973-79; dean U. Idaho Coll. Agr., 1979-85, v.p. for agr.; dean Coll. Agr. and Coll. Life Sci. U. Md., College Park, 1986-89, vice chancellor agr. and natural resources, 1989-91; pres. Md. Inst. for Agrl. and Natural Resources, 1991-93, prof. agronomy, 1986—; internat. expert in areas of agrl. sci. and edn. with spl. emphasis on Russia, former Soviet Union, East Europe. Author numerous papers in field. Pres. Idaho Rsch. Found., 1980-85; bd. govs. Agrl. Rsch. Inst., 1979-80; chmn. legis. subcom. Expt. Sta. Com. on Policy, 1981-82; chmn. bd. div. agr. Land Grant Assn., 1985-86; co-chmn. Nat. Com. Internat. Sci. Edn. Joint Coun., USDA, 1991-94; bd. dirs. C.V. Riley Found., 1985-93; chmn. budget com. Bd. Agr., Nat. Assn. State Univs. and Land Grant Colls., 1993. Grantee Internat. Congress Soil Sci., 1960, Purdue U. Research Found., summers 1960, 61. Fellow AAAS, Am. Soc. Agronomy, Soil Sci. Soc. Am.; mem. Internat. Soc. Soil Sci.,, Clay and Clay Minerals Soc., Am. Chem. Soc., Am. Soc. Plant Physiolotists, Elks, Lions, Sigma Xi, Phi Kappa Phi, Gamma Sigma Delta, Alpha Zeta. Home: 3319 Gumwood Dr Hyattsville MD 20783-1934 Office: HJ Patterson Hall Univ Md College Park College Park MD 20742

MILLER, REED, lawyer; b. Fairmont, W.Va., Dec. 1, 1918; s. Maurice Entler and Lillian Moore (Reed) M.; m. Emilie Morrison Crawford, Feb. 20, 1943; children: Michael Reed, George Crawford, Richard Clinton. AB, W.Va. U., 1939, LLB, 1941. Bar: W.Va. 1941, N.Y. 1945, D.C. 1946. Assoc. Arnold & Fortas, 1946-47; assoc. Arnold, Fortas & Porter, Washington, 1947-59, ptnr., 1959-65; ptnr. Arnold & Porter, Washington, 1965—; ret., 1995; mem. vis. com. Coll. Law, W.Va. U., 1981-86. Trustee N.Y. Ave. Presbyn. Ch., Washington, 1967-69, 88-91. Served to maj. U.S. Army, 1941-46. Mem. ABA, Fed. Communications Bar Assn. (pres. 1976, mem. exec. com.), Army Navy Country Club (Arlington, Va.), Columbia Country Club, Kenwood Golf and Country Club, Phi Beta Kappa, Beta Theta Pi. Avocation: skiing.

MILLER, REGINALD WAYNE, professional basketball player; b. Riverside, Calif., Aug. 24, 1965. Student, UCLA. Basketball player Indiana Pacers, 1987—. Named to NBA All-Star Team, 1990, 94, Dream Team II, 1994. Holder NBA Playoff record most three-point field goals in one quarter (5), 1994, co-holder NBA Playoff record most three-point field goals in one half (6), 1994, 95. *

MILLER, RENE HARCOURT, aerospace engineer, educator; b. Tenafly, N.J., May 19, 1916; s. Arthur C. and Elizabeth M. (Tobin) M.; m. Marcelle Hansotte, July 16, 1948 (div. 1968); children: Christal L., John M.; m. Maureen Michael, Nov. 20, 1973. B.A., Cambridge U., 1937, M.A., 1954. Registered profl. engr., Mass. Aero. engr. G.L. Martin Co., Balt., 1937-39; chief aero. and devel. McDonnell Aircraft Corp., St. Louis, 1939-44; mem. faculty aero. engring. MIT, Cambridge, 1944—, prof., 1957-86, Slater prof. flight transp., 1962-86; head dept. aeros. and astronautics MIT, 1968-78, prof. emeritus, 1986—; v.p. engring. Kaman Aircraft Corp., Bloomfield, Conn., 1952-54; mem. tech. adv. bd. FAA, 1964-66; mem. Aircraft panel Pres.'s Sci. Adv. Com., 1960-72, Army Sci. Adv. Panel, 1966-73; chmn. Army Aviation Sci. Adv. Group, 1963-73; mem. Air Force Sci. Adv. Bd., 1959-70; com. on aircraft aerodynamics NASA, 1960-70. Contbr. articles to profl. jours. Recipient U.S. Army Decoration for Meritorious Civilian Service, 1967, 70; recipient L.B. Laskowitz award N.Y. Acad. Scis., 1976. Fellow Am. Helicopter Soc. (hon. tech. dir. 1957-59, editor jour. 1957-59, Klemin award, Hon. Nikolski lectr. 1983), AIAA (hon., pres. 1977-78, Sylvanus Albert Reed award), Royal Aero. Soc. (Great Britain); mem. Nat. Acad. Engring., Internat. Acad. Astronautics, Academie National de L'Air et de L'Espace France. Home: San Jose New Rd, Penzance Cornwall TR18 4PN, England Office: MIT Dept Aeros & Astronautics 33-411 Cambridge MA 02139

MILLER, REUBEN GEORGE, economics educator; b. Phila., Mar. 28, 1930; s. George and Edna (Fuchs) M.; m. Sylvia Raigla, June 9, 1955. B.A., LaSalle Coll., 1952; diploma, U. Stockholm, 1954; M.A., U. Mont., 1956; Ph.D., Ohio State U., 1966. Asst. instr. Ohio State U., 1954-57; acting asst. prof. Oberlin (Ohio) Coll., 1957-58; asst. prof. U. Mass., Amherst, 1959-67; assoc. prof. econs. Smith Coll., Northampton, Mass., 1967-70; Charles A. Dana prof. econs., chmn. dept. Sweet Briar Coll., 1970—, chmn. div. social scis.; mem. adv. staff Computer Sci. Corp., Washington; cons. Dept. Def.; Fulbright-Hayes lectr. econs. Coll. Law, Nat. Taiwan U., Republic China, 1965-66. Contbr. articles to profl. jours. Am.-Scandinavian Found. fellow, 1952-53; Research Tng. fellow Social Sci. Research Council, 1958-59. Mem. Am. Econ. Assn., Am. Fin. Assn., Royal Econ. Soc. Office: Sweet Briar Coll Dept Econs Sweet Briar VA 24595

MILLER, RICHARD ALAN, lawyer, former merger and acquisition and forest products company executive; b. Cleve., July 29, 1939; s. Joshua Spencer and Martha (Harris) M.; m. Virginia Bell McCully, June 23, 1962; children: Cynthia Lynn (dec.), Alexander James. B.B.A., U. Mich., 1961, J.D., 1964. Bar: Ariz. 1964, Ill. 1989, Wis. 1989, Fla. 1994; lic. real estate broker, Ill., Wis. Assoc. Fennemore, Craig, von Ammon and Udall (now Fennemore Craig), Phoenix, 1964-69; ptnr. Fennemore, Craig, von Ammon and Udall (now Fennemore Craig), 1970-71; exec. v.p. Southwest Forest Industries, Inc., Phoenix, 1972-86; pres., chief exec. officer Knox Lumber Co., St. Paul, 1986; v.p. F.H. Fin. Corp., Milw., 1987-88; owner Hammett, Williams & Miller, Delavan, Wis., 1989-91; of counsel Brennan, Steil, Basting & MacDougall, S.C., Delavan, 1991—. Mem. Ariz. Bar Assn., Ill. Bar Assn, Wis. Bar Assn., Fla. Bar Assn.

MILLER, RICHARD ALAN, economist, educator; b. Springfield, Ohio, Feb. 25, 1931; s. Ross and Beatrice Miller; m. Joan Taylor Walton, July 7, 1956; children: Carol Elizabeth, Jean Anne, Eric Ross. BA, Oberlin Coll., 1952; MA, Yale U., 1957; MA (hon.), Wesleyan U., 1972; PhD, Yale U., 1962. Mem. faculty Wesleyan U., Middletown, Conn., 1960—, chmn. dept. econs., 1968-69, 71-73, 75-76, 92-94, Andrews prof., 1995—; vis. lectr. Yale U., New Haven, 1961-62, vis. assoc. prof., 1967-68, vis. prof., 1973, 83, 85, 95; vis. assoc. prof. U. Calif., Berkeley, 1969-70; vis. prof. U. Adelaide, Australia, 1981; vis. lectr econs. U. Conn., Storrs, 1983; economist Econ. Policy Office, Antitrust Div., U.S. Dept. Justice, Washington, 1973-74, cons., 1974-75; cons. antitrust sect. State Conn., 1980, 82; dir. Kawanhee, Inc., Maine, 1975-81, 82-86. Contbr. articles on indsl. orgn. and antitrust econs. to profl. jours. Mem. cert. adv. coun. Dept. Edn., State Conn., 1982-86; mem. coms. Bd. for State Acad. Awards. State Conn., 1978-97; dean faculty of Cons. Examiners., 1985-87; trustee Conn. Joint Coun. Econ. Edn., 1982-85. Served to lt. (j.g.) USNR, 1952-55. Ford Found. fellow Yale U., 1958-59; NSF fellow MIT, 1964-65, Wesleyan U., 1965-69; Shelby Cullom Davis Found. grantee Wesleyan U., 1979-82; Fulbright fellow N.Z. Inst. Econ. Research, 1986, 88. Mem. Am. Econs. Assn., Am. Law and Econs. Assn., Indsl. Orgn. Soc., So. Econ. Assn. Congregationalist. Home: 83 Paterson Dr Middletown CT 06457-5138 Office: Wesleyan U Dept Econs Middletown CT 06459

MILLER, RICHARD HAMILTON, lawyer, broadcasting company executive; b. Cleve., July 18, 1931; s. Ray Thomas and Ruth (Hamilton) M.; m. Ernestine Bowman, Aug. 25, 1985; children: James M., Suanne R., Elizabeth M., Judith K., William P., Matthew W. A.B., U. Notre Dame, 1953, J.D., 1955. Bar: Ohio 1955. Since practiced in Cleve. as mem. firm Miller & Miller; asst. prosecutor Cuyahoga County, 1957-60; pres. Cleve. Broadcasting, Inc., 1966-70, Searles Lake Chem. Corp., Los Angeles, 1966-69, Miller Broadcasting Co., Cleve., 1970-87, Hollywood Bldg. Systems, Inc., Meridian, Miss., 1974-86; mng. partner Miller & Co., Cleve., 1974—; former owner, dir. Cleve. Profl. Basketball Co., Cleve. Baseball, Inc. Dir. gen. counsel Mail Marketing Inc., 1974—, R.W. Sidley, Inc., 1966—; gen. chmn. N.E. Ohio March of Dimes, 1971-73; adv. council Catherine Horstman Home Retarded Children, 1969-73; mem. Cuyahoga Democratic Exec. Com., 1955-66. Served to capt. AUS, 1956-57. Named Irishman of the Yr., City Counsel of Cleve., 1995. Mem. Ohio, Cuyahoga County, Cleve. bar assns., Cleve. Citizens League. Clubs: K.C. (Cleve.), Variety (Cleve.), Notre Dame (Cleve.) (pres. 1964-65), Cleve. Athletic (Cleve.) (dir. 1971-74); Shaker Heights (Ohio) Country. Office: The Park 1700 E 13th St Apt 20T Cleveland OH 44114-3223

MILLER, RICHARD IRWIN, education educator, university administrator; b. Fairbury, Nebr., Feb. 1, 1924; s. Carl W. and Iva Mae (Wilburn) M.; m. Peggy J. McLaren, June 25, 1955; children: Joan Marie, Diane Lee, Janine Louise. B.S., U. Nebr., 1947; M.Ed., Springfield Coll., 1948; Ed.D., Columbia U., 1958. Instr. Pa. State U., 1957-58; observer UN, 1958-60; assoc. dir. project on instrn. NEA, 1960-63; assoc. dir. Ctr. Study of Instrn., 1963-64; prof. edn. U. Ky., Lexington, 1964-69, chmn. dept. social philosophy Founds. in Edn., 1967-69, dir. program for ednl. change, 1964-69; v.p. acad. affairs, dean Baldwin-Wallace Coll., Berea, Ohio, 1970-72; assoc. dir. Ill. Bd. Higher Edn., Springfield, 1972-77; prof. higher edn., v.p. for ednl. services SUNY, Brockport, 1977-80; vis. fellow Cornell U., Ithaca, N.Y., 1980-81; v.p. for acad. affairs, prof. S.W. Tex. State U., San Marcos, 1981-84; prof., coordinator higher edn. Ohio U., Athens, 1984—; ednl. advisor ABA, 1959-63; mem. adv. bd. Ctr. for Info. on Am., 1965-70; dir. nat. evaluation program Elem. and Secondary Edn. Act Title III, 1967-68; exec. sec. Pres.'s Nat. Adv. Council Supplementary Ctrs. and Services, 1968-69; cons. Com. Econ. Devel., U.S. Office Edn., 1967-70; cons. edn. Mead Ednl. Service, Inc. div. Mead Corp., also coordinator spl. ednl. seminars. Author: Dag Hammarskjod and Crisis Diplomacy, 1961, Education in a Changing Society, 1963, Teaching About Communism, 1966; editor: (with Ole Sand) Schools for the Sixties, 1963, ESEA Title III: Catalyst for Change, 1967, The Nongraded School, 1968, Perspectives on Educational Change, 1967, Evaluating Faculty Performance, 1972, Developing Programs for Faculty Evaluation, 1974, Assessment of College Performance, 1979, Institutional Assessment for Self-Improvement, 1981, Evaluating Faculty for Promotion and Tenure, 1987, (with Ed Holzapfel) Issues in Personnel Management, 1988; editor: Evaluating Major Components in Two-Year Colleges, 1988, Major American Higher Education Issues and Challenges in the Nineties, 1990; editor, chpt. contbr.: Applying the Deming Method to Higher Education, 1991. Served with USAF, 1942-43. Recipient Nat. Pacesetter award in edn. Nat. Coun. Supplementary Ctrs. and Svcs., 1968, Kathryn G. Moore higher edn. mgmt. award Coll. and Personnel Assn., 1994. Mem. Cosmos Club (Washington), Rotary. Presbyterian. Home: 17 Briarwood Dr Athens OH 45701-1302

MILLER, RICHARD JACKSON, lawyer; b. Milw., July 17, 1946; s. Wayne D. and Margarite M. (Von Sitany) M.; m. Irene Nikki Tsacoyeanes, May 28, 1972; children: Nicole Elizabeth, Andrew James, Katherine M., Penelope Constance. BA, U. N.C., 1968; JD, U. Va., 1971. Bar: N.Y. 1973, U.S. Dist. Ct. (so. dist.) N.Y. 1975, U.S. Ct. Appeals (2d cir.) 1975, Fla. 1988. Assoc. Brown and Wood, N.Y.C., 1971-78, Wood and Dawson, N.Y.C., 1978-82; ptnr. Alexander and Green, N.Y.C., 1982-86, Mudge, Rose, Guthrie, Alexander & Ferdon, West Palm Beach, Fla., 1986-95, Edwards and Angell, Palm Beach, Fla., 1995—; Contbr. articles to profl. jours., chpt. to book. Capt. USAR, 1972-79. Mem. ABA, Fla. Bar Assn., N.Y. State Bar Assn., Palm Beach County Bar Assn., University Club (N.Y.C.). Episcopalian. Avocations: golf, tennis. Office: Edwards & Angell 250 Royal Palm Way Ste 300 Palm Beach FL 33480-4317

MILLER, RICHARD JEROME, bank executive; b. Erie, Pa., May 8, 1939; s. Richard A. and Irene (Strahl) M.; children by previous marriage: Edward Scott, Lisa Ann, Sondra Lynn; m. Suzanne Marie Johnson, Oct. 22, 1983. BS, Lehigh U., 1961; MA, New Sch. N.Y.C., 1964; postgrad. NYU, 1964-68. With Chase Manhattan Bank, N.Y.C., 1961-82, v.p., 1974-82; v.p. E.F. Hutton Credit Corp./Chrysler Capital Corp., Greenwich, Conn., 1982-88, The CIT Group, N.Y.C., 1988-90; dir. Miller/Davis & Assocs., N.Y.C., 1991—; v.p. Nat. Westminster Bank, N.Y.C., 1991-97. Mem. Waldwick Bd. Edn., N.J., 1968-72, v.p., 1971-72; pres. Columbia Condominium. Mem. Am. Econ. Assn., Western Fin. Assn., Fin. Mgmt. Assn. Republican. Roman Catholic. Office: Miller Davis & Assocs 60 E 42nd St Rm 1440 New York NY 10165-1499

MILLER, RICHARD KEITH, engineering educator; b. Fresno, Calif., June 12, 1949; s. Albert Keith and Gloria Mae (Pittman) M.; m. Elizabeth Ann Parrish, July 10, 1971; children: Katherine Elizabeth, Julia Anne. BS in Aerospace Engring., U. Calif., Davis, 1971; MS in Mech. Engring., MIT, 1972; PhD in Applied Mechanics, Calif. Inst. Tech., Pasadena, 1976. Asst. prof. mech. engring. U. Calif., Santa Barbara, 1975-79; assoc. prof. civil engring. U. So. Calif., L.A., 1979-85, prof., 1985-92, assoc. dean engring., 1989-92; prof., dean Coll. Engring., U. Iowa, 1992—; cons. Astro Aerospace Corp., The Aerospace Corp., Jet Propulsion Lab. Contbr. numerous articles to sci. and profl. jours. Mem. ASCE, Am. Soc. Engring. Edn. Office: U Iowa Coll Engring Office of Dean 3100 EB Iowa City IA 52242-1527

MILLER, RICHARD KIDWELL, artist, actor, educator; b. Fairmont, W.Va., Mar. 15, 1930; s. Maurice Entler and Lillian (Reed) M.; m. Teresa Marie Robinson, Apr. 27, 1957. Student, Pa. Acad. Fine Arts, 1948-49; BA, Am. U., Washington, 1953; MFA, Columbia U., 1956. Instr. painting Scarsdale (N.Y.) Community Sch., 1970-75; asst. prof. Kansas City Art Inst., 1968-69. Participated extensively in profl. theater as actor and singer including roles in Broadway Prodn. Baker Street; actor stock cos. including Fiddler on the Roof; one man art shows include Trans-Lux Gallery, Washington, 1951, Bader Gallery, Washington, 1954, Balt. Mus. Art, 1955, Graham Gallery Ltd., N.Y.C., 1960, 62, 65, Argas Gallery, Madison, N.J., 1966, Jefferson Place Gallery, Washington, 1966, Albrecht Gallery Art, St. Joseph, Mo., 1969, L.I. U., 1973, Aaron Berman Gallery N.Y.C., 1983, Westbeth Gallery, N.Y.C., 1982; group shows include Corcoran Gallery Art., 1950-51, 53, Pa. Acad. Fine Arts, 1951, 64, Carnegie Internat., 1961, Salon de National, Paris, 1954, Whitney Mus., 1958, U. Nebr., 1963, Martha Jackson Gallery, N.Y.C., 1973, Nat. Acad. Design, N.Y.C., 1996, Art of the Northeast, New Caanan, Conn., 1996, others; represented in permanent collections Hirshorn Mus. and Sculpture Garden, Washington, Phillips Collection, Washington, Rochester Mus. Art, Albrecht Gallery U. Ariz., also numerous private collections; featured in Jan. edit. Am. Artist Mag., 1988, Christian Sci. Monitor, 1990,, World Artists (Claude Marks), 1991. Washington Times Herald scholar, 1944, 45, 46; Gertrude Whitney scholar, 1948-53, 55-56; Fulbright fellow, 1953-54. Address: 222 West 83d St Apt 8C New York NY 10024 *I have an insatiable need to express myself—I suppose I was born with it. I was given more than one talent to satisfy this need, and for that I thank God. I have endeavored to use these talents to the absolute best of my ability. I can do no more than that. Some times I have succeeded, and many times I have failed, but the real joy and meaning is in the doing. All the pain has been worth it.*

MILLER, RICHARD L., architectural executive; b. Salina, Kans., Jan. 31, 1941; s. L. William and Inez Corine (DeMars) M.; m. Sharalena Miller, June 22, 1963; children: Lora Miller Vinson, Scott Miller. Student, Kansas Wesleyan U., 1959-61; BArch, U. Kans., 1966, postgrad., 1966-67. Registered architect, 38 states and V.I. Assoc. Earl Swensson Assocs., Nashville, 1967-73, pres., 1973—; mem. hosp. licensure task force State of Tenn. Dept. Pub. Health, 1975, Ambulatory Surg. Treatment Ctr. Act Task Force, 1976-77, SCARAB, Hon. Archtl. Frat., Nursing Home Task Force, 1977-78; participant Internat. Pub. Health Seminar, Budapest, 1984; speaker Fla. HRS seminars, 1986, 90; mem. ann. faculty health care forum on health facilities design, 1990; speaker numerous confs. in field, including World Workplace, 1995, NeoCon '95 World's Trade Fair, 1995, Health Facility Inst. Fifth Ann. Conf., 1994. Co-author: New Directions in Hospital and Healthcare Facility Design, 1995. Mem. Leadership Nashville, 1993-94. Mem. Am. Inst. Architects (mem. com. architecture for health 1980), Tenn. Soc. Architects (mem. ad hoc fire com. 1975). Mem. Christian Ch. Avocations: golfing, kite flying, sailing. Office: Earl Swensson Assocs 2100 W End Ave Ste 1200 Nashville TN 37203-5225

MILLER, RICHARD MCDERMOTT, sculptor; b. New Philadelphia, Ohio, Apr. 30, 1922; s. J. Harry and Clela Belle (McDermott) M.; m. Audrey F. Miller, 1942; 1 dau., Sue Ann (Mrs. Kenneth Hartz); m. Gloria B. Bley, Mar. 18, 1961. Student, Cleve. Inst. Art, 1940-42, 49-51. Prof. emeritus Queens Coll., CUNY. One man shows include Peridot Gallery, N.Y.C., 1964, 66, 67, 69, Washburn Gallery, N.Y.C., 1971, 74, 75, 77, Canton (Ohio) Art Inst., 1980, 20-yr. retrospective Artists Choice Mus., N.Y.C., 1984, Springfield (Mo.) Mus. Art, 1985, Friends of Figurative Sculpture Gallery, N.Y.C., 1987-97, Philharm. Ctr., Naples, Fla., 1991, J.J. Brookings Gallery, San Francisco, 1997; represented in numerous pub. and pvt. collections; author: Figure Sculpture in Wax and Plaster, 1971. Served with AUS, 1942-46. Mem. NAD (pres. 1989-92), Sculptors Guild, Nat. Sculpture Soc. (pres. 1997—), Century Assn. Address: 53 Mercer St New York NY 10013-2617

MILLER, RICHARD SHERWIN, legal educator; b. Boston, Dec. 11, 1930; s. Max and Mollie (Kruger) M.; m. Doris Sheila Lunchick, May 24, 1956; children: Andrea Jayne Armitage, Matthew Harlan. B.S.B.A., Boston U., 1951, J.D. magna cum laude, 1956; LL.M., Yale U., 1959. Bar: Mass. 1956, Mich. 1961, Hawaii 1977. Pvt. practice law Boston, 1956-58; assoc. prof. law Wayne State U., Detroit, 1959-62, prof., 1962-65; prof. Ohio State U., Columbus, 1965-73, dir. clin. and interdisciplinary program, 1971-73; prof. U. Hawaii, Honolulu, 1973-95, prof. emeritus, 1995—, dean, 1981-84; vis. prof. law USIA/U. Hawaii, Hiroshima U. Affiliation Program, Japan, fall 1986, Victoria U., Wellington, N.Z., spring 1987; del. Hawaii State Jud. Conf., 1989-92. Author: Courts and the Law: An Introduction to our Legal System, 1980; editor: (with Roland Stanger) Essays on Expropriations, 1967; editor-in-chief: Boston U. Law Rev., 1955-56; contbr. articles to profl. jours. Mem. Hawaii Substance Abuse Task Force, 1994-95; arbitrator Hawaii Ct. Annexed Arbitration Program, 1995—; bd. dirs. Drug Policy Forum Hawaii, 1996—. 1st lt. USAF, 1951-53. Sterling-Ford fellow Yale U., 1958-59; named Lawyer of Yr. Japan-Hawaii Lawyers Assn., 1990. Mem. ABA, Hawaii State Bar Assn., Hawaii ACLU, Am. Inn of Ct. IV (founding mem., master of the bench), Am. Law Inst., Honolulu Cmty-Media Coun. (pres. 1994—). Office: U Hawaii Richardson Sch Law 2515 Dole St Honolulu HI 96822-2328

MILLER, RICHARD STEVEN, lawyer; b. Mt. Vernon, N.Y., Dec. 5, 1951; s. Norman and Mildred (Curtis) M. BA, U. Pa., 1974; JD, NYU, 1977. Bar: N.Y. 1978, U.S. Dist. Ct. (so. and ea. dists.) N.Y. 1978, U.S. Ct. Appeals (2d cir.) 1978. Asst. dist. atty. Kings County, N.Y., 1977-79; with Hahn & Hessen, N.Y.C., 1979-82, Levin & Weintraub & Crames, N.Y.C., 1982-87; counsel, then ptnr. Rogers & Wells, N.Y.C., 1987-91; ptnr. Dewey Ballantine, N.Y.C., 1991—. Mem. ABA, Internat. Bar Assn., Am. Bankruptcy Inst. Office: Dewey Ballantine 1301 Avenue Of The Americas New York NY 10019-6092

MILLER, RICHARDS THORN, naval architect, engineer; b. Jenkintown, Pa., Jan. 31, 1918; s. Herman Geistweit and Helen Buckman (Thorn) M.; B.S. in Naval Architecture and Marine Engring., Webb Inst. Naval Architecture, 1940; Naval Engr., MIT, 1951; m. Jean Corbat Spear, Sept. 13, 1941; (dec.); children: Patricia (Mrs. Charles G. Fishburn), Linda (Mrs. John X. Carrier); m. 2d, Alice Johnson Houghton, May 19, 1984. Reg. profl. engr. Commd. ensign U.S. Navy, 1940, advanced through grades to capt., 1960; head preliminary design br. Bur. Ships, 1960-63; dir. Mine Def. Lab., Panama City, Fla., 1963-66; dir. ship design Naval Ship Engring. Ctr., 1966-68; specialized work design oceanographic research ships, mine sweepers, torpedo boats, destroyers; ret., 1968; mgr. ocean engring. Oceanic div. Westinghouse Electric Corp., 1969-75, adv. engr., 1975-79; cons. naval architect and engr., 1968—; arbitrator admiralty and ship building contract cases, 1978—; mem. com. naval architecture Am. Bur. Shipping, 1960-63, mem. tech. com., 1978-92; mem. ship structure com., 1966-68. Decorated Navy Legion of Merit; recipient William Selkirk Owen award Webb Alumni Assn., 1983. Fellow Soc. Naval Architects and Marine Engrs. (chmn. S.E. sect. 1965-66, chmn. marine systems com. 1970-77, chmn. tech. and rsch. steering com. 1977-78, chmn. small craft com. 1983-87, v.p. tech. and rsch. 1979-81, hon. v.p. (life), 1981—, mem. coun. 1976—, mem. exec. com. 1977-81; Capt. Joseph H. Linnard prize 1964, Disting. Svc. award 1988); mem. Am. Soc. Naval Engrs. (mem. council 1976-78), U.S. Naval Inst., N.Y. Yacht Club, Annapolis Yacht Club, Sailing Club of the Chesapeake, Sigma Xi. Author: (with R.G. Henry) Sailing Yacht Design, 1963, (with K.L. Kirkman) Sailing Yacht Design-A New Appreciation, 1990; also sects. in books, articles. Home and Office: 957 Melvin Rd Annapolis MD 21403-1315

MILLER, RICK FREY, emergency physician; b. Peoria, Ill., July 27, 1946; s. Richard Ross and Mildred (Frey) M.; m. Cheryl Kay Hasty, June 1, 1968; children: Richard Andrew, Jennifer Caroline, Heidi Sue. BS in Math., BS in Chemistry, Bradley U., 1969; MD, U. Ill., 1974. Bd. cert. emergency medicine and pediats. Program dir. emergency medicine St. Francis Med. Ctr., Peoria, Ill., 1980-88, med. dir. Life Flight, 1985-91, chmn. dept. emergency medicine, dir. emergency med. svcs., 1988—. Contbr. book chpt.: Emergency Medicine Clinics of North America, 1992. Bd. dirs. Prevent Child Abuse-Ill., Springfield, 1991—, Mental Health Assn. of Illinois Valley, Peoria, 1996—; co-lay dir. Teens Encounter Christ, Peoria, 1997. Recipient Ptnrs. in Peace award Ctr. for Prevention of Abuse, 1996. Fellow Am. Coll. Emergency Physicians, Am. Acad. Pediats.; mem. Soc. Acad. Emergency Medicine. Avocations: skiing, bicycling. Office: St Francis Med Ctr 530 NE Glen Oak Ave Peoria IL 61637-0001

MILLER, RITA, personnel consultant, diecasting company executive; b. Bklyn., Jan. 15, 1925; d. Joseph and Etta M.; BA, Bklyn. Coll., 1947; MA, Boston U., 1949; children: Erika Greenwald, Roy Barnet Glickman. Personnel officer, sec. to pres. Marine Elec. Corp., Bklyn., 1943-47; script writer Song Debut, Boston, 1949-50; dir. Writers' Workshops, interviewer pub. opinion surveys, New Rochelle, N.Y., 1962-64; mgr. employee relations Dynacast div. Coats & Clark, Inc., Yorktown Heights, 1966-89. Mem. Am. Soc. Personnel Adminstrn., Westchester Personnel Mgmt. Assn. (dir.), Personnel Council New Rochelle, Bus. and Profl. Women U.S.A., Nat. Sociology Hon. Soc. Editor: The Management Consultant (George Kenning), 1965; contbr. articles to profl. jours. Home: 16 Congress St New Rochelle NY 10801-1902

MILLER, ROBERT, advertising executive; b. N.Y.C., June 2, 1923; s. Samuel and Adele (Elswit) M.; m. Frances Fitzgerald, June 10, 1944 (dec. 1978); children: Marc Robert, William Fitzgerald, Daniel Bates, Ellen Minette (Mrs. John Meyer); m. Sandra Gold Patelmo, 1980. Student, NYU, 1940-42, Syracuse U., 1943. Newsroom employee N.Y. Daily Mirror, 1942; with Miller Advt. Agy., Inc., N.Y.C., 1946—, v.p., 1948-54, chmn. bd., 1954-57, pres., 1958—; pres. Miller Advt. Service Corp., 1956-62; pres. Miller Advt. Agy. Ill., Inc., 1965-73, also bd. dirs.; bd. dirs. Hereford Ins. Co., Inc., 1988-94. Contbg. editor Madison Avenue mag., 1975-78. Bd. govs. Roslyn Democratic Club, 1957-61, 68-73; mem. Nassau County Dem. Com., 1958-61, 68-73; Bd. dirs. Shalom Peace Found. Served to 1st lt. USAAF, 1942-46. Mem. Am. Legion, Jewish War Vets. Home: 301 E 52nd St New York NY 10022-6319 also: 17 Shelly Dr Ellenville NY 12428-1809 Office: Miller Advt Agy Inc 71 5th Ave New York NY 10003-3004

MILLER, ROBERT ALLEN, hotel executive; b. Chgo., Nov. 26, 1945; m. Diana Marie Hall, Dec. 29, 1967; children: David, Allison, Brian. BSBA, U. Fla., 1967. CPA, Fla. Auditor, acct. Arthur Young & Co., Tampa, Fla., 1967-72; chief fin. officer Fleetwing Corp., Lakeland, Fla., 1972-78; pres. Am. Resorts Corp., Lakeland, 1978-84; v.p. Marriott Internat., Bethesda, Md., 1984—. Office: Marriott Internat 1 Marriott Dr Washington DC 20058-0001

MILLER, ROBERT ALLEN, software engineer, consultant; b. Batavia, N.Y., Aug. 18, 1946; s. Wilford Earl and Mildred A. (Faith) M. BA, DePauw U., 1968. Cert. data processor, cert. systems profl. Software engr. AT&T, Alpharetta, Ga., 1972-95, instr. Bell Labs. Tech. Edn. Ctr., 1988-94. Vol. ARC, Atlanta, 1992. Sgt. USAF, 1968-72. Mem. Assn. for Computing Machinery. Office: AT&T 300 N Point Pkwy Alpharetta GA 30005-4116

MILLER, ROBERT ARTHUR, state supreme court chief justice; b. Aberdeen, S.D., Aug. 28, 1939; s. Edward Louis and Bertha Leone (Hitchcox) M.; m. Shirlee Ann Schlim, Sept. 5, 1964; children: Catherine Sue, Scott Edward, David Alan, Gerri Elizabeth, Robert Charles. BSBA, U. S.D., 1961, JD, 1963. Asst. atty. gen. State of S.D., Pierre, 1963-65; pvt. practice law Philip, S.D., 1965-71; state atty. Haakon County, Philip, 1965-71; city atty. City of Philip, 1965-71; judge State of S.D. (6th cir.), Pierre, 1971-86, presiding judge, 1975-86; justice S.D. Supreme Ct., Pierre, 1986—, now chief justice; bd. dirs. Nat. Conf. of Chief Justices; trustee S.D. Retirement Sys., Pierre, 1974-85, chmn., 1982-85; mem. faculty S.D. Law Enforcement Tng. Acad., 1975-85. Mem. S.D. State Crime Commn., 1979-86; mem. adv. commn. S.D. Sch. for the Deaf, 1983-85, Communications Svcs. to Deaf, 1990—; cts. counselor S.D. Boy's State, 1986—. Mem. State Bar of S.D., S.D. Judges' Assn. (pres. 1974-75). Roman Catholic. Lodge: Elks. Avocations: golf, hunting. Office: SD Supreme Ct 500 E Capitol Ave Pierre SD 57501-5070*

MILLER, ROBERT BRANSON, JR., retired newspaper publisher; b. Battle Creek, Mich., Aug. 10, 1935; s. Robert Branson and Jean (Leonard) M.; m. Pattricia E. Miller; children: Melissa Ann, Gregory Allen, Jennifer Lynn, Jeffrey William. Grad., Hotchkiss Sch., Lakeville, Conn., 1953; BA, Mich. State U., 1959. Advt. salesman State Jour., Lansing, Mich., 1959-61; circulation sales rep. State Jour., 1961-62, reporter, 1962-65, nat. advt. mgr., 1965-66; asst. to pub. Idaho Statesman, Boise, 1966-69, pub., 1971-79; pub. Daily Olympian, Olympia, Wash., 1969-71; pub. Battle Creek Enquirer, 1979-90, chmn., 1990-91. Mem. adv. bd. Battle Creek chpt. ARC, Big Bros./Big Sisters, Neighborhoods Inc.; sr. advisor United Way; trustee Cheff Ctr. for Handicapped, Miller Found., Battle Creek. With USNR, 1956-58.

MILLER, ROBERT CARL, library director; b. May 9, 1936; m. Jeanne M. Larson. BS in History and Philosophy, Marquette U., 1958; MS in Am. History, U. Wis., 1962; MA in Libr. Sci., U. Chgo., 1966. Head telephone reference Library of Congress, Wash., 1959-60; reference librarian Marquette U., Milw., 1960-62, acquisition librarian, 1962-66; head tech. services/librarian Parsons Coll., Fairfield, Iowa, 1966-68; head acquisitions dept. U. of Chgo. Library, Ill., 1968-71; assoc. dir (reader services) U. of Chgo. Library, 1971-73; assoc dir (gen. service) U. of Chgo., 1973-75; dir. of libraries U. Mo., St. Louis, 1975-78; dir of libraries U. of Notre Dame, Ind., 1978-97, ret., 1997; vis. prof. IBIN-U. Warsaw, Poland, 1992, 93, 97. Contbr. to prof. jour. Fellow Woodrow Wilson Found. (sr.), Coun. on Libr. Resources; mem. ALA, Polish Inst. of Arts and Letters of Am. Roman Catholic. Home: 4540 W Binner Dr Chandler AZ 85226

MILLER, ROBERT CARMI, JR., microbiology educator, university administrator; b. Elgin, Ill., Aug. 10, 1942; s. Robert C. and Melba I. (Steinke) M.; m. Patricia A. Black, Aug. 29, 1964; children: Geoffrey T., Christopher J. BS in Physics, Trinity Coll., Hartford, Conn., 1964; MS in Biophysics, Pa. State U., 1965; PhD in Molecular Biology, U. Pa., 1969. USPHS trainee U. Pa., Phila., 1966-69; postdoctoral fellow U. Wis., Madison, 1969-70; rsch. assoc., Am. Cancer Soc. postdoctoral fellow MIT, Cambridge, 1970-71; asst. prof. U. B.C., Vancouver, 1971-79, prof. microbiology, 1980—, head dept. microbiology, 1982-85, dean sci., 1985-88, v.p. rsch., 1988-95, univ. senate, 1985-88; assoc. vice provost for rsch., dir. technology transfer U. Wash., Seattle, 1995—; vis. prof. Inst. Molecular Biology, U. Geneva, Switzerland, 1976; mem. grants com. on genetics Med. Rsch. Coun., 1980-82; mem. Grants Panel A Nat. Cancer Inst., 1981-85; biotech. com. B.C. Sci. Coun., 1981-87, univ./industry program grant com., 1987-92; biotech. com. Med. Rsch. Coun., 1983; assoc. com. for biotech. NRC, 1983-86; strategic grant com. biotech. NSERC, 1985-87; bd. dirs. Paprican, Discovery Found., Sci. Coun. B.C., TRIUMF. Assoc. editor Virology, 1974-85, Jour. Virology, 1975-84; contbr. 100 articles to profl. jours.; author research papers. Recipient gold medal Nat. Sci. Coun. B.C., 1993; grantee Natural Sci. and Engring. Rsch. Coun., 1971-96, Med. Rsch. Coun., 1981, 86-89, Nat. Cancer Inst., 1982-86. Office: Office Technology Transfer Univ Wash 1107 NE 45th St Seattle WA 98105-4631

MILLER, ROBERT CHARLES, retired physicist; b. State College, Pa., Feb. 2, 1925; s. Lawrence P. Miller and Eva Mae (Gross) Wiedemann; m. Virginia Callaghan, Aug. 30, 1952; children: Robin Kingon Storey, Jeffrey Lawrence Miller, Lauren Wray Lynch. AB, Columbia U., 1948, MA, 1952, PhD, 1956. Staff mem. Johns-Manville Research Ctr., Finderne, N.J., 1948-49; teaching asst. in physics Columbia U., N.Y.C., 1949-51, lectr. in physics, 1951-53; mem. tech. staff Bell Telephone Labs., Murray Hill, N.J., 1954-63, head solid state spectroscopy research dept., 1963-67; staff mem. Inst. Defense Analyses, Arlington, Va., 1967-68; head optical elec. research dept. Bell Telephone Labs., Murray Hill, 1968-77; mem. tech. staff AT&T Bell Labs., Murray Hill, 1977-84, disting. mem. tech. staff, 1984-88, ret., 1988; cons. Office of Sec. Def., Arlington, Va., 1968-75. Inventor (with Dr. J.A. Giordmaine) Optical Parametric Oscillator, 1965 (co-recipient R.W. Wood prize, 1986); contbr. articles to profl. jours. Served with U.S. Army, 1943-46, ETO. RCA predoctoral fellow Columbia U., 1953-54. Fellow Am. Phys. Soc.; mem. AAAS, N.Y. Acad. Scis., Sigma Xi. Avocations: sailing, sports cars, tennis. Home: 65 Eaton Ct Cotuit MA 02635-2908

MILLER, ROBERT EARL, engineer, educator; b. Rockford, Ill., Oct. 4, 1932; s. Leslie D. and Marcia V. (Jones) M. B.S., U. Ill., 1954, M.S., 1955, Ph.D., 1959. Asst. prof. theoretical and applied mechanics U. Ill., Urbana, 1959-61; asso. prof. U. Ill., 1961-68, prof., 1968-94, prof. emeritus, 1994—; cons. in field to industry U.S. Army; in various positions in industry, summers, 1963-68. Contbr. articles to profl. jours. Mem. AIAA, Am. Soc. Engring. Edn. (Disting. Engring. award 1991), ASCE. Office: U Ill 216 Talbot Lab 104 S Wright St Urbana IL 61801-2935

MILLER, ROBERT FRANCIS, physiologist, educator; b. Eugene, Oreg., Nov. 30, 1939; s. Irvin Lavere and Ettie (Graham) M.; m. Rosemary F. Fish, June 12, 1968; children: Derek, Drew. MD, U. Utah, 1967. Head neurophysiology Naval Aerospace Med. Rsch. Lab., Pensacola, Fla., 1969-71; asst. prof. physiology SUNY, Buffalo, 1971-76, assoc. prof. physiology, 1976-78; assoc. prof. ophthalmology Washington U. Sch. Medicine, St. Louis, 1978-83, prof. ophthalmology, 1983-88; 3M Cross prof., head physiology dept. U. Minn., Mpls., 1988—; Mem. VISA 2 NEI study sect. NIH, 1986—. Mem. editorial bd. Jour. Neurophysiology, 1986—. Lt. comdr. USN, 1969-71. Recipient Merit award NIH, 1988, award for med. rsch. Upjohn, 1967, Rsch. to Prevent Blindness Sr. Scientists award, 1988; James S. Adams scholar, 1982, Robert E. McCormick scholar, 1977-78. Mem. AAAS, Assn. Rsch. in Vision and Ophthalmology, Assn. Chmn. Depts. Physiology, N.Y. Acad. Scis., Neurosci. Soc. Achievements include discovery of major new excitatory amino acid receptor, discovery that the electroretinogram in generated by glia. Home: 4613 Golf Ter Edina MN 55424-1512 Office: U Minn Dept Physiology 6-255 MIllard Hall 435 Delaware St SE Minneapolis MN 55455-0347

MILLER, ROBERT FRANK, retired electronics engineer, educator; b. Milw., Mar. 30, 1925; s. Frank Joseph and Evangeline Elizabeth (Hamann) M.; m. La Verne Boyle, Jan. 10, 1948 (dec. 1978); children: Patricia Ann, Susan Barbara, Nancy Lynn; m. Ruth Winifred Drobnic, July 26, 1980. BSEE, U. Wis., 1947, MSEE, 1954, PhD in Elec. Engring., 1957. Profl. engr., Wis. Instr. physics Milw. Sch. Engring., 1949-53; sr. engr. semicondr. Delco Electronics/GMC, Kokomo, Ind., 1957-67, asst. chief engr., 1967-70, mgr. product assurance, 1970-73, dir. quality control, 1973-85; asst. prof. elec. engring. tech. Purdue U., Kokomo, 1986-90; ret., 1990; ind. cons., Kokomo, 1990—; mem. Ind. Microelectronics Commn., Indpls., 1987—. Author tech. papers; co-author lab. manuals. Bd. dirs. Howard Community Hosp. Found., Kokomo, 1974—; trustee YMCA, Kokomo, 1990—, bd. dirs., 1967-90. Named Disting. Alumnus U. Wis., Madison, 1980, 90. Mem. IEEE (life), Am. Soc. Quality Control (bd. dirs. sect. 0918, advisor Cen. Ind. sect. bd. 1988—), Sigma Xi, Tau Beta Pi, Phi Kappa Phi, Eta Kappa Nu. Presbyterian. Home: 3201 Susan Dr Kokomo IN 46902-7506

MILLER, ROBERT G., retail company executive; b. 1944. With Albertson's Inc., 1961-89, exec. v.p. retail ops., 1989-91; chmn. bd., CEO Fred Meyer Inc., Portland, Oreg., 1991—. Office: Fred Meyer Inc 3800 SE 22nd Ave Portland OR 97202-2918*

MILLER, ROBERT HAROLD, otolaryngologist, educator; b. Columbia, Mo., July 2, 1947; s. Harold Oswald and Ruth Nadine (Ballew) M.; m. Martha Guillory, Apr. 18, 1981; children: Morgan Guillory, Reed Thurston. BS in Biology, Tulane U., 1969, MD, 1973; cert. in otolaryngology-head/neck surg., UCLA Med. Ctr., 1978; MBA, Tulane U., 1996. Diplomate Am. Bd. Otolaryngology. From asst. prof. to assoc. prof. otolaryngology-HNS Baylor Coll. Medicine, Houston, 1978-87; prof., chmn. otolaryngology-HNS Tulane Sch. Medicine, New Orleans, 1987—; bd. dirs. Am. Bd. Otolaryngology; chief of staff Tulane Hosp., 1995-96. Mem. editl. bd. Archives of Otolaryngology, 1986—, Head & Neck Surgery, 1987—, Larynoscope '96. Named Outstanding Young Man, Houston C. of C., 1980; Robert Wood Johnson Health Policy fellow, 1996-97. Fellow ACS, Am. Soc. Head & Neck Surgery, Am. Acad. Oto-Head & Neck Surgery (Disting. Svc. award 1994, Honor award 1991), Triological Soc. (exec. sec. 1992-97). Avocations: tennis, computers. Home: 205 Brockenbraugh Ct Metairie LA 70005-3319 Office: Tulane U Sch Medicine 1430 Tulane Ave New Orleans LA 70112-2699

MILLER, ROBERT HASKINS, retired state chief justice; b. Columbus, Ohio, Mar. 3, 1919; s. George L. and Marian Alice (Haskins) M.; m. Audene Fausett, Mar. 14, 1943; children: Stephen F., Thomas G., David W., Stacey Ann (dec.). A.B., Kans. U., 1940, LL.B., 1942; grad., Nat. Coll. State Trial Judges, Phila., 1967. Bar: Kans. 1943. Practice in Paola, 1946-60; judge 6th Jud. Dist. Kans., Paola, 1961-69; U.S. magistrate Kans. Dist., Kansas City, 1969-75; justice Kans. Supreme Ct., Topeka, 1975-88, chief justice, 1988-90, ret., 1990; chmn. Kans. Jud. Coun., 1987-88. Contbg. author: Pattern (Civil Jury) Instructions for Kansas, 2d edit, 1969. Served with AUS, 1942-46. Mem. Kans. Bar Assn., Wyandotte County Bar Assn., Shawnee County Bar Assn., Am. Legion, Phi Gamma Delta, Phi Delta Phi. Presbyterian. Office: Supreme Ct Kans-Jud Ctr 301 SW 10th Ave Topeka KS 66612-1502

MILLER, ROBERT JAMES, educational association administrator; b. Mansfield, Ohio, Jan. 27, 1926; s. Dennis Cornelius and Mabel (Snyder) M.; m. Jerri Ann Burran, June 5, 1952; children: Robert James Jr., Dennis Burran. Student, Heidelberg Coll., 1946-47; BS, U. N.Mex., 1950, MA, 1952; postgrad., Miami U., Oxford, Ohio, 1951-55; MBA, Fla. Atlantic U., 1978. Asst. exec. sec. Phi Delta Theta Hdqrs., Oxford, 1951-54, adminstrv. sec., 1954-55, exec. v.p., 1955-91; pres. Phi Delta Theta Found., Oxford, 1984—; bus. mgr. The Scroll, Oxford, 1955-91; dir. Interfrat. Found., 1995—. Editor: Phikeia—The Manual of Phi Delta Theta, 1951, 19 edits., 1989, Phis Sing, 1958, Constitution and General Statutes of Phi Delta Theta, Fraternity Education Foundations, 1962, Directory of Phi Delta Theta, 1973. Chmn. United Appeal, Oxford, 1960; bd. dirs. U. N.Mex. Alumni Assn., 1961-68; pres. Fedn. of Clubs, Oxford, 1964, McGuffey PTA, 1971, Miami U. Art Mus., 1993-94, McCullough-Hyde Hosp., Oxford, 1966, chmn. endowment adv. com., 1988-89; vol. leader Boy Scouts Am., Oxford, 1966-79. Recipient citizen of yr. award City of Oxford, 1968, citation Theta Chi, 1967, Order of Interfrat. Svc. Lambda Chi Alpha, 1994, interfrat. leadership award Sigma Nu, 1994, accolate for intrafraternity svc. Kappa Alpha, meritorious svc. award Boy. Scouts Am., 1977, others; Interfrat. Inst. fellow Ind. U., 1988. Mem. Nat. Intrafraternity Conf. (various coms. 1954—, cert. of svc. 1981, 85, gold medal 1992), Am. Soc. Assn. Execs. (cert.), Cin. Soc. Assn. Execs., Fraternity Execs. Assn. (pres. 1962-63, svc. citations 1980, 85, 90, disting. svc. award 1991), Edgewater Conf. (pres. 1978-79), Summit Soc., Country Club Oxford (bd. dirs.), Order of Symposiarchs, Order of Omega, Rotary (founder Oxford club 1965, pres. 1966, merit award 1974, dist. gov. S.W. Ohio 1978-79, study group exch. leader South Africa 1992), Blue Key, Phi Delta Kappa, Omicron Delta Kappa. Home: 170 Hilltop Rd Oxford OH 45056-1572 Office: Phi Delta Theta Ednl Found 1210 Avenue M South Houston TX 77587-5042

MILLER, ROBERT JAMES, lawyer; b. Dunn, N.C., Jan. 14, 1933; s. Robert James and Edith (Crockett) M.; m. Patricia L. Shaw, Sept. 29, 1984; children: Patricia Ann, Susan Ballantine, Nancy Crockett. B.S., N.C. State U., 1956; M.F., Yale U., 1962, M.S., 1965, Ph.D., 1967; J.D., N.C. Central U., 1984. Registered land surveyor. Forester W.Va. Pulp & Paper Co., 1956-59, Tilghman Lumber Co., 1959-61; asst. in instrn. and research Yale U., New Haven, 1962-65; assoc. prof. biology Radford (Va.) Coll., 1965-67, prof., chmn. biology dept., 1967-68, dean div. natural scis., 1968-71, v.p. for acad. affairs, 1971-73; prof. law, dean of coll. St. Mary's Coll., Raleigh, N.C., 1973-85; atty. Patton, Boggs & Blow, Raleigh, N.C., 1985-89; pvt. practice, 1989—; mediator N.C. Gen. Ct. of Justice; ecol. cons.; arbitrator Am. Arbitration Assn., Better Bus. Bur.; lectr. comml. law Tomsk (Russia) State U. Author: The Assimilation of Nitrogen Compounds by Tree Seedlings, 1967, Some Ecological Aspects of Dry Matter Production, 1962, Liberal Arts and the Individual, 1972, Liberal Arts: An Educational Philosophy, 1973, Laboratory Notebook: General Biology, 1976, Educational Malpractice, 1984, Issues in International Commercial Mediation, 1995. Mem. Am. Soc. Plant Physiologists, Ecol. Soc. Am., ABA, Am. Immigration Lawyers Assn., N.C. Acad. Trial Lawyers, N.C. Bar Assn., Sigma Xi, Phi Kappa Phi, Xi Sigma Pi. Episcopalian. Lodges: Masons; Shriners. Home: 3404 Lake Boone Trl Raleigh NC 27607-6756

MILLER, ROBERT JOSEPH, governor, lawyer; b. Evanston, Ill., Mar. 30, 1945; s. Ross Wendell and Coletta Jane (Doyle) M.; m. Sandra Ann Searles, Oct. 17, 1949; children: Ross, Corrine, Megan. BA in Polit. Sci., U. Santa Clara, 1967; JD, Loyola U., Los Angeles, 1971. First legal advisor Las Vegas (Nev.) Met. Police Dept., 1973-75; justice of the peace Las Vegas Twp., 1975-78; dep. dist. atty. Clark County, Las Vegas, 1971-73, dist. atty., 1979-86; lt. gov. State of Nev., 1987-89, acting gov., 1989-90, gov., 1991—. Chmn. Nev. Commn. on Econ. Devel., Carson City, 1987-91, Nev. Commn. on Tourism, Carson City, 1987-91; mem. Pres. Reagan's Task Force on Victims of Crime, 1982; chmn. Nev. divsn. Am. Cancer Soc., 1988-90. Mem. Nat. Dist. Attys. Assn. (pres. 1984-85), Western Govs. Assn. (chmn. 1993-94), Nat. Govs. Assn. (vice chmn. exec. com. 1995-96, chmn. 1996-97, past chmn. com. on justice and pub. safety, chmn. legal affairs com. 1992-94, lead gov. on transp. 1992—), Nev. Dist. Attys. Assn. (pres. 1979, 83). Democrat. Roman Catholic. Home: Gov Mansion 606 N Mountain St Carson City NV 89703-3955 Office: State of Nev Office of Gov Capitol Bldg Carson City NV 89710*

MILLER, ROBERT L., JR., federal judge; b. 1950; m. Jane Woodward. BA, Northwestern U., 1972; JD, Ind. U., 1975. Law clk. to presiding justice U.S. Dist. Ct. (no. dist.) Ind., 1975; judge St. Joseph Superior Ct., South Bend, Ind., 1975-86, chief judge, 1981-83; judge U.S. Dist. Ct. (no. dist.) Ind., South Bend, Ind., 1985—. Office: US Dist Ct 325 Fed Bldg 204 S Main St South Bend IN 46601-2122*

MILLER, ROBERT LOUIS, university dean, chemistry educator; b. Chgo., Jan. 26, 1926; s. Sam P. and Ida (Reich) M.; m. Virginia Southard, Oct. 26, 1947 (dec. Sept. 1973); children: Ruth, Stephen, Martin, Andrew; m. Bonnie Seay Berard, Nov. 28, 1975; children: Edouard, Derek. Ph.B., U. Chgo., 1947, B.S., 1949, M.S., 1951; Ph.D., Ill. Inst. Tech.; Ph.D. (NSF Sci. faculty fellow), 1963. Mem. faculty U. Ill. Chgo. Circle Campus, 1953-67, asst. dean Coll. Liberal Arts and Scis., 1963-65, assoc. dean Coll. Liberal Arts and Scis., 1965-67; prof. chemistry U. N.C.-Greensboro, 1968—, dean arts and scis., 1968-85, acting dean Grad. Sch., 1989-91, spl. asst. to the provost, 1993-94, acting assoc. provost, 1994-96, spl. asst. to provost, 1996—; Am. Council Edn. adminstrv. intern SUNY-Binghamton, 1967-68. Mem. exec. com. of com. environ. affairs Piedmont Council Govts., 1971-76; mem. Greensboro Task Force on Energy; chmn. residential and transp. subcom Greensboro Energy Commn.; mem. Bd. Edn., Oak Park, Ill., 1965-66; bd. dirs. Hospice at Greensboro, 1981-87, pres., 1982-84, vol. 1988-89; vol., mem. bd. dirs. Cities in Schs., 1988-92; bd. dirs. Gilbert Pearson Audubon Soc., Greensboro Civil Liberties Union, Weatherspoon Gallery, 1981-85. Served with AUS, 1944-46, ETO. Mem. AAAS, Sigma Xi (treas. chpt.). Home: 4020 Watauga Dr Greensboro NC 27410

MILLER, ROBERT NOLEN, lawyer; b. Monmouth, Ill., May 30, 1940; s. Robert Clinton and Doris Margaret (Nolen) M.; m. Diane Wilmarth, Aug. 21, 1965; children: Robert Wilmarth, Anne Elizabeth. BA, Cornell Coll., Mt. Vernon, Iowa, 1962; JD, U. Colo., 1965. Bar: Colo. 1965. Assoc. firm M. Quiat, Denver, 1965-66, Fischer & Beaty, Ft. Collins, Colo., 1969-70; dist. atty. Weld County Dist. Atty's. Office, Greeley, Colo., 1971-81; U.S. atty. U.S. Dept. Justice, Denver, 1981-88; chief counsel litigation and security US West Inc., Englewood, Colo., 1988-93; of counsel Patton, Boggs & Blow, Denver, 1993-94, LeBoeuf, Lamb, Greene & Mac Crae, Denver, 1994—; instr. bus. law Am. U., U. S.C., Myrtle Beach, 1966-69. Co-author: Deathroads, 1978. Bd. dirs. Boys Club, Greeley, 1974-78, 1st Congl. Ch., Greeley, 1975-78; Rep. candidate for atty. gen. Colo., 1977-78. Capt. USAF, 1966-69. Recipient Citizen of Yr. award Elks Club, Greeley. Mem. Fed. Bar Assn. (pres. Colo. chpt. 1983-84), Colo. Dist. Atty's Coun. (pres. 1976-77), Colo. Bar Assn., Weld County Bar Assn., Rotary (pres. local chpt. 1980-81). Republican. Avocations: fishing, hunting, golf, tennis, reading. Office: LeBoeuf Lamb Greene MacRae 633 17th St Ste 2800 Denver CO 80202-3660

MILLER, ROBERT REESE, trade association executive; b. Cin., Nov. 14, 1934; s. Louis and Lucille D. (Cantwell) M.; m. Jimmie Lorraine Mote, Aug. 15, 1965; children: Tracy Lou, Kimberly Kristin. BS, U. Okla., 1959. Ter. mgr. Walker div. Tenneco, Shreveport, La., 1961-64; dist. mgr. Garlock, Inc., Chgo., 1964-68; regional mgr. Ideal Corp., Bklyn., 1968-69, nat. sales mgr., 1970-73, v.p., 1973-74; group v.p. Parker Hannifin Automotive, Bklyn., 1975-86; pres. Gen. Automotive Splty., North Brunswick, N.J., 1986-89; v.p. Wagner div. Cooper Industries, Parsippany, N.J., 1989-91; chmn. Motor and Equipment Mfrs. Assn., Englewood Cliffs, N.J., 1985-87; pres., CEO, Motor and Equipment Mfrs. Assn., Research Triangle Park, N.C., 1991—; chmn. Automotive Anti-Counterfeiting Task Force, 1983-87; mem. auto parts adv. com. U.S. Dept. Commerce, Washington, 1993-95; responsible for achieving passage of trade mark counterfeit bill making product counterfeiting a criminal offense. Contbr. articles to profl. publ. Recipient Pursuit of Excellence award Automotive Warehouse Distbrs. Assn., 1991. Mem. Automotive Sales Coun. (pres. 1985-87), Fedn. N.Am. Automotive Parts Mfrs. (sec.-gen. 1993-95), Durham C. of C. (bd. dirs. 1995—), Treyburn Country Club, Univ. Club, Detroit Soc. Clubs. Avocations: reading, golf, deep sea fishing, tennis. Office: Motor-Equipment Mfrs Assn 10 Laboratory Dr Box 13966 Research Triangle Park NC 27709-3966

MILLER, ROBERT SCOTT, mental health administrator, social worker; b. Seattle, Dec. 12, 1947; s. Bert Lester and Carol Theresa (Gustafson) M.; m. Karen Ann Staake, Nov. 12, 1977; children: Sarah, Megan, Emily. BA in Sociology cum laude, Seattle Pacific U., 1970; AM in Social Work, U. Chgo., 1972; MA in Human Resources Mgmt., Pepperdine U., 1977. Cert. social worker, Wash. Br. supr. Wash. State Dept. Social and Health Svcs., Oak Harbor and Anacortes, 1975-78; supr. casework Wash. State Dept. Social and Health Svcs., Everett, 1973-75; lectr., coord. rural community mental health project U. Wash., Seattle, 1978-83; exec. dir. Armed Svcs. YMCA, Oak Harbor, 1984-86; area dir. United Way of Island County, Oak Harbor, 1986-88, exec. dir., 1988-92; exec. dir. Saratoga Community Mental Health, Coupeville, Wash., 1992-93; outpatient therapist, attention-deficit/hyperactivity disorder mental health specialist Cath. Cmty. Svcs. Northwest, Oak Harbor, Wash., 1993-96; dir. Cath. Cmty. Svcs. Northwest, Oak Harbor and Mount Vernon, Wash., 1996—, Island and Skagit Counties; part-time instr. sociology Chapman U. Naval Air Sta. Whidbey Island, Orange, Calif., 1988-95; mem. adv. bd. Island Family Health Ctr., Oak Harbor, 1990-91; project mgr. risk mgmt. Com. Associated Provider Network. Contbr. articles to profl. jours. Bd. dirs. Puget Sound chpt. Huntington's Disease Soc. Am., 1989-93, pres., 1991, fundraising chmn., 1989-91, v.p., 1990; mem. adv. bd. United Ways Wash., 1991-92; chmn. Island County bd. emergency food and shelter program Fed. Emergency Mgmt. Agy.; vice chmn. Cmty. Resource Network, Oak Harbor, 1991; mem. steering com. Greater Oak Harbor Econ. Summit, 1991; mem. strategic planning com. Whidbey Gen. Hosp., Coupeville, 1992-93; mem. exec. com. Mt. Baker coun. Boy Scouts Am., 1993; bd. dirs. Opportunity Coun., Bellingham, 1993-94; bd. dirs. Concerts on the Cove, Coupeville, 1993-96, v.p., 1994-95; mem. Oak Harbor Citizen's Comprehensive Plan Task Force, 1994; mem. Readiness to Learn Coupeville Cmty. Team, 1996; project mgr., risk mgmt. com. Associated Provider Network, 1997—, risk mgmt. subcom. chair 1997—. Recipient outstanding svc. award Armed Svcs. YMCA of U.S., Dallas, 1985, two program merit awards McDonald's Corp., Oak Harbor, 1986; named Alumni of a Growing Vision, Seattle Pacific U., 1991, Diplomat of Yr. Greater Oak Harbor C. of C., 1991. Mem. NASW (bd. dirs. Wash. chpt. 1982-85), Wash. Assn. Social Welfare (pres. 1975-76), Acad. Cert. Social Workers, Rotary. Lutheran. Avocations: reading, genealogy, camping, fishing, computers. Home: 2450 S Rocky Way Coupeville WA 98239-9610 Office: Cath Community Svcs NW 1121 SE Dock St Oak Harbor WA 98277-4067

MILLER, ROBERT STEVEN, secondary school educator; b. Van Nuys, Calif., Aug. 9, 1963; s. Frederick Earl and Mary (Brash) M. AA, L.A. Valley Coll., 1984; BSBA, Calif. State U., 1987, MA in History, 1990. Cert. substitute tchr., 1993-96. Study group leader, study skills researcher Ednl. Opportunity Program Calif. State U., L.A., 1989-93, faculty mem. History Dept., lectr., 1990-92; sec., treas. Agate/Amethyst World, Inc., Van Nuys, Calif., 1986-91, v.p., 1992—; with Summer Bridge Program Calif. State U., L.A., 1994—; tchr. history Chatsworth (Calif.) H.S., 1996—. Mng. editor (jour.) Perspectives, 1990, editor-in-chief, 1991. Jake Gimbel scholar, 1989. Mem. Am. Historians Assn., The Soc. for Historians of Am. Fgn. Rels., Phi Alpha Theta (v.p. 1990, pres. 1991, Eta Xi chpt., Ledeboer Family scholar 1989), Pi Sigma Epsilon (v.p. 1986-87, pres. 1988 Phi chpt.), Mu Kappa Tau (pres. and founder 1989, Calif State U. LA chpt.). Democrat. Roman Catholic. Home: 13750 Runnymede St Van Nuys CA 91405-1515 Office: Chatsworth HS 10027 Lurline Ave Chatsworth CA 91311-3153

MILLER, ROBERT STEVENS, JR., finance professional; b. Portland, Oreg., Nov. 4, 1941; s. Robert Stevens and Barbara (Weston) M.; m. Margaret Rose Kyger, Nov. 9, 1966; children: Christopher John, Robert Stevens, Alexander Lamont. AB with distinction, Stanford U., 1963; LLB, Harvard U., 1966; MBA, Stanford U., 1968. Bar: Calif. bar 1966. Fin. analyst Ford Motor Co., Dearborn, Mich., 1968-71; spl. studies mgr. Ford Motor Co., Mexico City, 1971-73; dir. fin. Ford Asia-Pacific, Inc., Melbourne, Australia, 1974-77, Ford Motor Co., Caracas, Venezuela, 1977-79; v.p., treas. Chrysler Corp., Detroit, 1980-81, exec. v.p. fin., 1981-90, vice chmn., 1990-92; sr. ptnr. James D. Wolfensohn, Inc., N.Y.C., 1992-93; chmn. bd. dirs. Morrison Knudsen Corp., 1995-96; bd. dirs. Fed.-Mogul, Fluke, Pope & Talbot, Coleman, Symantec, Morrison Knudsen.

MILLER, ROBERT WILLIAM, personal property appraiser, writer; b. Phila., Apr. 28, 1922; s. Stuart Parmalee and Ruth Anne (Mills) M.; m. Judith Bayard Wood, Sept. 1948 (div. Feb. 1951); m. Bettie Lucy Hays, Apr. 28, 1962. Student, NYU, 1945-46, Fenster Sch. Writing, N.Y.C., 1945-47, Dickinson Coll., 1948-49. Copywriter Ruthraff & Ryan, N.Y.C., 1944-46; writer various publs., 1944-60; ind. personal property appraiser N.W. Fla., 1960—; writer Wallace-Homestead Book Co., Des Moines, 1971-86; lectr., mus. cons. on antiques, Gt. Britain, France, Italy, Fed. Republic Germany, 1963—; cons. McClung Mus., Knoxville, Tenn., 1968-72, Houston Mus., Chattanooga, 1970-78. Host TV talk show Antiques and Collectibles, PBS, 1968-72; author 34 books on antiques and collectibles. Dir. Swim Program for Handicapped, Oak Ridge, Tenn., 1954-68; scoutmaster, cubmaster Boy Scouts of Am. Troop #120, Oak Ridge, 1962-68. Vol. Am. Field Svc., 1943-44, CBI. Decorated 1939-45 Star, Burma Star, War Medal (Gt. Britain); recipient Nat. award Nat. Recreation Assn., 1960. Mem. Appraisers Assn. Am., Nat. Geog. Soc. Presbyterian. Avocations: scuba diving, fishing, collecting antique cars. Home: 100 Greenwood Dr Panama City FL 32407

MILLER, ROBERTA BALSTAD, science administrator; b. Mpls., June 25, 1940; d. Gerhard Oliver and Laverne K. (Anderson) Balstad; m. Gary David Lange, Nov. 26, 1959 (div. 1968); m. Floyd John Miller, June 15, 1969; 1 child, Aaron Gerhard. BA, U. Minn., 1964, MA, 1970, PhD, 1973. Rsch. assoc. AIA, Washington, 1974; staff assoc. Social Sci. Rsch. Coun., Washington, 1975-81; exec. dir. Consortium Social Sci. Assns., Washington, 1981-84; divsn. dir. NSF, Washington, 1984-93; pres., CEO Consortium for Internat. Earth Sci. Info. Network (CIESIN), University Center, Mich., 1993—; adj. prof. natural resources policy and behavior U. Mich., 1993—; guest scholar Woodrow Wilson Internat. Ctr. Scholars, 1994; sr. assoc. mem. St. Anthony's Coll., U. Oxford, Eng., 1991-92; mem. chmn. NATO adv. panel on Advanced Sci. Insts./Advanced Rsch. Workshops, Brussels, 1988-91; mem. exec. com. Space Studies Bd. Nat. Rsch. Coun., 1995—; mem. U.S.

Nat. Com. IIASA, 1995—; chmn. adv. bd. Luxembourg Income Survey, 1987-91. Author: City and Hinterland, 1979; editor (with Harriet Zuckerman) Scientometrics, 1979; contbr. articles to profl. jours.; translator poetry of Jorge Luis Borges, 1989, 90, 91. Bd. trustees Newport Schs., Kensington, Md., 1986-91, St. Anthony's Coll. Trust, 1994—; adv. trustee Environ. Rsch. Inst. Mich., 1995—. Recipient NSF Meritorious Svc. award, 1993. Mem. AAAS (com. mem., chmn. 1987—), U.S. Man in the Bioshphere Program (mem. com., chmn. 1989-91), Internat. Social Sci. Coun. (mem. com. 1991—, v.p. 1992-94), Am. Hist. Assn., Am. Lit. Translators Assn., Coun. on Fgn. Rels., Cosmos Club. Lutheran. Home: 3909 Jocelyn St NW Washington DC 20015-1905 Office: CIESIN 2250 Pierce Rd University Center MI 48710

MILLER, ROBERTA DAVIS, editor; b. Oklahoma City, Aug. 18, 1931; s. Robert Rutter and Lenora (Baldwin) Davis; children: Wendy, Jane, Elisabeth. Student, Okla. U., 1948-50, Central State U., 1950-51. Editor Golden Books, Western Pub. Co., 1963-71; pub. Sesame St. Mag., Electric Co. Mag., Children's TV Workshop, N.Y.C., 1971-76; editor-in-chief Pizzazz Mag., Cadence Pub. Co., N.Y.C., 1976-78; v.p., dir. lit. properties United Media, N.Y.C., 1978-85, v.p. internat. pub., 1986-93, v.p., dir. pub., 1993-94; prin. Roberta D. Miller Assoc., N.Y.C., 1994—. Mem. Authors Guild, Newswomen's Club N.Y. Office: 42 E 12th St New York NY 10003-4640

MILLER, RONALD ALFRED, family physician; b. Orange, Calif., Sept. 27, 1943; s. Alfred Casper and Inez Geraldine (Gunderson) M.; m. Jean Ilene Andrews, June 18, 1966; children: Jon, Lauri, Bryan. BA, Pacific Luth. U., 1965; MD, U. Wash., 1969. Diplomate Am. Bd. Family Practice (bd. dirs. 1985-90, pres. bd. 1989-90). Intern in medicine Parkland Meml. Hosp., Dallas, 1969-70; gen. practice residency USPHS Gallup Indian Med. Ctr., Gallup, N.Mex., 1970-72; prin. Medical Doctor Family Physicians' Clinic, Whitefish, Mont., 1972—; clin. prof. U. Wash., Seattle, 1975—; coord. community clin. unit in family medicine, U. Wash., Whitefish, 1975—; bd. dirs. Utah Med. Ins. Assn., Salt Lake City, 1987—. Bd. dirs. Whitefish Housing Authority, 1977-82; mem. alumni bd. Pacific Luth. U., Tacoma, 1976-81, pres., 1979-80; mem. Glacier Community Chorale, Whitefish, 1984—, bd. dirs., 1990-92. Lt. comdr. USPHS, 1970-72. Mem. Am. Acad. Family Physicians (com. on continuing med. edn. 1977-81, com. on edn. 1984-89, Mead Johnson award Grad. Edn. in Family Practice 1972), Mont. Acad. Family Physicians (bd. dirs., sec./treas, v.p., pres. 1982-83, del. nat. congress 1978-84), Rotary, Alpha Omega Alpha. Republican. Lutheran. Avocations: hunting, fishing, skiing, backpacking, choral singing. Home: 721 Iowa Ave Whitefish MT 59937-2338 Office: Family Physicians Clinic 401 Baker Ave Whitefish MT 59937-2435

MILLER, RONALD BAXTER, English language educator, author; b. Rocky Mount, N.C., Oct. 11, 1948; s. Marcellus Cornelius and Elsie (Bryant) M.; m. Jessica Garris, June 5, 1971; 1 child, Akin Dasan. BA magna cum laude, N.C. Ctrl. U., 1970; AM, Brown U., 1972, PhD, 1974. Asst. prof. English Haverford Coll., Haverford, Pa., 1974-76; assoc. prof. English, dir. Black lit. program U. Tenn., Knoxville, 1977-81, prof. English, dir. Black lit. program, 1982-92, Lindsay Young prof. liberal arts and English, 1986-87; prof. English, dir. Inst. for African Am. Studies U. Ga., Athens, 1992—; instr. summer sch. Roger Williams Coll., Bristol, R.I., 1973; lectr. SUNY, 1974; Mellon prof. Xavier Univ., New Orleans, 1988; Irvine Found. visiting scholar Univ. San Francisco, 1991. Author: (reference guide) Langston Hughes and Gwendolyn Brooks, 1978, The Art and Imagination of Langston Hughes, 1989 (Am. Book award, 1991), (monograph) Southern Trace in Black Critical Theory: Redemption of Time, 1991; editor, contbr.: Black American Literature and Humanism, 1981, Black American Poets Between Worlds, 1940-60, 1986; co-editor: Call and Response The Riverside Anthology of African American Literary Experience, 1997; mem. editl. bd. Tenn. Studies in Lit., 1991-93, Black Fiction Project (Yale-Cornell-Duke-Harvard), 1985—, U. Ga. Press, 1994-97; contbr. numerous articles and revs. to profl. jours. Recipient award Am. Coun. of Learned Socs., 1978, Golden Key Faculty award Nat. Golden Key, 1990, 95, Alpha award for disting. svc. U. Ga. Athens, 1993; Lilly Sr. Teaching fellow U. Ga. Athens, 1994, Nat. Rsch. Coun. sr. fellow, 1986-87, NDEA fellow, 1970-72, Ford Found. fellow, 1972-73, NEH fellow, 1975; Nat. Fellowships Fund dissertation grantee, 1973-74, others. Mem. MLA (exec. com. Afro-Am. Lit. Discussion Group 1980-83, chair 1982-83, mem. del. assembly 1984-86, 97-99, com. on langs. and lits. of Am. 1993-97, chair 1996), Langston Hughes Soc. (pres. 1984-90). Office: U Ga Inst African Am Studies Athens GA 30602

MILLER, RONALD EUGENE, regional science educator; b. Seattle, Sept. 1, 1933; s. Eugene H. and Nellie A. (Myers) M. B.A., Harvard U., 1955; M.A., U. Wash., 1957; Ph.D., Princeton U., 1961. Asst. prof. regional sci. U. Pa., Phila., 1962-65; assoc. prof. U. Pa., 1965-71, prof., 1971-95, chmn. dept., 1981-84, prof. emeritus, 1995—. Author: Input-Output Analysis, 1985; Dynamic Optimization and Economic Applications, 1979; Modern Mathematical Methods for Economics and Business, 1972; also articles; editor Jour. Regional Sci., 1965—. Mem. Regional Sci. Assn. Home: 137 Elfreths Aly Philadelphia PA 19106-2005 Office: U Pa Regional Sci Dept 3718 Locust Walk Philadelphia PA 19104-6209

MILLER, RONALD GRANT, journalist; b. Santa Cruz, Calif., Feb. 28, 1939; s. Fred Robert and Evelyn Lenora (Mosher) M.; m. Darla-Jean Irene Rode, Nov. 2, 1963. AA, Monterey Peninsula Coll., 1958; BA, San Jose State U., 1961. Reporter Santa Cruz (Calif.) Sentinel, 1959-62; reporter, chief news bur. San Jose (Calif.) Mercury News, 1962-77, editor T.V., 1977—; syndicated TV columnist Knight Rider Syndicate, 1978—; commentator, critic Sta. KLOK, San Jose, 1981-83; panelist, guest speaker various orgns., 1978—; nat. judge Cableace awards, 1987. Author: (foreword) Les Brown's Encyclopedia of Television, 1992; co-author: Masterpiece Theatre, 1995, Author: Mystery! A Celebration, 1996 (Agatha award nominee for Best Non-Fiction Book 1996); contbr. articles and short fiction to various mags. Recipient Nat. Spot News Photo award Sigma Delta Chi, 1961, Outstanding Alumnus award San Jose State U. Dept. Journalism and Mass Comm., 1985, Nat. Headline award Press Club Atlantic City, 1994. Mem. TV Critics Assn. (nat. pres. 1981). Democrat. Home and Office: 1554 Arbor Ave Los Altos CA 94024-5913

MILLER, RONALD M., manufacturing executive; b. Bklyn., Aug. 30, 1944; s. Samuel L. and Kitty M.; m. Carole J. Schaps, June 9, 1966; children: Elisa, Deborah. BSEE, Poly. Inst., Bklyn., 1966, MS in Ops. Rsch., 1969. Sr. electronic engr. Grumman Aerospace Corp., Bethpage, N.Y., 1966-72; dir. program mgmt. Gould Inc., Simulation Systems div., Melville, N.Y., 1972-81; v.p. ops. EMS Devel., Farmingdale, N.Y., 1981-85; pres., chief exec. officer Marks Polarized Corp., Deer Park, N.Y., 1985-89, also chmn. bd. dirs., 1985—; pres., chief exec. officer Marks Polarized Corp., Hauppauge, N.Y., 1989—; pres., chmn. bd. dirs. Upward Tech. Corp., 1989-92, sec., COO, bd. dirs., 1989-96; pres. Image Analytics Corp., Hauppauge, N.Y., 1992—; adj. lectr. Hofstra U. Hempstead, N.Y., 1969-70; bus. cons. Aerospace Industry, Long Island, N.Y., 1978—. Sr. arbitrator Better Bus. Bur., Farmingdale, 1981—; arbitrator Am. Arbitration Assn., Garden City, N.Y., 1980—. Mem. L.I. Forum for Tech. (v.p., bd. dirs. 1987-92), Navy League of U.S. (life), Am. Def. Preparedness Assn. (life). Avocations: amateur radio. Home: 38 Fairfield Dr Dix Hills NY 11746-7137 Office: Marks Polarized Corp 275 Marcus Blvd # D Hauppauge NY 11788-2022

MILLER, ROSS HAYS, retired neurosurgeon; b. Ada, Okla., Jan. 30, 1923; s. Harry and Helen (Rice) M.; m. Catherine Railey, May 2, 1943; children—Terry Hays, Helen Stacy. B.S., East Central State Coll., Ada, 1943; M.D., U. Okla., 1946; M.S. in Neurosurgery, U. Minn., 1952. Diplomate: Am. Bd. Neurol. Surgery (chmn. exam. com. 1978-84). Intern St. Luke's Hosp., Cleve., 1946-47; fellow in neurosurgery Mayo Clinic, Rochester, Minn., 1950-54; instr. in neurosurgery Mayo Med. Sch., 1954-63, asst. prof. neurosurgery, 1963-73, asso. prof., 1973-75, prof., chmn. dept. neurosurgery, from 1975, now ret.; vis. prof. neurol. surgery Med. U. S.C., Med. Coll. Ga., Augusta. Contbr. numerous articles to med. publs. Trustee East Central State U. Found. Served as capt., M.C. U.S. Army, 1947-49, Korea. Named to Okla. Hall of Fame, 1977, Athletic Hall of Fame, East Central U. Okla., 1977; recipient Disting. Alumnus award East Central U. Okla., 1974, Mayo Found. Disting. Alumnus award, 1992. Mem. AMA, ACS, Am. Assn. Neurol. Surgeons (chmn. com. profl. practice 1976-79, dir. 1976-79, v.p. 1979, rep. to Council Med. Splty. Socs. 1980-84), Congress Neurol. Surgeons (exec. com. 1963-65), Minn. Soc. Neurol. Scis., Neurosurg. Soc. Am. (v.p. 1975), Soc. Neurol. Surgeons (v.p. 1983), Sigma Xi.

MILLER, SAM SCOTT, lawyer; b. Ft. Worth, July 26, 1938; s. Percy Vernon and Mildred Lois (MacDowell) M.; m. Mary Harrison FitzHugh, May 10, 1969. BA, Mich. State U., 1960; JD, Tulane U., 1964; LLM, Yale U., 1965. Bar: La. 1965, N.Y. 1966, Minn. 1969. Assoc. Simpson Thacher & Bartlett, N.Y.C., 1965-68; sr. counsel Investors Diversified Services, Mpls., 1968-73; ptnr. Ireland Gibson Reams & Miller, Memphis, 1973-74; gen. counsel Paine Webber Group, Inc., N.Y.C., 1974-87, sr. v.p., 1976-87; ptnr. Orrick, Herrington & Sutcliffe, N.Y.C., 1987—; adj. prof. NYU Law Sch., 1986-90; vis. lectr. Yale Law Sch., 1980-85, Inst. for Internat. Econs. and Trade, Wuhan, China, 1983, U. Calif., 1986; trustee Omni Mut., Inc., 1988-; ombudsman Kidder Peabody Group, 1988-, Charles Schwab & Co., 1991-, Gruntal & Co., 1995-. Contbr. articles to profl. jours.; editor-in-chief: Tulane Law Rev, 1964-65; bd. editors Securities Regulation Law Jour., 1982—. Bd. dirs. Guthrie Theatre Found., Mpls., 1971-74; bd. dirs. Minn. Opera Co., 1971-74, Yale U. Law Sch. Fund., 1981—; bd. govs. Investment Co. Inst., 1980-87. Mem. ABA (vice chmn. com. fed. regulation of sec. 1995-, chmn. subcom. market regulation 1985-93), Assn. Bar City N.Y. (treas. and mem. exec. com. 1994-96, chmn. broker-dealer investment co. and regulations subcom. 1982-83), Internat. Bar Assn., Securities Industry Assn. (chmn. fed. regulation com. 1976-78), Down Town Assn., Knickerbocker Club, Order of Coif, Omicron Delta Kappa. Democrat. Baptist. Office: Orrick Herrington et al 666 Fifth Ave New York NY 10103

MILLER, SAMUEL MARTIN, apparel company finance executive; b. N.Y.C., Jan. 31, 1938; s. Irving Nathaniel and Estelle (Furman) M.; m. Kay Shapiro, Dec. 23, 1963; children: Jennifer, Suzanne. BBA magna cum laude, CCNY, 1964. With Coopers & Lybrand, N.Y.C., 1964-72; supervising sr. acct. Coopers & Lybrand, 1968-69, audit mgr., 1969-72; corp. controller Manhattan Industries, Inc., Glen Rock, N.J., 1972-74; v.p., corp. controller Manhattan Industries, Inc., 1974-76, v.p., treas., controller, 1976-83, v.p., sec.-treas., controller, 1983-88; sr. v.p. fin., CFO, mem. leadership coun. and exec. coun. Liz Claiborne Inc., North Bergen, N.J., 1988—; bd. dirs. XM Net, Inc. Served with USN, 1957-59. Recipient Haskin's award N.Y. State Uniform C.P.A. Exam. Mem. AICPA, Am. Arbitration Assn., Am. Apparel Mfrs. Assn. (chmn. fin. mgmt. com.), Fin. Execs. Inst. (CFO adv. com.), Nat. Assn. Accts., N.Y. State Soc. CPAs (chief fin. officer com.), Beta Gamma Sigma, Beta Alpha Psi. Office: Liz Claiborne Inc One Claiborne Ave North Bergen NJ 07047

MILLER, SANDRA PERRY, middle school educator; b. Nashville, Aug. 3, 1951; d. James Ralph and Pauline (Williams) Perry; m. William Kerley Miller, June 22, 1974. BS, David Lipscomb U., 1973; MEd, Tenn. State U., 1983, cert. in spl. edn., reading splty., 1986. Cert. tchr., Tenn. Tchr. Clyde Riggs Elem. Sch., Portland, Tenn., 1973-86; tchr. social studies Portland Mid. Sch., 1986—; adv. bd. tech. and comm. in edn. Sumner County Sch. Bd., Gallatin, Tenn., 1990—; co-dir., cons. Tenn. Students-at-Risk, Nashville, 1991—; assoc. edn. cons. Edn. Fgn. Inst. Cultural Exch., 1991-92; fellow World History Inst., Princeton (N.J.) U., 1992—; awards com. Tenn. Dept. Edn., Nashville, 1992; U.S. edn. amb. E.F. Ednl. Tours, Eng., France, Germany, Belgium, Holland, 1991; ednl. cons. HoughtonMifflin Co., Boston; apptd. Tenn. Mini-Grants award com., Tenn. 21st Century Tech. Com.; mem. Tenn. Textbook Com., 1995, Think-Tank on 21st Century Edn., Tenn. and Milliken Nat. Educator Found.; apptd. to Gov.'s Task Force Commn. on 21st Schs., Gov.'s Task Force for Anti-Drug and Alcohol Abuse Among Teens; mem. nat. com. for instnl. tech. devel. Milken Family Found. Nat. Edn. Conf., 1996; apptd. to Instrnl. Tech. Devel.-Project Strand, 1996 Milken Family Found., Nat. Edn. Conf.; appointed curriculum com. Bicentennial WW II Meml., 1996-97; developed State Model Drop-Out Prevent Program, 1996-97. Author curriculum materials; presenter creative crafts segment local TV sta., 1990-93; producer, dir. documentary on edn. PBS, Corona, Calif., 1990. Performer Nashville Symphony Orch., 1970-73; leader Sumner County 4-H Club, 1976-86; mem. Woodrow Wilson Nat. Fellowship Found. on Am. History, Princeton U., 1994; nat. com. Instructional Tech. Devel. Project Strand of the 1996 Milken Family Found. Nat. Edn. Conf., L.A., 1996. Recipient Excellence in Teaching award U. Tenn., 1991-92, 92-93, award for Outstanding Teaching in Humanities Tenn. Humanities Coun., 1994; named Tchr. of Yr. Upper Cumberland dist. Tenn. Dept. Edn., 1991-92, 92-93, Mid. Tenn. Educator of Yr. Tenn. Assn. Mid. Schs., 1991, Tenn. Tchr. of Yr. Tenn. Dept. Edn., 1992, Nat. Educator of Yr. Milken Family Found., 1992; recipient grant Tenn. Dept. Edn. for Devel. of Model Drop Out Prevention Program, 1996. Mem. NEA, ASCD, Sumner County Edn. Assn. (sch. rep. 1973—, Disting. Tchr. of Yr. 1992), Tenn. Edn. Assn. (rep. 1973—), Nat. Geographic Tenn. Alliance (rep. 1990—, grantee 1990), Tenn. Humanities Coun. (rep. 1990—), Nat. Coun. Social Studies. Baptist. Avocations: crafts, doll collecting, reading, music, fashion modeling. Office: Portland Mid Sch 922 S Broadway Portland TN 37148-1624

MILLER, SARAH PEARL, librarian; b. Wilkensburg, Pa., Aug. 31, 1938; d. Samuel Henry and Anna Deborah (Shirley) Lyons; m. Paul Victor Miller, Apr. 15, 1989; children: Cheryl, Michael, Daniel, Lorel. BS, Indiana U. of Pa., 1960; MREM, Denver Conservative Bapt. Sem., 1965; MA, U. Denver, 1966. Libr. Denver Conservative Bapt. Sem., 1966—. Mem. Am. Theol. Libr. Assn. (bd. dirs. 1978-81, 90-91, index bd. 1983-90). Home: 15707 E Grand Ave Aurora CO 80015-1708

MILLER, SCOTT JOSEPH, software executive; b. Milw., Feb. 15, 1964; s. James Russell and Gloria (Welter) M.; m. Jeanette Luczko, Aug. 9, 1986; children: Nicholas Scott, Maxine Loren. AA in Applied Scis., Milw. Sch. Engring., 1984, BS in Elec. Engring. Tech., 1986. MIS dir. ArcRon Ltd., Menomonee Falls, Wis., 1986; application engr. ICOM, Inc., West Allis, Wis., 1986-88, support engr., 1988-90; prodn. mgr., 1990-91; pres. WM Investments, Inc., Milw., 1992-93; ops. mgr. ICOM, Inc., West Allis, 1991-94, ICOM, Inc./Rockwell Software Inc., 1994—, Rockwell Software Inc., Milw., 1994—. Mem. IEEE, Consumer Electronics Soc., Computer Soc., Engring. Mgmt. Soc. Home: 98N 9435 W Huntington Dr Mequon WI 53092

MILLER, SHELBY ALEXANDER, chemical engineer, educator; b. Louisville, July 9, 1914; s. George Walter and Stella Katherine (Cralle) M.; m. Jean Adele Danielson, Dec. 26, 1939 (div. May 1948); 1 son, Shelby Carlton; m. Doreen Adare Kennedy, May 29, 1952 (dec. Feb. 1971). BS, U. Louisville, 1935; PhD, U. Minn., 1943. Registered profl. engr., Del., Kans., N.Y. Asst. chemist Corhart Refractories Co., Louisville, 1935-36; teaching, rsch. asst. chem. engring. U. Minn., Mpls., 1935-39; devel. engr., rsch. chem. engr. E.I. duPont de Nemours & Co., Inc., Wilmington, Del., 1940-46; assoc. prof. chem. engring. U. Kan., Lawrence, 1946-50; prof. U. Kan., 1950-55; Fulbright prof. chem. engring. King's Coll. Durham U., Newcastle-upon-Tyne, Eng., 1952-53; prof., chem. engring. U. Rochester, 1955-69, chmn., 1955-68; assoc. lab. dir. Argonne (Ill.) Nat. Lab., 1969-74; dir. Ctr. Ednl. Affairs, 1969-79, sr. chem. engr., 1969-84; ret. sr. chem. engr., cons., 1984—; vis. prof. chem. engring. U. Calif., Berkeley, 1967-68; vis. prof. U. of Philippines, Quezon City, 1986. Editor: Chem. Engring. Edn. Quar, 1965-67; sect. editor: Perry's Chem. Engrs.' Handbook, 7th edit., 1997; contbr. to McGraw-Hill Ency. Sci. and Tech., 7th edit., 1992; contbr. articles to tech., profl. jours. Sec. Kans. Bd. Engring. Examiners, 1954-55; mem. adv. com. on tng. Internat. Atomic Energy Agy., 1975-79; treas. Lawrence (Kans.) League for Practice Democracy, 1950-52; sec. Argonne Credit Union, 1994-97. Fellow AAAS, Am. Inst. Chemists, Am. Inst. Chem. Engrs. (past chmn. Kansas City sect.); mem. Am. Chem. Soc. (past chmn. Rochester sect.), Soc. Chem. Industry, Am. Soc. Engring. Edn. (past chmn. grad. studies div.), Am. Nuclear Soc., Filtration Soc., Triangle, Sigma Xi, Sigma Tau, Phi Lambda Upsilon, Tau Beta Pi, Alpha Chi Sigma. Presbyn. Home: 825 63rd St Downers Grove IL 60516-1962 Office: Argonne Nat Lab Chem Tech Divsn Argonne IL 60439-4837

MILLER, STANFORD, reinsurance exeuctive, arbitrator, lawyer; b. Kansas City, Mo., Nov. 15, 1913; s. Hugh and Gertrude Anna (Kraft) M.; m. Gloria Goble, July 11, 1942 (div. 1958); 1 child, Hans Hugh; m. Beverly Breuer, Apr. 19, 1962; 1 son, Bradford Channing. B.A., U. Kans., 1934; J.D., U. Chgo., 1938. Bar: Mo. 1938. lectr. in field. Author: (with Robert D. Brown) Health Insurance Underwriting, 1962; also articles. Bd. dirs. Kansas City, Boy Scouts Am., Community Living Opportunities; trustee emeritus U. Kansas City. Mem. Mo. Bar Assn., Reins. Assn. Am. (past chmn.), Health Ins. Assn. Am. (former sec., dir.), Am. Arbitration Assn. (panel of arbitrators), Phi Alpha Delta, Alpha Tau Omega. Clubs: Rotary, Profl. Men's, Mission Hills Country. Home: 2709 Tomahawk Rd Shawnee Mission KS 66208-1827 Office: 6700 Antioch Rd Ste 400 Shawnee Mission KS 66204-1200

MILLER, STANLEY CUSTER, JR., physicist, retired educator; b. Kansas City, Mo., July 30, 1926; s. Stanley Custer and Verda (Storer) M.; m. Elene G. Josephson, Nov. 27, 1957 (dec.); children: Gloria Diane, James Kenneth, Richard Eric (dec.). BS in Engring. Physics, U. Colo., 1948; PhD in Physics, U. Calif. at Berkeley, 1953. Mem. faculty U. Colo., Boulder, 1953-90; prof. physics U. Colo., 1961-90. Author: Principles of Physics, 2 vols, 1966, Irreducible Representations of Space Groups, 1967, Principles of Modern Physics, 1970, Kronecker Product Tables, 1979. Served with USNR, 1944-46. Mem. Am. Phys. Soc. Home: 2570 S Dayton Way Apt 306A Denver CO 80231-3944

MILLER, STEPHEN BRYAN, social worker, marriage counselor; b. Clare, Mich., Aug. 1, 1951; s. Bryan David and Shirley Jean (Dull) M.; m. Nancy Marie Brandau, Aug. 24, 1974; children: Jennifer Marie, Adam Bryan. AA, Ferris State U., Big Rapids, Mich., 1972; BS, Western Mich. U., 1974, MSW, 1978. Lic. marriage counselor. Social worker Ionia (Mich.) Intermediate Schs., 1974-76, Sanilac County Dept. Social Svcs., Sandusky, Mich., 1976; clin. social worker Caro (Mich.) Regional Mental Health Ctr., 1978; sch. social worker Tuscola Intermediate Schs., Caro, 1978-81, Allegan (Mich.) County Schs., 1981-83, Thornapple-Kellogg Pub. Schs., Middleville, Mich., 1983—; field instr. Western Mich. U., Kalamazoo, 1988—; pvt. marriage counselor, Kentwood, Mich., 1989—; family and marriage cons. John Knox Presbyn. Ch., Grand Rapids, Mich., 1989—. Chairperson Kentwood Activities Com., 1988-89; deacon John Knox Presbyn. Ch., Grand Rapids, 1987-90. Mem. NASW, Acad. Cert. Social Workers (cert.), Mich. Nat. Edn. Assn. (region IX del. 1986-88), Mich. Assn. Tchrs. of Emotionally Disturbed Children. Democrat. Home: 5642 Juanita Dr SE Grand Rapids MI 49508-6427 Office: Thornapple-Kellogg Schs 3385 Bender Rd Middleville MI 49333-9262

MILLER, STEPHEN RALPH, lawyer; b. Chgo., Nov. 28, 1950; s. Ralph and Karin Ann (Olson) M.; children: David Williams, Lindsay Christine. BA cum laude, Yale U., 1972; JD, Cornell U., 1975. Bar: Ill. Assoc. McDermott, Will & Emery, Chgo., 1975-80, income ptnr., 1981-85, equity ptnr., 1986—, mgmt. com. mem., 1992-95; mem. spl. task force on post-employment benefits Fin. Acctg. Standards Bd., Norwalk, Conn., 1987-91. Contbr. articles to profl. jours. Mem. Chgo. Coun. on Fgn. Rels., 1978—; trustee police pension bd., Wilmette, Ill., 1992—; bd. trustees Seabury We. Theol. Sem., Evanston, Ill., 1994—. Mem. ABA, Ill. Bar Assn., Yale Club Chgo., Mich. Shores Club, Chgo. Athletic Assn., Hundred Club Cook County, Legal Club of Chgo. Avocations: sailing, water skiing, cross-country skiing. Office: McDermott Will & Emery 227 W Monroe St Ste 3100 Chicago IL 60606-5018

MILLER, STEVEN DOUGLAS, federal agency executive; b. Chateauroux, France, Jan. 30, 1960; came to U.S., 1960; s. Frank Lee and Athalee Evelyn (Bailey) M. BA, Evergreen State Coll., Olympia, Wash., 1981; MPA, U. Tex., 1987. Budget analyst IRS, Washington, 1987-90; budget examiner Dept. of Treasury, Washington, 1990-92; budget officer Bur. of the Pub. Debt, Parkersburg, W.Va., 1992-96; acting dir. divsnl. fin. mgmt. Bur. of the Pub. Debt, Parkersburg, 1996—. Delegation mem. Citizen Amb. Program (Russia), Spokane, Wash., 1994; bd. dirs. Family Crisis Intervention Ctr., Parkersburg, 1993-94, pres. bd. dirs., 1995—. Mem. Am. Assn. for Budget and Program Analysis, Am. Soc. for Pub. Adminstrn., Evergreen State Coll. Alumni Assn. (bd. dirs. 1983-84). Democrat. Roman Catholic. Avocations: golf, reading. Home: 1511 Park Ave Parkersburg WV 26101 Office: Bureau of the Public Debt 200 3rd St Rm 201 Parkersburg WV 26101-5312

MILLER, STEVEN H., museum director; b. Phila., 1947; m. Jane McClure Pelson; children: Andrew Steven, Katherine Ann. BA, Bard Coll., 1970; cert. in conservation sci., Internat. Ctr. for Study of Preservation and Restoration of Cultural Property, Rome, 1978. Asst. to sr. curator Mus. of City of N.Y., N.Y.C., 1971-72, asst. curator paintings, prints and photographs, 1973-77, curator prints and photographs, 1977-79, curator, dept. head fine art collections, history and spl. collections, 1979-85, sr. curator, 1985-87; asst. dir. Maine State Mus., 1987-91; dir. of mus. Western Res. Hist. Soc., Cleve., 1991-95; exec. dir. The Bennington (Vt.) Mus., 1995—; adj. prof. mus. studies Case Western Res. U., 1991-94; lectr. NYU, 1978-87, Columbia U., N.Y.C., 1981, 82, New Sch. for Social Rsch., N.Y.C., 1978, 83, Maine State Mus., 1987-91. Author catalogs; contbr. articles to profl. jours. Bd. govs. Bard-St. Stephen's Alumni Assn.; mem. fellowship gift com., bd. trustees Hist. Deerfield, Mass.; bd. dirs. Vt. Mus. and Gallery Alliance; former mem. landmarks preservation com. Shaker Heights, Ohio; charter and former mem. hist. preservation com. City of Gardiner, Maine; former mem. adv. com. Blaine House Restoration, Maine; former mem., art adv. com. Gracie Mansion Conservancy, N.Y.C.; former mem. adv. coun. Mus. Moving Image, Astoria, N.Y. Mem. Am. Assn. Mus. (mem. mus. advocacy team, mem. mus. accreditation vis. com.), Maine Assn. Mus. (co-founder, charter coun. mem.), Nat. Arts Club. Home: 5 Appletree Ln Bennington VT 05201-2210

MILLER, STEVEN MAX, humanities educator; b. Portland, Ind., Feb. 9, 1950; s. J. Max and Belva Kathryn (Kitty Booher) M.; m. Fran Felice Koski, May 30, 1985 (div. Aug. 7, 1992). BA in Eng., Coll. of William and Mary, 1972; MA in English Lang. and Lit., Ind. U., 1975, PhD in English Lang. and Lit., 1985. Sr. libr. asst. cataloger rare books and spl. collections Lilly Libr., Bloomington, Ind., 1972-76; assoc. instr. English Ind. U., Bloomington, 1975-82; asst. prof. English Millersville (Pa.) U., 1985-94; assoc. prof. English Millersville (Pa.) U., 1994—; faculty sponsor Iota Phi chpt. Sigma Tau Delta Millersville (Pa.) U., 1986—; asst. prof. English Murray (Ky.) State U., 1989-90; cons. women writers project Brown U., Providence, 1990-95; reader nat. tchg. exam. Ednl. Testing Svc., Princeton, N.J., 1990-92. Editor (Re)Soundings jour.; contbr. articles to profl. jours. Grantee NEH, 1991, 92. Mem. MLA, John Donne Soc. Am., Spenser Soc., English Assn. Pa. State Univs. (nominating com. 1987), Bibliog. Soc. Am. Episcopalian. Avocation: gardening. Office: Millersville U Dept English Chryst PO Box 1002 Millersville PA 17551

MILLER, STEVEN SCOTT, lawyer; b. N.Y.C., May 28, 1947; s. Stanley Irwin and Corinne (Mass) M.; m. Nina Catherine Augello, Apr. 24, 1983. BA cum laude, U. Pa., 1967; JD cum laude, NYU, 1970. Bar: N.Y. 1971, U.S. Dist. Ct. (so. and ea. dists.) N.Y. 1972, U.S. Ct. Appeals (2d cir.) 1974. Law clk. to judge U.S. Dist. Ct. (so. dist.) N.Y., N.Y.C., 1970-71; assoc. Proskauer Rose Goetz & Mendelsohn, N.Y.C., 1971-78; assoc. Rosenman & Colin, N.Y.C., 1978-81, ptnr., 1981-92; v.p., asst. gen. counsel Chase Manhattan Bank (formerly Chemical Bank), N.Y.C., 1992—. Editor NYU Law Rev., 1968-70. Mem. N.Y. State Bar Assn. Home: 135 E 83rd St New York NY 10028-2408 Office: Chase Manhattan Bank 25th Fl 1 Chase Manhattan Plz Fl 25 New York NY 10081-1000

MILLER, SUSAN ANN, school system administrator; b. Cleve., Nov. 24, 1947; d. Earl Wilbur and Marie Coletta (Hendershot) M. BS in Edn., Kent State U., 1969; MEd, Cleve. State U., 1975; PhD, Kent State U., 1993. Cert. supt.; cert. elem. prin., cert. elem. supervisor; cert. Learning Disabled/Behavior Disabled tchr.; cert. tchr. grades 1-8; cert. sch. counselor; lic. counselor. Tchr., guidance counselor, interim prin. North Royalton City Schs., Ohio, 1969-84; dir. elem. and spl. edn., acting supt., asst. supt. Cuyahoga County Bd. Edn., Valley View, Ohio, 1984—. Contbr. articles to profl. jours. Grantee Latchkey Program, State Dept. Edn., North Coast Leadership Forum. Mem. ASCD, Coun. Exceptional Children, Phi Delta Kappa. Home: 14508 Cross Creek Ln Cleveland OH 44133-4811 Office: Department Education 5700 W Canal Rd Valley View OH 44125-3326

MILLER, SUSAN HEILMANN, publishing executive; b. Yuba City, Calif., Jan. 13, 1945; d. Paul Clay and Helen Christine (Sterud) Heilmann; m. Allen Clinton Miller III, June 24, 1967. BA, Stanford U., 1966; MS, Columbia U., 1969; PhD, Stanford U., 1976. Info. officer Montgomery County Schs., Rockville, Md., 1970-71, Palo Alto Schs., Calif., 1969-70, 71-73; news-features editor Bremerton Sun, Wash., 1976-80; night city editor Peninsula

Times Tribune, Palo Alto, 1980-81; exec. editor News-Gazette, Champaign, Ill., 1981-85; dir. editorial devel. Scripps Howard Newspapers, Cin., 1985-90, v.p. editorial, 1990-93; pres., editor The Monterey (Calif.) County Herald, 1993—. Contbr. articles to profl. jours. Bd. dirs. Vol. Illini Projects, U. Ill., 1983-85, Washington Journalism Ctr., 1985-90, New Directions for News, 1988-91; mem. Pulitzer Prize Nominating Jury, 1986-87, accrediting com. Accrediting Council on Journalism and Mass Communication, 1986-89; active YWCA of Monterey Peninsula, 1997; world affairs coun. United Way Monterey Peninsula, 1997—. Mem. Am. Soc. Newspaper Editors (bd. dirs. 1985-92), Newspaper Assn. Am., Nat. Press Found. (assoc.), Internat. Newspaper Fedn. Newspaper Pub. (mem. newspaper mktg. bureau 1991-93), Assoc. Press Mng. Editors (bd. dirs.1984-91), Ill. AP Mng. Editors (bd. dirs. 1984-85). Clubs: Executive (Champaign, Ill.) (bd.dirs. 1984-85). Office: PO Box 271 8 Upper Ragsdale Dr Monterey CA 93940-0271

MILLER, SUZANNE MARIE, law librarian, educator; b. Sioux Falls, S.D., Feb. 25, 1954; d. John Gordon and Dorothy Margaret (Sabatka) M.; 1 child, Altinay Marie. B.A. in English, U. S.D., 1975; M.A. in Library Sci., U. Denver, 1976; postgrad. in polit. sci. U. LaVerne, 1980, postgrad. in law, 1984. Librarian II, U. S.D. Sch. of Law, Vermillion, 1977-78; law libr. U. LaVerne, Calif., 1978-85, instr. in law, 1980-85; asst. libr. tech. svcs. McGeorge Sch. Law, 1985—, prof. advanced legal rsch., 1994—. Co-author (with Elizabeth J. Pokorny) U.S. Government Documents: A Practical Guide for Library Assistants in Academic and Public Libraries, 1988; contbr. chpt. to book, articles to profl. jours. Recipient Am. Jurisprudence award Bancroft Whitney Pub. Co., 1983. Mem. Am. Assn. Law Librs., So. Calif. Assn. Law Libs. (arrangements com. 1981-82), Innovacq Users Group (chairperson, 1986-88), No. Calif. Assn. Law Librs. (mem. program com., inst. 1988), Western Pacific Assn. Law Librs. (sec. 1990-94, pres. elect 1994-95, pres. 1995-96, local arrangements chair 1997). Roman Catholic. Home: 4030 Jeffrey Ave Sacramento CA 95820-2551 Office: U of the Pacific McGeorge Sch Law Library 3200 5th Ave Sacramento CA 95817-2705

MILLER, TAMARA DEDRA, psychologist; b. Cleve., Jan. 13, 1961; d. Taswill Taylor and Ethel (Midgett) M.; stepd. Gwendolyn (Hicks) M. BA in Psychology, Wittenberg U., 1982; D in Psychology, Wright State U., 1987. Lic. clin. psychologist, Ohio. Chief psychol. svc. USAF, Altus, Okla., 1987-89; chief psychol. testing USAF, Dayton, Ohio, 1989-92; dir. PTSD program Dept. VA, Dayton, 1992—; clin. prof. Wright State U., Dayton, 1992—; cons. Jackson County Youth, Altus, 1987-89, Ctr. for Retardation, Altus, 1987-89; adj. prof. Ctrl. State U., Wilberforce, 1991—; mem. panel Women's Fed. Program, Dayton, 1991; clin. advisor Les Femmes Concerned Citizens for Cancer, Dayton, 1992—. Consulting editor: Professional Psychology: Research and Practice, 1994. Capt. USAF, 1986-89. Mem. Nat. Coun. Negro Women Inc., VA Psychologists, Delta Sigma Theta. Avocations: reading, theatre, dance, aerobics, modeling. Home: 5670 Olive Tree Dr Dayton OH 45426-1313 Office: Dept VA Affairs Med Ctr 4100 E 3rd St Dayton OH 45403-2244

MILLER, TERRY ALAN, chemistry educator; b. Girard, Kans., Dec. 18, 1943; s. Dwight D. Miller and Rachel E. (Detjen) Beltram; m. Barbara Hoffmann, July 16, 1966; children: Brian, Stuart. BA, U. Kans., 1965; PhD, Cambridge (Eng.) U., 1968. Disting. tech. staff Bell Telephone Labs, 1968-84; vis. asst. prof. Princeton U., 1968-71; vis. lectr. Stanford U., 1972; vis. fgn. scholar Inst. Molecular Sci., Okazaki, Japan, summer 1983; Ohio eminent scholar, prof. chemistry Ohio State U., Columbus, 1984—; chair Molecular Spectroscopy Symposium, Columbus, 1992—. Mem. editl. bd. Jour. Chem. Physics, 1978-81, Jour. Molecular Spectroscopy, 1982-87, Laser Chemistry, 1986—, Rev. of Sci. Instruments, 1986-89, Jour. Phys. Chemistry, 1989-95, Jour. Optical Soc. Am., 1989-95, Chemtracts, 1989-90, Ann. Revs. Phys. Chemistry, 1989-94, Jour. Molecular Structure, 1996—; contbr. more than 250 articles to profl. jours. Marshall fellow Brit. Govt., 1965-67, NSF fellow, 1967-68; William F. Meggard Awd., 1993, Optical Soc. Am. Fellow Optical Soc. Am. (Meggars award 1993), Am. Phys. Soc.; mem. Am. Chem. Soc. (councilor), Coblentz Soc. (Bomen-Michaelson award 1995). Office: Ohio State U 120 W 18th Ave Columbus OH 43210-1106

MILLER, TERRY MORROW, lawyer; b. Columbus, Ohio, Mar. 11, 1947; s. Robert E. and Elizabeth Jane (Morrow) M.; m. Martha Estella Johnson, Mar. 20, 1976; 1 child, Timothy. BS, Ohio State U., 1969, JD, 1975. Bar: Ohio 1975, U.S. Ct. Appeals (6th cir.) 1979, U.S. Supreme Ct. 1980. Asst. atty. gen. State of Ohio, Columbus, 1975-77; ptnr. Miller & Noga, Columbus, 1977-81; assoc. Vorys, Sater, Seymour and Pease, Columbus, 1981-85; ptnr. Vorys, Sater, Seymour & Pease, Columbus, 1986—. Sgt. U.S. Army, 1969-71, Okinawa. Mem. Ohio State Bar Assn., Columbus Bar Assn. Avocations: golf, Ohio history. Home: 288 E North Broadway Columbus OH 43214-4114 Office: Vorys Sater Seymour et al PO Box 1008 52 E Gay St Columbus OH 43215-3161

MILLER, THEODORE ROBERT, surgeon, educator; b. Phila., Mar. 13, 1907; s. Robert and Regina (Ramspacher) M.; m. Helen E. Reiser, July 31, 1934. Student, Swarthmore Coll., Yale, Stockholm U.; MD, Temple U., 1933. Diplomate Am. Bd. Surgery. Intern Hackensack (N.J.) Hosp., 1933-34, resident, 1934-36, asst. attending surgeon, chief tumor clinic, 1936-39, adj. cons. neoplastic diseases, 1947-52, cons. in surgery, 1959—; asst. attending surgeon City Hosp., N.Y.C.; asst. resident, fellow Meml. Hosp., N.Y.C., 1939-42; clin. asst. surgeon gastric and mixed tumor services Meml. Hosp., 1947-49, asst. attending surgeon, gastric and mixed tumor services, 1949-59, asso. attending surgeon, 1959-64, attending surgeon chief bone tumor service, 1964-74, sr. attending surgeon, 1974-77, emeritus surgeon, 1977—, chief spl. surgery service, 1964-70; fellow Am.-Scandinavian Found., 1946-47; assoc. surgeon Pack Med. Group, N.Y.C., 1947-69; instr. surgery Cornell U. Med. Coll., 1952-62, clin. asst. prof., 1962-64, clin. assoc. prof. surgery, 1964-70, clin. prof. surgery, 1970-78, emeritus clin. prof., 1978—; clin. prof. surgery Rutgers U. Med. Coll. Contbr. articles to profl. publs. Served from capt. to lt. col. M.C. AUS, 1942-46. Fellow ACS, AMA, AAAS, N.Y. Acad. Medicine; mem. N.Y. State, County N.J. State, Middlesex County med. socs., Am. Radium Soc. (pres. 1959-60), N.Y. Cancer Soc., Del. Valley Ornithol. Club, N.Y. Surg. Soc., James Ewing Soc. (pres. 1967-68), N.Y. Acad. Scis., Academia Peruana de Cirguia (corr.), Sociedad Venezolana de Cirugia (corr.), Academia de Zulia (Venezuela) (corr.), Yale Club (N.Y.C. and Princeton), Phi Sigma Kappa. Home: 3 David Brainerd Dr Jamesburg NJ 08831-1927

MILLER, THOMAS HULBERT, JR., former marine corps officer; b. San Antonio, June 3, 1923; s. Thomas Hulbert and Dora S. (Bartlett) M.; m. Ida Mai Giddings, May 11, 1943; children: Jacqueline Mai, Jo Ann. Student, U. Tex. Lic. comml. single and multi-engine pilot; lic. flight instr. Commd. 2d lt. USMC, 1943, designated naval aviator, 1943, advanced through grades to lt. gen., 1975; service in Pacific, Korea; chief staff 3d Amphibious Force Vietnam, 1970; comdg. gen. 2d Marine Aircraft Wing, 1972; dep. comdr., later comdg. gen. Fleet Marine Forces Pacific, 1975; dep. chief staff aviation Hdqrs. USMC, 1975-79, ret., 1979; cons. Applied Physics Lab., Johns Hopkins U., Nat. Acad. Sci., Def. Sci. Bd.; pres. mem. FAA Blue Ribbon Panel on Civil Pilot and Maintenance Pers. Availability; pres. Seniram II, Inc. Chmn. joint bd. U.S. Space Camp and Astronaut Scholarship Found.; mem. exec. bd. Astronaut Scholarship Found.; mem. exec. bd. Washington Airports Task Force, Air & Space Heritage Coun. Decorated Disting. Svc. medal Legion of Merit (2), D.F.C. (4), Air medal (15), Navy Commendation medal; recipient Grey Eagle award; Silver Hawk award; Am./Brit. John Curtis Wilkinson Sword award for Anglo/Am. aerospace contbn.; Paul E. Haueter award Am. Helicopter Soc.; named one of Va.'s Pioneers of Aviation. Mem. Soc. Exptl. Test Pilots, Marine Corps Aviation Assn., Assn. Naval Aviation, Naval Aviation Mus. Found., Daedalians, Golden Eagles, Am. Radio Relay League, Masons, USMC Hist. Found. Presbyterian. Holder 500 kilometer closed course world speed record F4H-1 Phantom II aircraft, 1960; first American to fly British Harrier aircraft, 1968. Home: 3689 N Harrison St Arlington VA 22207-1843 *I believe a balanced life must include equal emphasis on moral, professional (work) and recreational activity. This activity must be guided by a strong Christian faith, moral and professional integrity, loyalty and a humble recognition of others rights. And, although we all are imperfect, we should strive to achieve perfection in these characteristics and never accept or receive those things that we do not work for.*

MILLER, THOMAS J., state attorney general; b. Dubuque, Iowa, Aug. 11, 1944; s. Elmer John and Betty Maude (Kross) M.; m. Linda Cottington, Jan. 10, 1981; 1 child, Matthew. B.A., Loras Coll., Dubuque, 1966; J.D., Harvard U., 1969. Bar: Iowa bar 1969. With VISTA, Balt., 1969-70; legis. asst. to U.S. rep.John C. Culver, 1970-71; legal edn. dir. Balt. Legal Aid Bur., also mem. part-time faculty U. Md. Sch. Law, 1971-73; pvt. practice McGregor, Iowa, 1973-78; city atty. McGregor, 1975-78, Marquette, Iowa; atty. gen. of Iowa, 1979-91, 95—; ptnr. Faegre & Benson, Des Moines, 1991-95. Pres. 2d Dist. New Democratic Club, Balt., 1972. Mem. Am. Bar Assn., Iowa Bar Assn., Common Cause. Roman Catholic. Office: Office of the Atty Gen Hoover State Office Bldg 2nd Fl Des Moines IA 50319*

MILLER, THOMAS ROBBINS, lawyer, publisher; b. Chgo., Mar. 8, 1938; s. William Whipple and Helen (Robbins) M.; m. Tran Tuong Nhu, July 3, 1974; children: Toby, Teddy, Nathalie, Gabriella. BA, Yale U., 1960; LLB, Stanford U., 1965; cert., Parker Sch. Fgn. and Comparative Law, Columbia U., 1966. Bar: N.Y. 1966, Calif. 1974. Assoc. Webster & Sheffield, N.Y.C., 1965-68; sole practice N.Y.C., 1968-74, Berkeley, 1974-89; pub. Lancaster Miller Pubs., Berkeley, 1974-89; sr. ptnr. Miller & Ngo, PLC, Oakland, Calif., 1989—; founder, pres. Internat. Children's Fund, Berkeley, 1974—; cons. Peace Corps, Washington, 1961, Ctr. for Constl. Rights, UNICEF, N.Y.C., 1973-76; dep. dir. Calif. Rural Legal Assistance, San Francisco, 1977-79. Named 1 of 10 Outstanding Young Men in U.S., U.S. Jaycees, 1974. Democrat. Office: 725 Washington St Oakland CA 94607-3924

MILLER, THOMAS WILLIAMS, former university dean; b. Pottstown, Pa., July 2, 1930; s. Franklin Sullivan and Margaret (Williams) M.; m. Edythe Edwards, Dec. 20, 1952; children: Theresa, Thomas, Christine, Stefanie. B.S. in Music Edn, West Chester (Pa.) State Coll., 1952; M.A., East Carolina U., Greenville, N.C., 1957; Mus.A.D. (Univ. fellow), Boston U., 1964. Dir. instrumental music Susquenita (Pa.) High Sch., 1955-56; instr. trumpet East Carolina U., 1957-61; asst. dean East Carolina U. (Sch. Music), 1962-68, dean, 1969-71; vis. prof. U. Hawaii, Honolulu, 1968; dean Sch. Music Northwestern U., Evanston, Ill., 1971-89; dean emeritus Northwestern U., Evanston, Ill. Contbr. articles to profl. jours. Assoc. Nat. Arts, 1989. Served with AUS, 1952-55. Named Distinguished Alumnus West Chester State Coll., 1975. Mem. Nat. Arts Assn., Music Educators Nat. Conf. (life), Nat. Assn. Schs. Music (hon. life, grad. commr. 1974-79, v.p. 1979-82, pres. 1982-85, chmn. grad. com. 1985-86, bd. dirs. 1986-89), Coll. Music Soc., Pi Kappa Lambda (hon. life regent, nat. pres. 1976-79), Phi Mu Alpha Sinfonia (hon. mem., Orpheus award 1989), Sigma Alpha Iota. Home: 3121 Walden Ln Wilmette IL 60091-1139 Office: Sch of Music Northwestern U Evanston IL 60208*

MILLER, THORMUND AUBREY, lawyer; b. Pocatello, Idaho, July 14, 1919; s. Roy Edmund and Lillian (Thordarson) M.; m. Hannah A. Flansburgh, Feb. 10, 1946; children: Karen Lynette Van Gerpen, Christine Alison Westall. BA, Reed Coll., 1941; LLB, Columbia U., 1948; grad., Advanced Mgmt. Program, Harvard Bus. Sch., 1961. Bar: Calif. 1949, D.C. 1951, U.S. Supreme Ct. 1960. Assoc. McCutchen, Thomas, Matthews, Griffiths & Greene, San Francisco, 1948-50; atty. So. Pacific Transp. Co., Washington, 1950-56; asst. gen. atty. So. Pacific Transp. Co., 1956-59, gen. atty., 1959-66; sr. gen. atty. So. Pacific Transp. Co., San Francisco, 1966-75, gen. solicitor, 1975-79, gen. commerce counsel, 1979-83, dir., mem. exec. com., 1983-87, v.p., gen. counsel, 1983-89; gen. counsel So. Pacific Communications Co., San Francisco, 1970-79, dir., 1970-81; pvt. practice law Atherton, Calif., 1989-96. Pres. Wood Acres Citizens Assn., Bethesda, Md., 1955-56; mem. exec. com. Holbrook Palmer Recreation Park Found., 1979—, pres., 1982-84; bd. dirs. Atherton Civic Interest League, 1981—, pres., 1992-94; mem. Atherton Park and Recreation Commn., 1991-95; mem. alumni bd. Reed Coll., 1971-72, trustee, 1987—, campaign com., 1995—; bd. dirs. Assocs. of U. Calif. Press, 1994—; mem. San Mateo Civil Grand Jury, 1997. Mem. ABA, Calif. Bar Assn., World Trade Club. Presbyterian.

MILLER, TICE LEWIS, theatre educator; b. Lexington, Nebr., Aug. 11, 1938; s. Tice M. and Thyra V. (Lewis) M.; m. Carren J. Miller, Sept. 6, 1963; children: Dane, Graeme. BA, Kearney State Coll., 1960; MA, U. Nebr., 1961; PhD, U. Ill., 1968. Instr. Kansas City (Mo.) Jr. Coll., 1961-62; asst. prof. U. West Fla., Pensacola, 1968-72; from assoc prof. to prof., chair U. Nebr., Lincoln, 1972—; chair commn. on accreditation Nat. Assn. Schs. of Theatre, 1997—. Author: Bohemians and Critics, 1981; co-editor: Shakespeare Around the Globe, 1986, Cambridge Guide World Theatre, 1988 (Hewitt award 1989), Cambridge Guide American Theatre, 1993, The American Stage, 1993. Bd. dirs., ATHE, 1987-89, Lincoln Midwest Ballet Co., 1989-91, Theatre Arts for Youth, Lincoln, 1975-76, Pensacola Theatre, 1970-71. Lt. comdr. USNR 1963-65. Am. Theatre fellow. Fellow Great Plains Assn.; mem. Am. Soc. for Theatre Rsch. Democrat. Unitarian. Office: U Nebr Dept Theatre Arts Danc Lincoln NE 68588

MILLER, TOM POLK, retired architect; b. Houston, Nov. 17, 1914; s. Enoch Lester and Willie Elvie (Chumley) M.; m. Isabel Mount, Aug. 10, 1947; children: Crispin Mount, Abigail Mount. BA, Rice U., 1936, BS in Arch., 1937. Registered architect, Tex., Calif. Draftsman, designer Salisbury & McHale, Houston, 1937-38, Nunn & McGinty, Houston, 1939-40, Robert & Co., Corpus Christi, Tex., 1940-41; assignee Civilian Pub. Service, Ark., Calif., Ind., Fla. and Oreg., 1942-46; draftsman, designer Kemper Nomland, Los Angeles, 1946-47, 48-49, Frick & Frick, Pasadena, Calif., 1950-51, Walter Reichardt, Los Angeles, 1951-52, De Witt & Swank, Dallas, 1952-54; prin. Mount-Miller, Houston, 1947-48, Denton, Tex., 1954-89; prin. Mount Miller McCain, Denton, 1989—. Editor The Illiterati and The Untide Press, 1945-52, The Denton Voice, 1970-74, Arkwork Rev., 1979-83; contbr. articles to profl. jours. Mem. Denton County Dem. Com., 1960-67; mem. Denton Hist. Landmark Commn., 1980-92, vice chmn., 1980-82; mem. The Fine Arts at Waldport, 1944-46, exec. sec. 1945, Am. Inst. Architects, 1957—, Anthropology Group Dallas, 1953—, The Forum, Denton, 1968—. Recipient Community Arts Recognition award Greater Denton Arts Council, 1982, State Service Recognition award Tex. Civil Liberties Union, 1986. Mem. AIA (emeritus), Interfaith Forum for Religion Art and Architecture (emeritus), Soc. Archtl. Historians, Nat. Trust for Hist. Preservation, Am. Solar Energy Soc., ACLU, War Resisters League, Fellowship of Reconciliation, Nat. Ataxia Found. Democrat. Unitarian Universalist. Avocations: music, piano, writing, travel, photography. Home and Office: 711 W Sycamore St Denton TX 76201-5919

MILLER, TRAVIS MILTON, association executive, accountant; b. Jasper, Tex., May 18, 1946; s. Clinton E. and Estelleen (Odom) M.; m. Mary E. Griffin, May 24, 1970; children: Tamera, Christianne. BS in Edn., Tex. A&M U., 1970; MS in Accountancy, U. Houston, 1976. CPA, Tex. Contr., then regional contr. Stewart Title Co., Houston, 1975-81; v.p. Griffin's Jewelers, Longview, Tex., 1981-89; contr. Hydrolex, Inc., Longview, 1989-91; pvt. practice, acctg., Arlington, Tex., 1991-94; exec. dir. Nat. Assn. of Women in Constrn. Edn. Found., Ft. Worth, 1994—. 1st lt. U.S. Army, 1970-74. Mem. Am. Soc. Assn. Execs. Methodist. Avocations: theater, choral music, golf. Home: 744 Glenhaven Dr Hurst TX 76054 Office: NAWIC Edn Found 327 S Adams St Fort Worth TX 76104-1002

MILLER, VEL, artist; b. Nekoosa, Wis., Jan. 22, 1936; d. Clarence Alvin Krause and Celia Mae (Houston) Clark; m. Warren Eugene Miller, Apr. 30, 1955; children: Jennifer, Andrea, Matthew, Stuart. Student, Valley Coll., Art League L.A. Exhbns. include Stamford (Tex.) Art Found., Haley Libr., Midland, Tex., Peppertree Ranch, Santa Ynez, Calif., Trappings of Am. West, Flagstaff, Ariz., Mountain Oyster Club, Tucson, Cowboy Classic, Phoenix, Cowboy Gathering, Paso Robles, Phoenix, Cattlemans Show, San Luis Obispo, Calif.; represented in permanent collections at Home Savings and Loan L.A., Glendale (Ariz.) Coll., Cavalry Mus., Samore, France; also pvt. collections. Recipient Best of Show award San Fernando Valley Art Club, San Gabriel Art Assn., Death Valley Invitational Show, numerous others. Mem. Am. Woman Artist (founder), Oil Painters Am.

MILLER, VICTORIA LOREN, marketing and communications design executive; b. San Francisco, May 25, 1957; d. Leon and Malvina (Hoffman) M. BFA, UCLA, 1979; postgrad., Art Ctr. Coll. Design, Pasadena, Calif., 1979, 80, UCLA, 1980-82, Otis/Parsons, L.A., 1981. Freelance designer, art dir. Bright and Assocs., L.A., 1979-80; designer Richard Runyon Design, L.A., 1980-83; art dir. Grey Entertainment Media, Santa Monica, Calif., 1984; prin. Victoria Miller Design, Santa Monica, Calif., 1984—. Label designer for Grand Cru Vineyards (Clio award 1985); designs represented in permanent collection Libr. Congress; pub. in Print Regional Ann., ADLA Ann., Am. Corp. Identity, Letterheads 5, Vision mag.; contbr. articles to profl. publs.; pckg. designer for Mattel, Disney, Macromedia, others. Mem. Am. Inst. Graphic Arts, Mus. Contemporary Art (photography coun.), Art Dirs. Club. Jewish. Avocations: contemporary art, photography, dance, tennis, cycling. Home and Office: 10650 Kinnard Ave # 311 Los Angeles CA 90024-5983

MILLER, VINCENT PAUL, JR., geography and regional planning educator; b. Swissvale, Pa., May 11, 1932; s. Vincent Paul and May Eleanor (Reed) M.; m. Alida Field Ward, July 21, 1960; 1 child, Bradley Cleland. BS, Muskingum Coll., 1954; MS, Pa. State U., 1957; PhD, Mich. State U., 1970. Social sci. asst. Quartermaster R&D Comdt., Natick, Mass., 1957-59; instr. Coll. of Wooster, Ohio, 1959-60; asst. instr. Mich. State U., East Lansing, 1961; assoc. prof. Indiana (Pa.) U., 1962-70, prof., 1970—. Author: Project Ebenezer: Modeling Holistic Missions, 1981, Central Place Hierarchy & Access to Services, 1985; editor/author: The Future at the Bicentennial, 1977, Planning Issues in Marginal Areas, 1991, Technology, Landscape, and Arrested Development: Essays on the Geography of Marginality, 1997; editor: The Pa. Jr. Geographer, 1965-66, The Pa. Geographer, 1966-75. Dir. rsch. Ministries in Action, Miami, Fla., 1980—; bd. mem. Birthright, Indiana, United Ministry Indiana U. of Pa.; mem. com. Diaconal Ministries Com., Kiskiminitas Presbytery, Rural Valley, Pa. Ctrl. Pl. Rsch. grantee, 1985, Travel grantee U. Presbyn. Ch., 1995. Mem. Assn. Am. Geographers (chair rural devel. specialty group 1984-88, sec. treas. 1984-86, pres. 1986-88), Assn. Pub. Justice, Pa. Geog. Soc. (pres. 1979-80). Avocations: music, writing, photography, yard work. Home: 111 View St Indiana PA 15701 Office: Indiana U of Pa Dept Geography & Regional Planning Indiana PA 15705

MILLER, W. MARSHALL, II, insurance consultant; b. Roanoke, Va., Feb. 3, 1953; s. Warren M. and Anne (Cooper) M. BA, Coll. William and Mary, 1975. CLU, ChFC. Agt. Prudential Ins. Co., Newport News, Va., 1976—; owner and pres. Ins. Consultants of Va., Inc., Newport News, 1979—. Mem. Nat. Assn. Life Underwriters, Advanced Assn. Life Underwriters, Internat. Assn. Fin. Planners, Peninsula Estate Planning Coun., Peninsula Chartered Life Underwriters (v.p. 1982-83), PRUSER Group, Million Dollar Round Table. Lutheran. Avocations: golf, photography, travel, gardening, bridge. Office: Ins Consultants of Va Inc 11818 Rock Landing Rd Ste 103 Newport News VA 23606-4273

MILLER, WALTER JAMES, English and humanities educator, writer; b. McKee City, N.J., Jan. 16, 1918; s. Walter Theodore and Celestia Anna (Simmons) M.; m. Bonnie Elizabeth Nelson, July 9, 1969 (div.); children: Naomi, Jason, Robin, Jared, Elizabeth. BA, CUNY, 1941; MA, Columbia U., 1952. Instr. English Poly. Inst. Brooklyn, N.Y., 1946-53, asst. prof., 1953-55; asst. prof. English and modern langs. Colo. State U., Ft. Collins, 1955-56; assoc. prof. English NYU, N.Y.C., 1958-66, prof. English, 1966-84, prof. emeritus, 1984—; Dir. Summer Writers Conf. Hofstra U., Hempstead, N.Y., 1972-79, NYU, N.Y.C., 1983-85. Author: 1001 Ideas for English Papers, 1994, Making an Angel: Poems, 1977, Engineers as Writers, 1953; author, translator: Annotated Jules Verne, 1995; editor, translator: Verne's 20,000 Leagues Under the Sea, 1993; contbg. editor Simon and Schuster, 1969—. Recipient Spl. award Engrs. Coun. Profl. Devel., 1966, Charles Angoff award The Lit. Rev., 1983, Gt. Tchr. award NYU Alumni Assn., 1980. Democrat. Avocations: hiking, fishing, traveling. Home: 100 Bleecker St Apt 17E New York NY 10012-2205 Office: NYU 50 W 4th St New York NY 10012-1106

MILLER, WALTER NEAL, insurance company consultant; b. N.Y.C., Nov. 26, 1929; s. Morton and Kathryn (Gersten) M.; m. Nancy Louise Clapp, Sept. 11, 1954; children—Scott, Timothy, David, Kathryn, Amy. B.A., Swarthmore Coll., 1951. With N.Y. Life Ins. Co., N.Y.C., 1951-86; v.p., actuary Prudential Ins. Co., Newark, 1986-93; sr. v.p., chief actuary Prudential Preferred Fin. Svcs., Liberty Corner, N.J., 1993-94; pvt. practice cons., 1994—. Author: (with others) Analysis of Actuarial Theory for Variable Life Insurance, 1969; contbr. (with others) articles to profl. jours. Mem. Soc. Actuaries, Am. Acad. Actuaries. Home: 470 Grandview Ave Wyckoff NJ 07481-2546

MILLER, WARREN EDWARD, political scientist; b. Hawarden, Iowa, Mar. 26, 1924; s. John Carroll and Mildred Ovedia (Lien) M.; m. Ruth S. Jones, May 1981; children by previous marriage: Jeffrey Ralph, Jennifer Louise. B.S., U. Oreg., 1948, M.S., 1950; Ph.D., Maxwell Sch. Citizenship and Public Affairs, Syracuse U., 1954; Ph.D. (hon.), U. Goteborg, Sweden, 1972. Asst. study dir. Survey Research Ctr., Inst. Social Research, U. Mich., 1951-53, study dir., 1953-56, research assoc., 1956-59, program dir., 1959-68, research coordinator polit. behavior program, 1968-70, prin. investigator nat. election studies, 1977—; dir. Ctr. Polit. Studies, Inst. Social Research, 1970-81; program dir. Ctr. Polit. Studies, 1982-93; asst. prof. polit. sci. Ctr. Polit. Studies, Inst. Social Research, 1956-58, asso. prof., 1958-63, prof., 1963-93, Arthur W. Bromage prof. polit. sci., 1981-82; prof. polit. sci. Ariz. State U., 1981—; fellow Ctr. Advanced Study in Behavioral Scis., 1961-62; exec. dir. Inter-univ. Consortium for Polit. and Social Rsch., 1962-70, assoc. dir., 1978—; vis. prof. U. Tilburg, Netherlands, 1973, U. Geneva, 1973, European U. Inst., Florence, Italy, 1979; vis. Disting. prof. Ariz. State U., 1981; trustee Inst. Am. Univs., 1970—; Regents' prof., Ariz. State U., 1988—. Author: (with others) books including The Voter Decides, 1954, American Voter, 1960, Elections and the Political Order, 1966, (with T.E. Levitin) Leadership and Change: Presidential Elections from 1952-1976, 77, (with M.K. Jennings) Parties in Transition, 1986, Without Consent, 1988, (with others) The American National Election Studies Data Sourcebook, 1952-1978, 80, The American National Election Studies Data Sourcebook, 1952-86, 89; (with J. Merrill Shanks) The New American Voter, 1996; contbr. (with others) articles to profl. publs.; editl. bd.: (with others) Am. Polit. Sci. Rev, 1966-71, Computers and the Humanities, 1969-71, Social Science History, 1976-91, Social Science Rev., 1973; editorial adv. bd.: (with others) Sage Electoral Studies Yearbook, 1974. Served with USAAF, 1943-46. Recipient Disting. Alumnus award Maxwell Sch. Citizenship and Public Affairs, Syracuse U., 1974, Disting. Faculty Achievement award U. Mich., 1977; honored in the creation of the Warren E. Miller award for Intellectual Accomplishment and Svc. Am. Polit. Sci. Assn. sect. on Elecions, Pub. Opionion and Voting Behavior, 1995, creation of the Warren E. Miller award for Meritorious Svc. to Social Scis. Inter-Univ. Consortium for Polit. and Social Rsch., 1993. Fellow Am. Acad. Arts and Scis.; mem. AAAS, Am. Polit. Sci. Assn. (pres. 1979-80), Internat. Polit. Sci. Assn. (coun. 1969-73), M.W. Polit. Sci. Assn., Internat. Soc. Polit. Psychology, So. Polit. Sci. Assn., Social Sci. History Assn. (pres. 1979-80), Norwegian Acad. Sci. and Letters. Office: Ariz State U Dept Polit Sci Tempe AZ 85287

MILLER, WARREN LLOYD, lawyer; b. Bklyn., July 18, 1944; s. Allan and Ella (Faecher) M.; m. Jana Lee Morris, May 13, 1978; children: Lindsey Beth, Alan Gregory, William Brett. BA with high univ. honors, Am. U., 1966; JD with honors, George Washington U., 1969. Bar: Va., 1969, D.C., 1969, U.S. Supreme Ct., 1981. Law clk. to Hon. Edward A. Beard Superior Ct. D.C., 1968-69; asst. U.S. atty. for D.C., 1969-74; ptnr. Stein, Miller & Brodsky, 1974-85; pres. Warren L. Miller, P.C., 1986—; of counsel Reed, Smith, Shaw & McClay, 1986-93; lectr. Georgetown U. Law Sch., 1970-71, Am. U., 1971-72; guest spkr. various TV programs and legal forums; mem. Jud. Conf. D.C. Cir., 1984—; pres. Asst. U.S. Attys. Assn. of D.C., 1983-84. contbr. articles to profl. jours. Parliamentarian credentials and rules coms. Rep. Nat. Conv., 1984, mem. D.C. Law Revision Commn., 1987-91 (apptd. by Pres. Reagan), U.S. Commn. for Preservation of Am.'s Heritage Abroad, 1992— (apptd. by Pres. Bush, reapptd. by Pres. Clinton 1996); bd. dirs. Found. for Buchenwald and Mittelbau-Dora Memls., 1994—; spkr. ceremonies commemorating 50th anniversary of liberation of Buchenwald, Garmeny, 1995; spkr. U.S. Holocaust Meml. Mus., 1995; fundraiser Rep. Nat. Com. and Pres. Bush, 1988-92; co-chmn. dinner for V.P. Bush, 1988; vice-chmn. Pres.'s Dinner, 1989; co-chmn. Pres.'s Club, Washington, 1990-92; co-chmn. fundraiser for U.S. Senator Christopher Bond, 1992; chmn., fundraiser U.S. Senator John Warner, 1996; vice-chmn., fundraiser Senator Bob Dole, 1996. Mem. Congl. Country Club (Bethesda, Md.), Phi Delta Phi, Omicron Delta Kappa, Pi Gamma Mu. Office: 2300 N St NW Ste 600 Washington DC 20037-1122

MILLER, WILBUR HOBART, business diversification consultant; b. Boston, Feb. 15, 1915; s. Silas Reuben and Muriel Mae (Greene) M.; m. Harriett I. Harmon, June 20, 1941; children: Nancy Iber Miller Harray, Warren Harmon, Donna Sewall Miller Davidge. B.S., U. N.H., 1936, M.S., 1938; Ph.D., Columbia U., 1941. Rsch. chemist Am. Cyanamid Co., Stamford, Conn., 1941-49, Washington tech. rep., 1949-53, dir. food industry devel., 1953-57; tech. dir. products for agr. Cyanamid Internat. Am. Cyanamid Co., N.Y.C., 1957-60; sr. scientist Dunlap & Assos., Darien, Conn., 1960-63, sr. assoc., 1963-66; coord. new product devel. Celanese Corp., N.Y.C., 1966-67, mgr. comml. rsch., 1967-68, dir. corp. devel., 1969-84; bus. diversification cons., 1984—; lectr. on bus. and soc. Western Conn. State Coll., 1977-79. Contbr. sci. papers to profl. jours.; patentee in field. Chmn. Stamford Forum for World Affairs, 1954-87, hon. chmn., 1987—; mem. adv. bd. Ctr. for Study of Presidency, 1980—; bd. dirs. Stamford Symphony, 1974-80, v.p., 1978-80; bd. dirs. Stamford Hist. Soc., 1988, v.p., 1991-92, pres., 1993-95; pres. Coun. for Continuing Edn. Stamford, 1963, bd. dirs., 1960-70; elder United Presbyn. Ch., nominating com., 1960-63; pres. Interfaith Coun. of Stamford, 1973; internat. fellow U. Bridgeport, 1985-88; mem. pres.'s coun. U. N.H., 1982—. Recipient outstanding achievement award Coll. Tech., U. N.H., 1971, Am. Design award, 1948, Golden Rule Award J.C. Penney & Co., 1986; Univ. fellow Columbia U., 1940-41. Fellow AAAS, Am. Inst. Chemists (councillor N.Y. chpt. 1984-85); mem. Am. Chem. Soc. (news svc. adv. bd., 1948-53), N.Y. Acad. Scis., Société de Chimie Industrielle (v.p. fin. Am. sect. 1980-84, dir. 1984—), Inst. Food Tech., Soc. for Internat. Devel., Am. Acad. Polit. and Social Scis., Stamford Hist. Soc., Chemists Club (N.Y.C., treas. 1982-84), Sigma Xi, Alpha Chi Sigma, Phi Kappa Phi. Home: 19 Crestview Ave Stamford CT 06907-1906

MILLER, WILBUR RANDOLPH, university educator and administrator; b. Elsberry, Mo., Nov. 12, 1932; s. Charles Clifton and Pauline Jean (Dryden) M. Student, SE Mo. U., 1951-53; BEd, U. Mo., 1954, MEd, 1955, EdD, 1960. Cert. secondary tchr., Mo. Tchr. indsl. arts Hazelwood Sch. Dist., St. Louis, 1955-56, U. Lab. Sch., Columbia, Mo., 1956-60; indsl. tchr. educator Purdue U., West Lafayette, Ind., 1960-63; asst. prof. U. Mo., Columbia, 1963-67, assoc. prof. and chmn. dept. coll. edn., 1967-76, prof. and assoc. dean coll. edn., 1976-86, dean coll. edn., 1986-91, prof., dean emeritus, 1992; cons. Rep. of Turkey, 1993, 94; v.p. for devel. Auburn U., 1996—; chmn. adv. coun. Fed. Rsch. Ctr. in Vocat. Edn., Ohio State U., Columbus, 1981-84; internat. edn. cons. 1992—; edn. adv. bd. DeVry Inc., Oakwood Terrace, Ill., 1986—; mem. pvt. post-sec. tech. sch. accreditation commn. ACCSET, 1994—. Author: Teaching Children Through Construction Activities, 1985, Instructors and Their Jobs, 1990, The Golf Primer, 1991, Handbook for College Teaching, 1997; editor: (series) Basic Industrial Arts, 1978; contbr. more than 40 articles to profl. jours. Pres., bd. dirs. Lenoir Inc., Columbia, 1977-84; mem. Woodhaven Sch. Bd., Columbia, 1982-83. With USNR, 1955-63. Recipient U. Faculty/Alumni award, 1985. Mem. Nat. Assn. Indsl. Tchr. Educators (pres., officer 1965-74), Am. Indsl. Arts Assn. (v.p. 1980), Mo. Vocat. Assn. (pres. 1974-75), Mo. Assn. Colls. for Tchr. Edn. (pres. 1987-90), Am. Vocat. Assn. (Outstanding Svc. award 1979). Mem. Disciples of Christ Ch. Club: Faculty (Columbia) (officer 1977-82). Lodge: Kiwanis. Avocations: golf, travel, home maintenance. Office: PO Box 2683 Auburn AL 36831-2683

MILLER, WILLARD, JR., mathematician, educator; b. Ft. Wayne, Ind., Sept. 17, 1937; s. Willard and Ruth (Kemerly) M.; m. Jane Campbell Scott, June 5, 1965; children—Stephen, Andrea. S.B. in Math., U. Chgo., 1958; Ph.D. in Applied Math, U. Calif.-Berkeley, 1963. Vis. mem. Courant Inst. Math. Scis., NYU, 1963-65; mem. faculty U. Minn., 1965—, prof. math., 1972—, head Sch. Math., 1978-86; co-prin. investigator Inst. Math. and its Applications, 1980-94, assoc. dir., 1987-94; assoc. dean Inst. of Tech., 1994—; acting dean Inst. of Tech., 1995. Author: Lie Theory and Special Functions, 1968, Symmetry Groups and Their Applications, 1972, Symmetry and Separation of Variables, 1977; assoc. editor Jour. Math. Physics, 1973-75, Applicable Analysis, 1978-90. Mem. AAAS, Soc. Indsl. and Applied Math. (mng. editor Jour. Math. Analysis 1975-81), Am. Math. Soc., Sigma Xi. Home: 4508 Edmund Blvd Minneapolis MN 55406-3629 Office: Univ Minn Sch Math Minneapolis MN 55455

MILLER, WILLIAM, library administrator; b. Phila., Jan. 9, 1947; s. Julius and Norma (Frank) M.; m. Anne Hendry Hickok, July 20, 1983; children: Jessica, Miriam. BA, Temple U., 1968; PhD, U. Rochester, 1974; MLS, U. Toronto, Ontario, Canada, 1976. Reference libr. Albion (Mich.) Coll., 1976-80; head reference and govt. documents Mich. State U. Libr., East Lansing, Mich., 1980-84; assoc. dean of librs. Bowling Green (Ohio) State U., 1984-87; dir. librs. Fla. Atlantic U., Boca Raton, 1987-90, dir. librs. and learning resources, 1990—. Editor: College Librarianship, 1981; contbr. articles to profl. jours. Recipient Ontario Libr. Assn. Prize, Toronto, 1976, Libr. Instrn. Grant, Earlham Coll., Nat. Sci Found., Richmond, Ind., 1978. Mem. ALA (chair editorial bd. Choice mag. 1980-82, other offices), MLA, Assn. for Integrative Studies. Home: 8595 Brody Way Boca Raton FL 33433-7647 Office: Fla Atlantic U Libr PO Box 3092 Boca Raton FL 33431-0992

MILLER, WILLIAM ALVIN, clergyman, author, lecturer; b. Pitts., Jan. 1, 1931; s. Christ William and Anna Ernestine (Wilhelm) M.; m. Marilyn Mae Miller, Aug. 8, 1953; children: Mark William, Eric Michael. BA, Capital U., 1953; MDiv, Luth. Theol. Sem., Columbus, Ohio, 1957; MST, Andover Newton Theol. Sch., Newton Centre, Mass., 1958, D of Ministry, 1974. Ordained to ministry Luth. Ch.; lic. marriage & family therapist, Minn. Pastor St. James Luth. Ch., Balt., 1958-66; chaplain Fairview Hosp., Mpls., 1966-73, dir. dept. religion & health, 1973-87; instr. Fairview Sch. Nursing, Mpls., 1967-75, Luther Northwestern Theol. Sem., St. Paul, 1973-85; pres. Woodland Pub. Co., Wayzata, Minn., 1979—; dir. Woodland Pastoral Assocs., Mpls., 1987-96; assoc. pastor Cen. Luth. Ch., Mpls., 1989-94; chair bd. dirs. Luth. Social Svcs. Md., Balt., 1963-65; adminstr. Dialogue 88, Mpls., 1987-88. Author: Why Do Christians Break Down?, 1973, Big Kids' Mother Goose, 1976, When Going to Pieces Holds You Together, 1976, You Count, You Really Do!, 1976, Mid Life, New Life, 1978, Conversations, 1980, Make Friends With Your Shadow, 1981, Prayers at Mid Point, 1983, The Joy of Feeling Good, 1986, Your Golden Shadow, 1989, 91, Meeting the Shadow, 1991; assoc. editor Jour. Pastoral Care, Decatur, Ga., 1984-88, editl. cons., 1988—; contbr. articles to profl. jours. Chaplain, Jr. C. of C., Randallstown, Md., 1962-64; bd. dirs. Am. Protestant Health Assn., Schaumburg, Ill., 1983-89. Fellow Coll. Chaplains (pres. 1985-87), Assn. Mental Health Clergy (Anton T. Boisen award 1989); mem. Assn. Clin. Pastoral Edn. (supr.). Avocations: cabinetmaking, skiing, publishing, construction. Home and Office: 2005 Xanthus Ln N Minneapolis MN 55447-2053

MILLER, WILLIAM CHARLES, lawyer; b. Jacksonville, Fla., Aug. 6, 1937; s. Charles and Mary Elizabeth (Kiger) M.; m. Hadmut Gisela Larsen, June 10, 1961; children: Monica Lee, Charles Andreas. BA, Washington and Lee U., 1958, LLB, 1961; LLM, NYU, 1963; postgrad., Harvard U., 1978. Bar: Fla. 1961, Calif. 1984, Ind. 1987, U.S. Supreme Ct. 1968. Counsel to electrochem., elastomers and internat. depts. E.I. duPont de Nemours & Co., Wilmington, Del., 1963-66; counsel S. Am. ops. Bristol-Myers Co., N.Y.C., 1967-69; internat. counsel Xerox Corp., Stamford, Conn., 1969-79; assoc. gen. counsel Xerox Corp., Stamford, 1979-80; v.p., gen. counsel, sec. Max Factor & Co., Hollywood, Calif., 1981-85, Boehringer Mannheim Corp., Indpls., 1985-92; v.p., gen. counsel Collagen Corp., Palo Alto, Calif., 1992-95, Gen. Probe Inc., San Diego, 1995-96, Safeskin Corp., San Diego, 1996—. Bd. dirs. Southwestern Legal Found., 1975-85. Fulbright scholar, 1959-60; Ford Found. fellow, 1961-62; Hague Acad. fellow, 1963; German Govt. grantee, 1962-63; Kappa Sigma scholar, 1959. Mem. Internat. Bar Assn., ABA, Calif. Bar Assn., Fla. Bar Assn., Ind. Bar Assn., Masons, Elks, Phi Beta Kappa, Phi Eta Sigma, Delta Theta Phi. Republican. Mem. Christian Ch. Home: 3516 Villanova Ave San Diego CA 92122-2313

MILLER, WILLIAM CHARLES, college dean, architect; b. San Francisco, May 11, 1945; s. Francis Leland and Ethel Lorene (Britt) M.; m. Beverly Jean McConnell, Dec. 22, 1968; children: Britt A., David A. BArch, U. Oreg., 1968; MArch, U. Ill., 1970. Registered architect, Ariz., Kans., Utah. Architect various firms, San Francisco, Sacramento, Calif., Tucson and Oak Harbor, Wash.; asst. prof. Coll. Architecture U. Ariz., Tucson, 1970-73, 74-77; assoc. prof. dept. architecture Kans. State U., Manhattan, 1977-86, prof., 1986-92, head dept., 1990-92; dean, prof. Grad. Sch. Architecture U. Utah, Salt Lake City, 1992—; guest lectr. over 36 schs. architecture; presenter to more than a dozen profl. socs. and orgns.; dir. west ctrl. region Assn. Collegiate Schs. Architecture, 1988-91, chair theme paper sessions ann. meeting, San Francisco, 1990, chair regional paper sessions ann. meeting, Washington, 1991, co-chair adminstrv. conf., Milw., 1995; bd. dirs. Nat. Archtl. Accrediting Bd., 1996—. Author: Alvar Aalto: An Annotated Bibliography, 1984; co-editor: The Architecture of the In-Between, 1990, Architecture: Back to Life, 1991; contbr. articles to profl. jours., chpts. to books. Bd. dirs. Assist, Inc., Artspace, Inc., Contemporary Arts Group. Recipient Svc. awards Assn. Collegiate Schs. Architecture, Nat. Coun. Archtl. Registration Bds. Fellow AIA (architects in edn. com., com. on design, Kans. profl. edn. com., pres-elect Flint Hills, treas. Utah, exec. com., treas., exec. com. Western Mountain region, elected coll. of fellows 1997); mem. Am.-Scandinavian Found., Soc. for Advancement Scandinavian Studies, Tau Sigma Delta. Office: U Utah Grad Sch Architecture Salt Lake City UT 84112

MILLER, WILLIAM FREDERICK, research company executive, educator, business consultant; b. Vincennes, Ind., Nov. 19, 1925; s. William and Elsie M. (Everts) M.; m. Patty J. Smith, June 19, 1949; 1 son, Rodney Wayne. Student, Vincennes U., 1946-47; BS, Purdue U., 1949, MS, 1951, PhD, 1956; D.Sc., 1972. Mem. staff Argonne Nat. Lab., 1955-64, assoc. physicist, 1956-59, dir. applied math. div., 1959-64; prof. computer sci. Stanford U., Palo Alto, Calif., 1965—; Herbert Hoover prof. pub. and pvt. mgmt. Stanford U., 1979—, assoc. provost for computing, 1968-70, v.p. for research, 1970-71, v.p., provost, 1971-78; mem. Stanford Assocs., 1972—; chmn. bd. Who Where?, Inc.; pres., chief exec. officer SRI Internat., Menlo Park, Calif., 1979-90; chmn. bd., chief exec. officer SRI Devel. Co., Menlo Park, David Sarnoff Research Ctr., Inc., Princeton, N.J.; bd. dirs. Borland Internat., Inc., 1996—; chmn. bd. dirs. Whowhere, Inc., 1997; professorial lectr. applied math. U. Chgo., 1962-64; vis. prof. math. Purdue U., 1962-63; vis. scholar Ctr. for Advanced Study in Behavioral Scis., 1976; bd. dirs. Wells Fargo and Co., McKenna Group; mem. adv. coun. BHP Internat.; mem. computer sci. and engring bd. NAS, 1968-71; mem. Nat. Sci. Bd., 1982-88; mem. corp. com. computers in edn. Brown UU., 1971-79; mem. policy bd. EDUCOM Planning Coun. on Computing in Edn., 1974-79, chmn., 1974-76; mem. ednl. adv. bd. Guggenheim Meml. Found., 1976-80; mem. com. postdoctoral and doctoral rsch. staff NRC, 1977-80, mem. computer sci. and telecom. Assoc. editor: Pattern Recognition Jour, 1968-72, Jour. Computational Physics, 1970-74. Served to 2d lt. F.A. AUS, 1943-46. Recipient Frederic B. Whitman award United Way Bay Area, 1982, Sarnoff Founders medal, 1997. Fellow IEEE, Am. Acad. Arts and Scis., AAAS; mem. Am. Math. Soc., Am. Phys. Soc., Soc. Indsl. and Applied Math., Assn. Computing Machinery, Nat. Acad. Engring., Sigma Xi, Tau Beta Pi. Office: Stanford U Grad Sch Bus Stanford CA 94305

MILLER, WILLIAM GREEN, ambassador; b. N.Y.C., Aug. 15, 1931; m. Suzanne Lisle; 2 children. BA, Williams Coll., Oxford U., U.K.; MA, Oxford U., U.K.; postgrad., Harvard U. Tutor Winthrop House Harvard Univ., 1956-59; with Fgn. Svc., 1959; vice consul, polit. officer Isfahan, Iran, 1959-62; polit. officer Tehran, Iran, 1962-64; line officer, exec. secretariat Dept. of State, 1965-66; mem. Sr. Interdepartmental Group, 1966-67; spl. asst. fgn. affairs and def. Senator John Sherman Cooper, 1967-73; staff dir. Senate Select Com. Emergency Powers, 1973-75, Senate Select Com. to Study Govtl. Ops. with Respect to Intelligence Communities, 1975-76, Senate Select Com. Intelligence, 1976-81; assoc. dean, adj. prof. internat. politics Fletcher Sch. Law and Diplomacy, 1981-83, rsch. assoc., 1983-85; faculty assoc. Harvard Ctr. Middle Eastern Studies, 1983-86; pres. Am. Com. U.S.-Soviet Rels., 1986-92; U.S. amb. to Ukraine, 1993—; cons. D.H. Sawyer and Assocs., Ltd., N.Y.C., 1985; bd. dirs. Internat. Found., pres. 1986-92; pres. Com. Am.- Russian Rels., cons. Catherine T. MacArthur Found., 1992-93. Contbr. articles to profl. jours. Rsch. fellow Harvard Ctr. Sci. and Internat. Affairs, 1984-86, John F. Kennedy Sch. of Govt. fellow Harvard U., 1986. Fellow Rsch. Inst. of Politics; mem. Nat. Acad. Pub. Diplomacy, Nat. Acad. Pub. Adminstrn., Internat. Inst. Strategic Studies, Coun. Fgn. Rels., Children of the 21st Century, Middle East Inst., Embassy of the U.S. America. Office: 10 Yuria Kotsyubinskovo, 252053 Kiev 53, Ukraine

MILLER, WILLIAM HUGHES, theoretical chemist, educator; b. Kosciusko, Miss., Mar. 16, 1941; s. Weldon Howard and Jewel Irene (Hughes) M.; m. Margaret Ann Westbrook, June 4, 1966; children: Alison Leslie, Emily Sinclaire. B.S., Ga. Inst. Tech., 1963; A.M., Harvard U., 1964, Ph.D., 1967. Jr. fellow Harvard U., 1967-69; NATO postdoctoral fellow Freiburg (Germany) U., 1967-68; asst. prof. chemistry U. Calif., Berkeley, 1969-72, assoc. prof., 1972-74, prof., 1974—, dept. chmn., 1989-93; fellow Churchill Coll., Cambridge (Eng.) U., 1975-76; hon. prof. Shandong U., People's Republic of China, 1994. Alfred P. Sloan fellow, 1970-72; Camille and Henry Dreyfus fellow, 1973-78; Guggenheim fellow, 1975-76, Christensen fellow St. Catherine's Coll., Oxford, 1993; recipient Alexander von Humboldt-Stiftung U.S. Sr. Scientist award, 1981-82, Ernest Orlando Lawrence Meml. award, 1985, Hirschfelder prize in theoretical chemistry, U. Wis., 1996, Alumni Achievement award Ga. Inst. Tech., 1997. Fellow AAAS, Am. Acad. Arts and Scis., Am. Phys. Soc. (Irving Langmuir award 1990); mem. NAS, Am. Chem. Soc. (Theoretical Chemistry award 1994, Ira Remsen award 1997), Internat. Acad. Quantum Molecular Sci. (Ann. prize 1974). Office: U Calif Dept Chemistry Berkeley CA 94720

MILLER, WILLIAM LEE, JR., minister; b. Mammoth Spring, Ark., Dec. 27, 1926; s. William L. and Janie Katherine (Murrell) M.; m. Marion Evelyn O'Neal, Mar. 23, 1947 (div. 1976); children: Georgia Katherine Miller Beach, William Lee III; m. Judith Ann Bell, Nov. 28, 1977. AB, Phillips U., 1950, LittD, 1968; postgrad., U. Ark., 1951-52, Tex. Christian U., 1958, U. Ky., 1961; BD, Lexington Theol. Sem., 1961. Ordained to ministry Christian Ch. (Disciples of Christ), 1950. Pastor 1st Christian Ch., Rogers, Ark., 1952-59, Rogers Heights Christian Ch., Tulsa, 1961-62; v.p. Bd. Higher Edn., Indpls., 1962-68; pres. Bd. Higher Edn. Christian Ch. (Disciples of Christ), 1968-77; v.p. devel. Nat. City Christian Ch. Corp., Washington, 1977-82; upper Midwest regional min., pres. Christian Ch. (Disciples of Christ), Des Moines, 1982-93; pres. Miller Devel. Assocs.; dir. Christian Ch. Found., Indpls., 1968-77, 84-93; trustee Bethany Coll., W.Va., 1972-85, Culver Stockton Coll., 1970-77, 82—, Tougaloo Coll., Jackson, Miss., 1970-76, Christian Theol. Sem., Indpls., 1987-94. Precinct committeeman Dem. Party, Indpls., 1968-72; mem. Reagan First Inaugural Religious Com.; bd. dris. St. Louis Christian Home, 1956-59; chmn. Coop. Coll. Registry, Washington, 1963-70; mem. Disciples of Christ Ch., Disciples Soc. for Faith & Reason; bd. dirs., exec. com. Christian Ch. D.C., N.C., 1995—; pres. Friends of Dare County (N.C.) Librs., 1997—; v.p. North Dare County Ministerial Assn. Mem. Disciples of Christ Hist. Soc., Coun. Christian Unity (exec. com. 1968-77), Nat. Evangelitic Assn. (bd. dirs. 1983-86), Am. Assn. Higher Edn., Masons, KT, Sigma Chi. Disciples of Christ and Presbyterian. Home: 113 Kellam Ct Manteo NC 27954 Office: Miller Devel Assocs PO Box 194 Manteo NC 27954-0194

MILLER, WILLIAM NAPIER CRIPPS, lawyer; b. Long Branch, N.J., June 7, 1930; adopted s. Julia (Erwin) M.; m. Carolyn Anderson, Jan. 19, 1951 (div. 1963); children: Bruce Douglass, Jennifer Erwin; m. Hannelore Steinbeck, Dec. 4, 1970;. A.A., Coll. Marin, 1949; student, U. Calif.-Berkeley, 1949-51, J.D., 1955. Bar: N.Y., Calif. 1956, U.S. Supreme Ct. 1983. Assoc. Mudge, Stern, Baldwin & Todd, N.Y.C., 1955-58; assoc. Pillsbury, Madison & Sutro, San Francisco, 1959-65, ptnr., 1966—; staff NYU Law Sch., 1957-58; ct. adv. com. Calif. State Assembly Judiciary Com., 1979-80. Bd. dirs. Laguna Honda Hosp., San Francisco, 1966—; bd. visitors U. Calif.-Hastings Law Sch. Served with USAF, 1951-52. Recipient Bur. Nat. Affairs award U. Calif.-Hastings, 1955; recipient Thurston Soc. award, 1953. Fellow Am. Coll. Trial Lawyers; mem. ABA, San Francisco Bar Assn., Order of Coif, St. Francis Yacht Club, Silverado Country Club. Home: 16 George Ln Sausalito CA 94965-1890 Office: Pillsbury Madison & Sutro PO Box 7880 San Francisco CA 94120-7880

MILLER, WILLIAM RICHEY, JR., lawyer; b. Oklahoma City, Apr. 4, 1947; s. William Richey and Edna Rosalind (Nielsen) M.; m. Susan Hammond, Aug. 2, 1970; children: Brooke, Karen. BA, Pomona Coll., Claremont, Calif., 1969; MA, Claremont Grad. Sch., 1972; JD, Lewis and Clark Coll., 1975. Bar: Oreg. 1975, U.S. Dist. Ct. Oreg. 1976, U.S. Ct. Appeals (9th cir.) 1976. Staff atty. Oreg. Ct. Appeals, Salem, 1975-76; with firm Griffith, Bittner, Abbott & Roberts, Portland, Oreg., 1976-83; ptnr. Davis Wright Termaine, Portland, 1983—; adj. prof. Lewis and Clark Law Sch., 1975-78. Bd. dirs. Portland Civic Theatre, 1988-91, Am. Lung Assn. Oreg., Portland, 1985-88, Oreg. Bus. Com. for the Arts, Portland, 1991-93. Mem. Oreg. State Bar (sect. chair 1990-91), Comml. Fin. Assn., Oreg. Bankers Assn., Lewis and Clark Alumni Assn. (bd. dirs. 1989-92). Presbyterian. Home: 843 Lakeshore Rd Lake Oswego OR 97034-3704 Office: Davis Wright Tremaine 1300 SW 5th Ave Ste 2300 Portland OR 97201-5667

MILLER, YVONNE BOND, state senator, educator; b. Edenton, N.C.; d. John and Pency Bond. BS, Va. State Coll., Petersburg, 1956; postgrad., Va. State Coll., Norfolk, 1966; MA, Columbia U., 1962; PhD, U. Pitts., 1973; postgrad., CCNY, 1976. Tchr. Norfolk Pub. Schs., 1956-68; asst. prof. Norfolk State U., 1968-71, assoc. prof., 1971-74, prof., 1974-88, head dept. early childhood/elem. edn., 1984-87; mem. Va. Ho. Dels., Richmond, 1984-87, mem. edn. com., health, welfare and instns. com., militia and police com., 1983-87; mem. Va. Senate, Richmond, 1987—; now mem. commerce and labor com., gen. laws com., transp. com., rehab. and social svcs. com. Va. Senate, now chair rehab. and social svcs. com., mem. rules com.; Va. Dems. vice chair; mem. Nat. Dem. Com.; cons. to chs., parent orgns. and community groups. Commr. Ea. Va. Med. Authority; adv. bd. Va. Div. Children; active C.H. Mason Meml. Ch. of God in Christ. 1st black woman to be elected to Va. Legislature, 1983, 1st black woman to be elected to Va. Senate, 1987. Mem. Nat. Alliance Black Sch. Educators (bd. dirs.), Va. Assn. for Early Childhood Edn., Nat. Assn. Dem. Chairs, Zeta Phi Beta (past officer). Office: 960 Norchester Ave Norfolk VA 23504-4038 also: Norfolk State U 2401 Corprew Ave Norfolk VA 23504-3907 also: Va Senate Gen Assembly Bldg Rm 365 Richmond VA 23219

MILLER, ZELL BRYAN, governor; b. Young Harris, Ga., Feb. 24, 1932; s. Stephen Grady and Birdie (Bryan) M.; m. Shirley Carver, Jan. 14, 1954; children: Murphy Carver, Matthew Stephen. Student, Young Harris Coll.; AB, MA, U. Ga. Dir. Ga. Bd. Probation, 1965-66; dep. dir. Ga. Dept. Corrections, 1967-68; exec. sec. to gov. Ga., 1968-71; mem. State Bd. Pardons and Paroles, Atlanta, 1973-75; lt. gov. State of Ga., 1975-90, gov., 1990—; prof. polit. sci. and history U. Ga., Young Harris Coll., 1959-64. Author: The Mountains Within Me, Great Georgians, They Heard Georgia Singing. Mem. Ga. Senate, 1960-64; mayor Young Harris, 1959; exec. dir. Democratic Com. Ga., 1971-72; pres. Coun. State Govts., 1991—; vice chmn. So. Gov.'s Assn., 1991—; bd. dirs. Towns County Hosp. Authority. Served with USMC, 1953-56. Mem. Ga. Sch. Food Services Assn. (life), Ga. Peace Officers Assn. (life), Gridiron Soc. U. Ga., Blue Key, Lions Club. Methodist. Office: Office of Governor State Capitol Rm 203 Atlanta GA 30334*

MILLER, ZOYA DICKINS (MRS. HILLIARD EVE MILLER, JR.), civic worker; b. Washington, July 15, 1923; d. Randolph and Zoya Pavlovna (Klementinovska) Dickins; m. Hilliard Eve Miller, Jr., Dec. 6, 1943; children: Jeffrey Arnot, Hilliard Eve III. Grad. Stuart Sch. Costume Design, Washington, 1942; student Sophie Newcomb Coll., 1944, New Eng. Conservatory Music, 1946, Colo. Coll., 1965; grad. Internat. Sch. Reading, 1969. Instr. Stuart Summer Sch. Costume Design, Washington, 1942; fashion coord. Julius Garfinckel, Washington, 1942-43; fashion coord., cons. Mademoiselle mag., 1942-44; star TV show Cowbelle Kitchen, 1957-58, Flair for Living, 1958-59; model mags. and comml. films, also nat. comml. recs., 1956—; dir. devel. Webb-Waring Inst. for Biomedical Rsch., Denver, 1973—. Contbr. articles, lectures on health care systems and fund raising. Mem. exec. com., bd. dirs. El Paso County chpt. Am. Lung Assn., Colo., 1954-63; mem. exec. com. Am. Lung Assn. Colo., 1965-84, bd. dirs. 1965-87, chmn. radio and TV coun., 1963-70, mem. med. affairs com., 1965-70, pres., 1965-66, procurer found. funds, 1965-70; developer nat. radio ednl. prodns. for internat. use Am. Lung Assn., 1963-70, coord. statewide pulmonary screening programs Colo., other states, 1965-72; chmn. benefit fund raising El Paso County Cancer Soc., 1963; co-founder, coord. Colorado Springs Debutante Ball, 1967—; coord. Nat. Gov.'s Conf. Ball, 1969; mem. exec. com. Colo. Gov.'s Comprehensive Health Planning Coun., 1967-74, chmn., 1971-72; chmn. Colo. Chronic Care Com., 1969-73, chmn. fund raising, 1970-72, chmn. spl. com. congl. studies on nat. health bills, 1971-73; mem. Colo.-Wyo. Regional Med. Program Adv. Coun., 1969-73; mem. Colo. Med. Found. Consumers Adv. Coun., 1972-78; mem. decorative arts com. Colorado Springs Fine Arts Ctr., 1972-75; founder, state coord. Nov. Noel Pediatrics Benefit Am. Lung Assn., 1973-87; founder, chmn. bd. dirs. Newborn Hope, Inc., 1987—; mem. adv. bd. Wagon Wheel Girl Scouts, 1991—, Cmty. in Schs., 1995—. Zoya Dickins Miller Vol. of Yr. award established Am. Lung Assn. of Colo., 1979; recipient James J. Waring award Colo. Conf. on Respiratory Disease Workers, 1963, Nat. Pub. Rels. award Am. Lung Assn., 1979, Gold Double Bar Cross award, 1980, 83, Jefferson award Am. Inst. Pub. Svc., 1991, Thousand Points of Light award The White House, 1992, Recognition award So. Colo. Women's C. of C., 1994, Silver Spur Community award Pikes Peak Range Riders, 1994, Silver Bell award Assistance League Colorado Springs, 1996, Svc. to Mankind award Centennial Sertoma Club, 1997, Help Can't Wait award Pikes Peak chpt. ARC, 1997; named Humanitarian of Yr., Am. Lung Assn. of Colo., 1987, One of 50 Most Influential Women in Colorado Springs by Gazette Telegraph Newspaper, 1990, One of 6 Leading Ladies Colo. Homes & Lifestyles Mag., 1991. Lic. pvt. pilot. Mem. Colo. Assn. Fund Raisers, Denver Round Table for Planned Giving, Nat. Soc. Fund Raising Execs., Nat. Cowbell Assn. (El Paso county pres. 1954, TV chmn., chmn. nat. Father of Yr. contest Colo. 1956-57), Broadmoor Garden Club. Home: 74 W Cheyenne Mountain Blvd Colorado Springs CO 80906-4336

MILLER-CHERMELY, DOROTHY L., sales executive; b. Hof, Bavaria, Germany, Nov. 30, 1947; d. Furman C. and Hilde (Weigold) Alderman; m. Kenneth Eugene Miller, Oct. 8, 1966 (div. 1972); m. Ronald Joseph Chermely, Feb. 14, 1993. AAS in Bus. Adminstrn., Corning Community Coll., 1973; BS in Indsl. and Labor Rels., Cornell U., 1975. Lic. real estate broker, Fla. Exec. sec. Corning (N.Y.) Bldg. Co., 1967-73; personnel adminstr. Xerox Corp., Rochester, N.Y., 1975-77; supt., constrn. mgr. U.S. Home Corp., Port Richey, Fla., 1979-80, sales cons., 1981-82, exec. v.p., 1982-83, v.p., sales mgr., 1990-94, v.p. project mgr., 1995; constrn. supt. Charles Rutenberg Corp., Clearwater, Fla., 1983-85. Vol., mem. self-sufficiency subcom. Health and Rehab. Svcs., Port Richey, Fla., 1993; vol. Salvation Army Spouse Abuse Ctr.; vol. AIDS/HIV instr. ARC; pres. bd. dirs. Unity Ch., sec. Women of Unity, coord. fundraising. Mem. NOW, Fla. Trust for Hist. Preservation, Nat. Trust for Hist. Preservation, Pasco C. of C. (rep. 1990-93), Pasco Builders Assn. (rep. 1990-93), Optimist Club (sec. 1993-94, v.p. 1994—). Avocations: arts and crafts, antiquing, historic preservation, travel. Home: 8806 Planters Ln New Port Richey FL 34654-4200

MILLER DAVIS, MARY-AGNES, social worker; b. Montgomery, Ala., Jan. 21; d. George Joseph and Mollie (Ingersoll) M.; m. Edward Davis, Sept. 20, 1941. BA, Wayne State U., 1944; MSW, U. Mich., 1970. Lic. social worker, Mich. Social caseworker Cath. Family Ctr., Detroit, 1946-48; foster homes worker Juvenile Ct., Detroit, 1953-57; youth svc. bur. League of Cath. Women, Detroit, 1957-59; mayor's community action for youth com. worker City of Detroit, 1963; instr. urban sociology Madonna Coll., Livonia, Mich., 1968; pers. cons. Edward Davis Motor Sales, Detroit, 1963-70; exec. cons. Edward Davis Assocs., Inc., Detroit, 1975—; founder Co-Ette Club, Inc., Detroit, 1941—, Met. Detroit Teen Conf. Coalition, Detroit, 1983—; program chair Wayne State U.-Merrill Palmer Inst., Detroit, 1976—. Editor Girl Friends, Inc. Mag., 1960-62; contbr. numerous articles to profl. publs. Life mem. NAACP, League of Cath. Women; charter mem. Meadowbrook Summer Music Festival, com. of Oakland (Mich.) U.; adv. bd. Women for the Detroit Symphony Orch.; mem./patron Founder's Soc. the Detroit Inst. of Arts; bd. dirs., other offices ARC, Detroit, 1974—; mem. The Detroit Hist. Soc., Heart of Gold Coun., Women for United Found. (named to Heart of Gold coun. 1968), Friends of the Detroit Libr., Mich. Opera Theatre; mem. nat. hon. com./nat. vol. week United Cmty. Svc. and Nat. Vol. Ctr., Washington, 1990—; former bd. dirs. United Community Svcs. Women's Com., Campfire Girls, LWV, Neighborhood Svcs. Orgn., Cath. Interracial Coun. and others; founder Met. Detroit Teen Conf. Coalitions Merrill Palmer Inst. Wayne State U. Recipient Nat. Community Leadership award Nat. Coun. Women of U.S., Inc., 1984, Am. Human Resources award Am. Bicentennial Rsch. Inst., 1976, Heart of Gold award United Way, 1968, Nat. Leadership award United Negro Coll. Fund, 1963, Recognition award Westin Hotel, 1991, Top Ladies of Distinction award, 1994; named One of Mich. Outstanding Women City of Detroit, 1976, Heart of Gold 25th Anniversary honoree United Way Southeastern Mich., 1992; Vassar Summer

Seminar scholar NCCJ, 1953, Notre Dame Summer Seminar scholar, 1960. Mem. NASW, ARC (bd. dirs. 1973—), Nat. Conf. of Social Work, The Cons. Club of Detroit (adv. bd. edn. com.), Detroit Econ. Club (mem. adv. com.). Home: 2020 Chicago Blvd Detroit MI 48206-1783

MILLER-LANE, BARBARA See LANE, BARBARA MILLER

MILLETT, KATE (KATHERINE MURRAY MILLETT), political activist, sculptor, artist, writer; b. St. Paul, Sept. 14, 1934; m. Fumio Yoshimura, 1965. BA magna cum laude, U. Minn., 1956; postgrad. with 1st class honors, St. Hilda's Coll. Oxford, Eng., 1956-58; PhD with distinction, Columbia U., 1970. Instr. English U. N.C. at Greensboro, 1958; file clk. N.Y.C., kindergarten tchr., 1960-61; sculptor, Tokyo, 1961-63; tchr. Barnard Coll., 1964-70; tchr. English Bryn Mawr (Pa.) Coll., 1970; disting. vis. prof. Sacramento State Coll., 1972-73; founder Women's Art Colony Farm, Poughkeepsie, N.Y. Author: Sexual Politics, 1970, The Prostitution Papers, 1973, Flying, 1974, Sita, 1977, The Basement, 1979, Going to Iran, 1982, The Loony Bin Trip, 1990, The Politics of Cruelty, 1994, A.D., 1995; co-prodr., co-dir. film Three Lives, 1970; one-woman shows Minami Gallery, Tokyo, Judson Gallery, N.Y.C., 1967, Noho Gallery, N.Y.C., 1976, 79, 80, 82, 84, 86, 93, Women's Bldg., L.A., 1977; drawings Andre Wanters Gallery, Berlin, 1980, Courtland Jessup Gallery, Provincetown, Mass., 1991, 92, 93, 94, 95. Mem. Congress of Racial Equality; chmn. edn. com. NOW, 1966; active supporter gay and women's liberation groups, also mental patients liberation and political prisoners. Mem. Phi Beta Kappa. Office: 295 Bowery New York NY 10003-7104

MILLETT, RALPH LINWOOD, JR., retired newspaper editor; b. Memphis, Oct. 30, 1919; s. Ralph Linwood and Alice (Campbell) M.; m. Mary Virgina Smith, Dec. 10, 1944; children—Mary Jo, Alice Virginia, Jan Vasco, Ralph Linwood III. Student, U. Wyo., 1938-40; B.J., U. Mo., 1942. Copy reader, copy desk chief, news editor Knoxville (Tenn.) News-Sentinel, 1947-66, editor, 1967-84; ret., 1984. Served to lt. USNR, 1942-45. Mem. Am. Soc. Newspaper Editors, Sigma Chi, Sigma Delta Chi, Kappa Tau Alpha. Presbyterian. Club: Cherokee.

MILLEY, JANE ELIZABETH, academic administrator; b. Everett, Mass., May 20, 1940; d. Walter R. and Florence (Leach) M. MusB, Boston U., 1961; MA in Music, Columbia U., 1966; PhD in Higher/Post Sec. Edn.-Adminstrn., Syracuse (N.Y.) U., 1977. Coord., founder, pianist Elmira (N.Y.) Coll. Fine Arts Trio, 1967-75; instr. music Elmira Coll., 1967-70, asst. prof. music, 1970-75, dir. arts and scis. program, 1974-75; rsch. assoc. Syracuse U., 1975-76, adminstrv. asst. to dean Coll. Arts and Scis., 1976-77; div. dean humanities and fine arts Sacramento City Coll., 1977-80; assoc. dean sch. fine arts, prof. music Calif. State U., Long Beach, 1980-81, interim dean, sch. fine arts, prof. music, 1981-82, dean, sch. fine arts, prof. music, 1982-84; arts advisor to chancellor Calif. State Univ. System, 1983-84; chancellor N.C. Sch. Arts U. N.C., Winston-Salem, 1984-89; cons. to pres. Sonoma State U., Rhonert Park, Calif., 1989-90; sr. fellow Am. Assn. State Colls. and Univs., Santa Rosa, Calif., 1989-90; provost, v.p. acad. affairs SUNY, Oswego, 1990-94; provost Simmons Coll., Boston, 1994-95; exec. dir. Cranberry Partnership, Inc., South Weymouth, Mass., 1995—; speaker, cons. in field. Author: (with J. Sturnick and C. Tisinger) Women at the Helm, 1991; contbr. articles to profl. jours. Ex officio bd. dirs. Regional Arts Found., 1982-84, N.C. Scenic Studios, 1984-89, N.C. Dance Theatre, 1984-89, N.C. Shakespeare Festival, 1984-89; bd. dirs. Sacramento Film Festival, 1979-80, Long Beach Grand Opera, 1980; charter mem., founder Sacramento Exptl. Theatre, 1978-84. Commendation for outstanding svc. Los Rios Community Coll. Bd. Trustees, 1980, Sacramento City Coll., 1980. Mem. AAUW (found. adv. com. 1987-89), Am. Assn. State Colls. and Univs. (chmn. arts com. 1986-89), Nat. Assn. State Univs. and Land Grant Colls. (U. N.C. rep. commn. on arts 1986-89), Internat. Coun. Fine Arts Deans, N.C. Women's Forum, N.Y. Edn. Consortium, N.Y. State Sea Grant Inst. (bd. govs. 1991-95), Oswego County Opportunities (bd. dirs. 1991-95), Kappa Delta Pi, Pi Kappa Lambda. Office: 33 Union St Ste 20 South Weymouth MA 02190-2314

MILLGATE, JANE, language professional; b. Leeds, Eng., June 8, 1937; d. Maurice and Marie (Schofield) Barr; m. Michael Millgate, Feb. 27, 1960. B.A. with honors, Leeds U., Eng., 1959, M.A., 1963; Ph.D., U. Kent, Eng., 1970. Instr. U. Toronto, Ont., 1964-65, lectr., 1965-70, asst. prof., 1970-72, assoc. prof., 1972-77, prof. English, 1977—, vice-dean arts and scis., 1983-87; mem. bd. regents Victoria U., Toronto, 1981-86. Author: Macaulay, 1973, Walter Scott, 1984, 2d edit., 1987, Scott's Last Edition: A Study in Publishing History, 1987. Editor: Editing 19th Century Fiction, 1978. Contbr. articles to profl. jours. Doctoral fellow Can. Council, 1968-70; research fellow Can. Council, 1972, 74-75, Social Scis. and Humanities Research Council Can., 1980-81, 85-87, 88-90, 91-94, 95—, Connaught Rsch. fellow, 1995-96. Fellow Royal Soc. Can., Royal Soc. Edinburgh; mem. Victorian Studies Assn. (pres. 1978-80), Assn. Can. Univ. Tchrs. English (pres. 1980-82), Can. Fedn. for Humanities (exec. 1981-83, 95-96), Assn. Scottish Studies, Soc. for History of Authorship, Reading and Pub., Bibliog. Soc. Home: 75 Highland Ave, Toronto, ON Canada M4W 2A4 Office: Victoria Coll, U Toronto, Toronto, ON Canada M5S 1K7

MILLGATE, MICHAEL (HENRY), retired English educator; b. Southampton, Eng., July 19, 1929; arrived in Can., 1964; s. Stanley and Marjorie Louisa (Norris) M.; m. Jane Barr, Feb. 27, 1960. BA, Cambridge U., 1952, MA, 1956; postgrad., U. Mich., Ann Arbor, 1956-57; PhD, U. Leeds, 1960. Tutor Workers' Ednl. Assn., Eng., 1953-56; lectr. English lit. U. Leeds, 1958-64; prof., chmn. dept. English York U., Ont., Can., 1964-67; prof. English U. Toronto, 67-94, univ. prof., 87-94, univ. prof. emeritus, 1994—; Carpenter lectr. Ohio Wesleyan U., 1978; vis. scholar Meiji U., 1985. Author: William Falulkner, 1961, American Social Fiction, 1964, The Achievement of William Faulkner, 1966, Thomas Hardy: His Career as a Novelist, 1971, Thomas Hardy: A Biography, 1982, Testamentary Acts: Browning, Tennyson, James, Hardy, 1992; editor: Tennyson: Selected Poems, 1963, Thomas Hardy: The Life and Work of Thomas Hardy, 1985, William Faulkner Manuscripts, 20 (4 vols.), 21 (2 vols.), 22 (4 vols.), 23 (2 vols.), 1986, New Essays on Light in August, 1987, Thomas Hardy: Selected Letters, 1990, Letters of Emma and Florence Hardy, 1996, Faulkner's Place, 1997; co-editor: Transatlantic Dialogue, 1966, Lion in the Garden, 1968, The Collected Letters of Thomas Hardy, Vol. I, 1978, Vol. II, 1980, Vol. III, 1982, Vol. IV, 1984, Vol. V, 1985, Vol. VI, 1987, Vol. VII, 1988, Thomas Hardy's Studies, Specimens, Etc. Notebook, 1994. Can. Coun. leave fellow, 1968-69, S.W. Brooks fellow U. Queensland, 1971; Killam sr. rsch. scholar, 1974-75; Guggenheim Meml. fellow, 1977-78, Connaught sr. fellow, 1979-80; Social Sci. and Humanities Rsch. Coun. Can. leave fellow, 1981-82, grantee, 1977—; Can. Coun. grantee, 1973-77; Killam rsch. fellow, 1986-88. Fellow Royal Soc. Lit., Royal Soc. Can.; mem. MLA (adv. com. Ctr. for Edit. Am. Authors 1971-74, com. on scholarly edits. 1985-89), Victorian Studies Assn. Ont. (pres. 1970-72), Thomas Hardy Soc. (v.p. 1973—), Bibliog. Soc. Am., Soc. for Study So. Lit. (exec. coun. 1972-76, 81-83), Soc. Textual Scholarship, Tennyson Soc. Home: 75 Highland Ave, Toronto, ON Canada M4W 2A4

MILLHAUSER, GLENN LAWRENCE, biochemist, educator; b. L.A., Mar. 1, 1956. BS in Chemistry with honors, Calif. State U., 1980; MS in Chemistry, Cornell U., 1982, PhD of Phys. Chemistry, 1985. Postdoctoral fellow NIH Cornell U., Ithaca, N.Y., 1985-88; asst. prof. chemistry and biochemistry U. Calif. Santa Cruz, 1988-93, assoc. prof., assoc. dean natural scis., 1993—; lectr. in field. Contbr. articles to profl. jours. Mem. AAAS, Am. Chem. Soc., Biophys. Soc. Home: 1606 King St Santa Cruz CA 95060 Office: Dept Chemistry & Biochem Univ California Santa Cruz CA 95064

MILLHAUSER, STEVEN, writer; b. N.Y.C., Aug. 3, 1943. BA, Columbia Coll., 1965; postgrad., Brown U., 1968-71. Author: The Barnum Museum, 1991, Little Kingdoms, 1993, Martin Dressler: The Tale of an American Dreamer, 1996; contbr. short stories to periodicals. Recipient Pulitzer Prize for fiction, 1997. *

MILLIAN, KENNETH YOUNG, public policy consultant; b. Washington, Sept. 29, 1927; s. John Curry and Myrtle (Young) M.; m. Alva Randolph Clarke, Sept. 10, 1949; children: J. Randolph, Kenneth Y. Jr., Kathleen M. Gilbert, Elizabeth W. Allen. BA, U. Md., 1951; MA in Internat. Rels., George Washington U., 1969; Diploma, Nat. War Coll., Washington, 1969; MS in Bus., Columbia U., 1980. Officer U.S. Fgn. Svc., 1951-76; corp. exec. W.R. Grace & Co., N.Y.C, 1976-93; corp. v.p., dir. govt. rels. W.R. Grace & Co., Washington, 1982-88; corp. v.p., dir. environ. policy W.R. Grace & Co., N.Y.C., Fla., 1988-93; ret., 1993; pres. Millian Assocs., Washington, 1993—; pres. Found. for Pres. Pvt. Sector Survey on Cost Control, 1986-92. Bd. govs. Wesley Sem., Washington, 1988—. Democrat. Methodist. Avocations: sailing, golf. Office: Millian Assocs 3rd Fl 1090 Vermont Ave NW Ste 3 Washington DC 20005-4905

MILLIARD, ALINE, social worker; b. Portage, Maine, Nov. 18, 1937; d. Alderic and Ida (Dionne) M. MSW, Adelphi U., 1976; diploma social work supervision, Hunter Coll., 1986. Bd. cert. diplomate, clin. cert. social worker. Nurses' aide Good Samaritan Hosp., West Islip, N.Y., 1964-65, admitting office clk., 1965-70, social svc. asst.; intake worker Maryhaven Diagnostic & Guidance Ctr., Port Jefferson, N.Y., 1972-74; coord. marriage counseling program Diocesan Human Rels. Svcs., Portland, Maine, 1977, family svc. worker, 1977-79; sch. social worker Sanford (Maine) Pub. Sch. Dept., 1979-81; campus social worker Green Chimneys Childrne Svcs., Brewster, N.Y., 1982-85, dir. group homes, 1985-88; social worker Fletcher Allen Health Care, Burlington, 1989—. Mem. Acad. Cert. Social Workers, NASW. Home: 64 1/2 Howard St Burlington VT 05401-4814 Office: FAHC Colchester Ave Burlington VT 05401

MILLICHAP, JOSEPH GORDON, neurologist, educator; b. Wellington, Eng., Dec. 18, 1918; came to U.S., 1956, naturalized, 1965; s. Joseph P. and Alice (Flello) M.; m. Mary Irene Fortey, Feb. 25, 1946 (dec. Oct. 1969); children: Martin Gordon, Paul Anthony; m. Nancy Melanie Kluczynski, Nov. 7, 1970 (dec. Apr. 1995); children: Gordon Thomas, John Joseph. M.B. with honors in Surgery, St. Bartholomew's Med. Coll., U. London, Eng., 1946, M.D. in Internal Medicine, 1951, diploma child health, 1948. Diplomate: Am. Bd. Pediatrics, Am. Bd. Neurology and Child Neurology, Am. Bd. Electroencephalography. Intern, resident St. Bartholomew's Hosp., 1946-49, Hosp. Sick Children, London, 1951-53, Mass. Gen. Hosp., Boston, 1958-60; pediatric neurologist NIH, 1955-56; USPHS fellow neurology Mass. Gen. Hosp., Boston, 1958-60; cons. pediatric neurology Mayo Clinic, 1960-63; pediatric neurologist Children's Meml. Hosp., Northwestern Med. Center, Chgo., 1963—; prof. neurology and pediatrics Northwestern U. Med. Sch., 1963—; Cons. surgeon gen. USPHS; mem. med. adv. bds. Ill. Epilepsy League, Muscular Dystrophy Found., Cerebral Palsy Found., 1963—; vis. prof. Gt. Ormond St. Hosp., U. London, 1986-87. Author: Febrile Convulsions, 1967, Pediatric Neurology, 1967, Learning Disabilities, 1974, The Hyperactive Child with MBD, 1975, Nutrition, Diet and Behavior, 1985, Dyslexia, 1986, Progress in Pediatric Neurology, 1991, Vol. II, 1994, Vol. III, 1997, Environmental Poisons in Our Food, 1993, A Guide to Drinking Water, Hazards and Health Risks, 1995; editor Jour. Pediatric Neurology Briefs; contbr. articles to profl. jours., chpts. to books. Chmn. research com. med. adv. bd. Epilepsy Found., 1965—. Served with RAF, 1949-51. Named New Citizen of Year in Met. Chgo., 1965; recipient Americanism Medal D.A.R., 1972; USPHS research grantee, 1957. Fellow Royal Coll. Physicians; mem. Am. Neurol. Assn., Am. Pediatric Soc., Am. Soc. Pediatric Research, Am. Acad. Neurology, Am. Soc. Pharmacology and Exptl. Therapeautics, Soc. Exptl. Biology and Medicine, Am. Bd. Psychiatry and Neurology (asst. examiner 1961—), A.M.A. Episcopalian. Home: PO Box 11391 Chicago IL 60611-0391 Office: Northwestern Meml Med Ctr PO Box 11391 Chicago IL 60611-0391

MILLIE, HAROLD RAYMOND, editor; b. Mpls., July 19, 1930; s. Odin Larsen and Aagot (Skaftun) M.; B.A., Claremont Men's Coll., 1955, M.A., 1960; m. Elena Gonzalez, Aug. 8, 1969. Resident teaching fellow Brown U., Providence, 1961-63; research asso. Nat. Planning Assn., Washington, 1964-65; ops. research analyst Nat. Bur. Standards, Washington, 1965-70, GSA, Washington, 1971-73; editor Bur. Mines, Dept. Interior, Washington, 1974-79; internat. petroleum trade specialist U.S. Dept. Energy, 1979—. Served with U.S. Army, 1949-50. Mem. AIME. Episcopalian. Editor: Minerals and Materials/A Monthly Survey, 1976-79. Home: 4725 River Rd Bethesda MD 20816-3034 Office: 1000 Independence Ave SE Washington DC 20585-0001

MILLIGAN, ARTHUR ACHILLE, retired banker; b. Oxnard, Calif., Oct. 29, 1917; s. John Leslie and Julia (Levy) M.; m. Jeanne Welch, Dec. 12, 1942; children: Michael S., Marshall C. BA, Stanford U., 1938. Pres., CEO Bank of A. Levy, Oxnard, Calif., 1955-82, chmn. bd. dirs., 1982-87, chmn. exec. com., 1988-95; dir. Oxnard Frozen Foods Corps., 1958-90; chmn. Real Estate Investment Trust of Calif., Santa Monica, 1968-87. Lt. USN, 1942-45. Mem. Ind. Bankers So. Calif. (pres., 1958), Western Ind. Bankers (pres. 1961), Calif. Bankers Assn. (pres. 1964), Am. Bankers Assn. (pres. 1978), Valley Club (Montecito, bd. dirs. 1969-73, 85-87, 88—, pres. 1990-92), Elks, Rotary (pres. 1949—). Republican.

MILLIGAN, GLENN ELLIS, retired psychologist; b. Emporia, Kans., Nov. 12, 1919; s. Ellis S. and Clara (Kriete) M.; m. Phyllis Eaton, Aug. 26, 1945 (div.); children: Douglas, Gregory, David; m. Janice Barron Dawes, Oct. 10, 1970; 1 step-dau., Virginia. BS, Kans. State Tchrs. Coll., 1941, MS, 1942; postgrad., U. Chgo., 1943-44; Ed.D., Colo. State Coll., 1951. Head dept. edn. Findlay (Ohio) Coll., 1946-55; psychologist Columbus (Ohio) Pub. Schs., 1955-56; asso. prof. edn. Ohio Wesleyan U., Delaware, 1956-60; exec. dir. Am. Assn. Mental Deficiency, Columbus, 1960-65; cons. mental retardation Vocat. Rehab. Adminstrn., HEW, 1965-67; psychologist spl. edn. Montgomery County Pub. Schs., Rockville, Md., 1967-96; ret., 1996; Lectr. Catholic U. Am. Editor: (1st) Mental Retardation, 1963-64, (with others) Directory of Residential Facilities for the Mentally Retarded, 1965. Fellow Am. Assn. Mental Deficiency; mem. Am. Psychol. Assn., NEA (life). Home: 5208 Elsmere Ave Bethesda MD 20814-5731

MILLIGAN, JOHN DRANE, historian, educator; b. N.Y.C., Oct. 11, 1924; s. Carl Glover and Hazel Gray (Drane) M.; m. Joyce Mary Jervis, Nov. 16, 1946; children: Jacqueline M., Paula J., Mary M., Elizabeth Y. BA, U. Mich., 1952, MA, 1953, PhD, 1961. Tchg. asst. U. Mich., 1951-52, tchg. fellow, 1954-56; from asst. prof. to prof. history SUNY, Buffalo, 1962—, dir. grad. programs in history, 1963-68, 94-95, dir. undergrad. programs in history, 1979-86, acting dept. chmn., summers, 1977, 78-80, 88; vis. prof. McMaster U., Hamilton, Ont., Can., summer 1964, 69-70. Author: Gunboats Down the Mississippi, 1965, From the Fresh-Water Navy, 1861-1864, 1970; also chpts. in books, articles in jours., encys. Mem. Ann Arbor chpt. NAACP, exec. bd., 1956-61; mem. ACLU, exec. bd., 1959-61; mem. campaign coms. for various candidates for local and nat. office, 1960-76; mem. Buffalo NAACP, Buffalo Housing Opportunities Made Equal, Citizens Council on Human Relations, Physicians for Social Responsibility, Common Cause, Amnesty Internat.; faculty chmn. United Fund dr., 1977; active Foster Parents Plan, 1955—; adoptive parent Internat. Social Services; founder charitable trust for minority coll. scholarships. Served with USAAF, 1943-46, USAFR, 1946-56. James B. Angell scholar U. Mich.; grantee Research Found. SUNY; grantee U.S. Naval Inst.; Citation of Civil War Round Table; Moncado Award of Am. Mil. Inst. Mem. Am. Hist. Assn., Assn. Am. Historians, So. Hist. Assn., Buffalo and Erie County Hist. Soc., Afro-Am. Hist. Soc., Soc. Civil War Historians, Buffalo Coun. for Responsibility in Fgn. Policy (founding), Soaring Soc. Am., Aircraft Owners and Pilots Assn., Niagara Soaring Club, Cambria Flying Soc., Silver Wings Assn., Civil War Round Table, SUNY Buffalo Pres.'s Assocs., SUNY Buffalo Founders' Soc., Tau Sigma Delta, Phi Kappa Phi, Phi Alpha Theta. Home: 21 Allenhurst Rd Buffalo NY 14214-1201 Office: SUNY History Dept Buffalo NY 14260 *If an individual cannot influence for the better the course of humankind, one can sometimes influence for the better the life of another individual.*

MILLIGAN, LAWRENCE DRAKE, JR., consumer products executive; b. Lake Forest, Ill., Apr. 6, 1936; s. Lawrence Drake Sr. and Mary Catherine (Cliggit) M.; m. Lucy Shepard, Oct. 20, 1962; children: Michael D., Carolyn S. BA, Williams Coll., 1960. Nat. sales mgr. Bar Soap and Household Cleaning Products div. Procter & Gamble, Cin., 1974-78; gen. mgr. spl. products Procter & Gamble, Cin., 1979-80, gen. mgr. food service and lodging products, 1980-84, v.p. food service and lodging products, 1984, v.p. food products, 1984-87, v.p. sales in Europe, 1987-89, v.p. sales, customer devel. internat., 1989—; sr. v.p. worldwide sales Procter & Gamble, 1990—. Served as sgt. USMC, 1955-58. Republican. Home: 7475 Old Hickory Ln Cincinnati OH 45243-1454 Office: Procter & Gamble Co 1 Procter And Gamble Plz Cincinnati OH 45202-3315

MILLIGAN, MANCIL WOOD, mechanical and aerospace engineering educator; b. Shiloh, Tenn., Nov. 21, 1934; s. Mancil Abernathy and Ivy (Wood) M.; m. Arlys Joyce Cushman, Sept. 15, 1956; children: Mancil Wood, Matthew Wayne. B.S., U. Tenn., 1956, M.S., 1958, Ph.D., 1963; postgrad., U. Wash., 1958, Stanford U., 1964. Research engr. Boeing Co., Seattle, 1956-57, 58-59; instr. mech. engring. U. Tenn., Knoxville, 1957-58; prof. mech. and aerospace engring. U. Tenn., 1959—, head mech. and aerospace engring., 1973-82; cons. to more than 100 industries, 1959—. Mem. ASME, AIAA, Am. Soc. Engring. Edn., Tech. Soc. Knoxville, Pi Tau Sigma, Tau Beta Pi, Sigma Gamma Tau. Home: 10214 Emory Rd Luttrell TN 37779-2942

MILLIGAN, SISTER MARY, theology educator, religious consultant; b. Los Angeles, Jan. 23, 1935; d. Bernard Joseph and Carolyn (Krebs) M. BA, Marymount Coll., 1956; Dr. de l'Univ., U. Paris, 1959; MA in Theology, St. Mary's Coll., Notre Dame, Ind., 1966; STD, Gregorian U., 1975; D. honoris causa, Marymount U., 1988. Tchr. Cours Marymount, Neuilly, France, 1956-59; asst. prof. Marymount Coll., Los Angeles, 1959-67; gen. councillor Religious of Sacred Heart of Mary, Rome, 1969-75, gen. superior, 1980-85; asst. prof. Loyola Marymount U., Los Angeles, 1977-78, provost, 1986-90, prof., 1990—, dean liberal arts, 1992—; pres. bd. dirs. St. John's Sem., Camarillo, Calif., 1986-89; mem. exec. com. Internat. Union Superiors Gen., Rome, 1983-85; mem. planning bd. spiritual renewal program Loyola Marymount U., Los Angeles, 1976-78. Author: That They May Have Life, 1975; compiler analytical index Ways of Peace, 1986; contbr. articles to profl. jours. Vis. scholar Grad. Theol. Union, Berkeley, 1986. Mem. Calif. Women in Higher Edn., Coll. Theology Soc., Cath. Biblical Assn. Democrat. Roman Catholic. Office: Loyola Marymount U 7900 Loyola Blvd Los Angeles CA 90045-2659

MILLIGAN, MICHAEL EDWARD, insurance services company executive; b. Fullerton, Calif., Aug. 28, 1952; s. Edward Scott Milligan and Patricia Ann (Shirk) Madson; m. Diane Marie Mascaro, June 21, 1974; children: Robert Michael, Lauren Alicia, Stefanie Diane. BS, U.S. Mil. Acad., 1974; MS, U. So. Calif., 1979. Commd. 2d lt. U.S. Army, 1974, advanced through grades to capt., 1979; comdr. U.S. Army, Europe, 1974-79; resigned, 1979; various positions to group leader product devel. Procter & Gamble, Cin., 1979-85; mgr. product devel. and tech. svcs., then div. mgr. engring. Pepsi Cola USA, Purchase, N.Y., 1985-87; div. mgr. stratetic planning ops. Pepsi Cola Co., Somers, N.Y., 1987-88; dir. mktg., sales and devel. Gen. Analysis Corp., Norwalk, Conn., 1988-89; dir. market planning and devel. Ins. Svcs. Office subs. ISOTEL, N. Y.C., 1989-91; asst. v.p. mktg. and product devel. Ins. Svcs. Office, Inc., N. Y.C., 1991—. Republican. Roman Catholic. Avocation: golf. Home: 14 Patti Pl Hopewell Junction NY 12533-6814 Office: Ins Svcs Office Inc 7 World Trade Ctr New York NY 10048-1102

MILLIKAN, CHARLES REAGAN, pastor; b. Houston, Feb. 8, 1946; s. Herman Charles and Eva Geraldine (Isbell) M.; m. Laura Nan Jackson, Aug. 7, 1970; children: Kevin, Kristin, Katy. BA, Southwestern U., 1968; ThM, So. Meth. U., 1971; D of Ministry, Drew U., 1984. Youth min. Marvin United Meth. Ch., Tyler, Tex., 1968-70; pastor Winona (Tex.) United Meth. Ch., 1970-72, Friendship United Meth., Porter, Tex., 1972-76, Wesley United Meth. Ch., Tyler, 1976-81; sr. pastor St. Peters United Meth. Ch., Katy, Tex., 1981-85, Seabrook (Tex.) United Meth. Ch., 1985-88, Pollard Meml. United Meth. Ch., Tyler, 1988-93, Moody Meml. 1st United Meth. Ch., Galveston Island, Tex., 1993—; bd. trustees Tex. Wesleyan U., Ft. Worth, 1992—, Southwestern U., Georgetown, Tex., 1995—, Permanent Endowment Fund-Moody Meml. 1st United Meth. Ch., Galveston Island, 1993—; bd. dirs. Meth. Retirement Cmtys., The Woodlands, Tex. Recipient David Knox Porter award Southwestern U., 1968, Bishops award Tex. Ann. Conf., 1995. Mem. Rotary, Galveston Country Club, Toastmasters (Outstanding Club Pres. dist. 25 1977, Disting. Toastmaster 1981). Avocation: golf. Office: Moody Meml 1st United Meth Ch 2803 53rd St Galveston TX 77551-5914

MILLIKAN, CLARK HAROLD, physician; b. Freeport, Ill., Mar. 2, 1915; s. William Clarance and Louise (Chamberlain) M.; m. Gayle Margaret Gross, May 2, 1942 (div. Apr. 1966); children: Terri, Clark William, Jeffry Brent; m. Janet T. Holmes, July 21, 1966 (div. Dec. 1987); m. Nancy Futrell, Dec. 28, 1987. Student, Parsons (Kans.) Jr. Coll., 1935; MD, U. Kans., 1939. Diplomate Am. Bd. Psychiatry and Neurology. Intern St. Luke's Hosp., Clev., 1939-40, asst. resident medicine, 1940-41; from resident neurology to asst. prof. neurology State U. Iowa, Iowa City, 1941-49; staff Mayo Clinic, Rochester, Minn., 1949—, cons. neurology, 1958—; dir. Mayo Center for Clin. Research in Cerebrovascular Disease; prof. neurology Mayo Sch. Medicine; physician-in-chief pro tem Cleve. Clinic, 1970; prof. neurology U. Utah Sch. Medicine, Salt Lake City, 1976-87, U. Miami (Fla.) Sch. Medicine, 1987-88; scholar in residence, dept. neurology Henry Ford Hosp., Detroit, 1988-92; prof. neurology Sch. of Medicine Creighton U., Omaha, 1992-94; clin. prof. neurology Med. Coll. Ohio, Toledo, 1994—; Asst. chmn., editor trans. 2d Princeton Conf. Cerebrovascular Disease, 1957, chmn. confs., 1961, 64; chmn. com. classification and nomenclature cerebrovascular disease USPHS, 1955-69; mem. council Nat. Inst. Neurologic Diseases and Blindness, NIH, USPHS, 1961-65, div. regional med. program, 1965-68; A.O.A. lectr. Baylor U., Waco, Tex., 1952; James Mawer Pearson Meml. lectr., Vancouver, B.C., Can., 1958; Conner Meml. lectr. Am. Heart Assn., 1961; Peter T. Bohan lectr. U. Kans., 1965, 73. Editor: Jour. Stroke, 1970-76, assoc. editor, 1976—. Recipient Outstanding Alumnus award U. Kans., 1973. Fellow ACP, Am. Acad. Neurology (founding chmn. sect. on stroke and vascular neurology 1994), Royal Soc. Medicine; mem. AMA, AAUP, AAAS, Assn. Rsch. Nervous and Mental Disease (pres. 1961), Am. Neurol. Assn. (1st v.p. 1969-70, pres. 1973-74), Minn. Med. Assn., Four County Med. Soc. South Minn., Cen. Neuropsychiat. Assn., N.Y. Acad. Sci., Am. Heart Assn. (chmn. coun. cerebrovascular disease 1967-68, Gold Heart award 1976, Spl. Merit award 1981), Nat. Stroke Assn. (pres. 1986, editor Jour. Stroke and Cerebrovascular Disease 1990—), Sigma Xi.

MILLIKAN, JAMES ROLENS, cleaning service executive, musician, composer; b. Beaumont, Tex., Jan. 15, 1950; s. George Lee and Gertrude Louise (Mann) M.; m. Dorothy Jane Albright, Apr. 22, 1989. BFA, U. Houston, 1968; MFA, Juilliard Sch., 1971. Mgr., ptnr. Edward, Bankers & Co., Houston, 1971-73; prop. gen. Max M. Kaplan Properties, San Antonio, 1973-75; gen. bldg. mgr. Property Mgmt. Systems, Atlanta, 1975-79; dir. real estate Sun Life Group Am., Atlanta, 1979-81; prin. The Millikan Cos., Atlanta, 1981-85, J.R. & Co., Atlanta, 1985-87; sr. v.p., gen. mgr. east coast Nat. Cleaning Contractors, Inc., Atlanta, 1987-93; prin., pres. Master Bldg. Cleaners Inc., Atlanta, 1993—; cons., Sun Life Group Am., 1982-84, McFaddin Ventures, Houston, 1983-84. Composer: Crystal Blue Persuasion (gold record 1969), Crimson & Clover (gold record 1969), Mony Mony (gold record 1969), I Love You More Today than Yesterday (gold record 1970), 1900 Yesterday (gold record 1971), others; instrumentalist for orchs. of Duke Ellington, Count Basie, Buddy Rich, Woody Herman and Glenn Miller, 1965-68; drummer, arranger, conductor for recording artist Petula Clark, 1968-71, leader J.R. and Co., Jazz Ensemble. Founder, pres., St. Luke's Econ. Devel. Corp., Atlanta, 1979, bd. dirs.; bd. dirs. St. Jude's House, Atlanta, 1984, Am. Suicide Found., chmn. Southeastern Divsn. Nat. Bd. Mem. Am. Suicide Found.; mem. Home Bldg. with Habitat for Humanity. With U.S. Army, 1970-76. Mem. Bldg. Owners and Mgrs. Atlanta, Am. Mktg. Assn., Am. Suicide Found. (bd. dirs.), Bldg. Svc. Contractors Assn. Internat. Democrat. Episcopalian. Avocations: music, golfing, skiing, white water rafting. Home and Office: Master Bldg Cleaners Inc 4600 Runnemede Rd NW Atlanta GA 30327-3461

MILLIKAN, LARRY EDWARD, dermatologist; b. Sterling, Ill., May 12, 1936; s. Daniel Franklin and Harriet Adeline (Parmenter) M.; m. Jeanine Dorothy Johnson, Aug. 27, 1960; children: Marshall, Rebecca. B.A., Monmouth Coll., 1958; M.D., U. Mo., 1962. Intern Great Lakes Naval Hosp., Ill., 1962-63; housestaff in tng. U. Mich., Ann Arbor, 1967-69, chief resident, 1969-70; asst. prof. dermatology U. Mo., Columbia, 1970-74, assoc. prof., 1974-81; chmn. dept. dermatology Tulane U., New Orleans, 1981—; cons. physician Charity Hosp., New Orleans, Tulane U. Hosp., New Orleans, Huey B. Long Hosp., Pineville; mem. bd. trustees Sulzberger Inst. for Dermatological Edn.; chmn. cont. med. edn. com. La. State Med. Soc., 1994-95. Assoc. editor Internat. Jour. Dermatology, 1980—; mem. editorial bd. Current Concepts in Skin Disorders, Am. Jour. Med. Scis., Postgrad. Medicine; contbr. articles to med. jours. Bd. dirs. Women's Dermatol. Assn.

With USN, 1960-67. Recipient Andres Bello awrd Govt. of Venezuela, 1989, citation of merit Sch. Medicine, U. Mo., 1993; named Disting. Alumnus, Monmouth Coll., 1990; Nat. Cancer Inst. grantee, 1976-84. Fellow ACP; mem. AAAS, AMA, Am. Acad. Dermatology (bd. dirs. 1986-90), Am. Dermatol. Assn., Am. Dermatol. Soc. for Allergy and Immunology (pres., bd. dirs.), Soc. for Investigative Dermatology (past pres. South sect.), So. Med. Assn. (vice chmn. dermatology sect. 1984, chmn. 1994), Coll. Physicians Phila., Assn. Profs. Dermatology (bd. dirs. 1984-86), Orleans Parish Med. Soc., La. Med. Soc., Pam Am. Med. Assn., Internat. Soc. Dermatology (asst. sec. gen. 1989—), Mo. Allergy Assn. (past pres.), Am. Coll. Cryosurgery, Assn. Acad. Dermatol. Surgeons, Internat. Soc. Dermatol. Surgery, Dermatol. Found. Leaders Soc. (state chmn. 1993-96). Office: Tulane Univ Sch Medicine Dept of Dermatology 1430 Tulane Ave # 73 New Orleans LA 70112-2699

MILLIKEN, JOHN GORDON, research economist; b. Denver, May 12, 1927; s. William Boyd and Margaret Irene (Marsh) M.; m. Marie Violet Machell, June 13, 1953; children: Karen Marie, Douglas Gordon, David Tait, Anne Alain. BS, Yale U., 1949, BEng, 1950; MS, U. Colo., 1966, PhD, 1969. Registered profl. engr., Colo. Engr. U.S. Bur. Reclamation, Denver, 1950-55; asst. to plant mgr. Stanley Aviation Corp., Denver, 1955-56; prin. mgmt. engr., dept. mgr. Martin-Marietta Aerospace Divsn., Denver, 1956-64; mgmt. engr. Safeway Stores, Inc., Denver, 1964-66; sr. rsch. economist, prof., assoc. div. head U. Denver Rsch. Inst., 1966-86; pres. Univ. Senate, 1980-81; prin. Milliken Chapman Rsch. Group, Inc., Littleton, Colo., 1986-88, Milliken Rsch. Group, Inc., Littleton, 1988—; vis. fellow sci. policy rsch. unit U. Sussex, Eng., 1975-76; bd. dirs. Sci. Mgmt. Corp.; cons. mgmt. engr. Author: Aerospace Management Techniques, 1971, Federal Incentives for Innovation, 1974, Recycling Municipal Wastewater, 1977, Water and Energy in Colorado's Future, 1981, Metropolitan Water Management, 1981, Technological Innovation and Economic Vitality, 1983, Water Management in the Denver, Colorado Urban Area, 1988, Benefits and Costs of Oxygenated Fuels in Colorado, 1990, Water Transfer Alternatives Study, 1994, Colorado Springs Water Resources Plan Alternative Assessment Study, 1995; contbr. articles to profl. jours. Bd. dirs. S.E. Englewood Water Dist., 1963—, South Englewood San. Dist., 1965—; bd. dirs. South Suburban Pk. and Recreation Dist., 1971-96, chmn., 1990-92; chmn. Dem. Com. of Arapahoe County, 1969-71, 5th Congl. Dist. Colo., 1972-73, 74-75; mem. exec. com. Colo. Faculty Adv. Coun., 1981-85; mem. Garrison Diversion Unit Commn., 1984; trustee Colo. Local Govt. Liquid Asset Trust, 1986—, chmn., 1991-93; bd. dirs. Colo. Spl. Dist. Assn. Property and Liability Pool, 1989—, pres. 1997—. With M.C., U.S. Army, 1945-46. Recipient Adlai E. Stevenson Meml. award, 1981, hon. title "Amicus Universitatis," U. Denver, 1994, Disting. Svc. award Spl. Dist. Assn. Colo., 1995; Milliken Park named in his honor for svcs. to Littleton cmty., 1996. Mem. Acad. Mgmt., Nat. Assn. Bus. Economists, Yale Sci. and Engring. Assn., Am. Water Works Assn., Sigma Xi, Tau Beta Pi, Beta Gamma Sigma, Sigma Iota Epsilon. Congregationalist. Home and Office: 6502 S Ogden St Littleton CO 80121-2561

MILLIKEN, ROGER, textile company executive; b. N.Y.C., Oct. 24, 1915; s. Gerrish and Agnes (Gayley) M.; m. Justine V. R. Hooper, June 5, 1948; children: Justine, Nancy, Roger, David, Weston. Student, Groton Sch., 1929-33; A.B., Yale U., 1937; LL.D. (hon.), Wofford Coll., Rose-Hulman Inst. Tech., Phila. Coll. Textiles and Sci., Brenau Coll., The Citadel; D. Textile Industry (hon.), Clemson U.; D.H.L. (hon.), Converse Coll. CEO Milliken & Co., N.Y.C., 1947-83, chmn., chief exec. officer, 1983—; chmn. bd. Inst. Textile Tech., 1948-97, chmn. emeritus, 1997—; bd. dirs. Am. Textile Mfrs. Inst., S.C. Textile Mfrs. Assn. Chmn. Greenville-Spartanburg Airport Commn.; trustee Wofford Coll., S.C. Found. Ind. Coll. Mem. Bus. Council, Textile Inst. (Eng.) (companion mem.). Clubs: Union League, Links, Augusta Nat. Golf, Yeamans Hall. Office: Milliken & Co PO Box 3167 Spartanburg SC 29304

MILLIMET, ERWIN, lawyer; b. N.Y.C., Oct. 7, 1925; s. Maurice and Henrietta (Cohen) M.; m. Mary Malia; children: Robert, James, Rachel, Sarah. BA magna cum laude, Amherst Coll., 1948; LLB cum laude, Harvard U., 1951. Bar: N.Y. 1952. Formerly sr. ptnr., chmn. exec. com. Stroock & Stroock & Lavan, N.Y.C., ret. 1991. Mem. bd. visitors U. San Diego Law Sch.; mem. faculty Grad. Sch. Mgmt., U. Mass.; active Nat. Support Group for Africa; founder Citizens for Am., Washington, 1984; mem. Rep. Presdl. Task Force; mem. Rep. Club, N.Y.C. and Washington. Served with inf. U.S. Army, 1943-46. Mem. N.Y. State Bar Assn., Assn. of Bar of City of N.Y., Fed. Bar Assn., Phi Beta Kappa.

MILLIMET, JOSEPH ALLEN, retired lawyer; b. West Orange, N.J., July 23, 1914; s. Morris and Dorothy (McBlain) M.; m. Elizabeth Gray Gingras, Jan. 10, 1942 (dec. 1995); children: Madlyn Ann (Mrs. Angus Deming), Lisa Gray (Mrs. Silas Little, III), Rebecca Allen (Mrs. Stacey Petersen), Peter Joseph (dec.). A.B., Dartmouth Coll., 1936; LL.B., Yale U., 1939; LLD (hon.), U. N.H., 1992. Bar: N.H. 1939. Pvt. practice Concord and Manchester, N.H.; sr. ptnr. Devine, Millimet, Stahl & Branch, and predecessors (now Devine Millimet & Branch), Manchester, 1947-93, ret.; with FCC, 1941-42. Mem. N.H. Bd. Bar Examiners, 1953-61, legislative counsel to, gov. N.H., 1963-66; chmn. Commn. to Revise N.H. Constn., 1964, 74, 84; mem. Commn. Uniform State Laws, 1965-73. Served with USCG, 1942-45. Fellow Am. Coll. Trial Lawyers; mem. N.H. Bar Assn. (pres. 1962-63), ABA. Democrat. Home: 1655 N River Rd Manchester NH 03104-1645 Office: Devine Millimet & Branch 111 Amherst St Manchester NH 03101-1809

MILLING, BERT WILLIAM, JR., federal judge; b. Mobile, Ala., Mar. 5, 1946; s. Bert William and Marjorie Ann (Smith) M.; m. Priscilla Pitman, Apr. 15, 1966; children: Brooks Pitman, Jeremy Bacon, Maran Celeste. AB in Philosophy, Coll. William and Mary, 1968; JD, U. Ala., 1971. Bar: Ala. 1971. Legal officer 212th Arty. Group, Fort Lewis, Wash., 1971-72; legal asst. officer Judge Advocate Gen.'s Office, Ft. Sill, Okla., 1972-74; spl. asst. atty. gen. Dist. Atty.'s Office, Mobile, 1974-75, asst. dist. atty., 1977-78; assoc. Sintz, Pike, Campbell & Duke, Mobile, 1975-77; ct. referee Juvenile Div. of Cir. Ct., Mobile, 1978-81; counsel U.S. Senate Com. on Jud., Subcom. on Security & Terrorism, Washington, 1981-83; asst. U.S. atty. Justice Dept., Mobile, 1983-86; U.S. magistrate judge U. S. Dist. Ct. So. Dist. Ala., Mobile, 1986—. Capt. U.S. Army, 1971-74. Mem. Ala. Bar Assn., Mobile Bar Assn. Episcopalian. Avocations: jogging, reading. Office: US Courthouse 113 Saint Joseph St Mobile AL 36602-3606

MILLING, MARCUS EUGENE, SR., geologist; b. Galveston, Tex., Oct. 8, 1938; s. Robert Richardson and Leonora Mildred (Currey) M.; m. Sandra Ann Dunlay, Sept. 21, 1959; 1 child, Marcus Eugene Jr. BS in Geology, Lamar U., 1961; MS in Geology, U. Iowa, 1964, PhD in Geology, 1968. Cert. petroleum geologist. Rsch. geologist Exxon Prodn. Rsch. Co., Houston, 1968-76; prodn. geologist Exxon Co. U.S.A., Kingsville, Tex., 1976-78; dist. explt. geologist Exxon Co. U.S.A., New Orleans, 1978-80; mgr. geol. rsch. Arco Oil and Gas Co., Plano, Tex., 1980-86; chief geologist Arco Oil and Gas Co., Dallas, 1986-87; assoc. dir. Bur. Econ. Geology U. Tex., Austin, 1987-92; exec. dir. Am. Geol. Inst., Alexandria, Va., 1992—; vice-chmn. Offshore Tech. Conf., Dallas, 1984-87; dir. Geosci. Inst. for Oil and Gas Recovery Rsch., Austin, 1988-91. NSF fellow, 1966. Fellow Geol. Soc. Am. (councilor 1986-89); mem. Am. Assn. Petroleum Geologists, Soc. Petroleum Engrs., Am. Inst. Profl. Geologists, Blue Key, Sigma Xi. Home: 11457 Hollow Timber Ct Reston VA 20194-1980 Office: Am Geol Inst 4220 King St Alexandria VA 22302-1507

MILLION, KENNETH RHEA, management consultant; b. Trenton, Ohio, July 3, 1939; s. Clara (Poff) Gardner; divorced; 1 child, Kimberley Rhea Stang. BSBA, U. Cin., 1963. With human resources mgmt. dept. Bendix Corp., Hamilton, Ohio, 1962-65, Cin., 1965-69; dir. pers. Lunkenheimer Co., Cin., 1969-73; v.p. human resources Clopay Corp., Cin., 1973-75; pres. Mgmt. Performance Inc., Cin., 1975-78; pres., owner Million & Assocs., Inc., Cin., 1978—. Internat. amb. People to People and Am. Soc. Pers. Adminstrn., 59 countries. Mem. Kiwanis (v.p. Cin. 1985-86). Republican. Home: 135 Garfield Pl # 619 Cincinnati OH 45202 Office: 1831 Carew Tower Cincinnati OH 45202

MILLIS, ROBERT LOWELL, astronomer; b. Martinsville, Ill., Sept. 12, 1941; married, 1965; 2 children. BA, Ea. Ill. U., 1963; PhD in Astronomy, U. Wis., 1968. Astronomer Lowell Obs., Flagstaff, Ariz., 1967-86, assoc. dir., 1986-90, dir., 1990—. Mem. Am. Astron. Soc., Internat. Astronomy Union, Divsn. Planetary Sci. (sec.-treas. 1985-88, chmn. 1994-95). Achievements include research in planetary satellites and ring systems; occultation studies of solar system objects; research on comets. Office: Lowell Observatory 1400 W Mars Hill Rd Flagstaff AZ 86001-4470

MILLMAN, BRUCE RUSSELL, lawyer; b. Bronx, N.Y., June 4, 1948; s. Meyer and Garie (Solomon) M.; m. Lorrie Jan Liss, Aug. 12, 1973; children—Noemi, Avi. A.B., Princeton U., 1970; J.D., Columbia U., 1973. Bar: N.Y. 1974, U.S. Dist. Ct. (ea. and so. dists.) N.Y. 1975, U.S. Ct. Appeals (2d cir.) 1978, U.S. Supreme Ct. 1978. Assoc. Rains & Pogrebin and predecessors Rains, Pogrebin & Scher, Mineola, N.Y., 1973-79, ptnr., 1980—; arbitrator Nassau County Dist. Ct., Mineola, 1981-83. Contbr. New York Employment Law, 1995, Labor and Employment Law for the Corporate Counselor and General Practitioner, 1994, Updating Issues in Employment Law, 1986, Public Sector Labor and Employment Law, 1988. Bd. dirs. West Side Montessori Sch., N.Y.C., 1984-90, sec. 1985-87, pres. 1987-90. Harlan Fiske Stone scholar Columbia U. Law Sch., N.Y.C., 1971, 73. Mem. ABA, N.Y. State Bar Assn. (chair-elect labor & employment law sect.), Nassau County Bar Assn., Indsl. Rels. Rsch. Assn. (bd. dirs. L.I. chpt. 1984—, pres. 95-96). Home: 60 Riverside Dr New York NY 10024-6108 Office: Rains & Pogrebin PC 210 Old Country Rd Mineola NY 11501-4218 also: 375 Park Ave New York NY 10152

MILLMAN, JODE SUSAN, lawyer; b. Poughkeepsie, N.Y., Dec. 28, 1954; d. Samuel Keith and Ellin Sadenberg (Bainder) M.; m. Michael James Harris, June 20, 1982; children: Maxwell, Benjamin. BA, Syracuse U., 1976, JD, 1979. Bar: N.Y. 1980, U.S. Dist. Ct. (so. and ea. dists.) N.Y. 1982, U.S. Supreme Ct. 1983. Asst. corp. counsel City of Poughkeepsie, 1979-81; assoc. Law Office of Lou Lewis, Poughkeepsie, 1981-85; pvt. practice Poughkeepsie, 1985—; staff counsel City of Poughkeepsie Office of Property Devel., 1990—; gen. mgr. WCZX-Communicatons Corp. Contbg. author: Kaminstein Legislative History of the Copyright Law, 1979. Pres. Dutchess County (N.Y.) Vis. Bur., 1980-82; bd. dirs. Poughkeepsie Ballet Theater, 1982, Jewish Comty. Ctr., 1988; mem. assigned counsel program Dutchess County Family Ct., 1985—; trustee Greater Poughkeepsie Libr. Dist., 1991-94, Poughkeepsie Day Sch., 1995—. Mem. ABA, N.Y. State Bar Assn., Dutchess County Bar Assn. (chmn. pub. rels. 1991—), Mid-Hudson Women's Bar Assn., Poughkeepsie Area C. of C. (econ. devel. com. 1994—). Democrat. Jewish. Office: 97 Cannon St Poughkeepsie NY 12601-3303

MILLMAN, RICHARD GEORGE, architect, educator; b. St. Johns, Mich., Feb. 12, 1925; s. Harold Fildew and Elizabeth Hill (Van Deusen) M.; m. Mary Louise Manley, June 17, 1950; children: John Richard, Ruth Barbara. BArch, U. Mich., 1951, MArch, 1962. Registered architect, Mich., Ohio, Ala. Job capt. Smith Hinchman & Grylls, Detroit, 1951-52; designer assoc. Eliot Robinson, AIA, Birmingham, Mich., 1952-55; designer Eero Saarinen Assocs., Bloomfield Hills, Mich., 1955-56; assoc. Chas. W. Lane Assocs. Inc., Ann Arbor, Mich., 1956-59; prin. Kainlauri, MacMullan, Millman, Ann Arbor, 1959-62; assoc. prof. Ohio U., Athens, 1962-68; prof. Auburn (Ala.) U., 1968—, head architecture dept., 1968-73, 84-85, head indsl. design dept., 1988-89; prof. Mid. East Tech. U., Ankara, Turkey, 1966-67,King Faisal U., Dammam, Saudi Arabia, 1979-81. One man shows include Dhahran Art Group, Saudi Arabia, 1981, Peet Gallery, Auburn U., 1983, 91; author: Washtenaw Community Coll., 1962, Auburn U. Tour Guide, 1990. With U.S. Army, 1943-46, ETO, PTO. Recipient Cert. of Honor Ala. Hist. Commn., 1977; Alumni scholar U. Mich., 1961; Fulbright lectr. Exch. Com., Mid. East Tech. U., 1966. Mem. AIA (treas. Ala. coun. 1969, v.p. 1970, pres. 1972, emeritus 1990, Auburn chpt. pres. 1970, emeritus), Nat. Coun. Archtl. Registration Bd. (cert.), Auburn Arts Assn. Avocations: painting, photography. Home: 736 Brenda Ave Auburn AL 36830-6038 Office: Auburn U Architecture Dept 104 Dudley Hall Auburn AL 36849-5121

MILLNER, ROBERT B., lawyer; b. N.Y.C., Apr. 20, 1950; s. Nathan and Babette E. (Leventhal) M.; m. Susan Brent, June 5, 1983; children: Jacob, Daniel, Rebecca. BA, Wesleyan U., 1971; JD, U. Chgo., 1975. Bar: Ill. 1975. Law clk. to Hon. George C. Edwards U.S. Ct. Appeals for 6th Cir., Cin., 1975-76; with Sonnenschein Nath & Rosenthal, Chgo., 1976—, ptnr., 1982—; mem. Panel of Bankruptcy Trustees, Chgo., 1992—. Editorial bd. Jour. Corp. Disclosure and Confidentiality, 1989-92; contbr. articles to profl. jours. Trustee Anshe Emet Synagogue, Chgo., 1990-93; mem. gov. coun. Am. Jewish Cong. midwest region, 1989—. Fellow Am. Bar Found.; mem. ABA (co-chair bankruptcy and insolvency com. litigation sect. 1992-95), Am. Bankruptcy Inst., Shakespearean Assn. Am. (v.p. Stratford chpt. 1992—), Chgo. Bar Assn., Comml. Bar Assn. (hon. overseas mem.), Legal Club, Std. Club, Wesleyan Alumni Club Chgo. (pres. 1988-90), Phi Beta Kappa. Office: Sonnenschein Nath & Rosenthal 8000 Sears Tower Chicago IL 60606-6328

MILLNER, WALLACE B., III, banker; b. Charlotte, N.C., Aug. 1, 1939; s. Wallace B. and Virginia (Reed) M.; m. Nancy Jean Bost, Aug. 25, 1961; children—Wallace Michael, Christopher Bost. AB, Davidson Coll., N.C., 1961; MBA, U. N.C., Chapel Hill, 1962. Asst. v.p., dir. investment rsch. Bank of Va. Co., Richmond, 1971-72, treas., 1973-74, v.p., treas., 1974-76, sr. v.p., treas., 1976-80, chief fin. officer, 1980-85; exec. v.p., chief fin. officer Signet Banking Corp., 1985-88, sr. exec. v.p., CFO, 1988—, vice chmn., CFO, 1996—. Chmn. bd. dirs. Family and Children's Svcs., 1984-86; pres. Richmond (Va.) Symphony, 1994-96. 1st lt. U.S. Army, 1962-64. Decorated Army Commendation medal. Mem. Richmond Soc. Fin. Analysts (pres. 1984-85), Inst. Chartered Fin. Analysts, Fin. Analysts Fedn. (bd. dirs. 1986-91, chmn. 1990), Bankers Roundtable, Assn. Investment Mgmt. and Rsch. (bd. govs. 1990-91), Country Club of Va., Commonwealth Club. Republican. Episcopalian. Avocations: tennis, art. Home: 314 Summit Ln Richmond VA 23221-3711 Office: Signet Banking Corp PO Box 25970 Richmond VA 23260-5970

MILLON, HENRY ARMAND, fine arts educator, architectural historian; b. Altoona, Pa., Feb. 22, 1927; s. Henri Francois and Louise (de Serent) M.; m. Emily Dees, June, 1953; m. Judith Rice, Dec. 27, 1966; children: Henri, Hadrian, Phoebe, Aaron. BA, Tulane U., 1947, BS, 1949, BArch, 1953; AM, Harvard U., 1954, MArch, 1955, PhD, 1964; LHD (hon.), Tulane U., 1995. Asst. prof. MIT, Cambridge, 1960-69, prof., 1969-80, vis. prof., 1981—, pres. univ. Film Study Ctr., 1972-73, trustee Film Study Ctr., 1967-73; dean Ctr. for Advanced Study in Visual Arts, Nat. Gallery Art, Washington, 1979—; mem. bd. visitors Fine Arts Sch. Boston Mus., 1972-78; mem. rsch. grants panel NEH, 1972-73, rsch. tools panel, 1983; dir. Am. Acad. in Rome, 1974-77, trustee, 1977—, vice chmn., 1982—; mem. adv. coun. Sch. Architecture, Princeton U., 1970-73, adv. coun. dept. art and archeology, 1972-73, 80-84; mem. cons. com. Nat. Survey Historic Sites and Bldgs., Nat. Pk. Svc. div. U.S. Dept. Interior, 1969-80; vice chmn. Boston Landmarks Commn., 1970-73; panelist Gladys Kriebel Delmas Found., 1979—; chmn. adv. bd. architecture and design TV series Guggenheim Prodns., 1980-88; vis. com. Dept. Fine Arts Harvard U., 1982-84, Sch. Hist. Studies Inst. Advanced Study, 1978, Arthur M. Sackler Gallery Smithsonian Instn., 1986-92; mem. U.S. Nat. Com. History of Art, 1980—; alt. del. Internat. Com. History of Art, 1981-85, del., 1985—, sci. sec. working group Thesaurus Artis Universalis, 1983-89; hon. mem. Boston Archtl. Ctr., 1982—; chmn. sr. fellows com. history of landscape architecture program Dumbarton Oaks, 1983-89, convenor archtl. drawing adv. group, 1983—; mem. adv. com. Getty Art Hist. Info. Program, 1983-91, mem. internat. repertory of lit. of art history, 1985-90, adv. com. Bibliography of the History of Art, 1986—; vice chmn. Coun. Am. Overseas Rsch. Ctrs., 1984-90; pres. Found. for Documents of Architecture, 1987-93; trustee Nat. Bldg. Mus., 1988-94. Author: Baroque and Rococco Architecture, 1962, Key Monuments of the History of Architecture, 1964, Filippo Juvarra: Drawings from the Roman Period, 1704-1714, 1984, (with Craig H. Smyth) Michelangelo Architect, 1988; editor: (with Linda Nochlin) Art and Architecture in the Service of Politics, 1978, Studies in Italian Art and Architecture 15th through 18th Centuries, 1980; co-editor: The Renaissance From Brunelleschi to Michelangelo: The Representation of Architecture, 1994. With USNR, 1944-46. Recipient citation for excellence Internat. Archtl. Book Publ., AIA, 1994, Prix Hercule Catenacci, Inst. de France, 1995, A.H. Barr award Coll. Art Assn., 1996, Centennial medal Am. Acad. in Rome, others; named Hon. Mem. Accademia di San Luca, 1995; Fulbright fellow, Italy, 1957, Am. Acad. Rome fellow, 1957-60. Mem. Soc. Archtl. Historians (pres. 1968-70), Coll. Art Assn. (bd. dirs. 1982-85), AIA Found. (mem. octagon com. 1986-88), Renaissance Soc., Am. Acad. Arts and Scis., Am. Philos. Soc., Deputazione Subalpina di Storia Patria, Soc. Preservation New Eng. Antiquities, Am. Inst. Archeology, Am. Soc. 18th Century Studies, Academia delle Scienze di Torino. Home: 8051 Parkside Ln NW Washington DC 20012-2252

MILLOY, FRANK JOSEPH, JR., surgeon; b. Phoenix, June 26, 1924; s. Frank Joseph and Ola (McCabe) M.; BS, Notre Dame U., 1946; MS, Northwestern U., 1949, M.D., 1947. Intern, Cook County Hosp., Chgo., 1947-49, resident, 1953-57; practice medicine, specializing in surgery, Lake Forest, Ill., 1958—; asso. attending staff Presbyn.-St. Lukes Hosp.; attending staff Cook County Hosp.; mem. staff U. Ill. Rsch. Hosp.; clin. asso. prof. surgery, U. Ill. Med. Sch.; asso. prof. surgery Rush Med. Sch. Cons. West Side Vet. Hosp. Served as apprentice seaman USNR, 1943-45; lt. M.C., USNR, 1950-52; PTO. Diplomate Am. Bd. Surgery and Thoracic Surgery. Mem. A.C.S., Chgo. Surg. Soc., Internat. Soc. Surgery, Am. Coll. Chest Physicians, Soc. Thoracic Surgeons, Phi Beta Pi. Clubs: Metropolitan, University (Chgo.). Home: 574 Jackson Ave Glencoe IL 60022-2036

MILLS, AGNES EUNICE KARLIN, artist, printmaker, sculptor; b. N.Y.C., Apr. 2, 1915; d. Herman Karlin and Celia (Ducoffe) Karlin; m. Saul Mills, May 10, 1910 (dec. Nov. 1993); children: Karen, Marghe Mills Thysen. Grad., Cooper Union Art Sch., N.Y.C., 1938; BFA, Pratt Inst., 1975; student, NYU. One-woman shows include Carus Gallery, N.Y.C., Unitarian Soc., Manhasset, N.Y., Harbor Gallery, Cold Spring Harbor, N.Y., North Truro Art Gallery, Cape Cod, Mass., Alfredo Valente Gallery, N.Y.C., Robbins Gallery, East Orange, N.J., Nuance Galleries, Tampa, Friends of Tampa Ballet, Graphic Eye Coop Gallery, Pt. Washington, N.Y., City Ctr. Gallery, N.Y.C., Lincoln Ctr. Art Gallery, N.Y.C., North Shore Cmty. Arts Ctr., Great Neck, N.Y., Delray Beach Works in Progress Gallery, Boca Raton Cmty. Ctr., Palm Beach Pub. Libr., Gramercy Park Armory, N.Y.C.; exhibited in group shows at Alfredo Valente Gallery, N.Y.C., Audubon Soc., N.Y.C., Bowdoin Coll. Mus. Art, Brunswick, Maine, Brandeis U., Waltham, Mass., Bklyn. Mus. Art, Brown U., Providence, Butler Inst. Am. Art, Youngstown, Ohio, Colgate U. Libr., Hamilton, N.Y., Cornell U., Ithaca, N.Y., East Hampton (N.Y.) Guild Artists, Gallery K, Woodstock, N.Y., Graphic Eye Coop Gallery, Port Washington, N.Y., Heckscher Mus., Huntington, N.Y., Hunterdon County Mus., Clinton, N.J., Joan Avnet Gallery, Great Neck, N.Y., Lincoln Ctr. Libr. Performing Arts, N.Y.C., Madison Gallery, N.Y.C., Boca Raton City Hall, Boca Raton Cmty. Ctr., Boca Raton Libr.; represented in permanent collections at Boca Raton Mus. Art, Nat. Women in the Arts Mus. Home and Studio: 1070 SW 22d Ave #3 Delray Beach FL 33445

MILLS, BELEN COLLANTES, early childhood education educator; s. Ricardo and Epifania (Tomines) C.; children: Belinda Mills Keiser, Roger A. BSE, Leyte Normal Coll., Tacloban, Leyte, Philippines, 1954; MS in Edn., Ind. U., 1955, EdD, 1967. Prof. early childhood edn. Fla. State U., Tallahassee; early childhood cons. to ednl. agys. and orgns. Author books on early childhood edn. and acad. readiness computer programs; contbr. articles to profl.jours. Smith-Mundt Fulbright scholar. Mem. Nat. Assn. for the Edn. of Young Children, Nat. Assn. of Early Childhood Tchr. Edn., World Coun. for Curriculum and Instruction, Assn. of Childhood Edn. Internat. Home: PO Box 20023 Tallahassee FL 32316-0023

MILLS, BRADFORD, merchant banker; b. N.Y.C., Dec. 16, 1926; s. Dudley Holbrook and Louise (Morris) M.; m. Cheryl Ann Di Paolo; children: Elizabeth Lee, Bradford Alan, Barbara Louise, Ross Dudley. BA cum laude in Econs, Princeton U., 1948; postgrad., Oxford (Eng.) U., 1950-51. Asst. to dir. overseas ters. div. ECA, Paris, 1948-50; assoc. corp. fin. dept. F. Eberstadt & Co., N.Y.C., 1954-62; ptnr. F. Eberstadt & Co., 1960-62; mng. ptnr. N.Y. Securities Co., 1962-70; chmn., dir. Specialized Svcs., Inc., Atlanta, 1968-85; pres., CEO Overseas Pvt. Investment Corp., Washington, 1971-73; dir. Overseas Pvt. Investment Corp., 1971-75; chmn. bd., dir. F. Eberstadt & Co. Internat., 1973-74; mng. ptnr. Bradford Assocs., 1974-92; ltd. ptnr. Bradford Investment Ptnrs. Ltd., 1992-96; past chmn. Diamond Glass, MMX Corp., HWC Corp., Chgo. Stock Tab Corp., Filtration Scis., Overseas Pvt. Investors Ltd., Overseas Pvt. Equities, Overseas Equity Investors, Inc; chmn. U.S. Precision Glass Inc.; bd. dirs. Papel Freelance, Inc., DentureCare, Inc., The Princeton Packet, Treflow Med., Princeton Investment Group, Inc. Pres. Mills Found.; trustee, treas. Millbrook (N.Y.) Sch., 1978—; trustee Med. Ctr. Princeton, 1995—. Mem. Coun. Fgn. Rels., Blooming Grove Club (Pa.), Links Club, Leash Club, Anglers Club N.Y., Nassau Club, Bedens Brook Club, Amwell Valley Conservancy, Inc. Home: 15 Van Kirk Rd Princeton NJ 08540-4214 Office: Bradford Investment Group Inc 44 Nassau St Ste 365 Princeton NJ 08542-4511

MILLS, CAROL MARGARET, business consultant, public relations consultant; b. Salt Lake City, Aug. 31, 1943; d. Samuel Lawrence and Beth (Neilson) M.; BS magna cum laude, U. Utah, 1965. With W.S. Hatch Co., Woods Cross, Utah, 1965-87, corp. sec., 1970-87, traffic mgr., 1969-87, dir. publicity, 1974-87; cons. various orgns., 1988—; dir. Hatch Svc. Corp., 1972-87, Nat. Tank Truck Carriers, Inc., Washington, 1977-88; bd. dirs. Intermountain Tariff Bur. Inc., 1978-88, chmn., 1981-82, 1986-87; bd. dirs. Mountainwest Venture Group. Fund raiser March of Dimes, Am. Cancer Soc., Am. Heart Assn.; active senatorial campaign, 1976, gubernatorial campaign, 1984, 88, congl. campaign, 1990, 92, 94, vice chair voting dist., 1988-90, congl. campaign, 1994; chmn. 1990-92, chmn. party caucus legis. dist.; witness transp. com. Utah State Legislature, 1984, 85; apptd. by gov. to bd. trustees Utah Tech. Fin. Corp., 1986—, corp. sec., mem. exec. com., 1988—; mem. expdn. to Antarctica, 1996, Titanic '96 expdn. Recipient svc. awards W.S. Hatch Co., 1971, 80; mem. Pioneer Theatre Guild, 1985—; V.I.P. capt. Easter Seal Telethon, 1989, 90, recipient Outstanding Vol. Svc. award Easter Seal Soc. Utah, 1989, 90. Mem. Nat. Tank Truck Carriers Transp. Club Salt Lake City, Am. Trucking Assn. (mem. pub. rels. coun.), Utah Motor Transport Assn. (bd. dirs. 1982-88), Internat. Platform Assn., Traveler's Century Club, Titanic Internat., Beta Gamma Sigma, Phi Kappa Phi, Phi Chi Theta. Home and Office: 77 Edgecombe Dr Salt Lake City UT 84103-2219

MILLS, CELESTE LOUISE, hypnotherapist, professional magician; b. L.A., May 16, 1952; d. Emery John and Helen Louise (Bradbury) W.; m. Robert Richardson Feigel, Apr. 11, 1971 (div. 1973); m. Peter Alexander Mills, June 12, 1991, (div. 1992). BBA, Western State U., Doniphan, Mo., 1987; PhD in Religion, Universal Life Ch. Univ., 1987; grad., Hypnotism Tng. Inst., Glendale, Calif., 1990. Cert. hypnotherapist. Credit mgr. accounts receivable Gensler-Lee Diamonds, Santa Barbara, Calif., 1973-74, Terry Hinge and Hardware, Van Nuys, Calif., 1975-78; credit mgr., fin. analyst Peanut Butter Fashions, Chatsworth, Calif., 1978-82; personal mgr. Charter Mgmt. Co., Beverly Hills, Calif., 1982-83; co-owner, v.p. Noreen Jenney Communicates, Beverly Hills, 1983-85; corp. credit mgr., fin. analyst Cen. Diagnostic Lab., Tarzana, Calif., 1985-89; credit mgr., fin. analyst Metwest Clin. Lab., Inc., Tarzana, Calif., 1989-90; pvt. practice, 1990—; cons. Results Now, Inc., Tarzana, 1986-87. Prodr., host (TV) Brainstorm, 1993—. Media spokesperson Am. Cancer Soc., 1990—. Mem. NAFE, NOW, Nat. Humane Ednl. Found., Credit Mgrs. Assn. Trade Groups (bd. govs. 1988-89), Nat. Clin. Lab. Trade Group (chmn. 1988-89), Med. and Surg. Suppliers Trade Group (vice chmn. 1988-89, chmn. 1989-90), Soc. Am. Magicians, Acad. Magical Arts, Internat. Brotherhood of Magicians, Assn. Advanced Ethical Hypnosis, Am. Coun. Hypnotist Examiners. Avocations: scuba diving, sailing.

MILLS, CHARLES GARDNER, lawyer; b. Griffin, Ga., Feb. 29, 1940; s. Charles G. and Marguerite (Powell) M. AB, Yale U., 1962; JD, Boston Coll., 1967. Bar: N.Y. 1967, U.S. Dist. Ct. (so. and ea. dists.) 1972, U.S. Ct. Appeals (2d cir.) 1975, U.S. Supreme Ct., 1977, U.S. Ct. Claims 1991, U.S. Ct. Vets. Appeals 1996, U.S. Ct. Appeals (fed. cir.) 1997. Assoc. Smart & McKay, N.Y.C., 1967-68, Smart & Mills, N.Y.C., 1969-71, Eaton & VanWinkle, N.Y.C., 1971-82, Payne, Wood & Littlejohn, Glen Cove and Melville, N.Y., 1982-91; pvt. practice, Glen Cove, 1991—. With U.S. Army, 1962-64, ETO. Mem. N.Y. State Bar Assn., Assn. Bar City N.Y., Nassau County Bar Assn., Rotary (pres. Glen Cove Club 1989-90), Am. Legion (comdr. Locust Valley, N.Y. post 1988-90, comdr. Nassau County com.

1995-96), Soc. Colonial Wars, SCV, Order of the Arrow. Republican. Roman Catholic. Office: 56 School St Glen Cove NY 11542-2512

MILLS, CYNTHIA SPRAKER, association executive; b. Williamsburg, Va., June 11, 1962; d. Charles E. and Marceil H. (Harris) Spraker; m. John E. Mills, Oct. 18, 1986. BA in History and Psychology, Queens Coll., 1984; MA in Medieval Studies, U. of York, Eng., 1986. Cert. assn. exec., 1996. Fin. aid officer Rutledge Edn. Sys., Charlotte, N.C., 1987-88; assoc. dir. Programming & Sys., Inc., Charlotte, 1988-90; asst. exec. dir. Nat. Assn. Coll. Aux. Svcs., Staunton, Va., 1990-93; exec. dir. Pilot Internat. & Pilot Internat. Found., Macon, Ga., 1993—; presenter in field. Contbr. articles to profl. publs. Chair Pacesetters divsn. United Way of Staunton/West Augusta County, 1992; mem. adv. bd. Edn. Exch., Ind., 1991-93; mem. Commonwealth/Cmty. Alliance for Drug Rehab. and Edn. of Staunton/Augusta County, Inc., 1991-93. Rotary Found. scholar, 1984-85, Queens Coll. Presdl. scholar, 1980-84. Mem. Ga. Soc. Assn. Execs. (v.p. fin. 1996-97, staff mgmt. com. 1994-96, chair tech. spl. interest group 1994-95, bd. dirs. 1995—), Am. Soc. Assn. Execs. (cert., membership com. 1991—, Notable Accomplishment award 1991, mem. Chmn.'s Honor Roll 1992, mem. Chmn.'s Round Table for Membership Recruitment 1994), Am. Biog. Inst. (rsch. bd. advisors), Nat. Ctr. for Nonprofit Bds., Svc. Club Leaders Conf. Republican. Lutheran. Office: Pilot Internat & Found PO Box 4844 244 College St Macon GA 31208

MILLS, DANIEL QUINN, business educator, consultant, author; b. Houston, Nov. 24, 1941; s. Daniel Monroe and Louise (Quinn) M.; divorced; children: Lisa Ann, Shirley Elizabeth. BA, Ohio Wesleyan U., 1963; MA, Harvard U., 1965, PhD, 1968. Prof. MIT, Cambridge, 1968-75, Harvard Bus. Sch., Boston, 1976—; impartial umpire Plan to Settle Disputes in Constrn., 1973-79, Trans-Alaska Pipeline, 1975-78, AFL-CIO Internal Disputes Plan, 1975-82; commr. Nat. Commn. on Employment Policy, Washington, 1982-86. Author: Industrial Relations in Construction, 1971, Labor, Government and Inflation, 1975, Labor-Management Relations, 1978, 5th edit., 1993, Construction Industry, 1979, The New Competitors, 1985, Not Like Our Parents: The Baby-Boom Generation, 1987, The IBM Lesson, 1988, The Rebirth of the Corporation, 1990, The GEM Principle, 1994, Broken Promises: What Went Wrong at IBM, 1996. Mem. Am. Econ. Assn., Indsl. Relations Research Assn., Phi Beta Kappa. Mem. United Ch. of Christ. Office: Harvard U Harvard Bus Sch Soldiers Field Rd Allston MA 02163

MILLS, DAVID HARLOW, psychologist, association executive; b. Marshalltown, Iowa, Dec. 26, 1932; s. Harlow Burgess and Esther Winifred (Brewer) M.; m. Janet Louise Anderson, June 15, 1957 (div. 1984); children: Ross Harlow, Anne Louise; m. Susan S. Greene, Aug. 3, 1984. BS, Iowa State U., 1955, MS, 1957; PhD, Mich. State U., 1964. Postdoctoral fellow USPHS U. Ill., Champaign, 1964-65; from asst. prof. psychology to assoc. prof. Iowa State U., Ames, 1965-69; asst. dir. counseling ctr. Iowa State U., 1967-69; faculty U. Md., College Park, 1969-81; prof. psychology U. Md., 1972-81, asst. dir. counseling center, 1969-81; adminstrv. officer Am. Psychol. Assn., Washington, 1981-86; pvt. practice Bangor, Maine, 1989—, Blue Hill, Maine, 1990—; cons. Iowa Women's Reformatory, 1966-69, VA, Rockwell City, Iowa, 1966-69; rsch. assoc. Nat. Register Health Svcs. Providers in Psychology; mgmt. cons. Ctr. Creative Leadership U. Md., 1980—; mem. Maine Bd. Psychologists; mem. examination com. Assn. State and Provincial State Psychology Bds., 1995—. Contbr. articles to profl. jours. Pres. Woodmoor-Pinecrest Citizens Assn., Silver Spring, Md., 1973-74; mem. com. higher edn. Allied Civic Group Montgomery County, 1974, sr. fellow Consortium of Univs. of the Washington D.C. Met. Area., 1987—. Served with U.S. Army, 1957-61. Fellow APA (bd. dirs. 1986-90, dir. ethics 1986—, ethics cons. 1990—); mem. Internat. Assn. Counseling Svcs. (accrediting bd. 1972-74, v.p. 1975-77, pres. 1977-79). Democrat. Unitarian. Home: RR 1 Box 323A Little Deer Isle ME 04650-9801 Office: Greens Hill Box 1015 Blue Hill ME 04624

MILLS, DON HARPER, pathology and psychiatry educator, lawyer; b. Peking, China, July 29, 1927; came to U.S., 1928; s. Clarence Alonzo and Edith Clarissa (Parrett) M.; m. Lillian Frances Snyder, June 11, 1949; children: Frances Jo, Jon Snyder. BS, U. Cin., 1950, MD, 1953; JD, U. So. Calif., 1958. Diplomate Am. Bd. Law in Medicine. Intern L.A. County Gen. Hosp., 1953-54, admitting physician, 1954-57, attending staff pathologist, 1959—; pathology fellow U. So. Calif., L.A., 1954-55, instr. pathology, 1958-62, asst. clin. prof., 1962-65, assoc. clin. prof., 1965-69, clin. prof., 1969—, clin. prof. psychiatry and behavioral sci., 1986—; asst. in pathology Hosp. Good Samaritan, L.A., 1956-65, cons. staff, 1962-72, affiliating staff, 1972-91; dep. med. examiner Office of L.A. County Med. Examiner, 1957-61; instr. legal medicine Loma Linda (Calif.) U. Sch. Medicine, 1960-66, assoc. clin. prof. humanities, 1966-95; cons. HEW, 1972-73, 75-76, Dept. of Def., 1975-80; bd. dirs. Am. Bd. Law in Medicine, Inc., Chgo., 1980-86; med. dir. Profl. Risk Mgmt. Group, 1989—. Column editor Newsletter of the Long Beach Med. Assn., 1960-75, Jour. Am. Osteopathic Assn., 1965-77, Ortho Panel, 1970-78; exec. editor Trauma, 1964-88, mem. editl. bd., 1988—; mem. editl. bd. Legal Aspects of Med. Practice, 1972-90, Med. Alert Comms., 1973-75, Am. Jour. Forensic Medicine and Pathology, 1979-87, Hosp. Risk Control, 1981-96; contbr. numerous articles to profl. jours. Bd. dirs. Inst. for Med. Risk Studies, 1988—. Recipient Ritz Heerman award Calif. Hosp. Assn., 1986, Disting. fellow Am. Acad. Forensic Scis., 1993, Genesis award Pacific Ctr. for Health Policy and Ethics, 1993, Founder's award Am. Coll. Med. Quality, 1994. Fellow Am. Coll. Legal Medicine (pres. 1974-76, bd. govs. 1970-78, v.p. 1972-74, chmn. malpractice com. 1973-74, jour. editl. bd. 1984—), Am. Acad. Forensic Sci. (gen. program chmn. 1966-67, chmn. jurisprudence sect. 1966-67, 73-74, exec. com. 1971-74, 84-88, v.p. 1984-85, pres. 1986-87, ethics com. 1976-86, 91—, chmn. ethics com. 1994—, strategic planning com. 1990—, jour. editl. bd. 1965-79); mem. AMA (jour. editl. bd. 1973-77), AAAS, ABA, Calif. Med. Assn., L.A. County Med. Assn., L.A. County Bar Assn., Am. Soc. Hosp. Attys., Calif. Soc. Hosp. Attys. Home: 700 E Ocean Blvd Unit 2606 Long Beach CA 90802-5039 Office: 911 N Studebaker Rd Ste 250 Long Beach CA 90815-4900

MILLS, DONALD MCKENZIE, librarian; b. Virden, Man., Can., Feb. 25, 1946; s. Earl Townsend and Mable Elizabeth (Davies) M.; m. Kathrine Ann Richards, Aug. 26, 1968; children—Jennifer, Susan. B.A., U. Winnipeg, Man., Can., 1968; M.L.S., U. B.C., Vancouver, Can., 1972. Chief librarian St. Albert Pub. Library, Alta., Can., 1972-75; children's coordinator Kamloops Pub. Library, B.C., Can., 1975-78; chief librarian West Vancouver Pub. Library, B.C., Can., 1978-82, Winnipeg Pub. Library, Man., Can., 1982-87, Mississauga (Ont.) Pub. Library, 1987—. Mem. ALA, Can. Library Assn., Ontario Libr. Assn. Office: Mississauga Libr Sys, 301 Burnham Thorpe Rd, Mississauga, ON Canada L5B 3Y3

MILLS, DOROTHY ALLEN, investor; b. New Brunswick, N.J., Dec. 14, 1920; d. James R. and Bertha Lovilla (Porter) Allen; m. George M. Mills, Apr. 21, 1945; children: Dianne, Adele, Dorothy L. BA, Douglass Coll., New Brunswick, N.J., 1943. Investment reviewer Cen. Hanover Bank, N.Y.C., 1943-44; asst. to dir. of admissions and sec. undergrad. yrs. Douglass Coll., New Brunswick, 1944-45; sec., regional dir. O.P.A., Ventura, Calif., 1945-46; corp. sec. George M. Mills Inc., Highland Park, N.J., 1946-75; pvt. investor N. Brunswick, N.J., 1975—. Sr. v.p. Children Am. Revolution, N.J., 1965; active alumni com. Douglass Coll., 1990—. Recipient Douglass Alumni award, 1992. Mem. AAUW, New Brunswick Hist. Soc., DAR, English Speaking Union, Rutgers Alumni Faculty Club, Woman's League of Rutgers U., Princeton-Douglass Alumni Club, N. Brunswick Women's Club, Auxiliary Robert Wood Johnson Hosp. and Med. Sch. Republican. Mem. Dutch Reformed Ch. Avocations: travel, gardening, bridge. Home: 1054 Hoover Dr New Brunswick NJ 08902-3244

MILLS, ELIZABETH ANN, librarian; b. Cambridge, Mass., Apr. 1, 1934; d. Ralph Edwin and Sylvia Elizabeth (Meehan) McCurdy; m. Albert Ernest Mills, July 6, 1957; 1 child, Karen Elizabeth. BA, Duke U., 1956; MS, Simmons Coll., 1973; postgrad. Boston Coll., Framingham State U., Bridgewater State U. Sec. Lowell House, Harvard U., Cambridge, Mass., 1956-57; substitute libr., tchr. Wellesley (Mass.) H.S., 1972-73, Needham (Mass.) H.S., 1972-73; libr. Tucker Sch. Media Ctr., Milton (Mass.) Pub. Schs., 1973-94, chmn. computer curriculum com., 1982, mem. computer study com., 1988-91, bldg. coordinator gifted program, 1981-94; libr. Milton (Mass.) H.S., 1994—. Contbr. articles to profl. jours. Active Girl Scouts U.S.A., U.S. Power Squadron, Gt. Blue Hill, Mass., 1974—. Mem. ALA, Am. Assn. Sch. Librarians, Assn. Library Service Children, Mass. Assn. Ednl. Media, Mass. Sch. Libr. Assn., Beta Phi Mu, Kappa Delta, Delta Kappa Gamma. Republican. Episcopalian. Home: 177 Jarvis Cir Needham MA 02192-2034 Office: Milton HS 451 Centre St Milton MA 02186-4118

MILLS, ELIZABETH SHOWN, genealogist editor, writer; b. Cleve., Miss., Dec. 29, 1944; d. Floyd Finley Shown and Elizabeth Thulmar (Jeffcoat) Carver; m. Gary Bernard Mills, Apr. 15, 1963; children: Clayton Bernard, Donna Rachal, Daniel Garland. BA, U. Ala., 1980. Cert. genealogist, geneal. lectr. Profl. geneal. writer, educator, 1972-86; editor Nat. Geneal. Soc. Quar., Arlington, Va., 1987—; faculty Samford U. Inst. of Genealogy and Hist. Rsch., Birmingham, Ala., 1980-97, trustee Assn. for Promotion of Scholarship in Genealogy, N.Y., 1984-90, contract dir., cons. U. Ala., 1985-92, faculty Nat. Inst. of Geneal. Rsch., 1985-97. Author, editor, translator Cane River Creole Series, 6 vols.; author: Evidence: Citation and Analysis for the Family Historian, 1997; contbr. articles to profl. jours. Mem. adv. bd. Assn. for Preservation of Historic Natchitoches, La., 1972-80, bd. mem. Friends of La. State Archives, Baton Rouge, 1976-77, Tuscaloosa (Ala.) Preservation Soc., 1984-85, chair Hist. Records Task Force Ala. State Archives, Montgomery, 1984-85; trustee Nat. Bd. Certification Genealogists, 1984-89, v.p., 1989-94, pres., 1994-96. Named Outstanding Young Women of Am. Jaycees, Gadsden, 1976, Outstanding Alumna award U. Ala. New Coll., Tuscaloosa, 1990. Fellow Am. Soc. of Geneal. (sec. 1992-95, v.p. 1995—), Nat. Geneal. Soc., Utah Geneal. Assn.; mem. Assn. of Profl. Geneal. (Smallwood Svc. award, 1989). Republican. Roman Catholic. Home: 1732 Ridgedale Dr Tuscaloosa AL 35406-1942 Office: Nat Geneal Soc 4527 17th St N Arlington VA 22207-2378

MILLS, EUGENE SUMNER, college president; b. West Newton, Ind., Sept. 13, 1924; s. Sumner Amos and Lela (Weatherly) M.; m. Dorothy Frances Wildman, Oct. 22, 1945; children: David Walden, Sara Anne. A.B., Earlham Coll., 1948; M.A., Claremont Grad. Sch., 1949, Ph.D., 1952; Spl. Postdoctoral Auditor, Harvard, 1958-59; LLD (hon.), N.H. Coll., 1979, U. N.H., 1988; LHD (hon.), Earlham Coll., 1987. Instr. psychology Whittier (Calif.) Coll., 1950, asst. prof., chmn. dept., 1952-55, assoc. prof., chmn. dept., 1955-60, prof. psychology, chmn. dept., 1960-62; faculty U. N.H., Durham, 1962-79; prof. psychology U. N.H., 1962-79, chmn. dept., 1962-65, dean Grad. Sch., coordinator research, 1963-67; dean U. N.H. (Coll. Liberal Arts), 1967-70, acad. v.p., 1970-71, provost, 1971-74, provost, acting pres., 1974, pres., 1974-79; pres. Whittier (Calif.) Coll. and Whittier Coll. Sch. of Law, 1979-89; prof. psychology Whittier (Calif.) Coll., 1979-89, emeritus prof. psychology, pres. emeritus, 1989—; vis. prof. U. Victoria, B.C., summers 1958, 60; bd. dirs. Elderhostel, Inc., 1977—, chmn., 1984-90, vice chmn., 1996-97; bd. dirs. Fedco Inc., 1988—, vice-chmn., 1996—; interim pres. Earlham Coll., 1996-97; bd. dirs. New Eng. Bd. Higher Edn., 1974-79; mem. N.H. Psychol. Assn., 1962-79, pres., 1969-70, bd. dirs., 1967-70; trustee Earlham Coll., 1966-69. Author: George Trumbull Ladd: Pioneer American Psychologist, 1969, The Story ofElderhostel, 1993; contbr. articles to profl. jours. Danforth Found. grantee; NSF grantee. Fellow Am. Psychol. Assn.; mem. Western Psychol. Assn., Sigma Xi, Phi Kappa Phi., Omicron Delta Kappa. Mem. Soc. of Friends.

MILLS, FREDERICK VANFLEET, art educator, watercolorist; b. Bremen, Ohio, June 5, 1925; s. Frederick William and Juanita Ellen (VanFleet) M.; m. Lois Jean Rademacher; children: Mark Steven (dec.), Michael Sherwood, Mollie Sue, Merre Shannon, Randal Dean, Susan Lynn, Todd Patrick, Shondra Marie. BS, Ohio State U., 1949; MS, Ind. U., 1951, EdD, 1956; postgrad., U.S. Army Staff and Command Coll., 1973-76. Tchr. art, supr. Celina (Ohio) Pub. Schs., 1949-51; instr. univ. h.s. Ind. U., 1951-55; prof. art, art edn., chmn. dept. art edn. Ind. U., Bloomington, 1959-65; vis. prof. U. Tex.-Austin, 1965; chmn. dept. related arts, crafts and interior design U. Tenn., Konxville, 1966-68; prof. art, chmn. dept. art Ill. State U., 1968-85, prof. emeritus, 1985—; prof. art Lincoln Coll., Normal, 1986—; rsch. reader humanities HEW, 1968-69; resource person arts, edn. and Ams. panel Rockefeller Report Am Coun. Arts in Edn., 1977-78; cons. Latin Am. Fulbright Scholarship Program Harvard U., 1981-82; mem. com. Ill. Fine Arts Rev. for Capital Devel. Bd., 1987—, planning com. Nat. Inst. Advanced Studies in Art and Design and Archives of Am. Art Sch., 1988—, rsch. com. Nat. Sch. Art and Design. One-man shows include McLean County Arts Ctr., Bloomington, Ill., Lincoln (Ill.) Coll., Ill. Agriculture Assn. Credit Union Art Exhbn. Series, Bloomington, Suzette Schochet Gallery, Newport, R.I.; represented in permanent collections Wonderlin Gallery, Normal, Ill., State Farm Ins. Co., Kemper Fin. Securities/Kemper Fin. Fund, First of Am. Bank, Ill., Diamond Star Motors Corp., Easter Seal Assn., City of Vladimir, Russia, City of Asahikawa, Hokkaido, Japan, County of McLean, City of Bloomington, Town of Normal; author, editor: The Status of the Visual Arts in Higher Education, 1976, New Perspectives in Visual Arts Administration, 1977, Issues in the Administration of Visual Arts, 1978, Politics and the Visual Arts, 1979, The Visual Arts in the Ninth Decade, 1980; editor Western Arts Bull., 1958-62; featured in 12 part ser. As An Artist Sees local pub. access; contbr. to profl. jours. Pres. Ill. Alliance Art Edn., 1975-77, Ill. Task Force for Arts Edn. in Gen. Edn., 1976-77; mem. Tenn. Arts Commn., 1967-68, Nat. Alliance Arts Edn./Kennedy Ctr., 1975-77; charter trustee Ill. Summer Sch. for Arts, v.p., v.p. Found. Bd., 1988-94; bd. dirs., co-founder Sugar Creek Arts Festival, Normal, 1985—; chair major gifts com. Normal Theater Restoration Project, 1992—; bd. dirs., v.p. McLean County Arts Ctr., Bloomington, 1980-90, sponsor Skilled Crafts award, 1968—. Served to maj. USAR; Col. Ill. Militia. Recipient Recognition award Alliance for Arts Edn., 1984, Outstanding Svc. award Ill. Alliance Arts Edn., 1984, 1994 Ornament of Yr./Artist of Yr. award; subject articles, TV interviews. Mem. Nat. Council Art Adminstrs. (charter, sr. rsch. editor bd. dirs. 1973-81), Nat. Assn. Schs. Art (instnl. del. 1974-84, nominating com. 1977-78, rsch. com. 1976-77), Western Arts Assn. (pres. 1962-64), Coll. Art Assn., Nat. Art Edn. Assn. (dir. 1964-66), Scabbard and Blade, Phi Delta Kappa, Delta Tau Delta, Delta Phi Delta. Club: Rotary Internat. Home: K 162 Lake Bloomington RR 2 Box 60 A Hudson IL 61748 *As I reflect on my life and career up to this point, I feel that consistency and humaneness are two words that come to mind. It seems extremely important to be consistent when a person relates to others, and if that is coupled with humaneness and consideration of the value of others, being aware of their strengths and weaknesses, their likes and dislikes, it becomes easier to relate to them in this most complex world of ours.*

MILLS, GARY BERNARD, history educator; b. Marshall, Tex., Sept. 10, 1944; s. Harold Garland and Hazel Cecilia (Rachal) M.; m. Elizabeth Shown; children: Clayton Bernard, Donna Rachal, Daniel Garland. BA in History and Bus. Adminstrn., Delta State U., 1967; MA in History, Miss. State U., 1969, PhD in History, 1974. Instr. history McNeese State U., Lake Charles, La., 1969-72, U. Ctr., Jackson, Miss., 1972-75; asst. prof. U. Ala., Gadsden, 1976-79, assoc. prof., 1979-82; assoc. prof. U. Ala., Tuscaloosa, 1982-83, prof. history, 1984Ö; cons. in field. Author numerous books; co-editor Nat. Geneal. Soc. Quar., 1987Ö; contbr. numerous articles to profl. jours. Del. Am.-Russian Archival Adv., Washington, Moscow, Minsk, 1989-91; mem. adv. bd. Archive Am. Minority Cultures, U. Ala., 1983-90. Fellow Huntington Libr., San Marino, Calif., 1988. Fellow Grady McWhiney Hist. Rsch. Found. (sr.); mem. Nat. Geneal. Soc., Am. Hist. Assn., Ala. Hist. Assn., La. Hist. Assn. (bd. dirs. 1972-94), Orgn. Ala. Historians, So. Hist. Assn. (various coms. 1981-86), St. George Tucker Soc. (fellow 1992Ö). Independent. Roman Catholic. Avocations: music, genealogy. Home: 1732 Ridgedale Dr Tuscaloosa AL 35406-1942 Office: U Ala PO Box 870212 Tuscaloosa AL 35487

MILLS, GEORGE ALEXANDER, retired science administrator; b. Saskatoon, Sask., Can., Mar. 20, 1914; s. George Robison and Leafa (Johnson) M.; m. Roberta Walker Mills, June 15, 1940; children: Richard, Sandra, Marilyn, Janice. B.Sc., U. Sask., 1934, M.Sc., 1936; Ph.D., Columbia U. Instr., Dartmouth Coll., 1939-40; with Houdry Process Co., 1940-68; with U.S. Bur. Mines, 1968-75, chief coal div., 1968-75; dir. fossil energy research ERDA, 1975-77; dir. internat. programs fossil energy Dept. Energy, Washington, 1977-81; exec. dir. Ctr. Catalytic Sci. and Tech., U. Del., Newark, 1981-84, sr. scientist Ctr. Catalytic Sci and Tech., 1984-95. Contbr. numerous articles to profl. jours. Mem. Nat. Acad. Engring., Am. Inst. Chemists (Pioneer award), Am. Chem. Soc. (Storch award, Murphree award), AAAS, Am. Inst. Chem. Engring., Catalysis Soc. Presbyterian. Patentee in field. Home: Cokesbury Village # 48 726 Loveville Rd Hockessin DE 19707-1515

MILLS, GEORGE MARSHALL, insurance and financial consultant; b. Newton, N.J., May 20, 1923; s. J. Marshall and Emma (Scott) M.; m. Dorothy Lovilla Allen, Apr. 21, 1945; children: Dianne (Mrs. Thomas McKay III), Dorothy L.A. (Mrs. Edward Sphatt). BA, Rutgers U., 1943; MA, Columbia U., 1951. CLU, CPCU; chartered fin. cons.; cert. govt. fund mgr. Pres. George M. Mills Inc., North Brunswick, N.J., 1946-75; pres. CORECO, Inc., Newark, 1960-78; risk mgr. N.J. Hwy. Authority, Woodbridge, 1976-95; pres. Assoc. Risk Mgmt., North Brunswick, N.J., 1995—; cons. Govs.'s Com. on Bus. Efficiency in Pub. Schs., 1979-80; cons. Risk Mgmt. Ins., Real Estate. Bd. dirs. Alpha Chi Rho Ednl. Found., vice-chmn. 1991—; workshop Easter Seal Soc.; mem. Gov.'s Task Force on Sound Mcpl. Govt., 1981-82; pres. Nat. Interfrat. Conf., 1979-80. With USNR, 1943-46. Mem. Am. Coll. Life Underwriters, Am. Coll. Property Liability Underwriters, Internat. Bridge Tunnel and Turnpike Assn. (chmn. risk mgmt. com. 1980-95, mem. bus. ins. risk mgmt. bd. 1988-95, Matthew J. Lenz Jr. medal 1989, Paul K. Addams award 1992), New Brunswick Hist. Soc., English Speaking Union, Rutgers U. Alumni-Faculty Club, Alpha Chi Rho (nat. councillor 1964-70, nat. pres. 1970-73, nat. treas. 1975-78), Kappa Kappa Psi, Tau Kappa Alpha, Phi Delta Phi. Mem. Reformed Ch. Am. Home: 1054 Hoover Dr New Brunswick NJ 08902

MILLS, GORDON LAWRENCE, financial executive; b. N.Y.C., Feb. 21, 1933; s. Dudley H. and Louise M. (Morris) M.; m. Margaret Devereux Aydelotte, Dec. 13, 1958 (div. 1993); children: Julia H., Thomas B.; m. Signa Lynch Read, Nov. 9, 1993. AB cum laude, Princeton U., 1954; MBA, Harvard U., 1958. Chartered fin. analyst. Sr. analyst White Weld & Co. (now Merrill Lynch), N.Y.C., 1958-62; v.p. Mut. Life Ins. Co., N.Y.C., 1962-74; gen. mgr. pension The Continental Group (formerly Continental Can), Stamford, Conn., 1974-81; v.p. Lipper Analytical Service, Greenwich, Conn., 1981-83; mgr. benefit plans fin. mgmt. Texaco Inc., White Plains, N.Y., 1983-90; chmn. bd. advisors S.E.I. Internat., Greenwich, 1991-96; mng. ptnr. Manchester (Vt.) Capital Mgmt., 1994—; Vt. state sen. cand. Natural Law Party, 1994; lectr. Fin. Mgmt. of Multinat. Corps., N.Y.C., 1975-80, Cornell Sch. Indsl. Rels., 1978, Internat. Counsel Adv. Bd. Can. Assn. Pension Mgmt., 1976; pres. Am. Capital Corp., Greenwich, 1981-83; cons. Venture Capital Partnerships, N.Y.C., 1981-83. Author: Pension Management-AMA, 1983; editor of Conn. Venture Group newsletter, Stamford, 1981-83. Profl. magician UN Hospitality Com., 1979; bd. dirs. N.Y.C. Mission Soc., Soc., 1963-85, exec. com. mem., investment com. chmn., United Hosp. Fund Greater N.Y., 1974-80, Nat. Audubon Soc. Greenwich, 1979-86, Allegheny Power Systems Inc, 1973-81, Home for Old Men and Aged Couples, N.Y.C., 1974-80; fin. com. chmn., Amsterdam House. 1st lt., arty. U.S. Army, 1954-56. Mem. Sentinel Pension Inst. (bd. advs., lectr. 1975—), Pension Group East (founding mem., lectr., Internat. counsel adv. bd. Can. Assn. Pension Mgmt. 1975-78), The Links Club (N.Y.C.), Clove Valley Rod and Gun Club, Holland Lodge. Office: Box 416 Brookside Bldg Hist Rte 7A Manchester VT 05254

MILLS, INGA-BRITTA, artist; b. Eskilstuna, Sweden, Sept. 14, 1925; came to U.S., 1954; d. Gerhard Valdemar and Märta Kristina (Söderberg) Stenhäll; m. Mogens Schiött, June, 1950 (div. 1952); m. Victor Moore Mills, June 6, 1956; children: Karl-Olof, Victoria Inga Kristina. Attended, U. Gothenburg, Sweden, 1946-48; BA, MA, Montclair State Coll., 1979; postgrad., Temple U., 1980-82. Sec. to port dir. Port Authority, Gothenburg, Sweden, 1952-54; adminstrv. asst. UN, N.Y.C., 1954-55. One-person shows include Montclair Pub. Libr., 1977, UN Food and Agr. Orgn., Rome, 1979, Libr. Arts Ctr., Newport, N.H., 1984, Ariel Gallery, Soho, N.Y.C., 1986, Stamford Mus. and Nature Ctr., 1989, Burnham Libr., Bridgewater, Conn., 1991, Westover Sch., Middlebury, Conn., 1993, Roxbury Libr., 1995, Gallery AE, Gothenburg, Sweden, 1995, Conn. Housing Fin. Authority, Rockyhill; exhibited in group shows including Am. Women's Assn. of Rome, 1982, Marian Graves Mugar Gallery, Colby-Sawyer Coll., New London, N.H., 1984, Artworks Gallery, Hartford, Conn., 1986, Greene Gallery, Guilford, Conn., 1989, The Discovery Mus., Bridgeport, Conn., 1990, Silvermine Galleries, New Canaan, Conn., 1990, Ward-Nasse Gallery, Soho, 1991, 92, Internat. Juried Print Exhibit, Somers, N.Y., 1992, Grand Prix Fine Art de Paris, 1993, Stamford Hist. Soc., 1993, Montserrat Gallery, Soho, 1994, Internat. Print Biennial, Cracow, Poland, 1994, Trenton (N.J.) State Coll., 1995, New Haven Paint and Clay Club, 1995, Conn. Women Artists, New Britain Mus. Am. Art, 1995, Internat Print Triennial, Cracow, Polant, 1997, 4th Ann. Internat. Graphics Addiction, Stockholm, 1997; represented in collections Conning & Co., N.Y.C., New Haven Paint and Clay Club, Somerstown Gallery, Somers; represented in pvt. collections, U.S., Europe, Japan, and Australia. Recipient Marjorie Frances Meml. award Stamford (Conn.) Mus. and Nature Ctr., 1990, Faber-Birren Color award Stamford Art Assn., 1990. Mem. Wash. Art Assn. Democrat. Avocations: gardening, reading, music, theatre.

MILLS, JAMES SPENCER, author; b. Milw., May 20, 1932; s. Ralph Erskine and Elisabeth Amsden (Stevens) M. Student, Erskine Coll., 1950-51; BA, Princeton U., 1956. Reporter Worcester (Mass.) Telegram and Evening Gazette, summer 1955, Corpus Christi (Tex.) Caller Times, 1958, UPI, 1959; reporter, corr., writer, editor Life mag., 1960-66. Author: The Panic in Needle Park, 1966, The Prosecutor, 1969, Report to the Commissioner, 1972, One Just Man, 1974, On the Edge, 1975, The Seventh Power, 1976, The Truth about Peter Harley, 1979, The Underground Empire: Where Crime and Governments Embrace, 1986, The Power, 1990, Haywire, 1995. Served with USNR, 1956-58. Address: care Marvin Kalickstein 2547 Joel Pl Oceanside NY 11572-1331

MILLS, JAMES STEPHEN, medical supply company executive; b. Chgo., Sept. 29, 1936; s. Irving I. and Beatrice (Shane) M.; m. Victoria L. Krisch, Mar. 23, 1973; children: Charles, Donald, Margaret. B.S. in Bus., Northwestern U. Vice pres. sales Mills Hosp. Supply Co., Chgo., 1961-66; pres. Medline Industries Inc., Northbrook, Ill., 1966-75, chmn. bd., 1975—. Served with AUS, 1958-64. Jewish. Home: 500 N Green Bay Rd Lake Forest IL 60045-2146 Office: Medline Industries Inc 1 Medline Pl Mundelein IL 60060-4485

MILLS, JERRY WOODROW, lawyer; b. Springfield, Mo., July 17, 1940; s. Woodrow Wilson and Billie Louise M.; m. Marion Cargile, Mar. 27, 1964; children: Eric E., Brendon W. BSEE, Tex. A&M U., 1963; JD, Georgetown U., 1967. Bar: Tex. 1967, U.S. Patent Office 1967. Ptnr. Richards, Harris & Hubbard, Dallas, 1970-82, Baker, Mills & Glast, Dallas, 1982-90; sr. ptnr. Baker & Botts, Dallas, 1990—; adj. prof. So. Meth. U. Law Sch., 1994—. Bd. dirs. Dallas Legal Svcs. Project, 1972-75. Fellow Tex. Bar, Dallas Bar; mem. ABA, Tex. State Jr. Bar Assn. (treas. 1975, dir.), Dallas Jr. Bar Assn. (pres. 1971, Outstanding Young Lawyer award 1975), Dallas Bar Assn. (bd. dirs. 1983-85). Methodist. Home: 5316 Montrose Dr Dallas TX 75209 Office: Baker & Botts 800 Trammell Crow Ctr 2001 Ross Ave Dallas TX 75201-8001

MILLS, JOHN JAMES, research director; b. Motherwell, Scotland, May 12, 1939; came to U.S., 1966; s. John Thompson King and Esther Houston (Leitch) M.; m. Dorothea Becker, Mar. 27, 1971; children: Jennifer, Julia, Janine, Ian. BS in Physics, U. Glasgow, Scotland, 1961; PhD in Applied Physics, U. Durham, Eng., 1965. Rsch. fellow dept. elec. engring. Imperial Coll., London, 1964-66; from scientist to sr. scientist IIT Rsch. Inst., Chgo., 1966-71; sr. fellow Inst. Silicatforschung der Fraunhofergesellschaft, Fed. Republic of Germany, 1972-73; sect. leader Inst. Werkstofftechnic, Rosenthal AG, Fed. Republic of Germany, 1973-75; sr. scientist Martin Marietta Labs., Balt., 1975-79, mgr. aluminum fabrication R&D, 1979-84, mgr. mfg. tech. R&D, 1984-88, project dir., 1988-90; dir. Automation & Robotics Rsch. Inst., U. Tex. at Arlington, 1990—, Agile Aerospace Mfg. Rsch. Ctr. Automation/Robotics Rsch., 1994—; bd. dirs. Coalition of Intelligent Mfg. Systems, Washington. Mem. editorial bd. Agility & Global Competition; contbr. chpt. to book, articles to profl. jours. Recipient rsch. fellowship British Oxygen Co., 1964-66, A. von Humboldt fellowship Inst. Silicatforschung der Fraunhofergesellschaft, 1972-73, Outstanding Achievement award Martin Marietta Labs., 1981. Mem. ASME (at-large mem. mfg. tech. operating group bd. 1993-96), Soc. Mfg. Engring., Am. Soc. Metals, Am. Inst. Mining and Metall. Engring., Am. Phys. Soc., Ft. Worth C. of C. (bd. dirs. East Area Coun. 1991-97). Avocations: wine making, rowing, cabinet making. Office: Automation and Robotics Rsch 7300 Jack Newell Blvd S Fort Worth TX 76118-7115

MILLS, JON K., psychologist, educator, philosopher. AS in Criminal Justice, Parkland Coll., 1985; BS in Psychology with honors, So. Ill. U., 1987, MA in Rehab. Counseling with honors, 1988; PsyD, Ill. Sch. Profl. Psychology, 1992; postgrad., Vanderbilt U., 1994-96. Cert. rehab. counselor. Crisis intervention trainer, hotline supr. Synergy Crisis Intervention Agy., Carbondale, Ill., 1986-87, individual and family counselor, 1987; individual and group therapist Evaluation and Devel. Ctr., Carbondale, Ill., 1987-88, Youth Options: Substance Abuse Svcs., Marion, Ill., 1988; intern Jackson County Community Mental Health Ctr., Carbondale, 1988; diagnostic extern Elgin (Ill.) State Mental Health Ctr., 1989-90; staff therapist Davis Ctr. for Emotional Devel., Glen Ellyn, Ill., 1989-90; therapy extern Roosevelt U., Chgo., 1990—; counselor coord. Copley Weight Mgmt. Copley Meml. Hosp., Aurora, Ill., 1989—; predoctoral intern Michael Reese Hosp. and Med. Ctr., Chgo., 1991; asst. prof. dept. psychology Lewis U., Romeoville, Ill., 1992—; staff psychologist Inst. for Behavioral Svcs., Oak Brook, Ill., 1993—; teaching asst. for tests and measurements Rehab. Inst., So. Ill. U., 1987-88; teaching asst. Ill. Sch. of Profl. Psychology, Chgo., 1989-90; adj. faculty dept. of psychology Waubonsee Community Coll., Sugar Grove, Ill., 1990—, Coll. of Dupage, Naperville, 1989—; faculty mem. social sci. dept. Joliet (Ill.) Jr. Coll., 1990—. Contbr. numerous articles to profl. jours. Vol. Crisis Hotline Jackson County Community Mental Health Ctr., Carbondale, 1987. Tchg. fellow Vanderbilt U. Dept. Philosophy, Nashville, 1994—; Fulbright scholar U. Toronto, York U., 1996-97, others. Mem. APA, Ill. Group Psychotherapy Soc., Chgo. Assn. for Psychoanalytic Psychology, Phi Kappa Phi, Gamma Beta Phi. Avocations: vocal, guitar, harmonica. Home: 2112 Augusta Dr Springfield IL 62704-3103

MILLS, KATHLEEN CLAIRE, anthropology and mathematics educator; b. Pitts., Dec. 27, 1948; d. Clair I. and Ruth (McDowell) Wilson; m. William G. Mills, May 27, 1978; 1 child, David Lee. AS, Kilgore Coll., 1968; BS, Met. State Coll., Denver, 1982; MA in Secondary Edn., U. Colo., 1987, MA in Anthropology, 1989. Mem. staff U.S. Geol. Survey, Denver, 1980-82; computer application specialist Petroleum Info., Englewood, Colo., 1982-83; entry level geologist La. Land and Exploration, Denver, 1983-86; prof. anthropology and math. C.C. of Aurora, 1987—, GED coord., 1996—; prof. anthropology Red Rocks C.C., 1994—; excavation supr. Caesarea Maritima, Israel, 1989—. Drafter U.S. Oil and Gas Map, 1981. Mem. Am. Schs. Oriental Rsch., Denver Natural History Mus., Archaeol. Inst. Am. Colo. Archaeol. Soc., Nat. Geog. Soc. Avocations: bicycling, reading, hiking, travel. Home: 7946 E Mexico Ave Denver CO 80231-5687 Office: Community Coll Aurora 16000 E Centretech Pky Aurora CO 80011-9057

MILLS, KEVIN LEE, government executive; b. Frederick, Md., Oct. 21, 1951; s. John Lee and Doris Jean (Comer) M.; m. Karen June Davis, Dec. 30, 1972; children: Colin Walter, Elizabeth Anne. BS in Polit. Sci. and Econs., Frostburg (Md.) State U., 1973; MS in Tech. Mgmt., Am. U., 1979; PhD in Info. Tech., George Mason U., 1996. Sr. computer analyst System Devel. Corp., McLean, Va., 1976-81; project mgr. Tesdata Systems Corp., McLean, 1981-82; computer scientist Nat. Bur. of Stds., Gaithersburg, Md., 1982-84; group leader Nat. Bur. of Stds., Gaithersburg, 1984-87; divsn. chief Nat. Inst. Stds. and Tech., Gaithersburg, 1987-95; program mgr. Def. Advanced Rsch. Projects Agy., Arlington, Va., 1996—; adj. faculty George Mason U., 1996—; cons. in field, 1980-82. Contbr. articles to profl. jours. Capt. USMC, 1972-78. Mem. IEEE (sr.), Assn. for Computing Machinery. Avocations: hiking, writing, reading.

MILLS, KEVIN PAUL, lawyer; b. Detroit, Oct. 1, 1961; s. Raymond Eugene and Helene Audry M.; m. Holly Beth Fechner, June 15, 1986. BA, Oberlin Coll., 1983; JD, U. Mich., 1987. Bar: Mich. 1988. High sch. tchr., asst. dir. summer environ. inst. The Storm King Sch., Cornwall-on-Hudson, N.Y., 1983-84; staff atty. E. Mich. Environ. Action Coun., Birmingham, Mich., 1987-90; assoc. Tucker & Rolf, Southfield, Mich., 1988-89; sr. atty., pollution prevention program dir. Environ. Def. Fund, Washington, 1990—; low-level radioactive waste cons. State Mich., Lansing, 1988; founder Pollution Prevention Alliance, 1991, co-founder Great Printer's Project, 1992—, staff to co-chair eco-efficiency Pres. Coun. Sustainable Devel., 1993-95, Auto Pollution Prevention adv. group, 1994—, EPA Auto Mfr. CSI, 1994—; adv. bd. Nat. Pollution Prevention Roundtable, 1996—; mem. Nat. Adv. Coun. on Environ. Policy and Tech., 1997—. Contbr. articles to profl. jours. Bd. dirs., v.p. Ea. Mich. Environ. Action Coun., Birmingham, 1985-87; pres. Environ. Law Soc., Ann Arbor, Mich., 1986-87. Mem. State Bar Mich. Office: Environ Def Fund 1875 Connecticut Ave NW Washington DC 20009-5747

MILLS, LAWRENCE, lawyer, business and transportation consultant; b. Salt Lake City, Aug. 15, 1932; s. Samuel L. and Beth (Neilson) M. BS, U. Utah, 1955, JD, 1956. Bar: Utah 1956, ICC 1961, U.S. Supreme Ct. 1963. With W.S. Hatch Co. Inc., Woods Cross, Utah, 1947-89, gen. mgr., 1963-89, v.p., 1970-89, also dir.; bd. dirs. Nat. Tank Truck Carriers, Inc., Washington, 1963—, pres., 1974-75, chmn. bd., 1975-76; mem. motor carrier adv. com. Utah State Dept. Transp., 1979—; keynote speaker Rocky Mountain Safety Suprs. Conf., 1976; mem. expedition to Antartica, 1996, Titanic Expedition, 1996. Contbr. articles to legal publs. Del. to County and State Convs., Utah, 1970-72; v.p. Utah Safety Coun., 1979-82, bd. dirs., 1979—, pres., 1983-84; mem. Utah Gov's Adv. Com. on Small Bus.; capt. Easter Seal Telethon, 1989, 90; state vice chmn. High Frontier, 1987—; mem. adv. com. Utah State Indsl. Commn., 1988—, chmn. com. studying health care cost containment and reporting requirements 1990—; mem. expdn. to Antarctica, 1996, Titanic '96 expedition. Recipient Safety Dir. award Nat. Tank Carriers Co., 1967, Outstanding Svc. and Contbn. award, 1995, Trophy award W.S. Hatch Co., 1975, Disting. Svc. award Utah State Indsl. Commn., 1992, Outstanding Svc. award Utah Safety Coun., 1994. Mem. Salt Lake County Bar Assn., Utah Motor Transport Assn. (dir. 1967—, pres. 1974-76, Outstanding Achievement Award 1989), Utah Hwy. Users Assn. (dir. 1981—), Indsl. Rels. Coun. (dir. 1974—), Salt Lake City C. of C., U.S. Jaycees (life Senator 1969—, ambassador 1977—, pres. Utah Senate 1979-80, Henry Giessenbier fellow 1989), Nat. Petroleum Coun., Utah Associated Gen. Contractors (assoc. 1975-77, 88—), Silver Tank Club, Hillsdale Coll. President's Club, Traveler's Century Club. Home and Office: 77 Edgecombe Dr Salt Lake City UT 84103-2219 *Personal philosophy: Excessive government regulation stifles individual initiative. We should learn from the downfall of communism.*

MILLS, LINDA S., public relations executive; b. San Antonio, June 26, 1951; d. Frank M. and Betty A. (Young) M. BA, St. Mary's U., 1971. Asst. dir. Paseo Del Rio Assn., San Antonio, 1971-74; mktg. officer Frost Nat. Bank, San Antonio, 1974-79; account exec. Fleishman-Hillard Inc., St. Louis, 1979-81, v.p., sr. ptnr., 1981-85, exec. v.p., sr. ptnr., 1985—, dir. corp. planning, 1986—; bd. dirs. Fleishman-Hillard U.K. Ltd., London, Fleishman-Hillard France, Paris. Mem. adv. bd. St. John's Mercy Med. Ctr. Mem. Pub. Relations Soc. Am., Noonday Club. Office: Fleishman Hillard Inc 200 N Broadway Saint Louis MO 63102-2730

MILLS, LISTON OURY, theology educator; b. Wilmington, N.C., Aug. 7, 1928; s. Leonard Liston and Ruby Preston (Oury) M.; m. Jennie Ellen Windsor, Dec. 28, 1962; 1 child, Sarah Elizabeth. BA, Davidson Coll., 1950; BD, So. Bapt. Theol. Sem., 1953, ThM, 1957, ThD, 1964. Ordained to ministry So. Bapt. Conv., 1953. Asst. pastor 5th Ave. Bapt. Ch., Huntington, W.Va., 1957-58; pastor Kent (Ind.) Bapt. Ch., 1960-62; successively instr., asst. prof., assoc. prof. Vanderbilt U. Div. Sch., Nashville, Oberlin Alumni prof. pastoral theology and counseling, 1962—, Alexander Heard disting. svc. prof., 1991-92, acting dean, 1989; vis. prof. Earlham Grad. Sch. Theology, Richmond, Ind., 1965, St. Luke's Sch. Theology, Sewanee, Tenn., 1972, 73, 74, 85, So. Bapt. Theol. Sem., 1980, Lexington (Ky.) Theol. Sem., 1981; vis. lectr. Yale U. Div. Sch., New Haven, 1969; cons. Tenn. Dept. Mental Health, Nashville, 1964-65, Tenn. Personnel Dept., Nashville, 1967-68, VA Med. Ctr., Nashville, 1972—, Chief of VA Chaplains, Washington, 1975, 78; Ingersoll lectr. Harvard U., Cambridge, Mass., 1971; Upperman lectr. Tenn. Technol. U., Cookeville, 1973; Stringfellow lectr. Drake U., Des Moines, 1974. Editor: Perspectives on Death, 1969; assoc. editor: Dictionary of Pastoral Care and Counseling, 1990; editor Pastoral Psychology, 1974-82; contbr. articles to jours. Bd. dirs. Family and Children's Svc., Nashville, 1978-81, Tenn. Pastoral Counseling Ctrs., Nashville, 1984-91, 93—, St. Thomas Home Health Care, Nashville, 1986-89. 1st lt. U.S. Army, 1953-55. Recipient Obert Kempson award for disting. svc. S.E. Region Assn. for Clin. Pastoral Edn., 1994; named Alumni Educator of Yr., Vanderbilt U., 1984, Pastoral Theologian of Yr., Pastoral Psychology Jour., 1994; fellow So. Bapt. Theol. Sem., 1959-62, Assn. Theol. Schs., 1968-69. Mem. Soc. for Sci. Study of Religion, Assn. for Profl. Edn. for Ministry (pres. 1972-74), Assn. for Clin. Pastoral Edn., Soc. for Pastoral Theology, Omicron Delta Kappa. Office: Vanderbilt U Div Sch Nashville TN 37240

MILLS, LOIS JEAN, company executive, former legislative aide, former education educator; b. Chgo., Oct. 20, 1939; d. Martin J. and Annabelle M. (Hrabik) Rademacher; m. Frederick V. Mills, Dec. 1, 1974; children: Todd, Susan, Randal, Merre, Mollie, Michael, Mark (dec.). BS in Edn., Ill. State U., Normal, 1962, MS in Edn., 1969. Lectr. elem. curriculum Ill. State U., 1973-90; in-svc. advisor for elem., gifted, critical thinking and study skills, coop. learning Title I State Bd. Edn., Springfield, Ill., 1969-90; elem. tchr., supr. Metcalf Lab. Sch. Ill. State U., 1962-72; legis. aide to Asst. Majority Leader Senator John Maitland, Jr., Ill. Gen. Assembly, 1990-95; pres., ptnr. Mills Design Assocs., 1996—; mem. state rep. Dan Rutherford's house task force for statute repeal, 1995—, adv. roundtable, 1995—, legis. task force for cmty. residential svcs. deaf adults, 1995—; campaign coord. Asst. Majority Leader Senator John Maitland, Jr., 1995—; county campaign coord. for Ill. Comptroller Loleta Didrickson, 1994—. Contbr. articles to profl. jours. Pres. Leadership Ill., 1994—, pres.-elect, 1993-94; past pres. governing bd. Lake Bloomington Assn., v.p., 1993-94, pres., 1994-95; mem. mgmt. com. McLean County 21st Century commn., 1991-92, vice chair cmty. rels., 1991-92; commr. McLean County Regional Planning commn., vice chair 1994-95; charter bd. govs. Ill. Lincoln Excellence in Pub. Svc. Series, 1994—, other civic activities; mem. Ill. steering com. Beijing-UN Women's Conf. One Yr. Later, 1996. Recipient Exemplary Tchr. awards Ill. State U. Student Elem. Edn. Bd., Women of Distinction award YWCA of McLean County. Mem. NAFE, Ill. State U. Alumni Assn. (bd. dirs. 1982—, nat. pres. 1992-94, past nat. pres. 1994—), McLean County Rep. Women's Club (v.p. 1986, pres. 1987, past pres. 1988), Ill. Rep. Committeewoman's Roundtable, Ill. Fedn. Rep. Women, Nat. Fedn. Rep. Women, Internat. Platform Assn. Home: K-162 Lake Bloomington RR 2 Box 60A Hudson IL 61748-9414

MILLS, MICHAEL JAMES, architect; b. Streator, Ill., Feb. 18, 1951; s. Harry Nelson and Ruth Ludia (Piel) M.; m. Kathryn Louise Brewington, June 6, 1974 (div. Feb. 1977); m. Beverly Jane Ballard, Mar. 14, 1981; children: Kevin Charles, Jeffrey Ross, Caroline Ruth. BA, Princeton U., 1973; cert., ICCROM, 1979; MS, Columbia U., 1980. Registered architect, N.J., S.C., N.Y., D.C., Pa., Mich.; lic. profl. planner, N.J. Draftsman John Milner Assocs., West Chester, Pa., 1973-74, John Diehl & Assocs., Princeton, N.J., 1974-75; project mgr. Heritage Studies, Princeton, N.J., 1975-76; draftsman Short and Ford Architects, Princeton, N.J., 1976-78; apprentice architect The Ehrenkrantz Group, N.Y.C., 1979-80; apprentice architect Short & Ford & Ptnrs., Princeton, 1980-83, assoc., 1983-87; partner Short & Ford & Ptnrs. (name changed to Ford, Farewell, Mills and Gatsch Architects 1992), Princeton, 1987-92, 1992—; cons. Burlington County Hist. Dist. Commn., Burlington, N.J., 1983-93. Contbr. articles to profl. jours. Chmn. Hopewell Planning Bd., 1985-89. Excellence in Architecture N.J. Soc. Architects, 1989, 92, hon. mention, 1983. Mem. AIA, Assn. Preservtion Tech., Nat. Trust for Hist. Preservation, N.J. Soc. Architects, U.S.-Internat. Coun. on Monuments and Sites. Presbyterian. Avocations: guitar, photography, tennis. Office: Ford Farewell Mills and Gatsch Architects 864 Mapleton Rd Princeton NJ 08540-9538

MILLS, MIKE, popular musician; b. Macon, Ga.. Student, U. Ga. Bass guitarist R.E.M., 1980—. Rec. albums include Chronic Town, 1982, Murmur, 1983 (Gold record, Rolling Stone Critics Poll Best Album of Yr. 1983), Reckoning, 1984 (Gold record), Fables of the Reconstruction, 1985 (Gold record), Life's Rich Pageant, 1986 (Gold record), Dead Letter Office, 1987 (Gold record), Document, 1987 (Platinum record), Eponymous, 1988 (Platinum record), Green, 1988 (Platinum record), Out of Time, 1991 (Platinum record, 7 Grammy nominations, Best Pop Vocal Group Grammy award 1992), Automatic for the People, 1993 (4 Grammy nominations), Monster, 1994; appeared on Robbie Robertson's album, Storyville, 1991; perfomed on "Backbeat" soundtrack, 1994, Murmur, 1995, New Adventures in Hi-Fi, 1996. Named Rolling Stong Artist of Yr., 1992. *

MILLS, NANCY ANNE, elementary education educator; b. Madisonville, Ky., Oct. 2, 1937; d. Leslie Owen and Ruby A. (Baker) Hawkins; m. Orton Leroy Mills, May 11, 1957; children: Charles Leroy, Roy Leslie. BS in Edn., Ind. U., South Bend, 1970, MS in Edn., 1972; Edn. Specialist dergree, Ind. U., 1978. Cert. elem. tchr., Ind. Tchr. elem. South Bend Schs., 1972—; gifted cadre' Purdue U-For Ind., Lafayette, 1988—; presenter workshops; cons. econ. edn.; started gifted program South Bend Schs. Chmn. new ch. com. Nazarene Ch., South Bend, 1990; supr. students with Student Exch., France, 1991-96. Named Woman of Yr., Profl. and Bus. Womans Club, 1989; Inst. for Chem. Edn. grantee, 1989. Mem. Ind. Coun. Econ. Edn. (cons. 1987—, Tchr. of Yr. for State of Ind. 1992), Delta Kappa Gamma. Avocations: sewing, travel. Home: 16320 Wellington Pky Granger IN 46530-8309 Office: Muessel Sch 1213 California Ave South Bend IN 46628-2701

MILLS, NANCY STEWART, chemistry educator; b. Osceola, Nebr., Mar. 31, 1950; d. Robert Lees and Margaret Eva (Stewart) M.; m. Mark Alan Hurd, Aug. 20, 1977; children: Caroline Margaret Mills Hurd, William Clark Mills Hurd. BA, Grinnell Coll., 1972; PhD, U. Ariz., 1976. Asst. prof. Carleton Coll., Northfield, Minn., 1977-79; asst. prof. Trinity U., San Antonio, 1979-83, assoc. prof., 1983-89, prof., 1979—, chmn. chemistry dept., 1990-93; mem. dept. rev. team Bowdoin Coll., Brunswick, Maine, 1986, Macalester Coll., St. Paul, 1989, Albion Coll., 1991, Hamilton Coll., 1996; mem. Coun. on Undergrad. Rsch., 1991—, chair chemistry divsn., 1996—. Contbr. articles to profl. jours. Grantee NSF, Welch Found., Petroleum Rsch. Fund, Rsch. Corp., 1977—; Camille and Henry Dreyfus Found. scholar, 1994; recipient Outstanding Teaching and Campus Leadership award Sears Roebuck Found., 1990, Z.T. Scott Fellowship for outstanding teaching Trinity U., 1992. Mem. AAUP, Sigma Xi. Avocations: backpacking, reading, sewing, singing. Home: 137 Alta Ave San Antonio TX 78209-4508 Office: Trinity U 715 Stadium Dr San Antonio TX 78212-3104

MILLS, OLAN, II, photography company executive; b. 1930; married. Grad., Princeton U., 1952. With Olan Mills, Inc., Chattanooga, 1950—, now chmn., sec., also bd. dirs. Office: Olan Mills Inc PO Box 23456 Chattanooga TN 37422 also: 4325 Amnicola Hwy Chattanooga TN 37406-1014*

MILLS, PATRICIA JAGENTOWICZ, political philosophy educator, writer; b. Newark, Mar. 18, 1944; d. Alexander A. and Louise A. (Breunig) Jagentowicz; 1 child, Holland Mills. BA, Rutgers U., 1973; MA, SUNY, Stony Brook, 1975; PhD, York U., Toronto, Ont., Can., 1984. Lectr. U. Toronto, 1984-85, vis. scholar, 1985-86, asst. prof. philosophy, 1986-88; asst. prof. polit. theory U. Mass., Amherst, 1988-91, assoc. prof. polit. theory, 1991—; lectr. philosophy dept. Smith Coll., spring 1992; manuscript referee Social Scis. and Humanities Rsch. Coun. Can., 1985-86, 87-88, 91-92, Polity: Jour. of Northeastern Polit. Sci. Assn., 1990, 91; invited spkr. NEH seminar, Mt. Holyoke Coll., 1992, U. Pitts., 1993, Antigone Conf., SUNY Buffalo, 1997, Coll. Holy Cross, 1991, New Sch. for Social Rsch., 1990. Author: Woman, Nature, and Psyche, 1987; editor: Feminist Interpretations of G.W.F. Hegel, 1996; author, contbr.: (book chpts.) The Sexism of Social and Political Theory: Women and Reproduction from Plato to Nietzsche, 1979, Ethnicity in a Technological Age, 1988, Taking Our Time: Feminist Perspectives on Temporality, 1989, Renewing the Earth: The Promise of Social Ecology, 1990, The Future of Continental Philosophy and the Politics of Difference, 1991, Ecological Feminist Philosophies, 1996; contbr. articles to profl. jours. Dir. Drop-In Ctr., Newark, 1972-73; mem. N.J. Abortion Project, 1971-73; mem. Fortune Soc., N.J., 1972; grassroots organizer against the war in Vietnam, N.J., 1970-71; grassroots organizer women's movement, N.J. and N.Y., 1971-73. Recipient Disting. Tchg. award Pi Sigma Alpha Honor Soc., 1996-97, Disting. Faculty award Delt Lambda chpt., U. Mass., 1997; postdoctoral fellow Social Scis. and Humanities Rsch. Coun. Can., 1983-85; scholar York U., 1975; faculty grantee for tchg. U. Mass., 1991-92. Mem. Am. Philos. Assn. (conf. presenter 1995 meeting), Soc. for Phenomenology and Existential Philosophy (presenter conf. papers 1988, 91, 92), Hegel Soc. Am., Soc. for Women in Philosophy, Nat. Women's Studies Assn. Avocation: Aikido. Office: U Mass Thompson Hall Dept Polit Sci Amherst MA 01003

MILLS, PETER RICHARD, advertising executive; b. Nanango, Queensland, Australia, Mar. 28, 1939; s. Frederick Richard and Muriel Estelle (Fischer) M.; m. Nicole Poulin, July 2, 1982; children: Duncan, David, Alexander, Maxine. Student, York U., Toronto, 1964-65. Copy/contact Jackson Wain Publicity Ltd., Brisbane, Australia, 1957-60; copywriter T. Eaton Co., Toronto, Can., 1960-62; bus. mgr. Southam Publs. Inc., Toronto, 1962-66; account exec. J. Walter Thompson, Vancouver, Toronto, 1966-70; gen. mgr. J. Walter Thompson, Montreal, Can., 1970-75; chief oper. office J. Walter Thompson, Toronto, Can., 1975-79; gen. mgr. J. Walter Thompson, N.Y.C., 1979-82; chmn., chief exec. officer J. Walter Thompson, Australia, 1982-88; pres., chief exec. officer Comcore/BBDO, Toronto, Can., 1986-91; pres., No. Am. div. BBDO Worldwide Inc., Southfield, Mich., 1991-93; chmn., pres., CEO Roy Ross Comms. Inc., Bloomfield Hills, Mich., 1993—. Mem. Nat. Yacht Club, Toronto. Avocations: scuba diving, sailing, skiing, reading. Office: Roy Ross Comms Inc 100 Bloomfield Hills Pkwy Bloomfield Hills MI 48304-2949

MILLS, RICHARD HENRY, federal judge; b. Beardstown, Ill., July 19, 1929; s. Myron Epler and Helen Christine (Greve) M.; m. Rachel Ann Keagle, June 16, 1962; children: Jonathan K., Daniel Cass. BA, Ill. Coll., 1951; JD, Mercer U., 1957; LLM, U. Va., 1982. Bar: Ill. 1957, U.S. Dist. Ct. Ill. 1958, U.S. Ct. Appeals 1959, U.S. Ct. Mil. Appeals 1963, U.S. Supreme Ct. 1963. Legal advisor Ill. Youth Commn., 1958-60; state's atty. Cass County, Virginia, Ill., 1960-64; judge Ill. 8th Jud. Cir., Virginia, 1966-76, Ill. 4th Dist. Appellate Ct., Springfield, Ill., 1976-85, U.S. Dist. Ct. (cen. dist.) Ill., Springfield, 1985—; adj. prof. So. Ill. U. Sch. Medicine, 1985—; mem. adv. bd. Nat. Inst. Corrections, Washington, 1984-88, Ill. Supreme Ct. Rules Com., Chgo., 1963-85. Contbr. articles to profl. jours. Pres. Abraham Lincoln coun. Boy Scouts Am., 1978-80. With U.S. Army, 1952-54, Korea, col. res.; maj. gen. Ill. Militia. Recipient George Washington Honor medal Freedoms Found., 1969, 73, 75, 82, Disting. Eagle Scout Boy Scouts Am., 1985. Fellow Am. Bar Found.; mem. ABA (joint com. profl. sanctions), Nat. Conf. Fed. Trial Judges (exec. com.), Ill. Bar Assn., Chgo. Bar Assn., Cass County Bar Assn. (pres. 1962-64, 75-76), Sangamon County Bar Assn., 7th Cir. Bar Assn., Am. Law Inst., Fed. Judges Assn., Army and Navy Club (Washington), Sangamo Club, Masons (33 degree). Republican. Home: 2112 Augusta Dr Springfield IL 62704-3103 Office: US Dist Ct 600 E Monroe St Ste 319 Springfield IL 62701-1626

MILLS, RICHARD P., state agency administrator. BA with honors, Middlebury Coll., 1966; MA in Am. History, Columbia U., 1967, MBA, 1975, EdD, 1977. Planning assoc. N.J. Dept. of Edn., 1975-78, dir. policy analysis, 1978-80, dep. asst. commr., 1980-82, spl. asst. to the commr., 1982-84; spl. asst. to Gov. Thomas H. Kean of N.J., 1984-88; commr. of edn. State of Vt., 1988-95, State of N.Y., 1995—; adj. asst. prof. Columbia Univ. Tchrs. Coll., 1977; adj. assoc. prof. Rider Coll., N.J., 1979; cons. task force to oversee fiscal reform in Newark, 1975; tchr. The Dalton Sch., N.Y.C., 1967-71, Elizabeth Seeger Sch., N.Y.C., 1971-73; mem. Carnegie Task Force on Learning in the Primary Grades; chair mgmt. group Nat. Alliance for Restructuring Edn.; bd. New Stds. Project; mem. bd. Nat. Ctr. on Edn. and the Economy. Contbr. articles to profl. jours. U.S. rep. to standing com. European Ministers of Edn., 1987. Office: Univ of the State of NY NY State Edn Dept Edn Bldg Washington Ave Albany NY 12234*

MILLS, ROBERT A., lawyer; b. Kansas City, Mo., Jan. 20, 1934; s. William N. and Mary Aileene (Arnold) M.; m. Jan. 14, 1956 (div. Apr. 1978); children: Thomas B., James A., John M.; m. Anita Hickey, Feb. 12, 1983; 1 child, Christopher Robert. BS, U. Mo., 1955; LLB, Washington U., St. Louis, 1960. Bar: Calif. Trial atty. U.S. Dept. Justice, Washington, 1960-62; assoc. Lewis & Roca, Phoenix, 1962-65, McCutchen Doyle Brown & Enersen, San Francisco, 1965-70; ptnr. McCutchen Doyle Brown & Enersen, 1970—; Editorial cons. Calif. Legal Systems, Wills and Trusts, 1983-95. Served to 1st lt. U.S. Army, 1955-57. Fellow Am. Coll. Trust & Estate Counsel; mem. ABA, State Bar of Calif. (chmn. probate and trust law com. 1975-76), Fed. Bar Assn. (chpt. pres. 1964), Internat. Acad. Estate and Trust Law (Pres. 1988-90), The Pacific-Union Club, Olympic Club of San Francisco. Home: 15 Rancheria Rd Kentfield CA 94904 Office: McCutchen Doyle Brown & Enersen 3 Embarcadero Ctr San Francisco CA 94111-4003

MILLS, ROBERT HARRY, church administrator; b. Moncton, N.B., Can., Mar. 3, 1933; s. Harry Earl and Evelyn Perl (Cosman) M.; m. Karen Barbara Keirstead, Dec. 26, 1953 (dec. June 1991); children: Deborah Karen, Michael Robert, Stephen Gordon, David Richard, Katrina Marie; m. Helga Kutz-Harder, July 1, 1995. BA, Mt. Allison U., Sackville, N.B., 1954; diploma in theology, Pine Hill Divinity Hall, Halifax, N.S., Can., 1956. Ordained to ministry United Ch. Can., 1956. Minister religion Port Mouton (N.S.) Pastoral Charge, 1956-59, Tatamagouche (N.S.) Pastoral Charge, 1959-65, St. Andrew's United Ch., Wolfville, N.S., 1965-67, Bridgewater (N.S.) United Ch., 1967-75, Wesley United Ch., St. John's, Nfld., Can., 1975-82, Fairview United Ch., Halifax, N.S., 1982-89; exec. sec. maritime conf. United Ch. Can., Sackville, 1989-95; interim gen. sec. Can. Coun. Chs., Toronto, Ont., 1995—; sec. settlement com. maritime conf. United Ch. Can., 1963-67, chmn., 1967-71, chmn. transfer com. gen. coun., 1970-71, chmn. staff com. Newfound and Labrador conf., 1978-82, sec. Halifax Presbyn., 1983-87. Avocation: music. Office: 40 St Clair Ave E Ste 201, Toronto, ON Canada M4T 1M9

MILLS, ROBERT LAURENCE, physicist, educator; b. Englewood, N.J., Apr. 15, 1927; s. Frederick Cecil and Dorothy Katherine (Clarke) M.; m. Elise Ackley, July 21, 1948; children—Katherine, Edward, Jonathan, Susan, Dorothy. A.B., Columbia Coll., 1948; B.A., Cambridge (Eng.) U., 1950, M.A., 1954; Ph.D., Columbia, 1955. Research asso. Brookhaven Nat. Lab., Upton, N.Y., 1953-55; mem. Sch. Math. Inst. for Advanced Study, Princeton U., 1955-56; asst. prof. physics Ohio State U., Columbus, 1956-59, assoc. prof., 1959-62, prof., 1962-95, prof. emeritus, 1995—. Author: Propagators for Many-Particle Systems, 1969, Space, Time and Quanta, 1994. Recipient (with C. N. Yang) Rumford prize for devel. of generalized gauge invariant field theory (Yang-Mills Theory), 1980; Fulbright scholar Republic of Ireland, 1995-96. Mem. Am. Phys. Soc., AAUP, Fedn. Am. Scientists. Home: 2825 Neil Ave Apt 816 Columbus OH 43202-2077

MILLS, ROBERT LEE, president emeritus; b. Erlanger, Ky., Nov. 13, 1916; s. John Clifford and Dixie Lee (Morris) M.; m. Mildred Sizer, June 24, 1942; children: Robert Lee, Dixie Louise, Barbara Jean. A.B. in Math. and Physics, U. Ky., 1938, M.A. in Edn.l. Adminstrn, 1941, Ed.D., 1951; LLD, William Jewell Coll., 1971. Tchr. Covington (Ky.) pub. schs., 1938-41; head hydraulics br. Air Force Tech. Sch., Lincoln, Nebr., 1942-44; mem. supervisory staff electromagnetic plant Oak Ridge, 1944-48; research asst. U. Ky., Lexington, 1948-51; dean admissions, registrar U. Ky., 1954-57; dir. research, head bur. adminstrn. and finance Ky. Dept. Edn., 1951-54; chmn. dept. ednl. adminstrn. U. Tex., Austin, 1957-59; pres. Georgetown (Ky.) Coll., 1959-78, chancellor, 1978-86, pres. emeritus, 1987—; exec. sec. Ky. Adv. Commn. Ednl. Policy, 1952-54; v.p. Ky. Assn. Colls. and Secondary Schs., 1962-63, exec. com., 1959-64, pres., 1963-64; chmn. exec. com. Ky. Ind. Coll. Found.; mem. Ky. Commn. on Higher Edn., 1967-70, Ky. Govt. Council, 1968-72; adviser Texas Assn. Sch. Bds., 1957-59. Contbr. articles to profl. jours. Cons. Pres.' Com., White House Conf. Edn., 1955; mem. Ky. Devel. Council, 1961-65, Ky. Constn. Revision Assembly, 1964-66. Recipient Distinguished Alumni award U. Ky., 1963, Centennial award, 1964. Mem. Nat., Ky. edn. assns., Newcomen Soc., So. Assn. Bapt. Colls. (pres. 1965-66), Bapt. World Alliance (mem. exec. com. 1965-70, chmn. men's dept. 1965-67), So. Assn. Colls. and Schs. (commn. on colls. 1971-77), Kappa Delta Pi, Phi Delta Kappa, Phi Kappa Tau. Democrat. Baptist. Lodge: Kiwanis.

MILLS, RUSSELL ANDREW, newspaper publisher; b. St. Thomas, Ont., Can., July 14, 1944; s. Gerald Armond and Phyllis Marie (Hulse) M.; m. Judith Elizabeth Zimmerman, Mar. 25, 1967; children: Lara, Colin, Patrick. BA, U. Western Ont., London, 1967, MA, 1968. Reporter London (Ont.) Free Press, 1964-67; city editor The Oshawa (Ont.) Times, 1970; asst. city editor, night editor, asst. mng. editor The Ottawa (Ont.) Citizen, 1971-85, exec. editor, 1975-76, editor, 1977-84, gen.mgr., 1984-86, pub., 1986-89, pres., publ., 1992—; pres. Southam Newspaper Group, Toronto, Ont., 1989-92. Office: Ottawa Citizen, 1101 Baxter Rd, Ottawa, ON Canada K2C 3M4

MILLS, S. LOREN, product safety manager, engineer; b. Manassas, Va., Oct. 31, 1946; s. James Bryan and Charlatta Ruth (Holland) M.; m. Nancy Jane Mathews, Apr. 7, 1979; children: Tyler, Mitchell, Molly. BS, Western Mich. U., Kalamazoo, 1975. Cert. product safety mgr. Internat. Product Safety Mgmt. Cert. Bd. Sr. staff engr. Clark Equipment Co., Battle Creek, Mich., 1966-86; engring. mgr. Hayes Machine Co., Marshall, Mich., 1986-88; product safety cons. Mills Cons., Marshall, Mich., 1988-89; product safety mgr. Van Dorn Demag Corp., Strongsville, Ohio, 1989—; v.p., bd. dirs. Insulation Wholesale Supply Co., Battle Creek, 1981—. Co-author: Product Safety Management Handbook, 1994. Mem. Nat. Safety Coun., 1995—. With U.S. Army, 1968-74. Mem. ASME (ANSI B56.1 stds. devel. com. 1981—), Soc. Plastics Industry (chmn. risk mgmt. com. 1992—), Assn. Mfg. Tech. (mem. capital goods stds. coalition U.S. Tag ISO/TC199 com. 1992—), Am. Soc. Plastics Industry (mem. ANSI B151.1 stds. devel. com. 1989—, ANSI B151.27 stds. devel. com. 1991—), Nat. Elec. Mfrs. Assn. (ANSI Z535 stds. devel. com. 1991—, ANSI/NFPA 79 std. devel. com. 1997—), Soc. Automotive Engrs., Am. Soc. Safety Engrs., Nat. Safety Coun. Avocations: tennis, boating, fishing. Home: 19813 Winding Trl Strongsville OH 44136-8741 Office: Van Dorn Demag Corp 11794 Alameda Dr Strongsville OH 44136-3011

MILLS, SAMUEL DAVIS, JR., professional football player; b. Neptune, N.J., June 3, 1959. Student, Montclair State U. With Cleve. Browns, 1981, Toronto Argonauts, CFL, 1982, Phila. Stars, USFL, 1982; linebacker New Orleans Saints, 1986-95, Carolina Panthers, 1995—. Named USFL All-Star Team Inside Linebacker by Sporting News, 1983, 85, NFL All-Pro Team Inside Linebacker by Sporting News, 1991-92. Played in Pro Bowl, 1987, 88, 91, 92. Office: Carolina Panthers 800 S Mint St Charlotte NC 28202-1518*

MILLS, STEPHEN NATHANIEL, computer software company executive; b. Boston, Apr. 18, 1942; s. Nathaniel and Alice Mary (Lerner) M.; m. Lorraine Hill Ransom, Mar. 27, 1966 (div. Apr. 1993); children: Nathaniel Stephen, George Robert, Beman Ransom (dec.), Priscilla Alden; m. Patricia Punch Meadows, Mar. 5, 1994 (div. Dec. 1995); m. Marcia Ann Perry Brandes, May 4, 1997. Student, MIT, 1959-61; BS, Regents Coll., 1989. Programmer analyst Cambridge (Mass.) Computer Assocs., 1966-68; sr. programmer, analyst Computer Fulfillment, Winchester, Mass., 1968-69; pres. Software Engring., Inc., Norton, Mass., 1969-73; product devel. mgr. Pecan Software Corp., Roswell, Ga., 1987-88; pres. Software Eclectics, Inc., Alpharetta, Ga., 1988—; cons. in field; mem. Lang. Test Mgmt. Coun., Inst. Cert. Computer Profls., Des Plaines, Ill., 1994—; adj. faculty Gwinnett Tech. Inst., Lawrenceville, Ga., 1992, Chattahoochee Tech. Inst., Marietta, Ga., 1992. Sgt. USAR, 1964-70. Mem. IEEE Computer Soc., Southeastern Software Assn., Data Processing Mgmt. Assn. (Atlanta bd. dirs. 1992-93), Assn. Computing Machinery, Mensa (Boston chpt. pres. 1967-68, Little Rock newsletter editor 1978). Avocation: aviation. Office: Software Eclectics Inc Ste 401 3894 Vicar Ct Atlanta GA 30360-1321

MILLS, SYLVIA JANET, secondary education educator; b. Chgo., Oct. 5, 1954; d. Clarence Thomas and Janet Lucille (Curry) Mills; children: Ean O'Harrel Gay Mills, Raymond Ear Echols II. BA in Journalism, Columbia Coll., Chgo., 1979; MA in Instructional Design, U. Iowa, 1993, secondary tchg. cert. in journalism, 1996. Edn. Beat reporter Chgo. Daily Defender Newspapers, 1979-80; tech. writer/editor, data mgmt. supr., ops./planning analyst Sonicraft, Inc., Chgo., 1983-88; sec. and pub. rels. officer Female Entrepreneurs of Chgo., 1988-89; adminstrv. asst./editor Student Devel. Office, City Colls. of Chgo., 1989-91; rsch. intern Am. Coll. Testing, Inc., Iowa City, Iowa, 1991-93; grad. asst. U. Iowa Grad. Coll., Iowa City, 1993-95; rsch. asst. Ctr. for Evaluation and Assessment, U. Iowa, 1995-96. Bd. dirs. All in a Kid's Day Summer Immersion Program, Iowa City, 1994; mem. PTA Beasley Acad. Ctr., Chgo., 1988-90, PTO, Iowa City, 1992-93. Mem. ASCD, Alpha Kappa Alpha (treas., dean of pledges 1973—). Avocations: reading, writing. Home: 1416 Orleans Ave Keokuk IA 52632

MILLS, THOMAS COOKE, psychiatrist; b. San Francisco, Nov. 24, 1955; s. Willard Cooke and Billie Dee (Hunt) M. BS, MIT, 1977; MD, U. Ill., Chgo., 1981; MPH, U. Calif., Berkeley, 1991. Diplomate Am. Bd. Psychiatry and Neurology. Resident in psychiatry U. Calif., San Francisco, 1981-85, asst. clin. prof., 1985-91, assoc. clin. prof., 1991—; med. dir. Jail Psychiat. Svcs., San Francisco, 1985-88; pvt. practice San Francisco, 1985-88; staff psychiatrist Dept. Vets. Affairs, San Francisco, 1988-93, psychiat. authorizing physician, 1991-93; postdoctoral fellow U. Calif., Berkeley, 1990-91. Fellow NIMH, 1990-91. Mem. Am. Psychiat. Assn., No. Calif. Psychiat. Soc. Office: PO Box 460520 San Francisco CA 94146-0520

MILLS, WILLIAM HAROLD, JR., construction company executive; b. St. Petersburg, Fla., July 24, 1939; s. William Harold and Caroline (Bonfoey) M.; m. Sylvia Ludwig, Jan. 4, 1962 (div. 1975); children—William Harold III, Robert Michael, Leslie Anne; m. Kimberly Keyes, May 4, 1985 (div. 1988); m. Gigi Alice Schmidt, Aug. 1, 1990. Grad., Woodberry Forest Sch., 1954-57; B.S. in Civil Engring., U. Fla., 1961. Cert. Class A gen. contractor, Fla. V.P. bus. devel. Mills & Jones Constrn., St. Petersburg, Fla., 1964-68; v.p. Wellington Corp., Atlanta, 1968-71; exec. v.p. Mills & Jones Constrn., St. Petersburg, Fla., 1971-79; pres., chmn. Federal Constrn. Co., St. Petersburg, 1979-88, vice chmn., 1988—; pres., chair Univ. Housing Svcs., Inc., St. Petersburg; mem. adv. com. St Petersburg Port, 1993—. Pres. St. Petersburg Progress, Inc., 1986-87; active mem. Suncoasters, St. Petersburg, 1974—, St. Anthony's Devel. Found., St. Petersburg, 1983-86; past chmn. Pinellas Marine Inst., St. Petersburg, Blue Ribbon Zoning Com., City of St. Petersburg; former mem. Pinellas County Constrn. Licensing Bd., Tampa Bay Aviation Adv. Com., United Fund Pinellas County; former mem. U. South Fla. Campus Adv. Bd. Named Hon. Royal Navy Liaison Officer Her Majesty's Royal Navy, 1984—. Mem. ASCE, NSPE, Am. Mgmt. Assn., Mensa, St. Petersburg Area C. of C. (bd. govs. 1983-85), Fla. Sports Adv. Coun., Order of Salvador/Salvador Dali Mus., St. Petersburg Yacht Club, Dragon Club, Les Ambassadeurs Club (London), Vinoy Croquet Club (pres.), Annabel's Club (London), Useppa Island Club (bd. govs.), Sigma Alpha Epsilon, U.S. Croquet Assn., Univ. Fla. Pres.'s Coun. (life). Republican. Episcopalian. Home: 1260 Brightwaters Blvd NE Saint Petersburg FL 33704-3728 Office: 1325 Snell Isle Blvd NE Ste 201 Saint Petersburg FL 33704-2455

MILLS, WILLIAM HAYES, lawyer; b. Gordo, Ala., Mar. 30, 1931; s. Early S. and Bama (Cameron) M. LL.B., U. Ala., 1956. Bar: Ala. 1956. Since practiced in Birmingham; partner Rogers, Howard, Redden & Mills, 1961-79, Redden, Mills & Clark, 1979—; arbitrator Fed. Mediation and Conciliation Service, Am. Arbitration Assn. Served with AUS, 1948-50, 50-51. Mem. ABA, Ala., Birmingham bar assns., Am., Ala. trial lawyers assns. Baptist. Home: 2105 Williamsburg Way Birmingham AL 35223-1740 Office: Redden Mills & Clark 940 1st Alabama Bank Bldg Birmingham AL 35203

MILLS (KUTZ-HARDER), HELGA, religious organization executive. BA (hon.), U. Western Ont., 1959; MA, U. B.C., Vancouver, 1965; PhD in English Renaissance Lit., U. N.C., 1976. Specialist instr. English, German Fisher Ph. H.S., Ottawa, Can., 1959-63; sessional instr. to instr. dept. English U. B.C., 1964-67; sessional instr. to prof. dept English U. Windsor, Windsor, Ont., 1970-78, 82-85; missionary United Ch. Can., Tokyo, 1978-82; United Ch. Can.; program cons. United Ch. Can., Windsor, 1985-91; exec. sec. United Ch. Can. Toronto Conf., 1991-94; prin. St. Paul's United Coll., U. Waterloo, Ont., Ont., 1994—. Contbr. to articles to religious mags. Gov. Gen. Gold medalist, 1959; Deutsche Acad. Austauschdienst scholar, 1961, Can. Coun. scholar, 1963, U. B.C. grad. scholar, 1964. Office: U Waterloo St Paul's United Coll, Westmount Rd, Waterloo, ON Canada N2L 3G5

MILLSAPS, FRED RAY, investor; b. Blue Ridge, Ga., Apr. 30, 1929; s. Samuel Hunter and Ora Lee (Bradshaw) M.; m. Audrey Margaret Hopkins, June 22, 1957; children: Judith Gail, Stephen Hunter, Walter Scott. A.B., Emory U., 1951; postgrad., U. Wis. Sch. Banking, 1955-57, Harvard Bus. Sch., 1962; LLD, Fla. So. Coll., 1991. Auditor Fed. Res. Bank, Atlanta, 1953-58, asst. v.p., 1958-62, v.p., 1962-64; fin. v.p. Fla. Power & Light Co., 1965-69; pres., dir. First Nat. Bank of Ft. Lauderdale, Fla., 1969-73; chmn., pres. Landmark Banking Corp. of Fla., Ft. Lauderdale, 1971-78; chmn. Landmark Union Trust Bank of St. Petersburg, Fla., 1976-78; bd. dirs. Franklin Templeton Mut. Funds. Chmn. com. of 100 Broward County Indsl. Devel. Bd., 1972-77; chmn. South Fla. Coordinating Coun., 1976-78, WPBT Community TV Found. of South Fla., 1973-75, Fla. So. Coll., Lakeland, Broward Performing Arts Authority, Honda Classic, Broward Workshop, Holy Cross Health Corp.; mem. Fla. Coun. of 100. Mem. Tower Club, Inverrary Club, Coral Ridge Country Club. Methodist.

MILLSON, RORY OLIVER, lawyer; b. Capetown, Republic of South Africa, Nov. 26, 1950; s. Harry E. and Fay Leonard (Liesching) M.; m. Linda Ellen Rodd, June 15, 1985; children: Helen Fay, John Rodd, Henry Francis. BA, Yale U., 1973, JD, 1977; MA, Oxford (Eng.) U., 1975. Bar: N.Y. 1978, U.S. Dist. Ct. (so. and ea. dists.) N.Y. 1978, U.S. Ct. Appeals (D.C. cir.) 1990, U.S. Ct. Appeals (2d cir.) 1991, U.S. Supreme Ct. 1991. With Cravath, Swaine & Moore, N.Y.C., 1976—, ptnr., 1984—. Office: Cravath Swaine & Moore 825 8th Ave New York NY 10019-7416

MILLSPAUGH, MARTIN LAURENCE, real estate developer, urban development consultant; b. Columbus, Ohio, Dec. 16, 1925; s. Martin Laurence and Elisabeth (Park) M.; m. Meredith Plant, May 10, 1952; children: Elisabeth, M. Laurence, Meredith, Thomas. AB summa cum laude, Princeton U., 1949. Reporter, columnist Richmond News Leader, Va., 1949-53; urban affairs writer Balt. Evening Sun, 1953-57; asst. commr. Urban Renewal Adminstrn., Washington, 1957-60; dep. gen. mgr. Charles Ctr., Balt., 1960-65; pres., chmn., chief exec. officer Charles Ctr.-Inner Harbor Mgmt., Inc., 1965-85; exec. v.p., pres., vice chmn. Enterprise Devel. Co., Columbia, Md., 1985—, also bd. dirs.; pres. Enterprise Internat. Devel. Co., Columbia, 1988-91, vice chmn., 1991—; vice chmn. Enterprise Real Estate Svcs., Inc., 1996—; cons. to pvt. developers and local pub. agys., Mass., Va., S.C., Fla., Calif., Sydney, 1981—; conducted seminars in Nagasaki and Kagoshima, Japan, 1991-92; lectr. Columbia U., Princeton U., Johns Hopkins U., U. Md., U. New Orleans, NYU, Acad. Polit. Sci., AAAS, Lambda Alpha Internat., 1991, 95, U.K. Inst. Travel and Tourism, 1993, Can. Water Resources Assn., 1991, Nat. Bldg. Mus., 1995, Internat. Property Market, Cannes, 1996, and numerous other profl. confs. and seminars; appeared on USIA Worldnet TV Dialogue, Montevideo, Uruguay, 1990, Recife and Rio de Janeiro, 1995. Author: (with others) The Human Side of Urban Renewal, 1958; author, editor (monograph) Baltimore's Charles Center, 1964; author (newspaper series) Design for Living (hon. mention Heywood Broun award 1957); profl. appearances include VOA, 1994, CBS Sunday News, 1994; contbr. articles to profl. jours. Trustee Enoch Pratt Free Libr., Balt., 1965-85, Gilman Sch., 1975-80, Bryn Mawr Sch. for Girls, 1978-81; bd. dirs. Planned Parenthood Assn. Md., 1962-65, Roland Park Civic League, 1962-64, sec., 1963-64, Blue Cross of Md., Inc., 1970-80, Balt. Symphony Orch. Assn., 1974-78, YMCA of Greater Balt. area, 1977-81; Md. Internat. Coun., Balt., 1992-96, mem. long range planning com., 1994-96, sec., 1995-96; mem. chair nominating com. World Trade Ctr. Inst., 1996—; mem. task force Twentieth Century Fund, N.Y.C., 1984-85; mem. adv. coun. real estate devel. program Columbia U. Grad. Sch. Architecture and Planning, 1985-94; mem. bd. advisors Fight-Blight Fund, Balt., 1961-62, Waterfront Ctr., Washington, 1987-90; mem. adv. bd. Nat. Aquarium, Balt., 1988—, Sch. Bus. Mgmt. Morgan State U., 1993-94, Real Estate Inst., Sch. Continuing Studies Johns Hopkins U., 1994—; mem. pres.'s adv. bd. U. Md. Balt. County, 1989-94; mem. adv. panel Ctr. Strategic and Internat. Studies, Washington, 1993-94; mem. Md. Transp. Real Estate Adv. Group, 1996; active U.S. Senate Productivity Award Selection Com. for Md., 1987. Served to sgt. USAF, 1944-46, PTO. Recipient Disting. Svc. award U.S. Housing and Home Fin. Agy., Washington, 1960, Urban Planning award The Waterfront Ctr., 1995. Mem. Urban Land Inst. (hon., exec. group internat. coun., 1989—, vice chmn. internat. coun. 1995-96, award of excellence, 1980, chair adv. panel for city of Harrisburg, Pa., 1984, internat. com. 1987-88, 96—, Balt. dist. coord. 1987-91, vice-chmn. dist. coun. com. 1991-94; mem. adv. panel for Oklahoma City, 1995, awards com. 1995—), Greater Balt. Com. (urban affairs coun. 1982-84, J. Jefferson Miller award for civic accomplishment 1981), Coun. on Urban Econ. Devel., Internat. Downtown Assn., Internat. New Town Assn. (mem. adv. panel for waterfront devel. for City of Malmo, Sweden 1987), Phi Beta Kappa, Lambda Alpha. Democrat. Episcopalian. Clubs: Center, Balt., 14 W Hamilton St (Balt.); Ivy (Princeton, N.J.). Home: 203 Ridgewood Rd Baltimore MD 21210-2538 Office: Enterprise Devel Co 600 American City Bldg Columbia MD 21044

MILLSTEIN, DAVID J., lawyer; b. N.Y.C., Apr. 15, 1953; s. Stanley and Irma (Klein) M. AB, U. Calif., Berkeley, 1975, JD, 1979. Bar: Calif. 1979, U.S. Dist. Ct. (no. dist.) Calif. 1979, U.S. Dist. Ct. (ea. dist.) Calif. 1984. Assoc. Bostwick & Tehin, San Francisco, 1991-93; asst. dist. atty. San Francisco Dist. Atty.'s Office, 1993—; pvt. practice San Francisco, 1982-95, 97—; ptnr. Millstein & Doolittle, San Francisco, 1996—; chief asst. dist. Atty. City and County of San Francisco, 1996; judge pro tem San Francisco Mcpl. Ct., 1983—; probation monitor Calif. State Bar, 1995—; panelist Calif. Psychol. Assn.; lectr. San Francisco Gen. Hosp., Stanford U., 1994, Boalt Hall Sch. of Law, U. Calif., Berkeley, 1995—; adj. prof. Hastings Coll. Law, San Francisco, 1993—, co-chair advocacy sect., 1994—; legal analyst KBO-ABC News, San Francisco, 1995—, KTVV-Fox News, Oakland, Calif., 1994—; chief asst. dist. atty. City and County of San Francisco, 1996. Author supplement to How to Prepare For, Take and Use a Deposition, 1995; contbr. articles to law jours. Office: 580 California St Ste 500 San Francisco CA 94104-1000

MILLSTEIN, IRA M., lawyer, lecturer; b. N.Y.C., Nov. 8, 1926; s. Harry M. and Birdie E. (Rosenbaum) M.; m. Diane G. Greenberg, July 3, 1949; children: James Eliot, Elizabeth Jane. B.S., Columbia U., 1947, LL.B., 1949. Bar: N.Y. 1949, U.S. Supreme Ct. 1973. Atty. antitrust div. Dept. Justice, Washington, 1949-51; assoc. firm Weil Gotshal & Manges, N.Y.C., 1951-57, ptnr., 1957—; chmn. bd. advisors Ctr. for Law and Econ. Studies, Columbia U., 1987—; fellow faculty govt. John F. Kennedy Sch. Govt., Harvard U., 1983-87; Eugene F. Williams Jr. vis. prof. in competetive enterprise and strategy Yale Sch. Mgmt., 1996—, Sloan fellow, 1982-83, Disting. fellow Yale U.Sch. Orgnl. Mgmt., 1992-96; mem. coun. Adminstrv. Conf. U.S., 1978-81. Author: (with Katsh) The Limits of Corporate Power, 1981; contbr. articles to profl. jours. Mem. Nat. Commn. on Consumer Fin., 1969-72, chmn., 1971-72; chmn. N.Y.C.'s Spl. Com. on Inquiry into Energy Failures, 1977-82, N.Y. State Energy Planning Bd., 1978-82, Gov. Cuomo's Task Force on Pension Fund Investment, 1988—; vice chmn. bd. overseers Albert Einstein Coll. Medicine, Yeshiva U., Bronx, N.Y., 1981—; chmn. bd. trustees Cen. Pk. Conservancy. Decorated chevalier Nat. Order of Merit, France. Fellow Am. Acad. Arts and Scis.; mem. ABA (chmn. antitrust law sect. 1977-78, chmn. antitrust law sect.'s task force report on antitrust div. 1988-89), N.Y. State Bar Assn. (chmn. antitrust law sect. 1967-68), Nat. Assn. Corp. Dirs. (bd. dirs. 1994—), Met. Club, Quaker Ridge Golf Club. Home: 1240 Flagler Dr Mamaroneck NY 10543-4601 Office: Weil Gotshal & Manges 767 5th Ave New York NY 10153-0001

MILLSTONE, DAVID J., lawyer; b. Morgantown, W.Va., 1946. AB, Johns Hopkins U., 1968; JD, U. W.Va., 1971. Bar: W.Va. 1971, Ohio 1971, Fla. 1980. Ptnr. Squire, Sanders & Dempsey LLP, Cleve. Mem. ABA (internat. coord. labor and employment practice). Office: Squire Sanders & Dempsey 4900 Key Tower 127 Public Sq Cleveland OH 44114-1216

MILMAN, DORIS HOPE, pediatrics educator, psychiatrist; b. N.Y.C., Nov. 17, 1917; d. Barnet S. and Rose (Smoleroff) Milman; m. Nathan Kreeger, June 15, 1941; 1 child, Elizabeth Kreeger Goldman. BA, Barnard Coll., 1938; MD, NYU, 1942. Diplomate Am. Bd. Pediats.; lic. physician, N.Y. Intern Jewish Hosp., Bklyn., 1942-43, resident, 1944-46, fellow in pediat., 1946-47; postgrad. extern in psychiatry Bellevue Hosp., N.Y.C., 1947-49; attending pediat. psychiatrist Jewish Hosp., Bklyn., 1950-56; asst. prof. pediat. Health Sci. Ctr. at Bklyn. SUNY, 1956-67, assoc. prof., 1967-73, prof., 1973-93, prof. emeritus, 1993—, acting chmn. dept. pediat., 1973-75, 82; pvt. practice child and adolescent psychiatry, Bklyn., 1950-90; vis. prof. Ben Gurion U. of the Negev, Beersheva, Israel, 1977. Mem. adv. bd. N.Y. Assn. for the Learning Disabled, N.Y.C., 1975-80. Recipient Disting. Alumna award Barnard Coll., 1986, Solomon R. Berson Achievement award NYU Sch. Medicine, 1991; Grace Potter Rice fellow Barnard Coll., 1938-39. Fellow Am. Acad. Pediat. (emeritus), Am. Psychiat. Assn. (life); mem. AAAS, Am. Orthopsychiat. Assn. (life), Am. Pediat. Soc. (emeritus), N.Y. Pediat. Soc. (emeritus). Home: 126 Westminster Rd Brooklyn NY 11218-3444 Office: Health Sci Ctr at Bklyn SUNY Box 49 450 Lenox Rd Brooklyn NY 11203-2020

MILMOE, PATRICK JOSEPH, lawyer; b. Oct. 2, 1939; s. Hugh A. Milmoe and Mary Frances (O'Connell) Steenken; m. Carolyn Mann, Nov. 30, 1963; children: Mary Kaye Chrysicas, Caroline Pugh, Hugh. BA, Coll. William and Mary, 1959; JD, U. Va., 1962. Bar: N.Y. 1962, Va. 1962, Fla. 1989. With Davis & Polk, N.Y.C., 1965-72; ptnr. Hunton & Williams, Richmond, Va., 1972—; chmn. DARE Marina, Inc., Grafton, Va., 1992—, States Roofing Corp., Norfolk, Va., 1994—, Virginia Beach Marlin Club, Inc., 1980—. Trustee Village of Atlantic Beach, N.Y., 1965-72; bd. dirs. St. Joseph's Villa, Richmond, Va., 1985-91. Capt. U.S. Army, 1963-65. Mem. Am. Coll. Real Estate Lawyers. Avocations: boating, fishing. Office: Hunton & Williams 951 E Byrd St Richmond VA 23219-4040

MILNE, EDWARD LAWRENCE, biomedical engineer; b. Ottawa, Ont., Can., June 20, 1948; came to U.S., 1985; s. Roderick Francis and Mary Angela (Massiah) M.; m. Pamela Mary Sklenka, Aug. 23, 1975; children: Marc Aaron, Adam Daniel. BSc, Dalhousie U., 1971. Rsrch. asst. Tech. U. N.S., Halifax, Can., 1973-76; technologist Dalhousie U., Halifax, 1976-85; biomed. engr. Mt. Sinai Med. Ctr., Miami Beach, Fla., 1986—. Contbr. articles to profl. jours. Avocations: computers, reading, fresh water fishing, gardening. Office: Mt Sinai Med Ctr 4300 Alton Rd Miami FL 33140-2800

MILNE, JAMES, secretary of state; b. Barre, Vt., July 8, 1950; m. Judith Garigliano; children: Honah Lee, Heather, Joseph, Elizabeth. BS in Pharmacy, Mass. Coll. Pharmacy, 1974. City clk., treas. City of Barre (Vt.), 1988-94; sec. of state State of Vt., 1995—; pharmacist, mgr. Allan Milne Pharmacy, 1974-88. Mem. Aldrich Pub. Libr. (bd. trustees), Nat. Ski Patrol, Mutuo, Inc.; chair Barre Basketball Tournament Com.; dir. Granite Mutual Ins. Co. Mem. Vt. Municipal Clks. and Treas. Assn., Vt. Jaycees (pres. 1979-80), U.S. Jaycees (nat. v.p. 1980-81), Barre Elks Lodge, Barre Country Club, Barre Rotary Club (pres. 1985-86). Republican. Office: PO Box 992 Barre VT 05641-0992 also: Off of Sec of State 109 State St Montpelier VT 05609-0001

MILNER, BRENDA ATKINSON LANGFORD, neuropsychologist; b. Manchester, Eng., July 15, 1918; emigrated to Can., 1944; d. Samuel and Leslie (Doig) Langford. BA, Cambridge (Eng.) U., 1939, MA, 1949, ScD, 1972; PhD, McGill U., 1952; DSc (hon.), 1991;, LLD (hon.), Queen's U., 1980; ScD (hon.) U. Manitoba, 1982, U. Lethbridge, 1986, Mt. Holyoke Coll., 1986, U. Laval, 1987, U. Toronto, 1987; LHD (hon.), Mt. St. Vincent U., 1988; Hon. D. U. de Montréal, 1988; DSc (hon.) Wesleyan U., 1991, Acadia U., 1991, U. St. Andrews, 1992, U. West Hartford, 1997. Exptl. officer U.K. Ministry of Supply, 1941-44; prof. agrégé Institut de Psychologie, Université de Montréal, 1944-52; rsch. assoc. psychology dept. McGill U., Montreal, 1952-53, lectr. dept. neurology and neurosurgery, 1953-60, asst. prof., 1960-64, assoc. prof., 1964-70, prof. psychology, 1970-93; Dorothy J. Killam prof. Montreal Neurological Inst., 1993—; head neuropsychology rsch. unit Montreal Neurol. Inst., 1953-90; Clothworkers fellow Girton Coll., Cambridge, 1972-73. Mem. editorial bd. Neuropsychologia, 1973-93, Behavioral Brain Rsch., 1980-88, Hippocampus, 1990-96. Decorated officer Order of Can., officier l'Ordre Nat. du Que., 1985; Career investigator Med. Rsch. Coun. Can., 1964—; recipient Kathleen Stott prize Newnham Coll., 1971, Karl Spencer Lashley award Am. Philos. Soc., 1979, Izaak Walton Killam Meml. prize Can. Coun., 1983, Hermann Von Helmholtz prize Cognitive Neuroscience Inst., 1984, Penfield award Can. league Against Epilepsy, 1984, William James fellow Am. Psychol. Soc., 1989, Wilder Penfield prize Province of Quebec, 1993, Neural Plasticity prize Fondation IPSEN, Paris, Met. Life Found. award, 1996; named Great Montrealer, 1987; named to Can. Med. Hall of Fame, 1997. Fellow APA (Disting. Contbn. award 1973), AAAS, Royal Soc. London, Royal Soc. Can. (McLaughlin medal 1995), Can. Psychol. Assn.; mem. NAS (fgn. assoc.), Am. Epilepsy Soc. (William G. Lennox award 1974, 95), Am. Neurol. Assn., Association de Psychologie Scientifique de Langue Française, Brit. Soc. Exptl. Psychology, Exptl. Psychol. Soc., Psychonomic Soc., Eastern Psychol. Assn., Internat. Neuropsychology Symposium, Internat. Brain Rsch. Orgn. (exec. sec. 1993-97), Soc. Neurosci. (Ralph W. Gerard prize 1987), Am. Acad. Neurology (assoc.), Assn. Rsch. in Nervous and Mental Diseases (assoc.), Royal Soc. Medicine (affiliate), Sigma Xi. Office: Montreal Neurol Inst, 3801 University St, Montreal, PQ Canada H3A 2B4

MILNER, CLYDE A., II, historian; b. Durham, N.C., Oct. 19, 1948; s. Charles Fremont and Eloyse (Sargent) M.; m. Carol Ann O'Connor, Aug. 14, 1977; children: Catherine Carol, Charles Clyde. AB, U. N.C., 1971; MA, Yale U., 1973, MPhil, 1974, PhD, 1979. Admissions counselor Guilford Coll., Greensboro, N.C., 1968-70; acting instr. Yale U., New Haven, Conn., 1974-75; research fellow McNickle Ctr., Chgo., 1975-76; instr. Utah State U., Logan, 1976-79, asst. prof., 1979-82, assoc. prof., 1982-88, prof., 1988—; dir. Mountain West Ctr. for Regional Studies, 1997—; reader of manuscripts History Book Club, Inc., 1986—. Author: With Good Intentions, 1982; editor: Major Problems in the History of the American West, 1989, co-editor 2d edit., 1997; editor: A New Significance: Re-envisioning the History of the American West, 1996; assoc. editor The Western Hist. Quar., 1984-87, co-editor, 1987-89, editor, 1990—; co-editor: Churchmen and the Western Indians, 1985, Trails: Toward a New Western History, 1991, Oxford History of the American West, 1994 (Western Heritage award for non-fiction Nat. Cowboy Hall of Fame 1994, Caughey Western History Assn. award for best book on history of Am. West 1995). Recipient Paladen Writing award The Montana Mag. Western History, 1987, Faculty Svc. award Associated Students Utah State U., 1987, Outstanding Social Science Researcher award Utah State U., 1983, (with Carol A. O'Connor) Charles Redd prize Utah Acad. Scis., Arts and Letters, 1996. Mem. Western History Assn., Orgn. Am. Historians, Phi Alpha Theta, Phi Beta Kappa. Society of Friends. Home: 1675 E 1400 N Logan UT 84341-2975 Office: Utah State U Dept of History Logan UT 84322

MILNER, HAROLD WILLIAM, hotel executive; b. Salt Lake City, Nov. 11, 1934; s. Kenneth W. and Olive (Schoettlin) M.; m. Susan Emmett, June 19, 1959 (div. 1976); children—John Kenneth, Mary Sue; m. Lois Friemuth, Aug. 14, 1977; 1 dau., Jennifer Rebecca. B.S., U. Utah, 1960; M.B.A., Harvard, 1962. Instr. Brigham Young U., Provo, Utah, 1962-64; v.p. Gen. Paper Corp., Mpls., 1964-65; dir. finance Amalgamated Sugar Co., Ogden, Utah, 1965-67; corp. treas. Marriott Corp., Washington, 1967-70; pres., chief exec. officer, trustee Hotel Investors, Kensington, Md., 1970-75; pres., chief exec. officer Americana Hotels Corp., Chgo., 1975-85, Kahler Corp., Rochester, Minn., 1985-97; pres., CEO The Kensington Co., Salt Lake City, 1997—. Author: A Special Report on Contract Maintenance, 1963. Served as lt. AUS, 1960. Mem. Minn. Bus. Partnership (dir. 1991—). Mem. Ch. Jesus Christ Latter-day Saints. Home: 4010 Mayowood Rd SW Rochester MN 55902-4255 Office: Kahler Corp 20 2nd Ave SW Rochester MN 55902-3013

MILNER, HOWARD M., real estate developer, international real estate financier; b. L.A., Sept. 21, 1937; s. David Daniel and Rose (Devron) M.; m. Shirley Glogow, Oct. 24, 1964 (div. 1978); children: Mara Lynn, Debra Faye. AA in Architecture, L.A. City Coll., 1960; cert. real estate, UCLA, 1962; Doctorate (hon.), London Inst. Applied Rsch., 1994; PhD in Philanthropy, Pepperdine U., 1995. Sr. store planner Broadway Dept. Stores, L.A., 1959; exec. v.p. Palm Properties Inc., Van Nuys, Calif., 1959-69; v.p. Network Cinema Corp., L.A., 1969-79, Hesa Global Investments Ltd., Beverly Hills, Calif., 1979-86; pres., CEO Lyons Internat. Realty and Devel. Inc., L.A., 1986-87, Howard M. Milner and Assocs., North Hollywood, Calif., 1987—; sr. cons. Swiss-Am. Investment Trust, North Hollywood, 1979—; adj. sr. assoc. Visa Enterprises Inc., Beverly Hills., 1986—; sr. assoc. cons. AMF Roadmaster Mfg. Co., North Hollywood, 1986—; developed nat. expansion Internat. House Pancakes, Copper Penny Coffee Shops, Fotomat Corp., Jerry Lewis Cinema Theatres, K-Mart Shopping Ctrs.; lectr. in field. Contbr. articles on real estate to profl. jours. Life mem., fin. sec. City of Hope, L.A.'s mem. Mayor's Comml. Devel. Com., Brea, Calif., Mayor's Redevel. Com., L.A. and Hollywood; active City of Hope Cancer Rsch. Found., Duarte, Calif. With U.S. Army, 1957-59. Recipient Eagle Scout award Boy Scouts Am., 1952, Disting. Citizen award and Disting. Eagle award Boy Scouts Am., Civic Appreciation award Mayor of L.A., 1987; Architecture scholar Ford Motor Co., 1954, Architecture scholar East L.A. Coll., 1955. Mem. AIA, Am. Inst. Indsl. Engrs., Am. Inst. Plant Engrs., Am. Soc. Mil. Engrs., Calif. Apt. and Motel Mgrs. Assn., Calif. Notary Assn., Calif. Real Estate Assn., Constrn. Specifications Inst., Inst. Real Estate Mgmt., Internat. Coun. Shopping Ctrs., Internat. Real Estate

Fedn., Nat. Home Builders Assn. Am., Nat. Franchise Assn. Am., Real Estate Cert. Inst., Young Home Builders Coun. Am., L.A. C. of C., San Fernando C. of C., Saugus-Newhall C. of C., Van Nuys C. of C., Toastmasters, Masons (32 degree), Shriners. Democrat. Jewish. Avocations: walking, jogging, racquetball, golf, cooking. Office: Wells Fargo Bank Bldg 4605 Lankershim Blvd # 413 North Hollywood CA 91602-1818

MILNER, IRVIN MYRON, lawyer; b. Cleve., Feb. 5, 1916; s. Nathan and Rose (Spector) M.; m. Zelda Winograd., Aug. 15, 1943. A.B. cum laude, Western Res. U. (now Case Western Res. U.), 1937, J.D., 1940, LL.M., 1970. Bar: Ohio 1940, U.S. Dist. Ct. (no. dist.) Ohio 1946. Pvt. practice Cleve., 1946—; exec. sec., counsel Men's Apparel Club Ohio, Cleve., 1947-48; adj. instr. Sch. Law, Case Western Res. U., 1965-66; spl. counsel Ohio Office Atty. Gen., 1960-70; legal counsel Korean Am. Assn. Greater Cleve., 1973-95. Mem. Cleve. Fgn. Consular Corps., 1970-96, hon. consul Rep. of Korea for Cleve., 1970-96; bd. dirs. Internat. Human Assistance Programs, Inc., 1973-79, voting corp. mem., 1980-88. Served with U.S. Army, 1941-45, ETO. Decorated Order Diplomatic Svc. Merit-Heung-in medal (Republic of Korea), 1975; named to Disting. Alumni Hall of Fame, Cleveland Heights (Ohio) High Sch., 1983. Fellow Internat. Consular Coll., Ohio Bar Found.; mem. ABA (small bus. com., corp. bus. law sect. 1971-74), Greater Cleve. Bar Assn., Cuyahoga County Bar Assn. (pres. 1975-76, co-chmn. jud. standards com. 1987-88, life trustee, award of Special Merit 1976, Pres.' award 1988), Ohio State Bar Assn. (coun. dels., 1976-86, com. on legal ethics and profl. conduct 1984-97), Cuyahoga County Bar Found. (sec.-treas. 1980-84, bd. dirs. 1984—), Cuyahoga County Coun. Ohio VFW (comdr. 1958, Merit award 1958), Am. Security Coun. (nat. adv. bd.), Cleve. Coun. on World Affairs, Western Res. Coll. Alumni Assn. (bd. dirs. 1982-88). Tau Epsilon Rho (chancellor Cleve. Grad. chpt. 1987-88), Delta Phi Alpha. Republican. Jewish. Club: Cleve. City. Lodges: Masons 32 degree.

MILNER, MAX, food and nutrition consultant; b. Edmonton, Alta., Can., Jan. 24, 1914; came to U.S., 1939, naturalized, 1944; s. Morris Abram and Rose (Lertzman) M.; m. Elizabeth Banen, Aug. 9, 1942; children—Ruth Sharon, Marcia Ann. B.Sc., U. Sask., 1938; LL.D. (hon.), 1979; M.S., U. Minn., 1941, Ph.D., 1945. Research chemist Pillsbury Mills Inc., Mpls., 1939-40; prof. grain sci. and industry Kans. State U., Manhattan, 1947-59; sr. food technologist UNICEF, N.Y.C., 1959-71; chief nutrition br. AID, 1966-67; dir. secretariat protein calorie adv. group UN, 1971-75; assoc. dir. internat. nutrition program M.I.T., 1975-78; exec. officer Am. Inst. Nutrition, Bethesda, Md., 1978-84; mem. U.S. Wheat Industry Council, 1980-83; mem. expert evaluation panel Bd. Internat. Food and Agrl. Devel., 1983—; chmn. Gordon Research Conf. Food and Nutrition, 1968; Gen. Food Co. (Can.) disting. internat. lectr., 1975. Co-author: Protein Resources and Technology, 1978, Postharvest Biology and Biotechnology, 1978; Editor: Protein-enriched Cereal Foods for World Needs, 1969, Nutrition Improvement of Food Legumes by Breeding, 1975; Contbr. articles to profl. jours., chpts. to monographs. Bd. dirs., exec. com. Meals for Million/Freedom From Hunger Found., 1975-83, cons. in field. Fellow AAAS, Inst. Food Technologists (Internat. award 1968, lectr. sci. series 1971-72, Disting. Food Service award N.Y. sect. 1975), Am. Inst. Nutrition; mem. Am. Chem. Soc., Am. Assn. Cereal Chemists. Home: 10401 Grosvenor Pl Apt 721 Rockville MD 20852-4635 *As a child of immigrant parents with minimal formal education, my career, like that of many Americans with this kind of background, is a testimonial to the unique role of the Canadian and American system of open higher education, available to all able to qualify for admission. It is to such institutions that I owe a profound debt.*

MILNER, PETER MARSHALL, psychology educator; b. Silkstone Common, Eng., June 13, 1919; s. David William and Edith Anne (Marshall) M.; m. Susan Walker, Oct. 13, 1970; 1 son, David Elliot. B.S., Leeds U., 1941; M.S., McGill U., Ph.D., 1954. Sr. sci. officer U.K. Ministry Supply, 1941-48; research asso. physics McGill U., 1948-50, research asst., prof. dept. psychology, 1950-92, prof. emeritus, 1992—, chmn. dept., 1980-83. Author: Physiological Psychology. Fellow Am. Psychol. Assn., Canadian Psychol. Assn.; mem. Sigma Xi. Home: 1050 Amesbury Ave #729, Montreal, PQ Canada H3H 2S5 Office: McGill U Dept Psychology, 1205 Dr Penfield Ave, Montreal, PQ Canada H3A 1B1

MILNES, ARTHUR GEORGE, electrical engineer, educator; b. Heswall, Eng., July 30, 1922; came to U.S., 1957, naturalized, 1964; s. George and Marion (Teasdale) M.; m. Mary Laverne Wertz, Dec. 4, 1955; children: Sheila Rae, Brian George, John Teasdale. BSc, U. Bristol, Eng., 1943, MSc, 1947, DSc, 1956. With Royal Aircraft Establishment, 1943-57, prin. sci. officer, 1952-57; mem. faculty Carnegie-Mellon U., Pitts., 1957-87; prof. elec. engring. Carnegie-Mellon U., 1960-87, assoc. head dept., 1966-69, Buhl prof., 1973-87; prof. emeritus Carnegie-Mellon U., Pitts., 1987—; cons. to industry on semiconductor devices, 1957. Author: Transductors and Magnetic Amplifiers, 1957, (with D.L. Feucht) Heterojunctions and Metal-Semiconductor Junctions, 1972, Deep Impurities in Semiconductors, 1973, Semiconductor Devices and Integrated Electronics, 1979; contbr. articles to profl. jours. FOA rsch. fellow NAS-Royal Soc. London, 1954. Fellow IEEE (J.J. Ebers award 1982, van der Ziel award 1993), Am. Phys. Soc., Instn. Elec. Engrs. (London). Home: 1417 Inverness St Pittsburgh PA 15217-1157

MILNES, SHERRILL E., baritone; b. Downers Grove, Ill., Jan. 10, 1935; s. James Knowlton and Thelma (Roe) M.; m. Maria Zouves, Dec. 19, 1996; children by previous marriage—Eric, Erin, Shawn. Student, North Central Coll.,, Ill.; B in Music Edn., Drake U., 1957, M in Music Edn., 1958; postgrad., Northwestern U., 1958-61; studied with Boris Goldovsky, Rosa Ponselle, Andrew White, Hermanes Baer; postgrad. hon. degree, Ripon Coll., Drake U., Coe Coll., Westminster Choir Coll., SUNY, Potsdam. Disting. prof. Yale U. Sch. Music. Operatic debut Goldovsky Opera Co., N.Y.C., 1960; leading baritone N.Y.C. Opera Co., Met. Opera Co., 1965—; European debut in Macbeth, Vienna, 1970; appearances major world opera cos. including Covent Garden, London, L'Opera, Paris, Staasoper, Vienna, Austria, Teatro Colon, Argentina, La Scala, Milan, Hamburg, Munich, Salzburg, Frankfurt, Berlin, Zurich, as well as continued appearances in the U.S. in San Antonio, Cin., Miami, Houston, Pitts., Chgo., Balt.; numerous TV, concerts, recitals, recordings (RCA, Deutsche Grammophon, Angel/EMI, London, Decca, Philips, CBS). Decorated Order of Merit (Italy); chevalier of French Republic; Ford Found. awardee, 1962. Mem. Tucker Found. (v.p.), Phi Mu Alfa Sinfonia (life). Office: care Herbert Barrett 1776 Broadway Ste 1610 New York NY 10019-2002

MILNIKEL, ROBERT SAXON, lawyer; b. Chgo., Aug. 17, 1926; s. Gustav and Emma Hazel (Saxon) M.; m. Virginia Lee Wylie, July 26, 1969; children: Robert Saxon Jr., Elizabeth Wylie. AB, U. Chgo., 1950, JD, 1953. Bar: Ill. 1953, U.S. Dist. Ct. 1954. Assoc. Traeger, Bolger & Traeger, Chgo., 1953-57, Heineke, Conklin & Schrader, Chgo., 1958-66; ptnr. Peterson & Ross, Chgo., 1966—. With USN, 1944-46, PTO. Mem. Beta Theta Pi (pres. chpt. and alumni assn.), Cliffdwellers Club (bd. dirs. Arts Found.). Republican. Lutheran. Home: 601 Ridge Rd Kenilworth IL 60043-1042 Office: Peterson & Ross 200 E Randolph St Ste 7300 Chicago IL 60601-7012

MILNOR, WILLIAM ROBERT, physician; b. Wilmington, Del., May 4, 1920; s. William Robert and Virginia (Sterling) M.; m. Gabriella Mahaffy, Aug. 19, 1944; children—Katherine Alexander, William Henry. A.B., Princeton U., 1941; M.D., Johns Hopkins U., 1944. Diplomate: Am. Bd. Internal Medicine. Intern, resident Johns Hopkins Hosp., 1944-46; research fellow Nat. Heart Inst., 1949-51; physician-in-charge heart sta. Johns Hopkins Hosp., 1951-60, physician, 1952—; mem. faculty Johns Hopkins Med. Sch., 1951—, prof. physiology, 1969—; vis. fellow St. Catherine's Coll., Oxford (Eng.) U., 1968; mem. med. adv. panel Am. Inst. Biol. Scis., 1971—; assessor Nat. Med. Research Council of Australia, 1976—. Author: Hemodynamics, 2d edit., 1989, Cardio-vascular Physiology, 1990; contbr. articles to med. textbooks, med. jours. Served to capt. M.C. USAAF, 1946-48. Fellow A.C.P.; mem. Am. Physiol. Soc., Am. Fedn. Clin. Research, Biomed. Engring. Soc., Am. Heart Assn. (chmn. research com. 1966), Heart Assn. Md. (past pres.). Clubs: L'Hirondelle, Princeton, 14 W Hamilton St. Office: Johns Hopkins Med Sch 725 N Wolfe St Baltimore MD 21205-2105

MILONAS, MINOS, artist, designer, poet; b. Heraklion, Crete, Greece, Apr. 28, 1936; came to U.S., 1964, naturalized, 1968; s. Stavros and Maria (Kaplantzis) M.; m. Arlene Watson, Dec. 23, 1963 (div. 1970); m. Sarah Brown, Dec. 1973 (div. 1974); m. Elaine Mauceli, May 26, 1988. BA, Calif. State U., Northridge, 1970; MFA with hons., U. Wash., Seattle, 1972. Freelance writer and poet Athens, 1960-64; freelance artist L.A., 1964-66; instr. U. Wash., 1971-72, Studio Milonas, Seattle, 1972-76; artist Studio Milonas, N.Y.C., 1977—, textile designer, 1984-94. One man shows include Second Story Gallery, Seattle, 1971, Henry Art Gallery, Seattle, 1972, Polly Friedlander Gallery, Seattle, 1973, Stavrakakis Gallery, Crete, Greece, 1977, West Broadway Gallery, N.Y.C., 1979, 81, 82, Heraklion Art Gallery, Crete, 1983, Kreonides Gallery, Athens, 1983, 84, Doma Gallery, N.Y.C., 1988, Hellenic Cultural Ctr., N.Y., 1990, 93, Cypriot Consulate, N.Y.C., 1990; exhibitions in group shows at Calif. State U., Northridge, 1968-69, Mcpl. Art Gallery, L.A., 1969, U. Wash. Libr., Seattle, 1971, 72, Panaca Gallery, Bellevue, Wash., 1973, Mercer Island Art Gallery, Seattle, 1973, Henry Art Gallery, Seattle, 1973, Tacoma Art Mus., 1973, 75, N.W. Watercolor Soc., 1974, Gordon Woodside Gallery, Seattle, 1974, Coll. of the Cisciyous, Calif., 1975, Laguna Gloria Art Mus., Austin, Tex., 1975, Redmonds (Wash.) Arts Festival, 1975, Univ. Dist. Arts Festival, Seattle, 1976, Bellevue Art Mus., 1976, Sunne Savage Gallery, Boston, 1976, Cretan Artists, Stavrakakis Gallery, Heraklion, Crete, 1978, Internat. Drawing Biennale, Cleveland, Eng., 1981-82, Bowes Mus., Barnard Castle, Eng., 1982, Shipley Art Gallery, Gateshed, Eng., 1982, House of Commons, London, 1982, Haggin Mus., Stockton, Calif., 1985-86, U. N.D., Grand Forks, 1987, Greek Cultural Ctr., Springfield, Mass., 1987, 89, Del Bello Gallery, Toronto, Ont., Can., 1987, Ball State U., Muncie, Ind., 1989, Morin-Miller Galleries, N.Y.C., 1989-90, Columbia (Md.) Coll., 1989, Grand Prospect Hall, Bklyn., 1990, Kenneth Raymond Gallery, Boca Raton, Fla., 1993-96; author: The Small Caravan, 1962; author of short stories; author of numerous poems; videos include Multimedia Artist, 1988, 500 Definitions--Art Is, 1991. Recipient 4 Sculpture awards Summer Art Festivals, 1970-76, 2 Merit awards Greek Cultural Ctr., 1987; U. Wash. grantee, 1970; U. Wash. scholar, 1971. Mem. Nat. Artists Equity Assn., Inc., N.Y. Artists Equity Assn., Inc., Poetry Soc. Am., Greek-Am. Writers Assn. Democrat. Home and Office: 790 11th Ave Apt 39A New York NY 10019-3521

MILONE, ANTHONY M., bishop; b. Omaha, Sept. 24, 1932. Grad., North American Coll. (Rome). Ordained priest Roman Catholic Ch., 1957. Ordained titular bishop of Plestia and aux. bishop Diocese of Omaha, 1982; apptd. bishop Mont. Diocese, Great Falls-Billings, 1987—. Office: PO Box 1399 121 23rd St S Great Falls MT 59403-1399*

MILONE, JAMES MICHAEL, occupational health-safety engineering executive, evironmental engineer; b. Welfare Island, N.Y., Sept. 1, 1942; s. Michael James and Winifred Patricia (Rhenos) M.; m. Lois Esther Polinsky, Sept. 30, 1967; 1 child, Michelle Elena Milone. ABA, St. John's U., 1963; MPH Engring., MS in Environ. Scis., La Salle U., 1993, PhD in Indsl. Hygiene and Environ. Policy for Resource Mgmt., 1994. Registered indsl. hygienist, constrn./re-engring. occupl. health & safety engr., occupational health & safety engr., Integrated Pest Mgmt. expert; cert. environ. auditor/insp., environ./food sanitarian, environ./hazardous materials and waste mgmt. mgr. cons., econ./biol. entomologist; lic. air sample technologist, remediation supr., project monitor, mgmt. planner, integrated pest mgmt. cons.; cert. comml. applicator, profl. mgr. bldgs. and grounds. Sales, mktg. and bus. devel. cons., sales mgr. Profl. Porter Svc., Lynbrook, N.Y., 1963-69; dir. environ. svcs. Cross and Brown Co., N.Y.C., 1969-71; v.p., gen. mgr. Cert. Bldg. Maintenance Corp., N.Y.C., 1971-76; gen. mgr. Orkin Ext. Co., Inc., L.I., N.Y., 1976-80; sr. v.p., gen. mgr., environ.-occupl. health-safety engr., sr. project mgr., dir. constrn. sys., safety and loss prevention, risk mgmt. Envirotronics Ltd., Wilmington, Del., 1980—, human resources mentor, trainer; adj. faculty/prof. Nat. and Internat. Diplomate for LaSalle U., Kent Coll., Southland Law Sch., Nova U., LaSalle U. Internat. Practical Tng. Program U.S. Dept. Edn., Coun. on Post Secondary Christian Edn.; cons. Fed. Govt., Gen. Svcs. Adminstr., Dept. VA, Ben Gilman House of Reps., Sen. Joseph Holland/N.Y., others; corp. risk mgr., profl. cons., sys. safety mgr. Author/lectr.: Integrated Pest Management Systems In A Government Hospital Metroplex, 1994. Served with U.S. Army, 1961-69. Mem. Am. Indsl. Hygiene Assn., Am. Soc. Safety Engrs., Environ. Mgmt. Assn., Entomol. Soc. Air and Waste Mgmt., Am. Assn. for Standards and Testing of Materials, Products, Svcs. and Systems, numerous other environ., occupl. health, safety assns. and orgns. Roman Catholic. Achievements include invention of non-toxic biodegradeable odor counteractant and the development of an inter-disciplinary building maintenance green building system. Home: Ste # 3C 161-51 Jewel Ave Flushing NY 11365-4353

MILORO, PROTOPRESBTER FRANK, church official, religious studies educator; b. Wilmington, Del., Jan. 26, 1947; m. Constance Ann Evanisko, Apr. 20, 1969; children: Alexandra, Stephanie, Christopher. Grad. summa cum laude, Saviour Sem., 1969; grad. with high honors, St. Vincent Coll., 1972; attended, U. Pitts. Ordained to Diaconate and Priesthood, 1969. Assigned St. John's Ch., Ligonier, Pa., 1969-72, St. Stephen's Ch., Latrobe, Pa., 1969-72, St. John's Ch., Rahway, N.J., 1972-76; dir. Camp Nazareth, diocesan dir. youth, 1976-86; dean Christ the Saviour Sem.; elevated to dignity of Very Rev., 1985, sec. to bishop, instr. homiletics and parish administrn.; diocesan chancellor Am. Carpatho-Russian Orthodox Diocese, 1990—; dean Christ the Savior Cathedral, 1997—; chaplain Ea. Orthodox residents Polk Ctr., Commonwealth Pa., established chapel. Assoc. editor The Ch. Messenger. Office: 312 Garfield St Johnstown PA 15906-2122

MILOSZ, CZESLAW, poet, author, educator; b. Lithuania, June 30, 1911; came to U.S., 1960, naturalized, 1970; s. Aleksander and Weronika (Kunat) M. M Juris, U. Wilno, Lithuania, 1934; LittD (hon.), U. Mich., 1977; honoris causa, Brandeis U., 1985, Harvard U., 1989, Jaqellonian U., Poland, 1989, U. Rome, Italy, 1992. Programmer Polish Nat. Radio, 1935-39; diplomatic service Polish Fgn. Affairs Ministry, Warsaw, 1945-50; vis. lectr. U. Calif., Berkeley, 1960-61; prof. Slavic langs. and lits. U. Calif., 1961-78, prof. emeritus, 1978—. Author: The Captive Mind, 1953, Native Realm, 1968, Post-War Polish Poetry, 1965, The History of Polish Literature, 1969, Selected Poems, 1972, Bells in Winter, 1978, The Issa Valley, 1981, Separate Notebooks, 1984, The Land of Ulro, 1984, The Unattainable Earth, 1985, Collected Poems, 1988, Provinces, 1991, Beginning With My Streets, 1992, A Year of the Hunter, 1994, Facing the River, 1995, A Book of Luminous Things, 1996, Striving Towards Being, 1996. Recipient Prix Littéraire Européen Les Guildes du Livre, Geneva, 1953, Neustadt Internat. prize for lit. U. Okla., 1978, citation U. Calif., Berkeley, 1978, Nobel prize for lit., 1980, Nat. Medal of Arts, 1990; Nat. Culture Fund fellow, 1934-35; Guggenheim fellow, 1976. Mem. AAAS, Am. Acad. Arts and Scis., Am. Acad and Inst. Arts and Letters, Polish Inst. Letters and Scis. in Am., PEN Club in Exile. Office: U Calif Dept Slavic Langs Lits Berkeley CA 94720

MILSOM, ROBERT CORTLANDT, banker; b. Butler, Pa., Dec. 15, 1924; s. Robert C. and M. Ethel (Leyland) M. BS, John Carroll U., 1948. With PNC Bank (formerly Pitts. Nat. Bank), 1948-90; asst. sec., asst. cashier customer relations div. PNC Bank, 1953-56, asst. v.p. loan div., 1956-60, v.p. charge comml. loan group, 1960-65, sr. v.p. charge comml. banking div., 1965-68, exec. v.p., 1968-72, pres., 1972-85, chmn., CEO, 1985-90, also bd. dirs., 1972—; vice chmn., dir. PNC Bank Corp, 1972-90; bd. dirs. PNC Bank N.A., PNC Equity Mgmt. Corp., Exec. Svc. Corps., Foxwall Med. Svc.; chmn. bd. trustees Mercy Hosp. Pitts., 1994—. Bd. dirs. Pitts. Mercy Health System, Inc., Pitts. Ballet Theatre, Regional Indsl. Devel. Corp.; hon. trustee John Carroll U., Cleve.; mem. adv. bd. Mon Valley Renaissance program California U. Pa. Mem. Duquesne Club of Pitts., Fox Chapel Golf Club of Pitts., Laurel Valley Golf Club, Rolling Rock Club. Office: PNC Bank 5th Ave & Wood St Pittsburgh PA 15222 Office: PNC Bank NA P1-POPP-23-3 1 PNP Plz 249 Fifth Ave Pittsburgh PA 15222-2707

MILSOME, DOUGLAS, cinematographer. Cinematographer: (TV movies) Family of Spies, Hollywood Detective, Spies, Diana: Her True Story, Following the Heart, (TV mini-series) Great Expectations, Dirty Dozen, Lonesome Dove, Lonesome Dove II-The Return, Old Curiosity Shop, Buffalo Girls, (cable movie) Seasons of the Heart, (films) Race for the Yankee Zephyr, Wild Horses, Full Metal Jacket (British Critics Cir. award 1987, Oscar nomination 1987), Hawks, The Beast, Desperate Hours, If Looks Could Kill-Teenagent, Robin Hood-Prince of Thieves, Last of the Mohicans, (1st 7 weeks of the 1st Unit principal photography), Sunset Grill, Body of Evidence, Rumpelstulskin, Sunchaser. Office: Smith/Gosnell/Nicholson & Assoc PO Box 1166 1515 Palisades Dr Pacific Palisades CA 90272

MILSTED, AMY, medical educator. BSEd, Ohio State U., 1967; PhD, CUNY, 1977. Lectr. Hunter Coll./CUNY, 1970-76; instr. Carnegie-Mellon U., Pitts., 1976-77; postdoctoral fellow Muscular Dystrophy Assn./Carnegie-Mellon U., Pitts., 1978-79; rsch. assoc. Case Western Res. U., Cleve., 1979-82; rsch. chemist VA Med. Ctr., Cleve., 1982-87; project staff The Cleve. Clin. Found., 1987-89; asst. staff dept. brain and vascular rsch. Cleve. Clinic Found., 1989-93; grad. faculty Sch. Biomed. Scis. Kent (Ohio) State U., 1995—; assoc. prof. dept. biology U. Akron, Ohio, 1993—; adj. faculty biology dept. Cleve. State U., 1991—. Contbr. articles to profl. jours. Mem. Am. Heart Assn., Inter-Am. Soc. Hypertension, Am. Chem. Soc., Endocrine Soc., AAAS, Assn. Women in Sci. Office: University of Akron Dept of Biology ASEC 279 Akron OH 44325-3908

MILSTEIN, ELLIOTT STEVEN, legal educator, academic administrator; b. Hartford, Conn., Oct. 19, 1944; s. Samuel M. and Mildred K. Milstein; m. Bonnie Myrun, Oct. 1, 1967 (div. Oct. 1992); 1 child, Jacob. BA, U. Hartford, 1966; JD, U. Conn., 1969; LLM, Yale U., 1971. Bar: Conn. 1969, D.C. 1972, U.S. Dist. Ct. Conn. 1969, U.S. Ct. Appeals (D.C.) 1972. Lectr. in law U. Conn. Clin. Program. 1969-70; staff atty. New Haven Legal Assistance Assn., 1971-72; asst. prof. law, dir. clin. programs Washington coll. law Am. U., 1972-74, assoc. prof., dir. clin. programs, 1974-77, prof., dir. clin. programs, 1977-88, interim dean, 1988-90, dean, 1990—, assoc. dean Law Sch., 1977-78, interim pres., 1993-94; dean. Washington Coll. Law Am. Univ., 1994-95, prof. law, 1995—; co-dir. Nat. Vets. Law Ctr., 1978-84; cons. Calif. Bar Bd. of Bar Admissions, Nat. Conf. of Bar Examiners, lawyer tng. Practising Law Inst., N.Y.C.; chmn. D.C. Law Students in Ct. Program, 1982-83; mem. Law Tchrs. for Legal Svcs. Bd. dirs. Alliance for Justice, 1996—. Ford Urban Law fellow, 1971-72. Mem. Soc. Am. Law Tchrs., Assn. Am. Law Schs. (chmn. sect. clin. edn. 1982, mem. accreditation com. 1984-86, chmn. standing com. clin. edn. 1993—, exec. com. 1996—), ABA (skills tng. com. 1983-85, govt. rels. com. 1992—), ACLU. Democrat. Home: 3216 Brooklawn Ct Bethesda MD 20815-3941 Office: Am U Washington Coll Law 4400 Massachusetts Ave NW Washington DC 20016-8001

MILSTEIN, LAURENCE BENNETT, electrical engineering educator, researcher; b. Bklyn., Oct. 28, 1942; s. Harry and Sadie (Kaplan) M.; m. Suzanne Barbara Hirschman, Oct. 3, 1969; children—Coreen Roxanne, Renair Marissa. B.E.E., CUNY, 1964; M.S.E.E., Poly. Inst. Bklyn., 1966, Ph.D. in Elec. Engring., 1968. Mem. tech. staff Hughes Aircraft Co., El Segundo, Calif., 1968-69, staff engr., 1969-72, sr. staff engr., 1972-74; asst. prof. Rensselaer Poly. Inst., Troy, N.Y., 1974-76; asst. prof. U. Calif.-San Diego, La Jolla, 1976-79, assoc. prof., 1979-82, prof. elec. engring., 1982—, chmn. dept., 1984-88; rons. Hughes Aircraft Co., Culver City, Calif., 1976-78, Lockhead Missiles & Space Co., Sunnyvale, Calif., 1978-93, Motorola Satellite Comm., 1992—, InterDigital Comm. Corp, 1992-96, Golden Bridge Tech., 1995—, various govt. agys., pvt. cos., 1975—. Co-editor: Tutorials in Modern Communications, 1983; Spread Spectrum Communications, 1983; contbr. articles to profl. jours. Recipient Outstanding Tchr. award Warren Coll., U. Calif.-San Diego, La Jolla, 1982; grantee Army Rsch. Office, 1977-80, 81-84, 86-89, 91-94, 95—, Office of Naval Rsch., Arlington, Va., 1982—, TRW, San Diego, 1983-89, 92-97, NSF, 1993-96. Fellow IEEE, IEEE Coms. Soc. (bd. govs. 1983, 85-87, 93-95, v.p. for tech. activities 1990-91), IEEE Info. Theory Soc. (bd. govs. 1989-94). Jewish. Office: U Calif-San Diego Dept Elec and Computer Engring La Jolla CA 92093

MILSTEIN, RICHARD CRAIG, lawyer; b. N.Y.C., July 16, 1946; s. Max and Hattie (Jacobson) Worchel; children: Brian Matthew, Rachel Helanie. AA with honors, Miami-Dade Jr. Coll., 1966, AB cum laude, U. Miami, Fla., 1968, JD, 1973. Bar: Fla. 1974, U.S. Dist. Ct. Fla. 1974, U.S. Ct. Appeals (5th cir.) 1974, U.S. Supreme Ct. 1977, U.S. Ct. Appeals (11th cir.) 1982. Assoc., August, Nimkoff & Pohlig, Miami, Fla., 1974-76; mng. ptnr. Jepeway, August, Gassen & Pohlig, Miami, 1976-78, August, Gassen, Pohlig & Milstein, Miami, 1978-80, August, Pohlig & Milstein, P.A., Coral Gables, Fla., 1980-83; sr. ptnr. Milstein & Wayne, Coral Gables, 1983-85; ptnr. Tescher & Milstein, PA, Coral Gables, 1986-90, Akerman, Senterfitt & Eidson, P.A. 1990—. Co-founder Dade County Vol. Lawyers for Arts; mem. Met. Dade County Ind. Rev. Panel, 1984-86; councilor Metro Dade County Cultural Affairs Coun., 1986-91; sec./treas. Ops. SafeDrive, 1988; bd. dirs. South Fla. Mediation Ctr., 1982-89, chmn. bd. dirs., 1985-86; bd. dirs. Ptnrs. for Youth, 1981-91, Bet Shira Congregation, 1986—, pres., 1985-86, South Fla. Inter-Profl. Council Inc., 1986-87, v.p., 1985-86, sec. 1984-85, bd. dirs., 1983—; bd. dirs. Dance Umbrella Inc., 1983-87, Miami Coalition Inc., 1988-94; Fla. bar elder law sect., chair U. Miami, 1996-97; chair Dade County Cultural Alliance, 1993—. Fellow Am. Coll. Trust and Estate Counsel, Nat. Acad. Elder Law, Nat. Coun. Aging; mem. ABA, Am. Trial Lawyers Assn., Dade County Bar Assn. (dir. 1980-83, treas. 1983-84, sec. 1984-85, v.p. 1985-87, pres.-elect 1987-88, pres. 1988-89,), Coral Gables Bar Assn., Fla. Bar Assn. (professionalism com. guest lectr. real property and probate sect., Pro Bono awards 1986), Acad. Fla. Trial Lawyers (City of Miami Beach transition team), U. Miami Law Alumni (pres. 1997—), Phi Theta Kappa, Delta Theta Mu, Omicron Delta Kappa, Phi Alpha Theta, Kappa Delta Pi, Phi Kappa Phi, Alpha Kappa, Zeta Epsilon Nu. Democrat. Home: North Bay Island 1311 Bay Ter North Bay Village FL 33141-4002 Office: Akerman Senterfitt & Eidson One SE 3rd Ave Fl 28 Miami FL 33131

MILSTEIN, RICHARD SHERMAN, lawyer; b. Westfield, Mass., May 9, 1926; s. Abraham and Sarah (Yudman) M. BA, Harvard U., 1948; JD, Boston U., 1952. Bar: Mass. 1952, U.S. Supreme Ct. 1959. Ptnr. Ely & King, Springfield, Mass., 1954-95, Chaplin & Milstein, Boston, 1984-91; sr. counsel Robinson, Donovan, Madden & Barry P.C., Springfield, 1995—; dir. Mass. Continuing Legal Edn., 1969-80; cons. dir., 1980—. Commr. Springfield Parking Authority, 1984-90; trustee Comty. Music Sch., Springfield, 1994-96, Springfield Symphony Orch., 1995—, Springfield Libr. Mus. Assn.; overseer Mass. Supreme Jud. Ct. Hist. Soc., 1995—; trustee, life mem. Sta. WGBY-TV, pub. TV, Springfield; mem. adv. com. Springfield Fine Art Mus., 1988—, chmn., 1988-90; trustee Baystate Hosp., v.p., 1995—; vice chmn. Westfield Acad.; chmn. Horace Smith Fund, 1977-93. Lt. comdr. USCGR, 1952-64. Fellow Am. Coll. Trust and Estate Counsel, Mass. Bar Found. (life); mem. Am. Law Inst. (life), Am. Bar Found. (life). Home: 47 Mattoon St Springfield MA 01105-1715 Office: Robinson Donovan et al 1500 Main St Springfield MA 01115-0001 also: Mass Continuing Legal Edn 10 Winter Pl Boston MA 02108-4733

MILSTEN, ROBERT B., lawyer; b. Tulsa, Nov. 6, 1932; s. Travis I. and Regina (Jankowsky) M.; m. Jane Herskowitz, June 24, 1956; children: Stuart Paul, Leslie Jane. B.S., Ind. U., 1954; LL.B., U. Okla., 1956; postgrad., So. Meth. U., 1959. Bar: Okla. 1956, U.S. Ct. of Appeals 1956, U.S. Tax Ct 1956. Practiced in Oklahoma City, 1962—; govt. atty. Office Chief Counsel, IRS, 1958-62; atty. Fuller, Smith, Mosburg & Davis, 1962-63; atty. Andrews, Davis, Legg, Bixler, Milsten & Price, Inc. (and predecessor firm), 1964—, mem. firm, 1966—, dir., 1977-82, 96—; mem. S.W. region IRS/Bar Liaison Com., 1994—. Past pres., trustee Temple B'nai Israel. Served as lt., JAGC USAF, 1956-58. Mem. ABA (com. civil and criminal tax penalties sect. taxation 1962—), Okla. Bar Assn., Oklahoma County Bar Assn., Fed. Bar Assn. (2d v.p. local chpt. 1976), Econ. Club Okla., Quail Creek Golf and Country Club, Men's Dinner Club , Phi Delta Phi (treas. 1955-56). Office: 500 W Main St Oklahoma City OK 73102-2253

MILTON, CATHERINE HIGGS, public service entrepreneur; b. N.Y.C., Jan. 6, 1943; d. Edgar Homer and Josephine (Doughty) Higgs; m. A. Fenner Milton (div.); m. Thomas F. McBride, Aug. 25, 1974; children: Raphael McBride, Luke McBride. BA, Mt. Holyoke Coll., 1964, PhD (hon.), 1992. Reporter, travel writer Boston Globe, 1964-68; with Internat. Assn. Chiefs Police, Washington, 1968-70; asst. dir. Police Found., Washington, 1970-75; spl. asst. U.S. Treasury Dept., Washington, 1977-80; project staff Spl. Com. Aging/Senate, Washington, 1980-81; spl. asst. to pres., founder/exec. dir. Stanford (Calif.) U. Haas Ctr. for Public, 1981-91; exec. dir. Commn. for Nat. and Cmty. Svc., Washington, 1991-93; v.p. Corp. for Nat. Svc., Washington, 1993-95; exec. dir. Presidio Leadership Ctr., 1995-96; exec. dir. U.S. Programs Save the Children, Westport, Conn., 1996—; mem. U.S. Atty. General's Task Force on Family Violence, 1981-82; chair nat. forum Kellogg Found., 1990. Author: Women in Policing, 1972, Police Use of Deadly Force, 1976; co-author: History of Black Americans, 1965, Team Policing, Little Sisters and the Law, 1970. Bd. mem. Youth Svc. Calif., L.A., 1986-91, Trauma Found., San Francisco, 1982-90; spl. advisor Campus Compact, 1986-91. Nat. Kellogg Found. fellow, Battle Creek, Mich., 1985-88;

recipient Dedication and Outstanding Efforts award Bd. Suprs., Santa Clara, Calif., 1989, Outstanding Vol. Contbn. award Strive for Five, San Francisco, 1991, Dinkelspiel award Stanford U., 1991; named Outstanding Campus Adminstr. COOL, 1987. Avocations: backpacking, skiing, hiking, travel. Home: 59 Whitney St Westport CT 06880 Office: Save the Children PO Box 950 Westport CT 06881

MILTON, CHAD EARL, lawyer; b. Brevard County, Fla., Jan. 29, 1947; s. Rex Dale and Mary Margaret (Peacock) M.; m. Ann Mitchell Bunting, Mar. 30, 1972; children: Samuel, Kathleen, Kelsey. BA, Colo. Coll., 1969; JD, U. Colo., 1974; postgrad., U. Mo., 1976-77. Bar: Colo. 1974, Mo. 1977, U.S. Dist. Ct. Colo. 1974, U.S. Dist. Ct. (we. dist.) Mo. 1977. Counsel Office of Colo. State Pub. Defender, Colo. Springs, 1974-76; pub. info. officer, counsel Mid-Am. Arts Alliance, Kansas City, Mo., 1977-78; claims counsel Employers Reinsurance Corp., Kansas City, Mo., 1978-80; sr. v.p., asst. gen. counsel Media/Profl. Ins., Kansas City, Mo., 1981—; reporter, photographer, editor Golden (Colo.) Daily Transcript, 1970; investigator, law clk. Office of Colo. State Pub. Defender, Denver, Golden, 1970-74; assoc. Gage, Tucker, Hodges, Kreamer, Kelly & Varner (now Lathrop & Gage), Kansas City, 1973; participant Annenberg Project on the Reform of Libel Laws, Washington, 1987-88; adj. prof., comm. and advt. law Webster U., 1989-93; lectr. in field. Pres. bd. dirs. Folly Theater, 1992-94. Mem. ABA (chair intellectual property law com. of the torts and ins. practice sect., forum com. on comm. law), Mo. Bar Assn., Kansas City Met. Bar Assn., Libel Def. Resource Ctr. (editorial bd., exec. com.). Avocations: tennis, golf, skiing, sailing, antique maps. Home: 8821 Alhambra St Shawnee Mission KS 66207-2357 Office: Media/Profl Ins 2 Pershing Sq 2300 Main St Ste 800 Kansas City MO 64108-2415

MILTON, CHRISTIAN MICHEL, insurance executive; b. London, Nov. 13, 1947; came to U.S., 1978; s. Frank Harry and Gismonde Marie Susini; m. Rana Nikpour, Mar. 31, 1985. Claims clk. Stewart Smith Co., London, 1966-67; mgr. reins. claims Henry Head & Co., London, 1967-73; asst. v.p. reins. div. Airco, Hamilton, Bermuda, 1974-78, Nat. Union Fire Ins. Co., Pitts., 1980-81; asst. v.p. reins. div. Am. Internat. Group Inc., N.Y.C., 1978-80, 81-85, v.p. reins. div., 1985—; bd. dirs. Nat. Union Fire Ins. Co., N.Y.C., Am. Home Ins. Co., N.Y.C.; lectr. reins. Ins. Soc. N.Y., 1988—. Avocation: reading. Office: Am Internat Group Inc 70 Pine St New York NY 10270-0002

MILTON, CORINNE HOLM, art history educator; b. Nogales, Ariz., Oct. 16, 1928; d. Walter and Louise (Oates) Holm; m. Lee B. Milton, July 17, 1950 (dec. Oct. 1986); children: Bruce, Marina, Alan, Stuart. BA in Polit. Sci., U. Ariz., 1951, MLS, 1982; tchg. cert., U. N.Mex., 1973. Cert. secondary sch. tchr., Ariz., C.C. tchr., Ariz., Calif. Real estate sales agt. Walter Holm & Co., 1951-67; French and history tchr. Dept. State Overseas Schs., Washington, 1968-76; Sci. Tran Sci. Translating Co., Santa Barbara, Calif., 1976-78; libr. City of Nogales, 1982-83, City of Tucson, 1990-93; lectr. U. Ariz. Extension, Tucson, 1984—; Spanish instr. Pima Coll., Tucson, 1990-93; mem. Ariz.-Sonora Gov.'s Commn., Phoenix, 1993—; evaluator Ariz. Coun. for Humanities. Author, abstracter ABC Clio Press, 1976-78. Mem. Ariz. Opera Guild, 1989-96; bd. dirs. Hilltop Gallery, Nogales, 1989—; hostess, translator Tuscon Internat. Vis. Coun., 1994-96; lectr. on art history to cmty. schs. and retirement homes, Tucson, 1989—. Mem. UN Coun., Tucson Mus. Art (docent 1989—), Sunbelt World Trade Assn., Pimeria Alta Hist. Soc., Sierra Club. Democrat. Episcopalian. Avocations: hiking, raising greyhounds. Home: 6981 E Jagged Canyon Pl Tucson AZ 85750

MILTON, JOHN CHARLES DOUGLAS, nuclear physicist; b. Regina, Sask., Can., June 1, 1924; s. William and Frances Craigie (McDowall) M.; m. Gwendolyn Margaret Shaw, Oct. 10, 1953; children: Bruce F., Leslie J.F., Neil W.D., Theresa M. A.M. in Music, U. Man., 1943, B.Sc. with honors, 1947; M.A., Princeton U., 1949, Ph.D. in Physics, 1951. Asst. research officer Atomic Energy Can., Ltd., Chalk River, Ont., 1951-57; assoc. research officer Atomic Energy Can., Ltd., 1957-62, sr. research officer, 1962-70, prin. research officer, 1970—, head nuclear physics br., 1967-83, dir. physics div., 1983-85, v.p. physics and health scis., 1986-90, researcher emeritus, 1990-97; vis. scientist Lawrence Berkeley Lab., 1960-62, Centre de Recherches, Strasbourg & Bruyeres-le-Chatel, 1975-76; chmn. nuclear physics grants Natural Sci. and Engring. Research Council, 1977-82. Fellow Royal Soc. Can., Am. Phys. Soc.; mem. Can. Assn. Physicists (pres. 1992). Home: 3 Alexander Pl, Deep River, ON Canada K0J 1P0 Office: Chalk River Nuclear Lab, Chalk River, ON Canada K0J 1J0

MILTON, JOSEPH PAYNE, lawyer; b. Richmond, Va., Oct. 24, 1943; s. Hubert E. and Grace C. M.; children: Michael Payne, Amy Barrett, David King.; m. Cela Cabler Milton, Apr. 8, 1989. BS in Bus. Adminstrn., U. Fla., 1967, JD, 1969. Bar: Fla. 1969, U.S. Ct. Appeals (5th cir.) 1971, U.S. Supreme Ct. 1972, U.S. Ct. Appeals (11th cir.) 1981. Assoc. Toole, Taylor, Moseley & Gabel, Jacksonville, 1969-70; ptnr. Toole, Taylor, Moseley, Gabel & Milton, Jacksonville, 1971-78, Howell, Liles, Braddock & Milton, Jacksonville, 1978-89; Milton & Leach, Jacksonville, 1990-95; Milton, Leach & D'Andrea, Jacksonville, 1996—. Mem. Mayor's Blue Ribbon Task Force; pres. Civic Round Table of Jacksonville, 1980-81; campaign chmn. NE Fla. chpt. March of Dimes, 1973-74, v.p., 1974-75; pres. Willing Hands, 1974-75; chmn. attys.' div. United Way, 1977; mem. exec. com. Jacksonville Area Legal Aid, Inc., 1982-83; mem. Law Center Coun., U. Fla. Coll. Law, 1972-78; chmn. pvt. bar involvement com. Legal Aid Bd. dirs., 1982-83. Recipient Outstanding Service award for Individual Contbns. in Support of Legal Services for the Poor, 1981. Fellow Am. Bar Found., Internat. Soc. Barristers; Southeastern Admiralty Law com.; dir. Port, Jax, 1996; mem. ABA, Am. Bd. Trial Advocates (charter, pres.-elect Jacksonville chpt. 1996, pres. 1997), Jacksonville Bar Assn. (pres. 1980-81, pres. young lawyers sect. 1974-75), Fla. Bar (4th jud. cir. nominating commn. 1980-82, grievance com. 1975-77, chmn. 1976, mem. exec. coun. for trial sect. 1982-89, chmn.-elect 1986-87, chmn. 1987, 88, voluntary bar liaison com. 1982-83, bd. govs. 1988-90), Jacksonville Assn. Def. Counsel (pres. 1981-82, lectr. CLE programs, guest lectr. U. Fla., NARTC), Fla. Coun. Bar Assn. Pres. (exec. com. 1982-88, v.p. 1984, pres. 1985-86), Nat. Assn. R.R. Trial Counsel (v.p. southeastern region 1984-86, exec. com. 1979—, pres. elect 1989-90, pres. 1990-91), Maritime Law Assn. U.S., Acad. Fla. Trial Lawyers, Assn. Trial Lawyers Am., Am. Judicature Soc. Republican. Clubs: San Jose Country (Jacksonville), University, Gulf Life Tower (Jacksonville), Country Club Sapphire Valley. Home: 4655 Corrientes Cir N Jacksonville FL 32217 Office: Milton Leach & D'Andrea 1660 Prudential Dr Ste 200 Jacksonville FL 32207-8185

MILTON, LEONHARDA LYNN, elementary and secondary school educator; b. Minneota, Minn., Apr. 7, 1924; d. John and Mathilde (Bockman) Hinderlie; m. John Ronald Milton, Aug. 3, 1946; 1 child, Nanci. BA, U. Minn., 1949. Cert. tchr., Minn., Colo., S.D. Visual art tchr. Humboldt High Sch., St. Paul, 1949-57, Vermillion (S.D.) Middle Sch., 1972—; tchr. Kuns Miller Jr. High Sch., Denver, 1960-61; occupational therapist N.D. State Hosp., Jamestown, 1959-60. Exhibited prin. works in numerous shows in Minn., N.D., S.D. Mem. Nat. Art Edn. Assn. (State Art Educator award 1983), S.D. Art Educators (pres. 1980-83), S.D. Alliance for Art Edn. (pres. 1985-88). Democrat. Lutheran. Avocations: reading, visual artwork, travel. Home: 630 Thomas St Vermillion SD 57069-3631 Office: Vermillion Mid Sch Princeton St Vermillion SD 57069

MILTON, RICHARD HENRY, retired diplomat, children's advocate; b. Bowling Green, Ky., Sept. 30, 1938; s. Lester Thomas and Rose Ann (Jesse) M.; m. Evy M. Miller, Aug. 28, 1964; children: Christopher, Ann. Student, W.Va. U., 1956-57; BA, Marshall U., 1960, MA, 1964. Tchr. Columbus, Ohio, 1960-61; tchr. Sidney, Ohio, 1964-65; fgn. svc. officer U.S. Dept. State, Washington, 1965-94; dep. asst. dir. ACDA, Washington, 1982-83; consul gen. U.S. consulate gen., Guayaquil, Ecuador, 1984-87; polit. advisor U.S. Space Command, Peterson AFB, Colo., 1987-90, 92-94; v.p. Am. Fgn. Svc. Assn., U.S. Dept. State, Washington, 1990-91; vis. prof. USCG Acad., New London, Conn., 1977-79. Pres. Community Welfare Assn., Warsaw, Poland, 1975; ct. apptd. spl advocate Colo. 4th Jud. Dist., 1993—, Cmty. Partnership for Child Devel., 1995—, Protect our Children Coalition, 1996. Served to 1st lt. U.S. Army, 1961-63. Congl. fellow Am. Polit. Sci. Assn., 1974-75. Mem. Am. Fgn. Svc. Assn., Consular Officers Assn. (pres. 1983-84). Avocation: antique automobiles. Home: 2022 Devon St Colorado Springs CO 80909-1618

MILTON, ROBERT MITCHELL, chemical company executive; b. St. Joseph, Mich., Nov. 29, 1920; s. Clare Leon and Frances Thornton (Mitchell) M.; m. Mary Wills Bridges, June 22, 1946; children: Mrs. M. Gillian Sanders (dec.), Mrs. Suzanne M. Padilla, David Wills. B.A., Oberlin Coll., 1941; M.A., Johns Hopkins U., 1943, Ph.D., 1944. C.Y. War Project Johns Hopkins U., Balt., 1943-45, rsch. assoc., 1945-46; with Union Carbide Corp., 1946-85, rsch. chemist, 1946-51, rsch. supr., 1951-54, mgr. devel. lab., 1954-58, asst. mgr. new products, 1958-59, asst. dir., then dir. rsch. Linde div., 1959-73, exec. v.p. Showa UNOX, Showa Union Gosei div., 1973-77, dir. agrl. bus. devel., v.p. Keystone Seed Co. div., 1977-79; assoc. corp. dir. product safety and liability Union Carbide Corp., Danbury, Conn., 1980-85; pres. R. Milton Assocs., Inc., 1986—; cons. U.S. Naval Tech. Mission to Europe, 1945; mem. adv. bd. hyperbaric medicine SUNY, 1966-73; mem. NRC panel on environ. protection, safety and hazardous materials of Com. on Chem. Engring. Frontiers, 1985-87. Inventor Linde molecular sieve adsorbents and catalysts, hi-flux tubing; patentee in field. Mem. AAAS, Am. Chem. Soc. (Jacob F. Schoellkopf medal 1963), Am. Inst. Chemists (dir.-at-large 1982-87, pres. elect 1988-89, pres. 1990-91, chmn. bd. dirs. 1992-93, Chem. Pioneer award 1980), Wawashkamo Golf Club (pres. emeritus), Mackinac Island Yacht Club, Johns Hopkins Club, Phi Beta Kappa, Sigma Xi. Home and Office: # 310 19800 US Hwy # 1 Tequesta FL 33469 also: PO Box 326 Mackinac Island MI 49757-0326

MILUNAS, J. ROBERT, health care organization executive; b. Aug. 7, 1947; s. Joseph John M.; m. Glenetta Graham; children: Amy, Joseph, Anna Kate. BS, Tulane U., 1969; postgrad., Samford U., 1973; MBA, Ga. State U., 1977. Mgr. internal and govt. reporting, corp. contr.'s staff Arvin Industries Inc., Columbus, Ind., 1977-80; mgr. consol. acctg., corp. contr.'s staff Mattel Inc., Hawthorne, Calif., 1980-82; asst. contr. Times Mirror Cable TV Inc., Irvine, Calif., 1982-83; Western Div. contr. SCA, Santa Ana, Calif., 1983-84; v.p., corp. contr. Tchrs. Mgmt. Investment Corp., Newport Beach, Calif., 1984-86; v.p., chief fin. officer Beech St. Inc., Irvine, 1987-89; v.p. fin. and adminstrn. ConsumerHealth Inc., Newport Beach, Calif., 1989-93; pres. Aegis Consulting Svcs., Laguna Niguel, Calif., 1993—. 1st lt. U.S. Army Transp. Corps., 1969-71. Decorated Bronze Star. Home: 28331 Las Cabos Laguna Niguel CA 92677-7562 *Life is a precious gift to be nurtured daily through interaction with friends and family and helping others achieve their potential.*

MIMS, EDWARD TROW, electronics industry executive; b. Pittsburgh, Calif., Feb. 29, 1948; s. Arthur Trow and Marjorie (Fisher) M.; m. Verna Lynne Daubert, Jan. 23, 1981; 1 child, Matthew Edward. Student, U. Tex., 1966-70. Profl. baseball player Houston Astros Sports Assn., 1970-75; dist. mgr. Team Electronics, Mpls., 1976-80; regional mgr. Bose Corp., Framingham, Mass., 1980-85, mgr. nat. field sales, 1985-86, mgr. nat. accounts, 1986-90, dir. spl. markets, 1990-91, dir. sales N.Am., 1991-93; dir. sales N.Am. Cerwin-Vega! Inc., Simi Valley, Calif., 1993-96; exec. dir. worldwide sales and mktg. Cerwin-Vega! Inc., Simi Valley, 1996—.

MIMS, WILLIAM CLEVELAND, state legislator, lawyer; b. Harrisonburg, Va., June 20, 1957; s. David Lathan and Lurleen Shirley (Stovall) M.; m. Jane Ellen Rehme, Dec. 20, 1980; children: Katherine Grace, Emily Anne, Sarah Joy. AB, Coll. of William & Mary, 1979; JD, George Washington U., 1984; LLM, Georgetown U., 1986. Bar: Va. Legis. asst. Congressman Paul Trible, Washington, 1981-82; dep. legis. dir. Senator Paul Trible, Washington, 1983-85; chief of staff Congressman Frank Wolf, Washington, 1986-87; atty. Hazel & Thomas, P.C., Leesburg, Va., 1987-91, Worcester, Mims & Atwill, P.C., Leesburg, 1993—; mem. Va. Gen. Assembly, Richmond, 1991—; Va. Housing Study Commn., 1994—. Bd. dirs. Dulles Area Transp. Assn., Herndon, Va., 1994—, Marshall Home Preservation Fund, Leesburg, 1992—, Youth for Tomorrow, 1995—; treas., bd. dirs. Loudoun Bar Assn., Leesburg, 1988-89; chmn. Loudoun Rep. Com., Leesburg, 1988-91; dist. rep. Nat. Eagle Scout Assn., 1992—. Recipient commendation Com. for Dulles, 1986; named outstanding local chmn. Rep. Party of Va. 1991, Flemming fellow, 1995-96. Mem. Va. Bar Assn., Va. Trial Lawyers Assn., Christian Legal Soc., Loudoun C. of C. Republican. Episcopalian. Office: Worcester Mims & Atwill PC PO Drawer 741 Leesburg VA 20178

MIN, NANCY-ANN, federal agency administrator; b. Rockwood, Tenn.. BA with highest honors, U. Tenn.; BA in Politics and Econs., Balliol Coll.; MA in Polits. and Econs., Oxford U.; JD, Harvard U., 1983. Staff asst. Sarah Weddington, Pres. Carter's Asst. for Polit. Liaison; jud. intern to Mark Cannon Adminstrv. Asst. to Chief Justice Warren Burger Supreme Ct.; law clk. Chief Judge Gilbert Merritt, U.S. Ct. Appeals 6th Cir.; comml. litigation ptnr. Bass, Berry & Sims, Nashville; cabinet mem. Commr. of the Dept. Human Svcs., Tenn.; lawyer Covington & Burling, Washington; assoc. dir. health Office of Mgmt. Budget, Washington, 1993—; adj. prof. Vanderbilt U. Office: Health & Personnel Old Executive Ofc Bldg Washington DC 20503*

MINAHAN, DANIEL FRANCIS, manufacturing company executive, lawyer; b. Orange, N.J., Dec. 3, 1929; s. Alfred A. and Katherine (Kelly) M.; m. Mary Jean Gaffney, May 2, 1953; children: Daniel F. Jr., John A. AB magna cum laude, U. Notre Dame, 1951; JD magna cum laude, U. Conn., 1964; grad., Advanced Mgmt. Program, Harvard, 1975. Bar: Conn. 1964, U.S. Supreme Ct. 1964, U.S. Ct. of Appeals (2d cir.), U.S. Dist. Ct. Conn. 1967. Mgr. indsl. engring. Uniroyal, Inc., Naugatuck, Conn., 1952-59, mgr. indsl. relations, 1959-64; dir. labor relations Uniroyal, Inc., N.Y.C., 1964-66; v.p. indsl. relations and labor counsel Phillips Van Heusen Corp., N.Y.C., 1966-69; v.p. personnel-adminstrn. Broadway-Hale Stores, Inc., Los Angeles, 1969-70; v.p. employee relations, sec. Magnavox-N.Am., Philips Corp., 1970-73, v.p. ops., group exec., 1973-83, sr. v.p. adminstrn., 1984-89, exec. v.p., 1989-93, vice chmn., 1991-93; vice chmn. nat. found. bd. Robert Anderson Sch. Mgmt., U. N.Mex., 1993—; mem. trustees adv. coun., Fairfield U., mem. dean's coun. Grad. Sch. Bus. Co-author: The Developing Labor Law, 1971. Chmn. bd. Internat. Fedn. Keystone Youth Orgns., London and Chgo., 1984-88; trustee U. Conn. Law Sch.; vice-chmn. nat. found. bd. Anderson Sch. Mgmt., U. N.Mex., 1993—. With USMC. Mem. ABA, Conn. Bar Assn., NAM, Harvard Advanced Mgmt. Assn., Washington Internat. Corp. Circle, Harvard Club, Club Internat. (Chgo.), Belfrey Club (London). Office: c/o Office of the Dean U N Mex Robert Anderson Sch Bus Albuquerque NM 87131

MINAHAN, JOHN C., JR., federal judge; b. Melbourne, Australia, Mar. 1, 1943; came to U.S., 1946; s. John C. and Mavis V. (Monahan) M.; children: Keith, Eliot. BS, U. Calif., Berkeley, 1965; JD, Creighton U., 1973; LLM, Harvard U., 1976. Bar: Nebr. 1973, U.S. Dist. Ct. Nebr. 1973, U.S. Ct. Appeals (8th cir.) 1984. Prof. Vt. Law Sch., South Royalton, Vt., 1974-77; ptnr. Kutak Rock & Campbell, Omah, 1977-82; prin. Dixon Dixon & Minahan, P.C., Omah, 1982-87; bankruptcy judge U.S. Dist. Ct. Nebr., Lincoln, 1987—; adj. prof. U. Nebr. Sch. of Law, Lincoln, 1987—. Contbr. articles to profl. jours. Capt. USMC, 1965-69, Vietnam. Mem. Fed. Bar Assn., Nebr. Bar Assn., Lincoln Bar Assn., Nat. Conf. of Bankruptcy Judges, Am. Legion. Avocations: skiing, shortwave radio, competitive shooting. Office: US Bankruptcy Ct 463 Federal Bldg 100 Centennial Mall N Lincoln NE 68508-3804

MINAHAN, JOHN ENGLISH, author; b. Albany, N.Y., Apr. 30, 1933; s. John English and Constance Madeline (Langdon) M.; m. Verity Ann Hill, Apr. 27, 1966. Student, Cornell U., 1955-57, Harvard U., 1958-59, Columbia U., 1959-60. Staff writer Time mag., 1960-61; chief TV writer J. Walter Thompson Co., N.Y.C., 1961-65; free-lance writer N.Y.C., 1965-73, L.A., 1976-79, Miami, 1981-95; editor, pub. American Way mag., N.Y.C., 1973-76; contbg. editor L.A. mag., 1978-79; dir. corp. comms. The Wackehut Corp., Coral Gables, Fla., 1990-95; free-lance writer Palm Springs, Calif., 1995—; cons. Universal-MCA Inc., 1976-79; instr. novel writing workshop Harvard U. Ctr. Lifelong Learning, 1987-89. Author: (novels) A Sudden Silence, 1963, The Passing Strange, 1965, Jeremy, 1973, Sorcerer, 1977, Nine/Thirty/Fifty-Five, 1977, Almost Summer, 1978, Nunzio, 1978, The Complete American Graffiti, 1979, Eyewitness, 1981, The Great Hotel Robbery, 1982, The Great Diamond Robbery, 1984, Mask, 1985, The Face Behind the Mask, 1986, The Great Pyramid Robbery, 1987, The Great Harvard Robbery, 1988, The Great Grave Robbery, 1989; (biographies) The Dream Collector, 1972, The Quiet American: A Biography of George R. Wackenhut, 1994; translation from French: The Fabulous Onassis, 1972; screenplays: A Sudden Silence, 1965, The Passing Strange, 1979; TV play: First Flight, 1968; contbg. editor book and theater revs., Miami Herald, 1983-95; also articles in N.Y. Times, Saturday Rev., Time-Life Spl. Reports. Recipient Doubleday award, 1960. Mem. Nat. Soc. Lit. and Arts, Alpha Delta Phi. Club: Harvard of Miami, Faculty of Harvard U. Home and Office: 5289 E Cherry Hills Dr Palm Springs CA 92264-5903

MINAKER, GEORGE, Canadian provincial official; b. Morris, Manitoba, Can.. BSEE, U. Manitoba, 1960. Numerous engring. positions Winnipeg, 1961-84; mem. for Winnipeg-St. James House of Commons, 1984-88; mem. Nat. Transp. Agy., Ottawa, Ont., Can., 1990-96; mem. fin. com. House of Commons, energy, mines and resources com. Mem. city coun. St. James, St. James-Assiniboia and Winnipeg, 1967-73; mem. Manitoba Legislative Assembly, St. James, 1973-81, Min. of Cmty. Svcs. and Corrections. Mem. Assn. Profl. Engrs. Ont. and Manitoba. Office: Nat Transp Agy, Ottawa, ON Canada K1A 0N9

MINAMI, ROBERT YOSHIO, artist, graphic designer; b. Seattle, May 1, 1919; s. Kichitaro and Suma (Fujita) M.; m. Shizu Tashiro, May 30, 1953; 1 child, Ken. Artist; student, Art Inst., Chgo., 1957, Am. Acad. Art, Chgo., 1980-81. Graphic artist Filmack Studios, Chgo., 1945-48, S. Taylor & Leavitt Assocs., Chgo., 1949-50; head graphic designer NBC-TV, Chgo., 1950-82; fine artist Robert Minami's Studio, Oceanside, Calif., 1983—; artist Goodman Theatre Design, Chgo., 1955-56; mem. Oceanside Mus. Art Exhbn. Com.; art instr. Mus. Sch. Art, Oceanside, 1997-98. Exhibits include Oceanside Mus. Art, 1996. Active Supporters for City Couns., Oceanside, 1984—. Recipient Merit award Artist Guild Chgo., 1956, People's Choice award Carlsbad Oceanside Art League, 1986, Dick Blick award, 1992, 1st place award Mixed Media Collage, 1993, Nat. Watercolor award Watercolor West, 1994. Mem. San Diego Watercolor Soc., United Scenic Artists (life), Am. Fine Art Connection, San Diego Art Inst., Nat. Watercolor Soc. (assoc.), Watercolor West Juried Assn. Avocations: painting, travel, movies, concerts, opera.

MINARD, EVERETT LAWRENCE, III, journalist, magazine editor; b. Seattle, Nov. 19, 1949; s. Everett Lawrence Jr. and Nancy M.; m. Elizabeth Anne Bailey, Sept. 15, 1979. BA in Econs., Trinity Coll., Hartford, Conn., 1972; postgrad., New Sch. for Social Rsch., 1972-74. Reporter, staff writer, mgr. European, West Coast/Asia burs. Forbes mag., 1974-89; mng. editor Forbes mag., N.Y.C., 1989—. Mem. Seattle Yacht Club, Heights Casino Club, Lawrence Beach Club. Office: Forbes Inc 60 5th Ave New York NY 10011-8802*

MINARDI, RICHARD A., JR., lawyer; b. Mobile, Ala., Aug. 15, 1943; s. Richard A. and Martha F. (Beck) M.; m. Frances Archer Guy, Oct. 21, 1989. BA, Yale U., 1965, LLB, 1968. Bar: Va. 1969. Assoc. McGuire Woods & Battle, Richmond, Va., 1968-71; ptnr. Staples, Greenberg Minardi & Kessler, Richmond, 1971-86, Mays & Valentine, Richmond, 1986—. Mem. ABA, Va. Bar Assn., Richmond Bar Assn. Home: 211 Santa Clara Dr Richmond VA 23229-7152 Office: Mays & Valentine PO Box 1122 Richmond VA 23208-1122

MINARIK, ELSE HOLMELUND (BIGART MINARIK), author; b. Aarhus, Denmark, Sept. 13, 1920; d. Kaj Marius and Helga Holmelund; m. Walter Minarik, July 14, 1940 (dec.); 1 child, Brooke Ellen; m. Homer Bigart, Oct. 3, 1970 (dec.). BA, Queens Coll., 1942. Tchr. 1st grade, art Commack (N.Y.) Pub. Schs., 1950-54. Author children's books: Little Bear, 1957, Father Bear Comes Home, 1959, Little Bear's Friend, 1960, Little Bear's Visit, 1961, No Fighting, No Biting, 1958, Cat and Dog, 1960, The Winds That Come From Far Away, 1960, The Little Giant Girl and the Elf Boy, 1963, A Kiss for Little Bear, 1968, What If, 1987, Percy and the Five Houses, 1988, It's Spring, 1989, The Little Girl and the Dragon, 1991, Am I Beautiful, 1992. Mem. PEN Club. Home: Parker Ridge HC 64 Box 270 Blue Hill ME 04614

MINARIK, JOSEPH JOHN, economist, researcher; b. Lancaster, Pa., July 27, 1949; s. Joseph John and Helen Elizabeth M.; m. Eileen Marie Dowds; children: Mara Christina, Sara Elizabeth. B.A., Georgetown U., 1971; M.A., Yale U., 1972, M.Phil., 1973, Ph.D., 1974. Rsch. assoc. Brookings Instn., Washington, 1974-81; dept. asst. dir. Congl. Budget Office, Washington, 1981-84; sr. rsch. assoc. Urban Inst., Washington, 1984-88; exec. dir. Joint Econ. Com. U.S. Congress, Washington, 1988-90; exec. dir. for policy, chief economist House Budget Com., 1991-93; assoc. dir. econ. policy Office Mgmt. and Budget, 1993—. Author: Making Tax Choices, 1985, Making America's Budget Policy, 1989; contbr. articles to profl. jours. Fellow NSF, 1971-74, Yale U., 1971. Mem. Am. Econ. Assn., Nat. Tax Assn. Democrat. Home: 11656 Mediterranean Ct Reston VA 22090-3401 Office: Economic Policy 244 Old Executive Bldg Washington DC 20503

MINASI, ANTHONY, software company executive; b. N.Y.C., July 9, 1948; s. Dominic A. and Mary (De Rosa) M.; m. Patricia Ann Gallagher, Oct. 3, 1976; children: Christopher, Marie Elizabeth. BA, Hunter Coll., 1971; MBA with distinction, Pace U., 1982, postgrad., 1988. Bus. analyst Am. Internat. Group, N.Y.C., 1971-75; systems mgr., officer Fiduciary Trust Co., N.Y.C., 1975-79; systems mgr. Flexivan Leasing, N.Y.C., 1979-84; group mgr., v.p. Drexel Burnham, N.Y.C., 1984-89; mng. dir. tech. Vista Concepts, Inc., N.Y.C., 1989-93; sr. prin., mgr. N.Am. investment industry sales/svc. Am. Mgmt. Systems, Inc., N.Y.C., 1994-95; practice mgr. Investment Industry Group, N.Y.C., 1996-97, v.p., engagement mgr. corp. banking and securities practice, 1997—. Avocations: photography, tennis, woodworking. Office: American Management Sys 1 Chase Plz New York NY 10005

MINC, HENRYK, mathematics educator; b. Lodz, Poland, Nov. 12, 1919; came to U.S., 1960, naturalized, 1966; s. Izrael and Haja (Zyngler) M.; m. Catherine Taylor Duncan, Apr. 16, 1943; children: Robert Henry, Ralph Edward, Raymond. MA with honors, Edinburgh U. (Scotland), 1955, PhD, 1959. Tchr. Morgan Acad., Dundee, Scotland, 1956-58; lectr. Dundee Tech. Coll., Scotland, 1957-58, U. B.C., Vancouver, Can., 1958-59, asst. prof., 1959-60; assoc. prof. U. Fla., Gainesville, 1960-63; vis. prof. Technion Israel Inst. Tech., Haifa, 1969-80; prof. U. Calif.-Santa Barbara, 1963-90, emeritus, 1990—; referee and reviewer for math. jours. Author: A Survey of Matrix Theory and Matrix Inequalities, 1964, translated into Russian, 1972, Chinese, 1990; Introduction to Linear Algebra, 1965, translated into Spanish, 1968; Modern University Algebra, 1966; Elementary Linear Algebra, 1968, translated into Spanish, 1971; New College Algebra, 1968; Elementary Functions and Coordinate Geometry, 1969; Algebra and Trigonometry, 1970; College Algebra, 1970; College Trigonometry, 1971; Integrated Analytic Geometry and Algebra with Circular Functions, 1973; Permanents, 1978, translated into Russian, 1980, Chinese, 1991; Nonnegative Matrices, 1988, trans. into Chinese, 1991; contbr. over 80 research papers to profl. jours. 2d. lt. Polish Army, 1940-48. France, U.K. Recipient Lester Ford award Math. Assn. Am., 1966, rsch. contract Office Naval Rsch., 1985-88. Air Force Office Sci. Rsch. grantee, 1960-83, Lady Davis fellow, 1975, 78. Fellow Soc. Antiquaries of Scotland; mem. Am. Math Soc., , Burns Fedn. (hon. pres.), Inst. Antiquity and Christianity, Scottish Soc. Santa Barbara (past chieftain), Scots Lang. Soc., Saltire Soc., Assn. for Scottish Lit. Studies, James Hogg Soc., Santa Barbara Elks Lodge, Clan Fraser Soc. N.Am. Democrat. Home: 4076 Naranjo Dr Santa Barbara CA 93110-1213 Office: U Calif Dept Math Santa Barbara CA 93106

MINCER, JACOB, economics educator; b. Tomaszow, Poland, July 15, 1922; came to U.S., 1948; s. Isaac and Dora (Eisen) M.; m. Flora Kaplan, 1951; children—Deborah, Carolyn. B.A., Emory U., 1950; Ph.D., Columbia U., 1957; LLD honoris causa, U. Chgo., 1991. Asst. prof. CUNY, 1954-59; assoc. prof. Columbia U., N.Y.C., 1960-62; prof. econs. Columbia U., 1962—; Mem. research staff Nat. Bur. Econ. Research, N.Y.C., 1960—. Author: Schooling, Experience and Earnings, 1974, Studies in Human Capital, 1993, Studies in Labor Supply, 1993; author, editor: Economic Forecasts and Expectations, 1969. Contbr. numerous articles to profl. publs. Postdoctoral fellow U. Chgo., 1957-58; Guggenheim fellow, N.Y.C., 1971. Fellow Am. Statis. Assn., Econometric Soc., Am. Econ. Assn. (Disting.); mem. Am. Acad. Arts and Scis., Nat. Acad. Edn. Home: 448 Riverside Dr New York NY 10027-6818 Office: Columbia U Dept Econs 118th St at Amsterdam Ave New York NY 10027

MINCKLER, LEON SHERWOOD, forestry and conservation educator, author; b. New Milford, N.Y., May 7, 1906; s. Walter Harmon and Eva Lena (Williams) M.; m. Althea Mae Singleton, Mar. 31, 1929 (dec. 1946); children: L. Sherwood, C. Christine, E. Maxine; m. Edith Adair Springer, Mar. 7, 1947; children: Sandra Gayle, Walter David; adopted children: William, Jean. BS in Forestry, N.Y. State Coll. Forestry, 1928, PhD in Plant Physiology, 1935. Jr. forester U.S. Forest Svc., Kans., Okla., Tex., 1935-36; rsch. forester U.S. Forest Svc., Asheville, N.C., 1936-45; rsch. ctr. leader U.S. Forest Svc., Buckingham, Va., 1945-46; forester U.S. Forest Svc., Carbondale, Ill., 1946-68; prof. agr. Va. Poly. Forestry Coll., Blacksburg, Va., 1968-70; adj. prof. forestry SUNY, Syracuse, 1970-77; cons., writer Blacksburg, 1977-91; adj. prof. So. Ill. Forestry Coll., Carbondale, 1991-97; retired, 1997. Author: Woodland Ecology, 1975, 2nd edit., 1980; contbr. over 170 articles to profl. jours. Recipient 50 Yr. Award of Merit, N.Y. State Coll. Forestry. Fellow AAAS; mem. Soc. Am. Foresters, Nat. Parks and Conservation Assn. (bd. dirs. 1970-80). Democrat. Unitarian. Avocation: earth ethics and human cooperation with natural laws. Home: 1510 Hollyhill Pl Blacksburg VA 24060-6200

MINDELL, EARL LAWRENCE, nutritionist, author; b. St. Boniface, Man., Can., Jan. 20, 1940; s. William and Minerva Sybil (Galsky) M.; came to U.S., 1965, naturalized, 1972; BS in Pharmacy, N.D. State U., 1963; PhD in Nutrition, Pacific We. U., 1985; masner herbalist Dominion Herbal Coll., 1995; m. Gail Andrea Jaffe, May 16, 1971; children: Evan Louis-Ashley, Alanna Dayan. Pres. Adanac Mgmt. Inc., 1979—; instr. Dale Carnegie course; lectr. on nutrition, radio and TV. Mem. Beverly Hills, Rancho Park, Western Los Angeles (dir.) regional chambers commerce, Calif., Am. pharm. assns., Am. Acad. Gen. Pharm. Practice, Am. Inst. for History of Pharmacy, Am. Nutrition Soc., Internat. Coll. Applied Nutrition, Nutrition Found., Nat. Health Fedn., Orthomolecular Med. Assn., Internat. Acad. Preventive Medicine. Clubs: City of Hope, Beverly Hills Rotary, Masons, Shriners. Author: Earl Mindell's Vitamin Bible, Parents Nutrition Bible, Earl Mindell's Quick and Easy Guide to Better Health, Earl Mindell's Pill Bible, Earl Mindell's Shaping Up with Vitamins, Earl Mindell's Safe Eating, Earl Mindell's Herb Bible, Mindell's Food as Medicine, Earl Mindell's Soy Miracle, 1995, Anti-Aging Bible, 1996, Secret Remedies, 1997; columnist Let's Live mag., The Vitamin Supplement (Can.), The Vitamin Connection (U.K.), Healthy N' Fit; contbr. articles on nutrition to profl. jours. Fellow Brit. Homeopathic Inst., Scottish Inst. Homeopathy. Home: 244 S El Camino Dr Beverly Hills CA 90212-3809 Office: 107 S Beverly Dr Beverly Hills CA 90212-3002

MINDELL, EUGENE ROBERT, surgeon, educator; b. Chgo., Feb. 24, 1922; s. Leon and Tillie (Rosenthal) M.; m. June A. Abrams, Sept. 19, 1945; children: Barbara, Ruth, David, Douglas. BS, U. Chgo., 1943, MD, 1945. Diplomate Am. Bd. Orthopaedic Surgery (bd. dirs. 1977-84, pres. 1983-84). Resident in orthopaedic surgery U. Chgo. Clinics, 1948-52; instr. U. Chgo., 1952; mem. faculty dept. orthopaedic surgery Sch. Medicine SUNY, Buffalo, 1953—, prof. Sch. Medicine, 1964—; chmn. dept. SUNY Sch. Medicine, Buffalo, 1964-88, dir. orthopaedic oncology Sch. Medicine, 1988—; mem. bd. mgrs. Erie County Med. Ctr., 1990-96. Assoc. editor Jour. Bone and Joint Surgery, 1984-88, trustee, 1991—; contbr. articles to profl. jours. Lt. (j.g.) M.C. USNR, 1946-48. Eugene R. Mindell Chair of Orthopaedic Surgery established in his honor SUNY, Buffalo, 1996; recipient Disting. Svc. award Alumni U. Chgo. Sch. Medicine, 1990; NRC fellow, 1949-50/. Fellow ACS; mem. Am. Acad. Orthopaedic Surgeons (bd. dirs. 1991), Am. Orthopaedic Assn. (v.p. 1990-91), Assn. Orthopaedic Chmn., Am. Assn. Surgery of Trauma, Am. Orthopaedic Rsch. Soc. (pres. 1972-73, residency rev. com. 1985-91), Musculoskeletal Tumor Soc. (pres. 1989-90), Coun. Musculoskeletal Specialty Socs. (chmn. elect 1991, chmn. 1992). Jewish. Home: 85 Depew Ave Buffalo NY 14214-1509 Office: 100 High St Buffalo NY 14203-1126

MINDES, GAYLE DEAN, education educator; b. Kansas City, Mo., Feb. 11, 1942; d. Elton Burnett and Juanita Maxine (Mangold) Taylor; BS, U. Kans., 1964; MS, U. Wis., 1965; EdD, Loyola U., Chgo., 1979; m. Marvin William Mindes, June 20, 1969 (dec.); 1 son, Jonathan Seth. Tchr. pub. schs., Newburgh, N.Y., 1965-67; spl. educator Ill. Dept. Mental Health, Chgo., 1967-69; spl. edn. supr. Evanston (Ill.) Dist. 65 Schs., 1969-74; lectr. Northeastern Ill. U., Chgo., 1974, Loyola U., Chgo., 1974-76, Coll. St. Francis, Joliet, Ill., 1976-79, North Park Coll., Chgo., 1978; cons. Chgo. Head Start, 1978-79; asst. prof. edn. Oklahoma City U., 1979-80; vis. asst. prof., rsch. assoc. Roosevelt U. Coll. Edn., Chgo., 1983-87, prof., dir. R&D, dir. tchr. edn., dir. early childhood, dir. grad. edn. ctr., Roosevelt U. Coll., Albert A. Robin campus, 1993; prof. sch. edn. De Paul U., 1993—, assoc. dean sch. edn., 1996—, mem. search com. multicultural student affairs, v.p. advancement; chair Roosevelt U. Senate, 1986-89; co-chair ILAEYC Bldg. Bridges; cons. Ill. Resource Ctr., Arts Coun. Oklahoma City, Indian Affairs Commn., 1979-80, Bensenville Pub. Schs., Lincolnwood (Ill.) Pub. Schs., Chgo. Pub. Schs., Atwood Sch. Dist, Chgo. Assn. Retarded Citizens, Nat. Assn. Tech. Tng. Schs., Ill. State Bd. Edn., Itasca Pub. Schs., Decatur Pub. Schs., Robin Scholarship Found., 1982—, Rasho Media, Ill. Facilities Fund for Childcare; alt. rep. faculty coun. Sch. Edn. DePaul U., mem. faculty adv. com. to univ. plan. and info. tech., also mem. panel on grievances, 1995—, mem. comprehensive pers. devel. com., 1995—; mem. tng. sub-com. adv. Ill. Dept. Children & Family Svcs., 1993-95; mem. panel of advisers comprehensive pers. devel. sys. Ill. State Bd. Edn., 1995—; mentor, cons. to partnerships project tng. early intervention svcs. U. Ill., Champaign; early childhood panelist Ill. Initiative for Articulation between Ill. Bd. Higher Edn. and Ill. Cmty. Coll. Bd.; education panelist for Early Childhood Assessment System. Assoc. editor Ill. Sch. R & D; Ill. Div. Early Childhood Edn. Adv. Com. to Ill. Bd. Edn.; co-chair early childhood panelist for early childhood assessment system, Bansenville Pub. Schs.; editor: Depaul U. Sch. Edn. Newsletter. Co-author: Planning a Theme Based Curriculum for 4's or 5's, 1993, Assessing Young Children, 1996; contbr. articles to profl. jours. Bd. dirs. North Side Family Day Care, 1981; northside affiliates Mus. Contemporary Art, 1991-96; trustee Roosevelt U., 1987-93; mem. edn. adv. com. Okla. Dept. Edn., 1979-80; mem. adv. bd. bilingual early childhood program Oakton Community Coll.; mem. adv. bd. early childhood tech. assistance project Chgo. Pub. Schs., Lake View Mental Health, 1986-90; mem. planning com. Lake View Citizens Coun. Day Care Ctr., 1978-79, local planning coun. Ill. Dept. Child and Family Svcs., childcare block grant tng. sub. com.; co-chair Ill. Assn. for Edn. Young Children Building Bridges Project; chmn. teen com. Florence G. Heller JCC, membership com.; mem. adv. bd. Harold Washington Coll. Child Devel., regional tech. assistance grant LICA; mem. parents com. Francis W. Parker Sch. Cerebral Palsy Assn. scholar, 1965; U. Wis. fellow in mental retardation, 1964-65; U. Kans. scholar, 1960. Fellow Am. Orthopsychiat. Assn.; mem. AAUP, ASCD, AAUW, Assn. Children with Learning Disabilities, Nat. Assn. for Edn. Young Children (tchr. edn. bd. 1990-94), Am. Ednl. Rsch. Assn., Coun. for Exceptional Children, Ill. Coun. for Exceptional Children (mem. multicultural affairs com. divsn. early childhood), Ill. Assn. for Edn. Young Children, Coun. on Children with Behavioral Disorders, Soc. for Rsch. in Child Devel., Foun. for Excellence in Teaching (selection com. Golden Apple 1989-94), Alpha Sigma Nu, Phi Delta Kappa, Pi Lambda Theta. Office: DePaul Univ Sch Of Edn Chicago IL 60614

MINDLIN, PAULA ROSALIE, retired reading educator; b. N.Y.C., Nov. 27, 1944; d. Simon S. and Sylvia (Naroff) Bernstein; m. Alfred Carl Mindlin, Aug. 14, 1965; 1 child, Spencer Douglas. BA in Edn., Bklyn. Coll., 1965; MS in Edn., Queens Coll., 1970, Specialist Sch. Adminstrn, 1973. Tchr. Dist. 16 Pub. Sch., Bklyn., 1965-68; reading tchr. Dist. 29 Pub. Sch. and Dist. 16, Bklyn., 1968-85; instr. insvc. courses Comty. Sch. Dist. 29, Queens Village, N.Y., 1984-93; reading coord. Reading/Comms. Arts Program Comty. Sch. Dist. 29, Queens, N.Y., 1985-90; dir. reading Cmty. Sch. Dist. 29, Queens Village, N.Y., 1990-94; adj. lectr. York Coll., 1989; dir. chpt. 1 program U.S. Sec. Edn., 1993 (Nat. Recognition award). Recipient Educator of Yr. award Qeensboro Coun. Reading, N.Y. State Reading Assn. Coun. Svc. award, 1996. Mem. ASCD, Internat. Reading Assn., Nassau Reading Coun., Queensboro Reading Coun. (pres. 1994-96, Educator of Yr. award 1994), Phi Delta Kappa. Avocations: reading, gardening, boating.

MINDLIN, RICHARD BARNETT, market research executive; b. Kansas City, Mo., Apr. 9, 1926; s. Harold Saul and Ann (Copeland) M.; m. Susan Dorothy Weinberg, Feb. 6, 1954; children: Steven, Edward, Andrew. Student, U. of South, 1943-46, Columbia U., 1947-48. Mdse. mgr. Kaufmann's Dept. Store, Pitts., 1951-54; founder, pres. Coach House Stores, Kansas City, Mo., 1955-76, Richard B. Mindlin Assocs., mktg. and new product research and devel., Shawnee Mission, Kans., 1963—. Author books and articles to profl. jours. Chmn. bd. dirs. Bacchus Charity, 1960; bd. dirs. Kaw council Boy Scouts Am., 1964-66; pres. bd. trustees Kansas City Mus. History and Sci.; trustee Menorah Med. Center, Kansas City, Mo. Served to lt. (j.g.) USNR, 1943-45. Club: Oakwood Country (Kansas City, Mo.) (dir. 1981-84). Home and Office: 4101 W 90th St Shawnee Mission KS 66207-2325

MINE, HILARY ANNE, telecommunications company executive, consultant; b. Portland, Oreg., Aug. 21, 1961; d. Lewis Stuart Keizer and Ann Christina (Kelly) Mine; m. Jon Charles Evans, Jan. 10, 1997; 1 child, Kelly Anne. BA in Econs., Reed Coll., 1983; MBA in Bus. Analysis, San Francisco State U., 1990. Analyst Berkeley Roundtable on Internat. Economy, U. Calif., Berkeley, 1984-85, program mgr. Engring. Sys. Rsch. Ctr., 1985-88; project mgr., computer cons. San Francisco State U., 1988-89; bus. planning analyst Chips and Techs., Inc., 1989-90; rsch. dir. info. techs. Frost & Sullivan, 1990-92; prin. Info. Techs. Cons., 1992-94; dir. global cons. No. Bus. Info./Datapro, 1994-96; sr. v.p. Probe Rsch., Inc., Folsom, Calif., 1996—. Tutor St. John's Tutoring Ctr., 1988; asst. edn. coord. Planned Parenthood, 1990-91. Mem. IEEE, NAFE. Avocations: cooking, kayaking, travel, Simcity. Office: Probe Rsch Inc 9580 Oak Avenue Pkwy Ste 7-170 Folsom CA 95630-1888

MINE, KATSUTOSHI, instrumentation educator; b. Fukuoka-ken, Japan, Apr. 28, 1928; s. Tsuneo and Chiyoko (Yoshimura) M.; m. Kazuko Yamauchi, Feb. 5, 1956; 1 child, Satoshi. Diploma, Meiji Tech. Coll., Kitakyushu, Japan, 1949; D of Engring., Kyoto (Japan) U., 1978. Engr. Mitsubishi Chem. Co. Ltd., Kitakyushu, 1949-50, Dantani Plywood Co. Ltd., Kitakyushu, 1955-56; assoc. prof. Ube (Japan) Tech. Coll., 1962-72, prof., 1972-80; prof. Kyushu Inst. Tech., Kitakyushu, 1980-92; prof. Kyushu Kyoritsu U., Kitakyushu, 1992—, gen. mgr. libr., 1996—. Author: T.EMC, IEEE, 1994; inventor in field. Recipient Acad. award Fukuhara Gakuen U. Consortium, Kitakyushu, 1993. Mem. IEEE (reviewer indsl. electronics 1992), IEEE Japan, Soc. Instrumentation and Control Engrs. (bd. dirs. 1990-92), Japan Soc. Med. and Biol. Engrs. (gen. chmn. 6th conf. 1991-92, bd. dirs. 1993—, congress 1992), Kitakyushu Med. and Engring. Coop. Assn. (pres. 1989-93), Kitakyushu Techno-coop. Assn. (bd. dirs. 1992—), N.Y. Acad. Sci. Avocations: classical music, skiing, hiking. Home: 296-2 Mushiozu, Onga-cho Fukuoka 811-43, Japan Office: Kyushu Kyoritsu Univ, 1-8 Jiyugaoka Yahatanishiku, Kita-Kyushu 807, Japan

MINER, A. BRADFORD, journalist; b. Columbus, Ohio, Oct. 30, 1947; s. Robert Bradford and Margaret L. (Earnhart) M.; m. Sydny H. Weinberg, Apr. 29, 1984; children: Robert Bradford II, Jonathan Frederick. BA, Ohio U., 1970. Mgr., Gaylord Enterprises, Columbus, 1974-77; sales planning mgr. Bantam Books, N.Y.C., 1977-80, sr. editor, 1980-84; editor hardcover and paperback books Harper & Row, N.Y.C., 1984-86; nat. sales mgr. Sea-Tex Inc. div. Balson-Hercules Group, N.Y.C., 1987-89; lit. editor National Review, 1989-91; co-editor Nat. Rev. Coll. Guide, 1991, rev. 1993; Olin prof. Adelphi U., 1994—. Editor Good Order, 1994; author: Concise Conservative Encyclopedia, 1996; pres. Religion Pub. Group, N.Y.C., 1983-84. Mem. Fulton J. Sheen Soc. (trustee), Authors Guild. Republican. Roman Catholic. Club: N.Y. Athletic.

MINER, EARL HOWARD, retired trust banker; b. Donnellson, Iowa, Jan. 26, 1923; s. T. Ralph and Carrie T. (Talbot) M.; m. Marian Aumann, May 30, 1944; children: Marcia, Susan, Scott. B.A., Iowa Wesleyan Coll., 1947; J.D., U. Iowa, 1948. Bar: Iowa 1948, Mich. 1965. Atty. Mt. Pleasant, Iowa, 1948-55; trust officer Nat. Bank Burlington, Iowa, 1955-57; v.p. 1st Trust Co., St. Joseph, Mo., 1957-62; investment editor Trusts & Estates Mag., N.Y.C., 1962-64; v.p., trust officer Chem. Bank, Midland, Mich., 1964-70; v.p., sr. trust officer Old Kent Bank and Trust Co., Grand Rapids, Mich., 1970-72; sr. v.p. Old Kent Bank and Trust Co., 1972-79, Citizens Trust Co., Ann Arbor, Mich., 1979-88; ret., 1988; instr. Iowa Wesleyan Coll., part-time 1949-50; county atty., Henry County, Iowa, 1951-55. Chmn. bd. dirs. Mary Free Bed Hosp., Grand Rapids, 1977-79; pres. Green Valley Cmty. Coordinating Coun., 1995—. With USAAF, World War II. Decorated D.F.C., Air medal with 2 oak leaf clusters. Mem. Iowa Bar Assn., State Bar Mich., Mich. Bankers Assn. (chmn. trust div. 1970-71, 86-87), Lambda Chi Alpha, Phi Alpha Delta. Republican. Presbyterian (elder). Home: 1473 W Via De La Gloria Green Valley AZ 85614-5009

MINER, EARL ROY, literature educator; b. Marshfield, Wis., Feb. 21, 1927; s. Roy Jacob and Marjory M.; m. Virginia Lane, July 15, 1950; children: Erik Earl, Lisa Lane. B.A. summa cum laude, U. Minn., 1949, M.A., 1951, Ph.D., 1955. Instr. English Williams Coll., 1953-55; mem. faculty dept. English UCLA, 1955-72, prof., 1964-72; prof. English Princeton U., 1972-74, Townsend Martin Class of 1917 Prof. English and comparative lit., 1974—; vis. fellow U. Canterbury, 1985; mem. joint com. for Japanese Studies Social Sci. Rsch. Coun., 1979-83; disting. vis. prof. Emory U., 1989; vis. prof. UCLA, 1990, Stanford U., 1994; mem. Com. on Scholarly Communications with Peoples Republic China, 1983-87. Author numerous books including The Japanese Tradition in British and American Literature, 1958, The Metaphysical Mode from Donne to Cowley, 1969, The Restoration Mode from Milton to Dryden, 1974, The Princeton Companion to Classical Japanese Literature, 1985, Comparative Poetics, 1991, Naming Properties, 1996; co-author: Literary Transmission and Authority, 1993; assoc. editor: The New Princeton Ency. of Poetry and Poetics, 1993; assoc. gen. editor: Calif. edit. Works of John Dryden, 1964-72, editor 3 vols.; author articles. Am. Coun. Learned Socs. fellow, 1962-63; Guggenheim Found. fellow, 1977-78; fellow Woodrow Wilson Internat. Ctr. for Scholars, 1982-83, U. Calif. Humanities Res. Inst. fellow, 1990; vis. prof. Internat. Rsch. Ctr. for Japanese Studies, 1993-94; recipient Yamagata Banto Prize Osaka Prefectural Govt., 1987, Koizumi Yakumo prize, 1991; decorated Order of the Rising Sun with Gold Rays and Neck Ribbon Japanese Govt., 1994. Mem. Am. Soc. for 18th Century Studies (pres. 1981-82, Clifford lectr. 1997), Milton Soc. Am. (pres. 1982-83), Am. Comparative Lit. Assn. (adv. bd. 1977-80, 86-89), Internat. Comparative Lit. Assn. (exec. coun. 1986-88, pres. 1988-91). Office: Princeton U 22 McCosh Hall Princeton NJ 08540-5627

MINER, JACQUELINE, political consultant; b. Mt. Vernon, N.Y., Dec. 10, 1936; d. Ralph E. and Agnes (McGee) Mariani; B.A., Coll. St. Rose, 1971, M.A., 1974; m. Roger J. Miner, Aug. 11, 1975; children: Laurence, Ronald Carmichael, Ralph Carmichael, Mark. Ind. polit. cons., Hudson, N.Y.; instr. history and polit. sci. SUNY, Hudson, 1974-79. Rep. county committeewoman, 1958-76; vice chmn. N.Y. State Ronald Reagan campaign, 1980; candidate for Rep. nomination for U.S. Senate, 1982; co-chair N.Y. state steering com. George Bush for Pres. campaign, 1986-88; vice chmn. N.Y. State Rep. Com., 1991-93; del. Rep. Convention, 1992; chmn. Coll. Consortium for Internat. Studies; mem. White House Outreach Working Group on Central Am.; co-chmn. N.Y. State Reagan Roundup Campaign, 1984-86; mem. nat. steering com. Fund for Am.'s Future, 2d cir. Hist. Com. Mem. U.S. Supreme Ct. Hist. Soc., P.E.O. Address: 1 Merlin's Way Camelot Heights Hudson NY 12534

MINER, JOHN BURNHAM, industrial relations educator, writer; b. N.Y.C., July 20, 1926; s. John Lynn and Bess (Burnham) M.; children by previous marriage: Barbara, John, Cynthia, Frances; m. Barbara Allen Williams, June 1, 1979; children: Jennifer, Heather. AB, Princeton U., 1950, PhD, 1955; MA, Clark U., 1952. Lic. psychologist, N.Y. Rsch. assoc. Columbia U., 1956-57; mgr. psychol. svcs. Atlantic Refining Co., Phila., 1957-60; faculty mem. U. Oreg., Eugene, 1960-68; prof., chmn. dept. orgnl. sci. U. Md., College Park, 1968-73; rsch. prof. Ga. State U., Atlanta, 1973-87; pres. Orgnl. Measurement Systems Press, Eugene, Oreg., 1976—; prof. Human Resources SUNY, Buffalo, 1987-94, chmn. dept. orgn. and human resources, 1989-92; profl. practice Eugene, Oreg., 1995—; cons. McKinsey & Co., N.Y.C., 1966-69; vis. lectr. U. Pa., Phila., 1959-60; vis. prof. U. Calif., Berkeley, 1966-67, U. South Fla., Tampa, 1972; researcher on orgnl. motivation, theories of orgn., human resource utilization, bus. policy and strategy, entrepreneurship. Author many books and monographs including Personnel Psychology, 1969, Personnel and Industrial Relations, 1969, 73, 77, 85, The Challenge of Managing, 1975, (with Mary Green Miner) Policy Issues Personnel and Industrial Relations, 1977, (with George A. Steiner) Management Policy and Strategy, 1977, James A. Hamilton-Hosp. Adminstrs. Book award 1982, 86), (with M.G. Miner) Employee Selection Within the Law, 1978, Theories of Organizational Behavior, 1980, Theories of Organizational Structure and Process, 1982, People Problems: The Executive Answer Book, 1985, The Practice of Management, 1985, Organizational Behavior: Performance and Productivity, 1988, Industrial-Organizational Psychology, 1992, Role Motivation Theories, 1993, (with Donald P. Crane) Human Resource Management: The Strategic Perspective, 1995, The 4 Routes to Entrepreneurial Success, 1996, (with Michael H. Capps) How Honesty Testing Works, 1996; contbr. numerous articles, papers to profl. jours. Served with AUS, 1944-46, ETO. Decorated Bronze Star, Combat Infantryman's Badge; named Disting. Prof. Ga. State U., 1974. Fellow APA, Acad. of Mgmt. (editor Jour. 1973-75, pres. 1977-78), Soc. for Personality Assessment, Am. Psychol. Soc.; mem. Soc. for Human Resource Mgmt., Indsl. Rels. Rsch. Assn., Internat. Coun. for Small Bus., Strategic Mgmt. Soc., Internat. Pers. Mgmt. Assn., Human Resource Planning Soc. Republican. Home and Office: 34199 Country View Dr Eugene OR 97408

MINER, JOHN RONALD, bioresource engineer; b. Scottsburg, Ind., July 4, 1938; s. Gerald Lamont and Alice Mae (Murphy) M.; m. Betty Katheron Emery, Aug. 4, 1963; children—Saralena Marie, Katherine Alice, Frederick Gerald. B.S. in Chem. Engring., U. Kans., 1959; M.S.E. in San. Engring, U. Mich., 1960; Ph.D. in Chem. Engring. and Microbiology, Kans. State U., 1967. Lic. profl. engr., Kans., Oreg. San. engr. Kans. Dept. Health, Topeka, 1959-64; grad. research asst. Kans. State U., Manhattan, 1964-67; asst. prof. agrl. engring. Iowa State U., 1967-71, assoc. prof., 1971-72; assoc. prof. agrl. engring. Oreg. State U., 1972-76, prof., 1976—, head dept., 1976-86, acting assoc. dean Coll. Agrl. Sci., 1983-84, assoc. dir. Office Internat. Research and Devel., 1986-90, extension water quality specialist, 1991—; environ. engr. FAO of UN, Singapore, 1980-81; internat. cons.; cons. to livestock feeding ops., agrl. devel. firms. Co-author book on livestock waste mgmt.; author 3 books of children's sermons; contbr. numerous articles on livestock prodn., pollution control, control of odors associated with livestock prodn. to profl. publs. Mem. Am. Soc. Agrl. Engrs. (bd. dirs. 1985-87), Water Pollution Control Fedn., Sigma Xi, Gamma Sigma Delta, Alpha Epsilon, Tau Beta Pi. Presbyterian. Office: Oreg State U Dept Bioresource Engring Corvallis OR 97331

MINER, MARY ELIZABETH HUBERT, retired secondary school educator; b. Provident City, Tex., Mar. 25, 1921; d. Fred Edward and Charlotte Alice (Haynes) Hubert; m. Daniel Bowen Miner, Jan. 29, 1945 (dec. Aug. 1979); children: Charlotte Martelia Miner Williams, Daniel Bowen Jr., Mary Elizabeth Miner Martinez, Joseph Frederick, William McKinley. BA, Rice U., 1942; postgrad., U. Houston, East Tenn. State U., 1959, U. Tenn., 1961. Cert. tchr. math., English, French, history, Tex., 8th grade, math., English, French, Am. history grades 9-12. Math. tchr. Crosby (Tex.) H.S., 1942-43; office mgr. Uvalde Rock Asphalt, Houston, 1943-44; tchr. math., English, health Rogersville (Tenn.) H.S., 1947-49, 55-78; tchr. math., English, French Ch. Hill. (Tenn.) H.S., 1949-51, 53-55; tchr. 8th grade Rogersville (Tenn.) City Schs., 1951-53; tchr. math. Cherokee Comprehensive H.S., Rogersville, 1978-84; chmn. math. and sci. planning com., Hawkins County, Tenn., 1977-79; pvt. tutor, Rogersville. Tchr. ladies Bible class Rogersville United Meth. Ch., 1952—, mem. choir, 1979—, sec., 1967-96, sec. adminstr. bd. dirs.; blood donor ARC, Rogersville, 1974-75. Lt. Women's Corps USNR, 1944-47. Recipient Apple award Sta. WKGB, 1956. Mem. NEA (life), Tenn. Edn. Assn. (life), Rogersville Bus. and Profl. Women (pres. 1953-55, treas. 1948-53), Am. Legion Aux. (pres.), Delta Kappa Gamma (Alpha Iota chpt. pres.), Hawkins Ret. Tchrs. Assn. (pres. 1984-85). Republican. Avocations: bridge playing, playing piano, teaching, sewing, visiting children.

MINER, MICHAEL E., neurosurgery educator; b. Louisville, July 25, 1943; s. Gerald Lamont and Alice Mae (Murphy) M.; m. Mildred Elizabeth Kennedy, 1972 (dec. July, 1978); children: Caroline, Matthew, Amanda, Nicholas; m. Mary Ann Bruton, 1980 (dec. Dec., 1992). BS, U. Kans., Lawrence, 1965; MD, U. Kans., Kansas City, 1969, PhD, 1975. Diplomate in neurological surgery Am. Bd. Psychiatry and Neurology. Prof. Ohio State U., 1975—; dir. divsn. neurosurgery Ohio State U., Houston, 1984—; neurosurg. dir. Por Cristo, Boston, 1983—. Author: Neurotrauma, 1986; contbr. articles on neurosurg. disorders to profl. jours. Chmn. Houston Child-Safe Com., 1986—. Served to capt. U.S. Army, 1965-75. Grantee NIH, 1983-87; named Outstanding Tchr., U. Tex., 1984. Mem. Peruvian Surg. Soc., Am. Assn. Neurol. Surgeons (cert.), Soc. Neurol. Surgeons, Ohio State Neurosurg. Soc. (pres. 1995-96). Avocations: running, Civil War history. Office: Univ of Tex Med Sch at Houston Dept of Immunology & Organ Transplant 6431 Fannin St # 148 Houston TX 77030-1501 also: Ohio State Univ Hosps Neurol Dept Columbus OH 43210*

MINER, ROBERT GORDON, creative promotional consultant, auctioneer, writer, publisher, actor, educator; b. Blue Island, Ill., Jan. 29, 1923; s. Glen Ernest and Catherine (Leytze) M.; m. Betty Anne Clegg, May 23, 1944; children: Patricia L. Miner Jolin, Stephen C., David N. Student, Knox Coll., 1941-42; M.B.A., U. Chgo., 1950; grad., U.S. Army Command and Gen. Staff Coll., 1968. Payroll auditor Employers Group Ins. Cos., 1946-49; advt. salesman Cole & Mason (pubs. reps.), 1949-54, partner, 1955-56; asst. pub. Flower Grower mag., Williams Press, 1956-61, pub., 1961-67; owner Media Design Assos., Westport, Conn., 1967-71; pres. Early Am. Soc., Inc. (pub. Early Am. Life), Harrisburg, Pa., 1971-81; owner, pub. Old Main Books, 1981-87; creative promotional cons., auctioneer, appraiser St. Thomas, V.I., 1987—; adj. prof. humanities U. V.I., 1994-96. Author: Handbook of Gardening, 1966; Complete Gardening Guide, 1969, Flea Market Handbook, 1981, rev., updated edit., 1990; columnist V.I. Islands Daily News, 1990-95. Served from 2d lt. to capt. AUS, 1942-46; col. Res. ret. Decorated Bronze Star. Republican. Episcopalian. Clubs: St. Thomas Yacht, Navy League. Home: 8-24 Estate Nazareth 6501 Red Hook Plz Ste 201 Saint Thomas VI 00802

MINER, ROGER JEFFREY, federal judge; b. Apr. 14, 1934; s. Abram and Anne M.; m. Jacqueline Mariani; 4 children. BS, SUNY; LLB cum laude, N.Y. Law Sch., 1956, LLD, 1989; postgrad., Bklyn. Law Sch., Judge Advocate Gen.'s Sch., U. Va.; LLD (hon.), N.Y. Law Sch., 1989, Syracuse U., 1990, Albany Law Sch./Union U., 1996. Bar: N.Y. 1956, U.S. Ct. Mil. Appeals 1956, Republic of Korea 1958, U.S. Dist. Ct. (so. and ea. dists.) N.Y. 1959. Ptnr. Miner & Miner, Hudson, N.Y., 1959-75; justice N.Y. State Supreme Ct., 1976-81; judge U.S. Dist. Ct. (no. dist.) N.Y., 1981-85, U.S. Ct. Appeals (2d cir.), Albany, N.Y., 1985—; corp. counsel City of Hudson, 1961-64; asst. dist. atty. Columbia County, 1964, dist. atty., 1968-75; adj. assoc. prof. criminal law State U. System, N.Y., 1974-79; adj. prof. law N.Y. Law Sch., 1986-96; lectr. state and local bar assns.; lectr. SUNY-Albany, 1985; N.Y. Law Sch. Bd. Trustees, 1991-96; mem. jud. coun. 2d Cir., 1992-96; 2d Cir. Com. on Hist. and Commemorative Events, 1989-94; Cameras in the Courtroom Com., 1993-96, No. Dist. Hist. Com., 1981-85; State, Fed. Jud. Coun. of N.Y., 1986-91, chmn., 1990-91; Jud. Conf. of U.S. com. on fed.-state jurisdiction, 1987-92; trustee Practicing Law Inst. Mng. editor N.Y. Law Sch. Law Rev.; contbr. articles to law jours. 1st lt. JAGC, U.S. Army, 1956-59, capt. USAR ret. Recipient Dean's medal for Disting. Profl. Svc., N.Y. Law Sch., Disting. Alumnus award, Charles W. Froessel award for Valuable Contbn. to Law. Albany Jewish Fedn. award, Abraham Lincoln award, Community Svc. award Kiwanis, others; named Columbia County Man. of Yr., 1984, Ellis Island medal of Honor. Mem. ABA, N.Y. State Bar Assn., Assn. of Bar of City of N.Y., Columbia County Bar Assn., Am. Law Inst., Am. Judicature Soc., Fed. Judges Assn., Fed. Bar Coun., Am. Soc. Writers on Legal Subjects, Assn. Trial Lawyers Am., Columbia County Magistrates Assn., Supreme Ct. Hist. Soc., Columbia County Hist. Soc., N.Y. Law Sch. Alumni Assn. (hon. mem., bd. dirs.), B'nai Brith, Elks (past exalted ruler). Jewish. Office: US Ct Appeals 445 Broadway Ste 414 Albany NY 12207-2926

MINER, THOMAS HAWLEY, international entrepreneur; b. Shelbyville, Ill., June 19, 1927; s. Lester Ward and Thirza (Hawley) M.; m. Lucyna T. Minciel, July 22, 1983; children: Robert Thomas, William John. Student, U.S. Mil. Acad., 1946-47; BA, Knox Coll., 1950; JD, U. Ill., 1953. Bar: Ill. 1954. Atty. Continental Ill. Nat. Bank & Trust Co., Chgo., 1953-55; pres. Harper-Wyman Internat. (S.A.), Venezuela and Mex., 1955-58, Hudson Internat. (S.A.), Can. and Switzerland, 1958-60, Thomas H. Miner & Assoc., Inc., Chgo., 1960—; chmn. Miner, Fraser & Gabriel Pub. Affairs, Inc., Washington, 1982-88, Miner Systems, Inc., 1981—; bd. dirs. Lakeside Bank; chmn. Ill. dist. export coun. U.S. Dept. Commerce, 1971-76; sec. Consular Corps Chgo., 1986-88. Chmn. bd. dirs. Sch. Art Inst. Chgo., 1977-81; bd.

govs., life mem., sustaining fellow Art Inst. Chgo.; former chmn. UN Assn., Chgo.; founder, chmn. Mid-Am. Com., 1968—; former mem. bd. dirs. UNICEF, NAM, Internat. Trade Policy Com. and Working Group on Commonwealth of Ind. States and Ea. Europe; trustee 4th Presbyn. Ch., Chgo., Roosevelt U., 1996; bd. advisors Mercy Hosp.; vice chmn. Chgo. Sister Cities; mem. adv. bd. Internat. Inst. Edn.; bd. dirs. Internat. Sister Cities. With USNR, 1945-46; mem. Pres. Coun. U. Ill. Found. Capt. U.S. Army, 1946-47. Decorated commendatore Ordine al Merito della Repubblica Italiana; recipient Alumni Achievement award Knox Coll., 1974, Gold Medallion award Internat. Visitors Ctr. Chgo., 1989; named One of Chgo.'s 10 Outstanding Young Men, 1962, Chicagoan of Year Chgo. Assn. Commerce and Industry, 1968, Alumni of Month Coll. Law U. Ill., Nov. 1970, Aug. 1984; hon. consul Republic of Senegal, 1970-88. Mem. Am. Mgmt. Assn., Chgoland C. of C., Mid-Am. Arab C. of C. (founder, former pres.), Chgo. Bar Assn., Chgo. Com., Chgo. Coun. Fgn. Rels. (past dir.), Coun. of the Ams., Internat. Trade Club (past dir., pres.), Japan-Am. Soc., Nat. Coun. U.S.-China Trade, Nat. Acad. Scis. (pres. coun.), English Speaking Union (dir., past chmn.) Trade and Econs. Coun. USA-CIS (dir.), U.S.-Russia Bus. Coun., Mus. Contemporary Art, Newcomen Soc. N.Am., U.S.-China Bus. Coun., U.S.-Arab C. of C. (bd. dirs.), U.S.-Mex. C. of C. (bd. dirs.), Thomas Minor Soc., Chgo. Club, Econ. Club, Grant Park Concerts Soc., Chgo. Farmers Club, Mid-Am. Club, Univ. Club (Washington), Univ. Club (Milw.), Hillsboro Club (Fla.), Tryall Golf and Beach Club (Jamaica), Rotary, Phi Delta Phi, Phi Gamma Delta. Office: 150 N Michigan Ave Chicago IL 60601-7524 also: 2400 Virginia Ave NW Washington DC 20037-2612 also: Miner Farms Shelbyville IL 62565

MINES, HERBERT THOMAS, executive recruiter; b. Fall River, Mass., Jan. 30, 1929; s. Abraham and Fanny (Lepes) M.; B.S. in Econs., Babson Coll., 1949; M.S. in Indsl. and Labor Relations, Cornell U., 1954; m. Barbara Goldberg, Oct. 23, 1960; 1 child, Susan. Supr., asst. buyer, employment supr. G. Fox & Co., Hartford, Conn., 1949-52; adminstr. div. tng.-exec. devel. and orgn. planning R.H. Macy & Co., N.Y.C., 1954-66; v.p. personnel Neiman Marcus Co., Dallas, 1966-68, sr. v.p. personnel, 1968-70; v.p. personnel Revlon, Inc., N.Y.C., 1970-73; pres. Bus. Careers, Inc., 1973-78, chmn., 1978-81; pres. Exec. Search and Cons. Div., Wells Mgmt. Corp., 1978-81; pres. Herbert Mines Assocs., Inc., 1981-93, chmn., CEO 1993—. Bd. dirs. Fashion Inst. Tech., Am. Jewish Com., Assn. of Exec. Search Cons. Contbr. articles to trade publs.; mem. editl. bd. Commentary Mag., bd. dirs. Office: 399 Park Ave New York NY 10022

MINETA, NORMAN YOSHIO, aerospace transportation exescutive, former congressman; b. San Jose, Calif., Nov. 12, 1931; s. Kay Kunisaku and Kane (Watanabe) M.; m. Danealia; children: David, K., Stuart S. B.S., U. Calif.-Berkeley, 1953; D of Pub. Svc., Santa Clara U., 1989; HHD (hon.), Rust Coll., 1993. Agt./broker Mineta Ins. Agy., San Jose, 1956-89; mem. adv. bd. Bank of Tokyo in Calif., 1961-75; mem. San Jose City Council, 1967-71; vice mayor City of San Jose, 1969-71, mayor, 1971-75; mem. 94th-104th Congresses from 13th (now 15th) Calif. dist., 1975-95; subcom. surface transp., 1989-92, former dep. Dem. whip, ranking minority mem. transp. and infrastructure com.; sr. v.p., mng. dir. transp. sys. & srvs. Lockheed Martin, Washington, 1995—; chmn. fin. com. Santa Clara County (Calif.) Council Chs., 1960-62; commr. San Jose Human Relations Commn., 1962-64, San Jose Housing Authority, 1966—. Precinct chmn. Community Theater Bond Issue, 1964; mem. spl. gifts com. Santa Clara County council Boy Scouts Am., 1967; sec. Santa Clara County Grand Jury, 1964; bd. dirs. Wesley Found., San Jose State Coll., 1956-58, Pacific Neighbors, Community Council Cen. Santa Clara County, Japan Soc., San Francisco, Santa Clara County chpt. NCCJ, Mexican-Am. Community Services Agy.; mem. exec. bd. No. Calif.-Western Nev. dist. council Japanese Am. Citizens League, 1960-62, pres. San Jose chpt., 1957-59; bd. regents Smithsonian Instn., 1979-95 ; chmn. Smithsonian vis. com. for Freer Gallery, 1981-95; mem. bd. regents Santa Clara U. Served to lt. AUS, 1954-56. Mem. Greater San Jose C. of C., Nat. Assn. Indsl. Ins. Agts., Calif. Assn. Indsl. Ins. Agts., San Jose Assn. Ind. Ins. Agts. (dir. 1960-62), North San Jose Optimists Club (pres. 1956-58), Jackson-Taylor Bus. and Profl. Assn. (dir. 1963). Methodist. Office: Lockheed Martin 1200 K St NW Fl 12 Washington DC 20005-4029 *Personal philosophy: My two greatest responsibilities are accountability and accessibility to everyone I represent, and to anyone who comes to me for help.*

MING, SI-CHUN, pathologist, educator; b. Shanghai, China, Nov. 10, 1922; came to U.S., 1949, naturalized, 1964; s. Sian-Fan and Jan-Teh (Kuo) M.; m. Pen-Ming Lee, Aug. 17, 1957; children—Carol, Ruby, Stephanie, Michael, Jeffrey, Eileen. M.D., Nat. Central U. Coll. Medicine, China, 1947. Resident in pathology Mass. Gen. Hosp., Boston, 1952-56; assoc. pathologist Beth Israel Hosp., Boston, 1956-67; asst. prof. pathology Harvard U. Med. Sch., 1965-67; assoc. prof. U. Md., 1967-71; prof. Temple U., Phila., 1971-93, prof. emeritus, 1993—, acting chmn. dept. pathology, 1978-80, dep. chmn. dept. path., 1980-86; mem. Internat. Study Group on Gastric Cancer; mem. coun. Internat. Gastric Cancer Assn.; U.S. rep. WHO Collaborating Ctr. for Primary Prevention, Diagnosis and Treatment of Gastric Cancer; hon. prof. Tianjin Med. Coll., Shanghai Second Med. U., Fourth Mil. Med. U., China, 1988—. Author: Tumors of the Esophagus and Stomach, 1973, supplement, 1985, Precursors of Gastric Cancer, 1984, Pathology of the Gastrointestinal Tract, 1992. Nat. Cancer Inst. sr. fellow Karolinska Inst. Stockholm, 1964-65; named hon. prof. Tianjin Med. U., Shanghai Second Med. U. and Fourth Mil. Med. U., China, 1988—. Mem. AAAS, U.S. Canadian Acad. Pathology, Am. Soc. Investigative Pathology, Am. Gastroenterol. Assn., N.Y. Acad. Scis. Achievements include development of classification method for stomach carcinoma based on the growth pattern of the cancer. Office: 3400 N Broad St Philadelphia PA 19140-5104

MINGE, DAVID, congressman, lawyer, law educator; b. Clarkfield, Minn., 1942; m. Karen Aaker; children: Erik, Olaf. BA in History, St. Olaf Coll., 1964; JD, U. Chgo., 1967. Atty. Faegre & Benson, Mpls., 1967-70; prof. law U. Wyo., 1970-77; atty. Nelson, Oyen, Torvik, Minge & Gilbertson, 1977-93; mem. 103d-105th Congresses from 2nd Minn. Dist., 1993—; mem. agrl. com.; cons. Ho. Jud. Com., Subcom. Adminstrv. Law U.S. Congress, 1975; formerly atty. Minn. Valley Coop. Light and Power Assn., 1984-93; chair Agrl. Law Sect., Minn. State Bar Assn. 1990-92, adv. bd. Western Minn. Legal Svcs., 1978-84; bd. dirs. Legal Advice Clinics, Ltd., Hennepin County, Western Minn. Vol. Atty. Program. Clk. Montevideo Sch. Bd., 1989-92; dir. Montevideo Community Devel. Corp.; steering com. Clean Up the River Environ., 1992 ; co-coord. Montevideo area CROP Walk for the Hungry, Multi-church Vietnamese Refugee Resettlement Com., Montevideo, 1978-90; bd. dirs. Montevideo United Way, Model Cities Program, Kinder Kare; chair AFS Montevideo chpt. Mem. Minn. Bar Assn., Chippewa County Bar Assn. (chair), Montevideo C. of C., Kiwanis (pres.). Office: 1415 Longworth HOB Washington DC 20515-2302*

MINGER, TERRELL JOHN, public administration institute executive; b. Canton, Ohio, Oct. 7, 1942; s. John Wilson and Margaret Rose M.; m. Judith R. Arnold, Aug. 7, 1965; 1 child, Gabriella Sophia. BA, Baker U., 1966; MPA, Kans. U., 1969; Urban Exec. Program, MIT, 1975; Loeb fellow Harvard U., 1976-77; Exec. Devel. Program, Stanford U., 1979; MBA, U. Colo., 1983. Asst. dir. admissions Baker U., 1966-67; asst. city mgr. City of Boulder, Colo., 1968-69; city mgr. City of Vail, Colo., 1969-79; pres., chief exec. officer Whistler Village Land Co., Vancouver, B.C., Can., 1979-81; v.p., gen. mgr. Cumberland S.W. Inc., Denver, 1981-83; exec. asst., dep. chief of staff to Gov. Colo., 1983-87; pres., chief exec. officer Sundance (Utah) Inst. for Resource Mgmt., 1986—; pres., chief exec. officer Sundance Enterprises Ltd., 1988-91; adj. prof. grad. sch. pub. affairs U. Colo., 1983—, Sch. Bus. U. Denver, 1992—; bd. dirs. Colo. Open Lands, Inc., 1986—; participant UN Conf. on Environment and Devel., Rio de Janeiro, 1992; chmn. environ. adv. bd. Wal-Mart, Inc., 1990—; bd. dirs. Piton Found., 1996. Editor: Greenhouse/Glasnost—The Global Warming Crisis, 1990. Spl. del. UN Habitat Conf. Human Settlements, spl. rep. to UN Environment Program, 1992, coord. UN Global Youth Forum, 1993, 94, co-chmn. conf. on environment and marketing, N.Y.C., 1993; founder Vail Symposium; co-founder, bd. dirs. Colo. Park Found., 1985—; founding mem. Greenhouse/Glasnost U.S./USSR Teleconf. with Soviet Acad. Scis., 1989—; mem. pres. task force Commn. on Sustainable Devel., 1994—; co-chmn. Golf and Environ. Conf., Pebble Beach, Calif., 1995; founder, pres. Western Rendezvous, 1995—. Nat. finalist White House Fellowship, 1978; named one of B.C.'s Top Bus. Leaders for the '80's, 1980. Mem. Urban Land Inst., Colo. Acad. Pub. Adminstrn. (charter, founding mem. 1988), Colo. City Mgmt. Assn., Internat. City Mgrs. Assn. (Mgmt. Innovation award 1974-76), Western Gov.'s Assn. (staff coun., chmn. adv. com. 1985-86), Flatirons Athletic Club. Editor: Vail Symposium Papers, 1970-79; author, editor: Growth Alternatives for Rocky Mountain West, 1976; Future of Human Settlements in the West, 1977. Home: 785 6th St Boulder CO 80302-7416 Office: Ctr for Resource Mgmt 1410 Grant St Ste 307C Denver CO 80203-1846

MINGLE, JAMES JOHN, lawyer. AB in English, St. Joseph's Coll., Phila., 1968; JD, U. Va., 1973. Bar: Md. 1974, Va. 1990, N.Y. 1996. Asst. to pres. Frostburg State Coll., 1973-77, adj. prof. bus. law, 1975-77; asst. atty. gen. State of Md., 1977-89; chief counsel state univ. and coll. sys. U. Md., 1981-89; gen. counsel U. Va., Charlottesville, 1989-95, lectr. law, 1994-95; univ. counsel, sec. corp., lectr. law Cornell U., Ithaca, N.J., 1995—; adj. prof. law U. Md., 1984-88; asst. to bus. mgr. Phila. 76ers NBA Club, 1968-69; city atty. City of Frostburg, Md., 1974-76. Mem. Nat. Assn. Coll. and Univ. Attys.

MINGLE, JOHN ORVILLE, engineer, educator, lawyer, consultant; b. Oakley, Kans., May 6, 1931; s. John Russell and Beulah Amelia (Johnson) M.; m. Patricia Ruth Schmitt, Aug. 17, 1957; children: Elizabeth Lorene, Stephen Roy. B.S., Kans. State U., Manhattan, 1953, M.S., 1958; Ph.D., Northwestern U., 1960; J.D., Washburn U., 1980. Bar: Kans., Wyo., U.S. Patent Office; registered profl. engr., Kans. Tng. engr. Gen. Electric Co., Schenectady, 1953-54; mem. faculty Kans. State U., 1956-90, prof. nuclear engring., 1965-90, prof. emeritus, 1990—, Black & Veatch Disting. prof., 1973-78; dir. Inst. Computational Research in Engring., 1969-88; exec. v.p., patent counsel Kans. State U. Research Found., 1983-88; instr. Northwestern U., 1958-59; vis. prof. U. So. Calif., 1967-68; cons. to govt. and industry. Author: The Invarient Imbedding Theory of Nuclear Transport, 1973; also articles. Bd. dirs. Laramie Regional Airport, 1994—. Officer AUS, 1954-56. Mem. ABA (chairperson sci. and tech. phys. scis. com. 1982-92), NSPE (sect. exec. com. 1985-87, chmn. 1985-86), Am. Nuclear Soc. (sect. pres. 1976-77), Am. Inst. Chem. Engrs. (profl. devel. com. 1982-95), Am. Soc. Engring. Edn. (chmn. Midwest sect. 1984-87, exec. com. 1984-87), Profl. Engrs. in Edn. (vice chmn. 1978-80, workshop chairperson 1983), Kans. Engring. Soc. (past chpt. pres.), Kans. Bar Assn., Licensing Execs. Soc., Sigma Xi (past chpt. pres., lectr.), Soc. Univ. Patent Adminstrs. (exec. com. 1985-87, v.p. cen. region 1985-87). Home: 1409 Downey St Laramie WY 82070-1867 *In times past workaholic behavior produced prudent contributions. Now in our world of paradox, the philosophy has been turned on its head, and an iota of "wisdom work" often overshadows everything else.*

MINGO, JAMES WILLIAM EDGAR, lawyer; b. Halifax, N.S., Can., Nov. 25, 1926; s. Edgar Willard and Lila Theresa (McManus) M.; m. Edith Peppard Hawkins, July 6, 1953; children: Sarah M. (Mrs. J.P. Camus), James A., Johanna E., Nancy S., Charles H. B.A., Dalhousie U., Halifax, 1947, LL.B., 1949; LL.M., Columbia U., 1950; LL.D. (hon.), St. Mary's U., 1981. Bar: N.S. 1950, Queen's counsel 1966. Ptnr. Stewart, McKelvey, Stirling & Scales (and predecessors), Halifax, 1958—, assoc., 1950-57, chmn. exec. com., 1979-92; pres., dir. Canning Investment Corp. Ltd., Halifax; dir. Sun Life Assurance Co. Can., Toronto, Ont., Maritime Tel&Tel Co. Ltd., Halifax, Eastern Telephone & Telegraph Co., Halifax, Minas Basin Pulp & Power Co. Ltd., Hantsport, N.S., Minas Basin Holdings Ltd., Hantsport, The Great Eastern Corp. Ltd., Charlottetown, P.E.I. and Halifax, Onex Corp., Toronto, Crossley Carpet Mills Ltd., Truro, N.S., Oxford Frozen Foods Ltd., Oxford, N.S., CBA Law for the Future Fund; trustee Forum for Young Canadians, Found. for Legal Research. Mem. Halifax-Dartmouth Port Commn., 1955-83, chmn., 1960-83; chmn. Halifax Grammar Sch., 1971-73; mem. Halifax Port Authority, 1972-84; chmn. nat. treasury com. Liberal Party Can., 1976-85; dir. N.S. Legal Aid, 1977-80; mem. Med. Research Council Working Group on Human Experimentation, 1977-78. Mem. Can. Bar Assn. (exec. com. 1973-76, spl. com. on legal ethics 1969-75, 84-87), N.S. Barristers Soc. (pres. 1975-76), Law Found. N.S. Clubs: Halifax, Saraguay, Royal N.S. Yacht Squadron. Office: Box 997 Tower I, Purdy's Wharf, Halifax, NS Canada B3J 2X2

MINGO, JOE LOUIS, elementary school educator; b. Kershaw, S.C., Nov. 14; s. John L. and Ella (Wilson) M. BA in Elem. Edn., U. S.C., 1980, MEd, 1982, postgrad., 1994—. Cert. tchr. elem. edn., early childhood edn. Singer operator Springs Industries, Lancaster, S.C., 1972-79; with BJH Realty, Columbia, S.C., 1980-81, Carabo Inc., Columbia, 1980-85; tchr. 3d grade Sumter County (S.C.) Sch. Dist. #2, 1982-86, tchr. 4th grade, 1986-94, tchr. math, 1994—; lead tchr. math Shaw Heights Elem. Sch., Shaw AFB, S.C., 1993—; Author poetry in New Voices in Am. Poetry, 1986, 88. With USAF, 1984—, Desert Storm. Avocation: writing. Office: High Hills Elem Sch 4971 Frierson Rd Shaw AFB SC 29152-1400

MINICHELLO, DENNIS, lawyer; b. Cleve., June 9, 1952; s. Ernest Anthony and Mary Theresa (Rocci) M.; m. Janine Stevens, Feb. 14, 1987. BA in Econs., Ohio U., 1974, MA in Econs., 1974; JD, Northwestern U., 1978. Bar: U.S. Dist. Ct. (no. dist.) Ill., U.S. Ct. Appeals (7th cir.), Supreme Ct. Ill., U.S. Supreme Ct. Assoc. Haskell & Perrin, Chgo., 1978-84; ptnr. Tribler & Marwedel, Chgo., 1984-89, Keck, Mahin & Cate, Chgo., 1989—. Contbr. articles to profl. jours. Bd. dirs. Great Lakes Naval and Maritime Mus. Fulbright scholar, 1974-75. Mem. ABA, Ill. State Bar Assn., Chgo. Bar Assn. (mem. transp. com.), Maritime Law Assn. (proctor), Casualty Adjusters Assn. Chgo., The Propeller Club U.S. (pres. 1983-84), Port Chgo., Met. Club. Roman Catholic. Avocations: sailing, reading, running. Office: Keck Mahin & Cate 77 W Wacker Dr Chicago IL 60601

MINICK, MICHAEL, publishing executive; b. Albany, N.Y., Mar. 26, 1945; s. Jason and Ruth Isabelle (Solomon) M. Student, U. Va., 1963-66; BA in History, L.I. U., 1968. Editorial dir. Mag. Mgmt., N.Y.C., 1969-73; mng. editor Gentlemen's Quarterly, N.Y.C., 1975-76; pub., ptnr. Beauty Digest, N.Y.C., 1978-90; pub. Pa. Ofcl. Wine and Liquor Quar., N.Y.C., 1985—, Ohio Liquor Quar., 1990—. Author: The Kung Fu Exercise Book-Health Secrets of Ancient China, 1974, The Wisdom of Kung Fu, 1974; contbr. numerous articles to popular mags. Mem. 25 Yr. Club of Ind. Distbrs., Pa. Wine and Spirit Assn. Democrat. Home: 146 7th Ave Pelhon NY 10803 Office: Wine and Liquor Quars Inc 146 7th Ave Pelham NY 10803-1302

MINICUCCI, RICHARD FRANCIS, lawyer, former hospital administrator; b. N.Y.C., Jan. 16, 1947; s. Daniel Michael and Marie Felice (Trotta) M.; m. Nancy Jean Moran, Aug. 16, 1969; children: Jonathan, Elizabeth, Richard. BA, Rutgers Coll., 1969; MHA, Duke U., 1971; JD, Memphis State U., 1976. Bar: Tenn. 1977, N.Y. 1978. Adminstrv. asst. Duke Hosp., Durham, N.C., 1971; health planner Mid-South Med. Ctr. Coun., Memphis, 1971-73; dir. adminstrn. Memphis & Shelby County Hosp. Authority, 1973-77; assoc. Hayt Hayt & Landau, Great Neck, N.Y., 1977-81, ptnr., 1981-89; ptnr. Nixon Hargrave Devans & Doyle, LLP, Garden City, N.Y., 1989—; lectr. various health law assns. Editor: New York Environmental Law Handbook, 2d edit.; author: Residency Training Program Accreditation, 1st-5th edits.; editor-in-chief Accreditation Alert. Co-chmn. fund raising Luth. High Sch., Brookville, N.Y., 1991. Capt. U.S. Army, 1971-79. Mem. Am. Acad. Hosp. Attys., N.Y. State Bar Assn., Nassau Bar Assn., Nat. Health Lawyers Assn. Republican. Roman Catholic. Avocations: tennis, skiing, hockey, travel. Office: Nixon Hargrave Devans & Doyle LLP 990 Stewart Ave Garden City NY 11530-4838

MINICUCCI, ROBERT A., business executive; b. Waterbury, Conn., May 7, 1952; s. Arnold A. and Mary (Garafola) M.; m. Jill Hanau, June 18, 1988; children: Robert A. Jr., Alexandra H. BA, Amherst (Mass.) Coll., 1975; MBA, Harvard U., 1979. CPA. Staff acct. Price Waterhouse, Boston, 1975-77; assoc. Lehman Bros., N.Y.C., 1979-82; v.p. Lehman Bros., 1982-85, sr. v.p., 1985-88, mng. dir., 1988-91; sr. v.p., treas. Am. Express Co., 1991-92; CFO First Data Corp., N.Y.C., 1992-93; gen. ptnr. Welsh, Carson, Anderson & Stowe, N.Y.C., 1993—; bd. dirs. Attachmate Corp., Global Knowledge Network Inc., Servantis Sys. Inc., Strategic Mortgage Svcs., Inc., Seer Techs., Inc., Alliance Data Systems, Inc. Home: 7 Hilltop Rd S Norwalk CT 06854-5001 Office: Welsh Carson Anderson Stowe 320 Park Ave Ste 2500 New York NY 10022-6815

MINIEAR, J. DEDERICK, software company executive, consultant; b. Columbia City, Ind., Oct. 10, 1959; s. Gary Allen and Mallory Virgean (Dederick) M.; m. Lisa Anne Lattimer, July 30, 1983 (div. May 1991); 1 child, Andrew Ross. BA in Econs. and Computer Studies, Northwestern U., 1982. Head data processing Holcomb & Hoke, Mfg., Indpls., 1982-85; systems engr. Elec. Data Systems, Kokomo, Ind., 1985-87; cons. Healthcare Adminstrv. Systems, Indpls., 1987-89, Software Synergy Inc., Indpls., 1989-90, Indecon, Inc., Indpls., 1990-94, Source Cons., Indpls., 1994—; founder, owner, CEO Aerosoft, Inc., Indpls., 1989—; computer cons. Ind. Basketball Hall of Fame, New Castle, 1989-90. Author, found. mem.: Northwestern Rev., 1982; author PC graphics, advt. diskettes, fitness log, screen saver software and video. Pvt. promoter Pres.'s Coun. on Phys. Fitness and Sport, Indpls., 1991—, Nat. Assn. Gov.'s Couns. on Phys. Fitness and Sports, Fellowship Christian Athletes, 1996. Mem. Assn. of Shareware Profls., Christian Coalition (press liaison 1995—), Full Gospel Businessmen Fellowship Internat. (local sec. 1991—). Methodist. Avocations: jogging, weight-lifting, basketball. Office: Aerosoft 4912 Sunview Cir Apt 1027 Indianapolis IN 46237-4621

MINISH, ROBERT ARTHUR, lawyer; b. Mpls., Dec. 25, 1938; s. William Arthur and Agnes Emilia (Olson) M.; m. Marveen Eleanor Allen, Sept. 16, 1961; 1 children: Roberta Ruth. BA, U. Minn., 1960, JD, 1963. Bar: Minn. 1963. Assoc. Popham, Haik, Schnobrich & Kaufman, Ltd., Mpls., 1963-67, ptnr., 1967—; bd. dirs. Braas Co., Mpls. Mem. ABA, Minn. Bar Assn. Avocations: fishing, traveling. Home: 331 Pearson Way NE Minneapolis MN 55432-2418 Office: Popham Haik Schnobrich & Kaufman 3300 Piper Jaffray Tower 222 S 9th St Minneapolis MN 55402-3389

MINISI, ANTHONY JOSEPH, cardiologist, educator; b. Phila., May 9, 1954; m. Margaret Joan Conroy, May 23, 1980; children: John Anthony, Karen Margaret. BA cum laude, U. Pa., 1976, MD, 1980. Diplomate Am. Bd. Internal Medicine, Am. Bd. Cardiovascular Disease, Nat. Bd. Med. Examiners. Intern in internal medicine Med. Coll. Va., Richmond, 1980-81, resident, 1981-83, clin. fellow cardiology div., 1984-86, clin. instr. dept. medicine, 1983-84, instr., 1987-88, asst. prof., 1989—; mem. clin. attending staff cardiology div. McGuire VA Med. Ctr., Richmond, 1986-87, clin. attending in cardiology-Cardiac Catheterization Lab., 1987-88, attending staff, 1988-90, assoc. dir. Cardiac Catheterization Lab., 1989-93; dir. Cardiac Catheterization Lab., Richmond, 1993—. Co-author: (with others) Reflex Control of the Circulation, 1991, Cardiovascular Reflex Control in Health and Disease, 1993, Cardiovascular Reflex Control in Health and Disease, 1993; contbr. articles to profl. jours. Tng. grantee NIH, 1986. Fellow Am. Coll. Cardiology; mem. Am. Fedn. Clin. Rsch., Am. Heart Assn. Home: 7609 Dell Dr Richmond VA 23235-6303 Office: McGuire VA Med Ctr Div Cardiology Box 111J-1 1201 Broad Rock Blvd Richmond VA 23249-0001

MINISI, ANTHONY S., lawyer; b. Newark, Sept. 18, 1926; s. Anthony F. and Leonora (Petoia) M.; m. Rita Marie Hentz, Jan. 8, 1949; children: Claire, Anthony J., Joseph J., Brian A. BS, U. Pa., 1948, JD, 1952. Player, N.Y. Giants, NFL, 1948; law clk. to presiding judge Ct. of Common Pleas #6, Phila., 1952-54; counsel Wolf, Block, Schorr and Solis-Cohen, Phila., 1954—; past pres., vice chmn. Robert E. Maxwell Meml. Football Club, Eastern Assn. Intercoll. Football Ofcls. Past chmn. Com. of Seventy, Phila.; former mem., past pres. Bd. of Edn., Tredyffrin/Easttown Joint Sch. Dist.; mem., chmn. bd. supr. Easttown Twp.; past v.p. Cmty. Svcs. Planning Coun., Phila.; trustee U. Pa.; trustee, mem. exec. com. U. Pa. Health Sys.; chmn. Clin. Care Assocs. U. Pa. Health Sys.; former mem., vice-chmn. Pa. State Bd. Law Examiners. Served to maj. USAR. Mem. ABA (ho. of dels.), Pa. Bar Assn., Phila. Jr. Bar Assn. (past pres.), Def. Lawyers Am., Assn. Trial Attys. Am., Phila. Bar Assn. (bd. of govs., past chmn.), Phila. Trial Lawyers Assn., Fed. Bar Assn., Phila. Trial Lawyers Assn. Republican. Roman Catholic. Clubs: Lawyers (past pres.), Justinian Soc., Union League (Phila.). Office: Wolf Block Schorr & Solis-Cohen SE Corner 15th & Chestnut Sts Philadelphia PA 19102

MINISTER, KRISTINA, speech communication educator; b. Dayton, Ohio, Aug. 27, 1934; d. Roy J. and Margaret (Chatterton) Arndt; m. Edward Minister, Mar. 1959 (div. 1972); children: Matthew, Margaret; m. Hal W. Howard, Sept. 10, 1977 (dec. Sept. 1993). BFA, Ohio U., 1958; MA, Columbia U., 1962; PhD, Northwestern U., 1977. Instr. speech St. John's U., Bklyn., 1962-65, Bowdoin Coll., Brunswick, Maine, 1969-71; asst. prof. speech communication U. Ariz., Tucson, 1974-77, Calif. State U., Northridge, 1978-79; vis. asst. prof. communication Ariz. State U., Tempe, 1979-82; oral historian Oral History Ctr., Inc., Phoenix, 1982-89; prof. comm. Midway (Ky.) Coll., 1989—; cons. oral history to bus., families, mus. and schs., 1982-89. Author: Oral History: The Privilege You Inherit, 1985; contbr. scholarly essays to various publs. Actor Cmty. Profl. Theatre. Mem. Women in Comm., Inc., Speech Comm. Assn., Oral History Assn., Am. Folklore Soc. Democrat. Episcopalian. Avocations: race walking, community theater, arts, travel. Office: Midway Coll 512 E Stephens St Midway KY 40347-1112

MINK, JOHN ROBERT, dental educator; b. Peru, Ill., Sept. 8, 1927; s. Monte Franklin and Marcella (White) M.; m. Barbara Joanne Merrell, June 21, 1952; children: Sarah, Teresa, Kathleen, Mary, James, Elizabeth. BA, Ind. U., 1951; DDS with honors, 1956, MS in Pedodontics, 1961. Diplomate Am. Bd. Pedodontics (bd. examiners). Instr. Ind. U., Indpls., 1957-60, asst. prof., 1960-62; dir. dental Clinic Handicapped Children, James Whitcomb Riley Hosp. for Children, Indpls., 1957-62; mem. faculty U. Ky., Lexington, 1962—, chmn. dept. pedodontics, 1962-74, prof. pedodontics, 1966—, asst. dean clin. affairs Coll. Dentistry, 1974-80, assoc. dean clin. affairs, 1980-85; prof., chmn. dept. pediatric dentistry U. Ky. and U. Louisville, 1985-88; dir. U. Ky. Med. Plaza Dental Clinic, 1985-89; cons. pedodontics USPHS, 1969-72, U.S. Army, Fort Knox, 1969—, ADA, 1972—, Ft. Jackson, 1987—, Ft. Lewis, 1989. Pres. Vols. Bur. Lexington, Ky., 1972-73; bd. dirs. Vol. Action Ctr., 1978—; bd. dirs. Margaret Hall Sch., Versailles, Ky., chmn. bd., 1976—; pres. Margaret Hall Found., 1980—. Served with AUS, 1946-47. Fellow Am. Acad. Pedodontics, Internat. Coll. Dentists (dep. regent 1990—); mem. Am. Soc. Dentistry for Children (pres. Ky. chpt. 1967—), Ky. Assn. Pediat. Dentists (sec.-treas. 1979—), Am. Assn. Dental Schs., Blue Grass Dental Soc. (pres. 1985-86), Pierre Fauchard Acad., Ind. U. Pediat. Dentistry Alumni Assn. (pres. 1993—), Delta Upsilon, Delta Sigma Delta (Delta Epsilon chpt. sec.-treas. 1992-94, pres.-elect 1994, pres. 1995), Omicron Kappa Upsilon. Home: 5411 Parkers Mill Rd Lexington KY 40513-9711 Office: U Ky Coll Dentistry Chandler Med Ctr Lexington KY 40504

MINK, PATSY TAKEMOTO, congresswoman; b. Paia, Maui, Hawaii, Dec. 6, 1927; d. Suematsu and Mitama (Tateyama) Takemoto; m. John Francis Mink, Jan. 27, 1951; 1 child, Gwendolyn. Student, Wilson Coll., 1946, U. Nebr., 1947; BA, U. Hawaii, 1948; LLD, U. Chgo., 1951; DHL (hon.), Chaminade Coll., 1975, Syracuse U., 1976, Whitman Coll., 1981. Bar: Hawaii. Pvt. practice Honolulu, 1953-65; lectr. U. Hawaii, 1952-56, 59-62, 79-80; atty. Territorial Ho. of Reps., 1955; mem. Hawaii Ho. of Reps., 1956-58, Ter. Hawaii Senate, 1958-59, Hawaii State Senate, 1962-64, 89th-94th Congresses from 2nd Hawaii dist., 101st-105th Congresses from 2d dist. Hawaii, 1990—; mem. econ. and ednl. opportunity com., mem. budget com.; mem. U.S. del. to UN Law of Sea, 1975-76, Internat. Woman's Yr., 1975, UN Environ. Program, 1977, Internat. Whaling Commn., 1977; asst. sec. of state U.S. Dept. State, 1977-78. Charter pres. Young Dem. Club Oahu, 1954-56, Ter. Hawaii Young Dems., 1956-58; del. Dem. Nat. Conv., 1960, 72, 80; nat. v.p. Young Dem. Clubs Am., 1957-59; v.p. Ams. for Dem. Action, 1974-76, nat. pres., 1978-81; mem. nat. adv. com. White House Conf. on Families, 1979-80; mem. nat. adv. coun. Federally Employed Women. Recipient Leadership for Freedom award Roosevelt Coll., Chgo., 1968, Alii award 4-H Clubs Hawaii, 1969, Nisei of Biennium award, Freedom award Honolulu chpt. NAACP, 1971, Disting. Humanitarian award YWCA, St. Louis, 1972, Creative Leadership in Women's Rights award NEA, 1977, Human Rights award Am. Fedn. Tchrs., 1975, Feminist of Yr. award Feminist Majority Found., 1991, Margaret Brent award ABA, 1992, Outstanding Woman of Yr. award Nat. Assn. Profl. Am. Women, 1992, Environ. Leadership award Nat. League Conservation Voters, 1993, Jessie Bernard Wise Women award Ctr. for Women Policy Studies, 1993, Hawaii's Health Mother award, 1994, Hispanic Health Leadership award, 1995, Women Work! Nat. Network for Women's Employment, 1995, Women at Work Pub. Policy award, 1995, Justice in Action award Asian Am. Legal Def. and Edn. Fund, 1996, Daniel K. Inouye award Hawaii Psychol. Assn., 1996, Indsl. Union Dept. Lewis-Murray-Reuther Social Justice award AFL-

CIO, 1996, Top Rating for Global Internat. Trade Watch, Pub. Citizens/ Nat. Farmers Union/Friends of the Earth, 1996, award Inferfaith IMPACT for Justice and Peace, 1996, Hawaii Coun. on Lang. Planning and Policy cert. for opposition to English-only legislation, 1996, Hawai'i Women Lawyers Lifetime Achievement award 1997, Legis. Leadership award Nat. Assn. of WIC Dirs., 1997. Office: US Ho of Reps 2135 Rayburn HOB Washington DC 20515

MINKEL, HERBERT PHILIP, JR., lawyer; b. Boston, Feb. 11, 1947; s. Herbert Philip and Helen (Sullivan) M. AB, Holy Cross Coll., 1969; JD, NYU, 1972. Bar: Mass. 1973, N.Y. 1976, U.S. Dist. Ct. Mass. 1973, U.S. Dist. Ct. (so. dist.) N.Y. 1976. Law clk. U.S. Dist. Ct. Mass., Boston, 1972-73; assoc. Milbank, Tweed, Hadley & McCloy, N.Y.C., 1973-79; ptnr. Fried, Frank, Harris, Shriver & Jacobson, N.Y.C., 1979-94; adj. assoc. prof. NYU Law Sch., 1987-94; mem. adv. com. on bankruptcy rules Jud. Conf. U.S., 1987-93. Contbg. editor 5 Collier on Bankruptcy, 15th edit. 1979-96; contbr. articles to profl. jours.; co-author American Bankers Association Bankruptcy Manual, 1979. Bd. visitors Boston U. Grad. Sch. Dentistry; bd. advisors Spl. Olympics, Spl. Smiles. Root-Tilden scholar, NYU, 1969-72. Mem. ABA, Nat. Bankruptcy Conf., Mass. Bar Assn. Home: 85 E India Row Boston MA 02110 Office: Ste 3200 Exch Pl 53 State St Boston MA 02109-2804

MINKER, JACK, computer scientist, educator; b. Bklyn., July 4, 1927; s. Harry and Rose (Lapuck) M.; m. Rita Goldberg, June 24, 1951 (dec. Oct. 11, 1988); children: Michael Saul, Sally Anne; m. Johanna Cartee Weinstein, Jan. 19, 1997; m. Johanna Carlee Weinstein, Jan. 19, 1997. B.A. cum laude with honors in Math., Bklyn. Coll., 1949; M.S. in Math., U. Wis., 1950; Ph.D. in Math., U. Pa., 1959. Grad. teaching asst. U. Wis., 1949-50; tchr. math. Erasmus Hall High Sch., Bklyn., 1950-51; engr. Bell Aircraft Corp., Buffalo, 1951-52; mgr. info. tech. sect. RCA, Bethesda, Md., 1952-63; dir. tech. staff Auerbach Corp., Washington, 1963-67, tech. cons., 1967-72; mem. Faculty NIH Grad. Sch., 1965-66; vis. mem. faculty U. Md., 1967-68, assoc. prof. computer sci., 1968-71, prof., 1971—, 1st chmn. dept. computer sci., 1974-79; cons., speaker, lectr. in field; cons. NSF, 1979-82, chmn. adv. bd. on computer sci., 1980-82; prof. Inst. Advanced Computer Studies, 1986—; vice-chmn. Com. Concerned Scientists, 1973—; past mem. U.S. Nat. Com. for Fedn. Info. Documentalists. Author: (with H. Gallaire and J.M. Nicolas) Logic and Data Bases a Deductive Approach, 1984; editor: (with H. Gallaire and J.M. Nicholas) Advances in Data Base Theory, vol. 1, 1980, vol. 2, 1984, (with H. Gallaire) Logic and Data Bases, 1978, Foundations of Deductive Databases and Logic Programming, 1988, (with J. Lobo and A. Rajasekar) Foundations of Disjunctive Logic Programming, 1992; contbr. numerous articles to profl. publs.; publs. reviewer; mem. editl. bd. numerous jours. Vice chmn. Com. Concerned Scientists, 1972—. With U.S. Army, 1945-46. Recipient U. Md. Presdl. medal, 1996; named Disting. Scholar-Tchr. U. Md., 1997-98. Fellow AAAS, ACM, IEEE (editl. bd. Expert Info. Sys. jour.), Am. Assn. Artificial Intelligence (founding); mem. Assn. Computing Machinery (chmn. nat. program com. 1968-69, vice chmn. com. on sci. freedom and human rights 1979-89, Outstanding Contbn. award 1985, vice chmn. com. concerned scientists 1972—). Jewish. Office: U Md Dept Computer Sci Inst Advanced Computer Studies College Park MD 20742

MINKOFF, ALICE SYDNEY, interior designer, showroom owner; b. Washington, Jan. 29, 1948; d. Lawrence and Ellen (Altman) Glassman; children: Adam Pollin, Shane Pollin, Jacob, Sam. Student, U. Md. Owner Fredrick, Miley & Assocs., Inc., 1983—, Showroom at Washington Design Ctr.; interior designer for homebuilders, 1975-82; interior designer high end residential homes and hotel interiors, 1980—. Vol. Food and Friends, Washington, 1991—; chair Heartstrings, Washington, 1990—; active AIDS awareness; mem. Leadership Coun. of the Retreat, East Hampton, N.Y.; mem. human rights campaign Amagansett Village Improvement Soc. Mem. NOW, ACLU, Nat. Trust Hist. Preservation, Nature Conservancy. Avocations: gourmet cooking, antique collecting, dolls, quilts. Home: PO Box 7064 Amagansett NY 11930 Office: Matches at Miley 300 D St SW Ste 440 Washington DC 20024-4703

MINKOFF, JACK, economics educator; b. N.Y.C., Jan. 29, 1925; s. Isidore and Yetta (Fine) M.; m. Anne B. Johnson, June 19, 1948; children—Ellen, Paul. A.B., Cornell U., 1948; A.M., Columbia U., 1950, Ph.D. (Ford Found. fellow), 1960. Instr. econs. Western Res. U., 1952-53; instr. econs. Sarah Lawrence Coll., 1959-60; prof. econs., chmn. dept. social sci. Pratt Inst., Bklyn., 1960—; acting dean Sch. Liberal Arts and Scis. Pratt Inst., 1985-86, dean, 1986-93, acting provost, 1993-95; prof. econs., 1996—. Served with USAAF., 1943-45. Fellow Social Sci. Research Council, 1950-51. Mem. Phi Beta Kappa. Home: 57 Ruxton Rd Great Neck NY 11023-1528 Office: Pratt Inst Economics Dept Brooklyn NY 11205

MINKOWITZ, MARTIN, lawyer, former state government official; b. Bklyn.; s. Jacob and Marion (Kornblau) M.; m. Carol L. Ziegler; 1 son from previous marriage, Stuart Allan. AA, Bklyn. Coll., 1959, BA, 1961; JD, Bklyn. Law Sch., 1963, LLM, 1965. Bar: N.Y. 1963, U.S. Supreme Ct. 1967, U.S. Tax Ct. 1974, all four U.S. Dist. Cts. N.Y. Ptnr. firm Minkowitz, Hagen & Rosenbluth, N.Y.C., 1964-76; gen. counsel State of N.Y. Workers' Compensation Bd., N.Y.C., 1976-81; gen. counsel, dep. supt. State of N.Y. Ins. Dept., N.Y.C., 1981-88; instr. CUNY, 1975; ptnr. Stroock & Stroock & Lavan, N.Y.C., 1988—; mem. adv. bd. Coll. Ins., 1987-90; adj. prof. law N.Y. Law Sch., N.Y.C., 1982—; lectr. ABA, N.Y. C. of C., Practicing Law Inst., N.Y. State Bar Assn., Nat. Assn. Ins. Commrs., Nat. Conf. Ins. Legis.; hearing officer N.Y.C. Transp. Dept., 1970-75; cons. City Council, N.Y.C., 1969. Author: (with others) Rent Stabilization and Control, 1973; (with others) Handling the Basic Workers' Compensation Law Case, 1982, 85, 87; co-author: Workers Compensation Insurance and Law Practice-The Next Generation, 1989; commentaries to McKinney's Consol. Laws, 1982—; mem. editorial bd. Jour. Occupational Rehabilitation U. Rochester, 1991—; contbr. numerous articles to profl. jours. Bd. dirs., sec. Kingsbay YM-YWHA, Bklyn., 1978—; pres. bd. dirs. Shore Terrace Co-op., Bklyn., 1982-83; co-chmn. exec. bd., met. council, nat. v.p. Am. Jewish Congress, N.Y.C., 1983-91; bd. dirs. Met. Coord. Coun. on Jewish poverty, 1993—, Nat. Conf. Christians and Jews (bd. dir. N.Y. divsn. 1994, nat. bd. trustees 1995—). Recipient cert. meritorious service Bklyn. Law Sch., 1963, Outstanding Pub. Service award Ind. Ins. Agts. Assn., 1988, citation outstanding performance State of N.Y. Workers' Compensation Bd., 1981, Disting. Leadership award N.Y. Claims Assn., 1986, City of Peace award State of Israel Bonds, 1986, Brotherhood award NCCJ, 1994. Fellow N.Y. State Bar Found.; mem. N.Y. County Lawyers Assn. (chmn. unlawful practice of law com. 1982-86, mem. profl. ethics com. 1985-91, chair worker's compensation com. 1988-91, chair adminstrv. law com. 1996—), N.Y. State Bar Assn. (chmn. unlawful practice of law com. 1981-83, mem. com. on profl. ethics 1981-84, chmn. com. profl. discipline 1988-92, Sustaining Mem. of Yr. award 1995), Soc. Ins. Recievers, Bklyn. Law Sch. Alumni Assn. (v.p. bd. dirs. 1984-92, pres. elect 1993-94, pres. 95-96). Office: Stroock Stroock & Lavan 180 Maiden Ln New York NY 10038-4925

MINKOWYCZ, W. J., mechanical engineering educator; b. Libokhora, Ukraine, Oct. 21, 1937; came to U.S., 1949; s. Alexander and Anna (Tokan) M.; m. Diana Eva Szandra, May 12, 1973; 1 child, Liliana Christine Anne. B.S. in Mech. Engring., U. Minn., 1958, M.S. in Mech. Engring., 1961, Ph.D. in Mech. Engring, 1965. Asst. prof. U. Ill., Chgo., 1966-68, assoc. prof., 1968-78, prof., 1978—; cons. Argonne Nat. Lab. Ill., 1970-82, U. Hawaii, Honolulu, 1974—. Founding editor-in-chief Jour. Numerical Heat Transfer, 1978—; editor Internat. Jour. Heat and Mass Transfer, 1968—, Internat. Communications in Heat and Mass Transfer Jour., 1974—; editor book series: Computational and Physical Processes in Mechanics and Thermal Sciences, 1979—, Advances in Numerical Heat Transfer, 1996—; editor: Rheologically Complex Fluids, 1972, Handbook of Numerical Heat Transfer, 1988; contbr. articles to profl. jours. Recipient Silver Circle for Excellence in Teaching, U. Ill.-Chgo., 1975, 76, 81, 86, 90, 94, Harold A. Simon award Excellence in Teaching, 1986, Ralph Coats Roe Outstanding Tchr. award Am. Soc. Engring. Edn., 1988, U. Ill. Disting. Tchr. award, 1989. Fellow ASME (Heat Transfer Meml. award 1993); mem. Sigma Xi, Pi Tau Sigma. Republican. Ukrainian Catholic. Office: U Ill Dept Mech Engring Mail Code 251 842 W Taylor St Chicago IL 60607-7021

MINKUS, RAYMOND DAVID, communications and public relations executive; b. Chgo., Aug. 8, 1953; s. Fred and Roslyn Minkus; BS in Journalism, U. Mo., Columbia, 1975; m. Sara Anthony, June 26, 1977; children: Stephanie Raye, Evan Andrew. Reporter, asst. sect. editor Fairchild Publs., N.Y.C., 1975, Chgo.-Midwest editor, 1976; fin. news columnist Milw. Sentinel, 1976-78; sr. communications specialist, mgr. media rels. Miller Brewing Co. Milw., 1978-81; pres. Weiser Minkus Walek Communications, 1981-91; pres. Minkus & Dunne Communications, Inc., 1992—; chmn. ArakNet Comm., 1995—. Bd. dirs. Future Milw., 1980-81; mem. mktg. com. Milw. United Performing Arts Fund, 1980-81; communication task force Chgo. Area Cen. Com., 1984—; legis. asst. Mo. Ho. of Reps., 1974-75; bd dirs. Mental Health Assn. Ill., 1993—, Cystic Fibrosis Found., 1986-92. Recipient Outstanding Corp. Publ. award Bus. and Profl. Adv. Assn. Milw. Mem. Chgoland C. of C. (bd. dirs.), Pub. Rels. Soc. Internat. Assn. Bus. Communicators. Am., Chgo. Assn. Commerce and Industry (communications com., bd. dirs., exec. coms., div. v.p., Vol. of Yr. 1988). Contbr. articles to Common Stock Reporter, Women's Wear Daily, Chgo. Tribune, Commerce Mag., Prentice-Hall Exec. Action Report, others. Home: 2292 Sheridan Rd Highland Park IL 60035-2015 Office: Minkus & Dunne COmmunications, Inc. 150 S Wacker Dr Chicago IL 60606-4103

MINNER, RUTH ANN, state senator; b. Milford, Del., Jan. 17, 1935; m. Roger Minner. Student Del. Tech. and Community Coll. Office receptionist Gov. of Del., 1972-74; mem. Del. Ho. of Reps., 1974-82; mem. Del. Senate, 1982-92; lt. gov. State of Del., Dover, 1993—; mem. Dem. Nat. Com., 1988. Home: RD 3 Box 694 Milford DE 19963 Office: Office Lt Gov Tatnall Bldg 3rd Fl Dover DE 19901*

MINNERLY, ROBERT WARD, retired headmaster; b. Yonkers, N.Y., Mar. 21, 1935; s. Richard Warren and Margaret Marion (DeBrocky) M.; m. Sandra Overmire, June 12, 1957; children: Scott Ward, John Robert, Sydney Sue. AB, Brown U., 1957; MAT, U. Tex., Arlington, 1980. Tchr., coach Rumsey Hall Sch., Washington, Conn., 1962-64; tchr., coach Berkshire Sch., Sheffield, Mass., 1964-70, asst. head, 1969-70, headmaster, 1970-76; dir. Salisbury (Conn.) Summer Sch. Reading and English, 1970; prin. upper sch. Ft. Worth Country Day Sch., 1976-86; headmaster Charles Wright Acad., Tacoma, Wash., 1986-96; ednl. cons. The Educators' Group, 1996—; cons. Tarrant County Coalition on Substance Abuse, 1982-84; mem. mayor's task force Tacoma Edn. Summit, 1991-92. Contbr. articles to profl. jours. Bd. dirs. Tacoma/Pierce County Good Will Games Art Coun., 1989; mem. exec. com. Am. Leadership Forum, 1991-95; bd. dirs. Broadway Ctr. for Performing Arts, Tacoma, 1988-94, 96-97, mem. exec. com., 1990-93; elected Wash. State Bd. Edn., 1996—. Named Adminstr. of Yr. Wash. Journalism Edn. Assn., 1991. Mem. Pacific N.W. Assn. Ind. Schs. (chmn. long-range planning com. 1989-92, exec. com. 1990-92, 91, v.p. 1994). Republican. Presbyterian. Home and Office: 4214 39th Avenue Ct NW Gig Harbor WA 98335-8029

MINNERS, HOWARD ALYN, physician, research administrator; b. Rockville Center, N.Y., Sept. 1, 1931; s. Howard A. and Marie Henriette (Soberski) M.; m. Gretchen Paffenbarger, Oct. 25, 1958; children: Todd, Bradford. AB, Princeton U., 1953; MD, Yale U., 1957; MPH, Harvard U., 1960. Diplomate Am. Bd. of Preventive Medicine; cert. Nat. Bd. of Med. Examiners. Commd. 2d. lt. USAF, 1956; intern Wilford Hall USAF Hosp., San Antonio, 1957-58; resident Sch. of Aerospace Medicine, USAF, Brooks AFB, Tex., 1960-62; advanced through grades to maj. USAF, 1966; advanced through grades to rear adm. USPHS, ret., 1987; dir. office rsch. promotion and devel. WHO, Geneva, Switzerland, 1977-80; dir. Office of Sci. Advisor Agy. Internat. Devel., Washington, 1981-91; dep. dir. Office Internat. Health USPHS and Asst. Surgeon Gen., 1980-81; assoc. dir. NIH Nat. Inst. of Allergy and Infectious Diseases, 1966-77. Pres. Model A Ford Found., 1994—. Fellow World Acad. Art and Sci., Am. Coll. Preventive Medicine; mem. AAAS, Internat. Found. Sci. Stockholm (pres., chmn. bd. trustees 1991—). Avocations: antique automobile restoration, advertising history.

MINNICH, DALE E., religious administrator. Assoc. gen. sec. Gen. Svcs. Commn. Office: Ch of the Brethren 1451 Dundee Ave Elgin IL 60120-1674*

MINNICH, DIANE KAY, state bar executive; b. Iowa City, Feb. 17, 1956; d. Ralph Maynard Minnich and Kathryn Jane (Obye) Tompkins. BA in Behavioral Sci., San Jose State U., 1978. Tutorial program coord./instr. Operation SHARE/La Valley Coll., Van Nuys, Calif., 1979-81; field exec. Silver Sage Girl Scout Coun., Boise, Idaho, 1981-85; continuing legal edn. dir. Idaho State Bar/Idaho Law Found. Inc., Boise, 1985-88, dep. dir., 1988-90, exec. dir., 1990—. Mem. Assn. CLE Adminstrs., Chgo., 1985-90; bd. dirs. Silver Sage coun. Girl Scouts, Boise, 1990-93, nominating com. mem., 1990-94, 97-97, chair nominating com., 1991-92. Named one of Outstanding Young Women in Am., 1991. Mem. Nat. Orgn. Bar Execs. (membership com. 1992-97), Zonta Club Boise (pres. 1991-92, bd. dirs. 1989-93, chair long range planning com.), Rotary Club Boise (chair mem. com. 1994-97, bd. dirs. 1996-97). Avocations: soccer, softball, jogging, golf. Office: Idaho State Bar/Idaho Law Found PO Box 895 525 W Jefferson St Boise ID 83702-5931

MINNICH, JOSEPH EDWARD, tourist railway consultant; b. Swanton, Ohio, Sept. 13, 1932; s. Charles and Leila (Gaiman) M.; m. Frances Katherine Searcy, Feb. 6, 1977; children: Christopher, Susan, Teresa. Student, U. Toledo, 1956-58, Am. U., 1969. Ins. broker Wright Russell & Bay Co., Toledo, 1961-67; ch. adminstr. St. Paul's Luth. Ch., Toledo, 1968-80; pres. Toledo Lake Erie & Western R.R., 1978-81, Heritage R.R. Co., 1981-83; exec. v.p. Centennial Rail, Ltd., Denver, 1981-94, chmn. bd. dirs., 1994—; v.p. Airpower West Ltd., 1992-95. Author: Steam Locomotives in the United States, 1985, Historic Diesels in the United States, 1988; editor Trainline mag., 1979-95. V.p. Airpower West, Ltd., 1992-95. Sgt. USAF, 1951-55. Nat. Assn. Ch. Bus. Adminstrs. fellow, 1971. Mem. Tourist Ry. Assn. (bd. dirs. 1984-95, Disting. Svc. award 1991), Colo. Ry. Mus. Republican. Lutheran. Home: 3641 S Yampa St Aurora CO 80013-3527 Office: Centennial Rail Ltd PO Box 460393 Aurora CO 80046-0393

MINNICH, NELSON HUBERT JOSEPH, historian, educator; b. Cin., Jan. 15, 1942; s. Hubert Jakob Matthäus and Alberta Mary Rosella (Pfadt) M. AB in Philosophy, Boston Coll., 1965, MA in History, 1969; STB in Theology, Gregorian U., 1970; PhD in History, Harvard U., 1977. Instr. Loyola Acad., Wilmette, Ill., 1966-68; teaching fellow, asst. Harvard U., Cambridge, Mass., 1972-73, 74-76; instr. Cath. U. of Am., Washington, 1977, asst. prof., 1977-83, assoc. prof., 1983-93, prof., 1993—. Co-editor: Studies in Catholic History in Honor of John Tracy Ellis, 1985; author: The Fifth Lateran Council (1512-17): Studies on Its Membership, Diplomacy, and Proposals for Reform, 1993, The Catholic Reformation: Council, Churchmen, and Controversies, 1993; assoc. editor The Cath. Hist. Rev., 1977-90, adv. editor, 1991—; editor Melville Studies in Church History, 1988—; contbr. chpts to books, numerous articles to profl. jours. and encys. Grantee, Societas Internationalis Historiae Conciliorum Investigandae, 1982, 84, 86, 87, 90, 97, Am. Philos. Soc., 1984, NEH, 1978, Am. Coun. Learned Socs., 1986, Cath. Univ. Am. faculty rsch., 1981, 90, 93-95; recipient fellowship Harvard U., 1972-73, 73-74, Villa I Tatti: The Harvard U. Ctr. for Italian Renaissance, 1979, Am. Acad. in Rome, 1979-80, Am. Coun. Learned Socs., 1979-80, 1990, NEH, 1986; recipient scholarship Harvard U., 1971-73, 74-76, Richard Krautheimer, 1980, Carl Meyer prize, 1977. Mem. Am. Cath. Hist. Assn., Gesellschaft zur Herausgabe des Corpus Catholicorum, Erasmus of Rotterdam Soc., Sixteenth Century Studies Conf. Avocations: dancing, local politics, gardening, travel, genealogy. Home: 5713 37th Ave Hyattsville MD 20782-3821 Office: Cath U of Am 423 Caldwell Hall Washington DC 20064

MINNICK, MALCOLM DAVID, lawyer; b. Indpls., July 5, 1946; s. Malcolm Dick and Frances Louise (Porter) M.; m. Heidi Rosemarie Klein, May 24, 1972. BA, U. Mich., 1968, JD, 1972. Bar: Calif. 1972, U.S. Dist. Ct. (cen. dist.) Calif. 1972, U.S. Ct. Appeals (9th cir.) 1984, U.S. Dist. Ct. (no. dist.) Calif. 1986, U.S. Supreme Ct. 1986. Assoc. Lillick McHose & Charles, Los Angeles, 1972-78; ptnr. Lillick & McHose, Los Angeles, 1978-91, Pillsbury, Madison & Sutro (formerly Lillick & McHose), San Francisco, 1991—; group mgr. Creditors Rights and Bankruptcy Group, 1993—; panelist Calif. Continuing Edn. of Bar, L.A., 1982-86, 88, Practicing Law Inst., 1992, 93, 94; bd. govs. Fin. Lawyers Conf., L.A., 1981-84; mem. exec. com. Lillick & McHose, 1982-85. Co-author: Checklist for Secured Commercial Loans, 1983. Mem. ABA (corp., banking and bus. law sect.), Calif. Bar Assn. (Uniform Comml. Code com. 1983-86), L.A. County Bar Assn. (exec. com. comml. law and bankruptcy sect. 1987-90), Bar Assn. San Francisco (comml. law and bankruptcy sect.), L.A. Country Club, Univ. Club (bd. dirs. 1983-86, pres. 1985-86). Avocation: golf. Office: Pillsbury Madison & Sutro 235 Montgomery St Fl 14 San Francisco CA 94104-2902

MINNICK, MALCOLM L., JR., clergy member, church administrator. Exec. dir. Division for Outreach of the Evangelical Lutheran Church in America, Chicago, Ill. Office: Evangelical Lutheran Church Am 8765 W Higgins Rd Chicago IL 60631-4101*

MINNIE, MARY VIRGINIA, social worker, educator; b. Eau Claire, Wis., Feb. 16, 1922; d. Herman Joseph and Virginia Martha (Strong) M. BA, U. Wis., 1944; MA, U. Chgo., 1949, Case Western Reserve U., 1956. Lic. clin. social worker, Calif. Supr. day care Wis. Children Youth, Madison, 1949-57; coordinator child study project Child Guidance Clinic, Grand Rapids, Mich., 1957-60; faculty, community services Pacific Oaks Coll., Pasadena, Calif., 1960-70; pvt. practice specializing in social work various cities, Calif., 1970-78; ednl. cons. So. Calif. Health Care, North Hollywood, Calif., 1978—; med. social worker Kaiser Permanente Home Health, Downey, Calif., 1985-87; assoc. Baby Sitters Guild, Inc., 1987-94; cons. Home Health, 1987-90; pres. Midwest Assn. Nursery Edn., Grand Rapids, 1958-60; bd. dirs., sec. So. Calif. Health Care, North Hollywood; bd. dirs., v.p. Baby Sitters Guild Inc., South Pasadena, 1986-94; cons. project Head Start Office Econ. Opportunity, Washington, 1965-70. Mem. Soc. Clin. Social Workers, Nat. Assn. Social Workers, Nat. Assn. Edn. Young Children (1960-62). Democrat. Club: Altrusa (Laguna Beach, Calif.) (pres. 1984-87). Avocations: music, travel, tennis, swimming, walking. Home and Office: 2225 Silver Oak Way Hemet CA 92545-8126

MINNIGH, JOEL DOUGLAS, library director; b. Greenville, Pa., Apr. 9, 1949; s. Wendell Ellsworth and Frances Alene (Hyde) M.; m. Margaret Beth Crowther, Dec. 26, 1972; children: Bradley Dean, Douglas Knox. BA, Allegheny Coll., 1971; MLS, U. Pitts., 1975. Cert. libr., Pa. Asst. libr. Wilkinsburg (Pa.) Pub. Libr., 1976-77, head libr., 1977—. Bd. dirs. Goodwill Industries Pitts., 1980-90; vice chmn. bd. dirs. Bach Choir Pitts., 1984-87; sec., bd. dirs. United Meth. Ch. Union, Pitts., 1987-88; elder, deacon Fox Chapel Presbyn. Ch., 1987—; v.p. Friends of Music Libr.-Carnegie Libr., 1988—. Recipient honor Goodwill Industries Pitts., 1990, citation Pa. Senate, 1991. Mem. Pa. Libr. Assn. (treas. S.W. chpt. 1988-89), Allegheny County Libr. Assn. Republican. Avocations: travel, cooking, gardening, music, reading. Home: 1009 Blackridge Rd Pittsburgh PA 15235-2719 Office: Wilkinsburg Pub Libr 605 Ross Ave Pittsburgh PA 15221-2145

MINNIX, BRUCE MILTON, television and theatre director; b. Hendersonville, N.C., Apr. 26, 1923; s. Bruce Milton and Jane Irene (Leverett) M.; m. Corinne McClure, Aug. 5, 1950; 1 child, Tracy Logue. B.A., U. N.C., 1948. mem. faculty New Sch., N.Y.C., 1977-80; adj. prof., Bklyn., 1985; AT&T sales tng. program, 1987. Dir. numerous TV shows including: U.S. Steel Hour, 1961-62, Merchant of Venice, 1962, Essay on Doors, 1963, Never Too Young, 1965-66, On Being Black, 1969, The Haggadah Oratorio, 1981, Search for Tomorrow, 1968-74, All My Children, 1978-79, Another World, 1981, Texas, 1981-82, Body Talk, 1983, As the World Turns, 1985-86; The Cradle Will Rock, 1986 (Emmy nomination), Minolta Tng. series Minolta Info. Network, 1980-81; dir. Citibank, 1984, N.J. Bell (AT&T), 1985; dir. Victorian Cape May A Video Visit to a Town out of Time, 1988 (medal Houston Film Festival), dir. Pitney Bowes Copier Intro 1992, Time Warner Cable 1991; producer, writer: Mt. Washington Valley, A Video Visit in Four Seasons, 1990; Actor: Music Video by Little Texas What Might Have Been, 1993. Mayor, City of Cape May, N.J., 1972-76; founding mem., 3-term pres. Mid-Atlantic Center for Arts. Served with USN, 1943-45. Mem. Dirs. Guild Am.

MINOCHA, ANIL, physician, educator, researcher; b. India, Feb. 4, 1957; Came to U.S., 1982; s. Ram Saroop and Kamla Devi M. Pre-med. diploma, Punjab U., India, 1974; MD, Med. Coll., Rohtak, India, 1980; postgrad. studies in pharmacology, Baylor Coll. Medicine, 1982-84. Diplomate Am. Bd. Internal Medicine, Am. Bd. Gastroenterology, Am. Bd. Forensic Medicine, Am. Bd. Geriatric Medicine. House officer depts. ophthalmology and dermatology Med. Coll. Hosp., Rohtak, India, 1980-81; med. officer State Health Svcs. Govts. of Punjab and Haryana, India, 1981-82; rsch. asst. Baylor Coll. Med., Houston, 1982-84; fellow clin. pharmacology U. Va., Charlottesville, 1984-86; resident physician Franklin Square Hosp., Balt., 1986-89; fellow gastroenterology Mich. State U., East Lansing, 1989-91; asst. prof. U. Louisville, 1991-95; assoc. prof. medicine U. Okla., Oklahoma City, 1995—; instr. dept. medicine Mich. State U., 1989-91; staff physician dept. medicine VAA Med. Ctr., Louisville, 1991-95; mem. credentials com. Humana Hosp., U. Louisville, 1992, other coms., 1992-94; mem. R&D com. VA Hosp., 1992-95; presenter in field; mem. PPT Com. Heartland Health Plan, Oklahoma City, 1996—; mem. R&D com. VA Med. Ctr., Oklahoma City, 1996—, chmn. med. record com., 1996—; mem. Formulary Adv. Coun. of the Okla. State Bd. of Nursing, 1997—. Contbr. numerous articles to profl. jours. Prin. investigator Gulf Biosystems, Charlottesville, 1985; biomed. rsch. grantee Mich. State U., 1990; sch. medicine rsch. grantee U. Louisville, 1993. Fellow ACP, Am. Coll. Gastroenterology, Am. Coll. Forensic Examiners; mem. Am. Gastroenterol. Assn., Am. Assn. for Study of Liver Disease. Office: U Okla Divsn Digestive Dis UH7NP Rm #526 800 NW 13th St Oklahoma City OK 73106-6827

MINOGUE, JOHN P., academic administrator, priest, educator; b. Chgo.. B in Philosophy, St. Mary's Sem.; MDiv, Deandreis Inst. Theology, 1972; M in Theology, DePaul U., 1975; D in Ministry, St. Mary of the Lake Sem., 1987. Ordained Vincentian priest, 1972. Vincentian priest Congregation of the Mission; instr. theology, dir. clin. pastoral placement programs St. Thomas Sem., Denver, 1972-76; instr. grad. theology, asst. then acad. dean DeAndreis Inst., 1976-83; pres. DePaul U., Chgo., 1993—; trustee DePaul U., 1991—; bd. mems. DePaul U. Corp., 1981-91; adj. prof. Sch. New Learning DePaul U., 1984—, instr. law and med. ethics Coll. Law DePaul U., 1989—; asst. prof. clin. ob.-gyn. Northwestern U.; instr. health care ethics St. Joseph Coll. Nursing, Joliet, Ill., Northwestern Sch. Nursing, Chgo.; cons. nat. heatlh care ethics, patient decision-making. Office: De Paul U 25 E Jackson Blvd Chicago IL 60604-2201*

MINOGUE, ROBERT BROPHY, retired nuclear engineer; b. Covington, Ky., Jan. 31, 1928; s. Joseph and Catherine Ann (Brophy) M.; m. Marie Joan Clarke, June 12, 1954; children: Patrick, Margaret, Marie, Francis. B.S., Thomas More Coll., 1949; M.S., U. Cin., 1951; grad., Oak Ridge Sch. Reactor Tech., 1952. Registered profl. engr., Calif. Nuclear engr., then head nuclear tech. sect. naval reactors br. AEC, Washington, 1952-56; head research reactor design and enngring., then head nuclear power plant engring. sect. Gen. Atomic div. Gen. Dynamics Corp., 1957-67; chief spl. projects br. div. reactor standards AEC, Washington, 1967-72, asst. dir., then dep. dir. regulatory standards, 1972-74; dir. office standards devel. Nuclear Regulatory Commn., Washington, 1975-80, dir. office research, 1980-86; pvt. practice Temecula, Calif., 1986—; U.S. mem. sr. adv. group Safety Standards IAEA, 1974-86; mem. Com. on Interagy. Radiation Research and Policy Coordination, 1982-86. Author: Reactor Shielding Design Manual, 1956; patentee: Triga Research Reactor. Served with AUS, 1946-48. Recipient Bernard F. Langer award, ASME, 1982. Mem. ASTM (dir. 1975-76, 77-80). Roman Catholic. Home and Office: 29743 Marhill Cir Temecula CA 92591-1809

MINOR, CHARLES DANIEL, lawyer; b. Columbus, Ohio, May 28, 1927; s. Walter Henry and Helen Margaret (Bergman) M.; m. Mary Jo Klinker, Dec. 27, 1950; children: Elizabeth, Daniel, Amy. B.S. in Bus. Adminstrn, Ohio State U., 1950, J.D. summa cum laude, 1952. Bar: Ohio 1952. Mem. firm Vorys, Sater, Seymour and Pease, Columbus, 1952—, ptnr., 1957-93, of counsel, 1993—; bd. dirs. Inland Products, Inc., Worthington Industries, Inc. Served with USNR, 1945-46. Mem. Columbus, Ohio State bar assns., The Columbus Club, Double Eagle Club, Scioto Country Club. Republican. Office: Vorys Sater Seymour & Pease 52 E Gay St Columbus OH 43215-3108

MINOR, GEORGE GILMER, III, drug and hospital supply company executive; b. 1940; married. BA, Va. Mil. Inst., 1963; MBA, U. Va., 1966. With Owens & Minor, Inc., Richmond, Va., 1963—, mgr. sales Acme Candy Co. div., 1966-68, mgr. retail mktg., 1968-73, div. mgr. wholesale drug br., 1973-77, v.p., 1977-80, exec. v.p., 1980-81, pres., chmn., CEO, 1981—, also bd. dirs. Office: Owens & Minor Med Inc 4800 Cox Rd Glen Allen VA 23060-6292*

MINOR, JOSEPH EDWARD, civil engineer, educator; b. Corpus Christi, Tex., June 2, 1938; s. William Smoot Jr. and Irene (Schiller) M.; m. Treva Ann Edmiston, Sept. 3, 1960; children: Joseph Edward Jr., Sharon Diane. BSCE, Tex. A&M U., 1959, M of Engring., 1960; PhD, Tex. Tech U., 1974. Registered profl. engr., Tex., Mo., Fla. Sr. rsch. engr. Southwest Research Inst., San Antonio, 1962-69; P. Whitfield Horn prof. Tex. Tech U., Lubbock, 1969-88; Thomas Reese prof., chmn. dept. civil engring. U. Mo., Rolla, 1988-93, rsch. prof., 1993—; pres. Insulating Glass Cert. Council, N.Y., 1986-89. Contbr. articles to profl. jours. Served with USAR. Recipient Disting. Engr. award Tex. Tech U., 1989; Nat. Def. fellow, 1959-60; Fulbright scholar, 1978. Fellow ASCE (pres. Tex. sect. 1984-85); mem. Nat. Soc. Profl. Engrs., Am. Meteorol. Soc. Presbyterian. Avocation: fishing. Office: Joseph E Minor PE Consulting Engineer PO Box 603 Rockport TX 78381-0603

MINOR, MARK WILLIAM, allergist; b. Steubenville, Ohio, May 19, 1956; s. Garland Edgar Minor and Norma Jean McKenzie Shidock; m. Rachael Anne Hatfield, Aug. 15, 1987; children: Megan, Emily. BS in Biology magna cum laude, U. Miami, 1978; MD, W.Va. U., 1982. Resident in internal medicine W.Va. U., Charleston; fellow in allergy/immunology U. So. Fla., Tampa; staff physician Holmes Regional Hosp., Melbourne, Fla.; clin. asst., prof. medicine U. South Fla.; physician Osler Med., Melbourne, Fla., 1987—. Contbr. articles, referee Jour. Allergy and Clin. Immunology, So. Med. Jour. Fellow Am. Coll. Allergy and Immunology, Am. Coll. Physicians; mem. Am. Acad. Allergy and Immunology, Alpha Omega Alpha. Office: Osler Medical 930 S Harbor City Blvd Melbourne FL 32901-1963

MINOR, MARY ELLEN, civilian military employee; b. Konawa, Okla., Jan. 11, 1947; d. Tom Loye and Barbara Anna (Wheeler) Bounds; 1 child, Rose Mary Minor Wright. BS in Math., East Ctrl. State U., Ada, Okla., 1968; MS in Math., U. Ark., 1970; postgrad., U. Utah, 1970-72. Ops. rsch. analyst U.S. Army Comm. Command, Ft. Huachuca, Ariz., 1974-78; mathematician U.S. Dept. Treasury, Washington, 1978-79; ops. rsch. analyst U.S. Army Concepts Analysis AG., Bethesda, Md., 1979-80, Office Chief of Staff of Army, Washington, 1980-82; program integration specialist U.S. Army Materiel Command, Alexandria, Va., 1982-88, supervisory ops. rsch. analyst, 1988-93; supervisory ops. rsch. analyst U.S. Army Logistics Integration Agy., Alexandria, 1993—. Parent sponsor Girl Scouts U.S., Annandale, Va., 1981-84. Mem. Am. Def. Preparedness Assn. Avocations: gardening, beachcombing, reading, movies. Home: 20583 Snowshoe Sq Apt 302 Ashburn VA 20147-3964 Office: US Army Logistics Integration Agy 5001 Eisenhower Ave Alexandria VA 22304-4841

MINOR, ROBERT ALLEN, lawyer; b. Washington, Oct. 20, 1948; s. Robert Walter and Joan (Allen) M.; m. Sue Ellyn Blose, June 13, 1981; children: Robert Barratt, Sarah Allen. AB in English, Duke U., 1970; JD, Ohio State U., 1975. Bar: Ohio 1975, U.S. Dist. Ct. (so. dist.) Ohio 1976, D.C. 1979. Assoc. Vorys, Sater, Seymour & Pease, Columbus, Ohio, 1975-82, ptnr., 1982—. Author seminar articles. With U.S. Army, 1970-72. Mem. ABA, Ohio Bar Assn., Columbus Bar Assn., Athletic Club Columbus, Scioto Country Club. Republican. Presbyterian. Office: Vorys Sater Seymour & Pease PO Box 1008 52 E Gay St Columbus OH 43216-1008

MINOR, RONALD RAY, minister; b. Aliceville, Ala., Nov. 3, 1944; s. Hershel Ray and Minnie Ozell (Goodson) M.; m. Gwendolyn Otella Newsome, July 25, 1970; 1 child, Rhonda Rene. BA in Ministerial, Southeastern Bible Coll., 1971, BA in Secondary Edn., 1973; DDiv, Southern Bible Coll., 1984. Ordained to ministry Pentecostal Ch. of God, 1968. Gen. sec. Pentecostal Ch. of God, Joplin, Mo., 1979—; dist. supt. Pentecostal Ch. of God, Philadelphia, Miss., 1975-79; pastor Pentecostal Ch. of God, Bartow, Fla., Orient Park Tabernacle, Tampa, Fla.; pres. Pentecostal Young People's Assn., Fla. and Miss.; sec. Gen. Bd. Pentecostal Ch. of God, Joplin, 1979; bd. dirs. Nat. Assn. Evangs., Wheaton, Ill., 1981-96; adv. coun. Am. Bible Soc., N.Y.C., 1979—; sec. Commn. Chaplains, Washington, 1991-95. Home: 2625 E 13th St Joplin MO 64801-5353 Office: Pentecostal Ch of God 4901 Pennsylvania Ave Joplin MO 64804-4947

MINOW, JOSEPHINE BASKIN, civic worker; b. Chgo., Nov. 3, 1926; d. Salem N. and Bessie (Sampson) Baskin; m. Newton N. Minow, May 29, 1949; children: Nell, Martha, Mary. BS, Northwestern U., 1948. Asst. to advt. dir. Mandel Brothers Dept. Store, Chgo., 1948-49; tchr. Francis W. Parker Sch., Chgo., 1949-50; vol. in civil and charitable activities, 1950—; bd. dirs. Juvenile Protective Assn., Chgo., 1958—; pres. Juvenile Protective Assn., 1973-75; bd. dirs. Parnham Trust, Beaminster, Dorset, Eng. Author: Marty the Broken Hearted Artichoke, 1997. Founder, coord. Children's div. Hospitality and Info. Svc., Washington, 1961-63; mem. Caucus Com., Glencoe, Ill., 1965-69; co-chmn. spl. study on juvenile justice Chgo. Community Trust, 1978-80; chmn. Know Your Chgo., 1980-83; bd. dirs. Chgo. Coun. Fgn. Rels.; trustee Chgo. Hist. Soc., Ravinia Festival Assn.; mem. women's bd. Field Mus., U. Chgo.; founding mem., v.p. women's bd. Northwestern U., 1978; bd. govs. Chgo. Symphony, 1966-73, 76—; mem. Citizens Com. Juvenile Ct. of Cook County, 1985-96; exec. com. Northwestern U. Libr. Coun., 1974-96; grandparents' adv. com. Chgo. Children's Mus. Recipient spl. award Chgo. Sch. and Workshop for Retarded, 1975, Children's Guardian award Juvenile Protective Assn., 1993. Mem. Hebrew Immigrant Aid Soc. (bd. dirs. 1977—, award 1988), Friday Club, Northmoor Country Club. Democrat. Jewish. Office: Chgo Hist Soc Clark St at North Ave Chicago IL 60614

MINSHALL, DREXEL DAVID, retired manufacturing company executive; b. Bridgeport, Nebr., Nov. 1, 1917; s. Charles D. and Minnie C. (Nordell) M.; m. Betty Jane Tesdell, Feb. 12, 1938 (dec. June 1971); children—Drexel David, Carol J. Minshall Preston; m. Roylynn Hurlburt McAllister, Apr. 19, 1974. Student, Colo. U., 1934-38. Sales mgr. Gates Rubber Co., Denver, 1939-61; v.p. mktg. Perfect Circle Corp., Hagerstown, Ind., 1961-65; pres. Dana Parts Co. div. Dana Corp., Toledo, Ohio, 1965-67, group v.p., 1967-73, sr. group v.p., 1973-79; pres. Service Parts Worldwide, 1979-81; chmn. bd. Dana Western Hemisphere Trade Corp., Toledo, 1970-81; dir. Dana World Trade Corp., Ludwig Motors Corp., Corp. HZ, Caracas, Venezuela, Arcamsa, Rosario, Argentina, Brown Bros. Ltd., London, Eng.; pres. Double D Mktg. Corp. Bd. dirs. Community Chest, 1972-75; trustee Toledo Boys Club, 1967-82. Mem. Automotive Service Industries Assn. (past pres.), Automotive Hall of Fame (past chmn.), Automotive Acad., Nat. Inst. Automotive Service Excellence (bd. dirs. 1972-86, past chmn.), Nat. Automotive Parts Assn. (bd. dirs. mfrs. council 1971-81, past chmn.), Motor and Equipment Mfrs. Assn. (product v.p. 1972-75), Alpha Tau Omega. Clubs: Toledo, Inverness; Atlantis Golf (Fla.). Lodges: Masons, Shriners. Contbr. articles to profl. jours. Home: 620 Estates Way Atlantis FL 33462

MINSKER, ROBERT STANLEY, consultant, former industrial relations executive; b. Pitts. Jan. 1, 1911; s. Theodore Kühne and Isabella Lavinia (Trumbor) M.; BS, U. Ill., 1934; postgrad. Pa. State U., 1938-39; m. Marion Elizabeth Warner, May 29, 1937; children: Norma (Mrs. Leo Jerome Brown II), Robert S., James. D. With Owens-Ill., Inc., Toledo, Ohio, 1934-76, pers. dir. Clarion (Pa.) plant, 1936-40, per. dir. Columbus (Ohio) plant, 1940-44, mgr. indsl. rels. Alton, 1945-72, adminstr. workmen's compensation, safety and health Ill. and pub. affairs Ill. Plants, 1972-76; dir. Germania Fin. Corp., 1963-82, Germania Bank 1953-82, hon. dir., 1982-91; assoc. faculty So. Ill. U., 1959-64; chmn. bd. dirs. Midwestern Comm., Inc., CEO, 1992-96; chmn. bd. dirs. Riverview, Inc., 1992—; cons. Chmn. Madison County Savs. Bond Campaign, 1959-61; active Boy Scouts Am.; pres. Piasa Bird Coun., 1949-51, mem. exec. bd., 1945-90; mem. grievance com. panel State of Ill. Dept. Pers., 1967-80; vice chmn. Higher Edn. Coordinating Coun. Met. St. Louis, 1966-70; founder Board Pride, Inc., 1966—. Mem. Bd. Edn., 1957-70, pres. 1961-70. Bd. dirs., treas., sec., exec. com. Alton Meml. Hosp., 1969-88, dir. emeritus 1988—, bd. dirs. Alton Meml. Hosp. Found., 1986-91; Jr. Achievement, United Fund.; bd. dirs. Cmty. Chest, v.p., 1949-54, 61-66, gen. chmn., 1949-50; adminstr., sec., Alton Found., 1955—; trustee Lewis and Clark C.C., sec. bd., 1970-77; bd. dirs. McKendree Coll., 1981—, Madison County Urban League, 1990-96; mem. pres. coun. U. Ill. Found., Alton Police Chief Adv. Com., 1994—. Recipient Silver Beaver award Boy Scouts of Am., 1951, Achievement award U.S. Treasury Dept., 1951, Hall of Fame award Piasa Bird Coun., 1969, Alton Citizens' award, 1988, Southwestern Ill. Leadership Coun. award, 1989, Lovejoy Human Rights award, 1989, Pride Outstanding Citizen award, 1988; named to Lewis and Clark Hall of Fame, 1977, Impact Cmty. Svc. award, 1992, Ill. State Bd. Edn. Cmty. mem. award of excellence, 1995, Marquett H.S. Svc. Leadership award, 1995, Boys & Girls Club Man and Youth award, 1996, Urban League chmn.'s award, 1996. Mem. Alton C. of C. (chmn. pub. rels. 1951-54), U. Ill. Varsity "I" Assn., U. Ill. Alumni Assn., Acacia, Alpha Phi Omega. Methodist. Clubs: Masons, (32 deg.), K.T., Shriners. Home: 2018 Chapin Pl Alton IL 62002-4631

MINSKY, BRUCE WILLIAM, lawyer; b. Queens, N.Y., Sept. 28, 1963; m. Jill R. Heinter, May 1992; children: Aryeh Hanan, Elisheva Yael. BA in Polit. Sci., Boston U., 1985; JD, Southwestern U., 1988; postgrad., Boston U., 1989. Bar: Calif. 1988, Conn. 1989, N.Y. 1990, U.S. Dist. Ct. (ea. and so. dist.), U.S. Ct. Appeals. Assoc. Quirk & Bakalor, N.Y.C., 1989-91; house counsel, v.p. Banco Popular de P.R., N.Y.C., 1991—; house counsel Banco Popular, FSB, N.J., 1995—. Atty. Monday Night Law Pro Bono Svcs., N.Y.C. Mem. Assn. of Bar of City of N.Y. (mem. young lawyers com. 1993-95). Avocations: music, sports, literature. Office: 7 W 51st St New York NY 10019-6910

MINTER, DAVID LEE, English literature educator; b. Midland, Tex., Mar. 20, 1935; s. Kenneth Cruse and Frances (Hennessey) M.; m. Cynthia Caroline Sewell, Dec. 22, 1957; children: Christopher Sewell, Frances Elizabeth. B.A., N. Tex. State U., 1957, M.A., 1959; B.D., Yale U., 1961, Ph.D., 1965. Univ. lectr. Hamburg (W. Ger.) U., 1965-66; lectr. Yale U., 1966-67; asst. prof. Rice U., Houston, 1967-69, assoc. prof., 1969-74, prof., 1974-80; prof. English Emory U., Atlanta, 1981-89, Asa G. Candler prof. Am. lit., 1989-90, dean Coll. Arts and Scis., 1981-90, v.p. arts and scis., 1984-90; Libbie Shearn Moody prof. English Rice U., Houston, 1990—. Author: The Interpreted Design as a Structural Principle in American Prose, 1969, William Faulkner: His Life and Work, 1980, 82, 91, 97, A Cultural History of the American Novel: Henry James to William Faulkner, 1994, 96; editor: Twentieth-Century Interpretations of Light in August, 1969, The Norton Critical Edit. of The Sound and the Fury, 1987, 93; co-editor: The Harper American Literature, 1986, 93, 96, 97, The Columbia Literary History of the United States, 1987 (Italian edit. 1990, Chinese edit. 1994, Japenese edit. 1997); also articles and revs. Fulbright Travel fellow, 1966; Nat. Endowment for Humanities fellow, 1969-70; Am. Council Learned Socs. grantee, 1975; Fred Harris Daniels fellow, 1980. Mem. MLA, Am. Lit. Group, Am. Studies Assn., Phi Beta Kappa. Methodist. Home: 2145 Swift Houston TX 77030-1215 Office: Rice U Dept English PO Box 1892 Houston TX 77251-1892

MINTER, JERRY BURNETT, electronic component company executive, engineer; b. Ft. Worth, Oct. 31, 1913; s. Claude Joe and Roxie (Ayers) M.; m. Monica Rose Hanlon, Mar. 2, 1940; children: Claude, Mark (dec.), Byron, Claire, Maureen. BSEE, MIT, 1934. Engr., Boonton (N.J.) Radio Corp., 1935-36, Ferris Instruments Co., Boonton, 1936-39; v.p., chief engr. Measurements Corp., Boonton, 1939-53; pres. Components Corp., Denville, N.J., 1946—. Contbr. numerous articles to tech. jours.; patentee in field. Pilot, CAP, Morristown, N.J., 1947-50. Fellow IEEE (life, past chmn. no. N.J. sect.), Audio Engring. Soc. (past pres.), Radio Club Am. (life, pres. emeritus, past pres., Armstrong Medal 1968); mem. Am. Soc. for Metals (life), Am. Inst. Aero. and Astronautics, N.Y. Acad. Scis., Soc. Motion Picture TV Engrs. (life), Internat. Soc. Photo-Optical Instrumentation Engrs., Quiet Birdmen. Home: 48 Normandy Heights Rd Morristown NJ 07960-4613 Office: Components Corp 6 Kinsley Pl Denville NJ 07834

MINTER, JIMMIE RUTH, accountant; b. Greenville, S.C., Sept. 28, 1941; d. James C. and Lois (Williams) Jannino; BS Acctg., U. S.C., 1962; m. Charles H. Minter, Nov. 3, 1972; 1 child, Regina M.; stepchildren: Rhonda, Julie, Gregg; adopted child, Michael Minter. Asst. controller Package Supply & Equipment Co., Greenville, 1964-70, Olympia Knitting Mills, Spartanburg, S.C., 1970-72; controller Diacou Knitting Mills, Spartanburg, 1972-74; adminstr. Atlanta Med. Specialists, P.C., Riverdale, Ga., 1974-79; adminstr., corp. sec. David L. Cooper, M.D. P.C., Riverdale, 1979-89; acct. Ted L. Griffin Enterprises, Jonesboro, Ga., 1988-93; chief tax acct. Clayton County Tax Commn., Jonesboro, 1993—. Program chmn. 4th of July Celebration and Beauty Pageant, City of Riverdale; mem. exec. com. Clayton County Dem. Party, 1987—; Ga. State Dem. treas.; active Clinton Campaign Com.; active local and state election campaign fund raising; bd. dirs. Clayton County Human Rels. Com. Mem. Am. Bus. Women's Assn. (chpt. Bus. Woman of Yr. 1969), Nat. Assn. Female Execs. Am. Cancer Soc. (silent auction com.), Clayton County Alzheimers Assn. (bd. dirs.). Home: 1244 Branchfield Ct Riverdale GA 30296-2148 Office: PO Box 1119 Riverdale GA 30274-1119

MINTER, PHILIP CLAYTON, retired communications company executive; b. Sydney, Australia, Aug. 9, 1928; cme to U.S., 1957; s. Roy Dixon and Adeline Claire (Bradly) M.; m. Mary Bashford Schettler, Jan. 24., 1959; children: Elizabeth C., Margaret S. BSc with honours, U. Sydney, 1951; MS, U. Wyo., 1958; PhD, U. Wis., 1960. Tchr. King's Sch., Parramatta, Australia, 1951-57; mng. dir. Motivational Rsch. Assocs., Sydney, 1960-62; dir. rsch. Nat. Fund Raising Coun., Sydney, 1962-65; project dir. USDA, Ft. Collins, Colo., 1965-67; chief info. pesticides program USPHS, Atlanta, 1967-68; mgr. data bases div. Pa. Rsch. Assocs., Phila., 1968-70; pres. Ednl. Communications Inc., King of Prussia, Pa., 1970-94; pres. Svc. Tng. Ltd., Kenilworth, Eng., 1976-88; cons. Westinghouse Learning Corp., 1972. Author: Handbook for Pesticide-Chemicals Program Coordinators, 1967. Recipient Terry Magill award Australia Soc., N.Y., 1994. Mem. Soc. Automotive Engrs., Sci. Rsch. Soc. Am., Royal Heritage Soc. (bd. dirs.), U. Wis. Alumni Assn. (bd. dirs. Delaware Valley br.), Australian/Am. C. of C. Phila. (exec. dir.), Union League, Brit. Officers Club Phila. (pres. 1992-93), Sloane Club (London), Sigma Xi. Republican. Episcopalian. Home: 141 Orchard Ct Blue Bell PA 19422 Office: PO Box 248 Blue Bell PA 19422-0248

MINTER, STEVEN ALAN, foundation executive, social worker; b. Akron, Oct. 23, 1938; s. Lawrence L. and Dorothy (Knox) M.; m. Dolores Kreicher, Apr. 8, 1961; children: Michele, Caroline, Robyn. BA in Edn., Baldwin-Wallace Coll., 1960, LHD (hon.), 1974; M in Social Adminstrn., Case Western Reserve U., 1963, LHD (hon.), 1989; LHD (hon.), Findlay (Ohio) Coll., 1984, Kent (Ohio) State U., 1988, Oberlin Coll., 1988, Lake Erie Coll., 1990. Lic. social worker. Dir. Cuyahoga County Welfare Dept., Cleve., 1969-70; commr. Mass. Dept. Pub. Welfare, Boston, 1970-75; assoc. dir., program officer The Cleve. Found., 1975-80, 1981-83, exec. dir., 1984—; under sec. U.S. Dept. Edn., Washington, 1980-81; bd. dirs. Goodyear Tire and Rubber Co., Akron, Ohio, Key Corp Svc. Corp., Cleve., Consol. Natural Gas, Pitts., Rubbermaid Inc., Wooster, Ohio. Contbr. articles to profl. jours. Trustee Coll. of Wooster, Ohio, 1977—, Found. Ctr., 1990—, Leadership Cleve.; bd. dirs. Am. Assn. for Higher Edn., 1993—, Cleve. Initiative for Edn., 1991—. Recipient Disting. Svc. award Jr. C. of C. of Cleve., 1969, Disting. Svc. award Case Western Res. U. Sch. Applied Social Svcs., 1985, Ohio Govs. award, 1991; named Black Profl. of the Yr., Cleve. Black Profl. Assn., 1985. Mem. Nat. Acad. Pub. Adminstrs., NAACP (life), Assn. Black Found. Execs., NASW, Pepper Pike (Ohio) Club, Union. Democrat. Presbyterian. Home: 2878 Woodbury Rd Cleveland OH 44120-2426 Office: The Cleve Found 1422 Euclid Ave Ste 1400 Cleveland OH 44115-2001

MINTON, DWIGHT CHURCH, manufacturing company executive; b. North Hills, N.Y., Dec. 17, 1934; s. Henry Miller and Helen Dwight (Church) M.; m. Marian Haven Haines, Aug. 4, 1956; children: Valerie Haven, Daphne Forsyth, Henry Brewster. B.A., Yale U., 1959; M.B.A., Stanford U., 1961. With Church & Dwight Co., Inc., Princeton, N.J., 1961—; asst. v.p. Church & Dwight Co., Inc., 1964-66, v.p., 1966-67, pres., 1967-81, chief exec. officer, 1969-95, chmn., 1981—, dir., 1966—; bd. dirs. Crane Corp., Medusa Cement Corp., First Brands Corp. Trustee Atlanta U., 1971-88, Morehouse Coll., 1971—, Spelman Coll., 1971-80; v.p., bd. dirs. Greater Yellowstone Coalition, 1991—. With U.S. Army, 1956-57. Mem. Chem. Mfrs. Assn. (bd. dirs. 1980-83), Grocery Mfrs. Am. (dir. 1983-87). Clubs: Seawanhaka Corinthian Yacht, Racquet and Tennis, Yale, Lotos. Office: Church & Dwight Co Inc 469 N Harrison St Princeton NJ 08540-3510

MINTON, JERRY DAVIS, lawyer, former banker; b. Ft. Worth, Aug. 13, 1928; s. Robert Bruch and Anna Elizabeth (Davis) M.; m. Martha Drew Fields, Nov. 28, 1975; children: Marianne, Martha, John Morgan. B.B.A., U. Tex., Austin, 1949, J.D., 1960; grad. cert., Nat. Trust Sch., Northwestern U., 1960. Of counsel Michener, Larimore, Swindle, Whitaker, Flowers et al., 1991—; vice chmn. 1st Nat. Bank Ft. Worth, 1982-84; chmn. & CEO 1st City Bank Ft. Worth, 1986-91. Pilot USAF, 1951-55, pilot Tex. Air N.G., 1955-57; capt. USAFR Ret.). Decorated D.F.C., Air medal with 3 oak leaf clusters. Mem. SAR, State Bar Tex., Tarrant County Bar Assn. (former chmn.), Ft. Worth C. of C. Found., Mil. Order World Wars, Soc. Descendants of Washington's Army at Valley Forge, Mil. Order Stars and Bars, Sons of Confederate Vets., River Crest Country Club, Breakfast Club, Sigma Iota Epsilon, Phi Delta Phi. Episcopalian. Home: 5404 El Dorado Dr Fort Worth TX 76107-3236 Office: 301 Commerce St Ste 3500 Fort Worth TX 76102-4135

MINTON, JOHN DEAN, historian, educator; b. Cadiz, Ky., July 29, 1921; s. John Ernest and Daisy Dean (Wilson) M.; m. Betty Jo Redick, June 8, 1947; children—John Dean, James Ernest. A.B. in Edn, U. Ky., 1943, M.A. in History, 1947; Ph.D., Vanderbilt U., 1959. Instr. history U. Miami, Fla., 1951; tchr. Broward County Pub. Sch. System, U. Miami evening div., 1951-53; prin. Trigg County (Ky.) High Sch., 1953-58; prof. history Western Ky. U., Bowling Green, 1958-86, ret., dean Grad. Coll., 1964-71, v.p. for adminstrv. affairs, 1970-79, interim pres., 1979, v.p. for student affairs, 1981-86, part-time prof., 1986—. Author: The New Deal in Tennessee, 1932-1938, 1979; contbr. articles to profl. jours. Mem. Gen. Bd. Discipleship, United Meth. Ch.; mem. Louisville Bd. Discipleship; lay speaker Louisville Conf. Meth. Ch.; bd. dirs. Higher Edn. Found., Meth. Ch., Jesse Stuart Found. Served with USNR, 1943-46. Mem. NEA, Ky. Edn. Assn., So. Hist. Assn., Ky. Hist. Soc., Bowling Green C. of C. (bd. dirs.), Civitan Club (pres. Cadiz 1956), Phi Alpha Theta, Phi Eta Sigma, Kappa Delta Pi. Home: 645 Ridgecrest Way Bowling Green KY 42104-3818

MINTON, JOSEPH PAUL, retired safety organization executive; b. Houston, Oct. 20, 1924; s. Joseph Marion and Stella (Fite) M.; m. Nancy Fettig, June 19, 1948; children: Joan M., Michael J., Jean A., Mary B., John E., Diane C. BS in Air Transp., Purdue U., 1949; Grad., U.S. Air Force Air Command and Staff Coll., 1958. Commd. 2d lt. USAF, 1944, advanced through grades to col., 1966; combat USAF, Burma, World War II; assignments in crew, staff and command USAF, ret., 1967; v.p. Purdue Airlines Inc., Lafayette, Ind., 1967-68, pres., CEO, 1969-71; mng. dir., chief exec. officer Saber Air Ltd., Singapore, 1971-73; sr. v.p. Brit. Caledonian Airways, N.Y.C., 1974-76; mng. dir. Nat. Transp. Safety Bd., Washington, 1977-78; exec. dir. Nat. Safety Coun., Washington, 1978-88. Decorated D.F.C. with oak leaf cluster, Air medal with 3 oak leaf clusters, 3 battle stars, Air Force Commendation medal with oak leaf cluster. Republican. Roman Catholic. Address: 1720 Lake Shore Crest # 15 Reston VA 20190-3243

MINTON, TORRI, journalist; b. San Rafael, Calif., Oct. 7, 1956; d. John and Mary. BA in Ethnic Studies, U. Calif., Berkeley, 1983; M of Journalism, Columbia U., 1984. Reporter Associated Press, San Francisco, 1984, Bay City News Svc., San Francisco, 1984-86, San Francisco Chronicle, 1986—; vice chmn. San Francisco Chronicle No. Calif. Newspaper Guild, 1992, 97; rep. assembly del., 1992, 93, 94, 95, 96. Community devel. vol. Oper. Crossroads Africa, Tiriki, Kenya, 1979. Mem. Phi Beta Kappa. Office: San Francisco Chronicle 901 Mission St San Francisco CA 94103-2905

MINTON, YVONNE FAY, mezzo-soprano; b. Sydney, Australia; d. Robert Thomas and Alice Violet M.; m. William Barclay, Aug. 24, 1965; children—Malcolm Alexander, Alison Elizabeth. Ed., Sydney Conservatorium of Music, 1960-61. Mezzo-soprano with all maj. orchs. in, Australia, 1958-61; moved to, London, 1961, joined, Royal Opera House, Covent Garden, 1965-70, guest artist, Cologne (W. Ger.) Opera, 1969—, U.S. debut as Octavian in Der Rosenkavalier, 1970; appeared, with Lyric Opera, Chgo., 1970, Met. Opera, N.Y.C., 1973, San Francisco Opera, 1974, Paris Opera, 1974, Bayreuth, 1974, Salzburg, 1978; sings regularly with maj. symphony orchs. throughout world, 1968—; recs. include The Knot Garden, 1970, Cosi Fan Tutte, 1971, Lulu, 1979; maj. vocal works include Mahler songs with, Chgo. Symphony. Comdr. Order Brit. Empire, 1980. Hon. mem. Royal Acad. Music. Office: care Ingpen & Williams, 26 Wadham Rd, London SW15 2LR, England

MINTS, GRIGORI EFROIM, specialist in mathematical logic; b. Leningrad, USSR, June 7, 1939; s. Efroim B. and Lea M. (Novick) M.; m. Maryanna Rozenfeld, July 21, 1987; 1 child, Anna. Diploma, Leinigrad U., 1961, PhD, 1965, ScD, 1989. Rsch. assoc. Steklov Inst. Math., Leningrad, 1961-79; with Nauka Pubs., Leningrad, 1979-85; sr. rsch. assoc. Inst. Cybernetics, Tallinn, Estonia, 1985-91; prof. dept. philosophy Stanford (Calif.) U., 1991—; mem. adv. bd. Jour. Symbolic Logic, 1987-90; mem. editorial bd. Jour. Symbolic Computation, 1983-96, Jour. of Functional Programming, 1990-95; mem. program orgn. com. Logic in Computer Sci., 1991-94, ASL mtg. March 1997, Conf. on Automated Deduction, Logic Programming and Automated Reasoning. Editor: Mathematical Investigation of Logical Deduction, 1967, COLOG-88, 1989, Logic Colloquium, 1996; Jour. Logic and Computation, 1991—; contbr. articles to profl. jours. Mem. Assn. Symbolic Logic (mem. coun. 1990-93), Internat. Union History and Philosophy and Sci. (assessor 1991-95), Annals of Pure and Applied Logic (mem. editorial bd. 1980-89).

MINTZ, ALBERT, lawyer; b. New Orleans, Oct. 19, 1929; s. Morris and Goldie (Goldblum) M.; m. Linda Barnett, Dec. 19, 1954; children—John Morris, Margaret Anne. B.B.A., Tulane U., 1948, J.D., 1951. Bar: La. bar 1951. Since practiced in New Orleans; ptnr. Montgomery, Barnett, Brown, Read, Hammond & Mintz, Hurwitz-Mintz Realty Cos., New Orleans.; bd. dirs. Sunbelt Mfg., Inc., Strauss Distbrs., Avrico, Inc. Mem. adv. bd. Law Sch. Tulane U.; chmn., dir. adv. bd. Tulane Summer Lyric Theater; bd. dirs. Tulane Ctr. Stage Talent and Shakespearean Theatre; bd. dirs. Jewish Cmty. Ctr., New Orleans, 1965-72, Jewish Fedn., 1968—, Home for Jewish Aged, 1968-71, Jewish Family Svc., New Orleans, 1968-72; trustee, bd. mgrs. Touro Infirmary Hosp. and Found.; trustee Jewish Endowment Found.; charter mem. La. Hist. Assn. Mem. ABA, La. Bar Assn. (lectr., publ. on corp., tax, real estate law), New Orleans Bar Assn. (exec. com. 1971-74), Am. Law Inst., U.S. Hist. Assn., New Orleans C. of C. (chmn. com. civic affairs and state legis. 1968-69), City Energy Club, Phi Delta Phi, Omicron Delta Kappa, Zeta Beta Tau. Jewish. Home: 2017 Jefferson Ave New Orleans LA 70115-5618 Office: 3200 Energy Ctr 1100 Poydras St New Orleans LA 70163-1101

MINTZ, DALE LEIBSON, health education executive; b. Bronx, July 28, 1944; d. Jack and Martha (Tobin) Leibson; m. Stephen Allan Mintz, June 19, 1966; children: Eric Michael, Jaclyn Leibson. BA, SUNY, Purchase, 1982; MPA, Bernard M. Baruch Coll., 1991. Cert. health edn. specialist. Corp. art cons. Merryl Wilson Assoc., N.Y.C., 1982-85; asst. to CEO New Am. Libr., N.Y.C., 1985-86; estates coord. Sotheby's, N.Y.C., 1986-87; program dir. Am. Heart Assn., Purchase, 1987-94; field svcs. exec. Nat. Hemophilia Found., N.Y.C., 1994-95; nat. health edn. dir. Hadassah, Women's Zionist Orgn. of Am., N.Y.C., 1995—; chair task force COMMIT, Yonkers, N.Y., 1988-93. Trustee Comty. Synagogue, Rye, N.Y., 1975-78, Rye Arts Ctr., 1980-89, Rye Hist. Soc., 1994-97. Mem. Nat. Assn. Exec. Women, Assn. Women's Health Profls., N.Y. State Profl. Health Educators. Avocations: reading, volunteering. Office: Hadassah 50 W 58th St New York NY 10019-2505

MINTZ, DANIEL HARVEY, diabetologist, educator, academic administrator; b. N.Y.C., Sept. 16, 1930; s. Jacob A. and Fannie M.; m. Dawn E. Hynes, Jan. 15, 1961 (dec.); children: David, Denise, Debra; m. Marge K Peiman, Nov. 30, 1996. B.S. cum laude, St. Bonaventure Coll., 1951; M.D., N.Y. Med. Coll., 1956. Diplomate: Am. Bd. Internal Medicine. Intern Henry Ford Hosp., Detroit, 1956-57; resident Georgetown med. div. D.C. Gen. Hosp., Washington, 1957-59, Georgetown U. Hosp., Washington, 1958-59; fellow medicine Nat. Inst. Arthritis and Metabolic Diseases, 1959-60, Am. Diabetes Assn., 1960-61; practice medicine, specializing in internal medicine Miami, Fla.; asst. prof. medicine Georgetown U. Sch. Medicine, 1963-64; assoc. prof. medicine U. Pitts. Sch. Medicine, 1964-69; prof. medicine U. Miami Sch. Medicine, 1969—, Mary Lou Held prof. medicine, 1981—, chief div. endocrinology and metabolism, dept. medicine, 1969-80,

Sci. dir. Diabetes Research Inst., 1980—; chief of service Georgetown U. Med. div. D.C. Gen. Hosp., Washington, 1963-64; chief of medicine Magee-Women's Hosp., Pitts., 1964-69; guest prof. U. Geneva, 1976-77. Contbr. articles to profl. jours. Fellow ACP; mem. Endocrine Soc., Am. Diabetes Assn. (program dir. 1972), Am. Fedn. Clin. Research, Am. Soc. Clin. Investigation, Central Soc. Clin. Investigation, So. Soc. Clin. Investigation., Am. Assn. Physicians. Office: U Miami Diabetes Rsch Inst PO Box 016960 R-134 Miami FL 33101-6960

MINTZ, DONALD EDWARD, psychologist, educator; b. N.Y.C., July 19, 1932; s. Irving and Pauline Lynore (Arenson) M.; children: Peter Graham, Hayley Ilana. AB, Columbia U., 1954, PhD, 1961. Rsch. assoc. Princeton U., 1959-63; asst. prof. psychology City Coll., CUNY, 1963-67, assoc. prof., 1967-73, chmn. dept., 1971-74, prof., 1973-95, prof. emeritus, 1995—, acting dean Sch. Architecture and Environ. Studies, 1982-85; pvt. practice psychotheraphy N.Y.C., 1979—. Author: Dynamics of Response, 1965; contbr. articles to profl. jours. Served to lt. USN, 1954-57. NSF predoctoral fellow, 1957. Fellow N.Y. Acad. Sci.; mem. Am. Psychol. Assn., AAAS, Psychonomic Soc., Assn. Advancement Behavior Therapy, Eastern Psychol. Assn., N.Y. Acad. Scis., Phi Beta Kappa, Sigma Xi. Democrat. Jewish. Club: Stuyvesant Yacht. Home: 10 W 15th St New York NY 10011-6838 Office: CCNY Psychology Dept New York NY 10031

MINTZ, JEFFRY ALAN, lawyer; b. N.Y.C., Sept. 15, 1943; s. Aaron Herbert and Lillian Betty (Greenspan) M.; m. Susan Politzer, Aug. 22, 1979; children: Jennifer, Melanie, Jonathan. AB, Tufts U., 1964; LLB, Rutgers U., 1967; postgrad. U. Pa. Law Sch., 1968-70. Bar: D.C. 1968, N.Y. 1970, U.S. Supreme Ct. 1972, N.J. 1973, Pa. 1983. Law clk. to judge U.S. Ct. Appeals, New Orleans, 1967-68; asst. defender Defender Assn. Phila., 1968-70; asst. counsel NAACP Legal Def. and Ednl. Fund, N.Y.C., 1970-74; dir. Office Inmate Advocacy, N.J. Dept. Pub. Advocate, Trenton, 1974-81; pvt. practice Haddonfield and Medford, N.J., 1982; ptnr. Stein & Shapiro, Medford, 1982-83, Cherry Hill, N.J., 1983-84, Mesirov, Gelman, Jaffe, Cramer & Jamieson, Cherry Hill, also Phila., 1984-90, Schlesinger, Mintz & Pilles, Mt. Holly, N.J., 1990-92; pvt. practice atty., Mt. Holly, 1992—. Trustee Congregation M'Kor Shalom, Cherry Hill, 1990-97; Mem. Burlington County and Mt. Laurel Dem. Coun. Com., 1993-95; chair Moorestown Dem. Com., 1995—. Mem. ABA, ATLA, N.J. Bar Assn. (del., gen. coun. 1986-88, 89-91), D.C. Bar Assn., Camden County Bar Assn., Burlington County Bar Assn. (trustee 1989-92), Assn. Trial Lawyers N.J. (bd. govs. 1990-95). Jewish. Home: 224 Quakerbridge Ct Moorestown NJ 08057-2823 Office: 129 High St Mount Holly NJ 08060-1401

MINTZ, KENNETH ANDREW, librarian; b. Plattsburgh, N.Y., Mar. 15, 1951; s. Max Manuel and Mildred Patricia (O'Rourke) M.; m. Melinda Lou Harris, Jan. 12, 1974 (div. Oct. 31, 1975). BA, U. Redlands, 1973; MLS, So. Conn. State U., 1978. Cert. profl. libr., N.J. Temporary cataloger Medford (Mass.) Pub. Libr., 1980; libr. Bayonne (N.J.) Pub. Libr., 1980-88; cataloger Hoboken (N.J.) Pub. Libr., 1991—; book reviewer Libr. Jour., N.Y.C., 1988-93; head drama group Community Ch. of N.Y., N.Y.C., 1993—. Author: The Holy Ghost, 1980; newsletter editor Unitarian Soc. Rutherford, N.J., 1984-85; asst. newsletter editor First Unitarian Soc. New Haven, 1979-80; contbr. book revs. to Am. Book Rev., Wilson Libr. Bulletin, Libr. and Culture. Mem. ch. coun. Community Ch. of N.Y., 1988-90. Recipient Quill Poetry award Quill Books, 1991, Essay prize Hudson County Writing Festival, Bayonne, 1994, Bayonne Writers Legion of Honor award, 1989, Editor's Choice award Nat. Libr. Poetry, 1989, 96, awards N.J. Superbowl of Writing, Halloween Story, 1995, Playwriting, 1995, Essay, 1996; named Poet of Yr., 1994, Writer of Yr., 1995; named to Bayonne Writers' Wall of Fame, 1996. Mem. ALA, N.J. Libr. Assn., Poetry Soc. of Am., Bayonne Writers Group (v.p. 1986), Acad. of Am. Poets, Hoboken Creative Alliance, N.Y. Acad. Scis. Democrat. Unitarian-Universalist. Avocations: history, piano, chess, bowling, fishing. Office: Hoboken Pub Libr 500 Park Ave Hoboken NJ 07030-3906

MINTZ, M. J., lawyer; b. Phila., Oct. 29, 1940; s. Arthur and Lillian (Altenberg) M.; children: Robert A., Christine L.; m. Judith E. Held. B.S., Temple U., 1961, J.D., 1968. Bar: D.C.; C.P.A., Pa., D.C. Atty. adv. to judge U.S. Tax Ct., Washington, 1968-70; asst. gen. counsel Cost of Living Coun., Exec. Office of Pres., Washington, 1971-73; ptnr. Dickstein, Shapiro & Morin, Washington, 1973—; adj. prof. George Mason U. Law Sch., Va., 1974-78; adv. to U.S. sec. of labor Employee Ret. Income Security Act of 1974, Adv. Coun., Washington, 1982-85. Contbr. articles to profl. jours. Apptd. by Pres. Ronald Reagan to advisory com. Pension Benifit Guaranty Corp., 1987; reapptd. and designated chmn. by Pres. George Bush; apptd. by Gov. George Allen of Va., Bd. of the Va. Pub. Bldg. Authority, 1996—; rep. candidate Fairfax County Bd. of Suprs., 1971. Fellow Nat. Assn. Watch & Clock Collectors; mem. ABA, AICPA, Antiquarian Horological Soc. (London), Cosmos Club, Belle Haven Country Club, Met. Club (Washington), Chappaquiddick Beach Club. Avocation: antiquarian horologist.

MINTZ, MARSHALL GARY, lawyer; b. Detroit, May 28, 1947. BA, UCLA, 1968, JD, 1971. Bar: Calif. 1972. Law clk. appellate dept L.A. County Superior Ct., 1971-72; ptnr. Kelly Lytton Mintz & Vann, L.A., Calif., 1995—; moderator, panelist Calif. Continuing Edn. of Bar, 1980—; mem. arbitration adminstrv. com. L.A. County Superior Ct., 1979, mem. 1984 Olympics spl. settlement panel. Mem. ABA, State Bar Calif., L.A. County Bar Assn. (arbitrator arbitration and client rels. com. 1978-90), Assn. Bus. Trial Lawyers (bd. govs. 1976-77, program chmn. 1976). Office: Kelly Lytton Mintz & Vann Ste 1450 1900 Avenue Of The Stars Los Angeles CA 90067-4405

MINTZ, MORTON ABNER, author, former newspaper reporter; b. Ann Arbor, Mich., Jan. 26, 1922; s. William and Sarah (Solomon) M.; m. Anita Inez Franz, Aug. 30, 1946; children—Margaret Ruth, Elizabeth Diane (dec.), Roberta Joan, Daniel Robert. A.B. in Econs, U. Mich., 1943. Reporter St. Louis Star-Times, 1946-50; reporter, asst. city editor St. Louis Globe-Democrat, 1951-58; reporter Washington Post, 1958-88. Author: The Therapeutic Nightmare, 1965, By Prescription Only, 1967, The Pill: An Alarming Report, 1969, At Any Cost: Corporate Greed, Women, and the Dalkon Shield, 1985, (with Jerry S. Cohen) America, Inc.: Who Owns and Operates the United States, 1971, Power, Inc.; Public and Private Rulers and How to Make Them Accountable, 1976, (with others) In the Name of Profit: Profiles in Corporate Irresponsiblity, 1972, More Bucks, Less Bang: How the Pentagon Buys Ineffective Weapons, 1983. Recipient Heywood Broun, Raymond Clapper, George Polk awards for journalism, 1962, A.J. Liebling award, 1974, Worth Bingham Meml. award, 1976, Columbia Journalism award, 1983, Hugh M. Hefner First Amendment award for lifetime achievement, 1996.

MINTZ, NORMAN NELSON, investment banker, educator; b. N.Y.C., Sept. 18, 1934; s. Alexander and Rebecca (Nelson) M.; m. Marcia Lynn Belford, Aug. 27, 1960; children: Geoffrey Belford, Douglas Nelson. AB, Bucknell U., 1955; PhD, NYU, 1966. Asst. gen. mgr. Ross Products Inc., N.Y.C., 1957-59; media analyst Benton & Bowles Inc., N.Y.C., 1960; asst. prof. fin. Syracuse U., 1965-69; asst. prof. econs. Columbia U., N.Y.C., 1968-72; assoc. dean Grad. Sch. Arts and Scis. Columbia U., 1972-77, dep. provost, 1977-80, acting provost, 1978-79, sr. v.p., 1980-82, exec. v.p. for acad. affairs, 1982-89, exec. v.p., ret., 1990—; mng. dir. Loeb Ptnrs. Corp., 1990—; economist U.S.-P.R. Commn. on Status of P.R., 1965-66; bd. dirs. Sr. Network, Inc., Inncom, Inc., Comm. Mgmt. Sys., Inc., Exxel/Atmos, Inc., Acutus-Gladwin Corp., Bernal Internat., Inc., Evare, Ltd., Primacor, Inc., CreditCom Svcs., L.L.C. Author: Monetary Union and Economic Integration, 1970; contbr. articles to profl. jours. Dir. Conf. on Jewish Social Studies, 1975-94, N.Y.C. Coun. on Econ. Edn., 1993—. Served with Signal Corps U.S. Army, 1955-57. Earhart Found. fellow, 1963-65. Mem. Am. Econ. Assn., Am. Fin. Assn., Royal Econ. Soc., India House Club, Phi Beta Kappa, Omicron Delta Epsilon. Office: care Loeb Ptnrs 61 Broadway New York NY 10006-2701

MINTZ, RICHARD I., federal official; b. Bklyn., Aug. 10, 1961; s. Walter and Sandra (Ullman) M.; m. Helaine Greenfeld, Sept. 1, 1991. BA in Internat. Rels., Union Coll., 1983. Assoc. prodr. CBS News, 1983-85; press sec. N.E.-Midwest Congrl. Coalition, 1985-86; media dir. Nat. Abortion Rights Action League, 1986-88; v.p. Ogilvy, Adams & Rinehart, 1988-91; dir. staff Hillary Rodham Clinton, dep. mgr. Clinton-Gore Campaign, Calif., 1991-92; dir. comm. Presdl. Inaugural Com., 1992-93; dir. pub. affairs Dept. Transp., Washington, 1993—; s.r. v.p. Ogilvy, Adams & Rinehart, Washington. Office: Ogilvy, Adams & Rinehart 1901 L St NW Ste 300 Washington DC 20036-3515

MINTZ, RONALD STEVEN, lawyer; b. Bklyn., Aug. 16, 1947; s. Herbert and Phoebe (Gilman) M.; children: Raymond, Gloria. JD, Western State U., Fullerton, Calif., 1978. Bar: Calif. 1978, U.S. Dist. Ct. (no., so., ea. and cen. dists.) Calif. 1978, U.S. Ct. Appeals (9th cir.) 1979, U.S. Supreme Ct. 1982. Pvt. practice law Berkeley, Calif., 1978-80, Canyon Country, Calif., 1980-83, Chino, Calif., 1983-84, Ontario, Calif., 1984-88, Pomona, Calif., 1988-91, San Fernando, Calif., 1991-92; pvt. practice, pvt. practice, L.A., 1992-93, Joshua Tree, Calif., 1993-94, Hollywood, Calif., 1994; founder legal aid orgn. to protect civil rights Tactical Law Command. Producer film on air pollution: State of Emergency, 1971, videotape documentary: America-A True Glimpse, 1987; publisher opposition newspaper: Ten Penny Press. Recipient Am. Jurisprudence awards Bancroft Whitney Law Book Pub. Co., 1977, 78. Mem. Lawyers in Mensa (charter), State Bar Calif. (criminal law sect. 1983-84, police misconduct lawyer referral service), Mensa. Avocations: photography, film, video, guns, cars. Office: 5858 Hollywood Blvd Ste 306A Los Angeles CA 90028-5619

MINTZ, SEYMOUR STANLEY, lawyer; b. Newark, Mar. 7, 1912. A.B., George Washington U., 1933, J.D., 1936. Bar: D.C. 1936. Atty. Office of Undersec. of Treasury, 1937-38, Office of Chief Counsel, IRS, 1938-42; assoc. Hogan & Hartson, Washington, 1946-49; ptnr. Hogan & Hartson, 1949-84, counsel, 1985—. Contbr. articles to profl. jours. Fellow Am. Coll. Tax Counsel; mem. ABA, D.C. Bar Assn., Am. Law Inst., Order of Coif. Office: Hogan & Hartson 555 13th St NW Washington DC 20004-1109

MINTZ, SHLOMO, conductor, violist, violinist; b. Moscow, Oct. 30, 1957; came to U.S., 1974; s. Abraham and Eve (Labko) M.; m. Corina Ciacci; children: Eliav David, Alexander. Studied with Ilona Feher; Diploma, Juilliard Sch. Music, 1979. judge internat. Tchaikovsky Competition, Moscow, 1990; juror queen Elisabeth Internat. Music Competition, Brussels, 1993. Concerto debut with Israel Philharm.; violin solo recordings include Violin Concertos by Mendelssohn and Bruch (Grand prix du Disque Diapason d'or), 1981, Complete Sonatas and Partitas for Solo Violin by J.S. Bach, The Miraculous Mandarin-Two Portraits (with Abbado/Chicago Symphony Orchestra) by Bartok, Compositions and Arrangements (with Clifford Benson, piano) by Kreisler, Violin Concerto; also Bruch: Violin Concerto Number 1 (with Abbado/Chgo. Symphony Orchestra) by Mendelssohn, Twenty-Four Caprices by Paganini, Two Violin Concertos (with Abbado/London Symphony Orchestra) by Prokofiev, The Four Seasons (with Stern, Perlman, Mehta) by Vivaldi, Vivaldi violin concertos, Vols. I & II (with Israel Chamber Orch.), 1992, Collection String Symphonies, Vol. III to X, (with Israel Chamber Orch., 1992, Violin and Viola Sonatas by Chostakovich (with V. Postnikova); apptd. music advisor, chief condr., soloist Israel Chamber Orch., 1989-93; artistic advisor, prin. guest condr. Limburg Symphony Orch., Maastricht, The Netherlands, 1994; condr. London Symphony Orch., Berlin Radio Symphony, Balt. Symphony, Detroit Symphony, Rotterdam Philharm.; soloist with Montreal Symphony, Nat. Symphony, Washington, Carnegie Hall, Tonhalle Orch. of Zurich, Spanish Nat. Orch., Israel Philharm., others. Recipient Premio Accademia Musicale, Chigiana Siena, Italy, 1984. Uses Zahn violin made by Stradivarius, and a Carlo-Guiseppe Testrove viola. Office: ICM Artists Inc 40 W 57th St New York NY 10019-4001 Address: care Irma de Jong, Postbox 402, NL-6200 AL Maastricht The Netherlands

MINTZ, SIDNEY WILFRED, anthropologist; b. Dover, N.J., Nov. 16, 1922; s. Solomon and Fromme Leah (Tulchin) M.; m. June Mirken, May 1952 (div. Dec. 1962); children: Eric Daniel, Elizabeth Rachel; m. Jacqueline Wei, June 6, 1964. BA, Bklyn. Coll., 1943; PhD, Columbia U., 1951; MA, Yale U., 1963. Mem. faculty dept. anthropology Yale U., New Haven, 1951-74; prof. Yale U., 1963-74; prof. anthropology Johns Hopkins U., Balt., 1974—; vis. prof. anthropology MIT, 1964-65, Princeton U., 1975-76; directeur d'études associé E.P.H.E., Paris, 1970-71; professeur associé. Coll. de France, Paris, 1988; editor Yale U. Press Caribbean Series, 1957-74; Lewis Henry Morgan lectr. U. Rochester, 1972; Christian Gauss lectr. Princeton U., 1979; Harry Hoijer lectr. UCLA, 1981; Duijker Found. lectr., Amsterdam, 1988; Rodney lectr. U. Warwick, 1993. Author: (with others) People of Puerto Rico, 1956, Worker in the Cane, The Life History of a Puerto Rican Sugar Cane Worker, 1960, Caribbean Transformations, 1974, Sweetness and Power, 1985, (with Richard Price) The Birth of African-American Culture, 1992, Tasting Food, Tasting Freedom, 1996. Served with USAAF, 1943-46. Recipient William Clyde DeVane medal Yale U., 1972, Huxley medalist Royal Anthrop. Inst., 1994, disting. lectr. award Am. Anthrop. Assn., 1996; named Social Sci. Rsch. Coun. Faculty Rsch. fellow, 1958-59, Guggenheim fellow, 1957, Fulbright fellow, 1966-67, 70-71, NEH fellow, 1978-79, Smithsonian Inst. Regents' fellow, 1986-87. Fellow Am. Anthrop. Assn.; mem. Am. Ethnol. Soc. (v.p., pres.-elect 1967-68), Royal Anthrop. Soc. Gt. Britain and Ireland, Am. Acad. Arts and Scis., Sigma Xi. Office: Johns Hopkins U Dept Anthropology Baltimore MD 21218

MINTZ, STEPHEN ALLAN, real estate company executive, lawyer; b. N.Y.C., May 21, 1943; s. Irving and Anne (Medwick) M.; m. Dale Leibson, June 19, 1966; children: Eric Michael, Jaclyn Leibson. AB, Cornell U., 1965; JD cum laude, Harvard U., 1968. Bar: N.Y. 1969. Assoc. Proskauer, Rose, Goetz & Mendelsohn, N.Y.C., 1968-76, ptnr., 1976-80; v.p. Integrated Resources, Inc., N.Y.C., 1980-84, 1st. v.p., 1984-86, sr. v.p., 1986-89, exec. v.p., 1989-94; chmn. Resources Hotel Mgmt. Svc. Inc., 1986-94; pres. Resources High Equity, Inc., 1991-94, Stemin Assocs., Rye, N.Y., 1994—. Mem. ABA, N.Y. State Bar Assn. Democrat. Jewish. Home & Office: 11 Eve Ln Rye NY 10580-4113

MINTZ, SUSAN ASHINOFF, menswear manufacturing company executive; b. N.Y.C., Dec. 7, 1949; d. Lawrence Lloyd and Thelma B. (Rubens) A.; m. Robert Beier Mintz, June 18, 1983; children: Geoffrey Harrison, Tyler Edward Richard. BA, Finch Coll., 1971; MPA, NYU, 1977. Menswear advt. asst. New Yorker Mag., N.Y.C., 1971-72; assoc. Staub, Warmbold & Assocs., Inc., exec. search co., N.Y.C., 1972-80; exec. v.p. Muhammad Ali Sportswear, Ltd., N.Y.C., 1980-81; pres. Forum Sportswear, Ltd., N.Y.C. and Portsmouth, Va., 1981—; group v.p. Coronet Casuals, Inc., Portsmouth, 1985—, also bd. dirs. Trustee Dean Jr. Coll. Named to Outstanding Young Women Am., U.S. Jaycees, 1980. Mem. Nat. Assn. Men's Sportswear Buyers, Men's Apparel Guild Calif., Beacon Hill Club. Office: 2615 Elmhurst Ln Portsmouth VA 23701-2736

MINTZ, WALTER, investment company executive; b. Vienna, Austria, Feb. 23, 1929; came to U.S., 1938, naturalized, 1945; s. Maximilian and Ilse (Schueller) M.; m. Sandra Jane Earl, Aug. 27, 1971. B.A., Reed Coll., 1950; postgrad. in econs, Columbia U., 1950-51, 53-54. Asso. editor Barrons mag., 1951-53, 54-56; with Shearson Hammill Co., 1956-70, dir. research, 1962-69, exec. v.p. charge investment div., 1965-70; partner Cumberland Assocs., investment mgmt., 1970-85; spl. ltd. ptnr. Cumberland Ptnrs., investment ptnrship., 1982—; bd. dirs. Merrill Lynch Phoenix Fund, Merrill Lynch Fed. Securities Trust, Merrill Lynch Retirement Series Fund. Trustee Reed Coll., 1971—, vice chmn. bd. trustees, 1991—; trustee Manhattan Inst., 1990—, vice chmn., 1994—; bd. dirs. Citizens Union of N.Y.C., 1980—. Mem. N.Y. Soc. Security Analysts (bd. dirs. 1969-75). Home: 2 E 88th St New York NY 10128-0555 Office: Cumberland Assocs 1114 Avenue Of The Americas New York NY 10036-7703

MINTZBERG, HENRY, management educator, researcher, writer; b. Montreal, Que., Can., Sept. 2, 1939; s. Myer and Irene M.; children: Susan, Lisa. B.Eng., McGill U., 1961; B.A., Sir George Williams U., 1962; S.M., M.I.T., 1965, Ph.D., 1968; hon. degree, U. Venice, 1983, U. Lund, 1989, U. Lausanne, 1991, U. Montreal, 1993, U. Geneva, 1995, U. Liege, 1996. Operational research analyst Can. Nat., 1961-63; mem. faculty mgmt. McGill U., Montreal, 1968—, Cleghorn prof. Mgmt. Studies, 1996—; mem. faculty mgmt. INSEAD, Fontainebleau, France, 1994—; vis. prof. Carnegie-Mellon U., 1973, Universite d'Aix-Marseille, 1974-76, Ecole des Hautes Etudes Commerciales de Montreal, 1977-78, London Bus. Sch., 1990, INSEAD, France, 1992, 93-94. Author: The Nature of Managerial Work, 1973, The Structuring of Organizations, 1979, Power In and Around Organizations, 1983, The Strategy Process, 1988, Mintzberg on Management, 1989, The Rise and Fall of Strategic Planning, 1994, The Canadian Contition, 1995; contbr. articles to profl. jours. Fellow Royal Soc. Can., Acad. Mgmt., Internat. Acad. Mgmt.; mem. Strategic Mgmt. Soc. (pres. 1988-91). Office: McGill U Faculty Mgmt, 1001 Sherbrooke W, Montreal, PQ Canada H3A 1G5

MINTZER, DAVID, physics educator; b. N.Y.C., May 4, 1926; s. Herman and Anna (Katz) M.; m. Justine Nancy Klein, June 26, 1949; children: Elizabeth Amy, Robert Andrew. B.S. in Physics, Mass. Inst. Tech., 1945, Ph.D., 1949. Asst. prof. physics Brown U., 1949-55; research asso. Yale U., 1955-56, assoc. prof., dir. lab. marine physics, 1956-62; prof. mech. engring. Northwestern U., Evanston, 1962-91, prof. physics and astronomy, 1968-91, prof. emeritus mech. engring., prof emeritus physics and astronomy, 1991—; assoc. dean McCormick Sch. Engring. and Applied Sci., 1970-73, acting dean, 1971-72, v.p. for rsch., dean sci., 1973-86, spl. asst. to pres., 1986-87, prof. emeritus mech. engring., physics and astronomy, 1991—; mem. mine adv. com. Nat. Acad. Sci.-NRC, 1963-73; mem. Ill. Gov.'s Commn. on Sci. and Tech., 1987-88; mem. adv. bd. Applied Rsch. Lab. Pa. State U., 1976-82, chmn., 1980-81. Contbr. numerous chpts. to books, papers to profl. publs. Trustee EDUCOM interuniv. communications coun., 1975-83, vice chmn., 1977-78, chmn., 1978-81; trustee Adler Planetarium, 1976-92, life trustee, 1992—; bd. dirs. Rsch. Park, Inc., Evanston, 1986-92, treas., 1986-91; trustee Ill. Math. and Sci. Acad., 1986—, mem. exec. com., 1989-95, chmn. alliance coun., 1991-93; chmn. bd. dirs. Heartland Venture Capital Network, Inc., 1987-90; bd. dirs. Tech. Innovation Ctr., Inc., 1990-92, treas., 1990-92. Fellow Am. Phys. Soc., Acoustical Soc. Am.; mem. ASME, Am. Astron. Soc., Sigma Xi, Tau Beta Pi, Pi Tau Sigma. Research on underwater acoustics and rarefied gas dynamics. Office: 990 N Lake Shore Dr #16A Chicago IL 60611-1343

MINUDRI, REGINA URSULA, librarian, consultant; b. San Francisco, May 9, 1937; d. John C. and Molly (Halter) M. BA, San Francisco Coll. for Women, 1958; MLS, U. Calif.-Berkeley, 1959. Reference libr. Menlo Park (Calif.) Pub. Libr., 1959-62; regional libr. Santa Clara County (Calif.) Libr., 1962-68; project coord. Fed. Young Adult Libr. Svcs. Project, Mountain View, Calif., 1968-71; dir. profl. services Alameda County (Calif.) Libr., 1971, asst. county libr., 1972-77; libr. dir. Berkeley Pub. Libr., 1977-94; lectr. U. San Francisco, 1970-72, U. Calif., Berkeley, 1977-81, 91-93; lectr. San Jose State U., 1994—; cons., 1975—; adv. bd. Miles Cutter Ednl., 1992—. Bd. dirs. No. Calif. ACLU, 1994-96, Cmty. Memory, 1989-91, Berkeley Cmty. Fund, 1994—, chair youth com., 1994—, Berkeley Pub. Libr. Found. Bd., 1996—; mem. bd. mgrs. cen. br. Berkeley YMCA, 1988-93. Recipient proclamation Mayor of Berkeley, 1985, 86, 94, Citation of Merit Calif. State Assembly, 1994; named Woman of Yr. Alameda County North chpt. Nat. Women's Polit. Caucus, 1986, Outstanding Alumna U. Calif. Sch. Libr. and Info. Scis., Berkeley, 1987. Mem. ALA (pres. 1986-87, exec. bd. 1980-89, coun. 1979-88, 90-94, Grolier award 1974), Calif. Libr. Assn. (pres. 1981, coun. 1965-69, 79-82), LWV (dir. Berkeley chpt. 1980-81, v.p. comm. svcs. 1995—). Author: Getting It Together, A Young Adult Bibliography, 1970; contbr. articles to publs. including School Libr. Jour., Wilson Libr. Bull. Office: Reality Mgmt 836 The Alameda Berkeley CA 94707-1916*

MINYARD, LIZ, food products executive. BBA, Tex. Christian U., 1975. CEO Minyard Food Stores, Coppell, Tex., 1976—; dir. consumer affairs Minyard Food Stores Inc., Coppell, Tex., v.p. consumer affairs, 1980, v.p. corp. rels., 1983, also vice-chmn. bd. dirs., also co-chmn. bd. dirs. Chmn. United Way Dallas and Tarrant Counties, 1978, 83-95, Tarrant County sect. chmn., 1983-84, merchants divsn. chmn. Dallas County, 1987, Dallas County bd. dirs., 1995; bd. mem. Goodwill Industries of Dallas, Inc., 1981-94, mem. exec. com., 1987-88, 93-95, vice-chmn., 1992-94, chmn., 1995; mem. YWCA Dallas campaign drive spring 1982, chmn. campaign, 1983-85, co-chmn. of capital campaign, 1995, mayor's summer youth employment commn. co-chmn., 1994, chmn., 1995, bd. dirs., 1995; v.p. Dallas Urban League, 1989-91, bd. dirs., 1985-95, chmn. bd. dirs., 1992-93, bldg. com. chmn., 1995; mem. Dallas Citizens Coun., 1988-94, bd. dirs. exec. com., 1992-95; bd. dirs. Leukemia Assn. of North Ctrl. Tex., 1988-95; mem. Dallas Assembly, 1989-95; bd. dirs. Baylor Hosp. Found., 1989-95; mem. Dallas Summit, 1992-95, Dallas Together Forum, 1993-95, Dallas Women's Forum, 1994-95; bd. dirs. Zale Lipshy Hosp., 1993-95, Am. Heart Assn., 1991-94; chmn. City of Dallas Bond Program, 1995; nat. trustee Boys and Girls clubs of Am., 1995, and numerous others. Recipient Dallas/Ft. Worth Dist. Women in Bus. Advocate of Yr. award U.S. Small Bus. Adminstrn., 1995, Tex. Family Bus. of Yr.-Cmty. Involvement award Tex. Inst. Family Bus., 1995, Bus. award for Cmty. Involvement Martin Luther King, Jr. Cmty. Ctr., 1995, Contbrs. award Black State Employees Assn. of Tex., 1995, Art of Achievement award Nat. Fedn. of Women Bus. Owners, 1995. Mem. Food Mktg. Inst. (mem. consumer coun. 1977-88, mem. steering com. 1982, mem. pub. affairs com. 1989-90, bd. dirs. 1991-95), Tex. Food Mktg. Assn. (v.p. 1981-82, pres. 1982-84), North Tex. Food Bank (founding bd. mem., sec. 1981-83, bd. mem. 1982-95, pres. 1984, v.p. devel. 1987, chmn. hunger link program 1989-90), Second Harvest (Chgo., bd. dirs. 1992-95), CIES The Food Bus. Forum (ann. congress com. mem. 1996), North Tex. Commn. (bd. dirs. 1992-95), Greater Dallas C. of C. (mem. leadership program 1982-83, bd. dirs. 1994-95, bd. dirs. 1987-90, mem. women's bus. issues exec. com. 1994-95, women's convenant diamond cutters award 1995). Home: PO Box 518 Coppell TX 75019 Office: Minyard Food Stores Inc PO Box 518 Coppell TX 75019-0518

MIRABELLO, FRANCIS JOSEPH, lawyer; b. Ft. Lauderdale, Fla., Mar. 2, 1954; s. Frank Guy and Mary (Sorce) M.; m. Marianna Hay O'Neal, Aug. 5, 1978; childen: Diana H., A. Paul. BS in Civil Engring., Princeton U., 1975; JD, Harvard U., 1978. Bar: Calif. 1978, Pa. 1981, Fla. 1983. Assoc. Irell & Manella, Los Angeles, 1978-81; ptnr. Morgan, Lewis & Bockius, Phila., 1981—; lectr. law Villanova (Pa.) U. Law Sch., adj. prof. law U. Pa., Phila. Mem. ABA (chmn. tax sect. subcom.). Club: Martins Dam, Merion Cricke. Avocation: tennis. Office: Morgan Lewis & Bockius 2000 One Logan Sq Philadelphia PA 19103

MIRABELLO, MARK LINDEN, history educator; b. Toledo, May 6, 1955; s. Paul Joseph and Regina Joan (Baranski) M. BA, U. Toledo, 1977; MA, U. Va., 1979; PhD, U. Glasgow (Scotland), 1988. Instr. honors program U. Toledo, 1984-87; sr. instr. European history Shawnee State U., Portsmouth, Ohio, 1987-88, asst. prof. European history, 1988-93, chair honors program, 1990—, assoc. prof. European History, 1993—; vis. assoc. prof. European history Nizhni Novgorod State U., Russia, 1994; dir. Ian B. Cowan Award for Outstanding Work in Hist. Studies, Shawnee State U., Portsmouth, 1990—; cons. The Open Air, Shawnee State U. newspaper, Portsmouth, 1992—, The Univ. Chronicle Shawnee State Univ. Newspaper, Portsmouth, 1992—; co-founder, advisor Ar Tyr Ar Fraternity Shawnee State U., Portsmouth, 1992—. Author: The Odin Brotherhood: A True Narrative of a Dialogue with a Mysterious Secret Society, 1992, The Crimes of Jehovah: A Brief Selection from the Bible, 1996. Co-founder, adviser Delta Tau Omega fraternity, Shawnee State U., Portsmouth, 1992—. Honored by Asatru Sogulega Bokasafn, 1996. Mem. Am. Hist. Assn., Ohio Acad. History, Fortean Soc. (London), Internat. Fortean Orgn., Planetary Soc.. Avocation: Fortean research. Home: 940 2nd St Portsmouth OH 45662-4347 Office: Dept History Shawnee State U Portsmouth OH 45662

MIRABILE, CAROLYN ROSE, lawyer; b. Norristown, Pa., June 12, 1966; d. Paul Joseph and Norma Jean (DiFerdinando) M.; m. Richard Lawrence Giles, Sept. 26, 1992. BA in Polit. Sci., Villanova U., 1988, JD, 1991. Bar: Pa. 1991, N.J. 1991. Assoc. Gultanoff & Lynch, Norristown, 1992-93, Gultanoff Lynch & Tornetta, Norristown, 1993-94; ptnr. Lynch Tornetta & Mirabile, Norristown, 1994-96, Lynch & Mirabile, Norristown, 1996—; assoc. Montgomery County Family Law Com., 1991—, Doris Jonas Freed Am. Inn. of Ct., 1994—; co-chair Montgomery County Law Day, Norristown, 1993, 94, 95, Family Law Practicum, 1996. Avocation: golf. Office: Lynch & Mirabile 617 Swede St Norristown PA 19401-3901

MIRACLE, GORDON ELDON, advertising educator; b. Olympia, Wash., May 28, 1930; s. Gordon Tipler and Corine Adriana (Orlebeke) M.; m. Christa Stoeter, June 29, 1957; children: Gary, Gregory, Glenn. BBA, U. Wis., 1952, MBA, 1958, PhD, 1962. Case officer, civilian intelligence analyst U.S. Army, Fed. Republic Germany, 1955-57; instr. commerce U. Wis. Grad. Sch. Bus., Madison, 1958-60; instr., then asst. prof. mktg. U. Mich., Ann Arbor, 1960-66; assoc. prof. advt. Mich. State U., East Lansing, 1966-70, chmn. PhD program in mass media, 1973-74, chmn. dept., 1974-80, prof.

advt., 1970—; vis. prof. mktg. mgmt. N. European Mgmt. Inst., Oslo, 1972-73; cons., lectr. in field. Author: Management of International Advertising, 1966; co-author: International Marketing Management, 1970, Advertising and Government Regulation, 1979, Instructor's Manual for International Marketing Management, 1971, European Regulation of Advertising: Supranational Regulation of Advertising in the European Economic Community, 1986, Voluntary Regulation of Advertising: A Comparative Analysis of the United Kingdom and the United States, 1987, (in Korean) Cultures in Advertising: Advertising in Cultures, 1990; contbr. articles to scholarly and profl. jours.; editor: Marketing Decision Making: Strategy and Payoff, 1965, Sharing for Understanding, Proc. Ann. Conf. Am. Acad. Advt., 1977. Served with AUS, 1952-55. Recipient first Biennial Excellence in Advt. award, U. Ill., 1995; Ford Found. fellow, 1961-62, 64, Am. Assn. Advt. Agys. fellow Marsteller, Inc., 1967, Advt. Ednl. Found. fellow McCann-Erickson Hakuhodo, 1985, Fulbright rsch. fellow Waseda U., Tokyo, 1985; recipient numerous grants. Fellow Am. Acad. Advt. (treas., exec. com. 1978-79); mem. Acad. Internat. Bus. (sec., exec. com. 1973-75), Am. Mktg. Assn., Internat. Advt. Assn. (ednl. accreditation com. 1993-95, internat. advt. edn. group 1996—), Adcraft Club Detroit. Home: 10025 Oak Island Dr Laingsburg MI 48848-8718 Office: Mich State U Dept Advt East Lansing MI 48824

MIRACLE, ROBERT WARREN, retired banker; b. Casper, Wyo.; m. Maggie Zanoni; children—Mark, John. BS in Law, U. Wyo., 1951; grad. with honors, Pacific Coast Banking Sch., 1960. With Wyo. Nat. Bank (now Norwest Bank Casper N.A.), 1954-91; exec. v.p. Wyo. Nat. Bank of Casper, 1967; pres., chief exec. officer Wyo. Nat. Bank of Casper (now Norwest Bank Casper N.A.)ú, 1968-87; chmn. Wyo. Nat. Bank of Casper (formerly Norwest Bank Casper N.A.), 1983-91, also bd. dirs.; pres., chief exec. officer, dir. Wyo. Nat. Bancorp. (formerly Affiliated Bank Corp Wyo.), Casper, 1970-91; instr. bank mgmt. U. Colo., 1971-75. Bd. dirs. United Fund of Natrona County, Wyo., 1963-85, campaign co-chmn., 1973-78; trustee The Myra Fox Skelton Found., 1963—, Goodstein Found., 1992—; bd. dirs., pres. Investment in Casper, 1967-70; Wyo. treas. Radio Free Europe, 1967-72; trustee Casper Coll. Foun., 1967-91, pres., 1973-75, 85-91; trustee U. Wyo. Found., 1972-87; chmn. Casper Downtown Improvement Assn., 1974-75; bd. dirs. Cen. Wyo. Fair Bd., 1974-79, pres., 1977-78; dir. Mountain States Employers Coun., 1979-91. Capt. USMC, 1951-53. Recipient James C. Scarboro Meml. award Colo. Sch. Banking., 1977; Disting. Service in Bus. award U. Wyo. Coll. Commerce and Industry, 1980. Mem. Wyo Bankers Assn. (chmn. legis. com. 1969-80, pres. 1974-75), Am. Bankers Assn. (mem. governing coun. 1974-75, 81-83), Am. Mgmt. Assn., Rocky Mountain Oil and Gas Assn., Newcomer Soc. in N.Am., Casper C. of C. (pres. 1965-66, Disting. Svc. award 1981), VFW, Casper Petroleum Club, Casper Country Club (pres. 1993-94), Masons, Lions.

MIRAGEAS, EVANS JOHN, record company executive; b. Ann Arbor, Mich., Nov. 17, 1954; s. Xenophon John and Constance (Collins) M. BA, U. Mich., 1976. Producer WUOM, Ann Arbor, Mich., 1973-82; sr. prodr. WFMT, Chgo., 1982-89; artistic adminstr. Boston Symphony, 1989-94; sr. v.p. artists and repertoire Decca Records Ltd., London, 1994—. Bd. mem. Classical Action, N.Y.C., 1992—. Greek Orthodox. Office: Decca Records Ltd, 347-353 Chiswick High Rd, London W4 4HS, England

MIRAND, EDWIN ALBERT, medical scientist; b. Buffalo, July 18, 1926; s. Thomas and Lucy (Papier) M. B.A., U. Buffalo, 1947, M.A., 1949; Ph.D., Syracuse (N.Y.) U., 1951; D.Sc. (hon.), Niagara (N.Y.) U., 1970, D'Youville Coll., Buffalo, 1974. Successively undergrad. asst., grad. asst., instr. U. Buffalo, 1946-48; teaching fellow Syracuse U., 1948-51; instr. Utica (N.Y.) Coll., 1950; mem. staff Roswell Park Meml. Inst., Buffalo, 1951—; head W. Seneca labs., 1961—, assoc. inst. dir., head dept. edn., 1967—, dir. cancer rsch., 1968-73, head dept. viral oncology, 1970-73, head dept. biol. recources, 1973—; rsch. prof. biology Grad. Sch., prof. biochem. pharmacology Sch. Pharmacy, SUNY, Buffalo, 1955—, dean Roswell Park grad. div. SUNY, 1967—; rsch. prof. biology Grad. Sch.; mem. human cancer virus task force, clin. cancer edn. com. NIH. Mem. editorial bd. Jour. Surg. Oncology, Cancer Rsch., Jour. Cancer Edn., Cancer jour.; contbr. articles to profl. jours. Mem. U.S. nat. com. Union Internat. Contra Cancer; profl. edn. com. cancer control Nat. Cancer Inst; liaison mem. Pres.'s Nat. Cancer Adv. Bd.; mem. N.Y. State Health Research Council; mem. Gov.'s AIDS Adv. Council, 1982—; sec. N.Y. State Cancer Programs, Inc., 1984—; bd. dirs. Network in Aging of Western N.Y., Inc., 1986—. Recipient Billings Silver medal AMA, 1963, Margaret Hays Edwards award in edn., SUNY, Buffalo, 1993, Citation award in sci. coll. arts and scis., 1964, award sci. rsch. mammalian tumor viruses Med. Soc. State N.Y., 1963. Life mem., fellow N.Y. Acad. Sci.; fellow AAAS; mem. Am. Cancer Soc. (state pub. edn. com. 1982—, nat. adv. com. on research personnel 1985—), Assn. Gnotobiotics (pres. 1968-69, dir. 1975-78), Internat. Assn. for Gnotobiology (pres. 1981-84), Assn. Am. Cancer Insts. (sec.-treas. 1968—), Am. Assn. Cancer Research, Radiation Research Soc., Am. Soc. Zoologists, Soc. Exptl. Biology and Medicine, Am. Assn. for Cancer Edn., Buffalo Acad. Medicine, Am. Soc. Hematology, Internat. Soc. Hematology, Pub. Health Cancer Assn. Am., Internat. Union Against Cancer (chmn. U.S. nat. com. 1979—, sec.-gen. 13th Internat. Cancer Congress), Hematology Soc., Am. Soc. Preventive Oncology, Buffalo Hist. Soc. (life), Buffalo Fine Arts Acad. (life), Sigma Xi. Home: S-6178 Hunters Creek Rd South Wales NY 14139 Office: Roswell Park Meml Inst 666 Elm St Buffalo NY 14263-0001

MIRANDA, CARLOS SA, food products company executive; b. Fall River, Mass., Nov. 16, 1929; s. Carlos Sa and Annette (Pratt) M.; m. Natalie Cardoso, Jan. 5, 1949; children—Carla, Lucy, John. B.S. in Mech. Engring., Marquette U., 1956. With internat. div. Kellogg Co., Battle Creek, Mich., 1964-65, gen. mgr., Brazil, 1965-80, gen. mgr. Kellogg's Spain, 1983-84, v.p. Kellogg Internat., Battle Creek, 1980-89, country dir. internat. exec. svc. corps., Costa Rica, 1990-91; mediator Fla. County Cts., 1994—. Recipient Pero Vaz Caminha award, Brazil, 1976; conferred title Comdr. of Legion of Honor of Marshal Rondon, Brazil, 1971. Mem. ASME. Republican. Roman Catholic. Home: Apt 614 988 Boulevard Of The Arts Sarasota FL 34236-4840

MIRANDA, CONSTANCIO FERNANDES, civil engineering educator; b. Raia-Goa, India, Dec. 4, 1926; came to U.S., 1960, naturalized, 1966; s. Alex Fernandes and Maria Marcelina (Viegas) M.; m. Joan Mary Menezes, Mar. 3, 1957; children: Steven Alex, Christopher Gerard, Kenneth Michael, Marie Lynn. Student, Karnatak Coll., Dharwar, 1944-46; B Engring. (civil), U. Bombay, 1949; MS in Civil Engring, U. Notre Dame, 1962; PhD in Structural Engring, Ohio State U., 1964; MA in Math, U. Detroit, 1974. Registered profl. engr., Ind., N.C. With civil engring. projects Govt. Bombay, 1950-60; teaching asst., then instr. U. Notre Dame, 1960-62; instr., rsch. assoc. Ohio State U., 1962-64; mem. rsch. staff U. N.Mex., 1964-65; mem. faculty U. Detroit, 1965-88, prof. civil engring., 1966-88, chmn. dept., 1965-72, prof. structural and systems engring., 1973-88, assoc. dean Coll. Engring., acting dean, 1972-73, ret., 1989; cons. civil, structural, systems engring., applied maths. and computer applications, 1989—; bd. dir. Profl. Adv. Svc. Ctr., 1973-75; staff engr. EPA, N.C., 1976-77. Contbr. profl. jours. Named Engring. Tchr. of Yr. Engring. Joint Coun., U. Detroit, 1967, 76; Distinguished Alumnus Ohio State U., 1973. Mem. ASCE, Am. Soc. Engring. Edn., Sigma Xi, Chi Epsilon, Tau Beta Pi, Pi Mu Epsilon. Home: 100 Silvercliff Trl Cary NC 27513-2803

MIRANDA, MICHELE RENEE, optometrist; b. Springfield, Mass., Jan. 6, 1960; d. Vincent Michael and Lucy Theresa (Scibelli) M. BS, Springfield Coll., 1982; DO, New Eng. Coll. Optometry, 1986. Diplomate Internat. Assn. Bd. Examiners in Optometry. Resident VA Med. Ctr., Roxbury/Brockton, Mass., 1988; optometrist Med. Eye Care Assoc., Norwood, Mass., 1987-95, Bassett Healthcare, Cooperston, N.Y., 1995-96, Baystate Eye Care, Springfield, Mass., 1996—; liaison New Eng. Coun. Optometrists, Boston, 1989-91, bd. corporators, 1991-93; spkr. in field. Recipient Alumni Assn. award New Eng. Coll. Optometry, 1986, Barnes Hind Student Recognition award New Eng. Coll. Optometry, 1986. Mem. Am. Optometric Assn., N.Y. State Optometric Assn., Mass. Soc. Optometrists (pres. 1990-91), Beta Sigma Kappa. Office: Baystate Eye Care 275 Bicentennial Hwy Springfield MA 01118-1965

MIRANDA, ROBERT NICHOLAS, publishing company executive; b. Bklyn., July 9, 1934; m. Marilyn H. Pils, May 25, 1958; children: Marilyn, Robert, Susan, Lori, Jennifer. A.A. in Acctg. and Bus. Adminstrn., SUNY-Farmingdale. Pres. Pergamon Press, Inc., Elmsford, N.Y., 1965-92; chmn., chief exec. officer Cognizant Communication Corp., Elmsford, 1992—; bd. dirs., exec. v.p., vice chmn. Soc. and Assoc. Svc. Corp., McLean, Va., 1979-82; bd. dirs., chmn. electronics com. Copyright Clearance Ctr., 1984-93. Pub. Acupuncture and Electro Therapeutics Research, Analgesia, Bird Behavior, Cancer Prevention International, Festival Management and Event Tourism, Gene Expression, Life Support and Biosphere Science, Oncology Rsch., Tourism Analysis, Technology: Jour. of Franklin Inst., Failure & Lessons Learned in Information Technology, Pacific Tourism Review, SSA Jour.-Jour. of Semi-Conductor Safety Assn. Served with USNR, 1954-59. Mem. Council Sci. Editors, Internat. Soc. Intelligent Systems (founder, bd. dirs., fin. dir. 1992—). Avocations: hunting; fishing; horseback riding. Office: Cognizant Comm Corp PO Box 217 Croton On Hudson NY 10520-0217

MIRANTE, ARTHUR J., II, real estate company executive; b. Hackensack, N.J., Aug. 25, 1943; s. Arthur J. and Mildred (Spaluzzi) M.; m. Elizabeth McMillan, Oct. 2, 1993; children: Arthur, Claudia, Matthew. BS, Coll. of the Holy Cross, 1965; JD, St. John's U., 1968. Bar: 1968. Sole practice N.Y.C., 1966-71; asst. to gen. counsel Cushman & Wakefield, N.Y.C., 1971-77, gen. counsel, 1977-81, nat. dir. asset mgmt., 1981-82, exec. v.p., dir. N.Y. area, 1982-84, pres., chief exec. officer, 1984—. Home: 211 E 70th St New York NY 10021 Office: Cushman & Wakefield Inc 51 W 52nd St New York NY 10019-6119

MIRCHANDANEY, ARJAN SOBHRAJ, mathematics educator; b. Hydrabad, Sind, India, Aug. 13, 1923; s. Sobhraj Gurmukhdas and Jamuna Mohanlal (Advani) M.; m. Padma Kalachand Lalwani, Oct. 20, 1958; 1 child, Haresh. BS, U. Bombay, India, 1943; MS, U. Bombay, 1946; PhD, U. Conn., 1984. Asst. prof. math. D.G. Nat. Coll., U. Bombay, 1943-47; lectr. Jai Hind Coll. U. Bombay, 1949-60, lectr. postgrad. classes, 1953-78, prof. math. Jai Hind Coll., 1960-69, prof., head dept. math. Jai Hind Coll., 1969-78; asst. prof. math. No. Ill. U., DeKalb, 1979-80, Knox Coll., Galesburg, Ill., 1982-85; prof. math. Defiance (Ohio) Coll., 1986—; coord. math. coll. sci. improvement program for Bombay colls., 1971-74; vis. prof. math. St. Lawrence U., Canton, N.Y., 1978; vis. asst. prof. Cornell U., Ithaca, N.Y., 1985-86; postgrad. lectr. U. Bombay, 1953-78; external examiner Shivaji U., Kolhapur, India, 1972-74; presenter Internat. Congress on Relativity and Gravitation, Munich, 1988, Internat. Congress History of Sci., Munich, 1989, Internat. Conf. on Space, Time, Gravitation, St. Petersburg, Russia, 1996. Author: A Course in Elementary Trigonometry, 1954, 3d edit., 1965; contbr. articles, papers to profl. jour., chpt. to book. Mem. Nat. Ctr. for Performing Arts, Bombay, 1969-78. Grantee Defiance Coll., 1989. Mem. Am. Math. Soc., Math. Assn. Am. Achievements include research in field theory of electromagnetics and photic field theory. Home: 700 Ralston Ave Apt 36 Defiance OH 43512-1567 Office: Defiance Coll 701 N Clinton St Defiance OH 43512-1610

MIRELS, HAROLD, aerospace engineer; b. N.Y.C., July 29, 1924; s. Hyman and Lily (Efron) M.; m. Nell Segal, Oct. 4, 1953; children: Lily, Laurence Franklin, Jeremy Mark. BSME, Cooper U., 1944; MSME, Case Inst. Tech., 1949; PhD in Aero. Engring., Cornell U., 1953. Sect. head NACA, Cleve., 1944-57; br. chief NASA, Cleve., 1957-61; dept. head Aerospace Corp., El Segundo, Calif., 1961-78, assoc. dir., 1978-84, prin. scientist, 1984-93; cons., 1993—. Co-inventor continuous wave chem. laser. Recipient Tech. Achievement award Cleve. Tech. Socs., 1960. Fellow AIAA (Fluid and Plasmadynamics award 1988), Am. Phys. Soc.; mem. Nat. Acad. Engring. Home: 3 Seahurst Rd Palos Verdes Peninsula CA 90274-3700

MIRENBURG, BARRY LEONARD, publisher, company executive, educator; b. N.Y.C., Feb. 16, 1952; s. Fred and Mildred (Solomon) M. BS, Mercy Coll., 1979; BFA, Cooper Union, 1980; MBA, N.Y. Inst. of Tech., 1983; MA, Columbia U., 1983, postgrad., 1983—; MFA, Syracuse U., 1990. Pres., pub. Barlenmir House, N.Y.C., 1972—; pres., owner Barlenmir House Theatres, Inc., N.Y.C., 1978—; head Design Graphics N.Y. Inst. of Tech., N.Y.C., 1979—; pres., creative dir. The Corp. Communications Group, N.Y.C., 1985—, Mirenburg & Co., N.Y.C., 1985—; instr. unranked Parsons Sch. of Design, N.Y.C., 1979—, coord. computer graphics, 1990-91; asst. prof. Fashion Inst. of Tech., N.Y.C., 1979-81; corp. art dir. Music Sales/Quick Fox, N.Y.C., 1982-85; adj. assoc. prof. Grad. Sch. Coll. of New Rochelle, N.Y., 1985—; chmn. Restaurants Internat. Inc., 1993—; cons. in field. Recipient more than 125 awards and honors for art and design; Fulbright scholar, 1991. Mem. AAUP, Nat. Coun. Art Adminstrs., Am. Inst. Graphic Arts, Soc. Publ. Designers, Am. Ctr. for Design, Art Dirs. Club, Soc. Indsl. Designers, Coll. Art Assn., Mensa. Home and Office: 301 E 38th St New York NY 10016-2750

MIRICK, HENRY DUSTIN, architect; b. Washington, Aug. 6, 1905; s. Henry Brown and Blanche Mitchell (Swope) M.; m. Marion Winsor, June 24, 1933; children: Marion Mirick Dick, Henry Dustin, Heath Mirick Kennedy, Richard. B.A., Princeton, 1927; B. Arch., U. Pa., 1930, M. Arch., 1931. Ptnr. Mirick, Pearson, Batcheler, Phila., 1935—. Works include monograph on large baths Hadrians Villa, Trivoli, Italy; works include Pennwalt, Nat. Bd. Med. Examiners bldgs., Friends Cen. Shipley Sch., Agnes Irwin Sch., Haverford Sch., Episcoal Schs., Pa. State U. natatorium and labs., Bryn Mawr Hosp., Lankeneau Hosp., Jefferson Hosp., U. Pa. Hosp., Medford Leas, Dunwoody, Cathedral Village retirement communities, Mus. Dr. Albert Barnes, Phila., Nat. Scis. Phila. auditorium and labs., James Murphy House, Episcopal Acad., St. Christopher's Ch., Parish House, Ch. of the Redeemer, Bryn Mawr, Humming Bird house, African Plains, Bear Mountain, Phila. Zoo, Sunnybrook, Buena Vista and Whitemarsh country clubs. Pres. Lower Merion Bd. Hist. Review, 1963-66; mem. Lower Merion Planning Commn., 1955-69; Trustee Acad. Natural Scis., 1965-78, emeritus, 1985—; bd. dirs. Pa. Environ. Council, Phila. Zool. Soc., 1963—Harriton Assn., Wharton Community Center, 1951-63; bd. dirs., treas. Phila. com. World Wildlife Fund; treas. Conservation Projects Inc.; chmn. bd. Montgomery Country Day Sch., 1965-67; bd. dirs. Dunwoody Retirement Community, 1976-82, emeritus, 1986—; mem. vestry Ch. of the Redeemer, Bryn Mawr, 1977-80; overseer Strawbery Banke, Portsmouth, N.H., 1981-84. Served to lt. col. AUS, 1942-45 (commendation medal). Recipient Rome prize in architecture, 1930, AIA merit citations; fellow Am. Acad. Rome, 1933. Fellow AIA (pres. Phila. 1970, chmn. Phila. charitable trust 1971-74); mem. Pa. Soc. Architects, Phila. C. of C. (bd. dirs. 1970-75), Pa. Hort. Soc. (pres. 1959-62), Pa. Soc. Promoting Agr. (v.p. 1980-83, pres. 1983-84), Am. Arbitration Assn., Shakspere Soc., Delaware Valley Ornithol. Club, Tau Sigma Delta, Delta Psi. Clubs: Merion Cricket, Philadelphia, Rittenhouse, Art Alliance Phila., Princeton, Pohoqualine Fish Assn., Wilderness (Phila.); Quadrangle (Princeton), Am. Alpine Club. Home: 101 Cherry Ln Ardmore PA 19003

MIRICK, ROBERT ALLEN, military officer; b. Kingston, N.Y., June 26, 1957; s. Harry Lawrence and Jean Alice (Erickson) M.; m. Pamela Ann Warburton, July 24, 1982; children: Kristen E., Kathryn A., Meredith W., Abigail S. BS in Oceanography, U.S. Naval Acad., 1979; MS in Engring. Acoustics, Naval Postgrad. Sch., 1989. Commd. ensign USN, 1979, cmmdr., 1994; navigator, propulsion asst. USS McCandless, 1979-82; diving and deck officer USS Pigeon, 1983-85; exec. officer, navigator USS Bolster, 1985-87; commdg. officer USS Hoist, 1990-92; cmty. mgr., assignment and placement officer USN Spl. Ops., 1993-95; exec. officer U.S. Naval Activities, Guam, 1995-97, Comnavmarianas Support Activity, 1997—; vol. staff diver Monterey (Calif.) Bay Aquarium, 1987-89; field asst. Scripps Inst., San Diego, 1985. Contbr. article to Jour. of Acoustical Soc. Am. Pres. Parents Assn. of L.A., San Pedro, Calif., 1986. Decorated Meritorious Svc. medal USN, 1992, 95. Mem. Acoustical Soc. Am., Am. Soc. Naval Engrs., U.S. Naval Inst., Soc. Colonial Wars. Republican. Achievements include research in sediment acoustics; development of apparatus to determine the complex mass of a viscous fluid contained in a rigid porous solid from acoustic pressure measurements; contributor to certification of USN MK2 Mod1 Deep Diving System to 850 feet. Office: Commander US Naval Forces Marianas Psc 489 Box 14 APO AP 96536-0091

MIRIKITANI, ANDREW KOTARO, lawyer; b. N.Y.C., Aug. 25, 1955; s. Carl Mamoru and Hisa (Yoshimura) M. BA magna cum laude, U. So. Calif., 1978; JD, U. Santa Clara, 1982. Bar: Hawaii 1984, U.S. Dist. Ct. Hawaii 1984, U.S. Ct. Appeals (9th cir.) 1984. Law clk. to chief judge James S. Burns Intermediate Ct. of Appeals, State of Hawaii, Honolulu, 1985-86; atty. Case, Kay & Lynch, Honolulu, 1986-87; mem., vice chmn. Honolulu City Coun., 1990—; atty. Char Hamilton Campbell & Thom, Honolulu, 1988-92; v.p. Am. Beltwrap Corp. Honolulu, 1986—. Editor Santa Clara Law Rev., 1982; patentee in field. Trustee Carl K. Mirikitani Meml. Scholarship Fund, Honolulu, 1984—; pres. East Diamond Head Community Assn., Honolulu, 1988-89; chmn. Waialae-Kahala Neighborhood Bd., Honolulu, 1988-89; bd. dirs. Legal Aid Soc. of Hawaii, 1988-90, Protection ad Advocacy Agy., Honolulu, 1989; del. Dem. Party of Hawaii, Honolulu, 1990-92; pres. Save Diamond Head Beach, Honolulu, 1993—; mem. Nat. Women's Polit. Caucus, Hawaii Women's Polit. Caucus. Mem. ABA, Hawaii Bar Assn., am. Trial Lawyers Assn., Hawaii Women Lawyers Assn., Advocates for Pub. Interest Law, Phi Beta Kappa, Alpha Mu Gamma. Democrat. Office: City Council Honolulu Hale Honolulu HI 96813

MIRIKITANI, JOHN MASA, foundation administrator; b. Honolulu, Nov. 24, 1962; s. Clifford Kunio and Helene M. AB, U. Calif., Berkeley, 1985; JD, U. Mich., 1990; postgrad., U. Hawaii. Policy analyst intern Sloan Found. for Pub. Policy and Mgmt./U. Calif., Berkeley, 1984; policy analyst legis. bus. devel. com. State of Hawaii, Honolulu, 1988-89; founder, pres. John and Clifford Mirikitani Found., Honolulu, 1988—; sponsor Mirikitani Lectrs. in law and econs. edn., U. Hawaii, Manoa, Honolulu, 1989—. Candidate for State Bd. Edn., State Hawaii, 1992, 94. Recipient fellowship Harvard Kennedy Sch. of Govt., 1985. Mem. Am. Law and Econs. Assn., Phi Beta Kappa. Avocations: internat. investing, chess, weightlifting, nutrition, ichthyology. Home: 2336 Oahu Ave Honolulu HI 96822-1965

MIRISCH, LAWRENCE ALAN, motion picture agent; b. Los Angeles, CA, Oct. 10, 1957; s. Walter and Patricia (Kahan) M. BA Radio & TV, Film, Calif. State U., Northridge, 1980. Apprentice film editor, 1975-77, 2nd asst. dir., 1978-81; agent The Gersh Agency, Los Angeles, CA, 1982-84, Adams, Ray & Rosenberg, Los Angeles, CA, 1984, Triad Artists, Los Angeles, CA, 1984-92; pres. The Mirisch Agency, Los Angeles, CA, 1992—; mem. Mot. Picture Editors Guild, 1975; Directors Guild of Amer., 1978; Academy of Motion Pictures Arts & Sciences, 1987; Amer. Cinema Editors, 1988; adv. bd., Amer. Film Inst., 1990; special products comm., Dir. Guild of Amer., 1991. bd. of governors, Cedars Sinai Hosp., 1991. Office: The Mirisch Agency 10100 Santa Monica Blvd Suite 700 Los Angeles CA 90067

MIRISCH, MARVIN ELLIOT, motion picture producer; b. N.Y.C., Mar. 19, 1918; s. Max and Josephine (Urbach) M.; m. Florene Smuckler, Dec. 28, 1941; children—Donald, Carol, Lynn. B.A., Coll. City N.Y., 1940. With contract and print depts., then office mgr. Grand Nat. Films, Inc., N.Y.C., 1936-40; organized theatre concession bus. Theatres Candy Co., Inc., Milw., 1940; exec., corporate officer Allied Artists Pictures Corp., Hollywood, Calif., 1953-57; co-organizer Mirisch Co., Inc. (motion picture producers), Hollywood, Calif., 1957; v.p., dir. Mirisch Co., Inc. (motion picture producers), 1957—; chmn., chief exec. officer Mirisch Prodns., Inc., 1968—; Chmn. permanent charities com. Motion Picture and TV Industries. (Recipient Best Picture of Year award Acad. Motion Picture Arts and Scis. for The Apartment, 1961, West Side Story, 1962, In the Heat of the Night 1968, Producer of Year award Nat. Assn. Theatre Owners 1972). Bd. govs. Cedars-Sinai Med. Ctr. Mem. Assn. Motion Picture and TV Producers Am. (dir., vice-chmn.), Los Angeles Art Inst., Acad. Motion Picture Arts and Scis. (bd. govs., 1st v.p.). Jewish. Clubs: Motion Picture Pioneers, Hillcrest Country. Office: Office 100 Universal C Plz North Hollywood CA 91606

MIRISCH, WALTER MORTIMER, motion picture producer; b. N.Y.C., Nov. 8, 1921; s. Max and Josephine (Urbach) M.; m. Patricia Kahan, Oct. 11, 1947; children: Anne, Andrew, Lawrence. Student, CCNY, 1938-40; BA, U. Wis., 1942, LHD (hon.), 1989; I.A., Harvard Grad. Sch. Bus., 1943. Producer, exec. producer Allied Artists Pictures Corp., 1946-57; producer, v.p. charge prodn. Mirisch Co., Inc., Los Angeles, 1957—; pres.-exec. head prodn. Mirisch Corp., Inc., 1969—. Prodns. include The Magnificent Seven, In the Heat of the Night (Acad. award for best picture of yr. 1968), Two for the Seesaw, The Hawaiians, The Organization, Toys in the Attic, Mr. Majestyk, Midway, Gray Lady Down, Same Time Next Year, Romantic Comedy, Prisoner of Zenda, 1979, Dracula, 1979, Some Like It Hot, West Side Story, The Apartment, The Great Escape, The Pink Panther, Fiddler on the Roof, others. Pres., bd. dirs. Motion Picture Permanent Charities, 1960-61; bd. dirs. Ctr. Theatre Group, L.A., Cedars-Sinai Med. Ctr.; bd. govs. The L.A. Music Ctr. Decorated Order Arts et Lettres (France); recipient UCLA medal, 1989. Mem. Acad. Motion Picture Arts and Scis. (pres. 1973-77, gov. 1964-70, 72—, Motion Picture Acad. Jean Hersholt award 1983, Motion Picture Acad. Irving Thalberg award 1977), Producers Guild Am. (pres., dir. 1959-62), Motion Picture Assn. Am. (dir. 1961—), Wis. Alumni Assn. (dir. 1967-73).

MIRISOLA, LISA HEINEMANN, air quality engineer; b. Glendale, Calif., Mar. 25, 1963; d. J. Herbert and Betty Jane (Howson) Heinemann; m. Daniel Carl Mirisola, June 27, 1987; 1 child, Ian Cataldo. BSME, UCLA, 1986. Cert. engr.-in-tng., Calif. Air quality engr. South Coast Air Quality Mgmt. Dist., Diamond Bar, Calif., 1988—. Chancellor's scholar UCLA, 1981. Mem. ASME, NSPE, Soc. Women Engrs. Office: South Coast Air Quality Mgmt Dist 21865 Copley Dr Diamond Bar CA 91765-4178

MIRKIN, ABRAHAM JONATHAN, surgeon; b. Flushing, N.Y., Aug. 17, 1910; s. Samuel and Anna (Jaffe) M.; m. Miriam G. Klawan, Jan. 26, 1936; children: Louise, Lawrence Stanley. A.B., Cornell U., 1931; M.D., NYU, 1935. Diplomate: Am. Bd. Surgery. Intern, then resident Sinai Hosp., Balt., 1935-41; mem. surg. staff Meml. and Sacred Heart hosps., both Cumberland, Md; pres. med. staff Meml. Hosp., 1966-67; instr. Traffic Inst., Northwestern U., 1964, 68, 72, 74, 76, 78, 80, 82; med. adv. bd. Fla. Dept. Hwy. Safety and Motor Vehicles, 1977—; mem. Com. on Uniform Laws and Ordinances, 1969-72. Gen. chmn. Nat. Conf. on Aging Drivers, 1974. Served to maj. M.C. AUS, 1942-46. Fellow A.C.S. (chmn. hwy. safety com. Md. chpt. 1967-68), Southeastern Surg. Congress; mem. AMA (past chmn. med. aspects automotive safety), Allegany County Med. Soc. (pres. 1947-48), Assn. for Advancement of Automotive Medicine (bd. dirs. 1957-60, 79-81, pres. 1957-59), Soc. Automotive Engrs. (com. on automotive safety), Med.-Chirurg. Faculty Md. (subcom. on traffic safety 1970-76), Fla. Med. Assn., Palm Beach County Med. Soc., Allegany County (Md.) Med. Soc. (pres. 1948-50). Home and Office: 2003 N Ocean Blvd Ph 203 Boca Raton FL 33431-7854

MIRKIN, BERNARD LEO, clinical pharmacologist, pediatrician; b. Bronx, N.Y., Mar. 31, 1928; s. Max and Esther M.; m. Phyllis Korduner, Aug. 1954 (dec. 1982); children: Lisa Mia, Mara Rebecca; m. Sarah Solotaroff, 1986; stepchildren: Jennifer, Rachel, Jacob. AB, NYU, 1949; PhD, Yale U., 1953; MD, U. Minn., 1964. Asst. prof. pharmacology SUNY, Downstate Med. Center, 1954-60; Ford Found. postdoctoral fellow Karolinska Inst., Stockholm, 1960-61; USPHS post-doctoral fellow Yale U., 1961-62; resident in pediatrics U. Minn. Hosp., Mpls., 1964-66; asst. prof. U. Minn. Med. Sch., Mpls., 1966-67; asso. prof. U. Minn. Med. Sch., 1967-72; prof. pediatrics and pharmacology, dir. div. clin. pharmacology U. Minn. Health Sci. Ctr., 1972-89; prof. pediatrics and pharmacology Northwestern U. Med. Sch., Chgo., 1989—; head, dir. rsch. Children's Meml. Inst. for Edn. and Rsch., Children's Meml. Hosp., Chgo., 1989—; assoc. dean Rsch. Northwestern U. Med. Sch., 1994—; cons. NIH, Office of Technology Assessment, U.S. Congress, WHO, U.S. Pharmacopeia, Pharm. Rsch. and Mfrs. of Am. Found., Nat. Inst. Health; vis. fellow Jesus Coll., Oxford U., 1974. Author: Perinatal Pharmacology and Therapeutics, 1976, Clinical Pharmacology: A Pediatric Perspective, 1978. postdoctoral fellow Karolinska Inst. Stockholm 1960-61. Served with M.C. U.S. Army, 1954-56. Mem. Am. Fedn. Clin. Research, Soc. Pediatric Rsch., Am. Assn. Cancer Rsch., Am. Pediatrics Soc., Am. Soc. Pharm. Exptl. Therapeutics. Home: 427 Greenleaf St Evanston IL 60202-1328 Office: Childrens Meml Inst Edn and Rsch Mailcode # 117 2300 N Childrens Plz Chicago IL 60614-3318

MIRKIN, DAVID, television producer; b. Phila.. Exec. prodr., writer, dir. Newhart, 1984-88 (Emmy award for writing 1987); exec. prodr., co-creator, dir. Get A Life, 1990-92; writer The Tracey Ullman Show; exec. prodr. The Simpsons, 1990— (Emmy award 1995), dir., Romy and Michele's High School Reunion. Office: Fox Broadcasting Co PO Box 900 Beverly Hills CA 90213

MIRMAN, IRVING R., scientific adviser; b. Syracuse, N.Y., July 29, 1915; s. Saniel I. and Rebecca (Raichlin) M.; m. Beatrice Wolff, Aug. 14, 1942; children—Robert, Marsha, Kenneth. B.E.E., N.Y. U., 1942; postgrad., Harvard-Mass. Inst. Tech., 1942-43, Poly. Inst. Bklyn., 1947-51, Air U., 1952, 56, 59, George Washington U., 1956, Colgate U., 1957, Syracuse U., 1958, Am. U., 1964-65. Registered profl. engr., Mass. Elec. engr. Central N.Y. Power Co., Syracuse, 1937-41; project engr. Watson Labs., Red Bank, N.J., 1946-50; mem. tech. staff Rome Air Devel. Ctr., N.Y., 1950-51; chief program staff Rome Air Devel. Ctr., 1951-55, asst. sci. dir., 1955-57, assoc. dir. R & D, 1957-59; dir. tech. planning and ops. Capehart Corp., N.Y., 1959-60; v.p. Capehart Corp., 1960-63; sci. cons. Anser Corp., Baileys Cross Roads, Va., 1963; sci. adviser, dep. chief staff research and devel. in sci. and tech. Dept. Air Force, Washington, 1963-66; sci. adviser S.E. Asia matters Dept. Air Force, 1966-72; spl. asst. to comdr. Hdqrs. Air Force System Command, 1966-76; dep. dir. SHAPE Tech. Center, The Hague, Netherlands, 1976-80; pres. Decision Process Systems, Washington, 1980—. Served to capt. USAF, 1942-46. Recipient Meritorious Civilian award Dept. Air Force, 1958, also Distinguished Civilian award, 1976. Fellow A.A.A.S.; sr. mem. IEEE; mem. Am. Inst. Aeros. and Astronautics, N.Y. Acad. Sci., Research Engring. Soc. Am. Home: 5729 Fairway Pk Dr #20-203 Boynton Beach FL 33437-1764

MIRMAN, JOEL HARVEY, lawyer; b. Toledo, Dec. 3, 1941; s. Benjamin and Minnie (Krapifko) M.; m. Denise M. Dembinski, June 12, 1982; children: Lisa, Julie, Benjamin. BBA, Ohio U., 1963; JD, Ohio State U., 1966. Bar: Ohio 1966, U.S. Dist. Ct. (so. dist.) Ohio 1966, U.S. Supreme Ct. 1972. Ptnr. Topper, Alloway, Goodman, DeLeone & Duffey, Columbus, Ohio, 1966-85, Benesch, Friedlander, Coplan & Aronoff, 1986-93; shareholder Buckingham, Doolittle & Burroughs, Columbus, Ohio, 1994—; lectr. Ohio CLE Inst., Columbus, 1972—. Author direct examination CLE materials; contbr. articles to profl. jours. Mem. Ohio Elections Commn., 1976-80, vice-chmn. 1980. Mem. Capital Club, Worthington Hills Country Club, Worthington Hills Civic Assn. (pres. 1992-93), Assn. Trial Lawyers Am. (chmn. family law sects. 1993-94). Office: Buckingham Doolittle & Burroughs 88 E Broad St Ste 1600 Columbus OH 43215-3506

MIRONOVICH, ALEX, publisher; b. Brooklyn, N.Y., Nov. 30, 1952; s. Peter Mironovich and Olga Sachrina; m. Cynthia Ann Wuss, July 23, 1983; children: Britany, Nicholas. BA in psychology, City U., N.Y.C., 1970-74. Sales rep. House Beautiful mag., N.Y.C., 1976-79, Sawyer Ferguson Walker, N.Y.C., 1979-82, Creative Ideas for Living, N.Y.C., 1982-83, Parents mag. G and J, N.Y.C.; assoc. pub. Y.M. Gruner and Jahr, N.Y., 1986-88; pub. Y.M. Gruner and Jahr, 1988, Better Homes and Gardens, N.Y.C. Office: Better Homes and Gardens 125 Park Ave New York NY 10017*

MIROWSKI, PHILIP EDWARD, economics educator; b. Jackson, Mich., Aug. 21, 1951; s. Edward and Elizabeth Mirowski; m. Pamela Margaret Cook, June 14, 1986. BA, Mich. State U., 1973; MA in Econs., U. Mich., 1976, PhD in Econs., 1979. Asst. prof. U. Santa Clara, Calif., 1978-81; asst. prof. Tufts U., Medford, Mass., 1981-84, assoc. prof. econs., 1984-90; Carl Koch prof. econs. and history and philosophy of sci. U. Notre Dame, Ind., 1990—; vis. assoc. prof. Yale U., New Haven, 1987-88; vis. prof. Tinbergen Inst., Erasmus U., Rotterdam, Holland, 1991, U. Paris, 1997. Author: Reconstruction of Economic Theory, 1986, Against Mechanism, 1988, More Heat Than Light, 1989; Rowman & Littlefield series editor Studies in Worldly Philosophy; editor: Natural Images in Economics, 1994, Edgeworth on Chance, 1994; mem. editorial bd. History Polit. Econ., Duke U., 1986—, Social Concept, 1988-94, Review of Polit. Economy, 1994—; contbr. articles to profl. jours. Mem. Am. Econs. Assn., History Sci. Soc., History Econs. Soc., Soc. for Social Studies of Sci., Philosophy of Sci. Assn. Office: U Notre Dame Dept Econs Notre Dame IN 46556

MIRRA, SUZANNE SAMUELS, neuropathologist, researcher; b. N.Y.C., Feb. 16, 1943. BA, Hunter Coll., 1962; MD, SUNY, Bklyn., 1967. Instr. pathology Yale U. Sch. Medicine, New Haven, 1971-73; staff pathologist Atlanta VA Med. Ctr., Decatur, Ga., 1973-97; asst. prof. pathology Emory U. Sch. Medicine, Atlanta, 1973-80, assoc. prof. pathology, 1981-93, prof. pathology, 1993-97; dir., prin. investor Emory Alzheimer's Disease Ctr., Atlanta, 1991-97. Mem. editl. bd. Arch Pathol. Lab. Med., 1988—, Jour. Neuropathology Exptl. Neurology, 1991-95, Brain Pathology, 1995—, Alzheimer's Disease Reviews, 1995—. Recipient Albert E. Levy Sci. Faculty Rsch. award Emory U., 1987, Disting. Alumnus Achievement award SUNY, 1992; named to Hunter Coll. Hall of Fame, 1996. Fellow Coll. Am. Pathologists (Presdl. award 1987,89, Herbert Lansky award 1990, chair neuropathology commn. 1992-95); mem. Am. Assn. Neuropathologists (v.p. profl. affairs 1992-97), Alzheimer's Assn. (bd. dirs. Atlanta chpt. 1987-97). Office: VA Med Ctr 113 Emory U 1670 Clairmont Rd Decatur GA 30033-4004

MIRREN, HELEN, actress; b. London, 1946. First appeared with Nat. Youth Theatre; appeared as Cleopatra in Antony and Cleopatra, Old Vic, 1965; joined Royal Shakespeare Co., 1967; appeared as Castiza in The Revenger's Tragedy and Diana in All's Well That Ends Well; other roles include: Cressida in Troilus and Cressida, Royal Shakespeare Co., Stratford, Eng., 1968; Hero in Much Ado About Nothing, Stratford, 1968; Win-the-Fight Littlewit in Bartholomew Fair, Aldwych, 1969; Lady Anne in Richard III, Stratford, Ophelia in Hamlet, Julia in The Two Gentlemen of Verona, Stratford, 1970 (last part also at Aldwych); Tatyana in Enemies, Royal Shakespeare Co., Aldwych, 1971; title role in Miss Julie, Elynae in The Balcony, The Place, 1971; with Peter Brook's Centre Internationale de Recherches Theatrales, Africa and U.S., 1972-73; Lady Macbeth, Royal Shakespeare Co., Stratford, 1974, and Aldwych, 1975; Maggie in Teeth 'n' Smiles, Royal Ct., 1975; Nina in The Seagull and Ella in The Bed Before Yesterday, Lyric for Lyric Theatre Co., 1975, Antony and Cleopatra, The Roaring Girl, Henry VI-Parts 1, 2, 3, 1977-78, Measure for Measure, 1979, The Duchess of Malfi, 1980-81, Faith Healer, 1981, Royal Shakespeare Co., Barbican, 1983, Extremities, 1984, Madame Bovary, 1987, Two Way Mirror, 1988, Sex Please We're Italian, 1991, A Month in the Country, 1994 (Tony nominee - Lead Actress in a Play, 1995); films include: Age of Consent, 1969, Savage Messiah, O Lucky Man!, 1973, Caligula, 1977, The Long Good Friday, Excalibur, 1981, Cal, 1984 (Best Actress award Cannes Film Festival 1984), 2010, 1984, White Knights, 1984, Heavenly Pursuits, 1985, The Mosquito Coast, 1986, Pascali's Island, 1987, When The Whales Came, 1988, Bethune, Making of a Hero, 1988, The Cook, The Thief, His Wife, and Her Lover, 1989, The Comfort of Strangers, 1990, Where Angels Fear to Tread, 1991, The Gift, 1991, The Hawk, 1991, The Prince of Jutland, 1991, The Madness of King George, 1994 (Acad. award nominee for Best Supporting Actress), Critical Care, 1996; TV appearances include: Behind the Scene, Cousin Bette, Coffin for the Bride, Jackanory, The Changeling, Bellamira, The Philanthropist, Mussolini And Claretta Petacci, The Collection, The Country Wife, Blue Remembered Hills, The Serpent Son, Quiz Kids, Midsummer Night's Dream, After the Party, Cymbeline, Coming Through, Cause Celebre, Miss Julie, The Apple Cart, The Little Minister, As You Like It, Mrs. Reinhardt, Soft Targets, 1982, Heavenly Pursuits, 1985, Red King White Knight, 1988, Prime Suspect, 1991 (Best Actress award BAFTA 1991), Prime Suspect 2, 1992, Prime Suspect 3, 1993 (Emmy award 1994), Prime Suspect 4, 1994 (Emmy award 1996), Prime Suspect 5, 1996, Chase in Losing Chase, 1995, Some Mothers Son, 1995, A Month in the Country, 1995. Mem. PTO. Office: Ken McReddie Ltd, 91 Regent St, London WIR 7TB, England

MIRRIELEES, JAMES FAY, III, publishing executive; b. Cin., Nov. 2, 1939; s. James Fay and Alicia Lucille (Beatty) M.; m. Gillian C. Hanlon, July, 1986; 1 child, Hillary Evan, from previous marriage. BA, U. Cin. Editorial dir. McGraw-Hill Coll. Pub. Co., N.Y.C., 1975-77; v.p. Holt-Rinehart & Winston, N.Y.C., 1977-79; pres. CBS Coll. Pub., N.Y.C., 1979-81, 83-85, CBS Internat. Pub., 1981-83; mng. dir. European ops. Ashton-Tate, London, 1985-86; pres. Somerset House Edn. and Profl. Pubs., 1986-87; chief exec. officer Raintree Pub. Inc., 1987-88; chmn., pres. Raintree I Ltd. Partnership, 1988-91; pres. Coronet/MTI Film & Video, Deerfield, Ill., 1991-93; v.p. mktg. Edunetics Corp., Arlington, Va., 1993-95; v.p. bus. devel. Jennings & Keefe Media, 1995; pres. Blue Aegean Media, Arlington, Va., 1996—. Democrat. Home: 2175 N Pierce St Arlington VA 22209-2505 Office: 2175 N Pierce St Arlington VA 22209-1110

MIRSE, RALPH THOMAS, former college president; b. Carrsville, Ky., Aug. 8, 1924; s. Ralph Thomas and Rubye Catherine (Morris) M.; m. Blanche Allen, May 10, 1945; children: Ralph Allen, Deborah Lynn, Sally Ann. BA, Asbury Coll., Wilmore, Ky., 1943; ThM, Asbury Theol. Sem., 1946; PhD, Boston U., 1962; LHD (hon.), Lakeland Coll., Sheboygan, Wis., 1977; LLD (hon.), Buena Vista Coll., Storm Lake, Iowa, 1978; LittD (hon.), Heidleberg Coll., Tiffin, Ohio, 1981; DEd (hon.), Sungshin Women's U., Seoul Korea, 1983; DFA (hon.), Columbia Coll., 1988; DD (hon.), Oklahoma City U., 1988. Ordained to ministry United Methodist Ch., 1947; pastor Meth. Chs., in Ky., 1947-57; exec. sec. New Eng. Conf. United Meth. Ch., 1960-65, exec. sec. nat. div., 1965-70; v.p. Baker U., Baldwin, Kans., 1970-74; pres. Lakeland Coll., 1974-77, Columbia Coll., 1977-88, ret., 1989; part-time dir. ednl. devel. U. S.C., Hilton Head, 1989—; mem. Gov. S.C. Adv. Bd. Social Services, S.C. Adv. Council Pvt. Colls.; chmn. bd. S.C. Ptnrs. of Ams. Author: The Methodist Minister, 1960, The Self-Image of the Methodist Minister, 1962, The Changing Face of New England, 1964, Community Planning Studies, 1970. Decorated Order of Ky. Col., 1979, Order of the Palmetto, 1986. Mem. Am. Assn. Higher Edn., Counc. Advancement and Support Edn., Am. Acad. Polit. and Social Sci., Nat. Conf. Small Pvt. Colls. (pres., dir.), S.C. Found. Pvt. Colls., S.C. Coll. Counc., Internat. Assn. Univ. Pres.' (exec. com.), Am. Coun. on Edn., Rotary. Republican. Clubs: Forest Lake, Summit (Columbia); Univ. (N.Y.C.); Hyannis (Mass.) Yacht. Lodges: Rotary, Shrine. Office: 10 Office Park Rd Hilton Head Island SC 29928-7535

MIRSEPASSI-TOLOUI, SHIRLEY SHIRIN, pathologist, educator; b. Tehran, Iran, Apr. 13, 1944; came to U.S., 1972; d. Morteza and Esmatelmolook (Bahrami) Mirsepassi; m. Gerald Javad Toloui, Apr. 23, 1970; children: Kenneth, Sam. MD, Tehran U., 1969. Diplomate Am. Bd. Anatomic and Clin. Pathology and Cytopathology. Asst. prof. N.Y. Med. Coll., Valhalla, 1990—; assoc. pathologist St. Vincent's Hosp., Staten Island, N.Y., 1994—. Fellow Coll. Am. Pathologists, Am. Soc. Clin. Pathologists. Republican. Avocation: classical music. Office: St Vincent's Hosp 355 Bard Ave Staten Island NY 10310-1664

MIRSKY, ALLAN FRANKLIN, psychologist, researcher; b. N.Y.C., Feb. 2, 1929; s. Harry Leroy and Charlotte (Copans) M.; m. Carol Patricia Vogel, June 24, 1951 (dec. 1983); children: Laura Ann, Richard Daniel; m. Constance Catharine Duncan, July 4, 1986. BS, City Coll. N.Y., 1950; MS, Yale U., 1952, PhD, 1954. Diplomate Am. Bd. Profl. Psychology; cert. clin. Neuropsychology. Rsch. psychologist Nat. Inst. Health, Bethesda, Md., 1954-61; asst. prof. to prof. Boston U., Mass., 1961-80; chief lab. of psychology and psychopathology NIH, Bethesda, Md., 1980-95, chief sect. on clin. and exptl. neuropsychology, 1995—; cons. NIH, NSF, NRC, Washington, 1965-93, WHO, 1992—; adj. prof. Johns Hopkins U., Balt., 1987—. Editor, author: Education and The Brain, 1978, Elements of Petit Mal Epilepsy, 1988. Comdr. USPHS, 1954-61. Rsch. grant NSF, NIH, 1961-80; recipient Career award NIMH, 1961-80, Outstanding Achievement in Psychology City Coll. N.Y., 1989. Fellow AAAS, Am. Psychology Assn. (pres. divsn. comp. and physiol. psychology 1982-83), Am. EEG Soc., Am. Am. Coll. Neuropsychopharmacology; mem. Internat. Neuropsychological Soc. (pres. 1972), Cosmos Club. Achievements include contributions to the neuropsychology of attention, schizophrenia and petit mal epilepsy. Home: 6204 Perthshire Ct Bethesda MD 20817-3348 Office: NIMH/Bldg 15-K 15 North Dr # 2668 Bethesda MD 20814-1507

MIRSKY, ARTHUR, geologist, educator; b. Phila., Feb. 8, 1927; s. Victor and Dorothy M.; m. Patricia Shorey, Dec. 22, 1961; 1 dau., Alexis Catherine. Student, Bklyn. Coll., 1944-45, 46-48; BA, U. Calif., 1950; MS, U. Ariz., 1955; PhD, Ohio State U., 1960. Cert. geologist, Ind. Field uranium geologist AEC, S.W. U.S., 1951-53; cons. uranium geologist Albuquerque, 1955-56; asst. dir. Inst. Polar Studies, Ohio State U., 1960-67; from asst. prof. geology to prof. Ind. U.-Purdue U., Indpls., 1967-94, prof. emeritus, 1994—, coord. geology, 1967-69, chmn. dept. geology, 1969-93; adj. asst. prof. Ohio State U., 1964-67. Contbr. articles to profl. jours. Served with USN, 1945-46. Mem. AAAS, AAUP, Am. Inst. Profl. Geologists, Geol. Soc. Am., Nat. Assn. Geosci. Tchrs., Am. Geol. Inst., Soc. Sedimentary Geology, Ind. Acad. Sci., Sigma Xi. Office: Indiana U-Purdue U Dept Geology 723 W Michigan St Indianapolis IN 46202-5191

MIRSKY, JEFFREY, science foundation administrator. Pres., COO Nat. Diagnostics, Inc. Address: 305 Patton Dr Atlanta GA 30336

MIRSKY, PHYLLIS SIMON, librarian; b. Petach Tikva, Israel, Dec. 18, 1940; d. Allan and Lea (Prizant) Simon; m. Edward Mirsky, Oct. 21, 1967; 1 child, Seth (dec.). BS in Social Welfare, Ohio State U., 1962; postgrad., Columbia U., 1962-63; AMLS, U. Mich., 1965. Caseworker field placement Children's Aid Soc., N.Y.C., 1962-63; hosp. libr. hosp. and instns. divsn. Cleve. Pub. Libr., 1963-64; reference libr. UCLA Biomed. Libr., 1965-68, reference/acquisitions libr., 1968-69, head cons./continuing edn. Pacific S.W. Regl. Med. Libr. Sv., 1969-71, asst. dir. Pacific S.W. Regl. Med. Libr. Sv., 1971-73, faculty coord. Biomed. Libr. program Cen. San Joaquin Valley Area Health Edn. Ctr., 1973-77, assoc. dir. Pacific S.W. Regl. Med. Libr. Sv., 1973-79; head reference sect., coord. libr. assoc. program Nat. Libr. of Medicine, Bethesda, Md., 1979-81; asst. univ. libr., scis. U. Calif.-San Diego, La Jolla, 1981-86, acting univ. libr., 1985, 92-93, asst. univ. libr. adminstrv. and pub. svcs., 1986-87, assoc. univ. libr. adminstrv. and pub. svcs., 1987-92, assoc. univ. libr., 1993-95; dep. univ. libr., 1995—; guest lectr. Libr. Schs. UCLA and U. So. Calif., 1967-78, Grad. Sch. Libr. Sci. Cath. U., Washington, 1980, Grad. Sch. Libr. and Info. Sci. UCLA, 1984; mem. task force on role of spl. libr. nationwide network and coop. programs Nat. Commn. on Libr. and Info. Svcs./Spl. Libr. Assn., 1981-83; facilitator AASLD/MLA Guidelines Scenario Writing Session, L.A., 1984; mem. users coun. OCLC Online Computer Libr. Ctr., Inc., 1991-94; U. Calif.-San Diego rep. Coalition for Networked Info., 1992—; instr. Assn. Rsch. Librs., Office Mgmt. Studies, Mgmt. Inst., 1987; peer reviewer Coll. Libr. Tech. and Cooperation Grant Program U.S. Dept. Edn., 1988-94; cons. Nat. Libr. Medicine, Bethesda, Md., 1988, San Diego Mus. Contemporary Art Libr., La Jolla, Calif., 1993, Salk Inst., 1995; mem. Libr. of Congress Network Adv. Com., 1994-96, chair steering com., 1995-96. Contbr. articles to profl. jours. and bulls. NIH fellow Columbia U., 1962-63; sr. fellow UCLA/Coun. on Libr. Resources, 1987. Fellow Med. Libr. Assn. (bd. dirs. 1977-80); mem. ALA (site visitors panel com. on accreditation 1990-92, libr. adminstrn. and mgmt. assn. 1990-92), Med. Libr. Group Soc. Calif. and Ariz. (sec. 1970-71, v.p. 1971-72, pres. 1972-73), Documentation Abstracts, Inc. (bd. dirs. 1985-90, vice chair bd. dirs. 1988-90), Med. Libr. Assn. (pres. 1984-85), U. Mich. Sch. Libr. Sci. Alumni Assn. Office: U Calif-San Diego Univ Libr 0175G 9500 Gilman Dr La Jolla CA 92093-5003

MIRSKY, SONYA WOHL, librarian, curator; b. N.Y.C., Nov. 12, 1925; d. Louis and Anna (Steiger) Wohl; m. Alfred Ezra Mirsky, Aug. 24, 1967 (dec. June 1974). B.S. in Edn., CCNY, 1948; M.S.L.S., Columbia U., 1950. Asst. libr. Rockefeller U., N.Y.C., 1949-60, assoc. libr., 1960-77, univ. libr., 1977-91, univ. libr. emeritus, 1991—; trustee Med. Libr. Ctr. N.Y., 1965-91, v.p., 1980-88; cons. libr. mgmt. Mem. Bibliog. Soc. Am., Bibliog. Soc. Can., Bibliog. Soc. Gt. Britain, Soc. Bibliography of Natural History. Home: Sutton Ter 1161 York Ave Apt 4F New York NY 10021-7945 Office: Rockefeller U Libr 1230 York Ave New York NY 10021-6307

MIRVIS, DAVID MARC, health administrator, cardiologist, educator; b. Hampton, Va., Dec. 20, 1945; s. Allan and Lena (Sear) M.; m. Arlynn Shara Katz, June 30, 1968; children: Simcha Zev, Tova Aliza, Shoshana Fruma. Student, Yeshiva Coll., N.Y.C., 1966, MD, 1970. Diplomate Am. Bd. Internal Medicine. Intern U. Tenn., Memphis, 1970-71, fellow, resident, 1973-75, asst., assoc. prof., 1973-83, prof., 1983—; assoc. dean U. Tenn., Memphis, 1987—; fellow, cardiovascular physiology NIH, Bethesda, Md., 1971-73; chief of cardiology Memphis VA Med. Ctr., 1983-87, chief of staff, 1987—; pres. Rsch., Inc., 1990—; dir. Health Svcs. Rsch. Divsn., The Univs. Prevention Ctr. Author, editor: Body Surface Electrocardiographic Mapping, 1988; author: Electrocardiography: A Physiologic Approach; contbg. editor Jour. Electrocardiology, 1984—, Am. Jour. Noninvasive Cardiology, 1986—. Com. chair Anshei Sphard Synagogue, Memphis, 1987—. Grantee NIH, 1975-89. Fellow Am. Heart Assn. (coun. on circulation), Am. Coll. Cardiology; mem. Am. Soc. Clin. Investigation, Am. Acad. Med. Dirs., Internat. Soc. Computerized Electrocardiography, So. Soc. Clin. Rsch. Democrat. Home: 5676 Redding Ave Memphis TN 38120-1848 Office: U Tenn 956 Court Ave Memphis TN 38103-2814 also: U Tenn 66 N Pauline Memphis TN 38105

MIRZA, DAVID BROWN, economist, educator; b. Dayton, Ohio, Feb. 28, 1936; s. Youel Benjamin and Althea (Brown); m. Leona Lousin, June 20, 1965; children: Sara Anush, Elizabeth Ann. AB, Earlham Coll., 1958; PhD, Northwestern U., 1973. Instr. Dartmouth Coll., Hanover, N.H., 1961-63, Kalamazoo (Mich.) Coll., 1963-69; assoc. prof. econs. Loyola U., Chgo., 1969—, chmn. dept. econs., 1978—, dir. Inst. Futures Trading, 1973—. Trustee Earlham Coll., Richmond, Ind., 1988-95, mem. found. bd., 1991—. Mem. Am. Econ. Assn. Mem. Soc. of Friends. Home: 795 Lincoln Ave Winnetka IL 60093-1920 Office: Loyola Univ Chgo 820 N Michigan Ave Chicago IL 60611-2103

MIRZA, MUHAMMAD ZUBAIR, product development company executive, researcher, engineering consultant, inventor; b. Jhelum, Punjab, Pakistan, Nov. 13, 1949; came to U.S., 1971; s. Muhammad Siddique and Shehr (Bano) M.; m. Tahira Beena, Aug. 12, 1977; children: Sarah, Nadia, Sana. Grad., Cadet Coll., Hasan Abdal, Pakistan, 1967; AS in Respiratory Therapy, St. Joseph/VA Hines Hosps., Chgo., 1974; BS in Biology, Sangamon State U., Springfield, Ill., 1976; MS in Product Design for Health Care, U. Ill., Chgo., 1978. Respiratory therapist St. Joseph Hosp., Chgo., 1974-79; assoc. engr. J.G.G. & Assocs., Woodbridge, N.J., 1979; product devel. engr. Becton-Dickinson Respiratory Sys., Lincoln Park, N.J., 1979-82; biomed. product devel. cons. M. Zubair Mirza Cons., Saddle Brook, N.J., 1982-86; co-founder, v.p. R & D, bd. dirs. Critichem, Inc. (acquired by Becton-Dickinson Corp. 1986), Little Falls, N.J., 1982-86; mgr. advanced devel. engring. Becton-Dickinson, Critichem Group, Fairlawn, N.J., 1986-88; dir. biomed. engring./tech. and equipment planning Shifa Internat. Hosp., Islamabad, Pakistan, 1989-90; pres. M. Zubair Mirza Cons., Wyckoff, N.J., 1988—, Ameer, Natural Solutions, Inc., Wyckoff, 1991—; rsch. asst. Sch. Medicine, So. Ill. U., Springfield, 1976; rsch. assoc. Office of Spl. Edn., Springfield, 1975-76, designer spl. edn. facility; rsch. assoc. to sr. cons. WHO, Geneva, 1977-78, designer self-health care kit. Author: Islamization of Business, 1994; patentee on respiratory monitor, 1992, respiratory monitoring device, 1993, trocar system, 1994; patents pending on electronic spirometer, surg. (laparotomy) trocar and insertion sys, Transportable Sign or Message Holder. Trustee, v.p. Islamic Edn. Found. N.J., 1995—, active Muslim, Jewish & Christian Dialogues, 1994—. Islam. Avocations: inventing, writing, reading, camping. Office: 570 Farview Ave Wyckoff NJ 07481-1140

MIRZA, SHAUKAT, engineering educator, researcher, consultant; b. Bhopal, India, Aug. 1, 1936; s. Mirza Afaq Beg and Birjees Jahan; m. Ferzana Beg, June 24, 1967; children: Sabah Jahan, Mazin. BS in Engring., Aligarh U., 1956; MS in Civil Engring., U. Wis.-Madison, 1960, PhD in Engring. Mechanics, 1962. Sr. lectr. Delhi Coll. Engring., India, 1962-64; prof. Indian Inst. Tech., New Delhi, 1964-69; prof. mech. engring. U. Ottawa, Ont., Can., 1969-96, vice dean R & D faculty engring, 1991-94; vis. engr. Westinghouse Nuclear Europe, Brussels, 1976-77; vis. engr. Def. Rsch. Establishment, Ottawa, 1987-88; cons. Govt. of India, New Delhi, 1967-68, Atomic Energy Can., 1974-80, Bell No. Research, Ottawa, 1981-82. Vis. prof. Worcester (Mass.) Polytech. Inst., 1994-95s 96s, Ecole Nat. Superieur d'Ingeneur de Const. Aero., Toulouse, France, 1994; disting. vis. prof. mech. engring. Worcester (Mass.) Poly. Inst., 1996—; emeritus prof. mech. egring. U. Ottawa, Can. Invited keynote speaker various internat. profl. confs.; contbr. rsch. articles, tech. reports to publs. Recipient Pres.'s gold medal, Roorkee U., India, 1958. Mem. ASME, Assn. Profl. Engrs. Ont. Office: Worcester Polytech Inst Dept Mech Engring 100 Institute Rd Worcester MA 01609-2247

MISA, KENNETH FRANKLIN, management consultant; b. Jamaica, N.Y., Sept. 24, 1939; s. Frank J. and Mary M. (Soszka) M.; BS cum laude in Psychology, Fairfield U., 1961; MS in Psychology, Purdue U., 1963; PhD in Psychology (Fellow 1963-66), St. John's U., 1966. Staff psychologist Rohrer, Hibler & Replogle, Los Angeles, 1966-67; assoc. A.T. Kearney, Inc., Los Angeles, 1968-71, sr. assoc., 1972-74, prin., 1975-78, v.p., partner, 1979-86; pres. HR Cons. Group, 1987—. Cert. mgmt. cons.; lic. psychologist, Calif. Mem. Am. Psychol. Assn., Am. Psychol. Soc., Calif. State Psychol. Assn., Soc. for Human Resources Mgmt., Human Resources Planning Soc., Indsl. Rels. Rsch. Assn., Soc. for Indsl. and Organizational Psychology, World Affairs Coun. of L.A., Town Hall of So. Calif., Glendale C. of C., Jonathan Club. Republican. Roman Catholic. Home: 924C S Orange Grove Blvd Pasadena CA 91105-1741 Office: HR Cons Group 100 N Brand Blvd Ste 200 Glendale CA 91203-2614

MISCHER, DONALD LEO, television director and producer; b. San Antonio, Mar. 5, 1940; s. Elmer Frederick and Lillian Alma. B.A., U. Tex., 1961, M.A., 1963. Mem. faculty U. Tex., 1962-63; producer/dir. USIA, Washington, 1965-68; with Charles Guggenheim Prodns., 1969-71; pres. Don Mischer Prodns., pres. Mischer Enterprises, Inc., Beverly Hills, Calif., prodr., dir., and program packager for network television programs, 1971—. Television programs include: The Opening and Closing Ceremonies of the 1996 Centennial Olympic Games, Atlanta, The Kennedy Center Honors: A Celebration of the Performing Arts (Emmy Awards 1981, 87); The Tony Awards (Emmy Awards 1987-88); Michael Jackson's Super Bowl XXVII Halftime Show; Baryshnikov by Tharp (Emmy Award 1985); Gregory Hines, Tap Dance America; Carnegie Hall: Live at 100; It's Garry Shandling's Show; Mowtown 25: Yesterday, Today, Tomorrow (Emmy Award 1983); The Muppets Celebrate Jim Henson; Motown Returns to the Apollo (Emmy Award 1985); Baryshnikov in Hollywood, Goldie and Liza Together, Shirley MacLaine—Illusions, Making Television Dance with Twyla Tharp, An Evening with Robin Williams, Am. Film Inst. Salute to Gene Kelly; producer additional programs with Bob Hope (Bob Hope: The First 90 Years - Emmy award Outstanding Variety, Music or Comedy Special, 1993), Barbara Walters, Goldie Hawn, others. Recipient: Primetime Emmy awards (10), Director's Guild awards for Outstanding Directorial Achiement (8), NAACP Image awards (3), Peabody award, Golden Rose of Montreux award, Gabriel award, Ohio State award. Mem. Dirs. Guild Am., Nat. Acad. TV Arts and Scis. Gov., Am. Film Inst. Office: Brillstein-Grey Entertainment 9150 Wilshire Blvd Ste 350 Beverly Hills CA 90212-3430

MISCHKE, CARL HERBERT, religious association executive, retired; b. Hazel, S.D., Oct. 27, 1922; s. Emil Gustav and Pauline Alvina (Polzin) M.; m. Gladys Lindloff, July 6, 1947; children: Joel, Susan Mischke Blahnik, Philip, Steven. B.A., Northwestern Coll., Watertown, Wis., 1944; M.Div., Wis. Luth. Sem., Mequon, 1947. Ordained to ministry Evang. Lutheran Ch. Parish pastor Wis. Synod, 1947-79; pres. Western Wis. Dist. Evang. Luth. Ch., Juneau, 1964-79; v.p. Wis. Luth. Synod, Milw., 1966-79, pres., 1979-93; retired, 1993.

MISCHKE, CHARLES RUSSELL, mechanical engineering educator; b. Glendale, N.Y., Mar. 2, 1927; s. Reinhart Charles and Dena Amelia (Scholl) M.; m. Margaret R. Bubeck, Aug. 4, 1951; children: Thomas, James. BSME, Cornell U., 1947, MME, 1950; PhD, U. Wis., 1953. Registered mechanical engr. Iowa, Kans. Asst. prof. mech. engring. U. Kans., Lawrence, 1953-56; assoc. prof. mech. engring. U. Kans., 1956-57; prof., chmn. mech. engring. Pratt Inst., N.Y.C., 1957-64; prof. mech. engring. Iowa State U., Ames, 1964—, Alcoa Found. prof., 1974. Author: Elements of Mechanical Analysis, 1963, Introduction to Computer-Aided Design, 1968, Mathematical Model Building, 1972; editor: Standard Handbook of Machine Design, 1986, 1996, Mechanical Engineering Design, 5th edit., 1989, 8 Mechancal Designers Workbooks, 1990, Fundamentos de Diseno Mechanico, 4 vols., 1994. Scoutmaster Boy Scouts Am., Ames. With USNR, 1944-75, mem. Res. ret. Recipient Ralph Teetor award Soc. Automotive Engrs., 1977, best book award Am. Assn. Pubs., 1986, Legis. Teaching Excellence award Iowa Assembly, 1990, Ralph Coates Roe award Am. Soc. for Engring. Edn., 1991. Fellow ASME (life, Machine Design award 1990); mem. Am. Soc. Engring. Edn. (Centennial cert. 1993), Am. Gear Mfrs. Assn., Scabbard and Blade, Cardinal Key, Sigma Xi, Phi Kappa Phi, Pi Tau Sigma. Avocations: model bldg., railway history. Office: Iowa State U Dept Mech Engring Ames IA 50011

MISCHKE, FREDERICK CHARLES, manufacturing company executive; b. Benton Harbor, Mich., Sept. 21, 1930; s. Fred William and Clara Adeline (Ruhno) M.; m. Kathleen Ann Schultz, Nov. 19, 1955 (dec. Aug. 1980);

children: Stephanie Ann, Michael Frederick (dec. Oct. 12, 1996), Eric William; m. Lori Ann Leonard, Dec. 23, 1983. AA, Lake Mich. Coll., 1956; BBA, Western Mich. U., 1958. CPA, Ind., Mich. Staff acct. Lybrand, Ross Bros. & Montgomery, Chgo., 1958-63; supr. acctg. Lybrand, Ross Bros. & Montgomery, Niles, Mich., 1963-65; v.p., treas. Skyline Corp., Elkhart, Ind., 1965-91, ret., 1991. Vol. Svc. Corps. Ret. Execs., 1992—, local v.p., 1993—; chmn. Meml. Endowment Fund Luth. Ch., 1995—. Mem. AICPA, Ind. Assn. CPAs (Civic Achievement award, 1976), Mich. Assn. CPAs, Fin. Execs. Inst. (Michiana chpt. pres. 1974-75), Nat. Assn. Accts., U.S. Power Squadron. Republican. Lutheran. Club: Elcona Country (pres. 1975). Lodge: Rotary (local pres. 1976-77). Avocations: photography, boating, golf, bowling. Home: 23322 Greenleaf Blvd Elkhart IN 46514-4508

MISER, HUGH JORDAN, systems analyst, operations researcher, consultant; b. Fayetteville, Ark., May 23, 1917; s. Wilson Lee and Nellie (Pyle) M.; m. Josephine Spence Lehmann, June 24, 1944; children: James Spence, Wendel Lee, Andrew Lehmann, Emily Margaret. BA magna cum laude, Vanderbilt U., 1938; MS, Ill. Inst. Tech., 1940; PhD, Ohio State U., 1946. Tchr. math. Ill. Inst. Tech., Chgo., 1938-40, 42-44, Ohio State U., Columbus, 1940-42, 45-46; acting chmn. dept. math. Lawrence Coll., Appleton, Wis., 1944; ops. analyst Hdqrs. 20th Air Force, Washington and Guam, 1945; asst. prof. math. Williams Coll., Williamstown, Mass., 1946-49; ops. analyst Hdqrs. USAF, Washington, 1949-59, dep. asst. ops. analysis, 1951-59, acting asst. for ops. analysis, 1958-59; dir. operational scis. lab. Rsch. Triangle Inst., Durham, N.C., 1959-60; dir. applied sci. div. ops. evaluation group MIT, Cambridge, Mass., 1960-62; asst. to dir. systems planning and rsch. Mitre Corp., Bedford, Mass., 1962-65; v.p. Travelers Rsch. Ctr., Inc., Hartford, Conn., 1965-69; with U. Mass., Amherst, 1969—, prof. indsl. engrng. and ops. rsch., 1969-80, acting head dept. indsl. engrng. and ops. rsch., 1975-76, head dept., 1976-79, prof. emeritus, 1980—; leader craft of systems analysis, exec. editor publs. Internat. Inst. Applied Systems Analysis, Laxenburg, Austria, 1979-82, acting head communications, 1980-81; cons., sec., chief of staff USAF, 1967-68; cons. ops. analysis office hdqrs. USAF, 1968-71; mem. NAS Evaluation Panel for Inst. Applied Tech., Nat. Bur. Standards, 1969-72, Evaluation Panel for Tech. Analysis Div., 1967-69, 72-73, chmn. 1969-72; mem. commerce tech. adv. bd. Panel on Noise Abatement, 1968-71; cons. info. systems programs NSF Office Sci. Info. Svc., 1969-74, Ctr. for the Environment and Man Inc., Hartford, 1970-79, Rensselaer Poly. Inst. of Conn., Hartford, 1970, Am. Acad. Arts and Scis., Cambridge, 1983-85; chmn. rsch. adv. com. Ins. Inst. for Hwy. Safety, Washington, 1967-69; cons., mem. systems and program analysis panel Gen. Acctg. Office, Washington, 1972-76. Co-author: Basic Mathematics for Engineers, 1944, Basic Mathematics for Science and Engineering, 1955; co-editor: Handbook of Systems Analysis, Vol. 1, 1985, Vol. 2, 1988; editor: Vol. 3, 1995. Moderator First Ch. of Christ, Congl., Farmington, Conn., 1986-88; pres. New World Chamber Ensemble, Inc., Simsbury Conn., 1986-88, 90-92, 93-94. Recipient Arthur S. Flemming award U.S. Jr. C. of C., 1952. Fellow AAAS; mem. Ops. Rsch. Soc. Am. (founding mem. 1952, sec. 1958-61, v.p. 1961-62, pres. 1962-63, rep. to NRC 1967-73, editor Bull. 1959-61, editor Ops. Rsch. 1968-74, George E. Kimball medal 1975), Inst. Mgmt. Scis., Can. Operational Rsch. Soc. (Harold Larnder prize 1990), Am. Math. Soc., Math. Assn. Am., Soc. for Indls. and Applied Math., Inst. Math. Stats., Am. Statis. Assn., Conn. Acad. Sci. and Engrng. (founding mem. 1976), Ops.-Rsch./Mgmt.-Sci. Found. Inc. (pres. 1987-91), Operational Rsch. Soc., Assn. Pub. Policy and Mgmt., Phi Beta Kappa, Sigma Xi. Home and Office: 199 South Rd Farmington CT 06032-2522

MISH, FREDERICK CRITTENDEN, editor; b. Hagerstown, Md., Feb. 11, 1938; s. Joseph Dubbs and Edith Louise (Crittenden) M.; m. Judith Elizabeth Solberg, Mar. 15, 1969; children—Stephen Crittenden, Andrew Dubbs, David Rogneby. BA, Yale U., 1959; MA, U. Minn., 1967, PhD, 1973; LHD (hon.), York Coll., 1995. Instr. English, Severn Sch., Severna Park, Md., 1959-61; chmn. dept. English Severn Sch., 1963-65; teaching assoc. U. Minn., Mpls., 1965-71; asst. editor G & C Merriam Co., Springfield, Mass., 1973-74, assoc. editor, 1974, sr. editor, 1974-75, joint editorial dir, 1975-78; editorial dir. Merriam-Webster Inc., 1978-93, v.p., editor-in-chief, 1993—. Editor-in-chief: The Merriam-Webster Book of Word Histories, 1976, 6,000 Words: A Supplement to Webster's Third, 1976, Webster's School Dictionary, 1980, Webster's Beginning Dictionary, 1980, Webster's Vest Pocket Dictionary, 1981, Webster's Ninth New Collegiate Dictionary, 1983, Merriam Webster's Collegiate Dictionary, 10th Edit., 1993, 9,000 Words: A Supplement to Webster's Third, 1983, 12,000 Words: A Supplement to Webster's Third, 1986, Webster's Intermediate Dictionary, 1986, Webster's Word Histories, 1989, The New Merriam Webster Dictionary, 1989, Addenda Section 1993: A Supplement to Webster's Third, The Merriam-Webster Dictionary, 1994. Advisor Noah Webster Found., 1979—; trustee Davis and Elkins Coll., 1986-95, 96—. With U.S. Army, 1961-63. S. H. Monk teaching fellow, 1971-72. Mem. MLA, Nat. Coun. Tchrs. English (commn. on English lang. 1981-83), Linguistic Soc. Am., Am. Dialect Soc., Am. Name Soc., Dictionary Soc. N.Am. Home: 45 Harwich Rd Longmeadow MA 01106-1207 Office: Merriam Webster Inc 47 Federal St PO Box 281 Springfield MA 01102-0281

MISHELEVICH, DAVID JACOB, medical company executive, consultant; b. Pitts., Jan. 26, 1942; s. Benjamin and Sarah (Bachrach) M.; m. Bonnie Gray McKim, Dec. 6, 1981; 1 child, Cory Jane. BS in Physics, U. Pitts., 1962; MD, Johns Hopkins U., 1966, PhD in Biomed. Engring., 1970. Lic., Md., Tex. Intern in medicine Balt. City Hosps., 1966-67; staff assoc. Nat. Inst. Neurol. Diseases and Stroke, NIH, Bethesda, Md., 1967-69; exec. v.p. Nat. Ednl. Consultants, Balt., 1971-72; prof., dept. chairperson, dir. med. computing resources ctr. U. Tex. Health Sci. Ctr., Dallas, 1972-82; attending physician/sr. attending physician internal med. Dallas County Hosp., Dist. Parkland Meml. Hosp., 1973-82; v.p. computer and software tech. EANTECH, Mountain View, Calif., 1983-84; CEO Garden Gate Software, Cupertino, Calif., 1984-86; dir., then v.p. and gen. mgr. applications and rsch. divsn. IntelliCorp, Inc., Mountain View, 1986-89; v.p. mktg. and sales Viewpoint Engring., Mountain View, 1989-90; v.p. engring. AirWays Med. Techs., Inc., Palo Alto, Calif., 1991-93; dir., then v.p. R&D, chief tech. officer Circadian, Inc., San Jose, Calif., 1993-95, v.p., gen. mgr. AirWays Asthma Ctrs. divsn., 1995-96; CEO Sterling Healthcare Outcomes, Inc., Cupertino, 1996—; pres. Mishelevich Assocs., Dallas, 1982-83, Cupertino, 1990-91; mem. biomed. libr. rev. com. NIH-Nat. Libr. Medicine, 1978-82; cons. in field. Former tech. reviewer IBM Sys. Jour., Jour. of AMA; contbr. numerous articles to profl. jours.; patentee in field. V.p. Dallas chpt. Am. Jewish Congress, 1980-84, Am. Jewish Fund, 1980-81. Fellow Am. Coll. Med. Informatics; mem. AAAS, IEEE and IEEE Computer Soc. (exec. bd. tech. com. on computational medicine 1981-83), Am. Assn. for Artificial Intelligence, Assn. for Computing Machinery (chair Dallas chpt. 1974-75), Am. Med. Informatics Assn., Internat. Tandem Users Group (past pres.), Phi Beta Kappa, Omicron Kappa. Democrat. Jewish. Home and Office: 20902 Garden Gate Dr Cupertino CA 95014

MISHELL, DANIEL R., JR., physician, educator; b. Newark, May 7, 1931; s. Daniel R. and Helen Mishell; m. Carol Goodrich; children: Sandra, Daniel III, Tanya. BA, Stanford U., 1952, MD, 1955. Diplomate Am. Bd. Ob-Gyn. (examiner 1975-95, bd. dirs., dir. subspecialty divsn. reproductive endocrinology 1985-89, pres. 1986-90, chmn. 1990-94). Intern L.A. County Harbor Gen. Hosp., Torrance, 1955-56; resident in ob-gyn. Bellevue Hosp., N.Y.C., 1956-57, UCLA-Harbor Gen. Hosp., Torrance, 1959-63; rsch. fellow Univ. Hosp., Uppsala, Sweden, 1961-62; asst. prof. dept. ob-gyn. Sch. Medicine, UCLA, 1963-68, assoc. prof., 1968-69; prof. U. So. Calif., L.A., 1969—, assoc. chmn. dept., 1972-78, chmn. dept., 1978—. Editor-in-chief Contraception, 1969—; editor Jour. Reproductive Medicine, 1982—, Year Book of Obstetrics and Gynecology, 1987—, Year Book of Infertility, 1989-96; adv. com. Core Jours. in Ob-gyn., 1982—; mem. editl. bd. New Trends in Gynecology and Obstetrics, 19985—. Capt. USAF, 1957-59. Recipient Lester T. Hibbard award U. So. Calif., L.A., 1983, Joseph Bolivar DeLee Humanitarian award Chgo. Lying-In Hosp., 1985, Arthur and Edith Wippman Sci. Rsch. award Planned Parenthood Fedn. Am., 1992, Disting. Scientist award Soc. Gynecologic Investigation, 1994. Mem. Am. Gyn-Ob Soc., Am. Fertility Soc., Am. Coll. Obstetricians and Gynecologists, Am. Fedn. Clin. Rsch., Endocrine Soc., Soc. for Gynecologic Investigation (pres. 1985-86), L.A. Ob-Gyn. Soc. (v.p. 1984-85, pres. 1985-86), Assn. Profs. Gynecology and Obstetrics (exec. coun. 1982-85), Pacific Coast Fertility Soc. (pres. 1973-74), Salerni Collegium, L.A. Athletic Club, Phi Beta Kappa, Alpha Omega Alpha. Avocations: tennis, fishing. Office: U So Calif Dept Ob-Gyn 1240 N Mission Rd Los Angeles CA 90033-1078

MISHKIN, MORTIMER, neuropsychologist; b. Fitchburg, Mass., Dec. 13, 1926; married; 2 children. AB, Dartmouth Coll., 1946; MA, McGill U., Montreal, Can., 1949, PhD, 1951. Asst. in research and physiology and psychiatry Yale U. Med. Sch., New Haven, Conn., 1949-51; research assoc. Inst. of Living, Hartford-Conn. and NYU Bellevue Med. Ctr., N.Y.C., 1951-55; research psychologist, sect. on neuropsychology NIMH, Bethesda, Md., 1955-75, research physiologist, Lab. of Neuropsychology, 1976-78, chief, sect. on cerebral mechanisms, Lab. of Neuropsychology, 1979-80, chief Lab. of Neuropsychology, 1980—, assoc. dir. basic rsch. DIRP, 1994—; part-time instr. psychology Howard U., 1956-58; vis. scientist Nencki Inst. Exptl. Biology, Warsaw, Poland, winter 1958, 68, Tokyo Met. Inst. Neuroscis., summer 1978, Oxford U. Dept. Exptl. Psychology, summer 1979; mem. psychol. scis. panel NIH, 1959-61, exptl. psychology study sect., 1965-69; mem. NIMH Assembly of Scientists Council, 1962-64, 72-74; mem. NIMH Scientist Promotion Rev. Com., 1984-86; mem. adv. com. Cognitive Neurosci. Inst., 1982-86; mem. NIH Fogart Internat. Scholars-in-Residence Adv. Panel, 1985-89; adv. bd. McDonnell-Pew Program Cognitive Neurosci., 1989-94; review com. Brain rsch., Human Frontier Sci. program, 1992-94, chmn. 1993—. Cons. editor Jour. Comparative and Physiol. Psychology, 1963-73, Exptl. Brain Rsch., 1965—, Brain Rsch., 1974-78, Neuropsychologia, 1963, mem. editl. bd., 1963-92; mem. editl. bd. Human Neurobiology, 1981-87, Exptl. Brain Rsch., 1965—, Brain Rsch., 1974-78, Human Neurobiology, 1981-87, Jour. Cognitive Neurosci., 1989—, Jour. NIH Rsch., 1989—, Cerebral Cortex, 1990-95, Advances in Neurobiology, 1990—, Handbook Behavioral Neurology, 1991—, Behavioral and Neural Biology, 1992—; reviewing editors Sci., 1985-93; assoc. editor Neuroreport, 1990—; contbr. numerous articles to profl. jours., also abstracts and book revs. Served to lt. (j.g.) USNR. Fellow AAAS (chair-elect 1990-91, chair 1991-92, past chair 1992-93), Am. Psychol. Assn. (officer, divsn. 6 mem. at large 1964-66, coun. rep. 1967-69, pres. 1968-69); mem. NAS (officer, sect. 52 chmn. 1989-92), Ea. Psychol. Assn., Internat. Brain Research Orgn. (officer, rep.-at-large governing coun. 1993—), Internat. Neuropsychol. Soc., Internat. Neuropsychol. Symposium, Internat. Primatological Soc., Internat. Soc. Neuroethology, Soc. Exptl. Psychologists, Soc. Neurosci. (officer, pres.-elect 1985-86, pres. 1986-87, past pres. 1987-88), Sigma Xi, Phi Beta Kappa. Achievements includes research in behavioral and cognitive neuroscience in primates. Office: NIMH Lab Neuropsychology Bldg 49 Rm 1B80 49 Convent Dr MSC 4415 Bethesda MD 20892-4415

MISHKIN, PAUL J., lawyer, educator; b. Trenton, N.J., Jan. 1, 1927; s. Mark Mordecai and Bella (Dworetsky) M.; m. Mildred Brofman Westover; 1 child, Jonathan Mills Westover. AB, Columbia U., 1947, JD, 1950; MA (hon.), U. Pa., 1971. Bar: N.Y. State bar 1950, U.S. Supreme Ct. bar 1958. Mem. faculty Law Sch. U. Pa., Phila., 1950-72; prof. law U. Calif., Berkeley, 1972-75, Emanuel S. Heller prof., 1975—; Cons. City of Phila., 1953; reporter study div. jurisdiction between state and fed. cts. Am. Law Inst., 1960-65; mem. faculty Salzburg Seminar in Am. Studies, 1974; Charles Inglis Thompson guest prof. U. Colo., 1975; John Randolph Tucker lectr., 1978, Owen J. Roberts Meml. lectr., 1982; vis. fellow Wolfson Coll., Cambridge U., 1984; vis. prof. Duke U. Law Sch., 1989. Author: (with Morris) On Law in Courts, 1965, (with others) Federal Courts and the Federal System, 2d edit, 1973, 3d edit, 1988; contbr. articles to profl. jours. Trustee Jewish Publ. Soc. Am., 1966-75; mem. permanent com. Oliver Wendell Holmes Devise, 1979-87. With USNR 1945-46. Rockefeller Found. rsch. grantee, 1956; Center for Advanced Study in Behavioral Scis. fellow, 1964-65; recipient Russell Prize for Excellence in Teaching, 1996. Fellow Am. Acad. Arts Scis., Am. Bar Found.; mem. Am. Law Inst., Order of Coif, Phi Beta Kappa. Home: 91 Stonewall Rd Berkeley CA 94705-1414 Office: U Calif Sch Law Boalt Hall Berkeley CA 94720

MISHLER, CLIFFORD LESLIE, publisher; b. Vandalia, Mich., Aug. 11, 1939; s. Nelson Howard and Lily Mae (Young) M.; m. Sandra Rae Knutson, Dec. 21, 1963 (dec. July 8, 1972); m. Sylvia M. Leer, Feb. 27, 1976; children: Sheila, Sharon, Susan. Student, Northwestern U., 1957-58. Author, pub. ann. edits. Ann. Studies U.S. and Can. Commemorative Medals and Tokens, 1958-63; assoc. editor Numismatic News, Krause Publs., Iola, Wis., 1963-64; editor Numismatic News, Krause Publs., 1964-66, numismatic editor all publs., 1966-75, exec. v.p., pub. all numismatic publs., 1975-78, exec. v.p., pub. all products, 1978-88, sr. v.p., pub. all Numismatic products, 1988-89, sr. v.p. ops., 1989-90; pres. Krause Publs., Iola, Wis., 1991—; bd. dirs. First State Bank Iola, 1972-83, Scandinavia Telephone Co., 1981—; ex-officio dir. Iola Old Car Show, Inc., 1985—; mem. coins and medals adv. panel Am. Revolution Bicentennial Commn., 1970-75; mem. ann. assay commn. U.S. Mint, 1973. Co-author: Standard Catalog of World Coins, ann. 1972—; contbr. articles New Book Knowledge, ann. 1969-81. Bd. dirs. William R. Higgins, Jr. Found., 1991—. Fellow Am. Numismatic Soc. (life mem.); mem. Am. Numismatic Assn. (life mem., medal of merit 1983, Farran Zerbe meml. disting svc. award 1984, Glen Smedley meml. dedicated svcs. award 1991), Token and Medal Soc. (life mem., pres. 1976-78, editor jour. 1964-68, disting. svc. award 1966, 80), Numismatists Wis. (life mem., pres. 1974-76, meritorious svc. award 1972), Soc. Internat. Numismatics (award of excellence 1981), Blue Ridge Numismatic Assn. (life mem., hall of fame 1994), Tex. Numismatic Assn. (life mem., hall of fame 1993), Ind. State Numismatic Assn. (life mem., founders award 1993), Ctrl. States Numismatic Soc. (life mem., medal of merit 1984), Iola Lions (Melvin Jones fellow 1996). Home: 100 Island Dr Iola WI 54945-9485 Office: 700 E State St Iola WI 54990-0001

MISHLER, JACOB, federal judge; b. N.Y.C., Apr. 20, 1911; s. Abraham and Rebecca M.; m. Lola Mishler, Sept. 1, 1936; m. Helen Mishler, Aug. 26, 1970; children: Alan, Susan Lubitz; stepchildren: Bruce Shillet, Gail Shillet Unger. Degree, NYU, 1931, JD, 1933. Pvt. practice L.I. City, N.Y., 1934-50; ptnr. Mishler & Wohl, 1950-59, 60; judge N.Y. State Supreme Ct., 1959; sr. judge U.S. Dist. Ct. (ea. dist.), Uniondale, N.Y., 1961—; mem. U.S. Jud. Conf., Dist. Judge Rep., 2nd cir., 1974-77. Office: US Dist Ct LI Courthouse Rm 311 2 Uniondale Ave Uniondale NY 11553-1259*

MISHLER, JOHN MILTON (YOCHANAN MENASHSHEH BEN SHAUL), natural sciences educator, academic administrator; b. Cairo, Ill., Sept. 25, 1946; s. John Milton and Mary Jane (Woodbury) M.; m. Mary Therese Stember, Apr. 15, 1972 (div. Nov. 1981); m. Sigrid Ruth Elizabeth Fischer, Dec. 15, 1981; 1 child, Joshua Evan. AA with honors, Orange Coast Coll., Costa Mesa, Calif., 1966; AB in Molecular Biology, U. Calif., San Diego, 1969, ScM in Engring. Scis., 1971; DPhil in Immunohematology, St. John's Coll., Oxford U., 1978. Cert. community coll. instr., Calif. Clin. coord. McGaw Labs., Costa Mesa, 1972-78; rsch. fellow Royal Postgrad. Med. Sch., Eng., 1977-78, Med. U., Cologne, Fed. Republic Germany, 1978-80; br. chief Nat. Heart, Lung and Blood Inst. NIH, Bethesda, Md., 1980-82; prof. med., basic life scis. and pharmacol. U. Mo., Kansas City, 1983-89, asst. vice chancellor, 1983-85, dir. div. basic med. scis., 1985-86, assoc. vice chancellor, 1985-89; prof. nat. scis. U. Md. Ea. Shore, Princess Anne, 1989-94, dean grad. studies and rsch., 1989-91; prof. biology Delaware Valley Coll. Sci. and Agrl., Doylestown, Pa., 1994—, dean of Coll., 1994-95; frequent nat. and internat. lectr.; chmn. 13 nat. and internat. meeting sects. Author: Pharmacology of Hydroxyethyl Starch. Use in Therapy and Blood Banking, 1982; editor or co-editor 6 sci. monographs; mem. editorial rev. bd. Jour. Soc. Rsch. Adminstrs., 1987-91; book rev. editor Grants Mag., 1987-89; contbr. more than 100 articles to profl. jours. Bd. dirs. Ctr. for Bus. Innovation, Inc., 1987, Bucks Assn. for Retarded Citizens, 1995-96. Sr. rsch. fellow Alexander von Humboldt Foun. (West Germany), 1978-80; recipient Outstanding Adminstrn. Svc. award U. Mo., Kansas City, 1987, Excellence award Soc. Rsch. Adminstrn., 1989, Cert. Appreciation, 1991. Fellow Internat. Soc. Haematology, Royal Coll. Pathologists; mem. Am. Soc. Hematology, German Soc. Hematology, Nat. Coun. Univ. Rsch. Adminstrn., Nat. Assn. State Univs. and Land-Grant Colls. (mem. exec. com. coun. on rsch. policy and grad. edn. 1990-91), Coun. Grad. Schs., N.Y. Acad. Scis., Sigma Xi. Jewish. Avocations: reading, abstract art painting, writing, music. Home: 475 North Street Apt 6-F Doylestown PA 18901 Office: Delaware Valley Coll 700 E Butler Ave Doylestown PA 18901-2607

MISHLER, WILLIAM, II, political science educator; b. Miami, Fla., Oct. 14, 1947; s. William Thomas Earle and Marie Katheryn (Schmitz) M.; m. Mary Catherine Tanner, Aug. 5, 1972. BA, Stetson U., 1969; MA, Duke U., 1972, PhD, 1973. Asst. prof. Duke U., Durham, N.C., 1972-78; assoc. prof. SUNY, Buffalo, 1978-82, prof., chmn., 1984-86; dir. polit. sci. program NSF, Washington, 1982-84; prof., chmn. U. S.C., Columbia, 1986-89, prof., 1989-97, James F. and Maude B. Byrnes prof. govt., 1995-97; prof., head dept. polit. sci. U. Ariz., Tucson, 1997—; vis. prof. U. Strathclyde, Glasgow, Scotland, 1976-77; vis. scientist, dir. polit. sci. program NSF, Washington, 1990-91. Author: Influence in Parliament, Political Participation in Canada, Representative Democracy in the Canadian Provinces, Resurgence of Conservatism, Controversies in Political Economy; mem. editorial bds. Jour. Politics, 1982-88, Legis. Studies Quar., 1988-91. Capt. U.S. Army, 1972. Mem. Am. Polit. Sci. Assn., So. Polit. Sci. Assn., Midwest Polit. Sci. Assn., Can. Polit. Sci. Assn., Internat. Studies Assn., Assn. Can. Studies (U.S. chpt.). Office: U Ariz Dept Polit Sci Tucson AZ 85721

MISIEK, DALE JOSEPH, oral and maxillofacial surgeon; b. Hartford, Conn., Dec. 10, 1952; s. Joseph John and Jadwiga Magdelena (Wojtowicz) M.; m. Patricia Ann Munson, June 28, 1975; children: Matthew Bryan, Stacy Lynne, Michael Stephen. BA magna cum laude, U. Conn., Storrs, 1974; DMD, U. Conn., Farmington, 1978; cert. advanced tng. oral and maxillofacial surgery, La. State U., 1982. Diplomate Am. Bd. Oral and Maxillofacial Surgery. Resident oral surgery Charity Hosp. of La., New Orleans, 1978-82, mem. clin. surgery com., 1984-86, mem. surgery com., 1986—, mem. credentials com., 1988—; asst. prof. dept. oral and maxillofacial surgery Sch. Dentistry, La. State U., New Orleans, 1984-87, assoc. prof., 1987-94; prof. dept. oral and maxillofacial surgery Sch. Dentistry La. State U., New Orleans, 1994—; also mem. various coms. Sch. Dentistry, La. State U., New Orleans; practice dentistry specializing in oral surgery New Orleans, 1982-84; mem. staff Ear, Eye, Nose and Throat Hosp., New Orleans, 1982—, chmn. dental dept., also mem. exec. com., credentials com. and instrument com., 1983-84; mem. staff East Jefferson Gen. Hosp., Metairie, 1982, chmn. dental dept., 1990-94, med. records com., 1983-85, credentials com., 1994—; mem. staff Univ. Hosp., New Orleans, 1982—; courtesy staff Children's Hosp., New Orleans, 1982—, Mercy Hosp., New Orleans, 1982—, So. Bapt. Hosp., New Orleans, 1983—, Our Lady of the Lake Regional Med. Ctr., Baton Rouge, 1985, Kenner (La.) Regional Med. Ctr., 1986—, Dr.'s Hosp., Metairie, 1986—; cons. VA Med. Ctr., New Orleans, 1984—; lectr. in field. Contbr. articles and abstracts to profl. jours. Recipient C.V. Mosby Book award. Fellow Am. Assn. Oral and Maxillofacial Surgeons (mem. spl. com. for devel. stds. and criteria for care 1986—, spl. com. on oral and maxillofacial surgery self-assessment program 1990), Am. Coll. Oral and Maxillofacial Surgeons; mem. ADA (cons. commn. on dental accreditation 1986—), Am. Bd. Oral and Maxillofacial Surgery (adv. com. 1990-95), La. Dental Assn., New Orleans Dental Assn. (mem. sci. program com. 1983-84), La. Soc. Oral and Maxillofacial Surgeons (mem. anesthesia com. 1983-85, mem. advanced cardiac life support com. 1986-88, sec./treas. 1991-95, v.p. 1996—), Internat. Assn. Oral and Maxillofacial Surgery, Acad. Osseointegration, Internat. Assn. Dental Rsch., Am. Assn. Dental Rsch., Orleans Parish Med. Soc., Am. Heart Assn. (instr.), Phi Beta Kappa, Phi Kappa Phi, Omicron Kappa Upsilon. Republican. Roman Catholic. Avocations: baseball, weightlifting, fishing. Office: La State U Med Ctr Sch Dentistry Dept Oral Surgery 1100 Florida Ave # 220 New Orleans LA 70119-2714

MISIOREK, MARY MADELYN, social worker; b. Mt. Holly, N.J., Sept. 7, 1950; d. Frank and Anna (Dudek) M. BA, Trenton (N.J.) State Coll., 1972; MSW, Rutgers U., 1993. Social worker State of N.J., Pemberton, 1973-79; psychiat./med. social worker Rancocas Hosp., Willingboro, N.J., 1980-95; clin. mgr. The Counseling Program, Marlton, N.J., 1995—. Mem. NASW, LCSW, ACSW, Alpha Beta Mu. Office: The Counseling Program Clinical Dept Marlton NJ 08053

MISKIEWICZ, SUSANNE PIATEK, elementary education educator; b. Elizabeth, N.J., Nov. 19, 1947; d. Edward Walter and Charlotte Teresa (Kardel) Piatek; m. Randall Lee Grover; 1 child, Michelle Lee Grover Domenico; m. Raymond Richard Miskiewicz; children: Lisa Marie, Raymond Edward. BA, Newark State Coll., 1972; MA, Kean Coll., 1976. Cert. prin./supr., supr., reading specialist, elem. edn., nursery sch., N.J. Tchr. Linden (N.J.) Bd. Edn., 1973-79, 87-90; tchr. Linden Adult Sch., 1981-88, dir., 1988-90; tchr. Roselle (N.J.) Bd. Edn., 1991; tchr. New Providence (N.J.) Bd. Edn., 1991-96, dept. head lang. arts K-12, 1996—; cons., trainer N.J. Dept. Edn., Trenton, 1987-90; cons. Am. Guidance Svc., Minn., 1979—; mem. bd. edn. Linden, 1991-94, v.p., 1993-94; presenter NJEA Conv., 1976, Edn. Fair, Washington, 1973. Reviewer: Prep, Keymath, You and Your Small Wonder, Books 1 and 2, 1979-88. sec., treas., v.p. PTA, Linden, 1984-92; mem., v.p. Gen. Pulaski Com., Linden, 1985—; mem., sec., v.p., treas. Linden Summer Theatre, 1978-85; trustee St. Teresa' Ch., Linden, 1970-73; advisor St. Elizabeth's Ch. Altar Server Soc., 1994—; leader Girl Scouts Am., Linden, 1987-91. Mem. ASCD, N.J. ASCD, Internat. Reading Assn., N.J. Reading Assn., N.J. Edn. Assn., NEA, New Providence Edn. Assn. (pres. 1995—). Roman Catholic. Avocations: reading, crafts, golf. Home: 43 Palisade Rd Linden NJ 07036-3828 Office: New Providence Bd Edn 35 Pioneer Dr New Providence NJ 07974-1515

MISKOWSKI, LEE R., retired automobile executive; b. Stevens Point, Wis., Mar. 27, 1932; s. Paul P. and Marie Grace (Glazer) M.; m. Billie Poulson, 1963; children: Christine, Katherine. BBA, U. Wis., 1954, MBA, 1957. V.p. Ford of Europe Ford Motor Co., Cologne, Fed. Republic Germany, 1977-80; gen. mktg. mgr. Ford div. Ford Motor Co., Dearborn, Mich., 1980-83, v.p., gen. mgr. parts and svc. div., 1989-91, v.p., gen. mgr. Lincoln-Mercury div., 1991-94; ret. Ford Motor Co., 1994; bd. dirs. Autocraft, Inc., Adco Techs., Inc., Lear Corps., Bradford Equities. Trustee Hospice of S.E. Mich., Detroit, 1988-94, chmn.; chmn. Hospice of Mich., 1996; chmn. bd. dirs. Mich. Parkinson Found., Detroit, 1992-94. With U.S. Army, 1954-56. Mem. Oakland Hills Country Club. Roman Catholic. Avocations: tennis, snow skiing, reading, extensive travel.

MISKUS, MICHAEL ANTHONY, electrical engineer, consultant; b. East Chicago, Ind., Dec. 10, 1950; s. Paul and Josephine Miskus; BS, Purdue U., 1972; AAS in Elec. Engring. Tech., Purdue U., Indpls., 1972, MA in Orgnl. Mgmt., U Phoenix, 1996, postgrad., 1997; cert. mgmt. Ind. U., 1972, Ind. Central Coll., 1974; MA in Orgnl. Mgmt. U. Phoenix, 1996; postgrad. Columbia U. Cert. plant engr.; registered environ. assessor REA, Calif. Service engr. Reliance Electric & Engring. Co., Hammond, Ind., 1972-73; maintenance supr., maintenance mgr. Diamond Chain Co./AMSTED Industries, Indpls., 1973-76; primary and facilities elec. engr. Johnson & Johnson Baby Products Co., Park Forest South, Ill., 1976-81; prin. Miskus Cons., indsl./comml. elec. cons., 1979—; plant and facilities engring. mgr. Sherwin Williams Co., Chgo. Emulsion Plant, Chgo., 1981-85; with Miscon Assocs., Riverside, Calif., 1985—; acting dir. plant and facilities engring. Bourns Inc., 1982-90; facility mgr. Cardiovascular Devices Inc., 3M Healthcare, 1990—; mgr. Metrology and Corp. Metrology Lab & ISO 9000, 3M, St. Paul; facility mgr. Press Enterprise, Riverside, 1997—; instr., lectr. EET program Moraine Valley C.C., Palos Hills, Ill., 1979; instr. cert. program plant engring. U. Calif.; lectr. energy engring., bldg. automation systems Prairie State Coll., Chicago Heights, Ill., 1980—; mem. adj. faculty, faculty adv. bd. Orange Coast Coll., Costa Mesa, Calif.; commr., chmn. Riverside Energy Commn., 1988—; mem. Elec. Industry Evaluation Panel. Mem. faculty adv. bd. Moraine Valley C.C., 1980—. Mem. IEEE, Am. Inst. Plant Engrs. (pres. Pomona chpt. 1989—, chmn. western region VI membership, chmn. nat. coun. stds. labs. region II Twin Cities sect. 1995—), Assn. Facility Engrs. (pres. chpt. III 1997—), Assn. Energy Engrs., Assn. Energy Engrs. (sr., So. Calif. chpt.), Assn. Profl. Energy Mgrs. (bd. dirs. Orange County chpt. 1992), Illuminating Engring. Soc. N.Am., Internat. Platform Assn., 3M Global plant engring. steering com., ops. subcom.; Riverside C. of C. Club: Purdue Alumni Org. of L.A. (v.p. Inland chpt.), Perdue Club L.A. (v.p. Inland Empire sect.). Office: PO Box 55525 Riverside CA 92517-0525

MISLOW, KURT MARTIN, chemist, educator; b. Berlin, Germany, June 5, 1923; came to U.S., 1940, naturalized, 1946; s. Max and Ida (Bingen) M.; m. Jacqueline Ford, 1966; children: Christopher, John. B.S., Tulane U., 1944, D.Sc. (hon.), 1975; Ph.D., Calif. Inst. Tech., 1947; D. honoris causa, Free U., Brussels, 1974, Uppsala U., 1977; Düsseldorf U., 1994. Instr. NYU, 1947-51, asst. prof., 1951-56, asso. prof., 1956-60, prof., 1960-64; Hugh Stott Taylor prof. chemistry Princeton, 1964-88, chmn. dept. chemistry, 1968-74, prof. emeritus, 1988—; vis. prof. Stanford U., 1960, Calif. Inst. Tech., 1994; M.S. Kharasch vis. prof. U. Chgo., 1989; Univ. lectr. U. London, 1965; J.A. McRae Meml. lectr. Queen's U., 1967; H.A. Iddles lectr. U. N.H., 1972; Solvay lectr. and medalist Free U. Brussels, 1972; E.C. Lee lectr. U. Chgo.; A.A. Vernon lectr. Northeastern U., 1976; PPG lectr. Ohio U., 1977; J. Musher Meml. lectr. Hebrew U. Jerusalem, 1978; North Country lectr., 1978; Honor lectr. Ariz. State U., 1981; E. Ritchie meml. lectr. Sydney U.,

1983; Fuson lectr. U. Nev., 1983; Research Scholar lectr. Drew U., 1983; McGregory lectr. Colgate U., 1984; Sandia lectr. U. Alta., 1984; Purves lectr. McGill U., 1985; Arnold lectr. So. Ill. U., 1985; Bergmann lectr. Yale U., 1986; H.C. Brown lectr. Purdue U., 1988; Irvine lectr. U. St. Andrews, 1988; Eyring lectr. Ariz. State U., 1989; Disting. Scientist lectr. Bard Coll., 1991; Syntex Disting. lectr. Colo. State U., 1991; Disting. scientist lectr. Bard Coll., 1991; J.W.T. Spinks lectr. U. Saskatchewan, 1992; Bristol-Myers-Squibb disting. lectr. Syracuse U., 1992; Churchill fellow Cambridge U., 1974-75; mem. adv. panel chemistry NSF, 1963-66; mem. panel medical and organic chemistry NIH, 1963-66. Author: Introduction to Stereochemistry, 1965; also numerous articles; bd. editors: Jour. Organic Chemistry, 1965-70; mem. editl. adv. bd. Monatshefte für Chemie, Topics in Stereochemistry, Accounts of Chem. Rsch., Chem. and Engring. News, Bull des Sociétés Chimiques Belges, Symmetry, Jour. Math. Chemistry. Recipient Prelog medal, ETH Zurich, 1986, W.H. Nichols medal, 1987, Sci. Achievement award medal CCNY, 1988, Disting. Alumni award Calif. Inst. Tech., 1990, Chirality medal, 1993, Arthur C. Cope Scholar award Am. Chem. Soc. 1995; Guggenheim fellow, 1957-58, 74-75, Alfred P. Sloan fellow, 1959-63, Sherman Fairchild disting. scholar Calif. Inst. Tech., 1990, 91, 94. Fellow AAAS, Am. Acad. Arts and Scis.; mem. Nat. Acad. Scis., Am. Chem. Soc. (James Flack Norris award 1975), Chem. Soc. London, AAUP, Phi Beta Kappa, Sigma Xi, Phi Lambda Upsilon.

MISNER, CHARLES WILLIAM, physics educator; b. Jackson, Mich., June 13, 1932; s. Francis deSales and Madge B. (Mee) M.; m. Susanne Elisabeth Kemp, June 13, 1959; children: Benedicte Elisabeth, Francis Frithjof, Timothy Charles, Christopher Kemp. B.S., U. Notre Dame, 1952; M.A., Princeton U., 1954, Ph.D., 1957. Instr. Princeton U., (N.J.), 1956-59, asst. prof., 1959-63; assoc. prof. physics U. Md., College Park, 1963-66, prof., 1966—; vis. fellow Inst. for Theoretical Physics, U. Calif., Santa Barbara, 1980-81, All Souls Coll., Oxford, Eng., 1973; vis. faculty Calif. Inst. Tech., 1972, Princeton U., 1969. Author: (with Wheeler and Thorne) Gravitation, 1973, (with Patrick J.Cooney) Spreadsheet Physics, 1991; contbr. articles to profl. jours. Recipient Sci. Centennial award U. Notre Dame, 1965, Dannie Heineman prize (with R. Arnowitt and S. Deser) for math. physics Am. Phys. Soc., 1994; NSF sr. postdoctoral fellow, 1966-67; Guggenheim fellow, 1972-73; Einstein Centennial lectr., 1979. Fellow Am. Phys. Soc., Royal Astron. Soc., AAAS; mem. Philosophy of Sci. Assn., Am. Math. Soc. Fedn. Am. Scientists. Democrat. Roman Catholic. Office: U Md Dept Physics College Park MD 20742-4111

MISNER, CHARLOTTE BLANCHE RUCKMAN, community organization administrator; b. Gifford, Idaho, Aug. 30, 1937; d. Richard Steele and Arizona (Hill) Ruckman; m. G. Arthur Misner, Jr., Aug. 29, 1959; children: Michelle, Mary, Jennifer. BS in Psychology, U. Idaho, 1959. Vol. numerous orgns. India, Mexico, The Philippines, 1962-70; sec., v.p., pres., trustee St. Luke's Hosp., Manila, 1970-84; founding mem., 3d v.p., pres. Am. Women's Club of Philippines, 1980-84; exec. dir. Friends of Oakland (Calif.) Parks and Recreation, 1986-92, 1992—. Active Lincoln Child Ctr., Oakland, 1984—. Recipient Vol. Svc. award Women's Bd. St. Luke's Hosp., 1977, Mid. Sch. Vol. award Internat. Sch.-Manila, 1980. Me. Alpha Gamma Delta (alumnae treas., pres. East Bay 1985-89, province dir. alumnae 1989—), Cum Laude Soc. (hon.). Home: 481 Ellita Ave Oakland CA 94610-4808 Office: Friends of Oakland Parks & Recreation 1520 Lakeside Dr Oakland CA 94612-4521

MISRA, JAYADEV, computer science educator; b. Cuttack, Orissa, India, Oct. 17, 1947; s. Sashibhusan and Shanty (Kar) M.; m. Mamata Das, Nov. 30, 1972; children: Amitav, Anuj. B Tech, Indian Inst. Tech., Kanpur, 1969; PhD, Johns Hopkins U., 1972. Staff scientist IBM, Gaithersburg, Md., 1973-74; from asst. prof. to prof. computer sci. U. Tex., Austin, 1974—, Regents chair in computer sci., 1992—; vis. prof. Stanford (Calif.) U., 1983-84; cons. on software and hardware design. Contbr. articles to profl. jours. Guggenheim fellow, 1988-89. Fellow IEEE, Assn. Computing Machinery (Samuel N. Alexander Meml. award 1970). Office: Univ Tex Dept Computer Sci Austin TX 78712-1188

MISRA, RAGHUNATH PRASAD, physician, educator; b. Calcutta, W. Bengal, India, Feb. 1, 1928; came to U.S., 1964; s. Guru Prasad and Anandi M.; m. Therese Rettenmund, Sept. 13, 1963; children: Sima, Joya, Maya, Tara. BSc with honors, Calcutta U., 1948; MBBS, Med. Coll., Calcutta, 1953; PhD, McGill U., Montreal, Que., 1965. Diplomate Am. Bd. Anatomical and Clin. Pathology. Asst. prof., dir. kidney lab. U. Louisville Sch. Medicine, 1964-68; asso. investigator and dir. kidney lab Mt. Sinai Hosp., Cleve., 1968-73; asst. prof. Case Western Reserve Med. Sch., Cleve., 1973-76; asst. prof., dir. kidney lab. La. State U., Sch. Medicine, Shreveport, 1976-80, assoc. prof., 1980-86; prof. La. State U., Sch. of Medicine, Shreveport, 1986—, dir. Ocular Pathology Lab., 1988—; cons. VA Med. Ctr., Shreveport, 1977—, EA Conway Meml. Hosp., Monroe, La., 1980—. Author: Atlas of Skin Biopsy, 1983. Pres. India Assn. of Shreveport, 1979, 81. Recipient Tallisman Fellowship, Mt. Sinai Hosp., 1970-73. Fellow Am. Coll. Pathologists, Am. Soc. Clin. Pathologists, Am. Coll. of Internat. Physicians, U. Calcutta Med. Alumni Assn. Am. (pres. 1992-93), Sigma Xi (pres. 1987-89). Democrat. Hindu. Avocations: photography, travel. Office: La State U Sch Medicine 1501 Kings Hwy Shreveport LA 71103-4228

MISRA, RAJ PRATAP, engineering educator, electrical engineer; b. Chhaperpur, India, Dec. 23, 1919; came to U.S., 1939; SB, MIT, 1941; MEE, Cornell U., 1945, PhD in Elec. Engring. & Indsl. Mgmt., 1955. Gen. mgr., chief engr. Hamara Radio & Gen. Industries Ltd., Delhi, India, 1947-50; instr. elec. engring. Cornell U., Ithaca, N.Y., 1950-52; mgr. reliability and high frequency Philco Corp., Lansdale, Pa., 1952-58; mgr. reliability rsch. and devel. Tex. Instruments, Dallas, 1958-62; prof. reliability N.J. Inst. Tech., Newark, 1962-90; disting. prof emeritus; cons. Tex. Instruments, 1962-93, v.p. cons. Soletron Inc., N.Y., Fla., 1966-69, Kertron, Reriera Beach, Fla., 1969-80; cons. reliability Astro Electronics Divsn. Westinghouse, Calif., 1962-65, Autonetics, Calif., 1965-66; vis. prof. U.S. Acad. Sci. to Romanian Acad., 1988-89, vis. prof., Indian Inst. of Tech., New Dehli, 1990, 93,. Fulbright scholar; Fulbright fellow Coun. Internat. Exch. Scholars, 1991-92. Fellow Indian Assn. Engrs.; mem. IEEE (chmn. reliability group 1965-68), ASTE (chmn. ref. planar diode task force 1955-59), Sigma Xi. Home: 1 Decamp Court West Caldwell NJ 07006 Office: NJIT Ctr for Reliability Rsch 323 Martin Luther KingJr Blvd Newark NJ 07102

MISRACH, RICHARD LAURENCE, photographer; b. L.A., July 11, 1949; s. Robert Laskin and Lucille (Gardner) M.; m. Debra Bloomfield, Jan. 18, 1981 (div. 1987); 1 son, Jacob Luke; m. Myriam Weisang, Apr. 17, 1989. A.B. in Psychology, U. Calif., Berkeley, 1971. Instr. Assoc. Students Studio, U. Calif., Berkeley, 1971-77; vis. lectr. U. Calif.-Berkeley, 1982; lectr. U. Calif.-Santa Barbara, 1984; juror Nat. Endowment Arts, 1986, Whitney Biennial, 1991. Exhbns. include Musée d'Art Moderne, Paris, 1979, Mus. Modern Art, N.Y.C., 1978, Whitney Mus. Am. Art, N.Y.C., 1981, Grapestake Gallery, San Francisco, 1979, 81, Young-Hoffman Gallery, Chgo., 1980, Oakland Mus., 1982, 87, San Francisco Mus. Modern Art, 1983, Centre Georges Pompidou, Paris, 1983, L.A. County Mus. Art, 1984, Fraenkel Gallery, San Francsico, 1985, 89, 91, 95, Min Gallery, Tokyo, 1975-87, Univ. Art Mus., Berkeley, Curt Marcus Gallery, 1995, 96, James Danziger Gallery, 1995, Melbourne Internat. Festival, Australia, 1995, numerous others; one person exhbns. at Art Inst. Chgo., 1988, Milw. Art Mus., 1988, Carpenter Ctr., Harvard U., 1988, Fotomanm, Inc., N.Y., 1989, 91, Photographers Gallery, 1990, Parco Gallery, Tokyo, 1990, Arles Festival, France, 1990, Jan Kesner Gallery, 1990, 91, 94, Houston Mus. Fine Arts, 1996, Ctr. Creative Photography, Tucson, 1996, Mus. Contemporary Art, Chgo., 1997; art commn. cover Time mag., July 4, 1988; books include Telegraph 3 A.M., 1974, Grapestake Gallery, 1979, (A Photographic Book), 1979, Hawaii protfolio, 1980, Graecism dye-transfer portfolio, 1982, Desert Cantos, 1987, (Internat. Ctr. of Photography award 1988), Bravo 20: The Bombing of the americna West, 1990 (Pen Ctr. U.S. A. West award for nonfiction 1991), Houston Ctr. for Photography, 1985, Light Gallery, N.Y.C., 1985, Richard Misrach, Minn. Gallery, 1988, Violent Legacies, Aperture, 1992, Crimes and Splendors, 1996. Guggenheim fellow, 1978; Ferguson grantee, 1976; NEA grantee, 1973, 77, 84, 92; AT&T commn., 1979; Eureka fellow, 1991; NEA fellow, 1992-93; recipient Koret Israel prize, 1992. *Photographs are the shadows of reality much like dreams. On the one hand, they appear to literally transcribe the real world, while on the other, they defy our linear concept of time and meaning. Because the primary illusion of photography is fact, it is the most powerful art medium of our time.*

MISS, ROBERT EDWARD, fundraiser; b. Frederick, Md., Oct. 14, 1937; s. Robert Edward Sr. and Anna Theresa (Pazdersky) M.; m. Lee Ann Menendez Devine, Nov. 23, 1964 (div. Feb. 1985); children: Stephen Patrick, David Edward, Sarah Ann; m. Judith F. Schwartz Millman, May 22, 1993. AB, Fordham U., 1963; MA, U. N.C., 1973. Asst. dir. pub. affairs Fordham U., Bronx, N.Y., 1963-65; editor Coun. for Advancement and Support of Edn., Washington, 1965-69; network dir. U. N.C.-TV, Chapel Hill, 1969-79; v.p. City Suburban Workshop, N.Y.C., 1979-81; dir. mktg. comm. Lighthouse, Inc., N.Y.C., 1981-86; ptnr. Mktg. Comm. Policy Group, N.Y.C.-various, 1986-89; v.p. Heartshare Human Svcs., Bklyn., 1989-95; sr. acct. exec. Semple & Bixel, Inc., Nutley, N.J., 1996-97; prin. Resource Devel. Coun., Dobbs Ferry, N.Y., 1997—. Author, editor: Teacher's Resources for ETV, 1973, Corp. Strategy for Issues of Aging, 1988; author of poems. Recipient Gilbert Poetry prize Women in the Moon Pubs., 1995. Mem. Nat. Soc. Fundraising Execs., Acad. Am. Poets, Westchester Assn. Devel. Officers. Democrat. Roman Catholic. Avocations: poetry writing, film/video producing, road racing. Home and Office: 37 Round Hill Rd Dobbs Ferry NY 10522

MISSAN, RICHARD SHERMAN, lawyer; b. New Haven, Oct. 5, 1933; s. Albert and Hannah (Hochberg) M.; m. Aileen Louise; children: Hilary, Andrew, Wendy. B.A., Yale U., 1955, J.D., 1958. Bar: N.Y. 1959, U.S. Dist. Ct. (so. and ea. dists.) N.Y. 1979, U.S. Ct. Appeals (2d cir.) N.Y. 1993. Assoc. Kaye, Scholer, Fierman, Hays & Handler, N.Y.C., 1962-67; ptnr. Schoenfeld & Jacobs, N.Y.C., 1968-78, Walsh & Frisch, N.Y.C., 1979-80, Gersten, Savage & Kaplowitz, N.Y.C., 1980-87, v.p., gen. counsel, Avis, Inc., 1987-88; pvt. practice, N.Y.C., 1988—; spl. prof. law Hofstra U., 1988—; mem. panel of mediators U.S. Dist. Ct. (ea. dist.) N.Y. Revision author: Corporations, New York Practice Guide (Business and Commercial). Mem. ABA, N.Y. State Bar Assn., Fed. Bar Council, Assn. of Bar of City of N.Y. (com. on corrections, chmn. subcom. on legis., com. on juvenile justice, chmn. subcom. on juvenile facilities, past com. corrections, com. on atomic energy, mem. com. on mcpl. affairs, com. on housing and urban devel.), Yale Club.

MISSAR, CHARLES DONALD, librarian; b. Cleve., July 16, 1925; s. Charles Frank and Genevieve Catherine (Buechele) M.; m. Margaret Mary du Fief, Feb. 17, 1962; children: Charles David, Stephen du Fief. Student, Sacred Heart Sem., Detroit, 1943-45, St. Mary's Sem., Cleve., 1945-49; BA, John Carroll U., 1951; MLS, Cath. U. Am., 1960. Referral specialist Libr. of Congress, Washington, 1963-66; ERIC info. specialist U.S. Office Edn., Washington, 1966-72; head Ednl. Reference Ctr. Nat. Inst. Edn., Washington, 1973-78, supervisory libr., 1978-85; sr. libr. U.S. Dept. Edn., 1985-86; sr. editor Computer Scis. Corp. Profl. Svcs. Group, 1986-94, Missar Assocs., Washington, 1994—; agy. rep. Fed. Libr. Com., Washington, 1978-86; ann. lectr. Fed. Libr. Resources Workshop, Catholic U. Am., Washington, 1981-96. Editor: Management of Federally Sponsored Libraries: Case Studies and Analysis, 1995; editor monthly jour. Tech. Abstract Bull., 1958-60; mem. editorial bd. Online Mag., 1977-80. Recipient Superior Svc. Group award U.S. Office Edn., 1968, Superior Performance award Nat. Inst. Edn., 1974, 84; inductee Spl. Libraries Assn. Hall of Fame, 1991. Mem. ALA, D.C. Libr. Assn. (treas. 1972-74), Spl. Librs. Assn. (chmn. edn. divsn. 1980-81, chmn. 1989-90), Am. Soc. Info. Sci. (chmn. info. svcs. for edn. group 1984-86), John Carroll Soc., Cleve. Club, Serra Club (pres. 1992-93, 94-96), Arimathean Club. Roman Catholic. Home: 5617 32nd St NW Washington DC 20015-1622 Office: Missar Assocs 5617 32nd St NW Washington DC 20015-1622

MISSIMER, THOMAS MICHAEL, geologist; b. Lancaster, Pa., Mar. 10, 1950; s. Jacob M. and Lorraine L. (Bilodeau) M.; A.B. in Geology, Franklin and Marshall Coll., 1972; M.S. in Geology, Fla. State U., 1973; PhD in Marine Geology and Geophysics, U. Miami, 1995. Hydrologist, U.S. Geol. Survey, Ft. Myers, Fla., 1973-75; research asso. sedimentology U. Miami, Coral Cables, Fla., 1975-76; pres. Missimer & Assocs., Inc., Cape Coral, Fla., 1976-91; vice chmn. ViroGroup, Inc., 1991-93; pres. Missimer Internat., Inc., 1993—, bd. Fla. Profl. Geologists, 1991—, vice chmn. 1993, chmn. 1994, 95; chmn. tech. adv. com. Govt. Com. for a Substantial South Fla., 1995—, chmn., (1996—). Mem. citizens planning adv. com. Bd. Lee County (Fla.), 1981-82, chmn., 1982-83. Registered profl. geologist, Fla., Ga., Ind., Va. Mem. Geol. Soc. Am., Am. Inst. Profl. Geologists (cert. profl. geol. scientist), Am. Water Resources Assn., Am. Water Works Assn., AAAS, Am. Inst. Hydrology (cert. profl. hydrogeologist), Am. Soc. Groundwater Engrs. and Scientists (cert. hydrogeologist), Fla. Acad. Scis. (chmn. earth and planetary sci. sect. 1973-74, 1995), Southeastern Geol. Soc. Republican. Author Water supply development for membrane water treatment facilities, 1994, Lender's Guide to environmental liability management, 1996; contbr. hydrogeol. and geol. studies of Southeastern U.S. to sci. jours. RecipientBest Paper award, Internat. Desalination Assoc., D.C., World Conf. on Desalination, 1991. Home: 3214 Mcgregor Blvd Fort Myers FL 33901-6723 Office: Missimer Internat Inc College Pkwy Ste 202 Fort Myers FL 33919

MISSIRIOTIS, IRENE, recreational activities director, artist; b. North Charleroi, Pa., Nov. 12, 1938; d. Alexander and Athena (Stirou) M. Diploma in fashion illustration, Art Inst. Pitts., 1960; BS in Psychology-English, writing cert., U. Pitts., 1976. Artist Livingston's, Youngstown, Ohio, 1961-63; layout artist O'Neils, Akron, Ohio, 1963-67; tchr. art Art Inst. Pitts., 1967-73; reporter, typographer, layout artist, illustrator Night Times, Pitts., 1973-76; art coord. Cmty. Human Svcs. Corp., Pitts., 1977-78; recreation leader Pitts. Parks and Recreation Dept., summers 1979-80; program mgr. United Cerebral Palsy Assn., Pitts., 1981; adult day care attendant Hill House Assn., Pitts., 1985-87; therapeutic recreation asst. Angelus Convalescent Ctr., Pitts., 1987-89; activities coord. Canterbury Place, Pitts., 1989-90; activities dir. The Woodwell, Pitts., 1991—; freelance watercolors artist, 1956—; designer brochures, booklets, flyers. Vol. Mondale-Ferraro Presdl. Campaign, Pitts., 1984; activist mem. NOW, 1974—. Mem. Pitts. Assn. for the Arts in Edn. and Therapy, Assn. for Women in Psychology, Nat. Mus. Women in the Arts (charter), Nat. Mus. Am. Indian (charter, cert. of appreciation), Waterford Soc. (charter), World Wildlife Fund, Alpha Sigma Lambda (charter). Democrat. Greek Orthodox. Avocations: singing, cooking, collecting pandas and shells, walking. Home: 4733 Centre Ave Apt 1A Pittsburgh PA 15213

MISTACCO, VICKI E., foreign language educator; b. Bklyn., Nov. 18, 1942; d. Anthony Sebastian and Lucia (Lalli) M. BA, NYU, 1963; MA, Middlebury Coll., 1964; M Philosophy, Yale U., 1968, PhD, 1972. Instr. French, Wellesley Coll., Mass., 1968-72, asst. prof. French, 1972-78, assoc. prof. French, 1978-84, prof. French, 1984—, chmn., 1978-81; mem. nat. adv. bd. Sweet Briar Jr. Yr. in France, Va., 1978—. Contbr. articles to profl. jours. Fulbright fellow, 1963-64; Woodrow Wilson fellow, 1964-65, 1966-67; NEH fellow, 1983-84, 94-95. Mem. MLA, N.E. MLA, Am. Assn. Tchrs. French, Phi Beta Kappa. Democrat. Roman Catholic. Avocations: photography; travel. Office: Wellesley Coll Dept French 106 Central St Wellesley MA 02181-8203

MISTHAL, HOWARD JOSEPH, accountant, lawyer; b. Bklyn., Feb. 16, 1940; s. Max and Evelyn (Glass) M.; m. Angela Marie Giorgio, May 7, 1975; children: Barry Jay, Robin Lyn, Sara Ann. BBA cum laude, CCNY, 1961; LLB cum laude, NYU, 1967, LLM, 1972. CPA, N.Y.; bar: N.Y. 1968. From staff mem. to sr. tax ptnr. David Berdon & Co., LLP, CPAs, N.Y.C., 1961—; dir., chmn. audit and loan com. The Apple Bank for Savs.; lectr. Sch. of Law Summer Continuing Ednl. Program, NYU, 1990-95. Mem. AICPAs (tax sect.), N.Y. State Soc. CPAs, N.Y. State Bar Assn. (trust and estates sect.). Avocations: bicycling, hiking, swimming, travel. Office: David Berdon & Co LLP 415 Madison Ave New York NY 10017-1111

MITBY, NORMAN PETER, college president; b. Cashton, Wis., May 21, 1916; s. Chester M. and Margaret (Murray) M.; m. Luvern J. Jensen, June 15, 1941; children: John C., Margaret N. BS, Whitewater (Wis.) State Coll., 1938; postgrad., U. Wis., 1947-48; MS, Stout State U., 1949. Tchr. high sch., vocat. sch. Cornell, Wis., 1938-41, Antigo, Wis., 1941-46; asst. dir. LaCrosse (Wis.) Vocat. and Adult Schs., 1946-54; dir. vocat. and adult sch. Oshkosh, Wis., 1954-55, Green Bay, Wis., 1955-60, Madison, Wis., 1960-67; dist. dir. tech. and adult edn. dist. Madison Area Tech. Coll., 1967, pres., 1967-88; prof. Stout State U. Grad. Sch., Menomonie, Wis.; mem. adv. council U. Wis. Schs. Edn., Madison and Milw., 1961-64; cons., examiner North Central Assn. Colls. and Secondary Schs., 1970-88; mem. pres.'s adv. com. Assn. Community Coll. Trustees, 1978-79; mem. joint adminstrv. com. on acad. programs U. Wis. Vocat., Tech. and Adult Edn. System, 1985-88. Mem. Community Welfare Council Madison, 1960-63, mem. needs and priorities com., 1964; sponsor Wis. Heart Assn.; chmn. pub. employees div. Cancer Fund drive, 1963; mem. Mayor's Com. for Employment Handicapped, 1964-68, Nat. Adv. Com. on Health Occupations Tng., 1964-68; chmn. gov.'s adv. com. Title I, Higher Edn. Act, 1965-74; mem. adv. council Midwest Community Coll., Leadership Council, 1968-73; mem. Wis. Gov.'s Adv. Council on Vocat. Edn., 1969-74, Wis. Gov.'s Health Planning and Policy Task Force, 1971-73; adv. com. Wis. State Bd. Nursing, 1972-74; mem. Wis. Council Safety, 1960-73; bd. dirs. Madison Civic Music Assn., 1960-88, Oakwood Found. Inc., 1990-97. Recipient Disting. Svc. Alumni award U. Wis.-Whitewater, Spl. award NAACP, 1987, cert. recognition Phi Delta Kappa-U. Wis. chpt., 1987, Rotary Sr. Svc. award, 1992; named to Madison Area Tech. Coll. Athletic Hall of Fame, 1989. Mem. Am. Assn. Community and Jr. Colls. (dir. 1975-78, Leadership award 1988), Am. Vocat. Assn. Merit award Region 3 1988), Wis. Assn. for Vocat. and Adult Edn. (Disting. Svc. award 1988), Wis. Assn. Dirs. Vocat. and Adult Edn. (pres. 1960-61), Sigma Tau Gamma, Epsilon Pi Tau, Delta Pi Epsilon. Clubs: Rotarian, Elk, Nakoma Golf. Home: 4413 Waite Ln Madison WI 53711-2845

MITCH, WILLIAM EVANS, nephrologist; b. Birmingham, Ala., July 22, 1941; s. William Evans and Mary Elizabeth (Ackerman) M.; m. Frances Alexandra Fisher, Aug. 21, 1965; children: Eleanor Baylor, William Armistead. BA, Harvard Coll., 1963; MD, Harvard Med. Sch., 1967. Intern Brigham & Women's Hosp., Boston, 1967-68; resident Brigham & Women's Hosp., 1968-69; clin. assoc. Nat. Inst. Health, Bethesda, Md., 1969-72; resident Johns Hopkins Hosp., Balt., 1972-73, Brigham & Women's Hosp., 1973-74; asst. prof., assoc. prof. Johns Hopkins U. Dept. Pharm., Balt., 1974-78; assoc. prof. medicine Harvard Med. Sch., Boston, 1978-87; prof. medicine Emory U. Sch. Medicine, Atlanta, 1987—; pres. region II Nat. Kidney Found., 1990-92; study sect. NIH, 1988-92. Editor: The Progressive Nature of Renal Disease, 1986, 2d edit., 1992, Nutrition and the Kidney, 1988, 2d edit., 1993. With USPHS, 1969-72. Grantee NIH, 1979—. Mem. Am. Soc. Clin. Investigation, Assn. Am. Physicians, Internat. Soc. Nephrology (treas. 1997—). Office: Emory U Sch Medicine 1364 Clifton Rd NE Atlanta GA 30322-1059

MITCHAM, JULIUS JEROME, accountant; b. Pine Bluff, Ark., Jan. 2, 1941; s. James Vernon and Bertha Lee (Robertson) M.; m. Janet Claire Berry, Mar. 31, 1970 (div. Sept. 1981); m. Marsha Lee Henderson, Oct. 22, 1983; 1 child, Timothy John. BBA, U. Cen. Ark., 1971. CPA, Ark.; cert. healthcare fin. mgr. Br. mgr. Comml. Nat. Bank, Little Rock, 1961-66; auditor, acctg. supr. Ark. Blue Cross and Blue Shield, Little Rock, 1971-77; controller Riverview Hosp., Little Rock, 1977-81; pvt. practice acctg. Little Rock, 1981-82; controller Henryetta (Okla.) Med. Ctr., 1982-83; fin. report supr. Am. Med. Internat., Inc., Houston, 1983; dir. corp. acctg. Ft. Myers (Fla.) Community Hosp., 1984-86; controller Med. Ctr. of Southeast Okla., Durant, 1986-87; chief fin. officer Gulf Coast Community Hosp./Qualicare of Miss., Inc., 1987-88; asst. adminstr. fin. S.W. Gen. Hosp., San Antonio, 1988-89; pvt. practice San Antonio, 1989-90; CFO Bapt. Meml. Hosps. of Mississippi County, Blytheville, Ark., 1991-94, Med. Arts Hosp., Texarkana, Tex., 1994-96, Healthsouth Rehab. Hosp., Texarkana, Tex., 1997—. Served with USN, 1959-61. Mem. AICPA, Ark. Soc. CPAs, Healthcare Fin. Mgmt. Assn. (cert. fellow), Lions (sec. 1985-86, 2d v.p. 1995-96), Masons. Republican. Baptist. Office: 515 W 12th St Texarkana TX 75501-4416

MITCHEL, F(REDERICK) KENT, retired food company executive; b. Orange, N.J., June 2, 1927; s. E. Kent and Arlene (Lee) M.; m. Elizabeth L. Rich, June 25, 1955 (div. 1990); children: Pamela, Peter; m. Susan Holden Colcock, 1990. AB, Dartmouth Coll., 1950; postgrad., Harvard U., 1970. With Gen. Foods Corp., 1950-86; v.p. mktg., then v.p. corp. comm. Gen. Foods Corp., White Plains, N.Y., 1970-79; v.p. mktg. staffs Gen. Foods Corp., 1979-86; pres. Mktg. Sci. Inst., Cambridge, Mass., 1987-89, chmn., 1990-91; pres. Fair Tide Assocs. Ltd., Sandwich, N.H., 1987-95; past chmn. Assn. Nat. Advertisers; trustee Mktg. Sci. Inst., chmn., 1990-91; past chmn. Nat. Advt. Rev. Coun., Advt. Coun. Bd. dirs. Squam Lakes Assn., 1989-91. Mem. Univ. Club (N.Y.C.), Harvard Club Boston. Episcopalian.

MITCHELHILL, JAMES MOFFAT, civil engineer; b. St. Joseph, Mo., Aug. 11, 1912; s. William and Jeannette (Ambrose) M.; BS, Northwestern U., 1934, MSCE, 1935; m. Maurine Hutchason, Jan. 9, 1937 (div. 1962); children: Janis Maurine Mitchelhill Leas, Jeri Ann Mitchelhill Riney; m. Alicia Beuchat, 1982; registered profl. engr., Mont., P.R., Tex.; Engring. dept. C., M., St. P. & P.R.R. Co., Chgo. and Miles City, Mont., 1935-45; asst. mgr. Ponce & Guayama R.R. Co., Aguirre, P.R., 1945-51, v.p., gen. mgr., 1969-70; mgr. Cen. Cortada, Santa Isabel, P.R., 1951-54; r.r. supt. Braden Copper Co., Rancagua, Chile, 1954-63; staff engr. Coverdale & Colpitts, N.Y.C., 1963-64; asst. to exec. v.p. Central Aguirre Sugar Co., 1964-67; v.p., gen. mgr. Coddea, Inc., Dominican Republic, 1967-68; asst. to gen. mgr. Land Adminstrn. of P.R., La Nueva Central Aguirre, 1970-71, for Centrals Aguirre Lafayette and Mercedita, 1971-72; asst. to gen. mgr. Corporacion Azucarera de P.R., 1973-76, asst. to exec. dir., 1977-79, asst. exec. dir. for environ., 1979-82; engring. cons., 1982-92, 97—; Kendall County engr., 1985-97; county engring. cons., 1997—. Fellow ASCE; mem. Am. Ry. Engring. Assn., Colegio de Ingenieros y Agrimensores de P.R., Explorers Club, Circumnavigators Club, Travellers Century Club, Sigma Xi, Tau Beta Pi. Home: PO Box 506 Boerne TX 78006-0506 Office: 12 Staudt St Boerne TX 78006-1820

MITCHELL, ADA MAE BOYD, legal assistant; b. Nov. 23, 1927; d. Allen T. Boyd and Marjorie (Bigger) Boyd Mills; 1 child, Joseph W. Student, NYU, 1972-73. Supr. Faberge, Inc., Mahwah, N.J.; mgr. Demostration Svcs. and Promotional Monies; mgr. accounts receivables, credit mgr. Faberge, Inc., Mahwah, N.J.; legal asst. Wright Patterson Med. Ctr., Dayton, Ohio, 1990—. Pres. Urban League Guild, Bergen County, N.J., 1982—, bd. dirs. 1982-83; treas. Bethany Presbyn. Ch., Englewood, N.J., 1975, fin. sect., 1966-67, chairperson bldg. and renovation com., 1978-81, choir mem., elder, 1979—; 1st Black woman moderator Presbytery of Palisades-Presbyn. Ch., 1986; mem. self devel. of people com. Presbyn. Ch. Miami Presbytery, Dayton; dtr. Isis Akbar Ct. # 33, 1995—; vol. WPAFB, Ohio-Legal Office/Med. Group, 1990—. Mem. NAFE, NAACP, Order Eastern Star (Queen of Sheba chpt. 4, Worthy Matron 1972-73).

MITCHELL, ALLAN EDWIN, lawyer; b. Okemah, Okla., May 13, 1944; m. Neva G. Ream; children: Brian, Amy. BA in Mass. Comm., Northwestern Okla. State U., Alva, 1991; JD, U. Okla., 1994. Bar: Okla. 1994, U.S. dist. ct. (we. and no. dists.) 1994. Asst. state mgr. Oklahomans for Right to Work, Oklahoma City, 1967-68; exec. dir. London Sq. Village, Oklahoma City, 1968-73; dist. mgr. Farmland Ins. Svc., Oklahoma City, 1974-80, Nat. Farmers Union, Oklahoma City, 1980-85; dist. agt. Prudential Ins., Cherokee, Okla., 1985-89; atty. Hughes & Grant, Oklahoma City, 1994-96, Collins & Mitchell, Cherokee, Okla., 1996—. Mem. Cherokee Bd. Edn., 1985-90; mem. fin. com. Rep. Party of Okla., 1995, state com., 1997—; scoutmaster, 1981-86; adult advisor Girl Scouts Am.; pres. United Way Cherokee, 1984; mem. Okla. Sch. Bd. Mems. Legis. Network, 1985-90; vol. Okla. Spl. Olympics, 1996, 97. Mem. Ch. of the Nazarene. Avocations: public speaking, politics, civic activities. Office: Collins & Mitchell 214 S Grand Ave Cherokee OK 73728-2030

MITCHELL, ANDREA, journalist; b. N.Y.C., Oct. 30, 1946; d. Sydney and Cecile Mitchell. B.A., U. Pa., 1967. Polit. reporter KYW Newsradio, Phila., 1967-76; polit. corr. Sta. KYW-TV, Phila., 1972-76; corr. Sta. WTOP-TV, Washington, 1977-78; gen. assignment and energy corr. NBC News, Washington, 1978-81; White House corr. NBC News, 1981-88, chief congl. corr., 1989-92, chief White House corr., 1993-94; chief fgn. affairs corr. NBC News, Washington, 1995—, 1994—; instr. Gt. Lakes Colls. Assn., 1974-76; co-anchor Summer Sunday, USA, NBC-TV News, 1984, substitute anchor Meet the Press, 1988—. Overseer, Sch. of Arts and Scis., U. Pa., 1989-95, trustee, 1995—; mem. nat. adv. bd. Girl Scouts U.S. Recipient award for pub. affairs reporting Am. Polit. Sci. Assn., 1969, Pub. Affairs Reporting award AP, 1976, AP Broadcast award, 1977; named Communicator of the Yr., Phila. chpt. Women in Comms., 1976, Woman of the Yr., Phila. chpt. Am. Women in Radio and TV, 1989, Lucretia Mott award Woman's Way,

1991. Mem. White House Corrs. Assn. Office: NBC News 4001 Nebraska Ave NW Washington DC 20016-2733*

MITCHELL, ARTHUR, dancer, choreographer, educator; b. N.Y.C., Mar. 27, 1934; s. Arthur and Willie Mae M. Student, Sch. Am. Ballet.; D. Arts (hon.), Columbia Coll., Chgo., 1975; cert. of competence, Peter U., 1978; DFA (hon.), City Coll., CUNY, 1979, N.C. Sch. Arts, 1981, L.I. U. Sch. Bus. Pub. Adminstrn., 1982, Fordham U., 1983, Princeton U., 1986, Williams Coll., 1986, Juilliard Sch., 1990; DHS (hon.), Urbana Coll., 1979; DA (hon.), Harvard U., 1987. With William Dollar's Ballet Theatre Workshop, 1954, John Butler Co., 1955; prin. dancer N.Y.C. Ballet, 1955-72; artistic dir., founder Am. Negro Dance Co., N.Y.C., 1966—; founder, dir., choreographer Dance Theatre of Harlem, N.Y.C., 1969—; former resident choreographer, artistic dir. Nat. Ballet Co., Brazil; tchr. dance Karel Shook Studio, Melissa Hayden Sch., Cedarhurst, L.I., Jones-Haywood Sch. Ballet, Washington. dancer in Kiss Me, Kate, Orpheus, Carmen Jones, Allegro, Creation of the World, Episodes, House of Flowers, numerous others; choreographer (with Rod Alexander) Newport Jazz Festival, Rhythmetron, 1971, Ode to Otis, 1969, Lil' Gal, 1969, Tones, 1970, Biosfera, 1970, Fun and Games, 1970, Holberg Suite, 1970, Manifestations, 1975, Concerto for Jazz Band and Orch., 1971, Fête Noire, 1971, Spiritual Suite: Dance In Praise of His Name, 1976, Breezin', 1977, The Greatest, 1977, El Mar, 1977, Doin' It, 1978, Porgy and Bess, 1985, Phoenix Rising, 1987, John Henry, 1988, Ribbon In The Sky, 1990, Bach Passacaglia, 1993; co-choreographer Broadway prodn. Shinbone Alley; dancer, choreographer, actor: Spoleto Festival of Two Worlds, 1960; TV prodns. A Streetcar Named Desire dance prodn., PBS, Songs of Mahler, Dance in America: Dance Theatre of Harlem, PBS, Stravinsky's Firebird, PBS, Creole Giselle, NBC, Fall River Legend, A&E. Active Nat. Conf. on Social Welfare, 1973, U.S. Dept. State Dance Adv. Panel, Pres. Task Force on Arts and Humanities, 1981, Commn. for Cultural Affairs, N.Y.C., 1982, Arts and Entertainment Adv. Bd. N.Y.C. Partnership, Inc., 1983, Nat. Coun. of Arts, 1987; named to Pres. Commn. on White House Fellowships, 1991. Recipient Changers award Mademoiselle Mag., 1970, North Shore Commn. Arts Ctr. award 1971, Capezio Dance award, 1971, Ann. Excellence award John F. Kennedy Ctr. for Performing Arts, 1980, Am. Dance Guild award, 1982, Ebony Mag. Am. Black Achievement award, 1983, Pres.'s Cabinet award U. Detroit, 1982, Paul Robeson award Actors Equity Assn., 1986, Lion of the Performing Arts award N.Y. Pub. Libr., 1986, Arnold Gingrich Meml. award, 1987, Banquet of Golden Plate, 1989, Harkness Disting. Artist award Adelphi U., 1990, Disting. Svc. to Arts award Am. Acad. of Arts and Letters, 1994, Zenith award for Fine Arts, 1994, Handel Medallion, City of New York, 1993, Barnard Medal of Distinction Barnard Coll., 1994, Lifetime Achievement award Sch. Am. Ballet, 1995, Nat. Medal of Arts Nat. Endowment for the Arts, 1995, Living Landmarks award N.Y. Landmarks Conservancy, 1995; named to NAACP Image Awards Hall of Fame, 1986; Kennedy Ctr. Honor for Lifetime Achievement, 1993; Conroy fellow St. Paul's Sch., Concord, N.H., 1982, MacArthur fellow, 1994. Office: Dance Theatre Harlem 466 W 152nd St New York NY 10031-1814*

MITCHELL, ARTHUR HARRIS, newspaper columnist; b. St. John, N.B., Can., Nov. 8, 1916; s. Stuart Campbell and Marjorie (Harris) M.; m. Mary Moliawko, Nov. 6, 1944; children: John Stuart, Marjorie Starr. Student, Columbia Sch. Journalism, 1945-46. Travelling freelance writer various U.S., Can. mags., 1946-48; syndicated newspaper columnist, 1971—; editor Mitchell Press Ltd., Vancouver, B.C.; founding editor Can. Pulp and Paper Industry mag., Western Homes & Living mag., 1948-66; editor Can. Homes mag., Southstar Publs. Ltd., Toronto, Ont., 1967-80; Can. cons. Time-Life Books, N.Y.C., 1976-82. Author: You Wanted to Know, 1971, Easy Furniture Finishing, 1974, The Basement Book, 1977. Served with Brit. and U.S. Mcht. Marine, 1940-45. Home: TH28 270 Timberbank Blvd, Scarborough, ON Canada M1W 2M1

MITCHELL, BERT BREON, literary translator; b. Salina, Kans., Aug. 9, 1942; s. John Charles and Bernita Maxine (Breon) M.; m. Lynda Diane Fink, July 21, 1965; children: Kieron Breon, Kerry Archer. BA, U. Kans., 1964; PhD, Oxford U., 1968. Asst. prof. German and comparative lit. Ind. U., Bloomington, 1968-71, assoc. prof., 1971-78, prof., 1978—, assoc. dean Coll. Arts and Scis., 1975-77, chmn. comparative lit., 1977-85, dir. Wells Scholars program, 1988—. Author: James Joyce and the German Novel, 1922-1933, 1976, Beyond Illustration; The Livre d'Artiste in the Twentieth Century, 1976, The Complete Lithographs of Delacroix's Faust and Manet's The Raven, 1981; editor: Literature and the Other Arts, 1978, Metamorphosis and the Arts, 1979, Paul Morand, Fancy Goods/Open All Night, 1984; translator: Heartstop (Martin Grzimek), 1984, Selected Stories (Siegfried Lenz), 1989, The Musk Deer and Other Stories (Vilas Sarang), 1990, Looking Back (Lou Andreas-Salomé), 1991, Shadowlife (Martin Grzimek), 1991, Laura's Skin (J.F. Federspiel), 1991, The Color of the Snow (Rüdiger Kremer), 1992, Knife Edge (Ralf Rothmann) 1992, In the Kingdom of Enki (Vilas Sarang), 1993, The Silent Angel (Heinrich Böll), 1994, On the Glacier (Jürgen Kross), 1996, The God of Impertinence (Sten Nadolny), 1997, The Mad Dog (Heinrich Böll), 1997. Rhodes scholar, 1964-68; Danforth fellow, 1964-68, Woodrow Wilson fellow, 1964, Alexander-von-Humboldt fellow, 1971, Translation fellow Nat. Endowment for Arts, 1989; recipient Frederic Bachman Lieber Meml. award for disting. teaching, 1974, hon. citation Columbia Translation Ctr., 1990, Theodore Christian Hoepfner award So. Humanities Rev., 1995. Mem. MLA (chair William Riley Parker prize selection com. 1994), P.E.N., Am. Comparative Lit. Assn., Am. Lit. Translators Assn. (pres. 1985-87, Alta prize for disting. translation 1992), Am. Translators Assn. (com. lit. transl. 1983-84, German Lit. prize for disting. translation 1987, chmn. honors and awards com. 1995), Nat. Coun. Tchrs. of English (chair com. on comparative and world lit. 1995—),James Joyce Found., Franz Kafka Soc., Samuel Beckett Soc., So. Comparative Lit. Assn., Brit. Comparative Lit. Assn., Internat. Comparative Lit. Assn. Office: BH402 Indiana University Bloomington IN 47405

MITCHELL, BETTIE PHAENON, religious organization administrator; b. Colorado Springs, Colo., June 6, 1934; d. Roy William and Laura Lee (Costin) Roberts; m. Gerald Mitchell, May 3, 1952; children: Michelle Smith, Laura Sweitz, Jennie Grenzer, Mohammad Bader. BS in Edn., Lewis & Clark Coll., 1954; postgrad., Portland State U., 1962-72; MA in Religion summa cum laude, Warner Pacific Coll., 1979. Cert. counselor, Oreg. Elem. tchr. Quincy Sch. Dist., Clatskanie, Oreg., 1955-56; substitute tchr. Beaverton (Oreg.) and Washington County Schs., 1956-77; tchr. of the Bible Portland (Oreg.) C.C., 1974-92; counseling and healing ministry, 1977-79; founder, exec. dir. Good Samaritan Ministries, Beaverton, 1979-88, founder, internat. exec. dir., 1988—; tchr. Christian Renewal Ctr. Workshops, 1977-85; spkr., presenter in field; leader tours in the Mid. East; developing counselor edn. programs Pakistan, Ukraine, Jordan, Egypt, Kenya, Uganda, Tanzania, Zambia, Malawi, South Africa, Nigeria, Burundi, Sierra Leone, India. Author: Who Is My Neighbor? A Parable, 1988, The Power of Conflict and Sacrifice, A Therapy Manual for Christian Marriage, 1988, Good Samaritan Training Handbook, 1989, Be Still and Listen to His Voice, The Story of Prayer and Faith, 1990, A Need for Understanding - International Counselor Training Manual, 1993. Mem. Israel Task Force, Portland, 1974-80; Leader Camp Fire Internat., 1962-73, elem. sch. coord., 1962-68; asst. dir. Washington County Civil Def., 1961-63; precinct committeewoman Rep. Party, 1960; bd. dirs. Beaverton Fish, 1966-74; v.p. NCCJ, Portland, 1983-85; chmn., speaker's bur. Near East Task Force for Israel; chmn. fire bond issue campaign City of Beaverton, mgr. mayoral campaign, 1960; sunday sch. tchr., speaker, organizer Sharing and Caring program Bethel Ch., 1974-79. Mem. AACA, Christian Assn. for Psychol. Studies, Oreg. Counseling Assn. Republican. Avocations: historical research, writing, photography, Biblical archaeology, correspondence. Home: 6550 SW Imperial Dr Beaverton OR 97008-5311 Office: Good Samaritan Ministries 7929 SW Cirrus Dr # 23 Beaverton OR 97008-5973

MITCHELL, BEVERLY ANN BALES, insurance agency owner, women's rights advocate; b. Fremont, Nebr., July 27, 1944; d. Richard Lee Roy Stillwell Bales and Thelma May (Nelson) Lemen (dec.). BA, Midland Luth. Coll., 1967; postgrad., U. Iowa, 1970, 71. Reporter, film columnist, entertainment sect. editor Fremont (Nebr.) Daily Guide and Tribune, 1961-66; tchr. H.S. English Cedar Bluffs (Nebr.) Valley PUb. Schs., 1967-71; dir. quality control, dir. field ops. Frank N. Magid Assocs., Marion, Iowa, 1971-76; employment specialist U.S. Dept. Labor, Cedar Rapids, Iowa, 1976-78; owner, gen. agy. Mitchell Ins., Cedar Rapids, 1978—. Founder, editor: (monthly periodical) Lilith Speaks, 1971-76, 88—; contbr.: Strong Minded Women, 1992. Co-founder, pres. Cedar Rapids (Iowa) Womens Caucus, 1971-76; commr. Cedar Rapids Civil Rights Commn., 1976-80, Cedar Rapids Charter Commn., 1995-96; pres. Linn County (Iowa) Women's Polit. Caucus, 1977-79; mem. Linn County Bd. Condemnation and Compensation, 1994—. Recipient Creighton By-Line award Creighton U., Omaha, 1963, Best Editorial award Nebr. Press Assn., Lincoln, 1963; named Women of the Yr., Cedar Rapids (Iowa) Women's Orgns., 1977. Mem. NRA, NOW (coord. Iowa state divsn. 1973-76, pres. Cedar Rapids chpt. 1994—), Bus. and Profl. Women (bd. dirs. 1994-95), Dodge County Humane Soc. Lutheran. Unitarian. Office: Mitchell Ins 1000 Maplewood Dr NE Cedar Rapids IA 52402-3807

MITCHELL, BRIANE NELSON, lawyer; b. Seattle, July 4, 1953; s. Robert Max and Frances Marie (Nelson) M.; m. Suzanne Harmatz; children: Brianne Nelson, Brittany Suzanne. AB, Columbia U., 1975; JD, U. Idaho, 1978. Law clk. U.S. Ct. Appeals (9th cir.), 1978-80; assoc. Debevoise & Plimpton, N.Y.C., 1980-84; assoc. Paul, Hastings, Janofsky & Walker, L.A., 1984-86, ptnr., 1986-93; with McCambridge, Deixler & Marmaro, L.A., 1993-95; ptnr. Shapiro, Hinds & Mitchell LLP, 1996—. Mem. ABA, Idaho Bar Assn., N.Y. State Bar Assn., Calif. Bar Assn.

MITCHELL, BRUCE TYSON, lawyer; b. San Francisco, Nov. 6, 1928; s. John Robert and Lorraine C. (Tyson) M.; m. Adrienne Means Hiscox, Oct. 14, 1951; 1 son, Mark Means. AB with great distinction, Stanford U., 1949, JD, 1951. Bar: Calif. 1952, U.S. Dist. Ct. (no. dist.) Calif 1952, U.S. Ct. Appeals (9th cir.) 1952, U.S. Supreme Ct. 1971. Estate adminstr. Crocker Nat. Bank, San Francisco, 1955-57; atty. Utah Internat. Inc., San Francisco, 1957-87; sec. Utah Internat. Inc., 1974-87, sr. counsel, 1961-87; mem. nonsecurities panel arbitrators N.Y. Stock Exch., Pacific Stock Exchange, NASD Bd. Arbitrators. Chmn. San Mateo County Rep. Cen. Com., 1964-70; mem. Calif. Rep. Central Com., 1964-74, 77-83; alt. del. Rep. Nat. Conv., 1968; co-chmn. San Mateo (Calif.) County Pres. Ford Com., 1976; mem. bd. visitors sch. law Stanford U., 1980-83; exec. v.p., bd. dirs. San Francisco Jr. C. of C., 1961; bd. dirs. No. Calif. chpt. Arthritis Found., 1972-85, 1987-92, St. Francis Hosp. Found., San Francisco. Lt. (j.g.) USNR, 1952-55, Japan. Mem. ABA, Calif. Bar Assn., San Francisco Bar Assn., Am. Judicature Soc., Am. Soc. Corp. Secs. (v.p. 1976-77, dir. 1976-79), Assn. Former Intelligence Officers, Commonwealth Club of Calif. (pres. San Francisco 1973), Pacific Union Club, Olympic Club, Capitol Hill Club, Travelers Century Club, Masons. Congregationalist. Home: 165 Redwood Dr Hillsborough CA 94010-6971 Office: 400 Montgomery St Ste 200 San Francisco CA 94104-1209

MITCHELL, BURLEY BAYARD, JR., state supreme court chief justice; b. Oxford, N.C., Dec. 15, 1940; s. Burley Bayard and Dorothy Ford (Champion) M.; m. Mary Lou Willett, Aug. 3, 1962; children: David Bayard, Catherine Morris. BA with honors, N.C. State U., 1966, DHL (hon.), 1995; JD, U. N.C., 1969. Bar: N.C. 1969, U.S. Ct. Appeals (4th cir.) 1970, U.S. Supreme Ct. 1972. Asst. atty. gen. State of N.C., Raleigh, 1969-72, dist. atty., 1973-77, judge Ct. Appeals, 1977-79, sec. crime control, 1979-82; justice Supreme Ct. N.C., Raleigh, 1982-94; chief justice Supreme Ct. of N.C., Raleigh, 1995—. Served with USN, 1958-62, Asia. Recipient N.C. Nat. Guard Citizen Commendation award, 1982. Mem. ABA, VFW, N.C. Bar Assn., Mensa, Am. Legion. Democrat. Methodist. Home: 820 Glen Eden Dr Raleigh NC 27612-5038 Office: Supreme Ct NC PO Box 1841 Raleigh NC 27602-1841

MITCHELL, CAROL ANN, nursing educator; b. Portsmouth, Va., Aug. 31, 1942; d. William Howell and Eleanor Bertha (Wesarg) M.; m. David Alan Friedman, June 17, 1971 (div. 1988). Diploma, NYU, 1963; BS, Columbia U., 1968, MA, 1971, EdM, 1974, EdD, 1980; MS, SUNY, Stony Brook, 1990. Charge nurse Nassau County Med. Ctr., East Meadow, N.Y., 1963-65; staff nurse Meml. Hosp., N.Y.C., 1965-68; head nurse, supr. Community Hosp. at Glen Cove (N.Y.), 1969-71; assoc. prof. dept. nursing Queensborough Community Coll. CUNY, Bayside, 1971-80; assoc. prof. Marion A. Buckley Sch. Nursing Adelphi U., Garden City, N.Y., 1981-88; ednl. cons. Nat. League for Nursing, N.Y.C., 1980-81; prof. sch. nursing SUNY, Stony Brook, 1988-92, chmn. adult nursing, 1988-92; prof. chair Coll. Nursing East Tenn. State U., 1992-95, mem faculty, 1995-96; geriatric nurse practitioner Vet. Affairs Med. Ctr., Mountain Home, Tenn., 1996—; mem. faculty Regents Coll. degrees in nursing program USNY, Albany, 1978-91, cons., 1978—; faculty cons. geriatrics Montefiore Med. Ctr., 1991-93. Editor emeritus: Scholarly Inquiry in Nursing Practice, 1983—; contbr. articles to profl. jours. Robert Wood Johnson clin. nurse scholar postdoctoral fellow U. Rochester (N.Y.), 1983-85. Mem. Am. Nurses Assn., Nat. League for Nursing, Gerontol. Soc. Am., N.Am. Nursing Diagnosis Assn., Soc. for Research in Nursing Edn. Avocations: reading, gardening, cycling, travel, cooking.

MITCHELL, CAROL ELAINE, publishing executive, writer, educator; b. Columbus, Aug. 11, 1949; d. William Earl and Betty Jane (Tyson) Johnson; m. Larry Lindsay Mitchell, Mar. 3, 1973; 1 child, Mark Lindsay. BS, Ohio State U., 1971. Cert. English tchr. 7-12. Pres. Sparrow House Pub., Columbus, 1990—; instr. adult edn. Columbus Pub. Schs., 1992—; judge Excellence in Writing Columbus Pub. Schs., 1992. Author: Paths of Blessings, 1991; editor, writer, prodr.: Columbus pub. schs. adult and juvenile literacy ednl. t.v., 1993. Mem. NAFE, Nat. Edn. Assn., Ohio Edn. Assn., Internat. Platform Assn. Home: 228 Sherbourne Dr Columbus OH 43219-2972 Office: 342 Sherbourne Dr Columbus OH 43219-2942

MITCHELL, CAROLYN COCHRAN, college official; b. Atlanta, Dec. 27, 1943; d. Clemern Covell and Agnes Emily (Veal) Cochran; m. W. Alan Mitchell, Aug. 30, 1964; 1 child, Teri Marie. AB magna cum laude, Mercer U., 1965, M in Svc. Mgmt., 1989. Caseworker Ga. Dept. Family & Children Svcs., Macon, 1965-67, Covington, 1967-69; presch. dir. Southwestern Theol. Sem., Ft. Worth, 1969-70; presch. tchr., dir. Noah's Ark Day Care, Bowden, Ga., 1970-72, First Bapt. Ch., Bremen, Ga., 1972-75, Roebuck Park Bapt. Ch., Birmingham, Ala., 1975-79; freelance office mgr. and bookkeeper Macon, 1979-84; asst. to pres. Ga. Wesleyan Coll., Macon, 1984—; exec. dir. Ga. Women of Achievement, 1991-95; dir. Macon Arts Alliance, 1981-91; mem. Cultural Plan Oversight Com., 1989-90. Mem. Get Out the Vote Task Force, Macon, 1981—, Macon Symphony Guild, 1986-91; dep. registrar Bibb County Bd. Elections, Macon, 1981-95. Mem. AAUW (bd. dirs. Ga. chpt., v.p. 1991-93, chair coll.-univ. rels. com. 1993-94, bylaws com. 1991-92, v.p., treas., historian, Macon chpt., Named Gift Honoree 1988), NAFE, NOW, Women's Network for Change, Am. Mgmt. Assn., Presdl. Assts. in Higher Edn., Religious Coalition for Reproductive Choice, The Interfaith Alliance, Women's Polit. Orgn. Macon, Sigma Mu. Democrat. Unitarian. Office: Ga Wesleyan Coll 4760 Forsyth Rd Macon GA 31210-4407

MITCHELL, CHARLES ARCHIE, financial planning consultant, engineer; b. Kodia Kanal, Madras, India, May 3, 1926; came to U.S., 1932; s. Charles Archie and Ethel Blanche (Nutter) M.; m. Betty Louise Johnson, June 15, 1947; children: Cynthia E., Charles Archie Jr., Susan L. BSEE, Worcester (Mass.) Poly. Inst., 1946; MBA, Harvard U., 1954; CFP, Coll. of Fin. Planning, 1974. Sales engr. Johnson Steel & Wire Co., Worcester, 1947-50; dist. sales mgr. GE, Plainville, Conn., 1954-61; v.p. mktg. Dictograph Co., Danbury, Conn., 1962-63; dir. corp. planning GCA Corp., Bedford, Mass., 1963-65; div. mgr. Polaroid Corp., Cambridge, Mass., 1965-66; rep. Hayden Stone, Inc., Boston, 1966-69; div. mgr. Westamerica Fin. Corp., Boston, 1971-77; officer, dir. MHA Mgmt. Corp., Braintree, Mass., 1977-89; pres., dir. Mitchell Fin. Corp., Falmouth, Mass., 1989—. Contbr. articles to profl. jours. Instr. Northeastern U., Boston, 1962-66, Mass. Dept. of Edn., Cambridge, 1966-69. Lt. USN, 1943-47, 51-53, Korea. Mem. Internat. Assn. Fin. Planners (treas., bd. dirs. 1975-76), Inst. Cert. Fin. Planners (ea. v.p. nat. bd. dirs. 1974-79), Nat. Assn. Life Underwriters, Cape Cod Estate Planning Coun., Cape Cod Curling Club, Woods Hole Yacht Club, Masons, Shriners. Avocations: sailing, curling, golf. Office: PO Box 550 Falmouth MA 02541-0550

MITCHELL, CHARLES F., lawyer; b. Washington, Oct. 18, 1963; s. John Joseph and Duane (Schwertner) M.; m. Sherrie Ilyse Braude, June 7, 1986; children: Matthew Ryan, Sydni Paige, Jake Bradley. BA, U. Md., 1985; JD, Georgetown U., 1989. Bar: Md. 1989, D.C. 1991, U.S. Ct. Md. 1990, U.S. Ct. Appeals (4th and fed. cirs.) 1991, U.S. Ct. Fed. Claims 1991. Assoc. Holland & Knight (formerly Dunnells & Duvall), Washington, 1989-93; gen. counsel John J. Kirlin, Inc., Rockville, Md., 1993—. Contbr. articles to profl. jours. Mem. Am. Inns of Ct., ABA (vice-chmn. subcontracts com. for constrn. industry 1995, mem. public contract law/litigation sects.). Avocations: golf, tennis. Home: 9814 Bald Cypress Dr Rockville MD 20850 Office: John J Kirlin Inc 643 Lofstrand Ln Rockville MD 20850-1389

MITCHELL, CHARLES PETER, library director; b. Bklyn., May 3, 1949; s. Charles S. and Anna B. Mitchell; m. Roberta Downing, Dec. 10, 1977. BA summa cum laude, Pace U., 1971; MLS, Pratt Inst., 1972. Jr./sr./prin. libr. Paterson (N.J.) Pub. Libr., 1972-80; libr. dir. Falmouth (Maine) Meml. Libr., 1980-93, Blue Hill (Maine) Pub. Libr., 1993-95, Millinocket (Maine) Meml. Libr., 1995—; tchr. adult edn. program Falmouth, Maine, 1992; lectr. Woman's Lit. Union, Westbrook Coll., 1986. Columnist book reviews: Katahdin Times, 1995—, Forecaster, Falmouth, Maine, 1984-92; contbr. articles to profl. jours. Chmn. So. Maine Libr. Dist., Portland, 1983-85, Libr. Prime, 1988-91, treas., 1986-88, 92-93. Recipient Nat. Libr. award, 1989. Mem. Maine Libr. Assn., Richard III Soc. Avocations: classical music, film history. Home: 25 Garden St Millinocket ME 04462-1812 Office: Millinocket Meml Library 5 Maine Ave Millinocket ME 04462-1416

MITCHELL, CLAYBOURNE, JR., retired utilities executive; b. Chgo., Jan. 13, 1923; s. Claybourne and Ethel Emma (Osby) M.; m. Isabella Ophelia Skerrett; 1 dau., Mary Faith. Assoc. in Engring. Sci., Flint Jr. Coll., 1948; B.S. in Physics, U. Mich., 1950, M.S. in Physics, 1959. Dir. research Controlled Power Corp., Farmington, Mich., 1968-74; gen. dir. engring. research dept. Detroit Edison, 1974-77, mgr. personnel services, 1977-79, asst. v.p. planning and research, 1979-80, v.p. planning and research, 1980-88. Inventor, patentee: system for periodically reversing elec. energy through a load; co-inventor photon detector sliderule; co-patentee resolution voltage controllable interferometer, micromeasurement apparatus, apparatus for infrared scanning. Served to master sgt. USAAF, 1943-46, PTO. Mem. Engring. Soc. Detroit, Detroit Sci. Ctr.

MITCHELL, DAVID CAMPBELL, inventor, corporate executive; b. Sacramento, Dec. 11, 1957; s. Alan Campbell and Lorraine May (Grant) M.; m. Lanette Pearson; children: David Kirk, Travis, Holly Ann. Student, U. Utah, 1973-74, Brigham Young U. Rsch. dir. Flex Inc., Williston, N.D., 1976-78; with Deseret Industries, Salt Lake City, 1978-81; head R&D Pro Biotiks Labs., Ogden, Utah, 1981—, Melaleuca, Idaho Falls, Idaho, 1987-89; pres., chmn. David C. Mitchell Med. Rsch. Inst., Salt Lake City, 1980—; rsch. cons. U. Utah Rsch. Park, Salt Lake City, 1981—; environ. cons. Hi-Valley Chem., Salt Lake City, 1988—; v.p. Mitchell Products, Orem, Utah, 1989—. Inventor, 125 patents in vitamins, cosmetics, pharmaceuticals, arthritis, cancer, psoriasis, scars and wounds, artificial sweeteners, pain killers, anti-depressants and related biochemistries. Vol. Freeman Inst., Salt Lake City, 1980-87; vol. supr. Granite Bakery (Feed the Poor), Salt Lake City, 1982-87; active rehab. handicapped Deseret Industries, Salt Lake City, 1978-81; pres., young adults rep. Latter-day Saints Ch., Salt Lake City, 1977-78. Scholar NSF, 1973; named one of Outstanding Young Men of Am., 1989. Fellow AAAS, ACS, N.Y. Acad. Scis. Home and Office: 3594 Little Cottonwood Ln Sandy UT 84092

MITCHELL, DAVID WALKER, lawyer; b. Oakland, Calif., Nov. 11, 1935; s. Theodore Boyd and Helen Louise (Walker) M.; m. Carolyn Hilliard Graves, July 29, 1961; children: Sarah M. Meyer, Betsy M. Kinney. AB in History, Stanford U., 1957; JD, Harvard U., 1960. Bar: Calif. 1961. Assoc. Kindel & Anderson, L.A., 1961-65, Weir, Hopkins, Donovan, San Jose, Calif., 1965-68; ptnr. Hopkins, Mitchell & Carley, San Jose, 1968-87, McCutchen, Doyle, Brown & Enersen, San Jose, 1987-93, Hoge, Fenton, Jones & Appel, San Jose, 1993—. Bd. dirs. Peninsula Open Space Trust, Menlo Park, Calif., 1982—, pres., 1984-92; bd. dirs. Santa Clara Community Found., San Jose, 1977-94; chair bd. trustees United Way Santa Clara County, 1983-85. Fellow Am. Bar Found., Am. Leadership Forum (sr.); mem. Santa Clara County Bar Assn. (trustee 1972-75), San Jose C. of C. (bd. dirs. 1975-80). Mem. United Ch. of Christ. Avocations: music, hiking. Office: Hoge Fenton Jones Appel 60 S Market St Ste 1400 San Jose CA 95113-2396

MITCHELL, DENNIS A., Olympic athlete, track and field; b. Feb. 20, 1966. Student, U. Fla. Olympic runner Barcelona, Spain, 1992. Recipient 4x100m relay Track and Field Gold medal, 100m Bronze medal, Olympics, Barcelona, 1992. Office: US Olympic Com 1750 E Boulder St Colorado Springs CO 80909-5724*

MITCHELL, DON, professional sports team executive; m. Michelle Mitchell; children: Jennifer, Julie, Jamie. AA, Paducah C.C., Ky.; B in Civil Engring. and Tech., U. Tenn. Player Cin. Reds, area scouting supr., 1986; midwest regional supr. Cleve. Indians, 1989-90; ea. regional supr. Pitts. Pirates, 1991-92; nat. supr. Atlanta Braves, 1992, asst. dir. scouting, 1993; dir. scouting Ariz. Diamondbacks. Office: Ariz Diamondbacks PO Box 2095 Phoenix AZ 85001*

MITCHELL, DONALD J., former congressman; b. Ilion, N.Y., May 8, 1923; m. Margaretta Wilson Levee, 1945; children: Gretchen, Cynthia, Allen. Student, Hobart and William Smith Coll., 1946-47, LLD (hon.); BS in Optometry, Columbia U., 1949, MA in Edn., 1950; LLD (hon.), Pa. Coll. Optometry; D Ocular Scis. (hon.), So. Coll. Optometry. Optometrist; mem. 93d-97th Congresses from, N.Y.; Councilman Town of Herkimer, 1954-56; mayor Village of Herkimer, 1956-59; mem. sr. assoc. faculty Nat. Emergency Tng. Ctr.; pres. Mohawk Valley Conf. Mayors, 1959; mem. N.Y. State Assembly, 1965-72, majority whip, 1968-72; bd. dirs. Comml. Travelers Mut. Ins. Co. Bd. dirs. Herkimer chpt. Cub Scouts, Cen. N.Y. Assn. for the Blind, Herkimer County United Fund, ea. chpt. Nature Conservancy. With USNR, 1942-45, 51-53. Named Optometrist of Yr. N.Y. State Optometric Assn., 1971; recipient Pub. Svc. award, 1965, award of distinction SUNY State Coll. Optometry Alumni Assn., Patriot of Yr. award N.Y. Res. Officers Assn., Nat. Security award U.S. Civil Def.; Jimmy Doolittle fellow Aerospace Edn. Found. of Air Force Assn. Mem. Nat. Soc. State Legis. (gov. 1971), Am. Civil Def. Assn. (pres. 1988—), Am. Legion, VFW. Republican. Methodist. Clubs: Rod and Gun, Masons, Elks, Kiwanis. Home: Herkimer NY 13350

MITCHELL, EARL NELSON, physicist, educator; b. Centerville, Iowa, Aug. 30, 1926; s. Earl Nelson and Nina (Swank) M.; m. Marlys Marie Panning, July 23, 1955. AB magna cum laude, U. Iowa, 1949, MS, 1951; PhD, U. Minn., 1955. Research scientist Sperry Rand Corp., St. Paul, 1955-58; asst. prof., then assoc. prof. physics U. N.D., Grand Forks, 1958-62; vis. assoc. prof., then assoc. prof. and prof. physics U. N.C., Chapel Hill, 1962-91, prof. emeritus, 1991—, asst. chmn. dept., 1968-76; lectr. Hamline U., 1956, 57; cons. Sperry Rand Corp., 1958-62. Contbr. articles to profl. jours.; author textbooks. Mem. Chapel Hill Planning Bd., 1970-71; pres. Chapel Hill Concert Series, 1967-70; mem. bd. for missions to deaf Luth. Ch. Mo. Synod, 1958-64. Served in USNR, 1945-46. Mem. AAAS, Am. Phys. Soc., Am. Assn. Physics Tchrs., Am. Soc. Enologists (bd. dirs. ea. sect. 1984-91, pres. elect 1988, pres. 1989, past pres. 1990), Soc. Wine Educators, N.C. Grape Coun., N.C. Wine Growers Assn. (pres. 1994—), Phi Beta Kappa, Sigma Xi, Phi Eta Sigma. Democrat. Office: U NC Physics Dept Chapel Hill NC 27599

MITCHELL, EARL WESLEY, clergyman; b. Excelsior Springs, Mo., Mar. 16, 1931; s. Earl Van and Ora Leah (Butterfield) M.; m. Mary Lou Bell, June 8, 1956; children: Susan Yvonne, Randall Bruce. Ordained to ministry Christian Union Ch., 1971. Min. Vibbard (Mo.) Christian Union Ch., 1962-69, Liberty (Mo.) Christian Ch., 1969-77, Barwick Christian Union Ch., Cameron, Mo., 1977-80, Independence (Mo.) Christian Union Ch., 1980-95; assoc. pastor Flack Meml. Christian Union Ch., Excelsior Springs, Mo., 1995-96; mem. state exec. bd. Christian Union Mo.; area rep. Mo. Christian Union USA; former mem. gen. exec. bd., former editor C.U. Witness. Sgt. USAF, 1951-55. Avocations: music, woodworking, painting, photography. Home and Office: 618 Henrie St Excelsior Springs MO 64024-2022

MITCHELL, EDWARD JOHN, economist, retired educator; b. Newark, Aug. 15, 1937; s. Edward Charles and Gladys (Werner) M.; m. Mary Josephine Osborne, June 14, 1958; children: Susan, Edward. B.A. summa cum laude, Bowling Green State U., 1960; postgrad. (Social Sci. Research Council fellow), Nuffield Coll., Oxford U., Eng., 1963-64, Ph.D. in Econs. (NDEA fellow 1960-63, NSF fellow 1964-65), 1966. Lectr. in econs. Wharton Sch., U. Pa., 1964-65; economist Rand Corp., 1965-68; mem. Inst. Advanced Study, Princeton, N.J., 1968-69; sr. economist Pres.'s Council Econ. Advs., Washington, 1969-72; vis. assoc. prof. econs. Cornell U., 1972-73; assoc. prof. bus. econs. U. Mich., 1973-75, prof., 1975-88, prof. emeritus bus. econs. and pub. policy, 1988—; pres. Edward J. Mitchell Inc., Ann Arbor, 1977—; dir. nat. energy project Am. Enterprise Inst., 1974-76; pres. Fountainhead Investment Co., 1984—. Author: U.S. Energy Policy: A Primer, 1974, Dialogue on World Oil, 1974, Financing the Energy Industry, 1975, Vertical Integration of the Oil Industry, 1976, The Deregulation of Natural Gas, 1983; contbr. articles to profl. jours. Home: 310 Penny Ln Santa Barbara CA 93108-2601 Office: Grad Sch Bus U Mich Ann Arbor MI 48109

MITCHELL, EHRMAN BURKMAN, JR., architect; b. Harrisburg, Pa., Jan. 25, 1924; s. Ehrman Burkman and Alice (DeCevee) M.; m. Hermine Strickler, Sept. 25, 1948; children: Eric Ehrman, Marianne. AB, U. Pa., 1947, BArch, 1948; LHD (hon.), Spring Garden Coll., 1989. Asso. architect Bellante & Clauss, 1951-58; partner Mitchell/Giurgola, Assocs., Phila., 1958-85; dir. Wyck Assn.; lectr. Ohio State U., U. Ariz., U. Utah, Cath. U. Am., Washington U., St. Louis, U. Notre Dame, Dartmouth Coll., U. Ky., U. Md., Temple U.; Phila. lectr. U. Nebr.; lectr. Calif. Poly. State U., U. Brasilia, Boston Archtl. Ctr., Pa. State U., Clemson U., Cornell U.; bd. overseers Temple U. Arch. Sch., U. Pa. Grad. Sch. Fine Arts; arch. design rev. panels U. Pa. Prin. works Nat. hdqrs. Am. Coll. Life Underwriters, Bryn Mawr, Pa. also, Adult Learning Research Center; office bldg. Penn Mut. Life Ins. Co., Phila., Ins. Co. N.Am., Phila.; U. Wash. Law Sch. and Library, Seattle, USIS Cultural Center, Brasilia, Brazil, A.B. Volvo Co. mfg. plant, Chesapeake, Va., New Parliament House, Canberra, Australia. Pres. Citizens Coun. Whitemarch Twp., Montgomery County, Pa., 1963-65, dir., 1963-67; mem. Del. Valley Citizens Transp. Com., 1964—, Citizens Coun. Montgomery County, 1964—; mem. archtl. rev. panel U.S. Fed. Res. System; bd. regents Am. Archtl. Found. With USNR, 1943-46. Recipient Gold medal Artists Guild Phila., Hazlett award Pa. Coun. Arts, 1985, plaque honor Mexican Fedn. Architects; fellow U. Pa. Mus. Fellow Royal Archtl. Inst. Can. (hon.), Royal Australian Inst. Architects; mem. AIA (chpt. dir. Phila. 1965-68, coll. fellows 1969—, nat. dir. 1973-75, v.p. 1977, 1st v.p. 1978, pres. 1979, gold medal Phila. chpt. 1964, 72, 74, silver medal 1973, Nat. Honor award 1974, 75, archtl. firm award 1976), Pa. Soc. Architects (dir. 1966—, sec. 1966, v.p. 1967, pres. 1968, silver medal 1974, 75, 77), Am. Inst. Mgmt. (pres.'s coun. 1967), Pa. Acad. Fine Arts, Pan Am. Fedn. Architects, Nat. Acad. Designs, Societe Arquitecto Mexicanos, Beta Theta Pi. Clubs: Philadelphia, Carpenter's Co., St. Andrew's Soc. (Phila.). Home: 600 E Cathedral Rd E101 Philadelphia PA 19128-1933

MITCHELL, ELIZABETH MARELLE, nursing educator, medical, surgical nurse; b. Bemis, Tenn., Dec. 2, 1937; d. William Columbus and Ruth Marelle (Wadley) Latham; m. Thomas Alton McNatt, June 20, 1953 (dec. Mar. 1984); children: Glenn McNatt, Craig McNatt, Chris McNatt; m. Charles Leon Mitchell, Sept. 7, 1985; stepchildren: Melanie Campbell, Mike, Allyson Flanagan. AA in Nursing, Union U., 1965; BSN, U. Tenn., Martin, 1994; MSN, FNP, U. Tenn., Memphis, 1996. RN, Tenn.; CNOR; cert. BCLS, BCLS instr., BCLS instr. trainer, ACLS, ACLS instr; cert. family nurse practitioner. Staff nurse med.-surg. units Jackson (Tenn.)-Madison County Gen. Hosp., 1965-66; physician 1st asst. Jackson Clinic Surgeons, 1966-74; nursing instr. Jackson Area Vo-Tech Sch., 1974-78, nursing instr. supr., 1978-81; supr. oper. rm. Jackson Splty. Hosp. (acquired by Jackson-Madison County Gen. Hosp. 1983), 1981-85; instr. nurse edn. Jackson-Madison County Gen. Hosp., 1985-96; family nurse practitioner Perry County Med. Ctr.; mem. nursing adv. bd. Jackson Area Vo-Tech Sch., 1987—; mem. task force nursing asst. curriculum devel. State of Tenn., Nashville, 1992; clin. skills judge Health Occupations Student Assn. Tenn. State Competition, Nashville, 1992. Tchr. Sunday sch. Malesus (Tenn.) Bapt. Ch., 1975-86. Mem. ANA, Am. Acad. Nurse Practitioners, Tenn. Nursing Assn., Assn. Oper. Rm. Nurses (del. to congress 1992, mem. program com. 1993, 94), Am. Soc. Healthcare Edn. and Tng. (svc. rep. West Tenn. 1988, Outstanding Regional Rep. Tenn. chpt. 1988), West Tenn. Healthcare Edn. and Tng. Conf. Group (pres. 1987, regional rep. 1988, sec. 1994), U. Tenn. Martin Nursing Honor Soc., Phi Theta Kappa. Avocations: reading, swimming, handicrafts. Home: RR 3 Box 378 Linden TN 37096-9544 Office: Jackson-Madison County Gen Hosp 708 W Forest Ave Jackson TN 38301-3901

MITCHELL, GARY EARL, physicist, educator; b. Louisville, July 5, 1935; s. Earl Raymond and Delma Kathlene (Lockard) M.; m. Carolyn Fey Stutz, Aug. 4, 1957; children: Scott Frederick, Karen Lee (dec.). BS, U. Louisville, 1956; MA, Duke U., 1958; PhD, Fla. State U., 1962. Research assoc. Columbia U., N.Y.C., 1962-64, asst. prof., 1964-68; assoc. prof. N.C. State U., Raleigh, 1968-74, prof. physics, 1974—, assoc. head physics dept., 1982-97. Contbr. numerous articles to sci. publs. Sr. scientist Alexander Von Humboldt Found., Bonn, Fed. Republic Germany, 1975, 97. Recipient Alumni Disting. Prof. award N.C. State U. Fellow Am. Phys. Soc.; mem. numerous sci. assns. Avocation: history. Home: 2913 Harriman Dr Durham NC 27705-5423 Office: NC State U Dept Physics PO Box 8202 Raleigh NC 27695-8202

MITCHELL, GEORGE ERNEST, JR., animal scientist, educator; b. Duoro, N.Mex., June 7, 1930; s. George Ernest and Alma Thyrza (Hatley) M.; m. Billie Carolyn McMahan, Mar. 14, 1952; children: Leslie Dianne, Karen Leigh, Cynthia Faye. B.S., U. Mo., 1951, M.S., 1954; Ph.D., U. Ill., 1956. Asst. prof. animal sci. U. Ill., 1956-60; assoc. prof. U. Ky., Lexington, 1960-67; prof. U. Ky., 1967—, dir. grad. studies in animal scis., 1964-96, coord. beef cattle and sheep, 1974-90. Contbr. articles to profl. jours. Served with USAF, 1951-53. Fulbright research scholar New Zealand, 1973-74; Rsch. scholar Japan Soc. for Promotion of Sci., Japan, 1989. Mem. Am. Soc. Animal Sci. (sec. 1969-70, v.p. 1970-71, pres. So. sect. 1971-72, rsch. fellow 1989, Disting. Svc. award 1994), Am. Dairy Sci. Assn., Am. Inst. Nutrition, AAAS, Council for Agrl. Sci. and Tech., Sigma Xi, Alpha Zeta, Gamma Sigma Delta, Omicron Delta Kappa. Democrat. Methodist. Home: 690 Hill N Dale Rd Lexington KY 40503-2164 Office: U Ky 809 W P Garrigus Bldg Lexington KY 40546

MITCHELL, GEORGE TRICE, physician; b. Marshall, Ill., Jan. 20, 1914; s. Roscoe Addison and Alma (Trice) M.; m. Mildred Aletha Miller, June 21, 1941; children: Linda Sue, Mary Kathryn. BS, Purdue U., 1935; MD, George Washington U., 1940. Intern Meth. Hosp., Indpls., 1940-41; gen. practice medicine Marshall, 1946—; mem. courtesy staff Union and Regional Hosps., Terre Haute, Ind.; clin. assoc. Sch. Basic Medicine U. Ill.; chmn. bd. dirs. First Nat. Bank, Marshall. Author: Dr. George-An Account of the Life of a Country Doctor, 1993. Mem. adv. coun. premedicine Eastern Ill. U., 1965-69; alt. del. Rep. Conv., 1968, del., 1972; trustee Lakeland Jr. Coll., 1978-92. Lt. col. USAAF, 1941-45. Named Health Practitioner of Yr. Ill. Rural Health Assn., 1993; recipient Disting. Svc. award, Lake Lund Coll., 1992, Purdue Alumni Assn. Citizenship award, 1996. Fellow Am. Acad. Family Physicians (Family Physician of Yr. 1993); mem. AMA, Ill. med. Soc. (2d v.p. 1980-81), Clark County Med. Soc. (pres.), Aesculapian Soc. of Wabash Valley (pres. 1965), Nat. Rural Health Assn. (Practitioner of Yr. 1995), Clark County Hist. Soc. (pres. 1968-70), Masons (32 degree), Shriners. Methodist. Home: RR 2 Marshall IL 62441-9802 Office: 410 N 2nd St Marshall IL 62441-1010

MITCHELL, GEORGE WASHINGTON, JR., physician, educator; b. Balt., Apr. 30, 1917; s. George Washington and Katharyne Eugenia (Diggs) M.; m. Anne Jenkins Shriver, Dec. 19, 1942 (div. 1954); children: Beverly Shriver, George Washington III, Anne Jenkins, Edward Diggs; m. Mary Elizabeth McKay, Sept. 14, 1957; children—Bruce McKay, Katharyne Wilcox. A.B., Johns Hopkins, 1938, M.D., 1942. Diplomate: Am. Bd. Ob-Gyn (dir.). Intern Johns Hopkins Hosp., 1942, resident, 1946-49; gynecologist in chief New Eng. Med. Center Hosp., Boston, 1950-81; prof. ob-gyn Tufts U. Sch. Med., 1954-81, prof. emeritus, 1981—, chmn. dept., 1956-81; prof. ob-gyn U. Tex., San Antonio, 1981—; chief of gynecology U. Tex. Health Scis. Center, San Antonio, 1981-92; cons. Surgeon Gen. Navy. Served with USNR, 1943-46. Recipient Pub. Svc. award USN, 1977; named to Soc. Scholars Johns Hopkins U., 1991. Fellow ACS, ACOG, Am. Gynecol. and Obstet. Soc.; mem. AMA, Am. Fertility Soc., Soc. Pelvic Surgeons, Mass. Med. Soc., Obstet. Soc. Boston, New Eng. Ob-Gyn. Soc., Soc. Gynecol. Oncologists, So. Atlantic, Tex. Ob-Gyn. Soc., N.Am. Ob-Gyn. Soc., S.W. Ob-Gyn. soc., Johns Hopkins Med. and Surg. Assn., Soc. of Scholars Johns Hopkins U. Office: Dept Obstetrics and Gynecology U Texas Health Sci Center San Antonio TX 78284

MITCHELL, GLORIA JEAN, elementary school principal, educator; b. Plant City, Fla., Oct. 14, 1945; d. Jessie Mae (Anderson) Smith; m. Thero Mitchell, Sept. 19, 1969; children: Tarra Shariss Patrick, Thero Jr. BS, Bethune-Cookman Coll., 1967; MA, U. Detroit, 1974; postgrad., U. Wash., 1990. Cert. tchr., adminstr. Wash. Tchr. Dade County Schs., Miami, Fla., 1967-71, Agana (Guam) Presch., 1971-72, Detroit Pub. Schs., 1973-76, Prince Williams Schs., Dale City, Va., 1976-81; counselor/tchr. State of Alaska, Ketchikan, 1981-85; tchr. Bellevue (Wash.) Schs., 1985-90, tchr., prin., 1992—; bd. dirs. YMCA Bothell, Wash., chair sustaining drive, 1994-95; bd. dirs. Cascadia C.C., Bothell. Recipient Golden Acorn award PTA-Lake Hills Schs., 1986, Golden Apple award KCTS TV, Seattle, 1994-95; named West Field Vol. of Yr., YMCA, Bothell, Wash., 1987, Woman of Yr., Woodinville (Wash.) Region II Prin. of Yr., Bellevue, 1994. Mem. ASCD, Nat. Alliance Black Sch. Educators, Wash. Alliance Black Sch. Educators,. Avocations: needle point, golf, cmty. volunteerism. Office: Bellevue Pub Schs 14220 NE 8th St Bellevue WA 98007-4103

MITCHELL, GRAHAM RICHARD, government engineering executive; b. Oxford, Eng., Sept. 14, 1938; came to U.S., 1968; s. David and Doris (Clarke) M.; m. Patricia Mary Garside, Jan. 11, 1963; children: Claire Helen, Iain Andrew. BSc, U. Westminster, London, 1962, PhD, 1968. Mgr. rsch., bus. devel. and engring. GE, Phila., 1968-76; cons. GE Corp. R&D Ctr., Schenectady, N.Y., 1976-80; dir. planning & forecasting GTE Labs., Waltham, Mass., 1980-93; asst. sec. of commerce for tech. policy U.S. Dept. Commerce, Washington, 1994—; bd. dirs. Indsl. Rsch. Inst. Contbr. articles to books and profl. jours.; patentee in field. Recipient Ayerton Premium Inst. of Elec. Engring., London, Maurice Holland award IRI, 1993. Mem. IEEE, Am. Mgmt. Assn. (mem. mgmt. coun. 1990—), Internat. Assn. for Mgmt. of Tech. (bd. dirs.). Home: 3909 Highwood Ct NW Washington DC 20007-2132 Office: US Dept Commerce Rm 4814C 14th & Constitution Ave NW Washington DC 20230-0002

MITCHELL, HERBERT HALL, former university dean, educational consultant; b. New Market, Ala., Dec. 10, 1916; s. Walter Hall and Vera Pearl (Johnston) M.; m. Audrey Elizabeth Taylor, Oct. 30, 1942; children: William Hall, Robert Michael, Richard Lee, Mary Ann. B.S., U. Ala., 1939, M.S., 1950; Ph.D., U. N.C., 1954. Asst. to dean of men U. Ala., 1939-42, asst. dean of men, 1942-43, asst. to dean of students, 1946-48; instr. U. N.C., 1948-51; asst. prof. Ala. Poly. Inst., 1951-55, assoc. prof., 1955-56; prof., head dept. bus. adminstrn. Miss State U., 1956-60; prof., chmn. dept. bus. adminstrn. Va. Poly. Inst., 1960-61, dean Sch. Bus., 1961-81, dean emeritus, 1981—; dean Coll. Commerce and Bus. Adminstrn. U. Ala., 1981-86, dean emeritus, 1986—; ednl. cons. and lectr., 1986—; vis. prof. finance grad. program in England and Germany U. Ark., 1972; mem. adv. bd. Intercollegiate Case Clearing House, Harvard U., 1973-76, 77-78. Contbr. articles to jours. Bd. dirs. Ala. Council Econ. Edn., 1982—; trustee Joint Council on Econ. Edn., 1982-86. Capt. Transp. Corps, AUS, 1943-46, col. Res., ret. Edn. fellow Joseph T. Ryerson & Son, Inc., Chgo., summer 1956. Mem. So Bus. Adminstrn. Assn. (pres. 1968-69), Am. Assembly Collegiate Schs. Bus. (dir. 1973-80, v.p. 1977, pres. 1978), Anderson Soc., Ret. Officers Assn., West Ala. Ret. Officers Club (pres. 1989), Indian Hills Country Club, Phi Eta Sigma, Delta Sigma Pi, Beta Alpha Psi, Omicron Delta Epsilon, Beta Gamma Sigma (nat. bd. govs. 1980-84), Omicron Delta Kappa (G. Burke Johnston award 1981), Mu Kappa Tau, Gamma Iota Sigma. Methodist. Home: 82 The Highlands Tuscaloosa AL 35404-2915

MITCHELL, HOWARD ESTILL, human resources educator, consultant; b. Indpls., Aug. 13, 1921; s. Estill and Emma (Howard) M.; m. Nadine Wilson Harris, July 21, 1946; 1 son, Howard Estill Jr. B.S., Boston U., 1943; Ph.D., U. Pa., 1950; D.F.A., Phila. Coll. Art, 1969. Asst. chief clin. psychologist VA Mental Hygiene Clinic, Phila., 1953-57; chief psychologist Lankenaw Hosp., Phila., 1957-59; asst. prof. family study in psychiatry U. Pa. Sch. Medicine, Phila., 1955-66; dir. U. Pa. Human Resources Ctr., 1964-84; prof. human resources U. Pa. Grad. Sch. Fine Arts, Phila., 1966-67, 1907 Found. Prof. urbanism and human resources, 1967-73; UPS prof. mgmt. and human resources Wharton Sch. U. Pa., 1974-92, emeritus UPS prof. mgmt. and human resources, 1992—; dir. U. Pa. Univ. Ctr. Transit Research and Mgmt. Devel., 1981-84; chmn. bd. Change Technologies, Inc., Phila., 1981-85; pres. Mitchell and Mitchell Assn., Phila, 1983—; cons. Barton-Aschman Assocs., Evanston, Ill., 1982-89 , IBM Human Resources Forum, Armonk, N.Y., 1983, Squibb Corp., 1984—, Skadden, Arps, 1985—, Ford Motor Co., 1986—, Gen. Motors Corp., 1986—, Covington & Burling, 1987—, others. Mem. bd. Com. of Seventy, Phila, 1975-78; mem. vestry Old Christ Ch., 1978-88; chieftain Segamores of the Wabash, State of Ind., 1989. Served to 1st lt. U.S. Army, 1943-46. Named Albert Hill Cup Prof. of Yr., Sigma Kappa Phi, 1983, 91; named to Hall of Fame, Boston U., 1996; W.T. Grant Found. fellow, 1950-51. Fellow Am. Psychol. Assn.; mem. Pa. Psychol. Assn. (pres. 1959-60, 50th Anniversary past pres. award 1983), Am. Acad. Mgmt., Am. Soc. Tng. and Devel., Am. Pub. Transp. Assn., Friars Sr. Soc. U. Pa. (hon. mem.). Democrat. Episcopalian. Club: Franklin Inn (Phila.). Office: Mgmt Dept Wharton Sch U Pa 3620 Locust Walk Philadelphia PA 19104-6302

MITCHELL, JACKIE WILLIAMS, state agency administrator, consultant; b. Madison, Miss., June 22, 1964; d. Fillmore and Annie Mae Williams; m. Johnny Lee Mitchell, Dec. 6, 1986. BS in Computer Sci., Jackson State U., 1986, MS in Ednl. Adminstrn. and Supervision, 1991, postgrad., 1992—; grad., Inst. Cmty. Devel., U. Ctrl. Ark. Cert. profl. cmty. developer. Computer sci. instr. Phillips Jr. Coll., Jackson, Miss., 1991-92; cmty. assistance specialist Miss. Dept. of Econ. and Cmty. Devel., Jackson, Miss., 1993—; del. White House Cmty. Empowerment Conf., 1996. Dir. cmty. events The Arts Alliance of Jackson & Hinds County, Jackson, 1987-93. Grantee Miss. Arts Commn., Jackson, 1992. Mem. ASPA (Miss. state coun. mem. 1995—), Cmty. Devel Soc. (Milw.), Toastmasters, Order Eastern Star (Prince Hall Affiliated). Home: 2503 Rutledge Ave Jackson MS 39213-5946 Office: Miss Dept Econ & Cmty Devel PO Box 849 Jackson MS 39205

MITCHELL, JAMES AUSTIN, insurance company executive; b. Cin., Dec. 16, 1941; s. James Austin and Jeannette Louise (Stiles) M.; 1 child, J. David. A.B., Princeton U., 1963. CLU; chartered fin. cons.; FSA. Various positions Conn. Gen. Life Ins. Co., Hartford, 1963-73, v.p., controller, 1973-77; v.p., chief fin. officer Aetna Ins. Co., Hartford, 1977-82; pres. Cigna RE Corp., Hartford, 1982-84; chmn., CEO IDS Life Ins. Co., Mpls., 1984—; dir. IDS Fin. Services and Affiliated Cos., Mpls. Mem. exec. com. Mpls. Inst. Arts, 1987—; bd. dirs. Mpls. YMCA. With U.S. Army, 1964-70. Fellow Soc. Actuaries; mem. Soc. C.L.U.s. Republican. Presbyterian. Club: Minneapolis. Avocations: tennis; skiing; reading. Home: 1314 Marquette Ave # 3404 Minneapolis MN 55403 Office: IDS Life Ins Co 2900 IDS Tower 10 Minneapolis MN 55474

MITCHELL, JAMES KENNETH, civil engineer, educator; b. Manchester, N.H., Apr. 19, 1930; s. Richard N. and Henrietta (Moench) M.; m. Virginia D. Williams, Nov. 24, 1951; children: Richard A., Laura K., James W., Donald M., David L. B.C.E., Rensselaer Poly. Inst., 1951; M.S., M.I.T., 1953; D.Sc., 1956. Mem. faculty U. Calif., Berkeley, 1958-93, prof. civil engring., 1968-89, chmn. dept., 1979-84, Edward G. and John R. Cahill prof. civil engring., 1989-92, Edward G. and John R. Cahill prof. civil engring. emeritus, 1993—; Berkeley citation, 1993; Via prof. civil engring. Va. Poly. Inst. and State U., Blacksburg, 1994—, Univ. Disting. prof., 1996—; geotech. cons., 1960—. Author: Fundamentals of Soil Behavior, 1976, 2d edit., 1993; contbr. articles to profl. jours. Asst. scoutmaster Boy Scouts Am., 1975-82; mem. Moraga (Calif.) Environ. Rev. Com., 1978-80. Served to 1st lt. AUS, 1956-58. Recipient Exceptional Sci. Achievement medal NASA, 1973, Berkeley Citation, 1993. Fellow ASCE (hon., Huber prize 1965, Middlebrooks award 1962, 70, 73, Norman medal 1972, 95, Terzaghi lectr. 1984, Terzaghi award 1985, pres. San Francisco sect. 1986-87); mem. Nat. Acad. Engring., Am. Soc. Engring. Edn. (We. Electric Fund award 1979), NRC (geotech. bd. chmn. 1990-94, bd. on infrastructure and constrn. environ. 1994-96, transp. rsch. bd. exec. com. 1983-87), Internat. Soc. Soil Mechanics and Found. Engring. (v.p. N.Am. 1989-94), Earthquake Engring. Rsch. Inst., Brit. Geotech. Soc. (Rankine lectr. 1991), Sigma Xi, Tau Beta Pi. Office: Va Tech Dept Civil Engring Blacksburg VA 24061-0105

MITCHELL, JANET BREW, health services researcher; b. N.Y.C., Oct. 20, 1949; d. Robert Moscrip Mitchell and Dorothy Brennan; m. Jerry Lee Cromwell, June 15, 1980; children: Alexander, Genevieve. BA with highest honors, U. Calif., San Diego, 1971; MSW, UCLA, 1973; PhD, Brandeis U., 1976. Rsch. asst. Brandeis U./Worcester Tng. Program in Social Rsch. & Psych., Waltham, Mass., 1973-75; sr. analyst Abt Assocs., Cambridge, Mass., 1975-77; asst. prof. Boston U. Sch. Medicine, 1977-80; pres. Ctr. for Health Econs. Rsch., Waltham, Mass., 1980—; mem. com. on monitoring access to health care svcs. Inst. Medicine, 1989-92; mem. nat. adv. com. Robert Wood Johnson Health Care Fin. Fellows, 1988-93; cons. VA, 1982-85, NIH, 1983-85, Health Care Financing Adminstrn., 1979—; advisor Physician Reimbursement Study, Congl. Budget Office, 1984-85; mem. adv. panel on physicians & med. tech. Office of Tech. Assessment, 1984-85; mem. health care tech. study sect. Nat. Ctr. for Health Svcs. Rsch., 1984-88; psychiat. social worker UCLA Med. Ctr., 1971-72; med. social worker U. So. Calif., 1972-73, Univ. Hosp. San Diego, 1973. Author (with F.A. Sloan & J. Cromwell) Private Physicians and Public Programs, 1978; contbr. chpts. to 8 books; contbr. numerous articles to profl. jours. Thesis grantee VA, 1976-77. Office: Ctr for Hlth Econ Rsch 300 5th Ave Waltham MA 02154-8705

MITCHELL, JOHN ADAM, III, banker; b. Wilmington, Del., May 26, 1944; s. John Adam and Carolyn Brown (Shomo) M.; m. Elizabeth Lenta Love, July 17, 1976; children—Christina Love, Jacqueline Elizabeth. B.S. in Elec. Engring., N.C. State U., 1966; M.B.A., U. N.C., 1968. Dir. market research Br. Banking & Trust Co., Wilson, N.C., 1966-70, regional credit adminstr., 1970-73, v.p., city exec., Lexington, 1974-76, sr. v.p., Wilson, N.C., 1977-79; exec. v.p. First Tulsa Bancorp., 1980-82; group exec. v.p. Northwestern Fin. Corp., North Wilkesboro, N.C., 1983-85; dir. advanced mgmt. program N.C. Sch. Banking, Chapel Hill, 1984-89; exec. v.p. First Union Nat. Bank, Greenville, S.C., 1986-87; dir. human resources First Union Corp., 1988-89; pres. First Union Nat. Bank, Jacksonville, Fla., 1990-92, also bd. dirs. 1990—, chmn. 1993—. Chmn. Mayor's commn. on housing, Jacksonville, 1990-93; bd. dirs. INROADS, Inc., Jacksonville, 1992—, chmn. 1992—; chmn. bd. dirs. Jacksonville Zool. Soc., 1995—; pres. bd. trustees Country Day Sch., Jacksonville, 1996—; vice chmn. bd. dirs. Enterprise Fla. Capital Devel. Bd., 1996—. Author: A General Credit Model: A Tool for Loan Officer Training and Decision Making, 1976. Bd. dirs. Jr. Achievement Tulsa, 1982; v.p. N.C. Phys. and Math. Scis. Found., Raleigh, 1984. Mem. Am. Bankers Assn. (banking advisor 1980-84), N.C. Bankers Assn. (dir. comml. lending com. 1983-84). Republican. Baptist. Office: First Union Nat Bank PO Box 2080 Jacksonville FL 32231

MITCHELL, JOHN CHARLES, business executive; b. Bedford, Ind., May 25, 1947; s. John Lewis and Mary Ellen (Rowe) M.; m. Marie Elizabeth Bruland, Aug. 21, 1971; 1 child, Allison Anne. BA in Econs., Va. Mil. Inst., 1969; MBA, Ind. U., 1975, JD, 1975. Bar: Ind., 1975, Fed. Cts., 1975. Brand mgr. Procter and Gamble Co., Cin., 1975-82; group product mgr. RJR/Del Monte, San Francisco, 1982-84; dir. mktg. RJR/Nabisco, Parsippany, N.J., 1984-87, v.p. mktg., 1987-88, v.p., gen. mgr., 1988-90, pres. sales and logistics Co., 1991-94; pres. Planters, Lifesavers co. RJR/Nabisco, Winston-Salem, N.C., 1994-96; v.p., gen. mgr. bus. printer divsn. Lexmark Internat., Inc., Lexington, Ky., 1997—. 1st lt. US Army, 1969-71. Inductee Va. Mil. Inst. Sports Hall of Fame, 1981. Mem. ABA. Republican. Methodist. Avocations: golf, skiing. Office: Lexmark Internat Inc 740 New Circle Rd NW Lexington KY 40511-1806

MITCHELL, JOHN DAVID, journalism educator; b. Chgo., Jan. 22, 1924; m. Mila Agnes Johnston, Sept. 12, 1947 (div. 1981); children: Justin, Alexandra. AB, Oberlin Coll., 1950; MS in Journalism, Kans. State U., 1959. Sports editor Elgin (Ill.) Courier-News, 1946-47; reporter/desk man Rockford Morning Star, Ill., 1950-52, Lima News, Ohio, 1952-56; temp. instr. Kans. State U., 1956-58; asst. prof., assoc. prof. Univ. Colo., 1958-73; mag. dept. acting chair Newhouse Sch., Syracuse (N.Y.) Univ., 1973-79, newspaper dept. chair, 1973-83, journalism divsn. acting asst. dean, 1980-81, journalism prof., 1973-94, prof. emeritus, 1994—; Fulbright lectr. Thammasat Univ., Bangkok, 1962-63; exec. sec. N.Y. State Soc. of Newspaper Editors, Syracuse, 1973-80. Co-author: Mass Communication Resources in Thailand, 1965; contbr. chpt. to The Asian Newspapers Reluctant Revolution, 1971; contbr. articles to profl. jours. Mem. Assn. for Edn. in Journalism and Mass Communication (charter mem. newspaper div., head 1976-79, minorities and communications div. charter mem., sec. 1977-79), Soc. Profl. Journalists, Syracuse Press Club (Svc. award 1984). Democrat. Avocations: sports, collecting jazz, country and western music, travel. Home: 101 Sun Harbor Dr Liverpool NY 13088-4323

MITCHELL, JOHN DAVID, ophthalmologist; b. Arlington, Va., Nov. 13, 1958; s. Joseph David and Janice Lynn (Funkhouser) M.; m. Mary Bell McPherson, Oct. 29, 1983; children: John David Fontaine, Thomas Barrick, Lewis Hopkins. BS in Biochemistry, Va. Tech., 1980; U. Va., 1985. Cert. Am. Bd. Emergency Medicine. Intern Med. Ctr. Del., Wilmington, 1985-86, resident, 1986-88; emergency medicine attending CMty. Hosp., Roanoke, Va., 1988-91, Emergency Rm. Assocs., Roanoke, Va., 1991-94; clin. asst. prof. U. Va., Roanoke, 1992-94; resident Washington Hosp. Ctr., 1994-97, residency program dir. dept. ophthalmology, 1997—; mem. adv. bd. Coll. Health Scis., Roanoke, 1989-91. Recipient Western Va. EMS Coun. Recognition award, 1989, 90, 91, Davis Cup award Washington Hosp. Ctr. Dept. Ophthalmology, 1996. Mem. Am. Acad. Ophthalmology. Republican. Episcopalian. Avocations: hunting, caving, mountaineering. Home: 15619 Meherrin Dr Centerville VA 20120 Office: Washington Hosp Ctr 110 Irving St NW Washington DC 20010-2931

MITCHELL, JOHN DIETRICH, theatre arts institute executive; b. Rockford, Ill., Nov. 3, 1917; s. John Dennis Royce and Dora Marie (Schroeder) M.; m. Miriam Pitcairn, Aug. 25, 1956; children: John Daniel, Lorenzo Theodore, Barbarina Mitchell Heyerdahl. BSS, Northwestern U., 1939, MA, 1941; EdD, Columbia U., 1956; HHD (hon.), Northwood U., 1986. Dir., producer Am. Broadcasting Co., N.Y.C., 1942-46; assoc. editor Samuel French, Pub., N.Y.C., 1946-48; assoc. prof. Manhattan Coll., N.Y.C., 1948-58; pres. Inst. for Advanced Studies in the Theatre Arts, N.Y.C., 1958—; founder, pres. Eaton St. Press, Key West, Fla., 1994; bd. dirs. Beneficia Found., Jenkintown, Pa. Author: Staging Chekhov, 1990, Actors Talk, 1991, Gift of Apollo, 1992, Staging Japanese Theatre: Noh and Kabuki, 1995, Men Stand on Shoulders, 1996; author: (aka Jack Royce) The Train Stopped at Domodossola, 1993, Murder at the Kabuki, 1994, Dressed to Murder, Way to the Towers of Silence, 1997. Trustee Northwood U., Midland, Mich., 1972-91; patron Met. Opera, N.Y.C.; mem. Cmty. Ch. Key West. Named Hon. conch Key West (Fla.) Commrs., 1994. Mem. Met. Mus., Key West Arts and Hist. Soc., Spencer Family Assn. Mayflower Soc., Key West Literary Seminar (emeritus), Nippon Club N.Y.C., N.Y. Athletic Club. Avocations: Tai Chi Chuan, swimming, collecting musical recordings, books. Home: 703 Eaton St Key West FL 33040-6843 also: Eaton Street Press 524 Eaton St # 30 Key West FL 33040-6881 Office: Inst Advanc Studies Theater 703 Eaton St Key West FL 33040-6843

MITCHELL, JOHN HENDERSON, retired army officer, management consultant; b. Atlanta, Sept. 9, 1933; s. William Lloyd and Jessie (Henderson) M.; m. Joan Ann Cameron, Apr. 8, 1961; children: John Cameron, Christopher Lloyd, Colin MacKenzie. BABA, St. Bonaventure U., 1956, PhD in Sci., 1991; MA in Pub. Adminstrn., Shippensburg State U., 1973. Commd. 2nd lt. U.S. Army, 1956, advanced through grades to maj. gen., 1982; comdr. 8th Bn., 6th Arty., 1st Inf. divsn. U.S. Army, Vietnam, 1968; chief officer assignments Field Arty. br. Officer Pers. Directorate, U.S. Army, Washington; chief of staff 8th divsn. U.S. Army, 1973-75; asst. dept. chief of staff for personnel, Hdqrs. U.S. Army Europe and 7th Army U.S. Army, Heidelberg, Germany, 1975-77; comdr. Arty. divsn., chief of staff 1st Inf. divsn. U.S. Army, Ft. Riley, Kans., 1977-79; comdr., Field Command, Def. Nuclear Agy. U.S. Army, Kirtland AFB, N.Mex., 1979-81; dir. Human Resources Devel. Office, dept. chief staff for pers. U.S. Army, Washington; U.S. comdr. Berlin, 1984-88; ret., 1989; pres. Intersys., Inc., Englewood, Colo., 1989-94, Pease, Orr, Mitchell Enterprises, Colorado Springs, Colo., 1994—. Bd. dirs. Nat. Safety Coun., 1982-84. Decorated D.S.M. with oak leaf cluster, Legion of Merit with oak leaf cluster, D.F.C. with oak leaf cluster, Bronze Star with oak leaf cluster and V., Air medals. Mem. Assn. U.S. Army, VFW, Army Navy Club, Army War Coll. Alumni, Soc. of First Inf. Div. Republican. Roman Catholic. Avocations: tennis, history, reading. Home: 375 Hidden Creek Dr Colorado Springs CO 80906-4386

MITCHELL, JOHN MCKEARNEY, manufacturing company executive; b. N.Y.C., Sept. 20, 1938; s. James William and Genevieve (McKearney) M.; AB, Dartmouth Coll., 1960; MBA, Amos Tuck Sch. Bus., 1961; m. Melinda Marsters, Aug. 25, 1962; children: Peter Marsters, Jeffrey Dewing. Acct., Ernst & Whinney, N.Y.C., 1962-64; asst. MIS mgr., mgr. acctg. Sperry Corp., Univac Internat. Div., N.Y.C., Bluebell, Pa., 1964-68; planning analyst, mgr. treas. ops., asst. contr. Sybron Corp., Rochester, N.Y., 1968-80; corp. contr. Condec Corp., Old Greenwich, Conn., 1980-83; exec. v.p. Powell Duffryn (U.S.A.) Ltd., 1983-86; pres. 1986-88; pres. Vt. Marble Co., Proctor, 1988-89, Pluess-Staufer Ind. Inc., 1990—; bd. dirs. Canadiagua Enterprises., Park Ridge Hosp., Greese, N.Y., 1971-80, Assoc. Ind. of Vt., 1990-94; chmn. bd. dirs. Conn. Ballet Theatre, Stamford, Conn., 1983-88. 1st lt., inf., U.S. Army, 1961-62. Mem. Fin. Execs. Inst. Republican. Home: Otis Ho RR 1 Box 257B Danby VT 05739-9754

MITCHELL, JOHN NOYES, JR., electrical engineer; b. Pownal, Maine, Dec. 16, 1930; s. John Noyes and Frances (Small) M.; m. Marilyn Jean Michaelis, Sept. 1, 1956; children: Brian John, Cynthia Lynn Mitchell Tumbleson, Stephanie Lee Mitchell Judson. BSEE, Milw. Sch. Engring., 1957. Registered profl. engr., Ohio. Elec. rsch. engr. Nat. Cash Register Co., Dayton, Ohio, 1957-65; sr. engr. Xerox Corp., Rochester, N.Y., 1965-70, area mgr., 1970-73; area mgr. Xerox Corp., Dallas, 1973-76; area mgr. Xerox Corp., El Segundo, Calif., 1976-79, tech. program mgr., 1979-85, competitive benchmarking mgr., 1985-92, quality mgr., 1992—. With USN, 1949-53. Mem. IEEE, Mason. Republican. Episcopalian. Home: 11300 Providencia St Cypress CA 90630-5351 Office: Xerox Corp ESC1-16W Xerox Centre Dr El Segundo CA 90245-4806

MITCHELL, JOSEPH PATRICK, architect; b. Bellingham, Wash., Sept. 29, 1939; s. Joseph Henry and Jessie Delila (Smith) M.; student Western Wash. State Coll., 1957-59; BA, U. Wash., 1963, BArch, 1965; m. Marilyn Ruth Jorgenson, June 23, 1962; children: Amy Evangeline, Kirk Patrick, Scott Henry. Assoc. designer, draftsman, project architect Beckwith Spangler Davis, Bellevue, Wash., 1965-70; prin. J. Patrick Mitchell, AIA & Assoc./Architects/Planners/Cons., Kirkland, Wash., 1970—. Chmn. long range planning com. Lake Retreat Camp, 1965-93; bldg. chmn. Northshore Baptist Ch., 1980-96, elder, 1984-90; mem. bd. extension and central com. Columbia Baptist Conf., 1977-83; Northshore Bapt. Ch. del. Bapt. World Alliance 16th Congress, Seoul, Korea, 1990, 17th Cong., Buenos Aires, Argentina, 1995; trustee Bakke Libr./Cultural Ctr., 1994-96; vice moderator Columbia Baptist Conf., 1995-96, moderator, 1996-97, ch. ministries overseer bd., 1997—; chartered mem., Cascade Cmty. Ch., 1997—. Recipient Internat. Architectural Design award St. John Vianney Parish, 1989. Cert. Nat. Council Archtl. Registration Bds. Mem. AIA, Constrn. Specification Inst., Interfaith Forum Religion, Art, and Architecture, Nat. Fedn. Ind. Bus., Christian Camping Internat., Wash. Farm Forestry Assn., Rep. Senatorial Inner Circle, Woodinville C. of C., Kirkland C. of C. Republican. Office: 12620 120th Ave NE Ste 208 Kirkland WA 98034-7511 *Personal philosophy: Look to God for inspiration and direction; pursue higher education; be a strong family person; plan wisely for today and the future; work hard yet take time to smell the roses; be firm yet kind; do it right the first time; take care of the details, and the big things will take care of themselves.*

MITCHELL, KENNETH D., physiologist, medical educator; b. Musselburgh, Scotland, Mar. 5, 1959; m. Maria Heavens, Sept. 30, 1995. BSc with upper 2d class honors, U. Edinburgh, Scotland, 1981, PhD in Physiology, 1986. Physiology tutor Univ. Med. Sch., Edinburgh, 1981-84; rsch. assoc. Dept. Physiology and Biophysics Nephrology Rsch. and Tng. Ctr. U. Ala., Birmingham, 1984-86, postdoctoral rsch. fellow, 1986-87, rsch. instr., 1987-88, scientist I, 1987-88; asst. prof. Dept. Physiology Tulane U. Sch. Medicine, New Orleans, 1988-95, assoc. prof., 1995—. Contbr. articles to profl. jours. Nat. Heart, Lung and Blood Inst. grantee, 1995—. Mem. Am. Physiological Soc., Am. Soc. Nephrology, Am. Heart Assn. (fellow Coun. High Blood Pressure Rsch. 1993—, Established Investigator award 1995—), Internat. Soc. Nephrology. Office: Tulane U Sch Medicine Dept Physiology SL39 1430 Tulane Ave New Orleans LA 70112-2699

MITCHELL, LANSING LEROY, federal judge; b. Sun, La., Jan. 17, 1914; s. Leroy A. and Eliza Jane (Richardson) M.; m. Virginia Jumonville, Apr. 18, 1938; children—Diane Mitchell (Mrs. Donald Lee Parker), Lansing Leroy. B.A., La. State U., 1934, LL.B., 1937. Bar: La. 1937. Pvt. practice Pontchatoula, 1937-38; spl. agt. FBI, 1938-41; atty. SEC, 1941-42; asst. U.S. atty. Eastern Dist. La., 1946-53; also engaged in pvt practice; ptnr. Deutsch, Kerrigan & Stiles., New Orleans, 1953-66; U.S. dist. judge Eastern Dist. La., 1966—. Chmn. nat. security com. New Orleans C. of C., 1963-66; vice chmn. New Orleans Armed Forces Day, 1964, 65, New Orleans Heart Fund campaign, 1959-60; mem. New Orleans Municipal Auditorium Adv. Com., 1957-61, New Orleans Municipal Com. Finance, 1955-67, Small Bus. Adv. Council La., 1963-66; pres. Camp Fire Girls Greater New Orleans, 1965-67; La. chmn. Lawyers for Kennedy-Johnson, 1960. Served to lt. col. AUS, 1942-46; col. Res. (ret.). Decorated Royal Order St. George Royal Order Scotland. Mem. ABA, Inter-Am. Bar Assn., La. Bar Assn., New Orleans Bar Assn., Maritime Law Assn. U.S., Judge Adv. Assn., Soc. Former Spl. Agts. FBI, Am. Legion, Mil. Order World Wars, V.F.W., Navy League, Assn. U.S. Army (pres. La. 1964-65, pres. New Orleans 1961-64, v.p. 4th Army region 1963-66), Soc. Mayflower Descendants in State of La. (assoc.), Scabbard and Blade, SAR, S.R., Soc. War 1812 La., Pi Kappa Alpha, Phi Delta Phi, Theta Nu Epsilon. Clubs: Mason (33 degree, New Orleans) (Shriner), Press (New Orleans), Paul Morphy Chess (New Orleans), Southern Yacht (New Orleans), Bienville, Pendennis (New Orleans); Tchefuncta Country (Covington, La.). Office: US Dist Ct C-508 US Courthouse 500 Camp St New Orleans LA 70130-3313 *To serve my country as a soldier, praying that I need never be called to arms again; to serve the people as a jurist, knowing that I too shall someday be judged; to serve my family as a shepherd, finding that my love for them begets greater loving.*

MITCHELL, LEE MARK, communications executive, investment fund manager, lawyer; b. Albany, N.Y., Apr. 16, 1943; s. Maurice B. and Mildred (Roth) M.; m. Barbara Lee Anderson, Aug. 27, 1966; children: Mark, Matthew. A.B., Wesleyan U., 1965; J.D., U. Chgo., 1968. Bar: Ill. 1968, D.C. 1969, U.S. Supreme Ct. 1972. Assoc. Leibman, Williams, Bennett, Baird & Minow, Chgo. and Washington, 1968-72; assoc. Sidley & Austin, Washington, 1972-74, ptnr., 1974-84, 92-94; exec. v.p. and gen. counsel Field Enterprises, Inc., Chgo., 1981-83, pres. and chief exec. officer, 1983-84; pres., chief exec. officer Field Corp., 1984-92; prin. Golder, Thoma, Cressey, Rauner, Inc., Chgo., 1994—; bd. dirs. Paging Network, Inc., Washington Nat. Corp., Chgo. Stock Exch., Inc., PTN Pub. Co., ERO, Inc., Am. Medserve Corp.; chmn. Learning Scis. Corp., NOTIS Systems, Inc., 1987-91. Author: Openly Arrived At, 1974, With the Nation Watching, 1979; co-author: Presidential Television, 1973. Mem. LWV PResdl. Debates Adv. Com., Washington, 1979-80, 82; U.S. del. Brit. Legis. Conf. on Covt. and Media, Ditchley Park, Eng., 1974; bd. visitors U. Chgo. Law Sch., 1984-86, Medill Sch. Journalism, Northwestern U., 1984-91; bd. govs. Chgo. Met. Planning Coun., pres., 1988-91; mem. midwest regional adv. bd. Inst. Internat. Edn., 1987—; trustee Ravinia Festival Assn., Northwestern U. Mem. ABA, Fed. Comm. Bar Assn., Econ. Mid-Am. Club (trustee), Chgo. Club, Comml. Club Chgo. Home: 135 Maple Hill Rd Glencoe IL 60022-1252 Office: Golder Thoma Cressey Rauner Inc 6100 Sears Tower Chicago IL 60606-6326

MITCHELL, LEONA PEARL, soprano; b. Enid, Okla., Oct. 13, 1949; d. Hulon and Pearl Olive (Leatherman) M.; married. BA, Oklahoma City U., 1971, MusD (hon.), 1979. With San Francisco Opera, spring, 1973, fall, 1974, 77. Appeared at Edinburgh (Scotland) Festival, 1977, Sacria Umbria Festival, Perugia, Italy, 1977, on concert tour, Australia, 1978; has sung with most maj. symphonies throughout U.S.; European debut Barcelona, Spain, 1974; Met. Opera debut as Micaela, 1975; also appeared films and TV shows; recs. include Porgy and Bess with Cleve. Orch., 1975. Winner San Francisco Opera auditions, 1971; named Ambassadress of Enid, 1978, Okla. Hall of Fame, 1983. Mem. Am. Guild Musicians Assn. Sigma Alpha Iota, Alpha Kappa Alpha. Mem. Ch. of God in Christ. Performed for Pres. Ford, 1976, Pres. Carter, 1978, 79. Office: Mitchell-Bush Agency 925 S Mason Rd Ste 10 Katy TX 77450-3838*

MITCHELL, MADELEINE ENID, nutritionist, educator; b. Jamaica, W.I., Dec. 14, 1941; came to U.S., 1963, naturalized, 1974; d. William Keith and Doris Christine (Levy) M. B.Sc. in Home Econs., McGill U., Montreal, Que., Can., 1963; M.S., Cornell U., 1965, Ph.D., 1968. Asst. prof. Wash. State U., Pullman, 1969-77, assoc. prof., 1978—, acting chmn. home econs. research ctr., 1981-83, asst. dir. Agri Research Ctr., Coll. Agr. and Home Econs., 1984-86; nutrition scientist U.S. Dept. Agr., Washington, 1980-81. Mem. Am. Dietetics Assn., Am. Soc. Clin. Nutrition, Am. Inst. Nutrition, Assn. Faculty Women, Sigma Xi, Phi Kappa Phi, Omicron Nu. Episcopalian. Avocations: genealogy, music. Office: Wash State U Human Nutrition Dept Food Sci Pullman WA 99164-6376

MITCHELL, MARGERY HOPE, lawyer; b. N.Y.C., Oct. 21, 1942; d. Lee and Florence Waxman; m. Willard H. Mitchell, Apr. 4, 1982. A.B., Smith Coll., 1964; J.D. with honors, George Washington U., 1967. Bar: D.C. 1968, U.S. Supreme Ct. 1971. Law clk. Honorable Spottswood W. Robinson III, U.S. Ct. Apls. for D.C. Cir., 1967-68; assoc. Covington & Burling, 1968-72; asst. gen. counsel Office Consumer Affairs, 1972-73; dep. gen. counsel Cost of Living Council, 1973-74; exec. asst. to chmn. FTC, 1975, asst. dir., dep. dir., acting dir. Bur. Consumer Protection, 1976-77, exec. dir., 1977-79; gen. counsel Office Personnel Mgmt., Washington, 1979-81; dep. gen. counsel Dept. Treasury, Washington, 1981-86; ptnr. Sidley & Austin, Washington, 1986-95, Mediation Coun., Washington, 1995—. Recipient Meritorious Rank award, 1980, Presdl. Disting. Rank award, 1985. Mem. ABA, Am. Law Inst., Fed. Bar Assn., D.C. Bar Assn., Womens Bar Assn. Office: Mediation Coun 3921 Idaho Ave NW Washington DC 20008-3107

MITCHELL, MARK-ALLEN BRYANT, state government administrator; b. La Jolla, Calif., July 25, 1954; s. Carl Thomas Mitchell and Dorothy (Utley) Franklin; m. Judith Dillen Pearce, May 17, 1980 (div. July 1987); 1 child, Mark-Allen Bryant Jr.; m. Teresa Jeanne Mielewski, Dec. 5, 1992. AA, Hudson Valley C.C., 1974; BBA, George Washington U., 1977, MBA, 1981. Acct. World Bank, Washington, 1978-81; contr. CEXEC, Inc., McLean, Va., 1981-82; gen. acctg. mgr. Penril Corp., Gaithersburg, Md., 1983-84; mgr. fin. and adminstrn. Computervision, Dallas, 1984-88; v.p. Currier Travel Agy., Inc., Albany, N.Y., 1989-93; fin. advisor Prudential Securities Inc., Albany, 1993-94; dir. internal audit N.Y. State Dept. Labor, 1994—. Pres., co-founder Sentinel Condominium Homeowners, Inc., Alexandria, Va., 1982-85; dir. Sentinel of Landmark Condominium, Alexandria, 1982-85; Republican committeeman, Town of Colonie, N.Y., 1992-95. Mem. Latham Area C. of C. (bd. dirs. 1993-95). Republican. Roman Catholic. Avocations: politics, religion, travel, photography. Home: Dutch Village Apts 9-CR Mohawk House Albany NY 12204

MITCHELL, MARTIN MORGAN, JR., advertising executive; b. N.Y.C., Aug. 14, 1937; s. Martin Morgan and Helen (Flood) M.; BA, Holy Cross Coll., 1959; MBA, N.Y. U., 1967; postgrad. in advanced mgmt. Harvard U., 1968; m. Ann Fogarty, Mar. 23, 1964; children: Martin, Leeann, Marguerite. Product mgr. Colgate Palmolive Co., N.Y.C., 1960-63; account exec. J. Walter Thompson Co., N.Y.C., 1963-68; acoount exec. Wells Rich Greene, N.Y.C., 1968-81, v.p., account supr., 1969-72, v.p., mgmt. supr., 1972-75, sr. v.p., 1975-80; pres. WRG Can., 1980-81; exec. v.p., gen. mgr. Sawdon and Bess div. Ted Bates Worldwide, N.Y.C., 1981-83, pres., COO, 1983-87; vice chmn. AC&R, 1987-94; pres., COO Burkhardt & Christy (name changed to Christy, MacDougall & Mitchell), N.Y.C., 1994—; assoc. prof. mktg. Pace U., pres. Collegiate Info. Svcs. 1994—; tchr. seminars various univs. Mem. communications bd. Jr. Achievement, 1977-80; pres. Philharmonic Virtuosi, 1987-90, chmn.,1990-94. Served with U.S. Army, 1959-60. Roman Catholic. Club: Westchester Country. Home: 118 Winfield Ave Harrison NY 10528 Office: Christy, MacDougal & Mitchell 304 E 45th St New York NY 10017-3425

MITCHELL, MAURICE MCCLELLAN, JR., chemist; b. Lansdowne, Pa., Nov. 27, 1929; s. Maurice McClellan and Agnes Stewart (Kerr) M.; m. Marilyn M. Badger, June 14, 1952. BS in Chemistry, Carnegie-Mellon U., 1951, MS in Chemistry, 1957, PhD in Phys. Chemistry, 1960. Group leader rsch. and devel. U.S. Steel Corp., Pitts., 1951-61; br. head phys. chemistry rsch. and devel. Melpar Inc., Falls Church, Va., 1961-64; group leader rsch. and devel. Atlantic Richfield Co., Phila., 1964-73; dir. rsch. and devel. Houdry div. Air Products and Chems., Inc., 1973-81; dir. rsch. and devel. Ashland (Ky.) Oil Inc., 1981-86, v.p. rsch. and devel., 1986-93; vis. lectr. dept. chem. Coll. Arts and Scis. Ohio U. Southern Campus, Ironton, 1993-96; cons. in field, 1996—. Contbr. articles to profl. jours.; patentee in field. Fellow Am. Inst. Chemists; mem. Am. Chem. Soc., Am. Inst. Chem. Engrs., Catalysis Soc. N.Am. (pres. 1985-89), AAAS, Sigma Xi. Home: 2380 Hickory Ridge Dr Ashland KY 41101-3604

MITCHELL, MICHAEL KIEHL, elementary and secondary education educator, minister; b. Phila., Pa., Oct. 27, 1932; s. Robert Bartow and Louise Rosm (Keyser) M.; m. Gloria (Nell) Wilburn, Nov. 12, 1960; children: Donald Kiehl, Robert Alan. B in Edn., U. Miami, 1955; MEd, Tex. A&M U., 1975, PhD, 1978; grad., Internat. Sch. Christian Comm. Cert. elem. and secondary edn., Fla., Tex., Alaska; lic. comml. pilot. Tchr. math. Dade County Pub. Schs., Miami Springs, Fla., 1955-60; tchr. elem. Greenwood Sch. Dist., Midland, Tex., 1961-63; from tchr. social studies, English to tng. coord. Midland (Tex.) Sch. Dist., 1963-75; prin. rsch. investigator Tex. A&M U., College Station, 1977-78; project dir. Edn. Profl. Devel. Consortium, Richardson, Tex., 1978-79; sr. rsch. scientist Am. Airlines, Dallas, 1979-83; pres. North Rsch. Inc., Anchorage, Alaska, 1983-84; vocat. edn. curriculum specialist Anchorage Sch. Dist., 1984-87; sci. tchr., dept. head McLaughlin Youth Ctr. Anchorage (Alaska) Sch. Dist., 1987—; adj. prof. U. Alaska, Anchorage, 1987-89; evaluation team N.W. Accreditation Assn., Anchorage, 1985; asst. min. United Meth. ch., 1990-94; min. Christian Cmty. Fellowship, 1994—; instr. Flight and Ground Sch. Dir., v.p. Anchorage Comty. Theater, 1984-89; marriage commr. 3d Jud. Dist. Alaska, Anchorage, 1989-93; vol. United Way, Anchorage, 1984-90, Tony Knowles for Gov. Campaign, Anchorage, 1990, 94, Mark Begich for Mcpl. Assembly Campaign, 1991, Cheryl Clementson for Mcpl. Assembly Campaign, 1993. With U.S. Army, 1946-47. Tex. Edn. Agy. fellow, Austin, 1975, Ednl. Profl. Devel. fellow, 1975-78. Mem. Am. Correctional Edn. Assn., Alaska Airmans Assn. (bd. dirs. 1983-89), Screen Actors Guild, Mensa, Am. Legion, Clowns of Am., Nat. Sci. Tchrs. Assn., Alaska Sci. Tchrs. Assn., Alaskan Aviation Safety Found., Tex. Assn. Aerospace Tchrs., Phi Delta Kappa, Phi Kappa Phi. Avocations: commercial pilot, professional acting, FAA accident prevention counselor. Home: 6626 Foothill Dr Anchorage AK 99504-2620 Office: McLaughlin Youth Cen High 2600 Providence Dr Anchorage AK 99508-4613 *Life has taught me: 1) Regret not the past. 2) Fear not the future. 3) Enjoy the moment.*

MITCHELL, MILTON, lawyer; b. Rochester, N.Y., Apr. 6, 1916; s. Mark and Pauline (Amberg) M.; m. Marion Irene Lieberman, Nov. 1, 1942; children: Mark, Martha. J.D. with honors, George Washington U., 1942. Bar: D.C. 1941, U.S. Supreme Ct. 1966. Atty. Bur. Customs, Washington, 1945-50; asst. chief protocol Dept. State, Washington, 1950-64, sr. atty., 1964-69; lectr., prof. internat. law Nat. Law Ctr., George Washington U., Washington, 1964-80; professional lectr. diplomatic and consular law; gen. counsel Accuracy in Media, Inc., Washington, 1973-90. Bd. dirs. Community Action Council, Rossmoor Leisure World, Silver Spring, Md., 1979-85. Served to lt. USNR/World War II. Mem. Fed. Bar Assn., D.C. Bar Assn., Am. Acad. Philately (dir., pres.), Soc. Philatelic Americans, Royal Philatelic Soc. Can. Republican. Clubs: Lawyer (Washington); Diplomatic and Consular Assn. Aspen Hill Tennis. Address: 3401 Hallaton Ct Silver Spring MD 20906-1833 *I have always felt that one of cardinal principles of my life was to tell it like it is— to have the courage to present my views on important subjects, no matter whether they met with agreement or disagreement. It was never my policy to curry favor with important people just to please them or to advance my station in life. I have always felt I first have to live with myself, and I have found that most people valued my sincerity, whether or not they agreed with my position.*

MITCHELL, ORLAN E., clergyman, former college president; b. Eldora, Iowa, Mar. 13, 1933; s. Frank E. and Alice G. (Brown) M.; m. Verlene J. Huehn, June 10, 1952; children: Jolene R., Stephen M., Nadene A., Timothy M., Mark E. B.A., Grinnell Coll., 1955; B.D., Yale U., 1959, M.Div., 1965; D.Min., San Francisco Theol. Sem., 1976. Ordained to ministry United Ch. of Christ, 1959; pastor chs. Sheridan Twp., Iowa, 1954-55, New Preston, Conn., 1956-59, Clarion, Iowa, 1959-69, Yankton, S.D., 1969-77; pres. Yankton (S.D.) Coll., 1977-96; conf. minister Iowa Conf. United Ch. Christ; ret., 1996; cons. in field. Mem. Sch. Bd., Clarion, Iowa, 1965-69, mem., Yankton, S.D., 1973-77, pres., 1976; bd. dirs. Lewis and Clark Mental Health Center. Mem. S.D. Found. Pvt. Colls., S.D. Assn. Pvt. Colls., Colls. of Mid-Am. Democrat. Lodges: Kiwanis; Masons. Office: 725 Park St Grinnell IA 50112-2235

MITCHELL, PAMELA ANN, airline pilot; b. Otis AFB, Mass., May 6, 1955; d. Gene Thomas and Rose Margaret (Jones) Mitchell; m. Robert Carroll Stephens, May 26, 1984 (div. Dec. 1992). BFA, Colo. State U., 1975; postgrad., Webster Coll., 1981. Lic. pilot Ill., comml. instr., airline transport pilot, jet rating, Boeing 747 and 727, Boeing 747-400. Flight attendant United Airlines, Chgo., 1976-80; charter pilot Air Aurora, Sugar Grove, Ill., 1978-80; owner, operator Deliverance, Unltd. Ferry Co., Aurora, Ill., 1978-81; flight test pilot Cessna Aircraft Co., Wichita, Kans., 1981-82, nat. spokeswoman, 1982-83; airline pilot Rep. Airlines, Mpls., 1983-84, Northwest Airlines, Mpls., 1985—; pres., prtnr., artist Aerographics Jacksonville, Fla., 1986-90. Mem. Safety Coun. Airline Pilots Assn., 99's Internat. Women Pilots Assn., Mooney Aircraft Pilots Assn., Internat. Soc. Women Airline Pilots (bd. dirs. 1994-96), Nat. Aviation Club, N.W. Airline Ski Team (capt. 1989-94), Kappa Kappa Gamma. Republican. Presbyterian. Avocations: piano, snow skiing, tennis, travel, golf. Home: 12502 Mission Hills Cir Jacksonville FL 32225 Office: Northwest Airlines Minn/St Paul Internat Airport Saint Paul MN 55111

MITCHELL, PAULA RAE, nursing educator; b. Independence, Mo., Jan. 10, 1951; d. Millard Henry and E. Lorene (Denton) Gates; m. Ralph William Mitchell, May 24, 1975. BS in Nursing, Graceland Coll., 1973; MS in Nursing, U. Tex., 1976; EdD in Ednl. Adminstrn., N.Mex. State U., 1996. RN, Tex., Mo.; cert. childbirth educator. Commd. capt. U.S. Army, 1972; ob-gyn. nurse practitioner U.S. Army, Seoul, Korea, 1977-78; resigned, 1978; instr. nursing El Paso (Tex.) C.C., 1979-85, dir. nursing, 1985—, acting div. chmn. health occupations, 1985-86, div. chmn., 1986—, curriculum facilitator, 1984-86; ob-gyn. nurse practitioner Planned Parenthood, El Paso, 1981-86, mem. med. com., 1986—; cons. in field. Author: (with Grippando) Nursing Perspectives and Issues, 1989, 93; contbr. articles to profl. jours. Founder, bd. dirs. Health-C.R.E.S.T., El Paso, 1981-85; mem. pub. edn. com. Am. Cancer Soc., El Paso, 1983-84, mem. profl. activities com., 1992-93; mem. El Paso City-County Bd. Health, 1989-91; mem. Govt. Applications Rev. Com., Rio Grande Coun. Govts., 1989-91; mem. collaborative coun. El Paso Magnet H.S. for Health Care Professions, 1992-94, co-chair, Unite El Paso Health and Human Svc. Task Force, 1996—. Decorated Army Commendation medal, Meritorious Svc. medal. Mem. Nat. League Nursing (mem. resolutions com. Assocs. Degree coun. 1987-89, accreditation site visitor, AD coun. 1990—, mem. Tex. edn. com. 1991-92, Tex. 3rd v.p. 1992-93), Am. Soc. Psychoprophylaxis Obstetrics, Nurses Assn. Am. Coll. Obstetricians & Gynecologists (cert. in ambulatory women's health care; chpt. coord. 1979-83, nat. program rev. com. 1984-86, corr. 1987-89), Advanced Nurse Practitioner Group El Paso (coord. 1980-83 legis. committee 1984), Am. Phys. Therapist Assn. (commn. on accreditation, site visitor for phys. therapist assistant programs 1991—), Orgn. Assoc. Degree Nursing (Tex. membership chmn. 1985-89, chmn. goals com. 1989—, mem nat. bylaws com., 1990-95), Am. Vocat. Assn., Am. Assn. Women Community & Jr. Colls., Tex. Orgn. Nurse Execs., Nat. Coun. Occupational Edn. (mem. articulation task force 1986-89, program standards task force 1991-93), Nat. Coun. Instructional Adminstrs., Tex. Soc. Allied Health Profls., Tex. Nurses Assn., Nat. Soc. Allied Health Profls. (mem. edn. com. 1993—), Sigma Theta Tau, Phi Kappa Phi. Mem. Christian Ch. (Disciples of Christ). Home: 4616 Cupid Dr El Paso TX 79924-1726 Office: El Paso C C PO Box 20500 El Paso TX 79998-0500

MITCHELL, PETER KENNETH, JR., educational consultant, association administrator; b. Bklyn., June 12, 1949; s. Peter Kenneth and Joan Marie (Hayes) M.; m. Susan Veitch Mitchell, June 25, 1983; 1 child, Elyse Alexandra. BA, SUNY, Geneseo, 1970; MS in French, L.I. U., 1975; cert. of French lang. proficiency, U. de Neuchatel, Switzerland, 1969. Tchr. French and Spanish Middle Country Sch. Dist., Selden, N.Y., 1972-81; tech. asst. to dir. internat. affairs dept. Am. Fedn. Tchrs., Washington, 1981-82; asst. to gen. sec. Internat. Fedn. of Free Tchrs. Unions, Amsterdam, 1982-90; exec. dir. Internat. Reading Assn., Newark, Del., 1990-91; owner Insights Out Assocs., Newark, Del., 1992—; dir. mktg. Jr. Achievement Del., 1994—. Author numerous ednl. publs. Mem. ACLU, Am. Soc. Assn. Execs., Blue and Gold Club, Washington U. Club, Amnesty Internat. Avocations: reading, music. Office: Insights Out Assocs PO Box 9652 Newark DE 19714-9652

MITCHELL, PETER WILLIAM, addictions counselor; b. Queens, N.Y., Sept. 2, 1950; s. James Francis and Margaret (Tiernan) M.; m. Mary Elizabeth Brett, May 15, 1976; children: Bryan Scott, Shannon Marie, Kevin James, Michael Ryan. BS in Mktg., Fordham U., 1972; MBA, Calif. Coast U., 1984. Cert. criminal justice specialist, master addictions counselor. Spl. agt. FBI, Washington, 1972-77; store co-mgr. First Nat. Stores, Inc., Somerville, Mass., 1977-78; area sales mgr. H.J. Heinz Co., Indpls., 1978-83; exec. sales rep. Sandoz Nutrition Corp., Mpls., 1983-91; regional sales mgr. Fresenius Pharma USA, Inc., New Brunswick, N.J., 1991-92; sales cons. Cardinal Health/Marmac Div., East Windsor, Conn., 1992-93; primary counselor, case mgr. Sunrise House Found., Lafayette, N.J., 1993—. Bd. mem. Vernon (N.J.) Twp. Little League, 1985-89, Vernon (N.J.) Bd. Ethics, 1991—. Recipient Capitol award Nat. Leadership Coun., Washington, 1991. Mem. Nat. Assn. Alcoholism and Drug Abuse Counselors, Am. Assn. Compulsive Gambling Counselors, Nat. Assn. Forensic Counselors. Republican. Roman Catholic. Avocations: softball, basketball, volleyball, golf. Home: 101 Greenhill Rd Hamburg NJ 07419 Office: Sunrise House Found PO Box 600 Lafayette NJ 07848-0600

MITCHELL, PHILIP MICHAEL, aerospace engineer, consultant; b. Mobile, Ala., Feb. 12, 1953; s. Philip Augustus and Betty J. (Hardy) M. BS in Aeros. magna cum laude, Embry-Riddle Aero. U., Daytona Beach, Fla., 1980, MS in Aeros., 1987; MBA in Ops. and Project Mgmt., Wright State U., 1997. Radar systems engr. ITT, Van Nuys, Calif., 1980-82; commd. 2d lt. USAF, 1982, advanced through grades to maj., 1994; bomber br. chief 42d Orgnl. Maintenance Squadron, Loring AFB, Maine, 1983-86; officer-in-charge weapons br. 520th Aircraft Generation Squadron, RAF Upper Heyford, Eng., 1986; asst. maintenance supr. 20th Equipment Maintenance Squadron, RAF, RAF Upper Heyford, 1986-87, 88-90; weapons safety officer 20th Tactical Fighter Wing, RAF Upper Heyford, 1986-87; chief standardization and tng. div. 42d Bomb Wing, Loring AFB, 1990-91; chief of maintenance 42d Maintenance Squadron, Loring AFB, Maine, 1991-92; maintenance mgmt. officer 42d BMW, 1992-94; dir. spl. projects and policies Aero. Sys. Ctr., Wright-Paterson AFB, Ohio, 1994-95; grad. rsch. asst. Wright State U., 1995—; adj. prof. European div. Embry-Riddle Aero. U., 1988-90; aerospace cons., 1987—. Recipient Meritorious Svc. medal with cluster, Commendation medal with one oak leaf cluster, Air Force Achievement medal. Fellow Brit. Interplanetary Soc.; mem. AIAA (sr.), Am. Soc. Quality Control, Soc. Logistics Engrs., Am. Prodn. and Inventory Control Soc., Air Force Assn., Royal Scottish Country Dance Soc., Masons (32 deg.), Scottish Rite, Sigma Iota Epsilon. Episcopal. Avocations: flying, skiing, Scottish country dancing. Home and Office: 6305 Longford Rd Dayton OH 45424-3573

MITCHELL, RICHARD BOYLE, advertising executive; b. St. Louis, June 20, 1947; s. Samuel West and Blair (Boyle) M.; m. Deborah Mead Boas, June 1, 1968; children: Rebecca, Jessica. BS in Mktg., NYU, 1969. Account exec. D.L. Blair Corp., N.Y.C., 1967-70, NW Ayer Advt. Agy., N.Y.C., 1970-74; sr. account exec. Ted Bates Agy., N.Y.C., 1974-75; sr. v.p. DKG Advt., N.Y.C., 1975-81, McCaffrey/McCall, N.Y.C., 1981-86; pres., CEO Marshall Jaccoma Mitchell Advt., N.Y.C., 1986-96; sr. ptnr. Poppe Tyson Advt., N.Y.C., 1996—. Commr. Wilton (Conn.) Police Dept., 1984—. Served with USAR, 1969-74. Democrat. Roman Catholic. Club: Wilton Riding. Avocations: mil. history, running, weight lifting. Home: 43 Collinswood Rd Wilton CT 06897-1811 Office: Poppe Tyson Advt 40 W 23rd St New York NY 10010-5200

MITCHELL, RICK, journalist, writer; b. San Jose, Calif., Nov. 27, 1952; s. Maurice Dale Mitchell and Mary Margaret (Woody) Gron; m. Lori Sumako, May 3, 1987; 1 child, Chelsea Pearl. BA in Am. Studies, Calif. State U., Fullerton, 1974. Music critic Oreg. Jour., Portland, 1978-82, Willamette Week, Portland, 1983, The Oregonian, Portland, 1984-85; music critic, sports columnist Willamette Week, 1986; freelance writer L.A., 1987; arts and entertainment reporter The Bakersfield Californian, 1988; music critic Houston Chronicle, 1989—. Author: Garth Brooks: One of A Kind, Workin' on A Full House, 1993; jazz columnist Request Mag., 1990—; contbr. New Country Music Mag., 1994—. Mem. adv. com. Houston Blues Soc.; mem. Houston Zen Cmty. Mem. Amnesty Internat. Avocations: athletics, reading.

MITCHELL, ROBERT ARTHUR, college president; b. N.Y.C., Jan. 19, 1926; s. George P. and Vera A. (Duffy) M. A.B. (summa cum laude), Woodstock Coll., 1949, AB summa cum laude, 1950; STL magna cum laude, Facultes S.J. de Louvain, Belgium, 1957; ThD, U. Strasbourg, France, 1965; (hon.), Le Moyne Coll., 1990, Loyola U., 1991; U. Detroit, 1992. Joined S.J., 1943, ordained priest, Roman Cath. Ch., 1956. Instr. in philosophy LeMoyne Coll., 1950-53, asst. prof. theology, 1958-59, acad. dean, 1959-63, assoc. prof. theology, acad. dean, 1965-66; pres. Loyola Coll., Shrub Oak, 1966; provincial N.Y. State Province (S.J.), 1966-72; pres. Jesuit Conf., chmn. Am. Jesuit Provincials, Washington, 1972-76; dir. Woodstock Theol. Ctr., 1976-79; pres. U. Detroit, 1979-90, chancellor, 1990-92; consultant, Higher Education to Jesuit U.S. Provincials, 1992—; acting pres. Le Moyne Coll., Syracuse, N.Y., 1993-94, pres., 1994—; bd. dirs. Economic Club of Detroit, 1979-92, Detroit Econ. Growth Corp., 1983-92, Detroit Symphony Orchestra, 1981-89, Woodstock Theological Ctr., 1977-83, Georgetown U., 1976-82, 1983-92; bd. trustees, Loyola Marymount U., 1986, St. Peter's Coll., 1992, U. Detroit, 1979, Sta. WTVS/Channel 56, 1979-86, 1988-92, Michigan Cancer Foundation, 1985-92, New Detroit, Inc., 1979-92, Fordham U., 1966-74, Le Moyne Coll., 1977-83, Boston Coll., 1966-90. Office: Le Moyne College Office of the Pres Syracuse NY 13214

MITCHELL, ROBERT CAMPBELL, nuclear consultant; b. West Point, N.Y., Mar. 28, 1940; s. Herbert V. and Beatrice Cheeseman (Campbell) M.; m. Mardeene Burr, Aug. 19, 1963 (div. Dec. 1983); children: Wendolyn, Dawnelle; m. Patricia Johnson, Aug. 17, 1987. B of Engring., Stevens Inst. Tech., 1962; MEE, Rensselaer Poly. Inst., 1965. Registered profl. engr., Calif. Design/ops. engr. Knolls Atomic Power Lab., Schenectady, N.Y., 1962-67; prin. tng. engr. Nuclear Energy Div. Gen. Electric Co., San Jose, Calif., 1967-72, project engr., 1972-75, mgr. advanced projects, 1975-77, project mgr., 1977-87, licensing mgr., 1987-95; pvt. cons. San Jose, 1995—. Contbr. articles to profl. jours. Nominee White House fellow Gen. Electric Co., San Jose, 1973. Mem. Elfun Soc. Republican. Avocations: photography, bridge, golf, computers. Home and Office: 2140 E Bighorn Mt Dr Tucson AZ 85737

MITCHELL, ROBERT DALE, consulting engineer; b. Worthington, Minn., Aug. 2, 1910; s. Karl V. and Margaret Dumont (Steigleder) M.; m. Carol Sherman Northrop, June 17, 1939; children—Constance Remington, Robert Brown. B.S., S.D. State U., 1932; S.M. (grad. fellow), Harvard U., 1939. Engr. J. Emberg, Madison, S.D., 1932-35; instr. S.D. State U., 1935-37; engr. Malcolm Pirnie, N.Y.C., 1939-42; project engr., partner Malcolm Pirnie, 1945-70, sr. v.p., sec., chief engr., 1970-75, cons., 1975—. Served to maj. San. Corps AUS, 1942-45. Recipient Distinguished Engr. award S.D. State U., 1977. Mem. ASCE, Am. Water Works Assn., Am. Cons. Engrs. Council, New Eng. Water Works Assn. (Commemorative award 1963). Home: 487 Brackett Rd Rye NH 03870-2204 Office: 102 Corporate Park Dr White Plains NY 10604-3802

MITCHELL, ROBERT EDWARD, urban planner, international development specialist, educator; b. Detroit, May 16, 1930; s. Arthur and Elizabeth (Wayne) M.; m. Sylvia Ann Sheppard, Aug. 26, 1950 (div. 1993); children: Anthony Edward, Maude Wayne, Adam Arthur. BA in Oriental Civilizations, U. Mich., 1952; M.A., Harvard U., 1955; Ph.D. in Sociology, Columbia U., 1962. Instr., project dir. Bur. Applied Social Research, Columbia U., 1956-62; coord. internat. rsch. program, dep. dir. Survey Research Center, U. Calif.-Berkeley, 1962-66; dir. Hong Kong Urban Family Life Survey, dir. Social Survey Research Centre, Chinese U., Hong Kong, 1966-69; chief tech. market rsch. adviser Grant Advt. of Hong Kong, 1967-70; prof. urban and regional planning, dir. Survey Data Center Fla. State U., Tallahassee, 1969-78; pvt. internat. devel. cons., 1995—; exec. dir. Fla. Gov.'s Task Force on Housing and Cmty. Devel., 1971-73; mem. UN Ad Hoc Meeting Experts on Social Aspects of Housing in Urban Areas, 1970; mem. tech. mission to Jordan Dept. State, 1973; behavioral sci. adv. urban devel. Nr. East Bur., Office Tech. Support, AID, Dept. State, Washington, 1979—, devel. ofcl., 1980-95; AID duty tours, Egypt, Yemen and Guinea-Bissau; cons. in field. Author: The Needs of Hong Kong Manufacturing Industry for Higher Level Manpower, 1968, Levels of Emotional Strain in Southeast Asian Cities: A Study of Individual Responses to the Stresses of Urbanization and Industrialization, Family Life in Urban Hong Kong, 1972, Pupil, Parent and School, 1972, Housing, Urban Growth, and Economic Development, 1972; Contbr. articles to profl. jours. Mem. Am. Sociol. Assn.

MITCHELL, ROBERT EVERITT, lawyer; b. Port Washington, N.Y., June 14, 1929; s. Everitt and Alice (Fay) M.; m. Anne Nordquist, Nov. 2, 1957; children: Anne C. Mitchell Coneys, Maura A. Kelly, Michael E. BS, U. Mich., 1952; JD, Georgetown U., 1956. Bar: N.Y. 1957, U.S. Dist. Ct. (so. dist.) N.Y. 1958, U.S. Supreme Ct. 1966. Assoc. Sullivan & Cromwell, N.Y.C., 1956-63; v.p., sec., gen. counsel Lambert & Co. Inc., N.Y.C., 1963-65; ptnr. Campbell & Mitchell, Manhasset, N.Y., 1965-80; asst. gen. counsel J.P. Stevens & Co. Inc., N.Y.C., 1980-82, gen. counsel, 1982-88; pvt. practice Peconic, N.Y., 1988—. Atty. Village Baxter Estates, Port Washington, 1967-83; Counsel Mobilized Community Resources, Roslyn, N.Y., 1969-80; asst. scout master Troop 1001 Boy Scouts Am., Port Washington, 1976-79; justice Village Sands Point, N.Y., 1966-85. Served to lt. USNR, 1952-55. Mem. ABA. Republican. Roman Catholic. Clubs: Manhasset Bay Yacht (Port Washington) (commodore 1972-73); N.Y. Yacht (N.Y.C.). Avocations: sailing, fishing, camping, platform tennis, music. Home and Office: 3905 Wells Rd Peconic NY 11958-1738

MITCHELL, ROBERT GREENE, industrial manufacturing executive, consultant; b. Abington, Pa., July 20, 1925; s. James Henry and Nellie Edna (Greene) M.; m. Alma Maerker Honsberger, Mar. 6, 1948; children: Scott Craig, Donna Lynn, Sandra Lee. B.S., Drexel U., 1948. Cert., CPIM. Dept. mgr. Internat. Playtex, Dover, Del., 1949-52, quality control mgr., 1952-59, mfg. mgr. Indsl. div., 1959-60; v.p. ops. The Wool "O" Co., Phila., 1960-65; mfg. mgr. Plymouth Rubber, Canton, Mass., 1965-68; chief indsl. engr., spl. projects Vanity Fair Mills, Monroeville, Ala., 1968-75; v.p. materials mgmt. The H.W. Gossard Co., Chgo., 1975-76; v.p. adminstrn., 1977; v.p. adminstrn., mem. exec. com. Knickerbocker Toy Co., Middlesex, N.J., 1977-79; pres. H&R Block, Prince Frederick, Md., 1979-85; sr. mfg. cons. Sperry Corp. (now UNISYS Corp.), Lutherville, Md., 1980-87, Hunt Valley, Md., 1987-89; ret., 1989. 1st lt. USAF, 1943-46. Mem. Am. Soc. Quality Control (cert. quality engr., chmn. textile div. 1959-60), Am. Prodn. and Inventory Control Soc. Lodge: Lions (dir. 1954-56, pres. 1955-56). Patentee in field. Home and Office: 22 Hillside Ct Huntingtown MD 20639-9406

MITCHELL, ROGER LOWRY, agronomy educator; b. Grinnell, Iowa, Sept. 13, 1932; s. Robert T. and and Cecile (Lowry) M.; m. Joyce Elaine Lindgren, June 26, 1955; children: Laura, Susan, Sarah, Martha. B.S. in Agronomy, Iowa State Coll., 1954; M.S., Cornell U., 1958; Ph.D. in Crop Physiology, Iowa State U., 1961. Mem. faculty Iowa State U., 1959-69, prof. agronomy, 1966-69, prof. charge farm operation curriculum, 1962-66; prof. agronomy, chmn. dept. U. Mo., Columbia, 1969-72, 81-83; dean agr., dir. expt. sta. U. Mo., 1983—, dean extension, 1972-75; v.p. agr. Kans. State U., Manhattan, 1975-80; exec. dir. Mid-Am. Internat. Agrl. Consortium, 1981; exec. bd. divsn. agr. Nat. Assn. State Univs. and Land Grant Colls., 1978-80, 85-90, chmn., 1988-89; mem. bd. agr. NRC/NAS, 1983-86. Author: Crop Growth and Culture, 1970; co-author: Physiology of Crop Plants, 1985. Served to 2d lt. USAAF, 1954-56. Danforth fellow, 1956-61; Acad. Adminstrn. fellow Am. Council Edn., 1966-67. Fellow AAAS (chmn. sect. O 1980-81), Am. Soc. Agronomy (pres. 1979-80), Crop Sci. Soc. (pres. 1975-76); mem. Soil Sci. Soc. Am., Coun. Agrl. Sci. and Tech., Sigma Xi, Gamma Sigma Delta, Alpha Zeta, Phi Kappa Phi. Home: 502 W Lathrop Rd Columbia MO 65203-2804

MITCHELL, RONNIE MONROE, lawyer; b. Clinton, N.C., Nov. 10, 1952; s. Ondus Corneilius and Margaret Ronie (Johnson) M.; m. Martha Cheryl Coble, May 25, 1975; children: Grant Stephen, Mitchell, Meredith Elizabeth Mitchell. BA, Wake Forest U., 1975, JD, 1978. Bar: N.C. 1978, U.S. Dist. Ct. (ea. dist.) N.C. 1978, U.S. Ct. Appeals (4th cir.) 1983, U.S. Supreme Ct. 1984. Assoc. atty. Brown, Fox & Deaver, Fayetteville, N.C., 1978-81; ptnr. Harris, Sweeny & Mitchell, Fayetteville, 1981-91, now Harris, Mitchell & Hancox, 1991—; adj. prof. law Norman Adrian Wiggins Sch. of Law, Campbell U; bd. dirs. Mace, Inc. Contbr. chpts. to books. Chmn. Cumberland County Bd. Adjustment, 1985—, Cumberland County Rescue Squad, 1986-93; bd. dirs. Cumberland County Rescue Squad, Fayetteville, 1983-91. Recipient U.S. Law Week award Bur. Nat. Affairs, 1978. Mem. ABA, ATLA, Twelfth Judicial Dist. Bar Assn. (pres. 1988-89), N.C. Bar Assn. (councillor Young Lawyers divsn. 1982-85), N.C. Legis. Rsch. Commn. (family law com. 1994), Cumberland County Bar Assn. (mem. family law com., N.C. State Bar Bd. legal specialization), N.C. Acad. Trial Lawyers, Fayetteville Ind. Light Infantry Club, Dem. Men's Club (pres. 1993-94), Moose, Masons. Home: RR 23 Box 108C Fayetteville NC 28301-9125 Office: Harris Mitchell & Hancox 308 Person St Fayetteville NC 28301-5736

MITCHELL, ROY DEVOY, industrial engineer; b. Hot Springs, Ark., Sept. 11, 1922; s. Watson W. and Marie (Stewart) M.; m. Jane Caroline Gibson, Feb. 14, 1958; children: Michael, Marilyn, Martha, Stewart, Nancy. BS, Okla. State U., 1948, MS, 1950; B of Indsl. Mgmt., Auburn U., 1960. Registered profl. engr., Ala., Miss. Instr. Odessa (Tex.) Coll., 1953-56; prof. engrng. graphics Auburn (Ala.) U., 1956-63; field engr. HHFA, Cmty. Facilities Adminstrn., Atlanta and Jackson, Miss., 1963-71; area engr. Met. Devel. Office, HUD, 1971-72, chief architecture and engring., 1972-75, chief program planning and support br., 1975, dir. archtl. br., Jackson, 1975-77, chief archtl. br. and engring. br., 1977-84, cmty. planning and devel. rep., 1984-88; prin. Mitchell Mgmt. and Engring., 1988—; cons. Army Balistic Missile Agy., Huntsville, Ala., 1957-58, Auburn Rsch. Found., NASA, 1963; mem. state tech. action panel Coop. Area Manpower Planning System; elected pub. ofcl., chmn. Bd. of Election Commrs., Rankin County, Miss. Mem. Cen. Miss. Fed. Personnel Adv. Council; mem. House and Home mag. adv. panel, 1977; trustee, bd. dirs. Meth. Ch., 1959-60; docent Miss. Mus. Art, 1993—; bd. dirs. Am. Heart Assn., Rankin County, 1994. Served with USNR, 1943-46. Recipient Outstanding Achievement award HUD, Commendation by Sec. HUD. Mem. NSPE, Am. Soc. for Engring. Edn., Miss. Soc. Profl. Engrs., Nat. Assn. Govt. Engrs. (charter mem.), Jackson Fed. Execs. Assn., Ctrl. Miss. Safety Coun., Am. Water Works Assn., Iota Lambda Sigma. Club: River Hills (Jackson). Home and Office: HUD 706 Forest Point Dr Brandon MS 39042-6220

MITCHELL, ROY SHAW, lawyer; b. Sherwood, N.Y., Jan. 16, 1934; s. Malcolm Douglas and Ruth Landon (Holland) M.; m. Nancy Elizabeth Bishop, Aug. 27, 1955; children: Mark E., Jeffrey B., Jennifer R. BS, Cornell U., 1957; JD with honors, George Washington U., Washington, D.C., 1959. Bar: D.C. 1959, Ohio 1960, Va. 1967, U.S. Ct. Fed. Claims 1963, U.S. Supreme Ct. 1965. Atty. Squire, Sanders & Dempsey, Cleve., 1960-61, Hudson & Creyke, Washington, 1961-67, Lewis, Mitchell & Moore, Vienna, Va., 1967-87, Morgan, Lewis & Bockius, Washington, 1987—; vice-chmn. Ameribanc Savs. Bank, Annandale, Va., 1980-95; trustee Ameribanc Investors Group, Annandale, 1980-95. Co-author: (with others) Handbook of Construction Law and Claims, 1982, 89; contbr. numerous articles to profl. jours. Fellow ABA (pub. contract law sect.), Am. Coll. Construction Lawyers, Va. Bar Assn., D.C. Bar Assn. Presbyterian. Avocation: boating. Home: 5 Jefferson Run Rd Great Falls VA 22066-3227 Office: Morgan Lewis & Bockius 1800 M St NW Washington DC 20036-5802

MITCHELL, RUSSELL HARRY, dermatologist; b. Erie, N.D., Oct. 19, 1925; s. William John and Anna Lillian (Sögge) M.; B.S., B.A., U. Minn., Mpls., 1947, B.M., M.D., 1951; postgrad. U. Pa. Med. Sch., 1968-69; m. Judith Lawes Douvarjo, May 24, 1968; children: Kathy Ellen, Gregory Alan, Jill Elaine, Crystal Anne. Intern Gorgas Hosp., C.Z., 1951-52; resident in dermatology U.S. Naval Hosp., Phila., 1967-70; asst. chief out-patient dept. Gorgas Hosp., 1955-64; chief med. and surg. wards Ariz. State Hosp., Phoenix, 1965; commd. lt. (j.g.) M.C., U.S. Navy, 1953, advanced through grades to capt., 1968; svc. in Vietnam; ret., 1981; pvt. practice specializing in dermatology, Leesburg, Va., 1978—; mem. staff Loudoun Health Ctr., 1975—; dermatologist Nat. Naval Med. Center, Bethesda, Md., 1973-81; asst. prof. Georgetown U. Med. Sch., 1975-85. Pres. Archaeol. Soc. Panama, 1962-64. Decorated Bronze Star with combat V; Vietnam Gallantry Cross with palm and clasp; Condecoratión Vasco Nuñez de Balboa in orden de Caballero (Panamá); diplomate Am. Bd. Dermatology. Fellow Am. Acad. Dermatology, Am. Acad. Physicians, Explorers Club; mem. AMA, Assn. Mil. Surgeons, Assn. Mil. Dermatologists (life), Am. Soc. Contemporary Medicine and Surgery, Soc. Am. Archaeology, Royal Soc. Medicine, Pan Am. Med. Assn., Loudoun County Med. Soc., Dermatology Found., Marine's Meml. Club (assoc.), Internat. Platform Soc., Phi Chi. Contbr. articles to med. and archaeol. publs. Home: 18685 Woodburn Rd Leesburg VA 20175-9008 Office: 823J S King St Leesburg VA 20175-3910

MITCHELL, TEDDY LEE, physician; b. Columbia, La., Feb. 24, 1962; s. Oliver Clayton and Mary Elizabeth (Johnston) M.; m. Janet Luisa Tornelli, Apr. 9, 1988; children: Mary Katherine, Oliver Charles. BS in Biology, Stephen F. Austin State U., 1983; MD, U. Tex. Med. Br., 1987. Diplomate Am. Bd. Internal Medicine, Cert. of Added Qualification-Sports Medicine. Intern U. Tex. Med. Br., Galveston, 1987-88, resident, 1988-90, 90-91; staff physician Cooper Aerobics Ctr., Dallas, 1991—, med. dir. wellness program, 1991—. Mem. Rep. Sen. Inner Cir., Washington, 1993, Heritage Found., Washington, 1993. Capt. U.S. Army Res. Med. Corps, 1988-96. Mem. AMA, Am. Coll. Sports Medicine, Am. Coll. Physicians (cert Merit 1990), Tex. Med. Assn., Dallas County Med. Soc. Methodist. Avocations: exercise, travel, music. Home: 3224 Lovers Ln Dallas TX 75225-7626

MITCHELL, TERENCE EDWARD, materials scientist; b. Haywards Heath, Sussex, Eng., May 18, 1937; came to U.S., 1963, naturalized, 1978; s. Thomas Frank and Dorothy Elizabeth (Perrin) M.; m. Marion Wyatt, Dec. 5, 1959; children: Robin Norman, Jeremy Neil. BA, St. Catharine's Coll., Cambridge (Eng.) U., 1958, MA, 1962, PhD in Physics, 1962; ScD, U. Cambridge, 1994. Research fellow Cavendish Lab., Cambridge, 1962-63; asst. prof. metallurgy Case Inst. Tech., 1963-66; assoc. prof. Case Western Res. U., 1966-75, prof., 1975-87, adj. prof., 1987—, chmn. dept., 1983-86, dir. high voltage electron microscopy facility, 1970-82, co-dir. materials research lab., 1982-83; vis. scientist NASA at Ames Lab., Stanford U. and Electric Power Research Inst., Palo Alto, Calif., 1975-76; scientist Ctr. Materials Sci. Los Alamos (N.Mex.) Nat. Lab., 1987—, lab fellow, 1991—; lab fellows chair Los Alamos (N.Mex.) Nat. Lab., 1993-95; chmn. steering com. Electron Microscopy Ctr. Argonne (Ill.) Nat. Lab., 1979-83; cons. in field; mem. vis. com. metals and ceramics div. Oak Ridge Lab., 1987-91; vis. com. solid state scis. div. Ames Lab., 1987-89; sci. adv. com. Sci. and Tech. Ctr. for Superconductivity, 1989-93. Materials sci. editor Microscopy Rsch. and Technique, 1986—; sr. editor North Am., 1994—; contbr. articles to profl. jours. Pres. Cleve. Ethical Soc., 1970-72; bd. dirs Am. Ethical Union, 1972-74; steward Los Alamos Unitarian Ch., 1992-94; mem. policy com. Univ. Materials Coun., 1986-89; mem. policy com. Argonne Electron Microscopy Steering Com., chmn. 1978-82. Electric Power Research Inst. fellow, 1975-76; NSF grantee, 1966-88; Dept. Energy grantee, 1970-86, 87—; NIH grantee, 1969-72; NASA grantee, 1974-77, 81-87; USAF Office Sci. Research grantee, 1974-85; U.S. Army Research Office grantee, 1970-75, 79-83, EPRI grantee, 1986-89. Fellow Am. Soc. Metals, Am. Phys. Soc., Am. Ceramics Soc. (assoc. editor jour.), Minerals, Metals & Materials Soc., Los Alamos Nat. Lab.; mem. Japan Soc. Promotion of Sci., Electron Microscopy Soc. Am. (program chmn. 1981-82, dir. 1984-86, pres.-elect 1994, pres. 1995, past pres. 1996), Materials Rsch. Soc., Soc. Francaise de Microscopie Electronique (sci. com. 1982-90). Office: Los Alamos Nat Lab Ctr Materials Sci Ms # K-765 Los Alamos NM 87545

MITCHELL, THEODORE R., academic administrator; b. San Rafael, Calif., Jan. 29, 1956; s. Theodore Robert and Genevieve Dolores (Doose) M.; m. Christine M. Beckman, July 8, 1995. BA, Stanford U., 1978, MA, 1980, PhD, 1983. Asst. prof. Dartmouth Coll., Hanover, N.H., 1981-86, assoc. prof., 1986-87, chair dept. edn., 1987-91; dep. to pres. and provost Stanford U., 1991-92; dean Sch. Edn. and Info. Studies UCLA, 1992-96, vice chancellor, 1996—; trustee Stanford U., 1985-90, Thetford (Vt.) Acad., 1989-91; bd. dirs. L.A. Edn. Partnership, L.E.A.R.N., L.A. Author: Political Education, 1985. Bd. dirs. Children Now, Oakland, Calif., 1994—, Gateway Learning Corp., 1996—. Office: UCLA Office Chancellor 405 Hilgard Ave Los Angeles CA 90095-9000

MITCHELL, THOMAS EDWARD, JR., communications cabling executive; b. Sacramento, Apr. 12, 1946; s. Thomas Edward and Violet Mae (Southall) M.; m. Terri Kathleen Vance, Apr. 20, 1969; children: Anthony E., Brian C. BA, Nat. U., 1987, MBA, 1988. Enlisted USMC, 1966, advanced through grades to maj., 1980, retired, 1989; sr. exec. Nat. Decision Sys., Encinitas, Calif., 1989-90, Equifax Mktg. Decision Sys., San Dieto, 1990-93; pres., COO Holocomm Sys. Inc., San Diego, 1993—; bd. dirs. Cal-Pacific Steel Structure Inc., Hawaii, Calif. Contbr. articles to profl. jours.; patentee in field. Dir. Toys for Tots, L.A./ORange Counties, Calif., 1974-77. Recipient Silver Star medal U.S. Pres., 1968, Meritorious Svc. medal, Joint Chiefs of Staff Commendation medal, others. Mem. World Trade Assn. (assoc. 1989—), Am. Legion, Internat. Platform Assn. Avocations: restoring old cars, racquetball, golf, history. Home: 3264 Chase Ct Oceanside CA 92056-3809 Office: Holcomm Sys Inc 6540 Lusk Blvd Ste C252 San Diego CA 92121-2766

MITCHELL, THOMAS SOREN, urologist; b. Santa Monica, Calif., Feb. 15, 1941; s. Cyril Louis and Florence Jeanette (Mortensen) M.; m. Michal Jane Lawrence, June 19, 1963; children: Thomas Soren Jr., Lee Delphine. BA, Loma Linda U., 1962, MD, 1966. Diplomate Am. Bd. Urology. Resident U. Wash. Hosp., Seattle, 1966-67, Loma Linda (Calif.) Univ. Hosp., 1967-68; resident in urology U. Calif. Hosp., San Diego, 1970-74; pvt. practice urology Santa Monica, Calif., 1974-96; chief urology St. John's Hosp., Santa Monica, 1990-94; asst. clin. prof. urology UCLA Med. Sch., 1976—. Capt. USAF, 1968-70, Vietnam. Mem. Pacific Oncology Soc. (exec. bd. dirs., sec. 1994—), Am. Urol. Assn., Bay Surg. Soc. Avocations: wine making, fly fishing, tennis, hiking. Office: 2021 Santa Monica Blvd Ste 510E Santa Monica CA 90404-2206

MITCHELL, TONJA KEASHAVEL, physical education educator, nutritional consultant; b. Miami, Fla., Dec. 15, 1963; d. Harold and Barbara-Jean (Underwood) King; m. Vernon Ray Lofton, Mar. 3, 1984 (div. 1991); 1 child, Shatana Mailis Lofton; m. Marco Antonio Mitchell, July 27, 1991; 1 child, Dominique Amir Mitchell. BS in Bus., Fla. Internat. U., 1989; BSN in Nutrition, Am. Coll. Nutrition, Birmingham, Ala., 1993; postgrad., Am. Coll. Nutrition, 1997—. Mgr. Amoco minimart, Miami, 1983-84; nail technician TKL Nails, Miami, 1988-90; office clk. Inst. Med. Specialties, Miami, 1990-91; nutritional cons. Quick Weight Loss Inc., Houston, 1993-95; assoc. Nature's Sunshine Products, Houston, 1993-94, Heart to Heart Nutritional Svc., 1995-96. Mem. NAFE, Am. Naturopathic Med. Assn. Baptist. Avocations: reading, traveling, arts & crafts, music, writing.

MITCHELL, VIRGINIA BRINKMAN, development associate; b. New Brunswick, NJ, Jan. 20, 1949; d. Douglas Haig and Mary Alice (Cullinane) Brinkman; divorced; 1 child, Michael Joseph Mitchell. Cert., Durham Bus. Coll., Houston; AA, Brevard C.C., Cocoa, Fla., 1995; B in Bus., Barry U., Miami Shores, Fla., 1997. Cert. profl. sec. Sec. ITT-Fed. Electric, Houston, 1968, Mullins Investments, Houston, 1968-69; exec. sec. U. Houston, 1969-79; adminstrv. asst. Tex. A&M U., Corpus Christi, 1979-88; sales coord. Hewlett-Packard, Corpus Christi, 1988-89; exec. sec., visitors svc. mgr. Tex. State Aquarium, Corpus Christi, 1989-91; office mgr. Unified Svcs., Inc., Kennedy Space Ctr., Fla., 1992-96; devel. assoc. Circles of Care, Inc., Rockledge, Fla., 1996—. Mem. Nat. Mgmt. Assn., Profl. Secs. Internat., Space Coast Pet Therapy Program, Phi Theta Kappa. Episcopalian. Avocations: landscaping, sailing, scuba diving, pet therapy. Home: 5575 Broad Acres Dr Merritt Island FL 32953-7507 Office: Circles of Care Inc 1770 Cedar St Rockledge FL 32955-3133

MITCHELL, WAYNE LEE, health care administrator; b. Rapid City, S.D., Mar. 25, 1937; s. Albert C. and Elizabeth Isabelle (Nagel) M.; m. Marie Galletti; BA, U. Redlands (Calif.), 1959; MSW, Ariz. State U., 1970, EdD, 1979. Profl. social worker various county, state, and fed. agys., 1962-70, Bur. Indian Affairs, Phoenix, 1970-77, USPHS, 1977-79; asst. prof. Ariz. State U., 1979-84; with USPHS, Phoenix, 1984—; lectr. in field. Bd. dirs. Phoenix Indian Cmty. Sch., 1973-75, ATLATL, 1995; bd. dirs. Phoenix Indian Ctr., 1974-79, Cmty. Svc. award, 1977; mem. Phoenix Area Health Adv. Bd., 1975; mem. Community Behavioral Mental Health Bd., 1976-80; mem. bd. trustees Heard Mus. of Anthropology, Phoenix, Ariz., 1996; mem. bd. dirs. Partnership for Cmty. Devel. Ariz. State U.-West, 1996—. Bd. dirs. Ctrl. Ariz. Health Sys. Agy., 1982-85; mem. Fgn. Rels. Com. Phoenix. With USCG, 1960-62. Recipient Cmty. Svc. award Ariz. Temple of Islam, 1980, Ariz. State U., 1996, Dir. Excellence award Phoenix Area IHS Dir., 1992, 93. Mem. NASW, NAACP, Fgn. Rels. Coun., Am. Hosp. Assn., Asia Soc., U.S.-China Assn., Kappa Delta Pi, Phi Delta Kappa, Chi Sigma Chi, Nucleus Club. Congregationalist. Democrat. Contbr. articles to publs. Home: PO Box 9592 Phoenix AZ 85068-9592 Office: 3738 N 16th St Phoenix AZ 85016-5947

MITCHELL, WILLIAM ALLEN, air force officer, political geography educator; b. Waco, Tex., Apr. 21, 1940; m. Joan Mary Woodill, May 31, 1958; children: Bill, Jim, John, Brian. BS in Geography and Bus., East Tex. State U., 1965; MA in Geography, UCLA, 1969; PhD in Geography, U. Ill., 1974. Commd. 2d lt. USAF, 1965, advanced through grades to col., 1986, ret., 1991; dir. intercultural edn. USAF Acad., 1980-83, prof., head geography, 1985-86, prof. nat. security affairs, 1986-88; seminar dir. Am. War Coll., 1987, Air War Coll.; assoc. prof. Baylor U., Waco, Tex., 1993; adj. faculty U. Md., 1970, U. Colo., Colorado Springs, 1975-80, Troy State U., Montgomery, 1979-80. Author: (with John Kolars) The Euphrates River and The Southeast Anatolia Development Project, 1991; contbr. articles to profl. jours. Decorated U.S. Legion of Merit, Bronze Star, Humanitarian award for Kurdish Relief Effort, Humanitarian award for Turkish relief effort, Orgn. Excellence award, Vietnam Cross of Gallantry with bronze palm, Humanitarian award for Armenian earthquake relief, Spl. Rsch. award for intercultural edn. Dept. Air Force; named one of Outstanding Young Men of Am., 1976; recipient rsch. and travel grants NSF Quick Response to Earthquakes, 1978, 80, 84, 92, 95, Inst. Turkish Studies, 1985, Atlantic Coun. of the U.S.-NATO Discussion Series Assoc. to Brussels, 1988, German Marshall fund grant to Turkey, 1988, others. Mem. Phi Kappa Phi. Baptist. Home: 501 Brint Ln Waco TX 76706-6207 Office: Baylor Univ PO Box 97276 Waco TX 76798-7276

MITCHELL, WILLIAM GRAHAM CHAMPION, lawyer, business executive; b. Raleigh, Dec. 24, 1946; s. Burley Bayard and Dorothy Ford (Champion) M.; children: William Graham, Margaret Scripture. AB, U. N.C., 1969, JD with highest hons., 1975. Bar: N.C. 1975, U.S. Dist. Ct. (ea., mid. and we. dists.) N.C. 1976, U.S. Ct. Appeals (4th cir.) 1978. Ptnr. Womble, Carlyle, Sandridge & Rice, Winston-Salem, 1975-87; sr. v.p. for external affairs RJR Nabisco, Atlanta, 1987-89; exec. v.p. R.J. Reynolds Tobacco Co., Winston-Salem, 1988-89; ptnr. Howrey & Simon, Washington, 1990-94; spl. counselor to chmn. bd. True North Comm., Inc., Chgo., 1996—; bd. dirs. Fed. Agrl. Mortgage Corp. Mem. Pres.'s Adv. Com. on Trade Policy and Negotiations, Indsl. Policy Adv. Com., Washington, 1991—; exec. com. Nat. Assn. Mfrs., Washington, 1988-89, Nat. Fgn. Trade Coun., 1988-89; chmn. Tobacco Inst., Washington, 1988-89; bd. dirs. Washington Performing Arts Soc., 1988-92; bd. advisors Dem. Leadership Coun., 1988—; founding trustee Progressive Policy Inst., 1988—; vice chmn. fin. Bush Campaign. Mem. ABA (vice chmn. antitrust sect., pvt. litigation com. 1987-89, chmn. subcom. of FTC com. 1986), Georgetown Club, City Club of Washington, Forsyth Country Club, Order of the Coif. Office: 20 S King St Ste 700 Leesburg VA 20175-3007

MITCHELL, WILLIAM J., dean, architecture educator. BArch, U. Melbourne, Victoria, Australia, 1967; M of Environ. Design, Yale U., 1969; MA, U. Cambridge, Eng., 1977. Architect Yuncken-Freeman Architects, Melbourne, Australia, 1967-68; asst. prof. architecture, urban design UCLA, 1970-74, head architecture, urban design program, 1973-77, assoc. prof. architecture, urban design, 1974-80, prof. architecture, urban design, program headž, 1980-86; pres. The Urban Innovations Group, L.A., 1973-74; founding ptnr. The Computer-Aided Design Group, Marina Del Rey, Calif., 1978-91; prof. architecture Harvard U., Cambridge, Mass., 1986-89, dir. Master in Design Studies Program, 1986-92, G. Ware and Edythe M. Travelstead prof. architecture, 1989-92; prof. architecture and media arts & scis. MIT, Cambridge, Mass., 1992—, dean Sch. of Architecture and Planning, 1992—; vis. critic Yale U., New Haven, 1970-75, Tulane U., New Orleans, 1981; lectr. dept. architecture U. Cambridge, Eng., 1978-80; vis. prof. U. Calif., Berkeley, 1982, Carnegie-Mellon U., Pitts., 1979-83, U. Sydney, NSW, Australia, 1985; disting. vis. scholar U. Adelaide, South Australia. Author: (book) Computer-Aided Architecture Design, 1983, (with others) The Art of Computer Graphics Programming, 1987, (with others) The Poetics of Gardens, 1988, (with others) The Electronic Design Studio: Architectural Knowledge and Media in the Computer Era, 1990, The Logic of Architecture: Design, Computation and Cognition, 1990, The Reconfigured Eye: Visual Truth in the Post-Photographic Era, 1992, (with others) Digital Design Media, 2d edit., 1991, City of Bits: Space, Place, and the Infobahn, 1995; contbr. numerous articles to profl. jours. Fellow Royal Australian Inst. Architecture. Office: MIT 77 Massachusetts Ave Cambridge MA 02139-4301*

MITCHEM, MARY TERESA, publishing executive; b. Atlanta, Aug. 31, 1944; d. John Reese and Sara Letitia (Marable) Mitchem. BA in History, David Lipscomb Coll., 1966. Sch. and library sales mgr. Chilton Book Co., Phila., 1972-79; dir. market devel. Baker & Taylor Co. div. W.R. Grace, N.Y.C., 1979-81; dir. mktg. R.R. Bowker Co. div. Xerox Corp., N.Y.C, 1981-83, dir. mktg. research, 1983-85; mktg. mgr. W.B. Saunders Co. div. Harcourt, Brace & Jovanovich, Phila., 1985-87; mktg. dir. Congl. Quarterly Inc., Washington, 1987-89; dir. mktg. rsch. and devel. Bur. Nat. Affairs, Inc., Washington, 1990-96; account exec. Hughes Rsch. Corp., Rockville, Md., 1996; ind. mktg. and rsch. cons. Canton, N.C., 1997—. Mem. Book Industry Study Group, Inc. (chairperson stats. com. 1984-86), Mktg. Research Assn., Soc. Competitive Intelligence Profls.

MITGANG, HERBERT, author, journalist; b. N.Y.C., Jan. 20, 1920; s. Benjamin and Florence (Altman) M.; m. Shirley Kravchick, May 13, 1945; children: Esther, Lee, Laura. LLB, St. John's Law Sch., 1942. Bar: N.Y. 1942. Sports stringer Bklyn. Eagle, 1938-39; screen writer Universal-Internat. Pictures, 1945; copy editor, reviewer N.Y. Times, N.Y.C., 1945-54; supervising editor Sunday Times drama sect., 1955-62; editorial writer, mem. editorial bd. N.Y. Times, 1963-64, 67-76, deputy editor Op-Ed page, 1970-76, publishing, cultural corr., book critic, 1976-94; asst. to pres., exec. editor CBS News, 1964-67; instr. English evening divsn. CCNY, 1948-49; vis. lectr. English, guest fellow Silliman Coll., Yale U., 1975-76; lit. advisor White House Libr, 1977-81. Writer, prodr.: (film documentaries) Henry Moore: Man of Form (Documentary Film award 1966), D-Day Plus 20 Years, Sandburg's Prairie Years, Degas' Racing World (Duke Ellington score), Ben-Gurion on the Bible, Anthony Eden on Vietnam; author: Lincoln As They Saw Him, 1956, (novel) The Return, 1959, The Man Who Rode the Tiger: The Life and Times of Judge Samuel Seabury, 1963 (Gavel award ABA), Working for the Reader, 1970, (novel) Get These Men Out of the Hot Sun, 1972, The Fiery Trial: A Life of Lincoln, 1974, (novel) The Montauk Fault, 1981, (novel) Kings in the Counting House, 1983, Dangerous Dossiers: The Secret War Against America's Authors, 1988, Words Still Count With Me: A Chronicle of Literary Conversations, 1995; editor: Washington, D.C., in Lincoln's Time, 1958, Civilians Under Arms: Stars and Stripes, Civil War to Korea, 1996, The Letters of Carl Sandburg, 1968, America at Random, 1969, Spectator of America, 1971, Selected Writings of Abraham Lincoln, 1992; (play) Mister Lincoln, 1980, Knight Errant, 1996; contbr. to the New Yorker, Art News, Am. Heritage, The Progressive, The Nation, Chicago Tribune, Newsday, New York Times, Washington Post. Mem. exec. bd. Newspaper Guild of N.Y., CIO, 1948-49. Served with counter-intelligence sect. 5th wing USAAF, 1942-43, MTO; Army corr., mng. editor Stars and Stripes, Oran-Casablanca and Sicily edits. 1943-45. Decorated six battle stars, Knight Order of Merit (Italy); recipient Human Rights award Newspaper Guild of N.Y., 1958, Broadcast Preceptor award San Francisco State Coll., 1970, N.Y. State Bar Assn. Media award, 1976, Lincoln award Civil War Roundtable of N.Y., 1981, George Polk Career award L.I. U., 1993, 25 Yr. News Achievement award Soc. of Silurians, 1993, Lit. Lions award N.Y. Pub. Libr. Fellow Soc. Am. Historians; mem. Authors League (council 1962—, pres. fund 1976-97, bd. dirs. 1997—), Dramatists Guild, Authors Guild (pres. 1971-75), Internat. P.E.N. (U.S. del. London). Jewish. Club: Century Assn. (N.Y.C.). Office: 203 E 72nd St New York NY 10021-4568

MITGANG, IRIS FELDMAN, lawyer, educator; b. Chgo., Sept. 2, 1937; d. Harry and Leanore (Nelson) Feldman; m. Robert Newton Mitgang, Sept. 9, 1956 (div. Dec. 1974); children: Alix Susan, Steven Ross, Jennifer Lynn. AB, U. Chgo., 1958; MA, U. Rochester, 1967; JD, U. Calif., Davis, 1976. Bar: Calif. 1976, U.S. Dist. Ct. (no. and ea. dists.) Calif.; cert. specialist family law. Ptnr. Dodge, Reyes, Brorby, Randall, Mitgang & Titmus, Walnut Creek, Calif., 1978-90; prin. Law Office Iris F. Mitgang, Walnut Creek, Calif., 1990—; instr. legal writing Sch. Law U. Calif., Davis, 1975-76; adj. prof. family law Sch. Law John F. Kennedy U., Walnut Creek, 1977-87, Sch. Law Golden Gate U., San Francisco, 1987; mem. pro tempore judges panel Contra Costa Superior Ct.; spkr. in field. Mem. editorial bd. Law Rev. U. Calif., Davis Sch. Law, 1976; contbr. various articles to profl. jours. Bd. dirs. Leadership Conf. Civil Rights, Washington, 1979-81, ACLU, Northern Calif.; founding mem. Rape Crisis Ctr. Contra Costa County. Recipient Woman of Yr. award Bus. and Profl. Women, 1979, Women's Leadership award State of Calif., 1980. Mem. State Bar Calif., Nat. Women's Polit. Caucus (nat. chair 1979-81, nat. adv. bd. chair 1981-85, vice chair 1977-79, politic. action chair 1977-79), Am. Acad. Family Mediators, Contra Costa Bar Assn. (co-chair fam. law mediation sect. 1992—), Calif. Women Lawyers, Alameda Contra Costa Trial Lawyers (bd. dirs. 1992-95, chair mentors program), Assn. Family and Conciliation Cts., Assn. Cert. Family Law Specialists, Calif. Dispute Resolution Coun., Soc. Profls. in Dispute Resolution. Democrat. Jewish. Office: Law Offices Iris F Mitgang 1850 Mount Diablo Blvd Ste 605 Walnut Creek CA 94596-4427

MITHOFF, RICHARD WARREN, lawyer; s. Richard Warren Sr. and Frances (Maas) M.; m. Virginia Lynn McTaggart; children: Michael Karl, Caroline Rebecca. BBA, U. Tex., 1968, JD, 1971. Bar: Tex., U.S. Supreme Ct. Law clk. U.S.Dist. (ea. dist.) Tex., Tyler, 1972-74; ptnr. Jamail, Kolius & Mithoff, Houston, 1974-83, Mithoff & Jacks, Houston, 1983—; guest speaker in U.S. and Can. Endowed Richard Warren Mithoff Professorship U. Tex. Fellow Houston Bar Found., Tex. Bar Found. (life), Am. Bd. Profl. Liability Attys.; mem. Am. Coll. Trial Lawyers, Internat. Soc. Barristers, Am. Bd. Trial Advocates, Houston Trial Lawyers Assn. (pres. 1986-87), Tex. Trial Lawyers Assn. (bd.dirs. 1982), Ass. Trial Lawyers Am., State Bar Tex. (com. pattern jury charges 1981—), Internat. Assn. Trial Lawyers. Office: Mithoff & Jacks Penthouse 1 Allen Ctr Houston TX 77002

MITHUN, RAYMOND O., advertising agency executive, banker, real estate and insurance executive; b. Warren, Minn., Mar. 20, 1909; s. Louis and Alma (Anderson) M.; m. Doris Berg, Aug. 9, 1932; children—Lewis, John, Raymond, Jr. A.B., U. Minn., 1930. From printers devil to editor Buffalo Jour., 1922; bus. mgr., 1924; editor Minn. Daily, 1929; pub. Wright Co. Press, 1929-30; city editor Mankato (Minn.) Free Press, 1930; copywriter, radio dir., account exec. Batten, Barton, Durstine & Osborn, Inc., 1930-32; founder, chmn. Campbell-Mithun, Inc., Mpls., 1933; chmn. Mithun Enterprises; owner State Bank of Chanhassen, Minn. Admitted to Advtg. Hall Fame, 1989. Mem. Delta Upsilon, Sigma Delta Chi (Journalism award 1930). Clubs: Minneapolis, Minikahda (Mpls.); Tavern (Chgo.); Minnesota (St. Paul); El Dorado (Palm Desert), Thunderbird (Palm Desert); Woodhill Country (Wayzata, Minn.). Home: 630 Indian Mound St Wayzata MN 55391-1759 Office: 900 Wayzata Blvd E Wayzata MN 55391-1836

MITRA, SANJIT KUMAR, electrical and computer engineering educator; b. Calcutta, West Bengal, India, Nov. 26, 1935; came to U.S., 1958; MS in Tech., U. Calcutta, 1956; MS, U. Calif., Berkeley, 1960, PhD, 1962; D of Tech. (hon.), Tampere (Finland) U., 1987. Asst. engr. Indian Statis. Inst., Calcutta, 1956-58; from teaching asst. to assoc. Univ. Calif., Berkeley, 1958-62; asst. prof. Cornell U., Ithaca, N.Y., 1962-65; mem. tech. staff Bell Telephone Labs., Holmdel, N.J., 1965-67; prof. U. Calif., Davis, 1967-77; prof. elec. and computer engring. U. Calif., Santa Barbara, 1977—, chmn. dept. elec. and computer engring., 1979-82; dir. Ctr. for Info. Processing Rsch., 1993-96; cons. Lawrence Livermore (Calif.) Nat. Lab., 1974-95; cons. editor Van Nostrand Reinhold Co., N.Y.C., 1977-88; mem. adv. bd. Coll. Engring. Rice U., Houston, 1986-89; mem. adv. coun. Rsch. Inst. for Math. and Computing Sci., U. Groningen, The Netherlands, 1995—. Author: Analysis and Synthesis of Linear Active Networks, 1969, Digital and Analog Integrated Circuits, 1980; co-editor: Modern Filter Theory and Design, 1973, Two-Dimensional Digital Signal Processing, 1978, Miniaturized and Integrated Filters, 1989, Multidimensional Processing of Video Signals, 1992, Handbook for Digital Signal Processing, 1993, Digital Signal Processing: A Computer-Based Approach, 1997. Named Disting. Fulbright Prof., Coun. for Internat. Exch. of Scholars, 1984, 86, 88, Disting. Sr. Scientist, Humboldt Found., 1989. Fellow AAAS, IEEE (Edn. award Crcts. and Systems Soc. 1988, disting. lectr. Crcts. and Systems Soc. 1991—, Tech. achievement award Signal Processing Soc. 1996), Internat. Soc. Optical Engring.; mem. Am. Soc. for Engring. Edn. (F.E. Terman award 1973, AT&T Found. award 1985), European Assn. for Signal Processing. Achievements include patents for two-port newtorks for realizing transfer functions; non-reciprocal wave translating device; discrete cosine transform-based image coding and decoding method; method and apparatus for multipath channel shaping; method and apparatus for multipath channel shaping. Office: Univ Calif Dept Elec Computer Eng Santa Barbara CA 93106

MITSAKOS, CHARLES LEONIDAS, education educator, consultant; b. Lowell, Mass., Oct. 17, 1939; s. Leonidas A. and Vasiliki (Sampatakakis) M.; m. Stella Martakos, June 23, 1963; children: Charles L. Jr., Andria Estelle. BS in Edn., Lowell State Coll., 1961; EdM, Boston U., 1963, EdD, 1977. Tchr., team leader, social studies curriculum specialist Lexington (Mass.) Pub. Schs., 1961-67; social studies coord., cons. Chelmsford (Mass.) Pub. Schs., 1967-78; asst. supt. of schs. Andover (Mass.) Pub. Schs., 1978-83; supt. of schs. Winchester (Mass.) Pub. Schs., 1984-92; clin. faculty supr. Sch. Edn., Boston Coll., Chestnut Hill, Mass., 1992-93; prof. edn., chair dept. edn. Rivier Coll., Nashua, N.H., 1993—; ednl. cons. to schs. and sch. dists. in 15 states, U.S. V.I., U.S. Dept. Def. Dep. Schs. and Ministries of Edn., 1970—; dir. Mid. Sch. Staff Devel. Inst. for Social Desegregation Program, Fairfield county, S.C., 1972; mem. staff, lectr. in team tchg. and social studies edn. NSF Insts., Stanford U., Ind. U., SUNY, Geneseo, Xavier U., U. N.C., Boston U., 1968-75; sr. lectr. sch. adminstrn. and curriculum devel. Sch. Grad. Studies, Rivier Coll., Nashua, N.H., 1977-93, numerous others. Author, gen. editor: (multimedia program for elem. sch.) The Family of Man Social Studies Program, 1971-77; co-author: (textbooks) America! America!, 1977, revised 2d edit., 1987, Ginn Social Studies, 1987; author: (workbook) America! America! Workbook, 1982, (textbook) Earth's Geography and Environment, 1991; others. Mem. Profl. Stds. Bd. N.H. Dept. Edn., Fin. Com. and Steering Com. So. N.H. Sch. to Careers Partnership; past chmn. task force on teenagers and religious edn. Greek Orthodox Archdiocese of North and South Am.; former trustee U. Lowell; chairperson affirmative action com., chairperson com. to oversee U. Lowell Rsch. Found.; former mem. ad hoc budget com. Town of Winchester; former mem. bd. dirs., chairperson nominating com. and search com. for resident dirs. Andover Com. for A Better Chance; fund-raising chairperson, mem. edn. com., former trustee, newsletter editor local ch. Recipient Disting. Alumni award U. Lowell, Coll. of Edn., 1987. Democrat. Greek Orthodox. Avocations: writing travel articles, mosaic iconography, travel, reading. Office: Rivier Coll 420 Main St Nashua NH 03060-5043

MITSCHER, LESTER ALLEN, chemist, educator; b. Detroit, Aug. 20, 1931; s. Lester and Mary Athelda (Pounder) M.; m. Betty Jane McRoberts, May 29, 1953; children: Katrina, Kurt, Mark. B.S., Wayne U., 1953, Ph.D., 1958. Research scientist, group leader Lederle Labs., Pearl River, N.Y., 1958-67; prof. Ohio State U., Columbus, 1967-75, U. Kans., Lawrence, 1975—; chmn. dept. medicinal chemistry U. Kans., 1975-92; intersearch prof. Victorian Coll. of Pharmacy, Monash U., Melbourne, Australia, 1975—; cons. NIH, Am. Cancer Soc., Abbott Labs., Searle Labs. Author: (with D. Lednicer) The Organic Chemistry of Drug Synthesis, Vol. 1, 1976, Vol. 2, 1980, Vol. 3, 1984, Vol. 4, 1990, The Chemistry of the Tetracycline Antibiotics, 1978; editor-in-chief Medicinal Research Reviews, 1995—; contbr. over 200 articles to profl. jours. Recipient Disting. Alumnus award Sch. Pharmacy, Wayne State U., 1980, Research Achievement award Acad. Pharm. Scis., 1980, 97, Volweiler research award Am. Assn. Colls. Pharmacy, 1985, Higuchi-Simmons award U. Kans., 1986. Fellow AAAS; mem. Am. Soc. Pharmacognosy (pres. 1992-93), Am. Chem. Soc. (former chmn. councilor medicinal chemistry divsn., Bristol-Myers Smissman rsch. award 1989), Chem. Soc. London, Japanese Antibiotics Assn., Soc. Heterocyclic Chemistry, Internat. Union of Pure and Applied Chemistry (commr. medicinal chemistry divsn.), Internat. Orgn. for Chemistry in Developing Countries (steering com.). Presbyterian. Office: Dept Medicinal Chemistry U Kans Lawrence KS 66045-2506

MITSEFF, CARL, lawyer; b. Detroit, Nov. 16, 1928; s. Frank H. and Katherine (Schaffer) M.; m. Phyllis Schlitters, June 28, 1952; children: C. Randall, Bradley Scott, Julie, Emily, Faye. B.S., Wayne State U., 1952, LL.B., 1955. Bar: Mich. 1956. Practiced in Detroit, 1956—; staff atty. Burroughs Corp., 1955-60; mem. firm LeVasseur, Mitseff, Egan & Capp, 1960-80, Mitseff & Baril, 1980-85, Fitzgerald, Hodgman, Cox, Cawthoren & McMahon, 1986-90, Cox & Hodgman, 1990—; spl. asst. atty. gen. State of Mich.; lectr. in field. Mem. ABA, State Bar Mich., Internat. Assn. Ins. Counsel, Internat. Assn. Indsl. Accident Bds. and Commns., Detroit Athletic Club (bd. dirs.), Beavers (pres.), Lochmoor Club, Grosse Pointe Yacht Club, Pi Kappa Alpha, Delta Theta Phi. Home: 612 N Brys Dr Grosse Pointe MI 48236-1247 Office: 1000 First Federal Bldg Detroit MI 48226

MITSIS, GEORGE, English language and literature educator; b. Indpls., Jan. 19, 1963; s. Kostas and Georgia (Gousia) M. BA, Ind. U., Indpls., 1986; MA, Butler U., Indpls., 1990; postgrad., Drew U., Madison, N.J., 1991—. Rsch. asst. Ind. U., Indpls., 1985-87; adj. instr. English Ind. Vocat. Tech. Coll., Indpls., 1990-91; rsch. asst. Drew U., 1992-94; adj. isntr. English Essex County Coll., West Caldwell, N.J., 1994—. Author articles and book revs. Drew U. scholar, 1991-93. Mem. MLA., N.E. MLA, South Atlantic MLA, Am. Soc. Eighteenth Century Studies, C.J. Jung Found. Greek Orthodox. Avocations: stamp collecting, music, movies. Home: 13 Park Ave Apt 2-D Madison NJ 07940

MITSTIFER, DOROTHY IRWIN, honor society administrator; b. Gaines, Pa., Aug. 17, 1932; d. Leonard Robert and Laura Dorothy (Crane) Irwin; m. Robert Mitchell Mitsifer, June 17, 1956 (dec. Aug. 1984); children: Kurt Michael, Brett Robert. BS, Mansfield U., 1954; MEd, Pa. State U., 1972, PhD, 1976. Cert. home economist. Tchr. Tri-County High Sch., Canton, Pa., 1954-56, Loyalsock Twp. Sch. Dist., Williamsport, Pa., 1956-63; exec. dir. Kappa Omicron Phi, Williamsport, Pa., 1964-86, Kappa Omicron Phi, Omicron Nu, Haslett, Mich., 1986-90, Kappa Omicron Nu, East Lansing, Mich., 1990—; prof. continuing edn. Pa. State U., University Park, 1976-80; prof. Mansfield (Pa.) U., 1980-86, pres.'s intern, 1984-86. Editor Kappa Omicron Nu Forum, 1986—; contbr. articles to profl. jours. Pres., bd. dirs. Profl. Devel. Ctr. Adv. Bd., Vocat. Edn., Pa. State U., 1980-86. Mem. ASCD, Am. Home Econs. Assn., Mich. Home Econs. Assn. (exec. dir. 1986-96), Am. Vocat. Assn., Am. Soc. Assn. Execs., Nat. Soc. Fund Raising Profls., Assn. Coll. Honor Socs. (sec.-treas. 1976—), Coll. Edn. Alumni Soc. Pa. State U. (pres. 1986-88, bd. dirs. 1980-90), Kappa Delta Pi. Avocations: sewing, camping, fishing. Home: 1425 Somerset Close St East Lansing MI 48823-2435 Office: Kappa Omicron Nu 4990 Northwind Dr Ste 140 East Lansing MI 48823-5031

MITTAL, MANMOHAN, electronic design automation engineer; b. Muzaffarnagar, India, Sept. 5, 1950; came to U.S., 1981; s. Keder Nath and Prakash (Wati) M.; m. Shashi Rani, Jan. 28, 1976; children: Vivek, Vibhav. BSEE, Inst. Tech. Banaras Hindu U., Varanasi, India, 1971; MASEE, U. Ottawa, Ont., Can., 1981; PhD in Elec. and Computer Engring., Wash. State U., 1984. Electronics engr. IIMS Banaras Hindu U., 1971-73; design engr. Bharat Heavy Elecs. Ltd., Haridwar, India, 1973-79; grad. rsch./teaching asst. Wash. State U., Pullman and U. Ottawa, 1979-84; DA mgr. CAE design automation Silicon Systems, Inc., Tustin, Calif., 1984-88; mgr. std. cell design automation Vitesse Semiconductor Corp., Camarillo, Calif., 1988-94; sole proprietor, cons. 2M Soft Tech. Group, Thousand Oaks, Calif., 1994-96; dir. corp. design automation C-Cube Micro Systems, Milpitas, Calif., 1996—. Contbr. tech. papers to profl. jours. U. medal Inst. Tech., Banaras Hindu U., 1972; fellow U. Ottawa, 1979-81; grantee Wash. State U., 1981-84. Mem. IEEE (sr., sec. exec. com. Orange County chpt. 1985-88, mem. tech. program. com., custom integrated cirs. conf. 1988-94, bipolar circuits and tech. conf. 1985-90), N.Y. Acad. Scis., Assn. Computing Machines, Sigma Xi, Tau Beta Pi. Hindu. Achievements include patent for Incremental Hierarchical Netlist Extraction Tool. Avocations: traveling, badminton, tennis. Office: C-Cube Micro Systems 1778 Mccarthy Blvd Milpitas CA 95035-7421

MITTEL, JOHN J., economist, corporate executive; b. L.I., N.Y.; s. John and Mary (Leidolf) M.; 1 child, James C. B.B.A., CUNY. Researcher econs. dept. McGraw Hill & Co., N.Y.C.; mgr., asst. to pres. Indsl. Commodity Corp., J. Carvel Lange Inc. and J. Carvel Lange Internat., Inc., 1956-64, corp. sec., 1958-86, v.p., 1964-80, exec. v.p., 1980-86; pres. I.C. Investors Corp., 1972—, I.C. Pension Adv., Inc., 1977—; bd. dir. several corps.; plan adminstr., trustee Combined Indsl. Commodity Corp. and J. Carvel Lange Inc. Pension Plan, 1962-86, J. Carvel Lange Internat. Inc. Profit Sharing Trust, 1969-86, Combined Indsl. Commodity Corp. and J. Carvel Lange Inc. Employees Profit Sharing Plan, 1977-86. Mem. grad. adv. bd. Bernard M. Baruch Coll., CUNY, 1971-72. Mem. Conf. Bd., Am. Statis. Assn., Newcomen Soc. N.Am. Club: Union League (N.Y.C.). Co-author: How Good A Sales Profit Are You, 1961, The Role of the Economic Consulting Firm. Office: 10633 Saint Andrews Rd Boynton Beach FL 33436-4714

MITTELSTADT, CHARLES ANTHONY, advertising executive; b. Eau Claire, Wis., Mar. 19, 1918; s. Frederick William and Pearl (White) M.; m. Angelica Farber, Feb. 20, 1957; children—Nancy Lee, Charles Anthony II, Monica, Simone. B.S., U. Wis., 1942, postgrad., 1945-47; grad., Advanced Mgmt. Program, Harvard, 1960. Radio announcer sta. WIBA, Madison, Wis., 1945-47; account exec. Foote, Cone & Belding, Chgo., 1948-52, Campbell-Mithun, Chgo., 1953-54; mktg. dir. Tatham-Laird, Chgo., 1955-56; exec. v.p. The Marschalk Co., N.Y.C., 1957-64, also bd. dirs.; chmn. plans bd., mgr. Interpub. Group Cos., Inc., Frankfurt, Germany, 1964-66; pres., CEO Erwin Wasey, Inc., Los Angeles, 1967-69; sr. v.p., mgr. Ctr. for Advt. Services Interpub. Group of Cos., Inc., 1969-92, cons., 1991—. Trustee, v.p. N.Y. Foundling Hosp., 1979—. Mem. Wis. Alumni Club, Harvard Alumni Club, N.Y. Athletic Club (N.Y.C.), Westchester Country Club, Am. Yacht Club. Home: 12 Griswold Rd Rye NY 10580-1802 *Be your own person, do your own thinking. Always give something back to those less fortunate.*

MITTEMEYER, BERNHARD THEODORE, urology and surgery educator; came to U.S., 1944, naturalized.; BS in Biology, Moravian Coll., 1952, LLD (hon.), 1982; MD, Temple U., 1956; DSc (hon.), William Jewell Coll., 1985. Diplomate Am. Bd. Urology, Am. Bd. Quality Assurance and Utilization Rev. Physicians. Rotation intern Santa Barbara (Calif.) Cottage and County Hosps., 1956-57; commd. officer U.S. Army, 1957; resident in gen. surgery Fitzsimons Army Med. Ctr., Denver, 1059-61; resident in urol. surgery Tripler Army Med. Ctr., Honolulu, 1962-65; asst. chief urol. surgery svc.-urol. residency tng. program Walter Reed Army Med. Ctr., Washington, 1965-68, 71-74, chief urol. surgery svc. and urol. residency tng. program, 1974-77, chief dept. surgery, 1976-77, comdg. gen., 1980-81; surgeon gen. Dept Army, Washington, 1981-85; ret., 1985; sr. v.p., corp. med. dir. Whittaker Health Svcs., L.A., 1985-86; prof. urology and surgery Tex. Tech U., Lubbock, 1986—, exec. v.p. Health Scis. Ctr., 1986-96, interim dean Sch. Medicine, 1988-90, 95-96, provost, 1988-96; clin. assoc. prof. urology George Washington U. Sch. Medicine, Washington, 1974-85; clin. prof. surgery (urology) Uniformed Svcs. U. Health Scis., Bethesda, Md., 1976—; vis. prof., guest lectr. urology U. Mo., U. Pitts., Korea U., Pa. State U., U. Mass., U. Va., Wake Forest U., Armed Forces Inst. Pathology, Walter Reed Army Inst. Rsch., 1975—; presenter in field; mem. ctrl. com. of pub.-acad. liaison Tex. Dept. Mental Health and Mental Retardation, 1990—; mem. managed health care adv. com. ex. Dept. Criminal Justice, 1993—. Contbr. articles to med. jours. Trustee Moravian Coll., 1982-86; bd. dirs. Sci. Spectrum, Lubbock, 1988—, Lubbock Symphony Orch., 1989-92, Lubbock Conv. and Visitors Bur., 1991-93. Decorated D.S.M., Legion of Merit with oak leaf cluster, DFC, Bronze Star with V device, Air medal with oak leaf cluster; recipient Comenius award Moravian Coll., 1978, Founders medal Assn. Mil. Surgeons, 1978, Alumni Achievement award in health policy Temple U. Sch. Medicine, 1988. Fellow ACS, Am. Coll. Physician Execs. (coun. fellows 1989—, v.p. bd. regents 1988), Am. Coll. Quality Assurance and Utilization Rev. Physicians; mem. AMA (ho. of dels. 1981-85), Am. Urol. Assn., Soc. Govt. Svc. Urologists, Soc. Univ. Urologists, Uniformed Svcs. U. Surg. Assocs., Am. Acad. Med. Dirs., Soc. Med. Cons. to Armed Forces, Assn. U.S. Army, Air Force Assn., Tex. Med. Assn. (cons. coun. on med. edn. 1987—, spl. com. on primary care 1994—), Lubbock-Crosby-Garza County Med. Soc., South Ctrl. Sect. Am. Urol. Assn., Lubbock C. of C. (armed svcs. com. 1988—). Home: PO Box 65285 Lubbock TX 79424-5285 Office: Tex Tech U Health Sci Ctr Med Office Plz 3502 9th St Ste 260 Lubbock TX 79415-3368

MITTEN, DAVID GORDON, classical archaeologist; b. Youngstown, Ohio, Oct. 26, 1935; s. Joe Atlee and Helen Louise (Boyd) M.; children: Claudia Antonia Sabina, Eleanor Elizabeth. BA, Oberlin Coll., 1957; MA in Classical Archaeology, Harvard U., 1958, PhD in Classical Archaeology, 1962. From instr. dept. fine arts to assoc. prof. Harvard U., Cambridge, Mass., 1962-69, James Loeb prof. classical art and archaeology, 1969—; curator ancient art Harvard U. Art Mus., Cambridge, Mass., 1976—, George M.A. Hanfmann curator ancient art, 1996—; assoc. dir. Harvard-Cornell Sardis Expdn., 1976—; Whitehead vis. prof. archaeology Am. Study of Classical Studies, Athens, Greece, 1990-91. Author: (with S.F. Doeringer) Master Bronzes from the Classical World, 1967, Classical Bronzes: Mus. Art, RISD, 1975, (with Arielle P. Kozloff) The Gods Delight: The Human Figure in Classical Bronze, Cleve. Mus. Art, 1988. Woodrow Wilson fellow Harvard U., 1958; Fulbright fellow Am. Sch. Classical Studies at Athens, 1959-60; Archaeol. Inst. Am. Olivia James fellow, 1969-70; John Simon Guggenheim Found. fellow, 1976-77. Mem. Archaeol. Inst. Am., Assn. Field Archaeology (co-founder), Am. Schs. Oriental Rsch., Brit. Sch. Archaeology (Athens, Greece), Am. Numismatic Soc. Office: Sackler Mus 316 Harvard Univ 485 Broadway Cambridge MA 02138-3802

MITTENDORF, ROBERT, physician, epidemiologist; b. Ironton, Ohio, Aug. 6, 1943; s. Robert William and Martha Jane (Whitley) M.; m. Marguerite Jean Herschel, Nov. 10, 1980; children: Jeffrey David, Robert William II, Inga. BS, Ohio State U., 1966; MD, U. Ky., 1974; MPH, Harvard U., 1987, D Pub. Health, 1991. Diplomate Am. Bd. Ob-Gyn. Attending physician St. Margaret's Hosp., Boston, 1977-87; chief of surgery Winthrop (Mass.) Hosp., 1986-88; project dir., collaborative breast cancer study Harvard U., Boston, 1989-91; dir. Office Clin. Rsch. Tufts Sch. Medicine, Boston, 1991-92; dir. health studies, dept. ob-gyn. U. Chgo., 1992—; mem. scientific adv. group anti-epileptic drugs in pregnancy, Research Triangle Park, N.C., 1993—; cons. Nat. Ctrs. for Disease Control and Prevention, Atlanta, 1994—; bd. dirs. U. Chgo. Health Plan, Chgo., Quadrangle Club, U. Chgo.; manuscript reviewer for Jour. of the AMA, Chgo., 1992—. Author: Control of Transmissible Diseases in Health Care, 1995; contbr. articles to profl. jours. Med. dir. Cambridge Econ. Opportunity Com., 1977-78. Capt. USAF, 1966-70. Mem. AMA, Soc. Perinatal Obs., Soc. Epidemiol. Rsch., U. Chgo. Quadrangle Club (bd. dirs.). Democrat. Achievements include devel. of a linear regression model that permits the more precise determination of the estimated date of confinement in pregnant women (Mittendorf-Williams Ruler); discovery that strenuous phys. activity is associated with a reduced risk of breast cancer, using a multivariate logistic regression model. Prin. investigator of the MAGnet Trial (magnesium and neurologic endpoints randomized control trial) to determine if using antenatal magnesium sulfate is associated with the prevention of severe cerebral palsy. Through statis. meta-analysis, discovered that certain prophylactic antibiotics are highly efficacious in preventing the serious infections associated with total abdominal hysterectomy. Home: 5244 S Greenwood Ave Chicago IL 60615-4316 Office: Chgo Lying-In Hosp MC2050 5841 S Maryland Ave # Mc2050 Chicago IL 60637-1463

MITTER, SANJOY K., electrical engineering educator; b. Calcutta, India, Dec. 9, 1933. PhD, Imperial Coll., Eng., 1965. Prof. elec. engring. MIT, Cambridge, 1973—, dir. Lab. Info. and Decision Systems, 1981-86, co-dir Lab. Info. and Decision Systems, 1986—, dir. Ctr. Intelligent Control Systems, 1986—. Fellow IEEE; mem. Nat Acad. Eng. Office: MIT Lab Info & Decision Systems Bldg 35 Rm 308 Cambridge MA 02139-4307

MITTERMILLER, JAMES JOSEPH, lawyer; b. Washington, Apr. 13, 1953; s. Jack and Alice Marie (Froeba) M.; m. Elizabeth Gaillard Simons, June 23, 1979; children: Samuel Stoney, Paul Andrew, Laurie Alice, Claire Mary. Student, U. Heidelberg, 1973-74; BA, Claremont Men's Coll., 1975; JD, U. Calif. Berkeley, 1978. Bar: Calif., U.S. Dist. Ct. (so., ctrl. and ea. dists.) Calif., U.S. Ct. Appeals (9th cir.), U.S. Supreme Ct. Assoc. Sheppard, Mullin, Richter & Hampton, L.A., 1978-86, ptnr., 1986—; panelist Calif. Continuing Edn. of Bar, L.A. and San Diego, 1984—. Dir. Legal Aid Soc. of San Diego, 1990—. Recipient Wiley Manuel Pro Bono award Calif. State Bar, 1992. Mem. Assn. Bus. Trial Lawyers, Am. Inns of Ct., Claremont McKenna Coll. Alumni Assn. San Diego (bd. dirs.). Avocations: swimming, surfing. Office: Sheppard Mullin Richter & Hampton 501 W Broadway Fl 19 San Diego CA 92101-3536

MITTLEBERG, ERIC MICHAEL, pharmaceutical administrator; b. N.Y.C., Nov. 7, 1951; s. Irving Ralph and Rose (Schnieder) M.; m. Jane Susan Baumoehl, Dec. 25, 1977; children: Alyson, Lauren. BS in Pharmacy, St. Johns U., Jamaica, N.Y., 1974, MS in Ind. Pharmaceutics, 1978, PhD in Pharmaceutics, 1982. Registered pharmacist, N.Y. Assoc. scientist Hoffmann-LaRoche Inc., Nutley, N.J., 1974-78; dept. head process improvement Lederle Labs, Pearl River, N.Y., 1978-83; mgr. mfg. devel. Key Pharm., Miami, Fla., 1983-86; dir. prodn., tech. svcs. Schering Labs, Miami, 1986-89; sr. dir. pharm. devel./tech. svcs. worldwide R.W. Johnson Pharm. Rsch. Inst., Raritan, N.J., 1989—. Mem. Internat. Soc. Pharm. Engrs., Acad. Pharm. Sci., Am. Pharm. Assn. Office: RW Johnson Pharm Rsch Inst Rt 202 Box 300 Raritan NJ 08869

MITTLER, DIANA (DIANA MITTLER-BATTIPAGLIA), music educator and administrator, pianist; b. N.Y.C., Oct. 19, 1941; d. Franz and Regina (Schilling) Mittler; m. Victor Battipaglia, Sept. 5, 1965 (div. 1982). BS, Juilliard Sch., 1962, MS, 1963; DMA, Eastman Sch. Music, 1974. Choral dir. William Cowper Jr. High Sch. and Springfield Gardens Jr. High Sch., Queens, N.Y., 1963-68, coordinator of music Flushing High Sch., Queens, 1968-79; asst. prin. music Bayside High Sch., Queens, 1979-86; assoc. prof. music Lehman Col. CUNY, 1986-87, prof., 1987—, choral dir., 1986—; dir. ednl. projects New World Records, 1987—; ednl. cons. Flushing Coun. on Culture and the Arts; cons. Sta. WNET; assoc. condr. Queens Borough-Wide Chorus, 1964-70; pianist, founder Con Brio Chamber Ensemble, 1978; faculty So. Vt. Music Festival, 1979-83; soloist with N.Y. Philharmonic, 1956; solo and chamber music appearances; examiner N.Y.C. Bd. Edn. Bd. Exams., 1985—. Author: 57 Lessons for the High School Music Class, 1983, Franz Mittler: Austro-American Composer, Musician and Humourous Poet, 1993. Choral dir. and accompanist various charitable, religious, mil., civic holiday functions. N.Y. State Regents scholar, 1958-62; scholarships, Juilliard Sch. and Eastman Sch. Music; recipient Excellence in Tchg. award, 1993, Prism award 1996. Contbr. articles to music publs.; performance Internat. Summer Acad. Mozarteum, Salzburg, Austria, 1995. Mem. Golden Key Soc., Am. Choral Dirs. Assn., Music Edn. Nat. Conf., Sonneck Soc. Democrat. Home: 10857 66th Ave Flushing NY 11375-2247 Office: Lehman Coll Music Dept Bedford Pk Blvd W Bronx NY 10468

MITTON, MICHAEL ANTHONY, environmental technology company executive; b. Bremen, Germany, Mar. 13, 1947; came to U.S., 1948 (parents Am. citizens); s. Ralph Walter and Aniela (Pilarz) M.; m. Lisa Van der Veer, Mar. 7, 1986 (div. 1991); m. Marilyn Kay Bowen, Sept. 18, 1993. BS, U. Wyo., 1970. Asst. mgr. ops. Moller Steamship Co., N.Y.C., 1970-72; investment analyst Moller Industries, N.Y.C., 1972-73; internal auditor Corning (N.Y.) Glass Works, 1973-75, supr. acctg., 1975-76; dir. acctg. Autotrain Corp., Washington, 1977-78; pres. RMA Ltd., Ft. Collins, Colo., 1978-81; contr. Purecycle Corp., Boulder, Colo., 1981-83; pres., chief exec. officer, treas. Synthetech Inc., Albany, Oreg., 1983-90, bd. dirs., chmn., 1990-95; ret., 1995; pres., CEO Chemical Biosensors, Inc., Beaverton, Oreg., 1992-95; technology entrepreneur, founder environ. tech. co., 1995—; co-chmn. Oreg. Biotech. Industry Coun., 1989-90. Mem. Gov.'s Task Force Tech. Transfer, 1992-94. Fellow Am. Leadership Forum; mem. Soaring Soc. Am., Oreg. Biotech. Assn. (bd. dirs., chmn. 1990-91, pres. 1991-92), Multnomah Athletic Club. Avocations: flying, squash, skiing, sailing. Home: 6300 Estate Frydenhoj #18 Saint Thomas VI 00802

MITZELFELD, JIM, commentor, legal assistant; b. Royal Oak, Mich., Apr. 26, 1961; s. Thomas Henry and Audrey Mae (Howard) M.; m. Lisa Jeanne Grayson, Sept. 28, 1985. BA in Journalism, Mich. State U., 1984; JD, U. Mich., 1996. Intern newspaper reporter The Times, Hammond, Ind., 1981; editor-in-chief The State News, East Lansing, Mich., 1982-83; intern reporter Democrat & Chronicle, Rochester, N.Y., 1983; newspaper reporter The Oakland Press, Pontiac, Mich., 1984-85, The Flint (Mich.) Jour., 1985-86, UP Internat., Lansing, 1986, AP, Lansing, 1986-88, The Detroit News, Dearborn, Mich., 1988-90; state capitol reporter The Detroit News, Lansing, 1990-93; intern law clk. to Judge David W. McKeague U.S. Dist. Ct. for We. Dist. Mich., 1994; summer assoc. Butzel Long, Lansing, 1994; law clk. Holland & Hart, Denver, 1995, Miller, Confield, Lansing, Mich., 1996; law clk. to Judge David W. McKeague U.S. Dist. Ct. (we. dist.) Mich., 1996—. Polit. commentator Off the Record Pub. TV, 1986-93. Recipient Nat. Best of Gannett Runner-up award, 1991, Top Well Done prize Best of Gannett, 1993, 2d place prize Mich. Associated Press, 1994, Pulitzer prize for beat reporting, 1994; honored by Mich. State Senate for pub. svc., 1993. Mem. Soc. Profl. Journalists (Journalist of Yr. Detroit Chpt. 1994), Mich. State U. Alumni Assn., State News Alumni Assn. (pres., co-founder 1991-93). Episcopalian. Avocations: travel, golf, photography, videography, hockey. Home: 5395 Wild Oak Dr East Lansing MI 48823-7252 Office: US Dist Ct 315 W Allegan St Rm 119 Lansing MI 48933-1514

MITZNER, DONALD H., cable television executive; b. N.Y.C., Nov. 17, 1940; s. Abraham E. and Beatrice (Silberbush) M.; m. Gail D. Schwartz, Aug. 24, 1963; children—Alan S., Jill R. BMechE, CCNY, 1963; MMechE, CCNY. 1966; M.Bus. Mgmt., C.W. Post Coll., 1969. Engr., Bendix Corp., Teterboro, N.J., 1963-66; project mgr. Fairchild Camera, Syosset, N.Y., 1966-68, Reeves Instrument, Westbury, N.Y., 1968-70; pres. Detwiler Corp., Westbury, 1976-81; sr. v.p. Group W Cable, N.Y.C., 1981-86; pres. Group W Satellite Communications, Stamford, Conn., 1986—; bd. dirs. The Discovery Channel, Landover, Md. Bd. dirs. Assn. for Children with Learning Disabilities, Westbury, N.Y., 1975-86, pres., 1987—; exec. v.p., trustee North Shore Jewish Ctr., Port Jefferson, N.Y., 1975-81; pres. bd. trustees Leeway Sch., Stony Brook, N.Y., 1972-76. Recipient Negev award State of Israel Bonds, 1982, Project Bus. award Jr. Achievement, N.Y.C., 1983. Mem. Cable TV Adminstrn. and Mktg. Soc., Nat. Acad. TV Arts and Scis., N.Y. State Cable TV Assn. (bd. dirs.). Jewish. Office: Nashville Network 250 Harbor Plaza Dr Box 10210 Stamford CT 06904 also: Westinghouse Broadcasting 888 7th Ave New York NY 10106*

MITZNER, KENNETH MARTIN, electrical engineering consultant; b. Bklyn., May 7, 1938; s. Louis Bernard and Dora (Sandler) M.; m. Ruth Maria Osorio, Dec. 26, 1968; children: Camille Lorena, Esther Jeannette, Sharon Michelle. BS, MIT, 1958; MS, Calif. Inst. Tech., 1959, PhD, 1964. Mem. tech. staff Hughes Aircraft, Malibu, Calif., 1959-64; prin. engr. B-2 divsn. Northrop Corp., Pico Rivera, Calif., 1964-94; owner Mitzner Sci. and Tech., Torrance, Calif., 1995—; instr. U. Calif., Santa Barbara, 1964-65; lectr. in field. Author: (handbook) Demonstrations Against Abortion & Death Selection, 1970; contbr. articles to profl. jours. Pres. Mobilization for the Unnamed, Torrance, Calif., 1970—; bd. dirs. Ams. United for Life, 1971-94, Nat. Right to Life Com., 1980-81, Jewish Life Issues Com., Solana Beach, 1983—; sec. Calif. Pro Life Coun., Sacramento, 1972; mem. L.A. County Select Citizens Com. on Life Support Policies, L.A., 1983-85;. Named Patron of Life Calif. Pro Life Coun., 1976, Pres's award, 1979; Howard Hughes fellow, 1959-64; grantee Fullbright Found., Govt. Italy, 1961-62. Fellow IEEE; mem. U.S. Nat. Commn. Internat. Union Radio Sci. (del. to 20th gen. assembly), Electromagnetics Acad. Avocations: historic research, stamp collecting.

MIURA, AKIO, quality assurance professional; b. Tokyo, Oct. 7, 1936; s. Takeshi and Sakiko (Andoh) M.; m. Takako Nakatani, Apr. 14, 1968; 1 child, Masahiro. BS, Waseda U., Tokyo, 1959. Cert. quality auditor, Internat. Register Cert. Auditors and Registrar Accreditation Bd.; registered ISO 9000 lead auditor. Staff mem. Mitsubishi Corp., Tokyo, 1959-75; mgr. indsl. machinery Mitsubishi Corp., 1975-78, asst. gen. mgr. indsl. machinery, 1984-90; exec. dir. Kinka Kikai Co., Gifu, Japan, 1978-84; sr. cons. N.C. Kist & Assocs., Inc., Naperville, Ill., 1990—; pres. Internat. Quality Sys., Inc., Tokyo, 1990—; chair Internat. QA Inst., 1991—. Author: Guide for Preparation of Quality Manual, 1992, Practice of ISO 9000, 1994.; contbr. articles to profl. jours. Mem. ASME, Am. Soc. Quality Control (sr.), Internat. Quality Inst. (chmn.). Avocations: baseball, chinese boxing, karate, fencing, classical music. Home and Office: 3-24-14-703 Shimo-meguro, Meguroku 153, Japan

MIURA, ROBERT MITSURU, mathematician, researcher, educator; b. Selma, Calif., Sept. 12, 1938; emigrated to Can., 1975; s. Richard Katsuki and Frances Yoneko (Yukutake) M.; m. Kathryn Bannai; children: Derek Katsuki, Brian Robert, Jared Bannai Nagae, Sean Takeo. BS, U. Calif.-Berkeley, 1960, MS, 1962; MA, Princeton U., 1964, PhD, 1966. Rsch. assoc. Princeton U. Plasma Physics Lab., 1965-67; assoc. rsch. scientist Courant Inst. Math. Sci., N.Y.C., 1967-68; asst. prof. math. NYU, 1968-71; assoc. prof. math. Vanderbilt U., 1971-75; assoc. prof. math. U. B.C., Vancouver, B.C., Can., 1975-78, prof., 1978—; chmn. joint com. on math. in life scis. Am. Math. Soc.-Soc. Indsl. and Applied Math., 1981-84; bd. dirs. Soc. for Math. Biology, 1995—. Editor: Backlund Transformations, 1976, Nonlinear Phenomena in Physics and Biology, 1981, Some Mathematical Questions in Biology-Neurobiology, 1982, Muscle Physiology, 1986, DNA Sequence Analysis, 1986, Plant Biology, 1986; assoc. editor Can. Applied Math. Quar.; adv. bd. Jour. Math. Biology; co-editor-in-chief Methods and Applications of Analysis; contbr. articles to profl. jours. Mem. steering com. Ctr. Math. Rsch., U. Montreal, 1990-94. John Simon Guggenheim fellow, 1980-81; U. B.C. hon. Killam fellow, 1980-81. Fellow Royal Soc. Can.; mem. AAAS, Am. Math. Soc., Soc. Indsl. and Applied Math., Can. Applied Math. Soc., Can. Math. Soc., Soc. Math. Biology, Pacific Inst. Math. Sci. (interim exec. bd. 1996), Sigma Xi. Office: U BC Dept Math, 1984 Mathematics Rd, Vancouver, BC Canada V6T 1Z2

MIXON, ALAN, actor; b. Miami, Fla., Mar. 15, 1933; s. James E. and Matilda (Beers) M. Student, U. Miami, 1951-52. Appeared in: premiere prodn. play Sweet Bird of Youth, Miami, 1956, N.Y.C., 1956; appeared in: premiere prodn. play View from the Bridge, Chgo. and San Francisco, 1957, 59, Royal Hunt of the Sun, Broadway and Hollywood, 1966; New York prodns. include Suddenly Last Summer, 1958, Desire Under the Elms, 1963, Trojan Women, 1963-64, The Alchemist, 1964, Sign in Sidney Brustein's Window, 1964-65, The Child Buyer, 1964-65, The Devils, 1965-66, A Whitman Portrait, 1966, Black Comedy, 1966-67, Unknown Soldier and His Wife, 1967, Iphegenia in Aulis, 1967-68, Love Suicide at Schofield Barracks, 1972, Small Craft Warnings, 1972, Mourning Becomes Electra, 1972, Equus, 1974-75, Benito Cereno, 1976; London prodn. Whitman Portrait, 1969; TV appearances include Theatre in America. Served with AUS, 1953-54.

MIXON, DEBORAH LYNN BURTON, elementary school educator; b. Charleston, S.C., Mar. 26, 1956; d. Harold Boyd and Peggy Wynell (Seagraves) Burton; m. Steven Douglas Schmidt (div. Mar. 1982); 1 child, Julie Ann Schmidt; m. Timothy Lamar Mixon, Oct. 11, 1982; children: Phillip Lamar, Catherine Elizabeth. BS in Edn., U. Ga., 1994. Cert. early childhood educator, Ga. Office coord. Morrison's Cafeteria, Athens, Ga., 1974-76; cashier Winn-Dixie, Athens, 1976-78; data entry clk. Athens Tech. Data Ctr., 1978-79; adminstrv. sec. U. Ga., Athens, 1980-86; sec. to plant mgr. Certain Teed Corp., Athens, 1986-87; s. adminstrv. sec. U. Ga., Athens, 1987-93; tchr. 4th grade Hall County Sch. Sys., Gainesville, Ga., 1994—. Leader Cub Scouts den Boy Scouts Am., 1993-94; troop vol. Girl Scouts U.S., 1992—; vol. leader 4-H Clarke County, Athens, 1992-94. Presdl. scholar U. Ga., 1993-94. Mem. Assn. for Childhood Edn. Internat., Profl. Assn. Ga. Educators, Golden Key, Kappa Delta Epsilon (perfect scholar 1994). Avocations: hiking, camping, swimming, canoeing, reading. Home: 171 Scottwood Dr Athens GA 30607-1338

MIYAKE, AKIO, biologist, educator; b. Kyoto, Japan, June 29, 1931; s. Yoshikazu and Yukie (Yamazaki) M.; m. Sadako Harada, Mar. 15, 1965 (dec. June 1986); children: Akiko, Toshio; m. Terue Harumoto, Dec. 30, 1988; 1 child, Yuka. BS, Kyoto U., 1953, D of Science, 1959. Asst. Osaka (Japan) City U., 1953-63; visiting scholar Ind. U., Bloomington, 1959-61; lectr. Kyoto (Japan) U., 1963-70; group leader Max-Planck Inst. for Molecular Genetics, West Berlin, 1970-74; visiting scholar U. Pisa, Italy, 1975-77, U. Münster, West Germany, 1978-83; prof. U. Camerino, Italy, 1983—. Contbr. articles on sexual reprodn. in microorganisms to profl. jours. and books. Recipient Zool. Soc. of Japan Prize, 1981. Mem. Zool. Soc. Japan, Genetics Soc. of Japan, AAAS, Soc. Protozoologists, Planetary Soc. Avocations: origin and evolution of life, Italian opera music. Home: Corso Italia 150, I-62022 Castelraimondo Italy Office: U Camerino Dept Cell Biol, Via F Camerini 2, I-62032 Camerino Italy

MIYAMOTO, CURTIS TRENT, medical educator; b. Bristol, Pa., Nov. 26, 1957; s. Sadao and Amy E. (Omoto) M.; m. Maria Amparo Gomez, Sept. 24, 1983; children: Maria Victoria, David James, Robert Paul. BS, Muhlenberg Coll., 1979; MD, U. Navarra, Pamplona, Spain, 1986. Lic. physician, Pa.; cert. radiation oncologist; bd. cert. radiation oncology Am. Bd. Radiology. Asst. prof. Allegheny Univ. Hosps., Phila., 1991—, co-founder Brain Tumor Ctr., 1994—; assoc. med. dir. Gynecologic Oncology Ctr., Phila., 1996—; bd. dirs. Richard Zaloga Found., Old Forge, Pa.; mem. radiation safety, credentials, surg. and invasive procedure rev., risk mgmt., quality improvement coms., instnl. rev. bd. Allegheny Univ. Hosps.; faculty Radiation Oncology Self Assessment Program. Author: (book chpt.) Management of Salivary Gland Lesions, 1992, Radioimmunoglobulins in Cancer Therapy, Principles and Practice of Radiation Oncology, 1996; co-author: (book chpt.) Radiobiology in Radiotherapy, 1988, Recent Results in Cancer Research-Systemic Radiotherapy with Monoclonal Antibodies, 1996, Radioimmunoglobulins in Cancer Therapy, Principles and Practice of Radiation Oncology, 1996; contbr. articles to profl. jours. including Am. Jour. Clin. Oncology, Internat. Jour. Radiation Oncology; mem. editl. bd. Radiation Oncology Investigations; article reviewer Am. Jour. Clin. Oncology. Mem. worship com. First Presbyn. Ch., Morristown, N.J., 1996; v.p. PTA, Glenolden, Pa., 1993. Outstanding scholar Hahnemann U., 1991. Fellow AMA (Physician's Recognition award 1994), Am. Cancer Soc.; mem. Interam. Coll. Physicians & Surgeons, Alpha Phi Omega (life), Sigma Xi. Republican. Presbyterian. Achievements include extensive work with biologic response modifiers. Home: 32 Parkdale Pl Marlton NJ 08053 Office: Allegheny Univ Hosps Ctr City Broad and Vine Sts Philadelphia PA 19102

MIYAMOTO, RICHARD TAKASHI, otolaryngologist; b. Zeeland, Mich., Feb. 2, 1944; s. Dave Norio and Haruko (Okano) M.; m. Cynthia VanderBurgh, June 17, 1967; children: Richard Christopher, Geoffrey Takashi. BS cum laude, Wheaton Coll., 1966; MD, U. Mich., 1970; MS in Otology, U.So. Calif., 1978. Diplomate Am. Bd. Otolaryngology. Intern Butterworth Hosp., Grand Rapids, Mich., 1970-71, resident in surgery, 1971-72; resident in otolaryngology Ind. U. Sch. Medicine, 1972-75; fellow in otology and neurotology St. Vincent Hosp. and Otologic Med. Group, L.A., 1977-78; asst. prof. Ind. U. Sch. Medicine, Indpls., 1978-83, assoc. prof., 1983-88; prof. 1988—; chmn. 1987—, chief Otology and Neurotology dept. Otolaryngology, Head and Neck Surgery, Ind. U., 1982—, chmn. dept. Otolaryngology, 1987—, Arilla DeVault prof., 1991; chief Otolaryngology, Head and Neck Surgery Wishard Meml. Hosp., 1979—. Mem. editorial bd. Laryngoscope, Am. Jour. of Otology, Otolaryngology-Head and Neck Surgery, European archives of Oto-Rhino-Laryngology, Anales de Otorrinolaringologia Mexicana; contbr. articles to profl. jours. Mem. adv. coun. Nat. Inst. Deafness and other communication disorders, 1989-94; mem. med. adv. bd. Alexander Graham Bell Assn. for the Deaf, The Ear Found. Served to maj. USAF, 1975-77. Named Arilla DeVault Disting. investigator Ind. U., 1983. Fellow Am. Acad. Otolaryngology (gov. 1982—), ACS, Am. Otological, Rhinological, and Laryngological Soc. (Thesis Disting. for Excellence award), Am. Neurotology Soc. Am. Auditory Soc. (mem. exec. com. 1985—); mem. Otosclerosis Study Group (coun. 1993—), Am. Otol. Soc. (coun. 1992—), Marines Meml. Assn., Wheaton Coll. Scholastic Honor Soc., Cosmos Club of Washington, Columbia Club of Ind., Royal Soc. Medicine London, Collegium Oto-Laryngologicum Amecitiae Sacrum; Alpha Omega Alpha. Office: Ind U Sch Med 702 Barnhill Dr Indianapolis IN 46202-5128

MIYARES, BENJAMIN DAVID, editor, publisher, consultant; b. Tampa, Fla., July 23, 1940; s. Benigno and Mary Carolyn (Dominguez) M.; m. Martha Suzanne Urban, May 14, 1966; children—David, Jeffrey, Beth. B.A. in Journalism, St. Bonaventure U., Olean, N.Y., 1962. News dir. radio sta. WSET, Glens Falls, N.Y., 1962-63; with subs. Edgell Communications, Inc. (magazines for industry), N.Y.C., 1963-89; editor Food and Drug Packaging mag., 1968-89, editorial dir. company, 1975-89, corp. v.p., 1977-80, exec. editor, 1980-89; publisher Candy Marketer, 1985-87, Instructor, 1987; pres. BDM Enterprises, Mktg./Communications Cons., Bay Village, Ohio, 1989—; cons. in packaging field. Pres. council Nat. Packaging Week, 1975; editorial com. Am. Bus. Press, 1973-74. Served with AUS, 1963. Fellow Inst. Packaging Profls. (v.p. 1976-78, pres. 1978-79). Office: BDM Enterprises 31408 Narragansett Ln Cleveland OH 44140-1068

MIYASAKI, GEORGE JOJI, artist; b. Kalopa, Hawaii, Mar. 24, 1935. BFA, Calif. Coll. Arts and Crafts, 1957, MFA, 1958. Asst. prof. art Calif. Coll. Arts and Crafts, Oakland, 1958-64; mem. faculty dept. art U. Calif., Berkeley, 1964-94; prof. emeritus U. Calif. John Hay Whitney fellow, 1957-58; Tamarind printing fellow, 1961; Guggenheim fellow, 1963-64; Nat. Endowment for Arts fellow, 1980-81, 85-86. Mem. Nat. Acad. of Design. Home: 2844 Forest Ave Berkeley CA 94705-1309

MIYASAKI, SHUICHI, lawyer; b. Paauilo, Hawaii, Aug. 6, 1928; s. Torakichi and Teyo (Kimura) M.; m. Pearl Takeko Saiki, Sept. 11, 1954; children: Joy Michiko, Miles Tadashi, Jan Keiko, Ann Yoshie. BSCE, U. Hawaii-Honolulu, 1951; JD, U. Minn., 1957; LLM in Taxation, Georgetown U., 1959; grad. Army War Coll., 1973. Bar: Minn. 1957, Hawaii 1959, U.S. Supreme Ct. 1980. Examiner, U.S. Patent Office, 1957-59; dep. atty. gen. State of Hawaii, 1960-61; mem., dir., sec./treas. Okumura Takushi Funaki & Wee, Honolulu, 1961-90; pvt. practice, Honolulu, 1991—; atty. Hawaii Senate, 1961, chief counsel ways and means com., 1962, chief counsel judiciary com., 1967-70; civil engr. Japan Constrn. Agy., Tokyo, 1953-54; staff judge adv., col. USAR, Ft. DeRussy, Hawaii, 1968-79; local legal counsel Jaycees, 1962; lectr. Nat. Assn. Pub. Accts. Hawaii Chpt. Ann. Conv., 1990, 94, Mid Pacific Inst. Found., Honolulu, 1990, Econ. Study Club of Hawaii, 1990, Meiji Life Ins. Co. Japan, 1992, Cent. YMCA, 1992. Legis. chmn. armed services com. C. of C. of Hawaii, 1973; instl. rep. Aloha council Boy Scouts Am., 1963-78; exec. com., sec., dir. Legal Aid Soc. Hawaii, 1970-72; state v.p. Hawaii Jaycees, 1964-65; dir., legal counsel St. Louis Heights Community Assn., 1963, 65, 73, 91-96; dir., legal counsel Citizens Study Club for Naturalization of Citizens, 1963-68; advisory bd. Project Dana Honolulu, 1991-96, vice chair 91, 92; life mem. Res. Officers Assn. U.S. Served to 1st lt., AUS, 1951-54. Decorated Meritorious Service medal with oak leaf cluster. Mem. ABA, Hawaii Bar Assn., U.S. Patent Office Soc., Hawaii Estate Planning Council, Rotary, Central YMCA Club, Waikiki Athletic Club, Army Golf Assn., Elks, Phi Delta Phi. Office: 1001 Bishop St Honolulu HI 96813-3429 *Personal philosophy: Study hard, work hard, play hard, love hard, have time for nonsense, help others and be fair to all concerned.*

MIYATA, GEN, history of religion educator; b. Kyoto, Japan, Feb. 11, 1933; s. Zenichiro and Ine (Yoshida) M.; m. Hiroko Fujiwara, Feb. 3, 1968; children: Kenichi, Mamoru, Teizo. BA, Tokyo U., 1956, MA, 1958. Lectr. Tenri (Japan) U., 1964-70, assoc. prof., 1970-79, prof., 1979—, chairperson dept. religious studies, 1981-87, 89-91, 92-93, dean faculty letters, 1987-89, 91-92, dean faculty human studies, 1993-96; vis. prof. Ind. U., Bloomington, 1980-81. Mem. Japanese Assn. for Am. Studies (councilor 1972—), Japanese Assn. for Religious Studies (dir. 1989—). Tenrikyo. Office: Tenri U, 1050 Somanouchi cho, Tenri Nara, Japan 632

MIZE, JOE HENRY, industrial engineer, educator; b. Colorado City, Tex., June 14, 1934; s. Kelly Marcus and Birtie (Adams) M.; m. Betty Bentley, Mar. 16, 1966; 1 dau., Kelly Jean. B.S. in Indsl. Engring, Tex. Tech. Coll., 1958; M.S. (Research Found. grantee) in Indsl. Engring, Purdue U., 1963, Ph.D., 1964. Registered profl. engr., Ala., Okla. Indsl. engr. White Sands Missile Range, N.Mex., 1958-61; grad. research asst. Purdue U., Lafayette, Ind., 1961-64; asso. prof. engring. Auburn (Ala.) U., 1964-69; dir. Auburn (Ala.) U. (Computer Center), 1965-66; prof. engring. Ariz. State U., Tempe, 1969-72; prof., head Sch. Indsl. Engring. and Mgmt. Okla. State U., Stillwater, 1972-80; dir. Univ. Ctr. for Energy Research Okla. State U., 1980-83, Regents prof., 1982—; cons. to Air War Coll., 1968-69, U.S. Army, Ops. Analysis Standby Unit, U. N.C., 1965-69, various mfg. firms, 1964—; program adv. Office of Mgmt. and Budget, Exec. Office of the President, Washington, 1974-79; adv. to NSF, 1974-79, Nat. Center for Productivity and Quality of Work Life, 1973-78; chmn. tech. adv. council So. Growth Policies Bd., 1975-77; accrediting visitor Engrs. Council for Profl. Devel., 1973-80. Author: (with J.G. Cox) Essentials of Simulation (translated into Japanese 1970), 1968, Prosim V.: Instructor's Manual, 1971, Student's Manual, 1971, (with C.R. White and George H. Brooks) Operations Planning and Control, 1971, (with J.L. Kuester) Optimization Techniques with Fortran, 1973, (with W.C. Turner and K.E. Case) Introduction to Industrial and Systems Engineering, 3d edit., 1993 (named Book of Yr., Am. Inst. Indsl. Engrs. 1979), Guide to Systems Integration, 1991; contrbr. articles to profl. jours., more. Recipient Disting. Engring. Alumnus award Purdue U., 1978. Mem. Am. Inst. Indsl. Engrs. (exec. v.p. 1978-80, pres. 1981-82, H.G. Maynard Innovative Achievement award 1977, Gilbreth Indsl. Engring. award 1990), Am. Soc. for Engring. Edn. (sec. govt. rels. com. 1975-76), Nat. Soc. Profl. Engrs., Okla. Soc. Profl. Engrs. (Outstanding Engring. Achievement award 1977, Outstanding Engr. in Okla. 1981), Inst. Mgmt. Scis., Coun. Indsl. Engring. Acad. Dept. Heads (chmn. 1975-76), NAE, Nat. Rsch. Coun., Sigma Xi, Tau Beta Pi, Alpha Pi Mu. Office: Oklahoma State U Indsl Engring Dept Stillwater OK 74078

MIZE, LARRY, professional golfer. Profl. golfer, 1981—; PGA tour victories include: Memphis Classsic, 1983, Masters, 1987, Northern Telecom Open, 1993, Buick Open, 1993. mem. U.S. Ryder Cup Team, 1987. Office: care PGA 100 Avenue Of Champions Palm Beach Gardens FL 33418*

MIZEL, MARK STUART, orthopedic surgeon; b. N.Y.C., May 23, 1945; s. Harold Henry and Irene (Adelman) M. BSME, Columbia U., 1966, MSME, 1968; MD, Tufts U., 1977. Diplomate Am. Bd. Orthopedic Surgery. Intern, George Washington U. Hosp., 1977-78, resident in surgery, 1978-79; resident Mass. Gen. Hosp., Boston, 1979-82; fellow in foot and ankle surgery Dr. Roger Mann, San Francisco, 1983; practice medicine specializing in orthopedic surgery Orthopedic Ctr. of Lake Worth, Fla., 1983-91; clin. assoc. prof. Orthopedics and Rehab. U. Miami, 1989-91; clin. asst. prof. orthopedic surgery, Tufts U., 1991-95; dir. Boston Foot & Ankle Ctr., 1991-95; asst. prof. orthopedic surgery Johns Hopkins, 1995—. Assoc. editor Foot & Ankle. Served as aviator USN, 1969-72; Vietnam. Fellow ACS, Am. Acad. Orthopedic Surgeons, Am. Orthopedic Foot and Ankle Soc. (membership com. 1988-90, orthotics and prosthetics com. 1990-91, chmn. regional rev. subcom., 1993-96). Office: Johns Hopkins Orthopedics Dept 601 N Caroline St Baltimore MD 21205-1809

MIZELL, ANDREW HOOPER, III, concrete company executive; b. Franklin, Tenn., Sept. 26, 1926; s. Andrew Hooper, Jr. and Jennie McEwen (Fleming) M.; B.A., Vanderbilt U., 1950; m. Julia Yolanda Mattei, Dec. 20, 1947; children—Andrew Hooper, Julia Fleming. Supt., Wescon Constrn. Co., Nashville, 1950-52; accountant McIntyre & Asso., Nashville, 1952-55; credit mgr. Ingram Oil Co., Nashville, 1955-56, v.p. and dir., 1956-62; v.p., dir. Comml. Sign & Advt. Co., Nashville, 1957-59; v.p. and dir. Gen. Properties Co., New Orleans, 1957-62; v.p. and dir. Minn. Barge & Terminal Co., St. Paul, 1957-62; mgr. real estate and devel. Murphy Corp., El Dorado, Ark., 1962-63, mgr. retail sales, 1962-63; pres. and chmn. bd. Transit Ready Mix, Inc., Nashville, 1963—; pres., Conco, Inc., Apollo Concrete Products, Inc.; ptnr. Mizell Riggs Enterprises. Active United Givers Fund, 1965-66; chmn. Concrete div. Office Emergency Planning, 1965—; mem. Nat. UN Day Com., 1978. Served with USNR, 1944-46. Named Ark. Traveler, 1966, Ky. Col., 1969. Mem. Nat. Ready Mix Concrete Assn. (chmn. membership com. Tenn. sect. 1971—, chmn. marketing com. Tenn. chpt. 1973—), Assn. Gen. Contractors, Tenn. Bldg. Material Assn., Nat. Fedn. Ind. Businessmen, Portland Cement Assn., Nat. Area Bus. and Edn. Radio, Asso. Builders and Contractors, Spl. Indsl. Radio Service Industry, Tenn. Road Builders, Boat Owners Assn. U.S., Nashville C. of C., U.S. C. of C., Am. Concrete Inst. Clubs: Nashville Yacht, Nashville City, Belle Meade Country, The Honors Course, Commodore Yacht (past commodore). Home: 4340 Beekman Dr Nashville TN 37215-4504

MIZGALA, HENRY F., physician; b. Montreal, Nov. 28, 1932; s. Louis and Mary (Ropeleski) M.; m. Pauline Barbara Delaney, Oct. 26, 1957; children: Paul Stephen, Cynthia Louise, Liane Mary, Melanie Frances Mizgala Dressler, Nancy Elizabeth Mizgala Lewis. B.A. magna cum laude, Loyola Coll., Montreal, 1953; M.D., C.M., McGill U., 1957. Rotating intern, then resident in medicine St. Mary's Hosp., Montreal, 1957-59; asst. physician St. Mary's Hosp., 1963-66; resident in medicine Royal Victoria Hosp., Montreal, 1959-60; Dazian fellow cardiology Mt. Sinai Hosp., N.Y.C., 1960-61, USPHS fellow cardiology, 1961-62; resident in cardiology Montreal Gen. Hosp., 1962-63, assoc. physician, 1966-74; asst. physician, cons. cardiology Lachine (Que.) Gen. Hosp., 1964-80; cardiologist Montreal Heart Inst., also dir. CCU, 1974-80; cons. Centre Hosp. Baie des Chaleurs, Gaspe, Que., 1975-80; hon. cons. Montreal Heart Inst., 1980—; prof. medicine U. B.C., 1980—; cardiologist The Vancouver (B.C.) Hosp. and Health Scis. Ctr.; cons. B.C. Cancer Agy., Vancouver, 1981—; cons. staff Univ. Hosp., U. B.C. site, 1981-94; mem. faculty McGill U. Med. Sch., Montreal, 1968-74; asso. prof. medicine McGill U. Med. Sch., 1973-74; assoc. prof., then prof. Montreal U. Med. Sch., 1974-81; prof. medicine, head div. cardiology U. B.C., 1980-87. Mem. editl. bd. Can. Jour. Cardiol. 1988—, Jour. Am. Coll. Cardiology, 1992-95; contbr. numerous articles to med. jours. Fellow Royal Coll. Phys. and Surg. Can., Am. Coll. Cardiology, Am. Heart Assn. (council clin. cardiology); mem. Can. Med. Assn., Can. Cardiovascular Soc. (treas. 1974-90), Que. Med. Assn., B.C. Med. Assn., B.C. and Yukon Heart and Stroke Found. (bd. dirs., sr. bd. dirs.), Alpha Omega Alpha. Office: U BC Div Cardiology Dept Med, 865 W 10th Ave, Vancouver, BC Canada V5Z 1L7

MIZRAHI, ABRAHAM MORDECHAY, retired cosmetics and health care company executive, physician; b. Jerusalem, Apr. 16, 1929; came to U.S., 1952, naturalized, 1960; s. Solomon R. and Rachel (Haliwa) M.; m. Suzanne Eve Glasser, Mar. 15, 1956; children: Debra, Judith, Karen. B.S., Manchester Coll., 1955; M.D., Albert Einstein Coll. Medicine, 1960. Diplomate: Am. Bd. Pediatrics, Nat. Bd. Med. Examiners. Intern U. N.C., 1960-61; pediatric resident Columbia-Presbyn. Med. Center, N.Y.C., 1961-63; NIH fellow in neonatology Columbia-Presbyn. Med. Center, 1963-65; assoc. dir. Newborn Service Mt. Sinai Hosp., N.Y.C.; also dir. Newborn Service Elmhurst Med. Center, 1965-67; staff physician Geigy Pharm. Corp., N.Y.C., 1967-69; head cardio-pulmonary sect. Geigy Pharm. Corp., 1969-71; sr. v.p. corp. med. affairs USV Pharm. Corp., Tuckahoe, N.Y., 1971-76; v.p. health and safety Revlon, Inc., N.Y.C., 1976-89, sr. v.p. human resources, 1989-94; ret., 1994; assoc. in pediatrics Columbia U., 1963-67; cons. in neonatology Misericordia-Fordham Med. Ctr., 1967-89; clin. affiliate N.Y. Hosp.; clin. asst. prof. Cornell U. Med. Coll., 1982—. Contbr. articles to profl. jours. Trustee Westchester (N.Y.) Jewish Center. Mem. AMA, N.Y. State and County Med. Soc., Am., N.Y. acads. medicine, Am. Soc. Clin. Pharmacology and Therapeutics, Am. Pub. Health Assn., Am. Occupational Med. Assn. Home: 7 Jason Ln Mamaroneck NY 10543-2108 *The principles that have guided my life are old Biblical concepts. Firstly, that God had created Adam and Eve and all Men are, therefore, brothers and sisters. Secondly, God created Man and, therefore every human being has a spark of God in him. It, therefore, follows that killing diminshes God's presence on earth and saving of a human being increases His presence.*

MIZRAHI, EDWARD ALAN, allergist; b. Tyler, Tex., Aug. 24, 1945. BS in Econs., U. Pa., 1967; MD, U. Fla., 1972. Diplomate Am. Bd. Internal Medicine, Am. Bd. Allergy and Immunology. Intern Med. Coll. Ga., Augusta, 1972-73, resident, 1973-75; fellow Nat. Jewish Hosp., U. Colo., Denver, 1975-77; pvt. practice Jacksonville, Fla., 1977—; physician Bapt. Med. Ctr., Jacksonville, Columbia Meml. Med. Ctr., Jacksonville, St. Luke's Med. Ctr., Jacksonville, St. Vincent's Med. Ctr., Jacksonville, Meth. Hosp., Jacksonville, Columbia Orange Park (Fla.) Med. Ctr. Mem. Am. Coll. Allergy, Asthma and Immunology, Am. Acad. Allergy, Asthma and Immunology, Fla. Med. Assn., Fla. Allergy and Immunology Soc., Duval County Med. Soc., Southeastern Allergy Assn. Office: 3636 University Blvd S Ste B2 Jacksonville FL 32216-4223

MIZRAHI, YVES, retail executive; b. Paris, France, Nov. 22, 1954; came to U.S., 1959; s. Maurice and Fanny (De Leon) M.; m. Deborah Anne Mizrahi, May 20, 1978; children: Lauren, Amanda. BA in Biology, U. Wash., 1977; MBA in Fin., U. Puget Sound, 1980. Registered real estate broker, Wash. Pers. officer U. Wash., Seattle, 1977-80; sr. treasury analyst ENI Exploration Co., Seattle, 1980-81; sr. fin. analyst Seafirst Bank, Seattle, 1981-83; sr. econ. cons. The NBBJ Group, Seattle, 1983-85; sr. investment analyst Composite Rsch., Seattle, 1985-86; v.p. Wahl & Assocs., Seattle, 1986-90; v.p. real estate and store development Starbucks Coffee, Seattle, 1990—. Mem. com. Downtown Seattle Assn., 1983-85; mem. fin. com. Villa Acad., Seattle, 1992-93. Mem. Internat. Conf. Shopping Ctrs., NACORE. Avocations: tennis, running, travel. Office: 2401 Utah Ave S Seattle WA 98134-1431

MLAY, MARIAN, government official; b. Pitts., Sept. 11, 1935; d. John and Sonia M.; A.B., U. Pitts., 1957; postgrad. (Univ. fellow) Princeton U., 1969-70; J.D., Am. U., 1977. Mgmt. positions HEW, Washington, 1961-70, dep. dir. Chgo. region, 1971-72, dir. div. consol. funding, 1972-73, dep. dir. office policy devel. and planning USPHS, Washington, 1973-77; dir. program evaluation EPA, Washington, 1978-79, dep. dir. Office of Drinking Water, 1979-84, dir. Office of Ground Water Protection, 1984-91, dir. Oceans and Coastal Protection, 1991-95; sr. rsch. assoc. Nat. Acad. Pub. Adminstrn. 1995—. Bd. dirs. D.C. United Fund, 1979-80. Recipient Career Edn. award Nat. Inst. Public Affairs, 1969. Mem. ABA, D.C. Bar (steering com. energy, environment and natural resources sect.). Author articles in field. Home: 3747 1/2 Kanawha St NW Washington DC 20015-1838 Office: Nat Acad Pub Adminstrn 1120 G St NW Ste 850 Washington DC 20005-3801

MLOCEK, SISTER FRANCES ANGELINE, financial executive; b. River Rouge, Mich., Aug. 4, 1934; d. Michael and Suzanna (Bloch) M. BBA, U. Detroit, 1958; MBA, U. Mich., 1971. CPA, Mich. Bookkeeper Allen Park (Mich.) Furniture, 1949-52, Gerson's Jewlery, Detroit, 1952-53; jr. acct. Meyer Dickman, CPA, Algaze, Staub & Bowman, CPAs, Detroit, 1953-58; acct., internal auditor Sisters, Servants of Immaculate Heart of Mary Congregation, Monroe, Mich., 1959-66, asst. gen. treas., 1966-73, gen. treas., 1973-76; internal auditor for parishes Archdiocese of Detroit, 1976-78; asst. to exec. dir. Leadership Conf. of Women, Silver Spring, Md., 1978-83; dir. of fin. Nat. Conf. of Cath. Bishops/U.S. Cath. Conf., Washington, 1989-94; CFO Sisters Servants of the Immaculate Heart of Mary, Monroe, Mich., 1994—; trustee Sisters, Servants of Immaculate Heart of Mary Charitable Trust Fund, Monroe, 1988—. Author: (manual) Leadership Conference of Women Religious/Confernce of Major Superiors of Men, 1981. Treas. Zonta Club of Washington Found., Washington, 1983-88, pres., 1992-93; bd. dirs. Our Lady of Good Counsel High Sch., Wheaton, Md., 1983-89. Mem. AICPA, D.C. Inst. CPAs (mem. not-for-profit com. 1992-94, CFOs com. 1990-94. Democrat. Roman Catholic. Office: Sisters Servants Immaculate Heart Mary 610 W Elm Ave Monroe MI 48162-7909

MLYNIEC, WALLACE JOHN, law educator, lawyer, consultant; b. Berwyn, Ill., July 10, 1945; s. Casimir Adele and Adeline Mary (Kaczka) M. BS, Northwestern U., 1967; JD, Georgetown U., 1970. Bar: D.C. 1971, Alaska 1971, U.S. Dist. Ct. D.C. 1971, U.S. Ct. Appeals (D.C. cir.) 1971, U.S. Supreme Ct. 1974. Exec. dir. ABA standards U.S. Cir. Jud. Conf. Project on ABA Standards, Washington, 1971-73; dir. Juvenile Justice Clinic, Georgetown U., Washington, 1973—, prof. law, 1973—; coord. clin. edn, 1986-89, assoc. dean, 1989—; cons. Nat. Adv. Com. on Juvenile Justice, Washington, 1979-80; cons. pvt. and pub. agys. on juvenile and criminal justice, 1974—; chmn. Juvenile Justice Adv. Group, D.C., 1980-82; mem. Nat. Resource Ctr. on Child Abuse and Neglect. Recipient Stuart Stillar Found. award, 1994; Meyer Found. grantee, 1980-82; Swedish Bicentennial fellow, 1985. Mem. Am. Assn. Law Schs. (mem. com. on polit. interference 1983-84, chair 1991, standing com. on clin. edn., William Pincus award 1996), ABA (mem. adv. com. on family ct. rules 1984), D.C. Bar Assn. (chmn. juvenile justice sect. 1973).

MNOOKIN, ROBERT HARRIS, lawyer, educator; b. Kansas City, Mo., Feb. 4, 1942; s. I.J. and Marion (Sittenfeld) M.; m. Dale Seigel, June 16, 1963; children: Jennifer Leigh, Allison Heather. A.B., Harvard U., 1964, LL.B., 1968. Bar: D.C. 1970, Calif. 1971. Fulbright scholar Econometric Inst., Netherland Sch. Econs., 1964-65; assoc. Howard, Prim, Smith, Rice & Downs, San Francisco, 1970-72; of counsel Howard, Prim, Smith, Rice & Downs, 1972-93; vis. prof. Stanford U. Sch. Law, 1980-81, prof. law, 1981-89, Adelbert H. Sweet prof. law, 1989-93; Samuel Williston prof. Harvard Law Sch., Cambridge, Mass., 1993—; dir. Harvard negotiation rsch. project Harvard U., Cambridge, 1993—, chair program on negotiation, 1993—; lectr. U. Calif., Berkeley, 1972, dir. childhood and govt. project, 1972-74, acting prof. law, 1973-75, prof. law, 1975-81; dir. Stanford Ctr. on Conflict and Negotiation, 1988-93; vis. fellow Wolfson Coll. and Centre for Socio-Legal Studies, Oxford, Eng., 1978; fellow Center for Advanced Studies in Behavioral Scis., 1981-82; vis. prof. Harvard Law Sch., 1990-91; arbitrator IBM-Fujitsu Arbitration, 1985—. Author: In the Interest of Children, 1985, Dividing the Child, 1992, Child, Family and State, 3d edit., 1995, Barriers to Conflict Resolution, 1995; contbr. articles to profl. jours. Mem. overseer's com. to visit Law Sch., Harvard U., 1972-78; trustee Berkeley Pub. Library, 1973-80, chmn., 1975-77, vice chmn., 1978-80. Fellow Am. Acad. Arts and Scis.; mem. ABA, Calif. Bar Assn. Home: 10 Follen St Cambridge MA 02138-3503 Office: Hauser 416 Harvard Law Sch Cambridge MA 02138

MO, LUKE WEI, physicist, educator; b. Shangtung, China, June 3, 1934; s. Si-leng and Shu-feng (Lo) M.; m. Doris Chang, Dec. 31, 1960; children: Curtis L., Alice. B.S. in Elec. Engring, Nat. Taiwan U., 1955; M.S. in Physics, Nat. Tsinghua U., Taiwan, 1959; Ph.D., Columbia U., 1963. Research asso. Columbia U., N.Y.C., 1963-64; research physicist Stanford (Calif.) Linear Accelerator, 1965-69; asst. prof. physics U. Chgo., 1969-76; prof. physics Va. Poly. Inst. and State U., Blacksburg, 1976—. Contbr. articles to profl. jours. Served with Taiwan Air Force, 1955-56. Recipient Alumni Research Excellence award Va. Poly. Inst. and State U., 1980, Guggenheim fellow, 1981, NSF grantee, 1969—. Fellow Am. Phys. Soc. Office: Va Poly Inst Physics Dept 315 Robeson Hall Blacksburg VA 24061-0435

MO, ROGER SHIH-YAH, electronics engineering manager; b. Shanghai, Rep. of China, Mar. 10, 1939; s. Maurice Chun-Dat and Mary (Shen) M.; m. Amy Chun-Muh Chang, June 21, 1964; 1 child, Karen Voong-Tsun. BSEE, MIT, 1962; MSEE, Northeastern U., Boston, 1964, PhD, 1967; MBA, Pepperdine U., 1980. Engr. Raytheon Corp., Sudbury, Mass., 1967-69; on tech. staff Xerox, El Segundo, Calif., 1969-74, mgr. memory, 1974-77, mgr. cirs. and subsystems, 1977-81, area mgr., 1981-87, program mgr., 1987-89, imaging systems mgr., 1989-92, systems design mgr., 1992—; sr. lectr. West Coast U., L.A., 1978-87, chmn. acad. standards com., 1981-82. Contbr. articles to profl. jours. Bd. dirs. The Wellness Community So. Bay Cities, 1989-96. Mem. IEEE, Chinese Am. Assn. of So. Calif. (bd. dirs. 1983-87). Democrat. Roman Catholic. Lodge: Flip Flap (local chmn. 1974, nat. chmn. 1976). Avocations: golf, table tennis, photography. Home: 6852 Verde Ridge Rd Palos Verdes Penin CA 90275-4638 Office: Xerox Corp 701 S Aviation Blvd El Segundo CA 90245-4806

MOAG, RODNEY FRANK, language educator, country music singer; b. Warsaw, N.Y., Oct. 15, 1936; s. Hugh Alexander and Imogene (Hodges) M.; m. Rachel Ann Foley, Feb. 9, 1964 (div. Aug. 1974); children: Robin Gray, Hugh Daniel, Jeffry Lee. BS, Syracuse U., 1961; MA, U. Wis., 1966, PhD, 1973. Dir. college preparatory program for visually impaired U. Mo., Columbia, 1974; vis. Fulbright prof. U. South Pacific, Suva, Fiji Islands, 1975-78; vis. assoc. prof. U. Mich., Ann Arbor, 1978-80, adj. prof., 1981, vis. assoc. prof., 1982; sr. lectr. U. Tex., Austin, 1981, 83-90, assoc. prof., 1990—. Author: (texts) Fiji Mindi, 1977, Malayalam, 1986; country music artist: several records, one CD, 1995. Mng. dir. Amateur Radio Repeaters of Washtenaw, 1984-86; pres. Mich. Repeater Coun., 1985-88; v.p. Austin Amateur Radio Club, 1993-94; vol. programmer, KO-OP. Mem. Ctrl. Tex. Bluegrass Assn., Austin Amateur Radio Club, Austin Repeater Orgn., Tex. VHF FM Soc. Avocations: amateur radio, country and bluegrass music. Home: 6909 Miranda Dr Austin TX 78752 Office: Univ Tex Dept Asian Studies Austin TX 78712

MOAKLEY, JOHN JOSEPH, congressman; b. Apr. 27, 1927; m. Evelyn Duffy, 1957. LLB, Suffolk U., 1956. Bar: Mass. 1957. Pvt. practice Boston, 1957-72; mem. 93rd-105th Congresses from 9th Mass. dist., 1973—; ranking minority mem. com. on rules. Chmn. com. on rules Mass. Senate, 1964-70; mem. Boston City Coun., 1971-72, chmn. appropriations and fin. com. With USNR, 1943-46. Office: US Ho of Reps 235 Cannon HOB Washington DC 20515*

MOATES, G. PAUL, lawyer; b. Los Angeles, May 26, 1947; s. Guy Hart and Virginia Rose (Mayolett) M.; m. Paulette Anita Minkus, Mar. 21, 1970; 1 child, Amanda Frances. B.A., Amherst Coll., 1969; J.D., U. Chgo., 1975. Bar: Ill. 1975, D.C. 1976, U.S. Ct. Appeals (D.C. cir.) 1976, U.S. Supreme Ct. 1980, U.S. Ct. Appeals (6th cir.) 1984, U.S. Ct. Appeals (3d cir.) 1991, U.S. Ct. Appeals (7th cir.) 1993. Assoc. firm Sidley & Austin, Washington, 1975-82, ptnr., 1982—. Contbr. articles to profl. jours. Served with U.S. Army, 1970-73. Mem. ABA, Ill. Bar Assn., D.C. Bar Assn. Office: Sidley & Austin 1722 I St NW Washington DC 20006-3705

MOAWAD, ATEF, obstetrician, gynecologist, educator; b. Beni Suef, Egypt, Dec. 2, 1935; came to U.S., 1959; s. Hanna and Baheya (Hunein) M.; m. Ferial Fouad Abdel Malek, Aug. 22, 1966; children: John, Joseph, James. Student, Cairo U. Sch. Sci., 1951-52; MB, BCh, Cairo U. Sch. Medicine, 1957; MS in in Pharmacology, Jefferson Med. Coll., 1963. Diplomate Am. Bd. Ob-Gyn; licentiate Med. Coun Can. Rotating intern Cairo U. Hosp., 1958-59, Elizabeth (N.J.) Gen. Hosp., 1959-60; resident in ob-gyn. Jefferson Med. Coll. Hosp., Phila., 1961-64; lect. dept. pharmacology U. Alta., Can., 1966; asst. prof. dept. ob-gyn. and pharmacology U. Alta., Can., 1967-70, assoc. prof., 1970-72; assoc. prof. dept. ob-gyn. and pharmacology U. Chgo., 1972-75, prof. dept. ob-gyn. and pediatrics, 1975—, co-dir. perinatal ctr., 1974-80; obstetrician-gynecologist, chief obstetrics, co-dir. perinatal ctr. The Chgo. Lying-in Hosp. U. Chgo., 1980—; vis. investigator dept. ob-gyn. U. Lund, Sweden, 1969. Co-author book chpts., jour. articles. Mem. perinatal adv. com. Chgo. March of Dimes, 1977—, health profl. adv. com., 1983—; mem. perinatal adv. bd. com. State of Ill., 1978—; mem. Chgo. Maternal Child Health Adv. Com., chmn., 1991—; mem. Mayor's Adv. Com. on Infant Mortality, 1991—. Fellow Jefferson Med. Coll., 1960-61, Case Western Reserve U., 1964-65; grantee Brush Found., 1966-67, Maternal Fetal Medicine Unites Network NIH, 1994; recipient award Phila. Obstet. Soc., 1964, Disting. Teaching award Am. Profs. Gynecology and Obstetrics, 1993. Fellow Am. Coll. Ob-Gyn. (Purdue-Frederick award 1978), Royal Coll. Surgeons (Can.); mem. Soc. for Gynecol Investigation, Pharmacol. Soc. Can., Am. Gynecol. and Obstet. Soc., Soc. Perinatal Obstetricians, N.Y. Acad. Scis., Chgo. Gynecol. Soc., Can. Med. Assn., Christian Med. Soc., Edmonton Obstetrics Soc. Office: U Chgo Dept Ob-Gyn 5841 S Maryland Ave Chicago IL 60637-1463

MOBBS, MICHAEL HALL, lawyer; b. Lawrenceburg, Tenn., Dec. 25, 1948; s. Hershel Leon and Doris (Davis) M.; m. Ellene Winn, June 19, 1976; children: Michael Hall Jr., Clifton Stevenson, Ellene Glenn. BA summa cum laude, honors with exceptional distinction in Russian studies, Yale U., 1971; JD, U. Chgo., 1974. Bar: Ala. 1974, D.C. 1978, U.S. Supreme Ct. 1980. Assoc. Bradley, Arant, Rose & White, Birmingham, Ala., 1974-77; assoc. Stroock & Stroock & Lavan, Washington, 1977-81, ptnr., 1990-93; ptnr. Squire, Sanders & Dempsey, 1994—, mng. ptnr. Moscow, 1995—; rep. of sec. def. to Strategic Arms Reduction Talks, Washington and Geneva, 1982-85; spl. counsel to head of del. and rep. of sec. def. to Negotiations on Nuclear and Space Arms, Washington and Geneva, 1985; asst. dir. of U.S. Arms Control and Disarmament Agy., Washington, 1985-87. Ford Fund scholar, 1967-71; Bates fellow, 1970; recipient Fellows' prize Jonathan Edwards Coll. Yale U., 1971. Mem. ABA (mem. com. on Ctrl. and Ea. European law initiatives), FBA, Am. Soc. Internat. Law, Ala. State Bar, D.C. Bar, Phi Beta Kappa. Democrat. Clubs: Yale of N.Y.C.; City Tavern (Washington). Author: (with George G. Lorinczi) An Importer's Roadmap to U.S. Import Restrictions, 1980, CBMs For Stabilizing the Strategic Nuclear Competition, 1986, Remarks on Verification of Arms Control Agreements, 1988, (with William J. Vanden Heuvel) Overview of the Laws Governing Foreign Investment in the USSR, 1990, On the Road in Eastern Europe, 1991, Environmental Protection in the CIS and Eastern Europe: Emerging Trends May Affect Your Business, 1993. Home: 636 E Capitol St NE Washington DC 20003-1233 Office: Squire Sanders & Dempsey PO Box 407 1201 Pennsylvania Ave NW Washington DC 20044-0407

MOBERG, DAVID OSCAR, sociology educator; b. Montevideo, Minn., Feb. 13, 1922; s. Fred Ludwig and Anna E. (Sundberg) M.; m. Helen H. Heitzman, Mar. 16, 1946 (dec. Oct. 16, 1992); children: David Paul, Lynette, Jonathan, Philip; m. Marlys Taege, July 23, 1994. AA, Bethel Jr. Coll., 1942; AB, Seattle Pacific Coll., 1947; MA, U. Wash., 1949; PhD, U. Minn., 1952. Assoc. instr. U. Wash., Seattle, 1948-49; faculty Bethel Coll., St. Paul, 1949-68, prof. sociology, 1959-68, chmn. dept. social scis., 1952-68; prof. sociology Marquette U., Milw., 1968-91, prof. emeritus, 1991—, chmn. dept. sociology and anthropology, 1968-77; cons. Nat. Liberty Found., 1970-71, Fetzer Inst., 1995—; cons. Nat. Interfaith Coalition on Aging, 1973-75, mem. nat. adv. bd., 1980-89; guest rschr. Sociology of Religion Inst., Stockholm, summer 1978; adj. prof. San Francisco Theol. Sem., 1964-73, McCormick Theol. Sem., 1975-78, 81-82; vis. prof. U. So. Calif., 1979, Princeton Theol. Sem., 1979, So. Bapt. Theol. Sem., 1982, Soc. for Care of Handicapped in the Gaza Strip of Palestine, 1995; mem. adv. bd. Ecumenical Ministry with Mature Adults, 1983-92; resource scholar Christianity Today Inst., 1985—. Author: The Church as A Social Institution, 1962, 2d edit. 1984, (with Robert M. Gray) The Church and the Older Person, 1962, 2d edit., 1977, Inasmuch: Christian Social Responsibility in the 20th Century, 1965, White House Conference on Aging: Spiritual Well-Being Background and Issues, 1971, The Great Reversal: Evangelism and Social Concern, 1972, 2d edit, 1977, Wholistic Christianity, 1985; also articles, chpts. in symposia.; editor: International Directory of Religious Information Systems, 1971, Spiritual Well-Being: Sociological Perspectives, 1979, Rev. Religious Research, 1968-72, Jour. Am. Sci. Affiliation, 1962-64, Adris Newsletter, 1971-76; co-editor Research in the Social Scientific Study of Religion, 1986—; assoc. editor: Social Compass, 1968—; mem. editl. bd. Christian Univ. Press, 1979-84, Perspectives on Sci. and Christian Faith, 1988—; consulting editor Calif. Sociologist, 1982—. Fulbright lectr. U. Groningen, Netherlands, 1957-58, Fulbright lectr. Muenster U., West Germany, 1964-65. Fellow Am. Sci. Affiliation (editor jour. 1962-64, publs. com. 1984-91, social ethics com. 1985-88, program chair 1995-96), Gerontol. Soc. Am.; mem. Am. Sociol. Assn., Internat. Sociol. Assn. (sociology of religion rsch. com. 1972—), Wis. Sociol. Assn. (pres. 1969-71), Midwest Sociol. Assn. (Wis. bd. dirs. 1971-73), Assn. Devel. Religious Info. Sys. (coord. ADRIS 1971—, editor ADRIS newsletter 1971-76), Religious Rsch. Assn. (editor Rev. Religious Rsch. 1968-72, contbg. editor 1973-77, assoc. editor 1983—, bd. dirs. 1959-61, 68-72, pres. 1981-82, H. Paul Douglass lectr. 1986), Assn. for Sociology of Religion (exec. coun. 1971-73, pres. 1976-77), Soc. for Sci. Study Religion (exec. coun. 1971-74, sr. editl. cons. SSSR-RRA History Project 1995—), Evangelicals for Social Action (planning com. 1973-75), Christian Sociol. Soc. (steering com. 1973-81, newsletter lit. reveiwer 1981-93), Family Rsch. Coun. (assoc. 1985-88, rsch. network 1989—), Psychologists Interested in Religious Issues (profl. affiliate 1984—), Midwest Coun. for Social Rsch. on Aging (fellow 1961-64, 87—), Am. Soc. on Aging, Forum on Religion and Aging, Fairview Elder Enterprises (bd. dirs. 1990—). Home: 7120 W Dove Ct Milwaukee WI 53223-2766 Office: Marquette U Dept Social & Cultural Sci Milwaukee WI 53201-1881 *As I try to live with eternity's values in view, my entire lifetime seems to grow ever briefer instead of longer.*

MOBERLY, DAVID LINDSEY, retired foundation executive; b. Irvine, Ky., Apr. 25, 1929; s. Earl and Blanche (Finney) M.; m. Peggy Compton, Dec. 30, 1951; children—Kent, Lynn. A.B., U. Ky., 1951; postgrad., Am. U., 1950; M.A., U. Ky., 1953; Ph.D., Kent State U., 1965. Tchr. Jefferson County Bd. Edn., Louisville, 1951-54; dean of boys Jefferson County Bd. Edn., 1954-55, asst. prin., 1955-57; ednl. adv. AID, U.S. State Dept., Tripoli, Benghazi, Libya, 1957-61; edn. program officer, research and survey team AID, U.S. State Dept., Nairobi, Kenya, 1961-62; instr., resident project coordinator in Tanzania Kent State U., 1962-65; supt. schs. Bd. Edn., Tallmadge, Ohio, 1966-67, Warren, Ohio, 1967-71, Cleve. Heights, 1971-74; supt. schs. Evanston (Ill.) Twp. High Sch., 1974-76, Seattle Sch. Dist. 1, 1976-81; pres. Seattle Found., 1981-84; nat. edn. mgr. Deloitte, Hoskins & Sells, 1984-89; asst. state supt. State of Wash., 1989-95; dep. supt. State of Washington, 1995-96, ret., 1996; spl. participant documentary on problems in edn. ABC-TV, 1976. Area chmn. Ohio's Right-to-Read project, 1969-71; chmn. alumni com. for edn. com. Kent State U., 1968-71; mem. nat. adv. bd. Corp. for Pub. Broadcasting; U.S. del. to World Orgn. of Teaching Profession, in Rome, Italy, 1958; Mem. Seattle council Boy Scouts Am.; bd. dirs. Jr. Achievement; trustee Pacific Sci. Center Found., Seattle; mem. Pvt. Sector's Initiative Bd., Seattle. Mem. NEA, Am. Assn. Sch. Adminstrs., Wash. Assn. Sch. Adminstrs., Mcpl. League, Seattle C. of C., Kappa Delta Pi, Phi Delta Kappa. Club: Rotarian. Home: 3045 44th Ave W Seattle WA 98199-2401

MOBERLY, LINDEN EMERY, educational administrator; b. Laramie, Wyo., Jan. 4, 1923; s. Linden E. and Ruth (Gathercole) M. BS, Coll. Emporia, 1952; MS, Kans. State Tchrs. Coll., 1954; m. Viola F. Mosher, Apr. 29, 1949. Tchr. sci., Florence, Kans., 1952-54, Concordia, Kans., 1954-56, Grand Junction, Colo., 1957-60; asst. prin. Orchard Mesa Jr. High Sch., Grand Junction, 1960-66, prin., 1967-84; field cons. Nat. Assn. Secondary Sch. Prins., 1985—. Sgt. USMC, 1941-46. Recipient Outstanding Secondary Prin. award Colo. Assn. Sch. Execs., 1978. Mem. NEA, VFW, Nat. Assn. Secondary Prins. (bd. dir. 1979-83), Colo. Edn. Assn. (bd.dir. 1968-71), Colo. North Central Assn. Colls. and Secondary Schs., Colo. Assn. Secondary Sch. Prins. (bd. dir. 1974-77), Lions, Sons of the Revolution, Marine Corps League (life), VFW (life), Masons (award of Excellence 1990). Home: 2256 Kingston Rd Grand Junction CO 81503-1221

MOBERLY, ROBERT BLAKELY, lawyer, educator; b. Madison, Wis., Sept. 17, 1941; s. Russell Louis and Hildegarde (Reimer) M.; m. Lynne Webb; children—Laura, Richard, Reed. B.S., U. Wis., 1963, J.D., 1966. Bar: Wis. 1966, Tenn. 1977, Fla. 1984 (faculty affiliate). Law clk. Wis. Supreme Ct., 1966-67; arbitrator, trial examiner, mediator Wis. Employment Relations Commn., 1968-71; practice law Milw., 1971-73; prof. U. Tenn. Coll. Law, Knoxville, 1973-77; prof., dir. U. Fla. Coll. Law, 1977—; vis. prof. U. Ill. Inst. for Labor Rels., 1973, U. Louvain, Belgium, 1975, Polish Acad. Scis., 1981; mem. arbitration panels, Fed. Mediation and Conciliation Svc., Am. Arbitration Assn., Nat. Mediation Bd.; prin. investigator U.S. Labor Dept., 1988; mem. com. on mediation and arbitration Fla. Supreme Ct., 1989—, chair arbitration subcom., standards of conduct subcom. Author: Public Employment Labor Relations, 1974, Arbitration and Conflict Resolution, 1979; contbr. articles to profl. jours. Mem. ABA, Fla. Bar Assn. (exec. council labor law sect. 1986-88), Nat. Acad. Arbitrators (chmn. S.E. region 1976-79), Indsl. Relations Rsch. Assn., Soc. Profls. in Dispute Resolution, Internat. Soc. Labor Law and Social Legislation (mem. exec. bd. 1989-92), Assn. Am. Law Schs. (chair labor law sect. 1989, chair alternative dispute resolution sect. 1997). Office: U Fla Coll Law PO Box 117625 Gainesville FL 32611-2038

MOBLEY, EMILY RUTH, library dean, educator; b. Valdosta, Ga., Oct. 1, 1942; d. Emmett and Ruth (Johnson) M. AB in Edn., U. Mich., 1964, AM in Libr. Sci., 1967, postgrad. Tchr. Ecorse (Mich.) Pub. Schs., 1964-65; adminstrv. trainee Chrysler Corp., Highland Park, Mich., 1965-66, engring. libr., 1966-69; libr. II Wayne State U., Detroit, 1969-72, libr. III, 1972-75; staff asst. GM Rsch. Labs. Libr., Warren, Mich., 1976-78, supr. reader svcs., 1978-81; libr. dir. GMI Engring. & Mgmt. Inst., Flint, Mich., 1982-86; assoc. dir. for pub. svcs. & collection devel., assoc. prof. libr. sci. Purdue U. Librs., West Lafayette, Ind., 1986-89, acting dir. librs., assoc. prof. libr. sci., 1989, dean librs., prof. libr. sci., 1989—; Esther Ellis Norton Disting. Prof. Libr. Sci. Purdue U., West Lafayette, Ind., 1997—; adj. lectr. U. Mich. Sch. Libr. Sci., Ann Arbor, 1974-75, 83-86; mem. editorial bd. Reference Svcs. Rev., 1989—; grants reader Libr. of Mich., 1980-81; project dir. Mideastern Mich. Region Libr. Cooperation, 1984-86; cons. Libr. Coop. of Macomb, 1985-86, Clark-Atlanta U., 1990, 91; mem. search com. for new dir. of libr. Smithsonian Instn., 1988; mem. GM Pub. Affairs Subcom. on Introducing Minorities to Engring. Author numerous publs.; mem. editl. bd. Infomanage, 1993—; presenter in field. Mem. corp. vis. com. for librs. MIT, 1990—; mem. Ind. Statewide Libr. Automation Task Force, 1989-90; mem. state tech. strategy subcom. on info. tech. & telecommunications Ind. Corp. for Sci. & Tech., 1989; mem. nat. adv. com. Libr. of Congress, 1988; trustee Libr. of Mich., 1983-86, v.p., 1986, long range plan com., 1979-82, task force on document access and delivery, 1977-79; info. project mem. Rep. Nat. Conv., 1980; bd. dirs. Small Farms Assn., Southfield, Mich. Recipient Bausch & Lomb award for Scientific Achievement, 1960, Cert. for Outstanding Performance in Acad. Achievement State of Mich. Ho. of Reps., 1976, Spl. Tribute for Outstanding Contbns. Libr. of Mich. Bd. Trustees, 1986, Disting. Alumnus award U. Mich. Sch. Info. & Libr. Studies, 1989; U. Mich. Regents Alumni scholar, 1960-64; CIC doctoral fellow in libr. sci., 1973-76. Mem. ALA (com. on accreditation, subcom. to rev. 1972, standards for accreditation 1988-89, OLOS minority internship com. 1988-89, nominating com. 1992-93, mem. coun. resolutions com. 1993-97), Assn.

Coll. & Rsch. Librs. (task force on libr. sch. curriculum 1988-89, com. on profl. edn. 1990-92), Libr. Adminstrn. & Mgmt. Assn., Assn. Rsch. Librs. (bd. dirs. 1990-93), Spl. Librs. Assn. (pres. 1987-88, fellow 1991, numerous coms. and other offices), Alpha Kappa Alpha. Office: Purdue U Librs Stewart Ctr West Lafayette IN 47907

MOBLEY, JOHN HOMER, II, lawyer; b. Shreveport, La., Apr. 21, 1930; s. John Hinson and Beulah (Wilson) M.; m. Sue Lawton, Aug. 9, 1958; children: John Lawton, Anne Davant. AB, U. Ga., 1951, JD, 1953. Bar: Ga. 1952, U.S. Dist. Ct., D.C. Ptnr. Kelley & Mobley, Atlanta, 1956-63, Gambrell & Mobley, 1963-83; sr. ptnr., Sutherland, Asbill & Brennan, 1983—. Chmn. Cities in Schs. of Ga.; dir. Cities in Schs. Capt. JAGC, USAF, 1953-55. Mem. ABA, D.C. Bar, State Bar Ga., Atlanta Bar Assn., Am. Judicature Soc., Atlanta Lawyers Club, Phi Delta Phi. Clubs: Atlanta Athletic, Atlanta Country, Commerce, Piedmont Driving, Georgian (Atlanta), N.Y. Athletic, Metropolitan (Washington). Home: 4348 Sentinel Post Rd NW Atlanta GA 30327-3910 Office: Sutherland Asbill & Brennan 999 Peachtree St NE Atlanta GA 30309-3964

MOBLEY, KAREN RUTH, art gallery director; b. Cheyenne, Wyo., Aug. 26, 1961; d. David G. and Marlene G. (Franz) M. BFA, U. Wyo., 1983; MFA, U. Oka., 1987. Sales assoc. Morgan Gallery, Kansas City, Mo., 1984-85; grad. asst. U. Okla. Mus. Art, Norman, 1985-87; dir. Univ. Art Gallery N.Mex. State U., Las Cruces, 1988-93; exec. dir. Nicolaysen Art Mus., Casper, Wyo., 1993—; guest artist Okla. City Community Coll., 1986. Paintings exhibited in numerous exhbns. including Phoenix Triennial, 1990, New Am. Talent, Laguna Gloria Art Mus., Austin, Tex., 1992, Adair Margo Gallery, El Paso, 1992, 93, 94, Wyo. Arts Coun. Gallery and Casper Coll., 1995, Mont. State U., 1996. Wyo. Arts Coun. Individual Artist grantee 1994, Lit. fellow, 1995, 96; named Outstanding Young Women Am. Mem. Am. Assn. Mus., Mountain Plains Mus. Assn., N.Mex. Mus Assn., Coll. Art Assn., Phi Beta Kappa, Phi Kappa Phi. Home: PO Box 1574 Casper WY 82602-1574 Office: Nicolaysen Art Mus 400 E Collins Dr Casper WY 82601-2815

MOBLEY, TONY ALLEN, university dean, recreation educator; b. Harrodsburg, Ky., May 19, 1938; s. Cecil and Beatrice (Bailey) M.; m. Betty Weaver, June 10, 1961; 1 child, Derek Lloyd. BS, Georgetown Coll., 1960; MS, Ind. U., 1962, D Recreation, 1965; MRE, So. Sem., Louisville, 1963. Chmn. dept. recreation and pks. Western Ill. U., Macomb, 1965-72, Pa. State U., University Park, 1972-76; prof., chmn. recreation and pks., dean Sch. Health, Phys. Edn. and Recreation Ind. U., Bloomington, 1976—; chair health adv. coun. White River Park Commn., State of Ind., 1979—; v.p Ind. Sports Corp., Indpls., 1983-89; bd. dirs. Nat. Inst. for Fitness and Sport, Indpls., 1984—; J.B. Nash scholar, lectr. Am. Assn. Leisure and Recreation, Reston, Va., 1985. Contbr. over 50 articles to profl. jours. Bd. dirs. Monroe County YMCA, Bloomington, 1984-88. Am. Coun. Edn. adminstrv. internship fellow, N.C. State U., 1970-71. Fellow Am. Acad. Pk. and Recreation Adminstrn. (pres. 1985-86); mem. Nat. Recreation and Pk. Assn. (pres. 1978-79, Nat. Disting. Profl. award 1981), Assn. Rsch., Adminstrn., Profl. Couns. and Socs. (pres. 1986-87, award 1987), Am. Alliance Health, Phys. Edn., Recreation and Dance (Coll. and Univ. Adminstrs. Coun. Honor award 1986), Soc. Pk. and Recreation Edn. (pres. 1974-75, award 1978), Ind. Pk. and Recreation Assn. (Outstanding Profl. award 1985). Avocations: golf, travel. Office: Ind U Sch Health Phys Edn & Rec Recreation Rm 111 Bloomington IN 47405

MOBLEY, WILLIAM HODGES, management educator, researcher; b. Akron, Ohio, Nov. 15, 1941. BA, Denison U., 1963; PhD, U. Md., 1971. Mgr. employee relations research PPG Industries, Pitts., 1971-73; prof. U. S.C., Columbia, 1973-80; head dept. of mgmt. Tex. A&M U., College Station, 1980-83, dean. coll. of bus. adminstrn., 1983-86, exec. dep. chancellor, 1986-88, pres., 1988-93; chancellor Tex. A&M U. Sys., College Station, 1993-94; prof. mgmt. Tex. A&M U., College Station, 1994-97; pres. PDI Global Rsch. Consortium, Ltd., Hong Kong, Dallas, 1996—; bd. dirs. AMMA Found., Pool Energy Svc., Medichi Sci. Co.; vis. fellow Cornell U., 1994, vis. prof. Hong Kong U. Sci. and Tech., 1995-97. Author: Employee Turnover, 1982. Bd. dirs. Amma Found., 1991—, Internat. Food and Agrl. Devel. and Econ. Coop., U.S. Agy. Internat. Devel., 1992-94; mem. tri-lateral task force on N.Am. Higher Edn. Coop., USIA, 1993-95; mem. Pres. Bush's Commn. on Minority Bus. Devel., 1990-92, U.S. com. of the Pacific Econ. Coop. Coun., 1995—. Fulbright scholar Found. for Scholarly Exchange, Republic China, 1978-79; recipient DAAD, Rep. Germany, 1984; Fellow NDEA U.S. Dept. of Edn., 1968-71. Fellow APA, Am. Psychol. Soc. Home: 4317 Fannin Dr Irving TX 75038 Office: PDI Global Rsch Ltd 600 Las Colinas Blvd E Irving TX 75039-5616

MOCCIA, MARY KATHRYN, social worker; b. Harrisburg, Pa.; d. John Joseph and Winifred Louise Trephan. BEd, U. Hawaii, 1978, MSW with distinction, 1980; postgrad., Fuller Theol. Sem., 1987. Diplomate clin. social work. Intern Koko Head Mental Health Clinic, Honolulu, 1978-79, Dept. Social Services and Housing, Honolulu, 1979-80; vol. worker, group coleader Waikiki Mental Health Ctr., Honolulu, 1979, social worker, 1980; workshop facilitator St. Louis-Chaminade Edn. Ctr. Dept. Insts. and Workshops, Honolulu, 1980-83; founding mem. Anorexia and Bulimia Ctr. Hawaii, Honolulu, 1983, pvt. practice psychotherapy and cons., 1983—; personal counselor Chaminade U. Honolulu, 1980-88; clin. social worker Queen's Med. Ctr., 1988—; practicum instr. U. Hawaii, 1992—; guest lectr. U. Hawaii Sch. Social Work, Honolulu, 1980-81; vol. telephone specialist Suicide and Crisis Ctr. and Info. and Referral Service, Honolulu, 1981-83; group leader obesity program Honolulu Med. Group, 1988-96; mem. Hawaii Coun. Self Esteem, 1993; condr. various workshops on anorexia and bulimia. Guest appearances on local tv and radio programs. Mem. Manoa Valley Ch. Mem. NASW, Nat. Assn. Christians in Social Work, Acad. Cert. Social Workers, Registry Clin. Social Workers, Mortar Bd. (pres., nat. del. 1978), Phi Kappa Phi, Pi Lambda Theta, Alpha Tau Delta (pres. 1970). Avocations: traveling, dancing, swimming, lifting weights, Bible study. Office: Queens Med Ctr Dept Social Work 1301 Punchbowl St Honolulu HI 96813-2413

MOCH, ROBERT GASTON, lawyer; b. Montesano, Wash., June 20, 1914; s. Gaston and Fleeta Belle (Metcalf) M.; m. Barbara M. Kent, Sept. 2, 1940 (dec.); children: Marilynn A., Michael K., Robert M.; m. LaVerne I. Miller, May 29, 1968. BA magna cum laude, U. Wash., 1936; JD, Harvard Coll., 1941. Bar: Mass. 1941, Wash. 1945. Asst. crew coach U. Wash., 1936-39; head crew coach Mass. Inst. Tech., 1939-44; practiced in Boston, 1941-44, Seattle, 1945—; asso. Herrick, Smith, Donald, Farley & Ketchum, 1941-44, Eggerman, Rosling & Williams, 1945-50, Weter, Roberts & Shefelman, 1950-53; ptnr. Roberts & Shefelman, 1953-87; of counsel Foster, Pepper & Shefelman, 1988—; Del. Nat. Conf. on Law and Poverty, 1965, Nat. Defender Conf., 1969; chmn. King County Pub. Defender Adv. Com., 1970. Mem. U. Wash. Crew, 1933-36. Recipient Olympic Gold medal, 1936; named to Helms Rowing Hall of Fame, U. Wash. Hall of Fame. Mem. ABA, Wash. Bar Assn., Seattle-King County Bar Assn. (past trustee, com. chmn.), U. Wash. Alumni Assn. (pres. 1978-79, Disting. Svc. award 1986), Wash. Alumni Advs. (pres. 1985-87), Rainier Club, Rotary, Phi Beta Kappa, Beta Gamma Sigma, Alpha Kappa Psi, Phi Delta Phi, Phi Gamma Delta. Mem. Christian Ch. Home: 22509 SE 42nd Ter Issaquah WA 98029-7229 Office: Foster Pepper & Shefelman 1111 3rd Ave Ste 3400 Seattle WA 98101-3299

MOCHEL, MYRON GEORGE, mechanical engineer, educator; b. Fremont, Ohio, Oct. 9, 1905; s. Gustave A. and Rose M. (Minich) M.; m. Eunice Katherine Steinicke, Aug. 30, 1930 (dec. Dec. 1982); children: Kenneth R., David G., Virginia June. BSME, Case Western Res. U., 1929; MSME, Yale U., 1930. Registered profl. engr. N.Y., Mass., Pa. Devel. engr. nitrogen div. Allied Chem. Corp., Hopewell, Va., 1930-31; devel. engr. R&D dept. Mobil Corp., Paulsboro, N.J., 1931-37; design and devel. engr. gearing div. Westinghouse Electric Corp., Pitts., 1937-43; rsch. assoc. underwater sound lab. Harvard U., Cambridge, Mass., 1943-45; supr. of tng. steam turbine div. Worthington Corp., Wellsville, N.Y., 1945-49; prof. mech. engr. Clarkson U., Potsdam, N.Y., 1949-71; prof. emeritus Clarkson U., Potsdam, 1971—; lect. U. Pitts., 1938-43, N.Y. State U. Adult Edn., Wellsville, 1946-49, Oswego, 1965, N.Y. State High Sch. Enrichment Program, Potsdam, 1962-71; cons. Designers for Industry, Cleve., 1953, rsch. engr. Morris Machine Works, Baldwinsville, N.Y., 1954, design engr. Racquette River Paper Co., Potsdam, 1955. Author: Fundamentals of Engineering Graphics, 1960, Pre-Engineering and Applied Science Fundamentals, 1962, Fortran Programming, Programs and Schematic Storage Maps, 1971; co-author: (with Eunice S. Mochel) Funds For Fun, 1983, (with Donald H. Purcell) Beyond Expectations, 1985; contbr. articles to profl. jours. Officer, vol. St. Lawrence Valley Hospice, 1983; pres. Mayfield Tenants Assn., 1989-91. Mem. ASME, Am. Soc. Engring. Edn. (advt. mgr. Jour. Engring. Graphics 1963-66, sec. 1966-67, high schs. laision on engring. graphics 1962-65, awards com. chmn. 1965-66), Am. Assn. Ret. Persons (founder St. Lawrence County chpt., income tax counselor 1988-89, medicare/medicaid assistance program counselor 1988—, pres. 1989-90). Republican. Mem. Unitarian Universalist Ch. Home and Office: 9C Mayfield Apt # 1 Potsdam NY 13676-1322

MOCHRIE, DOTTIE, professional golfer; b. Saratoga Springs, N.Y., 1966. Student, Furman University. Top ranked player LPGA Tour, 1992. 3 time NCAA All-American; recipient Rolex Player of the Year Award, 1992; recipient Vare Trophy, 1992; leading money winner LPGA, 1992. Winner tournaments including Mazda Classic, 1989, Crestar Classic, 1990, Nabisco Dinah Shore, 1992, Sega Women's Championship, 1992, Welch's Classic, 1992, Sun-Times Challenge, 1992, LPGA Leading Money Winner, 1992, Wendy's Three-Star Challenge, 1992, PING/Welch's Championship, 1995, JC Penney/LPGA Skins Game, McCall's LPGA Classic. Address: care LPGA Ste B 2570 W International Speedway Blvd Daytona Beach FL 32114-7103*

MOCHRIE, RICHARD D., physiology educator; b. Lowell, Mass., Feb. 17, 1928; s. William Blair and Helen (Stephens) M.; m. Helene Mary Buchanan, Aug. 19, 1950; children—Barbara Jean Washer, Steven Howard, Lois Ann Blair. B.S., U. Conn., 1950, M.S., 1953; Ph.D., N.C. State U., 1958. Research technician U. Conn., 1950-53; grad. asst. N.C. State U., 1953-54, instr., 1954-58, asst. prof., 1958-61, assoc. prof., 1961-72, prof. lactational physiology and nutrition, 1972-89, prof. emeritus, 1989—, faculty rep. athletics, 1983-88; U.S. organizer U.S.-Autralian Forage Workshop, also co-editor procs. Author: Lactation Laboratory Outline, 1971; contbr. numerous articles to sci. jours.; Ruminant Nutrition and Metabolism to Ency. Biochemistry, 1967. Precinct com. chmn., county conv. del. Cary and Wake County (N.C.) Dem. Party, 1972—; mem. Cary Recreation Commn., 1989-92, chmn., 1964-70; mem. Wake County Parks and Recreation Commn., 1977, chmn., 1978-83; bd. dirs. Raleigh YMCA; master track and field ofcl.; v.p. N.C. U.S.A. Track & Field, pres., 1992-94. With AUS, 1946-47. Recipient Upjohn Co. citation for contbn. to quality milk mgmt., 1978; inducted into Chelmsford (Mass.) H.S. Hall of Fame, 1995. Mem. Nat. Mastitis Coun. (dir. 1973-86, v.p. 1975, pres. 1976, disting. svc. award 1978), Am. Dairy Sci. Assn. Found. (charter), Assn. Ofcl. Analytical Chemists (assoc. referee), Interstate Milk Shippers, N.C. Recreators Found. (chmn. 1981-89), Nat. Recreation and Park Assn. (citizen bd. mem. divsn. 1984-94, bd. dirs. 1984-90), Atlantic Coast Conf. (pres. 1986), N.C. Recreation and Park Soc. (bd. dirs. 1981-85, Citation award 1986), N.C. State U. Faculty Club (bd. dirs. 1990-92, pres. 1991-92), Cary Exch. (pres. 1963-64), Dairy Shrine, Gamma Sigma Delta (cert. of merit 1978), Sigma Chi, Pi Alpha Sigma, Sigma Xi. Democrat. Presbyterian (deacon 1959-61). Home: 505 S Dixon Ave Cary NC 27511-3254

MOCK, DAVID CLINTON, JR., internist; b. Redlands, Calif., May 6, 1922; s. David Clinton and Eithel (Benson) M.; m. Marcella Enriqueta Fellin, Nov. 13, 1952. A.B., U. So. Calif., 1944; M.D., M.H.D., Hahnemann Med. Coll., 1948. Intern Hahnemann Hosp., Phila., 1948-49; resident San Mateo (Calif.) County Hosp., 1949-51, 54, VA Hosp., Oklahoma City, 1954-55; research fellow in exptl. therapeutics U. Okla., Oklahoma City, 1956-57, L.N. Upjohn fellow, 1958, dir. exptl. therapeutics unit, 1959-62; dir., preceptorship program, 1968-76; assoc. prof. medicine U. Okla., Oklahoma City, 1963-72, prof., 1972-84, emeritus prof. medicine, 1984—, assoc. dean med. student affairs, 1970-76, assoc. dean postdoctoral edn., 1976-82, dir. continuing med. edn., 1980-83, dir. Transitional Yr. program, 1980-84, dir. History of Medicine program, 1982-84; assoc. mem. Faculty of Homeopathy Royal London Homeopathic Hosp., Eng.; pres., dir. Coachella Valley Fruit Co., Inc., Indio, Calif. Lt. comdr. USPHS, 1951-53; now capt. Res. Fellow ACP; mem. Am. Fedn. Medical Rsch., N.Y. Acad. Scis. Unitarian. Home: 570 Alameda Blvd Coronado CA 92118-1617

MOCK, FRANK MACKENZIE, lawyer; b. South Bend, Ind., May 17, 1944; s. Frank Carlton and Julia (Baughmann) M.; m. Virginia Johns, Dec. 31, 1974 (div. Feb. 1991); children: Shannon, John, Bridget; m. Christine Mall, June 1995; 1 child, Mackenzie Ann. BA, Duke U., 1966, JD, 1969. Bar: Fla. 1969. Assoc. Mahoney, Adams, Criser, Jacksonville, Fla., 1969-74, ptnr., 1977-92; gen. counsel Builders Investment Group, Valley Forge, Pa., 1974-77; ptnr. Baker & Hostetler, Orlando, Fla., 1992—. Mem. ABA, Duval County Bar Assn., Orange County Bar Assn., Dade County Bar Assn., Palm Beach County Bar Assn., Turnaround Mgmt. Assn. Republican. Episcopalian. Avocations: hiking, fishing, reading. Home: 2147 Santa Antilles Rd Orlando FL 32806-1533 Office: Baker & Hostetler 200 S Orange Ave Orlando FL 32801-3410

MOCK, HENRY BYRON, lawyer, writer, consultant; b. Greenville, Tex., Feb. 1, 1911; s. Henry Byron and Ellena (Edmonds) M.; m. Mary Morris, Nov. 11, 1949. A.B., U. Ariz., 1933; J.D., Georgetown U., 1939, George Washington U., 1940. Asst. sec. to Congresswoman Isabella Greenway of Ariz., 1934-35; office mgr., legal research asst., recreation div. WPA, Washington, 1935-38; asst. atty. WPA, 1938; legal adv. President's Adv. Com. on Edn., 1938-39; asst. solicitor Dept. Interior, 1939-41; chief counsel U.S. Grazing Service, Salt Lake City, 1941-42; adminstr. region IV U.S. Bur. Land Mgmt., Colo., Utah, 1947-54; area adminstr. U.S. Bur. Land Mgmt., Idaho, Ariz., Utah, Nev., 1954-55; exec. resource cos., 1955—; adj. prof. law U. Utah, 1979—. Contbr. profl. publs. Chmn. Dept. Interior storm relief com. Western U.S., 1949; mem. U.S. Pub. Land Law Rev. Commn., 1964-70, vice chmn., 1965-70; mem. Interior Oil Shale Com., 1964. Served pvt. to capt. with AUS, 1942-46, MTO. Mem. D.C., Va., Utah bar assns. Bar Supreme Ct. of U.S., Am., Fed. bar assn., U.S. C. of C., Bar of Ct. Mil. Appeals, Am. Inst. Mining and Metall. Engrs., Am. Soc. Range Mgmt., Am. Soc. Pub. Adminstrn. (past Utah pres.), Western Polit. Sci. Assn., Am. Forestry Assn., Pi Kappa Alpha. Clubs: Rotary (Salt Lake City), Alta (Salt Lake City). Home and Office: 900 Donner Way Apt 101 Salt Lake City UT 84108-2107

MOCK, MELINDA SMITH, orthopedic nurse specialist, consultant; b. Austell, Ga., Nov. 15, 1947; d. Robert Jehu and Emily Dorris (Smith) Smith; m. David Thomas Mock, Oct. 20, 1969. AS in Nursing, DeKalb Coll., 1972. RN, Ga.; cert. orthopedic nurse specialist, orthopedic nurse. Nursing technician Ga. Baptist Hosp., Atlanta, 1967, staff nurse, 1979; asst. corr. Harcourt, Brace & World Pub. Co., Atlanta, 1968-69; receptionist-sec. Goodbody & Co., Atlanta, 1969-70; nursing asst. DeKalb Gen. Hosp., Decatur, Ga., 1970-71; staff nurse Doctor's Meml. Hosp., Atlanta, 1972-73; staff nurse Shallowford Cmty. Hosp., Atlanta, 1973, relief charge nurse, 1973, charge nurse, 1973-76, head nurse, 1976-79, orthopedic nurse specialist emergency room, 1979; rehab. specialist Internat. Rehab. Assocs., Inc., Norcross, Ga., 1981, sr. rehab. specialist, 1981, rehab. supr., 1981-82; cons., founder, propr. Healthcare Cost Cons., Alpharetta, Ga., 1982-83; cons., founder, pres. Healthcare Cost Cons., Inc., Alpharetta, 1983—; mem. legis. com. of adv. coun. Ga. Bd. Nursing, Atlanta, 1984-85; mem. adv. coun. Milton H.S. Coop. Bus. Edn., 1986-89; mem. Congressman Patrick Swindall Sr. Citizen Adv. Coun., 1988, Congressman Ben Jones Vets. Affairs Adv. Com., 1989-92, White House Conf. on Small Bus. (appointed by Newt Gingrich 1995), Nat. Fedn. Specialty Nursing Orgns. Task Force on Profl. Liability Ins., 1987-89, Dep. voter registrar Fulton County, Ga., 1983-87; Rep. treas. 23d house dist., mem. Fulton County Rep. Com., 1989—, nominating com., 1991, 92, 93, 95, 96, chmn. polit action com., 1993-95, asst. treas., 1994-95, sec., 1995—; treas. 41st House Dist. Rep. Party, 1993—; 1st vice chairwoman 6th Congl. Dist. Rep. Party, 1993-97, chmn., 1997—; mem. State Com. Ga. Rep. Party, 1993—; del. Fulton County Rep. Conv., 1991, 92, 94, 95, 96, 97, del. Ga. 4th Congrl. Dist., 1991, 92, parliamentarian, 1992, credentials com., 1992, Ga. Rep. Conv., 1991, 92, 93, 95, 96, 97, del. Ga. 6th Congrl. Dist. Rep. Party Convention, 1993, 95, 96, 97; alt. del.-at-large Nat. Rep. Conv., 1996; mem. Chattahoochee Rep. Women, 1989—, chmn. campaign com., 1992-94, rec. sec., 1995—; chmn. nominating com. House Dist. 23, 1990; mem. steering com. to re-elect state rep. Tom Campbell, 1990; mem. campaign staff to re-elect state senator Sallie Newbill, 1990, 92, 94; health advisor campaign to elect Matt Towery for lt. gov., 1990, health adv. compaign to elect Bob Barr U.S. Senate, 1991-92; mem. election com. Mark Burkhalter for State Rep.; vol. campaign staff to re-elect Congressman Newt Gingrich, 1992, 94, 96; mem. campaign staff to elect Jim Hunt as state rep., 1996; vol. campaign to elect Tom Price to state senate, 1996. Recipient Nat. Disting. Service Registry award, 1987; named one of Outstanding Young Women Am., 1984. Mem. NAFE, Nat. Assn. Orthopedic Nurses (nat. policies com. 1981-82, chmn. govt. rels. com. 1987-90, nat. treas. 1991-95, nurse Washington intern 1987, legis. contbr. editor news 1989, chmn. legis. workshop, 1989, co-chmn. legis. workshop, 1990, guest editl. Orthopaedic Nursing Jour. 1988, spkr. 1990, 92, 93, 94, Ann. Congress, del. 1982, 91, 92, 93, 94, 96, Pres's. award 1992, Outstanding Contbn. to NAON award 1996, chmn. budget and fin. com. 1991-95, nat. bylaws and policies com. 1995—, bylaws and policies com. Atlanta chpt. 1994—, pres.-elect Atlanta chpt. 1996—), Orthopedic Nurses Assn. (nat. bd. dirs. 1977-79, nat. treas. 1979-81, Coun. Splty. Nursing Orgns. Ga. (nominating com. 1976-77), Ga. Med. Auditors Assn., Nat. Nurses in Bus. Assn., Assn. Rehab. Nurses (bd. dirs. Ga. chpt. 1980-81, del. people-to-people program to China 1981), Nat. Fed. Ind. Bus. (guardian 1988—, adv. coun. 1990—, healthcare task force chmn. 1992—, vice-chmn./fed. liaison Ga. adv. coun. 1995—), Am. Bd. Nursing Specialities (chmn. nominating com. 1993-94, 94-95, chmn. com. on specialty bd. rev. 1993-95), Ga. Jaycees (dist. 4C rep. Ga. Jaycee Legis. 1984, 85), Ga. seatbelt coalition, Orthopaedic Nurses Cert. Bd. (bd. dir. 1991-96, pres. 1992-93, task force on advanced practice certification 1991-92), North Fulton C. of C. (vice chmn. health service effectiveness alliance 1984-85, chmn. 1985-86, co-chmn./editor periodical 1985, 3rd Quarter Workhorse award 1985), Alpharetta Jaycees (adminstrv. v.p. 1984-85, internal v.p. 1985-86), Alpharetta Jaycee Women (bd. dirs. 1983). Baptist. Avocations: reading, boating, cmty. svc. activities. Home: 424 Michael Dr Alpharetta GA 30201 Office: Healthcare Cost Cons Inc PO Box 466 St Alpharetta GA 30239

MOCK, ROBERT CLAUDE, architect; b. Baden, Fed. Republic of Germany, May 3, 1928; came to U.S., 1938, naturalized, 1943; s. Ernest and Charlotte (Geismar) M.; m. Belle Carol Bach, Dec. 23, 1952 (div.); children: John Bach, Nicole Louise; m. Marjorie Reubenfeld, Dec. 20, 1964. BArch, Pratt Inst., 1950; MArch, Harvard U., 1953. Registered architect, N.Y., Conn., N.J., Nat. Council Archtl. Registration Bds. Architect George C. Marshall Space Center, Huntsville, Ala., 1950-51; archtl. critic Columbia Sch. Architecture, N.Y.C., 1953-54; dir. facility design Am. Airlines, N.Y.C., 1955-60; founder Robert C. Mock & Assocs. (architects and engrs.), N.Y.C., 1960—; Mem. Mayor's Panel of Architects, N.Y.C. Prin. works include: Shine Motor Inn, Queens, N.Y., 1961 (recipient 1st prize motel category Queens C. of C. 1961), temporary terminal bldg. Eastern Air Lines , La Guardia Airport, N.Y.C., 1961, cargo bldgs United Airlines and Trans World Airlines, Kennedy Airport, N.Y.C., Bridgeport (Conn.) Airport, 1961, Eastern Air Lines Med. Ctr., Kennedy Airport, 1962, ticket office Trans World Airlines Fifth Ave., N.Y.C., 1962, terminal bldgs. Eastern Air Lines and Trans World Airlines , La Guardia Airport, N.Y.C., 1963, 7 bldgs. Mfrs. Hanover Trust Co. , 1964-66, kitchen and commissary bldg. Lufthansa German Airlines, 1964, Ambassador Club, La Guardia Airport, 1964, Happyland Sch., N.Y.C., 1965, cargo bldgs. Alitalia and Lufthansa German Airlines, Kennedy Airport, 1965, FAA-Nat. Prototype Air Traffic Control Tower, 1966; Lufthansa German Airlines; Irish Internat. Airlines, El Al Israel Airlines, Varig Brazilian Airlines; passenger terminals Kennedy Airport, 1970; Swiss Air Cargo Terminal, Lufthansa German Airlines, cargo terminals El Al Israel airline cargo terminal, Kennedy Airport, 1972, passenger terminal Aerolineas Argentina, 1974, N.Am. hdqrs. Aerolineas Argentinas, N.Y.C., 1974, corp. hdqrs. Am. Airlines, 1977, N.Am. hdqrs. Varig Brazilian Airlines, N.Y.C., 1977, Norel-Ronel Indsl. Pk., Hollywood, Fla., 1979, N.Am. hdqrs. Irish Internat. Airlines , N.Y.C., 1979, corp. hdqrs. Bankers Trust Co., N.Y.C., 1980, cargo terminal Air India, cargo terminal Flying Tiger, Kennedy Airport, 1982, 2 flight kitchen bldgs. Ogden Food Corp., Kennedy Airport, 1984, 88 and LaGuardia Airport, 1987, Greenwich Assn. Retarded Citizens Sch., 1983, passenger terminal extension Varig Brazilian Airlines , 1985, 3 restaurants La Guardia Airport, 1987, residences Palm Beach, Fla., 1989-92, Bethesda, Md., 1993, 97, Fenwick Island, Del., 1994, Potomac Falls, Md., 1995. Recipient United Way Vol. of Yr. award, 1984. Mem. Am. Arbitration Assn., Harvard Club, Admirals Cove Club. Office: 185 Byram Shore Rd Greenwich CT 06830-6909

MOCK, STANLEY CLYDE, financial planner, investment advisor; b. Seattle, Nov. 7, 1946; s. Darrell O. and Elsie (Broeckel) M.; m. Deloris J. Weis, June 4, 1967; children: Shannon Mock Frohardt, Kristin Ann Hagen. Student, Columbia Basin U., 1965-67; CFP, Coll. Fin. Planning, 1987. CFP; registered fin. advisor, registered investment advisor. Agt. Met. Life Ins. Co., Eugene, Oreg., 1969-73; sales mgr. Met. Life Ins. Co., Spokane, 1973-76; advanced underwriting advisor Met. Life Ins. Co., Bellevue, Wash., 1976; dist. sales mgr. Met. Life Ins. Co., Boise, Idaho, 1976-78; gen. agt. Ohio Nat. Cos., Boise, 1978—; fin. planner Fin. Planning Svcs., Boise, 1978—. Author: Life Insurance Selling, 1992; contbr. articles to mags. With USNR, 1967-69. Named One of Best Fin. Planners in Am., Money Mag., 1987. Mem. Internat. Assn. Fin. Planning (pres. 1988-89), Distributive Edn. Club Am. (pres. 1965), Rotary. Republican. Avocations: Corvettes, Harley-Davidson motorcycles, snowmobiles, shooting. Home: 10246 W Cranberry Ct Boise ID 83704-1999 Office: Fin Planning Svcs 3050 N Lakeharbor Ln Ste 200 Boise ID 83703-6243

MOCK, THEODORE JAYE, accounting educator; b. Traverse City, Mich., May 28, 1941; s. Raymond Doris and Georgeann (Lardie) M.; m. Mary Jo Icenhower, Mar. 25, 1962; children—Christopher, Cameron. B.S. in Math., Ohio State U., 1963, M.B.A. in Fin., 1964; Ph.D. in Bus. Adminstrn., U. Calif.-Berkeley, 1969. Dir. AIS Research Ctr. UCLA, 1969-73; dir. Ctr. Acctg. Research, Arthur Andersen Alumni prof. acctg. U. So. Calif., 1982—; vis. prof. Norwegian Sch. Econs. and Bus., Bergen, 1988, Bond U., Gold Coast, Australia, 1990, 92, So. Cross U., Lismore, Australia, 1994; adj. prof. U. Limburg, The Netherlands, 1991—; hon. prof. Hong Kong City U., 1995—; bd. dirs. Maastricht (The Netherlands) Acctg. Rsch. Ctr., U. Limburg, 1991—; Shaw prof. Nankang Tech. U., Singapore, 1997. Author: (monographs) Risk Assessment, 1985, Internal Accounting Control (Am. Acctg. Assn. Wildman medal), 1983, Measurement and Accounting Information Criteria, 1976, Impact of Future Technology on Auditing, 1988, Auditing and Analytic Review, 1989; mem. editorial bd. Auditing: A Jour. of Practice and Theory, 1983-86, 88-93, editor, 1993-96; mem. editorial bd. The Acctg. Rev., 1972-78. Recipient CPA Faculty Excellence award Calif. CPA Found. for Edn. and Rsch., 1983; Fulbright scholar U. Otago, Dunedin, New Zealand, 1988, U. Limburg, Maastricht, The Netherlands, 1993. Mem. Acctg., Orgns. and Soc. (editorial bd. 1978-93), Am. Acctg. Assn. (dir. rsch. 1982-84, acad. vice chmn. auditing sect. 1990-91, chair auditing sect. 1991-92). Office: U So Calif Sch of Acctg Los Angeles CA 90089-1421

MOCKARY, PETER ERNEST, clinical laboratory scientist, researcher; b. Zghorta, Lebanon, Jan. 6, 1931; came to U.S., 1953; s. Ernest Peter and Evelyn (Kaddo) M.; m. Yvette Fadlallah, Aug. 27, 1955; children: Ernest, Evelyn, Paula, Vincent, Marguerite. BA in Philosophy, Coll. des Freres, Tripoli, Lebanon, 1948; BA in Medicine, Am. U. Beirut, 1950, postgrad., 1950-52. Cert. clin. lab. technologist, Calif.; cert. clin. lab. scientist Nat. Certification Agy. Chief hematology unit VA Wadsworth Med. Ctr., West Los Angeles, Calif., 1956-81; CEO Phoenicia Trading Co., 1981-88; dir. Coagulation Lab., Orthopaedic Hosp., L.A., 1988—; lab. supr. Westside Hosp., L.A., 1964-79; lectr. hematology UCLA, West Los Angeles, 1970-78. Pres. World Lebanese Cultural Union, L.A., 1978-79. With U.S. Army, 1954-56. Recipient outstanding performance award lab. svc. VA Wadsworth Med. Ctr., 1972-76. Republican. Roman Catholic. Avocations: billiards, reading, classical music. Home: 3103 Gilmerton Ave Los Angeles CA 90064-4319 Office: Orthopaedic Hosp 2400 S Flower St Los Angeles CA 90007-2629

MOCKO, GEORGE PAUL, minister; b. Little Falls, N.Y., Feb. 15, 1934; s. George and Anna (Swancara) M.; m. Elizabeth Carol Davidson, Sept. 2, 1956; children: David, Paul, Kristopher, Elissa. BA, Hartwick Coll., 1956; BD, Phila. Sem., 1959, STM, 1972; DD (hon.), Gettysburg Coll., 1978. Ordained to ministry Evang. Luth. Ch. in Am., 1959. Pastor Jacob's and Outwood Chs., Pine Grove, Pa., 1959-62; assoc. pastor St Mark's Ch., Wilmington, Del., 1962-65, sr. pastor, 1965-78; sr. pastor Ascension Evang. Luth. Ch., Towson, Md., 1978-91; bishop Del.-Md. Synod Evang. Luth Ch.

in Am., Towson, 1991—. Author books; contbr. articles to profl. jours. Home: 501 Sussex Rd Baltimore MD 21286-7609 Office: Evang Luth Ch in Am 7604 York Rd Baltimore MD 21204-7508 *Colossians speaks of Christ as the one in whom "all things hold together". I know that Christ is the one who holds me together. Proclaiming and living his life, the church holds our society together.*

MOCKUS, JOSEPH FRANK, electrical engineer; b. Chgo., Nov. 17, 1965; s. Joseph John and Jean Frances (Widmar) M. BS Gen. Engring., Washington Nat. U., 1995. Cert. engr.-in-tng. Mich., cert. quality sys. auditor. Asst. engr. C. Cretors and Co., Chgo., 1987; dir. automotive programs Andrew Corp. Wireless Products Group, Itasca, Ill., 1989—. Patentee in field. Mem. ASTM, IEEE, Am. Soc. Quality Control (sr., cert. quality technician), Antennas and Propagation Soc., Vehicular Tech. Soc., Chgo. Deming Assn., Mensa. Achievements include U.S. patents on low cost, slot fed ultra high frequency glass mount antenna, 1995, 96. Avocations: tennis, literature, music. Home: 2321 S 11th Ave No Riverside IL 60546-1124 Office: 1100 Maplewood Dr Itasca IL 60143-3205

MODANO, MICHAEL, professional hockey player; b. Livonia, Mich., June 7, 1970. Right wing/center Minn. North Stars, 1988-93, Dallas Stars, 1993—; player World Hockey League East All-Star Game, 1988-89, NHL All-Rookie Game, 1989-90, NHL All-Star Game, 1993. *

MODE, CHARLES J., mathematician, educator; b. Bismarck, N.D., Dec. 29, 1927; s. Charles and Fannie E. (Hansen) M.; m. Eleanore L. Perdelwitz; 1 dau., Martha Lisa. B.S. in Genetics, N.D. State U., 1952; M.S. in Genetics, Kans. State U., 1953; Ph.D. in Genetics, U. Calif., Davis and Berkeley, 1956; postgrad. in stats. (Univ. fellow), N.C. State U., 1956-57. Asst. prof. math. Mont. State U., 1957-59, asso. prof., 1960-62, prof., 1963-66, mem. genetics group, 1957-66; asso. prof. math. stats. SUNY, Buffalo, 1966-70; prof. math. Drexel U., 1970—; cons. to industry. Author: Multitype Branching Processes - Theory and Applications, 1971, Stochastic Processes in Demography and their Computer Implementation, 1985; contbr. numerous articles to profl. publs.; assoc. editor: Math. Bioscis, 1975—. Mem. Inst. Math. Stats., Biometric Soc., Am. Math. Soc., AAAS, Population Assn. Am., Sigma Xi, Phi Kappa Phi, Pi Mu Epsilon. Lutheran. Home: 502 Balsam Rd Cherry Hill NJ 08003-3202 Office: Drexel Univ Dept Math Philadelphia PA 19104

MODE, PAUL J., JR., lawyer; b. Columbus, Ohio, Feb. 23, 1938; s. Paul J. and Dorothy O. Mode; m. Elaine Rush, June 13, 1961; children: Rebecca D., David B. BME with distinction, Cornell U., 1961; LLB magna cum laude, Harvard U., 1967. Bar: D.C., U.S. Supreme Ct. Assoc. Wilmer, Cutler & Pickering, Washington, 1967-70, 73-74, ptnr., 1975—, mem. mgmt. com., 1983-86, chmn. mgmt. com., 1987-95; chief counsel U.S. Senate Subcom. on Constl. Amendments, Washington, 1970-73; panelist Ctr. for Pub. Resources Panel of Disting. ADR Neutrals, 1989—. Author: (with others) Litigation, vol.12, No.4, 1986; mem. editorial bd. Harvard Law Rev., 1966-67, Alternatives to the High Cost of Litigation, 1991—; contbr. articles to profl. jours. Mem. issues staff Robert F. Kennedy Presdl. campaign, 1968. Lt. (j.g.) USN, 1961-64. Avocations: tennis, collecting antique maps. Home: 2750 Brandywine St NW Washington DC 20008-1040 Office: Wilmer Cutler & Pickering 2445 M St NW Washington DC 20037-1435

MODEL, PETER, molecular biologist; b. Frankfort, Germany, May 17, 1933; s. Leo and Jane (Ermel) M.; m. Pat Goldman, 1961 (div. 1981); 1 child Paul; m. Marjorie Russel, June 21, 1981; 1 child Sascha. BA, Stanford U., 1954; PhD, Columbia U., 1965. Rsch. assoc. Columbia U., N.Y.C., 1965-1967; fellow Rockefeller U., N.Y.C., 1967-69, mem. faculty, 1969—, prof., 1987—; bd. dirs. Biotechnica Inst., Cambridge, Mass., 1981-86. Mem. editorial bd. Jour. Virology, Virology; contbr. articles to profl. jours. Bd. dirs. United Help, N.Y., 1980, Self Help Community Svc., N.Y., 1980. 1st Lt. U.S. Army, 1954-56. Mem. Am. Soc. Virology, Am. Soc. Microbiology, Am. Soc. for Biochemistry and Molecular Biology. Democrat. Office: Rockefeller U Lab of Genetics 1230 York Ave New York NY 10021-6307

MODELAND, PHYLLIS JO, author; b. Carthage, Mo., Dec. 22, 1938; d. Howard Levi and Pauline (Crawford) Anderson; m. Dennis L. Rossiter, Mar. 30, 1968 (dec. Apr. 1992); 1 child, Eric Shawn; m. Vernon L. Modeland, May 29, 1996. Head libr. Trs. Regional Libr. Br., Odessa, Mo., 1979-83; editor, gen. mgr. Ozark County Times Newspaper, Gainesville, Mo., 1989; freelance writer, tchr., editor, lectr., photographer. Author: On the Scent of Danger, 1989, Moxie, 1990, A Living History of the Ozarks, 1992; contbr. articles to profl. jours., periodicals, short story anthologies. Mem. Soc. Children's Book Writers, Western Writers of Am., Women Writing the West, Rocky Mountain Fiction Writers, Ozarks Writers League (v.p. 1990, Dan Saults award 1988, 93), Mo. Writers Guild (Best Column. 1989, Best Book 1991, Best Major Work 1992). Avocations: photography, hand spinning. Home: Box 1299 Flippin AR 72634

MODELL, ARTHUR B., professional football team executive; b. Bklyn., June 23, 1925; m. Patricia Breslin, July 25, 1969; stepchildren: John, David. Owner, pres. Cleve. Browns football team(now Baltimore Ravens), 1961—; pres. Nat. Football League, 1967-70. Office: Baltimore Ravens 11001 Owings Mills Blvd Owings Mills MD 21117-2857*

MODELL, JEROME HERBERT, anesthesiologist, educator; b. St. Paul, Sept. 9, 1932; s. William and Frieda (Singer) M.; m. Shirley Graves, Nov. 25, 1977; children—Charles, Jack, Julie. B.A., U. Minn., 1954, B.S., 1957, M.D., 1957. Intern U.S. Naval Hosp., St. Albans, N.Y., 1957-58; resident U.S. Naval Hosp., 1958-60; practice medicine specializing in anesthesiology Gainesville, Fla., 1969—; attending staff U.S. Naval Hosp., St. Albans, 1960-61; chief anesthesiology U.S. Naval Hosp., Pensacola, Fla., 1961-63; asso. prof. dept. anesthesiology U. Miami (Fla.) Sch. Medicine, 1963-69; prof., chmn. dept. anesthesiology U. Fla. Coll. Medicine, Gainesville, 1969-92, sr. assoc. dean clin. affairs, 1990-95, exec. assoc. dean, 1996—; assoc. v.p. U. Fla. Health Sci. Ctr. Affiliations, 1992-96; assoc. v.p. U. Fla. Health Sci. Ctr. Affiliations, 1992-96. Author: The Pathophysiology and Treatment of Drowning and Near-Drowning, 1971, (with others) Introduction to Life Support, 1973; also numerous scientific articles. Served to lt. comdr. USN, 1957-63. Recipient NIH Research Career Devel. award. Mem. AMA, AAAS, Assn. U. Anesthetists, Am. Soc. Anesthesiologists, N.Y. Acad. Scis., Am. Coll. Chest Physicians. Home: PO Box 14347 Gainesville FL 32604-4347

MODELL, JOHN, historian, educator; b. N.Y.C., June 3, 1941; s. Walter and Merriam (Levant) M.; m. Judith Schachter, June 2, 1963; children: Jennifer, Matthew Thelonious. AB, Columbia U., 1962, MA, 1963, PhD, 1969; postgrad. (Social Sci. Research Council research tng. fellow), U. Pa., 1969-70. Research asst. Bur. Applied Social Research, Columbia U., 1962-65; lectr. Kingsborough Community Coll., 1965-66; dir. research Japanese Am. Research Project, UCLA, 1966-69; asst. prof. history U. Minn., 1969-72, assoc. prof., 1972-77, prof., 1977-83; prof. Carnegie Mellon U., 1983—, acting dean Coll. Humanities and Social Scis., 1985-87; Cardozo vis. prof. history Yale U., 1991; adj. prof. human devel. Brown U., 1996—; rsch. assoc. Phila. Social History Project, U. Pa., 1974-85; mem. adv., planning com. Ctr. for Coordination of Study of Social Indicators, Social Sci. Rsch. Coun., 1980-85; mem. com. child devel. rsch. and pub. policy NRC, 1981-86; mem. coun. Inter-Univ. Consortium for Polit. and Social Rsch., 1982-86; adv. com. Henry Murray Ctr. for Rsch. in Human Lives, Radcliffe Coll.; mem. MacArthur Found. Rsch. Network on Successful Pathways through Middle Childhood; mem. Network Program on Aging and Social Change, Nat. Inst. Aging. Author: The Economics and Politics of Racial Accommodation: The Japanese of Los Angeles 1900-1942, 1977, Into One's Own: From Youth to Adulthood in the United States, 1920-75, 1989, (with others) The Economic Basis of Ethnic Solidarity, 1981, Recent Social Trends in the United States 1960-90, 1991; editor, author: (with others) The Kikuchi Diary: Chronicle of an American Concentration Camp, 1973; editor: (with others) Theory, Method, and Practice in Social and Cultural History, 1992, Children in Time and Place: Developmental and Historical Insights, 1993; mem. editorial bd. Jour. Social History, 1985—, Historical Methods, 1985-87, Pub. Opinion Quar., 1987-91, Jour. of Research in Adolescence, 1990-93, The Historian, 1990-91. John Simon Guggenheim Meml. fellow, 1978-79. Home: 125 Morris Ave Providence RI 02906 Office: Carnegie Mellon U Dept History Pittsburgh PA 15213

MODER, JOHN JOSEPH, academic administrator, priest; b. St. Louis, Apr. 9, 1948; s. Helen (Freihaut) M. BA in English and Philosophy, St. Mary's U., San Antonio, 1970; MA in Philosophy, Fordham U., 1972, PhD in Philosophy, 1977; M Div, U. St. Michael's, 1979. Joined Soc. of Mary, ordained priest Roman Cath. Ch., 1979. Mem. faculty Assumption High Sch., East St. Louis, Ill., 1973-75, Vianney High Sch., St. Louis, 1975-77; faculty mem. Irish Christian Bros. Sch., Mono Mills, Ont., Can., 1977-79; asst. prof. philosophy St. Mary's U., San Antonio, 1979-86, assoc. prof. philosophy, trustee, co-chmn. peace commn., 1986-88, pres., 1988—. Bd. advisors Communities-in-Schs., San Antonio, 1988—. Mem. Am. Cath. Philos. Assn., Am. Cancer Soc., Hispanic Assn. Colls., World Affairs Coun., Greater San Antonio C. of C., Rotary Club of San Antonio. Avocations: hiking, reading, travel, running. Office: St Mary's U Office of Pres 1 Camino Santa Maria St San Antonio TX 78228-5433

MODERACKI, EDMUND ANTHONY, music educator, conductor; b. Hackensack, N.J., July 18, 1946; s. Edmund Joseph and Helen Theresa (Fisher) M. BA, Montclair State Coll., 1968, postgrad., 1970-71; MA, Hunter Coll., 1970, postgrad., 1970-72; postgrad., Newark State Coll., 1969-70, Seton Hall U., 1970, Rutgers U., 1976-78, Ctr. for Understanding Media, 1973. Tchr. music pub. schs. River Vale, N.J., 1968—; asst. condr. Ridgewood (N.J.) Symphony Orch., 1969—, trustee, pres., 1986-87, 94-95; asst. condr. Adelphi Chamber Orch., 1994-95; tuba soloist Rutherford Cmty. Band, Ridgewood Village Band, Waldwick Band, Ridgewood Concert Band, 1978—, Ridgewood Concert Band, 1983—; guest condr., 1985, 86, 88, 93; mgr. All Bergen High Sch. Band, 1994. Town historian River Vale; mem. steering com. Bergen County Teen Arts, 1991—. Recipient County Exec. Vol. award, 1991, Tchr. Recognition award Gov. of State of N.J., 1990; Bergen County PTA fellow, 1976. Mem. NEA, Music Educators Nat. Conf., N.J. Orch. Assn. (trustee 1981-85), N.J. Edn. Assn. (alt. del. assembly 1983-93, mem. state membership com. 1986—), Music Educators Bergen County (bd. mem. at-large 1995-97, treas. 1997—), River Vale Edn. Assn. (pres. 1981-83, 88-91), Brigade Am. Revolution (bd. dirs. at large 1991-95, info. officer 1989-95, adj. 1996—), Phi Mu Alpha Sinfonia, Kappa Delta Pi. Home: 531 Westwood Ave River Vale NJ 07675-5526 Office: Woodside Sch River Vale NJ 07675

MODEROW, JOSEPH ROBERT, package distribution company executive; b. Kenosha, Wis., 1948. Grad., Calif. State U., Fullerton, 1970; JD, Western State U., 1975. Bar: Calif. 1975, U.S. Dist. Ct. (cen. dist.) Calif. 1975, U.S. Supreme Ct. 1982. Now sr. v.p., sec., gen. counsel, dir. United Parcel Svc. Am., Inc., Atlanta, Ga. Office: United Parcel Svc of Am Inc 55 Glenlake Pkwy NE Atlanta GA 30328-3474

MODERY, RICHARD GILLMAN, marketing and sales executive; b. Chgo., Sept. 20, 1941; s. Richard Gustave Modery and Betty Jane (Gillman) Perok; m. Kay Francis Whitby, July 31, 1966 (div. July 1977); children: Stacey Lynn, Marci Kay; m. Anne-Marie Lucette Arsenault, Feb. 27, 1979. Student, Joliet (Ill.) Jr. Coll., 1959-61, Aurora (Ill.) Coll., 1963-65, Davenport Bus. Coll., Grand Rapids, Mich., 1969-71, Northwestern U., Evanston, Ill., 1987. Mktg. products mgr. Rapistan, Inc., Grand Rapids, 1964-75; mgr. estimating, project mgmt., customer svc. E.W. Buschman Co., Cin., 1975-78; exec. v.p. Metzgar Conveyor Co., Grand Rapids, 1979-84; mng. dir. Metzco Internat (cen. and S.Am.), Grand Rapids, Mich., 1981-84, Transfer Technologies, Inc., Grand Rapids, 1984-87; gen. ptnr., pres., chief exec. officer Nat. Monument Co., Grand Rapids, 1986—; v.p. Translogic Corp., Denver, 1987-88; corp. officer, v.p. mktg., field ops. and sales S.I. Handling Systems, Inc., Easton, Pa., 1988-91; v.p. mktg., sales and engring. Integrated Material Handling Co., Tomkins Industries, Inc., Oshkosh, Wis., 1991-93; pres. Handling Concepts, Inc., Chgo., 1993—, Modery Sys., Inc., Chgo., 1997—; agt. Muratec-Murata Automated Systems, Inc., Midwest, 1997—. Patentee in field. Commr. City of East Grand Rapids, Mich. Traffic Commn., 1983-86. Served with USNG, 1963-69. Mem. Internat. Material Mgmt. Soc., Am. Mgmt. Assn., Material Handling Inst. Am., Material Handling Inst. (speaker nat. confs.), Am. Mktg. Assn., Conveyor Equipment Mfrs. Assn., Material Handling Equipment Distbrs. Assn., Masons (32 degree). Avocations: tropical fish, photography, travel, power walking, golf. Home: 2255 Palmer Cir Naperville IL 60564-5672 Office: Handling Concepts Inc & Modery Systems Inc 2255 Palmer Cir Naperville IL 60564-5672

MODESTINO, JAMES WILLIAM, electrical engineering educator; b. Boston, Apr. 27, 1940; s. William and Mary Elizabeth (Dooley) M.; m. Leone Marie MacDougall, Aug. 25, 1962; children: Michele Marie, Lee Ann. BS, Northeastern U., 1962; MS, U. Pa., 1966; MA, Princeton U., 1968, PhD, 1969. Mem. tech. staff Gen. Telephone Electronics Labs., Waltham, Mass., 1969-70; asst. prof. Northeastern U., Boston, 1970-72; prof. Rensselaer Poly. Inst., Troy, N.Y., 1972-93, inst. prof., 1993—, dir. Ctr. for Image Processing Rsch., co-dir. Internat. Ctr. for Multimedia Edn.; vis. prof. U. Calif., San Diego, 1981-82; vis. faculty fellow GE Corp. R&D Ctr., 1988-89; vis. prof. MIT, Cambridge, Mass., 1995-96; pres. Modcom Inc., Ballston Lake, N.Y., 1981—; v.p. ICUCOM Inc., Troy, N.Y., 1986—. Recipient Sperry Faculty award Sperry Corp., 1986. Fellow IEEE (S.O. Rice Prize Paper award 1984, mem. bd. of govs. Info. Theory Soc. 1988-92). Avocations: sailing, jogging, tennis, skiing. Office: Rensselaer Poly Inst 110 8th St Troy NY 12180-3522

MODIANO, ALBERT LOUIS, gas, oil industry executive; b. N.Y.C., Sept. 10, 1953; s. Sam A. and Eve Modiano; m. Carolyn Elizabeth Barker, Sept. 29, 1979; children: Aaron, Sarah Anne. BA cum laude, Hobart Coll., 1975; MA, U. Chgo., 1977; postgrad., Harvard U., 1992. Mem. U.S. Senate, 1980-81; assoc. Am. Petroleum Inst., Washington, 1981-87; dep. dir. Office of Oil Policy U.S. Dept. Energy, Washington, 1987-89; dep. dir. U.S. Minerals Mgmt. Svc., Washington, 1989-93; v.p. Mid Continent Oil & Gas Assn., Washington, 1993—. Mem. Phi Beta Kappa. Office: Mid Continent Oil Gas Assn 801 Pennsylvania Ave NW Ste 840 Washington DC 20004-2615

MODIC, STANLEY JOHN, business editor, publisher; b. Fairport Harbor, Ohio, Dec. 29, 1936; s. Frank and Mary (Zakrajsek) M.; m. Albina DiMichele, May 27, 1961; children—Mark Francis, Laurel Marie. BS in Commerce, Ohio U., 1958. Reporter The Telegraph, Painesville, Ohio, 1960-63; city editor The Telegraph, 1964-65; asst. editor Steel Mag., Cleve., 1965-67; news editor Steel Mag., 1968-70; mng. editor Industry Week (formerly Steel Mag.), Cleve., 1970-72; exec. editor Industry Week (formerly Steel Mag.), 1972; editor Industry Week, 1972-86; sr. editor Industry Week (formerly Steel Mag.), 1986-89; editor-in-chief Purchasing World Mag., 1989-90; editor-in-chief Tooling and Prodn. Mag., 1990—, pub., editor in chief, 1991—. Mcpl. clk. Fairport Harbor, 1960-61; mem. Fairport Harbor Village Council, 1962-63, pres., 1962-63. Recipient G.D. Crane award Am. Bus. Press, 1991. Mem. Am. Soc. Bus. Press Editors, Am. Fedn. Musicians, Press Club (pres. Cleve. chpt. 1978-79), Am.-Slovenian Club, KC, Elks, Sigma Delta Chi (pres. Cleve. chpt. 1975-76). Clubs: K.C. (Cleve.), Press (Cleve.) (pres. 1978-79); Am.-Slovenian (Fairport Harbor). Home: 5842 Woodhill St Painesville OH 44077-5167 Office: 29100 Aurora Rd Cleveland OH 44139-1855

MODIGLIANI, FRANCO, economics and finance educator; b. Rome, June 18, 1918; came to U.S., 1939, naturalized, 1946; s. Enrico and Olga (Flaschel) M.; m. Serena Calabi, May 22, 1939; children: Andre, Sergio. D. Jurisprudence, U. Rome, 1939; D. Social Sci., New Sch. Social Rsch., 1944; LLD (hon.), U. Chgo., 1967; D. honoris causa, U. Louvain, Belgium, 1974, Istituto Universitario di Bergamo, 1979, Hartford U.; LHD (hon.), Bard Coll., 1985, Brandeis U., 1986, New Sch. Social Research, 1989; LLD, Mich. State U., 1989; D (hon.), U. Ill., 1990, U. Valencia, Spain, 1992. Instr. econs. and statistics N.J. Coll. Women, New Brunswick, 1942; instr., then asso. econs. and statistics Bard Coll., Columbia, 1942-44; lectr., asst. prof. math. econs. and econometrics New Sch. Social Rsch., 1943-44, 46-48; rsch. asso., chief statistician Inst. World Affairs, N.Y.C., 1945-48; rsch. cons. Cowles Commn. Rsch. in Econs. U. Chgo., 1949-54; asso. prof., then prof. econs. U. Ill., 1949-52; prof. econs. and indsl. adminstrn. Carnegie Inst. Tech., 1952-60; vis. prof. econs. Harvard U., 1957-58; prof. econs. Northwestern U., 1960-62; vis. prof. econs. MIT, 1960-61, prof. econs. and finance, 1962—, Inst. prof., 1970-88, Inst. prof. emeritus, 1988—; fellow polit. economy U. Chgo., 1948; Fulbright lectr. U. Rome, also, Palermo, Italy, 1955. Author: The Debate Over Stabilization Policy, 1986, Il Caso Italia, 1986, The Collected Papers of Franco Modigliani, 3 vols., 1980, 4th and 5th vols., 1989; co-author: National Incomes and International Trade, 1953, Planning Production, Inventories and Work Forces, 1960, The Role of Anticipations and Plans in Economic Behavior and Their Use in Economic Analysis and Forecasting, 1961, New Mortgage Designs for Stable Housing in an Inflationary Environment, 1975, (with Frank J. Fabozzi) Capital Markets: Institutions and Instruments, 1991, (with Frank J. Fabozzi) Mortgage and Mortgage-Backed Security Markets, 1992, (with Frank J. Fabozzi, Michael G. Ferri) Foundations of Financial Markets and Institutions, 1994. Recipient Nobel prize in econ. sci., 1985; Cavaliere Di Gran Croce Repubblica Italiana, 1985, Premio Coltura for Econs., Repubblica Italiana, 1988, Premio APE award, 1988, Graham and Dodd award, 1975, 80, James R. Killian Jr. Faculty Achievement award, 1985, Lord Found. prize, 1989, Italy Premio Columbus, 1989, Italy Premio Guido Dorso, 1989, Italy Premio Stivale D'oro, 1991, Italy Premio Campione D'Italia, 1992; named hon. citizen of Town of Modigliana, Italy, 1993, Hon. Citizen of Town of Chiavari, Italy, 1996, Jan Timbergen Meml. Lect., Rotterdam, 1994; named honorary citizen of the Town of Chivari, Italy, 1996. Fellow NAS, Am. Econ. Assn. (v.p. 1971, pres. 1976), Econometric Soc. (coun. 1960, v.p. 1961, pres. 1962), Am. Acad. Arts and Scis., Internat. Econ. Assn. (v.p. 1977-83, hon. pres. 1983—); mem. Am. Fin. Assn. (pres. 1981), Accademia Nazionale dei Lincei (Rome), Shadow Fin. Regulatory Com., 1992.

MODISETT, JEFFREY A., lawyer, consultant; b. Windfall, Ind., Aug. 10, 1954; s. James Richard and Diana T. (Tutewiler) M.; m. Jennifer Ashworth, June 9, 1990; 1 child, Matthew Hunter Ashworth. BA, UCLA, 1976; MA, Oxford (Eng.) U., 1978; JD, Yale U., 1981. Bar: Ind., Calif., D.C. Clk. to Hon. R. Peckham U.S. Dist. Ct. (no. dist.) Calif., San Francisco, 1981-82; asst. U.S. atty. Office U.S. Atty. (ctrl. dist.) Calif., L.A., 1982-88; issues dir. Evan Bayh for Gov., Indpls., 1988; exec. asst. to gov. State of Ind., Indpls., 1989-90; prosecutor Marion County, Indpls., 1991-94; sr. counsel Ice Miller Donadio & Ryan, Indpls., 1995-96; attorney genl. State of Ind., 1997—; chmn. Gov. Commn. for Drug Free Ind., Indpls., 1989—, Gov. Coun. on Impaired & Dangerous Driving, Indpls., 1989—; pres. Family Advocacy Ctr., Indpls., 1991-94, Hoosier Alliance Against Drugs, Indpls., 1993-96; dir. Cmty. Couns. of Indpls., 1991-93; chmn. Ind. Criminal Justice Inst., Indpls., 1989-90, dir., 1989—; vice chmn. Juvenile Justice and Youth Gang Study Com., Indpls., 1992-94; cons. Kato Inst., Indpls., 1993—; legal analyst Sta. WTHR-TV, Indpls., 1995—. Author: Prosecutor's Perspective, 1991-94; editor-in-chief Yale Jour. Internat. Law, 1980-81. Co-chair Ind. State Dem. Coordinated Campaign, Indpls., 1996. Recipient Spl. Enforcement award U.S. Customs, 1988; named Top Lawyer, Indpls. Monthly mag., 1993; named to Sagamore of Wabash, State of Ind., 1995. Mem. Ind. Bar Assn., Indpls. Bar Assn. Avocation: bicycling. Office: 402 W Washington St Rm C553 Indianapolis IN 46204*

MODLIN, GEORGE MATTHEWS, university chancellor emeritus; b. Elizabeth City, N.C., July 13, 1903; s. John William and Nannie E. (Matthews) M.; m. Virginia Pendleton Brinkley, June 2, 1928. A.B., Wake Forest (N.C.) U., 1924, LL.D., 1947; M.A., Princeton, 1925, Ph.D., 1932; Dr. Laws, Stetson U., 1962, Hampden-Sydney Coll., 1971, U. Richmond, 1971. Asst. in econs. Princeton U., 1927-28, instr., 1928-32, asst. prof., 1932-38; part- time lectr. econs. Rutgers U., 1936-38; prof. econs., dean Sch. Bus. Adminstrn. U. Richmond, Va., 1938-46, pres., 1946-71, chancellor, 1971-86, chancellor emeritus, 1986—; Mem. pub. panel War Labor Bd., 1943-45. Author: (with F.T. De Vyver) Development of Economic Society, 1936, rev., 1946, (with A.M. McIsaac) Social Control of Industry, 1938. Trustee Keesee Ednl. Fund, 1963—; trustee, v.p. Titmus Found., 1971—; trustee Va. Found. Ind. Colls., pres., 1956-58. Mem. Richmond C. of C. (pres. 1951), So. U. Conf. (pres. 1955), So Assn. Bapt. Schs. and Colls. (pres. 1952), Assn. Va. Colls. (pres. 1952), Assn. Am. Colls. (pres. 1962), Phi Beta Kappa, Kappa Alpha, Beta Gamma Sigma, Omicron Delta Kappa. Clubs: Country of Virginia, Commonwealth; University (N.Y.C.). Office: Univ of Richmond Richmond VA 23173

MODLIN, HOWARD S., lawyer; b. N.Y.C., Apr. 10, 1931; s. Martin and Rose Modlin; m. Margot S., Oct. 18, 1956; children: James, Laura, Peter. AB, Union Coll., Schenectady, 1952; JD, Columbia U., 1955. Bar: N.Y. 1956, D.C. 1973. Assoc., Weisman, Celler, Spett & Modlin, P.C., N.Y.C., 1956-61, ptnr., 1961-76, mng. ptnr., 1976-95, pres., 1996—; sec., dir. Gen. DataComm Industries, Inc., Middlebury, Conn.; dir. Am.-Book-Stratford Press, Inc., N.Y.C., Fedders Corp., Liberty Corner, N.J., Trans-Lux Corp., Norwalk, Conn. Chmn. bd. dirs. Daus. of Jacob Geriat. Ctr., Bronx, N.Y. Mem. ABA, Assn. of Bar of City of N.Y., D.C. Bar Assn. Office: Weisman Celler Spett & Modlin PC 445 Park Ave New York NY 10022-2606

MOE, ANDREW IRVING, veterinarian; b. Tacoma, Jan. 2, 1927; s. Ole Andrew and Ingeborg (Gordham) M.; BS in Biology, U. Puget Sound, 1949; BA, Wash. State U., 1953, DVM 1954; m. Dorothy Clara Becker, June 25, 1950; children: Sylvia Moe McGowan, Pamela Moe Barker, Joyce. Meat cutter Art Hansen, Tacoma, 1943-48; gen. practice as veterinarian Baronti Vet. Hosp., Eugene, Oreg., 1956-57; veterinarian, regulatory Calif. Animal Health br. Calif. Dept. Food and Agr. Resident veterinarian II, Modesto, Calif., 1957-64, acting veterinarian-in-charge Modesto Dist. Office (veterinarian III), 1976-77, ret., 1990—. Watersafety instr. ARC, 1958-61. Capt., Vet. Corps., 1954-56, 62; comdr. 417th Med. Svc. Flight Res. (AFRES), 1965-66, 71-73; lt. col. Biomed. Scis. Corps USAF, ret., 1982. Recipient Chief Veterinarian badge, 1975. Mem. VFW (life), AVMA, Calif. Vet. Med. Assn., No. San Joaquin Vet. Med. Assn. (pres. 1979), Calif. Acad. Vet. Medicine (charter), Res. Officers Assn. (life), Ret. Officers Assn. (life), Assn. Mil. Surgeons U.S. (life), U.S. Animal Health Assn., Sons of Norway, Shriners (bd. dirs., dir. Modesto Shrine 1995), Masons (Illustrious Master Modesto chpt. 1983, Allied Masonic degrees, pres. Modesto Masonic Luncheon Club 1991, Meritorious Svc. medal 1992), Scottish Rite, Internat. Order of the Rainbow for Girls, Theta Chi, Alpha Psi. Lutheran (del. 102d Synod 1961). Home: 161 Norwegian Ave Modesto CA 95350-3542 *Personal philosophy: Try to be comparatively good.*

MOE, CHESNEY RUDOLPH, physics educator; b. Ont., Can., Oct. 6, 1908; s. Oscar and Edith (Miller) M.; m. Berthe Newton, Aug. 24, 1935 (dec. Sept. 1950); 1 son, Ronald; m. Bernice Woolman, July 21, 1951 (dec. May 1993); 1 dau., Donna. A.B., Stanford, 1929, A.M., 1931; Ph.D., U. So. Calif., 1941. Registered profl. engr., Cal. Asst. in physics San Diego State U., 1929-30, instr., 1931-35, asst. prof., 1935-39, asso. prof., 1939-45, prof. physics, 1945—, chmn. dept. physics, 1948-51, 53-56, 61-64, asso. chmn. div. phys. scis., 1956-61; cons. in acoustics Tracor, San Diego, 1965-74, Jet Propulsion Lab., Pasadena, 1968-70; dir. Electronics Investment Corp., 1959-63. Served as comdr. USNR, 1942-46, 1951-54; capt. Res. ret. Fellow Acoustical Soc. Am. (contbr. to jour.); mem. Sigma Xi, Phi Delta Kappa, Sigma Pi Sigma, Kappa Sigma. Home: 900 Sante Fe Dr # 32 Encinitas CA 92024

MOE, ORVILLE LEROY, racetrack executive; b. Spokane, Wash., Nov. 26, 1936; s. Clarence Orville and Georgia Maria (Lombard) M.; m. Deonne Wesley Schultz, Jan. 11, 1953; children: Kathleen June, Susan Marie, Terry Ann. Co-owner Moe's Sudden Svc. Fuel Co., Spokane, Wash., 1956-74; sec. Gold Res. Mining Corp., Spokane, 1973-89, Bonanza Gold Corp., Spokane, 1973-85; pres., founder Spokane Raceway Park, Inc., 1971—; regional v.p. Am. Hot Rod Assn., Kansas, Mo., 1968-84, mktg. dir., 1978-84; co-producer Internat. Car Show Assn., Spokane, 1969-90. Co-producer Spokane Auto Boat Speed Show, 1964—. Mem. Nat. Rep. Senatorial Com., 1984—; mem., trustee Rep. Presdl. Task Force, mem. 1992 Presdl. Trust Rep. Nat. Com. Mem. ISCA, Eagles, Am. Hot Rod Assn. (exec. v.p. Spokane, Wash. 1986—), Internat. Footprint Assn., Am. Auto Racing Assn. (regional v.p.). Republican. Avocations: auto racing, mining, collecting and rebuilding autos, fishing, ice hockey. Office: Spokane Raceway Park Inc 101 N Hayford Rd Spokane WA 99224-9510

MOE, RICHARD PALMER, lawyer; b. Duluth, Minn., Nov. 27, 1936; s. Russell James and Virginia Mary (Palmer) M.; m. Julia Neimeyer, Dec. 26, 1964; children—Eric Palmer, Andrew Neimeyer, Alexandra Julia. B.A., Williams Coll., 1959; LL.B., U. Minn., 1966. Bar: Minn. 1967, D.C. 1979, N.Y. 1991. Adminstrv. asst. to mayor City of Mpls., 1961-62; to lt. gov. State of Minn., 1963-66; fin. dir. Minn. Democratic Farmer-Labor Party, 1967-69, chmn., 1969-72; adminstrv. asst. to Sen. Walter F. Mondale of Minn., Washington, 1972-76; chief of staff Vice Pres. Walter F. Mondale, 1977-81; counsel Davis Polk & Wardwell, Washington, 1981-85, ptnr., 1985-

92; pres. Nat. Trust for Hist. Preservation, Washington, 1992—. Office: Nat Trust for Hist Preservation 1785 Massachusetts Ave NW Washington DC 20036-2117

MOE, RONALD CHESNEY, public administration researcher; b. San Diego, May 28, 1937; s. Chesney R. and L. Bernice (Weston) M.; m. Carolyn Carr, May 18, 1962 (div. Feb. 1974); children: Steven, Cynthia; m. Grace Tyler, Apr. 30, 1976. BA, Claremont Coll., 1959; MA, Columbia U., 1962, PhD in Pub. Law and Govt., 1968. Asst. prof. San Diego State U., 1967-70; sr. policy advisor Office of Econ. Opportunity, Exec. Office of the Pres., Washington, 1970-71, Cost of Living Coun., Exec. Office of the Pres., Washington, 1971-73; specialist govt. orgns. and mgmt. Congl. Rsch. Svc. Libr. of Congress, Washington, 1973—; cons. OECD, Paris, 1996—. Contbr. chpts. in books, articles to profl. jours. Mem. exec. bd. Congregational Chs. of Am., Milw., 1985-89. Capt. U.S. Army Res., 1961-63. Ctr. Study of Am. Govt. fellow Johns Hopkins U., Washington, 1993—; recipient ASPA Louis Brownlow award, 1988, 91, 95-96. Fellow Nat. Acad. Pub. Adminstrn.; mem. Acad. Polit. Sci., Cosmos Club (Washington), Phi Beta Kappa. Republican. Home: 4700 Connecticut Ave NW 407 Washington DC 20008 Office: Congl Rsch Svc Libr of Congress Washington DC 20540

MOE, SCOTT THOMAS, chemist; b. Webster City, Iowa, Dec. 14, 1964; s. John Harry and Betty Ann Moe; m. Veronica Vovides, May 17, 1990. BS in Chemistry, Winona State U., 1986; PhD of Pharmacy, U. Iowa, 1990. Rsch. fellow Nat. Inst. Drug Abuse, Mpls., 1990-91, U. Minn., Mpls., 1992; asst. rsch. scientist, assoc. Medicinal Chemistry NPS Pharm., Inc., Salt Lake City, 1993—. Patentee in field; contbr. articles to profl. jours. Recipient Hon. Sci. award Bausch & Lomb Pharms., 1983. Mem. Am. Chem. Soc. (divsn. Medicinal Chemistry, Organic Chemistry, Outstanding Undergrad. Achievement award 1986). Methodist. Avocations: molecular graphics, numismatics, philately, marine aquaculture. Office: NPS Pharms Inc 420 Chipeta Way Salt Lake City UT 84108-1256

MOE, STANLEY ALLEN, architect, consultant; b. Fargo, N.D., May 28, 1914; s. Ole Arnold and Freda Emily (Pape) M.; m. Doris Lucille Anderson, May 25, 1937; children: Willa Moe Crouse, Myra Moe Galther. BArch, U. Minn., 1936; D of Engring. (hon.), U. N.D., 1993. lic. architect several states; NCARB cert. Project architect several firms in Midwest, 1936-42; project architect U.S. Army Corps Engrs., Africa, 1942-43; ptnr. H.S. Starin, Architects & Engrs., Duluth, Minn., 1943-47; sr. ptnr. Moe & Larsen, Architects & Engrs., L.A., 1947-54; ptnr., gen. mgr., exec. v.p. Daniel, Mann, Johnson & Mendenhall, L.A., 1954-71, corp. v.p., 1972-79; prin. Stanley A. Moe, AIA, L.A., 1979—; dir. design of major mil. projects in Eritrea, Sudan, Egypt, Yemen for Allied Forces, 1942-43; chmn. control com. DMJM & Assocs., 1958-63; project dir. Space Shuttle facilities Kennedy Space Ctr., 1973; project dir. for design of aircraft maintenance complex Iranian Aircraft Industries, 1978; project mgr. for design of major med. facility program Min. of Def. and Aviation, Saudi Arabia, 1975-76; project mgr. design of Boufarik Internat. Airport, Algeria, 1983. Pres. San. Fernando Valley Young Reps., 1952, Van Nuys (Calif.) Jaycees, 1950. Recipient Dsiting. Svc. award for cmty. svc. Van Nuys Jaycees, 1949, Sioux award U. N.D. Alumni Assn., 1985, Trustees Soc. award U. Minn., 1992. Mem. AIA (Calif. coun.), Delta Tau Delta. Republican. Presbyterian. Avocations: world travel, hunting, fishing, historic restoration, woodworking. Home and Office: 447 S Plymouth Blvd Los Angeles CA 90020-4706

MOE, TOMMY (THOMAS SVEN MOE), skier, former Olympic athlete; b. Missoula, Mont., 1970. Gold medalist, men's Downhill alpine skiing Olympic Games, Lillehammer, Norway, 1994; Silver medalist, men's Super-G alpine skiing Olympic Games, 1994; skier Fedn. Ski World Cup Circuit. Office: US Skiing Assn PO Box 100 Park City UT 84060-0100*

MOECK, WALTER F., conductor, music director; b. Milw., Mar. 18, 1922; s. Walter Ernst and Verena Helen (Klein) M.; m. Barbara Conklin; children: Karen, Richard, Stephen. MusB in Trumpet, Eastman Sch. Music, 1947; studies with Pierre Monteux, L'Ecole Monteux, 1951-53; MA in Conducting, U. Iowa, 1955; D in Fine Arts & Music (hon.), London Inst. Applied Rsch., 1993. Instr. brass Univ. Ala., Tuscaloosa, 1947-54, condr. symphony, 1950-54; assoc. condr. Birmingham (Ala.) Symphony, 1948-60; condr. Southeastern Composers Symphony, Tuscaloosa, 1950-54; mus. dir. Birmingham Ballet Co., 1955-62; mus. dir., condr. Ala. Pops Symphony, Birmingham, 1955-73, L.A. Repertoire Orch., 1975-88, San Fernando Valley Theater of Performing Arts, L.A., 1977-88, Am. Philharmonia New Project, L.A., 1978—; instr. Birmingham Southern Coll., Samford U., Montevallo U., Indian Springs Sch., 1954-68; cons., judge various mus. orgns., L.A. and Birmingham, 1947—; tchr. writing various groups and individuals, L.A., 1968—; guest condr. New Orleans Philharm., 1980, Burbank (Calif.) Symphony Orch., 1972, Bakersfield (Calif.) Philharm., 1971, Phila. Symphony Orch., 1953; condr., musical dir. Fine Arts Orch. Scottsdale/ Phoenix, Sun City Concert Band. Composer: Trumpet Etudes (2 vols.), 1980, various warm-up exercises for all brass instruments, 1980; contbr. articles to Brass Warm-Ups, 1974. Mayor, pres. Town of Hoover, Ala., 1966; pres. Ch. Coun., L.A., 1973-74; mem. Pres. George Bush's Presdl. Task Force, Nat. Rep. Senatorial Com., Nat. Rep. Congrl. Com., Nat. Rep. Com. With U.S. Army, 1943-46. Recipient Key to City of Birmingham, 1986, Merit medal Pres. Bush, 1990, Man of the Yr. award Internat. Biog. Centre of Cambridge, Eng., 1993; Walter Moeck Week proclaimed in his honor musicians of Birmingham, 1986. Fellow Internat. Inst. of Arts and Letters (life); mem. Calif. Symphony Assn. Republican. Roman Catholic. Avocations: golf, reading, hiking. Home: 14507 W Trading Post Dr Sun City West AZ 85375-5794 Office: Fine Arts Orch Scottsdale Coll 9000 E Chaparral Rd Scottsdale AZ 85250-2614

MOECKEL, BILL REID, retired university dean; b. Pekin, Ill., Sept. 2, 1925; s. Willis E. and Daisy M. M.; m. Pauline C. Fox, Sept. 1, 1946; children—Steven, Cindy, Nancy. B.S., U. Ill., 1948, M.S., 1949, Ph.D., 1953. Instr. mktg. U. Mo., 1949-51; asst. prof. Ga. State U., 1953-54; asso. dean Sch. Bus., Ohio State U., 1954-67; dir. USAF Sch. Logistics, 1958-65; dean Sch. Bus., Miami U., Oxford, Ohio, 1967-87. Served with AUS, 1943-46. Mem. Am. Assembly Collegiate Schs. Bus. (nat. pres. 1981-82), Air Force Inst. Tech. Assn. Grads, Beta Gamma Sigma (nat. pres. 1976-78), Alpha Delta Sigma, Omicron Delta Kappa, Alpha Kappa Psi, Pi Sigma Epsilon, Mu Kappa Tau, Beta Alpha Psi.

MOEHLMAN, MICHAEL SCOTT, lawyer; b. Columbus, Ohio, Apr. 11, 1938; s. Arthur Henry and Marguerite Caroline M.; m. Carol Jean Shafer, Sept. 28, 1963; 1 son, Matthew. B.A., Harvard U., 1960; LL.B., U. Tex., 1963. Bar: Tex. 1963. Ptnr. Baker & Botts, Houston, 1963—. Bd. dirs. St. Martin's Episcopal Children's Ctr. Mem. ABA (com. bank securities, com. bus. bankruptcy, com. savs. instns.) Tex. Bar Assn. (com. revision corp. law), Houston Bar Assn. (judicature com.), Am. Judicature Soc., Houston Bar Found. (chmn. bd. dirs.), Phi Delta Phi. Episcopalian. Clubs: Houston (chmn. fin. com., bd. dirs., pres.), Houston Racquet, Houston Yacht, Harvard (Boston), St. Charles Bay Hunting. Office: Baker & Botts 1 Shell Plz 30th Fl Houston TX 77002

MOEHRING, FRED ADOLF, fastener distribution company executive; b. Bklyn., Nov. 4, 1935; s. Fred Henry Christian and Elsa Martha (Klein) M.; m. Marilyn Agnes Rieber, June 7, 1958; 1 child, Donna. Grad. high sch., Jamaica, N.Y. Salesman Miller-Charles and Co., Mineola, N.Y., 1956-63, Century Fasteners Corp., Elmhurst, N.Y., 1963-65; gen. mgr. Stewart Air Industries, Syosset, N.Y., 1965-70; salesman Supreme Lake Mfg. Co., Plantsville, Conn., 1971, Allmetal Screw Products Inc., Garden City, N.Y., 1971-72; cab driver Scull's Angels, Flushing, N.Y., 1972-74; gen. mgr. Empire Fasteners, L.I.C., N.Y., 1974-83, Mar-Lin Sales, Bklyn., 1983—. Mem. ASME, ASTM, NRA, ASM Internat., Soc. Automotive Engrs., Met. Fastener Distbrs. Assn. (pres. 1991-92), Steuben Soc. Am., United German-Am. Com. of U.S.A., Inc., German-Am. Steuben Parade Com. Republican. Lutheran. Avocations: bowling, golf. Office: Mar-Lin Sales 208 N 8th St Brooklyn NY 11211-2008

MOELING, WALTER GOOS, IV, lawyer; b. Quantico, Va., Feb. 16, 1943; s. Walter Goos III and Dorothy (Tritle) M.; m. Nell Frances Askew, Aug. 27, 1965; children: Charles H., Christine E. BA, Duke U., 1965, JD, 1968. Bar: Ga. 1968. Assoc. Powell, Goldstein, Frazer & Murphy, Atlanta, 1968-75, ptnr., 1975—. Bd. dirs. So. Banking Law and Policy Conf., 1989-96, Southeastern Conf. for Bank Dirs., 1996—, Children's Rehab. Ctr., Atlanta, 1982—, Gatchell Home, Atlanta, 1983—; bd. dirs. REACH, Inc., 1989—, chmn. bd. dirs., 1993. Mem. ABA (mem. banking com. 1986—), Ga. Bar Assn., Ga. Bankers Assn. (assoc., chairperson bank counsel sect. 1992-95), Cmty. Bankers Assn. (assoc.), Capital City Club, Willow Point Country Club. Democrat. Unitarian. Avocations: golf, fly-fishing. Office: Powell Goldstein Frazer & Murphy 191 Peachtree St NE Ste 16 Atlanta GA 30303-1740

MOELLEKEN, WOLFGANG WILFRIED, Germanic languages and literature educator; b. Jan. 14, 1934; s. August and Emmy (d'Oliva) M.; m. Melita Anne Hildebrandt, Dec. 27, 1958; children: Brent Roderick Wilfred, Alan Patrick Wilfred, Sonja Melita Clarice. Student, U. Cologne, 1955-57; BE, U. B.C., 1961; MA, U. Wash., 1962, PhD, 1965. Asst. prof. U. Calif., Riverside, 1964-67; assoc. prof. U. Va., 1967-68, SUNY, Stony Brook, 1968-69; prof. U. Calif., Davis, 1969-77; prof. Germanic langs. and lits., head dept. fgn. langs. and lits. Purdue U., 1977-79; prof. Germanic langs. SUNY, Albany, 1979—, chmn. dept., 1979-82, 88-92; vis. prof. Univ. Augsburg, Univ. Marburg; dir. Ctr. for German Speech Islands in Am.; corr. mem. Rsch. Ctr. on Multilingualism, Brussels. Author numerous books and monographs; editor: German Lang. and Lit. Monographs, 1976—; founding editor: Purdue U. Monographs in Romance Langs., Davis Medieval Texts and Studies; contbr. articles to profl. jours. Calif. Humanities Inst. grantee and fellow; Regents fellow; Am. Council Learned Socs. grantee; Am. Philos. Soc. grantee; SUNY Research Found. fellow; Austrian Govt. fellow; Deutsche Forschungsgemeinschaft research and teaching prof.; NEH grantee; Fulbright sr. research fellow. Mem. Belgian Rsch. Assn. (rsch. prof.). Office: SUNY Dept Germanic Langs Li Albany NY 12222

MOELLER, ACHIM FERDINAND GERD, art dealer, curator, consultant, publisher; b. Heidelberg, Germany, July 21, 1942; came to U.S., 1967; s. Friedrich Hermann and Liselotte Gerda Emilie (Kehrer) M.; m. Danièle Poli, Mar. 24, 1971 (div. 1978); children: Frèdèric, Bèatrice; m. Colette Jeannine Estiveau, Aug. 11, 1986; 1 child, Stephanie. Baccalauréat, Lycée Français, Sarrebruck, Germany, 1961; student econs., Wildenstein & Co., N.Y.C., 1966-67. Asst. mgr. Kunsthaus Lempertz, Cologne, Germany, 1964-66; dir., v.p. Marlborough-Gerson Gallery, N.Y.C., 1967-71; pres. Achim Moeller Ltd., London, 1971-84, Achim Moeller Fine Art Ltd, N.Y.C., 1983—; curator in chief John C. Whitehead Collection, Washington, N.Y.C., 1981—; expert Lyonel Feininger, N.Y.C., 1980—. Pub., editor, author: (exhbn. catalogs) Lyonel Feininger, 1969, 75, 85, 86, 90, (book catalogs) Kirchner-Heckel, 1975, Kandinsky, 1977, Ph. Guston, 1977, Julius Bissier, 1987, John C. Whitehead Collection, 1987, Feininger-Tobey, The Complete Correspondence, 1991, Feininger in Paris, 1892-1911, 1992, The Whitehead Collection, 1997. Trustee Lacoste (France) Sch. of the Arts. Mem. Am. Art Dealers Assn., French Nat. Syndicate of Art Dealers, Confedn. Internat. de Negociants en Oeuvres d'Art, Rotary Internat. (Paul Harris fellow), Am. Coun. of Germany, Nat. Arts Club. Avocations: violin, literature, chess, photography, contemporary art. Office: 167 E 73rd St New York NY 10021-3510

MOELLER, AUDREY CAROLYN, energy company executive, corporate secretary; b. Pitts., May 10, 1935; d. Nicholas William and Edith Tecla (Russman) M. Grad. high sch., Pitts. Legal sec. Equitable Resources Inc., Pitts., 1955-72, asst. corp. sec., 1972-80, corp. sec., 1980-86, v.p., corp. sec., 1986—; also corp. sec. Equitable Resources Inc. subs.; dir. EOT Capital Corp., ERI Investments, Inc. Com. mem. United Way Allegheny County, Pa., 1978, United Way Southwestern Pa., 1984. Mem. Loyal Christian Beneift Assn. (nat. coun. 1993), Am. Soc. Corp. Secs. (asst. sec., chmn. membership Pitts. chpt. 1995, treas. 1996, v.p. and program chmn. 1997), Pa. Assn. Notaries. Democrat. Roman Catholic. Avocations: choral singing, golf. Home: 1015 Edward Dr Pittsburgh PA 15227-3917 Office: Equitable Resources Inc 420 Blvd Of The Allies Pittsburgh PA 15219-1301

MOELLER, DADE WILLIAM, environmental engineer, educator; b. Grant, Fla., Feb. 27, 1927; s. Robert A. and Victoria (Bolton) M.; m. Betty Jean Radford, Oct. 7, 1949; children: Garland Radford, Mark Bolton, William Kehne, Matthew Palmer, Elisabeth Anne. BSCE, Ga. Inst. Tech., 1947, MS in Environ. Engring., 1948; PhD in Nuclear Engring., N.C. State U., 1957. Commd. jr. asst. san. engr. USPHS, 1948, advanced through grades to san. engr. dir., 1961; rsch. engr. Los Alamos Sci. Lab., 1949-52; staff asst. Radiol. Health Program, Washington, 1952-54; rsch. assoc. Oak Ridge Nat. Lab., 1956-57; chief radiol. health tng. Taft San. Engring. Ctr., Cin., 1957-61; officer charge Northeastern Radiol. Health Lab., Winchester, Mass., 1961-66; assoc. dir. Kresge Center Environ. Health, Harvard Sch. Pub. Health, 1966-83, prof. engring. in environmental health, head dept. environmental health scis., 1968-83, dir. Office of Continuing Edn., 1982-84, assoc. dean continuing edn., 1985-93; environ. cons., 1993—; pres. Dade Moeller & Assocs., Inc., 1993—; cons. radiol. health. Author: (textbook) Environmental Health, 2d edit., 1997; contbr. articles to profl. jours. Chmn. Am. Bd. Health Physics, 1967-70; mem. com. 4 Internat. Commn. on Radiol. Protection, 1978-85; chmn. nat. air pollution manpower devel. adv. com. U.S. EPA, 1972-75; mem. adv. com. reactor safeguards U.S. NRC, 1973-88, chmn., 1976, chmn. adv. com. nuclear waste, 1988-93. Fellow Am. Pub. Health Assn., Am. Nuclear Soc.; mem. AAAS, Am. Acad. Environ. Engrs., Nat. Coun. Radiation Protection and Measurements (hon.), Nat. Acad. Engring, Health Physics Soc. (pres. 1971-72). Home and Office: 147 River Island Rd New Bern NC 28562-3656

MOELLER, JAMES, state supreme court justice; b. Valley, Nebr., Nov. 14, 1933; s. Hans and Marie Grace (Shumaker) M.; m. Nancy Lee Kiely, Dec. 16, 1961; children: Amy Jo, Linda Anne. BA, Nebr. Wesleyan U., 1954; JD with high distinction, George Washington U., 1959. Bar: Ariz. 1959, U.S. Dist. Ct. Ariz. 1959, U.S. Ct. Appeals (9th cir.) 1961. Assoc. Lewis and Roca, Phoenix, 1959-64, ptnr., 1964-70; ptnr. Moeller Hover Jensen & Henry, Phoenix, 1970-77; judge Maricopa County Superior Ct., Phoenix, 1977-87; assoc. justice Ariz. Supreme Ct., Phoenix, 1987-92, vice chief justice, 1992-96, assoc. justice, 1996—. Editor-in-chief George Washington U. Law Rev., 1958-59. Bd. dirs. Found. for Blind Children, Scottsdale, Ariz., 1964-70, Ariz. Found. Prevention of Blindness, Phoenix, 1966-70; Rep. committeeman, Phoenix and Scottsdale, 1965-69. Served with U.S. Army, 1954-56. Mem. ABA, Am. Judicature Soc., Ariz. Bar Assn., Maricopa County Bar Assn. Methodist. Avocations: travel, puzzles, history. Office: Ariz Supreme Ct 432 Ariz Courts Bldg 1501 W Washington St Phoenix AZ 85007-3231

MOELLER, ROBERT JOHN, management consultant; b. Mpls., July 20, 1938; s. Ben G. and Catheryn D. M.; m. Sharon Lee Holmberg, Sept. 1, 1962; children: Mark Thomas (dec.), Maria Therese. BBA, U. Minn., 1962, MBA, 1965; grad. exec. mgmt. program, Columbia U., 1972; grad. exec. internat. mgmt., Mankato U., 1990. Asst. brand mgr. toiletries Procter & Gamble, Cin., 1965-68; group product mgr. No. div. Am. Can Co., Greenwich, Conn., 1968-71, dir. mktg. Dixie div., 1971-73; v.p. mktg. and sales Tonka Toy Co., Mpls., 1973-77; v.p. mktg. and sales Toro Co., Mpls., 1977-79, v.p. gen. mgr. outdoor appliance div., 1979-80, v.p. gen. mgr. irrigation div., 1980-84, exec. v.p. internat. and irrigation div., 1984-88; pres., chief oper. officer Mackay Envelope Corp., Mpls., 1988-90; sr. v.p. mktg. meat sector Cargill, Inc., 1991-94; pres. Moeller Mgmt. Cons., 1994—; bd. dirs. Vista Info. Solutions. Vice chair bd. trustees Voyageur Outward Bound Sch., 1993—; bd. dirs. State of Minn. Prison Industries, St. Paul, 1984—; commr. Chaska (Minn.) Planning Commn., 1988—; pres. Dist. 112 Ednl. Found., Chaska, 1987-92; pres. Chaska Civic Theatre, 1978-80; chmn. Jonathan Archtl. Rev. Commn., 1976-78. With USN, 1955-61. Recipient Crystal Achievement award for human svcs. First Nat. Bank of Chaska, 1996. Avocations: skiing, sailing, tennis, music, golf.

MOELLERING, JOHN HENRY, aviation maintenance company executive; b. Ft. Wayne, Ind., Feb. 4, 1938; s. Robert Charles and Irene Pauline (Nolde) M.; m. Karla Louise Fritzsche, Dec. 21, 1963; children: John Henry, Matthew C., Ann Elizabeth. BS, U.S. Mil. Acad., 1959; MS, U. Calif., Berkeley, 1962; postgrad., Army Command and Gen. Staff Coll., 1971-72, Army War Coll., 1976-77. Registered profl. engr., La. Commd. 2d lt. U.S. Army, 1959, advanced through grades to lt. gen., 1985; aide de camp Combat Devel. Command, 1961-63; command and staff 24th Inf. Div., Fed. Republic Germany, 1964-67; ops. officer Engr. Group, Vietnam, 1967-68; instr. civil engring., asst. prof. history U.S. Mil. Acad., 1968-71; with Office Army Chief of Staff, Pentagon, 1972-73; White House staff, 1973-74; bn. comdr. 101st Airborne Div., 1974-76; dist. engr. Vicksburg, Miss., 1977-79; exec. to Army Chief of Staff, Pentagon, 1979-81; asst. div. comdr. 9th Inf. Div., Ft. Lewis, Wash., 1981-82; commandant West Point, N.Y., 1982-84; comdg. gen. Ft. Leonard Wood, Mo., 1984-85; asst. to chmn. Joint Chiefs of Staff, Pentagon, Washington, 1985-87; corp. v.p. Automatic Data Processing, Inc., San Ramon, Calif., 1987-90; pres., chief exec. officer Lear Siegler Mgmt. Svcs. Corp., Oklahoma City, 1990-93; pres. UNC Aviation Svcs., Annapolis, Md., 1993—; bd. dirs. USAA Ins. Co. Editor, contbr.: Evolution of Modern Warfare, 1969, Battalion Commanders Speak Out, 1977. Chmn. Class of '59 fund com. U.S. Mil. Acad., 1984-89; bd. dirs. Last Frontier coun. Boy Scouts Am.; bd. dirs. U. Okla. Sch. Continuing Edn. and Pub. Svc.; v.p.Oklahoma County unit Am. Cancer Soc.; mem. Def. Sci. Bd., The Pentagon. Decorated Def. DSM, Army DSM, Legion of Merit, Bronze Star; White House fellow, 1973-74. Mem. Econ. Club Okla., Oklahoma City C. of C. (bd. dirs.), Phi Kappa Phi. Home: 1526 Shipsview Rd Annapolis MD 21401-5740 Office: 175 Admiral Cochrane Dr Annapolis MD 21401-7316

MOELLERING, ROBERT CHARLES, JR., internist, educator; b. Lafayette, Ind., June 9, 1936; s. Robert Charles and Irene Pauline (Nolde) M.; children: Anne Elizabeth, Robert Charles, Catherine Irene; m. Mary Jane Ferraro, July 11, 1987. BA, Valparaiso U., 1958, DSc, 1980; MD cum laude, Harvard U., 1962. Diplomate: Am. Bd. Internal Medicine. Intern Mass. Gen. Hosp., Boston, 1962-63, resident, 1963-64, postdoctoral fellow in infectious diseases, 1967-70, resident, 1966-67, mem. infectious disease unit and asst. physician, 1970-76, assoc. physician, 1976-83, hon. physician, 1983—, cons. bacteriology, 1972-87; instr. medicine Harvard U. Med. Sch., Boston, 1970-72, asst. prof., 1972-76, assoc. prof., 1976-80, prof., 1980—; chmn. dept. medicine, physician-in-chief New Eng. Deaconess Hosp., 1981-96; pres., CEO Deaconess Profl. Practice Group, 1995—; Shields Warren-Mallinckrodt prof. clin. rsch. Harvard U. Med. Sch., Boston, 1981-89, Shields Warren-Mallinckrodt prof. med. rsch., 1989—; assoc. physician-in-chief Beth Israel Deconess Med. Ctr., 1996—; mem. subcom. on susceptibility testing Nat. Com. for CLin. Lab. Standards, 1976-88; mem. subcom. on antimicrobial agts. and chemotherapy, 1978-80; subcom. on antimicrobiol disc. diffusion suceptibility testing, 1980-88; pres., CEO Harvard Faculty Physicians Beth Israel Deaconess Med. Ctr., 1997—. Mem. editl. bd. Antimicrobial Agts. and Chemotherapy, 1977-81, editor, 1981-85, editor-in-chief, 1985-95; editor European Jour. Clin. Microbial Infectious Diseases, 1990—; consulting. editor Infectious Disease Clinics N.Am., 1986—; editor Les Infections, 1983; editl. bd. New Eng. Jour. Medicine, 1977-81, European Jour.Clin. Microbiology, 1981—, Jour. Infectious Diseases, 1981-85, 89-93, Infectious Disease Alert, 1981-92, Pharmacotherapy, 1982—, Antimicrobial Agts. Ann., 1984-87, Zentralblatt Fur Bacteriologie, Microbiologie and Hygience, 1984—, Jour. of Infection, 1986—, Innovations, 1986-90, Residents Forum in Internal Medicine, 1988-90, Diagnostic Microbiology and Infectious Disease, 1989-90, Internat. Jour. Antimicrobial Agts., 1990—, Infectious Diseases in Clin. Practice, 1991-92, Jour. Infection and Chemotherapy, 1995—. Served with USPHS, 1964-66. Grantee USPHS, NIH. Fellow ACP, Am. Acad. Microbiology, Infectious Diseases Soc. Am. (v.p. 1988-89, pres. elect 1989-90, pres. 1990-91, past pres. 1991-92); mem. Am. Soc. Microbiology, Am. Clin. and Climatol. Assn., Internat. Soc. Chemotherapy, Am. Soc. Clin. Investigation, Assn. Am. Physicians, European Soc. Clin. Microbiology, Am. Fedn. Clin. Rsch., Assn. Profs. Medicine, Roxbury Clin. Records Club, Mass. Med. Soc. (councilor), Brit. Soc. Antimicrobial Chemotherapy, Coun. Biology Editors, Alpha Omega Alpha, Phi Kappa Psi. Home: 49 Longfellow Rd Wellesley MA 02181-5220 Office: New Eng Deaconess Hosp Dept Medicine 110 Francis St Boston MA 02215-5501

MOELY, BARBARA E., psychology researcher, educator; b. Prairie du Sac, Wis., July 17, 1940; d. John Arthur and Loretta Ruth (Giese) M.; children: John Jacob Moely Wiener, David Andrew Moely Wiener. Student Carroll Coll., 1958-60; BA, U. Wis., 1962, MA, 1964; PhD, U. Minn., 1968. Asst. prof. U. Hawaii, Honolulu, 1967-71; rsch. psychologist UCLA, 1971-72; asst. prof. Tulane U., New Orleans, 1972-75, assoc. prof. psychology, 1975-85, prof., 1985—, dept. chmn., 1992-96. Contbr. articles to profl. jours. Grantee U.S. Office Edn., Handicapped Pers. Preparation, 1977-80, Tulane U., 1973, 75, 77, 78, 83-84, Inst. for Mental Hygiene, City of New Orleans, 1983-84, Nat. Inst. Edn., 1983-84, La. Edn. Quality Support Fund, 1988, 89, 91, 92, 96, HUD, 1997, Annenberg, 1997. Mem. AAUP (v.p. La. conf. 1992-93, sec. 1993—, pres. Tulane 1992-94), APA, Soc. Rsch. in Child Devel., Am. Ednl. Rsch. Assn., Southwestern Soc. for Rsch. in Human Devel. (pres. 1986-88), Phi Beta Kappa (pres. Alpha chapter La. 1981-82, sec. 1995—). Office: Tulane Univ Dept Psychology New Orleans LA 70118

MOEN, RODNEY CHARLES, state senator, retired naval officer; b. Whitehall, Wis., July 26, 1937; s. Edwin O. and Tena A. (Gunderson) M.; m. Catherine Jean Wolfe, 1959; children: Scott A., Jon C. (dec.), Rodd M., Catherine J., Daniel M. Student Syracuse U., 1964-65; BA, U. So. Calif., 1972; postgrad. Ball State U., 1975-76. Contbg. editor Govt. Photography, 1970-74; gen. mgr. Western Wis. Communications Coop., Independence, Wis., 1976-83; mem. Wis. Senate, 1983—, mem. health, human svcs. and aging com., 1983—. Lt. USN, 1955-76, Vietnam. Home: 18775 Dewey St Whitehall WI 54773-0215 Office: State Capitol PO Box 7882 Madison WI 53707-7882

MOENS, PETER B., biology researcher and educator; b. Sukabumi, Indonesia, May 15, 1931; s. Pieter B. and Anneke D. (Ritsema van Eck) M.; m. Marja Schroder, May 8, 1953; children: Richard, Theodore, Vivian, Cecilia, Francis. B.S. in Forestry, U. Toronto, 1959, M.A., 1961, Ph.D., 1963. Lectr. biology York U., Downsview, Ont., Can., 1963-64; asst. prof. York U., 1964-67, asso. prof., 1967-71, prof., 1971—, chmn. dept. biology, 1981-84. Editor: Genome; Chromosoma, 1988—. Fellow Royal Soc. Can.; mem. Genetics Soc. Am., Can. Soc. Cell Biology, Genetics Soc. Can. (pres. 1979), Am. Soc. Cell Biology. Office: York U, Dept Biology, Downsview, ON Canada M3J 1P3

MOERBEEK, STANLEY LEONARD, lawyer; b. Toronto, Ont., Can., Nov. 12, 1951; came to U.S., 1953; s. John Jacob and Mary Emily (Giroux) M.; m. Carol Annette Mordaunt, Apr. 17, 1982; children: Sarah, Noah. BA magna cum laude, Calif. State U., Fullerton, 1974; student, U. San Diego-Sorbonne, Paris, 1977; JD, Loyola U., 1979. Bar: Calif. 1980; cert. in internat. bus. transactions, bankruptcy and bus. rehab., and civil trial practice. From law clk. to assoc. McAlpin Doonan & Seese, Covina, Calif., 1977-81; assoc. Robert L. Baker, Pasadena, Calif., 1981-82, Miller Bush & Minnott, Fullerton, 1982-83; prin. Law Office of Stanley L. Moerbeek, Fullerton, 1984—; judge pro tem Orange County Superior Ct., Calif., 1984—; notary pub., lt. gov. 9th cir. law student divsn. ABA, 1979. Mem. Heritage Found., Washington, 1989—. Calif. Gov.'s Office scholar, 1970; recipient Plaque of Appreciation, Fullerton Kiwanis, 1983. Mem. Calif. Assn. Realtors (referral panel atty. 1985—), Orange County Bar Assn. (Coll. of Trial Advocacy 1985), Orange L.A. County Bar Assns., Calif. C. of C., Phi Kappa Phi. Roman Catholic. Avocations: history, politics, sports. Office: 1370 N Brea Blvd Ste 210 Fullerton CA 92835-4128

MOERDLER, CHARLES GERARD, lawyer; b. Paris, Nov. 15, 1934; came to the U.S., 1946, naturalized, 1952; s. Herman and Erna Anna (Brandwein) M.; m. Pearl G. Hecht, Dec. 26, 1955; children: Jeffrey Alan, Mark Laurence, Sharon Michele. BA, L.I.U., 1953; JD, Fordham U., 1956. Bar: N.Y. 1956, U.S. Supreme Ct. 1962. Asso. firm Cravath, Swaine & Moore, N.Y.C., 1956-65; spl. counsel coms. City of N.Y. and judiciary N.Y. State Assembly, 1960-61; commr. bldgs. City of N.Y., 1966-67; sr. ptnr., chmn. litigation dept. Stroock & Stroock & Lavan, N.Y.C., 1967—; bd. dirs., gen. counsel, dir. N.Y. Post Co., Inc., 1987-92; cons. housing, urban devel. and real estate to Mayor of N.Y.C., 1967-73; mem. com. on character and fitness of applicants for admission to Bar, Appellate div. 1st Dept., N.Y., 1977—; commr. N.Y. State Ins. Fund, 1978—, vice chmn., 1986-94, chmn., 1995—; mem. Mayor's Com. on Judiciary, 1994—. Mem. editorial bd. N.Y. Law Jour., 1985—; assoc. editor Fordham Law Rev., 1956. Asst. dir. Rockefeller nat. presdl. campaign com., 1964; adv. bd. Sch. Internat. Affairs Columbia U., 1977-80; bd. govs. L.I.U., 1966, trustee, 1985-91; chmn. Cmty. Planning Bds. 8 and 14, Bronx County, 1977-78; nat. bd. govs. Am. Jewish Congress, 1966; bd. overseers Jewish Theol. Sem. Am., 1993-95; trustee St. Barnabas Hosp., Bronx, N.Y., 1985—. Recipient Walker Metcalf award L.I. U., 1966. Mem. Am. Bar Assn., N.Y. State Bar Assn., N.Y. County Lawyers Assn.,

Internat. Bar Assn., Assn. of Bar of City of N.Y., Free Sons of Israel, World Trade Ctr. Club, Metro. Club. Home: 7 Rivercrest Rd Bronx NY 10471-1236 Office: Stroock Stroock & Lavan 7 Hanover Sq New York NY 10004-2616

MOERDYK, CHARLES CONRAD, school system administrator; b. Kalamazoo, Sept. 4, 1948; s. Vernon Frank and Eileen Marie (Riverside) M.; m. Cheryl Ann Rudge, July 29, 1967 (div. 1984); children: Paulette Ann, Carie Ann; m. Cynthia Marie Peters, Sept. 1, 1984. BBA, Western Mich. U., 1970; M of Edn. Adminstrn., Northern Mich. U., 1990. CPA Mich. 1974. Acct. J.R. Rugg & Co., Grand Rapids, Mich., 1970-71; controller Newman Visual Edn. Inc., Grand Rapids, Mich., 1971-73; asst. auditor gen. State of Mich., Lansing, 1973-74; ptnr. Goodman deMink & Cerutti, Kalamazoo, 1974-79; cons. pvt. practice, Kalamazoo & Crystal Falls, Mich., 1980-85; interim dir. support svcs. Planned PArenthood Assn., Chgo., 1981-82; bus. mgr. Breitung Twp. Schs., Kingsford, Mich., 1985-89, Alma (Mich.) Pub. Schs., 1989-96; adj. prof. Davenport Coll., Alma, 1991—; dir., treas. Gra Co Fed. Union, Alma, 1991-94; pres. Anselara, Ltd., 1996—. Mem. World Future Soc., pres. Anselara, Ltd., 1996—. Avocations: singing, aviation. Home: PO Box 305 Alma MI 48801-0305 Office: Anselara Ltd 7726 N Alger Rd Alma MI 48801-9320

MOESCHL, STANLEY FRANCIS, electrical engineer, management consultant; b. Cin., Mar. 14, 1931; s. Stanley F. and Matilda F. (Trenkamp) M.; m. Kathleen K. Koebel, Aug. 21, 1954; children: Stanley, Melissa, Deborah, Karen. BSEE, Purdue U., 1957. Engr. Honeywell Space Div., St. Petersberg, Fla., 1957-60; engring. mgr. Honeywell Space Div., St. Petersberg, 1960-69, program mgr., 1969-77; dir. engring. Honeywell Avionics Div., Mpls., 1977-80; v.p. gen. mgr. Honeywell Space Div., St. Petersberg, 1980-82, Honeywell Avionics Div., Mpls., 1982-88; pres. Sundstrand Data Control, Redmond, Wash., 1988-92; bd. mem. Com. of 100, St. Petersberg, 1980-82, Wash. Round Table, Seattle, 1989-92. Bd. dirs. Jr. Achievement, Mpls., 1983-86, Seattle, 1989-92. With USCG, 1951-54, Korea. Mem. IEEE, AIEE, Eta Kappa Nu, Tau Beta Pi. Home: 4575 S Landings Dr Fort Myers FL 33919-4635

MOESCHLER, JOHN BOYER, physician, educator; b. Omaha, Mar. 14, 1950; s. William Joseph and Norma Rose (Boyer) M.; children: Kate, Emily. BS, Creighton U., 1972; MD, U. Nebr., 1975. Bd. cert. Am. Bd. Pediatrics, Am. Bd. Med. Genetics. Intern Univ. Nebr. Med. Ctr., Omaha, 1975-76, resident, 1976-78; fellow Univ. Wash., Seattle, 1978-80; asst. prof., dept. pediatrics Univ. Nebr. Med. Ctr., Meyer Children's Rehab. Inst., Omaha, 1980-83; asst. prof., dept. pediatrics, sect. med. genetics W.Va. Univ. Med. Sch., Morgantown, 1983-85; asst. prof., dept. maternal and child health Dartmouth Med. Sch., Dartmouth-Hitchcock Med. Ctr., Hanover, N.H., 1985-88; assoc. prof., dept. maternal and child health Dartmouth Med. Sch., Dartmouth-Hitchcock Med. Ctr., Hanover, 1988—; dir. Clin. Genetics & Child Devel. Ctr. Dartmouth-Hitchcock Med. Ctr., Hanover, 1988—; med. dir., Clinic for Children with Neuromotor Disabilities Dept. Health & Human Svcs., Bur. Spl. Med. Svcs., N.H., 1985—; med. dir., Genetic Svcs. Program Dept. Health & Human Svcs., Bus. of Spl. Med. Svcs., N.H., 1988—; bd. dirs. Planned Parenthood of No. New England; attending physician Children's Orthopedic Hosp., Seattle, 1978-80; assoc. dir. Birth Defects Clinic, Children's Meml. Hosp., Omaha, 1982-83; cons. Nebr. State Svcs. for Crippled Children, 1980-83; dir. pediatric rehab. MCRI and Univ. Nebr. Hosp., Omaha, 1982-83; steering com. New England Regional Genetics Group, 1988—; presenter in field. Contbr. articles to Jour. Pediatrics, Am. Jour. Med. Genetics, Am. Jour. Disabled Child, Jour. Ment. Def. Rsch., Jour. Ultrasound Med., Dysmorphology and Clin. Genetics, Jour. Clin. Dysmorphology, Prenatal Diagnosis, Am. Jour. Diseases Children, Devel. Medicine and Child Neurology, Clin. Genetics, and others. Fellow Am. Acad. Pediatrics, Am. Acad. Cerebral Palsy & Devel. Medicine; mem. Soc. for Devel. Pediatrics, Am. Soc. Human Genetics (info. and edn. com. 1990—), Am. Assn. on Mental Retardation, N.H. State Med. Soc., Grafton County Med. Soc. Home: 9 Woodside Rd Durham NH 03824-2120 Office: Clin Genetics Dartmouth-Hitchcock Med Ctr Child Development Ctr Hanover NH 03756*

MOESE, MARK DOUGLAS, environmental consultant; b. Jersey City, Aug. 3, 1954; s. Harold Francis and Mary Frances (Wilk) M.; m. Elizabeth Renker Cozine, Apr. 20, 1991; children: Elizabeth Renker, Kevin Harold. BS, Fairleigh Dickinson U., 1976, MS, 1979; PhD, NYU, 1988. Rsch. asst. West Indies Lab., St. Croix, U.S.V.I., 1978-79, NYU Med. Ctr., Tuxedo, N.Y., 1980-86; staff scientist Hazen and Sawyer, P.C., N.Y.C., 1982-85; supr. risk assessment EBASCO Environ., Lyndhurst, N.J., 1986-94, Foster Wheeler Environ., Lyndhurst, 1994-96, Betterchem Corp., Campbell Hall, N.Y., 1996; environ. cons. Louis Berger & Assocs., Inc., East Orange, N.J., 1996—; cons. Taiwan Power Co., Taipei, 1987, 89, Hub River Power Co., Fauji Corp., Karachi, Pakistan, 1991-92, Chinese Rsch. Acad. Environ. Scis., 1993; human and environ. risk assessments profl. Ebasco Environ., 1986-94, Foster Wheeler Environ., Lydnhurst, N.J., 1994-96, Betterchem Corp., 1996; cons. to pharm. industry, Louis Berger & Assocs., 1996—. Contbr. articles to profl. jours. Sigma Xi grantee-in-aid, 1978; grad. fellow NYU Med. Ctr., 1980-86. Mem. ASTM (voting mem., mem. E-47 com., mem. sediment toxicity subcom.), Soc. for Risk Analysis, Soc. Environ. Toxicology and Chemistry. Office: Louis Berger Assocs 100 Halsted St East Orange NJ 07018-2612

MOESER, ELLIOTT, principal. Prin. Nicolet High Sch., Glendale, Ill. Recipient Blue Ribbon Sch. award, 1990-91. Office: Nicolet High Sch 6701 N Jean Nicolet Rd Glendale WI 53217-3701*

MOESSNER, HAROLD FREDERIC, allergist; b. Lincoln, Nebr., Mar. 29, 1945; s. Samuel Frederick and Helen Lucy (Larson) M.; m. Linda McLeod, Apr. 30, 1972; children: Annie Larson, John Christopher, Sarah Elizabeth. BS with distinction, U. Nebr., 1967; MD, U. Minn., 1971. Diplomate Am. Bd. Pediatrics, Am. Bd. Allergy and Immunology. Intern VA Hosp., Dallas, 1971-72; resident in pediatrics Children's Med. Ctr., Dallas, 1972-74; commd. 2d lt. U.S. Army, 1974-78, advanced through the grades to col., 1980-87; pediatrician Fort Ritchie, Md., 1974-75, U.S. Army Hosp, Augsburg, Germany, 1975-78; fellow in adolescent medicine U. Tex. Health and Sci. Ctr., Dallas, 1978-79; asst. prof. pediatrics Uniformed Svcs., U. Health Scis., Bethesda, Md., 1980-83; fellow allergy and immunology Walter Reed Army Med. Ctr., Washington, 1983-85; chief allergy immunology svc., chief dept. medicine Blanchfield Army Hosp., Fort Campbell, Ky., 1985-87; pvt. practice Nashville, 1987—; staff hosp. courtesy appointment Williamson Med. Ctr., Franklin, Tenn., Maury Regional Hosp., Columbia, Tenn. Contbr. to profl. jours. Fellow Am. Bd. Pediats., Am. Bd. Allergy and Immunology; mem. Am. Acad. Allergy and Immunology, Montgomery County Med. Soc., Tenn. Soc. Allergy, Tenn. State Med. Assn., Nashville Allergy Soc., Phi Beta Kappa. Home: 5304 Otter Creek Ct Brentwood TN 37027-4126 Office: 1909 Mallory Ln Ste 308 Franklin TN 37067-8230 also: 1754 Madison St Ste 2 Clarksville TN 37043-4913

MOFENSON, HOWARD C., pediatrician, toxicologist; b. N.Y.C., Jan. 26, 1925; s. Jack L. and Theresa (Cohen) M.; m. Lois Stugart, July 26, 1947; children: Lynne, Jeffrey, Dayna. MD, Jefferson Med. Coll., 1951. Intern Nassau County Med. Ctr., 1951-52; resident Bklyn. Hosp., 1952-53, L.I. Coll. Hosp., 1953-54; attending Winthrop U. Hosp., Mineola, N.Y., 1954—, Nassau County Med. Ctr., East Meadow, N.Y., 1954—; prof. pediatrics SUNY, Stony Brook, N.Y., 1973—, prof. emergency medicine, 1990—; prof. clin. pharmacy St. John's Sch. Pharmacy, Queens, N.Y., 1982—; prof. of toxicology N.Y. Coll. Osteo., 1985—; Acting dean SUNY. Contbr. articles to profl. jours. With U.S. Army, 1942-46. Decorated Purple Heart (2), Bronze Star (2). Mem. Am. Assn. Poison Control (pres.), Am. Acad. Pediatrics, Am. Diabetes Assn. Avocations: writing, photography, art. Home: 160 Emory Rd Mineola NY 11501 Office: LI Regional Poison Control Ctr Winthrop Univ Hosp Mineola NY 11501

MOFFAT, JOHN WILLIAM, physics educator; b. Copenhagen, Denmark, May 24, 1932; s. George William and Esther (Winther) M. PhD, Trinity Coll., Cambridge (Eng.) U., 1958; DSc, U. Winnipeg, 1989. Sr. research fellow Imperial Coll., London, Eng., 1957-58; scientist Research Inst. Advanced Studies, Balt., 1958-60; prin. scientist Research Inst. Advanced Studies, 1961-64; scientist CERN, Geneva, Switzerland, 1960-61; asso. prof. dept. physics U. Toronto, Ont., Can., 1964-67; prof. U. Toronto, 1967—. Contbr. articles to profl. jours. Dept. Sci. and Indsl. Research fellow, 1958-60; NRC Can. grantee, 1965. Fellow Cambridge Philos. Soc. (Eng.); mem. N.Y. Acad. Scis., Can. Astron. Soc., Internat. Union Astronomers. Office: Univ of Toronto, Dept Physics, Toronto, ON Canada

MOFFATT, HUGH MCCULLOCH, JR., hospital administrator, physical therapist; b. Steubenville, Ohio, Oct. 11, 1933; s. Hugh McCulloch and Agnes Elizabeth (Bickerstaff) M.; m. Ruth Anne Colvin, Aug. 16, 1958; children: David, Susan. AB, Asbury Coll., 1958; cert. in phys. therapy, Duke U., 1963. Lic. in phys. therapy and health care adminstrn. Commd. officer USPHS, 1964, advanced through grades to capt.; therapist USPHS, N.Y.C., 1964-66, Sitka, Alaska, 1970-72; therapist cons. USPHS, Atlanta, 1968-70; clinic adminstr. USPHS, Kayenta, Ariz., 1972-73; hosp. dir. USPHS, Sitka, 1973-78; therapist cons. Idaho Dept. Health, Boise, 1966-68; contract health officer USPHS, Anchorage, 1978-89, ret., 1989; phys. therapy cons. Ocean Beach Hosp., Ilwaco, Wash., 1989—, Harbors Home Health Svcs., Aberdeen, Wash., 1990—; therapist cons. Our Lady of Compassion Care Ctr., Anchorage, 1979—, Alaska Native Med. Ctr., Anchorage, 1988—. With U.S. Army, 1955-57. Mem. Am. Phys. Therapy Assn., Commd. Officers Assn. USPHS, Res. Officers Assn., Ret. Officers Assn., Am. Assn. Individual Investors, Am. Assn. Ret. Persons, Eagles. Avocations: automobile repairs, woodworking, camping, fishing, church choir.

MOFFATT, JOYCE ANNE, performing arts executive; b. Grand Rapids, Mich., Jan. 3, 1936; d. John Barnard and Ruth Lillian (Pellow) M. BA in Lit., U. Mich., 1957, MA in Theatre, 1960; HHD (hon.), Profl. Sch. Psychology, San Francisco, 1991. Stage mgr., lighting designer Off-Broadway plays, costume, lighting and set designer, stage mgr. stock cos., 1954-62; nat. subscription mgr. Theatre Guild/Am. Theatre Soc., N.Y.C., 1965-67; subscription mgr. Theatre, Inc.-Phoenix Theatre, N.Y.C., 1963-67; cons. N.Y.C. Ballet and N.Y.C. Opera, 1967-70; asst. house mgr. N.Y. State Theater, 1970-72; dir. ticket sales City Ctr. of Music and Drama, Inc., N.Y.C., 1970-72; prodn. mgr. San Antonio's Symphony/Opera, 1973-75; gen. mgr. San Antonio Symphony/Opera, 1975-76, 55th St. Dance Theater Found., Inc., N.Y.C., 1976-77, Ballet Theatre Found., Inc./Am. Ballet Theatre, N.Y.C., 1977-81; v.p. prodn. Radio City Music Hall Prodns., Inc., N.Y.C., 1981-83; artist-in-residence CCNY, 1981—; propr. mgmt. cons. firm for performing arts N.Y.C., 1983—; exec. dir. San Francisco Ballet Assn., 1987-93; mng. dir. Houston Ballet Assoc., 1993-95; gen. mgr. Chgo. Music and Dance Theater, Inc., 1995—; cons. Ford Found., N.Y. State Coun. on Arts, Kennedy Ctr. for Performing Arts.; mem. dance panels N.Y. State Coun. on Arts, 1979-81; mem. panels for Support to Prominent Orgns. and Dance, Calif. Arts Coun., 1988-92. Appointee San Francisco Cultural Affairs Task Force, 1991; chmn. bd. dirs. Tex. Inst. for Arts in Edn., 1994—; trustee Internat. Alliance of Theatrical Stage Employees Local 16 Pension and Welfare Fund, 1991-94. Mem. Assn. Theatrical Press Agts. and Mgrs., Actors Equity Assn., United Scenic Artists Local 829, San Francisco Visitors and Conv. Bur. (bd. dirs.), Argyle Club (San Antonio). Office: Chicago Music & Dance Theater Mezz Level 203 N La Salle St Chicago IL 60601-1210

MOFFATT, KATY (KATHERINE LOUELLA MOFFATT), musician, vocalist, songwriter; b. Ft. Worth, Nov. 19, 1950; d. Lester Huger and Sue-Jo (Jarrott) M. Student, Sophie Newcomb Coll., 1968, St. John's Coll., 1969-70. Rec. artist Columbia Records, 1975-79, Permian/MCA Records, 1982-84, Enigma Records, L.A., 1985, Wrestler Records, L.A., 1987-88, Red Moon Records, Switzerland, 1988-93, Philo/Rounder Records, 1989-93, Round Tower Music, U.K., Ireland, Europe, 1993—, Watermelon Records, U.S., 1994—. Folksinger, Ft. Worth, 1967-68; musician, vocalist, songwriter, rec. artist: (films) Billy Jack, 1970, Hard Country, 1981, The Thing Called Love, 1993; prodn. asst. film, Sta. KIII-TV, Corpus Christi, 1970, audio engr., Sta. KRIS-TV, Corpus Christi, 1970; musician, vocalist in blues band, Corpus Christi, 1970; receptionist, bookkeeping asst., copywriter, announcer, Sta. KFWT, Ft. Worth, 1971, musician, vocalist, songwriter, Denver, 1971-72, on tour, 1973, 75—, Denver, 1974, on tour, 1976-79, European tour, 1977, Can. tour, 1984-85, on tour in Europe, U.S., Can. and Asia, 1985—; albums include Katy, 1976, Kissin' In The California Sun, Am. release, 1977, internat. release, 1978, A Town South of Bakersfield, 1985, Walkin' on the Moon, European release, 1988, U.S. release, 1989, Child Bride, 1990, (duet album with brother Hugh) Dance Me Outside, 1992, (Switzerland only) Indoor Fireworks, 1992, The Greatest Show On Earth A.K.A. The Evangeline Hotel, 1994, Hearts Gone Wild, 1994, Tulare Dust, 1995, (duet album with Kate Brislin) Sleepless Nights, 1996, Midnight Radio, 1996; singles include Take it as it Comes, 1981, Under Loved and Over Lonely, 1983; songs include The Magic Ring, 1971; Gerry's Song, 1973, Kansas City Morning, 1974, Take Me Back To Texas, 1975, (Waitin' For) The Real Thing, 1975, Didn't We Have Love, 1976, Kissin' in the California Sun, 1977, Walkin' on the Moon, 1989. Recipient Record World Album award, 1976; named one of 4 Top New Female Vocalists, Cashbox Singles Awards, 1976; nominee for Top New Female Vocalist, Acad. Country Music, 1985; winner best singer-songwriter category Ft. Worth Weekly Mag. Music awards, 1997. Mem. AFTRA, SAG, NARAS, Am. Fedn. Musicians.

MOFFATT, MICHAEL ALAN, lawyer; b. Indpls., Feb. 22, 1964; s. James L. Kelso and Peggy A. Tackett; m. Nancy Norman, Sept. 23, 1989; children: Patricia Margaret, Michael Alan, Nicole Elizabeth. BA in Polit. Sci., Depauw U., 1986; JD, Ind. U., 1989. Bar: Ind. 1989, U.S. Dist. Ct. (so. and no. dists.) Ind. 1989, U.S. Ct. Appeals (7th cir.) 1991. Law clk., atty. White & Raub, Indpls., 1987-94; atty. Wooden McLaughlin & Sterner, Indpls., 1994-95, Barnes & Thornburg, Indpls., 1995—; lectr. litigation, paralegal program, Ind. U./Purdue U., Ind. CLE Forum & labor/employment seminars. Contbr. articles to legal jours. Cons. pediatric ethics com. Meth. Hosp., Indpls., 1990-92; co-chmn. Keep Am. Beautiful, Greencastle, Ind., 1986, bd. dirs., sec., 1990-94; mem. devel. control com. Geist Harbors Property Owerns' Assn., Indpls., 1993-94, cons., 1994, pres., 1997—. Mem. Fed. Bar Assn., Ind. State Bar Assn., Ind. Defense Lawyers Assn., Indpls. Bar Assn. (coun. labor law sect.), Exch. Club. Avocations: golf, basketball, war gaming, softball. Office: Barnes & Thornburg 1313 Merchants Bank Bldg 11 S Meridian St Indianapolis IN 46204-3506

MOFFET, HUGH LAMSON, pediatrician; b. Monmouth, Ill., Jan. 6, 1932; s. Victor Logue and Helen (Sipfle) M.; m. Donna Mae Pienschke, Sept. 20, 1984; children: Cynthia, Sandra, Douglas. AB, Harvard U., 1953; MD, Yale U., 1957. Instr. Bowman Gray Sch. Medicine, Winston-Salem, N.C., 1957-60; asst. prof. Northwestern U., Chgo., 1963-68, assoc. prof., 1968-71; assoc. prof. U. Wis., Madison, 1971-75, prof., 1975—; head div. infectious diseases Children's Meml. Hosp., Chgo., 1963-71. Author: (book) Clinical Microbiology, 1975, 2d rev. edit., 1980, Pediatric Infectious Diseases, 1975, 3d rev. edit., 1989. Capt. USAR, 1953-68.

MOFFETT, CHARLES SIMONTON, museum director, curator, writer; b. Washington, Sept. 19, 1945; s. Charles Simonton M. and Faith Atherton Locke Phelps; m. Jane Pettigrew Daniels, July 28, 1979; children: Kate Serena, Charles Locke. B.A., Middlebury Coll., 1967; M.A., NYU, 1970. Ford Found. fellow Nelson Gallery Art, Kansas City, Mo., 1969-70; expert Sotheby Parke Bernet, N.Y.C., 1970-71; guest asst. curator Met. Mus., N.Y.C., 1974-75, assoc. curator, 1976-81, curator European paintings, 1981-83; curator-in-charge Fine Arts Mus. San Francisco, 1983—, chief curator, summer 1987; sr. curator paintings Nat. Gallery Art, Washington, 1987-92; dir. The Phillips Collection, Washington, 1992—; organizer mus. exhbns., author catalogues; mem. spl. exhbns. panel Nat. Endowment for Arts, 1987; project dir. publs. grant from J. Paul Getty Trust to Fine Arts Mus. San Francisco, 1987; fellow conf. on econs. of arts, presenter Salzburg (Austria) Conf., 1993; grad. Mus. Mgmt. Inst., 1990, sr. mus. assoc., 1994—. Trustee San Francisco Day Sch., 1987, Middlebury Coll., 1987-90, Sterling and Francine Clark Art Inst., 1996—. Andrew Mellon fellow Met. Mus. Art, 1975; travel grantee Met. Mus. Art, 1980; recipient award for best exhbn. Soho News Arts Awards, 1978; co-recipient Prix Bernier for Manet 1832-1883, 1983, recipient Alumni Achievement award Middlebury Coll., 1985, Kaufman award Nat. Gallery Art, 1989. Episcopalian. Office: The Phillips Collection 1600 21st St NW Washington DC 20009-1003

MOFFETT, J. DENNY, lawyer; b. Atlanta, Sept. 20, 1947; s. James Denny Moffett Jr. and Dorothy (Mckenzie) McCall; m. Mary F. Ray, June 6, 1987; children: David, Jenny. BA, U. Okla., 1969; JD with honors, George Washington U., 1972, LLM in Taxation, 1974. Bar: Okla. 1972, U.S. Tax Ct. 1973. Legis. asst. U.S. Senate, Washington, 1973-74; ptnr. Conner & Winters, Tulsa, 1974-90, McKenzie, Moffett, Elias & Books, Tulsa, Oklahoma City, 1990—; adj. faculty U. Tulsa Law Sch., 1978; arbitrator Nat. Assn. Securities Dealers. Commr. Ark.-Okla. River Compact Commn., 1990-94; pres. Nicholas Club Tulsa, 1984; endowment com. Trinity Episcopal Ch., 1990—. 2d lt. U.S. Army, 1972-74; bd. dirs. Am. Cancer Soc., Tulsa, 1991-94. Mem. Am. Arbitration Assn., Tulsa Tax Club (pres. 1981, 94). Republican. Home: 2132 E 32d Pl Tulsa OK 74105 Office: McKenzie Moffett et al 1000 Philtower Bldg Tulsa OK 74103

MOFFETT, THOMAS DELANO, music educator; b. Smiths, Ala., Sept. 19, 1942; s. Early Moffett and Estella Sparks; m. Gloria Jean Marshall, Dec. 22, 1968; children: Stephanie Viloria, Marlon Delano. BS, Fla. A&M U., 1963; MEd, Auburn U., 1972, EdD, 1981. Cert. tchr., Ga. Band dir. Drake High Sch., Auburn, Ala., 1963-66, Talbotton Rd. Jr. High Sch., Columbus, Ga., 1966-78; asst. prin. Waddell Elem. Sch., Columbus, Ga., 1978-81; prin. St. Mary's Elem. Sch., Columbus, Ga., 1981-90, Dimon Elem. Sch., Columbus, Ga., 1990; music supr. Muscogee County Sch. Dist., Columbus, Ga., 1990-93; assoc. prof. music Troy (Ala.) State U., 1993—. Active membership drive YMCA, Columbus, 1991; mem. adv. bd. Boy Scouts Am. Pack 120, Columbus, 1981-89. Recipient citation Achievement in Edn., Omega Psi Phi, 1981, Past President's award Muscogee Elem. Prins. Assn., 1989, Outstanding Alumni award Fla. A&M, 1987; named Boss of Yr., Muscogee Assn. Edn. Office Personnel, 1989. Mem. NEA, Music Educators Nat. Conf., Ala. Music Educators Assn., Troy State Educators Assn., Phi Delta Kappa, Phi Mu Alpha. Democrat. Methodist. Avocations: golf, bowling, singing, saxophone. Home: PO Box 5501 Columbus GA 31906-0501 Office: Troy State U Smith Hall Troy AL 36082

MOFFITT, CHARLES WILLIAM, insurance sales executive; b. Altoona, Pa., Mar. 24, 1932; s. Charles William and Beatrice Jeanette (Shellenberger) M.; m. Marianne Foley Potter, May 23, 1980 (dec.); children: Michelle Ann Hunt, Charles William III, Deborah K.; stepchildren: Christopher Potter, Kimberly Bryan. B.A., Pa. State U., 1957. Examiner Pa. R.R., Buffalo, 1957-62; asst. to pres. White Cross Stores, Inc., Monroeville, Pa., 1962-65; sec. White Cross Stores, Inc., 1965-70, v.p. adminstrn., sec., 1970-72; dir. labor relations and legal affairs Revco D.S., Inc., Cleve., 1972-75; asst. v.p. personnel Revco D.S., Inc., 1974-75; pres. Fashion Wearhouse, Inc., Altoona, Pa., 1975-87; owner Omega Advt. Co.; pres. Olympus I, Inc., 1980-87; agt. Prin. Fin. Group, 1988-90, Variable Annuity Life Ins. Co., 1990—. Co-author: Mincemeat Cartoons, Altoona Mirror Newspaper. Bd. dirs. Bedford Springs Music Festival, 1984-87, Blair County Arts Found., 1987-91. Republican. Roman Catholic. Home and Office: 2033 Southpoint Dr Hummelstown PA 17036-8944

MOFFITT, DAVID LOUIS, lawyer, county and state official; b. Alexandria, Va., June 8, 1953; s. Otis Breheon and Lillian Vlasta (Svatik) M.; m. Kathleen Ann Brata, Aug. 20, 1988; children: David Lachlan, Drake Lorne. BA in Philosophy, U. Mich., 1976; JD, U. Detroit, 1979. Assoc. Plunkett, Cooney, Rutt, Watters, Stanczyk and Pedersen, P.C., Detroit, 1979-80, Kitch, Suhreheinrich, Smith, Saurbier and Drutchas, P.C., Detroit, 1980-81, Alan R. Miller, P.C., Birmingham, Mich., 1981-83; pvt. practice Birmingham, 1983—; lectr. real estate law U. Mich. Grad. Sch. Bus. Adminstrn./Mich. Assn. Realtors. Contbr. articles to profl. jours. em. Oakland County Bd. Commrs., 1985—, pers. com., 1985-94, vice chmn. pub. svcs. com., 1988-89, majority party caucus, 1987-89, vice chmn. planning and bldg. com., 1989-91, pers. appeals bd., 1992-93; chmn. Oakland County Zoning Coordinating Bd., 1991, 93, vice chmn., 1992; mem. exec. coun. Southeast Mich. Coun. Govts., 1993—; mem. Pub. Lands Nat. Policy Steering Com., Nat. Assn. Counties, 1996—, vice chmn. Payment In Lieu of Taxation subcom., 1997—; mem. Environ., Energy & Land Use Nat. Policy Steering Com., 1992-96; pub. hearing officer Oakland County Road Commn., 1983-85; adminstr. emeritus David L. Moffit Scholarships for Outstanding Legal Editl. Achievement and Outstanding Achievement in Legal Journalism, U. Detroit Sch. Law; apptd. to Mich. State Hazardous Waste Site Rev., Bd., 1995—. Named Clarence M. Burton/ Dean's scholar U. Detroit, 1979; recipient Most Disting. Brief to Mich. Supreme Ct. award Thomas M. Cooley Law Sch., 1988. Office: 30600 Telegraph Rd Ste 3250 Bingham Farms MI 48025-4533

MOFFITT, DONALD EUGENE, transportation company executive; b. Terre Haute, Ind., May 22, 1932; s. James Robert and Margaret Mary (Long) M.; m. Billie Duffy, Feb. 21, 1989; 1 child, Jaime. BA, Ind. State U., 1954; postgrad., Ind. U., 1956; grad., Advanced Mgmt. Program, Harvard U., 1972. Acct. Foster Freight Lines, Indpls., 1955-56; with Consol. Freightways Inc., San Francisco, 1956-88, v.p. planning, 1961-69; v.p. fin., motor carrier subs. Consol. Freightways Corp. Del., 1969-75; v.p. fin., treas. parent co. Consol. Freightways Inc., San Francisco, 1975-81; exec. v.p. Consol. Freightways Inc., Palo Alto, Calif., 1981-86; vice chmn. parent co. bd. Consol. Freightways, Inc., Palo Alto, Calif., 1986-88; chmn., CEO Circle Express, Indpls., 1988-90; pres., CEO Consol. Freightways, Inc., Palo Alto, Calif., 1990-96, chmn., CEO, 1995-96, also bd. dirs.; chmn. bd. dirs. all subsidiaries CNF Transport, 1990—; chmn., pres., CEO CNF Transp. Inc., 1996—. Bd. dirs. Bay Area Coun., Calif. Bus. Roundtable, Conf. Bd., Boy Scouts Am., ARC; bd. dirs., exec. com. Hwy. Users Fedn.; bd. trustees Automotive Safety Found.; bus. adv. coun. Northwestern U. Transp. Ctr. Mem. Nat. C. of C. (Washington) (bd. dirs.). Office: Consol Freightways Inc 3240 Hillview Ave Palo Alto CA 94304-1201

MOFFITT, GEORGE, JR., retired foreign service officer; b. N.Y.C., June 18, 1918; s. George and Margaret (Buchanan) M.; m. Lois Anderson, July 7, 1946; children: Katherine M., Margaret Louise. Student, U. Wis., 1950-51. With indsl. firm, 1937-39; fgn. service officer in Haiti, Iraq, Can., Belgium, Burma, Netherland Antilles, Cyprus,, Washington 1939—; counselor of embassy Brussels, 1966-71; polit. adviser to comdr.-in-chief Allied Forces, So. Europe, 1971-76; ret. Bd. dirs. Fulbright Found. for Belgium and Luxembouurg; vice chmn. Burlington Bicentennial Commn.; chmn. Cen. Conn. Adv. Coun. on Aging, 1979-80, Conn. Coalition on Aging, 1979-80; bd. dirs. Conn. Assn. for Human Svcs., 1980-81, Cen. Conn. Regional Planning Agy., 1985-87; corporator Wheeler Clinic; mem. Conn. Gov.'s Commn. on Energy Assistance, 1987—, Bristol (Conn.) Bd. Pub. Welfare, 1988-92; hon. pres. Burlington Libr. Assn., mem., 1979-88. Home: 2 Chimney Crest Ln Bristol CT 06010-7969

MOFFLY, JOHN WESLEY, IV, magazine publishing executive; b. Phila., Aug. 5, 1926; s. John W. III Moffly and Audrey (Kane) Chancellor; m. Donna Jeanette Clegg, July 11, 1959; children: Jonathan Wesley, Audrey Kane. BA, Princeton U., 1949. With Woodrow Wilson Sch. Time Inc., Cleve., 1954-62; N.Y. advt. mgr. House & Home Mag. Time Inc., N.Y.C., 1962-66, N.Y. advt. mgr. LIFE Mag., 1967-73, v.p. selling areas mktg. divsn., 1973-87; pub., owner GREENWICH (Conn.) mag., 1987—. Hon. trustee Greenwich Hist. Soc.; bd. dirs. Boys and Girls Club Greenwich, Community Answers, Greenwich, United Way, Greenwich Emergency Med. Svc., Greenwich Adult Day Care, Greenwich Green & Clean; mem. Amb.'s Round Table-Foru, World Affairs. With USAAF, 1944-45. Mem. Greenwich C. of C. (Small Businessman of Yr. 1991), Riverside Yacht Club, Cruising Club Am., Indian Harbor Yacht Club. Republican. Episcopalian. Avocations: sailing, tennis, clay bird shooting, skiing, international studies. Home: 100 Meadow Rd Riverside CT 06878-2520 Office: GREENWICH mag 39 Lewis St Greenwich CT 06830-5553

MOGABGAB, WILLIAM JOSEPH, epidemiologist, educator; b. Durant, Okla., Nov. 2, 1921; s. Anees and Maude (Jopes) M.; m. Joy Roddy, Dec. 24, 1948 (div. July 1988); children: Robert (dec.), Ann, Kay, Edward R., Jean, Robert M. Berryman, William J.M. Berryman; m. Rose Warren Berryman, July 18, 1988. B.S., Tulane U., 1942, M.D., 1944. Diplomate Am. Bd. Internal Medicine, Am. Bd. Microbiology. Intern Charity Hosp. La., New Orleans, 1944-45, resident, 1946-49, vs. physician, 1949-51, sr. vis. physician, 1971-75; cons., 1976—; mem. faculty Tulane U. Sch. Medicine, 1948—, prof. medicine, 1962-92; cons. infectious diseases, epidemiology, internal medicine New Orleans Dept. Health, 1992—; vis. investigator, asst. physician Hosp. Rockefeller Inst. Med. Research, N.Y.C., 1951-52; chief infectious disease VA Hosp., Houston, 1952-53; asst. prof. medicine Baylor U. Coll. Medicine, 1952-53; head virology div. NAMRU 4, USNTC, Great Lakes, Ill., 1953-55; cons. infectious disease VA Hosp., New Orleans, 1956—; cons. FDA Orphan Products Devel. Grants Program, 1984—. Assoc. mem. commn. influenza Armed Forces Epidemiological Bd., 1959-71; mem. New Orleans Mayor's Health Adv. Com., 1983—. With UNS, 1945-46; comdr. USNR, ret. 1981. Fellow Nat. Found. Infantile Paralysis, 1951-52. Fellow ACP, Am. Acad. Microbiology, Infectious Disease Soc. Am., Am. Coll. Epidemiology; mem. Soc. Exptl. Biology and Medicine, So., Central socs. clin. research, Am. Fedn. Clin. Research, Am. Soc. Cell Biology, Am. Soc. Microbiology, Am. Soc. Clin. Investigation, Tissue Culture Assn., Am. Pub. Health Assn., Am. Soc. Internal Medicine, Am. Soc. Clin. Pharmacology and Therapeutics, So. Med. Soc., AMA, AAAS, Am. Soc. Internal Medicine, Southwestern Assn. Clin. Biology, Soc. Epideniol. Research, Am. Soc. Virology. Research, publns. agts. of and vaccines for respiratory infections, viruses, mycoplasma, new antibiotics. Home: 3 Fortress Rd New Orleans LA 70122-1336

MOGEL, LEONARD HENRY, author; b. Bklyn., Oct. 23, 1922; s. Isaac and Shirley (Goldman) M.; m. Ann Vera Levy, Oct. 23, 1949; children: Wendy Lynn, Jane Ellen. B.B.A., Coll. City N.Y., 1947. Salesman N.Y. Printing Co., N.Y.C., 1946-48; sales mgr. Pollak Printing Co., N.Y.C., 1948-52; advt. dir. Diners Club, Inc., N.Y.C., 1952-56; pub. Diners Club for Signature and Bravo mags., 1956-67; pres. Leonard Mogel Assos., Inc. (nat. advt. reps.), N.Y.C., 1952-67; prin. owner San Francisco Warriors Profl. Basketball Team, 1963-64; pres. Twenty First Century Communications Inc., N.Y.C., 1967-72; pub. Cheetah and Weight Watchers mags., 1967-75; dir. Regents Pub. Co. div. Simon & Schuster, 1960-67; advt. cons. Harvard Lampoon, 1968; pub. Nat. Lampoon, 1970-86, Liberty mag., 1971-73, Ingenue mag., 1973-75, Heavy Metal mag., 1977-86; adj. prof. NYU Sch. Continuing Edn., 1973-78; panelist Folio Mag. Pub. Conf., 1975-76; pres. Perfect World Entertainment, 1996. Exec. prodr.: (feature films) Heavy Metal, 1981; author: Everything You Need to Know to Make It in the Magazine Business, 1979, Making It in the Media Professions, 1988, Making It in Advertising, 1993, Making It in Public Relations, 1993, Making It in Broadcasting, 1994, Making It in Book Publishing, 1996. Sponsor Albert Einstein Med. Coll., Birch Wathen Sch., N.Y.C. Served with AUS, 1942-46, CBI.

MOGEL, WILLIAM ALLEN, lawyer, educator, author; b. N.Y.C., Mar. 7, 1942; s. Harry H. and Therese M.; m. Judith; children: Elisabeth, Andrew. B.A. cum laude, Hobart Coll., 1963; LL.B., U. Pa., 1966. Bar: D.C. 1967, Md. 1971. Ptnr., Morley Caskin, Washington, 1991—; adj. instr. Am. U., Washington, 1982—; active Washington Bd. Trade. Author: Transportation & Marketing of Natural Gas, 1985, 86, Natural Gas: Current Federal and State Developments, 1987; editor-in-chief: Energy Law Jour., 1980—; editor: Natural Gas Yearbook, 1988-92; co-editor: Energy Law & Transactions; contbr. articles to profl. jours. Trustee Hobart Coll., 1983-88. Served to capt. U.S. Army, 1966-69. Mem. Fed. Energy Bar Assn. Home: 4701 Willard Ave Apt 736 Chevy Chase MD 20815 Office: Mogel & Russell 1225 I St NW Washington DC 20005-3914

MOGELEVER, BERNARD, public relations executive; b. Newark, Oct. 15, 1940; s. Louis J. and Kate (Rosenblatt) M.; m. Diane Hinkley, Feb. 1966; children: Elisa, Jonathan G. BA, Rutgers U., New Brunswick, N.J., 1962. News & feature writer S.I. Advance, N.Y., 1965-66; pub. rels. writer The Nat. Found., N.Y.C., 1966-68; exec. A.A. Schechter Assocs., N.Y.C., 1968-73; sr. v.p. Harshe-Rotman & Druck, Inc., N.Y.C., 1973-82; exec. v.p. Ruder Finn & Rotman, N.Y.C., 1982-85; sr. v.p. Burson-Marsteller, 1985-91; pres. Mogelever Comm., Inc., N.Y.C., 1991—. Lt. USAF, 1962-65.

MOGELGAARD, MICHAEL, creative director. Owner Mogelgaard & Assocs. Advt. Agy., 1975-90; co-chmn., creative dir. EvansKraft Advt., Seattle, 1990—. Named Mktg. Man of Yr. 1989; recipient emmy, and addies. Avocations: photographer, professional announcer, professional magician. Office: EvansGroup EvansGroup Bldg 190 Queen Anne Ave N Seattle WA 98109-4968

MOGERMAN, SUSAN, state agency administrator. CEO, dir. State of Ill. Historic Preservation Agy., Springfield. Office: State Ill-Hist Preservation Agy Old State Capitol Springfield IL 62701

MOGHADAM, AMIR, consultant, educational administrator. BSME, U. London, 1983; PhD in Aeronautical Engring., U. Cambridge, 1987. Rsch. assoc. U. Calif., Santa Barbara, 1987-88; asst. prof. Northrop U., L.A., 1988-92, v.p. faculty senate, 1990-91; assoc. prof. Northrop-Rice Aviation Inst. of Tech., Inglewood, Calif., 1992-94, dir. engring. tech., 1994-95, dean of academics, prof. engring. tech., 1995-96, dean/campus dir., 1996—; pres., CEO Aeronautics Innovation Inc., Marina del Rey, Calif., 1993—; ind. cons., Woodland Hills, Calif., 1988-93. Contbr. articles to profl. jours. Mem. AIAA, ASME, Soc. Automotive Engrs., Am. Soc. Engring. Edn., Sigma Xi, Tau Alpha Pi, Tau Beta Pi, Sigma Gamma Tau. Office: Northrop-Rice Aviation Inst Tech 8911 Aviation Blvd Inglewood CA 90301-2904

MOGHISSI, KAMRAN S., obstetrician, gynecologist, educator; b. Tehran, Iran, Sept. 11, 1925; came to U.S., 1959, naturalized, 1965; s. Ahmad and Monireh (Rohani) M.; m. Ida Laura Tedeschi, Jan. 2, 1952; children: Diana J., Soraya R. ChB, MB, U. Geneva, 1951, MD, 1952. Diplomate Am. Bd. Ob-Gyn., Am. Bd. Reproductive Endocrinology. Intern, Univ. Hosp., Geneva, 1951-52, Horton Gen. Hosp., United Oxford Hosps., Banbury, Eng., 1952-53; resident in ob-gyn. Gloucestershire Royal Hosp., Eng., 1953-54, St. Helier Hosp., London, 1954-55, Leeds Regional Hosp. Bd., Yorkshire, Eng., 1955-56, Detroit Receiving Hosp., 1961, attending gynecologist, 1962; assoc. prof. ob-gyn. U. Shiraz Med. Sch., Iran, 1957-59; rsch. assoc. ob-gyn. and physiol. chemistry, Wayne State U., Detroit, 1959-61, asst. prof., 1962-66, assoc. prof., 1966-70, prof., 1970—, dir. div. reproductive endocrinology and infertility, 1970-94; vice chmn., 1983-88, chmn. dept. ob-gyn., 1988-91; sr. attending physician ob-gyn. Hutzel Hosp., Detroit, 1963, vice chief, 1978-82, 83-89, chief, 1982-83, 88-91, chief of staff, 1991-93, attending surgeon, chief ob-gyn. Harper-Grace Hosp., 1983-84; obstetrician, gynecologist, chief, Detroit Med. Ctr., 1988-91; cons. and lectr. in field. Contbr. chpts. to books, articles to profl. jours. Developer exhibits in medicine, movies and teaching prodns.; mem. numerous editorial bds.; cons. in field. Fellow ACS, Am. Coll. Ob-Gyn. Am. Gynecol. and Obstetric Soc.; mem. AMA (ho. of dels. 1992—), AAAS, Am. Soc. Reprodn. Medicine (formerly Am. Fertility Soc., pres. 1990-91), Soc. Study Reprodn., Am. Soc. Andrology, Wayne County Med. Soc., Mich. Soc. Ob-Gyn, Central Assn. Ob-Gyn., N.Y. Acad. Scis., Soc. Reproductive Endocrinologists (charter mem., pres. 1990), Soc. Reproductive Surgeons (charter mem.), Soc. for Assisted Reproductive Tech. (charter mem.), Lochmoor Club (Grosse Pointe), Renaissance Club (Detroit). Home: 56 Moorland Dr Grosse Pointe MI 48236-1112 Office: Hutzel Hosp 4707 Saint Antoine St Detroit MI 48201-1427

MOGIELSKI, PHYLLIS ANN, health association administrator, psychotherapist; b. Chgo., Mar. 5, 1964; d. Edward John and Carmella (Iovino) M. BA, Coll. St. Francis, Joliet, Ill., 1986; MS, Ill. Benedictine Coll., 1990. Cert. drug and alcohol abuse counselor. Sr. counselor PEER Svcs., Inc., Evanston, Ill., 1987-90; project mgr. Am. Acad. Pediatrics, Elk Grove Village, Ill., 1991—; youth worker Dept. Youth Svcs., Highland Park, Ill., 1989; supr., dir. social svcs. Bonaventure House, Chgo., 1989-91, instr. Moraine Valley C.C., Palos Hills, Ill., 1991; assoc. psychotherapist Healy & Assocs., Naperville, Ill., 1991-92, Brook Clinic Assocs., Oak Brook, Ill., 1992—. Mem. NASW, Employee Assistance Profls. Assn., Inc., Ill. Alcohol and other Drugs Profl. Cert. Assn., Inc. Avocations: reading, walking, theatre.

MOGIL, H(ARVEY) MICHAEL, meteorologist, educator; b. N.Y.C., July 9, 1945; s. Nathan and Linda (Balansky) M.; m. Sheila Rose Schleiderer, Mar. 13, 1965 (div. 1987); children: Fredrika Sharon, Allyn Keith; m. Barbara G. Levine, Feb. 6, 1988. BS in Meteorology, Fla. State U., 1967, MS in Meteorology, 1969. Cert. cons. meteorologist. Cons. How the Weatherworks, Rockville, Md., 1979—; trainer NOAA, Washington, 1985-95; instr. U. Mo., Columbia, 1989-92, Loyola Coll., Balt., 1992—; tchr. 5th grade math. and sci. Sandy Spring Friends Sch., 1995-96; co-chair Project "Sky Awareness Week", Rockville, 1991—; adv. bd. Rockville Consortium for Sci., 1990—. Co-author: Weather Study Under a Newspaper Umbrella, 1989, The Amateur Meteorologist, 1993, Anytime Weather Everywhere, 1996; creator video tape tchr. guide Our Sea of Clouds, 1992, A Hurricane: Through the Eyes of Children, 1993; contbr. numerous articles to profl. jours. Mem. Nat. Sci. Tchrs. Assn. (reviewer 1983—), Nat. Earth Sci. Tchrs. Assn., Nat. Weather Assn. (chmn. tng. com. 1986-89, Mem. of the Yr. 1988), Am. Meteorol. Soc. Avocations: biking, reading, gardening, travel.

MOGILNY, ALEXANDER, professional hockey player; b. Khabarovsk, Russia, Feb. 18, 1969. With Buffalo Sabres, 1988-95, capt., 1993-95; with Vancouver Canucks, 1995—; mem. gold-medal winning USSR Olympic Team, 1988. Played in NHL All-Star Game, 1992-94; named to Sporting News All-Star Second Team, 1992-93, NHL All-Star Second Team, 1992-93. Office: Vancouver Canucks, 800 Griffiths Way, Vancouver, BC Canada

MOGK, JOHN EDWARD, law educator, association executive, consultant; b. Detroit, Feb. 10, 1939; s. Clifford Anthony and Evelyn Lenore (Paselk) M.; m. Lylas Heidi Good, Aug. 23, 1964; children: Marja, Tenley, Matthew. BBA, U. Mich., 1961, JD with distinction, 1964; diploma in comparative law, U. Stockholm, 1965. Bar: N.Y. 1966, Mich. 1970. Assoc. atty. Shearman & Sterling, N.Y.C., 1964-68; mem. faculty Wayne State U. Sch. Law, 1968—, dir. grad. studies, 1990-95; pres. MERRA Rsch. Corp., 1974-94; cons. econ. and urban devel., arbitrator. Editor Michigan International Lawyer and Utilities Law Rev.; contbr. articles to profl. jours. Chmn. Mich. TOP Task Force, 1972; vice chmn. Mich. Constrn. Code Commn., 1973; mem. exec. com. Southeastern Mich. Coun. Govts., 1970; chmn. Detroit Sch. Boundary Commn., 1970, Downtown Detroit Vacant Bldg. Com., 1991-93; mem. Detroit Bd. Edn., 1970; mgr. Detroit Empowerment Zone Proposal, 1994; project exec. New Detroit Stadium, 1995. Named Outstanding Wayne State U. Assoc. Prof., 1971, Outstanding Wayne Law Sch. Prof., 1977, 83, 93, 97, Outstanding Young Man in Detroit, 1972, One of Ten Outstanding Young Men in U.S., 1973, One of Four Outstanding Vols. in U.S., 1974; recipient Presdl. citation Wayne State U., 1977, State of Mich., 1988, 94; Am.-Scandinavian fellow, 1965; vis. fellow U. Warwick, Eng., 1985-86. Mem. ABA, Mich. Bar Assn., Assn. of Bar of City of N.Y. Home: 1000 Yorkshire Rd Grosse Pointe MI 48230-1432

MOHAIDEEN, A. HASSAN, surgeon, healthcare executive; b. Ramanathapuram, India, Aug. 14, 1940; s. Abdul and Mariam (Pitchai) Kader; m. Zarina M. Meera, May 30, 1965 (dec. July 1986); children: Ahamed, Mariam, Najeeba, Azeema; m. Laurie J. Kucich, June 23, 1989; children: Yasmin Sara, Leila Jahan. MD, U. Madras, India, 1965; MBA, Wagner Coll., 1996. Diplomate Am. Bd. Surgery, Am. Bd. Quality Assurance and Utilization. Intern Govt. Stanley Hosp., Madras, 1965-66, Good Samaritan Hosp., West Islip, N.Y., 1967-68; resident in gen. and vascular surgery L.I. Coll. Hosp., Bklyn., 1968-73, asst. attending surgeon, 1973-76, assoc. attending surgeon, 1976-78, attending surgeon, 1978—, chief divsn. vascular surgery, 1980-93, dir. vascular lab., 1981-93; v.p. Bklyn.-Caledonian Hosp. Ctr. (affiliate of NYU), 1994-95; sr. v.p., managed care and exec. vice-chmn. dept. surgery The Bklyn.-Caledonian Hosp. Ctr. (affiliate of NYU), 1995-96; asst. surgeon G.H.Q. Hosp., Ramnad, India, 1966-67; assoc. attending surgeon Meth. Hosp., Bklyn., 1982-90, attending surgeon, 1991; asst. attending surgeon Bklyn. Caledonian Med. Ctr., 1973-85, mem. courtesy staff, 1985-94, attending surgeon, 1994—; attending physician Victory Meml. Hosp., Bklyn., 1982—; vis. physician Kings County Hosp. Ctr., Bklyn., 1973—; clin. instr. in surgery Downstate Med. Ctr., SUNY, Bklyn., 1973-78, clin. asst. prof. surgery, 1978—; mem. exec. com. of med. staff L.I. Coll. Hosp., Bklyn., 1979-93, treas. med. staff, 1982-85, pres., 1985-87, med. chmn. Guild Ball com., 1981, mem. quality assurance com. dept. surgery, 1988-94, chmn. credentials com., 1990-93, quality assurance and risk mgmt. com., 1990-93; bd. dirs. Aetna Health Plans of N.Y., AIDS adv. com., 1987—, stds. com., 1986-94, quality assurance com.; bd. dirs. Aetna-U.S. Healthcare, 1997—; mem. credentials com. Prucare, 1988-92; sr. v.p. managed care Bklyn. Hosp., 1995-96; mem. quality mgmt. com. Oxford Health Plans, 1995—; mem. quality improvement com. Chubb Health, N.Y., 1994—; exec. dir. Mayan Health, PPO. Contbr. articles to med. jours. Fellow ACS (com. on Long Island dist. applicants, 1988—), Royal Coll. Physicians and Surgeons Can. (cert.), Internat. Coll. Surgeons; mem. AMA (Physician's Recognition award), AAAS, Am. Coll. Physician Execs., Med. Soc. of State of N.Y., N.Y. State Soc. of Surgeons, N.Y. Acad. of Scis., Med. Soc. of County of Kings (mediation com., 1979-85), Bklyn. Surg. Soc., Soc. for Non-Invasive Vascular Technicians, Kings Physicians I.P.A. (pres./med. dir., 1985-95), Bklyn. Physicians I.P.A. (v.p., 1985-96, pres.). Avocations: photography, computers, walking. Office: 705 86th St Brooklyn NY 11228-3219

MOHALLEY, PATRICIA JOANN, library media specialist; b. Lafayette, Ind., Aug. 24, 1951; d. Robert Dean and Alta Mae (Hancock) Clerget; m. Jeremiah J. Mohalley, Mar. 17, 1979; Sarah Frances and Jeremiah J. Jr. BA in Edn., Purdue U., 1973, MS in Edn., 1978. Cert. edn.-libr. media specialist, Ind., Tex. Tchr. grade 5 Crown Point (Ind.) Sch. Corp., 1973-74; tchr. grades 5 and 6 South Newton Sch. Corp., Kentland, Ind., 1974-77; dir. elem. librs. Community Sch. Corp. of Ea. Hancock County, Wilkinson, Ind., 1977-80; libr. media specialist Met. Sch. Dist. of Lawrence Twp., Indpls., 1980-81, Spring Br. Ind. Sch. Dist., Houston, 1981-89, Klein (Tex.) Ind. Sch. Dist., 1989—. Active Cypress Creek Friends Libr., Spring, Tex., 1988—; life mem. Tex. PTA, 1989—. Mem. ALA, Tex. Libr. Assn. Avocations: reading, traveling, baking. Home: 7814 Springberry Ct Spring TX 77379-4084

MOHAMED, JOSEPH, real estate broker, developer, engineering contractor; b. Omar, W.Va., Mar. 19, 1928; s. Mose and Minnie Elizabeth (Martin) M.; m. Patricia Louise Olmstead, Apr. 11, 1947 (div. 1972); children: Joseph Jr., John W., James R., Leslie Louise; m. Shirley Ida Medeiros, June 22, 1979. AA in Bus. Adminstrn., Sacramento City Coll., 1950; BBA Personnel, Sacramento State U., 1952; postgrad. U. Pacific, U. Calif., Davis, Am. River Coll. Farmer, 1949—; founder comml. trucking operation, Calif., 1949-52, Baja, Calif., Mex., 1953; founder Mexican Co. of Agr. and Livestock, Ltd., Ensenada, Baja, Calif., Mex., 1953-57; owner Quintair, Inc., Calif., 1954—; contractor, real estate developer, 1949—; owner Joseph's Landscape Svc., Sacramento, 1952-72, Joseph Mohamed Enterprises, 1972—; pest control adviser, Calif., 1970—. Mem. Rep. Nat. Com., Rep. Presdl. Task Force, Sacramento Regional Arts Coun., 1965—, Govs.' Emergency Drought Task Force, 1977, Civil Affairs Assn., Calif. Rental Assn., 1975—, Sacramento Apartment Assn., Calif. Apartment Assn., Nat. Apartment Assn.; dir. McClellan Aviation Museum Found., Sacramento County Sheriff's Mounted Posse, 1961—. Served with U.S. Army, 1946-48, USAR, 1949-78. Decorated Legion of Merit; recipient Master Aviator Badge. Mem. Sacramento U. Alumni Assn., Sacramento State Horseman's Assn., Calif. State Horseman's Assn., Sacramento Metro. C. of C., Navy League of U.S., Reserve Officer's Assn., Assn. of U.S. Army, Elk Grove C. of C., Sacramento Bd. of Realtors, Calif. Assn. Realtors, Nat. Assn. Realtors. Clubs: Comstock (Sacramento), Commonwealth (San Francisco). Lodges: Masons, Shriners, Elks.

MOHAN, CHANDRA, research biochemistry educator; b. Lucknow, India, Aug. 3, 1950; came to U.S., 1977; s. Prithivi Nath and Tara Rani (Sharma) Shastri; m. Nirmala Devi Sharma, July 23, 1978; children: Deepak, Naveen. BS, Bangalore (India) U., 1970, MS, 1972, PhD, 1976. Research assoc. U. So. Calif. Med. Sch., Los Angeles, 1977-83, asst. prof., 1983-93; dir. tech. svc., sr. tech. writer CalBioChem Corp., San Diego, 1993—. Assoc. editor Biochem. Medicine, Los Angeles, 1986—; contbr. articles to profl. jours. Recipient BRSG award U. So. Calif., 1983. Mem. AAAS, Am. Diabetes Assn., N.Y. Acad. Scis., Soc. Exptl. Biology and Medicine, Am. Inst. Nutrition. Hindu. Avocations: photography, coin collecting. Home: 13638 Dicky St Whittier CA 90605-2949 Office: CalBioChem Corp 10394 Pacific Center Ct San Diego CA 92121-4340

MOHAN, JOHN J., lawyer; b. St. Louis, May 22, 1945; s. John Joseph and Virginia Loretta (Durkin) M.; m. Elaine Bronwyn Lipe, May 29, 1982; children: Bryn Elizabeth, John Burke. BS Indsl. Engring., St. Louis U., Sch. Engring. and Earth Scis., 1967; JD, St. Louis U., 1971. Bar: Mo. 1971, Ill. 1971, U.S. Dist. Ct. (we. dist.) Mo. 1971, U.S. Dist. Ct. (ea. dist.) Mo. 1980, U.S. Dist. Ct. (so. dist.) Ill. 1981, U.S. Ct. Appeals (8th cir.) 1987. Asst. prosecuting atty. St. Louis County, 1971-72; asst. cir. atty. St. Louis Cir. Atty's. Office, 1972-74; spl. asst. state's atty. St. Clair County Atty's. Office, Belleville, Ill., 1974—; assoc. Lashley, Caruthers, Theis, Rava & Hamel, St. Louis, 1979-80; ptnr. Schreiber, Tueth & Mohan, Clayton, Mo., 1981-83, Danis, Reid, Murphy, Tobben, Schreiber & Mohan, Ladue, Mo., 1983-87, Hinshaw & Culbertson, St. Louis, 1987—. Mem. U. Mo. Law Sch. Found. Scholarship. Mem. ABA, Am. Arbitration Assn. (cert. mediator, arbitrator 1988—), U.S. Arbitration and Mediation Midwest (cert. mediator, arbitrator 1985—), Ill. State Bar Assn., Mo. Bar, Bar Assn. Metropolitan St. Louis, St. Clair County Bar, St. Louis County Bar, Defense Rsch. Inst., Mo. Orgn. Defense Lawyers, Maritime Law Assn., Phi Delta Phi. Home: 529 Big Horn Basin Ct Ballwin MO 63011-4818 Office: Hinshaw & Culbertson 1010 Market St Ste 350 Saint Louis MO 63101-2000

MOHANTY, BINAYAK PRASAD, hydrologist, environmental engineer; b. Bhubaneswar, Orissa, India, June 23, 1964; came to U.S., 1989; s. Harish Chandra and Indulata Mohanty; m. Deepanwita Mohanty, July 14, 1991. B in Engring., Orissa U. Agr. and Tech., 1985; M in Engring., Asian Inst. Tech., 1987; PhD, Iowa State U., 1992. Instr. Orissa U. Agr. and Tech., Bhubaneswar, India, 1985; rsch. assoc. Asian Inst. Tech., Bangkok, Thailand, 1987-88; rsch. asst., postdoctoral rschr. Iowa State U., Ames, 1989-93; rsch. scientist U.S. Salinity Lab. USDA-ARS, Riverside, Calif., 1993—. Assoc. editor: Paddy Field Engineering, 1988, 92; contbr. articles to profl. jours. Mem. Am. Geophys. Union, Am. Soc. Agrl. Engrs., Soil Sci. Soc. Am., Agronomy Soc. Am., Nat. Ground Water Assn., Soil and Water Conservation Soc., Alpha Epsilon, Gamma Sigma Delta. Achievements include multidimensional physical process based spatial analysis techniques, integration of GIS, MODFLOW, and crop water stress models, discovery of hysteresis in spatio-temporal variability of soil temperature, discovery of multimodal hydraulic conductivity functions in unsaturated soil, ground truthing of remotely-sensed soil moisture data, pedo transfer of soil, landscape, and vegetation information to soil hydraulic and thermal properties, development and improvement of hydraulic conductivity measurement techniques for dual porosity media. Office: US Salinity Lab 450 W Big Springs Rd Riverside CA 92507-4617

MOHIUDDIN, SYED MAQDOOM, cardiologist, educator; b. Hyderabad, India, Nov. 14, 1934; came to U.S., 1961, naturalized, 1976; s. Syed Nizamuddin and Amat-Ul-Butool Mahmoodi; m. Ayesha Sultana Mahmoodi, July 16, 1961; children: Sameena J., Syed R., Kulsoom S. M.B., B.S., Osmania U., 1960; M.S., Creighton U., Omaha, 1967; D.Sc., Laval U., Que., Can., 1970. Diplomate: Am. Bd. Internal Medcine (cardiovascular disease). Intern Altoona (Pa.) Gen. Hosp., 1961-62; resident in cardiology Creighton Meml. Hosp., also St. Joseph Hosp., Omaha, 1963-65; mem. staff Creighton Meml. Hosp., also St. Joseph Hosp., 1965—; prof. adjoint Laval U. Med. Sch., 1970; practice medicine specializing in cardiology Omaha, 1970—; prof. Creighton U. Med. Sch., 1977—, assoc. dir. div. cardiology, 1983-96; prof. pharmacy practice Creighton U. Sch. Pharmacy, 1986—; dir divsn. cardiology, 1996—; cons. Omaha VA Hosp. Research fellow Med. Research Council Can., 1968; grantee Med. Research Council Can., 1970; grantee NIH, 1973. Fellow ACP, Am. Coll. Cardiology (gov. for Nebr. 1987-90), Am. Coll. Clin. Pharmacology, Am. Coll. Chest Physicians; mem. AAAS, Am. Heart Assn. (fellow coun. clin. cardiology, bd. dirs. 1973-75), Am. Fedn. Clin. Rsch., Nebr. Heart Assn. (chmn. rsch. com. 1974-76, dir. 1973—), Gt. Plains Heart Com. (Nebr. rep. 1976-84, pres. 1977-78), N.Y. Acad. Scis., Nebr. Cardiovascular Soc. (pres. 1980-81). Democrat. Islam. Home: 12531 Shamrock Rd Omaha NE 68154-3529 Office: Cardiac Ctr Creighton U 3006 Webster St Omaha NE 68131-2100

MOHIUDDIN, YASMEEN NIAZ, economics educator; b. Aligarh, India, Feb. 25, 1948; came to U.S., 1974, naturalized, 1994; d. Niaz Ahmed Siddiqui and Bismillah Niaz Ahmed; m. Muhammad Mohiuddin Siddiqi, July 29, 1972; children: Umar Mohiuddin Siddiqi, Nazia Mohiuddin Siddiqi. BA, U. Karachi, Pakistan, 1965, MA, 1967; MA, Vanderbilt U., Nashville, 1978, PhD, 1983. Staff economist Inst. Devel. Econs., Karachi, Pakistan, 1967-69; asst. prof., assoc. prof. U. Karachi, Pakistan, 1969-74, 78-81, 83-85, prof., 1991; teaching asst. Vanderbilt U., Nashville, Tenn., 1977-78; instr., asst. prof. U. of the South, Sewanee, Tenn., 1981-83, 85-90, assoc. prof., 1990-96, prof., 1996—; cons. World Bank, Washington, D.C., 1988—, World Food Program, Rome, Italy, 1989—; vis. prof. Vanderbilt Univ., summer, 1988; cons. Internat. Labor Orgn., Karachi, 1983-85, Internat. Fund for Agrl. Devel., Rome, Italy, 1991—; assoc. exec. editor Jour. Asian Econs., N.J., 1989—; keynote speaker Soc. for Internat. Devel., Bangladesh, 1990; lecturer in the field. Contbr. numerous articles to profl. jours. Adv. bd. mem. Tenn. Network for Cmty. Econ. Devel.; bd. dirs. Appalachian Women's Guild, Cumberland Ctr. for Justice and Peace, 1994—; panelist AAUW. Internat. Labor Orgn. travel grantee, 1985, Soc. Internat. Devel. travel grantee, 1985, 91, Can. Internat. Devel. Agy. travel grantee, 1985, U. of South Rsch. grantee, 1986-89, 90—, U. Ky. travel grantee, 1987, 90, 95, Ford Found. fellow, 1974-78, 81, Ford Found. travel grantee, 1992, U Wis. Women's Studies fellow, 1983, fellow Transfer of Knowledge Through Expatriate Nat. UNDP programme. Mem. LWV, NOW (co-pres. Sewanee chpt. 1988-89), Nat. Social Sci. Assn., Ea. Econ. Assn., Soc. for Internat. Devel., Pakistan Fedn. of U. Women, Am. Com. on Asian Econ. Studies, Toastmasters Internat. Club, Bread for the World, Pakistan Women's Assns. Moslem. Avocations: community development work, clogging, travel, chess, reading. Home: Maxon Ln # 114 Sewanee TN 37375-2000 Office: U of the South Dept Econs Sewanee TN 37383-1000

MOHL, ALLAN S., social worker; b. Passaic, N.J., Feb. 10, 1933; s. Milton and Ruth (Meisler) M.; m. Judith Klein, Dec. 21, 1958; children: Barbara, Eric, Adam. BA, NYU, 1954, MA, 1956, MSS, 1960; PhD, Columbia Pacific U., 1991. Diplomate Clin. Social Work. Dir. resdl. social svcs. Queens Soc. for Prevention of Cruelty of Children, Queens, N.Y., supvr. of incest; psychotherapist in pvt. practice Ardsley, N.Y.; cons. Tip Neighborhood House, Bronx; dir. family svcs. Tip Neighborhood House; sch. social worker Com. on Spl. Edn., Dist. 28, N.Y.C.; condr. workshop on incestuous families and child sexual abuse; unit dir. Children's Village, Dobbs Ferry, N.Y.; cons. Parents Anonymous, South Bronx, N.Y. Contbr. articles to profl. jours. Former chmn. Gen. Social Svcs. Adv. Coun. # 6; active participant Bronx Task Force on Child Abuse and Neglect; group leader Project Enable, South Bronx, N.Y.; sponsor Parents' Anonymous group, Bronx. With U.S. Army, 1956-58. NIMH grantee. Mem. NASW, Am. Assn. Marriage and Family Therapy, Am. Orthopsychiat. Assn., N.Y. State Soc. Clin. Social Wk. Psychotherapists, Internat. Assn. Counselors and Therapists, Am. Group Psychotherapy Assn. (assoc. clin. mem.). Home: 8 Shorthill Rd Ardsley NY 10502-2020

MOHLEJI, SATISH CHANDRA, electrical engineer; b. New Delhi, India, Aug. 16, 1940; came to U.S. 1970; s. Raghbir Singh and Kashmiro Devi (Sharma) M.; m. Manjula Sharma, Apr. 5, 1972; children: Anjali, Shalini, Nandita. BE with hons., U. Bombay, India, 1962; M.Engring., Tech. U. N.S., Can., 1967; PhD, U. Windsor, Can., 1970; MS in Mgmt. Sci., Am. U., Washington, 1988. Registered profl. engr., Ont., 1967-79. Asst. engr. World Wide Engrs. pvt. Ltd., New Delhi, 1962-63, Dodsal Pvt. Ltd., New Delhi, 1963-64; engr. trainee Richard Zimmerman, K.G., Stuttgart, Germany, 1964; engr. Std. Elec. Lorenz, Stuttgart, 1964-65, Lear Siegler, Inc., Grand Rapids, Mich., 1970-71; prin. engr. MITRE Corp., McLean, Va., 1971—. Contbr. articles to profl. jours. Mem. rsch. adv. panel Aviation Wk. and Space Tech. Pub., 1986-87. Fellow AIAA (assoc., chmn. aircraft ops. tech. com.); mem. IEEE (sr.) Internat. Fedn. Automatic Control (chmn. air traffic control automation tech. com.) RTCA (spl. com. SC-166 tech. working group, chmn. 1989-92). Avocations: photography, gardening. Home: 12324 Ox Hill Rd Fairfax VA 22033-2407 Office: The MITRE Corp 1820 Dolley Madison Blvd Mc Lean VA 22102-3401

MOHLER, BRIAN JEFFERY, diplomat; b. Niskayuna, N.Y., May 28, 1948; s. Donald and Rosemary (Brown) M. BA, Johns Hopkins U., 1970, MA, 1972. Economist Congl. Rsch. Svc. Libr. of Congress, Washington, 1973-74; staff asst. Bur. Econ. Affairs, Washington, 1974-76, economist, 1979-82; consul Am. Consulate Gen., Strasbourg, France, 1976-78; desk officer European community affairs Bur. European Affairs, Washington, 1982-84; petroleum attache Am. Embassy, Riyadh, Saudi Arabia, 1986-88, counselor for econ. affairs, 1988-90; dep. chief of mission Am. Embassy, Abu Dhabi, United Arab Emirates, 1990-93; desk officer Japanese affairs Bur. East Asian and Pacific Affairs, Washington, 1984-86, dep. dir. of econs. for Japanese affairs, 1993-95; counselor for econ. affairs Am. Embassy, Tokyo, 1995—. 2d lt. U.S. Army, 1972, capt. USAR, 1972-85. Recipient Superior Honor award Dept. of State, 1993, Meritorious Honor award, 1987. Mem. Am. Fgn. Svc. Assn., Confrerie de la Chaine des Rotisseurs, Sigma Nu. Roman Catholic.

MOHLER, GEORGIA ANN, geriatrics nurse practitioner; b. Iowa Falls, Iowa, Mar. 11, 1941; d. George Edward and Norma Dorothy (Wolf) M. Diploma, Meth.-Kahler, Rochester, Minn., 1962; BSN, U. Wash., 1971. RN, Wash.; cert. geriatric nurse practitioner. Relief charge nurse, team leader Swedish Hosp., Seattle, 1963-72; pub. health nurse Vis. Nurse Svc., Seattle, 1971-72; relief charge nurse and medicare coord. Restorative Care Ctr., Seattle, 1972-81; unit coord. Tacoma Luth. Home and Retirement Ctr., Tacoma, 1981-82; nurse practitioner Tacoma Luth. Home, 1983—, dir. home health agy. and nurse practitioner, 1993—. Contbr. to profl. jours. Mem. Pierce County Nurse Practitioner Group, Nat. Conf. Gerontol. Nurse Practitioners. Lutheran. Home: 909 N I St Apt 401 Tacoma WA 98403-2136

MOHLER, MARIE ELAINE, nurse educator; b. Norma, N.D., Mar. 2, 1946; d. Ervin and Katie M. (Nichol) Hansen; children: Zane, Tracy, KyLynn, Todd, Lynnette. Diploma in nursing, Trinity Hosp. Sch. Nursing, Minot, 1967; BSN, Mont. State U., 1969, M in Nursing, 1970; diploma nurse midwifery, SUNY, Bklyn., 1973. RN, N.D.; cert. nurse midwife Am. Coll. Nurse Midwifes. Staff nurse pediatrics Trinity Hosp., Minot, 1967; resident nurse girl's dormitory Mont. State U., Bozeman, 1967-68; staff nurse med.-surg. wards Bozeman (Mont.) Deaconess Hosp., 1969; relief nurse Student Health Ctr. Mont. State U., Bozeman, 1970; camp nurse Camp Pinemore Minoqua, Wis., 1971; part-time staff nurse labor & delivery-maternity-newborn Bannock Meml. Hosp., Pocatello, Idaho, 1972-75; cons. maternal-newborn, pediatric wards Bannock Meml. Hosp., Pocatello, 1972-75; staff nuse maternity-newborn ward John Moses Hosp., Minot, 1977; part time staff nurse maternal-newborn ward St. Joseph's Hosp., Minot, 1978-81; nurse assessor Luth. Social Svc. N.D. and Family Care Network, 1991-93; instr. Ariz. State U., Tempe, 1971-72, No. Ariz. U., Flagstaff, 1972, Idaho State U., Pocatello, 1972-75; asst. prof. Minot (N.D.) State Coll. divsn. Allied Health, 1975-76; instr. medicine U. Miss. Med. Ctr., Jackson, 1976-77; assoc. prof. Minot (N.D.) State U. Coll. Nursing, 1977—; pres. coun. coll. faculties N.D. U. Sys., 1993-94, chair faculty compensation com., 1993-94, 96—, others; mem. budget and salary com., constl. rev. com. Minot State U., 1993-94, others. Author of various videotapes and slide series. Recipient Minot C. of C. Disting. Prof. award, 1986; Burlington No. Found. Faculty Achievement award, 1987; grantee in field. Mem. Assn. Women's Health, Obstetric and Neonatal Nurses (chair legis. chpt.), Mabel Meug Honor Soc., Alpha Tau Delta. Office: Minot State Univ Coll Nursing 500 University Ave W Minot ND 58707-0001

MOHLER, MARY GAIL, magazine editor; b. Milaca, Minn., Dec. 15, 1948; d. Albert and Deane (Vedders) M.; m. Paul Rodes Trautman, June 5, 1976 (div. 1994); children: Elizabeth Deane, David Albert Rodes, Theodore DeForest Lloyd. B.A., U. Calif.-Davis, 1974; M.A. in Lit., SUNY-Stony Brook, 1976. Asst., then editor-reporter Family Circle Mag., N.Y.C., 1979-81; editorial coordinator Ladies' Home Jour., N.Y.C., 1981, assoc. articles editor, 1982, mng. editor, 1982-93, sr. editor, 1994—; editor in chief Ladies' Home Jour. Parent's Digest. Medieval philosophy fellow SUNY-Binghamton, 1978. Mem. MLA, Am. Soc. Mag. Editors, Phi Beta Kappa. Clubs: Medieval; Overseas Press. Office: Ladies Home Jour 125 Park Ave New York NY 10017-5529

MOHLER, RICHARD ALBERT, JR., academic administrator, theologian; b. Lakeland, Fla., Oct. 9, 1959; s. Richard Albert Sr. and Janet Rae (Johnson) M.; m. Mary Ann Kahler, July 16, 1983; children: Mary Katherine, Christopher Albert. BA magna cum laude, Samford U., 1980; MDiv, So. Bapt. Theol. Sem., Louisville, 1983, PhD, 1989; postgrad., St. Meinrad Sch. Theology, 1985, Oxford (Eng.) U., 1986. Ordained min. So. Bapt. Ch. Pastor Union Grove Bapt. Ch., Bedford, Ky., 1982-87; asst. to pres., coord. found. support, dir. capital funding So. Bapt. Theol. Sem., Louisville, 1983-89, pres., 1993—; editor The Christian Index, Atlanta, 1989-93; prof. christian theology, 1996—; assoc. dir. The So. Sem. Found., 1983-89; lectr. in field. Assoc. editor Preaching, 1985-93, contbg. editor, 1993—; gen. editor: The Gods of the Age of the God of the Ages?, 1993; contbr. articles to profl. jours. Named one of 40 Rising Evangelical Leaders, Christianity Today, 1996, One of 96 Southerners to Watch, Atlanta Jour. and Constitution, 1996. Mem. Am. Acad. Religion, Soc. Biblical Lit., Evangelical Theol. Soc., So. Bapt. Hist. Soc., Bapt. Pub. Rels. Assn., So. Bapt. Press Assn., Evangelical Press Assn., Nat. Assn. Evangelicals, Ga. Bapt. Hist. Soc., Rotary Internat., Phi Kappa Phi, Omicron Delta Kappa. Named one of 50 young leaders under 40 years of age TIME Mag. Office: So Bapt Theol Sem 2825 Lexington Rd Louisville KY 40280-0001

MOHLER, RONALD RUTT, electrical engineering educator; b. Ephrata, Pa., Apr. 11, 1931; s. David Wealand and Elizabeth (Rutt) M.; m. Nancy Alice Strickler, May 6, 1950; children: Curtis Gene, Pamela Louise, Susan Lynn, Anita Marie, John Scott, Andrew Thomas, Jennifer Lee, Lisa Nancy. B.S. (scholarship), Pa. State U., 1956; M.S., U. So. Calif., 1958; Ph.D., U. Mich., 1965. Designer, trainee Textile Machine Works, Rockwell Internat. Corp., Reading, Pa., 1949-56; staff mem. Hughes Aircraft Co., Culver City, Calif., 1956-58, Los Alamos Sci. Lab., 1958-65; asso. prof. elec. engring. U. N.Mex., Albuquerque, 1965-69; prof. elec. engring./aerospace, mech. and nuclear engring. U. Okla., 1969-72, prof., chmn. info. and computing scis., 1970-72; dir. Systems Research Center, 1969-72; adj. prof. elec. engring. and nuclear engring. U. N.Mex., Los Alamos Grad. Center, 1959-65; cons. Sandia Corp., Albuquerque, 1966-69, Aerojet-Gen. Corp., Sacramento, 1966; vis. assoc. prof. system sci. UCLA, 1968-69; cons. community health project OEO, Oklahoma City, 1970-71; prof. elec. and computer engring. Oreg. State U., Corvallis, 1972—; head dept. Oreg. State U., 1972-79, 90; pres. Pace Tech., Inc., 1982—; vis. prof. U. Rome, 1973, 75, Imperial Coll., London, 1978-79, U.S. Naval Postgrad. Sch., 1983-85, Australian Nat. U., 1988, Sydney U., 1995; cons. Optimization Software, L.A., 1973—, Bonneville Power Adminstrn., 1975—, Internat. Inst. Applied Systems Analysis, 1988—. Author: Optimal Control of Nuclear Reactors, 1970, Bilinear Control Processes, 1973, Nonlinear Systems: Dynamics and Control, vol. 1, 1991, Applications to Bilinear Control, vol. II, 1991, Disease Dynamics, 1993; editor: Theory and Application of Variable Structure Systems, 1972, Variable Structure Systems with Application to Biology and Economics, 1975, Recent Developments in Variable Structure Systems, Economics and Biology, 1979, Nonlinear Time Series and Signal Processing, 1988, assoc. editor Annals of Nuclear Energy, 1973—; contbr. jours. Chmn. St. Stephens Sch. Bd., Norman, 1970-72. Recipient NATO award, 1979; rsch. grantee NSF, 1966—, Sandia Labs., 1966-68, ONR, 1981-92, NASA, EPRI, BPA, 1990—; AEC fellow, 1961-65, Hughes fellow, 1956-58; Acad. Sci. exch. scientist to USSR and China, 1980, US-CIS (USSR) Commn. on Engring. Edn., 1991—. Fellow IEEE (life, local chmn. 1975); mem. Am. Soc. Engring. Edn., Control System Soc., Sigma Xi, Tau Beta Pi, Pi Tau Sigma. Democrat. Pioneer rsch. on bilinear systems and worldwide collaboration. Home: 2050 NW Dogwood Dr Corvallis OR 97330-1102

MOHLER, STANLEY ROSS, physician, educator; b. Amarillo, Tex., Sept. 30, 1927; s. Norton Harrison and Minnie Alice (Ross) M.; m. Ursula Luise Burkhardt, Jan. 24, 1953; children: Susan Luise, Stanley Ross, Mark Hallock. B.A., U. Tex., 1953, M.A., 1953, M.D., 1956. Diplomate: Am. Bd. Preventive Medicine. Intern USPHS Hosp., San Francisco, 1956-57; med. officer Center Aging Research, NIH, Bethesda, Md., 1957-61; dir. Civil Aeromed. Rsch. Inst., FAA, Oklahoma City, 1961-66; chief aeromed. applications div. Civil Aeromed. Rsch. Inst., FAA, Washington, 1966-78; prof., vice chmn. dept. community medicine, dir. aerospace medicine Wright State U. Sch. Medicine, Dayton, Ohio, 1978—; rsch. assoc. prof. preventive medicine and pub. health U. Okla. Med. Sch., 1961—; vice chmn. Am. Bd. Preventive Medicine, 1978—, sec.-treas., 1980—. Co-editor: Space Biology and Medicine (5 vol. series), 1995 (Life Scis. Book award Internat. Acad. Astronautics); contbr. articles to profl. jours. Bd. dirs. Sr. Citizens Assn. Oklahoma City, 1962—, Flying Physicians Assn., 1961—. Served with AUS, 1946-48. Recipient Gail Borden Rsch. award, Boothby award Aerospace Med. Assn., 1966, FAA Meritorious Svc. award, 1974; co-recipient Life Scis. Book award in space, biology and medicine Internat. Acad. Astronautics, 1995. Fellow Geriatrics Soc., Aerospace Med. Assn. (pres. 1983, Harry G. Moseley award 1974, Lyster award 1984), Am. Coll. Preventive Medicine, Gerontol. Soc.; mem. AMA, Aircraft Owners and Pilots Assn. (Sharples award 1984, Hubertus Strughold award 1991), Alpha Omega Alpha. Home: 6539 Reigate Rd Dayton OH 45459-3214 Office: Wright State U Sch Medicine PO Box 927 Dayton OH 45401-0927

MOHN, MELVIN PAUL, anatomist, educator; b. Cleve., June 19, 1926; s. Paul Melvin and Julia (Jacobik) M.; m. Audrey Faye Lonergan, June 28, 1952; children—Shorey Faye, Andrew Paul. A.B., Marietta Coll., 1950; Sc.M., Brown U., 1952, Ph.D. in Biology, 1955. Instr. SUNY Downstate Med. Ctr., Bklyn., 1955-59, asst. prof., 1959-63; asst. prof. anatomy U. Kans. Sch. Medicine, Kansas City, 1963-65, assoc. prof., 1965-72, prof., 1972-89, prof. emeritus, 1989—; cons. Nat. Med. Audiovisual Ctr., Atlanta, 1972; vis. lectr. U. Miami Sch. Medicine, Fla., 1966. Bd. dirs. U. Kans. Med. Ctr. Credit Union, 1968-77, Kansas City Youth Symphony, 1972-77; mem. U.S. Pony Club, 1964-71, Med. Arts Symphony, 1965-71, 90—, Spring Hill Chorale, 1990—. Served with USN, 1944-46, PTO. McCoy fellow, 1950, Arnold biology fellow, 1954. Fellow AAAS; mem. Am. Soc. Zoologists, Am. Assn. Anatomists, Am. Inst. Biol. Sci., Phi Beta Kappa, Sigma Xi, Beta Beta Beta. Republican. Methodist. Club: Lions, Rotary, Lodge: Masons. Home: Yankee Bit Farm 23595 W 223rd St Spring Hill KS 66083-4029 Office: U Kans Med Ctr Dept Anatomy 39th and Rainbow St Kansas City KS 66103

MOHNEY, RALPH WILSON, minister; b. Paris, Ky., May 20, 1918; s. Silas Phillip and Clarine (Wilson) M.; m. Nell Marie Webb, Dec. 31, 1948; children—Richard Bentley, Ralph Wilson. B.A., Transylvania Coll., 1940; B.D., Vanderbilt U., 1943; S.T.M., Boston U., 1945; postgrad., Harvard, Garrett Bibl. Inst.; D.D., Emory and Henry Coll., 1959. Ordained elder Meth. Ch., 1944; pastor Winter Street Congl. Ch., Bath, Me., 1943-45, Manker Meml. Meth. Ch., Chattanooga, 1945-50, Washington Pike Meth. Ch., Knoxville, 1950-56; supt. Kingsport dist. Holston Conf. Meth. Ch., 1956-59; pres. Tenn. Wesleyan Coll., 1959-65; sr. minister Centenary Meth. Ch., 1965-66, First Centenary United Meth. Ch., Chattanooga, 1967-81, First Broad St. United Meth. Ch., Kingsport, Tenn., 1981-87; asst. dir. Growth Plus Ministries Gen. Bd. Discipleship, Chattanooga, 1988-92, Disting. evangelist in residence, 1991-96; staff mem. Large Ch. Initiative, 1988-89; Staley Disting. lectr. Columbia Coll., 1973, Emory and Henry Coll., 1975, Pfeiffer Coll., 1976, Union Coll., 1977; del. World Conf. Christian Youth, Oslo, Norway, 1947; adult counselor Meth. Youth Caravan to Poland., 1947; chmn. Holston Conf. Commn. on World Peace, 1952-56; leader Annual Lenten Pilgrimage to Holy Land, 1973-80; pres. Holston Council on Finance and Administrn., 1968-76, mem., 1976-84; mem. Gen. Council Finance and Adminstrn., 1976-84, mem. exec. com., 1976-80; chmn. Commn. on Christian Higher Edn., 1956-59; res. del. Gen. Conf. Meth. Ch., del. jurisdictional conf. Meth. Ch., 1960, 68; del. Meth. Ch. (Gen. Conf.), 1976; mem. Gen. Bd. Christian Social Concerns, 1960-72, World Council Meth. Ch., 1966-70; mem. steering com. United Meth. TV Presence and Ministry, 1979-81; mem. S.E. radio and film commn. Meth. Ch., 1968-76; dir. Holston Conf. Found., 1984-92; exchange minister Eng., 1984, New Zealand, 1987. Co-author: Parable Churches, 1989, Churches of Vision, 1990, Vision 2000: Planning for Ministry Into the Next Century, 1991. Bd. dirs. E. Tenn. State Coll. Wesley Found., 1955-59, U. Tenn. Wesley Found., 1956-62; pres. Athens United Fund, 1965, Affiliated Ind. Colls. Tenn., 1963-65, Chattanooga Meth. Ministers Assn., 1966-67, Chattanooga Clergyman's Assn., 1968. Mem. Pi Kappa Alpha, Pi Kappa Delta. Club: Kiwanis. Home: 1004 Northbridge Ln Chattanooga TN 37405-4214

MOHOLY, NOEL FRANCIS, clergyman; b. San Francisco, May 26, 1916; s. John Joseph and Eva Gertrude (Cippa) M.; grad. St. Anthony's Sem., Santa Barbara; STB, Faculte de Theologie, Universite Laval, Quebec, Que., Can., 1944, STL, 1945, STD, 1948; Joined Franciscan Friars, 1935; ordained priest Roman Catholic Ch., 1941; tchr. fundamental theology Old Mission Santa Barbara, 1942-43, sacred theology, 1947-58; tchr. langs. St. Anthony's Sem., 1943-44; Am. adminstr. (handling affairs of the cause in U.S.) Cause of Padre Junipero Serra, 1950-55, vice postulator, 1958—; retreat master San Damiano Retreat, Danville, Calif., 1964-67. Mem. Ann. Assay Commn. U.S. Mint, 1964. Occupied numerous pulpits, assisted in several Franciscan Retreat Houses; condr. series illustrated lectrs. on cause of canonization of Padre Junipero Serra to students of all Franciscan study houses in U.S., summer 1952, also speaker in field at various clubs of Serra Internat. in U.S., Europe and Far East, on NBC in documentary with Edwin Newman, Padre Serra, Founding Father, 1985, PBS on Firing Line with William F. Buckley: Junipero Serra—Saint or Sinner, 1989, CBS, ABC broadcasts and conducted own local TV series. Mem. Bldg. Com. for Restoration Hist. Towers and Facade of Old Mission Santa Barbara, 1950-53; exec. dir., treas. Old Mission Restoration Project, 1954-58; mem. Calif. Hist. Landmarks Adv. Com., 1962-71, Calif. Hist. Resources Commn., 1971-76, Calif. Bicentennial Celebration Commn., 1967-70; pres. Serra Bicentennial commn., 1983-86, dir. Old Spanish Days in Santa Barbara, Inc., 1950-58, Nat. and internat. authority on Saint Irenaeus, mariology, Calif. history (particularly history of Father Serra). Decorated Knight comdr. Order of Isabella la Catolica, 1965. Pres. Father Junipero Serra 250th Anniversary Assn., Inc., 1964—. Named hon. citizen Petra de Mallorca, 1969, Palma de Mallorca, 1976; recipient Cross of Merit Sovereign Mil. Order of Knights Malta, 1989. Mem. Mariol. Soc. Am., Native Sons Golden West, Associacion de los Amigos de Padre Serra, K.C., Calif. Missions Study Assn. Author: Our Last Chance, 1931; Saint Irenaeus; the Father of Mariology, 1952; The California Mission Story, 1975; The First Californian, 1976; co-author (with Don DeNevi) Junipero Serra, 1985; producer phonograph records Songs of the California Missions, 1951, Christmas at Mission Santa Barbara, 1953, St. Francis Peace Record, 1957; producer VCR The Founding Father of the West, 1976. Home: The Old Mission 2201 Laguna St Santa Barbara CA 93105-3611 Office: Serra Cause The Old Mission Santa Barbara CA 93105-3611

MOHR, EILEEN THERESA, environmental geologist; b. Buffalo, Feb. 21, 1957; d. Jacob Carl and Marjorie Mary (McDonald) M. BA magna cum laude in geology, SUNY, Buffalo, 1979; MS summa cum laude, Kent State U., 1983. Cert. profl. geologist, hazardous materials mgr.; lic. profl. geologist, Pa. Intern U.S. Geol. Survey, Flagstaff, Ariz., 1978; grad. tchg. asst. Kent (Ohio) State U., 1979-81; geologist Ohio Environ. Protection Agy., Twinsburg, 1982-87, project mgr., 1990—; co-facilitator H.M. Environ. Reflection Action Group, Villa Maria, Pa., 1989-91. Head coach Challenger Baseball, Streetsboro, Ohio, 1994—; vol. AIDS Holistic Health Svcs., Akron, Ohio, 1990—, H.M. Life Opportunity Svcs., Akron, 1990—, Villa Maria Organic Farm, 1995—, various others. Recipient 1st and 2nd place Randolph Portage County Fair photography contest, 1986. Mem. N.E. Ohio Cert. Hazardous Materials Mgr.'s chpt., Kent State Newman Ctr. Democrat. Roman Catholic. Avocations: photography, bicycling, camping, social justice issues, Native Am. spirituality and traditions. Office: Ohio Environ Protection Agy 2110 E Aurora Rd Twinsburg OH 44087-1924

MOHR, GARY ALAN, physician; b. Erie, Pa., Aug. 17, 1952; s. Arthur John and Sue (Richardson) M.; children: Benjamin, Nathan, Elizabeth, Katelyn, Eric. BS, Pa. State U., 1975; MD, Jefferson Med. Coll., 1979. Pvt. practice Canon City, Colo., 1982—. Founder, treas. Jefferson Soc., Fremont County, Colo., 1991. Mem. Mensa. Lutheran. Avocations: hiking, climbing, rafting, skiing. Office: 730 Macon Ave Canon City CO 81212-3314

MOHR, JAY PRESTON, neurologist; b. Mar. 5, 1937; s. John G. and Marguerite F. Mohr; A.B., Haverford Coll., 1958; M.S., U. Va., 1963, M.D., 1963; m. Joan L. Seal, Mar. 10, 1962; children—Thea, Gregory. Intern, then asst. resident in medicine Mary Imogene Bassett Hosp., Cooperstown, N.Y., 1963-65; asst. resident in neurology N.Y. Neurol. Inst., Columbia-Presbyn. Med. Ctr., N.Y.C., 1965-66; fellow in neurology Mass. Gen. Hosp., Boston, 1966-69; instr. neurology Johns Hopkins U. Med. Sch., also U. Md. Med. Sch., 1969-71; assoc. neurologist Mass. Gen. Hosp., also asst. prof. Harvard U. Med. Sch., 1972-78; prof. neurology, chmn. dept. U. South Ala. Med. Sch., Mobile, 1978-83; Sciarra prof. clin. neurology Columbia U. Coll. Physicians and Surgeons, N.Y.C., 1983—; dir. cerebrovascular research N.Y. Neurol. Inst., N.Y.C., 1983—. Served as maj. M.C., U.S. Army, 1969-72. Diplomate Am. Bd. Neurology and Psychiatry. Fellow Am. Acad. Neurology; mem. Am. Neurol. Assn., Am. Heart Assn. (stroke council), Sigma Xi. Democrat. Quaker. Contbr. articles to med. jours. Home: PO Box 1014 Shelter Island Heights NY 11965-1014 Office: NY Neurol Inst 710 W 168th St New York NY 10032-2603 also: Presbyn Hosp Columbia-Presbyn Med Ctr New York NY 10032-3784

MOHR, JOHN LUTHER, biologist, environmental consultant; b. Reading, Pa., Dec. 1, 1911; s. Luther Seth and Anna Elizabeth (Davis) M.; m. Frances Edith Christensen, Nov. 23, 1939; children: Jeremy John, Christopher Charles. AB in Biology, Bucknell U., 1933; student, Oberlin Coll., 1933-34; PhD in Zoology, U. Calif., Berkeley, 1939. Research asso. Pacific Islands Research, Stanford, 1942-44; rsch. assoc. Allan Hancock Found., U. So. Calif., 1944-46, asst. prof., 1946-47, asst. prof. dept. biology, 1947-54, asso. prof., 1954-57, prof., 1957-77; chmn. dept., 1960-62, prof. emeritus, 1977—; vis. prof. summers U. Wash. Friday Harbor Labs., 1956, '57; rsch. assoc. vertebrate zoology Natural History Mus., Los Angeles County, 1996—; marine borer and pollution surveys harbors So. Calif., 1948-51, arctic marine biol. research, 1952-71; chief marine zool. group U.S. Antarctic research ship Eltanin in Drake Passage, 1962, in South Pacific sector, 1965; research deontology in sci. and academia; researcher on parasitic protozoans of anurans, crustaceans, elephants; analysis of agy. and industry documents, ethics and derelictions of steward agy., sci. and tech. orgns. as they relate to offshore and coastal onshore oil activities, environ. effects of oil spill dispersants and offshore oil industry discharges and naturally occurring radioactive material NORMs. Active People for the Am. Way; mem. Biol. Stain Commn., 1948-80, trustee, 1971-80, emeritus trustee, 1981—, v.p., 1976-80. Recipient Guggenheim fellowship, 1957-58. Fellow AAAS (coun. 1964-73), So. Calif. Acad. Scis., Sigma Xi (exec. com. 1964-67, 68, 69, chpt.-at-large bd. 1968-69); mem. Am. Micros. Soc., Marine Biol. Assn. U.K. (life), Am. Soc. Parasitologists, Western Soc. Naturalists (pres. 1960-61), Soc. Protozoologists, Soc. Integrative and Comparative Biology, Ecol. Soc. Am., Calif. Native Plant Soc., Assn. Forest Svc. Employees Environ. Ethics, Common Cause, Huxleyan, Sierra Club, Phi Sigma, Theta Upsilon Omega. Home: 3819 Chanson Dr Los Angeles CA 90043-1601

MOHR, L. THOMAS, newspaper executive; b. Endicott, N.Y., Dec. 25, 1955; s. Lionel Charles and Anne (Tredwell) M.; m. Pageen Rogers, July 13, 1985; children: Mary Catherine, Jack. BA with honors, Queens U., Kingston, Ont., Can., 1979; MBA, U. Calif., Berkeley, 1987. Gen. mgr. Foster City (Calif.) Progress, 1981-82; classified advt. mgr. Peninsula Times Tribune, Palo Alto, Calif., 1982-85, mktg. mgr., 1985-86, advt. sales dir., 1986-87; dir. mktg. and advt. sales Bakersfield Californian, 1987-90; classified advt. dir. Star Tribune, Mpls., 1990-93, v.p., 1993-96, sr. v.p., gen. mgr., 1996—. Bd. dirs. March of Dimes, Mpls., 1994—. Mem. Newspaper Assn. Am. (bd. dirs. classified fedn. 1993—), New Media Fedn. (bd. dirs.). Republican. Roman Catholic. Avocations: running, tennis, golf, cross country skiing. Home: 3080 Quinwood Ln N Plymouth MN 55441-2807 Office: Star Tribune 425 Portland Ave Minneapolis MN 55415-1511

MOHR, LAWRENCE CHARLES, physician; b. S.I., N.Y., July 8, 1947; s. Lawrence Charles Sr. and Mary Estelle (Dawsey) M.; m. Linda Johnson, June 14, 1970; 1 child, Andrea Marie. AB with highest honors, U. N.C., 1975, MD, 1979. Diplomate Am. Bd. Internal Medicine. Commd. 2d lt. U.S. Army, 1967, advanced through grades to col., 1989; med. intern Walter Reed Army Med. Ctr., Washington, 1979-80, resident in medicine, 1980-82, chief resident, 1982-83, attending physician, 1984-86, pulmonary fellow, 1986-87; command surgeon 9th Inf. Div., Ft. Lewis, Wash., 1983-84; med. cons. Madigan Army Med. Ctr., Tacoma, 1983-84; physician The White House, Washington, 1987-93; asst. prof. medicine Uniformed Svcs. U. of the Health Scis., Bethesda, Md., 1984-91; assoc. prof. medicine Uniformed Svcs. U. Health Scis., Bethesda, Md., 1991-94; assoc. clin. prof. medicine George Washington U., Washington, 1990-94; prof. medicine Med. U. S.C., Charleston, 1994—, dir. environ. hazards assessment program, 1995—; attending physician Med. U. Hosp., Charleston, 1994—, Charleston Meml. Hosp., 1994—; mem. Working Group on Disability in U.S. Presidents, 1995—. Contbr. articles to profl. jours. and books. Bd. dirs. Internat. Lung Found., Washington; mem. adv. bd. Nat. Mus. Health and Medicine, Washington. Decorated Silver Star, Bronze Star with 2 V devices and 3 oak leaf clusters, Purple Heart, Meritorious Svc. medal with oak leaf cluster, Air medal, Army Commendation medal with oak leaf cluster, D.S.M.; recipient Erskine award Walter Reed Army Med. Ctr., 1982; named Outstanding Med. Resident, 1982. Fellow ACP, Am. Coll. Chest Physicians; mem. AMA, Army and Navy Club, Order Mil. Med. Merit, Harbour Club, Phi Beta Kappa. Episcopalian. Avocations: mountain climbing, skiing. Home: Ste 11-R 310 Broad St Charleston SC 29401 Office: Med U S C Environ Hazards Assess Prgm 171 Ashley Ave Charleston SC 29425-0001

MOHR, ROGER JOHN, advertising agency executive; b. Milw., Sept. 8, 1931; s. Reinhold and Clara (Meissner) M.; m. Pauline Spicuzza, Oct. 18, 1958; children: Gregory, Mary Margaret, Kristin, Thomas, Kathleen. B.S. in Speech, Marquette U., 1953; postgrad. radio and TV, Northwestern U., 1955-56. Staff announcer radio sta. WBKB, West Bend, Wis., 1952, WCAN, Milw., 1952-54; with Arthur Meyerhoff Assos., Inc., Chgo., 1956-80; pres. Arthur Meyerhoff Assos., Inc., 1965-80; pres. BBDO, Chgo., 1980-82, chmn., 1982-90, vice chmn. internat., 1991-93; retired, 1996. Chmn. Lake Bluff (Ill.) Plan Commn., 1972-75; mem. Lake Forest (Ill.) Plan Commn., 1994—; bd. dirs. Chgo. City Ballet, 1982-84, Off the Street Club, 1976-78; mem. adv. coun. Marquette U. Sch. Comm., 1993—. Served with AUS, 1954-55. Mem. Am. Assn. Advt. Agys. (chmn. Chgo. coun. 1966-67, sec., treas., nat. bd. dirs. 1976-77), Evans Scholars Alumni Assn. (pres. 1964-65), Western Golf Assn. (bd. dirs. 1980—, v.p. 1994—), Knollwood Club (bd. govs. 1980-85, 89-92), Tavern Club (bd. govs., v.p. 1988-94). Home: 2000 Knollwood Rd Lake Forest IL 60045-1137

MOHR, SELBY, retired ophthalmologist; b. San Francisco, Mar. 11, 1918; s. Selby and Henrietta (Foorman) M.; AB, Stanford U., 1938, MD, 1942; m. Marian Buckley, June 10, 1950; children—Selby, John Vincent, Adrianne E., Gregory P. Asst. resident in ophthalmology U. Calif. Hosp., 1942-43; pvt. practice ophthalmology, San Francisco, 1947-88; mem. past pres. med. staff Marshall Hale Meml. Hosp.; mem. staff Mt. Zion Hosp., St Francis Meml. Hosp. Dir. Sweet Water Co., Mound Farms, Inc., Mound Farms Oil & Gas, Inc. Lt. (j.g.) USNR, 1943-46; PTO. Diplomate Am. Bd. Ophthalmology. Fellow Am. Acad. Ophthalmology; mem. AMA, Calif., San Francisco Med. Socs., Pan-Pacific Surg. Soc., Pan-Am. Assn. Ophthalmology. Home: 160 Sea Cliff Ave San Francisco CA 94121-1125

MOHRAZ, JUDY JOLLEY, college president; b. Houston, Oct. 1, 1943; d. John Chesler and Mae (Jackson) Jolley; m. Bijan Mohraz; children: Andrew, Jonathan. BA, Baylor U., 1966, MA, 1968; PhD, U. Ill., 1974. Lectr. history Ill. Wesleyan U., 1972-74; asst. prof. history So. Meth. U., Dallas, 1974-80, coord. women's studies, 1977-81, assoc. prof. history, 1980-94, asst. provost, 1983-88, assoc. provost for student academics, 1988-94; pres. Goucher Coll., Towson, Md., 1994—; cons. Ednl. Testing Svc., Princeton, N.J., 1984-93, Nat. Park Svcs., Seneca Falls, N.Y., 1992-93; bd. dirs. Balt. Equitable Soc.; bd. visitors U.S. Naval Acad., 1996—. Trustee The Lamplighter Sch., 1991-94, St. Mark's Sch. Tex., 1993-94; adv. bd. U. Tex. Southwestern Med. Sch., 1992-94; active Leadership Dallas, 1994. Recipient Disting. Alumni award Baylor U., 1993; named Woman of Merit, Omicron Delta Kappa, 1993. Office: Goucher Coll Office of Pres 1021 Dulaney Valley Rd Baltimore MD 21204-2753

MOHRFELD, RICHARD GENTEL, heating oil distributing company executive; b. Camden, N.J., Dec. 30, 1945; s. Herbert Henry and Elizabeth Weldon (Gentel) M.; m. Ann Bacon, June 20, 1971 (div. 1975); m. Janice Lee Strickland, July 1, 1978; children: Kathryn Elizabeth, Christopher Hall. BSc in Geology, Dickinson Coll., 1971. Staff geologist Temple U., Phila., 1971-74; pres. Mohrfeld Inc., Collingswood, N.J., 1974—; bd. dirs. South Jersey Savs. & Loan Assn., Turnersville, N.J., 1984—. Bd. dirs. Boy Scouts Am., Camden County, N.J., 1985—; trustee, treas. Knight Park Trustees, Collingswood, 1986—; trustee Health Care Support Found., Inc., 1994—. Sgt. USAF, 1969-71. Mem. Air Conditioning Contractors Am. (pres. 1986-88), Fuel Mchts. Assn. N.J. (pres. 1992-94), Rotary (pres. Collingswood 1980-81). Episcopalian. Avocations: travel, photography. Home: 47 Treaty Elm Ln Haddonfield NJ 08033-3413 Office: 24 Lees Ave Collingswood NJ 08108-1926

MOHRMAN, KATHRYN, academic administrator. Pres. The Colo. Coll., Colo. Springs. Office: Colorado College Office of the President 14 E Cache La Poudre St Colorado Springs CO 80903-3243

MOHRMANN, LEONARD EDWARD, JR., chemist, chemical engineer; b. Winston Salem, N.C., June 14, 1940; s. Leonard E. and Helen (Bean) M.; m. Sue Ross, June 18, 1966; children: Leonard III, Vaden, Nelwyn Ann. BS in Chemistry, U. Tex., 1963; PhD in Chemistry, Fla. State U., 1971; BSChemE, Tex. A&M U., 1980. Tech. lab. coord. Tex. A&M U., College Station, 1971-81, rsch. assoc., 1981-82; chemist, chemical engr. Tex. Dept. Health, Austin,

1982-92, Tex. Water Commn., Austin, 1992-93, Fugro Environ., Inc. formerly Fugro McClelland, Houston, 1993-95, Tex. Dept. Health, Austin, 1995—. Contbr. articles to sci. jours. Active Mathcounts program Tex. Soc. Profl. Engrs., Austin, 1991-92, Jr. Achievement Program, Houston, 1994-95. Recipient Appreciation cert. Tex. Soc. Profl. Engrs., 1993. Achievements include development of Texas regulations for special waste disposal, medical waste handling and disposal, special waste program for municipal waste. Office: Tex Dept Health Bur Labs 1100 W 49th St Austin TX 78756-3101

MOILANEN, THOMAS ALFRED, construction equipment distributor; b. Hancock, Mich., Sept. 3, 1944; s. A. Edward and Elsie E. (Karkanen) M.; m. Kathleen Ann Maibach, Sept. 18, 1965; children: Todd Alan, Karl Edward. Cert., Wayne State U., 1967. Licensed funeral dir., Mich. Funeral dir. Ross B. Northrop & Son, Inc., Redford, Mich., 1967-68; sales mgr. Cloverdale Equipment Co., Oak Park, Mich., 1971; v.p., gen. mgr. Cloverdale Equipment Co., Oak Park, 1972-78, pres., chief exec. officer, bd. dirs., 1978—; pres., chief exec. officer, bd. dirs. Hasper Equipment Co., Muskegon, Mich., 1980—, SunBelt Crane & Equipment, Sarasota, Fla., 1982-90, Armstrong/Cloverdale Equipment Co., Columbia, S.C., 1987-89; pres. Air Cloverdale, Inc., 1996—. Treas., bd. dirs. Livonia Hockey Assn., 1981-82. Mem. Associated Equipment Distbrs. Am. (equipment distbn. com. 1984, lt. dir. region 7 1993), Mich. Constrn. Equipment Dealers Assn. (pres. 1983, 88, 94), Concrete Improvement Bd. (bd. dirs. 1978-79), Kiwanis (bd. dirs. Redford 1967-69, pres. 1969-70), Skyline Club (Southfield, Mich.). Republican. Avocations: hunting, golf, aviation. Home: 18332 Laraugh Dr Northville MI 48167-3504 Office: Cloverdale Equipment Co 13133 Cloverdale St Oak Park MI 48237-3205

MOIR, ALFRED KUMMER, art history educator; b. Mpls., Apr. 14, 1924; s. William Wilmerding and Blanche (Kummer) M. A.B. cum laude, Harvard U., 1948, A.M., 1949, Ph.D., 1953. From instr. to assoc. prof. Newcomb Coll., Tulane U., 1952-62; mem. faculty U. Calif., Santa Barbara, 1962-91, prof. art history, 1964-91, prof. emeritus, 1991—, chmn. dept., 1963-69; dir. Edn. Abroad Program U. Calif., Italy, 1978-80; cons. for acquisitions Isaac Delgado Mus. Art, 1953-57; v.p. Friends La. State Mus., 1959-62, Friends New Orleans Pub. Libr., 1959-62; pres. So. Calif. Art Historians, 1964-66, 67-69; chmn. Tri-Counties Com. to Rescue Italian Art, 1967-68; art historian in residence Am. Acad. Rome, 1969-70, 80; cons. NEH, 1971-78; vis. prof. U. Minn., 1973; hon. curator of drawings U. Calif.-Santa Barbara Art Mus., 1985-94, cons. curator of drawings, 1997—. Author: (with others) Art in Italy, 1600-1700, 1965, The Italian Followers of Caravaggio, 2 vols, 1967, Caravaggio's Copyists, 1976, Caravaggio, 1982, Van Dyck, 1994; editor: (with others) Seventeenth Century Italian Drawings in the Collection of Janos Scholz, 1974, European Drawings in the Santa Barbara Museum of Art, 1976, Regional Styles of Drawing in Italy 1600-1700, 1977, Old Master Drawings from the Feitelson Collection, 1983, Old Master Drawings from the Collection of John and Alice Steiner, 1985, (with others) Van Dyck's Antwerp, 1991. Trustee Santa Barbara Free Sch., 1968-71; gov. Brooks Inst. Art Gallery, 1968-69. Served with AUS, 1943-46. Named hon. alumnus Tulane U., 1963, Outstanding Alumnus of 1993, The Blake Sch., Mpls., 1993. Mem. Coll. Art Assn., Medieval Acad. Am., Soc. Archtl. Historians, Renaissance Acad. Am., Soc. Fellows of Am. Acad. in Rome, Ateneo Veneto (fgn. mem.). Clubs: Harvard (La. pres. 1959-62, Boston), University Calif. at Santa Barbara Faculty (pres. 1968). Office: U Calif Dept Art History Santa Barbara CA 93106

MOISE, EDWIN EVARISTE, mathematician, educator; b. New Orleans, Dec. 22, 1918; s. Edwin Evariste and Annie Josephine (Boatner) M.; m. Mary Lorena Leake, May 28, 1942 (div. 1980); children: Edwin Evariste, Claire Mary. Student, La. State U., 1935-37; BA, Tulane U., 1940; PhD in Pure Math., U. Tex., 1947; MA (hon.), Harvard U., 1960. Instr. math. U. Mich., 1947-49, from asst. prof. to prof. math., 1951-60; James Bryant Conant prof. edn. and math. Harvard U., 1960-71; vis. prof. Centro de Investigación y de Estudios Avanzados, Instituto Politecnico Nacional, Mexico City, 1970-71; Disting. prof. Queens Coll., CUNY, 1971-80, 81-87, now emeritus; Hudson prof. Auburn U., 1980-81; Temp. mem. Inst. Advanced Study, Princeton, 1949-51, 56-57; mem. writing team Sch. Math. Study Group, summers 1958-60. Author: Elementary Geometry from an Advanced Standpoint, 1963, (with Floyd L. Downs, Jr.) Geometry, 1964, Number Systems of Elementary Mathematics, 1965, Calculus: Part I, 1966, Calculus: Part II, 1967, Geometric Topology in Dimensions 2 and 3, 1977, Introductory Problem Courses in Analysis and Topology, 1982. With USNR, 1942-46. Mem. Am. Math. Soc. (mng. editor bull. 1958-63, v.p. 1973-74), Math. Assn. Am. (v.p. 1965, pres. 1967-68), Phi Beta Kappa. Home: 77 Bleecker St Apt 323E New York NY 10012-1553

MOIZE, JERRY DEE, lawyer, government official; b. Greensboro, N.C., Dec. 19, 1934; s. Dwight Moody and Thelma (Ozment) M.; m. Margaret Ann Wooten, Aug. 13, 1976; 1 child, Jerry Dee Jr. AB cum laude, Elon (N.C.) Coll., 1957; JD, Tulane U., New Orleans, 1960; diploma, Army Command & Gen. Staff Sch., USAR, 1981. Bar: Colo. 1961, U.S. Dist. Ct. Colo. 1961, U.S. Ct. Mil. Appeals 1962, U.S. Supreme Ct. 1965, N.C. 1965. Legal clk. Air Def. Commd., Colorado Springs, Colo., 1960-61, assistance officer, 1962-63; chief legal assistance divsn. 2d Army, Ft. Meade, Md., 1964-65; staff JAG, Indiantown Gap Mil. Reservation, 1965; law clk. to hon. Eugen Gordon U.S. Dist. Ct. (mid. dist.) N.C., Winston-Salem, 1965-66; dir. Legal Aid Soc. Forsyth County, Winston-Salem, 1966-69; exec. dir. Forsyth Bail Project, Winston-Salem, 1968-69, Lawyer Referral Svc. of Bar of 21st Jud. Dist., Winston-Salem, 1968-69; staff atty. office of gen. counsel FAA, Washington, 1969-70, acting chief admin. & legal resources, 1970-71; staff atty. office of gen. counsel Dept. Housing & Urban Devel., Washington, 1971; area counsel Jackson (Miss.) field office Dept. Housing & Urban Devel., 1971-83, chief counsel Jackson (Miss.) field office, 1983-94; chief counsel Office Gen. Counsel Miss., Jackson, 1994—; lectr. U. W.Va. Conf. on Poverty Law, 1968. Editor N.C. Legal Aid Reporter, 1968-69, N.C. Legal Aid Directory, 1968, Avlex Legal Index (2d supplement), 1971, developed Miss. low income housing financing mechanism 1975-76; contbr articles to profl. jours., articles to splty. mags. Dem. candidate N.C. Ho. of Reps., Guilford County, 1964; mem. mil. com. Forsyth County N.C. Red Cross, 1967-68; pack leader Andrew Jackson coun. Boy Scouts Am., 1986-92; active Project Adv. Group U.S. Office Econ. Opportunity Legal Svcs. Program, 1968-69, Adv. Com. on Housing & Urban Devel., Miss., Law Rsch. Inst., 1980-81, Pilot Mountain Preservation & Park Com., Winston-Salem, 1968-70; mem. Race Com. Whitworth Hunt Races, 1973-76; Am. Master of Foxhounds Assn., 1976-79. Capt. AUS, 1960-65; ret. lt. col. USAR, 1966-87. Decorated Meritorious Svc. medal, Army Commendation medal with one oak leaf cluster, Army Res. Forces Achievement medal with three oak leaf clusters, Nat. Def. Svc. medal, Armed Forces Res. medal. Mem. Fed. Bar Assn., N.C. State Bar, Miss. Hist. Assn., Miss. Track Club, Iron Bridge Hunt (v.p. 1964-65), Whitworth Hunt (founder, master of foxhounds 1975-76), The Austin Hunt (joint master of foxhounds 1976-79), Caledonian Soc. Miss., Sons of Confederate Vets., Order Eastern Star, Freemasons, Shriners, Pi Gamma Mu. Republican. Episcopal. Avocations: riding to hounds, running, book collecting. Home: Ivanhoe 935 Bellevue Pl Jackson MS 39202 Office: Dept Housing & Urban Devel Miss State Office 9th Fl Fed Bldg 100 W Capitol Jackson MS 39269

MOJICA, AGNES, academic administrator. Chancellor Internat. Am. U. of PR, San German, P.R.; chair governing bd. Hispanic Assn. Colls. and Univs., 1995-96, co-chair leadership group. Mem. Consortium of Presidents and Chancellors for the Prevention of the Use and Abuse of Drugs and Alcohol. Mem. Assn. Industrialists of P.R., Western C. of C., Am. Assn. Higher Edn., Assn. Profl. Women, Club de Roma (P.R. chpt.), Altrusa, Rotary (hon.), Alpha Delta Kappa, Phi Delta Kappa. Office: Inter Am U Office of the Chancellor San German PR 00753

MOJTABAI, ANN GRACE, author, educator; b. N.Y.C., June 8, 1937; d. Robert and Naomi (Friedman) Alpher; m. Fathollah Mojtabai, Apr. 27, 1960 (div. 1966); children: Chitra, Ramin. B.A. in Philosophy, Antioch Coll., 1958; M.A. in Philosophy, Columbia U., 1968, M.S. in L.S., 1970. Lectr. philosophy Hunter Coll., CUNY, 1966-68; librarian CCNY, 1970-76; fellow Radcliffe Inst. Ind. Study, Cambridge, Mass., 1976-78; Briggs-Copeland lectr. in English Harvard U., 1978-83; writer-in-residence U. Tulsa, 1983—, Yaddo Found., Saratoga, N.Y., 1975, 76. Author: Mundome, 1974, The 400 Eels of Sigmund Freud, 1976, A Stopping Place, 1979, Autumn, 1982, Blessed Assurance, 1986, Ordinary Time, 1989, Called Out, 1994. Recipient Richard and Hinda Rosenthal award Am. Acad. and Inst. Arts and Letters, 1983, Lillian Smith award So. Regional Council, 1986, Lit. Acad. award AAAL, 1993; Guggenheim fellow, 1981-82. Mem. PEN, Mark Twain Soc., Tex. Inst. Letters, Phi Beta Kappa. Home: 2102 S Hughes St Amarillo TX 79109-2212 Office: U Tulsa Dept English 600 S College Ave Tulsa OK 74104-3126

MOK, CARSON KWOK-CHI, structural engineer; b. Canton, China, Jan. 17, 1932; came to U.S., 1956, naturalized, 1962; s. King and Chi-Big (Lum) M.; B.S. in Civil Engring., Chu Hai U., Hong Kong, 1953; M.C.E., Cath. U. Am., 1968; m. Virginia Wai-Ching Cheng, Sept. 19, 1959. Structural designer Wong Cho Tong, Hong Kong, 1954-56; bridge designer Michael Baker Jr., Inc., College Park, Md., 1957-60; structural engr., chief design engr., asso. Milton A. Gurewitz Assos., Washington, 1961-65; partner Wright & Mok, Silver Spring, Md., 1966-75; owner Carson K.C. Mok, Cons. Engr., Silver Spring, 1976-81, pres., 1982—; facility engring. cons. Washington Met. Area Transit Authority, 1985-86; pres. Transp. Engring. and Mgmt. Assocs., P.C., Washington, 1986—; adj. asst. prof. Howard U., Washington, 1976-79, adj. assoc. prof., 1980-81; bd. dirs. U.S. Pan Asian Am. C. of C. Sec., N.Am. bd. trustees, China Grad. Sch. Theology, Wayne, Pa., 1972-74, pres., 1975-83, v.p., 1984-91; elder Chinese Bible Ch. Md., Rockville, 1978-80; chmn. Chinese Christian Ch. Greater Washington, 1958-61, 71, elder, 1972-76; dir. Evergreen Family Friendship Svc., Inc., A Pub. Benefit Corp., Palm Springs, Calif., 1993—. Recipient Outstanding Standard of Teaching award Howard U., 1980; registered profl. engr., Md., D.C. Mem. ASCE, ASTM, Constrn. Specification Inst., Nat. Assn. Corrosion Engrs., Concrete Reinforcing Steel Inst., Am. Concrete Inst., Am. Welding Soc., Prestressed Concrete Inst., Post-Tensioning Inst., Soc. Exptl. Mechanics., Internat. Assn. Bridge and Structural Engring., Pui Ching Mid. Sch. Alumni Assn. (pres. nation's capital chpt. 1991—) Contbr. articles to profl. jours. Home: 4405 Bestor Dr Rockville MD 20853-2137 Office: 9001 Ottawa Pl Silver Spring MD 20910-2257

MOKODEAN, MICHAEL JOHN, lawyer, accountant; b. Canton, Ohio, Dec. 24, 1923; s. Michael and Elizabeth (Stroia) M.; m. Jean Cristea, Apr. 17, 1950 (dec.); children: Michael Dan, Christine Ann; m. Josephine Woodward, Jan. 28, 1995. B.S. in Edn, Kent (Ohio) State U., 1948; J.D., William McKinley Sch. Law, Canton, 1955. Bar: Ohio 1955; C.P.A., Ohio. Agt. IRS, Canton, 1950-56; self-employed atty. C.P.A., Canton, 1957-69; tax accountant Elmer Fox & Co., Las Vegas, Nev., 1969; mgr. tax and ins. Diebold, Inc., Canton, 1969-74; sec., house counsel Diebold, Inc., 1974-78, v.p. legal, 1978-87, cons., 1987-89; part-time instr. tax accounting Walsh Coll., N. Canton, 1963-64, bd. advisers, 1976—; bd. advisers Stark Tech. Coll., Canton, 1972-76. Bd. advisers Doctors' Hosp., Massillon, Ohio, 1986-93. With AUS, 1943-46. Mem. Brookside Country Club. Roman Catholic. Home: 2607 Charing Cross Rd NW Canton OH 44708-1588

MOKRASCH, LEWIS CARL, neurochemist, educator; b. St. Paul, May 9, 1930; s. Lewis and Anna (Dvorak) M.; m. Jane Carolyn Church, Apr. 20, 1974. B.S. magna cum laude, Coll. St. Thomas, 1952; Ph.D., U. Wis., 1955. Research assoc. dept. psychiatry and neurology La. State U. Med. Center, New Orleans, 1956-57; assoc. prof. dept. biochemistry La. State U. Med. Center, 1971-76, prof., 1976-92, prof. emeritus, 1992—, acting head dept., 1978-79; instr. medicine U. Kans. Med. Center, Kansas City, 1957-59, assoc. in medicine, dir. neurochemistry lab., 1959-62; asst. biochemist McLean Hosp., Belmont, Mass., 1960-64, assoc. biochemist, 1964-71; assoc. dept. biol. chemistry Harvard Med. Sch., Boston, 1964-67; asst. prof., 1967-71; adj. assoc. prof. biology Hellenic Coll., Brookline, Mass., 1969-71; staff scientist Neurosciences Research Programs, Brookline, 1970-71; vis. prof. neurology Duke U. Med. Center, 1981-82; lectr. in field. Author book written on myelin; contbr. articles to profl. jours.; book reviewer for jours. Sci. and FASEB. Pres. Belmont Preservation Soc., 1969; candidate Bd. Selectman, Belmont, 1969; active Met. Opera Guild, Piedmont Opera Guild, Winston Salem Piedmont Triad Symphony Guild, Reynolda Ho. Mus. Am. Art, Reynolda Gardens, Sr. Svcs. Program, Winston Salem, Citizens Quality Nursing Home Care, 1991-92. Grantee NIMH, 1973-74, Nat. Inst. Neurol. Disability and Blindness, 1957-90, Schlieder Found., 1971-72, 83-84, La. Bd. Regents, 1986-88. Fellow Am. Assn. Clin. Chemists; mem. AAUP, Am. Soc. Neurochemistry (local chmn. 1974), Am. Soc. Biol. Chemists, Soc. Neurosci. (founder, pres. local chpt. 1974-75), Soc. Rsch. Adminstrs. (membership chmn. New Eng. sect.), Nat. Citizens Coalition Nursing Home Reform, Nat. Taxpayers Union, N.C. Taxpayers United, Am. Assn. Individual Investors (founder, past pres. Piedmont chpt.),Peoples Med. Soc. Libertarian. Achievements include first demonstration of adaptive enzyme regulation in animals and allosteric control of fructose bisphosphatase, of incorporation of hydrouracil into transfer RNA, of thermogenic mechanism for arousing hibernators, of metabolic control in hibernation, of altered hydrophobic proteins in neurological disorders, of biosynthesis of hydrophobic proteins and mitochondrial proteins in brain in vitro, of altered transport processes in cells of neurological disease victims, of defective transport of acetylcholine precursors into cells of Alzheimer's victims and that such transport is modulatable; development of coestimation method for ketoses, aldoses, and pentoses; first isolation in pure form of receptor hydrophobic proteins from mammalian brain. Home: 1422 Reynolda Rd Winston Salem NC 27104-1016 *Before I entered Science, I regarded it as a Priesthood of individuals dedicated to the service of humanity, whose common goal was the enhancement of human life and the remedying of its ills. After 30 years in Science, I hold this thesis more strongly and have found many colleagues who agree with it. I am certain now that the failures and abuses of Science derive from the use of it for the goals of wealth, fame and power.*

MOKRISKI, J. CHARLES, lawyer; b. Hartford, Conn., Oct. 14, 1942. BA magna cum laude, Yale U., 1964, MA, 1966, M in Philosophy, 1968, JD, 1971. Bar: Conn. 1972, Mass. 1992. Lawyer Day, Berry & Howard, Boston. Chmn. Hartford Housing Authority, 1976-1980, Office of Arbitration Archdiocese of Hartford, 1976-82; Bd. Trustees St. Thomas More House Catholic Chapel at Yale, 1978—. Mem. Bosto Bar Assn. (vice chmn. ethics com.). Office: Day Berry & Howard 260 Franklin St Ste 21 Boston MA 02110-3112

MOLAND, KATHRYN JOHNETTA, computer scientist, software engineer; b. Tallahassee, Nov. 5, 1961; d. John and Kathryn Vastavia (Gadson) M. BS in Sociology, Fla. A&M U., 1982; MS in Computer Sci., Southern U., 1987; PhD in Info. Systems, Nova Southeastern U., 1997. Programmer, summer intern IBM, Lexington, 1985; mem. tech. staff Bell Communications Rsch., Piscataway, N.J., 1986; programmer Logos Corp., Mount Arlington, N.J., 1987-88, Telecommunications Inds., Vienna, Va., 1988; systems analyst Advanced Tech., Inc., Reston, Va., 1988; project leader Advanced Tech., Inc., Aiken, S.C., 1989-90; sr. systems analyst, project leader Westinghouse Savannah River Co., Aiken, S.C., 1990-94; devel. mgr. SCT Utility Systems, Inc., Columbia, S.C., 1994-97; mng. prin. Metasys Inc., Charlotte, N.C., 1997—; tech. mem. Occurrence Reporting Spl. Interest Group, Oak Ridge, Tenn., 1991-94. Bd. govs. Am. Biog. Inst. Rsch. Assn. Mem. IEEE (treas. 1991-92, vice chair 1992-93, chair 1993-94, mem. tech. coun. software engring.), NAFE, Nat. Mgmt. Assn., Project Mgmt. Inst., Assn. Computing Machinery. Avocations: bowling, tennis, reading. Home: PO Box 981 Irmo SC 29063 Office: Metasys Inc 2550 W Tyvola Rd Charlotte NC 28217-4543

MOLDEN, A(NNA) JANE, retired counselor; b. Weeping Water, Nebr.. BS, Schauffler Coll.; MA, Princeton (N.J.) Theol. Sem. Cert. adminstr., Iowa. Dir. outreach Chgo. City Union; campus minister Iowa Congl Chs., Ames; dir. Christian edn. 1st Congl. Ch., Ames; dir. community outreach Congl. Chs., Kansas City, Mo.; ctrl. regional dir. Am. Friends Svc., Des Moines; dir. acad. support counseling Grand View Coll., Des Moines; dir. Consortium of Higher Edn., Des Moines; mem. Health Planing Coun. Ctrl. Iowa; mem. Gov.'s Vocat. Rehab. Adv. Coun., 1993—mem. Protection and Adv. Pair Adv. Coun., 1993—. Dir. Grand View Coll. Dems., 1971-93; active devel. com. for handicapped HUD, Des Moines; bd. dirs. Plymouth Pl.; mem. Dr. Martin Luther King Com., Des Moines, Internat. Black Children's Conf., Iowa Vocat. Rehab. Coun., Iowa Protection and Adv. Coun.; chair Des Moines Human Rights Commn.; mem. study com. LWV; past pres. Citizens Disability Coun.; mem. community adv. bd. McKinley Sch.; mem. George Washington Carver com. Simpson Coll.; bd. dirs. Bernie Lorenz House, Community Focus, Greater Des Moines YWCA, Christian Ednl. Plymouth Congl. Ch. Named Outstanding Educator Jack and Jill, Inc., Des Moines, Supporting Friend, Learning Disability Coun. Ctrl. Iowa. Mem. AACD, Torch Club Internat. (pres.), Delta Kappa Gamma. Democrat. Mem. United Ch. of Christ. Home: 1611 27th St 212 Des Moines IA 50310

MOLDEN, HERBERT GEORGE, publisher; b. Taunton, Mass., June 14, 1912; s. Ernest William and Edith (Parker) M.; m. Eleanor Caswell, Aug. 26, 1935; children: Marilyn (Mrs. Robert Erb), Parker C. Ph.B., Brown U., 1934. Head history dept. Storm King Sch., Cornwall on Hudson, N.Y., 1934-44; salesman, promotion mgr., exec. editor Macmillan Co., 1944-60; v.p. McCormick-Mathers Pub. Co., Inc., Wichita, Kans., 1960-61; with Am. Book Co., 1961-69, pres., 1968—; pres. Cambridge Book Co., 1970-78, H.G. Molden Co. Inc., Fairfield, Conn., 1978—; v.p., dir. N.Y. Times Media Co., 1971-76. Mem. Phi Beta Kappa.

MOLDENHAUER, JUDITH A., graphic design educator; b. Oak Park, Ill., Feb. 28, 1951; d. Raymond L. and Jean Marie (Carqueville) M. BFA, U. Ill., 1973; MA, Stanford U., 1974; MFA, U. Wis., 1977. Design supr. N.E. Mo. State U., Kirksville, Mo., 1977-79; asst. prof. design, design dept. Kans. City Art Inst., Mo., 1979-83; asst. prof. art, graphic design Sch. Art U. Mich., Ann Arbor, 1983-92; vis. lectr. Wayne State U., 1990-92, asst. prof. graphic design, 1992—, area coord. graphic design, 1992—; free-lance designer The Detroit Inst. Arts, Toledo (Ohio) Mus. Art, Burroughs Corp. (Unisys) Detroit, Detroit Focus Gallery; vis. designer N.S. Coll. Art and Design, 1986; juror Ohio Mus. Assn., 1986, Collaborator Presdl. Initiative "Healthy Start": prenatal and pre-conceptional booklets and ednl. modules designs, 1992—. Contbr. articles to profl. jours. Recipient award of distinction, merit award Am. Assn. Museums, 1985, 86, Excellence Design award Beckett Paper Co., 1991, gold award for softcover books Printing & Pub. Competition, 1994, Am. Graphic Design award, 1996; Rackham grantee U. Mich., 1987, grantee Nat. Endowment for Arts, 1988. Mem. Am. Ctr. Design, Univ. and Coll. Designers Assn. (merit award 1979, gold award 1979), Coll. Art Assn. (chmn. panel 1991), Women's Caucus for Art (panel chmn. 1987), Amnesty Internat., Women in Design (excellence award Chgo. 1985, Sierra Club, Audubon Soc. Lutheran. Office: Wayne State U Dept Art and Art History 150 Art Bldg Detroit MI 48202

MOLDENHAUER, WILLIAM CALVIN, soil scientist; b. New Underwood, S.D., Oct. 27, 1923; s. Calvin Fred and Ida (Killam) M.; m. Catherine Ann Maher, Nov. 26, 1947; children—Jean Ann, Patricia, Barbara, James, Thomas. B.S., S.D. State U., 1949; M.S., U. Wis., 1951, Ph.D., 1956. Soil surveyor S.D. State U., Brookings, 1948-54; soil scientist U.S. Dept. Agr., Big Spring, Tex., 1954-57; soi. scientist U.S. Dept. Agr., Ames, Iowa, 1957-72, Morris, Minn., 1972-75; rsch. leader Nat. Soil Erosion Rsch. Lab., Agrl. Rsch. Svc. U.S. Dept. Agr., West Lafayette, Ind., 1975-85; prof. dept. agronomy Purdue U., West Lafayette, 1975-85, prof. emeritus, 1985—. Contbr. articles to profl. jours. Served with U.S. Army, 1943-46. Fellow Am. Soc. Agronomy, Soil Sci. Soc., Soil Conservation Soc. Am. (pres. 1979), World Assn. Soil and Water Conservation (pres. 1983-85, exec. sec. 1985—). Home and Office: 317 Marvin Ave Volga SD 57071-2011

MOLDOVAN, LEONARD MICHAEL, chemist; b. Bronx, Nov. 2, 1950; s. Michael M. and Anne M. (Piliero) M. BA, NYU, 1974; AAS, Bronx C.C., 1990; AAS in Data Processing. Rschr. laser initiated chem. reactions and coal gasification CCNY Data Processing, N.Y.C., 1974; tutor phys. chemistry Bronx C.C., N.Y.C., 1975-76; researcher CCNY Phys. Dept., N.Y.C., 1977-80; computer aide Mayor's Office Bus. Devel., N.Y.C., 1983; chemist JAcob-Winston Labs., N.Y.C., 1984; computer aide N.Y.C. Transit Authority, Bklyn., 1985; office aide III N.Y.C.E.R.S., 1986-93; tutor Cert. Tutoring Svc., Bklyn., 1994-93. Mem. exec. com. Benjamin Franklin Dem. Club, 1993—. Regents scholar. Mem. AAAS, Am. Chem. Soc., N.Y. Acad. Scis., I.U.P.A.C. Roman Catholic. Avocations: chess, horseback riding, snow mobiling, water skiing, tennis. Home: 234 Naples Ter Apt 4A Bronx NY 10463-5426

MOLE, RICHARD JAY, accounting company executive; b. Berea, Ohio, Aug. 10, 1951; s. Wells Warren Jr. and Helen Irene (Buse) M.; m. Kathleen Ann Brennan, Oct. 28, 1978; children: Kevin Michael, Eileen Anne. BBA, U. Notre Dame, 1973; MBA, U. Pitts., 1974. CPA, Ohio, Pa.; CMA, CFM. Staff acct. James P. Ross, CPA, Elyria, Ohio, 1974-75; mgr. acctg. Dean J. Benshoff, PA, Mogadore, Ohio, 1975-77, John P. Hyland, CPA, Cleve., 1980; fin. adminstr. St. Joseph Ch. and Sts. Joseph and John Interparochial Sch., Strongsville, Ohio, 1977-80; v.p., contr. Citadel Alarm, Inc. div. Revco Drug Stores, Inc., Cleve., 1980-82; pres. Richard J. Mole, CPA, Inc., Andover, Ohio, 1982—; instr. Lorain County Cmty. Coll., 1975. Chmn. bldg. com., v.p. Andover Pub. Libr., 1983—; mem. Ashtabula County Bd. Mental Retardation, Ashtabula, Ohio, 1987-89; chmn. fin. com. parish coun. Our Lady of Victory Cath. Ch., Andover, 1985-90; bd. dirs. Ashtabula County 503 Corp., 1986-92, pres., 1990-92; bd. dirs. Ashtabula County Revolving Loan Fund, 1986-92, pres., 1990-92; treas. Civic Devel. Corp. Ashtabula County, 1994—; mem. Leadership Ashtabula County, 1989, grad. charter class; bd. dirs. Pymatuning Area Indsl. Devel. Corp., Andover, pres., 1986-88, 93-94; chmn. Andover Twp. Zoning Commn., 1989-94, mem., 1995, sec., 1996; treas. Andover Civic Improvement Corp., 1992-96, pres., 1996-97; treas. Andover Found., Inc., 1993—; coach, mgr. Pymatuning Area Youth Orgn., 1987-91, 95, pres., 1991-92. Recipient leadership award Civic Devel. Corp., Ashtabula, 1985, Quality of Living award Pymatuning Area Indsl. Devel. Corp., 1986, Best of County award Ashtabula County Growth Partnership, 1992, Leadership award State of Ohio, 1993. Fellow AICPA, Ohio Soc. CPAs, Pa. Inst. CPAs; mem. Nat. Assn. Accts., Rotary Internat. (bd. dirs. Andover 1984—, pres. 1985-86, 96-97, treas. 1988-96, Paul Harris fellow 1993), Andover C. of C. (v.p. 1983-85, treas. 1985-87). Republican. Office: Richard J Mole CPA Inc 124 S Main St Andover OH 44003-9601

MOLEN, JOHN KLAUMINZER, lawyer; b. Gary, Ind., June 13, 1952; s. Franklin B. and Jane Anne (Klauminzer) M.; m. Susan Wilson Blair, Aug. 10, 1985; children: Mary Wilson, Elisabeth Blair. AB with honors, U. N.C., 1974, MBA, 1978, JD with honors, 1978. Bar: Ala. 1978. Assoc. Bradley Arant Rose & White LLP, Birmingham, Ala., 1978-84; ptnr. Bradley, Arant, Rose & White, Birmingham, Ala., 1984—. Mem. Rotary Club Birmingham-Sunrise. Presbyterian. Avocations: sailing, swimming. Office: Bradley Arant Rose & White LLP 2001 Park Pl Ste 1400 Birmingham AL 35203-2700

MOLER, EDWARD HAROLD, lawyer; b. Oklahoma City, May 26, 1923; s. Harold Stanley and Rosemary (Callahan) M.; m. Donna Blocksom Cram, Sept. 12, 1964; children: John Frederick, Shelley Elizabeth, Christopher Bryan. BA, U. Okla., 1947, LLB, 1948. Bar: Okla. 1948, U.S. Supreme Ct. 1951. Pvt. practice law Oklahoma City, 1948-52, 61—, asst. mcpl. counselor, 1952-59, mcpl. counselor, 1959-61; spl. justice Okla. Supreme Ct., 1977. Trustee Oklahoma City Mcpl. Improvement Authority, 1960-61; bd. dirs. Mummers Theatre, Inc., 1969—; bd. dirs. Greater Oklahoma City YMCA, 1981-91. 2d lt. USAAF, 1943-45. Mem. ABA, Okla. Bar Assn., Oklahoma County Bar Assn. (bd. dirs. 1963-67, pres. 1968), Rotary, Phi Delta Phi, Phi Gamma Delta (pres. local chpt. 1946, pres. Nu Omega Housing Assn. 1963-65). Home: 2540 NW Grand Blvd Oklahoma City OK 73116-4110 Office: City Pl Oklahoma City OK 73102

MOLER, ELIZABETH ANNE, federal agency administrator, lawyer; b. Salt Lake City, Jan. 24, 1949; d. Murray McClure and Eleanor Lorraine (Barry) M.; m. Thomas Blake Williams, Oct. 19, 1979; children: Blake Martin Williams, Eleanor Bliss Williams. BA, Am. U., 1971; postgrad., Johns Hopkins U., 1972; JD, George Wash. U., 1977. Bar: D.C. 1978. Chief legis. asst. Senator Floyd Haskell, Washington, 1973-75; law clk. Sharon, Pierson, Semmes, Crolius & Finley, Washington, 1975-76; profl. staff mem. com. on energy and natural resources U.S. Senate, Washington, 1976-77, counsel, 1977-86, sr. counsel, 1987-88; commr. FERC, Washington, 1988-93, chair, 1993—. Mem. ABA, D.C. Bar Assn. Democrat. Home: 1537 Forest Ln Mc Lean VA 22101-3317 Office: FERC 888 1st St NE Ste 11A Washington DC 20426-0001

MOLER, JAMES CLARK, marketing research executive; b. West Union, Ohio, Nov. 17, 1930; s. Joseph Adam and Kathryn Susan (Clark) M.; m. Barbara Lucille Painter, Sept. 14, 1953 (div. 1973); children: Kathy, James. BBA, U. Cin., 1953. Various positions Burgoyne, Inc., Cin., 1956-

62, v.p. client svc., 1962-65, exec. v.p., 1965-69; pres. J.C. Moler and Assocs., Cin., 1969-71, B&B Rsch. Svcs., Inc., Cin., 1971—. Lt. USN, 1953-56. Mem. Am. Mktg. Assn., Mkgt. Rsch. Assn. Avocations: woodworking, stamp collecting, tennis. Office: B&B Rsch Svcs Inc 8005 Plainfield Rd Cincinnati OH 45236-2500

MOLES, RANDALL CARL, orthodontist; b. Gary, Ind., Mar. 13, 1946; s. Ben and Sonia Moles; children: Brant Randall, Justin Hunter, Joelle Renae, Alexandria Rosemarie. DDS, Marquette U., 1970, MS, 1974. Lic. orthodontist; diplomate Am. Acad. Pain Mgmt. Pvt. practice Racine, Wis., 1974—, Milw., 1993—; asst. prof. orthodontics Marquette U., Milw., 1974-76; internat. lectr. orthodontics TMJ. Author: Ending Head and Neck Pain: The TMJ Connection, 1989; inventor Seacure custom scuba mouthpiece; exec. prodr. Windchill Prodns. Lt. USPHS, 1972-74. Mem. ADA, Am. Assn. Orthodontists, Wis. Soc. Orthodontists (pres. 1994-95), Ill.-Wis. Orthodontic Study Club (pres. 1990-91), Racine County Hist. Soc. (dir., pres. 1990-91), Rotary Internat. (dir., pres. local chpt. 1995-96). Avocations: sailing, skiing, diving, reading. Office: 5801 Washington Ave Racine WI 53406-4057

MOLFENTER, DAVID P., electronics executive; b. 1945. CEO Hughes Def. Comm., Fort Wayne, Ind. Office: Hughes Def Comm 1313 Production Rd Fort Wayne IN 46808-1164*

MOLGAT, GILDAS L., Canadian government official; b. Ste. Rose du Lac, Man., Can., Jan. 25, 1927; s. Louis and Adele (Abraham) M.; m. Allison Malcom, July 31, 1958; children: Anne Marie, Mathurin Paul. B.Comm. with honors, U. Man., 1947. Elected M.L.A. Man., 1953, re-elected, 1958, 59, 62, 1966, 69; leader Liberal Party in Man., 1961-68, leader opposition, 1961-68; summoned to Senate of Can., 1970—, dep. spkr., 1983-84, 89-91, spkr., 1994—; joint chmn., spl. joint com. Senate and House of Commons on constn. of Can., 1971, on Reform of the Senate of Can., 1982; apptd. dep. leader Opposition in Senate, 1991, dep. leader govt., 1993, chmn. com. of whole on Meech Lake Constnl. Accord, 1987-88, task force on Meech Lake Constnl. Accord and Yukon and N.W. Territories, 1987-88, chmn. submissions group, 1988; chmn. Man. Lib. Fed. campaign, 1972; govt. whip, 1973; elected pres. Liberal Party of Can., 1973. Founding chmn. St. Boniface Hosp. Rsch. Found., 1971. Served with Royal Winnipeg Rifles, 1946-66, hon. lt. col., 1966, hon. col., 1985. Mem. Royal United Svcs. Inst. Man. (hon. pres. 1990), Army, Navy and Air Force Vets. of Can. (Winnipeg Unit #1 hon. pres. 1992), Man. Army Cadet League (founding pres. 1971), Army Cadet League Can. (pres. 1977-79), Can. Corps Commissionaires, Royal Can. Legion, Société Franco-Manitobaine, St. Andrew's Soc. Roman Catholic. Office: Spkr Senate of Canada, Parliament Bldg Rm 280-F Ctr Block, Ottawa, ON Canada K1A 0A4

MOLHO, EMANUEL, publisher; b. N.Y.C., Jan. 27, 1936; s. Isaac Emanuel and Alvira (Altchek) M.; m. Brenda Nadel, Sept. 25, 1965; children—Deborah Rochelle, Brian Emanuel. B.A., N.Y. U., 1957; M.B.A., Wharton Sch., U. Pa., 1960. Pres. French & European Publs., Inc., N.Y.C., 1961—, French & Spanish Book Corp., 1967—; pres. Librairie de France, Inc., 1961—. Recipient Orden de Merito Civil Spain, 1975. Mem. Am. Booksellers Assn., French-Am. C. of C. in U.S. (exec. com.), Paris Am. Club. Office: Librairie de France Rockefeller Center Promenade 610 5th Ave New York NY 10020-2403

MOLHOLM, KURT NELSON, federal agency administrator; b. Denver, June 24, 1937; s. Ervin Maurice and Helen Pauline (Nelson) M.; m. Sonja Dell Williams, Aug. 17, 1967; children: Kevin William, Paul Nelson. BS, U. Oreg., 1959; MS, George Washington U., 1974; grad., Indsl. Coll. Armed Forces, 1974. Computer specialist D.L.A. Adminstrv. Support Ctr., Alexandria, Va., 1963-65; with Hdqrs. Def. Logistics Agy., Alexandria, 1965-85, chief planning and policy office, 1975-76, chief ADP/T tech. div., 1984-85; adminstr. Def. Tech. Info. Ctr., Alexandria, 1985—; pres. Nat. Fedn. Abstracting and Info. Svcs., Phila., 1993-94, treas., 1990-93; del. Va. Govs. Conf. Librs. Info. Svcs., 1990, Fed. Libr. Pre-White House Conf. On Librs. Info. Sci., 1990; vice chmn. Fed. Libr. and Info. Ctr. Com., 1992-93; chmn. Commerce, Energy, NASA, NLM, Def. Info. Group, 1991-94; mem. NATO Agard Tech. Info. Panel, 1985-91, Internat. Coun. Sci. and Tech. Info., 1993—, Info. Infrastructure Task Force, 1993—. 1st lt. U.S. Army, 1960-63. Recipient Meritorious award William A. Jump Meml. Found., 1973. Methodist. Office: Ctr 8725 John J Kingman Rd Fort Belvoir VA 22060-6218

MOLHOLT, PAT, academic administrator, associate dean; b. Fond du Lac, Wis., Oct. 19, 1943; d. Elmore Harrison and Leona Ann (Reschke) Leu; divorced; children: Rebecca Marie, Stephanie Anne. BS, U. Wis., 1966, MLS, 1970; PhD, Rensselaer Poly. Inst., 1996. Library intern Milw. Pub. Library, 1966-67; astronomy librarian, dept. astronomy U. Wis., Madison, 1970-73; physics librarian U. Wis. Libraries, Madison, 1973-77; asst. prof., dir. U. Wyo. Sci. and Tech. Library, Laramie, 1977-78; assoc. dir. Rensselaer Poly. Inst. Libraries, Troy, N.Y., 1978-92, affirmative action advisor to pres., 1988-92; asst. v.p., assoc. dean scholarly resources Columbia U., N.Y.C., 1992—; co-dir. art and architecture thesaurus program J. Paul Getty Trust, Williamstown, Mass., 1983-86; rsch. analyst U.S. Dept. Edn., Washignton, 1987-88; pres. Universal Serials and Book Exch., 1988-89; trustee Capital Dist. Libr. Coun., 1986-89; bd. visitors U. Pitts. Sch. Libr. and Info. Studies, 1993-95; mem. adv. bd. libr. sci. program Wayne State U., Detroit, 1992-95; mem. IBM Higher Edn. Custome Adv. Coun., 1995—; mem. Biomed. Libr. rev. com. Nat. Libr. of Medicine, 1995—. Contbr. articles to profl. jours. Mem. adv. bd. Sch. Info. and Pub. Policy, SUNY-Albany, 1989; mem. steering com. N.Y. Gov.'s Conf. on Libr. and Info. Svcs., 1989-90; active N.Y. State Regent's Vis. Com. on State Archives, 1991—. Fellow Spl. Librs. Assn. (pres. 1983-84, John Cotton Dana award 1989); mem. ALA, NSF (mem. adv. bd., divsn. networking comm. rsch. and infrastructure 1991-92), Am. Soc. Info. Sci. (chair tech. program com. mid-yr. meeting, 1994). Office: Columbia U Health Scis 701 W 168th St Rm 201 New York NY 10032-2704

MOLINA, MARIO JOSE, physical chemist, educator; b. Mexico City, Mexico, Mar. 19, 1943; came to U.S., 1968; s. Roberto Molina-Pasquel and Leonor Henríquez; m. Luisa Y. Tan, July 12, 1973; 1 child, Felipe. Bachillerato, Acad. Hispano Mexicana, Mexico City, 1959; Ingeniero Químico, U. Nacional Autónoma de México, 1965; postgrad., U. Freiburg, Fed. Republic Germany, 1966-67; Ph.D., U. Calif., Berkeley, 1972. Asst. prof. U. Nacional Autónoma de México, 1967-68; research assoc. U. Calif.-Berkeley, 1972-73; research assoc. U. Calif.-Irvine, 1973-75, asst. prof. phys. chemistry, 1975-79, assoc. prof., 1979-82; sr. rsch. scientist Jet Propulsion Lab., 1983-89; prof. dept. earth, atom and planet sci., dept. chemistry MIT, Cambridge, 1989—, Martin prof. atmospheric chemistry. Recipient Tyler Ecology award, 1983, Esselen award for chemistry in pub. interest, 1987, Max-Planck-Forschungs-Preis, Alexander von Humboldt-Stiftung, 1994, Nobel Prize in Chemistry, 1995. Mem. NAS, Am. Chem. Soc., Am. Phys. Soc., Am. Geophys. Union, Pres.'s Com. on Advisors on Sci. and Tech., Sigma Xi. Achievements include discovering the theory that fluorocarbons deplete ozone layer of stratosphere. Home: 8 Clematis Rd Lexington MA 02173-7117 Office: MIT Dept of EAPS 77 Massachusetts Ave # 54-1312 Cambridge MA 02139-4301 *We have to understand our environment to find out if we are tampering with it. One of our accomplishments has been to call attention to society's potential altering of the atmosphere.*

MOLINARI, SUSAN, congresswoman; b. S.I., N.Y., Mar. 27, 1958; d. Guy V. and Marguerite (Wing) M.; m. Bill Paxon, 1994. BA, SUNY, Albany, 1980, MA, 1982. Former intern for State Senator Christopher Mega; former rsch. analyst N.Y. State Senate Fin. Com.; former fin. asst. Nat. Rep. Gov.'s Assn.; ethnic community liaison Rep. Nat. Com., 1983-84; minority leader N.Y.C. Council, 1986-90; mem. 101st-104th Congresses from 14th (now 13th) N.Y. dist., 1990—; vice-chair House Rep. Conf., mem. budget com., chmn. transp. and infrastructure subcom. on railroads. Roman Catholic. Office: US Ho of Reps 2411 Rayburn HOB Washington DC 20515

MOLINARO, VALERIE ANN, lawyer; b. N.Y.C, Oct. 21, 1956; d. Albert Anthony and Rosemary Rita (Zito) M.; m. Howard Robert Birnbach; 1 child, Michelle Annalise Birnbach. BA with honors, SUNY, 1978; JD, Syracuse U., 1980, MPA, 1980. Asst. counsel. New York State Housing Finance Agy., N.Y.C., 1980-82; assoc. counsel, asst. secy. N.Y. State Urban Devel. Corp., N.Y.C., 1982-85; assoc. Mudge Rose Guthrie Alexander & Ferdon, N.Y.C., 1985-87, Bower & Gardner, N.Y.C., 1988, Hawkins, Delafield & Wood, N.Y.C., 1988-91; of counsel McKenzie, McGhee & Harper, N.Y.C., 1991—. Author: Am. Bar Assn. Jour., 1981. Mem. N.Y.C. Commn. on Status of Women, 1995—. Mem. N.Y. State Bar Assn., (tax exempt fin. com.), Assn. Bar City of N.Y., Nat. Assn. Bond Lawyers, N.Y.C. Commn. on the Status of Women (legis. chmn.). Office: McKenzie McGhee et al 888 7th Ave Ste 1809 New York NY 10019-3201

MOLINDER, JOHN IRVING, engineering educator, consultant; b. Erie, Pa., June 14, 1941; s. Karl Oskar and Carin (Ecklund) M.; m. Janet Marie Ahlquist, June 16, 1962; children: Tim, Karen. BSEE, U. Nebr., 1963; MSEE, Air Force Inst. Tech., 1964; PhD EE, Calif. Inst. Tech., 1969. Registered profl. engr., Calif. Project officer Ballistic Systems Div., Norton AFB, Calif., 1964-67; sr. engr. Jet Propulsion Lab., Pasadena, Calif., 1969-70; prof. engrng. Harvey Mudd Coll., Claremont, Calif., 1970—; prin. engr. Qualcomm Inc., 1996-97; part-time lectr. Calif. State U., Los Angeles, 1970-74; mem. tech. adv. panel Kinemetrics, Pasadena, 1985-86; part-time mem. tech. staff Jet Propulsion Lab., Pasadena, 1974—, rep. NASA Hdqrs., Washington, 1979-80; vis. prof. elec. engrng. Calif. Inst. Tech., 1982-83. Contbr. articles to profl. jours. Served to capt. USAF, 1963-67. Mem. IEEE. Avocations: bicycling, reading, computers. Office: Harvey Mudd Coll Dept of Engrng 301 E 12th St Claremont CA 91711-5901

MOLINE, JON NELSON, philosopher, educator, college president; b. Ft. Worth, May 12, 1937; s. Paul Ross and Elsie Virginia (Nelson) M.; m. Sandra Lois Reininger, Aug. 13, 1960; children: Kevin, Eric. AB, Austin Coll., 1960, LHD, 1995; PhD, Duke U., 1964. Asst. prof. U. Wis., Madison, 1964-69, assoc. prof., 1969-73, prof. philosophy, 1973-86, prof. environ. studies, 1974-86, nat. humanities faculty advisor, 1976-82; v.p., dean St. Olaf Coll., Northfield, Minn., 1987-94; pres. Tex. Luth. U., Seguin, 1994—; vis. asst. prof. U. Ill., Chgo., 1969; vis. assoc. prof. U. Tex., Austin, 1971-72; fellow Nat. Humanities Ctr., 1979-80. Pres. Madison Symphony Orch., 1975-77; bd. dirs. Fund for Improvement Post-Secondary Edn., 1985-91; mem. Nat. Coun. on the Humanities, 1991—, vice-chair, 1993—. Vis. fellow Inst. for Research in Humanities, 1973, 75-76; Spencer Found. fellow, 1974; Rockefeller Found. humanities fellow, 1975-76. Office: Texas Lutheran Univ 1000 W Court St Seguin TX 78155-5978

MOLINE, SANDRA LOIS, librarian; b. San Antonio, Dec. 13, 1938; d. Udo F. and Olivia Marie (Link) Reininger; m. Jon Nelson Moline, Aug. 13, 1960; children: Kevin, Eric. BA in Chemistry, Austin Coll., 1960; postgrad., Duke U., 1962-64; MA in History of Sci., U. Wis., 1976, MLS, 1977. Tchr. chemistry and physics Durham (N.C.) High Sch., 1960-64; head physics libr. U. Wis., Madison, 1977-88; head reference svcs. Sci. and Engrng. Libr. U. Minn., Mpls., 1988-94; libr., assoc. prof. Luth. Univ., Seguin, 1994—. Bd. dirs. Mid-Tex. Symphony, 1995—; trustee Seguin-Guadalupe County Pub. Libr., 1996—. Mem. Spl. Librs. Assn. (physics, astronomy, math, sci.-tech. divsns.), Librs. Assembly (sec., treas. 1980, pres. 1983), Madison Acad. Staff Assn. (steering com. 1980-83, pres. 1982). Home: 605 Fleming Dr Seguin TX 78155-3413

MOLINEAUX, CHARLES BORROMEO, lawyer, arbitrator, columnist, poet; b. N.Y.C., Sept. 27, 1930; s. Charles Borromeo and Marion Frances (Belter) M.; m. Patricia Leo Devereux, July 2, 1960; children: Charles, Stephen, Christopher, Patricia, Peter, Elizabeth. BS cum laude, Sch. Fgn. Service, Georgetown U., 1950; JD, St. John's U., N.Y.C., 1959. Bar: N.Y. 1959, Mass. 1981, D.C. 1988. Assoc., then ptnr. Nevius, Jarvis & Pilz and successor firms, N.Y.C., 1959-77; ptnr. Gadsby & Hannah, N.Y.C., 1978-80; v.p., gen. counsel Perini Corp., Framingham, Mass., 1980-87; pvt. practice, Washington, 1987—; mem. adj. faculty Internat. Law Inst., Washington, 1989—. Author numerous poems. Committeeman Republican Party, Nassau County, N.Y., 1965-71, Fairfax County, Va. Mem. exec. com., 1969. Served to 1st lt. U.S. Army, 1954-56. Fellow Am. Bar Found.; mem. ASCE, Am. Arbitration Assn. (constrn. ADR task force 1994—), Chartered Inst. Arbitrators, Fedn. Internat. des Ingénieurs-Conseils (Assoc. Gen. Contractors del. constrn. contract com., Louis Prangey award for svc. to profession cons. engrng. 1996), Del. Hist. Soc., London Ct. Internat. Arbitration, Fellowship Cath. Scholars. Roman Catholic. Home: 8321 Weller Ave McLean VA 22102-1717 Office: 8100 Boone Blvd Vienna VA 22182-2642

MOLINO, THOMAS MICHAEL, retired career military officer; b. Bklyn., Feb. 16, 1947; s. Angelo Thomas and Jean (Tepedino) M.; m. Mary Ellen Thomas, June 3, 1973; children: T. Andrew, Sara Catherine. BA, St. Peter's Coll., 1968; MA, Loyola U., 1979. Commd. 2d lt. U.S. Army, 1968, advanced through ranks to col.; comdr. HHT 11th Cavalry Regiment U.S. Army, Dian, Vietnam, 1970-71; cmdr. 2d Squadron 2d Cavalry Regiment U.S. Army, Bamberg, Germany, 1983-85; spl. asst. to vice chmn. Joint Chiefs of Staff, Pentagon, 1987-89; exec. asst. to cmdr. in chief U.S. Army Europe U.S. Army, Heidelberg, Germany, 1990-93; cmdr. 2d Cavalry Regiment U.S. Army, Ft. Lewis, Wash. and Ft. Polk, La., 1992-94; chief strategic planning U.S. Army, Washington, 1995-96, ret., 1997; sr. def. analyst Sci. Applications Internat. Corp., 1997—. Decorated DSM, Def. Superior Svc. medal, 3 Legion of Merit awards, 2 bronze stars for combat, Republic of Vietnam Honor medal, Air medal, others. Mem. Assn. U.S. Army, U.S. Armor Assn., VFW, Army-Navy Country Club. Roman Catholic. Avocation: golf. Office: 1710 Goodridge Dr Mc Lean VA 22102-3701

MOLINOFF, PERRY BROWN, biologist, science administrator; b. Smithtown, N.Y., June 3, 1940; s. Henry Charles and Thelma (Brown) M.; m. Marlene Sirota, 1963; children: Jeffrey, Sharon. BS, Harvard U., 1962, MD, 1967. Intern U. Chgo. Hosp. & Clinics, 1967-68; research assoc. NIMH, Bethesda, Md., 1968-70; vis. fellow Univ. Coll., London, 1970-72; asst. prof. U. Colo. Health Sci., Denver, 1972-76; assoc. prof. U. Colo. Health Sci., 1976-80, prof., 1980-81; A.N. Richards prof., chmn. U. Pa., Phila., 1981-94; v.p. C.N.S. Drug Discovery Bristol-Myers Squibb, Wallingford, Conn., 1995—. Editor: Basic Neurochemistry, 1989, Biology of Normal and Abnormal Brain Function, 1990, Goodman and Gilman: The Pharmacological Basis of Therapeutics, 1996; editl. adv. bd. Molecular Pharmacology, 1976—. Med. adv. bd. Dysautonomia Found., 1977—. Lt. comdr. USPHS, 1968-70. Mem. Soc. Neurosci. (membership com., treas.), Am. Heart Assn. (rsch. com.), John Morgan Soc. (sec.-treas. 1988—), Pa. Heart Assn. Home: 10 Broad St Weston CT 06883-2911 Office: Bristol-Myers Squibb 5 Research Pkwy PO Box 5100 Wallingford CT 06492-7600

MOLINSKY, BERT, tax consultant; b. Bronx, N.Y., Feb. 25, 1938; s. Joseph and Ida G. (Rosenberg) M.; m. Donna L. Thurman, June 26, 1964; children: Avery, Lucy, Lois, Sarah. Student, U. Ariz., 1956-61, Diablo Valley Coll., 1986-88, Calif. State U., Hayward, 1988-92. CFP; CLU; ChFC; Enrolled Agt. Field supt. INA Life, Phoenix, 1968-72; regional life mgr. Sentry Life Ins. Co., Oklahoma City, 1972-73, Mpls., 1973-75, San Francisco, 1975-78; mgr. Acacia Mutual Life, Oakland, Calif., 1978-80; gen. agt. Am. United Life, Concord, Calif., 1980-82; owner East Bay Triple Check Tax Svcs., Walnut Creek, Calif., 1982—, Triple Check Tax and Fin. Svc., Peoria, Ariz., 1993—; instr. Golden Gate U. CPD, San Francisco, 1983-93, Mt. Diablo Sch. Dist., Concord, 1986-93; faculty Coll. for Fin. Planning, Denver, 1983—; bd. dirs. Triple Check Licensee Coun. Contbr. articles to profl. jours. Nat. dir. U.S. Jaycees, Phoenix, 1967; pres. Bnai Brith Coun. of Lodges, San Francisco, 1986. With USNR, 1955-72. Named Jaycee of Yr. Ariz. Jaycees, 1967. Fellow Nat. Tax Practice Inst.; mem. Enrolled Agts., East Bay Assn Life Underwriters (pres. 1985-86), Nat. Assn. Enrolled Agts., Peoria Sunset Lions (pres. 1996—), Ariz. State Enrolled Agts. Assn. (v.p. 1996—). Avocation: sports. Office: Plaza Del Rio Ctr 9401 W Thunderbird Rd Ste 140 Peoria AZ 85381-4817 also: PO Box 100 Peoria AZ 85380-0100

MOLITOR, GRAHAM THOMAS TATE, lawyer; b. Seattle, Apr. 6, 1934; s. Robert Franklin and Louise Margaret (Graham) M.; m. Carlotta Jean Crate, July 30, 1960; children: Graham Thomas Tate, Anne Therese, Christopher Robert. BS, U. Wash., 1955; LLB, Am. U., 1963. Bar: D.C. 1963. Rsch. asst. U. Wash., Seattle, 1957; bailiff U.S. Criminal Ct. D.C., 1958-59; legis. counsel U.S. Ho. of Reps., Washington, 1961-63; dir. candidate rsch. Rockefeller for Pres. Com., 1963-64, 68; D.C. counsel, asst. dir. govt. rels. Nabisco, Inc., Washington, 1964-70; dir. govtl. rels. Gen. Mills, Inc., Washington, 1970-77; pres., CEO Pub. Policy Forecasting, Inc., Potomac, Md., 1977—; prin. ptnr. Pub. Policy Communicators, 1989-91; prin., ptnr. Pub. Policy Action Inst., Potomac; adv. bd. Creative Bus. Strategies, Inc.; adj. prof. Grad. Sch. Bus., Am. U., Washington, 1969-75, 79-85, Montgomer Coll., Rockville, Md., 1987-88; dir. rsch. White House Conf. on Indsl. World Ahead, 1971-72; mem. White House Adv. Com. on Social Indicators, 1975-76; chmn. Commn. on the Future of Montgomery County, 1986-88; guest lectr. numerous univs.; del. White House Confs. on Food, Nutrition and Health, 1969-71, White House Conf. on Youth, 1970; bd. dirs. First Global Conf. on the Future, Inc., Can., 1980—. Contbg. editor Food Tomorrow Newsletter, 1976-77; co-editor, chmn. editl. bd. Ency. of the Future, 1991-96; chmn. editl. bd. Future Survey, 1995—; mem. bd. editors Hudson Inst. Study of World Food Problems, 1975-77; mem. editl. bd. Bus. Tomorrow Newsletter, 1977-79; mem. bd. advisors New Mktg. Techs. Monitor, 1983-85; polit. editor: On the Horizon, 1993-95; contbr. articles to profl. jours. Mem. Food Adv. Bd., N.Y.C., 1980-86. Served to 1st lt. U.S. Army, 1958-61. Recipient Disting. Service award Grocery Mfrs. Am., 1973-74, Disting. Service award Nat. Consumer Info. Center, 1974, Disting. Service award Am. Mgmt. Assn., 1975. Mem. Washington Bus.-Govt. Rels. Coun., Washington Indsl. Roundtable, E.D. Export Coun., World Future Soc. (gen. chmn. 2d Gen. Assembly 1975, v.p., dir. 1981-94, v.p., legal counsel 1994—, Disting. Svc. award 1975), Univ. Club, Phi Kappa Sigma, Phi Alpha Delta. Republican. Presbyterian. Home and Office: 9208 Wooden Bridge Rd Rockville MD 20854-2416

MOLITOR, KAREN ANN, lawyer; b. Chgo., Apr. 20, 1953; d. Edward William and Elizabeth M. (Schmolke) Swanson; m. Patrick John Molitor, Apr. 26, 1971; children: Elizabeth Ann, Patrick John Jr. BS with honors, U. Ark., 1986, JD, 1990. Bar: Conn. 1990, U.S. Dist. Ct. Conn. 1990, U.S. Ct. Appeals (2d cir.) 1994. Assoc. atty. Shipman & Goodwin, Hartford, Conn., 1990-93; asst. atty. gen. Conn. Atty. Gen.'s Office, Storrs, Conn., 1993-94; gen. coun. The Meadows Music Theatre, Hartford, 1994—; gen. counsel Martin Media, Hartford, Conn., 1996—. Mem. ABA, Conn. Bar Assn., Nat. Assn. Coll. and Univ. Attys., Phi Beta Kappa. Roman Catholic. Avocations: bicycling, reading, physical fitness. Home: 28 Sunset Ter West Hartford CT 06107-2738 Office: Martin Media 32 Midland St Windsor CT 06095-4334

MOLITOR, SISTER MARGARET ANNE, nun, former college president; b. Milford, Ohio, Sept. 19, 1920; d. George Jacob and Mary Amelia (Lockwood) M. B.A., Our Lady of Cin. Coll., 1942; M.Ed., Xavier U., 1950; LL.D.; M.A., Catholic U. Am., 1963, Ph.D., 1967. Joined Sisters of Mercy, 1943; tchr. elementary schs. Cin., 1946-50, secondary schs., Cin. and Piqua, Ohio, 1951-60; faculty Edgecliff Coll., Cin., 1962-73; pres. Edgecliff Coll., 1973-80; archivist Cin. Province Sisters of Mercy; research cons. various religious communities. Bd. dirs. Citizens Com. on Youth; trustee Chatfield Coll., Clermont Mercy Hosp., Mercy St. Theresa Retirement Ctr.; mem. Area Coun. Planning Task Force, Cin. Community Devel. Adv. Coun.; pres. Better Housing League of Greater Cin. Recipient Woman of Year award Cin. Enquirer, 1977, 200 Greater Cincinnatians Bicentennial award, 1988. Mem. Greater Cin. Consortium Colls. and Univs. (pres. 1980). Address: 2335 Grandview Ave Cincinnati OH 45206-2219

MOLITOR, MICHAEL A., entrepreneur, consultant; b. Bklyn., Nov. 7, 1965; s. Henry J. and Janet A. (Monti) M.; m. Michele A. Emery, July 8, 1995. BS, Siena Coll., 1987. Cert. Fin. Planner, Accredited Tax Prepared. Fin, aid counselor Janet's Coll. Tuition Aid, Massapequq Park, N.Y., 1987-92; income tax acct. Michael A. Molitor, Massapequa, N.Y., 1988—; owner, fin. aid counseling svc. Molitor Coll. Aid Counseling, Massapequa, 1992—; money mgr. Molitor Money Mgmt., Massapequa, 1992—; cons. Alive-To-Thrive, Inc., Westchester, N.Y., 1992—, cons., adv. bd. Orphan's Aid Soc., Douglaston, N.Y., 1994—. Author: You Can Afford A College Education, 1992; contbr. articles to profl. jours., various TV talk shows. Con. to Guidance Dept. Massapequa Sch. Dist., Massapequa, 1998—, mem. Long Island Assn., Hauppauge, N.Y., 1990-92. Recipient Top Producer-Pres. Club Transamerica Funds, Houston, 1993, 94, mem. signature Club Oppenheimer Funds, Denver, 1995. Mem. Internat. Assn. Fin. Planning, N.Y. Fin. Air Adminstr. Assn., NAt. Assn. Fin. Aid Adminstr., BMW Car Club Am., Porsche Club Am. Mem. Christian Ch. Avocation: golf, drumming, track driving. Office: Molitor Money Mgmt Inc 5550 Merrick Rd Ste 305 Massapequa NY 11758-6238

MOLITOR, PAUL LEO, professional baseball player; b. St. Paul, Aug. 22, 1956; m. Linda Kaplan; 1 child, Blaire. Student, U. Minn., 1975-77. With Milw. Brewers, 1978-92, Toronto Blue Jays, 1992-95, Minnesota Twins, Mpls., 1996—; mem. Am. League All-Star Team, 1980, 85, 88, 91-94. Named Am. League Rookie of Yr. Sporting News, 1978, Sporting News Coll. All-America Team, 1977; recipient Silver Slugger award, 1987, 88, 93, World Series MVP award, 1993, Midwest League MVP award. Office: Minnesota Twins 34 Kirby Puckett Pl Minneapolis MN 55415-1523*

MOLITORIS, BRUCE ALBERT, nephrologist, educator; b. Springfield, Ill., June 26, 1951; s. Edward and Joyce (Tomasko) M.; m. Karen Lynn Wichterman, June 16, 1973; children: Jason, Jared, Julie. BS, U. Ill., 1973, MS in Nutrition, 1975; MD, Wash. U., 1979. Resident Sch. Medicine U. Colo., Denver, 1979-81, nephrology fellow, 1981-84, asst. prof. medicine, 1984-88, assoc. prof. medicine, 1988-93, prof., 1993; dir. nephrology Ind. U. Med. Sch., Indpls., 1993—; vis. scientist U. Colo., MCDB, Boulder, 1989-90, Max Planck Inst., Federal Republic of Germany, 1984-85; NIH reviewer, 1991-94; dir. home dialysis Denver VA Ctr., 1984-93. Mem. editl. bd. Am. Jour. Physiology, 1989—, Am. Jour. Kidney Diseases, 1991, Am. Jour. Kidney Disease, 1996; assoc. editor Jour. Ivnestigative Medicine, 1994—; contbr. articles to profl. jours. Pres. Cherry Creek Village South Homeowners Assn., 1989-90; v.p. Our Father Luth. Ch., Denver, 1989-90; coach Cherry Creek Soccer Assn., Greenwood Village, 1988-91, Centennial little league Titans Basketball; bd. dirs. CSSA, 1993. Recipient Upjohn Achievement award, 1979, Liberty Hyde Bailey award, 1973. Mem. Am. Soc. Nephrology, Internat. Soc. Nephrology, N.Y. Acad. Sci., Am. Soc. Clin. Investigation, Am. Fedn. for Clin. Rsch. (nat. counselor 1991-94), Western Assn. Physicians. Avocations: bridge, fishing, antiques, hiking. Office: Indiana Univ Med Ctr Fesler Hall 115 1120 South Dr Indianapolis IN 46202-5135*

MOLITORIS, JOLENE M., federal agency administrator. BA, Cath. U. Am.; MA, Case Western Res. U. From asst. liaison officer to exec. dir. Ohio Rail Transp. Authority, 1977-83; dep. dir. Ohio Dept. Transp., 1984-92; adminstr. Fed. Railroad Adminstrn., Washington, 1993—; former chair Region 1 Nat. Conf. State Rail Ofcls. Recipient Pres. award for outstanding achievement Maglev/High Speed Rail Assn., 1989, 92. Office: Fed Railroad Adminstrn 1120 Vermont Ave NW Fl 7 Washington DC 20005-3523*

MOLL, CLARENCE RUSSEL, retired university president, consultant; b. Chalfont, Pa., Oct. 31, 1913; s. George A. and Anna A. (Schmidt) M.; m. Ruth E. Henderson, Nov. 19, 1941; children: Robert Henderson, Jonathan George. BS, Temple U., 1934, EdM, 1937; LHD, Pa. Mil. Coll., 1949; PhD, NYU, 1955; LLD, Temple U., 1963; ScD, Chungang U., Seoul, Korea, 1969; LLD, Swarthmore Coll., 1970, Gannon U., 1981; LittD, Delaware Valley Coll., 1976; Ped D, Widener U., 1981. Instr. physics and chemistry Conshohocken (Pa.) H.S., 1935-37; instr. sci. Freehold (N.J.) H.S., 1937-38; instr. physics, chemistry Meml. H.S., Haddonfield, N.J., 1938-42; instr. electronics and radar USN, Phila., 1942-43; assoc. prof. physics and elec. engrng. Pa. Mil. Coll., Chester, Pa., 1943-45; registrar, coord. engrng. program Pa. Mil. Coll., 1945-47, dean admissions, student pers., prof. edn., 1947-56, v.p., dean pers. svcs., 1956-59, pres. coll., 1959-72; pres. Widener U. (formerly PMC Colls.), 1972-81, chancellor, 1981-88, pres. emeritus, 1988—; pres. RC Assocs., Inc., 1981—; instr. electronics Temple U., 1944-46; headmaster Pa. Mil. Prep. Sch., 1945-47; bd. dirs. Fedders Corp., Ironworkers Savs. Bank. Contbr. numerous mag. articles. on history of Pa. Mil. Coll. Chmn. Pa. Commn. Ind. Colls., 1969, Found. for Ind. Colls. Pa., 1970; chmn. Com. for Financing Higher Edn. in Pa., 1975; trustee Pa. Inst. Tech., 1985—; commr. Am. Assn. Homes for Aging Cont. Care Accrediting Commn., 1985-95. Recipient Horatio Alger award, 1962, Disting. Alumnus award Temple U., 1964, B'nai B'rith Citizen Service award, 1966, Distinguished Citizen award, 1971, Themis award Del. County Bar, 1976, Good Citizenship award Phila. Bar, 1976, Exec. of Yr. award Soc. Advancement Mgmt., 1978. Mem. Assn. Mil. Colls. and Schs. (pres. 1969), Pa. Assn. Colls. and Univs. (chmn. 1970, Sheepskin award 1982), Am. Soc. Engrng. Edn., Springhaven Club (Wallingford, Pa.), Univ. Club (Wilmington, Del.), Tau Beta Pi, Phi Delta Kappa,

Alpha Sigma Lambda, Phi Kappa Phi. Lutheran. Home: 1960 Dog Kennel Rd Media PA 19063-1008 Office: Widener U Pres Emeritus Office Chester PA 19013

MOLL, CURTIS E., manufacturing executive; b. 1933. Diploma, Wesleyan Coll., 1961, So. Meth. U., 1963. Chmn., CEO MTD Products Inc. Office: MTD Products Inc PO Box 368022 Cleveland OH 44136*

MOLL, JOHN LEWIS, electronics engineer, retired; b. Wauseon, Ohio, Dec. 21, 1921; s. Samuel Andrew and Esther (Studer) M.; m. Isabel Mary Sieber, Oct. 28, 1944; children: Nicolas Josef, Benjamin Alex, Diana Carolyn. B.Sc., Ohio State U., 1943, Ph.D., 1952; Dr. h.c., Faculty Engring., Katholieke U. Leuven, (Belgium), 1983. Elec. engr. RCA Labs., Lancaster, Pa., 1943-45; mem. tech. staff Bell Telephone Labs., Murray Hill, N.J., 1952-58; mem. faculty Stanford U., 1958-69, prof. elec. engring., 1959-69; tech. dir. optoelectronics Fairchild Camera and Instrument Corp., 1969-74; dir. integrated circuits labs. Hewlett-Packard Labs., Palo Alto, Calif., 1974-80; dir. IC structures research, sr. scientist Hewlett-Packard Labs., 1980-87, dir. Superconductivity Lab., 1987-90, mem. tech. staff, 1990-96; ret., 1996. Author: Physics of Semi Conductors, 1964; co-author Computer Aided Design and VLSI Device Development, 1985, rev. edit., 1988; inventor (with Ebers) first analytical transistor model, 1953, still valid and useful for circuit design. Recipient Howard N. Potts medal Franklin Inst., 1967, Disting. Alumnus award Coll. Engring., Ohio State U., 1970, Benjamin C. Lamme medal Coll. Engring., Ohio State U., 1988, Vladimir Karapetoff award Eta Kappa Nu, 1995; Guggenheim fellow, 1964. Fellow IEEE (Ebers award 1971, Thomas A. Edison medal 1991), Am. Acad. Arts and Scis.; mem. Am. Phys. Soc., Nat. Acad. Engring., Nat. Acad. Scis., N.Y. Acad. Scis. Home: 1 W Edith Ave #A105 Los Altos CA 94022-2711

MOLL, JOSEPH EUGENE, chemical engineer, chemical company executive; b. Evansville, Ind., Sept. 3, 1950; s. Jacob Eugene and Mary Ann (Zenthoefer) M., m. Karen Jean Pennington, Aug. 20. 1977; children: Laura, Angela, Jared. BS in Chem. Engring., Purdue U., 1972. Cert. ofcl. USS Swimming. Mem. mfg. mgmt. staff GE, Selkirk, Danville, N.Y., Ill, 1972-74; product devel. engr. GE, Pittsfield, Mass., 1974-75; tech. specialist Betz Labs., Kokomo, Ind., 1975-78; account mgr. Betz Labs., Evansville, Ind., 1978-88; account exec. Betz Indsl., Evansville, 1988-90, area mgr., 1990—; mem. Mayor's Tech. Adv. Com., Mt. Vernon, Ind., 1983—. Instr. ARC, Evansville, 1971-73; ofcl. Ill. High Sch. Assn., Danville, 1972-73; min. of the word St. Matthew's Ch., Mt. Vernon, Ind., 1980—; amb. Promise Keepers Men's Ministry, 1994—, Sunday sch. tchr., 1996—; asst. cubmaster Boy Scouts Am., 1993-96, asst. scoutmaster, 1997—. Mem. AICE (v.p. 1971-72), Tech. Assn. of Pulp and Paper Industry, Am. Water Works Assn., Purdue Alumni Assn. (life), John Purdue Coaches Club, Elks, Omega Chi Epsilon, Triangle Fraternity. Roman Catholic. Avocations: golf, weight tng., swimming, bible study group. Home: 28 Parkridge Dr Mount Vernon IN 47620-9405 Office: Betzdearborn 2843 Brownsboro Rd Ste 111 Louisville KY 40206-1274

MOLL, LLOYD HENRY, banker; b. Reading, Pa., June 26, 1925; s. Lewis J. and Katie (Rothermel) M.; m. Luise G. Keiper, Oct. 25, 1947; children: Lloyd E., Darryl M. BA, Albright Coll., Reading, 1952. Aircraft engine installer War Dept., 1942-47; tire inspector Firestone Tire & Rubber Co., Pottstown, Pa., 1947-48; asst. mgr. Household Fin. Corp., Reading, 1952-57; v.p. Meridian Asset Mgmt. Inc. and Meridian Trust Co. (formerly Am. Bank & Trust Co. of Pa.), Reading, 1957-94; v.p. sales and mktg. Investors Trust Co., Wyomissing, Pa., 1995—; co-founder, past dir. Estate Planning Council of Berks County. Served with AUS, 1945-47. Mem. Am. Inst. Banking. (dir., chmn. bank relations Berks County chpt., pres. 1972-73), Toastmasters (pres. Reading club 1992), Optimists (pres. Reading club 1978-79). Democrat. Home: 213 W 39th St Crestwood Reading PA 19606 Office: Investors Trust Co 2201 Ridgewood Rd #180 Wyomissing PA 19610-1190 *Although it has been known to fail me on occasion I try to live by my understanding of the "Golden Rule". When it does fail me I'm usually able to discount such failure by recounting in my mind the many times it has been a two-way street or by convincing myself that I didn't try hard enough in this particular instance. All too often it comes to me much later that the other fellow's interpretation of the "Golden Rule" was far superior to mine. When this happens I have added to my learning. When it does not happen, it forces me to try that much harder to avoid "PERFECTION".*

MOLLARD, JOHN DOUGLAS, engineering and geology executive; b. Regina, Sask., Can., Jan. 3, 1924; s. Robert Ashton and Nellie Louisa (McIntosh) M.; m. Mary Jean Lynn, Sept. 18, 1952; children: Catherine Lynn, Jacqueline Lee, Robert Clyde Patrick. BCE, U. Sask., 1945; MSCE, Purdue U., 1947; PhD, Cornell U., 1952; LLD (hon.), U. Regina, 1995, U. Regina, 1995. Registered profl. engr., profl. geologist Sask., Alta. and B.C., Can. Resident constrn. engr. Sask. Dept. Hwys and Transp., 1945; grad. asst. Purdue U., West Lafayette, Ind., 1946-47; rsch. engr. sch. civil engring. Cornell U., Ithaca, N.Y., 1950-52; air surveys engr., soil and water conservation and devel. Prairie Farm Rehab. Adminstrn., Govt. of Can., 1947-50; chief, airphoto analysis and engring. geology divsn. Prairie Farm Rehab. Adminstrn., Govt. of Can., Regina, 1953-56; pres. J.D. Mollard and Assocs. Ltd., Regina, 1956—; aerial resource mapping surveys tech. adv. Colombo plan, Govts. Ceylon and Pakistan, 1954-56; advisor Shaw Royal Commn. on Nfld. Agr.; Disting. lectr. series Ea. Can. Geotech. Soc., 1969; Cross Can. disting. lectr. Can. Geotech Soc., 1993; C.J. Mackenzie Disting. Grad. Meml. lectr. Coll. Engring. U. Sask., 1994; guest lectr., vis. lectr., instr. over 50 short courses on remote sensing interpretation aerial photos and satellite imagery numerous univs., cities and provinces in Can., also Cornell U., Ithaca, N.Y., Harvard U., Cambridge, Mass., U. Calif., Berkeley, U. Wis., Madison, U. Hawaii, 1952—. Author: Landforms and Surface Materials of Canada, 7 edits.; co-author: Airphoto Interpretation and the Canadian Landscape, 1986; contbr. over 100 articles to profl. pubs. Organizer, canvasser United Appeal campaigns; former bd. dirs. Regina Symphony Orch. Recipient Engring. Achievement award Assn. Profl. Engrs. Sask., 1984, Massey medal Royal Can. Geog. Soc., 1989. Fellow ASCE, Geol. Soc. Can., Geol. Soc. Am., Am. Soc. Photogrammetry and Remote Sensing (award for contbns. airphoto interpretation and remote sensing 1979), Internat. Explorers Club; mem. Engring. Inst. Can. (Keefer medal 1948), Assn. Cons. Engrs. Can., Can. Geotech. Soc. (1st R.M. Hardy Meml. Keynote lectr. 1987, Thomas Roy award with engring. geology divsn. 1989, R.F. Legget award 1992), Regina Geotech. Soc., Geol. Soc. Sask., Can. Soc. Petroleum Engrs., Regina YMCA (former dir.), Rotary (former dir. Regina club). Mem. United Ch. of Can. Avocations: jogging, reading, golf, tennis, nature study. Home: 2960 Retallack St, Regina, SK Canada S4S 1S9 Office: JD Mollard/Assoc 810 Avord Tower, 2002 Victoria Ave, Regina, SK Canada S4P 0R7

MOLLEN, EDWARD LEIGH, pediatrician, allergist and clinical immunologist; b. Richmond, Va., May 13, 1946; s. Irving Roth and Ruth (Damsky) M.; m. Mary Viola Jeffrey, Dec. 14, 1975; children: Shawn, Michael, Eric, Christopher. BS in Chemistry, Coll. William and Mary, 1968; MD, Med. Coll. Va., 1972. Diplomate Am. Bd. Pediatrics, Am. Bd. Allergy and Immunology. Resident in pediatrics Med. Coll. Va., Richmond, 1972-75, fellow in allergy and immunology, 1975-77; practice allergy and pediatric allergy and clin. immunology Allergy Assocs. of Richmond, 1977-85; pvt. practice allergy/pediatric allergy and clin. immunology Richmond, 1985—. Fellow Am. Acad. Allergy and Immunology, Am. Acad. Pediatrics; mem. Med. Soc. Va., Richmond Acad. Medicine, Am. Thoracic Soc., Va. Allergy Soc. Avocations: bicycling, running, gardening. Office: 5855 Bremo Rd Ste 702 Richmond VA 23226-1926

MOLLENAUER, LINN FREDERICK, physicist; b. Washington, Pa., Jan. 6, 1937. B of Engring. Physics, Cornell U., 1959; PhD in Physics, Stanford U., 1965. Asst. prof. physics U. Calif., Berkeley, 1965-72; rsch. staff mem. Bell Labs./Lucent Techs., Holmdel, N.J., 1972—. Co-editor: (with J.C. White) Tunable Lasers, 1987. Recipient Rank prize in Photonics, 1991, Ballantine medal Franklin Inst., 1986. Fellow AAAS, IEEE, Optical Soc. Am. (R.W. Wood prize 1982, Charles Hard Townes award 1997), Am. Phys. Soc.; mem. NAE. Office: Bell Labs Lucent Technologies Rm 4C-306 Crawfords Corner Rd Holmdel NJ 07733

MOLLER, HANS, artist; b. Wuppertal-Barmen, Germany, Mar. 20, 1905; came to U.S., 1936, naturalized, 1944; s. Ernst and Auguste (Heer) M.; m. Helen Rosenblum, Feb. 28, 1933. Student, Art Sch., Barmen, Germany, 1919-27, Berlin Acad., 1927-28. tchr. graphic design and painting Cooper Union, N.Y.C., 1944-56. One man shows include Bonestell Gallery, N.Y.C., 1942-43, Arts Club Chgo., 1945, U. Mich., 1945, Kleeman Galleries, N.Y.C., 1945, 47, 48, 49, 50, Pen and Palette Gallery, St. Louis, 1949, Grace Borgenicht Gallery, N.Y.C., 1951, 53, 54, 56, Fine Arts Assocs., 1957, Otto Gerson Gallery, 1960, Albert Landry Gallery, N.Y.C., 1962, Midtown Gallery (now Midtown Payson Galleries), 1964, 67, 70, 73, 76, 79, 81, 84, 87, Allentown Art Mus., Pa., 1969, 80, 93, Norfolk Mus., Va., 1970, Muhlenberg Coll., Allentown, 1977, Lehigh U., 1977, Madison (Conn.) Gallery, 1987, Hobe Sound (Fla.) Gallery, 1989, Baum Sch. Art, Allentown Art Mus., 1995, Torsteu Bröhan Gallery, Düsseldorf, Germany, 1995; exhibited in group shows at Colby Coll., F.A.R. Coll., Durand-Ruel Galleries, N.Y.C., Nierendorf Gallery, N.Y.C., Pa. Acad., Phila., Chgo. Art Inst., Whitney Mus. and Met. Mus., N.Y.C., Nat. Acad. N.Y., Bklyn. Mus., Corcoran Gallery, Washington, Va. Mus. Fine Arts, Richmond, Walker Art Center, Mpls., Worcester Mus., Mass., Phila. Print Club, Nat. Inst. Arts and Letters, N.Y.C., Maine Coast Artists, Rockport, 1991, Forty Years Maine Painting, 1952-92; included in, Mass. Pepsi Cola Show, N.Y.C., 1946; represented in permanent collections NAD, N.Y.C, Pa. Acad., Phila., The Michener Found., Mus. Modern Art, N.Y.C., Bklyn. Mus., Nat. Gallery Victoria, Australia, Staedtisches Mus., Wuppertal, Fed. Republic Germany, Walker Art Center, Mpls., Yellowstone Art Center, Billings, Mont., Phillips Meml. Gallery, Washington, Whitney Mus., N.Y.C., Detroit Inst. Art, Cummer Gallery, Jacksonville, Fla., N.Y. Pub. Library, Allentown Art Mus., Princeton U., Butler Inst. Am. Art, Youngstown, Ohio, Sunrise Found., Charleston, W.Va., Portland Mus. Art, Maine, Guggenheim Mus., N.Y.C., Nat. Mus. Am. Art, Washington, Va. Mus. Fine Art, Richmond, also univ. assns., pvt. collections, retrospective exhbn., 1926-56, 1956-62, Olsen Found. at U. Bridgeport, Bennington Coll., Dartmouth Coll., Trinity Coll., Mt. Holyoke Coll., Middlebury Coll., U. Vt., Portland Sch. Art, Bates Coll., U. Maine. Recipient first purchase prize Nat. Religious Art Exhbn., 1964, Edwin Palmer Meml. prize N.A.D., 1968, 80, Samuel Finley Breese Morse medal, 1969, Murry Kupferman prize Audubon Artists, 1973, Andrew Carnegie prize N.A.D., 1974, Hibbard Meml. award, 1975, purchase prize Childe Hassam Fund, 1966, 70, 76, 1st prize and merit medal Butler Inst. Am. Art, 1978, Edwin Palmer Meml. prize Nat. Acad. N.Y., 1980, 92, Andrew Carnegie prize, 1985. Mem. NAD, Audubon Artists Inc. (Gold medal and prize 1992). Home: 2207 W Allen St Allentown PA 18104-4327*

MOLLIGAN, PETER NICHOLAS, lawyer; b. New Orleans, Mar. 8, 1938; s. Peter Nicholas and Violet Augusta (Scheeler) M.; children: Liza J., Jessica L., Rene N. BA, La. State U., 1960; JD, San Francisco Law Sch., 1970. Bar: Calif. 1970. Claims mgr. Govt. Employees Ins. Co., San Francisco, 1963-70; trial atty., pres., CEO Molligan, Cox & Moyer, San Francisco, 1970—; pro-tem judge San Francisco Supreme Ct., 1989—. Lt. (j.g.) USN, 1960-65. Fellow Am. Coll. Trial Lawyers; mem. Am. Bd. Trial Advocates, Nat. Bd. Trial Advocates, ATLA, Calif. Trial Lawyers Assn. Avocations: tennis, chess. Office: Molligan Cox & Moyer 703 Market St San Francisco CA 94103-2102

MOLLMAN, JOHN PETER, book publisher, consultant electronic publishing; b. Belleville, Ill., Feb. 8, 1931; s. Kenneth John and Maurine (Farrow) M.; children—Sarah Chase, Eric Cleburne. BA, Washington U., St. Louis, 1952. Advt. specialist Gen. Electric Co., Schenectady and Boston, 1952-54; mgr. Enterprise Printing Co., Millstadt, Ill., 1956-66; gen. mgr. Monarch Pub. Co., N.Y.C., 1966-67; dir. prodn. Harper & Row Pubs., N.Y.C., 1967-74; pub. Harper's Mag. Press, N.Y.C., 1971-74; v.p. prodn. Random House Inc., N.Y.C., 1974-81; sr. v.p. World Book-Childcraft Inc., Chgo., 1981-88; pres. World Book Pub., 1988-91; pub. cons., 1991-92; dir. intellectual property devel. Multimedia Publishing Microsoft, 1992-96; cons. in electronic pub. Carmel, Calif., 1996—. Mem. vis. com. Washington U.; mem. pub. com. Art Inst. Chgo. With U.S. Army, 1954-56. Mem. Assn. Am. Pubs., Siwanoy Club (Bronxville, N.Y.), Sigma Delta Chi, Omicron Delta Kappa. Unitarian. Home: 25340 Vista Del Pinos Carmel CA 93923

MOLLO, JOHN, film costume designer, military historian; b. London, Mar. 18, 1931; s. Eugene Simonovitch and Ella Clara (Cockell) M.; m. Margaret Ann Mollo, Apr. 4, 1956 (div. 1966); m. Louise Alexandra Mary Mollo, Aug. 12, 1968; 1 child, Thomas Frederick George. Student, Farnham Sch. Art, 1947-49. Ptnr. Hist. Rsch. Unit, London, 1964-70, Mollo Publs., London, 1970-90, John Mollo Assocs., Hungerford, Eng., 1981—. Costume designer for films Star Wars, 1977 (Academy award best costume design 1977), Alien, 1978, The Empire Strikes Back, 1978, Outland, 1980, Gandhi, 1982 (Academy award best costume design 1982), The Lords of Discipline, 1982, Greystoke, 1983, King David, 1984, Revolution, 1985, Cry Freedom, 1986, White Hunter, Black Heart, 1989, Chaplin, 1991, Rudyard Kipling's Jungle Book, 1994, Event Horizon, 1996, others; mil. adviser The Jewel in the Crown, 1981; hist. advisor The Charge of the Light Brigade, Barry Lyndon, others; author: Military Fashion, 1972, Uniforms of the American Revolution, 1975,. Acting capt., Inf. Brit. Army, 1950-56, Hong Kong and Eng. Recipient Acad. award for Star Wars, 1978, for Gandhi, 1982, also 2 nominations, 5 nominations Brit. Acad. Film and TV Arts. Mem. Soc. for Army Hist. Rsch., Acad. Motion Picture Arts and Scis. Avocations: painting, listening to music, collecting watercolors and militaria.

MOLLO-CHRISTENSEN, ERIK LEONARD, oceanographer; b. Bergen, Norway, Jan. 10, 1923; came to U.S., 1951, naturalized, 1955; s. Axel and Helga (Holmboe) Mollo-C.; m. Johanna D. Waller, Nov. 20, 1948; children—Jan E., Peter E., Anne. S.B. in Aero. Engring, Mass. Inst. Tech., 1948, S.M., 1949, Sc.D., 1954. With Norwegian Def. Research Establishment, 1949-51, sr. sci. officer, 1951; grad. student, then research assoc. Mass. Inst. Tech., 1951-55, prof. aeronautics, 1955-84, prof. meteorology, 1964-73, prof. oceanography, 1973-84; chief oceanography divsn. NASA/Goddard Space Flight Ctr., 1983-90, assoc. dir. earth scis., 1990-91, ret., 1991; cons. to industry, from 1955. Guggenheim fellow, 1957. Fellow Am. Phys. Soc.; mem. AIAA (Von Karman award 1970), Am. Meteorol. Soc., Am. Geophys. Union., Am. Acad. Arts and Scis. Home: 10 Barberry Rd Lexington MA 02173-8026

MOLLOFF, FLORENCE JEANINE, speech and language therapist; b. St. Louis, Aug. 28, 1959; d. Lawrence Allan and Rietta Gertrude (Fiegenbaum) M. BS, Fontbonne Coll., St. Louis, 1983; MEd summa cum laude, Nat. Louis U., St. Louis, 1989; student, Project ACCESS Inst., 1992, Judevine Ctr. Autistic Children Tng., 1992. Cert. speech correctionist, Mo. Intern St. Louis State Sch. for Profoundly Retarded, 1983-84; speech therapist St. Louis Pub. Schs., 1984—; Judvine Ctr. for Autistic Children Tng., 1992; speech/lang. therapist St. Louis Pub. Schs./Autism Program, 1992-93; speech/lang. therapist Michael Sch. Medically Fragile and Multiply Handicapped Michael Sch. Medically Fragile and Multiply Handicapped, 1993-96; speech, lang. therapist St. Louis Pub. Schs./Michael Sch. for Medically Fragile and Multiply Handicapped, 1993—; ednl. cons. program devel. Mo. Coalition for Environ., St. Louis, Columbia, Kansas City, 1990—; cons., trainer in puppetry Kids on the Block, St. Louis Pub. Schs., 1988—; vol. grant writer West End Restoration Corp.; speech/lang. therapist Mid. Sch. for Medically Fragile and Multiply Handicapped, 1993-96. Author, creator transition curriculum: Consultative Resource Program, 1989; creator puppet program: Save Our Astonishing Plantet, 1990; ednl. cons. program devel. young St. Louis audiences (adapted program for severe to profoundly handicapped children "Arabian Nights", 1994; editor: Strides Newsletter, St. Louis, 1996—; contbr. artist St. Louis Internat. Jazz Mus.; vol. grant writer West End Restoration Corp. Educator, lobbyist Coalition for the Environ., St. Louis, 1990; activist, lobbyist Housing Now, St. Louis, 1989; foster parent Christian Children's Fund, 1986—; activist Habitat for Humanity Internat., 1994—; mem., fundraiser Gateway I Have a Dream Found., 1995—; mem. nat. steering com. (hon.) Pres. Clinton's Re-election, 1995; contbg. mem. Dem. Nat. Com., 1995—; vol. grant writer West End Restoration Corp.; mem. Emily's List. Mem. AAUW, Coun. Exceptional Children (state rep. Mo. divsn. for children with communicative disorders 1988-89, presenter nat. conv. 1989), Internat. Platform Assn., Am. Fedn. Tchrs. (bldg. rep. 1992), Nat. Arbor Day Found., Nat. Parks and Conservation Assn., Nat. Women's Polit. Caucus, Mo. Assn. for Augmentative Comm. Systems, Met. St. Louis Women's Polit. Caucus, Emily's List, Am. Med. Writers Assn., Soc. for Technical Communication, NEA (editor Strides newsletter 1996—, grantee Internet project, elected sec. 1997—), Mo. NEA, Amnesty Internat. Democrat. Avocations: puppetry, profl. clowning, running track, film, debate, graphic arts. Home: 9823 Lullaby Ln Saint Louis MO 63114-2510

MOLLOHAN, ALAN B., congressman, lawyer; b. Fairmont, W.Va., May 14, 1943; s. Robert H. and Helen (Holt) M.; m. Barbara Whiting, Aug. 7, 1976; children: Alan, Robert, Andrew, Karl, Mary Kathryn. AB in Polit. Sci., Coll. William and Mary, 1966; JD, W.Va. U., 1970. Assoc. law firm, 1970-82; mem. 98th-104th Congresses from 1st W.Va. dist., 1983—; mem. appropriations com., budget com. Mem. ABA, W.Va. Bar, Moose, Elks. Baptist. Office: US Ho of Reps Office of Postmaster 2346 Rayburn Ho Office Bldg Washington DC 20515

MOLLOY, JOSEPH A., professional sports team executive; b. Mar. 13, 1961; m. Jessica Molloy; children: Elizabeth, Jennifer, Robert Joseph. Grad., St. Leo Coll. Educator, coach St. Lawrence Cath. Sch., Tampa; with N.Y. Yankees, 1987—, sec./treas., v.p., 1989-92, chief adminstrv. officer, gen. ptnr., 1992—. Office: NY Yankees Yankee Stadium E 161st St & River Rd Bronx NY 10451*

MOLLOY, SYLVIA, Latin American literature educator, writer; b. Buenos Aires, Argentina, Aug. 29, 1938; came to U.S. 1967; d. Herbert Edward and Margarita Berta (Chasseing) M. Licence es Lettres, U. Paris, 1960, Diplome D'Etudes Superieures, 1961, Doctorat de U. Paris, 1967. Asst. prof. Spanish SUNY, Buffalo, 1967-69; asst. prof. Spanish Vassar Coll., Poughkeepsie, N.Y., 1969-70; asst. prof. Spanish Princeton U., Princeton, N.J., 1970-73, assoc. prof., 1973-81, Emory L. Ford prof., 1981-86; prof. Spanish Yale U., New Haven, 1986-90; ALbert Schweitzer prof. of Humanities NYU, 1990—. Author: La Diffusion de la Litterature Hispanoamericaine en France, 1972, Las Letras de Borges, 1979, En Breve Carcel, 1981, At Face Value: Autobiographical Writing in Spanish America, 1991; co-author Women's Writing in Latin America, 1991; author short stories and contbr. articles to profl. jours.; cons., editorial bd. Revista Iberoamericana, 1979-81, 1985—, Latin Am. Literary Rev., 1985—, Revista de Filología, Buenos Aires, 1985—. fellow Am. Philos. Soc., 1970, NEH, 1976; Social Sci. Research Council grantee, 1983; Guggenheim Found. fellow, 1986-87. Mem. MLA, Asociacion Internacional de Hispanistas, Instituto Internacional de Literatura Iberoamericana.

MOLNAR, DONALD JOSEPH, landscape architecture educator; b. Springfield, Ill., Dec. 24, 1938; s. Joseph and Mabel Irene (Woods) M.; m. Carol Jeanette Smith, Aug. 22, 1958; children: Elaina Deanne, Amy Lynn, Holly Suzanne. BFA in Landscape Architecture, U. Ill., 1960, MFA in Landscape Architecture, 1964. Landscape architect Simonds and Simonds, Pitts., 1961-63; landscape architect campus planning U. Ill., Urbana, 1963-72; asst. dir., planner capital programs U. Ill., Urbana and Chgo., 1971-81; assoc. prof. landscape architecture Purdue U., West Lafayette, Ind., 1981-85, dir. landscape architecture coop. program, 1983—, prof. landscape architecture, 1985—, chair landscape architecture program, 1987—, dir. internat. exch. landscape architecture, 1988—; cons. to architect, engrs., park agys., 1964—, MObile Homes Mfr. Assn., Chgo., 1966-76. Author: Anatomy of a Park, 2d edit., 1986; illustrator: Anatomy of a Park, 1971, Visual Approach to Park Design, 1980; developer software CompuPave, 1992. Mem., program coord. Champaign (Ill.) Devel. Coun., 1966-78. Named Hon. Parks Commr., Champaign Park Dist., 1981. Fellow Am. Soc. Landscape Architects (licensing com. Ill. chpt. 1968-70, registration com. Ind. chpt. 1982-85, pres. 1991-92, award 1982). Avocations: travel, computers. Office: Purdue U Landscape Architecture Prog 1165 Horticulture Bldg West Lafayette IN 47907-1165

MOLNAR, THOMAS, philosophy of religion educator, author; b. Budapest, Hungary, June 26, 1921; s. Alexander and Aurelie (Blon) M. M.A. in French Lit., Université de Bruxelles, 1948, M.A. in Philosophy, 1948; Ph.D., Columbia U., 1952; PhD honoris causa, U. Mendoza (Argentina), 1986. Prof. French and world lit. Bklyn. Coll., 1957—; prof. philosophy of religion U. Budapest, 1991—; adj. prof. European intellectual history L.I. U., 1967—; guest prof. polit. philosophy Potchefstroom U., South Africa, 1969; guest prof. philosophy Hillsdale Coll., Mich., 1973-74; vis. prof. Yale U., 1983; vis. prof. philosophy U. Dijon, France, 199p; prof. philosophy of religion U. Budapest, 1991—, permanent vis. prof. philosophy of religion dept. philosophy, 1991—. Author: Bernanos, His Political Thought and Prophecy, 1960, The Future of Education, 1961, The Decline of the Intellectual, 1962, The Two Faces of American Foreign Policy, 1962, Africa, A Political Travelogue, 1965, Utopia, The Pernennial Heresy, 1967, Sartre, Ideologue of Our Time, 1968, Ecumenism or New Reformation?, 1968, The Counter-Revolution, 1969, La Gauche vue d'en face 1970, L'Animal politique, 1974, The European Dilemma, 1974, God and the Knowledge of Reality, 1974, Le Socialisme sans visage, 1976, Authority and Its Enemies, 1976, Christian Humanism, A Critique of the Secular City and Its Ideology, 1978, Le Modèle défigurè, l'Amerique de Tocqueville à Carter, 1978, Theists and Atheists, A Typology of Non-Belief, 1980, Politics and the State: A Catholic View, 1982, Le Dieu Immanent, 1982, Tiers-Monde, Idèologie Rèalitè, 1982, L'Eclipse du Sacré, 1986, The Pagan Temptation, 1987, Twin Power: Politics and the Sacred, 1988, L'Europe entre Parenthèses, 1990, Philosophical Grounds, 1991, The Church, Pilgrim of Centuries, 1991, L'Amèicanologie, Le triomphe du modèle planètaire?, 1991, Az Ideális èllam kritikája, 1991, L'Hègèmonie libèrale, 1992, The Emerging Atlantic Culture, 1994, Archetypes of Thought, 1995, Return to Philosophy, 1996, La modernite et ses antidotes, 1996; also numerous articles in Am. and European scholarly jours. Relm Found. grantee for travel and study in French-speaking Africa, 1963-64, for travel in S.Am., 1966, for writing Sartre, Ideologue of Our Time, 1967; Earhart Found. grantee, 1992. Home: 238 Heights Rd Ridgewood NJ 07450-2414

MOLNAU, CAROL, state legislator; b. Sept. 17, 1949; m. Steven F. Molnau; 3 children. Attended, U. Minn. Mem. Minn. Ho. of Reps., 1992—. Active Our Saviors Luth. Ch., 4-H, Chaska City Coun. Mem. Agrl. Com., Econ. Devel., Infrastructure & Regulation Fin.-Transportation Fin. Divsn., Fin. Inst. & Ins.: Internat. Trade & Economic Devel. Republican. Home: 495 Pioneer Trl Chaska MN 55318-1151 Office: State Capitol 287 State Office Bldg Saint Paul MN 55155

MOLO, STEVEN FRANCIS, lawyer; b. Chgo., June 30, 1957; s. Steven and Alice (Babinski) M.; m. Mary Wood, Dec. 31, 1986; children: Alexander, Madeline, Julia, Allison. BS, U. Ill., 1979, JD, 1982. Bar: Ill. 1982. Asst. atty. gen. criminal pros. and trial divsn. Chgo., 1982-86; assoc. Winston & Strawn, Chgo., 1986-89, ptnr., 1989—; adj. prof. Loyola U. Law Sch., Chgo., 1988-93,. Northwestern U. Law Sch., Chgo., 1989—; mem. faculty Nat. Inst. Trial Advocacy, Chgo., 1989—; lectr. on trial advocacy, appellate advocacy, and evidence to various orgns. Co-author: Corporate Internal Investigations, 1993, updated annually, 1993—; bd. editors Bus. Crimes Bull: Litigation and Compliance, 1994—; contbr. articles to legal jours. Spl. counsel Ill. Jud. Inquiry Bd., 1986-90; spl. reapportionment counsel Cook County Judiciary, 1988-89, spl. reapportionment counsel to Rep. leadership Ill. Ho. of Reps. and Senate, 1991-92. Named one of World's Leading White Collar Crime Lawyers, Euromoney PLC, 1995, Leading Ill. Attys. Comml. Litigation and Criminal Law, 1996, Crain's Chicago Bus. "40 Under 40" Chicago Leaders, 1997. Mem. ABA, FBA, Ill. Bar Assn., Chgo. Bar Assn., Theodore Roosevelt Assn., Chgo. Athletic Assn., Econ. Club Chgo., Tavern Club, Chgo. Inn of Ct. (master of bench, pres. 1997-98). Office: Winston & Strawn 35 W Wacker Dr Chicago IL 60601-1614

MOLOFF, ALAN LAWRENCE, army officer, physician; b. Bklyn., Sept. 29, 1954; s. Louis Rubin and Muriel (Trabeck) M. BS, U. Vt., 1976; DO, U. N.J., 1983; MPH, Harvard U., 1988; student, U.S. Army Command/Gen. Staff Course, 1994-95. Diplomate Am. Bd. Preventive Medicine; bd. cert. aerospace medicine, undersea medicine. Commd. platoon leader U.S. Army, 1976, advanced through grades to lt. col., 1993; intern Fitzsimons Army Med. Ctr., Aurora, Colo., 1983-84; med. officer lst Battalion 10th Spl. Forces Group, Bad Tolz, Fed. Republic of Germany, 1984-87; resident in aerospace medicine Harvard U., Boston, 1987-89; chief spl. ops. forces divsn. Acad. Health Scis., San Antonio, 1989-92; command surgeon Spl. Forces Command, Ft. Bragg, N.C., 1992-93; dep. surgeon U.S. Army Spl. Ops. Command, Ft. Bragg, N.C., 1993-94; with command and gen. staff coll. U.S. Army, 1994-95; dep. surgeon 30th Med. Brigade, Heidelberg, Germany, 1995-96; SE TAF surgeon, 1995-97; dep. U.S. Army Europe Fwd Surgeon, Hungary, 1995-96; surgeon V Corps, Heidelberg, Germany, 1996-97; setaf surgeon, 1995-97; lectr. advanced trauma life support NOAA, Aerospace Med. Assn. Contbr. articles to profl. jours. Active in civic activities. Decorated Meritorious Svc. medal with 2 oak leaf clusters, Joint Svc. Commendation medal, S.W. Asian Svc. medal, Army Commendation medal with oak leaf cluster, Army Achievement medal, Armed Forces Svc. medal, NATO medal, Kuwait Liberation medal, German Paratrooper badge, Pathfinder badge, Expert Field Med. badge, Order of Mil. Med. Merit, Master Parachutist award. Fellow Am. Coll. Preventive Medicine, Aerospace Med. Assn. (assoc.); mem. Am. Osteo. Assn., Aerospace Med. Assn., Assn. Mil. Surgeons of U.S., Assn. Mil. Osteo Physicians and Surgeons, Undersea and Hyperboric Medicine Soc., Soc. U.S. Army Flight Surgeons (life). Avocations: skiing, scuba diving, weightlifting, military history. Home: 67 Im Emmertsgrund, Emmertsgrund Germany Office: HHC 30th Med BDE V Corps Surgeon Unit 29218 Box 246 APO AE 09102-9218

MOLONEY, STEPHEN MICHAEL, lawyer; b. L.A., July 1, 1949; s. Donald Joseph and Madeline Marie (Sartoris) M.; m. Nancy Paula Barile, Jan. 15, 1972; children: Michael, John, Kathleen. Student, St. John's Sem., Camarillo, Calif., 1967-69; BS, U. Santa Clara, 1971, JD, 1975. Bar: Calif. 1975, U.S. Dist. Ct. (cen. dist.) Calif. 1976, U.S. Supreme Ct. 1990. Assoc. Gilbert, Kelly, Crowley & Jennett, L.A., 1975-80, from ptnr. to sr. ptnr., 1980—; arbitrator, settlement officer Los Angeles Superior Ct., 1985—. Contbr. articles to profl. jours. Dir. Calif. Def. Polit. Action Com., Sacramento, 1991—. With USAR. Recipient Svc. award to Pres. of So. Calif. Def. Counsel, Def. Rsch. Inst., Chgo., 1992. Mem. Assn. So. Calif. Def. Counsel (pres. 1992-93), Calif. Def. Counsel (dir. 1991—), L.A. County Bar Assn. (vols. in parole, 1976-77, exec. com. alternative dispute resolution com. 1992—), Jonathan Club, Oakmont Country Club, La Quinta Hotel Golf Club. Democrat. Roman Catholic. Avocations: politics, golf, reading, travel. Office: Gilbert Kelly Crowley & Jennett 1200 Wilshire Blvd Ste 6 Los Angeles CA 90017-1908

MOLONEY, THOMAS E., lawyer; b. Rockville Ctr., N.Y., Jan. 9, 1949. BS, U. Dayton, 1971; JD, U. Notre Dame, 1974. Bar: Ohio 1974. Ptnr. Baker & Hostetler, Columbus, Ohio. Office: Baker & Hostetler Capital Sq 65 E State St Ste 2100 Columbus OH 43215-4213

MOLONEY, THOMAS JOSEPH, lawyer; b. Bklyn., Oct. 14, 1952; s. Thomas J. and Grace (Nelson) M.; m. Molly K. Heines, Dec. 26, 1976. AB, Columbia U., 1973; JD cum laude, NYU, 1976. Bar: N.Y. 1977, U.S. Dist. Ct. (so. dist.) N.Y. 1977, U.S. Dist. Ct. (ea. dist.) N.Y. 1978, U.S. Ct. Appeals (2d cir.) 1981. Assoc. Cleary, Gottlieb, Steen & Hamilton, N.Y.C., 1976-84, ptnr., 1984—; bd. dirs. N.Y. Lawyers for Pub. Interest, N.Y.C., 1986-91; mediator U.S. Bankruptcy Ct. for So. Dist. N.Y., 1995. Asst. counsel Gov.'s Jud. Nominating Com., N.Y.C., 1981-85; chmn. bus. adv. coun. Washington Irving H.S., 1994—. Mem. ABA, Am. Bankruptcy Inst., Assn. of Bar of City of N.Y. (bankruptcy, corp. reorganization coms. 1983-86, chair com. legal assistance), Order of Coif. Avocations: chess, golf, dance, travel, wine. Office: Cleary Gottlieb Steen & Hamilton 1 Liberty Plz New York NY 10006-1404

MOLONY, MICHAEL JANSSENS, JR., lawyer; b. New Orleans, Sept. 2, 1922; s. Michael Janssens and Marie (Perret) M.; m. Jane Leslie Waguespack, Oct. 21, 1951; children: Michael Janssens III (dec.), Leslie, Megan, Kevin, Sara, Brian, Ian, Duncan. JD, Tulane U., 1950. Bar: La. 1950, D.C. 1979, U.S. Dist. Ct. (ea. and mid. dists.) La. 1951, U.S. Ct. Appeals (5th cir.) 1953, U.S. Supreme Ct. 1972, U.S. Dist. Ct. (we. dist.) La. 1978, U.S. Ct. Appeals (11th and D.C. cirs.) 1981. Ptnr., Molony & Baldwin, New Orleans, 1950; assoc. Jones, Flanders, Waechter & Walker, 1951-56; ptnr. Jones, Walker, Waechter, Poitevent, Carrere & Denegre, 1956-75, Milling, Benson, Woodward, Hillyer, Pierson & Miller, 1975-91, Chaffe, McCall, Phillips, Toler & Sarpy, 1991-92, Sessions & Fishman, 1993—; instr., lectr. Med. Sch. and Univ. Coll. Tulane U., 1953-59; mem. Eisenhower Legal Com., 1952. Bd. commrs. Port of New Orleans, 1976-81, pres., 1978; mem. bd. rev. Associated Br. Pilots, 1990-96; bd. dirs. La. World Expn. Inc., 1974-84; bd. dirs., exec. com. New Orleans Tourist and Conv. Commn., 1971-74, 78, chmn.; family attractions com. 1973-75; chmn. La. Gov.'s Task Force on Space Industry, 1971-73; chmn. La. Gov.'s Citizens' Adv. Com. Met. New Orleans Transp. and Planning Program, 1971-77; mem. La. Gov.'s Task Force Natural Gas Requirements, 1971-72; mem. La. Gov.'s Proaction Commn. for Higher Edn., 1995; mem. Goals Found. Coun. and ex-officio mem. Goals Found., Met. New Orleans Goals Program, 1969-72, vice chmn. ad hoc planning com. Goals Met. New Orleans, 1969-73; vice chmn. Port of New Orleans Operation Impact, 1969-70, mem. Met. Area Com., New Orleans, 1970-84; trustee, Pub. Affairs Rsch. Coun. La., 1970-73, mem. exec. com. Bus./Higher Edn. Coun., U. New Orleans, 1980-94, bd. dirs., 1980—, v.p. 1986-88, pres., 1988-90, chmn. Task Force on Pub. Higher Edn. Funding, 1990-95, chmn. governmental affairs, 1995—, Task Force on Edn./Econ. Devel. Alliances, 1993-95; mem. Mayor's Coun. on Internat. Trade and Econ. Devel., 1978; mem. Mayor's Transition Task Force Econ. Devel., 1994; bd. dirs. La. Partnership for Tech. and Innovation, 1989—; bd. dirs. Acad. Sacred Heart, 1975-77, Internat. House, 1985-86, adv. coun. 1985—; bd. dirs. U. New Orleans Found., 1991—; mem. vis. com. Sch. Bus. Adminstrn., Loyola U., New Orleans, 1981—, trustee Loyola U., 1985-91, vice chmn. bd. trustees, 1990-91; mem. Dean's Coun. Tulane U. Law Sch., 1988-96, vice chmn. building com., 1991-95; bd. dirs., mem. exec. com. Internat. Trade Mart, chmn. internat. bus. com., 1983-85; World Trade Ctr.-New Orleans (bd. dirs. 1983—, mem. Port Activity com. 1985-91, transp. com. 1991-95, govt. affairs com. 1996—); chmn. Task Force on Internat. Banking, 1982; mem. Mayor's Task Force on Drug Abuse, 1989-90. Capt. JAGDR, USAAF, 1942-46, PTO, Recipient Leadership award AIAA, 1971, Yenni award Loyola U., New Orleans, 1979, New Orleans Times Picayune Loving Cup, 1986, First Citizen of the Learning Soc. Dean's award UNO Met. Coll, 1992; also various civic contbn. awards; co-recipient Silver Anvil award Pub. Rels. Soc. Am., 1991. Fellow Coll. Labor and Employment Law; mem. ABA (labor and employment law and litigation sects., com. equal opportunity law, chmn. regional com. liaison with equal opportunity commn., office of fed. contract compliance programs), D.C. Bar Assn., Fed. Bar Assn., La. Bar Assn. (past sec.-treas., bd. govs. 1957-60, editor jour. 1957-59, sec. spl. supreme ct. com. on drafting code jud. ethics), New Orleans Bar Assn. (dir. legal aid bur. 1954, chmn. standing com. legis. 1968, vice chmn. standing com. pub. rels. 1970-71), Am. Judicature Soc., La. Law Inst. (asst. sec.-treas. 1958-70), Am. Arbitration Assn. (bd. dirs., 1995—, chmn. reg. adv. coun., chmn. reg. adv. coun. employment law cases, mem. spl. panel large complex arbitration/mediation cases, Whitney North Seymour Sr. award 1991), So. Inst. Mgmt. (founder), AIM, U.S. C. of C. (urban and regional affairs com. 1970-73), La. C. of C. (bd. dirs. 1963-66), New Orleans and River Region C. of C. (v.p. met. devel. and urban affairs 1969, past chmn. labor rels. coun., bd. dirs. 1970-78, pres.-elect 1970, pres. 1971, dir., exec. com. 1972, ex officio mem., bd. dirs. 1979—), Bienville Club, English Turn Golf and Country Club, Pickwick Club, Plimsoll Club, Serra Club, So. Yacht Club, Sigma Chi (pres. alumni chpt. 1956). Roman Catholic. Home: 3039 Hudson Pl New Orleans LA 70131-5337 Office: Sessions & Fishman 201 Saint Charles Ave New Orleans LA 70170-1000

MOLPUS, DICK H., resource management company executive; b. Philadelphia, Miss., Sept. 7, 1949; s. Richard and Frances (Blount) M.; m. Sally Nash, May 27, 1971; children—Helen Nash, Richard Gregory. BBA, U. Miss., 1971. V.p. mfg. Molpus Co., Phila., 1971-80; exec. dir. Gov's Office Fed.-State Programs, Jackson, Miss., 1980-83; sec. of state State of Miss., Jackson, 1984-96; pres. Molpus Co. and Woodlands Resource Mgmt. Group, Phila., 1996—; dir. Citizens Bank and Trust Co. Vice pres. Miss. Agr. and Forestry Mus., 1979; campaign dir., chmn. bd. United Givers Fund, Nehshoba County, Miss., 1979-80; bd. dirs. Miss. PTA, 1980—; founder Parents for Pub. Schs. orgn., 1989. Recipient Friends of Children award Miss. Assn. Elem. Sch. Adminstrs., 1984, Pub. Ofcl. of Yr. award Miss. chpt. Am. Soc. for Pub. Adminstrn., 1985. Mem. Miss. Forestry Assn. (bd. dirs. 1980-87), Nat. Assn. Secs. of State (pres. 1992), Nature Conservancy (bd. dirs. Miss. chpt.), Sigma Chi, Omicron Delta Kappa, Pi Sigma Alpha (Theta Beta chpt.). Avocations: hiking, tennis, running, reading. Office: PO Box 59 Philadelphia MS 39350-0059

MOLSON, ERIC H., beverage company executive; b. Montreal, PQ, Can., Sept. 16, 1937; s. Thomas Henry Pentland and Celia Frances (Cantlie) M.; m. Jane Mitchell, Apr. 16, 1966; 3 children. AB, Princeton U., 1959. With The Molson Cos. Ltd., Montreal, chmn. bd., 1988—. Office: The Molson Cos Ltd, 1555 Notre Dame St E, Montreal, PQ Canada H2L 2R5

MOLTZ, JAMES EDWARD, brokerage company executive; b. Williamsport, Pa., July 25, 1932; s. George N. and Margaret L. (Abell) M.; m. Barbara Vance, Sept. 8, 1956; children: George Wilson, James Clay, John Thomas. BS, Williams Coll., 1954; MBA, Wharton Sch., U. Pa., 1956. Chartered fin. analyst. Fin. analyst Cyrus J. Lawrence Inc., N.Y.C., 1957-62, rsch. dir., 1962-64, gen. ptnr., 1964-71, mng. ptnr., 1971-73; chmn., pres. C.J. Lawrence/Deutsche Bank Securities Corp., N.Y.C., 1973-95; chief investment officer Deutsche Morgan Grenfell, 1996—. Mem. fin. com. Williams Coll.; trustee Sterling and Francine Clark Art Inst., Darien (Conn.) Libr.; hon. trustee Williamsport-Lycoming Found.; elder Noroton (Conn.) Presbyn. Ch.; trustee Woods Hole Oceanographic Inst., Charles Culpepper Found. Mem. Fin. Analysts Fedn., N.Y. Soc. Security Analysts (former dir.), Rockefeller Ctr. Club, Union League Club (N.Y.C.), Wee Burn Country Club (dir.), Windsor Club (Vero Beach). Home: 29 Indian Spring Trl Darien CT 06820-2109 Also: Deutsche Morgan Grenfell 31 W 52nd St New York NY 10019-6118

MOLTZ, MARSHALL JEROME, lawyer; b. Chgo., May 22, 1930; s. Nathan and Rose (Nathanson) M.; m. Rita G., Dec. 26, 1954; m. 2d, Mary Ann, Nov. 4, 1967; children: Alan J., Michelle S. Yastrow, Marilyn F. Moltz-Hohmann, Julie A., Steven E., Rachel N. BS, Northwestern U., 1951, JD, 1954. Bar: Ill. 1954, U.S. Assoc., John B. Moser, Chgo., 1957; assoc. Goldberg, Devoe, Shadur & Mikva, Chgo., 1957-58; assoc. Lester Plotkin, Chgo., 1958-59; sole practice, Chgo., 1959-65; ptnr. Moltz & Spagat, Chgo., 1966-67; sole practice, Chgo., 1967-68; ptnr. Moltz & Wexler, Chgo., 1968-80; sole practice Chgo. 1980—; pres. Mercury Title Co.; faculty mem. profl. liab. in real estate transactions ABA Regional Inst., 1993; mem. Blue Ribbon com. Cook County Recorder of Deeds; speaker real estate law; atty. Counseling Ctr. of Lake View Mental Health Orgn., Chgo. With M.I., U.S. Army, 1955-56; ETO. Recipient Louden Wigmore prize Northwestern U. Law Sch., 1954. Mem. ABA, Am. Coll. Real Estate Lawyers, Ill. State Bar Assn., Chgo. Bar Assn. (mem. real property law com. 1958—, chmn. Torrens sub-com. 1968-75, vice chmn. real property law com. 1974-75, chmn. real property law com. 1975-76, speaker and faculty mem. various seminars 1993-96, faculty mem. residential real estate seminar, 1995, 96), VFW, Phi Alpha Delta (law fraternity). Author course outlines Ill. Inst. Continuing Legal Edn., 1972, 73; editorial bd. Northwestern U. Law Rev., 1953-54. Home: 112 Harvard Ct Glenview IL 60025-5917 Office: 77 W Washington St Ste 1620 Chicago IL 60602-2903

MOLTZON, RICHARD FRANCIS, manufacturing executive; b. Bklyn., Nov. 20, 1941; s. Arthur G. and Joan (Paladino) M.; m. Susan A. Anderson, Feb. 15, 1981; children: Paige, Kimberly, Michael, Keir. BS in Info. Systems Mgmt., U. Md., 1970. Various positions IBM Corp., various locations, 1965-70; plant mgr. Telex Terminal Communications, Inc., Raleigh, N.C., 1970-75, Carnes Co. div. Wehr Steel, Sanford, N.C., 1975-76; dir., gen. mgr. Modular Computer Systems, Inc., Ft. Lauderdale, Fla., 1980-87; v.p. ops. Profile Corp., Pompano Beach, Fla., 1987-88; dir. mfg. AMF, Inc., Herndon, Va., 1976-79, Documation, Inc., Melbourne, Fla., 1979-80, Concurrent Computer Corp., Oceanport, N.J., 1988-89; v.p. mfg. Internat. Tech. Corp., Clearwater, Fla., 1989-90; pres. The Realty Authority, Inc., 1990-92; ops. mgr. Combustion Tec, Inc., Orlando, Fla., 1992—. With U.S. Army, 1961-64. Mem. KC (chancelor 1987, 88), Omicron Delta Kappa. Roman Catholic. Avocations: golf, jogging, writing, scuba diving, exotic birds. Office: Combustion Tec Inc PO Box 607693 Orlando FL 32860-7693

MOLYNEAUX, DAVID GLENN, newspaper travel editor; b. Marion, Ind., Oct. 16, 1945; s. Glenn Ingersol and Barbara Wingate (Draudt) M.; m. Ann Louise Geery, Aug. 8, 1970; children: Miles David, Rebecca Susan. BS in Econs., Miami U., Oxford, Ohio, 1967. Reporter The Plain Dealer, Cleve., 1967-75, city editor, 1976-78, assoc. editor, 1979-80, editorial page editor, 1980-82, travel editor, 1982—. Editor: 75 Years-An Informal History of Shaker Heights, 1987. Trustee Shaker Heights Pub. Libr., 1987—. With U.S. Army, 1968-70. Mem. Cleve. Press Club. Office: Plain Dealer 1801 Superior Ave E Cleveland OH 44114-2107*

MOLZ, REDMOND KATHLEEN, public administration educator; b. Balt., Mar. 5, 1928; d. Joseph T. and Regina (Barry) M. B.S., Johns Hopkins U., 1949, M.A., 1950; M.A.L.S., U. Mich., 1953; D.L.S., Columbia U., 1976. Librarian I and II Enoch Pratt Free Library, Balt., 1953-56; pub. relations officer Free Library of Phila., 1958-62; editor Wilson Library Bull. H.W. Wilson Co., Bronx, N.Y., 1962-68; chief planning staff Bur. Libraries and Learning Resources U.S. Office Edn., Washington, 1968-73; prof. library sci. Sch. Library Service Columbia U., N.Y.C., 1976-80, Melvil Dewey prof., 1980-93; prof. pub. affairs Sch. Internat. and Pub. Affairs, Columbia U., N.Y.C., 1993—; cons. U.S. Nat. Commn. Libraries and Info. Sci., Washington, 1974-75, U.S. Adv. Commn. Intergovtl. Relations, Washington, 1979-80. Author: Federal Policy and Library Support, 1976 (Ralph R. Shaw award 1977), National Planning for Library Service, 1935-75, 1984, Library Planning and Policy Making: The Legacy of the Public and Private Sector, 1990, The Federal Roles in Support of Public Library Services, 1990, The Federal Roles in Support of Academic and Research Libraries, 1991; co-editor: The Metropolitan Library (anthology), 1972; author TV script Portraits in Print, 1959. Recipient Leadership Tng. award Fund for Adult Edn., 1956-57; recipient Disting. Alumnus award Sch. Library Sci. U. Mich., 1969, George Virgil Fuller award Columbia U., 1975, Johns Hopkins U. scholar, 1949-50, Horace H. Rackham fellow U. Mich., 1952-53, Columbia U. scholar, 1974-76, Tangley Oaks fellow, 1975-76; Council Library Resources Inc. Officers' grantee, 1974. Mem. ALA (councilor 1972-74, 76-80, exec. bd. 1976-80, chmn. legis. com. 1985-86), Freedom to Read Found. (dir. 1972-79, pres. 1977-79). Office: Columbia U Sch Internat & Pub Affairs New York NY 10027

MOLZ, ROBERT JOSEPH, manufacturing company executive; b. Yonkers, N.Y., Mar. 15, 1937; s. Philip and Maria Hilda (Geist) M.; m. Diane Ruth Horowitz, July 31, 1960; children—Jennifer Ann, Erica Beth. B.S., CCNY, 1960, M.A., 1966; Ph.D., N.Y. Med. Coll., 1969. Tech. services supr. E.I. DuPont de Neumours Co. Inc., Wilmington, Del., 1971-73, product mgr., 1973-75, quality assurance mgr. clin. systems div., 1976, research and devel. mgr. clin. systems div., 1976-84, asst. dir. research and devel. div. agrl. chem. dept., 1984-86, dir. departmental plans div., med. products dept., 1986-88, dir. med. scis. programs, cen. R&D, 1988-91, dir. new bus. devel., Cen. R&D, 1991-92, exec. dir. rsch. support, 1992-96. Roman Catholic. Home: 306 Dove Dr Newark DE 19713-1212

MOLZEN, CHRISTOPHER JOHN, lawyer; b. Manhattan, Kans., Sept. 5, 1961; s. Gilbert John and Janice Molzen; m. Robin Larson. BA in Polit. Sci., U. Mo., 1983, JD, 1987. Bar: Mo. 1987, U.S. Dist. Ct. (we. dist.) Mo. 1987, U.S. Tax Ct. 1994, U.S. Supreme Ct. 1994. Assoc. Shughart Thomson & Kilroy, Kansas City, 1995—. Co-author, editor The Judicial Handbook of Kansas City, 1993. Pegasus scholar Inner Temple, London, 1991, William L. Bradshaw scholar, 1982. Mem. ATLA, Mo. Assn. Trial Attys., Kansas City Met. Bar Assn., Young Lawyer's (pres. 1996—), Federalist Soc., Ross T. Roberts Inn of Ct., Order of Barristers, Phi Delta Phi. Home: PO Box 6938 Lees Summit MO 64064-6938 Office: Shughart Thomson & Kilroy Twelve Wyandotte Plz 120 W 12th St Kansas City MO 64105-1917

MOLZEN, DAYTON FRANK, consulting engineering executive; b. Newton, Kans., Jan. 6, 1926; s. Walter N. and Ionia Maude (Gordon) M.; m. Margaret Jean Hanna, Aug. 13, 1949; children: George Walter, Lucena Ann. B.S., Kans. State U., 1950. Project engr. Kans. Hwy. Commn., Garden City, 1950-51; design engr. Wilson & Co., Engrs., Albuquerque and Salina, Kans., 1953-60; civil engr., pres. D.F. Molzen and Assocs., Inc., Albuquerque, 1960-74; pres. Molzen-Corbin & Assos., Albuquerque, 1974-96; founding prin., 1996—. Served with A.C. U.S. Army, 1942-45; Served with USAF, 1951-53. Fellow Am. Cons. Engrs. Coun. (nat. bd. dirs. 1982-85, exec. dir. N.Mex. 1985-93); mem. ASCE, Cons. Engrs. Coun. (past pres.), Am. Pub. Works Assn. Clubs: Masons, Shriners, Rotary, Appaloosa Horse (past pres. N.Mex., nat. dir.). Home: 3216 Calle De Estella NW Albuquerque NM 87104-3003 Office: 2701 Miles Rd SE Albuquerque NM 87106-3228

MOMAH, ETHEL CHUKWUEKWE, women's health nurse; b. Iyi-Enu, Onitsha, Nigeria, May 28, 1934; d. Zaccheus C. and Victoria U. (Orizu) Obi; m. Christian C. Momah, Nov. 21, 1959; children: Chukwudi, Adaora, Azuka. SRN, Harrow Hosp., Middlesex, U.K., 1956; SCM, Mothers Hosp., London, 1957; MTD, Midwife Tchrs. Coll., Surrey, U.K., 1964; BS, Upsala Coll., 1988. Cert. inpatient obstetric nurse Nat. Cert. Corp. Nurse-midwife Guy's Hosp., London, 1959; nursing sister, head nurse labor/delivery Univ. Coll. Hosp., Ibadan, Nigeria, 1960-62; midwife tutor Lagos (Nigeria) Island Maternity Hosp., 1963-66; nurse-midwife Brit. Hosp., Paris, 1966, Hosp. Cantonal, Geneva, Switzerland, 1967-78; patient care coord. St. Peter's Med. Ctr., New Brunswick, N.J., 1985-90, antenatal testing nurse, 1990—. Mem. breast health task force Middlesex County unit N.J. divsn. Am. Cancer Soc. Mem. Assn. of Women's Health, Obstetric and Neonatal Nurses. Office: St Peters Med Ctr New Brunswick NJ 08901

MOMEYER, DOUGLAS H., lawyer; b. Donora, Pa., Mar. 30, 1944. BA, Northwestern U., 1966, JD, 1969. Bar: Ill. 1969. Mem. Hinshaw & Culbertson, Chgo. Mem. ABA, Chgo. Bar Assn., Ill. State Bar Assn., Soc. Trial Lawyers, Defense Rsch. Inst. Office: Hinshaw Culbertson 222 N La Salle St Ste 300 Chicago IL 60601-1013

MOMMSEN, KATHARINA, retired German language and literature educator; b. Berlin, Sept. 18, 1925; came to U.S., 1974, naturalized, 1980; d. Hermann and Anna (Johannsen) Zimmer; m. Momme Mommsen, Dec. 23, 1948. Dr.phil., U. Tübingen, 1956; Dr. habil., Berlin Free U., 1962. Collaborator Acad. Scis., Berlin, 1949-61; assoc. prof. Free U., Berlin, 1962-70; prof. German Carleton U., Ottawa, Can., 1970-74; Albert Guerard prof. lit. Stanford U., 1974-94, ret., 1995; vis. prof. U. Giessen, Tech. U. Berlin, 1965, State U. N.Y., Buffalo, 1966, U. Calif., San Diego, 1973. Author over 150 publs. on 18th-20th century German and comparative lit.; editor: Germanic Studies in America. Mem. Internat. Assn. Germanic Langs. and Lit., Goethe Soc., Schiller Soc. Home: 980 Palo Alto Ave Palo Alto CA 94301-2223

MONA, STEPHEN FRANCIS, golf association executive; b. N.Y.C., June 9, 1957; s. Francis Joseph and Lucille (Croce) M.; m. Mary Jo Abate, May 31, 1983 (div. 1990); 1 child, Meredith Iris. BA in Journalism, San Jose State U., 1980. Sports writer Tri-Valley News, Danville, Calif., 1977-78, Tri-Valley Herald, Livermore, Calif., 1978-80; tournament dir. Northern Calif. Golf Assn., Pebble Beach, Calif., 1980-81; asst. mgr., press relations U.S. Golf Assn., Far Hills, N.J., 1981-83; exec. dir. Ga. State Golf Assn., Atlanta, 1983—. Bd. dirs. Ga. Turf Grass Found., Norcross, Ga., 1988—; treas. Ga. Jr. Golf Found., Atlanta, 1986—. Named Golf Writer of the Yr., Northern Calif. PGA, Calif. 1980; Sports Story of the Yr., Contra Costa Press Club, Walnut Creek, Calif., 1977, 1978. Mem. Ga. Soc. Assn. Execs. (bd. dirs. 1988—), Internat. Assn. Golf Adminstrs. (pres. 1990), Am. Soc. Assn. Execs., Rivermont Country Club, Pinetree Country Club. Republican. Roman Catholic. Avocations: golf, reading, yardwork. Office: GCSAA 1421 Research Park Dr Lawrence KS 66049-3858 Address: 2012 Palmer Dr Lawrence KS 66047-2044

MONACELLI, AMIETO, professional bowler. Top money leader, top average Pro Bowlers Assn., 1990. Office: c/o Pro Bowlers Assn 1720 Merriman Rd Akron OH 44313-5252*

MONACELLI, GIANFRANCO, publishing executive; b. Milan; came to U.S., 1965; s. Rodolfo and Isabella (Paolillo) M.; m. Eugenia Hyman; children: Nurit, Fausto, Alexander. Dr., U. Turin, Italy, 1963, Acad. Santa Cecilia, Italy, 1964; BS, Mannes Coll., 1967; postgrad., Columbia U., 1969. Gen. mgr. Rizzoli Internat. Bookstore, N.Y.C., 1969-72, v.p., 1972-75; exec. v.p. Rizzoli Internat., Milan, 1975-78; pres., chief exec. officer Rizzoli Internat. Publs., Inc., N.Y.C., 1975-93, Rizzoli Internat. Bookstores, Inc., N.Y.C., 1975-92, Rizzoli Editore Corp., N.Y.C., 1975-89; sr. v.p. RCS Rizzoli Corp., N.Y.C., 1989-93; pres. USITAL Ltd., N.Y.C., 1993—, The Monacelli Press, Inc., N.Y.C., 1994—; v.p. Epikos Security Printing S.A., N.Y.C., 1997—. Trustee Mannes Coll., N.Y.C., 1979-81; pres. Weathersfield Music Festival, Vert., 1993—; mem. vis. com. U. Miami, Coral Gables, Fla., 1988-89. Recipient Met. Home Deesign 100 award, 1997; named Pub. of Yr., AIA, 1996. Mem. Century Assn., Am.-Italy Soc. (pres. 1993-94).

MONACO, ANTHONY PETER, surgery educator, medical institute administrator; b. Phila., Mar. 12, 1932; s. Donoto Charles and Rose (Consalvi) M.; m. Mary Louise Oudens, June 4, 1960; children: Anthony Peter, Marck Churchill, Christopher Donoto, Lisa Oudens. B.A. in Chemistry, U. Pa., 1952; M.D. magna cum laude, Harvard U., 1956. Diplomate Am. Bd. Surgery, Am. Bd. Thoracic Surgery. Prof. surgery Harvard Med. Sch., Boston, 1977-95, Peter Medawar prof. transplantation surgeyr, 1995—, mem. bd. acad. advisors, 1974-83; chief transplantation div. Sears Surg. Research Lab. Boston City Hosp., 1967-73; sci. dir. Cancer Research Inst., New Eng. Deaconess Hosp., Boston, 1980—; chief div. organ transplantation Cancer Research Inst., New Eng. Deaconess Hosp., 1975—; Peter Medacor prof. transplantation surgery Harvard Med. Sch., 1995; mem. surgery study sect. NIH, 1973-77, mem. clin. sci. study sect., 1983— ; mem. adv. com. endstage renal disease Bur. Quality Assurance, HEW, 1975-76; mem. merit rev. bd. immunology VA, Washington, 1977-80. Author: Biology of Tissue Transplantation, 1964; editor: Transplantation Procedures, 1970, 81; jour. Transplantation, 1969—. Trustee New Eng. Organ Bank, Boston, 1970—, chmn., 1981—; bd. dirs. Kidney Found. Mass., 1978-81; mem. Harvard Med. Sch. Alumni Council, 1979-81. Recipient nat. scholar Harvard Med. Sch., 1952-56; recipient Henry Asbury Christian award Harvard Med. Sch., 1956, Lederle Med. Faculty award Harvard Med. Sch., 1968. Mem. Transplantation Soc. (charter, v.p. 1971-74, pres. 1985, internat. pres. 1986), Am. Soc. Transplant Surgeons (charter, treas. 1982-85, pres. 1985—), Am. Surg. Assn., Soc. Univ. Surgeons, ACS (pres. Mass. chpt. 1985). Club: Harvard (Boston). Home: 25 Farlow Rd Newton MA 02158-2407 Office: Harvard Med Sch-Surgery Boston MA 02218

MONACO, JOHN J., molecular genetics research educator. Prof. U. Cin. Sch. of Medicine; investigator Howard Hughes Med. Inst. Recipient Eli Lilly and Co. Rsch. award in Microbiology and Immunology, Am. Soc. Microbiology, 1995, Investigators award Pharmagen/Am. Assn. Immunologists, 1997.. Office: Howard Hughes Med Inst U Cin Sch Medicine Dept Molecular Genetics 231 Bethesda Ave Cincinnati OH 45229-2827

MONACO, PAUL, academic administrator, educator, artist, writer; b. Niskayuna, N.Y., Sept. 11, 1942; s. Angelo M. and Birdena (O'Melia) M.; m. Victoria O'Donnell, 1993. BS, Columbia U., 1965; MA, U. N.C., 1966; PhD, Brandeis U., 1974. Asst. prof. hist. Brandeis U., Waltham, Mass., 1973-75; prof. arts and humanities U. Tex., Dallas, 1975-85, dir. grad. studies arts and humanities, 1976-80; dept. head, prof. media and theatre arts Mont. State U., Bozeman, 1985—; bd. dirs. U. Film and Video Assn., 1988-91, 95-96, Bozeman Film Festival, 1985— (pres. 1987-90); mem. Hist. Preservation Com., Bozeman, 1988-90, Mont. Com. for Humanities, Missoula, 1989-93; regional coord. Nicholls Screenwriting Awards, 1989-91. Author: Cinema and Soc., Modern Europe Culture..., 1993, Ribbons in Time, 1988 (ALC Outstanding Acad. Book award 1988); prodr., dir.: Montana: 2d Century, 1990-96 (Mont. broadcasters award 1991), Bison in the Killing Fields, 1996; prodr., dir., co-writer: Home to Montana, 1988; dir. I Often Thought of Berlin, 1989, Women, War and Work, 1997, Way of the Trout, 1994, Gary Strobel: A Portrait, 1996. Bd. dirs. Mont. Ballet Co., Bozeman, 1986-90; mem. selection com. Fulbright Found., Germany, 1996, 97. Recipient Fulbright Prof. award U.S., Germany, 1982-83, 92. Home: 290 Low Bench Rd Gallatin Gateway MT 59730-9741 Office: Mt State Univ Visual Communications Bldg Bozeman MT 59717

MONACO, ROBERT ANTHONY, radiologist; b. N.Y.C., July 5, 1945; s. Edmond V. and Jean (DeSena) M.; m. Susan Margaret Thompson; children: Kevin, Robert, Christopher, Sarah. BS, Siena Coll., 1967; MD, N.J. Coll. Medicine, 1971. Diplomate Am. Bd. Radiology, Am. Bd. Nuclear Medicine. Radiology resident N.J. Coll. Medicine, Newark, 1971-75; fellow in nuclear medicine med. ctr. NYU, N.Y.C., 1975-76; attending radiologist Med. Ctr. Ocean County, Point Pleasant, N.J., 1976-87, dir. dept. radiology, 1987—; gen. ptnr. Point Pleasant Radiology Group, 1987—; bd. dirs. Found. Med. Ctr. Ocean County, Mid-Coastal IPA, 1997—. Capt. USAR, 1972-76. Mem. Am. Coll. Radiology, Am. Coll. Nuclear Medicine, Radiol. Soc. N.J. Roman Catholic. Avocations: tennis, fishing, swimming. Home: 1545 Oakshire Ln Manasquan NJ 08736-2519 Office: Point Pleasant Radiology Group Rt 88 and Lakewood Rd Point Pleasant NJ 08742

MONAGHAN, EILEEN, artist; b. Holyoke, Mass., Nov. 22, 1911; d. Thomas F. and Mary (Doona) Monaghan; m. Frederic Whitaker. Student, Mass. Coll. Art. Represented in collections NAD, Okla. Mus. Art, Hispanic Soc., High Mus. Art, Atlanta, Norfolk museums, U. Mass., Springfield (Mass.) Mus. Fine Art, Reading (Pa.) Art Mus., Charles and Emma Frye Art Mus., Seattle, Kans. State U., Wichita, St. Lawrence U., N.Y., NAD, also in numerous pvt. collections, ann. exhbns., nat. and regional watercolor shows; author: Eileen Monaghan Whitaker Paints San Diego, 1986. Recipient Wong award Calif. Watercolor Soc., Ranger Fund purchase Nat. Acad. Design, Allied Artists Am., DeYoung Mus. show award, Soc. Western Artists award, 1st award Springville (Utah) Mus., William P. and Gertrude Schweitzer prize for excellence in a watercolor NAD, 1996, numerous others. Mem. NAD (academician, Obrig prize, Walter Biggs Meml. award), Am. Watercolor Soc. (Silver medal, Dolphin fellow), Watercolor West Soc. (hon.), San Diego Watercolor Soc. (hon.), Providence Watercolor Club (award), Phila. Watercolor Club. Address: 1579 Alta La Jolla Dr La Jolla CA 92037-7101

MONAGHAN, MATTHEW JOHN, lawyer; b. Portland, Maine, June 14, 1961; s. Thomas Francis and Anne Marie (Perry) M.; m. Karen Ellen Hopkins, Aug. 10, 1985; children: Erin, Casey. BA, Bowdoin Coll., 1984; JD, Lewis & Clark Coll., 1987. Bar: Maine 1987, U.S. Dist. Ct. Maine, 1987, U.S. Ct. Appeals (1st cir.) 1991, U.S. Supreme Ct., 1991. Assoc. Monaghan, Leahy, Hochadel & Libby, Portland, 1987-92, ptnr., 1992—. Bd. dirs., v.p. Am. Heart Assn., Maine affil., 1993-96; deacon Woodfords Congregational Ch., Portland, 1994-97. Mem. Maine State Bar Assn., (co-chmn. legal edn. and admission com. 1991-95); Maine Trial Lawyers, ABA. Office: Monaghan Leahy Hochadel & Libby 95 Exchange St Portland ME 04101-5037

MONAGHAN, MICHAEL SEAN, pharmacist. PharmD, Creighton U., 1989. Diplomate Am. Bd. Pharmacy, Pharmacotherapy Specialist. Asst. prof. pharmacy U. Ark. Med. Scis., Little Rock, Ark., 1990-96, assoc. prof. pharmacy practice, 1996; assoc. prof. pharmacy Creighton U., Omaha, 1996—; cons., mem. pharmacy and therapeutics com. Pharmacy Assoc., Inc., Little Rock, 1994—. Contbr. articles to profl. jours. Bd. dirs. Ark. affiliate Am. Diabetes Assn., 1995—. Recipient numerous grants; named Most Outstanding Clin. Faculty in Dept. Med. Practice, Class of 1996, Tchr. of Yr. U. Ark. Coll. Pharmacy Student Body, 1995-96. Mem. Am. Assn. Coll. Pharmacy, Am. Coll. Clin. Pharmacy (assoc.), Am. Soc. Health-System Pharmacists, Kappa Psi. Office: Creighton Univ Sch of Pharm and Health 2500 California Plz Omaha NE 68178-0001

MONAGHAN, THOMAS JUSTIN, prosecutor. U.S. atty. Dept. Justice, Omaha, 1993—. Office: US Attys Office PO Box 1228 Omaha NE 68101-1228

MONAGHAN, THOMAS STEPHEN, restaurant chain executive; b. Ann Arbor, Mich., Mar. 25, 1937; m. Marjorie Zybach, Aug. 25, 1962; children—Mary, Susan, Margaret, Barbara. Student, Ferris State Coll., U. Mich.; Ph.D. (hon.), Cleary Coll., 1982, Madonna Coll., 1983, Eastern Mich. U., 1984, So. Fla. U., 1985. Ptnr. Dominick's Pizza, Ypsilanti, Mich., 1960-65; pres., chmn. bd., founder, CEO Domino's Pizza, Inc., Ann Arbor, Mich., 1960—; owner Detroit Tigers, 1983-92. Author: (autobiography) Pizza Tiger. Bd. dirs. Cleary Coll., Ypsilanti, Henry Ford Hosp., Detroit, Detroit Renaissance, U. Steubinville, Ohio, St. Joseph's Hosp. Devel. Bd., Ann Arbor. Served with USMC, 1956-59. Named Entrepreneur of Yr. Harvard U. Bus. Sch., 1984, Pizzaman of Yr. Nat. Assn. Pizza Owners, 1984; recipient Golden Plate award Am. Acad. Achievement, 1984, Golden Chain award Multi Unit Franchise Svc. Orgn., 1986, Horatio Alger award, 1986, Restaurant Bus. Leadership award, 1986, Pope John Paul II Family Fidelity award 1988, Pine Mission's Knights of Charity award, 1990, Semper Fidelis award USMC, 1990. Mem. Internat. Franchise Assn. (Entrepreneur of Yr. 1986), Nat. Restaurant Assn. (Silver Plate award 1985), Mich. Restaurant Assn., Ypsilanti C. of C., U. Mich. Pres.'s Club, Ann Arbor Pres.'s Assn., Missionary Vehicle Assn. (bd. dirs.), AIA (hon.), Mich. Soc. Architects (hon.). Club: Barton Hills Country (Ann Arbor). Lodge: K.C. Avocations: collecting Frank Lloyd Wright furniture and memorabilia, classic cars. Office: Domino's Pizza Inc 30 Frank Lloyd Wright Dr Ann Arbor MI 48105-9755*

MONAGHAN, WILLIAM EDWARD, II, financial services company executive. BA magna cum laude, Duke U., 1985; MBA, U. N.C., 1991. Acctg. supr. Shawmut Bank of Boston, 1985-87; acct. mgr. State St. Bank and Trust Co., Boston, 1987-88; ops. officer The Boston Co. Advisors, Inc., 1988-89; mgmt. cons. intern Price Waterhouse, N.Y.C., 1990; asst. v.p. The Boston Co. Advisors, Inc., 1991-92, v.p., 1992-94; v.p. First Data Investor Svcs. Group, Boston, 1994-95, State St. Bank and Trust Co., Boston, 1995—. Mem. Boston Security Analysts Soc., Assoc. for Investment Mgmt and Rsch., Iron Dukes, Duke Club, Yale Club, Carolina Club, Inst. Chartered Fin. Analysts, Delta Kappa Epsilon. Office: State St Bank & Trust Co 225 Franklin St Boston MA 02110-2804

MONAHAN, EDWARD CHARLES, academic administrator, marine science educator; b. Bayonne, N.J., July 25, 1936; s. Edward C. and Helen G. (Lauenstein) M.; m. Elizabeth Ann Eberhard, Aug. 27, 1960; children: Nancy Elizabeth, Carol Frances, Eilis Marie. B of Engring. Physics, Cornell U., 1959; MA, U. Tex., 1961; PhD, MIT, 1966; DSc, Nat. U. Ireland, Dublin, 1984. Rsch. asst. Woods Hole (Mass.) Oceanographic Inst., 1964-65; asst. prof. physics No. Mich. U., Marquette, 1965-68; asst. prof. oceanography Hobart and William Smith Coll., Geneva, N.Y., 1968-69; asst. prof. dept. meteorology, oceanography U. Mich., Ann Arbor, 1969-71, assoc. prof. dept. atmosphere and ocean sci., 1971-75; dir. edn. and rsch. Sea Edn. Assn., Woods Hole, 1975-76; statutory lectr. phys. oceanography U. Coll., Galway, Ireland, 1976-86; prof. marine scis. U. Conn., Avery Point, 1986—; dir. Conn. Sea Grant Coll. Program, Avery Point, 1986—. Editor: Oceanic Whitecaps and Their Role in Air-Sea Exchange Processes, 1986, Climate and Health Implications of Bubble-Mediated Sea-Air Exchange, 1989; co-editor: (with B. Jähne) Air-Water Gas Transfer, 1995; contbr. numerous articles to profl. jours. Recipient more than 115 rsch. grants, 1966—. Fellow Royal Meteorol. Soc., Am. Meteorol. Soc. (Editor's award 1997); mem. AAUP, Am. Geophys. Union, Am. Soc. Limnology and Oceanography, Acoustical Soc. Am., Internat. Assn. Theoretical and Applied Limnology, Irish Meteorology Soc., Irish Marine Sci. Assn., European Geophys. Soc., The Oceanography Soc. (life). Avocation: recreational sculling.

MONAHAN, FRANCES DONOVAN, nursing educator; b. Lawrence, Mass., Aug. 29, 1943; d. Francis Jeremiah and Isabel Rita (Torpey) Donovan; m. William Thomas Monahan; children: Michael McCain, Kerryane Torpey. AB in Psychology, Emmanuel Coll., 1964; BS in Nursing, Columbia U., 1966; MS in Med. Surg. Nursing, Boston U., 1968; PhD in Nursing, NYU, 1980. RN, N.Y. Staff nurse Lawrence Gen. Hosp., 1967, Columbia Presbyn. Hosp., N.Y.C., 1969; instr. Beth Israel Hosp. Sch. Nursing, N.Y.C., 1969-71; from asst. to assoc. prof. Dept. Nursing Rockland Community Coll., Suffern, N.Y., 1971-82, prof., chmn., 1983—; staff nurse Columbia-Presbyn. Hosp., N.Y.C., 1969; camp nurse Model Cities Program, Highland Falls, N.Y., summers 1972-73, Ladycliff Coll., 1971-74; mem. adj. faculty SUNY, New Paltz, 1985-86, fall 1987; mem. faculty Regents Coll., 1992—; chmn. bd. rev. Coun. Assoc. Degree Programs, 1995-96. Co-author: Writing Across the Curriculum Handbook of Strategies, 1983, Pocket Companion to Nursing Care of Adults, 1994, A Practical Guide to Health Assessment, 1997; editor: Nursing Care of Adults, 1994; contbg. author Pathophysiology; contbr. articles to profl. jours. Mem. adv. bd. Nursing Coll. New Paltz, 1984—; bd. dirs. Orange County Ballet, 1988-90. Recipient Disting. Alumna award in Nursing Edn. Columbia Sch. of Nursing, 1995, Excellence in Practice award Rockland County Nurse Recognition Day, 1995. Mem. ANA, Am. Nursing Dianosis Assn. (charter), Nat. League for Nursing (site visitor for accreditation 1987, mem. bd. rev. assoc. degree coun. 1992-96, initiating commr. accrediting commn. 1997), Mid-Atlantic Regional Nursing Assn., N.Y. State Assn. Degree Nursing Coun., NYU Alumnae Assn., Sigma Theta Tau. Avocations: reading, computing, crocheting, gardening. Office: Rockland C C 145 College Rd Suffern NY 10901-3611

MONAHAN, JOHN T., law educator, psychologist; b. N.Y.C., Nov. 1, 1946; s. John Joseph and Dorothy (King) M.; m. Linda Costa, Aug. 24, 1969; children: Katherine, John. BA, SUNY, 1968; PhD, Ind. U., 1972. Asst. prof. U. Calif., Irvine, 1972-80; prof. U. Va., Charlottesville, 1980-84, Doherty prof., 1985—; dir. mental health law MacArthur Found., Chgo., 1988—. Author: Predicting Violent Behavior, 1981 (Guttmacher award 1981), Social Science in Law, 1994. Recipient Disting. Contbn. Pub. Policy award APA, Washington, 1990. Mem. APA (Isaac Ray award 1996). Home: 939 Rosser Ln Charlottesville VA 22903-1645 Office: U Va Sch Law 580 Massie Rd Charlottesville VA 22903-1738

MONAN, JAMES DONALD, university administrator; b. Blasdell, N.Y., Dec. 31, 1924; s. Edward Roland and Mary Gertrude (Ward) M. AB, Woodstock Coll., 1948, PhL, 1949, STL, 1956; PhD, U. Louvain, 1959; post-doctoral research, Munich, Oxford, Paris; LHD (hon.), Le Moyne Coll., 1973, St. Joseph's Coll., 1973, New Eng. Sch. Law, 1975, Northeastern U., 1975, U. Mass., 1984; LLD (hon.), Harvard U., 1982, Loyola U., Chgo., 1987, Nat. U. Ireland, 1991, Boston Coll., 1996, U. Mass., 1997. Prof. philosophy Le Moyne Coll., Syracuse, N.Y., 1960-68; v.p., acad. dean Le Moyne Coll., 1968-72; pres. Boston Coll., Chestnut Hill, Mass., 1972-96, chancellor, 1996—; cons. to N.Y. Jesuit Provincial for Higher Edn., 1966-72; dir. First Nat. Bank Boston, Bank of Boston Corp., 1976-96; interim pres. Assn. Jesuit Colls. and Univs., 1996-97. Author: The Philosophy of Human Knowing, 1952, A Prelude to Metaphysics, 1967, Moral Knowledge and Its Methodology in Aristotle, 1968. Chmn. edn. div. Boston United Way, 1974; chmn. steering com. of coll. pres. under phase II of ct.-ordered desegregation Boston Pub. Sch. System, 1974-76, Coun. for Aid to Edn., 1985-96, The Partnership, 1984-94, Sr. Thea Bowman Black Cath. Ednl. Found., 1989-96, Gov.'s Internat. Trade Adv. Bd., 1992; bd. dirs. Nat. One to One, 1991—; co-chair Greater Boston One-to-One, 1992—; trustee Le Moyne Coll., 1961-69, 1995—, Fordham U., 1969-75, Boston Coll., 1972-96, Canisius Coll., 1976-82, Georgetown U., 1979-84, Sta WGBH, 1972-96; exec. com. Boston Higher Edn. Ptnrship, 1988-96; mem. com. to Review and Implement Apostolic Constitution Ex Corde Ecclesiae, 1991-96. Mem. Assn. Jesuit Colls. and Univs. (dir., chmn. exec. com. 1983-86), Assn. Ind. Colls. and Univs. Mass. (exec. com. 1988-91, chmn. 1977-78), Nat. Assn. Ind. Colls. and Univs., Harvard Bd. Overseers (com. to visit grad. sch. bus. adminstrn., 1987-93), Nat. Collegiate Athletic Assn. (pres.'s commn. 1984-88), Metaphys. Soc. Am., Jesuit Philos. Assn., Soc. Phenomenology and Existential Philosophy, Soc. Ancient Greek Philosophy. Home: Boston Coll Chestnut Hill MA 02167

MONASEE, CHARLES ARTHUR, retired healthcare foundation executive; b. Gary, Ind., Apr. 29, 1924; s. Sam Hasell and Phyllis (Kresham) M.; m. Lyra Ann Halper, Jan. 28, 1950; children—Pam, Lisa. B.S., U. Chgo., 1944. With Am. Cmty. Stores, 1955-80, pres., 1968-80; pres. Am. Community Stores Corp., Omaha, 1971-80; exec. v.p. parent co. Cullum Companies, 1976-80; group pres. Riekes Group, ALCO Standard Corp., 1980-84; pres. Health Future Found., 1984-96. Pres., bd. dirs. United Way Midlands, 1977-78; bd. dirs. Omaha Symphony Assn., 1968-94, Boys Town, 1973-79, Creighton U., Omaha, 1976—, Ctr. Human Nutrition, 1987—; past chmn. bd. Joslyn Mus.; trustee Nebr. Meth. Hosp., 1974-86, Temple Israel, Omaha; nat. trustee NCCJ, 1986-89; bd. govs. Boys Clubs Omaha, 1975—; past mem. adv. coun. U. Nebr. Med. Ctr., 1978-88; pres. Omaha Jewish Cmty. Ctr., 1972-75; active SAC Hdqs. Consultation Com., 1976-92. Lt.col. USAF, 1943-55. Decorated Bronze Star. Mem. Air Force Assn., Plaza Club. Home: 9977 Spring St Omaha NE 68124-2654

MONAT, WILLIAM ROBERT, university official; b. Biwabik, Minn., Oct. 9, 1924; s. William Stephen and Milda Aleta (Sundby) M.; m. Josephine Ann Sclafani, Sept. 9, 1951; children: Lise Ann, Kathryn, Margaret, William Michael, Eric. A.A., Virginia (Minn.) Jr. Coll., 1947; B.A. magna cum laude, U. Minn., 1949, Ph.D., 1956; postgrad., Wayne U., 1949-50. Asst. prof. Wayne U., 1954-57; exec. asst. to Gov. Mich., 1957-60; asso. prof. Pa. State U., 1960-65, prof. polit. sci., 1965-69; asso. dir. Inst. Pub. Adminstrn., 1962-69; majority budget dir. Pa. Ho. of Reps., 1968-69; prof., chmn. dept. polit. sci. No. Ill. U., De Kalb, 1969-71, provost, 1976-78, Regency prof., 1986-92; Regency prof. emeritus, 1992—; pres. No. Ill. U., De Kalb, 1978-84; chancellor Ill. Bd. Regents, 1984-86; prof., dean faculties Baruch Coll., City U. N.Y., 1971-74, v.p. acad. affairs, 1974-76; cons. USPHS, 1958, Office of Sec. Dept. Labor, 1963-64, Bur. Labor Stads., 1966, Office of Gov. Pa., 1968; bd. dirs. 1st Nat. Bank DeKalb, Castle Bancgroup, Inc., Castle Mortgage Co., Castle Finance Co. Author: Labor Goes to War, 1965, The Public Library and its Community, 1967, Politics, Poverty and Education, 1968; Editor: Public Adminstration in Era of Change, 1962; Contbr. articles to profl. jours. Mem. Gov.'s Commn. on Sci. and Tech., 1983-87; trustee Grad. Sch. Polit. Mgmt., N.Y., 1986—. With AUS, 1943-46. Recipient Outstanding Achievement award U. Minn., 1981; decorated Bronze Star medal. Mem. Am. Polit. Sci. Assn., Am. Soc. Pub. Adminstrn., Phi Beta Kappa. Home: 1605 Mayflower Dr De Kalb IL 60115-1723

MONBERG, JAY PETER, management consultant; b. N.Y.C., Aug. 19, 1935; s. Carl-Johannes and Maria Anna Sophie (Haugwitz-Hardenberg-Reventlow) Hammerich-Monberg; B.B.A., Northwestern U., 1962, M.B.A., 1968. Corp. controller Furnas Elec. Co., Batavia, Ill., 1966-67; sr. v.p., dir. Logan Mfg. Co., Chgo., 1967-72; exec. v.p. Moser Industries, Inc., Naperville, Ill., after 1972; pres., chief exec. officer, dir. Wickman Machine Tools Inc., Elk Grove Village, Ill., also sector exec. John Brown Co., Ltd., London, 1977-80; internat. mgmt. cons., 1980—. Mem. dean's council Grad. Sch. Mgmt., Northwestern U., 1973— . Fellow Inst. Dirs. of U.K., , Inst. Mktg., British Inst. Mgmt.; mem. European Planning Fedn., Inst. of Mktg., Strategic Planning Soc., Internat. Soc. Planning and Strategic Mgmt., Am. Mgmt. Pres. Assn. Scandinavian-Am. Found., Rebild Nat. Park Soc. (v.p.), Dania Soc., Danish Nat. Com. (trustee), Sheffield Hist. Soc., Danish Am. Lang. Found. (pres.), Danish-Am. C. of C. (v.p., dir.), Chgo. Council on Fgn. Relations, Chgo. Com., Internat. Trade Club of Chgo. Clubs: Execs., Mid-Am., Internat., 100 Club of Cook County, Union League (Chgo.); The Am. Club (London, Eng.), The English Speaking Union (London). Home: 5201 S Torrey Pines Dr Unit 1249 Las Vegas NV 89118 also: 1 Passage du Cedre Saint Marceau, 45100 Orleans France Office: 100 Kenilworth Rd, Coventry CV4 7AH, England also: Lerchenborgvej 1 Vanlose, Copenhagen Denmark

MONCHARSH, PHILIP ISAAC, lawyer; b. N.Y.C., May 27, 1948; s. Bernard J. and Betty R. (Chock) M.; m. Karen L. Fellows, Nov. 1, 1981; children: Rachael, Anna. BA, Yale U., 1970; JD, Columbia U., 1973. Bar: Calif. 1973, U.S. Dist. Ct. (cen. dist.) Calif. 1979, U.S. Ct. Appeals (9th cir.) 1981. Trial dep. L.A. County Pub. Defender, L.A., 1973-78; assoc. Strote & Whitehouse, Beverly Hills, Calif., 1978-81, Ghitterman, Hourigan, et al, Ventura, Calif., 1981-86, Heily & Blase, Ventura, Calif., 1986-87; of counsel Hecht, Diamond & Greenfield, Pacific Palisades, Calif., 1988; ptnr. Benton, Orr, Duval & Buckingham, Ventura, 1988-89, Rogers & Sheffield (now Rogers Sheffield & Herman), Santa Barbara, Calif., 1989—; arbitrator, judge pro tem Superior and Mcpl. Cts., Ventura and Santa Barbara, 1986—. Pres. Ojai Valley (Calif.) Land Conservancy, 1988-94. Mem. Calif. Trial Lawyers Assn., Santa Barbara Trial Lawyers Assn., Ventura Trial Lawyers Assn., L.A. Trial Lawyers Assn., Assn. Trial Lawyers Am., Consumer Attys. of Calif., Consumer Attys. of L.A., Yale Club Santa Barbara, Ventura and San Luis Obispo Counties (pres.). Avocations: hiking, backpacking, travel. Office: Rogers Sheffield & Herman 427 E Carrillo St Santa Barbara CA 93101-1401

MONCREIFF, ROBERT P., lawyer; b. Evanston, Ill., Mar. 26, 1930; s. W. Philip and Maxine E. M.; m. Elisabeth M.; children: Anne, Philip, Jane. BA, Yale U., 1952; MA, Oxford U., Eng., 1954; LLB, Harvard U., 1957. Bar: Mass. 1957. Assoc. Palmer & Dodge, Boston, 1957-62, ptnr., 1963-95, of counsel, 1995—. City councillor, Cambridge, Mass., 1970-74. Office: Palmer & Dodge 1 Beacon St Boston MA 02108-3107

MONCRIEF, WILLIAM ALVIN, JR., oil and gas producer; b. Little Rock, Mar. 27, 1920; d. William Alvin and Elizabeth (Bright) M.; m. Deborah Beggs, Jan. 30, 1947; children: William A. III, R.W., C.B., T.O. B.S. in Petroleum Engring., U. Tex., Austin, 1942. Registered profl. engr., Tex. Ptnr. Moncrief Oil, Ft. Worth, 1945—; dir. First Republic Bank, Dallas. Regent, U. Tex. system. Served to ensign USNR, 1944-45, PTO. Named Disting. Engring. Grad. U. Tex.-Austin, 1983. Republican. Episcopalian. Clubs: Shady Oaks of Ft. Worth (pres.); Eldorado (Indian Wells, Calif.); Brookhollow (Dallas). Office: Moncrief Oil Moncrief Bldg 9th And Commerce St Fort Worth TX 76102

MONCURE, JAMES ASHBY, historian; b. Abingdon, Va., June 4, 1926; s. Walter R.D. and Harriet Ashby (Ogburn) M.; m. Jennie Bruce Belk, June 15, 1952; 1 son, James Ashby. BA, U. Richmond, 1949; MA, Columbia U., 1954-74, PhD, 1960. Mem. faculty U. Richmond, 1954-74, prof. English history, 1967-74; dean U. Richmond (Univ. Coll.), 1968-74, dir. univ. summer sch. study abroad program, 1963-70; v.p. for acad. and student affairs Elon Coll., 1974-83, prof. history, 1974-87; Pres. Richmond Experiment Internat. Living, 1957-59, Duntreath Community Assn., 1959-61, Richmond Internat. Council, 1967-69. Editor white paper on activities of Va. Gen. Assembly, 1958, 60, 62 for Va. C. of C., Research Guide to European Historical Biography, 1991, 93, 8 vols. Bd. dirs. English Speaking Union, YMCA, Experiment Internat. Living, E.R. Patterson Edn. Found. Served with inf., M.C. AUS, 1944-46, 50-51. Decorated Bronze Star medal, Combat Inf. badge; Richmond Community ambassador to Eng., 1954. Mem. Experiment Nat. Alumni Assn. (bd. dirs.), Am. Hist. Assn., Archeol. Inst. Am., Conf. Brit. Studies, Va. Social Sci. Assn., Omicron Delta Kappa, Pi Sigma Alpha, Phi Alpha Theta, Cross Keys. Baptist (chmn. bd. deacons). Home: 3336 Seven Lks West End NC 27376

MONCURE, JOHN LEWIS, lawyer; b. Houston, Nov. 4, 1930; s. Walter Raleigh Daniel and Margaret (Atkins) M.; m. Norma Steed, Dec. 29, 1954 (dec. June 1982); children—John Carter, Michael Lewis, Douglas Lee, Stuart Richard, Mary Margaret; m. Margaret Edmonston, Nov. 12, 1983. B.B.A., U. Houston, 1953; J.D., U. Tex., 1956. Bar: Tex. 1956. Assoc. Butler, Binion, Rice, Cook & Knapp, Houston, 1956-68; ptnr. Prappas, Moncure & Eidman, Houston, 1969-86, John L. Moncure and Assocs., Houston, 1987—; lectr. bus. law U. Houston, 1958-59, 68-69. Mem. sch. bd. St. Thomas Episcopal Sch., Houston, 1965-78; mem. vestry St. Thomas Episc. Ch., 1975-78. Named Distinguished Alumni Coll. Bus., U. Houston, 1968. Fellow Am. Coll. Probate Counsel; mem. Am., Tex., Houston bar assns., Assn. Christian Schs. (trustee), Coll. Bus. Alumni Assn. U. Houston (pres., dir.), U. Houston Alumni Fedn. (treas., dir.), Sigma Alpha Epsilon. Democrat. Home: 1100 Richmond Ave Apt 10 Houston TX 77006-5447 Office: 1200 River Oaks Tower 3730 Kirby Dr Houston TX 77098-3905

MONDALE, JOAN ADAMS, wife of former vice president of United States; b. Eugene, Oreg., Aug. 8, 1930; d. John Maxwell and Eleanor Jane (Hall) Adams; m. Walter F. Mondale, Dec. 27, 1955; children—Theodore, Eleanor Jane, William Hall. BA, Macalester Coll., 1952. Asst. slide librarian Boston Mus. Fine Arts, 1952-53; asst. in edn. Mpls. Inst. of Arts, 1953-57; weekly tour guide Nat. Gallery of Art, Washington, 1965-74; hostess Washington Whirl-A-Round, 1975-76. Author: Politics in Art, 1972. Mem. bd. govs. Women's Nat. Dem. Club; hon. chmn. Fed. Coun. on Arts and Humanities, 1978-80; bd. dirs. Associated Coun. of Arts, 1973-75, Reading Is Fundamental, Am. Craft Coun., N.Y.C., 1981-88, J.F.K. Center Performing Arts, 1981-90, Walker Art Ctr., Mpls., 1987-93, Minn. Orch., Mpls., 1988-93, St. Paul Chamber Orch., 1988-90, Northern Clay Ctr., 1988-93, St. Paul, 1988-93, Nancy Hauser Dance Co., Mpls., 1989-93, Minn. Landmarks, 1991-93; trustee Macalester Coll., 1986—. Presbyterian. Office: Unit 45004 Box 200 APO AP 96337-5004

MONDALE, WALTER FREDERICK, former vice president of United States, diplomat, lawyer; b. Ceylon, Minn., Jan. 5, 1928; s. Theodore Sigvaard and Claribel Hope (Cowan) M.; m. Joan Adams, Dec. 27, 1955;children: Theodore, Eleanor, William. BA cum laude, U. Minn., 1951, LLB, 1956. Bar: Minn. 1956. Law clk. Minn. Supreme Ct.; pvt. practice law, 1956-60; atty. gen. State of Minn., 1960-64; U.S. senator from Minn., 1964-77, v.p. of U.S., 1977-81; mem. Nat. Security Council, 1977-81; mem. firm Winston & Strawn, 1981-87; ptnr. Dorsey & Whitney, Mpls., 1987-93; U.S. amb. to Japan Tokyo, 1993-96. Author: The Accountability of Power—Toward a Responsible Presidency, 1975; mem. Minn. Law Rev. Dem. nominee for Pres. U.S., 1984. With U.S. Army, 1951-53. Mem. Minn. Law Review. Presbyterian.

MONDAY, JON ELLIS, music publishing company executive; b. San Jose, Calif., Oct. 6, 1947; s. John Lang Monday and Marjorie (Meinecke) Licht; m. Anna Genia Hochman, Nov. 6, 1968; 1 child, Rachel. V.p., gen. mgr. Takoma Records, L.A., 1970-79; dir. mktg. Chrysalis Records, Inc., L.A., 1979-82; v.p. product devel. Romox, Inc., Campbell, Calif., 1982-85; v.p. mgmt. info. systems Epyx, Inc., Redwood City, Calif., 1985-89; pres., co-founder MusicWriter, Inc., Los Gatos, Calif., 1989—. Producer various records including Gospel Nights, 1979, Last Chance..., 1978, A Christmas Yet to Come, 1975; co-inventor NoteStation music distribution system. Mem. Vedanta Soc. (bd. dirs.). Office: MusicWriter Inc 170 Knowles Dr Ste 203 Los Gatos CA 95030-1833

MONDESI, RAUL, professional baseball player; b. San Cristobal, Dominican Republic, Mar. 12, 1971. Grad. H.S., Dominican Republic. Outfield L.A. Dodgers, 1993—. named N.L Rookie of The Yr., Baseball Writers' Assn. Am., 1994, N.L Rookie of Yr., The Sporting News, 1994; selected to N.L. All-Star Team, 1995. Office: LA Dodgers 1000 Elysian Park Ave Los Angeles CA 90012-1112*

MONDLIN, MARVIN, retail executive, antiquarian book dealer; b. Bklyn., July 1, 1927; s. Samuel and Thelma (Schultz) M.; m. Phyllis Grossman, Oct. 23, 1962 (div. 1968); 1 child, Gerri; m. Irene Szmulewicz, Sept. 4, 1970. Student, Cornell U., 1945; student of Aesthetic Realism, with Eli Siegel, 1945-68; student, CCNY, 1948, Bklyn. Coll., 1969-71. Ptnr. Amory Books, N.Y.C., 1953-59; clk. Strand Book Store, N.Y.C., 1951, estate book buyer, 1959-71, 74-76, sr. exec. v.p., 1976—; bus. mgr. Definition Press., N.Y.C., 1957; cataloger U. Cath. de Louvain, Belgium, 1972. Author: Appraisals: A Guide for Bookmen, 1997; proofreader, copy editor Dover Publs., N.Y.C., 1958; editor Yearbook of Internat. Assocs., 1974. Mem. Antiquarian Booksellers Assn. Am., Appraisers Assn. Am., Bibliog. Soc. Am., Bibliog. Soc. London, Am. Photog. Hist. Soc., European Soc. History of Photography. Avocations: photography, non-silver processes lab. work, natural history, horticulture, music. Home: 889 Broadway New York NY 10003-1212 Office: Strand Book Store 828 Broadway New York NY 10003-4805 *Lectures and writes articles on rare books; diverse related activities in publishing and editing; speaks French; reads Spanish; some acquaintance with German, Russian, other major European languages. Appearances in numerous major American newspapers (e.g. 2 column front page article in Wall Street Journal: August 21, 1986) and journals abroad in Germany, Switzerland, Finland, Sweden, etc. Plans availability as consultant in used and rare book field. Marvin Mondlin is willing to speak on serious book-related television and radio talk shows; is presently at work on a centennial, pictorial and anecdotal history of New York City's Fourth Avenue book trade: 1890-1990.*

MONDSCHEIN, LAWRENCE GEOFFREY, medical products executive; b. New Brunswick, N.J., Nov. 3, 1957; s. Harold and Florence (Kaplovsky) M.; m. Ellen Laurie Hirschhorn, Aug. 17, 1995. BS, Rutgers U., 1980, MLS, 1985, PhD, 1988. Regulatory asst. Janssen Pharmaceutica, Piscataway, N.J., 1983-84, database adminstr., 1984-86; rsch. adminstr. Janssen Rsch. Found., Piscataway, 1986-89; mgr. chem. info. Johnson & Johnson World Hdqrs., New Brunswick, N.J., 1989—; mem. planning panel on toxicology & environ. health Nat. Libr. Medicine, Bethesda, Md., 1992. Contbr. articles to profl. jours. Trustee Essex Skating Club of N.J., sec., 1984-88, v.p., 1988-90, pres., 1990-93. Mem. U.S. Figure Skating Assn. (nat. judge 1992—, sectional vice chmn. for judges 1993-95, bd. dirs. 1995—), Am. Soc. for Info. Sci. Avocations: figure skating (gold medalist in figures, free skating and ice dancing). Office: Johnson & Johnson 1 Johnson And Johnson Plz New Brunswick NJ 08933-0001

MONE, MICHAEL EDWARD, lawyer; b. Brockton, Mass., May 15, 1942; s. Edward Patrick and June Elizabeth (Kelliher) M.; m. Margaret E. Supple, Sept. 11, 1965; 1 child, Michael E., Jr. B.A., Middlebury Coll., 1964; J.D., Boston Coll., 1967. Bar: Mass. 1967, U.S. Dist. Ct. Mass. 1968. U.S. Ct. Appeals (1st cir.) 1968. Trial atty. Schneider & Reilly, Boston, 1967-73, ptnr., 1969-73; trial lawyer Esdaile, Barrett & Esdaile Boston, 1973—, ptnr., 1976—; instr. Boston Coll. Law Sch., 1981. Chmn. Zoning Bd. Appeals, Brockton, Mass., 1976-78. Fellow Am. Coll. Trial Lawyers (bd. regents

1995—); mem. ABA, Am. Trial Lawyers Assn. (bd. govs. 1975-78), Mass. Bar Assn. (pres. 1993-94), Mass. Acad. Trial Lawyers (pres. 1981-84, joint bar com. on judicial nominations 1986-90). Office: Esdaile Barrett & Esdaile 75 Federal St Boston MA 02110-1913

MONE, ROBERT PAUL, lawyer; b. Columbus, Ohio, July 23, 1934; s. Henry P. and Ann E. (Freedlund) M.; m. Lucille L. Willman, May 3, 1960; children: Robert, Maria, Andrew, Richard. BA, U. Dayton, 1956; JD, U. Notre Dame, 1959. Bar: Ohio 1959. Law clk.to presiding judge U.S. Dist. Ct. (no. dist.) Ohio, Cleve., 1960-62; assoc. George, Greek, King, et al, Columbus, 1962-66, ptnr., 1966-79; ptnr. McConnaughey, Stradley, et al, Columbus, 1979-81, Thompson Hine & Flory LLP, Columbus, 1981—. Cpl. U.S. Army, 1959-60. Mem. ABA, Ohio State Bar Assn., Fed. Energy Bar Assn., Columbus Bar Assn., Nat. Generation and Transmission Coop. Lawyers Assn. (1st pres.), Rotary. s. Home: 2300 Tremont Rd Columbus OH 43221-3706 Office: Thompson Hine & Flory LLP 10 W Broad St Columbus OH 43215-3418

MONEGRO, FRANCISCO, psychology educator, alternative medicine consultant; b. La Vega, Dominican Republic, Apr. 20, 1949; s. Francisco Monegro-Fdez and Ana A. (Pena) Monegro. Grad. cum laude, Pontifical U., Santiago, Dominican Republic, 1973; grad. psychology, Autonomous U. Santo Domingo, 1978, MD, 1986; MA in Ednl. Psychology, Tech. Inst. Santo Domingo, 1981; PhD in Nutrition, LaSalle U., Mandeville, La., 1993. Cert. natural health profl., hypnotherapist, profl. biofeedback profl.; diplomate in behavioral medicine, diplomate in pain mgmt.; lic. in psychology Autonomous U. Santo Domingo, 1978. Tchr. Peace H.S., Santo Domingo, Dominican Republic, 1975-76; dir. dept. psychology Holy Trinity Ednl. Ctr., Santo Domingo, 1978-80; prof. Sch. Medicine Tech. Inst. Santo Domingo, 1986-87; dir. dept. psychology Interam. U., Santo Domingo, 1988-89; prof. psychology and medicine Autonomous U. Santo Domingo, 1978-89, psychologist, counseling dept., 1979-84; staff mem. spl. edn. Bd. Edn. Dist. X, Bronx, N.Y., 1991-93; founder, chmn. N.Y. Inst. for Holistic Life, N.Y.C., 1991—; prof. psychology CUNY at HCC, Bronx, 1990—; founder, pioneer in behavioral medicine Behavioral Medicine Clinic, Santo Domingo, 1987-94. Author: Biofeedback-Bio-retroalimentacion, 1988, Holistic Behavioral Medicine, 1993, Biomagnetic Medicine: Secrets and Power of Magnetic Energy, 1996, Psychology and Life Mind, Body and Society, 1997; editor, pub.: BOEST, 1978, Dominican Bull. Behavioral Medicine, 1987, Holistic Life/Vida Holistica, 1991, others. Mem. Dominican Psychol. Assn. (treas. 1978-79), Soc. Behavioral Medicine, Assn. for Advancement of Behavior Therapy, Am. Acad. Pain Mgmt., Assn. for Applied Psychophysiology and Biofeedback. Democrat. Roman Catholic. Avocations: computers, golf, basketball, swimming, travel. Home: PO Box 302 Bronx NY 10458 Office: NY Inst for Holistic Life 336 Fort Washington Ave Ste 1-a New York NY 10033-6803

MONEO, JOSÉ RAFAEL, architecture educator; b. Tudela, Navarra, Spain, May 9, 1937; s. Rafael and María Teresa (Vallés); m. Belén Feduchi; children: Belén, Teresa, Clara Matilde. Degree in architecture, Madrid, 1961, DArch, 1963; DArch (hon.), Harvard U., 1986. Postgrad. fellow Spanish Acad., Rome, 1963-65; prof. architecture Barĉelona, Spain, 1971-80, Madrid, 1981-84; prof. architecture Sch. Design, Harvard U., Cambridge, Mass., 1985—, chmn. dept. architecture, 1985—. Prin. works include Bankinter, Madrid, Logronó Hall, Merida Roman Art Mus., Atocha Sta., Madrid, Seville (Spain) Airport, Auditorium of Barcelona, Auditorium of San Sebastian, Thyssen-Bornemesza Mus., Madrid, Wellesley Coll. Davis Mus., Miro Collection Mus., Mallorca, Diagonal Bldg., Barcelona. Recipient Arnold W. Brunner Mem. prize in Architecture, Am. Acad. Arts and Letters, 1994. Office: Harvard U Dept Arch 48 Quincy St Cambridge MA 02138*

MONEY, JOHN WILLIAM, psychologist; b. Morrinsville, N.Z., July 8, 1921; came to U.S., 1947, naturalized, 1962; s. Frank and Ruth (Read) M. MA with honors, Victoria U. Coll., N.Z., 1943; postgrad., U. Pitts., 1947; PhD, Harvard U., 1952; DHL (hon.), Hofstra U., 1992. Jr. lectr. philosophy and psychology U. Otago, N.Z., 1945-47; part-time vis. lectr. Bryn Mawr Coll., Pa., 1952-53; mem. faculty Johns Hopkins U., 1951—, prof. med. psychology, 1972-86, assoc. prof. pediatrics, 1959-86, prof. emeritus med. psychology and pediatrics, 1986—; psychologist Johns Hopkins Hosp., 1955—, founder psychohormonal research unit, 1951, founding mem. gender identity com., 1966—; vis. prof. pediats. Albert Einstein Coll. Medicine, 1969, U. Nebr. Coll. Medicine, 1972; vis. prof. endocrinology Harvard U., 1970; vis. prof. ob-gyn. U. Conn., 1975; Rachford lectr. Children's Hosp., Cin., 1969; bd. dirs. Sex Info. and Edn. Coun. U.S., 1965-68, Neighborhood Family Planning Ctr., 1970-82; mem. task force homosexuality NIMH, 1967-69; mem. study sect. devel. and behavioral scis. NIH, 1970-74; mem. task force on nomenclature Am. Psychiat. Assn., 1977-79, 85-87; pres. Am. Found. Gender and Genital Medicine and Sci., 1978—; bd. advisors Elysium Inst., 1980—; mem. adv. bd. Internat. Coun. Sec. Edn. and Parenthood, 1981—; mem. external com. for rev. of Inst. for Sex Rsch., Ind. U., 1980; mem. sci. adv. bd. The Kinsey Inst. for Rsch. in Sex, Gender and Reprodn., 1982—; hon. chmn. internat. adv. bd. Nat. Inst. Rsch. in Sex Edn., Counseling and Therapy, 1991; Kan Tongpo vis. prof. dept. psychiatry U. Hong Kong, 1994. Mem. editl. bd. numerous jours.; field editor Medicine and Law: an Internat. Jour., 1982—. Recipient Hofheimer prize Am. Psychiat. Assn., 1956, Gold medal Children's Hosp., Phila., 1966, citation Am. Urol. Assn., 1975, Harry Benjamin medal of honor Erickson Ednl. Found., 1976, Outstanding Contbn. award Md. Psychol. Assn., 1976, Lindemann lectr. pediatrics Cornell U., 1983, Bernadine Disting. lectr. U. Mo., 1985, Maurice W. Laufer Meml. lectr. Bradley Hosp. and Brown U., 1986, Disting. Scholar award Harry Benjamin Internat. Gender Dysphoria Assn., 1987, Outstanding Rsch. Accomplishments award Nat. Inst. Child Health and Human Devel., 1987, Gloria Scientae award, 1991, Lifetime Outstanding Sci. Contbn. award Internat. Cmty. Profls. for Treatment of Sex Offenders, 1991, Richard J. Cross award Robert Wood Johnson Med. Sch., 1992, Career Achievement award N.Y. Soc. Forensic Scis., 1994, Coun. of Sex Edn. and Parenthood Internat. award, 1994; named Sexologist of Yr. Polish Acad. Sex. Sci., 1988; James McKeen Cattell fellow Am. Psychol. Soc., 1993; subject of book John Money: A Tribute (E. Coleman, editor), 1991. Fellow AAAS (life), Soc. Sci. Study Sex (charter, pres. 1974-76, award 1976, Past Pres. award 1987, Kinsey award western regional chpt. 1996), Harriet Lane Alumni Soc., Nat. Inst. Rsch. Sex Edn., Counseling and Therapy (hon.); mem. APA (master lectr. 1975, Disting. Sci. award 1985), Deutsche Gesellschaft für Sexualforschung, Internat. Orgn. Study Human Devel., Soc. Pediat. Psychology, Lawson Wilkins Pediat. Endocrine Soc. (founder), Am. Assn. Sex Educators, Counselors and Therapists (hon. mem., awards 1976, 85), European Soc. Pediat. Endocrinology (corr.), Internat. Acad. Sex Rsch. (charter, award 1991), Assn. Sexologists (life), Columbian Sexol. Soc. (hon.), Internat. Soc. Psychoneuroendocrinology, N.Y. Acad. Scis., Md. Soc. Med. Rsch., Internat. Coll. Pediats., Czechoslovak Sexology Soc. (hon., mem. internat. adv. bd. 1995), New Zealand Soc. on Sexology (hon., life), Sociedad Brasileira de Sexologia (hon.), Sociedad Andaluza de Sexologia (hon.), Can. Sex Rsch. Forum (hon.), Asian Fedn. for Sexology (hon.), Assn. de Especialistas en Sexologia (hon.). Home: 2104 E Madison St Baltimore MD 21205-2337 Office: Johns Hopkins Hosp Baltimore MD 21205 *It has always been my policy to combine research with clinical care, academic teaching and public education. I have combined a lifelong interest in world travel and in research by lecturing on all continents except Antarctica.*

MONEY, RUTH ROWNTREE, child development specialist, consultant; b. Brownwood, Tex.; m. Lloyd Jean Money; children: Jeffrey, Meredith, Jeannette. BA in Biology, Rice U., 1944; MA in Devel. Psychology, Calif. State U., Long Beach, 1971; BA in Early Childhood Edn., U. D.C., 1979. Rsch. psychologist Early Edn. Project, Capitol Heights, Md., 1971-73; lectr. No. Va. C.C., Anandale, 1973-74; tchr. preschs. Calif. and Va., 1979-81; dir. various preschs., Washington and Va., 1981-85; instr. guided studies Pacific Oaks Coll., Pasadena, Calif., 1986-88; cons. parent/infant programs Resources for Infant Educarers, L.A., 1986—; founder, dir. South Bay Infant Ctr., Redondo Beach, Calif., 1988-92; instr. child devel. Harbor Coll., L.A., 1992-93; bd. dirs. Resources for Infant Educarers, 1986—; pres. bd. dirs. South Bay Infant Ctr., Redondo Beach, 1988-94, treas., 1994—. Producer (ednl. videos) Caring for Infants, 1988—. Mem. League of Women Voters, 1956—, v.p., 1972-76. Mem. Nat. Assn. for Edn. of Young Children, Assn. for Childhood Edn. Internat. Avocations: traveling, hiking. Home: 904 21st St Hermosa Beach CA 90254-3105 Office: Resources for Infant Educarers 1550 Murray Cir Los Angeles CA 90026-1644

MONEYPENNY, EDWARD WILLIAM, petroleum exploration and production executive; b. Long Branch, N.J., Jan. 28, 1942; s. Edward Henry and Eleanor Kathleen (O'Hagen) M.; BS in Acctg., St. Joseph's U., 1964; MS in Acctg. Sci., U. Ill., 1967; m. Connie Wills, Feb. 19, 1966; children—Matthew, Jonathan, Christopher. Audit mgr. Coopers & Lybrand, Phila., 1970-76; mgr. corp. acctg. Sun Co., Inc., Radnor, Pa., 1976-78; v.p. fin. adminstrn. Sun Prodn. Co., Dallas, 1978-81; v.p. fin. and CFO Oryx Energy Co. (formerly Sun Exploration & Prodn. Co.), Dallas, 1981-91; sr. v.p. fin., CFO Oryx Energy Co, Dallas, 1992-94, exec. v.p. fin., bd. dir. and CFO, 1994—; mng. gen. ptnr. Sun Energy Ptnr. L.P. Bus. adv. coun. U. Ill. Sch. Bus., 1994—. Bd. dirs. Hesbic Inc. of Dallas, 1984—. 1st lt. U.S. Army, 1967-70. CPA, Tex. Mem. AICPA, Fin. Execs. Inst., Tex. Soc. CPAs. Home: 4712 Stoneholow Way Dallas TX 75287-7524 Office: Oryx Energy Co 13155 Noel Rd Dallas TX 75240-5090

MONFILS-CLARK, MAUD ELLEN, analyst; b. Amstelveen, The Netherlands, June 7, 1955; d. Wouter William Frederic and Jeane Albertina (Verbauwen) Monfils; m. Harry Carl Clark, Nov. 26, 1983 (div. 1993). BSBA, Calif. State U., L.A., 1990. Physicians assocs. mgr. L.A. County Health Dept., L.A., 1990-92, fin. mgr., 1992-93, health planning analyst, 1993-95; contract officer Gen. Relief Health Care Program, 1995—; active Comm. Strategy Group, L.A., 1994—, Workforce Devel., L.A., 1994—; mem. staff Stragetic Planning Leadership Team, L.A., 1994—, High Desert Hosp. Strategic Planning Com., L.A., 1994—. Co-recipient Nat. Assn. Counties award, 1994, Pub. Svc. Excellence award, 1994. Avocations: gardening, needlepoint, writing, reading.

MONG, ROBERT WILLIAM, JR., publisher; b. Fremont, Ohio, Jan. 22, 1949; s. Robert William and Betty (Dwyer) M.; m. Carla Beth Sweet, July 25, 1975 (div. 1979); m. Diane Elizabeth Reischel, Jan. 23, 1988; children: Eric Robert, Elizabeth Diana. BA, Haverford (Pa.) Coll., 1971. Reporter Cin. Post, 1973-75, Capital Times, Madison, Wis., 1975-77; city editor Madison Press Connection, 1977-79; asst. city editor Dallas Morning News, 1979-80, bus. editor, 1980-81, projects editor, 1981-83, asst. mng. editor, 1983-88, dep. mng. editor, 1988-90, mng. editor, 1990-96; pub. Owensboro Messenger-Inquirer, 1996—. Mem. Am. Soc. Newspaper Editors, Newspaper Assn. Am. Office: Messenger-Inquirer PO Box 1480 1401 Frederica St Owensboro KY 42302-1480*

MONGAN, JAMES JOHN, physician, hospital administrator; b. San Francisco, Ca., Apr. 10, 1942; s. Martin and Audrey Vera (Cunningham) M.; m. Jean Trotter Holmes, Apr. 22, 1972; children—John Holmes, Sarah Holmes. Student, U. Calif., Berkeley, 1959-62; BA, Stanford U., 1963, MD, 1967. Intern Kaiser Found. Hosp., San Francisco, 1967-68; med. officer USPHS, Denver, 1968-70; profl. staff mem. U.S. Senate Fin. Com., Washington, 1970-77; dep. asst. sec. for health HEW, Washington, 1977-79; assoc. dir. human resources Domestic Policy Staff, White House, 1979-81; asst. surgeon gen. USPHS, 1979-81; exec. dir. Truman Med. Center, U. Mo., Kansas City, 1981—; dean sch. medicine U. Mo., Kansas City, 1987-96; pres., COO Mass. Gen. Hosp., 1996—; prof. healthcare policy, prof. medicine Harvard Med. Sch. Commr. Dept. Vets. Affairs Commn. on Future Structure of Vets. Health Care, 1990-91; mem. Pew Health Profesions Commn., Kaiser commn. on Future of Medicaid, Joint Commn. Users Adv. Group; trustee Pembroke Hills Sch., Kansas City, Mo.; bd. dirs. Midwest Rsch. Ins., Kansas City, Mo. Med. officer USPHS, 1968-70, asst. surgeon gen., 1979-81; trustee Kaiser Family Found.; chmn. Commonwealth Fund Health Adv. Com. Mem. NAS (Inst. Medicine), Am. Hosp. Assn. (trustee 1988-91), Am. Assn. Teaching Hosps. (bd. dirs. coun. teaching hosps. 1984-90). Home: 135 Crafts Rd Chestnut Hill MA 02167-1825 Office: Massachusetts General Hospital 32 Fruit St Boston MA 02114-2620

MONGE, JAY PARRY, lawyer; b. N.Y.C., Mar. 15, 1943; s. Joseph Paul and Dorothy Emma (Oschmann) M.; m. Julia T. Burdick, 1966 (div. 1994); children: Justin Parry, Lindsay Newton; m. Elizabeth Ann Tracy, 1994. AB, Harvard U., 1966; LLB, U. Va., 1969. Bar: Ill. 1969, N.Y. 1981. Assoc. Mayer, Brown & Platt, Chgo., 1969-75, ptnr., 1976-79; ptnr. Mayer, Brown & Platt, N.Y.C., 1980—, mng. ptnr., 1981-94. Contbr. legal commentaries Ill. Inst. Continuing Legal Edn., 1974, 78, 81, 84, 87, 93, 96. Trustee Wagner Coll., 1996—. Mem. ABA, Assn. Bar City N.Y., Chgo. Club, Onwentsia Club, Sky Club. Office: Mayer Brown & Platt 1675 Broadway New York NY 10019-5820

MONHOLLON, LELAND, lawyer; b. Corbin, Ky., Nov. 8, 1925; s. Lewis Tom and Thelma (Prewitt) M.; m. Gawinna Owens, 1946 (div. 1969); 1 child, Patricia Lynn; m. Alice Faye Burden, July 3, 1970. JD, U. Ky., 1952. Bar: Ky. 1952. Supervising adjustor Travelers Ins. Co., Louisville, 1955-69; pvt. practice law Madisonville, Ky., 1969—. With USN, 1943-46, PTO, USNR, 1963-69. Mem. Ky. Bar Assn., Hopkins County Bar Assn., Am. Legion, VFW. Republican. Baptist. Home: 185 Threadneedle Dr Madisonville KY 42431-6439 Office: 111 S Main St Madisonville KY 42431-2555

MONIA, JOAN, management consultant; b. Teaneck, N.J., Mar. 20, 1938; d. James Anthony and Anne Linden (Cairns) McCaffrey; m. Charles Anthony Monia, Dec. 30, 1961; 1 child, Clare Ann Woodman. BA, Ohio Dominican U., 1960. Info. specialist Battelle Meml. Inst., Columbus, Ohio, 1960-62; project leader Douglas Aircraft Corp., Huntington Beach, Calif., 1962-64; programmer analyst McDonnell Aircraft Corp., St. Louis, 1965-66; project mgr. Sanders Assocs., Nashua, N.H., 1968-70; database adminstrn. project leader Mass. Blue Cross, Boston, 1970-74; data strategist Factory Mut. Engring. Corp., Norwood, Mass., 1974-78; mgr. data resource planning Digital Equipment Corp., Maynard, Mass., 1978-84; sr. mem. tech. staff GTE Govt. Systems Corp., Needham, Mass., 1984-91; prin. DMR Group, Inc., Waltham, Mass., 1991-96; cons. Marlborough, Mass., 1997—. Recipient Sci. medal Bausch & Lomb, 1956. Avocation: painting. Home: 175 Anderson Rd Marlborough MA 01752-1474

MONICAL, ROBERT DUANE, consulting structural engineer; b. Morgan County, Ind., Apr. 30, 1925; s. William Blaine and Mary Elizabeth (Lang) M.; m. Carol Arnetha Dean, Aug. 10, 1947 (dec. 1979); children: Mary Christine, Stuart Dean, Dwight Lee; m. Sharon Kelly Eastwood, July 13, 1980; 1 stepson, Jeffrey David Eastwood. B.S.C.E., Purdue U., 1948, M.S.C.E., 1949. Engr. N.Y.C. R.R., Cin., 1949-51, So. Rwy., Cin., 1951; design engr. Pierce & Gruber (Cons. Engrs.), Indpls., 1952-54; founder, partner Monical & Wolverton (Cons. Engrs.), Indpls., 1954-63; founder, partner Monical Assocs., Indpls., 1963—, pres., 1975—; v.p. Zurwelle-Whittaker, Inc. (Engrs. and Land Surveyors), Miami Beach, Fla., 1975-90; Mem. Ind. Adminstrv. Bldg. Council, 1969-75; chmn., 1973-75; mem. Meridian St. Preservation Commn., 1971-75, Ind. State Bd. of Registration for Profl. Engrs. and Land Surveyors, 1976-84, chmn., 1979, 83. Served with USNR, 1943-46, USAR, 1948-53. Mem. ASCE (Outstanding Civil Engr. award Ind. sect. 1987), Cons. Engrs. Ind. (pres. 1969, Cons. Recognition award 1986), Am. Cons. Engrs. Council (pres. 1978-79), Ind. Soc. Profl. Engrs. (Engr. of Yr. 1980), Nat. Soc. Profl. Engrs., Prestressed Concrete Inst., Am. Concrete Inst., Post-Tensioning Inst., Am. Inst. Steel Constrn., Am. Arbitration Assn., Indpls. Sci. and Engring. Found. (pres. 1992-93), Am. Legion, Lions, Masons, Shriners. Mem. Christian Ch. Home and Office: 14238 Skipper Ct Carmel IN 46033-8715

MONIS, ANTONIO, JR. (TONY MONIS), electric industry executive. Pres. Consolidated Electrical Distributors, Thousand Oaks, Calif. Office: Consolidated Electrical Distrs 31356 Via Colinas Thousand Oaks CA 91362-3915*

MONISMITH, CARL LEROY, civil engineering educator; b. Harrisburg, Pa., Oct. 23, 1926; s. Carl Samuel and Camilla Frances (Geidt) M. BSCE, U. Calif., Berkeley, 1950, MSCE, 1954. Registered Civil Engr., Calif. From instr. to prof. of civil engring. dept. civil engring. U. Calif., Berkeley, 1951—, chmn. dept. civil engring., 1974-79, Robert Horonjeff prof. civil engring., 1986—; cons. Chevron Rsch. Co., Richmond, Calif., 1957-93, U.S. Army CE Waterways Expt. Sta., Vicksburg, Miss., 1968—, B.A. Vallerga, Inc., Oakland, Calif., 1980—, ARE, Austin, Tex. and Scotts Valley, Calif., 1978-92; cons. Bechtel Corp., San Francisco, 1982-86. Contbr. numerous articles to profl. jours. Served to 2d lt. U.S. Army Corps Engrs., 1945-47. Recipient Rupert Myers medal U. NSW, 1976; named Henry M. Shaw Lectr. in Civil Engring., N.C. State U., 1993; sr. scholar Fulbright Found., U. NSW, 1971; named Disting. Engring. Alumnus, Coll. Engring., U. Calif., Berkeley, 1996. Fellow AAAS, NAE; mem. ASCE (hon. mem., pres. San Francisco sect. 1979-80, ednl. activities com. 1989-91, State of Art award 1977, James Laurie prize 1988), ASTM, Assn. Asphalt Paving Technologies (hon., pres. 1968, W.J. Emmons award 1961, 65, 85), Transp. Rsch. Bd. (assoc., chmn. pavement design sect. 1973-79, K.B. Woods award 1972, 1st disting. lectureship 1992, Roy W. Crum award 1995), Am. Soc. Engring. Edn., Internat. Soc. for Asphalt Pavements (chmn. bd. dirs. 1988-90), Asphalt Inst. (roll of honor 1990), U. Calif. (Berkeley citation 1996). Avocations: swimming, stamp collecting. Office: U Calif Dept Civil Engring 115 McLaughlin Hall Berkeley CA 94720

MONIZ, ERNEST JEFFREY, physics educator; b. Fall River, Mass., Dec. 22, 1944; s. Ernest Perry and Georgina (Pavao) M.; m. Naomi Hoki, June 9, 1973; 1 child, Katya. B.S., Boston Coll., 1966; Ph.D., Stanford U., 1971. Prof. physics MIT, Cambridge, Mass., 1973—; dir. Bates Linear Accelerator Ctr. MIT, Middleton, Mass., 1983-91, head physics dept., 1991-95, 97—; cons. Los Alamos Nat. Lab., 1975-95; assoc. dir. for sci. Office of Sci. and Tech. Policy, Exec. Office of the Pres., 1996-97. Contbr. numerous articles to profl. jours. Office: MIT Dept Physics 6-113 Cambridge MA 02139

MONJAN, ANDREW ARTHUR, health science administrator; b. N.Y.C., Feb. 9, 1938; s. Victor Momjian and Sonia (Sherinian) Dardarian; m. Susan Vollenweider, July 1961 (div. Nov. 1965); m. Usha Bose, Aug. 14, 1969; children: Matthew, Vanessa. BSc, Rensselaer Poly. Inst., 1960; PhD, U. Rochester, 1965; MPH, Johns Hopkins U., 1970. Rsch. asst. Sterling-Winthrop Rsch. Inst., Rensselaer, N.Y., 1960; USPHS rsch. fellow Ctr. for Brain Rsch. U. Rochester, N.Y., 1964-66; asst. prof. depts. psychology and physiology U. Western Ont., London, Can., 1966-69; from asst. prof. to assoc. prof. dept. epidemiology Sch. Hygiene and Pub. Health Johns Hopkins U., Balt., 1971-83; expert epidemiology extramural programs br. NIH, Bethesda, Md., 1983-85; chief neurobiology/immunology programs physiology aging br. NIH, Bethesda, 1985-87, acting assoc. dir., 1987, chief neurobiology, acting chief neuropsychology brs., 1987—; exec. sec. Nat. Commn. on Sleep Disorders Rsch., 1990-92; presenter in field. Contbr. articles to profl. jours. N.Y. State Regents scholar, 1955-59; N.Y. State Regents Grad. Tchg. fellow, 1960-62, USPHS rsch. fellow, 1962-64, 64-66. Mem. Soc. for Neurosci., Sigma Xi. Office: Nat Inst Aging Ste 3C307 7201 Wisconsin Ave # 9205 Bethesda MD 20814-4810

MONK, ALLAN JAMES, baritone; b. Mission City, B.C., Can., Aug. 19, 1942; m. Marlene Folk; 3 children. Student, Elgar Higgin and Boris Goldovsky. Operatic debut in Old Maid and the Thief San Francisco, 1967; joined touring co., later main co. San Francisco Opera; appeared with Tulsa Opera, Pitts. Opera, Edmonton Opera, Vancouver Opera, So. Alta. Opera, Chgo. Opera, Balt. Opera, Miami Opera, Colo. Opera, Mont real Opera, Hawaii Opera Theatre, Portland Opera.;, 1976. Met. Opera debut as Schaunard in La Boheme, 1976, sang title role in Wozzeck, Wolfram in Tannheuser, Dr. Malatesta in Don Pasquale, Rodrigo in Don Carlo, Sharpless in Madame Butterfly, Herald in Lohengrin; sang with Can. Opera Co. as Abelard in Heloise and Abelard, Macbeth, Rigoletto, Belcore in L'Elisir D'Amoure, Jago in Otello, as Ford in Falstaff, four villains in Les Contes d'Hoffman; with Nat. Arts Ctr. Opera Festival, Ottawa, Ont., Can., title role in Don Giovanni, Almaviva in Le Nozze Di Figaro, gulielmo in Cossi Fan Tutti, Tomsky in Pique Dame, Marcello in La Boheme; Carnegie Hall debut as Vladislav in Dalibor, 1977; European debut as Wozzeck, 1980; solo recitalist; toured with Nat. Arts Ctr. Orch. in USSR, Poland, Italy, 1973; movie debut as Baron Douphol in La Traviata, 1983. Named Artist of Yr. Can. Music Council, 1983, laureat Order of Can., 1985. Office: 97 Woodpark Close SW, Calgary, AB Canada T2W 6H1

MONK, DEBRA, actress. Stage appearances include (Broadway) Steel Pier Company, Nick & Nora, Prelude to a Kiss, Pump Boys and Dinettes (also co-author), Redwood Curtain (Tony award featured actress in play 1993), Picnic (Tony nomination featured actress 1994), (off-Broadway) Death Defying Acts, 3 Hotels (Helen Hayes award leading actress 1994), Assassins, Man in His Underwear, The Innocent's Crusade, Molieère in Spite of Himself, Oil City Symphony (co-author, Drama Desk award Best Ensemble 1988); TV appearances include Ellen Foster. Office: Gage Group 315 W 57th St Frnt 4H New York NY 10019-3158

MONK, DIANA CHARLA, artist, stable owner; b. Visalia, Calif., Feb. 25, 1927; d. Charles Edward and Viola Genevieve (Shea) Williams; m. James Alfred Monk, Aug. 11, 1951; children: Kiloran, Sydney, Geoffrey, Anne, Eric. Student, U. Pacific, 1946-47, Sacramento Coll., 1947-48, Calif. Coll. Fine Arts, San Francisco, 1948-51, Calif. Coll. Arts & Crafts, Oakland, 1972. Art tchr. Mt. Diablo Sch. Dist., Concord, Calif., 1958-63; pvt. art tchr. Lafayette, Calif., 1963-70; gallery dir. Jason Aver Gallery, San Francisco, 1970-72; owner, mgr. Monk & Lee Assocs., Lafayette, 1973-80; stable owner, mgr. Longacre Tng. Stables, Santa Rosa, Calif., 1989—. One-person shows include John F. Kennedy U., Orinda, Calif., Civic Arts Gallery, Walnut Creek, Calif., Vallery Art Gallery, Walnut Creek, Sea Ranch Gallery, Gualala, Calif., Jason Aver Gallery, San Francisco; exhibited in group shows at Oakland (Calif.) Art Mus., Crocker Nat. Art Gallery, Sacramento, Le Salon des Nations, Paris. Chair bd. dirs. Walnut Creek (Calif.) Civic Arts, 1972-74, advisor to dir., 1968-72; exhibit chmn. Valley Art Gallery, Walnut Creek, 1977-78; juror Women's Art Show, Walnut Creek, 1970, Oakland Calif. Art. Home and Office: Longacre Tng Stables 1702 Willowside Rd Santa Rosa CA 95401-3922

MONK, MEREDITH JANE, artistic director, composer, choreographer, film maker, director; b. N.Y.C., Nov. 20, 1942; d. Theodore G. and Audrey Lois (Zellman) M. BA, Sarah Lawrence Coll., 1964; ArtsD (hon.), Bard Coll., 1988, U. of the Arts, 1989. Artistic dir., founder House Found. for Arts, N.Y.C., 1968—. Prin. works include Vessel, 1971, Quarry, 1976, Turtle Dreams, 1983, Recent Ruins, 1979, The Games, 1983, Book of Days, 1988, Facing North, 1990, Atlas, 1991, Three Heavens and Hells, 1992, Volcano Songs, 1994, American Archeology, 1994, The Politics of Quiet, 1996. Guggenheim fellow, 1972, 86, Norton Stevens fellow, 1993-94; Recipient Obie award Village Voice, 1972, 76, 85, Creative Arts award Brendeis U., 1974, Deutches Kritiker Preis for best record, 1981, 86, Bessie award N.Y. Dance and Performance awards, 1985, Nat. Music Theatre award, 1986, Dance Mag. award, 1992, John D. and Catherine T. MacArthur award, 1995, 1st Sarah Lawrence Alumna Achievement award, 1995, Samuel Scripps award, 1996. Fellow MacDowell Colony (Sigma Phi Omega award 1987); mem. ASCAP. Office: House Found for Arts 131 Varick St New York NY 10013-1410

MONK, NANCY DINA, artist, educator; b. Mpls., Aug. 1, 1951; d. Dale Bertram and Jean Ellen (Groettum) M. BFA, Colo. State U., 1973; MFA, U. Minn., 1976. Instr. Pasadena (Calif.) City Coll., 1989-95. One-woman shows include U. Calif., Irvine, 1981, Koplin Gallery, L.A., 1982, L.A. Jr. Arts Ctr., L.A., 1984, Polytechnic Sch., Pasadena, 1990, Gosdick-Nelson Gallery, Alfred, N.Y., 1991, Robert Lehman Gallery, Bklyn., 1993, Claremont (Calif.) Grad. Sch. East Gallery, 1993, Jan Kesner Gallery, L.A., 1996; exhibited in group shows at Mpls. Inst. Arts, 1977, Corning (N.Y.) Glass Mus., 1979, L.A. Mcpl. Art Gallery, 1979, Mandell Gallery, L.A., 1980, Baxter Gallery, Pasadena, 1981, Spark Gallery, Denver, 1982, Reria Internat. de Ceramica Vidrio, Valencia, Spain, 1982, Limbo Gallery, Southampton, N.Y., 1985, Moderne Internat. Glaskunsi, Ebeltoft, Denmark, 1986, Heller Gallery, N.Y.C., 1987, Long Beach (Calif.) Art Mus., 1988, Gallery Functional Art, Santa Monica, Calif., 1989, Kavesh Gallery, Ketchum, Idaho, 1990, L.A. C. of C., 1992, Armory Ctr. for Arts, Pasadena, 1993, Hunsaker/Schlesinger, L.A., 1995, others. NEA grantee, 1986, 90, City of PAsadena Arts grantee, 1992.

MONK, RICHARD FRANCIS, air force officer, health care administrator; b. Washington, Feb. 9, 1947; s. Leslie G. and Doris Coleman (White) M.; m. Rhonda Lee Wise, Mar. 24, 1978; children: Ryan Michael, Robyn Lynn. BA in Chemistry, N.C. Wesleyan Coll., 1969; postgrad., Med. Coll. Va., 1969-72; MS, Trinity U., San Antonio, 1975. Assoc. adminstr. French Hosp., San Francisco, 1977-78; adminstr. Mono Gen. Hosp., Bridgeport, Calif., 1978-79, Polk Cmty. Hosp., Dallas, Oreg., 1979-80, San Cruval,

Green Valley, Ariz., 1980; commd. officer USAF, 1981, advanced through grades to maj., 1991; CFO, March Regional Hosp., Riverside, Calif., 1981-85; asst. prof. Uniformed Svcs. U. Health Scis., Bethesda, Md., 1985-88; squadron comdr. 15th Med. Group, Honolulu, 1988-91; hosp. comdr. Homestead (Fla.) AFB, 1992; assoc. adminstr. 355th Med. Group, Tucson, 1992-94; ops. officer 355th Med. Support Squadron, Tucson, 1994-95; regional med. planner Ft. Sam Houston, Tex., 1995-96. 1st counselor LDS Ch., Tucson, 1994-95. Fellow Am. Coll. Health Care Execs.; mem. Internat. Brotherhood Magicians (v.p. ring 172). Libertarian. Avocations: magic, hiking, weight training. Home: 14239 Butlers Bridge San Antonio TX 78232-5490 Office: Epidemiol Rsch Divsn 2601 W Gate Rd Ste 114 Brooks AFB TX 78235-5237

MONK, SUSAN MARIE, physician, pediatrician; b. York, Pa., May 7, 1945; d. John Spotz and Mary Elizabeth (Shelly) M.; m. Jaime Pacheco, June 5, 1971; children: Benjamin Joaquin, Maria Cristina. AB, Colby Coll., 1967; MD, Jefferson Med. Coll., 1971. Diplomate Am. Bd. Pediatrics. Pediatrician Children's Med. Ctr., Dayton, Ohio, 1975—; assoc. clin. prof. pediatrics Wright State U., Dayton. Mem. bd. dirs. Children's Med. Ctr., Dayton, 1991-96, chief-of-staff, 1992-94. Mem. Am. Acad. Pediatrics, We. Ohio Pediatric Soc., Pediatric Ambulatory Care Soc. Avocations: reading, gardening, travel, movies, theater. Office: Childrens Health Clinic 536 Valley St Dayton OH 45404-1845

MONLUX, ANDREW W., educator, veterinarian; b. Algona, Iowa, Jan. 29, 1920; s. Delos David and Elvira Ulrica (Seastream) M.; m. Jean Eleanor Hauser, Aug. 20, 1950; children—Roy David, Laura Joan. D.V.M., Iowa State U., 1942, M.S., 1947; Ph.D., George Washington U., 1951. Pvt. practice Woden, Iowa, 1942; asst. vet. hygiene Iowa State U., 1946-48; Am. Vet. Med. Assn. fellow Armed Forces Inst. Pathology, Washington, 1948-51; veterinarian USDA, 1951-56; prof. vet. pathology, chmn. dept. Coll. Vet. Medicine, Okla. State U., Stillwater, 1956-72, Regents prof. vet. pathology, 1972-85, prof. emeritus, 1985—; pres. Southwest Vet. Labs., Stillwater, 1985—. Co-author: Principles of Veterinary Pathology, 7th edit, 1965, Atlas of Meat Inspection Pathology, 1972. Served to maj. AUS, 1942-46. Mem. Am., Okla. vet. med. assns., Research Workers in Animal Diseases in N.Am., Animal Disease Research Workers So. States, Vet. Cancer Soc., Sigma Xi, Phi Zeta, Phi Kappa Phi, Gamma Sigma Delta. Research on neoplastic diseases of cattle, dogs and cats, photosensitivity diseases of cattle; lead toxicity in cattle, dogs, rats; kidney diseases of dogs. Home: 2202 Black Oak Dr Stillwater OK 74074-2124

MONMONIER, MARK, geographer, graphics educator, essayist; b. Balt., Feb. 2, 1943; s. John Carroll and Martha Elizabeth (Mason) M.; m. Margaret Janet Kollner, Sept. 4, 1965; 1 child, Jo Kerry. BA, Johns Hopkins U., 1964; MS, Pa. State U., 1967, PhD, 1969. Asst. prof. U. Rhode Island, Kingston, 1969-70, SUNY, Albany, 1970-73; assoc. prof Syracuse U., N.Y., 1973-79, prof., 1979—; cons. N.Y. State, Albany, 1974-93, Nat. Geog. Soc., 1987, Microsoft Corp., 1993—, AT&T Rsch., 1996—; rsch. geographer U.S. Geol. Survey, Reston, Va., 1979-84; dep. dir. N.Y. Ctr. for Geographic Info. and Analysis, 1989-90; Robinson vis. fellow George Mason U., 1985; Ida Beam Disting. vis. prof. U. Iowa, 1985; mem. adv. bd. GIS Law and Policy Inst.; adv. bd. Philip Lee Philips Soc. Author: Maps, Distortion and Meaning, 1977, Computer-assisted Cartography, 1982, Technological Transition in Cartography, 1985, Maps with the News, 1989, How to Lie with Maps, 1991, 2d edit. 1996, Mapping It Out, 1993, Drawing the Line, 1995, Cartographies of Danger, 1997; co-author: The Study of Population: Elements, Patterns, Processes, 1982, Map Appreciation, 1988; assoc. editor: The American Cartographer, Falls Church, Va., 1977-82, editor, 1982-84; assoc. editor Mapping Scis. and Remote Sensing, 1987—; contbg. editor Cartographica, 1984—. Statistician, Police Dept, Syracuse, 1978-80. Fellow John Simon Guggenheim Meml. Found., 1984; recipient Chancellor's citation for Disting. Acad. Achievement, 1993. Mem. Assn. Am. Geographers, Am. Cartographic Assn. (pres. 1983-84), Authors Guild, Can. Cartographic Assn., N.Am. Cartographic Info. Soc., Pa. Acad. Sci. (editl. bd. 1979—), Philip Lee Phillips Soc., Soc. for History of Technology, Sigma Xi, Pi Tau Sigma, Tau Beta Pi. Roman Catholic. Home: 302 Waldorf Pky Syracuse NY 13224-2240 Office: Syracuse U Dept Of Geography Syracuse NY 13244

MONNINGER, ROBERT HAROLD GEORGE, ophthalmologist, educator; b. Chgo., Nov. 5, 1918; s. Louis Robert and Katherine (Lechner) M.; m. Anna Evelyn Turnen, Sept. 1, 1944; children—Carl John William, Peter Louis Philip. A.A., North Park Coll., 1939; B.S., Northwestern U., 1941, M.A., 1945; M.D., Loyola U., Chgo., 1953, Sc.D. (hon.), 1968. Diplomate Am. Bd. Cosmetic Plastic Surgery. Intern St. Francis Hosp., Evanston, Ill., 1953-54; resident Presbyterian-St. Luke's, U. Ill. Research and Eye, Va. hosps., 1954-57; mem. leadership council Ravenswood Hosp. Med. Ctr.; instr. chemistry Lake Forest Coll., Ill., 1946-47; instr. biochemistry, physiology Loyola U. Dental Sch., 1948-49; clin. assoc. prof. ophthalmology Stritch Sch. Medicine, Loyola U., Maywood, Ill., 1957-72; practice medicine specializing in ophthalmology Lake Forest, 1957—; clin. prof. ophthalmology Finch U. Health Scis./Chgo. Med. Sch.; guest lectr. numerous univs. med. ctrs. U.S., Can., Europe, Central and S.Am., Orient; resident lectr. Klinikum der Goethe-Universitat, Fed. Republic Germany, 1981; mem. panel Nat. Disease and Therapeutic Index; cons. Draize eve toxicity test revision HEW, cons. research pharm. cos. Nat. Assoc. Smithsonian Instn.; bd. dirs. Eye Rehab. and Research Found.; postgrad. faculty Internat. Glaucoma Congress; lectr. Hopital Dieu, Paris; lectr. postgrad. courses for developing nations physicians WHO; life mem. Postgrad. Sch. Medicine U. Vienna; cons. Nat. Acad. Sci.; adv. bd. Madera Del Rio Found. Cons. author Textbook of Endocrinology. Editorial bd. Clin. Medicine, 1958—, EENT Digest, 1958—, Internat. Surgery, 1972—, profl. jours. Served with USMCR, 1941-44. Recipient citation Gov. Bahamas, 1960, Ophthalmic Found. award, 1963, Sci. Exhibit award Ill. State Med. Soc., 1966, Franco-Am. Meritorious citation, 1967, Paris Post No. 1 Am. Legion award, 1967, citation Pres. Mexico, 1968, Sightsaving award Bausch & Lomb, 1968, exhibit award Western Hemisphere Congress Internat. Surgeons, 1968, Research citation Japanese Soc. Ophthalmology, 1969; Barraquer Gold Medallion; Physician's Recognition award AMA, Bicentennial citation Library of Congress Registration Book; Pres.'s medal of merit; meritorious citation Gov. Ill., citation and medal Lord Mayor of Rome, also Pres. of Italy, 1981, Civic Ctr. of Evanston, Ill., 1981, commendation and citation Ill. Gen. Assembly, 1982, cert. of accomplishment Loyola U. Alumni Assn., Chgo., 1983; Catherine White Scholarship fellow, 1945-46. Fellow Internat. Coll. Surgeons (postgrad. faculty continuing edn.), Am. Coll. Angiology, Oxford Ophthal. Congress and Soc. (lectr. 1960-61), Royal Soc. Health, Internat. Acad. Cosmetic Surgery (editorial bd.), Sociedad Mexicana Ortopedia (hon.), C. Puestow Surg. Soc.; mem. AAAs, Internat. Soc. Geog. Ophthalmology (program course coordinator, lectr. ocular electrophysiology VI Internat. Congress, Rio de Janiero), Pan Am. Assn. Ophthalmology, Assn. for Research Ophthalmology, Am. Assn. Ophthalmology, Am. Soc. Contemporary Ophthalmology, Internat. Glaucoma Soc., Ill. Soc. for Med. Research, Ill. Assn. Ophthalmology, Internat. Soc. clin. electrophysiology of Vision (hon., lectr. 1978), Brazilian Soc. Ophthalmology (hon. corr.), German Ophthal. Soc., Internat. Fedn. Clin. Chemists (lectr.), Primum Forum Ophthalmologicum (lectr.), European Ophthal. Soc. (lectr.), Internat. Congress Anatomists (lectr.), Assn. des Diabetologues Francise (lectr.), German Soc. for Internal Medicine (lectr.), Met. Opera Guild, Fedn. Am. Scientists, N.Y. Acad. Scis., Ill. Acad. Scis., AAUP, Nat. Soc. Lit. and Arts, Nat. Hist. Soc., Rush Med. Sch.-Presbyn. St. Luke's Alumni Assn., Sociedad Poblana Oftalmologia (hon, silver placue, commemorative prestige lectr. 1982) (Mex.), Internat. Platform Assn., Cousteau Soc., Sigma Xi, Sigma Alpha Epsilon, Phi Beta Pi, Theta Kappa Psi.

MONOPOLI, DANIEL MARCO, computer company executive; b. Cranston, R.I., Sept. 15, 1939; s. Donato and Santa (Tedeschi) M.; 1 child, Jennifer Marie. Student, R.I. Coll., 1961-62, U. R.I., 1962-68. Svc. technician Voicewriter div. McGraw Edison, Cranston, 1962-63; non-destructive testing specialist Gen. Dynamics/Electric Boat, Groton, Conn., 1963-64; mgr. employee rels. ITT Hammel-Dahl, Warwick, R.I., 1964-66; pers. mgr. Clifton div. Litton Industries, Fall River, Mass., 1966-68; dir. indsl. rels. Revenue Control Systems div., N.Y.C., 1968-70; v.p. ops. Symphonic Electronic, Lowell, Mass., 1970-73; pres. Marc Enterprises, Wheeling, Ill., 1973-77; v.p. mktg./adminstrv. svcs. ECM Motor Co., Schaumburg, Ill., 1977-82; pres. User Systems, Inc., Ringwood, Ill., 1982-86, Integrated Computer Concepts, Inc., 1986-96; asst. to pres. HTE Corp., Orlando, 1997; reg. mgr. Coded Comms. Corp., Carlsbad, Calif., 1997—. With USNR, 1958-61. Home and Office: 773 Cold Stream Ct Winter Spgs FL 32708-4953

MONOS, DIMITRIOS, medical educator, researcher. BS in Biology, U. Patras, Greece, 1975; PhD in Biochemistry and Immunology, Georgetown U., 1981. Vis. fellow lab. tumor immunology & biology Nat. Cancer Inst. NIH, Bethesda, Md., 1982-84; immunopathology fellow dept. pathology & lab. medicine U. Pa., Phila., 1984-86, rsch. assoc. immunology, 1986-88, asst. prof., 1990-96, assoc. prof., 1996—; vis. scholar dept. biochemistry & molecular biology Harvard U., 1988-90; dir. immonogenetics lab. dept. pathology Children's Hosp. Phila., 1996; lectr. in field. Editl. bd. CLin. and Diagnostic Lab. Immunology; ad hoc reviewer Cancer Rsch., Diabetes, Human Immunology, Jour. Immunology, New Eng. Jour. Medicine; contbr. articles to profl. jours. With Greek Army, 1988. Recipient New Investigator Rsch. award NIH, 1986, Rsch. award Am. Diabetes Assn., 1995; grantee NIH, 1986—, U. Pa., 1987-88, 95, Diabetes Rsch. & Edn. Found., 1990, Juvenile Diabetes Found., 1990-92, Nat. Marrow Donor Program, 1992-94, ADA, 1995-96; Fogarty Internat. fellow NIH, 1982. Mem. Am. Assn. Immunologists, Am. Soc. Histocompatibility & Immunogenetics, Acad. Clin. Lab. Physicians & Scientists, Sigma Xi. Office: Children's Hosp Phila Dept Pediats Abramson Rsch Bldg 1208B 34th St & Civic Ctr Blvd Philadelphia PA 19104

MONRAD, ERNEST EJNER, trust company executive; b. Little Falls, N.Y., May 30, 1930; s. Karl J. and Augusta (Olsen) M.; m. Elizabeth Ann Haffenreffer, June 15, 1951; children: Ernest Scott, Elizabeth, Bruce H. AB in Econs, Harvard U., 1951; LLB, U. Va., 1956. Bar: Mass. 1956. Assoc. firm Herrick & Smith, Boston, 1956-59; treas. H.P. Nichols, Inc., Boston, 1960-64; v.p. Alsace Corp., Boston, 1964-67; trustee Northeast Investors Trust, Boston, 1960-69, chmn. trustees, 1969—; v.p., bd. dirs., clk. Furman Lumber Co., Inc., Boston, 1971—; trustee, corporator Boston 5 Cent Savs. Bank, 1972—, mem. bd. investment, 1976—; trustee Century Shares Trust, 1976—, Ostrander High Income Res. fund, 1988-90; bd. dirs. New Am. High Income Fund, Inc. Trustee Simmons Coll., acting chmn., 1991-92; trustee Harvard Coll. Fund, chmn., 1987-89; pres. bd. trustees Fessenden Sch., West Newton, Mass., 1971-78; mem. com. on univ. resources Harvard U., 1978; corporator Mass. Gen. Hosp., Boston, 1980-90; bd. overseer Mus. Fine Arts, 1990—; commr. trust fund Town of Weston, Mass., 1975. 2d lt. U.S. Army, 1951-53. Mem. Boston Security Analysts Soc. (dir. 1973-75). Home: 91 Dean Rd Weston MA 02193-2709 Office: Northeast Investors Trust 50 Congress St Boston MA 02109-4002

MONROE, BROOKS, investment banker; b. Greenville, S.C., July 24, 1925; s. Clarence Jenningsand Edith Cabot (Johnson) M.; m. Hilda Marie Meredith, June 30, 1956. B.S. in Commerce, U. Va., 1948, J.D., 1951; grad., Inst. Investment Banking, U. Pa., 1959. Dir. pub. relations Scott, Horner & Co., Lynchburg, Va., 1951-53; sales mgr. Scott, Horner & Co., Richmond, Va., 1953-56; v.p., gen. sales mgr. Scott, Horner & Co., Lynchburg, 1956-59; sales mgr. nat. and underwriting Francis I. duPont & Co., N.Y.C., 1959-61; gen. partner Francis I. duPont & Co., 1961-66, Paine, Webber, Jackson & Curtis, N.Y.C., 1966-69; pres., chief exec. officer Brooks Monroe & Co., Inc., N.Y.C., 1969—; chmn. HHM Corp., Wilmington and Beverly Hills, Calif., 1969—, Bargeland Corp., Phila., 1970—, IGAS Corp., Pitts., 1975—; chmn. PPM Internat., Inc., Spartanburg; S.C.founder, chmn. Execs. Guardian Co., N.Y.C., 1971—; Tchr. U. Va., 1949-51; asso. mem. Am., N.Y. stock exchanges, 1961-72; mem. Pacific Stock Exchange, 1962-66, Chgo. Bd. Trade, 1962-66. Bd. dirs. McIntire Sch. Commerce U. Va. Served with USAAF, 1943-46, PTO. Mem. U. Va. Alumni Assn. (N.Y. pres. 1978-81), Sigma Chi, Delta Sigma Rho, Pi Delta Epsilon, Omicron Delta Kappa, Delta Theta Pi. Republican. Presbyterian. (trustee). Clubs: Boar's Head Sport, (Charlottesville, Va.), Farmington Country (Charlottesville); Bond, City Midday, Union League (N.Y.C.); Quogue (N.Y.) Field, Quogue Beach; Clan Munro (Scotland and U.S.). Home: Ednam Forest Charlottesville VA 22903 Office: PO Box 5246 2 Boars Head Pl Charlottesville VA 22905

MONROE, FREDERICK LEROY, chemist; b. Redmond, Oreg., Oct. 13, 1942; s. Herman Sylvan Monroe and Mary Roberta (Grant) Monroe Emery; B.S. in Chemistry, Oreg. State U., 1964; M.S. in Environ. Engring., Wash. State U., 1974. Control specialist Air Pollution Control Authority, Centralia, Wash., 1969-70; asst. chemist Wash. State U., 1970-74; environ. engr. Ore-Ida Foods, Inc., Idaho, 1974-77; cons., Idaho, 1977-78; applications engr. AFL Industries, Riviera Beach, Fla., 1979-80; mgr. chem. control PCA Internat., Matthews, N.C., 1980-85; quality assurance mgr. Stork Screens Am., Charlotte, N.C., 1985-93, environ. mgr., 1993—, grade IV N.C. wastewater treatment operator; instr. electroplating and literacy. Developed lit. materials for adults in workplace. Pres. Unity Ch., 1982-84. Served with USAF, 1964-68, maj. Res. ret.; served with N.G., 1973-78. Decorated Air Force Commendation medal; recipient Blue Thumb award Charlotte-Mecklenburg Utility Dist., 1993. Fellow AIChE; mem. Am. Chem. Soc. Republican. Home: 1008 Autumnwood Ln Charlotte NC 28213-5722 Office: Stork Screens Am Service Rd 3001 N Interstate 85 Charlotte NC 28269-4493

MONROE, HASKELL M., JR., university educator; b. Dallas, Mar. 18, 1931; s. Haskell M. and Myrtle Marie (Jackson) M.; m. Margaret Joan Phillips, June 15, 1957; children: Stephen, Melanie, Mark, John. B.A., Austin (Tex.) Coll., 1952, M.A., 1954; Ph.D., Rice U., Houston, 1961. From instr. to prof. Tex. A&M U., 1959-80; asst. dean Tex. A&M U. (Grad. Sch.), 1965-68, asst. v.p. acad. affairs, 1972-74, dean faculties, 1974-80, assoc. v.p. acad. affairs, 1977-80; pres. U. Tex., El Paso, 1980-87; chancellor U. Mo., Columbia, 1987-91; prof. history U. Mo., 1987-97, chancelor emeritus, prof. history, 1997—; dean faculties emeritus, div. devel. Tex. A&M U., College Station, 1997—; instr. Schreiner Inst., Kerrville, Tex., summer 1959; vis. lectr. Emory U., summers 1967, 72; faculty lectr. Tex. A&M U., 1972; alumni lectr. Austin Coll., 1980; bd. dirs. Southwestern Bell Corp., Boone County Nat. Bank. Contbr. articles, revs.; editor: Papers of Jefferson Davis, 1964-69; adv. editor: Texana, 1964-71; bd. editorial advisers: Booker T. Washington Papers, 1965-85 . Bd. dirs. Brazos Valley Rehab. ctr., 1975-77, Salvation Army, El Paso, 1984-87, Columbia, Mo., 1988—, Crime Stoppers of El Paso, United Way Columbia, 1988-94; trustee Bryan Hosp., 1976-79, chmn., 1979; bd. ch. visitors Austin Coll., 1977-78; deacon First Presbyn. Ch., Bryan, 1961-63, elder, 1965-67, 69-71, 73-74, clk. of session, 1973-74, chmn. pulpit nominating com., 1971-72; mem. presbytery's com. Presbytery of Brazos, 1969-71, mem. resources for the 80s steering com., 1978-80; elder 1st Presbyn. Ch., El Paso, 1984-87, 1st Presbyn. Ch., Columbia, 1994-96; mem. exec. bd. Grat Rivers coun. Boy Scouts Am., 1990—; mem. Pres. Coun. NCAA, 1986-87; chmn. Jefferson Davis award com. Confederate Mus., 1996—; bd. dirs. Salvation Army, 1989—. Recipient Citation of Appreciation, LULAC, 1982, also numerous achievement awards; grantee Social Sci. Rsch. Coun., Tex. A&M U., Huntington Libr., Intrafraternity and Sorority Outstanding Tchr. award, 1997. Mem. Am. Hist. Assn., Orgn. Am. Historians, So. Hist. Assn. Hist. Found. Presbyn. and Reformed Chs. (pres. 1970-72), Coll. Football Assn. (chmn. bd. 1989-90, bd. dirs.), Truman Scholarship Panel, Soc. Conf. Deans Faculties and Acad. V.P.s (pres. 1978), Rotary (El Paso, hon. Columbia, Mo.). Home: 1005 Sonoma College Station TX 77845 Office: Tex A&M U Rudder Tower College Station TX 77843

MONROE, HELEN LEOLA, nurse, consultant, educator; b. Alma, Ga., Jan. 30, 1931; d. Silas Leo Monroe and Thelma (Fussell) Smith; 1 child, Reavena M. M. Oliver. BS, Fla. A&M U., 1954; MS, St. John's U., L.I., N.Y., 1959. Staff nurse Vis. Nurse Assn. Duval County, Jacksonville, Fla., 1954-55; instr. sch. nursing Fla. A&M U., Tallahassee, 1955-57, asst. prof., 1959-64; dir. nursing edn. Mississippi Valley State Coll., Itta Bena, Miss., 1964-67; asst. prof. Norfolk State Coll. Va., 1967-68; asst. prof., dir. nursing edn. Lincoln U., Jefferson City, Mo., 1968-80; pvt. practice nursing Jefferson City, 1981-85; pvt. practice achievement cons. Jacksonville, 1987—; cons. Jacksonville, 1987—; cons. nursing William Woods Coll., Fulton, Mo., 1972-73; established first edn. program for nonwhites to become RNs in Miss. Sec. Jefferson City chpt. NAACP, 1971-73; chmn. edn. com. Cancer Soc. Cole County, Jefferson City, 1972-74; v.p. Cole County Mental Health Assn., 1973; mem. fin. com. United Way Cole County, 1975. Recipient Outstanding Achievement award Citizens' Com. of Jefferson City, 1970, Woman of Achievement award AAUW, 1974, Permanent Royal Patronage from Principality of the Hutt River Province, 1994. Avocations: gardening, sewing, reading, bicycling, bowling. Home: 5436 Mays Dr Jacksonville FL 32209-2926

MONROE, JAMES WALTER, organization executive; b. Fairfax, S.D., Feb. 13, 1936; s. Sherman William and Frances (Burnett) M.; m. Dorothy Lou Gillette, Apr. 1, 1961; children—Steven James, David Walter, Melody Anne, Andrew Scott. Student, Huron (S.D.) Coll., 1954-56, U. Nebr., 1956-57; B.A., Nebr. Wesleyan U., 1960. Mgr. Belleville (Kans.) C. of C., 1960-61, Concordia (Kans.) C. of C., 1961-62; asst. chief Div. Nebr. Resources, 1962-65; dir. S.D. Indsl. Devel. Expansion Agy., 1965-67, Nebr. Dept. Econ. Devel., 1967-71; sec. Nebr. Resources Found., 1967-71; exec. dir. Omaha Econ. Devel. Council, 1971-76; pres. Kansas City (Mo.-Kans.) Area Devel. Council, 1976-90; pres., chief exec. officer New Orleans and the River Region C. of C., 1990-96, Metrovision Found., Econ. Devel. Coun. Metro, New Orleans; ret., 1996; mem. Am. Indsl. Devel. Council, 1965—, chmn. certification bd., 1981-82; sec. labor mgmt. council Greater Kansas City, 1979-90; mem. exec. com. Gov.'s Econ. Devel. Adv. Council, 1979-81. Bd. dirs. Am. Econ. Devel. Coun., 1992—. Served with AUS, 1957-59. Republican. Presbyterian. Home: 1735 Dexter North Seattle WA 98109 Office: New Orleans & River Reg 301 Camp St New Orleans LA 70130-2803

MONROE, KENDYL KURTH, retired lawyer; b. Clayton, N.Mex., Sept. 6, 1936; s. Dottis Donald and Helen (Kurth) M.; m. Barbara Sayre, Sept. 12, 1956; children: Sidney, Dean, Loren. AB, Stanford U., 1958, LLB, 1960. Bar: N.Y. 1961, Calif. 1961. Assoc. Sullivan & Cromwell, N.Y.C., 1960-67, ptnr., 1968-94; chmn. TEB Charter Svcs., Inc., Teterboro, N.J., Air Am. Inc., Santa Fe, N.Mex., El Valle Escondido Ranch Ltd. Co., Seneca, N.Mex., Highland Forests, Keeseville, N.Y.; bd. dirs. No. Minerals Co., Keeseville, N.Y. Chmn. Hope Entertainment, Inc., N.Y.C., Pub. Health Rsch. Inst., N.Y.C.; bd. dirs. N. Mex. First, Santa Fe, Greenwich Village Soc. Historic Preservation, N.Y.C., N.Y. Chamber Soloists, N.Y.C., Seamen's Ch. Inst., N.Y.C. Mem. Calif. State Bar Assn., Assn. Bar City N.Y., Met. Club (N.Y.C.). Home: Kenton Rte Seneca NM 88437

MONROE, KENNETH ANTHONY, facility and project management consultant; b. Chgo., June 16, 1951; s. Clarence Anthony and Edna Ruth (Waleski) M.; m. Cynthia Stearns, Mar. 26, 1988. BSME, Northwestern U., Evanston, Ill., 1975, M in Mgmt., 1983. Registered profl. engr., Ill. Staff engr. City of Chgo., 1975-77, Consoer, Townsend & Assocs., Chgo., 1977-78, FMC Corp., Itasca, Ill., 1978-80; project mgr. Michael Reese Hosp., Chgo., 1981-84; account mktg. rep. IBM, Chgo., 1984-89; project mgr. St. Francis Hosp., Evanston, 1990-93; asst. dir. engring. Victory Meml. Hosp., Waukegan, Ill., 1993-94; pres. MC Enterprises, Evanston, Ill., 1994—. Docent Chgo. Architecture Found., v.p., treas., 1991-92, pres., 1979-81, 90-91; Bus. Profl. Assn. Chgo. Symph. Orch., v.p. 1989-91, 93-94. Mem. ASME, ASHRAE (editor newsletter 1985-87), Internat. Facilities Mgrs. Assn. Roman Catholic. Avocations: photography, Corvettes, bicycling, trumpet, tennis. Home and Office: 904 Oakton St # 3 Evanston IL 60202-2849

MONROE, L. A. J., oil well drilling company executive; b. Springhill, Ark., Nov. 8, 1919; s. Eugene and Alma Edna (Collins) M.; m. Elizabeth Kirkland Moore, Apr. 18, 1942; children: Jamison, Mark Kirkland. B.S., Tex. Christian U., 1942. With Nat. Supply Co., 1945-65; regional mgr. Nat. Supply Co. (Gulf Coast), 1960-62, gen. mgr. sales, domestic and Can. cos., 1962-65; with Dixilyn-Field Drilling Co., Houston, 1965-83; pres., chief exec. officer Dixilyn-Field Drilling Co., 1971-83, chmn. bd., 1978-83; ptnr. Monroe & Bruner, Inc., 1983-92, chmn., 1983-92; chmn. Monroe & Monroe, Inc., Houston, 1992—; dir. First City Bank of Highland Village. Trustee Tex. Christian U.; adminstrv. bd. Chapelwood United Meth. Ch., Houston. Served with U.S. Navy, 1942-45. Named Most Valuable Alumnus Tex. Christian U., 1974, named to Hall of Fame Tex. Christian U., 1991. Mem. Internat. Assn. Drilling Contractors, Nat. Ocean Industry Assn., Mid-Continent Oil and Gas Assn. Republican. Baptist. Clubs: River Oaks Country, Ramada, Petroleum (past dir.), Houston; Les Ambassador (London). Office: Monroe & Monroe Inc 415 Brown Saddle St Houston TX 77057-1411

MONROE, MELROSE, retired banker; b. Flowery Branch, Ga., Apr. 13, 1919; d. Willis Jeptha and Leila Adell Cash; m. Lynn Austin, June 14, 1942. AB in Edn., Ga. State U., 1968. Negotiator Trust Co. Bank, Atlanta, 1962-89, ret., 1989. Mem. Nat. Women's C. of C. (pres. 1987-88), Atlanta Women's C. of C. (dir. 1965-66, pres. Fidelis SS class 1962-63), Am. Legion Aux. (pres. 5th dist. 1986-87, Ga. state chaplain 1989-90, state historian 1991-92, state 2d v.p. 1992-93, 1st v.p. 1993-94, pres. 1994-95), Order of Ea. Star (worthy matron 1951-52). Democrat. Home and Office: 6243 Spout Springs Rd Flowery Branch GA 30542-5032

MONROE, MURRAY SHIPLEY, lawyer; b. Cin., Sept. 25, 1925; s. James and Martha (Shipley) M.; m. Sally Longstreth, May 11, 1963; children: Tracy, Murray, Courtney, David. BE, Yale U., 1946, BS, 1947; LLB, U. Pa., 1950. Bar: Ohio 1950, U.S. Dist. Ct. (so. dist.) Ohio 1954, U.S. Dist. Ct. (mid. dist.) Tenn. 1981, US Dist. Ct. (mid. dist.) N.C. 1974, U.S. Dist. Ct. (mid. dist.) Pa. 1986, U.S. Dist. (ea. dist.) Pa. 1960, U.S. Dist. Ct. (we. dist.) Mo. 1974, U.S. Dist. Ct. Mass. 1978, U.S. Dist. Ct. (ea. dist.) La. 1979, U.S. Dist. Ct. (no. dist.) Ill. 1980, U.S. Ct. Appeals (4th cir.) 1984, U.S. Ct. Appeals (6th cir.) 1969, U.S. Supreme Ct. 1977, U.S. Ct. Appeals (3d cir.) 1990. Assoc. Taft, Stettinus & Hollister, Cin., 1950-58, ptnr., 1958-96; of counsel, 1997—; mem. lawyers com. Nat. Ctr. for State Cts., 1985—; faculty Ohio Legal Ctr. Inst., 1970-93. Contbr. articles to profl. jours. Trustee, treas. The Coll. Prep. Sch., 1972-76; trustee The Seven Hills Schs., 1982-88, chmn. bd., 1982-85. 2d lt. USNR, 1943-46. Recipient award Seven Hills Schs., 1985. Fellow Ohio Bar Found.; mem. ABA (speaker symposiums), Ohio Bar Assn. (coun. dels. 1977-82, bd. govts. antitrust sect. 1960-95, dir. emeritus 1995—, chmn. bd. govs. 1973-75, Merit award 1976, speaker symposiums), Bankers Club (Cin.), Cin. Country Club, Tau Beta Pi. Republican. Episcopalian. Avocations: sailing, tennis.

MONROE, ROBERT RAWSON, engineering construction executive; b. Oakland, Calif., Sept. 25, 1927; s. Robert Ansley and Muriel Estelle (Burnham) M.; m. Charlotte Boies Anderson, Oct. 16, 1951; children: Robert Anderson, Nancy Lynn Monroe Sims, Susan Leslie Monroe Gordon. BS in Naval Sci., U.S. Naval Acad., 1950; MA in Internat. Rels., Stanford U., 1962. Commd. ensign USN, 1950, advanced through grades to vice-admiral, 1977; dir. Navy Systems Analysis, 1972-73, comdr. South Atlantic Force, 1973-74; comdr. Operational Test and Evaluation Force USN, 1974-77; dir. Def. Nuclear Agy., 1977-80, dir. Navy Rsch., Devel., Test and Evaluation, 1980-83, ret., 1983; joined Bechtel Nat., Inc., San Francisco, 1984, mgr. def. and space, 1984-89, v.p., 1985, sr. v.p., ptnr., 1987, mgr. mktg. and govt. ops., 1989-91, mgr. spl. projects, 1992-93; mgr. govt. ops. Bechtel Nat., Inc., Washington, 1993—; mem. nat. security adv. bd. Los Alamos (N. Mex.) Nat. Lab., 1983-88; mem. tech. evaluation panel U.S. Dept. Energy, 1983-88; mem. engring. adv. com. Oak Ridge (Tenn.) Nat. Lab., 1986-89, Rensselaer Poly Inst., 1990-91; mem. bd. advisors Office Tech. Assessment, Washington, 1987-89, Nat. Contract Mgmt. Assn., 1986-91; mem. task forces Def. Sci. Bd., Washington, 1983-89; corp. mem. Charles Stark Draper Lab., Cambridge, Mass., 1983—; affiliate mem. Ctr. for Internat. Security and Arms Control, Stanford U., 1989-93; chmn. space transp. subcom. NASA's Aeros. & Space Transp. Tech. Adv. Com., 1995—; mem. strategic adv. bd. Nev. Test Site, 1995—, Nat. Security adv. bd., Sandia Nat. Lab, 1996—. Decorated Def. D.S.M., USN D.S.M., Legion of Merit, Bronze Star medal with combat device, Joint Svcs. Commendation medal, USN Commendation medal with combat device; Legion of Honor (France). Mem. AIAA, Nat. Security Indsl. Assn., Soc. Am. Mil. Engrs., Am. Def. Preparedness Assn., U.S. Naval Inst. Avocations: tennis, golf, hiking, reading. Home: 2313 Sawdust Rd Vienna VA 22181-3044 Office: Bechtel Nat Inc 1015 15th St NW Ste 700 Washington DC 20005-2605

MONROE, RUSSELL RONALD, psychiatrist, educator; b. Des Moines, June 7, 1920; s. Ronald Russell and Mildred (Schmidt) M.; m. Lillian Constance Brooks, June 23, 1945; children—Constance Ellen Monroe Teevan, Nancy Brooks Monroe Amoss, Russell Ronald Jr. B.S., Yale U., 1942, M.D., 1944; cert. in psychoanalysis, Columbia U., 1950. Intern New Haven Hosp., 1944-45; resident Rockland State Hosp., Orangeburg, N.Y., 1947-50; from asst. to assoc. prof. psychiatry Tulane U. Sch. Med., New Orleans, 1950-60; prof. U. Md. Sch. Med., Balt., 1960—; chmn. dept. U. Md. Sch. Med., 1976-85; dir. Inst. Psychiatry and Human Behavior U. Md., 1976-85; vis. prof. Am. U., Beirut, Lebanon, 1966-67; mem. adv. commn. Nat. Inst. Law Enforcement and Criminal Justice, 1977-80. Author: Episodic Behavioral Disorders, 1970, Brain Dysfunction in Aggressive

Criminals, 1978, Creative Brainstorms, 1992. Served to capt. AUS, 1945-47. Commonwealth fellow, 1966-67, NIMH fellow, 1966-67; grantee NIMH. Fellow Am. Psychiat. Assn., Am. Coll. Psychiatrists; mem. Am. Acad. Psychoanalysis (charter). Clubs: Hamilton St., So. Yacht. Home: 236 W Lafayette Ave Baltimore MD 21217-4210 Office: U Md Sch Medicine 645 W Redwood St Baltimore MD 21201-1542

MONROE, THOMAS EDWARD, industrial corporation executive; b. Ironton, MO, Nov. 19, 1947; s. Donald Mansfield and Edwina Frances (Carr) M.; children: Thomas Edward II, Katherine Jenna. B.A., Drury Coll., 1969; postgrad., Washington U. Sch. Bus. Adminstrn., St. Louis, 1970. Acctg. mgr., asst. controller Am. Transit Corp., St. Louis, 1970-74; mgr. corp. devel., asst. treas. Chromalloy Am. Corp., St. Louis, 1974-77, v.p. fin., 1977-78, exec. v.p., 1978-82; dir. Chromalloy Fin. Corp., 1976-82, Am. Universal Ins. Co., 1978-82; chmn. Capital Assocs. Corp., 1982—, Fed. Air Ambulance, The Safe Deposit Co., CompuVault, Inc., James Flying Svc., Inc., Lindbergh Leasing, Inc. Mem. Algonquin Club. Presbyterian. Office: Capital Assocs Corp 515 S Lindbergh Blvd Saint Louis MO 63131-2731

MONROE, WILLIAM LEWIS, human resources executive; b. Detroit, May 11, 1941; s. Lewis Stewart and Ada Jeanette (Williams) M.; m. Sharon Lynne Kahal, June 30, 1967; children: Andrea M. Dunk, William J. BA, Western Mich. U., 1963, MA, 1964. Rsch. analyst Chrysler Corp., Detroit, 1965-72, labor economist, 1972-77, mgr. retirement, savs. and unemployment benefit plans, 1977-81; dir. employee benefits W. R. Grace & Co., N.Y.C., 1981-87, v.p. human resources, 1987—, bd. trustee, v.p. coun. on employee benefits, 1989—, pres. coun. on employee benefits, 1995-96; corp. bd. dirs. Internat. Found. Employee Benefits, 1986-88; mem. bus. rsch. adv. coun. to U.S. Dept. Labor/Bur. Labor Stats., 1987—; mem. Human Resources Policy Inst. Boston U., 1993-96. Co-chmn. closing com. PTSA Sch., Birmingham, Mich., 1977; chmn. personnel com. Wilton Presbyn. Ch., Wilton, Conn., 1982-86; officer, bd. dirs. Forest Hills Property Owners Assn. Birmingham, 1974-80; mem. exec. bd. Gulf Stream coun. Boy Scouts Am., 1993—. Served with USAR, 1965-71. Mem. Soc. for Human Resources & Mgmt., Boca Raton (Fla.) Resort and Club, Princeton Club N.Y.C. Republican. Presbyterian. Avocations: tennis, golf. Office: W R Grace & Co 1 Town Center Rd Boca Raton FL 33486-1010

MONROY, GLADYS H., lawyer; b. N.Y., Aug. 29, 1937; d. Henry B. and Leonora E. (Low) Chu; m. Jaime L. G. Monroy (div.); m. C. Lawrence Marks, Nov. 29, 1980. BA, Hunter Coll., N.Y., 1957; MS, NYU, 1968, PhD, 1973; JD, U. San Francisco, 1986. Bar: Calif. Lab. technician Sloan-Kettering Inst., N.Y., 1957-60; lab. technician Pub. Health Rsch. Inst., N.Y., 1960-63, rsch. asst., 1963-68; post doctoral fellow Albert Einstein Coll. Medicine, Bronx, N.Y., 1973-77; asst. prof. N.Y. Med. Coll., Valhalla, 1977-79; acquisitions editor Acad. Press, Inc., 1979-81; reseach assoc. U. Calif., San Francisco, 1981-83; atty. Irell & Manella, Menlo Park, Calif., 1986-90, ptnr., 1990-91; ptnr. Morrison & Foerster, Palo Alto, Calif., 1991—. Contbr. articles to profl. jours. Mem. bd. dirs. Project Hogar De Los Ninos, Menlo Park, Calif., 1987, mem. Profl. Women's Network, San Francisco, 1988—; mem. bd. dirs. Child Advocates of Santa Clara and San Mateo Counties, 1995—. Mem. ABA, Am. Intellectual Property Law Assn., Am. Soc. Human Genetics, Am. Chem. Soc., Calif. Bar Assn., San Francisco Intellectual Property Law Assn. (chair patent com. 1992-94), Peninsula Patent Law Assn. (program chair 1993-94, treas. 1994-95, sec. 1995-96, v.p. 1996—), Am. Soc. Microbiology, Phi Alpha Delta. Avocations: swimming, bicyle riding, skiing, reading, opera. Office: Morrison & Foerster 755 Page Mill Rd Palo Alto CA 94304-1018

MONROY, VICTOR M., polymer scientist; b. Tampico, Tamaulipas, Mexico, Aug. 8, 1953; s. Mario and Maria Luisa (Soto-Serdan) M.; m. Deborah Costley, Dec. 27, 1980; children: Mario Alexander, Stephanie Claire Anais, Sebastian John Philip. BS Chem. Engring., Inst. Tech. Cd. Madero, Mexico, 1975; PhD in Macromolecular Phys. Chem., Inst. Charles Sadron CNRS, Strasbourg, France, 1983. Deve. engr. Hules Mexicanos, S.A., Altamira, Tamps., Mexico, 1976-77; R&D engr. Industrias Negromex, S.A. de C.V., Mexico City, 1984-85, R&D supr., 1985-86, analytical instrumentation mgr., 1987, rsch. mgr., 1988-90; rsch. assoc. General Tire, Inc., Akron, Ohio, 1993, mgr., 1994; rsch. dir. Continental Gen. Tire, Inc., Akron, 1995-96; dir. materials rsch. and USA-Europe rsch. coord. Continental AG, Hanover, Germany, 1996—; vis. scientist, prof. The U. Akron, 1990-93; cons. General Tire, Inc., 1991-92, COPERBO, Cabo, Brazil, 1992-93; chemistry adv. bd. UNCC. Author Kirk-Othmer Ency. of Chem. Tech., 1995; contbr. articles to profl. jours.; patentee in field. Nat. researcher Sistema Nacional de Investigadores, Mexico City, 1989; grantee Nat. Coun. Sci. and Tech., Mexico City, 1977, Edison Polymer Innovation Corp., Akron, 1990. Fellow Am. Inst. Chemists; mem. Indsl. Rsch. Inst., Am. Chem. Soc. Roman Catholic. Avocations: jogging, soccer, reading, music. Home: Haseluener Str 29, 30539 Hannover Germany Office: Continental AG, Postfach 169, 30001 Hannover Germany

MONSARRAT, NICHOLAS, newspaper editor, writer; b. Norwalk, Conn., Dec. 26, 1941; s. John and Margaret Jane (Cashatt) M.; m. Barbara Ann Curcio, Feb. 25, 1995; children: Sean, Andrea, J. Alexander. BA in Journalism, Washington and Lee U., 1963. Reporter, editor The Times Argus, Barre, Vt., 1969-85; mng. editor The Rutland (Vt.) Daily Herald, 1985-88; adj. prof. journalism St. Michael's Coll., Colchester, Vt., 1988-92, assoc. prof. journalism, 1992-95, writer, adj. prof. journalism, 1996—; editl. page editor Burlington (Vt.) Free Press, 1995-96; participant Am. Press Inst., Reston, Va., 1986, New Eng. Writers Workshop, Boston, 1989. Co-chmn. U.S.-Soviet Editors Exch. Program, New London, N.H., 1982, mem., Moscow, Leningrad, 1983, Middlebury, Vt., 1987. Staff sgt. USAF, 1963-67. Recipient Allan B. Rogers award for editl. writing UPI, 1981. Mem. New Eng. Soc. Newspaper Editors (pres. 1982-83), New Eng. Press Assn. (bd. dirs. 1986-91). Episcopalian. Home and Office: 3834 Mt Philo Rd Charlotte VT 05445

MONSEN, ELAINE RANKER, nutritionist, educator, editor; b. Oakland, Calif., June 6, 1935; d. Emery R. and Irene Stewart (Thorley) Ranker; m. Raymond Joseph Monsen, Jr., Jan. 21, 1959; 1 dau., Maren Ranker. B.A., U. Utah, 1956; M.S. (Mead Johnson grad. scholar), U. Calif., Berkeley, 1959, Ph.D. (NSF fellow), 1961; postgrad. NSF sci. faculty fellow, Harvard U., 1968-69. Dietetic intern Mass. Gen. Hosp., Boston, 1956-57; asst. prof. nutrition, lectr. biochemistry Brigham Young U., Provo, Utah, 1960-63; mem. faculty U. Wash., 1963—, prof. nutrition and medicine, 1984—, prof. nutrition, adj. prof. medicine, 1976-84, chmn. div. human nutrition, dietetics and foods, 1977-82, dir. grad. nutritional scis. program, 1994—, mem. Council of Coll. Arts and Scis., 1974-78, mem. U. Wash. Press com., 1981—; chmn. Nutrition Studies Commn., 1969-83; vis. scholar Stanford U., 1971-72; mem. sci. adv. com. food fortification Pan-Am. Health Orgn., São Paulo, Brazil, 1972; tng. grant coordinator NIH, 1976-97. Editor Jour. Am. Dietetic Assn., 1983—; mem. editorial bd. Coun. Biology Editors, 1992-96; author research papers on lipid metabolism, iron absorption. Bd. dirs. A Contemporary Theatre, Seattle, 1969-72; trustee, bd. dirs. Seattle Found., 1978-95, vice chmn., 1987-91, chmn., 1991-93; pres. Seattle bd. Santa Fe Chamber Music Festival, 1984-85; mem. Puget Sound Blood Ctr. Bd., 1996—. Grantee Nutrition Found., 1965-68, Agrl. Rsch. Svc., 1969-84; recipient Disting. Alumnus award U. Utah, F. Fischer Meml. Nutrition Lectr. award, 1988, L.F. Cooper Meml. Lectr. award, 1991, L. Hatch Meml. Lectr. award, 1992. Mem. Am. Inst. Nutrition, Am. Soc. Clin. Nutrition (sec. 1987-90), Am. Dietetic Assn., Soc. Nutrition Edn., Am. Soc. Parenteral and Enteral Nutrition, Wash. Heart Assn. (nutrition council 1973-76), Phi Beta Kappa, Phi Kappa Phi. Office: U Wash 306 Raitt Hall Box 353410 Seattle WA 98195

MONSEN, RAYMOND JOSEPH, JR., economist, educator, art patron; b. Payson, Utah, Mar. 13, 1931; s. Raymond Joseph and Lucile (Monsen); m. Elaine Ranker, Jan. 21, 1959; 1 dau., Maren Ranker. B.S., U. Utah, 1953; M.A., Stanford U., 1954; Ph.D., U. Calif. at Berkeley, 1960. Asst. prof. econs. Brigham Young U., 1960-63; cons. to govt. and banking industry, 1962-63; assoc. prof. Coll. of Bus., U. Wash., Seattle, 1963-65; prof. U. Wash., 1966-86, prof. dept. mgmt., 1986, chmn. dept. bus., govt. and society, 1966, 73-81, prof. emeritus, 1986—; dir. research Coll. of Bus., U. Wash. (Grad. Sch. Bus.), 1964-68; Guggenheim fellow, dept. econs. Harvard U., 1968-69; vis. prof. Grad. Sch. Bus., Stanford U., 1971-73; vis. prof. U. Calif., Berkeley, Spring 1985. Author: Modern American Capitalism: Idealogies and Issues, 1963, (with Mark Cannon) American Power Groups and Their Ideoloies, 1965, Business and the Changing Environment, 1973, (with others) Management, Systems, and Society, 1976, (with K. Walters) Nationalized Companies: Capitalism Challenged, 1983; editor: (with B. Saxberg) The Business World, 1967; contbr. over 50 articles to profl. jours.; photographic and ceramic collections exhibited at Portland Crafts Ctr., 1968, U. Wash. Art Gallery, 1969, 79, 86, 94-95, San Francisco Art Mus., 1973, Seattle Art Mus., 1974, 76, Portland Art Mus., 1977, La Jolla (Calif.) Mus., 1989, San Francisco Friends of Photography, 1995, Pontiac Art Mus., Portland Art Mus., Maine, 1995-96, U. Calif. at San Diego Art Mus., 1996. Past pres. contemporary art coun. Seattle Art Mus., 1967, trustee, 1968-85; mem. vis. com. U. Pugent Sound Law Sch., 1981-88; mem. vis. com. Met. Mus. Art, N.Y.C., 1992-96; founder-trustee Seattle Opera Assn.; founder Henry Art Gallery Assn., U. Wash.; past trustee Salt Lake Art Ctr., Pacific N.W. Art Assn.; established Monsen Photography collection U. Wash. Art Mus., 1978. Mem. Am. Econs. Assn., Seattle Tennis Club. Avocation: art patron.

MONSERRATE, JENNIFER KRATZER, healthcare administrator; b. Macomb, Ill., May 4, 1968; d. David Edwin and Judith Ann (Lochmann) Kratzer; m. Steven Monserrate, Oct. 12, 1996. BA, U. Ky., 1990, MBA, 1993. Acct. rep. Humana Health Plans, Lexington, Ky., 1992-94; dir. mktg. & admission Horizon Health Care, Las Cruces, N.Mex., 1994; from network devel. specialist to mgr. network devel. Humana Health Plans, Dallas, 1994-96; dir. ops. Physicians Care Mgmt. Co., Dallas, 1996—. Mem. Tex. HMO Assn., Managed Care Peer Forum (bd. dirs.). Lutheran. Avocations: soccer, art. Home: 6314 Martel Ave Dallas TX 75214

MONSKY, JOHN BERTRAND, investment banking executive; b. Montgomery, Ala., May 17, 1930; s. Harry and Belle (Golding) M.; m. Joan Gilbert, June 8, 1952; children: Leslie Joy, John Richard, Harry Robert. B.A., Yale, 1952; M.B.A., Harvard, 1954. Sec. Devoe & Raynolds Co., Inc., Louisville, Ky., 1956-65; v.p., dir. Universal Marion Corp., Jacksonville, Fla., 1965-69, pres., chmn. bd., chief exec. officer, 1969-71, cons., 1971—; vice chmn. ServAmerica, Inc., Jacksonville, 1972-74, co-chmn. bd. dirs., 1974-80, chmn. bd. dirs., 1980—; pres., chmn. bd. dirs. First Fla. Capital Corp., 1985—; dir. Fla. Wire & Cable Co., Jacksonville, 1975-82. Past pres. bd. trustees Jacksonville Country Day Sch.; bd. dirs. Jacksonville Art Mus.; trustee Bolles Sch., Jacksonville, Jacksonville Symphony Assn. Served with USAF, 1954-56. Mem. Jacksonville Area C. of C. (com. of 100), Jackson County Citizen Involvement Clubs, Harvard Bus. Sch. Club of Ky. (exec. com. 1964-65), Phillips Acad. Andover Alumni Club of Ky. (pres. 1963-64), Epping Forest Cmty. Master Assn. (bd. dirs. 1994—), Yale Club N.E. Fla. (bd. dirs. 1987—), Yale Club of N.Y.C., Harvard Club (Jacksonville), Assn. Yale Alumni (del. 1996—), River Club, Ponte Vedra Club, Epping Forest Yacht Club. Home: Epping Forest 7015 Gaines Ct Jacksonville FL 32217-2672 Office: 300 Wharfside Way # B Jacksonville FL 32207-8153

MONSMA, MARVIN EUGENE, library director; b. Prairie City, Iowa, May 14, 1933; s. John and Johanna Hester (Branderhorst) M.; m. Elaine Gross, Aug. 2, 1963; children: Kristy Lynne Monsma De Vos, Kimberly Sue Monsma Rottschafer, Michelle Eileen Monsma Haan. AB, Calvin Coll., 1957; AM in Secondary Edn., Mich. State U., 1961; AMLS in Librarianship, U. Mich., 1967. English tchr. Muskegon (Mich.) Christian Sch., 1957-60, Grand Rapids (Mich.) Christian H.S., 1960-63, Unity Christian H.S., Hudsonville, Mich., 1963-65; asst. libr. Calvin Coll. & Sem., Grand Rapids, 1965-67, head gen. svcs., 1967-68, asst. libr. dir., 1968-69, acting libr. dir., 1969-70, libr. dir., 1970—. Orthodox Presbyterian. Avocations: classical music, gardening, nature. Office: Calvin Coll and Sem Hekman Libr 3207 Burton St SE Grand Rapids MI 49546-4301

MONSMA, ROBBIE ELIZABETH, lawyer, mediator, arbitrator, real estate executive; b. L.A., Nov. 4, 1952; d. Robert Euart and Bessie Esadean Cook; m. Thomas H. Tyrell Jr., Jan. 11, 1970 (div. 1977); 1 child, Trace; m. Durham J. Monsma, Aug. 12, 1979; children: Ian, Mallory. BA, Calif. State U., 1976; JD, UCLA, 1979; postgrad., Fuller Theol. Seminary, 1997. Bar: Colo. 1994. Law clk. The Times Mirror Co., L.A., 1977-78; assoc. Cox, Castle & Nicholson, L.A., 1979-81; corp. counsel, v.p., sec. Becket Investment Corp., Santa Monica, Calif., 1981-85; corp. counsel, sr. v.p. SoPac Real Estate Group, Pasadena, Calif., 1985-94; corp. counsel, exec. v.p. PacificUS Real Estate Group, Pasadena, 1990—; ptnr. Stott Monsma & Assoc. Conflict Mgmt Tng. and System Design, 1993—; receiver panel mem. L.A. Superior Ct., 1992-94; mem. jud. arbitration panel, L.A. and Ventura Counties, 1992-94; vol. settlement officer, L.A. County, 1992-94; vol. judge protem Pasadena Sml. Claims Ct., 1992-94; cert. vol. mediator The Mediator Ctr., Irvine, Calif., 1992, Christian Concilitation Svc., Hollywood, Calif., 1992; trainer Dispute Resolution Svcs., L.A., 1992; cert. conciliator Inst. for Christian Conciliation, 1993—. Bd. mem. Westside Legal Svcs., Santa Monica, Calif., 1983-84; pro bono advisor I Love La Cañada (Calif.) Flintridge Com., 1989-91; mem. bd. dir. Concerned Citizens of La Cañada Flintridge, 1987-91, Hill an' Dale Family Learning Ctr., Santa Monica, 1984-85, West L.A. Bapt. Sch. Parent-Tchr. Club, West Los Angeles, Calif., 1984-85, Ctr. Leadership Devel., 1996—; mem. stewardship bd. Mission Hills Ch., 1995—; bd. dirs. Peacemaker Ministries, 1996—. Mem. Soc. Profls. Dispute Resolution, Constrn. Industry Dispute Resolution Task Force.

MONSON, ARCH, JR., fire alarm manufacturing company executive; b. Thorntown, Ind., Nov. 10, 1913; s. Arch and Mabel (Miller) M.; m. June Hammersmith, Jan. 10, 1959; children—Eminel, Arch III, Dwight, Jay. Grad. high sch. Pres. Monson-Pacific Inc., San Francisco, 1935—; pres. Monson Electric Co. div. Monson-Pacific Inc., San Francisco, 1935—; West coast mgr. Autocall div. Fed. Signal Corp., Blue Island, Ill., 1945—; owner, operator St. George Ranch, Geyserville, Calif., 1959—; dir. Ampex Corp., Redwood City, Calif., Signal Cos. Inc., Beverly Hills, Calif. Chmn. Nat. Jamboree Boy Scouts Am., 1973, v.p. nat. exec. bd., 1973-74, pres., 1975-77; Trustee Pacific Med. Center, San Francisco, 1964—, mem. exec. com., 1969—; trustee Golden Gate U., YMCA of San Francisco, Salvation Army. Recipient Silver Beaver award Boy Scouts Am., 1968, Silver Antelope award, 1968, Silver Buffalo award, 1971. Mem. San Francisco Electric Club, Pacific Coast Elec. Assn., Nat. Elec. Contractors Assn., San Francisco Conv. and Visitors Bur., Internat. Assn. Fire Chiefs, Internat. Municipal Signal Assn. Republican. Presbyn. (elder). Clubs: Mason (Shriner, 33 deg.), Rotarian, Bohemian (pres. 1962, 63), Olympic, The Family. Home: 2825 Broadway San Francisco CA 94115-1060

MONSON, CAROL LYNN, osteopath, physician, psychotherapist; b. Blue Island, Ill., Nov. 3, 1946; d. Marcus Edward and Margaret Bertha (Andres) M.; m. Frank E. Warden, Feb. 28, 1981. B.S., No. Ill. U., 1968, M.S., 1969; D.O., Mich State Coll. Osteo. Medicine, 1979. Lic. physician, Mich., diplomate Am. Bd. Osteo., Am. Bd. Family Physicians, Am. Bd. Osteo. Gen. Practice, diplomate MSUCOM. Expeditor-psychotherapist H. Douglas Singer Zone Ctr., Rockford, Ill., 1969-71; psychotherapist Tri-County Mental Health, St. Johns, Mich., 1971-76; pvt. practice psychotherapy, East Lansing, Mich., 1976-80; intern Lansing Gen. Hosp., Mich., 1979-80, residency dir. family practice, 1988—; pvt. practice osteo. medicine, Lansing, 1980—; mem. staff Ingham Med. Hosp., Lansing Gen. Hosp. (now Mich. Capital Med. Ctr.), chmn. gen practice, 1987-89; field instr. Sch. Social Work, U. Mich., 1973-76; clin. instr. Central Mich. Dept. Psychology, 1974-75; clin. prof. Mich. State U., 1980-88, asst. prof., 1988—, tng. supr. family medicine residency, 1988—, residency dir. family medicine, 1994—; mem. adv. bd. Substance Abuse Clearinghouse, Lansing, 1983-85, Kelly Health Care, Lansing, 1983-85, Americor Health Svcs., Lansing, 1984-88, Lansing Home Care, 1988-94. Mem. Am. Osteo. Assn., Am. Acad. Family Practice, Internat. Transactional Analysis Assn., Mich. Assn. Physicians and Surgeons (program com. 1992—, governance coun., 1996—), Ingham County Osteo. Assn. (pres. 1993-95, 96—), Nat. Assn. Career Women (conv. com. 1984—), Lansing Assn. Career Women, Soc. Tchrs. of Family Medicine, Mich. Assn. Osteo Family Physicians (pres.-elect 1994, pres. 1995-96), Am. Coll. Family Physicians (residency insp. 1991—), Zonta (chmn. service com. Mid Mich. Capital Area chpt.). Avocations: gardening; orchid growing; antique collecting. Office: 2445 Jolly Rd Ste 400 Okemos MI 48864-4572

MONSON, DAVID CARL, school superintendent, farmer, state legislator; b. Langdon, N.D., July 30, 1950; s. Carl Arthur and Shirley Jean (Klai) M.; m. Mary Kathryn Greutman, July 8, 1972; children: Cordell Carl, Cale David, Jared Arthur. Cert. tchr., adminstr., N.D. Sci. tchr. Hankinson (N.D.) Pub. Sch., 1972-75; tchr. Nekoma (N.D.) Pub. Sch., 1975-76; tchr., prin. NeKoma (N.D.) Pub. Sch., 1976-79; tchr., supt. Nekoma (N.D.) Pub. Sch., 1979-80; tchr., prin. Milton (N.D.)-Osnabrock High Sch., 1981-84; supt. Adams (N.D.) Pub. Schs., 1984-88; ins. agt. N.Y. Life, Fargo, N.D., 1988-95; self-employed ins. agt., Osnabrock, 1988—, farmer, 1975—; mem.. N.D. Ho. of Reps., Bismarck, 1993—; supt. Edinburg (N.D.) Pub. Schs., 1995—. Mem. sch. bd. dirs. Osnabrock Sch. Bd., 1989—; leader Bobcats 4-H Club, 1988—. Mem. N.D. Farm Bur., N.D. Coun. Sch. Adminstrs., Eagles, KP (grand sec. N.D. and Sask. 1985-93, award 1990). Republican. Lutheran. Avocations: skiing, gardening, hunting, coin collecting.

MONSON, DAVID SMITH, accountant, former congressman; b. Salt Lake City, June 20, 1945; s. Smith Weston and Dorothy (Brammer) M.; m. Julianne Johnson, Feb. 4, 1971; children: David Johnson, Traci Lyn, Marianne, Kari, Smith Douglas. BS in Acctg., U. Utah, 1970. C.P.A., Utah. Acct. Elmer Fox and Co., Salt Lake City, 1970-72; auditor State of Utah, Salt Lake City, 1973-76; lt. gov. State of Utah, 1977-84; mem. 99th Congress, 1985-87; v.p. I Corp., 1987-91; bus. cons. and acct., 1992—; mem. exec. com. Nat. Conf. Lt. Govs., 1978-84 mem. State Bd. Regents, 1981-84. Bd. dirs. Utah Soc. to Prevent Blindness, 1976-83; chmn. Utah Cancer Crusade, 1979-80, chmn. Bd. Salt Lake County Am. Cancer Soc., 1980-81; govt. group chmn. United Way, 1979, assoc. campaign chmn., 1981, campaign chmn. 1982; treas. Utah Reps., 1975-76; trustee Ballet West, 1977-81, Travis Found., 1977-84, bd. dirs. Osmond Found., 1982-84, Utah Opportunities Industrialization Ctrs., Inc., 1988-91; sec. bd. dirs. Utah Sports Found., Inc., 1988-91. Recipient Outstanding Young Man Am. award, 1977, 81; named One of 3 Outstanding Young Men Utah Jaycees, 1980-81. Mem. Council State Govts. (v.p. Western conf. 1974-75). Republican. Mem. Ch. Jesus Christ Latter Day Saints. Home: 792 Northview Dr Salt Lake City UT 84103-4027 *Two principles have been the overriding factors in motivating the actions I have taken throughout my life—a strong desire to be the successful leader and provider of a stable family unit and a faith in and a desire to follow the teachings of a loving God.*

MONSON, DIANNE LYNN, literacy educator; b. Minot, N.D., Nov. 24, 1934; d. Albert Rachie and Iona Cordelia (Kirk) M. BS, U. Minn., 1956, MA, 1962, PhD, 1966. Tchr., Rochester Pub. Schs. (Minn.), 1966-59, U.S. Dept. Def., Schweinfurt, W.Ger., 1959-61, St. Louis Park Schs. (Minn.), 1961-62; instr. U. Minn., Mpls., 1962-66; prof. U. Wash., Seattle, 1966-82; prof. literacy edn. U. Minn., Mpls., 1982—, chmn. Curriculum and Instrn., 1986-89. Co-author: New Horizons in the Language Arts, 1972; Children and Books, 6th edit., 1981; Experiencing Children's Literature, 1984; (monograph) Research in Children's Literature, 1976; Language Arts: Teaching and Learning Effective Use of Language, 1988; Reading Together: Helping Children Get A Good Start With Reading, 1991; assoc. editor Dictionary of Literacy, 1995. Recipient Outstanding Educator award U. Minn. Alumni Assn., 1983, Alumni Faculty award, 1991. Fellow Nat. Conf. Rsch. in English (pres. 1990-91); mem. ALA, Nat. Coun. Tchrs. English (exec. com. 1979-81), Internat. Reading Assn. (dir. 1980-83, Arbuthnot award 1993, Reading Hall of Fame 1997), U.S. Bd. Books for Young People (pres. 1988-90). Lutheran. Home: 740 River Dr Saint Paul MN 55116 Office: U Minn 350 Peik Hall Minneapolis MN 55455

MONSON, JAMES EDWARD, electrical engineer, educator; b. Oakland, Calif., June 20, 1932; s. George Edward and Frances Eleanor (Fouche) M.; m. Julie Elizabeth Conzelman, June 25, 1954; children—John, Jamie, Jennifer. BSEE, Stanford U., 1954, MSEE, 1955, PhD in Elec. Engring., 1961. Mem. tech. staff Bell Telephone Labs., Murray Hill, N.J., 1955-56; devel. engr. Hewlett-Packard Co., Palo Alto, Calif., 1956-61; Robert C. Sabini prof. engring. Harvey Mudd Coll., 1961—. Mem. governing bd. Claremont Unified Sch. Dist., 1966-71, pres., 1969-70; pres. Claremont Civic Assn., 1974-75; bd. dirs. Claremont YMCA, 1978-82. Fellow NSF, 1954-55, Japan Soc. Promotion Sci., 1984; Fulbright Rsch. grantee, 1975-76; Fulbright sr. lectr., 1980. Fellow IEEE; mem. AAUP, Magnetics Soc. Japan, Phi Beta Kappa, Sigma Xi, Tau Beta Pi. Home: PO Box 453 Pioneertown CA 92268 Office: Harvey Mudd Coll 301 E 12th St Claremont CA 91711-5901

MONSON, JOHN RUDOLPH, lawyer; b. Chgo., Feb. 4, 1941; s. Rudolph Agaton and Ellen Louise (Loeffler) M.; m. Susan Lee Brown, May 22, 1965; children: Elizabeth Louisa, Christina Lee, Donald Rudolph. BA with honors, Northwestern U., 1963; JD with distinction, U. Mich., 1966. Bar: Ill. 1966, N.H. 1970, Mass. 1985. Atty. assoc. Chapman & Cutler, Chgo., 1966-68, Levenfeld, Kanter, Baskes & Lippitz, Chgo., 1968-70, Nighswander, Martin & Mitchell, Laconia, N.H., 1970-71; mem., ptnr. Wiggin & Nourie, P.A., Manchester, N.H., 1972—; pres. Wiggin & Nourie, P.A., Manchester, 1991-94; sec., gen. counsel Rock of Ages Corp., 1996—. Mem. N.H. Fish and Game Commn., Concord, 1980-94, chmn., 1983-93; sr. bd. dirs. Brown-Monson Found., 1991—; incorporator Cath. Med. Ctr., 1988-95, Optima Health, 1994—. Fellow Am. Coll. Trust and Estate Counsel. Republican. Avocations: skiing, hunting, running. Home: 24 Wellesley Dr Bedford NH 03110-4531 Office: Wiggin & Nourie PA 20 Market St Manchester NH 03101-1931

MONSON, THOMAS SPENCER, church official, publishing company executive; b. Salt Lake City, Aug. 21, 1927; s. George Spencer and Gladys (Condie) M.; m. Frances Beverly Johnson, Oct. 7, 1948; children—Thomas L., Ann Frances, Clark Spencer. BS with honors in mktg, U. Utah, 1948; MBA, Brigham Young U., 1974, LLD (hon.), 1981. With Deseret News Press, Salt Lake City, 1948-64; mgr. Deseret News Press, 1962-64; mem. Council Twelve Apostles, Ch. of Jesus Christ of Latter Day Saints, 1963-85, mem. first presidency, 1985—, bishop, 1950-55; pres. Canadian Mission, 1959-62; chmn. bd. Deseret News Pub. Co., 1977-96; vice chmn. Deseret Mgmt. Corp.; pres. Printing Industry Utah, 1958; bd. dirs. Printing Industry Am., 1958-64; mem. Utah exec. bd. U.S. West Communications. Mem. Utah Bd. Regents; mem. nat. exec. bd. Boy Scouts Am.; trustee Brigham Young U.. With USNR, 1945-46. Recipient Recognition award, 1964, Disting. Alumnus award U. Utah, 1966; Silver Beaver award Boy Scouts Am., 1971; Silver Buffalo award, 1978; Bronze Wolf award World Orgn. of the Scout Movement, 1993. Mem. Utah Assn. Sales Execs., U. Utah Alumni Assn. (dir.), Salt Lake Advt. Club, Alpha Kappa Psi. Club: Exchange (Salt Lake City). Office: LDS Ch 47 E South Temple Salt Lake City UT 84150-1005

MONTAG, JOHN JOSEPH, II, librarian; b. Omaha, Jan. 8, 1948; s. John Joseph and Ruth Helen (Johnston) M.; m. Linda Kay Lubanski, Apr. 8, 1971; children: Nicole Elizabeth, Megan Kristine. BA, Midland Luth. Coll., 1970; postgrad., Wash. State U., 1970-74; MA, U. Iowa, 1976; postgrad., U. Nebr., 1982-84. English tchr. pub. schs., Nebr., Iowa, 1972-75; reference librarian Concordia Coll., Moorhead, Minn., 1976-81; asst. prof. library sci. U. Nebr., Lincoln, 1981-84; dir. Office of Info. State Library Iowa, Des Moines, 1984-86, state librarian, 1986-87; dir. Thomas Library Wittenberg U., 1987-95; dir. Cochrane-Woods Libr. Nebr. Wesleyan U., Lincoln, 1995-97, dir. libr. and computer svcs., 1997—; trustee Bibliog. Ctr. for Research, Denver, 1986-87; adv. bd. No. Lights Library Network, Detroit Lakes, Minn., 1980-81; chair Southwest Ohio Consortium Higher Edn. Libr. Coun., 1991-94. Contbr. articles to profl. jours. Univ. Found. library improvement grantee, U. Nebr., 1983; Challenge grantee NEH, 1992. Mem. ALA, Assn. Coll. and Research Libraries. Office: Cochrane Woods Libr Nebr Wesleyan U 5000 Saint Paul Ave Lincoln NE 68504-2760

MONTAGNA, BERNICE DONNA, education educator; b. Bridgeport, Conn., Mar. 31, 1953; d. Philip Romano and Catherine (MacDaniel) Echinger; m. Robert John Montagna, June 9, 1979; children: Cariann, Robert. AA, Broward Community Coll., 1974; BS, Southern Conn. State U., 1977, degree in ednl. leadership, 1996; MAT, Sacred Heart U., 1992. Cert. tchr. Conn. Substitute tchr. East Haven (Conn.) Bd. Edn., 1981-82, instructional aide, 1985-92; tchr. North Haven (Conn.) Bd. Edn., 1992—. Leader Girl Scouts Am., North Haven, 1989-91. Mem. NEA, Conn. Reading Assn., Conn. Edn. Assn., Kindergarten Assn. Conn., North Haven Edn. Assn., Assn. Supervision & Curriculum Devel. Avocations: reading, cooking, arts/crafts. Home: 10 Rance Ct North Haven CT 06473-3454

MONTAGU, ASHLEY, anthropologist, social biologist; b. London, June 28, 1905; came to U.S., 1927, 30; naturalized, 1940; s. Charles Ehrenberg and Mary (Plotnick) M.; m. Helen Marjorie Peakes, Sept. 18, 1931; children: Audrey, Barbara, Geoffrey. Spl./student, U. London, 1922-25; student, U. Florence, 1928-29; Ph.D., Columbia U., 1937; D.Sc. (hon.), Grinnell Coll.,

1967, U. N.C., 1987; D.Litt. (hon.), Ursinus Coll., 1972. Research asso. Brit. Mus. Natural History, London, 1926-27; curator phys. anthropology Wellcome Hist. Med. Mus., 1929-30; asst. prof. anatomy N.Y. U., 1931-38; asso. prof. anatomy Hahnemann Med. Coll. and Hosp., Phila., 1938-49; chmn. dept. anthropology Rutgers U., 1949-55; vis. lectr. dept. social sci. Harvard, 1945; sr. lectr. VA Postgrad. Tng. Program Psychiatry and Neurology, 1946—; lectr. New Sch. Social Research, 1931-59; vis. prof. U. Del., 1955; Regents prof., U. Calif., Santa Barbara, 1962; lectr. Princeton U., 1978-83; dir. Inst. Natural Philosophy, 1979-81; fellow Stevenson Hall, Princeton U., 1978—; dir. rsch. N.J. Com. Phys. Devel. and Health, 1953-57; family affairs editor, anthrop. adv. NBC-TV, 1954; chmn. Anisfield-Wolf Award Com., 1954-95; co-chmn. Attach, 1992—; responsible for drafting statement on race for UNESCO, 1949-50, cons., 1949; a drafter NSF Bill, 1946-47, co-drafter constn. Am. Assn. Human Genetics, 1949; hon. corr. mem. anthrop. socs. Paris and Florence; pres. Phila. Anthrop. Soc., 1942-48. Produced, financed, wrote and directed: film One World or None for, Nat. Commn. on Atomic Info. and Am. Fedn. Sci. Workers, 1946; Author: Coming into Being Among the Australian Aborigines, 1937, 2d edit., 1974, Man's Most Dangerous Myth: The Fallacy of Race, 1942, 5th edit., 1974, 6th edit., 1997 Edward Tyson, M.D., F.R.S., (1650-1708): and the rise of human and comparative anatomy in England, 1943, Introduction to Physical Anthropology, 1945, 3d edit., 1960, Adolescent Sterility, 1946, On Being Human, 1950, 2d edit., 1966, On Being Intelligent, 1951, Statement on Race, 1952, 3d edit., 1972, Darwin, Competition and Cooperation, 1952, The Natural Superiority of Women, 1953, 3d edit., 1992, The Direction of Human Development, 1955, 2d edit., 1970, Immortality, 1955, Biosocial Nature of Man, 1956, Anthropology And Human Nature, Man: His First Million Years, 1957, Man His First Two Million Years, 1969, The Reproductive Development of the Female, 1957, 3d edit., 1979, Education and Human Relations, 1958, The Cultured Man, 1958, Human Heredity, 1959, 2d edit., 1963, Handbook of Anthropometry, 1960, Man in Process, 1961, Prenatal Influences, 1962, The Humanization of Man, 1962, Race, Science, and Humanity, 1963, The Dolphin in History, (with John Lilly 1963), Life Before Birth, 1964, 2d edit., 1978, The Science of Man, 1964, (with E. Steen) Anatomy and Physiology, 1959, 2d edit., 1983, The Idea of Race, 1965, (with C.L. Brace) The Human Revolution, 1965, 2nd edit., 1977, Up the Ivy, 1966, The American Way of Life, 1967, The Anatomy of Swearing, 1967, (with E. Darling) The Prevalance of Nonsense, 1967, Man Observed, 1968, Man, His First Two Million Years, 1957, 3d edit., 1962, Sex, Man, and Society, 1969, (with E. Darling) The Ignorance of Certainty, 1970, Immortality, Religion, and Morals, 1955, 2nd edit., 1971, Touching, 1971, 3d edit., 1986, (with M. Levitan) Textbook of Human Genetics, 1971, 2d edit., 1977, The Elephant Man, 1971, 3d edit., 1996, America As I See It, 1971, (with S.S. Snyder) Man and the Computer, 1972, The Endangered Environment, 1974, The Nature of Human Aggression, 1976, (with C.L. Brace) Human Evolution, 2nd edit., 1977, (with Floyd Matson) The Human Connection, 1979, (with Floyd Matson) The Dehumanization of Man, 1983, Growing Young, 1981, What We Know About Race, 1985, Times Change...Do People?, 1985, The Peace of the World, 1986, Living and Loving, 1986, Humanity Speaking to Humankind, 1986, The World of Humanity, 1986, Coming into Being, 1988, the Story of People, 1988; editor Nat. Hist. Soc. Series, Classics of Anthropology; adv. editor Sci., Tech. and Humanities; anthropology editor Isis, 1936-56, publs. editor, 1937-45. Guardsman with Welsh Guards, 1919. Recipient 1st prize Morris Chaim prize Centennary 2d Dist. Dental Soc., 1936, Chgo. Forum Lit. contest, 1943, Rollo May award Saybrook Inst. Humanistic Studies, 1991, Verney award Pre-Perinatal Psychol. Assn. N.Am., 1993; recipient Disting Svc. award Assn. Childbirth at Home Internat., 1970, Am. Anthrop. Assn., 1984, Phi Beta Kappa, 1985, Inst. Human Behavior, 1986, Nat. Assn. Parents and Profls. Safe Alternatives in Childbirth, 1986, Am. Humanist of Yr. award, 1995, Assn. for Humananistic Psychol. Pathfinder award, 1995, Ashley Montagu Peace award Common Bond Inst. of U.S. and Harmony Inst. of Russia, 1995. Fellow AAAS; mem. Royal Soc. Medicine (affiliate), Internat. Soc. Study of Race Rels., Internat. Assn. Human Biologists, pres. Phila. Antropological Soc., Am. Assn. Anatomists, Am. Soc. Study of Child Growth and Devel., Am. Assn. Maternal and Child Health, Am. Assn. Phys. Anthropologists (Charles Darwin Lifetime Achievement award 1994), Sigma Xi. Expert forensic problems witness on legal, sci. problems relating to race and anthrop. matters, 1930. Home: 321 Cherry Hill Rd Princeton NJ 08540-7617 *To be kind, to be, to do, and to depart gracefully.*

MONTAGUE, BRIAN JOHN, consulting company executive; b. Washington, Oct. 9, 1951; s. H.C. and Dorothy (Brand) M.; m. Kathryn Valente, Oct. 2, 1993. B.A., Bridgewater Coll., 1973; student, St. Mary's (Md.) Coll., 1975, George Washington U., 1980, Miss. State U., 1981. Toxicology technician Hazelton Labs., Vienna, Va., 1973-74; asst. mgr. Chesapeake Sea Farms, Ridge, Md., 1974-76; tng. instr., program coord. Natural Resources Dept., Annapolis, Md., 1976-77; fishery biologist Nat. Aquarium, U.S. Fish and Wildlife Svc., Washington, 1977-82, curator aquarium, 1982-88; pres. Aquatic Images, Annapolis, 1989—; lectr. local interest groups. Office: Aquatic Images 740 Red Cedar Rd Annapolis MD 21401-6000

MONTAGUE, DROGO K., urologist; b. Alpena, Mich., Dec. 11, 1942; s. Frank Wright and Susan Alice (Kidder) M.; m. Margaret Mary Barrett; children: Mark Andrew, Lisa Joy. Student, U. Mich., 1963, MD cum laude, 1968. Diplomate Am. Bd. Urology. Intern Cleve. Clinic Hosp., 1968-69, resident in gen. surgery, 1969-70, resident in urology, 1970-73; assoc. staff urologist Cleve. Clinic Found., 1973-75, staff urologist, 1975—, head sect. prosthetic surgery, 1981—, urology residence program dir., 1985—, dir. Ctr. for Sexual Function, 1987—; prof. surgery Ohio State U. Coll. Medicine, 1992—; trainee cardiovascular rsch. tng. program NIH, 1962-68; trustee Am. Bd. Urology, 1989-95, mem. examination com., 1975-80, examiner cert. exam., 1980-88, rep. to Am. Bd. Med. Specialties, 1989-95. Reviewer various publs. in field; contbr. numerous articles to profl. publs., chpts. to books; editor: Disorders of Male Sexual Function, 1988, Surgical Treatment of Erectile Dysfunction, 1993; author audiovisual tapes in field. James B. Angell scholar, 1961, 62, Nat. Found. scholar, 1963-68; recipient Russell and Mary Hugh Scott Edn. award, 1989, Iowa Rsch. award, 1967. Fellow ACS; mem. Am. Urolog. Assn. (chmn. sci. exhibits com. North Cen. sect. 1977, mem. residency edn. com. 1979-83, vice chmn. audio visual com. 1989-95, mem. various coms., editor Am. Urolog. Assn. Video Libr. 1995—, chmn. audio visual com. 1996—), Am. Assn. Genitourinary Surgeons, Cleve. Urolog. Soc. (sec.-treas. 1978-80, v.p. 1980-81, pres. 1981-82, 94-95), Soc. for Study of Impotence (pres. 1995). Office: Cleve Clinic Found Dept Urology 9500 Euclid Ave Cleveland OH 44195-0001

MONTAGUE, EDGAR BURWELL, III (MONTY MONTAGUE), industrial designer; b. Charlotte, N.C., Aug. 6, 1958; s. Edgar B. Jr. and Mary Sue (Calhoun) M.; m. Nancy Oliver Stallworth, Feb. 25, 1984; children: Nancy Lea, Edgar Eubank. B Environ. Design cum laude, N.C. State U., 1980. Indsl. design Design/Joe Sonderman, Inc., Charlotte, 1980-85; design prin. Machen Montague, Inc., Charlotte, 1985-93, BOLT, Charlotte, 1994—. Holder 8 design and/or utility patents; work published in Product Design 1-6, Design for Humanity. Designer corp. identity program Habitat for Humanity, Charlotte, 1987 (logo design now used throughout world). Recipient ann. design award Internat. Design mag., 1988-93, ID-40 ID Mag., 1994. Mem. Indsl. Designer Soc. Am. (co-founder Carolina chpt., program chmn. 1981-83, vice chmn. 1984, 93, Kudo award for chpt. svc. 1982, Indsl. Design Excellence awards 1989-94). Avocations: travel, art, time with family. Office: BOLT 2221 Edge Lake Dr Ste 100 Charlotte NC 28217-4509

MONTANA, JOSEPH C., JR., former professional football player; b. New Eagle, Pa., June 11, 1956; s. Joseph C. Montana, Sr., and Theresa M.; m. 1st, Kim Monses, 1975 (div.); m. 2nd, Cass Castillo (div. 1983); m. 3rd, Jennifer Wallace, 1984; 2 children, Alexandra, Elizabeth. B.B.A. in Mktg., U. Notre Dame, 1978. Quarterback San Francisco 49ers, 1979-93; mem. Super Bowl Championship Team, 1982, 85, 90; named to Pro Bowl, 1981, 83, 84, 85, 87, 89, 90, 93; quarterback Kansas City Chiefs, 1993-95. Author (with Alan Steinberg): Cool Under Fire, 1989. Named MVP at Super Bowl, 1982, 85, MVP at NFL, 1989, Player of Yr., The Sporting News, 1989, Man of Yr., The Sporting News, 1989; named to Pro Bowl 1981, 83-85, 87, 89, 90, 93. Holds NFL career records for highest completion percentage (63.67), highest passer rating (93.5), NFL single-season record for highest passer rating (112.4), 1989, NFL record for most consecutive games with 300 or more yards passing (5), 1982, most consecutive passes completed (22), 1987. Office: care Internat Mgmt Group 1 Erieview Plz Ste 1300 Cleveland OH 44114-1715*

MONTANA, PATRICK JOSEPH, management educator; b. N.Y.C.; s. Joseph Paul and Constance (Frezza) M. B.S. cum laude, L.I. U., M.S. cum laude; Ph.D., N.Y. U., 1966; M.B.A., U. Cin., 1974. Asst. dean, asso. prof., dir. placement, chmn. mgmt. L.I. U., Bklyn., 1960-66; asso. prof. Drexel U., Phila., 1966-67; asst. dean N.Y. U. Grad. Sch. Bus. Adminstrn., N.Y.C., 1967-69; asst. v.p., dir. planning and human resources devel. Sperry & Hutchingson Co. (trading stamps and subsidiaries), N.Y.C., 1969-74; U.S. presdl. interchange exec., 1973; pres. Profl. Inst., Am. Mgmt. Assn., N.Y.C., 1974-76, Nat. Center Career Life Planning, 1975-80, 80—; prof. mgmt. Hofstra U. Sch. Bus.; adj. prof. mgmt. and mktg. Fordham U. Grad. Sch. Bus., N.Y.C., 1969-79; curriculum cons. U. P.R., 1968; guest lectr. Congress for Internat. Progress in Mgmt., 1965, IBM Corp. Mgmt. Sch., 1964-65, 76-77; mediator Pub. Employee Relations Bd., 1969; bd. dirs. Ednl. Systems and Publs., 1970-75. Author: The Marketing Executive of the Future, 1967, You Can Change Your Future, 1976, Managing Nonprofit Organizations, 1977, Marketing in Nonprofit Organizations, 1978, Career Life Planning for Americans, 1978, Overcoming Mid and Late Career Crises, 1978, Successful Teamwork—How Managers and Secretaries Achieve It, 1979, Managing Terrorism, 1982; Retirement Programs: How to Develop and Implement Them, 1985; Work Force Management in the Arabian Peninsula, 1986, Management, 1987, Preretirement Planning, 1988, Stepping Out, Starting Over, 1992, Managing Public and Nonprofit Organizations, 1994; contbr. numerous articles to profl. publs. Recipient achievement award Wall Street Jour., 1959-60, U.S. Sec. Labor's recognition award 1974, Disting. Alumnus award L.I. U.; fellow Ford Found., 1963-64. Mem. Am. Assembly Collegiate Schs. Bus. (accreditation com. 1970-72, standards com. 1973-75, govt. relations com. 1976-78), Am. Mktg. Assn. (awards com., continuing edn. com.), Beta Gamma Sigma, Eta Mu Pi. Office: Hofstra U Sch Bus Hempstead NY 11550

MONTCALM, NORMAN JOSEPH, lawyer; b. Trois-Rivieres, Que., Can., July 8, 1945; s. Aimé and Alida (Filion) M.; m. Marie Lanctôt, July 28, 1973; children: Julie, Valérie, Jean-François. BA, Collège des Trois-Riviéres, 1967; BCL, McGill U., 1971. Bar: Que. 1972. Legal counsel Hydro-Que., Montreal, 1972-79; v.p. legal affairs, sec. Civitas Corp., Montreal, 1979-83; legal counsel Imasco Ltd., Montreal, 1983-88, sec., legal counsel, 1988-89; ptnr. Legault Longtin Laurin Halpin, Montreal, 1992—. Mem. St. Justine Hosp. Found., Montreal, 1986—, Order of Que. Olympic Games, Montreal, 1988—. Mem. Can. Bar Assn., Que. and Montreal bar assns. (various coms.), Montreal C. of C., Mt. Royal Country Club (pres. 1995—), Nat. Circus Sch. Found. Montreal (bd. dirs. 1995—). Roman Catholic. Home: 221 Carlyle, Mount Royal, PQ Canada H3R 1T1 Office: Legault Longtin Laurin Halpin, 630 Blvd René-Lévesque W # 1800, Montreal, PQ Canada H3B 1S6

MONTE, BONNIE J., performing company executive, director, educator; b. Stamford, Ct., Nov. 27, 1954; d. Eugene N. and Ruth M. (Thompson) M. BA, Bethany Coll., 1976; diploma, Hartman Conservatory, Stamford, 1978. Assoc. artistic dir. Williamstown (Mass.) Theatre Festival, 1981-89; casting dir. Manhattan Theatre Club, N.Y.C., 1989-90; artistic dir. N.J. Shakespeare Festival, Madison, 1990—; mem. faculty Drew U., Madison, 1991—; guest artist, vis. asst. prof. U. Notre Dame, fall 1994. Grantee Lotte Crabtree Found., Boston, 1977. Democrat. Avocations: equerry, cycling, archery, writing, travel. Office: NJ Shakespeare Festival 36 Madison Ave Madison NJ 07940-1434

MONTECEL, MARIA ROBLEDO (CUCA ROBLEDO MONTECEL), educational association administrator; b. Laredo, Tex., Jan. 14, 1953; d. Ismael and Paula (Benavides) Robledo; m. Lucas Montecel, Aug. 18, 1979; children: Ismael Gavino, Xavier Mario. BSSW magna cum laude, Our Lady of Lake U., 1972; MEd, Antioch U., 1975; PhD in Urban Edn., U. Wis., 1985. Rsch. asst. D.C. Devel. Assocs., Inc., San Antonio, 1973-75; test designer Dissemination and Assessment Ctr. for Bilingual Edn. U. Tex., San Antonio, 1975-76; grad. rsch. asst. office rsch. Sch. Edn. U. Wis., Milw., 1980-81, program dir. Midwest NODAC dept. cultural founds. Sch. Edn., 1985; evaluator Ctr. for Mgmt. Innovation in Multicultural Edn. Intercultural Devel. Rsch. Assn., San Antonio, 1976-77, dir. bilingual edn. cost analysis project, 1977-78, dir. divsn. rsch., devel. and evalutation, 1978-80, rsch. specialist, 1982-85, dir. Ctr. for Prevention and Recovery Dropouts, 1985-88, 90-92, dir. tng. and tech. assistance, 1988-89, dir. valued youth program, 1988-90, dep. dir., 1992, exec. dir., 1992—; trustee Our Lady of Lake U. Mem. editorial bd. Tex. Rschr.; contbr. articles to profl. jours. Vol. advocate Alamo Area Rape Crisis Ctr.; mem. rsch. com. Hispanas Unidas; participant Leadership Tex. '85; invited mem. Tex. State Task Force Dropout Prevention; chmn. lifelong learning coun. San Antonio 2000; cons. edn. and immigrant students Mellon Found.; bd. dirs. Mex.-Am. Solidarity Found.; founding bd. dirs. CIVICUS World Alliance Citizen Participation; bd. dirs. community edn. leadership program Mott Found.; mem. nat. adv. coun. Race and Ethnic Studies Inst., Tex. A & M; mem. ednl. review bd. Tex. Ctr. Ednl. Rsch.; mem. nat. adv. bd. ERIC/CRESS, 1994. Recipient High Achievement Commendation, Antioch Coll., 1975, Peter F. Drucker award Coca-Cola Valued Youth Program; Women and Minority Rsch. fellow Nat. Inst. Edn., 1979, Title VII Doctoral fellow U. Wis., 1980-82. Mem. Am. Edn. Rsch. Assn., Nat. Assn. Bilingual Edn., Nat. Dropout Prevention Network (charter), Alphi Chi. Roman Catholic. Avocations: reading, writing, fishing, golf. Office: Intercultural Devel Rsch Assn 5835 Callaghan Rd Ste 350 San Antonio TX 78228-1125

MONTEFERRANTE, JUDITH CATHERINE, cardiologist; b. N.Y., Jan. 27, 1949; d. Stanley and Monica (Vinckus) Sosaris; m. Ronald J. (div. 1983); 1 child, Jason Paul; m. Roger E. Salisbury, Mar. 3, 1990. BS, Adelphi U., Garden City, 1970; MS, SUNY, Buffalo, 1973; MD, Mt. Sinai, N.Y.C., 1978. Cert. nuclear cardiology, CCNC (Certification Coun. of Nuclear Cardiology). Attending N.Y. Med. Coll., Valhalla, N.Y., 1983-84; pvt. practice White Plains, N.Y., 1984--.; past pres. Am. Heart Assn., 1984-86. Contbr. articles to profl. jours. Fellow ACP, Am. Coll. Cardiology, Coun. on Clin. Cardiology of AHA, N.Y. Cardiol.; mem. Am. Soc. of Nuclear Cardiology. Office: 222 Westchester Ave # 405 White Plains NY 10604-2906

MONTEIRO, GEORGE, English educator, writer; b. Cumberland, R.I., May 23, 1932; s. Francisco José and Augusta (Temudo) M.; m. Lois Ann Hodgins, Aug. 14, 1958 (div. 1992); children: Katherine, Stephen, Emily; m. Brenda Murphy, Mar. 25, 1995. AB, Brown U., 1954; AM, Columbia U., 1956; PhD, Brown U., 1964; DHL (hon.), U. Mass., Dartmouth, 1993. From instr. to assoc. prof. Brown U., Providence, 1961-72, prof. English, 1972—; vis. prof. Providence Coll., 1967-68; Fulbright prof. Am. lit. U. Sao Paulo, 1969-71. Author: Henry James and John Hay: The Record of a Friendship, 1965, The Coffee Exchange: Poems, 1982, Robert Frost and the New England Renaissance, 1988, Double Weaver's Knot: Selected Poems, 1989, The Presence of Camões, 1996; editor: The Man Who Never Was: Essays on Fernando Pessoa, 1982, The Correspondence of Henry James and Henry Adams, 1877-1941, 1992, Conversations with Elizabeth Bishop, 1996; translator: In Crete with the Minotaur and Other Poems, 1980, Fernando Pessoa: Self Awareness and Thirty Other Poems, 1988, A Man Smiles at Death with Half a Face, 1991. Decorated Order of Prince Henry the Navigator, govt. of Portugal, 1989. Office: Brown U Dept English Providence RI 02912

MONTEIRO, LOIS ANN, medical science educator; b. Central Falls, R.I., Mar. 22, 1934; d. William Henry and Martha Mae (Leach) Hodgins; m. George Monteiro, Aug. 14, 1958 (div. Feb. 1992); children: Katherine, Stephen, Emily. RN, Roger Williams Hosp., Providence, 1954; BA, Brown U., k1958, PhD, 1970; MS, Boston U., 1960. Asst. prof. Boston U., 1960-65; asst. prof. Brown U., Providence, R.I., 1971-77, assoc. prof., 1978-82, prof., 1983—, chmn. dept., 1985—, assoc. dean medicine, 1991—; vis. prof. U. Va., 1990; bd. dirs. Harvard Cmty. Health Plan, 1990-95, Harvard Pilgrim Health Care Plan, New Eng., 1995—. Author: Montoring Health Status, 1976, Cardiac Rehabilitation, 1980; contbr. articles to profl. jours. Mem. Commn. State of R.I., Providence, 1989—. NSF grantee, 1969, Robert W. Johnson Found. grantee, Princeton, N.J., 1983, NIH grantee, 1987; Bunting Inst. fellow, Cambridge, Mass., 1981. Mem. Am. Sociol. Assn., R.I. State Nurses Assn. (pres. 1974-76), Women in Medicine/Assn. Am. Med. Colls. Democrat. Presbyterian. Avocation: collecting books on nursing history. Office: Brown U Dept Med Sci Box G-A413 Providence RI 02912

MONTEITH, CLIFTON JAMES, artist; b. Detroit, July 8, 1944; s. James Elsworth and Shirley Alice (Bossardet) M.; m. Elizabeth Ann Sutherland, June 14, 1969 (div. Apr. 1985); 1 child, Matthew Fredrick; m. Nancy Louise Paepke, Sept. 29, 1986. BFA, Mich. State U., 1968, postgrad., 1973-74. Instr. painting, drawing and sculpture Mich., Conn., N.Y., 1968-84; twig furniture and sculpture designer and builder Lake Ann, Mich., 1985—; guest lectr. U. Mich. Sch. Art, Ann Arbor, 1987, instr. twig design and constrn. workshop, 1987, 90, 92; guest lectr. Calvin Coll., Grand Rapids, Mich., 1990, Parnham Coll., Dorset, Eng., 1993; lectr. So. Ohio Mus., Portsmouth, Ohio, 1993, Takumi-Jyuku wood working sch., Makigahora, Gifu, Japan, 1994, Far East Soc. Archs. and Engrs., Osaka, Japan, 1994, Osaka Designer's Coll., 1994, Artist's Forum, Internat. House of Japan, Tokyo, 1994, Dennos Mus., Traverse City, Mich., 1995; spkr. Organic Arch. Forum, Coll. Art Assn. Ann. Conf., N.Y.C., 1994. One man shows include Carl Hammer Gallery, Chgo., 1989, 91, Miami Univ. Mus., Oxford, Ohio, 1992; exhibited in group shows Carl Hammer Gallery, Chgo., 1988, 89, 90, 94, Design N.Y., N.Y.C., 1989, Joy Emery Gallery, Grosse Pointe Farms, Mich., 1989, 90, Artful Domain Gallery, Birmingham, Mich., 1990, Am. Primitive Gallery, N.Y.C., 1990, Judith Racht Gallery, Harbert, Mich., 1990, Perception Gallery, Grand Rapids, Mich., 1990, Columbus (Ohio) Cultural Arts Ctr., 1990, Muskegon (Mich.) C.C., 1990, Contemporary Arts Ctr., Cin., 1990, Columbia Coll. Art Gallery, Chgo., 1991, Joan Robey Gallery, Denver, 1991, Detroit Inst. Arts, 1991, The Westman Collection, Birmingham, 1991, Art Inst., Chgo., 1991, Ohio Designer Craftsman Traveling Exhbn., 1993, Gallery of Functional Art, Santa Monica, Calif., 1993; works included in publs. including Traverse the Mag., 1986, Detroit Monthly, 1988, Country Living, 1989, Chgo. Tribune, 1989, 91, La Architectura, Milan, 1989, N.Y. Times, 1990, Detroit News, 1990, Town and Country, 1990, Grand Rapids Press, 1990, Cin. Enquirer, 1990, Am. Craft, 1990, Antique Monthly, 1991, Making Rustic Furniture (Daniel Mack), 1992, U.S. News and World Report, 1992, Record Patriot, 1993, Rustic Traditions (Ralph Kylloe), 1993, The Japan Times, 1994, Record Eagle, 1995. Nat. Endowment of Arts fellow, 1992, Japan fellow U.S.-Japan Friendship Commn., 1994. Mem. Am. Craft Coun. Libr. Home: PO Box 9 20341 E Fowler Rd Lake Ann MI 49650*

MONTEITH, LARRY KING, university chancellor; b. Bryson City, N.C., Aug. 17, 1933; s. Earl and Essie (King) M.; m. Nancy Alexander, Apr. 19, 1952; children: Larry, Carol, Steve. BSEE, N.C. State U., 1960; MSEE, Duke U., 1962, PhDEE, 1965. Registered profl. engr., N.C. Mem. tech. staff Bell Telephone Labs., Burlington, N.C., 1960-62; mem. tech. staff Resch. Triangle Inst., Raleigh, 1962-66, group leader rsch. sect., 1966-68; adj. asst. prof. elec. engring. N.C. State U., Raleigh, 1965-68, assoc. prof., 1968-72, prof., 1972—, head dept. elec. engring., 1974-78, dean of engring., 1978-89, interim chancellor, 1989-90, chancellor, 1990—; bd. dirs. Microelectronics Ctr. N.C., Rsch. Triangle Inst. Contbr. articles to profl. jours. Trustee Nat. Tech. Univ., Triangle Univ. Ctr. Advanced Studies, Inc.; corp. mem. Underwriters Labs., Inc.; bd. visitors Air U. With USN, 1952-56. Recipient Disting. Engring. Alumnus award Duke U., 1984, Outstanding Engring. Achievement award N.C. Soc. Engrs., 1990. Fellow IEEE, Am. Soc. for Engring. Edn.; mem. NSPE (edn. adv. group), Raleigh C. of C. (bd. dirs.), Rotary Internat. (Paul Harris fellow Rotary Found. 1991), Phi Beta Kappa, Sigma Xi, Sigma Iota Rho, Phi Kappa Phi, Eta Kappa Nu, Tau Beta Pi, Sigma Beta Delta. Home: 1903 Hillsborough St Raleigh NC 27607-7348 Office: NC State U Chancellor's Office Box 7001 Raleigh NC 27695

MONTELEONE, PATRICIA, academic dean. Dean St. Louis U. Sch. Medicine. Office: St Louis U Sch Medicine 1402 S Grand Blvd Saint Louis MO 63104-1004

MONTELONGO, MICHAEL, career officer; b. N.Y.C.; m. Debra Tenison; 1 child, Amanda. BS in Nat. Security and Pub. Affairs, U.S. Military Acad.; MBA in Corp. Strategy and Fin., Harvard U., 1988; grad., Command and Gen. Staff Coll., 1992. Commd. 2d lt. U.S. Army, 1977, advanced through grades to lt. col., platoon leader, 1980, staff officer, 1982, ops. officer, company comdr., 1986; admissions officer U.S. Military Acad., West Point, N.Y., 1991, asst. prof. social scis. dept., 1991; rsch. analyst office economic and manpower analysis U.S. Army, 1991; adviser, spl. asst. Comdr.-in-Chief U.S. Southern Command, 1991; bat. exec. officer, bat. and brigade ops. officer U.S. Army, 1993; special asst. to U.S. Army chief of staff U.S. Army, Washington, 1994; senate legis. asst., 1995; sec. supervisory com. Ft. Bliss Fed. Credit Union, 1994; ch. music min., 1969—. Sec. Nat. Soc. Hispanic MBA, 1995; Mex.-Am. legal Def. and Ednl. Fund Advanced Legal Program, 1993, Leadership El Paso Program, 1993; trustee Unite El Paso, 1993. U.S. Army Advanced Civil Schooling fellow, 1986, Inter-Univ. Seminar on Armed Forces and Soc. fellow, 1990, Congl. Hispanic Caucus Inst. fellow, 1992, Army Congl. fellow, 1995. Home: 5589 Anne Peake Dr Fairfax VA 22032-3132 Office: 283 Senate Russell Bldg Washington DC 20510-4304

MONTEMAYOR, CARLOS R., advertising executive; b. San Antonio, Nov. 21, 1945; s. Raul Martin and Mary (Lyall) M.; m. Marina Cara Cook, Sep. 21, 1967 (div. Dec. 1978); m. Barbara Kay Volmer, Dec. 23, 1979; 1 child, Justin Norman. BBA in Mktg., U. Tex., 1967; MS in Journalism, Northwestern U., 1968. Account exec. Campbell-Ewald Co., Detroit and Cin., 1968-72, Ross Roy Inc., Detroit, 1972-74, Pitluk Group, San Antonio, 1974-76; v.p. GSD&M Advt., San Antonio, 1976-78; mktg. mgr. Church's Fried Chicken, San Antonio, 1978-81; v.p. Ed Yardang & Assocs., San Antonio, 1981-83; pres. Montemayor y Asociados, San Antonio, 1983—; bd. dirs. USAA Fed. Savs. Bank, Witte Mus., San Antonio Zoo; sec. Fiesta San Antonio Commn. 2d Lt. USAR, 1968-74. Mem. S.W. Found. Biomed. Rsch. (bd. govs.), Club Giraud, Argyle Club, Friends of McNay Club. Republican. Roman Catholic. Avocations: collecting classic cars, traveling, racquet ball. Home: 563 Elizabeth Rd San Antonio TX 78209-6132 Office: Montemayor Y Asociados Inc 70 NE Loop 410 San Antonio TX 78216-5842

MONTENEGRO, JEAN BAKER, English language educator; b. Syracuse, N.Y.; d. Ernest Monroe and Lucy Maebelle (Atkins) Baker; m. Roberto Carranza Montenegro, June 21, 1991; 1 child, Al H. Johnson Fr. BA, U. Ky., 1955; MA, No. Ariz. U., 1975, Azusa Pacific U., 1982. Cert. adminstr., supr.; cert. tchr. lang. arts, phys. edn., health edn., journalism. Sr. high sch. phys. edn. instr. San Francisco Unified, 1964, Grossmont Unified, San Diego, 1964-66; prof. phys. edn., recreation, health edn. Imperial (Calif.) Valley Coll., 1966-81, prof. journalism, 1981-88, prof. English, 1981—; staff devel. coord. Imperial Valley Coll., 1988-94, gender equity coord., 1990-91; coord. Am. Assn. Women in Cmty. and Jr. Colls., San Diego and Imperial County, 1988-90; elected to serve 3 yr. term on Acad. Senate, Imperial Valley Coll., 1994-96. City editor Imperial Valley Press, summer 1989, copy editor, summers 1989, 91; editor Downtown El Centro Assn. newsletter, ARCHES editor Calif. Women for Agriculture Imperial Valley chpt. newsletter Food for Thought; editor Pvt. Industry Coun. newsletter Ptnrs. Pres. Substance Abuse Adv. Bd. Imperial County, 1976-78; v.p. Imperial Valley Methodone Bd. Dirs., 1974-80; v.p. Imperial County Alcohol Adv. Bd., 1978-80; recreation commr. City of Brawley, 1976-78; auditor Rep. Women, 1990-96; sec. S.W. Rep. Women, 1997; head judge Literacy Vols. Am. Spelling Bee; elected sec. Imperial County Rep. Ctrl. Commn., 1997. Recipient Arab award Imperial Valley Coll. Student Body, 1989; named Vol. of Yr., Imperial Juvenile Justice Commn., 1982, Woman of Yr., Imperial County, 1995; apptd. to commn. State of Calif. C.C. League, 1990. Mem. Journalism Assn. So. Calif. (sec. 1988), Pvt. Industry Coun.-Imperial Valley Downtown El Centro Assn., Sunrise Optimists Club (dir. pub. rels.). Presbyterian. Avocations: jogging, walking, reading. Office: Imperial Valley Coll PO Box 158 Imperial CA 92251-0158

MONTERO, DARREL MARTIN, sociologist, social worker, educator; b. Sacramento, Mar. 4, 1946; s. Frank and Ann Naake; m. Tara Kathleen McLaughlin, July 6, 1975; children: David Paul, Lynn Elizabeth, Laura Ann, Emily Kathryn. AB, Calif. State U., 1970; MA, UCLA, 1972, PhD, 1974. Postgrad. researcher Japanese-Am. Research Project UCLA, 1971-73, dir. research, 1973-75; assoc. head Program on Comparative Ethnic Studies, Survey Research Ctr. UCLA, 1973-75; asst. prof. sociology Case Western Res. U., Cleve., 1975-76; asst. prof. urban studies, research sociologist Pub. Opinion Survey, dir. urban ethnic research program U. Md., College Park, 1976-79; assoc. prof. Ariz. State U., Tempe, 1979—; cons. rsch. sect. Viewer Sponsored TV Found., Los Angeles, Berrien E. Moore Law Office, Inc., Gardena, Calif., 1973, Bur. for Social Sci. Research, Inc., Washington,

Friends of the Family, Ltd., Nat. Sci. Found. Author: Japanese Americans: Changing Patterns of Ethnic Affiliation Over Three Generations, 1980, Urban Studies, 1978, Vietnamese Americans: Patterns of Resettlement and Socioeconomic Adaptation in the United States, 1979, Social Problems, 1988; mem. editorial bd. Humanity and Society, 1978-80; contbr. articles to profl. jours. Served with U.S. Army, 1966-72. Mem. Am. Sociol. Assn., Am. Assn. Pub. Opinion Research (exec. council, standards com.), Am. Ednl. Research Assn., Council on Social Work Edn., Soc. Study of Social Problems, D.C. Sociol. Soc., Am. Soc. Pub. Adminstrn., Nat. Assn. Social Workers, Pacific Sociol. Assn. Office: Ariz State Univ Sch Social Work Tempe AZ 85281

MONTERO, FERNAN GONZALO, advertising executive; b. Buenos Aires, May 22, 1948; came to U.S., 1952; s. Adolfo and Donne (Strang) M.; m. Cheryl Bowman, Dec. 30, 1976. BBA, U. Wis., 1971; M. Journalism in Advt., Northwestern U., 1972. With Young & Rubicam Inc., 1972-82; pres. Young & Rubicam Argentina, Buenos Aires, 1982-85; dep. area mgr. Young & Rubicam Latin Am., Sao Paulo, Brazil, 1985-87; sr. v.p., dir. bus. devel. Young & Rubicam Inc., N.Y.C., 1987-91, chmn., CEO Latin Am., 1991-92; chmn., CEO Europe Young & Rubicam Inc., London, 1993—. Office: Young & Rubicam, Greater London House, Hampstead Rd London NW1, England

MONTFORD, CLAUDIAN HAMMOND, gifted and talented education educator; b. Bainbridge, Ga., Jan. 31, 1947; d. Eugene and Ruth Lee (Clark) Hammond; m. Redolphus Montford, Dec. 21, 1968; children: Randolph Eugene, Rodolph Levell. BA in Early Childhood and Elem. Edn., Newark State-Kean Coll., Union, N.J., 1969; MA in Scis. Edn., Fairleigh Dickinson U., 1996. Cert. tchr., N.J. Cashier Sears, Roebuck and Co., Watchung, N.J., 1965-68; tchr. sci. Camp Crusades, Plainfield, N.J., 1969; tchr. cons. Bank Street Coll., N.Y.C., 1973; tchr. gifted and talented edn. Plainfield Bd. Edn., 1969-72, 74—, tchr. dir. Title I compensatory reading program, 1970-72, tchr. advisor instrnl. coun., 1981-83, elem. coord. sci. fair, 1990-92; playground dir. Plainfield Recreation Dept., 1967-68. Fundraiser Black United Fund N.J., 1990, chmn., 1991, 92, 93; elem. coord. Science Fair, Plainfield, 1990-93. Recipient 1st gov.'s tchr. recognition N.J. Dept. Edn., 1986, Excellence in Edn. award Frontiers Internat., 1988; grantee N.J. Dept. Edn., 1983, tech. grantee AT&T, 1996; New Zealand Study Tour scholar Plainfield Bd. Edn., 1993. Mem. NEA, N.J. Edn. Assn., Union County Edn. Assn., Plainfield Edn. Assn., Evergreen Edn. Assn. Seeking Ednl. Equity and Diversity Project. Democrat. Baptist. Avocations: reading, sewing and dress designing, macrame, horticulture, computer programming. Office: Evergreen Sch 1033 Evergreen Ave Plainfield NJ 07060-2613

MONTFORD, JOHN THOMAS, state legislator, academic administrator, lawyer; b. Ft. Worth, June 28, 1943; s. Thomas L. and Jewell F. (Coursey) M.; m. Pamela Jacobs, June 3, 1966 (div.); 1 child, Melinda; m. Debra Kay Mears, Dec. 24, 1975; children: Melonie, John Ross. BA, U. Tex.-Austin, 1965, JD, 1968; LLD (hon.), Lubbock (Tex.) Christian U., 1989. Bar: Tex. 1968. Pvt. practice law, Lubbock, Tex., 1971-78; criminal dist. atty. Lubbock County, Tex., 1979-82; state senator Dist. 28, Lubbock, 1983-96; chancellor Health Scis. Ctr., Tex. Tech U., 1996—. Trustee S. Park Hosp., Lubbock, 1981-82; bd. dirs., trustee Tex. Boys Ranch, Lubbock, 1982—; chmn. profl. div. United Way, Lubbock, 1980; energy com. So. Legis. Conf., 1983; senate appointee So. Growth Policies Bd., 1983; chmn. adv. coun. Lubbock Substance Abuse Prevention Partnership; mem. bd. govs. West Tex. Chpt. Multiple Sclerosis. Mem. dean's roundtable U. Tex. Sch. Law, 1988; mem. Lubbock Symphony Orch. Bd., 1997—. Maj. USMC, 1968-71. Recipient Outstanding Young Man of Lubbock award Jaycees, 1973, Headliner of Yr. award Greater Lubbock Press Club, 1979, Man of Yr./Law Enforcement award Lubbock Optimist Club, 1979, Boss of Yr. award Legal Secs. Assn., 1980, Exec. of Yr., Lubbock Sales Exec. Assn., 1981; named Finest Freshman, Tex. Bus. Mag., 1983, Outstanding State Senator Tex. Youth Commn., 1988, Legislator of Yr. Tex. Pub. Health Assn., 1988, Legislator of Yr. Tex. Pub. Employees Assn. and State Employees, 1989, Outstanding Tex. Leader award John Ben Shepperd Pub. Leadership Forum, 1989, Best New Legislator award Tex. Monthly mag., 1983,, Disting. Alumni, L.D. Bell High Sch., 1984, Lubbock's Man of the Yr. League of Women Voters and Am. Diabetes Assn., 1987, Disting. Svc. award Tex. C. of C., 1989, Outstanding Legislator in State of Tex. Epsilon Sigma Phi, 1989, Legislator of Yr. award Tex. Soc. Profl. Surveyors, 1989, Legislator of Yr. award 71st Legislature, Tex. Mcpl. League, 1989, Tree of Life award Jewish Nat. Fund, 1989; named one of the Ten Best Legislators 71st Legislature, Dallas Morning News, Tex. Monthly, 1989, 72d Legislature, 1991, Tex. Monthly, 1989, 91, Outstanding Legislator Epsilon Sigma Phi, 1989, Legislator of Yr. 71st Legislature Tex. Soc. Profl. Surveyors, 1989, Tex. Mcpl. League, 1989; recipient Outstanding Svc. award Tex. Electric Coops., 1989, Pub. Ofcl. award Tex. Pub. Power Assn., 1990, George Woods award in politics NAAACP, 1990, Legislative Leadership award 72d Legislator Tex. C. of C., 1992, One of the Seven Best Legislators 73d Legislature Dallas Morning News, 1993, 74th Legislature Dallas Morning News, 1995, One of the Ten Best Legislators 73d Legislature Tex. Monthly, 1993, 74th Legislature Tex. Monthly, 1995, Legislator of the Yr. Tex. Public Employees Assn., 1993, Bowie award Tex. State Guard Assn., 1993, award Lubbock Arts Festival, 1994, award Tex. Mental Health Assn., 1994, honor award Tex. Commn. on the Arts, 1994, Cmty. Statesman award Heritage of Odessa Found., 1995, Legislator of Yr. award Tex. Game Warden's Assn., 1995, Judy Coyle Tex. Liberty award Assn. Tex. Profl. Educators, 1995, Man of Yr. in Tex. Agriculture award Texas County Agrl. Agts. Assn., 1995, Mirabeau B. Lamar medal-Leadership in Learning award Assn. Tex. Colls. & Univs., 1995, Outstanding Legislator award Tex. Police Chiefs Assn., 1995, One of Top Ten, Harte-Hanks Comm., Inc., 1995, Newsmaker of 1995, Lubbock Avalanche Jour., One of Friends of Bus. 74th Legislature, Tex. Bus. Mag., 1995, Outstanding Legislator, Tex. Jr. Coll. Tchrs. Assn., 1995, Integrated Pest Mgmt. award in Excellence, Nat. Found. Integrated Pest Mgmt. Edn., 1996, and numerous others. Mem. State Bar Tex. (com. admissions), Tex. Criminal Def. Lawyers Assn., Tex. Dist. and County Attys. Assn. (life, legis. com.), Western States Water Council, Tex. Assn. Community Schs. (hon. life), Tex. Heart Inst. (nat. adv. coun. 1991), Lubbock C. of C. (Disting. Svc. award 1996), Order of Coif (hon.), Omicron Delta Kappa, Delta Theta Phi. Club: Jaycees (v.p. 1974), Mert. Rotary, Lubbock Lions. Office: PO Box 1709 Lubbock TX 79408-1709

MONTGOMERIE, COLIN, professional golfer; b. Glasgow, Scotland, June 23, 1963; m. Elmear Montgomerie; 1 child, Olivia Rose. Profl. golfer, 1987—; mem. Walker Cup Team, 1985, 87, Ryder Cup Team, 1991, 93, Dunhill Cup Team, 1988, 91, 92, World Cup Team, 1988, 91. Winner Scottish Stroke Play, 1985, Scottish Amateur Championship, 1987, European Tour Rookie of Yr., 1988, Portuguese Open, 1989, Scandinavian Masters, 1991, Heineken Dutch Open, 1993, Volvo Masters, 1993, Spanish Open, 1994, English Open, 1994, German Open, 1994; leader European Tour Merit, 1993, European Order of Merit, 1994. Avocations: music, cars. Office: care PGA 100 Avenue Of Champions Palm Beach Gardens FL 33418-3653*

MONTGOMERY, ANDREW STUART, financial advisor; b. Decorah, Iowa, May 25, 1960; s. Henry Irving and Barbara Louise (Hook) M. Student bus. adminstrn., Escola Rua de Jardim, Sao Paulo, Brazil, 1978-79; BA in Econs. and Bus. Adminstrn. magna cum laude, Coe Coll., 1983. CFP. Registered rep. 1st Investors Corp., Mpls., 1983-84; fin. adviser Planners Fin. Svcs., Inc., Mpls., 1984—, asst. to pres., 1984-85, dir. computer dept., 1984-87, investment analyst, 1985—, chairperson investment mgr. selection com., 1986—, v.p., 1989-93, exec. v.p., 1993-94, pres., 1994—. Mem. editl. rev. bd. Jour. Fin. Planning. Active Mpls. Estate Planning Coun., pres., 1992-93, program chairperson, 1991-92. Mem. Inst. CFP (cert. program v.p. local chpt. 1993-94, program adv. 1995-96, mem. lic. practitioner divsn.), Nat. Assn. Life Underwriters, Internat. Assn. Fin. Planning, Toastmasters (sec. Mpls. chpt. 1986, treas. 1987), Audubon Soc., Phi Beta Kappa, Phi Kappa Phi. Avocations: sailing, birding, Borzoi hounds, gardening. Office: Planners Fin Svcs Inc 7710 Computer Ave Ste 100 Minneapolis MN 55435-5417

MONTGOMERY, ANNA FRANCES, elementary school educator; b. Spokane, Wash., Nov. 5, 1945; d. Carl Jacob and Edna Frances (Evans) Kuipers; m. William Lee Montgomery Jr., Oct. 7, 1989. AA, Mid. Ga. Coll., 1965; BS in Elem. Edn., Woman's Coll. of Ga., 1966; MEd, Ga. Coll., 1969, specialist in edn., 1973. Cert. elem. tchr., Ga. Classroom tchr. Muscogee County Sch. Dist., Columbus, Ga., 1966—, reading tchr. Title 1 tutorial program, summer 1975, instr. staff devel. program, 1977-80; social sci. lead tchr. Wesley Heights Elem. Sch., Columbus, 1992—; tennis and athletic instr. Camp Tegawitha, Tobyhanna, Pa., summer 1970; presenter workshop Chattahoochee Valley Coun. for Social Studies, 1977; mem. social studies textbook adoption com. Muscogee County Sch. Dist., 1977-78, 82-83, sick leave com., 1993-95; judge Columbus Regional Social Sci. Fair, 1977, 93-96; mem. basic skills program comprehensive planning task force Muscogee County Sch. Dist., 1995-96, mem. com. to revise the basic skills program in social studies, 1980; presenter in field. Editor: Muscogee County School District's Handbook for Beginning Teachers, 1979. Treas. Wesley Heights PTA, 1983-86; vol. Med. Ctr. Aux., Columbus, 1975-79; pres. pastor's Bible study class St. Luke United Meth. Ch., 1993-94, 96, 97, mem. Sarah cir., cir. #11, sec., 1969-71, 78-80, co-chmn., 1976-78; mem. Bessie Howard Ward Handbells Choir; devel. chmn. Ga. state divsn. Centennial/fellowships com. AAUW, 1974-76. Recipient Valley Forge Tchrs. medal Freedoms Found. at Valley Forge, 1975, Outstanding Tchr. of Yr. award Wesley Hts. Elem. Sch., 1975, Muscogee County Sch. Dist., 1979; named Very Important Lady award Girl Scouts Am., Columbus, 1976, Outstanding Young Woman Am., 1982. Mem. AAUW (chmn. centennial fellowship com. Columbus br. 1973-75), Ga. PTA (hon. life), Profl. Assn. Ga. Educators (bldg. rep. Muscogee County chpt. 1983—, sec. 1992-94, treas. 1994—), Nat. Coun. Social Studies (mem. hostess and registration coms. ann. meeting 1975), Ga. Coun. for Social Studies, Ga. Sci. Tchrs. Assn., Valley Area Sci. Tchrs. (corr. sec. 1996-97), Ga. Coll. Alumni Assn., Mid. Ga. Coll. Alumni Assn., Order of Amaranth (charity com. 1991-93, 95, assoc. conductress 1996, conductress 1997), Scottish Rite Ladies Aux., Alpha Delta Kappa (Rho chpt., sec. 1975-76, pres.-elect 1976-78, pres. 1978-80, chaplin, 1996—), Delta Kappa Gamma (Beta Xi chpt., pres. 1980-82, chmn. pubs. and publicity 1976-78, chmn. profl. affairs 1978-80, nominations com. chair 1980-82, chmn. world fellowship and fund raising 1984-86, 96—, chmn. fin. 1990-92, chmn. membership 1994-96), Wesley Heights Elem. Sch. PTA. Avocations: reading, gardening, travel, fishing, playing clarinet and handbells. Home: 5134 Stone Gate Dr Columbus GA 31909-5573

MONTGOMERY, BETTY DEE, state official, former state legislator. BA, Bowling Green State U.; JD, U. Toledo, 1976. Former criminal clk. Lucas County Common Pleas Ct.; asst. pros. atty. Wood County, Ohio, pros. atty., 1980-88; pros. atty. City of Perrysburg, Ohio; mem. Ohio Senate, 1989-94; atty. gen. State of Ohio, Columbus, 1995—. Mem. Nat. Dist. Atty. Assn., Ohio Bar Assn., Toledo Bar Assn., Wood County Bar Assn. Office: Attorney Generals Office State Offical Tower 30 E Broad St Columbus OH 43215-3414

MONTGOMERY, CHARLES BARRY, lawyer; b. Latrobe, Pa., Apr. 17, 1937. BA cum laude Muskingum Coll., 1959; JD U. Mich., 1962. Bar: Ill. 1962, U.S. Dist. Ct. (no. dist.) Ill., 1982, U.S. Supreme Ct. 1971. Atty. Jacobs & McKenna, 1962-67; founder, ptnr. Jacobs, Williams and Montgomery, Ltd., 1967-85; sr. ptnr. Williams and Montgomery, Ltd., Chgo., 1985—; instr. advocacy inst. U. Mich., Ann Arbor, 1985, advanced program Nat. Inst. Trial Advocacy, 1986, trial acad. Internat. Assn. Def. Counsel, 1987, law inst. program Def. Rsch. Inst; pub. speaker ins. litigation; contbr. articles to profl. jours. Fellow Internat. Acad. Trial Lawyers; mem. ABA (vice-chair medicine and law com. 1989-90), Am. Arbitration Assn., Chgo. Bar Assn., Def. Rsch. Inst., Ill. Assn. Def. Trial Counsel, Ill. Assn. Hosp. Attys., Ill. State Bar Assn., Internat. Assn. Def. Counsel, Nat. Assn. R.R. Trial Counsel, Soc. Trial Lawyers, Legal Club of Chgo., Trial Lawyers Club of Chgo. Office: Williams and Montgomery Ltd 20 N Wacker Dr Chicago IL 60606-2806

MONTGOMERY, CHARLES HARVEY, lawyer; b. Spartanburg, S.C., Jan. 28, 1949; s. Dan Hugh and Ann Louise (Gasque) M.; m. Renée Jean Gubernot, Mar. 27, 1971; children: Charles Scott, Marie Renée. BA, Duke U., 1971; JD, Vanderbilt U., 1974. Bar: N.C. 1974, U.S. Dist. Ct. (ea. dist.) N.C. 1974, U.S. Supreme Ct. 1979, U.S. Dist. Ct. (mid. dist.) N.C. 1991. Assoc. Jordan Morris & Hoke, Raleigh, N.C., 1974-75; atty. Wake County Legal Svcs., Raleigh, 1975-76; pvt. practice Raleigh, 1977; ptnr. Montgomery & Montgomery, Cary, N.C., 1978-79, Sanford Adams McCullough & Beard, Raleigh, 1979-86, Adams McCullough & Beard, Raleigh, 1986-89, Toms Reagan & Montgomery, Cary, 1989-92, Toms & Montgomery, Cary, 1992-93; pvt. practice Cary, 1993—; bd. dirs. Br. Bank and Trust, Cary; pres. Family Law Mediation, Inc. Councilman Town of Cary, 1977-81, 83-87; vice-chmn. Wake County Dem. party, Raleigh, 1991-92; commr. Wake County, Raleigh, 1992; bd. dirs. East Cen. Cmty. Legal Svcs., Inc., 1997—. Mem. ABA, N.C. Bar Assn. (chmn. pub. info. com. 1994-96, dir. family law coun. 1994—), Wake County Bar Assn., N.C. Acad. Trial Lawyers (chmn. family law sect. 1996—). Methodist. Avocation: sailing. Office: PO Box 1325 1135 Kildare Farm Rd # 315 Cary NC 27511

MONTGOMERY, CHARLES HOWARD, retired bank executive; b. Bloomington, Ill., Mar. 23, 1930; s. Dewey H. and Madeline (Wonderlin) M.; m. Diane Dickerson Cohen, Aug. 30, 1978 (dec. Oct. 1996); children: Alison, Douglas. A.B., Ill. Wesleyan U., 1951; M.S., U. Ill., 1960. CPA, Ill. Auditor Lybrand Ross Bros. & Montgomery, Rockford, Ill., 1955-59; with Abbott Labs., North Chicago, Ill., 1959-67; controller Abbott Labs., 1965-67; v.p. finance Anchor Coupling Co., Libertyville, 1967-69; v.p., comptroller First Nat. Bank Chgo., 1969-73, sr. v.p., 1973-75, exec. v.p., 1976-88, comptroller, 1973-88; comptroller First Chgo. Corp.; ret.; past chmn. Inter-Assn. Com. Bank Acctg. Served with AUS, 1952-53. Mem. Fin. Execs. Inst., AICPA, Ill. Soc. CPAs, Tau Kappa Epsilon, Phi Kappa Phi, Univ. Club (Chgo.). Home: 5490 S South Shore Dr Chicago IL 60615-5984

MONTGOMERY, DAVID BRUCE, marketing educator; b. Fargo, N.D., Apr. 30, 1938; s. David William and Iva Bernice (Trask) M.; m. Toby Marie Franks, June 11, 1960; children: David Richard, Scott Bradford, Pamela Marie. BSEE, Stanford U., 1960, MBA, 1962, MS in Stats., 1964, PhD in Mgmt. Sci., 1966. Asst. prof. mgmt. MIT, 1966-69, assoc. prof., 1969-70; assoc. prof. mktg. and mgmt. sci. Stanford U., 1970-73, prof., 1973-78, Robert A. Magowan prof. mktg., 1978-92, Sebastian S. Kregge prof. mktg. strategy, 1992—; prin. The MAC Group Inc., 1969-91; mem. adv. bd. LEK Partnership, London; mem. sci. adv. bd. Univ. Connection, Bonn, Germany; acad. trustee Mktg. Sci. Inst., 1994—, exec. dir., 1995—. Author: (with Glen L. Urban) Management Science in Marketing, 1969, (with Massy and Morrison) Stochastic Models of Buying Behavior, 1970, (with Day et al) Planning: Cases in Computer and Model Assisted Marketing, 1973, (with others) Consumer Behavior: Theoretical Sources, 1973, (with G. J. Eskin) Data Analysis, 1975; editor 4 books; contbr. over 70 articles and tech. reports. Trustee Family Service Assn. of Mid Peninsula, 1972-73. Recipient citation for outstanding contbns. to use of computers in mgmt. edn. Hewlett Packard, 1977, Best Paper award for outstanding contbn. to strategic mgmt. Strategic Mgmt. Soc., 1996. Fellow Royal Statis. Soc.; mem. Inst. Mgmt. Scis., Am. Mktg. Assn., Econometric Soc., Am. Inst. Decision Scis., Tau Beta Pi. Republican. Congregational. Home: 960 Wing Pl Stanford CA 94305-1028 Office: Stanford U Grad Sch Bus Stanford CA 94305

MONTGOMERY, DAVID CAMPBELL, physicist, educator; b. Milan, Mo., Mar. 5, 1936; s. Merrill Edward and Ruth E. (Campbell) M.; m. Shirley Arlene Imig, July 20, 1957; children: Kathleen Montgomery Sutton, Elizabeth. Student, U. Mo., 1953-55; B.S., U. Wis., 1956; M.A., Princeton, 1958, Ph.D., 1959; D honoris causa, Eindhoven U. of Tech., The Netherlands, 1996. Research assoc. Princeton U., 1959-60; instr. U. Wis., 1961-62; asst. prof. U. Md., 1962-65; assoc. prof. U. Iowa, Iowa City, 1965-70; prof. U. Iowa, 1970-77; prof. physics Coll. William and Mary, Williamsburg, Va., 1977-84; prof. Dartmouth Coll., Hanover, N.H., 1984-88, Eleanor and A. Kelvin Smith prof. physics, 1988—; vis. prof., rschr. U. Colo., 1966, U. Alaska, 1968, U. Calif.-Berkeley, 1969-79, Bell Labs., 1971, U. Wis., 1989; lectr. Internat. Summer Sch. Theoretical Physics, Les Houches, France, 1972, U. Wis., Madison, 1973; vis. prof. Hunter campus CUNY, 1973-74, U. Nagoya, Japan, 1983, Columbia U., N.Y.C., 1985, Tech. U., Eindhoven, The Netherlands, spring 1992; vis. scientist Nat. Ctr. Atmospheric Rsch., Boulder, Colo., summers 1975, 76, 79, 87; cons. NASA Hdqs., Washington, 1977-82, JET Joint Undertaking, Culham, U.K., fall 1991; vis. rsch. prof. U. Md., 1977-84; mem. vis. staff Los Alamos Sci. Lab., summers 1977, 78, 79, 80, 81, 86, 91, 92, 94; cons., collaborator, vis. staff mem. Los Alamos Sci. Lab.; former cons. Oak Ridge Nat. Lab., NASA; vis. rschr. Los Alamos Nat. Lab., 1987-88; J.M. Burgers prof. Eindhoven Tech. U., The Netherlands, 1995-96, 97, U. Md., 1997. Former assoc. editor: Physics of Fluids, Internat. Jour. Engring. Sci.; contbr. more than 150 rsch. articles to profl. publs.; also monographs. Fellow Am. Phys. Soc.; mem. N.Y. Acad. Scis., Phi Beta Kappa, Sigma Xi, Pi Mu Epsilon, Phi Mu Alpha. Achievements include introduction of modern fluid turbulence methods into space and controlled fusion theory; developed maximum entropy, or "most probable" states, method of describing coherent structures achieved as a product of turbulent relaxation. Home: 46 River Rd Hanover NH 03755-6612 Office: Dartmouth College Physics Dept Hanover NH 03755

MONTGOMERY, DAVID PAUL, professional baseball team executive; b. Phila.; m. Lyn Sagendorph. BA in History, U. Pa., 1968; MBA, Wharton Sch., U. Pa., 1970. With Phila. Phillies, 1971—, successively mem. sales dept., dir. mktg., dir. sales, exec. v.p., COO. Office: Phila Phillies PO Box 7575 Philadelphia PA 19101-7575*

MONTGOMERY, DONALD RUSSELL, labor consulting firm executive; b. Canora, Sask., June 8, 1920; s. Milton Templeton and Margaret Genva (Culbert) M.; m. Lu Eirene Huggard, May 20, 1954; children—Charmeine, Donald Kirk. Student, Turner Bus. Coll. With United Steelworkers of Am., 1940—; steelworkers area supr. Toronto-Barrie area, 1953-74; sec.-treas. Toronto and Lakeshore Labour Coun., 1953-64, pres., 1964-74; sec.-treas. Can. Labour Congress, 1974-84; cons. union adminstrn., indsl. rels., Ottawa and Toronto; pres., chief exec. officer MertoLabour Cons. Inc., Toronto, 1989—; pres. LueDon Properties, Toronto; founding mem. Labor Coun. Devel. Found.; former mem. Export Trade Devel. Bd., adv. com. Aviation Unions; bd. dirs. GSW Ltd. (formerly Gen. Steel Wares Ltd.); cons. in field to labor unions, govts. and employers. Contbr. numerous papers on unions, labor edn. to profl. jours. Mem. Assn. Comml. and Tech. Employees. Home: 19 Baby Point Rd, Toronto, ON Canada M6S 2E8 Office: LueDon Properties, PO Box 25033, 421 Jane St, Toronto, ON Canada M6S 2Z7

MONTGOMERY, GEORGE CRANWELL, lawyer, former ambassador; b. Chattanooga, Aug. 24, 1944; s. George Donaldson and Mary Elizabeth (Cranwell) M.; m. Carol Lanfear, 1 child, Erynn Elizabeth. BA, U. Va., 1966; JD, Vanderbilt U., 1975. Bar: U.S. Ct. Appeals (D.C. cir.) 1976. Mem. legis. staff Senator Howard Baker, Washington, 1975-80; spl. counsel Senate Majority Leader, Washington, 1980-85; U.S. amb. to Oman, 1985-89; ptnr. Baker, Donelson, Bearman and Caldwell, Washington, 1989—; bd. visitors Georgetown U. Sch. of Bus. Mem. Coun. on Fgn. Rels. With USN, 1966-72, capt. Res. Mem. ABA, D.C. Bar Assn., Sigma Chi. Office: Baker Donelson Bearman & Caldwell 801 Pennsylvania Ave NW Ste 800 Washington DC 20004-2615

MONTGOMERY, GILLESPIE V. (SONNY MONTGOMERY), former congressman; b. Meridian, Miss., Aug. 5, 1920; s. Gillespie M. and Emily (Jones) M. B.S., Miss. State U. Mem. Miss. Senate, 1956-66, 90th-104th Congresses from 3rd Miss. Dist., 1967-96; chmn. vets. affairs com., 1981-94; mem. vets. affairs com., chmn. spl. com. on S.E. Asia 90th-102d Congresses, 1978-96; ranking minority mem., 1994-96; mem. armed services. com. 90th-103d Congresses, chmn. select com. on missing persons in southeast Asia, 1975-96; mem. vets. affairs com.; mem. Woodcock Commn., 1977; CEO, pres. The Montgomery Group, Alexandria, Va., 1997—. Pres. Miss. N.G. Assn., 1959; pres. Miss. Heart Assn., 1967-68. Served with AUS, World War II, Korea, ret. maj. gen. Miss N.G. Decorated Bronze Star medal, Combat Inf. Badge; recipient Miss. Magnolia award, 1966, Lifetime Achievement award Mil. Educators & Counselors Assn., 1992. Mem. VFW, Am. Legion 40 and 8, Congl. Prayer Breakfast Group (pres. 1970). Episcopalian. Lodges: Masons; Shriners; Scottish Rite. Office: The Montgomery Group 11 Canal Center Plz Ste 104 Alexandria VA 22314

MONTGOMERY, GRETCHEN GOLZÉ, secondary education educator; b. Washington, Sept. 16, 1941; d. Alfred Rudolph and Marjorie (Lodge) Golzé; m. Charles Williams, Jan. 25, 1963 (div. Oct. 1975); children: Rebecca, Matthew; m. Jerry L. Montgomery, May 14, 1977. BA, Marietta Coll., 1963. Cert. tchr., Ohio. Tchr. Warren Local Sch. Dist., Vincent, Ohio, 1963-67; dir. Betsey Mills Club, Marietta, Ohio, 1975-80; tchr. Wolf Creek Sch. Dist., Waterford, Ohio, 1980—; mem. lang. arts course of study com. Washington County, Marietta, 1985—, mem. competency based edn. testing com., 1985—; mem. ednl. planning com. Wolf Creek Edn., Waterford, 1988-91, mem. testing com., 1988—, mem. textbook com., 1989-90; mentor tchr. Washington County, 1991—, mentor tchr. trainer, 1994—. Jennings scholar Martha Holden Jennings Found., 1982. Mem. NEA, Nat. Coun. Tchrs. English, Ohio Coun. Tchrs. English Lang. Arts, Wolf Creek Local Tchrs. Assn. (sec. 1985—), Ohio Edn. Assn., Ohio Tchr. Leader Network. Avocations: reading, gardening, spectator sports, theater. Home: 105 Rathbone Ter Marietta OH 45750-1443 Office: Wolf Creek Schs PO Box 45 Waterford OH 45786-0045

MONTGOMERY, HENRY IRVING, financial planner; b. Decorah, Iowa, Dec. 18, 1924; s. Harry Biggs and Martha Grace (Wilkinson) M.; m. Barbara Louise Hook, Aug. 14, 1948; children: Barbara Ruth, Michael Henry, Kelly Ann, Andrew Stuart. Student U. Iowa, 1942-43, 47-48; BBA, Tulane U., 1952, postgrad., 1952; postgrad. U. Minn., 1976. CFP, Colo. Field agt. OSS, SSU, CIG, CIA, Ctrl. Europe, 1945-47; pres. Nehi Bottling Co., Decorah, Iowa, 1952-64; prin. Montgomery Assocs., Mktg. Cons., Trieste, Italy and Iowa, 1965-72; pres. Planners Fin. Svcs., Inc., Mpls., 1972-95, chmn., 1995—; prin. Montgomery Investment Mgmt., 1992—. Author: Race Toward Berlin, 1945. Served with U.S. Army, 1943-46; ETO. Decorated Bronze Star. Mem. Inst. Cert. Fin. Planners (bd. dirs. 1977-82, pres. 1980-81, chmn. 1981-82, Cert. Fin. Planner of Yr. 1984, chmn. Fin. Products Standards Bd. 1984-88), Nat. Assn. Securities Dealers (mem. dist. 8 com. 1988-91, vice chmn. 1990), Internat. Assn. Fin. Planning (internat. dir. 1976-81), Mpls. Estate Planning Coun., Met. Tax Planning Group (pres. 1984-87), Twin City Fin. Planners (pres. 1976-78), Twin Cities Soc. of Inst. Cert. Fin. Planners, Am. Legion, Elks (Decorah), Beta Gamma Sigma. Avocations: Italian and German languages. Office: Planners Fin Svcs Inc 7710 Computer Ave Ste 100 Minneapolis MN 55435-5417

MONTGOMERY, JAMES EDWARD, JR., lawyer; b. Champaign, Ill., Feb. 8, 1953; s. James Edward Sr and Vivian M.; m. Linda C.; children: James III, Anne, Heather, Leslie. AB Polit. Sci., Duke U., 1975; JD, So. Meth. U., 1978. Bar: Tex., 1978, Md., 1994; U.S. Dist. Ct. (ea. dist.) Tex. 1978, U.S. Dist. Ct. (we. dist.) Tex., 1985, U.S. Dist. Ct. (so. dist.) Tex. 1986, U.S. Dist. Ct. (no. dist.) Tex. 1987, U.S. Dist. Md., 1994; U.S. Ct. Appeals (5th cir.) 1979; U.S. Supreme Ct., 1993. Assoc. Strong, Pipkin, Nelson & Parker, Beaumont, Tex., 1978-81; owner Sibley & Montgomery, Beaumont, 1981-85; assoc. Law Offices of Gilbert Adams, Beaumont, 1985; prin. James E. Montgomery, Beaumont, 1985-88; ptnr. Montgomery & Kontiuszcy, Beaumont, 1988-89; assoc. Sawtelle, Goode, Davidson & Troilo, San Antonio, Tex., 1989-91; shareholder Davidson & Troilo, San Antonio, 1991-94; pres. Montgomery & Assocs., San Antonio, 1994-97; prin. Soules & Wallace, San Antonio, 1997—. Editor: Fifth Cir. Reporter, 1983-86. Bd. dirs. Boys and Girls Clubs of San Antonio, 1995—; dist. chmn. Boy Scouts, San Antonio, 1994. Mem. ABA, State Bar of Tex., San Antonio Bar Assn., Rotary (pres. Alamo Hts. chpt. 1997-98), 5th Cir. Bar Assn. (bd. dirs. 1983-86), Jefferson County Bar Assn. (treas. 1986). Avocations: tennis, skiing, golf, reading. Office: Soules & Wallace Frost Bank Tower 100 W Houston St San Antonio TX 78205-1400

MONTGOMERY, JAMES FISCHER, savings and loan association executive; b. Topeka, Nov. 30, 1934; s. James Maurice and Frieda Ellen (Fischer) M.; m. Diane Dealey; children: Michael James, Jeffrey Allen, Andrew Steven, John Gregory. BA in Acctg., UCLA, 1957. With Price, Waterhouse & Co., C.P.A.'s, Los Angeles, 1957-60; controller Conejo Valley Devel. Co., Thousand Oaks, Calif., 1960; asst. to pres. Gt. Western Fin. Corp., Beverly Hills, Calif., 1960-64; pres. United Financial Corp of Calif., Los Angeles, 1964-75; chmn., CEO Great Western Financial Corp., Chatsworth, Calif., 1975-96, now chmn. bd. dirs.; fin. v.p., treas. United Fin. Corp., Los Angeles, 1964-69, exec. v.p., 1969-74, pres., 1975; pres. Citizens Savs. & Loan Assn., Los Angeles, 1970-75. Served with AUS, 1958-60. Office: Great Western Fin Corp 9200 Oakdale Ave Chatsworth CA 91311-6519*

MONTGOMERY, JAMES HUEY, state government administrator, consultant; b. New Albany, Miss., Dec. 2, 1942; s. James Columbus and Ethel Louise (Todd) M.; divorced; children: Angela Lee, Leslie Louise. B degree,

Wayne State U., 1991. Border patrol agt. U.S. Border Patrol, Calexico, Calif., 1964-66, Miami, Fla., 1969-71; spl. agt. U.S. Immigration and Naturalization, San Francisco, 1971-75, Chgo., 1975-76; spl. agt. U.S. Immigration and Naturalization, Ft. Snelling, Minn., 1976-78, asst. regional commr., 1978-82; dist. dir. U.S. Immigration and Naturalization, Detroit, 1982-93, ret., 1993; pres. Guard Well Inc., 1994—; dir. comml. enforcement Office Comml. Svcs. Mich. Dept. Consumer and Industry Svcs., Lansing, 1995—. Mem. Leadership Detroit, 1991—; mem. Mich. polit. leadership program Mich. State U., 1993—. 1st lt. U.S. Army, 1966-69. Recipient Appreciation award Korean Soc. Detroit, 1987, Chaldean Fedn. Am., 1988, Chaldean Kiwanis Club, 1988, Cmty. Appreciation award TV Orient, 1993, Appreciation award Arab Am. Chaldean Assn., 1993. Mem. Immigration Dirs. Assn. (chmn. 1988-91, dep. chmn. 1985-88), Internat. Border Assn. (pres. 1986, bd. dirs. 1982-93), Southeastern Mich. Chiefs of Police, Golden Key, Fed. Exec. Bd. (policy com. 1985-93, quality mgmt. com. 1992-93), Arab Am. C. of C. Detroit (bd. dirs. 1994), Internat. Inst. of Detroit (bd. dirs. 1995-96, adv. bd. 1996—). Baptist. Avocations: photography, golf, computers. Home and Office: 2516 Royce Ct East Lansing MI 48823-2965

MONTGOMERY, JAMES MORTON, public relations, marketing executive, association executive; b. Birmingham, Ala., July 4, 1931; s. Hugh Nelson and Sidney Tazewell (Morton) M.; m. Helen Patton Martin, June 12, 1954 (div. Oct. 1987); children: Louis Martin, Caroline Montgomery Brown, Helen Montgomery DeBevoise, Fleta Montgomery Edwards; m. Helen Preston Tapp, Jan. 29, 1994. AB, U. Ala., 1953, MBA, 1958. Mktg. instr. U. Ala., Tuscaloosa, 1953-54, 56-57; dir. publs. Gulf States Paper Corp., Tuscaloosa, 1957-60, advt. dir., 1960-63, pub. rels. mgr., 1963-71, corp. communications mgr., 1971-76; v.p. pub. info. Am. Forest Inst., Washington, 1976-77; v.p. regions Am. Forest Inst., Atlanta, 1980-86; exec. v.p. So. Forest Inst., Atlanta, 1977-86; pres. Montgomery & Assocs., pub. rels. and mktg., Atlanta, 1986—; comms. cons., Atlanta, 1973-86; guest, adj. lectr. various univs. in Ala. and Ga., 1965—; coord. Advt. Coun. Smokey Bear, N.Y.C., 1970-76. Mem. adv. bd. Metro Atlanta Salvation Army, 1993—; v.p. U. Ala. Nat. Alumni Assn., 1974-75; mem. State Rep. Exec. Com., Ala., 1962-70. 1st lt. USAF, 1954-56. Named to Ga. Pub. Rels. Hall of Fame, Order of the Phoenix. Fellow Pub. Rels. Soc. Am. (accredited, chpt. pres. 1972, nat. assembly 1973-76, 80-81), Clan Montgomery Soc. Internat. (pres. 1993-95), Phoenix Soc. (trustee 1984-85), Burns Club Atlanta (pres. 1990-91), Kiwanis Internat. (pres. Tuscaloosa Club 1972-73), Altanta Club, Soc. Profl. Journalists, Beta Gamma Sigma, Omicron Delta Kappa, Delta Tau Delta. Presbyterian.

MONTGOMERY, JEFFREY THOMAS, professional baseball player; b. Wellston, Ohio, Jan. 7, 1962. BS Computer Sci., Marshall Coll., 1984. With Cin. Reds, 1983-88, Kansas City Royals, 1988—; mem. Am. League All-Star Team, 1992-93, 96. Names Am. League Fireman of Yr., Sporting News, 1993. Office: Kansas City Royals PO Box 419969 Kansas City MO 64141-6969*

MONTGOMERY, JERRY LYNN, education educator; b. Owensville, Ind., Apr. 21, 1935; s. Philip Matthew and Lois Caroline (Anderson) M.; m. Murelyn Ann Rogers, Sept. 21, 1957 (div. Apr. 1976); stepchildren: Rebecca Williams Slominski, Matthew Williams; m. Gretchen Wendelroth Golze, May 14, 1977; children: Robin Montgomery, Lori Abbott, Vicki Randolph. BS, Purdue U., 1957; MA, Ball State U., 1964, EdD, 1969. Vocat. agrl. Milton (Ind.) Pub. Schs., 1957-58, Carthage (Ind.) Pub. Schs., 1958-61; sci. tchr. Angola (Ind.) City Schs., 1961-66; edn. prof. Marietta (Ohio) Coll., 1969—; sci. educator Project Discovery, Athens, Ohio, 1994—; goal #4 com. Marietta (Ohio) City Schs., 1993—, grade 4 profiency test com. Ohio Dept. of Edn., Columbus, Ohio, 1994—; mem. young engrs. and scientists Marietta Telesis Group, Marietta, 1992—. Recipient Outstanding Educator Martha Holden Jennings Found., 1989. Mem. Assn. of Tchr. Educators (credentials com. 1991—), Nat. Sci. Tchrs. Assn., Sci. Edn. Coun. Ohio, Ohio Acad. of Sci., Phi Delta Kappa. Avocations: reading, canoeing, traveling, fishing, camping. Home: 105 Rathbone Ter Marietta OH 45750-1443 Office: Marietta Coll 215 5th St Marietta OH 45750-4033

MONTGOMERY, JOHN ATTERBURY, research chemist, consultant; b. Greenville, Miss., Mar. 29, 1924; s. Daniel Cameron and Ruth (Atterbury) M.; m. Jean Kirkman, July 19, 1947; children: John Jr., Elaine Porter, Kirkman, Ruth Adrianne. AB cum laude, Vanderbilt U., 1946, MS in Organic Chemistry, 1947; PhD in Organic Chemistry, U. N.C., Chapel Hill, 1951. Research chemist So. Research Inst., Birmingham, Ala., 1952-56; dir. organic chemistry So. Research Inst., 1956-74, v.p., 1974-81, sr. v.p., dir. Kettering Meyer Lab., 1981-90, disting. scientist rsch., 1990—; exec. v.p., dir. rsch., chief scientific officer Biocryst, 1990—; adj. prof. Birmingham So. Coll., 1957-62; adj. sr. scientist U. Ala., Birmingham, 1978—; bd. dirs. Am. Assn. Cancer Research, Assn. Am. Cancer Insts.; mem. Pres. Reagan's Cancer Panel. Author over 600 rsch. papers; editor profl. books; mem. editl. bd. numerous profl. jours. Recipient T.O. Soine Meml. award U. Minn., 1979. Fellow N.Y. Acad. Scis.; mem. Am. Chem. Soc. (councilor 1971-86, recipient Herty medal 1974, So. Chemist award 1980, Burger award 1986, Edward E. Smissman Bristol-Myers Squibb Award, 1995), Am. Assn. Cancer Research (Cain Meml. award 1982), Am. Soc. Pharmacology and Exptl. Therapeutics, Internat. Soc. Heterocyclic Chemistry (adv. bd. 1982-83), Sigma Xi, Alpha Chi Sigma. Republican. Episcopalian. Clubs: Country of Birmingham, The Club (Birmingham) Lodge: Rotary. Home: 2215 Brookshire Pl Birmingham AL 35213-2032 Office: So Research Inst PO Box 55305 Birmingham AL 35255-5305 also: BioCryst Pharmaceuticals 2190 Parkway Lake Dr Birmingham AL 35244-1803

MONTGOMERY, JOHN DICKEY, political science educator; b. Evanston, Ill., Feb. 15, 1920; s. Charles William and Lora Kathryn (Dickey) M.; m. Jane Ireland, Dec. 19, 1954; children—Faith, Patience, John. A.B., Kalamazoo Coll., 1941, A.M., 1942, LL.D., 1962; A.M., Harvard, 1948, Ph.D., 1951. Dir. devel. research center African studies program Boston U., 1961-63; prof. pub. adminstrn. Harvard U., 1963-86, Ford Found. prof. internat. studies, 1986—, chmn. dept. govt., 1980-84; dir. Pacific Basin Rsch. Ctr. Soka U. Am., L.A., 1991—. Author: The Purge in Occupied Japan, 1953, Forced to be Free, 1957, The Politics of Foreign Aid, 1962, Foreign Aid in International Politics, 1967, Technology and Civic Life, 1974, Aftermath, Tarnished Outcomes of American Foreign Policy, 1986, Bureaucrats and People, 1988; co-editor: (with Dennis Rardinelli) Great Policies, Strategic Innovations in Asia and the Pacific Basin, 1995. Home: 36 Hyde Ave Newton MA 02158-2311 Office: Harvard U 79 Jfk St Cambridge MA 02138-5801

MONTGOMERY, JOHN RICHARD, pediatrician, educator; b. Burnsville, Miss., Oct. 24, 1934; s. Guy Austin and Harriet Pauline (Owens) M.; m. Dottye Ann Newell, June 26, 1965; children: John Newell, Michelle Elizabeth. BS, U. Ala., 1955, MD, 1958. Intern U. Miss., Jackson, 1958-59, resident in pediatrics, 1959-60; resident in pediatrics Baylor Coll. Medicine, Houston, 1960-61, 63-64, fellow in pediatric infectious diseases and immunology, 1964-66, asst. prof. pediatrics, 1966-70, assoc. prof. pediatrics, 1970-75, prof. pediats., 1975—, chief pediatric programs U. Ala. Sch. Medicine, Huntsville, 1975-95. Served with AUS, 1961-62; Korea, col. USAR (ret.). Mem. Soc. Pediatric Rsch., Am. Assn. Immunologists, Infectious Diseases Soc. Am., N.Y. Acad. Scis., Am. Acad. Pediatrics (pres. Ala. chpt. 1991-93), Sigma Xi, Phi Beta Kappa. Contbr. articles to books and profl. jours.; assisted in devel. of germ-free environ. bubble to protect patient with no natural immunity (patient later subject of movie The Boy in The Bubble).

MONTGOMERY, JOHN WARWICK, law educator, theologian; b. Warsaw, N.Y., Oct. 18, 1931; s. Maurice Warwick and Harriet (Smith) M.; m. Joyce Ann Bailer, Aug. 14, 1954; children: Elizabeth Ann, David Warwick, Catherine Ann; m. Lanalee de Kant, Aug. 26, 1988. AB with distinction in Philosophy, Cornell U., 1952; BLS, U. Calif., Berkeley, 1954, MA, 1958; BD, Wittenberg U., 1958, MST, 1960; PhD, U. Chgo., 1962; Docteur de l'Université, mention Théologie Protestante, U. Strasbourg, France, 1964; LLB, LaSalle Extension U., 1977; diplôme cum laude, Internat. Inst. Human Rights, Strasbourg, 1978; M. Phil. in Law, U. Essex, Eng., 1983. Bar: Va. 1978, Calif. 1979, D.C. 1985, Wash. 1990, U.S. Supreme Ct. 1981, Eng. 1984; lic. real estate broker Calif.; cert. law librarian; diplomate Med. Library Assn.; ordained to ministry Luth. Ch., 1958. Librarian, gen. reference service U. Calif. Library, Berkeley, 1954-55; instr. Bibl. Hebrew, Hellenistic Greek, Medieval Latin Wittenberg U., Springfield, Ohio, 1956-59; head librarian Swift Libr. div. and Philosophy, mem. federated theol. faculty U. Chgo., 1959-60; assoc. prof., chmn. dept. history Wilfred Laurier U. (formerly Waterloo Luth. U.), Ont., Can., 1960-64; prof., chmn. div. ch. history, history of Christian thought, dir. European Seminar program Trinity Evang. Div. Sch., Deerfield, Ill., 1964-74; prof. law and theology George Mason U. Sch. Law (formerly Internat. Sch. of Law), Arlington, Va., 1974-75; theol. cons. Christian Legal Soc., 1975-76; dir. studies Internat. Inst. Human Rights, Strasbourg, France, 1979-81; founding dean, prof. jurisprudence, dir. European program Simon Greenleaf U. Sch. Law, Anaheim, Calif., 1980-88; Disting. prof. theology and law, dir. European program Faith Evang. Luth. Sem., Tacoma, Wash., 1989-91; prin. lectr. in law Luton U., Eng., 1991-92, reader in law, 1992-93, prof. law and humanities, dir. Ctr. Human Rights, 1993-97, emeritus prof., 1997—; prof. apologetics and law, v.p. for U.K. and European ops. Trinity Coll. and Theol. Sem., Newburgh, Ind., 1997—; vis. prof. Concordia Theol. Sem., Springfield, Ill., 1964-67, DePaul U., Chgo., 1967-70; hon. fellow Revelle Coll., U. Calif., San Diego, 1970; rector Freie Fakultaten Hamburg, Fed. Republic Germany, 1981-82; lectr. Rsch. Scientists Christian Fellowship Conf. St. Catherines Coll., Oxford U., 1985, Internat. Anti-Corruption Conf., Beijing, China, 1995; Pascal lectr. on Christianity and the Univ., U. Waterloo, Ont., Can., 1987; A. Kurt Weiss lectr. biomed. ethics U. Okla., 1997; adj. prof. Puget Sound U. Sch. Law, Tacoma, 1990-91; numerous other invitational functions. Author: The Writing of Research Papers in Theology, 1959; A Union List of Serial Publications in Chicago Area Protestant Theological Libraries, 1960; A Seventeenth-Century View of European Libraries, 1962; Chytraeus on Sacrifice: A Reformation Treatise in Biblical Theology, 1962; The Shape of the Past: An Introduction to Philosophical Historiography, 1962, rev. edition, 1975; The Is God Dead Controversy, 1966; (with Thomas J.J. Altizer) The Altizer-Montgomery Dialogue, 1967; Crisis in Lutheran Theology, 2 vols., 1967, rev. edit., 1973; Es confiable el Christianismo?, 1968; Ecumenicity, Evangelicals, and Rome, 1969; Where is History Going?, 1969; History and Christianity, 1970; Damned Through the Church, 1970; The Suicide of Christian Theology, 1970; Computers, Cultural Change and the Christ, 1970; In Defense of Martin Luther, 1970; La Mort de Dieu, 1971; (with Joseph Fletcher) Situation Ethics: True or False?, 1972; The Quest for Noah's Ark, 1972, rev. edit., 1974; Verdammt durch die Kirche, 1973; Christianity for the Toughminded, 1973; Cross and Crucible, 2 vols., 1973; Principalities and Powers: The World of the Occult, 1973, rev. edit., 1975; How Do We Know There is a God?, 1973; Myth, Allegory and Gospel, 1974; God's Inerrant Word, 1974; Jurisprudence: A Book of Readings, 1974, 4th edit., 1992; The Law Above the Law, 1975; Cómo Sabemos Que Hay un Dios?, 1975; Demon Possession, 1975; The Shaping of America, 1976; Faith Founded on Fact, 1978; Law and Gospel: A Study for Integrating Faith and Practice, 1978, 3rd edit., 1994; Slaughter of the Innocents, 1981; The Marxist Approach to Human Rights: Analysis & Critique, 1984; Human Rights and Human Dignity, 1987, Wohin marschiert China?, 1991, Evidence for Faith: Deciding the God Question, 1991, Giant in Chains: China Today and Tomorrow, 1994, Law and Morality: Friends or Foes?, 1994, Jésus: La Raison Rejoint L'Histoire, 1995, (with C.E.B. Cranfield and David Kilgour) Christians in The Public Square, 1996; editor: Lippincott's Evangelical Perspectives, 7 vols., 1970-72; International Scholars Directory, 1973, Simon Greenleaf Law Rev., 7 vols., 1981-88; contbg. editor: Christianity Today, 1965-84, New Oxford Review, 1993-95; films: Is Christianity Credible?, 1968; In Search of Noah's Ark, 1977; Defending the Biblical Gospel, 1985 (11 videocassette series); (TV series) Christianity on Trial, 1987-93; contbr. articles to acad., theol., legal encys. and jours., chpts. to books. Nat. Luth. Ednl. Conf. fellow, 1959-60; Can. Council postdoctoral sr. research fellow, 1963-64; Am. Assn. Theol. Schs. faculty fellow, 1967-68; recipient Angel award Nat. Religious Broadcasters, 1989, 90, 92. Fellow Trinity Coll. (Newburgh, Ind.), Royal Soc. Arts (Eng.), Victoria Inst. (London), Acad. Internat. des Gourmets et des Traditions Gastronomiques (Paris), Am. Sci. Affiliation (nat. philosophy sci. and history sci. commn. 1966-70); mem. European Acad. Arts, Scis. and Humanities (Paris), Lawyers Christian Fellowship (hon. v.p. 1995—), Nat. Conf. U. Profs., Calif. bar Assn. (human rights commn. 1980-83), Internat. Bar Assn., ALA, World Assn. Law Profs., Mid. Temple and Lincoln's Inn (barrister mem.), Am. Soc. Internat. Law, Union Internat. des Avocats, Nat. Assn. Realtors, Tolkien Soc. Am., N.Y. C.S. Lewis Soc., Am. Hist. Assn., Soc. Reformation Rsch., Creation Rsch. Soc., Tyndale Fellowship (Eng.), Stair Soc. (Scotland), Presbyn. Hist. Soc. (North Ireland), Am. Theol. Libr. Assn., Bibliog. Soc. U. Va., Evang. Theol. Soc., Internat. Wine and Food Soc., Soc. des Amis des Arts (Strasbourg), Chaine des Rôtisseurs (commandeur), Athenaeum (London), Wig and Pen (London), Players' Theatre Club (London), Sherlock Holmes Soc. London, Soc. Sherlock Holmes de France (hon.), Club des Casseroles Lasserre (Paris), Ordre des chevaliers du Saint-Sepulcre Byzantin (commandeur), Phi Beta Kappa, Phi Kappa Phi, Beta Phi Mu. Office: 4 Crane Ct # 9, Fleet St, London EC4A 2EJ, England also: 2 rue de Rome, 67000 Strasbourg France

MONTGOMERY, KEITH NORRIS, SR., insurance executive, state legislator; b. Natchez, Miss., Sept. 22, 1951; s. Charles Norris Jr. and Miriam (Marron) M.; m. Joan Marie Bishop; children: Keith Jr., Mason, Brenton. BBA, U. Miss., 1974. Sales rep. Boyle-Midway, Monroe, La., 1975-77, Am. Nat. Ins., Jackson, Miss., 1977-79; owner Exec. Benefits, Clinton, Miss., 1979—; state rep. Miss. Ho. of Reps., Jackson, 1993—. City councilman City of Clinton, 1985-93. Master sgt. USAR, 1972—. Mem. Am. Legis. Exch. Coun., Miss. Econ. Coun., Jackson Assn. Health Underwriters (bd. dirs. 1992-94), Clinton C. of C. Republican. Methodist. Home: 104 Countrywood Cir Clinton MS 39056-5717 Office: PO Box 2204 Clinton MS 39060-2204

MONTGOMERY, LESLIE DAVID, biomedical engineer, cardiovascular physiologist; b. Otterbein, Ind., Sept. 4, 1939; s. Gerald Wesley and Doris Elnora (Sosbe) M.; m. Patricia Ann Trigg, Aug. 25, 1971; children: Gerald Wesley, Nathaniel Brendon, David Patrick. BA, Monmouth Coll., 1962; MS in Engring., Iowa State U., 1963; PhD in Engring., UCLA, 1972. Rsch. engr. N.Am./Rockwell, L.A., 1963-73; owner LDM Assocs., San Jose, Calif., 1973—; rsch. engr. SRI Internat., San Mateo, Calif., 1980-85; dir. rsch. Ctr. for Neurodiagnostic Study, Inc., 1987-91; sr. rsch. engr. Bionetics Corp., 1994-95, Lockheed Martin Engring. Svcs., 1995—; NRC postdoctoral fellow NASA-Ames, Calif., 1973-75; NRC sr. postdoctoral fellow Wright Patterson AFB, Ohio, 1986-88, NASA-Ames Rsch. Ctr., 1992-94. Contbr. articles to profl. jours.; author presentations on physiology and biomed. engring. Fellow Aerospace Med. Assn. (assoc.); mem. Biomed. Engring. Soc. Republican. Presbyterian. Avocations: woodwork, computer programming. Home and Office: 1764 Emory St San Jose CA 95126-1910

MONTGOMERY, LINDA STROUPE, county official; b. Havaco, W.Va., Feb. 12, 1943; d. James Allen Stroupe and Opal Marie (Daugherty) Leif; m. James R. Sutliff, Aug. 9, 1960 (div. Feb. 1982); children: Mark S., Debra Lynn, Amy Sutliff Sweckard; m. Paul L. Montgomery, Apr. 23, 1983. Student, S.W. Mo. State U., 1979-93. Sec. Va. Poly. Inst., Blacksburg, 1961-64; office mgr., parlegal William H. Wendt, Springfield, Mo., 1973-84; office adminstr. Greene County Commn., Springfield, 1984-94; recorder of deeds Greene County, 1995—; mem. legis. com. Local Area Govt. Employees Retirement Sys., State of Mo., 1993—; dist. dir. Mo. Assn. Counties, 1997—. Bd. dirs. Springfield-Greene County Libr. Dist., 1991—, also past pres.; mem. allocations com., sect. chmn. United Way Ozarks, Springfield, 1990—; committeewoman, legis. chmn. Greene County Rep. Ctrl. Com., 1987—. Mem. ALA, Internat. Assn. Clks., Recorders, Election Ofcls. and Treas., Recorder's Assn. Mo., Mo. Libr. Assn., Springfield Area C. of C., Grand Order Pachyderms (past pres.), Phi Kappa Phi. Methodist. Avocations: reading, needlework, antiques. Home: 5209 S Shari Ln Rogersville MO 65742-9474 Office: Greene County Govt 940 N Boonville Ave Springfield MO 65802-3850

MONTGOMERY, MARTHA M., nursing educator; b. Kalkaska, Mich., Feb. 23, 1934; d. Alvah James Montgomery and Genevieve (Ragan) Shaffer. Dipl., Henry Ford Hosp., Detroit, 1955; BSN, Wayne State U., 1962, MSN, 1964. Cert. orthopedic nurse. Staff nurse, head nurse Henry Ford Hosp., Detroit, 1955-59; faculty, staff nurse Evang. Deaconess Hosp., Detroit, 1961-65; staff nurse, rsch. asst. Wayne State U., Detroit, 1963, 75-76; cmty. health nurse Vis. Nurse Assn., Detroit, 1988—; instr. nursing Henry Ford C.C., Dearborn, Mich., 1964—. Instrl. designer and formative evaluator (tv prodn.) Newer Media Approaches to Edn. for Nursing, 1968-71; coauthor, editor, cons. in design (brochure) The Curriculum Master Plan, 1981. Grantee Helene Fuld Health Trust, 1990, 93. Mem. ANA, N.Am. Nursing Diagnosis Assn., Am. Fedn. Tchrs., Assn. Ednl. Comm. and Tech., Assn. for Devel. Computer-Based Instrl. Sys., Nat. Assn. Orthopedic Nurses, Sigma Theta Tau (Lambda chpt.). Avocations: hiking, backpacking, camping, travel, golf. Office: Henry Ford Cmty Coll 5101 Evergreen Rd Dearborn MI 48128-2407

MONTGOMERY, MARVIN, musical producer. Mem. band Light Crust Doughboys, 1935—; prodr., leader Light Crust Doughboys, mus. orgn., Mesquite, Tex., 1947—; mem. touring act. State of Tex. Commn. on Arts. Originator western swing music. Named to Tex. Western Swing Hall of Fame; named ofcl. music amb. Tex. Ho. of Reps. Office: Light Crust Doughboys 105 Broad St Mesquite TX 75149

MONTGOMERY, MICHAEL DAVIS, hotelier, advanced technology consultant; b. San Luis Obispo, Calif., June 4, 1936; s. Herold Ray and Elva Dee (Davis) M.; m. Rita Martin, Dec. 28, 1957 (div. Sept. 1975); children: Jeanne, Gwen, Michele. MSEE, Stanford U., 1959; PhD, U. N.Mex., 1967. Group leader Max Planck Inst. for Astrophysics, Munich, 1974-76; group leader advanced concepts Los Alamos (N.Mex.) Nat. Labs., 1976-83; program mgr. for simulation Maxwell Labs. Inc., San Diego, 1983-84, dep. for DNA programs, 1984-85, v.p. rsch. and devel., 1986-91, sr. v.p. applied tech., 1991-92; sr. cons., 1993-96; owner Casa Del Mar Inn, Santa Barbara, Calif., 1991—. Assoc. editor Jour. Geophys. Research; contbr. articles to sci. jours. Served to lt. comdr. USN, 1959-62. Recipient Sr. Scientist award Alexander Von Humboldt Found., 1972. Mem. AAAS, Am. Phys. Soc., Phi Beta Kappa, Sigma Xi, Tau Beta Pi. Avocations: amateur radio. Home: 18 Bath St Santa Barbara CA 93101-3803 Office: Casa Del Mar Inn 18 Bath St Santa Barbara CA 93101-3803

MONTGOMERY, PARKER GILBERT, investment banker; b. Norwood, Mass., July 30, 1928; s. Spencer Bishop and Eleanor Carrie (Gilbert) M.; children: Parker Jr., Carol, John B., William W., Kathryn. A.B., Harvard U., 1949, LL.B., 1953. Bar: Mass. 1953, N.Y. 1956. Assoc. Heminway & Barnes, Boston, 1953; assoc. Dewey, Ballantine, Bushby, Palmer & Wood, N.Y.C., 1956; with Baker, Weeks & Co., investment bankers, N.Y.C., 1957; founder Cooper Labs., Inc., N.Y.C., Calif., 1958; chmn. bd., pres. Cooper Devel. Co., Carpinteria, Calif.; spl. Asst. to Sec. of State Dept. State, 1959-61, vice chmn. Task Force on Internat. Pvt. Enterprise, 1983-84; mem. Investment Policy Adv. Com. U.S. Trade Rep., 1990-94; alt. U.S. rep. 47th Session Gen. Assembly U.N., 1992-93. Councilman Town of Bedford, 1971-75; bd. dirs. and exec. com. Santa Barbara Med. Found. Clinic; mem. vis. com. JFK Sch. Govt. Harvard U. Lt. USNR, 1945-46, 54-55. Mem. Coun. Fgn. Rels. (N.Y.C.), Econ. Club (N.Y.), Harvard Club (N.Y.C), Pacific Union Club, River Club (N.Y.C.), Royal Thames Yacht Club (London), Bedford Golf and Tennis Club, The Valley Club of Montecito, Coral Casino Club of Santa Barbara. Office: Cooper Devel Co 1110 Eugenia Pl Carpinteria CA 93013-2060

MONTGOMERY, PAULA KAY, publisher; b. Omaha, Sept. 23, 1946; d. Floyd Woodrow and Adelyn Ann (Peterson) M. BA in English, Fla. State U., 1967, MLS in Libr. Sci., 1968; PhD in Reading Edn., 1989. Sch. libr. Montgomery County Pub. Sch., Rockville, Md., 1969-72, libr. specialist, 1972-79; chief sch. libr. Md. State Dept. Edn., Balt., 1979-88; pub. Sch. Libr. Media Activities Monthly, Balt., 1984—; del. Gov.'s Conf. on Librs., Balt., 1990. Author: Teaching Library Media Skills, 1983, Thematic Approaches to Literature, 1991, Subject Approaches to Literature, 1991, Subject Approaches to Literature, 1991, Literary Forms Approach to Literature, 1995, The Bookmark Book, 1995; editor: (book series) Library Media Skills, 1982—. Mem. ALA, Nat. Assn. State Ednl. Media Profls. (pres. 1987), Assn. Edn. Communication and Tech. Lutheran. Office: 17 E Henrietta St Baltimore MD 21230-3910

MONTGOMERY, REX, biochemist, educator; b. Halesowen, Eng., Sept. 4, 1923; came to U.S., 1948, naturalized, 1963; s. Fred and Jane (Holloway) M.; m. Barbara Winifred Price, Aug. 9, 1948 (dec.); children: Ian, David, Jennifer, Christopher. BSc, U. Birmingham, Eng., 1943, PhD, 1946, DSc, 1963. Rsch. assoc. U. Minn., 1951-55; mem. faculty U. Iowa, Iowa City, 1955—; prof. biochemistry U. Iowa, 1963—, assoc. dean U. Iowa Coll. Medicine, 1974-95, v.p. rsch., 1989-90; vis. prof. Nat. Australian U., 1969-70; mem. physiol. chemistry study sect. NIH, 1968-72; mem. drug devel. contract rev. com., 1975-87; chmn. com. biol. chemistry NAS, 1961-64; pesticide and fertilizer adv. bd. Iowa Dept. Agr., 1990-91; bd. dirs. Wallace Tech. Transfer Found., 1989-93; chmn. bd. dirs. Neurotron Inc., 1990-95; mem. rsch. com. Iowa Corn Promotion Bd., 1995—; rsch. dir. Biotech. Byproducts Consortium, 1989—; cons. in field. Author: Chemical Production of Lactic Acid, 1949, Chemistry of Plant Gums and Mucilages, 1959, Quantitative Problems in Biochemical Sciences, 2d edit., 1976, Biochemistry: A Case-Orientated Approach, 6th edit., 1996; mem. editl. adv. bd. Carbohydrate Rsch., 1968-80; mem. editl. bd. Molecular Biotherapy, 1988-92; contbr. articles to profl. jours. Postdoctoral fellow Ohio State U., 1948-49; fellow Sugar Research Found., Dept. Agr., 1949-51. Home: 701 Oaknoll Dr Iowa City IA 52246-5168 Office: U Iowa Coll Medicine Dept Biochemistry Iowa City IA 52242

MONTGOMERY, ROBERT F., state legislator, retired surgeon, cattle rancher; b. Ogden, Utah, May 13, 1933; s. William Floyd and Adrianna (Van Zweden) M.; m. Jelean Skeen, June 24, 1953; children: Lance, Dana, Kristen, Keri, Tanya. AS, Weber State U., 1953; BS, Brigham Young U., 1957; MD, U. Utah, 1961. Pvt. practice Anaheim, Calif., 1966-88; senator Utah State Senate, 1992—; chief surgery Anaheim Gen. Hosp., 1970, Anaheim Meml. Hosp., 1972-74. Rep. chmn. Weber County, Utah, 1991-93; pres. Am. Cancer Soc., Salt Lake City, 1992-93. Sgt. U.S. Army, 1953-55, Korea. Mem. Rotary, Utah Elephant Club, Traveler's Century Club. Mormon. Avocations: traveling, reading, hunting, fishing, golfing. Home: 1825 Mountain Rd Ogden UT 84414-2903

MONTGOMERY, ROBERT HUMPHREY, JR., lawyer; b. Boston, Apr. 1, 1923; s. Robert Humphrey and Mary (Murray) M.; m. Henriette de Sieyes, 1952; children: Margaret, Anne (dec.), Samuel Bishop. AB, Harvard U., 1947; LLB, Columbia U., 1950. Bar: N.Y. 1953, D.C. 1978. Ptnr. Paul, Weiss, Rifkind, Wharton & Garrison, N.Y.C., 1950-93, of counsel, 1994—. Chmn. Alliance for the Arts, N.Y.C., 1985—; trustee Vassar Coll. Sgt. U.S. Army, 1943-46. Mem. Century Assn., Groucho Club (London). Democrat. Home: 31 E 79th St New York NY 10021-0101 Office: Paul Weiss Rifkind Wharton & Garrison 1285 Avenue Of The Americas New York NY 10019-6028

MONTGOMERY, ROBERT MOREL, JR., lawyer; b. Birmingham, Ala., June 9, 1930; s. Robert Morel and Ella Bernice (Smith) M.; m. Mary Lemerle McKenzie, Mar. 6, 1953; 1 child, Courtnay Elizabeth. B.S., U. Ala., 1952; LL.B., U. Fla., 1957. Bar: Fla. 1957; diplomate Acad. Fla. Trial Lawyers. With Howell & Kirby Attys at Law, Jacksonville, Fla., 1957-59; ptnr. Howell, Kirby, Montgomery, Sands & D'Aiuto, Jacksonville, Fla., 1959-66, Howell, Kirby, Montgomery, D'Aiuto, Dean & Hallowes, West Palm Beach, Fla., 1966-75, Montgomery, Lytal, Reiter, Denny & Searcy, West Palm Beach, Fla., 1976-85, Montgomery Searcy & Denny, West Palm Beach, Fla., 1986-89; sr. ptnr. Montgomery & Larmoyeux, West Palm Beach, Fla., 1989—; civil trial adv. Nat. Bd. Trial Advocacy. Chmn. Palm Beach Opera; vice chmn. Kravis Ctr., Palm Beach Cultural Coun. 1st lt. AUS, 1952-54. Named Alumnus of Yr. U. Fla. Law Rev., 1983, Philanthropist of Yr. Nat. Assn. Fund Raising Execs., 1990, Honoree for Yr. City of Hope, 1991; recipient Learned Hand award Am. Jewish Com., 1985, Pub.'s award honor for contbg. most to improving quality of life in Broward and Palm Beach counties, 1992, Great Am. Traditions award B'nai B'rith, 1996. Mem. ABA, Fla. Bar Assn. (lectr. continuing edn.), Palm Beach County Bar Assn., Trial Lawyers Assn. Am., Inner Circle Advs. Home: 1800 S Ocean Blvd Palm Beach FL 33480-5104 Office: PO Box 3086 West Palm Beach FL 33402-3086

MONTGOMERY, ROBERT RENWICK, medical association administrator, educator; b. New Castle, Pa., June 3, 1943. BS in Chemistry, Grove City Coll., 1965; MD, U. Pitts., 1969. Diplomate Am. Bd. Pediatrics. Intern Childrens Hosp. Phila. U. Pa., 1969-70; resident Harriet Lane Svc. Johns Hopkins Hosp., 1972-73, fellow, 1972-73; fellow U. Colo., 1973-76, Scripps Clinic and Rsch. Found., 1976-77; gen. med. officer USPHS, Chinle, Ariz., 1970-71; dep. chief pediatrics USPHS, Tuba City, Ariz., 1971-72; rsch. clin fellow in pediatric hematology U. Colo., 1973-76; rsch. fellow in molecular immunology Scripps Clinic and Rsch. Found., 1976-77; acting dir. Mountain States Regional Hemphilia Program U. Colo., 1977-78, asst. prof. dept. pediatrics, 1977-80, co-dir. coagulation rsch. labs., asst. dir. mountain sates regional hemophilia program, 1978-80; asst. prof. dept. pediatrics Med. Coll. Wis., 1980-81; dir. homeostasis program Milwaukee Children's Hosp., 1980-84; med. dir. Great Lakes Hemophilia Found., 1980-84; dir. regional homeostasis reference lab. The Blood Ctr. Southeastern Wis., 1981—; cons. hemostasis lab., dept. pathology The Children's Hosp. Wis., 1981—; assoc. prof. dept. pediatrics Med. Coll. Wis., 1981-84; sr. investigator The Blood Ctr. Southeastern Wis., 1982—, section head hemostasis rsch.; scientific dir. Great Lakes Hemophilia Found., 1984—; assoc. dir. rsch. The Blood Ctr. Southeastern Wis., 1984-86; assoc. clin. prof. dept. pediatrics Med. Coll. Wis., clin. prof. dept. pediatrics, 1986-96; dir. rsch. The Blood Ctr. Southeastern Wis., 1986—; acting sect. head coagulation lab., dept. pathology Med. Coll. Wis., 1986-87; faculty med. tech. Marquette U., Milw., 1986-92; clin. prof. dept. pathology Med. Coll. Wis., 1987—; v.p., dir. rsch. The Blood Ctr. Southeastern Wis., 1988-96; mem. med. adv. com. Great Lakes Hemophilia Found., 1980-96; mem. libr. com., human rsch. rev. com. The Blood Ctr. Southeastern Wis., 1981—, mem. rsch. mgmt. group, rsch. strategic planning com., 1983—; mem. subcom. FVII and von Willebrand factor Internat. Congress Thrombosis and Haemostasis, 1984—; mem. radiation safety com. The Blood Ctr. Southeastern Wis., 1984—; ad hoc reviewer Heart Lung and Blood Inst., NIH, 1984—; mem. Inst. Biosafety com. The Blood Ctr. Southeastern Wis., 1985—; chmn. rsch. review com. Nat. Hemophilia Found., 1987-96; ad hoc reviewer com. B Nat. Heart, Lung and Blood Inst., 1991—; chmn. von Willebrand subcom. Hemophilia Rsch. Soc., 1990-97; pres. Hemophilia Rsch. Soc., 1990-93; mem. scientific adv. com. Nat. Hemophilia Found., 1992-95; mem. bd. dirs. Wis. Sickle Cell Disease Comprehensive Ctr., 1992-94; chair med. adv. coun. Great Lakes Hemophilia Found., Milw., 1992-96; mem. blood diseases and resources adv. com. Nat. Heart, Lung, and Blood Inst., 1992-95; prof. pediat. Med. Coll. Wis., 1996—. Sr. asst. surgeon USPHS, Indian Health Svc., 1971-72. Recipient Nat. Rsch. Svc. award Heart Lung and Blood Inst., NIH, 1975-77, Young Investigator award, 1978-81, Established Investigator award Am. Heart Assn., 1982-87, Jack Kennedy Alumni Achievement award Groce City Coll., 1985, Dr. Murray Thelin award Nat. Hemophilia Found., 1991. Mem. AAAS, Am. Soc. Clin. Investigators, Am. Soc. Pediatric Hematology/Oncology, Am. Soc. Hematology, Am. Fedn. Clin. Rsch., Am. Heart Assn., N.Y. Acad. Sci., Western Soc. Pediatric Rsch., Internat. Soc. Thrombosis and Hemostasis, Soc. Pediatric Rsch., Hemophilia Rsch. Soc. Office: Blood Center of SouthEastern Wis Blood Research Institute 1701 W Wisconsin Ave Milwaukee WI 53233-2113

MONTGOMERY, ROBIN VERA, realtor; b. Boise, Idaho, July 21, 1928; d. Bruce Cameron and Grace Evangeline (Matthews) M.; m. Lewis Robert Goldberg, June 10, 1956 (div. June 1978); children: Timothy, Holly, Randall. BA in Journalism, U. Mich., 1957; BArch, U. Oreg., 1972. Architect Robin's Roost, Eugene & Florence, Oreg., 1972-82; realtor Exclusive Realtors, L.A., 1989—. Program chair Hadassah, Eugene, 1968; pres. Elec. Wires Underground, Eugene, 1967. With USN, 1949-53. Mem. Calif. Assn. Realtors, Theta Sigma Phi. Democrat. Avocations: hiking, films, writing, concerts. Home: 1334 S Carmelina Ave Apt 7 Los Angeles CA 90025-1919

MONTGOMERY, ROGER, dean; b. N.Y.C., May 28, 1925; s. Graham Livingston and Ann Katharine (Cook) M.; m. Mary Elizabeth Hoyt, Apr. 23, 1949 (dec. Feb. 1980); children: Richard W., Thomas V., John L., Peter G. Student, Oberlin Coll., 1942-44, 47, N.C. State U., 1953-55; MArch, Harvard U., 1957. Architect Zeller & Hunter, Springfield, Ohio, 1948-53; assoc. prof. architecture Washington U., St. Louis, 1957-64, prof. architecture, 1964-67; architect, planner Anselevicius & Montgomery, St. Louis, 1957-70; prof. U. Calif., Berkeley, 1967—, assoc. dean environ. design, 1976-79, 81-84, acting dean, 1988-89, dean, 1989—; emeritus prof., 1995—, emeritus dean, 1996—; pres. Calif. Council on Archtl. Edn., 1986, bd. dirs., 1983-87. Co-author: Architecture in State of Washington, 1980; co-editor: Housing in America, 1979, Housing Policy for the 1980's; contbr. articles to profl. jours. mem. Redevel. Commn., Berkeley, 1978-80, pres. 1980. Served with U.S. Army, 1945-47. Mem. AIA, Am. Planning Assn., Urban Land Inst., Planners Network. Office: U Calif 228 Wurster Hall Berkeley CA 94720-1851

MONTGOMERY, ROY DELBERT, retired gas utility company executive; b. Indpls., Apr. 24, 1926; s. Lloyd Sipes and Nona Mae (Brummett) M.; m. Barbara Ann Reno, Apr. 21, 1946; children: Stephanie, Rebecca, Jeffrey, Laura. Student, Purdue U., 1950-51; M.E., Internat. Corr. Schs., 1953; A.S. in Mgmt. and Adminstrn., Ind. U., 1973. Registered profl. engr. Ind. Engr. Citizens Gas & Coke Utility, Indpls., 1952-59, supt., 1959-60, dir., 1960-73, exec. dir., 1973-78, v.p., 1978-82, sr. v.p., 1982-86, cons., 1986-88. Contbr. articles to profl. jours. Vice pres. exploring Crossroads of Am. Coun. Boy Scouts Am., Ind., 1978; corp. rep. Jr. Achievement Ind., 1970-82; pres. Fairway Trace at Pendia I, 1994—, Fairway Trace Home Owners Assn., 1995—. Recipient Bronze Big Horn award Boy Scouts Am. Explorer Div., Ind., 1978. Mem. Am. Gas Assn. (merit award 1966), Ind. Gas Assn., Scientec Club Ind., Kiwanis. Republican. Avocations: oil painting, boating, golf, genealogy.

MONTGOMERY, RUTH SHICK, author; b. Sumner, Ill.; d. Ira Whitmer and Bertha (Judy) Shick; m. Robert H. Montgomery, Dec. 26, 1935 (dec. 1993). Student, Baylor U. and Purdue U.; LL.D., Baylor U., 1956, Ashland Coll., 1958. Former news reporter Waco (Tex.) News-Tribune; women's editor Louisville Herald-Post; feature writer St. Louis Post-Dispatch, Indpls. Star; news reporter Detroit Times, Detroit News, Chgo. Tribune; Washington corr. N.Y. Daily News, 1944-55; fgn. corr. S.Am., Europe, Far and Middle East, intermittently 1946-68; spl. Washington corr. Internat. News Service, 1956-58; syndicated columnist Capital Letter King Features, Hearst Headline Service, 1958-68. Author: Once There Was a Nun, 1962, Mrs. LBJ, 1964, A Gift of Prophecy, 1965, A Search for the Truth, 1966, Flowers at the White House, 1967, Here and Hereafter, 1968, Hail to the Chiefs, 1970, A World Beyond, 1971, Born to Heal, 1973, Companions Along The Way, 1974, The World Before, 1976, Strangers Among Us, 1979, Threshold to Tomorrow, 1983, Aliens Among Us, 1985; subject of book Ruth Montgomery: Herald of the New Age, 1986. Recipient Pall Mall Journalism award, 1947; Front Page award Indpls. Press Club, 1957; George Holmes Journalism award, 1957; best non-fiction award Ind. U., 1966; Most Valuable Alumna award Baylor U., 1967; inducted into Journalism Hall of Fame (Ind.), 1993. Mem. White House Corrs. Assn., State Dept. Corrs. Assn., Theta Sigma Phi (Woman of Year award 1966), Alpha Chi Omega, Kappa Kappa Kappa. Clubs: Nat. Press (pres. 1950-51, gov. 1951-54). Only woman selected to cover Pres. Roosevelt's funeral, 1945. Home: Penthouse 2 3115 Gulf Shore Blvd N Naples FL 34103

MONTGOMERY, SETH DAVID, retired state supreme court chief justice; b. Santa Fe, Feb. 16, 1937; s. Andrew Kaye and Ruth (Champion) M.; m. Margaret Cook, Oct. 29, 1960; children: Andrew Seth, Charles Hope, David Lewis. AB, Princeton U., 1959; LLB, Stanford U., 1965. Bar: N.M. 1965. Ptnr. Montgomery & Andrews, P.A., Santa Fe, 1965-89, of counsel, 1994—; justice N.Mex. Supreme Ct., 1989-94, chief justice, 1994; adj. prof. law U. N.Mex. Sch. Law, Albuquerque, 1970-71; chmn. N.Mex. adv. coun. Legal Svcs. Corp., Santa Fe, 1976-89. Bd. visitors Stanford U. Sch. Law, 1967-70, 82-85, U. N.Mex. Sch. Law, 1982-89; pres., chmn. Santa Fe Opera, 1981-86; pres. Santa Fe Opera Found., 1986-89; chmn., vice chmn. Sch. Am. Rsch., Santa Fe, 1985-89; bd. dirs. New Vistas, Santa Fe, 1986-89, First Interstate Bank of Santa Fe, 1977-89, Old Cienega Village Mus., 1980-89. Lt. (j.g.) USN, 1959-62. Named Citizen of Yr., Santa Fe C. of C., 1986, Sunwest Bank of Santa Fe, 1994; recipient Disting. Cmty. Svc. award Anti-Defamation League, 1991, Western Area Outstanding Achievement award Nat. Multiple Sclerosis Soc., 1992, award for advancement of law N.Mex. Trial Lawyers, 1994, Award for Outstanding Judge Albuquerque Bar Assn., 1994. Fellow Am. Coll. Trial Lawyers, Am. Coll. Trust and Estate Counsel, Am. Bar Endowment, N.Mex. Bar Assn. (bd. bar commrs. 1986-89, sec., treas. 1988-89, Professionalism award 1993); mem. ABA, Am. Judicature Soc. Democrat.

MONTGOMERY, THEODORE ASHTON, physician; b. Los Angeles, Oct. 27, 1923; s. Wayne A. and Hazel (Osmer) M. MD, U. So. Calif., 1947; MPH cum laude, Harvard U., 1955. Diplomate: Am. Bd. Preventive Medicine, Am. Bd. Pediatrics. Intern Los Angeles County Gen. Hosp., 1946-48; intern Los Angeles Children's Hosp., 1948; resident Los Angeles Childrens' Hosp., 1950-51, St. Louis Childrens' Hosp., 1951-52; asst. in pediatrics Washington U., St. Louis, 1951-52; instr. pediatrics U. So. Calif., 1952-55; practice medicine specializing in pediatrics Los Angeles, 1952-54; lectr. pub. health U. Calif., Berkeley, 1960-83; cons. child health Calif. Dept. Pub. Health, 1954-60, chief maternal and perinatal health, 1960-61, acting chief bur. maternal and child health, 1961-63, asst. chief div. preventive med. services, 1963-66, chief, 1966-68, chief preventive medicine program, 1968-69, dep. dir. of Dept., 1969-73; chief div. disease control Alameda County Health Care Services Agy., 1973-74; cons. maternal and child health Calif. Dept. Health, Berkeley, 1974-78; chief maternal and child health br. No. Calif. Regional Office, Calif. Dept. Health Services, 1978-83; WHO fellow med. care adminstrn., Europe, 1966; co-chmn. Calif. Inter-agy. Council on Tb, 1966-72; vice chmn. Calif. Drug Research Adv. Panel, 1969-70;; White House Conf. Mental Retardation, 1963; Gov's. chmn. Calif. Regional Hemodialysis Rev. Com., 1968-73; exec. sec. Gov.'s Population Study Commn., 1966; mem. com. on Tb, Calif. Lung Assn., 1973-74. Author: (with others) Standards and Recommendations for Public Prenatal Care, 1960, Guide to Hearing Testing of School Children, 1961; contbr. articles to med. jours. Bd. dirs. Calif. Interagy. Coun. on Family Planning, 1970-73; chmn. Calif. State Interdepartmental Com. on Food and Nutrition, 1977-79, pres. Clan Montgomery Soc. Internat., 1981-84, regional commr., 1985-91. With M.C. AUS, 1948-50. Fellow Am. Acad. Pediatrics (chmn. Calif. com. Indian health 1973-76, mem. nat. com. on Indian health 1963-79, vice chmn. 1977-79), Am. Pub. Health Assn. (chmn. task force on population policy 1971-72); mem. Alpha Epsilon Delta, Delta Omega. Home: 85 Wildwood Gdns Piedmont CA 94611-3831

MONTGOMERY, THOM MATHEW, health program administrator, counselor; b. Delaware, Okla., Dec. 30, 1942; s. Francis Thomas and Ellen Grace (Whelan) M.; m. Dinah Lee Hicks, Feb. 4, 1961 (div. 1964); 1 child, Laura Diane. Student, Highlands U., 1960-61, Tulsa U., 1961-64, U. Calif., Irvine, 1980-81. Lic. counselor, Calif. Brokerage mgr. John Hancock Life Ins. Co., Boston, 1964-70; mng. editor Renown Publs., Reseda, Calif., 1970-77; publs. dir. Am. Pub. Health Found., Corona Del Mar, Calif., 1977-79; program adminstr. Life Plus Martin Luther Hosp., Anaheim, Calif., 1979-92; program dir. Rehab. Alcohol Programs, Pomona, Calif.; pres. Montgomery Counseling Assocs., Orange, 1986—. Author: A Party for Laura Lee, 1973; contbr. articles to profl. jours. Founding mem. Task Force on Alcohol & Drug Abuse for Disabled, Orange County, 1981, Sobriety Faire, Orange County, 1982. Fellow Am. Pub. Health Found.; mem. Nat. Coun. on Alcoholism, Nat. Assn. Alcohol and Drug Abuse Counselors, Calif. Assn. Alcohol and Drug Abuse Counselors. Republican. Presbyterian. Avocations: chess, hiking, swimming, poetry, drama. Home: 22371 Village Way Dr Canyon Lake CA 92587-7588 Office: Twin Town Saint Josephs Hosp 1100 W Stewart Dr Orange CA 92669

MONTGOMERY, WILLIAM ADAM, lawyer; b. Chgo., May 22, 1933; s. John Rogerson and Helen (Fyke) M.; m. Jane Fauver, July 28, 1956 (div. Dec. 1967); children: Elizabeth, William, Virginia; m. Deborah Stephens, July 29, 1972; children: Alex, Katherine. AB, Williams Coll., 1955; LLB, Harvard U., 1958. Bar: D.C. 1958, Ill. 1959, U.S. Ct. Appeals (7th cir.) 1959, U.S. Supreme Ct. 1977. Atty. civil div., appellate sect. Dept. Justice, Washington, 1958-60; assoc. Schiff Hardin & Waite, Chgo., 1960-68, ptnr., 1968-93; v.p., gen. counsel State Farm Ins. Cos., Bloomington, Ill., 1994—. Author: (39 corp. practice series) Tying Arrangements, 1984, also articles. Fellow Am. Coll. Trial Lawyers; mem. ABA (coun. antitrust sect. 1989-92), Chgo. Bar Assn., Seventh Cir. Bar Assn. (pres. 1988-89), Legal Club Chgo., Law Club Chgo., Econ. Club Chgo. Avocations: skiing, woodturning. Office: State Farm Ins Cos 1 State Farm Plz Bloomington IL 61710-0001

MONTGOMERY, WILLIAM D., ambassador; b. Carthage, Mo., Nov. 8, 1945; m. Lynne Germaine Montgomery; 3 children. BA, Bucknell U.; MA, George Washington U.; student, Nat. War Coll., 1986-87. With Fgn. Svc., 1974; econ. officer Fgn. Svc., Belgrade, Yugoslovia, 1975-78; comml. then polit. officer Fgn. Svc., Moscow, 1979-81; line officer, secretariat staff then exec. asst. to under sec. polit. affairs Dept. State, 1981-84, exec. asst. to dep. sec., 1991-93; dep. chief mission Dar es Salaam, Tanzania, 1984-85, Sofia, Bulgaria, 1988-91; U.S. ambassador Bulgaria, 1993-96; spl. advisor to Pres. and sec. state for Bosnia peace implementation of the Bosnia peace plan, 1996—. Decorated Bronze Star, Commendation medal with V device; decorated Order of the Horseman of the Madara, Order of the Stara Planina (Bulgaria). Mem. Am. Fgn. Svc. Assn. Office: US Dept State Rm 6219 2201 C St NW Washington DC 20521

MONTGOMERY, WILLIAM J., finance company executive; b. 1930; married. BA, Dartmouth Coll., 1952. Sales rep. IBM Corp., 1954-59; div. mgr. Security Leasing Co., 1959-62; v.p. U.S. Leasing Corp., 1962-68; pres. Computer Property Corp., 1968-70, Singer Leasing Corp., 1970-74, Chase Manhattan Leasing Corp., 1974-79; chmn., chief exec. officer, dir. Xerox Credit Corp., Stamford, Conn., 1979-91; chmn., CEO Am. Fin. Group, Boston, 1991-93; ptnr. The Alta Group, Hanover, N.H., 1993-97; pres., CEO Dell Fin. Svcs., L.P., Austin, Tex., 1997—. Office: Dell Fin Svcs LP 1 Dell Way RR 2 Box 44 Austin TX 78664

MONTGOMERY, WILLIAM WAYNE, surgeon; b. Proctor, Vt., Aug. 20, 1923; s. Charles Lynn and Ann (Jones) M. AB, Middlebury (Vt.) Coll., 1944; MD, U. Vt., 1947. Diplomate: Am. Bd. Otolaryngology. Intern Mary Fletcher Hosp., Burlington, Vt., 1947-48; gen. practice medicine W. Rutland, Vt., 1948-50; resident otolaryngology Mass. Eye and Ear Infirmary, 1952-55, mem. staff, 1956—, sr. surgeon in otolaryngology, 1966—; mem. staff Mass. Gen. Hosp., 1956—, surgeon otolaryngology, 1966-86; prof. Harvard Med. Sch., 1986-94, John W. Merriam prof. otology and laryngology, 1994—, med. dir. voice lab., 1993. Author: Surgery of the Upper Respiratory System, vol. I, II, The Mustache that Walks Like a Man, 1995; contbr. articles to med. jours. Served as batallion surgeon USMCR, 1950-52, Korea. Decorated Purple Heart, Bronze Star, Commendation medal; recipient Disting. Alumni award U. Vt. Med. Sch., 1968, Alumni Achievement award Middleburg Coll., 1985. Fellow ACS; mem. AMA, Am. Acad. Ophthalmology and Otolaryngology (instr. 1963-67), Am. Broncho-Esophagological Assn., Am. Laryngol. Assn. (James E. Newcomb award 1990), Am. Otologic Soc., Am. Laryngol., Rhinol. and Otol. Soc. (Cert. of merit 1990), Pan Am. Med. Assn., Mass. Med. Soc. (program chmn. 1966—), Suffolk Med. Soc., Am. Triological Soc. (Mosher award 1963, v.p. 1987), New Eng. Otolaryngol. Soc. (pres. 1977-78), Am. Soc. Head and Neck Surgery, Am. Acad. Facial Plastic and Reconstructive Surgery. Spl. research paranasal sinuses and laryngeal surgery. Home: 20 Hilltop Rd Chestnut Hill MA 02167-1846 Office: 243 Charles St Boston MA 02114-3002

MONTLE, PAUL JOSEPH, entrepreneur; b. Medford, Mass., Aug. 28, 1947; s. Joseph Frederick and Frances Elizabeth (Fogarty) M.; m. Elizabeth Anne Rusch, Mar. 3, 1973 (div. 1997); children: Alexis Elizabeth, Daphne Caroline. BA in Econs., Tufts U., 1969; postgrad., Boston U., 1969-70. Pres., chief exec. officer Killebrew, Montle Internat. Inc., Boston, 1971-73; v.p. Burgess & Leith, Boston, 1973-75, Hawthorne Securities Corp., 1975-76; founder, pres. First New Eng. Securities Corp., Boston, 1976-80, chmn., 1980-83; founder, pres. The Yankee Cos. Inc., Boston, 1977-88, chmn., chief exec. officer, 1988-89; founder, pres. Montle Internat., Boston, Houston, Hong Kong, London, 1987—, Am. Pacific Properties, Inc., Houston, 1990-92, Glenville Properties Inc., Houston, 1990—; chmn., CEO Teleconcepts, Inc., 1992-93, founder, chmn., CEO LS Capital Corp., 1992—; founder, gen. ptnr. Travis Ptnrs. G.P., 1991—, Great So. Capital Ptnrs. G.P., 1994—; also bd. dirs., pres. Viral Testing Systems Corp., 1992-94, also bd. dirs., Motion Media Techs. Corp., 1991-92, also bd. dirs.; chmn., CEO 1st Response Med. Inc., 1993; trustee, treas. Derby Acad., Hingham, Mass., 1985-90; bd. dirs. South Shore Playhouse Assn., Cohasset, Mass., 1987-90; internat. bd. overseers Tufts U., 1993—. Mem. Houston Club, Woods Hole Golf Club, Houston Racquet Club. Avocations: sailing, golf, tennis. Office: LS Capital Corp 15915 Katy Fwy Ste 250 Houston TX 77094-1700

MONTO, ARNOLD SIMON, epidemiology educator; b. Bklyn., Mar. 22, 1933; s. Jacob and Mildred (Kaplan) M.; m. Ellyne Gay Polsky, June 15, 1958; children: Sarah D. Monto Maniaci, Jane E., Richard L., Stephen A. BA in Zoology, Cornell U., Ithaca, N.Y., 1954; MD, Cornell U., N.Y.C., 1958. Diplomate Am. Coll. Epidemiology. Intern, asst. resident in medicine Vanderbilt U. Hosp., Nashville, 1958-60; USPHS postdoctoral fellow in infectious disease Stanford U. Med. Ctr., Palo Alto, Calif., 1960-62; mem. staff virus diseases sect. mid. Am. rsch. unit Nat. Inst. Allergy and Infectious Disease, Panama Canal Zone, 1962-65; from asst. prof. to prof. epidemiology U. Mich. Sch. Pub. Health, Ann Arbor, 1965—, chmn. dept. population planning and internat. health, 1993—, dir. Ctr. for Population Planning, 1993—; vis. scientist Clin. Rsch. Ctr., Northwick Park Hosp., Harrow, Eng., 1976; scholar-in-residence bd. on sci. and tech. for internat. devel. NAS and Inst. Medicine, Washington, 1983-84; vis. scientist div. communicable diseases WHO, Geneva, 1986-87; mem. pulmonary diseases adv. com. Nat. Heart, Lung and Blood Inst., Bethesda, Md., 1979-83; mem. nat. adv. coun. Nat. Inst. Allergy and Infectious Diseases, Bethesda, 1989-93,. Contbr. articles to med. jours. Recipient career devel. award NIH. Fellow Am. Coll. Epidemiology, Infectious Diseases Soc. Am.; mem. APHA (governing coun. 1978-80), Am. Epidemiol. Soc. Achievements include research on respiratory viral infections in the community; demonstration of effectiveness of influenza vaccine in severe disease in the elderly; prevention of spread of influenza virus and treatment of illness, occurrence, causes and treatment of common cold. Office: U Mich Sch Pub Health 109 Observatory St Ann Arbor MI 48109-2029

MONTONE, LIBER JOSEPH, engineering consultant; b. Apr. 21, 1919; s. Vito and Philomena (Carnicelli) M.; m. Clara Elisabeth Edwards, June 1, 1945; 1 child, Gregory Edwards. MS, Temple U., 1961; PhD (hon.), 1994. Registered profl. engr., Pa. Quality control supr. Haskell Electronic and Tool Corp., Homer, N.Y., 1950-53; researcher IBM Airborne Computer Lab., Vestal, N.Y., 1954-56; devel. engr. Western Electric Co. and Bell Labs., Laureldale, Pa., 1956-61; sr. devel. engr. Western Electric Co. Inc., Reading, Pa., 1961-65, sr. staff engr. R&D, 1965-82; cons. Naples, Fla., Fenwick Island, Del., 1983—; biomed. engr., cancer rsch. projects pathology and clin. lab. St. Joseph's Hosp., Reading, 1961-80; tech. cons. Reading Hosp., 1961-78. Contbr. articles to profl. jours. including The Engr., Am. Assn. Clin. Scientists Symposium. Capt. USAAF, 1942-45, ETO. Recipient Outstanding Paper award Engring. Rsch. Ctr., Princeton, N.J., 1963. Mem. NSPE, Fla. Engring. Soc., Res. Officer's Assn. (life). Achievements include patents in field; invention (with others) diagnostic cystic fibrosis capillary conduction test method. Office: 4242 Vanderbilt Dr Naples FL 33963

MONTORIO, JOHN ANGELO, magazine editor; b. Montclair, N.J., June 26, 1948; s. John Daniel and Lorraine (DiVita) M.; m. Lois Ann Marco, May 15, 1977; children—John Nicholas, Nicholas Ross. B.A. cum laude in English, Seton Hall U., 1970; M.A. in English, U. Va., 1972. Sr. editor Gralla Pubs., N.Y.C., 1973-74; assoc. editor Lebhar-Friedman Pubs., N.Y.C., 1974-76; asst. editor Fairchild Pubs., N.Y.C., 1976-77; Sunday mag. editor Washington Star, 1977-81; asst. bus.-fin. editor, dep. home editor N.Y. Times, N.Y.C., 1981-83; Sunday mag. editor Newsday, L.I., N.Y., 1983—. Recipient pubs. award Newsday Inc., 1984. Democrat. Roman Catholic. Office: The NY Times Co 229 W 43rd St New York NY 10036-3913*

MONTOYA, VELMA, federal agency administrator; b. L.A., Apr. 9, 1938; d. Jose Gutierrez and Consuelo (Cavazos) Montoya; m. Earl A. Thompson; 1 child, Bret L. Thompson. BA in Diplomacy and World Affairs, Occidental Coll., 1959; MA in Internat. Rels., Fletcher Sch. of Law and Diplomacy, 1960; MS in Econs., Stanford U., 1965; PhD in Econs., U. Calif., L.A., 1977. Asst. prof. Econs. Calif. State U., L.A., 1965-68; vis. assoc. prof. U. So. Calif., 1979; instr. U. Calif., L.A., 1981-82; staff economist The Rand Corp., Santa Monica, Calif., 1973-82; asst. dir. for strategy, White House Office of Policy Devel. Exec. Office of the Pres., 1982-83; expert economist, Office of Regulatory Analysis, Occupational Safety and Health Adminstrn. U.S. Dept. of Labor, 1983-85; dir. of Studies in Pub. Policy and Assoc. Prof. of Political Economy, Sch. of Bus. Mgmt. Chapman U., 1985-87; adj. prof., Sch. of Bus. Mgmt. Pepperdine Univ., 1987-88; pres. Hispanic-Am. Pub. Policy Inst., 1984-90; assoc. prof. of Fin., Sch. of Bus. Adminstrn. Calif. State Polytechnic Univ., Pomona, 1988-90; commr. Occupational Safety and Health Review Commn., 1990—; cons. Urban Inst., 1974, Mexican-Am. Study Project UCLA, 1966, Graduate and Profl. Fellowships to the Office of Post Secondary Education, U.S. Dept. of Edn.; editorial referee Contemporary Policy Issues, Economic Inquiry, Policy Analysis, The Journal of Economic Literature; discussion leader Am. Assembly on Rels. Between the U.S. and Mex.; pres. del. White House Conf. on Aging, 1981; reader of 1988 proposals for the U.S. Dept of Edn. for the Improvement and Reform of Schs. and Teaching; research participant U.S. Dept. of Edn. Delphi Assessment of Drug Policies for Use in Minority Neighborhoods, 1989; mem. hispanic adv. panel Nat. Commn. for Employment Policy, 1981-82; lectr. Brookings Inst. Seminars for U.S. Bus. Leaders; bd. adv. Close-Up Found., 1982-83; discussant Western Economic Assn. Meetings, 1985, 93; bd. adv. Nat. Rehab. Hosp., 1991-94; mem. nat. exec. adv. bd. Harvard Jour. of Hispanic Policy, 1993-95. Mem. census adv. com. on hispanic population for 1990 census, Washington, D.C., 1988-93, Senate Rep. Conf. Task Force on Hispanic Affairs, Washington, D.C., 1991—. Named One of the 100 U.S. Hispanic Influentials Hispanic Bus. Mag., 1982, 90, Woman of the Yr. Mex.-Am. Oportunity Found., 1983, The East L.A. Com. Union, 1979, Marshall scholar, Fulbright scholar; recipient Freedom Found. at Valley Forge Honor Econ. Edn. Excellence Cert., 1986, Univ. fellow Stanford Univ., Internat. Rels. fellow Calif. PTA, John Hay Whitney Opportunity fellow; Calif. State Univ. Found. Faculty Rsch. grantee. Mem. ASTM (com. on rsch. and tech. planning 1985-87), Am. Econ. Assn. (session chair ann. meetings 1995), Nat. Coun. of Hispanic Women, State Bar of Calif., Calif. State Bar Ct. (exec. com. 1987-89, disciplinary bd. 1986-89), Western Econ. Assn., Indsl. Rsch. Inst. for Pacific Nations (adv. bd. 1988-89), Salesian Boys and Girls Club (bd. dirs. 1989—), Vets. in Com. Svc. (adv. com. 1989-94), Bd. of Regents U. Calif., 1994—, Phi Beta Kappa, Omicron Delta Epsilon, Phi Alpha Theta. Home: 6970 Los Tilos Rd Los Angeles CA 90068-3107

MONTROSE, DONALD W., bishop; b. Denver, May 13, 1923. Grad., L.A. Coll., 1943; student, St. John's Sem., Camarillo. Ordained priest Roman Cath. Ch., 1949. Tchr. Mater Dei H.S., Santa Ana, Calif., 1960-64, prin., 1960-64; supt. Cath. H.S. Archdiocese of L.A., 1964-77; adminstr. Resurrection Parish, 1970-73, pastor, 1973—; Aux. bishop Roman Cath. Ch., Los Angeles, 1983; bishop Diocese of Stockton, Calif., 1985—. Office: Diocese of Stockton PO Box 4237 1105 N Lincoln St Stockton CA 95203-2410

MONTROSS, ERIC SCOTT, professional basketball player; s. Scott and Janice M.; m. Laura, Aug. 27, 1994. Student in Speech Comm., U. N.C. Ctr. Boston Celtics, 1994-96, N.J. Nets, 1996—. Named All-Am. Second team AP, All-ACC First team, All-Tournament teams ACC, NCAA East Region, NCAA Final Four, All-Rookie Second team, Schick, 1994-95. Avocations: reading, bass fishing, skeet shooting, travel, country music. Office: NJ Nets 405 Murray Hill Pkwy East Rutherford NJ 07073*

MONTY, CHARLES EMBERT, utility company executive; b. Plainfield, Conn., Mar. 9, 1927; s. Arthur Ovila and Mary Louise (Bromley) M.; children: Charles E., Mary, Janice, Nathan, Marcia. BSEE, Northeastern U., 1950; MBA, U. Maine, 1969. Registered profl. engr., Maine. Chmn. bd. dirs. Maine Yankee Atomic Power Co., 1988-92; chief oper. officer Cen. Maine Power Co., 1984-89, also bd. dirs.; energy cons., 1989—; mem. mgmt. com. New Eng. Power Pool, 1982-86. Mem. IEEE, Maine Assn. Engrs. Republican. Mem. United Chs. of Christ.

MONTY, GLORIA, television producer; b. Union City, N.J.; d. Joseph and Concetta M. (Mango) Montemuro; m. Robert Thomas O'Byrne, Jan. 8, 1952. BA, NYU; MA, Columbia U. Dir. New Sch. Social Rsch., N.Y.C., 1952-53; dir. Old Towne Theatres, Smithtown, N.Y., 1952-56, Abbey Theatre Workshop, N.Y.C., 1952-56; cons. ABC. Dir. numerous TV programs, including Secret Storm, 1956-72, Bright Promise, numerous episodes ABC Wide World Entertainment; exec. prodr. General Hospital, 1977-86, 90-92, The Hamptons, 1983-85; made-for-TV movies, including Confessions of a Married Man, 1982, The Imposter, 1984; exec. prodr. in devel. for primetime TV 20th Century Fox, 1987-90; head cons. daytime TV ABC, 1987-90; prin. Gloria Monty Prodns. for new ABC daytime drama devel.; co-exec. prodr. While My Pretty One Sleeps, 1994-95, CBS Remember Me, FAMILY CHANNEL, 1995-97, Let Me Call You Sweetheart, 1997—, Moonlight Becomes You, 1997—; made-for-TV movies in assn. with Grosso-Jacobson. Chair Film Commn., State of N.J. Recipient Emmy awards, 1982, 84, Am. Soc. Lighting Dirs. award, 1979, Most Successful TV Show in

History of TV award ABC, 1982, Spl. Editors award Soap Opera Digest, 1984, numerous others; named Woman of Yr., Paulist Choristers So. Calif., 1986. Mem. Women in Film, Dirs. Guild Am. (mem. exec. com.), Stuntman's Assn. (hon.), Thunderbird Country Club (Rancho Mirage, Calif.), Bel Air Country Club (Calif.), Deal Country Club, Navesink Country Club.

MONTZ, FLORENCE STOLTE, church official; b. Lowden, Iowa, June 7, 1924; d. Emil L. and Emma Marie (Meier) Stolte; m. C. R. Montz, June 15, 1947; children: Jennifer Montz Rechlin, Fredrick John. BS, RN, U. Iowa, 1947; LLD (hon.), Concordia Coll., Bronxville, N.Y., 1984; LHD (hon.), Concordia Coll., St. Paul, 1988. RN, Iowa. V.p., then pres. N.D. dist. Luth. Women's Missionary, Luth. Ch.-Mo. Synod, Bismarck, 1960-68, 1st v.p. internat., 1967-71, pres., 1971-75; editor Better Health mag. Luth. Ch.-Mo. Synod, Bismarck, 1983—, also bd. dirs.; Parish nurse instr. Trinity Hosp., Minot, S.D., 1995—. Mem. Assn. Lutheran Older Adults (pres. 1996—), Sigma Theta Tau. Home: PO Box 1293 Bismarck ND 58502-1293

MONYPENY, DAVID MURRAY, lawyer; b. Jackson, Tenn., Apr. 29, 1957; s. Kent Brooks Monypeny and Kathryn (Warner) Sadowski. BBA, U. Okla., 1980; JD, U. Memphis, 1983. Bar: Tenn. 1983; CPA. Atty. Glankler, Brown et al, Memphis, 1983-85; CPA Frazer, Thomas & Tate, Memphis, 1985-87; atty. Diamond, Finklestein, Monypeny, Memphis, 1987-88, Lawrance & Monypeny, Memphis, 1988-94, Monypeny, Simpson et al, Memphis, 1994—; atty., cons., bus. mgr. Jerry Lee Lewis, Nesbit, Miss. Author: (video) Wiping Out Tax Debt You Can't Afford to Pay, 1993. Mem. Bellevue Ch., Memphis, 1983-96; campaign fin. chair Neil Small Chancellor, Memphis, 1990. Republican. Baptist. Avocations: music, video. Office: Monypeny Simpson Walker & Schatz 6256 Poplar Ave Memphis TN 38119-4713

MOODY, CHERYL ANNE, social services administrator, social worker, educator; b. Winston-Salem, N.C., July 31, 1953; d. Fred Bertram and Mary Edna (Weekley) M. BSW with honors, Va. Commonwealth U., 1975; MSW, U. Mich., 1979. Social worker Family Svcs., Inc., Winston-Salem, 1974-77; sch. social work intern Huron Valley Jr. H.S., Milford, Mich., 1977-78; children's social work intern Downriver Child Guidance Clinic, Allen Park, Mich., 1978-79; children's svcs. specialist Calhoun County Dept. Social Svcs., Battle Creek, Mich., 1979-81; children's psychiat. social worker Eastern Maine Med. Ctr., Bangor, 1981-82, sr. med. social worker, 1982-85; clin. social worker Ctr. for Family Svcs. in Palm Beach County, Inc., West Palm Beach, Fla., 1988-89, Jupiter, Fla., 1989-91; dir. children's programs Children's Home Soc. of Fla., West Palm Beach, 1985—; asst. prof. social work Fla. Atlantic U., Boca Raton, 1993—. Vol. group leader Lupus Found., Boca Raton, 1994—. Mem. NASW, Acad. Cert. Social Workers. Democrat. Methodist. Avocations: reading, knitting, drawing. Home: 6212 62nd Way West Palm Beach FL 33409-7130 Office: Children's Home Soc of Fla 3600 Broadway West Palm Beach FL 33407-4844

MOODY, EVELYN WILIE, consulting geologist; b. Waco, Tex.; d. William Braden and Enid Eva (Holt) Wilie; children: John D., Melissa L., Jennifer A. Student, Baylor U., 1934-35; BA with honors in Geology and Edn. U. Tex., 1938, MA with honors in geology, 1940. Cert. profl. geologist; cert. permanent tchr., Tex. Geologist Ark. Fuel Oil Co., Shreveport, La., New Orleans and Houston, 1942-45; teaching asst. Colo. Sch. Mines, Golden, 1946-47; exploration cons. geologist Gen. Crude Oil Co., Houston, 1975-77; ind. cons. geologist, Houston, 1977—; exploration cons. geologist Shell Oil Co., Houston, 1979-81; faculty dept. continuing edn. Rice U., Houston, 1978. Contbr. articles to profl. jours.; editor: The Manual for Independents, 1983, The Business of Being a Petroleum Independent (A Road Map for the Self Employed), 1987; co-author: How (to Try) To Find An Oil Field, 1981. Mem. Am. Assn. Petroleum Geologists (del. Houston chpt. 1986-89, 89-91, 91-94, 94—), Soc. Ind. Profl. Earth Scientists (hon. Houston chpt., sec. 1978-79, vice chmn. 1979-80, chpt. chmn. 1980-81, nat. dir. 1982-85, chpt. award for Outstanding Svc. 1986, editor SIPES Bull., 1983-85, treas. SIPES Found. 1984, pres. 1985, Nat. award for Outstanding Svc. 1988, SIPES Found. award 1994, hon. mem. in SIPES Houston chpt., 1994), Geol. Soc. Am., Watercolor Soc. Houston, Art Students League N.Y.C., Art Assn., Am. Inst. Profl. Geologists, Houston Geol. Soc. (chmn. libr. com. 1978—), Soc. Econ. Paleontologists and Mineralogists, Pi Beta Phi (nat. officer 1958-60, 66-68), Pi Lambda Theta. Republican. Presbyterian.

MOODY, FLORENCE ELIZABETH, education educator, retired college dean; b. Penn Yan, N.Y., Sept. 29, 1932; d. James William Southby and Rebecca (Worrall) M.; B.S., SUNY, Geneseo, 1954; M.S., Syracuse (N.Y.) U., 1961; Ed.D. (NDEA fellow), U. Rochester (N.Y.), 1969. Elem. sch. tchr., N.Y. State, 1954-64, 66-68; coord. profl. devel. Eastern Regional Inst. Edn., Syracuse, 1969-71; mem. faculty SUNY, Oswego, 1971-92, prof. elem. edn., 1978-92, assoc. dean profl. studies, 1980-85, dean, 1985-92; mem. N.Y. State Tchr. Edn. Cert. and Practice Bd., 1983-89; mem. Tchr. Edn. Conf. Bd., 1982-84. Nat. sec. Nat. Women's Party, 1974-76; bd. dirs. Oswego County Extension Service, 1974-76. Danforth asso., 1978—. Mem. Am. Assn. Colls. Tchr. Edn. (pres. N.Y. State chpt. 1983-84), Assn. Tchr. Educators, Assn. Supervision and Curriculum Devel., Am. Ednl. Research Assn., N.Y. State Assn. Tchr. Educators (sec., exec. bd. 1976-78), Kappa Delta Pi, Pi Lambda Theta, Phi Delta Kappa, Delta Kappa Gamma. Presbyterian. Club: Order Eastern Star. Home: 44 Franklin Ave Oswego NY 13126-1711

MOODY, FREDERICK JEROME, mechanical engineer, consultant thermal hydraulics; b. Aurora, Ill., Apr. 2, 1935; s. Frederick J. and Ruth K. (King) M.; m. Phyllis Arlene Ivemeyer, Aug. 27, 1955; children: David, John, Paul, Daniel. B.S. in Mech. Engring., U. Colo., 1958; M.S. in Mech. Engring., Stanford U., 1965, Ph.D. in Mech. Engring., 1971. Engr., GE, San Jose, Calif., 1958-78, prin. engr., 1978-81, cons. engr., 1981—; adj. prof. San Jose State U., 1971—; consulting engr. thermal-hydraulics GE, 1958—. Author: Introduction to Unsteady Thermofluid Mechanics, 1990; co-author: The Thermal-Hydraulics of a Boiling Water Nuclear Reactor, 1977, 2nd edit., 1993. Sunday Sch. tchr. Calvary Baptist Ch., Los Gatos, Calif., 1960—; chmn. bd. dirs. Med. Inst. Chaplains, San Jose, 1984. Fellow ASME (George Westinghouse Gold Medal 1980). Republican. Home: 2265 Sunrise Dr San Jose CA 95124-2640 Office: Gen Electric Co Mail Code 747 175 Curtner Ave San Jose CA 95125-1014

MOODY, GENE BYRON, engineering executive, small business owner; b. Calhoun, Ga., Aug. 29, 1933; s. Denzel Elwood and Mary Edna (Hughes) M.; m. Willie Earline Chauncey, Sept. 1, 1955; children: Byron Eugene, Iva Marie Levy. BSCE, U. Tenn., 1956. Registered profl. engr., Ala., Ark., Ga., La., Miss., Tex. V.p. S.I.P. Engring. Corp., Baton Rouge, 1968-70; project engr. S.I.P., Inc., Houston, 1970-73; dir. of engring. Jacus Assoc., Mpls., 1972-73; dir. of civil engring. Barnard & Burk, Baton Rouge, 1973-79; project mgr. Process Svcs., Baton Rouge, 1979-80, Salmon & Assoc., Baton Rouge, 1980-81; chief engr. Minton & Assoc., Lafayette, La., 1982; mgr. Assoc. Engr. Cons., Baton Rouge, 1982-86; owner Gene B. Moody, P.E., Baton Rouge, 1986—. Author: Good Homemakers, 1988, Deliverance Manual, 1989; contbr. articles to profl. jours. Deacon South Side Bapt. Ch., Baton Rouge, 1974; tchr. Hamilton Bible Camp, Hot Springs, Ark., 1981-91; trustee Manna Bapt. Ch., Baton Rouge, 1989-91. With U.S. Army, 1957. U. Chattanooga scholar, 1951, U. Tenn. scholar, 1953. Fellow ASCE; mem. Am. Soc. Safety Engrs., La. Soc. Profl. Surveyors, Soc. Automotive Engrs., Inst. Transp. Engrs., La. Engring. Soc., Transp. Res. Rsch. Bd. Mem. Christian Ch. (minister). Home and Office: 9852 Hillyard Ave Baton Rouge LA 70809-3109

MOODY, GRAHAM BLAIR, lawyer; b. Roswell, N. Mex., July 20, 1925; s. Graham Blair and Vinnie Charlotte (Burton) M.; m. Linda Alden Swanson, Apr. 11, 1970 (div.); children: Graham Blair III, Stuart, Katherine, Charlotte, Douglas, Margaret. BA, Yale U., 1947; MBA, Harvard U., 1947; LLB, U. Calif., Berkeley, 1955. Bar: Calif. 1956, U.S. Dist. Ct. (no. dist.) Calif. 1956, U.S. Ct. Appeals (9th cir.) 1956, U.S. Supreme Ct. 1963. Asst. to dist. mgr. producing dept. Standard Oil of Calif., L.A., 1948-52; head law clk. to chief justice U.S. Supreme Ct., Washington, 1955-56; assoc. McCutchen, Doyle, Brown & Enersen, San Francisco, 1956-64; ptnr. McCutchen, Doyle, Brown & Enersen, 1964-85, of counsel, 1985-86; ptnr. Moody & Moody, 1987-94. Vestryman St. Clement's Episc. Ch., then All Souls Episc. Ch., 1960-68, Ch. of Our Savior, 1988-90; bd. dirs., 1st pres. Eugene O'Neill Found., Tao House, Danville, Calif., 1975-76; bd. dirs. League to Save Lake Tahoe, 1978—, pres., 1980-82, 88-90, mem. exec. com., 1980-93; bd. dirs. Trauma Found., 1988—, Point Reyes Bird Obs., Stinson Beach, Calif., 1991—, mem. exec. com. vice chair, 1996—, chair, 1997—; bd. dirs. Calif. Kidney Cancer Found., 1994—, chair, 1997—; bd. dirs. Henry Ohloff House, San Francisco, 1994—, Friends of Redwoods, Mill Valley, Calif., 1991-92. Supply officer USN. Mem. ABA, Am. Law Inst. (life), Yale Club (past pres. local club).

MOODY, JAMES L., JR., retail food distribution company executive; b. Manchester, N.H., 1931; married. AB, Bates Coll., 1953. With Gen. Electric Co., 1955-59; with Hannaford Bros. Co., Scarborough, Maine, 1959—; treas. Hannaford Bros. Co., 1961-69, pres., 1969-84, chief exec. officer, 1973-92, chmn., 1992—, also bd. dirs.; dir. Penobscot Shoe Co., UNUM Corp., Sobey's Stores Ltd., Can., Staples, Inc., IDEXX Labs., Inc., Colonial Group of Funds, Mass. Served with U.S. Army, 1953-55. Office: Hannaford Bros Co PO Box 1000 Portland ME 04104

MOODY, JAMES T(YNE), federal judge; b. LaCenter, Ky., June 16, 1938; s. Harold B. and Dorothy M. (Simmons) M.; m. Kay A. Gillett, Dec. 26, 1960; children: Patrick, Jeffrey, Timothy, Kathleen. BA, Ind. U., 1960, JD, 1963. Bar: Ind. 1963, U.S. Dist. Ct. (no. and so. dists.) Ind. 1963, U.S. Supreme Ct. 1972. Atty. Cities of Hobart and Lake Station, Ind., 1963-73; sole practice Hobart, 1963-73; judge Lake County (Ind.) Superior Ct., 1973-79; magistrate U.S. Dist. Ct. (no. dist.) Ind., Hammond, 1979-82, judge, 1982—; mem. faculty bus. law Ind. U., 1977-80. Republican. Office: US Dist Ct 128 Fed Bldg 507 State St Hammond IN 46320-1503*

MOODY, LAMON LAMAR, JR., retired civil engineer; b. Bogalusa, La., Nov. 8, 1924; s. Lamar Lamon and Vida (Seal) M.; BS in Civil Engring., U. Southwestern La., 1951; m. Eve Thibodeaux, Sept. 22, 1954 (div. 1991); children: Lamon Lamar III, Jennifer Eve, Jeffrey Matthew. Engr., Tex. Co., N.Y.C., 1951-52; project engr. African Petroleum Terminals, West Africa, 1952-56; chief engr. Kaiser Aluminum & Chem. Corp., Baton Rouge, 1956-63; pres., owner Dyer & Moody, Inc., Cons. Engrs., Baker, La., 1963-94, also chmn. bd., dir.; ret., 1994. Chmn., Baker Planning Commn., 1961-63. Trustee La. Coun. on Econ. Edn., 1987-93. Served with USMCR, 1943-46. Decorated Purple Heart; registered profl. engr., La., Ark., Miss., Tex.; registered profl. land surveyor, La., Tex. Fellow ASCE, Am. Congress Surveying and Mapping (award for excellency 1972); mem. La. Engring. Soc. (dir., v.p. 1980-81, pres. 1982-83, Charles M. Kerr award for public relations 1971, A.B. Patterson medal 1981, Odom award for disting. svc. to engring. profession, 1986), Profl. Engrs. in Pvt. Practice (state chmn. 1969-70), La. Land Surveyors Assn. (pres. 1968-69, Land Surveyor of Yr. award 1975), Cons. Engrs. Coun., Pub. Affairs Rsch. Coun. of La. (exec. com., trustee 1983—), Good Roads and Transp. Assn. (bd. dirs. 1984-96), Baker C. of C. (pres. 1977, Bus. Leader of Yr. award 1975), NSPE (nat. dir. 1982-83), DAV (cmdr. Capital City Post 5, comdr. Baton Rouge cht. 1997—), Blue Key, Mil. Order Purple Heart (officer Red Stick chpt. 177). Republican. Baptist. Clubs: Masons (32 deg., K.C.C.H. 1986), Kiwanis (dir. 1964-65), Disabled Am. Vets. (comdr.). Home: 451 Ray Weiland Dr Baker LA 70714-3353 Office: 2835 Ray Weiland Dr Baker LA 70714-3247

MOODY, LIZABETH ANN, law educator; b. Johnson City, Tenn., July 11, 1934; d. Robert Alexander and Clara Pauline (Fine) M.; m. Alan Paul Buchmann, Sept. 5, 1959. AB, Columbia U., 1956; LLB, Yale U., 1959. Bar: Conn. 1959, Ohio 1960, U.S. Dist. Ct. Conn. 1960, U.S. Supreme Ct. 1977, U.S. Dist. Ct. (no. dist.) Ohio 1961. Assoc. Goldstein & Peck, Bridgeport, Conn., 1959-60, Slough & Slough, Cleve., 1960-61, 63-66, Ginsberg, Guren & Meritt, Cleve., 1962; ptnr. Metzenbaum, Gaines, Finley & Stern, Cleve., 1967-71; assoc. prof. Cleve. State U., 1970-73, prof., 1973-94, interim dean and prof., 1987-88; vis. prof. U. Toledo, Ohio, 1976-77; v.p., dean Coll. Law, prof. Stetson U., 1994—; rev. authority on civil rights HEW, Washington, 1973-79; vis. prof. Nat. Law Ctr. George Washington U., 1981-82, U. Hawaii, Honolulu, 1988. Author: (books) Smith's Review of Corps, 1987, Smith's Review of Estates, 1987; contbr. articles to profl. jours. Pres. Cuyahoga County Econ. and Community Devel., Cleve., 1984-88, Task Force on Violent Crime, Cleve., 1987-88; chmn. audit com. Law Sch. Admission Coun., New Town, Pa., 1988-89, bd. trustees Law Sch. Admission Svc., 1989-94, exec. dir., 1991-93, pres. Law Sch. Admission Svc., 1991-93; commr. Ohio Ethics Commn., Columbus, Ohio, 1988-91, Ohio Pub. Defender Commn.; v.p., trustee Gt. Lakes Theatre Festival, Cleve., 1972-90; dir. Cleve. Growth Assn., 1987-88. Recipient New Frontier award Ams. for Dem. Action, 1977, YWCA Women of Distinction award, 1988, Josephine Irwin award, 1990; Day named in her honor, May 8, 1990, Cleve. Mem. ABA (chair non-profit corp. com. 1987-91, house of dels. 1994—, accreditation com. 1994—, bus. law sect., Glass Cutter award 1997), Assn. Am. Law Schs. (exec. com. 1977-81), Ohio State Bar Assn. (coun. of dels. 1981-91, Ohio Bar medal 1992, 93), Cleve. Bar Assn. (pres. 1987-88, meritorious svc. award 1987), Assn. Univ. Profs., Univ. Club, English Speaking Union (trustee 1986-89). Office: 1401 61st St S Saint Petersburg FL 33707-3246

MOODY, PATRICIA ANN, psychiatric nurse, artist; b. Oceana County, Mich., Dec. 16, 1939; d. Herbert Ernest and Dorothy Marie (Allen) Baesch; m. Robert Edward Murray, Sept. 3, 1960 (div. Jan. 1992); children: Deanna Lee Cañas, Adam James Murray, Tara Michelle Murray, Danielle Marie Murray; m. Frank Alan Moody, Sept. 26, 1992. BSN, U. Mich., 1961; MSN, Washington U., St. Louis, 1966; student, Acad. of Art, San Francisco, 1975-78. RN; lic. coast guard, ocean operator. Psychiat. staff nurse U. Mich., Ann Arbor, 1961-62, Langley-Porter Neuro-Psychiat. Inst., San Francisco, 1962-63; instr. nursing Barnes Hosp. Sch. Nursing, St. Louis, 1963; psychiat. nursing instr. Washington U., St. Louis, 1966-68; psychiat. nurse instr. St. Francis Sch. Nursing, San Francisco, 1970-71; psychiat. staff nurse Calif. Pacific Med. Ctr., San Francisco, 1991—; psychiat. staff nurse Charter Heights Behavioral Health Sys., Albuquerque, 1996-97; owner, cruise cons. Cruise Holidays Albuquerque, 1995—. Oil and watercolors included in various group exhbns., 1982-93. V.p. Belles-Fundraising Orgn., St. Mary's Hosp., San Francisco, 1974; pres. PTO, Commodore Sloat Sch., 1982. Recipient Honor award Danforth Found., 1954, Freshman award Oreon Scott Found., 1958; merit scholar U. Mich., 1957. Mem. San Francisco Women Artists (Merit award for oil painting 1989), Artist's Equity (bd. dirs. No. Calif. chpt. 1987-89, pres. No. Calif. chpt. 1990), Met. Club. Republican. Lutheran. Avocations: cycling, hiking, sailing, photography, piano. Home: 219 Spring Creek Ln NE Albuquerque NM 87122 Office: Cruise Holidays Albuquerque 11032 Montgomery Blvd NE Albuquerque NM 87111-3962

MOODY, RICK, collegiate basketball coach; b. Mobile, Ala., May 27, 1954; m. Sandra Morgan, 1976; 1 child, Ben. AA, Patrick Henry State C.C., 1974; BS, Troy State U., 1976; MA in Phys. Edn., U. Ala., 1982. Ninth grade basketball coach Clifford Meigs Jr. H.S., Shalimar, Fla., 1976-77; jr. varsity basketball coach Choctawhatchit H.S., Ft. Walton Beach, Fla., 1977-79; varsity boys basketball coach Ft. Walton Beach H.S., 1979-81; asst. women's basketball coach U. Ala., Tuscaloosa, 1981-84; varsity boys' basketball coach Guntersville (Ala.) H.S., 1984-89; head coach women's basketball U. Ala., 1989—. Named to Exch. Club Outstanding Alabamians Ct. Honor, 1994; coach of yr. Sporting News, 1996-97; gold medal winner U.S. Sports Festival, 1995. Avocations: fishing, public speaking, hunting. Office: U Ala PO Box 870393 Tuscaloosa AL 35487

MOODY, ROBERT ADAMS, neurosurgeon; b. b1. Swampscott, Mass., Oct. 1, 1934; s. George F. and Florence P. M.; m. Claudia; children: Robert Adams, II, Cathy, Paul, Lisa, Sherri. B.A., U. Chgo., 1955, B.S., 1956, M.D., 1960. Intern Royal Victoria Hosp., Montreal, Que., Can., 1960-61; resident in neurosurgery U. Vt. Affiliated Hosps., 1961-66; fellow Lahey Clinic, Boston, 1963-64; asst. prof. neurol. surgery U. Chgo. Med. Sch., 1966-71; sr. clin. instr., then asst. clin. prof. Tufts U. Med. Sch., 1972-74; prof. neurosurgery Abraham Lincoln Med. Sch., U. Ill., Chgo., 1975-81; chmn. div. neurosurgery Cook County Hosp., Chgo., 1974-81; assoc. chmn. dept. surgery Cook County Hosp., 1976-81; clin. prof. neurosurgery SUNY-Binghamton, 1983—; chmn. neurosurgery Guthrie Clinic, Sayre, Pa., 1981-95; ret., 1995. Contbr. articles med. jours. USPHS fellow, 1957-58. Mem. ACS, Am. Assn. Neurol. Surgeons, Pa. Neurosurg. Soc. (councillor 1986-87, pres.-elect 1988, pres. 1989), Mid-Atlantic Neurosurg. Soc., Ctrl. Neurosurg. Soc. (pres. 1978-79), Alumni Assn. Lahey Clinic Found., Sigma Xi. Office: Guthrie Clinic Guthrie Sq Sayre PA 18840

MOODY, ROBERT M., bishop; b. Balt., July 23, 1939; m. Lance Baty Martin; children: Leanne Moody Stoufer, Sharon Ruth Schechtel, Christian, Elizabeth. Grad., Rice Univ., 1962; postgrad. in law, U. Tex.; MDiv, Va. Theol. Seminary, 1966, DD, 1988. Rector St. James Ch., Riverton, Wyo., 1970-75, Grace Ch., Alexandria, Va., 1975-88; elected Bishop Coadjutor Diocese Okla., Oklahoma City, 1988-89, 4th diocesan bishop, 1989—. Office: 924 N Robinson Ave Oklahoma City OK 73102-5814*

MOODY, ROLAND HERBERT, retired librarian; b. Manchester, N.H., July 17, 1916; s. Louis and Alice (Heath) M.; m. Ethel Corwin, Aug. 20, 1939; children—Jonathan Corwin, Ellen Jane. A.B., Dartmouth, 1938; B.S. in L.S, Columbia, 1941. Asst. res. desk Dartmouth Library, 1938-39; asst. reference and circulation librarian Middlebury (Vt.) Coll. Library, 1939-40; gen. asst. Harvard Coll. Library, 1941-43, keeper collections, 1946-48; circulation librarian Lamont Library, 1948-53; dir. Northeastern U. Library, 1953-83, dean libraries and learning resources, 1975-83. Served with inf. AUS, 1943-45, ETO. Decorated Bronze Star. Mem. Am., Mass. library assns., Am. Assn. U. Profs. Conglist. (deacon).

MOODY, STANLEY ALTON, entrepreneur, financial consultant; b. Portland, Maine, Oct. 16, 1939; s. Alton Elwood and Mary Gwendolyn (Young) M.; m. Jo-Ann Newton Vercoe, Dec. 15, 1975 (dec. Apr. 1992); children: Karen Elizabeth, Kirt Edward, Leslie Ann; m. Barbara Marie Katkus, June 28, 1992; 1 child, Jonathan Edwards. BSEE, U. Maine, 1962; postgrad., George Washington U., 1963-66; MA in Theol. Studies, Gordon-Conwell Theol. Sem., 1994; postgrad., Trinity Theological Sem., 1995—. Ordained to ministry Am. Bapt. Chs. U.S.A., 1996. Various positions Eastman Kodak Co., Kelsey-Hayes Co., Components, Inc., 1962-73; prin. Stan Moody Assoc., Augusta, Maine, 1973—; pres. Newton and Moody, Inc., Portland, Maine, 1980-84, Family Bookstores of New Eng., Portland, 1973—; dir. bus. cons. Maine Devel. Found., 1984-86. Author: Entrepreneurship in Maine, 1985, Telecommunications Design Strategy for Maine, 1986, No Turning Back, 1989, I Will Walk Again, 1993. Candidate for Gov. Maine, 1978; pastor North Manchester Meeting House, 1994—; chmn. Greater Portland C. of C. Energy Awareness Task Force, 1977; budget com. Town of Manchester, 1995—; chmn. Manchester Comm. awards Spirit of Am. Found., 1996. Mem. Safari Club Internat. Maine (v.p. 1993, pres. elect 1994), N. Am. Hunt Club (life). Republican. Avocations: hunting, fly fishing, writing. Home: PO Box 240 Manchester ME 04351-0240 Office: Stan Moody Assoc 7 N Chestnut St Augusta ME 04330-5012

MOODY, WILLARD JAMES, SR., lawyer; b. Franklin, Va., June 16, 1924; s. Willie James and Mary (Bryant) M.; m. Betty Glenn Covert, Aug. 2, 1948; children: Sharon Paige Moody Edwards, Willard J. Jr., Paul Glenn. AB, Old Dominion U., 1946; LLB, U. Richmond, 1952. Bar: Va. 1952. Pres. Moody, Strople & Kloeppel Ltd., Portsmouth, Va., 1952—; commr. Chancery, Portsmouth, 1960—, Accounts, 1960—. Del. Va. Ho. of Reps., Portsmouth, 1956-68; senator State of Va., 1968-83; chmn. Portsmouth Dems., 1983—. Recipient Friend of Edn. award Portsmouth Edn. Assn., 1981. Mem. ABA, Va. Bar Assn., Portsmouth Bar Assn. (pres. 1960-61, lectr. seminars), Va. Trial Lawyers Assn. (pres. 1968-69), Hampton Roads C. of C. (bd. dirs. 1983-86), Portsmouth C. of C. (bd. dirs. 1960-61), Inner Circle Advs., VFW, Cosmopolitan Club, Moose. Home: 120 River Point Cres Portsmouth VA 23707-1028 Office: Moody Strople & Kloeppel Ltd 500 Crawford St Portsmouth VA 23704-3844

MOOERS, CHRISTOPHER NORTHRUP KENNARD, physical oceanographer, educator; b. Hagerstown, Md., Nov. 11, 1935; s. Frank Burt and Helen (Miner) M.; m. Elizabeth Eva Fauntleroy, June 11, 1960; children: Blaine Hanson MacFee, Randall Walden Lincoln. BS, U.S. Naval Acad., 1957; MS, U. Conn., 1964; PhD, Oreg. State U., 1969. Postdoctoral fellow U. Liverpool, Eng., 1969-70; assoc. prof. U. Del., Newark, 1976-78, prof., 1978-79; prof., chmn. dept. oceanography Naval Postgrad. Sch., Monterey, Calif., 1979-86; dir. Inst. Naval Oceanography, Stennis Space Ctr., Miss., 1986-89; sci. advisor to dir. Inst. for Naval Oceanography, 1989; rsch. prof. U. N.H., Durham, 1989-91; asst. prof. U. Miami, Fla., 1970-72, assoc. prof., 1972-76; prof., chmn. divsn. applied marine physics U. Miami, Fla., Fla., 1991-93, dir. Ocean Pollution Rsch. Ctr., 1992—; coord. Coastal Ocean Scis. Program, 1991—. Editor Jour. Phys. Oceanography, 1991-96; mng. editor Coastal and Estuarine Studies, 1978—. With USN, 1957-64. NSF fellow, 1964-67; NATO fellow, 1969-70; Sr. Queen Elizabeth fellow, 1980. Mem. AAAS, The Oceanography Soc. (interim councilor 1987-88), Am. Geophys. Union (pres. ocean sci. sect. 1982-84), Ea. Pacific Oceanic Conf. (chmn. 1979-86), U.S. Nat. Com. Internat. Union Geodesy and Geophysics (chmn. 1996—), U. Nat. Oceanog. Lab. Sys./Fleet Improvement Com. (chair 1994-97), Am. Meteorol. Soc. (chmn. sci. and tech. activities com. on the meteorology and oceanography of the Coastal Zone 1996—), Marine Tech. Soc., Sigma Xi. Achievements include pioneering direct observation of transient coastal ocean currents and fronts plus mesoscale and coastal ocean prediction rsch. Home: 2521 Inagua Ave Coconut Grove FL 33133-3811 Office: U Miami Divsn Applied Marine Physics RSMAS 4600 Rickenbacker Cswy Miami FL 33149-1031 *My central goal is to understand the ocean as a physical system by combining the interpretation of observations with dynamical theory and numerical models. Special emphasis has been on the dynamics of coastal oceans (continental shelf regions), now the scientific basis for practical mesoscale ocean prediction applied to marginal and semi-enclosed seas.*

MOOG, DONALD ANDREW, professional hockey player; b. Penticton, B.C., Can., Feb. 18, 1960. Hockey player Edmonton (Can.) Oilers, 1980, Boston Bruins, 1988-93, Dallas Stars, 1993—. Played in NHL All-Star game, 1985, 86, 91; co-recipient William M. Jennings trophy, 1989-90; mem. Stanley Cup championship teams, 1984, 85, 87. Office: care Dallas Stars 211 Cowboys Pkwy Irving TX 75063-5931

MOOMAW, RONALD LEE, economics educator; b. Orkney Springs, Va., Aug. 1, 1943; s. Leo V. and Vivian (Fansler) M.; m. Juliana Pendleton, Dec. 27, 1971; children: Sara Christina, Kate Winston. BS with highest distinction, U. Va., 1964; PhD, Princeton (N.J.) U., 1976. Vis. asst. prof. U. Va., Charlottesville, 1968-72; asst. prof., assoc. prof. econs. Okla. State U., Stillwater, 1972-83, prof., 1983—, head dept., 1987-93; sr. rsch. assoc. Urban Inst., Washington, 1980-81; vis. assoc. prof. U. B.C., Vancouver, Can., 1983-84; prof. bus. adminstrn. CBA Assocs., 1994—. Co-author: Profile of Oklahoma, 1977, Economics and Contemporary Issues, 1996; asst. editor Jour. of Econs., 1991—, Jour. of Regional Sci., 1994—; editl. bd. Internat. Regional Sci. Rev., 1995—; contbr. articles to profl. jours. Vestryman St. Andrew's Episcopal Ch., Stillwater, 1979-80, treas., 1990—; mem. budget com. Diocese of Okla., 1994—. Woodrow Wilson fellow, 1964, NSF fellow, 1964-66. Mem. Am. Econ. Assn., So. Econ. Assn. (bd. trustees 1989-91), Regional Sci. Assn., So. Regional Sci. Assn. (exec. com. 1985-87), Missouri Valley Econ. Assn. (pres.-elect 1995-96, pres. 1996-97). Office: Coll Bus Okla State U Stillwater OK 74078

MOON, DEBORAH JOAN, paralegal; b. Pine Bluff, Ark., Apr. 20, 1956; d. Fletcher Leon and Joann Talley (Shepherd); m. David Carlton Taylor, Apr. 7, 1989. BA in Sociology, U. So. Ill., Edwardsville, 1979; BS in Paralegal Studies, U. So. Ill., Carbondale, 1984. Paralegal/intern Kionka & Assocs, Carbondale, 1984; paralegal Roath & Brega, Denver, 1985-86, Bridges Young Matthews & Drake PLC, Pine Bluff, 1987—; Mem. S.E. Ark. Paralegal Adv. Com., 1996—. Vol. Area Agy. on Aging of S.E. Ark. Inc., Pine Bluff, 1992—; mem. pub. health and welfare com. City of Pine Bluff, 1997—; pres., bd. dirs. Jefferson County Humane Soc., 1996—. Mem. ABA, Nat. Assn. Legal Assts. (profl. devel. com. 1993-94, 96—, Affiliates award 1995), Ark. Assn. Legal Assts. (chmn. regional and membership coms. Ark chpt. 1991-94, 2d v.p. 1992-93, mem. exec. bd. dirs. 1991—, liaison to Nat. Assn. 1993-94, 1st v.p. 1994—, chmn. edn. and seminar com. 1994—, region 5 dir. 1996—), Ark. Assn. Bankruptcy Assts., Ark. Bar Assn. (paralegal com. 1996—). Avocation: raising and handling AKC boxers. Office: Bridges Young Et Al PO Box 7808 315 E 8th St Pine Bluff AR 71611

MOON, HARLEY WILLIAM, veterinarian; b. Tracy, Minn., Mar. 1, 1936; s. Harley Andrew Moon and Catherine Mary (Engesser) Lien; m. Irene Jeannette Casper, June 9, 1956; children: Michael J., Joseph E. Anne E. Teresa J. BS, U. Minn., 1958, DVM, 1960, PhD, 1965. Diplomate Am. Bd. Veterinary Pathologists. Instr. Coll. Vet. Medicine U. Minn., St. Paul, 1960-62, NIH postdoctoral fellow, 1963-65; vis. scientist Brookhaven Nat. Lab.,

Upton, N.Y., 1965-66; assoc. prof. Coll. Vet. Medicine U. Sask., Saskatoon, Can., 1966-68; rsch. vet. Nat. Animal Disease Ctr. Agrl. Rsch. Svc., USDA, Ames, Iowa, 1968-88, ctr. dir., 1988—; Franklyn Ramnsey chair in veterinary medicine & prof. Ames, Iowa; assoc. prof. Iowa State U., Ames, 1970-73, prof. 1973-74; cons. U. N.C., Chapel Hill, 1985-92, Pioneer Hy-Bred Internat., Johnson, Iowa, 1986-92. Contbr. articles reporting rsch. on animal diseases. Recipient Superior Svc. award USDA. Mem. NAS, Am. Coll. Vet. Pathologists, AVMA, Am. Soc. Microbiologists, AAAS, NAS, Sigma Xi, Phi Zeta. Avocation: farming. Home: 800 Shagbark Dr Nevada IA 50201-2702 Office: Iowa State University Veterinary Medicine Research Institute 1802 Elmwiid Dr Ames IA 50011*

MOON, HENRY, dean. BA in Geography, Va. Poly. Inst. and State U., 1978; MS in Geography, U. Ala., 1984; PhD in Geography, U. Ky., 1986. Edn. advisor Toledo Indsl., Recreation and Employee Svcs. Coun., Inc., 1995—; acad. advisor The Buckeye Ctr., 1994—; prof. geography and planning U. Toledo, 1986—, dean Univ. Coll., 1995—; cons., presenter and rschr. in field. Author: Environmental Geography Lab Manual, 1986, Environment Geography Lab Manual, 2d edit., 1990; co-author: A Workbook in Human Geography, 1987; contbr. chpts. to books and articles to profl. jours.; jour. article reviewer; software reviewer; manuscript reviewer; book reviewer; grant program reviewer, others. Advisor Area Growth Com., 1986-90, Ashland Ave. Revitalization Com., 1986—, Buckeye Basin Mgmt. Team, 1986—, City of Toledo, 1986—, Toledo Met. Area Coun. Govts., 1986—, Viva! Toledo, 1986-90, Collingwood Springs Redevel. Corp., 1987—, Com. of 100, 1987—, Heritage South Comml. Revitalization Assn., 1987—, Toledo-Lucas County Port Authority, 1987—, Archbold Area Schs., 1991—; mem. Toledo Met. Area Coun. of Govts. N.W. Ohio Strategic Planning Conf./Gen. Assembly, 1989; chair Toledo Met. Area Coun. Govts. Com. One, 1989-91, Toledo Met. Area Coun. Govts. Citizen Adv. Com., 1990-92, N.W. Ohio Passenger Rail Task Force, 1993; mem. Toledo Express Airport Master Planning Com., 1991-92, City of Toledo and Lucas County, Overall Econ. Devel. Planning Com., 1995—, City of Toledo Competitive Coun., 1995; trustee Arrowhead Park Assn.; trustee Arrowhead Park Assn., 1995—, Greater Toledo Conv. and Visitors Bur., 1996—. Recipient Most Outstanding Paper award 62nd Annual Meeting of the Ala. Acad. Sci., 1984, GM Vol. Spirit award, 1995, Buick Vol. Spirit award, 1995; grantee U. Ala. Student Govt. Assn., 1984, Ala. Acad. Sci., 1984, Collingwood Springs Redevel. Corp., 1987, U. Toledo Office of Rsch., 1987, Toledo-Lucas County Port Authority, 1988, Toledo Met. Area Coun. Govts., 1988, U.S. Dept. Energy, 1991, 92, 94, Williams County Econ. Devel. Corp., 1994, Environ. Sys. Rsch. Inst., Inc., 1995, Nat. Aero. and Space Adminstrn., 1996, many others. Mem. Ohio Acad. Sci. (v.p. geography sect. 1990-92), Assn. Am. Geographers (chair East Lakes divsn.), Am. Land Resource Assn. (charter mem. 1985-87), Toledo Area C. of C. (advisor 1986—). Office: Office of the Dean U Toledo Univ Coll 401 Jefferson Ave Toledo OH 43604-1063

MOON, JOHN HENRY, SR., banker; b. Van Buren, Ark., Aug. 19, 1937; s. B.R. and Alma (Witte) M.; m. Agnes Rose Dickens, Aug. 16, 1958; children: John Henry, Randall Allen. AA, Delmar Coll., Corpus Christi, 1956; BBA cum laude, Tex. A&M Univ., Kingsville, 1958. Sr. acct. Tex. Eastern Transp. Co. and subs., 1958-63; exec. v.p., dir. Houston Research Inst., 1963-68; sr. v.p., asst. to chmn. bd., dir. Main Bank, 1968; vice chmn. bd., dir. N.E. Bank, 1969; CEO, chmn. bd., dir. Pasadena (Tex.) Nat. Bank, 1970-81; gen. ptnr. Moon and Assocs., Ltd., 1977—; chmn. bd., pres. Interservice Life Ins. Corp., Phoenix, Cmty. Bank, Houston, 1975-81, Interstate Bank, Houston, 1977-81; chmn. bd., pres. Cmty. Capital Corp., Pasadena, 1975—, Peoples Bank, Houston, 1983-93; chmn. bd. Cmty. Nat. Bank, Friendswood, Tex., 1981-93; chmn. bd. Peoples Nat. Bank, Pasadena, Tex., 1984-93; dir. San Jacinto River Authority, 1991-93; chmn., pres. Sam Houston Pky. Transp. Corp., 1991—; bd. dirs. Harris County Indsl. Devel. Corp., 1996—, Pro Technologies, Inc., 1987-96. Past bd. dirs. Pasadena Heart Assn., Salvation Army, Tex. Assn. Prevention of Blindness; past chmn. City of Pasadena Bd. Devel.; past chmn. adv. bd. Pasadena Civic Ctr.; past dir. S.E. Econ. Devel., Inc. Named Outstanding Young Man of Yr., Pasadena Jr. C. of C., 1973; named to Pasadena Hall of Fame, 1988. Mem. AICPA, Pasadena C. of C. (bd. dirs. S.E. Econ. Devel., Citizen of Yr. 1994), Tex. Soc. CPAs, Tex. Bankers Assn., Rotary. Home: 3914 Peru Cir Pasadena TX 77504-2320 Office: PO Box 910 Pasadena TX 77501-0910

MOON, RONALD T. Y., state supreme court chief justice; b. Sept. 4, 1940; m. Stella H. Moon. B in Psychology and Sociology, Coe Coll., 1962; JD, U. Iowa, 1965. Bailiff, law clk. to Chief Judge Martin Pence U.S. Dist. Ct., 1965-66; dep. prosecutor City and County of Honolulu, 1966-68; assoc. Libkuman, Ventura, Ayabe, Chong & Nishimoto (predecessor firm Libkuman, Ventura, Moon & Ayabe), Honolulu, 1968-72, ptnr., 1972-82; judge 9th div. 1st cir., Cir. Ct., State of Hawaii, Honolulu, 1982-90; assoc. justice Supreme Ct., State of Hawaii, Honolulu, 1990-93; chief justice Supreme Ct., State of Hawaii, 1993—; apptd. arbitration judge 1st cir. cir. ct.; adj. prof. law U. Hawaii, 1986, 87, 88; lectr., guest spkr. numerous events. Mem. ABA, Hawaii Bar Assn., Assn. Trial Lawyers Am., Am. Bd. Trial Advocates (pres. 1986-93, nat. sec. 1989-91), Am. Inns of Cts. IV (bencher 1983—), Am. Judicature Soc.$DHawaii Trial Judges' Assn. (seminar orgn. com. 1987, exec. com. 1985-90, liaison supreme ct. 1990). Office: Supreme Ct Hawaii 417 S King St Honolulu HI 96813-2902

MOON, SAMUEL DAVID, medical educator; b. Westminster, S.C., June 14, 1949; s. David Smithson and Beverly Baines (Cook) M.; m. Jean Gibert, Aug. 10, 1971 (div. 1974); m. Robin Allene Dennett, Dec. 22, 1979; children: Miriah Michael Teeter, Ezra Smithson. BS, Wofford Coll., 1971; MD, Med. Coll. Va., 1975; MPH, U. N.C., 1990. Diplomate Am. Bd. Preventive Medicine, Am. Bd. Pain Medicine. mem. adv. bd. N.C. Ergonomics Resource Ctr., Raleigh, 1995—; mem. clin. faculty scis. coun. Duke U., Durham, N.C., 1995—; mem. adj. faculy dept. indsl. engring. N.C. State U. Editor: Beyond Biomechanics, 1996. Fellow Am. Acad. Family Physicians. Office: Duke U Med Ctr Box 2914 Durham NC 27710

MOONEY, JAMES DAVID, JR., security consultant; b. Anderson, Ind., May 20, 1921; s. James David and Jane (Watson) M.; m. Christine Mott, Dec. 29, 1944 (div. 1957); children: Barbara, James II, Richard; m. Gloria van Bomel Schoninger, Dec. 8, 1972. Student, U.S. Naval Acad., 1940-43; naval aviator, USN Flight Sch., 1943; BS in Engring., Princeton U., 1947. Cert. protection profl. Am. Soc. for Indsl. Security; lic. comml. pilot FAA. Supply mgr. Willys-Overland Motors, Inc., Maywood, Calif., 1947-50; contr. F.L. Jacobs Co. Inc., Detroit, 1953-55; spl. rep. U.S. Steel Export Co., Washington, 1956-61; mgr. internat. ops. Armour Rsch. Found., Chgo., 1962-65; v.p. CDC Sys., Elizabeth, N.J., 1972-74; pres. Cash Control Corp., Mineola, N.Y., 1974-77; cons. J.D. Mooney Assoc., Oyster Bay, N.Y., 1978—. Author: Long Range Planning, 1967. Police commr. Village of Centre Island, Oyster Bay, 1979-83, mayor, 1983-89. Lt. USN, 1940-45, 51-53. Mem. Internat. Assn. Chiefs of Police, N.Y. State Conf. Mayors, Aircraft Owners and Pilots Assn., Cove Neck Tennis Club, Piping Rock Club, N.Y. Yacht Club. Roman Catholic. Avocations: tennis, sailing. Home: 527 Centre Island Rd Oyster Bay NY 11771

MOONEY, JAMES HUGH, newspaper editor; b. Pitts., Aug. 18, 1929; s. James H. and Kathryn A. (Hall) M.; m. Eileen Jane Casey, July 30, 1960; children: Mark Hall, Sean Francis, Annina Marie, James Matthew, Lorelei Jane, Paul Adam, Kathryn Celeste. B.A. in Journalism, Duquesne U., Pitts., 1957. With advt. dept., then editorial dept. Pitts. Post-Gazette, 1953-61; writer-editor Nat. Observer, 1961-77, Nat. Geographic, 1977-79; editor Found. News mag., Washington, 1979-81; press sec. Congressman Mickey Edwards of Okla., Washington, 1982; asst. nat. editor Washington Times, 1982-83; editor Status Report, 1983-92; dir. info. resources Ins. Inst. for Hwy. Safety, 1992-93; editor Western Pa. Medicine, Johnstown, 1993-95, Embassy Flash, Aspen Hill, Md., 1995-96. Mem. editorial adv. bd. Nat. Study Ctr. Trauma and Emergency Med. Systems. Served with AUS, 1951-53. Mem. European Assn. Sci. Editors, Washington Automotive Press Assn., Nat. Press Club. Home: 13820 N Gate Dr Silver Spring MD 20906-2215

MOONEY, JOHN BRADFORD, JR., oceanographer, engineer, consultant; b. Portsmouth, N.H., Mar. 26, 1931; s. John Bradford and Margaret Theodora (Akers) M.; m. Martha Ann Huntley, Dec. 25, 1953 (dec. May 1990); children: Melinda Jean, Pamela Ann, Jennifer Joan; m. Jennie Marie Duca, Nov. 24, 1990. BS, U.S. Naval Acad., 1953; postgrad., George Washington U., 1970, 71, 76; grad. sr. execs. nat./internat. security, Harvard U., 1980. Commd. ens. USN, 1953, advanced through grades to rear adm., 1979; chief staff officer Submarine Devel. Group 1, 1971-73; commdr. Bathyscaphe Trieste II, 1964-66, Submarine Menhaden, 1966-68; comdg. officer Naval Sta., Charleston, S.C., 1973-75; dep. dir. Deep Submergence Systems Div., Office Chief Naval Ops., Washington, 1975-77; comdr. Naval Tng. Ctr., Orlando, Fla., 1977-78; dir. Total Force Planning Div., Office Chief Naval Ops., Washington, 1978-81; oceanographer USN, 1981-83, chief naval rsch., 1983-87, ret., 1987; pres. Harbor Br. Oceanographic Instn., Inc., Ft. Pierce, Fla., 1989-92, marine bd., 1991-94; mem. marine programs adv. coun. grad. sch. oceanography U. R.I., Narragansett, 1989—; chmn. study panel on undersea vehicles and nat. needs Nat. Rsch. Coun., 1993-96, mem. adv. com. for postdoctoral and sr. rsch. associateship programs, 1995—; mem. panel to visit the former Soviet Union to evaluate undersea tech. for U.S. govt., 1993, chair, 1995. At controls of Trieste II when hull of Thresher was found on floor of Atlantic, 1964; coordinated deep search and recovery of hydrogen bomb lost off coast of Spain, 1966; condr. recovery operation from depth of 16,400 feet in Mid-Pacific, 1972. Decorated Legion of Merit with 1 gold star; recipient spl. citation Armed Forces Recreation Assn., 1975, Dist. Eagle Scout award, 1986. Fellow Marine Tech. Soc. (pres. 1991-93), Explorers Club; mem. NAE, Am. Soc. Naval Engrs., U.S. Naval Inst., Nat. Geog. Soc., Smithsonian Assocs., Masons, Shriners, Order of DeMolay (Legion of Honor), Tau Beta Pi. Avocations: racquetball, sailing. Home and Office: 2111 Jeff Davis Hwy #1009S Arlington VA 22202

MOONEY, MARILYN, lawyer; b. Pitts., July 29, 1952; d. James Russell and Mary Elizabeth (Cartwright) M. BA summa cum laude, U. Pa., 1973, JD, 1976. Bar: Mass. 1977, D.C. 1985, Pa. 1990, U.S. Dist. Ct. D.C. 1985, U.S. Ct. Appeals (D.C. cir.) 1985, U.S. Supreme Ct. 1986. Atty. E. I. du Pont de Nemours & Co., Wilmington, Del., 1976-84, Washington, 1985; assoc. Fulbright & Jaworski L.L.P., Washington, 1985-90, ptnr., 1990—. Contbr. articles to profl. jours. Mem. ABA, Am. Soc. Corp. Secs., Fed. Regulation of Securities Com. (subcom. registration statements-1933 Act 1986—), Internat. Bar Assn. Office: Fulbright & Jaworski LLP 807 Pennsylvania Ave SE Washington DC 20003-2155

MOONEY, MICHAEL EDWARD, lawyer; b. Beloit, Wis., Jan. 21, 1945; s. William C. and Edith (Slothower) M. BA in Econs., St. Norbert Coll., 1966; JD, Boston Coll., 1969. Bar: Mass. 1969, Maine 1969, U.S. Tax Ct. 1975, U.S. Ct. Internat. Trade 1986. Assoc. Nutter, McClennen & Fish, LLP, Boston, 1969-77, sr. ptnr., 1978-89; mng. ptnr. Nutter, McClennen & Fish, Boston, 1989—; mem. exec. com. Fed. Tax Inst. New Eng., 1987—, v.p. and exec. dir., 1996—; spkr., lectr. numerous seminars. Co-editor: Considerations in Buying or Selling a Business, 1985; mem. bd. editors Accounting for Law Firms, 1988—. Bd. dirs. Lincoln and Therese Filene Found., Boston, 1991-97, Alliance Francaise of Boston, 1997, Internat. Bus. Ctr. New Eng., 1986-89; clk. U.S.S. Constn. Bicentennial Salute, Inc. Fellow Am. Coll. Tax Counsel; mem. Boston Bar Assn. (chmn. tax highlights com. 1986-95, mem. fin. com. 1990-92), Boston Tax Forum, Boston Ptnrs. in Edn. (lawyers fund com.), Artery Bus. Com. Office: Nutter McClennen & Fish 1 International Pl Boston MA 02110-2602

MOONEY, MICHAEL JOSEPH, college president; b. Evansville, Ind., Dec. 15, 1942; s. Joseph Thomas and Marie Louise (DeJean) M.; children: Susanne, Julia. AB summa cum laude, St. Meinard Coll., 1964; STL magna cum laude, Univ. Innsbruck, Austria, 1968; M in Philosophy, Columbia U., 1973, PhD, 1982. Lectr. dept. religious studies, St. Mary's U., Halifax, N.S., Can., 1968-70, Union Theol. Sem., N.Y.C., 1972-74; project coord. Columbia U., N.Y.C., 1973-74, preceptor dept. religion, 1975-76, spl. asst. to exec. v.p. for acad. affairs, 1976-77, asst. provost, 1977-79, assoc. provost, 1979-82, dep. provost, 1982-89; pres. Lewis and Clark Coll., Portland, Oreg., 1989—; visitor Inst. for Advanced Study, Princeton, N.J., 1984; trustee Jour. Philosophy, 1982—; bd. dirs. Nat. Asssn. Ind. Colls. and Univs., 1995—; mem. exec. com. NAICU, 1997; mem. Commn. Women in Higher Edn., Am. Coun. Aging, 1997—; mem. Commn. on Internat. Edn., Am. Coun. on Edn., 1993-95; bd. dirs. Reid Hall, Inc., N.Y.C. and Paris, 1977-89, v.p., 1983-89. Author: Vico in the Tradition of Rhetoric, 1985 (Gottschalk prize Am. Soc. 18th Century Studies 1985); editor: Renaissance Thought and Its Sources, 1979; co-editor: Toward a Theology of Christian Faith: Readings in Theology, 1968, Vico and Contemporary Thought, 1976, Small Comforts for Hard Times: Humanists on Public Policy, 1977. Bd. dirs. Roothbert Fund, 1980-92, Portland Opera Assn., 1992-93; trustee Scuola d'Italia, N.Y.C., 1986-90, World Affairs Coun., 1992—, Oreg. Ballet Theater, 1992—; mem. adv. com. Chamber Music N.W., 1990—. Recipient Rome prize Am. Acad. in Rome, 1989; Roothbert Fund fellow, 1970, Kent fellow Danforth Found., 1972, Woodrow Wilson fellow, 1972, Presdl. fellow Columbia U., 1972, F.J.E. Woodbridge Disting. fellow Columbia U., 1973; NEH grantee, 1984; Cavaliere Ufficiale, Order Merit, Republic of Italy, 1991. Fellow Italian Acad. for Advanced Studies in Am. (sr.); mem. Soc. for Values in Higher Edn., Am. Soc. for Eighteenth-Century Studies, Internat. Soc. for History of Rhetoric, Renaissance Soc. Am., Am. Acad. Religion, Am. Philos. Assn. Office: Lewis & Clark Coll Office of Pres 0615 SW Palatine Hill Rd Portland OR 97219-7879

MOONEY, RICHARD EMERSON, writer; b. Plainfield, N.J., Mar. 31, 1927; s. Wandell M. and Alice (Joy) M.; m. Elizabeth B. Coleman, Oct. 30, 1954; children: James C., Stephen E., John B. BA, Yale U., 1947; postgrad. (Nieman fellow), Harvard U., 1955-56. Writer United Press, N.Y.C., 1948-51; econ. reporter United Press, Washington, 1951-56, N.Y. Times, Washington, 1957-63; European econ. correspondent N.Y. Times, Paris, 1963-67; econ. reporter N.Y. Times, N.Y.C., 1967; asst. to exec. editor N.Y. Times, 1968, asst. to mng. editor, 1969, dep. fgn. editor, 1970-72, asst. fin. editor, 1972-76, mem. editl. bd., 1982-95; contbg. editor, 1995-96; v.p. Hartford Courant, 1976-81, exec. editor, 1976-81, dir., 1977-81. Author: (with Edwin L. Dale, Jr.) Inflation and Recession, 1959. Trustee Hartford Courant Found., 1977-81. Served with USNR, 1944-48. Mem. Yale Club (N.Y.). Home: 130 E 67th St New York NY 10021-6136 Office: NY Times 229 W 43rd St New York NY 10036-3913

MOONEY, ROBERT MICHAEL, ophthalmologist; b. Mt. Vernon, N.Y., July 25, 1945; s. Robert Michael and Marie Evelyn (sabatini) M.; m. Dorothy May Kazmaier, Feb. 21, 1981. BS in Biology, Fordham U., 1966; MD, U. Bologna, Italy, 1972. Diplomate Am. Bd. Ophthalmology. Intern Grasslands Hosp., Valhalla, N.Y., 1972-73; resident in surgery Grasslands Hosp., 1973-74; resident in ophthalmology N.Y. Med. Coll., Valhalla, 1974-76; chief resident ophthalmology N.Y. Med. Coll., 1976-77; acting dir. dept. ophthalmology Westchester County Med. Ctr., Valhalla, 1980-86; pvt. practice Katonah-Mt. Kisco, N.Y., 1979—; asst. clin. prof. ophthalmology N.Y. Med. Coll., Valhalla, 1982—. Fellow Am. Acad. Ophthalmology, Am. Coll. Surgeons; mem. Med. Soc. State of N.Y., Westchester County Med. Soc., Westchester Acad. Medicine (chmn. sect. ophthalmology 1987-89), MENSA. Republican. Roman Catholic. Avocations: travel, photography. Office: 51 Bedford Rd Katonah NY 10536-2135

MOONEY, WILLIAM PIATT, actor; b. Bernie, Mo., May 2, 1936; s. Lowell E. and Louise S. M.; m. Valorie Shaw Goodall, Jan. 13, 1962; children: Sean Goodall, William Norvell. Student Am. theater wing, U. Colo. pres. William Mooney Assocs., cons. to industry for exec. presentations. Appeared in continuing role of Paul Martin on TV series All My Children, 1972-85; one-man show Half Horse, Half Alligator & Damn Everything But the Circus; stage appearances: Brownsville Raid, We, A Man for All Seasons, Lolita; films: The Next Man, Network, A Flash of Green, Beer, Second Sight, C.A.T. Squad; author/star mus. play Banjo Reb and the Blue Ghost; co-author: ASAP-The Fastest Way to Create a Memorable Speech, 1992, Ready-to-Tell Tales, 1994, A Storyteller's Guide, 1995, (PBS) With a Dog's Eyes, 1997; recording artist: Why the Dog Chases the Cat, 1997 (ALA Notable Parent's Choice Gold and Naird awards). Dir. jazz mus. Jam. Grammy nominee, 1995. Address: 8 Brookside Ct East Brunswick NJ 08816-2611

MOONIE, CLYDE WICKLIFFE, financial consultant; b. San Francisco, May 23, 1918; s. William B. and Vivienne (Selby) M.; m. Liana Maria Gabrielli, June 18, 1949; children: Gregory James, Barbara Marie. M.B.A., U. Chgo., 1941. C.P.A., Calif. C.P.A., N.Y. Mgr. Arthur Andersen & Co., C.P.A.s, 1941-58; adminstrv. mgr. Marcona Mining Co. S.A., 1958-62; controller Minerals & Chems. Philipp Corp., 1962-67; v.p., controller Engelhard Minerals & Chems. Corp, N.Y.C.; (merger Minerals & Chems. Philipp Corp. and Engelhard Industries, Inc.), 1967-73, sr. v.p., 1973-76, exec. v.p., 1976-80; exec. v.p. Phibro-Salomon Inc. (formerly Engelhard Minerals & Chems. Corp.), 1981-82; exec. dir. Fin. Acctg. Standards Adv. Council, 1983-86; fin. cons., 1982—; mem. panel arbitrators Am. Arbitration Assn. Served to capt. AUS, 1942-45. Recipient Forbes gold medal Calif. C.P.A. Soc., 1945. Mem. Am. Inst. C.P.A.s, Fin. Execs. Inst. Home and Office: 4 Lafayette Ct Apt Ph Greenwich CT 06830-5301

MOONVES, LESLIE, television company executive; b. N.Y.C., Oct. 6, 1949; s. Herman and Josephine (Schleifer) M.; m. Nancy Wiesenfeld, Dec. 17, 1978; children: Adam, Sara, Michael. BA, Bucknell U., 1971. Devel. exec. Catalina Prodns., Burbank, Calif., 1980-81; v.p. devel. Saul Ilson Prodns. Columbia Pictures TV, Burbank, 1981-82; v.p. movies and miniseries 20th Century Fox, L.A., 1982-85, Lorimar, Inc., Culver City, 1985-87; exec. v.p. creative affairs Lorimar-Telepictures, Culver City, 1987-90; pres. Lorimar TV, Burbank, 1990-93, Warner Bros. TV, Burbank, 1993-95, CBS Entertainment, Los Angeles, 1995—. Developer, producer TV series including Dallas, Dark Justice, Guns of Paradise, Knots Landing, Midnight Caller, Sisters, Family Matters, Full House, Perfect Strangers, Family Man, I'll Fly Away, Reasonable Doubts, Step by Step, Hangin' with Mr. Cooper, the Jackie Thomas Show, Crossroads, Homefront, Going to Extremes, Shaky Ground, It Had to Be You, Time Trax, Against the Grain, Lois & Clark: The Adventures of Superman, Cafe Americain, How'd They Do That, Living Single, Family Album, Getting By. Bd. dirs. L.A. Free Clinic. Mem. Acad. TV Arts and Scis. (exec. com.), Hollywood Radio & TV Soc. (bd. dirs. 1988-91, pres. 1991). Democrat. Jewish. Office: CBS Entertainment 7800 Beverly Blvd Los Angeles CA 90036-2165*

MOOR, ANNE DELL, education director; b. Atlanta, Mar. 29, 1947; d. Kenneth Orman and Lida Louise (Springer) Dupree; m. Philip Ellsworth Moor, June 6, 1970; children: Andrew, Laura. BA, La Grange Coll., 1968. Cert. elem. edn. tchr., Tenn. Tchr. DeKalb County Bd. Edn., Atlanta, 1968-71, Briarcliff Bapt. Presch., Atlanta, 1972-73, Tates Sch., Knoxville, 1973-76; dir. after sch. care Cedar Springs Presbyn., Knoxville, 1993—. Discussion leader Bible Study Fellowship, Knoxville, 1980-93. Mem. Assn. for Childhood Edn. Internat., Tenn. Assn. for Young Children, Knoxville Area Assn. for Young Children. Presbyterian. Avocations: watercolor, hiking, needlework, vocal soloist. Office: Cedar Springs Presbyn Ch 9132 Kingston Pike Knoxville TN 37923-5227

MOOR, ROB, professional basketball team executive; b. Geneva, Switzerland; came to U.S., 1966; Degree, U. Calif., Irvine. Staff in distribution MGM Studios; staff in royalties, licensing and profits Twentieth Century Fox Studios; exec. v.p. Los Angeles Kings NHL; pres. Minn. Timberwolves, 1994—. Mem. Greater Minneapolis C. of C. (bd. dirs.). Office: Minn Timberwolves 600 1st Ave N Minneapolis MN 55403-1400*

MOOR, ROY EDWARD, finance educator; b. Riverside, Calif., Oct. 11, 1924; s. Hugh Erin and Clara Viola Moor; m. Beverly A. Colbroth, Aug. 29, 1959; children—Cynthia Ann, Sheryl Lynn. B.A., UCLA, 1949; Ph.D., Harvard U., 1958. Vice pres., chief economist Fidelity Bank, Phila., 1965-68; vice pres., chief economist Drexel Firestone, Phila., 1968-71, Warburg Paribas Becker, N.Y.C., 1971-81; sr. v.p., chief economist First Chgo. Corp., 1981-86; prof. fin. Ill. Inst. Tech., Chgo., 1986—; dir. Nat. Bur. Econ. Research, Cambridge, Mass. Author: Federal Budget as an Economic Document, 1962. Fellow Nat. Assn. Bus. Economists (pres. 1973). Home: 1013 Woodrush Ct Westmont IL 60561-8823 Office: Ill Inst Tech 10 W 31st St Chicago IL 60616-3729

MOORADIAN, ARSHAG DERTAD, physician, educator; b. Aleppo, Syria, Aug. 20, 1953; came to U.S., 1981; s. Dertad and Araxie (Halajian) M.; m. Deborah Lynn Miles, June 25, 1985; children: Arshag Dertad Jr., Ariana Araxie. BS, Am. U., Beirut, 1976, MD, 1980. Diplomate Am. Bd. Internal Medicine. Asst. prof. medicine UCLA, 1985-88; assoc. prof. U. Ariz., Tucson, 1988-91; prof. St. Louis U., 1991. Contbr. articles to Jour. Endocrinology, Diabetes, Jour. Gerontology, Neurochemistry Rsch. VA grantee, 1985—. Mem. Am. Fedn. Clin. Rsch., Gerontol. Soc. Am., Endocrine Soc., Am. Diabetes Assn. (chmn. task force on micronutreints 1990-91). Mem. Armenian Orthodox Ch. Achievements include identification of a potential biomarker of aging; research on age-related changes in the blood-brain barrier, on age-related changes in thyroid hormone action, on diabetes related changes in the central nervous system. Office: Saint Louis U Med Sch 1402 S Grand Blvd Saint Louis MO 63104-1004

MOORE, ACEL, journalist; b. Phila., Oct. 5, 1940; s. Jerry A. and Hura Mae (Harrington) Acel M.; m. Carolyn Weaver, June 1964 (div. 1974); 1 child, Acel; m. Linda Wright Avery, Aug. 6, 1988. Student, Settlement Music Sch., 1958, Charles Morris Price Sch., 1966-67. Copyboy Phila. Inquirer, 1962-64, editorial clk., 1964-68, staff reporter, 1968-80, editorial writer/columnist, 1980-81, assoc. editor, 1981—, also mem. edit. bd.; co-producer Black Perspective on the News (Nat. PBS weekly news program), 1972-78. Served with U.S. Army, 1959-62. Recipient Pulitzer prize, 1977, Robert F. Kennedy Journalism prize, 1977, Heywood Broun prize, 1977, Pa. Prison Soc. award, 1977, Humanitarian award House of Umoja, 1977, Community Service award Youth Devel. Center, 1976, Journalism award Phila. Party, 1977, Phila. Bar Assn. award, 1970, Ann. Paul Robeson award, 1977, Clarion award, 1977, Media award Mental Health Assn., 1977; Nieman fellow Harvard U., 1979-80. Mem. Nat. Assn. Black Journalists, Phila. Assn. Black Journalists (pres.), Am. Soc. Newspaper Editors, Sigma Delta Chi (Phila. chpt. Pub. Service awards 1972, 77, Reporting award 1977). Office: Phila Inquirer PO Box 8263 400 N Broad St Philadelphia PA 19101-4015*

MOORE, ALBERT CUNNINGHAM, lawyer, insurance company executive; b. Miami, Fla., May 31, 1931; s. Elias Richard and Virginia Adelaide (Thompson) M.; m. Anne Cambreleng Bonynge, Aug. 24, 1957; children: Emily Robinson French, Barbara Raffield Walton, Catherine Anne Bonynge Wells. A.B., U. N.C., 1953; J.D., U. Va., 1959. Bar: N.Y. 1960. Atty. White & Case, N.Y.C., 1959-69; corporate sec. Studebaker-Worthington, Inc., N.Y.C., 1969-72; sr. v.p., gen. counsel Crum & Forster, 1973-87. Former trustee N.J. Shakespeare Festival; former bd. dirs. DeBordieu Property Owners Assn., Debordieu Arch. Rev. Bd. With USNR, 1953-56. Mem. ABA, Wilton Ctr. Tennis Club (N.H.), DeBordieu Club (S.C.), Phi Alpha Delta, Chi Phi. Home: 1318 Debordieu Blvd Georgetown SC 29440

MOORE, ALBERT LAWRENCE, investment company executive, investment broker; b. Marion, Ind., Feb. 12, 1956; s. John Calvin and Alta Marie (Glandt) M.; m. Diane Kay Poe, Feb. 28, 1982; children: Wesley Calvin, Lisa Michelle. BA, Ind. U., Kokomo, 1978. Claims rep. Social Security Adminstrn., 1978-83; from investment broker to v.p. J.J.B. Hilliard W.L. Lyons, Inc., Greensburg, Ind., 1983—. Pres. Decatur County Dem. Club, Greensburg, 1984-89, Decatur County United Fund, 1989-90; chmn. Greensburg Dem. Com., 1987; vice chmn. Decatur County Dem. Ctrl. Com., 1993-97; bd. dirs. Decatur County Meml. Hosp., chmn. bd., 1991-94, vice chair, 1996—; mem. Decatur County Election Bd., 1990—; mem. local coordinating com. Gov.'s Coun. for Drug Free Ind., 1991-93. Mem. Masons, Scottish Rite, Indpls. Urban League, Interfaith Alliance. Presbyterian. Avocations: stamp collecting, politics, investments, European history. Home: 807 E Erdmann Rd S Greensburg IN 47240-8661 Office: JJB Hilliard WL Lyons Inc 101 E Main St Greensburg IN 47240-2031

MOORE, ALDERINE BERNICE JENNINGS (MRS. JAMES F. MOORE), association and organization administrator; Sacramento, Apr. 17, 1915; d. James Joseph and Elise (Thomas) Jennings; BA, U. Wash., 1941; m. James Francis Moore, Aug. 14, 1945. Sec. to div. Plant supr. Pacific Tel. & Tel. Co., Sacramento, 1937-39; exec. sec. Sacramento Community Chest Fund Raising Dr., 1941; sec. USAAF, Mather Field, Sacramento, 1942; statistician Calif. Western States Life Ins. Co., 1943; treas. Women's Aux. Stranger's Hosp., Rio de Janeiro, Brazil, 1964-65. Vice pres. Douglaston (N.Y.) Women's Club, 1955; mem. Douglaston Garden Club, 1951-55; pres. Nina Opland chpt. Women's Cancer Assn. U. Miami, 1960-61; corr. sec. Coral Gables (Fla.) Garden Club, 1960-62; pres. Miami Alumnae Club of Pi Beta Phi, 1961-62; mem. Putnam Hill chpt. D.A.R., Greenwich Conn., 1967-75, Palm Beach chpt., 1978—; mem. Woman's Club, Greenwich, Conn., 1967-75; mem. Women's Panhellenic Assn., Miami, 1961-62; internat. treas.

Ikebana Internat., Tokyo, Japan, 1966-67, parliamentarian Tokyo chpt., 1966-67, N.Y. chpt., 1968-69; mem. Coll. Women Assn. Japan, 1965-66; mem. Tchrs. Assn. Sogetsu Sch. Japanese Flower Arranging, 1966—, Atlantis Golf Club. Served to 1st.lt. WAVES, 1943-45. Mem. Internat. Platform Assn., AAUW, Pi Beta Phi (local v.p. alumnae club 1969-71). Baptist. Club: Steamboat Investment (pres. 1972-73). Home: 316 Fairway Ct Atlantis FL 33462

MOORE, ALFRED ANSON, corporate executive; b. Muttontown, N.Y., Oct. 1, 1925; s. Benjamin Moore and Alexandra (Emery) McKay; m. Sarah Carolyn Rush, July 1954 (div. 1973); m. Betty Ruth Teipel, July 19, 1974; children: Jeremiah, Alexandra. BA, Yale U., 1946; postgrad., Harvard U., 1946-47. Reporter, re-writer Bergen Evening Record, Hackensack, N.J., 1948-49; v.p. Emery Kunston, Cin., 1961-62; pres. Profl. Realty Service, Cin., 1967, Emery Realty, Cin., 1969; dir. Thomas Emery's Sons, Inc., Cin., 1949—; pres. Chelsea Moore Corp., N.Y. and Cin., 1953-91, chmn. bd., 1979—; trustee various personal trusts, Ohio, Maine, Pa., 1969—, ptnr. various real property devels., Ohio, S.C., Colo., 1964—; executor Estate of Alexandra E. McKay, Monticello, Fla., 1983-89; co-chmn. Emery Ctr. Corp., 1987—. Chmn. bd. Contemporary Arts Ctr., Cin., 1977-80, trustee, 1972—; chmn. Save the Terminal, Cin., 1972-73; trustee, sec. Community Improvement Corp., Cin., 1975—; trustee Am. Farm Sch., Thessaloniki, Greece, 1980-83, Seven Hills Sch., 1987-92, Nat. Dropout Prevention Fund., 1988-90; trustee, v.p. Miami Purchase Assn., Cin., 1962-67, 87-90. Lt. (j.g.) USNR, 1943-46, ETO, PTO. Named Benefactor, City Mgr., Cin., 1968. Mem. Soc. Colonial Wars, Camargo Club, Racquet Club, Mason. Republican. Avocations: squash, shooting, fishing. Office: Carew Tower 2300 Carew Tower 441 Vine St Cincinnati OH 45202-2800

MOORE, AMY NORWOOD, lawyer; b. Durham, N.C., Sept. 24, 1953. AB summa cum laude, Mt. Holyoke Coll., 1976; MA, U. Va., 1978, JD, 1983. Bar: D.C. 1984, U.S. Ct. Appeals (D.C. and 6th cirs.) 1985. Law clk. to Frank M. Coffin, U.S. Ct. Appeals (1st cir.), 1983-84; ptnr. Covington & Burling, Washington. Articles editor Va. Law Rev., 1982-83. Mem. Phi Beta Kappa. Office: Covington & Burling PO Box 7566 1201 Pennsylvania Ave NW Washington DC 20044-7566

MOORE, ANDREA S., state legislator; b. Libertyville, Ill., Sept. 2, 1944. Attended, Drake U. m. William Moore; 3 children. Mem. Ill. Ho. of Reps., 1993—; mem. com. on elections and state govt., mem. com. on aging, mem. cities and villages com., mem. environ. and energy com., mem. labor and commerce com., mem. com. on healthcare, mem. revenue and commerce com. Republican. Home: 361 S Saint Marys Rd Libertyville IL 60048-9407 Office: Ill Ho of Reps State Capitol Springfield IL 62706 also: 2014-H Stratton Bldg Springfield IL 62706 also: 733 N Milwaukee Ave Libertyville IL 60048-1913*

MOORE, ANDREW GIVEN TOBIAS, II, investment banker, educator; b. New Orleans, Nov. 25, 1935; m. Ann Elizabeth Dawson, June 5, 1965; children—Cecily Elizabeth, Marianne Dawson. B.B.A., Tulane U., 1958, J.D., 1960. Bar: La. 1960, Del. 1963. Law clk. to chief justice Del. Dover, 1963; assoc. firm Killoran & Van Brunt, Wilmington, Del., 1964-70; partner Killoran & Van Brunt, 1971-76; partner firm Connolly, Bove & Lodge, Wilmington, 1976-82; justice Del. Supreme Ct., Wilmington, 1982-94; sr. mng. dir. Wasserstein Perella & Co., Inc., N.Y.C., 1994—; mem. Del. Bar Examiners, 1975-82; mem. Del. Gen. Corp. law com., 1969-83; chmn. joint com. Del. Bar Assn.-Del. Bankers Assn., 1978-79; chmn. Del. Jud. Proprieties Com., 1983-94, Del. Bench and Bar Conf., 1988-94; trustee Del. Bar Found., 1984-94; faculty Tulane Inst. European Legal Studies, Paris Inst., 1990—; adj. prof. law Georgetown U. Law Ctr., Widener U. Sch. Law, U. Iowa Coll. Law; guest lectr. law Tulane U., U. Toronto, Can., U. Tex., Villanova U., Washington U., St. Louis, U. Iowa, George Mason U., DeVrije U. van Brussel, Cath. U. Louvain La Neuve; mem. pres.'s coun. Tulane U., 1990—; chmn. Tulane Corp. Law Inst., 1988-95; Lehmann disting. vis. prof. law Washington U., St. Louis, 1994, 96; Mason Ladd disting. vis. prof. U. Iowa, 1995; disting. vis. prof. law St. Louis U., 1995, 96. Trustee Del. Home and Hosp. for Chronically Ill, Smyrna, 1966-70, chmn., 1966-69; mem. New Castle County Hist. Rev. Bd., Wilmington, 1974-82; mem. Del. Ctrs. Planning Com., 1982-94; dean's coun. Tulane U. Law Sch., 1988—; bd. visitors Walter F. George Sch. Law, Mercer U., 1985-91, chmn., 1988-90. With JAGC, USAF, 1960-63. Mem. ABA, La. Bar Assn., Del. Bar Assn. (v.p. 1976-77, exec. com. 1982-83), Am. Judicature Soc. (bd. dirs. 1982-86), Order Barristers, Phi Delta Phi, Delta Theta Phi (hon.), Omicron Delta Kappa. Democrat. Presbyterian. Office: Wasserstein Perella & Co 31 W 52nd St New York NY 10019-6118

MOORE, ANDREW TAYLOR, JR., banker; b. Tarboro, N.C., June 17, 1940; s. Andrew Taylor and Mary Dare (Allsbrook) M. BA in History, Duke U., 1962; LLB, U.Va., Charlottesville, 1965. Asst. sec. Signet Banking Corp., Richmond, 1965-71, asst. v.p., corporate sec., 1971-75, v.p., corporate sec., 1975-82, sr. v.p., corporate sec., 1982-94. Bd. dirs. Theatre IV, Richmond, Va., 1981—, Va. State YMCA adv. coun., Lynchburg, 1988—; trustee Hist. Richmond Found., 1993—. With U.S. Army, 1967. Mem. Va. Hist. Soc. (pres. coun. 1995—), Commonwealth Club. Presbyterian. Avocations: jogging; gardening; travel. Home: 2011 Hanover Ave Richmond VA 23220-3539

MOORE, ANN S., magazine publisher; b. McLean, VA, 1950; d. Monty and Bea Sommovigo; m. Donovan Moore; 1 son, Brendan. MBA, Harvard U., 1978. With Time, Inc., New York, NY, 1978—; founding publisher Sports Illustrated For Kids, 1989-91; publisher People Weekly, 1991-94, pres., 1994—. Office: People Magazine Rockefeller Ct Time & Life Building New York NY 10020-1393*

MOORE, ANNE, physician; b. N.Y.C., Apr. 28, 1944; d. John D.J. and Mary Foote Moore; m. Arnold L. Lisio, Sept. 6, 1969; children: Philip Moore, Mary Foote. BA, Smith Coll., 1965; MD, Columbia U., 1969. Diplomate Am. Bd. Internal Medicine, Am. Bd. Hematology (chmn. 1996), Am. Bd. Oncology. Intern dept. medicine N.Y. Hosp., N.Y.C., 1969-73, assoc. attending physician, 1981-95, attending physician, 1996—; postdoctoral fellow Rockefeller U., 1972-73, hematology-oncology fellow, 1973-75; asst. prof. medicine Cornell U. Med. Coll., N.Y.C., 1975-91, assoc. prof. clin. medicine, 1981-95, prof. clin. medicine, 1996—; cons. Strang Cancer Prevention Ctr.; lectr., cons., in field. Author: Patient's Guide to Breast Cancer Treatment, 1992, rev. edit., 1997; ad hoc reviewer Am. Jour. Clin. Oncology, 1994, New Eng. Jour. Medicine, 1994, 96, 97; contbr. articles to profl. jours., chpts. to books. Trustee St. David's Sch., 1983-89, HealthCare Chaplaincy, Inc., 1991—; bd. dirs. Camilli Found., 1990—, Cure Myeloma Fund, 1988—. Recipient award SHARE, 1992, Wholeness of Life award Hosp. Chaplaincy, 1992, Alumnae award Oak Knoll Sch., 1994, Eileen Dreyer Meml. Lectureship award Sass Found. for Med. Rsch., 1996, Commendation award Office of Exec. Nassau County, 1996. Mem. Am. Soc. Hematology, Am. Soc. Clin. Oncology, N.Y. Acad. Scis., Soc. for Study of Blood (membership chmn. 1979-80), N.Y. Met. Breast Cancer Group (membership chmn. 1992-93, sec.-treas. 1993-95, v.p. 1995-96), Soc. for Study of Breast Disease, N.Y. Cancer Soc. Office: Cornell U Med Coll 428 E 72nd St New York NY 10021-4635

MOORE, BEATRICE, religious organization administrator; b. Somerville, Mass., Oct. 6, 1928; d. George and Christina Turner; m. Wendell Moore, May 9, 1953; children: Karl C., Linda Moore Flewelling, Diane Pearl, Larry. BS in Theology and English, Berkshire Christian Coll., Lenox, Mass., 1950. Pres. The Woman's Home and Foreign Mission Society, Loudon, N.H.; nat. pres. The Woman's Home and Foreign Mission Society, Charlotte, N.C. Sunday sch. tchr., deaconess Loudon Ridge Family Bible Ch.; active Women's Home and Fgn. Mission Soc., Loudon, past pres. N.H. Soc., past pres. ea. region; hostess, contact chmn., Bible club guide Stonecroft Ministries; past leader 4-H Club. Office: Woman's Home & Foreign Mission 845 Loudon Ridge Rd Loudon NH 03301-1712

MOORE, BENJAMIN, theatrical producer; b. Boston, Oct. 25, 1945; s. Charles Frederick and Adeline Reeves (Nichols) M.; m. Mary Bradford Paine, May 31, 1969 (div. Jan. 1982); children: Alexandra Paine, Brendan Adams; m. Barbara Ann Dirickson, June 25, 1983; children: Lillian, Richard Braden. BA, Dartmouth U., 1967; MFA, Yale U., 1970. Asst. mng. dir. Yale Repertory Theatre, New Haven, 1969-70; gen. mgr. Westport (Conn.) Country Playhouse, 1970; prodn. dir. Am. Conservatory Theatre, San Francisco, 1970-79, gen. mgr., 1979-81, mng. dir., 1981-85; mng. dir., bd. dirs. Seattle Repertory Theatre, 1985—. Active Seattle Arts Commn., 1986-90, chair, 1989. Mem. Wash. State Arts Alliance (bd. dirs. 1985—), League Resident Theatres (mem. exec. com. 1986—), Rainier Club. Office: Seattle Repertory Theatre 155 Mercer St Seattle WA 98109-4639*

MOORE, BETTY JEAN, retired education educator; b. L.A., Apr. 4, 1927; d. Ralph Gard and Dora Mae (Shinn) Bowman; m. James H. Moore, Nov. 25, 1944 (div. 1968); children: Barbara, Suzanne, Sandra; m. George W. Nichols, Oct. 15, 1983. BA, Pasadena Coll., 1957; MA, U. Nev., 1963; PhD, U. Ill., 1973. Tchr. Calif. Elem. Schs., 1953-63; sec. tchr. Calif. pub. schs., 1963-68; asst. prof. Ea. Ill. U., Charleston, 1968-71; grad. teaching asst. U. Ill., Champaign, 1971-73; asst. prof. to assoc. prof. S.W. Tex. State U., San Marcos, 1973-83, prof. edn., 1983-89, ret., 1989, prof. emeritus, 1995—; sch. evaluator; cons. in field; reading clinic dir. S.W. Tex. State U., 1974-85; cons. Min. Edn., Rep. of Singapore, 1980, 97. Contbr. articles to profl. jours.; author: Teaching Reading, 1984; producer/dir. 5 ednl. videos. Active fund raising various charitable orgns. Mem. Internat. Reading Assn. (chpt. pres. 1964-65), Nat. Council Tchrs. English, AAUP. Presbyterian. Avocations: reading, writing, swimming, cooking. Office: Southwest Tex State U C & I Dept San Marcos TX 78666

MOORE, BEVERLY COOPER, lawyer; b. Greensboro, N.C., Dec. 8, 1909; s. Adolphus Greene and Georgia (Cooper) M.; m. Irene Warren Mitchell, July 10, 1943; children: Beverly Cooper Jr., Irene Warren Moore Miller. AB, U. N.C., 1931; JD, Yale U., 1934. Bar: N.C. 1934, U.S. Dist. Ct. N.C. 1934, U.S. Ct. Appeals (4th cir.) 1954, U.S. Supreme Ct. 1945. Practice law Greensboro, 1934—; ptnr. Smith, Helms Mulliss & Moore (and predecessors), 1946-94, ptnr. emeritus, 1995—; mem. N.C. Gen. Assembly, 1941-42. Contbr. to legal publs. Trustee Consol. U. N.C., 1967-72; chmn. bd. trustees U. N.C.-Greensboro, 1972-75. Served with USAAF, 1942-45. Fellow Am. Bar Found.; mem. ABA (ho. of dels. 1962-68, 73-75, 76-80, bd. govs. 1970-73), N.C. Bar Assn. (pres. 1958-59), Greensboro Bar Assn. (pres. 1949-50), Assn. of Bar of City of N.Y., Internat. Bar sssn., Am. Coll. Trial Lawyers, Practising Law Inst. (trustee 1965-72), Am. Judicature Soc. (bd. dirs. 1964-67), Am. Law Inst., Fed. Jud. Conf., Am. Counsel Assn. (pres. 1970-71), Inst. Jud. Adminstrn., Nat. Center Adminstrv. Justice (dir. 1979-81, chmn. 1981-82), Southeastern Legal Found. (chmn. legal adv. bd. 1979-87), SAR, Phi Beta Kappa, Selden Soc. (London). Episcopalian. Clubs: Sedgefield Country, Greensboro City, Greensboro Country. Home: 906 Country Club Dr Greensboro NC 27408-5602 Office: PO Box 21927 Greensboro NC 27420-1927

MOORE, BOB STAHLY, communications executive; b. Pasadena, Calif., July 3, 1936; s. Norman Hastings and Mary Augusta (Stahly) M. Student, U. Mo., 1954-58, MIT, 1958-62. News dir. WPEO, Peoria, Ill., 1958-60, KSST, Davenport, Iowa, 1960-62, WIRE, Indpls., 1962-64, WCFL, Chgo., 1964-67; White House corr. Metromedia, Inc., Washington, 1967-71; news dir. Gateway Communications, Altoona, Pa., 1972-74; Washington Bur. chief MBS, 1974-76; v.p. news MBS, Arlington, Va., 1976-78; White House corr. MBS, 1978-81; dir. communications Fed. Home Loan Bank Bd., Washington, 1981-85; spl. asst. to bd. govs. Fed. Res. System, Washington, 1985—. Active ARC. Served with USAF, 1961-63. Recipient profl. awards Ind. News Broadcasters, 1963, Ill. News Broadcasters, 1965, UPI, 1960, 63, 65, AP, 1956, 58, 61, 65, 67, Mo. News Broadcasters, 1956, 61. Mem. Radio and Television News Dirs. Assn. (Profl. award), White House Corrs. Assn., State Dept. Corrs. Assn., Radio-Television Corrs. Gallery (U.S. Capitol), Chgo. Council on Fgn. Relations, Pub. Relations Soc. Am., Nat., Washington, Chgo. press clubs, U.S. Jr., Mo., Ill. chambers commerce, Sigma Delta Chi. Presbyterian. Home: 817 Crescent Dr Alexandria VA 22302-2214 Office: 20th and Constitution NW Washington DC 20551

MOORE, BOBBIE FAY, geriatrics nurse practitioner, nurse administrator; b. Woodward, Okla., Jan. 21, 1943; d. Marion Byron and Lelah Catherine (Anderson) Carey; m. Donald Kent Strickland, Apr. 2, 1959 (div. June 1968); children: Donald, Michael; m. Myrl Lynn Moore, Apr. 15, 1988. ADN, N.Mex. State U., Carlsbad, 1983; geriatric nurse practitioner, U. Colo., Denver, 1985. Cert. geriatric nurse practitioner, Am. Nurses Credentialing Ctr., N.Mex. Charge nurse Landsun Homes, Carlsbad, 1971-76; office nurse Dr. C. Munkers, Marquette, Mich., 1976-78; staff and treatment rm. nurse Guadalupe Med. Ctr., Carlsbad, 1978-83; nursing supr., nurse practitioner Landsun Homes, Carlsbad, 1985—, lic. nursing home adminstr., 1990—; mem. nursing adv. bd. N.Mex. State U., 1985—. Tchr. Sunday sch. Meth. Ch., Carlsbad; treas. Continuing Edn. Commn., Carlsbad, 1988—; counselor Boy Scouts Am., Carlsbad, 1989—; youth spnosor 1st United Meth. Ch., Carlsbad, 1990—. Mem. N.Mex. Nurse Practitioner Coun. Avocations: reading, walking. Home: 1401 Chico Dr Carlsbad NM 88220-5231

MOORE, BOBBY See RASHAD, AHMAD

MOORE, BRADFORD L., lawyer; b. Brownfield, Tex., Feb. 9, 1952; s. Billie Buell and Jimmy (Green) M.; m. Carmelita Chaffin, June 20, 1971; children: April V., Ashli F. BA, Tex. Tech U., 1974, JD, 1977. Bar: Tex. 1978, U.S. Dist. Ct. (no. dist.) Tex. 1978, U.S. Dist. Ct. (we. dist.) Tex. 1987, U.S. Supreme Ct. 1987. V.p. McGowan & McGowan PC, Brownfield, 1978-90; pvt. practice, Brownfield, 1990—. Pres. Brownfield Little Girls Basketball, 1987-90. Recipient award for outstanding representation of abused children Tex. Dept. Human Svcs., 1984. Mem. Brownfield Bar Assn. (social chmn. 1980—), Rotary (sgt.-at-arms Brownfield 1980-81), Kiwanis (pres. Brownfield 1984-86). Office: PO Box 352 Brownfield TX 79316-0352

MOORE, BRIAN, writer; b. Belfast, No. Ireland, Aug. 25, 1921; came to U.S., 1960; s. James Bernard and Eileen (McFadden) M.; m. Jean Denney, Oct. 1967; 1 son, Michael. Author: The Lonely Passion of Judith Hearne, 1955, The Feast of Lupercal, 1957, The Luck of Ginger Coffey, 1960, An Answer From Limbo, 1962, The Emperor of Ice-Cream, 1965, I Am Mary Dunne, 1968, Fergus, 1970, The Revolution Script, 1971, Catholics, 1972, The Great Victorian Collection, 1975, The Doctor's Wife, 1976, The Mangan Inheritance, 1979, The Temptation of Eileen Hughes, 1981, Cold Heaven, 1983, Black Robe, 1985, The Color of Blood, 1987, Lies of Silence, 1990, No Other Life, 1993, The Statement, 1995, The Magician's Wife, 1997, (screenplays) Catholics, The Luck of Ginger Coffey, Torn Curtain, Control, The Blood of Others, Black Robe. Recipient Que. Lit. prize, 1958, U.S. Nat. Arts and Letters award, 1961, Fiction award Gov.-Gen. Can., 1961, 75, W.H. Smith award, 1973, James Tait Black Meml. award, 1975, Heinemann award Royal Soc. Lit., 1986, Sunday Express Book of Yr. award, 1987, Lifetime Achievement award L.A. Times, 1994; Guggenheim fellow, 1959; Can Coun. sr. fellow, 1962, 76; Scottish Arts Coun. Internat. fellow, 1983. Office: care Curtis Brown 10 Astor Pl New York NY 10003-6935

MOORE, BROOKE NOEL, philosophy educator; b. Palo Alto, Calif., Dec. 2, 1943; s. Ralph Joseph and Dorothy Louise (Noll) M.; children: Sherry, Bill. BA, Antioch Coll., 1966; PhD, U. Cin., 1973. Asst. prof. Calif. State U., Chico, 1970-74, assoc. prof., 1974-79, prof., 1980—. Author: Philosophical Possibilities Beyond Death, 1981; co-author: Critical Thinking, 1987, 5th edit., 1997, The Power of Ideas, 1990, 3rd edit., 1995, The Cosmos, God and Philosophy, 1992, Moral Philosophy, 1993, The Power of Ideas: A Brief Edition, 1995, Making Your Case, 1995; mem. editl. bd. Tchg. Philosophy, 1972. Mem. Am. Philos. Assn. Office: Calif State U Chico Dept of Philosophy Chico CA 95929

MOORE, C. BRADLEY, chemistry educator; b. Boston, Dec. 7, 1939; s. Charles Walden and Dorothy (Lutz) M.; m. Penelope Williamson Percival, Aug. 27, 1960; children—Megan Bradley, Scott Woodward. B.A. magna cum laude, Harvard U., 1960; Ph.D., U. Calif., Berkeley, 1963. Predoctoral fellow NSF, 1960-63; asst. prof. chemistry U. Calif., Berkeley, 1963-68, assoc. prof., 1968-72, prof., 1972—, vice chmn. dept., 1971-75, chmn. dept. chemistry, 1982-86, dean Coll. Chemistry, 1988-94; professeur associé Faculté des Scis., Paris, 1970, 75; Miller Rsch. Prof. U. Calif., Berkeley, 1972-73, 87-88; vis. prof. Inst. for Molecular Sci., Okazaki, Japan, 1979, Fudan U., Shanghai, 1979, adv. prof., 1988—; vis. fellow Joint Inst. for Lab. Astrophysics, U. Colo., Boulder, 1981-82; faculty sr. scientist Lawrence Berkeley Nat. Lab., 1974—; mem. editl. bd. Jour. Chem. Physics, 1973-75, Chem. Physics Letters, 1980-85, Jour. Phys. Chemistry, 1981-87, Laser Chemistry, 1982—. Editor: Chemical and Biochemical Applications of Lasers; assoc. editor Annual Review of Physical Chemistry, 1985-90; contbr. articles to profl. jours. Trustee Sci. Svc., Inc., 1995—. Recipient Coblentz award, 1973, E.O. Lawrence Meml. award U.S. Dept. Energy, 1986, Lippincott award, 1987, 1st award Inter-Am. Photochem. Soc., 1988; nat. scholar Harvard U., 1958-60; fellow Alfred P. Sloan Found., 1968, Guggenheim Found., 1969, Humboldt Rsch. award for Sr. U.S. Scientists, 1994. Fellow AAAS, Am. Acad. Arts and Scis., Am. Phys. Soc. (Plyler award 1994); mem. NAS (chmn. com. undergrad. sci. edn.), Am. Chem. Soc. (past chmn. divsn. phys. chemistry, Calif. sect. award 1977). Avocation: cycling. Home: 936 Oxford St Berkeley CA 94707-2435 Office: U Calif Dept Chemistry 211 Lewis Hall Berkeley CA 94720-1460

MOORE, CALVIN C., mathematics educator, administrator; b. N.Y.C., Nov. 2, 1936; s. Robert A. and Ruth (Miller) M.; m. Doris Lienhard, Sept. 14, 1974. A.B. summa cum laude, Harvard U., 1958, M.A., 1959, Ph.D. in Math., 1960. Research instr. U. Chgo., 1960-61; asst. prof. U. Calif. at Berkeley, 1961-65, asso. prof., 1965-66, prof. math., 1966—, dean phys. scis., 1971-76, chair dept. math., 1996—; dir. Center Pure and Applied Math, 1977-80; dep. dir. Math. Scis. Research Inst., 1981-85; asst. v.p. acad. planning and personnel U. Calif. Systemwide Adminstrn., 1985-86, assoc. v.p. acad. affairs, 1986-94; mem. Inst. for Advanced Study, 1964-65; mem. at large NRC, 1971-73; mem. Math. Sci. Edn. Bd., 1991-93, mem. exec. com.; mem. Pres.'s Com. on Nat. Medal Sci., 1979-81; chair task force on rewards and recognition in math. scis. Joint Policy Bd. for Math., 1993-95. Chmn. bd. govs.: Pacific Jour. Math., 1972-76; editor: Mathematische Zeitschrift, Ill. Jour. Math, Pacific Jour. Math.; exec. editor research announcements; mng. editor: Bull. Am. Math. Soc.; contbg. editor: Advances in Mathematics; contbr. articles to profl. jours. Fellow Am. Acad. Arts and Scis.; mem. Am. Math. Soc. (exec. com., council mem. at large, v.p., chmn. bd. trustees). Home: 1408 Eagle Point Ct Lafayette CA 94549-2328 Office: U Calif at Berkeley Dept Math Evans Hall Berkeley CA 94720

MOORE, CARL GORDON, chemist, educator; b. Zanesville, Ohio, Feb. 7, 1922; s. Henry Carl and Hilda Marie (Oberfield) M.; m. Sheila Marie O'Toole, Nov. 2, 1951; children: Carl, Patrick, Martina, Michael, Maureen, Regina, Madeleine, Terence. BS in Chem. Engring., Ga. Inst. Tech., 1947; MS in Chem. Engring., Carnegie Mellon U., 1948, postgrad., 1948-51; postgrad., U. Newark, Del., 1973-74. Cert. tchr., Pa., Del. Chemist Manhattan Project, Oak Ridge, Tenn., 1944-46; chem. engr. Koppers Co., Pitts., 1946-47; rsch. chemist E.I. DuPont de Nemours & Co., Wilmington, Del., 1951-73; tchr. Chester (Pa.)-Upland Sch., 1974-78; tutor Del. Tutoring, Wilmington, 1981-88; instr. Del. Tech. and Community Coll., Wilmington, 1982-90, U. Del., Newark, 1984—. Author tech. reports on hydrogen over voltage of titanium and zirconium. Adult leader Wilmington area Boy Scouts Am., 1953-73; tchr. Sunday sch., Wilmington, 1962-67; group leader U.S. Census Bur., 1980. Sgt. U.S. Army, 1943-46. Mem. Am. Chem. Soc., Sigma Xi. Achievements include 13 patents, production of TiO_2 Rutile by chloride process, 100% oxygen oxidation of $TiCl_4$, 100% anatase by chloride process. Home and Office: 1913 Oak Lane Rd Wilmington DE 19803-5237

MOORE, CARLETON BRYANT, geochemistry educator; b. N.Y.C., Sept. 1, 1932; s. Eldridge Carleton and Mabel Florence (Drake) M.; m. Jane Elizabeth Strouse, July 25, 1959; children—Barbara Jeanne, Robert Carleton. BS, Alfred U., 1954, DSc (hon.), 1977; PhD, Cal. Inst. Tech., 1960. Asst. prof. geology Wesleyan U., Middletown, Conn., 1959-61; mem. faculty Ariz. State U., Tempe, 1961—; nat. rsch. coun. rsch. assoc. NASA Ames Rsch. Ctr., 1974; prof., dir. Ctr. for Meteorite Studies Ariz. State U., Regents' prof., 1988—; vis. prof. Stanford U., 1974; Prin. investigator Apollo 11-17; preliminary exam. team Lunar Receiving Lab., Apollo, 12-17. Author: Cosmic Debris, 1969, Meteorites, 1971, Principles of Geochemistry, 1982, Grundzügeder Geochemie, 1985; editor: Researches on Meteorites, 1961, Jour. Meteoritical Soc.; contbr. articles to profl. jours. Fellow Ariz.-Nev. Acad. Sci. (pres. 1979-80), Meteoritical Soc. (life hon., pres. 1966-68), Geol. Soc. Am., Mineral. Soc. Am., AAAS (council 1967-70); mem. Geochem. Soc., Am. Chem. Soc., Am. Ceramic Soc., Sigma Xi. Home: 507 E Del Rio Dr Tempe AZ 85282-3764 Office: Ariz State U Ctr for Meteorite Studies Tempe AZ 85287

MOORE, CAROLE IRENE, librarian; b. Berkeley, Calif., Aug. 15, 1944. AB, Stanford U., 1966; MLS, Columbia U., 1967. Reference libr. Columbia U., N.Y.C., 1967-68; reference libr. U. Toronto, Can., 1968-80, head cataloguing, 1980-85, assoc. libr., 1985-86, chief libr., 1986—; mem. nat. adv. bd. Nat. Libr. Can., Ottawa, 1991-94; bd. dirs. Rsch. Librs. Group. 1994—, U. Toronto Press, 1994—. Recipient Disting. Alumni award Columbia U., 1989. Mem. ALA, Can. Libr. Assn., Can. Assn. Rsch. Librs. (pres. 1989-91). Avocation: gardening. Office: U Toronto Libr, 130 Saint George St, Toronto, ON Canada M5S 1A5

MOORE, CAROLYN LANNIN, video specialist; b. Hammond, Ind., Aug. 14, 1945; d. William Wren and Julia Audrey (Mathews) Lannin; m. F. David Moore, Oct. 21, 1967; children: Jillian Winter Moore Mirise, Douglas Mathew, Owen Glen. BA, Ind. U., 1967; MA, Purdue U., 1991. Stockholders corr. Sears Roebuck and Co., Chgo., 1967-68; caseworker Lake County Dept. of Pub. Welfare, Hammond, Ind., 1968-71; field dir. Campfire Girls Inc., Highland, Ind., 1975-77; project dir. Northwest Ind. Pub. Broadcasting, Highland, 1984-85, interim exec. dir., 1985-87; cons. Telecom. and Grant Writing, Munster, Ind., 1981-85; prin. Carolyn Moore and Assocs.-Laughing Cat Prodns., Munster, Ind., 1987—; instr. Purdue U.-Calumet, Ind., 1989; instr. Valparaiso (Ind.) U., 1990-91; lectr. in field. Prodr. TV series Visclosky Viewpoint, 1985-87; video prodr. A Kid's Eye View of the Symphony, 1987; vol. on-air talent Sta. WYIN Channel 56; co-host This Week in Munster. Mem. Munster Cable TV Commn., 1984—; bd. dirs. N.W. Ind. Literacy Coalition, Inc.; mem. Lake County Master Gardeners; bd. dirs. Ednl. Referral Ctr.. Mem. AAUW, NAFE, Alliance for Cmty. Media, Assn. Ind. Video and Filmmakers Inc., Munster C. of C., Communicators N.W. Ind. (treas. 1996, pres. 1997—), N.W. Ind. World Trade Coun. (bd. dirs.), Ind. U. Alumni Assn., Scherwood Ladies Golf Leagues, Wicker Park Ladies Golf League (pres.). Democrat. Catholic. Avocations: golf, reading, sailing. Home and Office: Carolyn Moore & Assocs Laughing Cat Prodns 9604 Cypress Ave Munster IN 46321-3418

MOORE, CHARLES AUGUST, JR., psychologist; b. Medford, Oreg., Feb. 22, 1944; s. Charles August and Bernadine (Newlun) M. BS, Lewis and Clark Coll., 1965; MA, U. Colo., 1967, PhD, 1972. Lic. psychologist, Calif., Oreg. Teaching asst. U. Colo., Boulder, 1965-66, 70-71, rsch. asst., counselor, practicum supr., 1966-67, 71-72; asst. psychologist State Home and Tng. Sch., Grand Junction, Colo., 1967; intern in psychology Camarillo (Calif.) State Hosp., 1968-69; psychology assoc., program psychologist Camarillo Drug Abuse Program (The Family), 1969-70; intern in psychology Oxnard (Calif.) Mental Health Ctr., 1969; clin. psychologist, dir. intern tng. Rural Clinics, Reno, 1972; clin. psychologist Kern County Mental Health Svcs., Bakersfield, Calif., 1972-74; clin., cons. psychologist San Diego County Mental Health Svcs., 1974-88; pvt. practice La Jolla (Calif.) Clinic, 1976-78; August Ctr., Chula Vista, Calif., 1978-85; staff psychologist Dept. Vet.'s Affairs Domiciliary, White City, Oreg., 1988—; guest lectr. Calif. State Coll., Bakersfield, 1973-74; mem. Health Systems Agy. Mental Health Task Force, 1979; mem. doctoral dissertation com. U.S. Internat. U., 1975-76; mem. mental health task force San Diego County Bd. Suprs., 1979. Contbr. articles to profl. jours. Mem. Univ. City Community Coun., San Diego, 1976-78; bd. dirs. Pub. Employees Assn., 1976-77. Recipient Experiment in Internat. Living European Study award Lewis and Clark Coll., 1962; USPHS fellow, 1967-68; U. Colo. Grad. Sch. Rsch. grantee, 1971; recipient Hands and Heart award Dept. Vets. Affairs, 1989-90, Domiciliary Spl. Contbn. and Outstanding Performance awards, 1990, 91. Mem. APA, Am. Psychology and Law Soc., Calif. Psychol. Assn., Western Psychol. Assn., San Diego County Psychol. Assn., Assn. County Clin. Psychologists San Diego, San Diego Psychology and Law Soc., San Diego Soc. Clin. Psychologists. Office: Dept VA Domiciliary Psychology Svc 8495 Crater Lake Hwy White City OR 97503-3011

MOORE, CHARLES HEWES, JR., industrial and engineered products executive; b. Coatesville, Pa., Aug. 12, 1929; s. Charles Hewes and Jane Richards (Scott) M.; m. Judith L. McClellan, June 23, 1971; children: Charles Hewes III, James, David, Susan, Kevin, Christopher, Margery, Brian, Amanda. BME, Cornell U., 1952. With Lenape Forge Co. div. Gulf

& Western Industries, West Chester, Pa., 1952-73; pres. Lapp div. Interpace Corp., Le Roy, N.Y., 1973-77; pres., chief exec. officer Allied Thermal Corp. subs. Interpace, 1978-79; sr. v.p., dir. Interpace, 1979-80; exec. v.p., dir. Interpace Corp., Parsippany, N.J., 1980-81; pres., chief exec. officer, dir. Clevepak Corp., 1981-83, 84-86, chief exec. officer, vice chmn. bd., dir., 1983-84; mng. dir. Peers & Co., 1987-88; chief exec. officer Peers Mgmt. Resources, Inc., 1987-88; pres., chief exec. officer Ransburg Corp., Indpls., 1988-92; pres. ITW Finishing Systems and Products, Indpls., 1990-92; exec. v.p. Ill. Tool Works Inc., Glenview, 1991-92; vice-chmn. Advisory Capital Ptnrs., Inc., Greenwich, Conn., 1993-94; CEO, chmn. bd. dirs. Xpander Pak Inc., 1995—; athletic dir. Cornell U., 1994—; bd. dirs. Turner Corp., Elcotel, Inc. Mem. mgmt. policy coun., mem. adv. bd. Fundamental Mgmt.; chmn. audit com., pub. sector dir. U.S. Olympic Com. Recipient Gold medal in 400 meter hurdles, 1952 Olympics, Herbert Adams Meml. award for advancement of Am. sculpture, Nat. Sculpture Soc., 1985. Mem. Pine Valley Golf Club (N.J.), Royal and Ancient Golf Club St. Andrews (Scotland). Republican. Episcopalian. Office: Cornell U Teagle Hall Campus Rd Ithaca NY 14853-6501

MOORE, CHRISTINE HELEN, critical care nurse; b. Johnstown, Pa., Mar. 20, 1964; d. Conrad David and Dorothy Emily (Michalides) M. Diploma, Conemaugh Valley Meml. Hosp. Sch. Nursing, 1986; BS in Nursing, U. Pitts., 1991; MS in Nursing, Gannon U., 1997. RN, Pa.; cert. register nurse anesthetist. Staff nurse, med. surg. unit Windber (Pa.) Hosp.; staff nurse, intensive/coronary care unit Conemaugh Valley Meml. Hosp., Johnstown, Pa., 1988-97. Home: 320 W 7th St Apt 3 Erie PA 16502-1401

MOORE, CHRISTOPHER HUGH, writer; b. Stoke-on-Trent, Eng., June 9, 1950; arrived in Can., 1954; s. M. Vincent and Kathleen A. (Lennox) M.; m. Louise A. Brophy, May 7, 1977; children: Elizabeth, Kate. BA with honors, U. B.C., Vancouver, 1971; MA, U. Ottawa, Ont., Can., 1977. Staff historian Nat. Historic Pks. Svc., Louisbourg, N.S., Can., 1972-75; sec. to bd. Heritage Can. Found., Ottawa, 1977-78; writer, historian Toronto, Ont., 1979—. Author: Louisbourg Portraits, 1982, The Loyalists, 1984, 94, Eighteen Sixty-Seven, 1997; co-author: Illustrated History of Canada, 1987, The Story of Canada, 1992. Recipient Gov. Gen.'s Lit. award Can., 1983, Sec. of State Prize Govt. Can., Ottawa, 1985, Mr. Christie's Prize Christie-Brown Ltd., Toronto, 1993. Mem. Writers' Union of Can. (chair contracts com. 1990-94, mem. nat. coun. 1995-97), Can. Hist. Assn. Office: 396 Pacific Ave # 202, Toronto, ON Canada M6P 2R1

MOORE, CHRISTOPHER ROBERTSON KINLEY, petroleum geologist; b. Manchester, Eng., Sept. 28, 1954; came to U.S., 1989; s. James Robertson Kinley and Irene (Mason) M.; m. Marian Isabel Pope, Sept. 3, 1977; children: Andrew Christopher, Scott David. BA, U. Cambridge, 1975, MA, 1979. Geologist Brit. Petroleum Co., Scotland, England, Tunisia, 1975-80; sr. geologist Tricentrol Oil Corp., London, 1980-88; planning mgr. ARCO Brit. Ltd., London, 1988-89; from exploration planning advisor to dir. exploration ARCO Internat. Oil & Gas Co., Plano, Tex., 1989—. Fellow Geol. Soc. London; mem. Am. Assn. Petroleum Geologists, Soc. Petroleum Engrs., Geol. Soc. Am. Home: 2133 Country Club Dr Plano TX 75074 Office: Arco Internat Oil & Gas Co 2300 W Plano Pkwy Plano TX 75075-8427

MOORE, DAN STERLING, insurance executive, sales trainer; b. Lincoln, Nebr., June 27, 1956; s. Jack Leroy and Carolyn Marie (Bachman) M.; m. Marla Janine Collister, June 2, 1979; children: Tyler David, Anna Rose. Student, Red Rocks Coll., 1977. Lic. ins. exec. Asst. mgr. European Health Spa, Englewood, Colo., 1975-78; sales mgr. Colo. Nat. Homes, Westminster, 1979-80; sales assoc. Dale Carnegie, Denver, 1981; sales mgr. Paramount Fabrics, Denver, 1981-84; sales assoc. Mighty Distbg., Arvada, Colo., 1984-87; dist. mgr. Nat. Assn. for Self Employed/United Group Assn., Englewood, Colo., 1987—; dist. mgr. Communicating for Agr. Assn., 1993—, Am. Soc. Women Entrepreneurs, 1997—. Leader, trainer Alpine Rescue Team, Evergreen, Colo., 1971-74; minister Jehovah's Witnesses, 1972—. Mem. Am. Soc. Women Entrepreneurs (dist. mgr. 1997—). Avocations: golf, skiing, backpacking, scuba diving, tennis. Home: 892 Nob Hill Trl Franktown CO 80116-8716 Office: Nat Assn Self Employed/United Group 10579 W Bradford Rd Ste 100 Littleton CO 80127-4247

MOORE, DAN TYLER, writer; b. Washington, Feb. 1, 1908; s. Dan T. and Luvean Jones (Butler) M.; m. Elizabeth Valley Oakes, Mar. 12, 1932; children: Luvean O. (Mrs. Owens), Elizabeth Oakes (Mrs. Thornton), Harriet (Mrs. Lester Ballard), Dan Tyler III. BS, Yale, 1931. Chief counter-intelligence OSS, Middle East, 1943-44; pres. Middle East Co., Cleve., 1946-48, China Co., Cleve., 1946-48; asst. to pres. Intercontinental Hotels Corp., Istanbul, Turkey, 1948-50; freelance writer Cleveland Heights, Ohio, 1950—. Author: The Terrible Game, 1957, Cloak and Cipher, 1962, Wolves, Widows and Orphans, 1966, Lecturing For Profit, 1967, (movie) Gymkata 1988; contbr. articles and stories to popular mags. Pres. Greater Cleve. Muscular Dystrophy Assn., 1952-65; mem. exec. com. Cuyahoga County Dem. Party, 1951-70, mem. state exec. com., 1962-65; commr. Ohio Fed. Jury, 1961-68; trustee, bd. dirs. Cleve. Mus. Natural History; bd. dirs. Near East Coll. Assn., Karamu Theatre, Cleve. Served with AUS, 1942-44. Mem. Internat. Platform Assn. (dir. gen. emeritus). Clubs: Met. (Washington, D.C.); Yale (N.Y.C.); Union, Tavern, Skating and Rowfant (Cleve.). Home: 2564 Berkshire Rd Cleveland OH 44106-3365

MOORE, DANIEL CHARLES, physician; b. Cin., Sept. 9, 1918; s. Daniel Clark and May (Strebel) M.; m. Betty Maxine Tobias, Aug. 5, 1945 (div. 1988); children: Barbara, Nancy, Daniel, Susan. Grad., Amherst (Mass.) Coll., 1940; M.D., Northwestern U., 1944. Diplomate: Am. Bd. Anesthesiologists. Intern Wesley Meml. Hosp., Chgo., 1944; resident Wesley Meml. Hosp., 1945; dir. anesthesia Va. Mason Hosp., Seattle, 1947-72; anesthesiologist (Mason Clinic), 1947-72, sr. cons. in anesthesia, 1972-83; clin. prof. U. Wash. Sch. Medicine, 1963—. Author: Regional Block, 1953, Stellate Ganglion Block, 1954, Complications of Regional Anesthesia, 1955, Anesthetic Techniques for Obstetrical Anesthesia and Analgesia, 1964, also papers. Served as capt. M.C. AUS, 1945-47. Recipient Ralph M. Waters award Ill. Soc. Anesthesiologists, Carl Koller Gold medal European Soc. Regional Anaesthesia, 1995. Mem. Am. Soc. Anesthesiologists (1st v.p. 1953-54, 2d v.p. 1954-55, pres. 1958-59, distinguished service award 1976), AMA (sec. anesthesiology sect. 1956-58), Am. Acad. Anesthesiology, Am. Soc. Regional Anesthesia (adv. bd., Gaston Labat award 1977), Wash. Soc. Anesthesiologists (pres. 1949-50), Wash. Med. Soc., King County Med. Soc., Faculty Anaesthetists Royal Coll. Surgeons (hon.), Northwest Forum, Beta Theta Pi, Nu Sigma Nu. Home: Madison Park Pl # 103 2000 43rd Ave E Seattle WA 98112-2704 Office: PO Box 900 Seattle WA 98111-0900

MOORE, DANIEL EDMUND, psychologist, educator, retired educational administrator; b. Pitts., Dec. 31, 1926; s. John Daniel and Alma Helen (Goehring) M.; m. Rose Marie Blunkosky, Nov. 11, 1949; children: Catherine Chiodo, Claire Marie Moore Caveney, Mary Moore Brilmyer, Suzanne Moore Gray, Elizabeth Moore Sullivan. BSEd, Duquesne U., 1949, MEd, 1952; postgrad., California (Pa.) State Coll., 1954-56, U. Pitts., 1958-59, Mt. Mercy Coll., 1959-60, Cath. U. Am., 1966, W.Va. U., 1970-72. Lic. psychologist; cert. sch. psychologist. Tchr. math. Cecil Twp. Sch. Dist., McDonald, Pa., 1949-52, Pitts. Public Schs., 1952-53; with Mt. Lebanon Twp. (Pa.) Sch. Dist., 1953-88, psychologist, 1954-71, dir. pupil personnel svcs., 1988; psychol cons. Peters Twp. Sch. Dist., McMurray, Pa., 1961-88, Blackhawk Sch. Dist., Beaver, Pa., 1989—, Quaker Valley Sch. Dist., Sewickley, Pa., 1989-90; lectr., supr. Grad. and Undergrad. Sch. Edn. Duquesne U.; psychologist DePaul Inst., Pitts., 1992—; lectr. ednl. psychology Grad. Sch. Edn., Duquesne U., 1957-92, supr. student tchrs., 1989-92; ednl. cons. St. Francis Sch. Nursing, New Castle and Pitts., 1959-91; mem. test adv. bd. Ednl. Records Bur., 1976-86; hearing officer Right to Edn. Office, Dept. Edn., Harrisburg, Pa., 1975—; in-svc. adv. bd. Pa. Dept. Edn. Hearing Officers. Mem. Chartiers Valley Sch. Dist. Bd., 1963-94, pres., 1971, v.p., 1991; mem. Pkwy. West Tech. Sch. Bd. 1965-67; bd. dirs. secondary sch. rsch. program Ednl. Testing Svc., Princeton, 1971-85; bd. dirs. Robert E. Ward Home for Children, 1975-87, St. Agatha Parish Coun., 1988—, Pathfinder Sch., 1989, v.p., 1990-94, pres. sch. bd., 1991-92; vol. Bridgeville Area Food Bank, 1988—; chairperson Parish 100 Jubilee Ceremony, Goodwill Villa Bd., Goodwill Plaza, Inc., Goodwill Villa Bd. of Incorporators, 1992—; pres. bd. dirs. Goodwill Plaza, 1992—; jubilee chairperson St. Agatha's, Bridgeville, Pa. With USNR, 1945-48. Henry C. Frick grantee, 1970, 73; named Jaycee Educator of Yr. for South Hills Area, Ward Home Outstanding Community Leader, 1984. Mem. Am., Pa. psychol. assns., Coun. Exceptional Children (pres. 1957), Phi Delta Kappa (pres. chpt. 1974-75, chmn. lay awards com. 1979—, Svc. Key award 1985). Roman Catholic. Home: 213 Station St Bridgeville PA 15017-1806 Office: 428 Forbes Ave Pittsburgh PA 15219-1603

MOORE, DAVID GRAHAM, sociologist, educator; b. Norwich, Conn., May 9, 1918; s. Royal Tolman and Alta Gladys (Jenkin) M.; children by previous marriage: Barbara E., Linda C. Turbyville; m. Margaret Louise Rider, Dec. 2, 1950; children: David G., Kathryn R. (Mrs. T.J. Miller). B.A., U. Ill., 1940, M.A., 1943; Ph.D., U. Chgo., 1954. Personnel research Western Electric Co., 1940-41; mem. personnel staff Sears, Roebuck and Co., 1941-43, 46-50; personnel dir. Am. Flange & Mfg. Co., 1943-46; asst. prof. sociology, indsl. relations U. Chgo., 1950-55, asso. prof. bus. adminstrn., sociology, dir. exec. program, 1955-56; prof. mgmt. Mich. State U., 1956-58, head dept. personnel and prodn. adminstrn., 1958-61, prof. mgmt., sociology, 1961-63; dean N.Y. State Sch. Indsl. and Labor Relations, Cornell U., 1963-71; sr. v.p. Conf. Bd., N.Y.C., 1971-73; exec. v.p. Conf. Bd., 1973-79; prof., chmn. dept. bus. adminstrn. U. North Fla., 1979-86, prof. bus. adminstrn., 1986-89, asst. to pres., 1983-84; vis. Ford Found. prof. behavioral scis. U. Wis., fall 1962. Co-author: Human Relations in Industry, 4th edit, 1964, SRA Employee Inventory, 1951, The Enterprising Man, 1964. Mem. Am. Sociol. Assn., Soc. Applied Anthropology, Acad. Mgmt., Indsl. Relations Research Assn. Home: 91 San Juan Dr Apt D-1 Ponte Vedra Beach FL 32082-1336 Office: U North Fla PO Box 17074 Jacksonville FL 32245-7074

MOORE, DAVID LOWELL, dentist; b. Hartshorne, Okla., Apr. 3, 1930; s. David Lee and Zula (Winslow) M.; m. Mary Janell Stewart, Sept. 7, 1962; children—David Lee, Andrew Stewart. B.S., Okla. State U., 1949; M.S., M.A., U. Mo., 1964, D.D.S., 1955. Asst. prof. dentistry U. Mo. Dental Sch., Kansas City, 1958-61; teaching fellow U. Mo. Dental Sch., 1961-63, assoc. prof., 1963-64, prof., chmn. dept. restorative dentistry, 1964—; cons. VA hosps., Leavenworth, Kans., Topeka, Kansas City and Columbia, Mo.; mem. faculty VA Physician and Dentist in Residence Program; mem. test constrn. com. Nat. Bd. Dental Exams. Author articles in field, chpt. in textbook; editorial rev. bd. Jour. Prosthetic Dentistry. Deacon Nall Ave. Baptist Ch., Shawnee, Kans., 1970—. Served with USAF, 1955-58. Recipient Univ. Alumni Achievement award; trustees faculty fellow. Mem. ADA, Omicron Kappa Upsilon, Phi Kappa Phi, Omicron Delta Kappa, Psi Omega. Home: 10705 W 52nd Cir Shawnee KS 66203-1817 Office: U Mo Dental Sch 650 E 25th St Kansas City MO 64108-2716

MOORE, DAVID ROBERT, lawyer; b. Champaign, Ill., Jan. 1, 1959; s. Robert P. and Barbara L. (James) M. BA, Butler U., 1980; JD, Ind. U., 1982. Bar: Ill. 1983, Ind. 1983, U.S. Dist. Ct. (ctrl. dist.) Ill. 1983, (so. dist.) Ind. 1988. Assoc. Moore & Assocs., Champaign, 1983-90; ptnr. David R. Moore, P.C., Urbana, Ill., 1990-93, Follmer & Moore, Urbana, 1993—. Mem. Ind. State Bar Assn., Ill. State Bar Assn., Dram Shop Def. Bar Assn. Office: 1717 Philo Rd Urbana IL 61802-6044

MOORE, DEMI (DEMI GUYNES), actress; b. Roswell, N.Mex., Nov. 11, 1962; d. Danny and Virginia Guynes; m. Bruce Willis, Nov. 21, 1987; 3 daughters: Rumer Glenn, Scout LaRue, Tallulah Belle. Studies with Zina Provendie. Actress: (feature films) Choices, 1981, Parasite, 1981, Young Doctors in Love, 1982, Blame it on Rio, 1984, No Small Affair, 1984, St. Elmo's Fire, 1985, About Last Night..., 1986, Wisdom, 1986, One Crazy Summer, 1987, The Seventh Sign, 1988, We're No Angels, 1989, Ghost, 1990, Mortal Thoughts, 1991 (also co-producer), The Butcher's Wife, 1991, Nothing But Trouble, 1991, A Few Good Men, 1992, Indecent Proposal, 1993, Disclosure, 1994, The Scarlet Letter, 1995, Now and Then, 1995 (also prodr.), Undisclosed, 1996, Striptease, 1996, The Juror, 1996; (TV series) General Hospital, 1982-83; (TV movies) If These Walls Could Talk, 1996 (also exec. prodr.); (voice) The Hunchback of Notre Dame, 1996, G.I. Jane, 1997. Office: Creative Artists Agy Inc 9830 Wilshire Blvd Beverly Hills CA 90212-1804*

MOORE, DIANNE J. HALL, insurance claims administrator; b. Wadsworth, Ohio, June 9, 1936; d. Glenn Mackey and Dorothy Laverne (Broomall) Hall; widowed; children: Christine M. Gardner Fiocca, Jon R. Gardner. BA in Speech, Heidelberg Coll., Tiffin, Ohio, 1958. Receptionist Buckeye Union Ins. Co., Akron, Ohio, 1966-67; adjuster Liberty Mut. Ins. Co., Akron, 1967-69; claims liaison Ostrov Agy., Akron, 1969-70; underwriter Clark Agy., Wadsworth, 1971-72; adjuster Celina Group, Wadsworth, 1972-73, Nationwide, Canton, Ohio, 1973-77; asst. claim mgr. Motorist Mut. Ins. Co., Akron, 1977-87; claim rep. Ohio Casualty Ins. Co., San Diego, 1987-88; claims adminstr. Riser Foods, Inc. Risk Mgmt., Bedford Heights, Ohio, 1989—. Mem. Ohio Hist. Soc., Friends of Gettysburg. Mem. Assn. for Preservation of Civil War Sites Inc., Ohio State Claims Assn., Akron Claims Assn. (pres. 1985). Avocations: Civil War history, genealogical research, reading, painting. Office: Riser Foods Inc 5300 Richmond Rd Bedford OH 44146-1335

MOORE, DONALD FRANCIS, lawyer; b. N.Y.C., Dec. 14, 1937; s. John F. and Helen A. (McLoughlin) M.; m. Alice L. Kalmar; children: Christina M., Marianne, Karen L., Alison A. AB, Fordham U., 1959; JD, St. John's U., Bklyn., 1962. Bar: N.Y. 1962, D.C. 1970, U.S. Supreme Ct. 1993. Assoc. Paul, Weiss, Rifkind, Wharton & Garrison, N.Y.C., 1962-70, ptnr., 1970—. Editor in chief St. John's U. Law Rev., 1962. Served to 1st lt. U.S. Army, 1962-64. Mem. N.Y. State Bar Assn., Assn. of Bar of City of N.Y. Roman Catholic. Avocation: fishing. Home: 7 Wedgewood Ct Glen Head NY 11545-2229 Office: Paul Weiss Rifkind Wharton & Garrison 1285 Avenue Of The Americas New York NY 10019-6028

MOORE, DORSEY JEROME, dentistry educator, maxillofacial prosthetist; b. Boonville, Mo., Feb. 8, 1935; s. Lloyd Elliott Moore and Mary Elizabeth (Day) Katemann; m. Mary Louise Foote, May 2, 1959; children: Elizabeth L., David J. DDS, U. Mo., Kansas City, 1959. Diplomate Am. Bd. Prosthodontics. Commd. ensign USN, 1955, advanced through grades to capt., 1973; gen. practice dentistry various naval stas., 1959-63; practice in prosthodontics USS Proteus AS-19, 1963-66; resident in prosthodontics and maxillofacial prosthetics Naval Dental Sch., Bethesda, Md., 1966-69, chief maxillofacial prosthetics div., 1969-70; sr. dental advisor Naval Adv. Group, Comdr. Naval Forces, Saigon, Vietnam, 1970-71; chief maxillofacial prosthetics div. Nat. Naval Dental Ctr., 1971-76; chief maxillofacial prosthetics br. Naval Regional Med. Ctr., Great Lakes, Ill., 1976-79, ret., 1979; vis. lectr. U. Mo. Sch. Dentistry, Kansas City, 1976-79, H.G.B. Robinson prof., chmn. dept. removable prosthodontics, 1979—; assoc. prof. U. Saigon Sch. Dentistry, 1970-71; advisor to Min. of Health, Saigon, 1970-71; prof. lectr. George Washington U., Washington, 1971-76; clin. assoc. prof. surgery U. Kans. Sch. Medicine, 1987—; cons. maxillofacial prosthetics NIH Treatment Ctr., 1973—, Nat. Cancer Inst., 1973—, VA Hosp., North Chicago, Ill., 1976—, ADA Couns. Dental Edn., Hosp. Dental Svc. and Commn. on Accredition, 1978—; vice chancellor Devel. Adv. Com., 1983—; examiner Mo. Specialty Bd. Prosthodontics, 1982—; internat. cir. course lectr. Am. Prosthetics Soc., Indonesia, 1974, Guatelmala, 1975, N.Z., 1976, S.Africa, 1981; nat. cons. U.S. Naval Dental Sch., Bethesda, 1991—. Author: Practical Oral Rehabilitation of the Edentulous Patient, 8th edit., 1995; mem. editorial bd. Cancer of the Head and Neck: A Comprehensive Review of the Literature, 1982—; contbr. over 40 articles and abstracts to profl. jours. Mem. adminstrv. ch. bd. Cen. Methodist Ch., 1981-88, pres. official ch. bd., 1983-85; bd. dirs. Ednl. Rsch. Found. Prosthodontics, 1982—, chmn. 1988—; bd. dirs. Penn Valley Fitness Trail Assn., 1982—. Decorated Legion of Merit with combat V, other awards; Navy Cross of Gallantry with palm (Republic of Vietnam). Fellow Am. Acad. Maxillofacial Prosthetics (bd. dirs. 1972-75, mem. exec. com. 1973-76, pres. 1978-79, mem. exec. coun. 1979-82), Am. Coll. Prosthodontics (charter), Acad. Denture Prosthetics, Internat. Coll. Dentist, Midwest Acad. Prosthodontics; mem. ADA. Avocations: jazz musician, string bassist. Office: U Mo-Kans City Sch Dentistry 650 E 25th St Kansas City MO 64108-2716

MOORE, DUDLEY STUART JOHN, actor, musician; b. Dagenham, Essex, Eng., Apr. 19, 1935; s. John and Ada Francis (Hughes) M.; m. Suzy Kendall, 1966 (div.); m. Tuesday Weld, 1975 (div.); 1 child: Patrick; m. Brogan Lane (Denise Brogan), Feb. 21, 1988 (div.); m. Nicole Rothschild, April 16, 1994. Student, Guildhall Sch. Music; BA, Oxford (Eng.) U., 1957, MusB, 1958. Author: Dud and Pete: The Dagenham Dialogues, 1971; stage debut with Oxford U. Drama Soc., 1955; other stage appearances include Beyond the Fringe, London, 1960-62, Broadway, 1962-64, Play It Again Sam, 1970, Good Evening, 1973-75; appeared with Vic Lewis, John Dankworth Jazz Band, 1959-60; composed incidental music Royal Ct. Theatre, 1958-60; appeared in own BBC-TV series with Peter Cook Not only...but also, 1964, 66, 70; Royal Command Performance, ITV, 1965, Goodbye Again, ITV, 1968; appeared on BBC-TV series It's Lulu, not to mention Dudley Moore, 1972, Dudley, 1993, Daddy's Girls, 1994—; toured U.S., 1975; appeared on various TV and radio shows with jazz piano trio; actor (films) The Wrong Box, 30 is a Dangerous Age, Cynthia, Alice in Wonderland, Those Daring Young Men in their Jaunty Jalopies, Bedazzled, The Bed Sitting Room, The Hound of the Baskervilles, Foul Play, 10, Wholly Moses, Arthur (Golden Globe award 1983, Acad. award nomination 1983), Six Weeks, Lovesick, Romantic Comedy, Unfaithfully Yours, Best Defense, Mickey & Maude (Golden Globe award 1985), Santa Claus The Movie, Like Father, Like Son, Arthur on the Rocks, (voice over) The Adventures of Milo and Otis, 1989, Crazy People, 1990, Blame it on the Bellboy, 1991, A Weekend in the Country, The Pickle, 1994; (TV) Daddy's Girls, 1995; also various TV shows.; composer (film music) 30 is a Dangerous Age, Cynthia, Inadmissible Evidence, The Staircase, Six Weeks; rec. artist (albums) The Other Side of Dudley Moore, Today, Genuine Dud, Derek and Clive - Live, Beyond the Fringe and All That Jazz, Dudley Moore Trio - Down Under, Bedazzled, Songs Without Words, 1992, others. Named Male Star of Yr. N.A.T.O., 1983; Organ scholar Oxford U., 1958. Mem. St. James's Club, Annabel's Club, Harry's Bar, Tramp Club. Office: care Mr Lou Pitt 8942 Wilshire Blvd Beverly Hills CA 90211-1934 also: Dennis Selinger I.C.M., Oxford House 76 Oxford St, W1R 1RB London England*

MOORE, DUNCAN THOMAS, optics educator; b. Biddeford, Maine, Dec. 7, 1946; s. Thomas Fogg Moore and Virginia Robinson Wing; m. Gunta Liders, July 1995. BA in Physics, U. Maine, 1969, DSc (hon.), 1995; MS in Optics, U. Rochester, 1970, PhD in Optics, 1974. Asst. prof. U. Rochester, N.Y., 1974-78, assoc. prof., 1978-86, prof., 1986—, Kingslake prof., 1993—, dean engring. and applied sci., 1995—; pres., founder Gradient Lens Corp., Rochester, 1980; dir. N.Y. State Ctr. Advanced Optical Tech., Rochester, 1987-94; vis. scientist Nippon Schlumberger, Tokyo, 1983; Congl. fellow Am. Phys. Soc., Washington, 1993-94; sci. advisor to Sen. John D. Rockefeller IV, W. Va., 1993-94; bd. dirs. Amarel Precision Instruments, Inc. Contbr. numerous articles to profl. jours.; patentee in field. Chmn. Hubble Indpendent Rev. Panel, 1990-91; mem. adv. bd. high tech. Rochester C. of C., 1988—. Recipient Disting. Inventor of Yr. award Rochester Intellectual Property Law Assn., 1993, Grin Optics award Japanese Applied Physics Soc., 1993, Sci. and Tech. award Greater Rochester C. of C., 1992. Mem. Lasers and Electro-Optics Soc. of IEEE, NRC, Am. Ceramic Soc., Am. Soc. Precision Engring., Optical Soc. Am. (editor Applied Optics 1989-92, bd. dirs. 1987-89, 92-97, v.p. 1994, pres. 1996), Am. Assn. Engring. Soc., Materials Rsch. Soc. (bd. govs. 1995-97), Coun. Scientific Socs. (pres.'s co-chair govt. affairs com. 1996—), Forum on Physics and Soc. (exec. com. 1996—). Home: 4 Claret Dr Fairport NY 14450-4610 Office: U Rochester Inst Optics 305 Lattimore Hall Rochester NY 14627

MOORE, E. HARRIS, bishop. Bishop Western Mo. Ch. of God in Christ, Kansas City. *

MOORE, EDWARD FORREST, computer scientist, mathematician, former educator; b. Balt., Nov. 23, 1925; s. James Bernard and Edith (Thorn) M.; m. Elinor Constance Martin, July 30, 1950; children—Nancy, Shirley, Martha. BS in Chemistry, Va. Poly. Inst., 1947; MS in Math., Brown U., 1949, PhD in Math., 1950. Asst. prof. math. U. Ill., 1950-51; mem. tech. staff Bell Tel. Labs., Murray Hill, N.J., 1951-61, 62-66; vis. prof. elec. engring. Mass. Inst. Tech., 1961-62; vis. lectr. applied math. Harvard, 1961-62; prof. computer scis., math. U. Wis.-Madison, 1966-85; now ret. Author: Sequential Machines, 1964. Membership chmn. Fair Housing Com. of Chathams, N.J., 1964; treas. Francis Wayland Found., 1970-73; bd. dirs. Madison Campus Ministry, 1970-75. Served with USNR, 1944-46. Mem. AAAS, Nat. Speleological Soc., Wis. Speleological Soc., Am. Math. Soc., Soc. Indsl. and Applied Math., Math. Assn. Am., Bat Conservation International, N.Y. Acad. Scis., State Hist. Soc. Wis., Sigma Xi, Phi Kappa Phi, Phi Lambda Upsilon. Baptist. Home: 4337 Keating Ter Madison WI 53711-1563

MOORE, EDWARD TOWSON, electronics company executive, electrical engineer; b. Wytheville, Va., Feb. 26, 1937; s. Robert Brent and Jane Courtney (Oewel) M.; m. Linda Ernette Lunsford, June 27, 1965; children: Alan Towson, Jennifer Lynn. BSEE, Va. Poly. Inst. and State U., 1958; PhD in Elec. Engring., Duke U., 1963. Elec. engr. Sperry Farragut Co., Bristol, Tenn., 1958-59; rsch. assoc. Duke U., Durham, N.C., 1963-64; pres. Wilmore Electronics, Inc., Hillsborough, N.C., 1963—, Energy Dynamics, Inc., Yanceville, N.C., 1986—; cons. various indsl. cos. Contbr. over 12 articles to profl. jours; patentee in field. Bd. dirs. Goodwill Industries of Research Triangle Area, Durham, 1968-69; trustee Durham Tech. C.C., 1977-86. 1st lt. U.S. Army, 1958-59. Mem. IEEE, Sigma Si. Presbyterian. Avocations: flying, saltwater fishing. Office: Wilmore Electronics Co Inc PO Box 1329 Hillsborough NC 27278

MOORE, ELLIS OGLESBY, retired public affairs consultant; b. N.Y.C., May 12, 1924; s. Francis Lee and Gertrude (Ellis) M.; m. Peggy Sorrells, June 21, 1944; children: Ellis Oglesby, Jane Elizabeth Avallone, Kathleen Arnett, John Francis, Michael William. Student, Washington and Lee U., 1941-43. Reporter Pine Bluff (Ark.) Coml., 1946-47, Memphis Comml. Appeal, 1947-52; writer, exec. press and publicity NBC, N.Y.C., 1952-63; pub. relations exec. Standard Oil Co. (N.J.), N.Y.C., 1963-66, Am. Broadcasting Cos. Inc., N.Y.C., 1966-85; v.p. pub. relations Am. Broadcasting Cos. Inc., 1972-79, v.p. corp. relations, 1979-82, v.p. pub. affairs, 1982-85; pub. affairs cons., 1985-90. Served with AUS, 1943-46. Recipient Nat. Headliners award, 1950. Home: 984 Esplanade Pelham NY 10803-2904

MOORE, EMILY ALLYN, pharmacologist; b. Evansville, Ind., Apr. 3, 1950; d. Otis Barton and Helen Louise (Felker) Allyn; m. Robert Alan Yount, Nov. 25, 1972 (div. Feb. 1986); 1 child, Joseph Taylor; m. Robert E. Moore Jr., Aug. 11, 1990; 1 child, Alexander Allyn. AB in Chem. Biology, Ind. U., Bloomington, 1971; MS in Applied Computer Sci., Purdue U., Indpls., 1985; PhD in Pharmacology, Ind. U., Indpls., 1976. Vis. asst. prof. biology Ind. U., Bloomington, 1979; rsch. assoc. in biochemistry Ind. U., Indpls., 1979-81, rsch. assoc., 1982-83, computer programmer for med. genetics, 1983-85, asst. scientist. med. genetics, 1985-87; tech. assessment specialist Boehringer Mannheim Corp., Indpls., 1987, mgr. sci. info., 1987-89; mgr. Tech. Assess, Indpls., 1989-93, quality process analyst, 1993-94. Contbr. articles to profl. jours. Officer or bd. dirs. LWV, Hendricks County, Ind., 1977-84; elder St. Luke's United Ch. of Christ, Speedway, Ind., 1983-85; mem. adv. bd. Operation SMART, Indpls., 1989-90. Achievements include participation in creation of first DNA bank for storage of DNA samples for future use in diagnosis of genetic diseases.

MOORE, EMMETT BURRIS, JR., physical chemist; b. Bozeman, Mont., June 14, 1929; s. Emmett Burris and Iris Marie (Brown) M.; m. Diane Elizabeth Girling, Oct. 1, 1960; children: Karen Elizabeth, Robin Diane. B.S. in Chemistry, Wash. State U., 1951; Ph.D. in Phys. Chemistry (Shell fellow), U. Minn., 1956. Teaching asst. U. Minn., Mpls., 1951-55; asst. prof. physics U. Minn., Duluth, 1957-59; mem. staff Boeing Sci. Research Labs., Seattle, 1959-73; lectr. chemistry Seattle U., 1973; dir. power plant siting Minn. Environ. Quality Bd., St. Paul, 1973-76; gen. mgr. Richland (Wash.) Divsn. Olympic Engring. Corp., 1976-78; staff scientist Pacific N.W. Nat. Lab., 1978-96; mem. environ. engring. rev. panel EPA, 1989—; alt. mem. Hanford Adv. Bd., 1995—; adj. prof. environ. sci. Wash. State U., 1990—. Contbr. articles to profl. jours. Trustee Mid-Columbia Symphony Soc., 1978-85, v.p., 1980-81, pres., 1981-83; trustee Richland Light Opera Co., 1984-88, bus. mgr., 1984-88. Fellow AAAS; mem. Am. Phys. Soc., Am. Chem. Soc. (chmn. Pauling award com. 1971, sec. Puget Sound sect. 1971-73, mem. energy panel of com. on chemistry and pub. affairs 1983-86), Am. Assn. Physics Tchrs. (v.p. Wash. sect. 1965-66, pres. 1966-67), N.W. Sci. Assn., Phi Beta Kappa, Phi Kappa Phi, Phi Eta Sigma, Alpha Chi Sigma, Phi Lambda Upsilon, Sigma Alpha Epsilon (v.p. province 1972-73). Episcopalian (vestryman 1967-69, 76-79, 91, sr. warden 1969, del. diocesan conv.

1969-72). Home: 2323 Greenbrook Blvd Richland WA 99352-8427 Office: Wash State U 100 Sprout Rd Richland WA 99352-1641

MOORE, ERNEST EUGENE, JR., surgeon, educator; b. Pitts., June 18, 1946; s. Ernest Eugene Sr. and Mary Ann (Burroughs) M.; m. Sarah Van Duzer, Sept. 2, 1978; children: Hunter Burroughs, Peter Kitrick. BS in Chemistry, Allegheny Coll., 1968; MD, U. Pitts., 1972. Surg. resident U. Vt., Burlington, 1972-76; chief of trauma Denver Health Med. Ctr., 1976—; chief dept. surgery Denver Gen. Hosp., 1984—; chief div. of emergency med. svcs. U. Colo., Denver, 1984—, prof. surgery, vice chmn. dept., 1985—; dir. rsch. Colo. Trauma Inst., Denver, 1984—. Editor: Critical Decisions in Trauma, 1987, Trauma, 1988, rev. edits., 1991, 96, Early Care of the Injured, 1989; assoc. editor Jour. Trauma, Am. Jour. Surgery, Surgery-Problem Solving Approach, 2d edit., 1994, others; patentee retrohepatic vena cava shunt. Fellow ACS (com. on trauma, vice chair 1990), Soc. Univ. Surgeons (pres. 1989), Am. Assn. Surgery of Trauma (pres. 1993), Internat. Assn. Surgery of Trauma and Surg. Intensive Care (pres.-elect 1995), Pan Am. Trauma Assn. (pres. 1991), Southwestern Surg. Congress (v.p. 1996, pres. elect 1997), Western Trauma Assn. (pres. 1989). Republican. Avocations: skiing, hockey, hunting, marathons, fishing, camping. Home: 2909 E 7th Avenue Pky Denver CO 80206-3839 Office: Denver Health Med Ctr Dept Surgery Denver CO 80204

MOORE, F. RICHARD, music educator; b. Uniontown, Pa., Sept. 4, 1944; s. Franklin L. and Anna Jane (White) M.; children: Amanda, Dariel, Marick. BFA in Music Composition, BFA Music Performance, Carnegie-Mellon U., 1966; postgrad., U. Ill., 1966-67; MSEE, Stanford U., 1975, PhD, 1977. Acoustics researcher AT&T Bell Labs., Murray Hill, N.J., 1967-79; music prof. U. Calif.-San Diego, La Jolla, 1979—, dir. comuter audio research lab., 1979—, dir. ctr. for music experiment, 1982-92, chair dept. music, 1996—; percussionist Pitts. Symphony, 1964-66. Author: Programming in C with a Bit of UNIX, 1985, Elements of Computer Music, 1990; contbr. articles to profl. jours. Grantee for computer music research System Devel. Found., 1982-88, NEA, 1979—, Rockefeller Found., 1978, Ford Found., 1982. Mem. IEEE, Audio Engring. Soc., Acoustical Soc. Am. Avocations: aviation, amateur radio, skiing. Office: U Calif San Diego Dept Music La Jolla CA 92093-0037

MOORE, FAYE ANNETTE, social services professional; b. Glasgow, Mont., Feb. 21, 1938; d. Chester Oliver and Viola Adelaide (Skalet) Baker; m. Russell Dale Guthrie, July 1, 1961 (div. Nov. 1975); children: Tamia Lee, Owen Bradley; m. William Bateman Moore, Jan. 6, 1979. BA Sociology, Mont. State U., 1959; MA Social Work, U. Chgo., 1961; MBA, N. Mex. State U., 1984, PhD Ednl. Adminstrn., 1989. Social worker Ill. Childrens Home and Aid Soc., Chgo., 1961-63; social worker Divsn. Social Svcs., Fairbanks, Alaska, 1964-72, supr. social worker, 1972-74, staff mgr., 1974-75; regl. mgr. Divsn. Family and Youth Svcs., Anchorage, Alaska, 1976-80, regl. adminstr., 1991-96; adminstr. Rsch. Ctr. N.Mex. State U. Coll. Bus., Las Cruces, 1984-86; instr. Golden Gate U., Holloman AFB/Alamogordo, N.Mex., 1989-91, Webster U., Ft. Bliss, El Paso, Tex., 1989-91; ret., 1996—; presenter confs. in field. Contbr. articles to profl. jours. Recipient Supervisory Employee of the Year Commissioner's award Dept. of Health and Social Svcs., 1993. Mem. NASW, Realtor Assn. N.Mex. (state dir. 1990-91, chmn. state edn. com. 1991), Las Cruces Assn. Realtors (v.p. 1991), Am. Bus. Comm. Assn., Beta Gamma Sigma, Phi Kappa Phi. Avocations: gardening, walking, knitting, sewing. Home: PO Box 6162 Spring Hill FL 34611-6162 Office: Divsn Family and Youth Svcs 550 W 8th Ave Ste 304 Anchorage AK 99501-3572

MOORE, FLETCHER BROOKS, engineering company executive; b. Heiberger, Ala., June 15, 1926; s. Amzi Wallace and Mary Elizabeth (May) M.; m. Margaret Marian Foreman, Sept. 5, 1954; children—Larry Brooks, Ronald Howell. B.S. in Electronic Engring, Auburn U., 1948; M.S. in Electronic Engring, Ga. Inst. Tech., 1949. With U.S. Navy Mine Counter-Measures Sta., Panama City, Fla., 1949-52, Army Ballistic Missile Redstone Arsenal, Ala., 1952-60; with Marshall Space Flight Ctr., NASA, Huntsville, Ala., 1960-81; dir. Astrionics Lab. NASA Marshall Space Flight Ctr., 1968-81; chief missile system Teledyne Brown Engring., Huntsville, 1981-83; v.p. Control Dynamics Co., Huntsville, 1983-91; pres. Logicon Control Dynamics, Inc., Huntsville, 1991-94; divsn. dir. Control Dynamics, a Divsn. of bd. Systems, Huntsville, 1994—. Past chmn. alumni engring. coun. Auburn U.; mem. Auburn U. rsch. coun.; vice chairman. Ala. Indsl. Coun. on Engring. Edn.; mem. adminstrv. sci. adv. coun. U. Ala., Huntsville. Mem. AIAA, Inst. of Navigation, NASA Alumni League (past pres. Marshall Space Flight Ctr. chpt.). Home: 119 Sherwood Dr SE Huntsville AL 35802-2430

MOORE, FRANKLIN HALL, JR., lawyer; b. Camden, N.J., Sept. 6, 1937; s. Franklin H. and Dorothy (Jones) M.; m. Mary Ellen Toye, Sept. 10, 1960; children: Holly T., Christopher M. AB, Bucknell U., 1959; LLB, Yale U., 1962. Bar: N.Y. 1964. Assoc. Shearman & Sterling, N.Y.C., 1962-70, ptnr., 1971—. Mem. N.Y. State Bar Assn., Assn. of Bar of City of N.Y. Home: 440 E 56th St New York NY 10022

MOORE, GARY ALAN, academic administrator, educator; b. Indianola, Iowa, Jan. 23, 1946; s. Robert Lincoln and Ruby Marie Moore; B.S., Nebr. Wesleyan U., 1968; M.A. (grad. teaching asst. 1971-74), U. Nebr., Lincoln, 1973, Ph.D., 1974; m. Annemarie Neubecker; 1 son, Adrian David. Prof. bus. and econs. SUNY, Geneseo, 1985—, head Jones Sch. Bus., 1990—; mediator, factfinder N.Y. Public Employment Relations Bd., Albany, 1977—; mediator, arbitrator N.Y. Bd. Mediation, Albany, 1980—. Served with USAR, 1970. Grantee SUNY, N.Y. Com. Work Environment and Productivity. Mem. Am. Econ. Assn., Indsl. Relations Research Assn., Acad. Legal Stud. Bus., Blue Key, Omicron Delta Epsilon, Pi Gamma Mu. Author: (with R. Elkin) Labor and the Economy, 1983, (with A. Magaldi and J. Gray) Legal Environment of Business, 1987; contbr. research papers to profl. jours. Office: Sch Bus SUNY Geneseo NY 14454

MOORE, GEOFFREY HOYT, economist; b. Pequannock, N.J., Feb. 28, 1914; s. Edward H. and Marian (Leman) M.; m. Ella C. Goldschmid, July 12, 1938 (dec. June 2, 1975); children: Stephen, Peter, Kathleen, Pamela; m. Melita H. Riley, Sept. 28, 1975. BS, Rutgers U., 1933, MS, 1937; PhD, Harvard, 1947. Assoc. prof. econs. NYU, 1947-48; assoc. dir. Nat. Bur. Econs. Rsch., N.Y.C., 1948-64, dir. rsch., 1965-67, v.p. rsch., 1968, 73-75, dir. bus. cycle rsch., 1975-79; commr. labor stats. Dept. Labor, 1969-73; dir. Ctr. for Internat. Bus. Cycle Rsch., Columbia U., N.Y.C., 1979-96, EC Cycle Rsch. Inst., N.Y.C., 1996—; instr. agrl. econs. Rutgers U., 1936-42; sr. rsch. fellow Hoover Instn., Stanford U., 1973-78; adj. scholar Am. Enterprise Inst., 1975-80; vis. lectr. Columbia U., 1953-54, sr. rsch. scholar, 1983—. Author: (with W. A. Wallis) A Significance Test for Time Series, 1941, Production of Industrial Materials in World Wars I and II, 1944, Statistical Indicators of Cyclical Revivals and Recessions, 1950, The Diffusion of Business Cycles, 1955, Measuring Recessions, 1958, Business Cycle Indicators, 1961, Tested Knowledge of Business Cycles, 1962, (with J. Shiskin) Indicators of Business Expansions and Contractions, 1966, (with P. Klein) The Quality of Consumer Instalment Credit, 1967, The Anatomy of Inflation, 1969, The Cyclical Behavior of Prices, 1971, How Full is Full Employment, 1973, Slowdowns, Recessions and Inflation, 1975, An Inflation Chronology, 1977, Business Cycles, Inflation and Forecasting, 1983, (with P. Klein) Monitoring Growth Cycles in Market-Oriented Countries, 1985, (with M. Moore) International Economic Indicators: A Sourcebook, 1985, The Service Industries and the Business Cycle, 1987, Leading Indicators for the 1990's, 1989, (with K. Lahiri) Leading Economic Indicators, 1991, (with E. Boehm and A. Banerji) Using Economic Indicators to Reduce Risk in Stock Market Investments, 1992. Mem. N.Y. State Coun. Econ. Advisers, 1973-74. Subject of book edited by Philip A. Klein, Analyzing Modern Business Cycles: Essays Honoring Geoffrey H. Moore, 1990. Fellow Am. Statis. Assn. (pres. 1968), Nat. Assn. Bus. Economists, Am. Econs. Assn. (disting. fellow); mem. Nat. Economists Club, Forecasters Club N.Y., Cosmos Club, Phi Beta Kappa, Alpha Zeta. Home: 1171 Valley Rd New Canaan CT 06840-2428 Office: EC Cycle Rschg Inst 420 Lexington Ave Rm 1645 New York NY 10170-1699

MOORE, GEORGE CRAWFORD JACKSON, lawyer. BA, U. Fla., 1963; PhB in Soviet Law, U. St. Andrews, Scotland, 1966; MA in English Law with honors, Cambridge U., Eng., 1968, LLM in Internat. Law, 1969. Bar: Eng. (Barrister, Inner Temple) 1970, Jamaica 1971, Fla. 1973, Turks & Caicos Islands 1974, Antigua and Barbuda, Brit. V.I., Grenada, Montserrat, St. Lucia 1977; U.S. Supreme Ct. 1976. Legis. asst. to U.S. sen. Washington, 1970-72; asst. pub. defender Palm Beach County, Fla., 1973; pvt. practice West Palm Beach, Fla., 1973—; chmn. Fla. Export Coun. of U.S. Dept. Commerce, 1991-92; chmn. Fla. Coun. Internat. Devel., 1983-84, chmn. emeritus, 1990—; chmn. Fla. Gov.'s Conf. on World Trade and Investment, 1989; founding pres. World Trade Coun. of Palm Beach County, 1981—. Editor spl. issues Fla. Bar Jour., 1982, 87, chmn. editorial bd., 1988-89; mem. editorial bd. The Internat. Lawyer jour. of ABA, 1979-84; contbr. articles to profl. jours. Chmn. Fla. Econ. Growth and Internat. Devel. Commn., 1989-90. Fellow Soc. Internat. Bus. Fellows, Ctr. for Internat. Legal Studies; mem. ABA, Fla. Bar (chmn. internat. law sect. 1994—). Office: 105 S Narcissus Ave Ste 812 West Palm Beach FL 33401-5530

MOORE, GEORGE ELLIOTT, management consultant; b. Pilot, N.C., Nov. 20, 1935; s. Woodrow Wilson and Kate Nell Moore; m. Barbara Jean Spivey, Aug. 29, 1958; children: Sharon Lynne, Todd Elliott. BA, U. N.C., 1962. Exec. dir. Sci. and Humanities Symposium, Duke U., Durham, N.C., 1962-66; dir. fed. programs Roanoke (Va.) City Schs., 1966-68; dir. devel. Hollins (Va.) Coll., 1968-80; assoc. vice chancellor N.C. State U., Raleigh, 1980-83; exec. v.p., chief exec. officer N.C. Med. Soc., Raleigh, 1983-93; sr. cons. Mgmt. Concepts, Inc., Raleigh, 1994—; treas. Carolina Drs. Care, Inc., Raleigh, 1987-93, also bd. dirs.; bd. dirs. Med. Soc. Svcs., Inc., Raleigh, State Med. Jour. Advt. Bur., Inc., Chgo.; trustee, officer N.C. Med. Soc. Found., Inc., 1988-93. Contbg. author: Corporate Foundation Support for Public Institutions, 1985, Multiple Foundations: Advantages and Problems, 1986. Mem. adv. bd. Kate B. Reynolds Health Care Trust, Winston-Salem, N.C., 1983-93; committeeman N.C. Citizens for Bus. and Industry, Raleigh, 1984-94; bd. dirs. N.C. Forum for Rsch. and Econ. Edn., Raleigh, 1988-93; sec. bd. trustees Hollins Coll., 1968-80. Sgt. USMC, 1954-58. Recipient Grand award Alumni Programs, U.S. Steel Found., Pitts., 1978, Award for Excellence in Publs., Time Inc., N.Y.C., 1979, 80. Mem. Am. Soc. Assn. Execs., Am. Assn. Med. Soc. Execs., N.C. Inst. Medicine, Assn. Execs. N.C. (bd. dirs. 1983-93), Capital City Club, Raleigh Country Club, Pine Valley Country Club. Avocations: golf, carpentry and restoration, reading.

MOORE, GEORGE EMERSON, JR., geologist, educator; b. Lebanon, Mo., Jan. 2, 1914; s. George Emerson and Dorothea Louisa (Niewohner) M.; m. Wilma Corrine Leonard, May 20, 1939; children: George E. III, Dana Corinne, Craig G. A.B., U. Mo., 1936, M.A., 1938; Ph.D., Harvard U., 1947. Instr. U. Mo., 1938-39; teaching asst. Harvard U., 1940-42, 1946-47; geologist A.P. Green Fire Brick Co., Mexico, Mo., 1942-46; instr. Ohio State U. at Columbus, 1947-48, asst. prof., 1948-57, assoc. prof., 1957-64, prof., 1964-84, prof. emeritus, 1984—; geologist U.S. Geol. Survey, 1952-83. Fellow Geol. Soc. Am.; mem. Phi Beta Kappa, Sigma Xi. Home: 58 Mulberry Dr Wakefield RI 02879-1416

MOORE, GEORGE EUGENE, surgeon; b. Minn., Feb. 22, 1920; s. Jesse and Elizabeth (MacRae) M.; m. Lorraine Hammell, Feb. 22, 1945; children—Allan, Laurie, Linda, Cathy, Donald. B.A., U. Minn., 1942, M.A., 1943, B.S., 1944, B.M., 1946, M.D., 1947, Ph.D. in Surgery, 1950. Intern surgery U. Minn. Hosps., 1946-47; med. fellow gen. surgery, 1947, dir. tumor clinic, 1951-53; sr. research fellow USHPS, 1947-48; faculty U. Minn. Med. Sch., 1948-53, cancer coordinator, 1951-53; chief surgery Roswell Park Meml. Inst., Buffalo, 1953-72; dir. Roswell Park Meml. Inst., 1953-67; dir. pub. health research N.Y. State Health Dept., Albany, 1967-73; clin. prof. surgery State U. N.Y. at Buffalo, 1962-73, also prof. research biology, 1955-69; dir. surg. oncology Denver Gen. Hosp., 1973—; prof. surgery U. Colo., 1973—. Author: Diagnosis and Localization of Brain Tumors, 1950, Cancerous Diseases, 1970; contbr. 660 articles to profl. jours. Recipient Outstanding Citizen award Buffalo Evening News, 1958, Outstanding Sci. Achievement award, 1959, Disting. Achievement award Modern Medicine mag., 1962, Chancellor's medal U. Buffalo, 1963, Charles Evans Hughes award pub. adminstrn. Albany, 1963, Bronfman prize Am. Pub. Health Assn., 1964, Tchr. of Yr. award Dept. Surgery, U. Colo., 1977, Disting. Svc. award U. Colo., 1990, Meritorious Svc. Regents award U. Colo., 1990. Mem. Soc. U. Surgs., Halsted Soc., Am. Surg. Assn., Colo. Oncology Found. (pres.). Home: 12048 S Blackhawk Dr Conifer CO 80433-7107 Office: Denver Gen Hosp 645 Bannock St PO Box 1806 Denver CO 80204 *Individuals are miraculous temporal genetic patterns whose accomplishments will always transcend those of any committee, consensual group, or political assembly; society must provide special early educational opportunities for creative youngsters and those with genius. I hope to see the practical development of cell therapy for the infectious and cancerous diseases and genetic corrections of inherited disorders.*

MOORE, GORDON E., electronics company executive; b. San Francisco, Jan. 3, 1929; s. Walter Harold and Florence Almira (Williamson) M.; m. Betty I. Whittaker, Sept. 9, 1950; children: Kenneth, Steven. BS in Chemistry, U. Calif., 1950; PhD in Chemistry and Physics, Calif. Inst. Tech., 1954. Mem. tech. staff Shockley Semicondr. Lab., 1956-57; mgr. engring. Fairchild Camera & Instrument Corp., 1957-59, dir. research and devel., 1959-68; exec. v.p. Intel Corp., Santa Clara, Calif., 1968-75; pres., chief exec. officer Intel Corp., 1975-79, chmn., chief exec. officer, 1979-87, chmn., 1987—; bd. dirs. Varian Assocs. Inc., Transamerica Corp. Fellow IEEE; mem. Nat. Acad. Engring., Am. Phys. Soc. Office: Intel Corp 2200 Mission College Blvd Santa Clara CA 95054-1537*

MOORE, HAL G., mathematician, educator; b. Vernal, Utah, Aug. 14, 1929; s. Lewis Henry and Nora (Gillman) M.; m. D'On Empey, July 20, 1956; children: David, Nora (Mrs. Bret C. Hess), Alison (Mrs. Samuel M. Smith). BS, U. Utah, 1952, MS, 1957; PhD, U. Calif., Santa Barbara, 1967. Tchr. Salt Lake City Public Schs., 1952-53; instr. math. Carbon Jr. Coll., also Carbon High Sch., Price, Utah, 1953-55, Purdue U., Lafayette, Ind., 1957-61; adminstrv. asst. dept. math Purdue U., 1960-61; from asst. prof. math. to assoc. prof. math. Brigham Young U., Provo, 1961-71, prof., 1971-95; prof. emeritus, 1995—; assoc. chmn. dept. Math. Brigham Young U., 1986-89. Author: Precalculus Mathematics, 2d edit, 1977, (with Adil Yaqub) Elementary Linear Algebra With Applications, 1980, College Algebra and Trigonometry, 1983, A First Course in Linear Algebra, 1992; contbr. articles to profl. jours. Mem. High Coun., Ch. of Jesus Christ of Latter Day Saints, 1985-91, MTC br. pres., 1991-94, Bishop, 1958-61, 78-82. NSF faculty fellow U. Calif., Santa Barbara, 1964-66. Mem. Am. Math Soc., Math Assn. Am. (bd. govs. 1989-92), Utah State Math. Coalition (planning dir. 1990, bd. dirs. 1991-92), Sigma Xi (dir. 1974-80, 82-85, com. chmn. 1982-90), Phi Kappa Phi. Home: 631 W 650 S Orem UT 84058-6027 Home and Office: 631 W 650 S Orem UT 84058-6027 *Revelation and reason can work together to bring human beings closer to the truth of their existence and place in the universe. But charity and love and dedication are as necessary to the success of this union as they are to all others.*

MOORE, HAROLD BLAINE, middle school educator; b. Cleveland, Tenn., Sept. 29, 1955; s. Harry Lee and Glenna Jacqueline (Hawkins) M.; m. Sandra Lee Wyatt, Dec. 15, 1978. BA, Tenn. Tech. U., 1979. Tchr., coach Glenn L. Martin Jr. High Sch., Crossville, Tenn., 1979—. Mem. Cumberland County Edn. Assn. (assn. rep. 1989—, chief negotiator 1990-92). Avocations: puzzle-solving, reading novels, sports. Office: Glenn L Martin Jr High Sch 314 Miller Ave Crossville TN 38555-4037

MOORE, HENDERSON ALFRED, JR., retired savings and loan executive; b. Hattiesburg, Miss., May 28, 1912; s. Henderson Alfred and Lucy Alice (Currie) M.; m. Mary Cleo Barnes, June 16, 1946 (dec. Dec. 1976); children: Betty Barnes Moore McKenzie, H.A., Lucy Currie Moore Pledger (dec.); m. 2d, Dot Marie R. Evans, Oct. 24, 1979. BA, U. Miss., 1934, LLB, 1936, JD, 1968. Bar: Miss. 1936. Mem. Moore and Jones, Hattiesburg, 1961-77, of counsel, 1977—; exec. v.p. Magnolia Fed. Bank for Savs. (formerly First Magnolia Fed. Savs. and Loan Assn., and formerly First Fed. Savs. and Loan Assn. of Hattiesburg), Hattiesburg, 1961-68, pres., 1968-77, chmn. bd., chief exec. officer, 1977-84, chmn. emeritus, 1984—; city pros. atty., 1938-41, 47-49; city judge, 1941-42, city atty., 1949-53. Mem. Forrest County Indsl. Bd., 1965-77; mem. Hattiesburg Redevel. Authority, 1981-87, vice chmn., 1984, chmn., 1985. Miss. Econ. Council, 1960-84. Lt. USN, 1942-46. Mem. Inst. Fin. Edn., Miss. Bar Found., ABA, South Central Bar Assn., Miss. State Bar, Newcomen Soc. N.Am., Miss. Econ. Council (dir. 1960-84), U.S. League of Savs. Assn. (dir. 1968-71, 74-77), Fed. Home Loan Bank (dir. 1973-74), Miss. Savs. and Loan League (past pres.), Southwestern Savs. and Loan Conf. (dir. 1965-67), Miss. Folklore Soc., Hattiesburg Civic Assn., Soc. War of 1812, SAR, Miss. Hist. Soc., Hattiesburg C. of C., U. So. Miss. Found., U. So. Miss. Alumni Assn. (Alumni Hall of Fame 1995), U. Miss. Alumni Assn., Pi Kappa Alpha, Phi Alpha Delta, Phi Kappa Phi, Hattiesburg Country Club, Elks. Home: 2312 Carriage Rd Hattiesburg MS 39402-2526 Office: 100 W Front St Hattiesburg MS 39401-3460

MOORE, HENRY ROGERS, consulting engineer, retired railroad executive; b. Chatham, Va., Jan. 15, 1916; s. Charles Anderson and Lillian (Moon) M.; m. Billie Henslee, Mar. 26, 1949; 1 child, Mary James Moore Quillen. BSCE with honors, Va. Poly. and State U., 1940. Various positions So. Ry., southeastern U.S., 1939-52, div. supt., 1952-56; asst. chief engr. Washington, and chief engr. MWS, So. Ry., Charlotte, N.C., 1956-64; gen. supt. transp. Atlanta, 1965-68, gen. mgr., 1968-82; cons. AMTRAK, 1983-86; exec. v.p., chief oper. officer AMTRAK, Washington, 1986-88; pres. R.R. Transp. Cons. Inc., Atlanta, 1982—. Mem. Atlanta Athletic Club. Methodist. Home and Office: PO Box 98208 Atlanta GA 30359-1908

MOORE, J. SCOTT, materials engineer; b. Detroit, Sept. 27, 1952; s. James Brown and Marguerite Louise (Loyselle) M.; m. Soon Ki Lee, Apr. 15, 1987; 1 child, Ross Lee. BS, Rensselaer Poly. Inst., 1974, MS, 1977, PhD, 1981. From engr. to sr. contracts adminstrn. IBM, E. Fishkill, N.Y., 1982-88, Yorktown Heights, N.Y., 1988-95; pvt. practice Mt. Kisco, N.Y., 1995—. Mem. IEEE, Sigma Xi. Avocations: Buddhism, vedanta, yoga, new media. Home and Office: 25-107 Barker St Mount Kisco NY 10549

MOORE, JACQUELYN CORNELIA, labor union official, editor; b. Balt., Dec. 25, 1929; d. James C. and Harriette I. (Conaway) Thomas; m. Clarence Carbin Moore, Jan. 19, 1947 (dec. Feb. 1970); children: Clarence Joseph, Janet Elizabeth Moore Marshall. Mail clk. U.S. P.O., Phila., 1966-93; editor Local 509 Newsletter, Nat. Alliance of Postal and Fed. Employees, Washington, 1969-74, editorial newsletter chmn., 1969-74, sec. Dist. 5, 1972-74, nat. editor Nat. Alliance, 1974—, mem. exec. bd., 1974—, union photographer, 1974—, dir. 202 Housing for Elderly Corp. bds., Chattanooga, New Orleans, 1981—, Atlanta, 1988—, sec. supervisory com. Nat. Fed. Credit Union, 1977-82, 84-94, chair 1994—. Vol. D.C. Voting Rights Corp., Washington, 1979—; sustaining mem. Dem. Nat. Com., 1977—. Mem. Coalition of Labor Union Women, Nat. Bus. and Profl. Women's Club, Nat. Press Club. Roman Catholic. Home: 1102 R St NW Washington DC 20009-4364 Office: 1628 11th St NW Washington DC 20001-5011

MOORE, JAMES ALFRED, ski company executive, lawyer; b. Madisonville, Ky., Oct. 20, 1915; s. Virgil Yandell and Dorothy Ina (Price) M.; m. Lucile Carpenter, June 29, 1970; children by previous marriage: Marjorie M. Eickel, James Kelly, Kathleen M. Marozzi; m. Judith Gallen, June 10, 1995. A.B., U. Ky., 1936; LL.B., Harvard U., 1939. Bar: Pa. 1940, D.C. 1969, Va. 1978. Assoc. firm Pepper, Hamilton & Scheetz, Phila., 1940-51; partner Pepper, Hamilton & Scheetz, 1951-69; partner firm Pepper, Hamilton & Scheetz, Washington, 1969-77; pres. Camelback Ski Corp., Tannersville, Pa., 1963-86, chmn., bd. dirs., 1986-93, chmn. emeritus, 1993—. Contbr. articles to various law revs. Bd. dirs. Phila. Soc. for Crippled Children and Adults, 1959-69. Served from ensign to lt. comdr. USNR, 1942-45. Mem. Am. Bar Assn., Am. Law Inst. Republican. Methodist. Club: Merion Cricket (Haverford, Pa.). Home: PO Box 1241 Front Royal VA 22630-1241 Office: Camelback Ski Corp PO Box 168 Tannersville PA 18372-0168

MOORE, JAMES E., state supreme court justice; b. Laurens, S.C., Mar. 13, 1936; s. Roy Ernest and Marie (Hill) M.; m. Mary Alicia Deadwyler, Jan. 27, 1963; children—Erin Alicia, Travis Warren. B.A., Duke U., 1958, J.D., 1961. Bar: S.C. 1961, U.S. Dist. Ct. S.C. 1961. pvt. practice, Greenwood, S.C., 1961-76; cir. judge 8th Jud. Cir. S.C., Greenwood, 1976-1991; Assoc. Justice S.C. Supreme Ct., 1992—; Mem. S.C. Ho. of Reps., Columbia, 1968-76. Mem. S.C. Bar Assn., ABA, Am. Judicature Soc. Baptist. Home: 148 Amherst Dr Greenwood SC 29649-8901 Office: PO Box 277 Greenwood SC 29648-0277

MOORE, JAMES MENDON, industrial engineering educator, consultant; b. Winchester, Mass., Apr. 25, 1925; s. Mendon Preston and Fannie Judith (Merrill) M.; m. Lenna Mary Maguire, June 10, 1950; children: Thomas P., Richard M., Terry R., Alan M. B.S., Rensselaer Poly. Inst., 1950; M.S., Cornell U., 1956; Ph.D., Stanford U., 1964. Instr. Cornell, Ithaca, N.Y., 1952-56; asst. prof. mech. engring. Clarkson Coll. Tech., Potsdam, N.Y., 1956-59; instr. Stanford U., 1959-60; prof., chmn. indsl. engring. dept. Northeastern U., Boston, 1961-73; head dept. indsl. engring. and ops. research Va. Poly. Inst. and State U., Blacksburg, 1973-75, prof., 1976-90; pres. Moore Productivity Software, Blacksburg, 1976—; Lucas vis. prof. engring. prodn. U. Birmingham, Eng., 1975-76; sr. Fulbright lectr. Tech. U. Finland, Helsinki, 1968-69; dir. rsch. Hefei U., China, 1988, County Bd. Suprs., 1990—; chmn. bd. Internat. Found. Prodn. Rsch., 1991-93. Author: Plant Layout and Design, 1962; Co-author: Computer Aided Layout: A User's Guide, 1978, Applications of Graph Theory Algorithms, 1979, An Engineer's Guide to Spreadsheets, Word Processors & Data Base Managers, 1986; co-editor: The Production System: An Efficient Integration of Resources; assoc. editor: Internat. Jour. Prodn. Research, 1973-1983. Served with AUS, 1943-45. Decorated Bronze Star, Purple Heart. Fellow Am. Inst. Indsl. Engrs. (pres. chpt. 1963-64), Royal Soc. Home: 1607 Greenwood Dr Blacksburg VA 24060-5937

MOORE, JAMES R., lawyer; b. Longview, Wash., Sept. 14, 1944; s. James Carlton and Virginia (Rice) M.; m. Patricia Riley, Aug. 25, 1967 (div. 1978); 1 child, Katherine M.; m. Christine M. Monkman, July 14, 1979 (div. 1996); stepchildren: Amy McKenna, John McKenna; 1 foster child, Zia Sunseri; m. Kathryn Lindquist, Aug. 26, 1996; stepchildren: Matthew Elggren, Adam Elggren, Erin Elggren, David Heilner. BA, Whitman Coll., 1966; JD, Duke U., 1969. Bar: Wash. 1970, U.S. Ct. Appeals (4th cir.) 1972, U.S. Supreme Ct. 1973, U.S. Ct. Appeals (9th cir.) 1974, D.C., 1995. Law clk. to Hon. J. Barnes U.S. Ct. Appeals (9th cir.), L.A., 1969-70; trial atty. pollution control, land/natural resources div. U.S. Dept. Justice, Washington, 1970-74; asst. U.S. atty. U.S. Atty.'s Office, Seattle, 1974-82; regional counsel U.S. EPA Region 10, Seattle, 1982-87; counsel Perkins Coie, Seattle, 1987-88, ptnr., 1989—; trainer, speaker on environ. litigation, negotiation and law. Contbr. articles to profl. jours. Bd. dirs. Environ. Law Inst., 1995—; chair audit com. Whitman Coll., 1994—. Mem. ABA (sect. natural resources 1987—), Wash. State Bar Assn. (environ. and land use sect. 1974—, spl. dist. coun. 1988-95). Democrat. Office: Perkins Coie 1201 3rd Ave Ste 4100 Seattle WA 98101-3000 also: 607 14th St NW Washington DC 20005-2007

MOORE, JANE ROSS, librarian; b. Phila., Apr. 24, 1929; d. John William and Mary (McClure) Ross; m. Cyril Howard Moore, Jr., June 1, 1956 (div. Mar. 1967). A.B., Smith Coll., 1951; M.S. in L.S, Drexel U., 1952; postgrad., Columbia U.; M.B.A. with distinction, NYU, 1965; Ph.D., Case Western Res. U., 1974. Cataloguer, Yale U. Library, 1952-54; chief tech. processes librarian Lederle Labs., Am. Cyanamid Co., Pearl River, N.Y., 1954-58; chief serials catalog librarian Bklyn. Coll. Library, 1958-65, asst. prof., chief catalog div., 1965-70, asso. prof., chief catalog div., 1971-73, asso. prof. asso. librarian adminstrv. services, 1973-76; prof., chief librarian Mina Rees Libr., Grad. Sch. and Univ. Center, CUNY, 1976-91, prof., chief libr. emerita, 1991—; lectr. Syracuse U. Grad. Sch. Libr. Sci., summer 1967, 69, Queens Coll. Grad. Sch. Libr. and Info. Studies lectr., 1967-69; adj. assoc. prof., 1974-76, adj. prof., 1977-86; HEW Title IIB fellow Case Western Res. U. Sch. Library Sci., 1970-72; trustee N.Y. Met. Reference and Rsch. Libr. Agy., 1984-93, 2d v.p., 1985-88, v.p., 1988-90, treas. 1991-93; mem. chancellor's task force on librs. CUNY, 1979-81. Bd. dirs. Vis. Nurse Assn. of Bklyn., 1984—, mem. exec. com., 1987—; elder, clk. of session, pres. of corp. Presbyn. Ch. Mem. N.Y. Library Assn. (pres. 1979-80, pres. resources and tech. services sect. 1966-67, councilor 1966-67, 75-76, 78-81, sec.-treas. acad. and spl. libraries sect. 1973-75), ALA (membership com. 1967-71, chmn. council regional groups, resources and tech. services div. 1968-69, dir. div. 1968-70, 75-76, chmn. div. cataloging and classification sect. 1975-76), N.Y. Tech. Services Librarians (pres. 1963-64, award 1976), Assn. Coll. and Research Libraries (chmn. univ. libraries sect. 1983-84), N.Y. Library Club (sec. 1964-66, pres. 1980-81, council 1966-70, 73-77, 79-82), OCLC Users Council (SUNY del. 1981-85), AAUP, AAUW, Am. Printing History Assn., Am. Soc. Info. Sci., Archons of Colophon, Library Assn. of Great Brit., Spl. Libraries Assn., The Typophiles (sec.-treas. 1996—), NYU Grad. Sch. Bus.

Adminstrn. Alumni Assn. (rec. sec. 1967-69, dir. 1969-70, 75-79), Smith Coll. Club Bklyn. (pres. 1966-67, 67-68, class treas. 1976-81), Smith Coll. Club N.Y., Princeton Club N.Y., Phi Kappa Phi. Home: 35 Schermerhorn St Brooklyn NY 11201-4826 Office: Mina Rees Libr Grad Sch & U Ctr CUNY 33 W 42nd St New York NY 10036-8003

MOORE, JAY WINSTON, director cytogenetics laboratory; b. Madison, Wis., Apr. 20, 1942; s. Millard Harold and Leona J. (Miller) M.; m. Nancy E. Shimits; children: Meredith, Steven. BS, Cedarville Coll., 1964; MS, U. Nebr., 1966; PhD, U. Mass., 1970. Diplomate Am. Bd. Med. Genetics. From asst. prof. to prof. Eastern Coll., St. David's, Pa., 1970-84; fellow pediatric genetics Johns Hopkins Sch. of Medicine, Balt., 1984-86; asst. dirs. cytogenetics U. Iowa, Iowa City, 1986-90; dir. cytogenetics lab. Children's Hosp., Columbus, Ohio, 1990—; asst. clin. prof. Ohio State U., Columbus, 1991—. Fellow Am. Coll. Med. Genetics; mem. Am. Soc. Human Genetics. Office: Childens Hosp Cytogenetics Lab 700 Childrens Dr Columbus OH 43205-2664

MOORE, JEANNE, arts educator and administrator; b. L.A., Aug. 28, 1932; d. George E. and Ellen Kearny (Patrick) M. AA, Pasadena (Calif.) City Coll., 1952; BA with honors, UCLA, 1954; MM, U. So. Calif., 1965, DMA, 1970. Music tchr. Arvin (Calif.) H.S., 1955-60, Santa Maria (Calif.) H.S., 1960-65, Arroyo H.S., El Monte, Calif., 1965-66; asst. prof. edn. U. Victoria, B.C., Can., 1968-70; asst. prof. music edn. Bowling Green (Ohio) State Coll., 1970-71; prof. music West Chester (Pa.) State Coll., 1971-72; lectr. music San Jose (Calif.) State U., 1972-73; asst. prof. music Madison Coll., Harrisonburg, Va., 1974-76; coord. fine arts W.Va. Dept. Edn., Charleston, 1977—; choral dir. Santa Maria Choral Soc., 1963-64, Silver Lake Presbyn. Ch., L.A., 1966-67, Wesley United Meth. Ch., San Jose, 1972-74; contbr./cons. Nat. Study of Sch. Evaluation, Falls Church, Va., 1983-85, 89. Author, editor more than 40 books/monographs; editor, project coord.: (6 books, audio and video) West Virginia Music Test Item Bank, K-4, 1989, (2 books, slides and video) West Virginia Museum Resources for Teaching Art, 1991; co-author: Beyond the Classroom: Informing Others, 1987. Staff mem. Gov.'s Task Force on Arts Edn., W.Va., 1990-94. Nat. Endowment for Arts grantee, 1989-90, 91-92. Mem. Nat. Art Edn. Assn., Nat. Coun. State Suprs. Music (pres. 1984-86), Music Educators Nat. Conf., W.Va. Music Educators Assn. (bd. dirs. 1977—, Presdl. award 1990), W.Va. Art Edn. Assn. (bd. dirs. 1986—, Outstanding Adminstr. award 1991, 92, 93), Phi Delta Kappa, Pi Kappa Lambda, Mu Phi Epsilon. Episcopalian. Home: 102 Brammer Dr Charleston WV 25311-1738 Office: WVa Dept Edn 1900 Kanawha Blvd E Rm B-330 Charleston WV 25305-0009

MOORE, JEANNETTE AILEEN, animal nutrition educator; b. Bellflower, Calif., Jan. 6, 1957; d. Harry Joseph Jr. and Alba Aurora (Celaya) M.; m. Matthew Henry Poore, Oct. 2, 1982. BS in Animal Scis., Calif. State Polytechnic U., 1980; MS in Animal Scis., U. Ariz., 1983, PhD in Nutritional Scis., 1987. Cert. nutrition specialist. Postdoctoral rsch. assoc. U. Ariz., Tucson, 1988-90; postdoctoral rsch. assoc. N.C. State U., Raleigh, 1990-92, coord. Spend-A-Day-At-State program, 1994-97, chair dept. info. tech. com., mem. coll. acad. computing adv. com., undergrad. tchg. coord., 1997—; vis. asst. prof. N.C. State U., Raleigh, 1992—, faculty advisor Animal Sci. Club, 1992—, advisor Acad. Quadrathlon Team, 1993-94, advisor Rodeo Club, 1994—, World Wide web coord. Dept. Animal Sci., 1994—. Author: (computer spreadsheet) Ruminant Animal Diet Evaluator, 1993; mem. editl. bd. Jour. Animal Sci., 1995—. Supt. jr. ewe show, N.C. State Fair, Raleigh, 1992—; vol. N.C. Sci. and Math Partnership, Wake county, N.C., 1991—. Mem. Am. Soc. Nutritional Scis., Am. Soc. Animal Sci., Am. Dairy Sci. Assn., Am. Coll. Nutrition, Nat. Assn. Colls. and Tchrs. Agr., Coun. Agrl. Sci. and Tech., Alpha Zeta. Avocations: horseback riding, aerobics, reading, travel. Office: NC State U Dept Animal Sci Box 7621 Raleigh NC 27695-7621

MOORE, JERRY, religious organization administrator. Exec. sec. Home Mission Bd. of the Nat. Baptist Convention, USA, Washington, D.C. Office: Home Mission Bd 4606 16th St NW Washington DC 20011-4329*

MOORE, JOAN ELIZABETH, human resources executive, lawyer; b. Valleyfield, Que., Can., Apr. 29, 1951. BS in Social Scis., Mich. State U., 1973; JD, Case Western Res. U., 1976. Bar: Ohio 1977. Pers. exec. Ford Motor Co., Dearborn, Mich., 1976-80; cons. James Lash & Co., Southfield, Mich., 1980-83; pres., owner The Arbor Cons. Group, Inc., Plymouth, Mich., 1983—; owner Integrated Pers. Systems Inc., Plymouth, 1986—. V.p., bd. dirs. Pvt. Industry Coun., Wayne County, Mich., 1985-87; grad. Leadership Detroit VII, 1986, active alumni bd.; mem. computer subcom. Mich. Tech. Coun., 1986—; bd. dirs. Am. Cancer Soc. Mem. ABA, Ohio Bar Assn., Soc. for Human Resources Mgmt. (cert. Sr. Profl. in Human Resources), Leadership Detroit Alumni, Ann Arbor Art Assn. (bd. dirs.), Children's Aid Soc. (pers. advisor), Human Resources Assn. Greater Detroit (pres. 1996). Office: The Arbor Cons Group 711 W Ann Arbor Trl Plymouth MI 48170-1631

MOORE, JOANNE IWEITA, pharmacologist, educator; b. Greenville, Ohio, July 23, 1928; d. Clarence Jacob and Mary Edna (Klepinger) M. A.B., U. Cin., 1950; Ph.D., U. Mich., 1959. Rsch. asst. Christ Hosp. Inst. Med. Rsch., Cin., 1950-55; rsch. asst. U. Mich., Ann Arbor, 1955-57, teaching fellow, 1957-59; postdoctoral fellow in pharmacology Emory U., Atlanta, 1959-61; asst. prof. pharmacology U. Okla. Coll. Medicine, Oklahoma City, 1961-66, assoc. prof., 1966-71, acting chmn., 1969-71, prof., interim chmn., 1971-73, prof., chmn. dept., 1973—, David Ross Boyd prof., chair, 1993; mem. gen. rsch. support rev. com. NIH, 1975-79, mem. biomed. scis. study sect., 1986-90; mem. adv. bd. Fogarty Internat. Ctr., 1992-94. Contbr. articles to profl. jours. USPHS grantee, 1963-69, 72-74, 79-87. Mem. AAAS, Am. Soc. Pharmacology and Exptl. Therapeutics, Assn. Med. Sch. Pharmacology, Am. Heart Assn. (bd. dirs. Okla. affiliate 1973-88, pres. 1979-80, chmn. bd. 1983-85, bd. dirs. Oklahoma City div. 1988-91, pres. 1989-90), Sigma Xi. Office: U Okla Coll Medicine Dept Pharmacology 753 BMSB OUHSC Oklahoma City OK 73190

MOORE, JOHN CORDELL, retired lawyer; b. Winchester, Ill., July 20, 1912; s. John Clayton and Winifred (Peak) M.; m. Pauline Ruyle, July 29, 1939 (dec. 1979); m. Wilma K. Smith Jackson, Aug. 1981. A.B., Ill. Coll., 1936, LL.D., 1967; LL.B., Georgetown U., 1949, J.D., 1967; postgrad. in geology, Am. U., 1955-57. Bar: Tenn., U.S. Supreme Ct. Rep. Universal Credit Co., St. Louis, 1937-39; tchr. Capitol Page Sch.; also clk. to mem. Ho. of Reps., 1939-41; examiner Metals Res. Co., 1941-42; exec. dir. Fgn. Liquidation Commn. for S. and C. Am., Balboa, C.Z., 1946-47; with Office Alien Property, Dept. Justice, 1947-50; asst. dir. property mgmt. Interior Dept., 1950-52, dir. security for dept., 1952-61; adminstr. Oil Import Adminstrn., 1961-65, asst. sec. for mineral resources, 1965-69; ret.; U.S. rep. oil and energy com. OECD, Paris, 1965-69; former dir. Clark Oil, Milw. Served to comdr. USNR, 1942-46; capt. Res. Mem. Am. Legion, Scott County (Winchester, Ill.) Hist. Soc. (life), Delta Theta Phi, Elks, Army-Navy Club, Nat. Lawyers Club (Washington), Jacksonville Country Club.

MOORE, JOHN EDWIN, JR., college president; b. Aurora, Mo., Nov. 7, 1942; s. John Edwin and Emma Lou (Harback) M.; children: John E. III, Catherine Porter. BA cum laude, Yale U., 1964, MA in Teaching, 1965; EdD, Harvard U., 1971. Tchr. N.C. Advancement Sch., Winston-Salem, 1965-66; rsch. asst. Tech. Edn. Rsch. Ctr., Cambridge, Mass., 1969-70; adminstrv. asst., treas. Kirkwood Sch. Dist. R-VII, St. Louis, 1970-73, asst. supt., treas., 1973-74; adj. prof. U. Mo., St. Louis, 1973-74; v.p. Athens (Greece) Coll., 1974-75; asst. commr. edn. Dept. Elem. and Secondary Edn., Jefferson City, Mo., 1975-83; pres. Drury Coll., Springfield, Mo., 1983—; part-time instr. Far-East div. U. Md., 1967-68. Bd. dirs. United Way Ozarks, campaign chmn., 1988; bd. dirs. Mo. Colls. Fund, chmn., 1988-89; bd. dirs. Make-A-Wish Found. With U.S. Army, 1966-68. Recipient Vincent Conroy Meml. award Harvard Grad. Sch. Edn., 1971; named one of Outstanding Young Men Am., 1973. Mem. Springfield Area C. of C. (v.p. 1988, bd. dirs. Springfieldian of Yr. 1989), Nat. Assn. Intercollegiate Athletics (coun. pres.'s), Rotary (pres. Springfield chpt. 1988-89). Presbyterian (elder). Avocations: hunting, fishing, gardening, conservation. Home: 1234 N Benton Ave Springfield MO 65802-1902 Office: Drury Coll 900 N Benton Ave Springfield MO 65802-3712

MOORE, JOHN GEORGE, JR., medical educator; b. Berkeley, Calif., Sept. 17, 1917; s. John George and Mercedes (Sullivan) M.; m. Mary Louise Laffer, Feb. 8, 1946; children: Barbara Ann, Douglas Terence, Bruce MacDonald, Martha Christine. B.A., U. Calif., Berkeley, 1939; M.D., U. Calif., San Francisco, 1942. Diplomate: Am. Bd. Ob-Gyn (pres. 1974-78, chmn. 1978-82). Asst. prof. U. Iowa, 1950-51; asso. prof. UCLA, 1951-65, prof., chmn. dept. ob-gyn, 1968-88; prof., chmn. dept. ob-gyn Columbia U. Coll. Physicians and Surgeons, N.Y.C., 1965-68; chief of gynecology VA Hosp., Sepulveda, Calif., 1988-94. Contbr. articles to profl. jours. Served to maj. M.C. U.S. Army, 1942-46. Decorated Silver Star, Bronze Star, Purple Heart.; NIH grantee U. Copenhagen; Royal Postgrad. Sch. Medicine, London. Mem. ACS, ACOG, Soc. Gynecol. Investigation (pres. 1967), Assn. Profs. Gynecology and Obstetrics (pres. 1975), Western Assn. Gynecol. Oncologists (pres. 1976), Am. Gynecol. Soc., Pacific Coast Ob-Gyn. Soc., L.A. Ob-Gyn. Soc., Pepperdine U. Assocs. Home: Tamarron Unit 843 PO Box #3131 Durango CO 81302-3131

MOORE, JOHN HEBRON, history educator; b. Greenville, Miss., Feb. 26, 1920; s. John Pressley and Cora (Hebron) M.; m. Margaret Burr DesChamps, Dec. 20, 1955; 1 child, John Hebron Jr. BS in Aero-engring., Miss. State U., 1946; MA in History, U. Miss., Oxford, 1951; PhD, Emory U., 1955. Asst. prof. Delta State U., Cleveland, Miss., 1955-56; asst. prof. U. Miss., Oxford, 1956-57, assoc. prof., 1957-62, prof., 1962-70, chmn. history dept., 1966-69; prof. Fla. State U., Tallahassee, 1970-93, chmn. history dept., 1975-80; prof. emeritus, 1993—. Author: Agriculture in Antebellum Mississippi, 1958, Andrew Brown and Cypress Lumbering in the Old Southwest, 1967, The Emergence of the Cottom Kingdom in the Old Southwest: Mississippi, 1770-1860, 1988. With U.S. Army, 1941-43, USAAF, 1943-45, ETO, PTO. Mem. Agrl. History Soc. (pres. 1985), So. Hist. Assn., Miss. Hist. Soc. Presbyterian. Home: 2529 Blarney Dr Tallahassee FL 32308-3152

MOORE, JOHN JOSEPH, lawyer; b. West New York, N.J., Jan. 24, 1933; s. George Thomas and Dorothy (Zimmer) M.; m. Carmela Macrini, Mar. 10, 1957; children: Christine, John Joseph. B.S., Jersey City State Coll., 1956; LL.B., N.Y. Law Sch., 1961; LL.M., NYU, 1970. Bar: N.Y. 1961. Since practiced in N.Y.C.; assoc. with firm Dwyer & Lawler, after 1961; then mem. firm Reid, Devlin, Grubbs & Moore (now Alio & McDonough); chmn. bd. Leber Inc., 1983-93; mem. Barry McTierman and Moore, 1970—; guest lectr. disclosure Fordham U.; tchr. social studies pub. schs., Union City, N.J.; Sponsor, coach local Biddy Basketball Team, 1972—. Author: Discovery and Inspection, 1969, Legal Significance, 1975; editor: Defendant, 1969-73, 1987-92. Trustee devel. fund Jersey City State Tchrs. Coll., 1973-81; trustee Jersey City State Coll., 1982, vice chmn. bd. trustees, 1983-87, chmn., 1989—; chmn. governing bds. Assn. State Colls. N.J., 1985-87; chair Civilian Rev. Complaint Bd., Teaneck, N.J., 1992—; mem. Bd. Higher Edn. State N.J., 1985-87, Coun. N.J. State Colls., 1984-85; mem. governing bds. Assn. State Colls. N.J., 1985-89. With AUS, 1956-58. Mem. ABA, Am. Arbitration Assn. (arbiter 1968—), N.Y. State Bar Assn., N.Y. County Bar Assn., Def. Assn. N.Y. (pres. 1973-74, chmn. bd. 1974-75), Assn. State Colls. N.Y. (gov. bd. 1985-93), Cath. Ins. Guild (pres. 1972-73, chmn. bd. 1973-74), Def. Rsch. Inst. (regional v.p. 1983-86), Downtown Athletic Club (N.Y.C.), Manhattan Club, Oritani Field Club (Hackensack, N.J.), Hackensack Golf Club. Roman Catholic (dir. mus. group). Home: 573 Standish Rd Teaneck NJ 07666-2605 Office: 25 Broadway New York NY 10004-1010

MOORE, JOHN LEO, JR., journalist, writer, editor; b. Providence, R.I., June 24, 1927; s. John Leo and Annabelle Cecilia (Eastwood) M.; m. Dorothy Dolores Drankwicz, 1952; children: John Leo III, Christopher, Meredith Margaret Moore Poffenberger. AB, Brown U., 1950. Reporter Pawtucket (R.I.) Times, 1950-66, Providence (R.I.) Jour.-Bulletin, 1966; correspondent Carpenter News Svc., Washington, 1966-69; assoc. editor Nat. Jour., Washington, 1969-74; asst. mng. editor Congl. Quarterly, Washington, 1974-78, asst. dir. books, 1978-90; freelance writer, editor Washington, 1990—; cons. World Bank Internat. Monetary Fund, Washington, 1990—. Editor: (books) Guide to U.S. Elections, 2nd edit. 1985, 3rd rev. edit. 1994, CQ's Washington Guidebook, 1990, Congressional Ethics, 1992; author: Speaking of Washington, 1993. Committeeman Boy Scouts Am. Troop 15, Pawtucket, 1946-50, Troop 12, 1964-66; pres. Local 185 Newspaper Guild, Pawtucket, 1964-66; v.p. Community Assn., Severna Forest, Md., 1976-78. Named Eagle Scout, 1943; recipient salute Pawtucket C. of C., 1965, resolution of praise Pawtucket City Coun., 1966; cited for disting. reporting pub. affairs Am. Polit. Sci. Assn., 1961. Mem. Soc. Profl. Journalists. Roman Catholic. Avocations: photography, home improvement, lawn and garden work, reading, walking. Home and Office: 807 Cottonwood Dr Severna Park MD 21146-2813

MOORE, JOHN NEWTON, retired natural science educator; b. Columbus, Ohio, Apr. 2, 1920; s. Lawrence Newton and Grace C. (Jones) M.; m. Wilma Marie Proctor, Aug. 30, 1941; children—Douglas Warren, Donald Norman. A.B., Denison U., Granville, Ohio, 1941; M.S., Mich. State U., E. Lansing, 1943, Ed.D., 1952. Grad. asst. botany Mich. State U., 1941-43, instr. math., 1943-44, mem. faculty, 1946-82, prof. natural sci., 1970-82, prof. emeritus, 1982—; vis. prof. edn. Tenn. Temple Coll., summer 1974; bd. dirs. Creation Research Soc., 1963-86. Author: Questions and Answers on Creation/Evolution, 1976, How to Teach Origins, 1983; co-editor: Biology: A Search for Order in Complexity, rev. edit, 1974; mng. editor: Creation Research Soc. Quar, 1965-77; author chpts. in books. Served to lt. (j.g.) USNR, 1944-46. Fellow Creation Research Soc.; mem. Lambda Chi Alpha, Beta Beta Beta. Address: 119 Edward Ave Lehigh Acres FL 33972-5411

MOORE, JOHN NORTON, lawyer, diplomat, educator; b. N.Y.C., June 12, 1937; s. William Thomas and Lorena (Norton) M.; m. Barbara Schneider, Dec. 12, 1981; children: Victoria Norton, Elizabeth Norton. AB in Econs., Drew U., 1959; LLB with honors, Duke U., 1962; LLM, U. Ill., 1965; postgrad., Yale U., 1965-66. Bar: Fla. 1962, Ill. 1963, Va. 1969, D.C. 1972, U.S. Supreme Ct. 1972. Walter L. Brown prof. law, dir. Ctr. Oceans Law and Policy Ctr. for Nat. Security Law, U. Va., 1965-72, 76—; counselor on internat. law Dept. State, Washington, 1972-73; chmn. Nat. Security Coun. Task Force on Law of Sea and dep. spl. rep. of Pres. and amb. Law of Sea Conf., 1973-76; fellow Woodrow Wilson Internat. Ctr. for Scholars, Washington, 1976; adj. prof. Georgetown Law Ctr., 1978—; mem. Nat. Adv. Com. on Oceans and Atmosphere, 1984-85; mem. U.S. del. Conf. Security and Coop. in Europe, 1984; spl. counsel, dep. agt. for U.S. to World Ct.; former cons. to the Pres.'s Intelligence Oversight Bd., Arms Control and Disarmament Agy., U.S. Info. Agy.; chmn. bd. dirs. U.S. Inst. Peace; co-chmn. with the U.S. dep. atty. gen. Moscow Seminar on the Rule of Law, 1990; legal advisor during Gulf crisis for Kuwait's Amb. to U.S., including legal adviser to the Kuwait Rep. to UN Boundary Commn., 1991-94. Author: Law and the Indo-China War, 1972 (Phi Beta Kappa award); editor: Law and Civil War in the Modern World, 1976, Readings in International Law, 1979, The Arab-Israeli Conflict, 3 vols., 1976, 4th vol., 1991, Nat. Security Law, 1990, Crisis in the Gulf, 1992, Nat. Security Law Documents, 1995; contbr. articles on oceans policy, nat. security, internat. law, congl.-exec. rels. in fgn. policy and democracy-building to profl. jours. Sesquicentennial assoc. Ctr. Advanced Studies, U. Va., 1971-72; mem. adv. bd. on law of sea State Dept., 1977-80, mem. adv. bd. on internat. law, 1982; chmn. bd. dirs. U.S. Inst. Peace, 1986-89, 89-91; chmn. oceans policy com. Rep. Nat. Com.; mem. Consortium on Intelligence. Recipient Alumni award in arts Drew U., 1976; Compass Disting. Achievement award for significant contbns. to art and sci. of oceanography and marine tech., 1994; NIH fellow Yale U., 1965-66. Mem. ABA (past vice-chmn. sect. internat. law and past 5-term chmn. com. on law and nat. security), Am. Law Inst., Am. Oceanic Orgn. (exec. coun.), Marine Tech. Soc. (exec. coun.), Coun. Fgn. Rels., Order of Coif, Cosmos Club, N.Y. Yacht Club, Freedom House (bd. dirs.), Phi Beta Kappa. Republican. Episcopalian. Home: 824 Flordon Dr Charlottesville VA 22901-7810 Office: U Va Sch Law North Grounds Charlottesville VA 22901 *Life offers opportunity to pursue many worthwhile interests. In selecting among them it has seemed most useful to focus on those issues of sufficiently broad general significance as to justify the efforts of a lifetime. For me that has meant focus on promoting democracy and the rule of law, improving the functioning of government, controlling and reducing international conflict, and the policy choices of the ocean frontier.*

MOORE, JOHN PLUNKETT DENNIS, publisher; b. Mexico, Mo., Mar. 2, 1931; s. Dennis Talmage and Vona Mae (Vance) M.; m. Lydia Benz Ahern, Aug. 15, 1959; children: Alison Ahern, Lydia Benz, John Talmage, Maude Ahern, Meredith Coleman. Student, Princeton U., 1948-51, U.S. Naval Acad., 1951-53; B.A., U. Mo., Columbia, 1953; postgrad., Harvard Law Sch., 1955-56. Coll. traveler The Dryden Press, Inc., N.Y.C., 1957-59; coll. traveler The Macmillan Co., N.Y.C., 1959-60; editor The Macmillan Co., 1960-67; assoc. exec. editor Columbia U. Press, N.Y.C., 1968-74; editor in chief Columbia U. Press, 1974-80, pres., 1980-97, also bd. dirs.; bd. dirs., pres. Columbia U. Music Press; bd. dirs. Univ. Presses of Calif., Columbia and Princeton, Chichester, West Sussex, Eng., 1979—, chmn., 1981-83, 85-87, 96-97; trustee Composer's Recordings, Inc., 1984-97, Columbia U. Press, 1980-97. Author: A Historical Sketch, 1893-93; Editl. bd. N.Y. Acad. Scis., 1993—. Bd. dirs. Greenwich (Conn.) Health Assn., 1970-75; bd. dirs. assoc. The Family Ctr., Greenwich, 1975—; trustee Princeton Libr. in N.Y.c., 1984—; mem. vestry St. Barnabas Ch., Greenwich, 1995—. With U.S. Army, 1953-55. Mem. Assn. Am. Univ. Presses (chair internat. com. 1994-96, bd. dirs. 1996-97). Episcopalian. Clubs: Publishers Lunch (N.Y.C.), Princeton (N.Y.C.), Faculty House Columbia U. (N.Y.C.), Century Assn. (N.Y.C.); Nassau (Princeton, N.J.), the Book Table (N.Y.C.).

MOORE, JOHN RONALD, manufacturing executive; b. Pueblo, Colo., July 12, 1935; s. John E. and Anna (Yesberger) M.; m. Judith Russelyn Bauman, Sept. 5, 1959; children: Leland, Roni, Timothy, Elaine. BS, U. Colo., 1959; grad. advanced mgmt. program, Harvard Grad. Sch. Bus., 1981. Mgmt. trainee Montgomery Ward & Co., Denver, 1960-65; distbn. mgr. Midas Internat. Corp., Chgo., 1965-71; v.p., gen. mgr. Midas, Can., Toronto, Ont., 1972-75; pres. Auto Group Midas Internat. Corp., Chgo., 1976-82, pres., chief exec. officer, 1982—, also bd. dirs.; bd. dirs. Midas Australia Pty. Ltd., Melbourne. Served with U.S. Army, 1953-55. Mem. Ill. Mfr.'s Assn., Motor Equipment Mfrs. Assn. (pres.'s council 1982—), Internat. Franchising Assn., Econ. Club of Chgo., Comml. Club Chgo., Harvard Bus. Sch. Alumni Assn., U. Colo. Alumni Assn. Republican. Office: Midas Internat Corp 225 N Michigan Ave Chicago IL 60601-7601 *There is very little we accomplish in our lifetime that results from effort we alone expend. All of us should have the wisdom to express our appreciation to our families and associates who have helped us attain our goals and accomplishments—for failure to do so tarnishes our successes and breeds selfishness.*

MOORE, JOHN RUNYAN, agricultural and resource economics educator; b. Columbus, Ohio, Sept. 30, 1929; s. Lawrence Levi and Hazel Marie (Runyan) M.; m. Marjorie Ann Coy, June 14, 1953; children: Lee, Andrew. BSc in Agriculture, Ohio State U., 1951; MSc in Agrl. Econs., Cornell U., 1955; PhD in Agrl. Econs., U. Wis., Madison, 1959. County 4-H Club agt. Ohio Coop. Extension Svc., Steubenville, 1951; grad. rsch. asst. Cornell U., Ithaca, N.Y., 1953-55, U. Wis., Madison, 1955-58; asst. prof. Mich. State U., East Lansing, 1958-62; mktg. specialist, econ. cons. Ford Found., New Delhi, 1968-70; assoc. prof. U. Md., College Park, 1962-68, prof. in world food situation and food mktg., 1968-95, prof. emeritus, 1995—; econ. cons. FTC, Washington, 1963-64, World Bank, India and Nigeria, 1971-74, U.S. AID, Indonesia, Malawi, Haiti, Liberia and Egypt, various dates, FAO, Beijing, 1990. Co-author: (book) Market Structure of Agriculture Industries, 1964, U.S. Investment In Latin American Food Processing, 1966, Indian Food Grain Market, 1972. Trustee S.E. Consortium for Internat. Devel., 1978-95; commr. City College Park Housing Authority, 1996—. Lt. (j.g.) USNR, 1951-53. Recipient Internat. Honor award USDA, Washington, 1985, Cert. of Appreciation, 1986. Mem. Am. Agrl. Econ. Assn. (Thesis award 1960), Am. Econ. Assn., Internat. Agrl. Econ. Assn., Trees for the Future (trustee), Rotary (v.p. 1997—). Avocations: photography, travel, gardening, golf.

MOORE, JOHN STERLING, JR., minister; b. Memphis, Aug. 25, 1918; s. John Sterling and Lorena (Bounds) M.; m. Martha Louise Paulette, July 6, 1944; children: Sterling Hale, John Marshall, Carolyn Paulette. Student, Auburn U., 1936-37; AB, Samford U., 1940; ThM, So. Bapt. Theol. Sem., 1944. Ordained to ministry So. Bapt. Conv., 1942. Pastor chs. Pamplin, Va., 1944-48, Amherst, Va., 1949-57; pastor Manly Meml. Bapt. Ch., Lexington, Va., 1957-84, pastor emeritus, 1984—; mem. Hist. Commn., So. Bapt. Conv., 1968-75; pres. Va. Bapt. Pastor's Conf., 1963. Author: History of Broad Run Baptist Church, 1762-1987, 1987; co-author: Meaningful Moments in Virginia Baptist Life, 1715-1972, 1973; editor Va. Bapt. Register, 1972—; contbr. articles to profl. jours. Chmn. Lexington Mayor's Com. on Race Rels., 1962-65; bd. dirs. Stonewall Jackson Hosp., 1967-72, pres., 1969-71; treas. Rockbridge Mental Health Clinic, 1971-84. Recipient Disting. Svc. award Hist. Commn., So. Bapt. Conv., 1988. Mem. Am. Soc. Ch. History, So. Bapt. Hist. Soc. (bd. dirs. 1972-91, pres. 1975-76, sec. 1977-85), Va. Bapt. Hist. Soc. (exec. com. 1963—, pres. 1984-85), Va. Hist. Soc., Masons. Home: 8709 Gayton Rd Richmond VA 23229-6331

MOORE, JOHN W., academic administrator. Pres. Ind. State U., Terre Haute. Office: Indiana State U Office of President Terre Haute IN 47809

MOORE, JOHN WARD, chemistry educator; b. Lancaster, Pa., July 17, 1939; s. Joseph D. and Lillian B. M.; m. Elizabeth Augustin, Aug. 26, 1961. AB, Franklin & Marshall Coll., 1961; PhD, Northwestern U., 1965. Asst. prof. Ind. U., Bloomington, 1965-71; assoc. prof. Eastern Mich. U., Ypsilanti, 1971-76, prof., 1976-89; prof. U. Wis., Madison, 1989—; cos. Ecology Ctr. of Ann Arbor, 1979-81; vis. prof. U. Wis., Madison, 1981-82; vis. assoc. prof. U. Nice, France, 1987—; dir. Project SERAPHIM, 1982—, Inst. for Chem. Edn., 1989—. Editor Jour. Chem. Edn.: Software, 1988-96, Jour. Chem. Edn., 1996—; contbr. articles to profl. jours. Recipient Disting. Faculty award for rsch., publ. and svc. Ea. Mich. U., 1977, sci. faculty profl. devel. award NSF, 1979, Disting. Faculty award Mich. Assn. Governing Bds., 1982, Catalyst award Chem. Mfg. Assn., 1982, silver medal CASE Prof. Yr., 1986, George C. Pimentel award in chem. edn. Am. Chem. Soc., 1991, James Flack Norris award in chem. edn., 1991, Upjohn award for excellence in tchg., 1993, Underkofler award for excellence in tchg. Wis. Power & Light Co., 1995. Home: 3995 Shawn Trl Middleton WI 53562-3521 Office: U Wis Dept Chemistry Dept Chemistry 1101 University Ave Madison WI 53706-1322

MOORE, JOHN WILLIAM, university president; b. Bayonne, N.J., Aug. 1, 1939; s. Frederick A. and Marian R. (Faser) M.; m. Nancy Baumann, Aug. 10, 1968; children: Matthew, Sarah, David. BS in Social Sci. and Edn., Rutgers U., 1961; MS in Counseling and Student Pers. Svcs., Ind. U., 1963; EdD, Pa. State U., College Station, 1970. Asst. to dean Coll. Edn. Pa. State U., University Park, 1968-70; asst. to dean students U. Vt., Burlington, 1970-71, asst. prof. edn. adminstrn., 1973-76, asst. v.p. acad. affairs, 1973-76, assoc. v.p. acad. affairs, 1976-77; v.p. policy and planning Old Dominion U., Norfolk, Va., 1977-78, exec. v.p., 1982-85; pres. Calif. State U., Stanislaus, Turlock, 1985-92, Ind. State U., 1992—. Author: (with others) The Changing Composition of the Work Force: Implications for Future Research and Its Application, 1982, also articles, papers presented at profl. meetings. Pres. United Way, Modesto Calif., 1989; campaign chair United Way Wabash Valley, Terre Haute, Ind.; bd. dirs. Pvt. Industry Coun., Modesto, 1989, Union Hosp., Swope Mus., Am. Assn. Colls. and Univs.; bd. dirs., exec. com. Alliance for Growth and Progress, Terre Haute, Ind., 1992—, Terre Haute C. of C., Wabash Valley United Way, Bus. and Modernization Tech. Corp., Ind. Econ. Devel. Commn., PSI Energy. Recipient Disting. Svc. award Old Dominion U. Alumni Assn., 1985, Hispanic C. of C., 1982; recipient Community Svc. award Norfolk Commn. Edn., 1985, Leadership award United Way,1 986, Svc. award Pvt. Industry Coun., 1989; Alumni fellow Pa. State U., 1990. Mem. Am. Assn. State Colls. and Univs. (rep. Calif. chpt. 1988-92, bd. dirs. 1994—), Gould Med. Found. (bd. dirs. 1988-92, trustee 1988-92), Modesto Symphony Orch. Assn. (bd. dirs. 1990-92), Am. Coun. Edn., Commn. on Women in Higher Edn., Turlock C. of C. (bd. dirs. 1988-92), Rotary. Methodist. Avocations: fitness training, skiing, coaching youth sports. Office: Ind State U Condit House Terre Haute IN 47809

MOORE, JOHN WILSON, neurophysiologist, educator; b. Winston-Salem, N.C., Nov. 1, 1920; s. John Watson and Marjorie (MacAlpine) M.; m. Natalie Bayless, May 6, 1944 (div. 1977); children: John Reid, Marjorie Lee, Stephen Wilson; m. Ann E. Stuart, Apr. 2, 1978; 1 son, Jonathan Watson Stuart-Moore. B.S. in Physics, Davidson (N.C.) Coll., 1941; M.S., U. Va., 1942, Ph.D. in Physics, 1945. Asst. prof. physics Med. Coll. Va., 1946-50; biophysicist Naval Med. Research Inst., 1950-54, Lab. of Biophysics, Nat. Inst. Nervous Diseases and Blindness, NIH, 1954-61; mem. faculty Duke U., 1961—, prof. physiology and pharmacology, 1965-88, prof. neurobiology, 1988—; vis. prof. dept. neurobiology Harvard U. Med. Sch., 1978-79.

Trustee, mem. exec. com. Marine Biol. Lab., Woods Hole, Mass. DuPont fellow, 1941-46; Nat. Neurol. Research Found. scientist, 1961-66. Mem. IEEE, AAAS, Am. Physiol. Soc., Biophys. Soc. (coun., Cole award 1981), Soc. Neurosci., Marine Biol. Lab. Corp., Soc. Gen. Physiologists, Phi Beta Kappa, Omicron Delta Kappa. Office: Duke Univ Dept Neurobiology PO Box 3209 Duke Univ Med Ctr Durham NC 27710-0001

MOORE, JUDY KAY, media relations specialist; b. Mt. Clemens, Mich., July 20, 1963; d. Elmer Michael and Sharon Ann (Moore) Zurakowski. BA, Albion Coll., 1985. News reporter Green Bay (Wis.) News-Chronicle, 1985-87; chief legislative aide Wis. State Leg., Madison, 1987-90; sr. media relations specialist Univ. Wis. Hosp. Medical Sch., Madison, 1990—. Cons. Am. Heart Assn. Fundraiser, Madison, 1995; co-chair campaign State Rep. Mary Lou Van Dreel, Green Bay, 1988; mem. publicity com. Health Emotions Rsch. Inst. U. Wis., 1996, Med. Flight Critical Care Helicopter 10th Anniv. U. Wis., 1995. Recipient Merit for PR Campaign award Wis. Pub. Rels. Soc. of Am., 1995, Newswriting award Wis. Newspaper Assn., 1986. Mem. Women in Communications (membership com. 1995—), Wis. Communicators Council, Inc., Wis. Healthcare Pub. Rels. and Mktg. Soc. Avocations: reading, travel. Office: Univ Wis Hosp Medical Sch 610 Walnut St Rm 758 Warf Madison WI 53705-2336

MOORE, JULIA ALICE, federal government executive; b. Jersey City, N.J., Sept. 10, 1950; d. John Richard and Jean (Alexander) M.; mm. Harry C. Blaney III, Feb. 14, 1976. BS in Fgn. Svc., Georgetown U., Washington, 1972. Analyst Washington Analysis Corp., Washington, 1972-73; assoc. dir. Joseph S. White & Assoc., Washington, 1973-75; dep. dir. Arms Control Assn., Washington, 1982-84; legis. & pub. affairs officer U.S. Dept. of State, Washington, 1975-86; v.p. communications World Wildlife Fund, Washington, 1986-90; sr. assoc. Ogilvy & Mather Pub. Affairs, Washington, 1990-91; exec. dir. Physicians for Social Responsibility, Washington, 1991-95; dir. legis. and pub. affairs NSF, Arlington, Va., 1995—. Author: OP-EDS. Mem. Coun. on Fgn. Rels. Named Rusk Fellow, Georgetown U., 1985. Mem. Nat. Press Club, Internat. Inst. for Strategic Studies, Arms Control Assn. Episcopalian. Home: 4700 Connecticut Ave NW 601 Washington DC 20008-5629 Office: NSF 4201 Wilson Blvd Arlington VA 22230-0001

MOORE, KAREN NELSON, judge; b. Washington, Nov. 19, 1948; d. Roger S. and Myrtle (Gill) Nelson; m. Kenneth Cameron Moore, June 22, 1974; children—Roger C., Kenneth N., Kristin K. A.B. magna cum laude, Radcliffe Coll., 1970, J.D. magna cum laude, Harvard U., 1973. Bar: D.C. 1973, Ohio, 1976, U.S. Ct. Appeals (D.C. cir.) 1974, U.S. Supreme Ct. 1980, U.S. Ct. Appeals (6th cir.) 1984. Law clk. Judge Malcolm Wilkey, U.S. Ct. Appeals (D.C. cir.), 1973-74; law clk. Assoc. Justice Harry A. Blackmun, U.S. Supreme Ct., Washington, 1974-75; assoc. Jones, Day, Reavis & Pogue, Cleve., 1975-77; asst. prof. Case Western Res. Law Sch., Cleve., 1977-80, assoc. prof., 1980-82, prof., 1982-95; judge U.S. Ct. Appeals (6th cir.), Cleve., 1995—; vis. prof. Harvard Law Sch., 1990-91. Mem. Harvard Law Rev., 1971-73. Contbr. articles to legal publs. Trustee Lakewood Hosp., Ohio, 1978-85, Radcliffe Coll., Cambridge, 1980-84. Fellow Am. Bar Found.; mem. Cleve. Bar Assn. (trustee 1979-82), ABA (standing com. jud. selection, tenure and compensation 1978-82), Am. Law Inst., Am. Assn. Law Schs. (chmn. civil procedure sect. 1985, academic freedom and tenure com. 1985-89, chmn. 1987-89), Harvard Alumni Assn. (bd. dirs. 1984-87), Phi Beta Kappa. Office: US Ct Appeals 6th Cir 328 US Courthouse 201 Superior Ave E Cleveland OH 44114-1201

MOORE, KATHLEEN, dancer; b. Chgo.. Student with Sonia Arova, Thor Sutowski, Ala. Sch. Fine Arts; student, Sch. Am. Ballet, Am. Ballet Theatre Sch. Joined ABT II, 1980; mem. corps de ballet Am. Ballet Theatre, N.Y.C., 1982-88, soloist, 1988-91, prin. dancer, 1991—. Repertoire includes Dark Elegies, Don Quixote (Kitri's Wedding), Fall River Legend, Fancy Free, Giselle, Rodeo, Romeo and Juliet, The Leaves Are Fading, Nine Sinatra Songs, Everlast, Enough Said, Gaite Parisienne, The Rite of Spring, Pillare of Fire, The Informer, Brief Fling, Duets, Sinfonietta, Sunset, Les Liasons Dangereuses, Manon, Undertow, others; created roles in Agnes de Mille's The Informer, Mark Morris' Drink to Me Only With Thine Eyes. Office: Am Ballet Theatre 890 Broadway New York NY 10003-1211*

MOORE, KATHRYN MCDANIEL, education educator; d. Lawrence W. and Doris K. McDaniel; m. Dan Emery Moore, Aug. 20, 1966; children: Todd Lawrence, Jason Emery. BA and BS, Ohio State U., 1965, MA, 1966; PhD, U. Wis., 1972. Project asst. office of dean of students U. Wis., Madison, 1966-68, asst. to assoc. dean Coll. Letters and Sci., 1970-71; asst. prof., assoc. prof. edn. dept. Cornell U., 1971-77; assoc. prof. ctr. study of hogher edn. Pa. State U., 1977-84, prof., sr. rsch. assoc. ctr. study of higher edn., 1984-86, dir., prof. ctr. study of higher edn., 1986-88; prof. edn. policy and leadership dept. ednl. adminstrn. Mich. State U. Coll. Edn., East Lansing, 1988—, chmn., 1991-96, dir. Ctr. for Advanced Learning Sys., 1996—; speaker and reviewer in field. Mem. editl. bd. Rev. Higher Edn., 1991-94, Innovative Higher Edn., 1991—, Am. Ednl. Rsch. Jour., 1989-92, Jour. Higher Edn., 1995—; mem. adv. bd. Higher Edn. Abstracts, 1984—; contbr. to monographs, books and articles to profl. jours. Grantee in field; recipient Disting. Alumni award Ohio State U., 1987. Mem. Am. Ednl. Rsch. Assn., (various coms.), Am. Assn. Higher Edn., Nat. Ctr. Edn. Statistics (nat. adv. bd. 1977-81, other coms.), Assn. for Study of Higher Edn. (pres. 1983, various coms.), History of Edn. Soc. (nominations com., bd. dirs. 1981-83, Henry Barnard prize com. 1977-85, chair 1980-81), Ohio State Alumni Assn. (bd. dirs. 1990-95, chair 1995-97), Ohio State U. Commn. on Women (alumni rep. 1991-92), Golden Key Soc. (hon. mem.), Phi Beta Kappa, Phi Kappa Phi. Office: Mich State U Ednl Adminstrn 418 Erickson Hall East Lansing MI 48824-1034

MOORE, KENNETH CAMERON, lawyer; b. Chgo., Oct. 25, 1947; s. Kenneth Edwards and Margaret Elizabeth (Cameron) M.; m. Karen M. Nelson, June 22, 1974; children: Roger Cameron, Kenneth Nelson, Kristin Karen. BA summa cum laude, Hiram Coll., 1969; JD cum laude, Harvard U., 1973. Bar: Ohio 1973, U.S. Dist. Ct. Md. 1974, U.S. Ct. Appeals (4th cir.) 1974, D.C. 1975, U.S. Dist. Ct. (no. dist.) Ohio 1976, U.S. Ct. Appeals (6th cir.) 1977, U.S. Ct. Appeals (D.C. cir.) 1979, U.S. Supreme Ct. 1980. Law clk. to judge Harrison L. Winter, U.S. Ct. Appeals, 4th Cir., Balt., 1973-74; assoc. Squire, Sanders & Dempsey, Washington, 1974-75, Cleve., 1975-82, ptnr., 1982—, mem. fin. com., 1990—, profl. ethics ptnr., 1996—. Chmn. Ohio Fin. Com. for Jimmy Carter presdl. campaign, 1976; del. Dem. Nat. Conv., 1976; chief legal counsel Ohio Carter-Mondale Campaign, 1976; mem. Cleve. com., Cleve. Coun. World Affairs; mem. bd. advisors The Environ. Counselor; trustee Hiram Coll., 1997—. Served with AUS, 1970-76. Mem. ABA, Fed. Bar Assn., Ohio Bar Assn., Greater Cleve. Bar Assn., Cleve. City Club. Home: 15602 Edgewater Dr Cleveland OH 44107-1212 Office: Squire Sanders & Dempsey 4900 Society Ctr 127 Public Sq Cleveland OH 44114-1216

MOORE, KENNETH EDWIN, pharmacology educator; b. Edmonton, Alta., Can., Aug. 8, 1933; came to U.S., 1957, naturalized, 1966; s. Jack and Emily Elizabeth (Tarbox) M.; m. Barbara Anne Stafford, Sept. 19, 1953; children—Grant Kenneth, Sandra Anne, Lynn Susan. B.S., U. Alta., 1955, M.S., 1957; Ph.D., U. Mich., 1960. Instr. pharmacology Dartmouth Med. Sch., Hanover, N.H., 1960-61; asst. prof. Dartmouth Med. Sch., 1962-66; assoc. prof. pharmacology Mich. State U., East Lansing, 1966-70; prof. Mich. State U., 1970—, chmn. dept. pharmacology and toxicology, 1987—; vis. scholar Cambridge (Eng.) U., 1974; instr. Lansing Community Coll., 1975-81; cons. NIH, also pharm. industry. Author 1 book; contbr. articles to profl. jours. Fellow Am. Coll. Neuropsychopharmacology; mem. Am. Soc. Pharmacology and Exptl. Therapeutics (chmn. bd. publs. trustees 1992-96), Soc. Exptl. Biology and Medicine, Soc. Neurosci. Home: 4790 Arapaho Trl Okemos MI 48864-1402 Office: Dept Pharmacology Mich State U East Lansing MI 48824

MOORE, KENNETH JAMES, agronomy educator; b. Phoenix, June 6, 1957; s. George Taylor and Barbara Joyce (Amy) M.; m. Gina Marie McCarthy Aug. 11, 1979; children: Ellyn Elizabeth, David Taylor, Mark Daniel. BS in Agr., Ariz. State U., 1979; MS in Agronomy, Purdue U., 1981, PhD in Agronomy, 1983. Asst. prof. agronomy U. Ill., Urbana, 1983-87; assoc. prof. N.Mex. State U., Las Cruces, 1988-89; rsch. agronomist Agrl. Rsch. Svc., USDA, Lincoln, Nebr., 1989-93; prof. Iowa State U., Ames, 1993—; adj. assoc. prof. U. Nebr. Lincoln, 1989-93, prof., 1993-96. Author: Crop Science Laboratory Manual, 1988; assoc. editor Agronomy Jour., 1989-93, tech. editor, 1994—; assoc. editor Crop Sci., 1994; contbr. chpts. to books. Bd. dirs. Lincoln Children's Mus., 1991-93, Children's Svcs. of Ctrl. Iowa, 1997—; mem. mgmt. com. N.E. YMCA, Lincoln, 1991-93; mem. youth policy forum Lincoln YMCA, 1991-92. Recipient Point of Light award USDA, 1991. Fellow Am. Soc. Agronomy, Crop Sci. Soc. Am. (divsn. chmn. 1990-92, Young Crop Scientist award 1993); mem. Am. Forage and Grassland Coun. (Outstanding Young Scientist award 1982, merit award 1991), Am. Soc. Animal Sci., Am. Dairy Sci. Assn. Republican. Presbyterian. Avocations: swimming, fishing, music. Office: Iowa State U Agronomy Dept 1567 Agronomy Hall Ames IA 50011

MOORE, KEVIN MICHAEL, federal judge; b. 1951. BA, Fla. State U.; JD, Fordham U. Bar: Fla. 1976. U.S. atty. no. dist. State of Fla., Tallahassee, 1987-89; dir. U.S. Marshals Svc., Arlington, Va., 1989-92; judge US. Dist. Ct. So. Dist. Fla., Miami, 1992—. Office: US Dist Ct Federal Justice Bldg 99 NE 4th St Rm 1168 Miami FL 33132-2139*

MOORE, LARRY GALE, lawyer; b. Ogden, Utah, Dec. 11, 1954; s. Lawrence Gale and Ivy (Blalock) M.; married. BA, Brigham Young U., 1977; JD, Columbia U., 1980. Bar: Utah 1980, U.S. Dist. Ct. Utah 1980. Ptnr. Ray, Quinney & Nebeker, Salt Lake City, 1986—; faculty Am. Banker's Inst., 1981-83; lectr. Mortgage Banker's Assn., 1986—. Harlan Fiske Stone scholar. Office: Ray Quinney & Nebeker 500 Deseret Bldg Salt Lake City UT 84111

MOORE, LAURENCE JOHN, business educator; b. Greeley, Colo., May 7, 1938; s. John Harold and Ruth Anderson M.; m. Nancy Kay Hibbert, Aug. 31, 1963; children: Rebecca Ann, John Andrew, Stefani Ruth. BA in Econs., Monmouth Coll., Ill., 1962; MS in Econs., Ariz. State U., 1965, DBA in Mgmt. Sci., 1970. Dist. mktg. rep. Standard Oil Co. (Ind.), Chgo., 1962-63; sr. analyst long range and capital planning, 1964-66; head quantitative studies Continental Ill. Bank, Chgo., 1966-67; mem. faculty dept. mgmt. sci. Coll. Bus. Va. Poly. Inst. and State U., Blacksburg, 1970—; prof. Coll. Bus. Va. Poly. Inst. and State U., 1977-85, C&P Disting. prof. bus., 1985—, head dept. Coll. Bus., 1976-83, dir. univ. fin. planning and analysis, 1983-84; dir. univ. planning Va. Poly. Inst. and State U., Blacksburg, 1988-89; cons. in field. Author: (with S.M. Lee, B.W. Taylor) Management Science, 1981, 4th edit., 1993, (with S.M. Lee) Introduction to Decision Sciences, 1975, (with E.R. Clayton) GERT Modeling and Simulation: Fundamentals and Applications, 1976. Served with U.S. Army, 1957-59. Recipient Disting. Service award SE region Am. Inst. Decision Scis., 1977. Fellow Am. Inst. Decision Scis. (pres. 1983-84, Disting. Svc. awrd 1986); mem. Inst. Mgmt. Sci. (Disting. Svc. award SE region), Inst. for Ops. Rsch. and Mgmt. Sci., Inst. Indsl. Engrs., Alpha Iota Delta, Beta Gamma Sigma, Omicron Delta Epsilon, Sigma Iota Epsilon. Presbyterian. Home: PO Box 11134 Blacksburg VA 24062-1134 Office: Va Poly Inst and State U Dept Mgmt Sci 1007 Pamplin Hall Blacksburg VA 24061-5102

MOORE, LAWRENCE JACK, lawyer; b. Brownwood, Tex., Jan. 24, 1926; s. Lawrence Houston and Lena Emily (Grantham) M.; m. Eloise Camille Dickinson, May 24, 1947; children: John L., James D., Jane E. Moore Horner. Student Howard Payne U., 1946-47, Tarleton State U., 1942-43; LLB, U. Tex., 1949. Bar: Tex. 1949, N.Y. 1980. Pvt. practice, 1949-57; city atty., Ballinger, Tex., 1950, 55-57; county atty. Runnels County, Tex., 1951-54; atty. Texaco Inc., 1957-70, assoc. gen. counsel, 1970-79; v.p., gen. counsel Caltex Petroleum Corp., Dallas, 1979-89; mem. Johnson & Gibbs, P.C., Dallas, Houston, Austin, Tex., Washington, 1989-91; pvt. practice, 1992—; adv. bd. Internat. and Comparative Law Ctr., Internat. Oil and Gas Ctr. of Southwestern Legal Found.; mem. devel. bd., U. Tex., Dallas, 1986-91; dir. Nat. Fgn. Trade Coun., N.Y., 1985-93. Served to cpl. AUS, 1944-46. Mem. ABA, State Bar Tex., University Club (N.Y.C.), Country Club of Darien (Conn.), Petroleum Club (Dallas), Horseshoe Bay Country Club, Barton Creek Country Club (Lakeside), Masons. Republican. Methodist. Office: PO Box 8510 Horseshoe Bay TX 78657-8510

MOORE, LINDA KATHLEEN, personnel agency executive; b. San Antonio, Tex., Feb. 18, 1944; d. Frank Edward and Louise Marie (Powell) Horton; m. Mack B. Taplin, May 25, 1963 (div. Feb. 1967); 1 child, Mack B.; m. William J. Moore, Mar. 8, 1967 (div. Nov. 1973). Student, Tex. A&I Coll., 1962-63. Co-owner S.R.O. Internat., Dallas, 1967-70; mgr. Exec. Girls Pers. & Modeling Svcs., Dallas, 1970-72, Gen. Employment Enterprises, Atlanta, 1972-88; owner, mgr. More Pers. Svcs., Inc., Atlanta, 1988-94, pres., chmn. bd., 1994—; Contbr. short story to Writer's Digest. Mem. NAFE, Nat. Fedn. Bus. and Profl. Women, Am. Soc. Profl. and Exec. Women, Women Bus. Owners, Nat. Assn. Women Cons., Nat. Assn. Personnel Svcs., Ga. Assn. Personnel Svcs., Women's Clubs, Atlanta C. of C. (speaker's bur.), Better Bus. Bur., Cobb County C. of C. Office: More Pers Svcs Inc 4501 Circle 75 Pkwy SE # 75 Pkwy Atlanta GA 30339-3025

MOORE, LOIS JEAN, health science facility administrator; married; 1 child. Grad., Prairie View (Tex.) Sch. Nursing, 1957; BS in Nursing, Tex. Woman's U., 1970; MS in Edn., Tex. So. U., 1974. Nurse Harris County (Tex.) Hosp. Dist., 1957—; pres., chief exec. officer Harris County Hosp.; adminstr. Jefferson Davis Hosp., Houston, 1977-88, exec. v.p., chief ops. officer, 1988—; Mem. adv. bd. Tex. Pub. Hosp. Assn. Contbr. articles to profl. jours. Mem. Mental Health Needs Council Houston and Harris County, Congressman Mickey Leland's Infant Mortality Task Force, Houston Crack-down Com., Gov.'s task force on health care policy, 1991; chairperson Tex. Assn. Pub. and Nonprofit Hosps., 1991, subcom. of Gov.'s task force to identify essential health care svc., 1992; bd. dirs. ARC, 1991—, Greater Houston Hosp. Coun., March of Dimes, United Way. Recipient Pacesetter award North-East C. of C., 1991; named Nurse of Yr. Houston Area League Nursing, 1976-77, Outstanding Black Achiever YMCA Century Club, 1974, Outstanding Women in Medicine YWCA, 1989. Mem. Am. Coll. Hosp. Adminstrs., Tex. Hosp. Assn. (chmn. pub. hosp. com.), Young Hosp. Adminstrs., Nat. Assn. Pub. Hosps. (bd. dirs., mem. exec. com. Tex. assn.), License Vocat. Nurses Assn., sigma Theta Tau. Home: 3730 S MacDreyon Way Houston TX 77021 Office: Harris County Hosp Dist PO Box 66769 Houston TX 77266-6769

MOORE, LORETTA WESTBROOK, banker; b. Cameron, Tex., Jan. 2, 1938; d. Merrill Holman and Gladys Evangeline (Strelsky) Westbrook; m. Joe Gregg Moore Jr., Sept. 22, 1956; children: Terri Lynn, Joe Gregg III. Grad. high sch., Hearne, Tex. With Planters & Merchants State Bank, Hearne, Tex., 1956—, v.p., cashier, 1980—, also bd. dirs.; group pres. Nat. Assn. Bank Women (now Fin. Women Internat.), Waco, Tex., 1980-81. Vocat. adv. coun. Hearne Pub. Schs., 1984—. Named Hon. Chpt. Farmer Future Farmers Am., 1984, Notable Women of Tex., 1984. Mem. Bank Adminstrn. Instn. (pres. Brazos Valley chpt. 1983-84), Am. Inst. Banking (bd. dirs. Brazos Valley chpt., charter), Order Eastern Star (past matron). Methodist. Avocations: travel, ranching with husband, grandchildren. Home: RR 1 Box 395 Hearne TX 77859-9617 Office: Planters & Mchts State Bank 122 E 4th St Hearne TX 77859

MOORE, MALCOLM FREDERICK, manufacturing executive; b. Kankakee, Ill., Sept. 19, 1950; s. Robert Dunham and Josephine Frances (Jones) M.; m. Patricia Claudine Bennert, June 13, 1971; children: Michael Dunham, Emily Suzanne, Marjorie Nicoll. BSBA, Am. U., 1972; M of Mgmt., Northwestern U., 1982. Internat. mktg. mgr., product mgr. FMC Corp., Chgo., 1973-84, mktg. and engring. mgr., 1985-90; cons. Frank Lynn & Assoc., Chgo., 1984-85; v.p., gen. mgr. Lindberg unit of Gen. Signal, Watertown, Wis., 1990-93; pres. Abar Ipsen Industries, Inc., Bensalem, Pa., 1993-96, Centorr Vacuum Industries, Nashua, N.H., 1993-96, Linac Holdings, Inc., Rockford, Ill., 1994-96; pres., CEO Pangborn Corp., Hagerstown, Md., 1996—. Inventor material handling equipment. Mem. The Exec. Com., The Mfrs. Alliance. Episcopalian. Office: Pangborn Corp Pangborn Blvd Hagerstown MD 21741-0380

MOORE, MARC ANTHONY, university administrator, writer, retired military officer; b. Dallas, July 15, 1928; s. Edward Clark and Mary Cathrine (Spake) M.; m. Mary Joan Donahue, Sept. 5, 1953; children—Daniel, Mary Ellen, Virginia, Andria. B.A., So. Meth. U., 1951; M.A., George Washington U., 1970; grad., Amphibious Warfare Sch., 1960, Nat. War Coll., 1974; LHD (hon.), Philippine Women's U., 1987. Served as enlisted man U.S. Marine Corps, 1946-48, commd. 2d lt., 1951, advanced through grades to maj. gen., 1978; regtl. comdr. Camp Pendleton, Calif., 1971; regtl. exec. officer Vietnam, 1970; with Joint Chief Staff Ops., Washington, 1977-78; asst. dir. Marine Command and Staff Coll., 1972-73; dir. div. English and history U.S. Naval Acad., 1974-76; comdg. gen. 4th Marine Div., New Orleans, 1978-80; chief of staff U.S. Forces, Japan, from 1980, now ret.; former chancellor San Diego campus, v.p. for devel. Nat. U., 1990-91; teaching asst. dept. psychology George Washington U., 1974; instr. dept. behavioral sci. U.S. Naval Acad., 1975-76; adj. faculty Nat. U., 1983. Co-founder Leadership 2000; mem. coun. advisors Calif. State U., San Marcos, 1993-96; mem. bd. advisors Marine Mil. Acad., 1983-95; founder, bd. advisors Command Mus. and Warfare Leadership Ctr., Marine Recruit Depot, San Diego, 1984—. Decorated Legion of Merit, Bronze Star with oak leaf cluster, Air medal, D.S.H., Order Sacred Treasure (Japan); recipient Disting. Alumni award So. Meth. U., 1981, Superior Svc. medal, Dept. Def., Meritorious Svc. medal Dept. Def. Mem. Marine Corps Assn., Phi Delta Theta. Roman Catholic. Home: 3611 Lago Sereno Escondido CA 92029-7902

MOORE, MARGARET BEAR, American literature educator; b. Zhenjiang, China, Mar. 14, 1925; came to U.S., 1929; d. James Edwin Jr. and Margaret Irvine (White) Bear; m. Rayburn S. Moore, Aug. 30, 1947; children: Margaret Elizabeth Moore Kopcinski, Robert Rayburn. BA, Agnes Scott Coll., 1946; MA, U. Ga., 1973. Book rev. editor East Ark. Record, Helena, Ark., 1947-50; bibliographer Perkins Libr. Duke U., Durham, N.C., 1950-52; instr. in English Hendrix Coll., Conway, Ark., 1955-56, U. Ctrl. Ark., Conway, 1958-59; editor Inst. Cmty. & Area Devel. U. Ga., Athens, 1974-79; tchr. Latin Athens Acad., 1980-81; ind. scholar Athens, 1981—. Author (book revs.) Am. Lit., 1989, 94, Nathaniel Hawthorne Rev., 1992, The Salem World of Nathaniel Hawthorne, 1997; contbr. articles to profl. jours. Tchr. Presbyn. Ch., Va., Ark., N.C. and Ga., 1945—; deacon, elder First Presbyn. Ch., Athens, 1974—. Mem. MLA, Am. Lit. Assn., Philol. Assn. Carolinas, Soc. for Study So. Lit., South Atlantic MLA, Nathaniel Hawthorne Soc. (exec. com. 1987-90, sec. 1997—), William Gilmore Simms Soc., Peabody Essex Mus., House of Seven Gables, Va. Hist. Soc., Mortar Bd., Phi Beta Kappa, Phi Kappa Phi. Avocations: reading, walking, travel. Home: 106 Saint James Dr Athens GA 30606-3926

MOORE, MARIANNA GAY, law librarian, consultant; b. La Grange, Ga., Sept. 12, 1939; d. James Henry and Avanelle (Gay) M. AB in French, English, U. Ga., 1961; MLS, Emory U., 1964; postgrad., U. Ga., 1965-66, U. Ill., 1967-68. Asst. law libr. U. Ga., Athens, 1964-66; asst. libr. Yavapai Coll. Libr., Prescott, Ariz., 1969-72; libr. U. Ill. Law Libr., Urbana, 1966-68; law libr. Leva, Hawes, Symington, Washington, 1972-75; libr. project coord. Wash. Occupational Info. Svc., Olympia, 1976-80, Wash. State Health Facilities Assn., Olympia, 1981-82; mgr. Wash. State Ret. Tchrs. Assn., Olympia, 1982-83, exec. dir., 1984-89; exec. dir. Wash. State Retired Tchrs. Found., Olympia, 1986-89; law libr. Solano County Law Libr., Fairfield, Calif., 1989—; libr. LIBRARY/USA N.Y. World's Fair, N.Y.C., 1965; consulting law libr. Dobbins, Weir, Thompson & Stephenson, Vacaville, Calif., 1989—; law libr. cons. Coconino County Law Libr., Flagstaff, Ariz., 1968-70. Author: Guide to Fin. Aid for Wash. State Students, 1979; tng. package to introduce librs. to Wash. State Info. Svc., 1980. Bd. dirs. Thurston County Sr. Ctr., Olympia, 1976-84, Thurston-Mason Nutrition Program, Olympia, 1977-79, Wash. Soc. Assn. Execs., Edmonds, 1987-89. Mem. Am. Assn. Law Librs., No. Calif. Assn. Law Librs., Calif. Coun. of County Law Librs. Avocations: reading, tatting, travel, music, calligraphy, cats. Office: Solano County Law Libr Hall of Justice 600 Union Ave Fairfield CA 94533-6324

MOORE, MARILYN PATRICIA, community counselor; b. Nashville, Jan. 16, 1950; m. Roy Allen Moore; children: Christopher Manuel, Christina Marilyn, Catrina Marilyn. Merchandising cert., Bauder Coll., 1969; BS, Tenn. Wesleyan Coll., 1975; MEd., Tenn. Tech., 1979, EdS, 1981. Lic. profl. adminstr. and tchr., Tenn. Head resident/counselor Tenn. Wesleyan Coll., Athens, 1974-75; tchr. Rhea County Dept. Edn., Dayton, Tenn., 1975-81; prin. Rhea County Dept. Edn., 1981, 84-86; adj. coll. instr. Tenn. Tech. U., Cookeville, 1981—; coord. off campus program Tenn. Tech. U., 1981-86; tchr. Rhea County Dept. Edn., Dayton, 1982-83; prin. Rhea County Dept. Edn., 1983-86, supt. schs., 1986-90; evaluator, community intervention counselor Behavioral Health Svcs., Kingsport, Tenn., 1992-94, cmty. intervention counselor, 1994—; voting mem. Rhea County Purchase and Fin., Dayton, 1986—; adj. faculty East Tenn. State U., 1991, Holston Svcs., 1991. Chairperson Polit. Action Com. for Edn., Dayton, 1978-81; bd. dirs. Battered Women, Inc., Crossville, Tenn., 1987—; chairperson allocations United Way, Dayton, 1987-88; mem. Tenn. Sheriff's Assn., Nashville, 1988—; aide-de-camp Rep. Shirley Duer, Nashville, 1987; life mem. Presdl. Task Force, 1991—. Recipient Cert. Appreciation, Am. Legion, 1988, Cert. Participation, Very Spl. Arts, 1989, Am. Fedn. of Police Edgar Hoover award, 1991, John Edgar Hoover Meml. Gold medal, 1991; named Hon. Mem. Staff, Senator Anna Belle O'Brien, Nashville, 1987. Mem. NEA (past del.), Tenn. Edn. Assn., Tenn. Orgn. Sch. Supts., Alliance for a Drug Free Tenn. (chairperson 1987-91), Women Hwy. Safety Leaders Tenn. (county leader 1989—), USAF Aux. Aerospace (capt. 1987—), Tenn. Assn. Sch. Bus. Officials, Dayton C. of C., Nat. Police Assn. (Am. Patriotism award 1993). Republican. Methodist. Avocations: workshops, classes, readings on law and the Am. legal system. Home: 205 Santa Fe Dr Bristol TN 37620-6441 Office: Kingsport Med Ctr 441 Clay St Ste 3 Kingsport TN 37660-3654

MOORE, MARK HARRISON, criminal justice and public policy educator; b. Oak Park, Ill., Mar. 19, 1947; s. Charles Eugene and Jean (McFeely) M.; m. Martha Mansfield Church, June 15, 1968; children—Phoebe Sylvina, Tobias McFeely, Gaylen Williams. Student, Phillips Acad., 1962-65; B.A., Yale U., 1969; M.Public Policy, Harvard U., 1971, Ph.D., 1973. Teaching fellow, instr. public policy J.F. Kennedy Sch. Govt., Harvard U., Boston, 1971-73; asst. prof. J.F. Kennedy Sch. Govt., Harvard U., 1973-74, 75-76, assoc. prof., 1976-79, Guggenheim prof. criminal justice policy and mgmt., 1979—; spl. asst. to adminstr., chief planning officer Drug Enforcement Adminstrn., U.S. Dept. Justice, Washington, 1974-75; cons. U.S. Dept. Justice, 1975-76, 81. Author: Buy and Bust: The Effective Regulation of an Illicit Market in Heroin, 1977, Creating Public Value: Strategic Management in Government, 1995, (with others) Dangerous Offenders, 1985, From Children to Citizens: Vol. 1, The Mandate for Juvenile Justice, 1987, (with Malcolm K. Sparrow) Ethics in Government, 1990, (with Malcolm K. Sparrow and David Kennedy) Beyond 911: A New Era for Policing, 1991; editor: (with Joel Fleishman and Lance Leibman) Public Duties, 1980, (with Dean Gerstein) Alcohol and Public Policy, 1981. Mem. Assn. Schs. Public Policy and Mgmt., Phi Beta Kappa. Home: 331 Waverley St Belmont MA 02178-2418 Office: JF Kennedy Sch Govt Harvard U 79 Jfk St Cambridge MA 02138-5801

MOORE, MARSHA LYNN, elementary education educator; b. Washington, May 19, 1946; d. Marshall Alexander and Doris Virginia (Diggs) M. BA, Howard U., 1967; MEd, U. Md., 1973. Cert. sch. counseling K-12; cert. tchr. grades 1-6. Counselor Balt. County Schs., Towson, Md., 1972-77; fashion coord., mgr. Wallach's Ladies' Store, Nanuet, N.Y., 1977-80, Livingston, N.J., 1977-80; adult edn. cons., counselor East Orange (N.J.) Adult High Sch., 1980-83; minority counselor Essex County Community Coll., Newark, 1984-85; equal opportunity fund counselor, instr. Kean Coll., Union, N.J., 1985-87; elem. tchr. Washington Pub. Schs., 1967-72, 87—; coord. counselor Summer Youth Employment Program, East Orange, 1982; career fair coord. East Orange Adult H.S., 1981, Essex County C.C., 1985; math. tutorial coord., sch. newspaper coord. Brookland Sch., Washington, 1990-92, readers/writers club coord., 1992-93, chairperson restructuring team, 1992-93, restructuring team mem., 1993-94, 96-97, student coun. coord., 1993-95, 96—, 5th grade chairperson, 1996-97; mem. discipline com. PTA, 1996—. Chmn. Teen Lift, N.J., Delteens, Washington; 2d v.p. Washington Pan-Hellenic Coun., 1994-96, fin. sec. 1996—, co-chair Greek Forum, 1996-97. Mem. AFT, Howard U. Alumni Assn. (N.J. coord. 1980-87, v.p. Washington 1989-91, pres. 1991-93, reunion planning com. 1967), Friends of Andrew Rankin Chapel (adj. sec. 1994—, newsletter co-chairperson), Delta Sigma Theta. Episcopalian. Avocations: tennis, gardening, swimming, travel, cooking. Office: Washington Pub Schs 415 12th St NW Washington DC 20004-1905

MOORE, MARTIN, educator; b. Wilson, Ark., June 16, 1934; s. Martin Williams and Grace Watson (Adams) M. BA, U. Miss., 1958. Tchr. Latin

Peekskill (N.Y.) Mil. Acad., 1959-65; tchr. Latin, French The Browning Sch. for Boys, N.Y.C., 1965-66; tchr. English, Latin Hobbs (N.Mex.) High Sch., 1966-67; tchr. Latin, ancient history Bklyn. Friends Sch., 1967—. Poll watcher South Bklyn. Dem. Club, 1974; mem. Met. Coun. Housing, Bklyn., 1986—; tour dir. Ch. of St. Mary the Virgin, N.Y.C., 1978-82. Mem. Classical Assn. of the Empire State, Classical Assn. of the Atlantic States, N.Y. Classical Club (pres. 1991-92, scholar 1987). Democrat. Episcopalian. Avocations: music, theater, running, tennis, reading. Home: 80 Livingston St Brooklyn NY 11201 Office: Bklyn Friends Sch 375 Pearl St Brooklyn NY 11201-3706

MOORE, MARY FRENCH (MUFFY MOORE), potter, community activist; b. N.Y.C., Feb. 25, 1938; d. John and Rhoda (Teagle) Walker French; m. Alan Baird Minier, Oct. 9, 1982; children: Jonathan Corbet, Jennifer Corbet, Michael Corbet. BA cum laude, Colo. U., 1964. Ceramics mfr., Wilson, Wyo., 1969-82, Cheyenne, Wyo., 1982—; commr. County of Teton (Wyo.), 1976-83, chmn. bd. commrs., 1981, 83, mem. dept. pub. assistance and social svc., 1976-82, mem. recreation bd., 1978-81, water quality adv. bd., 1976-82. Bd. dirs. Teton Sci. Sch., 1968-83, vice chmn., 1979-81, chmn., 1982; bd. dirs. Grand Teton Music Festival, 1963-68, Teton Energy Coun., 1978-83, Whitney Gallery of Western Art, Cody, Wyo., 1995—; mem. water quality adv. bd. Wyo. Dept. Environ. Quality, 1979-83; Dem. precinct committeewoman, 1978-81; mem. Wyo. Dem. Cen. Com., 1981-83; vice chmn. Laramie County Dem. Cen. Com., 1983-84, Wyo. Dem. nat. committewoman, 1984-87; chmn. Wyo. Dem. Party, 1987-89; del. Dem. Nat. Conv., 1984, 88, mem. fairness commn. Dem. Nat. Com., 1985, vice-chairwoman western caucus, 1986-89; chmn. platform com. Wyo. Dem. Conv., 1982; mem. Wyo. Dept. Environ. Quality Land Quality Adv. Bd., 1983-86; mem. Gov.'s Steering Com. on Troubled Youth, 1982, dem. nat. com. Compliance Assistance Commn., 1986-87; exec. com. Assn. of State Dem. Chairs, 1989; mem. Wyo. Coun. on the Arts, 1989-95, chmn., 1994-95, Dem. Nat. Com. Jud. Coun., 1989—; legis. aide for Gov. Wyo., 1985, 86; project coord. Gov.'s Com. on Childrens' Svcs., 1985-86; bd. dirs. Wyo. Outdoor Coun., 1984-85; polit. dir., dep. mgr. Schuster for Congress, 1994-95. Recipient Woman of Yr. award Jackson Hole Bus. and Profl. Women, 1981, Dem. of Yr. Nellie Tayloe Ross award, Wyo. Dems., 1990. Mem. Alden Kindred of Am., Jackson Hole Art Assn. (bd. dirs., vice chmn. 1981, chmn. 1982), Assn. State Dem. Chairs, Soc. Mayflower Descendents, Pi Sigma Alpha. Home: 8907 Cowpoke Rd Cheyenne WY 82009-1234

MOORE, MATTHEW EMERSON, environmental program planning management specialist; b. Tuscaloosa, Ala., Aug. 5, 1964; s. Charles Thomas Moore Sr. and Annabel (Owens) Moore Allen; m. Anne Goldthwaite Dorr, March 20, 1993. BS, No. Ariz. U., 1987; MA, Claremont Grad. Sch., 1989. Mem. policy clinic team Ctr. for Politics and Policy, Claremont (Calif.) Grad. Sch., 1987-89; rsch. asst. Rose Inst. State and Local Govt., Claremont, 1989; analyst, asst. planner LSA Assocs., Inc., Irvine, Calif., 1989-90; project mgr. Urban Vision, Irvine, 1991-93; regional water quality mgmt. planning coord. Ariz. Dept. Environ. Quality, Phoenix, 1994; sr. air quality analyst Idaho Divsn. Environ. Quality, Boise, 1994—; mem. Sch. Renewable Natural Resources master's thesis com. U. Ariz., Tucson, 1994. Author: Lead Agency CEQA Procedures Survey Results, 1991; co-author: Taxes, Trees and Transit; California's Response to CO2-Induced Climate Change, 1990, Curbing Air Pollution in the South Coast Air Basin, 1989; editor-at-large: Multiple Resource Mgmt. Plan for El Cipres, Ensenada, Mex., 1994. Founding pres. Explorer Post 477, Boy Scouts Am., Tempe, Ariz., 1980-82; interpretive specialist Walnut Canyon Nat. Monument, Flagstaff, Ariz., 1987; mem. drought planning adv. bd. City of Claremont, 1988-89; mem. leadership coun. First United Meth. Ch., Boise. Mem. Am. Planning Assn., Am. Polit. Sci. Assn., Nat. Assn. Environ. Profls., Internat. Assn. Impact Assessment. Methodist. Avocations: sailing, surfing, reading, hiking, biking.

MOORE, MATTHEW SCOTT, publisher, deaf advocate, author; b. Indpls., Dec. 31, 1958; s. Scott Moore and JoNelle (Painter) Giegerich. BA in Social Work, Rochester Inst. Tech., 1983. Founder, pres. MSM Prodns., Ltd., Rochester, N.Y., 1984—; pub., co-editor-in-chief Deaf Life, Rochester, 1986—; chmn. Third N.Y. State Conf. for Sign-Lang. Instrs., Rochester, 1992; lectr., spkr. in field. Co-author: For Hearing People Only, 1992, Great Deaf Americans, 2nd edit., 1996. Co-dir. Flying Words Project, Rochester, 1989—; bd. dirs. Lights On! Deaf Cmty. Theater, 1992-95; founder Deaf Rochesterians' Cmty. Ctr. Core Team, 1992. Recipient Recognition cert. World Recreation Assn. of Deaf, 1990, Humanitarian award Delta Sigma Phi, 1991, Pres. award Am. Sign Lang. Tchrs. Assn. Lilac chpt., 1993, Outstanding Alumni award NTID, 1993, Tex. Deaf Caucus award, 1993, Alice Cogswell award Gallaudet U., 1994, Printing Week award, 1995, Disting. Alumni Modern ERA award Ind. Sch. Deaf, 1997. Avocations: writing, performing, collecting birdhouses, Plains Indian artifacts, theater. Office: MSM Prodns Ltd Box 23380 Rochester NY 14692

MOORE, MCPHERSON DORSETT, lawyer; b. Pine Bluff, Ark., Mar. 1, 1947; s. Arl Van and Jesse (Dorsett) M. BS, U. Miss., 1970; JD, U. Ark., 1974. Bar: Ark. 1974, Mo. 1975, U.S. Patent and Trademark Office 1977, U.S. Dist. Ct. (ea. dist.) Mo. 1977, U.S. Ct. Appeals (8th, 10th and Fed. cirs.). Design engr. Tenneco, Newport News, Va., 1970-71; assoc. Rogers, Eilers & Howell, St. Louis, 1974-80; ptnr. Rogers, Howell, Moore & Haferkamp, St. Louis, 1981-89; ptnr. Armstrong, Teasdale, Schlafly & Davis, St. Louis, 1989-95; ptnr. Polster, Lieder, Woodruff & Lucchesi, St. Louis, 1995—. Bd. dirs. Legal Services of Eastern Mo., 1984—. With USAR, 1970-76. Mem. ABA, Bar Assn. Met. St. Louis (chmn. young lawyers sect. 1981-82, sec. 1984-85, v.p. 1985-86, chmn. trial sect. 1986-87, pres. 1988-89), Ark. Bar Assn., St. Louis Bar Found. (sec. 1984-85, v.p. 1988-89, pres. 1989-90), The Mo. Bar (chmn. patent, trademark and copyright law com. 1992-94, co-chmn. 1994-95), St. Louis County Bar Assn., Women Lawyers Assn., Am. Intellectual Property Law Assn., Mound City Bar Assn., Phi Delta Theta Alumni (treas. St. Louis chpt. 1987-88, sec. 1988-89, v.p. 1989-90). Episcopalian. Club: Univ. (St. Louis). Home: 33 Deerfield Rd Saint Louis MO 63124-1412 Office: Polster Lieder Woodruff & Lucchesi 763 S New Ballas Rd Saint Louis MO 63141-8704

MOORE, MECHLIN DONGAN, communications executive, marketing consultant; b. N.Y.C., May 21, 1930; s. Albere Ethier and Pamela (Robinson) M.; m. Elizabeth Ann Tonkin, Feb. 11, 1956 (dec. 1992); children: Lansing, Pamela; m. Valery Ann Shields, July 14, 1995. AB, Harvard U., 1952. Reporter Washington Post, 1955-59; dir. build Am. better com. Nat. Assn. Real Estate Bds., D.C., 1960-64; dir. info. Urban Land Inst., D.C., 1964-66; exec. v.p. Central Assn. Seattle, 1966-70; asst. to pres. United Airlines, Inc., Chgo., 1971-72, sr. v.p. external affairs, 1972-74, group v.p. mktg., 1975-76, sr. v.p. pub. affairs, 1976-79; pres. Ins. Info. Inst., N.Y.C., 1979-91; pvt. practice Naples, Fla., 1991—; pres. Eagles Mere Water Co., 1993-96; bd. dirs. Automobile Protection Corp.; bd. electors Ins. Hall of Fame; bd. govs. Internat. Ins. Seminars. Contbg. author publs. Nat. Assn. Real Estate Bds.; assoc. editor Jour. Property Mgmt. Adv. bd. mem. Traffic Inst. Northwestern U.; past mem. St. George's Vestry, N.Y.C. 1st lt. U.S. Army, 1952-54. Recipient Disting. Service award Central Assn. Seattle, 1972. Mem. Univ. Club, Pelican Marsh Golf Club. Republican. Episcopalian. Home: 1273 Grand Isle Ct Naples FL 34108

MOORE, MICHAEL, film director. Films include Silver City, 1951, Stalag 17, 1953, Pony Express, 1953, Little Boy Lost, 1953, Jamaica Run, 1953, The Desperate Hours, 1955, Hot Dog...The Movie, 1984, Secret Admirer, 1985, Paper Hearts, 1993; actor, dir., prodr. Roger and Me, 1989; actor, dir. prodr., writer Canadian Bacon, 1994; TV movies include Convicted, 1986, Gypsy, 1993; dir., creator, host TV Nation, 1994— (Outstanding Informational Series Emmy award, 1995); dir. films include Paradise Hawaiian Style, 1965, An Eye for an Eye, 1966, The Fastest Guitar Alive, 1967, The Frontiersman, 1968, Buckskin, 1968; prodr., writer Clay Farmers, 1988. Office: CAA 9830 Wilshire Blvd Beverly Hills CA 90212-1804*

MOORE, MICHAEL THOMAS, mining executive; b. Bklyn., Oct. 10, 1934; s. Michael Joseph and Lucille M. (Wild) M.; m. Beatrice Lorraine Quinto, Sept. 10, 1960; children: Teresa, Stephanie, Jennifer, Elisabeth. BS in Bus., Indiana U. of Pa., 1956; postgrad., U. Pitts., 1959-63, Am. U., 1963-64, NYU, 1964-66. Fin. analyst, supr. U.S. Steel Corp., Duquesne, Pa., 1956-63; plant controller Am.-Standard, Balt., 1963-64; sr. fin. analyst Celanese Corp., N.Y.C., 1964-66; asst. controller to controller Cleve.-Cliffs Inc., 1966-72, v.p. controller, 1972-75, sr. v.p., 1975-83, exec. v.p., CFO, 1983-86, pres., dir., 1986, pres., dir., CEO, 1987, pres., CEO, 1987—, chmn., CEO, 1988—; bd. dirs. KeyCorp, LTV Corp. Bd. dirs. Cleve. Tomorrow, 1989—; trustee Fairview Health Sys., Cleve., 1990—. With U.S. Army, 1957-58. Named Outstanding Alumnus Indiana U. of Pa., 1981, Mining Industry CEO of Yr., 1993. Mem. Am. Iron and Steel Inst. (bd. dirs. 1987—), Nat. Mining Assn. (bd. dirs. 1987—), Bus. Roundtable, Am. Iron Ore Assn. (bd. dirs. 1987—), Union Club, The Fifty Club, Westwood Country Club, Pepper Pike Club, Rolling Rock Club, Quail Creek Country Club, Laurel Valley Golf Club. Office: Cleveland Cliffs Inc 1100 Superior Ave E Cleveland OH 44114-2518

MOORE, MICHAEL WATSON, musician, string bass, educator; b. Cin., May 16, 1945; s. Clarence Watson and Jeannette Elizabeth (Gardner) M.; m. Renee Allyn White, Oct. 23, 1993; children: Benjamin Butler, Matthew Satyavan. Attended, Cin. Coll. Conservatory of Music, 1964-65. Bass instr. Summer Stage Bank Clinic, 1969, Eastman Sch. of Music, Rochester, N.Y., 1974-87, U. Bridgeport, Bridgeport, Conn., 1981-83, L.I. U., Bklyn., 1993-96, William Patterson U., Wayne, N.Y., 1994-95. String bass player with Cal Collins Trio, Cin., 1965, Woody Evans Trio, Cin., 1965, Woody Herman Band, USO, Africa, Ea. Europe, 1966-67, Marion McPartland Trio, N.Y.C., 1968, Freddie Hubbard Quintet, N.Y.C., 1969-70, Jack Wilkins Trio, N.Y.C., 1971, Chet Baker Quartet, N.Y.C., 1972-73, Phil Woods Quartet, N.Y.C., 1972, Gene Bertoncini Duo, N.Y.C., 1972—, Stan Getz Quartet, N.Y.C., 1973, Tony Bennett, N.Y.C., 1973, Ruby Braff, George Barnes Quartet, N.Y.C., 1973-75, Gerry Mulligan Quartet, N.Y.C., 1974, Benny Goodman Sextet, N.Y.C., 1974-76, Lee Konitz Quartet, N.Y.C., 1975, Teddy Wilson Duo, N.Y.C., 1977, Jim Hall Trio, N.Y.C., 1977, Bill Evans Trio, N.Y.C., 1978, Bob Brookmeyer Quintet, N.Y.C., 1978, Mike Abene, Michael Moore Quintet, N.Y.C., 1978, Zoot Sims Quartet, N.Y.C., 1979, Gary Burton Quartet, N.Y.C., 1981-82, Louis Belson Quartet, N.Y.C., 1982, Roger Kellaway Duo and Trio, N.Y.C., 1980s, Jimmy Rowles Duo, N.Y.C., 1980s, Jon Scoffield Duo and Quartet, N.Y.C., 1980s, Lew Tabackin Trio, N.Y.C., 1980s, Hank Jones Trio, N.Y.C., 1980s, Shelly Mann Trio, N.Y.C., 1980s, Pepper Adams Quartet, N.Y.C., 1980s, Lou Levy Duo, N.Y.C., 1980s, Al Cohen Trio, N.Y.C., 1980s, Jake Hanna Quartet, N.Y.C., 1980s, Rosemary Clooney, N.Y.C., 1987-88, Louis Stewart Trio, Ireland and U.K., 1990, Howard Alden Trio, N.Y.C., 1990s, Warren Vache Trio, N.Y.C., 1990s, Harry Allen Trio, N.Y.C., 1990s, Ken Peplowski Trio, N.Y.C., 1990s, Charlie Byrd Quartet, N.Y.C., 1990s; co-leader duo with Rufus Reid, 1995, with Chris Potter, 1995; leader duo with Bill Charlap, 1995; composer: Rio Pindare, 1986, Wake Me When It's Over, 1988, The Lilter, 1989, The Old New Waltz, 1992, Zoot's Suite, 1995, Just Me, Just Me, 1995; recs. Michael Moore Trio Plays Gershwin, 1993, Michael Moore/Bill Charlap, 1995 (One of the Best Jazz CDs of 95, The New Yorker, 1996), Michael Moore/Rufus Reid Doublebass Delights, 1996 (One of the Best Jazz CDs of 96, The New Yorker, 1997); author: Improvising in the Thumb Position: Method for Improvisation for the String Bass, 1986; performer: (with Weslia Whitfield) The White House, 1996. Councilman Borough of Bangor, Pa., 1987-88. Mem. ASCAP. Avocation: piano. Home and Office: 5 E 22nd St Apt 15M New York NY 10010-5325

MOORE, MIKE, state attorney general; m. Tisha Moore; 1 child, Kyle. Grad., Jackson County Jr. Coll., 1972; BA, U. Miss., 1974, JD, 1976. Asst. dist. atty. State of Miss., 1977-78, dist. atty., 1979, atty. gen., 1988—. Mem. ABA, Miss. State Bar Assn. Office: Office of Atty Gen PO Box 220 Jackson MS 39205-0220*

MOORE, MIKE, baseball league executive; married Barbara Moore. Degree in bus. adminstrn., U. Tampa, 1963. Sports info. dir. U. Tampa, 1963-65; sports reporter Sta. WTVT-TV, Tampa, 1965-74; v.p., gen. mgr., part-owner Tampa Tarpons, 1971-88; chief adminstrv. officer Nat. Assn. Profl. Baseball Leagues, Inc., 1988-91, pres., 1991—. Office: Nat Assn Profl Baseball Leagues PO Box A Saint Petersburg FL 33731

MOORE, MILO ANDERSON, banker; b. Orange, N.J., Aug. 26, 1942; s. Milo H. and Helen (Wiley) M.; m. Judith J. Colosimo, May 4, 1968; children: Milo Robert, Matthew Wiley, Marykate Bartlett. BS, Ithaca Coll., 1964; MBA, Rutgers U., 1971. Traffic supt. N.Y. Tel. Co., N.Y.C., 1964-71; trust officer Midlantic Nat. Bank, Newark, 1971-76; v.p. Shearson Loeb Rhoades, N.Y.C., 1976-80; sr. v.p. Donaldson Lufkin & Jenrette, N.Y.C., 1980-85; sr. mng. dir. Bear, Stearns & Co., 1985-92; v.p. Chase Manhattan Pvt. Bank, Morristown, N.J., 1992—. Advisor Jr. Achievement, Bronx, N.Y., 1967-68; pres. Chatham Jaycees, N.J., 1974; big bros. Morris County Big Bros., Morristown, 1971-81; pres. Stanley Congl. Ch., Chatham, N.J., 1995-97; trustee SAGE Inc., 1994—. Mem. Securities Industry Assn. (tax shelter com. 1982-85), Glenburnie Club (pres. 1989—), Canoe Brook Country Club (Summit, N.J.), Beta Gamma Sigma. Office: Chase Manhattan Pvt Banking 225 South St Morristown NJ 07960-5336

MOORE, NICHOLAS G., finance company executive; m. Jo Anne Moore; children: Kelly, Garrett, Patrick, Katy. BS in Acctg., St. Mary's Coll.; JD, U. Calif., Berkeley. With Coopers & Lybrand, 1968—; prin. tax practice Coopers & Lybrand, San Jose, Calif., 1974-81; coun. Coopers & Lybrand, N.Y.C., 1984, exec. com., 1988, vice chmn. west region, 1991-92, client svc. vice chmn., 1992-94, chmn., CEO, 1994—. Bd. bus. coun. N.Y. State, bd. trustees coms. for econ. devel.; bd. dirs. Co-Operation Ireland; mem. Bus.-Higher Edn. Forum, U.S. C. of C. Ctr. for Workforce Preparation, N.Y.C. Partnership; vice chmn. bus. com. Met. Mus. of Art; adv. coun. Weissman Ctr. for Internat. Bus. Baruch Coll.; bd. regents St. Mary's Coll., Calif. Mem. AICPA, Calif. Bar Assn., Calif. Soc. CPAs, N.Y. State Soc. CPAs. Office: 1251 Avenue Of The Americas New York NY 10020-1104*

MOORE, OLIVER SEMON, III, publishing executive, consultant; b. Jersey City, July 26, 1942; s. Oliver S. and Ann Loy (Spies) M.; m. Dina Downing DuBois, Feb. 23, 1961 (div. 1974); 1 child, Deborah; m. Christine Laine Meyers, May 12, 1990; 1 child, Kathryn Laine. BA, U. Va., 1964. Chief bur. Richmond (Va.) Times-Dispatch, 1964-66; corr. Time mag., N.Y.C., 1966-67, contbg. editor, 1967-68; assoc. editor Newsweek, N.Y.C., 1969-71; freelance writer, 1972-75; mng. editor Motor Boating and Sailing, N.Y.C., 1976-78, editor, 1980-82; exec. editor US Mag., N.Y. Times Co., 1978-80; dep. editor Town & Country Mag., N.Y.C., 1982-84; editor Sci. Digest Mag., N.Y.C., 1984-86; pub. dir. Yachting Mag., N.Y.C., 1986-95; editorial dir. Outdoor Life, N.Y.C., 1993-95; v.p. The Outdoor Co., N.Y.C., 1994-95; editor-at-large Motor Boating & Sailing, 1995—; pres. Alamo Pub. Svcs., Inc., Detroit, 1995—. Author: (poems) Voices International, 1969; contbg. editor Sports Afield, 1996—; photographer (mags.) Motor Boating and Sailing, Yachting, Working Woman, (books) Lines to a Little Girl, Rancho Paradiso. Recipient Merit award Art Dirs. Club, 1981, award of merit Soc. Publ. Designers, 1981, Excellence in Media award Nat. Arbor Day Found., 1985. Mem. Nat. Marine Mfrs. Assn., Am. Soc. Mag. Editors, Mag. Pubs. Assn. (nat. mag. award 1995), N.Y. Yacht Club, Grosse Pointe (Mich.) Club, Bayview (Mich.) Yacht Club, The Huntsman (Mich.). Republican. Episcopalian. Avocations: sailing, antique cars. Office: Alamo Pub Svcs Inc 3645 Crooks Rd Troy MI 48084-1642

MOORE, OMAR KHAYYAM, experimental sociologist; b. Helper, Utah, Feb. 11, 1920; s. John Gustav and Mary Jo (Crowley) M.; m. Ruth Garnand, Nov. 19, 1942; 1 child, Venn. BA, Doane Coll., 1942; MA, Washington U., St. Louis, 1946, PhD, 1949. Instr. Washington U., St. Louis, 1949-52; teaching assoc. Northwestern U., Evanston, Ill., 1950-51; rsch. asst., prof. sociology Tufts Coll., Medford, Mass., 1952-53; researcher Naval Rsch. Lab., Washington, 1953-54; asst. prof. sociology Yale U., New Haven, 1954-57, assoc. prof. sociology, 1957-63; prof. psychology Rutgers U., New Brunswick, N.J., 1963-65; prof. social psychology, sociology U. Pitts., 1965-71, prof. sociology, 1971-89, prof. emeritus, 1989—; scholar-in-residence Nat. Learning Ctr.'s Capital Children's Mus., Washington, 1989-90; pres. Responsive Environ. Found., Inc., Estes Park, Colo., 1962—; assessor of rsch. projects The Social Scis. and Humanities Rsch. Coun. Can., 1982—; adj. prof. U. Colo., Boulder, 1992—. Contbg. editor Educational Technology; contbr. numerous articles to profl. jours.; patentee in field; motion picture producer and director. Recipient Award The Nat. Soc. for Programmed Instruction, 1965, Award Doane Coll Builder Award, 1967, Ednl. Award Urban Youth Action, Inc., 1969, Award House of Culture, 1975, Cert. of Appreciation, 1986, Cert. of Appreciation D.C. Pub. Schs., 1987, da Vinci Award Inst. for the Achievement of Human Potential, 1988, Cert. of Appreciation Capital Children's Museum, 1988, award Jack & Jill of America Found., 1988, Cert. of Appreciation U.S. Dept. of Edn., 1988, Cert. of Appreciation D.C. Pub. Schs., 1990, Person of Yr. in Ednl. Tech. award Ednl. Tech. mag., 1990. Mem. AAAS, Am. Math. Soc., Am. Psychol. Assn., Internat. Sociol. Assn., Am. Sociol. Assn., Assn. for Symbolic Logic, Assn. for Anthrop. Study of Play, Philosophy Sci. Assn., Psychonomics Soc., Soc. for Applied Sociology, Soc. for Exact Philosophy, Math. Assn. Am. Republican. Avocation: mountaineering. Home and Office: 2341 Upper High Dr PO Box 1673 Estes Park CO 80517

MOORE, PAT HOWARD, engineering and construction company executive; b. Laredo, Tex., Sept. 16, 1930; s. Howard Warren and Odette Evelyn (Bunn) M.; m. Elsie Mae Crossman, Mar. 23, 1954; children: Linda Marie Ford, Margaret Ann, Andrew Patrick. BA, Rice U., 1952, BS in Civil Engring., 1953; postgrad., Tulane U., 1956-58. Registered profl. engr., Tex., La. Spl. investigator Army Counter Intelligence Corps., Houston, 1954-56; div. engr. McDermott Inc., Morgan City, La., 1956-58; pres., dir. Navasota Tel. Co., Tex., 1958-63; project mgr. Brown & Root, Inc., Houston, 1963-67, exec. v.p., chief fin. officer, dir., 1990-95; pres., dir. Fluor Ocean Svcs., Houston, 1968-80; sr. v.p. Raymond Internat., Inc., Houston, 1980-86; pres., dir. Martin Moore Inc., Bellaire, Tex., 1986-90; dir. Charter Builders, Inc., Dallas, 1988-90; mgmt. cons. Bellaire, 1996—; adv. dir. Tex. Commerce Bank, Houston, 1985-96; lectr. ethics Rice U., 1996—; dir. United Scaffolding, Houston, 1997—. Bd. govs. Rice U., 1984-88. With U.S. Army, 1954-56. Fellow ASCE. Lodge: Kiwanis (pres. 1960). Home: 5251 Birdwood Rd Houston TX 77096-2503 Office: PO Box 1156 Bellaire TX 77402-1156

MOORE, PATSY SITES, food service consultant; b. San Marcos, Tex., Mar. 29, 1939; d. Sam W. and Hilda (Wiede) Sites. BS in Home Econs. Edn., S.W. Tex. State U., 1970. Owner, operator Westoner Kindergarten and Nursery Sch., San Marcos, 1965-68; food svc. dir. San Marcos Consol. Ind. Sch. Dist., 1975-97; cons. to food svc. industry, San Marcos, 1997—; cons. in field., 1997—. Mem. steering com. Play Scape/Children's Park, San Marcos, 1992. Mem. Am. Sch. Food Svc. Assn., Tex. Sch. Food Svc. Assn., Ctrl. Tex. Sch. Food Svc. Dirs. Assn. (founder, past pres.), Order Eastern Star. Lutheran. Avocations: gardening, oil painting, lapadary. Home and Office: 285 Hilliard Rd San Marcos TX 78666-8905

MOORE, PAUL, JR., bishop; b. Morristown, N.J., Nov. 15, 1919; s. Paul and Fanny Weber (Hanna) M.; m. Jenny McKean, Nov. 26, 1944 (dec.); children: Honor, Paul III, Adelia, Rosemary, George Mead, Marian Shaw, Daniel Sargent, Susanna McKean, Patience; m. Brenda Hughes Eagle, May 16, 1975. Grad., St. Paul's Sch., Concord, N.H., 1937; B.A., Yale U., 1941; S.T.B., Gen. Theol. Sem., N.Y.C., 1949, S.T.D. (hon.), 1960; D.D. (hon.), Va. Theol. Sem., 1964, Berkeley Divinity Sch., 1971; PhD (hon.), City Coll. N.Y. Ordained to ministry Episcopal Ch., 1949. Mem. team ministry Grace Ch., Jersey City, 1949-57; dean Christ Ch. Cathedral, Indpls., 1957-64; suffragan bishop Washington, 1964-70; bishop coadjutor Diocese, N.Y., 1970-72; bishop Diocese, 1972-89; lectr. St. Augustine's Coll., Canterbury, Eng., 1960; chmn. commn. Delta ministry Nat. Coun. Chgs., 1964-67; mem. urban divsn., nat. exec. coun. Episcopal Ch., 1952-68; dep. to Gen. Conv., 1961, Anglican Congress, 1963; chmn. com. 100; legal def. fund NAACP. Author: The Church Reclaims the City, 2d edit, 1970, Take A Bishop Like Me, 1979. Trustee Bard Coll.; former trustee Gen. Theol. Sem., Trinity Sch., Berkeley Div. Sch. at Yale U., N.Y.C.; mem. Human Rights Watch; mem. adv. coun. Gov.'s Com. on AIDS, 1983-87; chmn. The Timor Project, Project on Religion and Human Rights. Capt. USMCR, 1941-45, PTO. Decorated Navy Cross, Silver Star, Purple Heart.; recipient Margaret Sanger award Planned Parenthood, 1984, Frederick Douglas award North Star Fund, 1989, Freedom of Worship medal Franklin and Eleanor Roosevelt Inst., 1991; Yale Corp. sr. fellow, 1964-90. Mem. Century Club (N.Y.C.), Knickerbocker Club (N.Y.C.). Home and Office: 55 Bank St New York NY 10014-2146

MOORE, PEARL B., nurse; b. Pitts., Aug. 25, 1936; d. Hyman and Ethel (Antis) Friedman; diploma Liliane S. Kaufmann Sch. Nursing, 1956; BS in Nursing, U. Pitts., 1968, M. Nursing, 1974; 1 child, Cheryl. Staff nurse Allegheny Gen. Hosp., Pitts., 1957-60; instr. Liliane S. Kaufman Sch. Nursing, Pitts., 1960-70, asst. dir., 1970, dir., 1970-72; cancer nurse specialist Montefiore Hosp., Pitts., 1974-75; coordinator Brain Tumor Study Group, Pitts., 1975-83; adj. asst. prof. U. Pitts., 1983—. Fellow Am. Acad. Nursing; mem. Am. Nurses Assn., Oncology Nursing Soc. (exec. dir. 1983—, Disting. Svc. award 1995), Am. Soc. Clin. Onoclogy, Am. Soc. Assn. Execs., Nurses Alumnae U. Pitts., Sigma Theta Tau. Contbr. articles in field to profl. publs. Home: 4221 Winterburn Ave Pittsburgh PA 15207-1101 Office: 501 Holiday Dr Pittsburgh PA 15220-2749

MOORE, PENELOPE, school librarian; b. Sylacauga, Ala., Apr. 16, 1937; d. Frank Durward and Dorothy (Roberts) M. BA, Birmingham-So., 1959; MA, U. Miss., Oxford, 1960; MLS, U. Ala., Tuscaloosa, 1973. English tchr. Sylacauga (Ala.) High Sch., 1960-62, Lee High Sch., Huntsville, Ala., 1962-68; office mgr. Bell and Lang Law Firm, Sylacauga, 1969-72; libr. Mountainview Elem. Sch., Sylacauga, 1973—. Bd. dirs. Sylacauga Arts Coun., 1980—, Isabel A. Comer Mus. and Arts Ctr., Aylacauga, 1982-88, A Plus, Montgomery, Ala., 1992—; founder Sylacauga Community Chorus, 1976; active Ala. Libr. Media Leadership Group. Recipient Outstanding Achievement award Sylacauga Arts Coun., 1989; named Sylacauga Woman of the Yr. by Sylacauga Exchange Club, 1983, Ala. State Tchr. of Yr., 1992, Outstanding Vol. by United Way of Sylacauga, 1993. Mem. Ala. Libr. Assn., Ala. Instrl. Media Assn., Libr. and Media Profl. Orgn. (Outstanding Svc. to Ala. Librs. 1992), S.E. Regional Vision for Edn., Alpha Delta Kappa. Republican. United Methodist. Home: PO Box 479 Sylacauga AL 35150-0479 Office: Mountainview Elem School 100 Fluker St Sylacauga AL 35150-2291*

MOORE, PETER BARTLETT, biochemist, educator; b. Boston, Oct. 15, 1939; s. Francis Daniels and Laura Benton (Bartlett) M.; m. Margaret Sue Murphy, Jan. 30, 1966; children: Catherine, Philip. BS, Yale U., 1961, MA (hon.); PhD, Harvard U., 1966. Postdoctoral fellow U. Geneva, 1966-67, MRC Lab. of Molecular Biology, Cambridge, Eng., 1967-69; asst. prof., then assoc. prof. dept. molecular biophysics Yale U., New Haven, 1969-76, assoc. prof. dept. of chemistry, 1976-79, prof., 1979—, chmn. dept. chemistry, 1987-90. Contbr. numerous articles to profl. publs. Guggenheim Found. fellow, 1979-80. Fellow AAAS; mem. Am. Chem. Soc., Am. Soc. Biol. Chemists and Molecular Biologists, Biophys. Soc. Office: Yale U Dept of Chemistry 225 Prospect Ave New Haven CT 06512-1958

MOORE, PHILIP WALSH, appraisal company executive; b. Burmont, Pa., Aug. 1, 1920; s. Louise J.F. and Florence (Walsh) M.; m. Katherine Shean, Dec. 26, 1967 (div.); children: Jourdan, Thomas, Philip, Edward; m. Marya Phaedra Cocalis; children: Stuart, Kristina. AB, Princeton U., 1942; MBA, NYU, 1950. Security analyst First Boston Corp., N.Y.C., 1946-48, v.p. gen. adminstrn., 1967-70; asst. to pres. Schroder Rockefeller and Co., N.Y.C., 1948-50; pres. First Rsch. Co., Miami, Fla., 1950-67, chmn., CEO, 1971-84; pres. J&W Seligman Valuations Corp., N.Y.C., 1984-96; chmn. Moore Associates. Valuations, Inc., N.Y.C., Ponte Vedra Beach, Fla., 1997—; founder, then bd. dirs. Flagship Banks (now Sun Trust Banks), Miami, 1964. Author: Florida Real Estate, 1960, Branch Banking Strategy, 1964, National Image of Economic South, 1976, Valuation Revisited, 1987, Blockage Redux, 1992; author, editor: Internat. Banking Services, 1981. Trustee Ransom Everglades Sch., Miami, 1956-82; mem. adminstrv. com. Lincoln Ctr. Performing Arts, N.Y.C., 1969-75; mem. devel. council U. Hosp., Jacksonville, Fla., 1985—. Served to lt. USN, 1942-46, ETO, PTO. Mem. Inst. Bus. Appraiser, Nat. Assn. Bus. Economists, Am. Soc. Appraisers, Investment Assn. N.Y.C. (pres. 1948-50), So. Assn. Sci. and Industry (trustee, chmn. 1955-72), Overseas Mgmt. Internat. (bd. dirs. 1972-80), Down Town Club (N.Y.C.), River Club (Jacksonville, Fla.), Ponte Vedra Club, Phi Beta Kappa. Republican. Roman Catholic. Avocations: tennis, gardening, reading. Home: 78 San Juan Dr Ponte Vedra Beach FL 32082

MOORE, POWELL ALLEN, former government official, consultant; b. Milledgeville, Ga., Jan. 5, 1938; s. Jere N. and Sarah (Allen) M.; m. Katherine Southward, Oct. 14, 1961; children: Frances Moore Preston, Powell Allen Jr. B.A. in Jounalism, U. Ga., 1959. Press sec. to Richard Russell, U.S. Senate, Washington, 1966-71; dep. dir. pub. info. Dept. Justice, Washington, 1971-72; dep. spl. asst. to Pres. for legis. affairs The White House, Washington, 1973-75, dep. asst. to Pres. for legis. affairs, 1981-82;

cons. pub. affairs Washington, 1975-81; asst. sec. for congl. rels. Dept. State, Washington, 1982-83; v.p. legis. affairs Lockheed Corp., Washington, 1983-85, Ginn, Edington, Moore and Wade, Washington, 1985-90; pres. ASL Internat., Washington, 1990-93; sr. prin., mng. dir. Capitoline, MS&L, Washington, 1993—. Dir. press Com. to Re-elect the Pres., Washington, 1972; cons. Pres. Ford Com., 1976, Reagan-Bush Com., 1980. Served to capt., inf. U.S. Army, 1959-62. Mem. Belle Haven Country Club, Capitol Hill Club, Met. Club. Republican. Episcopalian.

MOORE, RAYBURN SABATZKY, American literature educator; b. Helena, Ark., May 26, 1920; s. Max Sabatzky and Sammie Lou (Rayburn) M.; m. Margaret Elizabeth Bear, Aug. 30, 1947; children: Margaret Elizabeth Moore Kopcinski, Robert Rayburn. A.B., Vanderbilt U., 1942, M.A., 1947; Ph.D., Duke U., 1956. Script writer King Biscuit Time, Interstate Grocer Co., KFFA, 1947-50; Vice pres. Interstate Grocer Co., Helena, 1947-50; research and grad. asst. Duke U., 1952-54; asst. prof. English, Hendrix Coll., Conway, Ark., 1954-55; asso. prof. Hendrix Coll., 1955-58, prof., 1958-59; asso. prof. U. Ga., Athens, 1959-65; prof. U. Ga., 1965-90, prof. emeritus, 1990—, chmn. Am. studies program, 1968-90, chmn. div. lang and lit., 1975-90; vis. scholar Duke U., 1958, 64. Author: Constance Fenimore Woolson, 1963, For the Major and Selected Short Stories of Constance Fenimore Woolson, 1967, Paul Hamilton Hayne, 1972, A Man of Letters in the Nineteenth-Century South: Selected Letters of Paul Hamilton Hayne, 1982; sr. editor: History of Southern Literature, 1985, Selected Letters of Henry James to Edmund Gosse (1882-1915): A Literary Friendship, 1988, The Correspondence of Henry James and the House of Macmillan, 1877-1914: All the Links in the Chain, 1993; mem. editorial bd. U. Ga. Press, 1972-74, Ga. Rev., 1974-82, chmn., 1980-82; contbr. articles, revs. to profl. jours. Mem. troop com. Boy Scouts Am., Athens, 1973-75; deacon, elder Presbyterian Ch., 1962—; mem. Lamar Meml. Lectures com. Mercer U., 1984-91. Served to capt. U.S. Army, 1942-46, PTO. Mem. MLA (exec. com. Gen. Topics VI 1972-75), Soc. Study So. Lit. (exec. com. 1968, 74-79, 85-88, 91-94, v.p. 1981-82, pres. 1983-84), South Atlantic Grad. English Coop. Group (exec. com. 1969-79, chmn. 1971-72), South Atlantic Modern Lang. Assn. (exec. com. 1975-77, nominating com. 1985-87), William Gilmore Simms Soc. (exec. com. 1993—, pres.-elect 1993-95, adv. bd. Letters of Henry James complete edit. 1995—, editl. bd. 1997—), Blue Key, Phi Beta Kappa, Sigma Chi. Office: U Ga Dept English Park Hall Athens GA 30602

MOORE, RAYMOND A., consultant, retired agriculture educator; b. Britton, S.D., Nov. 16, 1927; s. Arthur L. and Anna (Schuur) M.; m. Marlys Schiefelbein, Jun 17, 1951; children: Craig, Jay, Kent, Jeff. BA in Agrl. Edn. and Econs., S.D. State U., 1951, MS in Agronomy, 1958; PhD in Crop Physiology and Ecology, Purdue U., 1963. Instr. vocat. agriculture Bennett County H.S., Martin, S.D., 1951-56; instr., prof., adminstr. S.D. State U., Brookings, 1956-94, dir. emeritus agrl. expt. sta., 1994—; cons. Coop. States Rsch. Svcs. USDA, Washington, Producers Renewable Products, St. Paul. Contbr. chpts. to books, articles to profl. jours. With USN, 1945-47. Nat. Sci. Faculty fellow forage & pasture mgmt. CSRS/U.S. Dept. Agriculture, 1965; Citizens Ambassador Program People to People Internat. travel grantee, U.S. Dept. Agriculture travel grantee. Mem. Am. Soc. Agronomy, Kiwanis Internat., Sigma Xi, Gamma Sigma Delta. Avocations: hunting, fishing, gardening, farming. Home: 207 17th Ave Brookings SD 57006-2609 Office: SD State U PO Box 2207 Brookings SD 57007

MOORE, REBECCA ANN RUCKER, marketing executive; b. Little Rock, Aug. 29, 1952; d. Thurman K. and Wilibel (Hester) Rucker; m. Thomas Daniel Moore, Oct. 2, 1976 (div. July 1985); 1 child, Lauren Elizabeth. BA in Speech-Hearing and Lang. Pathology, Baylor U., 1974, postgrad., 1976; postgrad., Henderson State U., 1988. Lic. speech-hearing-lang. pathologist, Tex., Ark. Speech therapist Dripping Springs Kindergarten, Waco, Tex., 1974-76, Oakwood Early Childhood, Waco, 1976-80, Gurley Elem. Sch., Waco, 1981-82, Connelly Northcrest Elem. Sch., Waco, 1982-83, Connelly High Sch., Waco, 1982-83; dir. curriculum First Bapt. Ch., Waco, 1984-86; coord. early childhood edn. First Bapt. Ch., Arkadelphia, Ark., 1986-89; speech therapist Gurdon (Ark.) Ind. Schs., 1989-92, Popham Elem., Del Valle, Tex., 1992-95; pvt. bus. owner BLM Assocs., 1995—; vis. lectr. Weekday Early Edn. Conv., Little Rock, 1987, 88, 89. Mem. steering com. weekday early edn. program So. Bapt. Conv., Little Rock, 1986-88; mem. pre-sch. coordinating com. Dawson Ednl. Corp., Arkadelphia, 1988-89. Home: 7212 Chimney Cors Austin TX 78731-2147

MOORE, RICHARD ALAN, landscape architect; b. St. Louis, Jan. 17, 1930; s. Ira Mack and Helen Adoline (Fakes) M.; m. Patricia Ruth Burke, Mar. 15, 1952 (div. 1967); children: Sheryl Louise, Richard Dennis, Sara Lynn, Sandra Lee. BS, U. Mo., 1951; MLA, U. Oreg., 1957. Registered landscape architect, Calif., Hawaii. Asst. prof., head dept. landscape architecture Calif. State Poly. Coll., Pomona, 1957-61; assoc. prof., head dept. landscape architecture N.C. State U., Raleigh, 1962-67; pvt. practice landscape architecture Pomona, Calif., 1957-61; dir. land devel. and planning Oceanic Properties Inc., Honolulu, 1967-69; pvt. practice Honolulu, 1969-70, 79—; dir. ops. Eckbo, Dean, Austin & Williams, Honolulu, 1970-71, v.p. ops., 1971-73; pres. EDAW, Inc., San Francisco, 1973-76, chmn. bd., 1976-78; prof. landscape architecture Tex. A&M U., Bryan, 1977-79. Prin. works include Whispering Pines Motor Lodge, N.C., 1964 (award of merit N.C. chpt. AIA 1964), North Shore Devel. Plan, Kauai, Hawaii, 1973, Comprehensive Zoning Ordinance, County of Kauai, 1973 (Am. Soc. Landscape Architects honor award 1973, HUD honor award 1974), Lihue Devel. Plan, Kauai, 1975, Koloa, Poipu, Kalaheo Devel. Plan, Kauai, 1978, Gen. Plan Update, Kauai, 1982, Mililani Town Devel. Plan, 1967-69 (Am. Soc. Landscape Architects merit award 1970), Lanai Land Mgmt. and Devel. Study, 1969 (Am. Soc. Landscape Architects merit award 1970), Wailea Master Devel. Plan, 1971, Kukuiula Devel. Plan, 1983, Lanai Project Dist. Master Plan, 1983-89, Maliu Ridge Devel. Plan, North Kohala, 1985, Mililani Mauka Devel. Plan, 1988, Devel. Plan, Lanai City Comml. Dist., 1990, Dandan Golf Course, Guam, 1991. 1st lt. U.S. Army, 1951-53, Korea. Fellow Am. Soc. Landscape Architects; mem. Masons. Avocations: sports, drawing, painting.

MOORE, RICHARD ALLAN, mathematics educator; b. Mansfield, Ohio, Jan. 11, 1924; s. Robert Allan and Ruth (Miller) M.; m. Ruth Marguerite Neuhoff, July 30, 1949; children—Peter Allan, Susan Rebecca Moore McJunkin, Sarah Marguerite. A.B., Washington U., St. Louis, 1948, M.A. in Math, 1950, Ph.D., 1953. Instr. math. U. Nebr., 1953-54, Yale, 1954-56; mem. faculty Carnegie-Mellon U., Pitts., 1956-87; prof. math. Carnegie-Mellon U., 1967-87, prof. emeritus, 1987—, assoc. head dept., 1965-71, 75-85, chmn. dept., 1971-75; vis. lectr. Pa. Dept. Pub. Instrn., 1968-70; cons. in field, 1967—. Author. Mem. sch. bd. Churchill Area Schs., 1963-71; sch. bd. Eastern Area Spl. Schs., 1964-69. Served with AUS, 1943-45. Recipient Ryan Teaching award, 1969. Mem. Am. Math. Soc., Math. Assn. Am., Math. Coun. Western Pa. (bd. dirs. 1962-70), Pa. Coun. Tchrs. Math. (bd. dirs. 1966-68), Sigma Xi, Phi Kappa Phi. Episcopalian. Research papers, textbook ordinary differential equations. Home: 165 Fieldcrest Dr Pittsburgh PA 15221-3742

MOORE, RICHARD CARROLL, JR., family physician; b. Balt., Nov. 24, 1946; s. Richard Carroll and Virginia Mae (Clark) M.; m. Jeremy Pierson, Jan. 27, 1973; children: Peter Gregory, Laura Alexandra. BA, Johns Hopkins U., 1968, MPH, 1981; MD, UCLA, 1972. Diplomate Am. Bd. Family Practice. Intern South Balt. Gen. Hosp., 1972-73; commd. med. officer USPHS, 1976, ret., 1997; chief med. div. USCG Aviation Tng. Ctr., Mobile, Ala., 1976-80; chief med. ops. USCG, Washington, 1980-86; sr. med. officer USCG Yard, Curtis Bay, Md., 1986-88; dir. Health Unit # 1, USPHS, 1988-97; staff physician Piedmont Prime Care, Danville, Va., 1997—; mem. exec. bd. Emergency Med. Svcs. Coun., Mobile County, 1979, Med. and Chirurg. Faculty Md. Mem. editorial bd. MD Med. Jour., 1995—. Bd. dirs. Midway Fed. Credit Union, 1989-96, pres., 1991-96. With USN, 1973-76. Mem. Aerospace Med. Assn., So. Med. Assn, Soc. U.S. Naval Flight Surgeons, Johns Hopkins U. Alumni Assn., Commd. Officers Assn. USPHS, UCLA Alumni Assn., Alpha Omega Alpha, Sigma Phi Epsilon,. Republican. Home: 1927 Halifax Rd Apt 33 Danville VA 24540 Office: Piedmond PrimeCare 1429 S Boston Rd Danville VA 24540

MOORE, RICHARD EARL, communications creative director; b. Pontiac, Mich., Nov. 3, 1940; m. Noriko Negishi, Feb. 1, 1966. B.F.A., Art Ctr. Coll. Design, Los Angeles, 1968. Sr. designer Lippincott & Margulies, N.Y.C., 1969-71; prin. Richard Moore Assocs., N.Y.C., 1972-76; vice chmn., co-founder Muir Cornelius Moore, N.Y.C., 1976-90; prin. Richard Moore Assocs., N.Y.C., 1990—; juror frequent internat. advt. competitions; chmn. frequent internat. seminars on mktg. comm. Recipient numerous creative awards. Mem. Am. Inst. Graphic Art, Art Directors Club, Type Directors Club. Avocations: mountaineering; wilderness photography, scuba diving, skiing.

MOORE, RICHARD HARLAN, biology educator, university official; b. Houston, Sept. 16, 1945; s. Russell Lewis and Hazel Dean (Harlan) M.; m. Robin Morris, May 14, 1977; 1 child, Merlin R. Morris-Moore. BA in Gen Biology, Vanderbilt U., 1967; MA in Zoology, U. Tex., 1970, PhD in Marine Zoology, 1973. Staff scientist Environment Cons. Inc., Dallas, 1973-74; asst. prof. biology Coastal Carolina U., Conway, 1974-77, assoc., 1977-86, chmn. sci. div., 1978-79, dean Sch. Sci., 1979-87, prof., 1986—, asst. vice chancellor for rsch., 1987-93, asst. v.p., 1993—; rsch. assoc. Belle W. Baruch Inst. for Marine Biology and Coastal Rsch., Columbia, S.C., 1974—. Author: (with H.D. Hoese) Fishes of the Gulf of Mexico, 1977, 97; contbr. articles to profl. jours. Leader Boy Scouts Am., Port Aransas, Tex., 1980-82; com. chmn. S.C. Crawfish Festival Assn., Pawleys Island, 1980—, chmn. bd. dirs., 1995—. Recipient NSF grants 1975, 77. Mem. Am. Soc. Ichthyologists and Herpetologists, Am. Fisheries Soc., Ecological Soc. Am., Southeastern and Gulf Estuarine Rsch. Socs., Southeastern Fishes Coun. Office: Coastal Carolina U PO Box 261954 Conway SC 29528-1954

MOORE, RICHARD KERR, electrical engineering educator; b. St. Louis, Nov. 13, 1923; s. Louis D. and Nina (Megown) M.; m. Wilma Lois Schallau, Dec. 10, 1944; children: John Richard, Daniel Charles. BS, Washington U. at St. Louis, 1943; PhD, Cornell U., 1951. Test equipment engr. RCA, Camden, N.J., 1943-44; instr. and rsch. engr. Washington U., St. Louis, 1947-49; rsch. assoc. Cornell U., 1949-51; rsch. engr., sect. supr. Sandia Corp., Albuquerque, 1951-55; prof., chmn. elec. engring. U. N.Mex., 1955-62; Black and Veatch prof. U. Kans., Lawrence, 1962-94; prof. emeritus, 1994—; dir. remote sensing lab. U. Kans., 1964-74, 84-93; pres. Cadre Corp., Lawrence, 1968-87; cons. cos., govt. agys. Author: Traveling Wave Engineering, 1960; co-author: (with Ulaby and Fung) Microwave Remote Sensing, Vol. I, 1981, Vol. II, 1982, Vol. III, 1986; contbr. to profl. jours. and handbooks. Lt. (j.g.) USNR, 1944-46. Recipient Achievement award Washington U. Engring. Alumni Assn., 1978, Outstanding Tech. Achievement award Geosci. and Remote Sensing Soc., 1982, Louise E. Byrd Grad. Educator award U. Kans., 1984, Irving Youngberg Rsch. award U. Kans., 1989, Australian prize, 1995. Fellow AAAS, IEEE (sect. chmn. 1960-61, Outstanding Tech. Achievement award coun. oceanic engring. 1978); mem., NAE, AAUP, Am. Soc. Engring. Edn., Am. Geophys. Union, Internat. Sci. Radio Union (chmn. U.S. commn. F 1984-87, internat. vice chmn. commn. F 1990-93, chmn. 1993), Kiwanis, Sigma Xi, Tau Beta Pi. Presbyterian (past elder). Achievements include research in submarine communications, radar altimetry, radar as a remote sensor, radar oceanography; patent for polypanchromatic radar. Home: 1712 Carmel Dr Lawrence KS 66047-1840 Office: U Kans R S & Remote Sensing Lab 2291 Irving Rd Lawrence KS 66044-7541

MOORE, RICHARD LAWRENCE, structural engineer, consultant; b. Rocky Ford, Colo., Feb. 7, 1934; s. Lawrence and Margaret Kathryn (Bolling) M.; m. Donna St. Clair, Mar. 26, 1972 (div. 1983); 1 child, Andrew Trousdale; m. Margaret Ann Guthrie, May 4, 1984. BSCE, U. Colo., 1957; MS, Princeton U., 1963; PhD, Calif. Western U., Santa Ana, 1975. Registered profl. engr., Mass., Maine, Colo., Pa., Iowa, Nebr., N.Mex., Wyo., Ill., Ark., Mo., N.D., Mich., Okla., Mont. Structural engr. Cameron Engrs., Denver, 1964-66; v.p. Moore Internat., Jeddah, Saudi Arabia, 1967-78; asst. to pres. C.H. Guernsey Co., Oklahoma City, 1979-82; pres. R.L. Moore Co., Boston, 1983—; v.p., dir. Isolink Ing., Basel, Switzerland, 1990—; nat. chmn. Roof Cons. Inst., Raleigh, N.C., 1988-92; prof. Episcopal Sch. Theology, Denver, 1967-71. Patentee in field. Member Mound City (Mo.) Libr. Bd., 1963-64; pres. Dist. Rep. Party, Boston, 1988—; sr. warden St. John Chrysostom Epis. Ch., Denver, 1966-71. Danforth Found. scholar, 1962. Mem. ASCE, NSPE, Am. Concrete Inst., Nat. Forensic Ctr. Avocations: golf, travel, antique pocket watch collecting. Home and Office: RL Moore Co 534 E Broadway Boston MA 02127-4407

MOORE, RICHARD THOMAS, state legislator; b. Milford, Mass., Aug. 7, 1943; s. Thomas James and Helen Eliza (Andrew) M.; m. Joanne Bednarz, May 26, 1979. BA in History, Clark U., 1966; MA in Student Pers., Colgate U., 1967; postgrad., Clark U., 1967-70, U. Mass., 1981-85. Cert. tchr. secondary level social studies. Assoc. dean students Assumption Coll., Worcester, Mass., 1967-69; asst. to pres. Bentley Coll., Waltham, Mass., 1969-77; mem. Mass. Ho. of Reps., Boston, 1977-94; assoc. dir. mitigation Fed. Emergency Mgmt. Agy., Washington, 1994-96; senator Mass. Senate, Boston, 1996—, chmn. senate com. on pub. svc., 1997—; pres. Mass. Selectmen's Assn., Boston, 1975-76; chmn. House Com. on Election Laws, Boston, 1992-94, House Com. on Taxation, Boston, 1983-85, House Com. on State Adminstrn., Boston, 1983. Chmn. Blackstone Nat. Heritage Corridor Commn., Uxbridge, Mass., 1988-90; presdl. elector Mass. Electoral Coll., Boston, 1992; chmn. Mass. Dem. Leadership Coun., Boston, 1990-93. Named Outstanding Legislator Mass. Town Clks. Assn., Boston, 1993, New Dem. of Yr. Mass. Dem. Leadership Coun., Boston, 1994; recipient Disting. Svc. award Fed. Emergency Mgmt. Agy., 1996. Mem. Am. Soc. Pub. Adminstrn. (mem. bd. Mass. chpt. 1981-85), Nat. Emergency Mgmt. Assn. Roman Catholic. Avocations: politics, collecting political items. Office: State House Rm 416B Boston MA 02133

MOORE, ROB, professional football player; b. N.Y.C., Oct. 27, 1968. BS in Psychology, Syracuse U., 1990. With N.Y. Jets, 1990-94; wide receiver Ariz. Cardinals, Phoenix, 1994—. Named to Sporting News Coll. All-Am. Team, 1989, NFL Pro Bowl Team, 1994. Office: Ariz Cardinals 8701 S Hardy Dr Tempe AZ 85284-2800*

MOORE, ROBERT CONDIT, civil engineer; b. Newark, July 27, 1921; s. Ira Condit and Mildred A. (Gill) M.; m. Betty Aierstock, Sept. 21, 1946; children—Robert Condit, Patricia, Margaret. B.S. in Civil Engring. with honors, Lehigh U., 1943. Registered profl. engr., N.J., Mass., Pa., Conn., Vt. Jr. engr. Dravo Corp., Pitts., 1943; with Elson T. Killam Assos., Inc., 1946-80; exec. v.p., sec. Elson T. Killam Assos., Inc., Millburn, N.J., 1970-75; sr. v.p. Elson T. Killam Assos., Inc., 1976-80; cons. environ. engr., 1980-90, ret., 1990. Contbr. articles to profl. jours. Chmn. bd. dirs. Meml. Ctr. for Women, West Orange, N.J., 1974-92; elder First Presbyn. and Trinity Ch., South Orange, N.J. With U.S. Army, 1943-46. Fellow ASCE (Samuel A. Greeley award 1971), Am. Cons. Engrs. Coun. (nat. v.p. 1981-82); mem. ASTM (chmn. com. on asbestos cement products 1980-86), Am. Water Works Assn., Water Pollution Control Fedn., Am. Acad. Environ. Engrs. (diplomate), Cons. Engrs. Coun. of N.J. (pres. 1975, nat. dir. 1976-78), Rock Spring Club, Rotary, Kappa Alpha. Home: 75 Silver Springs Rd Short Hills NJ 07078-3120 also: Landmark, Southampton Bermuda SB-04

MOORE, ROBERT EDWARD, retired electronics executive; b. Winsted, Conn., July 29, 1923; s. Alfred Edward and Elizabeth (Clark) M.; m. Georgiana Muriel Moore, Dec. 22, 1946; children—Kathleen Moore Roberson, Brian Robert, John Craig. B.S. in Mech. Engring, U. Wis., 1948. Registered profl. engr., D.C. Chief insp. Rockwell-Standard Corp., Newark, Ohio, 1948-51; sec.-treas. A.E. Moore Co., Oshkosh, Wis., 1951-53; v.p. John I. Thompson & Co., Washington, 1953-65; founder, chmn., pres. Potomac Rsch., Inc. (merged with Electronic Data Systems Corp. 1979), Alexandria, Va., 1965-79, cons., 1979-81; chmn. Potomac Rsch. Internat., Fairfax, Va., 1981-96; ret. Served with U.S. Army, 1943-46. Mem. ASME. Episcopalian. Home: 11171 Crest Hill Rd Marshall VA 20115-2712

MOORE, ROBERT HENRY, insurance company executive; b. Madisonville, Ky., Sept. 16, 1940; s. William Lee Moore and Robbie (Pritchett) Ruby; m. Diana Churchill, Aug. 17, 1963 (div. 1978); children: Randall Lee, Robin Churchill; m. Patricia Mary George, Oct. 4, 1981; 1 child, Christopher Robert. BA, Davidson (N.C.) Coll., 1962; MA, U. N.C., 1964; PhD, U. Wis., 1972. Asst. dir. admissions Davidson Coll., 1963-64; teaching asst. U. Wis., Madison, 1965-68; staff and faculty U.S. Mil. Acad., West Point, N.Y., 1968-70; lectr., asst. prof. U. Md., College Park, 1970-76, assoc. prof., 1976; cons. U.S. Congress, Washington, 1976-77; emerging issues coordinator The Conf. Bd., N.Y.C., 1977-79; dir. govt. relations Benefacts, Inc., Washington, 1977-78; v.p. Alexander & Alexander, Inc., Washington, 1978-81; v.p. Alexander & Alexander Svcs. Inc., N.Y.C., Washington, 1981-85, sr. v.p. corp. rels., 1985-95, sr. v.p. (inactive), 1995—; chmn., pres. A & A Govt. and Industry Affairs Inc., Washington, 1990-94; del. Nat. Security Affairs Conf., Washington, 1978-82; mem. adv. bd. Career Opportunities Inst., U. Va., Charlottesville, 1982-86, Ctr. for New Am. Work Force, 1992—, co-chair rsch., 1995—; mem. corp. adv. bd. Queens Coll., CUNY, 1985—; mem. V.P.'s Forum, 1989-94; mem. coun. Conf. Bd. Corp. Comm. Execs., 1990-94; mem. Pub. Rels. Sem., 1993—. Co-author: (with others) School for Soldiers: West Point and the Profession of Arms, 1974 (NYT award 1974); contbr. articles to profl. jours.; contbr. interviews to nat. mags., newspapers, radio and TV. Mem. kitchen cabinet Points of Light Found., 1991-95; active Fairfax Unitarian Ch. With U.S. Army, 1968-70, capt. USAR, 1970-72. Ops. Crossroads Africa fellow, 1960; U. Md. rsch. grantee, 1972, 76; Inter-Univ. Seminar on Armed Forces and Society fellow. Fellow Internat. Ins. Soc., Soc. Risk Analysis; mem. Nat. Assn. Ins. Brokers (exec. com., bd. dirs. 1987, pres. 1985-86, chmn. past presidents adv. coun. 1989-93), Inst. Dirs. (London), U.S. C. of C. (civil justice action group 1985-87), The Tysons Club.

MOORE, ROBERT LOWELL, JR. (ROBIN MOORE), author; b. Boston, Oct. 31, 1925; s. Robert Lowell Sr. and Eleanor (Turner) M.; m. Joan Friedman, Sept. 15, 1952 (div. 1955); 1 child, Margo Joan; m. Mary Olga Troshkin, Feb. 17, 1973. AB, Harvard U., 1949. European corr. Boston Globe, 1947; ind. TV prodr. N.Y.C., 1949-52; dir. pub. rels. Sheraton Corp. Am., Boston, 1952- 54, dir. advt. and pub. rels., 1954-56, bd. dirs., 1954-62. Author: Pitchman, 1956, The Devil to Pay, 1961, The Green Berets, 1965, The Country Team, 1967, Fiedler, 1968, The French Connection, 1969, Court Martial, 1970, The Khaki Mafia, 1971, The Fifth Estate, 1974, Compulsion, 1982; (with Xaviera Hollander) The Happy Hooker, 1972, The Treasure Hunter, 1975, Dubai, 1976, Mafia Wife, 1977, The Banksters, 1977, Rhodesia, 1978, The Big Paddle, 1978, Search and Destroy, 1978, The Washington Connection, 1979; (with Milt Machlin) The Family Man, 1985, Force nine, 1987, The Man Who Made It Snow, 1990, The White Tribe, 1991, The Moscow Connection, 1994; screenwriter: The Green Berets, 1967, The French Connection, 1971, The Happy Hooker, 1973, Inchon, 1979, Hoffa, 1985, The Sparrowhood Curse, 1996. With USAAF, 1944-46, ETO. Decorated Air medal with two bronze oak leaf clusters. Mem. Met. Club (N.Y.C.). Developed pvt. TV closed circuit network for hotels. Home: 179 Nashawtuc Rd Concord MA 01742-1634

MOORE, ROBERT MADISON, food industry executive, lawyer; b. New Orleans, June 21, 1925; s. Clarence Greer and Anna Omega (Odendahl) M.; m. Evelyn Eileen Varva, Apr. 11, 1953; children: Eileen Alexandria Moore Wynne, John Greer. B.B.A., Tulane U., 1943; J.D., U. Va., 1952; LL.M. (Food Law Inst. fellow), NYU, 1953. Bar: La. 1956, Calif. 1972. Asst. to pres., gen. counsel Underwear Inst., N.Y.C., 1953-55; pvt. practice law New Orleans, 1955-56; asst. gen. atty., dir. Legal services, sec. and gen. atty. Standard Fruit & Steamship Co., New Orleans, 1957-72; v.p., gen. counsel Castle & Cooke Foods, 1972-81; v.p., gen. counsel Castle & Cooke, Inc., 1973-81, sr. v.p. law and govt., 1981-82; pres. Internat. Banana Assn., 1983—; dir. Ferson Optics of Del., Inc., 1958-69, Baltime Securities Corp., Pan American Devel. Found. Asst. atty. gen., La., 1958-63. Served with AUS, 1943-46. Mem. ABA, Calif. Bar Assn., La. Bar Assn., SAR (sec. 1960-61), Essex Club, Cosmos Club, Phi Delta Phi, Alpha Tau Omega. Democrat. Roman Catholic. Home: 3323 R St NW Washington DC 20007-2310 Office: 1929 39th St NW Washington DC 20007-2110

MOORE, ROBERT WILLIAM, professional organization executive; b. Claysburg, Pa., June 4, 1924; s. Frank B. and Sarah A. (Edelbute) M.; m. Helen Lingenfelter, July 17, 1948; children: Thomas R., Priscilla Jane. B.A., Pa. State U., 1948. With Price Waterhouse & Co., Pitts., 1948-62; mgr. Price Waterhouse & Co., 1955-62; asst. contr. Con-Gas Svc. Corp., Pitts., 1962-65, Consol. Natural Gas Svc. Co., Inc., Pitts., 1966-72; contr. Consol. Natural Gas Svc. Co., Inc., 1972-78, Consol. Natural Gas Co., Pitts., 1972-78; pres. Fin. Execs. Inst., Morristown, N.J., 1978-89, pres. emeritus, 1989—; mem. Fin. Acctg. Standards Adv. Coun., 1978-89. Bd. dirs. Central Blood Bank, Pitts., 1960-78, treas. corp., 1962-68, chmn. finance com., 1962-68, chmn. bd., 1969-72; mem. exec. bd. Pa. State U. Alumni Council, 1975-83; mem. exec. com. Campaign for Pa. State U., bd. vis.; pres. Pa. State Coll. Bus. Adminstrn. Soc., 1981-83. Served with AUS, 1943-45. Mem. Am., Pa. insts. C.P.A.s, Nat. Assn. Accountants, Fin. Execs. Inst., Pa. State U. Alumni Assn., Pa. Soc., Beta Alpha Psi (nat. forum), Delta Tau Delta. Episcopalian. Clubs: University (dir., pres. 1975-76), Valley Brook Country (dir. 1968-70, v.p. bd. 1970), Duquesne (Pitts.), University, St. Clair Country, Morris County Golf, Morristown (N.J.).

MOORE, ROBERT YATES, neuroscience educator; b. Harvey, Ill., Dec. 5, 1931; s. Raymon Irwin and Marie Louise (Fischer) M.; children: Elizabeth Allen, Matthew McCormick, Joshua Gilbert, Thomas Douglas. BA magna cum laude, Lawrence U., 1953; MD with honors, U. Chgo., 1957, PhD, 1962; MD (hon.), Lund (Sweden) U., 1974. Diplomate: Am. Bd. Psychiatry and Neurology. Intern Univ. Hosp., Ann Arbor, Mich., 1958-59; resident U. Chgo., 1959-64, asst. prof. neurology and anatomy, 1964-66, assoc. prof., 1966-70, prof., 1970-74; prof. neurosci. U. Calif., San Diego, 1974-79; prof., chmn. dept. neurology SUNY, Stony Brook, 1979-90; prof. psychiatry, neurology and neurosci. U. Pitts., 1990—, chmn. dept. neurology, 1996—; cons. Contbr. numerous articles to profl. jours. Recipient numerous grants. Fellow Am. Acad. Neurology; mem. Am. Neurol. Assn., Soc. Neurosci., Internat. Brain Research Orgn., Am. Assn. Anatomists. Office: U Pitts Ctr for Neurosci Biomed Sci Tower W 1656 Pittsburgh PA 15261

MOORE, ROGER ALBERT, JR., archaeologist; b. Tampa, Fla., Dec. 18, 1946; s. Roger Albert Moore and Frieda E. (Heil) Hutchison; m. Susan Kay Waters, Sept. 8, 1978; children: Tabitha Rose, Roxie Ann. BA in Anthropology, Ohio State U., 1972; student, U. Tenn., 1974-75; MA in Anthropology, Ea. N.Mex. U., 1981. Lic. archael. surveyor, N.Mex., Colo., Utah, Wyo., Ariz. Crew chief, field foreman U. Tenn., Knoxville, 1973-74, excavator, lab. asst., 1974-75; excavator, lab. asst. Cahokia Mounds State Park, Collinsville, Ill., 1974; lithic analyst Ea. N.Mex. U., Portales, 1975-78; lab. dir. U. Colo., Cortez, 1978-79; field dir. ESCA-Tech, Inc., Ridgeway, Colo., 1980; lab. dir. Navajo Nat. Archaeology Dept., Farmington, N.Mex., 1980-82; supervisory archaeologist San Juan County Mus. Assn., Bloomfield, N.Mex., 1982-88; owner, prin. investigator Moore Anthropol. Rsch., Aztec, N.Mex., 1988—; owner Southwest Archaeol. Svcs., Aztec, N.Mex., 1996—; instr. San Juan Coll., Farmington, 1983; mem. strategic action team Aztec Mcpl. Sch. Dist., 1995. Co-author: Old Dallas Historical Archaeology Project, 1987; contbr. articles to profl. jours. Vol. Portales (N.Mex.) Food Coopr., 1976-78, Salmon Ruin Mus., Bloomfield, 1982-88, Bonds for Books Plus Com., Aztec, 1994; mem. lithic dictionary com. N.Mex. Archaeol. Coun., 1989—; chmn. com. B.L.M. Cultural Adv. Group, Farmington, 1991—; mem. Aztec H.S. parent adv. com., 1996-97. Mem. Soc. Am. Archaeology (life), N.Mex. Archaeol. Coun., Archaeol. Soc. N.Mex. (cert., Archaeol. Achievement award 1994), Ariz. Archaeol. and Hist. Soc., Tenn. Anthropol. Assn. (life), San Juan County Mus. Assn. (bd. dirs. 1993-95), Nat.Trust for Hist. Preservation, Aztec C. of C. (bd. dirs. 1995—), San Juan Archaeol. Soc., Phi Kappa Phi. Republican. Presbyterian. Avocations: running, hiking, tennis, reading. Office: Moore Anthropol Rsch 102 N Main St Aztec NM 87410-1924

MOORE, ROY DEAN, judge; b. Chickasha, Okla., Jan. 15, 1940; s. Frank B. and Delia Pauline (Morgan) M.; m. Carolyn Kaye Wood, Aug. 10, 1962; children—Darla Kaye, Jared Dean, Amy Darise. B.A., Central State U., 1962, M. Teaching, 1966; J.D., Oklahoma City U., 1970; grad., Nat. Coll. State Trial Judges, 1972. Bar: Okla. 1970. Coach debate, instr. dramatics Kingfisher (Okla.) High Sch., 1962-67; instr. English and journalism, head dept. lang. arts. Jarman Jr. High Sch., Midwest City, Okla., 1967-70; pros. atty. City of Lawton, Okla., 1970; spl. dist. judge 5th Jud. Dist. Okla., 1971-72; pvt. practice law Lawton, 1973-90; dist. judge 5th Jud. Dist. Okla., 1990—. Pres. Swinney PTA, 1975-76; Editor: Problems in Teaching in the Secondary School, 1966. Pres. Comanche County Mental Health Assn., 1973-74, bd. dirs., 1972-76; co-chmn. Kingfisher County Reps. for Congressman James V. Smith, 1966; mem. state exec. com. Okla. Republican Com., 1973-74, chmn. auditing com., 1977-78; del. Rep. Nat. Conv., 1976; chmn. cts. com. Assn. South Central Okla. Govts. Crime Commn.; chmn. Comanche County Reps. for Reagan for Pres., 1973-83; mem. adv. bd. Jim

Taliferro Mental Health Center, 1977-78; del. Nat. Mental Health Assn. Conv., 1975; bd. dirs. Lawton Campfire Girls; elder N.W. Ch. of Christ, 1977—; dir. Back to Bible Campaigns, 1976—. Mem. Am., Okla., Comanche County bar assns., Okla. Trial Lawyers Assn., Lawton Antique Auto Club, Ford Retractible Club Am., Alpha Psi Omega, Delta Theta Phi. Republican. Mem. Ch. of Christ (elder). Clubs: Fraternal Order of Police, Lion. Home: 2114 NW Atlanta Ave Lawton OK 73505-3923

MOORE, SANDRA BUCHER, mathematics educator; b. Norfolk, Va., Jan. 5, 1946; d. Clayton Merrill and Helen (Wilson) Bucher; m. Robert Curtis Moore, Aug. 1, 1970; children: Kimberley Anne, Tara Elayne. BS, Radford Coll., 1968; MS, Old Dominion U., 1988. Cert. profl. tchr., Va. Elem. tchr. Hampton (Va.) City Schs., 1968-89, Title I math. specialist, 1989—; math. text reviewer McGraw-Hill Pubs., N.Y., 1985; reader of Eisenhower Proposals, U.S. Dept. of Edn., Washington, 1991; curriculum writer CII WHRO-TV, Hampton Rds., 1987-90. Author: (lesson plan) Computer Teacher Contest, 1987 (1st Pl. award 1987). Mem. Hampton Fedn. Tchrs., AFT, 1981-94, Womans Club, 1969-91; officer Poquoson H.S. Band Boosters, 1990-94. Recipient Tech. Educator of Yr. award CII-WHRO-TV, 1989. Mem. AFT (treas. 1988-92, 3d v.p. 1992-94), Va. Ednl. Computer Assn., Va. Coun. Tchrs. Math., Peninsula Coun. Tchrs. of Math. Democrat. Methodist. Avocations: crafts, sewing, gardening, spectator sports. Home: 9 Far St Poquoson VA 23662-2115

MOORE, SANDRA KAY, counselor, administrator; b. Sellersville, Pa., June 28, 1943; d. Sheldon Ellsworth and Olive (Moyer) McElroy; m. Thomas Van Moore, June 8, 1963; children: Thomas Shawn, Tara Quinn, Tammy Colleen, Thador Shelby. Student, East Stroudsburg (Pa.) U., 1961-63; BA, Gwynedd-Mercy Coll., 1986; MS, Chestnut Hill Coll., 1990. Cert. in student assistance program. Crisis counselor Archbishop Ryan H.S., Phila., 1989-90; guidance counselor Mt. St. Joseph Acad., Flourtown, Pa., 1990-93; dir. guidance Mt. St. Joseph Acad., Flourtown, 1993—; lectr. Gwynedd-Mercy Coll., Gwynedd, Pa., 1995—; lectr. in field. Author: So You Want to Go to College, 1994. Bd. dirs. Today, Inc., Hilltown, Pa., 1976-80; mem. Hilltown (Pa.) Civic Assn., 1975-85; pres. Bux-Mont Neighbors, Souderton, Pa., 1985, John M. Grasse Home and Sch. Assn., Perkasie, Pa., 1981; chairwoman Christian Edn. Com., Perkasie, 1994. Mem. APA, Ind. Counselors Assn., Nat. Assn. for Coll. Admissions Counselors, Specialists in Schs., Pa. Assn. Secondary Sch. and Coll. Admission Counselors. Democrat. Lutheran. Avocations: horseback riding, reading, writing, travel, collecting antique Santa Claus'. Office: Mount Saint Joseph Academy 120 W Wissahickon Ave Flourtown PA 19031-1802

MOORE, SCOTT, state official; b. York, Nebr., 1960; m. Danene Tushar, 1989. BA in Polit Sci., U. Nebr. Legis. aide Nebr. Legislature, 1981-86, mem., 1986-94, chair appropriations com.; sec. of state State of Nebr., 1995—; with Moore & Sons. Office: State Capitol # 2300 PO Box 94608 Lincoln NE 68509-4608 Address: 2616 Woodsdale Blvd Lincoln NE 68502-5044 also: State Legislature State Capital Lincoln NE 68516*

MOORE, SEAN, pathologist, educator; b. Belfast, No. Ireland, Nov. 24, 1926; arrived in Can., 1951; s. James Bernard and Eileen (McFadden) M.; m. Cynthia Balch, Oct. 1957; children: John Brian, Martha Ailish, Patrick Balch. MB, BChir, Queen's U., Belfast, 1950. From asst. to assoc. pathologist Montreal Gen. Hosp., Que., Can., 1958-69; pathologist-in-chief Jewish Gen. Hosp., Montreal, 1969-71; chmn. dept. pathology McMaster U., Hamilton, Ont., Can., 1972-78, dir. labs. med. cen., 1972-84; pathologist-in-chief Royal Victoria Hosp., Montreal, 1984-94; chmn. dept. pathology, Strathcona prof. pathology McGill U., Montreal, 1984-94. Editor: Vascular Injury and Atherosclerosis, 1981; mng. editor: Experimental and Molecular Pathology; contbr. articles to profl. jours. Fellow Royal Coll. Physicians & Surgeons (Can.). Home: 522 Clarke Ave, Montreal, PQ Canada H3Y 3C9 Office: McGill U Dept Pathology, 3775 University St, Montreal, PQ Canada H3A 2B4

MOORE, SHERYL STANSIL, medical nurse; b. Birmingham, Ala., May 17, 1963; d. Willie Caesar and Irene (Fisher) Stansil; m. Kyle R. Moore, Aug. 5, 1994; children: Tyler Christina, Danladi, William. BSN, Dillard U., 1987; MSN in Trauma Nursing, U. Ala. in Birmingham, 1992. Clin. instr. BSN program Coppin State Coll., Balt., Colo., 1997—; staff nurse Progressive Care Ctr., Terrace Gardens, Colo., 1995-96; instr. clin. nursing Beth-El Coll. Nursing, 1995; staff nurse Balt. VA Med. Ctr., 1996—, Nursefinders of Balt., 1996—; past instr. clin. nursing Beth-El Coll. Nursing; beauty cons. Mary Kay Cosmetics, 1996—. Named one of Outstanding Young Women of Am., 1988. Mem. ANA, AACN, State Nurses Assn., AMSN. Home: 5281 Brook Way Columbia MD 21044

MOORE, SHIRLEY THROCKMORTON (MRS. ELMER LEE MOORE), accountant; b. Des Moines, July 4, 1918; d. John Carder and Jessie (Wright) Throckmorton; student Iowa State Tchrs. Coll., summers 1937-38, Madison Coll., 1939-41; M.C.S., Benjamin Franklin U., 1944; CPA, Mc.; m. Elmer Lee Moore, Dec. 19, 1946; children: Fay, Lynn Dallas. Asst. bookkeeper Sibley Hosp., Washington, 1941-42, Alvord & Alvord, 1942-46, bookkeeper, 1946-49, chief accountant, 1950-64, fin. adviser to sr. ptnr., 1957-64; dir. Allen Oil Co., 1958-74; pvt. practice acctg., 1964—. Mem. sch. bd. Takoma Acad., Takoma Park, Md., 1970—; mem. hosp. bd. Washington Adventist Hosp., 1974-85; chmn. worthy student fund Takoma Park Seven Day Adventist Ch., 1987—; trustee Benson Found., 1963—; vol. Am. Women's Voluntary Svc., 1942-45. Recipient Disting. Grad. award Benjamin Franklin U., 1961. Mem. Am., D.C. (pub. rels. com. 1976—) insts. CPAs, Am. Women's Soc. CPAs, Am. Soc. Women Accts. (legislation chmn. 1960-62, nat. dir. 1952-53, nat. treas. 1953-54), Bus. and Profl. Women's Club (treas. D.C. 1967-68), Benjamin Franklin U. Alumni Assn. (Disting. Alumni award 1964, charter, past dir.), D.A.R., Md. Assn. CPAs (charter chmn. membership com. Montgomery Prince George County 1963-64, chmn. student rels. com. 1964-67, pres. 1968-69, mem. fed. tax com. 1971-73). Mem. Seventh Day Adventist Ch. Contbr. articles to profl. jours. Home and Office: 1007 Elm Ave Silver Spring MD 20912-5839

MOORE, STANLEY RAY, lawyer; b. Dallas, July 20, 1946; s. Elzey and Heloise (Dillon) M.; children—Natalie, William. B.S.M.E., So. Meth. U., 1969, J.D., 1973. Bar: Tex. 1973; U.S. Dist. Ct. (no. dist.) Tex. 1974. Assoc. Clegg, Cantrell, Crisman, Dallas, 1973-75; ptnr. Crisman & Moore, Dallas, 1975-80, Schley Cantrell & Moore, Dallas, 1980-83, Schley, Cantrell, Kice & Moore, Dallas, 1983-87, Johnson & Wortley, P.C., 1987-94, Jenkens & Gilchrist, 1995—. Patentee in field. Foster parent Hope Cottage, Dallas, 1982-90; fund raiser Am. Heart Assn., Republican Party. Recipient Outstanding Leadership commendation ASME, 1969. Mem. Dallas Bar Assn., ABA, Am. Patent Law Assn. Baptist. Home: 1 Victoria Cir Rowlett TX 75088-6059 Office: Jenkens & Gilchrist 1445 Ross Ave Ste 3200 Dallas TX 75202-2770

MOORE, STEPHEN JAMES, lawyer; b. Kansas City, Mo., Aug. 9, 1947; s. James Andrew and Frances Clare (Kennedy) M. BSBA, Rockhurst Coll., 1969, BA, 1975; JD, U. Mo., Kansas City, 1977, postgrad., 1990—. Bar: Mo. 1978, U.S. Dist. Ct. (we. dist.) Mo. 1978, U.S. Ct. Appeals (8th cir.) 1980, U.S. Ct. Appeals (10th cir.) 1981, U.S. Claims Ct. 1991. Law intern Mo. Atty. Gen.'s Office, Kansas City, 1976-77, asst., 1978; assoc. Popham, Conway, Sweeny, Fremont & Bundschu PC, Kansas City, 1978-84, Freilich, Leitner & Carlisle, P.C., Kansas City, 1985, Herrick, Feinstein, Kansas City, 1985-86, Freilich, Leitner, Carlisle & Shortlidge, Kansas City, 1986-90; ptnr. Freilich, Leitner & Carlisle, Kansas City, Dallas, L.A., 1987—, Aspen, Colo., 1987—; adj. prof. law U. Mo., Kansas City, 1995—. Mem. Friends of Art, Nelson-Atkins Mus. Art, Kansas City, 1988—, Smithsonian Inst., Washington, 1985—, Nat. Trust for Historic Preservation, Washington, 1988—, Libr. of Congress Assocs., The Federalist Soc. Mem. ABA, Assn. Trial Lawyers Am., Kansas City Metro Bar Assn., Sports Car Club Am., Am. Mus. Nat. History, Porsche Club Am., Lake Ozarks Yacht Assn., Boat Owners Assn. U.S., Delta Theta Phi, Tau Kappa Epsilon. Roman Catholic. Avocations: vintage sportscars, boating. Home: 5840 Mcgee St Kansas City MO 64113-2132 Office: Freilich Leitner & Carlisle 4600 Madison Ave Ste 1000 Kansas City MO 64112-3012

MOORE, TERRY WAYNE, high technology venture management consultant; b. North Kingston, R.I., Feb. 26, 1957; s. Robert Wendell and Marilyn (Rose) M. BS in Engring., U. Fla., 1981; MBA, U. San Diego, 1993; postgrad., U. Calif., San Diego, 1994. Sr. materials engr. U.S. Dept. Def., Alameda, Calif., 1981-85, program mgr., 1985-87; staff engr., scientist Gen. Atomics, La Jolla, Calif., 1987-89, project mgr., 1989-92, mktg. program mgr., 1992-93; owner Moore Consulting Co., San Diego, 1994—; entrepreneur Venture Mgmt., Moore Cons. Co., San Diego, 1990—; new high tech. ventures cons. for emerging growth and start up cos., 1991—; mem. dirs. database com. Internat. Forum Corp. Dirs., 1995—, program com., 1995—, membership com., 196—, improving dir. effectiveness cert.; mem. San Diego Regional Tech. Alliance, Calif. State Office Strategic Tech. Devel. Trade and Commerce; mem. Team Dennis Conner's Am.'s Cup Syndicate, 1995, crew mem. Stars and Stripes, winner Pacific Class Nat. Championships, 1995. Judge San Diego Sci. Fair, 1989—; rep. Neighborhood Watch, La Costa, Calif., 1989—; vol. fund raiser Am. Cancer Soc., Epilepsy Soc., United Way, U. Calif. San Diego Cancer Ctr. Found. Mem. Am. Soc. for Materials Internat. (sec.-treas. 1990-92, vice chmn. 1993-94, chmn. 1994-95, past chmn. 1995-96, bd. dirs. 1989—, nat. chpt ops. com., chmn. computer subcom. 1991—, chmn. 1994-95), Project Mgmt. Inst. (sec. 1993-94, treas. 1994-95, bd. dirs. 1993—), Nat. Bd. Cert. Project Mgmt. Profl. (cert.), San Diego Engring. Soc. (program chmn. bd. dirs. 1995-96), Soc. Advancement of Material and Process Engring., San Diego Venture Mgmt. Group, MIT Enterprise Forum (mem. panel selection com.), Found. for Enterprise Devel., San Diego Yacht Club. Republican. Presbyterian. Avocations: financial investments, ocean yacht racing, reading, triathlons, private pilot. Home and Office: 905 Orchid Way Carlsbad CA 92009-4830

MOORE, THOMAS CARROL, botanist, educator; b. Sanger, Tex., Sept. 22, 1936; s. Thomas M. and Willie Mae M.; m. Arvida Inmon DePriest, Sept. 1, 1956; children—Cynthia, Linda, Alan. B.A. in Biology, U. N. Tex., Denton, 1956; M.A. in Botany, U. Colo., 1958, Ph.D. (Outstanding Grad. Student in Biology award 1960, USPHS predoctoral fellow 1960-61), 1961. Instr. biology, then part-time instr. U. Colo., 1958-60; asst. prof. Ariz. State Coll., Flagstaff, 1961-63; mem. faculty Oreg. State U., Corvallis, 1963-93, prof. botany, 1971-93, prof. emeritus, 1993—, chmn. dept. botany and plant pathology, 1973-86, asst. to v.p. for rsch. and grad. studies, 1972-73; vis. prof. Colo. State Coll., 1963. Mem. editorial bd. Plant Physiology, 1981-86; editor in chief Jour. Plant Growth Regulation; contbr. articles to profl. jours. Recipient Mosser award outstanding undergrad. teaching Oreg. State U., 1966. Mem. Am. Soc. Plant Physiologists, Bot. Soc. Am., Am. Phytopathol. Soc., Internat. Plant Growth Substances Assn., Plant Growth Regulator Soc. Am., Sigma Xi. Democrat. Lodge: Elks. Home: 560 NW Merrie Dr Corvallis OR 97330-6524 Office: 2082 Cordley Hall Oreg State Univ Corvallis OR 97331

MOORE, THOMAS DAVID, academic administrator; b. Rochester, N.Y., July 26, 1937; s. Robert Franklin and Hilda (Kennedy) M.; m. Virginia Muller, June 13, 1959; children: Kathleen Mary, Michael David, Thomas David. BSS, St. John Fisher Coll., 1959; MS, SUNY, Brockport, 1962; EdD, Rutgers U., 1966. Tchr. Rochester City Schs., 1959-62; grad. asst. Rutgers U., New Brunswick, N.J., 1963-65; from asst. to full prof. Kent (Ohio) State U., 1965-93, asst. v.p. acad. affairs, 1976-83, v.p. faculty affairs and personnel, 1984-86, provost, v.p. acad. and student affairs, 1987-91; provost, v.p. acad. affairs Ctrl. Washington U., 1993-97. Roman Catholic. Avocations: sports, film, public affairs, music.

MOORE, THOMAS E., biology educator, museum director; b. Champaign, Ill.; s. Gerald E. and Velma (Lewis) M.; m. E. Eleanor Sifferd, Feb. 4, 1951; children: Deborah S., Melinda S. BS, U. Ill., 1951, MS, 1952, PhD, 1956. Tech. asst. Ill. Natural History Survey, Urbana, 1950-56; instr. zoology U. Mich., Ann Arbor, 1956-59, asst. prof. zoology, 1959-63, assoc. prof. zoology, 1963-66, prof. biology, 1966—, curator insects, 1956—, dir. exhibit mus., 1988-93; vis. prof. Orgn. for Tropical Studies, San Jose, Costa Rica, 1970, 72; bd. dirs. Orgn. Tropical Studies, San Jose, 1968-79; mem. steering com. tropical biome U.S. Internat. Biol. Program, 1969-72; mem. conf. planning com. Nat. Inst. for Environment, 1991-92; mem. steering com. Univ. Colloquium on Environ. Rsch. and Edn., 1991-93. Co-editor: Lectures on Science Education, 1991-1992, 1993; Cricket Behavior and Neurobiology, 1989; author movie 17-Year Cicadas, 1975. County rep. Huron River Watershed Coun., Ann Arbor, 1987-95; mem. Mich. H.S. Accreditation Adv. Com., Ann Arbor, 1988-92; mem. U. Mich. Senate Adv. Com. on Univ. Affairs, 1993-96, vice chair, 1995-96; bd. mem. U. Mich. Acad. Freedom Lecture Fund, 1995—, treas., 1995-98; cons. NSF Visual Tech. in Environ. Curricula, 1994-97. Rsch. grantee NSF, 1963-66, 66-69, 96-97, rsch. equipment grantee, 1984-86. Fellow AAAS, AAUP (pres. U. Mich. chpt. 1996—, exec. bd. Mich. conf. 1996—), Royal Entomol. Soc. London, Linnaen Soc. London; mem. Assn. Tropical Biology (pres. 1973-75), Sigma Xi (pres. U. Mich. chpt. 1994-96, coun. 1993—). Home: 4243 N Delhi Rd Ann Arbor MI 48103-9485 Office: Mus of Zoology U Mich Ann Arbor MI 48109-1079

MOORE, THOMAS GALE, economist, educator; b. Washington, Nov. 6, 1930; s. Charles Godwin and Beatrice (McLean) M.; m. Cassandra Chrones, Dec. 28, 1958; children: Charles G., Antonia L. B.A., Geroge Washington U., 1957; M.A., U. Chgo., 1959, Ph.D., 1961. Fgn. research analyst Chase Manhattan Bank, N.Y.C., 1960-61; asst. prof. econs. Carnegie Inst. Tech., 1961-65; assoc. prof., then prof. econs. Mich. State U., East Lansing, 1965-74; sr. staff economist Council Econ. Advisers, 1968-70; hon. research fellow Univ. Coll., London, 1973-74; adj. scholar Am. Enterprise Inst., 1971—, CATO Inst., 1982—; sr. fellow Hoover Inst. on War, Revolution and Peace-Stanford U., 1974—, dir. domestic studies program, 1974-85; mem. Council Econ. Advisers, Washington, 1985-89; mem. Nat. Critical Materials Council, 1985-89; mem. econ. adv. bd. Dept. Commerce, 1971-73; mem. adv. com. RANN, 1975-77, NSF, 1975-77; cons. Dept. Transp., 1973-74, 81-83; mem. adv. panel Synthetic Fuels Corp., 1982; mem. adv. bd. Reason Found., 1982—; dir. Stanford Savs. & Loan, 1979-82, chmn., 1982. Author: The Economics of American Theater, 1968, Freight Transportation Regulation, 1972, Trucking Regulation: Lessons from Europe, 1976, Uranium Enrichment and Public Policy, 1978; co-author: Public Claims on U.S. Output, 1973; contbr. articles to profl. jours. Served with USN, 1951-55, Korea. Fellow Earhart Found., 1958-59; fellow Walgreen Found., 1959-60, Hoover Instn., 1973-74. Mem. Am. Econ. Assn., Mont. Pelerin Soc., Chevy Chase Club. Home: 3766 La Donna Ave Palo Alto CA 94306-3150 Office: Stanford U Hoover Instn Stanford CA 94305

MOORE, THOMAS JOSEPH, financial company executive; b. Kalamazoo, Jan. 5, 1943; s. John Joseph and Bernita (Ryan) M.; m. Laura Leigh Johnson, Aug. 1, 1975; children: Ryan Michael, Janelle Marie, Darcie Kathleen. BBA, Western Mich. U., 1965; MBA, So. Meth. U., 1990. Various sales and mktg. positions IBM Corp., Southfield, Mich., 1968-79; exec. v.p., owner Carsonville (Mich.) Metal Products Corp., 1976-79; assoc. prof. Oakland Coll., Farmington Hills, Mich., 1977-78; group mgr. industry mktg. Recognition Equipment Inc., Dallas, 1979-81; mgmt. cons. APC Skills div. Alexander Proudfoot Co., Palm Beach, Fla., 1982-83; pres., chief exec. officer Lumentech of Am., Inc., Dallas, 1983-85; v.p., prin. Capital Alliance Corp., Dallas, 1985—; chmn., CEO, Laura Leigh Stores, Inc., Plano, Tex., 1993—; vis. lectr. Baylor U., Waco, Tex., 1986-89, sponsor, CEO roundtable, 1989-93. Pres. Bent Tree Homeowners Assn., Dallas, 1981-83; co-chair Jesuit Coll. Prep. Sch. Challenge Dr., 1992-95; chair car raffle Ursuline Acad. of Dallas, chmn. maj. donor campaign, 1994-95, co-chair bridge the gap campaign, 1995-96, chair underwriting, 1996. Mem. M&A Internat., So. Meth. U. Exec. MBA Alumni Assn. (bd. dirs. 1990-92). Republican. Roman Catholic. Avocations: running, reading, racquetball. Home: 4402 Cobblers Ln Dallas TX 75287-6732 Office: Capital Alliance Corp 2777 N Stemmons Fwy Ste 1220 Dallas TX 75207-2271

MOORE, THOMAS KAIL, chief judge; b. Idaho Falls, Idaho, Jan. 15, 1938; s. Burton L. and Clara E. (Kail) Moore; m. Judith Diane Gilman, July 30, 1966; children: David T., Jonathan G. AB in Phys. Scis., Harvard U., 1961; JD, Georgetown U., 1967. Bar: D.C., V.I., Va. Law clk. to Hon. John A. Danaher U.S. Ct. Appeals (D.C. Cir.), 1967-68; staff atty. Office Gen. Coun., Office Sec. Dept. Transp., Washington, 1968-69; assoc. Stanford, Reed & Gelenian, Washington, 1969-70; asst. U.S. Atty. U.S. Attys. Office, Washington, 1970-71; asst. U.S. Atty. U.S. Attys. Office (ea. dist.), Va., 1971-76. prin. asst. Alexandria office, 1974-76; asst. U.S. Atty. U.S. Attys. Office (V.I. dist.), 1976-78; pvt. practive St. Thomas, V.I., 1978-81; shareholder Hoffman & Moore, P.C., St. Thomas, 1981-87; ptnr. Grunert, Stout, Moore & Bruch, St. Thomas, 1987-92; chief judge U.S. Dist. Ct. (V.I. dist.), 1992—. Editor-in-chief Georgetown Law Journal, 1966-67. Scoutmaster Antilles Sch. Troop; trustee V.I. Montessori Sch. Capt. USAF, 1961-64, USAFR. Mem. ABA, V.I. Bar Assn. (judicial), V.I. C. of C., St. Thomas Yacht Club. Avocations: tennis, swimming, sailing. Office: Dist Ct of VI 5500 Veterans Dr Ste 310 Charlotte Amalie VI 00802-6424

MOORE, THOMAS LLOYD, librarian; b. Springfield, Ill., Oct. 4, 1942; s. Edward Joseph and Dorothy A. (Menezes) M.; m. Ann Mary Walsh, Aug. 29, 1971; children: Sean Christopher, Martin Thomas, Kathleen Adele. AA, Springfield Coll., 1963; BA, Cardinal Glennon Coll., St. Louis, 1968; MA in Library Sci., Rosary Coll., 1973. Tchr. Little Flower Grade Sch., Springfield, 1963-66; head of adult services Elk Grove Village (Ill.) Pub. Library, 1973-74; dir. Northlake (Ill.) Pub. Library Dist., 1974-75, Danville (Ill.) Pub. Library, 1975-78; adminstrv. librarian Palatine (Ill.) Pub. Library Dist., 1978-81; dir. Wake County Dept. of the Pub. Library, Raleigh, N.C., 1981—. Bd. dirs. Commit to a Healthier Region, 1991-93, Planned Parenthood of the Capital & Coast, 1993—, sec., 1994; bd. dirs. Pirates Cove Homeowners Assn., 1992—, v.p., 1993-94, pres., 1995-96; mem. Libr. Power Adv. Com., 1993-95, Facilitatators Orgnl. Devel. Group, 1995—, ASSIST Wake to Health Coalition, 1992-94. Mem. ALA, N.C. Library Assn. Democrat. Roman Catholic. Office: Wake County Pub Libr 4020 Carya Dr Raleigh NC 27610-2913

MOORE, THOMAS PAUL, broadcast executive; b. Danville, Ill., Feb. 29, 1928; s. Lester Rufus and Mabel Ellen (Jackson) M.; m. Jean LaVonne Sather, Aug. 31, 1952; children: Randyl Ellen, Patricia Kay, Gregory Sather. BA, North Cen. Coll., Naperville, Ill., 1952; postgrad., Denver U., 1952-53. Newscaster Sta. KFEL-AM-FM-TV, Denver, 1952-54; sales rep. Sta. KGMC, Englewood, Colo., 1954-56; sales mgr. Sta. KDEN-AM-FM, Denver, 1956-62; pres. Stas. WBCO, WQEL, Bucyrus, Ohio, 1962—; bd. dirs. First Fed. Savings and Loan, Bucyrus, 1990—. Lay leader, mem. program council Ohio Sandusky Conf., United Methodist Ch., 1966-69 (pres. gen. laity bd. and laymen's found. 1968-72); mem. Gen Council on Ministries, 1980-84, N.W. Ohio Water Devel. Adv. Com., 1967-69, Sandusky River Basin Water Pollution Study Com., 1968-69; v.p., bd. mgrs. EUB Men, Evang. United Brethren Ch., 1958-68; pres. Rocky Mountain Conf., 1957-61; mem. gen. bd. Nat. Council Christian Chs. Am., 1968-72; charter pres. Bucyrus Bratwurst Festival, Inc., 1968; adv. bd. Bucyrus Salvation Army, 1964-68; mem. planning com. East Ohio Conf., 1972-76 (chmn. comm. on minimum salaries, 1968-72, lay leader, 1972-76); vice chmn. council ministries, mem. episcopal com., 1972-76, head. del. to gen. conf., Portland, Oreg., 1976, Balt., 1984; head del. to Jurisdictional Conf., Sioux Falls, 1976, Duluth, Minn., 1984; pres. United Meth. Communications, 1972-76, mem. gen. council fin. and adminstrn., 1976-80; mem. communications commn. Nat. Council Chs., 1972-76; mem. communications con. Ohio Council Chs.; mem. Episc. com., chmn. New Vision Task Group, both East Ohio Conf., North Cen. Jurisdiction, United Meth. Ch.; mem. exec. com. Council on Ministries, 1980-86; mem. World Meth. Council, 1986-91, World Meth. Conf., 1996; trustee United Theol. Sem., 1972-80; trustee Ohio Northern U., 1986—, mem. exec. com., 1991—, chair student affairs com., 1991-95, chair, 1995—; mem. exec. com. East Ohio del. to United Meth. Gen. Conf. and Jurisdictional Conf., 1987-91; v.p. Community Improvement Corp., Bucyrus, 1989-91; mem. Overall Econ. Devel. Com. of Crawford County, 1992-96; chmn. Crawford County Traffic Safety Council, 1979-89, 96—; pres. Crawford County Econ. Devel. Adv. Coun., 1992-96; mem. Crawford County Devel. Bd., Inc.; mem. exec. com. of del. to 1988 Gen. Conf. United Meth. Ch., St. Louis; bd. dirs. Bucyrus Community Hosp., 1992-96, mem. fin. com., 1993-96, chair nominating com., 1993-96, campaign dir., chair fundraising com., 1993-96, v.p. bd. dirs., 1994-96; mem. N. Ctrl. Ohio Health Sys., 1996—. Served with USN, 1946-48. Named a Civic Leader of Am., 1968. Mem. Nat. Assn. Broadcasters (legis. liaison 1984-91, mem. small market radio com.), Ohio Assn. Broadcasters (pres. 1982-85), North Ctrl. Ohio Broadcasters Assn. (pres. 1983-84, 96—, v.p. 1985-96), Bucyrus Area C. of C. (chmn. airport study com. 1967-68, bd. dirs. 1964-67, pres. 1989-91), Rotary (pres. Bucyrus chpt. 1992-93). Office: WBCO-WQEL Radio 403 E Rensselaer St Bucyrus OH 44820-2438

MOORE, THOMAS RONALD (LORD BRIDESTOWE), lawyer; b. Duluth, Minn., Mar. 27, 1932; s. Ralph Henry and Estelle Marguerite (Hero) M.; m. Margaret C. King, Sept. 10, 1955; children: Willard S., Clarissa, Charles R.H. BA magna cum laude, Yale U., 1954; JD, Harvard U., 1957. Bar: N.Y. 1958, U.S. Supreme Ct. 1958. Instr. Internat. Program in Taxation Harvard Law Sch., 1956-57; assoc. Dewey Ballantine, N.Y.C.; ptnr. Breed, Abbott & Morgan, N.Y.C., Finley Kumble & Wagner, N.Y.C., Hawkins, Delafield & Wood, N.Y.C.; Law Offices of Thomas R. Moore, N.Y.C.; lectr. on law Cornell Law Sch., NYU, So. Fed. Tax Inst., Atlanta, U. Hartford, Practising Law Inst., N.Y.C., Las Vegas, New Orleans; lectr. N.Y.C., San Antonio, Tampa, L.A., Moscow, Charlottesville, Va., Washington, Kansas City. Author: Plantagenet Descent, 31 Generations from William the Conqueror to Today, 1995; co-author: Estate Planning and the Close Corporation; editor-in-chief Gastronome; bd. editors: The Tax Lawyer; contbr. articles to profl jours., popular press and TV commentaries. Bd. dirs. exec. com. Citymeals on Wheels; pres. bd. dirs. Nat. Soc. to Prevent Blindness, 1973-81, chmn., 1981-83, now hon. pres.; sec.-treas., trustee A.D. Henderson Found., Del.; trustee, Fla.; bd. dirs. Phoenix Theatre Inc., Inst. Aegean Prehistory, Found. Future of Man, Am. and Internat. Friends of Victoria and Albert Mus., London; conservator N.Y. Pub. Libr.; trustee Found. for Renaissance of St. Petersburg (Russia), Malcolm Wiener Found., Lawrence W. Levine Found. Recipient Coat of Arms and created Knight of St. John by Queen Elizabeth II, Order of Crown of Charlemagne, Order of Plantagenet, Order of Barons of Magna Charta; recipient Key to Kansas City by Mayor of Kansas City, Mo., 1989; Yale scholar of House, 1954; honoree Thomas R. Moore Disting. Pub. Servant award Nat. Soc. to Prevent Blindness. Mem. ABA, N.Y. State BAr Assn. (exec. com.), Assn. of Bar City of N.Y., Confrerie de la Chaine des Rotisseurs (nat. pres., dir., exec. com. world coun. Paris), Chevalier du Tastevin, Nat. Wine Coalition (bd. dirs. 1989—), Pilgrims Club, Knights of St. John Club, Downtown Assn., Univ. Club, Church Club, Delta Sigma Rho. Republican. Episcopalian. Office: 730 5th Ave Ste 900 New York NY 10019-4105

MOORE, THOMAS SCOTT, lawyer; b. Portland, Oreg., Nov. 17, 1937; s. Harry Alburn and Geraldine Elizabeth (Scott) M.; m. Saundra L. Wagner, Sept. 7, 1957 (div. 1974); children: Cindy, Kristin, Thomas, Victoria, Wendy; m. Alice H. Zeisz, Nov. 5, 1976; 1 child, Alice G. BA, Willamette U., 1959, JD cum laude, 1962. Bar: Oregon 1962. Pvt. practice Portland, 1962—. Contbr. articles to law jours. Republican. Avocation: tennis. Office: 4512 SW Kelly Ave Portland OR 97201-4257

MOORE, THURSTON ROACH, lawyer; b. Memphis, Dec. 10, 1946; s. Richard Charlton Moore and Halcyon Hall (Roach) Lynn; m. Grace Branch, Nov. 8, 1969. BA with distinction, U. Va., 1968, JD, 1974. Bar: Va. 1974. Rsch. analyst Scudder, Stevens & Clark, N.Y.C., 1968-71; ptnr. Hunton & Williams, Richmond, Va., 1974—; bd. dirs. Exec. Info. Sys., Inc., Darien, Conn., Met. Advantage Corp., Richmond. Bd. dirs. Met. Bus. Found., Richmond, Mary Morton Parsons Found., Charlottesville, Va., The Nature Conservancy, Charlottesville, vice chmn. Va. chpt.; trustee Va. Aerospace Bus. Roundtable, Hampton, 1989—, Va. Ea. Shore Sustainable Devel. Corp., 1995—. Mem. ABA (bus. law sect., chmn. ptnrs. com. 1992-96, mem. fed. regulation security com.), Va. Bar Assn., Va. State Bar. Office: Hunton & Williams 951 E Byrd St Richmond VA 23219-4040

MOORE, TOM, film and theater director; b. Meridian, Miss., Aug. 6, 1943; s. Heustis T. and Maryanne (Moody) M. B.A., Purdue U., 1965; M.F.A., Yale U., 1968; DFA, Purdue Univ., 1995. Tchr. Am. Dramatic Inst., U. London, 1968; guest dir. SUNY-Buffalo, 1968, Brandeis U., Boston, 1968; artistic dir. Peterborough Players (N.H.), 1971; lectr. Seminar Am. Studies, Salzburg, Austria, 1974. Dir. Broadway plays: Grease (one of the longest-running shows in history of Broadway), 1972-80, Over Here, 1974-75, Once in a Lifetime, 1978, Division Street, 1980, Frankenstein, 1981, 'night Mother, 1983 (Pulitzer Prize) (dir. film by same name 1986), The Octette Bridge Club, 1985, A Little Hotel on the Side, Nat. Actors Theatre, 1992, Moon over Buffalo, 1995-96; off-Broadway play: Welcome to Andromeda, 1973; plays Am. Conservatory Theatre, San Francisco, 1977-81, Williamstown (Mass.) Theatre Festival, 1976, 79, 93, Mark Taper Forum, Los Angeles, 1980, 82, 83, 84, 86, 91, Tyrone Guthrie Theatre, Mpls., 1975, Arena Stage, Washington, 1975, Old Globe Theatre Festival, San Diego, 1982, 85, Ahmanson Theatre, Los Angeles, 1983, Am. Repertory Theatre, Cambridge, Mass.,

1982, 84, La Jolla (Calif.) Playhouse, 1990; film Journey, 1972; co-dir. Fridays, ABC-TV; dir. thirtysomething, ABC-TV, LA Law, NBC-TV (Emmy nominee 1991), Almost Grown, CBS-TV, Wonder Years, ABC-TV (Humanitas prize for Square Dance episode, 1990), Cheers, NBC-TV, Northern Exposure, CBS-TV, Picket Fences, CBS-TV, Civil Wars, ABC-TV, Class of '96, Fox TV, Mad About You, NBC-TV; TV movies Maybe, Baby, and Fine Things, NBC, 1990; TV pilots The Flamingo Kid, 50 Minute Man. Recipient Tony award nomination 1974, 83, Golden Knight award Malta Film Festival, 1973, Cine Golden Eagle award, 1973, 6 Dramalogue awards, 1981-86, Emmy nominee, 1993. Fellow Am. Film Inst. *

MOORE, TOM O., program administrator; b. Trinidad, Colo., Nov. 24, 1948; s. M.C. and Leola Dell (Floyd) M.; m. Diane Lamkin, Feb. 17, 1966 (div. Oct. 1988); children: Stephen S., Dione D.; m. Sandra Raye Beaumont, Apr. 21, 1989; children: Robert Tyler, James Brandon. Grad. H.S., Los Alamos, N.Mex. Cert. indsl. hygiene technologist; cert. occupl. safety and health technologist, N.Mex. Indsl. hygiene technician Los Alamos Nat. Lab., 1969-74, respiratory protection tng. specialist, 1974-77, indsl. hygienist, 1977-79, indsl. hygienist, respiratory protection supr., 1979-81, respiratory protection program coord., 1981-96, facility mgmt., environ., safety and health officer, 1996—; cons., instr. Harvard Sch. Pub. Health, Boston, Colo. State U., Ft. Collins, U. N.Mex., Los Alamos, 1980-89; adv. instr. Nuclear Emergency Search Team, Los Alamos Base Worldwide Response, 1986-96, accident response group advisor Accident Response Group, 1986-96. Co-author: (tng. manual) Respiratory Protection Training Manual, 1974. Coach Young Am. Football League, Los Alamos, 1976, 76-79, Sandy Colfax Baseball, Los Alamos, 1979, 80, 90, 91, Little League Baseball, 1974-78; publicity dir. Mens Softball Assn., Los Alamos, 1977-85. Mem. Am. Indsl. Hygiene Assn., Bd. Cert. Safety Profls. Republican. Episcopalian. Office: Los Alamos Nat Lab PO Box 1663 MS-E536 Los Alamos NM 87545

MOORE, TRESI LEA, lawyer; b. Brownwood, Tex., Dec. 3, 1961; d. Dean Moore and Patsy Ruth (Evans) Adams. BA in Fgn. Svc., BA in French, Baylor U., 1984, JD, 1987. Bar: Tex. 1987, U.S. Dist. Ct. (no. dist.) Tex. 1988, U.S. Ct. Appeals (5th cir.) 1989. Atty. Richard Jackson & Assocs., Dallas, 1987-91, Amis & Moore (and predecessor firm), Arlington, Tex., 1992—. Vol. Legal Svcs. of North Tex., Dallas, 1988—, Dallas Com. for Fgn. Visitors, 1989-92; bd. dirs. Plano Internat. Presch., 1995-96. Recipient Pro Bono Svc. award Legal Svcs. of North Tex., 1989, 90, 91. Mem. AAUW (pub. policy dir. Plano, Tex. br. 1992, 93-94, v.p. 1994-95), State Bar Tex. (mem. mentor program for lawyers com. 1994—, mem. local bar svcs. com. 1994-96), Dallas Bar Assn., Dallas Women Lawyers Assn. (bd. dirs. 1989-90, v.p. 1992, pres. 1993). Avocations: scuba diving, reading, bicycling, hiking, growing herbs. Office: Amis & Moore 2301 E Lamar Blvd Ste 250 Arlington TX 76006-7425

MOORE, VERNON LEE, agricultural consultant, retired food products company executive; b. Creston, Iowa, Mar. 29, 1928; s. Newton and Eulalia Pearl (Lewis) M.; m. Lorene Shirley Moore, Jan. 29, 1949; children: Dianne, Nancy, Jack. BS in Agr., Iowa State U., 1951. Instr. vocat. agrl. Gowrie (Iowa) Sch. Dist., 1951-55; with Land O'Lakes, Inc., Mpls., 1955-88, sr. v.p., 1988, ret., 1988; pvt. practice agrl. cons., 1989—. Bd. dirs. exec. com. Agrl. Coop. Devel. Internat., Washington, 1972-89, Am. Inst. Coop., Washington, 1975-88, Minn. 4-H Found., Washington, 1980-91; bd. dirs. Vols. in OVerseas Coop. Devel., Washington, 1980-88, The Coop. Found., St. Paul, 1978-88; commr. Civil Svc. Commn., Columbia Hts., Minn., 1974—; mem. U. Minn. Adv. Com., St. Paul, 1984-91; various leadership positions Fridley United Meth. Ch., Minn., 1971—; dir. adminstrn. Russian Farm Cmty. Project. Recipient Internat. Coop. award Coop. Coordinating Group, 1987. Lodges: Rotary, Masons, Shriners. Avocations: photography, woodworking, gardening.

MOORE, WALTER PARKER, JR., civil engineering company executive; b. Houston, May 6, 1937; s. Walter Parker Sr. and Zoe Alma (McBride) M.; m. Mary Ann Dillingham, Aug. 19, 1959; children: Walter P. III, Melissa Moore Magee, Matthew Dillingham. BA in Civil Engring., Rice U., 1959, BS in Civil Engring., 1960; MS in Civil Engring., U. Ill., 1962, PhD in Civil Engring., 1964. Registered profl. engr., Ark., Ariz., Colo., Fla., Ga., Idaho, Ill., Ind., Kans., Maine, Md., Mich., Minn., Mo., Nev., N.H., N.Mex., N.Y., N.C., Okla., Oreg., Pa., R.I., Tex., Utah, Wash., Wis., Wyo. Rsch. asst. U. Ill., Urbana, 1960-64; design engr. Walter P. Moore & Assocs., Inc., Houston, 1966-70, sec., treas., 1970-75, exec. v.p., 1975-83, pres., chmn., 1983—, chmn., 1993—; engring. adv. coun. Rice U., 1970-74, adj. prof. architecture, 1975-82, archtl. adv. coun., 1988—; pres. Rice U. Alumni Assn., 1975; civil engring. vis. com. U. Tex. Austin, 1975-77; adv. com. effects of earthquake motions on reinforced concrete bldgs. U. Ill. Adv. Com., 1980; pres. Rice U. Engring. Alumni Assn., 1983, vis. lectr. Cornell U., 1986; mem. sesquicentennial com. State of Tex. Bus. and Fin. Com., 1986; vis. lectr. U. Ill., 1988, 89; engring. adv. coun. Tex. A&M U., 1990—; Thomas A. Bullock Endowed Chair Leadership and Innovation Coll. Arch., Dept. Civil Engring. Texas A&M U., 1994—, dir. Ctr. Bldg. Design and Constrn., dir. Ctr. Constrn. Edn. Group editor (monograph) Tall Building Systems and Concepts; mem. editorial adv. bd. Constrn. Bus. Rev., 1992—. Bd. dirs. Kiwanis Club Houston, 1974-76, Rice Design Alliance, 1976-79, Rice Ctr. for Community Design and Rsch., 1977-82, Harris County Heritage Soc., 1984-86, River Oaks Bank, 1983-91, Compass Bank, 1991-92; bd. dirs., v.p. The Forest Club, 1976-78; chmn. architects and engrs. United Way, 1985; mem. exec. com. River Oaks Bank, 1984-91. Capt. U.S. Army, 1964-66. Recipient Outstanding Civil Engring. Alumnus award U. Ill., 1992, Outstanding Engring. Alumnus award Rice U., 1993, Master Builder award Assoc. Gen. Contrs., Houston chpt., 1995. Fellow Am. Concrete Inst.; mem. AIA (hon. Houston chpt.), NAE, NSPE, ASCE (activities chmn. 1968-69, sec. structures group Tex. sect. 1976-77, vice-chmn. 1977-78, structural standards divsn., exec. com. 1989—, chmn. A7 com. 1988—, keynote speaker nat. conv. New Orleans 1986, Edmund Friedman award 1996, mem. bd. govs. Structural Engring. Inst. ASCE), Am. Cons. Engrs. Coun. (bd. dirs. CEC-T 1981-83, v.p. 1990-92), Internat. Assn. Bridge and Structural Engrs., Am. Concrete Inst. (mem. com. # 318, bd. direction 1989-91, Alfred E. Lindau award 1992), Soc. Am. Mil. Engrs., Coun. on Tall Bldgs. and Urban Habitat (mem. steering group 1971—, editor Com. 3 1975—, chmn. final plenary session Hong Kong Fourth World Congress, 1990, Hong Kong Forth World Congress, 1990, internat. and regional conference 1990—), Consulting Engrs. Coun. Tex. (bd. dirs. 1974-76, v.p. 1976-77, pres. 1977-78), Tex. Soc. Profl. Engrs. (Young Engr. of Yr. 1969-70, region IV Engr. of Yr., 1985), Post Tensioning Inst. (juror nat. awards 1983—), Structural Engrs. Assn. Tex. Episcopalian. Office: 2d Fl 3131 Eastside St Fl 2 Houston TX 77098-1935 also: Tex A&M U Dept Civil Engring CE/TTI Bldg Rm 710F College Station TX 77843-3136

MOORE, WARD WILFRED, medical educator; b. Cowden, Ill., Feb. 12, 1924; s. Cecil Leverett and Velma Leona (Frye) M.; m. Frances Laura Campbell, Jan. 29, 1949; children—Scott Thomas, Ann Gail, Brian Dean, Kevin Lee. A.B., U. Ill., 1948, M.S., 1951, Ph.D., 1952. Instr., rsch. assoc. U. Ill., 1952-54; asst. prof. Okla. State U., Stillwater, 1954-55, Ind. U., Bloomington, 1955-59; assoc. prof. Ind. U., 1959-66, prof. physiology, 1966-89, prof. physiology and biophysics emeritus, 1989—, acting chmn. dept. anatomy, 1971-73, assoc. dean basic med. scis., 1971-89, assoc. dean, dir. med. scis. program, 1976-89; vis. prof. Postgrad. Med. Center, Karachi, Pakistan, 1963-64; staff mem. Rockefeller Found., 1968-71; vis. prof., chmn. dept. physiology, faculty sci. Mahidol U., Bangkok, Thailand, 1968-71. Served with U.S. Army, 1943-46. Mem. Am. Physiol. Soc., Endocrine Soc., Am. Soc. Nephrology, Soc. Study Reproduction, Am. Assn. Anatomists, Soc. Exptl. Biology and Medicine, Am. Assn. Med. Colls., AAAS, Am. Inst. Biol. Scis., AAUP, Ind. Acad. Sci., Ind. Hist. Soc., Sigma Xi, Phi Sigma. Home: 3421 E Latimer Rd Bloomington IN 47401-4219 Office: Ind U Myers Hall # 203 Bloomington IN 47405

MOORE, WILLIAM B., lawyer; b. 1941. BA, Stanford U., 1963; JD, U. , 1966. Bar: Ill. 1966. Atty. Trans Union Corp., 1966-73, sr. atty., 1973- , sec., 1977-81, gen. counsel, 1979-81; corp. counsel IC Industries, 1982-86; ., dept. gen. counsel Whitman Corp., 1987-90, v.p., sec., gen. counsel. Mem. Am. Soc. Corp. Secs. Inc. (pres. Chgo. regional group 1979-80, dir. 1980-83). Office: Whitman Corp 3501 Algonquin Rd Rolling Meadows IL 60008-3103

MOORE, WILLIAM CULLEN, retired electronics company executive; b. Portland, Oreg., Nov. 17, 1912; s. William Cullen and Lillian (Rodé) M.; m. Helen Hays Edgar, Aug. 8, 1936; children: Shirley Carol, Ronald Cullen, Paul Alan, Katherine Leone. BA in Physics, Reed Coll., Portland, 1936; MA in Physics, Boston U., 1949. Electronics engr. United Airlines, Chgo., 1937-38; project leader Motorola, Inc., Chgo., 1938-47; sect. head govt. electronics group Motorola, Inc., Scottsdale, Ariz., 1958-78; ret.; project supr./instr. Upper Air Lab., Boston U., 1947-51; chief engr. Tracerlab, Inc., Boston, 1951-53; engring. mgr. Boonton (N.J.) Radio Corp., 1953-58; cons./facilitator (space) Motorola Mus. of Electronics, Schaumburg, Ill., 1987-90; investigator Apollo comms. NASA, Madrid, Spain, 1971. Contbr. articles to profl. jours. Mem. sch. bd. Lombard (Ill.) Sch. Dist., 1946-47, Mountain Lakes (N.J.) Sch. Dist., 1956-58; mem. allocations panels United Way, 1977-94. Fellow AIAA (assoc.; sect. chair 1963-64); mem. IEEE (sr.; sect. chair 1940—). Achievements include patents on coupling transformer; coded range signal responsive system (aviation); low level bridge discriminator; transponder for moving vehicle tracking system (space). Home: Apt 346 10015 W Royal Oak Rd Sun City AZ 85351-3186

MOORE, WILLIAM GROVER, JR., management consultant, former air freight executive, former air force officer; b. Waco, Tex., May 18; s. William Grover and Annie Elizabeth (Pickens) M.; student Kilgore (Tex.) Coll., 1937-39, Sacramento State Coll., 1951, George Washington U., 1962; grad. Air War Coll., Air U., 1957, Nat. War Coll., 1962; m. Marjorie Y. Gardella, Jan. 18, 1943; 1 dau., Allyson. Enlisted U.S. Army Air Force, 1940, commd. 2d lt., 1941, advanced through grades to gen., 1977; comdr. 777th Squadron, 15th AF, Italy, 1944-45, 3535th Maintenance and Supply Group, Mather AFB, Calif., 1951, 3d Bomb Group, Korea, 1952; chief bases and units div. Hdqrs. USAF, 1952-56; asst. dep. chief of staff ops. Hdqrs. USAF Europe, 1957-61; comdr. 314th Troop Carrier Wing, Sewart AFB, Tenn., 1962-63, 839th Air Div., 1963-65; asst. J3 U.S. Strike Command, 1965-66; comdr. 834th Air Div., Vietnam, 1966-67; dir. operational requirements Hdqrs. USAF, 1967-70; comdr. 22d AF, 1970-73, 13th AF, 1973; chief of staff Pacific Command, 1973-76; asst. vice chief of staff Hdqrs. USAF, 1976-77; comdr. in chief Mil. Air Lift Command, 1977-79; ret., 1979; pres., chief operating officer Emery Air Freight Corp., Wilton, Conn., 1981-83; bus. cons., 1983—; pres. Met. Nashville Airport Authority, 1984—. Decorated Def. D.S.M., Air Force D.S.M. with 2 oak leaf clusters, Legion of Merit with 4 oak leaf clusters, Silver Star, D.F.C. with oak leaf cluster, Air medal with 9 oak leaf clusters, AF Commendation medal with 10 oak leaf clusters (U.S.); Croix de Guerre with palm (France); Armed Forces Honor medal 1st class (Vietnam); Republic of China Cloud and Banner; Legion of Honor (Republic of Philippines); recipient L. Mendel Rivers award of excellence; Jimmy Doolittle fellow in aerospace edn., 1978; named to Minuteman Hall of Fame, 1979. Mem. Air Force Assn., Nat. Def. Transp. Assn., Am. Ordnance Assn. Home: 932 W Main St Franklin TN 37064-2730 Office: Nashville Internat Airport 1 Terminal Dr Ste 501 Nashville TN 37214-4110

MOORE, WILLIAM JASON, museum director; b. Asheboro, N.C., Aug. 4, 1938; s. Lonnie James and Pauline (Hamilton) M.; m. Jane Beane, Dec. 16, 1962; 1 son, William David. B.B.A., High Point Coll., 1960. Asst. to archeologist Town Creek Indian Mound, Mt. Gilead, N.C., 1959; dir. Greensboro Mus., (N.C.), 1963—; assessor Am. Assn. Mus., Washington, 1976—. Mem. N.C. Mus. Council (award 1976; pres. 1973-74), Am. Assn. Mus., Am. Assn. State and Local History. Episcopalian. Lodge: Rotary.

MOORE, WILLIAM JOHN MYLES, electrical engineer, researcher; b. Edinburgh, Scotland, May 3, 1924; arrived in Can., 1928; s. William Harold and Doris Kate (Paddon) M.; m. Ruth Elizabeth Duffy, Aug. 21, 1948; children: Roberta Louise, Marilyn Elizabeth. B in Applied Sci., U. B.C., Can., 1946; postgrad., NRC, Ottawa, Can., summer 1947; M in Engring., McGill U., 1948. Rsch. officer NRC Can., Ottawa, Ont., 1948-51, 55-88, sect. head power engring sect. elec. engring. div., 1988-90, ret., 1990; rsch. officer Can. Armament R&D Establishment, Valcartier, Que., 1951-52, head analysis sect., 1952-54, group leader analysis, control and simulation sects., 1954-55; cons. prof. Huazhong U. Sci. and Tech., Wuhan, Peoples Republic of China., 1988. Author: The Current Comparator, 1987; holder 10 patents. Fellow IEEE (chmn. Ottawa sect. 1966-67, chmn. Elec. and Electronic Measurement and Test Instrumentation Conf. and Instrumentation and Measurement Symposium 1969, pres. Group on Instrumentation and Measurement 1974, chmn. power systems instrumentation and measurement com. Power Engring. Soc. 1981-82, Morris E. Leeds award, 1987, Centennial medal 1984, A.G.L. McNaughton medal 1991), Assn. Prof. Engrs. Ont. Avocations: downhill skiing, personal computing. Home: 797 Dunloe Ave, Ottawa, ON Canada K1K 0K3

MOORE, WILLIAM LEROY, JR., career officer, physician; b. Savannah, Ga., June 1, 1934; s. William Leroy Sr. and Helen Louise (Robbins) M.; m. Anna Elizabeth Ballard, Mar. 15, 1958; children: William L., Christopher A., Mary Beth. Student, Ga. Inst. Tech., 1951-52; AB, Emory U., 1955; MD, Med. Coll. Ga., 1959; postgrad. mil. tng. courses, 1962-94. Diplomate Am. Bd. Internal Medicine, Am. Bd. Infectious Diseases. Commd. capt. U.S. Army, 1962, advanced through grades to maj. gen., 1991; intern Floyd Hosp., Rome, Ga., 1959-60; pvt. practice Rome, 1960-61; resident in internal medicine Brooke Gen. Hosp., Ft. Sam Houston, Tex., 1965-68; rsch. fellow in infectious diseases U. Tex. Southwestern Med. Sch., Dallas, 1968-70; resident in internal medicine Parkland Meml. Hosp., Dallas, 1968-70; gen. med. officer Martin Army Hosp., Ft. Benning, Ga., 1962, 5th Spl. Forces Group, Spl. Warfare Ctr., Ft. Bragg, N.C., 1962-63; gen. internist, group surgeon, commdg. officer 1st Spl. Forces Group, Spl. Action Force, Okinawa, Japan, 1963-65; asst. chief to chief infectious disease svc. Brooke Gen. Hosp., Ft. Sam Houston, Tex., 1970-74; chief internal medicine svc., chief dept. medicine, chief profl. svcs. Eisenhower Army Med. Ctr., Ft. Gordon, Ga., 1978-83; comdr. Frankfurt (Germany) Army Regional Med. Ct., 97th Gen. Hosp., 1983-86; project mgr. Office of Surgeon Gen., Washington, 1986-88; adj. faculty Nat. Def. U., Ft. Lesley J. McNair, Washington, 1986-88; vice comdr. Joint Mil. Med. Command, Randolph AFB, Tex., 1988-91; comdr. Brooke Army Med. Ctr., Ft. Sam Houston, Tex., 1988-91, U.S. Army Med. Dept. Ctr. & Sch., Ft. Sam Houston, Tex., 1991-94; state epidemiologist, dir. communicable & environ. disease Tenn. Dept. Health, 1995—; clin. prof. medicine divsn. infectious diseases Vanderbilt U. Sch. Medicine, Nashville, 1994—; clin. assoc. in medicine U. Tex. Southwestern Med. Sch., 1969-70; clin. assoc. prof. Medicine, U. Tex. Med. Sch., 1970-74; chief. sect. of infectious diseases, Med. Coll. Ga., 1974-75, assoc. prof., 1974-78, clin. prof., 1978-83; prin. investigator infectious disease rsch. VA Hosp., Augusta, Ga., 1974-78, asst. chief med. svc., 1974-75, dir. clin. microbiology lab., 1974-78, epidemiologist, 1974-78; head intenal medicine infectious disease 97th gen. Hosp., Frankfurt, 1983-86, Walter Reed Army Med. Ctr., 1986-88; clin. prof. medicine U. Tex. Health Sci. Ctr., San Antonio, 1989-94; mem. ref. panel on Am. Hosp. Formulary Svc. of Am. Soc. Hosp. Pharmacists, 1974-78; faculty Advisor Lane-Walker AMSA Free Clinic, Augusta, 1975-78; mem. various coms. and bds., VA Hosp., Augusta, 1974-78. Contbr. articles to profl. jours. Mem. Army Comty. Coun. San Antonio, 1988-94; dir., bd. dirs. Army Med. Dept. Mus. Found. Inc., 1989-94; bd. dirs. San Antonio Area chpt. ARC, 1989. Decorated Army Commendation medal, Meritorious Svc. medal (3), Legion of Merit with three oak leaf clusters, Disting. Svc. medal Army Med. Dept. Regiment, 1994, Order of Mil. Med. Merit; recipient Scholastic Excellence award C.V. Mosby Co., 1959, Laureate award, Am. Coll. Physician, 1996, Dirs. Commendation VA Hosp., Augusta, 1978, Surgeon Gen.'s A Profl. Designer fr Internal Med., 1982. Fellow ACP, Infectious Diseases Soc. Am.; mem. NAS (nat. rsch. coun. 1995-96), Assn. Mil. Surgeons U.S. (mem.-at-large exec. coun. Alamo chpt. 1989), Soc. Med. Cons. to Armed Forces (chmn. com. on cons. activities 1977-79), Am. Heart Assn. (bd. dirs. San Antonio divsn. 1988-89), San Antonio Rsch. Club (sec., pres. 1970-74), Tenn. Med. Assn., Nashville Acad. Medicine, Tenn. Pub. Health Assn., Coun.State and Territorial Epidemiologists. *Strict adherence to moral and ethical principles, willingness to work hard, use all of one's talents to benefit others and take advantage of all of the opportunities one finds to improve one's self while serving others are the elements of success in this life.*

MOORE, WILLIAM THEODORE, JR., judge; b. Bainbridge, Ga., May 7, 1940; s. William T. and Mary (Talbert) M.; m. Jane Hodges, July 18, 1964; children: Sarah S., Mary T. William T III. AA, Ga. Military Coll., 1960; JD, U. Ga., 1964; Law (hon.), Ga. Military Coll., 1978. Bar: Ga. 1964, U.S. Dist. Ct. (so. dist.) Ga. 1964, U.S. Ct. Appeals (5th and 11th cirs.) 1979, U.S. Supreme Ct. 1980. U.S. atty. So. Dist. Ga. U.S. Dept. of Justice, Savannah, 1977-81; ptnr. Corish, Smith, Remler & Moore, Savannah, 1967-77, Sparkman, Harris & Moore, Savannah, 1981-87, Oliver Maner & Gray, Savannah, 1988-94; atty. Savannah-Chatham County Bd. Pub. Edn., 1975-77, mem. U.S. Atty. Gen's. Adv. com. D.C. 1978-81. Recipient Spl. Appreciation award Ga. Bur. of Investigation, 1980, U.S. Dept. Treasury Bur. of Alcohol, Tobacco & Firearms, D.C., 1980; Extraordinary Svc. award Savannah Chapt. Fed. Bar Assn., 1980. Fellow Am. Bd. Criminal Lawyers (pres. 1993); mem. Nat. Assn. Criminal Def. Lawyers, Nat. Assn. Former U.S. Attys. (bd. dirs. 1984—), Ga. Assn. Criminal Def. Lawyers (v.p. 1986—), Ga. Bar Assn. Democrat. Episcopalian. Avocations: jogging, weight training. Office: US Dist Courthouse 125 Bull St PO Box 10245 Savannah GA 31412

MOORE, WILLIAM VINCENT, political science educator; b. Columbia, Mo., Apr. 13, 1944; s. Willis and Mabelle (Rogers) M.; m. Suzanne Shelton, July 14, 1967 (div. Feb. 1984); children: Mark, Laura. BA, So. Ill. U., 1966, MA, 1968; PhD, Tulane U., 1975. Instr. Fla. Meml. Coll., Miami, 1968-69, Xavier U., New Orleans, 1970-72; asst. prof. to assoc. prof. polit. sci. Coll. of Charleston, S.C., 1972-83, prof., 1983—, scholar-in-residence, 1976, dir. summer sessions, 1984-87, chmn. dept., 1987-93, dir., masters in pub. adminstrn. dept., 1993—; chmn. S.C. Interagy. Merit Coun., Columbia, 1987—; instr. jr. statesmen program Northwestern U., Evanston, Ill., 1996. Author: Political Extremism in the U.S.A., 1983; co-author: Politics and Government in South Carolina, 1994; contbr. articles to profl. jours. Recipient Disting. Teaching award Coll. of Charleston, 1981; grantee U. N.C., 1980; rsch. fellow U. S.C., 1983; NEH seminar Harvard U., 1995. Mem. Am. Polit. Sci. Assn., So. Polit. Sci. Assn., S.C. Polit. Sci. Assn. (pres. 1983-84), Phi Kappa Phi (chpt. pres. 1982-84), Pi Sigma Alpha (chpt. pres. 1987-93), Pi Alpha Alpha. Avocations: tennis, racquetball. Home: 1555 N Pinebark Ln Charleston SC 29407-3513 Office: Coll of Charleston Polit Sci Dept Charleston SC 29424

MOORE, WILLIS HENRY ALLPHIN, history and geography educator; b. N.Y.C., Dec. 14, 1940; s. Carl Allphin and Mary Catherine (Moody) M.; children: Patrick Kakela, Michael Kirby, Catherine Malia. BA Letters, U. Okla., 1962; MEd in Adminstrn., U. Hawaii, 1971. Teaching asst. dept. history U. Hawaii, 1962-64; dir. edn. Bernice P. Bishop Mus., Honolulu, 1967-76; pres. Hawaii Geog. Soc., Honolulu, 1976-78, exec. sec., editor, 1978—; mem. Hawaii Com. for Humanities, 1976-78; producer, narrator film-lecture programs Nat. Aududon Soc. and travelogue forums; instr. in history, geography and polit. sci. Chaminade U. of Honolulu, 1986—; lectr. elderhostel U. Hawaii, Hawaii Pacific U., Lewis and Clark State Coll., Idaho. Co-author/co-editor: Hawaii Parklands, Sociological History of Honolulu, Total Solar Eclipse over Hawaii, 1991; contbr. articles to Honolulu Advertiser, Pacific Daily News, Guam, Pacific Mag., Honolulu Star-Bull. Lay reader St. Andrew's Cathedral; active Nat. Mus. Am. Indian. Mem. Internat. Map Trade Assn., Am. Assn. State & Local History, Am. Mus. Assn., Pacific Sci. Assn., Hawaii Mus. Assn. (pres. 1972-74), Hawaii Pub. Radio, Am. Guild Organists, Soc. Prfs. Dispute Resolution, Sierra Club (chmn. Hawaii chpt. 1973-75), Hawaiian Hist. Soc., Nat. Soc. of Arts and Letters. Office: PO Box 1698 Honolulu HI 96806-1698

MOORE, WILLSON CARR, JR., lawyer; b. Honolulu, Nov. 24, 1928; s. Willson Carr and Jenna Vee (McMillan) C.; m. Sally Churchill, Apr. 25, 1952; children: Willson C. III, Brian C., Sharon Moore Fink. BA, U. Calif., Berkeley, 1950; JD, U. Calif., San Francisco, 1953. Law clk. to Hon. Jon Wiig U.S. Dist. Ct., Honolulu, 1953-54; dep. atty. gen. State of Hawaii, 1955-59; pvt. practice Moore & Moore, Honolulu, 1959-66; with Rush, Moore, Craven, Sutton, Morry & Beh, Honolulu, 1965—; bd. dirs. Hawaii Def. Lawyers, 1990-94, Def. Rsch. Inst., 1989-93; mem. appellate mediation panel Supreme Ct. State of Hawaii, 1995—; settlement master U.S. Dist. Ct. Hawaii, 1996—. Col. USAR, 1950-81. Fellow Am. Coll. Trial Lawyers; mem. ABA, Am. Bd. Trial Lawyers (adv.), Am. Judacature Soc., Assn. Def. Trial Attys. (pres. 1989-90, mem. exec. coun. 1983-91), Phi Alpha Delta. Office: Rush Moore Craven Sutton Morry & Beh 745 Fort Street Mall Ste 2000 Honolulu HI 96813-3820

MOORE, YVETTE M., artist, illustrator; b. Radville, Sask., Can., July 23, 1954; d. Raymond Joseph and Rosalie Marie (Bourassa) Paulhus; m. Richard Kevin Moore, May 12, 1972; children: Tyler, Rynette, Chantelle, Sarah. Diploma of tech., Sask. Tech. Inst., Moose Jaw, Sask., Can., 1988. Clk. Radville (Sask., Can.) Credit Union Ltd., 1973-75; owner, mgr. Hannigan's, Radville, 1981-85; archtl. technologist Arnott, Kelley & O'Connor, Regina, Sask., Can., 1988-89; artist Yvette Moore Fine Art & Designs, Moose Jaw, Sask., 1988-93, pres., 1993—; pres. Cranberry Rose Gallery, Ltd., 1995—. Illustrator: A Prairie Alphabet, 1992 (Mr. Christie Book award for illustration 1992), A Prairie Year, 1994. Bd. dirs. Moose Jaw Mcpl. Heritage, 1989-93, chmn., 1992-93. Recipient Merit cert. Art Dirs. Club N.Y., 1993. Mem. Can. Artists Representation, Sask. Writers Guild, Sask. Gymnastics Assn. (level III judge). Avocations: gardening, heritage restoration and preservation, decorations, reading, antiques. Home: 1101 Clifton Ave, Moose Jaw, SK Canada S6H 3L4

MOORE-BERRY, NORMA JEAN, secondary school educator; b. Hampton, Ark., Jan. 7, 1949; d. James E. and Alma Lee (McRae) Moore, Sr.; children: Rhemona Moore, Nerissa Moore. BA in English Edn., U. Ark., Pine Bluff, 1971; MA in Reading Edn., So. Ark. U., 1985; postgrad., Henderson State U., 1986, U. Ark., 1989-90. Cert. mid. and secondary English tchr., adult edn., all levels reading. Tchr. English Chidester (Ark.) Sch. Dist., 1971-73; tchr. English, adult edn. instr. Lewisville (Ark.) Sch. Dist., 1973-92, secondary tchr., 1973-93, reading tutor, 1991—; instr. adult edn. Texarkana (Ark.) Pub. Sch. Dist., 1984-91; tchr. English Ctrl. High Sch., 1984-93, Hall Sr. High Sch., Little Rock, 1987-90; chmn. English dept. Lewisville Sch. Dist.; instr. English Ctrl. High Sch., summer 1992; tchr. Ctrl. High Sch. Summer Sch., Little Rock Sch. Dist., summer 1994; English and reading secondary instr., 1994-95; reading tchr. Southeast Tech. Coll., Pine Bluff, Ark., 1996. Sponsor sr. class; active sch. charity fund-raising; organizer, sponsor Lewisville Reading Club, Lewisville English Club; mem. bible study group Bethel CME Ch., Stamps, Ark., sponsor, sec. ceo com. Ethnic Club Lewisville High Sch. Named Tchr. Yr., 1984, Lewisville Mid. Sch. Reading/English Tchr., Woman of Yr. ABI, 1993-94. Mem. ASCD, Nat. Coun. Tchrs. English, Ark. Edn. Assn., Ark. Tchr. Retirement Assn., Ark. Reading Coun. Assn. (lit. coun.), Lewisville Edn. Assn. (treas. 1993-94), Phi Delta Kappa. Home: 507 Hope Rd Stamps AR 71860-2017

MOOREFIELD, JENNIFER MARY, legislative staff member; b. Danville, Va., Nov. 10, 1950; d. Folger Lester and Mildred (Cox) M. BA in Psychology, Averett Coll., 1972; A in Applied Sci., Danville C.C., 1986; postgrad., Longwood Coll., 1995—. Social worker Henry County Social Svcs., Collinsville, Va., 1972-75, sr. social worker, 1975-80; clk. inventory control Dan River, Inc., Danville, Va., 1981-83; staff asst. U.S. Congressman Dan Daniel, Danville, 1984-88; staff asst. U.S. Congressman L.F. Payne, Danville, 1988-91, office mgr., casework supr., 1991-96; casework supr., office mgr. U.S. Congressman Virgil H. Goode, Jr., Danville, 1997—; office mgr. U.S. Congressman L.F. Payne, Danville, 1991-96. Bd. rec. sec. Danville Speech and Hearing Ctr., 1988; Sunday sch. tchr. Emmanuel Wesleyan Ch., Danville, 1975—; dir. Wesleyan Kids for Missions, Danville, 1993—, Ch. Vacation Bible Sch., Danville, 1993; sec. Danville Area Coun. on Cmty. Svcs., 1997—. Mem. Luncheon Pilot Club of Danville, Inc. (rec. sec. 1988-89, pres.-elect 1989-90, pres. 1990-91), Va. Dist.-Pilot Internat. (area fundraising leader 1990-91, dist. chaplain 1993-94), Va. Counselors Assn., Nat. Career Devel. Assn., Pinnacle. Avocations: reading, computers, music, photography, calligraphy. Home: 136 Brookview Rd Danville VA 24540-3408 Office: Office of Congressman Virgil H Goode Jr 437 Main St Danville VA 24541-1109

MOORE HUTTON, ANNE, museum consultant; b. Jan. 6, 1946; d. William Clifton and Frances Woods Moore; m. Michael P. Mezzatesta, Mar. 14, 1970 (div. 1987); children: Philip Moore, Alexander Woods, Marya Frances; m. Ernest Watson Hutton Jr., Apr. 20, 1996; stepchildren: Elizabeth, Elinor Hutton. BA in Art History, Columbia U., 1969, MA, 1971, MEd in Fine Arts, 1971, MA in Art History, 1982. Tchr. Manassas (Va.) High Sch., 1971-72, Poly. Prep. Country Day Sch., Bklyn., 1972-74; edn. instr. Kimbell Art Mus., Ft. Worth, 1980-83, rsch. assoc., lectr., 1983; assoc. mus. educator, outreach dir. Dallas Mus. Art, 1986-88; curator of edn., lectr. dept. art Oberlin (Ohio) Coll., 1988-90, curator acad. programs, lectr. dept. art, 1991-

92; dir., lectr. dept. art, museum cons. The Allen Meml. Art Mus. at Oberlin Coll., 1991-96. Bd. trustees Intermus. Conservation Assn. Mem. Assn. Art Mus. Dirs., Assn. Coll. and Univ. Mus. and Galleries, Am. Assn. Mus. (edn. com.), Ohio Mus. Assn., Coll. Art Assn. Office: 5 Union Sq W Ste 703 New York NY 10003-3306

MOORE MOIF, FLORIAN HOWARD, electronics engineer; b. Shelby, Ohio, Aug. 23, 1929; s. Carl Leslie and Mona Pearl (Dearth) M.; m. Dorothy Elizabeth Morse, Dec. 19, 1950. AA, Harvard U., 1974. Cert. indsl. maint. electrician; tchg. cert. indsl. electricity, indsl. electronics. With Diebold Inc., Boston, 1955-56; mem. electronics R & D staff Radio Corp. Am., Burlington, Mass., 1956-59; mem. electronics/mech. R & D staff MIT, Cambridge, 1959-74; mem. electricity/electronics/electromech. R & D staff Charles Stark Draper Labs., Cambridge, 1974-76; tchr. indsl. electronics Ashland County Joint Vocat. Sch., Ashland, Ohio, 1976-78; buyer Autocall divsn. Fed. Signal Corp., Shelby, 1978-79; journeyman electrician Excel Wire & Cable divsn. United Tech., Tiffin, Ohio, 1980-86; tchr. indsl. electricity Madison Comprehensive H.S., Mansfield, Ohio, 1986-88; pres., CEO Florian H. Moore & Assocs., Shelby, 1988—. Vol. Ohio Geneal. Libr., Mansfield; foster parent Commonwealth of Mass., 1962-82 (38 children). With USAF, 1948-52. Fellow Internat. Biog. Assn.; mem. Ohio Geneal. Soc. (v.p. Richland-Shelby gen. chpt. 1993-95, pres. 1995-97), Royal Lincolnshire Regtl. Assn. (life; Am. contingent, 10th foot), DAV (life), Order Internat. Fellowship (charter, U.S. rep. 1995), Masons (32 degree), Kappa Delta Phi (life). Avocations: history, snow skiing, sky diving, computer programming. Home and Office: 6234 State Route 61 N Shelby OH 44875-9575

MOORER, MICHAEL, professional boxer; b. Detroit, Mich., 1968; m. Bobbie; s. Michael, Jr. Champion World Boxing Assn., light heavyweight title, Pittburgh, Pa., 1990, World Boxing Assn. and Internat. Boxing Federation, heavyweight title, Las Vegas, Nev., 1994. Office: Main Event 811 Totowa Rd Totowa NJ 07512-1207*

MOORER, THOMAS HINMAN, retired naval officer; b. Mt. Willing, Ala., Feb. 9, 1912; s. Richard Randolph and Hulda (Hill) M.; m. Carrie Ellen Foy, Nov. 28, 1935; children: Thomas Randolph, Mary Ellen, Richard Foy, Robert Hill. B.S., U.S. Naval Acad., 1933; grad., Naval War Coll., 1953; LL.D. (hon.), Sanford U., Auburn U., Troy U., The Citadel. Commd. ensign U.S. Navy, 1933, advanced through grades to adm., 1957; held several fleet commands at sea; chief naval ops., 1967-70, chmn. joint chiefs of staff, 1970-74, ret., 1974; dir. Blount Inc., Montgomery, Ala., 1974—; dir. U.S. Life Ins. Corp., Arlington, Va., CACI, Arlington; adviser Center Strategic and Internat. Studies, The Citadel. Co-author: U.S. Overseas Bases: Problems of Projecting American Military Power Abroad, 1977, Sea Power and Strategy in the Indian Ocean, 1981. Chmn. Naval Aviation Mus. Found., Inc. Decorated Def. Dept. D.S.M. with oak leaf cluster, Navy D.S.M. with 4 stars, Army D.S.M., Air Force D.S.M., Silver Star, Legion of Merit, D.F.C., Purple Heart, others; recipient Forrestal award, 1975; named to Nat. Aviation Hall of Fame, 1987, Naval Aviation Hall of Honor, 1988. Mem. U.S. Naval Acad. Alumni Assn., U.S. Naval Inst., Ret. Officers Assn., Assn. Naval Aviation, Chevy Chase Club, Army-Navy Club. Republican. Baptist. Home: 6901 Lupine Ln Mc Lean VA 22101-1580 Office: 1800 K St NW Washington DC 20006-2202

MOORE-RIESBECK, SUSAN, osteopathic physician; b. Joliet, Ill., Jan. 23, 1963; d. Roy W. and Rita M. (Gondek) Moore; m. David E. Riesbeck. BS in Chemistry, Loyola U., Chgo., 1984; DO, Kirksville Coll. Osteo. Med., 1990. Diplomate Am. Bd. Family Practice. Chief resident in family practice Michiana Cmty. Hosp., South Bend, Ind., 1990-92, asst. residency dir., 1993—; med. dir. Transitional Health Svcs. Shamrock Gardens, South Bend, Ind., 1994—, Healthwin Nursing Home, South Bend, Ind., 1995—; Healthwin, South Bend; chair family practice dept. St. Mary Cmty. Hosp., South Bend, Ind., 1994-96; vice-chair family practice dept. Ancilla Health Care, 1997—. Ann Wright Hazen scholar, 1987-90, Quad City Osteo. Assn. scholar, 1987; recipient Janet M. Glasgow Meml. Achievement citation AMA, 1990. Mem. Am. Osteo. Assn., Ind. Assn. Osteo Physicians and Surgeons (orgnl. affairs com. 1996—), Am. Coll. Family Practitioners in Osteo. Medicine and Surgery, Phi Sigma Alpha. Office: 2515 E Jefferson Blvd South Bend IN 46615-2635 also: 150 W Angela South Bend IN 46617-1101

MOORES, JOHN, professional sports team executive; b. July 9, 1944; m. Becky Moores, 1963; children: Jennifer, John Jr. With IBM, Shell Oil; founder, CEO BMC Software, 1980-89, chmn., 1980-92; chmn., co-owner San Diego Padres, 1994—; owner Peregrine Sys., Inc., Del Mar, Calif.; founder Padres Found., 1995—, Padres Scholars Program, 1995—; chmn. JMI Svcs. Inc.; mem. adv. bd. San Diego Hall of Champions. Trustee Carter Ctr. of Emory U.; founder, chmn. River Blindness Found. Office: San Diego Padres PO Box 2000 San Diego CA 92112-2000

MOORE-SZEPESY, MARIANN LYDIA, health care executive; b. Jersey City, July 5, 1957; d. Thomas William and Eleanor Rita (Connolly) Moore; m. Kenneth Stephen Szepesy, June 3, 1995; 1 child, Alexis Noel. BSBA and Sociology summa cum laude, U. Md., 1979; MSW, Rutgers U., 1984. Lic. clin. soc. worker Acad. Cert. Soc. Workers. Social worker Jersey City Med. Ctr., 1979-86, coord. ob-gyn and pediatric soc. work svcs., 1986-88; project coord. Hudson County Maternal Health Project, Jersey City, 1988-91; exec. dir. Hudson Perinatal Consortium Inc., Jersey City, 1991—; cons. Robert Wood Johnson Found., Princeton, N.J., 1991—, Advanced Psychol. Assocs., Red Bank, N.J., 1989-91. Creator, contbr. video Sexual Abuse in Children, 1985; contbr. to documentary on pediatric AIDS, 1987. Mem. APHA, NASW, Am. Coll. Healthcare Execs., N.J. Women in Healthcare Execs., Soc. for Cmty. Assessment and Improvement (corr. sec.), Perinatal Assn. N.J. (v.p. 1994—, bd. dirs.), Maternal Child Health Advocacy Coalition (v.p. 1993-94), Phi Kappa phi. Democrat. Roman Catholic. Avocations: gardening, travel, cooking, singing, reading. Office: Hudson Perinatal Consortium 574 Summit Ave Jersey City NJ 07306-2702

MOORHEAD, CARLOS J., former congressman; b. Long Beach, Calif., May 6, 1922; s. Carlos Arthur and Florence (Gravers) M.; m. Valery Joan Tyler, July 19, 1969; children: Theresa, Catharine, Steven, Teri, Paul. BA, UCLA, 1943; JD, U. So. Calif., 1949. Bar: Calif. 1949, U.S. Supreme Ct. 1973. Pvt. practice law Glendale, Calif., 1949-72; dir. Lawyers Reference Service, Glendale, 1950-66; mem. 93d-104th Congresses from 22d (now 27th) Dist. Calif., 1973-96; mem. judiciary com., chmn. subcom. on cts. and intellectual property, vice chmn. commerce com., mem. subcom. on energy & power, subcom. on telecomm. & fin.; dean Calif. Congl. Rep. Delegation; apptd. to Fed. Cts. Study Com. Pres. Glendale Hi-Twelve Club; mem. Verdugo Hills council Boy Scouts Am.; mem. Calif. Assembly, 1967-72; mem. Calif. Law Revision Commn., 1971-72; pres. 43d Dist. Republican Assembly, Glendale Young Republicans; mem. Los Angeles County Rep. Central Com., Calif. Rep. Central Com.; pres. Glendale La Crescenta Camp Fire Girls, Inc. Served to lt. col. AUS, 1942-46. Recipient Man of Yr. award USO, 1979. Mem. Calif. Bar Assn. L.A. County Bar Assn., Glendale Bar Assn. (past pres.), Glendale C. of C., Masons, Shriners, Lions, Moose, VFW. Presbyterian. Office: 420 N Brand Blvd Ste 304 Glendale CA 91203-2300*

MOORHEAD, GERALD LEE, architect; b. Davenport, Iowa, Feb. 18, 1947; s. Wayne Lee and Marilou (George) M. BA, Rice U., 1969, BArch, 1971. Architect Middleton & Statton, El Paso, Tex., 1967, MA Floyd Assos., Houston, 1968, CRS Design Inc., Houston, 1969-70, Phillips & Peterson AIA, Houston, 1969-73; architect, v.p. Charles Tapley Assos., Houston, 1973-83; propr. Lloyd Jones Fillpot Assocs., 1986-87, Gerald Moorhead, Architect, 1983—. Photography exhibited in group shows Galveston Arts Coun., Tex., 1976, Jewish Community Center, Houston, 1977, Cronin Gallery, Houston, 1977; one-man photog. exhbns. include Autry House Gallery, Houston, 1979; contbg. editor Tex. Architect; contbg. editor Archtl. Record; contbr. articles on architecture to profl. publs.; exhbn. curator: Houston Mus. Natural Science, 1990, Mus. Fine Arts, Houston, 1991, FotoFest, Houston, 1996. Treas. Houston Ctr. for Photography, 1985-87. Recipient Spl. award Houston AIA/Houston Home & Garden, 1979, Honor award Houston AIA, 1979, Young Architect award Houston AIA, 1985, Internat. prize Union Architects of Kazakstan, 1991; named Architect Laureate of Kazakstan, 1992. Fellow AIA; mem. Soc. Archtl. Historians, Nat. Trust for Hist. Preservation, Tex. Soc. Architects (1st Honor award 1976, Interiors award 1986, Flowers Journalism award 1995), Rice Design Alliance. Home: 1842 Marshall St Houston TX 77098-2639

MOORHEAD, PAUL SIDNEY, geneticist; b. El Dorado, Ark., Apr. 18, 1924; s. Earle William and Ethel (Martin) M.; m. Betty Blanton Belk, June 8, 1949 (dec. 1989); children: Ann, Emily, Mary; m. Rebecca Otter, 1992. A.B., U. N.C., 1948, M.A. in Zoology, 1950; Ph.D., U. Tex., 1954. Research assoc. U. Tex. Med. Sch., Galveston, 1954-56, U. Pitts. Med. Sch., 1956-58; assoc. mem. Wistar Inst. Anatomy and Biology, Phila., 1959-69; assoc. prof. genetics and pediatrics U. Pa. Sch. Medicine, 1969-85, emeritus, 1985—; mem. rsch. staff Children's Hosp., Phila., 1974-85, mem. rsch. staff emeritus, 1985—. Contbr. numerous articles on genetics and cytology to sci. jours. Served to ensign USNR, 1942-46. Fellow AAAS; mem. Am. Soc. Human Genetics, AAUP, Environ. Mutagenesis Soc., Tissue Culture Assn. (pres. 1980-82), N.Y. Acad. Scis., Sigma Xi. Home and Office: PO Box 4 Claiborne MD 21624

MOORHEAD, SYLVESTER ANDREW, education educator retired; b. Denver, Feb. 23, 1920; s. Ray Rodney and Cora Margaret (Payne) M.; m. Katherine May Schlessman, July 21, 1945; children: Rodney A., Sylvia Kay, Kent A., Pamela Ann. B.A., U. No. Colo., 1942; Ph.D., Stanford U., 1950. Tchr. secondary sch. Redwood City, Calif., 1947-48, Sunnyvale, Calif., 1948-49; mem. faculty U. Miss., 1949—, prof. edn., 1955—, dean U. Sch. Edn., 1961-85, dean emeritus, 1985—. Contbr. articles profl. jours. Served with USAAF, 1942-45. Mem. NEA (life), Kappa Delta Pi, Phi Delta Kappa. Baptist. Lodge: Rotary. Home: 211 Vivian St Oxford MS 38655-2719

MOORHEAD, THOMAS BURCH, lawyer, pharmaceutical company executive; b. Evanston, Ill., May 3, 1934; s. John William and Jane (Hendrich) M.; m. Christie Barnard, Dec. 31, 1966 (div. June 1992); children: Merrell Hendrich, Hannah Christie, Rachel McGill. BA, Yale U, 1956; postgrad., The Hague Acad. Internat. Law, 1958; JD, U. Pa., 1959; LLM, NYU, 1964. Bar: N.Y. 1960, Conn. 1971, U.S. Supreme Ct. 1965. Assoc. Milbank, Tweed, Hadley & McCloy, N.Y.C., 1959-63; assoc. counsel, asst. sec. Hooker Chem. Corp., N.Y.C., 1963-68, dir. indsl. rels., 1968-69, v.p. indsl. rels., 1969-72; v.p. employee rels. Champion Internat. Corp., N.Y.C., 1972-74; v.p. adminstrn. Beker Industries Corp., Greenwich, Conn., 1974-76; v.p. corp. affairs Estée Lauder, Inc., N.Y.C., 1976-84, sr. v.p., 1984-87; v.p. human resources Carter-Wallace, Inc., N.Y.C., 1987—; bd. dirs., vice chmn. Transaction Billing Resources, Inc., 1991—; elected mem. Corp. Culinary Inst. of Am., 1993—. Mem. New Canaan (Conn.) Rep. Town Com., 1980-85; elected mem. New Canaan Town Coun., 1985—, vice chmn., 1989—; bd. dirs. Employment Policy Found., 1993—, Les Amis d'Escoffier Soc., 1990—, Les Amis d'Escoffier Found., 1990—, Yale U. Alumni Fund, 1987-92, Nat. Choral Coun., 1988-93, United Way Tri-State, Inc., 1986-89, United Way New Canaan, 1983-89, pres., 1986-87; mem. Conn. Oversight Commn., Metro-North Commuter R.R., 1985-89; U.S. del. ILO, 1985, 93, 94, 95, 96, head U.S. employer del., 1994, 95, 96. Mem. ABA, Assn. of Bar of City of N.Y., Am. Soc. Internat. Law, Met. Club, New Canaan Country Club, Gridiron Club of New Canaan (pres. 1990—), Yale Club. Home: 148 Ramhorne Rd New Canaan CT 06840-3007 Office: 1345 Avenue Of The Americas New York NY 10105-0302

MOORHEAD, THOMAS EDWARD, lawyer; b. Owosso, Mich., Aug. 27, 1946; s. Kenneth Edward and Lillian Jane (Becker) M.; BA in Communication Arts, Mich. State U., 1970; JD, Detroit Coll. Law, 1973; m. Marjorie E. Semans, Sept. 9, 1967; children: Robert Scott, Kristine Elizabeth. Admitted to Mich. bar, 1973; legal counsel Legis. Service Bur., State of Mich., Lansing, 1973-74; ptnr. firm Des Jardins & Moorhead, P.C., Owosso, 1974-85; sole practice, Owosso, 1985—; pres., founder Real Check Am., Inc. Pres., Bentley Sch. PTO, Owosso; chmn. adminstrv. bd. 1st United Meth. Ch., Owosso; bd. dirs. Shiawassee Arts Council; treas. Cub Scout Pack 67 Boy Scouts Am.; chmn. Community Leadership Prayer Breakfast, 1991; mem. Shiawassee County Rep. Exec. Com.; chmn. Shiawassee County Rep. Party; chmn. adminstrv. bd. 1st United Meth. Ch., 1991. Mem. Am. Bar Assn., Assn. Trial Lawyers Am., Shiawassee County Bar Assn. (past pres.), State Bar of Mich., Mich. State U. Alumni Assn., Owosso Jaycees (pres.; named Outstanding Local Pres. by state assn. 1977). Republican. Home: 1265 Ada St Owosso MI 48867-1664 Office: 204 W Exchange St Owosso MI 48867-2818

MOORING, F. PAUL, physics editor; b. Pitt County, N.C., Feb. 6, 1921; s. Benjamin Arthur and Amanda Elizabeth (Congleton) M.; m. Jean Louise Carpenter, Aug. 28, 1948; children: Cecily Hamm, Carol Larson, Margaret. BA, Duke U., 1944; PhD, U. Wis., 1951. Instr. Duke U., Durham, N.C., 1943-46; teaching asst. U. Wis., Madison, 1946-50, rsch. asst., 1950-51; physicist Argonne (Ill.) Nat. Lab., 1951-83; editor, cons. Am. Inst. Physics, Argonne, 1983—; adj. prof. St. Louis U., 1966-83. Contbr. articles to profl. jours. Pres. The Ill. Prairie Path, Wheaton, Ill., 1971-93, Ill. Audubon Soc., Wayne, Ill., 1978-81. Fulbright Rsch. fellow U. Helsinki, 1962-63. Mem. AAAS, Am. Phys. Soc. Democrat. Home: 295 Abbotsford Ct Glen Ellyn IL 60137-4803

MOORMAN, JOHN A., librarian; b. Humboldt, Nebr., Sept. 15, 1947; m. Ileen Mary Geiger, Dec. 20, 1968; children: Johanna, Jessica, John A. AB, Guilford Coll., Greensboro, N.C., 1969; MSLS, U. N.C., 1972; postgrad., U. N.C., Greensboro, 1974-75, U. Ill., 1994—. Pub. svcs. and circulation libr. Guilford Coll., 1972-75; dir. Elbert Ivey Meml. Libr., Hickory, N.C., 1975-80, Brazoria County Libr. System, Angleton, Tex., 1980-86, Oak Lawn (Ill.) Pub. Libr., 1986-88; exec. dir. Cumberland Trail Libr. System, Flora, Ill., 1989-92; city libr. Decatur (Ill.) Pub. Libr., 1992—. Author: Managing Small Library Collections in Businesses and Community Organizations: Advice for Non-Librarians, 1989. Mem. Econ. Devel. Coord. Com.; mem. exec. com. bd. dirs. Downtown Decatur Coun.; grad. Decatur Leadership Inst., 1993. Mem. ALA, Ill. Libr. Assn. (chmn. pub. policy com. 1993), Nat. Soc. Fund Raising Execs., Decatur C. of C. (small bus. coun. seminar com.), Decatur Civil War Round Table, Decatur Rotary Club. Quaker. Avocations: travel, reading, woodworking, sports. Home: 315 Hackberry Pl Decatur IL 62521-5503 Office: Decatur Pub Libr 247 E North St Decatur IL 62523-1128

MOORMAN, ROBERT LAWSON, real estate appraiser and broker; b. Waco, Tex., Sept. 2, 1951; s. George Robertson and Gladys Lee Billie (Scoggin) M.; m. Rebecca Ann Averitt, Sept. 9, 1983; children: Jason, Benjamin, Kate, William, Bethany, John. BBA, So. Meth. U., 1973; MS in Fin., Tex. A&M U., 1990; postgrad., Hawthorne U. CFP; cert. real estate appraiser; registered investment adviser; lic. real estate broker. Self-employed musician Austin, N.Mex., 1973-83; asst. v.p. Brenham (Tex.) Nat. Bank, 1983-85, First Nat. Bank, Navasota, Tex., 1985-87, First Savs. Assn., Brenham, 1987-89; asst. lectr. fin. Tex. A&M U., College Station, 1990-93; pres. RLM Fin. Group, Inc., Brenham, 1990—; co-owner Century 21-Lone Star Realty, 1997—. Editor: (book) Goals for Washington County, 1984. Dir. Brenham Opportunity Ctr., 1983-85; mem. Downtown Parking Com., Brenham, 1985; chmn. Parks Adv. Bd., Brenham, 1988-93; pres. Washington County Coalition, Brenham, 1993. Recipient Bookman Peters Banking fellowship Tex. A&M Grad. Sch. Bus., 1989, 90. Mem. SAR, Am. Soc. Appraisers, Appraisal Inst. (assoc.), Soc. Tex. A&M Real Estate Profls., Inst. of CFP, Internat. Assn. Fin. Planners, Nat. Assn. Realtors, Tex. Assn. Realtors, Greater Brenham-Bellville Assn. Realtors, Rotary. Avocations: guitar, jogging, nutrition, home repair and remodeling. Office: The RLM Fin Group Inc 200 W Masonic Dr Brenham TX 77833-5563

MOORMAN, ROSE DRUNELL, county administrator, systems analyst; b. Miami, Fla., May 13, 1945; d. Willie and Claudia (Fluker) M. BA in Mathematics, Fisk U., 1967; MSE in Computer and Info. Scis., U. Pa., 1976. Computer programmer GE, Valley Forge, Pa., 1967-70; programmer/analyst Price Waterhouse Co., Phila., 1970-72; sr. programmer/analyst Inst. Environ. Medicine U. Pa., Phila., 1972-77; systems analyst Honeywell, Ft. Washington, Pa., 1977-78; dir. tech. svcs. Gill Assocs., Inc., Washington, 1978-83; owner, CEO Computer and Info. Mgmt., Inc., Miami, 1983-88; mgr. tech. support City of Miami, 1988-94, coord. diversity, 1994-95; exec. adminstr. to county commr. Metro-Dade County, 1996—; facilitator Women in Info. Processing, Washington, 1979-83; computer edn. adv. panel Dade County Pub. Schs., 1984-88. Editor: (newsletter) Bits and Bytes, 1979-82; co-editor: (newsletter) Ebenezer Speaks, 1992—. Active Ebenezer United Meth. Ch., Miami, 1954—, treas., chair fin. com., 1992—, Family Christian Assn., 1989-94; troop leader Girl Scouts Am., 1990—; pres. Loran Park Sch. PTA, Miami, 1991-93; treas., bd. dirs. Overtown Cmty. Health Clinic, Miami, 1992—, New Miami Group, Inc., 1994—; mem. Dade Heritage Trust, Miami, 1994—; mem. Dade County Hist. Preservation Bd., 1996—. Recipient Leadership award ARC, 1957, 63, Bronze medallion for Community Svc. NCCJ, 1963, Svc. Excellence award Delta Sigma Theta, 1986. Meritorious Svc. award Fisk U., 1992. Mem. NAACP, Nat. Forum Black Pub. Adminstrs. (bd. dirs., 2d v.p. 1993—), Nat. Coun. Negro Women. Republican. Avocations: bridge, collecting cookbooks and kaleidoscopes, hunting, gardening, hist. preservation of structures and cultures. Home: 820 NW 172nd Ter Miami FL 33169-5305 Office: Metropolitan Dade County 111 NW 1st St Ste 220 Miami FL 33128-1903

MOORMAN, STEVE THOMAS, systems analyst; b. Lynchburg, Va., Apr. 6, 1959; s. Lloyd Woodie and Parke (English) M. AA in Computer Sci., Nat. Bus. Coll., 1984; postgrad., Liberty U., 1995—. Machine operator Burlington Industries, Altavista, Va., 1980-82; owner, mgr. Moorman's Body Shop & Garage, Gladys, Va., 1985-86; computer operator Lynchburg (Va.) Gen. Hosp., 1986-88; computer operator City of Lynchburg, 1988-89, computer programmer, 1989-91, systems analyst, 1991—. Republican. Methodist. Avocations: hunting, fishing, motorcycle riding. Office: City of Lynchburg PO Box 60 Lynchburg VA 24505-0060

MOOS, H. WARREN, physicist, astronomer, educator, administrator; b. N.Y.C., Mar. 26, 1936; s. Henry H. and Dorothy E. (Warren) M.; m. Doris Elaine McClure, July 13, 1957; children: Janet, Paul, Daniel, David. BS, Brown U., 1957; MA, U. Mich., 1959, PhD, 1962. Rsch. assoc. Stanford (Calif.) U., 1961-63; acting asst. prof. Johns Hopkins U., Balt., 1963-64, asst. prof., 1964-68, assoc. prof., 1968-71, prof., 1971—, dir. Ctr. for Astrophys. Scis., 1988-93, chmn. Physics & Astronomy, 1993-96; cons. in field; mem. com. on planetary and lunar exploration NRC/Nat. Acad. Sci., Washington, 1982-86; mem. space and earth sci. adv. com. NASA, Washington, 1984-87; vis. fellow Joint Inst. for Lab. Astrophysics, 1972-73, 80-81. Editor: Optical Properties of Ions in Crystals, 1967; contbr. over 250 articles to profl. jours. Sloan Found. fellow, 1965-69. Fellow Am. Phys. Soc.; mem. Am. Astron. Soc., Internat. Astron. Union. Achievements include prin. investigatorof far ultraviolet spectroscopic explorer; co-investigator of Apollo 17 ultraviolet spectrometer, of Hopkins Ultraviolet Telescope, of Voyager ultraviolet spectrometer, of space telescope imaging spectograph; research on ultraviolet astronomy and fusion plasma diagnostics. Home: 804 Post Boy Ct Baltimore MD 21286 Office: Dept Physics & Astronomy 34th & Charles Sts Baltimore MD 21218

MOOS, VERNA VIVIAN, special education educator; b. Jamestown, N.D., July 1, 1951; d. Philip and Violena (Schweitzer) M. BS in Edn., Valley City State U., 1973; MEd, U. So. Miss., 1983, EdS, 1988; AA, Minot State U., 1987; postgrad., East Tex. State U., U. Tex., N.D. State U., U. N.D., Kans. State U., McGill U. Supr. recreation Valley City (N.D.) Recreation Dept., 1969-73; tchr. Harvey (N.D.) Pub. Schs., 1973-75; tchr. spl. edn. Belfield (N.D.) Pub. Schs., 1975-77; edn. therapist N.D. Elks Assn., Dawson, 1976-77; tchr. spl. edn. Dickinson (N.D.) pub. Schs., 1977-87; ednl. technician ABLE, Inc., Dickinson, 1984-87; tchr. spl. edn. Pewitt Ind. Sch. Dist., Omaha and Naples, Tex., 1987—; tchr. adult edn. N.E. Tex. C.C., Mt. Pleasant, 1989—. Local and area dir. Tex. Spl. Olympics, Austin, 1988—; local, regional and state dir. N.D. Spl. Olympics, 1972-87; local coord. Very Spl. Arts Festival; mem. Am. Heart Assn., 1979-87, N.D. Heart Assn., 1979-87; mem. adminstrv. bd. First United Meth. Ch., Naples, Tex., 1994—. Named Dickinson Jaycees Outstanding Young Educator, 1979, Dickinson C. of C. Tchr. of Yr., 1985, Dallas area Coach of Yr., Tex. Spl. Olympics, 1993, Dir. of Yr., N.D. Spl. Olympics, 1985. Mem. NEA, Coun. Exceptional Children, Naples C. of C., Delta Kappa Gamma (scholar), Phi Delta Kappa, Kappa Delta Pi. Avocations: travel, reading, working, sports. Home: PO Box 788 Omaha TX 75571-0788 Office: Pewitt CISD PO Box 1106 Omaha TX 75571-1106

MOOSE, GEORGE E., government official; b. N.Y.C., June 23, 1944; s. Robert and Ellen Amanda Lane (Jones) M.; m. Judith Roberta Kaufmann, Jan. 3, 1981. BA, Grinnell Coll., 1966, LLD (hon.), 1990; postgrad., Syracuse U., 1967. Spl. asst. to under sec. for polit. affairs Dept. of State, Washington, 1977-78, dep. dir. for South Africa, 1978-79; internat. affairs fellow Coun. Fgn. Rels., N.Y.C., 1979-80; dep. polit. counselor U.S. Mission to UN Dept. of State, 1980-83; U.S. ambassador to Benin, 1983-86; dep. dir. mgmt. ops. Dept. of State, Washington, 1986-87, dir. mgmt. ops., 1987-88; U.S. ambassador to Senegal, 1988-91; U.S. alt. rep. UN Security Coun., 1991-92; diplomat in residence, Howard U. Dept. of State, Washington, 1992-93; asst. sec. African Affairs Dept. of State, 1993—. Recipient Superior Honor award Dept. of State, Grenada, 1974, 79, Meritorious Honor award, Washington, 1975, Presdl. Performance award, 1989, 94. Mem. Am. Fgn. Service Assn. Office: Bureau African Affairs Dept Of State Washington DC 20520

MOOSER, STEPHEN, author; b. Fresno, Calif., July 4, 1941; s. Joseph Nathan and Lillian Ruth (Davidson) M.; m. Etta Karlovec, Dec. 29, 1972 (div. Dec. 1994); children: Chelsea, Bryn. BA, UCLA, 1963, MA in Journalism, 1968. Reporter Dodge Svcs., L.A., 1964-66; freelance film maker Utah, 1966-68; author children's books SWRL, L.A., 1969-75; freelance author children's books L.A. and N.Y.C., 1975—. Author: New York Kids Book, 1979, 101 Black Cats, 1979, Elvis Is Back and He's in the Sixth Grade, 1994, many others. With U.S. Army, 1963-68. Mem. Soc. Childrens Book Writers and Illustrators (co-founder, pres. 1971—). Home and Office: 1342 Wellesley # 102 Los Angeles CA 90025

MOOSSA, A. R., surgery educator; b. Port Louis, Mauritius, Oct. 10, 1939; s. Yacoob and Maude (Rochecoute) M.; m. Denise Willoughby, Dec. 28, 1973; children: Pierre, Noel, Claude, Valentine. BS, U. Liverpool, Eng., 1962, MD (hon.), 1965; postgrad., Johns Hopkins U., 1972-73, U. Chgo., 1973-74. Intern Liverpool Royal Infirmary, 1965-66; resident United Liverpool Hosps. and Alder Hey Children's Hosp., 1966-72; from asst. prof. surgery to assoc. prof. U. Chgo., 1975-77, prof., dir. surg. rsch., chief gen. surgery svc., vice chmn. dept., 1977-83; chmn. dept. surgery U. Calif.-San Diego Med. Ctr., 1983—; Litchfield lectr. U., Oxford, Eng., 1978; praelector in surgery U. Dundee, Scotland, 1979; Hampson Trust vis. prof. U. Liverpool, Eng., 1992, G.B. Ong. vis. prof. U. Hong Kong, 1993, Philip Sandblon vis. prof. U. Lund, Sweden. Editor: Tumors of the Pancreas, 1982, Essential Surgical Practice, 1983, 3d edit., 1995, Comprehensive Textbook of Oncology, 1985, 2d edit., 1991, Gastrointestinal Emergencies, 1985, Problems in General Surgery, 1989, Operative Colorectal Surgery, 1993. Fellow Royal Coll. Surgeons (Hunterian prof. 1977); mem. ACS, Am. Surg. Assn., Soc. Univ. Surgeons, Am. Soc. Clin. Oncology. Office: U Calif San Diego Med Ctr 200 W Arbor Dr San Diego CA 92103-1911

MOOSSY, JOHN, neuropathologist, neurologist, consultant; b. Shreveport, La., Aug. 24, 1925; s. John Yazbeck and Rose (Ferris) M.; m. Yvonne Reese, Mar. 15, 1951; children: John Jefferson, Joan Marie. MD, Tulane U., 1950. Intern Charity Hosp. of New Orleans, 1950-51, neurology resident, 1951-53; neuropathology fellow Columbia U. Coll. of Physicians and Surgeons, N.Y.C., 1953-54; assoc., lectr. in neuropathology Tulane U. Sch. Medicine, New Orleans, 1954-57; asst. to prof. in pathology, neurology La. State U., New Orleans, 1957-65; prof. pathology, grad. faculty U. Pitts., 1965-67; prof. pathology neuropathology Bowman Gray Sch. of Medicine, Winston-Salem, N.C., 1967-72; prof. pathology and neurology, dir. div. neuropathology U. Pitts., Winston-Salem, N.C., 1972-93; emeritus prof. U. Pitts., 1993—; dir. Cerebrovascular Disease Study, World Fedn. of Neurology, Antwerp, Belgium, 1960-61; cons. Armed Forces Inst. of Pathology, Washington, 1977—, mem. sci. adv. bd., Washington, 1984-86. Editor: Cerebral Vascular Disease Seventh Conference, 1970, Cerebrovascular Diseases 12th Research Conference, 1981; editor-in-chief Jour. Neuropathology and Exptl. Neurology, 1981-91; mem. editorial bd. Archives Neurology, 1982-92. Recipient Excellence in Teaching award U. Pitts. Sch. of Medicine, 1987-88; named Commencement Speaker U. Pitts. Sch. of Medicine, 1989. Mem. Am. Acad. Neurology (sec.-treas. 1963-655), Am. Neurol. Assn. (v.p. 1977-78), Am. Assn. Neuropathologists (pres. 1974-75, Neuropathology award 1992), Internat. Soc. Neuropathology, Coun. Biology Editors.

MOOTE, A. LLOYD, history educator; b. Hamilton, Ont., Can., Mar. 22, 1931; s. Stanley Alanson and Esther Grace (Wood) M.; m. Barbara Brown,

Dec. 27, 1956 (div. 1982); children: Karen, Peter, Daphne, Robert; m. Dorothy Carter May, May 30, 1986. BA, U. Toronto, 1954; MA, U. Minn., Mpls., 1956, PhD, 1958. Tchg. asst. U. Minn., Mpls., 1955-58; lectr. U. Toronto, 1958-61; asst. prof. U. Cin., 1961-62; from asst. prof. to prof. history U. So. Calif., L.A., 1962-92; prof emeritus U. So. Calif., 1993—; vis. prof. Queen's U., Kingston, Ont., 1965-66; chmn. gen. edn. program U. So. Calif., 1978-81; mem. Inst. Advanced Study, Princeton, 1988-89; affiliated prof. Rutgers U., 1994—. Author: The Seventeenth Century, 1970, The Revolt of the Judges, 1971, The World of Europe: The Seventeenth Century, 1973, 2d edit., 1979, Louis XIII: The Just, 1989, paperback edit., 1991; co-editor, contbr. issue of French hist. studies on biography, 1996; mem. editl. bd. French Hist. Studies, 1971-74; internat. adv. bd. European History Quar., 1983—. Recipient William Koren prize Soc. French Hist. Studies, 1962, creative scholarship award U. So. Calif. Assocs., 1973, faculty book award U. So. Calif. chpt. Phi Kappa Phi, 1990; younger scholar NEH, 1969; grantee Am. Philos. Soc., 1962, Haynes Found., 1973, Wellcome Inst. for History Medicine, 1993-94, Burroughs-Wellcome Fund, 1996; Guggenheim fellow, 1976, fellow U. Essex, Eng., 1993-94, Rutgers Ctr. for Hist. Analysis, 1995-97. Mem. Am. Hist. Assn., Past and Present Soc., Soc. French Hist. Studies (pres. 1984-85), Western Soc. for French History, Soc. for Study French History (U.K.), Sixteenth-Century Studies Conf. Home: 149 Meadowbrook Dr Princeton NJ 08540-3664

MOOTY, BRUCE WILSON, lawyer; b. Mpls., May 27, 1955; s. John William and Virginia Mae (Nelson) M.; m. Ann Tracy Grogan, May 1, 1982; children: Katharine Grogan, Allison Taylor, Megan Ann. Student, Amherst Coll., 1973-74; BA summa cum laude, U. Minn., 1977, JD cum laude, 1980. Bar: Minn. 1980, U.S. Dist. Ct. Minn. 1980, U.S. Ct. Appeals 1983. Assoc., shareholder, officer, dir. Briggs & Morgan, P.A., Mpls., 1980-93; ptnr. Gray, Plant, Mooty, Mooty & Bennett, P.A., Mpls., 1993—; also bd. dirs. Pres., chmn. bd. dirs. A Better Chance Found., Edina, Minn., 1988, Minn. Amateur Baseball Found., Mpls., 1992; mem. coun. Colonial Ch. Edina, 1992. Mem. ABA, Minn. Bar Assn. (community rels. com. 1992—), Hennepin County Bar Assn., Ramsey County Bar Assn., Minikahda Club, Phi Beta Kappa, Phi Kappa Phi. Home: 7215 Lanham Ln Edina MN 55439-1823 Office: Gray Plant Mooty Mooty & Bennett 3400 City Ctr 33 S 6th St Minneapolis MN 55402-3601

MOOTY, JOHN WILLIAM, lawyer; b. Adrian, Minn., Nov. 27, 1922; s. John Wilson and Genevieve (Brown) M.; m. Virginia Nelson, June 6, 1952 (dec. 1964); children: David N., Bruce W., Charles W.; m. Jane Nelson, Jan. 15, 1972. B.S.L., U. Minn., 1943, LL.B., 1944. Bar: Minn. 1944. Ptnr. Gray, Plant, Mooty & Bennett, Mpls., 1945—; chmn. bd. Internat. Dairy Queen, Inc.; bd. dirs. Bur. of Engraving, Inc., Riverway Co. and subs., Rio Verde Svcs., Inc., Ariz., Turnquist, Inc. Author: (with others) Minnesota Practice Methods, 1956. Chmn. Gov.'s Task Force on Edn., 1981; pres. Citizens League Mpls., 1970; acting chmn. Republican Party of Minn., 1958. Mem. ABA, Minn. Bar Assn., Hennepin County Bar Assn., U. Minn. Alumni Assn. (pres. 1982). Clubs: Interlachen (Mpls.), Lafayette (Mpls.), Minikahda (Mpls.), Mpls. (Mpls.). Home: 6601 Dovre Dr Minneapolis MN 55436-1711 Office: 3400 City Ctr 33 S 6th St Minneapolis MN 55402-3601

MORA, FEDERICO, neurosurgeon; b. Guatemala, Guatemala, Jan. 11, 1926; came to the U.S., 1945; s. Carlos Federico and Rosa (Castaneda) M.; m. Natalie Viriginia Ramin, June 30, 1951; children: Federico, Clara Luz, Ana Maria, Claudia Ines, Juan Rafael. Student, Harvard Coll., 1945-46, MD, 1950. Diplomate Am. Bd. Neurol. Surgery. Pvt. practice neurol. surgery Guatemala and Albuquerque, 1958—; asst. prof. surgery and anatomy U. N.Mex. Sch. Medicine, Albuquerque, 1969-70. Capt. USAFR, 1954-56. Mem. Alpha Omega Alpha. Democrat. Avocations: scuba diving, nature studies. Home: 1809 Avenida Alturas NE Albuquerque NM 87110-4956

MORA, FRANCISCO, artist, printmaker; b. Uruapan, Mexico, May 7, 1922; s. Jose Maria and Clotilde (Perez) M.; m. Elizabeth Catlett, Oct. 31, 1946; children: Francisco, Juan, David. Student, Escuela de Pintura y Escultura La Esmeralda, 1941-46. Tchr. drawing Sch. Pub. Edn. Mexico, 1949-54; art adviser Mexican Acad. Edn., 1956—. Exhibited one-man shows Nitra, Prague, Czechoslovakia, 1971, Cite International de l'universite, Paris, 1972, Saxon Princes Palace, Dresden, 1973, Green Room Nat. Fine Arts Museum, Mexico, 1974-75, New Visions Gallery, San Diego, 1981, Atlanta, 1988, Salon de la Plastica, Mexico City, 1983, Tougaloo, Miss., 1986, U. Ariz. Mus., 1987, Kenkeleba Gallery, N.Y.C., 1988, In Faust Gallery, Hamburg, 1989, Miss. Mus. Art W. Catlett, 1990, Montgomery (Ala.) Mus. Art, 1991, Polk Mus. Art, Lakeland, Fla., 1991-92, Mus. African Am. Art, Detroit, 1992, Malcol Brown Gallery, Shaker Heights, Ohio, 1993, Isobel Neal Gallery, Chgo., 1994, Jame Lewis Mus., Balt., 1994-95, Queens' Coll. Mus., N.Y.C., Third World Mus., L.A., 1996, I-Space; illustrator books, pamphlets, mags. Mem. Salon de la Plastica Mexicana (founding mem.), Mexican Acad. Edn. (founding mem.). Home: Apartado Postal 694, 62000 Cuernavaca Morelos, Mexico

MORABITO, BRUNO PAUL, machinery manufacturing executive; b. Motticella, Italy, Feb. 10, 1922; s. Paul and Maria Antoinetta (Tedesco) M.; m. Therese Riccelli, June 29, 1946; 1 dau., Paula. B.C.E., Syracuse U., 1945. Application engr. Machinery and Systems div. Carrier Corp., Syracuse, N.Y., 1945-55; engring. mgr. Carrier Corp., 1955-66, mgr. centrifugal sales, 1966-69, mgr. machinery mktg., 1970-73, mgr. mktg., 1973-81; group v.p., gen. mgr. Environ. Systems Group Aeronca, Inc., Pineville, N.C., 1981-84; cons. Syracuse/Onondaga County Planning Agy., 1985—; pres. BPM Planning and Cons., 1988-93. Chmn. sewage disposal dist. com. and street lighting dist. com. of Syracuse Gardens Tract, 1951-52; vice chmn. Onondaga County Citizens Energy Com., 1996—. Recipient ASHRAE Wolverine Diamond Key award, 1961, Silver Knight of Mgmt. award Nat. Mgmt. Assn., 1978. Fellow ASHRAE (bd. dirs. 1970-78, v.p. 1974-76, pres. 1977-78); mem. Beaver Meadows Golf and Recreational Club (bd. dirs. 1973-80, 84-89). Roman Catholic. Home and Office: 302 Saltmakers Rd Liverpool NY 13088-6229

MORABITO, ROCCO ANTHONY, urologist; b. Huntington, W.Va., Nov. 23, 1950; s. Nicola F. and Theresa M. (Lobaldo) M.; m. Deborah Gayle Hall, 1973 (div. 1986); m. Brenda Kay Lyons, June 14, 1991; children: Shawn, Chris, Rocco Jr., Justin. BA, W.Va. U., 1972, MD, 1976. Diplomate Am. Bd. Urology, Nat. Bd. Med. Examiners. Surg. residency W.Va. U. Hosp., Morgantown, 1976-78, urol. residency, 1978-81; pres. Huntington (W.Va.) Urol. Assn., 1981—, Midwest Mobile Lithotripsy, Huntington, 1989-96, Tri-State Health Ptnrs., Huntington, 1994-96; pres. med. staff Cabell Huntington Hosp., Huntington, 1991-93, St. Mary's Hosp., 1997—; clin. asst. prof. urology, W.Va. U. Sch. Medicine, 1981—, Marshall U. Sch. Medicine, Huntington, 1981—. Fellow ACS; mem. AMA, Am. Urol. Assn., So. Med. Assn., W.Va. State Med. Assn., Cabell County Med. Soc., W.Va. U. Sch. Medicine Alumni Assn. (chmn. 1989-94). Republican. Roman Catholic. Avocations: tennis, boating, skiing, music. Home: 20 Kensington Lane Huntington WV 25705 Office: Huntington Urological Assn 2828 1st Ave Ste 305 Huntington WV 25702-1236

MORACZEWSKI, ROBERT LEO, publisher; b. Saint Paul, Nebr., May 13, 1942; s. Leo and Florence May (Wadas) M.; m. Virginia Kay Rohman, July 26, 1960; children—Mark, Matthew, Monika, Michael. BS in Agrl. Journalism, U. Nebr., 1964. Assoc. editor Farmer Mag. Webb Co., St. Paul, 1964-72; mng. editor Farm Industry News Webb Co., St. Paul, 1972-74; editor Big Farmer Mag., Chgo., 1974-75; editorial dir. Webb Agrl. Services, St. Paul, 1976; editor The Farmer, The Dakota Farmer Webb Co., St. Paul, 1983-89; group pub. Webb Co., St. Paul, 1989-90; v.p., 1990—; exec. dir. Minn. Agri-Growth Coun. Contbr. articles to profl. jours. Recipient numerous media awards. Mem. Am. Agrl. Editors Assn., Nat. Agrl. Mktg. Assn., Investigative Reporters and Editors Assn. Roman Catholic. Home: 26589 Everton Cir N Wyoming MN 55092-9008 Office: Webb Div Intertec Pub 7900 International Dr Minneapolis MN 55425

MORADI, AHMAD F., software company executive, consultant; b. Tehran, Persia, Mar. 21, 1955; came to U.S., 1973; s. Akbar and Afsar (Mokaram) M.; m. Lourdes Pernas; 1 child, Aimee. AS, Broward Community Coll., 1978; BA, Fla. Atlantic U., 1980, MBA, 1982; Phd, LaSalle U., 1987. Advisor restaurant industries Miami, Fla., 1974-78; pres. Octa-8, Inc., Ft. Lauderdale, Fla., 1980-82; mgmt. cons. MGI-MCG, Boca Raton, Fla., 1982-83; dir. ops. Datamation, Hollywood, Fla., 1983-85; pres. Software Intelligence Corp., Ft. Lauderdale, 1985—; with ARM Financial Corp., 1987-89; MIS dir., CIO Churchill Tech., Inc., Davie, Fla., 1992—; CEO Westmack Group Holding Co., Delray Beach, 1995—; prin. G4, Inc., Ft. Lauderdale, 1992—; lectr. South Fla. Bus. Jour., 1984-85, Victoria Hosp., Miami, Fla., 1985, Mt. Sinai Hosp., Miami, Fla., 1985, U. Miami, Fla., 1986, Chiropractic Today, 1989; cons., bus., mktg., internat. mktg. and telemarketing mgmt. Software Intelligence Corp., 1985—; systems analyst Softway, Inc., Ft. Lauderdale, 1986—. Mem. Data Processing Mgmt. Assn., Small Bus. Inst.

MORAFF, HOWARD, science foundation program director; b. N.Y.C.; m. Connie J. McClure; children: Kenneth, Judith, Steve. AB, Columbia U., BSEE, MSEE; PhD in Neurophysiology, Cornell U. Dir. vet. med. computing resources Cornell U., Ithaca, N.Y., 1967-82; dir. computing resources Merck Sharp & Dohme Rsch. Labs., Rahway, N.J., 1982-84; program dir. NSF, Washington, 1984—. Co-author: Electronics for Neurobiologists, 1973, Electronics for the Modern Scientist, 1982; contbr. articles to profl. jours. Capt. USAF. Mem. IEEE (sr.), IEEE Robotics and Automation Soc. (adminstrv. com. 1993-95, co-chair long range planning com. 1996—). Acad. Scis., Sigma Xi, Tau Beta Pi, Eta Kappa Nu, Phi Kappa Phi. Achievements include patent for transistor circuit; research in on-line laboratory automation and end-user computing. Office: NSF 4201 Wilson Blvd Arlington VA 22230-0001

MORAHAN, PAGE S., microbiologist, educator; b. Newport News, Jan. 7, 1940; d. Robert Bruce and Margaret (Coleman) S. BA, Agnes Scott Coll., Decatur, Ga., 1961; MA, Hunter Coll., N.Y.C., 1964; PhD, Marquette U., Milw., 1969. Asst. prof. microbiology Med. Coll. of Va., Richmond, 1971-74, assoc. prof., 1974-81, prof., 1981-82; prof. and chmn. dept. microbiology Med. Coll. Pa., Phila., 1982-93, assoc. dean faculty affairs, 1993-94, sr. assoc. provost faculty affairs, 1994—; adv. com. NCI Cancer Ctr. Rev. Com., Washington, 1986-90, mem. manpower rev. com., 1977-81; mem. test com. Nat. Bd. Med. Examiners, 1990-94, Hubbard award com., 1994-95, bd. dirs., 1995—; mem. AAMC Women in Medicine Coord. com., 1994-97; lectr. in field; conductor seminars in field. Editor Jour. of Reticuloendothelial Soc., 1982-88, Infection and Immunity, 1982-85; contbr. over 100 articles to profl. jours., chpts. to books. Sec., Spring Garden Historic Dist. Civic Assn., 1984-85, bd. dirs., 1985-86; mem.-at-large adminstrn. bd. First United Meth. Ch. of Germantown, 1990-95. Recipient rsch. career devel. award NIH, 1974-79, Lindback award, 1988; grantee NIMH, 1989-94, Nat. Inst. Arthritis and Infectious Disease, 1987-94, Nat. Cancer Inst., 1989-94; fellow Am. Coun. Edn., 1992-93; also others. Mem. AAAS, Am. Acad. Microbiology, Am. Assn. Immunologists, Am. Assn. for Cancer Rsch., Soc. for Exptl. Biology and Medicine, Soc. Virus Rsch., Reticuloendothelial Soc. (councilor 1981, chmn. membership com. 1984), Am. Soc. Microbiology (med. microbiology and immunology com. of pub. affairs bd. 1989-92), Assn. Med. Microbiology (pres. 1989, dir. 2d ednl. workshop 1988, adv. com. 3d, 4th, 5th ednl. workshops 1990, 92, 94), Phi Beta Kappa, Sigma Xi. Methodist. Office: Alleghney U Health Science Office Facilty Affairs Broad & Vine St Mail Stop 979 Philadelphia PA 19102-1192

MORALES, ARMANDO, artist; b. Granada, Nicaragua, Jan. 15, 1927. Student, Sch. Fine Arts, Managua, Pratt Graphic Art Ctr., N.Y.C. instr. advanced painting Cooper Union, N.Y., 1972, 73. Exhibited art at Bienal Modern Art, Sao Paulo, Brazil, 1953, 55, 59, Carnegie Inst., Pitts., 1958, 64, 67, Arte Am y Espana, Madrid, Barcelona, Rome and Berlin, 1961, Guggenheim Inst., N.Y., 1960, The Emergent Decade, Cornell U., Guggenheim Mus., 1966. Recipient Ernst Wolf award V Bienal, Sao Paulo, Brazil, 1959, award Arte Am y Espana, Madrid, 1963, J.L. Hudson award Carnegie Inst., 1964. Office: c/o Claude Bernard Gallery 900 Park Ave Fl 12 New York NY 10021-0231*

MORALES, CARLOTA ELOISA, principal; b. Havana, Cuba, Oct. 18, 1946; came to U.S., 1961; d. Jose Ramon and Rosa (Paradela) M. AA, Miami Dade Jr. Coll., 1964; BEd in Secondary Edn. Adminstrn., U. Miami, 1966, MEd, 1969, EdD in Adminstrn., 1984. Cert. Math. and langs. tchr., Fla. Tchr. Spanish Acad. of the Assumption, Miami, Fla., 1967-68; tchr. 6th grade Sts. Peter and Paul Sch., Miami, 1968-71, tchr. math., 1971-81, asst. prin., 1981-90; lectr. in Spanish Barry U., Miami Shores, Fla., 1981-82; prin. St. Agatha Sch., Miami, 1990—; judge literary contest Patronato de Cultura Pro-Cuba, Miami, 1973; judge Dade County Youth Fair, Miami, 1985-86; curriculum writer Archdiocese of Miami, 1983—; mem. vis. team Fla. Cath. Conf., Tallahassee, 1982—. Chairperson Sts. Peter and Paul Ann. Festival, Miami, 1971—. Mem. Assn. for Supervision and Curriculum Devel., Phi Delta Kappa. Roman Catholic. Avocations: travel, music, collecting porcelain flowers. Home: 1400 SW 14th Ave Miami FL 33145-1541 Office: Saint Agatha Sch 1111 SW 107th Ave Miami FL 33174-2506

MORALES, CYNTHIA TORRES, clinical psychologist, consultant; b. L.A., Aug. 13, 1952; d. Victor Jose and Lupe (Pacheco) Torres; m. Armando Torres Morales, June 30, 1989. BA, UCLA, 1975, M in Social Welfare, 1978, D in Counseling Psychology, 1986. Lic. psychologist, Calif. Clin. social worker VA, Brentwood, Calif., 1977-78; med. social worker Harbor-UCLA Med. Ctr., Carson, Calif., 1978-79; psychotherapist San Fernando Valley Child Guidance Clinic, Northridge, Calif., 1979-80; psychiat. social worker L.A. County Dept. Mental Health, 1980-81; child welfare worker L.A. County Dept. Children's Svcs., 1981-86; cons. psychologist, organizational devel. mgr. UCLA, 1986—; pvt. practice and consultation, 1992—; cons. Dept. Children Svcs., Health Svcs. Divsn., 1994—; cons. Hispanic Family Inst., L.A., 1989—, U. Calif., Calif. Youth Authority, Project Info.; mem. diversity com. UCLA, 1988—, mem. mental health emergency task force, 1986-89. Mem. Centro de Ninos Bd. Dirs., L.A., 1984-88; lobbyist self devel. people United Presbyn. Ch. Synod, L.A., 1982-88; chair Inner City Games Acad. Contest Hollenbeck Police Bus. Coun., L.A., 1992; co-chair Inner City Games Acad. Essay Contest, 1993; commr. L.A. County Commn. Children and Family Svcs., 2nd Supervisorial Dist. Recipient Cert. of Appreciation, Children's Bapt. Home, 1984, Cert. of Appreciation, Hollenbeck Police Bus. Coun. 1992, Spl. Recognition award Fed. Judge Takasugi, Pro Bono Bar Rev. and L.A. City Atty. 1993, Cert. of Appreciation, Hollenbeck Youth Ctr., 1992, commendation L.A. County Commn. for Children and Families, 1996. Mem. APA, L.A. County Psychol. Assn. Office: 1100 Glendon Ave Ste 1701 Los Angeles CA 90024-3521

MORALES, DAN, state attorney general. Grad. with honors, Trinity U., 1978; JD, Harvard U., 1981. Asst. dist. atty. Bexar County, 1983-85; former mem. Ho. of Reps. Tex.; atty. gen. State of Tex., Austin, 1991—. Bd. dirs. NCCJ, World Affairs Coun.; trustee So. Meth. U., Schreiner Coll., Kerrville; elder First Presbyn. Ch. Named one of Seven Best Legislators Dallas Morning News, Politician of Yr. San Antonio Express News; recipient Outstanding Svc. award Ind. Colls. and Univs., Outstanding Leadership award Texan's War on Drugs,. Mem. Tex. Lyceum Assn. Office: Office of Atty Gen PO Box 12548 Austin TX 78711-2548*

MORALES, JOHN MARK, cardiac surgeon; b. San Luis Potosi, Mex., June 25, 1961; (parents Am. citizens); s. Juan Manuel and Merlie (Vernoy) M.; m. Patti Lynn Fullerton, Sept. 2, 1994. BS, U. Autonoma San Luis Potosi, Mex., 1978; MD, U. Autonoma Guadalajara, Mex., 1982. Diplomate Am. Bd. Surgery with subspecialty in thoracic surgery. Intern Gen. Hosp., Mexico City, 1983; gen. practice Guadalajara State Clinic, Jalisco, Mex., 1984; fellow orthopedic surgery Berkshire Med. Ctr., 1985-86, PGY gen. surgery, 1986-90, PGY, chief gen. surgery, 1990-91; cardiothoracic resident W.Va. U., Morgantown, 1991-92; chief resident cardiothoracic surgery U. W.Va., Morgantown, 1992-93; sr. registrar in cardiothoracic surgery Hosp. for Sick Children, London, 1993-94; cardiac surgeon pvt. practice, Corpus Christi, Tex., 1994—; presenter in field. Contbr. numerous articles to profl. publs. Co-founder, provider Hearts for Tots, Inc. Fellow ACS (assoc.); mem. Soc. Thoracic Surgeons (candidate group). Roman Catholic. Avocations: sports, travel, reading, music, art. Office: 3533 S Alameda St Corpus Christi TX 78411-1721

MORALES, JULIO K., lawyer; b. Havana, Cuba, Jan. 17, 1948; came to U.S., 1960; s. Julio E. and Josephine (Holsters) M.; m. Suzette M. Dussault, May 31, 1970 (div. 1978); children: Julio E., Karel A.; m. Barbara A. Miller, July 14, 1979 (div. 1988); 1 child, Nicolas W. BA, Carroll Coll., 1969; JD, U. Mont., 1972. Bar: Mont. 1972, U.S. Dist. Ct. Mont. 1972, U.S. Ct. Mil. Appeals 1972, U.S. Ct. Appeals (9th cir.) 1980. Law clk. to presiding justice Mont. Supreme Ct., Helena, 1972; sole practice Missoula, Mont., 1973-78, 88—; sr. ptnr. Morales & Volinkaty, Missoula, 1978-88; pvt. practice law Morales Law Office, 1988—. Author: Estate Planning for the Handicapped, 1975. Pres. Rockmont, Inc., Missoula, 1985—. Served to 2d lt. U.S. Army, 1972. Named Boss of the Yr., Missoula chpt. Mont. Assn. Legal Secs., 1988. Mem. ABA (dist. rep. 1975-79, exec. coun. young lawyer divsn. 1977-79), Mont. Bar Assn. (chmn. law day 1974, 75, 77), Am. Judicature Soc., Assn. Trial Lawyers Am., World Assn. Lawyers, Missoula Soccer Assn. (pres. 1983-85), Mont. Sailing Assn. (bd. dirs. 1994—), Nat. Exch. Club (bd. dirs. Yellowstone dist. 1987-88, pres. 1990-91), Missoula Exch. Club, Phi Delta Phi. Roman Catholic. Avocations: sports, coaching youth, boating, skiing, golf. Office: PO Box 9311 430 Ryman St Missoula MT 59802-4208

MORALES, PABLO, Olympic athlete, swimmer. Olympic swimmer Barcelona, Spain, 1992. Recipient 100m Butterfly Gold medal Olympics, Barcelona, 1992. World record holder for 100 meter butterfly 52.84 seconds, set June 23, 1986, Orlando, Fla. Office: care US Olympic Com 1750 E Boulder St Colorado Springs CO 80909-5724*

MORALES-BORGES, RAUL HECTOR, physician; b. San Juan, P.R., Aug. 2, 1963; s. Raul and Sonia Margarita (Borges) M. BS, U. P.R., 1985; MD, San Juan Bautista Sch. Med., 1990. Diplomate P.R. Bd. Med. Examiners. Aux. sales rep. Borges Warehouse of Textiles, Gurabo, P.R., 1981-85; tutor Computer Lab. U. P.R., Cayey, 1984, asst. researcher Ecol. Lab., 1985; intern Henry Ford Hosp., Detroit, 1990-91, resident, 1991-93; fellow, medical oncology Providence Hosp./U. Mich., Mich., 1993-95; lectr. dept. pathology and physiology San Juan Bautista Sch. Medicine, San Juan, P.R., 1995—; chief fellow med. oncology, 1995; mem. prostate specific antigen clin. policy team Henry Ford Hosp., 1991-93, smoking cessation task force 1993; summer tutor Edn. Dept. P.R., Gurabo, 1986-87; mem. lung cancer working group Providence Hosp., 1993-95, leukemia/lymphoma working group, 1995, breast cancer working group 1995; pres. transfusion com. Fajardo Med. Ctr., 1997, tumor bd., 1997—; presenter in field. Organizer Com. of Profl. Assn., San Juan, 1988-90, Com. of San Jose Marathon, 1985-91. Mem. AMA, N.Y. Acad. Scis., Nat. Assn. Drs., Am. Soc. Blood and Marrow Transplant, Soc. for Nutritional Oncology Adjuvant Therapy, Ashford Healthcare Svcs., Inc., Medicina Dirigida, Inc., Am. Cancer Soc., Puerto Rican Soc. Hematology, Puerto Rico Coll. Physicians and Surgeons, Civic-socail Circle Gurabo. Roman Catholic. Achievements include research in tumor infiltrating lymphocytes in melanoma RCC, HLD-DR as a metastatic marker, adoptive immunotherapy, phase II trial of VP-16 and Miitoxantrone for metastatic breast cancer. Home: PO Box 873 Gurabo PR 00778-0873

MORALES-GALARRETA, JULIO, psychiatrist, child psychoanalyst; b. Trujillo, Peru, Dec. 1, 1936; came to U.S., 1973; s. Julio Morales-Fernandez and Lidia (Galarreta) Morales; (div.); children: Lourdes Lydia, Julio Fernando. MD, U. Trujillo, 1966; grad., St. Louis Psychoanalytic Inst., 1984, grad. in child psychoanalysis, 1985. Diplomate Am. Bd. Psychiatry and Neurology; cert. psychoanalyst.; cert. child psychoanalyst. Resident in psychiatry Ministry of Pub. Health, Peru, 1965-68; supr. psychiat. tng. program Ministry Pub. Health, Peru, 1970-72; physician and surgeon U. Trujillo, 1966; instr. psychaitry St. Marcos U., Peru, 1968-72; resident in psychiatry Fairfield Hills Hosp., Newtown, Conn., 1972-74; fellow in child psychiatry Washington U., St. Louis, 1974-76, instr. child psychiatry, 1976-82; dir. child devel. project St. Louis Psychonalytic Inst., 1982-94, dir. child and adolescent psychotherapy program, 1993—, dir. child psychoanalysis, 1996—; assoc. clin. prof. psychiatry and pediatrics St. Louis U., 1983-96, clin. prof. psychiatry and pediatrics, 1996—; faculty psychoanalysis and child analysis St. Louis Psychoanalytic Inst., 1984—, supervising analyst in child analyst, 1988, tng. and supervising analyst in adult and child psychoanalysis, 1991—. Fellow Peruvian Psychiat. Assn., Am. Psychiat. Assn., Am. Psychol. Assn.; mem. St. Louis Met. Med. Soc., Am. Acad. Child Psychiatry, Am. Psychoanalytic Assn., Am. Soc. Adolescent Psychiatry, Assn. Child Psychoanalysis. Avocations: classical music, biking, tennis. Home: 665 S Skinker Blvd Saint Louis MO 63105-2300 Office: 141 N Meramec Ave Saint Louis MO 63105-3750

MORAN, BARBARA BURNS, librarian, educator; b. Columbus, Miss., July 8, 1944; d. Robert Theron and Joan (Brown) Burns; m. Joseph J. Moran, Sept. 4, 1965; children: Joseph Michael, Brian Matthew. AB, Mount Holyoke Coll., S. Hadley, Mass., 1966; M.Librarianship, Emory U., Atlanta, 1973; PhD, SUNY, Buffalo, 1982. Head libr. The Park Sch. of Buffalo, Snyder, N.Y., 1974-78; prof. Sch. Info. and Libr. Sci. U. N.C., Chapel Hill, 1981—, asst. dean, 1987-90; dean Sch. Info. and Libr. Sci., U. N.C., Chapel Hill, 1990—; participant various seminars; evaluator various edn. progs.; cons. in field. Author: Academic Libraries, 1984; co-author: (with Robert D. Stueart) Library Management, 4th edit., 1993; contbr. articles to profl. jours., chpts. to books; mem. editl. bd. Jour. Acad. Librarianship, 1992-94, Coll. and Rsch. Libraries, 1996—. Coun. Libr. Resources grantee, 1985, Univ. Rsch. Coun. grantee, 1983, 89, others. Mem. ALA, Assn. for Libr. and Info. Sci. Edn., Popular Culture Assn., N.C. Libr. Assn., Beta Phi Mu. Home: 1307 Leclair St Chapel Hill NC 27514-3034 Office: Univ NC Sch Info & Libr Sci Chapel Hill NC 27599-3360

MORAN, CHARLES A., securities executive; b. Chgo., Feb. 7, 1943; s. Charles W. and Rose B. (Sutcher) M.; m. Donna L. Orbach, Sept. 3, 1967; children: Scott Alan, Erin Lizabeth. AB, Princeton U., 1964; JD, U. Mich., 1967; postgrad. advanced mgmt., Harvard U., 1982. CFP. With Chase Manhattan Bank, N.Y.C., 1967-70; pension trust officer, adminstrv. officer, officer in charge new bus. devel., pension div. Mfrs. Hanover Trust Co., N.Y.C., 1970-87, sr. v.p., officer-in-charge employee benefit trust div., 1979-80; chmn. bd., pres., CEO MH/Edie Investment Counsel (formerly Lionel D. Edie & Co.), N.Y.C., 1980-82, officer-in-charge corp. trust div., 1982-83, officer in charge-global securities group, 1983-87; pres. Govt. Securities Clearing Corp., N.Y.C., 1987-96; asst. prof. Coll. N.J., Trenton, 1996—; pres. Strategic Financial Adv., Montclair, N.J., 1996—; asst. prof. Harvard U., Cambridge, summer 1997—; bd. dirs. Mfrs. Hanover Trust Co. Calif., Mfrs. Hanover Data Svcs. Corp., Mortgage Backed Securities Clearing Corp., Nat. Securities Clearing Corp.; chmn. bd. dirs. Inform, Inc.; former lectr. bus. and econs. Bloomfield Coll.; former lectr. sociology and fin. employee benefits C.W. Post Coll., L.I. U.; cons. Urban Vol. Cons. Group, Inc.; mem. adv. coun. U.S. Dept. Labor; mem. adv. bd. BNA Pension Reporter; mem. Employees Retirement Income Security Act of 1974 Roundtable; mem. industry adv. com. Future Electronic Funds Payments Svcs. Fed. Res. Contbr. articles to profl. jours. Mem. AAUP, Am. Inst. Banking, Am. Pension Conf. (treas. 1976-79), N.Y. State Bankers Assn. (employees trust com.), Assn. Pvt. Pension and Welfare Plans (dir., mem. exec. com.), ERISA Industry Com. (pres., dir., mem. exec. com., treas.), Am. Bankers Assn. (chmn. employee benefit trust com. 1977-82), Internat. Found. Pension and Welfare Plans, Bank Adminstrn. Inst. (mem. tech. commn.), N.Y. C. of C. (task force on pub. pensions), The Inst. of Cert. Fin. Planners, N.J. Soc. Inst. Cert. Fin. Planners (bd. dirs.), Princeton Club, Havard Bus. Sch. Club of N.Y.

MORAN, DANIEL AUSTIN, mathematician; b. Chgo., Feb. 17, 1936; s. Austin Thomas and Violet Lillian (Johnson) M.; m. Karen Krull, Sept. 14, 1963; children: Alexander, Claudia. B.S. summa cum laude, St. Mary's of Tex., 1957; M.S., U. Ill., 1958, Ph.D., 1962. Research instr. U. Chgo., 1962-64; asst. prof. Mich. State U., 1964-68, assoc. prof., 1968-76, prof. math., 1976—; vis. scholar U. Cambridge, 1970-71, U. North Wales, 1978. Contbr. articles to profl. jours. Mem. Math. Assn. Am., Sigma Xi, Pi Mu Epsilon, Delta Epsilon Sigma, Kappa Mu Alpha. Roman Catholic. Home: 2633 Roseland Ave East Lansing MI 48823-3870 Office: Dept Math Michigan State Univ East Lansing MI 48824

MORAN, EDGAR M., physician, educator; b. Constantza, Romania, Apr. 28, 1928; came to U.S., 1965; s. Leon and Catty (Rosenblatt) M.; m. Huguette M. Moran; children: Daniel, Andre. BSc, St. Sava Coll., Bucharest, 1946; MD, U. Bucharest, 1952. From instr. to assoc. prof. medicine dept. medicine Franklin McLean Meml. Rsch. Inst./U. Chgo., 1968-76; dir. med. oncology City of Hope Nat. Med. Ctr., Duarte, Calif., 1976-78; prof. medicine U. Calif., Irvine, 1978—; chmn. cancer program VA Med. Ctr., Long Beach, Calif., 1978—. Editor Jour. Environ. Pathology, Toxicology and Oncology; contbr. more than 130 articles to profl. jours. Capt. res. Navy, Israel. Recipient Searle award Congress of Chemotherapy, Vienna, 1983, medal City of Besancon, France, 1987, gold medal City of

Brussels, 1989; named Outstanding New Citizen of Yr., Citizenship Coun. Met. Chgo., 1972. Mem. World Inst. Ecology and Cancer (pres. 1993—). Avocations: travel, photography, numismatics, music, history. Office: VA Med Ctr (11-T) 5901 E 7th St Long Beach CA 90822-5201

MORAN, EDWARD KEVIN, lawyer, consultant; b. N.Y.C., Mar. 4, 1964; s. Edward Joseph and Margaret Anne (Hauff) M.; m. Janet Athanasidy, Dec. 9, 1990. BA, SUNY, Binghamton, 1986; JD, N.Y. Law Sch., 1989. Bar: Conn. 1989, N.Y. 1990, N.J. 1990. Summer assoc. N.Y.C. Police Dept. Legal Bur., 1987; mng. atty. Landau, Miller and Moran, N.Y.C., 1990—; cons. Bottom Line Group, N.Y.C., 1992—. Editor-in-chief N.Y. Law Sch. Jour. Internat. and Comparative Law, 1988-89. Mem. Conn. Bar Assn., N.Y. State Bar Assn., Assn. Trial Lawyers Am., N.Y. State Trial Lawyers Assn. Office: Landau Miller and Moran 233 Broadway New York NY 10279

MORAN, JAMES BYRON, federal judge; b. Evanston, Ill., June 20, 1930; s. James Edward and Kathryn (Horton) M.; children: John, Jennifer, Sarah, Polly; stepchildren: Katie, Cynthia, Laura, Michael. AB, U. Mich., 1952; LLB magna cum laude, Harvard U., 1957. Bar: Ill. 1958. Law clk. to judge U.S. Ct. of Appeals (2d cir.), 1957-58; assoc. Bell, Boyd, Lloyd, Haddad & Burns, Chgo, 1958-66, ptnr., 1966-79; judge U.S. Dist. Ct. (no. dist.) Ill., Chgo., 1979—. Dir. Com. on Ill. Govt., 1960-78, chmn., 1968-70; vice chmn., sec. Ill. Dangerous Drug Adv. Coun., 1967-74; dir. Gateway Found., 1969—; mem. Ill. Ho. of Reps., 1965-67; mem. Evanston City Council, 1971-75. Served with AUS, 1952-54. Mem. Chgo. Bar Assn., Chgo. Council Lawyers, Phi Beta Kappa. Clubs: Law, Legal. Home: 117 Kedzie St Evanston IL 60202-2509 Office: US Dist Ct 219 S Dearborn St Chicago IL 60604

MORAN, JAMES J., JR., lawyer; s. James J. and Marilyn A. (Sullivan) M.; m. Mary Therese Stevens, Oct. 6, 1979; children: Sean M., James E., Matthew S. AB cum laude, Boston Coll., 1975, JD, 1978. Bar: Mass. 1978, U.S. Ct. Appeals (1st cir.) 1979, U.S. Dist Ct. Mass. 1979, U.S. Tax Ct. 1979, U.S. Supreme Ct. 1982; CPCU. Assoc. Haussermann, Davison & Shattuck, Boston, 1978-84; assoc. Morrison, Mahoney & Miller, Boston, 1984-87, ptnr., 1988—; mem. legal com. Commonwealth Automobile Reinsurers, 1988; mem. CLU/CPCU adv. com. Mass. Divsn. Ins., 1988-89; v.p., gen. counsel Ind. Property-Casualty Insurers Mass. Inc., 1991—; counsel Mass. Assn. Ins. Agts., 1985-96; ins. broker, Mass.; New Eng. regional regulatory counsel Alliance of Am. Insurers, 1994—; speaker in field. Contbr. articles to profl. jours. Bd. dirs. (gubernatorial appointee) Mass. Pollution Liability Reinsurance Corp., 1988-90. Recipient econ. leadership award Orgn. New Equality, 1997. Mem. ABA (Tort and Ins. practice sect.), Internat. Assn. Def. Coun., Mass. Bar Assn., CPCU Soc. (pres. Boston chpt. 1993-94), Fedn. Regulatory Coun., Ins. Libr. Assn. Boston (trustee 1983—, pres. 1989-90). Democrat. Roman Catholic. Office: Morrison Mahoney & Miller 250 Summer St Boston MA 02210-1134

MORAN, JAMES M., automotive sales executive; b. 1918; married. Owner Courtesy Motor Sales Inc. (formerly Hudson Motor Franchise Inc.), Chgo., 1947-68; chmn. JM Family Enterprises Inc., Deerfield Beach, Fla., 1969—. Office: JM Family Enterprises 100 NW 12th Ave Deerfield Beach FL 33442-1702*

MORAN, JAMES MICHAEL, JR., astronomer, educator; b. Plainfield, N.J., Jan. 3, 1943; s. James Michael and Martha (Algermissen) M.; m. Barbara Putney Smith, Nov. 30, 1974; children: Susan Harrison, Michael Putney. BS, U. Notre Dame, 1963; SM, MIT, 1965, PhD, 1968. Mem. staff MIT Lincoln Lab., Lexington, 1968-70; sr. radio astronomer Smithsonian Astrophys. Obs., Cambridge, Mass., 1970—; prof. practice of astronomy Harvard U., Cambridge, 1979-89, prof. astronomy, 1989—; assoc. dir. Harvard-Smithsonian Ctr. Astrophysics, 1987-92; dir. Submillimeter Array Project, 1996—; Jansky lectr. Nat. Radio Astronomy Obs., 1996; trustee N.E. Radio Obs. Corp., Cambridge, 1983—. Contbr. numerous articles on radio astronomy to profl. publs. Co-recipient Rumford prize Am. Acad. Arts and Scis., 1971; recipient Sr. award Alexander von Humboldt Soc., 1993. Fellow AAAS; mem. IEEE (sr.), Am. Astron. Soc. (Pierce prize 1978), Explorers Club. Avocations: photography, flying, hiking. Achievements include development of technique of very long baseline interferometry. Home: 93 Anson Rd Concord MA 01742-5704 Office: Harvard-Smithsonian Center for Astrophysics 60 Garden St Cambridge MA 02138-1516

MORAN, JAMES PATRICK, JR., congressman, stockbroker; b. Buffalo, N.Y., May 16, 1945; s. James Patrick and Dorothy (Dwyer) M.; m. Mary Craig, Dec. 27, 1967 (div. 1974); children: Jimmy, Mary; m. Mary Howard; children: Michael, Patrick, Dorothy. BA in Econs., Coll. of Holy Cross, Worcester, Mass., 1967; postgrad., CUNY, 1967-68; MA in Pub. Adminstrn., U. Pitts., 1970. Budget analyst HEW, Washington, 1969-74; budget and fiscal policy specialist, Congl. rsch. Libr. of Congress, Washington, 1974-76; sr. staff appropriations com. U.S. Senate, Washington, 1976-79; city councilman Alexandria, Va., 1979-91, vice-mayor, 1982-84, mayor, 1985-91; investment broker A.G. Edwards & Sons, Alexandria, Va., 1979—; mem. 102nd-105th Congresses from 8th Va. dist., Washington, D.C., 1991—; mem. govt. reform & oversight coms., appropriations coms.; ranking minority mem. civil svcs. subcom.; mem. internat. rels. on internat. ops. & human rights coms. Councilman, City of Alexandria, 1979-82, vice-mayor, 1982-84, mayor, 1985—; chmn. No. Va. Transportation Bd., 1988—, United Way, 1977-79; vice chmn. Mental Health Retard and Substance Abuse Bd., 1976-78, vice chmn. D.E.O., 1976-78;dir., Met. Area Council Govts., dir. No. Va. Transp. Commn., 1985—. Recipient Outstanding Citizenship award YMCA, 1983. Mem. C. of C. (dir. 1985-86). Democrat. Roman Catholic. Home: 205 Uhler Ter Alexandria VA 22301-1551 Office: US Ho of Reps 1214 Longworth Bldg Washington DC 20515-4608*

MORAN, JEFFREY WILLIAM, safety engineer; b. Sewaren, N.J., Mar. 3, 1954; s. Raymond A. and Margaret J. (Allen) M.; m. Karen M. Anderson, Oct. 15, 1988; children: Corey Francis, Megan Justine. BS, Morningside Coll., 1976; AAS, Middlesex County Coll., 1988. Rscher. Woodbridge (N.J.) Twp., 1977-79; safety technician, rscher. Selective, Inc., East Brunswick, N.J., 1979-82; safety engr., fire chief U.S. Metals Refining, Carteret, N.J., 1982; fire protection, safety cons. J.H. Merritt, N.Y.C., 1982-85; occupational safety cons. N.J. Dept. Labor, Trenton, 1985-89; fire capt. Woodbridge Fire Dept., 1989—; guest lectr. N.J. State Fire Coll., Cranford, 1986-87. Vice pres. Woodbridge G.O.P. Club, 1987-88; mem. county com. Middlesex County Rep. Party, 1989-93; exec. officer Woodbridge Emergency Squad, 1977-88. Mem. Nat. Fire Protection Assn., Am. Soc. Safety Engrs., Am. Assn. Indsl. Hygienists, N.J. State Safety Coun., N.J. Indsl. Fire Chiefs, Internat. Soc. Fire Svc. Instrs. Republican. Episcopalian. Avocations: skiing, scuba diving. Home: 900 Terrace Ave Woodbridge NJ 07095-3226 Office: Woodbridge Fire Hdqrs 418 School St Woodbridge NJ 07095-2935

MORAN, JERRY, congressman; m. Robba A. Moran. Senator dist. 37 State of Kans.; mem. 105th Congress from 1st Kans dist., 1997—. Republican. Home: 2758 Thunderbird Dr Hays KS 67601-1403 Office: 1217 Longworth Washington DC 20515-1601*

MORAN, JOAN JENSEN, physical education and health educator; b. Chgo., Sept. 25, 1952; d. Axel Fred and Mary J. (Maes) J.; m. Gregory Keith Moran. BS in Edn., Western Ill. U., 1974; MS in Edn., No. Ill. U., 1978. Cert. tchr., Ill. Tchr., coach East Coloma Sch., Rock Falls, Ill., 1974—; part-time recreation specialist Woodhaven Lakes, Sublette, Ill., 1975-79; cons. Ill. State Bd. Edn., Springfield, 1984—; instr. NDEITA, Ill., 1988—; facilitator Project Wild, Ill., 1990—. Instr. ARC, Rock Falls, 1978—, Am. Heart Assn., Rock Falls, 1978—; exec. bd. East Coloma Cmty. Club; fitness del. to Russia and Hungary, 1992; cons. Alcohol Awareness & Occupant Restraint Ill. State Bd. Edn., Substance Abuse Guidance Edn. Com., Rock Falls Drug Free Cmty. Grant com., Whiteside County CPR Coord. com. Recipient Western Ill. U. Alumni Achievement award, 1993, Western Ill. Master Tchr. award, 1993, Svc. award Ill. Assn. Health, Phys. Edn., Recreation and Dance, 1991, 92, Outstanding Young Woman award, 1986, Phys. Educator of Yr. award, 1988; named Mid. Sch. Phys. Edn. Tchr. of Yr. Midwest AAHPERD, 1993, Ill. Assn. Health, Phys. Edn., Recreation and Dance, 1992, Gov.'s Coun. Health and Phys. Edn. award, 1991, Am. Tchr. of Yr. award Walt Disney Co., 1993, Excel award ISBE, 1995, finalist Ill. Tchr. of Yr., 1996. Mem. AAHPERD, NEA, Ill. Assn. Health, Phys. Edn., Recreation and Dance (v.p. teenage youth 1988-90, pres. 1994, past pres., conv. coord. 1995, Honor Fellow award 1996), No. Dist. Ill. Assn. Health, Phys. Edn., Recreation and Dance, Ill. Edn. Assn. (newsletter editor 1984-85, exec. bd. 1985-90, treas. 1985-90), East Coloma Edn. Assn. (pres., pub. rels., v.p. 1993-94, Environ. Edn. Assn. Ill. Democrat. Lutheran. Avocations: skiing, hiking, biking, reading, traveling. Home: 1903 E 41st St Sterling IL 61081-9449

MORAN, JOHN, religious organization administrator; b. Oct. 4, 1935; m. Retha Jean Patrick; children: John II, James, Helen. Missionary, Nigeria, 1963-68; pastor, 1969-87; vice dist. supt. Missionary Ch., Ft. Wayne, Ind., 1977-81, pres., 1987—. Author: Joy in a Roman Jail and Taking the High Ground. Mem. Nat. Assn. Evang. (mem. exec. bd. 1987—), Nat. Assn. Evang./Nat. Black Evang. Assn. (com. on racial reconciliation 1995—). Office: Missionary Ch PO Box 9127 3811 Vanguard Dr Fort Wayne IN 46899-9127

MORAN, JOHN ARTHUR, oil company executive; b. L.A., Mar. 22, 1932; s. Benjamin Edward and Louise (Chisholm) M.; m. Mary Darlene Whittaker, Aug. 14, 1954 (div. Oct. 1984); children—Kelli, Marisa, Elizabeth. B.S., U. Utah, 1954; postgrad., NYU, 1958-59, U. So. Calif., 1959-60. Assoc. Blyth & Co., Inc, N.Y.C. and Los Angeles, 1958-64; v.p. Blyth & Co., Inc, Los Angeles, 1964-67; v.p. Dyson-Kissner Corp., N.Y.C., 1967-74, exec. v.p., 1974-75, pres., 1975-84, chmn., 1984-90; chmn. exec. com. Dyson-Kissner-Moran, N.Y.C., 1990-94; bd. dirs. Bessemer Securities, Rutherford Moran Oil Corp., The Coleman Co. Chmn. Rep. Nat. Fin. Com., 1993-95; mem. nat. adv. bd. U. Utah. Lt. USNR, 1955-58. Mem. Chief Execs. Orgn. Republican. Roman Catholic. Clubs: Metropolitan, Racquet and Tennis (N.Y.C.); Larchmont Yacht (N.Y.); Winged Foot Golf, (Mamaroneck, N.Y.), Vintage Club, Indian Wells Club (Calif.).

MORAN, JOHN BERNARD, government official; b. Saginaw, Mich., Nov. 26, 1936; s. Leo Lewis and Marie Katherine (Langley) M.; m. Diann Marie Markey, May 20, 1963 (div.); m. Barbara Jane Livingston, Aug. 18, 1978; children—Leslie Marie, Leanne Rene, Jeffrey John. B.S. in Metall. Engring., Ill. Inst. Tech., 1959. Sr. automotive specialist Dow Chem. Co., Midland, Mich., 1962-71; program dir. research EPA, Research Triangle Park, N.C., 1971-75; dir. monitoring tech. div. EPA, Washington, 1975-76; dir. div. safety research Nat. Inst. for Occupational Safety and Health, Ctrs. for Disease Control, USPHS, HHS, Morgantown, W.Va., 1976-77, 83-88; dir. research and devel. safety products div. Am. Optical Corp., Southbridge, Mass., 1977-80; v.p., dir. ops. Geomet, Inc., Rockville, Md., 1980-83; program dir. Hartford Engring. Tech., Inc., Windsor, Conn., 1988; assoc. dir. health and safety laborers Associated Gen. Contractors, 1988-89; dir. safety and health Laborers Health and Safety Fund, 1989-95; spl. asst. to dep. asst. sec. Worker Health and Safety U.S. Dept. Energy, Washington, 1995; dir. policy OSHA, U.S. Dept. Labor, Washington, 1996; expert cons. to asst. sec. OSHA, Washington, 1996—; mem. Nat. Mine Health Rsch. Adv. Com., Atlanta, 1980-84; govt. del. ILO, Geneva, 1985; mem. Nat. Adv. Com. on Constrn. Safety and Health, 1985-88, 92-95, Bur. Labor Stats. Rsch., 1991-95, hazardous material transp. info. com. NAS, 1991-93, Hazardous Materials Control Rsch. Inst.; chmn. lead subcom. Bldg. Constrn. Trades Dept., 1991-95; adj. asst. prof. mech. engring. W.Va. U., 1985-88; vis. ext. prof. U. Conn., Storrs, 1988-90; mem. Fed. Facilities Environ. Restoration Com., constrn. com. A 10 Am. Nat. Stds. Inst.; co-chair EPA-Labor Superfund Task Force, 1990-95; mem. nat. lead task force HUD, 1993-95; programs mgr. operating engrs. Nat. NAZMAT Progam, Beaver, W.Va., 1996—; cons., expert witness. Patentee; contbr. articles to profl. jours, chpts. to books. Mem. Task Force on Hazardous Materials, Rockville, Md., 1983. chmn. Nat. Inst. Health Sci., 1990. Served to capt. USMC, 1959-65. Recipient Bronze medal for commendable service EPA, 1974, Commitment to Life award Nat. Safe Workplace Inst., 1988. Mem. Internat. Soc. Respiratory Protection (pres. 1985-87, bd. dirs. 1987-89), Am. Conf. Govtl. Indsl. Hygienists. Roman Catholic. Home: 1605 Savannah Hwy North SC 29112-9625

MORAN, JOHN HENRY, JR., retired electrical engineer, consultant; b. Phila., Sept. 22, 1923; s. John Henry and Mary Joseph (Sheehan) M.; m. Jane Miriam Daly, June 29, 1946; children—Terrence, Kathleen, Michael, Patrick. B.S.E.E., Case Western Res. U., 1947. Profl. engr., N.Y., Ohio. Devel. engr. Allis-Chalmers, West Allis, Wis., 1947-55; engr. Lapp Insulator, LeRoy, N.Y., 1955-63, chief elec. engr., 1963-86, mgr. bushing engring., 1977-86; prin. cons., 1986—. Author: High Voltage Bushings, 1989; coauthor: Electrostatics and Its Applications, 1973; author tech. papers; patentee. Active Genesee Boy Scouts Am., 1936-88. Served with USN, 1942-46, U.S., ETO. Fellow IEEE (life); mem. Electrostatic Soc. Am. (founding, v.p. 1978-82). Republican. Roman Catholic. Home and Office: 9053 Roanoke Rd Stafford NY 14143-9524

MORAN, JOHN JOSEPH, retired food and beverage company executive; b. Scranton, Pa., Sept. 1, 1916; s. Edward Francis and Mary Ellen (Conlin) M.; divorced; children: Mary Anne Moran Greenall, Patricia, Cynthia (dec.). B.S., Rutgers U., 1942; grad., Advanced Mgmt. Program, Harvard, 1964. C.P.A., N.J. With Wiley, Block & White (C.P.A.'s), Paterson, N.J., 1937-42, Wright Aero. Corp., Paterson, 1933-37; br. chief War Assets Adminstrn., 1946-50; asst. controller J.P. Stevens & Co., 1950-59; controller Heublein Inc., 1959—, treas., 1968—, v.p., 1971-82, asst. to chmn., 1977-82, cons., 1982-86. Served to lt. comdr. USNR, 1942-46. Mem. Fin. Execs. Inst., Am. Inst. C.P.A.s, Harvard Advanced Mgmt. Assn. Catholic. Home: 3 Sawmill Xing Wethersfield CT 06109-1345 Office: 9 Potter Xing Wethersfield CT 06109-1327 *I've tried to run my life as follows: Do the best job possible: be honest, conscientious, and kind to people; try to help others, and stay healthy.*

MORAN, JOHN THOMAS, JR., lawyer; b. Oak Park, Ill., Mar. 15, 1943; s. John T. and Corinne Louise (Dire) M.; m. Catherine Casey Pyne, May 16, 1981; 1 child, Sean Michael Pyne-Moran. AB cum laude, U. Notre Dame, 1965; JD, Georgetown U., 1968. Bar: Ill. 1969, Colo. 1976, U.S. Supreme Ct. 1973. Chief appeals div. Pub. Defender Cook County, Ill., 1970-82; gen. counsel Pub. Defender Cook County, Chgo., 1984-86; chief litigation atty. Frank & Flaherty, Chgo., 1982; cons. ABA, Chgo., 1982-83; sole practice Chgo., 1986-93; founder Law Offices of John Thomas Moran;, 1993-95. Editor: Gideon Revisited, 1983. Bd. dirs. Lawyers for the Creative Arts, 1973—. Ford Found. grantee Internat. Common Law Colloquium, London, 1976, NEH grantee, Harvard Law Sch., 1977. Mem. Ill. State Bar Assn., Appellate Lawyers Assn., Nat. Legal Aid and Defenders Assn., Am. Soc. Internat. Law, Georgetown U. Law Ctr. Alumni Soc., Sorin Soc. U. Notre Dame. Avocation: sailing. Home: 930 Oakwood Ave Wilmette IL 60091-3320 Office: John T Moran & Assocs 309 W Washington St Ste 909 Chicago IL 60606-3200

MORAN, MARTIN JOSEPH, fundraising company executive; b. Bklyn., Nov. 3, 1930; s. Dominick and Mary (Lydon) M.; m. Mary Therese Schofield, June 5, 1954; children: Martin Joseph, John P., Maureen M., Thomas S., Robert P., William M., Maria M. BA, St. John's U., 1952. Profl. fundraising cons., 1956—; founder Martin J. Moran Co., Inc., N.Y.C., 1964, pres., 1964-74, chmn. bd., 1974—. Mem. Cardinal's Com. for Edn., N.Y.C., 1970-79, Cardinal's Com. for Laity Archdiocese N.Y., 1979—, Am. Revolution Bicentennial Commn., Oyster Bay, N.Y.; mem. Massapequa Park (N.Y.) Bd. Zoning Appeals, 1972-84, chmn., 1978-84; mem. Massapequa Park Ethics Commn., 1969-72; trustee Notre Dame Coll., S.I., 1969-72, La Salle Acad., N.Y.C., 1971-87; mem. pres.'s council Cath. U.P.R., Ponce, 1966-71. Served as aviator USMC, 1952-56. Decorated knight Order Holy Sepulchre, Pope Paul VI, 1968, Knight of Malta, Pope Paul VI, 1973; recipient Pietas medal St. John's U., N.Y., 1988; bd. councilors, sec., treas. Equestrian Order Holy Sepulchre of Jerusalem, 1990—, sec.-treas. 1990-93, pres., 1993—. Mem. Navy League, Navy Hist. Assn., St. John's U. Alumni Assn. (pres. 1987-94), Am. Assn. Fund Raising Counsel (bd. dirs. 1970—), Nassau County Hist. Soc., Friendly Sons of St. Patrick. Roman Catholic. Club: Madison Square Garden (N.Y.C.); Lost Tree Club (North Palm Beach, Fla.), Old Port Yacht Club. Lodge: KC. Home: 1300 Lakeshore Dr Massapequa Park NY 11762-1764 also: 677 Village Rd No Palm Beach FL 33408-3329 Office: Martin J Moran Co 1 Penn Plz New York NY 10119

MORAN, MICHAEL LEE, physical therapist, computer consultant; b. Batavia, N.Y., Sept. 26, 1955; s. John Henry and Jane Miriam (Daly) M.; m. Jeanne Marie Grunau, Oct. 14, 1978; children: Katie, Michael L. BS, SUNY, Stony Brook, 1978; MS, U. Scranton, Pa., 1983; ScD, Nova U., Ft. Lauderdale, 1990. Staff/chief phys. therapist Allied Svcs. for the Handicapped, Scranton, Pa., 1978-81; chief phys. therapist Mercy Hosp., Wilkes-Barre, Pa., 1981-83; staff phys. therapist Spinks & Violand, Monticello, N.Y., 1983-84; dir. phys. therapy Moran Phys. Therapy, Scranton, 1984-88, Manor Health Care, Inc., Kingston, Pa., 1988-92, Coll. Misericordia, Dallas, Pa., 1992—; cons. Phys. Therapy Online Network, Shawnee Mission, Kans., 1989-92; article abstractor Jour. Am. Phys. Therapy Assn., 1983—. Assoc. editor Issues on Aging, 1992-94, editor, 1994-96; contbr. articles to profl. jours. Mem. Nat. Eagle Scout Assn. Avocations: computers, fishing. Office: Coll Misericordia Dept Phys Therapy 301 Lake St Dallas PA 18612-1008

MORAN, PATRICIA EILEEN, special education educator; b. Abington, Pa., May 31, 1960; d. Francis Joseph Moran, Jr. and Kathryn Sydney Burness. BS, West Chester State U., 1983; MA in Reading, Calif. State U., San Bernardino, 1990; reading specialist credential, Calif. State U., 1992. Cert. spl. edn. tchr., Pa., Ca.; cert. reading specialist, Calif. Devel. specialist mentally handicapped Community Found., Perkasie, Pa., 1980-83, group home supr., 1983-84; tchr., seriously emotionally disturbed children Martin Luther King Sch., Plymouth Meeting, Pa., 1984-85; tchr. learning handicapped children Ramona Elem. Sch., Moreno Valley Unified Sch. Dist., Calif., 1985—; tchr. learning handicapped children Seneca Elem. Sch., Moreno Valley, Calif., 1993-96, 1st grade tchr., 1996—; mem. adv. bd. Pub. Edn. for Everyone in Regular Schs., Moreno Valley, 1990—, pilot adv. bd. Moreno Valley Unified Sch. Dist., 1992—; advisor, cons. Inclusion Model Pilot Program, Moreno Valley, 1991—. Choir mem. Newman Ctr., Riverside, Calif., 1990—. Mem. Inland Empire Coun. Internat. Reading Assn. (Reading award Teaching 1992), Internat. Reading Assn., Kappa Delta Pi. Democrat. Avocations: reading, travel, singing, horseback riding, photography. Home: 315B Sonora St Redlands CA 92373-6023 Office: Seneca Elem Sch 11615 Wordsworth Rd Moreno Valley CA 92557-8451

MORAN, PATRICIA GENEVIEVE, corporate executive; b. Evanston, Ill., July 26, 1945; d. James M.; children: Christine Coyle, Thomas Beddia, Donald Beddia. Attended, Marquette U. Pers. mgr. Sesco, 1983-84, dir. corp. transp., assoc. rels. dir., 1984-85, v.p. assoc. rels., 1985-88; group v.p. sales Southeast Toyota, Deerfield Beach, Fla., 1988-89, ceo., 1989-94; v.p. H.R. JM Family Enterprises, Inc., Deerfield Beach, pres., 1989-94, now CEO. Dir. Beacon Coun., Miami, Fla., 1992—, Broward Econ. Devel., Ft. Lauderdale, Fla., 1991—, Youth Automotive Tng. Ctr., Hollywood, Fla., 1985—. Named Top 50 Working Women by Working Woman's Mag. Mem. Ft. Lauderdale C. of C. (dir. 1991—), Tower Club, The Haven (adv. bd. 1994-95). Office: JM Family Enterprises 100 NW 12th Ave Deerfield Beach FL 33442-1702*

MORAN, PAUL JAMES, journalist, columnist; b. Buffalo, July 20, 1947; s. Paul James and Frances (Sciortino) M.; m. Kim Maldiner, Mar. 17, 1975 (div. July 1979); m. Colette Stass (div. Jan. 1997); 1 child, Heather. Student, SUNY, Buffalo, 1965-67, Millard Fillmore Coll., 1971-73. Sports editor Tonawanda News, North Tonawanda, N.Y., 1972-75; writer/columnist Fort Lauderdale (Fla.) News/Sun Sentinel, 1975-85, N.Y. Newsday, Melville, 1985—; cons. Green Country Racing Assn., Tulsa, 1983-85. Author: (with others) Crown Jewels of Thoroughbred Racing; contbr. articles to mags. and newspapers. Sgt. USAF, 1967-71. Recipient Eclipse award Thoroughbred Racing Assn., 1985, 90, Disting. Writing award Am. Soc. Newspaper Editors, 1990, Deadline Writing award Soc. Silurians, 1990, Deadline Reporting award L.I. Press Club, 1991, Disting. Sports Writing award N.Y. Newspaper Pubs. Assn., 1992, (with others) Journalism collection Best Newspaper Writing 1991. Mem. N.Y. Turf Writers' Assn. (pres. 1990-92, sec.-treas. 1992-94), Nat. Turf Writers' Assn. (bd. dirs. 1987-90). Republican. Avocations: photography, art collecting. Home: 40 Carnation Ave Floral Park NY 11001-2107 Office: Newsday 235 Pinelawn Rd Melville NY 11747-4226

MORAN, PHILIP DAVID, lawyer; b. Lynn, Mass., June 3, 1937; s. J. Francis and Margaret M. (Shanahan) M.; m. Carole A. Regan, May 12, 1962; children: Maura F., Philip David. A.B., Holy Cross Coll., 1958; Ed.M., Salem State Coll., 1961; J.D., Suffolk U., 1968. Bar: Mass. 1968, U.S. Dist. Ct. Mass., 1972, U.S. Supreme Ct., 1988, U.S. Ct. Appeals (1st cir.), 1993. House counsel Viatron Computer Systems Corp., Burlington, Mass., 1968-71; ptnr. Kane & Moran, Lynn, Mass., 1972-78; pvt. practice law Salem, Mass., 1978—; asst. dist. atty. Essex County (Mass.), 1974-78. Bd. dirs. Nat. Right to Life Inc., 1977-83, 87—, treas., 1981-83; Contbg. author: Encyclopedia of Biomedical Policy, 1995. Bd. dir. Mass. Citizens for Life, 1973—, pres. 1979-80, chmn. 1991-93. mem. Salem Conservation Commn., 1980-89, chmn., 1982-89; mem. pres.'s coun. Holy Cross Coll., 1985—; mem. Nat. Inst. Trial Advocacy U. Colo., 1973; gen. chmn bicentenary com. Maynooth Coll., Boston, 1994-96. With U.S. Army, 1960-66. Recipient Ignatius O'Connor Pro Life award, 1994, Gold medal St. Patrick Maynooth Coll., Ireland, 1996, Knight of Malta, 1997. Mem. Mass. Bar Assn., Salem Bar Assn., Lynn Bar Assn., Am. Trial Lawyers Assn., Nat. Acad. Elder Law Attys., Murray Inn of Ct., Pro Life Legal Def. Fund (pres. 1997), Hiberman Civil Rights Coalition (bd. dirs. 1997), Irish Am. Partnership. Roman Catholic. Avocations: swimming, reading, gardening, boating, photography. Home: 415 Lafayette St Salem MA 01970-5337 Office: 265 Essex St Salem MA 01970-3400

MORAN, RACHEL, lawyer, educator; b. Kansas City, Mo., June 27, 1956; d. Thomas Albert and Josephine (Portillo) M. AB, Stanford U., 1978; JD, Yale U., 1981. Bar: Calif. 1984. Assoc Heller, Ehrman, White & McAuliffe, San Francisco, 1982-83; prof. law U. Calif., Berkeley, 1984—; vis. prof. UCLA Sch. Law, 1988, Stanford (Calif.) U. Law Sch., 1989, N.Y.U. Sch. of Law, 1996, U. Miami Sch. Law, 1997; ann. civil rights lectr. Creighton U. Sch. Law, Omaha, 1989; Pirsig lectr. William Mitchell Coll. St. Paul, 1989, others; mem. steering com. Nat. Resource Ctr., Berkeley, 1988-89; chair Chicano/Latino Policy Project, 1993-96. Contbr. numerous articles to profl. jours. Grantee Joseph and Polly Harris Trust Inst. Govtl. Studies, Berkeley, 1987-89, Faculty Devel. U. Calif., Berkeley, 1985-86; recipient Disting. Tchg. award U. Calif. Mem. ABA, AAUP, Calif. Bar Assn., Phi Beta Kappa. Democrat. Unitarian. Avocations: jogging, aerobics, reading, listening to music. Office: U Calif Sch Law Boalt Hall Berkeley CA 94720

MORAN, ROBERT FRANCIS, JR., library director; b. Cleve., May 3, 1938; s. Robert Francis Sr. and Jeanette (Mulholland) M.; m. Judith Mary Pacer, Dec. 28, 1968; children: Mary Jeanette, Catherine, Margaret. BA, Cath. U. Am., Washington, 1961, MLS, 1965; MBA, U. Chgo., 1976. Head librarian St. Patrick's Sem., Menlo Park, Calif., 1965-69; coordinator and reference librarian U. Chgo., 1969-72; serials librarian U. Ill., Chgo., 1972-78, acquisitions librarian, 1977-80; dir. library services Ind. U. Northwest, Gary, 1980—, asst. vice chancellor tech., 1991—; v.p., sec., treas. Northwest Ind. Area Library Services Authority, Merrillville, 1982-91. Contbr. articles to profl jours. Mem. ALA, Libr. Adminstrn. and Mgmt. Assn. (com. chmn. 1981-86, sect. chmn. 1986-88, chmn. program com. 1988-91, chair nominating com. 1991-92, networked info. discussion group 1994—). Democrat. Roman Catholic. Office: Ind Univ NW Library 3400 Broadway Gary IN 46408-1101

MORAN, THOMAS FRANCIS, chemistry educator; b. Manchester, N.H., Dec. 11, 1936; s. Francis Leo and Mamie Marie (Morin) M.; m. Joan Elinor Belliveau, June 25, 1960; children: Dorothy, Michael, Linda, Mary. BA, St. Anselm's Coll., 1958; PhD, Notre Dame U., 1962. Teaching and rsch. fellow Notre Dame U., South Bend, Ind., 1958-62; USAEC postdoctoral fellow Brookhaven Nat. Lab., Upton, N.Y., 1962-64; staff scientist Brookhaven Nat. Lab., 1964-66; asst. prof. Ga. Inst. Tech., Atlanta, 1966-68; assoc. prof. Ga. Inst. Tech., 1968-72, prof. chemistry dept., 1972—. Contbr. articles to profl. jours. Danforth fellow Danforth Found. Mem. Am. Chem. Soc., Am. Physical Soc., Sigma Xi (award). Home: 2324 Annapolis Ct NE Atlanta GA 30345-3803 Office: Chemistry Dept Ga Inst Tech Atlanta GA 30332

MORAN, THOMAS HARRY, university administrator; b. Milw., Oct. 21, 1937; s. Harry Edward and Edna Agnes Moran; BS, U. Wis., 1964, MA, 1972, PhD, 1974; m. Barbara Ellen Saklad, June 10, 1969; children: David Thomas, Karen Ellen. Dir. capital budgeting Wis. Dept. Adminstrn., 1962-64; exec. dir. Wis. Higher Ednl. Aids Bd., 1964-69; spl. cons. tax policy Wis.

Dept. Revenue, 1973-74; dep. dir. Wis. Manpower Coun., Office of Gov., 1974-76; v.p. bus. and fin., treas. U. Detroit, 1976-78; exec. assoc. v.p. health affairs U. So. Calif., L.A., 1979-87; v.p. bus. affairs, 1988—. USN fellow, 1957-59; U.S. Office Edn. rsch. fellow, 1973. Mem. Am. Assn. Higher Edn., Phi Kappa Phi. Office: U So Calif 200 Town & Gown University Park Los Angeles CA 90007

MORAN, TIMOTHY, newspaper editor; b. N.Y.C., Jan. 1, 1952; s. Cyril Peter and Joan Marie (Gilbride) M.; m. Donna Marie Pasqualino, July 17, 1988; children: Derek, Christopher. BA, L.I. U., 1976, postgrad., 1976-78. Mng. editor Today's Office, Garden City, N.Y., 1977-85, Engring. Tools, Hasbrouck Heights, N.J., 1987-88; mng. editor EE Times, CMP Media Inc., Manhasset, N.Y., 1988-93, exec. editor EE Times, CMP, 1993-96; editor EE Times Online, 1996—. Office: CMP Media Inc 600 Community Dr Manhasset NY 11030-3847

MORAN, WILLIAM EDWARD, academic administrator; b. White Plains, N.Y., May 28, 1932; s. Frank Joseph and Margaret Mary (Farrell) M.; m. Barbara Carol Baillet, Apr. 20, 1963; children: Kathryn, Kevin, Colin, Christian. A.B., Princeton U., 1954; M.B.A., Harvard U., 1959; Ph.D., U. Mich., 1967. Mgmt. cons. Booz, Allen & Hamilton, N.Y.C., 1959-61; mem. adminstrv. staff Harvard U., Boston, 1961-63; asst. exec. v.p. SUNY-Stony Brook, 1966-71; chancellor Flint Campus U. Mich., 1971-79, U. N.C., Greensboro, 1979-94; sr. v.p. Connors Investor Svcs., Inc., 1994—; dir. J.P. Money Market Fund, Jefferson Pilot Money Market Fund, Greensboro, N.C. Connors Investor Services, Reading, Pa. Contbr. articles to profl. jours. Pres. So. Univ. Conf., 1987. Served with USN, 1954-57. Mem. N.C. Assn. Colls. and Univs. (pres. 1992), Princeton Club (N.Y.), Rotary. Home: 5206 Barnfield Rd Greensboro NC 27455 Office: Connors Investor Svcs Inc 1100 Berkshire Blvd Wyomissing PA 19610-1221

MORAN, WILLIAM MADISON, fundraising executive; b. Albany, Ky., Apr. 15, 1948; s. Marvin Madison and Eula Pickens (Duvall) M.; m. Mary Ruth Shanks, June 5, 1971; 1 child, Alice Janette. Student, U. Ky., 1966-68; BS, Tenn. Technol. U., 1971. Field rep. March of Dimes, Nashville, 1972-77; state dir. Nat. Found. March of Dimes, Nashville, 1977; dir. devel. East Tenn. Children's Hosp., Knoxville, 1977-84; exec. dir. St. Vincent's Found. Ala., Birmingham, 1984—; founding participant, Children's Miracle Network Telethon, 1982-84. Co-founder, bd. dirs. Ronald McDonald House, Knoxville, 1982-84; bd. dirs. Tanasi coun. Girl Scouts U.S.A., Knoxville, 1981-84, Cahaba coun. Girl Scouts U.S.A., Birmingham, 1986-94; bd. dirs. Cath. Housing Authority, Birmingham, 1989—, Seton Inst. for Internat. Devel., 1994—. Recipient Thanks badge Girl Scouts Am., 1992, 94. Fellow Assn. Healthcare Philanthropy (regional dir. 1986-88, bd. dirs. 1987-88, chmn. 1992 internat. conf.); mem. Soc. Fundraising Execs. (advanced cert., pres. Tenn. chpt. 1983, pres. Ala. chpt. 1989, 1990, bd. dirs. 1989-94, asst. treas. 1990, exec. com. 1990-94, chmn. fin. com. 1991, 92, 93, treas. 1992, 93, vice chair 1994, Outstanding Fundraising Exec. Ala. 1988), Optimists (Knoxville), Kiwanis (Birmingham), Phi Delta Theta. Methodist. Avocations: photography, flying, history of sci. and technology. Home: 3712 Spring Valley Rd Birmingham AL 35223-1526 Office: St Vincent's Found 2800 8th Ave N Ste 304 Birmingham AL 35203

MORAND, BLAISE E., bishop; b. Tecumseh, Ont., Can., Sept. 12, 1932. Ordained priest Roman Cath. Ch., 1958. Ordained coadjutor bishop Diocese of Prince Albert, Sask., Can., 1981, bishop, 1983—. Office: Diocese of Prince Albert, 1415 4th Ave W, Prince Albert, SK Canada S6V 5H1*

MORAND, PETER, investment company executive; b. Montreal, Que., Can., Feb. 11, 1935; s. Frank and Rose Alice (Fortier) M.; m. Dawn McKell, Oct. 10, 1957; children: Clifford, Tanya. BSc with honors, Bishop's U., Lennoxville, Que., 1956, DCL (hon.), 1991; PhD, McGill U., Montreal, 1959. NATO postdoctoral fellow Imperial Coll., London, 1959-61; sr. rsch. chemist Ayerst Labs., Montreal, 1961-63; asst. prof. chemistry U. Ottawa, Can., 1963-67, acad. asst. vice rector, 1968-71, dean sci.and engring., 1976-81, prof. chemistry, dir. rsch. svcs., 1981-87, vice rector univ. R&D, 1987-90; pres. Natural Scis. and Engring. Rsch. Coun., Ottawa, 1990-95; pres., CEO Can. Sci. and Tech. Growth Fund, 1996—; bd. dirs. Ottawa Life Scis. Coun., Can. Bacterial Diseases Network. Contbr. articles to profl. jours.; patentee in field. Trustee B.C. Applied Systems Inst., Vancouver, Can., 1990—. Natural Scis. and Engring. Rsch. Coun. grantee, 1964-90. Fellow Chem. Inst. Can.; mem. Soc. of Rsch. Adminstrs., Rideau Club, Cercle Univ. Office: 26 Central Ave, Ottawa, ON Canada K2P OM9

MORANDI, JOHN ARTHUR, JR., nursing administrator, educator, nurse; b. Mass., Feb. 26, 1952; s. John Arthur and Mary Elizabeth (DiPersio) M. AAS in Nursing, No. Va. Community Coll., 1974; BSN, DePaul U., 1984, MS in Nursing, 1988; postgrad. in edn., Va. Poly. Inst. and State U., 1990. RN, Va., D.C. Nursing supr., staff nurse Alexandria (Va.) Hosp.; part-time faculty mem. Marymount U., Arlington, Cath. U. Am., Washington. Mem. AACN, DePaul U. Nursing Alumni Assn., Sigma Theta Tau (scholar).

MORANG, DIANE JUDY, writer, television producer, business entrepreneur; b. Chgo., Apr. 28, 1942; d. Anthony Thomas Morang and Laura Ann Andrzejczak. Student, Stevens Finishing Sch., Chgo., 1956, Fox Bus. Coll., 1959-60, UCLA, 1967-69. Mem. staff Chgo. Sun Times, Daily News, 1957, Drury Ln. Theatre, Chgo., 1961-62, AM Show ABC-TV, Hollywood, Calif., 1970-71; chair, mem. judging panel Regional Emmy awards, 1989, judge 2 categories, 1985. Author: How to Get into the Movies, 1978; author, creator: The Rainbow Keyboard, 1991; creator: The Best Kids' Show in the World; contbr. numerous articles to newspapers, mags. Bd. dirs., mem. scholarship com. Ariz. Bruins UCLA Alumni Assn.; mem. Nat. Mus. Women in the Arts, Washington. Mem. NATAS (mem. Hollywood Emmy-award winning team Hollywood, Calif. 1971), Ariz. Authors Assn. (bd. dirs.). Roman Catholic.

MORANT, RICARDO BERNARDINO, psychology educator; b. New Britain, Conn., Feb. 13, 1926; s. J. Ramon and Rosario (Ciscar) M.; m. G. Francisca Giner, Dec. 26, 1955; children—Ramon, Francisca, Dolores, Ricardo. A.B., Harvard, 1948; postgrad., Wesleyan Coll., Middletown, Conn., 1948-49; M.A., Clark U., 1950, Ph.D., 1952. Faculty Brandeis U., Waltham, Mass., 1952—; prof. psychology Brandeis U., 1965—, Fierman prof. psychology, 1968—, chmn. dept., 1962-73; chmn. Sch. Social Scis., 1982-86, 94-96; chmn. Latin Am. Studies Brandeis U., 1984-91; Prin. investigator NIMH, Spencer Found., Rothman Found. 1960—; spl. research space perception, body orientation. Bd. dirs. Coun. Pub. Schs., 1970-73; mem. steering com. Sensory Aid Eval. and Devel. Ctr., MIT, 1963-67; chmn. bd. trustees Hiatt Ednl. Programs, 1982-94. Served with USNR, 1946-48. Fellow APA; mem. Ea. New Eng. Psychol. Assn., Psychonomic Soc. Home: 35 Cliff Rd Wellesley MA 02181-3001 Office: Brandeis Univ Waltham MA 02154

MORARDINI, MICHAEL ROBERT, professional baseball player; b. Kittanning, Pa., Apr. 22, 1966. Student, U. Ind. Second baseman Phila. Phillies Nat. League Baseball Team, 1990—. Mem. U.S. Olympic Baseball Team, 1988, Phila. Phillies Nat. League Champaions, 1993; named to Nat. League All-Star Team, 1995. Office: Phila Phillies PO Box 7575 Philadelphia PA 19101*

MORATH, INGE, photographer; b. Graz, Austria, May 27, 1923; d. Edgar Eugen and Mathilde (Wiesler) M.; m. Arthur Miller, Feb. 1962; 1 child, Rebecca Augusta. BA, U. Berlin; DFA (hon.), U. Hartford, 1984. Formerly translator and editor ISB Feature Sect., Salzburg and Vienna, Austria; later editor lit. monthly Der Optmist, Vienna and Austrian editor Heute Mag.; former free-lance writer for mags. and Red White Red Radio Network; with Magnum Photos, Paris and N.Y.C., 1952—; mem. Magnum Photos, 1953—; tchr. photography course Cooper Union, 2 years; lectr. at various univs. including U. Miami, U. Mich. Exhibited photographs one-woman shows Wuehrle Gallery, Vienna, 1956, Leitz Gallery, N.Y.C., 1958, N.Y. Overseas Press Club, 1959, Chgo. Art Inst., 1964, Oliver Woolcott Meml. Library, Litchfield, Conn., 1969, Art Mus., Andover, Mass., 1971, U. Miami, 1972, U. Mich., 1973, Carlton Gallery, N.Y.C., 1976, Neikrug Galleries, N.Y.C., 1976, 79, Grand Rapids (Mich.) Art Mus., 1979, Mus. Modern Art, Vienna, 1980, Kunsthaus, Zurich, Switzerland, 1980, Burden Gallery Aperture Inc., N.Y.C., 1987, Moscow Ctr. Photojournalists, 1988, Sala del Canal, Madrid, 1988, Cathedral, Norwich, Eng., 1989, Am. Cultural Ctr., Brussels, 1989, Kolbe Mus., Berlin, 1991, Mus. Rupertinum, Salzburg, 1991; retrospective Neue Galerie, Linz, Austria, Amerika House, Berlin, 1993, Hradčin, Prague, 1993, Royal Photographic Soc., Bath, Eng., 1994, Mus. Contemporary Art, Madrid, 1995, Book Fair, Frankfurt, 1995, Leica Gallery, N.Y.C., 1996, Mitsukosui Gallery, Tokyo, 1996; numerous group shows include Photokina, Cologne, Ger., World's Fair, Montreal, Que., Can.; represented in permanent collections Met. Mus. Art, Boston Mus. Art, Art Inst. Chgo., Bibliothèque Nationale, Paris, Kunsthaus, Zurich, Prague (Czechoslovakia) Art Mus., Rupertinum Mus., Salzburg, Austria; photographer for books Guerreà la Tristesse (Dominique Aubier), 1956, Venice Observed (Mary McCarthy), 1956, (with Yul Brynner) Bring Forth the Children (Yul Brynner), 1960, From Persia to Iran (Edouard Sablier), 1961, Tunisia (Claude Roy, Paul Sebag), 1961, Le Masque (drawings by Saul Steinberg), 1967, In Russia (Arthur Miller), 1969, East West Exercises (Ruth Bluestone Simon), 1973, Boris Pasternak: My Sister Life (O. Carlisle, translator), 1976, In the Country (Arthur Miller), 1977, Chinese Encounters (Arthur Miller), 1979, Salesman in Beijing (Arthur Miller), 1984, Images of Vienna (Barbara Frischmuth, Pavel Kohout, Andre Heller, Arthur Miller), 1981, Inge Morath: Portraits, 1987, In Our Time, 1990, Russian Journal (E. Yevtushenko, A. Voznesensky, O. Andreyev Carlisle), 1991, Inge Morath: Fotografien 1952-92, Inge Morath: Spain in the 50s, 1994, The Danube, 1995; editor, co-photographer books Paris/Magnum, Aperture Inc., biography Grosse Photographen unserer Zeit, 1975; contbr. numerous photographs to European, U.S., S. Am., Japanese mags., and to numerous anthologies including Life series on photography and photographic yearbooks. Recipient Great Austrian State Prize for photography, 1991, various citations for shows. Mem. Am. Soc. Mag. Photographers. Home: Tophet Rd 232 Tophet Rd Roxbury CT 06783 Office: Magnum Photos 151 W 25th St New York NY 10001-7204

MORATH, MAX EDWARD, entertainer, composer, writer; b. Colorado Springs, Colo., Oct. 1, 1926; s. Frederic Palmer and Gladys Hester Nancy (Ramsell) M.; m. Norma Loy Tackitt, Oct. 23, 1953 (div. 1992); children: Kathryn, Christine, Frederic; m. Diane Fay Skomars, May 24, 1993. BA in English, Colo. Coll., 1948; postgrad., Stanford NBC-Radio-TV Inst., Palo Alto, Calif., 1951; MA in Am. Studies, Columbia U., 1996. Touring nationally in concerts and theater The Ragtime Man, 1997—; recordings on Epic, RCA, Vanguard, SoloArt, Omega, Premier. Mem. Broadcast Music, Inc., Am. Fedn. Musicians, AFTRA, Screen Actors Guild, Actors Equity Assn. Home and Office: 100 Glen Rd Woodcliff Lk NJ 07675-7963

MORAVCSIK, JULIUS MATTHEW, philosophy educator; b. Budapest, Hungary, Apr. 26, 1931; came to U.S., 1949; s. Julius and Edith (Fleissig) M.; m. Marguerite Germain Truninger, Sept. 14, 1954; children: Adrian Clay, Peter Matthew. BA, Harvard U., 1953, PhD, 1959. Asst. prof. U. Mich., Ann Arbor, 1960-66, assoc. prof., 1966-68; prof. Stanford (Calif.) U., 1968—. Author: Understanding Language, 1975, Thought and Language, 1990, Plato and Platonism, 1992. Recipient Sr. Humanist prize Humboldt Found., 1983; fellow Ctr. Advanced Studies Behavioral Scis., 1986-87, Inst. Advanced Studies, 1988. Mem. Am. Philos. Assn. (pres. Pacific divsn. 1987-88), Am. Soc. Aesthetics (trustee 1988-92), Soc. Ancient Greek Philosophy (pres. 1989-91, bd. dirs. Jour. History Philosophy). Avocations: golf, tennis. Office: Stanford U Dept Of Philosophy Stanford CA 94305

MORAWETZ, CATHLEEN SYNGE, mathematics educator; b. Toronto, Ont., Can., May 5, 1923; came to U.S., 1945, naturalized, 1950; d. John Lighton and Elizabeth Eleanor Mabel (Allen) Synge; m. Herbert Morawetz, Oct. 27, 1945; children: Pegeen Morawetz Rubinstein, John Synge, Lida Morawetz Jeck, Nancy. BA, U. Toronto, 1945; SM, MIT, 1946; PhD, NYU, 1951; hon. degree, Ea. Mich. U., 1980, Smith Coll., 1982, Brown U., 1982, Princeton U., 1986, Duke U., 1988, N.J. Inst. Tech., 1988, U. Waterloo, 1993, U. Dublin, 1996, U. Toronto, 1996. Research assoc. Courant Inst., NYU, 1952-57, asst. prof. math., 1957-60, assoc. prof., 1960-65, prof., 1965—, assoc. dir., 1978-84, dir., 1984-88; chmn. bd. Sch. Theoretical Physics, DLAS. Editor Jour. Math. Analysis and Applications, Comms. in PDE; author articles in applications of partial differential equations, especially transonic flow and scattering theory. Trustee Princeton U., 1973-78, Sloan Found., 1980-94. Guggenheim fellow, 1967, 79; Office Naval Rsch. grantee, until 1990. Fellow AAAS; mem. NAS, Am. Math. Soc. (term trustee 1975-85, pres. 1995-97), Am. Acad. Arts and Scis., Soc. Indsl. and Applied Math. Office: 251 Mercer St New York NY 10012-1110

MORAWETZ, HERBERT, chemistry educator; b. Prague, Czechoslovakia, Oct. 16, 1915; came to U.S., 1945, naturalized, 1951; s. Richard and Frida (Glaser) M.; m. Cathleen Synge, Oct. 28, 1945; children: Pegeen Morawetz Rubinstein, John S., Lida Morawetz Jeck, Nancy B. B.A. Sci., U. Toronto, 1943, M.A. Sci., 1944; Ph.D., Poly Inst. Bklyn., 1951. With Bakelite Co., 1945-49; mem. faculty Poly. U. (formerly Poly. Inst. Bklyn.), 1951-81, prof. polymer chemistry, dir. Inst. Polymer Research, 1971-81; Inst. prof., 1981-86, Inst. prof. emeritus, 1986—; mem. materials research adv. com. NSF, 1977-80. Author: Macromolecules in Solution, 1965, rev. edit., 1975; Polymers: The Origins and Growth of a Science, 1985; mem. editorial bd. Jour. Polymer Sci., 1969-89; contbr. articles to profl. jours. Recipient Heyrovsky medal Czechoslovakia Acad. Sci., 1990; Case Centenary scholar, 1980; Whitby Meml. lectr. U. Akron, 1984. Fellow AAAS; mem. Am. Chem. Soc. (award in polymer chemistry 1986, assoc. editor Macromolecules 1991—). Home: 246 W 12th St New York NY 10014-1912 Office: 333 Jay St Brooklyn NY 11201-2907

MORAWITZ, HANS, physicist; b. Wiener Neustadt, Austria, Feb. 6, 1935; came to U.S., 1955; s. Johann and Josephine (Dinda) M.; m. Terry Lynn Langhorne, July 27, 1963; children: Werner, Dana. BS summa cum laude, Stanford U., 1956, PhD, 1963. Sr. lectr. Monash U., Melbourne, Australia, 1965-66; rsch. assoc. U. Vienna, Austria, 1966-67; staff mem. IBM Rsch. Div., San Jose, Calif., 1963-65, 67—; vis. prof. dept. physics Ulm (Fed. Rep. of Germany) U., 1982, 91, 92, 96, Inst. for Advanced Study, Nat. U., Canberra, Australia, 1984, Bayreuth (Fed. Rep. of Germany) U., 1986. Co-author: Mechanisms of Conventional and High Temperature Super Conductivity, 1993; co-editor: Vibrations at Surfaces, 1982; contbr. over 80 articles to profl. jours. Pres., bd. dirs. Ladera (Calif.) Community Assn., 1976-79, Ladera Recreation Dist., 1980-88, Com. for Green Foothills, Palo Alto, Calif. 1985—. NATO sr. fellow, 1993-96; Fulbright scholar, 1956; recipient award Dept. Supply, Canberra, 1965. Mem. Am. Phys. Soc., European Phys. Soc. Democrat. Achievements include development of quantum-electrodynamics near metal surfaces, of theory of photochemical holeburning in polymers; proposition of orientational peierls transition in organic conductors, of strong coupling phonon and layer plasmon pairing as explanation for the high superconducting transition temperatures in the cuprate superconductors. Home: 1981 Montecito Ave Apt 201 Mountain View CA 94043-4321 Office: IBM Almaden Rsch Ctr 650 Harry Rd San Jose CA 95120

MORBY, JACQUELINE, venture capitalist; b. Sacramento, June 19, 1937; d. Junior Jennings and Bertha (Backer) Collins; m. Jeffrey L. Morby, June 21, 1959; children: Andrew Jennings, Michelle Lorraine. BA in Psychology, Stanford U., 1959; M in Mgmt., Simmons Grad. Mgmt. Sch., Boston, 1978. Assoc. TA Assocs., Boston, 1978-81, gen. ptnr., 1982-89, mng. dir., 1989—; bd. dirs. Ontrack Computer Sys., Mpls., Axent Tech., Inc., Rockville, Md., Pivotpoint, Inc., Waltham, Mass., , NxTrend Techs., Inc., Colorado Springs, Colo., BLP Group, Inc., Fairlawn, N.J., Ansys, Inc., Houston, Pa., Pacific Mutual Life Ins., Co., Newport Beach, Calif. Trustee Chatham Coll.; mem. Mass. Gov.'s Coun. on Growth and Tech. Mem. Nat. Venture Capital Orgn. Avocations: theatre, reading, art, skiing, travel. Office: TA Assocs 125 High St Boston MA 02110-2704

MORCOTT, SOUTHWOOD J., automotive parts manufacturing company executive; b. 1939; married. Student, Davidson Coll.; MBA, U. Mich. Pres. Dana Corp., Toledo, 1963—; sales engineer, plant mgr. Dana Corp., Tyston, Ind., 1963-75; pres. Dana World Trade Corp., 1969; v.p. ops. Hayes Dana Ltd. Dana Corp., 1975-77, exec. v.p., gen. mgr., 1977-78, pres. Hayes-Dana Ltd., 1978-80, group v.p. Dana svc. parts group, 1980-84, pres. N.Am. ops., 1984-86, pres., chief operating officer, 1986-89, chief exec. officer, 1989—, also chmn., dir., 1990—. Office: Dana Corp 4500 Dorr St Toledo OH 43615-4040

MORDECAI, BENJAMIN, theatrical producer, drama educator; b. N.Y.C., Dec. 10, 1944; s. Allen Lewis Mordecai and Florence Doris (Goldman) Holl; m. Sherry Lynn Morley, July 20, 1974; 1 child, Rachel Elizabeth. BA, Buena Vista Coll., 1967; MA, Eastern Mich. U., 1968; postgrad., Ind. U., 1968-70. Founder, producing dir. Ind. Repertory Theatre, Indpls., 1971-82; mng. dir. Yale Repertory Theatre, New Haven, 1982-93; assoc. dean Yale Sch. Drama, New Haven, 1992—; mng. ptnr. Benjamin Mordecai and Assocs., New York, 1992—; cons. Found. for the Extension and Devel. of the Am. Profl. Theatre, N.Y.C., 1974; adj. prof. Yale Sch. of Drama, 1982—; ind. cons., New Haven, 1984—. Dir: (plays) Fables Here and Then, 1972, Dracula, 1973, Bird in the Hand, 1975; assoc. prodr.; (plays) Fences, 1987 (Tony award 1987), Joe Turner's Come & Gone, 1988 (N.Y. Drama Critics Circle award 1988), A Walk in the Woods, 1988; gen. mgr.; (play) A Walk in the Woods (USSR), 1989; exec. prodr.; (play) The Piano Lesson, 1990 (N.Y. Drama Critics Circle award 1990, Drama Desk award 1990), Two Trains Running, 1992, Angels in America (N.Y. Drama Critics award 1993, Tony award 1993, 94); prodr.: Redwood Curtain, 1993, Twilight: Los Angeles, 1992, 94; assoc.prodr.: The Kentucky Cycle, 1993; prodr.: Gate of Heaven (U.S. Holocaust Mus.), 1995, August Wilson's Seven Guitars, 1996 (N.Y. Drama Critics award 1996), Golden Child (Kennedy Ctr.). Recipient Disting. Svc. award Indpls. Jaycees, Indpls., 1979, spl. commendation City-County Coun., Inpls., 1982, Robert Whitehead award, 1993; named Outstanding Young Alumnus, Buena Vista Coll., 1987. Mem. League of Resident Theatres (exec. com. 1981-91), Assn. Arts Adminstrn. Educators (sec.-treas. 1984-88), Am. Theatre Exchange Initiative (bd. dirs. 1987—, pres. 1994—), Writers Theatre (bd. advisors 1983—), Stage Dirs. and Choreographers Found. (bd. dirs. 1990—), League Am. Theatres & Prodrs., Nat. Theatre Conf.

MORDEN, JOHN REID, Canadian government corporation administrator; b. Hamilton, Ont., Can., June 17, 1941; s. Warren Wilbert and Isabelle Gemmell (Reid) M.; m. Margaret Elizabeth Keens, June 27, 1964; children: Michael, Geoffrey. BA, Dalhousie U., Halifax, N.S., Can., 1962. Min., dep., permanent rep. Can. Mission UN, N.Y.C., 1980-82; counsellor Can. Embassy, Tokyo, 1975-78; dir. gen. Dept. External Affairs, Ottawa, Ont., 1982-84, asst. dep. min. trade policy, 1985-86; asst. dep. min. native claims Dept. Indian and No. Affairs, Ottawa, 1984-85; asst. sec. to cabinet Privy Coun. Office, Ottawa, 1986-87; dir. Can. Security Intelligence Svc., Ottawa, 1987-91; dep. min. of fgn. affairs, 1991-94; pres., CEO Atomic Energy Can. Ltd., Ottawa, 1994—; mem. internat. adv. bd. York U. Sch. Bus.; alt. gov. European Bank for Reconstrn. and Devel., 1991-94; bd. dirs. Can. Energy Coun., Red Cross Fractionation Corp. Mem. Can. Nuclear Assn., Nuclear Project Mgrs., Order St. Lazarus of Jerusalem, Rideau Club, Five Lakes Club. Avocations: reading, music, ballet,. Office: Atomic Energy Can Ltd, 2251 Speakman Dr, Mississauga, ON Canada L5K 1B2

MORDINI, MARILYN HEUER, physical education educator; b. Waukegan, Ill., Aug. 23, 1936; d. Lester and Evelyn (Scott) Heuer; m. Robert D. Mordini, Feb. 24, 1962; children: Robert Jr., Bruce, Beth. BS in Phys. Edn., Ill. State U., 1958; MS in Phys. Edn., Chgo. State U., 1984; MS in Adminstrn., Northeastern Ill. U., 1994. Tchr. phys. edn. Libertyville (Ill.) Pub. Schs., 1958-63, Highland Park (Ill.) Pub. Schs., 1978-81; tchr. phys. edn. North Chicago (Ill.) Sch. Dist. 187, 1981—, dir. intramural sports, 1985-92; tchr. phys. edn. Highland Park Summer Migrant Program, 1981-90; adv. bd. Park Dist. Highland Park, 1982-84. Rep. United Way, North Chicago, 1990-92; bd. dirs. Lake County divsn. Am. Heart Assn., 1992-96, chmn. Highland Park/Highwood br. Lake County divsn., 1995-96. Mem. AAHPERD, Ill. Assn. Health, Phys. Edn., Recreation and Dance (exec. bd. v.p. children 1997, pres. N.E. dist. 1995-96, Elem. Phys. Educator of Yr. 1991), Am. Fedn. Tchrs., Delta Kappa Gamma. Home: 2035 Grange Ave Highland Park IL 60035-1719

MORDY, JAMES CALVIN, lawyer; b. Ashland, Kans., Jan. 3, 1927; s. Thomas Robson and Ruth (Floyd) M.; m. Marjory Ellen Nelson, Nov. 17, 1951; children: Jean Claire Mordy Jongeling, Rebecca Jane Mordy King, James Nelson. AB in Chemistry, U. Kans., 1947; JD, U. Mich., 1950; postgrad., George Washington U., 1950-51. Bar: Kans. 1950, Mo. 1950; cert. in bus. bankruptcy law Am. Bankruptcy Bd. Cert. Assoc. Morrison, Hecker, Buck, Cozad & Rogers, Kansas City, Mo., 1950-59; ptnr. Morrison & Hecker, Kansas City, 1959-96, sr. counsel, 1996—. Contbg. author: Missouri Bar Insurance Handbook, 1968, Missouri Bar Bankruptcy Handbook, 1991, also supplements; contbr. articles to profl. jours. Chmn. bd. Broadway United Meth. Ch., Kansas City, 1964-70, chmn. bd. trustees, chmn. fin. com., 1988-90, 94; bd. dirs., exec. com. Della C. Lamb Neighborhood House, Kansas City, 1973-80; coun. mem. St. Paul Sch. Theology, Kansas City, 1986-97; del. 17th World Meth. Conf., Rio, 1996. Comdr. USNR, 1945-46, 51-53. Summerfield scholar, 1943-47; recipient Shepherd of the Lamb award Della C. Lamb Neighborhood House, 1980. Fellow Am. Coll. Bankruptcy, Am. Bar Found. (life); mem. ABA, Am. Judicature Soc., Am. Bankruptcy Inst., Mo. Bar Assn., Kans. Bar Assn., Kansas City Met. Bar Assn., Lawyers Assn. Kansas City, Workout Profs. Assn. Kansas City, Univ. Club (v.p., bd. dirs. 1983, 86), Barristers Soc., Phi Beta Kappa, Delta Tau Delta (pres. Kansas City alumni chpt. 1965-72, pres. U. Kans. House Corp. 1966-72), Alpha Chi Sigma, Phi Alpha Delta. Avocations: travel, geography (maps), history, music, theology. Home: 8741 Ensley Ln Leawood KS 66206-1615 Office: Morrison & Hecker 2600 Grand Blvd Kansas City MO 64108-4613

MORE, DOUGLAS MCLOCHLAN, lawyer; b. N.Y.C., Apr. 21, 1926; s. Morgan Berkeley and Lucinda (Bateson) M.; m. Pamela Bennett Marr, Aug. 6, 1954; children—Robin Maclachlan More Eddy, Alison Marr More Davies. Grad., Phillips Exeter Acad., 1943; B.A., Harvard U., 1947; LL.B., Columbia U., 1950. Bar: N.Y. State bar 1950, Conn. bar 1981, Fla. bar 1983. With N.Y. Trust Co., 1950-51; assoc. firm Bigham, Englar, Jones & Houston, N.Y.C., 1951-53; fin. analyst Johns-Manville Corp., 1953-54; assoc. firm Kissam & Halpin, N.Y.C., 1954-59; assoc. counsel Hooker Chem. Corp., 1959-63, gen. counsel, 1963-72, v.p., 1967-72; v.p. law Airco, Inc., 1972-75; gen. counsel Beker Industries Corp., 1975-81, v.p., 1975-78, sr. v.p., 1978-81; ptnr. firm More Phillips & Duncan, P.C., Greenwich, Conn., 1981-88, of counsel, 1988—. Served to lt. (j.g.) USNR, 1943-46. Mem. ABA, Conn. Bar Assn., Greenwich Bar Assn., Phi Delta Phi, Phoenix S-K Club, Hasty Pudding Inst. 1770 (Harvard). Home and Office: 27 Skylark Rd Greenwich CT 06830-4624

MORE, JOHN HERRON, lawyer, classicist; s. John Herron and Margaret (Rapp) M.; m. Livezey Hickenlooper, June 19, 1965; children: Anna Herron, Paul Livezey. BA, Yale U., 1964; PhD, Classical Philology, Harvard U., 1969, JD, 1979. Bar: D.C. 1979, U.S. Dist. Ct. D.C. 1979, U.S. Ct. Appeals (D.C. cir.) 1980. Asst. prof. classics Brown U., Providence, 1967-74, 75-76, Centro Univ per i Studi Classici, Rome, 1974-75; assoc. Covington & Burling, Washington, 1979-84, Shaw, Pittman, Potts & Trowbridge, Washington, 1984-88; counsel Shaw, Pittman, Potts & Trowbridge, 1989-92, Wiley, Rein & Fielding, 1992-93, Winston & Strawn, 1993-96; ptnr. Rogers & More, L.L.P., Washington, 1996—; lectr. classics Georgetown U., Washington, 1981-82. Contbr. to scholarly and profl. publs.; lectr. Bd. dirs. Cushings Island Conservation Corp., Portland, Maine, 1974—; co-chmn. ho. com. Washington Interfaith Network, Inc. Mem. ABA, Am. Soc. Internat. Law. Episcopalian. Office: Rogers & More LLP 1510 H St NW Ste 950 Washington DC 20005-1008

MORE, VISHWAS, engineering laboratory administrator; b. Kolhapur, India, July 5, 1936; came to U.S., 1958; s. Dattagi Jagtap and Parvati M.; m. Sheila More; children: Anil, Sanjiv, Dev, Sonya. BSME, U. Mich., 1951, MSME, 1953. Project engr. Air Conditioning Corp., Bombay, India, 1958-62; mech. engr. Abbott Lab., North Chgo., Ill., 1962-66; plant engr. Argonne (Ill.) Nat. Lab. U. Chgo., 1966-74; chief engr. Posotron Electron Project U. Calif., Stanford U., 1974-78; project mgr. Cell Culture Lab. U. Calif., 1979-80; plant engr., head dept. Lawrence Lab. U. Calif., Berkeley, 1978-83, project mgr., 1982-83, project mgr. Ctr. for Advanced Materials, 1984-93; ret.; cons. to various other nat. projects funded by Fed. Govt. Fund raising host for U.S. Senator and Gov. Pete Wilson; mem. Rep. Presdl. Task Force, Senatorial Inner Cir., 1989; apptd. by Gov. Pete Wilson to Fin. Aid Commn., State of Calif., 1993-94; bd. govs. Comty. Colls. State of Calif., 1994—, asst. chmn. fin. and budget, 1994-95, v.p., 1995-96, pres., 1996-97; mem. Task Force on Sch. to Career, 1996—; del. Rep. Nat. Conv., State of Calif., 1996; invited by Ednl. Ministry of Thailand to Master Plan Comty.

Coll. in Thailand, 1995. Mem. Prominent Indians in Am. (exec. v.p. 1982). Hindu. Avocations: travel, gardening. Home: 727 Evelyn Ct Alamo CA 94507

MOREHEAD, ANNETTE MARIE, disabled children's facility administrator, child advocate; b. San Diego; d. Michael Peter and Katherine Helen (Keegan) Russomondo; m. Peter James Morehead; children: Bradley Michael Caloca, Katherine Dana. Student, Southwestern Coll., Grossmont Coll. Dir. Rayito Day Care Ctr., San Diego, 1981-85; instrnl. asst. for children with disabilities San Diego City Schools, 1985-88; owner, operator Scripps Ranch Childcare Ctr. for Disabled Children, San Diego, 1990—; child advocate; speaker San Diego Bd. Edn., 1986, News Eight Local TV News, 1989, Miramar Coll., 1991, Scottish Rite Charities, 1992, U. Calif., San Diego, 1992, Exceptional Parents Found., 1993. Vol. Schweitzer Ctr. for Disabled Children, San Diego, 1985, Stein Edn. Ctr. for Autistic Children, San Diego, 1987-88; bd. dirs. San Diego Autism Soc., 1988-89, pres., 1989. Mem. Autism Soc. Am. (bd. dirs. 1988-89), Mensa. Democrat. Avocations: home, fine architecture. Home and Office: 7230 Blaisdell Ave Minneapolis MN 55423-3112

MOREHEAD, CHARLES RICHARD, insurance company executive; b. Independence, Mo., Jan. 25, 1947; s. Robert E. and Ruth Elizabeth (Taylor) M.; m. Donna Joyce Shores, Feb. 17, 1968 children: Grant, Blaine. BSBA, U. Mo., 1971. CPA, Fla. Mem. staff Peat, Marwick, Mitchell & Co., Kansas City, Mo., 1972-75; audit mgr. Peat, Marwick, Mitchell & Co., Jacksonville, Fla., 1976-83, audit ptnr., 1983-86; treas. Standard Havens, Inc., Kansas City, 1975-76; treas., CFO Am. Heritage Life Ins. Co., Jacksonville, Fla., 1986-94, exec. v.p., CFO, 1994—, also bd. dirs. Mem. AICPA, Fla. Soc. CPA's. Home: 4050 Chicora Wood Pl Jacksonville FL 32224 Office: Am Heritage Life Ins Co 1776 Am Heritage Life Dr Jacksonville FL 32224

MOREHEAD, JAMES CADDALL, JR., architect, educator; b. Bradenton, Fla., Oct. 29, 1913; s. James Caddall and Jeannette Dandridge (White) M.; m. Martha Petty Netting, Aug. 27, 1940; children: James Caddall, III, Naomi Willson, Kenneth Fielding. B.A., Princeton U., 1935; B.Arch., Carnegie Mellon U., 1939. Instr. math. Carnegie Mellon U., 1936-40; architecture, 1938-40; instr. architecture Rice U., 1940-42, 46, asst. prof., 1946-48, assoc. prof., 1948-51, prof., 1951-79, prof. emeritus, 1979—, head dept., 1953-61; registrar, 1964-79; asso. Wilson, Morris & Crain, Houston, 1951-55; past partner Morehead and Ransom (Architects); pvt. practice of architecture, 1960-90; dir. of permits City of Piney Point Village, Tex., 1954-81, 86-96. Author: (with J.C. Morehead, Sr.) Handbook of Perspective Drawing, 1952, Perspective and Projective Geometries, A Comparison, 1955, Elementary Structures, 2 vols, Intermediate Structures, ACSA Learning Packages, 1974, 75, A Walking Tour of Rice U., 1984, 2d edit., 1990. Dir. San Jacinto Girl Scouts, 1954-61; Mem. Study Commn. on Archtl. Edn. in South, So. Regional Edn. Bd., 1953, chmn. planning and zoning commn., Piney Point Village, Tex., 1954-81. Served as lt. col. F.A. AUS, 1942-46. Decorated Bronze Star with oak leaf cluster; recipient Alpha Rho Chi Medal in Architecture Carnegie Inst. Tech., 1939; Award of Merit Houston chpt. AIA, 1953. Fellow AIA (treas. Houston chpt. 1950-51); mem. Houston Philos. Soc. Scarab. Home: 354 Piney Point Rd Houston TX 77024-6506

MOREHOUSE, GEORGIA LEWIS, microbiologist, researcher; b. Guatamala City, Nov. 1, 1933; d. Bevan Blau and Margaret Julia (Ward) Lewis; m. Lawrence Glen Morehouse, Oct. 6, 1956; children: Timothy Lawrence, Glenn Ellen. BS, Purdue U., 1955. Microbiologist Purdue U., West Lafayette, Ind., 1955-60, Nat. Animal Disease Lab., Ames, Iowa, 1960-63; rsch. specialist dept. of dairy sci. U. Mo., Columbia, 1978-84; videographer, owner Great Moments in Video, Inc., Columbia, 1984-87; adminstr. auxiliary loan fund Mo. Vet. Med. Auxiliary, Columbia, 1987—. Contbr. articles to profl. jours. Chair of nom. com. and fund raising PTA Shepard Blvd. Sch., Columbia, 1968-78, co-chair Columbia Jr. Cotillion, Columbia, 1977-78; bd. dirs. Koinonia House, Columbia, 1978-82, vol. The Wardrobe, Columbia, 1972—, coord. latch key program Trinity Presbyn. Ch., Columbia, 1992-94; leader Boy Scouts Am., 1971-73, Girl Scouts Am., 1973-78; chair, bd. dirs. Friends of Music, U. Mo., 1996—; pres. Women's Symphony League Bd., Mo. Symphony Soc., Columbia, 1996—; tutor adult reading ctr. Columbia Pub. Schs., 1989—. Avocations: running, photography, reading, gardening, handiwork. Home: 916 Danforth Dr Columbia MO 65201-6164

MOREHOUSE, LAWRENCE GLEN, veterinarian, emeritus professor; b. Manchester, Kans., July 21, 1925; s. Edwy Owen and Ethel Merle (Glenn) M.; m. Georgia Ann Lewis, Oct. 6, 1956; children: Timothy Lawrence, Glenn Ellen. BS in Biol. Sci., Kans. State U., 1952, DVM, 1952; MS in Animal Pathology, Purdue U., 1956, PhD, 1960. Lic. vet. medicine. Veterinarian County Animal Hosp., Des Peres, Mo., 1952-53; supr. Brucellosis labs. Purdue U., West Lafayette, Ind., 1953-60; staff veterinarian lab. svcs. USDA, Washington, 1960-61; discipline leader in pathology and toxicology, animal health divsn. USDA Nat. Animal Disease Lab., Ames, Iowa, 1961-64; prof., chmn. dept. veterinary pathology U. Mo. Coll. Vet. Medicine, Columbia, 1964-69, 84-86, dir. Vet. Med. Diagnostic Labr., 1968-88, prof. emeritus, 1986—; cons. USDA, to comdg. gen. U.S. Army R & D Command, Am. Inst. Biol. Scis., NAS, Miss. State U., St. Louis Zoo Residency Tng. Program, Miss. Vet. Med. Assn., Okla. State U., Pa. Dept. Agr., Ohio Dept. Agr. Co-editor: Mycotoxic Fungi, Mycotoxins, Mycotoxicoses: An Encyclopedic Handbook , 3 vols., 1977; contbr. numerous articles on diseases of animals to profl. jours. Active Trinity Presbyn. Ch., Columbia, 1989-92; bd. dirs. Mo. Symphony Soc., Columbia, 1989-92. With USNR, 1943-46, PTO, U.S. Army, 1952-56. Recipient Outstanding Svc. award USDA, 1959, merit cert., 1963, 64, Disting. Svc. award U. Mo. Coll. Vet. Medicine, 1987, Dean's Impact award, 1996. Fellow Royal Soc. Health London; mem. Am. Assn. Vet. Lab. Diagnosticians (E.P. Pope award 1976, chmn. lab. accreditation bd. 1972-79, 87-90, pres. 1979-80, sec.-treas. 1983-87), World Assn. Vet. Lab. Diagnosticians (bd. dirs. 1984—), N.Y. Acad. Sci., U. S. Animal Health Assn., Am. Assn. Lab. Animal Sci., Mo. Soc. Microbiology, Am. Assn. Avian Pathologists, N.Am. Conf. Rsch. Workers in Animal Diseases, Mo. Univ. Retirees Assn. (v.p. 1996—). Presbyterian. Avocations: classic cars, boating, genealogy. Home: 916 Danforth Dr Columbia MO 65201-6164 Office: U Mo Vet Med Diagnostic Lab PO Box 6023 Columbia MO 65201

MOREHOUSE, RICHARD EDWARD, psychology educator; b. LaCrosse, Wis., May 21, 1941; s. Ervin Lenard and Anna Martha (Weiland) M.; m. Rita Spangler, Aug. 20, 1966; 1 child, Lyda Ann. BS, U. Wis., 1971, MST, 1973; PhD, The Union Inst., 1979. Teaching asst. U. Wis., LaCrosse, 1971-72; ednl. cons. Coop. Ednl. Svcs. Agy., LaCrosse, 1972-80; dir. coop. edn. Viterbo Coll., LaCrosse, 1980-85, from asst. to prof. psychology, 1985—; dept. chmn. Viterbo Coll., LaCrosse, 1986-93, chair 1995—; vis. prof. U. Turku, Finland, summer 1990; vis. scholar Tex. Wesleyan U., Ft. Worth, 1993-94. Co-author: Student Study Guide for Human Development Across the Lifespan, 1991, 94, Beginning Qualatative Research, 1994; co-editor: Analytic Teaching, 1991-96, Educator Analytic Teaching, 1996—. Gifted Edn. grantee Elem. and Secondary Edn. Act, 1976-79, Tchr. Tng., Cmty. Awareness grantee Wis. Humanities, 1982, Coll., Cmty. Symposium grantee, 1983. Mem. N.Am. Assn. for Cmty. Inquiry (founder, 1st pres. 1994), Am. Psychol. Soc. (charter mem.). Democrat. Unitarian. Home: 1131 Charles St La Crosse WI 54603-2508 Office: Viterbo Coll 815 9th St S La Crosse WI 54601-4777

MOREIRA, MARCIO MARTINS, advertising executive; b. Sao Paulo, Brazil, Nov. 20, 1947; came to U.S. 1980; naturalized, 1990; s. Guido Martins and Maria Rosa (Macrine) M.; children from previous marriage: Joaquim Pedro Rezende Martins Moreira; m. Maria Auxiliadora Godinho, Oct. 18, 1981; children: Eliana Maria Godinho Martins Moreira. Ed., U. Sao Paulo, Brazil, 1970. TV producer-copywriter McCann-Erickson, Sao Paulo, Brazil, 1967-71; creative dir. McCann-Erickson, Sao Paulo, 1974-77; group creative dir. McCann-Erickson, London, Lisbon and Frankfurt, 1971-74; executive creative dir. McCann-Erickson, Latin America, 1977-80; internat. creative dir. McCann-Erickson, N.Y.C., 1980-88; vice chmn., chief creative officer McCann Erickson Worldwide, N.Y.C., 1988—; vice chmn., regional dir. Asia-Pacific McCann-Erickson Worldwide, N.Y.C., 1995—; lectr. various univs. Author: Terraplenagem, 1968 Liquidacao, 1979; lyricist, 1968—; contbr. articles to profl. jours. U.S. judge, pres. jury Cannes Film Festival, 1989; chmn. bd. judges The New York Festivals. Recipient 5 Clio awards, 1976-89, Gold Lion, Silver Lion, Bronze Lion awards, Cannes, France, H.K. McCann award, Brazil, 1977, Paul Foley award Interpub. Group of Cos., 1983, Terence Cardinal Cooke medal for Disting. Svc. in Health Care, N.Y. Med. Coll., 1994. Mem. Brazilian-Am. C. of C. (bd. dir.). Republican. Roman Catholic. Avocations: cinema, songwriting, cars, speedwalking. Office: McCann-Erickson Worldwide 750 3rd Ave New York NY 10017-2703

MORELAN, PAULA KAY, choreographer; b. Lafayette, Ind., Nov. 24, 1949; d. Dickie Booth and Marian Maxine (Fetterhoff) M.; m. Kerim Sayan, Aug. 10, 1974. Student U. Utah, 1968-69; BFA, Tex. Christian U., 1972; postgrad., El Centro Coll., 1969-70. Tchr., Rosello Sch. Ballet, Dallas, 1972-74; mgr., tchr. Ballet Arts Ctr., Dallas, 1974-76; owner, tchr. Ballet Classique, Garland, Tex., 1976-87, Garland Ballet Acad., 1977-87; asst. to Mythra Rosello, Tex. Civic Ballet, Dallas, 1972-74; assoc. artistic dir. Dance Repertory Theatre Dallas, 1974-75; artistic dir. Dance Repertory Theatre Dallas, 1975-76, Garland (Tex.) Ballet Assn., 1977-90, Classical Ballet Acad., Performing Arts Sch., 1987-90; resident choreographer Garland Civic Theatre, 1988—. Recipient Leon Rabin award for Best Choreography, 1995-96.

MORELAND, ALVIN FRANKLIN, veterinarian; b. Morven, Ga., Sept. 5, 1931; s. Robert Hamilton and Laura Eloise (Edenfield) M.; m. Mary Ellen Hardee, Feb. 12, 1955; children: Ellen, Frank, Clyde. BS in Edn., Ga. Tchrs. Coll., 1951; MSEd, U. Ga., 1952, DVM, 1960. Diplomate Am. Coll. Lab. Animal Medicine. Asst. prof. U. Va. Sch. Medicine, Charlottesville, 1962-63; asst. prof. to prof. U. Fla. Coll. Vet. Medicine, Gainesville, 1963-95, prof. emeritus, 1995—; cons. vet. NASA, Kennedy Space Ctr., Fla., Bionetics Corp., 1983—. Contbr. articles to profl. jours. Served to lt. USNR, 1952-56. Mem. AVMA, Am. Assn. Lab. Animal Sci., Fla. Vet. Med. Assn. (Gold Star award 1976), Alachua Vet. Med. Assn., Internat. Assn. Aquatic Animal Medicine. Methodist.

MORELAND, DONALD EDWIN, plant physiologist; b. Enfield, Conn., Oct. 12, 1919; s. Albert Sinclair and Ruth (Cowan) M.; m. Verdie Brown Stallings, Nov. 6, 1954; 1 child, Donna Faye; stepchildren: Frank C., Paul Ziglar. BS in Forestry, N.C. State U., 1949, MS in Plant Physiology, 1950, PhD in Plant Physiology, 1953. Plant physiologist SUNY Coll. Forestry, Syracuse, 1952-53; plant physiologist USDA-Agrl. Rsch. Svc., Raleigh, N.C., 1953-71, rsch. leader, 1972-78, sr. exec., 1979-95, collaborator, 1996—; asst. prof. to prof. N.C. State U., Raleigh, 1953-95, prof. emeritus, 1996—; mem. toxicology study sect. NIH, USPHS, Bethesda, Md., 1963-67. Editor: Biochemical Responses Induced by Herbicides, 1982; mem. editorial bd. Pesticide Biochemistry and Physiology, 1971-97, Pesticide Sci., 1987-96; contbr. articles to profl. jours. 1st lt. U.S. Army, 1941-46. AEC predoctoral fellow, 1950-52. Fellow AAAS, Weed Sci. Soc. Am. (outstanding rsch. award 1973); mem. Am. Chem. Soc., Plant Growth Regulator Soc. Am., Am. Soc. Plant Physiologists, So. Weed Sci. Soc., Sigma Xi. Avocations: woodworking, surf fishing, square dancing. Home: 1508 Pineview Dr Raleigh NC 27606-2562 Office: USDA-Agrl Rsch Svc NC State U Crop Sci Dept 3127 Ligon St Raleigh NC 27607-5376

MORELLA, CONSTANCE ALBANESE, congresswoman; b. Somerville, Mass., Feb. 12, 1931; d. Salvatore and Mary Christine (Fallette) Albanese; m. Anthony C. Morella, Aug. 21, 1954; children: Paul, Mark, Laura; guardians of: Christine, Catherine, Louise, Rachel, Paul, Ursula. AA, Boston U., 1950, AB, 1954; MA, Am. U., 1967, D of Pub. Svc. (hon.), 1988; D of Pub. Svc. (hon.), Norwich U. and Dickinson Coll., 1989. Tchr. Montgomery County (Md.) Pub. Schs., 1956-60; instr. Am. U., 1968-70; prof. Montgomery Coll., Rockville, Md., 1970-86; mem. Md. Ho. Dels., Annapolis, 1979-86, 100th-104th Congresses from 8th Md. dist., 1987—; mem. civil svc., basic rsch., tech. coms.; adv. bd. Am. Univ., Washington; trustee Capitol Coll. Laurel, Md. Trustee Capitol Coll, Laurel, Md., 1977—; chair Sci. Com. Tech. Subcom., Basic Rsch. Subcom., coun. mem. Montgomery County United Way; adv. coun. Montgomery County Hospice Soc.; hon. bd. mem. Nat. Kidney Found; active Human Rights Caucus, co-chair Congressional Women's Caucus, Black Caucus; chair Gov. Reform and Oversight Com. Avocations: theatre, tennis, reading. Office: US Ho of Reps 2228 Rayburn Bldg Washington DC 20515-2008 also: 51 Monroe St Rockville MD 20850-2417*

MORELLO, CELESTE ANNE, historian, educator, criminologist; b. Norristown, Pa., July 22, 1958; d. Ann M. Morello. BA in Classics cum laude, BA in Art History magna cum laude, Chestnut Hill Coll., 1980; MS in Criminology, St. Joseph's U., Phila., 1994; postgrad., Temple U. Tchr. history, social studies, sci. Archdiocese of Phila., Phila., 1977-84; lectr. on ancient history of Sicily, 1982—; cons. criminologist in Mafia and LCN history Phila. Police and U.S. Atty.'s Office, 1993—; pioneer in criminal and Mafia history; petitioner, originator over 20 hist. sites Pa. Hist. and Mus. Commn. Hist. Marker Program, Phila. Author: Beyond History: The Times & Peoples of St. Paul's R.C. Church, 1843-1993, 1992; author numerous studies on Phila. Mafia/LCN, organized crime, Phila. social/ethnic history. Founder Sicilian Culture Collection Balch Inst. for Ethnic Studies. Mem. Moyamensing Hist. Soc. (founder). Roman Catholic. Home: 1234 S Sheridan St Philadelphia PA 19147

MORELLO, JOSEPH ALBERT, musician, educator; b. Springfield, Mass., July 17, 1928; s. Joseph Charles and Lilia (LaPalme) M.; m. Jean Ann Mehnert. Grad. high sch., Springfield. Ind. drummer Springfield, 1945-49; drummer Gil Melé, Stan Kenton, Tal Farlow, Johnny Smith, N.Y.C., 1953-55, Dave Brubeck Quartet, touring worldwide, 1955-68; clinician Selmer Ludwig Drum Co., Elkhart, Ind., 1957-92; leader Joe Morello Quartet, 1979—; clinician DW Drums, Oxnard, Calif., 1993—; rec. artist Digital Music Products Inc., 1993—. Rec. artist Savoy, Capitol, Norgran, Blue Note, Columbia, RCA labels; innovator finger control in jazz drumming; author: Joe Morello Drum Method, The Natural Approach to Technique, 1993, Joe Morello Drum Method 2, 1994, also New Directions in Rhythm, Rudimental Jazz, Off the Record, Master Studies; releases include (with Joe Morello Quartet) Going Places, 1993, Morello's Standard Time, 1994. Recipient New Star award Downbeat mag., 1955, Melody Maker mag. award, 1963-67, Jazz mag. award, 1964-67, Thomas A. Edison lifetime achievement award, 1990, record, CD and tape release RCA Bluebird Label, 1989, CD Joe Morello Quartet Going Places release DMP Label, 1990, Lifetime Achievement award Jersey Shore Jazz and Blues Found., 1996; poll winner Downbeat mag., 1963-65, Playboy mag., 1963-67; named to Hall of Fame, Modern Drummer mag., 1988, Percussive Arts Soc. Hall of Fame, 1993. Avocation: photography.

MORELLO, JOSEPHINE A., microbiology and pathology educator; b. Boston, May 2, 1936; married, 1971. BS, Simmons Coll., 1957; AM, Boston U., 1960, PhD in Microbiology, 1962. Cert. med. microbiologist Am. Bd. Microbiology. Inst. microbiology Boston U., 1962-64; rsch. assoc. Rockefeller U., 1964-66; resident med. microbiology Coll. Physicians & Surgeons Columbia U., N.Y.C., 1966-68, asst. prof. microbiology, 1968-69; dir. microbiology Harlem Hosp. Ctr., 1968-69; assoc. prof. pathology and medicine Coll. Physicians & Surgeons, Columbia U., 1973-78; prof. pathology and medicine U. Chgo., 1978—, dir. clinical microbiology, 1970—; vice-chair pathology, dir. hosp. lab. U. Chgo., 1994—. Editor Clin. Microbiology Revs., Clin. Microbiology Newsletter. Fellow Am. Acad. Microbiology; mem. Acad. Clin. Lab. Physicians and Scientists, Am. Soc. Microbiology (Sonnenwirth Meml. award 1991, Disting. Svc. award 1992), Am. Soc. Clin. Pathologists, Sigma Xi. Achievements include rsch. in improved methods clin. microbiology; epidemiology and characteristics pathogenic neisseria. Home: 425 Luthin Rd Oak Brook IL 60523-2770

MORENA, JOHN JOSEPH, manufacturing engineer, executive; b. Rockaway Beach, N.Y., Dec. 6, 1937; s. John Michael and Theresa (Verdoni) M.; children from a previous marriage: John Joseph, Stephen Scott, Todd Theodore; m. Diane Pizo, Feb. 9, 1990. Student, NYU, 1956-65, SUNY, 1956-65, Fla. Atlantic U., Boca Raton, Fla., 1988-91. Cert. mfg. engr. With AIL, Melville, N.Y., 1962-66, Maxson Electronics, Great River, N.Y., 1966-70, Airtron/Litton Inc., Morris Plains, N.J., 1970-72, Microlab/FXR, Livingston, N.J., 1972-74; v.p. Fibes Drums Inc., Farmingdale, N.Y., 1974-77; pres. Meam Inc., Farmingdale, 1977-79, GSU Inc., Farmingdale, 1976-80, Am. Composites Edn. Inc., Stuart, Fla., 1980—; tech. dir. Am. Composites Mfg. Learning Ctr., Stuart, Fla., 1983—; primary tech. advanced materials advisor Superconducting Super Collider, Dallas, 1988-94; exec. dir. Am. Maglev Star Orgn., Stuart, 1991—, dir. Maglev 2000, 1995—; bd. dirs. Maglev 2000 of Fla. Corp. Author: Advanced Composite Mold Making, 1988, World Composites Encyclopedia, 1992, Advanced Composites World Reference Dictionary, 1995; contbr. articles to profl. jours.; patentee in field. Avocations: instrumental music, painting, boating, sports, writing. Home: 4540 NE Sandpebble Trce Apt 104 Stuart FL 34996-1486 Office: Am Composite Edn Inc Am Composites Bldg 425 California Ave Stuart FL 34994-2917

MORENCY, PAULA J., lawyer; b. Oak Park, Ill., Mar. 13, 1955. AB magna cum laude, Princeton U., 1977; JD, U. Va., 1980. Bar: Ill. 1980, U.S. Dist. Ct. (no. dist.) Ill. 1980, U.S. Ct. Appeals (7th cir.) 1981, U.S. Ct. Appeals (5th cir.) 1990. Assoc. Mayer, Brown & Platt, Chgo., 1980-86, ptnr., 1987-94; ptnr. Schiff Hardin & Waite, Chgo., 1994—; adj. prof. trial advocacy Northwestern U. Sch. Law, Chgo. Author: Cross-Examination of a Franchise Executive, 1995, Insurance Coverage Issues in Franchise and Intellectual Property Litigation, 1996; contbg. author: Federal Litigation Guide Vol. 3, 1985. Mem. ABA (forum franchising litigation sect.), Chgo. Coun. of Lawyers (bd. govs. 1989-93). Office: Schiff Hardin & Waite 7200 Sears Tower Chicago IL 60606-6327

MORENO, CHRISTINE MARGARET, lawyer; b. Miami, Fla., Sept. 7, 1960; d. Arthur and Christine Moreno. BS magna cum laude, Barry U., 1981; JD cum laude, U. Miami, Coral Gables, Fla., 1984. Bar: Fla. 1984, D.C. 1985, U.S. Dist. Ct. (so. dist.) Fla. 1985, U.S. Dist. Ct. (mid. dist.) Fla. 1987, U.S. Tax Ct. 1987, U.S. Supreme Ct. 1988, U.S. Ct. Appeals (11th cir.) 1988; CPA, Fla. Law intern U.S. Securities Exch. Commn., Miami, Fla., 1984; assoc. atty. Ruden, Barnett, McCloskey, Ft. Lauderdale, Fla., 1984-85, Koppen, Watkins, Ptnrs. & Assocs., Miami, 1985-89; mayor city of North Miami, 1989-91; owner, atty., CPA Law Offices of Christine M. Moreno, North Miami, Stuart, Fla., 1989—; commr. Jensen Beach (Fla.) Cmty. Redevelopment Agy., 1994—; bd. dirs. North Miami Energy Adv. Bd.; life time dir. Mayor's Econ. Task Force, North Miami, 1989—. Co-author: (book) Senior Citizens Handbook, 1990; mem. staff U. Miami Law Review, 1982-84. Bd. dirs. Nat. League of Cities, Washington, 1990-91; v.p. polit. action Miami Dade Cmty. Coll. Alumni, 1991—. Mem. AICPA, North Dade Bar Assn. (bd. dirs.), Fla. Inst. CPAs, North Miami Jaycees (Jaycee of yr. 1993), Rep. Party Dade County (com. woman 1990-94), Phi Alpha Delta Internat. Law Fraternity (Miami alumni chpt. justice 1985—). Avocation: public service. Office: 13122 W Dixie Hwy North Miami FL 33161-4131 also: 630 SE Monterey Rd Stuart FL 34994-4410

MORENO, FEDERICO ANTONIO, federal judge; b. Caracas, Venezuela, Apr. 10, 1952; came to U.S., 1963; s. Francisco Jose and Rejane Genevieve (Nogues) M.; m. M. Cristina M. Morales-Gomez, May 31, 1977; children: Cristi, Ricky, Victoria. AB cum laude, U. Notre Dame, 1974; JD, U. Miami, 1974. Bar: Fla. 1978, U.S. Dist. Ct. (so. dist.) Fla. 1978, U.S. Ct. Appeals (5th cir.) 1979, U.S. Ct. Appeals (11th cir.) 1981, U.S. Supreme Ct. 1981, U.S. Dist. Ct. (mid. dist.) Fla. 1986. Ptnr. Thornton, Rothman & Moreno, Miami, 1982-86; judge Dade County Cir. Ct., Miami, 1986-90; dist. judge U.S. Dist. Ct. (so. dist.) Fla., Miami, 1990—. Recipient People Helping People award United Way, 1980, Pro Bono award Pub. Interest Law Bank, 1985. Mem. ABA, FBA, Fla. Bar Assn., Dade County Bar Assn., Trial Lawyer's Assn. Roman Catholic. Office: US Courthouse 99E N 4th St Rm 1061 Miami FL 33132-7702*

MORENO, G(ILBERTO) MARIO, federal agency administrator; b. Uvalde, Tex., Jan. 3, 1947; m. Susana Gomez; children: Christina Collins, Amielle. BA in Econs., Tex. A&M U., 1969; MA in Urban and Regional Planning, St. Mary's U., San Antonio, 1971, JD, 1981. Planning dir., asst. city mgr. City of Brownsville, Tex., 1972-78; exec. dir. AYUDA, Inc., Washington, 1982-84; regional counsel Mex. Am. Legal Def. and Edn. Fund, Washington, 1985-94; asst. sec. for intergovtl. and interagy. affairs U.S. Dept. Edn., Washington, 1994—. John L. Loeb fellow Harvard U. Grad. Sch. Design, 1978-79. Office: US Dept Edn Office Intergovtl/Interagy 600 Independence Ave SW Washington DC 20202-0004

MORENO, GLEN RICHARD, banker; b. San Jose, Calif., July 24, 1943; s. John and Ellen (Oberg) M.; m. Cheryl Lynne Eschbach, Mar. 26, 1966. B.A. with distinction, Stanford U., 1965; J.D., Harvard U., 1969. Group exec. Citicorp, N.Y.C., 1969-87; dir. Fidelity Internat. Ltd., Bermuda, 1987—; bd. dirs. ED&F Man Group PLC, India Fund., Rea Bros. PLC. Bd. govs. Ditchley Found., Oxford, Eng., 1983—. Mem. Bucks Club. Home: "Neala" RR 1 Box 73 Madison VA 22727-9729 also: 3 Whitehall Ct Flat 124A, London SW1A 2EL, England Office: Fidelity Investments, 25 Lovat Ln, London EC3, England

MORENO, MANUEL D., bishop; Educator U. of Calif., L.A., St. John's Sem., Camarillo, Calif. Ordained priest Roman Cath. church, 1961. Ordained aux. bishop of Los Angeles, titular bishop of Tanagra, 1977; installed as bishop of Tucson, 1982—. Office: PO Box 31 192 S Stone Ave Tucson AZ 85702*

MORENO, RITA, actress; b. Humacao, P.R., Dec. 11, 1931; m. Leonard I. Gordon, June 18, 1965; 1 child, Fernanda Luisa. Spanish dancer since childhood, night club entertainer; appeared on Broadway in The Sign in Sidney Brustein's Window, 1964-65, Gantry, 1969-70, The Last of the Red Hot Lovers, 1970-71, The National Health, 1974, The Ritz, 1975, Wally's Cafe, 1981, The Odd Couple, 1985; (off Broadway) After Play, 1995, (London prodn.) Sunset Blvd., 1996; motion picture debut, 1950, and appeared in numerous films including West Side Story, Carnal Knowledge, The King and I, Singing in the Rain, The Four Seasons, I Like it Like That, 1994, Angus, 1995, Wharf Rat, 1995. Recipient Acad. Award for best supporting actress, 1962; Grammy award for best rec., 1973; Antoinette Perry award for best supporting actress Broadway play, 1975; Emmy award, 1977, 78. In Guinness Book of World Records as only person to win Acad., Grammy, Tony and Emmy awards. Address: care Agency for Performing Arts 9000 W Sunset Blvd Los Angeles CA 90069-5801

MORENO, ZERKA TOEMAN, psychodrama educator; b. Amsterdam, The Netherlands, June 13, 1917; d. Joseph and Rosalia (Gutwirth) Toeman; m. Jacob L. Moreno (dec.); 1 child, Jonathan D.; 1 stepchild, Regina. Student, Willesden Tech. Coll., 1937-38, NYU, 1948-49. Cert. trainer, educator, practitioner of psychodrama and group psychotherapy Am. Bd. Examiners. Rsch. asst. Psychodramatic and Sociometric Insts., N.Y.C., 1942-51; pres. Moreno Inst., N.Y.C. and Beacon, N.Y., 1951-82; trainer in psychodrama Studiefrämjandet, Stockholm, 1976-83, Finnish Psychodrama Assn., Lahti, Finland, 1976-83; lectr., trainer, Gt. Britain, Australia, New Zealand, Norway, Sweden, Italy, Germany, Japan, 1976-96, Argentina, Brazil, Greece, The Netherlands, Denmark, Belgium, Spain, Israel, Korea and Taiwan, 1977—; hon. pres. Chinese Zerka Moreno Inst., Nanjing, China. Author: (book of poetry) Love Songs to Life, 1971, 93; co-author: Psychodrama, Vol. II, 1967, Vol. III, 1969. Named hon. citizen Comune di Roma, Assessorato Alla Cultura, 1983, Municipalidad de la Ciudad de Buenos Aires, 1984, Hon. Mem. Federacao Brasiliero de Psicodrama, Sao Paulo, 1996. Fellow Am. Soc. Group Psychotherapy and Psychodrama (pres. 1967-69, hon. pres. 1988—, sec.-treas. 1955-66); hon. mem. Internat. Assn. Group Psychotherapy (treas. 1974-76, bd. dirs. 1976-80), Soc. Psicodrama Sao Paulo (hon.), Sociedad Argentina Psicodrama (hon.). Home: 259 Wolcott Ave Beacon NY 12508-3711

MORENO-CABRAL, CARLOS EDUARDO, cardiac surgeon; b. Zacatecas, Mex., Nov. 4, 1951; s. Manuel Julio Moreno and Dominga Cabral; children: Rodrigo, Iza, Daniel. MD, Nat. U. Mex., 1976. Diplomate Am. Bd. Surgery, Am. Bd. Thoracic Surgery. Resident in gen. surgery U. Hawaii, 1977-80, Mich. State U., 1980-82; fellow in cardiac surgery Stanford (Calif.) U., 1982-84, 86-88; tng. in thoracic surgery SUNY, Bklyn., 1984-86; dir. cardiac transplant program St. Francis Hosp., Honolulu, 1989—. Author: Postoperative Management in Adult Cardiac Surgery, 1988. Fellow ACS; mem. Soc. Thoracic Surgeons. Avocation: photography. Office: 1380 Lusitana St Ste 912 Honolulu HI 96813-2448

MOREST, DONALD KENT, neuroscience educator; b. Kansas City, Mo., Oct. 4, 1934; s. F. Stanley and Clara Josephine (Riley) M.; m. Rosemary Richtmyer, July 13, 1963; children: Lydia, Claude. BA, U. Chgo., 1955; MD, Yale U., 1960. Sr. asst. surgeon USPHS, Bethesda, Md., 1960-63; asst. prof. U. Chgo., Ill., 1963-65; asst. to assoc. prof. Harvard Med. Sch., Boston, 1965-77; prof., dir. Ctr. for Neurol. Scis. U. Conn. Health Ctr., Farmington, 1977—; cons. NIH, Bethesda, 1975—. Contbr. articles to profl. jours. and books. Recipient Loeser award U. Conn. Health Ctr., Farmington, 1982; Career Devel. awardee NIH, 1971; named Javits neurosci. investigator NIH, 1984, Claude Pepper awardee, 1990. Mem. Am. Assn. Anatomists (C.Judson Herrick award 1966), Soc. for Neurosci., Assn. for Rsch. in Otolarynology, Conn. Acad. Sci. & Engring. (elected), Cajal Club (pres. 1980). Avocations: flute, badminton. Home: 18 Shady Ln West Simsbury CT 06092-2232

MORET, MARC, chemicals executive; b. Ménières, Switzerland, Nov. 15, 1923; married; 3 children. D Pub. Econs., U. Fribourg and Sorbonne, Paris, 1948. With practical indsl. tng. and assignments Swissair, Sulzer Bros., Nestlé S.A.; gen. mgr. Guigoz Internat.; from head of agro sales, to head agro and nutrition divsns. Sandoz Ltd., 1968, head finance dept., 1976, bd. dirs., 1977—, vice chmn. bd. dirs., 1980-85, pres., CEO, 1981-94, chmn. bd. dirs., 1985—. Office: Sandoz Ltd, Lichtstrasse 35, CH 4002 Basel Switzerland also: Sandoz Inc 608 Fifth Ave New York NY 10020-2303

MORETON, THOMAS HUGH, minister; b. Shanghai, China, Dec. 2, 1917; came to U.S., 1946; s. Hugh and Tsuru M; m. Olive Mae Rives, Apr. 1, 1947 (dec. Apr. 1986); children: Ann Rives Moreton Smith, Andrew Hugh, Margaret Evelyn Moreton Hamar; m. Selma Littig, June 7, 1986. LLB, 1939, BD, 1942, PhD, 1946; ThD, Trinity Sem., 1948; LittD, 1949. Ordained to ministry Bapt. Ch., Glasgow, Scotland, 1942. Min. various chs., also tchr. Seaford Coll. Eng., 1945-46; tchr. coll. and sem. level. div. courses various schs., Atlanta, Oklahoma City, 1946-51; founder Tokyo Gospel Mission, Inc., House of Hope, Inc., Tokyo, 1951—; also World Gospel Fellowship, Inc., Norman, Okla., 1967—; pastor chs., Moore, Okla., Shawnee, Okla., Ada., Okla., Del City, Okla., Tahlequah, Okla. and Oklahoma City, 1968—; preacher numerous fgn. countries; internat. tour dir., radio broadcaster. Contbr. articles to religious jours. Charter mem. Am.-Japan Com. for Assisting Japanese-Am. Orphans. Chaplain AUS, 1952-63. Recipient various awards Japanese govt. Fellow Royal Geog. Soc., Philos. Soc.; mem. Royal Soc. Lit., Am.-Japan Soc., Israel-Japan Soc.

MORETTI, AUGUST JOSEPH, lawyer; b. Elmira, N.Y., Aug. 18, 1950; s. John Anthony and Dorothy M. (De Blasio) M.; m. Audrey B. Kavka, Nov. 8, 1981; children: David Anthony, Matthew Alexander. BA magna cum laude, Princeton U., 1972; JD cum laude, Harvard U., 1975. Assoc. Heller, Ehrman, White and McAuliffe, San Francisco, 1976-82, ptnr., 1982—; lectr. bus. adminstrn. U. Calif. Berkeley, 1977-79; bd. dirs. AviGenics. Bd. dirs. Ann Martin Children's Ctr.; mem. adv. panel U. Calif. Berkeley Entrepreneur Program. Mem. ABA. Office: Heller Ehrman White & McAuliffe 525 University Ave Palo Alto CA 94301-1903

MOREY, CARL REGINALD, musicologist, academic administrator; b. Toronto, Ont., Can., July 14, 1934; s. Reginald Donald and Julia Beatrice (Mabey) M.; m. Lorna Ann Dalton, June 2, 1960 (dec.); 1 child, Rachel Adriana. MusB, U. Toronto, 1957; MusM, Ind. U., 1961, PhD, 1965. Asst. prof. Wayne State U., Detroit, 1962-63; assoc. prof. U. Windsor, Ont., 1964-70; prof. music U. Toronto, 1970—, dean faculty of music, 1984-90, Jean A. Chalmers prof., dir. Inst. for Can. Music, 1991—. Author: Music in Canada: A Research and Information Guide, 1997; editor: Works of Glenn Gould (Schott). Avocation: swimming. Home: 540 Palmerston Blvd, Toronto, ON Canada M6G 2P5 Office: U Toronto, Faculty of Music, Toronto, ON Canada M5S 1A1

MOREY, CHARLES LEONARD, III, theatrical director; b. Oakland, Calif., June 23, 1947; s. Charles Leonard Jr. and Mozelle Kathleen (Milliken) M.; m. Mary Carolyn Donnet, June 10, 1973 (div. 1975); m. Joyce Miriam Schilke, May 29, 1982; 1 child, William. AB, Dartmouth Coll., 1969; MFA, Columbia U., 1971. Artistic dir. Peterborough (N.H.) Players, 1977-88, Pioneer Theatre Co., Salt Lake City, 1984—; adj. asst. prof. theatre U. Utah, Salt Lake City, 1984—. Actor: N.Y. Shakespeare Festival, Playwrights Horizons, New Dramatists, ARK Theatre Co., Ensemble Studio Theatre, Cubiculo, Folger Theatre, Syracuse Repertory Theatre, Theatre by Sea, others; over 150 plays acted in or directed; guest dir. Ensemble Studio Theatre, ArK Theatre, Am. Stage Festivel, McCarter Theatre, Pioneer Theatre Co., PCPA Theatrefest, The Repertory Theater of St. Louis, Meadow Brook Theatre; author new adaptations Alexander Dumas' The Three Musketeers, Bram Stoker's Dracula, Charles Dickens' A Tale of Two Cities, Victor Hugo's The Hunchback of Notre Dame. Trustee Utah Arts Endowment, Inc.; panelist Nat. Endowment for Arts. Mem. Soc. Stage Dirs. and Choreographers, AEA, SAG, AFTRA, Salt Lake City C. of C. (Honors in the Arts award 1991), Utah Assn. Gifted Children (Community Svc. award 1991), Peterborough Players (Edith Bond Stearns award 1990). Democrat. Episcopalian. Office: Pioneer Theatre Co U Utah Salt Lake City UT 84112

MOREY, PHILIP STOCKTON, JR., mathematics educator; b. Houston, July 11, 1937; s. Philip Stockton and Helen Holmes (Wolcott) M.; m. Jeri Lynn Snyder, Sept. 5, 1964; children: William Philip, Christopher Jerome. BA, U. Tex., 1959, Ma, 1961, PhD, 1967. Asst. prof. math. U. Nebr., Omaha, 1967-68; assoc. prof. Tex. A&I U., Kingsville, 1968-76; prof. Tex. A&M U., Kingsville, 1976—; lectr. U. Tokyo, 1976, U. Hokkaido, 1977, 88. Contbr. articles to Tensor N.S., Internat. Jour. Engring. Sci, Tex. Jour. Sci. Recipient Researcher of Yr. awrd Tex. A&I Alumni Assn., 1985. Mem. Tex. Acad. Sci. (chmn. math. sect. 1982, '85), Am. Math. Soc., Tensor Soc., (Japan). Achievements include research in extensor analysis, tensor analysis, differential geometry, mathematical physics. Home: 1514 Lackey St Kingsville TX 78363-3199 Office: Tex A&M Univ Dept Math Kingsville TX 78362

MOREY, ROBERT HARDY, communications executive; b. Milw., Sept. 5, 1956; s. Lloyd W. and Ruby C. (McElhaney) M. AA, Ricks Coll., 1978; BA, Brigham Young U., 1983. Program dir. Sta. KABE-FM, Orem, Utah, 1982-83, sales mgr., 1983; nat. mgr. ops. Tiffany Prodns. Internat., Salt Lake City, 1983-84; account exec. Osmond Media Corp., Orem, 1984; corp. sec., bd. dirs. Positive Communications, Inc., Orem, 1984—, chief exec. officer, 1987—; gen. mgr. Sta. KSRR, Orem, 1985—; pres. K-Star Satellite Network, Orem, 1986—, Broadcast Media Svcs., Orem, 1989-93; gen. mgr. Sta. KMGR, Salt Lake City, 1993; ops. mgr. KQMB-FM, Salt Lake City, 1994-95, gen. mgr., 1995—; guest lectr. various colls. and univs., 1981—. Chmn. Rep. voting dist., Orem, 1984. Recipient Community Service award Utah Valley Community Coll., 1983; named one of Outstanding Young Men in Am. U.S. Jaycees, 1983. Avocations: reading, collecting stamps. Home: PO Box 828 Orem UT 84059-0828 Office: Sta KSRR Ventura Media Ctr 1240 E 800 N Orem UT 84097-4318

MORFOPOULOS, V., metallurgical engineer, materials engineer; b. Athens, Greece, Oct. 22, 1937. BS, Purdue U., 1958; MS, Columbia U., 1961, ScD in Engring. Sci., 1964. Rsch. assoc. metall. engring. Purdue U., 1957-60; rsch. engr. U.S. Steel Corp., 1961; instr. chem. CUNY, 1961-63; rsch. engr. Argonne Nat. Lab., 1963; rsch. engr. Am. Iron & Steel, Columbia U., 1964-65, sr. metall. sci., 1965-66; tech. dir. R&D testing Am. Standards Testing Bur., 1966—; cons. govt. and industry, 1966—; mem. Int. Commn. Chem. Thermodyn. & Kinetics; mem. Transp. Rsch. Bd., Nat. Rsch. Coun. Mem. AAAS, Am. Inst. Mining, Metall. Petroleum Engrs., Am. Soc. Engr. Edn., Assn. Cons. Chemists and Chem. Engrs., N.Y. Acad. Sci. Achievements include research and consulting in fields of corrosion and oxidation phenomena. low and high temperature thermodynamics, liquid metals and compounds, surface phenomena, electrometallurgy and electrode phenomena, electrical and magnetic properties of matter, failure and stress analysis, metal finishing, joining and working. Office: Am Standards Testing Bur Inc 40 Water St New York NY 10004-2605

MORFORD-BURG, JOANN, state senator, investment company executive; b. Miller, S.D., Nov. 26, 1956; d. Darrell Keith Morford and Eleanor May (Fawcett) Morford-Steptoe; m. Quinten Leo Burg, Nov. 12, 1983. BS in Agrl.-Bus., Comml. Econs., S.D. State U., 1979; cert. in personal fin. planning, Am. Coll., 1992. Agrl. loan officer 1st Bank System, Presho, S.D., 1980-82, Wessington Springs, S.D., 1982-86; agrl. loan officer Am. State Bank, Wessington Springs, 1986; registered investment rep. SBM Fin. Svcs. Inc., Wessington Springs, 1986-96; mem. S.D. State Senate, Wessington Springs, 1990—, majority whip, 1993-94, minority whip, 1995-96, mem., 1990-97; mem. S.D. State Senate, Miller, 1997; mem. senate appropriations com. 1993—; chair senate ops. and audit com. 1993, 94; mem. ops. and audit com., 1995—; vice chair Nat. Conf. State Legislators' Assembly of Fed. Issues Environ. Com., 1996—. Mem. Midwestern-Can. task force Midwest Conf., 1990-94; mem. transp. com., commerce com., taxation com. S.D. State Senate, Pierre, 1990-92; treas. twp. bd. Wessington Springs, 1990-92; mem. Wessington Springs Sch. Improvement Coun. Mem. Future Farmers Am. (adv. bd. Wessington Springs chpt.), S.D. State U. 4-H Alumni Assn., Nat. Life Underwriters Assn. (Huron chpt.), Order Ea. Star (various offices 1980—), Alumni Am. Coun. Young Polit. Leaders (China delegation 1996). Democrat. Methodist. Home and Office: PO Box 21 417 W 6th St Miller SD 57382-0021

MORGA BELLIZZI, CELESTE, editor; b. N.Y.C., Mar. 8, 1921; d. Louis and Emma (Macari) Morga; m. John J. Bellizzi, Sept. 1, 1942; children: John J., Robert F. Student, Columbia U., 1940-41, SUNY, Albany, 1970. Cert. med. lab. technician. Medical lab. technician USMC Hosp., N.Y.C., 1942, Woman's Hosp., N.Y.C., 1942-52; spl. investigator N.Y. State Atty. Gen.'s Office, Albany, 1958-65; editor Internat. Drug Report publ., The Narc Officer publ. Internat. Narcotic Enforcement Officers Assn., Albany, 1965—. Dir. Albany Inst. History and Art, 1988-90, N.Y. State Press Women, Albany, 1987; advisor UN Non-govtl. Orgns. Drug Com., N.Y.C., 1980-90, White House Conf. Drug Free Am., Washington, 1987; mem. com. Bethlehem Drug Prevention Program, Delmar, N.Y., 1987-90, Action Commn. Narc Edn., Delmar, 1984-90; v.p. Women's Rep. Party Albany, 1972. Recipient Pres.'s award INEOA, 1982, Disting. Svc. award Houston Police Dept., 1981. Mem. Nat. Fedn. Press Women, Nat. Press Club, Univ. Club, Albany Country Club, Aberdeen Country Club. Avocations: painting, golf, tennis. Office: Internat Narcotic Enforcement Officers Assn 112 State St Albany NY 12207-2005

MORGAN, ALAN DOUGLAS, state education official. B in Elem. Edn., N.Mex. Highlands U., 1969, MA in Guidance and Counseling, 1971; D in Edn. Leadership, U. Nev., 1995. State supt. education State of N.Mex., 1985—. Office: N Mex Edn Dept Edn Bldg 300 Don Gaspar Ave Santa Fe NM 87501-2752

MORGAN, ALAN VIVIAN, geologist, educator; b. Barry, Glamorgan, Wales, Jan. 29, 1943; emigrated to Can., 1964, naturalized, 1977; s. George Vivian Williams and Sylvia Nesta (Atkinson) M.; m. Marion Anne Medhurst, June 14, 1966; children: Siân Kristina, Alexis John. B.Sc. with honors in Geology and Geography, U. Leicester, Eng., 1964; M.Sc. in Geography, U. Alta., Calgary, Can., 1966; Ph.D. in Geology, U. Birmingham, Eng., 1970. Postdoctoral fellow U. Western Ont. and U. Waterloo, Ont., Can., 1970-71; asst. prof. earth scis. and man-environ. studies U. Waterloo, 1971-78, assoc. prof. earth scis., 1978-85, prof., 1985—; assoc. dir. Quaternary Scis. Inst. U. Waterloo, Ont., Can., 1992—; mem. Brit. Schs. Exploring Soc. Ctrl. Iceland Expdn., 1960; rep. Can. Geosci. Coun., 1977-83, exec. dir., 1988-94, adminstrv. dir., 1996—; mem. con. on global change Royal Soc. Can., 1988-91, mem. com. on pub. wareness of sci., 1989-94; coord. global change Geol. Survey Can.a, 1990-92. Author 6 field guides; editor newsletter OYEZ, 1990-94; contbr. articles to numerous profl. publs.; dir., prodr. documentary film The Heimaey Eruption, 1974. Recipient award for MS thesis Can. Assn. Petroleum Geologists, 1967, Bancroft award Royal Soc. Can., 1994, John H. Moss award Nat. Assn. Geology Tchrs., 1995, Wills Ambrose medal Geol. Assn. Can., 1997; Charles Lapworth scholar, 1970; Nat. Scis. and Engring. Rsch. Coun. Can. grantee, 1971—;. Fellow Geol. Assn. Can. (hon. life, sec.-treas. 1975-83, hon. disting. fellow, J. Willis Ambrose medal 1997), Geol. Soc. Am.; mem. Am. Quaternary Assn. (pres. 1990-92), Can. Quaternary Assn. (pres. 1987-89), Brit. Quaternary Research Assn., Internat. Union Quaternary Research (sec. gen. XII congress 1983-87). Office: U Waterloo, Dept Earth Scis, Waterloo, ON Canada N2L 3G1

MORGAN, ALFRED VANCE, management consulting company executive; b. Liberal, Kans., Apr. 13, 1936; s. Forrest Francis and Gertrude Irene (Henning) M.; m. Peggy Ann Riley, June 29, 1960; children: Trudie Marie, Vance Riley, Allen Forrest, Bradley Augustus, Kelly James. BBA, U. Kans., 1958; MBA, U. So. Calif., 1966; postgrad., Am. Inst. Banking, 1965. Asst. mgr. Fruehauf Trailer Co., L.A., Calif., 1960-61; asst. mktg. dir. Security Pacific Nat. Bank, 1961-65; mktg. exec. Doyle, Dane, Bernbach Advt., 1965-66; cons. Harbridge House, Inc., Boston, 1966-71; pres. Morgan Bus. Assocs., Inc., Santa Barbara and Boston, 1971; instr. bus. L.A. City Coll., 1971-72; instr. mgmt. Santa Barbara City Coll., 1973. Contbr. articles to profl. publs. With AUS, 1958-60. Mem. ASTD, Am. Mktg. Assn. L.A., Am. Soc. Profl. Cons., U. So. Calif. Grad. Sch. Bus. Alumni Assn. Office: 1676 E Valley Rd Santa Barbara CA 93108-2150

MORGAN, ANDREW WESLEY, artist, educator; b. Cleve., July 29, 1922; s. John B. and Bertha (Amersbach) M.; m. Dahlia Kaplow, May 18, 1973; children from previous marriage—Alexander, Vincent, Nicholas. B.A., Kenyon Coll., 1948; M.F.A., U. N.C., 1952; postgrad., N.Y.U., 1955-57; L.H.D. (hon.), Tarkio Coll. Head art dept. Greenwich (Conn.) Country Day Sch., 1952-59; chmn. dept. art, dir. gallery U. Miss., 1959-60; pres. Kansas City (Mo.) Art Inst., 1960-70; prof., chmn. art dept. U. Miami, Fla., 1970-87; Commr. Municipal Art Commn., Kansas City, 1965-70; co-chmn. Mid-Am. Urban Design Conf., 1966. One-man shows include Stanford (Conn.) Mus., 1958, Pietrantonio Gallery, N.Y.C., 1960, Lowe Mus., 1980, Viscaya Mus., Miami, Fla., 1984, Leedy-Voulkos Art Ctr., Kansas City, Mo., 1990, Polk Mus., Lakeland, Fla., 1991, New World Sch. for Arts Gallery, Miami, 1992, U. Miami, 1993, Art Mus. No. Ariz. U., 1993-94, one-person show Ctr. for Visual Comm., Coral Gables, Fla., 1995, Leedy-Voulkos Gallery, Kansas City, 1997; groups shows include Boston Arts Festival, 1960, Mid-South Annual, Memphis, 1961, Roko Gallery, N.Y.C., 1960, U. Miss., 1959, N.E. Ann. (Jury award oil prize), Silver Mine, Conn., 1958, Ctr. for Contemporary Art, 1989, Six Miami Painters, 1st Ave. Gallery, 1993, Fla. Landscape, 1994. Active Com. Econ. Devel., Kans., 1965-70; bd. dirs. Kansas City Regional Coun. Higher Edn.; pres. bd. dirs. Union Ind. Colls. Art, 1967-70; mem. visual arts bd. Nat. Found. for Arts, Miami, 1988; adv. bd. Vt. Studio Ctr., Johnson, 1989. With AUS, 1942-46. Mem. Nat. Assn. Schs. Art (dir.), Coll. Art. Assn. Home: 10331 SW 59th Ave Miami FL 33156-4114

MORGAN, ARLENE NOTORO, newspaper editor, reporter, recruiter; b. Phila., July 27, 1945; d. James Vincent and Mary Rose (Actis-Grande) Notoro; m. David J. Morgan, Mar. 3, 1948; children: Elizabeth, Lauren. BS in Journalism, Temple U., 1967. Reporter Delaware County Daily Times, Chester, Pa., 1967-69; reporter Philadelphia Inquirer, 1969—, dep. metro. editor, 1990-91, sr. editor, 1991—. Bd. dirs. Friends Hosp., Phila., 1978—. Recipient Community Service award Phila. chpt. VFW, 1983, Rafters Charities, Phila., 1982, Phila. Newspapers Inc. Employee Recognition award, 1987. Mem. Soc. Profl. Journalists. Roman Catholic. Avocations: ballet, travel, opera and art appreciation, advocate to the mentally ill. Office: Phila Inquirer 400 N Broad St Philadelphia PA 19130-4015*

MORGAN, AUDREY, architect; b. Neenah, Wis., Oct. 19, 1931; d. Andrew John Charles Hopfensperger and Melda Lily (Radtke) Anderson; m. Earl Adrian Morgan (div); children: Michael A. Morgan, Nancy Lee Morgan, Diana Lou Hansen, Susan Lynn Heiner. BA, U. Wash., 1955. Registered architect, Wash., Oreg.; cert. NCARB. Project mgr. The Austin Co., Renton, Wash., 1972-75; med. facilities architect The NBBJ Group, Seattle, 1975-79; architect constrn. rev. unit Wash. State Divsn. Health, Olympia, 1979-81; project dir., med. planner John Graham & Co., Seattle, 1981-83; pvt. practice architecture, Ocean Shores, Wash., 1983—, also health care facility cons., code analyst. Contbg. author: Guidelines for Construction and Equipment of Hospitals and Medical Facilities; Co-editor: Design Consideration for Mental Health Facilities; contbr. articles to profl. jours. and govt. papers; prin. works include quality assurance coord. for design phase Madigan Army Med. Ctr., Ft. Lewis, Wash.; med. planner and code analyst Rockwood Clinic, Spokane, Wash., Comprehensive Health Care Clinic for Yakima Indian Nation, Toppenish, Wash.; code analyst S.W. Wash. Hosps., Vancouver; med. planner Pacific Cataract & Lazer Inst. Chehalis & Kennewick, Wash; med. planner facilities for child, adult, juvenile and forensic psychiatric patients., States of Wash. and Oreg. expert witness litigation cases involving mental health facilities. Cons. on property mgmt. Totem council Girl Scouts U.S.A., Seattle, 1969-84, troop leader, cons., trainer, 1961-74; mem. Wash. State Bldg. Code Coun., tech. adv. group for non-residential bldgs., Barier Free Com. Tech. adv. group for Ams. with Disabilties Act; assoc. mem. Wash State Fire Marshals Tech. Adv. Group. Mem. AIA (nat. acad. architecture for health 1980—, subcoms. codes and standards, chair mental health com., 1989-92, and numerous other coms., founding mem. Wash. council AIA architecture for health panel 1981—, recorder 1981-84, vice chmn., 1987, chmn. 1988, bd. dirs. S.W. Wash. chpt. 1983-84), Nat. Fire Protection Assn., Soc. Am. Value Engrs., Am. Hosp. Assn., Assn. Western Hosps., Wash. State Hosp. Assn., Wash. State Soc. Hosp. Engrs. (hon.), Seattle Womens Sailing Assn., Audubon Soc., Alpha Omicron Pi. Lutheran. Clubs: Coronado 25 Fleet 13 (Seattle) (past sec., bull. editor); GSA 25 Plus. Home and Office: PO Box 1990 Ocean Shores WA 98569-1990 also: 904 Falls Of Clyde Loop SE Ocean Shores WA 98569-1990

MORGAN, BETTY MITCHELL, artist, educator; b. Raleigh, N.C., Apr. 17, 1948; d. Carlton Turner and Miriam Grace (Sexton) M.; m. Thomas Vance Morgan, June 24, 1972; children: David Vance, Thomas Mitchell. BS, Appalachian State U., 1970; MA in Art Edn., U. Ga., 1972; postgrad., Calif. State U., Northridge, 1983. Cert. tchr., Calif., Ga., N.J., N.C., Mass. Tchr. art Randolph Jr. High Sch., Charlotte, N.C., 1971-72, Oconee County Intermediate Sch., Watkinsville, Ga., 1972-77; tchr. English 1st Bapt. Day Sch., Van Nuys, Calif., 1982-83; freelance artist, tchr. Hillsborough, N.J., 1984-86; instr. Torrance Ctr. Creative Studies U. Ga., Athens, 1987-93; tchr. Benton Elem. Sch., Nicholson, Ga., 1988-89; tchr. art Jackson County Sch. System, Jefferson, Ga., 1989-93; instr. Danforth Mus. Sch., 1995—, DeCordova Mus. Sch., 1995—; art tchr. Eliot Sch., Needham, Mass.; lectr. art and civic assns., Ga., 1987-93, 95—; tchr. art Needham Pub. Schs., 1995—; freelance artist, 1976—; exhibiting mem. Loef Gallery, Athens, 1986-93; art editor Appalachian State U. Yearbook, Boone, N.C., 1970; coord. Japanese and Australian Children's Art Exch., 1992-93; presenter Mass. Music Tchrs. Assn. Conf. Cover illustrator Philanthropic Ednl. Orgn., 1991; exhibitor group and solo shows in N.J., Calif., N.C., Ga., and Mass., 1976—; works displayed in pvt. and pub. collections in U.S., Australia, Europe, corp. collections including AT&T Comm., Thomas Cook Travel Agy., Nat. Utilities, Inc., Trust Co. Bank N.E. Ga. Docent Art Appreciation in Schs., Hillsborough, N.J., 1984-86; cub den leader Athens and Hillsborough area Boy Scouts Am., 1985-88; mem. Am. Cancer Soc., Athens, 1987-89; vol. Am. Lung Assn., 1988. Selected for Tchr. to Japan program Japanese C. of C., 1992; winner 1st pl. award for artwork San Fernando Valley Artist Assn., Northridge, 1983; named Tchr. of Yr. by Benton Elem. Sch., 1992-93. Mem. Profl. Assn. Ga. Educators, Philanthropic Ednl. Orgn., Ga. Art Edn. Assn., Nat. Art Edn. Assn., Athens Art Assn., Mass. Art Edn. Assn. Avocations: painting, tennis, reading, hiking. Home: 14 Valley Rd Natick MA 01760-3415

MORGAN, BEVERLY, publishing company executive. Pres. Southex Exhbns., Inc., North Town, Ont., Can. Office: Southex Exhbns Inc, 1 Concord Gate Ste 800, North Town, ON Canada M3C 3M6*

MORGAN, BEVERLY CARVER, physician, educator; b. N.Y.C., May 29, 1927; d. Jay and Florence (Newkamp) Carver; children—Nancy, Thomas E. III, John E. M.D. cum laude (Mosby Scholar), Duke U., 1955. Diplomate Am. Bd. Pediatrics (oral examiner 1984-90, mem. written examination com. 1990—), Nat. Bd. Med. Examiners. Intern, asst. resident Stanford U. Hosp., San Francisco, 1955-56; clin. fellow pediatrics, trainee pediatric cardiology Babies Hosp.-Columbia Presbyn. Med. Center, N.Y.C., 1956-59; research fellow cardiovascular diagnostic lab. Columbia-Presbyn. Med. Center, N.Y.C., 1959-60; instr. pediatrics Coll. Physicians and Surgeons, Columbia U., 1960; dir. heart sta. Robert B. Green Meml. Hosp., San Antonio, 1960-62; lectr. pediatrics U. Tex., 1960-62; spl. research fellow in pediatric cardiology Sch. Medicine, U. Wash., Seattle, 1962-64; from instr. to prof. pediatrics Sch. Medicine, U. Wash., 1962-73, chmn. dept. pediatrics, 1973-80; mem. staff U. Wash. Hosp., chief of staff, 1975-77; mem. staff Harborview Med. Ctr.; mem. staff Children's Orthopedic Hosp. and Med. Ctr., dir. dept. medicine, 1974-80; prof., chmn. dept. pediatrics U. Calif., Irvine, 1980-88, prof. pediat. and pediat. cardiology, 1980—; pediatrician in chief Children's Hosp. Orange County, 1988; mem. pulmonary acad. awards panel Nat. Heart and Lung Inst., 1972-75; mem. grad. med. edn. nat. advisory com. to sec. HEW, 1977-80; mem. Coun. on Pediatric Practice; chmn. Task Force on Opportunities for Women in Pediatrics, 1982; mem. nursing rev. com. NIH, 1987-88. Contbr. articles to profl. jours.; mem. editorial bd. Clin. Pediatrics, Am. Jour. Diseases of Children, Jour. of Orange County Pediatric Soc., Jour. Am. Acad. Pediatrics, Los Angeles Pediatric Soc. Recipient Women of Achievement award Matrix Table, Seattle, 1974; Distinguished Alumnus award Duke U. Med. Sch., 1974; Ann. award Nat. Bd. Med. Coll. Pa., 1977; USPHS career devel. awardee, 1966-71. Mem. Am. Acad. Pediat. (chmn. com. on pediat. manpower 1984-86), Am. Coll. Cardiology, Soc. for Pediat. Rsch., Am. Fedn. Clin. Rsch., Am. Pediat. Soc., Assn. Med. Sch. Pediat. Dept. Chmn. (sec.-treas. 1981-87), Western Soc. for Pediat. Rsch., Alpha Omega Alpha. Home: 601 Lido Park Dr Newport Beach CA 92663-4411 Office: U Calif Irvine Med Ctr Dept Pediatrics 101 The City Dr S Orange CA 92868-3201

MORGAN, BEVERLY HAMMERSLEY, middle school educator, artist; b. Wichita Falls, Tex.; d. Vernon C. and Melba Marie (Whited) Hammersley; m. Robert Lewis Morgan, Sept. 21, 1957 (div. 1972); children: Janet Claire, Robert David. BA, So. Meth. U.; MA, U. Ala., 1980, AA certification, 1982; postgrad., U. Tex., 1991—. Cert. art tchr., Tex., Ala.; cert. elem. tchr., Ala. Art tchr. Ft. Worth Pub. Schs., 1955-60; English tchr. Lincoln County Schs., Fayetteville, Tenn., 1961-62; 6th grade tchr. Huntsville (Ala.) Pub. Schs., 1960-61, 62-68, art tchr., 1972-92, 93-94. One man shows include U. Ala., 1980, Huntsville Art League, 1981. Mem. Huntsville-Madison County Art Tchrs., Huntsville Mus. Art, Internat. Platform Assn., Am. Contract Bridge League. Republican. Avocations: bridge, travel, collector of Hammersley English bone china. Home: 12027 Chicamauga Trl SE Huntsville AL 35803-1544

MORGAN, BRUCE RAY, international consultant; b. Los Angeles, Oct. 28, 1932; s. Francis Raymond and Rose Hall (Black) M.; m. Bette Jeanne Moore, Oct. 7, 1957; children: Michael John, Brian Leo, Jeanne Ann. A.A., Sacramento Jr. Coll., 1952; B.S., U. Calif.-Berkeley, 1954, LL.B., 1957. Bar: Calif. 1957. Judge adv. USAF, Saudi Arabia and Morocco, 1958-61; atty. firm Thelen, Marrin, Johnson & Bridges, San Francisco, 1961-67; dep. dir. Peace Corps, Nepal, 1967-68, dir., 1968-70; exec. dir. Center Research and Edn., Denver, 1971-75; dir. U.S. representation to Saudi Arabia-U.S. Joint Commn. on Econ. Coop., Riyadh, 1975-76; pres. Bruce Morgan Assocs., Inc., Washington, 1976—. Editor: Calif. State Bar Jour. Legis. Rev, 1957. Served with USAF, 1958-61. Mem. U.S., Calif. bars. Office: Bruce Morgan Assocs 1010 N Glebe Rd Ste 500 Arlington VA 22201-4749

MORGAN, CAROL MIRÓ, marketing executive; b. Ancon, Republic of Panama, Jan. 31, 1942; d. Morton A. and Dora (Rebolledo) Blum; m. Edward J. Morgan, July 24, 1963 (div. Jan. 1972); children: Edward M., John G.; m. Doran J. Levy, Oct. 3, 1986. BS, Spring Hill Coll., 1962, Met. State U., 1986; MA, Kans. State U., 1966. Cert. tchr., La. Instr. Ohio State U., Columbus, 1966-67; staff writer Palm Beach (Fla.) Daily News, 1967-70; tchr. Isidore Newman Sch., New Orleans, 1972-77; dir. pub. rels. Hennepin County Med. Ctr., Mpls., 1977-79; mgr. pub. rels. Peavey Co., Mpls., 1979-81; owner, pres. Carol Morgan Assocs., Inc., Mpls., 1981-92, Strategic Directions Group, Inc., St. Paul, 1992—. Home: 1029 Lombard Ave Saint Paul MN 55105-3256 Office: Strategic Directions Group Inc 46 4th St E Ste 1100 Saint Paul MN 55101-1109

MORGAN, CAROLYN F., lawyer; b. Gadsden, Ala., Nov. 23, 1945; d. Sephes Jonah and Garnet Sylvia (Watson) M.; m. Galen Kennah, Dec. 16, 1967 (div. Nov. 1979); children: Jason, Jennifer; m. David Cummings, May 6, 1995. BS, Jacksonville State U., 1970; JD, Cumberland Sch. of Law, 1983. Bar: Ala., U.S. Dist. Ct. (no. dist.) Ala., U.S. Ct. Appeals (11th cir.), U.S. Supreme Ct. Social worker II State of Ala., Gadsden, Birmingham, 1969-80; asst. city atty. City of Gadsden, 1983-84; asst. dist. atty. State of Ala., Anniston, 1984-90; corp. counsel BE & K, Inc., Birmingham, 1990-95;

asst. gen. counsel BE&K Inc, Birmingham, 1995-96. Office: BE&K Inc VP Human Resources 2000 Internat Park Dr Birmingham AL 35243

MORGAN, CLYDE NATHANIEL, dermatologist; b. Bell County, Tex., Nov. 2, 1923; s. Xenophen William and Rhoda Ella (Deck) M.; m. Birdie Joyce Rich, Mar. 3, 1951; children: Clyde Nathaniel Jr., Reinette Jean, Nancy Elaine. BS, Abilene Christian Coll., 1948; MD, U. Tex. Galveston, 1953. Assoc. prof. biology Abilene (Tex.) Christian Coll., 1954-56; pvt. practice Abilene, 1954-67, dermatologist, 1969—. Contbr. articles to profl. jours. Mem. AMA, SAR (v.p. 1995-96, award 1995), Am. Coll. Cryosurgery, Internat. Soc. Cryosurgery, Tex. Med. Assn., Tex. Dermatologic Soc., Taylor-Jones-Haskell County Med. Soc. Republican. Mem. Ch. of Christ. Avocations: golf, fishing, hunting, cryogenics research. Home: 1718 Cedar Crest Dr Abilene TX 79601-3228 Office: 1166 Merchant St Abilene TX 79603-5014

MORGAN, DAVID ERNEST, computer and communications research executive; b. Terre Haute, Ind., Mar. 22, 1942; s. George Ernest and Barbara Marguerite (Lutz) M.; m. Judith Johanna Clement, July 2, 1966; children: Heidi Elizabeth, Gwendolen Anne. BS in Math, Rose Poly. Inst., 1964; MS in Math., U. Mich., 1965; PhD in Computer Sci., U. Waterloo, Ont., Can., 1971. Reporter, photographer WTHI Radio and TV, Terre Haute, 1961-64; mem. tech. staff Bell Telephone Labs., Holmdel, N.J., 1964-70; prof. computer sci. U. Waterloo, 1970-80, dir. networks rsch. lab., 1972-80; v.p. Telecom Network Tech., Toronto, Ont., 1975-80; mgr. arch. and tech. Digital Equipment Corp., Maynard, Mass., 1977-78, 80-84; dir. computer and networks lab. Indsl. Tech. Inst., Ann Arbor, Mich., 1984-86; v.p. rsch. Motorola Inc., Schaumburg, Ill., 1986—; pres. Mordata Ltd., Waterloo, 1973-86; dir., exec. com. Corp. of Open Systems, McLean, Va., 1986-94; vice chmn., adv. bd. Microelectronics and Computer Corp., Austin, Tex., 1992-93; mem. Ill. Gov.'s Task Force Comm., 1992-93; bd. dirs. Computer-Based Patient Record Inst., Chgo.; founder, chmn., bd. dirs. Healthcare Open Sys. Techs. and Trials (HOST Inc.), 1993—; speaker numerous confs. and seminars; vis. rsch. scientist MIT Media Labs, 1995—. Contbr. articles to profl. jours.; patentee/inventor in field. Weston-Wabash scholarship Westin-Wabash Found., 1960; fellowship IBM, 1970, grad. study fellowship Bell Labs., 1965. Mem. IEEE, Soc. Mfg. Engrs., Asynchronous Transfer Mode Forum, Assn. for Computing Machinery, Am. Nat. Stds. Inst. (X3 com. 1984-87, TI com. 1988-93), Tau Beta Pi. Avocations: vocal music, photography, travel. Office: 3436 N Kennicott Ave Ste 150 Arlington Heights IL 60004-7801

MORGAN, DAVID FORBES, minister; b. Toronto, Ont., Can., Aug. 3, 1930; came to U.S., 1954; s. Forbes Alexander and Ruth (Bamford) M.; m. Delores Mae Storhaug, Sept. 7, 1956; children—Roxanne Ruth, David Forbes II. BA, Rocky Mt. Coll.; ThB, Coll. of the Rockies, MDiv; postgrad. Bishop's Sch. Theology; LittD (hon.), Temple Coll., 1956, D.C. Nat. Coll. Ordained priest. Pres., Coll. of the Rockies, Denver, 1960-73; founder and rector Prior Order of Christ Centered Ministries, Denver, 1973—; canon pastor St. John's Cathedral, Denver, 1982-96, canon at large, 1996— ; bd. dir. Alpha Inc., Denver, 1981—. Author: Christ Centered Ministries, A Response to God's Call, 1973; Songs with A Message, 1956. Clubs: Oxford, Denver Botanic Garden. Home: 740 Clarkson St Denver CO 80218-3204 Office: St Johns Cathedral 1313 Clarkson St Denver CO 80218-1806

MORGAN, DENNIS RICHARD, lawyer; b. Lexington, Va., Jan. 3, 1942; s. Benjamin Richard and Gladys Belle (Brown) M. BA, Washington and Lee U., 1964; JD, U. Va., 1967; LLM in Labor Law, NYU, 1971. Bar: Ohio 1967, Va. 1967, U.S. Ct. Appeals (4th cir.) 1968, U.S. Ct. Appeals (6th cir.) 1971, U.S. Supreme Ct. 1972. Law clk. to chief judge U.S. Dist. Ct. Ea. Dist. Va., 1967-68; mem. Marshman, Snyder & Seeley, Cleve., 1971-72; dir. labor rels. Ohio Dept. Adminstrv. Svcs., 1972-75; asst. city atty. Columbus, Ohio, 1975-77; dir. Ohio Legis. Reference Bur., 1979-81; assoc. Clemans, Nelson & Assocs., Columbus, 1981; pvt. practice, Columbus, 1978-92; lectr. in field; guest lectr. Cen. Mich. U., 1975; judge moot ct. Ohio State U. Sch. Law, 1981, 83, grad. div., 1973, 74, 76, Baldwin-Wallace Coll., 1973; legal counsel Dist. IV Communications Workers Am., 1982-88; pers. dir. Pub. Utilities Commn. Ohio, 1989-91; asst. atty gen. State of Ohio, 1991—. Vice-chmn. Franklin County Dem. Party, 1976-82, dem. com. person Ward 58, Columbus, 1973-95; chmn. rules com. Ohio State Dem. Conv., 1974; co-founder, trustee Greater West Side Dem. Club; negotiator Franklin County United Way, 1977-81; regional chmn. ann. alumni fund-raising program U. Va. Sch. Law; commr. Greater Hilltop Area Commn., 1989—; pres. Woodbrook Village Condominium Assn., 1985—. Robert E. Lee Rsch. scholar, summer, 1965; recipient Am. Jurisprudence award, 1967. Capt. U.S. Army, 1968-70. Mem. Indsl. Rels. Rsch. Assn., ABA, Fed. Bar Assn., Am. Judicature Soc., Pi Sigma Alpha. Roman Catholic. Clubs: Shamrock, Columbus Metroplitan (charter). Home: 1261 Woodbrook Ln # G Columbus OH 43223-3243

MORGAN, DONALD CRANE, lawyer; b. Detroit, Sept. 17, 1940; s. Donald Nye and Nancy (Crane) M.; m. Judith Munro, June 23, 1962; children: Wendy, Donald. BA, Ohio Wesleyan U., 1962; JD, U. Mich., 1965. Bar: Mich. 1966, U.S. Dist. Ct. (ea. dist.) Mich. 1966, U.S. Ct. Appeals (6th cir.) 1967, U.S. Supreme Ct. 1971. Ptnr. Kerr, Russell and Weber, Detroit, 1965-87; of counsel Draugelis & Ashton, Plymouth, Mich., 1988-93; pvt. practice Plymouth, Mich., 1993—; twp. atty. Plymouth Twp., 1970-85, Northville Twp., 1972-85; city atty. City of Plymouth, 1995—; mediator Wayne County Mediation Tribunal, Detroit, 1981—, Oakland County Mediation Tribunal, Pontiac, Mich., 1992—; hearing panelist Mich. Atty. Discipline Bd., 1981—. Chmn. Wayne County II congl. Dist. Rep. Party, 1979-81; bd. dirs. Growth Works, Inc., treas., 1992-95, pres. 1995—; ruling elder 1st Presbyn. Ch., Plymouth, 1976-79, 90-93. Paul Harris fellow, 1980. Mem. ABA, Mich. Def. Trial Counsel, State Bar of Mich. (rep. assembly 1979-85, 89-95, chmn. medicolegal problems com. 1995-96), Detroit Assn. Def. Trial Counsel, Plymouth Rotary (pres. 1985-86), Plymouth Rotary Found., Inc. (sec. 1996—), Phi Alpha Delta, Sigma Alpha Epsilon. Republican. Presbyterian. Avocations: reading, travel, sports. Home: 1440 Woodland Pl Plymouth MI 48170-1569 Office: 134 N Main St Plymouth MI 48170-1236

MORGAN, DONNA JEAN, psychotherapist; b. Edgerton, Wis., Nov. 16, 1955; d. Donald Edward and Pearl Elizabeth (Robinson) Garey. BA, U. Wis., Whitewater, 1983, MS, 1985. Cert. psychotherapist, Wis.; cert. mental health and alcohol and drug counselor; nat. cert. alcohol and drug abuse counselor; lic. marriage and family therapist, Wis.; lic. ind. social worker; lic. clin. ind. social worker; nat. cert. counselor; lic. profl. counselor; lic. advanced practice social worker. Pvt. practice Janesville, Wis., 1988-91, New Focus, Waukesha and Mukwonago, Wis., 1996-97, William N. Watson MDSC & Assocs, Oconomowac, Wis., 1997—; clin. supr. Stoughton (Wis.) Hosp., 1985-88; prin. Morgan and Assocs., Janesville, Wis., 1991-96. Mem. underaged drinking violation alternative program Rock County, 1986-96; co-chmn. task force on child sexual abuse, 1989-91; mem. Rock County Multi-disciplinary Team on Child Abuse, 1990-96; mem. spkrs. bur. Rock County C.A.R.E. House, 1990—; adv. bd. Parents Place, Waukesha County, Wis., 1997—. Mem. APA, Am. Counseling Assn., Am. Profl. Soc. on the Abuse of Children, Wis. Profl. Soc. on the Abuse of Children (bd. dirs. 1994—), Rock County Mental Health Providers, Am. Assn. Mental Health Counselors, Wis. Assn. Mental Health Counselors, South Ctrl. Wis. Action Coalition, Am. Assn. Marriage and Family Therapy (clin. mem.), Am. Assn. Christian Counselors, Wis. Counseling Assn. Office: William N Watson MDSC & Assocs 888 Thackeray Trail Ste 210 Oconomowoc WI 53066 also: 2717 N Grandview Blvd #310 Waukesha WI 53188

MORGAN, E. A., church administrator. Chaplain Ch. of the Living God Exec. Bd. Office: Church of the Living God 735 S Oakland Dr Decatur IL 62522*

MORGAN, EDMUND SEARS, history educator; b. Mpls., Jan. 17, 1916; s. Edmund Morris and Elsie Sears (Smith) M.; m. Helen Theresa Mayer, June 7, 1939; children: Penelope, Pamela.; m. Marie Caskey, June 22, 1983. A.B., Harvard U., 1937, Ph.D., 1942. Instrument maker Radiation Lab., Mass. Inst. Tech., 1942-45; instr. U. Chgo., 1945-46; asst. prof. Brown U., 1946-49, asso. prof., 1949-51, prof., 1951-55, acting dean grad. sch., 1951-52; prof. Yale U., 1955-65, Sterling prof., 1965-86, prof. emeritus, 1986—; Research fellow Huntington Library, 1952-53; Johnson research prof. U. Wis., 1968-69. Author: The Puritan Family, 1944, Virginians at Home, 1953, (with Helen M. Morgan) The Stamp Act Crisis, 1953, The Birth of the Republic, 1956, The Puritan Dilemma, 1958, The Gentle Puritan, 1962, Visible Saints, 1963, Roger Williams, 1967, So What About History, 1969, American Slavery American Freedom, 1975, The Challenge of the American Revolution, 1976, The Meaning of Independence, 1976, The Genius of George Washington, 1980, Inventing the People, 1988; Mem. editorial bd.: N.E. Quar; Contbr. articles and revs. to hist. jours. Trustee Smith Coll., 1984-89. Mem. Organ. Am. Historianss (pres. 1971-72), Colonial Soc. Mass., Mass. Hist. Soc., Am. Antiquarian Soc., Am. Philos. Soc., Am. Acad. Arts and Scis., Conn. Acad. Arts and Scis., Brit. Acad., Royal Hist. Soc.

MORGAN, ELIZABETH, plastic and reconstructive surgeon; b. Washington, July 9, 1947; d. William James and Antonia (Bell) M.; children: 1 dau., Ellen. BA magna cum laude, Harvard U., 1967; postgrad. (fellow), Oxford U., Somerville Coll., 1967, 70; MD, Yale U., 1971; law student, Georgetown U., 1986-87; PhD in Psychology, U. Canterbury, Christchurch, New Zealand, 1995. Diplomate Am. Bd. Surgery, Am. Bd. Plastic Surgery. Intern Yale-New Haven Hosp., 1971-72, resident, 1972-73, 76-77; resident Tufts-New Eng. Med. Center, Boston, 1973-76, Harvard-Cambridge (Mass.) Hosp., 1977-78; columnist Cosmopolitan mag., 1973-80; practice medicine specializing in plastic and reconstructive surgery Washington, 1978-86, McLean, Va., 1978-86. Author: The Making of a Woman Surgeon, 1980, Solo Practice, 1982, Custody; A True Story, 1986, The Complete Book of Cosmetic Surgery for Men, Women and Teens, 1988. Fellow ACS, Am. Soc. Plastic and Reconstructive Surgeons; mem. APA, Internat. Soc. for Study Dissociation, New Zealand Psychol. Soc. Episcopalian.

MORGAN, ETHEL BRANMAN, accountant; b. N.Y.C., Jan. 16, 1914; d. Morris and Dina Branman; BS, U. Ala., 1964; m. Donald Arol Morgan, Mar. 14, 1936; children: Margaret Voelkel, Barbara Weeks, John T., Janet Katich, Ethel Lynn. Mathematician, Army Missile Command, Redstone Arsenal, Ala., 1964-67, computer specialist, 1967-71, lead engr. air def. system command control software, 1971-73; pvt. practice tax acctg., fin. cons., Huntsville, Ala., 1974—. Pres., Huntsville-Madison County Council on Aging, 1980-82; vice chmn. Citizens Adv. Com. to Small Claims Ct., 1980-83; bd. dirs. Madison County Sr. Center, 1979-83; bd. dirs. Madison County Council on Aging, 1978-82. Mem. AAUW, Nat. Soc. Pub. Accts., Nat. Assn. Enrolled Agts. Ala. Soc. Public Accts., Ala. Soc. Enrolled Agts. (treas. 1983-89), Phi Beta Kappa. Office: PO Box 4312 Huntsville AL 35815-4312

MORGAN, EVAN, chemist; b. Spokane, Wash., Feb. 26, 1930; s. Evan and Emma Anne (Klobucher) M.; m. Johnnie Lu Dickson, Feb. 14, 1959; 1 child, James. BS, Gonzaga U., 1952; MS, U. Wash., 1954, PhD, 1956. Staff chemist IBM Corp., Poughkeepsie, N.Y., 1956-60; group supr. Olin Mathieson Co., New Haven, 1960-64; assoc. prof. chemistry High Point (N.C.) Coll., 1964-65; sr. rsch. chemist Reynolds Metals Co., Richmond, Va., 1965-72; chemist Babcock & Wilcox, Lynchburg, Va., 1972-95, Lynchburg Tree Steward, Lynchburg, 1995—. Mem. Am. Chem. Soc. Home: 5128 Wedgewood Rd Lynchburg VA 24503-4208

MORGAN, FRANK, mathematics educator. BS, MIT, 1974; PhD, Princeton U., 1977; ScD (hon.), Cedar Crest Coll., 1995. Moore instr. to assoc. prof., Green prof. MIT, Cambridge, 1977-87, also chmn. undergrad. math. dept.; Meenan 3d Century prof., chmn. dept. math. Williams Coll., Williamstown, Mass., 1987—; vis. prof. Rice U., Houston, 1982-83, Stanford U., 1986-87; mem. Inst. Advanced Study, Princeton, N.J., 1990-91; vis. prof. disting. tchg. Princeton U., 1997—. Author: Geometric Measure Theory, 1988, Riemannian Geometry, 1993, Calculus Lite, 1995. Recipient Haimo award for disting. coll. or univ. tchg. of math. Math. Assn. Am., 1993. Office: Williams College Dept of Mathematics Williamstown MA 01267

MORGAN, FRANK EDWARD, II, lawyer; b. Burlington, Vt., May 16, 1952; s. Robert Griggs and Ruth (Jepson) M. First Class Cert. Merit, U. Edinburgh, Scotland, 1973; AB with honors, Brown U., 1974; LLM, Cambridge U., Eng., 1976; JD, U. Va., 1978. Bar: Mass. 1978, N.Y. 1990. Assoc. Gaston & Snow, Boston, 1978-82; v.p., gen. counsel Madison Fund, Inc. and Adobe Resources Corp., N.Y.C., 1982-87; ptnr. Gaston & Snow, N.Y.C., 1987-91, Mayer, Brown & Platt, N.Y.C., 1991-96, Dewey Ballantine, N.Y.C., 1996—. Mem. ABA, N.Y. State Bar Assn., Am. Soc. Internat. Law. Republican. Congregationalist. Home: 14 Sutton Place South New York NY 10022 Office: Dewey Ballantine 1301 Avenue Of The Americas New York NY 10019-6022

MORGAN, (GEORGE) FREDERICK, poet, editor; b. N.Y.C., Apr. 25, 1922; s. John Williams and Marion Haviland (Burt) M.; m. Constance Canfield, Dec. 20, 1942 (div. Aug. 1957); children: Gaylen, Veronica, George F.; m. Rose Fillmore, Aug. 14, 1957 (div. Aug. 1969); m. Paula Deitz, Nov. 30, 1969. A.B. magna cum laude, Princeton U., 1943. Founder The Hudson Rev., N.Y.C., 1947, editor, pres., 1947—; chmn. adv. council dept. Romance langs. and lits. Princeton U., N.J., 1973-91. Author: A Book of Change, 1972, Poems of the Two Worlds, 1977, The Tarot of Cornelius Agrippa, 1978, Death Mother and Other Poems, 1979, The River, 1980, Refractions, 1981, Northbook, 1982, Eleven Poems, 1983, The Fountain and Other Fables, 1985, Poems: New and Selected, 1987, Poems for Paula, 1995. Served with U.S. Army, 1943-45. Decorated chevalier de l'Ordre des Arts et des Lettres, Govt. of France, 1984. Clubs: Knickerbocker (N.Y.C.) (gov. 1981-89), University (N.Y.C.), Somerset (Boston). Office: The Hudson Review 684 Park Ave New York NY 10021-5043

MORGAN, GAYLIN F., public realtions executive; b. Cedar Falls, Iowa, Nov. 3, 1938. BS in Journ., Bus., Iowa State U., 1962. Creative dir. Reiman Assocs., 1965-75; pres. Morgan & Myers, Jefferson, Wis., 1976—. Office: Morgan & Myers 146 E Milwaukee St Jefferson WI 53549-1636

MORGAN, HENRY COKE, JR., judge; b. Norfolk, Va., Feb. 8, 1935; s. Henry Coke and Dorothy Lea (Pebworth) M.; m. Margaret John McGrail, Aug. 18, 1965; 1 stepchild, A. Robertson Hanckel Jr.; children: Catherine Morgan Stockwell, Coke Morgan Stewart. BS, Washington and Lee U., 1957, JD, 1960. Bar: Va. 1960, U.S. Dist. Ct. (ea. dist.) Va. 1961, U.S. Ct. Appeals (4th cir.) 1964. Asst. city atty. City of Norfolk (Va.), 1960-63; ptnr., chief exec. officer Pender & Coward, Virginia Beach, Va., 1963-92; vice chmn., gen. counsel Princess Anne Bank, 1986-92; judge U.S. Dist. Ct. (ea. dist.) Va. 1992—. Served with U.S. Army, 1958-59. Episcopalian. Office: US Dist Ct Eastern Dist VA Walter E Hoffman US Courthouse 600 Granby St Ste 329 Norfolk VA 23510-1915

MORGAN, HOWARD EDWIN, physiologist; b. Bloomington, Ill., Oct. 8, 1927; s. Lyle V. and Ethel E. (Bailey) M. Student, Ill. Wesleyan U., 1944-45; MD, Johns Hopkins U., 1949. Intern Vanderbilt U., Nashville, 1949-51; resident in ob-gyn. Vanderbilt U., 1951-53, instr., 1953-55, instr. physiology, 1957-59, asst. prof. physiology, 1959-62, assoc. prof., 1962-65, prof. physiology, 1965-67; Evan Pugh prof., chmn. physiology Pa. State U., Hershey, 1967-87; sr. v.p. rsch. Geisinger Clinic, Danville, Pa., 1987—; v.p. rsch. Am. Heart Assn., 1977-79; mem. Nat. Heart, Lung and Blood Adv. Coun., 1979-83. Editor: Physiol. Revs, 1973-79, Am. Jour. Physiology: Cell Physiology, 1981-84. With U.S. Army, 1955-57. Recipient award of Merit Am. Heart Assn., 1979, Carl Wiggers award, 1984; Howard Hughes scholar, 1982. Mem. Am. Physiol. Soc. (pres., Daggs award 1992), Am. Heart Assn. (pres., Disting. Achievement award 1988, Gold Heart award 1994), Am. Soc. Biol. Chemists, Biochem. Soc., Biophys. Soc., Internat. Soc. Heart Rsch. (pres., Peter Harris award 1995), Inst. Medicine of NAS. Office: Geisinger Clinic Weis Ctr for Rsch 100 N Academy St Danville PA 17822

MORGAN, HUGH JACKSON, JR., bank executive; b. Nashville, Aug. 10, 1928; s. Hugh Jackson and Robert Ray (Porter) M.; m. Ann Moulton Ward, Aug. 28, 1954; children—Ann, Grace, Caroline, Hugh. A.B., Princeton U., N.J., 1950; LL.B., Vanderbilt U., Nashville, 1956; A.M.P., Harvard Bus. Sch., 1976. Bar: Tenn. 1956. Practice law Miller & Martin, Chattanooga, 1956-60; atty. So. Natural Gas Co., Birmingham, Ala., 1961-65, gen. atty., 1966-70, v.p., 1971-78, pres., 1982-84, chmn. bd., 1984-87; v.p. Sonat Inc., Birmingham, Ala., 1973-78, sr. v.p., 1979-84, exec. v.p., 1984, vice chmn. bd., 1984-87; vice chmn. Nat. Bank of Commerce, Birmingham, Ala., 1987-90; chmn. Nat. Bank Commerce, Birmingham, Ala., 1990—, also bd. dirs.; bd. dirs. AlaTenn Resources, Inc., Ala.-Tenn. Nat. Gas Co., Blue Cross-Blue Shield Ala. Chmn. Birmingham Airport Authority, 1986—; trustee Episcopal High Sch., Alexandria, Va., Children's Hosp. Ala., Birmingham, 1974—. Served to lt. (j.g.) USN, 1950-53. Recipient Bennett Douglas Bell Meml. prize Vanderbilt Law Sch., 1956. Mem. Order of the Coif. Clubs: Mountain Brook (pres. 1972), Redstone, (Birmingham); Belle Meade (Nashville); Linville Golf (N.C.). Lodge: Rotary. Home: 3121 Brookwood Rd Birmingham AL 35223-2016 Office: Nat Bank of Commerce 1927 1st Ave N Birmingham AL 35203-4005

MORGAN, JACK M., lawyer; b. Portales, N.Mex., Jan. 15, 1924; s. George Albert and Mary Rosana (Baker) M.; BBA, U. Tex., 1948; LLB, 1950; m. Peggy Flynn Cummings, 1947; children: Marilyn, Rebecca, Claudia, Jack. Admitted to N.Mex. bar, 1950; sole practice law, Farmington, N.Mex., 1956—; mem. N.Mex. State Senate, 1973-88 . Served with USN, 1942-46. Mem. Am. Bar Assn., N.Mex. Bar Assn., S.W. Regional Energy Council (past chmn.), Kiwanis, Elks. Republican. Office: PO Box 2151 Farmington NM 87499-2151

MORGAN, JACOB RICHARD, cardiologist; b. East St. Louis, Ill., Oct. 10, 1925; s. Clyde Adolphus and Jennie Ella Henrietta (Van Ramshorst) M.; m. Alta Eloise Ruthruff, Aug. 1, 1953; children: Elaine, Stephen Richard. BA in Physics, BBA, U. Tex., 1953; MD, U. Tex., Galveston, 1957. Diplomate Am. Bd. Internal Medicine, Am. Bd. Cardiology. Ensign USN, 1944, advanced through grades to capt., 1969; intern U.S. Naval Hosp., Oakland, Calif., 1957-58; chief medicine U.S. Naval Hosp., Taipei, Republic of China, 1962-64; internal medicine staff San Diego, 1964-67, chief cardiology, 1969-73; ret., 1973; dir. medicine R.E. Thomas Gen. Hosp., El Paso, Tex., 1973-75; asst. clin. prof. medicine U. Calif., San Diego, 1970-73; prof. medicine, assoc. chmn. dep. Tex. Tech U. Sch. Medicine, Lubbock and El Paso, 1973-75; pvt. practice National City, Calif., 1976—; dir. cardiology Paradise Valley Hosp., National City, 1976-88; presenter in field. Contbr. articles on cardiology to sci. jours. Recipient Casmir Funk award, 1972. Fellow ACP, Am. Coll. Cardiology, Am. Coll. Chest Physicians, Am. Heart Assn. (coun. on clin. cardiology). Avocation: golf. Home: 9881 Edgar Pl La Mesa CA 91941-6833 Office: 2409 E Plaza Blvd National City CA 91950-5101

MORGAN, JACQUI, illustrator, painter, educator; b. N.Y.C., Feb. 22, 1939; d. Henry and Emily (Cook) Morganstern; m. Onnig Kalfayan, Apr. 23, 1967 (div. 1972); m. Tomás Gonda, Jan. 1983 (dec. 1988). B.F.A. with honors, Pratt Inst., Bklyn., 1960; M.A., Hunter Coll., CCNY, 1978. Textile designer M. Lowenstein & Sons, N.Y.C., 1961-62, Fruit of the Loom, N.Y.C., 1962; stylist-design dir. Au Courant, Inc., N.Y.C., 1966—; assoc. prof. Pratt Inst., Bklyn., 1977—; guest lectr. U. Que., Syracuse U., Warsaw TV & Radio, Poland, NYU, Parsons Sch. Design, N.Y.C., Sch. Visual Arts, N.Y.C., Va. Commonwealth U., others; mem. profl. juries; curator Tomás Gonda retrospective exhbn.; condr. workshops. One-person shows include Soc. Illustrators, N.Y.C., 1977, Art Dirs. Club, N.Y.C., 1978, Gallerie Nowe Miasto, Warsaw, 1978, Gallerie Baumeister, Munich, W.Ger., 1978, Hansen-Feuerman Gallery, N.Y.C., 1980; group shows include Mus. Contemporary Crafts, N.Y.C., 1975, Smithsonian Instn., Washington, 1976, Mus. Warsaw, 1976, 78, Mus. Tokyo, 1979, Nat. Watercolor Soc., 1989, Salmagundi Club, 1990, New Eng. Watercolor Soc. Open, 1990, Miss. Watercolor Grand nat., 1990, Illustration West 29, 1990, Adirondack Nat., 1990, Die Verlassenen Schuhe, 1993, N.Y. restaurant Sch., 1994, Lizan-Tops Gallery, 1996; represented in permanent collections: Smithsonian Instn., Mus. Warsaw; author-illustrator: Watercolor for Illustration; produced three of seven instrnl. watercolor videos; series of prints pub., 1995; series of plates publ., 1995; co-curator Tomas Gonda Retrospective, Va. Commonwealth U., Rutgers U., Carnegie Mellon U., others in U.S., Museo Del Arte Moderno, Buenos Aires/to be exhibited and become part of the permanent collection of the Ulmer Mus./HFG Archive; contbr. articles to profl. jours. Recipient more than 150 awards from various orgns. including Soc. Illustrators, Fed. Design Coun., Comm. Arts Mag., Am. Inst. Graphic Arts, N.Y. Art Dirs. Club, Print Design Ann. Mem. Graphic Artists Guild (dir. 1975-79), Soc. Illustrators, Women Artists of the West, Pa. Watercolor Soc. Studio: 692 Greenwich St New York NY 10014-2876 *Finally, I understand that it's the pleasure of the process and the internal knowledge of improvement that gives the greatest satisfaction.*

MORGAN, JAMES DURWARD, computer company executive; b. N.Y.C., Sept. 10, 1936; s. Durward Field and Harriet (Airey) M.; m. Ruth Ann Dobson, Jan. 14, 1967; children: Jennifer, Andrew. BEE, Yale U., 1961, MEE, 1962. Systems engr. Calspan Corp., Buffalo, 1962-68; v.p. Comptek Rsch. Inc., Buffalo, 1968-83, 90—, also bd. dirs.; v.p. Barrister Info. Systems Corp., Buffalo, 1983-90; also bd. dirs. Barrister Info. Systems Corp., 1983—. Mem. adv. coun. Erie C.C., Amherst, N.Y., 1985—, past chmn.; bd. dirs. Yale Alumni Bd., Buffalo, 1987—. Served with USN, 1959-61. Mem. IEEE, ACM (past chmn. local chpt.). Home: 34 Ironwood Ct East Amherst NY 14051-1628 Office: Comptek Rsch Inc 2732 Transit Rd Buffalo NY 14224-2523

MORGAN, JAMES EARL, librarian, administrator; b. Wheeling, W.Va., June 30, 1941; s. James H. L. and Ethel Irene (Goodwin) M.; m. Carman H. Head, Dec. 23, 1966; 1 child, Scott Andrew. B.S. in Edn., Ariz. State Coll., 1965; M.S.L.S., Fla. State U., 1966. Reference asst. social scis. Fla. State U., Tallahassee, 1965-66; head pub. services Ga. Coll., Milledgeville, 1967-69; dir. pub. services U. Tex. Med. Br., Galveston, 1969-73; dir. libraries U. Conn. Health Ctr., Farmington, 1973-76, Oreg. Health Sci. U., Portland, 1976—. Contbr. articles to profl. jours. Grantee Nat. Library Medicine, 1974-76, 78-81. Mem. ALA (life), Med. Libr. Assn. (chmn. Pacific N.W. chpt. 1981), Oreg. Health Scis. Librs. Assn., Pacific N.W. Libr. Assn., Spl. Libr. Assn., Oreg. Libr. Assn., Portland Area Spl. Librarians Assn., Assn. Coll. and Rsch. Librs., Am. Med. Informatics Assn., Nat. Rural Health Assn. Democrat. Office: Oreg Health Scis Univ Library Biomedical Info Comm Ctr 3181 SW Sam Jackson Park Rd Portland OR 97201-3011

MORGAN, JAMES EVAN, lawyer; b. Poughkeepsie, N.Y., Nov. 8, 1959; s. Evan and Johnnie Lu Morgan; m. Catherine Barr Altman, Sept. 21, 1991. BA, Lynchburg Coll., 1984; JD, N.Y. Law Sch., 1989. Bar: N.Y. 1993. Talk show host Sta. WLGM-AM Radio, Lynchburg, Va., 1982-86; legal editor Matthew Bender & Co., Inc., N.Y.C., 1989-91; ptnr. Morgan Cons., Chgo., 1992—; sr. investigator Chgo. Bd. Options Exch., 1993—. Editor: Bender's Federal Tax Service, 1989-91, Modern Estate Planning, 1989-91; pub., editor: Minerva, 1990. Mem. ABA (bus. law sect., com. on fed. regulation of securities, market regulation subcom. 1994—), Coun. on Fgn. Rels. Avocations: playing violin and viola, composing music. Office: Chgo Bd Options Exch 400 S La Salle St Chicago IL 60605-1023

MORGAN, JAMES NEWTON, research economist, educator; b. Corydon, Ind., Mar. 1, 1918; s. John Jacob Brooke and Rose Ann (Davis) M.; m. Gladys Lucille Hassler, May 12, 1945; children—Kenneth, Timothy, Salim, Janet. BA, Northwestern U., 1939; PhD, Harvard U., 1947. Asst. prof. econs. Brown U., Providence, 1947-49; Carnegie rsch. fellow U. Mich., Ann Arbor, 1949-51, asst. prof. econs., asst. program dir. Inst. Social Rsch., 1951-55; with Ctr. for Advanced Study in Behavior Sci., Palo Alto, Calif., 1955-56; prof. econs., program dir. Inst. Social Rsch. U. Mich., Ann Arbor, 1956-88, prof. emeritus, 1988—; bd. dirs. Consumers Union, Mt. Vernon, N.Y., 1955-82; com. on sci. and pub. policy NAS, 1983-86, report rev. com., 1987-91; com. on basic rsch. in behavior and social sci. NRC, Washington, panel on census requirements, 1992-95. Fellow Am. Statis. Assn., Am. Acad. Arts and Scis., Gerontol. Soc. Am., Wissenschaftskolleg zu Berlin; mem. NAS, Am. Econ. Assn. Methodist. Avocations: swimming; gardening. Home: 1217 Bydding Rd Ann Arbor MI 48103-3103 Office: Inst Social Research Thompson St Ann Arbor MI 48104

MORGAN, JAMES PHILIP, pharmacologist, cardiologist, educator; b. Cin., Jan. 13, 1948; s. James Weldon and Dorcas Adele (Meyer) M.; m. Kathleen Greive, Dec. 22, 1973; children: James Patrick, Jonathan Michael. BS, U. Cin., 1970, PhD, 1974, MD, 1976. Diplomate Am. Bd. Internal Medicine and Subspecialty Cardiovascular Disease. Fellow in internal medicine Mayo Clinic, Rochester, Minn., 1976-79, fellow in cardiovascular disease, 1979-83; asst. in medicine, Beth Israel Hosp., Boston, 1983—; instr. pharmacology U. Cin., 1975-76; asst. prof. pharmacology, instr. medicine, Mayo Clinic, 1981-83; asst. prof. medicine, Harvard U., Boston, 1983, assoc.

prof., 1988-96, Herman Dana prof. medicine, 1996—; affiliate faculty, dept. pharmacology, Harvard Med. Sch., 1986—; chief and prgram dir. cardiovascular divsn. Beth Israel Hosp., 1994—. Contbr. articles to profl. jours. Recipient Young Investigators award Am. Coll. Cardiology, 1982; Balfour award Mayo Clinic, 1983, Advanced Cardiac Life Support Spl Recognition award Mayo Clinic, 1983, Research Career Devel. award NIH, 1985-90. Mem. AMA, Am. Heart Assn., Biophys. Soc. Am. Soc. Pharmacology and Exptl. Therapeutics, Masons. Avocation: philatelics. Office: Beth Israel Deaconess Med Ctr 330 Brookline Ave Boston MA 02215-5400

MORGAN, JANE HALE, retired library director; b. Dines, Wyo., May 11, 1926; d. Arthur Hale and Billie (Wood) Hale; m. Joseph Charles Morgan, Aug. 12, 1955; children: Joseph Hale, Jane Frances, Ann Michele. BA, Howard U., 1947; MA, U. Denver, 1954. Mem. staff Detroit Pub. Libr., 1954-87, exec. asst. dir., 1973-75, dep. dir., 1975-78, dir., 1978-87; mem. Mich. Libr. Consortium Bd.; exec. bd. Southeastern Mich. Regional Film Libr.; vis. prof. Wayne State U., 1989—. Trustee New Detroit, Inc., Delta Dental Plan of Mich. (treas. Delta Dental Fund), Delta Dental Plan of Ohio; v.p. United Southwestern Mich.; pres. Univ.-Cultural Ctr. Assn.; bd. dirs. Rehab. Inst., YWCA, Met. Affairs Corp., Literacy Vols. Am., Detroit, Mich. Ctr. for the Book, Interfaith Coun.; bd. dirs., v.p. United Comty. Svcs. Met. Detroit; chmn. Detroiters for Adult Reading Excellence; chmn. adv. coun. libr. sci. U. Mich.; mem. adv. coun. libr. sci. U. Mich., mem. adv. coun. libr. sci. Wayne State U.; dir. Met. Detroit Youth Found.; chmn. Mich. LSCA adv. coun.; mem. UWA Literacy Com., Attys. Grievance Com., Women's Commn., Mich. Civil Svc. Rev. Com.; vice chair Mich. Coun. for Humanities; mem. Commn. for the Greening of Detroit; mem. adv. com. Headstart; mem. Detroit Women's Com., Detroit Women's Forum, Detroit Exec. Svc. Corps.; sec., treas. Delta Dental Fund. Recipient Anthony Wayne award Wayne State U., 1981, Summit award Greater Detroit C. of C.; named Detroit Howardite of Year, 1983. Mem. ALA, AAUW, Mich. Library Assn., Women's Nat. Book Assn., Assn. Mcpl. Profl. Women, NAACP, LWV, Women's Econ. Club, Alpha Kappa Alpha. Democrat. Episcopalian.

MORGAN, JOE LEONARD, investment company executive, former professional baseball player; b. Bonham, Tex., Sept. 19, 1943. Student, Oakland City (Ind.) Coll.; BA in Phys. Edn., Calif. State U.-Hayward, 1990. Infielder Houston Astros, 1962-71, 2nd baseman, 1980; 2nd baseman Cin. Reds, 1972-79, San Francisco Giants, 1981-82, Phila. Phillies, 1983, Oakland A's, 1984; pres. Joe Morgan Investments Inc., Oakland, 1984—; baseball analyst Sta. WLWT-TV, Cin., 1985; college baseball analyst ESPN, 1985-88, analyst ESPN Sunday Night Baseball, 1990—; analyst GiantsVision, 1986-90, ABC-TV, 1988, NBC-TV, 1994—; analyst Oakland Athletics Baseball Sports Channel, 1995—; owner, pres. Joe Morgan Beverage Co., 1988—. Named Most Valuable Player Tex. League, 1964; Rookie of Yr. in Nat. League Sporting News, 1965; Most Valuable Player Nat. League, 1975, 76; Maj. League Player of Year, Sporting News, 1975, 76; named to Nat. League All-Star Team, 1970, 72-79, Nat. League Comeback Player of the Year Sporting News, 1982, Nat. League Player of the Year Sporting News, 1975, Nat. League All Star Team Sporting News, 1972, 73-77; recipient Silver Slugger award Sporting News, 1982; elected to Baseball Hall of Fame, 1990; recipient CableACE award, 1990. player World Series, 1972, 75-76, 83. also: ESPN ESPN Plz Bristol CT 06010 Address: 3239 Danville Blvd #A Alamo CA 94507-1913*

MORGAN, JOHN BRUCE, hospital care consultant; b. Youngstown, Ohio, Oct. 25, 1919; s. John Benjamin and Ida May (Lane) M.; m. Marian Frampton, July 11, 1969; children: John B., Carolyn, Leonard, Suzanne (dec.). B.S., Miami U., 1941; M.B.A., Harvard U., 1946. Field rep. Gen. Motors Acceptance Corp., Youngstown, 1941; pres. Asso. Hosp. Service, Inc., Youngstown, 1947-74; pres. Hosp. Care Corp. (Blue Cross), Cin., 1974-83, cons., 1983—; pres. Health Maintenance Plan, Cin., 1974-83, Health Care Mutual, Cin., 1974-83; chmn. bd. govs., chmn. exec. com. Blue Cross Assn., Chgo., 1981-82; chmn. bd. Community Life Ins. Co., Worthington, Ohio, 1979-83; mem. joint exec. com. Blue Cross-Blue Shield Assns., mem. joint bds., Chgo.; mem. bus. adv. com. Miami U., Oxford, Ohio. Gen. chmn. United Fund campaign, Youngstown, 1965; pres. Cancer Soc., 1965; chmn. bd. trustees Ch. of the Palms, 1996. Served with AUS, 1942-46. Mem. Am.Hosp. Assn. (Justin Ford Kimball award 1983), Ohio Hosp. Assn., Ohio C. of C. (bd. dirs.), Youngstown Area C. of C. (pres. 1966-67), Delray Beach, Fla. C. of C., Youngstown Country Club, Delray Dunes Golf and Country Club (bd. dirs., v.p.), Rotary (bd. dirs. Delray Beach club, pres. 1992, Paul Harris fellow), Masons, Elks, Sigma Alpha Epsilon, Delta Sigma Pi. Mem. United Ch. of Christ. Home: 9 Slash Pine Dr Boynton Beach FL 33436-5524 Office: 1351 William Howard Taft Rd Cincinnati OH 45206-1721

MORGAN, JOHN DAVIS, consultant; b. Newark, Feb. 14, 1921; s. John Davis and Caroline Frommel (Schaller) M.; m. Leta Maude Bretzinger, June 27, 1953; children: John Davis III, Bret Zinger. B.S., Pa. State U., 1942, M.S., 1947, Ph.D., 1948, E.M., 1950; grad. extension course, Indsl. Coll. of Armed Forces, Washington, 1953. Asst. for materials and stockpile policies Nat. Security Resources Bd., Washington, 1948-51; dir. materials rev. div. DPA, Washington, 1951-53; materials expert ODM, Washington, 1953-56; mem. staff President's Cabinet Com. on Mineral Policy, 1953-54; cons. bus. and def. problems in metals, minerals and fuels Washington, 1956-71; mem. nat. def. exec. res. for ODM, 1956-58, OCDM, 1958-61, Office Emergency Planning, 1961-71, Emergency Minerals Adminstrn., 1972-95; mem. spl. stockpile advisory com. to ODM, 1957-58; com. on scope and conduct of materials research NAS, 1959-60, then, mem. com. on mineral sci. and tech., 1966-70; mem. Interagy. Adv. Com. on Mining and Mineral Research, 1977-95; head dept. sci. and math. Daytona Beach C.C., Fla., 1961-71; asst. dir. mineral position analysis U.S. Bur. Mines, Dept. Interior, Washington, 1971-74, acting dir. bur., 1973-74, 77-78, assoc. dir. mineral and materials supply/demand analysis, 1974-79, chief staff officer, 1979-95, Interior Dept. liaison to Coun. Internat. Econ. Policy Staff, 1973-77, to Econ. Policy Bd. Staff, 1974-77, to Dept. Def. Materials Steering Group, 1975-78, to FPA-FEMA Stockpile Com., 1975-88, to Winter Energy Emergency Planning Group of Dept. of Energy, 1977-81; alt. Interior rep. Trade Policy Rev. Group, 1975-81; chmn. minerals rev. com. Non-Fuel Minerals Policy Study, 1978; chmn. materials supply task force NSC Stockpile Study, 1983-87; liaison to Dept. Def. Stockpile Com., 1988—; mem. Def. Logistics Agy. Market Impact Com., 1988-95; mem. Def. Dept. Adv. Com. Operation and Modernization of Stockpile, 1993-95; U.S. rep. UN Sci. Conf. on Resources, 1949; lectr. numerous univs. including Nat. Def. U., War Coll., Indsl. Coll., Def. Intelligence Coll., Army War Coll., 1949—; hon. prof. Indsl. Coll., 1983—; invited spkr. nat. meetings sci. and engring. socs., 1949—. Author: Domestic Mining Industry of the U.S. in World War II, 1949; corr.: Mining Ann. Rev., London, 1958-95; contbr. articles to profl. jours. Served from 2d lt. to maj. Corps Engrs. AUS, 1942-46. Decorated Bronze Star; recipient Distinguished Service gold medal Interior Dept., 1976; named Meritorious Exec. Sr. Exec. Service, 1983. Fellow Soc. Am. Mil. Engrs.; mem. Sci. Research Soc. Am., Soc. Mining Engrs. (Disting. mem.), AIME (nat. Krumb lectr. 1973, Legion of Honor 1989), Mining and Metall. Soc. Am., Am. Def. Preparedness Assn., Sigma Xi, Tau Beta Pi, Sigma Tau, Pi Mu Epsilon, Phi Lambda Upsilon, Phi Kappa Phi, Phi Eta Sigma, Sigma Gamma Epsilon. Club: Cosmos (Washington). Home: 5013 Worthington Dr Bethesda MD 20816-2748

MORGAN, JOHN DERALD, electrical engineer; b. Hays, Kans., Mar. 15, 1939; s. John Baber and Avis Ruth (Wolf) M.; m. Elizabeth June McKneely, June 23, 1962; children: Laura Elizabeth, Kimberly Ann, Rebecca Ruth, John Derald. BSEE, La. Tech. U., 1962; MS, U. Mo., Rolla, 1965, Degree in Elec. Engring. (hon.), 1987; PhD, Ariz. State U., 1968. Registered profl. engr., forensic engr., Mo., N.Mex. Elec. engr. Tex. Eastman div. Eastman Kodak Co., 1962-63; instr. U. Mo., Rolla, 1963-65, Ariz. State U., 1965-68; asso. prof. elec. engring. U. Mo., Rolla, 1968-72; Alcoa Found. prof. elec. engring. U. Mo., 1972-75, chmn. elec. engring., 1978-85, assoc. dir. Ctr. Internat. Programs, 1970-78, Emerson Electric prof., 1975-85; dean engring. N.Mex. State U., 1985—; nat. adv. com. Engring. Explorer Post; cons. to industry. Author: Power Apparatus Testing Techniques, 1969, Computer Monitoring and Control of Electric Utility Systems, 1972, Control and Distribution of Megawatts Through Man-Machine Interaction, 1973, Electromechanical and Electromagnetic Machines and Devices, 1986; also articles. Pres. bd. trustees First Meth. Ch., Rolla, 1971-73; pres. adminstrv. bd. First United Meth. Ch. Rolla, 1978-79; v.p., mem. bd. adminstrn. People to People, 1976; bd. dirs., cubmaster Ozarks dist. Boy Scouts Am., 1968-79, asst. dist. commr., 1971-73, cubmaster Yucca coun., 1986-90, coun. commr., 1989-90, asst. scout master, 1990—, dist. com. Sushine Dist.; dist. chmn. Meramec dist., 1978-80; bd. dirs. Mo. Partners of the Americas. Recipient Scouters Key award and Scouter Tng. award Ozarks coun., Boy Scouts Am., 1971, Dist. award of merit 1977, Silver Beaver award, 1982, Cub Leader award, Webelos Leader award, Sunshine Dist. Yucca coun.; T.H. Harris scholar, 1959-61; John H. Horton scholar, 1961-62. Fellow IEEE (chmn. internat. practices subcom. 1972-79, sec. PSE com., vice chmn., chmn. 1979-85, chmn. ednl. resources subcom. 1973-78, selected award of Merit St. Louis sect., Educators award St. Louis sect., honor award St. Louis sect., Centennial award 1984), Nat. Acad. Forensic Engrs., ASTM; mem. NSPE (bd. govs., nat. dir., vice chmn., S.W. chmn. Profl. Engrs. in Edn.. v.p., mem. Steinman Coun.), N.Mex. Soc. Profl. Engrs. (N.Mex. Engr. of Yr. 1993), Am. Soc. Engring. Edn., Sigma Xi, Tau Beta Pi, Eta Kappa Nu, Omicron Delta Kappa, Phi Kappa Phi, Kappa Sigma (faculty and alumni advisor), Epsilon Gamma (grand master, grand procurator, PSI exec. of yr. 1993), Rotary Internat. (Paul Harris fellow 1997). Home: 2425 Janet Ann Ln Las Cruces NM 88005-5119 Office: NMex State U Main Campus Coll Engring PO Box 30001 Las Cruces NM 88003-8001

MORGAN, JOHN STEPHEN, state legislator, materials science researcher; b. Washington, Dec. 23, 1963; s. James Donald and Virginia Louise (Hendrickson) M.; m. Erin Denise Monica Pierce. BS, Loyola Coll., Balt., 1984; MS in Engring., Johns Hopkins U., 1988, PhD, 1990. Rsch. assoc. Johns Hopkins U., Balt., 1986-90; sr. engr. Johns Hopkins U., Laurel, Md., 1990—; mem. Md. Ho. of Dels., Annapolis, 1991—; mem. joint com. on legis. ethics Md. Gen. Assembly, Annapolis, 1995—; ranking minority mem. Commerce and Govt. Matters Com., Md. Ho. of Dels., 1995—. Chmn. adv. com. Bd. Edn. Howard County, Md., 1989-90; Dem. candidate U.S. House Reps. 5th Dist. Md., 1996. Recipient Charles Miller award Howard County Rep. Party, 1988. Mem. Am. Phys. Soc. (mem. panel on pub. affairs 1997—, Congl. Sci. fellow 1994-95), Materials Rsch. Soc., Kiwanis. Lutheran. Home: 7920 Ashford Blvd Laurel MD 20707-5874 Office: Md Gen Assembly Lowe House Office Bldg Annapolis MD 21401

MORGAN, LARRY RONALD, minister; b. Springhill, La., Mar. 12, 1936; s. Woodrow Wilson Morgan and Alma Elizabeth (Dunn) Burch; m. Elizabeth Dianne Baker, May 24, 1958; children: Elizabeth Denise Morgan Davis, Dennis Kevin. ADiv, Bapt. Missionary Assn. Theol. Sem., Jacksonville, Tex., 1990. Ordained to ministry Bapt. Ch., 1971. Clk., carrier U.S. P.O., Springhill, La., 1956-71; assoc. pastor Webb Chapel Bapt. Ch., Dallas, 1971-72, pastor, 1972—; clk., trustee Bapt. Missionary Assn. Sem., Jacksonville, 1983-86; chmn. bd. trustees Bapt. Progress, Dallas, 1984-87. Pres. PTA Browning Elem. Sch., Springhill, 1969-70. With USAR, 1959-66. Mem. Bapt. Missionary Assn. Am. (v.p. hdqrs. Little Rock 1985-86, pres. 1986-88, v.p. Am. 1996—), Dallas County Bapt. Assn. (moderator 1982-84). Home: 14517 Heartside Dr Dallas TX 75234-2152

MORGAN, LAWRENCE ALLISON, headmaster, educational administrator; b. Norman, Okla., June 12, 1935; s. Lawrence Nelson and Catherine (Edwards) Morgan; m. Nancy Catherine Somogyi, July 3, 1960; children: Michael Lawrence, Katherine Elizabeth, Thomas Leverett. AB, Harvard U., 1957; MA, Washington U.-St. Louis, 1969, Webster U., 1977. Faculty, Thomas Jefferson Sch., St. Louis, 1957-66, trustee, 1959—, dir. admissions, 1966-80, v.p., bd. trustees, 1966-80, headmaster, pres., 1980—; trustee Riverways Sch., 1986-87. Bd. dirs. Jefferson Twp., Dem. Club, 1971-72. Episcopalian. Clubs: Harvard Club (St. Louis, Boston, N.Y.C.). Avocations: travel; photography; camping; cycling; hiking. Home: 9112 Pardee Spur Saint Louis MO 63126-2718 Office: Thomas Jefferson Sch 4100 S Lindbergh Blvd Saint Louis MO 63127-1643

MORGAN, LEON ALFORD, retired utility executive; b. Washington, Dec. 29, 1934; s. Albert Lewis and Alice Viets (Alford) M.; children: David Richard, Sherry Alice; m. Jacqueline Jamieson, Feb. 14, 1993. BSEE, Worcester (Mass.) Poly. Inst., 1957. Registered profl. engr., Conn. With United Illuminating Co., New Haven, 1957-94; gen. ops. mgr., then v.p. ops. United Illuminating Co., 1973-76, exec. v.p., 1976-83, sr. v.p. fin., 1984-94. Republican. Episcopalian. Home: 43 Forest Brook Rd Guilford CT 06437-2245

MORGAN, LEWIS RENDER, retired federal judge; b. LaGrange, Ga., July 14, 1913; s. William Ellington and Bettie (Render) M.; m. Sue Phillips, July 29, 1944; children: Parks Healy, Sue Ann. Student, U. Mich., 1930-32; LLB, U. Ga., 1935; LLB (hon.), Atlanta Law Sch., 1963, La Grange Coll., 1977. Bar: Ga. 1935. Mem. Wyatt & Morgan, LaGrange, 1935-61; judge U.S. Dist. Ct. (no. dist.) Ga., 1961-68, chief judge, 1965-68; judge U.S. Cir. Ct. Appeals (5th and 11th cirs.), Newnan, Ga., 1968-96, sr. justice, to 1996; ret.; Mem. budget com. U.S. Courts, 1967—; Mem. Gen. Assembly Ga., 1937-39; exec. sec. A. Sidney Camp (congressman), 1939-42; Mem. visitors com. U. Ga. Law Sch., 1970-73; mem. spl. div. U.S. Ct. Appeals for D.C., 1978—; mem. Temporary Emergency Ct. Appeals, 1979—. Mem. Chi Psi, Phi Delta Phi. Presbyn. Home: Cameron Mill Rd La Grange GA 30240

MORGAN, LINDA J., federal agency administrator; m. Michael E. Karam; 1 child, Meredith Lyn. AB in Hispanic Studies, Vassar Coll., 1973; JD, Georgetown U., 1976; postgrad., Harvard U., 1991. Assoc. Welch & Morgan, Washington; staff counsel U.S. Senate Com. on Commerce, Sci. and Transp., 1978-86, gen. counsel; mem. Interstate Commerce Commn., Washington, 1994-96, chmn., 1995-96; chmn. Surface Transp. Bd., Washington, 1996—. Mem. D.C. Bar Assn., Women's Bar Assn., Women's Transp. Seminar. Office: Surface Transp Bd 1925 K St NW Mercury Bldg Washington DC 20423*

MORGAN, LORRIE (LORETTA LYNN MORGAN), country singer; b. Nashville, June 27, 1959; d. George Morgan; divorced; m. Keith Whitley (dec. 1989); children: Morgan, Jesse. Rec. artist RCA, 1989—. Albums: Leave the Light On, 1989, Something in Red, 1991, Watch Me, 1992, Merry Christmas from London, 1994, My Favorite Things, 1994, War Paint, 1994, Greatest Hits, 1995; (with Jon Randall) Greater Need, 1996; #1 Song: I Didn't Know My Own Strength; #1 gold single: Something in Red, 1991; TV movies include: Proudheart, 1993, ABC movie of the Week - The Enemy Within, 1995. Office: Lorrie Morgan Entertainment 1709 19th Ave S Nashville TN 37212-3701

MORGAN, LOU ANN, physical education educator; b. Andrews, N.C., Apr. 26, 1949; d. Jerry Myditt and Alice Josephine (O'Dell) Long; m. Frederick Wayne Morgan, July 9, 1972; children: Mandi Marie, Chad William. BS, Mars Hill Coll., 1971. Tchr. Farmer (N.C.) Elem. Sch., 1971-74, Flat Rock (N.C.) Jr. High Sch., 1974-81; craft dir. Camp Windy Wood, Tuxedo, N.C., 1981-84; tchr. weekday early edn. 1st Bapt. Ch., Hendersonville, N.C., 1983-84; phys. edn. specialist Dana (N.C.) Elem. Sch., 1984—. Co-author: (video) Outdoor Education ... Success for Everyon, 1993. Mem. scholarship com. 1st Bapt. Ch., Hendersonville, 1993—, mem. weekday early edn. com., 1985-86, mem. recreation/activities com., 1993-94. Named Outstanding Spring Vol. Henderson County Parks and Recreation, 1992; recipient Gov.'s Award for Fitness N.C. Gov.'s Coun. on Phys. Fitness and Health, 1994. Mem. AAHPERD, N.C. Assn. Health, Phys. Edn., Recreation and Dance (phys. edn. Western regional rep. 1994-95, Phys. Edn. Leadership Tng. steering com. 1989, 93, presider, presenter 1991, 94, Norm Leafe State Phys. Edn. Tchr. of Yr. 1990). Republican. Baptist. Avocations: painting, gardening, biking, fitness. Home: 447 Sunset Dr Hendersonville NC 28791 Office: Dana Elem Sch PO Box 37 Dana NC 28724-0037

MORGAN, LUCY W., journalist; b. Memphis, Oct. 11, 1940; d. Thomas Allin and Lucile (Sanders) Keen; m. Alton F. Ware, June 26, 1958 (div. Sept. 1967); children: Mary Kathleen, Andrew Allin; m. Richard Alan Morgan, Aug. 9, 1968; children: Lynn Elwell, Kent Morgan. AA, Pasco Hernando C.C., New Port Richey, Fla., 1975; student, U. South Fla., 1976-80. Reporter Ocala Star Banner, Fla., 1965-68; reporter St. Petersburg Times, Fla., 1967-86, capitol bur. chief, 1986—; assoc. editor and bd. dirs. Times Pub. Co. Recipient Paul Hansel award Fla. Soc. Newspaper Editors, 1981, First in Pub. Service award Fla. Soc. Newspaper Editors, 1982, First Place award in pub. service Fla. Press Club, 1982, Pulitzer award for investigative reporting Columbia U., 1985, First Place award in investigative reporting Sigma Delta Chi, 1985; named to Kappa Tau Alpha Hall of Fame, 1992. Home: 1727 Brookside Blvd Tallahassee FL 32301-6769 Office: Saint Petersburg Times 336 E College Ave Tallahassee FL 32301-1551

MORGAN, MARABEL, author; b. Crestline, Ohio, June 25, 1937; d. Howard and Delsa (Smith) Hawk; m. Charles O. Morgan, Jr., June 25, 1964; children—Laura Lynn, Michelle Rene. Ed., Ohio State U. Pres. Total Woman, Inc., Miami, Fla., 1970—; pub. speaker. Author: The Total Woman, 1973, Total Joy, 1976, The Total Woman Cookbook, 1980, The Electric Woman, 1985. Office: care Total Woman Inc 1300 NW 167th St Miami FL 33169-5738

MORGAN, MARIANNE, corporate professional; b. Muncie, Ind., Oct. 13, 1940; d. Clarence Wilson and Mary Estle (Shafer) M. BA, Calif. State U., Long Beach, 1962; MS, U. So. Calif., 1968. Lic. real estate salesperson, Fla. Lab. technician Ball Meml. Hosp. Pathology Lab, Muncie, 1956-61; sr. libr. asst. Anaheim (Calif.) Pub. Libr., 1963-68; coll. libr. Orange Coast Coll., Costa Mesa, Calif., 1968-73; exec. v.p. Brady Products, Inc., Clearwater, Fla., 1973—; bd. dirs. Brady Products, Inc., Clearwater, Suncoast Fluid Power, Inc., Clearwater. Fiction book reviewer, Libr. Jour., 1969-73; photography pub. in Irvine mag., 1973. Named Alice Miriam Kitselman Scholar, Kitselman Estate, Muncie, 1958. Mem. Nat. Water Well Assn., Boat Owners of the U.S., U.S. Tennis Assn., Eastlake Woodlands CountryClub, Sea Ray Boat Owners Club, RVing Women, Carefree Club. Republican. Avocations: boating, tennis, photography, travel, raising AKC Bulldogs. Home (summer): 17 Bee Tree Way Lake Toxaway NC 28747

MORGAN, MARILYN, federal judge; b. 1947; 1 child, Terrence M. Adamson. BA, Emory U., 1969, JD, 1976. Bar: Ga. 1976, Calif. 1977. Ptnr. Morgan & Towery, San Jose, Calif., 1979-88; bankruptcy judge U.S. Bankruptcy Ct. (no. dist.) Calif., 1988—; mem. bankruptcy adv. com. U.S. Dist. Ct., 1984-88; law rep. 9th Cir. Jud. Conf., 1987-88. Mem. adv. bd. Downtown YMCA, 1984-88; dir. The Women's Fund, 1987-88. Mem. Santa Clara County Bar Assn. (chmn. debtor and creditor and insolvency com. 1979, 81, treas. 1982, pres. 1985-86), Santa Clara County Bar Assn. Law Found. (trustee 1982, 86-88, pres. 1985, law related edn. trustee 1986-88), Nat. Assn. Bankruptcy Trustees (founding mem., v.p., sec. 1981-88), Rotary Club San Jose (bd. dirs. 1992—), Nat. Assn. Bankruptcy Trustees (founder). Office: US Bankruptcy Ct 280 S 1st St Rm 3035 San Jose CA 95113-3010*

MORGAN, MARY DAN, social worker; b. Tallulah, La., Nov. 30, 1943; d. Daniel Boone and Mary Louise (McLeod) M.; m. William Jefferson Day (div. Dec. 1995); 1 child, Forrest Jefferson Day. BA, La. Coll., 1965; MS in Libr. Sci., La. State U., 1968; MA in Edn., Murray State U., 1976; MS in Social Work, U. Louisville, 1992. Cert. social worker, Ky., Ind. Libr. Ascension Parish Schs., Donaldsonville, La., 1966-68, Jefferson County Schs., Louisville, 1968-75; tchr. Webster County Schs., Dixon, Ky., 1975-79; tchr. Hardin County Schs., Elizabethtown, Ky., 1979-82, dir. media ctr., 1982-87, tchr. day and residential juvenile facilities, 1987-91, tchr. mid. and sr. high alt. schs., 1991-93; social worker Hospice of Cen. Ky., Elizabethtown, 1993—; pres. Webster County Tchrs. Assn., Dixon, Ky., 1977-78; sec. Ky. Libr. Network Bd., Frankfort, 1986-87. Mem. NEA (life), NASW, AAUW, Filson Club. Office: Hospice of Cen Ky 105 Diecks Dr Elizabethtown KY 42701-2444

MORGAN, MARY LOU, retired education educator, civic worker; b. Chgo., Mar. 5, 1938; d. William Nicholas and Esther Lucille (Galbraith) Wanmer; m. James Edward Morgan, May 30, 1963. BA in Bus. Edn. and Econs., Wichita State U., 1971, MEd in Student Pers. and Guidance, 1974; postgrad., Kans. State U., 1986. Cert. bus. tchr., Kans. Reservationist Braniff, Wichita, Kans., 1961-62; stenographer, fin. analyst, clk.-typist Boeing Co., Wichita, 1962-68, tng., pers. and records positions, 1979-93; pers. cons. Rita Pers. Svc., Wichita, 1974-75; adminstrv. aide, manpower specialist, job developer City of Wichita, 1975-76; account exec., employment counselor Mgmt. Recruiters, 1976-77; pers. mgr., patient cons. Women's Clinic, 1977; vocat. rehab. counselor State of Kans., Parsons, 1977-79; pvt. detective Investigation Svcs., Wichita, 1981-84; instr. career devel. Wichita State U., 1988-90; paralegal asst. Turner & Hensley, Wichita, 1975. Precinct committeewoman Wichita Dem. Com., 1992-94; founder, 1st pres., v.p. program chmn. NOW, Wichita, 1969-93, asst. state coord. polit. action com., Wichita, 1993-95, at-large state bd., Joplin, 1994-95; mem. Jasper County-Newton County Dems., 1993—; coord. funding Women's Crisis Ctr., Wichita, 1975; docent Carver Mus., Hoover Mus.; bd. dirs. for City of Wichita, Wichita Commn. on Status of Women, 1988-91; vice chmn. Hist. Preservation Commn. Mem. AAUW, Am. Assn. Ret. Persons, Hillary Clinton Women's Dem. Club. Avocations: water skiing, boating, collecting Victorian clothing, travel.

MORGAN, MONROE, retired savings and loan executive; b. Long Beach, Calif., Sept. 4, 1921; s. Karle Barett and Ethel (Monroe) M.; m. Ann Betts, Sept. 30, 1949; children: Sarah Nell, Daniel, Marjorie Jane. BA, Pomona Coll., 1942. Cert. vol. counselor Health Ins. Counseling and Advocacy Program, Calif. Acctg. exec. Coast Fed. Savs. and Loan Assn., Los Angeles, 1945-50; sec., treas. Am. Savs. and Loan Assn., Whittier, Calif., 1952-56; sr. v.p. Gt. Western Fin. Corp., Beverly Hills, Calif., 1956-87; also officer subs. savs. and loan assns.; trustee Depositors Investment Trust, 1984-85; mem. investment mgmt. com. Internat. Found. Employees Plans, 1970-76; chmn. Thrift Industry Acctg. Com., 1976-78. Active Los Angeles County Art Mus.; chmn. Ethnic Arts Coun., 1977-80; dir. non-profit food distbn. orgn. Love Is Feeding Everyone, 1986-90, treas., 1981-94; bd. dirs. Amberjack, Ltd., Bloomington, Ill., 1985; mem. alumni coun. Pomona Coll., 1989-92, chmn. edn. com., 1992-94. Maj. USMCR, 1942-45, 50-51. Mem. Savs. and Loan Instns. (bd. govs. 1957-62), Fin. Mgrs. Soc. for Savs. Instns., Calif. Savs. and Loan League, Savs. Assns. Fin. Execs. (pres. 1968-75), Fin. Analysts Fedn. Home: 922 San Vicente Blvd Santa Monica CA 90402-2004

MORGAN, NEIL, author, newspaper editor, lecturer, columnist; b. Smithfield, N.C., Feb. 27, 1924; s. Samuel Lewis and Isabelle (Robeson) M.; m. Caryl Lawrence, 1945 (div. 1954); m. Katharine Starkey, 1955 (div. 1962); m. Judith Blakely, 1964; 1 child, Jill. AB, Wake Forest Coll., 1943. Columnist San Diego Daily Jour., 1946-50; columnist San Diego Evening Tribune, 1950-92, assoc. editor, 1977-81, editor, 1981-92; assoc. editor, sr. columnist San Diego Union-Tribune, 1992—; syndicated columnist Morgan Jour., Copley News Service, 1958—; lectr.; cons. on Calif. affairs Bank of Am., Sunset mag. Author: My San Diego, 1951, It Began With a Roar, 1953, Know Your Doctor, 1954, Crosstown, 1955, My San Diego 1960, 1959, Westward Tilt, 1963, Neil Morgan's San Diego, 1964, The Pacific States, 1967, The California Syndrome, 1969, (with Robert Witty) Marines of Margarita, 1970, The Unconventional City, 1972, (with Tom Blair) Yesterday's San Diego, 1976, This Great Land, 1983, Above San Diego, 1990, (with Judith Morgan) Dr. Seuss & Mr. Geisel, 1995; contbr. non-fiction articles to Nat. Geog., Esquire, Redbook, Reader's Digest, Holiday, Harper's, Travel and Leisure, Ency. Brit. Lt. USNR, 1943-46. Recipient Ernie Pyle Meml. award, 1957, Bill Corum Meml. award, 1961, Disting. Svc. citation Wake Forest U., 1966, grand award for travel writing Pacific Area Travel Assn., 1972, 78, Fourth Estate award San Diego State U., 1988, The Morgan award Leadership Edn. Awareness Devel. San Diego, 1993; co-recipient Ellen and Roger Revelle award, 1986; named Outstanding Young Man of Yr. San Diego, 1959. Mem. Authors Guild, Am. Soc. Newspaper Editors, Soc. Profl. Journalists, Explorers Club, Soc. of Am. Travel Writers, Bohemian Club, Phi Beta Kappa, Omicron Delta Kappa. Home: 7930 Prospect Pl La Jolla CA 92037-3721 Office: PO Box 191 San Diego CA 92112-4106

MORGAN, RAYMOND F., plastic surgeon; b. Pitts., Apr. 24, 1948; s. Edwin J. and Alberta (Hirt) M.; m. Sue Ann; children: Ryan Frederic, Alexander Evan, Elizabeth Anne. BS, U. Pitts., 1969, MEd, 1972, DMD, 1972; MD, W.Va. U., 1976. Diplomate Am. Bd. Plastic Surgery, Am. Bd. Hand Surgery. Intern Johns Hopkins U. Hosp., Balt., 1976-77, resident surgery, 1977-80, resident plastic surgery, 1980-82; resident hand surgery Union Meml. Hosp., Balt.; staff U. Va. Health Scis. Ctr., Charlottesville, M.T. Edgerton prof., chmn. dept. plastic surgery, 1988—. Mem. ACS, Soc. Univ. Surgeons, So. Surg. Assn., Am. Soc. for Surgery of the Hand, Am. Assn. Plastic Surgeons. Office: U of Va Dept of Plastic Surgery Charlottesville VA 22908

MORGAN, RAYMOND VICTOR, JR., university administrator, mathematics educator; b. Brownwood, Tex., May 10, 1942; s. Raymond Victor and Lovey Lucile (Tate) M.; m. Mary Jane Folks, Aug. 13, 1967; children: Jason Wesley, Jeremy Victor. BA, Howard Payne U., 1965; MA, Vanderbilt U., 1966; PhD, U. Mo., 1969. Asst. prof. So. Meth. U., Dallas, 1969-75; assoc. prof. Sul Ross State U., Alpine, Tex., 1975-82, math. dept. chmn., 1976-85, prof., 1982—, dean of scis., 1979-86, exec. asst. pres., 1985-90, pres., 1990—; bd. dirs. Tex. Internat. Edn. Consortium; bd. dirs. Southwestern Livestock Exposition, 1993—. Author textbook: Agricultural Mathematics, 1978; author articles. Founder, regional commr. Alpine Soccer League, 1984; v.p., coach Alpine Baseball League, 1983; pres. Alpine PTA, 1982-83; founder, pres. So. Meth. U. Faculty Club, 1973-75; mem. exec. com. Tex. Assn. Coll. and Univ. Student Personnel Adminstrs., 1990-92. NSF grantee, 1979. Mem. Am. Assn. Higher Edn., Tex. Assn. Coll. Tchrs. (chpt. v.p. 1978-79), Math. Assn. Am. (chmn. Tex. sect. 1985-86). Republican. Mem. Ch. of Christ. Clubs: Lions (pres. 1979-80, Lion of Yr. 1980, 83), Alpine Country. Avocations: motorcycling, golf, shooting. Home: PO Box 1341 Alpine TX 79831-1341 Office: Sul Ross State U E Highway 90 PO Box C114 Alpine TX 79831-0114

MORGAN, RICHARD ERNEST, political scientist, educator; b. Centre County, Pa., May 17, 1937; s. James Ernest and Helen Estelle (Hogge) M.; m. Jean Mary Yarbrough, 1996. A.B., Bowdoin Coll., Brunswick, Maine, 1959; A.M., Columbia U., 1961, Ph.D., 1967. Instr. in govt. Columbia U., 1962-63, 65-67, asst. prof. govt., 1967-68; asso. prof. govt. Bowdoin Coll., 1969-75, William Nelson Cromwell prof. constl. law and govt., 1975—; fellow in law and govt. Harvard U. Law Sch., 1968-69; research dir. Twentieth Century Fund Project on Polit. Surveillance in Am., 1975-79. Author: The Politics of Religious Conflict, 1968, The Supreme Court and Religion, 1972, (with others) American Politics: Directions of Change, Dynamics of Choice, 1979, Domestic Intelligence: Monitoring Dissent in America, 1980, Disabling America: The Rights Industry in Our Time, 1984, People, Power and Politics, 1994; contbr. articles to profl. publs.; editor: (with James E. Connor) The American Political System: Introductory Readings, 1971. Chmn. Spl. Commn. on Legis. Compensation, State of Maine, 1973-74; chmn. Maine adv. com. U.S. Commn. on Civil Rights, 1985-87. Served to 1st lt. U.S. Army, 1963-65. Mem. Am. Polit. Sci. Assn., New Eng. Polit. Sci. Assn. (pres. 1988-89). Republican. Episcopalian. Home: RR 2 South Harpswell ME 04079-9802 Office: Bowdoin Coll Brunswick ME 04011

MORGAN, RICHARD GREER, lawyer; b. Houston, Dec. 23, 1943; s. John Benjamin (stepfather) and Audrey Valley (Brickwede) Haus; children: Richard Greer, Jonathan Roberts. AB in History, Princeton U., 1966; JD, U. Tex., 1969. Bar: Tex. 1969, D.C. 1970, Minn. 1976, U.S. Ct. Appeals (D.C. cir.) 1970, U.S. Ct. Appeals (5th and 9th cirs., temporary emergency ct. appeals) 1976. Atty., advisor to commr. Lawrence J. O'Connor, Jr. Fed. Power Commn., Washington, 1969-71; assoc. Morgan, Lewis & Bockius, Washington, 1971-75; ptnr. O'Connor & Hannan, Washington, 1975-89, Lane & Mittendorf, Washington, 1989—; bd. dirs. Hexagon, Inc.; instr. law seminars; lectr. in field. Author: Gas Lease and Royalty Issues, Natural Gas Yearbook, 1989, 90, 91, 92; contbr. articles on energy law to profl. jours. Bd. dirs. Florence Crittenton Home, U. Tex. Law Sch. Found. Mem. ABA, Fed. Bar Assn. (bd. dirs.), Fed. Energy Bar Assn., D.C. Bar Assn., Princeton Alumni Council, Princeton Club Washington (exec. com., pres.). Home: 2772 Unicorn Ln NW Washington DC 20015-2234 Office: 919 18th St NW Fl 8 Washington DC 20006-5503

MORGAN, ROBERT ARTHUR, accountant; b. Decatur, Ill., Oct. 23, 1918; s. Robert Howard and Katherine (Massey) M.; m. Julia Ann Franklin, June 28, 1941; children: Robert A., Susan Ruth. BS, U. Ill., 1941. Acct. Pure Oil Co., 1941; acct. Caterpillar Tractor Co., Peoria, Ill., 1945-56, controller, 1956-78; mem. Fin. Acct. Standards Bd., Stamford, Conn., 1978-82; cons. Morton, Ill., 1982—. Contbr. articles to acctg. periodicals. Past mem. fin. acctg. standards adv. coun. Fin. Acctg. Found.; pres. bd. edn. Morton Twp. High Sch., 1960-61. Civilian auditor AUS, 1942-44. Mem. Nat. Assn. Accts. (nat. dir., nat. v.p. 1965-66, chmn. mng. practices 1974-75), Machinery and Allied Products Inst. (fin. coun. II 1956-78), Fin. Execs. Inst. (mem. com. corp. reporting 1977-78), Internat. Fedn. Accts. (chmn. com. fin. and mgmt. acctg. 1983).

MORGAN, ROBERT MARION, educational research educator; b. Ponca City, Okla., Feb. 5, 1930; s. Perry Harrison and Velma Beatrice (Stowe) M.; m. Constance Louise Claus, Jan. 3, 1963; children—Stephen, Melayne. B.S., Okla. State U., 1955, M.S., 1956; Ph.D., Ohio State U., 1958; LL.D., Dongah U., Pusan, Korea. Asst. prof. U. N.M., 1958-62; pres. Gen. Programmed Teaching Corp., Palo Alto, Calif., 1961-64; v.p. Ranchers Corp., Albuquerque, 1962-64; dir. ednl. systems Litton Industries, College Park, Md., 1964-66; dep. dir. div. vocational research U.S. Office Edn., Washington, 1966-68; prof., head dept. ednl. research Fla. State U., Tallahassee, 1968-74; dir. Center for Ednl. Tech., 1968-75, Learning Systems Inst., 1975—; Lectr. Catholic U. Am., 1966-68, Seoul (Korea) Nat. U., 1970-71; cons. AID, Republic of Brazil, Korea, Italian Air Force, Navy Dept., U.S. Naval Acad.; Chmn. Fla. Research and Devel., Council, 1969—; mem. sch. bd. U. Sch., Tallahassee, 1969-74. Author: Programmed Instruction—A Concept of Learning, 1963, An Educational Systems Analysis for the Republic of Korea, 1970; also articles. Bd. dirs. U.S. Coalition for Edn. for All, 1992—; trustee Aerospace Ednl. Found. With AUS, 1949-52. Fellow Royal Soc. Arts; mem. Am. Ednl. Research Assn., Am. Psychol. Assn., Nat. Soc. for Programmed Instrn., Am. Mgmt. Assn., Sigma Xi. Republican. Presbyterian. Lodge: Rotary. Home: 3322 Remington Run Tallahassee FL 32312-1462 Office: Fla State Univ 205 Dodd Hall Tallahassee FL 32306

MORGAN, ROBERT P., music theorist, educator; b. Nashville, July 28, 1934; s. Hugh J. and Robert (Porter) M.; m. Carole Ann Montgomery, June 12, 1965. BA, Princeton U., 1956, MFA, 1960, PhD, 1969; MA, U. Calif., 1958. Instr. U. Houston, 1963-67; asst. prof. Temple U., Phila., 1967-70, assoc. prof., 1970-75, prof., 1975-79; prof. U. Chgo., 1979-89, Yale U., New Haven, 1989—; vis. prof. U. Pa., Phila., 1976-78, Yale U., 1987; adv. bd. Fromm Music Found., Chgo., 1984-89. Author: Twentieth Century Music, 1991; mem. editorial bd. Critical Inquiry, 1980—, Studies in the Criticism and Theory of Music, 1981—, Composers of the Twentieth Century; composer orch., chamber ensemble, voice and piano works; articles in field. Grantee German Govt., 1960-62; Woodrow Wilson fellow, 1956-57, NEH sr. fellow, 1983-84. Mem. Am. Musicol. Soc. (council mem. 1982-85), Soc. for Music Theory (bd. dirs. 1985—), Coll. Music Soc., Yale Club (N.Y.C.). Democrat. Avocations: tennis, skiing. Office: Yale Univ Dept Of Music New Haven CT 06520-8310

MORGAN, ROBERT PETER, engineering educator; b. Bklyn., Feb. 26, 1934; s. Jack and Minna (Cohen) M.; m. Nancy Beverly Hutchins, Dec. 20, 1958; children: Thomas Albert, Jonathan Andrew. B.Ch.E., Cooper Union, 1956; S.M., MIT, 1959, Nucl.E., 1961; Ph.D., Rensselaer Poly. Inst., 1965. Asst. dir. MIT Practice Sch., Oak Ridge, 1958-59; instr. chem. engring. Rensselaer Poly. Inst., 1960-64; asst. prof. nuclear and chem. engring. U. Mo., 1964-68; assoc. prof. engring. Washington U., St. Louis, 1968-74, prof. tech. and human affairs, 1974-87, Elvera and William Stuckenberg prof. tech. and human affairs, 1987—, dir. Ctr. for Tech. Assessment and Policy, 1968—, chmn. dept. tech. and human affairs, 1976-83; sci. and pub. policy fellow Brookings Instn., 1982-83; council mem. Vols. in Tech. Assistance; chmn. adv. subcom. NASA Tech. Transfer Program, 1978-80; mem. nat. adv. bd. program on ethics and values in sci. and tech. NSF, 1977-79; mem. com. on research grants NRC, 1983-86; Sigma Xi nat. lectr., 1981-83; vis. sr. analyst Office of Tech. Assessment of U.S. Congress, 1989-90. Author: The Role of U.S. Universities in Science and Technology for Development, 1979, Renewable Resource Utilization for Development, 1981; Science and Technology for International Development: An Assessment of U.S. Policies and Programs, 1984; contbr. numerous articles to profl. publs.; mem. editorial bd. Telecommunications Policy, 1976-80, Sci., Tech. and Human Values, 1977-79, 81-88 . Recipient Disting. Faculty award Washington U., 1989; AEC fellow, 1959-60. Fellow AAAS (com. on sci., engring. and pub. policy 1977-80, program com. 1992—); mem. AAUP, Fedn. Am. Scientists, Am. Soc. Engring. Edn. (Chester F. Carlson award 1978), Tau Beta Pi. Office: Washington U Campus Box 1106 Saint Louis MO 63130

MORGAN, ROBERT STEVE, mechanical engineer; b. Oklahoma City, Oct. 10, 1945; s. Chester Steve and Madelein Ruth (Stowers) M.; m. Margaret Ann Groves, June 7, 1971; children: Jerri Dianna, Jamie Deann. Diploma, S.W. Tech. Inst., 1967. Chief draftsman R.L. Gilstrap Inc., Oklahoma City, 1966-67; mgr. print dept. Phelps-Spitz-Ammerman-Thomas Inc., Oklahoma City, 1967-68; sr. drafter GE, Oklahoma City, 1968-70; mech. designer Honeywell Inc., Oklahoma City, 1970-75; pvt. practice Oklahoma City, 1970—; sr. designer Control Data Corp., Oklahoma City, 1970-75; sr. designer, drafting coord., cad adminstr. BancTec Inc., Oklahoma City, 1984-96; design engr. Climate Master, Oklahoma City, 1996; contract design engr. Texas Instruments, Dallas, 1996-97; contract designer Lawrence Livermore (Calif.) Nat. Lab., 1997—. Patentee overlap document detector, double document detector, ribbon cartridge. Voter organizer Rep. Party, Oklahoma City, 1967; asst. leader Girl Scouts of Am., Yukon, Okla., 1984. Mem. Confederate Air Force (col.). Republican. Avocations: gun collecting, off road auto touring, coin collecting, bowling. Home: 704 Victoria Dr Yukon OK 73099-5341

MORGAN, ROBIN EVONNE, poet, author, journalist, activist, editor; b. Lake Worth, Fla., Jan. 29, 1941; 1 child, Blake Ariel. Grad. with honors, The Wetter Sch., 1956; student, pvt. tutors, 1956-59, Columbia U.; DHL (hon.), U. Conn., 1992. Free-lance book editor, 1961-69; editor Grove Press, 1967-70; editor, columnist World column Ms. Mag., N.Y.C., 1974-87, editor in chief, 1989-93, internat. cons. editor, 1993—; vis. chair and guest prof. women's studies New Coll., Sarasota, Fla., 1973; disting. vis. scholar, lectr. Ctr. Critical Analysis of Contemporary Culture, Rutgers U., 1987, U. Denver Grad. Sch. Internat. Affairs, 1996-97; invited spl. cons. UN com. UN Conv. to End All Forms Discrimination Against Women, Sao Paulo and Brasilia, Brazil, 1987; mem. adv. bd. ISIS (internat. network women's internat. cross-cultural exch.); spl. advisor gen. assembly conf. on Gender UN Internat. Sch., 1985-86; free-lance journalist, lectr. cons., editor, 1969—; invited speaker numerous confs., orgns., acad. meetings, U.S. and abroad. Author, compiler, editor: Sisterhood Is Powerful: An Anthology of Writings from the Women's Liberation Movement, 1970, Swedish edit., 1972, Sisterhood Is Global: The International Women's Movement Anthology, 1984, U.K. edit., 1985, Spanish edit., 1994, Feminist Press edit., 1996; author: (nonfiction) Going Too Far: The Personal Chronicle of a Feminist, 1978, German edit., 1978, The Anatomy of Freedom: Feminism, Physics and Global Politics, 1982, 2d edit., 1994, fgn. edits. U.K., 1984, Germany, 1985, Argentina, 1986, Brazil, 1992, The Demon Lover: On the Sexuality of Terrorism, 1989, U.K. edit., 1989, Japanese edit., 1992, The Word of a Woman: Feminist Dispatches 1968-91, 1992, 2d edit., 1994, U.K. edit., 1992, Chinese edit., 1996, A Woman's Creed, English, Arabic, French, Italian, Sanskrit, Hindi, Russian, Spanish, Portuguese, Chinese and Persian edits., 1995, (fiction) Dry Your Smile: A Novel, 1987, U.K. edit., 1988, The Mer-Child: A New Legend, 1991, German edit., 1995 (poetry) Monster: Poems, 1972, Lady of the Beasts: Poems, 1976, Death Benefits: Poems, 1981, Depth Perception: New Poems and a Masque, 1982, Upstairs in the Garden: Selected and New Poems, 1968-88, 1990, (plays) In Another Country, 1960, The Duel, 1979; co-editor: The Woman: Anthology, 1969; contbr. numerous articles, essays, book revs., poems to various publs.; presenter poetry readings, univs., poetry ctrs., radio, TV, others, 1970—. Mem. 1st women's liberation caucus CORE, 1965, Student Nonviolent Coordinating Com., 1966; organizer 1st feminist demonstration against Miss Am. Pageant, 1968; founder, pres. The Sisterhood Fund, 1970; founder, pres. N.Y. Women's Law Ctr., 1970; founder N.Y. Women's Ctr., 1969; co-founder, bd. dirs. Feminist Women's Health Network, Nat. Battered Women's Refuge Network, Nat. Network Rape Crisis Ctrs.; bd. dirs. Women's Fgn. Policy Coun.; adv. trustee Nat. Women's Inst. for Freedom of Press; founding mem. Nat. Mus. Women in Arts; co-founder Sisterhood is Global Inst. (internat. think-tank), 1984, officer, 1989—, co-organizer, U.S. mem. official visit Coalition of Philippines Women's Movement, 1988; chair N.Y. state com. Hands Across Am. Com. for Justice and Empowerment, 1988; mem. adv. bd. Global Fund for Women. Recipient Front Page award for disting. journalism, Wonder Woman award for internat. peace and understanding, 1982, Feminist of Yr. award Fund for Feminist majority, 1990; writer-in-residence grantee Yaddo, 1980; grantee Nat. Endowment for Arts, 1979-80, Ford Found., 1982, 83, 84. Mem. Feminist Writers' Guild, Media Women, N.Am. Feminist Coalition, Pan Arab Feminist Solidarity Assn. (hon.), Israeli Feminists Against Occupation (hon.). Office: Ms Mag 135 W 50th St New York NY 10020-1201

MORGAN, RONALD WILLIAM, sales executive; b. Redlands, Calif., May 9, 1951; s. Liberty W. and Eleanor L. (Creech) M.; m. Debra Ann Lein, Nov. 30, 1991. AA in Machine Shop, Valley Coll., 1973; BA in Bus., Calif. State U., San Bernardino, 1977. Sales mgr. Combined Ins., Redlands, 1976-77; ter. sales mgr. Bullard Safety, L.A., 1977-79; sales engr. H.E.S. Machine Tool, Whittier, Calif., 1979-81, Machinery Sales, L.A., 1981-89; regional mgr. Ingersoll Rand Water Jet, Yorba Linda, Calif., 1989-91; ter. sales mgr. Machinery Sales, L.A., 1991-93; dist. mgr. Ellison Machinery, L.A., 1993-94; regional mgr. Daewoo Machinery, L.A., 1995—. With USCGR. Mem. Soc. Mfg. Engrs., Sons Am. Revolution. Avocations: travel, boats, motorcycles. Office: Daewoo Machinery 10395 Slusher Dr Santa Fe Springs CA 90670

MORGAN, RUTH PROUSE, academic administrator, educator; b. Berkeley, Calif., Mar. 30, 1934; d. Ervin Joseph and Thelma Ruth (Prcesang) Prouse; m. Vernon Edward Morgan, June 3, 1956; children: Glenn Edward, Renée Ruth. BA summa cum laude, U. Tex., 1956; MA, La. State U., 1961, PhD, 1966. Asst. prof. Am. govt., politics and theory So. Meth. U., Dallas, 1966-70, assoc. prof., 1970-74, prof., 1974-95; prof. emeritus, 1995—; asst. provost So. Meth. U., Dallas, 1978-82, assoc. provost, 1982-86, provost ad interim, 1986-87, provost, 1987-93, provost emerita, 1993—; pres. RPM Assocs., 1993—; v.p. ABATECH, Inc., 1995—; Tex. state polit. analyst ABC, N.Y.C., 1972-84. Author: The President and Civil Rights, 1970; mem. editorial bd. Jour. of Politics, 1975-82, Presdl. Studies Quar., 1980—; contbr. articles to profl. jours. Active Internat. Women's Forum, 1987—; trustee Hockaday Sch., 1988-94; trustee The Kilby Awards Found., 1993-95; bd. dirs. United Way, Met. Dallas, 1993—; mem. adv. com. U.S. Army Command and Gen. Staff. Coll., 1994—; chmn. adv. com. Archives of Women of the Southwest, 1995—. Mem. Am. Polit. Sci. Assn., So. Polit. Sci. Assn. (mem. exec. coun. 1979-84), Southwestern Polit. Sci. Assn. (pres. 1982-83, mem. exec. coun. 1981-84), The Dallas Forum of Internat. Women's Forum (pres. 1996-98), Charter 100 Club (pres. 1991-92), Dallas Summit Club (pres. 1992-93), Phi Beta Kappa, Pi Sigma Alpha, Phi Kappa Phi, Theta Sigma Phi. Avocations: photography, travel.

MORGAN, SAMUEL P(OPE), physicist, applied mathematician; b. San Diego, July 14, 1923; s. Samuel Pope and Beatrice Marie (Summers) M.; m. Mary Caroline Annin, Jan. 23, 1948; children: Caroline Gail, Lesley Anne, Alison Lee, Diane Elizabeth. B.S., Calif. Inst. Tech., 1943, M.S., 1944, Ph.D. in Physics, 1947. Mem. tech. staff AT&T Bell Labs., Murray Hill, N.J., 1947-59; head dept. math. physics AT&T Bell Labs., 1959-67, dir. computing tech., 1969-70, dir. computing sci. research center, 1967-82, disting. mem. tech. staff, 1982-95; disting. mem. tech. staff Lucent Tech./Bell Labs., 1996—. Research, publs. on electromagnetic theory, applied math., queueing theory; patentee in field. Fellow IEEE; mem. AAAS, Am. Phys. Soc., Sigma Xi. Home: 9 Raleigh Ct Morristown NJ 07960-2535 Office: Lucent Tech Bell Labs New Providence NJ 07974

MORGAN, SCOTT ELLINGWOOD, publisher, lawyer; b. Kansas City, Kans., June 29, 1957; s. Ray Ellingwood and Mary Grace (Burkhardt) M.; m. Kathleen O'Leary, Oct. 8, 1983; children: Kelly, Calvin, Grace. BS in Journalism, U. Kans., 1979, JD, 1983. Bar: Kans. Mem. staff Senator Nancy Kassebaum, Washington, 1979-80; staff atty. U.S. Customs, Washington, 1983; staff counsel U.S. Senate Judiciary Com., Washington, 1983-86; rep. Fed. Election Com., Washington, 1986-87; chief counsel Bob Dole for Pres., Washington, 1987-88, Office of Gov., Topeka, Kans., 1988-91; atty. Schleicher, Latz, P.C., Kansas City, 1991-92; pres. Morgan Quitno Press, Lawrence, 1989—. Editor: State Rankings, 1990—, Health Care State Rankings, 1993—, Crime State Rankings, 1994—, City Crime Rankings, 1995—. Nominee U.S. Congress 2nd Dist. Kans., 1990; Rep. chmn. 2nd Dist. Kans., 1991. Congregationalist. Office: Morgan Quitno Press PO Box 1656 Lawrence KS 66044

MORGAN, STEPHEN CHARLES, academic administrator; b. Upland, Calif., June 2, 1946; s. Thomas Andrew and Ruth Elizabeth (Miller) M.; m. Ann Marie McMurray, Sept. 6, 1969; 1 child, Kesley Suzanne. BA, U. La Verne, 1968; MS, U. So. Calif., 1971; EdD, U. No. Colo., 1979. Devel. officer U. La Verne, Calif., 1968-71, asst. to pres., 1971-73, dir. devel., 1973-75, v.p. devel., 1975-76, pres., 1985—; dir. devel. U. So. Calif., L.A., 1976-79; exec. dir. Ind. Colls. No. Calif., San Francisco, 1979-85; dir. Ind. Colls. So. Calif., L.A., 1985—. Bd. dirs. Mt. Baldy United Way, Ontario, Calif., 1988—, McKinley Children's Ctr., San Dimas, Calif., 1989—; chair nat. com. on higher edn. Ch. of Brethren, Elgin, Ill., 1988-90; dir. Pomona Valley Hosp. Med. Ctr., 1992—, Inter Valley Health Plan, 1992-97. Mem. Assn. Ind. Calif. Colls. and Univs. (exec. com. 1989—, vice chair 1996—), L.A. County Fair Assn., Western Coll. Assn. (exec. com. 1992—, pres. 1996—), Pi Gamma Mu. Avocations: orchid culture, fly fishing, golf. Home: 2518 N Mountain Ave Claremont CA 91711-1579 Office: U of LaVerne Office of Pres 1950 3rd St La Verne CA 91750-4401

MORGAN, THOMAS BRUCE, author, editor, public affairs executive; b. Springfield, Ill., July 24, 1926; s. David Edward and Mabel Ariel (Wolfe) M.; m. Joan T. Zuckerman, Oct. 3, 1950 (div. 1972); children: Katherine Tarlow, Nicholas David; m. Mary Clark Rockefeller, May 4, 1974 (div. 1988); stepchildren: Geoffrey, Michael, Sabrina Strawbridge; m. Hadassah Teitz Brooks, Aug. 19, 1990; stepchildren: Shoshana Goldhill, Benjamin Brooks. BA, Carleton Coll., 1949. Assoc. editor Esquire Mag., N.Y.C., 1949-53; sr. editor Look Mag., N.Y.C., 1953-58; freelance writer N.Y.C., 1958-69; press sec. Mayor John V. Lindsay, N.Y.C., 1969-73; sr. editor New York Mag., 1974-75; editor The Village Voice, N.Y.C., 1975-76; publisher Politicks mag., N.Y.C., 1976-79; novelist, freelance writer, 1979-89; pres. WNYC Comm. Group, N.Y.C., 1990-94; pres., CEO UN Assn. of U.S.A., N.Y.C., 1994-95; freelance writer, 1996—; press sec. Stevenson for Pres., 1960, McCarthy for Pres., 1968. Author: Friends and Fellow Students, 1956, Self-Creations, 1965, (novel) This Blessed Shore, 1966, Among the Anti-Americans, 1967, (novel) Snyder's Walk, 1987; screenwriter documentary feature film Albert Schweitzer, 1957 (Acad. award); contbr. numerous articles to nat. mags. Trustee Carleton Coll., Northfield, Minn., 1975-79, 80—, WNYC Pub. Radio Found., 1996—. Mem. PEN, Authors Guild, Century Assn. Democrat. Jewish. Home and Office: 1155 Park Ave New York NY 10128

MORGAN, THOMAS OLIVER, bishop; b. Jan. 20, 1941; s. Charles Edwin and Amy Amelia (Hoyes) M.; m. Lillian Marie Textor, 1963; three children. BA, U. Sask., Can., 1962; BD, King's Coll., London, 1965; DD (hon.), Coll. of Emmanuel and St. Chad, Sask., 1986. Curate Ch. of the Saviour, Blackburn, Lancashire, Eng., 1966-69; rector Ch. of the Good Shepherd, Porcupine Plain, Sask., Can., 1969-73; rector Ch. of the Saviour, Kinistino, 1973-77, Shellbrook, 1977-83; Archdeacon Sask., 1983-85; bishop Diocese of Sask., Prince Albert, 1985-93, Diocese of Saskatoon, Sask., 1993—. Office: Diocese of Saskatoon, PO Box 1965, Saskatoon, SK Canada S7K 3S5*

MORGAN, THOMAS ROWLAND, retired marine corps officer; b. Allentown, Pa., Jan. 6, 1930; s. Harry Campbell and Olwen (Pierce) M.; m. Barbara A. Croze, June 29, 1957; children—Lynn A., Susan E., Beth E. B.A. in History, Colgate U., 1952; student, Marine Corps Command and Staff Coll., 1965-66; M.A. in Edn., U. Va., 1973. Commd. 2d lt. USMC, 1952, advanced through grades to gen., 1986; naval aviator Naval Air Sta., Pensacola, Fla., 1953-54; asst. maintenance officer 3d Marine Aircraft Wing, El Toro, Calif., 1954-55; personnel officer Marine Aircraft Group Western Pacific, 1954-55; dep. comdr. Fleet Marine Force, aide to comdg. gen. 1st Marine Aircraft Wing, Pacific, 1955; asst. ops. officer Marine Aircraft Group, Kaneohe Bay, Hawaii, 1956-57; squadron pilot, ground tng. officer Marine Attack Squadron, Hawaii, 1957-59; flight instr. Naval Air Sta., Olathe, Kans., 1959; personnel officer, aircraft maintenance officer Marine Fighter Squadron, Beaufort, S.C., 1959-61; exec. officer Hdqrs. and Maintenance Squadron, Atsugi, Japan, 1961-62; fleet liaison officer Marine Corps Air Sta., Yuma, Ariz., 1962-65; comdr. Marine Fighter Attack Squadron, Beaufort, 1966-67; group ops. officer, officer-in-charge DaNang DASC, Vietnam, 1968-69; exec. officer Marine Corps Air Sta., Quantico, Va., 1969-71; exec. officer Naval ROTC unit U. Va., 1971-73; chief war plans br. J-5 U.S. European Command Hdqrs., Stuttgart, Fed. Republic Germany, 1973-76; asst. to dep. chief of staff requirements and programs Hdqrs. U.S. Marine Corps, Washington, 1976-77; asst. div. comdr. 3d Marine Div., Okinawa, Japan, 1977-78; asst. chief of staff C-5 Combined Forces Command, Seoul, 1978-80; dep. comdr. FMF Pacific, Camp Smith, Hawaii, 1980-81; dep. chief of staff for requirements and programs Hdqrs. Marine Corps, Washington, 1981-85, dep. chief staff for plans, policies and ops., acting Chief of Staff, 1985-86, asst. commandant, 1986-88, ret. Decorated D.S.M., Def. Superior Service medal, Legion of Merit, Bronze Star medal, Meritorious Service medal, Air medal; Order of Nat. Security medal, Cheonsu medal (Korea). Mem. Am. Legion. Avocations: golf, skiing, water sports.

MORGAN, TIM DALE, physical education educator; b. Covington, Ky., Jan. 8, 1964; s. Thomas Benjamin and Audrey (Crider) M.; m. Shirley Mae Oliver, Nov. 9, 1992; children: Joshua David-Thomas, Andrew Jacob. BS in Phys. Edn., Ch. Recreation, Campbellsville Coll., 1991; MS in Phys. Edn., Ea. Ky. U., 1992, MS in Recreation and Park Adminstrn., 1993, MA in Allied Health, 1997; postgrad., U. Ky., 1997—; diploma in fitness and nutrition, Internat. Corr. Schs., 1992. Cert. in real estate, Ky. Asst. facility coord. Bapt. Student Union No. Ky. U., Highland Heights, 1986-88, supr. health ctr., 1986-87; dept. asst. Campbellsville (Ky.) Coll., 1988-91; mem. staff dept. phys. edn. Ea. Ky. U., Richmond, 1991-92, intramurals facility coord., 1992-93, phys. edn. instr., 1993—; survey coord. Champions Against Drugs, Campbellsville, 1990-91; adminstr. phys. testing Ky. State Police, Ea. Ky. U., Richmond, 1992-96. Fellowship dir. Bapt. Student Union, 1987-88, commuter coord., 1989, dir., adminstr. recreation, 1992; summer missionary So. Bapt. Conv. Home Mission Bd., Atlanta, 1987-89; vol. Christian Life Ctr., Campbellsville Bapt. Ch., 1990-91; music dir., tchr. coll. Sunday sch. Acton (Ky.) Bapt. Ch., 1990. Lance Cpl. USMC, 1982-88. Mem. AAHPERD, Ky. Assn. Health, Phys. Edn., Recreation and Dance. Democrat. Avocations: outdoor recreation, photography, volleyball, fitness and recreational activities. Home and Office: Ea Ky U 136 Oakland Ave Richmond KY 40475-1958

MORGAN, TIMI SUE, lawyer; b. Parsons, Kans., June 16, 1953; d. James Daniel and Iris Mae (Wilson) Baumgardner; m. Rex Michael Morgan, Oct. 28, 1983; children: Tessa Anne, Camma Elizabeth. BS, U. Kans., 1974; JD, So. Meth. U., 1977. Bar: Tex. 1977, U.S. Dist. Ct. (no. dist.) Tex. 1978, U.S. Ct. Appeals (5th cir.) 1979, U.S. Tax Ct. 1980; cert. tax law specialist. Assoc. Gardere & Wynne, Dallas, 1977-79; assoc. Akin, Gump, Strauss, Hauer & Feld, Dallas, 1979-83, ptnr., 1984-86; of counsel Stinson, Mag & Fizzell, Dallas, 1986-88; sole practice Dallas, 1988—; adj. lectr. law So. Meth. U., 1989-90, '92—. Bd. dirs. Dallas Urban League Inc., 1987-91. Mem. ABA (mem. taxation sect.), State Bar Tex. (mem. taxation sect.), Dallas Bar Assn., So. Meth. U. Law Alumni Coun. (sec. 1985-86), Order of Coif, Beta Gamma Sigma. Republican. Episcopalian. Home: 3719 Euclid Ave Dallas TX 75205

MORGAN, VIRGINIA, magistrate judge; b. 1946. BS, Univ. of Mich., 1968; JD, Univ. of Toledo, 1975. Bar: Mich. 1975, Federal 1975, U.S. Ct. Appeals (6th cir.) 1979. Tchr. Dept. of Interior, Bur. of Indian Affairs, 1968-70, San Diego Unified Schs., 1970-72, Oregon, Ohio, 1972-74; asst. prosecutor Washtenaw County Prosecutor's Office, 1976-79; asst. U.S. atty. Detroit, 1979-85; magistrate judge U.S. Dist. Ct. (Mich. ea. dist.), 6th circuit, Detroit, 1985—. Recipient Spl. Achievement award Dept. of Justice, Disting. Alumni award U. Toledo, 1993. Fellow Mich. State Bar Found.; mem. FBA (pres. 1996-97, bd. fed. jud. ctr. 1997), Nat. Assn. Women Judges, Mich. Bar Assn., Fed. Magistrate Judges Assn. (pres. 1995—). Office: US Courthouse 231 W Lafayette Blvd Detroit MI 48226-2720

MORGAN, WALTER, retired poultry science educator; b. Ledyard, Conn., Dec. 22, 1921; s. Walter Clifford and Margaret (Allyn) M.; m. Marcella Hodge, Dec. 28, 1948 (div. 1960); children: Nancy, Peggy, Beth; m. Helen Naden, May 14, 1966. BSc, U. Conn., 1946; MSc, George Washington U., 1949, PhD, 1953. Animal husbandman Nat. Cancer Inst., NIH, Bethesda, Md., 1946-49; rsch. assoc. Nevis Rsch. Sta., Columbia U., Irvington-on-Hudson, N.Y., 1950-53; asst. prof. U. Tenn., Knoxville, 1953-54; assoc. prof., prof. S.D. State U., Brookings, 1954-85; ret., 1985; fgn. expert on English and genetics People's Republic China, 1991; researcher biology div. Nuclear Energy Ctr., Mol, Belgium, 1968-69, genetics div. Commonwealth Sci. and Indsl. Rsch. Orgn., Sydney, Australia, 1975-76; cons., Kuala Lumpur, Malaysia, 1988, Europe, 1944, 69, 84, 95. Author: (poetry) Now and Then, 1982, Down Under, 1983, Hitchin' Around, 1985, Here and There, 1990, What's Good About China, 1992, In Europe 1944-1969-1994, 1995; contbr. over 100 articles to profl. jours. Former scoutmaster Boy Scouts Am., Brookings; pres. Men's Brotherhood, Brookings, 1974, U.S. Friends Fgn. Students, Brookings, 1986-97. Sgt. USAAF, 1942-45, ETO. Fellow AAAS; mem. Am. Genetics Assn., World Poultry Assn., N.Y. Acad. Scis., S.D. Acad. Sci. (pres.). Home: 1610 1st St Brookings SD 57006-2617

MORGAN, WAYNE PHILIP, art and popular culture exhibition producer; b. Dunnville, Ont., Can., Apr. 1, 1942. Cert., Sch. Art, Regina Coll., 1963; BA, U. Sask., Can., 1966; student, Emma Lake Artists Workshop, Sask., 1964-68, McGill U., Montreal, 1968, Art and Mass Culture Banff Ctr. for Arts, 1991. Community resident artist Weyburn (Sask.) Arts Council, 1967-70; dir., curator Dunlop Art Gallery, Regina (Sask.) Public Library, 1970-84; head curatorial services div. Winnipeg Art Gallery, Man., Can., 1984-85; ind. exhbn. prodr. specializing in popular culture, 1985—; mem. explorations jury Can. Coun., 1977-79; mem. secretariat Regina Arts Commn., 1979—; chmn. visual arts subcom. Ottawa-Carleton Adv. Com. for Arts. Mem. Western Can. Art Assn. (founding mem.), Sask. Mus. Assn. (bd. dirs. 1978-80, pres. 1982-84), Sask. Craft Coun. (founding mem.), Can. Mus. Assn. (bd. dirs. 1984-86, chmn. profl. devel. stds. com. 1985-86), Can. Ephemera Soc., Am. Ephemera Soc., Popular Culture Assn., Am. Culture Assn., Am. Game Collectors Assn., N.Y. State Hist. Assn. Home: 69 Main St E, Grimsby, ON Canada L3M 1N5

MORGAN, WILLIAM BRUCE, naval architect; b. Fairfield, Iowa, Dec. 20, 1926; s. Orville Burns and Mary Verle (Balderson) M.; m. Mary Maxine Gillam, June 21, 1950; children: Margaret Ann, Ann Elise. BS in Marine Engrng., U.S. Mcht. Marine Acad., 1950; MS in Hydraulic Engrng., U. Iowa, 1951; DEng in Naval Architecture, U. Calif., 1961. Hydraulic engr. David Taylor Model Basin, Bethesda, Md., 1951-52, naval architect, 1952-58, naval architect supr., 1958-62; head propeller br. David Taylor Model Basin, Bethesda, 1962-70; head hydromechanics div. David Taylor Naval Ship Research & Devel. Ctr. (formerly David Taylor Model Basin), Bethesda, Md., 1970-79; head hydromechanics directorate David Taylor Model Basin, Bethesda, Md., 1979—; chmn. exec. com. Am. Towing Tank Conf., 1983-86; mem. exec. com. Internat. Towing Tank Conf., 1984-90. Co-inventor ventilated propeller, supercavitating propeller with air ventilation; contbr. articles to profl. jours. Recipient Navy Superior Civilian Svc. award USN, 1974, Meritorious Exec. award Office of Pres., 1987, William Froude medal Royal Instn. Naval Architects, 1989, Capt. Robert Dexter Conrad award USN, 1993, Gibbs Bros. medal NAS, 1997. Fellow Soc. Naval Architects and Marine Engrs. (hon. life; exec. com. 1985—, Davidson medal 1986), ASME (chmn. fluids engrng. div. 1981-82); mem. NAE, Schiffbautechnische Gesellschaft, Am. Soc. Naval Engrs. (Gold Medal award 1993), Chinese Soc. Naval Architects and Marine Engrs. (hon.), Sigma Xi. Mem. Ch. of Brethren. Home: 110 Upton St Rockville MD 20850-1836 Office: David Taylor Model Bas Bethesda MD 20084-5000

MORGAN, WILLIAM J., accounting firm executive; b. Bklyn., Jan. 12, 1947; s. William J. and Emma T. (Kraft) M.; m. Patricia A. Maltz, Mar. 23, 1968; children: Michele, Jennifer. BS St. John's U., 1968. CPA, N.Y., Conn., N.J. Mng. ptnr. in charge Global Accounts, manufacturing, retailing and distbn. practice, audit staff KPMG Peat Marwick, N.Y.C., 1968-72, audit supr., 1972-74, audit mgr., 1974-77, ptnr.-in-charge pvt. bus. adv. service, N.Y.C., 1977-79, exec. office, ptnr.-in-charge recruiting, 1979-82, ptnr. comml. health care practice, Short Hills, 1982-91; ptnr.-in-charge N.J. audit practice, 1989-91, mng. ptnr. Fairfield/Westchester counties practice, 1991-94, ptnr. in charge metro N.Y. area, manufacturing retailing and distbn. practice, 1993-96; mem. Bus. Unit Planning Task Force, 1987-90, mem. compensation com., 1990-91, bd. dirs., 1991-95, chmn. profit distbn. com., 1991-95, mem. future direction com., 1991-93, pension task force, 1991-92; mem. acctg. adv. bd. Grad. Sch. Bus. Fordham U., 1979-82, mem. standardization com. Nat. Retail Mchts. Assn., 1979; bd. dirs.N.Y. chpt. small bus. fund drive ARC, 1978; trustee Tri County Scholarship Fund, 1984-91; chmn. Blackberry Hill Property Owners Assoc., 1986-87; v.p., exec. com., adv. bd. Fairfield coun. Boy Scouts Am., 1993-95; chmn. Fairfield County Info. Exchange, 1992-94; bd. dirs. S.W. Area Commerce and Industry Assn., 1994—, Inroads Fairfield and Westchester County chpt., 1992-95; mem. Bus. Execs. for Nat. Security, Ambs. Roundtable. Mem. Am. Inst. CPA's (small bus. devel. com. 1979-81, acctg. lit. awards com. 1983-86), N.J. Soc. CPA's (chmn. acctg. and auditing stds. com. 1988-90, trustee 1990-92, mem. pub. rels. task force, 1987, subcom. health care acctg. 1983-86), N.Y. State Soc. CPA's (retail acctg. com. 1975-78, com. on edn. in coll. and univs. 1978-82), Nat. Assn. Accts. (dir. manuscripts 1975-77, v.p. N.Y. chpt. 1977-81, pres. N.Y. chpt. 1981-82, nat. publs. com. 1982-83, com. acad. relations 1983-84, nat. dir. 1983-86, Disting. Service award 1975), Health Care Fin. Mgmt. Assn. (N.J. chpt. chmn. auditing com. 1982-83, legis. task force com. 1985-86, chmn. joint ventures com., 1987-88). Club: Fairmount Country (bd. govs., treas. 1987-90), Woodway Country, Conn. Golf, Landmark Club. Roman Catholic. Home: 14 Talmadge Hill Rd Darien CT 06820-2125 Office: KPMG Peat Marwick 3001 Summer St Stamford CT 06905-4317

MORGAN, WILLIAM LIONEL, JR., physician, educator; b. Honolulu, Nov. 18, 1927; s. William Lionel and Lucy Salisbury (Grimes) M.; m. Joan Brunjes, Apr. 10, 1954; children: Nancy Salisbury, Linda Pittman. B.A. cum laude, Yale U., 1948; M.D. magna cum laude, Harvard U., 1952. Diplomate: Am. Bd. Internal Medicine. (mem. bd. 1973-80, mem. residency review com. 1975-80, chmn. residency rev. com. 1979-80). Intern Mass. Gen. Hosp., Boston, 1952-53; resident in medicine Mass. Gen. Hosp., 1953-54, 56-57, fellow in cardiology, 1957-58; asso. physician div. cardiovascular disease Henry Ford Hosp., Detroit, 1958-62; asso. prof. medicine U. Rochester (N.Y.) Sch. Medicine and Dentistry, 1962-65, prof., 1966-89, prof. medicine emeritus, 1989—, asso. chmn. dept. medicine, 1966-89. Author: (with G.L. Engel) The Clinical Approach to the Patient, 1969. Served with USPHS, 1954-56. Mem. ACP (Master), Am. Clin. and Climatol. Assn., Phi Beta Kappa, Alpha Omega Alpha. Home: 160 Collingsworth Dr Rochester NY 14625-2024 Office: Dept Medicine Strong Meml Hosp 601 Elmwood Ave Rochester NY 14642

MORGAN, WILLIAM NEWTON, architect, educator; b. Jacksonville, Fla., Dec. 14, 1930; s. Thomas and Kathleen (Fiske) M.; m. Bernice E. Leimback, July 31, 1954; children: William Newton, Dylan Thomas. AB magna cum laude, Harvard Coll., 1952, MArch Grad. Sch. of Design, 1958. Pres. William Morgan Architects, P.A., Jacksonville, Fla., 1961—; critic various archtl. schs.; lectr. in field; adj. prof. of art history, Jacksonville U., U. North Fla., 1995-97. Prin. works include Fla. State Mus., Jacksonville Police Meml. Bldg., Pyramid Condominium, Ocean City, Fed. Cts. and Offices, Ft. Lauderdale, Fla., Westinghouse World Hdqs., Orlando, Fla., Neiman-Marcus store, Ft. Lauderdale, 1st Dist. Ct. Appeal, Tallahassee, Fla., Conf. Ctr., Tallahassee, U.S. Embassy, Khartoum, Sudan, U.S. Courthouse, Tallahassee; author; Prehistoric Architecture in the Eastern United States, 1980, Prehistoric Architecture in Micronesia, 1988, Ancient Architecture of the Southwest, 1994. Subject of The Architecture of William Morgan (Paul Spreiregen) 1987; Fulbright grantee, 1958-59; grantee Graham Found. Advanced Studies Arts; Lehman fellow Harvard U., 1957, Wheelwright fellow, fellow NEA, 1991; Sam Gibbons Eminent scholar Fla. A&M U. and U. South Fla. Fellow AIA (past chmn. com. design). Office: William Morgan Architects 220 E Forsyth St Jacksonville FL 32202-3320

MORGAN, WILLIAM RICHARD, mechanical engineer; b. Cambridge, Ohio, Mar. 27, 1922; s. Wilbur Alfred and Treva Beatrice (Minto) M.; m. Marjorie Eleanor Stevens, Feb. 17, 1946; children: Carol M. Morgan Dingledy, William R., Jr. BSME, The Ohio State U., 1944; MSME, Purdue U., 1950, PhD in Mech. Engrng., 1951. Lic. profl. engr., Ohio. Power plant design engr. Curtiss Wright Corp., Columbus, Ohio, 1946-47; instr., rsch. fellow Purdue U., West Lafayette, Ind., 1947-51; supr. exptl. mech. engrng. GE, Cin., 1951-55, mgr. controls analysis, devel. Aircraft Gas Turbine Divsn., 1955-59, mgr. XV5A vertical take-off and landing aircraft program, 1959-65, mgr. acoustic engrng. Flight Propulsion Divsn., 1965-69, mgr. quiet engine program Flight Propulsion Divsn., 1969-71; pres. Cin. Rsch. Corp., 1971-73; v.p., COO SDRC Internat., Cin., 1973-79; engrng. and mgmt. cons. Cin., 1979—. Author of papers presented at Brookhaven Nat. Lab., AEC Heat Transfer Symposium, 1954, ASME Fall Meeting, Thermal Conductivity of Insulation Material for Use in Nuclear Reactors, 1957, Am. Inst. Aero. Engrs. Ten-Ton V/STOL Lift Fan Transport, 1961, Dynamics Loads Symposium, XV5A Dynamic Load Characteristics, 1963, Joint Meeting of AGARD-Nato on Aircraft Engine Noise and Sonic Boom, 1969, ASME Meeting, Analytical Prediction of Fan/Compressor Noise, 1969. Lt. j.g. USNR, WWII. Westinghouse Rsch. fellow. Mem. ASME, Masons, Sigma Xi, Pi Tau Sigma, Pi Mu Epsilon. Achievements include patents in Humidity Detection and Indicating Instrument, Stall Prevention/Acoustic Tip Treatment, Acoustic Treatment, Inlet Noise Reduction Configuration. Home and Office: 312 Ardon Ln Cincinnati OH 45215-4102

MORGAN-FADNESS, CORRINA MAY, staff charge nurse; b. Longview, Wash., Jan. 12, 1963; d. Arthur Dallas and Dorothy Irene (Ellis) Miller; 1 child, Michael Patrick. AA, Lower Columbia Coll., 1982; BSN, U. Portland, 1987. RN, Wash.; cert. gerontol. nurse, cert. dir. nursing. Staff nurse Centralia (Wash.) Gen. Hosp., 1987; charge nurse Walker Care Ctr., Centralia, 1987-89, Park Royal Med. Ctr., Longview, Wash., 1987, 89; house supr. WHCC Riverside, Centralia, 1989-92; staff nurse Auburn (Wash.) Gen. Hosp., 1992—, WHCC Riverside, Centralia, 1996—; IV cons. on-call Evergreen Pharms., Inc., 1990—; unit mgr. Oakhurst Convalescent Ctr., Elma, Wash., 1992-93; patient care coord. Rehab. Sharon Care Ctr., Centralia, Wash., 1993—; staff nurse Morton (Wash.) Long Term Care, 1994-96; staff/charge nurse WHCC Riverside, Centralia, 1996—. Home: 403 2nd Ave NE Napavine WA 98565

MORGANROTH, FRED, lawyer; b. Detroit, Mar. 26, 1938; s. Ben and Grace (Greenfield) M.; m. Janice Marilyn Cohn, June 23, 1963; children: Greg, Candi, Erik. BA, Wayne State U., 1959, JD with distinction, 1961. Bar: Mich. 1961, U.S. Dist. Ct. (ea. dist.) Mich. 1961, U.S. Ct. Claims 1967, U.S. Supreme Ct. 1966; trained matrimonial arbitrator. Ptnr. Greenbaum, Greenbaum & Morganroth, Detroit, 1963-68, Lebenbom, Handler, Brody & Morganroth, Detroit, 1968-70, Lebenbom, Morganroth & Stern, Southfield, Mich., 1971-78; sole practice Southfield, 1979-83; ptnr. Morganroth & Morganroth P.C., Southfield, 1983-94, Morganroth, Morganroth, Alexander & Nye, P.C., Birmingham, Mich., 1994—. Mem. ABA (family law sect. 1987—), Mich. Bar Assn. (hearing panelist grievance bd. 1975—, Oakland County family law com. 1988—, vice chmn. 1992-93, chair 1993—), State Bar Mich. (mem. family law coun. of family law sect. 1990—, treas. 1993-94, chmn.-elect 1994-95, chmn. 1995-96), Detroit Bar Assn., Oakland Bar Assn. (cir. ct. mediator 1984—), Am. Arbitration Assn. (Oakland County family law com. 1985—, vice chmn. 1992-93, chmn. 1993-94, trained matrimonial arbitrator), Detroit Tennis Club (Farmington, Mich., pres. 1978-82), Charlevoix Country Club. Jewish. Avocations: comml. pilot, tennis. Home: 30920 Woodcrest Ct Franklin MI 48025-1435 Office: 300 Park St Ste 410 Birmingham MI 48009-3482

MORGANROTH, MAYER, lawyer; b. Detroit, Mar. 20, 1931; s. Maurice Jack Morganroth and Sophie (Reisman) Blum; m. Sheila Rubinstein, Aug. 16, 1958; children: Lauri, Jeffrey, Cherie. JD, Detroit Coll. Law, 1954. Bar: Mich. 1955, U.S. Dist. Ct. Mich. 1955, Ohio 1958, U.S. Dist. Ct. (no. dist.) Ohio 1958, U.S. Ct. Appeals (6th cir.) 1968, U.S. Supreme Ct. 1971, N.Y. 1983, U.S. Dist. Ct. N.Y. 1985, U.S. Tax Ct. 1985, U.S. Ct. Appeals (4th cir.) 1985, U.S. Ct. Claims 1986, U.S. Ct. Appeals (2d cir.) 1986, U.S. Ct. Appeals (fed. cir.), U.S. Ct. Appeals (8th cir.) 1994. Sole practice Detroit, 1955—, N.Y.C., 1983—; ptnr. Morganroth & Morganroth, 1989—; cons. to lending instns.; lectr. on real estate NYU, 1980—, bus. entities and structures Wayne State U., 1981—; trial atty. in fed. and state jurisdictions, nationwide. Served with USN, 1948-50. Mem. ABA, FBA, N.Y. State Bar Assn., Southfield Bar Assn., Oakland Bar Assn., Assn. Trial Lawyers Am., Assn. Trial Lawyers Mich., Am. Judicature Soc., U.S. Supreme Ct. Hist. Soc., Nat. Criminal Def. Assn., West Bloomfield (Mich.) Club, Fairlane Club (Dearborn, Mich.), Knollwood Country Club, Edgewood Athletic Club (pres. 1963-65). Democrat. Jewish. Office: 3000 Town Ctr Ste 1500 Southfield MI 48075-1186 also: 444 Madison Ave Ste 2801 New York NY 10022-6903

MORGANSTERN, MYRNA DOROTHY, lawyer; b. Chgo., June 12, 1946; d. Harry and Sarah (Fisher) Selwyn; m. Russell Jay Frackman, Aug. 3, 1980; children: Steven, Abigail. BA in English, U. Nev., 1967; MA in English, U. Calif., 1969; JD, U. Minn., 1975. Bar: Calif. 1976, U. S. Dist. Ct. (cen. dist.) Calif. 1977. Writer, researcher Calif. Cancer Control Project, L.A., 1975-77; deputy atty. gen. Atty. Gen. Calif., L.A., 1977-80; assoc. Gang, Tyre & Brown, L.A., 1980-81, Finley, Kumble, Wagner, Heine, Underberg & Manley, L.A., 1981-82; atty. U.S. Securities & Exch. Commn., L.A., 1984-88; atty., aide Mayor Larry Agran, Irvine, Calif., 1989-90; counsel George McGovern Exploratory Com., Irvine, Calif., 1991; chief counsel Agran for Pres. '92, Irvine, Calif., 1991-92; trial atty. U.S. Commodity Futures Trading Commn., 1996—; commr. L.A. County Rent Adjustment Commn., 1984-85; com. mem. Sci. Adv. Com., Irvine, 1989-91. Co-author: Cancer Control in the United States, 1977. Mem. ACLU, NAACP, Amnesty Internat. Avocations: travel, book collecting, piano, theatre, movies. Office: US Commodity Futures Trading Commn 10900 Wilshire Blvd Ste 400 Los Angeles CA 90024-6525

MORGANTE, JOHN-PAUL, state government training administrator; b. Yonkers, N.Y., June 26, 1962; s. Enzo and Teresa (DellaToffola) M.; m. Ellen Rothberger, May 26, 1984; children: Camden Anne, Bethany Nicole, Hailee Marie. BA, U. So. Calif., L.A., 1984. Ordained to ministry Christian Ch., 1987; cert. profl. in human resources. Adminstrv. dir. MCM Internat., Lomita, Calif., 1984-91; exec. dir. Champions for Christ, Austin, Tex., 1991-93; pres. Annimar Assocs., Austin, 1993-94; tng. supr. Harris Select Comms., 1994-95; tng. specialist Tex. Dept. Health, Austin, 1995—. Mem. ctrl. com. Orange County (Calif.) Reps., 1988-89; intern U.S. Rep. Robert Badham, Washington, 1983, campaign worker, 1984; intern Assemblyman Curt Pringle, Garden Grove, Calif., 1988; campaign worker U.S. Senator Chic Hecht, 1982, U.S. Rep. Robert Dornan, 1984, Reagan-Bush, 1984, Tex. State rep. Terry Keel, Austin, 1996; mem. solicitation bd. City of Austin, 1996—; del. Dist. 14 Rep. Conv., Austin, 1996; mem. nat. nominating com. Outstanding Young Ams., 1996—. Recipient Rep. Presdl. Legion of Merit, Presdl. Commemorative Honor Roll, 1991, Staff Mem. of Yr., 1987; commd. Hon. Texan by Gov. George Bush, 1995. Mem. ASTD, Soc. for Human Resource Mgmt., Internat. Platform Assn. Avocations: golf, travel. Office: Tex Dept Health 1100 W 49th St Austin TX 78756-3101

MORGANTI, AL, reporter; b. May 28, 1953. BS in Pub. Comms., Boston U., 1978. Corr. coll. and h.s. hockey Boston Globe, 1974-78; corr. Atlanta Flames Atlanta Constn., 1979; beat writer Miami Dolphins Ft. Lauderdale (Fla.) NEws, 1978; NHL corr. The Nat., 1990-91; beat writer Phila. Flyers Phila. Inquirer, 1979-89, corr. Winter Olympics, 1984, 88, corr. Summer Olympics, 1984, corr. Am.'s Cup, 1983, 87; columnist, sr. writer The Hockey News, 1988—; morning drive-time host Sta. WIP-AM, Phila., 1991—; host The Great Sports Debate roundtable discussion group PRISM Cable Network, Phila., 1990—; reporter Nat. Hockey Night telecast, NHL corr. ESPN, 1992—. Recipient Best Sports Story award AP, 1983, 85. Office: c/o ESPN ESPN Pla Bristol CT 06010

MORGEN, LYNN, public relations executive. Grad., CCNY. Former rep. Gruntal & Co., First Manhattan Co.; assoc. ECOM Cons., 1978-79, v.p. investor rels., 1979-82; founding ptnr Morgen-Walke Assocs., 1982—. Office: Morgen-Walke Assocs Inc 380 Lexington Ave Ste 5100 New York NY 10168-0002*

MORGENROTH, EARL EUGENE, entrepreneur; b. Sidney, Mont., May 7, 1936; s. Frank and Leona (Ellison) M.; m. Noella Nichols, Aug. 2, 1958; children: Dolores Roxanna, David Jonathan, Denise Christine. BS, U. Mont., 1961. From salesman to gen. mgr. Sta. KGVO-AM Radio, Missoula, Mont., 1958-65; sales mgr. Stas. KGVO-TV, KTVM-TV and KCFW-TV, Missoula, Butte, Kalispell, Mont., 1965-66, gen. mgr., 1966-68; gen. mgr. Sta. KCOY-TV, Santa Maria, Calif., 1968-69; v.p., gen. mgr. Western Broadcasting Co., Missoula, 1966-69, gen. mgr., pres., 1969-81; gen. mgr., pres. numerous cos., Mont., Calif. Idaho, P.R., Ga., 1966-84; pres., chmn. Western Broadcasting Co., Missoula, 1981-84, Western Communications, Inc., Reno, 1984-90; prin. Western Investments, Reno, 1984—; chmn. Western Fin., Inc., Morgenroth Music Ctrs., Inc., Mont., Band Instruments, Inc.; chmn. E & B Music Inc., Times Square, Inc., Willow Creek Ranches, LLC. Mem. Mont. Bank Bd., Helena; commencement spkr. U. Mont., 1988; bd. dirs. U. Mont. Found., 1985-95. With. U.S. Army, 1954-57. Named Boss of Yr. Santa Maria Valley J.C.s, 1968. Mem. U. Mont. Century Club (pres.), Missoula C. of C. (pres.), Rocky Mountain Broadcasters Assn. (pres.), Craighead Wildlife-Wildlands Inst. (bd. dirs.), Boone and Crockett Club (bd. dirs., v.p. comm.), Grizzly Riders Internat. (bd. dirs., v.p.), Bldg. A Scholastic Heritage (bd. dirs.). Republican. Methodist.

MORGENSEN, JERRY LYNN, construction company executive; b. Lubbock, Tex., July 9, 1942; s. J.J. and Zelline (Butler) M.; m. Linda Dee Austin, Apr. 17, 1965; children: Angela, Nicole. BCE, Tex. Tech U., 1965. Area engr. E.I. Dupont Co., Orange, Tex., 1965-67; div. engr. E.I. Dupont Co., La Place, La., 1967-73; project mgr. Hensel Phelps Constrn. Co., Greeley, Colo., 1973-78, area mgr., 1978-80, v.p., 1980-85, pres., CEO, 1985—. Office: Hensel Phelps Constrn Co 420 Sixth Ave PO Box O Greeley CO 80632*

MORGENSTEIN, WILLIAM, shoe company executive; b. Bklyn., Jan. 11, 1933; s. Samuel and Jeanne Marie (Mittentag) M.; m. Sylvia Dove, June 8, 1952; children: Lee Brian, David Barry. BS in Fin., U. Ala., 1955. Salesman Greenwald Shoe Co., Birmingham, Ala., 1954-56; sr. buyer Melville Shoe Corp., N.Y.C., 1958-67; pres. Kitty Kelly Shoe Co., N.Y.C., 1967-70; exec. v.p. A.S. Beck Shoes, N.Y.C., 1970-71, Sandia Internat., Englewood Cliffs, N.J., 1971-75; pres., chief exec. officer Marquesa Internat. Corp., Englewood, N.J., 1975-95; sales exec. Signature Group divsn. Montgomery Ward, 1995—; internat. cons. footwear exporting, 1965—. Served with U.S. Army, 1956-58. Mem. Footwear Distbrs. and Retailers Am. (vice chmn., bd. dirs., exec. com.), Internat. Footwear Assn. (chmn. 1989—, vice chmn. 1986—, exec. com. 1986—), 210 Assn. (Pres.' Circle 1987), Toastmasters (past pres. Teaneck, N.J. chpt.). Republican. Jewish. Avocations: history, golf.

MORGENSTERN, DAN MICHAEL, jazz historian, educator, editor; b. Munich, Germany, Oct. 24, 1929; came to U.S., 1947; s. Soma and Ingeborg Henrietta (von Klenau) M.; m. Elsa Schocket, Mar. 31, 1974; children: Adam Oran, Joshua Louis. Student, Brandeis U., 1953-56. Editorial asst. N.Y. Post, 1957-58; N.Y. corr. Jazz Jour., London, 1958-61; assoc. editor, then editor in chief Metronome mag., 1961; editor Jazz mag., 1962-64; assoc. editor Down Beat mag., 1964-67, editor, 1967-73; lectr. jazz history Peabody Instn., Balt., 1978-80; vis. prof., sr. research fellow in Am. Music, Bklyn. Coll., 1979; dir. Inst. Jazz Studies, Rutgers U., 1976—; bd. dirs. Jazz Inst. Chgo., N.Y. Jazz Mus. Producer ann. 10-concert series Jazz in the Garden, Museum Modern Art, N.Y.C., 1961-66; co-producer concert series Jazz on Broadway, 1963, Just Jazz; 10 program TV series, Public Broadcasting Service, 1971; author: The Jazz Story: An Outline History, 1973, Jazz People, 1976; translator, editor: (Joachim E. Berendt) The New Jazz Book, 1962, rev. edit., 1975; co-editor Ann. Rev. Jazz Studies, 1982—. Served with U.S. Army, 1951-53. Recipient Deems Taylor award ASCAP, 1977, Grammy award for best album notes 1973, 74, 76, 81, 91. Mem. NARAS (gov. 1971—, trustee 1976-79, 81-84, 85-89, 91—, v.p. 1979-83, 1st v.p. 1983-85), Nat. Endowment for Arts (chmn. jazz adv. panel 1971-73, cons. music programs 1973-80), Music Critics Assn., PEN, Authors Guild. Home: 365 W End Ave Apt 603 New York NY 10024-6563 Office: Rutgers U Dana Lib Inst Jazz Studies Newark NJ 07102*

MORGENSTERN, LEON, surgeon; b. Pitts., July 14, 1919; s. Max Samuel and Sarah (Master) M.; m. Laurie Mattlin, Nov. 27, 1967; 1 son, David Ethan. Student, CCNY, 1936-37; B.A. magna cum laude, Bklyn. Coll., 1940; M.D., N.Y. U., 1943. Diplomate: Am. Bd. Surgery. Intern Queens Gen. Hosp., Jamaica, N.Y., 1943-44; fellow, asst. resident in pathology Queens Gen. Hosp., 1947-48, resident in surgery, 1948-52; practice medicine, specializing in surgery Los Angeles, 1953-59, 60—, Bronx, N.Y., 1959-60; dir. surgery Cedars of Lebanon Hosp., Los Angeles, 1960-73; dir. surgery Cedars-Sinai Med. Center, Los Angeles, 1973-88, emeritus dir. surgery, 1989—; dir. Bioethics Program Cedars-Sinai Med. Ctr., L.A., 1995—; emeritus prof. surgery UCLA Sch. Medicine, 1973-85, prof. in residence, 1985—; dir. bioethics program Cedars-Sinai Med. Ctr., 1995—; asst. prof. surgery Albert Einstein Coll. Medicine, N.Y.C., 1959-60; adj. prof. bioethics U. Judaism, L.A., 1996—. Assoc. editor Mount Sinai Jour. Medicine, 1984-88; contbr. articles to profl. publs. Served to capt. M.C. U.S. Army, 1944-46. Mem. Soc. for Surgery Alimentary Tract, Soc. Am. Gastrointestinal Endoscopic Surgeons (hon.), Am. Gastroent. Assn., L.A. Surg. Soc. (pres. 1977), ACS (sec.-treas. 1976-77, pres. 1978, bd. dirs. So. Calif. chpt. 1976-78, gov.-at-large), Internat. Soc. Surgery, Western Surg. Assn., Pacific Coast Surg. Assn., AMA, Calif. Med. Assn., Los Angeles County Med. Assn., Am. Surg. Assn., others. Home: 5694 Calpine Dr Malibu CA 90265-3812

MORGENSTERN, LEWIS B., medical educator. Grad., U. Mich.; post-grad., U. Tex. Resident in neurology Johns Hopkins Hosp., Balt.; asst. prof. neurology U. Tex. Med. Sch., Houston, 1994—. Recipient Clinician Scientist award Am. Heart Assn., 1996. Mem. Alpha Omega. Office: U Tex Health Sci Ctr PO Box 20036 Houston TX 77225

MORGENSTERN, SHELDON JON, symphony orchestra conductor; b. Cleve., July 1, 1939; s. Irwin Arthur and Harriet Sue Morgenstern; m. Patricia Lou Bradshaw; 1 child, Sali Sharpe Hagan. BMus, Northwestern U., 1961; MMus, New Eng. Conservatory, 1966; DMA (hon.), Greensboro (N.C.) Coll., 1986. Mem. conducting staff New Eng. Conservatory, 1966-67; music dir. Greensboro Symphony Orch., 1967-74; prin. guest conductor Betica Philharmonic, Seville, Spain, 1978-82, Polish Radio Orch., Warsaw, Poland, 1990—; music dir. Ea. Music Festival, Greensboro, 1962—; music advisor Miss. Symphony Orch., 1985-86; bd. mem. Istanbul (Turkey) Internat. Festival, 1975—, Company for Televised Theatre; mus. cons. U.S. Dept. Interior for Wolf Trap Farm Park, 1972; mem. adv. bd. Avery Fisher Award, 1978—. Recipient O'Henry award City of Greensboro, 1980, Long Leaf Pine award State N.C., 1989, Nat. Alumni award Northwestern U., 1990. Home: Ferme Veudagne, Ch des Trois Noyers, 01210 Ferney-Voltaire France Office: Ea Music Festival PO Box 22026 Greensboro NC 27420-2026

MORGENTALER, ABRAHAM, urologist, researcher; b. Montreal, Quebec, Can., May 14, 1956; came to U.S., 1974; s. Henry Morgentaler and Chawa Rosenfarb; m. Susan Deborah Edbril, June 12, 1982; children: Maya Edbril, Hannah Edbril. AB, Harvard U., 1978, MD, 1982. Diplomate Am. Bd. Urology. Intern Harvard Surg. Svc.-N.E. Deaconess Hosp., Boston, 1982-83; resident Harvard Program in Urology, Boston, 1984-88; instr. surgery Harvard Med. Sch., Boston, 1988-92, asst. prof. surgery (urology), 1993—; staff urologist, dir. male infertility program and impotency Beth Israel Hosp., Boston, 1988—; dir. andrology lab. Beth Israel Hosp., 1990—. Author: The Male Body, 1993. Mem. AMA, Am. Urologic Assn., Am. Fertility Soc., Am. Soc. Andrology, Boston Fertility Soc., Am. Assn. Clin. Urologists. Achievements include detection of protein abnormalities in infertile sperm, detection of temperature dependent protein expression in mouse testis, use of investigational stents for treatment of benign prostatic hypertrophy, determination of relationship between serum testosterone levels risk of prostate cancer. Office: Beth Israel Hosp 330 Brookline Ave Boston MA 02215-5400

MORGENTHALER, ALISA MARIE, lawyer; b. St. Louis, June 3, 1960; d. Gerald Thomas and Mary Louise (Neece) M. BA, S.W. Mo. State U., 1982; JD, Cornell U., 1985. Bar: N.Y. 1986, D.C. 1988, Calif. 1990. Law clk. City of Springfield, Mo., 1981; bd. govs. FRS, Washington, 1984; staff atty. Fed. Res. System, Washington, 1985-86; assoc. Kirkpatrick & Lockhart, Washington, 1986-88, Stroock & Stroock & Lavan, Washington, 1988-89, Christensen, Miller, Fink, Jacobs, Glaser, Weil & Shapiro, L.A., 1989—. Mem. ABA, Calif. Bar Assn., D.C. Bar Assn., N.Y. Bar Assn., L.A. County Bar Assn., Beverly Hills Bar Assn., Century City Bar Assn., Women Lawyers Assn. of L.A. (bd. dirs.), 3019 Third St. Owners Assn. (bd. dirs.), Alpha Iota House Corp. (bd. dirs.), Order of Omega, Phi Alpha Delta, Rho Lambda, Phi Kappa Phi, Pi Sigma Alpha, Gamma Phi Beta. Office: Christensen Miller Et Al 2121 Ave of Stars 18th Fl Los Angeles CA 90067-5010

MORGENTHAU, ROBERT MORRIS, lawyer; b. N.Y.C., July 31, 1919; s. Henry Jr. and Elinor (Fatman) M.; m. Martha Pattridge (dec.); children: Joan, Anne, Elinor, Robert P., Barbara; m. Lucinda Franks, Nov. 19, 1977; children: Joshua, Amy. Grad., Deerfield (Mass.) Acad., 1937; BA, Amherst Coll., 1941, LLD (hon.), 1966; LLB, Yale U., 1948; LLD (hon.), N.Y. Law Sch., 1968, Syracuse Law Sch., 1976, Albany Law Sch., 1982, Colgate U., 1988. Bar: N.Y. 1949. Assoc. firm Patterson Belknap & Webb, N.Y.C., 1948-53; ptnr. Patterson Belknap & Webb, 1954-61; U.S. atty. So. Dist.

N.Y., 1961-62, 62-70; dist. atty. New York County, 1975—; former pres. N.Y. State Dist. Attys. Assn.; lectr. London Sch. Econs., 1993. Chmn. Police Athletic League; Dem. candidate for Gov. of N.Y., 1962; bd. dirs. P.R. Legal Def. and Edn. Fund; trustee Baron de Hirsch Fund, Federated Jewish Philanthropies, Temple Emanu-El, N.Y.C.; chmn. Gov.'s Adv. Com. on Sentencing, 1979; counsel N.Y. State Law Enforcement Coun.; mem. N.Y. exec. com. State of Israel Bonds; chmn. A Living Meml. to the Holocaust-Mus. of Jewish Heritage. Lt. comdr. USN, 1941-45. Recipient Emory Buckner award Fed. Bar Coun., 1983, Yale Citation of Merit, 1982, Fordham-Stein prize, 1988, Thomas Jefferson award in law U. Va., 1991, Brandeis medal U. Louisville, 1995, Omanut award Yeshiva U., 1995, Trumpeter award Nat. Consumers League, 1995. Fellow Am. Bar Found.; mem. ABA, N.Y. State Bar Assn., Assn. of the Bar of the City of N.Y., N.Y. County Lawyers Assn. (Disting. Pub. Svc. award 1993), Phi Beta Kappa. Office: Office Dist Atty One Hogan Pl New York NY 10013

MORGNANESI, LANNY M., journalist; b. Trenton, N.J., Sept. 21, 1951; s. Orlando John and Kathryn Theresa (Mercurio) M.; m. Lucille Heu, Nov. 27, 1987; 1 child, Dante Michael. BA in Liberal Arts, Millersville U., 1973; MA in Journalism, U. Mo., 1975. Reporter Bucke County Courier Times, Levittown, Pa., 1975-80, editl. page writer, 1980, assoc. editor, 1980-84; copy editor, advisor New China News Agy., Beijing, 1984-85; asst. city editor The Fla. Times-Union, Jacksonville, Fla., 1986-90, zoned editions editor, 1990-92, city editor, 1992-93; exec. editor The Intelligencer/Record, Doylestown, Pa., 1993—; exec. prodr., host cable TV show The Intelligencer Monthly, Suburban Cmty. TV, Doylestown, 1994—. Bd. dirs. Ctrl. Bucks Family YMCA, Doylestown, 1993—. Mem. Am. Soc. Newspaper Editors, Pa. Soc. Newspaper Editors, Pa. Newspaper Pubs. Assn. Office: The Intelligencer/Record 333 N Broad St Doylestown PA 18901-3407

MORGNER, AURELIUS, economist, educator; b. N.Y.C., May 23, 1917; s. Oscar A. and Anna G. (Hoffmeister) M. B.S. in Bus. Adminstrn., U. Mo., 1938, M.A. in Econs., 1940; Ph.D., U. Minn., 1955. Investigator Dept. Labor, 1941; project dir. Employment Stblzn. Research Inst., 1941-42; instr. bus. adminstrn. U. Minn., 1942-46; lectr. Northwestern U., 1946-47; assoc. prof. Tex. A&M U., 1947-56, prof., 1956-58; vis. prof. U. São Paulo, Brazil, 1958-60; dir. grad. social studies U. São Paulo, 1959-60; prof. econs. U. So. Calif., L.A., 1960—; chmn. dept. U. So. Calif., 1962-69; prof. internat. econs. Sch. Internat. Relations, 1960—; Pub. panel mem. Chgo. Regional War Labor Bd., 1943-45; pub. rep. minimum wage com. Dept. Labor, 1942,43; cons. Govt. Eucador, 1965-68, Govt. Guyana, 1968, state Nev., 1970, Philippines, 1971-72, Yemen Arab Republic, 1974-75; U.S. State Dept. vis. lectr., Brazil, summer 1966. Co-author: Local Labor Markets, 1948, Problems in Economic Analysis, 1948, Problems in the Theory of Price, 1954 (trans. Spanish 1965, Portuguese 1967). Ford faculty fellow Columbia U., 1954-55. Mem. So. Calif. Econ. Assn. (pres. 1965-66), Am. Econs. Assn., Western Econ. Assn., Am. Arbitration Assn., Internat. Studies Assn. Office: U So Calif Dept Econs Los Angeles CA 90089

MORGRIDGE, JOHN P., computer business executive; m. Tashia Morgridge; three children. BBA, DSc (hon.), U. Wis.; MBA, Stanford U. Mktg. profl. Honeywell Info. Systems, 1960-80; v.p. mkgt., sales and svc. Stratus Co., Inc., 1980-86; pres., chief ops. officer GRiD Systems (now part of Tandy Corp.), 1986-88; pres., CEO Cisco Systems, 1988—, chmn., 1995—. Office: Cisco Systems 170 W Tasman Dr San Jose CA 95134-1700

MORI, ALLEN ANTHONY, university dean, consultant, researcher; b. Hazleton, Pa., Nov. 1, 1947; s. Primo Philip and Carmella (DeNoia) M.; m. Barbara Epoca, June 26, 1971; 1 child, Kirsten Lynn. BA, Franklin and Marshall Coll., Lancaster, Pa., 1969; MEd, Bloomsburg U. Pa., 1971; PhD, U. Pitts., 1975. Spl. edn. tchr. White Haven (Pa.) State Sch. and Hosp., 1969-70, Hazleton Area Sch. Dist., 1970-71, Pitts. Pub. Schs., 1971-74; supr. student tchrs. U. Pitts., 1974-75; prof. spl. edn. U. Nev., Las Vegas, 1975-84; dean coll edn. Marshall U., Huntington, W.Va., 1984-87; dean sch. edn. Calif. State U., L.A., 1987—; hearing officer pub. law 94-142 Nev. Dept. Edn., Carson City, 1978—; mem. Nev. Gov.'s Com. on Mental Health and Mental Retardation, 1983-84; cons. Ministry Edn., Manitoba, Can., 1980-82; pres. Tchr. Edn. Coun. State Colls. and Univs., 1993-94. Author: Families of Children with Special Needs, 1983; co-author: Teaching the Severely Retarded, 1980, Handbook of Preschool, Special Education, 1980, Adapted Physical Education, 1983, A Vocational Training Continuum for the Mentally and Physically Disabled, 1985, Teaching Secondary Students with Mild Learning and Behavior Problems, 1986, 93; contbr. numerous articles, book revs. and monographs to profl. jours. Bd. dirs. Assn. Retarded Citizens San Gabriel Valley, ElMonte, 1989-94. Recipient grants U.S. Dept. Edn., 1976-91, Nev. Dept. Edn., W.Va. Dept. Edn., Calif. State U. Chancellor's Office. Mem. Assn. Tchr. Educators, Coun. for Exceptional Children (div. on Career Devel. exec. com. 1981-83), Nat. Soc. for Study of Edn., Kiwanis, Phi Beta Delta, Phi Delta Kappa, Pi Lambda Theta. Avocations: jogging, travel. Office: Calif State U 5151 State University Dr Los Angeles CA 90032-4226

MORIAL, MARC HAYDEL, mayor; b. New Orleans, Jan. 3, 1958; s. Ernest and Sybil M.; divorced; 1 child, Kemah. Bar: La. Legis. intern U.S. Sen. Russell Long, Washington, 1979; dir. U. Pa. Office of Supportive Svcs., Phila., 1979-80; summer assoc. U.S. Atty. U.S. Dist. Ct. (so. dist.) N.Y., 1982; legis. asst. U.S. Rep. George T. Leland, Washington, 1983; atty. Barham & Churchill, New Orleans, 1983-85; pvt. practice New Orleans, 1985—; mem. La. Senate, Baton Rouge, 1991-93, mem. revenue and fiscal affairs com., commerce com., labor and indsl. rels. com., select com. crime & drugs, intergovtl. rels. com., Pres. Clinton's action com. on crime & drugs, senate select com. on econ. devel.; mayor City of New Orleans, 1993—; adj. prof. law, polit. sci. Xavier U. La., New Orleans, 1988-90. Del. Nat. Rainbow Coalition Conv., 1986, La. State Dem. Conv., 1986, Dem. Nat. Conv., Atlanta, 1988; cooperating atty. NAACP Legal Def. Fund, mem. nat., New Orleans br.; gen. counsel La. Assn. Minority and Women Owned Businesses, Inc., La. Voter Registration/Edn. Crusade; cooperating atty. Minority Bus. Enterprise Legal Def. and Edn. Fund; divestment coord., legal advisor New Orleans Anti-Apartheid Coalition, 1983—; bd. dirs. La. ACLU, La. Spl. Olympics, Milne Boys Home; mem. project steering com. Voting Rights Law Reporter; mem. Young Leadership Coun., Friend of New Orleans Ctr. for Creative Arts. Recipient Chmns. award Congl. Black Caucus, 1989, Outstanding Svc. award Lutcher (La.) H.S., 1990, La. NAACP Cmty. Svc. award, 1988; named Legis. Rookie of Yr. Baton Rouge Bus. Report, 1992, All Rookie Team by polit. columnist John Maginnis, 1993, Legis. Newcome of Yr., 1992. Mem. ABA (standing com. on world order under law 1982-83), Nat. Bar Assn., La. State Bar Assn. (Pro Bono Pub. award 1988), La. Assn. Criminal Def. Attys., Nat. Conf. Black Lawyers, Amnesty Internat. USA, Transafrica, Louis A. Martinet Legal Soc. New Orleans, La. Trial Lawyers Assn. (pres. adv. coun.), Nat. Black Law Students Assn. (nat. bd. dirs. 1981-83), Alpha Phi Alpha. Office: Office of the Mayor 1300 Perdido St Ste 2E 10 New Orleans LA 70112-2188*

MORIARTY, DONALD WILLIAM, JR., banker; b. Amarillo, Tex., Sept. 15, 1939; s. Donald William and Lorraine Julia (Walck) M.; m. Rita Ann Giller, Nov. 28, 1964; children: Mary Kathleen, Jennifer Ann, Anne Marie, Kerry Lee, Erin Teresa. Student, St. Benedict's Coll., 1957-59, 60-61; B.Sc., Washington U., 1962; M.Sc., St. Louis U., 1965, Ph.D., 1970. Cost acct. Emerson Electric, St. Louis, 1959-63; grad. fellow in econs. St. Louis U., 1963-65, instr., 1965-68; asst. prof. U. Mo., St. Louis, 1968-70; with Fed. Res. Bank of St. Louis, 1968-83, v.p., 1971-74, sr. v.p., controller, 1974-77, 1st v.p., 1977-83; sr. v.p. Gen. Bancshares Corp., 1983-86; exec. v.p. Commerce Bancshares, Inc., 1986-87; bank cons., 1987-89; pres., CEO, bd. dirs. Duchesne Bank, St. Peters, Mo., 1989-95; sr. cons. Universal Fin. Group, Inc., 1996—; bd. dirs. Mid-Am. Payments Exchange, Duchesne Bank; vis. instr. Webster Coll., 1975-82; adviser City of Des Peres (Mo.), chmn. fin. com., 1976-78, chmn. mgmt. com., 1978-81, mem. personnel commn., 1978-81, mem. planning and zoning com., 1981-83. Mem. parent's coun. Creighton U., Omaha, 1995—; trustee, vice chmn. St. Joseph Hosp., 1982-93; mem. adv. bd. St. Joseph Acad., 1982-86; mem. pres.'s coun. St. Louis U., 1983—; bd. dirs. ea. Mo. region NCCJ, 1987-93; dist. chmn. Boy Scouts Am., 1991-93, vice chmn. 1994—. Recipient Alumni Merit award St. Louis U., 1979. Mem. Am. Econ. Assn., Am. Fin. Assn., Am. Mgmt. Assn., St. Peters C. of C., St. Charles C. of C., Beta Gamma Sigma, Alpha Kappa Psi. Club: Media.

MORIARTY, GEORGE MARSHALL, lawyer; b. Youngstown, Ohio, Sept. 16, 1942; s. George Albert Moriarty and Caroline (Jones) Bass; m. Elizabeth Bradley Moore, Sept. 11, 1965 (div. 1986); children: Bradley Marshall, Caroline Walden, Sarah Cameron. BA magna cum laude, Harvard U., 1964, LLB magna cum laude, 1968. Bar: Mass. 1969, U.S. Dist. Ct. Mass. 1973, U.S. Ct. Appeals (1st cir.) 1976, U.S. Ct. Appeals (D.C. cir.) 1984, U.S. Claims Ct. 1983, U.S. Supreme Ct. 1976. Law clk. to Hon. Bailey Aldrich U.S. Ct. Appeals (1st cir.), Boston, 1968-69; law clk. to Hon. Warren Burger, Hon. Hugo Black, Hon. Potter Stewart, Hon. Byron White U.S. Supreme Ct., Washington, 1969-70; spl. asst. to Hon. Elliot L. Richardson, Dept. Health, Edn. & Welfare, Washington, 1970-71, exec. asst., 1971-72; assoc. Ropes & Gray, Boston, 1972-77, ptnr., 1977—. Trustee Boston Athenaeum, Brigham & Women's Hosp., Ptnrs. Health Care Sys. Inc.; warden Trinity Ch. in City of Boston, vestryman. Mem. ABA, Am. Law Inst., Boston Bar Assn., Somerset Club, Tavern Club, Met. Club. Office: Ropes & Gray 1 Internat Pl Boston MA 02110

MORIARTY, JOHN, opera administrator, artistic director; b. Fall River, Mass., Sept. 30, 1930; s. John J. and Fabiola Marie (Ripeau) M. MusB summa cum laude, New Eng. Conservatory, 1952; D.M. New England Conservatory, 1992. Artistic adminstr. Opera Soc. of Washington, 1960-62, Santa Fe Opera, N.Mex., 1962-65; dir. Wolf Trap Co., Vienna, Va., 1972-77; chmn. opera dept. Boston Conservatory , 1973-89; chmn. opera dept. New Eng. Conservatory, 1989—; prin. condr. Central City Opera, Denver, 1978—, artistic dir., 1982—; panelist Nat. Inst. Music Theater, 1985, 86, 87, Conn. Arts Council, 1982, 84; adjudicator various contests including Met. Opera auditions, 1965—. Author: Diction, 1975. Trustee Boston Concert Opera; recs. on Cambridge Records and Newport Classics. Recipient Frank Huntington Beebe award, Boston, 1954, Disting. Alumni award New Eng. Conservatory Alumni Assn., 1982, Gold Chair award Cen. City Opera House Assn., 1988. Mem. Nat. Opera Assn., Sigma Alpha Iota, Delta Omicron, Pi Kappa Lambda. Office: New Eng Conservatory 290 Huntington Ave Boston MA 02115-5018 also: Cen City Opera House Assn 621 17th St Ste 1601 Denver CO 80293-1601

MORIARTY, RICHARD WILLIAM, pediatrician; b. Pitts., Oct. 4, 1939; s. Edwin Joseph and Catherine Bernadine (Binnie) M. BS, U. Pitts., 1961, MD, 1966. Chief pediatric resident Children's Hosp. Pitts., 1970-71; asst. prof. pediatrics U. Pitts. Sch. Medicine, 1971-77, assoc. prof., 1977—; assoc. dir. dept. pediatrics St. Francis Med. Ctr., 1987—; dir. Pitts. Poison Ctr., Children's Hosp. Pitts., 1971-87, Nat. Poison Ctr. Network, 1971-87; mem. adv. com. on hazardous chemicals, 1974-87; mem. tech. adv. com. poison prevention packaging Consumer Product Safety Commn., 1975-77; bd. dirs. Comprehensive Health Planning Com. Southwestern Pa., 1974-76; commr. Health Edn. Ctr., 1977-87. Named Man of Yr. in Medicine, 1977. Mem. Am. Acad. Pediatrics, Am. Assn. Poison Control Centers, Am. Acad. Clin. Toxicology, Am. Coll. Emergency Physicians (toxicology com. 1980-87), PGH Acad. of Medicine (pres. 1987-92), Longue Vue Club Pitts. Democrat. Club: University (Pitts.). Office: St Francis Med Office Bldg 4401 Penn Ave Ste 1400 Pittsburgh PA 15224

MORICE, JOSEPH RICHARD, history educator; b. Phila., Apr. 2, 1923; s. Joseph and Anna (Seary) M.; m. Josephine Tumminello, May 31, 1958; children—Ann Marie, Jacqueline. B.A., LaSalle Coll., 1947; M.A., Fordham U., 1951; M.Litt., U. Pitts., 1953, Ph.D., 1962. Mem. faculty Duquesne U., Pitts., 1948-89; prof. history Duquesne U., 1963-89, chmn. dept., 1965-69, dir. debate, 1955-89, emeritus prof. history, 1990—; mng. editor Duquesne Rev., 1956-73. Vol. Pub. Acct. Office, 1991-94, Pitts. Guild Blind, 1996—. With AUS, 1943-45. Mem. Orgn. Am. Historians, Cath. Host. Soc. W. Pa., Phi Kappa Phi, Phi Alpha Theta. Home: 1632 Worcester Dr Pittsburgh PA 15243-1534

MORIMOTO, CARL NOBORU, computer system engineer, crystallographer; b. Hiroshima, Japan, Mar. 31, 1942; came to U.S., 1957, naturalized, 1965; s. Toshiyuki and Teruko (Hirano) M.; m. Helen Kiyomi Yoshizaki, June 28, 1969; children: Matthew Ken, Justin Ray. BA, U. Hawaii, 1965; PhD, U. Wash., 1970. Research assoc. dept. chemistry Mich. State U., East Lansing, 1970-72; postdoctoral fellow dept. biochemistry and biophysics Tex. A&M U., College Station, 1972-75; sr. sci. programmer Syntex Analytical Instruments Inc., Cupertino, Calif., 1975-78; prin. programmer analyst, software engring. mgr. Control Data Corp., Sunnyvale, Calif., 1978-83; mem. profl. staff GE Aerospace, San Jose, Calif., 1983-93; prin. engr. GE Nuclear Energy, San Jose, 1993—. Mem. Am. Crystallographic Assn., Assn. Computing Machinery, Am. Chem. Soc., Sigma Xi. Am. Baptist. Home: 4003 Hamilton Park Dr San Jose CA 95130-1223

MORIN, CARLTON PAUL, private investments executive; b. Ashland, Maine, July 10, 1932; s. Leo Joseph and Leona (Nadeau) M.; children: Catherine Lee, Cynthia Ann, Bruce Carlton. AB, U. Maine, 1954; LLB, Seton Hall U., 1964. Tax acct. Internat. Nickel Co., Inc., N.Y.C., 1956-62; tax mgr. Abex Corp., N.Y.C., 1962-67; asst. to contr. Todd Shipyards Corp., N.Y.C., 1967-68; asst. treas. Interlake, Inc., Chgo., 1968-75, Congoleum Corp., Milw., 1975-77; treas. Congoleum Corp., 1977-79, v.p., treas., 1979-80, v.p. treasury and adminstrn., 1980-83, v.p. corp. devel., 1983-86; pvt. practice pvt. investor Portsmouth, 1986-92; chmn. Piscataqua Savs. Bank, 1991-92; bd. dirs. Kinderworks Corp., Casco Bay Gear and Apparel. With USMC, 1954-56. Office: PO Box 6676 Portsmouth NH 03802-6676

MORIN, JAMES CORCORAN, editorial cartoonist; b. Washington; s. Charles Henry and Elizabeth (Donnelly) M.; m. Danielle Flood; children: Elizabeth, Spencer. BFA, Syracuse U., 1975. Editorial cartoonist Beaumont (Tex.) Eeterprise, 1976-77, Richmnd (Va.) Times Dispatch, 1977-78, The Miami (Fla.) Herald, 1978—. Author, cartoonist: (books) Famous Cats, 1982, Jim Morin's Field Guide to Birds, 1985, Line of Fire, 1991 (Pulitzer prize 1996). Pulitzer Prize finalist, Columbia U., 1978, 90; Overseas Press Club award, 1990, Berryman award, 1996. Mem. Assn. of Am. Editorial Cartoonists, Nat. Cartoonists Soc. (award 1992), Soc. of Profl. Journalists (Green Eyeshade award). Avocations: oil painting, acoustic guitar playing, ice hockey. Office: The Miami Herald 1 Herald Plz Miami FL 33132-1609

MORIN, LOUIS, judge; b. Que., Can., Sept. 29, 1941; s. Paul-Emile and Jeanne Dechene) M.; m. Marthe Champoux, Sept. 12, 1970; children: Francois, Antoine, Brigitte. BA, Coll. Jesuites, 1962; LLL, U. Laval, 1965. Atty. Grondin LeBel Morin, Que., Can., 1966-77; judge Que. Labor Ct., 1977—, chief judge, 1990—; mem. Que. Jud. Coun., Montreal, 1992—; tchr. labor law U. Laval, Que., 1989. Mem. Can. Bar Assn., Que. Bar Assn., Que. Young Bar Assn. (pres. 1975-76), Que. Judge's Assn. (pres. 1989-90). Avocations: skiing, cycling. Home: 4070 Guerin, Quebec, PQ Canada G2A 1K7 Office: Que Labor Ct, 1245 Chemin St Foy Ste 340, Quebec, PQ Canada G1S 4W7

MORIN, PIERRE JEAN, retired management consultant; b. Quebec City, Que., Can., Aug. 5, 1931; s. Augustin Norbert and Yvonne (Gaudry) M.; m. Colette Poulin, Apr. 3, 1954; children: Anne, Gilles, Louis. B.S., Concordia U., Montreal, 1964; M.S., Laval U., Que., 1970, D.Sc., 1973. Quality control technician Dow Brevery, Montreal, Que., 1952-56; research assoc. Royal Victoria Hosp., Montreal, 1957-67; coordinator of research Que. Heart Inst., 1967-73; dir. research labs. Laval Hosp., Que., 1973-80, lectr. dept. medicine, 1973-77; dir. gen. Community Service Ctr., 1980-88; mgmt. cons., 1988-91, ret., 1991; cons. Que. Minister of Environ., 1975-84. Contbr. articles to profl. jours. and news media. Bd. dirs. St. mary's Hosp., Three Rivers, Que. Schering Travelling fellow, 1971. Mem. AAAS. Roman Catholic. Home: 336 Rg Castor, Leclercville, PQ Canada G0S 2K0 *Well assumed failure may be a must towards later success.*

MORIN, WILLIAM JAMES, management consultant; b. Kankakee, Ill., Aug. 5, 1939; s. Carl Wesley and Viola Grace (Seaberlie) M.; children: Mark, Timothy, Jason. BS, So. Ill. U., 1961, MS, 1963. Pres. Drake, Beam, Morin, N.Y.C., 1977-79, chmn., chief exec. officer, 1979-95; pres., CEO WJM Assocs., 1995—. Author: Successful Termination, Outplacement Techniques, Parting Company, Silent Sabotoge, 1995. Mem. Assn. Outplacement Cons. Firms (stds. com.).

MORIN, YVES-CHARLES, linguistics educator, researcher; b. St. Germain, Yvelines, France, Nov. 7, 1944; arrived in Can. 1972; s. Georges and Denise (Montaudouin) M.; 1 child, Yannig. Lic., U. Paris, 1967; Diploma in Engring., Ecole Centrale, 1967; M.A. in Linguistics, U. Mich., 1970, Ph.D. in Computer Sci., 1971. Engr. Mil. Radar Estab., Pontoise, France, 1971-72; asst. prof. U. Montreal, Montreal, Que., Can., 1972-76, assoc. prof., 1967-82, prof., 1982—, mem. exec. com. Faculty of Arts and Scis., 1984-86; invited prof. Bourguiba Inst., Tunis, Tunisia, 1977; mem. cons. bd. Humanities and Social Scis. Research Council of Canada, Ottawa, 1980-83; vis. scholar Centre d'Etudes Metriques de Nantes (France), 1994. Contbr. articles to profl. jours. Served to lt. Logistics-Radar, 1971-72; France. Harkness fellow Commonwealth Fund, 1967. Mem. Linguistic Soc. Am., Can. Linguistic Soc., Can. Jour. Linguistics, Société Asiatique, Sigma Xi, Phi Kappa Phi. Office: U Montreal Dept Linguistics, CP 6128, Montreal, PQ Canada H3C 3J7

MORING, JOHN FREDERICK, lawyer; b. Farmville, Va., Oct. 30, 1935; s. Scott O'Ferrall and Margaret Macon (Mitchell) M.; m. Margaret Ann Clarke, Mar. 30, 1959; children: Martha, Elizabeth, Scott, Lee. BS, Va. Poly. Inst., 1957; JD, George Washington U., 1961. Bar: Va. 1961, D.C. 1962, U.S. Supreme Ct. 1964. Assoc. Morgan, Lewis & Bockius, Washington, 1961-68, ptnr., 1969-78; ptnr. Jones, Day, Reavis & Pogue, Washington, 1978-79, Crowell & Moring, Washington and London, 1979—; sec. Associated Gas Distbrs., Inc., 1977—. Local gas utility columnist Nat. Gas Jour., 1989—; mem. editl. bd. Natural Gas Contracts, 1994—. Pres. Sterling Citizens Assn., Alexandria, Va., 1971-77; Rep. candidate 23d Dist./Va. Gen. Assembly, Alexandria, 1973; chmn. Alexandria Rep. Com. on Candidate Recruitment, 1974; bd. govs. St. Stephen's and St. Agnes Sch., Alexandria, 1989-95; pres. St. Stephen's Found., Inc., 1990-93; sr. warden Immanuel Ch. of the Hill, Alexandria, 1988, 89; trustee Ch. Schs. of Diocese of Va., 1996—. 2d lt. U.S. Army, 1958. Mem. ABA (natural resources law sect. 1982-86, coun.), Fed. Energy Bar Assn. (sec. 1963-66, pres. 1982-83), Belle Haven Country Club. Episcopalian. Avocations: golf, fishing, canoeing. Home: 509 Canterbury Ln Alexandria VA 22314-4747 Office: Crowell & Moring 1001 Pennsylvania Ave NW Washington DC 20004-2505 also: 2010 Main St Irvine CA 92614-7203 also: 180 Fleet St, London ECAA2 HD, England

MORIN-MILLER, CARMEN ALINE, writer; b. Montreal, Que., Can., Dec. 20, 1929; came to U.S., 1983; d. J. Gabriel Morin and Marie-Jeanne (Guay Morin) Vincent; m. Benoit H. Massicotte, July 28, 1951 (div. 1975); children: Andrée, Chantal, Joane, Claude, Anne; m. Jack Conway Miller, Sept. 9, 1983. Diploma, U. Laval, Que., 1950, C.I.M., 1974; diploma in art, Charles-Huot Sch., Que., 1978. Freelance writer, 1954—; info. officer Ministere des Communications of Quebec, Quebec City, 1974-83; gallery owner Equity Art Svcs., Collegeville, Pa., 1983—, Morin-Miller Galleries, N.Y.C., 1985-90; dir. Amities Culturelles, Beauport, Quebec City, 1968-75. Author: Lumiere, 1989, Conspiration, 1977; contbr. articles to Perspectives mag., other mags., newspapers. Pres. Assn. des Parents, Beauport, 1964-74. Mem. Nat. Geographic Soc., Am. Rhododendron Soc., Unon Ecrivaines et Ecrivains Quebecois, Club Jounalistes (pres. com. 1967-69), Assn. Morin d'Amerique (regional dir.). Avocations: reading, music, bridge, travel.

MORIS, LAMBERTO GIULIANO, architect; b. Siena, Tuscany, Italy, Mar. 29, 1944; came to U.S., 1972; s. Gualtiero Luigi and Giovanna (Avanzati) M.; m. Tracy P. Schilling, 1970 (div. 1985); children: Giacomo, Stefano; m. Beverly Chiang, Mar. 28, 1986; 1 child, Christopher. MA in Arch., U. Florence, Italy, 1970. Assoc. Marquis Assocs., San Francisco, 1972-78, prin., 1978-85; prin. Simon Martin-Vegue Winkelstein Moris, San Francisco, 1985—; tchr. San Francisco City Coll.; juror DuPont Antron Design Awards, 1989; mem. adv. com. Acad. of Art-Coll., San Francisco, 1991—. Mem. San Francisco Opera Guild. Fellow AIA (mem. Coll. Fellows, mem. interior arch. sect., juror Honor Award for interiors 1996); mem. Italingua Inst. (bd. dirs.), Oakland Met. C. of C., The Engrs. Club, Il Cenacolo Club. Roman Catholic. Avocations: coin collecting, skiing, travel. Office: Simon Martin-Vegue Winkelstein Moris 501 2nd St Ste 701 San Francisco CA 94107-1431

MORISATO, SUSAN CAY, actuary; b. Chgo., Feb. 11, 1955; d. George and Jessie (Fujita) M.; m. Thomas Michael Remec, Mar. 6, 1981. BS, U. Ill., 1975, MS, 1977. Actuarial student Aetna Life & Casualty, Hartford, Conn., 1977-79; actuarial asst. Bankers Life & Casualty Co., Chgo., 1979-80, asst. actuary, 1980-83, assoc. actuary, 1983-85, health product actuary, 1985-86, v.p., 1986-95, sr. v.p., 1996—, also bd. dirs.; participant individual forum Health Ins. Assn. Am., 1983; spkr. health forum Life Ins. Mgmt. Rsch. Assn., 1992, long-term care conf. Sharing the Burden, 1994. Mem. adv. panel on long term care financing Brookings' Inst. Fellow Soc. Actuaries (conf. spkr. 1988, 94, workshop leader 1990, 93, news editor health sect. news 1988-90); mem. Am. Acad. Actuaries, Health Ins. Assn. Am. (long term care task force 1988—, chair 1993-95, conf. spkr. 1990, 96, tech. adv. com. 1991-93, mem. health care reform strategy com. 1993-95, mem. supplemental ins. com. 1996—, mem. legis. policy com. 1996—, mem. nominating com. 1996—), Nat. Assn. Ins. Commrs. (ad hoc actuarial working group for long term care nonforfeiture benefits 1992), Am. Coun. Life Ins. (accelerated benefits/long term care com. 1997—), Chgo. Actuarial Assn. (sec. 1983-85, program com. 1987-89), Phi Beta Kappa, Kappa Delta Pi, Phi Kappa Phi. Office: Bankers Life & Casualty Co 222 Merchandise Mart Plz Chicago IL 60654-1103

MORISHIGE, FUKUMI, surgeon; b. Fukuoka, Japan, Oct. 24, 1925; s. Fukumatsu and Teruko M.; m. Fumie Osada, Apr. 18, 1954; children: Kyoko, Hisakazu, Noritsugu. MD, Kurume U., 1952, DMS, 1962; PhD, Fukuoka U., 1983. Intern Kurume U., 1951-52; asst. Kurume (Japan) U., Dept. Pathology, 1952-55, Kyoto (Japan) U. Inst. Chest Disease, 1955-58; v.p. Tachiarai Hosp., Fukuoka, Japan, 1959-67, Torikai Hosp., Fukuoka, Japan, 1968-80; chmn. Tachiarai Hosp., Fukuoka, Japan, 1980-84; dir. Nakamura Hosp., Fukuoka, Japan, 1984-86, supreme advisor, 1987—; dir. Morishige Cancer Clinic, Chiba, Japan, 1992—; resident fellow Linus Pauling Inst. of Sci. and Medicine, Palo Alto, Calif., 1976—; chemistry advisor Nissan Chem. Industries Ltd., Tokyo, 1983—. Author: Nutrition of Nucleic Acid, 1983, Brain Blood Circulation, 1986; contbr. articles to profl. jours. Fellow Linus Pauling Inst. Sci. and Medicine; mem. Japan Soc. Magnetic Resonance (founder, bd. dirs. 1978—, exec. sec. 1979—), Internat. Assn. for Vitamin & Nutritional Oncology (exec. com. 1983—), Japanese Cancer Assn., Japanese Assn. for Thoracic Surgery, Japan Surg. Soc. Democrat. Buddhist. Home and Office: Miyakono 2-10-13, Ooami-Shirasato-Machi, Sambu Chiba 299-32, Japan

MORISHITA, AKIHIKO, trading company executive; b. Osaka, Japan, Oct. 14, 1941; came to U.S., 1981; s. Sueyoshi and Toshiko Morishita; m. Fumiko Okamura; children: Shizuko, Kumiko, Okamura. BA in Econs., Wakayama U., Wakayama, Japan, 1965. Mgr. Hanwa & Co. Ltd., Osaka, 1965-80; cons. oil dept. Pacific Southwest Trading Co., San Diego, 1981-82; exec. Pacific Marine Bunkering, Inc., L.A., 1982—. Mem. Woodland Hills Country Club. Home: 4610 Don Pio Dr Woodland Hills CA 91364-4205

MORISON, JOHN HOPKINS, casting manufacturing company executive; b. Milw., June 29, 1913; s. George Abbot and Amelia (Elmore) M. m. Olga de Souza Dantas, July 29, 1944; children: Maria de Souza Dantas, John Hopkins III. AB, Harvard U., 1935; LLD, New Eng. Coll., 1973. Various positions Bucyrus-Erie Co., South Milwaukee, Wis., U.S. and Latin Am., 1935-49; pres., dir. Hitchiner Mfg. Co., Inc., Milford, N.H., 1949-93, chmn. bd., 1973-93, chmn. emeritus, 1994—; pres., treas. Upland Farm Inc., Peterborough, N.H.; chmn. RiverMead Retirement Community, Peterborough, N.H., 1991-96, trustee 1991—. Commr. N.H. Commn. on Arts, 1967-77; mem. regional exec. com. Boy Scouts Am., Framingham, Mass., 1970-76; mem. exec. com., pres., N.H. Coun. on World Affairs, 1955-76; trustee Canterbury Shaker Village, 1982-96; trustee Land Use Found. N.H., 1970-75, World Peace Found., 1962-90, Currier Gallery Art; pres. bd. dirs. Matthew Thornton Health Plan, 1972-82; bd. dirs. Forum on N.H.'s Future, 1979-81; pres., distbg. dir. N.H. Charitable Fund, 1968-79; mem. corp. MacDowell Colony; v.p. bd. govs. N.H. Public TV, 1979-89. Lt. (j.g.) USNR, 1943-46. Recipient Lifetime Achievement award N.H. Bus. and Industry Assn., 1993, N.H. High Tech. Coun., 1996, Granite State award U. N.H., 1994. Mem. Somerset Club. Unitarian. Home: RR 1 Box 326 Lyndeborough NH 03082-9734

MORISSETTE, ALANIS, musician; b. Ottawa, ON, Canada, June 1, 1974. Albums include Alanis, 1991, Now is the Time, 1992, Jagged Little

Pill, 1995. Recipient Grammy award for Album of Yr., Best Female Rock Vocal Performance, Best Rock Song, Best Rock Album, 1996. Office: Maverick Music Co 8000 Beverly Blvd Los Angeles CA 90048-4504 also: Fan Club Alanis Morissette care MSO 14724 Ventura Blvd Ste 410 Sherman Oaks CA 91403*

MORITA, RICHARD YUKIO, microbiology and oceanography educator; b. Pasadena, Calif., Mar. 27, 1923; s. Jiro and Reiko (Yamamoto) M.; m. Toshiko Nishihara, May 29, 1926; children—Sally Jean, Ellen Jane, Peter Wayne. B.S., U. Nebr., 1947; M.S., U. So. Calif., 1949; Ph.D., U. Calif., 1954. Microbiologist Mid-Pacific Expdn., 1950, Danish Galathea Deep-Sea Expdn., 1952, Trans-Pacific Expdn.; Postdoctoral fellow U. Calif., Scripps Inst. Oceanography, 1954-55; asst. prof. U. Houston, 1955-58; asst. prof., assoc. prof. U. Neb., 1958-62; prof. microbiology and oceanography Oreg. State U., Corvallis, 1962—; prog. dir. biochemistry NSF, 1968-69; Disting. vis. prof. Kyoto Univ.; cons. NIH, 1968-70; researcher in field. Contbr. articles to sci. lit. Patentee in field. Served with U.S. Army, 1944-46. Grantee NSF, 1962—, NIH, 1960-68, NASA, 1967-72, Office Naval Research, 1966-70, Dept. Interior, 1968-72, NOAA, 1975-82, Bur. Land Mgmt., 1982, EPA, 1986—; recipient awards including King Fredericus IX Medal and Ribbon, 1954, Sr. Queen Elizabeth II Fellowship, 1973-74, Hotpack lectr. and award Can. Soc. Fellow Japan Soc. for Promotion Sci.; mem. Am. Soc. Microbiology (Fisher award). Office: Oreg State U Dept Microbiology Corvallis OR 97331

MORITA, TOSHIYASU, technical manager; b. Tokyo, Feb. 8, 1967; s. Hiroshi and Fusako (Ishikawa) M. Grad. high sch., 1985. Programmer Origin Systems, Inc., Austin, Tex., 1987; engr. Cyclops Electronics, Boerne, 1988-90; programmer Taito R&D, Bothell, Wash., 1990; mgr. new tech. Lucas Arts Entertainment, San Rafael, Calif., 1990-93; tech. dir. Sega Tech. Inst., Redwood City, Calif., 1993-94, Sega of Am., Redwood City, 1994-96, SegaSoft, Redwood City, 1996—. Mem. IEEE Computer Soc. (affiliate), Mensa.

MORITSUGU, KENNETH PAUL, physician, government official; b. Honolulu, Mar. 5, 1945; s. Richard Yutaka and Hisayo Joan (Nishikawa) M.; children: Erika Lizabeth, Vikki Lianne. Student, Chaminade Coll. Honolulu, 1963-65; BA in Classical Langs. with honors, U. Hawaii, 1967; MD, George Washington U., 1971; MPH, U. Calif., Berkeley, 1975; DSc (hon.), Coll. Osteopathic Medicine, U. New Eng., 1988, Midwestern U., 1993; D Pub. Svc. (hon.), U. North Tex., 1994. Diplomate Am. Bd. Preventive Medicine (fellow); cert. correctional health profl. Intern USPHS Hosp., San Francisco, 1971-72, resident, 1972-75; commd. USPHS, 1968, advanced through grades to med. dir., 1979; promoted to rank of rear adm., asst. surgeon gen., 1988; staff med. officer USPHS Hosp., San Francisco, 1972-73; regional cons. med. manpower planning and devel. HEW, San Francisco, 1976-78; chief internat. edn. programs br. HEW, Washington, 1978; dep. dir. div. medicine HEW, 1978; dir. Bur. Health Professions, div. medicine HHS, Rockville, Md., 1978-83, dir. Nat. Health Service Corps, 1983-87, dep. dir. Bur. Health Professions, 1987; med. dir. Fed. Bur. Prisons Dept. Justice, Washington, 1987—. Decorated D.S.M.; recipient Commendation medal, Meritorious Svc. medal, Outstanding Svc. medal, Surgeon Gen.'s medallion, Surgeon Gen.'s medal, Dirs. award for Exceptional Svc., U.S. Marshal's Svcs., John D. Chase award for outstanding physician adminstrn., AMSUS, Nathan Davies award AMA (Disting. Svc. award ACHSA), others. Fellow Am. Coll. Preventive Medicine, Royal Soc. Health, Royal Soc. Medicine; mem. APHA, Assn. Tchrs. Preventive Medicine, Assn. Mil. Surgeons U.S., Res. Officers Assn., Mensa, Am. Guild Organists. Home: 726 Sonata Way Silver Spring MD 20901-5063 Office: US Dept Justice Fed Bur Prisons 320 1st St NW Ste 1000 Washington DC 20534-0002

MORITZ, CHARLES FREDRIC, book editor; b. Cleve., Jan. 23, 1917; s. Frederic and Alberta (Hartwig) M. B.A., Ohio State U., 1942; student, Harvard U., 1946-47, Columbia U., 1947-48; B.S. in L.S, Middlebury (Vt.) Coll., 1948, M.A., 1950. Asst. librarian rare book room and reference dept. Yale Library, 1948-50; mem. staff N.Y. Pub. Library, 1950-52; asst. prof. Grad. Sch. Library Service, Rutgers U., 1955-58; editor of Current Biography, 1958-92. Cons. editor Current Biography, 1993—; contbr. book revs. for Booklist, 1952-55; also articles. Served with AUS, 1942-45. Mem. ALA, Bibliog. Soc. Am. Democrat. Lutheran. Home: 3210 Arlington Ave 3-E Bronx NY 10463 Office: Current Biography 950 University Ave Bronx NY 10452-4224

MORITZ, DONALD BROOKS, mechanical engineer, consultant; b. Mpls., June 17, 1927; s. Donald B. and Frances W. (Whalen) M.; m. Joan Claire Betzenderfer, June 17, 1950; children: Craig, Pamela, Brian. B.S. in Mech. Engring., U. Minn., 1950; postgrad., Western Res. U., 1956-58. Registered profl. engr., Ill. Minn., Ohio. V.p., gen. mgr. Waco Scaffold Shoring Co., Addison, Ill., 1950-72; group v.p. Bliss and Laughlin Industries, Oak Brook, Ill., 1972-83; sr. v.p. AXIA Inc. (formerly Bliss and Laughlin Industries, Oak Brook, 1983-84, exec. v.p., chief operating officer, 1984-88; cons. Exec. Svc. Corps Chgo., 1988—; pres. Image-A-Nation, Unltd., 1988—; bd. dirs. Am. Photographic Acad. Patentee in field. Served with USN, 1945-46. Mem. ASME, Scaffold and Shoring Inst. (founder, past pres.), Mensa, Meadow Club. Office: Moritz and Assocs PO Box 305 Clarendon Hills IL 60514-0305

MORITZ, EDWARD, historian, educator; b. Columbia, S.C., Jan. 24, 1920; s. Edward and Edith (Jumper) M.; m. Betty Gene Reid, Apr. 8, 1946; children—Stephen Edward, John Reid, Richard Douglas, Sarah Anne. B.A., Miami U., Oxford, Ohio, 1949; M.A. (Taft scholar), U. Cin., 1950; Ph.D. (Knapp scholar), U. Wis., 1953. Instr. U. Wis., Madison, 1953-55; mem. faculty Kalamazoo (Mich.) Coll., 1955—, prof. history, 1963—, chmn. dept., 1965-88, prof. emeritus, 1988—; vis. prof. Oxford, Eng., 1971-72. Author: Winston Churchill, Parliamentary Career, 1908-12. Served with USAAF, 1942-46. Kellog fellow, 1971. Mem. Am. Hist. Assn., Conf. Brit. Studies, AAUP, Phi Beta Kappa, Phi Eta Sigma. Home: 420 Edgemoor Ave Kalamazoo MI 49001-4207 *This quote of the Earl of Montrose has influenced me over the years: He either fears his fate too much, or trusts it not at all; who will not put it to the touch--to win or lose it at all.*

MORITZ, JOHN REID, lawyer; b. Hamilton, Ohio, Nov. 30, 1951; s. Edward and Betty (Reid) M.; m. Darla F. Winter, July 26, 1986; children: Alexander R., Andrew F., Kathryn Ann. BA, Alma Coll., 1978; JD, Thomas M. Cooley Sch. Law, 1982. Bar: Mich. 1982. Law clk. Mich. 30th Jud. Cir., Lansing, 1981, Mich. 20th Jud. Cir., Grand Haven, 1982-83; legis. aide to rep. Mich. Ho. of Reps., Lansing, 1981-82; assoc. Swaney, Thomas & Moritz P.C., Holland, Mich., 1983—. With U.S. Army, 1973-76. Mem. ABA, Mich. Bar Assn., Ottawa County Bar Assn., Mich. Trial Lawyers Assn. Avocations: stamp collecting, antiques, tennis. Home: 4345 Lakeshore Dr N Holland MI 49424-5650 Office: Swaney Thomas & Moritz PC 30 E 9th St Holland MI 49423-3508

MORITZ, MICHAEL EVERETT, lawyer; b. Marion, Ohio, Mar. 30, 1933; s. Charles Raymond and Elisabeth Bovie (Morgan) M.; m. Lou Ann Yardley, Sept. 12, 1959; children: Ann Gibson, Jeffrey Connor, Molly Elisabeth, Catharine Morgan. BS, Ohio State U., 1958, JD summa cum laude, 1961. Bar: Ohio 1961, U.S. Tax Ct. 1970. Assoc. Dunbar, Kienzle & Murphey, Columbus, Ohio, 1961-65, ptnr., 1966-72; ptnr. Moritz, McClure, Hughes & Kerscher, Columbus, 1972-80, Baker & Hostetler, Columbus, 1980—; adj. prof. Capital U. Law Sch., Columbus, 1969-70; lectr. Ohio Legal Ctr. Inst., Columbus, 1967; chmn. legal div. United Appeal Franklin County, Columbus, 1964; pres. Capital City Young Rep. Club, Columbus, 1966; mem. Franklin County Rep. Exec. Com., Columbus, 1966—; mem. bd. dirs. The Ohio State U. Found., Ohio State U. Coll. Bus. Pacesetters Club; trustee Kenyon Festival Theatre, 1981-86, Players Theatre Columbus, 1986-88; commr. Ohio Elections Commn., 1993-95. With USN, 1954-56. Recipient Disting. Svc. award Columbus Jaycees, 1966. Mem. ABA, Ohio Bar Assn., Columbus Bar Assn., Am. Judicature Soc., Ohio State U. Faculty Club, Order of Coif, Phi Gamma Delta, Beta Gamma Sigma. Clubs: Muirfield Village Golf Club, Scioto Country, Capital, Columbus, Ohio State U. President's, Wedgewood Golf & Country Club, Jefferson Golf and Country Club, The Club at Seabrook Island. Office: Baker & Hostetler 65 E State St Columbus OH 43215-4213

MORITZ, MILTON EDWARD, security consultant; b. Reading, Pa., Sept. 5, 1931; s. Edward Raymond and Anna May M.; m. Elizabeth Ann Walls, June 6, 1952; children: Betsy Ann Moritz Koppenhaver, Stephen Edward, Sandra E. Student, U. Md., 1950-51, Fla. State U., 1959-60. Enlisted U.S. Army, 1949, chief warrant officer 3, 1968, spl. agt. M.I.; ret., 1970; safety and security dir. Harrisburg (Pa.) Hosp., 1970-72; security mgr. Sprint, Carlisle, Pa., 1972-94; prin. Moritz Assocs., Harrisburg, 1994—; lectr., instr. Harrisburg Area Community Coll.; mem. Indsl. Security Adv. Coun. Assoc. editor: Protection of Assets Manual. Pres. Greater Harrisburg Crime Clinic, 1974. Decorated Bronze Star with oak leaf cluster. Mem. Am. Soc. Indsl. Security (past pres., chmn. bd. dirs.), Assn. Former Intelligence Officers, Internat. Narcotic Enforcement Officers Assn., Pa. Crime Prevention Assn. (bd. dirs.). Republican. Lutheran. Home and Office: 7723 Avondale Ter Harrisburg PA 17112-3805

MORITZ, TIMOTHY BOVIE, psychiatrist; b. Portsmouth, Ohio, July 26, 1936; s. Charles Raymond and Elisabeth Bovie (Morgan) M.; m. Joyce Elizabeth Rasmussen, Oct. 13, 1962 (div. Sept. 1969); children: Elizabeth Wynne, Laura Morgan; m. Antoinette Tanasichuk, Oct. 31, 1981; children: David Michael, Stephanie Lysbeth. BA, Ohio State U., 1959; MD, Cornell U., 1963. Diplomate Am. Bd. Psychiatry and Neurology. Intern in medicine N.Y. Hosp., N.Y.C., 1963-64, resident in psychiatry, 1964-67; spl. asst. to dir. NIMH, Bethesda, Md., 1967-69; dir. Community Mental Health Ctr., Rockland County, N.Y., 1970-74, Ohio Dept. Mental Health, Columbus, Ohio, 1975-81; med. dir. psychiatry Miami Valley Hosp., Dayton, Ohio, 1981-82; med. dir. N.E. Ga. Community Mental Health Ctr., Athens, Ga., 1982-83, Charter Vista Hosp., Fayetteville, Ark., 1983-87; clin. dir. adult psychiatry Charter Hosp., Las Vegas, Nev., 1987-94; pvt. practice psychiatry Las Vegas, Nev., 1987—; prof. Wright State U., Dayton, Ohio, 1981-82; asst. prof. Cornell U., N.Y.C., 1970-73; cons. NIMH, Rockville, Md., 1973-83. Author: (chpt.) Rehabilitation Medicine and Psychiatry, 1976; mem. editorial bd. Directions in Psychiatry, 1981—. Dir. dept. mental health and mental retardation Gov.'s Cabinet, State of Ohio, Columbus, 1975-81. Recipient Svc. award Ohio Senate, 1981, Svc. Achievement award Ohio Gov., 1981. Fellow Am. Psychiat. Assn. (Disting. Svc. award 1981); mem. AMA, Nev. Assn. Psychiat. Physicians, Nev. State Med. Assn., Clark County Med. Soc., Cornell U. Med. Coll. Alumni Assn. Office: Timothy B Moritz MD 3815 S Jones Blvd # 7 Las Vegas NV 89103-2289

MORLAND, JOHN KENNETH, sociology and anthropology educator; b. Huntsville, Ala., July 4, 1916; s. Howard Cannon and Ethel Mae (Cowan) M.; m. Margaret Louise Ward, Feb. 26, 1949; children: Carol, Katherine, Evelyn. B.S., Birmingham So. Coll., 1938; B.D., Yale U., 1943; Ph.D., U. N.C., 1950. Instr. Yale in China Middle Sch., Changsha, Hunan, 1943-46; exec. sec. Yale in China Assn., New Haven, 1946-47; asst. prof. Coll. William and Mary, Williamsburg, Va., 1949-53; Charles A. Dana prof., chmn. dept. sociology and anthropology Randolph Macon Woman's Coll., Lynchburg, Va., 1953-87; rsch. analyst City of Lynchburg, 1989-94; cons. U.S. Dept. Edn., Dept. Commerce, NEH, So. Regional Coun. NSF, Ednl. and Rsch. Found., Lynchburg, Va. Author: Social Problems in the United States, 1975, Millways of Kent, 1958, (with John Williams) Race, Color and the Young Child, 1976, (with Jack Balswick) Social Problems: A Christian Understanding and Response, 1990; contbr., editor: The Not So Solid South, 1971. Pres. bd. nat. ministries Am. Bapt. Chs., USA, 1973-79. Named Eminent Laureate of Va., 1981; recipient Disting. Alumnus award Birmingham-So. Coll., 1985, Nat. Conf. Christians and Jews Humanitarian award, 1994; Fulbright scholar Chinese U., Hong Kong, 1966-67; grantee NSF, Taiwan, 1975, U.S. Dept. Edn., 1972, Liberty Bell award Lynchburg Bar Assn., 1997. Fellow Am. Anthropol. Assn.; mem. Am. Sociol. Assn., So. Sociol. Soc., Va. Social Sci. Assn. (pres. 1963), AAUP (pres. 1962). Home: 1619 Dogwood Ln Lynchburg VA 24503-1923 Office: Randolph Macon Woman's Coll Lynchburg VA 24503-1526

MORLAND, RICHARD BOYD, retired educator; b. Huntsville, Ala., June 27, 1919; s. Howard Cannon and Ethel May (Cowan) M.; A.B., Birmingham-So. Coll., 1940; M.Ed., Springfield Coll., 1947; Ph.D. (So. Fellowships Fund fellow 1957-58), N.Y. U. 1958; m. Jessie May Parrish, Mar. 17, 1949; 1 child, Laura. Phys. dir. YMCA, Frankfort, Ky., 1940-41; dir. athletics, head basketball coach Fla. So. Coll., 1947-50; lectr. in edn., N.Y. U., 1950-51; chmn. dept. phy. edn., Stetson U., Deland, Fla., 1952-60, head basketball coach, 1952-57, assoc. prof., 1958-63, prof. philosophy of edn., 1963-89, J. Ollie Edmunds prof., 1982-85, sr. active prof., 1989-90, chmn. grad. coun., 1962-69, chmn. dept. edn., 1969-75. Contbr. articles to profl. jours. Lt. USNR, 1941-45. Decorated 11 battle stars, USS Lexington. Named to Stetson U. Sports Hall of Fame; recipient McEniry award for Excellence in teaching, 1983; Richard B. Morland Distinguished Alumni award named in his honor; Bronze bust by Harry Messersmith dedicated, 1992. Mem. Philosophy of Edn. Soc. (pres. region 1963-64), Fla. Coun. Deans and Dirs. Tchr. Edn. (pres. 1974-75), Am. Ednl. Rsch. Assn., Am. Edn. Studies Assn., Soc. Profs. Edn., Fla. Founds. Edn. and Policy Studies Soc. (exec. bd. 1987-90), Univ. Profs. for Acad. Order, DeLand Country Club, Omicron Delta Kappa, Phi Alpha Theta, Kappa Delta Pi, Phi Delta Kappa (pres. region 1977-78, editorial bd. Phi Delta Kappan 1978-83, named Regional Educator of Yr. 1991), panel gallup poll on edn., 1995, Kappa Alpha. Democrat. Methodist. Home: 524 N Mcdonald Ave Deland FL 32724-3643

MORLEY, GEORGE WILLIAM, gynecologist; b. Toledo, June 6, 1923; s. Francis Wayland and Florence (Sneider) M.; m. Constance J. Morley, July 27, 1946 (dec. 1960); children: Beverly, Kathryn, George W. Jr.; m. Marcheta F. Morley, June 14, 1963. BS, U. Mich, 1944, MD, 1949, MS, 1955; cert. in Gynecologic Oncology, Am. Bd. Ob-Gyn., 1974. Diplomate Am. Bd. Ob-Gyn. Intern U. Mich. Hosp., 1949-50, asst. resident, 1950-51, resident, 1951-52, jr. clin. instr., 1952-53, sr. clin. instr., 1953-54; mem. faculty Sch. Medicine U. Mich., Ann Arbor, 1956—, dir. gynecology svc., 1973-85, dir. gynecologic oncology svc., 1964-86, 94-95, Norman F. Miller prof. dept. ob.-gyn., 1987—, assoc. chmn., 1987-91; Chmn. Mich. Jud. Commn., Lansing, 1988-92. Contbr. to med. publs. George W. Morley professorship established U. Mich., 1995. Fellow, ACS (bd. govs. 1986-91), Am. Coll. Ob.-Gyn. (pres. 1987); mem. Rotary. Republican. Presbyterian. Avocations: golf, music. Home: 1120 Chestnut St Ann Arbor MI 48104-2826 Office: U Mich Med Ctr 1500 E Medical Center Dr Ann Arbor MI 48109-0005

MORLEY, HARRY THOMAS, JR., real estate executive; b. St. Louis, Aug. 13, 1930; s. Harry Thomas and Celeste Elizabeth (Davies) M.; m. Nelda Lee Mulholland, Sept. 3, 1960; children: Lisa, Mark, Marci. BA, U. Mo., 1955; MA, U. Denver, 1959. Dir. men's student activities Iowa State Tchrs. Coll., 1955-57; dir. student housing U. Denver, 1957-60; pvt. practice psychol. consulting St. Louis, 1960-63; dir. adminstrn. County of St. Louis, Mo., 1963-70; regional dir. HUD, Kansas City, Mo., 1970-71; asst. sec. adminstrn. HUD, 1971-73; pres. St. Louis Regional Commerce and Growth Assn., 1973-78, Taylor, Morley, Inc., St. Louis, 1978—; teaching cons.-lectr. Washington U., St. Louis, 1962-70. Bd. dirs., mem. exec. com. St. Louis Coll. Pharmacy; past chmn. Better Bus. Bur.; chmn. Mo. Indsl. Devel. Bd., Mo. State Hwy. Commn.; bd. dirs. St. Luke's Hosps., St. Johns Hosp., Downtown St. Louis, Inc., Laclede's Landing Redevel. Corp. Served with USN, 1951-53. Mem. Am. C. of C. Execs., Nat. Assn. Homebuilders, St. Louis Homebuilders Assn. (pres.), St. Louis Advt. Club, Mo. Athletic Club, St. Louis Club, Noonday Club, Castle Oak Country Club, Round Table Club, Sunset Country Club. Republican. Methodist. Home: 14238 Forest Crest Dr Chesterfield MO 63017-2818 Office: 1224 Fern Ridge Pky Saint Louis MO 63141-4451

MORLEY, JOHN EDWARD, physician; b. Eshowe, Zululand, South Africa, June 13, 1946; came to U.S., 1977; s. Peter and Vera Rose (Phipson) M.; m. Patricia Morley, Apr. 4, 1970; children: Robert, Susan, Jacqueline. MB, BCh, U. Witwatersrand, Johannesburg, South Africa, 1972. Diplomate Am. Bd. Internal Medicine, subspecialty cert. endocrinology and geriatrics. Asst. prof. Mpls. VA Med. Ctr. and U. Minn., 1979-81; assoc. prof. U. Minn., Mpls., 1981-84; prof. UCLA San Fernando Valley, 1985-89; dir. GRECC Sepulveda (Calif.) VA Med. Ctr., 1985-89; Dammert prof. gerontology, dir. div. geriatric medicine St. Louis U. Med. Ctr., 1989—; dir. geriatric rsch., edn. and clin. ctr. St. Louis VA Med. Ctr., 1989—; mem. adv. panel of geriatrics and endocrinology U.S. Pharmacopeial Conv., Inc., Rockville, Md., 1990—. Author: (with others) Nutritional Modulation of Neuronal Function, 1988, Neuropeptides and Stress, 1988, Geriatric Nutrition, 1990, 2d edit., 1995, Medical Care in the Nursing Home, 1991, 2d edit., 1997, Endocrinology and Metabolism in the Elderly, 1992, Memory Function and Aging Related Disorders, 1992, Aging and Musculoskeletal Disorders, 1993, Aging, Immunity and Infection, 1994, Sleep Disorders and Insomnia in the Elderly, 1993, Quality Improvement in Geriatric Care, 1995, Focus on Nutrition, 1995, Applying Health Services Research to Long-Term Care, 1996, As We Age, 1996; mem. editl. bd. Peptides, 1983—, Internat. Jour. Obesity, 1986-89, Jour. Nutritional Medicine, 1990—, Clinics in Applied Nutrition, 1990-92; editor geriatrics sect. Yearbook of Endocrinology, 1987—, Nursing Home Medicine, 1992—, Clin. Geriatrics, 1992—, Sandwich Generation, 1997, others. Mem. adv. bd. Alzheimer's Assn., St. Louis, 1990-92; mem. adv. com. for physicians Mo. Divsn. Aging, Jefferson City, 1990—; bd. dirs. Mo. Assn. Long Term Care Physicians, 1991—, Long Term Care Ombudsman Program, St. Louis, 1992, Fund for Psychineuroimmunology, 1990—, Hamilton Hts. Health Resource Ctr., 1992—. Recipient Mead Johnson award Am. Inst. Nutrition, 1985. Cmty. Svc. award BREM, 1997. Mem. ACP (geriatrics subcom. 1991-92), Am. Soc. Clin. Investigation, Endocrine Soc., Am. Fedn. Clin. Rsch., Am. Acad. Behavioral Sci., Am. Geriatrics Soc. (assoc. editor jour. 1989-93, pres. Mo.-Kans. affiliate 1996—), Am. Fedn. Clin. Rsch., Gerontology Soc. Am., Am. Diabetes Assn., Am. Soc. Pharmacy and Therapeutics, Soc. for Neurosci., La Asociacion de Gerontologica y Geriatrica, A.C. (hon.), Assn. Dirs. Geriatric Acad. Programs. Office: Saint Louis U Sch Medicine 1402 S Grand Blvd Rm M238 Saint Louis MO 63104-1004

MORLEY, LAWRENCE WHITAKER, geophysicist, remote sensing consultant; b. Toronto, Feb. 19, 1920; s. George Whitaker and Mary Olive (Boyd) M.; divorced; children; Lawrence, Patricia, Chris, David; m. Beverly Anne Beckworth; step-children: Sandra Wellman, Stephen Burdett, Richard Burdett. BA, U. Toronto, 1946, MA, 1949, PhD, 1952; DSc (hon.), York U., Toronto, 1974. Dir. geophysics div. Geol. Survey Can., Ottawa, 1952-71; founding dir. gen. Can. Centre for Remote Sensing, Ottawa, 1971-80; founding exec. dir. Inst. for Space and Terrestrial Sci., Toronto, 1982-91; pres. Teledetection Internat., 1991—. Lt. Can. Navy, 1941-45. Fellow Royal Soc. Can.; mem. Can. Soc. Remote Sensing (founding pres. 1971-74), Am. Geophys. Union, Am. Soc. Phototogrammetry and Remote Sensing, Soc. Exploration Geophysicists, Can. Geophys. Union, Can. Geomatics Inst., Royal Can. Geog. Soc. Home and Office: 767 2d Ave W, Owen Sound, ON Canada N4K 4M2

MORLEY, LLOYD ALBERT, mining engineering educator; b. Provo, Utah, Oct. 28, 1940; s. John Jr. and Dorothea (Nielsen) M.; m. Jo Ann Bryant, Feb. 22, 1975; 1 child, Paul Loring. BS in Mining Engring., U. Utah, 1968, PhD in Mining Engring., 1972. Teaching asst., rsch. assoc. U. Utah, Salt Lake City, 1968-71; asst. prof. mining engring. Pa. State U., University Park, 1971-75, assoc. prof., 1975-80, prof., 1980-85; prof., head dept. mineral engring. U. Ala., Tuscaloosa, 1985-93, endowed chair mining engring., 1993—, prof. electrical engring., 1996—; cons. Jim Walter Resources, Inc., Brookwood, Ala., 1987—, Pitts. and Midway Coal Mining Co., Englewood, Colo., 1990—, Drummond Co., Inc., Birmingham, Ala., 1991—; engr. in tng., Utah. Author: Mine Power Systems, 1990; contbr. articles to profl. jours. Staff sgt. USNG, 1958-66. Recipient Wilson Outstanding Teaching award Pa. State U., 1980; Outstanding Rsch. Report awards U.S. Bur. Mines, 1983-84, grantee, 1971-87. Fellow IEEE (bd. dirs. 1991-92, 94, 97, v.p. publs. 1994, v.p. tech. activities 1997); mem. Industry Applications Soc. IEEE (Mining Best Paper awards 1984, 88, 90, pres. 1988, Disting. lectr. 1991, Disting. Svc. award 1995), Power Engr. Soc., Computer Soc. Republican. Episcopalian. Avocations: high-fidelity systems, classic sports cars, rose growing, music. Office: U Ala Dept Electrical and Computer Engring Box 870286 Tuscaloosa AL 35487-0286

MORLEY, MICHAEL B., public relations executive; b. Madras, India, Nov. 18, 1935; s. Gordon and Violet M.; m. Ingrid Hellman, Aug. 20, 1957; children: Andrew, Helen, Ann. Attended, Eastbourne Coll. Dir. Harris & Hunter Pub. Rels., 1960-67; mng. dir. Daniel J. Edelman, 1967; pres. Edelman Internat., 1970; dep. chmn. Edelman Worldwide, 1992—; pres. Edelman N.Y., 1994—. Comms. Advt. and Mktg. Edn. Found. fellow, 1981; decorated Knight of First Class, Order of Lion, Rep. Finland, 1978. Mem. Internat. Pub. Rels. Assn., Internat. Pub. Rels., Brit. C. of C., Japan Soc., Bus. Coun. Internat. Understanding, Inc., Korea Soc. Home: 1 Devon Pl Cresskill NJ 07626-1608 Office: Edelman Pub Rels Worldwide 1500 Broadway New York NY 10036-4015

MORLEY, ROGER HUBERT, company executive, consultant; b. Cleve., June 21, 1931; s. Hubert Patrick and Ayleen Marie (Mosier) M. BS in Indsl. Engring., Ohio U., 1953; MBA, Harvard U., 1957. Contr. Stromberg-Carlson, Rochester, N.Y., 1957-60; v.p., gen. mgr. GATX, Chgo., 1960-67; gen. mgr. Burndy Corp., Norwalk, Conn., 1967-68; exec. v.p., CFO, Gould Inc., Chgo., 1968-74; pres., vice chmn. Am. Express, N.Y.C., 1974-81; comng. dir. R&R Inventions, Eng., 1986—; bd. dirs. Lorraine Investments SA, Luxembourg, Bank of Am.-Ill., Biogen, Inc., Cambridge, Mass., Blyth Industries Inc., Artal SA, Luxembourg, Iris India Fund, Luxembourg, Blyth Industries, Greenwich, Conn.; assoc. lectr. U. Rochester, 1958-60; mem. U.S. adv. bd. European Inst. Bus. Adminstrn., 1975-81. Bd. dirs., mem. exec. com. Lincoln Ctr. for Performing Arts, 1974-81, chmn. consol. corp. fund drive, 1975-81; bd. dirs. Vis. Nurse Svc. N.Y., 1974-81, Sunny Bank Anglo-Am. Hosp., Cannes, France, 1985-87; trustee Darwin Trust Edinburgh, Scotland, 1991—; trustee, chmn. fin. com. Barnard Coll., 1976-80; v.p. Schiller Internat. U., Heidelburg, Germany, 1982—; mem. Com. de Jumelage, Ville de Grasse, 1983-87. Capt. USAF, 1953-55. Mem. Nat. Assn. Securities Dealers (gov.-at-large), Grasse Country Club (France), Links (N.Y.C.), Harvard Club N.Y.C., Univ. Club (Chgo.). Republican. Avocations: golf, tennis, travel, reading. Home and Office: L'Horizon, Clos Barnier Spéracèdes, 06530 Alpes Maritimes France

MORLOCK, CARL GRISMORE, physician, medical educator; b. Crediton, Ont., Can., Sept. 11, 1906; came to U.S., 1934, naturalized, 1939; s. Charles Edward and Emma (Grismore) M.; m. Katherine Ruth Mercer, Sept. 18, 1937; children: Anne Louise, William Edward. B.A., U. Western Ont., 1929, M.D., 1932; fellow internal medicine, Mayo Found., Grad. Sch. U. Minn., 1934-37; M.S. in Medicine, U. Minn., 1937. Intern Victoria Hosp., London, Ont., 1932-33; resident Victoria Hosp., 1933-34; practice medicine specializing in internal medicine and gastroenterology Rochester, Minn., 1934—; assoc.prof. internal medicine Mayo Found., 1949-62, prof. clin. medicine, 1962-72; prof. medicine Mayo Med. Sch., 1972—. Contbr. articles on gastrointestinal subjects to med. jours. Fellow ACP; mem. Am., Minn. med. assns., Osler Med. Soc., Am. Gastroent. Assn., Gideons Internat. Sigma Xi, Alpha Omega Alpha. Baptist. Home: 211 2nd St NW Apt 1303 Rochester MN 55901-2897 Office: Mayo Clinic 200 1st St SW Rochester MN 55902-3008

MORLOK, EDWARD KARL, engineering educator, consultant; b. Phila., Nov. 3, 1940; s. Edward Karl and Anna Marie (Kurtz) M.; m. Ottilia Angela Husz, Dec. 14, 1968 (div. July 1983); 1 child, Jessica Angela; m. Patricia Campbell Conboy, Mar. 23, 1991. BE, Yale U., 1962; PhD, Northwestern U., 1967; MA (hon.), U. Pa., 1973. Civil engr., transp. U.S. Dept. Commerce, Washington, 1966-67; from asst. prof. civil engring. to assoc. prof. Northwestern U., Evanston, Ill., 1967-73, asst. dir. rsch., transp. ctr., 1969-73; 1907 Found. assoc. prof. U. Pa., Phila., 1973-75, chmn., transp. grad. group, 1983-86, 91-95, UPS found. prof. transp., 1975—, chair systems grad. program, 1988-91; cons. nat. transp. policy study commn., Washington, 1978-79. Author: Analysis Transportation Technology and Network Structure, 1969, Introduction to Transportation Engineering and Planning, 1978; assoc. editor Transp. Rsch. Jour., 1975—; consulting editor series in transp. for McGraw-Hill Pub. Co., 1980—; contbr. more than 60 articles to profl. jours. Mem. Nat. Assembly Engring. panel on innovation in transp., Washington, 1979-80, panel on hazardous material transp., Washington, 1980-81. Recipient U.S. Sr. Scientist award Alexander von Humboldt Found., 1980-81; rsch. grantee Commonwealth of Pa., Consol. Rail Corp., K-Line Am., U.S. Dept. Transp., NASA, NSF. Mem. Inst. Ops. Rsch. and Mgmt., Transp. Rsch. Forum (v.p. 1974-75, pres. 1975-76, bd. disting. mems. 1983—), Transp. Rsch. Bd. (rec. com. of coun. of univ. transp. ctrs. 1985-88, coun. mem. 1988-90, chair freight transp. planning and mktg. com. 1994—, chair com. on policy options for intermodal freight trans. 1996-97).

Lutheran. Office: U Pa Dept Systems Engring 220 S 33rd St Philadelphia PA 19104-6315

MORNES, AMBER J. BISHOP, consultant, computer software trainer, analyst; b. Ft. Rucker, Ala., Oct. 20, 1970; d. David Floyd and Holly Brooke (Decker) Bishop; m. David Michael Mornes, May 22, 1993. BA in Psychology, U. Colo., Boulder, 1992. Asst. dir. admissions Rocky Mountain Coll. Art and Design, Denver, 1992-94, placement and alumni svcs. coord., 1995-96; computer software instr. Knowledge Alliance, Aurora, Colo., 1996—; analyst Andersen Cons., Denver, 1997—. Vol. Colo. Art Educator Assn., 1993—. Mem. APA (student affiliate), Nat. Art Edn. Assn., Colo. Art Edn. Assn. Home: 8288 S Emerson Way Littleton CO 80122 Office: Andersen Cons 1225 17th St Ste 3200 Denver CO 80202-5534

MORNING, JOHN, graphic designer; b. Cleve., Jan. 8, 1932; s. John Frew and Juanita Kathryn (Brannan) M.; m. Carole Ann Coleman, Jan. 24, 1964 (div. July 1984); children: Ann Juanita, John Floyd. BFA, Pratt Inst., 1955. Art dir. McCann-Erickson, Inc., N.Y.C., 1958-60; pvt. practice design N.Y.C., 1960—; bd. dirs. Dime Savings Bank N.Y. Bd. dirs. Repertory Theater Lincoln Ctr., 1970-73, N.Y. Landmarks Conservancy, Charles E. Culpepper Found., 1990—, Henry St. Settlement, chmn., 1979-86, Bklyn. Acad. Music, 1993, Lincoln Ctr. Inst., 1993; trustee Wilberforce U., com. on edn. Mus. Modern Art; chmn. bd. trustees Pratt Inst., Bklyn., 1988-92; bd. dirs. Mus. for African Art, N.Y.C., co-chair, 1991-94; vice chmn. N.Y.C. Cultural Affairs Adv. Commn., 1994—. With U.S. Army, 1956-58. Recipient Alumni medal Pratt Inst., 1972, Presdl. Recognition award Pres. of U.S., 1984, Lillian D. Wald Humanitarian award, 1992. Mem. Am. Inst. Graphic Arts, Am. Acad. Dramatic Arts (trustee 1988-95), Assn. Governing Bds. Colls. and Univs. (bd. dirs.). Republican.

MORNINGSTAR, RICHARD L., diplomat; married; 4 children. Degree with honors, Harvard Coll.; JD, Stanford Law Sch. Assoc. Peabody & Brown, Boston, 1970-81, ptnr., adminstr. dept. litig., 1976—; past chmn., CEO Costar Corp.; policy and investment sr. v.p. Overseas Pvt. Ivestment Corp., 1993-95; appt. amb., spl. advisor to pres., sec. state on assistance to new ind. states former Soviet Union Dept. States, Washington, 1995—; co-owner baseball team Lowell (Mass.) Spinners; past adj. prof. law Sch. Law Boston Coll.; past commr. Nat. Conf. Commrs. on Uniform State Laws; past advisor internat. trade and tech. Dept. Commerce; formerly active Econs. and Internat. Trade Cluster, preparation of analysis Trade and Devel. Agy. presdl. transition, 1992. Avocation: baseball. Office: Dept State Office Spl Advisor to Pres and Sec State 2201 C St NW Washington DC 20520-7512*

MOROLES, JESUS BAUTISTA, sculptor; b. Corpus Christi, Tex., Sept. 22, 1950. AA, El Centro Coll., Dallas, 1975; BFA, No. Tex. State U., 1978. bd. dirs. Internat. Sculpture Ctr., Washington; instr. Nat. Mus. Am. Art Symposium, 1992. One-person shows include Davis-McClain Gallery, Houston, 1982, 84, 86, 88, 90, 92, Janus Gallery, Santa Fe, 1984, 85, 86, 89, 90, 92, Marilyn Butler Gallery, Scottsdale, Ariz., 1986, 89, Richard Green Gallery, L.A., 1989, 91, N.Y., 1989, Santa Monica, Calif., 1990, Chgo. Internat. Art Exposition, Klein Art Works, Chgo., 1991, Mus. S.E. Tex., Beaumont, 1992, Wirtz Gallery, San Francisco, 1990, Escultura, 1991, Expositum, Polanco, Mex., 1991, Adams-Middleton Gallery, Dallas, 1992, Carl Schlosberg Fine Art, Sherman Oaks, Calif., 1992; commd. Tex. Commerce Bank, Dallas, 1983, Riata Devel., Houston, 1984, Siena Sq., Boulder, Colo., 1985, Nat. Health Ins. Co., Dallas, 1986, IBM, Raleigh, N.C., 1986; represented in permanent collections Albuquerque Mus., Mus. Fine Arts, Santa Fe, Old Jail Art Ctr., Albany, Tex., U. Houston, Mint Mus., Charlotte, N.C., Dallas Mus. Art, Nat. Mus. Am. Art, Smithsonian, Washington. Visual Art fellow Southeastern Ctr. Contemporary Art, Winston-Salem, N.C., 1982; Pres. Citation award U. No. Tex., 1992; Matching grnatee Nat. Endowment Arts, Birmingham Botanical Gardens, 1984. Office: Att Jesus B Moroles 73970 El Paseo Palm Desert CA 92260-4336*

MOROSANI, GEORGE WARRINGTON, real estate developer, realtor; b. Cin., July 20, 1941; s. Remy Edmond and Virginia Caroline (Warrington) M.; m. Judith Clontz, July 3, 1980; children by previous marriage: Katherine Carmichael, Elizabeth Warrington. BA, Rollins Coll., 1964, MBA, 1965. Fin. mgr. Lunar Orbitor and Minuteman Programs, Boeing Co., Cape Canaveral, Fla., 1965-68; controller Equitable Leasing Co., Asheville, N.C., 1968-69; founder, pres., treas. Western Carolina Warehousing Co., Asheville, 1969-87; co-founder, pres. Asheville Jaycee Housing, Inc., 1971-77; founder, pres., treas. A Mini Storage Co. (dba George's Stor-Mor), Asheville, N.C., 1976—; co-founder, treas. Accent on Living Co., Asheville, 1978-81; founder, pres., treas. G.M. Leasing, Asheville, N.C. 1986—, The Kingswood Co., Fletcher, N.C., 1986—; gen. partner Pine Needle Apts., Arden, N.C., 1978—, Pine Ridge Apts., Skyland, N.C., 1980—, Morganton Heights Apts., Morganton, N.C., 1981—, Maiden (N.C.) Apts., 1981—, Valley View Shopping Ctr., Candler, N.C., 1982-86, Meadow Garden Apts., Hendersonville, N.C., 1983—, Drexel Apts., N.C., 1983—, Heritage Hill Apts., Marion, N.C., 1983—, Cavalier Arms Apts., Waynesville, N.C., 1986—, Gwenmont Arms Apts., Murphy, N.C., 1986—, Nicol Arms Apts., Sylva, N.C., 1986—, Meadowwood Arms Apts., Gray, Tenn., 1986—, 4 Seasons Apts., Erwin, Tenn., 1986—, M. Realty LP, Asheville, 1986—, Woods Edge Apts., North Wilksboro, N.C., 1987—, Pond and Assocs., Asheville, 1992-94, Deer Park Apts., Cleve., N.C., 1987—; ptnr. Laurel Ridge Realty, Litchfield, Conn., 1973—, Laurel Properties, Rochester, Vt., 1978-94, Ashland Assocs., Asheville, N.C., 1985-88, Airport Assocs., Asheville, 1986-87; founder, owner George W. Morosani & Assocs., Asheville, 1981—, George's Rent-All, Asheville, N.C., 1988—; mgr. FI Realty I LLC, 1993—, Western Realty LLC, Asheville, 1994—, M Realty I LLC, 1994—, Sweeten Creek Realty LLC, 1994—, FI Realty I, LLC, 1994—, Patton Ave, LLC, 1995—, 3M Realty, LLC, 1995—, 3883 Sweeten Creek, LLC, 1997—. Bd. dirs. Jr. Achievement Greater Asheville Area, 1977—; mem. Regional Housing Adv. Com., 1981-86, Land-of-Sky Regional Coun., 1981-86, bd. dirs, 1990—; mem. Council Rural Housing and Devel., 1982-86, N.C. Real Estate Licensing Bd., S.C. Real Estate Commn., Tenn. Real Estate Commn., Ga. Real Estate Licensing Bd., Asheville Multiple Listing Svc., Hendersonville Multiple Listing Svc.; co-founder, treas. N.C. Council Rural Rental Housing, 1985—, sec., 1986-91; mem. Buncombe County Bd. Adjustment, 1988—, vice chmn., 1991—. Named Man of Yr., Asheville Jaycees, 1976. Mem. Sales and Mktg. Execs. Asheville (dir. 1974-76, 1982-84. chmn. membership com. 1976-77), Asheville Bd. Realtors, Hendersonville Bd. Realtors, Nat. Assn. Realtors, N.C. Assn. Realtors (property mgmt. div.). Mem. Asheville Comml. and Investment Realty Assn. (v.p. programs 1986-87, sec.-treas. 1987-92, 94—, pres., 1993), Nat. Mini-Storage Inst., W.N.C. Exchangers, Greater Asheville Apt. Assn. (chmn. membership com. 1988-89), Council Ind. Bus. Owners, Better Bus. Bur. Asheville/Western N.C. (dir. 1987—, second vice chmn. 1990, first vice chmn. 1991, chmn., 1992, chmn. nominating com., 1993), Econ. Devel. Assn. Western N.C., Self-Service Storage Assn., Asheville Area C. of C. (chmn. indsl. relations 1978-79), Hendersonville C. of C. Episcopalian. Clubs: Biltmore Forest Country, Asheville Downtown City. Lodge: Civitan (dir. 1975-77). Office: 932 Hendersonville Rd Asheville NC 28803-1761

MOROWITZ, HAROLD JOSEPH, biophysicist, educator; b. Poughkeepsie, N.Y., Dec. 4, 1927; s. Philip Frank and Anna (Levine) M.; m. Lucille Rita Stein, Jan. 30, 1949; children: Joanna Lynn, Eli David, Joshua Alan, Zachary Adam, Noah Daniel. BS, Yale U., 1947, MS, 1950, PhD, 1951. Physicist Nat. Bur. Stds., 1951-53, Nat. Heart Inst., Bethesda, Md., 1953-55; mem. faculty Yale U., 1955-88, assoc. prof. biophysics, 1960-68, prof. molecular biophysics and biochemistry, 1968-88, master Pierson Coll., 1981-86; mem. faculty George Mason U., Fairfax, Va., 1988—, Robinson prof. biology and natural philosophy, 1988—; dir. Krasnow Inst. for Advanced Study, 1993—; chmn. com. on models for biomed. rsch. NRC, 1983-85, mem. bd. on basic biology, 1986-92. Author: Life and the Physical Sciences, 1964, (with Waterman) Theoretical and Mathematical Biology, 1965, Energy Flow in Biology, 1968, Entropy for Biologists, 1970, (with Lucille Morowitz) Life On The Planet Earth, 1974, Ego Niches, 1977, Foundations of Bioenergetics, 1978, The Wine of Life, 1979, Mayonnaise and the Origin of Life, 1985, Cosmic Joy and Local Pain, 1987, The Thermodynamics of Pizza, 1991, Beginnings of Cellular Life, 1992, (with James Trefil) The Facts of Life, 1992, Entropy and the Magic Flute, 1993; editor Complexity, 1994—; contbr. articles to profl. jours. Mem. sci. adv. bd. Santa Fe Inst., 1991—. Mem. Biophys. Soc. (mem. exec. com. 1965), Nat. Ctr. for Rsch. Resources (mem. coun. 1987-92). Office: George Mason U Krasnow Inst Advanced Study Fairfax VA 22030

MOROZ, PAVEL EMANUEL, research scientist; b. Leningrad, Russia, 1928; came to U.S., 1976.; Degree in Medicine, Pavlov Med. Inst., Leningrad, 1952, MD in Cytology and Biophysics, 1960. Rsch. scientist various insts., Leningrad, 1952-75. Contbr. articles to profl. jours. Mem. N.Y. Acad. Scis. Achievements include research in the effects of the force of gravity and centrifugal force on the cell and development of centrifuge microscope. Home: 15-17 Willet St Apt 3K New York NY 10002

MORPHEW, DOROTHY RICHARDS-BASSETT, artist, real estate broker; b. Cambridge, Mass., Aug. 4, 1918; d. George and Evangeline Booth (Richards) Richards; grad. Boston Art Inst., 1949; children—Jon Eric, Marc Alan, Dana Kimball. Draftsman, United Shoe Machinery Co., 1937-42; blueprinter, advt. artist A.C. Lawrence Leather Co., Peabody, Mass., 1949-51; propr. Studio Shop and Studio Potters, Beverly, Mass., 1951-53; tchr. ceramics and art, Kingston, N.H., 1953—; real estate broker, pres. 1965-81; two-man exhbn. Topsfield (Mass.) Library, 1960; owner, operator Ceramic Shop, West Stewartstown, N.H. Served with USNR, 1942-44. Recipient Profl. award New Eng. Ceramic Show, 1975; also numerous certificates in ceramics. Home: 557 Palomino Trl Englewood FL 34223-3951 Studio: 57 Algonac Rd Cape Neddick ME 03909

MORPHY, JAMES CALVIN, lawyer; b. Pitts., Jan. 16, 1954; s. Robert Samson and Autumn (Phillips) M.; m. Priscilla Winslow Plimpton, July 11, 1981; children: Calvin, Katherine, Victoria. BA, Harvard U., 1976, JD, 1979. Bar: N.Y. 1980. Assoc. Sullivan & Cromwell, N.Y.C., 1979-86, ptnr., 1986—, mng. ptnr. gen. practice group, 1992—, mng. ptnr. M&A group, 1995—. Contbg. author New York and Delaware Business Entities: Choice Formation, Operation, Financing and Acquisitions. Mem. ABA (com. on fed. securities law 1992—), Assn. Bar of City of N.Y., Wianno Club (bd. govs.), Greenwich Country Club. Office: Sullivan & Cromwell 125 Broad St New York NY 10004-2400

MORREL, WILLIAM GRIFFIN, JR., banker; b. Lynchburg, Va., Aug 25, 1933; s. William Griffin and Virginia Louise (Baldwin) M.; m. Sandra Virginia Coats, Jan. 31, 1959; children: William Griffin, John Coats, Elisabeth White, Jere Coleman. BS, Yale U., 1955; postgrad. Rutgers U., 1965-67. With Md. Nat. Bank, Balt., 1955-84, asst. v.p., 1959, v.p., 1964, sr. v.p., 1975-84, mgmt. com. 1979-84, chmn. three lending coms., others; pres., bd. dirs. Md. Nat. Overseas Investment Corp.; chmn. bd. London Interstate Bank Ltd.; chmn. bd. dirs. Md. Internat. Bank; sr. v.p., chief operating officer Abu Dhabi Internat. Bank, Inc., 1984-86, pres., chief exec. officer Heritage Internat. Bank, 1986-89; dir., pres., CEO Madison Fin. Group, 1989—; chief exec. officer, chmn. The Valley Fin. Group, Balt., 1989—; pres., chief exec. officer Summit Bancorp, Balt., 1990-92; consul of the Netherlands at Balt., 1978-84. Mem. Balt. Consular Corps, 1978-84; chmn. Md. World Trade Efforts Commn., 1983-84; mem. Md. Trade Policy Council, 1985-88; vice chmn. Dist. Export Council, 1983—. Contbr. articles to profl. jours. Sr. fellow Ctr. for Internat. Banking Studies, Darden Grad. Bus. Sch. U. Va., 1978-91. Served with U.S. Army, 1956-58. Mem. Bankers Assn. for Fgn. Trade (bd. dirs. 1975-78), Robert Morris Assocs. (nat. bd. dirs. 1984-88), Internat. Lending Council (bd. dirs., chmn., 1978-80), Md. Hist. Soc. (trustee), Balt. Council Fgn. Relations (trustee), Econ. Devel. Council. Republican. Presbyterian. Clubs: Yale, Farmington Country, Elkridge, Md. Club. Home: 6 Beechdale Rd Baltimore MD 21210-2207 Office: The Madison Fin Group Inc PO Box 16265 Baltimore MD 21210-0265

MORRELL, ARTHUR ANTHONY, lawyer, state legislator; b. New Orleans, Mar. 22, 1943; s. Reynard and Mildred (Gray) M.; m. Cynthia Hedge; children: Todd, Matthew, Jean-Paul, Nicholas. BA, So. U., 1970, JD, 1978. Bar: La. 1978, all state and fed. cts. In-flight exec. rep. Ea. Airlines, New Orleans, 1968-72; ticket agt. Ea. Airlines, Chgo., 1972-75; passenger svc. agt. Ea. Airlines, New Orleans, 1968-70; fed. voters examiner Civil Svcs. Dept., New Orleans, 1975-77; pres., owner ACTMP Enterprises, New Orleans, 1982—; pvt. practice, New Orleans, 1982—; owner, breeder La. Horsemen, New Orleans, 1985—; mem. La. Ho. of Reps., New Orleans, 1984—. Mem. Very Spl. Arts; bd. dirs Total Cmty. Action. With Spl. Forces, U.S. Army, 1963-66. Mem. ABA, La. Trial Lawyers Assn., Assn. for Effective Govt., Am. Legion (Post 395), Delta Theta Pi. Democrat. Roman Catholic. Office: Ste 107-10 3200 Saint Bernard Ave New Orleans LA 70119-1929

MORRELL, DIANE MARIE, lawyer; b. Savannah, Ga., Jan. 26, 1966; d. Alice (Keyes) Morrell. BS in Criminal Justice, Armstrong State U., 1988; JD, Ga. State U., 1991. Bar: Ga. 1992, Ga. Ct. Appeals 1992, U.S. Dist. Ct. (so. dist.) Ga. 1992, U.S. Ct. Appeals (11th cir.) 1992. Assoc. Allen and Assocs., Savannah, Ga., 1991-92; ptnr. Allen & Morrell, Savannah, 1992-94; pvt. practice law, 1994—; judge protem Chatham County Recorder's Ct.; atty., coach mock trial competition Ga. State Bar. Bd. dirs. Hope House of Savannah, Greater Savannah Black Tourism Network, Frank Callen Boys Club; vol. Big Bros./Sisters, Davenport House. Mem. ABA, Assn. Trial Lawyers Am., Ga. Trial Lawyers Assn., Ga. Assn. Women Lawyers, State Bar Ga., Port City Bar Assn. Office: PO Box 9304 Savannah GA 31412-9304

MORRELL, GENE PAUL, liquid terminal company executive; b. Ardmore, Okla., Oct. 4, 1932; s. Paul T. and Etta L. (Weaver) M.; m. Jan A. Foster, Aug. 20, 1954; children: Jeffrey T., Kelly Ann, Rob Redman. BS in Geology, U. Okla., 1954, LLB, 1962. Bar: D.C. 1973. Geologist Gilmer Oil Co., Ardmore, Okla., 1957-59, atty.-geologist, 1962-63; sole practice, Ardmore, 1963-69; ofcl. Dept. Interior, Washington, 1969-72; v.p. Lone Star Gas Co., Washington, 1972-76; sr. v.p. United Energy Resources, Inc., Houston, 1976-86; vice chmn. Petro United Terminals, Inc., Houston, 1986—. Contbr. articles to profl. jours. Commr. City of Ardmore, 1967-69, vice-mayor, 1968. Mem. ABA, D.C. Bar Assn., Am. Assn. Petroleum Geologists, Phi Alpha Delta, Sigma Alpha Epsilon. Episcopalian. Clubs: City Tavern (Washington), Ramada-Tejas, Houston Artillery, Galveston Country, The Yacht Club (Galveston).

MORRILL, JOYCE MARIE, social worker, consultant; b. Rockland, Maine, Dec. 27, 1939; d. Henry Higgins and Julia Ellen (Philbrook) Thompson; BA, U. Hartford, 1964; MSW, Hunter Coll., 1972; m. Edward Morrill, Sept. 7, 1972; 1 son, Gregory Hodgman; step-son Shawn Morrill. Co-host Today in Conn. Program, Sta. WHNB-TV, Hartford, 1964-65; clin. social worker, field instr. Rehab. Inst., N.Y., 1972-78; dir., founder Wellness Svcs., Jamaica Estates, N.Y., 1979-95; pres. Morrill Support, 1996—. Mem. Nat. Assn. Social Workers, Inst. Noetic Scis., N.Am. Menopause Soc. Home and Office: 181-38 Midland Pky Jamaica Estates NY 11432-1400

MORRILL, RICHARD LELAND, geographer, educator; b. L.A., Feb. 15, 1934; s. Robert W. and Lillian M. (Riffo) M.; m. Joanne L. Cooper, 1965; children: Lee, Andrew, Jean. B.A., Dartmouth Coll., 1955; M.A., U. Wash., 1957, Ph.D., 1959. Asst. prof. geography Northwestern U., 1959-60; NSF research fellow U. Lund, Sweden, 1960-61; asst. prof. U. Wash., Seattle, 1961-65; asso. prof. U. Wash., 1965-69, prof., 1969—, chmn. dept. geography, 1974-83, asso. dir. environ. studies, 1974—; chmn. urban planning PhD program, 1992—; vis. asso. prof. U. Chgo., dir. Chgo. Regional Hosp. Study, 1966-67; cons. population, regional and urban planning. Author: Geography of Poverty, 1970, Spatial Organization of Society, 1973, Political Redistricting and Geographic Theory, 1981, Spatial Diffusion, 1987. Mem. King County Boundary Rev. Bd. Guggenheim fellow, 1983-84. Mem. Assn. Am. Geographers (Meritorious Contbn. award 1970, mem. coun. 1970-73, sec. 1979-81, pres. 1981-82), Regional Sci. Assn., Wash. Regional Sch. Assn. (pres. 1993-94), Population Assn. Am., Lambda Alpha. Office: Dept Geography U Wash Seattle WA 98195

MORRILL, RICHARD LESLIE, university administrator; b. Weymouth, Mass., June 4, 1939; s. Duncan Russel and Violet Erma (Gibson) M.; m. Martha Leahy, June 24, 1964; children: Katie, Amy. A.B. in History magna cum laude, Brown U., 1961; B.D. in Religious Thought, Yale U., 1964; Ph.D. in Religion, Duke U., 1968. Instr. Wells Coll., Aurora, N.Y., 1967-68; asst. prof. Chatham Coll., Pitts., 1968-74, assoc. prof., 1974-77, assoc. provost and asst. to pres., 1973-77; assoc. provost Pa. State U., University Park, 1977-79; pres. Salem Coll. and Acad., Winston-Salem, N.C., 1979-82, Centre Coll., Danville, Ky., 1982-88, U. Richmond, Va., 1988—; bd. dirs. Ctrl. Fidelity Banks, Inc.; v.p. So. Univ. Conf., 1993—; chmn. Assoc. Colls. of the South, 1993-94; v.p. So. Univ. Conf., 1993—; mem. governing coun. Wye Faculty Seminar, 1994—; mem. presdl. adv. com. KPMG Peat Marwick, 1989—; cons. edn. divsn. Lilly Endowment, 1990—. Author: Teaching Values in College, 1980; contbr. articles to profl. jours. Bd. dirs., mem. program com. Teagle Found., 1989—; mem. nat. bd. visitors Ind. U. Ctr. on Philanthropy, 1991—; mem. commn. on leadership devel. Am. Coun. on Edn., 1992-94; trustee Williamsburg Investment Trust, 1993—; mem. Richmond Symphony Coun., 1995—; mem. Va. Coun. for Internat. Edn., 1995-96; bd. dirs. Assn. Am. Colls. and Univs., 1996—. Woodrow Wilson fellow, 1961-62; James B. Duke fellow Duke U., 1964-67. Mem. Soc. for Values in Higher Edn. (dir. 1981-84), Am. Acad. Religion, Am. Soc. for Christian Ethics, Am. Assn. Higher Edn., So. Assn. Colls. and Schs. (commr. 1985—), Coll. Athletic Conf. (chmn. 1985-87), Council Ind. Ky. Colls. and Univs. (sec. 1984-86, v.p. 1986-88, exec. com. 1984-86), Assn. Presbyn. Colls. and Univs. (exec. com. 1984-86), Phi Beta Kappa. Club: University. Lodge: Rotary. Home: 7000 River Rd Richmond VA 23229-8532 Office: U Richmond Pres Office Maryland Hall Rm 203 Richmond VA 23173-1903*

MORRILL, THOMAS CLYDE, insurance company executive; b. Chgo., July 1, 1909; s. Walter and Lena Elpha (Haney) M.; m. Hazel Janet Thompson, Oct. 18, 1930; children: Dorothy Mae (Mrs. Gerald L. Kelly), Charles T. Student, Cen. Coll. Arts and Scis., Chgo., 1928-29, Northwestern U., 1929-30. With Alfred M. Best Co., Inc., 1929-45, assoc. editor, 1940-45; with N.Y. State Ins. Dept., 1945-50, dep. supt. ins., 1947-50; with State Farm Mut. Automobile Ins. Co., Bloomington, Ill., 1950-77, v.p., 1952-77; chmn. bd. State Farm Fire and Casualty Co., Bloomington, 1970-86, State Farm Gen. Ins. Co., Bloomington, 1970-91; cons. State Farm Ins. Cos., Bloomington, 1991—; founder, chmn., dir. Ins. Inst. for Highway Safety. Chmn. exec. subcom. Nat. Hwy. Safety Adv. Com., 1971-73; chmn. tech. com. on transp. White House Conf. on Aging, 1971; mem. Pres.'s Task Force on Hwy. Safety. Clubs: Union League (Chgo.); Union Hills Country, Lakes (Sun City, Ariz.).

MORRILL, WILLIAM ASHLEY, research executive; b. Bronxville, N.Y., Apr. 23, 1930; s. Ashley B. and Katharine A. (Anderson) M.; m. Lois Birrell, Dec. 27, 1953 (div. 1978); children: Margaret, Carolyn, Elizabeth, Janet; m. Nancy Porter, Aug. 26, 1978. B.A., Wesleyan U., 1952; M.P.A., Syracuse U., 1953. Mgmt. analyst, acting chief plans and policy Directorate of Manpower and Orgn., USAF, 1953-62; asst. div. chief AEC unit Bur. of Budget, Washington, 1962-65, Mil. Divsn. Bur. Budget, 1965-67; dep. dir. Nat. Security Programs div. Office of Mgmt. and Budget, 1967-71; dep. county exec. Fairfax County, Va., 1971-72; asst. dir. Office Mgmt. and Budget, Washington, 1972-73; asst. sec. for planning/evaluation HEW, 1973-77; mem. Energy Policy and Planning Office, White House, 1977; sr. fellow Mathematica Policy Research, Princeton, N.J., 1977-79, sr. v.p., 1979-80, pres., 1980-86; pres. Mathtech, Inc., 1985-95, chmn., 1985-96; sr. fellow, 1996—; mem. com. on child devel. rsch. and pub. policy NRC, 1978-87, chmn., 1983-87, com. on nat. stats., 1989-92, mem. Commn. on Behavioral and Social Scis. and Edn., 1990-96. Chmn. No. Va. Planning Dist. Commn., 1965-70, , 1986-89, William A. Jump Meml. Found. Recipient Meritorious award William A. Jump Meml. Found., 1966, Citizen of Yr. award for Fairfax County, Washington Star, 1970, Disting. Alumni award Maxwell Sch., Syracuse U., 1974, Disting. Svc. award Nat. Conf. on Social Welfare, 1976. Mem. Assn. Pub. Policy Analysis & Mgmt. (pres. 1982-83, mem. policy coun.), Nat. Acad. Pub. Adminstrn. (trustee 1984-93, vice-chmn. 1991-93), Coun. for Excellence in Govt. (bd. trustees 1983—, chmn. 1986-89). Home: PO Box 38 New Hope PA 18938-0038 Office: Mathtech Inc 202 Carnegie Ctr Ste 111 Princeton NJ 08540-6239

MORRIN, PETER PATRICK, museum director; b. St. Louis, Oct. 31, 1945; s. Kevin Charles and Helen Louise (Clanton) M.; m. Carolyn Brooks, Oct. 5, 1974; children: Matthew, Rebecca. AB, Harvard U., 1968; MFA, Princeton U., 1972. Asst. prof., dir. art gallery Vassar Coll., Poughkeepsie, N.Y., 1974-78; curator 20th century art High Mus. Art, Atlanta, 1979-86; dir. J.B. Speed Art Mus., Louisville, 1986—; panelist Nat. Endowment Arts. Contbr. articles to profl. publs. Served with USAR, 1968-74. Office: JB Speed Art Mus PO Box 2600 Louisville KY 40201-2600

MORRIN, THOMAS HARVEY, engineering research company executive; b. Woodland, Calif., Nov. 24, 1914; s. Thomas E. and Florence J. (Hill) M.; m. Frances M. Von Ahn, Feb. 1, 1941; children: Thomas H., Diane, Linda, Denise. *My wife, Frances, and I recently moved to the Gold Country Retirement Community, out of Placerville, California. We are gradually getting adjusted to the pleasant environment and prepared meals. We will look forward to visits by our four children and ten grandchildren .* BS, U. Calif., 1937; grad., U.S. Navy Grad. Sch., Annapolis, Md., 1941. Student engr. Westinghouse Electric Mfg. Co., Emeryville, Calif., 1937; elec. engr. Pacific Gas & Electric Co., 1938-41; head microwave engring. div. Raytheon Mfg. Co., Waltham, Mass., 1947-48; chmn. elec. engring. dept. Stanford Research Inst., 1948-52, dir. engring., research, 1952-60, gen. mgr. engring., 1960-64, vice pres. engring., sci., 1964-68; pres. University City Sci. Inst., Phila., 1968-69; pres., chmn. bd. Morrin Assos., Inc., Wenatchee, Wash., 1968-72. Trustee Am. Acad. Transp. Served as officer USNR, 1938-58, comdr. USN, 1945-48. Decorated Bronze Star; recipient Bank Am. award for automation of banking during 1950's, 1992. Fellow IEEE, AAAS; mem. Sci. Research Soc. Am., U.S. Naval Inst., Navy League, Marine Meml. Club (San Francisco). Home: Gold Country Retirement Cty 6081 Golden Center Ct # 115 Placerville CA 95667 *In my 82nd year I look back at the many accomplishments made in science and engineering and their contributions to business and industry as well as to many lives. However, when I look forward to the many things yet to come, I wish I were fifty years younger. In my 82nd year I feel privileged in having lived through the greatest advances made in the world: from the horse and buggy to people traveling 17,000 miles per hour in an earth orbit and sending probes throughout the solar system; from the pony express to world-wide instantaneous communications; from the one-room school to world-wide web. Although it has been a wonderful ride, as I expressed to my wife many years ago, our advances in technology have exceeded society's ability to match it with moral and cultural values. There is always such a time lag but in due time it always adjusts.*

MORRIONE, MELCHIOR S., management consultant, accountant; b. Bklyn., Dec. 31, 1937; s. Charles and Dionisia (Eletto) M.; m. Joan Finnerty, June 22, 1968; children—Karyn Morrione Frick, Nicole Morrione. BBA magna cum laude, St. John's U., 1959. CPA, N.J., N.Y. Tax ptnr. Arthur Andersen & Co., N.Y.C., 1959-91; mng. dir. MSM Consulting, LLC, Woodcliff Lake, N.J., 1992—; lectr. in field. Contbr. articles to profl. jours.; mem. editorial bd. Internat. Tax Jour. Served with U.S. Army, 1960-61. Mem. AICPAs, N.Y. State Soc. CPAs, N.J. Soc. CPAs, Internat. Fiscal Assn., Internat. Tax Assn. Republican. Roman Catholic. Clubs: Ridgewood Country (N.J.). Avocations: golf, tennis. Office: MSM Consulting LLC 11 Ginny Dr Woodcliff Lk NJ 07675-8115

MORRIS, ALBERT JEROME, pest control company executive; b. N.Y.C., Jan. 3, 1919; s. Peter and Minnie (Miller) M.; Barbara McLeod, Feb 6, 1943; children: Peter A., Lee Ellen Morris Guenther, Lisa Ann Morris Rasche. BS in Electronics, U. Calif., Berkeley, 1941; MS in Electronics, Stanford U., 1948, Degree of Engr., 1950. Registered profl. engr., Calif. Sr. v.p., co-founder Levinthal Elec. Products, Palo Alto, Calif., 1953-60; pres., dir. Radiation at Stanford, Palo Alto, 1960-63; pres., chief exec. officer Energy Systems Inc., Palo Alto, 1963-66, Genesys Systems Inc., Palo Alto, 1967-84; pres., chief exec. officer Biosys, Palo Alto, 1983-88, chmn. bd., 1989; also chmn. bd. TurboEnergy Systems, Phoenix, 1989-90; chmn. bd., chief exec. officer Neural Systems Corp., Palo Alto, 1991—; cons. to schs. of engring., Stanford U. and 18 other major univs.; chmn. San Francisco coun. Western Electronics Mfrs. Assn., 1965; chmn. bd. Western Electronics Show and Conv., Calif., 1961. Author over 50 papers on ship stabilization, high power electronics, med. electronics and continuing edn. Recipient Best Paper award IEEE/ASEE Frontiers in Edn. Conf., 1978. Fellow IEEE, Sigma Chi Iota; mem. AAAS. Avocation: tennis.

MORRIS, ANN HASELTINE JONES, social welfare administrator; b. Springfield, Mo., Feb. 3, 1941; d. Mansur King and Adelaide (Haseltine) Jones; m. Ronald D. Morris, Nov. 29, 1963 (div. 1990); children: David, Christopher. BA in Edn. and Art, Drury Coll., 1963. Art instr. Ash Grove (Mo.)/Bois D'Arc Pub. Sch. Dist., 1963-64; instr. Drury Coll., Springfield, 1966-67; tchr. Springfield R-12 Sch. Dist., 1974-86; exec. dir. S.W. Ctr. for Ind. Living, Springfield, 1986—; adv. com. Springfield R-12 Spl. Edn., 1993—; tech. cons. and alternative dispute resolution mediator Ams. with Disabilities Act EEOC, Dept. of Justice Network, 1993—. Bd. dirs. Ozark Greenways, 1991-93, Springfield Deaf Relay, 1988-90; adv. task force Allied Health Program Devel. S.W. Bapt Univ., 1988; mem. Drury Coll. Women's Aux., 1984—, conservator of the peace, handicap parking enforcement action team, 1991—; bd. treas. Mo. Parent Act, 1989-91, Diversity Network of the Ozarks, 1990—; svc. coord. Youthnet, 1990—; community adv. bd. Rehab. Svcs., St. John's Regional Health Care Ctr., 1988-91; mem. Springfield Homeless Network, 1989—, others; apptd. to Mo. Gov.'s Coun. on Disability; pres. Statewide Ind. Living Coun. Mem. NOW (sec. 1991), P.E.O., Mo. Assn. of Ctrs. for Ind. Living (v.p. 1990—), Mo. Assn. for Social Welfare (bd. treas. 1989-95), Nat. Assn. of Ind. Living Ctrs. (AIDS task force 1993—), Assn. of Programs for Rural Ind. Living, Nat. Soc. of Fund Raising Execs., Mo. Rehab. Assn., C. of C. (healthcare divsn.), Zeta Tau Alpha. Home: 1748 E Arlington Rd Springfield MO 65804-7742

MORRIS, ARLENE MYERS, marketing professional; b. Washington, Pa., Dec. 29, 1951; d. Frank Hayes Myers and Lula Irene (Slusser) Kolcun; m. John L. Sullivan, Feb. 17, 1971 (div. July 1982); m. David Wellons Morris, July 27, 1984. BA, Carlow Coll., 1974; postgrad., Western New England Coll., 1981-82. Sales rep. Syntex Labs., Inc., Palo Alto, Calif., 1974-77; profl. sales rep. McNeil Pharm., Spring House, Pa., 1977-78, mental health rep., 1978-80, asst. product dir., 1981-82, dist. mgr., 1982-85, new product dir., 1985-87, exec. dir. new bus. devel., 1987-89, v.p. bus. devel., 1989-93; v.p. bus. devel. Scios Inc., Mountain View, Calif., 1993-96, Coulter Pharma., 1996—. Mem. Found. of Ind. Colls., Phila., 1989. Mem. Pharm. Advt. Coun., Am. Diabetes Assn., Am. Acad. Sci., Healthcare Bus. Womens Assn., Lic. Execs. Soc. Home: 11701 Winding Way Los Altos CA 94024-6331 Office: Coulter Pharm 550 California Ave Palo Alto CA 94043-1107

MORRIS, BENJAMIN HUME, lawyer; b. Louisville, Sept. 25, 1917; s. Benjamin Franklin and Mary (Hume) M.; m. Lacy Hibbs Abell, July 7, 1942; children: Benjamin Hume, Lacy Wayne; m. Mary Frances Fowler Gatlin, Nov. 9, 1968. JD, U. Louisville, 1941. Bars: Ky. 1940, U.S. Supreme Ct. 1966. Assoc., Doolan, Helm, Stites & Wood, Louisville, 1941-50; atty. Brown-Forman Distillers Corp., Louisville, 1950-56; resident counsel, 1956-64, v.p., resident counsel, 1964-73, v.p., gen. counsel 1973-81, corp. sec. 1981; pres., dir. Can. Mist Distillers, Ltd., Collingwood, Ont., Can., 1971-81; of counsel Morris, Nicolas, Welsh & Vandeventer, Louisville, 1982-86, Ray & Morris, 1986-89, Ewen, Ray & Morris, 1989, Morris, Hawkins and Dutton, 1990-94, Morris & Dutton, 1995—. Trustee W. L. Lyons Brown Found., 1964—; trustee City of Riverwood, Ky., 1977-81; chmn. Jefferson County Social Svc. Adv. Com., 1959-62; bd. govs. Jefferson Alcohol and Drug Abuse Ctr., 1983-90; past. bd. dirs. Ky. C. of C., Better Bus. Bur. Louisville. Capt. USAF, 1941-45; col. Res. ret. Decorated Air medal with oak leaf cluster; recipient Disting. Alumni award, U. Louisville, 1981, medal of honor Nat. Soc., DAR, 1990. Fellow Am. Coll. Genealogists; mem. Ky. Bar Assn., Ky. Soc. SAR (pres., 1978), Nat. Soc. SAR (v.p. 1980, chancellor gen. 1982-83, sec. gen. 1984, pres. gen. 1985, Minuteman award 1984, Gold Good Citizenship medal 1986), Ky. Distillers Assn. (chmn. 1969), Distilled Spirits Council U.S. (pres. 1973, chmn. 1973-74, chmn. emeritus 1982—), Assn. Can. Distillers (bd. dirs. 1971-81), Soc. Colonial Wars, Soc. of the War of 1812 (v.p. gen. 1987-89, 1992-96, judge advocate gen., 1996, pres. Ky. soc. 1990-92), Soc. Sons and Daus. of the Pilgrims, Mil. Order of World Wars, Sons of the Revolution, Flagon and Trencher Soc., Sons Am. Colonists, Continental Soc., Sons Indian Wars, Americans of Royal Descent, Order of the Crown of Charlemagne in the U.S.. Republican. Presbyterian. Clubs: Louisville Boat, Filson, Reviser, Corp. sect. Banks-Baldwin's Ky. Legal Forms Book, 1982. Home: 2005 High Ridge Rd Louisville KY 40207-1125

MORRIS, BRUCE DORIAN, technical writer, literary historian, educator; b. San Francisco, July 10, 1947; s. William and Helen S. (Jorgensen) M. AA, Coll. San Mateo, Calif., 1968; BA in English and Linguistics, San Francisco State Coll., 1969; MA in English Lit., San Francisco State U., 1972; PhD, U. Denver, 1977. Grad. teaching fellow dept. English U. Denver, 1973-77; asst. instr. Pacific Crest Outward Bound Sch., Portland, Oreg., 1978; jr. tech. writer Harris-Farinon, San Carlos, Calif., 1979-82; sr. tech. writer Verilink Corp., San Jose, Calif., 1985-88, Tektronix Corp., Mountain View, Calif., 1988-90, MorComm Tech. Writing Svcs., Belmont, Calif., 1991—, MorComm Press, Belmont, Calif., 1992—; sr. tech writer Alpha Lab Telco Syss., Fremont, Calif., 1994-96. Author: Sport Climber's Guide to Skyline Boulevard, 1995; editor: Arthur Symons: Letters to Yeats, 1989. Calif. State grad. fellow. Mem. MLA, Internat. Platform Soc., Soc. for Tech. Comm., Irish-Am. Cultural Inst., Am. Alpine Club, Access Fun, Alpha Gamma Sigma. Avocations: rock climbing, bicycle racing. Home and Office: MorComm Press and Tech Writing Svcs 2221 Thurm Ave Belmont CA 94002-1547 Address: 443 Ventura Ave Apt 3 Palo Alto CA 94306

MORRIS, CALVIN CURTIS, architect; b. Champaign, Ill., Mar. 5, 1955; s. Charles Calvin Morris and Audrey Jane (Carr) Johnson; m. Monica Lynn Greco, May 16, 1987; children: Amanda Pauline, Leah Marie. BS in Archtl. Studies, U. Ill., Champaign, 1978. Registered architect, Ill., Mo.; cert. NCARB. Draftsman Archtl. Assocs. Inc., Collinsville, Ill., 1977-78; v.p. Archtl. Assocs. Inc., Collinsville, 1978-88, exec. v.p., 1988-89; prin. AAI/ Campbell, Inc., 1990-95, AAIC Inc., 1996—. Mem. Planning Comm., Collinsville, 1982-88, vice chmn., 1986-88; bd. dirs. Collinsville United Way, 1988-92, Downtown Devel. Commn., 1993-94; mem. Collinsville Econ. Devel. Commn., 1996—, Southwestern Ill. Leadership Coun., 1996—. Named one of Outstanding Young Men of Am. U.S. Jaycees, 1981. Mem. AIA, Nat. Coun. Archtl. Registration Bds., Nat. Trust for Historic Preservation, Soc. Am. Mil. Engrs., Collinsville C. of C. (bd. dirs. 1989-96), Collinsville Kiwanis Club (pres. 1983-85). Democrat. Lutheran. Avocations: camping, fishing, skiing, golf. Office: AAIC Inc 1 Design Mesa Collinsville IL 62234-4639

MORRIS, (WILLIAM) CARLOSS, lawyer, insurance company executive; b. Galveston, Tex., June 7, 1915; s. William Carloss and Willie (Stewart) M.; m. Doris Poole, Dec. 2, 1939; children: Marietta (Mrs. Morgan Maxfield), William Carloss III, Malcolm Stewart, Melinda Louise (Mrs. Glen Ginter). BA with distinction, Rice Inst., 1936; JD with highest honors, U. Tex., 1939. Bar: Tex. 1938. With Stewart Title Guaranty Co., Houston, 1939—, pres., 1951-75, chmn. bd. dirs., chief exec. officer, 1975-91; chmn. bd. dirs., co-chief exec. officer Stewart Info. Services Inc., 1975—; bd. dirs. Morris, Lendais, Hollrah and Snowden, Houston. Chmn. Interdisciplinary Commn. on Housing and Urban Growth, 1974-77; chmn. Star Hope Mission, 1951-90, hon., 1991—; pres. Tex. Safety Assn., 1950-51; bd. dirs. Goodwill Industries; bd. dirs., mem. exec. com. Billy Graham Evangelistic Assn.; chmn. Baylor Coll. Medicine, 1968, trustee, 1952—; trustee, deacon 1st Bapt. Ch., Houston, chmn. bd. deacons, 1987-89; trustee Baylor U., 1952-72, past vice chmn. bd. dirs.; trustee Oldham Little Ch. Found., B.M. Woltman Found. Recipient Book of Golden Deeds award Exch. Club of Houston, 1974, Disting. Svc. awrad Tex. Soc. Sons Am. Revolution, 1988, Gen. Maurice Hirsch award Soc. for Fund Raising Execs., 1988, George Washington Honor medal Freedoms Found. at Valley Forge, 1990; inducted into Tex. Bus. Hall of Fame, 1995. Fellow Am. Bar Found., State Bar Tex. Found.; mem. ABA (past chmn. younger lawyers sect.), Tex. Bar Assn., Tex. Young Lawyers Assn. (past pres.), Chancellors, Order of Coif, Phi Delta Phi, Alpha Tau Omega. Clubs: River Oaks Country, University. Lodge: Kiwanis. Office: 1980 Post Oak Blvd Ste 800 Houston TX 77056-3817

MORRIS, CHARLES ELLIOT, neurologist; b. Denver, Mar. 30, 1929; s. Jacob M. and Lillian Y. M.; m. Naomi Carolyn Minner, June 28, 1951; children: Jonathan E., David C. B.A., U. Denver, 1950, M.A. in Biochemistry, 1951; M.D., U. Colo., 1955. Diplomate: Am. Bd. Psychiatry and Neurology. Intern Los Angeles County Gen. Hosp., 1955-56; resident in neurology, teaching fellow neurology Harvard U. Med. Sch.-Boston City Hosp., 1956-59; mem. faculty U. N.C. Med. Sch., Chapel Hill, 1961-77; prof. neurology and medicine U. N.C. Med. Sch., 1976-77; attending neurologist Guam Meml. Hosp., Tamuning, also neurologist in charge Nat. Inst. Neurol. and Communicative Disorders and Stroke Rsch. Ctr., Agana, 1970-71; prof. neurology, 1976—, chmn. dept. Finch U. Health Scis. Chgo. Med. Sch., acting chief neurology svc. VA Med. Ctr., North Chgo., 1976-91; prof. dept. cell biology and anatomy, 1991-94; prof. neurosci., 1994—; vis. lectr. dept. neurol. scis. Rush Med. Coll., 1994—. Contbr. articles to profl. jours., chpts. to books. Served to lt. comdr. M.C., USNR, 1959-61. Mem. Am. Acad. Neurology, Assn. Rsch. in Nervous and Mental Diseases, AMA, AAAS, Am. Epilepsy Soc., So. Soc. Clin. Investigation, Ill. Med. Soc., Lake County Med. Soc., Sigma Xi, Alpha Omega Alpha, Phi Lambda Upsilon. Office: FUHS/Chgo Med Sch Dept Neurology 3333 Green Bay Rd North Chicago IL 60064-3037

MORRIS, CLAYTON LESLIE, priest; b. Eugene, Oreg., June 23, 1946; s. Joseph William Morris and Betty Fern (Rasmussen) Morris Darby; m. Mary Susan Pacquer, Dec. 30, 1968; children: Andrea Christine, Jonathan William. B Music, Willamette U., 1968; MA in Theology, Grad. Theol. Union, 1971, PhD in Theology, 1986; MDiv, Ch. Div. Sch., 1971. Ordained priest Episcopal Ch., 1971. Assoc. priest St. Andrew's Ch., Saratoga, Calif., 1971-74; rector St. Mark's Ch., King City, Calif., 1974-79; organist, choirmaster St. Paul's Ch., Oakland, Calif., 1979-80; teaching fellow, instr. Ch. Div. Sch., Berkeley, 1979-86; dir. music All Souls Ch., Berkeley, Calif., 1980-86; assoc. rector St. Mark's Ch., Palo Alto, Calif., 1986-91; staff officer liturgy and music Episc. Ch. Ctr., N.Y., 1991—. Mem. N.Am. Acad. Liturgy, Assn. Anglican Musicians, Assn. Diocesan Liturgy and Music Commns., Consultation on Common Texts, Associated Parishes Coun. Office: Episcopal Church Ctr 815 2nd Ave New York NY 10017-4503*

MORRIS, DANIEL KEARNS, journalist; b. Youngstown, Ohio, Jan. 14, 1954; s. John Mackey and Nancy Todd (Kearns) M.; m. Lisa Rachel Herrick, Aug. 25, 1984; children: Sarah Herrick, Nicholas Herrick. Student, Boston U., 1972-73; AB, U. Mich., 1978. VISTA vol. Winnebago (Nebr.) Indian Reservation, 1977-78; editor Pierian Press, Ann Arbor, Mich., 1979-81; pub., editor Alternative Rev. of Lit. and Politics mag., Ann Arbor, 1981-82; press sec. Richard Fellman for U.S. Congress campaign, Omaha, 1982; prodr., editor Nat. Pub. Radio, Washington, 1983-88; prodr. CBS News, Washington, 1988-91, ABC News Nightline, Washington, 1991—. Field organizer McGovern for President, Washington, 1972. Recipient Robert F. Kennedy Journalism award RFK Found., 1988, News and Documentary Emmy award 1994, 95. Home: 6208 31st St NW Washington DC 20015-1518 Office: ABC News 1717 Desales St NW Washington DC 20036-4401

MORRIS, DAVID, retired electrical engineer; b. N.Y.C., July 18, 1924; s. Morris Elia and Esther (Kohn) M.; m. Minnie Kramer, Feb. 2, 1957. BEE, CCNY, 1947, MEE, 1954. Elec. engr. Magnetic Amplifiers Inc., L.I., N.Y., 1951-53; chief engr. Square Root Mfg. Corp., Yonkers, N.Y., 1953-56; sect. head Poly. R&D, Bklyn., 1956-58; chief engr. Brach div. Gen. Bronze Corp., Newark, N.J., 1958-62; unit head Kearfott div. Singer Corp., Little Falls, N.J., 1962-70; group leader Monroe div. Litton Industries, Orange, N.J., 1970-72; sr. mem. tech. staff Lepel High Frequency Labs., Maspeth, N.Y., 1972-80, I.T.T. Avionics, Nutley, N.J., 1980-89; ret., 1989. Contbr. articles to profl. jours.; 7 patents in field. Mem. IEEE (life). Achievements include development of off line transistor switching regulator; radiation hardened hybrid electro-magnetic device for protection of semiconductor circuits; multi-winding power inductor; design of magnetic amplifiers for servo mechanisms used in the Ballistic Missile early warning system; power systems for N.Y. Fire Dept., T.F.X. fighter aircraft, AH64 Apache helicopter. Avocations: experimental physics, classical music, chess. Home: 806 Maple Hill Dr Woodbridge NJ 07095-4109

MORRIS, DESMOND, author; m. Ramona Morris; 1 son. Author: Biology of Art, 1962, Apes and Monkeys, 1965, Big Cats, 1965, Mammals: A Guide to the Living Species, 1966, The Naked Ape, 1968, The Human Zoo, 1969, Patterns of Reproductive Behavior, 1971, Intimate Behavior, 1971, Manwatching: A Field Guide to Human Behavior, 1977, The Soccer Tribe, 1981, The Book of Ages, 1983, The Art of Ancient Cyprus, 1985, Bodywatching: A Field Guide to the Human Species, 1985, The Illustrated Naked Ape, 1986, Catwatching, 1986, Dogwatching, 1986, The Secret Surrealist, 1987, Catlore, 1987, The Animals Roadshow, 1988, The Human Nestbuilders, 1988, Horsewatching, 1988, The Animal Contract, 1990, Animalwatching, 1990, Babywatching, 1991, Christmas Watching, 1992, The World of Animals, 1993, The Human Animal, 1994, Body Talk, A World Guide to Gestures, 1994, The Naked Ape Trilogy, 1994, Illustrated Cat Watching, 1994, Illustrated Babywatching, 1995, Illustrated Dogwatching, 1996, Catworld: A Feline Encyclopedia, 1996; co-author: (with Ramona Morris) Men and Snakes, 1965, Men and Apes, 1966, Men and Pandas, 1966, The Giant Panda, 1981, Gestures: Their Origins and Distribution, 1979; autobiography Animal Days, 1979; editor: Primate Ethology, 1969, (fiction) Inrock, 1983. Address: care Jonathan Cape, 20 Vauxhall Bridge Rd, London SWIV 2SA, England

MORRIS, DONALD, tax specialist; b. Chgo., Oct. 13, 1945; s. Donald Charles and Cathleen (Lautner) M.; m. Sue Morris, Nov. 9, 1990; children: Keith, Sarah. BA, Calif. State U., L.A., 1968; MA, De Paul U., 1972, MS in Taxation, 1987; PhD, So. Ill. U., 1978. CPA, Ill.; CFP. Prof. philosophy John A. Logan Coll., Carterville, Ill., 1972-79; tax mgr. Evans-Gries & Co. CPAs, Addison, Ill., 1980-83; sr. tax advisor Alexander Grant, CPA, Chgo., 1983-84; tax mgr. Evans & Co., Itasca, Ill., 1984-87; pvt. practice CPA Addison, 1987-88, Bloomingdale, 1988-93; Roselle, Ill., 1993-97; asst. prof. acctg. E. N.Mex. U., Portales, 1997—. Author: Dewey and the Behavioristic Context of Ethics, 1995; contbr. chpt. to book. Libertarian candidate for comptroller State of Ill., 1986. Mem. AICPA, Ill. CPA Soc., Am. Philos. Assn., Am. Acctg. Assn., Nat. Bus. Edn. Assn., Chgo. Area Runners Assn., Assn. Informal Logic and Critical Thinking. Avocations: distance running (4 marathons), tennis, wine making, woodworking. Home: 700 Scott Dr Elgin IL 60123-2634 Office: Ea New Mex U Coll of Business Portales NM 88130

MORRIS, DONALD ARTHUR ADAMS, college president; b. Detroit, Aug. 31, 1934; s. Robert Park and Margaret Lymburn (Adams) M.; m. Zella Mae Stormer, June 21, 1958; children: Dwight Joseph, Julie Adams. B.A., Wayne State U., 1961; M.P.A., U. Mich., 1966, Ph.D., 1970; LLD (hon.), Olivet Coll., 1987. Copy boy Detroit Times, 1952-55, reporter, 1955-57, edn. writer, 1957-60; adminstrv. asst. Wayne State U., Detroit, 1960-62; mng. editor news service U. Mich., 1962-64, mgr. spl. programs, 1964-68; mgr. Met. Detroit Devel. Program, 1968-71; v.p. for devel. Hobart and William Smith Colls., Geneva, N.Y., 1971-76; exec. v.p. Hobart and William Smith Colls., 1976-77; pres., prof. polit. sci. Olivet (Mich.) Coll., 1977-92; pres. emeritus Olivet Coll., Mich., 1992—, cons., 1992-93; trustee Mich. Intercollegiate Athletic Assn., 1977-92, Assn. Ind. Colls. and Univs. Mich., 1977-92, chair, 1984-85; cons. evaluator North Ctrl. Assn. Colls. and Schs., 1986-92; mem. Mich. Jud. Tenure Commn., 1991-94; mem. Newspaper Guild of Detroit, 1952-60, exec. bd., 1958-60. Contbr. articles to profl. jours. Trustee Olivet Coll., 1977-92, Mich. Coll. Found., 1977-92, exec. com., 1989-92; trustee Ecumenical Inst. Jewish-Christian Studies, 1988-89; mem. Mich. Higher Edn. Assistance and Student Loan Authorities, 1986—, chair, 1989-94; bd. dirs. Planned Parenthood of Finger Lakes, N.Y., 1973-77, pres., 1975-77; bd. dirs., treas. Genesee Regional Family Planning Program N.Y., 1975-77; trustee Coun. Higher Edn., United Ch. of Christ, 1977-92, mem. exec. com., 1982-92, chair, 1986-88; trustee Glen Lake Cmty. Libr. Bd., 1993—, pres., 1994—; mem. Sleeping Bear Noontiders, 1993—, sec., 1995, v.p. 1996-97, pres., 1997—, South Manitou Meml. Soc., 1980—, chair nominating com., 1997. Mem. Am. Assn. for Higher Edn., Sigma Delta Chi, Omicron Delta Kappa, Alpha Lambda Epsilon, Kappa Sigma Alpha, Gamma Iota Sigma, Alpha Mu Gamma, Phi Mu Alpha Sinfonia, Rotary (local pres. 1987-88, Paul Harris fellow). Congregationalist. Home: 8330 S Dunns Farm Rd Maple City MI 49664-8721 also: 6551 E Dorado Blvd Tucson AZ 85715-4705

MORRIS, DOROTHEA LOUISE, nurse midwife; b. Emporia, Kans., Oct. 30, 1944; d. Clarence Earl and Dorothy Ann (Draper) Richardson; m. David B. DeKalb, May 1, 1966 (div. Dec. 1981); children: Michele E. DeKalb, Cheryl L. Lines, David B. DeKalb Jr.; m. James Henry Morris, July 4, 1984. Diploma, Beth-El Sch. Nursing, Colorado Springs, Colo., 1966; BSN, Alaska Meth. U., 1975; MPA, Troy State U., 1988; MSN, U. N.Mex., 1990. RN Colo., N. Mex. Commd. 2d lt. USAF, 1977, advanced through grades to lt. col.; staff nurse Meml. Hosp., Colorado Springs, 1966-67; staff nurse, supr. Albany (Oreg.) Gen. Hosp., 1969; staff nurse, obstetrics Harrisonville (Mo.) Hosp., 1970, USAF Hosp., Anchorage, 1970-75; staff nurse, instr. BOCES, Verona, N.Y., 1976-77; staff nurse, instr. ADN program Mohawk Valley C.C., Utica, N.Y., 1976-77; staff nurse obstetrics Chanute AFB, Rantoul, Ill., 1977-79; nurse-midwife Homestead AFB (Fla.) Hosp., 1980-85, Weisbaden (Germany) Regional Med. Ctr., 1985-88; nurse-midwife, instr. Midwifery Sch., Andrews AFB, Md., 1990—; asst. dir. Air Force Nurse-Midwifery Program, Andrews AFB, 1991—; pres. CNM Svc. Dirs., Inc., 1995-97. Lt. col. USAF, 1977—. Mem. Am. Coll. Nurse Midwives (cert.), Nurses Assn. Obstetrics and Gynecology, NANP in Reproductive Health, Uniformed Nurse Practitioner Assn., Order Ea. Star. Baptist. Avocations: painting, knitting, crocheting. Home: 4024-2 Ashwood Cir Andrews AFB MD 20762 Office: SGHOM Malcolm Grow 89 MDOS/SGOGM Andrews Air Force Base MD 20762

MORRIS, DOUGLAS PETER, recording company executive; b. Far Rockaway, N.Y., Nov. 23, 1938; s. Walter and Mary (Lerner) M.; m. Monique Jequel, Mar. 20, 1964; children: Walter, Peter. B.A., Columbia Coll., 1960. Gen. mgr. Robert Mellin, Inc., N.Y.C., 1964-65; v.p., gen. mgr. Laurie Records, Inc., N.Y.C., 1965-69; owner Big Tree Records, N.Y.C., 1969-79; pres. Atlantic Records, N.Y.C., 1980—, chief oper. officer, 1989-94; chmn., CEO, COO, pres. Warner Music-U.S., 1994-95; chmn., CEO MCA Music Ent., N.Y.C.; cons. Ampex Records, 1968. Composer: songs Sweet Talkin Guys, 1968, Smoking in the Boys' Room, 1970. Served with U.S. Army, 1962-64. Recipient scholarship Paragon Oil, 1954, scholarship Columbia Coll., 1960; named Man of Yr. in Record Industry United Jewish Appeal, 1981. Mem. ASCAP. Office: MCA Music Ent 1755 Broadway 7th Flr New York NY 10019-6908*

MORRIS, EARLE ELIAS, JR., state official, business executive; b. Greenville, S.C., July 14, 1928; s. Earle Elias and Bernice (Carey) M.; m. Jane L. Boroughs, Apr. 12, 1958; children: Lynda Lewis, Carey Mauldin, Elizabeth McDaniel, Earle Elias III; m. Carol Telford, Oct. 4, 1972; 1 son, David Earle. BS, Clemson Coll., 1949, LLD; D.Pub. Svc. (hon.), U. S.C., 1980, S.C. State Coll., 1990; Dr. Med. Sci., U. S.C.; LLD (hon.), The Citadel, Cen. Wesleyan Coll.; HHD (hon.), Lander Coll., Francis Marion Coll., 1984, U. Charleston, 1992. Pres., chmn. bd. Morris & Co., Inc. (wholesale grocers), Pickens, S.C.; v.p., dir. Pickens Bank, 1956-69, Bankers Trust S.C., Pickens, 1968-75; pres. Gen. Ins. Agy., Pickens, 1970—; sec. Carolina Investors, Inc., chmn., 1993—; ptnr. Morris Realty Co., Pickens; mem. S.C. Ho. of Reps., 1950-54, S.C. Senate, 1954-70; lt. gov. State of S.C., 1971-75, comptr. gen., 1976—; chmn. bd. Santee Cooper Fisheries (Far East) Ltd., Hong Kong, Tai Pan Technologies, Ltd., Hong Kong; dir. Brunswick Worsted Mills, S.C. Devel. Corp., Pickens Savs. & Loan Assn. Pres. Clemson U. Found., 1984-85; state dir. Selective Svc. Sys. Served to brig. gen. S.C. N.G., maj. gen. S.C. S.G. Decorated Legion of Merit, Meritorious Svc. medals; recipient Algernon Sydney Sullivan award, 1980, Donald L. Scantlebury award, 1985, Nations Most Valuable Pub. Ofcl. award, 1993, Pub. Svc. award Am. Legion, 1993; named Disting. Alumnus, Clemson Coll. Mem. Nat. Assn. State Comptrollers (pres. 1982), Nat. Assn. State Auditors, Comptrollers and Treasurers (pres. 1988-89), S.C. Nat. Guard Assn. (pres. 1980-81), S.C. Jr. C. of C., S.C. Rehab. Assn. (v.p.), Govtl. Acctg. Standards Adv. Coun. (chmn. 1989-96), Fin. Acctg. Found. (trustee 1985-88, 96—), Blue Key, Palmetto Club, Faculty Club (Columbia), Poinsett Club (Greenville), Masons, Shriners, Lions, Order of Saint Stanislas (grand chancellor, Knight Grand Cross), Order of white Eagle of Saint Stanislas, Sovereign Mil. Order Swabia, Order of Polonia Restituta (knight comdr., 2d class), Knights of Malta, Order of Niadh Nask. Presbyterian (elder, former deacon, synod trustee). Home: 159 Lake Murray Ter Lexington SC 29072-9103 Office: Office of Comptr Gen State of SC Columbia SC 29211 *In my personal, public and professional life I have tried to follow the Biblical admonition of "loving mercy, doing justly, and walking humbly."*

MORRIS, EDWIN ALEXANDER, retired apparel manufacturing company executive; b. Concord, N.C., Aug. 13, 1903; s. William Lee M. and Martha Margaret (Ervin) M.; m. Mary Ella Cannon, Nov. 1, 1933; children: Joseph E., Mary Lou (dec.). BS in Commerce, Washington and Lee U., 1926. Joined Blue Bell, Inc., Greensboro, N.C., 1937; pres., chief exec. officer Blue Bell, Inc., 1948-66, chmn. bd., chief exec. officer, 1966-74, chmn. bd., 1974-81, dir., 1940-81. Bd. dirs. emeritus N.C. Citizens Assn., The Jesse Helms Ctr. Found., Wingate Coll, N.C.; trustee emeritus Wesley Long Hosp., Greensboro, 1958-83; bd. dirs. Nat. Taxpayers Union, Washington, Students for Am., Raleigh, N.C., 1990-94, The John Locke Found., Raleigh, 1992-94, N.C. Taxpayers United, Raleigh; bd. overseers Duke Comprehensive Cancer Ctr., Durham, 1985—. Presbyterian. Clubs: Greensboro Country, Greensboro City. Office: 400 W Market St Ste 408 Greensboro NC 27401-2241

MORRIS, EDWIN THADDEUS, construction consultant; b. N.Y.C., Jan. 13, 1912; s. Edwin T. and Helen (Hughes) M.; m. Winifred Walsh, Apr. 23, 1938; children: Edwin Thaddeus, Joan M., David M., Patrick J. Student, Manhattan Coll., 1928-30. Field engr. Madigan Hyland Cons. Engrs., 1936-37; supt. Raymond Concrete Pile Co., 1937-43; project mgr., gen. supt., officer subsidary Raymond Internat. Companies, 1946-58; v.p. Raymond Internat., Inc. (and subsidiaries), 1958-60, sr. v.p. overseas heavy constrn. div., 1960-66; pres., dir. Balt. Contractors, Inc., 1966-76; pres. Edwin T. Morris Constrn. Consultants, Inc., Towson, Md., 1976—. Served to lt., C.E. USNR, 1943-46. Clubs: Explorers (N.Y.C.), Moles (N.Y.C.). Home: 7927 Ruxway Rd Towson MD 21204-3515

MORRIS, ELIZABETH TREAT, physical therapist; b. Hartford, Conn., Feb. 20, 1936; d. Charles Wells and Marion Louise (Case) Treat; BS in Phys. Therapy, U. Conn., 1960; m. David Breck Morris, July 10, 1961; children: Russell Charles, Jeffrey David. Phys. therapist Crippled Children's Clinic No. Va., Arlington, 1960-62, Shriners Hosp. Crippled Children, Salt Lake City, 1967-69, Holy Cross Hosp., Salt Lake City, 1970-74; pvt. practice phys. therapy, Salt Lake City, 1975—. Mem. nominating com. YWCA, Salt Lake City. Mem. Am. Phys. Therapy Assn., Am. Congress Rehab. Medicine, Am. Alliance for Health Phys. Edn. Recreation & Dance, Nat. Speakers Assn., Utah Speakers Assn., Salt Lake Area C. of C., Friendship Force Utah, U.S. Figure Skating Assn., Toastmasters Internat., Internat. Assn. for the Study Pain, Internat. Platform Assn., World Confederation Phys. Therapy, Medart Internat. Home: 4177 Mathews Way Salt Lake City UT 84124-4021 Office: PO Box 526186 Salt Lake City UT 84152-6186

MORRIS, EUGENE JEROME, lawyer; b. N.Y.C., Oct. 14, 1910; s. Max and Regina (Cohn) M.; m. Terry Lesser, Mar. 28, 1934 (dec. Sept. 1993); 1 child, Richard S.; m. Blanche Bier Funke, June 22, 1994. B.S.S., CCNY, 1931; LL.B., St. John's U., 1934. Bar: N.Y. 1935. Practiced N.Y.C., 1935—; sr. and founding partner firm Demov, Morris & Hammerling, 1946-87; v.p., sr. counsel Ea. region Am. Title Ins. Co., N.Y.C., 1990-93; of counsel Spector & Feldman, 1991—; adj. prof. land use regulation NYU Grad. Sch. Pub. Adminstrn., 1978-81; adj. prof. legal issues in real estate, Real Estate Inst. NYU, 1988—; spl. master Supreme Ct. State of N.Y., 1979—; arbitrator Civil Ct. N.Y., 1994—. Editor weekly column N.Y. Law Jour., 1965-87, It's the Law, Real Estate Forum, 1982-87; editor-in-chief N.Y. Practice Guide: Real Estate, 4 vols., 1986, Real Estate Development, 4 vols., 1987; contbr. articles to profl. jours. Mem. N.Y. State Tax Revision Commn., 1977-80, N.Y.C. Rent Guidelines Bd., 1983-85. Served with AUS, 1943-45. Recipient Justice award N.Y. sect. Am. Jewish Congress, 1996. Mem. ABA (chmn. spl. com. housing and urban devel. 1970-73, coun. sect. real property, probate and trust law 1971-74, assoc. editor Real Property, Probate and Trust Jour. 1979-86, editor Real Property, Probate and Property mag., articles editor 1986-94), Am. Judges Assn., Assn. Bar City N.Y. (chmn. com. housing and urban devel. 1971-74, com. on lectures and continuing edn. 1980-83, coun. on jud. adminstrn. 1989-92), N.Y. State Bar Assn. (exec. com. 1980—, chmn. com. meetings and lectures 1982-92, CLE com. 1984-90, ho. of dels. 1986-95, co-editor Real Property Jour. 1995—), Citizens Union, Lambda Alpha (bd. dirs. 1990—, pres. N.Y. chpt. 1990-93, sec. 1993-95, treas. 1996—). Home: 200 Central Park S New York NY 10019-1415 *After 60 years of marriage and 62 years of practicing law, I feel I am ready for retirement. However, like the old fire horse when the bell rings I run; thus I am still teaching real estate law as an Adjunct Professor at the New York Universitsy Real Estate Institute, am counsel to my firm and stay active in bar associations, civic groups and fraternities.*

MORRIS, FLORENCE HENDERSON, auditor; b. Mobile, Ala., Sept. 8, 1964; d. Thomas Gordan Henderson and Joanne Elizabeth (Pfleger) Martin; m. Fred S. Morris, July 28, 1995. BS in Fin., U. Ala., 1986. Payment and receipt rep. SouthTrust Bank of Mobile, 1988-89; internal bank auditor SouthTrust Corp., Birmingham, 1989-90, compliance audit officer, 1990-92; prin. compliance auditor, asst. v.p. SouthTrust Corp. and SouthTrust Bank of Ga., Atlanta, 1992-95; compliance audit supr., v.p. SouthTrust Corp., Birmingham, 1995—. Mem. Inst. Internal Auditors, Bankers Adminstrn. Inst. (cert. bank compliance officer), Am. Bankers Assn., Ala. Fin. Assn., U. Ala. Alumna, Delta Sigma Pi. Office: SouthTrust Corp Audit Dept PO Box 2554 Birmingham AL 35290

MORRIS, FRANK EUGENE, banker; b. Detroit, Dec. 30, 1923; s. Frank and Beatrice (Perkins) M.; m. Geraldine Elizabeth Coltharp, Dec. 22, 1944; children—Susan, Lisa, Betsy. B.A., Wayne U., 1948; M.A., U. Mich., 1949, Ph.D. in Econs, 1955. Research dir. Investment Bankers Assn., Washington, 1955-61; asst. to sec. debt mgmt. Treasury Dept., 1961-63; v.p. Loomis Sayles and Co., Boston, 1963-68; pres. Fed. Res. Bank Boston, 1968-88; Peter Drucker prof. mgmt. Boston Coll., 1989-94; tchg. fellow U. Mich., 1949-51; bd. dirs. Thermo Electron Corp., Thermo Remediation Corp.; trustee SEI Mut. Funds. Served to 1st lt. USAAF, 1943-45.

MORRIS, G. RONALD, industrial executive; b. East St. Louis, Ill., Aug. 30, 1936; s. George H. and Mildred C. M.; m. Margaret Heino, June 20, 1959; children: David, Michele, James. B.S. in Metall. Engring, U. Ill., 1959. Metall. engr. Delco-Remy div. Gen. Motors Corp., 1959-60; factory metallurgist Dubuque Tractor Works, John Deere Co., Iowa, 1960-66; with Fed.-Mogul Corp., 1966-79, v.p., group mgr. ball and roller bearing group, 1979; pres. Tenneco Automotive div. Tenneco, Inc., Deerfield, Ill., 1979-82; pres., chief exec. officer PT Components, Inc., Indpls., 1982-88; vice-chmn. Rexnord Corp., Indpls., 1988-89; chmn., pres., chief exec. officer CTP Holdings Inc., 1986-88; chmn. Integrated Technologies, Inc., Indpls., 1990-92, also bd. dirs.; pres., chief exec. officer Western Industries, Inc., Milw., 1991—, also bd. dirs.; bd. dirs. Milnot Holding Corp., St. Louis, NN Ball & Roller, Inc., Erwin, Tenn.; corp. bd. dirs. Milw. Sch. of Engring. Mem. Pres.'s Coun., U. Ill.; corp. bd. dirs. Milw. Sch. of Engring. Mem. ASM, SAE, Meridian Hills Country Club (Indpls.), Exmoor Country Club (Highland Park, Ill.), The Landings Club (Savannah, Ga.), Blue Mound Golf and Country Club (Wauwatosa, Wis.), Elks, Masons. Republican. Presbyterian. Office: Western Industries Inc 1215 N 62nd St Milwaukee WI 53213-2915

MORRIS, GERALD DOUGLAS, newspaper editor; b. Boston, May 7, 1937; s. George Christopher and Lucy Bell (MacPhee) M.; m. Elaine Louise Owen, Nov. 13, 1964 (div. 1976); children: Laura Louise, Douglas Owen; m. Mary Elizabeth Simpson Stevens, Apr. 15, 1977; children: Jeffrey David Stevens Morris, Wendy Elizabeth Stevens Morris. Student, Boston U., 1959. Reporter Patriot Ledger, Quincy, Mass., 1961-66; copy editor Boston Globe, 1966—, travel editor, 1989—; syndicated columnist Globe-Trotting, 1970—. Author: Boston Globe Guide to Boston, 1989, New England under Sail, 1993, Epiten: Guide to Cape Cod, 1995. Chmn. Canton (Mass.) Cable Adv. Bd., 1990-92; bd. dirs. Lowell Thomas Found., 1997. With U.S. Army, 1959-61. Mem. Soc. Am. Travel Writers, Skal Club Boston, Lions (pres. Canton 1969-70, 80-81). Avocations: photography, travel. Home: 78 Cheney St Orange MA 01364-1603 Office: Globe Newspaper Co 135 Morrissey Blvd Boston MA 02125-3310

MORRIS, GRANT HAROLD, law educator; b. Syracuse, N.Y., Dec. 10, 1940; s. Benjamin and Caroline Grace (Judelson) M.; m. Phyllis Silberstein, July 4, 1967; children: Joshua, Sara. A.B., Syracuse U. (N.Y.), 1962, J.D., 1964; LL.M., Harvard U., 1971. Bar: N.Y. 1964. Atty. N.Y. Mental Hygiene Law Recodification Project, Inst. Public Adminstrn., N.Y.C., 1964-66; mem. faculty Wayne State U. Law Sch., 1967-73, prof. law, 1970-73, dean acad. affairs, 1971-73; prof. law U. San Diego Law Sch., 1973—, Univ. prof., 1996-97, acting dean, 1977-78, 88-89, assoc. dean grad. legal edn., 1978-81, interim dean, 1997—; prof. law in psychiatry Wayne State U. Med. Sch., 1970-73; adj. prof. U. Calif. San Diego Med. Sch., 1974-84, clin. prof., 19846; legal counsel Mich. Legis. Com. to Revise Mental Health Statutes, 1970-73; organizer law and psychiatry sect. Assn. Am. Law Schs., 1973, chmn., 1973-74; patients advocate, San Diego County, 1977-78; cons. Criminal Code Commn., Ariz. Legis., 1974; reporter task force on guidelines governing roles of mental health profls. in criminal process Am. Bar Assn. standing com. on assn. standards for criminal justice, 1981-84; cert. rev. hearing officer San Diego Superior Ct., 1984-90, ct. commr./judge pro tem, 1990-92, mental health hearing officer, 1992—; hearing officer San Diego Housing Commn., 1988-92; mem. exec. com. sect. law and mental disability Assn. Am. Law Schs., 1990—. Author: The Insanity Defense: A Blueprint for Legislative Reform, 1975; co-author: Mental Disorder in the Criminal Process: Stan Stress and the Vietnam/Sports Conspiracy, 1993; editor, contbr.: The Mentally Ill and the Right to Treatment, 1970. Mem. Phi Alpha Delta (faculty adv. 1970-73, 75-92). Home: 8515 Nottingham Pl La Jolla CA 92037-2125 Office: U San Diego Law Sch 5998 Alcala Park San Diego CA 92110-2429

MORRIS, GREG JAMES, advertising executive; b. Topeka, Jan. 25, 1956; s. James A. and Patricia A. (Souders) M.; m. Joyce L. Izynski, Feb. 25, 1978; children: Chad, Jason, Jonathon. BA in Telecomm., Ind. U., 1978. Account exec. WIBC Radio, Indpls, 1978-81, 85-88, WNDE Radio, Indpls, 1981-84; nat. sales mgr. WIBC/WKLR Radio, Indpls, 1988-89; gen. sales mgr. WKLR Radio, Indpls, 1989-91; advt. dir. Indpls. Bus. Jour., 1991—; v.p., dir. sales WTPI/WMYS, WZPL radio, Indpls., 1996—. Mem. Advt. Club Indpls., Phi Delta Theta. Republican. Avocations: tennis, golf, movies. Home: 11853 Stoney Bay Cir Carmel IN 46033-9501 Office: Indpls Bus Jour 431 N Pennsylvania St Indianapolis IN 46204-1806 Other Office: WTPI/WMYS/WZPL Radio 9245 N Meridian St Indianapolis IN 46260

MORRIS, HENRY ALLEN, JR., publisher; b. Moncks Corner, S.C., Feb. 9, 1940; s. Henry Allen Sr. and Edith Luther (Wall) M.; divorced; 1 child, Anthony Duane Allen. A in Acctg., Palmer Jr. Coll., Charleston, S.C., 1959; BA in English cum laude, Belmont Abbey Coll., N.C., 1974. Office mgr. Gas Engine and Electric Co., Charleston, 1959; cargo coord. S.C. State Ports Authority, Charleston, 1959-70; headmaster St. Stephen Acad., S.C., 1973-77; gen. mgr. The Berkeley Democrat, Moncks Corner, 1977-86, owner, 1989—; pub., editor Berkeley Ind., Moncks Corner, 1987—; pres. Berkeley Pub. Inc., Moncks Corner, 1987—. Author: (short story) The Easter Gift, 1973. Bd. dirs. Council of Govts. Regional Forum, Charleston, 1987, Winthrop Coll., 1983, Moncks Corner Downtown, Inc., 1986-87; mem. Moncks Corner City Council, 1983-88; mayor pro tem, 1986-88; commr. S.C. Vocat. Rehab. Agy.; treas. bd. dirs. Berkeley County YMCA; founder Charleston Opera Corp. Recipient Pres. award Berkeley Arts Council, 1985, Charleston Jaycees, 1971, Friend of Edn. award Berkeley County Sch. System, 1991; named Handicapped Man of Yr., Moncks Corner's Mayor's Com., 1990. Mem. Low County Soc. Profl. Journalists (pres.), S.C. Mcpl. Assn. (lesis. com.), Berkeley C. of C. (tourism com.), Moncks Corner Bus. Assn., Trident United Way (mem. exec. bd. 1983-91), Trident C. of C. (bd. dirs.), Rotary (past pres.). Episcopalian. Avocations: reading, painting, collecting art. Home: 117 Merrimack Dr Moncks Corner SC 29461-3580

MORRIS, HENRY MADISON, JR., education educator; b. Dallas, Oct. 6, 1918; s. Henry Madison and Ida (Hunter) M.; m. Mary Louise Beach, Jan. 24, 1940; children: Henry Madison III, Kathleen Louise, John David, Andrew Hunter, Mary Ruth, Rebecca Jean. BS with distinction, Rice Inst., 1939; MS, U. Minn., 1948, PhD, 1950; LLD, Bob Jones U., 1966; LittD, Liberty U., 1989. Registered profl. engr., Tex. Jr. engr. Tex. Hwy. Dept., 1938-39; from jr. engr. to asst. engr. Internat. Boundary Commn., El Paso, 1939-42; instr. civil engring. Rice Inst., 1942-46; from instr. to asst. prof. U. Minn., Mpls., also research project leader St. Anthony Falls Hydraulics Lab., 1946-51; prof., head dept. civil engring. Southwestern La. Inst., Lafayette, 1951-57, Va. Poly. Inst., Blacksburg, 1957-70; v.p. acad. affairs Christian Heritage Coll., San Diego, 1970-78, pres., 1978-80; dir. Inst. for Creation Rsch., 1970-80, pres., 1980-96, pres. emeritus, 1996—. Author: (with Richard Stephens) Report on Rio Grande Water Conservation Investigation, 1942, That You Might Believe, 1946, 2d edit., 1978, (with Curtis Larson) Hydraulics of Flow in Culverts, 1948, The Bible and Modern Science, 1951, rev. edit., 1968, (with John C. Whitcomb) The Genesis Flood, 1961, Applied Hydraulics in Engineering, 1963, The Twilight of Evolution, 1964, Science, Scripture and Salvation, 1965, 2d edit., 1971, Studies in The Bible and Science, 1966, Evoluation and the Modern Christian, 1967, Biblical Cosmology and Modern Science, 1970, The Bible has the Answer, 1971, Science and Creation: A Handbook for Teachers, 1971, (with J. M. Wiggert) Applied Hydraulics, 1972, A Biblical Manual on Science and Creation, 1972, The Remarkable Birth of Planet Earth, 1973, Many Infallible Proofs, 1974, 2d edit., 1996, Scientific Creationism, 1974, 2d edit., 1985, Troubled Waters of Evolution, 1975, The Genesis Record, 1976, Education for the Real World, 1977, 3d edit., 1991, The Scientific Case for Creation, 1977, The Beginning of the World, 1977, 2d edit., 1991, Sampling the Psalms, 1978, 2d edit., 1991, King of Creation, 1980, Men of Science, Men of God, 1982, 2d edit. 1988, Evolution in Turmoil, 1982, The Revelation Record, 1983, History of Modern Creationism, 1984, 2d edit., 1993, The Biblical Basis for Modern Science, 1984, Creation and the Modern Christian, 1985, Science and the Bible, 1986, Days of Praise, 1986, The God Who is Real, 1988, The Remarkable Record of Job, 1988 (with Martin Clark) The Bible Has the Answer, 2d edit., 1987; (with Gary E. Parker) What is Creation Science?, 1982, 2d edit., 1988, The Long War Against God, 1989, (with John D. Morris), Science, Scripture and the Young Earth, 1989, The Bible Science and Creation, 1991, Creation and the Second Coming, 1991, Biblical Creationism, 1993, The Defender's Bible, 1995, The Modern Creation Trilogy, 1996, Wonderful Words of Life, 1997. Fellow AAAS, ASCE, Am. Sci. Affiliation; mem. Am. Soc. Engring. Edn. (sec.-editor civil engring. divsn. 1967-70), Trans-Nat. Assn. Christian Schs. (pres. 1983-95), Creation Rsch. Soc. (pres. 1967-73), Am. Geophys. Union, Geol. Soc. Am., Am. Assn. Petroleum Geologists, Geochem. Soc., Gideons (pres. La. 1954-56), Phi Beta Kappa, Sigma Xi, Chi Epsilon, Tau Beta Pi. Baptist. Home: 6733 El Banquero Pl San Diego CA 92119-1129 *The Bible is the inerrant word of God and thus should be believed and obeyed in all things.*

MORRIS, HERBERT, lawyer, educator; b. N.Y.C., July 28, 1928; s. Peter and Minnie (Miller) M.; m. Virginia Ann Grenier, Apr.3, 1956 (div. Nov. 1977); children: Jacob Jeremy, Benjamin John.; m. Margery Ruth Maslon, June 8, 1980. A.B., UCLA, 1951; LL.B., Yale, 1954; D. Phil., Oxford (Eng.) U., 1956. Bar: Calif. 1958. Mem. faculty UCLA, 1956—, prof. philosophy and law, 1962—, dean div. humanities, 1983-92, interim provost Coll. Letters and Sci., 1992-93; rsch. clin. assoc. So. Calif. Psychoanalytic Inst., 1977-89; retired, 1994. Editor: Freedom and Responsibility, 1961, The Masked Citadel, 1968, Guilt and Shame, 1971, On Guilt and Innocence, 1976. Home: 233 S Medio Dr Los Angeles CA 90049-3911 Office: UCLA Sch Law 405 Hilgard Ave Los Angeles CA 90095-9000

MORRIS, JAMES ALOYSIUS, economist, educator; b. Lawrence, Mass., May 25, 1918; s. George Thomas and Elizabeth (Reardon) M.; m. Marjorie Leila Frampton, May 30, 1942 (dec. Jan. 1993); children: Stephen Frampton, Elizabeth Harvey; m. Frances Harvey Chalk, Sept. 24, 1994. B.A. with high honors, Northeastern U., 1942, LL.D., 1968; A.M., Harvard U., 1947, Ph.D., 1951; Litt.D., Coll. Charleston, 1970; L.H.D., Lander Coll., 1971, Francis Marion Coll., 1982. Adj. prof. U. S.C., Columbia, 1947-51; assoc. prof. U. S.C., 1951-56, prof. econs., dir. grad. studies, dir. Econ. Rsch. Bur., 1956-61, dean Sch. Bus. Adminstrn., 1961-66, v.p. advanced studies and research, dean Grad. Sch., 1966-68, chmn. faculty com. on admissions and athletics, Disting. prof., 1972-77; econ. cons., 1977—; commr. S.C. Commn. on Higher Edn., 1968-72, Edn. Commn. of the States, 1968-72, So. Regional Edn. Bd.; past chmn. bd. dirs., exec. com. S.C. Blue Cross-Blue Shield; past vice chmn. Gov.'s Productivity Coun.; past chmn. Charlotte br. Fed. Res. Bank, Rep. Nat. Bank; labor arbitrator Fed. Mediation Svcs., Am. Arbitration Assn., 1948—; vis. rsch. prof. Nuffield Coll., Oxford U., 1953-54; cons. to dir. ICA, 1955; spl. econ. adviser to dir. USOM, Turkey, 1956-57; past chmn. S.C. Regional Export Expansion Coun.; past mem. Nat. Export Expansion Coun.; past mem. Gov.'s Task Force on the Economy, Gov.'s Adv. Group on Health Planning; past chmn. Gov.'s Adv. Group on Mental Health Planning; past chmn. bd. S.C. Bd. Econ. Advisers, S.C. Law Inst.; adv. bd. dirs. Earth Sci. Rsch. Inst., Heathwood Hall Episc. Sch.; pres. Carolina Econ. Assocs. Inc., 1979—. Author: Woolen and Worsted Manufacturing in the Southern Piedmont, 1952; contbr. articles and revs. to profl. jours. Bd. dirs. United Comty. Svcs., S.C. Coun. Econs. Edn., 1988-94; pres. emeritus U. S.C. Ednl. Found.; past chmn. bd. dirs. Nat. Lab. Higher Edn.; past mem. corp., Northeastern U., mem. nat. coun., 1969—; trustee Episc. Divsn. Upper S.C., 1988—; bd. trustees Richland Meml. Hosp., 1995—; mem. adv. bd. Still Hopes Episcopal Home; mem. bd. The Heritage Assn., 1995—. Lt. col. U.S. Army, 1940-41, 42-46. Mem. Am. Econ. Assn., So. Econ. Assn., Nat. Assn. Bus. Economists, Am. Arbitration Assn., Forum Club, Forest Lake Country Club, Palmetto Club, Rotary. Episcopalian. Home: 1829 Senate St Columbia SC 29201-3837 Office: U SC Columbia SC 29208

MORRIS, JAMES CARL, architect; b. Richmond, Va., Sept. 2, 1930; s. James Carl and Florence Virginia (Hey) M.; m. Frances Parrott Wooten, June 9, 1952; children: James Carl Jr., David Palmer. Student, N.C. State U., 1948-50; BS in Bldg. Constrn., Va. Polytechnic Inst., 1952. Cert. Nat. Coun. Archtl. Registration Bds. Archtl. draftsman Va. Electric & Power Co., Richmond, Va., 1955-56, Marcellus, Wright & Son, Richmond, 1956-57; architect C.W. Huff, Jr., Richmond, 1957; ptnr. to prin./owner Huff-Morris Architects, Richmond, 1966—; pres. Point of Rocks Devel. Corp., Chesterfield, Va., 1986—; ptnr. Rivermont Assocs., Chesterfield, 1987—, JCM Partnership, Chesterfield, 1988—. Contbr. articles to profl. jours. Bd. dirs. Chesterfield Preservation Commn.; deacon Branch's Ch., Richmond, 1986-90; chmn. Va. Bapt. Extension Bd., Richmond, 1991—. With U.S. Army, 1953-54. Recipient award of Merit S.S. Bd. of So. Bapt., Nashville, Excellence in Masonry Design award Va. Masonry Coun., Richmond. Mem. AIA (past pres. Richmond chpt.), Interfaith Forum on Religion, Art & Architecture, Commonwealth Club of Va. Avocations: woodworking, fishing, hunting. Office: Huff-Morris Arch PC 8 N 1st St Richmond VA 23219-2102

MORRIS, JAMES MALACHY, lawyer; b. Champaign, Ill., June 5, 1952; s. Walter Michael and Ellen Frances (Solon) M.; m. Mary Delilah Baker, Oct. 17, 1987; children: James Malachy Jr., Elliot Rice Baker, Walter Michael. Student, Oxford U. (Eng.), 1972; BA, Brown U., 1974; JD, U. Pa., 1977. Bar: N.Y. 1978, U.S. Dist. Ct. (so. and ea. dists.) N.Y. 1978, Ill. 1980, U.S. Tax Ct. 1982, U.S. Supreme Ct. 1983; admitted to Barristers Chambers, Manchester, Eng., 1987. Assoc. Reid & Priest, N.Y.C., 1977-80; sr. law clk. Supreme Ct. Ill., Springfield, 1980-81; assoc. Carter, Ledyard & Milburn, N.Y.C., 1981-83; sole practice N.Y.C., 1983-87; counsel FCA, Washington, 1987—; acting sec., gen. counsel FCS Ins. Corp., McLean, Va., 1990—; cons. Internat. Awards Found., Zurich, 1981—, Pritzker Architecture Prize Found., N.Y.C., 1981—, Herbert Oppenheimer, Nathan & VanDyck, London, 1985—. Contbr. articles to profl. jours. Mem. ABA, Ill. Bar Assn., N.Y. State Bar Assn., N.Y. County Lawyers Assn., Assn. Bar City N.Y., Brit. Inst. Internat. and Comparative Law, Lansdowne Club (London), Decatur (Ill.) Club. Office: PO Box 1407 Mc Lean VA 22101-1407

MORRIS, JAMES MATTHEW, history educator; b. Reed City, Mich., July 13, 1935; s. Fred Michael and Florence C. (Weiland) M.; m. Nancy Christina Becker, Aug. 23, 1958; children: Patrick J., Anne C., Michael J., John E., Joseph A., Mary Jane. BA, Aquinas Coll., 1957; MA, Central Mich. U., 1962; PhD, U. of Cin., 1969. High sch. tchr. Mich., 1957-1962; instr.history Coll. Steubenville, Ohio, 1962-64; asst. prof. Providence Coll., R.I., 1967-71; prof. Christopher Newport U., Newport News, Va., 1971—, dept. chair, 1994—; host radio series Sta. WGH-FM, Hampton, Va., 1978-83; prodr., host Crossroads TV series Centex TV Network, Williamsburg, Va., 1982-83; orientation speaker Nat. Com. on U.S.-China Rels., Coll. William and Mary, Williamsburg, 1987-92. Author: Our Maritime Heritage, 1979, History of the U.S. Navy, 1984, History of the U.S. Army, 1986, America's Armed Forces: A History, 1991; sr. editor: America's Maritime Legacy, 1979. Recipent edn. award U.S. Dept. Edn., Washington, 1985, disting. prof. award, Alpha Chi, Zeta Chpt., Newport News, Va., 1985. Mem. U.S. Naval Inst., N.Am. Soc. for Oceanic Historians, Soc. for Mil. History. Roman Catholic. Home: 303 Woodroof Rd Newport News VA 23606-2211 Office: Christopher Newport U 50 Shoe Ln Newport News VA 23606-2949

MORRIS, JAMES PEPPLER, bass; b. Balt., Jan. 10, 1947; s. James Deal and Geraldine (Peppler) M.; m. Joanne Frances Vitali, Nov. 15, 1971; 1 child, Heather Frances; m. Susan Louise Quittmeyer, Jan. 3, 1987; children: (twins) Daniel Robert and Jennifer Louise. Student, U. Md., 1965-66, Peabody Conservatory, 1966-68, Acad. Vocal Arts, 1968-70. Recorded with Angel Records div. EMI and Deutche Grammophone, Sony, Phillips. Debut at Met. Opera, N.Y.C., 1971, singer, 1970—, opera and concert singer throughtou U.S., Can., S.Am., Europe, Australia, Japan, 1970—; recs. include Wotan in the New Ring Cycles. Recipient Grammy award for rec. of Wagner's Ring Cycle. Mem. Actors Equity (Can.), Am. Guild Mus. Artists. Office: care Colbert Artists Mgmt Inc 111 W 57th St New York NY 10019-2211

MORRIS, JANE ELIZABETH, home economics educator; b. Marietta, Ohio, Nov. 28, 1940; d. Harold Watson and LaRue (Graham) M. Student, U. Ky., 1960; BS, Marietta Coll., 1962, postgrad., 1963; MA, Kent State U., 1970, postgrad., 1985-87; postgrad., Coll. Mt. St. Joseph, 1984-86, John Carroll U., 1986, Ashland Coll., 1987. Cert. high sch. tchr., Ohio. Tchr. home econs. Chagrin Falls (Ohio) Mid. and High Sch., 1963-95; head cheerleading advisor Chagrin Falls H.S., 1970-80, freshman class advisor, 1981-82, head fine and practical arts dept., 1982-84, sophomore class advisor, 1982-85, 87-89, mem. prin.'s cabinet, 1987-88, tchr., adminstr. adv. coun., 1990-93. Vice chmn. The Elec. Women's Round Table, Inc., Cleve., 1968, chmn., 1969-71; treas. Trees Condominium Assn., 1981-83, pres., 1991-94; active Chagrin Falls chpt. Am. Heart Assn., Am. Cancer Soc., Geauga County Humane Soc., Valley Save a Pet. Mem. AAUW, NEA, Career Edn. Assn., Ohio Edn. Assn., Ohio Retired Tchrs. Assn., Chagrin Falls Edn. Assn. (bldg. rep. 1986-95, negotiating team 1990, negotiating com. 1993, commendation State of Ohio rep. assembly 1995), Alpha Xi Delta. Methodist. Avocations: swimming, interior design, sewing, gourmet cooking.

MORRIS, JASON, Olympic athlete. Mem. Olympic team Seoul, Korea, 1988; judo Barcelona, Spain, 1992; mem. Olympic team Atlanta, 1996. Recipient 172 lbs. Class Pan Am. Games champ, 1987, 91, 172 lbs. Class Judo Silver medal Olympics, Barcelona, 1992. Office: US Olympic Com 575 Swaggertown Rd Scotia NY 12302-9628

MORRIS, JEFFREY SELMAN, orthopedic surgeon; b. Johannesburg, South Africa, June 26, 1948; arrived in Can., 1979; came to U.S., 1990; s. Israel and Anna Riva (Belikoff) M.; m. Carol Parker, Jan. 21, 1973 (div. 1986); children: Amit, Leora. BSc, U. Witwatersrand, Johannesburg, 1970, B of Medicine, B of Surgery, 1973. Rotating intern Natalspruit Hosp., South Africa, 1974, surg. resident, 1975-76; resident in orthopedic surgery Cen. Emek Hosp., Afula, Israel, 1977-79, Queen's U., Kingston, Ont., Can., 1979-82; orthopedic surgeon Port Arthur Clinic, Thunder Bay, Ont., 1983-86, Joseph Brant Meml. Hosp., Burlington, Ont., 1986-90, Beachwood (Ohio) Orthopedic Assocs., 1990—; mem. staff Meridia South Pointe Hosp., Cleve.; assoc. staff Meridia Hillcrest Hosp., Cleve. Contbr. articles to profl. jours., chpt. to book. Med. advisor Arthritis Soc., Thunder Bay, 1983-86. Mem. ACS, Can. Med. Assn., Ont. Med. Assn., Can. Orthopedic Assn., Ont. Orthopedic Assn., Ohio Orthopedic Soc., Cleve. Orthopedic Soc., Cleve. Acad. Medicine, Royal Coll. Physicians and Surgeons (Can.), Can. Soc. Surgery of the Hand, Ohio Med. Assn. Jewish. Avocations: music, tennis, theatre, aviation. Office: Beachwood Orthopedic Assocs 23250 Mercantile Rd Beachwood OH 44122-5928

MORRIS, JERRY DEAN, academic administrator; b. Gassville, Ark., May 11, 1935; s. James Henry and Maud Idella (Taylor) M.; m. Marilyn Jo Pitman, June 11, 1955; children: Joseph, Neil, Laura, Kara. BS, U. Ark., 1960, MEd, 1964, EdD, 1971. Cert. sch. adminstr., Ark. High sch. tchr. Cotter (Ark.) Pub. Schs., 1959-60, high sch. prin., 1960-63; jr. high prin. Mountain Home (Ark.) Pub. Schs., 1963-66, high sch. prin., 1966-67, asst. supt., 1967-69; editor Ark. Sch. Bds. Newsletter, U. Ark., Fayetteville, 1969-70; dir. placement services Tex. A&M U.-Commerce (formerly East Tex. State U.), 1970-71, dean admissions & records, 1971-73, dean grad. sch., 1973-81, v.p. acad. affairs, 1982-86, pres., 1987—; cons. Ark. Basic Edn., 1970, U. Cen. Ark., Conway, 1972, coordinating bd. Tex. Colls. & Univs., Austin, 1981. Pres. Commerce C. of C., 1975; bd. dirs. Commerce Lions Club, 1977; chmn. Commerce United Way, 1978; mem. Commerce Indsl. Devel. Assn., 1974—. Named an Outstanding Young Man in Edn., Ark. Jaycees, 1966, Outstanding Young Man in Am., 1967. Mem. Tex. Assn. Coll. Tchrs., Assn. Tex. Grad. Schs. (pres. 1978-79), Coun. of So. Grad. Schs. (bd. dirs. 1976-79), Coun. of Grad. Schs. in U.S., Coun. of Pub. U. Pres. and Chancellors (exec. com. 1989-90, 1996-97), Assn. of Tex. Colls. and Univs. (exec. com. 1989-90), Tex. Internat. Edn. Consortium (exec. com. 1990—), Alliance for Higher Edn. (bd. dirs. 1986—), Phi Delta Kappa. Methodist. Avocations: jogging, gardening, reading, singing, travel. Home: ET Sta PO Box 3001 Commerce TX 75429-3001 Office: Tex A&M U-Commerce ET Station Commerce TX 75429

MORRIS, JOANN SEBASTION, federal agency adminstrator; b. Detroit, Sept. 24, 1944; d. Elmer John and Hazel (Jamieson) Sebastion. EdB, U. N.Mex., 1967; MA, UCLA, 1971. Cert. tchr., Calif. Social worker I Alameda County Welfare Dept., Oakland, Calif., 1967-68; social worker II L.A. County Dept. Pub. Social Svcs., 1968-69; project dir. Tribal Am./Tng. Cons. Associated, Burbank, Calif., 1971-74; pvt. practice cons. L.A., 1975-76; tchr. L.A. City Unified Sch. Dist., 1972-76, exec. dir. Am. Indian Edn. Commn., 1976-81; edn. policy fellow Office Intergovernmental and Interagency Affairs U.S. Dept. Edn., Washington, 1981-82; pvt. practice cons. Falls Church, Va., 1982-83; prin. investigator Minority Enterprise Svc. Assocs., Reston, Va., 1983-84; human resources coord. Nat. Congress Am. Indians, Washington, 1984-85; nat. coord., edn. secretariat Assembly First Nations, Ottawa, Ont., Can., 1985-88; dir. R&D Kipohtakaw Edn. Ctr., Alexander Res., Morinville, Alta., Can., 1988-91; sr. program assoc., dir. Nat. Origin Ctr. Ednl. Equity Mid-Continent Regional Ednl. Lab., Aurora, Colo., 1991-92, sr. program assoc., dir. Native Edn. Initiative, 1992-94; spl. asst. edn. Office Asst. Sec. Indian Affairs U.S. Dept. Interior, Washington, 1994-96, dir. Office Indian Edn. Programs, Bur. Indian Affairs, 1996—. Contbr. articles to profl. jours., and chpts. to books. Mem. Nat. Indian Edn. Assn., Nat. Indian Edn. Forum, Sault Ste. Marie Band Chippewa Indians, Upper Cayuga Band Six Nations Grand River Res. Home: 2924 Pine Spring Rd Falls Church VA 22042-1340 Office: Dept Interior Office Indian Edn Programs 1849 C St NW, MS 3512-MIB Washington DC 20240*

MORRIS, JOHN, composer, conductor, arranger; b. Elizabeth, N.J.; s. Thomas Arthur and Helen (Sherratt) M.; m. Francesca Bosetti; children: Evan Bosetti, Bronwen Helen. Student, Julliard Sch. Music, 1946-48, U. Wash., 1947, New Sch. Social Research, 1946-49. Composer mus. scores for (films) The Producers, The Twelve Chairs, The Gamblers, Blazing Saddles (nominated Acad. award 1976), The Bank Shot, Young Frankenstein, Sherlock Holmes Smarter Brother, Silent Movie, The Last Remake of Beau Geste, The In-Laws, The World's Greatest Lover, In God We Trust, High Anxiety, The Elephant Man (nominated Acad. award 1981), Table for Five, History of the World Part I, Yellowbeard, The Doctor and the Devils, Clue, To Be or Not To Be, Woman in Red, Johnny Dangerously, Haunted Honeymoon, Dirty Dancing, Spaceballs, Ironweed, The Wash, Stella, Life Stinks, (Broadway stage plays) My Mother, My Father and Me, Doll's House, Camino Real, (mus.) A Time for Singing, (off-Broadway) Take One Step, Young Andy Jackson, 15 scores for N.Y. Shakespeare Festival, Am. Shakespeare Festival, Stratford, Conn., (TV shows) Fresno, Katherine Anne Porter, Ghost Dancing, The Firm, The Mating Season, Splendor in the Grass, The Electric Grandmother, The Scarlet Letter, The Adams Chronicles, Georgia O'Keeffe, The Franken Project, The Tap Dance Kid (Emmy award 1986), Make Believe Marriage, ABC After Sch. Spl. Theme, Making Things Grow Theme, The French Chef Theme, The Desperate Hours, The Skirts of Happy Chance, Infancy and Childhood, The Fig Tree, The Little Match Girl, Our Sons, The Last to Go, The Last Best Year, The Sunset Gang, Coach Theme, Favorite Son, Journey Into Genius, When Lions Roared, Scarlett Mini Series, With God On Our Side, Ellen Foster, several documentary films; mus. supr., conductor, arranger numerous TV spls., Broadway and off-Broadway shows and recordings including Anne Bancroft Spl. #1 (Emmy award), 'S Lemmon 'S Gershwin 'S Wonderful (Emmy award), Hallmark Christmas Spls., (Broadway) Mack and Mabel, Much Ado About Nothing, Bells Are Ringing, (off-Broadway) Hair, (records) Wildcat, All-American, Bells Are Ringing, First Impressions, Bye-Bye Birdie, Kwamina, Baker Street, Rodgers and Hart, George Gershwin vols. I and II, Jerome Kern, Lyrics of Ira Gershwin, Cole Porter, others. Mem. ASCAP, Acad. Motion Picture Arts and Scis., Am. Fedn. Musicians. Avocations: computers, humorous poetry, cooking. Office: Alan Stein 270 Madison Ave New York NY 10016-0601

MORRIS, JOHN LUNDEN, global logistics and communications executive; b. Wilmington, Del., Feb. 26, 1943; s. Arthur Lunden and Carolyn Wilson (Bickell) M.; m. Sally Carolyn Wheeler, Mar. 9, 1967; children: Christopher Wheeler, Kevin Arthur. BA, U. Del., 1965; postgrad., Rutgers U., 1968-71. Ocean container specialist E.I. DuPont de Nemours & Co., Inc., N.Y.C., 1968-72; mgr. pricing U.S. gulf Seatrain Lines, Inc., Weehauken, N.J., 1972-73; dir. pricing Europe Seatrain Lines, Inc., Rotterdam, Holland, 1973-75; dir. market planning, advt. Seatrain Lines, Inc., Weehauken, 1975-76; dir. pricing Seatrain Agys., Inc., N.Y.C., 1976-80; dir. mktg. Prudential Lines, Inc., N.Y.C., 1980-85; dir. mktg. and rsch. Trans Atlantic Associated Freight Confs., N.Y.C., 1985-87; exec. dir. U.S. Atlantic and Gulf Venezuela Conf., Jersey City, 1987-91; chief exec. officer Inter-Am. Freight Conf., Jersey City, 1987-94; pres. INTRANSCO, Internat. Transp. Solutions, Inc., Upper Montclair, N.J., 1994—; dir. mktg. Mediterranean Shipping Co., N.Y.C., 1996—; mem. electronic systems adv. com. U.S. Customs Svc., Washington, 1988—; study com. Fed. Maritime Commn., Washington, 1987, 89-91, expert witness, Fed. Cts., Boston, N.Y.C.; spkr., presenter N.Y./N.J. Port Authority, World Trade Inst., Brazilian-Am. C. of C., Montclair C. of C. Mem. Twp. Transp. Adv. Com., Montclair, 1982-85; chmn. Upper Montclair troop 7 Boy Scouts Am., 1982-88; trustee Montclair Hist. Soc., 1996—. Mem. Transp. Rsch. Forum, Assn. for Corp. Computing Tech. Profl., Internat. Trade Users Assn., Christian Businessmen's Club. Presbyterian. Avocations: bicycling, golf, touring, art and architectural history. Office: Internat Transp Solutions PO Box 43479 Upper Montclair NJ 07043-0479 also: Mediterranean Shipping Co 420 Fifth Ave New York NY 10018-2702

MORRIS, JOHN SELWYN, philosophy educator, college president emeritus; b. Tonypandy, Wales, July 2, 1925; came to U.S., 1954, naturalized, 1993; s. Jenkin and Hannah M. (Williams) M.; m. Enid Elry Walters, Apr. 10, 1954; 1 child, Paul John. B.A., Univ. Coll. South Wales and Monmouthshire, 1951; M.A., Cambridge (Eng.) U., 1953; student, Union Theol. Sem., 1957-60; M.A., Colgate U., 1961; Ph.D., Columbia U., 1961; LL.D. (hon.), Hartwick Coll., 1979; LHD (hon.), Elmyra Coll., 1990; DLitt, Skidmore Coll., 1991. Ordained to ministry Presbyterian Ch., 1954; minister Vernon (N.Y.) and Vernon Center Presbyn. chs., 1954-57; instr. Colgate U., Hamilton, N.Y., 1960-63; asst. prof. Colgate U., 1963-66, asso. prof., 1966-70, prof. philosophy and religion, 1970-79, dir. div. humanities, 1970-72, dir. div. univ. studies, 1972-73, provost, dean of faculty, 1973-79, acting pres., 1977; prof. philosophy Union Coll., Schenectady, 1979-90, pres., chancellor Union U., 1979-90, pres. emeritus, rsch. prof. philosophy, 1990—; Leverhulme vis. fellow U. Exeter, Eng., 1968-69; chmn. Commn. Ind. Colls. and Univs., 1984-86; bd. dirs. Trustco N.Y. Bd. dirs. Schenectady Found.; trustee Skidmore Coll. With RAF, 1943-47. Recipient Disting. Svc. award Colgate U. Alumni Corp., 1978, Schenectady Patroon award, 1989. Mem. AAUP, Am. Philos. Assn., Am. Acad. Religion, Royal Inst. Philosophy, Soc. for Study Theology, Nat. Welsh Am. Found. (bd. advisors). Office: Union Coll Humanities Ctr Schenectady NY 12308

MORRIS, JOHN WOODLAND, II, businessman, former army officer; b. Princess Anne, Md., Sept. 10, 1921; s. John Earl and Allice (Cropper) M.; m. Geraldine Moore King, May 12, 1947; children: Susan K., John Woodland III. BS, U.S. Mil. Acad., 1943; MS, U. Iowa, 1947; postgrad., Army War Coll., 1961-62, U. Pitts., 1966. Commd. 2d lt. U.S. Army, 1943, advanced through grades to lt. gen., 1971; dep. dist. engr. Savannah, Ga., 1952-54; resident engr. Goose Bay, Labrador, 1955-57; staff officer Office Chief Engrs., 1957-60; comdg. officer 8th Engr. Bn., Korea, 1960-61; dist. engr. Tulsa, 1962-65; dep. comdt. U.S. Mil. Acad., 1965-67; dep. chief legis. liaison Office Sec. Army, Washington, 1967-69; comdg. gen. 18th Engr. Brigade, Vietnam, 1969-70; div. engr. Missouri River Div., Omaha, 1970-72; dir. civil works Office C.E., Washington, 1972-75; dep. chief engr. U.S. Army, 1975-76, chief engr., 1976-80; ret., 1980; exec. dir. Royal Volker Stevin, 1980-84; pres. J.W. Morris Ltd., 1981—; prof. U. Md., 1983-86; chmn. bd., chief exec. officer PRC Engring., 1986-88, cons.; cons., engr. advisor Zorc, Rissetto, Weaver & Rosen, 1988-92; engr. advisor Seltzer & Rosen, 1992—; bd. dirs. Air Water Tech., Morganti Constrn. Co., Search Techs. Inc. Mem. Indian Nations coun. Boy Scouts Am., 1962-65; chmn. Water Resources Congress, 1988-90; trustee U.S. Mil. Acad. Assn. Grads, 1986—; advisor dean engring. and math. U. Vt., 1990—. Decorated Legion of Merit with three oak leaf clusters, Army D.S.M., Def. D.S.M.; recipient Merit award Am. Cons. Engrs. Council; Palladium medal Audubon Soc., award of excellence Constrn. Industry Inst. Fellow ASCE; mem. AIA (hon.), Internat. Navigation Congress (v.p.), U.S. Soc. Mil. Engrs. (pres.), Nat. Acad. Engrs. (Founders award), U.S. Com. on Large Dams (past chmn. environ. effect com., named Constrn. Man of Yr. 1977, Navigation Hall of Fame 1990, Golden Beaver award for engring. 1995). Episcopalian. Home: 1329 N Lynnbrook Dr Arlington VA 22201-4918 Office: 3800 Fairfax Dr Apt 5 Arlington VA 22203-1703

MORRIS, JORDEN WALTER, dancer, educator; b. Banff, Alta., Can., Aug. 19, 1967; s. Walter Edgard Morris and Penny Ann (Stenton) Tilleniuss. Student, U. Winnipeg, 1993. Tchr./coach Royal Winnipeg Ballet, Can., 1985, 88—, mem. corps de ballet, 1987-89, soloist, 1989-92, prin. dancer, 1992—; asst. choregpgrapher Les Ballet Jazz De Montreal, Que., 1979; guest artist Banff (Alta.) Centre Sch. Fine Arts, 1984. Repertoire includes lead roles in Rodeo, Giselle, Romeo and Juliet, Four Last Songs, Lilac Garden, The Nutcracker, Swan Lake, Symphony in D, Stoolgame, Myth, Pas des Déeses, Dark Elegies, La Princesse et le Soldat; gala performer Canadian AIDS Benefit, Toronto, Ont., 1990. Recipient Alan Hooper scholarship Banff Centre Fine Arts, 1981, Larry MCkinnon scholarship Royal Winnipeg Ballet, 1984. Mem. Canadian Actors Equity Assn. (adv. com. 1990, union dep. 1995-96). Avocations: carpentry, guitars, mountain climbing, horse ranching. Home: 3H-440 Assiniboine Ave, 11-C 778 McMillan Ave, WPO, MB Canada R3M 0V3 Office: Royal Winnipeg Ballet, 380 Graham Ave, Winnipeg, MB Canada R3C 4K2*

MORRIS, JOSEPH ANTHONY, health science association administrator; b. nr. Marboro, Md., Sept. 6, 1918; s. Charles Lafayette and Essie (Stokes) M.; BS, Cath. U. Am., 1940, MS, 1942, PhD, 1947; m. Ruth Savoy, Nov. 1, 1942; children: Carol Ann, Marilyn T., Joseph A., Larry A. Asst. scientist Josiah Macy, Jr. Found., N.Y.C., 1943-44; virologist, Depts. Agr., Interior, Laurel, Md., 1944-47; virologist, chief hepatitis virus research Walter Reed Army Inst. Research, Washington, 1947-56; virologist, asst. chief, dept. virus and rickettsial diseases U.S. Army Med. Command, Japan, 1956-59; virologist chief sect. respiratory viruses, div. biologics standards NIH, Bethesda, Md., 1959—, dir. slow, latent and temperate virus br. FDA, Bethesda, 1972-76; lectr. dept. microbiology U. Md., College Park, 1977-79; vice-chmn. Bell of Atri, Inc., College Park, 1979-82, chmn., 1983; cons. Commn. on Influenza, Armed Forces Epidemiologic Bd., 1960—, Nat. Inst. Neurol. Diseases and Blindness, 1962—. Mem. Soc. Tropical Medicine and Hygiene, Soc. Am. Microbiologists, Soc. Exptl. Biology and Medicine, Am. Assn. Immunologists, N.Y. Acad. Sci. Discoverer of respiratory sycytial virus; research on infectious hepatitis, respiratory diseases of virus etiology and zoonosis. Home: 23E Ridge Rd Greenbelt MD 20770-0714

MORRIS, JUSTIN ROY, food scientist, consultant, enologist, research director; b. Nashville, Ark., Feb. 20, 1937; s. Roy Morris; m. Ruby Lee Blackwood, Sept. 5, 1956; children: Linda Lee, Michael Justin. BS, U. Ark., 1957, MS, 1961; PhD, Rutgers U., 1964. Rsch. asst. Rutgers U., New Brunswick, N.J., 1957-61, instr., 1961-64; extension horticulturist U. Ark., Fayetteville, 1964-67, from asst. to assoc. prof., 1967-75, prof., 1975-85; univ. prof., 1985—; dir. Inst. Food Sci. and Engring. Ctr. for Food Processing and Engring., 1995—; cons. viticulture sci. program Fla. A&M U., Tallahassee, 1979-81; cons. viticulture and enology program Grayson City Coll., Denison, Tex., 1987—; cons. J. M. Smucker Co., Orrville, Ohio, 1982-91. Co-author: Small Fruit Crop Management, 1990, Quality and Preservation of Fruits, 1991, Modern Fruit Science Text Book, 1995; assoc. editor: Am. Jour. Enology and Viticulture, 1985; contbr. more than 300 articles to sci. jours. Recipient rsch. award Nat. Food Processors Assn., 1982, Faculty Disting. Svc. award for rsch. and pub. svcs. U. Ark., 1993, Disting. Achievement award ea. sect. Am. Soc. Enology and Vitical Tace, 1995, Nat. Merit award Am. Soc. Enology & Viticultures, eastern sect., 1996, Spitze Land-grant U. Faculty award for excellence, 1997. Fellow Am. Soc. for Hort. Sci. (assoc. editor 1985, Gourley award 1979, Outstanding Rsch. award 1983), Inst. Food Tech.; mem. Ozark Food Processors Assn. (exec. v.p. 1988—), Coun. for Agrl. Sci. and Tech. (bd. dirs. 1987-93, chmn. nat. concerns 1987-91, pres.-elect 1993, pres. 1994, 95), Inst. Food Technologists (co-organizer fruit and vegetable divsn. 1987—), Gamma Sigma Delta. Achievements include development of mechanical cane fruit harvester, of mechanical strawberry harvester, of modified grape harvester for wine grapes, of mechanical shoot positioner for grapes; development of systems for the production, harvesting, handling, utilization, and marketing of grape juice and wine. Office: U Ark Dept Food Sci 272 Young Ave Fayetteville AR 72704-5585

MORRIS, KENNETH DONALD, lawyer; b. Montclair, N.J., Apr. 5, 1946; s. Thomas Almerin and Katherine Louise (Jacobs) M.; m. Susan Sauer, May 1, 1976; children: Ian, Jennifer. BA, Ohio Wesleyan U., 1968; MBA, George Washington U., 1971, JD, 1972. Bar: Pa. 1973, N.J. 1975, D.C. 1989. Atty. Westinghouse Electric, Pitts., 1972-74, Tenneco Chems., Inc., N.J., 1974-76; asst. corp. counsel Ronson Corp., Bound Brook, N.J., 1976-78; assoc. Walder, Sondak, Berkley & Brogan, Newark, 1978-81; sec., gen. counsel, mem. mgmt. com. NOR-AM Chem. Co. subs. Schering AG, Wilmington, Del., 1981-94, environ. com., 1987—, mem. fiduciary com., 1988—; sec., gen. counsel AgrEvo USA Co., Wilmington, 1994—. Incorporator, pres. Charter Oaks Assn.; mem. Gov.'s Internat. Trade Coun., Del. Wolcott Found. scholar, 1969. Mem. ABA (antitrust sect., corp. counsel com., banking and bus. law sect., multinational corps. subcom.), Am. Arbitration Assn. (panel arbitrators), Del. Bar Assn., Am. Corp. Counsel Assn. (dir. Delvacca chpt.), Def. Rsch. Inst. (corp. counsel com.), George Washington U. Sch. Govt. and Bus. Adminstrn. Alumni Assn. (Phila. chpt.), George Washington U. Nat. Law Ctr. Alumni Assn., European-Am. Gen. Counsel Assn., Fed. Bar Assn. Republican. Presbyterian. Avocations: classical music, running, sailing, tennis. Office: AgrEvo USA Co 2711 Centerville Rd Wilmington DE 19808-1643

MORRIS, LEIGH EDWARD, hospital executive officer; b. Hartford City, Ind., Dec. 26, 1934; s. Fredus Orlando and Martha (Malott) M.; m. Marcia Renee Meredith, Oct. 7, 1967; children: Meredith Anne, Curtis Paul. BS in Commerce, Internat. Coll., 1954; BSBA, Ball State U., 1958; M in Health Adminstrn., U. Minn., 1972. Mem. labor relations staff Borg-Warner Corp., Muncie, Ind., 1961-64; various positions then personnel mgr. Internat. Harvester Co., Ft. Wayne, Ind., 1964-70; pres. Huntington (Ind.) Meml. Hosp., 1972-78, La Porte (Ind.) Hosp., 1978—; bd. dirs. First of Am. Bank of Ind., Am. Hosp. Svcs., Inc.; chmn., bd. dirs. Am. Hosp. Pub. Co.; chmn. La Porte Devel. Corp., 1980-81. Chmn. La Porte chpt. ARC, 1984-86. With U.S. Army, 1958-60. Recipient Disting. Alumni award Ball State U., Muncie, Ind., 1968, James A. Hamilton award U. Minn., Mpls., 1972, Trustees award Am. Hosp. Assn., 1996. Fellow Am. Coll. Healthcare Adminstrn., Health Care Fin. Mgmt. Assn.; mem. APHA, Am. Hosp. Assn. (trustee, regional chmn. 1985-89), Soc. for Healthcare Planning and Mktg. (bd. dirs.), Ind. Hosp. Assn. (chmn. 1980-81), La Porte C. of C. (chmn. 1981-82), Constantian Soc., Masons. Republican. Presbyterian. Avocations: classic cars, civic affairs. Home: 1519 Indiana Ave La Porte IN 46350-5105 Office: La Porte Hosp Inc PO Box 250 La Porte IN 46352-0250

MORRIS, LOIS LAWSON, education educator; b. Antoine, Ark., Nov. 27, 1914; d. Oscar Moran and Dona Alice (Ward) Lawson; m. William D. Morris, July 2, 1932 (dec.); 1 child, Lavonne Morris Howell. B.A., Henderson U., 1948; M.S., U. Ark., 1951, M.A., 1966; postgrad. U. Colo., 1954, Am. U., 1958, U. N.C., 1968. History tchr. Delight High Sch., Ark., 1942-47; counselor Huntsville Vocat. Sch., 1947-48; guidance dir. Russellville Pub. Sch. System, Ark., 1948-55; asst. prof. edn. U. Ark., Fayetteville, 1955-82, prof. emeritus, 1982—; ednl. cons. Ark. Pub. Schs., 1965-78. Mem. Commn. on Needs for Women, 1976-78, Hist. Preservation Alliance Ark.; pres. Washington County Hist. Soc., 1983-85; pres. Pope County Hist. Assn.; mem. Ark. Symphony Guild; charter mem. Nat. Mus. in Arts; bd. dirs. Potts Inn Mus. Found. Named Ark. Coll. Tchr. of Year, 1972; recipient Plaque for outstanding svcs. to Washington County Hist. Soc., 1984. Contbr. articles to jours. Mem. LWV, AAUW, Ark. Coun. Social Studies (sec.-treas.), Washington County Hist. Soc. (exec. bd. 1977-80), NEA, Nat. Coun. Social Studies, Ark. Edn. Assn., Ark. Hist. Assn., Pope County Hist. Assn. (pres. 1991-92), The So. Hist. Assn., U. Ark. Alumni Assn., Sierra Club, Nature Conservancy, So. Hist. Assn., Ark. River Valley Arts Assn., Phi Delta Kappa, Kappa Delta Pi, Phi Alpha Theta. Democrat. Episcopalian. Address: 1601 W 3rd St Russellville AR 72801-4725 *I appreciate good teachers - the historian who taught research skills and forced me to write crisp, clear sentences; the botanist who unlocked plant life and pointed to tiny flowers growing in the grass; and the young artist who urged simplification through the use of light and big brushes. These teachings continue through retirement years.*

MORRIS, MAC GLENN, advertising bureau executive; b. Bessemer City, N.C., Jan. 24, 1922; s. Manly T. and Erin C. (Cline) M.; m. Janelle Connevey, July 27, 1946; children—Robert S., Janelle C., Patricia A., John Logan. A.B., Davidson Coll., 1942. Space salesman Progressive Farmer mag., N.Y.C., 1946-52; exec. v.p., advt. dir. This Week mag., 1952-68; pres. Newspaper One, N.Y.C., 1968-71; sr. v.p. nat. sales Newspaper Advt. Bur., N.Y.C., 1972-87; proprietor MGM Assocs., Princeton, N.J., 1987—; bd. dirs. Princeton Bank & Trust Co. divsn. Chem. Bank N.J., N.A., now owned by P.N.C. Bank, N.Y.C. Served to 1st lt., pilot USMCR, World War II. Decorated D.F.C. (2), Air medal (7). Mem. Newcomen Soc. in N. Am., Pi Kappa Phi. Presbyn. (deacon). Club: Springdale Golf (Princeton, N.J.) (bd. govs.). Home and Office: 417 Herrontown Rd Princeton NJ 08540-2932 *I am always an optimist at my work, with friends, and with my family.*

MORRIS, MALCOLM STEWART, title company executive, lawyer; b. Houston, May 8, 1946; s. Carloss M.; m. Rebecca Ann Simmons, June 14, 1969; children: Matthew William, Andrew James. BBA, So. Meth. U., 1968; JD, U. Tex., 1970, MBA, 1972. Bar: Tex. 1970. Legis. aid State of Tex., Sen. Charles Wilson, Austin, 1969-70; examiner Stewart Title Austin Inc., 1970-71; analyst Bank of the S.W., Houston, 1973-74; bus. mgr. Richard Hogue Evangelism, Inc., Houston, 1974-75; v.p. ops. Stewart Title Guaranty Co., Houston, 1975-87, sr. exec. v.p., asst. chmn., 1987-91, pres., CEO, 1991—; cons. Morris, Lendais, Hollrah & Snowden, Houston; mem. bd. Stewart Title Ins. Co., N.Y.C., Stewart Title Ins. Co. U.K. Deacon 1st Bapt. Ch., Houston, 1982—. Fellow Am. Bar Found., Houston Bar Assn.; mem. Phi Delta Phi. Baptist. Office: 1980 Post Oak Blvd Ste 800 Houston TX 77056-3817*

MORRIS, MARGRETTA ELIZABETH, government official; b. Oakland, Calif., Sept. 14, 1950; d. Joseph Francis and Mildred Ruth Madeo; m. Dennis W. Morris, July 22, 1972; children: Matthew B., Roseanna A. BA in Geography, Radford U., 1972. Exec. asst. John Hancock Life Ins., Pittsfield, Mass., 1972-79; paralegal Law Office of Henry F. Zwack, Stephentown, N.Y., 1980-91; exec. dir. Ea. Rensselaer County Waste Mgmt. Authority, Stephentown, 1991—; co-founder MDM Prodns., Stephentown, 1986—. Councilperson Town of Stephentown, 1987-92. Mem. N.Y. State Assn. for Solid Waste Mgmt. (rec. sec. 1992—), N.Y. State Assn. for Reduction, Reuse and Recycling (treas. 1992—), Coalition of N.E. Govs. (capital dist. regionalization task force 1994—), Fedn. N.Y. Solid Waste Assns. (chmn. 1997—), Gamma Theta Upsilon. Republican. Roman Catholic. Avocations: cross-country skiing, hiking. Office: Ea Rensselaer County Solid Waste Mgmt Authority 21428 NY 22 Hoosick Falls NY 12090

MORRIS, MARK WILLIAM, choreographer; b. Seattle, Wash., Aug. 29, 1956; s. William and Maxine (Crittenden) M. Studied with, Verla Flowers and Perry Brunson. Artistic dir. Mark Morris Dance Group, N.Y.C., 1980—, Théâtre Royal de la Monnaie, Brussels, 1988—; choreographer White Oaks Dance Project, 1990; performed with Lar Lubovitch Dance Co., Hannah Kahn Dance Co., Laura Dean Dancers and Musicians, Eliot Feld Ballet, Koleda Balkan Dance Ensemble. Choreographer for Mark Morris Dance Group: Mythologies, 1986, L'Allegro, il Penseroso ed il Moderato, 1988, Dido and Aeneas, 1989, The Nutcracker, 1991, Lucky Charms, 1994, Rondo, 1994, The Office, 1994, others; choreographer: Mort Subite, Boston Ballet, 1986, Esteemed Guests, Joffrey Ballet, 1986, Drink to Me Only With Thine Eyes, Am. Ballet Theatre, 1988, Ein Herz, Paris Opera Ballet, 1990, Nixon in China, Houston Grand Opera, 1987, Orfée et Euridice, Seattle Opera, 1988, The Death of Klinghoffer, Théâtre de la Monnaie, 1991; (television) Great Performances/Dance in America: The Hard Nut, 1992; dir: Die Fledermaus, Seattle Opera, 1988. Recipient N.Y. Dance and Performance award, 1984, 90; Guggenheim fellow, 1986. Office: Mark Morris Dance Group 225 Lafayette St Rm 504 New York NY 10012-4015*

MORRIS, M(ARY) ROSALIND, cytogeneticist, educator; b. Ruthin, Wales, May 8, 1920; came to U.S., 1942, naturalized, 1954; d. Aneurin Edmund and Celia Charles (Evans) M. BS in Horticulture, Ont. Agrl. Coll., Guelph, Can., 1942; PhD in Plant Breeding and Genetics, Cornell U., 1947. Mem. faculty U. Nebr., Lincoln, 1947—, prof. agronomy, 1958-90, prof. emeritus, 1990—. Contbr. chpts. to textbooks, articles to sci. jours. U. Nebr. Johnson Faculty fellow, Calif. Inst. Tech., Pasadena, 1949-50; John Simon Guggenheim Found. fellow, Sweden and Eng., 1956-57. Fellow AAAS, Am. Soc. Agronomy, Crop Sci. Soc. Am.; mem. AAUW, Genetics Soc. Can., Nebr. Acad. Sci., Nebr. Ornithologists' Union (editor The Nebr. Bird Rev. 1992—), Lincoln Camera Club, Sigma Xi, Gamma Sigma Delta, Sigma Delta Epsilon. Avocations: bird watching, photography, writing. Office: U Nebr Dept Agronomy Lincoln NE 68583-0915

MORRIS, MAX KING, foundation executive, former naval officer; b. Springfield, Mo., Oct. 23, 1924; s. Lee Howard and Aldyth (King) M.; m. Mary Jane Bull, June 19, 1952; children: Jane, William, Mary. B.S., U.S. Naval Acad., 1947; M.A. in Internat. Law, Tufts U., 1960, M.A. in Internat. Econs., 1961, Ph.D., 1967. Commd. ensign U.S. Navy, 1947, advanced through grades to rear adm., 1972; carrier pilot with combat duty in Korea and Vietnam, 1947-71, comdr. jet squadron U.S.S. America, 1965-67, maj. command at sea, 1969-70, comdt. U.S. Naval Acad., 1971-73, Joint Chiefs of Staff rep. UN Law of Sea Conf., 1973-77, ret., 1977; pres. Thalassa Rsch. Co., Jacksonville, Fla., 1977—; trustee Arthur Vining Davis Founds., Fla. Author: Politico-Military Coordination in the Armed Forces, 1968; Contbr. numerous articles to naval and legal jours. Served with arty. U.S. Army, 1942-44. Decorated D.S.M., Legion of Merit (2), Air medal (5). Mem. Internat. Inst. Strategic Studies (London), Council on Fgn. Relations, Middle East Inst., U.S. Naval Inst. Clubs: N.Y. Yacht, Fla. Yacht; Belfry (London); Ponte Vedra (Fla.). Home: 4990 Vandiveer Rd Jacksonville FL 32210-8314

MORRIS, MICHAEL ALLEN, insurance executive; b. Beatrice, Nebr., Dec. 25, 1953; s. M.H. and Betty Ruth (Folkers) M.; m. Beverly Gail Raser, Nov. 26, 1977; children: Margaret Cantrell, Jessica Laine. BS in Bus., U. Nebr., 1976. CLU, ChFC. Cons. Woodmen Accident and Life, Lincoln, Nebr., 1976-83; sales rep. Tantillo and Miller, Topeka, 1983-88; sales mgr. The New Eng., Topeka, 1988-90; pres. Corp. Plan Mgmt., Topeka, 1990—, Retirement Plan Mgmt., Topeka, 1996—; registered investment advisor SEC, Topeka, 1986-88. Participant Leadership Greater Topeka, 1988, Leadership U. Nebr. Alumni, Lincoln, 1989; mem. leadership com. Kans. Pharmacy Found., Topeka, 1992—; pres. Retirement Plan Mgmt., Inc., 1996—; bd. mem. Topeka Conv. Visitors Bur., 1997—. Mem. Topeka Assn. Life Underwriters (chmn. pol. action com. 1993-94, pol. involvement com. 1993-94), Am. Soc. CLU's/ChFC's (Nekansas chpt. bd. dirs. 1988), Profl. Advisors Round Table (chmn. 1991), Million Dollar Round Table, Past Active 20-30 Club (various offices 1986—, pres. 1992), Greater Topeka C. of C. (vice chair 1997—), Shawnee Country Club (membership com. 1991-92), Golfers Unit-Arab Shrine (hon. mem., pres. 1987), Topeka C. of C. (chair seminar com. 1995-97). Republican. Methodist. Avocations: home computing, golf, community volunteering. Office: Corp Plan Mgmt Inc 2900 SW Wanamaker Dr Ste A Topeka KS 66614-4188

MORRIS, NAOMI CAROLYN MINNER, medical educator, administrator, researcher, consultant; b. Chgo., June 8, 1931; d. Morris George and Carrie Ruth (Auslender) Minner; m. Charles Elliot Morris, June 28, 1951; children: Jonathan Edward, David Carlton. BA magna cum laude, U. Colo., 1952, MD, 1955; MPH magna cum laude, Harvard U., 1959. Diplomate Am. Bd. Preventive Medicine. Rotating intern L.A. County Gen. Hosp., 1955-56; clin. fellow in pediats. Mass. Gen. Hosp., Boston, 1957; pub. health physician Mass. Dept. Health, Boston, 1957-58; clin. pediatrician Norfolk (Va.) King's Daus. Hosp., 1959-61; from asst. prof. to prof. and chair dept. maternal and child health Sch. Pub. Health, U. N.C., Chapel Hill, 1962-77; prof., dir. cmty. pediats. U. Health Scis., Chgo. Med. Sch., 1977-80; prof. Sch. Pub. Health, U. Ill., Chgo., 1980—, dir. cmty. health scis. divsn., 1980-95; mem. liaison com. with Lake County Med. Soc. 1978-80; resource person Ill. 1980 White Ho. Conf. on Children, 1979-80; mem. nursing divsn. adv. com. Lake County Health Dept., 1980—; participant Enrich-A-Life series Chgo. Dept. Health, 1984-85, Ill. Health and Hazardous Substance Registry Pregnancy Outcome Task Force, 1984-86; mem. profl. adv. bd. Beethoven Project Ctr. Child Devel., 1986—; mem. planning com. for action to reduce infant mortality Chgo. Inst. Medicine, 1986-89; founding mem. Westside Futures Infant Mortality Network, 1986; mem. Ill. vital stats. supplement Ill. Dept. Pub. Health, 1987; investigator and team leader Rev. Mo. Families Maternal and Child Health State Svcs., 1989; mem. children and youth 2000 task force MacArthur Found., 1992—; active Ill. Caucus on Teenage Pregnancies, 1978—, Chgo. Dept. Health Child Health Task Force, 1982-83, HSC Interprofessional Edn. Com., 1983-84, Med. Task Force Project Life, 1983-88, Women's Studies Curriculum Com., 1985-90, Com. Rsch. on Women, 1985-90, Mayor's Adv. Com. on Infant Mortality, 1986—, Gov. Adv. Coun. on Infant Mortality, 1988—, Ctr. for Rsch. on Women Fellowship Com., 1993—; cons. pediat. nursing resources group Ill. Dept. Pub. Health, 1983-84; cons. Cook County Hosp. Study of Preventive Childhood Obesity, 1983-84. Author 8 book chpts; contbr. articles to profl. jours. Mem. Ill. MCH Coalition, 1994, Voices for Ill. Children, 1993—. Fellow APHA (mem. task force on adolescence maternal and child health sect. 1977-85, sec. 1979-80, cons. manpower project 1982-83, mem. publ. bd. 1985-87, mem. coun. pediat. rsch. to Am. Acad. Pediats. 1985-92), Am. Coll. Preventive Medicine, Am. Acad. Pediats. (mem. Ill. chpt. com. on sch. health and com. adolescent health 1993—); mem. Ambulatory Pediat. Assn., Assn. Tchrs. Maternal and Child Health (mem. exec. com. 1981-87, mem. com. on tng. and continuing edn. needs of MCH/CCS dirs. 1982-83, mem. liaison com. to fed. DCMH office 1983-87, pres. 1983-85), Chgo. Pediat. Soc., Phi Beta Kappa, Alpha Omega Alpha, Delta Omega, Sigma Xi. Avocations: photography, swimming, reading, classical music, travel. Office: U Ill Chgo Sch Pub Health 2035 W Taylor St Chicago IL 60612-4246

MORRIS, NORVAL, criminologist, educator; b. Auckland, New Zealand, Oct. 1, 1923; s. Louis and Vera (Burke) M.; m. Elaine Richardson, Mar. 18, 1947; children: Gareth, Malcolm, Christopher. LLB, U. Melbourne, Australia, 1946, LLM, 1947; PhD in Criminology (Hutchinson Silver medal 1950), London Sch. Econs., 1949. Bar: called to Australian bar 1953. Asst. lectr. London Sch. Econs., 1949-50; sr. lectr. law U. Melbourne, 1950-58, prof. criminology, 1955-58; Ezra Ripley Thayer teaching fellow Harvard Law Sch., 1955-56, vis. prof., 1961-62; Boynthon prof., dean faculty law U. Adelaide, Australia, 1958-62; dir. UN Inst. Prevention Crime and Treatment of Offenders, Tokyo, Japan, 1962-64; Julius Kreeger prof. law and criminology U. Chgo., 1964—, dean Law Sch., 1975-79; chmn. Commn. Inquiry Capital Punishment in Ceylon, 1958-59; mem. Social Sci. Rsch. Coun. Australia, 1958-59; Australian del. confs. div. human rights and sect. social def. UN, 1955-66; mem. standing adv. com. experts prevention crime and treatment offenders. Author: The Habitual Criminal, 1951, Report of the Commission of Inquiry on Capital Punishment, 1959, (with W. Morison and R. Sharwood) Cases in Torts, 1962, (with Colon Howard) Studies in Criminal Law, 1964, (with G. Hawkins) The Honest Politicians Guide to Crime Control, 1970, The Future of Imprisonment, 1974, Letter to the President on Crime Control, 1977, Madness and the Criminal Law, 1983, Between Prison and Probation, 1990, The Brothel Boy and Other Parables of the Law, 1992, The Oxford History of the Prison, 1995. Served with Australian Army, World War II, PTO. Decorated Japanese Order Sacred Treasure 3d Class. Fellow Am. Acad. Arts and Scis. Home: 1207 E 50th St Chicago IL 60615-2908 Office: U Chgo Law Sch 1111 E 60th St Chicago IL 60637-2702

MORRIS, OWEN GLENN, engineering corporation executive; b. Shawnee, Okla., Feb. 3, 1927; s. Vestus and Myrtle (Lindsey) M.; m. Joyce Gast; children: Deborah Moree, Janine Inez. B.S. in Mech. Engring. U. Okla., 1947, M.Aero. Engring., 1948; postgrad., U. Va., 1952-53, Va. Poly. Inst., 1955-56, Coll. William and Mary, 1957-58. Aero., research scientist NASA, Langley Field, Va., 1948-61; mgr. mission engring. NASA (Apollo), Houston, 1961-64; mgr. reliability and quality assurance NASA (Apollo), 1964-66, chief project engr. lunar module, 1966-69, mgr. lunar module, 1969-72; mgr. NASA (Apollo Spacecraft Program), 1972-73; dep. mgr. NASA (Space Shuttle Orbiter), 1973-80; mgr. systems integration NASA (Space Shuttle), 1974-80; pres. Eagle Engring., 1980-86; pres., chief exec. officer Eagle Aerospace, Houston, 1987-90, chmn., chief exec. officer, 1990-93, chmn. bd., 1992—. Mem. Tex. Water Control Improvement Dist. Bd., 1969-76. Served with USNR, 1943-46. Recipient U.S. Medal of Freedom, 1972,

NASA Distinguished Service medal, 1973, NASA Exceptional Service medal, 1969. Asso. fellow Am. Inst. Aeros. and Astronautics; mem. Am. Asrronautical Soc., Am. Aviation Hist. Soc., Acad. Model Aeros., Tau Beta Pi, Tau Omega. Presbyterian (elder 1964—). Club: Rotary. Home: 14914 Timberland Ct Houston TX 77062-2922 Office: Eagle Aerospace 910 Gemini St Houston TX 77058-2704

MORRIS, PATRICIA SMITH, media specialist, author, educator; b. Franklin, N.J., Jan. 31, 1940; d. Joseph P. and Pauline C. (Lasinski) Smith; m. Carl W. Morris; children: Margaret, Sarah, Maureen. BA, Paterson State Coll.; MLS, Rutgers U. Media specialist Hanover Park (N.J.) Regional H.S. Bd. Edn. Author: Stepping into Research!, 1990; 6 Vols. of Young Adult Reading Activities Library, 1993. Exec. co-dir. N.J. Connection; mem. exec. bd. Highlands Regional Libr. Cooperative. Recipient N.J. Gov's. Tchr. Recognition award, 1989, Pres. award EMA, 1995; named Outstanding Ednl. Media Specialist of N.J., 1990. Mem. ALA, NEA, Am. Assn. Sch. Librs., N.J. Edn. Assn., Morris County Sch. Media Assn. (past pres.), Ednl. Media Assn. N.J. (exec. bd.). Office: Whippany Park HS Whippany Rd Whippany NJ 07981

MORRIS, PAUL FRANCIS, landscape architect; b. Corvallis, Oreg., June 29, 1960; s. Reginald and June Marie (Goumy) M.; m. LaVerna Kaye Skickler, June 12, 1982; 1 child, Ketan Joshua Sunil. B in Landscape Architecture, U. Oreg., 1984; grad. cert. in planning, Harvard U., 1987. Registered landscape arch., Oreg., Wash., Idaho; registered mediator, Oreg. Owner Paul Morris-Planning and Design, Eugene, 1980-84; cmty. planner City of Madras, Oreg., 1983-84; project mgr. Fred Glick Assocs., Inc., Portland, Oreg., 1984-86; design svcs. mgr. The Benkendorf Assocs. Corp., Portland, 1986-89; v.p., prin. McKeever/Morris, Inc., Portland, 1989—; adj. prof. landscape architecture U. Oreg., Eugene, 1992; juror awards program Oreg. Women of Distinction in Arch., 1994; juror annual awards program Oreg. Landscape Contractors Assn., 1996; spkr. in field. Contbr. articles to profl. jours. Active Met. Bus. Assn., Portland, 1989-93, Cascadia Native Landscape Ctr., Portland, 1989-93; bd. dirs. Hosford-Abernathy Neighborhood Assn., Portland, 1985-89, vice chair bd. dirs., 1988, chair bd. dirs., 1989; mem. Hales for City Commr. Polit. Campaign, Portland, 1992, Portland Parks Gen. Obligation Bond Measure Campaign, Portland, 1994, Columbia-Willamette Water Conservation Coalition, 1994-95, Met. Greenspaace Campaign Fund Raising Com., Portland, 1995, Blumenauer for U.S. Senate Campaign, Portland, 1996. Mem. Am. Soc. Landscape Archs. (mem.-at-large exec. com. Oreg. chpt. 1989-91, 91, 92, mem. annual meeting and awards program com. Oreg. chpt. 1990, v.p./pres. elect exec. com. Oreg. chpt. 1992-93, mem. nominating com. Oreg. chpt. 1992-95, many others, Presdl. awards Oreg. chpt. 1990, 92, Honor award Oreg. chpt. 1992, Profl. Leadership award Oreg. chpt. 1994, Sustainable Design award Oreg. chpt. 1994, Nat. Orchid award 1994, Nat. Honor award 1995), Am. Planning Assn. (mem. annual profl. awards com. Oreg. chpt. 1989, 93, Profl. Achievement awards Oreg. chpt. 1991, 93), Nat. Design Profls. Assn., Nat. Assn. Home Builders, Nat. Soc. for Park Resources, Oreg. Mediation Assn., Nat. Trust for Hist. Preservation, Hist. Preservation League Oreg. Avocations: acting, traveling, sailing, swimming. Office: McKeever/Morris Inc 209 SW Oak St Ste 200 Portland OR 97204-2729

MORRIS, PHILIP JOHN, aerospace engineering educator; b. Llandudno, Wales, Apr. 21, 1946; came to U.S., 1973; s. William Garnet and Dora (Butterworth) M.; m. Brenda Mary English, Aug. 24, 1968; children: Nicola Carol, Karen Elizabeth, Anthony Richard. BSc with honors, Southampton (Eng.) U., 1967, MSc, 1969, PhD, 1972. Rsch. assoc. U. Toronto, Ont., 1971-73; rsch. engr. Lockheed-Ga. Co., Marietta, 1973-77; asst. prof. Pa. State U., University Park, 1977-80; assoc. prof. Pa. State U., 1980-86, prof., 1986—, Boeing/ A.D. Welliver prof. aerospace engring., 1992—; cons., Lockheed Ga. Co., 1977-88. Contbr. to tech. publs. Fellow Am. Phys. Soc., AIAA (assoc., aeroacoustics tech. com. 1981-84, 89-95, chmn. 1993-95). Avocations: soccer, running. Office: Pa State U 233 Hammond Bldg # P University Park PA 16802-1401

MORRIS, PHYLLIS SUTTON, philosophy educator; b. Quincy, Ill., Jan. 25, 1931; d. John Guice and Helen Elizabeth (Provis) Sutton; m. John Martin Morris, Feb. 4, 1950; children: William Robert, Katherine Jill. Student, U. Mich., 1948-51; AB, U. Calif., 1953; MA, Colo. Coll., 1963; PhD, U. Mich., 1969. Instr. humanities Mich. State U., East Lansing, 1968-69; from lectr. to assoc. prof. Kirkland Coll., Clinton, N.Y., 1969-78; assoc. prof. Hamilton Coll., Clinton, 1978-83; adj. assoc. prof. LeMoyne Coll., Syracuse, N.Y., 1983-85; rsch. assoc. in philosophy Oberlin (Ohio) Coll., 1995—; vis. prof. philosophy Oberlin Coll., 1989-91, 93, 94-95, U. Mich., Ann Arbor, 1996. Author: Sartre's Concept of a Person, 1976; revs. editor Sartre Studies Internat. jour., 1995; contbr. articles to profl. jours. Travel grantee Am. Coun. Learned Socs., 1988, Summer Seminar grantee NEH, 1974, 82. Mem. Am. Philos. Assn., Sartre Cir., Sartre Soc. N.Am. (co-founder 1985, exec. com. 1985-91), Soc. for Phenomenology and Existential Philosophy, Soc. for Women in Philosophy. Democrat. Avocations: reading, walking, film watching. Home: 2116 Runnymede Blvd Ann Arbor MI 48103-5034

MORRIS, RALPH WILLIAM, chronopharmacologist; b. Cleveland Heights, Ohio, July 30, 1928; s. Earl Douglas and Viola Minnie (Mau) M.; m. Carmen R. Mueller; children: Christopher Lynn, Kirk Stephen, Timothy Allen and Todd Andrew (twins), Melissa Mary. BA, Ohio U., Athens, 1950, MS, 1953; PhD, U. Iowa, 1955; postgrad., Seabury-Western Theol. Sem., 1979-81, McHenry County Coll., 1986-88. Research fellow in pharmacology, then teaching fellow U. Iowa, 1952-55; instr. dept. pharmacology Coll. Medicine, 1955-56; asst. prof. dept. pharmacognosy and pharmacology Coll. Pharmacy, 1956-62, assoc. prof., 1962-69; prof. dept. pharmacodynamics Med. Center, U. Ill., 1969—; adj. prof. edn. Coll. Edn. U. Ill. at Chgo., 1976-85; vis. scientist San Jose State U., Calif., 1982-83, St. George Med. Sch., Grenada, 1994; mem. adv. com. 1st aid and safety Midwest chpt. ARC, 1972-83; cons. in drug edn. to Dangerous Drug Commn., Ill. Dept. Pub. Aid, Chgo., Ill. Dept. Profl. Regulataions, Ill. Dept. Corrections and suburban sch. dists. Referee and contbr. articles to profl. and sci. jours., lay mags., radio and TV appearances. Trustee Palatine (Ill.) Pub. Libr., 1967-72, pres., 1969-70; trustee N. Suburban Libr. System, 1968-72, pres. 1970-72, mem. long-range planning com., 1975-81; chmn. Ill. Libr. Trustees, 1970-72, intellectual freedom com.; mem. Title XX Ill. Citizens Adv. Coun., 1981-83; trusteee McHenry (Ill.) Pub. Libr. Dist., 1987-89, pres., 1987-89; trustee St. Gregory's Abbey, Three Rivers, Mich., 1989-96; bd. dirs. United Campus Ministry U. Ill. at Chgo., 1983-87; pres. R.W. Morris & Assocs., 1988—. Recipient Golden Apple Teaching award U. Ill. Coll. Pharmacy, 1966; cert. of merit Town of Palatine, 1972. Mem. AAAS, Am. Assn. Coll. Pharmacists, Internat. Soc. Chronobiology, European Soc. Chronbiology, Am. Soc. Pharmacology and Exptl. Therapeutics, Am. Library Trustee Assn., Ill. Library Trustee Assn. (v.p. 1970-72, dir. 1969-72), Sigma Xi, Rho Chi, Gamma Alpha. Episcopalian. Home: 584 Shoreline Dr Lake Barrington IL 60010-3883 Office: U Ill MC 865 833 S Wood St Chicago IL 60612-7229

MORRIS, REBECCA ROBINSON, lawyer; b. McKinney, Tex., July 27, 1945; d. Leland Howell and Grace Laverne (Stinson) Robinson; m. Jesse Eugene Morris, July 18, 1964; children: Jesse III, Susan, John. BBA in Acctg., So. Meth. U., 1974, JD, 1978. Bar: Tex. 1979, U.S. Dist. Ct. (no. dist.) Tex. Acct. Electronic Data Systems Corp., Dallas, 1975; assoc. atty. Dresser Industries, Inc., Dallas, 1978-81, staff atty., 1981-83, corp. atty., 1983-86, asst. sec., 1984-90, sr. atty. corp. adminstrn., 1986-87, corp. counsel, 1987—, sec., 1990—, v.p., 1994—. Trustee Plano (Tex.) Ind. Sch. Dist., 1979-91, 93-94, pres., 1980-85, sec., 1986-91; bd. dirs. Plano Futures Found., Inc., 1992—, pres., 1992-93, 96—. Mem. ABA, AICPA, Tex. State Bar, Dallas Bar Assn., Tex. Soc. CPAs, Am. Soc. Corp. Secs. (mem. securities law com. 1988—, proxy system com. 1990-93, exec. steering com. 1993-94, budget com. 1993—, chmn. 1995—, bd. dirs. 1991-94, chmn. mem. com. Dallas chpt. 1986, treas. 1987, v.p. 1988, pres. 1989), Am. Corp. Counsel Assn. (corp. and securities law com. 1991—), SMU Law Rev. Corp. Counsel Symposium (bd. advisors 1996—). Methodist. Home: 1718 14th Pl Plano TX 75074-6404 Office: Dresser Industries Inc 2001 Ross Ave Box 718 Dallas TX 75221-0718

MORRIS, RICHARD JEFFERY, plastic extrusion company executive; b. Peoria, Ill., Feb. 23, 1953; s. Gordon Dale and Selma Ann Morris; m. Patricia Ann Boarman, Apr. 23, 1977; children: Michael Christopher, Christine Elizabeth. BFA, U. Ill., 1975. Elec. engr. Hatfield Electric Co., Mossville, Ill., 1975-76; designer Internat. Paper Co., Peoria, 1976-79, Champion Internat., St. Paul, 1979-80; indsl. designer Liberty Diversified Industries, Mpls., 1980-81, rsch. specialist, 1981-82; gen. mgr. Diversi-Plast Products, Mpls., 1982-96, v.p., gen. mgr., 1996—; freelance artist, 1970-81; graphics instr. Ill. Cen. Coll., Peoria, 1978-79; com. mem. Home Ventilating Inst. Patentee bldg. and packaging methods. Mem. ch. coun. St. Mark Luth. Ch., Chillicothe, Ill., 1972; coach youth athletics, Mpls., 1987—, fundraiser Mpls. YMCA, Mpls. United Way; bd. dirs., dir. basketball Prior Lake Athletics for Youth. Mem. Soc. Plastics Engrs., Phi Theta Kappa. Avocations: coaching youth sports, basketball, fishing, gardening. Home: 15987 Island View Rd NW Prior Lake MN 55372-1606 Office: Diversi Plast Products 7425 Laurel Ave Minneapolis MN 55426-1501

MORRIS, RICHARD WARD, author; b. Milw., June 16, 1939; s. Alvin Harry and Dorothy Lydia (Wissmueller) M. BS, U. Nev., 1962, PhD, 1968; MS, U. N.Mex., 1964. Exec. dir. COSMEP, Inc., San Francisco, 1968-95. Author: Poetry Is a Kind of Writing, 1975, Light, 1979, The End of the World, 1980, The Fate of the Universe, 1982, Evolution and Human Nature, 1983, Dismantling the Universe, 1983, Time's Arrows, 1985, The Nature of Reality, 1987, The Edges of Science, 1990, Assyrians, 1991, (with others) The Word and Beyond, 1982, Cosmic Questions, 1993, Achilles in the Quantum Universe, 1997.

MORRIS, ROBERT CHRISTIAN, education educator; b. Anderson, Ind., Mar. 1, 1948; s. Robert Childs and Velma Jane (Vogley) M.; m. Linda Marie Butkus, Jan. 14, 1989. AB, Duke U., 1970; MS, Ind. State U., 1971, PhD, 1977. Cert. tchr.; lic. prin., supt. Profl. football player Houston Oilers, 1970; tchr. social studies Roanoke (Va.) Schs., 1970-71, 74-76; profl. football player New Orleans Saints, 1971-73; asst. prof. edn. Auburn (Ala.) U., 1976-81; assoc. prof. edn. U. S.C., Columbia, 1981-84, No. Ill. U., DeKalb, 1984-87; prof., head dept. edn., leadership, tech. and rsch. Ga. So. U., Statesboro, 1987-91; dean. sch. edn. U. Indpls., 1991-93; prof. edn. State U. West Ga., Carrollton, 1993—; cons. Mt. Morris (Ill.) Pub. Schs., Dixon Pub. Sch., 1986; cons., evaluator bi-lingual programs Dixon (Ill.) Pub. Schs. Author: A Resource Guide for Working with Youth-At-Risk, 1992, (pamphlet) A Field Practicum for Tchrs. of Gifted Children, 1982—; editor: Vantil on Education, 1978, Youth at Risk: A Resource Guide, 1991, Solving the Problems of Youth-At-Risk, 1992, Using What We Know About At-Risk Youth: Lessons From the Field, 1994; contbr. over 100 articles to profl. jours. Sponsor Sigma Nu Auburn U., 1977-81, Phi Kappa Sigma No. Ill. U., 1984-88, Alpha Tau Omega West Ga. Coll., 1993—; regional co-dir. Auburn Spl. Olympics, Auburn, 1977-81; games dir. S.C. Spl. Olympics, Columbia, 1982-84. Mem. ASCD, VFW, Am. Assn. Colls. for Tchrs. Edn., Am. Ednl. Rsch. Assn., John Dewey Soc. (exec. sec.-treas. 1982—), Profs. of Curriculum, Soc. Profs. of Edn., Phi Delta Kappa (former v.p. local chpt.), Phi Kappa Sigma (sponsor/advisor local chpt.), Kappa Delta Pi (sec.-treas., chpt. counselor), Civitan. Avocations: weightlifting, travel, painting. Home: 73 Mountain Oaks Dr Carrollton GA 30116-9028 Office: State U West GA Ednl Leadership and Founds Carrollton GA 30118-5160

MORRIS, ROBERT G(EMMILL), retired foreign service officer; b. Des Moines, July 20, 1929; s. Robert William and Iva May (Gemmill) M.; m. Beverly Schupfer, July 3, 1955; children: Robert William II, John Schupfer, Richard Edward. BS, Iowa State U., 1951; postgrad., Charles Francis U., Graz, 1951-52; MS, Calif. Inst. Tech., 1954; PhD, Iowa State U., 1957. Asst. prof. S.D. Sch. Mines and Tech., Rapid City, 1958-59, assoc. prof., 1959-62, prof., head dept. physics, 1962-68; phys. sci. officer Office of Naval Research, Washington, 1968-73, dir. electronics program, 1973-74; U.S. fgn. service officer U.S. Dept. State, Washington, 1974-78; counselor for sci. and technol. affairs U.S. Mission to OECD, Paris, 1978-82, U.S. Embassy, Bonn, Fed. Republic Germany, 1982-85; dep. asst. sec. of state for sci. and tech. affairs Washington, 1985-87; fgn. svc. officer U.S. Embassy, Buenos Aires, 1987-90, Madrid, 1990-92. Contbr. articles to profl. jours. Fulbright scholar, Austria, 1951; Swiss govt. fellow, Zurich, 1957. Fellow APS; mem. IEEE, Am. Fgn. Service Assn.

MORRIS, ROBERT JULIAN, JR., art gallery owner; b. Decatur, Ill., Jan. 12, 1932; s. Robert J. and M. Letitia (Ross) M.; m. J. Jean Nelson Morris, June 6, 1952; children: R. Thomas, Debora L., Charles A., Sandra J. BS in Chemistry, U. Ill., 1954; MS in Chemistry, Marshall U., 1961. Analytical chemist Union Carbide Chemicals, South Charleston, W.Va., 1954-61; sr. research chemist U.S. Gypsum Co., Des Plaines, Ill., 1961-63; research mgr. MacAndrews and Forbes Co., Camden, N.J., 1963-66; tech. dir. Nat. Can Corp., Chgo., 1966-73; v.p. corp. engring. Coachmen Industries Inc., Middlebury, Ind., 1973-74; pres. Coachmen Homes Corp., 1974-76; chmn. bd., chief exec. officer Medallion Plastics Inc., Elkhart, Ind., 1976-93; owner Robert Morris Gallery, Goshen, Ind., 1993—. Contbr. articles to profl. jours. Bd. dirs. Career Ctr., Elkhart, 1983-89, Ind. Voc. Tech. Coll., Plastics R&D Ctr. Ball State U., 1987-94. Mem. Rotary. Republican. Methodist. Avocations: fine art black and white photographic silver prints, travel. Home: 113 E Madison St Goshen IN 46526-3938 Office: Robert Morris Gallery 113 E Madison St Goshen IN 46526-3938

MORRIS, ROBERT LOUIS, management consultant; b. Phila., Aug. 24, 1932; s. Joseph Aloysius and Philomena Mary Ellen (Clauser) M.; BS, Drexel U., 1955; MS, U. Pa., 1957; postgrad. U. Cin., 1965-66, U. Chgo., 1969-71; m. Elizabeth Marie Smyth, Sept. 10, 1955; children—Robert L., Thomas J., Lawrence F., Elizabeth M., Mary Ellen, Richard B. Group leader Procter & Gamble Co., Miami Valley Labs., 1958-68; dir. computing services research and devel. div. Kraft, Inc., Glenview, Ill., 1968-71; dir. research and process devel. Continental Baking Co., Rye, N.Y. and St. Louis, 1971-77, v.p. tech. affairs, 1978-92; tech. dir. food and chem. products ITT Inc., N.Y.C., 1977-78; pres., Managing Tech., Inc., Williamsburg, Va., 1992—. Bd. dirs. Fundacion Chile, Santiago, 1978-79, 83-85; mem. Greenwich Rep. Town Meeting, 1977. Served with AUS, 1957. NSF fellow, 1955-56; Wilson S. Yerger fellow, 1956-57. Fellow Am. Inst. Chem. Engrs.; mem. Assn. Rsch. Dirs., Indsl. Rsch. Inst. (bd. dirs. 1988-91), Am. Chem. Soc., Am. Assn. Cereal Chemists, Inst. Food Techs. Roman Catholic. Clubs: Ford's Colony Golf. Patentee in field. Office: Managing Tech Inc PO Box 679 Lightfoot VA 23090-0679

MORRIS, ROBERT RENLY, minister, clinical pastoral education supervisor; b. Jacksonville, Fla., Feb. 15, 1938; s. Joseph Renly and Sybil (Stephens) M.; m. Lenda Smith, Dec. 7, 1963; children: Christopher Renly, Jennifer Kelly. BA, U. Fla., 1959; MDiv, Columbia Theol. Sem., Atlanta, 1962, ThM, 1967, D Ministry, 1990. Ordained to ministry Presbyn. Ch. (U.S.A.), 1962. Min. to students Ga. State Coll., Atlanta, 1959-60; asst. min. Trinity Presbyn. Ch., Atlanta, 1960-62; min. Clanton (Ala.) Presbyn. Ch., 1963-65, Kelly Presbyn. Ch., McDonough, Ga., 1965-67; pastoral counselor Ga. Assn. for Pastoral Care, Atlanta, 1966-68; coord. pastoral svcs. Winter Haven (Fla.) Hosp. and Community Health Ctr., 1969-79; min. Presbytery of Greater Atlanta, mem. div. pastoral care, 1984-86; dir. clin. pastoral edn. Emory Ct. for Pastoral Svcs., Atlanta, 1979—; adj. faculty Candler Sch. Theology, 1979-88. Contbr. book chpts., articles to profl. jours. Mem. AIDS Task Force, Atlanta, 1988-95, Task Force on Chem. Dependency, 1988. Mem. Am. Assn. Pastoral Counselors, Coll. Chaplains, Am. Assn. Marriage and Family Therapists (clin.), Assn. for Clin. Pastoral Edn. (cert. supr., gen. assembly nominating com. 1984, chmn. 1985, coord. ann. conf. 1986, long range planning com. of C com., standards com. S.E. region 1990-93), Beta Theta Pi. Democrat. Avocations: antique key collecting, canoeing, fishing, sailing. Home: 542 Cross Creek Pt Stone Mountain GA 30087-5328 Office: Emory U Hosp Dept Pastoral Svcs 1364 Clifton Rd NE Atlanta GA 30322-1059

MORRIS, ROBERT WARREN, physician assistant; b. Oakland, Calif., Mar. 28, 1948; s. Warren and Javine (Don Carlos) M.; children: Rebecca Lynn, Daniel Robert. BS, Old Dominion U., 1971; BS with honors, George Washington U., 1976; postgrad., N.Y. Med. Coll. Diplomate Nat. Bd. Med. Examiners; registered, N.Y. Physician asst. internal medicine Group Health Assn., Washington, 1976-81; physician asst. family practice Waddington (N.Y.) Med. Clinic, 1981-83; physician asst. internal medicine Northeast Permanente Med. Group, White Plains, N.Y., 1983—; mem. pharmacy and therapeutics com. Kaiser Health Plan, White Plains, 1986—, AIDS task force mem., 1989—, quality care com., 1986-90, health ctr. adminstr., Tarrytown, Yonkers, N.Y., 1985-90. Mem. Am. Assn. Physician Assts. Avocations: amateur astronomy, skiing, swimming, travel. Home: 2 Scenic Cir Croton on Hudson NY 10520 Office: Kaiser Found Health Plan 210 Westchester Ave White Plains NY 10604-2914

MORRIS, RONALD ANTHONY, county official; b. Wilmington, Del., Nov. 8, 1946; s. Elwood and Sophia (Ptak) M.; m. Barbara Marie Szostkowski, July 16, 1976. BS, U. Balt., 1970; MBA, Widener U., 1975. Cert. govt. fin. mgr. Cost acct. Atlas Chem. Industries, New Castle, Del., 1966-67; sr. cost acct. Bethlehem Steel Corp., Balt., 1967-70; sr. acct. J.K. Lasser & Co., CPAs, Wilmington, 1970-71; dep. dir. fin. City of Wilmington, 1971-74; acctg. supr. New Castle County, 1974-75, controller, 1975-80, budget and acctg. mgr., 1980—. Recipient Achievement award Nat. Assn. Counties, 1990, 92, 94, EXSL award Nat. Ctr. for Pub. Productivity, 1990, Award of Excellence, Nat. Assns. County Info. Officers, 1989. Mem. Del. Assn. Govtl. Fin. Officers (v.p. 1990-94), Am. Soc. Pub. Adminstrn., Del. Assn. for Pub. Adminstrn. (councilman 1980-82), Govt. Fin. Officers Assn., U.S. and Can. (com. mem. 1989—, Fin. Reporting Achievement award 1981-97, Disitng Budget Presentation award 1991-97), Am. Acctg. Assn., Nat. Assn. Accts. Avocations: classic cars, coins, currency. Home: 904 Wawaset St Wilmington DE 19806-3244

MORRIS, RUSSELL D., federal agency administrator; b. Columbus, Ohio, May 14, 1941; s. Russell F. and Helen Katherine (Rothwell) M.; m. Rebecca Ruth Rainer, Sept. 18, 1965; 1 child. BSc, Ohio State U., 1963, MBA, 1964, PhD, 1973. Officer Huntington Nat. Bank, Columbus, Ohio, 1964-68; grad. asst. Ohio State U., 1968-70; analyst Fed. Res. Bd., 1970-73, 1973-80; gen. mgr. U.S. Postal Svc., 1973-80, asst. commr., 1980-88, dep. commr., 1988-91; commr. fin. mgmt. svc. Dept. the Treasury, Washington, 1991—. Contbr. articles to profl. jours. Recipient Outstanding Achievement award Assn. Govt. Accts., 1979-80, Govt. Mgmt. Excellence award Pres. Coun. on Mgmt. Improvement, 1988, Presdl. Rank award, 1996. Mem. Phi Alpha Kappa, Phi Kappa Tau. Unitarian. Avocations: golf, tennis, blue grass banjo, Old testament research. Office: Dept of the Treasury Financial Mngmnt Service 401 14th St NW Washington DC 20227-0001

MORRIS, RUSTY LEE, architectural consulting firm executive; b. Glenwood Springs, Colo., Nov. 28, 1940; d. Raymond M. and Raylene Pearl Marie (Hendrick) Morris; m. Robert W. Sosa, Nov. 20, 1995; children: Thomas John, Michael Joseph (dec.), Michelle Renee Bentley. Student, York Christian Coll., 1974-75, U. Nebr., 1975-76, Mesa State Coll., 1992-95; BS in Orgnl. Mgmt. summa cum laude, Colo. Christian U., 1996; postgrad., Union Inst., 1996—; MS in Mgmt., Colo. Christian U., Cin., 1997. Specialist comm. security Martin-Marietta Corp., Larson AFB, 1962-63; communications security specialist classified def. project Boeing Aerospace Div., Larson AFB, Wash., 1963-64; with F.W. Sickles div. Gen. Instrument Corp., Chicopee, Mass., 1965-68; adminstr. judicial affairs J. Arthur Hickerson, Judge, Springfield, Mass., 1969-71; researcher Mont. United Indian Assn., Helena, 1970-72; adminstrv. asst. Vanderbilt U. Hosp., Nashville, 1980-82; paid bus. supr. Sears Svc. Ctr., Grand Junction, Colo., 1987-89; founder, chief exec. officer Vast Spl. Svcs., Grand Junction, 1988—; courier U.S. Census Bur., Grand Junction, 1990; spl. program coord. Colo. Dept. Parks and Recreation, Ridgway, 1990-91; acad. athletic program founder, coord. Mesa State Coll., 1992-93, math. and sci. rep., student govt., 1992—, athletic coun., 1993—, student health ctr. com., 1993—, faculty search com., 1993; founder, CEO Rolling Spokes Assn.; world cons. on archtl. contracts for structural and/or outdoor recreational facilities. Author: Abuse of Women with Disabilities, 1996. Vol. Easter Seals Soc., 1964-67, vol. instr. Adult Literacy Program, 1984-87; vol. T.V. host Muscular Dystrophy Assn. Am., 1975-94; bd. dirs. Independent Living Ctr., 1985-87, Handicap Awareness Week, 1989; trails com. Colo. State Parks and Outdoor Recreation, 1988—; condr. seminars Ams. With Disabilites Act, 1989—; cons. Bur. Reclamation, 1988—, Bur. Land Mgmt., 1989—; staff trainer Breckenridge Outdoor Recreation Ctr., 1989-90; emergency svcs. officer Colo. Civil Air Patrol, Thunder Mountain Squadron, 1989—; bd. dirs. Handicap Awareness, 1989; dir. com. Colo. State Trails Commn., 1989-90; mem. Dem. Nat. Com., 1991—; dist. com. Grand Junction Sch. Dist., 1992—; mem. Restore the Com., Avalon, 1993—; bd. dirs., presenter No. Colo. chpt. Colo. Orgn. of Victim Assistance; with victim assistance Mesa County Sheriff's Dept., 1993—. Recipient Hometown Hero award, 1993. Mem. AAUW, Internat. Platform Assn., Handicap Scholarship Assn. (bd. dirs. 1994, award 1993), Nat. Orgn. Victim Assistance (presenter 1988—), Nat. Coun. Alcoholism and Drug Abuse (vol. 1987—), Mother's Against Drunk Driver's (bd. dirs. Mesa County chpt., v.p. 1985—), Concerns of Policy Survivors, Club 20 of Western Colo. (mem. com. status), Great Outdoor Colo., Grand Junction C. of C., Grand Junction Symphony, Mus. Western Colo., Mesa State Coll. Geology Club, Toastmasters (Able Toastmaster, winner speech contests 1985-87). Home and Office: Vast Spl Svcs 612 N 15th St Grand Junction CO 81501-4422

MORRIS, SAMUEL CARY, environmental scientist, consultant, educator; b. Summit, N.J., Dec. 16, 1942; s. Samuel Cary Jr. and Roberta Ann (Griffiths) M.; m. Stephanie Margaret Rose, Aug. 13, 1966; children: Jennifer, Daniel, Laura. BSCE, Va. Mil. Inst., 1965; MS in Sanitary Engring., Rutgers U., 1966; ScD in Environ. Health, U. Pitts., 1973. Asst. prof. environ. sci. Ill. State U., Normal, 1971-72; rsch. assoc. U. Pitts., 1972-73; asst. scientist, then assoc. scientist Brookhaven Nat. Lab., Upton, N.Y., 1973-77, scientist, 1977—, dep. head div. analytic scis., 1990—; head Biomed. and Environ. Assessment Group, 1994—; adj. prof. Carnegie Mellon U., Pitts., 1976—; editl. bd. Environ. Internat., 1983—; lectr. SUNY-Stony Brook, 1992—. Author: Cancer Risk Assessment, 1990; mem. editl. bd. Environ. Modeling and Assessment, 1995—; contbr. chpts. to books, articles to profl. jours. Capt. U.S. Army, 1966-68. Mem. ASCE, Inst. for Ops. Rsch. and the Mgmt. Scis., Air and Waste Mgmt. Assn., Soc. Risk Analysis (coun. mem. 1984-86), Delta Omega. Office: Brookhaven Nat Lab Divsn Analytic Sciences Upton NY 11973

MORRIS, SANDRA JOAN, lawyer; b. Chgo., Oct. 13, 1944; d. Bernard and Helene (Davies) Aronson; m. Richard William Morris, May 30, 1965 (div. Jan. 1974); children: Tracy Michelle, Bretton Todd; m. William Mark Bandt, July 12, 1981; 1 child, Victoria Elizabeth. BA, U. Ariz., 1965; JD, Calif. Western U., 1969. Bar: Calif. 1970, U.S. Dist. Ct. (so. dist.) Calif. 1970; diplomate Am. Coll. Family Trial Lawyers. Ptnr. Morris & Morris, APC, San Diego, 1970-74; sole practice San Diego, 1974—; mem. Adv. Commn. on Family Law, Calif. Senate, 1978-79. Contbr. articles to profl. jours. Pres. San Diego Community Child Abuse Coordinating Coun., 1977; mem. human rsch. rev. bd. Children's Hosp., San Diego, 1977-92. Fellow Am. Acad. Matrimonial Lawyers (chpt. pres. 1987-88, nat. bd. govs. 1987-89, 93-94, parliamentarian 1989-91, treas. 1994—), Internat. Acad. Matrimonial Lawyers; mem. ABA (exec. com. family law marital property sect. 1982-83, 87-94), State Bar Calif. (cert. family law specialist 1980—), Lawyers Club San Diego (bd. dirs. 1973), San Diego Cert. Family Law Specialists (chair 1995-96). Republican. Jewish. Avocations: skiing, travel. Office: 3200 4th Ave San Diego CA 92103

MORRIS, SETH IRWIN, architect; b. Madisonville, Tex., Sept. 1, 1914; s. Seth Irwin and Carrie (Holleman) M.; m. Suzanne Kibler, Dec. 29, 1945; children: Mark Peter, Maria, David Kibler, Laura Houston, John Hampson. B.A., Rice Inst., 1935. Practice architecture Houston, 1935-87; ptnr. Wilson & Morris, 1938-87, Wilson, Morris & Crain, 1946-87, Wilson, Morris, Crain & Anderson, 1954-87; ptnr. S.I. Morris Assocs., 1972-87, cons., 1988—; ptnr. Morris/Aubry Architects, 1980-85, Morris Architects, 1986-87; cons. Jackson & Ryan, 1989—. Prin. works include Harris County Domed Stadium (Astrodome), 1965, Houston Pub. Library, 1975,. S.W. Home Office Texaco Inc., 1975, Prudential Ins. Co., 1977, One Houston Center, 1977, Brown and Root, Inc. hdqrs, 1978, Alfred C. Glassell, Jr. Sch. Art, 1979, 1st City Bank Tower, 1981, Wortham Theater Ctr., 1985. Chmn. bd. trustees Houston Mus. Fine Arts, 1961-63, 67-68, pres., 1967-68; chmn. bd. trustees Contemporary Arts Mus., 1988-89; bd. govs. Rice U., Houston.; bd. dirs. ARC Harris County. Served to comdr. USNR, 1942-46. Decorated Legion of Merit; Order Cloud and Banner China; recipient numerous archtl. honor awards Tex. Soc. Architects, numerous archtl. honor awards Houston chpt. AIA; nat. awards AIA, Gold medal Assn. Rice U. Alumni, 1991; named Disting. Alumnus Rice U., 1981. Fellow AIA; mem. Tex. Soc. Architects (Llewellen Pitts award 1992), Assn. Gen. Contractors (master builder awrd 1994), Houston C. of C. (dir. 1964-86). Presbyterian (elder). Home: 2 Waverly Ct Houston TX 77005-1842 Office: 2370 Rice Blvd Ste 210 Houston TX 77005-2660

MORRIS, STEPHEN ALLEN, elementary school educator; b. Garden Grove, Calif., Mar. 2, 1957; s. Eddie Melvin and Lesta Joy (Birdsall) M.; m. MariLynn Edith; stepchildren: Tyler, Trevor. BS in Phys. Edn., Calif. State U., Fullerton, 1987. Cert. tchr., Calif. Elem. tchr. Riverside (Calif.) Unified Sch. Dist., 1990—; lectr. Calif. Elem. Edn. Assn., Torrance, 1994—, The Edn. Ctr., Torrance, 1994—; cons. Inland Area Math. Project, Riverside, 1992—. Author: Everything You Wanted to Know About Division...In a Day!, 1993. Mem. Benjamin Franklin Elem. Sch. Site Coun., Riverside, 1992. Mem. ASCD, Nat. Coun. Tchrs. Math., Calif. Math. Coun. Baptist. Avocations: running, cycling, silkscreening. Home: 7245 Ayers Rock Rd Riverside CA 92508-6043 Office: Ben Franklin Elem Sch 19661 Orange Terrace Pky Riverside CA 92508-3256

MORRIS, STEPHEN BURRITT, marketing information executive; b. Morristown, N.J., Aug. 13, 1943; s. Grinnell and Cornelia Rogers (Kellogg) M.; m. Victoria Ann French, Feb. 18, 1967; children: Christopher Jackson, Robin Taylor. BA, Yale U., 1965; MBA, Harvard U., 1969. With product mgmt. Gen. Foods Corp., White Plains, N.Y., 1969-83, gen. mgr. Maxwell House Coffee div., 1983-85; v.p. Gen. Foods Corp., 1983-87, pres. Maxwell House div., 1986-87; founder, dir. Spectra Mktg. Systems Inc., Chgo., 1987-90; pres., CEO Vid Code Inc., Waltham, Mass., 1990-92; pres. The Arbitron Co., N.Y.C., 1992—; bd. dirs. John B. Stetson Co., 1991—. Trustee N.Y. Theatre Workshop, 1995—. Served to 2d lt. USMCR, 1965-66. Avocations: tennis; skiing; gardening. Home: 300 Mt Holly Rd Katonah NY 10536 Office: The Arbitron Co 142 W 57th St New York NY 10019-3300

MORRIS, STEVEN LYNN, career officer, aeronautical engineering educator; b. Dallas, Dec. 7, 1952; s. William Ira and Alta Faye (McCarley) M.; m. Jacqueline Ann Fenter, July 30, 1977; children: Steven Sean, Michael Wayne. BS in Engring. Scis., USAF Acad., 1975; MS in Aero. Engring, Air Force Inst. Tech., 1980; PhD in Aerospace Engring., Tex. A&M U., 1989. Commd. 2d lt. USAF, 1975, advanced through grades to lt. col.; assoc. prof., dep. head dept. aeronautics USAF Acad., Colo., 1989—. Named Outstanding Young Man Am., Jaycees, 1981. Mem. AIAA (sr. flight mechanics tech. com. 1991-94, dep. dir. for edn. region V 1992-94), USAF Acad. Assn. Grads., Am. Soc. for Engring. Edn., Tex. A&M U. Assn. Former Students. Baptist. Avocations: running, photography, hiking. Home: 6935 Snowbird Dr Colorado Springs CO 80918-1309 Office: Hdqs USAF Acad-DFAN U S A F Academy CO 80840

MORRIS, STEVLAND See WONDER, STEVIE

MORRIS, THOMAS QUINLAN, hospital administrator, physician; b. Yonkers, N.Y., Jan. 3, 1933; s. William Thomas and Mary Berenice (Quinlan) M.; m. Jacqueline Ingram, Sept. 12, 1959; children: Thomas, Amy, MaryAnne. BS, U. Notre Dame, 1954; MD, Columbia U., 1958. Diplomate Am. Bd. Internal Medicine. From instr. to assoc. prof. clin. medicine Coll. Physicians and Surgeons, Columbia U., N.Y.C., 1964-79, prof., 1979—, acting chmn. dept. medicine, 1978-82, assoc. dean academic affairs, 1979-82, vice dean faculty of medicine, 1982-84, vice chmn. dept. medicine, 1993-94, sr. assoc. v.p. for health scis., vice dean faculty medicine, 1994—; acting dir. Med. Services, Presbyn. Hosp., N.Y.C., 1978-82, pres., 1985-90; v.p. for programs N.Y. Acad. Medicine, 1990-94, advisor 1994—. Med. editor Complete Home Medical Guide, 1985. Trustee Mary Imogene Bassett Hosp., Cooperstown, N.Y., 1980—, chmn. 1994—; trustee Am. Univ. of Beirut, N.Y.C., 1985—. Served to capt. USAF, 1962-64. Fellow ACP; mem. Greater N.Y. Hosp. Assn. (bd. govs. 1985-90), League of Voluntary Hosps. and Homes (chmn. bd. dirs. 1985-89). Clubs: The Century, Harvey Soc. (N.Y.C.). Office: Coll Physicians and Surgeons 630 W 168th St New York NY 10032-3702 also: New York Acad Medicine 2 E 103rd St New York NY 10029-5207

MORRIS, THOMAS ROBBINS, college president, political science educator; b. Roanoke, Va., July 28, 1944; s. Robert Vaughan and Ethel (Robbins) M.; m. Barbara-lyn Belcher, July 23, 1966; children: Sheila Dawn, Tabbitha Lyn, Sharon Robbins, Rosa-lyn Vaughan. B.A. in History, Va. Mil. Inst., 1966; M.A., U. Va., 1969, Ph.D. in Govt., 1973; postgrad. Princeton Theol. Sem., 1966-67. Asst. prof. U. Richmond, Va., 1971-78, assoc. prof. polit. sci., 1978-87, prof., 1987-92, chair dept., 1981-84; polit. analyst WTVR-Channel 6 TV, Richmond, 1981-95; pres. Emory and Henry Coll., 1992—; vis. scholar U. Utah, 1986-87. Author: The Virginia Supreme Court: An Institutional and Political Analysis, 1975, Virginia Government and Politics: Readings and Comments, 3d edit., 1990. Bd. dirs. Housing Opportunities Made Equal, Richmond, Va., 1982-92. Liberal arts fellow Harvard Law Sch., Cambridge, Mass., 1976-77, NEH fellow U. Wis.-Madison, 1979-80; named Disting. Educator, U. Richmond, Va., 1982. Mem. Am. Polit. Sci. Assn., Omicron Delta Kappa. Methodist. Office: Emory & Henry Coll Office of Pres Emory VA 24327

MORRIS, THOMAS WILLIAM, symphony orchestra administrator; b. Rochester, N.Y., Feb. 7, 1944; s. William H. and Eleanor E. M.; m. Jane Allison, Aug. 7, 1965; children: Elisa L., Charles A., William H. A.B., Princeton U., 1965; M.B.A., Wharton Sch. U. Pa., 1969. Adminstrv. asst., Ford Found. fellow for adminstrv. interns in arts Cin. Symphony, 1965-67; payroll clk. bus. office Boston Symphony Orch., 1969-71, asst. mgr. bus. affairs, 1971-73, mgr., 1973-78, gen. mgr., 1978-86, v.p. spl. projects and planning, 1986; pres. Thomas W. Morris and Co., Inc., Boston, 1986-87; exec. dir. Cleve. Orch., 1987—; chmn. policy com. Maj. Orch. Mgrs., 1977-79; chmn. orch. panel Nat. Endowment for Arts, 1979—. Chmn. Cleve. Cultural Coalition, 1992-95; mem. Cleve. Bicentennial Commn., 1993—. Mem. Am. Symphony Orch. League (dir. 1977-79). Office: Cleve Orch Severance Hall 11001 Euclid Ave Cleveland OH 44106-1713

MORRIS, WILLIAM CHARLES, investor; b. St. Louis, Apr. 15, 1938; s. Barney Lockhart and Kathryn (Evers) M.; m. Susan VanAvery Follett, Aug. 26, 1961; children: Edward F., David L., Kenneth V. SB in Chem. Engring., MIT, 1960; MBA, Harvard Bus. Sch., 1963. Assoc. Mobil Chem. Co., N.Y.C., 1963-66, Lehman Bros., N.Y.C., 1967-72; mng. dir. Lehman Bros. Kuhn Loeb Inc. (and predecessor), N.Y.C., 1973-84; sr. advisor Shearson Lehman Bros., N.Y.C., 1985-87; chmn. Carbo Ceramics Inc., Dallas, 1987—; chmn., pres. J&W Seligman & Co., Inc., N.Y.C., 1988—; chmn. Tri-Continental Corp., N.Y.C., 1988—, The Seligman Group of Investment Cos., N.Y.C., 1988—; bd. dirs. Kerr McGee Corp., Oklahoma City, 1977—. Trustee Sarah Lawrence Coll., 1991—; mng. dir. Metro. Opera Assn., N.Y., 1995—. Served as ensign USCGR, 1961. Home: 5 Hampshire Cir Bronxville NY 10708-5803 Office: J & W Seligman & Co Inc 100 Park Ave Fl 8 New York NY 10017-5516

MORRIS, WILLIAM JOSEPH, paleontologist, educator; b. Balt., Oct. 14, 1923; s. Benjamin Moss and Aida (Ruble) M.; m. Ann Bates, Aug. 11, 1945; children—Lynn Ann (Mrs. Thomas W. Nadal), Carol Florence. B.A., Syracuse U., 1947; M.A., Princeton, 1948, Ph.D., 1950. Asst. prof. to asso. prof. geology Tex. A. and M. U., 1950-55; asso. prof. to prof. geology Occidental Coll., 1955—; also research asso. in vertebrate paleontology Los Angeles County Mus. Natural History, 1957—; Mem. Nat. Geog. Soc. expdn. to Baja, Calif., 1968-73. Contbr. articles profl. jours. Served with AUS, 1942-45. Recipient Arnold Guyot award Nat. Geog. Soc., 1968. Fellow Geol. Soc. Am., So. Calif. Acad. Scis. (pres. 1969-70, dir. 1958-70); mem. AAAS, Soc. Vertebrate Paleontologists, Soc. Study Evolution, Sigma Xi. Club: Explorers (N.Y.C.). Home: 707 S 3rd Ave Battle Ground WA 98604-3213 *I maintain that a commitment to intellectual and personal integrity is necessary for spiritual well-being. My rules are not complex. Honesty and an undeviating sense of responsibility to those who have offered opportunities and placed their trust in me are a part of my life. Intelligence appears necessary in order to contribute significantly to our society, but often lacking in those with adequate mental status is perseverance. One must be firm in belief and determination, and have a mature skepticism that can lead to invention.*

MORRIS, WILLIAM OTIS, JR., lawyer, educator, author; b. Fairmont, W.Va., Dec. 2, 1922; s. William Otis and Flora Helois (Preston) M.; m. Hazel Irene Kolbus, May 28, 1948; children: Barbara Ann, Melinda Lou. Student, Fairmont State Coll., 1940-41; AB, Coll. William and Mary, 1944; LLB, U. Ill., 1946, JD, 1968; D of Honorable Causes, Nicolaus Copernicus U., Torun, Poland, 1992; DHC, Nicholas Copernicus U., Torun, Poland, 1992. Bar: Va. 1945, Ill. 1946, U.S. Supreme Ct. 1949. Prof. bus. law U. Ill., 1947-55; assoc. prof. law Stetson U., 1955-58; prof. law W.Va. U., Morgantown, 1958-94, prof. emeritus law, 1994—; vis. U. Vienna, Austria, Nat. U., Singapore, Nat. U., Seoul, Korea, U. Sydney, Australia, East China Inst. of Law and Politics, U. Thessaloniki, Greece. Author: Dental Litigation, 1972, 2d edit., 1977, The Law of Domestic Relations in West Virginia, 1975, Veterinarian in Litigation, 1976, Revocation of Professional License, 1985, Handbook of Dental Law, 1994, The Dentist's Legal Advisor, 1994; mem. bd. editors Jour. Law and Ethics in Dentistry, Med. Malpractice Prevention, Clin. Jour.; contbr. articles to profl. jours. Decorated Merit medal (Poland); recipient Spl. award Nat. U. Seoul, Old Guard Medallion Coll. William and Mary, 1994, Lifetime Achievement Award Dentistry, 1994. Fellow Cleve. Clinic Med. Inst.; mem. Va. Bar, Ill. Bar, Am. Trial Lawyers Assn., W.Va. Trial Lawyers Assn., Order of Coif, Order of White Jackets. Republican. Lutheran. Home: 644 Bellaire Dr Morgantown WV 26505-2421

MORRIS, WILLIAM SHIVERS, III, newspaper executive; b. Augusta, Ga., Oct. 3, 1934; s. William Shivers Jr. and Florence (Hill) M.; m. Mary Sue Ellis, Jan. 18, 1958; children: William Shivers IV, John Tyler, Susie Blackmar. A.B. in Journalism, U. Ga., 1956. Asst. to pres., pub. Southeastern Newspapers and Augusta Newspapers, 1956-60; v.p., dir. Savannah Newspapers, Inc. and Savannah News-Press, Inc., Ga., 1960-63; v.p., dir. Southeastern Newspapers Corp., 1963-65, chmn. bd., chief exec. officer; chmn. bd., chief exec. officer Banner-Herald Pub. Co., Athens, Ga., 1965, Morris Communications Corp., Augusta, Southwestern Newspapers Corp., N. Am. Publs., Inc., Fla. Pub. Co., Jacksonville; chmn. bd., chief exec. officer, pub. Augusta Chronicle, Athens Star, and Augusta Herald, Ga., 1966-94, Augusta Chronicle and Athens Star, Ga., 1966—; pub. Juneau Empire; dir. Ga. Power Co., Atlanta, So. Co., Atlanta, Associated Press. Trustee Augusta Coll. Found.; bd. regents Univ. System Ga., 1967-73. Served to capt. USAF, 1956-58. Hon. mem. Golden Quill Soc., 1960. Mem. Am. Newspaper Pubs. Assn., Southeastern Newspaper Pubs. Assn. (dir. 1966—), So. Newspaper Pubs. Assn., Internat. Press Inst. Presbyterian (elder). Clubs: Pinnacle (Augusta) (pres.); University (N.Y.C.); Oglethorpe (Savannah); Commerce (Atlanta). Office: Morris Communications Corp PO Box 936 Augusta GA 30903-0936 also: Amarillo Globe-News Div PO Box 2091 Amarillo TX 79166-0001*

MORRIS, WILLIE, author, editor; b. Jackson, Miss., Nov. 29, 1934; s. Henry Rae and Marion (Weaks) M.; m. Celia Ann Buchan, Aug. 30, 1958 (divorced 1969); 1 child, David Rae; m. JoAnne Shirley Prichard, Sept. 14, 1991. BA, U. Tex., 1956; BA (Rhodes scholar 1956), New Coll., Oxford (Eng.) U., 1959, M.A., 1960; Ph.D. (hon.), Grinnell Coll., 1967, Gettysburg Coll., 1968. Assoc. editor Tex. Observer, Austin, 1960; editor in chief Tex. Observer, 1960-62; assoc. editor Harper's mag., 1963-65, exec. editor, 1965-67, editor in chief, 1967-71; v.p. Harper's Mag., Inc., 1967-71; writer-in-residence U. Miss., 1980-91; hon. fellow Silliman Coll., Yale. Author: The South Today, 100 Years After Appomattox, 1965, (autobiography) North Toward Home (Carr P. Collins nonfiction award, Houghton-Mifflin lit. award 1967), Yazoo: Integration in a Deep Southern Town, 1971, (children's fiction) Good Old Boy, 1971, (novel) The Last of the Southern Girls, 1973, (memoir) James Jones: A Friendship, 1978, (essays) Terrains of the Heart and Other Essays, 1981, (nonfiction) The Courting of Marcus Dupree, 1983 (Christopher medal), (essays) Always Stand in Against the Curve, 1983, Homecomings, 1989 (Miss. Disting. Book award), (children's fiction) Good Old Boy and the Witch of Yazoo, 1989, Faulkner's Mississippi, 1990, (stories) After All, It's Only a Game, 1992, (autobiography) New York Days, 1993 (Gov.'s artistic achievement award 1994, Best Book of 1993 Miss. award Miss. Inst. Arts and Letters), My Dog Skip, 1995, Introductory Essay Official Games and Souvenir Program for 1996 Centennial Olympics Richard Wright medal for literary excellence 1996. Mem. P.E.N. Club, Soc. Rhodes Scholars, ACLU, Phi Beta Kappa, Phi Eta Sigma, Sigma Delta Chi, Delta Tau Delta.

MORRIS, WRIGHT, novelist, critic; b. Central City, Nebr., Jan. 6, 1910; s. William H. and Grace (Osborn) M.; m. Mary E. Finfrock, 1934 (div. 1961); m. Josephine Kantor, 1961. Student, Pomona Coll., 1930-33; hon. degrees, Westminster Coll, U. Nebr., Pomona Coll. Prof. San Francisco State U., 1962-75. Author: My Uncle Dudley, 1942, The Man Who Was There, 1945, The Inhabitants, 1946, The Home Place, 1948, The World in the Attic, 1949, Man and Boy, 1951, The Works of Love, 1952, The Deep Sleep, 1953, The Huge Season, 1954, The Field of Vision, 1956 (Nat. Book award 1957), Love Among the Cannibals, 1957, The Territory Ahead, 1958, Ceremony in Lone Tree, 1960, The Mississippi River Reader, 1961, What a Way to Go, 1962, Cause for Wonder, 1963, One Day, 1965, In Orbit, 1967, A Bill of Rites, a Bill of Wrongs, a Bill of Goods, 1968, God's Country and My People, 1968, Wright Morris: A Reader, 1970, Fire Sermon, 1971, War Games, 1971, Love Affair: A Venetian Journal, 1972, Here is Einbaum, 1973, A Life, 1973, About Fiction, 1975, Real Losses, Imaginary Gains, 1976, The Fork River Space Project, 1977, Earthly Delights, Unearthly Adornments: The American Writer as Image Maker. 1978, Plains Song, 1980 (Am. Book award 1981), Will's Boy, 1981, Photographs and Words, 1982, Solo: An American Dreamer in Europe, 1933-34, 1983, A Cloak of Light, 1985, Collected Stories, 1986, Time Pieces: Word and Image, 1989, Writing My Life: An Autobiography, 1992, Three Easy Pieces, 1993, Two for the Road, 1994. Recipient Robert Kirsch award for body of work, 1981, Life Achievement award Nat. Endowment for Arts, 1986; Guggenheim fellow, 1942, 46, 54. Mem. Nat. Inst. Arts and Letters, Am. Acad. Arts and Scis. (Whiting award 1982). Office: care Harper & Collins Pubs 10 E 53rd St New York NY 10022-5244

MORRISETT, LLOYD N., foundation executive; b. Oklahoma City, Nov. 2, 1929; s. Lloyd N. and Jessie Ruth (Watson) M.; m. Mary Frances Pierre, June 10, 1952; children: Sarah, Julie. BA, Oberlin Coll., 1951, LHD (hon.), 1971; postgrad., U. Calif., 1951-53; PhD, Yale U., 1956; hon. degree, Northwestern U., 1975, RAND Grad. Sch., 1995. Instr. U. Calif., 1956-57, asst. prof., 1957-58; staff mem. Social Sci. Research Council, 1958-59; exec. asst. Carnegie Corp. of N.Y., 1959-61, exec. assoc., 1961-63, exec. assoc. and asst. to pres., 1963-65, v.p., 1965-69; v.p. Carnegie Found. for Advancement Teaching, 1965-69; pres. Markle Found., 1969—; trustee Sys. Devel. Found., 1970-88; trustee N.Y. Rand Inst., 1969-75, chmn. bd., 1972-75; trustee Riverside Rsch. Inst., 1971-74, Rsch. Triangle Inst., 1970-79, Ednl. Testing Svc., 1983-87; trustee Oberlin Coll., 1972-88, chmn. bd., 1975-81; trustee Rand, 1973-83, 85-95, 96—, chmn. bd., 1986-95; chmn. bd. trustees Children's TV Workshop, 1970—; bd. dirs. The Multi Media Corp., 1990-97, Classroom, Inc., 1992—, Infonautics Corp.; mem. adv. bd. Walt Whitman Ctr., Rutgers U., 1993—; mem. bd. WEBS, 1996—, overseers Darmouth Sch. Medicine, 1995—. Mem. Coun. on Fgn. Rels., 1968—; mem. N.Y. State Commn. on Quality, Cost and Financing Elem. and Secondary Edn., 1969-72; bd. dirs. Sys. Devel. Corp., 1966-70; mem. vis. com. Office for Info. Tech., Harvard, 1974-80; mem. Am. Coun. on Germany, 1975-79; bd. dirs. Haskins Labs., 1976—; mem. steering com. NRC, 1994-95. Fellow NSF, 1956. Fellow APA, AAAS; mem. N.Y. Acad. Scis., Sigma Xi. Home: 12 Castle Rd Irvington NY 10533-2017 Office: The Markle Found 75 Rockefeller Plz Rm 1800 New York NY 10019-6908

MORRISEY, MARENA GRANT, art museum administrator; b. Newport News, Va., May 28, 1945. BFA in Interior Design, Va. Commonwealth U., 1967, MA Art History, 1970. With Orlando (Fla.) Mus. Art, 1970—, exec. dir., 1976—; former v.p., chmn. mus. svcs. com., mem. ad hoc com. on collections sharing and long range planning com., past chmn. exhbns. and edn. com. Am. Fedn. Arts; former mem. nat. adv. coun. George Washington U. Clearinghouse on Mus. Edn.; former mem. accreditation com. Nat. Found. for Interior Design Edn. Rsch. Former mem. strategic planning adv. coun. Orange County Sch. Dist.; former mem. advt. rev. bd. BBB; former mem. Orlando Pub. Art Adv. Bd., Orlando Leadership Coun., Orlando Hist. Bldg. Commn.; former chmn. art selection com. Orlando Internat. Airport; former mem. bd. dirs. Sta. WMFE-TV. Named Orlando's Outstanding Woman of Yr. in Field of Art; recipient Fla. State of Arts award. Mem. Am. Assn. Mus. (former mem. governing bd., accreditation commn., profl. stds. and practices com., internat. com. on mus.), Assn. Art Mus. Dirs., Southeastern Mus. Conf. (past pres.), Fla. Art Mus. Dirs. Assn. (past pres.), Fla. Assn. Mus. (former bd. dirs.), Greater Orlando C. of C. (past mem. steering com. Leadership Orlando, former mem. Project 2000), Jr. League Orlano-Winter Park, Rotary Club Orlando (program com. Orlando, membership com., chmn. found. com., Paul Harris fellow). Office: Orlando Museum of Art 2416 N Mills Ave Orlando FL 32803-1426

MORRISH, ALLAN HENRY, electrical engineering educator; b. Winnipeg, Man., Can., Apr. 18, 1924; s. Stanley and Agnes (Payne) M.; children: John Stanley, Allan Richard. B.Sc. with Honors, U. Man., 1943; M.A., U. Toronto, 1946; Ph.D., U. Chgo., 1949. Mem. faculty U. B.C., Vancouver, Can., 1949-52; research asst. Radiation Lab., McGill U., Montreal, Que., Can., 1952-53; with dept. elec. engring. U. Minn., Mpls., 1953-64; prof. dept. elec. engring. U. Minn., 1959-64; prof. U. Man., Winnipeg, 1964—; head dept. physics U. Man., 1966-87, disting. prof., 1984—; vis. prof. Monash U., Clayton, Victoria, Australia, 1971-72, U. Calif., Davis, 1978, Ariz. State U., Tempe, 1984, U. Wash., Seattle, 1984, Tex. A&M U., College Station, 1989, Iowa State U., Ames, 1991; cons. Honeywell, Inc., Hopkins, Minn., 1956-57, 59-63. Author: The Physical Principles of Magnetism, 1965, Canted Antiferromagnetism: Hematite, 1994; also articles. NRC Can. postdoctoral fellow U. Bristol, Eng., 1950-51; Guggenheim fellow U. Oxford, Eng., 1957-58. Fellow Royal Soc. Can., Inst. of Physics (Eng.); mem. Am. Phys. Soc., Can. Assn. Physicists (pres. 1974-75, medal for achievement in physics 1977), Sigma Xi. Research on magnetic materials using superconducting solenoids. Home: 71 Agassiz Dr, Winnipeg, MB Canada R3T 2K9

MORRISH, THOMAS JAY, golf course architect; b. Grand Junction, Colo., July 6, 1936; s. Wilbur Merle and Margaret Beula (Cronk) M.; m. Louise Ann Dunn, Apr. 2, 1965; children: Carter J., Kimberly L. Coder. AA, Mesa Coll., Grand Junction, 1956; BS in Landscape and Nursery Mgmt., Colo. State U., 1964. Golf course arch. Robert Trent Jones, Montclaire, N.J., 1964-67, George Fazio, Jupiter, Fla., 1967-69, Desmond Muirhead, Newport Beach, Calif., 1969-72, Jack Nicklaus, North Palm Beach, Fla., 1972-83; prin. Jay Morrish & Assocs. Ltd., Flower Mound, Tex., 1983—. Prin. golf course designs include: Troon Golf & Country Club, Scottsdale, Ariz., Las Colinas Sports Club, Irving, Tex., Mira Vista, Ft. Worth, Foothills Golf Course, Phoenix, Forest Highlands, Flagstaff, Ariz. (One of 100 Top Golf Courses in World, Golf mag., Golf Digest), Bentwater on Lake Conroe, Houston, Shadow Glen Golf Club, Olathe, Kans. (Best New Private Course, Golf Digest 1989), Troon North Golf & Country Club, Scottsdale (One of 100 Top Courses in U.S., Golf mag.), Harbor Club on Lake Oconee, Greensboro, Ga., Loch Lomond, Scotland, The Country Club of St. Albans, Mo., Broken Top, Bend, Oreg., Dauble Eagle Club, Galena, Ohio (one of Top 100 Courses in World, Golf Mag.), Buffalo Creek Golf Course, Rockwall, Tex., La Cantera, San Antonio (Best New Pub. Course of 1995, Golf Digest Mag.), numerous others. Edn. grantee State of Colo., 1961-64; Trans-Miss. golf scholar, 1962-64. Mem. Am. Soc. Golf Course Archs., Nat. Golf Found., Safari Club Internat., Dallas Safari Club. Republican. Avocation: hunting. Office: 3700 Forums Dr Ste 207 Flower Mound TX 75028-1847

MORRISON, ANGUS CURRAN, aviation executive; b. Toronto, Ont., Can., Apr. 22, 1919; s. Gordon Fraser and Mabel Ethel (Chalcraft) M.; m. Carlotta Townsend Munoz, Mar. 1, 1947; children—Sandra, James, Christian, Mark. Student, Upper Can. Coll., Bishop's Coll. Sch. Pres. Atlas Aviation, Ltd., Ottawa, Ont., 1946-51; sec. Air Industries and Transport Assn. Can., Ottawa, 1951-62; pres., chief exec. officer Air Transport Assn. Can., 1962-85; ret., 1985—; v.p., dir. Munoz Corp., Montclair, N.J., 1969-73. Councillor Town of Almonte, Ont., 1960-65. Served with Royal Can. Armoured Corps, 1939-46. Recipient Diplome Paul Tissandier Fedn. Aeronautique Internationale, 1977, Casi C.D. Howe award, 1987, Companion of Order of Flight, 1989; named to Can.'s Aviation Hall of Fame, 1989. Assoc. fellow Can. Aeronautics and Space Inst.; mem. Internat. N.W. Aviation Coun., Chartered Inst. Transport. Anglican. Clubs: Rideau, Wings. Home: Burnside, PO Box 609, Almonte, ON Canada K0A 1A0

MORRISON, ASHTON BYROM, pathologist, medical school official; b. Northern Ireland, Oct. 13, 1922; came to U.S., 1955; s. Samuel and Henrietta (Good) M.; m. Claire Morris, M.D.; 1 dau., Mary Claire. MB, Queen's U, Belfast, No. Ireland, 1946; PhD, Queens U., Belfast, No. Ireland, 1950, MD (hon.), 1988; MD, Duke U., 1946. Intern Royal Victoria Hosp., Belfast, 1947; asst. lectr. Queens U., 1947-52; registrar dept. exptl. medicine Cambridge U., 1952-55, dir. med. studies Corpus Christi Coll., 1954-55; assoc. Duke U., N.C., 1955-58; asst. prof. pathology U. Pa. Sch. Medicine, 1958-61; assoc. prof. U. Rochester Sch. Medicine, 1961-65; prof. pathology, chmn. dept. Rutgers U. Med. Sch., 1965-80; v.p. acad. affairs Eastern Va. Med. Authority, 1980-83; dean Eastern Va. Med. Sch., 1980-83; prof. pathology Robert Wood Johnson Med. Sch.-U. Medicine and Dentistry N.J., Camden, 1983-93; assoc. dean in charge Robert Wood Johnson Med Sch.-U. Medicine and Dentistry N.J., Camden, 1983-89, prof. pathology emeritus, 1994-96, prof. pathology and lab. medicine emeritus, 1997—; prof. pathology Ea. Va. Med. Sch., 1994—; 22nd Scott Heron lectr. Royal Victoria Hosp., Belfast, No. Ireland, 1978. Recipient Disting. Alumnus award Duke U. Med. Sch., 1987. Mem. Am. Assn. Investigative Pathologists (emeritus), Am. Physiol. Soc. (emeritus), Soc. Exptl. Biology and Medicine (emeritus), Am. Soc. Nephrology (emeritus). Home: 215 Brooke Ave Apt 306 Norfolk VA 23510 Office: Eastern Va Med Sch 358 Mowbray Arch Ste 108 Norfolk VA 23507-2219

MORRISON, BRUCE ANDREW, government executive, former congressman; b. N.Y.C., Oct. 8, 1944; s. George and Dorothea A. (Meyer) M.; m. Nancy A. Wanat, Sept. 22, 1991; 1 child, Drew. S.B., MIT, 1965; M.S., U. Ill., 1970; J.D., Yale U., 1973; Litt.D. (hon.), Quinnipac Coll. Staff atty. New Haven Legal Assistance Assn., 1973-74, mng. atty., 1974-76, exec. dir., 1976-81; mem. 98th-101st Congresses from 3d Conn. dist., 1983-90; Dem.-at-Large whip, mem. banking com., judiciary com., D.C. Com., select com. on children, youth and families, vet. affairs, 1983-91, chmn. L.I. Sound Caucus, chmn. Third World Debt Caucus; chmn. Fed. Housing Fin. Bd., 1995—; chmn. judiciary subcom. on immigration, refugees, and internat. law U.S. Ho. of Reps.; co-chmn. ad hoc com. on Irish affairs; mem. U.S. commn. on immigration reform; chair Irish Ams. for Clinton-Gore, 1992, 96; chair Ams. for a New Irish Agenda, 1993-95. Bd. dirs. U. Limerick (Ireland) Found. Mem. ABA, Conn. Bar Assn., New Haven County Bar Assn., Am. Immigration Lawyers Assn. Lutheran. Office: Federal Housing Finance Bd 1777 F St NW Washington DC 20006-5210

MORRISON, CLINTON, banker; b. Mpls., Mar. 26, 1915; s. Angus Washburn and Helen (Truesdale) M.; m. Mary K. Morrison. B.A., Yale U., 1937; M.B.A., Harvard U., 1939. With Shell Oil Co., N.Y.C., St. Louis, 1939-41; with Vassar Co., Chgo., 1946-48, Holding Co., Mpls., 1948, First Nat. Bank, Mpls., 1955-80; former vice chmn. bd., chmn. trust com. First Nat. Bank; former dir. Gt. No. Ins. Co., Minn. Title Fin. Corp., Munsingwear, Inc.; Dep. regional dir. Far East Fgn. Operations Adminstrn. for U.S. Govt., 1953- 55; mem. Internat. Pvt. Investment Adv. Council to AID, Dept. State, 1967-68, Nat. Adv. Council on Minority Bus. Enterprise, 1968-72. Life trustee Mpls. Art Inst., Mpls. Coll. Art and Design; former trustee Lakewood Cemetery Assn. Served to maj. Q.M.C. AUS, 1942-46. Mem. U.S. C. of C. (chmn. 1975-76), Bankers Assn. (exec. com. trust div. 1969-72), Twin Cities Soc. Security Analysts, Mpls. Econ. Roundtable. Home: 2400 Cedar Point Dr Wayzata MN 55391-2618 Office: 601 2nd Ave S Ste 4940 Minneapolis MN 55402-4321

MORRISON, DARREL GENE, landscape architecture educator; b. Orient, Iowa, June 20, 1937; s. Raymond Delbert and Rosy Christina (Mensing) M.; m. Dawna Lee Hauptman, June 29, 1963 (div. Sept. 1987); children: Jon David, Scott Darrel. B.S.L.A., Iowa State U., 1959; M.S.L.A., U. Wis., 1969. Landscape architect Md. Nat. Capital Park and Plan Commn., Silver Spring, 1962-64, T.D. Donovan & Assocs., Silver Spring, Md., 1964-66, City Washington, 1966-67; research asst. U. Wis., Madison, 1967-69, mem. faculty, 1969-83; John Bascom prof. U. Wis., 1978; dean environ. design U. Ga., Athens, 1983-92, prof. environ. design, 1992—. Co-editor: Landscape Jour., 1981-88. Served with U.S. Army, 1960-62. Recipient Disting. Tchg. award U. Wis., 1976, Bracken medal Pa. State U., 1996; named Outstanding Educator Coun. Educators in Landscape Architecture, 1977, 94. Fellow Am. Soc. Landscape Architects (v.p. 1987-89). Office: Sch of Environtl Design Univ Ga Athens GA 30602

MORRISON, DAVID, science administrator; b. Danville, Ill., June 26, 1940; s. Donald Harlan Morrison and Alice Lee (Douglass) Guin; m. Nancy Dunlap, June 19, 1966 (div. 1977); m. Janet L. Irick, Aug. 23, 1981. BA, U. Ill., 1962; PhD, Harvard U., 1969. Prof. astronomy U. Hawaii, Honolulu, 1969-88, vice chancellor rsch., 1983-85, dir. IRTF telescope, 1985-88; dep. assoc. adminstr. NASA OFfice Space Sci., Washington, 1981; chief space sci. div. NASA Ames Rsch. Ctr., Moffett Field, Calif., 1988-96, dir. space, 1996—; pres. Astron. Soc. of the Pacific, San Francisco, 1982-84; chmn. Divsn. for Planetary Scis., Washington, 1980-81; councillor Am. Astron. Soc., Washington, 1982-85; pres. Internat. Astron. Union Commn. on Planets, 1991-94. Author: Exploration of the Universe, 1987, 91, 95, The Planetary System, 1988, 96, Cosmic Catastrophes, 1989, Exploring Planetary Worlds, 1993, Voyages Through the Universe, 1996; editor: Satellites of Jupiter, 1982; contbr. articles to profl. jour. Fellow AAAS, 1982, Com. for Sci. Investigation of Claims of Paranormal, 1983, Calif. Acad. Sci. Mem. Cosmos Club. Achievements include advanced research for Voyager and Galileo planetary exploration missions. Home: 14660 Fieldstone Saratoga CA 95070 Office: NASA Ames Rsch Ctr # N200-7 Moffett Field CA 94035

MORRISON, DAVID CAMPBELL, immunology educator; b. Stoneham, Mass., Sept. 1, 1941; s. Walter Howard and Grace Falkner (May) M.; m. Pamela Wentworth, May 9, 1981; children: Michael Lawrence, Jenilee Angelica. BS magna cum laude, U. Mass., 1963; PhD, Yale U., 1969. Assoc. NIH, Bethesda, Md., 1969-71; assoc. Research Inst. Scripps Clinic, La Jolla, Calif., 1971-74, asst. prof., 1974-78, assoc. prof., 1978-80; assoc. prof. Emory U., Atlanta, 1980-81, prof., 1981-85; prof. Kans. U., Kansas City, 1985—; chmn. dept. microbiology Med. Ctr. Kans. U., Kansas City, 1985-91; assoc. dir. Cancer Ctr. Kans. U., Kansas City, 1991-95; cons. EPA, Washington, 1976-80, NIH bacteriology and mycology study sect., Bethesda, 1986-90; mem. NIAID allergy immunology and transplant rsch. com. NIH, 1995—; vis. scientist Max Planck Inst., Freiburg, Fed. Republic Germany, 1975. Editor Immunology Letters, 1991-95, Infection and Immunity, 1992-94, Jour. Endotoxin Rsch., 1993—. Recipient Rsch. Career Devel. award NIH, 1975, Merit award, 1990, Disting. Prof. of Cancer Rsch. Kansas Masons, 1994—. Fellow Infectious Disease Soc. Am.; mem. Am. Assn. Immunologists, Am. Soc. Exptl. Pathology, Am. Soc. Microbiology, Am. Acad. Microbiology, Am. Soc. Biochemistry and Molecular Biology, Internat. Endotoxin Soc. (pres). Avocations: gardening, banjo. Home: 6235 Mission Dr Mission Hills KS 66208-1252 Office: U Kans Med Ctr Cancer Ctr Kansas City KS 66160

MORRISON, DAVID FRED, freight company executive; b. Columbus, Ohio, Aug. 15, 1953; s. Fred Liew and Sophie Ann (Snider) M.; 1 child, Ian. BA, Stanford U., 1975; MBA, U. So. Calif., 1978. Sr. corp. planning analyst Tiger Internat., L.A., 1978-80, mgr. new bus. devel., 1980-81; dir. planning and controls Hall's Motor Transit Co., Mechanicsburg, Pa., 1981-82; mng. dir., gen. mgr. Consol. Freightways Export-Import Svc., San Francisco, 1984-86; asst. treas. McKesson Corp., San Francisco, 1987-90, treas., 1990-91; dir. strategic planning Consol. Freightways, Inc., Palo Alto, Calif., 1982-84, 86-87, v.p., treas., 1991-96; exec. v.p., CFO Consol. Freightways Corp., 1996—. Bd. dirs. Am. Sports Inst., Mill Valley, Calif., 1992—. Fellow State of Calif., 1977, Commerce Assocs., 1977. Mem. Nat. Assn. Corp. Treas., Fin. Execs. Inst. (silver medal 1978), Turnaround Mgmt. Assn, San Francisco Treas. Club (pres.). Avocations: cycling, scuba, skiing. Office: Consol Freightways Inc 175 Linfield Dr Menlo Park CA 94025-3750

MORRISON, DAVID LEE, librarian, educator; b. New London, Conn., Aug. 28, 1948; s. Samuel and Beatrice (Kinslinger) M. BA in Classics with highest honors, U. Calif., Santa Barbara, 1979; MLS, U. Ariz., 1986. Documents libr. Marriott Libr., U. Utah, Salt Lake City, 1987—, instr. libr. literacy course, 1990—; patent fellowship libr. U.S. Patent and Trademark Office, 1996-97; workshop presenter in field; guest lectr. U. Ariz. Grad. Libr. Sch., fall 1988-94; participant confs. in field. Fay and Lawrence Clark Powell scholar U. Ariz., 1983. Mem. ALA (govt. docs. round table info. tech. com. 1987-89), Utah Libr. Assn. (GODORT bylaws com. 1987-88, 91-92, chmn. nominating com. 1987-88, continuing edn. com. 1987-89, vice chmn., chmn.-elect 1992-93, chmn. GODORT 1993-94), Patent and Trademark Depository Libr. Assn. (fin. com. 1988-97, sec.-treas. 1989-90, 92—), Patent Documentation Soc. Home: Apt 518 S 2111 Jefferson Davis Hwy Arlington VA 22202 Office: U Utah Documents Div Marriott Libr Salt Lake City UT 84112

MORRISON, DEBORAH JEAN, lawyer; b. Johnstown, Pa., Feb. 18, 1955; d. Ralph Wesley and Norma Jean (Kinsey) Morrison; m. Ricardo Daniel Kamenetzky, Sept. 6, 1978 (div. Nov. 1991); children: Elena Raquel, Julia Rebecca. BA in Polit. Sci., Chatham Coll., 1977; postgrad., U. Miami, Fla., 1977-78; JD, U. Pitts., 1981. Bar: Pa. 1981, Ill. 1985. Legal asst. Klein Y Mairal, Buenos Aires, Argentina, 1978-79; legal intern Neighborhood Legal Svcs., Aliquippa, Pa., 1980-81; law clk. Pa. Superior Ct., Pitts., 1981-84; atty. John Deere Credit Co., Moline, Ill., 1985-89; sr. atty. Deere & Co., Moline, Ill., 1989-96, counsel, 1996—. Mem. ABA, Pa. Bar Assn., Phi Beta Kappa, Order of the Coif. Democrat. Mem. United Methodist. Office: Deere & Co John Deere Rd Moline IL 61265-8098

MORRISON, DONALD FRANKLIN, statistician, educator; b. Stoneham, Mass., Feb. 10, 1931; s. Daniel Norman and Agnes Beatrice (Packard) M.; m. Phyllis Ann Hazen, Aug. 19, 1967; children: Norman Hazen, Stephen Donald. B.S. in Bus. Adminstrn, Boston U., 1953, A.M., 1954; M.S., U. N.C., 1957; Ph.D., Va. Poly. Inst. and State U., 1960; M.A. (hon.), U. Pa., 1971. Mem. staff Lincoln Lab., M.I.T., 1956; cons. math. statistician NIMH, Bethesda, Md., 1956-63; mem. tech. staff Bell Labs., Holmdel, N.J., 1967; mem. faculty, dept. stats. Wharton Sch., U. Pa., 1963—, prof. stats., 1973—, chmn. dept., 1978-85. Author: Multivariate Statistical Methods, 3d edit., 1990, Applied Linear Statistical Methods, 1983; editor: The American Statistician, 1972-75; assoc. editor: Biometrics, 1972-74; contbr. articles to profl. jours. Served with USPHS, 1956-58. NSF grantee, 1966. Fellow Am. Statis. Assn., Inst. Math. Stats.; mem. AAAS, Internat. Statis. Inst., Biometric Soc., Royal Statis. Soc., Psychometric Soc., B&M R.R. Hist. Soc., Nat. R.R. Hist. Soc. Democrat. Home: 118 E Brookhaven Rd Wallingford PA 19086-6327 Office: U Pa Wharton Sch Philadelphia PA 19104-6302

MORRISON, DONALD GRAHAM, business educator, consultant; b. Detroit, Feb. 26, 1939; s. Roderick and Ethelyne (Murray) M.; m. Sherie Leaver, Sept. 12, 1964; children: Heather Margaret Cloonan, Tracey Michelle Oliva. B.S.M.E., MIT, 1961; Ph.D. in Ops. Research, Stanford U., 1965. Instr. Stanford U., Calif., 1965-66, vis. prof., 1982-97; mem. faculty Columbia U., N.Y.C., 1966-87, prof., 1973-87, Armand G. Erpf prof. bus., 1985-87; William E. Leonard prof. Anderson Grad. Sch. Mgmt., UCLA, 1987—; vis. prof. U. Calif., Berkeley, 1970-71; cons. in field, UCLA faculty athletic rep. to NCAA. Editor in chief Mgmt. Sci., 1983-90; founding editor Mktg. Sci., 1980-82. Elder Hitchcock Presbyn. Ch., Scarsdale, N.Y., 1978-84, Westwood Presbyn. Ch., L.A., 1991-94, 95—; treas. Scarsdale Jr. H.S. PTA, 1977-78; acad. trustee Mktg. Sci. Inst., 1986-92; mem. Decision, Risk and Mgmt. Sci. rev. bd. NSF, 1989-91. Mem. Inst. Mgmt. Sci. (pres. 1990-92), Ops. Rsch. Soc. Am., Am. Statis. Assn. Presbyterian. Avocations: golf; jogging; bridge. Office: UCLA Anderston Grad Sch Mgmt 110 Westwood Plz Los Angeles CA 90095-1481

MORRISON, DONALD WILLIAM, lawyer; b. Portland, Oreg., Mar. 31, 1926; s. Robert Angus and Laura Calista (Hodgson) M.; m. Elizabeth Margaret Perry, July 25, 1953; children: Elizabeth Laura, Carol Margaret. B.S.E.E., U. Wash., 1946; LL.B., Stanford U., 1950. Bar: Oreg. 1950, Calif. 1950, N.Y. 1967, Ill. 1968, Ohio 1974. Assoc. Pendergrass, Spackman, Bullivant & Wright, Portland, 1950-57; ptnr. Pendergrass, Spackman, Bullivant & Wright, 1957-60; gen. atty. Pacific N.W. Bell, Portland, 1960-66; atty. AT&T, N.Y.C., 1966-68; counsel Ill. Bell Telephone Co., Chgo., 1968-74; v.p., gen. counsel Ohio Bell Telephone Co., Cleve., 1974-91; of counsel Arter & Hadden, Cleve., 1991—. Trustee Citizens League Rsch. Inst., Health Trustees Inst., Cleve.; vice chair, mem. exec. com. Cleve. Coun. on World Affairs; mem. adv. com. Cleve. Play House; adv. com., trustee Cleve. Bot. Garden; mem. vis. com. Cleve. State U. Law Sch.; mem. Holden Parks Trust Commn. With USN, 1943-50. Recipient various bar and civic appreciation awards. Mem. ABA, Ohio State Bar Assn., Bar Assn. Greater Cleve., Oreg. State Bar Assn., Calif. Bar Assn., The Country Club, Rowfant Club. Office: Arter & Hadden 1100 Huntington Bldg Cleveland OH 44115

MORRISON, ELLEN M., writer, researcher; b. Marysville, Calif., Apr. 17, 1954; d. Louis Arch and Mildred Claire (Hansen) Morrison; m. Kenneth William Lann, Jun. 26, 1976; 1 child, Mallory. BA, UCLA, 1977; MA, U. Chgo., 1982, PhD, 1979-87. Rsch. asst. U. Chgo., 1980-82, rsch. analyst, 1982-84; project dir. Northwestern U., Evanston, Ill., 1984-87; postdoctoral fellow U. Calif., San Francisco, 1988-90; program dir. Inst. for the Future, Menlo Park, Calif., 1990-95; author San Carlos, Calif., 1995—. Co-author: Strategic Choices For America's Hospitals (book of the year 1990), 1990; Contbr. articles to profl. jours. Mem. NOW, Amnesty Internat., Greenpeace. Democrat. Avocations: public education support, community theatre, jogging, skiing, tennis. Home and Office: 142 Plymouth Ave San Carlos CA 94070-1621

MORRISON, FRANCIS SECREST, physician; b. Chgo., July 29, 1931; s. Clifton B. and Marie B. (LaPierre) M.; m. Dorothy Daniels, Nov. 29, 1957; children: Francis, Thomas, Kenneth. Student, U. Ill., Chgo., 1949-51; B.S. with honors, Miss. State U., 1954; M.D., U. Miss., 1959. Diplomate: Am. Bd. Internal Medicine. Intern Hosp. of U. Pa., Phila., 1959-60; resident in internal medicine Hosp. of U. Pa., 1960-62; trainee in hematology Blood Research Lab., Tufts-New Eng. Med. Center, Boston, 1962-64; research fellow Blood Research Lab., Tufts-New Eng. Med. Center, 1964-65; vis. investigator St. Mary's Hosp., London, 1966; attending physician, dir. div. hematology and oncology Univ. Hosp., Jackson, Miss., 1969-80; dir. div. hematology Univ. Hosp., 1980-92, dir. blood transfusion service, 1974-92, chief of staff, 1986; cons. in hematology Miss. Meth. Rehab. Ctr., Jackson, 1976; asst. prof. medicine U. Miss., Jackson, 1969-70, dir. div. hematology, 1969-92, assoc. prof., 1970-76, prof., 1976-95, prof. emeritus medicine, 1995—, med. dir. MetraHealth Gov. Programs, 1995—; mem. faculty U. Miss. Grad. Sch. Medicine, 1971-80; profl. adv. Jackson Community Blood Bank, Inc., 1973-75; dir. regional cancer program, also regional blood program Miss. Regional Med. Program, 1971-75; exec. dir. Miss. Regional Blood Ctr., 1975-79; mem. adv. bd. Jackson-Hinds Comprehensive Health Ctr., 1973-78; rsch. cons. Alcorn A. and M. Coll., 1973-74; med. cons. Travelers Medicare Miss. 1994-95; guest lectr. various health orgns. and TV programs; mem., chmn. hemophilia adv. bd. Miss. Bd. Health, 1974-90; chmn. task force on regionalization Am. Blood Commn., 1978-80; mem. Miss. Gov.'s Council on Aging, 1976-88; bd. dirs. Lake Lorman Corp., 1983-87, pres., 1987-88; commr. Lake Lorman Utility Dist., 1983-90, sec., treas., 1984-89, pres., 1989-91. Contbr. numerous articles on hematology and oncology to med. jours. Pres. parish coun. St. Peter's Cathedral, Jackson, 1972-74; chmn. Natchez-Jackson Diocesan Com. Community Svcs., 1972-76; bd. dirs. Miss. Opera Assn., 1973-78; bd. dirs. Miss. Found. for Med. Care, 1993—, vice chmn., 1996—; pres. bd. St. Joseph High Sch., 1974-75; bd. dirs. Med. Alumni of U. Miss., 1987-96, mem. exec. com., 1990—, pres., 1992, mem. dean's med. alumni adv. com., 1987-96. Served to comdr. M.C., USN. Fellow ACP; mem. Am. Assn. Blood Banks (sci. workshop com. 1975-78, Component Therapy com. 1987-90, sci. program com. 1988-90, extracorporeal therapy com. 1989-93, S. Cen. dist. adv. group 1985-93), Internat. Soc. Blood Transfusion, Am., Internat. socs. hematology, Jackson Acad. Medicine (pres. 1976), Am. Coll. Nuclear Medicine (alt. del. Miss. 1975), Am. Assn. Cancer Edn. (exec. com. 1978-81), Am. Assn. Cancer Rsch., N.Y. Acad. Scis., Miss. Acad. Scis., World Fedn. Hemophilia, Internat. Soc. Thrombosis and Haemostasis, Cen. Med. Soc., So. Med. Assn., So. Assn. Oncology (founding mem. 1988), Miss. Med Assn. (com. on blood transfusion 1976-77, ho. of dels. 1985-96, fin. com. 1985-90), Am. Soc. Nuclear Medicine, Am. Soc. Clin. Oncology, S.W. Oncology Group (prin. investigator), Soc. Cryobiology, Am. Cancer Soc. (dir. 1971-82, pres. Miss. div. 1977, chmn. exec. com. 1978, nat. del. 1981-82), South Central Assn. Blood Banks (hon. life, bd. dirs. 1974-89, program chmn. 1975, v.p. 1977-79, pres. 1987-88, pres. found. 1992-94), So. Blood Club (pres. 1977), Council Community Blood Centers (trustee 1975-79), Am. Soc. for Apheresis (bd. dirs. 1987-93, sec. treas, 1987-88, v.p. 1988-89, pres. 1990, program com., fin. com., internat. affairs com. 1990-96, chmn. 1992-92), World Apheresis Assn (bd. dirs. 1990—, pres.-elect 1993, pres. 1994), Internat. Platform Assn., Chain des Rotisseurs (founding Jackson Bailli, 1994, conseiller l'ordre mondial), Sigma Xi, Phi Kappa Phi, Omicron Delta Kappa. Home: 173 Lakeshore Dr Jackson MS 39213-9473 Office: Metrahealth 775 Woodlands Pky Ridgeland MS 39157-5212

MORRISON, FRED BEVERLY, real estate consultant; b. Gt. Neck, N.Y., May 21, 1927; s. Fred B. and Beverly (Fitzgerald) M.; m. Janet Thornton Johnson, May 22, 1948; children—Jane, Susan, Martha, James, Ann, David. BA, Columbia U., 1948, LLB, 1951. Bar: D.C. 1952. Asst. gen. counsel ARC, Washington, 1951-54; nat. exec. sec., voluntary home mortgage program Housing and Home Fin. Agy., Washington, 1954-57; investment v.p. mortgages Met. Life Ins. Co., N.Y.C., 1957-67; pres. Lomas & Nettleton Co., Dallas, 1967-76; pres., CEO Western Mortgage Corp., L.A., 1976-78; exec. v.p. real estate industries div. Crocker Nat. Bank, L.A., 1978-84; pres. Pearce, Urstadt, Mayer & Greer, N.Y.C., 1984-89; real estate cons., 1989—; bd. dirs. Guardian Life Ins. Co., MetLife Internat. Real Estate Equity Shares; chmn. Fed. Nat. Mortgage Assn. Adv. Com., 1981. Mem. Mortgage Bankers Assn. Am. (gov. 1979-84). Club: Union League (N.Y.C.). Home: 947 Post Rd Wakefield RI 02879-7521

MORRISON, FRED LAMONT, law educator; b. Salina, Kans., Dec. 12, 1939; s. Earl F. and Madge Louise (Glass) M.; m. Charlotte Foot, Dec. 27, 1971; children: Charles, Theodore, George, David. AB, U. Kans., 1961; BA, Oxford (Eng.) U., 1963, MA, 1968; PhD, Princeton U., 1966; JD, U. Chgo., 1967. Bar: Minn. 1973. Asst. prof. law U. Iowa, Iowa City, 1967-69; assoc. prof. law U. Minn., Mpls., 1969-73, prof. law, 1973-90, prof., 1990—, acting dean, 1994-95, Oppenheimer Wolff and Donnelly prof., 1990—; counselor on internat. law U.S. State Dept., Washington, 1982-83; of counsel Popham, Haik, Schnobrich & Kaufman, Mpls., 1983—. Mem. adv. com. on internat. law U.S. Dept. State, Washington, 1987-89; mem. internat. adv. bd. Inst. on Internat. Law, Kiel, Germany, 1989—. Home: 1412 W 47th St Minneapolis MN 55409-2204 Office: U Minn Law Sch 229 19th Ave S Minneapolis MN 55455-0400

MORRISON, GEORGE HAROLD, chemist, educator; b. N.Y.C., Aug. 24, 1921; s. Joseph and Beatrice (Morel) M.; m. Annie Foldes, Oct. 19, 1952; children—Stephen, Katherine, Althea. B.A., Bklyn. Coll., 1942; Ph.D., Princeton, 1948. Instr. chemistry Rutgers U., 1948-50; research chemist AEC, 1949-51; head inorganic and analytical chemistry Gen. Tel. & Electronic Labs., 1951-61; prof. chemistry Cornell U., 1961—; chmn. com. analytical chemistry NAS-NRC, 1965-77; Internat. Francqui chair U. Antwerp, Belgium, 1989. Editor Analytical Chemistry, 1980-91; contbr. articles to profl. jours. Served with AUS, 1943-46. Recipient Benedetti-Pichler award Am. Microchem. Soc., 1977, Ea. Analytical Symposium Jubilee award, 1986, Pitts. Analytical Chemistry award Soc. for Analytical Chemists of Pitts., 1990; NSF sr. fellow U. Calif., San Diego, 1967-68, Guggenheim fellow, U. Paris, Orsay, 1974-75, NIH sr. fellow Harvard Med. Sch., 1982-83. Mem. Am. Chem. Soc. (award analytical chemistry 1971), Soc. Applied Spectroscopy (award 1975), Sigma Xi. Office: Cornell Univ Baker Lab Chemistry Ithaca NY 14853

MORRISON, GORDON MACKAY, JR., investment company executive; b. Boston, Jan. 18, 1930; s. Gordon Mackay and Alice (Blodgett) M.; m. Barbara J. Lee, June 15, 1954; children: Lee, Leighton, Faith. AB, Harvard U., 1952, MBA, 1954. Regional mgr. Bankers Leasing Corp., Boston, 1965-68; portfolio mgr. Loomis, Sayles and Co., Boston, 1969-71; sr. v.p. Ft. Hill Investors Mgmt., Boston, 1972-75; chmn. bd. Bradford Gordon, Inc., Boston, 1976—; trustee East Boston Savs. Bank, 1962-91, Meridian Mut. Holding Co., 1991—. Bd. dirs. The New Eng. Hosp., 1961-96, emeritus, 1996—. Republican. Congl. Club: Harvard. Lodge: Masons. Home: 5 Neptune Ln Fortunes Rocks Biddeford ME 04005 Office: Bradford Gordon Inc 50 Congress St Boston MA 02109-4002

MORRISON, H. ROBERT, writer, editor, politician; b. Pitts., Apr. 7, 1938; s. Hugh and Gertrude Mary (Gehenio) M.; m. Meredith Wollenberg, Dec. 8, 1979; children: Hugh Robert Jr., Justin William, Elizabeth Jeanne. BA in English, Howard U., 1969. Cert. govtl. treas. Writer Nat. Geog. Soc., Washington, 1969-73, editor ednl. filmstrips, 1973-77, sr. writer, 1977-88, mng. editor nat. geography bee, 1988-89; elected treas. City of Falls Church, Va., 1993—; pres. Morrison & Reeve Sys., Inc., 1996—; bd. dirs. Falls Church Cable Access Corp., pres. 1990-93; bd. dirs. Treas. Assn. Va.; bd. dirs., pres. Morrison & Reeve Systems, Inc., 1996—. Contbg. author to numerous books including America's Seashore Wonderlands, 1985, America's Wild Woodlands, 1985, Exploring America's Valleys, 1984, America's Hidden Corners, 1983, America's Magnificent Mountains, 1980, America's Majestic Canyons, 1979, Mysteries of the Ancient World, 1979, The Ocean Realm, 1978, As We Live and Breathe, 1971; co-author: America's Atlantic Isles, 1981. Vice chmn. Falls Church (Va.) Dem. Com., 1988-89; treas. City of Falls Church, 1994—. With U.S. Army, 1961-64. Mem. Mcpl. Treas.' Assn. U.S. and Can., Treas.' Assn. Va. (bd. dirs. 1996—), Clan Morrison N.Am. (life), St. Andrew's Soc. Washington. Avocations: reading, personal computing, photography, TV production, historic preservation. Home: Bonnie Briar 502 Walden Ct Falls Church VA 22046-2628 Office: City Hall 300 Park Ave Falls Church VA 22046-3332

MORRISON, HARRY, chemistry educator, university dean; b. Bklyn., Apr. 25, 1937; s. Edward and Pauline (Sommers) M.; m. Harriet Thurman, Aug. 23, 1958; children: Howard, David, Daniel. BA, Brandeis U., 1957; PhD, Harvard U., 1961. NATO-NSF postdoctoral fellow Swiss Fed. Inst., Zurich, 1961-62; rsch. assoc. U. Wis., Madison, 1962-63; asst. prof. chemistry Purdue U., West Lafayette, Ind., 1963-69, assoc. prof., 1969-76, prof., 1976—, dept. head, 1987-92, dean Sch. Sci., 1992—; acad. adv. com. Indsl. Rsch. Inst., 1993-96; bd. dirs. Lilly Industries. Contbr. numerous articles to profl. jours. Bd. fellows Brandeis U. Mem. Am. Chem. Soc., Am. Soc. Photobiology, Internat. Photochem. Soc., Coun. for Chem. Rsch. (chmn. 1995), Phi Beta Kappa, Sigma Xi. Office: Purdue U Sci Adminstrn Sci Adminstrn Math Bldg West Lafayette IN 47907-1390

MORRISON, HOWARD IRWIN, computer services executive; b. Bklyn., Aug. 16, 1929; s. Philip Oscar and Anne Sylvia (Eisler) M.; m. Barbara May Kraut, Aug. 8, 1936 (dec. 1967); children: Peter, Scott, Dina; m. Joyce Elaine White, June 18, 1977. BA in Govt., George Washington U., 1951. Dir. computer divsn. CEIR Inc., Arlington, Va., 1956-61; pres. Computer Concepts, Silver Spring, Md., 1961-64; sr. v.p. Computer Applications Inc., N.Y.C., 1964-70; exec. v.p. Auerbach Pubrs., Inc., Phila., 1971-76; chmn. Delphi Sys. Inc., Burlington, Mass., 1976-80; pres. Arthur D. Little Sys., Burlington, Mass., 1976-80, Morrison Assocs., Sudbury, Mass., 1981-82; sr. v.p. Datacom Sys., Inc., N.Y.C., 1982-83; pres. PC Telemart Inc., Fairfax, Va., 1983-84; sr. v.p. Centel Info. Sys., Reston, Va., 1984-88; sr. v.p. comml. sales C3, Inc., Herndon, Va., 1989-90; prin. Morrison Assocs. Inc., Herndon, 1990-93; sr. v.p. C.S.A. Inc., Rockville, Md., 1994-96; pres. Sistex, Inc., Rockville, 1996—, Ctr. 2000, 1997—. Author: A Computer Executives View of USSR, 1972. With USN, 1948-53. Democrat. Jewish. Home: 118 Monroe St Rockville MD 20850

MORRISON, IAN A(LASTAIR), foundation executive; b. Glasgow, Scotland, Apr. 22, 1924; came to U.S., 1932, naturalized, 1937; s. William John and Alexandrina (Smith) M.; m. Naida Brown, Apr. 19, 1946; children: Craig William, Sheila Elise. BA, Wagner Coll., S.I., N.Y., 1948, LHD, 1968; MA, Columbia U., 1950, MS, 1958, EdD, 1961; LHD, Bard Coll., 1968. Assoc. prof. history, dean students Wagner Coll., 1949-56; exec. Inter Royal Corp., N.Y.C., 1956-57; exec. sec. Greer Sch., Millbrook, N.Y., 1958-61; exec. dir. Greer Sch., Millbrook, 1961-72; pres. Greer-Woodycrest Children's Found., N.Y.C., 1972-89, The Greer Inst. of Group Care Cons., 1979-90; pres. Greer Crest retirement community, N.Y.C., 1984-89, pres. emeritus, 1989-95. Author: Higher Education in World War II, 1950, American Political Parties, Political Science Handbook, 1953, Foster Care in the United States, 1975; editor NAHC Pub. Affairs Bull., 1975-87, Continuing Care Retirement Communities: Social, Political and Financial Issues; pub. Resdl. Group Care quar.; contbr. articles to profl. jurs.; author pub. affairs newsletter. Pres. Eastchester (N.Y.) Bd. Edn., 1962-66, Unionvale (N.Y.) Bd. Edn., 1969-87; mem. adv. coun. Dutchess C.C.; mem. long-range com. Columbia U. Divsn. Geriatrics and Gerontology; trustee emeritus St. Francis Hosp., Poughkeepsie, N.Y., 1981-90, chmn., 1990; bd. dirs. Bank Millbrook N.Y., 1973-90, Palma Sola Bot. Park, Bradenton, Fla., 1994—, Anna Maria Island Orch. and Chorus, 1995—. With AUS, WWII, ETO, POW, Germany. Decorated Purple Heart with oak leaf cluster, Prisoner of War medal, Bronze Star; Grad. fellow 1948 Wagner Coll., 1948. Mem. N.Y. State Assn. Child Care Agencies (pres. 1969), N.Y. State Assn. Children's Inst. (chmn. edn. com. 1961-68, pres. 1968), Nat. Assn. Homes for Children (hon. life mem., dir. 1975-89, pres. 1977-79, chmn. pub. affairs com. 1975-87, bd. dir. 1975-87, author code of ethics, 1976), Nat. Assn. Sr. Living Industry (founding mem.), Child Welfare League Am., Fgn. Policy Assn., St. Andrews Soc., Caledonia Soc. (bd. dirs. Sarasota), Nat. Assn. Homes for Children, Am. Assn. Homes for Aged, Nat. Assn. Fundraising Execs., Union League Club (N.Y.C.), Millbrook (N.Y.) Golf and Tennis Club, Columbia U. Club (N.Y.C.), Bradenton Country Club (Fla.).

MORRISON, JAMES FRANK, optometrist, state legislator; b. Colby, Kans., Apr. 11, 1942; s. Lloyd Wayne and Catherine Louise (Beckner) M.; m. Karen Jean Carr, Aug. 25, 1963; children: Mike, Jeff, Scott. Student, U. Kans., 1960-64; BS, So. Coll. Optometry, 1967, OD, 1967. Pvt. practice, 1969-75; founder, chief staff N.W. Kans. Ednl. Diagnostic and Referral Ctr. Children, Inc., Colby; asst. chief engr. Sta. KXXX-FM, 1977-80, chief engr., 1980-82; prof. vision dept. Colby Community Coll., 1979-84; mem. Kans. Ho. Reps., Topeka, 1992—. Cubmaster pack 140 Cub Scouts Am., 1970-80, dist. chmn., 1977-79. Fellow Am. Acad. Optometry, Coll. Optometrists in Vision Devel.; mem. Am. Optometric Assn., Am. Soc. Broadcast Engrs., Kans. Soc. Broadcast Engrs. (founder, pres. 1970-71), Kans. Optometric Assn., Kans. Assn. Children with Learning Disabilities, Mo. Optometric Assn., Thomas County Assn. Retarded Children, Rotary, Lions , Kiwanies (pres. 1971-72), Masons, Shriners. Rotary. Mem. Assemblies of God. Ch. Avocations: amateur radio, photography, astronomy. Home: 3 Cottonwood Dr Colby KS 67701-3902 Office: Morrison Optometric Assocs 180 W 6th St Colby KS 67701-2315

MORRISON, JAMES FREDERICK, management consultant; b. Evanston, Ill., Aug. 12, 1933; s. Paul Leslie and Carolyn Lola (Rosemeier) M.; m. Myra Val Wokoun, June 22, 1957; children: Myra Hollie Morrison Nielsen, Cynthia Leslie Morrison Karlsson. BA, Northwestern U., 1955, MBA, 1958. CPA, Wis. Accounting mgr. Froedtert Malt Corp., Milw., 1958-61; asst. controller, asst. v.p. Northwestern Nat. Ins. Co., Milw., 1961-65; controller Eutectic Welding Alloys Corp., Flushing, N.Y., 1965-68; internal auditor Sterling Drug, N.Y.C., 1968-69; controller Internat. Flavors and Fragrances, N.Y.C., 1970-76; mng. dir., v.p. Europe Internat. Flavors and Fragrances, London, 1977-80; v.p. new bus. group U.S. Internat. Flavors and Fragrances, N.Y.C., 1981-84; v.p. export and communications U.S. Internat. Flavors and Fragrances, Hazlet, N.J., 1984-96, cons., 1996—. Co-chmn. Milw. Festival of Arts, 1964-65; mem. Manhasset (N.Y.) Bd. Edn., 1970-75, v.p., 1975; bd. dirs. United Way Monmouth County, 1991—, chmn. priorities com., 1992, 93, strategic planning com., 1995-97; bd. dirs. Monmouth Ocean Found. for Ednl. Enhancement, 1996—; elder First Presbyn. Ch., Red Bank, N.J., 1996—. 1st lt. USAF, 1955-57. Mem. AICPA, Fin. Execs. Inst. (pres. L.I. chpt. 1975-76), Internat. Trade Facilitation Coun. (vice-chmn. 1991—), Wis. Soc. CPA's, Internat. Commerce Club N.J., Systems and Procedures Assn. (pres. Milw. chpt. 1965), Eastern Sr. Golf Assn. (treas. 1994—), Rumson Country Club (bd. dirs. 1996—), Beta Gamma Sigma. Presbyterian. Avocation: golf. Home: 14 Circle Dr Rumson NJ 07760-1112 Office: Internat Flavor & Fragrances 600 State Hwy 36 Hazlet NJ 07730

MORRISON, JAMES R., retired banker; b. Duluth, Minn., May 1, 1924; s. Earl Angus and Jessie (McLean) M.; m. Clarice Mae Wolf, June 5, 1949; children—Kenneth, Alan, Jane, Richard. M.B.A., U. Chgo., 1976. Br. mgr. Parkersburg State Bank, Iowa, 1947-49; asst. cashier Bank of Sparta, Wis., 1949-50; cashier Tobacco Exchange Bank, Edgerton, Wis., 1950-53; sr. v.p. Fed. Res. Bank Chgo., 1953-89, ret.; bd. dirs. Bank of Tokyo-Mitsubishi Chgo.; chmn. subcom. on credits and discounts Fed. Res. Sys., Chgo., 1984-86; mem. Mt. Prospect Fin. Commn., 1989—. Served with U.S. Army, 1943-46, ETO.

MORRISON, JAMES WILLIAM, JR., lobbyist, government relations consultant; b. Bluefield, W.Va., Jan. 14, 1936; s. James William and Winnie Ella (Hendricks) M.; B.A., W.Va. State Coll., 1957; M.P.A., U. Dayton (Ohio), 1970; m. Marva Elizabeth Tillman, Aug. 8, 1957 (div.); children: Traquita Renee, James William, III. Inventory mgr. Dayton Air Force Depot/Def. Electronics Supply Center, 1959-63; mgmt. specialist Air Force Logistics Command, Dayton, 1963-72; exec. asst. to dir. mgmt. systems NASA, Washington, 1972-74; sr. mgmt. asso. Exec. Office of Pres., Office

Mgmt. and Budget, 1974-79; asst. dir. econ. and govt. U.S. Office Personnel Mgmt., 1979, dir. congl. rels., 1979-81, assoc. dir. compensation, 1981-87; sr. mgr. CNA Ins. Co., 1987-88; pres. Morrison Assocs., 1988—; vis. lectr. pub. exec. project State U. N.Y., Albany, 1974-76. Mem. adv. com. Dayton Bd. Edn., 1971. Served to 1st lt. U.S. Army, 1957-59. Recipient Sustained Superior Performance award Def. Supply Agy., 1963; Exceptional Service award Exec. Office Pres., Office Mgmt. and Budget, 1977; Disting. Service award U.S. CSC, 1978; Presdl. cert. of Appreciation, 1979; award for meritorious service Office of Personnel Mgmt., 1980; Presdl. rank award meritorious exec., 1983; award for disting. service Office Personnel Mgmt., 1984; Presdl. Rank award-Disting. Exec., 1985. Mem. Alpha Phi Alpha, Pi Delta Phi, Pi Alpha Alpha. Democrat. Presbyterian. Contbr. articles to profl. jours. Home: 11311 Morning Gate Dr North Bethesda MD 20852 Office: 1000 Potomac St NW Ste 401 Washington DC 20007-3551

MORRISON, JEANETTE HELEN See LEIGH, JANET

MORRISON, JOEL LYNN, cartographer, geographer; b. Johnsville, Ohio, July 19, 1940; s. James Everett Morrison and Janet Maxine Rogers Rumpf; m. Carolyn Lee Coffman McVey, June 23, 1962 (div. May 1972); Ashley Scott, Anja Lynne; m. Beverly Sargent, Dec. 14, 1974; stepchildren: Anne Marie Hudson, Jane Elizabeth Hudson. BA cum laude, Miami U., Oxford, Ohio, 1962; MS, U. Wis., 1964, PhD, 1968. From instr. to prof. U. Wis., Madison, 1968-83, chmn. dept. geography, 1977-80; sr. sci. advisor for geography Nat. Mapping div. U.S. Geol. Survey, Reston, Va., 1983-86, asst. div. chief for rsch., 1986-95; geography divsn. chief U.S. Bur. Census, Washington, 1995—; adj. prof. U. Md., College Park, 1983-87; fellow Newberry Libr., 1974; adv. editor Rand McNally Corp., 1971—; chmn. U.S. Bd. on Geog. Names, 1995—; mem. bd. direction Internat. Union Surveying and Mapping, 1985-87, Nat. Ctr. for Geog. Info. and Analysis, 1990-94; mem. U.S. nat. com. for internat. geog. union NAS, NRC, 1985-92; pres. Am. Congress on Surveying and Mapping, 1981-82, pres. Internat. Cartographic Assn., 1984-87; speaker and presenter in field. Sr. author: Elements of Cartography, 6th edit., 1995; chief editl. cons. Atlas of North America, 1985; editor-in-chief Mapping Scis. and Remote Sensing, 1984—; sr. cons. Goode's World Atlas, 19th edit., Rand McNally Co., Chgo., 1995co-editor, coauthor: Elements of Spatial Data Quality, 1995; contbr. chpts. to books, numerous articles to profl. jours. NDEA Title IV fellow, 1962-65. Mem. URISA, Assn. Am. Geographers, Am. Congress on Surveying and Mapping, AM/FM Internat., Cosmos Club, Phi Beta Kappa, Omicron Delta Kappa, Phi Eta Sigma, Pi Mu Epsilon. Home: 2022 Turtle Pond Dr Reston VA 22091 Office: US Bur Census Washington DC 20233-7400

MORRISON, JOHN HADDOW, JR., engineering company executive; b. Bozeman, Mont., Aug. 24, 1933; s. John Haddow Sr. and Rosalie (Lehrkind) M.; m. Shirley Easbey, Sept. 11, 1954; children: Robert, Richard. BS, Mont. State U., 1955. Registered profl. engr., Mont., Nev., Utah, Ariz., Oreg., Calif.; registered land surveyor, Mont. Project engr. Morrison-Maierle, Inc., Helena, Mont., 1957-64, chief airport design, 1967-73, chief exec. officer, 1973-88, chmn., 1988—, also bd. dirs. Bd. dirs. Mont. State U. Found., Inc., 1983—, chmn. 1992-94; sec.-treas. Helena YMCA, 1977-80. With U.S. Army 1955-57. Mem. ASCE, NSPE (pres. Helena chpt. 1968-69, Outstanding Young Engr., Helena chpt. 1965), Cons. Engrs. Council Mont. (past sec., past v.p., pres. 1986-87). Methodist. Lodges: Kiwanis, Masons. Avocations: golf, photography. Home: 201 N Hannaford St Helena MT 59601-4725 Office: Morrison Maierle Inc 910 Helena Ave PO Box 6147 Helena MT 59604

MORRISON, JOHN HORTON, lawyer; b. St. Paul, Sept. 15, 1933. BBA, U. N.Mex., 1955; BA, U. Oxford, 1957, MA, 1961; JD, Harvard U., 1962. Bar: Ill. 1962, U.S. Supreme Ct. 1966. Assoc., Kirkland & Ellis, Chgo., 1962-67, ptnr., 1968—. Named Officer Most Excellent Order Brit. Empire, 1994; Rhodes scholar. Mem. ABA, Ill. Bar Assn., Internat. Bar Assn., Chgo. Bar Assn. Home: 2717 Lincoln St Evanston IL 60201-2042 Office: Kirkland & Ellis 200 E Randolph St Chicago IL 60601-6436

MORRISON, JOHN MARTIN, lawyer; b. McCook, Nebr., June 18, 1961; s. Frank Brennor and Sharon Romain (McDonald) M.; m. Catherine Helen Wright, Aug. 17, 1991; children: Allison Kay, Amanda Grace. BA, Whitman Coll., 1983; JD, U. Denver, 1986. Bar: Mont. 1987, U.S. Dist. Ct. Mont. 1988, U.S. Ct. Appeals (9th cir.) 1989, U.S. Supreme Ct., 1996. Legis. asst., legal counsel U.S. Senate, Washington, 1987-88; ptnr. Morrison Law Offices, Helena, Mont., 1988-93, Meloy & Morrison, Helena, 1994—. Contbr. articles to profl. jours. Alt. del. Dem. Nat. Conv., N.Y.C., 1980; del. Dem. Nat. Platform Com., 1992. Recipient Lewis F. Powell/ACTL/Bur. of Nat. Affairs Advocacy awards, 1986. Mem. ATLA, Mont. Bar Assn., Mont. Trial Lawyers Assn. (pres.-elect, bd. dirs. 1991—), Western Trial Lawyers Assn. (bd. govs. 1990-95), Trial Lawyers Pub. Justice (chair 1989-90). Avocations: skiing, fly fishing, mountain climbing, river rafting, running. Office: Meloy & Morrison 80 S Warren St Helena MT 59601-5700

MORRISON, JOSEPH YOUNG, transportation consultant; b. Flushing, N.Y., Jan. 4, 1951; s. William Barrier and Barbara Helen (Lowe) M.; m. Sally Jo Ormston, Dec. 19, 1976; children: Susan Parker, Travis Barrier. AS, Montreat (N.C.)-Anderson Coll., 1971; BA, Oglethorpe U., 1989. Dept. head J.C. Penny & Co., Atlanta, 1971-74; uniform patrol officer City of Atlanta, 1974-80; spl. agt. U.S. Dept. Transp., Atlanta, 1980-82; group dir. safety and ins. Western Express, Atlanta, 1982-85; dir. safety Taylor Maid Transp., Albany, Ga., 1985-86; v.p. risk mgmt. Burlington Motor Carriers, Inc., Daleville, Ind., 1986-96; pres. Motor Carrier Safety Cons. Inc., Noblesville, Ind., 1996—. Contbg. author: Guide to Handling Hazardous Material, 1986. Mem. Am. Trucking Assn. (hazardous materials com. 1982-86, chmn. injury control com. 1984-88, safety mgmt. coun. 1982—, interstate carrier conf. 1985—, nat. freight claims and security coun. 1985—, Safety Improvement awards, Accident Reduction awards, Injury Reduction awards), Kenilworth Civic Club (treas. Stone Mountain Ga. chpt. 1981-83, pres. 1983-84), Sertoma Club, Sigma Alpha Epsilon. Methodist. Avocations: home remodeling, restoring old cars. Home: 7111 Oakview Cir Noblesville IN 46060-9419 Office: Motor Carrier Safety Cons 136 S 9th St PO Box 2067 Noblesville IN 46060

MORRISON, KENNETH DOUGLAS, author, columnist; b. Mpls., Apr. 1, 1918; s. Kenneth Mortimore and Florence Myrtle (Sutton) M.; m. Helen Curtis, Feb. 25, 1943; children: Kenneth D., Sally, Steven C., Mary. A.B., Carleton Coll., 1940; grad. study, U. Miami, 1940-41, U. Minn., 1941. Free lance writer Mpls., 1941; editor publs. Minn. Dept. Conservation, 1942-47; Minn. rep. to Nat. Audubon Soc., 1947-49, dir. pub relations, editor Audubon mag., 1949-56, v.p., 1955-56; dir. Mountain Lake Sanctuary and Singing Tower Am. Found., 1956-80, dir. environ. concerns, 1980-82, fellow, 1982-83; syndicated nature-conservation newspaper columnist 4 papers, 1985—; Audubon tour lectr., 1958-63; interviewer naturalists Wildlife Unltd., TV sta. WOR-TV, N.Y.C., 1951- 52; Mem. Minn. Bird Commn., 1951-54; trustee emeritus Fla. Nature Conservancy; trustee Fla. Conservation Found.; v.p., trustee Conservation 70's; mem. Gov. Fla. Natural Resources Com., State Parks Adv. Council, 1971-79. Author: Favorite Birds of America, 1951, Favorite Animals of America, 1951, Mountain Lake Almanac, 1984; Compiler: (with Mrs. M. E. Herz) Where to Find Birds In Minnesota, 1950. Bd. dirs. Defenders Wildlife; adv. bd. Webber Coll., 1969—. Recipient Gov. Fla. Wildlife Conservation award, 1960, Gulf Oil Conservation award, 1982, Feinstone Environ. award SUNY, 1987, Carleton Coll. Disting. Achievement award, 1990, Grassroots Leadership award Fla. Nature Conservancy, 1996. Mem. Wilson Ornithol. Soc., Wilderness Soc., Cornell U. Ornithol. Lab., Fla. Audubon Soc. (pres., Award of Merit 1964, Cruickshank Conservation award 1993), Hawk Mountain Sanctuary Assn. (bd. sponsors), Nature Conservancy, Sierra Club, Friends of Earth, Pi Delta Epsilon. Methodist. Home: 1351 Hollister Rd Babson Park FL 33827-9684 *We ought to keep in mind that we are mammals and that we need to renew regularly our contact with the basic, simple life of soil, sun, water, animals and trees.*

MORRISON, MABLE JOHNSON, business technology educator; b. Carthage, Miss., July 13, 1930; d. Horace Lawrence and Mable Barnette Johnson; children: Lisa Susan Stone, Rayburn Holmes Bates Jr. BS in Commerce, U. Miss., 1952; MEd, Miss. State U., 1976. Cert. tchr. bus. edn., mktg. Bus. tchr. Clinton (Miss.) Pub. Schs., 1952-53; sec. Jackson (Miss.) Pub. Schs., 1954-64, tchr. bus., 1964-69, tchr., coord. mktg., 1971-78; instr. bus. Jones County Jr. Coll., Ellisville, Miss., 1978-84; instr. bus. tech. Miss. Gulf Coast C.C., Gautier, 1984-92. Mem. Am. Vocational Assn., Delta Kappa Gamma, Phi Beta Lambda (adviser, Outstanding Adviser 1991). Episcopalian. Avocations: gardening, volunteer work. Home: 3100 Phil Davis Rd Ocean Springs MS 39564-9076

MORRISON, MANLEY GLENN, real estate investor, former army officer; b. Weston, W.Va., July 29, 1915; s. Henry Frank and Alice (Riffle) M.; m. Ida Lerlene Johnson, Dec. 12, 1942 (dec. 1982); children: Manley James (dec.), Richard Glenn, Sandra Lynn.; m. Samma Annette Muffley, July 30, 1983. B.S., U. Md., 1958; M.A., Am. U., 1960; postgrad., U. Pitts., 1961, Ind. U., 1968; grad., Command and Gen. Staff Coll., Ft. Leavenworth, Kans., 1956, Army War Coll., Carlisle Barracks, Pa., 1960, DeVry Inst. Tech., 1974; D.H.L., Mass. Coll. Optometry, 1973. Table waiter Mills Cafeteria, Columbus, Ohio, 1935-36; mgr. Speer's Cafe, Twin Falls, Idaho, 1937-38; exec. chef steward U.P. R.R., Sun Valley, Idaho, 1939-42; commd. 2d lt. U.S. Army, 1942, advanced through grades to brig. gen., 1969; chief statis. analysis Hdqrs. EUCOM and USAREUR, Berlin, Nurnberg, Heidelberg, 1948-52; chief Manpower Div., Office Surgeon Gen., Washington, 1952-55; comptroller Walter Reed Army Med. Center, Washington, 1956-59; dir. adminstrn. and asst. exec. officer Office Surgeon Gen., Washington, 1960-62; chief of systems analysis Office of Mgmt., dep. chief of staff for logistics Dept. Army Gen. Staff, Washington, 1962-64; exec. officer, dir. personnel and adminstrn. Office of Surgeon, Hdqrs. U.S. Army Europe, Heidelberg, 1964-67; exec. officer Office of Comptroller, Office Army Surgeon Gen., Washington, 1967-69; chief of Army Med. Service Corps, Washington, 1969-73; ret., 1973, self-employed as real estate investor, 1973—. Community Scout leader, Heidelberg, 1948-52; bd. dirs. Teen Clubs, Am. Youth Assocs., Heidelberg, 1967; chmn. Residents' Coun. Freedom Pla., Peoria, Ariz. Decorated D.S.M., Legion of Merit, Bronze Star, Commendation medal with oak leaf cluster. Mem. Assn. Mil. Surgeons U.S., Alumni Assn. Army War Coll., Fed. Health Care Execs. Inst. Alumni Assn., Baylor U. Alumni Assn., Phi Kappa Phi, Pi Sigma Alpha. Republican. Club: Union Hills Country (Sun City, Ariz.) (bd. dirs. 1985-86, pres.). Lodge: Masons. Home: 13373 N Plaza Del Rio Blvd #7764 Peoria AZ 85381-4874 *I have sincerely tried to assess each problem and challenge in a positive manner. Once the decision has been made and an objective plan established, I have attempted to achieve the objectives while avoiding what I consider the most Common Mistakes of Man: (1) the delusion that individual advancement is made by crushing others, (2) the tendency to worry about things that cannot be changed or corrected, (3) insisting that a thing is impossible because we cannot accomplish it, (4) neglecting development and refinement of the mind and not acquiring the habit of reading and studying, (5) refusing to set aside trivial preference, (6) attempting to compel other persons to believe and live as we do, (7) attempting to quantify in mathematical terms the depth of human experience.*

MORRISON, MARCY, state legislator; b. Watertown, N.Y., Aug. 9, 1935; m. Howard Morrison; children: Liane, Brenda. BA, Queens Coll., 1957; student, Colo. Coll., U. Colo. Mem. Colo. Ho. of Reps., 1992—, mem. judiciary, health, environ., welfare and instns. coms. Mem. Manitou Springs (Colo.) Sch. Bd., 1973-83, pres., 1980-82, County Park Bd., 1976-83, State Bd. Health, 1985-93, pres., 1988-90, Mountain Scar Commn., 1989, Future Pub. Health, 1989-90, Health Policy Commn., 1990-92; commr. El Paso County, 1985-92, chmn., 1987-89; active Citizens Goals, United Way. Named Outstanding Sch. Bd. Mem., Pikes Peak Tchrs. Assn., 1978, Woman of Spirit, Penrose-St. Francis Hosp. Sys., 1991. Mem. LWV, Health Assn. Pikes Peake Area, Women's Edn. Assn., El Paso Mental Health Assn. Republican. Jewish. Home: 302 Sutherland Pl Manitou Springs CO 80829-2722 Office: Colo Ho of Reps State Capitol Denver CO 80203*

MORRISON, MARGARET LOUISE, artist; b. Atlanta, Oct. 6; d. Watson Russell Sr. and Eva (Darnell) Morrison. BS in Edn., U. Ga., 1970. Cert. tchr., Ga. Tchr. City of Decatur, Ga., 1970-71; supr. KPMG Peat Marwick, Atlanta, 1971-97. Exhbns. include Coastal Ctr. for the Arts, St. Simons Island, Ga., Gallery One, St. Simons Island, Coastal Ctr. for the Arts, Jekyll Island, Ga., Decatur (Ga.) Arts Alliance, Acad. Midi, Paris, The Glynn County Art Assn., L'Orangerie Mus., Paris. Royal patron Hutt River Province, Queensland, Australia, 1995; active High Mus. Art, Atlanta, 1989—; bd. govs. Internat. Biog. Ctr.; adv. bd. Am. Biog. Inst. Fellow Acad. Midi (hon.); mem. NAFE, AAUW, Internat. Platform Assn., Nat. Mus. Women in Arts, Allied Artists of Ga., Pen and Ink, U. Ga. Alumni Soc.

MORRISON, MARTIN (EARL), computer systems analyst; b. Oakland, Calif., Mar. 28, 1947; s. Raymond Earl and June (Cabral) M. AB with distinction, U. Calif., Berkeley, 1967, MA, 1969, postgrad., 1969-73. Certified (life) nat. tournament dir.; cert. jr./community coll. tchr. (life), Calif. Instr. classics and English composition U. Calif. at Berkeley, 1967-73; instr. legal argument Boalt Hall Law Sch., 1972; with exec. office CF Air Freight, Inc., 1979-83, asst. to traffic mgr. for spl. projects, 1982-83, computer systems mgr., 1982-83; computer systems analyst Qantel Bus. Computers, 1983-86, sr. computer systems analyst, 1986-92; sr. tech. writer Shared Med. Systems, 1992-96, supr. tech. writing, 1996—. Author: Writing Argument, 1972, USCF Yearbooks, 1974-76, Official Rules of Chess, 1975, 77, Chess Competitor's Handbook, 1980, Latin Works for Transparent Language Computer Program, 1992-93; editor: Chess Voice, 1968-73, Keeping Ancient Rome Alive, 1987-89; chess editor: Oakland Tribune, 1965-66; columnist Via Lorenzo, 1987-88, Metric Today, 1985—; pub., bus. mgr. Chess Life & Rev., 1977-78. Asst. concertmaster Berkeley Chamber Chorus and Orch., 1980-83; concertmaster Oakland Philharm., 1987-90, bd. dirs., corp. sec., 1988-90; 1st violin Albany Trio, 1987—; vol. staff Chabot Sci. Ctr., 1981-84, chmn. computer system mgmt. staff; sec., treas. AstroSoft, 1983-87. Schola Gregoriana San Francisco, 1989-92, Schola Cantemus, 1992-95, St. John Schola, 1995—. Fellow U.S. Metric Assn. (chmn. consumer edn. com. 1984—, Spl. Citation 1986, cert. advanced metrication specialist 1987); mem. Am. Philol. Assn., Am. Classical League, Eastbay Astron. Soc. (bd. dirs. 1981-84, v.p. 1983-84), Internat. Assn. Chess Press (v.p. 1973-77), Chess Journalists Assn. (pres. 1972-75), World Chess Fedn. (internat. life arbiter, mem. rules com. 1973-78, chmn. 1976-78), U.S. Chess Fedn. (bd. dels. 1968-78, 1st v.p. Pacific Region 1972-73, nat. sec. 1972-75, tech. dir. 1973-76, exec. dir. 1976-78, Spl. Svc. award 1985, Disting. Svc. award 1995), Calif. Alumni Assn. (life, scholarship com., chmn. 1987-93, Disting. Chmn. award 1990), San Lorenzo Garden Homes Assn. (v.p./sec. 1985-86, pres. 1986-92), Phi Beta Kappa. Home: 136 Loma Verde San Lorenzo CA 94580-1782

MORRISON, MICHAEL GORDON, university president, clergyman, history educator; b. Green Bay, Wis., Mar. 9, 1937; s. Gordon John and Gertrude (Crilly) M. A.B., St. Louis U., 1960, M.A., 1965, Ph.L., 1965, S.T.L., 1969; Ph.D., U. Wis., 1971. Ordained priest Roman Catholic Ch., 1968. Joined S.J., 1955; asst. v.p. acad. affairs Marquette U., Milw., 1974-77; v.p. acad. affairs Creighton U., Omaha, 1977-81, acting pres., 1981, pres., 1981—, dir.; mem. governing bd. Creighton Prep. Sch., 1993—. Bd. dirs. Health Future Found., 1983—, Xavier U., 1992—, Omaha 100 Inc., 1991—; mem. cons. com. SAC, 1988—; mem. adv. bd. Salvation Army, 1992—; trustee Duchesne Acad. of Sacred Heart, 1995—. Recipient Human Rights award Anti-Defamation League, 1982, Humanitarian award Nat. Conf. Christians and Jews, 1989. Mem. Assn. Jesuit Colls. and Univs. (bd. dirs.), Assn. Ind. Colls. and Univs. Nebr. (bd. dirs. 1981—), Nat. Assn. Ind. Colls. and Univs. (bd. dirs. 1993—),Greater Omaha C. of C. (bd. dirs. 1993—), Alpha Sigma Nu, Beta Alpha Psi. Office: Creighton U 2500 California Plz Omaha NE 68178-0001

MORRISON, PATRICE B., lawyer; b. St. Louis, July 8, 1948; d. Frank J. and Loretta (S.) Burgert; m. William Brian Morrison, Aug. 12, 1969; 1 child, W. Brett. AB, U. Miami, 1971, MA, 1972; JD, Am. U., 1975; LLM in Taxation, Georgetown U., 1978. Bar: Fla. 1975, D.C. 1977, N.Y. 1983. Atty. U.S. Dept. Treas., Washington, 1975-79; atty., ptnr. Nixon Hargrave Devans & Doyle, LLP, Palm Beach County, Fla., 1980-89, Nixon, Hargrave, Devans & Doyle, LLP, Rochester, N.Y., 1989—; bd. dirs. Cloverwood Devel., Inc. Author: (jour.) The Practical Lawyer, 1986, 91. Bd. dirs. Alzheimer's Assn., Rochester, 1990-95, Nat. Women's Hall of Fame, 1990-92; mem. Rochester Women's Network; mem. exec. com. Estate Planning Coun. Rochester, 1992-95. Mem. Am. Immigration Lawyers Assn. Republican. Office: Nixon Hargrave Devans & Doyle LLP PO Box 1051 Clinton Sq Rochester NY 14603

MORRISON, PATRICIA KENNEALY, author; b. N.Y.C., Mar. 4, 1946; d. Joseph Gerard and Genevieve Mary (McDonald) Kennely; m. James Douglas Morrison, June 24, 1970 (dec. July 3, 1971). Student, St. Bonaventure U., 1963-65; BA, Harpur Coll., 1967. Editor Jazz & Pop Mag., N.Y.C., 1968-71; sr. copywriter RCA Records, N.Y.C., 1971-73; copy dir. CBS Records, N.Y.C., 1973-79, New Sch., N.Y.C., 1979-81; author, pres./CEO Lizard Queen Prodns., Inc., N.Y.C., 1984—. Author: (novels) The Copper Crown, 1984, The Throne of Scone, 1986, The Silver Branch, 1988, The Hawk's Gray Feather, 1990, The Oak Above the Kings, 1994, The Hedge of Mist, 1996, Blackmantle, 1997; (autobiography) Strange Days: My Life With and Without Jim Morrison, 1992; contbr.: Rock She Wrote, 1995; tech. advisor, actress The Doors, 1990-91. Mem. Mensa, Ordo Supremus Militaris Templi Hierosolymitani (dame, preceptor 1995). Democrat. Avocation: Celtic studies. Office: Lizard Queen Prodns Inc 151 1st Ave Ste 120 New York NY 10003-2906 also: Henry Morrison Inc PO Box 235 Bedford Hills NY 10507

MORRISON, PERRY DAVID, librarian, educator; b. Mpls., Nov. 30, 1919; s. Arthur D. and Vera Mae (Perry) M.; m. Catherine Jean Gushwa, Apr. 22, 1946 (dec. Oct. 1991). A.A., Pasadena City Coll., 1940; A.B., Whittier Coll., 1942, M.A., 1947; B.L.S., U. Calif., Berkeley, 1949, D.L.S., 1961. Asst. Huntington Library, San Marino, Calif., 1947-48; asst. univ. librarian, head social sci. librarian U. Oreg., Eugene, 1949-63; prof. Sch. Librarianship U. Oreg., 1967-82, prof. emeritus, 1982—, dean Sch. Librarianship, 1970-73, coordinator library research, univ. library, 1978-82, part-time reference librarian, 1982-89, acting asst. univ. librarian, 1979-80; retired; coll. librarian, dir. library sci. program Sacramento State Coll., 1963-65; assoc. prof. U. Wash. Sch. Librarianship, 1965-67; cons. Monash U. Library, Australia, 1975-76, Central Oreg. Community Coll., 1977, Victoria State Coll., Toorak, Melbourne St. Coll., Kevin Grove St. Coll., Australia, 1980, Portland Community Coll., 1981, Treaty Oak Ednl. Dist., Oreg., 1983; dir. various Office Edn. Insts., 1968-75; mem. grant award appraisal panels Office Edn., Washington, 1972-74. Author: Career of the Academic Librarian, 1969; contbr. numerous articles, revs. to profl. jours.; editorial bd. Serials Libr., 1978-92, Social and Behavioral Scis. Libr., 1978-92; issue editor: Libr. Trends. 1981; compiler: A Journey Through Time: The Oregon Library Association, 1940-90. Mem. adv. bd. Lane County Law Libr., 1986-92; treas. Residents Assn. Cascade Manor, Eugene, Oreg., 1993-95; active Learning in Retirement Program com. U. Oreg., 1993-95. Capt. U.S. Army, 1942-46. Mem. ALA (life), Spl. Librs. Assn. (hon. life, pres. Oreg. chpt. 1974-75), Oreg. Libr. Assn. (hon. life, pres. 1961-62), Pacific N.W. Libr. Assn. (editor and bus. mgr. jour. 1967-71), Assn. Coll. and Rsch. Librs. Assn. (coms.), Lane County Assn. Oreg. Pub. Employees Retirement System (pres. 1985-86), U. Oreg. Ret. Profs. Assn., Faculty Club U. Oreg. (treas. 1981-82). Democrat. Mem. United Ch. of Christ. Home: 65 W 30th Ave Apt 416 Eugene OR 97405-3373 Office: Library U Oreg Eugene OR 97403

MORRISON, PORTIA OWEN, lawyer; b. Charlotte, N.C., Apr. 1, 1944; d. Robert Hall Jr. and Josephine Currier (Hutchison) M.; m. Alan Peter Richmond, June 19, 1976; 1 child, Anne Morrison. BA in English, Agnes Scott Coll., 1966; MA, U. Wis., 1967; JD, U. Chgo., 1978. Bar: Ill. 1978. Ptnr. Rudnick & Wolfe, Chgo., 1978—, also chmn. real estate dept., mem. governing policy com.; lectr. in field. Bd. dirs. Girl Scouts of Chgo. Mem. ABA, Am. Coll. Real Estate Lawyers, Chgo. Bar Assn. (real property com., subcom. real property fin., alliance for women), Pension Real Estate Assn., Chgo. Fin. Exch., Chgo. Real Estate Women. Office: Rudnick & Wolfe 203 N La Salle St Ste 1800 Chicago IL 60601-1225

MORRISON, ROBERT LEE, physical scientist; b. Omaha, Nov. 22, 1932; s. Robert Alton and Lulu Irene (Ross) M.; m. Sharon Faith Galliher, Feb. 19, 1966; children: Dennis, Karyn, Cheryl, Tamara, Traci. BA, U. Pacific, Stockton, Calif., 1957, MS, 1960. Chief chemist Gallo Winery, Modesto, Calif., 1957-66; rsch. scientist Lawrence Livermore Nat. Lab., Livermore, Calif., 1966-69, sr. rsch. scientist, 1973-93; pres. Poolinator, Inc., Gardena, Calif., 1970-72; owner R.L. Morrison Techs., Modesto, 1993—; cons., speaker, presenter in field. Contbr. numerous articles to profl. jours.; patentee in field. Recipinet Excellence in Nuclear Weapons award U.S. Dept. Energy, 1990, others. Mem. Am. Chem. Soc. Avocations: flying, skiing, scuba diving, photography. Home: 1117 Springcreek Dr Modesto CA 95355-4820

MORRISON, ROBERT TOWNSEND, nephrologist; b. Boston, Dec. 26, 1951; s. Robert Stier and Marie Day (Townsend) M.; m. Margaret Lou Dougherty, July 10, 1976; children: Sarah Marie, Samuel Thomas. BS, Rensselaer Poly. Inst., 1976; student, Columbia U., 1981; MD, Albany Med. Coll., 1985. Assoc. Herbert F. Gold and Assocs., Brookline, Mass., 1976; ins. claims adjuster GAB Adjustment Corp., Boston, 1976-78; lab. technician Rockefeller U., N.Y.C., 1980-81; resident in internal medicine USAF Med. Ctr., Wright-Patterson AFB, Ohio, 1985-88; fellow in nephrology Wilford Hall USAF Med. Ctr., Lackland AFB, Tex., 1988-90; chief nephrology svc. 13th Air Force Med. Ctr., Republic of Philippines, 1990-91, David Grant USAF Med. ctr., Travis AFB, Calif., 1991-94; med. dir., CEO, chief nephrology GMH Dialysis Ctr., Xenia, Ohio, 1994—; nephrologist, internist Med. Svc. Assocs., Xenia, 1994—; chmn. dept. internal medicine Greene Meml. Hosp., Xenia, 1996—; asst. clin. prof. medicine U. Calif. at Davis, Sacramento, 1991-94, Wright State U. Sch. Medicine, Dayton, 1995—; nephrology cons. Pacific Air Command, USAF, Clark AB, The Philippines, 1990-91; instr. Uniformed Svcs. U. Health Scis., 1988-90. Author jour. articles and abstracts. Co-chair combined fed. campaign United Way of Solano County, 1993-94; chmn. drives ARC, Albany, N.Y., 1982-83; chmn. Hunger Task Force of Riverside Ch., 1979-81. Maj. USAF, 1985-94, Res., 1994—. Mem. AMA, ACP, Nat. Kidney Found. (mem. profl. edn. com. Miami Valley chpt.), Soc. Air Force Physicians, Am. Soc. Nephrology, Greene County Med. Soc. (bd. dirs.), Ohio Med. Assn., Sigma Chi (pres. chpt. 1975-76). Democrat. Avocations: running, camping, carpentry, theater, hockey. Home: 126 W North College St Yellow Springs OH 45387-1563 Office: Med Svc Assocs 386 N Detroit St Xenia OH 45385-2233

MORRISON, ROGER BARRON, geologist; b. Madison, Wis., Mar. 26, 1914; s. Frank Barron and Elsie Rhea (Bullard) M.; BA, Cornell U., 1933, MS, 1934; postgrad. U. Calif., Berkeley, 1934-35, Stanford U., 1935-38; PhD, U. Nev., 1964; m. Harriet Louise Williams, Apr. 7, 1941 (deceased Feb. 1991); children: John Christopher, Peter Hallock and Craig Brewster (twins). Registered profl. geologist, Wyo. Geologist U.S. Geol. Survey, 1939-76; vis. adj. prof. dept. geoscis. U. Ariz., 1976-81, Mackay Sch. Mines, U. Nev., Reno, 1984-86; cons. geologist; pres. Morrison and Assocs., Ltd., 1978—; prin. investigator 2 Landsat-1 and 2 Skylab earth resources investigation projects NASA, 1972-75. Fellow Geol. Soc. Am.; mem. AAAS, Internat. Union Quaternary Rsch. (mem. Holocene and paleopedology commns., chmn. work group on pedostratigraphy), Am. Soc. Photogrammetry, Am. Soc. Agronomy, Soil Sci. Soc. Am., Internat. Soil Sci. Soc., Am. Quaternary Assn., Am. Water Resources Assn., Colo. Sci. Soc. Author 3 books, co-author one book, co-editor 2 books; editor: Quaternary Nonglacial Geology, Conterminous U.S., Geol. Soc. Am. Centennial Series, vol. K-2, 1991; mem. editorial bd. Catena, 1973-88; contbr. over 150 articles to profl. jours. Research includes Quaternary geology and geomorphology, hydrogeology, environ. geology, neotectonics, remote sensing of Earth resources, paleoclimatology, pedostratigraphy. Office: 13150 W 9th Ave Golden CO 80401-4201

MORRISON, SAMUEL FERRIS, secondary school educator; b. Glasgow, Scotland, Oct. 7, 1941; came to U.S., 1949; s. Thomas Green and Susan (McCaskill) M.; m. Kathryn Emily Schnaible, Aug. 14, 1971; 1 child, Ian James. BA, U. Wyo., 1968, MEd, 1985. Tchr. social studies Platte County Sch. Dist. 1, Wheatland, Wyo., 1968—, athletic dir., 1987—. With U.S. Army, 1963-65. Mem. NEA, Wyo. Edn. Assn., Platte County Edn. Assn. (pres. 1972-73). Democrat. Presbyterian. Avocations: golf, woodworking, photography. Home: 200 Front Rd Wheatland WY 82201-9158 Office: Wheatland Jr High Sch 13 And S Oak St Wheatland WY 82201

MORRISON, SCOTT DAVID, computer company executive; b.Duluth, Minn., May 8, 1952; s. Robert Henry and Shirley Elaine (Tester) M.; m. Jana Louise Bergeron, May 29, 1976; children: Robert Scott, Matthew John. Cert. in welding, Duluth Area Inst. Tech., 1971; student U. Wis.-Superior, 1976-77, A in Mfg. Mgmt. N. Hennepin C.C., 1985, BA Concordia Coll., 1988, St. Paul, Minn., MBA St. Thomas U., St. Paul, Minn., 1991. Cert. in quality tech., Am. Soc. Quality Control and St. Paul Tech. Vocat. Inst., 1985; lic. vocat. instr.; cert. welder Litton Ship Systems, Pascagoula, Miss., 1971-72, Barko Hydraulics, Superior, Wis., 1972-76; cert. welder Am. Hoist and Derrick Co., Mpls., 1977-89, cert. level II non-destructive exam. instr., 1979-80; quality supr. Colight Inc., Mpls., 1980, Tol-O-Matic, Inc., Mpls., 1980-82; quality assurance engr. ADC Telecommunications, Mpls., 1982-84, design assurance engr., 1985-86, product assurance engr., 1986-1987, sr. product assurance engr., quality improvement facilitator, 1987-88, product engring supr. 1988-90, mgr. design assurance, quality assurance, component engring., 1990-92; dir. quality and reg. affairs Waters Instruments, Inc., 1992-96, sr. quality engr., 1996, corp. quality sys. mgr., 1996—; mgr. corp. mfg. and quality Compaq Computer Corp., Houston, Texas, 1996—; Judge, U.S. Amateur Boxing Fedn., Mpls., 1978-87, 95—; examiner Minn. Quality Award Minn. Coun. for Quality, 1993, 95, Tex. Quality Award, 1997—; mem. quality coun. Am. Electronics Assn., 1994-95; mem. bd. dirs. Rochester Quality Coun., 1994-95; examiner Malcolm Baldridge Nat. Quality award Nat. Inst. Standards and Technology, 1994-95, sr. examiner, 1996—; reviewer fellowship grant applications ASQC, 1996—; adj. instr. Riverland Technical Coll., Rochester, Minn., 1995; lic. profl. boxing judge Tex. Dept. Licensing and Regulation, 1996—; cert. lead auditor British Standards Instn., 1996; facilitator Malcolm Baldridge Nat. Quality Award Regional Conf., 1997. Recipient Technical Excellence award ADC Telecomms., 1987, 88. Mem. ASTM, Am. Soc. Quality Control (cert. quality engr. cert. quality auditor, cert. quality mgr., chmn. host and attendance subcom. 1986-87), Am. Welding Soc., Soc. Mfg. Engrs., Internat. Platform Assn. Roman Catholic. Office: Compaq Computer Corp 20555 SH 249 MS 040210 Houston TX 77070

MORRISON, SHELLEY, actress; b. N.Y.C., Oct. 26, 1936; d. Maurice Nissim and Hortense (Alcouloumre) Mitrani; m. Walter R. Dominguez, Aug. 11, 1973. Student, L.A. City Coll., 1954-56. Actress: (films) Interns, 1962, The Greatest Story Ever Told, 1964, Castle of Evil, 1965, Divorce, American Style, 1965, How to Save a Marriage, 1966, Funny Girl, 1967, Three Guns for Texas, 1969, Man & Boy, 1971, Blume in Love, 1972, McKenna's Gold, 1967, Breezy, 1973, People Toys, 1973, Rabbit Test, 1975, Max Dugan Returns, 1982, Troop Beverly Hills, 1988, Fools Rush In, 1996, (TV movies) Three's a Crowd, 1969, Once an Eagle, 1974, The Night That Panicked America, 1975, Kids Don't Tell, 1984, Cries From the Heart, 1994, (TV series) Laredo, 1965-67, The Flying Nun, 1966-70, First and Ten, 1987, I'm Home, 1990, The Fanelli Boys, 1990, Love, Lies and Murder, 1990, Playhouse 90, Dr. Kildare, The Fugitive, Gunsmoke, Marcus Welby, and many others, 1960-70, Man of the People, Sisters, 1991, 92, Murder She Wrote, 1992, Johnny Bago, 1993, Columbo, 1993, L.A. Law, 1994, Live Shot, 1995, Courthouse, numerous others, (stage prodns.) Pal Joey, 1956, Bus Stop, 1956, Only in America, 1960, Orpheus Descending, 1960, Spring's Awakening, 1962, over 65 other prodns., 1956-1970; prodr., writer live shots, 1975—. Condr. seminars (with husband Walter Dominquez) about Native Americans to keep traditions and ceremonies flourishing. Honored (with husband Walter Dominguez) for work with homeless City of L.A., 1985, for work during L.A. riots, 1992. Mem. SAG, AFTRA, Actors Equity Assn. Democrat.

MORRISON, SHIRLEY MARIE, nursing educator; b. Stuttgart, Ark., June 13, 1927; d. Jack Vade Wimberly and Mabel Claire (Dennison) George; m. Dana Jennings Morrison, Mar. 12, 1951 (dec. Dec. 1995); children: Stephen Leslie, Dana Randall, William Lee, Martha Ann Morrison Carson. Diploma, Bapt. Hosp. Sch. Nursing, Nashville, 1949; BSN, Calif. U., Fullerton, 1977; MSN, Calif. U., L.A., 1980; EdD, Nova Southeastern U., 1987. RN, Tex., Calif.; cert. pub. health nurse, Calif.; cert. secondary tchr., Calif. Staff nurse perinatal svcs. Martin Luther Hosp., Anaheim, Calif., 1960-77, relief 11-7 house supr., 1960-77; dir. vocat. nursing program Inst. Med. Studies, 1978-81; mem. faculty BSN program Abilene (Tex.) Intercollegiate Sch. Nursing, 1981-92, dir. ADN program, 1992—; mem. profl. adv. bd. Nurse Care, Inc., Abilene, 1988—. Mem. adv. bd. parent edn. program Abilene Ind. Sch. Dist., 1985—; active Mar. Dimes, Abilene, 1990—, Ednl. Coalition for Bob Hunter, Abilene, 1994; bd. dirs. Hospice Big Country, Abilene, 1987—. Grantee NIH, 1992. Mem. Nat. Orgn. Assn. Degree Nurses (mem. program com. 10th anniversary nat. conv.), Tex. Orgn. Assoc. Degree Nurses, So. Nursing Rsch. Soc. (rsch. presenter), Health Edn. Resource Network Abilene (founding mem., pres. elect, pres. 1995-96). Democrat. Methodist. Avocations: traveling, reading. Home: PO Box 2583 Abilene TX 79604 Office: Abilene Intercollegiate Sch Nursing PO Box 2583 Abilene TX 79604-2583

MORRISON, STACY LYNNE, magazine editor; b. Jenkintown, Pa., Jan. 17, 1969; d. Robert Isaac and Sharon Lee (Wiley) Morrison; m. Christopher Cole Shannon, Oct. 1, 1994. BA, Washington & Lee U., 1990. Editl. asst. Mirabella mag., N.Y.C., 1991-92, asst. editor, 1992-93, assoc. features editor, 1993-95; mng. editor J. Crew Group Inc., N.Y.C., 1995, Time Out New York, N.Y.C., 1995—. Office: Time Out New York 627 Broadway Fl 7 New York NY 10012-2612

MORRISON, STEPHEN GEORGE, lawyer; b. Pasadena, Calif., Aug. 10, 1949; s. Ira George and Virginia Lee (Zimmer) M.; m. Gail Louise Moore, June 10, 1972; 1 child, Gregory Stephen. BBA, U. Mich., 1971; JD, U. S.C., 1975. Ptnr. Nelson, Mullins, Riley & Scarborough, Columbia, S.C., 1975—; adj. prof. U. S.C., Columbia, 1973-75, 82—; pres. Defense Rsch. Inst., 1995-96; exec. v.p., gen. counsel, sec., chief adminstrv. officer Policy Mgmt. Sys. Corp.; presenter in field. Author/editor: Products Liability Pretrial Notebook, 1989, South Carolina Appellate Practice Handbook, 1986. Bd. dirs. S.C. Com. Humanities, Columbia, 1986—, S.C. Gov. Sch. Arts, Columbia, 1988-95; pres., bd. dirs. Richland County Pub. Defender Assn., Columbia, 1991-95. Fellow S.C. Bar Found.; mem. Internat. Assn. Defense Coun., Lawyers for Civil. Justice (bd. dirs. 1995—, pres. elect 1997—). Democrat. Episcopalian. Avocations: fishing, country music, chamber music, physics, history. Home: 2626 Stratford Rd Columbia SC 29204 Office: Nelson Mullins Riley & Morrison 1330 Lady St Fl 3 Columbia SC 29201-3300

MORRISON, TONI (CHLOE ANTHONY MORRISON), novelist; b. Lorain, Ohio, Feb. 18, 1931; d. George and Ella Ramah (Willis) Wofford; m. Harold Morrison, 1958 (div. 1964); children: Harold Ford, Slade Kevin. B.A., Howard U., 1953; M.A., Cornell U., 1955. Tchr. English and humanities Tex. So. U., 1955-57, Howard U., 1957-64; editor Random House, N.Y.C., 1965—; assoc. prof. English SUNY, Purchase, NY, 1971-72; Schweitzer Prof. of the Humanities SUNY, Albany, NY, 1984-89; Robert F. Goheen Prof. of the Humanities Princeton Univ., Princeton, NJ, 1989—; Visiting prof., Yale Univ., 1976-77, Bard Coll., 1986-88. Author: The Bluest Eye, 1969, Sula, 1973 (National Book award nomination 1975, Ohioana Book award 1975), Song of Solomon, 1977 (National Book Critics Circle award 1977, American Acad. and Inst. of Arts and Letters award 1977), Tar Baby, 1981, (play) Dreaming Emmett, 1986, Beloved, 1987 (Pulitzer Prize for fiction 1988, Robert F. Kennedy Book award 1988, Melcher Book award Unitarian Universalist Assn. 1988, National Book award nomination 1987, National Book Critics Circle award nomination 1987), Jazz, 1992, Playing in the Dark: Whiteness and the Literary Imagination, 1992, Nobel Prize Speech, 1994, Birth of a Nation'hood: Gaze, Script & Spectacle in the O.J. Simpson Trial, 1997; editor: The Black Book, 1974, Race-ing Justice, En-Gendering Power: Essays on Anita Hill, Clarence Thomas, and the Construction of Social Reality, 1992; lyricist: Honey and Rue, 1992. Recipient New York State Governor's Art award, 1986; Washington College Literary award, 1987; Elizabeth Cady Stanton award National Organization for Women; Nobel prize in Literature Nobel Foundation, 1993. Mem. Author's Guild (council). Office: Princeton U Dept Creative Writing 185 Nassau St Princeton NJ 08544-2003 also: care Suzanne Gluck Internat Creative Mgmt 40 W 57th St New York NY 10019-4001*

MORRISON, VAN, musician, songwriter; b. Belfast, Ireland, Aug. 31, 1945; s. George and Violet Morrison; 1 child, Shana. Founder, lead singer rock group Them, 1964-67, albums include Them, 1965, Them Again, 1966, Them featuring Van Morrison, 1972; solo career, 1967—; albums include Blowin' Your Mind, 1967, Astral Weeks, 1968, Moondance, 1968, Best of Van Morrison, 1970, His Band and Street Choir, 1970, Tupelo Honey, 1971, St. Dominic's Preview, 1972, Hard Nose the Highway, 1973, It's Too Late To Stop Now, 1974, TB Sheets, 1974, Veedon Fleece, 1974, This Is Where I Came In, 1977, A Period of Transition, 1977, Wavelength, 1978, Into the Music, 1979, Common One, 1980, Beautiful Vision, 1982, Inarticulate Speech of the Heart, 1983, Live at the Grand Opera House Belfast, 1984, A Sense of Wonder, 1985, No Guru, No Method, No Teacher, 1986, Poetic Champions Compose, 1987, (with The Chieftains) Irish Heartbeat, 1988, Live for Ireland, 1988, Avalon Sunset, 1989, Enlightenment, 1990, The Best of Van Morrison, 1990, Hymns to the Silence, 1991, Bang Masters, 1991, The Best of Van Morrison, 1993, Too Long in Exile, 1993, A Night in San Francisco, 1994, Days Like This, 1995, The Healing Game, 1997, Tell Me Something, 1997 ; composer numerous hit singles including Gloria, 1965, Brown Eyed Girl, 1967, Moondance, 1968, Domino, 1970, Wild Night, 1971. *

MORRISON, WALTON STEPHEN, lawyer; b. Big Spring, Tex., June 16, 1907; s. Matthew Harmon and Ethel (Jackson) M.; m. Mary Lyon Bell, Dec. 19, 1932. Student Tex. A&M U., 1926-28; J.D., U. Tex., 1932. Bar: Tex. 1932. Asso., Morrison & Morrison, Big Spring, 1932-36, ptnr., 1939, 46; atty. County of Howard, 1937-39, judge, 1941-42, 47-48; atty. City of Big Spring, 1949-58; sole practice, Big Spring, 1953—; lectr. Am. Inst. Banking. Served with USAF, 1942-46. Fellow Tex. Bar Found., Am. Coll. Probate Counsel; mem. Tex. City Attys. Assn. (pres. 1955-56), Am. Judicature Soc., Tex. Bar Assn., ABA. Baptist. Clubs: Rotary (pres. 1949), Masons, Shriner. Home: 1501 E 11th Pl Big Spring TX 79720-4903 Office: PO Box 792 113 E 2nd St Big Spring TX 79720-2502

MORRISON, WILLIAM DAVID, lawyer; b. Phila., Aug. 19, 1940; s. Maxey Neal and Mary Fuller (Chase) M.; m. Barbara Heath, Aug. 25, 1962 (div.); children: David Conrow, Stephen Munro, John Pomeroy; m. Sandra Elizabeth Butter, Mar. 16, 1983; children: Charles, Nicholas, Sophie Natasha. BA, Princeton U., 1962; LLB, Yale U., 1965. Bar: N.Y. 1966, Calif. 1975. Assoc. Winthrop, Stimson, Putnam & Robert, N.Y.C., 1965-74; ptnr. Erickson & Morrison, and predecessor firms, Los Angeles, 1974-78, LeBoeuf, Lamb, Leiby & Macrae, N.Y.C., 1978-88, Bryan Cave, St. Louis, 1988—; lectr. on Saudi Arabian law. Active Internat. Inst. for Strategic Studies, Royal Geog. Soc. Mem. ABA, Assn. Bar City of N.Y., Calif. Bar Assn., Internat. Bar Assn., The Pilgrims, Brooks, Marks Club, Whites, Annabel's, RAC Club (London), Princeton Club (N.Y.C.). Author chpt. in Saudi Arabia: Keys to Business Success, 1981; contbr. articles to profl jours. Home: 34 Norland Sq, London England Office: Bryan Cave, 29 Queen Anne's Gate, London SW1H 9BU, England

MORRISS, FRANK, film editor. Editors: (TV movies) Duel, 1971, The Law, 1974, The Execution of Pvt. Slovik, 1974, (films) Charley Varrick, 1973, Ode to Billy Joe, 1976, First Love, 1977, I Wanna Hold Your Hand, 1978, Youngblood, 1978, Hometown, U.S.A., 1979, Inside Moves, 1980, Whose Life Is It, Anyway?, 1981, The Earthling, 1981, (with Edward Abroms) Blue Thunder, 1983 (Academy award nomination best film editing 1983), (with Donn Cambern) Romancing the Stone, 1984 (Academy award nomination best film editing 1984), American Flyer, 1985, Short Circuit, 1986, Hot to Trot, 1988, (with Dallas Puett) Disorganized Crime, 1989, (with Puett) Bird on a Wire, 1990, Short Time, 1990, (with Tony Lombardo) The Hard Way, 1991, Point of No Return, 1993, Another Stakeout, 1993. Office: care Motion Picture Editors 7715 W Sunset Blvd Ste 220 Los Angeles CA 90046-3912*

MORRISS, FRANK HOWARD, JR., pediatrics educator; b. Birmingham, Ala., Apr. 20, 1940; s. Frank Howard Sr. and Rochelle (Snow) M.; m. Mary J. Hagan, June 29, 1968; children: John Hagan, Matthew Snow. BA, U. Va., 1962; MD, Duke U., 1966. Diplomate Am. Bd. Pediatrics, Am. Bd. Perinatal and Neonatal Medicine. Intern Duke U. Med. Ctr., Durham, N.C., 1966-67, resident in pediatrics, 1967-68, fellow in neonatology, 1970-71; fellow in neonatology U. Colo., Denver, 1971-73; asst. prof. to prof. U. Tex. Med. Sch., Houston, 1973-86; prof. U. Iowa Coll. Medicine, Iowa City, 1987—, chmn. dept., 1987—. Editor: Role of Human Milk in Infant Nutrition and Health, 1986; contbr. numerous articles to profl. jours, chpts. to books. Lt. comdr. USN, 1968-70. NIH grantee, 77-87, 90—. Mem. Am. Pediatric Soc., Soc. Pediatric Rsch., Am. Acad. Pediatrics, Soc. Gynecol. Investigation, Midwest Soc. Pediatric Rsch., Assn. Med. Sch. Pediatric Dept. Chmn. Methodist. Avocation: tennis. Office: U Iowa Hosps & Clinics Dept Pediatrics Iowa City IA 52242

MORRISSETTE, BRUCE ARCHER, Romance languages educator; b. Richmond, Va., Apr. 26, 1911; s. James Archer and Mary (Bell) M.; m. Dorothy Behrens, Oct. 12, 1940; 1 child, James. B.A., U. Richmond, 1931, Litt.D., 1975; Docteur d'Université, Clermont-Ferrand, France, 1933; Ph.D., Johns Hopkins U., 1938. Jr. instr. French Johns Hopkins U., 1934-38; from asst. prof. to prof. Romance langs. Washington U., St. Louis, 1938-62; vis. prof. U. Wis., 1962; prof. French lit. U. Chgo., 1962—, mem. bd. publs., 1963-66, chmn. dept. Romance langs. and lits., 1967-70, 73-76, Bernard E. and Ellen C. Sunny Disting. Service prof., 1974—; vis. prof. U. Ill. at Urbana, 1967-68, U. Calif. at Los Angeles, 1969; Fulbright lectr. U. Western Australia, 1969; lectr. colls., univs. Author: L'Esthétique symboliste, 1933, Life and Works of Mlle Desjardins, 1947, The Great Rimbaud Forgery, 1956, La Bataille Rimbaud, 1959, Les Romans de Robbe-Grillet, 1963, Alain Robbe-Grillet, 1966, The Novels of Robbe-Grillet, 1975, Intertextual Assemblage from Topology to the Golden Triangle, 1979, Novel and Film: Essays in Two Genres, 1985; also numerous articles; assoc. editor: French Rev. and Symposium, 1963-69, Modern Philology, 1974-79, Critical Inquiry, 1976—. Mem. Christian Gauss Prize Award Com., 1967-69. Decorated chevalier Ordre des Palmes Academiques, France, 1962; chevalier Ordre du Mérite National France, 1980. Mem. Modern Lang. Assn. Am. (exec. council 1962-66), AAUP, Am. Assn. Tchrs. French, Soc. des Professeurs Francais, Assn. Internat. des Etudes Francaises, Soc. des Rosettes et Rubans de France. Address: PO Box 167 Harbert MI 49115-0167

MORRISSEY, CHARLES THOMAS, historian, educator; b. Newton, Mass., Nov. 11, 1933; s. Leonard Eugene and Margaret (McCarthy) M. AB, Dartmouth Coll., 1956; MA, U. Calif., Berkeley, 1957. Instr. Dartmouth Coll., Hanover, N.H., 1961-62; oral historian Harry S. Truman Library, Independence, Mo., 1962-64; chief John F. Kennedy Libr. Oral History Project, Washington, 1965-66; dir. Vt. Hist. Soc., Montpelier, 1966-71, 73-75, Ford Found. Oral History Project, 1971-73; adj. prof. history U. Vt., Burlington, 1969-73, 75-85; vis. summer instr. in oral history Portland State U., 1979-82, 84—, Vt. Coll., Montpelier, 1985—; cons., dir. oral history and archives office Baylor Coll. Medicine, Houston, 1985-96, cons., 1996—; bd. advisors Who's Who in the East; lectr. in field. Author: Vermont: A Bicentennial History, 1981, (with others) Vermont, 1985; editor: Oral History Assn. Newsletter, 1968-71, Vermont History, 1966-71, 73-76, Internat. Jour. Oral History, 1985-89; contbg. editor: Vermont Life mag., 1969-81, editor, 1982-83; also articles; radio commentator Sta. WDEV, Waterbury, Vt., 1982—. Recipient Harvey Kantor award New England Assn. Oral Historians, 1980. Fellow Ctr. for Research on Vt.; mem. Soc. Am. Archivists, Acad. Cert. Archivists, Oral History Assn. (pres. 1971-72), Am. Assn. for History of Medicine, Nat. Coun. on Public History (coun. 1980-82), Sharpshooters Club (North Fayston, Vt.), Cosmos Club (Washington).

MORRISSEY, DOLORES JOSEPHINE, investment executive; b. N.Y.C., July 22; d. Joseph Lawrence and Madeleine Catherine (Curran) M. B.S., NYU, 1963, M.B.A., 1968. Sr. v.p., treas. Bowery Savs. Bank, N.Y.C., 1958-87; exec. v.p. Mut. of Am., N.Y.C., 1987-94, Mut. of Am. Capital Mgmt., N.Y.C., 1994-96; pres., CEO Mutual of Am. Securities Corp., N.Y.C., 1996—; bd. dirs. Mut. of Am., N.Y.C., 1972-85; pres. Mut. of Am. Investment Corp., 1989—; pres., CEO Mut. of Am. Instnl. Fund, 1996—; mem. adv. commn. N.Y. State Comptroller Investment Adv. Com., N.Y.C., 1979-87. Dir. Yorkville Christian-Jewish Coun., N.Y.C., 1978—; past pres. Soroptimist Internat. of N.Y., N.Y.C. Mem. Money Marketeers of NYU, NYU Bus. Forum, Women's Bond Club, Women's Econ. Round Table, Alpha Kappa Delta. Roman Catholic. Avocations: travelling; photography; opera. Home: 180 East End Ave New York NY 10128-7763 Office: Mutual of America 320 Park Ave New York NY 10022-6815

MORRISSEY, EDMOND JOSEPH, classical philologist; b. N.Y.C., June 5, 1943; s. William J. and Anne K. (Gaffney) M.; m. Patricia M. Hanlon, Oct. 11, 1987; children: William, Edmond, Kathleen, Patrick, Jennifer, Lisa, Paula. A.B. summa cum laude, Boston Coll., 1965; B.A., U. Oxford, 1967, M.A., 1971; M.A., Harvard U., 1969, Ph.D., 1974. Seminarian Pope John XXIII Nat. Sem., Weston, Mass., 1974-77; collaborator prof. Sterling Dow Harvard U., Cambridge, Mass., 1977-95; cons. in pub. and photoreprodn. Author: Studies in Inscriptions Listing the Agonistic Festivals, 1974, A Quinquagesimal History of the Church of St. Bernadette, 1987; contbr. articles to profl. jours. Pres., chmn. adminstrn. fin., St. Bernadette's Ch., Archdiocese of Boston, 1980—; founding dir. Theol. Lectures Series, Randolph, Mass., 1978—, Randolph Hist. Commn., 1988—; staff vol. Cardinal Medeiros Program for Handicapped, 1980-82; treas., bd. dirs. Randolph Community Food Pantry, 1994—. Marshall scholar, 1965-67; Wilson scholar, 1965—; Gen. Motors scholar, 1962-65; Ford Found. fellow, 1967-69; Harvard U. fellow, 1969-71. Mem. Am. Inst. Archaeology, Am. Philol. Assn., Alumni Assn. Harvard, Oxford U. Alumni Assn., Boston Coll. Alumni Assn. Democrat. Roman Catholic. Home: 4 Bennington St Randolph MA 02368-2106

MORRISSEY, JOHN CARROLL, lawyer; b. N.Y.C., Sept. 2, 1914; s. Edward Joseph and Estelle (Caine) M.; m. Eileen Colligan, Oct. 14, 1950; children: Jonathan Edward, Ellen (Mrs. James A. Jenkins), Katherine, John, Patricia, Richard, Brian, Peter. BA magna cum laude, Yale U., 1937, LLB, 1940; JSD, N.Y. U., 1951; grad., Command and Gen. Staff Sch., 1944. Bar: N.Y. State 1940, D.C. 1953, Calif. 1954, U.S. Supreme Ct. 1944. Asso. firm Dorsey and Adams, 1940-41, Dorsey, Adams and Walker, 1946-50; counsel Office of Sec. of Def., Dept. Def., Washington, 1950-52; acting gen. counsel def. Electric Power Adminstrn., 1952-53; atty. Pacific Gas and Electric Co., San Francisco, 1953-70; assoc. gen. counsel Pacific Gas and Electric Co., 1970-74, v.p., gen. counsel, 1975-80; individual practice law San Francisco, 1980—; dir. Gas Lines, Inc. Bd. dirs. Legal Aid Soc., San Francisco; chmn. Golden Gate dist. Boy Scouts Am., 1973-75; commr. Human Rights Commn. of San Francisco, 1976-89, chmn., 1980-82; chmn. Cath. Social Svc. of San Francisco, 1966-68; adv. com. Archdiocesean Legal Affairs, 1981—; regent Archdiocesan Sch. of Theology, St. Patrick's Sem., 1994—; dir. Presidio Preservation Assn., 1995—. Served to col. F.A. U.S. Army, 1941-46. Decorated Bronze star, Army Commendation medal. Mem. NAS, AAAS, ABA, Calif. State Bar Assn., Fed. Power Bar Assn., N.Y. Acad. Scis., Calif. Conf. Pub. Utility Counsel, Pacific Coast Electric Assn., Pacific Coast Gas Assn., Econ. Round Table of San Francisco, World Affairs Council, San Francisco C. of C., Calif. State C. of C., Harold Brunn Soc. Med. Rsch., Electric Club, Serra Club, Commonwealth Club, Yale Club of San Francisco (pres. 1989-90), Pacific-Union Club, Sometimes Tuesday Club, Sovereign Mil. Order Malta, Phi Beta Kappa. Roman Catholic. Home: 2030 Jackson St San Francisco CA 94109-2840 Office: PO Box 77000 123 Mission St Rm 1709 San Francisco CA 94177

MORRISSEY, PETER A., public relations executive; b. Boston, Jan. 15, 1953; s. Edward William and Margaret Francis (L'Heureaux) M.; m. Carey S. Sherman; children: Halley, Jack, Cara. BS, Boston U., 1987; cert. in mgmt. program, Harvard U., 1990. Account exec. Prudential Ins. Co. Am., Boston, 1977-78; account exec. Clarke and Co., Boston, 1978-82, v.p., 1982-84, pres., chief exec. officer, 1984—; mng. ptnr. WORLDCOM. editor, pub.: The Boston Marathon, 1980-82. Dir. Multiple Sclerosis Soc., Morgan Meml. Goodwill Industries. Named one of Ten Outstanding Young Leaders Boston Jaycees, 1985. Mem. Pub. Rels. Soc. Am. (counselors acad.), Boston C. of C. (bd. dirs.). Roman Catholic. Office: Clarke & Co Pub Rels 535 Boylston St Boston MA 02116-3720

MORRISSEY, THOMAS JEROME, investment banker; b. Racine, Wis.; s. Patrick William and Lillian (Mitchell) M.; PhB, U. Wis., 1940; postgrad. U. Ill., 1942, U.S. Naval Acad., 1942; m. Clovene Marie Nogel, Feb. 21, 1957. Merchandising trainee Vick Chem. div. Richardson-Merrill, Inc., N.Y.C., 1940-41, sales promotion asst., 1941-42, mgr. mil. sales, 1942; pvt. practice mktg. and fin. cons., N.Y.C., 1952-54; dir. mktg. rsch. Pharmacraft Labs. div. Seagrams Distillers, Inc., N.Y.C., 1946-48, mgr. sales promotion, 1948-49, gen. sales mgr., 1949-52; asst. to pres. Turner-Smith Drug Co., N.Y.C., 1954-55, sales mgr., Smithtown, L.I., N.Y., 1955-57; mgr. advt. and sales Denver Chem. Mfg. Co., Stamford, Conn., 1957-58, N.Y.C., 1958-59; v.p., dir. mktg., account exec. Ralph Allum Advt. Agy., N.Y.C., 1959-67; v.p. Community Sci., Inc., 1959-67; account exec. Walston & Co., Inc., N.Y.C., 1967-74, Harris, Upham & Co., Inc., 1974-76; sr. account exec., v.p. Smith Barney Harris Upham & Co., 1976—. Lt. USNR, 1942-46. Decorated Silver Star; knighted Knight of Grace Soverign Orthodox Order of St. John of Jerusalem, Knights Hospitaller. Mem. The Marketeers (pres. 1963-67), Astoria Park Tennis Assn. (pres. 1967-70), Ea. Lawn Tennis Assn. (del. 1967-69), Met. Badminton Assn. (del. 1968- 4), Vet. Corps of Artillery of State of N.Y. (commd. major 1989) Mil. Order of Foreign Wars (bd. govs.), St. George's Soc., New Eng. Soc., Sigma Chi. Clubs: Dutch Treat (chmn. 1960-61), Army and Navy (pres.), Cen. Badminton (pres. 1971-83), Badminton Club of City of N.Y. (sec. 1985-97), West Side Tennis (Forest Hills), Princeton U. Club, St. George's Soc., New England Soc. Rsch. in field. Home: 865 United Nations Plz New York NY 10017-1803 Office: care Smith Barney Inc 40 W 57th St Fl 19 New York NY 10019-4001

MORRONE, FRANK, electronic manufacturing executive; b. Marano Marchesato, Cosenza, Italy, May 13, 1949; s. Luigi and Emma (Molinaro) M.; m. Katherine Ann Kuehn, Feb. 1, 1975; children: Louis H., Cecilia E., Joseph V. BSEE, U. Wis., 1972; M in Mgmt., Northwestern U., 1993. Project engr. 3M Co., St. Paul, 1972-73; product engr., mgr. Eaton Corp., Kenosha, Wis., 1973-79; chief elec. engr. Tree Machine Tool, Racine, Wis., 1979-80; v.p. engring. MacPower divsn. Manu-Tronics, Inc., Kenosha, 1980-84, exec. v.p., 1984—, bd. dirs., sec., 1988—. Mem. exec. bd. southeast coun. Boy Scouts Am., Racine, 1987—; bd. dirs. Kenosha Libr., 1987—. Mem. IEEE, Kenosha County Club (bd. dirs.). Office: Manu-Tronics Inc 8701 100th St Kenosha WI 53142-7718

MORROW, ANDREW NESBIT, interior designer, business owner; b. Fremont, Nebr., Feb. 22, 1929; s. Hamilton N. and May (Oberg) M.; m. Margaret M. Stoltinberg; children: Megan Beth, Molly Jean, Andrew C. BFA, U. Nebr., 1950. Interior designer Hardy Furniture, Lincoln, Nebr., 1950-61, Morrow Interiors, Lincoln, 1961—; bd. visitors Found. for Interior Design Edn. and Rsch., 1976-84; mem. standards com. Found. for Interior Design Edn. and Research, N.Y.C. Exhibitor Fremont Art Gallery, 1986, Haymarket Art Gallery, 1984. Pres. First Luth. Ch., Lincoln, 1987-90; bd. dirs. Lincoln Symphony, 1988-91, Nebr. Republicans for Choice, 1992, Luth. Family Svcs. of Nebr., 1994, Luth. Family Svc. Nebr. Found., 1995—; treas. NCID, 1992—. Fellow Am. Soc. Interior Designers (bd. dirs. Nebr.-Iowa chpt. 1974-78, pres. 1986-88); mem. Interior Design Educators Council (hon.). Republican. Avocations: gardening, horseback riding, cross-country skiing. Home: 1531 Kingston Rd Lincoln NE 68506-1524 Office: Morrow Interiors Inc 1010 K St Lincoln NE 68508-2851

MORROW, BARRY NELSON, screenwriter, producer; b. Austin, Minn., June 12, 1948; s. Robert Clayton and Rose Nell (Nelson) M.; m. Beverly Lee McKenzie, Mar. 3, 1969; children: Clayton McKenzie, ZoeAnna Rachel. BA, St. Olaf Coll., 1970; DHL (hon.), U. La Verne, Calif., 1990. Media specialist U. Iowa, Iowa City, 1974-81; freelance screenwriter Los Angeles, 1981-90; pres. Morrow-Heus Prodns., 1990—. Storywriter (TV film) Bill, 1981 (Emmy award 1982); screenwriter: (TV films) Bill: On His Own, 1983, Conspiracy of Love, 1987, Silent Victory, 1988, The Karen Carpenter Story, 1989, (feature film) Rain Man, 1988 (co-recipient Acad. award Best Original Screenplay 1989); screenwriter, exec. prodr.: Christmas on Division Street, 1991; exec. prodr.: Switched at Birth, 1991 (Emmy nomination), Gospa, 1995; screenwriter, prodr. Race the Sun, 1996; monologist: Bill for Short, 1992. Recipient Pres.'s award Am. Acad. for Devel. Medicine, 1978, Outstanding Contbn. award Mid-Am. Congress on Aging, 1983, SI award NASW, 1991, Pope John XXIII award Viterbo Coll., 1992. Mem. Writers Guild Am. West, Acad. TV Arts and Scis., Acad. Motion Picture Arts and Scis.

MORROW, CHARLES TABOR, aerospace consulting engineer; b. Gloucester, Mass., May 3, 1917; s. Charles Harvey and Melissa Luella (Tabor) M.; m. Julia Buxton Brown, June 4, 1949; children: Hope Elizabeth, Anne Barbara. AB, Harvard U., 1937, SM, 1938, SD, 1946. Sr. project engr. Sperry Gyroscope Co., Great Neck, N.Y., 1946-51; research physicist Hughes Aircraft Co., L.A., 1951-55; mgr. sci. and engring. relations Ramo Wooldridge Co., L.A., 1955-60; mgr. tech. relations Aerospace Corp., L.A., 1960-67; staff scientist LTV Research Ctr., Anaheim, Calif. and Dallas, 1967-76; cons. in field., Dallas and Encinitas (Calif.), 1977—. Author: Shock and Vibration Engineering, 1963; also numerous articles to profl. jours. Pres. Covey Aux. San Diego Mus. Natural History, 1983-85. Fellow

Acoustical Soc. Am., Inst. Environ. Scis. (Vigness award 1971), AIAA (assoc.); mem. IEEE (life), Inst. Noise Control Engring. (founding), Am. Soc. Engring. Edn., Sigma Xi. Avocations: music, photography, natural history, travelling. Home and Office: 1345 Cherrytree Ct Encinitas CA 92024-4011

MORROW, DAVID AUSTIN, III, veterinary medical educator; b. Arch Spring, Pa., Jan. 14, 1935; s. David Austin and Mary Harnish (Burket) M.; m. Sarah Linda MacDonough, Aug. 28, 1965; children: David Austin IV, Laurie Elizabeth, Melanie MacDonough. BS, Pa. State U., 1956; DVM, Cornell U., 1960, PhD, 1967. Postdoctoral fellow Cornell U., Ithaca, N.Y., 1965-68; assoc. prof. Mich. State U., East Lansing, 1968-81, prof. Coll. Vet. Medicine, 1981-90, prof. emeritus, 1990—; vet. cons., 1990—; vis. scientist Colo. State U., Ft. Collins, 1975-76. Editor: Current Therapy in Theriogenology, 1980, 2d edit., 1986. Elder Presbyn. Ch.; trustee Pa. State U., 1987—, chmn. bd. trustees phys. plant com., 1994-96, mem. presdl. selection com., 1995. Recipient Norden Disting. Teaching award Mich. State U., 1975, Outstanding Teaching award, 1979, 80, 84, 85, 86, Dairy Sci. Disting. Alumnus award Pa. State U., 1992, Hon. Lion Ambassador award Pa. State U., 1993, Hon. Alumnus award Mich. State U. Coll. Veterinary Medicine, 1993; coach 1st place team SCAUMA Nat. Intercollegiate Bovine Reporduction Contest, 1986, 88, 89, 90. Mem. AVMA (Borden award 1980, Am. Feed Mfg. award 1992), Am. Coll. Theriogenologists (charter diplomate), Pa. State U. Coll. Agr. Alumni Soc. (pres.-elect 1985-86, pres. 1987-89, past pres. 1989-91), Pa. State U. Alumni Coun. (exec. bd. 1983-95, pres.-elect 1989-91, pres. 1991-93, past pres. 1993-95), Phi Zeta (pres. 1977-79), Phi Kappa Phi (exec. bd.), Golden Key (hon.), Alpha Zeta (life, bd. dirs.), Sigma Xi. Republican. Avocations: skiing; gardening. Home and Office: 1060 Haymaker Rd State College PA 16801-6900

MORROW, DENNIS ROBERT, school system administrator, consultant; b. Viroqua, Wis., July 9, 1951; s. Clayton Stuart and W. Elaine (Kegley) M.; m. Patricia Lee Bergren, Aug. 4, 1973; children: Sarah Elizabeth, Gretchen Elaine, David Robert. BA, U. Minn., 1975, PhD, 1984; MA, Coll. St. Thomas, 1976. Tchr., dean Blaine Sr. High Sch., Mpls., 1975-78; asst. prin. Mounds View Pub. Schs., St. Paul, 1978-81; prin. Batavia (N.Y.) High Sch., 1981-83, Bklyn. Ctr. High Sch., Mpls., 1983-88, Hong Kong Internat. Sch., Tai Tam, 1988-90, Roseville Area Schs., St. Paul, 1990-91; asst. supt. Bklyn. Ctr. Schs., 1991-93, supt., 1993—; accreditation team leader North Cen. Assn. Schs. and Colls., Minn., 1986-88; forum lectr. Restructuring Edn., 1988-94. Contbr. articles to profl. jours. Bd. dirs. Hong Kong Community Drug Adv. Coun., 1988-90, North Hennepin Leadership Acad., 1992—, Leadership Mpls., 1987-88, Voyageur Outward Bound Sch., 1992—. LBJ fellow U.S. Ho. of Reps., 1977. Mem. Rotary Internat., Univ. Minn. Alumni Club. Republican. Avocations: mountaineering, sailing. Office: Bklyn Ctr Schs 6500 Humboldt Ave N Minneapolis MN 55430-1800

MORROW, ELIZABETH HOSTETTER, business owner, sculptress, museum association administrator, educator; b. Sibley, Mo., Feb. 28, 1947; d. Elman A. and Lorine (Hostetter) Morrow; married, 1970 (div. 1979); children: Jan Pawel, Lorentz Arthur. Student, William Jewell Coll., 1958-59, Colo. Coll., 1959-60, U. Okla., 1960-62; BFA, U. Kans., 1964, MFA, 1967; postgrad., U. Minn., 1965, U. Kans., 1968. Pres. E. Morrow Co., Kansas City, Mo., 1966-67; head dept. art U. Hawaii, Honolulu, 1968-69, Tarkio (Mo.) Coll., 1970-74; exec. dir. Pensacola (Fla.) Mus. Art, 1974-76; pres., owner Blair-Murrah Exhbns., Sibley, Mo., 1980—; pres. bd. trustees, chief exec. officer Blair-Murrah, Inc., 1991—; sec.-treas. Coun. for Cultural Resources, 1995—. Del. White House Conf. on Small Bus., 1986. Lew Wentz scholar U. Okla., 1960-62. Mem. AAUW, Internat. Coun. of Mus., Internat. Coun. Exhbn. Exch., Internat. Soc. Appraisers, Am. Assn. Mus., Nat. Orgn. of Women Bus. Owners, Nat. Assn. Mus. Exhibitions, Ft. Osage Hist. Soc., Friends Art, Internat. Com. Fine Arts, Internat. Com. Conservation, Internat. Sculpture Ctr., DAR, Delta Phi Delta. Republican. Avocations: historical and cultural activities, antique cars, midwest farm auctions. Home: Vintage Hill Orch Sibley MO 64088 Office: Blair-Murrah Vintage Hill Orch Sibley MO 64088 also: 7 rue Muzy, PO Box Nr 554, 1211 Geneva 6 Switzerland

MORROW, GEORGE LESTER, retired oil and gas executive; b. New Haven, Apr. 27, 1922; s. Lester W.W. and Esther (Morrow) M.; m. Mary L. Evenburg, Dec. 28, 1946; children: Susan Morrow Donaldson, William, John, Thomas. B.S., Rutgers U., 1943; M.B.A., U. Chgo., 1954. Registered profl. engr., Ill. With Peoples Gas Light and Coke Co., Chgo., 1947-77; v.p. ops. Peoples Gas Light and Coke Co., 1966-71, pres., 1971-77; also dir.; pres. Natural Gas Pipeline Co. Am., 1977-83; vice chmn., dir. Midcon Corp., 1983-87. Capt. AUS, 1943-46. Mem. Sarasota Yacht Club, Lake Zurich Golf Club. Presbyterian.

MORROW, GRANT, III, medical research director, physician; b. Pitts., Mar. 18, 1933; married, 1960; 2 children. BA, Haverford Coll., 1955; MD, U. Pa., 1959. Intern U. Colo., 1959-60; resident in pediat. U. Pa., 1960-62, fellow neonatology, asst. instr., 1962-63, instr., 1963-66, assoc., 1966-68, asst. prof., 1968-70, assoc. prof., 1970-72; assoc. prof. U. Ariz., 1972-74, prof., 1974-78, assoc. chmn. dept., 1976-78; med. dir. Columbus (Ohio) Children's Hosp., 1978-94; prof. neonatology and metabolism, chmn. dept. Ohio State U., 1978-94; med. dir., dir. divsn. molecular and human genetics Children's Hosp. Rsch. Found., Columbus, 1994—. Mem. Am. Pediat. Soc., Am. Soc. Clin. Nutrition, Soc. Pediat. Rsch. Achievements include research on children suffering inborn errors of metabolism, mainly amino and organic acids, patients on total parental nutrition. Office: Children's Hosp Rsch Found 700 Childrens Dr Columbus OH 43205-2664

MORROW, JAMES BENJAMIN, retired sea products company executive; b. Halifax, N.S., Can., 1926. Grad., Dalhousie U., 1948, Tech. U. N.S., 1950; doctoral degree (hon.), Tech. U. N.S., 1978. Exec. v.p. Nat. Sea Products Ltd., Halifax; past pres. Assoc. Prof. Engrs. of Novascotia; pres. Lunenburg Mutual Ins. Co., Lunenburg Mutual Relief Assn., Laubach Literacy of Can.; hon. dir. Sea Food Producers Assn., Nat. Sea Products Ltd. Past pres. Fishermen's Meml. Hosp., Lunenburg, N.S. Mem. Lunenburg Yacht Club (past commodore). Home: PO Box 339, Lunenburg, NS Canada B0J 2C0

MORROW, JAMES FRANKLIN, lawyer; b. Shenandoah, Iowa, Oct. 23, 1944; s. Warren Ralph and Margaret Glee (Palm) M. BS, Kans. State U., 1967; JD, U. Ariz., 1973. Bar: Ariz. 1973, U.S. Dist. Ct. Ariz. 1973. Ptnr. Bilby, Shoenhair, Warnock & Dolph, Tucson, 1973-83, Streich Lang, P.A., Tucson, 1984—. Mng. editor U. Ariz. Law Rev., 1972-73. Past chmn. bd. trustees Palo Verde Mental Health Svcs.; past pres. U. Ariz. Alumni Assn.; past chmn. bd. Palo Verde Hosp., Ariz. Tech. Devel. Corp.; past pres. bd. Cath. Cmty. Svcs.; past chmn. bd. dirs. U. Ariz. Found. Capt. U.S. Army, 1967-70. Mem. Am. Coll. Real Estate Lawyers, Am. Coll. Mortgage Attys., State Bar Ariz. (cert. real estate specialist, adv. com. real estate specialists, past chmn. real estate property sect.), Pima County Bar Assn., Calif. Bar Assn. Democrat. Roman Catholic. Avocation: golf. Office: Streich Lang PA Ste 1700 One South Church Ave Tucson AZ 85701

MORROW, JASON DREW, medical and pharmacology educator; b. St. Louis, Mar. 30, 1957; s. Ralph Ernest and Vera Rowena (Cummings) M.; m. Lisa Lee Hyman, Mar. 26, 1983; children: Jeremy Nash, Stephanie Rose. BA magna cum laude, Vanderbilt U., 1979; MD, Washington U., St. Louis, 1983. Diplomate Am. Bd. Internal Medicine, Am. Bd. Infectious Diseases. Med. intern, resident Vanderbilt U. Hosp., Nashville, 1983-86, Hugh J. Morgan chief med. resident, 1987-88, rsch. fellow in clin. pharmacology, 1988-91; sr. rsch. fellow dept. pharmacology Vanderbilt U., Sch. Medicine, Nashville, 1991-94, asst. prof. pharmacology and medicine, 1994-95; assoc. prof. Vanderbilt U., Nashville, 1995—, dir. Eicosanoid Core Lab. dept. pharmacology, 1992—, dir. tng. program in clin. pharmacology, 1996—; clin. fellow in infectious diseases Barnes Hosp./Washington U., 1986-87; staff physician in medicine and infectious diseases VA Med. Ctr., Nashville, 1991—; mem. internat. adv. com. 9th Internat. Conf. on Prostglandins and Related Compounds, Florence, Italy, 1994, 10th Conf., Vienna, Austria, 1996. Ad hoc reviewer Jour. Biol. Chemistry, Prostglandins, numerous other sci. publs.; contbr. over 160 articles, abstracts, revs. and papers to sci. jours., chpts. to books. Physician Nashville Union Rescue Mission, 1988—. Recipient Physician-Scientist award NIH, 1990-91, grantee; recipient Rsch. Found. Devel. award Internat. Life Scis. Inst., 1992-96; Centennial Clin. Pharmacology fellow Boehringer-Ingelheim, 1990-91, Howard Hughes Med. Inst. Physician rsch. fellow, 1991-94. Mem. AMA, ACP, AAAS, Am. Fedn. Clin. Rsch., So. Soc. Clin. Investigation, Infectious Diseases Soc. Am., Am. Soc. Pharmacology Exptl. Therapeutics, Phi Beta Kappa. Avocations: running, fishing, outdoors. Home: 6129 Montcrest Dr Nashville TN 37215-5621 Office: Vanderbilt U Dept Pharmacology 23rd and Pierce Aves Nashville TN 37232-6602

MORROW, JENNIFER LEIGH See LEIGH, JENNIFER JASON

MORROW, PAUL EDWARD, toxicology educator; b. Fairmont, W.Va., Dec. 27, 1922; s. Paul Reed and Imogene (Tench) M.; m. Anne Kelly, June 14, 1947; children—Robert Randolph, William David. BS in Chemistry, U. Ga., 1942, MS in Chemistry, 1947; PhD in Pharmacology, U. Rochester, N.Y., 1951. Diplomate Am. Bd. Indsl. Hygiene. Indsl. hygienist Tenn. Eastman Corp., Kingsport, 1942-43; instr. pharmacology and toxicology U. Rochester, 1952-56, asst. prof. radiation biology and pharmacology, 1956-60, assoc. prof. radiation biology and pharmacology, 1960-66, prof. radiation biology and pharmacology, 1967-85, assoc. prof. pharmacology and toxicology, 1967-69, prof. pharmacology and toxicology, 1969-85, emeritus prof. toxicology, 1985—, acting chmn. dept. radiation biology and biophysics, 1975-77; NIH-USPHS fellow U. Göttingen, Germany, 1959-60, U. Zurich, Switzerland, 1960-61; mem. Internat. Commn. for Radiol. Protection Com., 1967-77; space sci. bd. Nat. Acad. Scis., 1967; adv. com. NRC, 1968, toxicology info. program com., 1979-82; mem. Nat. Coun. for Radiation Protection, 1977-87. Contbg. author: Inhalation Carcinogenesis, 1970, Environmental Factors in Respiratory Disease, 1972, Respiratory Defense Mechanisms, 1978, Pulmonary Diseases and Disorders, 1978; editor: Assessment of Airborne Particles, 1972, Polluted Rain, 1980, Occupational and Industrial Medicine: Concepts and Methods, 1984, Aerosols in Medicine, 1985, 93, others; contbr. numerous articles to profl. jours. Advisor particulate matter control criteria Nat. Air Pollution Control Adminstrn., Nat. Acad. Scis. Health Effects of Fossil Fuel Combustion Products, 1968-69; cons. Comitato Nazionale Per L'Energia Nucleare, Casaccia Center, Rome, Italy, 1968-69; mem. temporary staff Med. Research Council, Carshalton, Eng., 1968-69; chmn. com. air pollution Rochester Com. Sci. Info., 1972—; chmn. com. environ. health planning Genesee Region Health Planning Council, 1970-74. Served with USNR, 1943-45. Recipient Aerosol Rsch. award Internat. Soc. Aerosols Med., 1988, Founders award Chem. Industry Inst. Toxicology, 1989, Mercer award Am. Assn. Aerosol Rsch. and Internat. Soc. of Aerosols in Medicine, 1995. Fellow AAAS, N.Y. Acad. Scis., Acad. Toxicology Scis.; mem. Am. Indsl. Hygiene Assn., Am. Inst. Biol. Scis., Radiation Research Soc., Am. Coll. Toxicology, Health Physics Soc., Soc. Toxicology (Inhalation Toxicology Speciality Sect. Achievement award 1985), Am. Thoracic Soc., Am. Assn. Aerosol Research, Gesellschaft für Aerosolforschung, Soc. of Leukocyte Biology, Internat. Soc. Aerosols in Med., Am. Acad. Hygiene. Home: 200 Laney Rd Rochester NY 14620-3018 Office: U Rochester Dept Environ Medicine Box EHSC Rochester NY 14642

MORROW, RALPH ERNEST, historian, educator; b. Marshall County, Ind., Sept. 16, 1920; s. Ralph E. and Myrtle (Parrish) M.; m. Vera Cummings, June 4, 1949; children: Jason Drew, Leslie Ellen. B.S., Manchester (Ind.) Coll., 1943; A.M., Ind. U., 1948, Ph.D., 1953. Instr. Ind. U., 1948-50, Mich. State U., 1953-55; mem. faculty Washington U., St. Louis, 1955—, prof. history, 1963—, chmn. dept., 1960-65, from 1967, dean Grad. Sch., 1967-79, dean Faculty Arts and Scis., 1979-84, provost, 1984-86, prof. emeritus, historian of the univ., 1986-96; cons. on call Danforth Found. Author: Northern Methodism and Reconstruction, 1956, Washington University in St. Louis: A History, 1996. Served to lt. (j.g.) USNR, 1943-46, PTO. Guggenheim fellow, 1959-60. Mem. Am. Hist. Assn. (chmn. com. coll. and univ. tchg. 1967-70), Orgn. Am. Historians. Presbyterian.

MORROW, RICHARD MARTIN, retired oil company executive; b. Wheeling, W.Va., Feb. 27, 1926; married. B.M.E., Ohio State U., 1948. With Amoco Corp., 1948-91; v.p. Amoco Prodn. Co., 1964-66; exec. v.p. Amoco Internat. Oil Co., 1966-70; exec. v.p. Amoco Chem. Corp., 1970-74, pres., 1974-78; pres. Amoco Corp., 1978-83, chmn. chief exec. officer, 1983-91; ret., 1991; bd. dirs. Potlatch Corp., Marsh & McLennan Cos., Inc., Seagull Energy Corp. Trustee U. Chgo. and Rush-Presbyn. St. Luke's Med. Ctr. Office: Amoco Corp 200 E Randolph St Ste 7909 Chicago IL 60601-7704

MORROW, RICHARD TOWSON, lawyer; b. Glendale, Calif., Aug. 3, 1926; s. Ray Leslie and Marion Elizabeth (Towson) M.; m. Virginia Alice Kaspar, June 28, 1947; children: Kathleen Ann, Randall Ray, Nancy Lynn. Student, Occidental Coll., 1944-45; BA, UCLA, 1947; LLB, U. So. Calif., 1950. Assoc. Musick & Burrell, Los Angeles, 1950-53; lawyer Walt Disney Prodns. (now Walt Disney Co.), Burbank, Calif., 1953-64; v.p. Walt Disney Prodns., Burbank, Calif., 1964-69, v.p., gen. counsel, 1969-85, dir., 1971-84; ptnr. Hufstedler, Kaus & Beardsley, Los Angeles, 1985-90, of counsel, 1990-91; ret., 1991; trustee Roy Disney Family Found., Burbank. Former pres., bd. dirs. Glendale YMCA, Calif.; former mem. adv. bd. Glendale Salvation Army; former trustee Glendale Cmty. Found., 1991-94. Served to lt. (j.g.) USNR, 1944-46. Mem. ABA (chmn. corp. law dept. com. 1982-84, coun. bus. law sect. 1984-88), Calif. Bar Assn., L.A. County Bar Assn. (corp. law dept. sect. chair 1973-74, trustee 1969-85, 1st recipient Outstanding Corp. Counsel award 1984), Glendale Bar Assn., Calif. Club, Chancery Club (L.A.), Lakeside Golf Club (North Hollywood, Calif.), Alisal Men's Golf Club (Solvang). Republican. Presbyterian. Avocation: golf. Home: 665 Hillside Dr Solvang CA 93463-2157

MORROW, ROB, actor; b. New Rochelle, N.Y., Sept. 21, 1962; s. Murray and Diane Francis (Markowitz) M. mem. Ensemble Studio Theatre. Stage appearances include Escape from Riverdale, 1984, The Return of Pinnochio, 1988, The Chosen, 1987-88, The Substance of Fire, 1990; TV series Tattingers, 1988, Northern Exposure, 1990-94 (Lead Actor in TV Drama Emmy award nominee 1991, 92, 93, Lead Actor in TV Drama Golden Globe nominee 1991, 92, 93), Mother, 1996; films: Private Resort, 1985, Quiz Show, 1994, Last Dance, 1995. Mem. Naked Angels (co-founder). Jewish. *

MORROW, SCOTT DOUGLAS, choreographer, educator; b. N.Y.C., Jan. 29, 1954; s. Alfred Lionel and Lorraine (Power) M. Grad., High Sch. Performing Arts, N.Y.C., 1972; BFA in Dance, SUNY, Purchase, 1976; MA in Choreography, UCLA, 1986. Prin. instr. Phil Black Dance Studio, N.Y.C., 1969-77; dir. dance div. No. Ill. U., DeKalb, 1976-78; artistic dir., resident choreographer No. Ill. Repertory Dance co., 1976-78; artistic dir. Scott Morrow Dance Theatre Co. and Sch., L.A., 1978-85; prin. instr. Mary Tyler Moore Los Angeles Dance Ctr., 1979-80; resident dance master South Coast Repertory Acting Conservatory, Calif., 1979-82; vis. prof. Wright State U., Ohio, 1981; ballet master, resident choreographer Empire State Ballet, Buffalo, 1984-85; asst. prof. U. Kans., Lawrence, 1985-88; resident choreographer Kans. U. Dance Co., Lawrence, 1985-88; choreographer Morrow Dance Theatre-in-Residence, U. Kans., 1985-88, 92d St. Dancer Ctr., YMHA and YWHA, N.Y.C., 1989; assoc. dir., dir. edn. pub. sch. dance programs K-12, Bronx Dance Theatre Performing Arts Ctr., N.Y.C., 1990-93; mem. faculty Internat. Summer Sch. Royal Acad. Dancing, N.Y.C., 1991, 92; dance specialist State Edn. Dept. Summer Inst. on Assessment in Arts, N.Y., 1992; founder, dir. in chief Inst. Advancement Edn. Dance, N.Y.C., 1992—; adv. bd. Internat. Found. for Performing Arts Medicine, 1992—; mem. faculty Calif. State U. Sys. Summer Inst. for Tchg. and Learning, 1994; advisor Performing Arts Medicine Ctr., Kessler Inst. Rehab., N.J., 1995—; Walter H. Annenberg disting. vis. artist-scholar The Renaissance Sch., N.Y.C., 1995—; cons. presenting and commissioning program Nat. Endowment for Arts, 1993-95; peer rev. panel Fund for Innovation in Edn. U.S. Edn. Dept., 1993-94; co-chmn. dance edn. com. World Dance Allliance: Americas Ctr., 1993—. Choreographer: (mus. theater) Broadway Musical Classics on International Tour, (film musicals) Chestnuts, Rainbows Edn., (teleseries) Adventures of Hans Christen Andersen, (indsl. show) Le Parfum Salvador Dali; performance and lecture, Scott Morrow Dance Theatre, Ghana Broadcasting TV, West Africa, 1997; world premieres presented at numerous festivals including Morningside Dance Festival, N.Y.C., Mid Am. Dance Festival, L.A. Dance Kaleidoscope Festival, Middfest Internat., Ohio, Smithsonian Instn's Duke Ellington Festival, Washington, Marche Internat. de Disque et de l'Edition Musicale, Cannes, France; creator over 40 ballets. Nat. Festival for the Performing Arts Choreographers fellow, 1989; Josephine & Randolph Stewart African Heritage Fund Edn. & Rsch. grantee; named Choreographer of the Yr., Kaymore Found. for Arts, 1984, Master Educator and Disting. Fellow, Am. Bd. Master Educators, 1987; Alvin Ailey scholar, Sch. Am. Ballet scholar, Harkness House for Ballet Arts scholar; recipient Grand Prize for Choreography, Ann. Internat. Artistic Impression Competition, 1991, citation U.S. Edn. Dept., 1993, contbns. to growth and advancement of performing arts award, U.S. Art1 Coun. Co-op, 1993, instrnl. approach recognized as an ednl. innovation Internat. Bur. Edn., UNESCO, 1996; grantee Josephine and Randolph Stewart African Heritage Fund for Edn. and Rsch., 1997, also numerous founds., corps., univs. Office: Lorraine Prodns Ste 8 28-04 33rd St Astoria NY 11102

MORROW, WALTER EDWIN, JR., electrical engineer, university laboratory administrator; b. Springfield, Mass., July 24, 1928; s. Walter Edwin and Mary Elizabeth (Ganley) M.; m. Janice Lila Lombard, Feb. 25, 1951; children—Clifford E., Gregory A., Carolyn F. S.B., M.I.T., 1949, S.M., 1951. Mem. staff Lincoln Lab., MIT, Lexington, Mass., 1951-55, group leader, 1956-65; head div. communications MIT Lincoln Lab., 1966-68, asst. dir., 1968-71, asso. dir., 1972-77, dir., 1977—. Contbr. articles to profl. publs. Recipient award for outstanding achievement Pres. M.I.T., 1963, Edwin Howard Armstrong Achievement award IEEE Communications Soc., 1976. Fellow IEEE, Nat. Acad. Engring. Achievements include patent for synchronous satellite, electric power plant using electrolytic cell-fuel cell combination. Office: MIT Lincoln Lab 244 Wood St PO Box 73 Lexington MA 02173

MORROW, WILLIAM CLARENCE, lawyer, mediator; b. Austin, Tex., Aug. 9, 1935; s. Theodore Faulkner and Gladys Lee (Ames) M.; 1 stepchild, Shana Lynn Barbee; m. Sandra Jean Scott, Jan. 19, 1959 (div. Feb. 1971); m. Sheila Beth Pfost, June 29, 1973. children: Scott Fitzgerald Morrow, Elizabeth Ann Rettig. BA, Baylor U., 1957; JD, So. Meth. U., 1962. Bar: Tex., 1962. Trial atty. SEC, Ft. Worth, 1963-65; former ptnr. Cotton, Bledsoe, Tighe, Morrow & Dawson, Lynch, Chappell, Alsup & Midland; exec. v.p. Magnatex Corp., Midland, 1980-86; v.p., gen. counsel and sec. Elcor Corp., Midland, 1986-88; pres. NG Resources, 1996—. Mem. Midland City Coun., 1992-95, mayor pro tem, 1994-95; former vice chmn. Tex. Rehab. Commn.; pres. Found. Mental Health and Mental Retardation Permian Basin; pres. United Way of Midland, 1985, Indsl. Found. Midland, 1987; trustee Midland Community Theatre, 1980—, chmn. 1995-96; elder 1st Presbyn. Ch., Midland. Mem. Tex. Bar Assn., Midland County Bar Assn., Midland C. of C. (past v.p.), Petroleum Club of Midland (past bd. dirs.), Phi Delta Phi. Home: 3110 Gulf Ave Midland TX 79705-8205 Office: 2500 N Big Spring St Midland TX 79705-6673

MORROW, WINSTON VAUGHAN, financial executive; b. Grand Rapids, Mich., Mar. 22, 1924; s. Winston V. and Selma (von Egloffstein) M.; m. Margaret Ellen Staples, June 25, 1948 (div.); children: Thomas Christopher, Mark Staples; m. Edith Burrows Ulrich, Mar. 2, 1990. AB cum laude, Williams Coll., 1947; JD, Harvard U., 1950. Bar: R.I. 1950. Assoc. atty. Edwards & Angell, Providence, 1950-57; exec. v.p., asst. treas., gen. counsel, bd. dirs. Avis, Inc. and subs., 1957-61; v.p., gen. mgr. Rent A Car div. Avis, Inc., 1962-64, pres., bd. dirs., 1964-75; chmn., chief exec. officer, bd. dirs. Avis, Inc. and Avis Rent A Car System, Inc., 1965-77; chmn., pres., bd. dirs. Teleflorists Inc. and subs., 1978-80; pres. Westwood Equities Corp., L.A., 1981-95, CEO, 1984-95, also bd. dirs.; chmn., pres., chief exec. officer Ticor Title Ins. Co., 1982-91, also bd. dirs.; chmn. TRTS Data Svcs. Inc., 1985-91; bd. dirs. AECOM Tech. Corp., L.A., 1990—; dir. William & Scott, Inc., 1994-96; mem. Pres.'s Industry and Govt. Spl. Travel Task Force, 1968, travel adv. bd. U.S. Travel Svcs., 1968-76, L.A. City-wide Airport Adv. Com., 1983-85; co-chmn. L.A. Transp. Coalition, 1985-91. Mem. juvenile delinquency task force Nat. Coun. Crime and Delinquency, 1985-86, L.A. Mayor's Bus. Coun., 1983-86, Housing Roundtable, Washington, 1983-85; chmn., pres. Spring St. Found., 1991—; bd. dirs. Police Found., Washington, 1983-91; trustee Com. for Econ. Devel., Washington, 1987-91. Decorated Stella Della Solidarieta Italy, Gold Tourism medal Austria). Mem. Fed. Bar Assn., R.I. Bar Assn., Car and Truck Rental Leasing Assn. (nat. pres. 1961-63), Am. Land Title Assn. (bd. govs. 1989-90), L.A. Area C. of C. (bd. dirs. 1983-90), Williams Club, L.A. Tennis Club, Phi Beta Kappa, Kappa Alpha. Home: 4056 Farmouth Dr Los Angeles CA 90027-1314 also: Meadowview Farm Cushing Corners Rd Freedom NH 03836-0221

MORSCH, THOMAS HARVEY, lawyer; b. Oak Park, Ill., Sept. 5, 1931; s. Harvey William and Gwenodyne (Maun) M.; m. Jacquelyn Casey, Dec. 27, 1954; children: Thomas H. Jr., Margaret, Mary Susan, James, Kathryn, Julia. BA, Notre Dame U., 1953; B.S.L., Northwestern U., 1953, J.D., 1955. Bar: Ill. 1955, D.C. 1955. Assoc. Crowell & Leibman, Chgo., 1955-62; ptnr. Leibman, Williams, Bennett, Baird & Minow, Chgo., IL, 1962-72, Sidley & Austin, Chgo., 1972—; bd. dirs. Chgo. Lawyers Com. for Civil Rights Under Law, chmn., 1982-83; bd. dirs. Pub. Interest Law Initiative, pres., 1993-95; No. Dist. Ill. Civil Justice Reform Com., 1991-95; mem. vis. com. Northwestern U. Law Sch., 1989-90. Pres. Republican Workshops of Ill., 1970; gen. counsel Ill. Com. to Re-elect the Pres., 1972; mem. LaGrange Plan Commn., Ill., 1972-80, LaGrange Fire and Police Commn., 1968-72; trustee LaGrange Meml. Hosp., 1983-89; adv. bd. Catholic Charities of Chgo., 1985—. Fellow Am. Coll. Trial Lawyers; mem. ABA, Ill. State Bar Assn., Chgo. Bar Assn. (bd. mgrs. 1979-81), D.C. Bar, Northwestern Law Sch. Alumni Assn. (pres. 1988-89), Chgo. Bar Found. (bd. dirs., pres. 1995-97). Roman Catholic. Clubs: Legal, Univ. (Chgo.), Mid Day (Chgo.); LaGrange Country, Palisades Park Country (Mich.), Point O'Woods Country (Mich.). Home: 301 S Edgewood Ave La Grange IL 60525-2153 Office: Sidley & Austin 1 First National Plz Chicago IL 60603-2003

MORSE, EDMOND NORTHROP, investment management executive; b. Balt., Dec. 31, 1922; s. Edmond Harris and Ethel (Dannenberg) M.; m. Sidney Harvey Phillips, June 5, 1948; children: Edmond H., David F., Judith B., Anne S., John B. BA, Brown U., 1944; M.B.A., Harvard, 1947. With Smith, Barney & Co. (investment bankers), N.Y.C., 1947-81; gen. partner Smith, Barney & Co. (investment bankers), 1961-64, v.p., dir., 1964-68, sr. v.p., dir., 1968-70, exec. v.p., dir., 1970-76; exec. v.p., dir. Smith Barney, Harris Upham, 1976-81; exec. v.p. First Manhattan Co., 1981-89; gen. ptnr. Morse Equity Ptnrs., Darien, Conn., 1989—; capt. ret., 1950; dir. First Century Ptnrs.; mem. Darien Pension Rev. Bd., 1989—. 1st lt. USMC, 1943-50, capt. USMCR, 1950. Mem. Wee Burn Country Club. Home: Ridge Acres Darien CT 06820 Office: 36 Old Kings Hwy S Darien CT 06820-4523

MORSE, EDWARD J., automotive executive; b. 1949. Pres. Morse Ops., Ft. Lauderdale, 1970—; pres., CEO Ed Morse Chevrolet, Inc., Ft. Lauderdale, Fla., 1979—. Office: Morse Operations Inc 6363 NW 6th Way Ste 400 Fort Lauderdale FL 33309-6119*

MORSE, EDWARD LEWIS, periodical publishing executive; b. N.Y.C., Jan. 5, 1942; s. Jonah Benjamin and Rebecca (Freiberg) M.; m. Linda Kasle Jones, Aug. 15, 1965; children: Michael Ari, Molly Rachel. BA, Johns Hopkins U., Balt., 1963; MA, Johns Hopkins U., Washington, 1966; PhD, Princeton U., 1969. Asst. prof. internat. politics Woodrow Wilson Sch. Princeton (N.J.) U., 1969-75; sr. rsch. fellow Coun. on Fgn. Rels., N.Y.C., 1975-78; exec. asst. to undersec. econ. affairs U.S. Dept. State, Washington, 1978-79, dep. asst. sec. for internat. energy policy, 1979-81; dir. internat. affairs Phillips Petroleum Co., Bartlesville, Okla., 1981-84; mng. dir. Petroleum Fin. Co., Ltd., Washington, 1984-96; pres., pub. The Oil Daily Co., 1996—; pres., publisher Petroleum Intelligence Weekly, N.Y.C., 1988—, The Oil Daily Co., N.Y.C., 1996—. Author: Foreign Policy and Interdependence in Gaullist France, 1973, Modernization and the Transformation of International Relations, 1976; contbr. articles to various publs. Home: 117 E 57th St # 30B New York NY 10022 Office: Energy Intelligence Group 575 Broadway New York NY 10012-3230

MORSE, JACK HATTON, management consultant; b. San Diego, June 4, 1923; s. John Henderson and Alberta (Peterson) M.; m. Kathleen Clark (div.); children: David Eugene, Steven Allen; m. Jean Larson. BA, San Diego State U., 1956, M in Bus. Sci., 1971. Exec. San Diego Gas & Electric, 1947-89; cons. Pub., contbr. Sea Power mag., 1987-89. Pres. Cystic Fibrosis Found., San Diego, 1980-83, Project Handclasp, 1991—; pres. Oceans Found., 1992-94, chmn., 1996—. Comdr. USNR, 1943-46, 52-54. Recipient Dr. Frederick Patterson award United Negro Coll. Fund, San Diego, 1989. Mem. IEEE, Pacific Coast Elec. Assn., Pacific Coast Gas Assn. (Silver medal

1981), Navy League U.S. (nat. pres., chmn. adv. com. 1987-89, Disting. Svc. award 1979, 88, 89), La Jolla Beach and Tennis Club, Masons. Republican. Mem. LDS Ch. Avocation: traveling. Home and Office: 6125 Terryhill Dr La Jolla CA 92037-6837

MORSE, JAMES L., state supreme court justice; b. N.Y.C., Sept. 11, 1940; m. Gretchen B, June 19, 1965; children: Rebecca Penfield, Rachel Lasell. AB, Dartmouth Coll., 1962; JD magna cum laude, Boston U., 1969. Bar: Vt. 1970, U.S. Dist Ct. Vt. 1970, U.S. Ct. Appeals (2d cir.) 1970, U.S. Supreme Ct. 1973. Law clk. to Judge Sterry R. Waterman U.S. Ct. Appeals (2nd cir.), 1969-70; pvt. practice Burlington, Vt., 1970-73, 75-76; asst. atty. gen. State of Vt., Montpelier, 1973-75, defender gen., 1976-81; judge Vt. Superior Ct., Montpelier, 1981-88; justice Vt. Supreme Ct., Montpelier, 1988—. Editor in chief Boston U. Law Rev., 1967-69. Lt. USNR, 1963-66. Mem. Vt. Bar Assn. Office: Vt Supreme Ct 109 State St Montpelier VT 05609-0001

MORSE, JOHN HARLEIGH, lawyer; b. Estherville, Iowa, Sept. 22, 1910; s. James W. and Winifred E. (Williams) M.; m. Marie A. Forrest, Nov. 11, 1936 (div. June 1962); children: James W. II, Bruce F.; m. Ann U. Stanton, May 23, 1964. B.A., State U. Iowa, 1930; M.B.A., Harvard U., 1932; JD, Yale U., 1935. Bar: N.Y. 1936. Since practiced in N.Y.C.; with firm Carter, Ledyard & Milburn, 1935; with firm Cravath, Swaine & Moore, 1936-76, ptnr., 1946-76; vice chair Nat. Forge Co., 1977-91. Pres. Forest Property Owners Assn., 1992-94. Mem. ABA (chmn. labor relations law sect. 1961-62), Forest Country Club, Phi Beta Kappa, Phi Gamma Delta. Home and Office: 16301 Fairway Woods Dr Fort Myers FL 33908-5333

MORSE, JOHN M., book publishing executive. Sr. v.p., publisher Merriam-Webster Inc., Springfield, Mass. Office: Merriam Webster Inc 47 Federal St Springfield MA 01105-3805

MORSE, JOHN MOORE, architect, planner; b. Brookline, Mass., Aug. 23, 1911; s. Arthur Moore and Helen (Stearns) M.; m. Emily Hall (dec. 1988); children: David Hall, Catherine Morse Wikkerink; m. Helen Taverniti, Aug. 5, 1989. AB, Harvard U., 1934, MArch, 1940. Registered architect, Wash. Tchr. Loomis Sch., Windsor, Conn., 1934-36; ptnr. Bassetti & Morse, Seattle, 1947-62; prin. John Morse & Assocs., Seattle, 1962-78; ptnr. Morse Stafford Ptnrship., Seattle, 1978-85; prin. John Morse Architect & Planner, Seattle, 1985—. Mem. King County (Wash.) Planning Commn., 1965-70, Design Rev. Bd., Mill Creek, Wash., 1987-89; chmn. Seattle Urban Design Bd., 1966; bd. dirs. Cornish Coll. Arts, Seattle, 1974-80. Fellow AIA (pres. Seattle chpt. 1969, Seattle chpt. medal, various local and nat. awards). Democrat. Office: 7027 32nd Ave NE Seattle WA 98115-5906

MORSE, JONATHAN KENT, religious organization administrator; b. Teaneck, N.J., Dec. 10, 1951; s. Alfred George and Agnes Marie (Lagatol) M.; m. Kathleen Zylinsky, May 10, 1980; children: Charlanne Marie, Justin George. BA, Cath. U., 1973, MRE, 1976; MA, Maryknoll Sem., 1978; PhD, Greenwich Sch. Theology, 1996. Ordained priest Ukrainian Cath. Ch., 1988. Instr. Manor Jr. Coll., Jenkintown, Pa., 1977-84; dir. religious edn. Maternity, Phila., 1984-89; adminstr. Sts. Peter and Paul, Spring Valley, N.Y., 1988-93; pres. Ukrainian Cath. Relief, Stamford, Conn., 1989—; dir. religious edn. Diocese of Stamford, 1990—, dir. youth ministry, 1989—, dir. family life, 1991—; asst. dir. religious edn. Archdiocese of Phila., 1982-88; adminstr. Sacred Heart Ch., Phila., 1982-88; bd. dirs. Ea. Christian Publs., Fairfax, Va., Hallel Missionaries, Sparkill, N.Y., Nat. Conf. Catechetical Leadership. Author: Ukrainian Catholics, 1987, Through the Son, vol. 1 and vol. 2, 1997; author, editor: Rich in Compassion, 1986; columnist: The Subtle Sense in The Way, 1982-88. Chaplain K.C., Pearl River, N.Y., 1989—, Columbiettes, Stamford, 1993—; presentor UN, N.Y.C., 1992. Mem. NAFSA, Serra Internat. (chaplain 1982-91), Ancient Order Hibernians, Pi Gamma Mu. Republican. Ukrainian Cath. Avocations: science fiction reading, travel. Home: 24 Hope St Stamford CT 06906-2603 Office: Ukrainian Cath Relief 14 Peveril Rd Stamford CT 06902-3019

MORSE, JOSEPH GRANT, chemistry educator; b. Colorado Springs, Colo., Oct. 16, 1939; s. Grant Addison and Faris Ellen (Winninger) M.; m. Karen Dale Williams, Apr. 6, 1963; children: Robert Grant, Geoffrey Easton. BS, S.D. State Coll., 1961; MS in Chemistry, U. Mich., 1963, PhD, 1966. Instr. U. Mich., Ann Arbor, 1965-66; asst. prof. Utah State U., Logan, 1968-74, assoc. prof., 1974-93; prof. Western Wash. U., Bellingham, 1993—, dir. sci. edn., 1996—. Councilman Cache County, Utah. Capt. U.S. Army, 1966-68. Fellow AAAS; mem. Am. Chem. Soc. Office: Western Wash U Chemistry Dept Bellingham WA 98225

MORSE, KAREN WILLIAMS, academic administrator; b. Monroe, Mich., May 8, 1940; m. Joseph G. Morse; children: Robert G., Geoffrey E. BS, Denison U., 1962; MS, U. Mich., 1964, PhD, 1967; DSc (hon.), Denison U., 1990. Rsch. chemist Ballistic Rsch. Lab., Aberdeen Proving Ground, Md., 1966-68; lectr. chemistry dept. Utah State U., Logan, 1968-69, from asst. to assoc. prof. chemistry, 1969-83, prof. chemistry dept., 1983-93, dept. head Coll. Sci., 1981-88, dean Coll. Sci., 1988-89, univ. provost, 1989-93; pres. Western Wash. U., Bellingham, 1993—; mem., chair Grad. Record Exam in chemistry com., Princeton, N.J., 1980-89, Gov.'s Sci. Coun., Salt Lake City, 1986-93, Gov.'s Coun. on Fusion, 1989-91, ACS Com. on Profl. Tng., 1984-92; cons. 1993; nat. ChemLinks adv. com. NSF, 1995; bd. advisor's orgn. com. 2008 summer Olympic Games, Seattle, 1995; faculty Am. Assn. State Colls. and Univs. Pres.'s Acad., 1995, 96; chair Wash. Coun. of Pres., 1995-96; bd. dirs. Whatcom State Bank. Contbr. articles to profl. jours. Mem. Cache County Sch. Dist. Found., Cache Valley, Logan, 1988-93; swim coach, soccer coach; trustee First United Presbyn. Ch., Logan, 1979-81, 82-85; adv. bd. Sci. Discovery Ctr., Logan, 1993, KCTS-TV, Bellingham, 1996—; mem. bd. dirs. United Way, Whatcom County, 1993—; exec. com. Bellingham-Whatcom Econ. Devel. Com., 1993—. Recipient Disting. Alumni in Residence award U. Mich., 1989. Fellow AAAS; mem. Am. Chem. Soc. (Utah award Salt Lake City and Cen. dists. 1988, Garvan-Olin medal 1997), Am. Assn. State Colls. and Univs. (mem. policy and purposes com. 1995, chair 1996), Bus. and Profl. Women Club (pres. 1984-85), Philanthropic Edn. Orgn., Phi Beta Kappa, Sigma Xi, Phi Beta Kappa Assocs., Phi Kappa Phi, Beta Gamma Sigma. Avocations: skiing, biking, photography. Office: Western Washington Univ Office of Pres Bellingham WA 98225-5996

MORSE, LEON WILLIAM, traffic, physical distribution and transportation management executive, consultant; b. N.Y.C., Nov. 13, 1912; s. Benjamin and Leah (Shapiro) M.; m. Goldie Kohn, Mar. 30, 1941; children: Jeffrey W., Saul J. BS, NYU, 1935; grad. Acad. Advanced Traffic, 1937, 1954; DBA, Columbia Pacific U., 1979. Registered practitioner STB, Fed. Maritime Commn. Individual bus., traffic mgmt. cons., Phila., 1950-58; gen. traffic mgr. W.H. Rorer, Inc., Ft. Washington, Pa., 1958-78; adj. prof. econs. of transp., logistics Pa. State U., Ogontz campus, 1960-82; owner Morse Assocs.; course leader seminars in freight traffic mgmt., phys. distbn. mgmt., transp. contract negotiations and freight claims for univs. in the U.S.; bd. dirs. Sr. Security Assocs., Inc.; Bd. trustees Temple B'rith Shalom. Author: Practical Handbook of Industrial Traffic Management, 1980, 87, (manuals) Job of the Traffic Manager, Effective Traffic Management, Fundamentals of Traffic Management, Transportation Contract Negotiations and Freight Claims. Capt. transp. corps, AUS, World War II. Recipient Del. Valley Traffic Mgr. of Yr. award, 1963. Mem. Traffic and Transp. Club of Phila., Traffic Club of Phila., Traffic Club of Norristown, Am. Soc. Internat. Execs. (past pres., bd. dirs., sec., cert.), Assn. Transp. Practitioners, Am. Soc. Transp. and Logistics (emeritus), Council Logistics Mgmt., Transp. Research Forum, Health & Personal Care Distribution Conf. (pres. 1973-75, chmn. bd. 1975-77), Sr. Security Assn., Inc. (bd. dirs.), Delta Nu Alpha Transp. Fraternity, Mason, Shriner.

MORSE, LOWELL WESLEY, banking and real estate executive; b. West Palm Beach, Fla., May 1, 1937; s. Alton and Blanche (Yelverton) M.; B.S., U. Santa Clara, 1968; grad. Def. Lang. Inst., Monterey, Calif., 1959; m. Vera Giacalone, June 22, 1958; children: Lowell Wesley, Stephen D., Michael S. Russian linguist U.S. Army Security Agy., 1957-60; asst. city mgr. City of Pacific Grove (Calif.), 1961-66; city mgr. Town of Los Altos Hills (Calif.), 1967-69; chmn. Morse & Assocs., Inc., Portland, Oreg., 1972—; founder, dir. Comerica Bank Calif., San Jose, 1979—; dir. Internat. Family Entertainment; chmn. Cypress Ventures Inc., Portland, The Bagel Basket, Inc.; chmn. bd. trustees Regent U. Served with U.S. Army, 1957-60. Home: 6205 SW Meridian Way Tualatin OR 97062-7711 Office: 5335 Meadows Rd Ste 365 Lake Oswego OR 97035-3114

MORSE, MARVIN HENRY, judge; b. Mt. Vernon, N.Y., July 19, 1929; s. Frank Irving and Lillian (Seeger) M.; m. Betty Anne Hess, Dec. 27, 1953; children: Martin Albert, Michael Howard, Lee Anne. AB, Colgate U., 1949; LLB, Yale U., 1952. Bar: N.Y. 1952, Ky. 1956, Md. 1964, U.S. Supreme Ct. 1960, U.S. Ct. Appeals (6th cir.), U.S. Dist. Ct. (we. dist.) Ky., U.S. Ct. Mil. Appeals, U.S. Ct. Claims, U.S. Ct. Appeals (D.C. cir.), U.S. Ct. Appeals (fed. cir.), U.S. Dist. Ct. (no. dist.) Tex., U.S. Dist. Ct. Hawaii. Pvt. practice Louisville, 1956-62; asst. counsel Office of Gen. Counsel Dept. Navy, Washington, 1962-65, Office of Gen. Counsel Office Sec. Def., Washington, 1965-68; asst. gen. counsel GSA, Washington, 1968-70, U.S. Postal Svc., Washington, 1970-73; adminstrv. law judge Fed. Energy Regulatory Commn., Washington, 1973-75, Postal Rate Commn., Washington, 1975-77, CAB, Washington, 1977-80; dir. adminstrv. law judges Office Pers. Mgmt., Washington, 1980-82; chief adminstrv. law judge SBA, Washington, 1982-87, asst. adminstr. office of hearings and appeals, 1985-87; adminstrv. law judge Exec. Office of Immigration Rev. Dept. Justice, Washington, 1987—; mem. Adminstrv. Conf. of U.S., 1980-84, govt. mem., 1985-86, 87-95, liaison mem.; faculty and faculty coord. The Nat. Jud. Coll., 1977, 79-80. Author: (with S. Groner) ABA Handbook chpt. on adminstrv. law, 1981. Trustee Washington area chpt. Am. Digestive Disease Soc., 1976-87. With JAGC, USAF, 1952-56, to col. USAFR, ret. 1979. Decorated USAF Legion of Merit; recipient Disting. Svc. award Am. Digestive Disease Soc., 1980. Mem. ABA (exec. com. 1977-82, 84-87, chmn. 1980-81, conf. adminstrv. law judges, del. ho. of dels. 1984-87, lawyers in govt. com. 1985-86, jud. selection, tenure and compensation com. 1987-93), Fed. Bar Assn. (nat. coun. 1976—, chmn. career svc. sect. 1983-86, chmn. judiciary sect. 1986-88, sect. coord. 1988-90, sec. 1991-92, del. to ABA ho. of dels. 1992-93, 97, v.p. 1993-94, pres.-elect 1994-95, pres. 1995-96), Am. Law Inst., Fed. Adminstrv. Law Judges Conf. (exec. com. 1975-77, 82-96), Nat. Assn. Adminstrv. Law Judges (hon.), Fed. Am. Inn of Ct. (coun. 1990-92, pres. 1992-94). Home: 8027 Cindy Ln Bethesda MD 20817-6912 Office: US Dept Justice 5107 Leesburg Pike Falls Church VA 22041-3234

MORSE, PETER HODGES, ophthalmologist, educator; b. Chgo., Mar. 1, 1935; s. Emerson Glover and Carol Elizabeth (Rolph) M. AB, Harvard U., 1957; MD, U. Chgo., 1963. Diplomate: Am. Bd. Ophthalmology. Intern U. Chgo. Hosp., 1963-64; resident Wilmer Inst. Johns Hopkins Hosp., Balt., 1966-69; fellow, retina service Mass. Eye and Ear Infirmary, Boston, 1969-70; asst. prof. ophthalmology, chief retina service U. Pa., 1971-75, assoc. prof., 1975; assoc. prof. U. Chgo., 1975-77; prof. ophthalmology, 1979-93, sec. dept. ophthalmology, 1976-77, chief retina service, prof., 1979-93; clin. prof. ophthalmology U. S.D. Sch. Medicine, Sioux Falls, 1993—; prof. La. State U., 1978; chmn. dept. ophthalmology, chief retina service Ochsner Clinic and Found. Hosp., New Orleans, 1977-78; clin. prof. Tulane U., 1978. Author: Vitreoretinal Disease: A Manual for Diagnosis and Treatment, 1979, 2d edit., 1989, Practical Management of Diabetic Retinopathy, 1985; co-editor: Disorders of the Vitreous, Retina, and Choroid; bd. editors Perspectives in Ophthalmology, 1976—, Retina, 1980—; contbr. articles to profl. jours. Served with USNR, 1964-66. Fellow ACS, Coll. Ophthalmologists Eng., Am. Acad. Ophthalmology, Royal Soc. Health (Eng.), Royal Coll. Ophthalmologists (Eng.); mem. AMA, La. Med. Soc., Orleans Parrish Med. Soc., New Orleans Acad. Ophthalmology, La. Ophthalmol. and Otolaryngol. Soc., Miss. Ophthalmol. and Otolaryngol. Soc., Assn. Rsch. Vision and Ophthalmology, Retina Soc., Soc. Heed Fellows, Ophthalmol. Soc. U.K., Pan Am. Assn. Ophthalmology, Oxford Ophthalmol. Congress, All-India Ophthalmol. Soc., Soc. Eye Surgeons, Vitreoretinal Soc. (India), Sigma Xi. Republican. Episcopalian. Home: 1307 S Holly Dr Sioux Falls SD 57105-0221 Office: Central Plains Clinic Dept Ophthalmology 1100 E 21st St Sioux Falls SD 57105-1020

MORSE, RICHARD, social scientist; b. Boston, Oct. 12, 1922; s. Stearns and Helen Ward (Field) M.; m. Romola Thomas Chowdhry, June 23, 1949; children: Ashok Daniel, Martha Sunita Kelly. A.B., Dartmouth Coll., 1946; postgrad., Banaras Hindu U., Aligarh Muslim U., Gokhale Inst. Politics and Econs., India, 1947, Columbia, 1950; A.M., ABD, Harvard, 1958. Edn. officer ECA, Burma, 1950-53; asst. rep. Ford Found., Burma, 1954-56; sr. internat. economist Stanford Research Inst., Menlo Park, Calif., 1958-64, 66-69; cons. Ford Found., India, 1964-66; indsl. devel. cons. Andover, Mass., 1969-74; rsch. assoc., sr. fellow, co-coord. Participatory Devel. Group East West Ctr., Honolulu, 1974-94; sr. fellow emeritus East West Ctr., Honolulu, 1994—; study dir. NAS and Nat. Acad. Engring. Internat. Panel on Internat. Industrialization Inst., 1972-73; chmn. bd. govs. Inst. Current World Affairs, 1972-74, trustee, 1988-91; bd. dirs. Inst. World Affairs, 1988-91, mem. adv. coun., 1992—; co-founder, dir. Hawaii Entrepreneurship Tng. and Devel. Inst., 1977—; mem. adv. com. Immigrant Ctr. Enterprise Project, Honolulu, 1992-96; ptnr.-founder Kalimat Moosilauke Pubs., 1996—. Co-author (with Eugene Staley): Modern Small Industry for Developing Countries, 1965, Village Voices in Rural Development and Energy Planning, 1987; co-editor: Grassroot Horizons: Connecting Participatory Development Initiatives East and West, 1995. Served with AUS, 1942-45. Fellow Inst. Current World Affairs, 1946-49; recipient certificate of honor Hawaii Ho. of Reps., 1994. Mem. Am. Econ. Assn., Am. Agrl. Econs. Assn., Am. Assn. Asian Studies, Economists Allied for Arms Reduction, UN Assn. (exec. bd. Hawaii divsn.). Home: 1621 Halekoa Dr Honolulu HI 96821-1126 Office: 1777 E West Rd Honolulu HI 96822-2323

MORSE, RICHARD JAY, human resources and organizational development consultant, manufacturers' representative company executive; b. Detroit, Aug. 2, 1933; s. Maurice and Belle Rosalyn (Jacobson) M. BA, U. Va., 1955; MA in Clin. Psychology, Calif. State U., L.A., 1967. Area pers. adminstr. Gen. Tel. Co. of Calif., Santa Monica, 1957-67; sr. v.p. human resources The Bekins Co., Glendale, Calif., 1967-83; pvt. cons. human resources and orgn. devel. Cambria, 1983—. Contbr. articles to profl. jours. Fund raiser various orgns., So. Calif., 1970—. Mem. Internat. Soc. Performance Improvement (founding mem. 1958—). Republican. Jewish. Avocations: travel, tennis, walking, swimming. Home and Office: 6410 Cambria Pines Rd Cambria CA 93428-2009

MORSE, RICHARD MCGEE, historian; b. Summit, N.J., June 26, 1922; s. William Otis and Marie (Zimmerman) M.; m. Emerante de Pradines, Dec. 30, 1954; children—Marise, Richard. Grad., Hotchkiss Sch., 1939; B.A. magna cum laude, Princeton U., 1943; M.A., Columbia U., 1947, Ph.D., 1952; M.A. (hon.), Yale U., 1963. Successively lectr., instr., asst. prof. history Columbia, 1949-58; dir. Inst. Caribbean Studies, U. P.R., 1958-61; vis. lectr. history Harvard U., 1960; prof. history, chmn. dept. SUNY-L.I., 1961-62; assoc. prof. history Yale U., 1962-63, prof., 1963-78, chmn. Council Latin Am. Studies, 1963-64, 65-70; William H. Bonsall prof. history Stanford U., Calif., 1978-84; sec. Latin Am. Program, Wilson Ctr., Washington, 1984-89; advisor U. Nuevo León Mex., 1958-60; L.Am. cons. to Ford Found., 1958-64, 73-75; vis. prof. El Colegio de Mex., 1981; sec. Interam. Found. Arts, 1963-68; disting. lectr. U. Guyana, 1975; Charles Phelps Taft Meml. lectr. history U. Cin., 1978; disting. Fulbright lectr. U. Rio de Janeiro, 1983; mem. selection com. Guggenheim Found., 1969-88, chmn. 1978-88; vis. scholar Getty Ctr., 1994. Author: From Community to Metropolis, A Biography of São Paulo, Brazil, 1958, The Bandeirantes, 1965, (with others) The Founding of New Societies, 1964, La Investigación urbana latino americana, 1971, Las Ciudades Latinoamericanas, 1973, Lima en 1900, 1973; play The Narrowest Street, 1945; El Espejo de Próspero, 1982, New World Soundings, 1989; also numerous articles; co-editor: Columbia Volumes on Contemporary Civilization, 1954-55; bd. editors Hispanic Am. Hist. Rev, 1960-65, 74-79; adv. editor Caribbean Studies, 1961-89, Jour. Urban History, 1973-90, Cuadernos Americanos, 1986—, Wilson Quarterly, 1989-92. Served to lt. USNR, 1943-46, PTO. Recipient Nat. Theatre Conf. prize play award, 1945, Conf. Latin Am. History prize essay award, 1962; Woodrow Wilson fellow, 1946-47; State Dept. fellow, 1947-48; Guggenheim fellow, 1964-65; Social Sci. Research Council fellow, 1964-65; fellow Center Advanced Studies Behavioral Scis., 1970-71; Stanford Humanities Ctr. fellow, 1983-84, Inst. Advanced Studies U. São Paulo, 1987; recipient medal of merit Getulio Vargas Found., 1975, Casa Rui Barbosa medal, 1992, Brazilian Order Cruzeiro do Sul, 1993, Brazilian Order Sci. Merit, 1996. Mem. Conf. Latin Am. History (chmn. 1969), Phi Beta Kappa. Home: 4412 Volta Pl NW Washington DC 20007-2019

MORSE, RICHARD VAN TUYL, manufacturing executive, consultant; b. N.Y.C., May 7, 1931; s. Norvell V. and Julie M. (Lamisha) M.; m. Florence Denby, June 21, 1953 (div. June 1983); children: Stuart V., Andrew D.; m. Emilie Atolli, Sept. 14, 1983. BS in Econs., U. Pa., 1953; MBA, NYU, 1958. Account supr. various advt. agys., N.Y.C., 1956-66; v.p., account supr. Wells, Rich, Greene, Inc., N.Y.C., 1960-70, Norman, Craig & Kummell, Inc., N.Y.C., 1970-74; sr. v.p., mgmt. supr. William Free & Co., N.Y.C., 1974-80; v.p. mktg. Canada Dry, Inc., N.Y.C., 1980-87; v.p. mktg. comm. Lithonia Lighting, Conyers, Ga., 1987—; dir. Pop Warner Football, N.Y.C., 1967-69. Contbr. articles to profl. jours. Elected Rep. rep. Union County, N.J., 1970-76. Capt. USAR. Mem. Am. Mktg. Assn., Nat. Lighting Bur. (bd. chmn., 1995-97), Bus. and Profl. Advt. and Mktg. Assn., Atlanta Shakespeare Co. (bd. chmn. 1986-92). Republican. Episcopalian. Avocations: trap and skeet shooting, travel, Brit. Victorian mil. history. Home: 7155 Roswell Rd NE # 53 Atlanta GA 30328-5419 Office: Lithonia Lighting PO Box A Conyers GA 30207-0067

MORSE, ROBERT HARRY, lawyer; b. Bklyn., May 25, 1941; s. Soll and Rachel Morse; m. Sandra Goldstein, July 22, 1967; children: Lisa Jennifer, Eric Jeffrey. BSEE with honors, MIT, 1963, MSEE with honors, 1964; JD, Harvard U., 1967. Bar: N.Y. 1968, D.C. 1978, Md. 1985. Assoc. Kenyon & Kenyon, Reilly, Carr & Chapin, N.Y.C., 1967-71; trial atty. Antitrust div. Dept. Justice, Washington, 1971-74, sr. trial atty., 1974-78; ptnr. Peabody, Lambert & Meyers, Washington, 1978-82, Galland, Kharasch, Morse & Garfinkle, Washington, 1982-97, Ropes and Gray, Washington, 1997—; dir. Earle Palmer Brown Cos. Mem. nat. area capital area coun. Boy Scouts Am., gen. counsel, 1991-94, exec. bd. dirs., 1990—. Recipient Spl. Achievement award, 1973, Meritorious award, 1976 (both Dept. Justice). Mem. ABA, D.C. Bar Assn., Pat. Bar, Nat. Alumni Assn. MIT (bd. dirs. 1986-88), Sigma Xi, Tau Beta Pi, Eta Kappa Nu. Club: MIT of Washington (sec. 1981-82, pres. 1983-84).

MORSE, ROBERT WARREN, research administrator; b. Boston, May 25, 1921; s. Walter L. and Ethel (Prince) M.; m. Alice Muriel Cooper, Jan. 25, 1943; children: Robert Warren, Pamela Morse Moschetti, James Prince. B.S., Bowdoin Coll., 1943, D.Sc. (hon.), 1966; Sc.M., Brown U., 1947, Ph.D., 1949. Mem. faculty Brown U., 1946-64, prof. physics, 1958-64, chmn. dept., 1960-62, dean coll., 1962-64; asst. sec. of navy, research and devel. Washington, 1964-66; pres. Case Inst. Tech., 1966-67, Case Western Res. U., Cleve., 1967-71; dir. research Woods Hole (Mass.) Oceanographic Instn., 1971-73, sr. scientist, 1973-83, scientist emeritus, 1983—, asso. dir., dean grad. studies, 1973-79; dir. PPG Industries, Research Corp. Tech.; Howard Found. fellow Royal Soc. Mond Lab., Cambridge (Eng.) U., 1954-55; mem. com. undersea warfare Nat. Acad. Scis., 1957-64, chmn., 1962-64; vis. lectr. U. Oslo, 1962; chmn. interagy. com. oceanography Fed. Council Sci. and Tech., 1964-66; chmn. bd. on human resources Nat. Acad. Scis., 1970-74, chmn. ocean affairs bd., 1971-76; vis. scientist Scripps Instn. Oceanography, La Jolla, Calif., 1982. Author articles on ultrasonics, superconductivity, properties metals, underwater acoustics. Overseer Bowdoin Coll., 1971-87. Served to lt. (s.g.) USNR, 1943-46. Recipient Navy Distinguished Pub. Service medal, 1966. Fellow Am. Phys. Soc. (chmn. divsn. solid state physics 1963-64), Acoustical Soc. Am. (pres. 1965-66), Am. Acad. Arts and Scis.; mem. Woods Hole Golf Club, Sigma Xi. Home: PO Box 574 North Falmouth MA 02556-0574

MORSE, SAUL JULIAN, lawyer; b. N.Y.C., Jan. 17, 1948; s. Leon William and Goldie (Kohn) M.; m. Anne Bruce Morgan, Aug. 21, 1982; children: John Samuel, Elizabeth Miriam. BA, U. Ill., 1969, JD, 1972. Bar: Ill. 1973, U.S. Dist. Ct. (so. dist.) Ill. 1976, U.S. Ct. Appeals (7th cir.) 1983, U.S. Supreme Ct. 1979, U.S. Tax Ct. 1982. Law clk. State of Ill. EPA, 1971-72; law clk. Ill. Commerce Commn., 1972, hearing examiner, 1972-73; trial atty. ICC, 1973-75; asst. minority legal counsel Ill. Senate, 1975, minority legal counsel, 1975-77; mem. Ill. Human Rights Commn., 1985-91; dir. Ill. Comprehensive Health Ins. Plan, treas., chair grievance com.; gen. counsel Ill. Legis. Space Needs Commn., 1978-92; sole practice, Springfield, Ill., 1977-79; ptnr. Gramlich & Morse, Springfield, Ill., 1980-85; prin. Saul J. Morse and Assocs., 1985-87; ptnr. Morse, Giganti and Appleton, 1987-92; v.p., gen. counsel Ill. State Medical Soc., 1992—; lectr. in continuing med. edn. 1986-90; counsel symposia; bd. dirs. Springfield Ctr. for Ind. Living, 1984-89, Ill. Comprehensive Health Ins. Plan Bd., United Cerebral Palsy Land of Lincoln, United Way Ctrl. Ill., Inc., 1991-97; dir. Hope Sch.; mem., bd. dirs. Springfield Jewish Fedn., 1992-95, mem. bd. dirs., Hope Sch. Springfield Ill.; mem. task force on transp. Republican Nat. Com., 1979-80, Springfield Jewish Community Rels. Coun., 1976-79, 82; mem. spl. com. on zoning and land use planning Sangamon County Bd., 1978. Named Disabled Adv. of Yr., Ill. Dept. Rehab. Svcs., 1985; recipient Chmn.'s Spl. award Ill. State Med. Soc., 1987, Susan S. Suter award as outstanding disabled citizen of Ill., 1990. Mem. Nat. Health Lawyers Assn., Am. Soc. Law and Medicine, ABA (vice chmn. medicine and law com. 1988-90, tort and ins. practice sect., forum com. on health law), Ill. State Bar Assn. (spl. com. on reform of legis. process 1976-82, spl. com. on the disabled lawyer 1978-82, young lawyers sect. com. on role of govt. atty. 1977-80, chmn. 1982, sect. council adminstrv. law, vice chmn. 1981-82), Sangamon County Bar Assn., Am. Soc. Med. Assn. Counsel, Phi Delta Phi. Home: 1701 S Illini Rd Springfield IL 62704-3301 Office: Ill State Med Soc 600 S 2nd St Ste 200 Springfield IL 62704-2542

MORSE, STEPHEN SCOTT, virologist, immunologist; b. N.Y.C., Nov. 22, 1951; s. Murray H. and Phyllis Morse; m. Marilyn Gewirtz, Feb. 1991. BS, CCNY, 1971; MS, U. Wis., 1974, PhD, 1977. NSF trainee dept. bacteriology U. Wis., Madison, 1971-72, rsch. asst., 1972-77; rsch. fellow Nat. Cancer Inst.-Med. Coll. Va./Va. Commonwealth U., Richmond, 1977-80, instr., 1980-81; asst. prof. microbiology Rutgers U., New Brunswick, N.J., 1981-85; rsch. assoc. Rockefeller U., N.Y.C., 1985-88, asst. prof., 1988-96; dir. program emerging diseases, asst. prof. Sch. Pub. Health Columbia U., 1996—; cons. U.S. Congress Office Tech. Assessment, Washington, 1989; chair conf. on emerging viruses NIH, 1989; cons. Inst. Medicine-NAS, mem. com. microbial threats to health, chair subcom. on viruses, 1990-92; chair Fedn. Am. Scientists (FAS) program for monitoring emerging diseases (ProMED), 1993—; program mgr. Def. Advanced Rsch. Projects Agy., 1996—. Editor: Emerging Viruses, 1993, Evolutionary Biology of Viruses, 1994; sect. editor Ctr. for Disease Control and Prevention Jour. "Emerging Infectious Diseases". Mem. Am. Soc. Microbiology, Am. Assn. Pathologists, Am. Assn. Immunologists, N.Y. Acad. Scis. (vice chair microbiology sect. 1994-96, chair 1996—), Marine Biology Lab., Sigma Xi. Office: Columbia U Sch Pub Health Divsn Epidemiology 600 W 168th St New York NY 10032-3702

MORSE, SUSAN EDWINA, film editor; b. Bklyn., Mar. 4, 1952; d. Rogers Watrous and Marian Edwina (Davis) M.; m. Jack Carter Richardson, July 11, 1987; 1 child, Dwight Rogers Richardson. BA, Yale U., 1974. Film editor Rollins & Joffe Prodns., N.Y.C., 1976-93, Sweetheart Prodns., N.Y.C., 1994—. Editor (films) Manhattan, 1979 (Brit. Acad. Award Nomination), Stardust Memories, 1980, Arthur, 1981, A Midsummer Night's Sex Comedy, 1982, Zelig, 1983 (Brit. Acad. Award Nomination), Broadway Danny Rose, 1984, The Purple Rose of Cairo, 1984, Hannah and Her Sisters, 1985 (Brit. Acad. Award Nomination, Oscar Nomination), Radio Days, 1986 (Brit. Acad. Award Nomination), September, 1987, Another Woman, 1988, New York Stories (Oedipus Wrecks), 1989, Crimes and Misdemeanors, 1989 (Brit. Acad. Award Nomination), Alice, 1990, Shadows and Fog, 1991, Husbands and Wives, 1992, Manhattan Murder Mystery, 1993, Bullets Over Broadway, 1994, Mighty Aphrodite, 1995, Everyone Says I Love You, 1996, Deconstructing Harry, 1997, (TV films) The Greatest Man in the World, 1978, Don't Drink the Water, 1994; co-editor (with Dennis Virkler) Miracles, 1985; assoc. editor (with David Holden) The Warriors, 1978, (with Thelma Schoonmaker) Raging Bull, 1979. Coach youth baseball team; referee youth soccer team. Mem. Acad. Motion Picture Arts and Scis., Am. Cinema Editors. Avocations: field hockey, music, theatre.

MORSON, PHILIP HULL, III, psychiatrist, osteopath; b. Tupelo, Miss., Oct. 1, 1948; s. Philip Hull and Jane Allen (McGee) M.; m. Brenda Lott, Aug. 28, 1970 (div. July 1986); children: Andrew Eugene, Benjamin Terrell; m. Katherine Ann Smith, Dec. 12, 1992; children: Bobbie Nichole, Samantha Grace. BA, Miss. State U., 1970; M of Combined Scis., U. Miss., Jackson, 1973; DO, U. Health Scis., Kansas City, Mo., 1978. Diplomate Nat. Bd. Osteo. Med. Examiners; cert. forensic physician. Brigade surgeon U.S.

Army, Fort Stewart, Ga., 1979-81; ranger bn. surgeon 1st Bn, 75th inf. U.S. Army, Savannah, Ga., 1981; chief outpatient clinic Winn Army Hosp., Ft. Stewart, Ga., 1981-82; chief emergency med. svcs. Winn Army Hosp., Ft. Stewart, 1982-83; pvt. practice Cleveland, Tenn., 1983-89, Bristol, Tenn., 1989-91; staff physician Western Mental Health Inst., Bolivar, Tenn., 1991—; chmn. treatment rev. com. Western Mental Helath Inst., 1991-96, vice chmn. pharmacy and therapeutics com., 1993-94, mem. exec. med. staff, 1994-96. Sponsor troop Girl Scouts Am., Bolivar, Tenn., 1992—; mem. PTA, Bolivar, 1992-94. Mem. Am. Osteo. Assn., Western Tenn. Osteo. Assn., Tenn. State Employees Assn. (treas. S.W. chpt. 1994-97, legis. com. 1994-95, long range planning com. 1996—, bd. dirs. 1997, Cora Redmond award 1996), Mensa, NRA. Republican. Unitarian. Avocations: theatre, sailing, piano playing, reading, body building. Home: 1915 Levy Ln Bolivar TN 38008 Office: Western Mental Health Inst 11000 Hwy 64 W Bolivar TN 38008

MORSS, LESTER ROBERT, chemist; b. Boston, Apr. 6, 1940; s. Sumner M. and Sylvia F. (Woolf) M.; m. Helaine Sue Gubin, June 19, 1966; children: Sydney, Benjamin, Rebecca, Alisa. BA, Harvard U., 1961; PhD, U. Calif., Berkeley, 1969. Postdoctoral rsch. assoc. Purdue U., West Lafayette, Ind., 1969-71; from asst. prof. to assoc. prof. Rutgers U., New Brunswick, N.J., 1971-80; chemist, sr. chemist Argonne (Ill.) Nat. Lab., 1980—; vis. prof. U. Liège, Belgium, 1978-79, U. Paris, Orsay, 1993. Author, co-editor: The Chemistry of the Actinide Elements, 1986, Syntheses of Lanthanide and Actinide Compounds, 1991; editor procs. Rare Earth Rsch. Conf., 1986—. Lt. USN, 1961-65, Atlantic and Mediterranean. Recipient Sr. Scientist award Alexander von Humboldt Found., 1992. Fellow AAAS; mem. Am. Chem. Soc. (sec. div. nuclear chemistry and tech. 1990-92), Am. Nuclear Soc., Sigma Xi (pres. Argonne chpt. 1988-89). Jewish. Home: 1S680 Verdun Dr Winfield IL 60190-1716 Office: Argonne Nat Lab Chem Dv Bldg 200 Argonne IL 60439

MORTENSEN, ARVID LEGRANDE, lawyer; b. Bremerton, Wash., July 11, 1941; s. George Andrew and Mary Louise (Myers) M.; m. Elaine Marie Mains, Aug. 2, 1968; children: Marie Louise, Anne Catherine, Joseph Duncan. BS in English and Psychology, Brigham Young U., 1965, MBA in Mktg. and Fin., 1967; JD cum laude, Ind. U., 1980. Bar: Ind. 1980, U.S. Supreme Ct. 1983, Mo. 1985, D.C. 1985; CLU, 1971; Accredited Estate Planner, 1995. Agt. Conn. Mut. Life Ins. Co., Salt Lake City, 1967-68, agt. and br. mgr., Idaho Falls, Idaho, 1968-74; with Rsch. and Rev. Svc. Am., Inc./Newkirk Assocs., Inc., Indpls., 1974-83, sr. editor, 1975-79, mgr. advanced products and seminars, 1979-80, sr. mktg. exec., 1980-83; tax and fin. planner, Indpls., 1980-85, St. Louis and Chesterfield, Mo., 1985-90, Tampa Bay, Fla., 1990-91, Orange County, Calif., 1991—. mem. sr. mgmt. com., v.p. Allied Fidelity Corp., 1983-85, Allied Fidelity Ins. Co., 1983-85, Tex. Fire and Casualty Ins. Co., 1983-85; v.p., bd. dirs. Gen. Am. Ins. Co., St. Louis, 1985-86; v.p. Gen. Am. Life Ins. Co., St. Louis, 1985-90; pvt. practice law, Indpls., 1980-85, St. Louis, Chesterfield and Bridgeton, Mo., 1985-90, Tampa Bay, 1990-91, Orange County, 1991—; active with Ch. Jesus Christ of Latter-day Saints, Denver, Idaho Falls, Idaho, Indpls., St. Louis, Chesterfield, Tampa Bay Area and Orange County, Calif., Profl. Assn. Diving Instrs. cert. Divemaster, 1989—; lic. amateur radio operator FCC, 1994—, amateur extra class, 1996. Mem. Assn. Advanced Life Underwriting, Mo. Bar Assn., Bar Assn. Met. St. Louis, D.C. Bar Assn., Ind. Bar Assn., Am. Soc. CLU's, Nat. Assn. Life Underwriters, Orange County,. Author: Employee Stock Ownership Plans, 1975, Fundamentals of Corporate Qualified Retirement Plans, 1975, 78, 80, Buy-Sell Agreements, 1988, The Key Executive Sale, 1989, (with Norman H. Tarver) The IRA Manual, 1975-87 edits., (with Norman H. Tarver) The Keogh Manual, 1975, 77, 78, 80 edits., (with Norman H. Tarver) The Section 403 (b) Manual, 1975, 77, 78, 80, 84, 85, 87 edits., sole author 1991,93 , 94, edit., (with Leo C. Hodges) The Life Insurance Trust Handbook, 1980; contbr. articles to profl. jours.; editor-in-chief various tax and fin. planning courses; bd. editors Ind. Law Rev., 1977-78. Office: 620 Newport Center Dr Ste 1100 Newport Beach CA 92660-8011 also: PO Box 6362 Laguna Niguel CA 92607-6362

MORTENSEN, CHRIS, sports analyst, reporter; b. Nov. 7, 1952. Student, El Camino Coll. Reporter South Bay (Calif.) Daily Breeze, 1969-83; reporter Atlanta Braves Atlanta-Jour. Constn., 1983-85, reporter Atlanta Falcons, 1985-86, reporter NFL, 1987-89; reporter NFL The Nat., 1989-90; analyst NFL draft ESPN, 1991, 92, reporter NFL Game Day, NFL Prime Monday, SportsCenter, 1991—, reporter Outside the Lines series, 1991—. Author: Playing for Keeps: A True Story about Football, Playoffs and the Mob; NFL columnist The Sporting News; contbg. writer Sport mag. Served with U.S. Army. Recipient George Polk award for reporting, 1987, 18 awards in journalism, Nat. Headliner award for investigative reporting, 1978; nominated for two Pulitzer Prizes. Office: c/o ESPN ESPN Pla Bristol CT 06010

MORTENSEN, EUGENE PHILLIPS, hospital administrator; b. N.Y.C., Mar. 28, 1941; s. Eugene Phillips and Mary (Hogarty) M.; m. Ellen Louise McDavitt, Aug. 8, 1964; children: Jeffrey Phillips, Jennifer-Kristine McDavitt. BA, Seton Hall U., 1963; MS in Mgmt., Frostburg State U., 1974; M in Profl. Studies, Cornell U., 1976. Commd. 2d lt. U.S. Army, 1963, advanced through grades to col., 1984; ret., 1994; med. budget advisor Office Army Surgeon Gen., Cholon, Vietnam, 1968-69; chief materials mgmt. br. and test and standards Office of Compt., Office Surgeon Gen., Washington, 1969-71; chief systems div. and health care system br. U.S. Army Health Svcs. Data Systems Agy., Ft. Detrick, Md., 1971-74, resigned, 1974; asst. adminstr. for gen. svcs. St. Joseph's Hosp. and Med. Ctr., Paterson, N.J., 1976-79, for clin. svcs., 1979-83, v.p. clin. svcs., 1983-89, exec. v.p., chief operating officer, 1989-92; sr. v.p. for operation, chief oper. officer Jersey City Med. Ctr., 1992—; chief op. officer Liberty Home Care Agency, 1994—; vice chair Hudson Perinatal Consortium, 1996—. Mem. editorial bd. Perinatal Newsletter, 1984-92. Coach Upper Saddle River (N.J.) Soccer Assn., 1986—; webelos den leader cub scouts, Boy Scouts Am., Upper Saddle River, 1986-90, asst. scoutmaster, 1990—; trustee N.J. Vis. Health Svcs., Totawa, 1988-92; trustee, mem. adv. bd. Passaic Valley Hospice, Totawa, 1986-92; bd. trustees Hudson County Occupational Ctr., 1993—. Decorated Bronze Star. Fellow Am. Coll. Healthcare Execs. (coun. regents); mem. Am. Hosp. Assn., N.J. Hosp. Assn. (coun. on govt. rels. 1992-94), Paterson C. of C. (bd. dirs. 1989-92). Republican. Roman Catholic. Home: 8 Iron Latch Ct U Saddle Riv NJ 07458-2005 Office: Jersey City Med Ctr 50 Baldwin Ave Jersey City NJ 07304-3154

MORTENSEN, GORDON LOUIS, artist, printmaker; b. Arnegard, N.D., Apr. 27, 1938; s. Gunner and Otillia Ernestine (Reiner) M.; m. Phoebe Hollis Hansen, Apr. 10, 1965 (div. 1968); m. Linda Johanna Sisson, Dec. 7, 1969. B.F.A., Mpls. Coll. Art and Design, 1964; postgrad., U. Minn., 1969-72. One-man shows include Minn. Mus., St. Paul, 1967, Concept Art Gallery Pitts., 1981, 83, 85, 87, 89, 91, 93, C.G. Rein Galleries, Mpls., 1978, 80, 85, 89, 91, 93, others; exhibited in group shows Miami U., Oxford, Ohio (1st place award 1977), Phila. Print Club (George Bunker award 1977), 12th Nat. Silvermine Guild Print Exhbn., New Canaan, Comm., 1976, 78, 80, 83, 86, 94 (Hearsch Mag. award 1978, Purchase award 1983, 86), 4th Miami Internat. Print Biennial (4th place award 1980), Rockford Internat., 1981, 85 (Juror's award 1981), Boston Printmakers Nat. Exhbn., 1977, 79, 80, 81, 83 (Purchase award 1977, 79, 83), others; represented permanent collections, Achenbach Found. Graphic Arts at Palace Legion of Honor, San Francisco, Bklyn. Mus., Phila. Mus. Art, Libr. of Congress, Minn. Mus. Art, Met. Mus. and Art Ctr., Miami, Fla., Mus. Am. Art, Washington, Art Inst. Chgo., Mus. Art at Carnegie-Mellon Inst., Pitts., Walker Art Ctr., Mpls., Dulin Gallery Art, Knoxville, Tenn., numerous corp. collections; profiled in numerous art jours. Served with USMC, 1957-60. Mem. Boston Printmakers, Phila. Print Club, L.A. Printmaking Soc., Albany Print Club. Home and Office: 4153 Crest Rd Pebble Beach CA 93953-3052

MORTENSEN, JAMES E., management consultant; b. Brayton, Iowa, Mar. 15, 1925; s. Axel C. and Mabel (Ide) M.; m. Genevieve Edsall, Nov. 8, 1946; 1 son, Arthur C. Student, U. Denver, 1946-48, Columbia Exec. Program, 1965. Gen. mgr. dog food div. Cargill, Inc., Mpls., 1949-56; exec. v.p. Battle Creek Dog Food Co., Mich., 1956-57; dir., vice chmn. bd., chief fin. officer pres. affiliates Young & Rubicam, Inc., N.Y.C., 1957-81; now ind. cons.; pres. Asbury Terrace, Inc., 1965-69; mem. adv. bd. NPD Group Inc., Port Washington, N.Y. Trustee Mus. of Fine Arts, St. Petersburg, Fla. Decorated Bronze Star, Purple Heart. Mem. Am. Radio Relay League (v.p.). Republican (pres. Irvington, N.Y. 1961-62). Home: PO Box 490 Indian Rocks Beach FL 33785-0328

MORTENSEN, PETER, banker; b. Ellwood City, Pa., Dec. 4, 1935; s. Norman Peter and Mary Letitia (Brown) M.; m. Collette; children: Linda V. Haning, Kelly J. Hebble, Nancy Sarah Patton, Karen Sue Harris. B.A., Coll. of Wooster, Ohio, 1956. With First Nat. Bank of Pa., Hermitage, Pa., 1959—; pres., chief exec. officer F.N.B. Corp., Hermitage, Pa., 1973—, chmn., 1987—. Mem. United Church of Christ. Avocation: hunting.

MORTENSEN, RICHARD EDGAR, engineering educator; b. Denver, Sept. 29, 1935; s. Edgar Steele and Frieda Amalie (Boecker) M.; m. Sarah Jean Raulston, Oct. 12, 1974 (div. 1978). BSEE, MIT, 1958, MSEE, 1958; PhD, U. Calif., Berkeley, 1966. Co-op. engr. GE Co., Schenectady, N.Y., 1955-57; mem. tech. staff Space Tech. Labs., L.A., 1958-61; rsch. asst. U. Calif., Berkeley, 1961-65; prof. engring. UCLA, 1965-91, prof. emeritus, 1991—; cons. TRW, Inc., Redondo Beach, Calif., 1966-70, Aerojet-Gen. Corp., Azusa, Calif., 1970-72, Applied Sci. Analytics, Inc., Canoga Park, Calif., 1980-82; guest lectr. Indian Inst. Sci., Bangalore, India, 1991. Author: Random Signals and Systems, 1987; contbr. to profl. publs. Team mem. Beyond War, Topanga, Calif., 1986-89; alcoholism counselor. Grantee NSF, 1987-90; named to Alumni Hall of Fame, Lambda Chi Alpha, 1996. Mem. IEEE, Soc. Indsl. and Applied Math., Sigma Xi, Tau Beta Pi, Eta Kappa Nu, Lambda Chi Alpha (Hall of Fame 1996). Avocations: hiking, yoga. Office: Dept Elec Engring 405 Hilgard Ave Los Angeles CA 90095-9000

MORTENSEN, ROBERT HENRY, landscape architect; b. Jackson, Mich., June 9, 1939; s. Henry and Charlotte Marie (Brown) M.; divorced; children: Phillip, Paul, Susan, Julia; m. Meta Jane Hearne Blakely, Nov. 1975; stepchildren: Laura, Kathryn. B Landscape Architecture, Ohio State U., 1961; M Landscape Architecture, U. Mich., 1965. Registered landscape architect, Ohio, Fla., Va., Md., Ohio. Landscape architect various firms, Louisville, 1960, 61-63; with Ohio Div. Parks, Columbus, 1960-61; landscape architect various firms, Toledo, 1963, 65-67; pvt. practice Ann Arbor, Mich., 1963-65; ptnr. firms Toledo, 1967-78; pres. Harvey Jones and Assocs., Clearwater, Fla., 1979-81; owner Mortensen Assocs., Toledo and Falls Church, Va., 1979-85; prin. Mortensen, Lewis & Scully, Inc., Vienna, Va., 1985-93; owner Mortensen Assocs., Vienna, Va., 1993—; assoc. prof. U. Mich. Grad. Sch., 1973; vis. lectr. Ohio State U., 1965—, Bowling Green (Ohio) State U., 1969—, U. Mich., 1971, Purdue U., 1971, Mich. State U., 1973—; mem. archtl. environ. rev. com. Ohio Arts Coun., 1974-78; adj. prof. Dept. Landscape Architecture, U. Md., 1992—. Editor: Handbook of Professional Practice, 1972, Marketing Landscape Architectural Services to the Federal Government, 1974. Mem. Ohio Bd. Unreclaimed Strip Mined Lands, 1973-76; mem. Lucas County facilities rev. com. Health Planning Assn. N.W. Ohio, 1972-76, chmn. maternal and child health subcom., 1972-74; bd. dirs. No. Va. Cmty. Appearance Alliance, 1988—, chair, 1991, pres., 1994. Recipient Disting. Svc. award Health Planning Assn. N.W. Ohio, 1973, Disting. Alumni award U. Mich. Sch. Natural Resources, 1985, Disting. Alumnus award Ohio State U. Coll. Engring., 1985. Fellow Am. Soc. Landscape Architects (trustee 1977-82, v.p. 1982-83, pres.-elect 1983-84, nat. pres. 1984-85, del. to Internat. Fedn. Landscape Architects 1987-92, del. Internat. Landscape Alliance 1994—); mem. Ohio Soc. Landscape Architects (pres. 1969-74), Toledo C. of C. (chmn. sts. and hwys. transit com. 1972-73), Greater Merrifield Bus. and Profl. Assn. (bd. dirs. 1993, pres. 1997), Washington Golf and Country Club, Ravines Golf and Country Club, Sigma Phi Epsilon. Home: 6843 Churchill Rd Mc Lean VA 22101-2822 Office: Mortensen Assocs 2787 Hartland Rd Falls Church VA 22043-3529 *One of the best continuing educational experiences for a practising professional is to teach students what you have learned. They respond in a critical and ever-so-fresh "so what" atmosphere, and demand more of you sometimes than you demand of yourself. Thus, there is learning on both sides of the lectern.*

MORTENSEN, WILLIAM S., banking executive; b. 1932. Chmn. bd., pres., CEO 1st Fed. Bank Calif., Santa Monica, 1955—, CEO, until 1997. Office: 1st Fed Bank Calif 401 Wilshire Blvd Santa Monica CA 90401-1416*

MORTENSEN-SAY, MARLYS (MRS. JOHN THEODORE SAY), school system administrator; b. Yankton, S.D., Mar. 11, 1924; d. Melvin A. and Edith L. (Fargo) Mortensen; BA, U. Colo., 1949, MEd, 1953; adminstrv. specialist U. Nebr., 1973; m. John Theodore Say, June 21, 1951; children: Mary Louise, James Kenneth, John Melvin, Margaret Ann. Tchr. Huron (S.D.) Jr. High Sch., 1944-48, Lamar (Colo.) Jr. High Sch., 1950-52, Norfolk Pub. Sch., 1962-63; sch. supt. Madison County, Madison, Nebr., 1963—. Mem. NEA (life), AAUW, Am. Assn. Sch. Adminstrs., Dept. Rural Edn., Nebr. Assn. County Supts., N.E. Nebr. County Supts. Assn., Assn. Sch. Bus. Ofcls., Nat. Orgn. Legal Problems in Edn., Assn. Supervision and Curriculum Devel., Nebr. Edn. Assn., Nebr. Sch. Adminstrs. Assn. Republican. Methodist. Home: 4805 S 13th St Norfolk NE 68701-6627

MORTENSON, THOMAS THEODORE, medical products executive, management consultant; b. Hallock, Minn., Dec. 18, 1934; s. Theodore William and Esther (Hanson) M.; m. Alice L. Girdvain, June 27, 1958; children: Kim M. Mortenson Zimmerman, Laura Dee Mortenson Pavlides. BSBA, U. N.D., 1956, postgrad., 1957-58. Sales rep. Johnson & Johnson, Detroit, 1960-66; tng. and product dir. Johnson & Johnson, New Brunswick, N.J., 1967-72; dir. market devel. C.R. Bard, Murray Hill, N.J., 1973-75; gen. mgr. MacBick, Murray Hill, 1976-78; dir. mktg. Bard Med. Systems, Murray Hill, 1979-81, dir. sales, 1982; dir. sales and mktg. Bac-Data Med. Info. Systems, Totowa, N.J., 1983-84; v.p. mktg. and sales United Med. Corp., Haddenfield, N.J., 1985-86; exec. v.p. Daltex Med. Scis., West Orange, N.J., 1987-92; assoc. ConMed Corp., Utica, N.Y., 1993—; guest lectr. Am. Mgmt. Assn., 1971, Mktg. Scis. Inc., N.Y.C., 1978, Internat. Novel Drug Delivery Techs., Tustin, Calif., 1987. With U.S. Army, 1957-58. Mem. Am. Mgmt. Assn. (instr. 1971), Berkeley Swim Club (Berkeley Heights, N.J.) (pres. 1979-82, bd. dirs. 1974-84). Avocations: woodworking, golf, volleyball, auto restoration. Home: 44 Ironwood Rd New Hartford NY 13413-3906 Office: 310 Broad St Utica NY 13501-1203

MORTHAM, SANDRA BARRINGER, state official; b. Erie, Pa., Jan. 4, 1951; d. Norman Lyell and Ruth (Harer) Barringer; m. Allen Mortham, Aug. 21, 1950; children: Allen Jr., Jeffrey. AS, St. Petersburg Jr. Coll., 1971; BA, Eckerd Coll. Cons. Capital Formation Counselors, Inc., Bellair Bluffs, Fla., 1972—; commr. City of Largo, Fla., 1982-86, vice mayor, 1985-86; mem. Fla. Ho. of Reps., 1986-94, Rep. leader pro tempore, 1990-92, minority leader, 1992-94; Sec. of State State of Fla., 1995—. Bd. dirs. Performing Arts Ctr. & Theatre, Clearwater, Fla.; exec. com. Pinellas County Rep. Com., Rep. Nat. Com. Named Citizen of Yr., 1990; recipient Tax Watch Competitive Govt. award, 1994, Bus. and Profl. Women "Break the Glass Ceiling" award, 1995, Fla. League of Cities Quality Floridian award, 1995, also numerous outstanding legislator awards, achievement among women awards from civic and profl. orgns. Mem. Am. Legis. Exch. Coun., Nat. Rep. Legislators Assn., Largo C. of C. (bd. dirs. 1987—, pres.), Largo Jr. Woman's Club (pres., Woman of Yr. award 1979), Suncoast Community Woman's Club (pres., Outstanding Svc. award 1981, Woman of Yr. award 1986), Suncoast Tiger Bay, Greater Largo Rep., Belleair Rep. Woman's, Clearwater Rep. Woman's. Presbyterian. Home: 6675 Weeping Willow Dr Tallahassee FL 32311 Office: Secretary of State The Capitol, PL-02 Tallahassee FL 32399-0250

MORTIMER, DAVID WILLIAM, communications engineer; b. Redding, Calif., June 8, 1962; s. Walter L. and Phyllis B. (Winters) M. BSEE, Brigham Young U., 1988; MBA, Syracuse U., 1997. Devel. engr. Scala Electronics, Medford, Oreg., 1988-89; asst. sta. mgr. Holzkirchen Radio Free Europe/Radio Liberty, Munich, 1989-90; asst. sta. mgr. Spain Radio Free Europe/Radio Liberty, Playa de Pals, 1990-93; ops. dir. Portugal Radio Free Europe/Radio Liberty, Lisbon, 1993-95; tech. asst. Radio Free Europe/Radio Liberty, Prague, Czech Republic, 1995; acting mng. dir. Portugal Radio Free Europe/Radio Liberty, Lisbon, 1995. Mem. IEEE, Nat. Eagle Scout Assn. (life).

MORTIMER, JAMES WINSLOW, analytical chemist; b. Mt. Kisco, N.Y., Mar. 11, 1955; s. James Winslow and Eileen Ruth (Cutting) M.; m. Dawn Romay Kania, Apr. 30, 1977. BA, Washington and Jefferson U., 1976. Tech. sales rep. Waters Assocs., Milford, Mass., 1978-82; dir. nat. accounts Zymark Corp., Hopkinton, Mass., 1982-89; v.p. Microflex Tech., Triadelphia, W.Va., 1989-90; mgr. mktg. Berthold Systems, Inc., Aliquippa, Pa., 1990-95; mktg. mgr. Fisher Sci., Pitts., 1995—; speaker at profl. confs. Author: Laboratory Robotics, 1987; cons. editor Lab. Robotics Jour., Hershey, Pa., 1990—; assoc. editor Lab. Robotics and Automation, 1988, 90; contbr. articles to tech. publs. Mem. TAPPI, Soc. Analytical Chemists (speaker 1978, 87), Masons. Achievements include development of cleavastat surgical instrument, beaker that will not cause vortexing action. Home: 113 Little John Dr Mc Murray PA 15317-2542 Office: Fisher Scientific 2000 Park Lane Dr Pittsburgh PA 15275-1126

MORTIMER, LAWRENCE PATRICK, sales executive; b. Chgo., Mar. 17, 1948; s. Evon Joseph and Lois Jean (Carlson) M.; m. Michele Marie Reese; 1 child, Kyle Patrick. BS in Journalism and Comms., Point Park Coll., Pitts., 1971. Newspaper pub.rep. Mathews, Shannon & Cullen, Cleve., 1972-76; regional sales mgr. Gannett Newspaper Advt. Sales, Atlanta, 1976-77; Midwest regl mgr. Gannett Newspapers, Chgo., 1977-82; Chgo. sales exec. USA Today, 1982-84; v.p., we. sales mgr. Gannett Media Sales, San Francisco, 1984-87; v.p., assoc. dir. advt. USA Weekend, Chgo., 1987-89; v.p., group sales mgr. ActMedia, Chgo., 1989—; bd. dirs., pres.-elect. Cmty. Youth Newspapers, Chgo., 1983-84; bd. dirs. Midwest Golf Nat. Pro-Am, Chgo., 1995. Bd. dirs. Spl. Olympics, St. Charles, Ill., 1995—. Served with U.S. Army, 1971-72/. Mem. Food Mktg. Inst., Promotional Mktg. Assn. Republican. Avocations: golf, sports memorabilia. Home: 1524 Falcon Dr Wheaton IL 60187-3044 Office: ActMedia 1011 E Touhy Ave Des Plaines IL 60018-5802

MORTIMER, PETER MICHAEL, lawyer; b. Detroit, May 20, 1943; s. Robert J. and Harriet C. (Evenson) M.; m. Sharon M. Olson, Aug. 20, 1966; children: Katherine, Trever, Peter. AB magna cum laude, Cornell U., 1965; JD cum laude, Harvard U., 1968. Bar: D.C. 1968, N.Y. 1970. Atty. Office Legal Adviser, U.S. Dept. State, Washington, 1968; assoc. Milbank, Tweed, Hadley & McCloy, N.Y.C., 1969-76, ptnr., 1977—, mem. compensation com., 1992—, co-practice group leader banking & instnl. investment group, 1995—; resident ptnr. Milbank, Tweed, Hadley & McCloy, Hong Kong, 1977-79, London, 1983-88. Fellow Frick Collection, N.Y.C., 1981—, Pierpont Morgan Libr., N.Y.C., 1980—, mem. coun., 1981-83. Decorated Order of Francisco de Miranda 1st class (Venezuela). Mem. D.C. Bar, Assn. of Bar of City of N.Y., Century Assn., Down Town Assn., Grolier Club, Short Hills Club, Baltusrol Golf Club, Phi Beta Kappa. Address: 57 Jefferson Ave Short Hills NJ 07078-3234 Office: Milbank Tweed Hadley & McCloy 1 Chase Manhattan Plz New York NY 10005-1401

MORTIMER, RICHARD WALTER, mechanical engineering educator; b. Phila., Dec. 7, 1936; s. Horace and Almira Duffield (Matthews) M.; m. Doris Claire Ridler, June 29, 1957; children: Patrick Lee, David Walter, James Matthew, Daniel Scott. BSME, Drexel U., 1962, MSME, 1964, PhD, 1967. Prof. Drexel U., Phila., 1967—, assoc. dean grad. sch., 1974-76, head dept. mech. engring., 1976-85, assoc. v.p. acad. affairs, 1985-89; mem. exec. com. Engring. Accreditation Com., N.Y.C., 1986-91. Contbr. over 40 articles to profl. jours. Pres. Haverford (Pa.) Twp. Sch. Dist., 1980-83. With U.S. Army, 1958-60. Recipient Achievement award Am. Soc. Nondestructive Testing, 1973, Best Tech. Paper award, 1973; fellow NASA, 1967, 68; grantee numerous orgns. including NASA, USAF, NSF, 1967-87; Fellow Members awd., Am. Soc. for Engineering Education, 1992. Fellow Am. Soc. Engring. Educators; mem. ASME (mem. numerous coms., bds. and chairs 1976-92). Republican. Episcopalian. Achievements include research in fields of structural dynamics and composite materials. Office: Drexel Univ 32D and Chestnut St Philadelphia PA 19104

MORTIMER, RORY DIXON, lawyer; b. Flint, Mich., Jan. 6, 1950; s. Kenneth N. and Phyllis (Rouleau) M.; m. Patricia Ann Amstadt, Sept. 18, 1971; children: Melissa Marie, Ryan Douglas. BA, Mich. State U., 1972, JD, 1978. Bar: S.C. 1978, Mich. 1979, U.S. Ct. Appeals (4th cir.) U.S. Tax Ct., U.S. Supreme Ct. 1979. Trust officer C&S Nat. Bank, Charleston, S.C., 1978-79; pvt. practice law Summerville, S.C., 1979-80; ptnr. Chellis & Mortimer, Summerville, 1980-85, Chellis, Mortimer & Frampton, Summerville, 1985-95; sr. ptnr. Mortimer, Leiendecker & Rose, Summerville, 1995—. Atty., Dorchester County Human Devel. Bd., 1987—. Mem. ATLA, S.C. Bar Assn., S.C. Trial Lawyers Assn., Mich. Bar Assn., Am. Soc. CLUs and ChFC (pres. 1989). Republican. Roman Catholic. Avocations: golf, tennis. Home: 105 Old Postern Rd Summerville SC 29483-3770 Office: Mortimer Leiendecker & Rose 1810 Trolley Rd Summerville SC 29485-8282

MORTIMER, WENDELL REED, JR., superior court judge; b. Alhambra, Calif., Apr. 7, 1937; s. Wendell Reed and Blanche (Wilson) M.; m. Cecilia Vick, Aug. 11, 1962; children: Michelle Dawn, Kimberly Grace. AB, Occidental Coll., 1958; JD, U. So. Calif., L.A., 1965. Bar: Calif. 1966. Trial atty. legal divsn. Legal div. State of Calif., L.A., 1965-73; assoc. Thelen, Marrin, Johnson & Bridges, L.A., 1973-76, ptnr., 1976-93; pvt. practice San Marino, Calif., 1994-95; judge L.A. Superior Ct., 1995—. With U.S. Army, 1960-62. Mem. ABA, Los Angeles County Bar Assn., Pasadena Bar Assn., Calif. Judges Assn., Am. Judicature Soc., Am. Judges Assn., Legion Lex. Home: 1420 San Marino Ave San Marino CA 91108-2042

MORTIMER, WILLIAM JAMES, newspaper publisher; b. Provo, Utah, June 26, 1932; s. William Earl and Margaret (Johnson) M.; m. Paula Ann Deline, Sept. 17, 1956; children: Jeffrey, David, Gregory, Bradley, Judy, William James II, Jennifer. BS, Utah State U, 1954; MS, Columbia U., 1957. Reporter Deseret News, Salt Lake City, 1957-59, pres., pub., 1985—; sales mgr. Deseret News Press, Salt Lake City, 1959-63; gen. mgr. Deseret News Press, 1979-80, Deseret Book Co., Salt Lake City, 1966-79; sr. account exec. Wheelwright Lithographing, Salt Lake City, 1963-66; dir. LDS Ch. Printing Svcs., Salt Lake City, 1980-85; v.p., dir. Newspaper Agy. Corp., Salt Lake City, 1985—; pres. Printing Industries of Utah, 1964-65, Utah Retail Mchts. Assn., Salt Lake City, 1977-79. Author: How Beautiful Upon the Mountains, 1963. Campaign chmn. Salt Lake Area United Way, 1987; hon. col. Utah N.G.; chmn. Utah Partnership Ednl. and Econ. Devel., 1995-97; mem. exec. com. Salt Lake Conv. and Visitors Bur.; chmn. bd. Pioneer State Theatre, 1990-93; bd. dirs. Utah Symphony; chmn. bd. dirs. Prevent Blindness, Utah. 1st lt. U.S. Army, 1954-56, Korea. Named Disting. Citizen of Yr., Salt Lake City, 1995. Mem. Utah-Idaho-Spokane AP Assn. (pres. 1993-94), Utah Press Assn. (pres. 1994-95), Salt Lake Area C. of C. (chmn. bd. 1988-89), Alta Club. Mem. LDS Ch. Avocations: music, reading, family activities. Home: 8763 Kings Hill Dr Salt Lake City UT 84121-6135 Office: Deseret News Pub Co PO Box 1257 Salt Lake City UT 84110-1257

MORTLOCK, ROBERT PAUL, microbiologist, educator; b. Bronxville, N.Y., May 12, 1931; s. Donald Robert and Florance Mary (Bellaby) M.; m. Florita Mary Welling, Sept., 1954; children—Florita M., Jeffrey R., Douglas P. B.S., Rensselaer Poly. Inst., N.Y., 1953; Ph.D., U. Ill., Urbana, 1958. Asst. prof. microbiology U. Mass., Amherst, 1963-68, assoc. prof. microbiology, 1968-73, prof. microbiology, 1973-78; prof. microbiology Cornell U., Ithaca, N.Y., 1978—. Editor: Microorganisms as Model Systems for Studying Evolution, 1984, The Evolution of Metabolic Function, 1992. Served to 1st lt. U.S. Army, 1959-61. Fellow Am. Acad. Microbiology; mem. AAAS, Am. Soc. Microbiology, Northeastern Microbiologists, Physiology, Ecology and Taxonomy (pres. 1984-91). Office: Cornell U Sect Microbiology Wing Hall Ithaca NY 14852

MORTOLA, EDWARD JOSEPH, academic administrator emeritus; b. N.Y.C., Feb. 5, 1917; s. John and Letitia (Pellarano) M.; m. Doris Slater, May 3, 1941; children: Doreen Mortola LeMoult, Elaine Mortola Clark. B.A., Fordham U., 1938, M.A., 1941, Ph.D., 1946, L.H.D. (hon.), 1964; postgrad., Columbia U., 1946; L.H.D. (hon.), Medaille Coll., 1980; LL.D. (hon.), Bryant Coll., 1965, Syracuse U., 1967, N.Y. Law Sch., 1968; Litt.D. (hon.), Manhattan Coll., 1967, Coll. St. Rose, 1971; LL.D. (hon.), Western State U., 1985; L.H.D. (hon.), Pace U., 1987. Grad. fellow, sch. edn. Fordham U., 1938-39, asst. registrar, 1939-41, asst. registrar, city hall div., lectr. grad. faculty, sch. edn., 1946-47; instr. math. Cooper Union and Townsend Harris High Sch., N.Y.C., 1941-42; mem. faculty St. Peter's Coll., Jersey City, part time 1946-47; with Pace U., N.Y.C., 1947—; asst. dean Pace U., 1947-49, dean, 1949-50, provost, 1950-54, v.p., 1954-60, pres., 1960-84, chancellor, 1984-90, chancellor emeritus, 1990—; mem. Community Planning Bd. 1, Borough Manhattan, 1954-66, chmn., 1956-58; mem., chmn. legis. com. Assn. Colls. and Univs. State N.Y., v.p., 1965-66, pres., 1967-68; mem. adv. council on higher edn. State Edn. Dept.; trustee, past pres. Com.

on Ind. Colls. and Univs.; mem. Middle States Assn. Colls. and Schs., N.Y. Gov.'s Commn. on Quality, Cost and Finance of N.Y. State Elementary and Secondary Edn., 1969-71, Westchester Planning Commn., 1966-73, Westchester County Assn., N.Y.C. Council on Econ. Edn., Commn. on Ind. Colls. and Univs. State N.Y., chmn., 1961-63; mem. council Fordham U.; mem. Mayor's Com. on Long-Term Fin. of N.Y.C.; former mem. adv. bd. Elizabeth Seton Coll.; past dir. and sec. Greater N.Y. Council Fgn. Students; chmn. bd. govs. Fordham U. Alumni Fedn., 1958-60; formerly trustee Rosemont Coll., St. Joseph's Sem., Yonkers, N.Y.; co-chmn. N.Y. State Edn. Dept. Task Force on Teaching Profession, 1987-88; chmn. Lincoln Ctr. Inst., 1987; bd. dirs. Lincoln Ctr., 1987—; hon. dir. N.Y.C. Partnership, 1987—. Bd. govs. New Rochelle Hosp.; hon. bd. govs. White Plains Hosp.; Downtown-Lower Manhattan Assn., Econ. Devel. Council; former trustee Instructional TV. Served with USNR, 1942-46; lt. comdr. Res. Decorated cavaliere, commendatore dell'Ordine Al Merito Republic of Italy., Knight of Malta; recipient Ann. Achievement award in edn. Fordham Coll., 1960, William O'Brien award Cardinal Newman Found., 1964, Ednl. and Youth Advancement award Westchester chpt. Am. Com. Italian-Immigration, 1969, James E. Allen Jr. Meml. award Disting. Svc. to Edn. Bd. Regents N.Y. State, 1977, Leadership in Edn. award Assn. Colls. and Univs. State of N.Y., 1986, Outstanding Achievement award 100 Yr. Assn. of N.Y., 1983, Big Bros. of N.Y. Achievement award, 1987, Distinguished Alumni award Fordham U. Sch. Edn. Alumni Assn., 1970, Outstanding Achievement award One Hundred Yr. Assn., 1983, Achievement award in edn. Big Bros. N.Y., 1987, Starr award Good Counsel Acad., 1991; named Man of Yr. B'nai B'rith Youth Services, 1975. Mem. N.Y. Acad. Pub. Edn. (pres. 1962-64, dir.), N.Y. C. of C. (chmn. edn. com. 1966-68, mem. exec. com.), Nat. Office Mgmt. Assn., NEA, N.Y. Adult Edn. Coun., Knights of Malta. Clubs: Metropolitan (N.Y.C.), Univ. (N.Y.C.); Larchmont Yacht Club, Old Port Yacht Club.

MORTON, BRIAN, writer, editor, educator; b. N.Y.C., July 8, 1955; s. Richard Paul and Tasha (Brisman) M. BA, Sarah Lawrence Coll., 1978. Tchr. grad. dept. English NYU, N.Y.C., 1992-94; tchr. 92d St. Y, N.Y.C., 1993—, The New Sch. for Social Rsch., N.Y.C., 1995—; exec. editor Dissent Mag., N.Y.C., 1994—. Author: The Dylanist, 1991; contbr. articles to profl. publs. including Dissent, The Nation, The New Leader, Lingua Franca; book rev. editor Dissent Mag., 1988—. Office: Dissent 521 5th Ave Ste 1700 New York NY 10175

MORTON, CLAUDETTE, education administrator; b. Billings, Mont., Jan. 21, 1940; d. Hugh Wesley and Timey Delacy (Hopper) M.; m. Larry Roy Johnson, July 5, 1959 (div. 1987); 1 child, Eric Roy Johnson; m. George Miller, Sept. 3, 1987. BA in Drama, U. Mont., 1963, MA in Drama, 1964, EdD in Edn., 1990. Cert. tchr., adminstrv., Mont. Tchr. English, supr. Moorhead (Minn.) State U., 1964-65; sub. tchr. Missoula and Glassgow (Mont.) Sch. Dists., 1965-70; English tchr., dir. speech, drama Glasgow H.S., 1970-78; English specialist, liaison to county supr. Office of Public Instrn., Helena, Mont., 1978-86; exec. sec. and state agy. dir. Bd. of Pub. Edn., Helena, 1986-90; dir. Mont. rural edn. ctr. and western Mont. coll. assoc. prof. edn. U. Mont., Dillon, 1990-96; exec. dir. Mont. Small Schs. Alliance, Helena, 1996—; mem. rural edn. adv. com. Northwest Reginal Edn. Lab., Portland, 1991-96, adv. bd. Ctr. for Study of Small and Rural Schs. U. Okla., 1993—; mem. Blue Ribbon Schs. Panel, U.S. Dept. Edn., 1994, 96—. Editor: Visions: Healthy Living for the 21 Century, 1992; contbr. articles to profl. jours. Mem. Ch. Pub. Policy Mont. Arts Coun., 1978-86, chair Mont. Cult. Advocacy, 1982-86; state. pres. AAUW, Mont., 1988-90, theatre content ch. arts assessment planning com. Coun. of Chief State Sch. Officers. Mem. Nat. Assessment Ednl. Progress (arts assessment, oversight com.), Nat. Rural Edn. Assn. (Howard A. Dawson award for svc. 1995), Nat. Coun. of Tchrs. of English, Am. Assn. Colls. of Tchr. Educators, Am. Edn. Rsch. Assn., Mont. Alliance for Arts Edn., Delta Kappa Gamma, Phi Delta Kappa. Democrat. Congregationalist. Avocations: travel, hiking, cross country skiing, politics. the arts. Office: Mont Small Schs Alliance 1 S Montana Ave Helena MT 59601-5178

MORTON, DAVID RAY, sales and marketing executive; b. Rockford, Ill., Dec. 7, 1948; s. Raymond Thomas and Nathalie Ilene (Hendricks) M.; m. Carol Lynn Pott, Apr. 1, 1972; children: Rebecca Lynn, Eric David. BS in Forestry, U. Ill., 1971; MBA, Ohio State U., 1983. Field svc. rep. So. Forest Products Assn., New Orleans, 1972-73; sales rep. chem. divsn. Ga. Pacific Corp., Columbus, Ohio, 1973-76; lumber broker Fireside Forest Industries, Columbus, 1976-77; sr. tech. sales & svc. rep. chem. divsn. Ga. Pacific Corp., Columbus, 1977-84; dir. mktg. Monitronix Corp., Columbus, 1984-85; dir. mktg. & sales Freeman Mfg. & Supply Co., Cleve., 1985-88; nat. sales and mktg. mgr. Hexcel Corp.-Resins Group, L.A., 1988-95; sales mgr. Hapco, Inc., Hanover, Mass., 1995-96, v.p. sales, 1996—; sales mgr. Conap, Olean, N.Y., 1996—. Del.-at-large Rep. Platform Planning Com., Avon Lake, Ohio, 1992. Sgt. maj. U.S. Army N.G., 1971—. Mem. Soc. Mfg. Engrs. (treas. 1982-84), Am. Foundrymen's Soc. (publ. chmn. 1992—), Ohio State Alumni Assn., U. Ill. Alumni Assn., Polyurethane Mfrs. Assn. (del. 1990—), Ohio N.G. Enlisted Assn., Enlisted Assn. N.G. U.S., Phi Kappa Sigma. Avocations: sailing, handball, tennis, woodworking. Home: 296 Chestnut Ct Avon Lake OH 44012-2141

MORTON, DONALD CHARLES, astronomer; b. Kapuskasing, Ont., Can., June 12, 1933; s. Charles Orr and Irene Mary (Wightman) M.; m. Winifred May Austin, Dec. 12, 1970; children: Keith James, Christine Elizabeth. BA, U. Toronto, 1956; PhD, Princeton U., 1959. Astronomer U.S. Naval Rsch. Lab., Washington, 1959-61; from rsch. assoc. to sr. rsch. astronomer with rank of prof. Princeton (N.J.) U., 1961-76; dir. Anglo-Australian Obs., Epping and Coonabarabran, Australia, 1976-86; dir. gen. Herzberg Inst. Atstrophysics, NRC of Can., Ottawa, Ont., 1986—. Contbr. numerous articles to profl. jours. Fellow Australian Acad. Sci.; mem. Internat. Astron. Union, Royal Astron. Soc. (assoc. 1980), Astron. Soc. Australia (pres. 1981-83, hon. mem. 1986), Royal Astron. Soc. Can., Am. Astron. Soc. (councilor 1970-73), Can. Astron. Soc. Australian Inst. Physics (Pawsey Meml. lectr. 1985), Can. Assn. Physicists, U.K. Alpine Club, Am. Alpine Club, Alpine Can. Club. Avocations: mountaineering, rock climbing, ice climbing, marathon running. Office: Herzberg Inst Astrophysics, NRC Can 5071 W Saanich Rd, Victoria, BC Canada V8X 4M6

MORTON, DONALD JOHN, librarian; b. Bklyn., Jan. 11, 1931; s. Ellwood Stokes and Gladys (Hassler) M.; m. Ann Mayo Tilden, Aug. 16, 1958; children—Saundra Kay, Donald John, Mary Ann. BS, U. Del., 1952; MS, La. State U., 1954; PhD, U. Calif. at Berkeley, 1958; MS in Libr. Sci., Simmons Coll., 1969, Dr. Arts in Library Sci, 1976. Asst. prof. botany N.M. State U., Las Cruces, 1957-58; asst. prof. plant pathology N.D. State U., Fargo, 1959-61; plant pathologist Agr. Dept., Tifton, Ga., 1961-65; asso. prof. plant pathology U. Del., Newark, 1965-68; librarian Northeastern U., Boston, 1968-70; head librarian, asst. prof. history of medicine U. Mass. Med. Sch., Worcester, 1970-74; dir. libr., assoc. prof. libr. sci. U. Mass. Med. Sch., 1974-94, libr. cons., 1994—; tchr. med. librarianship Worcester State Coll., 1974-94; libr. cons., 1994—; cons. in field; mem. adv. com. med. librarianship Simmons Coll., 1972-94; mem. task force com. New Eng. Regional Libr. Svc., 1971-94; mem. cooperating staff Worcester Found. Exptl. Biology, 1972-94; chmn. Coun. Developing Med. Librs., 1974; pres. North Atlantic Health Scis. Librs., 1974-75, Worcester Area Coop. Librs., 1974-75. Contbr. articles to profl. jours. Mem. Oliver Wendell Holmes endowment com. Boston Med. Libr., 1973-74, U. Mass. Bicentennial Com., 1973-75. Mem. Am. Assn. Univ. Adminstrs., Simmons Coll. Libr. Sch. Alumni Assn. (pres. 1975-76), Worcester Art Mus., Worcester Hist. Soc., Northboro Hist. Soc., Hampton Hist. Soc., N.H. Hist. Soc., Am. Soc. Info. Sci., ALA, Mass. Libr. Assn., Med. Libr. Assn. (chmn. New Eng. group 1974-75), Mycol. Soc. Am., Spl. Librs. Assn., New Eng. Coll. Librarians, Sigma Xi, Phi Kappa Phi, Phi Sigma, Delta Tau Delta. Home: 314 High St Hampton NH 03842-4004

MORTON, EDWARD JAMES, insurance company executive; b. Ft. Wayne, Ind., Nov. 8, 1926; s. Clifford Leroy and Clara Marie (Merklein) M.; m. Jean Ann McClernon, Apr. 30, 1949; children: Marcia Lynn, Anne; m. Matthild Schneider, Sept. 19, 1986; 1 child, Katherine. BA, Yale U., 1949. With John Hancock Mut. Life Ins. Co., Boston, 1949—, v.p., then sr. v.p., 1967-74, exec. v.p., 1974-82, pres., chief operating officer, 1982-86, chmn., chief exec. officer, 1987-92, also bd. dirs.; bd. dirs. John Hancock Mutual Life Ins. Co. Trustee Gettysburg Coll.; bd. dirs. Eisenhower World Affairs Inst., 1993;mem. vis. com. dept. Ancient Egyptian, Nubian and Near Eastern Art, Mus. Fine Arts, Boston; hon. life overseer Children's Hosp.; chmn. Boston Geog. Savs. Bond Campaign, 1991. Fellow Soc. Actuaries; mem. Nat. Assn. Security Dealers (prin.), Actuaries Club Boston, Comml. Club of Boston, Algonquin Club of Boston, Phi Beta Kappa. Office: John Hancock Mut Life Ins Co PO Box 111 Boston MA 02117-0111

MORTON, ERIC, liberal arts educator; b. Detroit, Feb. 24, 1934; s. Lee Jack and Theresa Magdalen (Leonard) M.; children: Tracey Lynn, Theresa Dallas. AA, Merritt Coll., 1992; BA, U. Calif., Berkeley, 1992; M of Profl. Studies, Cornell U., 1994; grad., SUNY, Binghamton, 1994—. Internat. organizer Am. Fedn. of State, County, Mcpl. Employees, Calif., 1970-73; field rep. State Senator Nicholas Petris, Oakland, Calif., 1973-75; mktg. adminstr. Safegate Aviation Systems, Oakland, 1975-80; asst. to dir. recreational sports U. Calif., 1980-92; grad. tchg. asst. Africana Studies and Rsch. Ctr., Cornell U., 1992-94; rschr., tchr. SUNY, Binghamton, 1994—; mem., multicultural core group Cornell U., 1992-94. Compiler (book) Mississippi Black Paper, 1965; contbr. articles to profl. jours. Active polit. campaigns; project mgr. Ctr. for Ind. Living, Berkeley, 1975-77. With U.S. Army, 1951-54. Recipient Award Met. Trans. Commn., 1973. Avocations: photography, reading. Home: 2019 Stuart St Berkeley CA 94703-2237

MORTON, FREDERIC, author; b. Vienna, Austria, Oct. 5, 1924; s. Frank and Rose (Ungvary) M.; m. Marcia Colman, Mar. 28, 1957; 1 dau., Rebecca. B.S., Coll. City N.Y., 1947; M.A., New Sch. Social Research, 1949. Author: The Hound, 1947, The Darkness Below, 1949, Asphalt and Desire, 1952, The Witching Ship, 1960, The Schatten Affair, 1965, Snow Gods, 1969, An Unknown Woman, 1976, The Forever Street, 1984, Crosstown Sabbath, 1987, (biography) The Rothschilds, 1962 (nominated for Nat. Book award), A Nervous Splendor-Vienna 1888/9, 1979 (nominated for Nat. Book award), Thunder at Twilight-Vienna 1913/14, 1989; books translated into 14 langs.; actor (documentary made in English and German) Crosstown Sabbath, 1995 (broadcast in Austria, Germany, Switzerland, U.S.); contbr. to publs. including Martha Foley's Best Am. Short Stories and other anthologies, N.Y. Times, Harper's mag., Atlantic mag., Nation, Playboy, Esquire, N.Y. Mag., Hudson Rev., Wall Street Jour., Vanity Fair, also others; columnist Village Voice, Conde-Nast Traveler, Wall Street Jour. Recipient Author of Year award Nat. Anti-Defamation League, B'nai B'rith; Hon. Professorship award Republic of Austria, 1980, Tom Osborne Disting. lectureship U. Nebr., 1989; Dodd, Mead Intercollegiate Lit. fellow, 1947; Yaddo residence fellow, 1948, 50; Breadloaf Writers' Conf. fellow, 1947; Columbia U. fellow, 1953; recipient Golden Merit award City of Vienna, 1986. Mem. Author's Guild (exec. council), P.E.N. Home: 110 Riverside Dr New York NY 10024-3715 Office: The Lantz Office 888 7th Ave New York NY 10106 *As a writer I'm trying to tell the truth interestingly.*

MORTON, HARRISON LEON, forestry educator; b. St. Paul, Oct. 19, 1938; m. 1962; 5 children. BS, U. Minn., 1961, MS, 1964, PhD in Plant Pathology, 1967. Chmn. fisheries, forestry and wildlife Sch. Natural Resources U. Mich., Ann Arbor, 1972-75, asst. prof., assoc. prof. pathology, forestry and wildlife, 1972-78, prof., 1978—; dir. Nichol's Arboretum, 1987—, assoc. dean, 1990—. Mem. Internat. Soc. Arboriculture, Am. Assn. Bot. Gardens and Arboreat, Forestry and Park Assn. Office: U Mich Sch Natural Resources Dana Bldg Ann Arbor MI 48109-1115

MORTON, HERBERT CHARLES, editor, economist; b. Mpls., July 19, 1921. B.A., U. Minn., 1942, M.A., 1950, Ph.D., 1964. Info. specialist War Assets Adminstrn., 1946-47; staff writer, telegraph news editor St. Paul Pioneer Press & Dispatch, 1947-53; rsch. editor, asst. prof. Amos Tuck Sch., Dartmouth Coll., 1953-56; dir. publs. Brookings Instn., Washington, 1956-68; dir. Office Publs. U.S. Bur. Labor Stats., 1968-70, assoc. commr., 1971-75; dir. pub. affairs Resources for Future, Washington, 1975-80; sr. fellow Resources for Future, 1981-82; cons. Russell Sage Found., 1980-84; dir. Office Scholarly Communication, Am. Coun. Learned Socs., 1984-87; cons. Ford Found., 1964-65, Internat. Inst. Applied Systems Analysis, 1978, Nat. Commn. on Unemployment Stats., 1978, Nat. Enquiry into Scholarly Communication, 1978-79, vis. lectr. Amos Tuck Sch., 1966, Am. U., 1970. Author: Public Contracts and Private Wages, 1965, The Story of Webster's Third, 1994; co-author: An Introduction to Economic Reasoning, 1956, 5th edit., 1979, Scholarly Communication: The Report of the National Enquiry, 1979, Energy Today and Tomorrow, 1983, The ACLS Survey of Scholars, 1989; editor: Brookings Papers on Public Policy, 1965; co-editor: The American Business Corporation, 1972, Writings on Scholarly Communication, 1988; cons. editor Scholarly Publishing, 1984-92; mem. editl. bd. Book Research Quarterly, 1985-94; contbr. articles to profl. jours. Trustee Joint Coun. Econ. Edn., 1960-68; bd. dirs. Am. U. Press Svcs. Inc., 1966-68. Served with Signal Corps AUS, 1942-46. NEH fellow, 1989. Mem. Soc. Scholarly Pub. (bd. dirs. 1988-92), Dictionary Soc. N.Am., Am. Dialect Soc. Home: 7106 Laverock Ln Bethesda MD 20817-4734

MORTON, JAMES CARNES, JR., public relations executive; b. Duncan, Okla., May 8, 1945; s. James Carnes and Syble Lyda (Looney) M.; m. Susan Phillips, May 25, 1968; children: James III, Terrissa Anne, Scott Thomas. BA, Westminster Coll., 1967; JD, U. Mo., 1972. Bar: Mo. 1972, S.C., 1991. Tax acct. Arthur Andersen Co., St. Louis, 1972-74; tax atty. Gen. Dynamics Corp., St. Louis, 1974-76; asst. gen. counsel Michelin Tire Corp., Greenville, S.C., 1976-86; gen. counsel Michelin Tire Corp. and Michelin Tires (Can.) Ltd., Greenville, S.C., 1990-92; dir. pub. rels. and govt. affairs Michelin Tire Corp., Greenville, S.C., 1986-92; exec. dir. external rels. Michelin N.Am., Greenville, S.C., 1992-96; v.p. pub. rels. and govt. rels. Michelin N.Am., Inc., 1996—. Bd. dirs. Ednl. Resources Found., 1992—, Greenville Symphony Orch., 1986-89, United Way Greenville, 1987-88, Greenville YMCA, 1988-89, S.C. Ednl. Resources Found., 1992—; mem. bd. trustees S.C. Gov.'s Sch. for Sci. and Math., 1996—; mem. bd. visitors and fin. com. Christ Ch. Episcopal Sch., Greenville, 1991—. Capt. U.S. Army, 1967-70, Vietnam. Mem. ABA, Rubber Mfrs. Assn. (bd. dirs. 1995—, govt. affairs com., tire mgmt. com.), Mo. Bar Assn. (nonresident), S.C. C. of C. (bd. dirs., pres. 1993-94, chmn. 1994-95, exec. com. 1981-84, 86-95, Svc. Recognition award 1982), Greater Greenville C. of C. (chmn. govt. affairs com. 1990, chmn. legis. affairs com. 1996—, bd. dirs. 1990-93), Greenville Country Club, Commerce Club, Faculty House Club (U.S.C.). Presbyterian. Avocation: golf. Office: Michelin NAm PO Box 19001 Greenville SC 29602-9001

MORTON, JAMES DAVIS, lawyer; b. Pitts., Jan. 30, 1928; s. Roy S. and Magdeline M. (Meeder) M.; m. Ann Medved, Sept. 7, 1957; children: Timothy, Ann, Gary. BS in Bus. Administrn., U. Pitts., 1951, Dr. of Laws, 1954. Bar: Pa. 1955, Fla. 1979. Assoc. Brown, Critchlow, Flick, Peckham & Miller, Pitts., 1954-55; shareholder Buchanan Ingersoll, P.C. (and predecessor firms), Pitts., 1955—; dir. Indsl. Sci. Corp., Pitts. Dir. Civic Light Opera, Pitts., 1985—; del. Pa. Constl. Conv., Harrisburg, 1967-68. Fellow Am. Coll. Trial Lawyers; mem. Acad. Trial Lawyers Allegheny County (past pres.), U.S. Dist. Ct. West. Dist. Pa. (com. mem. civil justice adv. group), Edgewood Country Club (past pres.). Republican. Episcopalian. Office: Buchanan Ingersoll PC 1 Oxford Centre 301 Grant St Ste 20 Pittsburgh PA 15219-1408

MORTON, JAMES IRWIN, hospital administrator; b. Chulumani, Sud Yungas, Bolivia, Feb. 28, 1935; came to U.S., 1952; s. Harrison Cecil and Flossie Mae (Irwin); m. Beverly Jean Nash, June 9, 1957; c1 child, Linda Kathleen. BA, Andrews U., 1957; MHA, U. Mich., 1959. Commd. 2nd lt. USAF, 1959, advanced through grades to col., 1988.; adminstr. Whitfield (Miss.) Med. Surg. Hosp., 1988—; pres. coun. Jackson-Vicksburg Hosp., 1992-93; cons. to surgeon gen. USAF, Washington, 1980-88. Charter mem. The Miss. Chorus, 1989—, bd. dirs., treas., 1990-93. Decorated Legion of Merit. Fellow Am. Coll. Healthcare Execs. (pres. Miss. affiliates 1991-92, Miss. Regent 1994-99). Avocations: singing, computers, photography, reading. Office: Whitfield Med Surg Hosp Whitfield MS 39193

MORTON, JAMES PARKS, priest; b. Houston, Jan. 7, 1930; s. Vance Mulock and Virginia (Parks) M.; m. Pamela Taylor, Dec. 30, 1954; children: Pamela Mary Morton Burton, Hilary Morton Shontz, Sophia, Mary Anastasia. AB magna cumlaude, Harvard Coll., 1951; MA, Trinity Coll., Cambridge, Eng., 1953; STB, STM, Gen. Theol. Sem., 1954, DD (hon.), 1996; DD (hon.), New Sem., 1992. Ordained to ministry Episcopal Church. Assoc. priest-in-charge team ministry Grace Ch., Jersey City, 1954-62; coord. joint urban program Exec. Coun. Episcopal Ch., N.Y.C., 1962-64; dir. Urban Tng. Ctr., Chgo., 1964-72; dean Cathedral of St. John the Divine, N.Y.C., 1972-96; pres. Interfaith Ctr. of N.Y., N.Y.C., 1997—; co-chair Global Forum of Spiritual and Parliamentary Leaders, 1985-93; canon St. George's Cathedral, Jerusalem, 1997—; co-chair exec. com. Joint Appeal by Religion and Sci. for Environ., 1989—; co-chair Parliamentary Earth Summit, Rio de Janeiro, 1992; chaplain The Big Apple Circus, 1995—; co-chair UN Conf. on World Settlement, 1996. Contbr. articles to profl. publs., foreword Internatonal Competition for the Cathedral of St. John the Divine, 1981. Chmn. Lindsfarne Assn., 1994—, Homes for the Homeless, N.Y.C., 1985—; pres. Temple of Understanding, 1985—; bd. dirs. Ann Frank Ctr. U.S.A., Aubrey Cartwright Found., N.Y., Coun. for a Parliament of the World's Religions, Chgo., Earth Charter Project, Ecumenical Trust, Fountain for Youth, Freedom Inst., Global Green Coun. Advisors, Greyston Family Inn, Zenn Cmty. of N.Y., Horizon Comms., West Cornwall, Conn., N.Y. Sch. of Circus Arts, N.Y. Therapeutic Cmtys. Ocean Arks Internat., Inc., Oomoto Sch. Traditional Japanese Arts, Kameoka, Japan, Promises, Rainforest Alliance, N.Y., Rocky Mountain Inst., Urasenke Chanoyu Ctr., N.Y., U.S. Interreligious Com. for Peace in Mid. East; mem. N.Am. adv. bd. UN Environ. Programme; mem. Urban Homesteading Assistance Bd., N.Y. Fiske fellow, 1951-53; recipient John Phillips award Phillips Exeter Acad., 1982, award of merit AIA, 1995, Inst. of Honor award AIA, 1986, Anderson medal Anderson Soc. Am., 1996, Spirit of the Cathedral award Cathedral of St. John the Divine, 1996, Audubon medal, 1996; named to 100 Young U.S. Leaders, Time Mag., 1975, 50 Young World Leaders, Time Mag., 1975. Mem. Phi Beta Kappa. Office: Interfaith Ctr N.Y. 570 Lexington Ave New York NY 10022-6837

MORTON, JEFFREY BRUCE, aerospace engineering educator; b. Chgo., Apr. 25, 1941; s. Max E. and Tillie (Forman) M.; m. Judy Gail Moss, June 14, 1964; children: Jonathan, Amy, Michael. BS, Mass. Inst. Tech., 1963; PhD, Johns Hopkins U., 1967. Sr. scientist U. Va., Charlottesville, 1967-68, asst. prof., 1968-72, assoc. prof., 1972-80, prof., 1980—; lectr. U. Va., 1967-68; pres. M.J. Systems Inc., Charlottesville, 1976-96, chmn. bd., 1996—. Contbr. articles to profl. jours. Assoc. Fellow AIAA; mem. Am. Soc. Engring. Edn. (southeast sect. rsch. award 1981), Am. Physical Soc., Sigma Xi. Office: U Va Dept Mech Aerospace Engring Charlottesville VA 22901

MORTON, JEROME HOLDREN, school psychologist; b. Duluth, Minn., July 30, 1942; s. Jerome Raefield and Svea (Holdren) M.; m. Anna Mary Moore, June 9, 1964; children: Scot, Jeanette. BA, Centre Coll., 1964; MS, Miami U., Oxford, Ohio, 1966; PhD, U. Tenn., 1973. Psychologist Pinellas County Sch. System, Clearwater, Fla., 1969-71; dir. psychol. and spl. edn. svcs. Little Tenn. Valley Ednl. Coop., Lenoir City, Tenn., 1973-76, exec. dir., 1977—; pres. and bd. dirs. Psychol. and Ednl. Cons., P.C., Knoxville, Tenn., 1985—; dir. Knoxville Alternative Ct. for Learning, 1985-91; rsch. assoc. spl. svcs. dept. Coll. Edn. U. Tenn., Knoxville, 1991-93; due process hearing officer State Tenn. Dept. Edn., Nashville, 1974-85; hon. asst. prof. psychology dept. U. Tenn., Knoxville, 1978—; mem. bd. advisors Big South Fork Regional Assn., Outdoor Adventure and Rsch. Ctr., 1991-93; bd. dirs. Mental Health Assn. Knox County, 1990-92, v.p. pub. policy, 1991-92; bd. dirs. East Tenn. Spl. Tech. Access Ctr, 1989-96, chmn. bd. dirs., 1993-95. Co-author: Students at Risk And Intervention Strategies, 1989; contbr. author Dropouts: Who Drops Out and Why-And The Recommended Action, 1990; contbr. articles to profl. jours. Co-chmn. East Tenn. Coalition for Children, 1983-84, chmn., 1984-85. Served with U.S. Army, 1966-69. Recipient Best Principal/Best School award Knoxville C. of C., 1989, Above and Beyond award E. Tenn. Found., 1995. Mem. APA, Tenn. Assn. Psychology in Schs. (pres. 1976-77), Tenn. Psychol. Assn. (v.p. 1976-77), Nat. Assn. Sch. Psychology, Internat. Speakers Network, Inc. Office: 1432 E Lee Hwy Loudon TN 37774-6440

MORTON, JOHN H., surgeon, educator; b. New Haven, Jan. 15, 1923; s. John J. and Nancy Barnard M.; m. Ruth Mitchell Irland, Oct. 15, 1949; children: John I., Nancy L., Peter S., Bruce J. BA, Amherst Coll., 1945; MD, Yale U., 1946. Diplomate Am. Bd. Surgery. Instr. surgery Sch. Medicine U. Rochester, N.Y., 1953-57, asst. prof. surgery, 1957-62, assoc. prof. surgery, 1962-67, prof., 1967—; pres. N.Y. State Bd. Med. Examiners, 1970-71, 72-73, bd. dirs., 1967-77; pres. Fedn. State Med. Bds. U.S., Ft. Worth, 1976-77, bd. dirs., 1971-78; vice chmn. Nat. Bd. Med. Examiners, Phila., 1975-79, mem. exec. com., 1974-83. Contbr. articles to profl. jours. Bd. dirs. Neighborhood Health Ctrs. Monroe County, Rochester, N.Y., 1969-73, Med. Scholarship Fund Med. Soc. County Monroe, 1969—; pres. Monroe Plan for Med. Care, Rochester, 1971-73; elder Third Presbyn. Ch., Rochester, 1958-61, 67-69, 80-83. Lt. (j.g.) USN, 1947-49. Recipient Edward Mott Moore award Med. Soc. County Monroe, 1975, Merit award Rochester Acad. Medicine, 1977, Disting. Svc. award Nat. Bd. Med. Examiners, 1983, Disting. Svc. award Fed. State Med. Bds. U.S., 1989, Henry I. Fineberg award Med. Soc. State N.Y., 1990. Mem. Am. Coll. Surgeons (gov. 1984-90), Am. Surg. Assn., Ctrl. Surg. Assn. Avocations: hiking, birdwatching, travelling. Home: 179 Maybrooke Rd Rochester NY 14618-1719 Office: U Rochester Sch Medicine 601 Elmwood Ave Rochester NY 14642-0001

MORTON, LAUREL ANNE, elementary education educator; b. Cin., July 27, 1954; d. James William and Rosemary (Danner) M. BA in Social Sci., Calif. State U.-Stanislaus, Turlock, 1978; teaching credential, Calif. State Polytech U., Pomona, 1986; MA in Edn., Calif. State Poly. U., Pomona, 1992. Cert. tchr., Calif., Colo. Sr. loan clk. Shearson Am. Express Mortgage Corp., Newport Beach, Calif., 1978-82; adminstrv. asst. Investco Corp., Santa Barbara, Calif., 1982-83; supr. loan servicing dept. County Savs. Bank, Santa Barbara, 1983-84; comm. asst. Fuller Theol. Sem., Pasadena, Calif., 1984-85; elem. tchr. Howard Sch., Ontario, Calif., 1986-91; tchr. Bon View Elem. Sch., Ontario, 1992—, 4th grade team leader, 1993-94, track leader, 1995-96. Tchr. sponsor Performing Arts Club, Bon View Elem. Sch., 1996-97. Mem. Nat. Honor Soc., Phi Kappa Phi, Zeta Tau Alpha. Avocations: tennis, theater, dancing, travel, museums or venues of educational interest. Home: 1919 Stonehouse Rd Sierra Madre CA 91024-1409 Office: Bon View Elem Sch 2121 S Bon View Ave Ontario CA 91761-5530

MORTON, LINDA, mayor; b. Dec. 7, 1944; married; 2 children. BA with honors, U. Nebr., 1966. Lic. real estate broker. Tchr. Sunnyvale (Calif.) Elem. Sch., 1967-69, Jefferson County (Colo.) Sch. Dist., 1966-67, 69-70; real estate agt. Crown Realty, Lakewood, Colo., 1979-82, Van Schaack & Co., Lakewood, 1982-83, Re-Max Profls., Lakewood, 1983-91. Mem. city coun. City of Lakewood, 1981-91, mayor, 1991—; chair Denver Metro Mayors Caucus; appts. by Gov. to Blue Ribbon Panel on State Transp. Needs, 1995; represented Lakewood on Bd. Denver Regional Coun. of Govts., from 1981, chair, 1986-87; chair Jefferson City C. of C., 1989-90; apptd. by Gov. Colo. to Met. Air Quality Coun., 1985; bd. dirs. Nat. Assn. Regional Coun. Govts., 1986-90, CML, 1993—. Office: City of Lakewood 445 S Allison Pky Lakewood CO 80226-3106*

MORTON, MARILYN MILLER, genealogy and history educator, lecturer, researcher, travel executive, director; b. Water Valley, Miss., Dec. 2, 1929; d. Julius Brunner and Irma Faye (Magee) Miller; m. Perry Wilkes Morton Jr., July 2, 1958; children: Dent Miller Morton, Nancy Marilyn Morton Driggers, E. Perian Morton Dyar. BA in English, Miss. U. for Women, 1952; MS in History, Miss. State U., 1955. Cert. secondary tchr. Tchr. English, speech and history Starkville (Miss.) H.S., 1952-58; part-time instr. Miss. State U., 1953-55; mem. spl. collection staff Samford U. Libr., Birmingham, Ala., 1984-92; lectr. genealogy and history, instr. Inst. Genealogy & Hist. Rsch., Samford U., Birmingham, 1985-93, assoc. dir., 1985-88, exec. dir., 1988-93; founding dir. SU British and Irish Inst. Genealogy & Hist. Rsch. Samford U., Birmingham and British Isles, 1986-93; owner, dir. Marilyn Miller Morton Brit-Ire-U.S. Genealogy, Birmingham, also British Isles, 1994—; instr. genealogy classes Samford U. Metro Coll., 1989-94; lectr. nat. conf. Fedn. of Geneal. Socs. Contbr. articles and book revs. to profl. jours. Active Birmingham chpt. Salvation Army Aux., 1982—. Inducted into Miss. U. for Women Hall of Fame, 1952. Fellow Irish Geneal. Rsch. Soc. London; mem. Internat. Soc. Brit. Genealogy and Family History, Nat. Geneal. Soc. (mem. nat. program com. 1988—, lectr. nat. mtgs.), Assn. Profl. Genealogists, Soc. Genealogists London, Antiquarian Soc. Birmingham (sec., 2d v.p. 1982-84), DAR (regent Cheaha chpt. 1977-78), Daus. Am. Colonists (regent Edward Waters chpt. 1978-79), Nat. League of Am. Penwomen, Phi Kappa Phi (charter mem. Samford U. chpt. 1972). Avocations: reading, travel, bridge, public speaking, chess. Home and Office: 3508 Clayton Pl Birmingham AL 35216-3810

MORTON, MICHAEL RAY, retail company consultant; b. Memphis, Nov. 10, 1952; s. James Ray and Margaret Regina (Stevens) M.; m. Mary Elizabeth Harkness; children: Mary Harkness, Margaret Jeanne, Molly Ray. BBA, U. Miss., 1973; MBA, U. Denver, 1975. Cost acct. Dover Corp., Memphis, 1975-76; internal auditor W.R. Grace and Co., Memphis, 1976-78; sr. fin. analyst W.R. Grace and Co., N.Y.C., 1979-80; v.p. Handy Dan div. W.R. Grace and Co., San Antonio, 1981-82; chief fin. officer, sec., treas. Home Ctrs. Am., San Antonio, 1983; sr. v.p. Builders Square K-Mart Corp., San Antonio, 1984-89; pres. Orion Strategic Solutions, Inc., 1989-95; mng. ptnr. Critical Path Strategies, Boerne, Tex., 1996—; bd. dirs. Builders Design Inc., Dania, Fla., 1989-91, treas., 1985-87, Materials Evolution Devel. USA; bd. dirs., v.p. Tex. Ind. Newspapers, Inc., San Antonio; mem. exec. com. Home Ctr. Industry Conf. Mem. San Antonio C. of C. (amb. 1981), Home Ctr. Leadership Coun. Republican. Roman Catholic. Avocations: running, golf, reading. Home: 8060 Pimlico Ln Boerne TX 78006-4705

MORTON, ROBERT ALLEN, small business owner; b. Boston, Oct. 18, 1954; s. Ralph A. and A. Louise (Dibblee) M.; m. Cynthia Walpole, Apr. 19, 1980; children: Angela Walpole, Jared Walpole. Grad. high sch., Walpole, 1972. Machinist Foxboro (Mass.) Co., 1972-73, Bird Machine Co., South Walpole, 1973-75; v.p., treas. A&W Instruments, Inc., Walpole, 1976-88, pres., 1988—. Member Nat. Arbor Day Found., 1985—, Mass. Audubon Soc., 1988—, Nat. Parks & Conservation Assn., 1990—; life mem. Rep. Nat. Com., 1991—, Eisenhower Commn., 1995. Mem. Nat. Tooling and Machining Assn., Nat. Fedn. of Ind. Bus. (guardian mem. 1981—), U.S. C. of C., Neponset Valley C. of C. Roman Catholic. Avocations: golf, skiing, sports, boating, gardening. Office: A&W Instruments Inc 405 Street St Walpole MA 02081

MORTON, STEPHEN DANA, chemist; b. Madison, Wis., Sept. 7, 1932; s. Walter Albert and Rosalie (Amlie) M.; BS, U. Wis., 1954, PhD, 1962. Asst. prof. chemistry Otterbein Coll., Westerville, Ohio, 1962-66; postdoctoral fellow water chemistry, pollution control U. Wis., Madison, 1966-67; water pollution research chemist WARF Inst., Madison, 1967-73; head environ. quality dept., 1973-76; mgr. quality assurance Raltech Sci. Services, 1977-82; pres. SDM Cons., 1982—. Served to 1st lt. Chem. Corps, AUS, 1954-56. Mem. AAAS, Am. Chem. Soc. Author: Water Pollution—Causes and Cures, 1976. Home: 1126 Sherman Ave Madison WI 53703-1620

MORTON, WILLIAM GILBERT, JR., stock exchange executive; b. Syracuse, N.Y., Mar. 13, 1937; s. William Gilbert and Barbara (Link) M.; m. Margaret Halleron, Nov. 26, 1982; children: Andrew Baker, William Gilbert III, Sarah Ellsworth, Kate Spencer. BA, Dartmouth Coll., 1959; MBA, NYU, 1965. Asst. v.p. Discount Corp. N.Y., 1960-67; co-mgr. trading, sr. v.p., dir. Mitchell Hutchins Inc., 1967-79; mng. stock exch. floors, sr. v.p., dir. Dean Witter Reynolds Inc., 1979-85; chmn., chief exec. officer Boston Stock Exch. Inc., 1985—; chmn. allocation com. N.Y. Stock Exch., floor ofcl., 1976-81, various working coms., 1970-85; bd. dirs. Tandy Corp., Ft. Worth, Investment Funds, Morgan Stanley Asset Mgmt. Inc., N.Y. Bd. dirs. Vt. Acad., Saxton's River, Bostonian Soc., Nat. Football Found. and Coll. Hall of Fame, N.Y.; trustee search com. Dartmouth Alumni Coun., 1988-91. With USMC, 1959-65. Mem. Boston Econ. Club, Mass. Bus. Roundtable, Algonquin Club (Boston), Racquet and Tennis Club N.Y.C., Stratton Mt. Country Club (Vt.), Colo. Arlberg Club (Winter Park), Brae Burn Country Club (Newton), Ekwanok Country Club (Vt.), Royal Poinciana Club (Fla.), Theta Delta Chi. Republican. Presbyterian. Office: Boston Stock Exch 1 Boston Pl Boston MA 02108

MORTVEDT, JOHN JACOB, soil scientist; b. Dell Rapids, S.D., Jan. 25, 1932; s. Ernest R. and Clara (Halvorson) M.; m. Marlene L. Fodness, Jan. 23, 1955; children: Sheryl Mortvedt Jarratt, Lori Mortvedt Klopf, Julie Mortvedt Stride. BS, S.D. State U., 1953, MS, 1959; PhD, U. Wis., 1962. Soil chemist TVA, Muscle Shoals, Ala., 1962-87, sr. scientist, 1987-92, regional mgr. field programs dept., 1992-93; ext. soils specialist Colo. State U., Ft. Collins, 1994-95, ext. environ. and pesticide edn. specialist, 1996. Editor: Micronutrients in Agriculture, 1972, 2d edit., 1991; contbr. articles to profl. jours. 1st lt. U.S. Army, 1953-57. Fellow AAAS, Soil Sci. Soc. Am. (pres. 1988-89, editor-in-chief 1982-87, Profl. Svc. award 1991), Am. Soc. Agronomy (exec. com. 1987-90); mem. Internat. Soil Sci. Soc., Colombian Soil Sci. Soc. (hon.), Exch. Club (pres. Florence, Ala. chpt. 1987-88), Toastmasters (pres. Florence chpt. 1964-65), Phi Kappa Phi. Avocations: photography, golf. Office: Colo State U Dept Soil and Crop Scis Fort Collins CO 80523

MOSAVI, REZA KHONSARI, laser physicist; b. Tehran, Iran, Sept. 23, 1944; came to U.S., 1964; s. Fazlolah Khonsari and Ghodsi (Khonsari) M.; m. Margaret Carol Booze, July 13, 1968; children: Leila, Sara. BS in Physics, Miami U., Oxford, Ohio, 1968; MS in Physics, U. Mass., 1970; PhD in Nuclear Engring., U. Cin., 1974. Rsch. scientist Battelle Columbus (Ohio) Labs., 1973-75; mgr. laser tech. sect. Atomic Energy Orgn. Iran, Tehran, 1975-84; cons., Cin., 1984-85; mgr. laser ops. Chromalloy Rsch. & Tech., Orangeburg, N.Y., 1985-94; cons. in laser material processing Howmet Advanced Refurbishment and Coatings, North Haven, Conn., 1994-96; staff engr. Ethicon, Inc., Cornelia, Ga., 1996—; mem. nat. rev. and selection com. for allocation rsch. funds in engring. Iranian Ministry Sci. and Higher Edn., Tehran, 1983-84. Contbr. articles to profl. jours.; patentee in field. 1st lt. Iranian Army, 1975-77. Mem. Soc. Mfg. Engrs., Optical Soc. Am., Laser Inst. Am. Moslem. Avocations: reading, travel. Home: 478 Chandler Heights Dr Alto GA 30510

MOSBACHER, MARTIN BRUCE, public relations executive; b. N.Y.C., Nov. 4, 1951; s. Walter and Grete (Wolffs) M.; m. Andrea Dow, Jan. 25, 1981; children: Sarah Mariel, Rachel Helene. BA in Polit. Sci., CCNY, 1972, MS in Urban Planning, 1975. Spl. asst. to speaker N.Y. State Assembly, Albany, 1976-78; mgr. pub. rels. Sea-Land Corp., Menlo Park, N.J., 1979-83; dir. pub. rels. Commodity Exch., Inc., N.Y.C., 1983-86; prin. NYCOM Assocs., N.Y.C., 1986-88; chmn. Trimedia Inc., N.Y.C., 1988—. Del. Dem. Nat. Conv., Miami, Fla., 1972. Mem. Futures Industry Assn., Pub. Rels. Soc. Am. Office: Trimedia Inc 425 Madison Ave Fl 600 New York NY 10017-1110

MOSCA, CHRISTOPHER PATRICK, principal; b. Newton, Mass., July 2, 1957; s. Antonio and Nicoletta (Errico) M.; m. Gina Montini Mosca, July 20, 1991. BS, Trinity Coll., 1979; MEd, Plymouth State Coll., 1989; Cert. advanced grad. study, Castleton State Coll., 1993. Cert. tchr. and adminstr., Vt., N.H., Conn. Tchr., tutor Eagle Hill Sch., Hardwick, Mass., 1979-82; tchr., athletic coach Lalumiere Sch., LaPorte, Ind., 1982-85, Windsor (Vt.) High Sch., 1985-89; assoc. prin. Rutland (Vt.) High Sch., 1989-93; prin. Springfield (Vt.) High Sch., 1993-96, Goffstown (N.H.) Area H.S. Mem. Springfield Workforce Investment Bd. Mem. ASCD, NASSP, Phi Delta Kappa. Avocations: white water rafting, nordic and alpine skiing, travel, outdoor cooking.

MOSCATO, ANTHONY CHARLES, federal official; b. N.Y.C., Sept. 4, 1945; s. Charles Joseph and Anne (Antreassian) M.; m. Deborah Louise (Stackawitz), Feb. 10, 1973; children: Charles Joseph, Emily Clair. BA, Columbia U., 1967; JD, George Washington U., 1970. Trial atty. tax div. U.S. Dept. Justice, Washington, 1976-77, spl. asst. to asst. atty. gen. justice mgmt. div., 1977-79, dir. property mgmt. and procurement staff justice mgmt. div., 1979-81, dir. evaluation staff justice mgmt.div., 1981-84, dir. fin. staff justice mgmt. div., 1984, counselor to asst. atty. gen. justice mgmt. div., 1984-87, dep. asst. atty gen., adminstrn. justice mgmt. div., 1987-89, acting insp. gen. Office of Insp. Gen., 1989-90, dep. asst. atty. gen., adminstrn., justice mgmt. div., 1990-92, dir. exec. office U.S. attys., 1992-94; dir. exec. office Immigration Rev., 1994—. Recipient Atty. Gen.'s award for Disting. Svc., 1988, Atty. Gen's. Medallion, 1990, Presdl. Meritorious Exec. Rank award, 1991, Edmund Randolph award, 1993. Office: Exec Office Immigration Review 5107 Leesburg Pike Ste 2400 Falls Church VA 22041-3234*

MOSCHELLA, SAMUEL L., dermatology educator; b. East Boston, Mass., Apr. 22, 1921. BS, Tufts U., 1943, MD cum laude, 1946. Diplomate Am. Bd. Dermatology. Intern in medicine Boston City Hosp., 1946-47; resident in dermatology U.S. Naval Hosp., Phila., 1948, St. Albans, 1951; postgrad. in skin and cancer Bellevue Hosp., N.Y.C., 1952-53; chief dermatology U.S. Naval Hosp., Phila., 1953-54, chief dermatology, asst. chief medicine, Guantanamo Bay, Cuba, 1948-51, chief dermatology, Chelsea, Mass., 1956-62, chmn. dept. dermatology, Phila., 1962-67; chmn. dept. dermatology Lahey Clinic Med. Ctr., Burlington, Mass., 1969-82; clin. prof. dermatology Harvard U. Med. Sch., Boston, 1980-91, prof. emeritus, 1991—; cons. U.S. Pub. Health Leprasorium, Carville, La., 1968—, U.S. Naval Hosp., Phila., 1967-72, Bethesda, Md., 1976—; guest lectr. U. Pa. Grad. Sch., 1962-67, Harvard Sch. Tropical Medicine, 1975—. Author/editor: (with otherw) Dermatology, 3d edit., 1992; contbr. articles to profl. jours.; also papers, book chpts. Fellow ACP; mem. AMA, Am. Acad. Dermatology, Am. Dermatol. Assn., Am. Soc. Dermapathology, Internat. Leprosy Assn., Internat. Soc. Dermatology, New Eng. Dermatologic Soc., Mass. Acad. Dermatology, Boston Dermatology Soc., Mass. Med. Soc., soc. Investigative Dermatology. Home: 887 Commonwealth Ave Newton MA 02159-1036 Office: Lahey Clinic Med Ctr 41 Mall Rd Box 541 Burlington MA 01805

MOSCONA, ARON ARTHUR, biology educator, scientist; b. Israel, July 4, 1922; came to U.S., 1955, naturalized, 1965; s. David DeAbravanel and Lola (Krochmaal) M.; m. Malka Kempinsky, July 6, 1954; 1 child, Anne. M.Sc., Hebrew U., Jerusalem, 1947, Ph.D., 1950. Postgrad. fellow Strangeways Research Lab., Cambridge, Eng., 1950-52; vis. investigator Rockefeller Inst., N.Y.C., 1955-57; prof. biology U. Chgo., 1958—, Louis Block prof. biol. scis., 1972-92, Louis Block prof. emeritus, 1992—; chmn. Com. on Devel. Biology, 1969-76; vis. prof. Stanford U., 1959, U. Montreal, 1960, U. Palermo, Italy, 1966, Hebrew U., Jerusalem, 1972, Tel-Aviv (Israel) U., 1977, 79, Kyoto U., Japan, 1980. Author: (with A. Monroy) Introductory Concepts in Developmental Biology, 1979; founder, editor: Current Topics in Developmental Biology, 1965; past mem. editorial bd. Jour. Molecular Neurosci., New Biologist, Mechanisms of Aging and Development, Cell Differentiation, Cancer Research, Devel. Neurosci, Experimental Cell Research; contbr. 260 articles to profl. jours. Recipient Claude Bernard medal in exptl. medicine, 1962, Alcon prize in visual sci., 1990, Gold medal Azabu Univ., Japan, 1991. Fellow AAAS, Am. Acad. Arts and Scis., Lombardo Inst. (Milan), N.Y. Acad. Scis.; mem. NAS, Internat. Soc. Devel. Biology (pres. 1977-81), Am. Soc. Devel. Biology, Internat. Soc. Cell Biology, Am. Soc. Zoology, Sigma Xi.

MOSEBY, LEBARON CLARENCE, JR., mathematics and computer science educator; b. Phila., Oct. 8, 1944; s. LeBaron Clarence and Louise (Walker) M. BA in math., Harvard U., 1966, MA in math., 1967, D in edn., 1972. Asst. dean admissions and studies Harvard Grad. Sch. Edn., 1971-73; faculty Nat. Sci. Found. Project Simmons Coll., Boston, 1974; asst. prof. edn. and dir. student teaching Simmons Coll., Boston, 1973-76; acting chmn. edn. dept. Trinity Coll., Hartford, 1977-78, asst. prof. edn. and dir. student teaching, 1976-81; dir. social context teaching and learning program U. Tex., Austin, 1981-83; asst. prof. math. and computer sci. South West Tex. State U., 1983-86; tech. edn. con. and tech. edn. specialist Wang Labs., Lowell; Mass., 1987—; cons., writer Southern Assn. Colls. and Schs., 1968-69; dir., coord. Miles Coll., 1968-69. Contbr. articles to profl. jours. Cons. Capitol Region Edn. Coun., Hartford, 1979, Nat. Inst. Edn., Washington, 1979-83, Hartford Pub. Schs., 1980, New Eng. Ctr. Urban Rsch., Hartford, 1978-80, Ct. State Dept. Edn., 1980; reviewer Am. Edn. Rsch. Assn., 1979-83. Fellow in edn. Harvard U., 1970-71. Mem. IEEE, Math. Assn. Am., Phi Delta Kappa. Home: 89 Union Park St Apt 407 Boston MA 02118-2470

MOSELEY, CARLOS DUPRE, former music executive, musician; b. Laurens, S.C., Sept. 21, 1914; s. Carlos Roland and Helen Allston (DuPre) M. BA magna cum laude, Duke, 1935; postgrad., Phila. Conservatory Music, 1941-44; student piano with Harold Morris, Olga Samaroff, Sophia Rosoff; LHD (hon.), Wofford Coll., 1966, Duke U., 1985; MusD (hon.), Converse Coll., 1971; DFA (hon.), U. S.C., 1989; LHD (hon.), The Juilliard Sch., 1995. Head fgn. information research div. OWI, N.Y.C., 1944-45; chief music sect. State Dept., Washington, 1946-48; music officer Office Mil. Govt. for Bavaria, Munich, Germany, 1948-49; chief fine arts and exhibits sect. reorientation br. Army Dept., N.Y.C., 1949-50; dir. Sch. Music, prof. music U. Okla., 1950-55; dir. press and pub. relations N.Y. Philharmonic Symphony Soc., N.Y.C., 1955-59; assoc. mng. dir. N.Y. Philharmonic Symphony Soc., 1959-61, mng. dir., 1961-70, pres., 1970-78, vice chmn., 1978-83, chmn., 1983-85, chmn. emeritus, 1985—; U.S. del. to UNESCO Music Conf., Paris, 1948; U.S. del Internat. Music Coun., Paris, 1953; mem. music panel Nat. Endowment for Arts, 1967-69, N.Y. State Coun. on Arts, 1973-77, Nat. Coun. on Arts, 1985-91. Soloist, N.Y. Philharmonic Orch., N.Y.C. Symphony, Berkshire Music Center Orch., San Diego Symphony, Portuguese Nat. Symphony, Lisbon, Vt. Symphony, others. Trustee Fan Fox and Leslie R. Samuels Found., Eleanor Naylor Dana Charitable Trust, Charles A. Dana Found.; mem. Lincoln Ctr. coun. Lincoln Ctr. for Performing Arts, 1961-78; chmn. performing arts adv. com. Asia Soc., 1970-91; mem. Met. Opera Assn. Winner MacDowell Nat. Young Artists Competition, 1939; recipient N.Y.C. Mayor's medal of honor for arts and culture, 1978, Disting. Svc. citation U. Okla., 1989, Order of the Palmetto, State of S.C., Nat. citation Nat. Fedn. Music Clubs, 1991, Lifetime Achievement award S.C. Gov.'s Sch. of the Arts, 1995. Mem. Met. Opera Assn., Century Assn. (N.Y.C.), Piedmont Club (S.C.), Phi Beta Kappa, Mu Phi Epsilon, Pi Kappa Lambda, Phi Eta Sigma. Office: care Dana Charitable Trust 375 Park Ave New York NY 10152-0002

MOSELEY, CHRIS ROSSER, marketing executive; b. Balt., Apr. 13, 1950; d. Thomas Earl and Fern Elaine (Coleman) Rosser; m. Thomas Kenneth Moseley. BA with honors, The Coll. of Wooster, 1972. Asst. dir. advt. and promotion Sta. WBAL-TV, Balt., 1972-74; dir. pub. rels. Mintz & Hoke Advt. Inc., Hartford, Conn., 1974-75; promotion mgr. Sta. WFSB-TV, Hartford, 1975-77; audience promotion mgr. Sta. WTVJ-TV, Miami, Fla., 1977-78; pres. CMA Mktg. Cons., Hyde Park, N.Y., 1979-82; promotion mgr. Ind. Network News-Sta. WPIX-TV, N.Y.C., 1982-84; sr. v.p., mgmt. supr. Christopher Thomas Muller Jordan Weiss, N.Y.C., 1984-89, Earle Palmer Brown/N.Y., N.Y.C., 1989-90; sr. v.p. advt., promotion Discovery Networks, U.S., Bethesda, Md., 1990—. Recipient Best Bus.-to-Bus. award Art Direction mag., 1984, award of achievement in media rels. and edn. Nat. Resources Coun. Am., 1991, Best Editorial Excellence award Mag. Age, 1992, Best Overall Mktg. Campaign award MIP/MIPCOM, 1994, 1st Place Print award: Media Promotion, London Internat. Advt. awards, 1993, Gold award Broadcast Designers, 1993, Mktg. 100 award Ad Age, 1995, Cable Marketer of Yr. award Ad Age, 1995. Mem. CTAM (chair, Mark award 1995, 96, co-chair 1997, bd. dirs. 1997), NCTA (conv. com. 1995, 96, Vanguard award for mktg. 1996), WIC, AWNY, PROMAX Internat. (chair 1996-97), CTPAA. Democrat. Avocations: horticulture, travel. Home: PO Box 418 Riderwood MD 21139-0418 Office: Discovery Comms Inc 7700 Wisconsin Ave Bethesda MD 20814-3578

MOSELEY, JAMES FRANCIS, lawyer; b. Charleston, S.C., Dec. 6, 1936; s. John Olin and Kathryn (Moran) M.; m. Anne McGehee, June 10, 1961; children: James Francis Jr., John McGehee. AB, The Citadel, 1958; JD, U. Fla., 1961. Bar: Fla. 1961, U.S. Supreme Ct. 1970. Pres. Moseley, Warren, Prichard & Parrish, Jacksonville, Fla., 1963—; chmn. jud. nominating com. 4th Jud. Cir., 1978-80. Assoc. editor: American Maritime Cases; contbr. articles on admiralty, transp. and ins. law to legal jours. Pres. Jacksonville United Way, 1979; chmn. bd. dirs. United Way Fla., 1992-93, S.E. regional coun. United Way, 1992-96; trustee Jacksonville Cmty. Found.; chmn. bd. trustees Jacksonville Pub. Libr.; trustee Libr. Found., sec., 1987-91; trustee CMI Am. Found.; chmn. Jacksonville Human Svcs. Coun., 1989-91; chmn. bd. trustees United Way N.E. Fla., 1995-97; bd. govs. United Way Am., 1996—. Fellow Am. Coll. Trial Lawyers, Am. Bar Found.; mem. Jacksonville Bar Assn. (pres. 1975), Fla. Coun. Bar Pres. (chmn. 1979), Maritime Law Assn. U.S. (exec. com. 1978-81, chmn. navigation com. 1981-88, v.p. 1992-96, pres. 1996—), Comm. Maritime Internat. (titulary), Com. on Collision (Lisbon Rules), Fed. Ins. Corp. Counsel (chmn. maritime law sect.), Internat. Assn. Def. Counsel (chmn. maritime com. 1989-91), Am. Inns of Ct. (master of bench), Assn. of Citadel Men (bd. mem. 1989-93, exec. com. 1994, Man Yr. award 1992), Citadel Inn of Ct. (sr. bencher), Deerwood Club, River Club, India House (N.Y.C.), Army Navy Club (Washington), St. John's Dinner Club (pres. 1988). Home: 7780 Hollyridge Rd Jacksonville FL 32256-7134 Office: Moseley Warren Prichard Parrish 1887 Bldg 501 W Bay St Jacksonville FL 32202

MOSELEY, JOHN TRAVIS, university administrator, research physicist; b. New Orleans, Feb. 26, 1942; s. Fred Baker and Lily Gay (Lord) M.; m. Belva McCall Hudson, Aug. 11 1964 (div. June 1979); m. Susan Diane Callow, Aug. 6, 1979; children: Melanie Lord, John Mark, Stephanie Marie, Shannon Eleanor. BS in Physics, Ga. Inst. Tech., 1964, MS in Physics, 1966, PhD in Physics, 1969. Asst. prof. physics U. West Fla., Pensacola, 1968-69; sr. physicist SRI Internat., Menlo Park, Calif., 1969-75, program mgr., 1976-79; vis. prof. U. Paris, 1975-76; assoc. prof. U. Oreg., Eugene, 1979-81, dir. chem. physics inst., 1980-84, prof. physics, 1984—, head physics dept., 1984-85, v.p. rsch., 1985-94, v.p. acad. affairs, provost, 1994—; mem. exec. com., coun. on acad. affairs NASULGC, 1994—, chair, 1996—; bd. dirs. Oreg. Resource and Tech., Portland; mem. com. on Atomic and Molecular Sci., 1983-85. Contbr. numerous articles to profl. jours. Mem. So. Willamette Rsch. Corridor, Eugene, 1985—, Lane Econ. Devel. Com., Eugene, 1988—; bd. dirs. Eugene/Springfield Metro Partnership, 1985—, Oreg. Bach Festival, Eguene, 1987-94, Eugene Arts Found., 1995—. Recipient Doctoral Thesis award Sigma Xi, 1969; Fulbright fellow, 1975; numerous rsch. grants, 1969—. Fellow Am. Physical Soc.; mem. Am. Chem. Soc., Am. Assn. for Advancement Sci., Am. Assn. Univ. Prof. Avocations: skiing, backpacking. Home: 2140 Essex Ln Eugene OR 97403-1851 Office: U Oreg Office of VP Acad Affairs and Provost Eugene OR 97403-1258

MOSELEY, KAREN FRANCES F., retired school system administrator, educator; b. Oneonta, N.Y., Sept. 18, 1944; d. Albert Francis and Dorothy (Brown) Flanigan; m. David Michael McLaud, Sept. 8, 1962 (div. Dec. 1966); m. Harry R. Lasalle, Dec. 24, 1976 (dec. Feb. 1990); 1 child, Christopher Michael; m. Kel Moseley, Jan. 22, 1994. BA, SUNY, Oneonta, 1969, MS, 1970. Cert. secondary edn. tchr., Fla., Mass., N.Y. Tchr. Hanover (Mass.) Pub. Schs., 1970-80; lobbyist Mass. Fed. Nursing Homes, Boston, 1980-84; tchr., dept. chair Palm Beach County Schs., Jupiter, Fla., 1985-95; chair of accredidation Jupiter H.S., 1990-91; Fulbright tchr., Denmark, 1994-95. Author: How to Teach About King, 1978, 10 Year Study, 1991. Del. Dem. Conv., Mass., 1976-84; campaign mgr. Kennedy for Senate, N.Y., 1966, Tsongas for Senate, Boston, 1978; dir. Plymouth County Dems., Marshfield, Mass., 1978-84; Sch. Accountability Com., 1991-95; polit. cons. Paul Tsongas U.S. Senate, Boston, 1978-84, Michael Dukakis for Gov., Boston, 1978-84. Mem. AAUW, NEA (lifetime mem.), Nat. Honor Soc. Polit. Scientists, Classroom Tchrs. Assn., Mass. Coun. Social Studies (bd. dirs. Boston chpt. 1970-80), Mass. Tchrs. Assn. (chair human rels. com. Boston chpt. 1976-80), Plymouth County Social Studies (bd. dirs. 1970-80), Mass. Hosp. Assn. (bd. dirs. Boston chpt. 1980-84), Nat. Coun. for Social Studies, Fulbright Alumni Assn. Roman Catholic. Avocations: reading, fishing, traveling, art collector, boating. Home: 369 River Edge Rd Jupiter FL 33477-9350

MOSELEY, MARC ROBARDS, sales executive; b. L.A., July 14, 1954; s. Thomas Robards and Doris Cecile (Tye) M. Student, U. Ky., 1972-74, U. Ga., 1977-78; BA, La. Tech. U., 1985; postgrad., Western Mich. U., 1986. Svc. rep. Ky. Mortgage Co., Lexington, 1973; loan rep. Termplan Fin. Co., Atlanta, 1975-77; sr. cons. Co-Ordinated Planning Assocs., Atlanta, 1979-80; sales rep. Nat. Starch & Chem. Corp., Monroe, La., 1980-84; v.p. sales Ednl. Funding Svc., Monroe, 1984-85; tech. sales rep. polymer divsn. Ralston Purina, St. Louis, 1985-87; account mgr. Protein Techs. Internat. Polymer Group subs. Ralston Purina, St. Louis, 1988-90, sr. account mgr., 1990-92, area dir. market ops., 1992-96, dir. industry mgmt. and bus. devel., 1996—; v.p. sales and mktg. RANA Enterprises, Inc., Atlanta, 1991—; dir. Radiant Chem., Atlanta, 1992—; v.p., dir. Bishop Pharm. Co., Inc., West Monroe, La., 1994-96. Mem. TAPPI Greater Atlanta, U. Ky. Alumni Assn. (bd. dirs. 1991-97, exec. v.p. Ga. sect. 1992-94). Avocations: water and snow skiing, basketball, music, golf. Home: 440 Bluff Meadow Dr Ellisville MO 63021 Office: Protein Tech Internat Inc Checkerboard Square Saint Louis MO 63164

MOSELEY, MARY PRUDENCE, educator; b. Ft. Worth, Dec. 31, 1922; d. Alexander Thomas and Clara (Strong) M. BA, So. Meth. U., 1943; MS, State U. Iowa, 1945. Cert. lifetime profl. tchr., Tex. Supr. Penn Mutual Life Ins. Co., Phila., 1945-47; instr. math. So. Meth. U., Dallas, 1949-50; tchr. math. Corpus Christi (Tex.) Ind. Sch. Dist., 1950-54; mgr. office H. Raymond Strong and Assocs., Consulting Actuaries, Dallas, 1958-60; computer programmer Southwestern Life Ins. Co., Dallas, 1960-63, Republic Nat. Life Ins. Co., Dallas, 1964-66; actuarial technician Arthur Stedry Hansen Cons. Actuaries, Dallas, 1967; tchr. math. Carrollton-Farmers Branch (Tex.) Ind. Sch. Dist., 1967-69; clk. policy svc. Conn. Mut. Life Ins. Co., Dallas, 1970-75; policyholder svc. Peerless Life Ins. Co., Dallas, 1975-79; pers. asst. Allan McDonnell Found., Waco, 1980-86; tchr. substitute Waco (Tex.) Ind. Sch. Dist., 1986—. Mem. Am. Assn. Ret. Persons, Sigma Xi (assoc.). Bahá'í Faith. Avocations: reading, music, math puzzles, word puzzles, logic puzzles. Home: 4018 Homan Ave Waco TX 76707-1650

MOSELEY, SHERYL BUCK, nursing administrator; b. Greenville, N.C., Nov. 27, 1955; d. James Earl and Hilda Hatton (Johnston) Buck; m. William Earl Moseley, June 17, 1978; 1 child, Taylor Brianne. BSN, East Carolina U., 1978, MSN, 1993. Staff nurse rehab. Pitt County Meml. Hosp., Greenville, 1978-80, permanent charge nurse, 1980-81, head nurse rehab., 1981-87, nursing adminstr., 1988—. Co-coord. 514th MP Co. Family Support Group, Greenville, 1991, coord., 1992. Mem. ANA, Assn. Rehab. Nurses (cert.), N.C. Assn. Rehab. Nurses (sec. 1980-81, pres. 1985-86, bd. dirs. 1986-88), N.C. Nurses Assn., Nat. League for Nursing, N.C. Orgn. Nurse Execs., Am. Orgn. Nurse Execs., Sigma Theta Tau (Beta Nu chpt.). Baptist. Avocations: cross-stitching, sewing, reading, fishing. Address: 3278 Old Creek Rd Greenville NC 27834 Office: Pitt County Meml Hosp PO Box 6028 2100 Stantonsburg Rd Greenville NC 27835-6028

MOSELEY, THERESA, guidance counselor, actress; b. Ft. Bragg, N.C., Feb. 27, 1958; d. Clarence B. and Hazel Mae (Stinney) M. BA, Ga. State U., 1988; MEd, Bowie State U., 1994; postgrad., Am. U. Receptionist Brannell Coll., Atlanta, Ga., 1981-84; red coat Continental Airlines, Newark, N.J., 1988-93; counselor U. Md., College Park, 1994; counselor, tchr. Prince Georges County Sch., Upper Marlboro, 1995—; mem. Assn. for Multi-cult. counseling and devel., 1993—, Md. Assn. for Counseling and Devel., 1993—, v.p. Montgomery County Parent Policy Coun., Rockville, Md., 1994-95. vol. Dem. Convention, Atlanta, 1988. With U.S. Army, 1976-80. Recipient Career Day Appreciation award John Burrough Elem., Washington, 1995, others. Mem. ACA, Am. Sch. Counseling Assn., Nat. Assn. for the Edn. of Young Children, Md. Assn. for Counseling and Devel., Prince Georges County Edn. Assn., AFTRA, SAG, Chi Sigma Iota. Democrat. Protestant. Avocation: acting, singing, dancing, photography, travel. Home: 1131 University Blvd W Silver Spring MD 20902

MOSELEY-BRAUN, CAROL, senator; b. Chgo., Aug. 16, 1947; d. Joseph J. and Edna A. (Davie) Moseley; m. Michael Braun, 1973 (div. 1986); 1 child, Matthew. BA, U. Ill., Chgo., 1969; JD, U. Chgo., 1972. Asst. U.S. atty. U.S. Dist. Ct. (no. dist.) Ill., 1973-77; mem. Ill. Ho. of Reps., 1979-88; recorder of deeds Cook County, Ill., 1988-92; U.S. senator from Ill. Washington, 1993—; mem. fin. com., subcom. on social security and family policy, subcom. on medicare, long-term care and health ins., mem. com. on banking, housing and urban affairs, subcom. on HUD oversight and structure, subcom. on internat. fin. and monetary policy, subcom. on fin. instns. and regulatory relief. Office: US Senate 324 Hart Senate Office Bldg Washington DC 20510

MOSELY, LINDA HAYS, surgeon; b. New Orleans, Feb. 20, 1941; d. Charles Hodge Mosely and Florence (Morley) Mosely Williams. Student Emory U., 1959-61; BS, La. State U., 1963, MD, 1967. Diplomate Am. Bd. Surgery, Am. Bd. Plastic Surgery; lic. physician, Va., D.C., La. Rotating intern Charity Hosp., New Orleans, 1967-68, med. resident, 1968-69, gen. surgery resident, 1970-72; surgery resident Mt. Sinai Hosp., N.Y.C., 1969-70; hand surgery fellow Dr. Harold Kleinert, Louisville, 1972, 74; clin. surg. fellow U. Louisville Med. Ctr., 1972, gen. surgery resident, 1973; rsch. fellow Yale Med. Ctr., New Haven, 1975, plastic surgery resident, 1975-77; tutor specialist Middlemore Hosp., Auckland, N.Z., 1977-78; practice aesthetic surgery Clinica Planas, Barcelona, Spain, 1978-79; cons. plastic surgery John Fitzgerald Kennedy Hosp., Monrovia, Liberia, 1979; clin. and rsch. fellow Toronto Gen. Hosp., Ont., Can., 1979-80; pvt. practice medicine specializing in hand and plastic surgery, Alexandria, Va., 1980—. Mem. People to People Citizen Amb. Program-Soviet Union-Orthopedic Del., 1991. Contbr.

articles to med. jours. Mem. ACS, Am. Soc. for Plastic and Reconstructive Surgeons, Am. Soc. for Surgery of Hand, Met. Washington D.C. Soc. for Surgery of Hand (pres. 1997—), D.C. Met. Plastic Surgery Soc., Med. Soc. Va., Alexandria Med. Soc., Tysons Corner, Va., Georgetown Club, Washington. Home: 5318 Echols Ave Alexandria VA 22311-1309 Office: 2500 N Van Dorn St Apt 128 Alexandria VA 22302-1601

MOSEMANN, LLOYD KENNETH, II, government official; b. Lancaster, Pa., May 16, 1936; s. Lloyd Kreider and Beatrice Elizabeth (Frey) M.; m. Arlene K. White, Sept. 6, 1957; children—Gigi Renee Mosemann Falke, Lloyd Kenneth III, Douglas Lamar, Holly Joy. A.B. in Social Sci., U. Chgo., 1957, A.M. in Internat. Relations, 1959. Gen. supply officer Navy Electronics Supply Office, Great Lakes, Ill., 1958-62; inventory mgmt. specialist Def. Electronics Supply Ctr., Dayton, Ohio, 1962-63; head integrated-retail supply and support br. Naval Supply Systems Command, Washington, 1963-69; dep. chief logistics support analysis office Def. Logistics Agy., Alexandria, Va., 1969-71; dep. for supply and maintenance Office Sec. of Air Force, Washington, 1971-74; dep. asst. sec. for logistics and communications Dept. Air Force, Washington, 1974-91, dep. asst. sec. for comm., computers and logistics, 1991-93, dep. asst. sec. for comm., computers and support systems, 1993-96; software and acquisition cons., 1996-97; corp. v.p. corp. devel. Sci. Applications Internat. Corp., McLean, Va., 1997—; mem. Air Force Exec. resources Bd., 1981-95; bd. dirs. McCabe and Assocs. Decorated D.S.M.; recipient Meritorious Svc. medal Sec. Air Force, 1977, Exceptional Civilian Svc. medal sec. Air Force, 1979, 81, 82, 87, 96, Meritorious Sr. Exec. award Pres. of U.S., 1982, 87, Def. Meritorious Civilian Svc. medal, 1985. Mem. Soc. Logistics Engrs. (bd. advisers 1983—, Founders medal 1983, H. Mark Grove award for excellence in software mgmt. 1996, Govt. Computer News Hall of Fame 1996, Fed. Computer Week "100" award 1996), Am. Def. Preparedness Assn. (bd. dirs. 1974-83), Nat. Inst. for Urban Search and Rescue (exec. bd. dirs. 1990—). Home: 10300 Granite Creek Ln Oakton VA 22124

MOSER, C. THOMAS, lawyer; b. Seattle, Aug. 10, 1947; s. Carl Thomas and Helen Louise (Felton) M.; m. Deborah J. St. Clair, Sept. 25, 1976; children: Nicole, Lauren. BA, Cen. Wash. U., 1972; M in Pub. Adminstrn., George Washington U., 1974; JD, Gonzaga U., 1976. Bar: Wash. 1977, U.S. Dist. Ct. (we. dist.) Wash. 1977, U.S. Dist. Ct. (ea. dist.) Wash. 1980, U.S. Ct. Appeals (9th cir.) 1980, U. S. Supreme Ct. 1981. Dep. pros. atty. Skagit County Pros. Atty., Mount Vernon, Wash., 1976-77, chief civil dep., 1979-80, pros. atty., 1980-86; pros. atty. San Juan County Pros. Atty., Friday Harbor, Wash., 1977-79; pvt. practice Mount Vernon, 1987—; hearing examiner pro tem Skagit County, 1992—. Author: Gonzaga Law Review, 1975. Bd. dirs. Wash. Environ. Coun., Seattle, 1971-72, Padilla Bay Found., Skagit County, Wash., 1988; bd. trustees Wash. Assn. County Officials, Olympia, 1983; exec. bd. North Pacific Conf. Evang. Covenant Ch., vice sec. 1991-96. Sgt. U.S. Army, 1967-69, Korea. Recipient Silver Key award ABA Student Law Div., 1976, Legion of Honor award Internat. Order DeMolay, Kansas City, Mo., 1982, Chevalier award 1982. Mem. ATLA, Nat. Coll. Advocacy (advocate), Wash. State Trial Lawyers Assn. (bd. govs. 1990-92, 96—), Wash. Assn. Pros. Attys. (bd. dirs. 1983-85), Skagit County Bar Assn. (pres. 1995-96), Kiwanis Club Mt. Vernon, Affiliated Health Svc. (ethics com.), Christian Legal Soc. Democrat. Evangelical. Avocations: skiing, golf, jogging, woodworking. Office: 411 Main St Mount Vernon WA 98273-3837

MOSER, DEBRA KAY, medical educator. BSN magna cum laude, Humboldt State U., Arcata, Calif., 1977; M in Nursing, UCLA, 1988, D in Nursing Sci., 1992. RN, Calif.; Ohio; cert. pub. health nurse, Calif. Staff nurse, relief supr. med.-surg. fl. Mad River Cmty. Hosp., Arcata, 1977-78, staff/charge nurse intensive care/cardiac care unit, 1978-86; clin. nursing instr. Humboldt State U., Arcata, 1985-86; staff/charge nurse surg. ICU Santa Monica (Calif.) Hosp., 1987-88; spl. reader UCLA Sch. Nursing, 1990-91, rsch. assoc., 1986-91, clin. rsch. nurse, 1988-92, project dir., 1991-92, asst. prof., 1992-94; asst. prof. dept. adult health and illness Ohio State U. Coll. Nursing, Columbus, 1994—; mem. working group on ednl. strategies to Prevent Prehosp. Delay in Patients at High Risk for Acute Myocardial Infraction, Nat. Heart Attack Alert Program, NIH, Nat. Heart, Lung and Blood Inst., 1993-95; abstract grader sci. sessions program Am. Heart Assn., 66th Sci. Sessions, 1993, 96; grad. advisor Sigma Theta Tau-Gamma Tau chpt., 1993-94; mem. med. adv. com. Westside YMCA Cardiac Rehab. Program, 1993-94; mem. Task Force on Women, Behavior and Cardiovasc. Disease NIH, Nat. Heart, Lung and Blood Inst., 1991. Reviewer Am. Jour. Critical Care, 1992—, Heart and Lung, 1991—, Progress in Cardiovasc. Nursing, 1993—, Heart Failure: Evaluation and Care of Patients With Left-Ventricular Systolic Function, 1993, Intensive Coronary Care, 5th edit., 1994, Rsch. in Nursing & Health, 1995—, Jour. Am. Coll. Cardiology, 1995; co-editor Jour. Cardiovasc. Nursing, 1997—; mem. editl. bd. Am. Jour. Critical Care, 1994—, Jour. Cardiovasc. Nursing, 1995—; contbr. articles to profl. jours., chpts. to books. Recipient scholarship UCLA, 1988-90, scholarship Kaiser Permanente Affiliate Schs., 1990, Ednl. Achievement award LA-AACN, 1990, Alumni rsch. award UCLA, 1990, rsch. abstract award AACN-IVAC, 1993; grantee Sigma Theta Tau-Gamma Tau chpt., 1989-90, AACN, 1989-90, 92-93, NIH, Nat. Ctr. Nursing Rsch., 1990-92, UCLA Program in Psychneuroimmunology, 1992-93, UCLA Sch. Nursing, 1993, UCLA Acad. Senate, 1993-94, AACN/Sigma Theta Tau Internat., 1994-95, NIH, Nat. Inst. Nursing Rsch., 1991-96, Sigma Theta Tau Epsilon chpt., 1995, Ohio State U., 1995, Nat. Am. Heart Assn., 1995—. Mem. AACN, Am. Heart Assn. Coun. Cardiovasc. Nursing (New Investigator award 1995, Heart Failure Rsch. prize 1995), Sigma Theta Tau (mem. rsch. com. 1990-94, Excellence in Rsch. award Gamma Tau chpt. 1993). Home: 6871 Meadow Oak Dr Columbus OH 43235-4950 Office: Ohio State U Coll Nursing Dept Adult Health & Illness 1585 Neil Ave Columbus OH 43210-1216

MOSER, DONALD BRUCE, magazine editor; b. Cleve., Oct. 19, 1932; s. Donald Lyman and Kathryn (McHugh) M.; m. Penny Lee Ward, Dec. 20, 1975. BA, Ohio U., 1957; postgrad., Stanford U., 1957-58, U. Sydney, 1959-60. With Life mag., 1961-72, West Coast bur. chief, 1964-65, Far East bur. chief, 1966-69, asst. mng. editor, 1970-72; free-lance writer, 1972-77; exec. editor Smithsonian mag., Washington, 1977-80; editor Smithsonian mag., 1981—, editor-in-chief. Author: The Peninsula, 1962, The Snake River Country, 1974, A Heart to the Hawks, 1975, Central American Jungles, 1976, China-Burma-India, 1978; contbr. articles to numerous mags., jours. Served with U.S. Army, 1953-55. Stegner fellow, 1957-58; Fulbright scholar, 1959-60. Mem. Phi Beta Kappa. Office: Smithsonian Mag Arts & Indsl Bldg 900 Jefferson St NW Washington DC 20011-2906*

MOSER, GREGG ANTHONY, career officer; b. Holton, Kans., Aug. 6, 1954; s. Paul Robert and Ila Rose (Jenkins) M.; m. Shari Ann Larson, Nov. 3, 1984. BS in Constrn. Sci., Kans. State U., 1979; MS in Safety, Ctrl. Mo. State U., 1984. Commd. 2d lt. USAF, 1980, advanced through grades to maj., 1991. Mem. Air Force Assn. (pres. Lt. Erwin R. Bleckley chpt. 1992-93, Medal of Merit 1994), Lions (pres. Wichita Flying Lions chpt. 1992-93, zone 1 chmn. dist. 17-SE region II 1993-94, dir. Scott Comty. Lions Club 1994-95, v.p. Scott Comty. Lions Club 1995-96). Republican. Methodist. Avocations: photography, reading. Home: 625 W 5th St Holton KS 66436-1406 Office: 607th Air Support Squadron/LGS Osan AB ROK APO AP 96278-2047

MOSER, HAROLD DEAN, historian; b. Kannapolis, N.C., Oct. 31, 1938; s. Walter Glenn and Angie Elizabeth (Allen) M.; m. Carolyn Irene French, Mar. 28, 1964; children: Andrew Paul, Anna Elizabeth. A.A., Wingate Coll., 1959; B.A. cum laude, Wake Forest U., 1961, M.A. Univ. fellow, 1963; Ph.D. Ford fellow, U. Wis., 1977. Tchr. Robert B. Glenn High Sch., Winston-Salem, N.C., 1961-62; instr. history Chowan Coll., Murfreesboro, N.C., 1963-65; teaching asst dept. history U. Wis., Madison, 1967-69; Nat. Hist. Publ. Commn. fellow The Papers of Daniel Webster (Dartmouth Coll.), Hanover, N.H., 1971-72, asst. editor, 1972-73, assoc. editor, 1973-76, co-editor, 1976-77, editor corr. series, 1978-79; editor dir. The Papers of Andrew Jackson, 1979—; adv. bd. The Papers of Albert Gallatin, Baruch Coll., CCNY, 1987—; rsch. prof. history U. Tenn., Knoxville, 1987—. Contbr. articles to profl. jours. Mem. Am. Hist. Assn., So. Hist. Assn., Orgn. Am. Historians, Soc. Historians of Early Am. Republic, Assn. for Documentary Editing, Tenn. Hist. Soc., Phi Alpha Theta, Eta Sigma Phi, Phi Theta Kappa. Democrat. Episcopalian. Home: 9605 Tallahassee Ln Knoxville TN 37923-2737 Office: U Tenn Hoskins Library Knoxville TN 37996

MOSER, HUGO WOLFGANG, physician; b. Switzerland, Oct. 4, 1924; came to U.S., 1940, naturalized, 1943; s. Hugo L. and Maria (Werner) M.; m. Ann Boody, Dec. 28, 1963; children—Tracey, Peter, Karen, Lauren. M.D., Columbia U., 1948; A.M. in Med. Sci, Harvard U., 1956. Intern Columbia-Presbyn. Med. Center, N.Y.C., 1948-50; asst. in medicine Peter Bent Brigham Hosp., Boston, 1950-52; research fellow dept. biol. chemistry Harvard U., 1955-57; asst. resident, resident in neurology Mass. Gen. Hosp., 1957-59, asst. neurologist, 1960-67, assoc. neurologist, 1967-69, neurologist, 1969-76; teaching fellow neuropathology Harvard Med. Sch., 1959-60, instr. neurology, 1960-64, assoc. in neurology, 1964-67, asst. prof., 1967-69, asso. prof., 1969-72, prof., 1972-76; dir. research and tng. Walter E. Fernald State Sch., 1963-68, asst. supt., 1968-73, acting supt., 1973-74, supt., 1974-76; dir. Center for Research on Mental Retardation and Related Aspects of Human Devel., dir. univ. affiliated facilities for mentally retarded, 1965-74; co-dir. Eunice Kennedy Shriver Center for Mental Retardation, Inc., 1969-74; pres. John F. Kennedy Inst., Balt., 1976-88; prof. neurology and pediatrics Johns Hopkins U., 1976—. Author: (with others) Mental Retardation: An Atlas of Diseases with Associated Physical Abnormalities, 1972; Contbr. (with others) articles to med. jours. Served with AUS, 1943-44; to capt. U.S. Army, 1952-54. Recipient Hower award Child Neurology Soc., 1994. Mem. Am. Acad. Neurology, Am. Assn. Mental Deficiency, Am. Assn. Neuropathologists, Am. Neurol. Assn., Internat. Soc. Neurochemistry, Am. Pediatrics Soc., Sigma Xi, Alpha Omega Alpha. Home: 100 Beechdale Rd Baltimore MD 21210-2209 Office: Kennedy Inst Inc 707 N Broadway Baltimore MD 21205-1832

MOSER, JEFFERY RICHARD, state official; b. Miller, S.D., Feb. 8, 1961; s. Richard and Ardessa Joan (Yost) M. Student, U. Minn., 1979-84; cert., Lay Minister Study Program, S.D., 1990-92. Lab asst., intern U. Minn. Dept. Limnology, Mpls., 1980-81; exec. intern pub. affairs dept. Target Corp., Mpls., 1982; intern asst. for legis. and policy Minn. Agri-Growth Coun., Bloomington, 1984-85; field office asst. U.S. Congressman Thomas A. Daschle, Aberdeen, S.D., 1986; pvt. cons., 1986-89; notary pub. State of S.D., 1986—; small bus. owner, 1986—; exec. dir. S.D. Assn. Towns and Twps., 1990-95; dep. state treas. State of S.D., Pierre, 1995—; participant 4-H/UN/USAID Presdl. young adult exch. program to Kenya and Botswana, Africa, summer 1985. Gen. election poll watcher Hand County Rural precincts, 1988; past mem. Beadle County Dems., Hand County Dems., Brown County Dems., Hughes County Dems.; del. State Dem. Conv., 1990, 92, 94; Clinton for Pres., 1992; nom. Dem. candidate State Auditor, 1994; donor Dem. Nat. Com.; Dem. Nat. Senate Task Force; with Dem. Congl. Campaign Com. Dem. Nat. Conv., 1996, Clinton-Gore, 1996, mem. State Adv. Com., 1996; at. del. Dem. Nat. Conv., 1996; vol. leader, advisor, and state fair judge S.D. 4-H Program, 1981-94; bd. dirs. S.D. Rural Devel. Coun., 1993-95, S.D. State Adv. Com. for Green Thumb, Inc., 1993-95; mem. task force Nat. Urban Comparative Risk Environ., 1994, Common Cause S.D., 1991-94; dist. dir. S.D. Farmers Union, 1988-93; dir. Golden Razor Hair Salon, Inc., Mpls., 1983-84; mem. Rose Hill Presbyn. Ch., S.D. Com. for World Food Day, S.D. Bread for the World, S.D. Project Prosperity Coalition, S.D. Farmers Union, Dakota Rural Action, South Dakotans For the Arts, S.D. Health Care Reform Coalition, S.D. Artists Network, S.D. Hist. Soc.; sec. Presbytery of S.D. Advocacy Devel. Ministry unit, 1992-93, ch. camp dean, moderator soc. witness and action com., 1994—; vol. coord. Bread for the World Hunger Awareness event, Huron, 1993; mem. planning com. 1993 Regional 4-H Leaders Forum, Sioux Falls; past del. rep. S.D. Nat. 4-H Congress, Nat. Farmers Union Nat. conf., Presbyn. Ch. USA Gen. Assembly, Presbyn. Ch. USA Consultation on Sustainable Devel., 1995, Nat. 4-H Coun. Master Communicators Conf., Common Cause Nat. Leadership conf., Sharing Global Harvests Nat. Tng., Nat. Assn. Towns and Twps. Am.'s Town Meeting, strategic leadership course Duke U., 1995; bd. co-chair Huron Postal Customer Adv. Bd., 1993-95; bd. dirs. S.D. Peace and Justice Ctr., sec.-treas., 1994, v.p., 1995, dir. 1994—. Mem. E. River Sierra Club. Mem. Huron C. of C. (govt. affairs com. 1991), Phi Beta Kappa, Omicron Delta Kappa, Mortar Bd. Office: Office of State Treas SD State Capitol Bldg #212 500 E Capitol Ave Pierre SD 57501-5070

MOSER, KENNETH MILES, physician, educator; b. Balt., Apr. 12, 1929; s. Simon and Helene Joyce M.; m. Sara Falk, June 17, 1951; children: Gregory, Kathleen, Margot, Diana. BA, Haverford Coll., 1950; MD, Johns Hopkins U., 1954. Diplomate Am. Bd. Internal Medicine. Intern, resident in medicine D.C. Gen. Hosp., Georgetown Hosp., 1954-59; chief pulmonary and infectious disease svc. Nat. Naval Med. Ctr., Bethesda, Md., 1959-61; dir. pulmonary div. Georgetown U. Med. Ctr., Washington, 1961-68; prof. medicine, dir. pulmonary and critical care med. divsn. Sch. Medicine U. Calif., San Diego, 1968—; dir. Specialized Ctr. Rsch. U. Calif.-San Diego/Nat. Heart Lung and Blood Inst., 1978—. Author 15 books in field of pulmonary medicine and thrombosis.; contbr. articles to med. jours. Bd. dirs. Am. Lung Assn. of San Diego and Imperial Counties, 1969-76, Am. Lung Assn. of Calif., 1976-80; mem. manpower com. Nat. Heart, Lung and Blood Inst., bd. dirs. 1978—. With USN, 1959-61. Fellow ACP, AAAS, Am. Coll. Chest Physicians; mem. Am. Thoracic Soc. (exec. bd., pres. 1985-86), Am. Heart Assn. Coun. on Thrombosis, Am. Physiol. Soc. Office: U Calif San Diego Med Ctr 200 W Arbor Dr San Diego CA 92103-1911 *Participating in academic medicine and research is like being a member of a relay team engaged in a race of infinite length. Two forces keep one running through the often difficult terrain: the goal of improving health; and the privilege of passing the baton to many others who will seek that same goal.*

MOSER, LARRY EDWARD, marketing professional; b. Chgo., Oct. 29, 1952; s. Paul Edward and Catherine Molly (Sittner) M.; m. Michelle Ann Lorden, Sept. 21, 1974 (div. Jan. 1984); children: Jennifer, Jacqueline. BS in Mktg., No. Ill. U., 1974, MBA, 1976. CLU, CPCU. Statis. analyst Addressograph-Multigraph, Mt. Prospect, Ill., 1974-75; grad. asst., mktg. instr. No. Ill. U., DeKalb, 1975-76, 77; mktg. asst. Allstate Ins. Co., Northbrook, Ill., 1977-78; project coord. Allstate Ins. Co., Northbrook, 1978-80; agt. Allstate Ins. Co., West Dundee, 1980; mktg. project mgr. to sr. mktg. mgr. Allstate Ins. Co., Northbrook, 1981—; prin. coord. Allstate WYO flood ins. program Allstate Ins. Co., 1994—, mem. nat. flood ins. program mktg. com., 1995—; v.p. Flood Ins. Svc. Cos. Am., 1997—; chmn. Allstate Share (United Way) Campaign, Northbrook, 1982-83, Allstate Helping Hands Com., Northbrook, 1985-86, Allstate Family Day Sports, Northbrook, 1991-94; pres. Allstate Men's Softball League, 1984—; dir. Flood Ins. Svc. Cos. of Am., 1996—. Active Twinbrook YMCA parent/child prog., Schaumburg, Ill., 1983-90; commr. Schaumburg Athletic Assn. Girls Softball, 1990-92. Recipient Am. Mktg. Assn. Scholastic Achievement award No. Ill. Univ., DeKalb, 1974, James E. Bell Superior Promise & Scholarship in Mktg. Mgmt. No. Ill. Univ. Dept. Mktg., DeKalb, 1976, William J. Hendrickson award for Outstanding Contbn. From An Alumni, DeKalb, 1988. Mem. Am. Soc. CLU, CPCU Soc., Pi Sigma Epsilon (pres. 1975-76), Phi Kappa Sigma, Beta Gamma Sigma, Omicron Delta Kappa. Roman Catholic. Avocations: travel, golf, tennis, camping, softball. Home: 812 Krause Ave Streamwood IL 60107-3045 Office: Allstate Inst Co Ste CIS 2775 Sanders Rd Northbrook IL 60062-6110

MOSER, M(ARTIN) PETER, lawyer; b. Balt., Jan. 16, 1928; s. Herman and Henrietta (Lehmayer) M.; m. Elizabeth Kohn, June 14, 1949; children—Mike, Moriah, Jeremy. A.B., The Citadel, Charleston, S.C., 1947; LL.B., Harvard U., 1950. Bar: Md. 1950, U.S. Supreme Ct., U.S. Ct. Appeals (4th cir.), U.S. Dist. Ct. Md. Asst. states atty. City of Balt., 1951, 53-54; assoc. Blades Rosenfeld, Balt., 1950, 53-54; ptnr. Frank, Bernstein, Conaway & Goldman and predecessor firms, Balt., 1955-90, co-chmn. firm, 1983-86; counsel, 1991-92; of counsel Piper & Marbury, 1992—; instr. U. Balt. Law Sch., 1954-56, 86, U. Md. Law Sch., 1986-87. Contbr. articles to profl. jours. Del., chmn. local govt. com. Md. Constl. Conv., 1967-68; mem. Balt. City Planning Commn., 1961-66, Balt. Regional Planning Council, 1963-66, Md. Commn. to Study Narcotics Laws, 1965-67, Mayor's Task Force on EEO, 1966-67, Met. Transit Authority Adv. Council, 1962, Com. to Revise Balt. City Planning Laws, 1962, Com. to Revise Balt. City Charter Provision on Conflicts of Interest, 1969-70; mem. Citizens Adv. Com. on Dist. Ct., chmn., 1971, Dist. Adv. Bd. for Pub. Defender System for Dist. 1, 1973-85; mem. Atty. Grievance Commn. of Md., 1975-78, chmn. 82-86; chmn. Md. State Ethics Commn., 1987-89; bd. dirs. Sinai Hosp., 1983—, Ct. of Appeals Comm. to Study the Model Rules, 1983-86. Served with JAGC, U.S. Army, 1951-53. Fellow Am. Bar Found., Md. Bar Found.; mem. ABA (ho. of dels. 1978—, treas. 1993-96, bd. govs. 1984-87, 92-96, ethics com. 1981-84, 87-90, 96—, chmn. 1981-82, 87-90, scope and cor. com. 1987-92, chmn. 1990-91), Md. State Bar Assn. (pres. 1979-80), Balt. Bar Assn. (pres. 1971-72), Fed. Bar Assn., Am. Law Inst., Wednesday Law Club, Lawyers' Round Table Club, Hamilton St. Club. Democrat. Jewish. Office: Piper & Marbury 36 S Charles St Fl 8 Baltimore MD 21201-3020

MOSER, MARVIN, physician, educator, author; b. Newark, Jan. 24, 1924; s. Sol and Sophia (Markowitz) M.; m. Joy Diane Lipez, July 1, 1954; children: Jill, Stephen, John. A.B., Cornell U., 1943; M.D., Downstate Coll. Medicine, N.Y.C., 1947. Diplomate: Am. Bd. Internal Medicine, subbd. cardiovascular disease. Intern univ. div. Kings County Hosp., N.Y.C., 1947-48; resident in medicine Kings County Hosp., 1948-49, Montefiore Hosp., N.Y.C., 1949-50; Nat. Heart Assn. fellow Mt. Sinai Hosp., N.Y.C., 1950-51; charge vascular service Walter Reed Army Hosp. Med. Centre, Washington, 1951-53; practice medicine specializing in cardiology White Plains, N.Y., 1953-95; assoc. physician cardiology Montefiore Hosp., 1953-75, in charge hypertension sect., 1960-71; attending physician cardiology White Plains Hosp., 1968-95, chief cardiology, 1969-78; adj. physician in cardiology Grasslands Hosp., Valhalla, N.Y., 1953-60; attending physician in medicine in charge Hypertension Clinic, Westchester County Med. Center, Valhalla, 1974-84; asst. clin. prof. medicine Albert Einstein Coll. Medicine, 1965-75; clin. prof. medicine N.Y. Med. Coll., 1974-84, Yale U. Sch. Medicine, 1984—; sr. med. cons. nat. high blood pressure program NIH, 1975—, mem. nat. high blood pressure coordinating com., 1976—; chmn. Joint Nat. Com. Hypertension, 1975-76, vice-chmn., 1979, mem., 1984-88, 92, 96; mem. exec. com. Nat. Citizens for Treatment High Blood Pressure, 1976-78, vice chmn., 1978-88; mem. N.Y. State Adv. Com. on Hypertension, 1977-84; chmn. Nat. Conf. on High Blood Pressure Control, 1979; mem. select panel on hypertension in Am. Congl. Subcom. on Aging, 1978-79; cons. cardiology N.Y. State Dept. Health, Gen. Hosp., Saranac Lake, N.Y., 1980-90; med. dir. Westchester County Hypertension Program, N.Y., 1979-88. Author: (with A.M. Master, M. Moser. H. Jaffee) Cardiac Emergencies and Heart Failure, 2d edit., 1955, (with A. Goldman) Hypertensive Vascular Disease, 1967, Hypertension, A Practical Approach, 1975, Lower Your Blood Pressure and Live Longer, 198; co-editor, contbr. Yale University School of Medicine Heart Book, 1992, Week by Week to a Strong Heart, 1992, Heart Healthy Cooking for all Seasons, 1996, Clinical Management of Hypertension, 1996, Myths, Misconceptions and Heroics, the Story of the Treatment of Hypertension, 1997; assoc. editor Angiology, 1976-85; bd. editors Primary Cardiology, 1975-78, assoc. editor-in-chief, 1978-96. Chmn. Narcotics Guidance Coun., Scarsdale, 1968-72; trustee Scarsdale Bd. Edn., 1970-73, Trudeau Inst., 1992—, Third Ave. Value Fund, 1994—. Served U.S. Army, 1941-46; capt. M.C. USAF, 1951-53. Nat. Heart Inst. grantee, 1958-62; recipient Achievement award for contbns. to hypertension control Nat. High Blood Pressure Edn. Program, 1985. Fellow ACP, Am. Coll. Cardiology; mem. Am. Heart Assn. (fellow coun. clin. cardiology, coun. high blood pressure rsch. 1974—, coun. geriatric cardiology 1988—, v.p. 1994-96, pres. 1996—, chmn. N.Y. State com. on hypertension 1974-75), N.Y. Cardiol. Soc., Century Country Club. Home and Office: 13 Murray Hill Rd Scarsdale NY 10583-2829

MOSER, ROBERT HARLAN, physician, educator, writer; b. Trenton, N.J., June 16, 1923; s. Simon and Helena (Silvers) M.; m. Linda Mae Salsinger, Mar. 18, 1989; children from previous marriage: Steven Michael, Jonathan Evan. BS, Loyola U., Balt., 1944; MD, Georgetown U., 1948. Diplomate Am. Bd. Internal Medicine. Commd. 1st lt. U.S. Army, 1948, advanced through grades to col., 1966, intern D.C. Gen. Hosp., 1948-49, fellow pulmonary disease D.C. Gen. Hosp., 1949-50; bn. surgeon U.S. Army, Korea, 1950-51; asst. resident Georgetown U. Hosp., 1951-52; chief resident Georgetown U. Hosp. U.S. Army, 1952-53; chief med. service U.S. Army Hosp. U.S. Army, Salzburg, Austria, 1953-55, Wurzburg, Fed. Republic Germany, 1955-56; resident in cardiology Brooke Gen. Hosp. U.S. Army, 1956-57, asst. chief dept. medicine Brooke Gen. Hosp., 1957-59, chief Brooke Gen. Hosp., 1967-68, fellow hematology U. Utah Coll. Medicine, 1959-60, asst. chief U.S. Army Tripler Gen. Hosp., 1960-64, chief William Beaumont Gen. Hosp., 1965-67, chief Walter Reed Gen. Hosp., 1968-69, ret., 1969; chief of staff Maui (Hawaii) Meml. Hosp., 1969-73, chief dept. medicine, 1975-77; exec. v.p. Am. Coll. Physicians, Phila., 1976-86; v.p. med. affairs The NutraSweet Co., Deerfield, Ill., 1986-91; assoc. prof. medicine Baylor U., 1958-59; clin. prof. medicine Hawaii U., 1969-77, Washington U., 1970-77, Abraham Lincoln Sch. Medicine, 1974-75; adj. prof. medicine U. Pa., 1977-86, Northwestern U., 1987-91; adj. prof. Uniformed Svcs. U. Health Scis., 1979—; clin. prof. medicine U. N.Mex. Coll. Medicine, 1992-96, emeritus, 1996—; flight contr. Project Mercury, 1959-62; cons. mem. med. evaluation team Project Gemini, 1962-66; cons. Project Apollo, 1967-73, Tripler Gen. Hosp., 1970-77, Walter Reed Army Med. Ctr., 1974-86; sr. med. cons. Canyon Cons. Corp., 1991—; mem. cardiovasc. and renal adv. com. FDA, 1978-82; chmn. life scis. adv. com. NASA, 1984-87, mem. NASA adv. coun., 1983-88, chmn. gen. med. panel Hosp. Satellite Network, 1984-86; mem. adv. com. NASA Space Sta., 1988-93; mem. Dept. Def. Com. on Grad. Med. Edn., 1986-87; mem. Life Scis. Strategic Planning Study Group, 1986-88; mem. space studies bd. NRC, 1988-93, space exploration initiation study, 1990, NASA Space Sta. Commn., 1992-93, mem. com. adv. tech. human supp. space, 1996-97. Author: Diseases of Medical Progress, 1955, rev. edit., 1969, House Officer Training, 1970; co-author: Adventures in Medical Writing, 1970, Decade of Decision, 1992; editor, chief div. sci. publs. Jour. AMA, Chgo., 1973-75; contbg. editor Med. Opinion and Rev., 1966-75; chmn. editorial bd. Diagnosis mag., 1986-89; mem. editorial bd. Hawaii Med. Jour., Family Physicians, Archives of Internal Medicine, 1967-73, Western Jour. Medicine, 1975-87, Chest, 1975-80, Med. Times, 1977-84, Quality Rev. Bull., 1979-91, The Pharos, 1991—, Emergency Med., 1993—, Travel Medicine, 1994—; contbr. over 200 articles to med. sci. jours and med. books. Master ACP (exec. v.p. 1977-86); fellow Am. Coll. Cardiology, Royal Coll. Physicians and Surgeons Can. (hon.), Am. Clin. and Climatol. Assn.; mem. AMA (adv. panel registry of adverse drug reactions 1960-67, coun. on drugs 1967-73),), Am. Med. Writers Assn., Am. Therapeutic Soc., Am. Osler Soc., Inst. Med., Nat. Assn. Phys. Broadcasters, Chgo. Soc. Internal Medicine, Coll. Physicians Phila., Soc. Med. Cons. to Armed Forces, Alpha Sigma Nu, Alpha Omega Alpha. Democrat. Jewish. Avocations: hiking, international travel, white water rafting. Home and Office: Canones Rd # 616 Chama NM 87520

MOSER, ROBERT LAWRENCE, pathologist, health facility administrator; b. Passaic, N.J., Mar. 22, 1952; s. Robert George and Marjorie Ann (Frankenberger) M.; m. Rosemarie Scolaro, June 16, 1978; children: Rachel Ann, Alexander Robert. BA in Biology magna cum laude, Lafayette Coll., 1974; MD with honors Microbiol./Internal Med., Hahnemann Med. Coll., 1978. Diplomate Am. Bd. Pathology, Am. Bd. Anatomic Pathology, Am. Bd. Clin. Pathology. Intern, fellow dept. Pathology The Johns Hopkins Hosp., Balt., 1978-79, resident, fellow dept. Pathology, 1979-81, chief resident, fellow dept. Pathology, 1981-82, resident, fellow dept. Lab. Medicine, 1982-84; cons. pathologist Perry Point (Md.) VA Med. Ctr., 1983-84; pathologist Helene Fuld Med. Ctr., Trenton, N.J., 1984-88; med. dir. St Francis Med. Ctr., Trenton, 1988—; dir. clin. info. systems Franciscan Health Systems, 1995-96, Cath. Health Initiatives, 1996—; pres. Pathology Assocs., Lawrenceville, N.J., 1981—. Contbr. articles to profl. jours. Fellow Coll. Am. Pathologists, Coll. Physicians of Phila.; mem. Am. Med. Informatics Assn., Med. Soc. N.J., Mercer County Med. Soc., Ctrl. Jersey Ind. Physician Assn. (v.p. 1994-95, sec.-treas. 1995-96), Ea. Pathology Assocs. (v.p. 1996), Phi Beta Kappa. Avocations: golf, gardening, skiing.

MOSER, ROSEMARIE SCOLARO, psychologist; b. Hackensack, N.J., June 16, 1954; d. Giovanni Natale and Mary (Bellaera) Scolaro; m. Robert Lawrence Moser, June 4, 1978; children: Rachel Ann, Alexander Robert. Student, Lafayette Coll., 1972-74; BA with honors in psychology, U. Pa., 1976, MS, 1977, PhD, 1981. Diplomate Am. Bd. Med. Psychotherapists, Am. Bd. Forensic Examiners (chmn. subcom. on psychotherapy splty. 1997, mem. subcom. on neuropsychology splty. 1997), Am. Acad. Experts in Traumatic Stress; cert. Nat. Bd. Cert. Clin. Hypnotherapists, APA Coll. Profl Psychology in Treatment of Alcohol and Psychoactic Substance Use; lic. psychologist, N.J., Pa., Md.; cert. sch. psychologist, N.J., Pa., Del., Md.; mem. Nat. Register Health Svc. Providers in Psychology. Doctoral intern Towson (Md.) State U. Counseling Ctr., 1979-80; counseling psychologist U. Md., Balt., 1980-84; sch. psychologist Lawrence Pub. Schs., Lawrenceville, N.J., 1984-85, Mercer County Non-Pub. Schs., Hamilton Square, N.J., 1985; pvt. practice psychology Morrisville, Pa. and Lawrenceville, N.J., 1985—; dir. RSM Psychology Ctr., Lawrenceville, 1995—; lectr. U. Pa., Phila., 1985-87; staff psychologist Helene Fuld Med. Ctr., Trenton, N.J., 1986—, St.

Francis Med. Ctr., Trenton, 1990—; mem. cmty. faculty Trenton Psychiat. Hosp., 1989-90; mem. adj. faculty Widener U., 1992-94; various TV appearances. Contbr. articles on psychology in profl. jours. Mem. Mercer County Med. Soc. Aux., N.J., 1987—, pres., 1990-91. Act-Discover grantee, 1986-87, ACA profl. enhancement rsch. grantee, 1986-87. Fellow Pa. Psychology Assn.; mem. APA, N.J. Psychology Assn. (co-chmn. task force on neuropsychology 1997), N.J. Acad. Psychology (Psychologist Recognition award 1987-95), Ea. Psychol. Assn., Am. Assn. for Counseling and Devel. (project dir., grant recipient, 1987-88), Am. Soc. Clin. Hypnosis, Nat. Acad. Neuropsychology, N.J. Neuropsychology Soc. (membership chair 1997, bd. trustee 1996-97), Phila. Neuropsychology Soc., Mercer County Psychol. Assn. (sec. 1996-97), Phi Delta Kappa. Office: 3131 Princeton Pike Ste 5 Lawrenceville NJ 08648-2201

MOSER, ROYCE, JR., physician, medical educator; b. Versailles, Mo., Aug. 21, 1935; s. Royce and Russie Frances (Stringer) M.; m. Lois Anne Hunter, June 14, 1958; children: Beth Anne Moser McLean, Donald Royce. BA, Harvard U., 1957, MD, 1961; MPH, Harvard Sch. Pub. Health, Boston, 1965. Diplomate Am. Bd. Preventive Medicine (trustee), Am. Bd. Family Practice. Commd. officer USAF, 1962, advanced through grades to col., 1974; resident in aerospace medicine USAF Sch. Aerospace Medicine, Brooks AFB, Tex., 1965-67; chief aerospace medicine Aerospace Def. Command, Colorado Springs, Colo., 1967-70; comdr. 35th USAF Dispensary Phan Rang, Vietnam, 1970-71; chief aerospace medicine br. USAF Sch. Aerospace Medicine, Brooks AFB, 1971-77; comdr. USAF Hosp., Tyndall AFB, Fla., 1977-79; chief clin. scis. div. USAF Sch. Aerospace Medicine, Brooks AFB, 1979-81, chief edn. div., 1981-83, sch. comdr., 1983-85; ret., 1985; prof. dept. family and preventive medicine U. Utah Sch. Medicine, Salt Lake City, 1985—, vice chmn. dept., 1985-95; dir. Rocky Mountain Ctr. for Occupl. and Environ. Health, Salt Lake City, 1987—; cons. in occupational, environ. and aerospace medicine, Salt Lake City, 1985—; presenter nat. and internat. med. meetings. Author: Effective Management of Occupational and Environmental Health and Safety Programs, 1992; contbr. book chpts. and articles to profl. jours. Mem., past pres. 1st Bapt. Ch. Found., Salt Lake City, 1987-89; mem., chmn. numerous univ. coms., Salt Lake City, 1985—; bd. dirs. Hanford Environ. Health Found., 1990-92; mem. preventive medicine residency rev. com. Accreditation Coun. Grad. Med. Edn., 1991-97; mem. ednl. adv. bd. USAF Human Sys. Ctr., 1991-96; chmn. long-range planning com. Am. Bd. Preventive Medicine, 1992-95. Decorated Legion of Merit (2). Fellow Aerospace Med. Assn. (pres. 1989-90, chair fellows group 1994—, Harry G. Mosely award 1981, Theodore C. Lyster award 1988), Am. Coll. Preventive Medicine (regent 1981-82), Am. Coll. Occupl. and Environ. Medicine (v.p. med. affairs 1995-97, Robert A. Kehoe award 1996), Am. Acad. Family Physicians; mem. Internat. Acad. Aviation and Space Medicine (selector 1989-94, chancellor 1994—), Soc. of USAF Flight Surgeons (pres. 1978-79, George E. Schafer award 1982), Phi Beta Kappa. Avocations: photography, fishing. Home: 664 Aloha Rd Salt Lake City UT 84103-3329 Office: Dept Family & Preventive Med 50 N Medical Dr Salt Lake City UT 84132-0001

MOSER, WILLIAM OSCAR JULES, mathematics educator; b. Winnipeg, Can., Sept. 5, 1927; s. Robert and Laura (Fenson) M.; m. Beryl Rita Pearlman, Sept. 2, 1953; children—Marla, Lionel, Paula. B.Sc., U. Man., 1949; M.A., U. Minn., 1951; Ph.D., U. Toronto, 1957. Lectr. U. Sask., 1955-57, asst. prof., 1957-59; asso. prof. U. Man., 1959-64; asso. prof. McGill U., 1964-66, prof., 1966—. Author: (with H.S.M. Coxeter) Generators and Relations for Discrete Groups, 1957, 4th edit., 1980, (with E. Barbeau, M. Klamkin) 500 Mathematical Challenges, 1995; also research papers.; Editor: Can. Math. Bull, 1962-70, Can. Jour. Math., 1982-85. NRC fellow, 1951-53; Can. Council leave fellow, 1971. Mem. Am. Math. Soc., Can. Math. Soc. (pres. 1975-77), Math. Assn. Am. Office: McGill U Dept Math, 805 Sherbrooke St W, Montreal, PQ Canada H3A 2K6

MOSES, ABE JOSEPH, international financial consultant; b. Springfield, Mass., July 15, 1931; s. Mohammed Mustapha and Fatima (Merriam) M.; m. Donna C. Moses (dec.); children: James Douglas, John C., Peter J. BA, Amherst Coll., 1955; MA in Internat. Affairs, Johns Hopkins U., 1957. Legis. aide Sen. J.F. Kennedy, 1955-57; fgn. service officer Dept. State, 1960-65; v.p., gen. mgr. Libyan Desert Oil Co., Texfel Petroleum Corp., Tripoli, Libya, 1965-67; v.p. adminstrn., fin. Occidental Petroleum Corp., Libya, 1967-70; v.p. fin., dir. Northrop Corp., 1970-74; chmn. Transworld Trade Ltd., Washington, 1971—; v.p., mng. dir. world adv. group Chase Manhattan Bank, 1974-80; pres. Berkshire Properties, 1976-95, Grolier Internat., Inc., Danbury, Conn., 1980-82; chief exec. officer, dir. Galadari Bros., Dubai, United Arab Emirates, 1982-86; internat. bus. and fin. cons. Traxol, Dubai, 1986—; fin. cons. Govt. Costa Rica, 1986-89; chmn. Aviation Sys. Corp., Arlington, Va., 1974, Dillon Internat., Akron, Ohio, 1986—; mng. dir. Sheraton Suites Akron, Cuyahoga Falls, Ohio, 1990—; owner's rep. Monarch Sheraton Hotel, Springfield, Mass., 1993-95; bd. dirs., v.p. Morgan Freeport Co., Hudson, Ohio; bd. dirs. Seeds of Peace, Washington; gen. ptnr. BPM Ltd. Partnership, 1995—. Pres., bd. dirs. Riverside Comty. Urban Redevel. Corp.; mem. exec. com., bd. dirs. Near East Found., N.Y.C., 1978—; pres. Riverfront Ctr. Assn., Cuyahoga Falls, 1992-95. Capt. USAF, 1957-60. Ford Found. fellow Johns Hopkins U., 1955, Barr Found. fellow, 1955-57. Mem. Mid. East Inst. Democrat. Home: 15 Bagburn Rd Monroe CT 06468-1432 Office: Riverside CURC 1989 Front St Cuyahoga Falls OH 44221-3811

MOSES, ALFRED HENRY, lawyer; b. Balt., July 24, 1929; s. Leslie William and Helene Amelia (Lobe) M.; m. Carol Whitehill, Nov. 24, 1955; Barbara, Jennifer, David, Amalie. BA, Dartmouth, 1951; postgrad., Woodrow Wilson Sch., Princeton U., 1951-52; JD, Georgetown U., 1956. Bar: D.C. 1956. Assoc. Covington & Burling, Washington, 1956-65, ptnr., 1965-94; spl. advisor, spl. counsel Pres. Jimmy Carter, Washington, 1980-81; amb. to Romania U.S. Embassy, Bucharest, 1994—; legal advisor minority rights Dem. Nat. Com., Washington, 1969, DC Commision on Urban Renewal, 1972; lectr. Am. Law Inst., ABA, New Orleans, 1970, Am. Inst. CPAs, ABA, Washington, 1969, Georgetown U. Law Ctr., 1971, Tax Exec. Inst., Washington, 1967-68, Tulane Tax Inst., New Orleans, 1971; commr. Pub. Housing, Fairfax County, Va., 1971-72. Contbr. articles, commentaries to internat. jours. and press. Co-chmn. legal div. United Givers Fund, Washington, 1975-76; mem. Coun. Fgn. Rels., N.Y.C., 1977—; bd. dirs. Paralysis Cure Rsch. Found., 1978-81; trustee Phelps Stokes Fund, N.Y.C., 1978-84; pres. Nat. Children's Island, Washington, 1975-76; pres. Golda Meir Assn., 1986-88, nat. chmn., 1988-93; trustee Jewish Publ. Soc., 1989-94, Haifa U., 1988-90; pres. Am. Jewish Com., 1991-94; mem. bd. regents Georgetown U., 1986-92. Mem. ABA, D.C. Bar Assn., Met. Club. Democrat. Jewish. Home: PO Box 7566 Washington DC 20044 Office: Am Embassy, Bucharest Romania

MOSES, DANIEL DAVID, civil engineer; b. Courtois, Mo., May 28, 1949; s. Jewell Artie and Genevieve Alice (Wilson) M.; married, 1970 (div. 1984); 1 child, Daniel David Jr.; m. Delores Clara Leslie, June 29, 1985; 1 child, Christopher Daniel. AAS, Mineral Area Coll., Flat River, Mo., 1969. Registered profl. engr., Mo., Ill. Highway designer Mo. Highway and Transp. Dept., Kirkwood, 1969-79; civil engr. Harland Bartholomew & Assoc., St. Louis, 1979-83; sr. project engr. Booker Assoc., Inc., St. Louis, 1983-94, v.p., Ill. divsn. mgr., sr. project engr., 1994-96; pres. Booker Assoc., Inc. of Ill., Fairview Heights, 1996—. Bd. dirs. Nat. Kidney Found., St. Louis, 1994—, Leadership Coun. of Southwestern Ill., 1997—; active Belleville (Ill.) Econ. Progress, 1993—. Mem. NSPE, Am. Pub. Works Assn., Soc. Am. Mil. Engrs. (1st v.p., pres. 1990-95, bd. dirs. 1995—). Presbyterian. Avocation: pedal steel guitar. Home: 1349 Summerpoint Ln Fenton MO 63026-6928 Office: Booker Assoc Inc 6701 N Illinois St Fairview Heights IL 62208-2019

MOSES, EDWARD CROSBY, artist; b. Long Beach, Calif.; s. Alfonsus Lemuel and Olivia (Branco) M.; m. Avilda Peters, Aug. 11, 1959; children: Cedd, Andrew. BA, U. Calif., Long Beach, 1954, MA, 1956. lectr. painting, drawing UCLA, 1961, 75-76, U. Calif., Irvine, 1968-72, Bakersfield Coll., Calif., 1977; guest lectr. Oberlin Coll., Wichita Art Mus., Cranbrook Inst. Numerous one-man shows, 1958—, latest include Andre Emmerich Gallery, N.Y.C., 1974-75, L.A. County Mus. Art, 1976, Tex. Gallery, Houston, 1979, High Mus. Art, Atlanta, 1980, Janus Gallery, L.A., 1982, Dorothy Rosenthal Gallery, Chgo., 1982—, L.A. Louver Gallery, Venice, 1985—, Louver Gallery, N.Y.C., 1989-93, Galerie Georges Lavrov, Paris, Mus. Contemporary Art, L.A.; exhibited numerous group shows, 1958—, latest include Corcoran Gallery Art, Washington, 1979, High Mus., 1980, San Francisco Mus., 1980, San Francisco Art Inst., 1981, Mus. Modern Art, Paris, 1982, L.A. Mcpl. Gallery, 1982, Mus. Contemporary Art, L.A., 1983, 86, Nat. Gallery Art, Washington, 1984, Nat. Gallery of Modern Art, 1988, Smithsonian Instn., 1986, Galerie Koltontorvet, Copenhagen, Mus. Contemporary Art, L.A., 1986, Whitney Mus., 1991; represented in permanent collections U. Calif. Art Mus., Berkeley, Seattle Art Mus., San Francisco Art Mus., Mus. Modern Art, N.Y.C., San Francisco Art Inst., Chgo. Art Inst., Hirshhorn Mus., Phila., Akron Art Inst., Ohio, Harvard U., Cambridge, Mass., Yale U., New Haven, Walker Art Mus., Mpls., Corcoran Gallery Art, Whitney Mus. Am. Art, N.Y.C., Mus. Modern Art., N.Y.C., Los Angeles County Mus. Art, Nat. Mus. Am. Art at Smithsonian Inst., Washington, Phila. Mus. Art. Served with USN, 1944-46. Recipient Tamarind fellowship in lithography, 1968, Art in Pub. Places award Calif. Arts Coun., 1987; NEA grantee, 1976; Guggenheim fellow, 1980.

MOSES, EDWIN, former track and field athlete; b. Dayton, Ohio, 1955; m. Myrella Moses. Student, Morehouse Coll. Fin. cons. Robinson-Humphrey Co., Atlanta. Olympian hurdler; Worlds Top Ranked Intermediate Hurdler, 1976—. Chmn. USOC Substance Abuse Com., 1989—. Holder world record 400 meter hurdle; Olympic gold medalist, 1976, 84; 1st U.S. athlete to be voted delegate to Internat. Amateur Athletic Fedn.; named Sportsman of the Yr. U.S. Olympic Com.; named to U.S. Track & Field Hall of Fame, 1994. Mem. Internat. Amateur Athletics Assn. (pres.), U.S. Olympic Com. (exec. com.). Office: Robinson-Humphrey Co 3333 Peachtree Rd NE Atlanta GA 30326*

MOSES, ELBERT RAYMOND, JR., speech and dramatic arts educator; b. New Concord, Ohio, Mar. 31, 1908; s. Elbert Raymond Sr. and Helen Martha (Miller) M.; m. Mary Miller Sterrett, Sept. 21, 1933 (dec. Sept. 1984); 1 child, James Elbert (dec.); m. Caroline Mae Entenman, June 19, 1985. AB, U. Pitts., 1932; MS, U. Mich., 1934, PhD, 1936. Instr. U. N.C., Greensboro, 1936-38; asst. prof. Ohio State U., Columbus, 1938-46; assoc. prof. Ea. Ill. State U., Charleston, 1946-56; asst. prof. Mich. State U., E. Lansing, Mich., 1956-59; prof. Clarion (Pa.) State Coll., 1959-71, chmn. dept. speech and dramatic arts, 1959—, emeritus prof., 1971—; Fulbright lectr. State Dept. U.S. Cebu Normal Sch., Cebu City, Philippine Islands, 1955-56; vis. prof. phonetics U. Mo., summer 1968; hon. sec.'s advocate dept. of aging State of Pa., Harrisburg, 1980-81. Author: Guide to Effective Speaking, 1957, Phonetics: A History and Interpretation, 1964, Three Attributes of God, 1983, Adventure in Reasoning, 1988, Beating the Odds, 1992, In Pursuit of Life, 1996; poems included in Best Poems of the 90s, 1992, in two web pages; contbr. articles to profl. jours.. Del. 3d World Congress Phoneticians, Tokyo, 1976; mem. nat. adv. com. fng. students and tchrs. HEW; del. to Internat. Congress Soc. Logopedics and Phoniatre, Vienna, 1965; liaison rep. to Peace Corps; pres. County Libr. Bd.; past exec. dir. Clarion County United Way; commr. Boy Scouts Am., 1976-77; pres. Venango County Adv. Coun. for Aging, 1978-79. Maj. AUS, 1942-46, lt. col. AUS, ret. Recipient Ret. Sr. Vol. Program Vol. of Yr. award No. Ariz. Coun. Govts., 1989, Spl. award Speech Comm. Assn., 1989, Endowment Benefactor award, 1991; 6 Diamong Pin of Melvin Jones Found., Internat. Lions, Best Male Songwriter, Poet of Yr. awards Entertainer Network Nashville, 1994, Lifetime Achievement in Entertainer-Indi-Assn. as Most Consistent Golden Poet of Nashville, 1995, EIA Platinum Poet, 1995, 96, Best Legendary Poet, 1996; named to Internat. Poetry Hall of Fame. Fellow United Writers Assn.; mem. Ariz. Comm. Support System, Quarter Century Wireless Assn., Soc. Wireless Pioneers, Mil. Affiliate Radio System, Hospitalier Order of St. John of Jerusalem, Knights Hospitalier, Knightly and Mil. Order of St. Eugene of Trebizond (chevalier), Soverign and Mil. Order of St. Stephen the Matyr (comdr.), Knightly Assn. of St. George the Matyr, Ordre Chevaliers du Sinai, Hist. File, VFW (comdr.), Am. Legion (comdr.), Rotary (pres. 1966-67, dist. gov. 1973-74), Order of White Shrine of Jerusalem, Niadh Nask (Marshall of Kilbonane), Internat. Chivalric Inst., Confedn. of Chivalry (life, mem. grand coun.), Ordre Souverain et Militaire de la Milice du Saint Sepulcre (chevalier grand cross), Sovereign World Order of White Cross (lord of knights, dist. commdr. Ariz.), Prescott High Twelve Club (pres. 1990), Morse Telegraph Club, Inc., 21st Century Club (charter), The Old Old Timers Club, Phi Delta Kappa (Svc. Key 1978). Republican. Methodist. Avocation: ham radio. Home: 2001 Rocky Dells Dr Prescott AZ 86303-5685

MOSES, FRANKLIN MAXWELL, retired chemical marketing executive; b. Kansas, Ohio, Oct. 17, 1918; s. Otto Franklin and Edith Mary (Diller) M.; m. Elizabeth Fleming, Feb. 27, 1948; children: Steven F., Gregory F., Christopher R. (dec.), Elizabeth Ann. B.S., Ohio State U., 1941; postgrad., U. Pitts., 1941-42. Indsl. engr. U.S. Steel Corp., Pitts., 1941-42; pilot Pan Am. World Airways, San Francisco, 1946-53; exec. v.p. Wilson & Geo Meyer & Co., South San Francisco, Calif., 1954-84; pvt. practice mktg. cons. Portola Valley, CA, 1984-94; ret., 1994; dir. Portola Ranch Assn., WGM Hydro, San Francisco. Served to capt. USMCR, 1942-46. Decorated with two Distinguished Flying Crosses, seven Air Medals. Mem. Calif. Acad. Scis., Marine Corps Aviation Soc., Assn. Naval Aviation, Tailhook Assn., Calif. Hist. Soc., Am. Inst. Wine and Food, Disting. Flying Cross Soc., Ohio State U. Alumni Assn. (life), St. Francis Yacht Club (San Francisco), California Club (L.A.), Portola Valley Polo Club, Portola Club (founder), Los Altos Hunt Club, World Trade Club, Family Club, Shack Riders, Frontier Boys, Marines Meml. Club (San Francisco). Republican. Episcopalian. Home: 4 Coalmine Vw Portola Vally CA 94028-8016 *To be responsible - responsible to family, friends, country, work-place and to one's self. Offering the best you can all of the time.*

MOSES, HAMILTON, III, neurology educator, hospital executive, management consultant; b. Chgo., Apr. 29, 1950; s. Hamilton Jr. and Betty Anne (Theurer) M.; m. Elizabeth Lawrence Hormel, 1977 (dec. 1988); m. Alexandra McCullough Gibson, 1992. BA in Psychology, U. Pa., 1972; MD, Rush Med. Coll., Chgo., 1975. Clk. Nat. Hosp. for Nervous Diseases, London, 1974; intern in medicine Johns Hopkins Hosp., Balt., 1976-77, resident in neurology, 1977-79, chief resident, 1979-80, assoc. prof. neurology, 1986-94, vice chmn. neurology and neurosurgery, 1980-86, v.p., 1988-94, dir. Parkinson's Ctr., 1984-94; dir. neurol. inst., prof. neurology and neurosurgery and mgmt. U. Va., Charlottesville, 1994-97; sr. advisor Boston Cons. Group, 1995—; prof. Darden Sch. Bus. U. Va., Charlottesville, 1994—; founder several tech. bus. Editor, major author: Principles of Medicine, 1985-96; editor newsletter Johns Hopkins Health, 1988—; contbr. numerous articles to med. jours. Mem. com. on med. ministries Episcopal Diocese Md., Balt., 1987; bd. dirs. Valleys Planning Ct.; trustee McLean Hosp., Belmont, Mass., 1997—. Mem. Am. Acad. Neurology (sec. 1989-91), Am. Neurol. Assn., Md. Neurol. Soc. (pres. 1984-86), Movement Disorders Soc., Md. Club, Green Spring Valley Hunt Club (Garrison, Md.). Republican. Avocations: landscape photography, sailing. Office: PO Box 150 North Garden VA 22959-0150

MOSES, IRVING BYRON, architect; b. Chgo., Aug. 5, 1925; s. Morris and Dorothy (Berns) M.; m. Toby June Kornfeld, June 29, 1947; children: Barbara Moses Tarr, Jack Robert, Carol Lynn. BS in Architecture Design, U. Ill., 1950. Time, motion and material research Small Homes Council of Ill., 1947-48; archtl. designer Holsman, Holsman, Klekamp & Taylor, Chgo., 1950-51; architect, ptnr. Comm, Comm & Moses, AIA, Chgo., 1951-62; prin. I. Moses Assocs., AIA, Chgo., 1962-78, Moses Assocs., AIA, Chgo., 1978—; cons. architect A. Epstein & Sons, Chgo., 1974-75, Globe Engring. Co., Chgo., 1975-77, Slip & Fall Litigation, 1980—; judge, arbitrator, Am. Arbitration Assn., 1976—. Author: Chicago School Architecture, 1982, Doors, 1984. Chmn. Appearance Review Commn., Highland Park, Ill., 1976-86; commr. Zoning Bd. Appeals, Highland Park, 1987—. Served with USN, 1943-46. Mem. AIA (chmn. membership commn. 1984-86, Bldg. award, 1965, 70, 75, 85), Am. Registered Architects, Ill. Soc. Architects. Club: Cliffdwellers (Chgo.). Avocations: art, running. Home: 145 Blackhawk Rd Highland Park IL 60035-5266 Office: Moses Assocs AIA 225 W Ohio St Chicago IL 60610-4198

MOSES, JEFFREY MICHAEL, customer services executive; b. Nov. 16, 1945; s. George John and Mildred (Kronz) M.; m. Barbrae Danowsky, Apr. 24, 1976; children: Apryl Richelle, Heather Lorien. AA, Eckel's Coll., Phila. Sales supr. Internat. Tariff Svcs., Inc., Washington, 1970-71; transp. analyst to mgr. of tariff pub. Charles Donley & Assocs., Pitts., 1973-81; transp. mgr. Texas Aromatics, Houston, 1981-83; dir. customer svcs. ChemCoast, Inc., LaPorte, Tex., 1983-91, v.p., 1991-96; dir. svcs. United Surveyors of Chems.; pres. Compliance Packaging & Svcs., 1996—; dir. of svcs. United Surveyors of Chems., Inc., 1997; mem. adv. bd. Tex. Workers' Compensation Ins. Fund; dir. svcs. USC, Baytown. Mem. Internat. Hazardous Materials Inst. (chmn. bd. 1993, 94, cert. master transp. specialist), Am. Assn. Inspection and Lab. Cos. (chmn.).

MOSES, JOEL, computer scientist, educator; b. Petach Tikvah, Israel, Nov. 25, 1941; came to U.S., 1954, naturalized, 1960; s. Bernhard and Golda (Losner) M.; m. Margaret A. Garvey, Dec. 27, 1970; children: Jesse, David. B.A., Columbia U., 1962, M.A., 1963; Ph.D., M.I.T., 1967. Asst. prof. dept. elec. engring. and computer sci. M.I.T., 1967-71, assoc. prof., 1971-77, prof., 1977—, assoc. dir. Lab for Computer Sci., 1974-78, assoc. head computer sci. and engring., dept. elec. engring. and computer sci., 1978-81, head dept., 1981-89, D.C. Jackson prof., 1989—, dean Sch. Engring., 1991-95, provost, 1995—; vis. prof. Harvard Grad. Sch. Bus. Adminstrn., 1989-90; bd. dirs. Analog Devices, Inc., Coltec Industries Inc. Editor: The Computer Age: A Twenty Year View, 1979. Bd. dirs. Woods Hole Oceanog. Instn. Recipient Achievement award MIT Lab. for Computer Sci., 1985. Fellow IEEE, AAAS, Am. Acad. Arts and Scis.; mem. NAE, Assn. for Computing Machinery, Am. Soc. Engring. Edn. (Centennial Cert.). Office: MIT Dept Electrical Engring 3-208 Cambridge MA 02139

MOSES, LINCOLN E., statistician, educator; b. Kansas City, Mo., Dec. 21, 1921; s. Edward Walter and Virginia (Holmes) M.; m. Jean Runnels, Dec. 26, 1942; children—Katherine, James O'D., William C., Margaret, Elizabeth; m. Mary Louise Coale, 1968. A.B., Stanford, 1941, Ph.D., 1950. Asst. prof. edn. Columbia Tchrs. Coll., 1950-52; faculty Stanford U., 1952—, prof. stats., 1959—, exec. head dept., 1964-68; assoc. dean Stanford U. (Sch. Humanities and Scis.), 1965-68, 85-86, dean grad. studies, 1969-75; faculty Stanford U. (Med. Sch.), 1952—; adminstr. Energy Info. Adminstrn., Dept. of Energy, 1978-80; L.L. Thurstone disting. fellow U. N.C., 1968-69; com. mem. Am. Friends Svc. Com., intermittently 1954—, chmn. No. Calif. chpt., 1972-76, 84-88. Guggenheim fellow, 1960-61; fellow Ctr. for Advanced Study in Behavioral Scis., 1975. Fellow Am. Acad. Arts and Scis., Inst. Math. Statistics (council 1969-72); mem. Inst. of Medicine of Nat. Acad. Scis., Am. Stats. Assn. (council 1966-67), Biometric Soc. (pres. Western N. Am. region 1969), Internat. Statis. Inst. Office: Stanford U Med Ctr Divsn Biostats Stanford CA 94305

MOSES, MIKE, commissioner. Commr. Tex. Dept. Edn., Austin. Office: Office of Commr Tex Dept Edn 1701 Congress Ave Austin TX 78701-1402*

MOSES, RAPHAEL JACOB, lawyer; b. Girard, Ala., Nov. 6, 1913; s. William Moultrie and Anna (Green) M.; m. Marian Eva Beck, Aug. 22, 1938 (dec. Feb. 1976); 1 child, Marcia (Mrs. William S. Johnson); m. Fletcher Lee Westgaard, Jan. 20, 1979. A.B., U. Colo., 1935, J.D., 1937. Bar: Colo. 1938. Practiced in Alamosa, 1938-62, Boulder, 1962—; pres. Moses, Wittemyer, Harrison & Woodruff (P.C.), from 1970, now of counsel; spl. asst. atty. gen. Rio Grande Compact, 1957-58; mem. Colo. Water Conservation Bd., 1952-58, chmn., counsel, 1958-76, cons., 1976-77; research asso., faculty law U. Colo., 1962-66, vis. lectr., 1966-76, resident counsel, 1964-66, regent, 1973-74; grad. faculty Colo. State U., 1963-67; mem. Western States Water Council, 1965-77, chmn., 1966-70. Trustee Rocky Mountain Mineral Law Inst., 1964-66; bd. dirs. U. Colo. Found., 1977-97, chmn., 1977-79, mem. chancellor's adv. coun., 1981-97; bd. dirs. Colo. Open Lands, 1983-91, U. Colo. Improvement Corp., 1980-90, Colo. Endowment for Humanities, 1986-89; mem. adv. bd. Natural Resources Ctr., U. Colo. Sch. Law, 1983-92, chmn., 1986-88. Served to lt. (s.g.) USNR, 1942-45. Recipient William E. Knous award U. Colo. Sch. Law, 1971, Norlin award U. Colo., 1972; Raphael J. Moses Disting. Natural Resources professorship established U. Colo., 1994. Fellow Am. Bar Found. (life), Colo. Bar Found. (trustee 1977-90), Am. Coll. Trial Lawyers; mem. ABA (chmn. water rights com. sect. natural resources 1959-60), Colo. Bar Assn. (pres. 1959-60, Award of Merit 1972), San Luis Valley Bar Assn. (pres. 1942), Am. Counsel Assn., Order of Coif (hon.). Presbyterian (elder). Clubs: Univ. (Denver); Boulder Country; Garden of the Gods (Colorado Springs). Home: 7060 Roaring Fork Trl Boulder CO 80301-3635

MOSES, ROBERT EDWARD, lawyer; b. Syracuse, N.Y., Feb. 23, 1936; s. Robert Henry and Kathryn Anne (Schoeneck) M.; m. Virginia Joan Speno, July 23, 1970; children: Robert, Kathryn, Hope, Frank. Student, U. Fribourg, Switzerland, 1957; BS, Georgetown U., 1958, JD, 1960. Bar: N.Y. 1961, U.S. Ct. Appeals (2d cir.) 1966, U.S. Supreme Ct. 1967. Assoc. Bond, Schoeneck & King, Syracuse, 1960-70, mem., 1970-74, ptnr., 1974—. Bd. dirs. George Jr. Republic Assn., Inc., Freeville, N.Y., 1976-88; bd. govs. Georgetown U., Washington, 1983-89; bd. regents LeMoyne Coll., Syracuse, 1985—; mem. adv. bd., spl. counsel Nat. Sports Acad., Lake Placid, N.Y., 1990-93; bd. dirs. N.Y. State Regional Econ. Devel. Lt. (j.g.) USCG, 1961-66. Mem. ABA, N.Y. State Bar Assn. (chmn. young lawyers sect. 1971-72, mem. exec. com. 1971-72, ho. of dels. 1972-75), Onondaga County Bar Assn., Onondaga County Bar Found. (bd. dirs. 1978—, pres. 1988-89), Am. Judicature Soc., Am. Arbitration Assn. (panel arbitrators 1969—), N.Y. State Econ. Devel. Coun. (mem. state legis. com. 1983—, chmn. 1983), Ft. Orange Club, Skaneateles Country Club. Republican. Roman Catholic. Home: Otisco Lake West Lake Rd Marietta NY 13110 Office: Bond Schoeneck & King LLP Fl 18 1 Lincoln Ctr Fl 18 Syracuse NY 13202-1324

MOSES, RONALD ELLIOT, retired toiletries products executive; b. Chelsea, Mass., Dec. 29, 1930; s. Isadore Philip and Ida (Finstein) M.; m. Eleanor Antoinette Vitale, June 22, 1952; children: Judith Jeanne, Thomas Charles. AB, Harvard U., 1952; MS in Chemistry, Northeastern U., Boston, 1959. Chemist Gen. Foods Corp., Woburn, Mass., 1954-60; sr. chemist Gillette Safety Razor Co., Boston, 1960-65, project chemist toiletries div., 1965-70, sr. mgr. rsch. toiletries div., 1970-73, dir. product devel. toiletries div., 1973-78, dir. product devel. personal care div., 1978-83, v.p. R&D personal care div., 1983-87; v.p. R&D personal care group Gillette North Atlantic, Boston, 1987-90, dir. R&D shaving and personal care group, 1990-91, v.p. R & D Toiletries Techs. Lab., 1991-93. Co-patentee gelatin fining and preparation, shaving product composition, hair conditioning composition. Lt. (j.g.) USN, 1952. Fellow Am. Inst. Chemists; mem. Am. Chem. Soc., Soc. Cosmetic Chemists, Winthrop Golf Club. Jewish. Avocations: classical music, reading, golf, model ships, computer programming. Home: 1039 Shirley St Winthrop MA 02152-1442

MOSES, WINFIELD C., JR., state legislator, construction company executive; b. Ft. Wayne, Ind., Feb. 20, 1943; s. Winfield C. and Helen A. (O'Neil) M.; children: Elizabeth, Christopher. AB in Econs, Ind. U., 1964, MBA in Fin, 1966. Apt. builder Ft. Wayne, 1966—; mem. Ft. Wayne City Coun., 1972-79; mayor City of Ft. Wayne, 1980-87; mem. Ind. Ho. of Reps., Indpls., 1992—. Founding pres. Washington House, 1973-76, Citizen Energy Coalition, 1974-75; active Art Mus.; mem. Ind. Urban Enterprise Zone Bd., Ind. Bus. Modernization Bd. Mem. C. of C., Rotary. Democrat. Unitarian. Office: 6000 N Oak Blvd Fort Wayne IN 46818-2438

MOSES-FOLEY, JUDITH ANN, special education educator; b. Steubenville, Ohio, Sept. 1, 1936; d. Joseph and Katherine Ann (Pavich) Moses; m. John P. Foley, 1958 (div. 1986); children: Katherine Ann Foley, John Joseph Foley, Sean Michael Foley, Judith Kristina Foley; m. John H. Murphy, 1986 (dec. 1992). BS in Edn., Ohio U., 1958; MA in Ednl. Adminstrn., Fresno Pacific U., 1981; postgrad., Brigham Young U., 1982-84, U. San Francisco, 1985-86, U. N.Mex., 1993-94. Cert. in adminstrn., Calif.; tchr., N.Mex., Ohio; spl. edn., bilingual/TESOL, and as transition resource specialist, N.Mex. Adminstr., tchr. health and social sci., coach Madera (Calif.) Unified Schs., 1958-81; chair dept. phys. edn. Dos Palos (Calif.) H.S., 1963-64; prin. Chowchilla (Calif.) Elem. Schs., 1981-85; instr. phys. edn. Merced (Calif.) C.C., 1981-85; supt., prin. St. Luke's Sch., Merced, 1985-86; instr. polit. sci. and bus. adminstrn. West Hills C.C., Lemore, Calif., 1985-86; instr. phys. edn. Mohave C.C., Kingman, Ariz., 1989-90; transition resource specialist Silver Consol. Sch., Silver City, N.Mex., 1993—; adj. prof. early childhood edn. Western N.Mex. U., Silver City; spl. edn. resource specialist Silver H.S., Silver City, 1990—, coach U.S. acad. decathlon, 1991—; grant writer Circle of Life, 1994—; coord., grant writer R.E: Learning; mem. North Ctrl. Accreditation Steering Com., 1992-95; v.p. divsn. transition and curriculum devel. State of N.Mex., sch. to work grant writer, 1997—; mem. N.Mex. State Bd. com. U.S. Acad. Decathlon,

1993—; developer lang. arts, social studies transition curriculum 9-12 Silver Consolidated Schs., N.Mex. Pres. Bobby Sox Softball League, Madera, 1975-78; head coach track and field Jr. Olympics, Madera County, 1970-81; coord. Gathering of War Birds Airshow, Madera, 1976-79. Recipient Master Tchr. award Calif. State U., Fresno, 1978-79; recipient scholarships and grants. Mem. AAHPER, AAUW, Am. Assn. Ret. Persons, Coun. for Exceptional Children. Mem. ASCD. Avocations: flying, jewelry design, painting, water skiing, fishing. Home: PO Box 2 Buckhorn NM 88025-0002 Office: Silver Consol Schs 3200 N Silver St Silver City NM 88061-7283

MOSETTIG, MICHAEL DAVID, television producer, writer; b. Washington, July 21, 1942; s. Erich and Ann (Nelson) M.; m. Anne L. Groer. Student, Ind. U., 1960-61; BA in Polit. Sci., George Washington U., 1964; MA in European History, Georgetown U., 1968. Reporter Leslie E. Carpenter News Bur., Washington, 1961-65, Newhouse Nat. News Svc., Washington, 1965-69, UPI, London and Brussels, 1969-70; editor, reporter Nat. Jour., Washington, 1970-71; producer NBC News, Washington and N.Y.C., 1971-79; assoc. Grad. Sch. Journalism Columbia U., N.Y.C., 1979-83; prodr. MacNeil/Lehrer News Hour, 1983-85, sr. prodr. fgn. affairs and def., 1985-95; sr. prodr. fgn. affairs and def. New Hour with Jim Lehrer, 1995—; mem. Internat. Inst. for Strategic Studies, London, Coun. Fgn. Rels., N.Y. Author: DeGaulle and His Anglo-Saxon Allies, 1968, (with Ronald Müller) Revitalizing America, 1980. With USCGR, 1966-68, USNR, 1968-78. Herman Lowe Meml. scholar Washington chpt. Sigma Delta Chi; Joan Barone award Radio-TV Corrs. Assn. Mem. Overseas Writers, Cosmos Club. Home: 3340 Northampton St NW Washington DC 20015-1653

MOSHER, DONALD RAYMOND, chemical engineer, consultant; b. Mpls., Jan. 7, 1930; s. Cleveland Bert and Rose (Alkofer) M.; m. Jane Lucille Ryan, June 20, 1954 (div. Dec. 1989); children: Leslie Renee Mosher Goode, Lee David, Laura Ann Mosher Flanders, Jennifer Lynn Mosher Konzen, Jill Teresa, Jody Lavonne; m. Lurlie Elizabeth Amsler, Dec. 19, 1992. BSChemE, U. Minn., 1953, MS, 1954. Prodn. area engr. U.S. Chem. Corps., Edgewood, Md., 1955-57; mng. engr. Union Carbide Corp., South Charleston, W.Va., 1957-68; cons. in new ventures Union Carbide Linde Div., Tanawhonda, N.Y., 1968-69; chief engr. design Hess Oil Corp., Woodbridge, N.J., 1969-70; plant mgr. Stearns Roger Ops., Rapid City, S.D., 1970-72; mgr. engring. sect. Stearns Roger Corp., Denver, 1972-82; mgr. gas process and environ. Allis Chalmers Coal Gas Corp., Milw., 1982-88; cons. Ralston Internat. Trading Assn. Inc., Kingsport, Tenn., 1988—, W.L. Gore, 1994. Author conf. reports; contbr. articles to profl. jours. Chmn. South Hills Community Assn., Charleston, 1967; mem. sponsor's com. So. Ill. U., 1986. With U.S. Army, 1955-57. Univ. and AEC scholar, 1952-54. Mem. Am. Inst. Chem. Engrs. (treas. local sect. 1963), Am. Chem. Soc., Assn. Cons. Chemists and Chem. Engrs. (cons. 1989—), Rotary, Phi Kappa (v.p. 1952-54), Phi Beta Epsilon. Republican. Roman Catholic. Achievements include patent for oxidation of butane; invention of system for conserving energy while cleaning dirty gas, of system for removing oil and tar from water with no discharge. Office: D R Mosher Corp PO Box 6707 Maryville TN 37802

MOSHER, GEORGE ALLAN, distribution company executive; b. Detroit, June 21, 1939; s. Carroll Leonard and Susan (Harris) M.; m. Julie Zaber, Dec. 31, 1966; children: Karen, Holly, Robert. AB, Harvard U., 1961, MBA, 1963. With sales promotion dept. Look mag., 1963-65; pres. Bus. & Instl. Furniture Co., Milw., 1965-75, Nat. Bus. Furniture Co., Milw., 1975—; chmn. Bus. Mailers, 1976; pres. Alfax Mfg. Co., N.Y.C., 1984—, Office Furniture Ctr., Boston, 1986—, Dallas Midwest, 1990—. Bd. dirs. Milw. Pub. Affairs Coun., 1975-84, v.p., 1982-83; bd. dirs. Future Milw., 1979-82, Vol. Ctr., 1988-91, Communique, 1986-90, Nat. Hospitality Supply, 1990—, Milw. Bus. Forum, 1975—, Capital Commerce Bancorp, 1994—, Conney Safety Products, 1995—. Mem. Wis. Direct Mktg. (founder, pres. 1987-88. Marketer of Yr. award 1991), Univ. Club, River Tennis Club (treas. 1983-86), Harvard Bus. Sch. Club (pres. 1973), Rotary, Harvard Club (Milw., N.Y.C.). Home: 4706 N Wilshire Rd Milwaukee WI 53211-1262 Office: 735 N Water St Milwaukee WI 53202-4100

MOSHER, LAWRENCE FORSYTH, journalist; b. L.A., July 12, 1929; s. Jack Marsh and Alice (Forsyth) M.; m. Constance Bauerlein, 1963 (div. 1980); children: Kirsten Louise, Honor Forsyth. BA, Stanford U., 1952; B Fgn. Trade, Am. Grad. Sch. Internat. Mgmt., 1956. Reporter Bergen Record, Hackensack, N.J., 1958-59, N.Y. World-Telegram & Sun, N.Y.C., 1959-62; staff writer, then Beirut bur. chief Copley News Svc., San Diego, 1962-67; staff corr. The Nat. Observer, Silver Spring, Md., 1967-77; staff writer, then contbg. editor Nat. Jour., Washington, 1979-88; editor The Water Reporter, Washington, 1984-90; resident journalist Environ. Health Ctr., Washington, 1988-89; mng. editor Middle East Insight, Washington, 1989-90; editor High Country News, Paonia, Colo., 1990-91; Rocky Mountain corr. The Economist, 1991—; news dir. Sta. KVNF pub. radio Paonia, Colo., 1992-93; mem. Delta County planning commn., 1995—; writer-in-residence Fgn. Svc. Sch. Georgetown U., Washington, 1977-79, Ctr. for Contemporary Arab Studies. Contbr. chpts. to America's Wild and Scenic Rivers, 1983, Bordering on Trouble: Resources and Politics in Latin America, 1986, World Resources, 1987-89. Lt. (j.g.) USNR, 1952-54, Korea. Named Communicator of Yr., Nat. Wildlife Fedn., 1982. Mem. Nat. Press Club, Potomac Rowing Club. Democrat. Avocations: choral music, sailing, sculling, horseback riding, skiing. Home and Office: 323 4200 Dr Crawford CO 81415-9763

MOSHER, SALLY EKENBERG, lawyer; b. N.Y.C., July 26, 1934; d. Leslie Joseph and Frances Josephine (McArdle) Ekenberg; m. James Kimberly Mosher, Aug. 13, 1960 (dec. Aug. 1982). MusB, Manhattanville Coll., 1956; postgrad., Hofstra U., 1958-60, U. So. Calif., 1971-73; JD, U. So. Calif., 1981. Bar: Calif., 1982. Musician, pianist, tchr., 1957-74; music critic Pasadena Star-News, 1967-72; mgr. Contrasts Concerts, Pasadena Art Mus., 1971-72; rep. Occidental Life Ins. Co., Pasadena, 1975-78; v.p. James K. Mosher Co., Pasadena, 1961-82, pres., 1982—; pres. Oakhill Enterprises, Pasadena, 1984—; assoc. White-Howell, Inc., Pasadena, 1984—; real estate broker, 1984—; harpsichordist, lectr., composer, 1994—. Contbr. articles to various publs. Bd. dirs. Jr. League Pasadena, 1966-67, Encounters Concerts, Pasadena, 1966-72, U. So. Calif. Friends of Music, L.A., 1973-76, Calif. Music Theatre, 1988-90, Pasadena Hist. Soc., 1989-91, I Cantori, 1989-91; bd. dirs. Pasadena Arts Coun., 1986-92, pres., 1989-92, chair adv. bd., 1992-93; v.p., bd. dirs. Pasadena Chamber Orch., 1986-88, pres., 1987-88; mem. Calif. 200 Coun. for Bicentennial of U.S. Constn., 1987-90; mem. Endowment Adv. Commn., Pasadena, 1988-90; bd. dirs. Foothill Area Cmty. Svcs., 1990-95, treas., 1991, vice chair, 1992-94, chair, 1994-95. Manhattanville Coll. hon. scholar, 1952-56. Mem. ABA, Calif. Bar Assn., Assocs. of Calif. Inst. Tech., Athenaeum, Kappa Gamma Pi, Mu Phi Epsilon, Phi Alpha Delta. Home: 1260 Rancheros Rd Pasadena CA 91103-2759 Office: 711 E Walnut St Ste 407 Pasadena CA 91101-4403

MOSHER, WENDY JEAN, retail chain official; b. New Bedford, Mass., Feb. 10, 1966; d. Robert Milton and Judith Louise (Rayno) M. Student, Butera Sch. Art, Boston, 1984-85, U. Mass., 1995—. Cashier Sears, Roebuck & Co., North Dartmouth, Mass., 1984-88; sales mgr. trainee Sears, Roebuck & Co., Dedham, Mass., 1988-90, mgr. automotive svc., 1990-91; mgr. automotive ctr. Sears, Roebuck & Co., Concord, N.H., 1991-93, Sears, Roebuck and Co., Nashua, N.H., 1993—; human resource mgr. Sears Roebuck & Co., Taunton, Mass., 1996—. Mem. NAFE, Merchant's Assn. N.H. (bd. dirs.). Home: 21 Lakeside Ave Lakeville MA 02347-2416 Office: Sears Roebuck & Co 8 Galleria Mall Dr Taunton MA 02780-3758

MOSHIER, DAVID IRWIN, church administrator; b. Roanoke, Va., Sept. 14, 1954; s. Emery Irwin (dec.) and Evelyn Mae (Kunkel) M.; m. Bonnie Sharon Dailey, Feb. 13, 1982. STD, Am. Bible Inst., 1991. Ordained to ministry Am. Evang. Christian Chs., 1992, Reformed Presbyn. Ch., 1995. Rsch. asst. mktg. dept. Clarendon Bank & Trust, Arlington, 1974; collection agt., installment loan dept. Clarendon Bank & Trust, Arlington, Va., 1974-75; loan collection officer George Washington U., Washington, 1975-77, sr. loan collection officer, 1977-79; student loan collection coord. Hahnemann Med. Coll. and Hosp., Phila., 1979-80; prin. account clk. George Washington U., Washington, 1980-83; pastor The Wesleyan Ch., Waldorf, Md., 1983-86; asst. pastor Floor Meml. Wesleyan Ch., Arlington, 1986-89; pastor First Wesleyan Ch., Alexandria, Va., 1989-91; dir. govt. rels. Am. Evang. Christian Chs., Alexandria, 1992-93, moderator Mid-Atlantic region, 1992-95, nat. exec. dir., 1993; pastor Fredericksburg (Va.) Area Reformed Presbyn. Mission, 1995; stated clk. Reformed Presbyn. Ch., Hanover, 1996—; coord. Conf. Confessing Presbyn. Chs., 1996; bd. dirs. TransAmericas Transp. Info. Svcs., Inc., Falls Church, Va.; sec. ext. and evangelism Capital Dist. Wesleyan Ch., Great Falls, Va., 1986-88; spl. asst. Office Army Chief of Chaplains, Arlington, 1987-90, cemetery rep. Arlington Nat. Cemetery, 1996—; alumni coun. Flint Hill Sch., Oakton, Va., 1991—; supply pastor Cmty. Ch./Am. Rescue Workers, Capitol Heights, Md., 1992; ch. rels. cons. WABS Radio, Arlington, 1992-94; mem. adv. bd. Covered Bridge Ministries, Morristown, Ind., 1993—, others. Contbr. articles to profl. jours. Officer of election Electoral Bd., Alexandria, 1991-92, Arlington, 1992-93. Recipient Cert. of Commendation, Army Chief of Chaplains, Washington, 1988, 89, 90, Cert. of Civil Svc., Desert Shield-Storm/Hqrs. U.S. Army, Washington, 1992. Mem. George Washington U. Gen. Alumni Assn. Republican. Home: 5928H Coverdale Way Alexandria VA 22310-5412 Office: Arlington Nat Cemetery Arlington VA 22211-5003

MOSHIER, MARY BALUK, patent lawyer; b. Pitts., Aug. 20, 1905; d. Andrew and Johanna (Hlebasko) Baluk; m. Ross Warren Moshier; children: Thomas, Stephen. BA, U. Ark., 1929; postgrad., U. Chgo., 1945-46; JD, No. Ky. U., 1962. Bar: U.S. Patent Office 1944, Ohio 1962. Tchr. Gary (Ind.) Pub. Schs., 1930-35; tech. libr. Monsanto Co., Dayton, Ohio, 1936-41, patent chemist, 1942-45, agt., atty., 1949-66; patent adviser U.S. Office of Naval Rsch., San Francisco, 1948-49; patents cons., pvt. practice, 1969—. Co-author: Anydrous Aluminum Chloride in Organic Chemistry, 1941. Mem. AAAS, AAUW, NOW, Lawyers Club of Sun City, Nat. Assn. Ret. Fed. Employees, U.S. Chess Fedn., Phi Alpha Delta Legal Frat. Internat. Democrat. Episcopalian. Avocations: reading, bridge, chess, gardening. Home and Office: 17300 N 88th Ave Apt 238 Peoria AZ 85382-3505

MOSHMAN, JACK, statistical consultant; b. Richmond Hill, N.Y., Aug. 12, 1924; s. Morris and Sadye (Posner) M.; m. Annette Gordon, Aug. 10, 1947; children: Gordon, Marc, Sherri, Ira. BA, NYU, 1946; MA, Columbia U., 1947; PhD, U. Tenn., 1953. Instr. Queens Coll., Flushing, N.Y., 1946-47, U. Tenn., Knoxville, 1947-53; statistician AEC, Oak Ridge, Tenn., 1948-50; sr. statistician Oak Ridge (Tenn.) Nat. Labs., 1950-54; mem. tech. staff Bell Tel. Labs., Murray Hill, N.J., 1954-57; v.p. C-E-I-R Inc., Washington, 1957-66; mng. dir. EBS Mgmt. Cons., Washington, 1966-68; sr. v.p. Leasco Systems & Rsch., Bethesda, Md., 1968-69; pres. Moshman Assocs. Inc., Bethesda, Md., 1970—; adj. prof. Rutgers U., 1963-66; professorial lectr. George Washington U., 1959-62; chmn. Inst. for Safety Analysis, Rockville, Md., 1975-89. Editor: Faith, Hope & Parity, 1967; author Ency. sect. Computers & Politics, 1985, 90, 93; contbr. articles to profl. jours. Trustee Babbage Found., St. Paul, 1983-87. With U.S. Army, 1943-46, ETO. Fellow Am. Statis. Assn. (coun. 1956, 58); mem. Am. Fedn. Info. Processing Soc. Am. (bd. dirs., pres. 1986-87), Assn. for Computing Machinery (sec. 1956-64, v.p 1964), Inst. for Math. Stats., Inst. for Mgmt. Scis., Ops. Rsch. Soc. Am., Biometrics Soc. Avocation: psephology. Office: Moshman Assocs Inc 4340 E West Hwy Bethesda MD 20814-4411

MOSICH, ANELIS NICK, accountant, author, educator, consultant; b. Yugoslavia, Aug. 30, 1928; came to U.S., 1939, naturalized, 1951; s. Dinko and Josephine (Ursich) M.; m. Dorothy V. Rasich, June 15, 1958; children: Lori, Lisa, Jeffrey. BS, UCLA, 1951, MBA, 1953, PhD (fellow), 1963. CPA, Calif. Mem. faculty UCLA, 1955-63, Calif. State U., Northridge, 1963-64; examiner for Calif. State Bd. Accountancy, 1964-70; prof. acctg. U. So. Calif., Los Angeles, 1964-74; William C. Hallett prof. acctg. U. So. Calif., 1974-81, Ernst & Young prof., 1981-90, chmn. acctg. dept., 1970-74, 77-78, prof. emeritus, 1993; cons. various bus. orgns., 1953—; expert witness; bd. dirs. Western Waste Industries; guest speaker various profl. and bus. groups in Calif., Oreg., N.Y., Tex., Fla., and Hawaii, 1963-93. Author: Intermediate Accounting, rev. 6th edit., 1989, Financial Accounting, 1970, 75, Accounting: A Basis for Business Decision, 1972, Modern Advanced Accounting, 4th edit., 1988, The CPA Examination: Text, Problems and Solutions, 1978; editor: Education column Calif. CPA Quar., 1965-66; contbg. editor: Education and Professional Training column Jour. Accountancy, 1971-77; contbr. numerous articles to jours. and acctg. Mem. productivity commn. City of L.A., 1993-94. With U.S. Army, 1953-55. Recipient Dean's award Sch. Bus. Adminstrn., U. So. Calif., 1973, 78, Fred B. Olds Support Group award U. So. Calif., 1994. Mem. AICPA, Calif. Soc. CPAs. Office: U So Calif Sch Acctg University Park Los Angeles CA 90089-1421

MOSIER, ARVIN RAY, chemist, researcher; b. Olney Springs, Colo., June 11, 1945; s. Isaac James Ellen Rena (Ross) M.; m. Susan Minnick, Dec. 30, 1965; children: Andrew, Katherine. BS, Colo. State U., 1967, MS, 1967-68, PhD, 1974. Chemist agr. research services USDA, Ft. Collins, 1967—; Contbr. papers and book chpt. to profl. publ. Mem. AAAS, Am. Soc. Agronomy, Soil Sci. Soc. Am., Internat. Soil Sci. Soc., Council Agrl. Sci. Tech., Phi Kappa Phi, Sigma XI, Gamma Sigma Delta. Republican. Methodist. Club: Arsenal Competitive Soccer. Avocations: tennis, soccer. Home: 903 Hilldale Dr Fort Collins CO 80526-4345 Office: USDA Agrl Rsch Svc PO Box E Fort Collins CO 80522-0470

MOSIER, HARRY DAVID, JR., physician, educator; b. Topeka, May 22, 1925; s. Harry David and Josephine Morrow (Johnson) M.; m. Nadine Oclea Merilatt, Aug. 24, 1949; children: Carolyn Josephine Mosier Pohlmeyer, William David, Daniel Thomas, Christine Elizabeth Mosier Mahoney; m. Marjorie Knight Armstrong, Sept. 26, 1963. B.S. magna cum laude, U. Notre Dame, 1948; M.D., Johns Hopkins U., 1952. Diplomate Am. Bd. Pediatrics, Am. Bd. Pediatric Endocrinology. Intern Johns Hopkins Hosp., Balt., 1952-53; resident in pediatrics Los Angeles Children's Hosp., 1953-54, resident pediatric pathology, 1954-55; fellow pediatric endocrinology Johns Hopkins U., 1955-57; asst. prof. pediatrics UCLA, 1957-61, assoc. prof., 1961-63; dir. research Ill. State Pediatric Inst., Chgo., 1963-67; assoc. prof. U. Ill., 1963-67; prof. pediatrics, head div. pediatric endocrinology U. Calif.-Irvine, 1967—; staff Children's Hosp. Med. Center, Long Beach, Calif., 1970—, U. Calif. Irvine Med. Center, Orange, 1979—; dist. cons. Medical Bd. Calif., 1995—. Contbr. articles to med. jours. With AUS, 1943-46, col. U.S. Army Med. Corps, 1990-91, Persian Gulf War. USAR Med. Corps. 1952-62, 83-93 (ret.). Office: U Calif Dept Pediatrics 101 City Dr S Orange CA 92868-3201

MOSK, RICHARD MITCHELL, lawyer; b. L.A., May 18, 1939; s. Stanley and Edna M.; m. Sandra Lee Budnitz, Mar. 21, 1964; children: Julie, Matthew. AB with great distinction, Stanford U., 1960; JD cum laude, Harvard U., 1963. Bar: Calif. 1964, U.S. Supreme Ct. 1970, U.S. Ct. Mil. Appeals 1970, U.S. Dist. Ct. (no., so., ea., and cen. dists.) Calif 1964, U.S. Ct. Appeals (9th dist.) 1964. Mem. staff Pres.'s Commn. on Assassination Pres. Kennedy, 1964; research clk. Calif. Supreme Ct., 1964-65; ptnr. Mitchell, Silberberg & Knupp, L.A., 1965-87; prin. Sanders, Barnet, Goldman, Simons & Mosk, P.C., L.A., 1987—; spl. dep. Fed. Pub. Defender, L.A., 1975-76; instr. U. So. Calif. Law Sch., 1978; judge Iran-U.S. Claims Tribunal, 1981-84, 97—, substitute arbitrator, 1984-97; mem. Los Angeles County Jud. Procedures Commn., 1973-82, chmn., 1978; bd. dirs. Internat. Arbitration Commn.; mem. adv. coun. Asia/Pacific Ctr. for Resolution International. Trade Disputes, 1986—; chmn. Motion Picture Assn. Classification and Rating Adminstrn., 1994—. Contbr. articles to profl. jours. Mem. L.A. City-County Inquiry on Brush Fires, 1970; bd. dirs. Calif. Mus. Sci. and Industry, 1979-82, Vista Del Mar Child Ctr., 1979-82; trustee L.A. County Law Libr., 1985-86; bd. govs. Town Hall Calif., 1986-91; mem. Christopher Commn. on L.A. Police Dept., 1991; mem. Stanford U. Athletic Bd., 1991-95. With USNR, 1964-75. Hon. Woodrow Wilson fellow, 1960; recipient Roscoe Pound prize, 1961. Fellow Am. Bar Found.; mem. ABA (coun. internat. law sect. 1986-90), FBA (pres. L.A. chpt. 1972), L.A. County Bar Assn., Beverly Hills Bar Assn., L.A. Assn. Bus. Trial Lawyers, Internat. Bar Assn.; Am. Arbitration Assn. (comml. panel, large complex case panel, Asia/Pacific panel), Hong Kong Internat. Arbitration Ctr. (mem. panel 1986—), Am. Film Mktg. Assn. (arbitration panel), L.A. Ctr. Internat. Comml. Arbitration, B.C. Internat. Arbitration Ctr. (mem. panel), World Intellectual Property Orgn. (mem. arbitration panel), Ctr. Pub. Resources (mem. arbitration panel), Phi Beta Kappa. Office: Sanders Barnet Goldman Simons & Mosk 1901 Avenue Of The Stars Los Angeles CA 90067-6001

MOSK, STANLEY, state supreme court justice; b. San Antonio, Sept. 4, 1912; s. Paul and Minna (Perl) M.; m. Edna Mitchell, Sept. 27, 1937 (dec.); 1 child, Richard Mitchell; m. Susan Hines, Aug. 27, 1982 (div.); m. Kaygey Kash, Jan. 15, 1995. Student, U. Tex., 1931; PhB, U. Chgo., 1933; postgrad., U. Chgo. Law Sch., 1934; JD, Southwestern U., 1935; postgrad., The Hague Acad. Internat. Law, 1970, U. Pacific, 1970; LLD, U. San Diego, 1971, U. Santa Clara, 1976, Calif. Western U., 1984, Whittier Coll. Law, 1993, Pepperdine U., 1995, Western State U., San Diego, 1995. Bar: Calif. 1935, U.S. Supreme Ct. 1956. Practiced in Los Angeles, until 1939; exec. sec. to gov. Calif., 1939-42; judge Superior Ct. Los Angeles County, 1943-58; pro tem justice Dist. Ct. Appeal, Calif., 1954; atty. gen. Calif., also head state dept., justice, 1959-64; justice Supreme Ct. Calif., 1964—; mem. Jud. Coun. Calif., 1973-75, Internat. Commn. Jurists. Chmn. San Francisco Internat. Film Festival, 1967; mem. Dem. Nat. Com, Calif., 1960-64; mem. bd. regents U. Calif., 1940; pres. Vista Del Mar Child Care Svc., 1954-58; bd. dirs. San Francisco Law Sch., 1971-73, San Francisco Regional Cancer Found., 1980-83. With AUS, WWII. Recipient Disting. Alumnus award U. Chgo., 1958, 93. Mem. ABA, Nat. Assn. Attys. Gen. (exec. bd. 1964), Western Assn. Attys. Gen. (pres. 1963), L.A. Bar Assn., San Francisco Bar Assn., Am. Legion, Manuscript Soc., Calif. Hist. Soc., Am. Judicature Soc., Inst. Jud. Adminstrn., U. Chgo. Alumni Assn. No. Calif. (pres. 1957-58, 67), Order of Coif (hon.), B'nai B'rith, Hillcrest Country Club (L.A.), Commonwealth Club, Beverly Hills Tennis Club. Office: Supreme Ct Calif 303 2nd St San Francisco CA 94107

MOSK, SUSAN HINES, lawyer; b. Pitts., Dec. 14, 1946; d. William James and Catherine Elizabeth (Cook) Hines; m. Stanley Mosk, Aug. 27, 1982 (div. Jan. 1995). B in Music Edn., Fla. State U., 1968, M in Music Edn., 1970; JD, U. Calif., San Francisco, 1990. Bar: Calif. 1990, U.S. Dist. Ct. (no. dist.) Calif. 1990, U.S. Ct. Appeals (9th cir.) 1990. Assoc. Payne, Thompson & Walker, San Francisco, 1990-94; of counsel Knecht, Haley, Lawrence & Smith, San Francisco, 1994-95; prin. Law Offices of Susan H. Mosk, San Francisco, 1995—; commr. Jud. Nominees Evaluation Commn., 1992-96. Author/editor: Rainmaking Guide to Corporate Counsel, 1993. Mem. steering com. Women's Leadership Coun. for U.S. Senator Diane Feinstein, 1992—; chair No. Calif. Women's Cabinet for Kathleen Brown Gubernatorial Campaign, San Francisco, 1994; co-chair fin. Willie L. Brown Mayoral Campaign, 1995. Mem. State Bar of Calif., Calif. Women Lawyers (bd. govs. 1992-94, 1st v.p. 1993-94), Queen's Bench. Democrat. Avocations: music, skiing, traveling, reading. Office: Law Offices of Susan H Mosk 57 Post St Ste 604 San Francisco CA 94104-5023

MOSKAL, ANTHONY JOHN, former dean, professor, management and education consultant; b. South Amboy, N.J., May 31, 1946; s. Anthony Joseph and Jennie (Salamon) M.; m. Kathryn Jean Coakley, July 8, 1978; 1 child, Nicole Elizabeth. AB, Villanova (Pa.) U., 1968, MA, 1972; MEd, Ga. State U., 1974; PhD, Columbia Pacific U., San Rafael, Calif., 1987. Prin. instr. U.S. Army, Ft. Benning, Ga., 1969-71; research mgr. Blue Cross and Blue Shield, Columbus, Ga., 1972-74; sales rep. J.C. Penney Co., Parlin, N.J., 1974-76; dean of students Alliance Coll., Cambridge Springs, Pa., 1976-77; tchr. Sayreville (N.J.) pub. schs., 1977-79; county 4-H agt. Rutgers U., New Brunswick, 1979-86; pres. Eagle Assocs., South Amboy, N.J., 1985—; adj. faculty Georgian Ct. Coll., Lakewood, N.J., 1987—, U.S. Army Command and Gen. Staff Coll., Ft. Leavenworth, Kans., 1989—, Nat. Def. U., Washington, 1991; cons. in mgmt., leadership, edn., volunteerism, youth programs, career planning; spl. liason to Mcpl. Bd. Edn., Sayreville, 1991-95; area admissions rep. U.S. Mil. Acad., 1984-91. Contbr. articles to profl. jours. Mem. Boy Scouts Am.; dir. religious edn. Sacred Heart Parish, South Amboy, N.J., 1988-91; counselor Thomas A. Edison coun. Boy Scouts Am., 1982—; pres., bd. dirs. Vol. Action Ctr., Middlesex County, N.J., 1979-87; pres. Sayreville (N.J.) War Meml. H.S. Band Parents Assn., 1994-96; county committeeman, Middlesex County, N.J., 1990-94. With U.S. Army, 1969-71, 90-92, lt. col. USAR. Decorated Meritorious Svc. medal, Army Commendation medal (2); recipient Order of the Arrow award Boy Scouts Am., 1960; United Way of Ctrl. Jersey grantee, 1984, others. Mem. ASCD, Nat. Eagle Scout Assn., N.J. Assn. 4-H Agts. (pres. 1985-86, outstanding svc. citation 1981, 87), Nat. Assn. Extension 4-H Agts. (regional contact 1981-83, cert. appreciation 1983), Am. Fedn. Police (award of merit 1989, legion of honor 1990, St. Michael the Archangel award 1992, patriotism award 1993, J. Edgar Hoover meml. medal 1991), Res. Officers Assn., Mil. Police Regtl. Assn., Vietnam Vets. of Am. (honor guard), Holy Name Soc., Kiwanis, K. of C. (lectr., vol. coord. fife and drums corps, Knight of the Month), Am. Legion. Republican. Roman Catholic. Avocations: reading, music, recreational camping, travel, woodworking. Home: 166 Luke St South Amboy NJ 08879-2231 Office: Eagle Assocs PO Box 231 South Amboy NJ 08879-0231

MOSKAL, ROBERT M., bishop; b. Carnegie, Pa., Oct. 24, 1937; s. William and Jean (Popivchak) M. BA, St. Basil Coll. Sem., Stamford, Conn., 1959; lic. sacred theology, Cath. U. Am., 1963; student, Phila. Mus. Acad. and Conservatory of Mus., 1963-66. Ordained priest Ukrainian Cath. Ch. 1963. Founder, pastor St. Anne's Ukrainian Cath. Ch., Warrington, Pa., 1963-72; sec. Archbishop's Chancery, Phila., 1963-67; apptd. vice-chancellor Archeparchy of Phila., 1967-74; pastor Annunciation Ukrainian Cath. Ch., Melrose Park, Phila., 1972-74; named monsignor, 1974; chancellor archdiocese, pastor Ukrainian Cath. Cathedral of the Immaculate Conception, Phila., 1974-84; apptd. bishop, 1981; Ordained titular bishop of Agathopolis and aux. bishop Ukrainian-Rite Archeparcy of Phila., 1981-83; first bishop Diocese of St. Josaphat, Parma, Ohio, 1983—; pro-synodal judge Archdiocean Tribunal, Phila., 1965-67; founder Ukrainian Cath. Hour: God is with Us, Sta. WIBF-FM, Phila, 1972-77, Christ Among Us, Sat. WTEL, 1975—; mem. Ukrainian Cath. Ch. Liturgical Subcommn., 1980; host to His Holiness Pope John Paul II. Bd. dirs. Ascension Manor, Inc., Phila., 1964-84, sec.-treas., 1964-78, exec. v.p., 1977-84. Office: PO Box 347180 5720 State Rd Parma OH 44134-7180

MOSKIN, JOHN ROBERT, editor, writer; b. N.Y.C., May 9, 1923; s. Morris and Irma (Rosenfeld) M.; m. Doris Marianne Bloch, Oct. 7, 1948 (div. 1978); children: Mark Douglas, David Scott, Nancy Irma; m. Lynn Carole Goldberg, Apr. 10, 1986. Grad., Horace Mann Sch., 1940; B.S., Harvard U., 1944; M.A., Columbia U., 1947. Reporter Boston Post, 1941-42, Newark News, 1947-48; asst. to gen. mgr. N.Y. Star, 1948-49; editor Westport (Conn.) Town Crier, 1949; med. editor Look mag., N.Y.C., 1950-51; articles editor Look mag., 1951-53, sr. editor, 1956-66, fgn. editor, 1966-71; mng. editor Woman's Home Companion, 1953-56; sr. editor Collier's, 1956; editor at large Saturday Rev., 1972-75; sr. editor World Press Rev., 1976-87, contbg. editor, 1987-93; editorial dir. Aspen Inst. Humanistic Studies, 1977-83; editorial dir. Commonwealth Fund, 1984-87, sr. editorial advisor, 1987-93. Author: (with others) The Decline of the American Male, 1958, Morality in America, 1966, Turncoat, 1968, The U.S. Marine Corps Story, 1977, 82, 87, 92, Among Lions, 1982, (with Julia Vitullo-Martin) The Executive's Book of Quotations, 1994, Mr. Truman's War, 1996; mem. editorial adv. com. Dimensions mag, 1970-71, Present Tense, 1973-90. Trustee Scarsdale Adult Sch., 1965-72, chmn., 1969-70; mem. Dana Reed Prize com. Harvard, 1947—; mem. com. Class of 1944, 1943—; mem. communications screening com. Council Internat. Exchange of Scholars, 1974-77, President's Coun. Heritage Coll., 1995—; bd. dirs. SIECUS, 1972-80, Jerusalem Found., 1977—, Marine Corps Hist. Found., 1979-82, 89-95, Faculty for Continuing Med. Edn., 1983-86. Served with AUS, 1943-46. Recipient Benjamin Franklin gold medal for pub. service Woman's Home Companion, 1955, Page One award Newspaper Guild N.Y., 1965, Sidney Hillman Found. award, 1965, National Headliners award, 1967, Overseas Press Club award, 1969, citation for excellence, 1971, Disting. Svc. award Marine Corps Combat Corrs. Assn., 1978, Nat. Jewish Book award, 1983, Disting. Svc. award Marine Corps Hist. Found., 1996. Mem. Am. Hist. Assn., Soc. Mil. History, Authors Guild, Fgn. Editors Group (chmn. 1970-71), Nat. Press Club (Washington), Overseas Press Club (gov. 1975-79), Century Club, Harvard Club (N.Y.C.), Lotos Club, (bd. dirs. 1988-90, 94— pres. 1991-94), Sigma Delta Chi (mem. nat. freedom of info. com. 1964, 71). Home: 945 5th Ave New York NY 10021-2655 also: 157 Jerusalem Rd Tyringham MA 01264

MOSKIN, MORTON, lawyer; b. N.Y.C., Mar. 28, 1927; s. Barnett and Sonia (Burr) M.; m. Rita Lee Goldberg, June 15, 1952; children: Tina, Ilene, Jonathan. B.A., Pa. State Coll., 1947; LL.B., Cornell U., 1950. Assoc. White & Case, N.Y.C., 1950-61, ptnr., 1962-94, cons., 1995—; chmn. exec. com. Mallinckrodt Group (formerly IMCERA, previously Internat. Minerals & Chem. Corp.), St. Louis, 1988-91, chmn. corp. governance com., 1993—, also bd. dirs.; sec. BT Mortgage Investors, Garden City, N.J., 1975-82. Bd. dirs. Fedn. Employment and Guidance Svcs.; bd. dirs., pres. Henry M.

Blackmer Found., N.Y.C., Achievement Found., to 1994, Stamford, Conn.; bd. dirs. Jewish Cmty. Svcs. L.I., 1974-93, pres., 1984-87. Fellow Am. Bar Found.; mem. ABA, N.Y. State Bar Assn., N.Y. County Lawyers Assn. (dir. 1981-86), Norfolk (Conn.) Country Club, Cornell Club N.Y. Home: 1160 Park Ave Apt 15B New York NY 10128-1212 Office: White & Case 1155 Avenue Of The Americas New York NY 10036-2711

MOSKOS, CHARLES C., sociology educator; b. Chgo., May 20, 1934; s. Charles and Rita (Shukas) M.; m. Ilca Hohn, July 3, 1966; children—Andrew, Peter. B.A. cum laude, Princeton, 1956; M.A., UCLA, 1961, Ph.D., 1963; L.H.D. (hon.), Norwich U., 1992. Asst. prof. U. Mich., Ann Arbor, 1964-66; assoc. prof. sociology Northwestern U., Evanston, Ill., 1966-70, prof., 1970—; fellow Progressive Policy Inst., 1992—; mem. Presdl. Commn. on Women in the Mil., 1992. Author: The Sociology of Political Independence, 1967, The American Enlisted Man, 1970, Public Opinion and the Military Establishment, 1971, Peace Soldiers, 1976, Fuerzas Armadas y Societdad, 1984, The Military--More Than Just A Job?, 1988, A Call to Civil Service, 1988, Greek Americans, 1989, Soldiers and Sociology, 1989, New Directions in Greek American Studies, 1991, The New Conscientious Objection, 1993, All That We Can Be, 1996, Reporting War When There Is No War, 1996. Mem. bd. advisors Dem. Leadership Coun., 1989—; chmn. Theodore Saloutos Meml. Fund; mem. Archdiocesean Commn. Third Millenium, 1982-88. Served with AUS, 1956-58. Decorated D.S.M., Fondation pour les Etudes de Def. Nat. (France), S.M.K. (The Netherlands); named to Marshall rsch. chair ARI, 1987-88, 95-96; Ford. Found. faculty fellow, 1969-70; fellow Wilson Ctr., 1980-81, guest scholar, 1991; fellow Rockefeller Found. Humanities, 1983-84, Guggenheim fellow, 1992-93, fellow Annenberg Washington Program, 1995; grantee 20th Century Fund, 1983-87, 92-94, Ford Found., 1989-90; recipient Nat. Educator Leadership award Todd Found., 1997, Book award Washington Monthly, 1997. Mem. Am. Sociol. Assn., Internat. Sociol. Assn. (pres. rsch. com. on armed forces and conflict resolution 1982-86), Am. Polit. Sci. Assn., Inter-Univ. Seminar on Armed Forces and Soc. (chmn. 1987—). Greek Orthodox. Home: 2440 Asbury Ave Evanston IL 60201-2307

MOSKOVITZ, STUART JEFFREY, lawyer; b. Phila., Jan. 21, 1949; s. Martin and Jean (Sandler) M.; m. Toni Cheryl Gans, June 1, 1980; children: Lauren Michelle, Leanne Meredith, Lisa Morgan. BA, Hofstra U., 1970; JD, Boston U., 1973. Bar: Pa. 1973, U.S. Dist. Ct. (mid. dist.) Pa. 1974, U.S. Claims Ct. 1975, U.S. Supreme Ct. 1979, N.Y. 1981, U.S. Dist. Ct. (so. dist.) N.Y. 1982, U.S. Ct. Appeals (2d cir.) 1983, N.J. 1993, U.S. Dist. Ct. N.J. 1993. Asst. atty. gen. Pa. Dept. Transp., Harrisburg, 1973-79; atty. Westinghouse Electric Corp., Pitts., 1980-81; ptnr. Berman, Paley, Goldstein & Berman, N.Y.C., 1981-90, Tanner, Propp & Farber, N.Y.C., 1991-94, Stadtmauer Bailkin, L.L.P., N.Y.C., 1995—. Pres. Ivanhoe Village Homeowner's Assn., 1984; mem. Coun. Excellence in Govt., Washington, 1991-93, N.Y. Bldg. Congress, 1991-94. Mem. ABA (forum com. on constrn. industry), N.Y. State Bar Assn. (comml. fed. litigation sect. com. on constrn.), Assn. of Bar of City of N.Y., Pa. Bar Assn. (constrn. litigation subcom.), N.J. State Bar Assn. Office: Stadtmauer Bailkin 850 3rd Ave New York NY 10022-6222

MOSKOWITZ, ARNOLD X., economist, strategist, educator; b. N.Y.C., Jan. 27, 1944; s. Morris and Millie (Kozichovsky) M.; m. Sandra Moskowitz; children: Alex, Nicole. BS in Elec. Engring., CCNY, 1966; MS in Indsl. Mgmt., Poly. Inst. N.Y., 1970; MPhil, NYU, 1979, PhD in Econs. and Fin., 1985. Analyst Grumman Corp., N.Y.C., 1968-70; assoc. economist Dean Witter Reynolds, Inc., N.Y.C., 1970-74, first v.p., economist, 1975-82, sr. v.p., economist, 1983-89; sr. v.p., dir. investment strategy County NatWest U.S.A., N.Y.C., 1989-90; chmn. Moskowitz Capital Cons. Inc., N.Y.C., 1990—; lectr. New Sch. Social Research, 1978—; adj. assoc. prof. fin. Pace U., N.Y.C., 1980-82; pres. Money Marketers NYU, 1988-89. Contbr. articles to profl. jours.; chpts. to books, including Security Selection and Active Portfolio Management; contbr. to Ency. of Economics, How to Beat Wall Street. Mem. Am. Econ. Assn., Nat. Econ. Club, Nat. Assn. Bus. Economists, Atlantic Soc., Beta Gamma Sigma. Jewish. Office: Moskowitz Capital Cons Inc 250 W 57th St Ste 1517-6 New York NY 10107 *Our guidelines for success starts with our principles to provide the highest level of service to our customers and treat our employees as partners in the business. Our goal is to maintain the highest level of integrity in dealing with clients and workers in order to maximize our performances.*

MOSKOWITZ, HERBERT, management educator; b. Paterson, NJ, May 26, 1935; s. David and Ruth (Abrams) M.; m. Heather Mary Lesgnier, Feb. 25, 1968; children: Tobias, Rebecca, Jonas. BS in Mech. Engring., Newark Coll. Engring., 1956; MBA, U.S. Internat. U., 1964; PhD, UCLA, 1970. Rsch. engr. GE, 1956-60; systems design engr. Gen. Dynamics Convair, San Diego, 1960-65; asst. prof. Purdue U., West Lafayette, Ind., 1970-75, assoc. prof., 1975-79, prof., 1979-85, Disting. prof., 1985-87, James B. Henderson Disting. prof., 1987-91, Lewis B. Cullman Dist. prof. mfg. mgmt., 1991—, dir. ctr. mgmt. mfg. enterprises; cons. AT&T, Inland Steel Co., Abbott Labs., others; adv. panelist NSF, 1990—. Author: Management Science and Statistics Texts, 1975-90; assoc. editor Decision Scis. Jour., 1984-90, Jour. Behavioral Decision Making, 1986-90; contbr. articles to jours. in field. Bd. dirs. Sons of Abraham Synagogue, Lafayette, Ind., 1970—; mem. Lafayette Klezmorem, 1973—. Capt. USAF, 1956-60. Recipient Disting. Doctoral Student award UCLA Alumni Assn., 1969-70; Fulbright Rsch. scholar, 1985-86. Fellow Decision Scis. Inst. (sec. 1985-87, v.p. 1978-80); mem. Ops. Rsch. Soc. Am./Inst. Mgmt. Sci. (liaison officer 1977—, panel mem., advisor NSF and Fulbright Scholar program 1993—), Tau Beta Pi, Pi Tau Sigma. Jewish. Avocations: Jewish music, tennis. Home: 1430 N Salisbury St West Lafayette IN 47906-2420 Office: Purdue U Krannert Grad Sch Mgmt Ctr Mgmt Mfg ENterprises West Lafayette IN 47907-1310

MOSKOWITZ, JAY, public health sciences educator; b. N.Y.C., Jan. 9, 1943; s. Murray and Helene Moskowitz; m. Joanne Cathy Schindelheim, Dec. 27, 1970; children: Michael Bradley, Andrew Cory. B.S., Queens Coll., 1964; postgrad., CUNY, 1965; Ph.D., Brown U., 1969. Research assoc. in pharmacology NIH, 1969-71, grants assoc. div. research grants, 1971-72, acting chief spl. programs br., div. lung diseases, 1972-74; assoc. dir. program planning and evaluation Nat. Heart, Lung and Blood Inst., 1979-80, assoc. dir. sci. program ops., 1980-86, dir. office of program planning and evaluation, 1976-86; assoc. dir. for program planning and evaluation NIH, 1986-88, dir. Office Program Planning and Evaluation, Office of Dir., 1986-88, assoc. dir. for sci. policy and legislation, 1988-93; acting dir. Nat. Inst. on Deafness and Other Communication Disorders, 1988-90; dep. dir. for sci. policy & tech. transfer, prin. dep. dir. NIH, 1993; dep. dir. Nat. Inst. on Deafness and Other Communication Disorders, 1993-95; sr. assoc. dean for rsch. devel., prof. pub. health scis. Wake Forest U. Bowman Gray Sch. Medicine, Winston-Salem, N.C., 1995—. Contbr. articles to profl. jours. Served to lt. comdr. USPHS. Recipient Meritorious award William A. Jump Meml. Found., 1977, Dir.'s award NIH, 1978, Superior Svc. award USPHS, 1980, performance awards Sr. Exec. Svc., Presdl. Meritorious Exch. Rank award 1989, Disting. Svc. award HHS, 1991, Disting. Svc. award Nat. Inst. on Deafness and Other Comm. Disorders, 1994. Mem. Soc. Exptl. Biology and Medicine, AAAS. Jewish. Home: 7908 Lasley Forest Rd Lewisville NC 27023 Office: Wake Forest U Bowman Gray Sch Medicine Office Rsch Devel Winston Salem NC 27104

MOSKOWITZ, JOEL STEVEN, lawyer; b. N.Y.C., Jan. 14, 1947; s. Jack I. and Myra (Shor) M.; children: David, Michael, Ellen. BA, UCLA, 1967, JD, 1970. Bar: Calif. 1971, U.S. Ct. Appeals (9th cir.) 1971, U.S. Ct. Appeals (D.C. cir.) 1975, U.S. Supreme Ct. 1975, U.S. Ct. Appeals (2d cir.) 1979. Dep. atty. gen. Calif. Dept. Justice, Sacramento, 1970-83; dep. dir. Calif. Dept. Health Svcs., Sacramento, 1983-85; of counsel Gibson, Dunn & Crutcher, L.A., 1985-88, ptnr., 1988-96. Author: Environmental Liability in Real Property Transactions, 1995; contbr. articles to legal pubs. Mem. Phi Beta Kappa. Office: Moskowitz Wood Nyznyk LLP 2049 Century Park E Ste 1800 Los Angeles CA 90067-3120

MOSKOWITZ, MICHAEL ARTHUR, neuroscientist, neurologist; b. N.Y.C., May 26, 1942; s. Irving Lawrence and Clara (Dranoff) M.; m. Mary Henderson, May 18, 1991; 1 child, Jenna Rachel. AB, Johns Hopkins U., 1964; MD, Tufts U., 1968; MSc (hon.), Harvard U., 1992. Diplomate Am. Bd. Psychiaty and Neurology, Am. Bd. Internal Medicine. Intern Yale U. Dept. Medicine, 1968-69, resident, 1969-71; resident in neurology Peter Bent Brigham Children Hosp., 1971-74; asst. prof. Med. Sch., Harvard U., Boston, 1975-79, assoc. prof., 1979-92, prof., 1992—; established investigator Am. Heart Assn., 1980-85; assoc. neurophysiologist and neurologist Mass. Gen. Hosp., Boston, 1981—; H.J. Barnett lectr. Canadian Heart Assn., Queens U., Kingston, Ont., 1993—, Witter lectr. U. Calif., San Francisco, 1994—, Barraquer-LaFora lectr. Spanish Neurol. Soc., Barcelona, Spain, 1994—, Decade of the Brain lectr. Am. Acad. Neurology, 1995, Briggs lecture dept. pharmacology U. Tex., San Antonio, 1995; mem. sci. adv. bd. Max Plank Inst., KÖn; program project dir. various NIH program projects. Editl. bd. Stroke, Acta Neurol. Scandinavica Cephalalgia, Jour. Cerebral Blood Flow & Metabolism, Cerebrovascular Disease; contbr. over 270 articles to profl. jours. MIT postdoctoral fellow, 1974-76, Alfred Sloan Found. fellow, 1978-80; recipient Enrico Greppi award Italian Neurology Soc., 1986, 88, Tchr.-Investigator award Nat. Inst. Neurol. Disease and Stroke, 1975-80, Zülch prize Max-Planck Soc./Inst., 1996; rsch. grantee Bristol-Myers Squibb, 1993—, MGH Interdepartmental Stroke Ctr. Mem. Am. Heart Assn. (nat. rsch. com. 1991-96, exec. com. stroke coun. 1991-96), Am. Neurol. Assn., Am. Acad. Neurology, Am. Pain Soc., Soc. Neurosci., Internat. Soc. for Cerebral Blood Flow and Metabolism (bd. dirs.), Internat. Symposium Pharm. of Cerebral Ischemia. Achievements include research in neuroscientific, neurology literature including stroke and migraine. Office: Mass Gen Hosp Charleston Navy Yard 149 13th St Charlestown MA 02129-2020

MOSKOWITZ, ROLAND WALLACE, internist; b. Shamokin, Pa., Nov. 3, 1929. MD, Temple U., 1953. Intern Temple U. Hosp., Phila., 1953-54; fellow in internal medicine Mayo Clinic, Rochester, Minn., 1954-55, 57-60; mem. staff U. Hosps. Cleve.; prof. medicine Case Western Res. U. Sch. Medicine, Cleve. Mem. ACR, Alpha Omega Alpha. Office: U Hosps Cleve Divsn Rheum Diseases 11100 Euclid Ave Cleveland OH 44106-1736

MOSKOWITZ, SAM (SAM MARTIN), author, editor, publisher; b. Newark, June 30, 1920; s. Harry and Rose (Gerber) M.; m. Christine Elizabeth Haycock, July 6, 1958. Partner Taurasi & Moskowitz (lit. agts.), N.Y.C., 1941-42; sales mgr. Hazel Specialty Co., Newark, 1944-52; mng. editor Gernsback Publishers, N.Y.C., 1952-54, Frosted Food Field, 1954-55; editor, asso. pub. Quick Frozen Foods, N.Y.C., 1955-72; editor, co-pub. Quick Frozen Foods, 1974-80; asso. pub. Quick Frozen Foods Internat., 1980-85; pub. Private Label, 1981-85; editor Beverage Industry, 1972-74; instr. creative writing City Coll. N.Y., 1953-55; spl. cons. frozen foods, sci. fiction; sci. fiction historian and anthologist. Author: 60 books on sci. fiction, including The Immortal Storm, 1954, Explorers of the Infinite, 1963, Seekers of Tomorrow, 1966, Science Fiction by Gaslight, 1968, Under the Moons of Mars, 1970, The Man Who Called Himself Poe, 1969, The Crystal Man, 1973, Out of the Storm, 1975, Strange Horizons, 1976, Far Future Calling, 1979, Science Fiction in Old San Francisco, 1980, A Merritt: Reflections in the Moon Pool, 1985, H.P. Lovecraft and Nils H. Frome, 1989, After All These Years (autobiography), 1991, The Haunted Pampero, 1992, Terrors of the Sea, 1994; editor Hyperion Press Science Fiction Classics, 1974. Served with AUS, 1942-43. Guest of honor 13th World Sci. Fiction conv., Cleve., 1955; recipient Big Heart award Pitts. World Sci. Fiction conv., 1960; Author's award for sci. fiction N.J. Assn. English Tchrs., 1966; Sci. Fiction Hall of Fame award, 1974; named Lit. Luminary of N.J. N.J. Inst. Tech., 1977; named to N.J. Lit. Hall of Fame, 1979. Mem. Eastern Frosted Foods Assn. (dir. 1962-72), Eastern Sci. Fiction Assn. (pres. 1945-50, 80-87), Sci. Fiction Writers Assn., Mystery Writers Am., Fantasy Amatuer Press Assn., First Fandom. Home: 361 Roseville Ave Newark NJ 07107-1721 *Attracted to science fiction in my youth by its suggested answers to provocative mysteries of time and space, I have devoted much of my life to revealing and illuminating its fascinating development, which has reflected mankind's most far-reaching aspirations and sometimes replaced, in modern tense, the voices of the ancient prophets.*

MOSKOWITZ, STANLEY ALAN, financial executive; b. N.Y.C., June 8, 1956; s. Sol and Kate (Mermelstein) M.; m. Eve Kronenberger, Sept. 20, 1981; children: Alana, Kate. BA, Queens Coll., 1978; MBA in Fin., St. John's U., 1980. Sr. credit analyst Mfrs. Hanover Leasing Corp., N.Y.C., 1979-81; gen. ptnr. Exec. Leasing Co., N.Y.C., 1981-83; pres. Execulease Corp., Elmont, N.Y., 1983-97; bd. dirs. UFA/Fedn. of Greenwich, Conn., 1995—, treas., 1997—. Mem. Ea. Assn. Equipment Lessors (chmn. pub. rels. 1985-90, bd. dirs. 1988-92, Meretorious Svc. award 1986-87, chmn. ethics com. 1991-92), Omicron Delta Epsilon. Republican. Jewish. Avocations: reading, cycling. Office: Execulease Corp PO Box 31147 Greenwich CT 06831

MOSLER, JOHN, retired financial planner; b. N.Y.C., Sept. 24, 1922; s. Edwin H. and Irma M.; children: Bruce Elliot, John Edwin, Michele Andree. Student, Philips Exeter Acad., 1938-41, Princeton U., 1941-43; L.H.D., Fordham U., 1965; D.C.S., Duquesne U., 1968. With Mosler Safe Co., 1945-67, exec. v.p., 1948-61, pres., 1961-66, chmn., 1966-67; pres., dir. Mosler Lock Co., 1953-67, Mosler de Mexico S.A., 1953-67; exec. v.p., dir. Mosler Research Products, Inc., 1956-67; dir. 1st Caribbean Mainland Capital Co., Inc., 1962-68, chmn. bd., 1963-68, pres., 1966-68; v.p., dir. Am. Standard Inc., 1967-68; chmn. bd., dir., chief exec. officer Holmes Protection, Inc., 1968-73, Holmes Protection Services Corp., 1968-73; chmn. bd. Hidromex, S.A. de C.V., Mex., 1968—, Mosler N.V., Europe, 1973—; chmn. bd. Internat. Controls Corp., 1973-87, resigned, 1987; past chmn. bd. Royal Bus. Funds Inc.; pres. Mosler Investments. Mem. Mayor's Com. on Judiciary; pres. Am.-Romanian Flood Relief Com.; past dir. Jr. Achievement N.Y.; spl. U.S. amb. to Mauritius, to Zambia's Indpendence ceremony; vice chmn. N.Y. Rep. County Com.; chmn. John Mosler Found.; trustee, dir. Nat. Urban League; trustee Appeal of Conscience Found., Linden Hall Sch. for Girls, Lititz, Pa.; hon. trustee, past pres. N.Y. Urban League; founder Harlem Prep. Sch. With CIC, AUS, 1943-46. Decorated knight comdr. Ordo Supremus Militaris A. Lilio Regni Navarrae; Sovereign Order Hospitallers St. John of Jerusalem, Knights of Malta; comdt. L'Ordre Senegal; recipient Man of Conscience award Appeal of Conscience Found., 1969. Mem. Young Pres.'s Orgn. (past pres.), U.S. C. of C., N.Y. World Bus. Coun., Bankers of Mex. Club (Mex.), Princeton U. (N.Y.), Confrerie des Chevaliers du Tastevin, Manhattan, Real Nautico de Barcelona (Spain), Sag Harbor Yacht, Univ. Club, Wall St. Club.

MOSLEY, MARY MAC, retired librarian; b. Rome, Ga., Nov. 11, 1926; d. William McKinley and Mary (Caldwell) H.; m. Samuel A. Mosley, June 12, 1946 (div. 1964); children: Samuel A. Jr., Pamela Ann, James Irwin. Student, Ga. State Coll. for Women, 1943-45; BS, Auburn U., 1947; cert. in teaching, Athens Coll., 1963; M in Library, Emory U., 1968. Tchr. sci. Rome City Schs., 1964-66; extension libr. Tri-County Regional Libr., 1966-67; libr. Shorter Coll., 1967-68, assoc. prof. libr. sci., 1968-76, dir. libr. svcs., 1968-93. Corr. sec. Rome Symphony Women's Guild; pres., ch. historian, treas. Christian Women's Fellowship, 1st Christian Ch., 1992-94; corr. sec. Rome Symphony Women's Assn., v.p., 1996. Mem. ALA, AAUW (pres. Rome br.), N. Ga. Assn. Librs., Ga. Libr. Assn., Christian Women's Fellowship, Coosa Country Club, Delta Kappa Gamma. Democrat. Mem. Christian Ch. Avocations: piano, knitting, reading, gardening. Home: 205 Benton Dr Rome GA 30165-1728

MOSLEY, W. HENRY, medical educator. MD, U. Okla.; MPH, Johns Hopkins U. Resident Johns Hopkins Hosp., Balt.; head epidemiology divsn. Cholera Rsch. Lab. CDC, Dhaka, Bangladesh, 1965-71; prof., chmn. dept. population dynamics, dir. Population Ctr. Johns Hopkins U., Balt., 1971-77, prof. population dynamics, internat. health, infectious dis., 1985—, chmn. dept. population dynamics, 1985—; cons. WHO, NAS, UN Population divsn., World Bank, many others; dir. Cholera Rsch. Lab., Bangladesh, 1977-79; sr. assoc., Population Coun. and vis. prof. population studies U. Nairobi, Kenya, 1979-81; child survival program officer Ford Found., Jakarta, Indonesia, 1982-84. Contbr. over 120 articles to profl. jours. With USPHS, 1961-63. Mem. APHA, Internat. Epidemiol. Soc., Am. Epidemiol. Soc., Population Assn. Am. Office: Johns Hopkins University Sch Hygiene/Pub Health 615 N Wolfe St Baltimore MD 21205-2103

MOSORA, FLORENTINA IOANA, physics educator; b. Cluj, Romania, Jan. 7, 1940; arrived in Belgium, 1968; d. Oprea and Cornelia (Stanescu) M.; m. Stephan Stan, Jan. 22, 1977; 1 child, Guy Bart. B in Biol. Sci. with highest distinction, U. Bucharest, Romania, 1961, B in Phys. Sci. with highest distinction, 1967, PhD in Biophysics cum laude, 1971. Cert. biologist and physicist. Rsch. fellow U. Bucharest, 1967-71; rsch. fellow U. Liege, Belgium, 1971-74, maitre de conferences, 1974-75; head rsch. fellow Inst. Physics, U. Liege, Belgium, 1975-79, lectr., 1979-88, prof., 1988—. Author: Elements of General Physics and Biophysics, vol. 1, 1974, vol. 2, 1975, Introduction to the Mechanics of Physiologic Fluids, 1984-85, Mechanics of Microcirculation, 1990: Editor: Biomechanical Transport Processes, 1991. Mem. European Med. Rsch. Coun. Devel. of Resch. in Nutrition and Stable Isotopes, 1991—. Decorated officer Ordre of Leopold II, (Belgium), 1981, comdr. Ordre de la Couronne (Belgium, 1992; recipient Agathon de Potter prize Royal Acad. Belgium, 1982. Mem. Stareso Oceanographic Rsch. Calvi (sci. coun. 1987—), Isotopes Stables (v.p. 1987—), Inst. Recherches Marines et Interactions Air-Mer (pres. 1989—), Hemo Liege (founder), Belgian Soc. Biophysics, Internat. Soc. Rsch. Circulation and Environ. Diseases, N.Y. Acad. Scis. Roman Catholic. Avocations: swimming, gymnastics. Home: Residence Verdi, Av Blonden 7, 4000 Liege Belgium Office: U Liege, Inst Physics B5, 4000 Liege Belgium

MOSS, AMBLER HOLMES, JR., academic administrator, educator, lawyer, former ambassador; b. Balt., Sept. 1, 1937; s. Ambler Holmes and Dorothea Dandridge (Williams) M.; m. Serena Welles, May 6, 1972; children: Ambler H., Benjamin Sumner, Serena Montserrat, Nicholas George Oliver. B.A., Yale U., 1960; J.D., George Washington U., 1970. Bar: D.C., Fla. Joined Fgn. Service Dept. State, 1964; vice consul Barcelona, 1964-66; adviser U.S. del. to OAS, 1966-69; Spanish desk officer, 1968-70; assoc. firm Coudert Bros., Washington, 1971-73; resident atty. Coudert Bros., Brussels, Belgium, 1973-76; mem. U.S. Negotiating Team for Panama Canal treaties, 1977; dep. asst. Sec. of State, Washington, 1977-78; ambassador to Panama, 1978-82; of counsel Greenberg, Traurig, Askew, Hoffman, Lipoff, Quentel, Wolff P.A., 1982-87, 95—; prof., dir. N.S. Ctr. and former dean Grad. Sch. Internat. Studies U. Miami, Fla.; bd. dirs. Espirito Santo Bank of Fla. Mem. Panama Canal Consultative Com., bd. visitors U.S. Army Sch. of the Ams., Ft. Benning, Ga. Served with USN, 1960-64. Mem. ABA, Am. Soc. Internat. Law, Inter-Am. Bar Assn., Am. Fgn. Svc. Assn., Coun. Fgn. Rels., Am. Legion, Inter-Am. Dialogue (Washington), Navy League, Greater Miami C. of C. (gov. 1983-86), Royal Inst. Internat. Affairs (London), Internat. Inst. Strategic Studies (London), Army and Navy Club, Order of the Coif. Address: 5711 San Vicente St Coral Gables FL 33146-2724

MOSS, ARTHUR HENSHEY, lawyer; b. Reading, Pa., July 26, 1930; s. John Arthur and Christine Bracken (Henshey) M.; m. E. Leslie Fritz, Feb. 1982; 1 child by previous marriage, John Arthur. AB, Williams Coll., 1952; JD, U. Pa., 1955. Bar: Pa. 1956. Assoc. Montgomery, McCracken, Walker & Rhoads, Phila., 1960-69, ptnr., 1969—. Editor U. Pa. Law Review, 1953-55; chmn. Radnor-Haverford-Marple Sewer Authority, 1968-83: pres. Wayne Civic Assn., 1964-65; steward, deacon Wayne Presbyn. Ch., 1963-66, ruling elder, 1966-72, 79-84, 89-95, clk. of session, 1973-74, 78-89, trustee, 1987-93; commr. Gen. Assembly Presbyn. Ch. (U.S.A.), 1983; dir. John Bartram Assn., 1987—, treas. 1989—; trustee Presbytery of Phila., 1984, 94—, treas., 1996—. Lt. USN, 1955-60. Mem. ABA, Pa. Bar Assn., Phila. Bar Assn., Nat. Assn. Bond Lawyers, Radnor Hist. Soc. (dir., sec. 1978-90), The Athenaeum of Phila., Broadacres Trouting Assn., Merion Golf Club, The Union League of Phila., Edgemere Club. Editor: U. Pa. Law Rev., 1954-55. Contbr. articles to profl. jours. Home: 200 Walnut Ave Wayne PA 19087-3423 Office: Montgomery McCracken Walker & Rhoads 123 S Broad St Philadelphia PA 19109-1029

MOSS, ARTHUR JAY, physician; b. White Plains, N.Y., June 21, 1931; s. Abraham Loeb and Ida (Bank) M.; m. Joy Folkman, June 23, 1957; children: Katherine, Deborah, David. BA, Yale U., 1953; MD, Harvard U., 1957. Resident Mass. Gen. Hosp., 1957-58, 60-61; fellow in cardiology med. ctr. U. Rochester, N.Y., 1961-65, from asst. to assoc. prof. sch. medicine and dentistry, 1966-71, clin. assoc. prof., 1971-82, clin. prof., 1982-91, prof. medicine, 1991—, dir. heart rsch. follow-up program med. ctr., 1971—; mem. cardiology adv. com. Nat. Heart, Lung, and Blood Inst., NIH, 1980-82, chmn., 1982-84. Author: Antiarrhythmic Agents, 1973; editor: Clinical Aspects of Life-threatening Arrhythmias, 1984, QT Prolongation and Ventricular Arrhythmias, 1992, Noninvasive Electrocardiology, 1995; editor-in-chief Ann. Noninvasive Electrocardiology, 1996—; editl. bd. Am. Jour. Cardiology, 1988—. Lt. USNR, 1958-60. Mem. Alpha Omega Alpha. Home: 581 Claybourne Rd Rochester NY 14618-1224 Office: Univ Rochester Med Ctr PO Box 653 Rochester NY 14642-8653

MOSS, BEN FRANK, III, art educator, painter; b. Phila., Feb. 28, 1936; s. B. Frank Jr. and Helen Charlotte (Figge) M.; m. Jean Marilyn Russel, Aug. 26, 1960; children: Jennifer Kathleen, Benjamin Franklin IV. BA, Whitworth Coll., 1959; postgrad., Princeton Theol. Seminary, 1959-60; MFA, Boston U., 1963; MA (hon.), Dartmouth Coll., 1993; studied with Walter Murch, Karl Fortess and Herman Keys. Instr. Gonzaga U., Spokane, Wash., 1964-65; assoc. prof., dir. MFA and vis. artist program Fort Wright Coll., Spokane, 1965-72; acting dean, co-founder Spokane Studio Sch., 1972-74; prof. painting and drawing Sch. Art and Art History U. Iowa, Iowa City, 1975-88; George Frederick Jewett prof. art. Dartmouth Coll., Hanover, N.H., 1988—; chmn. studio art dept. Dartmouth Coll., Hanover, 1988-94, Vt. Studio Ctr., Johnson, 1990; area head painting U. Iowa, 1985; artist-in-residence Queens Coll., U. Melbourne, Australia, 1993-94; vis. artist, lectr. in field. Represented in permanent collections Kraushaar Galleries, N.Y.C., Susan Conway Galleries, Washington, Gallery 68, Belfast, Maine; one-man shows include Susan Conway Galleries, 1990, Dartmouth Coll., 1989, 94, Kraushaar Galleries, 1981, 83, 87, Swarthmore Coll., Pa., 1984, Stony Brook (N.Y.) Sch., 1982, Saint-Gaudens, Picture Gallery, Cornish, N.H., 1981, Kans. State U., 1980, Francine Seders Gallery, Seattle, 1979, 82, Hudson D. Walker Gallery, Fine Arts Work Ctr., Provincetown, Mass., 1978, Arnot Art Mus., Elmira, N.Y., 1977, Kirkland Coll., Clinton, N.Y., 1977, Juniper Tree Gallery, Spokane, 1975, Middlebury (Vt.) Coll., 1971, Seligman Gallery, Seattle, 1967, 69, Cheney Cowels Meml. Mus., Spokane, 1967, Loomis Chaffee Sch., 1995, Tasis England Am. Sch., 1994, Queens Coll., U. Melbourne, 1994, Houghton Coll., 1996, Gordon Coll., 1996, N. W. Mo. State U., 1996, Brattleboro Mus. and Art Ctr., 1995, Nat. Acad. and Design, 1995, Messiah Coll., 1995, Phillips Exeter Acad., 1995, Susan Conway Galleries, 1993, 96, Chase Gallery City Hall, Spokane, 1993, Colby-Sawyer Coll., New London, N.H., 1992, Idaho State U., Pocatello, 1972, Francine Seders Gallery, 1972, Kraushaar Galleries, 1978—, exhibited in group shows at Blair Acad., Blairstown, N.J., 1996, Albright Knox Gallery, Buffalo, N.Y., 1995-96, Smith Coll., North Hampton, Pa., 1996, Nat. Acad. Design, N.Y.C., 1995, Boston U., 1995, Brattleboro (Vt.) Mus. and Art Ctr., 1995, Susan Conway Galleries, 1989—, Middlebury Coll. Mus. Art, Babcock Galleries, N.Y.C., Albany Inst. History and Art, Owensboro (Ky.) Mus. Fine Art, Westmoreland Mus. Art, Greenburg, Pa., Md. Inst. & Coll. Art, 1993-94, Gallery 68, 1992, Vt. Studio Ctr. Visiting Critics, Vergennes, 1992, 79th Ann. Maier Mus. Art, Randolph, Macon Women's Coll., Lynchburg, Va., 1990, Del. Ctr. Contemporary Arts, Wilmington, 1988, U. Iowa, 1976, 78, 80, 82, 84, 86, 88, Bladen Meml. Mus., Fort Dodge, Iowa, 1987, Phila. Mus. Art, 1986, Union League Club, N.Y.C., 1986, Blackfish Gallery, Portland, 1986, Columbia (S.C.) Mus. Art, 1985, Columbus Mus. Art, 1982-86, Paine Art Ctr., Oshkosh, Wis., 1985, Burpee Art Ctr., Rockford, Ill., 1985, Ill. State U., Normal, 1985, Wilkes Coll., Wilkes-Barre, Pa., 1985, Albright-Knox Mus., Buffalo, N.Y., 1984, Ark. Art Ctr., Little Rock, 1984, Millersville (Pa.) U., 1983, Fairfield (Conn.) U., 1983, Marion Koogler McKay Inst., San Antonio, 1983, Boston City Hall Gallery, 1983, Cedar Rapids (Iowa) Mus. Art, 1982, Montclair (N.J.) Jr. League, 1981, Iowa Arts Coun., Des Moines, 1980-81, numerous others. Sr. Faculty fellow Va. Ctr. for Creative Arts, 1996, Dartmouth Coll., 1993, MacDowell Colony, 1992, Devel. grant U. Iowa, 1980, 86; Summer fellowship U. Iowa, 1979, Rsch. and Travel grantee Ford Found., 1979-80, Yaddo Found., 1965, 72, Travel grantee U. Iowa Found., 1986; recipient Disting. Alumni award Boston U., 1988. Mem. NAD (academician mem.), Coll. Art Assn. Independent. Presbyterian. Avocations: music, poetry, travel, tennis. Office: Dartmouth Coll Hb 6081 Studio Art Hanover NH 03755

MOSS, BETTY SMITH, social worker; b. Fairfield, Ala., Dec. 8, 1931; d. James William Clarke and Helen Sarah (McKelduff) Smith; m. Cameron Gresham, Nov. 1, 1952; children: James Michael, David Patrick, Catherine Alice Moss Hodges, Nancy Carol Moss Weaks. BSSW, U. Ala., Birmingham, 1983. Lic. social worker, Ala.; cert. AIDS counselor, Fla. Staff Cooper Green Hosp., Birmingham, Ala., 1983-86; vol. Medicare, Medicaid Advocacy prog. counselor AARP, Panama City, Fla., 1987; vol. chmn. of hosp. vols. ARC, Tyndall AFB, Panama City, Fla., 1987-88; case mgr. Bay County Coun. on Aging, 1988; discharge planner Bay Med. Ctr., Panama City, Fla., 1988-94; ret., 1994. Bd. dirs. Western Mental Health Clinic; com. mem. AIDS Task Force, Birmingham, 1985-86. Mem. Nat. Assn. Social Workers, Acad. of Cert. Baccalarate Social Workers, Omicron Delta Kappa, Phi Kappa Phi, Alpha Lambda Delta. Home: 3007 Whispering Pines Ln Fultondale AL 35068-1029

MOSS, BILL RALPH, lawyer, publisher; b. Amarillo, Tex., Sept. 27, 1950; s. Ralph Voniver and Virginia May (Atkins) M.; m. Marsha Kelman, Mar. 2, 1985; 1 child, Brandon Price. BS with spl. honors, West Tex. State U., 1972, MA, 1974; JD, Baylor U., 1976; cert. regulatory studies program, Mich. State U., 1981. Bar: Tex. 1976, U.S. Dist. Ct. (no. dist.) 1976, U.S. Tax Ct. 1979, U.S. Ct. Appeals (5th cir.) 1983. Briefing atty. Ct. Appeals 7th Supreme Jud. Dist. Tex., Amarillo, 1976-77; assoc. Culton, Morgan, Britain & White, Amarillo, 1977-80; hearings examiner Pub. Utility Commn. Tex., Austin, 1981-83; asst. gen. counsel State Bar Tex., Austin, 1983-87; founder, owner Price & Co. Publs., Austin, 1987—; instr., lectr. West Tex. State U., Canyon, Ea. N.Mex. U., Portales, 1977-80. Active All Saints' Episcopal Ch. Mem. ABA, Tex. Bar Assn. (speaker profl. devel. programs 1983—), Nat. Orgn. Bar Counsel, Internat. Platform Assn., Alpha Chi, Lambda Chi Alpha, Omicron Delta Epsilon, Phi Alpha Delta, Sigma Tau Delta, Pi Gamma Mu. Home and Office: 2719 Mountain Laurel Ln Austin TX 78703-1142 Office: PO Box 164002 506 Explorer Dr Austin TX 78716-4002

MOSS, CHARLES, advertising agency executive; b. Bklyn., Sept. 7, 1938; s. Samuel and Celia (Liebes) Moskowitz; m. Margo Jean Schekman, July 3, 1963 (div.); 1 child, Robert Evan; m. Susan Dukes Calhoun, Mar. 18, 1977; children: Mary Calhoun, Samuel Calhoun. BA cum laude, Ithaca Coll., 1961. Copywriter Doyle, Dane, Bernbach, N.Y.C., 1962-65; group copy supr. J. Tinker & Partners, N.Y.C., 1965-66; creative dir. Wells, Rich, Greene, Inc., N.Y.C., 1968-74; pres., chief operating officer Wells, Rich, Greene, Inc., 1971-76, vice chmn., corp. creative dir., 1976—, also bd. dirs.; now chmn. Moss/Dragoti (ptnr. co. Wells, Rich, Greene/BDDP), N.Y.C. Author (with Stan Dragoti); film Dirty Little Billy, 1971. Mem. adv. bd. NYU Sch. Continuing Edn.; mem. creative rev. bd. Com. for Drug Free Am. Served with AUS, 1962-68. Recipient Gold Key Copy Club, 1968, 1st prize Clio award, 1968, 1st prize Art Dirs. Club, 1968; Andy award N.Y. Advt. Club, 1968, spl. Tony award, Golden Apple award for I Love New York advt. campaign 1978, Clio Classic Hall of Fame award 1983, 86, Gold medal for Hertz Corp., Internat. Film Festival, 1995. Mem. Writers Guild Am., Screen Authors Guild, Vertical Club. Avocations: tennis, jogging. Office: Moss Dragoti 9 W 57th St New York NY 10019

MOSS, CRUSE WATSON, automobile company executive; b. Kent, Ohio, Apr. 7, 1926; s. Cruse Watson and Lucile (Shafer) M.; m. Virginia Ann Patton, Dec. 22, 1949; children: Stephen, Carol Susan, Michael. BS in Indsl. Engring., Ohio U., 1948, LLD (hon.), 1985. Pres. Kaiser Jeep Automotive div., also exec. v.p. Kaiser Jeep Corp., 1960-70; group v.p. Am. Motors Corp., 1970; pres., dir. AM Gen. Corp., Detroit, 1970-79; chmn., chief exec. officer, dir. White Motor Corp., Farmington Hills, Mich., 1979-81; chmn. bd., chief exec. officer Gen. Automotive Corp., Ann Arbor, Mich., 1981—; chmn. bd. dirs., chief exec. officer The Flxible Corp., Delaware, Ohio; bd. dirs. The Burnham Fund Inc., N.Y.C. Mem. founders soc. Detroit Inst. Arts; dir. The Burnham Fund, Inc., N.Y.C. With USNR, 1944-46. Mem. Soc. Automotive Engrs., Confrerie des Chevaliers du Tastevin, Chief Execs. Orgn., Beta Theta Pi, Tau Beta Pi. Presbyterian. Clubs: Circumnavigators, Barton Hills Country, Detroit Athletic, Travis Pointe Country. Office: Gen Automotive Corp 2015 Washtenaw Ave Ann Arbor MI 48104-3656

MOSS, DOUGLAS G., professional hockey team executive. CEO, pres. Buffalo Sabres. Office: Buffalo Sabres Marine Midland Arena One Main St Buffalo NY 14203*

MOSS, ERIC OWEN, architect; b. L.A., July 25, 1943. BA, UCLA, 1965; MArch with honors, U. Calif., Berkeley, 1968, Harvard U., 1972. Prof. design So. Calif. Inst. Architecture, 1974—; prin. Eric Owen Moss Archs., Culver City, Calif., 1975—; Eliot Noyes chair Harvard U., Cambridge, Mass., 1990; Eero Saarinen chair Yale U., New Haven, 1991; lectr. Hirshhorn Mus. Symposium, Washington, 1990, Nat. AIA Conv., 1990, Mus. Contemporary Art, L.A., 1991, N.Y. Archtl. League, 1991, Archtl. Assn. Ireland, Dublin, Archtl. Assn., London, 1991, Royal Coll. Art, London, 1991, Smithsonian Inst., Washington, 1992, U. Calif., Berkeley, 1992, Osterreichiaches Mus. fur Angewandte Kunst, Vienna, Austria, 1992, UCLA, 1992, Royal Danish Acad. Fine Arts, Copenhagen, 1993, U. Lund, Sweden, 1993, Mus. Finnish Architecture, Helsinki, 1993, Royal Acad. Arts, London, 1993, U. Pa., Phila., 1994, others; tchr. U. Tex., Austin, 1983, Wash. U., St. Louis, 1984, U. Ill., Chgo., 1985, Tulane U., New Orleans, 1985, U. Minn., Mpls., 1985, Columbia U., N.Y.C., 1986, Rice U., Houston, 1988; participant various confs. Exhbns. of work include World Biennial of Architecture, Sofia, Bulgaria, 1989, Salle des Tirages du Credit Foncier de France, Paris, 1990, Bartlett Sch. Architecture and Urban Design, London, 1991, Gallery of Functional Art, Santa Monica, Calif., 1992, GA Gallery, Tokyo, 1992, Mus. fur Gestaltung Zurich, Switzerland, 1993, Santa Monica (Calif.) Mus. Art, 1993, Fonds Regional D'Art Contemporain du Centre, 1993, Aspen (Colo.) Art Mus., 1993, Centro de Arte y Comunicacion, Buenos Aires, 1993, Contemporary Arts Ctr., Cin., 1993, Philippe Uzzan Galerie, Paris, 1993, Contemporary Arts Ctr., Tours, France, 1993, Internat. Exhbn. Contemporary Architecture, Havana, Cuba, 1994, others. Recipient Progressive Architecture Design award, 1978, 92, Winning Interior Archtl. Record award, 1984, Interiors Design award, 1991. Fellow AIA (L.A. awards 1977, 79, 83, 88, 90, Calif. Coun. awards 1981, 86, 88, L.A. Honor awards 1991, Nat. Honor awards 88, 89, Calif. Coun. Urban Design/Adaptive Re-Use awards 1991, Nat. Interior Design awards 1992, 94, L.A. Design awards 1992, 93). Subject of monographs and numerous articles in mags. and jours. Office: 8557 Higuera St Culver City CA 90232-2535*

MOSS, GERALD S., dean, medical educator; b. Cleve., Mar. 4, 1935; s. Harry and Lillian (Alter) M.; m. Wilma Jaback, Sept. 1, 1957; children: William Alan, Robert Daniel, Sharon Lynn. BA, Ohio State U., 1956, MD cum laude, 1960. Diplomate Am. Bd. Surgery (apptd. assoc. examiner com. 1989); lic. Ill. Intern Mass. Gen. Hosp., Boston, 1960-61, resident, 1961-65; from asst. prof. to assoc. prof. dept. surgery Coll. Medicine U. Ill., Chgo., 1968-72, prof., 1973-77, 89—, head dept. surgery, 1989, dean, 1989—; prof. dept. surgery Pritzker Sch. Medicine U. Chgo., 1977-89; prof. dept. surgery U. Ill., Coll. of Medicine, 1989—; tutor in surgery Manchester (Eng.) Royal Infirmary, 1964; asst. chief surgical svcs. VA West Side Hosp., Chgo., 1968-70; attending surgeon dept. surgery Cook County Hosp., Chgo. 1970-72, chmn. 1972-77; dir. surgical rsch. Hektoen Inst. for Med. Rsch., Cook County Hosp., 1972-77, Micheal Reese Hosp. and Med. Ctr., Chgo., 1977-89, chmn. dept. surgery, 1977-89, chief svc. 1989, trustee, 1981, and numerou coms.; appointed to Nat. Rsch. Coun., NAS, 1966-68, Ad Hoc Subcom., NAE, 1970, Ad Hoc Study Sect., 1970, del. to Third Joint U.S-USSR Symposium, 1983, Blood Diseases and Resources Adv. Com., 1984-88, Planning Com. for discussing key blood problems, Nat. Heart and Lung Inst., 1987, chmn. Plasma and Plasma Products Com., 1979, bd. dirs., 1983, v.p., 1985, Ad Hoc Transition Com., Am. Blood Commn., 1989, Panel on Rsch. Opportunities, Office Naval Rsch. Program, 1987, exec. com., coord. com., Nat. Blood Edn. Program, 1988, Tech. Adv. Task Force Am. Hosp. Assn., 1988, chmn. review panel contract proposals, NIH, 1975, program project site visit, 1976, chmn. site-visit review group, 1977, adv. com. Blood Resources Work group, 1978, Planning Com. for Consensus, 1987, Small Bus. Innovation Rsch., 1988, Med. Rsch. Scv. Merit Review Bd. VA, 1978-81, Liaison Com. Graduate Med. Edn. AMA, 1979, and numerous other coms. for various med. organizations; cons. Nat. Heart and Lung Inst., Transfusion Medicine Acad. Awardees Program; vis. prof. Montefiore Med. Ctr. Bronx, N.Y., 1986, Ohio State U., 1988, U. N.Mex., Albuquerque, 1989, Seton Med. Ctr., Austin, Tex., 1990, U. Ill. Coll. Medicine, Peoria, 1991; guest lectr., participant numerous meetings, symposiums; cons. in field. Contbr. numerous articles to profl. jours., chpts. to books.. With U.S. Army, 1965-68, Vietnam. Teaching fellow Harvard Med. Sch., 1962; receipient Stitt Lectr. award Assn. Mil. Surgeons U.S.A., 1981; grantee U.S. Navy, 1969-84, U.S. Army, 1971-74, 75-78, NIH, 1969, 83-84, Dept. Pub. Health, 1973, HEW, 1974-77, UpJohn, 1974, Northfield Labs. 1985-89. Fellow ACS (pre and postoperative care com. 1975-83, rep. Am. blood commn. 1977—, mem. various coms., speaker various symposiums), Am. Soc. Surgery Trauma; mem. Am. Surgical Assn. (rep. Nat. Soc. Med. Rsch. 1984-88), Am. Trauma Soc., Am. Physicians Fellowship (rep. Israel Med. Assn.), Assn. Acad. Surgery (chmn. membership selection com. 1973-75, pres. elect 1974-75, pres. 1975-76, exec. coun. 1977-79), Soc. Univ. Surgeons (rep. Nat. Soc. Med. Rsch. 1973-77, com. Surgical Edn. 1979-81), Ctrl. Surgical Soc. (rep. Nat. Soc. Med. Rsch. 1973-77), Shock Soc. (chmn. planning com. 1986, chmn. program com. 1986, pres. elect 1986-87, pres. 1987-88), Soc. for Surgery Alimentary Tract (mem. com. west north ctrl. region 1978-82), Internat. Soc. Blood Transfusion, SurgicalBiology Club II, Nat. Soc. for Med. Rsch., Collegium Internationale Chirugiae Digestivae, Societe Internationale de Chirugie, Sigma XI, Alpha Omega Alpha (faculty advisor 1972-73). Office: U Ill Coll Medicine 1853 W Polk St # C 784 Chicago IL 60612-4316

MOSS, JOE FRANCIS, sculptor, painter; b. Kincheloe, W.Va., Jan. 26, 1933; s. Thomas R. and Audra (Frazier) M.; m. Jean Elizabeth Marcrum, July 1, 1952 (dec.); children: Joe Marcum, Jon Eric, Jay Keith; m. Daphne Brauner, 1992. BA in Art, W.Va. U., 1955, MA in Art, 1960. Tchr. art Morgantown (W.Va.) High Sch., 1956-60; assoc. prof. art W.Va. U., Morgantown, 1960-70; prof. art U. Del., Newark, 1970—. One-man shows of sculpture Washington Gallery Modern Art, 1967, Russell Mus., Great Falls, Mont., 1973, Sculpture Now Gallery, N.Y.C., 1975, CUNY Grad. Center, 1975, J.B. Speed Mus., Louisville, 1977, Madison Sq. Park, N.Y.C., 1980, Marian Locks Gallery and Marian Locks East, Phila., 1981, Fine Arts Gallery U.M.B.C., Balt., 1986; 20-yr. retrospective Edison Fine Arts Gallery, Ft. Myers, Fla., 1985; exhibited in numerous group shows including, Mus. Modern Art, N.Y.C., 1966, Fischbach Gallery, N.Y.C., 1966, Fellows of the Center Exhbn., M.I.T., 1978, Sculpture Now, N.Y.C., 1979, Laumeier Sculpture Park, St. Louis, 1979, Neuberger Mus., Purchase, N.Y., 1981, Kunsthalle, Hamburg, Fed. Republic Germany, 1985, Robert Moses Plaza, N.Y.C., 1985-86, MIT, 1986 Lights Orot, Yeshiva U., N.Y.C., 1988-89, St. Mary's Coll., South Bend, Inc., 1989—, Hist. and Fine Arts Mus., Anchorage, 1987, Montreal, Can. 1988; traveling exhibits include Multiple Interaction, MIT, also Phila., N.Y.C., L.A., Sculpture 75 Exhbn., Phila., 1975, invitational exhibit, U. Tenn., Chattanooga, 1971; represented in permanent collections Arts and Humanities Council Huntington (W.Va.) Galleries, Polaroid Corp., Cambridge, Mass., Martin Fine Villa, Miami, Fla., Cedarcrest Coll., Allentown, Pa., Johnson Mus., Ithaca, N.Y., Urban Am., Washington, Bloomsburg (Pa.) State Coll., St. Louis Art Mus., Del. Art Mus., others, also pvt. collections; one-man shows of paintings Pa. State U., 1965, Pitts. Playhouse Gallery, 1965, W.Va. U., 1965; exhibited in group shows, Fifty Artists Fifty States, Burpee Mus., Rockford, Ill., 1965, Am. Fedn. Art, 1966-68, Bocour Collection, Keene (N.H.) State Coll., 1974, others, interviews, WTOP-TV, Washington, 1967, Voice of Am, 1967; speaker Internat. Sculpture Conf. Kans. U., Lawrence, 1974; feature CNN including Sci. Week in Rev. Grantee W.Va. U., 1963, 67, 68, U. Del. Research Found., 1971, 72, Dimer Found., 1976-77; vis. research fellow Ctr. for Advanced Visual Studies MIT, Cambridge, 1973, Nat. Endowment for Arts fellow, 1980-81, Del. State Arts Council fellow, 1980-81; recipient 1st prize Nat. Show Huntington Galleries Mus., 1963, Environmental Sculpture award Three Rivers Exhbn., 1968, sculpture award Appalachian Corridors Exhibit, 1968. Home: 801 Valley Rd Newark DE 19711-2585

MOSS, KATE, model; b. Croydon, England, Jan. 16, 1974. With Storm Agy., England, Women Model Mgmt., N.Y.; model Calvin Klein Jeans. Office: Women Model Mgt 107 Greene St Fl 2 New York NY 10012-3803*

MOSS, LAWRENCE KENNETH, composer, educator; b. L.A., Nov. 18, 1927; s. Oscar and Sadye (Jacobs) M.; m. Graydon Hindley, Mar. 29, 1958; children: Pamela Ann, Claramarie, Jonathan, Ruth. Student, Pomona Coll., 1945-47; AB, UCLA, 1949; AM, Eastman Sch. Music, 1950; PhD, U. So. Calif., 1957. Prin. studies with Leon Kirchner, 1951-53; asst. prof. music theory Yale U., 1960-65, asso. prof. music theory, 1965-69; prof. music composition U. Md., 1969—. Composer: String Quartet, 1958, Sonata for Violin and Piano, 1959; 1 act comic opera The Brute, 1960; Four Scenes for Piano, 1961; Fromm commn., Scenes for Small Orchestra, 1961; women's chorus and piano In Spring, 1962; brass quintet Music for Five, 1963; soprano and piano Three Rilke Songs, 1963; chamber ensemble Remembrances, 1964; 2 act opera The Queen and the Rebels, 1965, rev. for chamber ensemble, 1989; piano for 4 hands Omaggio, 1966; flute, clarinet, doublebass Windows; flute, clarinet, viola, piano Patterns, 1967; wood-winds brass, percussion Exchanges, 1968; (New Haven Symphony commn.) soprano and orch. Ariel; 2 violins and viola Elegy, 1970; violin, piano, percussion Timepiece, 1970; (U. Chgo. Symphony commn.) orch. Paths, 1970; woodwind quintet and tape Auditions, 1971; alto saxophone and tape Evocation and Song, 1972; Fantasy for Piano, 1973; chorus and tape Exercise, 1973; soprano, oboe, tape, slides, lights Unseen Leaves, 1975; String Quartet, 1975; oboe, percussion Toot-Sweet, 1976; trombone, piano B.P., A Melodrama, 1976; Symphonies for Brass Quintet and Chamber Orchestra, 1977; piano and tape Omaggio II, 1977; oboe, harpsichord Little Suite, 1978; soprano, flute, clarinet, violin, percussion, dancer, slides, tape Nightscape, 1978; piano Ballad, 1979; piano, tape Hands Across the C, 1979; brass quintet Flight, 1979; tuba and bass-baritone Tubaria, 1979; dancer, tape, slides and lights Dreamscape, 1980; Flute choir Chanson, 1980; (Kindler Found. Commn.) string quartet String Quartet No. 3, 1980; cello solo Espressivo, 1981; clarinet, tape, dancer Images, 1981; soprano, flute, guitar Somewhere Inside Me, 1981; conductor soprano, flute, clarinet, viola, harp, piano, Loves, 1982 (NEA Consortium commn.); conductor, flute, clarinet, percussion, violin, cello, piano Music of Changes, 1986; tape, slides, lights, dancers, Rites, 1983; soprano, tape, Darkharbor, 1983; flute, percussion Aprèsludes, 1983; soprano, flute, piano At Night, 1984; dancer, tape Song to the Floor, 1984; piano A Musical Trip, 1984; piano, tenor Portals, 1984; movie Installation ... Lament, 1984; tape, dance That Gong-Tormented Sea, 1985; tenor, flute, clarinet, cello, percussion, violin, viola Voyages, 1985, Videotape Ephemeral Art, 1985; singer, tape, dancer Lesbia's Sparrow, 1985; dancer, percussion Incidental Music, 1986; flute, clarinet, violin, cello, percussion, piano Music of Changes, 1986; baritone, piano Drumtaps, 1986; clarinet solo Nature Studies, 1987; viola, tape Violaria, 1988; clarinet, mime/dancer, tape Blackbird, 1987; woodwind quintet Various Birds, 1987; chorus and piano Grand Is the Seen, 1988; 2 flutes, trumpet, harp, percussion, string quintet Clouds, 1989; soprano, tape Summer Night on the Youghiheny River, 1989, baritone, harp Lovesongs, 1990, soprano, violin, clarinet piano 4-hands Songs of the Earth and Air, Piano 4-hands Hommage, 1991, flute, clarinet, double bass, Through A Window..., 1992, Quartet for flute, cello, percussion and piano, chorus and piano, alto saxophone and tape Saxpressivo, The Gate, 1992; soprano, piano 2 songs to poems by Emily Dickinson, 1993; tenor, harp, oboe 10 Miracles, 1993; alto saxophone, piano 6 Short Pieces, 1993; China for tape alone, 1994; full orch., oboe and baritone soloists From Dawn to Dawn, 1995; band Chinese Lullaby, 1995, Fantasia for Harp Solo, 1996, Raccordo for Piano Solo, 1996, Into the Night for Flute Solo and Tape, 1996. Served with AUS, 1954-56. Fulbright scholar Vienna, 1953-54; Guggenheim fellow Florence, 1959-60, 68-69; Morse fellow Yale U., to Rome, 1964-65; Nat. Endowment Humanities grantee, 1975, 77, 80; U. Md. Disting. Scholar/Tchr. award, 1982-83; composer-in-residence Rockefeller Cultural Ctr., Bellagio, Italy, 1986. Mem. ASCAP. Home: 220 Mowbray Rd Silver Spring MD 20904-1221 Office: U Md Dept Music College Park MD 20740

MOSS, LESLIE OTHA, philanthropist, criminal justice administrator; b. Detroit, Mar. 8, 1952; s. Lonnie and Emma (Robinson) M. BA, U. Mich., 1982, postgrad., 1990—. Technician oper. rm. Sinai Hosp., Detroit, 1972-75; nurses' technician Detroit Osteo. Hosp., 1976-83; supr. Southfield (Mich.) Placement Ctr., 1983-85; rsch. asst. Wayne County Commr.'s Office, Detroit, 1985-86; fin. aid counselor Wayne State U., 1986-87; probation officer Dept. Corrections State of Mich., 1988—; exec. asst. Human Rights Dept., City of Detroit; rsch. asst. Law Dept. City of Detroit, 1990; asst. pers. mgr. Detroit Osteo. Hosp., 1991-93, Highland Pk. C.C., 1991-93; mental health worker Mich. Health Ctr.-Adult Mental Health and New Ctr. Hosp., Detroit, 1992-94; legal technician Ptnrs. Against Crime, Detroit, 1994; social work technician, 1994; sgt. of arms Detroit Police Res., 1987—; intern, assoc. prodr. local TV sta., Detroit, 1993; mem. bd. advisors, mem. bd. govs. Am. Biog. Rsch. Inst., dep. gov., 1994; exec. cons. in field., 1993—; asst. pers. mgr., 1993—. Bd. advisors Am. Biog. Inst., 1994; active re-election com. Mayor Coleman A. Young, Detroit, 1989-93; patient care counselor; adv. various causes, including industrialized Am., higher edn., automotive quality. Recipient Twentieth Century Achievement award Biog. Centre, 1994, Spl. Recognition award Detroit Pub. Sch. Sys., 1992, Internat. Man of Yr. award, 1992-93; award for mass media svc. participation Barden Cable Vision, Detorit, 1991, Man of the Yr. award, 1996, Disting. Alumni Award Mumford H.S. Detroit, 1996; named Most Admired Man of Decade, 1994, Disting. Alumnus, Detroit Pub. Schs. Mich., 1995, Most Admired Man of the Yr., State of Mich., 1995. Mem. NAFE, NAACP (advisor 1989), Internat. Order of Merit, Assn. Pre-Med Students (cons. 1988—), Assn. Psychologists, Am. Biog. Rsch. Inst. Assn. (mem. bd. govs. 1993, dep. gov.), Internat. Platform Assn., U. Mich. Alumni Assn., Golden Key (life), Kappa Alpha Psi.

MOSS, MADISON SCOTT, editor; b. Charlotte, N.C., May 23, 1948; s. James Madison and Nellie Lee (Jenkins) M. BA in English, U. N.C., 1970. Editl. aide NASW, Inc., Washington, 1974, promotions specialist, 1974-79, assoc. editor, 1979-80, editor, 1980-90, mng. editor, 1990—. Creator numerous videos. Campaign coord. Eugene McCarthy for Pres., Rutherford County, N.C., 1968. Recipient award for Pub. Excellence Comms. Concepts, 1993, 94, 95, 96, Bronze award newspaper gen. excellence Soc. Nat. Assn. Publs., 1996. Mem. ACLU, U. N.C. Gen. Alumni Assn., Am. Found. AIDS Rsch. Democrat. Avocations: video producing, creating digital art and animations, reading. Office: NASW Inc 750 1st St NE Ste 700 Washington DC 20002-4241

MOSS, MELVIN LIONEL, anatomist, educator; b. N.Y.C., Jan. 3, 1923; s. Maurice and Ethel (Lander) M.; m. Letty Salentijn, Apr. 1970; children (by previous marriage)—Noel Morrow, James Andrew. A.B., N.Y. U., 1942; D.D.S., Columbia, 1946, Ph.D., 1954. Mem. faculty Columbia, 1954—, prof., 1967-93; prof. emeritus, 1993; also dean Columbia (Sch. Dental and Oral Surgery.). Recipient Lederle Med. Faculty award, 1954-56. Fellow AAAS, Royal Anthrop. Soc. Gt. Britain; mem. Am. Assn. Anatomists, Am. Assn. Phys. Anthropologists, Internat. Assn. Dental Research (craniofacial biology award), Am. Soc. Zoologists, Sigma Xi, Omicron Kappa Upsilon. Research, numerous publs. on skeletal growth and application of computer-assisted methods of numerical and graphic analysis of growth. Home: 560 Riverside Dr New York NY 10027-3202

MOSS, MYRA ELLEN (MYRA MOSS ROLLE), philosophy educator; b. L.A., Mar. 22, 1937; m. Andrew Frank Rolle, Nov. 5, 1983. BA, Pomona Coll., 1958; PhD, The Johns Hopkins U., 1965. Asst. prof. Santa Clara (Calif.) U., 1968-74; prof. Claremont McKenna Coll., 1975—, chmn. Dept. of Philosophy, 1992-95; assoc. dir. Gould Ctr. for Humanities, Claremont, Calif., 1993-94; adv. coun. Milton S. Eisenhower Libr./Johns Hopkins U., 1994-96. Author: Benedetto Croce Reconsidered, 1987; translator Benedetto Croce's Essays on Literature & Literary Criticism, 1990; assoc. editor Special Issues; Symposia Journal of Value Inquiry, 1991, 92, 93 (Honorable Mention, Phoenix award). Dir. Flintridge (Calif.) Riding Club, 1991. Mem. Am. Philos. Assn., Am. and Internat. Soc. for Value Inquiry, Soc. for Aesthetics, Phi Beta Kappa (hon.). Avocations: gardening, horseback riding. Office: Claremont McKenna Coll 890 Columbia Ave Claremont CA 91711-3901

MOSS, RICHARD B., pediatrician; b. N.Y.C., Oct. 30, 1949. MD, SUNY, Downstate, 1975. Intern Children's Meml. Hosp., Chgo., 1975-76, resident, 1976-77; fellow Stanford (Calif.) U. Med. Sch., 1977-79, 80-81; now pediatrician Lucile Salter Packard Children's Hosp., Palo Alto, Calif.; prof. pediats. Stanford U. Med. Sch. Office: Stanford U Sch Med Ctr Dept Pediats Stanford CA 94305-5119

MOSS, RICHARD L., physiology educator; b. Fond du Lac, Wis., Nov. 2, 1947; s. Robert C. and Lenore H. Moss; m. Susan L. Rusch, Aug. 17, 1968; 1 child, James P. BS in Biology, U. Wis., Oshkosh, 1969; PhD in Physiology and Biophysics, U. Vt., 1975. Rsch. assoc. Boston Biomed. Rsch. Inst., 1975-79; asst. prof. physiology U. Wis., Madison, 1979-83, assoc. prof., 1983-87, prof., 1987—, chair dept., 1988—; dir. U. Wis. Cardiovascular Rsch. Ctr., 1995—; mem. cellular pharmacology and physiology rsch. study com. Am. Heart Assn., Dallas, 1990-93, Established Investigator, 1981-86; mem. physiology study sect. NIH, 1994—. Mem. editl. bd. Biophys. Jour., 1985-92, Jour. Gen. Physiology, 1987-91, Am. Jour. Physiology: Cellular, 1990-96, Physiol. Revs., 1985-91, Jour. Physiology (London), 1995—; contbr. articles to Biophys. Jour., Circulation Rsch., Nature, Jour. Physiology. NRSA fellow NIH, 1976-78. Achievements include research on regulation of heart and skeletal muscle contraction by selective extraction and/or exchange of regulatory protein from permeabilized muscle preparations, implicating role of thick filament proteins (i.e. light chain-2 and C-protein) in regulation of tension and kinetics of contraction. Office: U Wis Med Sch 1300 University Ave Madison WI 53706-1510*

MOSS, ROBERT DREXLER, lawyer; b. Cleve., June 12, 1909; s. Morris and Rosa (Goldman) M.; m. Ruth K. Rivitz, Dec. 28, 1939; children: Kenneth H., Suzanne R. A.B., Case Western Res. U., 1931, LL.B., 1933, J.D., 1969. Bar: Ohio bar 1933, U.S. Supreme Ct 1960. Practice in Barberton, Ohio and Summit County, Ohio, 1937-95; ret., 1995; past chmn. Ohio Legal Services Fund. Pres. Barberton chpt. ARC, 1966-67;life mem. adv. bd. Salvation Army, Barberton Corps . Served to maj. USAAF, 1942-46. Decorated Bronze Star; recipient Outstanding Law Alumnus award Case Western Res. U., 1976, Sir Thomas More award Bishop Gilbert Sheldon, Vicar of Akron, Bishop for so. region of Cleve. diocese, 1990. Fellow Am. Bar Found. (life mem.); mem. ABA, Ohio State Bar Assn. (pres. 1968-69, Ohio Bar medal 1978), Akron Bar Assn. (pres. 1956-57), Ohio State Bar Assn. Found. (life), Summit County Legal Aid Soc. (pres. 1955). Jewish (past pres. temple). Clubs: Rotary (Barberton), Elks (Barberton), Masons (Akron) (32 deg.), Shriners (Akron), Akron City (Akron), Rosemont Country (Akron) (past pres.); Play House (Cleve.). Home: 1006 Bunker Dr Apt 301 Akron OH 44333-3079

MOSS, ROGER WILLIAM, JR., historian, writer, administrator; b. Zanesville, Ohio, Jan. 31, 1940; s. Roger William and Dorothy Elizabeth (Martin) M.; m. Gail Caskey Winkler, 1981; children by previous marriage: Elizabeth McQuiston, Victoria Stiles. BS in Edn., Ohio U., 1963, MA, 1964; postgrad., Attingham, Eng., summer 1966; PhD, U. Del., 1972. Curator of rare books Ohio U., 1962-64; lectr., dept. history U. Del., 1966-68, U. Md., 1967-68; exec. dir. Athenaeum of Phila., 1968—; adj. assoc. prof. architecture U. Pa., Phila., 1981—. Publs. include Morgan Collection, 1965, Master Builders, 1972, Century of Color, 1981, Biographical Dictionary of Philadelphia Architects, 1985, Philadelphia, 1986, Victorian Interior Decoration, 1986, Victorian Exterior Decoration, 1987, Lighting for Historic Buildings, 1988 (Joel Polsky prize 1989), The American Country House, 1990, House Museums of Philadelphia Vicinity, 1997; gen. editor Athenaeum Libr. of Nineteenth-Century Am. series, 1975—; editor: Paint in America, 1994; contbr. to profl. jours. Bd. dirs. Conservation Ctr. for Art and Hist. Artifacts, 1984-96, chmn., 1993-95, Woodlands Cemetery Co., 1990—, Rsch. Librs. Group, 1993-96; exec. com., Phila. Area Consortium Spl. Coll., Librs., 1988-93; sec. Christopher Ludwick Found., 1969—; bd. dirs. Brit. Cathedrals and Historic Chs. Found., sec.-treas., 1996—, bd. dirs. Abraham Lincoln Found., 1996—, bd. dirs., sec., treas. Victorian Soc. in Am., 1969-88; assoc. Nat. Preservation Inst., 1982-93; bd. dirs. Hist. House Assn. Am., 1978-83, Com. for Preservation of Archtl. Records, 1978-80, Phila. Area Cultural Consortium, 1977-82, also treas., Mus. Coun. Phila., 1976-78; sec. Hopkinson House Council, 1982-93, Clivden Coun., Nat. Trust for Hist. Preservation, 1974-81, 84-86, Harriton House, 1969-81, Friends of Laurel Hill, 1978-83, Franklin Inn Club, 1976-79. NEH grantee, 1983-85. Fellow Royal Soc. Arts; mem. Soc. Archtl. Historians, Soc. Preservation New Eng. Antiquities, Hist. Soc. Pa., Libr. Co., Rushlight Club. Office: Athenaeum of Phila 219 S 6th St Philadelphia PA 19106-3719

MOSS, STEPHEN B., lawyer; b. Jacksonville, Fla., July 14, 1943; s. Rudy and Betty (Sobel) M.; m. Rhoda Goodman, Nov. 24, 1984; children: Kurt, Shannon. BA, Tulane U., 1964; JD, Samford U., 1968. Bar: Fla. 1968, U.S. Dist. Ct. (so. dist.) Fla., U.S. Tax Ct. From assoc. to ptnr. Heiman & Crary, Miami, Fla., 1971-74; pvt. practice law So. Miami, Fla., 1974-75; ptnr. Glass, Schultz, Weinstein & Moss P.A., Coral Gables, Fla., 1975-78, Ft. Lauderdale, Fla., 1978-80; ptnr. Holland & Knight, Ft. Lauderdale, 1980—. Capt. U.S. Army, 1968-70, Vietnam. Named Outstanding Kiwanian, Miami, 1974; Olympic torchbearer, 1996. Fellow ABA, Fla. Bar Found.; mem. Fla. Bar Assn., Fla. C. of C. (bd. dirs. 1996-99), Greater Ft. Lauderdale C. of C. (gen. counsel 1991-92, chmn. bd. dirs., bd. govs. 1995, Chmn.'s award 1991), Tower Club, Tower Forum (pres. 1993-94). Democrat. Jewish. Avocations:

running, softball, hiking, family activities. Office: Holland & Knight Fl 13 1 E Broward Blvd Fort Lauderdale FL 33301-1804

MOSS, STEPHEN EDWARD, lawyer; b. Washington, Nov. 22, 1940; s. Morris and Jean (Sober) M.; m. Abigail Deady, Dec. 19, 1964; children: Aubrey, Hilary. BBA, Baldwin-Wallace Coll., 1962; JD with honors, George Washington U., 1965, LLM, 1968. Bar: D.C. 1966, Md. 1971. Assoc. Cole & Groner, Washington, 1965-70; pvt. practice law Bethesda, Md., 1971-80; pres. Stephen E. Moss, P.A., Bethesda, 1981-89, Moss, Strickler & Weaver, Bethesda, 1990-94, Moss, Strickler & Sachitano, P.A., Bethesda, 1995—; lectr. in family law and trial practice. Fellow Am. Acad. Matrimonial Lawyers (cert.), Internat. Acad. Matrimonial Lawyers; mem. Montgomery County Bar Assn. (chmn. family law sect. 1981). Office: Moss Strickler & Sachitano PA 4550 Montgomery Ave Ste 700 Bethesda MD 20814-3304

MOSS, SUSAN, nurse, retail store owner; b. Youngstown, Ohio, Aug. 17, 1940; d. Jarlath G. and Sara G. (Curley) Carney; divorced; children: John P., Jerri Ann Moss Williams. Lic. nurse, Choffin Sch., 1973; AS in Am. Bus. Mgmt., Youngstown State U., 1992. Surg. scrub nurse St. Elizabeth Hosp., Youngstown, 1972-78; office mgr. Moss Equipment Co., North Jackson, Ohio, 1978-83; pvt. duty nurse Salem, Ohio, 1979—; night nurse supr. Gateways for Better Living, Youngstown, 1982-84; owner Laura's Bride and Formal Wear, Salem, 1987—; CEO Strawberry Sunshine Svcs. Co., Salem, 1994—; cons. Edith R. Nolf, Inc., Salem. Author: (novelette) Turlaleen. Water therapy aide Easter Seal Soc., Youngstown, 1970-75, bd. trustees, 1973-75; mem. Hear, Now, Denver, 1989. Mem. LPN Assn. Ohio, Bus. and Profl. Women, Youngstown State U. Alumni Club, Short Hills Lit. Soc., Beta Sigma Phi (v.p., Silver Circle award 1986, Order of the Rose 1987). Democrat. Roman Catholic. Avocations: writing, painting, music, public speaking, traveling. Office: Lauras Bride & Formal Wear 1271 E Pidgeon Rd Salem OH 44460-4364

MOSS, THOMAS HENRY, science association administrator; b. Cleve., June 27, 1939; s. Joseph Harold and Elsa Margaret (Lemkau) M.; m. Kathleen Goddard, May 31, 1966; children: Ellen, Joseph, Cheryl, David. AB, Harvard U., 1961; PhD, Cornell U., 1965. Cons. analyst govtl. sci. policy U.S. Govt. Office Mgmt. and Budget, Washington, 1963-67; research physicist IBM Corp., Yorktown, N.Y., 1967-74, 75-76; staff dir., sci. advisor Office of Congressman George E. Brown, Washington, 1976-79; staff dir. subcom. sci., research and tech. Ho. of Reps., Washington, 1979-82; prof. physics, dean grad. studies and research Case Western Res. U., Cleve., 1982-96; exec. dir. Govt.-Univ.-Industry Roundtable, 1996—; with Nat. Acad. Scis, Washington; adj. prof. physics Columbia U., N.Y.C., 1966-76; mem. nat rev. com. Office of Nuclear Waste Isolation, Columbus, 1983—; bd. dirs. Univ. Tech. Inc., Cleve.; bd. dirs. Ctr. Great Lakes, Chgo., 1985—; v.p. Edison Poymer Innovation Corp., Independence, Ohio, 1986-90. Editor: The Three Mile Island Nuclear Accident-Lessons, 1981; asst. editor Environ. Profl. mag.; cons. editor Sci, Tech. and Human Values Environ. mag.; contbr. articles to profl. jours. Treas. Lake Bancroft Cmty. Assn., Falls Church, Va., 1980; mem. adv. bd. Small Bus. SBIR Program, Cleve., 1983-85; mem., v.p. Shaker Heights (Ohio) Bd. Edn., 1989-96; chmn. N.E. Region Ohio Systemic Statewide Initiative in Sci. and Math. Edn., 1992-95. ASME fellow, 1995-96, NSF fellow Nobel Instn., 1966-67. Fellow Am. Phys. Soc. (chmn. forum on physics and soc. 1990-91), Nat. Coun. Univ. Rsch. Adminstrs. (Nat. Innovation Program award 1987), Scientists Inst. Pub. Info. (Disting. Svc. award Harlem Prep. Sch. 1971); mem. AAAS (chmn. com. on sci., engrng. and pub. policy 1989-91). Avocations: gardening, camping. Office: NAS 2101 Constitution Ave NW Rm 340 Washington DC 20418-0007

MOSS, WILLIAM JOHN, lawyer; b. Duluth, Minn., Aug. 31, 1921; s. John Hugh and Mary (Quinn) M.; m. Kathryn Casale, June 14, 1947; children: Mary Moss Appleton, Katy Moss Warner, Elizabeth Bradley, Amy Moss Brown, John, Gerard, Hugh, Patricia Moss Sheng, Susan Moss Homola, Barbara Moss Bartol. A.B., Harvard U., 1947, LL.B., 1949. Bar: N.Y. 1950. Assoc. firm Cadwalader, Wickersham & Taft, N.Y.C., 1949-58, ptnr., 1959—. Served to maj. AUS, 1942-45. Republican. Roman Catholic. Home: RR 9D Garrison NY 10524 Office: Cadwalader Wickersham & Taft 100 Maiden Ln New York NY 10038-4818

MOSSAVAR-RAHMANI, BIJAN, oil and gas company executive; b. Tehran, Iran, June 14, 1952; came to U.S., 1978; s. Morteza and Fatemeh (Mohtashem-Nouri) Mossavar-R.; m. Sharmin Batmanghelidj, Oct., 1980. BA, Princeton U., 1974; MS, U. Pa., 1975; MPA, Harvard U., 1982. Oil and energy columnist Kayahan Group of Newspapers, Iran, 1975-78; energy policy analyst Govt. of Iran, 1976-78; vis. rsch. fellow The Rockefeller Found., N.Y., 1978-80; rsch. coord. internat. natural gas study Harvard U., Mass., 1982-85, asst. dir. internat. energy studies, 1985-87; pres. Apache Internat., Inc., Houston, 1988-96; bd. dirs. Apache Côte d'Ivoire Petroleum LDC, Tex., Compagnie des Énergies Nouvelles de Côte d'Ivoire; sr. exec. cons., dir. oil and gas studies Temple, Barker & Sloane, Inc., Mass., 1983-87; chmn. bd. Mondoil Corp., Mora, N.Mex., N.Mex., 1996—; chmn. Assocs. Harvard Internat. Energy Program, Cambridge, Mass., 1988-91; mem. Internat. Consultative Group on Mid. East. Author: Energy Policy in Iran, 1981; co-author: OPEC and the World Oil Outlook, 1983, World Natural Gas Outlook, 1984, The OPEC Natural Gas Dilemma, 1986, Energy Security Revisited, 1987, Natural Gas in Western Europe, 1987, Lower Oil Prices: Mapping the Impact, 1988, Competition and Realignment in Global Energy Markets, 1997; mem. editl. adv. bd. Offshore mag., 1992-94. Bd. dirs. U.S.-Angola C. of C., 1990-92; mem. coun. Internat. Exec. Svc. Corps, 1991—. Mem. Internat. Assn. of Energy Economists, Denver U. Club, Nassau Club, Ivy Club, Harvard Club of N.Y. Avocation: art collecting. Address: PO Box 744 Mora NM 87732-0744

MOSSAWIR, HARVE H., JR., retired lawyer; b. Morton, Miss., Aug. 9, 1942; s. Harve H. and Madeline (Price) M.; children: Anna Christine, Karen Elyse; m. Judy S. Bardugo, Aug. 5, 1985; 1 child, Leigh Sarah. BA with honors, U. Ala., 1964; MA in Econs., U. Manchester, 1965; JD with honors, U. Chgo., 1968. Bar: Calif. 1970. Asst. prof. U. Ala. Law Sch., Tuscaloosa, 1968-69; assoc. Irell & Manella, L.A., 1969-74, ptnr., 1974-94, of counsel, 1994-96. Mem. bd. editors U. Chgo. Law Rev., 1966-68; contbr. articles to profl. jours. Fulbright scholar, 1964-65, Floyd Russell Mecham scholar, 1965-68. Mem. Calif. Bar Assn. Republican.

MOSS BOWER, PHYLIS DAWN, medical researcher; b. Waco, Tex., Oct. 27, 1959; d. Phillip Carroll and Teloiv Anita (Marrs) Eddins; m. W. Taylor Moss, Mar. 22, 1980 (div. Aug. 1990); children: Amber Nikkole Moss, Beau Christian Moss; m. Kevin Eugene Bower, May 27, 1992 (div. Sept. 1994). Student, Tex. Tech. U., 1977-78, 4-C Bus. Coll., 1989-90. Tumor registry Scott & White Hosp., Waco, 1988-92; clin. rsch. in oncology LaGrange (Ill.) Hosp., 1992-93; clin. rsch. asst. pharm. Christie Clinic, Champaign, Ill., 1993-96; data entry, bill clk., office mgr. Restaurant Equipment & Supply Co., 1996—; spirit of Scott & White com. mem. Scott & White Hosp., Temple, Tex., 1992. Leader Girl Scouts USA, Waco, 1983; com. mem. Children's Miracle Network, Temple, 1988-92; breast cancer prevention team Nat. Surg. Adjuvant Bowel and Breast Protocol, LaGrange, 1992-93. Mem. Nat. Tumor Registrars Assn., Tex. Tumor Registrars Assn. (fin. com. mem. 1988-92, membership com. 1989-90), Soc. Clin. Rsch. Assn. (fin. com. mem. 1992—). Methodist. Avocations: calligraphy, embroidery, bowling, cooking, crafts. Home: 909 Front St Villa Grove IL 61956-1301

MOSSE, GEORGE LACHMANN, history educator, author; b. Berlin, Sept. 20, 1918; came to U.S., 1939, naturalized, 1945; s. Hans Lachmann-Mosse and Felicia M. Student, Cambridge (Eng.) U., 1937-39; B.S., Haverford Coll., 1941; Ph.D., Harvard U., 1946; D.Litt., Carthage Coll., 1973; D.H.L., Hebrew Union Coll., 1987; laurea honoris causa, U. Camerino, Italy, 1995. From instr. to assoc. prof. State U. Iowa, 1944-55; from assoc. prof. to prof. U. Wis., 1955-89, Bascom prof. history, 1964-83, Bascom-Weinstein prof. Jewish studies, 1983-89, prof. emeritus, 1989—; fellow Inst. for Advanced Studies Hebrew U., 1987; vis. prof. Stanford U., 1963-64, Hebrew U., 1969-70, 72, 74, 76, 78, Koebner prof., 1979-86, emeritus, 1986—, U. Munich, 1982-83, École des Hautes, Études, Paris, 1986; fellow Inst. Contemporary Jewry, Hebrew U., 1974—; vis. prof. Jewish Tehol. Sem. Am., 1977; sr. fellow Australian Nat. U., 1972, 79; Kaplan vis. prof. Jewish studies U. Cape Town (South Africa), 1980; vis. prof. U. Amsterdam, 1988, U. Tel Aviv, 1989, Pembroke Coll., Cambridge U., 1990, 91, 94, Cornell U., 1989, 92, A.D. White prof.-at-large, 1993—, U. San Marino, 1992, Shapiro Sr. scholar-in-residence U.S. Holocaust Meml. Mus., 1994-95. Author: The Struggle for Sovereignty in England, 1950, The Holy Pretence, 1957, The Reformation, 1953, 2d edit., 1963, The Crisis of German Ideology, 1964, The Culture of Western Europe, 1961, 3d edit., 1988, Nazi Culture, 1966, (with H. Koenigsberger) Europe in the Sixteenth Century, 1968, 2d edit., 1989, Germans and Jews, 1970, The Nationalisation of the Masses, Political Symbols and Mass Movements in Germany, 1975, Nazism, 1978, Towards the Final Solution: A History of European Racism, 1978, Masses and Men, Nationalist and Fascist Perceptions of Reality, 1980, German Jews Beyond Judaism, 1985, Nationalism and Sexuality: Respectability and Abnormal Sexuality in Modern Europe, 1985, Fallen Soldiers: Reshaping the Memory of the World Wars, 1990, Ebrei in Gerhania Fra Assimilazione i antisemitismo, 1991, Ich Bleibe Emigrant: Gespräche, 1991, Confronting the Nation: Jewish and Western Nationalism, 1993, The Image of Man, The Creation of Modern Masculinity, 1996; editor: Police Forces in History, 1975, International Facism, 1979; co-editor: Europe in Review, 1957, Jour. Contemporary History, 1966—, (with Bella Vago) Jews and Non-Jews in Eastern Europe, 1975 (with Jehuda Reinharz) The Impact of Western Nationalisms, 1992; contbr. New Cambridge Modern History. Bd. dirs. Wiener Library, London, 1974-92, Leo Baeck Inst., N.Y.C., 1978—; bd. overseers Tauber Inst., Brandeis U., 1980—. Recipient Premio Aqui Storia, 1975, Premio Prezzolini, Florence, 1985, Goethe Medallie, Goethe Inst., 1988. Mem. AAUP (chmn. Iowa conf. 1954-55), Am. Soc. Reformation Research (pres. 1962), Am. Soc. Ch. History (council 1969-73), Am. Hist. Assn. (Award for Scholarly Distinction 1996), Am. Acad. Arts and Scis., Am. Philos. Soc., Phi Beta Kappa, Phi Eta Sigma (hon.). Home: 36 Glenway St Madison WI 53705-5206

MOSSE, PETER JOHN CHARLES, financial services executive; b. Mtarfa, Malta, Sept. 8, 1947; came to U.S., 1977; s. John Herbert Charles and Barbara Haworth (Holden) M.; m. Christine Marielle St. Preux, Oct. 17, 1994. BA, Oxford U., 1969; MBA, U. Pa., 1971; MA, Oxford U., 1989. Bank officer N.M. Rothschild & Sons Ltd., London, 1971-76; spl. projects officer banking Bumiputra Mcht. Bankers Berhad, Kuala Lumpur, Malaysia, 1976-77; v.p., treas., sec. NMR Metals Incorp., N.Y.C., 1977-79, exec. v.p., 1979-83; sr. v.p. Rothschild, Inc., N.Y.C., 1983-90; v.p., CFO, The Arista Group Inc., N.Y.C., 1991-93; U.S. rep. Travelex Fin. Svcs. Ltd., London, 1994-95; ptnr. Creelman Fine Arts, N.Y.C., 1995—. Mem. Pilgrims of the U.S., St. George's Soc. N.Y. (life), Oxford U. Alumni Soc. (exec. com. 1994-96), The Gold Inst. (co. rep., bd. dirs. 1985-90), The Silver Inst. (co. rep., bd. dirs. 1989-90), The Copper Club, Commodity Exch., Inc. (co. rep. 1979-90). Episcopalian. Avocations: international travel, railroads. Home and Office: 353 E 72nd St Apt 33D New York NY 10021-4622

MOSSEL, PATRICIA L., opera executive; b. N.Y.C., Nov. 19, 1933; d. Burnet Thomas and Martha Camille (Leigh) Kraut; m. Allan A Fleischer, Dec. 30,. 1956 (div. 1987); children: Hillary Lee Wanser, Jason Allan; m. John W. Mossel, Sept. 4, 1993. BA, U. Rochester, 1955; MA, Yale U., 1956. Cert. fund raising exec. Tchr. Colby Coll., New London, N.H., 1956-57; editor Far Eastern Pub.-Yale U., New Haven, 1957-60; dir. devel. San Francisco Opera, 1979-84; dir. devel., mktg. and pub. relations The Wash. Opera, 1984-95, exec. dir., 1995—; mem. bd. San Francisco Symphony and Opera; bd. chmn., exec. dir. Mt. Diablo Rehabilitation Ctr.; co-founder Medi-Physics, Inc.; cons. D.C. Humanities Council, 1989—. Editor: Western Lit. on China, 1959. Mem. adv. council Fund Raising Sch., Indpls.; v.p. Nat. Soc. Fund Raising Exec. Found. bd. dirs., Washington, 1985-87. Mem. Nat. Soc. Fund Raising Execs. (named Fund Raising Exec. of Yr. 1986), Assocs. of Yale Alumni (del. 1988-91), Yale Club, Phi Beta Kappa. Republican. Presbyterian. Avocations: painting, writing, piano. Office: Washington Opera Kennedy Ctr Washington DC 20566-0012

MOSSINGHOFF, GERALD JOSEPH, patent lawyer, engineer; b. St. Louis, Sept. 30, 1935; m. Jeanne Carole Jack, Dec. 29, 1958; children: Pamela Ann Jennings, Gregory Joseph, Melissa M. Ronayne. BSEE, St. Louis U., 1957; JD with honors, George Washington U., 1961. Bar: Mo. 1961, D.C. 1965, Va. 1981. Project engr. Sachs Electric Corp., 1954-57; dir. congl. liaison NASA, Washington, 1967-73, dep. gen. counsel, 1976-81; asst. Sec. Commerce, commr. patents and trademarks U.S. Patent Office, 1981-85; pres. Pharm. Rsch. and Mfrs. Am., Washington, 1985-96; vis. prof. intellectual property law George Washington U., Washington, 1996—; sr. counsel Oblon, Spivak, McClelland, Maier & Neustadt, Washington, 1997—; amb. Paris Conv. Diplomatic Conf.; vis. prof. law George Washington U., 1996—; sr. counsel Oblon, Spivak, McClelland, Maier & Neustadt, 1996—. Recipient Exceptional Svc. medal NASA, 1971, Disting. Svc. medal, 1980, Outstanding Leadership medal, 1981, Disting. Alumnus George Washington U., 1996; granted presdl. rank of meritorious exec., 1980; Disting. Pub. Svc. award Sec. of Commerce, 1983. Fellow Am. Acad. Pub. Adminstrn.; mem. Reagan Alumni Assn. (bd. dirs.), Cosmos Club, Knights of Malta, Order of Coif, Eta Kappa Nu, Pi Mu Epsilon. Home: Penthouse 28 1530 N Key Blvd Arlington VA 22209-1532 Office: George Washington U Law Sch 720 20th St NW Washington DC 20006-4306

MOSSMAN, THOMAS MELLISH, JR., television manager; b. Honolulu, Nov. 20, 1938; s. Thomas Mellish and Marian (Ledwith) M.; children: Thomas Mellish III, James Michael; m. Jan Carla MacAlister, Dec. 31, 1989. Student, U. Hawaii, 1954-57; BA, U. Denver, 1958, MA, 1965. Producer-dir. KRMA-TV, Denver, 1960-64, KCET-TV, L.A., 1964-72; pres. Mosaic Films, L.A., 1972-73; prodn. and operations dir. KLCS-TV, L.A., 1973-78, station mgr., 1978-87, 96—; dept. dir. Archdiocese of L.A., 1987-96; sta. mgr. KLCS-TV, L.A., 1996—; instr. Calif. State U., Northridge, 1981—; chairperson, founder L.A. Community TV, 1987-95. Chmn. exec. bd. Regional Ednl. TV Adv. Coun., 1989-93; chmn., founding mem., chmn. Alliance for Distance Edn. in Calif., 1991-95; pres. Cath. TV Network, 1993-96; bd. dirs. L.A. Cable TV Access Corp. Mem. NATAS, Dirs. Guild Am., Alliance for Community Media. Episcopalian. Office: KLCS-TV 1061 W Temple St Los Angeles CA 90012-1513

MOSSO, DAVID, accountant; b. Pasadena, Calif., Aug. 13, 1926; s. Joseph Ernest and Marian (Ure) M.; m. Lee McVoy Peirce, June 11, 1955; children: Janet, Andrew, Jocelyn. B.B.A. magna cum laude, Washburn U., 1950, D in Commerce (hon.), 1982; M.A. in Econs, U. Minn., 1951. CPA, Va. With Santa Fe Ry., 1942-44; instr. econs. and acctg. Washburn U., 1954-55; with U.S. Treasury Dept., 1955-77, commr. accounts, 1971-73, dep. asst. sec. treasury, 1973-75, asst. sec., 1975-77; with Fin. Acctg. Stds. Bd., 1978-96; vice chmn. Fin. Acctg. Standards Bd., 1986-87, asst. dir. rsch., 1988-96; adj. prof. acctg. Fordham U., 1996—; chmn. Fed. Acctg. Stds. Adv. Bd., Stamford, 1997—. Contbr. articles to profl. jours. Mem. Comptr. Gen.'s Acctg. Stds. Adv. Coun., 1987-90; mem. charter revision commn. City of Stamford, 1986-87, Can.-U.S. Adv. Group on Fed. Reporting, 1984-86; alt. trustee Nat. Gallery Art, 1975-77; dir. Stamford Emergency Med. Svc., 1993-94. 1st lt. AUS, 1944-46, 51-53. Recipient Alexander Hamilton award Treasury Dept., 1977. Mem. AICPA (Elijah Watt Sells award 1962), Va. Soc. CPAs (Gold medal 1962), Assn. Govt Accts. (fed. fin. mgmt. standards bd. 1971-77, dir. Washington chpt. 1972-73, Disting. Leadership award 1977, Elmer Staats award 1990), Treasury Hist. Assn. (pres. 1978), Tau Delta Pi, Pi Gamma Mu, Phi Kappa Phi. Home: 111 Saddle Hill Rd Stamford CT 06903-2307 Office: 441 G St NW Rm 3b18 Washington DC 20548-0001

MOSSOP, GRANT DILWORTH, geological institute director; b. Calgary, Alta., Can., Apr. 15, 1948; s. Cyril S. and Freida E. (Dilworth) M.; m. Ruth Shaver, May 24, 1969; children: Jenny, Jonathan, David. BSc in Geology, U. Calgary, 1970, MSc in Geology, 1971; PhD, DIC in Geology, Imperial Coll., U. London, 1973. Postdoctoral fellow U. Calgary, Alta., Can., 1974; asst. rsch. officer Alta. Rsch. Coun., Edmonton, 1975-77, assoc. rsch. officer, 1977-80, head geol. survey dept., 1980-84, sr. rsch. officer, 1985-91; dir. Geol. Survey of Can., Calgary, 1991—; acad. visitor dept. earth sci. Oxford (Eng.) U., 1984-85. Project mgr., editor Geol. Atlas of Western Canada Sedimentary Basin. Fellow Geol. Assn. Can. (pres. 1986-87); mem. Can. Soc. Petroleum Geologists. Home: 68 Colleen Cres SW, Calgary, AB Canada T2V 2R3 Office: Geol Survey Can, 3303-33d St NW, Calgary, AB Canada T2L 2A7

MOSS-SALENTIJN, LETTY (ALEIDA MOSS-SALENTIJN), anatomist; b. Amsterdam, The Netherlands, Apr. 14, 1943; came to U.S., 1968; d. Ewoud and Johanna Maria (Schoonhoven) Salentijn; m. Melvin Lionel Moss, Apr. 17, 1970. DDS, State U., Utrecht, The Netherlands, 1967, PhD, 1976. Asst. prof. histology, State U., Utrecht, 1967-68; asst. prof. Columbia U., 1968-74, assoc. prof., 1974-86, prof., 1986—, dir. dental radiology, 1980-86, dir. grad. program dental sci., 1986—, dir. postdoctoral affairs, 1987-90, asst. dean postdoctoral programs, 1990-94, assoc. dean acad. affairs, 1994—. Author: Orofacial Histology & Embryology, 1972; Dental and Oral Tissues, 1980, 2d edit., 1984, 3d edit. 1990; contbr. chpts. to books, articles to profl. jours. Fellow Royal Microscopical Soc.; mem. Am. Assn. Anatomists, Internat. Assn. Dental Rsch., Am. Soc. Biomechanics, Sigma Xi. (chpt. sec. 1980-87, pres. 1987-89), Omicron Kappa Upsilon (pres. local chpt. 1987). Avocation: stained glass art. Home: 560 Riverside Dr Apt 20K New York NY 10027-3242 Office: Columbia U Assoc Dean Academic Affairs 630 W 168th St New York NY 10032-3702

MOST, JACK LAWRENCE, lawyer, consultant; b. N.Y.C., Sept. 24, 1935; s. Meyer Milton and Henrietta (Meyer) M.; children: Jeffrey, Peter; m. Irma Freedman Robbins, Aug. 8, 1968; children: Ann, Jane. BA cum laude, Syracuse U., 1956; JD, Columbia U., 1960. Bar: N.Y. 1960, U.S. Dist. Ct. (so. and ea. dists.) N.Y. 1963. Assoc. Hale, Grant, Meyerson and O'Brien, N.Y.C., 1960-66; dep. assoc. dir. OEO, Exec. Office of The Pres., Washington, 1965-67; asst. to gen. counsel C.I.T. Fin. Corp., N.Y.C., 1968-70; corp. counsel PepsiCo, Inc., Purchase, N.Y., 1970-71; v.p. legal affairs Revlon, Inc., N.Y.C., 1971-76; asst. gen. counsel Norton Simon, Inc., N.Y.C., 1976-79; ptnr. Rogers Hoge and Hills, N.Y.C., 1979-86; ptnr. Finkelstein Bruckman Wohl Most & Rothman LLP, N.Y.C., 1986—, mng. ptnr., 1990-93; corp. sec. Requa, Inc., Flowery Beauty Products, Inc., 1987—. Contbr. articles to profl. jour. and mags. Bd. dirs. Haym Salomon Home for the Aged, 1978-91, pres., 1981-91; bd. dirs. The Jaffa Inst. for Advancement Edn., 1994-95; bd. dirs. Jewish Fellowship of Hemlock Farms, 1995—, treas., 1996—; bd. dirs., pres. Haym Salomon Geriatric Found., 1992—; mem. bd. advisors Touro Coll. Health Scis., 1989-90. Mem. ABA (food, drug and cosmetic law com., trademark and unfair competition com.), N.Y. State Bar Assn. (food, drug and cosmetics sect.), Am. Soc. Pharmacy Law, YRH Owners Corp. (bd. dirs., pres. 1989-92), Lords Valley Country Club (bd. govs. 1984-90, 1st v.p. 1987-88, 2d v.p. 1988-90), Zeta Beta Tau, Omicron (trustee Syracuse chpt. 1988-91). Jewish. Home: 429 E 52nd St New York NY 10022-6430 Office: Finkelstein Bruckman Wohl Most & Rothman LLP 575 Lexington Ave New York NY 10022-6102

MOST, NATHAN, mutual fund executive; b. L.A., Mar. 22, 1914; s. Bernard and Bertha (Saltzman) M.; m. Evelyn Rosenthal, July 10, 1964; children—Stephen, John, Robert, Barbara. BA, UCLA, 1935. Exec. v.p. Getz Bros. & Co., San Francisco, 1945-60; pres. Carad Corp., Palo Alto, Calif., 1961-64; exec. v.p. James S. Baker Co., San Francisco, 1964-65, Pacific Vegetable Oil Corp., San Francisco, 1965-70, Am. Import Co., San Francisco, 1970-74; pres. Pacific Commodities Exchange, San Francisco, 1974-76; spl. asst. to chmn. Commodity Futures Trading Commn., Washington, May-Dec. 1976; pres. Amex Commodities Exch., N.Y.C., 1977-80; v.p. new products devel. Am. Stock Exch., 1980-91, sr. v.p., 1991-96; pres., chmn. bd. Webs Index Fund Inc. (formerly Foreign Fund, Inc.), Wilmington, Del., 1996—; pres. Amex Commodities Corp., Inc., N.Y.C., 1982-96; v.p. Calif. Council Internat. Trade, 1966-67; pres. Commodity Club San Francisco, 1970—; bd. dirs. San Francisco-Pacific Commodity Exch., 1970—, San Francisco World Trade Assn., 1970—, World Affairs Council No. Calif., 1953-65; pres. San Francisco World Trade Assn., 1956-58. Councilman Atherton, Calif., 1959-64. Mem. Export Mgmt. Assn. No. Calif. (pres. 1972—), San Francisco Commodity Club (dir.). Home: PO Box 193 Burlingame CA 94011-0193

MOSTELLER, FREDERICK, mathematical statistician, educator; b. Clarksburg, W.Va., Dec. 24, 1916; s. William Roy and Helen (Kelley) M.; m. Virginia Gilroy, May 17, 1941; children: William, Gale. ScB, Carnegie Inst. Tech. (now Carnegie-Mellon U.), 1938, MSc, 1939, DSc (hon.), 1974; AM, Princeton U., 1942, PhD, 1946; DSc (hon.), U. Chgo., 1973, Wesleyan U., 1983; D. of Social Scis. (hon.), Yale U., 1981; LLD (hon.), Harvard U., 1991. Research assoc. Office Pub. Opinion Research, 1942-44; spl. cons. research br. War Dept., 1942-43; research mathematician Statis. Research Group, Princeton, applied math. panel Nat. Devel. and Research Council, 1944-46; mem. faculty Harvard U., 1946—, prof. math. stats., 1951-87, Roger I. Lee prof., 1978-87, prof. emeritus, 1987—, chmn. dept. stats., 1957-69, 75-77, chmn. dept. biostats., 1977-81, chmn. dept. health policy and mgmt., 1981-87; dir. Tech. Assessment Group, 1987—; dir. Ctr. for Evaluation Am. Acad. Arts and Scis., 1994—; vice chmn. Pres.'s Commn. on Fed. Stats., 1970-71; mem. Nat. Adv. Council Equality of Ednl. Opportunity, 1973-78, Nat. Sci. Bd. Commn. on Pre-coll. Edn. in Math., Sci. and Tech., 1982-83; Fund for Advancement of Edn. fellow, 1954-55; nat. tchr. NBC's Continental Class-room TV course in probability and stats., 1960-61; fellow Center Advanced Study Behavioral Sciences, 1962-63, bd. dirs., 1980-86; Guggenheim fellow, 1969-70; Miller research prof. U. Calif. at Berkeley, 1974-75; Hitchcock Found. lectr. U. Calif., 1985. Co-author: Gauging Public Opinion (editor Hadley Cantril), 1944, Sampling Inspection, 1948, The Pre-election Polls, 1948, 49, Stochastic Models for Learning, 1955, Probability with Statistical Applications, 1961, Inference and Disputed Authorship, The Federalist, 1964, The National Halothane Study, 1969, Statistics: A Guide to the Unknown, 3d edit., 1988, On Equality of Educational Opportunity, 1972, Sturdy Statistics, 1973, Statistics By Example, 1973, Cost, Risks and Benefits of Surgery, 1977, Data Analysis and Regression, 1977, Statistics and Public Policy, 1977, Data for Decisions, 1982, Understanding Robust and Exploratory Data Analysis, 1983, Biostatistics in Clinical Medicine, 1983, 3d edit., 1994, Beginning Statistics with Data Analysis, 1983, Exploring Data Tables, Trends and Shapes, 1985, Medical Uses of Statistics, 1986, 2d edit., 1992, Quality of Life and Technology Assessment, 1989, Fundamentals of Exploratory Analysis of Variance, 1992, Meta-analysis for Explanation, 1992, Doing More Good Than Harm, 1993, Medicine Worth Paying For, 1995; author articles in field. Trustee Russell Sage Found.; mem. bd. Nat. Opinion Research Center, 1962-66. Recipient Outstanding Statistician award Chgo. chpt. Am. Statis. Assn., 1971, Boston chpt., 1989, named Sports Statistician of 1996; recipient Myrdal prize Evaluation Research Soc., 1978, Paul F. Lazarsfeld prize Council Applied Social Research, 1979, R.A. Fisher award Com. of Pres.'s of Statis. Socs., 1987, Medallion of Ctrs. for Disease Control, 1988. Fellow AAAS (chmn. sect. U 1973, dir. 1974-78, pres. 1980, chmn. bd. 1981), Inst. Math. Statistics (pres. 1974-75), Am. Statis. Assn. (v.p. 1962-64, pres. 1967, Samuel S. Wilks medal 1986), Social Sci. Research Council (chmn. bd. dirs. 1966-68), Math. Social Sci. Bd. (acad. governing bd. 1962-67), Am. Acad. Arts and Scis. (council 1986-88), Royal Statis. Soc. (hon.); mem. Am. Philos. Soc. (council 1986-88), Internat. Statis. Inst. (v.p. 1986-88, pres.-elect 1989, pres. 1991-93), Math. Assn. Am., Psychometric Soc. (pres. 1957-58), Inst. Medicine of Nat. Acad. Scis. (council 1978), Nat. Acad. Scis., Biometric Soc. Office: 1 Oxford St Cambridge MA 02138-2901

MOSTELLER, ROBERT P., law educator; b. 1948. BA, U. N.C., 1970; MA, Harvard U., 1975; JD, Yale U., 1975. Bar: N.C. 1975, D.C. 1976. Law clk. to Hon. Braxton Craven U.S. Ct. Appeals (4th cir.), Asheville, N.C., 1975-76; atty., chmn. trial div., tng. dir. D.C. Pub. Defender Svc., 1976-83; assoc. prof. Duke U., 1983-87, prof., 1987—, sr. assoc. dean, 1989-91. Mem. Phi Beta Kappa (pres. 1969-70). Office: Sch Law Duke U Durham NC 27708

MOSTELLO, ROBERT ANTHONY, chemical engineer; b. Newark, Dec. 20, 1937; s. Anthony Joseph and Josephine Maria (Guarino) M.; m. Raquel Luisa Martinez, May 22, 1965; children: Elizabeth, Laura, Carolyn, Maria. BSChE, Newark Coll. Engring., 1958; M of Chem. Engring., Stevens Inst. Tech., 1967, PhD in Chem. Engring., 1971. Chem. process engr. Air Reduction Co., Jersey City, 1960-62; sr. chem. engr. Am. Cryogenics Inc., O'Fallon, Ill., 1962-64, Air Reduction Co., Jersey City, 1964-65; chief chem. engr. Procedyne Corp., New Brunswick, N.J., 1969-73; sr. engr. Allied Chem. Corp., Morris Twp., N.J., 1973-76; staff engr. Exxon Chem. Co., Florham Park, N.J., 1976-82; asst. to v.p. ops. Jacobs Engring. Group, Mountainside, N.J., 1982; prin. engr. advisor BOC Process Plants, Murray Hill, N.J., 1983—. Author: (encys.) Encyclopedia of Chemical Process and Design, 1990, Inorganic Chemicals Handbook, 1993, (jour.) Can. Inst. Chem. Engring. Jour., (pub. report) Electric Power Res. Inst. Mem., sec. Welfare Bd., Somerville, N.J., 1987-90. Mem. AIChE (bd. dirs. and editor local chpt. 1974-75). Achievements include 12 patents in field of industrial gases production. Avocations: hiking, gardening, travel, reading. Office: BOC Process Plants 575 Mountain Ave New Providence NJ 07974-2097

MOSTER, MARY CLARE, public relations executive; b. Morristown, N.J., Apr. 7, 1950; d. Clarence R. and Ruth M. (Duffy) M.; m. Louis C. Williams, Jr., Oct. 4, 1987. BA in English with honors, Douglass Coll., 1972; MA in English Lit., Univ. Chgo., 1973. Accredited pub. rels. specialist. Editor No. Trust Bank, Chgo., 1973-75, advt. supr., 1975-77, communications officer, 1977-78; account exec. Hill & Knowlton, Inc., Chgo., 1978-80, v.p., 1980-83, sr. v.p., 1983-87, sr. v.p., mng. dir., 1987-88; staff v.p. comms. Navistar Internat. Corp., Chgo., 1988-93; v.p. corp. comms. Comdisco, Inc., Rosemont, Ill., 1993—; mem. bd. dirs. The Pegasus Players, 1993—. Author poetry, poetry translation. Bd. govs. Met. Planning Coun., Chgo., 1988-94; fellow Leadership Greater Chgo., 1989-90; bd. dirs. New City YMCA, Chgo., 1986-92; corp. devel. bd. Steppenwolf Theatre Co., Chgo., 1988-90; mem. The Chgo. Network, 1994—, bd. dirs., 1996—. Mem. Nat. Investor Rels. Inst. (bd. dirs. 1988-89, 90-93), Arthur W. Page Soc., Pub. Rels. Soc. Am., Internat. Women's Forum, Equipment Leasing Assn. Am. (mem. pub. rels. adv. com.). Avocations: sailing, cross-country skiing. Office: Comdisco Inc 6111 N River Rd Rosemont IL 60018-5158

MOSTERT, PAUL STALLINGS, mathematician, educator; b. Morrilton, Ark., Nov. 27, 1927; s. Johannes F.T. and Lucy (Stallings) M.; m. Barbara Bond; children: Paul Theodore, Richard Stallings, Kathleen, Kristina. A.B., Rhodes Coll, 1950; M.S., U. Chgo., 1951; Ph.D., Purdue U., 1953. Mem. faculty Tulane U., 1953-70, prof. math., 1962-70, chmn. dept., 1968-70; prof. math. U. Kans., 1970-91, prof. emeritus math., 1991—, chmn. dept., 1970-73; vis. prof. U. Tubingen, Germany, 1962-63; vis. prof. math. U. Ky., 1984-85; mem. Inst. Advanced Study, Princeton, 1967-68; chmn. Rhodes Coll. Sci. Initiative Task Force, 1989-90; pres. Equix, Inc., 1984-85, Pennfield Biomechanics Corp., Inc., 1985-89, Equix Biomechanics, 1989—. Co-author: Splitting in Topological Groups, 1963, 3d edit., 1993, Elements of Compact Semigroups, 1966, The Cohomology Ring of Finite and Compact Abelian Groups, 1974; editor: Proc. Conf. Transformation Groups at New Orleans, 1969, Questiones Mathematicae, 1973-95; co-founder, exec. editor: Semigroup Forum, 1970-85, mng. editor, 1967-85, editor, 1985-88. Mem. Ky. Statewide Exptl. Program to Stimulate Competetive Rsch. Com., 1994-96. With USNR, 1945-46. NSF sr. postdoctoral fellow, 1967-68. Mem. AAAS, Am. Math. Soc. (mem. at large coun. 1972-75, chmn. com. on acad. freedom, tenure and employment security 1973-76), Assn. Mems. of Inst. for Advanced Studies, Soc. Indsl. and Applied Math., Internat. Soc. for Optical Engring., Internat. Soc. for Neural Networks, Thoroughbred Owners and Breeders Assn. Office: Equix Biomechanics 870 Corporate Dr Ste 203 Lexington KY 40503-5418

MOSTILLO, RALPH, medical association executive; b. Newark, Apr. 11, 1944; s. Joseph and Antoinette (Cipriano) M. BA in Chemistry magna cum laude, Rutgers U., Newark, 1972; MA in Biochemistry, Princeton U., 1974, PhD in Biochemistry, 1978. NIH rsch. fellow Princeton (N.J.) U., 1972-78; sr. scientist drug regulatory affairs Hoffmann-La Roche, Inc., Nutley, N.J., 1979-85; founder, chmn., chief exec. officer Am. Cancer Assn., Nutley, 1986—. Assoc. editor U.S. Pharmacopoeia XX-Nat. Formulary XV, 1980-85. With USN, 1962-66, Vietnam. Mem. Am. Chem. Soc., Am. Mgmt. Assn., Am. Mktg. Assn., N.Y. Acad. Scis., Am. Legion, Vietnam Vets. of Am., Phi Beta Kappa. Achievements include research on molecular transport systems in E. coli as general models for drug delivery into cells. Home: PO Box 505 Nutley NJ 07110-0505 Office: Am Cancer Assn PO Box 87 Nutley NJ 07110-0087

MOSTOFF, ALLAN SAMUEL, lawyer, consultant; b. N.Y.C., Oct. 19, 1932; s. Morris and Ida (Goldman) M.; m. Alice Tamara Popelowsky, July 31, 1955; children: Peter Alexander, Nina Valerie. BS, Cornell U., 1953; MBA, N.Y.U., 1954; LLB, N.Y. Law Sch., 1957. Bar: N.Y. 1958, D.C. 1964. Assoc. Olwine Connelly Chase O'Donnell & Weyher, N.Y.C., 1958-61; atty. SEC, Washington, 1962-66, asst. dir. 1966-69, assoc. dir. 1969-72, dir. div. investment mgmt. regulation, 1972-76; ptnr. Dechert Price & Rhoads, Washington, 1976—; adj. prof. Georgetown U. Law Ctr., 1972-82; mem. Fin. Acctg. Standards Adv. Bd., 1982-86; mem. adv. bd. Investment Lawyer. Mem. ABA (chmn. internat. devel. sub-com., com. on devels. in investment svcs.), Assn. of Bar of City of N.Y., Fed. Bar Assn. (chmn. exec. coun. securities regulation com. 1990-92), Am. Law Inst. Home: 6417 Waterway Dr Falls Church VA 22044-1325 Office: Dechert Price & Rhoads 1500 K St NW Washington DC 20005-1209

MOSTOVOY, MARC SANDERS, conductor, music director; b. Phila., July 1, 1942; s. Ira and Floretta (Schiff)M. MusB, Temple U., 1963; postgrad. musicology U. Pa., 1964-66; pvt. study in U.S.A., France, 1950-66; MusD (hon.), Combs Coll. of Music, 1980; diploma, Academie of Musique, Nice, France. Conductor, music dir. Concerto Soloists of Phila., 1964—; also dir., 1964—; cultural advisor to gov., Commonwealth of Pa., Harrisburg, 1971-77; music dir. Mozart on the Square, Phila., 1980-91, also dir., 1980-91; music advisor Walnut St. Theater, Phila., 1970—; editor various music compositions. Mem. adv. com. arts and cultural council Greater Phila. C. of C., 1984-88; mem. program adv. com. Nat. Mus. Am. Jewish History, 1985-86; bd. dirs. Citizens for the Arts in Pa., 1984-86. Condr. numerous nat. and internat. concert tours with Concerto Soloists Chamber Orch. of Phila.; artistic dir. Laurel Festival of the Arts, Jim Thorpe, Pa., 1990-95; mem. music adv. panel Pa. Coun. on the Arts, 1991-92. Recipient Orpheus Club award, 1958; Gov.'s citation, Commonwealth of Pa., 1976; Mayor's citation City of Phila., 1984; Temple U. scholar, 1960-63. Mem. Mus. Fund Soc. of Phila., Greater Phila. C. of C. Jewish. Office: Concerto Soloists Chamber Orch 338 S 15th St Philadelphia PA 19102-4902

MOSTOW, GEORGE DANIEL, mathematics educator; b. Boston, July 4, 1923; s. Isaac J. and Ida (Rotman) M.; m. Evelyn Davidoff, Sept. 1, 1947; children: Mark Alan, David Jechiel, Carol Held, Jonathan Carl. B.A., Harvard U., 1943, M.A., 1946, Ph.D., 1948; DSc (hon.), U. Ill., Chgo., 1989. Instr. math. Princeton U., 1947-48; mem. Inst. Advanced Study, 1947-49, 56-57, 75, trustee, 1982-92; asst. prof. Syracuse U., 1949-52; asst. prof. math. Johns Hopkins U., 1952-53, assoc. prof., 1954-56, prof., 1957-61; prof. math. Yale U., 1961-66, James E. English prof. math., 1966-81, Henry Ford II prof. math., 1981—, chmn., 1971-74; vis. prof. Conselho Nat. des Pesquisas, Inst. de Matematica, Rio de Janiero, Brazil, 1953-54, 91, U. Paris, 1966-67, Hebrew U., Jerusalem, 1967, Tata Inst. Fundamental Rsch., Bombay, 1970, Inst. des Hautes Etudes Scientifiques, Bures-Sur-Yvette, 1966, 71, 75, Japan Soc. for Promotion of Sci., 1985, Eidgenossische Technische Hochschule, Switzerland, 1986; chmn. U.S. Nat. Com for Math , 1971-73, 83-85, Office Math. Scis., NRC, 1975-78; mem. sci. adv. coun. Math. Scis. Rsch. Inst., Berkeley, Calif., 1988-91, Weizmann Inst., Israel, Tel Aviv U.; mem. vis. com. dept. math. Harvard U., 1975-81, MIT, 1981-94; Ritt lectr. Columbia U., 1982, Bergman lectr. Stanford U., 1983, Sachar lectr. Tel Aviv U., 1985, Karcher lectr. U. Okla., 1986, Markert lectr. Pa. State U., 1993. Assoc. editor Annals of Math, 1957-64, Trans. Am. Math. Soc, 1958-65, Am. Scientist, 1970-82, Geometrica Dedicata, 1985-90, Jour. D'Analyse, 1994—; editor Am. Jour. Math, 1965-69; assoc. editor, 1969-79; author rsch. articles. Fulbright rsch. scholar, Utrecht U., The Netherlands; Guggenheim fellow, 1957-58. Mem. AAAS, NAS (chmn. sect. math. 1982-84), Am. Math. Soc. (pres. 1987-88, Steele prize for paper of lasting importance 1993), Internat. Math. Union (chmn. U.S. del. to gen. assembly Warsaw 1982, exec. com. 1983-86), Phi Beta Kappa, Sigma Xi. Home: 25 Beechwood Rd Woodbridge CT 06525-1309 Office: Yale Univ Dept Mathematics New Haven CT 06520

MOSZKOWICZ, VIRGINIA MARIE, quality administrator; b. Uniontown, Pa., July 6, 1952; d. Edward Louis and Theresa Elizabeth (Congelio) Olsavicky; m. Michael John Moszkowicz, Sept. 29, 1979. BA in Chemistry, Thiel Coll., 1974; MS in Organic Chemistry, Duquesne U., 1978; MS in Mgmt. Tech., MIT, 1987. Devel. chemist PPG Inds., Pitts., 1974-75; analytical chemist Bayer/Mobay Chem. Corp., Pitts., 1975-78; chem testing leader sensitized goods mfg. divsn. Eastman Kodak Co., Rochester, 1978-80, devel. engr. sensitized goods mfg. divsn., 1980-84, product mgr. motion picture film, 1984-86, unit dir., quality assurance orgn. mfg. supply & distbn., 1987-91; mid. mgr. quality and indsl. engring. Equipment Mfg. Divsn., Ro, 1991-94, quality leader mechanical products, 1995-96; project mgr. consumer cameras Eastman Kodak Co., Rochester, 1996; quality mgr. mfg. Xerox Corp., 1987—. Bd. dirs. Lifetime Assistance Inc. Mme. Am. Soc. Quality Control, Am. Chem. Soc., Rochester Soc. Engrs., Toastmasters Internat. (dist. gov. 1991, club pres. 1994, Toastmaster of Yr. 1981, Disting. Toastmaster 1987). Avocations: skiing, golf, travel, French and German langs.

MOSZKOWSKI, LENA IGGERS, secondary school educator; b. Hamburg, Mar. 8, 1930; d. Alfred G. and Lizzie (Minden) M.; m. Steven Alexander, Aug. 29, 1952 (div. Oct. 1977); children: Benjamin Charles, Richard David (dec. 1995), Ronald Bertram. BS, U. Richmond, 1948; MS, U. Chgo., 1953; postgrad., UCLA, 1958. Tchr. Lab. asst. U. Chgo. Ben May Cancer Research Lab., Chgo., 1951-53; biology, sci. tchrs. Bishop Conaty High Sch., Los Angeles, 1967-68; chemistry, sci. tchr. St. Paul High Sch., Santa Fe Springs, Calif., 1968-69; chemistry, human ecology tchr. Marlborough Sch., Los Angeles, 1969-71; tchr. biology and sci. ecology L.A. Unified Sch. Dist., 1971—. Author: Termite Taxonomy Cryptotermes Haviland and C. Krybi, Madagascar, 1955, Ecology and Man, 1971, Parallels in Human and Biological Ecology, 1977, American Public Education, An Inside Journey, 1991-92. Founder, adminstr., com. mem. UCLA Student (and Practical Assistance Cooperative Furniture), Los Angeles, 1963-67; active participant UCLA Earth Day Program, Los Angeles, 1970. Recipient Va. Sci. Talent Search Winner Va. Acad. of Sci., 1946; Push Vol. Tchr. award John C. Fremont High Sch., Los Angeles, 1978. Mem. Calif. Tchrs. Assn., United Tchrs. L.A., Sierra Club. Democrat. Jewish. Avocations: civil rights, workers rights, redirecting public education, photography, animals. Home: 3301 Shelburne Rd Baltimore MD 21208-5626

MOTAYED, ASOK K., engineering company executive. MS, Rutgers U., 1974. Pres. Sheladia Assoc., Inc., Rockville, Md., 1979—. Office: Sheladia Assoc Inc 15825 Shady Grove Rd Rockville MD 20850-4008

MOTE, CLAYTON DANIEL, JR., mechanical engineer, educator, administrator; b. San Francisco, Feb. 5, 1937; s. Clayton Daniel and Eugenia (Isnardi) M.; m. Patricia Jane Lewis, Aug. 18, 1962; children: Melissa Michelle, Adam Jonathan. BSc, U. Calif., Berkeley, 1959, MS, 1960, PhD, 1963. Registered profl. engr., Calif. Asst. specialist U. Calif. Forest Products Labs., 1961-62; asst. mech. engr., 1962-63; lectr. mech. engring. U. Calif., Berkeley, 1962-63, asst. prof., 1967-69, asst. research engr., 1968-69, assoc. prof., assoc. research engr., 1969-73, prof., 1973—, vice chmn. mech. engring. dept., 1976-80, 83-86, chmn. mech. engring. dept., 1987-91, vice chancellor univ. rels., FANUC chair mech. systems, 1991—; research fellow U. Birmingham, Eng., 1963-64; asst. prof. Carnegie Inst. Tech., 1964-67; vis. prof. Norwegian Inst. Wood Tech., 1972-73, vis. sr. scientist, 1976, 78, 80, 84, 85; cons. in engring. design and analysis; sr. scientist Alexander Von Humboldt Found., Fed. Republic Germany, 1988, Japan Soc. for Promotion of Sci., 1991; mem. adv. bd. for mech. engring. Ga. Inst. Tech., Carnegie Mellon U.; pres. U. Calif. Berkeley Found.; trustee Behring-Hofmann Ednl. Inst. Mem. editl. bd. Soma Jour. Sound and Vibration, Machine Vibration; contbr. articles to profl. jours.; patentee in field. NSF fellow, 1963-64; recipient Disting. Teaching award, U. Calif., 1971, Pi Tau Sigma Excellence in Teaching award, U. Calif., 1975, Humboldt Prize, Fed. Republic Germany, 1988, Frederick W. Taylor Rsch. medal. Soc. Mfg. Engrs., 1991, Hetenyi award Soc. Exptl. Mechanics, 1992. Fellow NAE, AAAS, ASME (Blackall award 1975, v.p. environ. and transp. 1986-90, nat. chmn. noise control and acoustics 1980-84, chmn. San Francisco sect. 1978-79, Disting. Svc. award 1991, Charles Russ Richards award 1994, Rayleigh lectr. 1994), Internat. Acad. Wood Sci., Acoustical Soc. Am.; mem. ASTM (com. on snow skiing F-27 1984-87), Am. Soc. Engring. Edn. (Ralph Coats Roe award 1997), Am. Acad. Mechanics, Am. Soc. Biomechanics, Orthopaedic Rsch. Soc., Internat. Soc. Skiing Safety (v.p., sec. 1977-85, bd. dirs. 1977—, chmn. sci. com. 1985—), Sigma Xi, Pi Tau Sigma, Tau Beta Pi. Office: U Calif 2440 Bancroft Way Berkeley CA 94704-1603

MOTE, MARIE THERESE, reference librarian; b. Madisonville, Ky., May 5, 1948; d. John H. and Mary Cecelia (Sullivan) M. BA, Lincoln Meml. U., 1973; MLS, Vanderbilt U., 1974. Children's libr. Harris County Libr. System, Houston, 1975-76; learning resource ctr. coord. Aldine Sch. Dist., Houston, 1976-81; reference libr. Bellaire (Tex.) City Libr., 1983—; poetry columnist Tazewell-New Tazewell Observer, 1969-74. Mem. ALA (social responsibility roundtable, intellectual freedom roundtable), Pub. Libr. Assn., Tex. Libr. Assn., Cherokee Cultural Soc., Alpha Chi, Phi Alpha Theta. Avocations: artist, poet, writing fiction. Home: PO Box 1752 Bellaire TX 77402 Office: Bellaire City Libr 5111 Jessamine St Bellaire TX 77401-4424

MOTES, JOSEPH MARK, cruise and convention promotion company executive; b. Leesburg, Fla., Oct. 12, 1948; s. Lewis Jackson and Yolanda (Fernandez) M. AA in Computer Sci., Miami-Dade Community Coll., 1976. Promoter Trekruise & Seatrek, 1975—; conv. promoter Trekon & Vulkon, Fla., 1977—; v.p. Seatrek Ent., Inc., Cooper City, Fla.; pres. Genesis Prodns., Inc., 1992—. Sgt. USMC, 1967-74, Vietnam. Mem. SAR, SCV. Republican. Roman Catholic. Avocations: water sports, travel, boating, photography. Home and Office: 12237 SW 50th St Fort Lauderdale FL 33330-5406 also: 8306 Mills Dr Miami FL 33183-4838

MOTHERSHEAD, J. LELAND, III, dean; b. Boston, Jan. 10, 1939; s. John L. Jr. and Elizabeth Rankin (Crossett) M.; m. Therese Petkelis, June 23, 1963; 1 child, John Leland VI. BA, Carleton Coll., 1960; MA in Tchg., Brown U., 1963. Tchr. Tabor Acad., Marion, Mass., 1962-63, Chadwick Sch., Rolling Hills, Calif., 1963-66; tchr., adminstr. Flintridge (Calif.) Prep. Sch., 1966-75, head lower sch., 1972-74, dir. student affairs, 1974-75; tchr. Southwestern Acad., San Marino, Calif., 1979-83, dean, 1983—. Mem. Rotary (pres. San Marino Club 1994-95). Avocation: building historic wooden ship models. Home: 1145 Oak Grove Ave San Marino CA 91108-1028 Office: Southwestern Acad 2800 Monterey Rd San Marino CA 91108-1780

MOTHKUR, SRIDHAR RAO, radiologist; b. Mothkur, India, Oct. 5, 1950; came to U.S., 1975; s. Venkat Rao and Laxmi Bai (Gundepally) M.; m. Sheila Rama Rao Paga, Nov. 30, 1973; children: Swathi, Preethi, Venkat Krishna. Student, Coll. Arts and Sci. Osmania U., Siddipet, India, 1966; MB, BS, Osmania U., Hyderabad, India, 1972, DPH, 1974. Diplomate Am. Bd. Radiology. Rotating intern Osmania Gen. Hosp., Hyderabad, 1972-73, internal medicine intern, 1973, resident in surgery, 1974-75; resident Resurrection Hosp., Chgo., 1975-76; resident in radiology Luth. Gen. Hosp., Park Ridge, Ill., 1976-79, chief resident radiology, 1978-79; with rotations in nuclear medicine, angiography and neuroradiology Rush-Presbyn. St. Luke's Med. Ctr., Chgo., 1978; chmn. and med. dir. dept. radiology Louise Burg Hosp., Chgo., 1979-85, Shriner's Hosp., Chgo., 1986-88; fellow in ultrasound and computed tomography U. Ill., Chgo., 1988-89, fellow in magnetic resonance imaging, 1988-89; staff radiologist St. Anthony and Meml. Hosp., Michigan City, Ind., 1989—; with Michigan City Radiologists, Inc., 1989—; staff radiologist Kingwood Hosp., Michigan City, 1989-94, Charter Hosp., Behavioral Health Sys. Ind., Michigan City, 1994-96; cons. radiologist Franklin Clinic and Med. Watch, Michigan City; spl. staff radiologist Christ Hosp. Med. Ctr., Oaklawn, Ill., 1988-89; med. dir. interventional radiology St. Anthony and Meml. Hosp., Michigan City, 1989-93, MRI Ctr., 1989—, med. dir. diagnostic imaging Meml. Hosp., Michigan City, 1994-97; clin. asst. prof. in radiology U. Ill., Chgo., 1990—; cons. radiologist Jasper County Meml. Hosp., Rensselaer, Inc., 1994—. Fellow Am. Coll. Internat. Physicians, Am. Coll. Angiology, Internat. Coll. Angiology; mem. AMA, Internat. Soc. Krishna Consciousness, Radiol. Soc. N.Am., Telugu Assn. N.Am., Am. Roentgen Ray Soc., Am. Assn. Physicians of Indian Origin, Am. Diabetes Assn., Am. Coll. Emergency Physicians, Am. Soc. Head and Neck Radiology, Am. Telugu Assn., Am. Coll. Radiology, Soc. Magnetic Resonance Imaging, Soc. Cardiovascular and Interventional Radiology, Soc. Magnetic Resonance in Medicine, Indian Radiol. and Imaging Assn., Tristate Telugu Assn., Ind. Interventional Radiol. Assn., Am. Assn. Radiologists of Indian Origin, India Med. Assn. N.W. Ind., Ill. Med. Soc., Ind. State Med. Soc., Chgo. Med. Soc., Telugu Assn. Greater Chgo., La Porte County Med. Soc. Republican. Hindu-Madhava Brahmin (Parashira). Home: 1457 Sand Creek Dr S Chesterton IN 46304-2268 Office: Michigan City Radiologists Inc 916 Washington St Michigan City IN 46360-3518

MOTIN, REVELL JUDITH, retired data processing executive; b. Bayonne, N.J., July 24, 1941; d. Charles and Belle (Laks) Motin; children from a previous marriage: Laura Mantell, Deborah Mantell. BS in Psychology cum laude, Bklyn. Coll. CUNY, 1969. Systems analyst Univac div. Sperry Corp., N.Y.C., 1961-66; programmer, analyst J.C. Penney Co., N.Y.C., 1966-67; systems and programming cons. Automated Concepts, Inc., N.Y.C., 1968-72; ind. systems and programming cons. N.Y.C., 1972-76; mgr. systems and programming Citibank, NA, N.Y.C., 1976-83; v.p. data processing Columbia Savs. Bank, Fair Lawn, N.J., 1983-96; ret., 1996. Mem. Fin. Mgrs. Soc., Mensa. Jewish. Home: 43 Riverside Ave Haverstraw NY 10927-2009

MOTLEY, CONSTANCE BAKER (MRS. JOEL WILSON MOTLEY), federal judge, former city official; b. New Haven, Sept. 14, 1921; d. Willoughby Alva and Rachel (Huggins) Baker; m. Joel Wilson Motley, Aug. 18, 1946; 1 son, Joel Wilson, III. AB, NYU, 1943; LLB, Columbia U., 1946. Bar: N.Y. bar 1948. Mem. Legal Def. and Ednl. Fund, NAACP, 1945-65; mem. N.Y. State Senate, 1964-65; pres. Manhattan Borough, 1965-66; U.S. dist. judge So. Dist. N.Y., 1966-82, chief judge, 1982-86, sr. judge, 1986—. Mem. N.Y. State Adv. Council Employment and Unemployment Ins., 1958-64. Mem. Assn. Bar City N.Y. Office: US Dist Ct US Courthouse 500 Pearl St New York NY 10007-1316

MOTLEY, JOHN PAUL, psychiatrist, consultant; b. Carbondale, Pa., July 5, 1927; s. Joseph Adrian and Lillian (McCormick) M.; BS, Georgetown U., 1951; MD, Hahnemann Med. Coll., Phila., 1955; children: Marianne, Patricia, Kathleen, John Paul, Elizabeth, Joseph A. III, Grace, Michael. Intern, Hahnemann Med. Coll. Hosp., Phila., 1955-56; resident in psychiatry Inst. of Living, Hartford, Conn., 1956-59; practice medicine specializing in psychiatry, Point Pleasant, N.J., 1961—; mem. staff Jersey Shore Med. Ctr., 1961-72, chief of psychiatry, 1970-72; mem. staff Point Pleasant Hosp., 1961—, chief of psychiatry, 1961—; cons. in forensic psychiatry to various cts. and agys. Served with U.S. Army, 1944-46, ETO. Diplomate Am. Bd. Psychiatry and Neurology. Fellow Am. Psychiat. Assn.; mem. AMA, Royal Coll. Psychiatry, Am. Coll. Psychiatry, N.J. Psychiat. Assn. (past pres.). Clubs: Springlake Golf. Republican. Roman Catholic. Office: 3822 River Rd Point Pleasant Beach NJ 08742-2067

MOTOYAMA, HIROSHI, science association administrator; b. Tonoshomachi, Japan, Dec. 15, 1925; arrived in U.S., 1977; parents Katsuji Takasaki and Sizue Yoshima; m. Kaoru Motoyama, June 28, 1960; children: Mitsuharu, Kazuhiro, Yasuko, Tamaki, Kohsei. Grad., Tokyo U. Lit. & Sci., 1951, PhD, 1962. Established Inst. Religious Psychology, Japan, 1960, Internat. Assn. Religion and Parapsychology, 1972; gen. sec. Japan Holistic Medicine Soc., 1984; advisor, bd. dirs. Brazil Internat. Assn. Advanced Therapies, 1988—; established So. Calif. Inst. Japan Br. Grad. Sch., 1991, Calif. Inst. Human Sci., 1992, Motoyama Inst. Human Sci., 1994; guest rschr. Duke U., 1962-64; vis. prof. Andhra U., India, 1969-70. Contbr. articles to profl. jours. Office: Calif Inst Human Sci 701 Garden View Ct Encinitas CA 92024-2464

MOTSETT, CHARLES BOURKE, sales and marketing executive; b. Peoria, Ill., Jan. 13, 1949; s. William James and Matilda (Robb) M.; m. Mary T. Werner, Aug. 26, 1972; children: Jon Bourke, Jill Suzanne, Brian Werner. BA in Polit. Sci., Econs. and Mktg., U. So. Fla., 1984. Product support mktg. analyst Caterpillar Tractor Co., 1974-75; parts and service sales rep. Caterpillar Ams. Co., Mexico City, 1976-79; product support rep. Caterpillar Tractor Co., Vancouver, B.C., Can., 1979-80; leadman remanufactured products Caterpillar Tractor Co., Peoria, 1981-84; mgr. parts and service sales Caterpillar Tractor Co., Jacksonville, Fla., 1984-85; v.p. sales and mktg. Multi Media Productions of Am., Inc., Jacksonville, 1985-86; v.p. sales and mktg. Consol. Indsl. Skills Corp., Jacksonville, 1987—, corp. officer, 1988-92; v.p., gen. mgr. Ogden CISCO Inc., Jacksonville, 1992-94; v.p. sales and mktg. CompuTown Technologies Corp., Miami, 1994—, Shred All, 1995; pres. Bus. Solutions, Inc., Jacksonville, 1996—; pres. Bus. Solutions Internat., Jacksonville. Author: If It Wasn't For The People...This Job Would Be Fun (Coaching For Buy-in and Results), 1996; contbr. articles to profl. jours. Vice pres. PTO, Dunlap, Ill., 1981-82; vice chmn. St. Anthony's Ch., Vancouver, 1979-80; chmn. St. Jude Ch., Dunlap, 1982-83, Bishop Kenny High Sch. PTO Polit. Action Com., 1989; mem. adv. coun. Sch. Bd. Vocat. Edn., 1991-92. Capt. U.S. Army, 1967-70, prisoner of war, Vietnam. Decorated Silver Star, Bronze Star with V device, Purple Heart, Air medal with V device., Combat Infantryman's Badge, Underwater Ops. Badge, Vietnamese Jump Wings, Commendation medal, Good Conduct medal. Mem. Soc. Automotive Engrs., Am. Soc. Naval Engrs., Soc. Naval Architects and Marine Engrs., Am. Inst. Plant Engrs. (bd. dirs., conf. presenter), Am. Nuclear Soc., Propellor Club. Republican. Roman Catholic. Avocations: scuba diving, sailing, reading, golf. Home: 4457 Barrington Oaks Dr Jacksonville FL 32257-5092

MOTSINGER, JOHN KINGS, lawyer, mediator, arbitrator; b. Winston-Salem, N.C., Aug. 13, 1947; s. Madison Eugene and Margaret Mary (Kings) M.; m. Elisabeth Sykes, June 18, 1989; children: Christian Sykes, Lissa Sykes, John, Jr. BA, Washington & Lee U., 1970; MS, Georgetown U., 1972; JD, Wake Forest U., 1983. Bar: N.C. 1983, U.S. Dist. Ct. (mid. dist.) N.C. 1984. Consumer affairs assoc. U.S Postal Svc., Washington, 1972-73; pres., gen. mgr. Sta. WIPS-Radio, Ticonderoga, N.Y., 1973-79; staff atty. United Guaranty Corp., Greensboro, N.C., 1983-86, Republic Mortgage Ins. Co., Winston-Salem, 1986-91; v.p. law RMIC Corp., Winston-Salem, 1988-91; exec. dir. Carolina Concilation Svcs. Corp., 1992—. Past pres. Unitarian-Universalist Fellowship of Winston-Salem, 1993-94. Mem. ABA, N.C. Bar Assn. (corp. counsel sect. councilor 1989-93), N.C. State Bar, Acad. of Family Mediators, Am. Arbitration Assn. Democrat. Unitarian-Universalist. Avocations: jogging, music, reading. Home: 204 W Cascade Ave Winston Salem NC 27127-2029 Office: Carolina Conciliation Svcs Corp 1001 S Marshall St Ste 65 Winston Salem NC 27101-5858

MOTT, PEGGY LAVERNE, sociologist, educator; b. Stephenville, Tex., Mar. 23, 1930; d. Artemis Victor Dorris and Tempie Pearl (Price) Hickman; m. J.D. Mott, Sept. 11, 1947 (dec. Apr. 1988); children: Kelly A. Wilcoxson, Kimberly S. Minesinger. BA, Southwest Tex. State U., 1980, MA, 1982. Cert. instr. ceramic arts Nat. Ceramic Art Inst., 1972. Instr. ceramics Arts & Crafts Ctr. Lackland AFB, San Antonio, 1969-72, dir. sales Arts & Crafts Ctr., 1972-77; asst. instr. S.W. Tex. State U., San Marcos, 1980-82; instr. sociology Palo Alto Coll., San Antonio, 1991—. Author: Screaming Silences, 1994, (poem) Concho River Rev., 1993, Inkwell Echos, 1989-95, Lucidity, The T.O.P. Hwupp, 1994-95, Hwap, Patchwork Poems, 1995. Vol. coord. Fisher Houses, Inc., Lackland AFB, 1992—; parliamentarian Artistic Expressions, 1996—. Named Vol. of Month, USAF, 1976, 77, 78, Vol. of Quarter, 1976, 77, 78, 84, Vol. of Yr., 1980. Mem. Internat. Soc. Poets, Clipper Ship Poets, San Antonio Poets Assn. (v.p. 1991-92, pres. 1992-93, Poet Laureate 1994-95), San Antonio Ethnic Arts. Avocations: reading, writing, needlework. Home: 1307 Canyon Ridge Dr San Antonio TX 78227-1727

MOTT, STEWART RAWLINGS, business executive, political activist; b. Flint, Mich., Dec. 4, 1937; s. Charles Stewart and Ruth (Rawlings) M.; m. Kappy Wells, Oct. 13, 1979; 1 child, Samuel Apple Axle. Grad., Deerfield (Mass.) Acad., 1955; B.S. in Bus. Adminstrn, Columbia, 1961, B.A. in Comparative Lit, 1961, postgrad. English lit., 1961-62. Exec. trainee various cos., 1956-63; English instr. Eastern Mich. U., 1963-64; corp. dir. U.S. Sugar Corp., Clewiston, Fla., 1965—; investor various diversified cos., 1968—. Founder Flint Community Planned Parenthood, 1963; pres., founder Spectemur Agendo (merged with S.R. Mott Charitable Trust 1989), N.Y.C. and Flint, 1965—; bd. dirs. Fund For Peace, N.Y.C., 1967—, S.R. Mott Charitable Trust, 1968—, Nat. Com. for Effective Congress, N.Y.C., 1968—, Planned Parenthood Fedn. Am., 1964-81, Am. Commn. on U.S.-Soviet Rels., 1977-92, Citizens Research Found., 1977—, Ams. for Dem. Action, 1978-90, Friends of Family Planning, 1979-84, Voters for Choice, 1979-89; bd. dirs., founder Fund Constl. Govt., 1974—; bd. dirs. Population Action Council, 1978-82; maj. donor McCarthy, McGovern, Anderson campaigns. Mem. Phi Beta Kappa. *At age 18 I realized that two problems confront planet earth that dwarf and aggravate all conventional problems: namely the threat of nuclear war and the continuing worldwide population explosion. Coming to grips with these realities, I decided to dedicate my life to help find solutions to these two problems through public service in philanthropy and politics.*

MOTT, VINCENT VALMON, publisher, author; b. Washington, La., Sept. 18, 1916; s. Lucius and Marie (LeDoux) M.; m. Margaret McDonald, June 19, 1948; children: Vincent Valmon, Helene Virginia, John Michael. AB, Xavier U., 1938; MA, Fordham U., 1947, PhD, 1956. Instr. social sci. U. Scranton, Pa., 1947-51; instr. econs. Seton Hall U., South Orange, N.J.,

1952-53; asst. prof. Seton Hall U., 1954-58, asso. prof., 1958-66, prof. mktg., 1966—; adj. asso. prof. sociology St. Peters Coll., Jersey City, 1955-60; Pres. Florham Park Press, Florham Park, N.J., 1957—; pres., prin. stockholder V.V.R.&D., Inc. Author: The American Matriarch, 1970, The American Consumer, 1972, (with N. Chirovsky) Philosophy in Economic Thought, 1972, Philosophical Foundations of Economic Doctrines, 1978, The Creole, 1991, Academia Revisited, 1994; editor: Jour. Bus., Seton Hall U., 1963-64. Mem. bd. advisers Scranton Inst. Indsl. Relations, 1949-50. Served with AUS, 1940-45. Home and Office: 12 Leslie Ave Florham Park NJ 07932-2165

MOTT, WILLIAM CHAMBERLAIN, lawyer, retired naval officer; b. Maplewood, N.J., Sept. 7, 1911; s. Raymond Louis and Helen (Chamberlain) M.; m. Rosemary Baker, Sept. 17, 1938 (div. 1947); children: Adam S., Janie B.; m. Edith Grace, Nov. 13, 1947; children: Diane B., Lucy A., Sarah G., William Chamberlain. B.S., U.S. Naval Acad., 1933; J.D., George Washington U., 1940; LL.D., John Marshall Law Sch., 1961, Rhode Island Coll., 1964. Bar: D.C. 1940. Patent examiner Washington, 1936-40; commd. lt. (j.g.) U.S. Navy, 1939, advanced through grades to rear adm., 1960; asst. naval aide to Pres. Roosevelt, 1942-43; assigned (Amphibious Forces Pacific), 1944-45; liaison (UN and Dept. of State), 1946-48; legal adviser comdr. in chief (Pacific Area Command), 1948-50; comdg. officer (Sch. Naval Justice), 1950-53; spl. asst., chmn. (Joint Chiefs Staff), 1954-58; dep. judge adv. gen. (Office Judge Adv. Gen., Dept. of Navy), 1958-60, judge adv. gen., 1960-64; exec. dir. (Council on Econs. and Nat. Security). Exec. v.p. U.S. Ind. Telephone Assn., 1964-77; pres. Capital Legal Found.; chmn. adv. com. Nat. Strategic Materials and Minerals Program. Decorated Legion of Merit. Fellow Am. Bar Found.; mem. Am. Soc. Internat. Law, Am. Bar Assn., Fed. Bar Assn. Episcopalian. Clubs: Army and Navy, Farmington, Chevy Chase. Home: 9 N Dogwood Ln Charlottesville VA 22901-1907

MOTTEK, FRANK, broadcaster, journalist; b. Irvington, N.J., Feb. 17, 1962; s. Peter Mottek and Brigitte (Seidler) Fuller. AA, Broward C.C., Ft. Lauderdale, Fla., 1985; B.Liberal Studies, Barry U., Miami, Fla., 1988. News dir./anchor WMJX-FM Radio, Miami, 1978-81; news anchor/reporter WINZ Radio, Miami, 1981-92; news anchor space shuttles CBS Radio Network, Kennedy Space Ctr., Fla., 1985-91; news anchor, reporter WTVJ-TV 4, Miami, 1986-92; bus. news anchor, reporter PBS-WPBT TV Nightly Bus. Report, Miami, 1989-91; news anchor, reporter KNX Radio/KCBS-TV, L.A., 1992—. Recipient 1st place excellence in med. journalism Fla. Med. Assn., 1985, 1st place for news series AP, Fla., 1988, 1st place nat. award for documentary UPI, Washington, 1989, 1st place for spot news, Golden Mike award, 1996, L.A. press Club 1st place spot news, 1996. Mem. AFTRA, Radio/TV News Dirs. Assn. (1st place regional documentary award 1992), Fla. Assoc. Press Broadcasters (pres. 1988-89, bd. dirs. 1986-92), Radio/TV News Assn. of So. Calif. Office: KNX/CBS Radio 6121 W Sunset Blvd Los Angeles CA 90028-6423

MOTTER, THOMAS FRANKLIN, medical products executive; b. Modesto, Calif., June 27, 1948; s. Thomas Dean and Beverley June (Mosier) M.; m. Wanda Lenice Parker, Feb. 9, 1968 (div. Jan. 1972); children: Eric Franklin, Katrina Lenice; m. Jerry Ann Averill, Oct. 24, 1976; children: Heidi Marika, Courtney Averill. AA, Cabrillo Jr. Coll., Santa Cruz, Calif., 1968; BA, Stephens Coll., 1970; MBA, Pepperdine U., 1975. Social worker County of Santa Cruz and Amador, 1970-77; nat. dir. mktg. Humphrey Instruments/SmithKline, San Leandro, Calif., 1978-88; internat. gen. mgr. HGM Med. Lasers, Salt Lake City, 1988-89; pres., CEO Paradigm Med. Industries Inc., Salt Lake City, 1989—. V.p. Sandy (Utah) Pony Baseball, 1994-95; coach Kearns (Utah) Am. Legion Baseball, 1995-96. Capt. U.S. Army, 1970-76. Named. Mem. Nat. Adult Baseball Assn. (mem. Nat. Championship team), Am. Legion, Sons of the Am. Revolution Utah State Chpt. Episcopalian. Avocations: skiing, hardball baseball, coaching, fly fishing, hunting. Office: Paradigm Med Industries Inc 1772 W 2300 S Salt Lake City UT 84119-2010

MOTTET, NORMAN KARLE, pathologist, educator; b. Renton, Wash., Jan. 8, 1924; s. Louis John and Amalia (Lentzner) M.; m. Nancy Noble, June 21, 1952; children: Gretchen, Kurt, Mark. BS summa cum laude, Wash. State U., 1947; MD, Yale U., 1952. Diplomate: Am. bd. Pathology. Postdoctoral fellow Strangeways Research Lab., Cambridge, Eng., 1952-53, vis. scientist, 1969-70; rotating intern, then intern in pathology Yale Med. Ctr., 1953-55, resident in pathology, 1955-56, mem. faculty med. Sch., 1951-52, 55-59; pathologist, dir. labs. Griffin Hosp., Derby, Conn., 1955-59; mem. faculty U. Wash. Med. Sch., Seattle, 1959—, prof. pathology, 1966—; dir. hosp. pathology Univ. Hosp. U. Wash. Med. Sch., Seattle, 1959-74; mem. extramural program council Fred Hutchinson Carcer Research Ctr., 1975. Contbr. articles to med. jours.; mem. editorial bds. Served with AUS, 1942-45. James Hudson Brown fellow, 1949-50; fellow nat. Found. Infantile Paralysis, 1952-53; recipient Keese prize Yale U., 1952; trainee pathology USPHS, 1954-55; spl. rsch. fellow USPHS, 1969-70. Fellow Am. Soc. Clin. Pathology, AAAS; mem. Am. Soc. Pathology, Tetatology Soc., Internat. Soc. Trace Element Research, Internat. Com. Occupational Health, Internat. Com. Trace Metals, Sigma Xi, Alpha Omega Alpha. Home: E 360 Old Olson Rd Shelton WA 98584 Office: U Wash Sch Medicine Dept Path Seattle WA 98195

MOTTL, RONALD M., state legislator, lawyer; b. Cleve., Feb. 6, 1934; s. Milton and Anna Huml; m. Debra Budan; children: Ronald Jr., Ronda, Ron Michael, Amanda L. BS, Notre Dame U., 1956, LLB, 1957. Asst. law dir. City of Cleve., 1958-60; councilman Ward 2 City Coun., Parma, Ohio, 1960-61; pres. Parma City Coun., 1961-66; mem. Ohio Ho. of Reps., Columbus, 1967-68, 87—, Ohio State Senate, Columbus, 1969-74, U.S. Ho. of Reps., Washington, 1975-82; pres. Parma Sch. Bd., 1985; ptnr. Cassidy & Mottl, Cleve. State rep. Ohio House of Reps., 1986—. With U.S. Army, 1957. Mem. ABA, Ohio Bar Assn., Cuyahoga Bar Assb., Cleve. Bar Assn., Parma Bar Assn. Roman Catholic. Home: 10626 Stone Hinge N Royalton OH 44133-1997 Office: Ron Mottl & Assocs 5454 State Rd Parma OH 44134-1258

MOTTO, JEROME ARTHUR, psychiatry educator; b. Kansas City, Mo., Oct. 16, 1921. MD, U. Calif., San Francisco, 1951. Diplomate Am. Bd. Neurology and Psychiatry. Intern San Francisco Gen. Hosp., 1951-52; resident Johns Hopkins Hosp., Balt., 1952-55; sr. resident U. Calif., San Francisco, 1955-56, from asst. prof. to prof. emeritus., 1956—. Contbr. articles to profl. jours. With AUS, 1942-46; ETO. Fellow Am. Psychiatric Assn. (life).

MOTTOLA, THOMAS, entertainment company executive. Pres., COO Sony Music Entertainment, N.Y.C. Office: Sony Music Entertainment 550 Madison Ave Fl 32 New York NY 10022-3211*

MOTULSKY, ARNO GUNTHER, geneticist, physician, educator; b. Fischhausen, Germany, July 5, 1923; came to U.S., 1941; s. Herman and Rena (Sass) Molton; m. Gretel C. Stern, Mar. 22, 1945; children: Judy, Harvey, Arlene. Student, Cen. YMCA Coll., Chgo., 1941-43, Yale U., 1943-44; BS, U. Ill., 1945, MD, 1947, DSc (hon.), 1982, MD (hon.), 1991. Diplomate Am. Bd. Internal Medicine, Am. Bd. Med. Genetics. Intern, fellow, resident Michael Reese Hosp., Chgo., 1947-51; staff mem. charge clin. investigation dept. hematology Army Med. Service Grad. Sch., Walter Reed Army Med. Ctr., Washington, 1952-53; research assoc. internal medicine George Washington U. Sch. Medicine, 1952-53; from instr. to assoc. prof. dept. medicine U. Wash. Sch. Medicine, Seattle, 1953-61, prof. medicine, prof. genetics, 1961—; head div. med. genetics, dir. genetics clinic Univ. Hosp., Seattle, 1959-89; dir. Ctr. for Inherited Diseases, Seattle, 1972-90; attending physician Univ. Hosp., Seattle; cons. Pres.'s Commn. for Study of Ethical Problems in Medicine and Biomed. and Behavioral Research, 1979-83; cons. various coms. NRC, NIH, WHO, others. Editor Am. Jour. Human Genetics, 1969-75, Human Genetics, 1969—. Commonwealth Fund fellow in human genetics Univ. Coll., London, 1957-58; John and Mary Markle scholar in med. sci., 1957-62; fellow Ctr. Advanced Study in Behavioral Scis., Stanford U., 1976-77, Inst. Advanced Study, Berlin, 1984. Fellow ACP, AAAS; mem. NAS, Internat. Soc. Hematology, Am. Fedn. Clin. Research, Genetics Soc. Am., Western Soc. Clin. Research, Am. Soc. Human Genetics, Am. Soc. Clin. Investigation, Am. Assn. Physicians, Inst. of Medicine, Am. Acad. Arts and Scis. Home: 4347 53rd Ave NE Seattle WA 98105-4938 Office: U Wash Divsn Med Genetics Box 356423 Seattle WA 98195-6423

MOTZ, DIANA GRIBBON, federal judge; b. Washington, July 15, 1943; d. Daniel McNamara and Jane (Retzler) Gribbon; m. John Frederick Motz, Sept. 20, 1968; children: Catherine Jane, Daniel Gribbon. BA, Vassar Coll., 1965; LLB, U. Va., 1968. Bar: U.S. Dist. Ct. Md. 1969, U.S. Ct. Appeals (4th cir.) 1969, U.S. Supreme Ct. 1980. Assoc. Piper & Marbury, Balt., 1968-71; asst. atty. gen. State of Md., Balt., 1972-81, chief of litigation, 1981-86; ptnr. Frank, Bernstein, Conaway & Goldman, Balt., 1986-91; judge Md. Ct. of Special Appeals, Md., 1991-94, U.S. Ct. Appeals (4th Cir.), 1994—. Mem. ABA, Md. Bar Assn., Balt. City Bar Assn. (exec. com. 1988), Am. Law Inst., Am. Bar Found., Md. Bar Found., Lawyers Round Table, Fed. Cts. Study Com., Wranglers Law Club. Roman Catholic. Office: 101 W Lombard St Ste 920 Baltimore MD 21201-2611

MOTZ, JOHN FREDERICK, federal judge; b. Balt., Dec. 30, 1942; s. John Eldered and Catherine (Grauel) M.; m. Diana Jane Gribbon, Sept. 20, 1968; children: Catherine Jane, Daniel Gribbon. AB, Wesleyan U., Conn., 1964; LLB, U. Va., 1967. Bar: Md. 1967, U.S. Ct. Appeals (4th cir.) 1968, U.S. Dist. Ct. Md. 1968. Law clk. to Hon. Harrison L. Winter U.S. Ct. Appeals (4th cir.), 1967-68; assoc. Venable, Baetjer & Howard, Balt., 1968-69; asst. U.S. atty. U.S. Atty.'s Office, Balt., 1969-71; assoc. Venable, Baetjer & Howard, Balt., 1971-75, ptnr., 1976-81; U.S. atty. U.S. Atty.'s Office, Balt., 1981-85; judge U.S. Dist. Ct. Md., Balt., 1985—. Trustees Friends Sch., Balt., 1970-77, 1981-88, Sheppard Pratt Hosp., 1987—. Mem. ABA, Md. State Bar Assn., Am. Bar Found., Am. Law Inst., Am. Coll. Trial Lawyers. Republican. Mem. Soc. of Friends. Office: US Dist Ct 101 W Lombard St Rm 510 Baltimore MD 21201-2607

MOTZ, KENNETH LEE, former farm organization official; b. Grand Junction, Colo., Mar. 6, 1922; s. Harold I. and Acquila (Ulmer) M.; m. Margaret Florence Mitchell, Oct. 9, 1948; children: Gwendolyn Ann, Stephen Mitchell. AA, Mesa Jr. Coll., 1942; BSBA, Denver U., 1947. Bookkeeper Farmers Union Mktg. Assn., Denver, 1942-43; asst. sec. Nat. Farmers Union, Denver, 1947-50, 59-66, sec.-treas., 1966-72, 85-86, treas., asst. sec., 1972-85, retired, 1987; treas. Green Thumb, Inc., 1980-85, sec.-treas., 1985-86, retired, 1987; ins. acct. Nat. Farmers Union Ins. Cos., Denver, 1952-59. sec. uniform pension com. Nat. Farmers Union, 1959-93; Dem. precinct committeeman, 1960-68; elder Calvary Presbyn. Ch. Maj. USMCR, ret. 1982. Mem. Masons, Delta Sigma Pi. Presbyterian. Home: 11186 E Baltic Dr Aurora CO 80014-1070

MOUCHLY-WEISS, HARRIET, business executive; b. N.Y.C., Aug. 12, 1942; d. Robert and Anita (Shawmut) Berg; m. Charles Weiss, Sept. 13, 1975; children: Noa, Yoav. BA, Muhlenberg Coll., 1960; MA in Clin. Psychology, Hebrew U., 1964. Clin. psychologist Hadassah Hosp., Israel, 1962-65; chmn. Ruder & Finn, Israel, 1968-80; sr. v.p. Ruder Finn & Rotman, N.Y.C., 1980-86; pres. GCI Internat., N.Y.C., 1986-92; mng. ptnr. Strategy XXI Group, Ltd., N.Y.C., 1993—. Bd. dirs. N.Y. State Gov.'s World Trade Coun., Com. for Econ. Growth Israel; bd. dirs. U. Haifa, Capital Circle, Israel Policy Forum; trustee Internat. Ctr. for Peace in the Mid East, Am. Acad. in Rome; State of the World Forum advisor; mem. Friends of the UN, The Chinese Found. of Culture and Arts for Children; mem. adv. bd. dirs. Visage Tech. Recipient cert. of appreciation, HUD. Mem. Women in Comms., Pub. Rels. Soc. Am., Itnernat. Pub. Rels. Assn., Com. of 200 (chair comm.). Avocations: art, art history, politics. Office: Strategy XXI Group Ltd 515 Madison Ave Fl 34 New York NY 10022-5403

MOUL, MAXINE BURNETT, state official; b. Oakland, Nebr., Jan. 26, 1947; d. Einer and Eva (Jacobson) Burnett; m. Francis Moul, Apr. 20, 1972; 1 child, Jeff. BS in Journalism, U. Nebr., 1969; DHL (hon.), Peru State Coll., 1993. Sunday feature writer, photographer Sioux City Iowa Jour., 1969-71; reporter, photographer, editor Maverick Media, Inc., Syracuse, Nebr., 1971-73, editor, pub., 1974-83, pres., 1983-90; grant writer, asst. coord. Nebr. Regional Med. Program, Lincoln, 1973-74; lt. gov. State of Nebr., Lincoln, 1991-93; dir. Dept. Econ. Devel., Lincoln, 1993—. Mem. Dem. Nat. Com., Washington, 1988-92, Nebr. Dem. State Ctrl. Com., Lincoln, 1974-88; del. Dem. Nat. Conf., 1972, 88, 92; mem. exec. com. Nebr. Dem. Party, Lincoln, 1988-93. Recipient Margaret Sanger award Planned Parenthood, Lincoln, 1991, Champion of Small Bus. award Nebr. Bus. Devel. Ctr., Omaha, 1991, Toll fellowship Coun. State Govts., Lexington, Ky., 1992. Mem. Bus. and Profl. Womem, Nebr. Mgmt. Assn. (Silver Knight award 1992), Nat. Conf. Lt. Govs. (bd. dirs. 1991-93), Nebr. Press Women, Women Execs. in State Govt., Cmty. Devel. Soc., U. Nebr.-Lincoln Journalism Alumni. Democrat. Avocations: reading, gardening. Office: State of Nebr PO Box 94666 Lincoln NE 68509-4666*

MOUL, WILLIAM CHARLES, lawyer; b. Columbus, Ohio, Jan. 12, 1940; s. Charles Emerson and Lillian Ann (Mackenbach) M.; m. Margine Ann Tessendorf, June 10, 1962; children—Gregory, Geoffrey. B.A., Miami U., Oxford, Ohio, 1961; J.D., Ohio State U., 1964. Bar: Ohio 1964, U.S. dist. Ct. (so. dist.) Ohio 1965, U.S. Ct. Appeals (2d cir.) 1982, U.S. Ct. Appeals (6th cir.) 1984, U.S. Ct. Appeals (3d cir.) 1985. Assoc., ptnr. George, Greek, King, McMahon & McConnaughey, Columbus, Ohio, 1964-79; ptnr. McConnaughey, Stradley, Mone & Moul, Columbus, 1979-81; ptnr.-in-charge Thompson, Hine & Flory, Columbus, 1981—. Chmn. Upper Arlington Civil Service Commn., Ohio, 1981-86. Mem. ABA,Ohio State Bar Assn. (labor sect. bd. 1983—), Columbus Bar Assn. (chmn. ethics com. 1980-82), Lawyers Club Columbus (pres. 1976-77), Athletic Club, Scioto Country Club, Wedgewood Country Club, Masons. Lutheran. Home: 2512 Danvers Ct Columbus OH 43220-2822 Office: Thompson Hine & Flory 10 W Broad St Ste 700 Columbus OH 43215-3419

MOULDER, T. EARLINE, musician; b. Buffalo, Mo., Oct. 11; d. Earl Young and Ruby M. (Philpott) M.; m. R. David Plank, Dec. 21, 1980; children: Jeannine Stanton, Jon Stanton, Timothy Stanton. AB in Biology and French, Drury Coll., 1973; studied piano with Soulima Stravinsky, 1961; M in Music magna cum laude, Ind. U., 1963; D in Musical Arts, U. Kansas, 1991; pvt. organ study, Andre Marchal, Paris, France, 1971. Organist St. Paul Meth. Ch., Springfield, Mo., 1961-81; concert organist U.S., Europe, Middle East, 1964—; exec. editor Drury Coll. Mirror, Springfield, Mo., 1971-73; journalist U.S. Naval Res., Springfield and Treasure Island, Calif., 1975-77; organist King's Way Meth. Ch., Springfield, Mo., 1983-93; chair organ dept. Drury Coll., Springfield, Mo., 1968—, coll. organist, 1991—; lectr. recitals on Jewish music, 1991—; translator, Profl. documents, 1990—. Author: Organ Works of Elsa Barraine, 1995; composer organ composition The Crucifixion, 1971-95; contbr. articles to profl. jours. Charter mem. Nat. Mus. Am. Indian, 1994—. Recipient Teaching fellow U. Kans., Drury Mirror award Rank I Mo. Coll. Newspaper Assn. Mem. Mortar Bd., Sigma Alpha Iota, Alpha Lambda Delta, Pi Delta Phi, Beta Beta Beta, Pi Kappa Lambda, Organ Hist. Soc., Am. Guild Organist. Home: 3563 E Linwood Dr Springfield MO 65809-2131 Office: Drury Coll 900 N Benton Springfield MO 65802

MOULDER, WILLIAM H., chief of police; b. Kansas City, Mo., Feb. 19, 1938; s. Roscoe B. and Charleen M. (Flye) M.; m. Louise M. Pollaro, Aug. 2, 1957; children: Deborah, Ralph, Robert. BA, U. Mo., Kansas City, 1971, MA, 1976. Cert. police officer, Mo., Iowa. From police officer to maj. Kansas City (Mo.) Police Dept., 1959-84; chief of police City of Des Moines, 1984—. Mem. Internat. Assn. Chiefs of Police, Police Exec. Rsch. Forum, Iowa Police Exec. Forum. Avocations: racquetball, travel. Office: Office of Police Chief 25 E 1st St Des Moines IA 50309-4800

MOULDS, JOHN F., federal judge; m. Elizabeth Fry, Aug. 29, 1964; children: Donald B., Gerald B. Student, Stanford U., 1955-58; BA with honors, Calif. State U., Sacramento, 1960; JD, U. Calif, Berkeley, 1963. Bar: U.S. Supreme Ct., U.S. Dist. Ct. (no. dist.) Calif., U.S. Dist. Ct. (ea. dist.) Calif. 1968, U.S. Ct. Claims 1982, U.S. Ct. Appeals (9th cir.) 1967, Calif. Rsch. analyst Calif. State Senate Fact-Finding Com. on Edn., 1960-61; adminstrv. asst. Senator Albert S. Rodda, Calif., 1961-63; staff atty. Calif. Rural Legal Assistance, Marysville, 1966-68; dir. atty. Marysville field office and Sacramento legis. adv. office Calif. Rural Legal Assistance, 1968-69; staff atty. Sacramento Legal Aid, 1968-69; ptnr. Blackmon, Isenberg & Moulds, 1969-85, Isenberg, Moulds & Hemmer, 1985; magistrate judge U.S. Dist. Ct. (ea. dist.) Calif., 1985—, chief magistrate jdnge, 1988—; moot ct. and trial practice judge U. Calif. Davis Law Sch., 1975—, U. of Pacific McGeorge Coll. Law, 1985—; part-time U.S. magistrate judge U.S. Dist. Ct. (ea. dist.) Calif., 1983-85; mem. 9th Cir. Capital Case Com., 1992—, U.S. Jud. Conf. Com. on the Magistrate Judge Sys., 1992—, Adv. Com. to the Magistrate Judges' Divsn. Adminstv. Office of U.S. Jud. Conf., 1989—. Author: (with others) Review of California Code Legislation, 1965, Welfare Recipients' Handbook, 1967; editor: Ninth Circuit Capital Punishment Handbook, 1991. Atty. Sacramento Singlemen's Self-Help Ctr., 1969-74; active Sacramento Human Relations Commn., 1969-75, chair, 1974-75; active community support orgn. U. Calif. at Davis Law Sch., 1971—; mem., atty. Sacramento Community Coalition for Media Change, 1972-75; bd. dirs. Sacramento Country Day Sch., 1982-90, Sacramento Pub. Libr. Found., 1985-87; active various polit. orgns. and campaigns, 1960-82. Mem. ABA, Fed. Bar Assn., Nat. Coun. Magistrates (cir. dir. 1986-88, treas. 1988-89, 2d v.p. 1989-90, 1st v.p. 1990-91), Fed. Magistrate Judges Assn. (pres.-elect 1991, pres. 1992-93), Calif. State-Fed. Jud. Coun. Conf. (panelist capital habeas corpus litigation 1992), Fed. Jud. Ctr. Training Conf. for U.S. Magistrate Judges (panel leader 1993), Milton L. Schwartz Inns of Ct. Office: 5054 US Courthouse 650 Capitol Mall Sacramento CA 95814

MOULE, WILLIAM NELSON, electrical engineer; b. Highland Park, Mich., Sept. 13, 1924; s. Hollis Creager and Kate DeEtte (Hill) M.; m. Barbara Ann Bagley, June 27, 1953; children: Janice Louise, Robert Hollis (dec.), Linda Anne, Nancy Lynn Moule Moles. BSEE, Mich. State U., 1949; MSEE, U. Pa., 1957. Reg. profl. engr., N.J. Design engr. Radio Corp. of Am., Camden, N.J., 1949-59; sr. design engr. Radio Corp. of Am., Moorestown, N.J., 1959-67; sr. engr. Emerson Elec. Co., St. Louis, 1967-70, Emerson Elec. Rantec Divsn., Calabasas, Calif., 1970; sr. staff engr. Raytheon Co., Santa Barbara, Calif., 1970-73, ITT Gilfillan, Van Nuys, Calif., 1973, Jet Propulsion Lab., Pasadena, Calif., 1973-79; sr. rsch devel. engr. Lockheed Advanced Devel. Co., Burbank, Calif., 1979—. Patentee numerous inventions, 1956—. Dir. nat. alumni bd. Mich. State U., East Lansing, 1984-87; pres. Big Ten Club of So. Calif., L.A., 1992. Staff sgt. USAAF, 1943-46. Mem. IEEE (sr., L.A. chpt. sec., treas. Antennas and Propagation soc. 1987-89, vice chmn. 1989-90, chmn. 1990-91), 305th Bombardment Group Meml. Assn. (life). Democrat. Presbyn. Avocations: travel, photography, genealogy. Home: 5831 Fitzpatrick Rd Calabasas CA 91302-1104 Office: Lockheed Martin Skunk Works 1011 Lockheed Way Palmdale CA 93599-0001

MOULTHROP, EDWARD ALLEN, architect, artist; b. Rochester, N.Y., May 22, 1916; s. Ray Josiah and Jetta (McDonald) M.; m. Mae Elizabeth Crotser, Jan 31, 1942; children: Mark, Philip, Samuel, Timothy. B.Arch., Western Res. U., 1939; M.F.A., Princeton, 1941. Asst. prof. architecture Ga. Inst. Tech., 1943-46, asst. prof. physics, 1944-46; chief designer Robert and Co. Asso. Architects and Engrs., Atlanta, 1948-72; prin. Edward Allen Moulthrop (architect and cons.), Atlanta, 1972—; 1st chmn. Ga. Art Commn., 1954-65. Exhibited in, Watercolor U.S.A., 1962, USIA traveling show to Russia, crafts, 1970, Wichita Nat. Decorative Arts and Ceramics Exhbn., 1972, Ga. artists exhibit, High Mus. Art, Atlanta, 1971, 72, 74, Vatican Mus., Italy, 1978; represented in permanent collections, Mus. Modern Art, N.Y.C., Boston Mus. Fine Arts, Met. Mus. Art, N.Y.C. Phila. Mus. Art (Recipient Nat. Design award Am. Inst. Steel Constrn. 1959, 67, 1st Purchase award for crafts Atlanta Arts Festival 1963, 64, 67, 72, 74, 77, 78, Craftsman U.S. award of merit 1966, Judges Choice award Western Colo. Center for Arts 1973, purchase award 1975, prize Marietta Coll. Crafts Nat. 1974, 76, Craftwork prize Am. Crafts Council 1976, 78, Ga. Gov.'s Award in Arts 1981), USIA traveling show to Europe, crafts, 1990-93, The Art of Woodturning, 1993—, Permanent Collection of the White House, 1993. Fellow AIA (pres. Ga. chpt. 1953), Am. Craft Coun., Am. Craft Coun.; mem. Ga. Engring. Soc. (pres. 1958, spl. hon. mem. 1969), Am. Craftsmens Coun. (Ga. rep. 1973-75), Ga. Designer Craftsmen (pres. 1975-76). Home and Office: 4260 Carmain Dr NE Atlanta GA 30342-3504

MOULTHROP, REBECCA LEE STILPHEN, elementary education educator; b. Lubbock, Tex., Mar. 5, 1944; d. Lee Edward and Geraldine (Lansford) Stilphen; m. John Stephen Martin Moulthrop, June 1967 (div. 1968); 1 child, Paul Martin. BS in edn., U. New Mex., 1966; MS in reading edn., Calif. State U., Fullerton, 1971; postgrad., U. LaVerne. Elem. tchr. Arnold Heights Elem. Sch., Moreno Valley, Calif., 1966-67, Hawthorn Elem. Sch., El Monte, Calif., 1968-69; chap. 1 reading specialist Posey Elem. Sch., Lubbock, 1971-72; elem. tchr. Arnold Heights Elem. Sch., Moreno Valley, 1972-74, Sunnymead Elem. Sch., Moreno Valley, 1974-80, Moreno Elem. Sch., Moreno Valley, 1980-88; chap. 1 program coord. Edgemont Elem. Sch., Moreno Valley, 1988-91; elem. tchr. Sunnymeadows Elem. Sch., Moreno Valley, 1991—; assertive discipline cons. Moreno Valley (Calif.) Unified Sch. Dist., 1979-85, mentor/tchr., 1985-89, adminstrn. designee/trainee, 1988-95; effective tchg./supervision coach Riverside (Calif.) County Sch. Office, 1984-87. Mem. NEA, Calif. Reading Assn., Internat. Reading Assn., Reading Edn. Guild, Delta Kappa Gamma, Phi Delta Kappa. Avocations: traveling, dancing, painting. Home: 12542 Peachleaf St Moreno Valley CA 92553-4764 Office: Moreno Valley Unif Sch Dist 13911 Perris Blvd Moreno Valley CA 92553-4306

MOULTON, DAVID AUBIN, library director; b. Portsmouth, N.H., Nov. 20, 1952; s. Howard Turner and Dorothy Margaret (McLaughlin) M. BA in History, U. New Hampshire, 1974; MLS, Simmons Coll., 1976. Asst. libr. Strayer Coll., Washington, 1976-83; dir. LRC Strayer Coll., Arlington, Va., 1983-86; dir. lbirs. Strayer Coll., Washington, 1987—; chair library networking com. Consortium for Continuing Higher Edn. in No. Va., 1987. Mem. covenants com. Parc East Condominium, Alexandria, Va, 1987-90. Mem. ALA, Dist. of Columbia Libr. Assn., Va. Libr. Assn. Avocation: collecting childrens and boy's books, 1820-1940. Office: Strayer Coll 1025 15th St NW Washington DC 20005-2601

MOULTON, DAWN G., English language educator; b. Manchester, Tenn., Sept. 22, 1961; d. Cecil Horace and Florence Marie (Farrell) Gibb; 1 child, Katy. AAS, Motlow State C.C., 1981; BS, Mid. Tenn. State U., 1984, MA, 1993. Cert. tchr. Tenn. Adult edn. instr. Tullahoma (Tenn.) City Schs., 1991-92; from writing ctr. instr., dir. to English instr. Motlow State C.C., Tullahoma, 1992—. Pres. Highland Rim Alzheimer's Assn., 1994-95, bd. dirs., 1993—; mem. PTA, Tullahoma, 1990—. Mem. Nat. Hist. Preservation Soc., AAUW, AAUP, MLA, Nat. Coun. Tchrs. English, Popular Culture Assn. South, South Ctrl. Conf. on Christianity and Lit. Avocations: bicycling, pencil drawing, writing, furniture refinishing, flower drying/arranging. Office: Motlow State CC Motlow Coll Rd Tullahoma TN 37388

MOULTON, EDWARD QUENTIN, civil engineer, educator; b. Kalamazoo, Nov. 16, 1926; s. Burt Frederick and Esther (Fairchild) M.; m. Joy Wade, Jan. 2, 1954; children: Jennifer Fairchild, Charles Wade, David Frederick II, Alison Joy. BS, Mich. State U., 1947; MS, La. State U., 1948; PhD, U. Calif., Berkeley, 1956; DSc (hon.), Wittenberg U., 1980; LLD (hon.), Xavier U., 1983, Wilmington Coll., 1983. Registered profl. engr., Ohio. Instr. civil engring Mich. State U., 1947; hydraulic engring. fellow La. State U., 1947-48; engr. U.S. Waterways Expt. Sta., Vicksburg, Miss., 1948; rsch. fellow U. Wis., 1948-49; asst. prof. civil engring. Auburn U., 1949-50; lectr. civil engring. U. Calif., Berkeley, 1950-54; asst. prof. civil engring. Ohio State U., 1954-58, assoc. prof., 1958-64; asst. dean Ohio State U. (Grad. Sch.), 1958-62, assoc. dean Grad. Sch., Coll. Arts and Scis., chmn. geodetic sci., 1962-64, dean off-campus edn., asso. dean faculties for personnel budget, prof. engring. mechanics, 1964-66; dir. Coll. Sci. and Engring. Dayton campus Miami U.-Ohio State U., 1963-66; pres. U. S.D., 1966-68; exec. asst. to pres. Ohio State U., 1968-69, sec. trustees, 1968-79, prof. civil engring., 1968-79, v.p. adminstrv. ops., 1969-70, exec. v.p. adminstrv. ops., 1970-71, exec. v.p., 1971-73, v.p. bus. and adminstrn., 1973-79, v.p., sec. emeritus, 1984—; chancellor Ohio Bd. Regents, 1979-83, chancellor emeritus, 1984—; exec. v.p. Cranston Securities Co., 1983-84; pres. Lake Erie Coll., 1985-86; pres., gen. mgr. Columbus Symphony Orchestra, 1986-88; cons. civil engring. 1954—. Author articles, reports, bulls. on environ. engring. and edn. Trustee Blue Cross Ctrl. Ohio, 1971-77, 80-82, Columbus Symphony Orch., 1980-85, Riverside Meth. Hosp., 1979-95, chmn. fin. and assets com., 1983-94, treas., 1988-94, vice-chmn., 1994-95; nat. adv. coun. for small bus. to U.S. Sec. Treasury, 1975-76; steering com. Devel. Com. Greater Columbus, 1970-1980, chmn., 1978-79; nat. adv. coun. SBA, 1973-76; bd. dirs. Columbus Safety Coun., 1970-79, Greater Columbus Arts Coun., 1970-78, Mid-Ohio Health Planning Commn., 1973-74, Am. Univs. for Rsch. in Astronomy, 1972-79, Ohio Transp. Rsch. Ctr., 1979-83, U.S. Health Corp., 1995—; chmn. Grant/Riverside Meth. Hosps., 1995—; vice-chmn. Ohio Higher Edn. facilities Commn., 1979-83; with Ohio Sch. and Coll. Bd. Registration, 1979-83, Ohio Ednl. TV Commn., 1979-83, Midwest Edn. Commn., 1979-85; chmn. Columbus Symphony Grand Ball, 1983; chmn. judging Internat. Sci. and Engring. Fair, 1984. With USN, 1945-46, PTO. Fellow ASCE; mem. Ohio Hist. Soc. (bd. dirs. 1979-83), State Higher Edn. Exec. Officers (exec. com. 1981-83), Ohio Commodore, Scioto Country Club, Faculty Club (Columbus), Athletic Club Columbus, Sigma Xi, Tau Beta Pi, Pi Mu Epsilon, Chi Epsilon, Delta Omega, Romophos, Sigma Alpha Epsilon. Congregationalist. Home: 1303 London Dr Columbus OH 43221-1541

MOULTON, GRACE CHARBONNET, physics educator; b. New Orleans, Nov. 1, 1923; d. Wilfred J. and Louise A. (Hellmers) Charbonnet; m. William Gates Moulton, June 1, 1947; children: Paul Charbonnet Moulton, Nancy Gates Moulton. BA, Tulane U., 1944; MS, U. Ill., 1948; PhD, U. Ala., 1962. Asst. prof. physics U. Ala., Tuscaloosa, 1962-65; asst. prof. physics Fla. State U., Tallahassee, 1965-74, assoc. prof. physics, 1974-80, prof. physics, 1980-91, prof. emerita, 1991—; cons. State Bd. Regents, Fla., 1984-85, Fla. Univ. System, 1989-90. Referee jour. articles Jour. Chem. Physics, Radiation Rsch.; contbr. many sci. rsch. articles to profl. jours. Four Yr. Undergrad. scholar Tulane U., scholar U. Ill.; rsch. grantee NIH. Mem. Am. Phys. Soc., (mem. coun. southeastern sect. 1988—). Avocations: gardening, music (classical and folk), snorkeling. Office: Fla State U Dept Physics Tallahassee FL 32304

MOULTON, PHILLIPS PRENTICE, religion and philosophy educator; b. Cleve., Dec. 24, 1909; s. E. Phillips and Myrtle (Skeel) M.; m. Mary Cochran, June 14, 1947; children: Katharine, Lawrence. A.B., Ohio Wesleyan U., 1931; postgrad., Marburg U., Germany, 1931-32, Princeton Theol. Sem., 1941-42; B.D., Yale U., 1942, Ph.D., 1949. Religious work sec. Cleve. YMCA, 1937-40; nat. dir. univ. work Fed. Council Chs., 1944-47; coordinator religious activities Chgo. U., 1948-51; lectr. religion in higher edn. Union Theol. Sem., N.Y., 1951-54; chmn. dept. philosophy, coordinator gen. edn. program Simpson Coll., Iowa, 1954-58; pres. Wesley Coll., prof. religion U. N.D., 1958-65, chmn. dept., 1963-65; prof. philosophy Adrian (Mich.) Coll., 1965-76; Danforth lectr. religion and higher edn. Boston U., Northwestern U., summers 1953, 54; dir. Nat. Meth. Gt. Books Project, 1957; T.W. Brown fellow postdoctoral research Haverford Coll., 1965, 67-68; vis. scholar Union Theol. Sem., N.Y.C., 1971-72, Center for Study Higher Edn., U. Mich., 1976-78, Mil. Study Group, 1984-92. Author: Experiment in General Education, 1957, Violence—Or Aggressive Nonviolent Resistance, 1971, The Living Witness of John Woolman, 1973, Enhancing the Values of Intercollegiate Athletics at Small Colleges, 1978, Ammunition for Peacemakers, 1986 (winner Pilgrim Press manuscript contest); editor: Community Resources in Cleveland, Ohio, 1937, The Journal and Major Essays of John Woolman, 1971 (Am. Assn. State and Local History award of merit). Pres. Midwest Faculty Christian Fellowship, 1957-58; U.S. del. Ecumenical Youth and Internat. YMCA Conf., 1939; chmn. Nat. Danforth Campus Workshop, 1957; speaker 14th Internat. Philosophy Congress, Vienna, 1968. Am. Philos. Soc. research grantee, 1968; Inst. Internat. Edn. fellow, 1931-32; Hough fellow in sociology, 1936-37; Taylor Theol. fellow, 1931-32; Univ. scholar Yale, 1944-45. Mem. Am. Acad. Religion (pres. Midwest region 1961-62), Civilian-Based Def. Assn. (bd. dirs. 1986-92), Phi Beta Kappa, Delta Sigma Rho, Omicron Delta Kappa, Beta Theta Pi. Methodist, Quaker. Home: 17208 Friends House Rd Sandy Spring MD 20860-1200 *At age 16 I discovered the most important thing in life - a strong Christian faith. This has given me motivation, stability, and direction. It has stimulated me to question generally-accepted values, to distinguish the significant from the trivial, the enduring from the temporal. I believe the Christian interpretation of life provides the perspective needed to make one's efforts worthwhile.*

MOULTON, WILBUR WRIGHT, JR., lawyer; b. Pensacola, Fla., Dec. 3, 1935; s. Wilbur Wright and Evelyn (Nobles) M.; m. Ann Arnow, Nov. 10, 1978; 1 child, Kelly Arnow. BA, Duke U., 1957; LLB, U. Va., 1959; LLM in Taxation, NYU, 1964. Bar: Fla. 1959; cert. tax lawyer, Fla. Assoc. Beggs & Lane, Pensacola, 1964-69; gen. counsel The Moulton Trust, Pensacola, 1970-74; pvt. practice, Pensacola, 1974-83; ptnr. Carlton, Fields, Ward, Emmanuel, Smith & Cutler, P.A., Pensacola, 1983—, also bd. dirs. Pres. Pensacola Heritage Found., 1971-72, Lakeview Ctr., Inc., Pensacola, 1975-77, dir. emeritus, 1984; chmn. bd. Lakeview Found., Inc., Pensacola; bd. trustees Pensacola Mus. Art. Lt. USNR, 1960-64. Mem. ABA, Fla. Bar Assn., Estate Planning Coun. N.W. Fla. (pres. 1978), Escambia-Santa Rosa Bar Assn. (pres. 1988-89), Rotary, Pensacola Country Club. Democrat. Episcopalian. Avocations: reading, running, traveling. Office: Carlton Fields Ward Emmanuel Smith & Cutler PA 25 W Cedar St Pensacola FL 32501-5945

MOULTRIE, FRED, geneticist; b. Albertville, Ala., Apr. 18, 1923; s. Walter Louis and Minnie Alma (Bodine) M.; m. Frances Grace Aldridge, May 28, 1947; children: Marilyn R. Moultrie Phillips, Elizabeth Anne Moultrie Becker, Janet Carol Moultrie Gauger. BS, Auburn U., 1948, MS, 1949; PhD in Genetics, Kan State U., 1953. Asso. prof. Auburn U., 1951-55, prof., 1955-56; geneticist Arbor Acres Farm, Inc., Glastonbury, Conn., 1956-59; research coordinator Arbor Acres Farm, Inc., 1959-62, v.p., dir. research, 1962-64, exec. v.p., 1964-72, pres. domestic div., 1972-73; pres. Corbett Breeders, Westover, Md., 1973-81; v.p., dir. research Corbett Enterprises, Inc., 1973-81, Kennebec Internat., 1981-84; geneticist Perdue Farms, Salisbury, Md., 1984-88; genetics cons., 1988—. Served with USCGR, 1942-46. Mem. World's Poultry Sci. Assn., Am. Poultry Sci. Assn., Poultry Breeders Am. (pres. 1967-68), Sigma Xi, Phi Kappa Phi, Alpha Zeta, Gamma Sigma Delta. Club: Masons. Home and Office: 4360 Coulbourn Mill Rd Salisbury MD 21804

MOUNES, JANICE ROSE MOORE, real estate broker; b. Phoenix, May 20, 1938; d. Jefferson Robert and Oveita (Lawrence) Moore; m. Harvey Lee Acridge, June 8, 1956 (div. Dec. 1968); children—Sharma L., Lainie A., Scott Michael; m. Richard Leo Behner, Oct. 27, 1973 (div. May 1991). Student Ariz. State U., 1961-62. Lic. real estate broker; cert. residential specialist. and cert. real estate brokerage mgr. Salesman Goebel Realty, Phoenix, 1969-71, Apollo Enterprises, Glendale, Ariz., 1971-73; pres. Metro Realty, Inc., Phoenix, 1974-78, Century 21 Metro, Phoenix, 1973-78; cofounder 50 States Real Estate franchise (doing bus. as 50 States Realty), Phoenix, 1978, broker 1978-83 sec., treas., 1978-87, pres. 1987—, dir., 1978—; owner Metro Movers, Phoenix, 1981—; cons. curriculum com. Glendale (Ariz.) Community Coll., 1978-89. Mem. Valley Cathedral, Phoenix, 1967—, Phoenix Bd. Realtors Grievance com., 1985-87. Mem. Women's Council Realtors (pres. 1983-84). Republican. Office: 50 States Realty 3504 W Peoria Ave Phoenix AZ 85029-4026

MOUNT, KARL A., manufacturing executive; b. Trenton, N.J., Feb. 15, 1945. BS in Commerce, Rider Coll., 1967. Sr. auditor S. D. Leidesdorf and Co., N.Y.C., 1967-75; contr. Alpha Metals Inc., Jersey City, N.J., 1975-83, v.p. fin., 1983-84, exec. v.p., 1984-87, pres., 1987-90; v.p. fin. Cookson Am. Inc., Providence, 1990-92; cons. J.F. Krahnert Assn., Edison, N.J., 1993-95; CFO Micro Ctrl., Inc., Old Bridge, N.J., 1995—; v.p. fin. & adminstrn. DTS, Inc., Woodbridge, N.J., 1995—. Office: 8998 Rte 18 N PO Box 1009 Old Bridge NJ 08857

MOUNT, THOMAS H(ENDERSON), motion picture and stage producer; b. Durham, N.C., May 26, 1948; s. Lillard H. and Bonnie M. Student, Bard Coll., 1968-70; MFA, Calif. Inst. Arts, 1973. Prodn. exec. Universal Studios, Universal City, Calif., 1975-79, pres. for prodn., 1976-84, ind. film producer, 1984—; adj. prof. Columbia U. Grad. Sch. Film, 1995-96. Prodr.: (films) My Man Adam, 1985, Roman Polanski's Pirates, 1985, Can't Buy Me Love, 1987, Frantic, 1987, Bull Durham, 1988, Stealing Home, 1988, Tequila Sunrise, 1988, Frankenstein Unbound, 1989, The Indian Runner, 1990, Death and the Maiden, 1994, Night Falls on Manhattan, 1996, (TV) Open Admissions, 1986, Cinemax Comedy Experiment (series) 1987, Son of the Morning Star, 1987, (stage) Death and the Maiden, 1993. Trustee Prodrs. Guild Am., 1995—, Calif. Inst. Arts, 1971-72, Bard Coll., 1980-93. Artist in residence NEH, Duke U., Durham, S.C., 1990.

MOUNT, WILLIE LANDRY, mayor; b. Lake Charles, La., Aug. 25, 1949; d. Lee Robert and Willia Veatrice (McCullor) Landry; m. Benjamin Wakefield Mount, Aug. 19, 1976. BS, McNeese State U., 1971. Geophys. asst. Lousiana Land and Exploration, Lake Charles, La., 1971-76; pharm. rep. Lederle, Lake Charles, 1976-80; realtor Mary Kay Hopkins, Lake Charles, 1976-87; co-owner Paper Place, Lake Charles, 1991-95; mayor City of Lake Charles, 1993—; mem. met. planning orgn. policy bd. IMCAL, Lake Charles, 1993—; Gov. Violent Crime & Homicide Task Force, Baton Rouge, 1993-95; mem. steering com. La. conf. Mayors bd. La. State Bar Assn. Guest condr. Lake Charles Symphony, 1992; v.p. dist. D. La. Mcpl. Assn., Baton Rouge, 1995-96; pres. Jr. League of Lake Charles; mem. adv. bd. S.W. La. Literacy Coalition; active First United Meth. Ch., La. Meth. Conf., McNeese State U. Found., United Way, Children's Miracle Network; exec. com. Coun. for a Better La. Recipient Spiritual Aims award Kiwanis Club, 1991, Cmty. Svc. award, 1995; Dorthea Combre award NAACP, 1994; named Woman of Yr., Quota Club, 1991, Citizen of Yr., Women's com. S.W. La., 1992, Woman of Yr., Pub. Ofcl. of Yr. Msgr. Cramers KC. Mem. LWV, S.W. La. Mayor's Assn. (chmn. 1993-94). Home: 205 Shell Beach Dr Lake Charles LA 70601-5933 Office: Office of Mayor PO Box 900 Lake Charles LA 70602-0900

MOUNTAIN, CLIFTON FLETCHER, surgeon, educator; b. Toledo, Apr. 15, 1924; s. Ira Fletcher and Mary (Stone) M.; children: Karen Lockerby, Clifton Fletcher, Jeffrey Richardson. AB, Harvard U., 1947; MD, Boston U., 1954. Diplomate Am. Bd. Surgery. Dir. dept. statis. rsch. Boston U., 1947-50; cons. rsch. analyst Mass. Dept. Pub. Health, 1951-53; intern U. Chgo. Clinics, 1954, resident, 1955-58, instr. surgery, 1958-59; sr. fellow thoracic surgery Houston, 1959; mem. staff U. Tex. Anderson Cancer Ctr.; asst. prof. thoracic surgery U. Tex., 1960-73, assoc. prof surgery, 1973-76, prof., 1976-94, prof. emeritus, 1995Ô, prof. surgery Sch. Medicine, 1987Ô, chief sect. thoracic surgery, 1970-79, chmn. thoracic oncology, 1979-84, chmn. dept. thoracic surgery, 1980-85, cons. dept. thoracic and cardiovascular surgery, 1996Ô, chmn. program in biomath. and computer sci., 1962-64, Mike Hogg vis. lectr. in S.Am., 1967; prof. surgery U. Calif., San Diego, 1996Ô; mem. sci. mission on cancer USSR, 1970-78, and Japan, 1976-84; mem. com. health, rsch. and edn. facilities Houston Cmty. Coun., 1964-78; cons. Am. Joint Com. on Cancer Staging and End Result Reporting, 1964-74, Tex. Heart Inst., 1994-96; mem. Am. Joint Com. on Cancer, 1974-86, chmn. lung and esophagus task force; mem. working party on lung cancer and chmn. com. on surgery Nat. Clin. Trials Lung Cancer Study Group, NIH, 1971-76; mem. plans and scope com. cancer therapy Nat. Cancer Inst., 1972-75, mem. lung cancer study group, 1977-89, chmn. steering com., 1973-75, mem. bd. sci. counselors divsn. cancer treatment, 1972-75; hon. cons. Shanghai Chest Hosp. and Lung Cancer Ctr., Nat. Cancer Inst. of Brazil; sr. cons. Houston Thorax Inst., 1994-96. Editor The New Physician, 1955-59; mem. editorial bd. Yearbook of Cancer, 1960-88, Internat. Trends in Gen. Thoracic Surgery, 1984-91; contbr. articles to profl. jours., chpts. to textbooks. Chmn. profl. adv. com. Harris County Mental Health Assn.; bd. dirs. Harris County chpt. Am. Cancer Soc. Lt. USNR, 1942-46. Recipient award Soviet Acad. Sci., 1977, Garcia Meml. medal Philippine Coll. Surgeons, 1982, Disting. Alumni award Boston U., 1988, Disting. Achievement U. Tex. M.D. Anderson Cancer Ctr., 1990, Disting. Svc. award Internat. Assn. for the Study of Lung Cancer, 1991, Disting. Alumnus award Boston U. Sch. of Medicine, 1992; named hon. pres. First Internat. Congress on Thoracic Surgery, 1997. Fellow ACS, Am. Coll. Chest Physicians (chmn. com. cancer 1967-75), Am. Assn. Thoracic Surgery, Inst. Environ. Scis., N.Y. Acad. Sci., Assn. Thoracic and Cardiovascular Surgeons of Asia (hon.), Hellenic Cancer Soc. (hon.), Chilean Soc. Respiratory Diseases (hon., hon. pres. 1982); mem. AAAS, Am. Assn. Carcer Rsch., AMA, So. Med. Assn., Am. Thoracic Soc., Soc. Thoracic Surgeons, Soc. Biomed. Computing, Am. Fedn. Clin. Rsch., Internat. Assn. Study Lung Cancer (pres. 1976-78), Am. Radium Soc., European Soc. Thoracic Surgeons, Pan-Am. Med. Assn., Houston Surg. Soc., Soc. Surg. Oncology, James Ewing Soc., Sigma Xi. Achievements include conception and development of program for application of mathematics and computers to the life sciences, of resource for experimental designs, applied statistics and computational support; first clinical use of physiologic adhesives in thoracic surgery; demonstration of clinical behavior of undifferentiated small cell lung cancer; first laser resection of lung tissue at thoracotomy; development of international system for staging of lung cancer.

MOUNTCASTLE, KATHARINE BABCOCK, foundation executive; b. Phila., Feb. 2, 1931; d. Charles H. and Mary (Reynolds) Babcock; m. Kenneth Franklin Mountcastle, Sept. 1, 1951; children: Mary Babcock, Laura Lewis, Kenneth Franklin, Katharine Reynolds. B.A., Sweet Briar (Va.) Coll., 1952. Dir., Internat. Social Service, N.Y.C., 1960-68; dir. Mary R. Babcock Found., Winston-Salem, N.C., 1954—; pres. Mary R. Babcock Found., Winston-Salem, 1980-85; trustee Z. Smith Reynolds Found., Winston-Salem, 1964—; pres. Z. Smith Reynolds Found., 1975-79; dir. NARAL Found., 1983-89. Trustee Sapelo Island Rsch. found., Ga.; bd. dirs. Fairfield County Cmty. Found., People for the Am. Way, 1982-84. Presbyterian. Address: 37 Oenoke Ln New Canaan CT 06840-4516

MOUNTCASTLE, KENNETH FRANKLIN, JR., retired stockbroker; b. Winston-Salem, N.C., Oct. 8, 1928; s. Kenneth Franklin and May M.; BS in Commerce, U. N.C., Chapel Hill, 1950; m. Mary Katharine Babcock, Sept. 1, 1951; children: Mary Babcock, Laura Lewis, Kenneth Franklin, Katharine Reynolds. With Mountcastle Knitting Co., Lexington, N.C., 1952-55, Reynolds & Co., N.Y.C., 1955-71; with Reynolds Securities Inc. (co. name changed to Dean Witter Reynolds 1978), N.Y.C., 1971-95, sr. v.p., 1974-95, ret., 1995. Trustee, New Canaan (Conn.) Country Sch., 1962-68, Ethel Walker Sch., Simsbury, Conn., 1973-85; trustee Coro Found., 1980—, nat. chmn., 1986-89; bd. dirs., past pres. Mary Reynolds Babcock Found., Winston-Salem, N.C.; former bd. visitors U. N.C., Chapel Hill; bd. dirs. Inform, N.Y.C., Fresh Air Fund, N.Y.C., The Giraffe Project Friends of Thirteen, Bus. Execs. for Nat. Security. Served with U.S. Army, 1950-52. Mem. Country Club of New Canaan, Wee Burn Country Club (Darien, Conn.), Old Town Club (Winston-Salem, N.C.), Racquet and Tennis Club, City Midday Club, Ocean Forest Golf Club (Sea Island, Ga.), Pine Valley Golf Club, Bond Club, Stock Exch. Luncheon Club. Home: 37 Oenoke Ln New Canaan CT 06840-4516 Office: Dean Witter Reynolds 2 World Trade Ctr Fl 17 New York NY 10048-0203

MOUNTCASTLE, VERNON BENJAMIN, neurophysiologist; b. Shelbyville, Ky., July 15, 1918; s. Vernon Mountcastle and Anne-Francis Marguerite (Waugh) M.; m. Nancy Clayton Pierpont, Sept. 6, 1945; children: Vernon Benjamin III, Anne Clayton, George Earle Pierpont. BS in Chemistry, Roanoke Coll., Salem, Va., 1938, DSc (hon.), 1968; MD, Johns Hopkins U., 1942; DSc (hon.), U. Pa., 1976, U. Minn., 1995; MD (hon.), U. Zurich, 1983, U. Siena, 1984, U. Santiago, Spain, 1990. House officer surgery Johns Hopkins Hosp., 1942-43; mem. faculty Johns Hopkins Sch. Medicine, 1946—, prof. physiology, 1959, dir. dept., 1964-80, Univ. prof. neurosci., 1980-92, prof. emeritus, 1992—; dir. Neurosci. Research Program, Rockefeller U., 1981-84; dir. Bard Labs. Neurophysiology Johns Hopkins U., Balt., 1981-91; pres. Neurosci. Research Found., 1981-85; spl. research physiology brain; chmn. physiology study sect., mem. physiology tng. com. NIH, 1958-61; adv. council Nat. Eye Inst., 1971-74; mem. sci. adv. bd. USAF, 1969-71; vis. com. dept. psychology Mass. Inst. Tech., 1966-75; bd. biology and medicine NSF, 1970-73; mem. commn. on neurophysiology Internat. Union Physiol. Sci. Editor-in-chief: Jour. Neurophysiology, 1961-64; assoc. editor: Bull. Johns Hopkins Hosp., 1954-62; editorial bd.: Physiol. Revs, 1957-59, Exptl. Brain Research, 1966-85; editor, contbr.: Med. Physiology, 12th edit, 1968, 13th edit., 1974, 14th edit., 1980, (with G.M. Edelman) The Mindful Brain, 1978; author articles in field. Served to lt. (s.g.) M.C. USNR, 1943-46. Recipient Lashley prize Am. Philos. Soc., 1974, F.O. Schmitt prize and medal MIT, 1975, Sherrington prize and gold medal Royal Acad. Medicine, London, 1977, Horowitz prize Columbia U., 1978, Fyssen Internat. prize, Paris, 1983, Lasker award, 1983, Helmholtz prize, 1982, Nat. Medal Sci., 1986, McGovern prize and medal AAAS, 1990, award in neurosci. Fidia Fedn., 1990, Australia prize, 1993. Mem. NAS (chmn. sect. on physiology 1971-74), AAAS, Am. Physiol. Soc., Am. Acad. Arts and Scis., Harvey Cushing Soc., Am. Neurol. Assn. (hon., Bennett lectr. 1978), Soc. Neurosci. (pres. 1970-72, Gerard prize 1980), Am. Philos. Soc. (councillor 1979-82), Nat. Inst. Medicine, Physiol. Soc. (London, hon.), Acad. Scis. (France, fgn.), Royal Soc. London (fgn.), Phi Beta Kappa, Alpha Omega Alpha, Phi Chi. Sigma Xi. Home: 15601 Carroll Rd Monkton MD 21111-2009

MOUNTCASTLE, WILLIAM WALLACE, JR., philosophy and religion educator; b. Hanover, N.H., July 10, 1925; s. William Wallace and Grace Elizabeth (Zottarelli) M.; m. Ila M. Warner (div.); children: Christine, Susan, Gregory, Eric; m. Barbara Kaye Griffin, Oct. 19, 1979; 1 child, Cathleena; stepdaughter, Dasha. BA, Whittier Coll., 1951; STB, Boston U., 1954, PhD, 1958. Ordained to ministry United Meth. Ch. Asst. prof. philosophy and religion High Point (N.C.) Coll., 1958-60; mem. So. Calif. Ann. Conf. United Meth. Ch., 1954-60; assoc. prof., head dept. philosophy Nebr. Wesleyan U., Lincoln, 1960-63, prof., head dept. philosophy, 1963-67; mem. Neb. Ann. Conf. United Meth. Ch., 1960-95; prof. philosophy Fla. So. Coll., Lakeland, 1967-69; assoc. prof. philosophy and religion U. W. Fla., Pensacola, 1969-79, prof. philosophy and religion, 1979—, M.L. Tipton prof. philosophy and religion, 1980—. Author: Religion in Planetary Perspective, 1979, Science Fantasy Voices and Visions of Cosmic Religion, 1996; contbr. articles to profl. jours. Fighter pilot USAAF, 1942-48, PTO. Mem. NEA/United Faculty Fla., Am. Assn. Religion, Am. Philos. Assn.,. Democrat. Home: 4549 Sabine Dr Gulf Breeze FL 32561-9253 Office: U West Fla Dept Phil-Religious Studies Pensacola FL 32514

MOUNTZ, LOUISE CARSON SMITH, retired librarian; b. Fond Du Lac, Wis., Oct. 20, 1911; d. Roy Carson and Charlotte Louise (Scheurs) Smith; m. George Edward Mountz, May 4, 1935 (dec. Oct. 3 1951); children: Peter Carson, Pamela Teeters Mountz McDonald. Student, Western Coll. for Women, 1929-31; AB, The Ohio State U., 1933; MA, Ball State U., 1962; postgrad., Manchester Coll., 1954, Ind. U., 1960-61. Cert. tchr., Ind. Tchr. Monroeville (Ind.) High Sch., 1953-54, Riverdale High Sch., St. Joe, Ind., 1954-55; libr. High Sch., Avilla, Ind., 1955-58; head libr. Penn High Sch., Mishawaka, Ind., 1958-67, Northwood Jr. High Sch., Ft. Wayne, Ind., 1967-69, McIntosh Jr. High Sch., Auburn, Ind., 1969-74; dir. Media Ctr. DeKalb Jr. High Sch., Auburn, Ind., 1974-78; ret., 1978; cons. media ctr. planning Penn-Harris-Madison Sch. Corp., Mishawaka, 1966-67. Author: Biographies for Junior High Schools and Correlated Audio-Visual Materials, 1970; contbr. articles to profl. jours. Bd. dirs. DeKalb County chpt. ARC, 1938-42, 51-53, DeKalb County Heart Assn., 1946-52, DeKalb County Cmty. Concert Assn., 1946-58, Am. Field Svc. Mishawaka chpt., 1960-67; active Ft. Wayne Philharmonic Orch. Assn., Ft. Wayne Art Mus., Ft. Wayne Hist. Soc., DeKalb County Hist. Soc., Garrett Hist. Soc., DeKalb County Genealogy Soc., Preservation of DeKalb County Heritage Assn., DeKalb Meml. Hosp. Women's Guild, also life mem. Mem. AAUW, ALA, NEA, World Confedn. Orgns. Teaching Professions, Nat. Coun. Tchrs. English, Ind. Sch. Librarians Assn. (dir. 1963-67), Internat. Assn. Sch. Librarianship, Ind. Assn. Ednl. Communication and Tech., Assn. Ind. Media Educators, Nat. Ret. Tchrs. Assns., Nat. Trust Hist. Preservation, Hist. Landmarks Found. Ind., Delta Kappa Gamma (charter mem., Beta Beta chpt.), Kappa Kappa Kappa (pr. officer 1941-45, pres. Alpha Chi chpt. 1938-40, organizer Garrett Assoc. chpt. pres. Garrett Assoc. chpt. 1971-73), Delta Delta Delta (house pres.). Methodist. Lodge: Order Ea. Star. Clubs: Greenhurst Country, Ft. Wayne Women's, Athena Lit. (hon. mem.), Ladies Lit. of Auburn. Home: 19 Castle Ct Auburn IN 46706-1439

MOUNTZ, WADE, retired health service management executive; b. Winona, Ohio, Nov. 19, 1924; s. Lowell J. and Ethel M. (Coppock) M.; m. Betty G. Wilson, June 3, 1946; children: David John, Timothy Wilson. BA, Baldwin-Wallace Coll., 1948; MHA, U. Minn., 1951; LHD (hon.), Ky. Wesleyan Coll., 1991. With Norton Meml. Infirmary, Louisville, 1951-69; adminstr. Norton Meml. Infirmary, 1958-69; pres. Norton-Children's Hosps., Inc., Louisville, 1969-81, NKC, Inc., Louisville, 1981-85; vice chmn. NKC, Inc., 1985-87, pres. emeritus, 1987—. Vice chmn. Comprehensive Health Planning Council Ky., 1968-73, chmn., 1973-79; bd. dirs. Louisville chpt. ARC, 1961-74; trustee Blue Cross Hosp. Plan, 1959-72; trustee Am. Hosp. Assn., 1971-76, chmn. bd., 1975. Served with A.C., USNR, 1943-45. Recipient Disting. Service award Ky. Hosp. Assn.; Disting. Layman award Ky. Med. Assn. Fellow Am. Coll. Hosp. Healthcare Execs. (gold medal), Masons. Home: 9 Muirfield Pl Louisville KY 40222-5074 Office: 4350 Brownsboro Rd Ste 110 Louisville KY 40207-1681

MOURA, JOSÉ MANUEL FONSECA, electrical engineering and computer science educator; b. Beira, Mozambique, Portugal, Jan. 9, 1946; s. José Saraiva and Maria José (Fonseca) M.; m. Maria Tereza Fernandes, 1969 (div. 1981); 1 child, Barbara Fernandes; m. Maria Manuela Veloso, 1982; children: André Veloso, Pedro Veloso. Engenheiro Electrotecnico, Instituto Superior Tecnico, Lisbon, 1969; M.S. in Elec. Engring., MIT, 1973, Sc. D. in Elec. Engring. and Computer Sci., 1975. Prof. auxiliar Instituto Superior Técnico, Lisbon, 1975-78, prof. aggregado, 1978, prof. catedrático, 1979-86; prof. Carnegie Mellon U., Pitts., 1986—; vis. assoc. prof. elec. engring. and computer sci. MIT, Cambridge, 1984-86; vis. scholar U. So. Calif., Los Angeles, summers 1978, 79, 80, 81. Editor: (with others) Nonlinear Stochastic Problems, 1983, Acoustic Signal Processing for Ocean Exploration, 1993. Contbr. articles to profl. jours.; editor-in-chief IEEE Trans. on Signal Processing, 1995—. Fellow IEEE; mem. NAS Portugal (corr. mem.), Am. Math. Soc., Soc. Indsl. and Applied Math., Ordem dos Engenheiros. Home: 6645 Woodwell St Pittsburgh PA 15217-1320 Office: Carnegie-Mellon U Dept Elec & Computer Engring 5000 Forbes Ave Pittsburgh PA 15213-3815

MOURA-RELVAS, JOAQUIM M.M.A., electrical engineer, educator; b. Aveiro, Portugal, May 9, 1926; s. Joaquim Moura and Maria Emilia Albuquerque (Branco de Melo) Relvas; m. Maria Alice Barata Portugal, May 9, 1953; children: Jose Pedro, Joao Paulo, Luis Filipe, Joaquim Jose, Francisco Manuel, Maria Isabel. Degree in Elec. Engr., U. Porto, Portugal, 1951. Asst. engr. CTT (State Telecomms.), Lisbon, Portugal, 1951-53; design engr. UEP (Elec. Power Co.), Porto, 1953-73; prof. U. Coimbra, Portugal, 1973-81; chief engr. EDP (Electricidade de Portugal), Lisbon, 1981-88; prof. Poly. Inst. of Gaya, Vila Nova de Gaia, Portugal, 1988—. Author: Introduction to Digital Electronics, 1971, Introduction to Microcomputers, 1981, Digital Electronics, 1986. Mem. AAAS, N.Y. Acad. Scis., Ordem dos Engenheiros, Planetary Soc. Avocations: swimming, walking, photography, home movies, historical books. Home: Av da Republica 1815, Vila Nova de Gaia 4430, Portugal Office: ISP Gaya, R Antonio R da Rocha 341, Vila Nova de Gaia 4430, Portugal

MOURNING, ALONZO, professional basketball player; b. Chesapeake, Va., Feb. 8, 1970. Student, Georgetown U. Center Charlotte Hornets, 1992—; now with Miami Heat; player All-Star Game, 1994. Named to NBA All-Rookie First Team, 1993, Dream Team II, 1994. Office: Miami Heat SunTrust Int'l Ctr One SE 3rd Ave Ste 2300 Miami FL 33131*

MOURTON, J. GARY, communications executive; b. Mena, Ark., Jan. 22, 1947; s. Malvin G. and Helen J. (Eckhardt) M.; m. J. Gayle Lay, June 29, 1968; children: Jennifer, Lindsay, Kimberly, Natalie. B.S.B.A., U. Ark., 1969. C.P.A., Okla. Audit mgr. Arthur Andersen & Co., Tulsa, 1969-80; fin. officer T/SF Comm. Corp. (formerly Swab-Fox Cos. and Midwest Energy Corp.), Tulsa, 1980—. Mem. Am. Inst. C.P.A.s, Okla. Soc. C.P.A.s, Fin. Execs. Inst. Republican. Office: T/SF Comm Corp 2407 E Skelly Dr Tulsa OK 74105-6006

MOUSER, GRANT EARL, III, retired foreign service officer; b. Marion, Ohio, July 11, 1923; s. Grant Earl M. and Hilda Kenyon (Gorham) Crenshaw; m. Lena Little, Feb. 12, 1955; 1 son, Grant Earl IV. B.A., Washington and Lee U., 1943, J.D., 1948; student, Mannix Walker Sch. Fgn. Service, 1949-50, U.S. Naval War Coll., 1966, Fed. Exec. Inst., 1973. Vice consul Am. consulate gen., Hamburg, W. Ger., 1950-53; econ., comml. officer Am. embassy, Tehran, Iran, 1953-56; Iranian desk officer Dept. State, Washington, 1957-60; polit. officer Am. embassy, Bonn, W. Ger., 1960-65; Indian desk officer Dept. State, 1968-70; polit. officer Am. embassy, New Delhi, India, 1970-73; fgn. service insp. Dept. State, worldwide, 1973-76; State Dept. rep. Armed Forces Staff Coll., Norfolk, Va., 1977-80; cons. gen. Am. consulate gen., Hamburg, W. Ger., 1980-85; exchange officer Dept. Def., Washington, 1966-68; ret., 1985; diplomat in residence Old Dominion U., Norfolk, Va., 1985—; vis. prof. Allegheny Coll., Meadville, Pa., 1976-77; lecturer Old Dominion U., Norfolk, 1985-86, William and Mary, Williamsburg, Va., 1986-93; site interpreter Jamestown Rediscovery, 1994—; dir. colonial capital br., trustee APUA. Bd. dirs. World Affairs Council, Norfolk, 1977-80; vice chmn. James City County Rep. com., 1991; layman Bruton Parish Ch., 1985-93. Served to lt. USNR, 1943-46. Recipient Superior Service award Dept. State, 1977; recipient Meritorious Honor award Dept. State, 1980, Joint Service Commendation medal Dept. Def., 1978.

Mem. SAR (pres. 1992), Am. Fgn. Service Assn., U.S. Naval Inst., Phi Gamma Delta, Rotary. Republican. Epicopalian. Avocations: map collecting, book collection, tennis. Home: 104 Clara Croker Williamsburg VA 23185-6504

MOUZON, ALPHONSE, actor, composer, record producer, instrumentalist; b. Charleston, S.C., Nov. 21, 1948; s. Flagner and Emma (Washington) M.; m. Allison Talley; 1 child, Emma Alexandra; children from previous marriage: Alphonse Philippe, Jean Pierre. Student, N.Y. City Coll., 1966-68, Manhattan Med. Sch., 1968-70. Cert. med. tech. Pres., chief exec. officer MPC Records/Tenacious Records/Mouzon Prodn. Co., Northridge, Calif. Co-founder band The 11th House; artist on record albums By All Means, 1981, Morning Sun, 1981, Distant Lover, 1982, The Sky's the Limit, 1985, Back to Jazz, 1986, Love Fantasy, 1987, Early Spring, 1988, As You Wish, 1990, The Survivor, 1992, On Top of the World, 1994, The Night is Still Young, 1996, Absolute Best of Alphonse Mouzon, 1997; original mem. band Weather Report; scored music for jazz nightclub scene, actor (film) That Thing You Do, 1996. Mem. ASCAP, SAG, Nat. Assn. Ind. Record Distributors, Nat. Assn. Recording Merchandisers, Recording Industry Assn. of Am. Avocations: tennis, basketball, jogging. Office: Mouzon Music Co/ MPC Records/ Tenacious Records PO Box 7595 Northridge CA 91327-7595

MOVIUS, ALISON WHITNEY BURTON (ALISON WHITNEY), writer, educator, publisher, speaker, poet, songwriter; b. Billings, Mont., Apr. 4, 1945; d. William Robert and Alice Whitney (Burton) Movius; divorced; children: David Lindley, Elisabeth Whitney Movius. BA in Humanities, U. Calif., Berkeley, 1967. Staff mem. Campus Crusade for Christ, various locations, 1967-78; dir. The Happy Place Nursery Sch., Ann Arbor, Mich., 1978-80; curriculum writer, children's songwriter, seminar spkr., 1976-85; founder, owner pub. co. Whitney Works!, La Jolla, Calif., 1992-97; writer, founder, pres. Abuse Survivor's Friendship Network, San Diego, 1992-97. Author: (workbook, lectures) The Challenge of Being a Woman, 1976, Poems that Tell a Story, 1997, Poems for Battered Women, 1996, When There's Abuse..., 1996, Happy Little Scripture Songs (for young children) , 1996, Valued and Loved, 1996, When Life is Hard, 1997, The All New Challenge of Being a Woman, 1997, The Challenge of Being a Woman Transition Course, 1997; songwriter 1,500 children's songs. Named to Outstanding Young Women of Am., 1978. Avocations: reading, running, music, movies, cooking. Office: Whitney Works PO Box 13191 La Jolla CA 92039-3191

MOVSHOVITZ, HOWARD PAUL, film critic, educator; b. Trenton, N.J., Dec. 30, 1944; s. Abraham H. and Helen (Peskin) M.; m. Janis Hallowell, Dec. 23, 1988; 1 child, Zoe. BA, U. Pa., 1966; PhD, U. Colo., 1977. Film critic Colo. Pub. Radio, Denver, 1976—; asst. prof. U. Colo., Denver, 1978-90; film critic The Denver Post, 1987-96; instr. U. Colo., Boulder, 1990—; reporter Nat. Pub. Radio, Washington, 1986—; film critic internet mag. Divein, 1997—. Mem. ACLU (bd. dirs. 1986-87). Office: Denver Post 1560 Broadway Denver CO 80202-6000

MOW, DOUGLAS FARRIS, former naval officer, consultant; b. Carbondale, Colo., Nov. 10, 1928; s. James Leroy and Marie (Gerkin) M.; m. Rosalie Stearns Johnson, June 16, 1951; children: Douglas Farris, Deborah, Laura, Nancy. B.S., U.S. Naval Acad., 1951; M.S. in Physics, U.S. Naval Postgrad. Sch., 1958; student, Armed Forces Staff Coll., 1964-65. Commd. ensign USN, 1951, advanced through grades to rear adm., 1977; night attack pilot San Diego, 1953-56; served with research and devel. div. (Def. Nuclear Agy.), Albuquerque, 1958-60; nuclear weapons employment officer (Carrier Air Wing 11), Naval Air Sta. Miramar, San Diego, 1960-62; pilot, ops. officer (Light Attack Squadron), Naval Air Sta. Lemoore, Calif., 1962-64; assigned to atomic energy div. (Office Chief of Naval Ops.), Washington, 1965-66; comdg. officer squadron Vietnam War, 1967-68; staff comdr. (7th Fleet), 1969; comdr. (Carrier Airwing 19), 1970-71, (Light Attack Wing One), Jacksonville, Fla., 1971-73; exec. asst./naval aide to Sec. Navy Washington, 1973-77; VSTOL program coordinator, 1977-80; comdr. (Tactical Wings Atlantic), Virginia Beach, Va., 1980-81; cons., 1982—. Decorated D.S.M., Silver Star, D.F.C. with 2 oak leaf clusters, Legion of Merit with 2 oak leaf clusters, Bronze Star with 2 oak leaf clusters, Air medal with 4 oak leaf clusters, Navy Commendation medal with 2 oak leaf clusters. Mem. U.S. Naval Inst. Republican. Episcopalian.

MOW, ROBERT HENRY, JR., lawyer; b. Cape Girardeau, Mo., Dec. 10, 1938; s. Robert H., Sr. and Ann Elise (Beck) M.; m. Jody K. Boggs, Aug. 29, 1987; children: Robert M., Brynn A., W.Brett, Rebecca M., W. Kirk, Allison M. Student, Westminster Coll., 1956-57; A.B. with distinction, U. of Mo., 1960; LL.B. magna cum laude, So. Meth. U., 1963. Bar: Tex. 1963, U.S. Dist. Ct. (no. dist.) Tex. 1965, U.S. Dist. Ct. (so. dist.) Tex. 1969, U.S. Dist Ct. (ea. dist.) Tex. 1976, U.S. Dist. Ct. (we. dist.) Tex. 1976, U.S. Ct. Claims 1973, U.S. Ct. Appeals (5th cir. 1972, U.S. Ct. Appeals (11th cir.) 1981, U.S. Ct. Appeals (Fed. cir.), 1994, U.S. Supreme Ct. 1978. Assoc., Carrington, Johnson & Stephens, Dallas, 1963-69; ptnr. Carrington, Coleman, Sloman, & Blumenthal, Dallas, 1970-85; Hughes & Luce, L.L.P., Dallas, 1985—. Editor-in-chief Southwestern Law Jour., 1962-63. Served to 1st lt. U.S. Army, 1963-65. Fellow Am. Coll. of Trial Lawyers, mem. Dallas Jr. Bar Assn. (pres. 1968), Dallas Assn. of Def. Counsel (chmn. 1976-77), Tex. Assn. of Def. Counsel (v.p. 1981-82), Am. Bd. of Trial Advocates (pres. Dallas chpt. 1983-84). Republican. Baptist. Office: Hughes & Luce LLP 1717 Main St Ste 2800 Dallas TX 75201-7342

MOW, VAN C., engineering educator, researcher; b. Chengdu, China, Jan. 10, 1939. B. Aero. Engring., Rensselaer Poly. Inst., 1962, Ph.D., 1966. Mem. tech. staff Bell Telephone Labs., Whippany, N.J., 1968-69; assoc. prof. mechanics Rensselaer Poly. Inst., Troy, N.Y., 1969-76, prof. mechanics and biomed. engring., 1976-82, John A. Clark and Edward T. Crossan prof. engring., 1982-86; prof. mechanical engring. and orthopedic bioengring. Columbia U., N.Y.C., 1986—; dir. Orthopedic Research Lab., Columbia-Presbyn. Med. Ctr., N.Y.C., 1986—; vis. mem. Courant Inst. Math. Sci., NYU, 1967-68; vis. prof. Harvard U., Boston, 1976-77; chmn. orthopaedics and musculoskeletal study sect. NIH, Bethesda, Md., 1982-84; hon. prof. Chengdu U. Sci. Tech., 1981, Shanghai Jiao Tong U., 1987; mem. grants rev. bd. Orthopaedic Rsch. Edn. Found., 1992-96; bd. dirs. Hoar Rsch. Found., 1993—; cons. in field. Assoc. editor Jour. Biomechanics, 1981—, Jour. Biomech. Engring., 1979-86; chmn. editorial adv. bd. Jour. Orthopedic Rsch., 1983-90; adv. editor Clin. Orthopedic Rel. Rsch., 1993—; contbr. numerous articles to profl. jours. Founder Gordon Research Conf. on Bioengring. and Orthopedic Sci., 1980. NATO sr. fellow, 1978; recipient William H. Wiley Disting. Faculty award Rensselaer Poly. Inst., 1981; Japan Soc. for Promotion Sci. Fellow, 1986, Fogarty Sr. Internat. fellow, 1987; Alza disting. lectr. Biomed. Engring. Soc., 1987; H.R. Lissner award ASME, 1987, Kappa Delta award AAOS, 1980, Giovani Borelli award, 1991. Fellow ASME (chmn. biomechanics divsn. 1984-85, Melville medal 1982), Am. Inst. Med. Biol. Engring.; mem. NAE, Orthopaedic Rsch. Soc. (pres. 1982-83), Am. Soc. Biomechanics (founding), Internat. Soc. Biorheology, U.S. Nat. Com. on Biomechanics (sec.-treas. 1985-90, chmn. 1991-94). Office: Columbia-Presbyn Med Ctr BB-1412 630 W 168th St New York NY 10032-3702

MOWAT, FARLEY MCGILL, writer; b. Belleville, Ont., Can., May 12, 1921; s. Angus McGill and Helen (Thomson) M.; m. Frances Elizabeth Thornhill, Dec. 21, 1947; children: Robert Alexander, David Peter; m. Claire Angel Wheeler, 1965. BA, U. Toronto, 1949, LLD, 1973; DLitt (hon.), Laurentian U., 1970; LLD, U. Lethbridge, Alta., 1973, U. P.E.I., 1979; DLitt, U. Victoria, B.C., 1982, Lakehead U., Thunder Bay, Ont., 1986; LHD (hon.), McMaster U., Hamilton, Ont., 1994; LLD (hon.), Queen's Univ., Kingston, Ont., 1995; DLitt (hon.), U. Coll. of Cape Breton, Sydney, Nova Scotia, 1996. Arctic exploration, sci. work, 1947-48, writer, 1950—. Author: People of the Deer, 1952, The Regiment, 1955, Lost in the Barrens, 1956, The Dog Who Wouldn't Be, 1957, Coppermine Journey, 1958, The Grey Seas Under, 1958, The Desperate People, 1959, Ordeal By Ice, 1960, Owls in the Family, 1961, The Serpent's Coil, 1961, The Black Joke, 1962, Never Cry Wolf, 1963, Westviking, 1965, The Curse of the Viking Grave, 1966, Canada North, 1967, The Polar Passion, 1967 (with John de Visser) This Rock Within the Sea, 1968, The Boat Who Wouldn't Float, 1969, The Siberians, 1971, A Whale for the Killing, 1972, Tundra, 1973, (with David Blackwood) Wake of the Great Sealers, 1973, The Snow Walker, 1975, Canada North Now, 1976, And No Birds Sang, 1979, The World of Farley Mowat, 1980, Sea of Slaughter, 1984, My Discovery of America, 1985, Woman in the Mist, 1987, The New Founde Land, 1989, Rescue the Earth, 1990, My Father's Son, 1992, Born Naked, 1993, Aftermath, 1995; author documentary script The New North (Gemini award 1989); film Sea of Slaughter (Conservation Film of Yr. award 1990, ACE award finalist 1990, award of Excellence Atlantic Film Festival 1990). Served to capt. inf. Canadian Army, 1939-45. Recipient Pres. Medal Univ. Western Ont., 1952, Anisfield Wolfe award, 1954, Gov. Gen.'s medal, 1957, Book of Yr. Medal Can. Library Assn., 1958, Hans Christian Anderson Internat. award, 1958, 65, Can. Women's Clubs award, 1958, Boys Clubs Am. award, 1962, Nat. Assn. Ind. Schs. award, 1963, Can. Centennial medal, 1967, Stephen Leacock medal for humor, 1970, Leacock Medal for Humour, 1970, Vicky Metcalf award, 1970, Mark Twain award, 1971, Book of Yr. award, 1976, Curran award, 1977, Queen Elizabeth II Jubilee medal, 1978, Knight of Mark Twain, 1980, Can. Author's award, 1981, 85, Can. Author of Year award, 1988, Can. Book of Yr. award, 1988, Torgi Can. Talking Book of Yr. award, 1989, Can. Achievers award Toshiba Can., 1990, Take Back the Nation award Coun. Cans., 1991, Authors award, Author of Yr. Found. for Advancement of Can. Letters, 1993; decorated officer Order of Can., 1981, L'Etoile de la Mer, 1972. Address: 18 King St, Port Hope, ON Canada L1A 2R4

MOWATT, E. ANN, women's voluntary leader, lawyer. BA in History, Dalhousie U., Halifax, Nova Scotia, 1982, LLB, 1985. Barrister, solicitor Patterson Palmer Hunt Murphy, 1986—. Bd. dirs. YMCA-YWCA of Saint John N.B., Can., 1987-93; also mem. exec., fin., social action, and camp coms., pres., 1991; bd. dirs. YWCA of Can., 1989—, also chair constn. task force, mem.-at-large, treas., v.p., pres., 1995-97, past pres., 1997—; bd. dirs. Coalition of Nat. Vol. Orgns., 1994—, now sec.; pres. Saint John chpt. Multiple Sclerosis Soc. Con., 1987-88, bd. dirs. Atlantic divsn., 1988—, mem. nat. bd. dirs., 1992-95, pres. Atlantic divsn., 1993-95. Mem. Can. Bar Assn. (mem. N.B. coun. 1986-89), Law Soc. N.B. (mem. legal aid com. 1989-92). Avocations: reading, films, camping, canoeing, theatre. Home: 1054 Mollins Dr Apt 3, Saint John, NB Canada E2M 4L8 Office: 590 Jarvis St 5th Fl, Toronto, ON Canada M4Y 2J4 also: PO Box 1324, Saint John, NB Canada E2L 4H8

MOWDAY, RICHARD THOMAS, management educator; b. Oakland, Calif., Sept. 4, 1947; s. Richard Walter and Jessie Elizabeth (Steet) M.; m. Mary Nelson; children: Graham Thomas, Garrett Nelson. BS in Manpower Adminstrn., San Jose State U., 1970; MS in Adminstrn., U. Calif., Irvine, 1972, PhD in Adminstrn., 1975. Asst. prof. U. Nebr., Lincoln, 1975-77; asst. prof. U. Oreg., Eugene, 1977-81, assoc. prof., 1981-86, prof. mgmt., 1986—, Holden Affilate prof. mgmt., 1988, Gerald B. Bashaw disting. prof. mgmt., 1990, assoc. dean, 1994-96; vis. scholar Tuck Sch. Mgmt. Dartmouth Coll., Hanover, N.H., 1983-84; Hanson vis. prof. U. Washington, 1991—. Co-author: Employee-Organization Linkages, 1982, Managing Effective Organizations, 1985; co-editor: Research in Organizations, 1979; editor Acad. Mgmt. Jour., 1988-90, cons. editor, 1984-87; internat. cons. editor Jour. Occupational Psychology, 1983-91; editl. rev. bd. Jour. Vocat. Behavior, Jour. Mgmt., Adminstrv.. Sci. Quar., Jour. Mgmt. Inquiry. Fellow APA, Acad. of Mgmt. (div. chmn. 1984-85, bd. govs., v.p., program chmn., pres. Best Rsch. Paper award, orgnl. behavior div. 1986), Am. Psychol. Soc.; mem. Internat. Fedn. Scholarly Assns. Mgmt. (coun. mem. 1996—), Western Acd. Mgmt., Soc. Orgnl. Behavior. Congregationalist. Avocations: cross country skiing, bicycling, running. Home: 5225 Miramar St Eugene OR 97405-4842 Office: U Oregon Coll Bus Adminstrn Eugene OR 97403

MOWE, GREGORY ROBERT, lawyer; b. Aberdeen, Wash., Feb. 23, 1946; s. Robert Eden and Jeannette Effie (Deyoung) M.; m. Rebecca Louise Nobles, June 14, 1969; children: Emily, Tom. BA, U. Oreg., 1968, MA, 1969; JD magna cum laude, Harvard Law Sch., 1974. Bar: Oreg. 1974, U.S. Dist. Ct. Oreg. 1974, U.S. Ct. Appeals (9th cir.) 1974. Assoc. atty. Stoel Rives Boley Jones & Grey, Portland, Oreg., 1974-79; ptnr. Stoel Rivis Boley Jones & Grey, Portland, 1979—. Pres. bd. dirs. Planned Parenthood of Columbia/Willamette, Portland, 1989-90. 1st lt. U.S. Army, 1969-71, Vietnam. Mem. ABA, Phi Beta Kappa. Office: Stoel Rives Boley Jones & Grey 900 SW 5th Ave Ste 2300 Portland OR 97204-1232

MOWER, ERIC ANDREW, communications and marketing executive; b. N.Y.C., Oct. 10, 1944; s. Jack Henry Mower and Doris (Bernfeld) Schecter; m. Judith Ann Cotey, May 28, 1967; 1 child, Hillary Beth. BA, Syracuse (N.Y.) U., 1966, MA, 1968. Prin. Eric Mower and Assocs., Syracuse, 1968—. Pres. Health Sci. Ctr. Found., SUNY, Syracuse, 1983-88; pres., bd. dirs. Syracuse Symphony Orch., 1988-90; chmn. Ctrl. N.Y. chpt. Nat. Kidney Found., 1987-88, Ctrl. N.Y. Regional Market Task Force, 1988-90, Partnership for Arts; bd. dirs. Met. Devel. Assn., Everson Mus., Nat. Advt. Rev. Bd., Bus. Coun. N.Y. State; past mem. bd. dirs. Syracuse Stage, Jr. Achievement, Ctrl. N.Y. coun. Boy Scouts Am., Sta. WCNY-TV-FM; trustee, vice-chair Syracuse U. Mem. Am. Assn. Advt. Agys. (chmn. N.Y. state coun. 1986, chmn. bd. govs. ea. region 1988-89, nat. bd. dirs. 1990—, sec.-treas. 1993-94), Greater Syracuse C. of C. (chmn. bd. dirs. 1992-93), Univ. Club (N.Y.C.), Friars Club, Century Club. Office: Eric Mower and Assocs Inc 500 Plum St Syracuse NY 13204-1401 also: Eric Mower and Assocs 360 Delaware Ave Buffalo NY 14202-1610 also: Eric Mower and Assocs 350 Linden Oaks Dr Rochester NY 14625 also: Eric Mower and Assocs 18 Corporate Woods Blvd Albany NY 12211 also: Eric Mower and Assocs Ste 550 3379 Peachtree Rd NE Atlanta GA 30326

MOWERY, ANNA RENSHAW, state legislator; b. Decatur, Tex., Jan. 4, 1931; d. Lafayette William and Early Virginia (Bobo) Renshaw; m. Wesley Harold Mowery, June 2, 1951; children: Jeanette Mowery Hefferman, Mark William, Timothy Dean, Marianne Mowery Fichera. BA, Baylor U., 1951; MA, Ctrl. State U,, 1967. Tchr. Ft. Hood (Tex.) Pub. Schs., 1951-52; petroleum landman Ft. Worth, 1979-82; dist. dir. U.S. Congl. Dist. 6 Joe Barton, Ft. Worth, 1985-86; polit. cons., pres. Trinity Assocs., Ft. Worth, 1987-88; state rep. Tex. House Reps., Ft. Worth, 1988—. Chmn. Tarrant County (Tex.) Rep. Party, 1975-77; mem. Tex. Rep. Exec. Com., Ft. Worth, 1980-84, Greater Ft. Worth Literacy Coun., 1990—; mem. adv. bd. Sr. Citizen Svcs./Tarrant County, Ft. Worth, 1988—. Recipient 4-H Clubs Am. Alumni award, 1990; nominee Newsmaker of Yr., Ft. Worth Press Club, 1974, 76. Mem. Tex. Women's Alliance, Women's Policy Forum. Republican. Baptist. Home: 4108 Hildring Dr W Fort Worth TX 76109-4722 District Office: Ste 534 Twr II 4100 International Plz Fort Worth TX 76109-4820 Office: Tex House of Reps State Capitol Austin TX 78768-2910

MOWRY, ROBERT DEAN, art museum curator, educator; b. Quinter, Kans., Sept. 27, 1945; s. Eugene Adrian and Pearl Helen (Kreft) M. BA with honors, U. Kans., 1967, MA with honors, 1974, MPhil. with honors, 1975. Curatorial asst. and translator Nat. Palace Mus., Taipei, Taiwan, 1975-77; asst. curator Oriental art Fogg Art Mus., Harvard U., Cambridge, Mass., 1977-80; curator Mr. and Mrs. John D. Rockefeller 3d collection Asia Soc., N.Y.C., 1980-86; curator Asian Art Harvard U. Art Mus., Cambridge, 1986-92; curator Chinese art and head dept. Asian art Harvard U. Art Mus., 1992—; lectr. dept. fine arts Harvard U., Cambridge, 1987-94; sr. lectr. Chinese and Korean art dept. fine arts Harvard U., 1994—; contbg. editor Art and Auction, N.Y.C., 1982-86; lectr. grad. program Cooper-Hewitt Mus., N.Y.C.; 1983-86, Inst. Asian Studies, N.Y.C., 1982—. Author: Handbook of the Mr. and Mrs. John D. Rockefeller 3d Collection, 1981, The Chinese Scholar's Studio: Artistic Life in the Late Ming Period, 1987, China's Renaissance in Bronze: The Robert H. Clague Collection of Later Chinese Bronzes 1100-1900, 1993, Ancient China, Modern Clay: Chinese Influences on Five Ceramic Artists, 1994, Hare's Fur, Tortoise Shell and Partridge Feathers: Chinese Brown and Black Glazed Ceramics, 400-1400, 1996, Worlds within Worlds: The Richard Rosenblum Collection of Chinese Scholars' Rocks, 1997; contbr. articles to profl. jours. Vol. U.S. Peace Corps, Seoul Nat. U., Republic of Korea, 1967-69. Hackney scholar Freer Gallery Art, Washington, 1975-76; fellow U. Kans., Lawrence, 1971-75, J.D. Rockefeller 3d Fund, N.Y.C., 1976-77, Samuel Kress Found., N.Y.C., 1975. Mem. Coll. Art Assn. Am., Assn. for Asian Studies, Am. Com. for South Asian Art, Am. Assn. Mus., Nat. Trust for Hist. Preservation. Avocations: movies, reading, theatre, dance, opera, concerts. Office: Harvard U Art Mus Asian Dept 485 Broadway Cambridge MA 02138-3802

MOWRY, ROBERT WILBUR, pathologist, educator; b. Griffin, Ga., Jan. 10, 1923; s. Roy Burnell and Mary Frances (Swilling) M.; m. Margaret Neilson Black, June 11, 1949; children: Janet Lee, Robert Gordon, Barbara Ann. B.S., Birmingham So. Coll., 1944; M.D., Johns Hopkins U., 1946. Rotating intern U. Ala. Med. Coll., 1946-47, resident pathology, 1947-48; sr. asst. surgeon USPHS-NIH, Bethesda, Md., 1948-52; fellow pathology Boston City Hosp., 1949-50; asst. prof. pathology Washington U., St. Louis, 1952-53; asst. prof. pathology U. Ala. Med. Ctr., Birmingham, 1953-54, assoc. prof. pathology, 1954-57; prof. U. Ala. Med. Center, Birmingham, 1958-89, prof. emeritus, 1989—, prof. health svcs. adminstrn., 1976-84, dir. Anat. Pathology Lab., 1960-64, dir. grad. programs in pathology, 1964-72; sr. scientist U. Ala. Inst. Dental Research, 1967-72, dir. autopsy services, 1975-79; vis. scholar dept. pathology U. Cambridge, Eng., 1972-73; cons. FDA, 1975-81. Author: (with J.F.A. McManus) Staining Methods: Histologic and Histochemical, 1960; mem. editorial bd. Jour. Histochemistry and Cytochemistry, 1960-75, Stain Tech., 1965-90, AMA Archives of Pathology, 1967-76, Biotechnics and Histochemistry, 1991—. Served with USPHS, 1948-52. Mem. Am. Soc. Investigative Pathology, Internat. Acad. Pathology, Biol. Stain Commn. (v.p. 1974-76, pres. 1976-81, trustee 1966—), Soc. for Glycobiology, Am. Assn. Univ. Profs. Pathology, Phi Beta Kappa, Sigma Xi, Delta Sigma Phi, Alpha Kappa Kappa. Presbyterian. Achievements include perfection of staining methods for complex carbohydrates (Alcian blue and colloidal iron) and insulin (Alcian blue-aldehyde fuchsin); showed the utility of these in diagnostic histopathology. Home: 4165 Sharpsburg Dr Birmingham AL 35213-3234

MOXLEY, JOHN HOWARD, III, physician; b. Elizabeth, N.J., Jan. 10, 1935; s. John Howard, Jr. and Cleopatra (Mundy) M.; m. Doris Banchik; children: John Howard IV, Brook, Mark. BA, Williams Coll., 1957; MD, U. Colo., 1961; DSc (hon.), Sch. Medicine Hannemann U. Bar: Diplomate Am. Bd. Internal Medicine. Intern Peter Bent Brigham Hosp., Boston, 1961-62, resident in internal medicine, 1962-66; with Nat. Cancer Inst., USPHS, 1963-65; asst. to dean, instr. medicine Harvard Med. Sch., Boston, 1966-69; dean Sch. Medicine, U. Md., 1969-73; vice chancellor health scis., dean Med. Sch., U. Calif.-San Diego, 1973-79; asst. sec. for health affairs Dept. Def., Washington, 1979-81; sr. v.p. Am. Med. Internat., Beverly Hills, Calif., 1981-87; pres. MetaMed. Inc., Playa Del Rey, Calif., 1987-89; mgr. dir. Korn/Ferry Internat., L.A., 1989—; cons. FDA, NIH; dir. Nat. Fund for Med. Edn., 1986—, chmn., 1993—; dir. Henry M. Jackson Found. for Adv. Mil. Medicine. Contbr. articles to profl. jours. Dir. Polyclinic Health Svcs. Games of XXIII Olympiad. Recipient gold and silver award U. Colo. Med. Sch., 1974, commr.'s citation for outstanding svc. to over-the-counter drug study FDA, 1977, spl. achievement citation Am. Hosp. Assn., 1983, Sec. of Def. medal for disting. pub. svc., 1981. Fellow ACP, Am. Coll. Physicians Execs. (Disting.); mem. Inst. Medicine NAS, AMA (chmn. coun. sci. affairs 1985), Calif. Med. Assn. (chmn. sci. bd. 1978-83, councilor), San Diego C. of C., Soc. Med. Adminstrs., Am. Hosp. Assn. (trustee 1979-81), Alpha Omega Alpha. Rotary. Office: Korn/Ferry Internat 1800 Century Park E Ste 900 Los Angeles CA 90067-1512

MOY, RICHARD HENRY, academic dean, educator; b. Chgo., Feb. 2, 1931; s. Henry B. and Gladys (Pope) M.; m. Caryl L. Towsley, Aug. 21, 1954; children: Philip B., Eric R. BA in Pre-Medicine with gen. honors, U. Chgo., 1953, BS in Pre-Medicine, 1954, MD in Pathology with honors, 1957. Diplomate Am. Bd. Internal Medicine. Intern U. Chgo. Hosps. and Clinics, 1957-58, resident, 1960-63; clin. assoc. Nat. Cancer Inst. NIH, Bethesda, Md., 1958-60; instr. dept. internal medicine U. Chgo., 1962-63, rsch. assoc., asst. prof., 1964-68, assoc. prof., 1968-70; prof. internal medicine, dean Sch. Medicine So. Ill. U., Springfield, 1970-93, dean emeritus, 1974-93, 1993—; mem. health care program com. Health Care Svc. Corp., 1978-79, 82—, exec. com., 1979-80, 82-83, 84-86, 88—, fin. com., 1981-82, bd. orgn. and nominating com., 1984—, ad hoc com. for long range planning, 1982-83, bd. dirs., 1971—; mem. ad hoc rev. group for start-up assistance grants HEW, 1976; del. People-to-People Med. Edn. Trip to Africa, 1982; mem. med. determination bd. Ill. Dept. Pub. Health, 1980-85, adv. com. family practice residency, 1978, health svc. corps task force, 1980-93; mem. task force on future of mental health in Ill., 1986-87; panelist, lectr., cons. S.C. Commn. on Higher Edn., 1990, other orgns. Contbr. articles to profl. jours. Mem. adv. bd. Ill. Emergency Svcs. and Disaster Agy., 1984-93, Ill. Geriatric Edn. Ctr., 1989-93; chair emergency med. care com. Gov.'s Task Force on Earthquake Preparedness, 1989-90; bd. dirs. Am. Heart Assn. Ill., 1982-84; mem. planning com. St. John's Hosp., 1976-93, Meml. Med. Ctr., 1980-93; mem. VA med. assistance rev. com., 1974-78; chmn. citizens' task force to pass tax referendum Springfield Pub. Sch. Dist. 186, 1984; mem. site visit team Marshall U., 1974, 82, Duke U., 1978, Creighton U., 1980, UCLA, 1981, U. Okla., 1985, Temple U., 1988, Vanderbilt U. Sch. Medicine, 1992; chmn. site visit team U. Calif. Sch. Medicine, 1975, East Tenn. U., 1990, Med. Coll. Pa., 1991, Mich. State U., 1992, Loma Linda U. Med. Sch., 1994. Recipient Disting. Svc. award Med. Alumni Assn. U. Chgo., 1979, Recognition award Soc. Tchrs. of Family Medicine, 1981, Pub. Svc. award So. Ill. U. Carbondale Alumni Assn., 1984, Golden Achievement award Nat. Sch. Pub. Rels. Assn., 1985, Gold Medallion for Humanitarian Svc., Am. Lung Assn., 1993; named rector for medicine and sci. Lincoln Acad. Ill., 1991. Fellow ACP; mem. Assn. Am. Med. Colls. (various coms. and offices), AMA (sect. med. schs. 1977-93), Am. Bd. Med. Spltys. (rep. Assn. Med. Colls. 1986-91), Ill. Coun. Med. Deans (pres. 1978-79), Ill. Hosp. Assn. (ad hoc study group funding med. edn.), Ill. State Med. Soc., Nat. Bd. Med. Examiners (chair composite com. for U.S. med. licensing examination 1990-92, comprehensive part I and part II coms. 1986-92, John F. Hubbard award com. 1987, mem. ednl. adv. com. Nat. Fund for Med. Edn. 1988-90, chmn. 1988), Sangamon County Med. Soc., Springfield Med. Club, Cen. Ill. Consortium for Health Manpower Edn. (pres. 1976-77), Ill. State Acad. Sci. (hon.), Alpha Omega Alpha, Sigma Xi. Presbyterian. Avocations: med. history, fishing, reading. Office: So Ill U Sch Medicine 801 N Rutledge PO Box 19230 Springfield IL 62794-9230*

MOY, RONALD LEONARD, dermatologist, surgeon; b. Stuttgart, Germany, June 10, 1957; s. Howard Leonard Stephen and Jenny (Yee) M.; m. Lisa Wing Lan Lin, Aug. 10, 1986; children: Lauren, Erin. Grad., Rensselaer Poly. Inst., 1977, Albany Med. Coll., 1981. Dir. Mohs micrographic surgery div. dermatology UCLA, 1988-93, dir. dermatologic surgery div. dermatology, 1988-93, co-chief div. dermatology, 1992-93; chief dermatologic surgery VA-West Los Angeles Med. Ctr., 1988—. Author: Atlas of Cutaneous Flaps and Grafts, 1990; editor: Principle and Practice of Dermatologic Surgery, 1993; editor-in-chief: Dermatologic Surgery; contbr. articles to profl. jours. Bd. dirs. L.A. Costal unit Am. Cancer Soc., 1988. Recipient J. Lewis Pipkin award in dermatology Nat. Student Rsch. Forum, 1981, Henry Christian award Am. Fedn. Clin. Rsch., T-cell and Cytokine Patterns in Skin Cancer award NIH, 1992. Fellow Am. Acad. Dermatology (Gold award 1986); mem. Am. Soc. Dermatologic Surgery (bd. dirs. 1993—), Am. Coll. Mohs Micrographic Surgery and Cutaneous Oncology (bd. dirs. 1992-95), Assn. Acad. Dermatologic Surgeons (bd. dirs. 1992-95). Roman Catholic. Office: UCLA Div Dermatology 100 UCLA Med Plz Ste 590 Los Angeles CA 90024-6970

MOY, SAMUEL YEW, psychologist; b. N.Y.C., July 27, 1959; s. Danny Ging Yui and Yen Hay (Eng) M.; m. Shirley Eng, May 24, 1980; children: Lauren, Karyn, Daniel, Katherine. BA, King's Coll., 1980; MA, Fuller Sem., 1986, PhD, 1987. Lic. psychologist, N.Y., Conn. Staff psychologist Klingberg Family Ctrs., New Britain, Conn., 1987-90; v.p. PATH, P.C., West Hartford, Conn., 1990-94, pres., 1995—; v.p. Pathwise Behavioral Health, Farmington, Conn., 1993—; cons. Dept. Children and Family, Hartford, Conn., 1989-91, New Opportunities of Waterbury, Conn., 1989-93. Pres. bd. dirs. Covenant to Care, Bloomfield, Conn., 1990-93. Mem. Am. Psychol. Assn., Conn. Psychol. Assn. Avocations: family activities, golf. Office: PATH PC 970 Farmington Ave West Hartford CT 06107-2126

MOYA, OLGA LYDIA, law educator; b. Weslaco, Tex., Dec. 27, 1959; d. Leonel V. and Genoveva (Tamez) M.; m. James Troutman Byrd, Aug. 24, 1985; children: Leanessa Geneva Byrd, Taylor Moya Byrd. BA, U. Tex., 1981, JD, 1984. Bar: Tex. 1984. Legis. atty. Tex. Ho. of Reps., Austin, 1985; atty. Tex. Dept. Agr., Austin, 1985-90; asst. regional counsel U.S. EPA, Dallas, 1990-91; asst. prof. law South Tex. Coll. of Law, Houston, 1992-95, assoc. prof. law, 1995—. Author: (with Andrew L. Fono) Federal Environmental Law: The User's Guide, 1997. Bd. dirs. Hermann Children's Hosp., Houston, 1993—; mem. Leadership Tex., Austin, 1991—; bd. dirs. Tex. Clean Water Coun., Austin, 1992; U.S. del. to UN Conf. on the Environ. for Latin Am. and the Caribbean, San Juan, P.R., 1995. Recipient Nat. Top 12 Hispanics in Law, Miller Brewing Co., 1996; Vol. of Yr. award George H. Hermann Soc., 1995, Hispanic Law Prof. of Yr. Hispanic Nat.

Bar Assn., 1995. Mem. ABA (environ. law sect.), Hispanic Bar Assn. (bd. dirs. 1992—, Excellence award 1995, 96), Mex.-Am. Bar Assn. Office: South Tex Coll of Law 1303 San Jacinto St Houston TX 77002-7013

MOYA, PATRICK ROBERT, lawyer; b. Belen, N.Mex., Nov. 7, 1944; s. Adelicio E. and Eva (Sanchez) M.; m. Sara Dreier, May 30, 1966; children: Jeremy Brill, Joshua Dreier. AB, Princeton U., 1966; JD, Stanford U., 1969. Bar: Calif. 1970, Ariz. 1970, D.C. 1970, U.S. Dist. Ct. (no. dist.) Calif. 1970, U.S. Ct. Claims 1970, U.S. Tax Ct. 1970, U.S. Ct. Appeals (D.C. cir.) 1970, U.S. Supreme Ct. 1973. Assoc. Lewis and Roca, Phoenix, 1969-73, ptnr., 1973-83; sr. ptnr. Moya, Bailey, Bowers & Jones, P.C., Phoenix, 1983-84; ptnr., mem. nat. exec. com. Gaston & Snow, Phoenix, 1985-91; ptnr., Ariz. legal practice coord. Quarles & Brady, Phoenix, 1991—; instr. sch. of law Ariz. State U., 1972; bd. dir. Bobby McGee's U.S.A., Inc., 1982-86. Mem. Paradise Valley Bd. Adjustment, 1976-80, chmn., 1978-80; mem. Paradise Valley Town Coun., 1980-82; bd. dirs. Phoenix Men's Arts Coun., 1973-81, pres., 1979-80; bd. dirs. The Silent Witness, Inc., 1979-84, pres., 1981-83; bd. dirs. Enterprise Network, Inc., 1989-94, pres., 1991-92; bd. dirs. Phoenix Little Theatre, 1973-75, Interfaith Counseling Svc., 1973-75; precinct committeeman Phoenix Rep. Com., 1975-77; dep. voter registrar Maricopa County, 1975-76; mem. exec. bd. dirs. Gov.'s Strategic Partnership for Econ. Devel.; pres. GSPED, Inc.; mem. of Steering Com. for Sonora, Ariz. Joint Econ. Plan; mem. Gov.'s Adv. Com., Ariz. and Mex., Ariz. Corp. Commn. Stock Exch. Adv. Coun., Ariz. Town Hall. Mem. ABA, Nat. Hispanic Bar Assn., Los Abogados Hispanic Lawyers Assn., Nat. Assn. Bond Lawyers, Ariz. Bar Assn., Maricopa County Bar Assn., Paradise Valley Country Club, Univ. Club. Office: Quarles & Brady 1 E Camelback Rd Ste 400 Phoenix AZ 85012-1668

MOYARS-JOHNSON, MARY ANNIS, university official; b. Lafayette, Ind., July 19, 1938; d. Edward Raymond and Veronica Marie (Quigg) Moyars; m. Raymond Leon Molter, Aug. 1, 1959 (div. 1970); children: Marilyn Eileen Molter Davis, William Raymond, Ann Marie; m. Thomas Elmer Johnson, May 25, 1973 (div. 1989); children: Thomas Edward, John Alan, Barbara Suzanne. BS, Purdue U., 1960; MA, Purdue U., West Lafayette, Ind., 1991, postgrad., 1985—. Grader great issues Purdue U., West Lafayette, 1960-63, writer ednl. films, 1962-65, publicity dir. convocations and lectures, 1969-74, devel. officer Sch. Humanities, 1979-88, asst. to dir. Optoelectronics Rsch. Ctr., 1989-90, mgr. indsl. rels. Sch. Elec. and Computer Engring., 1990—; tchr. English and math. Benton Community Schs., Fowler, Ind., 1966-69; pub. rels. dir. Sycamore Girl Scout Coun., Lafayette, Ind., 1974-78; dir. pub. info. Ind. Senate, Majority Caucus, Indpls., 1977-78; sr. script writer Walters & Steinberg, Lafayette, 1988-89. Author: Colonial Potpourri, 1975; co-author: Historic Colonial French Dress, 1982; contbr. articles to profl. jours. Bd. govs. Tippecanoe County Hist. Assn., Lafayette, 1981—. Mem. Women in Communications, Inc. (v.p. program, Pres. award 1983), Ctr. for French Colonial Rsch. (dir. 1986-89, editor 1988-89), Am. Hist. Assn., Germanna Found., Palatines to Am., Ind. History Assn., Ind. Hist. Soc., Minitrista Coun. for Great Lakes Native Am. Studies, French Colonial Hist. Soc. Roman Catholic. Avocations: history, genealogy, embroidery. Home: 924 Elm Dr West Lafayette IN 47906-2246 Office: Sch Elec Computer Engring Electrical Engring Bldg Purdue U West Lafayette IN 47907-1285

MOYE, CHARLES ALLEN, JR., federal judge; b. Atlanta, July 13, 1918; s. Charles Allen and Annie Luther (Williamson) M.; m. Sarah Ellen Johnston, Mar. 9, 1945; children: Henry Allen, Lucy Ellen. A.B., Emory U., 1939, J.D., 1943. Bar: Ga. 1943. Since practiced in Atlanta; partner firm Gambrell, Russell, Moye & Killorin (and predecessors), 1955-70; chief judge U.S. Dist. Ct. (no. dist.) Ga., 1979-87, judge, 1970-87, sr. judge, 1988—. Chmn. DeKalb County Republican Exec. Com., 1952-56; chmn. Rep. Exec. Com. 5th Congl. Dist. Ga., 1956-64; mem. Ga. Rep. Central Com., 1952-64; Rep. candidate for Congress, 1954; del. Rep. Nat. Conv., 1956, 60, 64; chmn. Rep. Exec. Com. 4th Congl. Dist., 1964, Rep. presdl. elector, 1964. Mem. ABA, Fed. Bar Assn., Atlanta Bar Assn., State Bar Ga., Lawyers Club Atlanta, Am. Judicature Soc., Am. Bar Found., Am. Law Inst., Atlanta Athletic Club, Delta Tau Delta. Congregationalist. Home: 1317 Council Bluff Dr NE Atlanta GA 30335-3309 Office: US Dist Ct 2342 US Courthouse 75 Spring St SW Atlanta GA 30303-3309*

MOYE, JOHN EDWARD, lawyer; b. Deadwood, S.D., Aug. 15, 1944; s. Francis Joseph and Margaret C. (Roberts) M.; children: Kelly M., Mary S., Megan J. BBA, U. Notre Dame, 1965; JD with distinction, Cornell U., 1968. Bar: N.Y. 1968, Colo. 1971. Prof. law U. Denver, 1972-78, assoc. dean Coll. Law, 1974-78; prof. law So. Meth. U., Dallas, 1973; ptnr. Moye, Giles, O'Keefe, Vermeire & Gorrell, Denver, 1976—; lectr. Harcourt Brace Jovanovich, Chgo., 1972-95, Profl. Edn. Group, Minnetonka, Minn., 1982-95, West Profl. Tng. Program, 1995—; chmn. Bd. Law Examiners, Denver, 1988-92. Chmn. Denver Urban Renewal Authority, 1988-93, Colo. Hist. Found., Denver, 1987—; pres. Downtown Denver, Inc., 1986-88; mem. Consumer Credit Commn., 1985—; mem. bd. Stapleton Devel. Corp., 1995—; Denver Botanic Gardens, 1996—. Named Prof. of Yr., U. Denver, 1972-74, 76-78, Outstanding Faculty Mem., 1975. Fellow Am. Bar Found.; mem. ABA, Colo. Bar Assn. (chmn. corp., banking and bus. sect. 1982-84, Young Lawyer of Yr. award 1980), N.Y. State Bar Assn., Denver Bar Assn. (Young Lawyer of Yr. award 1980), Law Club (pres. 1982-84). Republican. Roman Catholic. Office: 1225 17th St Denver CO 80202-5534

MOYER, ALAN DEAN, retired newspaper editor; b. Galva, Iowa, Sept. 4, 1928; s. Clifford Lee and Harriet (Jacques) M.; m. Patricia Helen Krecker, July 15, 1950; children: Virginia, Stanley, Glenn. BS in Journalism, U. Iowa, 1950. Reporter, copy editor Wis. State Jour., Madison, 1950-53; reporter, photographer Bartlesville (Okla.) Examiner-Enterprise, 1953; telegraph editor Abilene (Tex.) Reporter-News, 1954-55; makeup editor Cleve. Plain Dealer, 1955-63; mng. editor Wichita (Kans.) Eagle, 1963-70; exec. editor Wichita Eagle and Beacon, 1970-73; mng. editor Phoenix Gazette, 1973-82, Ariz. Republic, 1982-89; ret., 1989; pres., dir. Wichita Profl. Baseball, Inc., 1969-75; mem. jury Pulitzer Prizes, 1973-74, 85, 86, 88. Mem. AP Mng. Editors Assn. (dir. 1973-78), Am. Soc. Newspaper Editors, Wichita Area C. of C. (dir. 1970-72), Sigma Delta Chi. Office: Phoenix Newspaper Inc 200 E Van Buren St Phoenix AZ 85004-2238

MOYER, CALVIN LYLE, adult educator; b. Phila., Nov. 2, 1941; s. Edwin Forrest and E. Ruth (Alt) M.; m. Urve V. Moyer, June 1, 1963; children: Eric P., Lia I. BS, Ursinus Coll., 1963; MA, Harvard U., 1965, PhD, 1968. From chemist to human resource mgr. DuPont Co., Wilmington, Del., 1968-92; CEO Learning Arts, Hockessin, Del., 1992—; CEO Strategic Learning Sys., Inc., Hockessing, 1994—; bd. dirs. Impact Consortiums, Inc., Chadds Ford, 1994—. Mem. ASTD, Assn. Psychol. Type, Am. Creativity Assn. (exec. dir. 1996—), Del. Mgmt. Profls., Del. Creative Educators, Monroe Inst., Foulk Woods Civic Assn. (treas. 1976-80), Del. State Bridge Assn. (pres., bd. dirs. 1978-82), Skyline Orchard Civic Assn. (sec. treas. 1986-91). Avocations: education, writing, humor, archaeology, photography. Home and Office: Strategic Learning Systems Inc 367 Skyline Orchard Dr Ste E Hockessin DE 19707-9355

MOYER, F. STANTON, financial executive, advisor; b. Phila., June 7, 1929; s. Edward T. and Beatrice (Stanton) M.; m. Ann P. Stovell, May 16, 1953; 1 child, Alice E. B.S. in Econs., U. Pa., 1951. Registered rep. Smith, Barney & Co., Phila., 1951-54, Kidder, Peabody & Co., Phila., 1954-60; mgr. corp. dept. Blyth Eastman Dillon & Co., Inc. (formerly Eastman Dillon, Union Securities & Co.), Phila., 1960-65; instl. sales mgr. Blyth Eastman Dillon & Co., Inc. (formerly Eastman Dillon, Union Securities & Co.), 1965-67, gen. partner, 1967-71, 1st v.p., 1971-74, sr. v.p., 1974-80; v.p., resident officer Kidder, Peabody & Co. Inc., Phila., 1980-86; chmn. Pa. Mcht. Group Ltd., Radnor, 1987-88; exec. v.p. Rorer Asset Mgmt., Phila., 1990-92; chmn. Mercer Capital Mgmt., 1992-93, Global Mgmt. Group, Inc., 1993-95; mng. dir. Avonwood Capital Corp., 1995—. Trustee U. Pa., 1978-83, Hosp. of U. Pa., 1978-87; bd. dirs. Atwater Kent Mus., Phila., 1983—. Mem. Racquet Club (Phila.), St. Anthony Club (Phila.), Merion Cricket Club (Haverford, Pa.), Gulph Mills Golf Club (King of Prussia, Pa.), Edgartown (Mass.) Golf Club, Gulf Stream Golf Club (Fla.), Delta Psi. Republican. Episcopalian. Home: 445 Caversham Rd Bryn Mawr PA 19010-2901

MOYER, HOMER EDWARD, JR., lawyer; b. Atlanta, Nov. 20, 1942; s. Homer Edward and Mildred Joye (Wilkerson) M.; m. Beret Butter, July 6, 1974; children: Bronwen, Homer, Eli, Kaia Joye. BA, Emory U., 1964; LLB, Yale Law Sch., 1967. Bar: Ga. 1967, D.C. 1973. Assoc. Covington & Burling, Washington, 1973-76; dep. gen. counsel U.S. Dept. of Commerce, Washington, 1976-78, counsellor to sec., 1979, gen. counsel, 1979-81; ptnr. Miller & Chevalier, Washington, 1981—. Co-author: Export Controls as Instruments of Foreign Policy, 1988. Bd. visitors Emory U., Atlanta, 1987-91. Mem. ABA (chmn. internat. law and practice sect. 1990-91, chmn. trade com. 1984-86, chmn. Cen. and East European Law Initiative 1990—, chmn. Moscow conf. on law and bilateral econ. rels. 1990). Episcopalian. Office: Miller & Chevalier 655 15th St NW Washington DC 20005-5701

MOYER, JOHN HENRY, III, physician, educator; b. Hershey, Pa., Apr. 1, 1917; s. John Henry and Anna Mae (Gruber) M.; m. Mary Elizabeth Hughes; children: John Henry IV, Michael, Carl, Anna Mary, Nancy Elizabeth, Mary Louise, Matthew Timothy. BS, Lebanon Valley Coll., 1939, DSc (hon.), 1968; MD, U. Pa., 1943. Diplomate Am. Bd. Internal Medicine, Nat. Bd. Med. Examiners; lic. physician Mass., Pa., Tex. Intern Pa. Hosp., Phila., 1943; resident in Tb and contagious diseases Belmont Hosp., Worcester, Mass., 1944-45; asst. instr. Tb and contagious diseases U. Vt., 1944-45; chief resident in medicine Brooke Gen. Hosp., San Antonio, 1947; fellow in pharmacology and medicine Sch. Medicine, U. Pa., Phila., 1948-50; attending physician, then. sr. attending physician Jefferson Davis Hosp., Houston, 1950-57, Meth. Hosp., Houston, 1950-57; from asst. prof. to prof. internal medicine and pharmacology Coll. Medicine, Baylor U., Houston, 1950-56, prof., 1956-57; prof., chmn. dept. medicine Hahnemann Med. Coll. and Hosp., Phila., 1957-74, exec. v.p. acad. affairs, 1971-73; sr. v.p., dir. profl. and ednl. affairs Conemaugh Valley Meml. Hosp., Johnstown, Pa., 1974-88; emeritus dir. profl. and ednl. affairs Conemaugh Valley Meml. Hosp., Johnstown, 1988—; prof. Temple U., 1977—; dir. regional affairs Sch. Medicine Temple U., 1977-88; clin. prof. Coll. Medicine Pa. State U., Hershey, 1976—; adj. prof. natural scis. U. Pitts., Johnstown, 1982-88; adj. prof. physician asst. sci. St. Francis Coll., 1983-88, sr. cons. physician asst. program adv. com., 1985-88; vis. prof., lectr. various ednl. instns.; mem. Pa. State Bd. Med. Edn. and Licensure, 1977-86, sec. to bd., 1982-86; mem. task force on profl. edn., mem. hypertension info. and edn. adv. com. U.S. HEW, 1972-75; chmn. high blood pressure control adv. bd. to sec. health State of Pa., 1980-86; cons. numerous profl. orgns. Editorial cons. Am. Jour. Cardiology, 1960-72; editor-in-chief Cyclopedia of Medicine, Surgery and Specialties, 1963-65; mem. editorial adv. bd. Internal Medicine News, 1969-92; editor 16 multi-authored textbooks; contbr. more than 600 articles to profl. jours. Mem. bd. trustees Pa. Heart Assn., 1959-65, v.p. bd. trustees, 1965; mem. bd. govs. Heart Assn. Southeastern Pa., 1958-64, 67-72; bd. dirs. Houston Heart Assn., 1952-57; mem., then emeritus fellow med. adv. bd. coun. for high blood pressure Am. Heart Assn., 1954—, chmn., 1964-65, mem., then emeritus fellow cen. adv. bd. coun. on circulation; deacon, Salem United Ch. of Christ. Maj. U.S. Army, 1945-48. Recipient Susan and Theodora R. Cummings Humanitarian award, 1962, 65, 66, Presdl. citation Cultural Exchg. Program, U.S. State Dept., 1964, Honors Achievement award Angiology Rsch. Found., 1965; named Alumni of Yr., Lebanon Valley Coll., Annville, Pa., 1967. Fellow ACP (Laureate award for Western Pa. 1986), Am. Coll. Cardiology (trustee 1961-68), N.Y. Acad. Scis. (emeritus), Am. Coll. Chest Physicians (emeritus); mem. AMA (emeritus, mem. ho. dels. 1966-72, cons. coun. on drugs 1968-72, mem. sect. coun. on clin. pharmacology and therapeutics), AAAS (emeritus), Am. Soc. Clin. Pharmacology and Therapeutics (emeritus dir., hon. dir.), Am. Fedn. Clin. Rsch. (emeritus), Am. Soc. Pharmacology and Exptl. Therapeutics (emeritus), Assn. Am. Med. Colls., Am. Acad. Med. Dirs., Am. Soc. Internal Medicine, Pa. Soc. Internal Medicine (pres. 1992-94, Pressman award for lifetime of contbns. and commitment to internal medicine 1996), Sems. and Symposia (pres.), Assn. Hosp. Med. Edn., Assn. Former Chmn. Medicine, U.S. Pharmacopaeia Convention (pres. 1970-75, bd. trustees 1970-80), Sigma Xi, many others. Republican. Achievements include extensive research in cardiovascular diseases with a major emphasis on hypertension. Address: 1090 Miller Rd Palmyra PA 17078-9602

MOYER, KENNETH EVAN, psychologist, educator; b. Chippewa Falls, Wis., Nov. 19, 1919; s. John Evan and Margaret (Lashway) M.; m. Doris Virginia Johnson, May 29, 1943; children: Robert Stephen, Cathy Lita. A.B. with honors, Park Coll., 1943; M.A., Washington U., St. Louis, 1948, Ph.D., 1951. Mem. faculty Carnegie-Mellon U., Pitts., 1949—; prof. psychology Carnegie-Mellon U., 1961—; cons. on higher edn. Gov. Norway, 1954; mem. research adv. com. Pa. Commonwealth Mental Health Found., 1956—. Author: The Physiology of Hostility, 1971, You and Your Child: A Primer for Parents, 1974, The Psychobiology of Aggression, 1976, Physiology of Aggression and Implications for Control, 1976, A Reader's Guide to Aggressive Behavior, 1977, Neuroanatomy, 1980, Bibliography of Aggressive Behavior: A Reader's Guide to the Literature, Vol. II, Violence and Aggression, 1987. Recipient Carnegie Found. award for excellence in teaching, 1954. Fellow AAAS, Am. Psychol. Assn.; mem. Psychonomic Soc., So. Soc. Philosophy and Psychology, Pitts. Psychol. Assn. (past dir.), Sigma Xi, Theta Kappa Theta. Research, publs. endocrinology emotion, startle response avoidance behavior, physiology aggression; demonstrated young children have capacity for prolonged attention spans if proper toys are used, that adrenal glands are not essential for effects electroconvulsive shock on behavior; devel. physiol. theory aggressive behavior. Home: 1211 Ridgewood Dr Lillian AL 36549-5303

MOYER, THOMAS J., state supreme court chief justice; b. Sandusky, Ohio, Apr. 18, 1939; s. Clarence and Idamae (Hessler) M.; m. Mary Francis Moyer, Dec. 15, 1984; 1 child, Drew; stepchildren: Anne, Jack, Alaine, Elizabeth. BA, Ohio State U., 1961, JD, 1964. Asst. atty. gen. State of Ohio, Columbus, 1964-66; pvt. practice law Columbus, 1966-69; dep. asst. Office Gov. State of Ohio, Columbus, 1969-71, exec. asst., 1975-79; assoc. Crabbe, Brown, Jones, Potts & Schmidt, Columbus, 1972-75; judge U.S. Ct. Appeals (10th cir.), Columbus, 1979-86; chief justice Ohio Supreme Ct., Columbus, 1987—. Sec. bd. trustees Franklin U., Columbus, 1986-87; trustee Univ. Club, Columbus, 1986; mem. nat. council adv. com. Ohio State U. Coll. Law, Columbus. Recipient Award of Merit, Ohio Legal Ctr. Inst.; named Outstanding Young Man of Columbus, Columbus Jaycees, 1969. Mem. Ohio State Bar Assn. (exec. com., council dels.), Columbus Bar Assn. (pres. 1980-81), Critchon Club, Columbus Maennerchor Club. Republican. Avocations: sailing, tennis. Office: Ohio Supreme Ct 30 E Broad St Fl 3 Columbus OH 43215-3414*

MOYERS, BILL D., journalist; b. Hugo, Okla., June 5, 1934; s. John Henry and Ruby (Johnson) M.; m. Judith Davidson, Dec. 18, 1954; children: William Cope, Suzanne, John. BJ with honors, U. Tex., 1956; grad. student, U. Edinburgh, Scotland, 1956-57; MDiv with honors, Southwestern Baptist Theol. Sem., 1959; DFA (hon.), Am. Film Inst. Personal asst. to Senator Lyndon B. Johnson, 1960; assoc. dir. Peace Corps, 1961-62, dept. dir., 1963; spl. asst. to Pres. Johnson, 1963-67, press sec., 1965-67; pub. Newsday, Garden City, N.Y., 1967-70; editor-in-chief Bill Moyers Jour. (weekly pub. affairs program on pub. TV), 1971-76, 78-81; chief corr. CBS Reports, CBS-TV, 1976-78; sr. news analyst CBS News, CBS-TV, 1981-86; exec. editor Pub. Affairs TV, Inc., 1987—. Author: Listening to America, 1971, Report from Philadelphia, 1987, The Secret Government, 1988; editor: Joseph Campbell and the Power of Myth, 1988, A World of Ideas, 1989, 2d edit., 1990, Healing and the Mind, 1993, Genesis, 1996. Recipient over 30 Emmy awards, Ralph Lowell medal for contbn. to pub. TV, George Peabody award, 1976, 80, 85-86, 88-90, The Humanities prize, 1978, 86, 95, Silver Baton award DuPont-Columbia U., 1979, 86, 88, Sigma Delta Chi award for disting. svc. to journalism, 1980, Robert F. Kennedy Journalism award for coverage of disadvantaged, 1988, Gold baton award, 1991, George Polk award, 1981, 86, career achievement award Internat. Documentary Assn., Eric Barnouw award Orgn. Am. Historians, medal of excellence N.Y. State Bd. Regents, James Madison award Nat. Broadcasting Editl. Assn., spl. recognition Assn. for Continuing Higher Edn., Communicator of Decade award Religious Comm. Congress, Elmer Holmes Bibst award NYU, Religious Liberty award Am. Jewish Com., 1995, Walter Cronkite award for excellence in journalism, 1995, The Fred Friendly First Amendment award, 1995, NEH Charles Frankel prize for outstanding contbns. to cultural life, 1997; elected to TV Hall of Fame, 1995. Fellow Am. Acad. Arts and Scis. Office: Pub Affairs TV Inc 356 W 58th St New York NY 10019-1804

MOYERS, JUDITH DAVIDSON, television producer; b. Dallas, May 12, 1935; d. Henry Joseph and Eula E. (Dendy) Davidson; m. Bill D. Moyers; children: William Cope, Suzanne, John. BS, U. Tex., 1956; LittD (hon.), L.I. U., 1989, SUNY, 1990. Pres., exec. prodr. Pub. Affairs T.V., N.Y.C., 1987—; Bd. dirs. Paine Webber Mut. Funds, Ogden Corp. Exec. prodr. numerous T.V. documentaries (Emmy 1980, 93); contbr. articles to profl. jours., newspapers, mags. Trustee SUNY, 1976-90; commr. U.S. Commn. UNESCO, Washington, 1977-80, White House commn. Internat. Yr. of Child, Washington, 1978-80; mem. jud. selection com. State N.Y., 1992-93; dir. Pub. Agenda Found. Mem. Acad. TV Arts and Scis., Century Club. Mem. Congregational Ch. Office: Pub Affairs TV Inc 356 W 58th St New York NY 10019-1804

MOYLAN, JAY RICHARD, medical products executive; b. Greenfield, Mass., Dec. 20, 1950; s. Richard J. and Margaret M. (McCarthy) M.; m. Sharon J. Slater, June 18, 1976; children: Jaimee, Shauna. AA in Liberal Arts, Greenfield Community Coll., 1972; AS in Respiratory Therapy, Springfield Tech. Community C., 1975; BS in Health Care Mgmt., U. Mass., 1983. Staff respiratory therapist Mercy Hosp., Springfield, Mass., 1973-74; respiratory therapy supr. Brattleboro (Vt.) Meml. Hosp., 1974-75; dir. cardiopulmonary svc. Farren Meml. Hosp., Turners Falls, Mass., 1975-83; cardiopulmonary sales rep. Erich Jeager, Inc., Rockford, Ill., 1983-85; cardiovascular sales rep. Electro Catheter Corp., Rahway, N.J., 1985-86; cardiopulmonary sales specialist Sensor Medics Corp., Yorba Linda, Calif., 1986-95; sys. sales dir. OmniCell Technologies, Inc., Palo Alto, Calif., 1995—; chmn. Coun. Pulmonary Svc. Mgrs., Springfield, 1980-81. Chmn. Cath. Stewardship Appeal Holy Trinity Parish, Greenfield, 1989; bd. dirs. cen. Mass. chpt. Am. Lung Assn., 1981-83; treas. FMH Credit Union, 1980-83; councilor Mass. Thoracic Soc., 1995—. Recipient Achievement award Mass. Soc. Respiratory Care, 1989. Mem. Coun. Pulmonary Svc. Mgrs. (Lifetime Mem. award), Am. Coll. Sports Medicine, Am. Assn. Respiratory Care (registered, rev. com. 1991), Am. Registry Diagnostic Med. Sonographers (registered), Nat. Bd. Respiratory Care (cert.), Nat. Soc. Cardiopulmonary Tech. (cert.), Mass. Thoracic Soc., Mass. Lung Assn., New Eng. Soc. for Healthcare Materials Mgmt. Avocations: skiing, golf. Home: 53 Meadow Ln Greenfield MA 01301-9703

MOYLAN, JOHN L., secondary school principal. Prin. DeMatha Cath. High Sch., Hyattsville, Md. Recipient Blue Ribbon Sch. award U.S. Dept. Edn., 1983-84, 90-91, Disting. Prin. award Archdiocese of Washington, 1991, Sch. Adminstr. award Md. Music Educators Assn., 1992, Disting. Ednl. Leadership award Washington Post, 1993. Office: DeMatha Cath High Sch 4313 Madison St Hyattsville MD 20781-1692*

MOYLE, PETER BRIGGS, fisheries and biology educator; b. Mpls., May 29, 1942; s. John Briggs and Evelyn (Wood) M.; m. Marilyn Arneson, June 11, 1966; children—Petrea Ruth, John Noah. B.A., U. Minn., 1964; M.S., Cornell U., 1966; Ph.D., U. Minn., 1969. Asst. prof. Calif. State U. Fresno, 1969-72; from asst. prof. to prof. U. Calif., Davis, 1972—, chmn. dept. wildlife and fisheries, 1982-87; head, Delta Native Fishes Recovery Team, 1993-95. Author: Inland Fishes of California, 1976; Fishes: An Introduction to Ichthyology, 3d edit., 1996; Distribution and Ecology of Stream Fishes of Sacramento San Joaquin Drainage, 1982, Fish: An Enthusiast's Guide, 1993. Fellow Calif. Acad. Sci.; mem. Am. Fisheries Soc. (life, award of excellence West div. 1991, Outstanding Educator award 1995), Ecol. Soc. Am., Am. Soc. Ichthyologists and Herptologists, Soc. Conservation Biology, Natural Heritage Inst. (v.p. 1994—). Home: 612 Eisenhower St Davis CA 95616-3031 Office: Dept Wildlife, Fish & Conservation Biology U Calif Davis Davis CA 95616

MOYNAHAN, JOHN DANIEL, JR., retired insurance executive; b. Chgo., Dec. 10, 1935; s. John Daniel and Helen (Hurley) M.; m. Virginia Thomas, Oct. 10, 1959; children: Laura, Mark, Tricia, Kate. B.A. cum laude, U. Notre Dame, 1957. With Met. Life Ins. Co., N.Y.C., 1957—; regional v.p. Met. Life Ins. Co., from 1971, with nat. div. group nat. accounts, 1979-80, sr. v.p. group life and health ops., 1980-86, exec. v.p., 1986-97.

MOYNAHAN, JULIAN LANE, English language educator, author; b. Cambridge, Mass., May 21, 1925; s. Joseph Leo and Mary (Shea) M.; m. Elizabeth Rose Reilly, Aug. 6, 1945; children: Catherine (dec.), Brigid, Mary Ellen. A.B., Harvard U., 1946, A.M., 1951, Ph.D., 1957. Cataloguer, rare books asst. Boston Pub. Library, 1948-49, 51; teaching fellow Harvard U., 1951-53; instr. English Amherst Coll., 1953-55; instr., asst. prof. English Princeton, 1955-63; Fulbright lectr. Am. and English lit. Univ. Coll., Dublin, 1963-64; assoc. prof. English Rutgers U., 1964-66, prof., 1966-93, disting. prof., 1976-93, prof. emeritus, 1993—; vis. prof. U. Wyo., summer 1965, Harvard U., summer 1967, Bread Loaf Sch., 1969, NYU, 1997; NEH vis. prof. Manhattanville Coll., 1972; Gauss lectr. Princeton U., 1975; vis. scholar English dept. U. Utah, spring 1980. Author: Sisters and Brothers, 1960, The Deed of Life, A Critical Study of D.H. Lawrence, 1963, Pairing Off, 1969, Vladimir Nabokov, 1971, Garden State, 1973, Where the Land and Water Meet, 1979, Anglo-Irish: The Literary Imagination in a Hyphenated Culture, 1995; editor: (D.H. Lawrence) Sons and Lovers: Text, Criticism, Backgrounds, 1968, 77, The Viking Portable Thomas Hardy, 1977; contbr. revs. and criticism to N.Y. Times Book Rev., New Republic, T.L.S., Washington Post Book World, N.Y. Rev. Books, London Observer; contbr., mem. editl. bd. The Recorder, Jour. Am. Irish Hist. Soc., 1994—. Bicentennial preceptorship Princeton, 1960-63, grants-in-aid Am. Council Learned Socs., Am. Philos. Soc.; mem. Pulitzer Prize Fiction Jury, 1981, chmn., 1987. Served with AUS, 1943-44. 7500 creative writing award Nat. Found. Arts, 1966; Ingram-Merrill award, 1967; NEH fellow, 1975; Guggenheim fellow, 1983-84. Mem. MLA, AAUP, PEN, Harvard Club of Princeton. Democrat. Home: 3439 Lawrenceville Rd Princeton NJ 08540-4717 also: 405 W 23rd St Apt 9B New York NY 10011-1412

MOYNE, JOHN ABEL, computer scientist, linguist, educator; b. Yezd, Iran, July 6, 1920; s. Abul Kasim and Sogra (Afshar) M.; came to U.S., 1956, naturalized, 1965; BA, Georgetown U., 1959, MA, 1960; PhD, Harvard U., 1970; m. Claudia Wienert, July 4, 1963; children: David, Nicholas, Parvin. With Brit. Govt., Iran and India, 1943-52, market research officer, Tehran, 1952; linguist U.S. Govt., Cyprus, 1953-56; rsch. assoc. Georgetown U., Washington, 1960-63; mgr. applied linguistics dept. IBM Corp., Cambridge, Mass., 1963-71; prof., chmn. computer sci. dept. Queens Coll., CUNY, Flushing, 1971-81, chmn. div. math. and natural scis., 1978-81, chmn. univ. faculty for Ph.D. in Computer Sci., 1978-82, exec. officer Grad. Sch. Ph.D. Program in Linguistics, 1983-88; prof. linguistics and computer sci. CUNY, 1971-91, prof. emeritus linguistics and computer sci., 1991—. Grantee, EURATOM, AEC, NSF, City U. N.Y. Mem. Linguistic Soc. Am., Brit. Inst. Engring. Technology, The Acad. Am. Poets. Democrat. Episcopalian. Author, co-author: Hafiz of Shiraz, 1946; Life in India, 1949; Open Secret, 1984; Understanding Language: Man or Machine, 1985; Unseen Rain, 1986, Rumi: These Branching Moments, 1988; This Longing: Poetry, Teaching Stories, and Letters of Rumi, 1988, LISP: A First Language for Computing, 1991, Say I Am You, 1994; The Essential Rumi, 1995; contbr. articles to profl. jours., chpts. to books. Home: 40 Prospect Ave Sea Cliff NY 11579-1029 Office: CUNY PhD Program Linguistics Grad Ctr 33 W 42nd St New York NY 10036-8003

MOYNE, YVES M., water treatment executive; b. Jallieu, Isere, France, May 23, 1955; came to U.S., 1994; PhD, Hautes Etudes Commerciales, Paris, 1980; M in Econs., U. La Sorbonne, Paris, 1980. Sr. KPMG Peat Marwick, Paris, 1980-83; fin. controller Lyonnaise Des Eaux, Paris, 1983-86, mgr. orgn., 1986-88; group dir. for Hong Kong, China, Macau Lyonnaise Des Eaux, Hong Kong, 1988-91; exec. dir. The Macau Water Supply Co., 1988-91; v.p., fin. and adminstr. Degremont, Rueil, France, 1991-94; chmn., pres., CEO INFILCO Degremont, Inc., Richmond, Va., 1994—; chmn., CEO Aquasource North Am., Richmond, Va., 1996—; v.p. JOUD, Crolles, France, 1994; advisor to French Govt. for Fgn. Trade, 1995—; dir. Greater Richmond Tech. Coun., 1996—; prof. U. Paris IV, Creteil, 1981; lectr. pub. utility mgmt., S.E. Asia, and China. Author survey: For a Better Knowledge of The Consumers' Habits, 1978. With French Air Force, 1976-77, Istres, France. Mem. French Am. C. of C. (bd. dirs. 1996—; exec. v.p. Washington). Avocations: architecture, skiing. Office: INFILCO Degremont Inc 2924 Emerywood Pkwy Richmond VA 23294-3746

MOYNIHAN, DANIEL PATRICK, senator, educator; b. Tulsa, Mar. 16, 1927; s. John Henry and Margaret Ann (Phipps) M.; m. Elizabeth Therese Brennan, May 29, 1955; children: Timothy Patrick, Maura Russell, John McCloskey. Student, CCNY, 1943; BA cum laude, Tufts U., 1948; MA,

Fletcher Sch. Law and Diplomacy, 1949, PhD, 1961, LLD (hon.), 1968; Fulbright fellow, London (Eng.) Sch. Econs. and Polit. Sci., 1950-51; AM (hon.), Harvard U., 1966; LLD (hon.), Cath. U. Am., 1968, New Sch. Social Rsch., 1968, U. Notre Dame, 1969, Fordham U., 1970, St. Bonaventure U., 1972, Boston Coll., 1976, Yeshiva U., 1978, Rensselaer Polytech. Inst., 1983, Syracuse U. Sch. Law, 1984, Columbia U., 1987, U. Rochester, 1994; D in Pub. Adminstrn. (hon.), Hamilton Coll., 1968; DSI (hon.), Defense Intelligence Coll., 1984; numerous other hon. degrees. With Internat. Rescue Com., 1954; successively asst. to sec., asst. sec., acting sec. to gov. State of N.Y., 1955-58, mem. tenure commn., 1959-60, dir. Syracuse U. govt. rsch. project, 1959-61, spl. asst. to sec. labor, 1961-62, exec. asst. to sec., 1962-63, asst. sec. labor, 1963-65; dir. Joint Ctr. for Urban Studies MIT and Harvard U., 1966-69; prof. edn. and urban politics Kennedy Sch. Govt., Harvard U., 1966-73, sr. mem., 1966-77, prof. govt., 1973-77; asst. for urban affairs to Pres. U.S., 1969-70; counsellor to Pres. U.S., mem. Cabinet, 1969-70, cons. to Pres. U.S., 1971-73; mem. U.S. del. 26th Gen. Assembly, UN, 1971, Pres.'s Sci. Adv. Com., 1971-73; ambassador to India New Delhi, 1973-75; U.S. permanent rep. to UN, N.Y.C., 1975-76; U.S. senator from N.Y., 1977—, chmn. senate fin. com., 1993-94, ranking mem., senate fin. com., 1995—; chmn. commn. on Reducing and Protecting Govt. Secrecy, 1994-97,vice chmn. Pres.'s Temp. Commn. on Pennsylvania Avenue, 1964-73; chmn. adv. com. traffic safety dept. HEW; fellow Ctr. Advanced Studies, Wesleyan U., 1965-66; hon. fellow London Sch. Econs. and Polit. Sci., 1970—; sec. pub. affairs com. N.Y. State Dem. Com., 1958-60; alt. del. Dem. Nat. Conv., 1960, 76. Author: Maximum Feasible Misunderstanding, 1969, The Politics of a Guaranteed Income, 1973, Coping: On the Practice of Government, 1974, A Dangerous Place, 1978, Counting Our Blessings, 1980, Loyalties, 1984, Family and Nation, 1986, Came the Revolution: Argument in the Reagan Era, 1988, On the Law of Nations, 1990, Pandaemonium: Ethnicity in International Politics, 1993, Miles To Go: A Personal History Of Social Policy, 1996; co-author: Beyond the Melting Pot, 1963; editor: The Defenses of Freedom, 1966, On Understanding Poverty, 1969, Ethnicity: Theory and Experience, 1975, others; editorial bd. Pub. Interest; contbr. articles to profl. jours. Vice chmn. Woodrow Wilson Internat. Ctr. for Scholars, 1971-76; chmn. bd. trustees Joseph H. Hirshhorn Mus. and Sculpture Garden, 1971-85; mem. bd. regents Smithsonian Instn., 1987—. With USN, 1944-47. Recipient Meritorious Svc. award U.S. Dept. Labor, 1965, Centennial medal Syracuse U., 1969, Internat. League for Human Rights award, 1975, John LaFarge award for Interracial Justice, 1980, Medallion SUNY Albany, 1984, Henry medal Smithsonian Instn., 1985, SEAL Medallion, CIA, 1986, Meml. Sloan-Kettering Cancer Ctr. medal, 1986, Britannica award, 1986, Notre Dame U. Laetare medal, 1992, Thomas Jefferson award AIA, 1993. Mem. AAAS (vice chmn. 1971, dir. 1972-73), Am. Philos. Soc. (Hubert Humphrey award 1983, Thomas Jefferson medal 1993), Nat. Acad. Pub. Adminstrn., Am. Acad. Arts and Scis. (chmn. seminar on poverty), Century Club, Harvard Club. Office: US Senate 464 Russell Senate Bldg Washington DC 20510-3201

MOYNIHAN, GARY PETER, industrial engineering educator; b. Little Falls, N.Y., Mar. 5, 1956; s. Peter H. and Frances S. (Ferjanec) M.; m. Eleanor T. McCusker, Mar. 10, 1984; children: Andrew Ross, Keith Patrick. BS in Chemistry, Rensselaer Polytech. Inst., 1978, MBA in Opsl. Mgmt., 1980; PhD in Indsl. Engring., U. Ctrl. Fla., 1990. Prodn. supr. Am. Cyanamid, Bound Brook, N.J., 1978-79, Nat. Micronetics, Kingston, N.Y., 1980-81; assoc. mfg. engr. Martin Marietta Aerospace, Orlando, Fla., 1981-82, indsl. engr., 1982-85, sr. indsl. engr., 1985-87, group indsl. engr., 1987-90; asst. prof. indsl. engring. U. Ala., Tuscaloosa, 1990-96, assoc. prof., 1996—; cons. in field. Contbr. articles to profl. jours. Regents scholar N.Y. State Bd. Regents, 1974-78; rsch. fellow NASA, 1992-93; rsch. grant BellSouth Telecomm., 1994-96; recipient Outstanding Tchg. award AMOCO Found., 1993-94. Mem. IEEE, Inst. Indsl. Engrs. (sr. mem., chpt. dir. 1991-95, chpt. pres. 1996-97), Aerospace & Def. Soc. (v.p. fin. and adminstrn. 1994-97). Achievements include design and development of information systems applications for the aerospace and foundry industries; rsch. in the measurement and prediction of on-line information system failure costs. Office: U Ala Dept Indsl Engring Tuscaloosa AL 35487

MOYNIHAN, JAMES J., architectural firm executive. Pres., CEO Herry Internat., Atlanta. Office: Heery Internat 999 Peachtree St Atlanta GA 30309

MOYNIHAN, WILLIAM J., museum executive; b. Little Falls, N.Y., Apr. 8, 1942; s. Bernard J. and Mary A. (Flynn) M.; m. Irene A. Sheilds, July 2, 1966; children: Patricia, Erin, Sean. BA, SUNY, Binghamton, 1964; MA, Colgate U., 1966; PhD, Syracuse U., 1973. From asst. to assoc. prof. Colgate U., Hamilton, N.Y., 1973-77, from asst. to assoc. dean faculty, 1977-80, dean students, 1980-83, dean coll., 1983-88; v.p.m dir. Am. Mus. Natural History, N.Y.C., 1988-95; pres., CEO Milw. Pub. Mus., 1995—; bd. dirs. N.Y. State Mus.; adv. com. arts and culture Congressman J. Nadler, N.Y.C., 1993-95. Adv. editor Curator jour., 1991-95. Mem. Am. Mus. Assn., Am. Assn. Museums (mem. ethics com., bd. dirs.), Wis. Acad. of Scis., Arts and Letters (councillor-at-large 1995—), Univ. Club. Home: 203 W Coventry Ct Glendale WI 53217-3970 Office: Milw Pub Mus 800 W Wells St Milwaukee WI 53233-1404

MOYSE, HERMANN, JR., banker; b. Baton Rouge, Aug. 3, 1921; s. Hermann and Rosalie (Gottlieb) M.; m. Marie Louise Levy, June 4, 1942; children—Lewis Arthur, Hermann III, Marie Rosalie. B.A., La. State U., 1942. With City Nat. Bank of Baton Rouge, 1946—, v.p., 1962-70, exec. v.p., 1970-72, pres., 1972-81, chmn., 1981-94, chmn. emeritus, 1995—, also dir.; pres., dir. Bistineau-Webster Oil Co.; sec., dir. Baton Rouge Realty Co., Ltd., Lottie Land & Devel. Co., Inc., Melrose Devel. Corp.; chmn. bd. First Commerce Corp., 1992—; bd. dirs. Pan Am. Life Ins. Co., Bank of Zachary, 1971-93. Pres. Capital Area United Givers Fund, 1966-67; mem. exec. com. Pub. Affairs Rsch. Coun., 1968-70; exec. com. Perkins Radiation Ctr.; bd. dirs. La. State U. Found. Maj. F.A. AUS, 1942-46. Decorated Bronze Star. Mem. Am. Bankers Assn. (governing coun. 1975-77), La. Bankers Assn. (pres. 1967-68, Baton Rouge Country Club, City Club of Baton Rouge. Office: City Nat Bank PO Box 1231 Baton Rouge LA 70821-1231

MOYSE, HERMANN, III, banker; b. Baton Rouge, Dec. 28, 1948; s. Hermann Jr. and Marie Louise (Levy) M.; m. Janet Lee Doise; children: Allison Leze, David Hermann, Aaron Lewis. BA, Coll. of Emporia, 1970; MSW, La. State U., 1973. Asst. dir. Capital Area Health Planning Agy., 1973-74; research assoc. La. State U., Baton Rouge, 1974-78; trainee to v.p. City Nat. Bank, Baton Rouge, 1978—, sr. v.p., 1985-94, also bd. dirs., chmn., 1994—; sec.-treas. Melrose Devel. Corp., Baton Rouge, 1986-87. Mem. Istrouma Council Boy Scouts Am.; mem. Capital Area United Way Agy. Svcs. Div., Baton Rouge, 1979-86, 88-91, vice chmn. 1981, bd. dirs., 1987—, chmn., 1989-90; v.p. Arts Coun. Greater Baton Rouge, 1990—; 1st v.p. La. Arts & Sci. Ctr., Baton Rouge, 1985—, pres., 1988; mem. Community Funds for Arts, 1989-90; mem. Arts & Humanities Coun., 1990—, v.p., 1991—, treas., 1992; mem. Community Funds for the Arts, 1989—, vice chmn., 1992; pres. Cath. Community Life Office, Baton Rouge, 1981, Baton Rouge Speech and Hearing Found., 1986, pres. 1983, treas., 1981; mem. St. Joseph's Acad. Adv. Bd., v.p., 1986-88, pres., 1987-88; bd. dirs. St. James Place; treas. Baton Rouge Crisis Intervention Ctr., 1984-85, v.p., 1987, pres., 1987; sec. St. Joseph's Children's Home, 1980; bd. dirs. Crime Stoppers, Inc., 1986—, v.p., 1989, pres. 1991—; pres. Mid City Devel. Alliance, 1991-93, 97—; mem. adv. bd. Tau Ctr., 1990-93; trustee Episc. High Sch., 1990-92; treas. La. Delta Svc. Corps. Inc., 1995—; bd. trustees Gen. Health Sys., Inc, 1994; mem. Baton Rouge Crimestoppers, chmn. fin. com., 1997—; chmn. First Commerce Cmty. Devel. Corp., 1993—. Mem. La. Bankers Assn. (fed. affairs com. 1990—), La. Coun. Econ. Edn. (trustee 1987, regional v.p. 1990—, Community Vol. Activist award 1988), NCCJ (chpt. bd. dirs. 1988, treas. 1995), City Club, Baton Rouge Country Club. Democrat. Jewish. Office: City Nat Bank PO Box 1231 Baton Rouge LA 70821-1231

MOZIAN, GERARD PAUL, real estate company executive, business consultant; b. N.Y.C., Jan. 16, 1945; s. Gerard and Virginia (Chadik) M.; m. Mary Susan McKelvey, July 26, 1969. BMechE, Manhattan Coll., 1966; MBA, U. Pitts., 1967. Fin. adminstr. Philco-Ford Corp., Tehran, Iran, 1969-71; fin. analyst Gen. Waterworks Corp., Phila., 1971-73; regional contr. Gen. Waterworks Corp., Miami, Fla., 1973-75; v.p. fin. Gen. Devel. Utilities, Miami, 1975-78, sr. v.p. fin. and adminstrn., 1978-81, exec. v.p. ops., 1981-82, pres., 1982-87; sr. v.p. planning and fin. Gen. Devel. Corp., Miami, 1983-87; sr. v.p., chief fin. officer Gen. Devel. Corp., 1988-89; pres. Sugarmill Woods Inc., 1990-92; exec. v.p., CFO Montenay Internat. Corp., MIami, 1992—. Home: 7521 SW 113th St Pinecrest FL 33156-4548 Office: 3225 Aviation Ave Miami FL 33133-4741

MOZLEY, PAUL DAVID, obstetrics and gynecology educator; b. Decatur, Ala., Oct. 27, 1928; s. James Howard and Ruth Dianne (Brindely) M.; m. Mary Dale Goss, Aug. 30, 1983; children from previous marriage: Susan Ruth, Paul David Jr., Sally Robin. BA, U. Ala., 1950; MD, Med. Coll. Ala., 1955. Diplomate Am. Bd. Ob-Gyn, Am. Bd. Psychiatry and Neurology. Commd. lt. USN, 1955; advanced through grades to capt., 1970, resident ob-gyn, Corona (Calif.) and San Diego Naval Hosp., 1956-59; resident in psychiatry Bethesda, Md., 1964-66, Phila. Naval Hosp., 1969-70; staff gynecologist U.S. Naval Hosp., Yokosuku, Japan, 1959-62; chief gynecologist U.S. Naval Hosp., Memphis, 1962-64; dir. med. services U.S. Naval Hosp., Naples, Italy, 1966-68, comdg. officer, 1969; chmn. neuropsychiatry Naval Regional Med. Ctr., Portsmouth, Va., 1970-75; ret., 1975; assoc. prof. psychiatry Eastern Va. Med. Sch., Norfolk, 1975-77, prof., interim chmn. dept., 1977-78, vice chmn. psychiatry, 1978-79; prof., dir. undergrad. edn. Dept. Ob-Gyn Sch. Medicine, East Carolina U., Greenville, 1979-84; prof. ob-gyn, chmn. dept., Coll. Community Health Scis. U. Ala., Tuscaloosa, 1984—, prof. ob-gyn, assoc. chmn. dept., Sch. Medicine, 1984—; dir. psychiat. services Norfolk Gen. Hosp., 1975-79; chmn. dept. ob-gyn DCH Regional Med. Ctr., Tuscaloosa, 1986—; cons. med. liability law legal firms., Ala., Tenn., 1980—. Contbr. numerous articles to profl. jours. Mem. Regional Parental Adv. Council, Montgomery, Ala., 1986-87; sponsor Tuscaloosa Symphony Assn. Recipient Meritorious Service medal Pres. U.S., 1975, Surgeon Gen.'s Merit award, 1975, Attending of Yr. award Residents in Psychiatry, 1979, Clin. Sci. Course award Dept. Ob-Gyn grad. class, 1982, Eastern Va. Sch. Medicine; named one of Outstanding Young Men in Am., Jaycees, 1964. Fellow ACS, Am. Coll. Ob-Gyn (chmn. various programs 1974, 76, 77, Chmn.'s award clin. research 1969), Am. Psychiat. Assn. (Continuing Med. Edn. Standards award 1977); mem. AMA (Physician's Recognition award 1986), Am. Soc. Psychosomatic Ob-Gyn (founding mem., pres. 1979-80, chmn. nominating com. 1981, permanent steering com. 1982), Va. Ob-Gyn Soc., Assn. Acad. Psychiatry, Va. Med. Soc., N.C. Neuropsychiat. Assn., Pitt County Med. Soc., Med. Assn. Ala., Ala. Psychiat. Assn., LWV, Alpha Epsilon Delta. Democrat. Mem. Ch. of Christ. Club: Torch (Portsmouth). Avocations: cabinetry, goldsmithing. Home: 21 Beech Hls Tuscaloosa AL 35404-4959 Office: The Univ of Ala Dept of Ob-Gyn PO Box 870376 Tuscaloosa AL 35487-0376

MRACHEK, LORIN LOUIS, lawyer; b. Fairmont, Minn., Jan. 5, 1946; s. Louis L. and Kathleen (Loring) M.; m. Elizabeth Moss, Aug. 31, 1968; children: Kathleen Elizabeth, Louis Moss. BA with honors, Fla. State U., 1968; MBA, Columbia U., 1974, JD, 1974. Bar: Fla. 1974, Va. 1977, U.S. Ct. Mil. Appeals 1977, U.S. Supreme Ct. 1978; cert. civil trial law Fla. Bar Bd. Certification, bus. bankruptcy law Am. Bd. Bankruptcy Certification, cert. civil trial advocacy Nat. Bd. Trial Advocacy. Commd. 2d lt. USMC, 1969, advanced through grades to capt., 1974; chief defense counsel MCRD USMC, Paris Island, 1975-77; resigned USMC, 1977; spl. asst. to gen. counsel U.S. Railway Assn., Washington, 1977-78; shareholder Gunster, Yoakley, Valdes-Fauli & Stewart, West Palm Beach, Fla., 1978—. Editor-in-chief Columbia Jour. Law & Social Problems, 1973-74; contbr. articles to profl. jours. Mem. ABA, Am. Bankruptcy Inst., Fla. Acad. Trial Lawyers, So. Fla. Bankruptcy Bar Assn. Avocations: running, tennis, golf. Office: 777 S Flagler Dr Ste 500E West Palm Beach FL 33401-6124

MRAZEK, DAVID ALLEN, pediatric psychiatrist; b. Ft. Riley, Kans., Oct. 1, 1947; s. Rudolph George and Hazel Ruth (Schayes) M.; m. Patricia Jean, Sept. 2, 1978; children: Nicola, Matthew, Michael, Alissa. AB in Genetics, Cornell U., 1969; MD, Bowman Gray Sch. Medicine, 1973. Lic. psychiatrist, child psychiatrist, N.C., Ohio, Colo., D.C., Va., Md.; med. lic. N.C., Ohio, D.C., Va., Md. Lectr. child psychiatry Inst. of Psychiatry, London, 1977-79; dir. pediatric psychiatry Nat. Jewish Ctr. for Immunology and Respiratory Medicine, Denver, 1979-91; chmn. psychiatry Childrens Nat. Med. Ctr., Washington, 1991—; acting chair psychiatry and behavioral scis. George Washington U. Sch. medicine, 1996—; dir. Children's Rsch. Inst. Neurosci., 1995—; asst. prof. psychiatry U. Colo. Sch. Medicine, 1979-83, assoc. prof. psychiatry and pediatrics, 1984-89, prof., 1990-91; prof. psychiatry and pediatrics George Washington U. Sch. Medicine, 1991—. Contbr. articles and book chpts. on child devel. and asthma to profl. publs. Recipient Rsch. Scientist Devel. awards NIMH, 1983-88, 88-91. Fellow Am. Acad. Child Psychiatry, Royal Soc. Medicine, Am. Psychiat. Assn. (Blanche F. Ittleson award 1996), Royal Coll. Psychiatrists; mem. Am. Coll. Psychiatrists, Group for the Advancement of Psychiatry, Colo. Child and Adolescent Psychiatry Soc. (pres. 1984). Office: Childrens Nat Med Ctr Psychiatry Dept 111 Michigan Ave NW Washington DC 20010-2916

MRKONIC, GEORGE RALPH, JR., retail executive; b. Lawrence, Kans., July 13, 1952; s. George Ralph and Ruth (Clayton) M.; m. Barbara Machmer, June 22, 1974; children: Matthew George, John William, Kelsey Margaret. BA and MA in Econs., Stanford U., 1975; MBA, Harvard U., 1978. Fin. analyst WR Grace/Retail Group, N.Y.C., 1978-79, group mgr., 1979-80, dir. fin. planning, 1980-81, v.p., chief fin. officer, 1981; v.p., chief fin. officer Herman's Sporting Goods Inc., Carteret, N.J., 1981-85, sr. v.p., chief fin. officer, 1985-87; exec. v.p., dep. chief exec. officer Herman's Sporting Goods Inc., Carteret, 1986-87, pres., chief exec. officer, 1987; pres. Eyelab, Inc, River Edge, N.J., 1987-90; exec. v.p. splty. retailing K Mart Corp., Troy, Mich., 1990-94; pres. and vice chmn. Borders Group, Inc., Ann Arbor, Mich., 1994—; bd. dirs. Borders Group, Inc., Champion Enterprises, Comshare.

MRKVICKA, EDWARD FRANCIS, JR., financial writer, publisher, consultant; b. Aurora, Ill., Oct. 17, 1944; s. Edward Francis Sr. and Ruth Caroline (Phillips) M.; m. Madelyn Helen Rimnac, July 1, 1972; children: Edward Francis III, Kelly Helen. Cert. comml. pilot, U. Ill., 1965; diploma, Dept. Def., 1967, Bank Mktg. Assn., 1972; grad. cert., Bank Mktg. Assn., 1973. Mktg. officer Downers Grove (Ill.) Nat. Bank, 1964-72; asst. v.p. and mktg. officer Bank of Westmont, Ill., 1972-73; v.p. and cashier 1st State Bank Hanover Park, Ill., 1973-76; pres. 1st Nat. Bank Marengo, Ill., 1976-81, Reliance Enterprises, Inc., Fin. News Syndicate, Omni, Fin. Group, Eagle Publishing, Marengo, 1981—; pub. Money Insider newsletter; adv. coun. Am. Monetary Found., Fullerton, Calif., 1987; mem. panel of experts Boardroom Reports, 1990—. Pub.: (newletter) Money Insider; author: Battle Your Bank-And Win!, 1984, Moving Up, 1985; (with others) The Complete Book of Personal Finance, 1987, The Bank Book, 1989, 91, 94, 1,037 Ways to make or Save Up to $100,000 This Year Alone, 1991, The Rational Investor, 1992, Your Bank is Ripping You Off, 1997; contbr. numerous articles to profl. jours. and newspapers; fin. columnist Nat. Enquirer, 1996—. Bd. dirs. DuPage County Lung Assn., Downers Grove, Ill., 1970; mem. bd. Western Suburbs Combined Com. Appeal, Downers Grove, 1971; bd. dirs. McHenry County Easter Seals Clinic, Woodstock, Ill., 1979; v.p., treas. Marengo/Union Chamber, 1980; Am. rep. Cans. for Constitutional Money, 1990—. Sgt. USAF, 1965-69. Mem. Nat. Writers Union. Republican. Avocations: bowling, fishing. Office: Reliance Enterprises Inc PO Box 413 Marengo IL 60152-0413

MROCHEK, MICHAEL J., physician; b. Ames, Iowa, Mar. 3, 1960; m. Diana Jo Ayoub, June 27, 1987; children: Justin, Jenna. BA in Chemistry, U. Tenn., 1982; MD, U. Tenn., Memphis, 1986. Diplomate Am. Bd. Phys. Medicine and Rehab., Am. Bd. Electrodiagnostic Medicine. Commd. 2d lt. U.S. Army, 1982, advanced through grades to maj., 1992; intern William Beaumont Army Med. Ctr., 1986-87; resident Walter Reed Army Med. Ctr., 1988-91; chief phys. medicine and rehab. William Beaumont Army Med. Ctr., El Paso, Tex., 1992-94; outpatient med. dir. Rio Vista Rehab. Hosp., El Paso, 1994—. Fellow Am. Acad. Phys. Medicine and Rehab., Am. Assn. Electrodiagnostic Medicine; mem. AMA, Tex. Med. Assn., El Paso County Med. Soc. Avocations: hunting, fishing, hiking, camping, swimming. Office: 1700 Murchison Dr El Paso TX 79902-2918

MROZ, JOHN EDWIN, political scientist; b. Lowell, Mass., May 1, 1948; s. Edwin T. and Margaret Mary (Little) M.; m. Karen Linehan, June 17, 1972; children: Jonathan E.R., Jessica, Jeffrey. BA, cert. Soviet and East European studies, U. Notre Dame, 1970; AM, Northeastern U., 1972; MA, MALD, Tufts U., 1974. Exec. sec. UN Assn. Greater Boston, 1971-73; exec. v.p., dir. Middle East Studies, Internat. Peace Acad., Inc., N.Y.C., 1976-81; pres. Inst. East-West Studies, N.Y.C., 1981—; cons., U.S. Govt. intermediary in Middle East, U.S. Dept. State, 1981-82; cons. Fgn. Svc. Inst., Dept. State, 1977-81; cons. Coun. of Europe, Strasbourg, Fed. Republic Germany, 1989—, East European govts., 1990—. Author: Beyond Security: Private Perceptions Among Arabs and Israelis, 1980. Contbr. articles to profl. jours. Teaching fellow NSF, 1971-72. Decorated Officer's Cross of Order of Merit Fed. Republic of Germany, 1991. Mem. Coun. on Fgn. Rels., Internat. Inst. Strategic Studies. Republican. Avocations: travel, falconry. Office: Inst East West Studies 700 Broadway New York NY 10003-9536

MRUK, CHARLES KARZIMER, agronomist; b. Providence, Sept. 23, 1926; s. Charles and Anna (Pisarek) M. BS in Agr., U. R.I., 1951, MS in Agronomy, 1957. Soil scientist soil conservation svc. Dept. Agr., Sunbury, Pa., 1951; insp. Charles A. McGuire Co., Providence, 1952; claims insp. R.R. Perishable Inspection Agy., Boston, 1953-55; asst. in agronomy U. R.I., 1955-57; agronomist Hercules Inc., 1957-79, tech. salesman, 1957-79; sr. tech. sales rep. BFC Chems., Inc., 1981-82; are devel. supr. Ea. States, 1982-84, ret., 1984; cons. turf maintenance Olympic Stadium and Grounds, Mexico City, 1968, Fenway Park, Boston, 1963-70; bd. mem. L. Troll/ G.C.S.A.N.E. Turf Rsch. Fund; advisor Mass. TurfGrass Conf. and Trade Show, Chicopee. author and editor articles on turf culture and fertilizers, 1960-81. Mem. Rep. Ward Com., Providence, 1963-76. With USN, 1944-46. U.S. Golf Assn. Green Sect. grantee, 1955-57. Mem. Am. Soc. Agronomy, New Eng. Sports Turf Mgrs. Assn. (life), R.I. Golf Course Supts. Assn., Mass. Turf and Lawn Grass Coun. (dir., mem. planning com., chmn. fin. com., 1987, pres., 1987-89), VFW, Am. Registry Cert. Profls. in Agronomy (cert. agronomist), Sigma Xi, Alpha Zeta. Mem. Polish National Ch. Home: 75 Burdick Dr Cranston RI 02920-1517

MTEWA, MEKKI, foundation administrator; b. Sungo, Mangochi, Malawi, Apr. 13, 1946; m. Sekina Batuli; 1 child, Natasha. BA, Chapman Coll., 1974; MA in Polit. Sci., Calif. State U., Fullerton, 1975; postgrad., Miami U., Oxford, Ohio, 1975-76; diploma in exec. law and leadership studies, LaSalle Extension U., Chgo., 1977; PhD in Pub. Adminstrn. and Pub. Policy, Claremont Grad. Sch., 1979; postdoctoral in legal studies, Vrije U., Brussels, 1985-86. Regional adminstrv. sec. Agrl. Devel. and Mktg. Corp., Limbe, Malawi, 1964-66; adminstrv. sec. United Transport (Malawi) Ltd., Blantyre, 1966-67; legal asst. Lilley, Wills & Co., Limbe, 1968-70; exec. dir., founder Assn. for Advancement Policy, Research and Devel. in the Third World, 1981—; exec. v.p., dep. dir. POS Inst., Washington, 1982—; chmn., chief exec. officer Internat. Devel. Found. Inc., 1984—; chmn. Malawi Inst. Internat. Affairs, 1987—; sec.-gen. AFORD Alliance for Democracy, 1993; research asst. Calif. State U., Fullerton, 1974-75, adj. prof., spring 1978-79; research asst. Polit. Sci. Dept. Miami U., Oxford, Ohio, 1975-76; adj. asst. prof. polit. sci. and mgmt. U. D.C., 1982-85; asst. prof. polit. sci. Howard U., Washington, 1979-85; cons. in field; lectr. in field. Author: Public Policy and Development Politics: The Politics of Technical Expertise in Africa, 1980, The Consultant Connexion: Evaluation of the Federal Consulting Service, 1981, Malawi Democratic Theory and Public Policy: A Preface, 1986; editor: Science Technology and Development: Options and Policies, 1982, Perspectives in International Development, 1986, Contemporary Issues in African Adminstration and Development Politics, 1987, International Development and Alternative Futures: The Coming Challenges, 1988, Internat. Science and Technology: Theory, Philosophy and Policy, 1990; contbr. articles to profl. jours., chpts. to books; mem. adv. bd. CHANGE: The Internat. Tech. newspaper; guest editor Jour. Ea. African Research and Devel.; various TV and radio appearances; subject of articles. Dep. br. sec. Malawi Congress party, 1965-66; com. chair S.W. Scholarship Fund, S.S. Neighborhood Assembly, Washington; chair election com. Rosemary Coop. Housing project; sec.-gen. Alliance for Democracy in Malawi, 1993; parliamentary candidate Mangochi Centre Constituency in Malawi, 1994. Grantee Sci. and Tech. in So. Africa Devel. Coordination Conf., 1982, Peace Corps Coll. project, 1982; fellow Midwestern U. Consortium, Miami U., Alpha Assn. Phi Beta Kappa Alumni in So. Calif.; recipient Seminar award Fgn. Student Council. Mem. Internat. Services Assn. (bd. dirs.), Sci. Soc. Chile (bd. dirs.), Lions, Phi Sigma Alpha. Avocation: travel. Office: Internat Devel Found 1730 K St NW Ste 304 Washington DC 20006-3839

MUCCI, GARY LOUIS, lawyer; b. Buffalo, Nov. 12, 1946; s. Guy Charles and Sally Rose (Battaglia) M.; m. Carolyn Belle Taylor, May 4, 1991. BA cum laude, St. John Fisher Coll., 1968; JD, Cath. U., 1972. Bar: N.Y. 1972. Law clk. to Hon. John T. Curtin U.S. Dist. Ct., Buffalo, 1972-74; assoc. atty. Donovan Leisure Newton & Irvine, N.Y.C., 1974-75; assoc. atty. Saperston & Day P.C., Buffalo, 1975-80, sr. ptnr., 1980—. Chmn. bd. Buffalo Philharm. Orch., 1985-86; pres. Hospice Buffalo, 1986-87; mem. N.Y. State Coun. on the Arts, 1987; chmn. Citizens Com. on Cultural Aid, Buffalo, 1992—; trustee St. John Fisher Coll. Recipient Brotherhood award NCCJ, Buffalo, 1983; named Man of Yr. William Paca Soc., 1984. Mem. Erie County Bar Assn., N.Y. State Bar Assn. Home: 27 Tudor Pl Buffalo NY 14222-1615 Office: Saperston & Day PC 3 Fountain Plz Ste 1100 Buffalo NY 14203-1414

MUCCI, PATRICK JOHN, financial consultant, realtor, commercial loan broker; b. Albany, N.Y., July 5, 1947; s. Philip and Angelina (Patrella) M.; m. Beverly Ann Scully, June 8, 1968; children: Philip Michael, Angelina Maria. AAS, Hudson Valley Community Coll., Troy, N.Y., 1967; BS, SUNY, Albany, 1977; MBA, Fairleigh Dickinson U., 1979. Cert. review appraiser, comml. investment mgr., real estate broker, internat. financier; registered mortgage underwriter; lic. ins. broker for life and accident ins. Adminstrv. asst. Nat. Savs. Bank, Albany, 1973-76; asst. v.p. Heritage Savs. Bank, Kingston, N.Y., 1976-78, Home Savs. Bank, Albany, 1978-81; v.p. Home Savs. Bank, 1981, Home & City Savs. Bank, Albany, 1981-83; sr. v.p. lending Home & City Savs. Bank, 1983-90; pres., chmn. bd., founder Greenbush Assocs., Inc., Rensselaer, N.Y., 1990—; chmn. bd., founder, pres. Patrician Funding, Inc., Rensselaer; bd. dirs. Vec Tech., Inc., Cycletech Inc. Active Italian-Am. Community Ctr.; mem. City of Albany Stratigic Planning Com., 1986; treas., bd. dirs. Theater Voices, 1990; bd. dirs. Albany League Arts, Discovery Ctr. Capital Region, 1990, N.Y. State Mus. Inst., Capital Affordable Housing Funding Com., Albany County Affordable Housing Corp.; mem. Rensselaer County Com. Sewer & Water Authority, 1993-94. Staff sgt. USAF, 1969-72. Mem. Nat. Assn. Mortgage Brokers, N.Y. State Mortgage Brokers Assn., N.Y. State Assn. Comml. and Indsl. Brokers, Soc. Internat. Financiers, Worldwide Network, N.E. Assn. Mtge. Bankers. Avocations: bicyclist, travel, reading, photography, computers. Home: 296 Luther Rd East East Greenbush NY 12061

MUCHA, JOHN FRANK, information systems professional; b. Ludlow, Mass., Sept. 12, 1950; s. Joseph Walter and Sophie (Chrusciel) M.; m. Anne Virginia Casey, Sept. 1, 1973 (div. Feb. 1989); m. Anna C. Isaacs, Sept. 17, 1994. BA in Polit. Sci., U. Mass., 1972; MBA in Tech. and Profl. Comm., Frostburg State U., 1985. Cert. computing profl. Computer programmer IRS, Washington, 1974-79, computer sys. programmer, 1979-81; computer sys. programmer IRS, Martinsburg, W.Va., 1981-86; staff sys. programmer fed. systems divsn. IBM, Gaithersburg, Md., 1986-87; chief tech. support IRS Martinsburg Computing Ctr., 1987-91; staff asst. to projects dir. info. sys. devel. IRS, Washington, 1991-92, computer specialist transition mgmt. office, 1992-95, sect. chief, 1995-97; team leader oversight team Govt. Program Mgmt. Office, New Carrollton, Md., 1997—. Contbr. articles to profl. jours. Team mem., bd. dirs. Beginning Experience of Balt., 1989-96; pres. Cath. Single Again Coun. of Balt., Inc., 1991-95, bd. dirs. Mem. IEEE, Computer Soc. of IEEE, Assn. for Computing Machinery, Assn. Info. Tech. Profls., Project Mgmt. Inst., Inst. for Certification of Computer Profls., Moose. Libertarian. Roman Catholic. Avocations: reading, instrumental music, travel, single again ministry. Home: 2482 Warm Spring Way Odenton MD 21113-1542

MUCHIN, ALLAN B., lawyer; b. Manitowoc, Wis., Jan. 10, 1936; s. Jacob and Dorothy (Biberfeld) M.; m. Elaine Cort, Jan. 28, 1960; children: Andrea Muchin Leon, Karen, Margery Muchin Goldblatt. BBA, U. Wis., Manitowoc, 1958, JD, 1961. Gen. counsel IRS, Chgo., 1961-65; assoc. Altman, Kurlander & Weiss, Chgo., 1965-68, ptnr., 1968-74; co-mng. ptnr. Katten Muchin & Zavis, Chgo., 1974—, chmn. bd., 1995—; bd. dirs. Adrco, Inc., Chgo., Chgo. Bulls, Chgo. White Sox, Sportmart, Inc., Wheeling, Ill., Globe Glass & Mirror, Chgo., Alberto-Culver Co. Trustee Ravinia Music Festival, Highland Park, Ill., 1992—, Lyric Opera Chgo., 1993—; mem. adv.

com. Loyola Family Bus. Ctr., Chgo., 1991—; co-com. chmn. Am. Com. for Weizmann Inst. of Sci., Chgo., 1991—. Mem. Econ. Club Chgo., Econ. Devel. Commn. (com. mem.), Comml. Club Chgo. Avocations: travel, tennis, reading. Office: Katten Muchin & Zavis 525 W Monroe St Ste 1600 Chicago IL 60661-3629

MUCHMORE, DENNIS C., governmental affairs consultant; b. Charleston, Ill., Nov. 23, 1946; s. Maurice Leo and Rose Catherine (Driscoll) M.; 1 child from previous marriage, Shane. BS in Edn., Ea. Ill. U., 1968; M in Pub. Adminstrn., Mich. State U., 1982. Tchr. Fitzgerald Pub. Schs., Warren, Mich., 1969-73; pres. Fitzgerald Edn. Assn., Warren, 1969-73; cons. Mich. State Senate, Lansing, 1975-77, adminstrv. asst., 1973-80; mgr. of tax and labor Mich C. of C., Lansing, 1980; v.p. Mich. C. of C., Lansing, 1980-84; cons. GCSI, Lansing, 1984-88; prin. Dennis Muchmore & Assoc., Lansing, 1988-93; pres. Muchmore Harrington Smalley & Assocs., Lansing, 1993—. Bd. dirs. Ea. Ill. U. Found., Charleston, 1992-95, Lansing C.C. Found., Lansing, 1993—, Lansing Symphony Orch., 1992-95; host com. Am. Legis. Exch. Coun., Lansing, 1993-94; mem. adv. bd. Mid Mich. Opera Theatre, Lansing, 1994-97. Mem. Am. Assn. of Polit. Cons., Mountain Men, Am. Soc. of Pub. Adminstrs. (bd. dirs. Capital chpt. 1982-86, 97—). Roman Catholic. Avocations: skiing, fly fishing. Home: PO Box 20114 Lansing MI 48901-0714 Office: Muchmore Harrington Smalley & Assocs 500 Michigan Nat Tower Lansing MI 48933

MUCHMORE, DON MONCRIEF, museum, foundation, educational, financial fund raising and public opinion consulting firm administrator, banker; b. Wichita, Kans., Dec. 26, 1922; s. Floyd Stephen and Ivy Fay (Campbell) M.; m. Virginia Gunn, June 18, 1949 (div. Dec. 1978); children—Melinda, Marcia. B.A., Occidental Coll., Los Angeles, 1945; postgrad., U. So. Calif. Law Sch., 1945; postgrad. polit. sci., UCLA. Intern Nat. Inst. Pub. Affairs, Washington, 1944; exec. asst. to congressman Washington, 1946-48; teaching asst. UCLA, 1949-50; mem. faculty San Diego State U., 1950-51; asst. prof., adminstr. Calif. State U., Long Beach, 1951-56; pres., chief exec. officer The Campbell Found., L.A., 1956—; spl. asst. to supt. pub. instrn. Calif. Dept. Edn., Sacramento, 1956-57; exec. mus. dir. Calif. Mus. Sci. and Industry, L.A., 1957-62, 82-88; exec. v.p., chief exec. officer Calif. Mus. Found., L.A., 1957-62, 82-89; dep. dir. (on loan from mus.) Calif. Dept. Fin., Sacramento, 1960; exec. vice chancellor Calif. State Colls. and Univs. System, Long Beach, 1962-64; first exec. asst. to chmn. and chief exec. officer Calif. Fed. Savs. and Loan Assn., L.A., 1964-66; sr. v.p. Calif. Fed. Savs. and Loan Assn, L.A., 1966-82; pres., CEO PE Conservation Svcs., Inc., 1990-94; chmn. bd. dirs., CEO Opinion Rsch. of Calif., Opinion Surveyors, The State Poll and Mkt. Surveys, Inc., Long Beach, 1948-71, syndicated by L.A. Times, 1961-70, also M-R Assocs. campaigns; cons. in pub. opinion mus. mgmt. and fund raising, 1948-71; chmn., CEO, cons. DMM & Assocs., Long Beach, 1961—; sec., treas. EVENUP for the Homeless, 1994—, Am. Mus., 1994—; mem. Inst. Mus. Svcs., 1983-88. Contbr. chpts. to books. Participant in pub. opinion work Dem. and Rep. campaigns, 1954-72; mem., chmn. 4 presdl. commns., 1970-82, Just Say No Internat., 1989-91, Reading is Fundamental, 1989—, The Buckley Sch., 1989-90; cons. overseas traveling sci. exhibit, planning mus., 1984-96, sr. adminstr., advisor, cons. to PCS (South Ctrl. L.A.) Sr. Citizens, 1995-96; cons. Long Beach Com. Improvement League, 1995-96; lead cons. New Solution to Homeless, 1993—; prin. officer Peruvians Cultural Exhibit, 1988-96; prin. cons. cultural exhibit Wonders of World, 1992—, Queensway Bay, Long Beach, 1992—; bd. dirs. Bus. Tele Network, 1995—; active Even Up for the Homeless, 1996—. Recipient Highest Mus. Edn. award Sigma Alpha Epsilon, 1992, Chpt. Advisor of Yr. (6), Citizen of Yr. award and numerous other awards from nat., state and local groups; named Pollster of Yr., Newsweek, 1962; Elks Nat. scholar. Mem. Am. Assn. Mus., Calif. Mus. Assn. (pres. 1960, bd. dirs. 1982-88), Assn. Sci. and Tech. Ctrs. (bd. dirs. 1988-88), Am. Assn. Pub. Opinion Rsch., Am. Polit. Sci. Assn., AAAS. Home: 525 E Seaside Way #209 Long Beach CA 90802 Office: The Campbell Found DMM & Associates 525 E Seaside Way Unit 209 Long Beach CA 90802-8001

MUCHMORE, ROBERT BOYER, engineering consultant executive; b. Augusta, Kans., July 8, 1917; s. Ray Boyer and Charlotte (McPherron) M.; m. Betty Vaughan, Jan. 29, 1944; children: Andrew Vaughan, Douglas Boyer. BS, U. Calif., Berkeley, 1939; degree in Elec. Engring., Stanford U., 1942. Project engr. Sperry Gyroscope Co., Garden City, N.Y., 1942-46; sr. mem. tech. staff Hughes Aircraft, Culver City, Calif., 1946-54; v.p., chief scientist TRW Systems, Redondo Beach, Calif., 1954-73; cons. TRW Systems, Sonoma, Calif., 1973—; lectr. in engring. UCLA, 1954-58. Author: Essentials of Microwaves, 1952. Fellow IEEE; mem. AAAS, Assn. Computing Machinery, Sierra Club. Home: 4311 Grove St Sonoma CA 95476-6046

MUCHMORE, WILLIAM BREULEUX, zoologist, educator; b. Cin., July 7, 1920; s. Oliver Charles and Ruby (Breuleux) M.; m. Marjorie Murrin, Aug. 15, 1943; children—Susan Jane, Patricia Ann. B.A., Oberlin Coll., 1942; Ph.D. in Zoology, Washington U., St. Louis, 1950. Instr. biology U. Rochester, N.Y., 1950-52; asst. prof. U. Rochester, 1952-58, asso. prof., 1958-70, prof., 1970-85, prof. emeritus, 1985—, asst. chmn. dept. biology, 1964-66, assoc. chmn., 1974-78; vis. prof. U. Hull, Eng., 1963-64; research assoc. Fla. State Collection Arthopods, 1974—. Contbr. articles to profl. jours. Served with U.S. Army, 1943-46. NSF grantee, 1958-69, 73-76; Fulbright travel grantee, 1963-64; Office Naval Research grantee, 1979-81. Fellow Rochester Acad. Sci., Nat. Speleological Soc.; mem. Am. Arachnological Soc., Am. Micro. Soc., Brit. Arachnological Soc., Centre Internat. de Documentation Arachnologique. Office: Dept Biology Univ of Rochester Rochester NY 14627

MUCHNICK, RICHARD STUART, ophthalmologist; b. Bklyn., June 21, 1942; s. Max and Rae (Kozinsky) M.; BA with honors. Cornell U., 1963, MD, 1967; m. Felice Dee Greenberg, Oct. 29, 1978; 1 child, Amanda Michelle. Intern in medicine N.Y. Hosp., N.Y.C., 1967-68, now assoc. attending ophthalmologist, chief Pediatric Ophthalmology Clinic; resident in ophthalmology, 1970-73; practice medicine, specializing in ophthalmology, notably strabismus and ophthalmic plastic surgery N.Y.C., 1974—; attending surgeon, chief Ocular Motility Clinic, Manhattan Eye, Ear and Throat Hosp., N.Y.C.; clin. assoc. prof. ophthalmology Cornell U., N.Y.C., 1984—. Served with USPHS, 1968-70. Recipient Coryell Prize Surgery Cornell U. Med. Coll., 1967. Diplomate Am. Bd. Ophthalmology, Nat. Bd. Med. Examiners. Fellow A.C.S., Am. Acad. Ophthalmology; mem. Am. Soc. Ophthalmic Plastic and Reconstructive Surgery, Am. Assn. Pediatric Ophthalmology and Strabismus, Internat. Strabismological Assn., N.Y. Soc. Clin. Ophthalmology, AMA, N.Y. Acad. Medicine, Manhattan Ophthal. Soc., N.Y. Soc. Pediatric Ophthalmology and Strabismus, Alpha Omega Alpha, Alpha Epsilon Delta. Clubs: Lotos, 7th Regt. Tennis. Clin. researcher strabismus, ophthalmic plastic surgery, 1973—. Office: 69 E 71st St New York NY 10021-4213

MUCKENFUSS, CANTWELL FAULKNER, III, lawyer; b. Montgomery, Ala., Apr. 25, 1945; s. Cantwell F. and Dorothy (Dauphine) M.; m. A. Angela Lancaster, June 25, 1978; children: Alice Paran Lancaster, Cantwell F. IV. BA, Vanderbilt U., 1967; JD, Yale U., 1971. Bar: N.Y. 1973, D.C. 1976. Law clk. to presiding justice U.S. Ct. Appeals (6th cir.), 1971-72; atty., project developer Bedford Stuyvesant D and S Corp., Bklyn., 1972-73; spl. asst. to the dir. FDIC, Washington, 1974-77, counsel to the chmn., 1977-78; sr. dep. comptroller for policy Office of the Comptroller of the Currency, Washington, 1978-81; ptnr. Gibson, Dunn & Crutcher, Washington, 1981—; mem. editorial adv. bd. Issues in Bank Regulation, Rolling Meadows, Ill., 1977-91, Electronic Banking Law and Commerce Report, 1996—; mem. bd. advisors Rev. Banking and Fin. Svcs., N.Y.C., 1985—; bd. dis. Fair Tax Edn. Fund, Washington, 1987-90. Served with USNG, 1968-70, USAR, 1970-74. Recipient Spl. Achievement award U.S. Dept. Treasury, 1979, Presdl. Rank award U.S. Govt., 1980. Mem. ABA, Fed. Bar Assn. Democrat. Episcopalian. Clubs: Kenwood Country (Bethesda, Md.); Yale (N.Y.C.). Office: Gibson Dunn & Crutcher 1050 Connecticut Ave NW Ste 900 Washington DC 20036-5320

MUCKENHOUPT, BENJAMIN, retired mathematics educator; b. Newton, Mass., Dec. 22, 1933; s. Carl Frederick and Sarah Joanna (Boell) M.; m. Mary Kathryn Heath, Aug. 29, 1964; children: Margaret, Carl Edward. A.B., Harvard U., 1954; M.S., U. Chgo., 1955, Ph.D., 1958. Instr. DePaul U., Chgo., 1958-59; asst. prof. math. DePaul U., 1959-60; faculty Rutgers U., New Brunswick, N.J., 1960-91; prof. math. Rutgers U., 1970-91; vis. assoc. prof. Mt. Holyoke Coll., 1963-65; visitor Inst. Advanced Study, Princeton, N.J., 1968-69, 75-76; vis. prof. SUNY-Albany, 1970-71. Contbr. articles to profl. jours. NSF rsch. grantee, 1965-88; Rutgers Rsch. Coun. fellow, 1968-69. Mem. Am. Math. Soc., Math. Assn. Am., Phi Beta Kappa, Sigma Xi. Home: 196 Woodfern Rd Neshanic Station NJ 08853-4054

MUCKERMAN, NORMAN JAMES, priest, writer; b. Webster Groves, Mo., Feb. 1, 1917; s. Oliver Christopher and Edna Gertrude (Hartman) M. B.A., Immaculate Conception Coll., 1940, M. in Religious Edn., 1942. Ordained priest Roman Catholic Ch., 1942. Missionary Redemptorist Missions, Amazonas, Para, Brazil, 1943-53; procurator missions Redemptorist Missions, St. Louis, 1953-58; pastor, adminstr. St. Alphonsus Ch., Chgo., 1958-67, St. Gerard, Kirkwood, Mo., 1967-71; mktg. mgr. circulation Liguori Pubs., Liguori, Mo., 1971-76; editor Liguorian Mag., Liguori, Mo., 1977-89. Author: How to Face Death Without Fear, 1976, Redemptorists on the Amazon, 1992; contbg. editor Liguorian, 1989-95. Recipient Nota Dez award Caixa Fed. Do Para, Brazil, 1958. Mem. Cath. Press Assn. (cons. 1971-95, bd. dirs. 1976-85, pres. 1981-84, St. Francis De Sales award 1985), St. Louis Press Club. Avocations: golf; travel; reading.

MUCKLER, JOHN, professional hockey coach, professional team executive; b. Midland, Ont., Can.; married; 5 children. Profl. hockey player, Ea. Hockey League, Baltimore, also Long Island Ducks; coach, gen. mgr. Long Island Ducks; 1st pres. N.Y. Jr. Met. League; coach, gen. dir. player pers., mgr. New York Rangers affiliate team, Am. Hockey League, Providence, R.I.; formerly head coach Minnesota North Stars; with Edmonton Oilers, 1981—, formerly co-coach; head coach Edmonton Oilers, 1989-1991; head coach Buffalo Sabres, 1991-94, gen. mgr., 1994—. Office: Buffalo Sabres Marine Midland Arena One Main St Buffalo NY 14202-4110*

MUDD, JOHN O., lawyer; b. 1943. BA, Cath. U., 1965, MA, 1966; JD, U. Mont., 1973; LLM, Columbia U., 1986, DS of Law, 1994. Bar: Mont. 1973. Ptnr. Mulroney, Delaney, Dalby & Mudd, Missoula, Mont., 1973-79; lectr. U. Mont., Missoula, 1973-74, 75-76, prof. law, dean, 1979-88; ptnr. Garlington, Lohn & Robinson, Missoula, 1988—; pres. Mid-Continent Assn. Law Schs., 1982-83. Bd. dirs. St. Patrick Hosp., 1985-90, Providence Svcs. Corp., 1992—; elected Dem. candidate U.S. Senate, 1994; chmn. Mont. Commn. Future of Higher Edn., 1989-90. With U.S. Army, 1967-73. Mem. ABA, Am. Judicature Soc. (bd. dirs. 1985—), State Bar Mont. Editor Mont. Law Rev., 1972-73. Office: Garlington Lohn & Robinson PO Box 7909 Missoula MT 59807-7909

MUDD, JOHN PHILIP, lawyer; b. Washington, Aug. 22, 1932; s. Thomas Paul and Frances Mary (Finotti) M.; m. Barbara Eve Sweeney, Aug. 10, 1957; children: Laura, Ellen, Philip, Clare, David. BSS, Georgetown U., 1954; JD, Georgetown Law Center, 1956. Bar: Md. 1956, D.C. 1963, Fla. 1964, Calif. 1973. Pvt. practice Upper Marlboro, Md., 1956-66; v.p., sec., gen. counsel Deltona Corp., Miami, Fla., 1966-72; sec., gen. counsel Nat. Community Builders, San Diego, 1972-73; gen. counsel Continental Advisers (adviser to Continental Mortgage Investors), 1973-75, sr. v.p., gen. counsel, 1975-80; sr. v.p., gen. counsel Am. Hosp. Mgmt. Corp., Miami, 1980-89; legal coord. Amerifirst Bank, Miami, 1989-92; v.p., legal counsel Cartaret Savs. Bank, Morristown, N.J., 1991-93, cons., 1991-92; gen. counsel Golden Glades Hosp., Miami, 1992-93, Bank of N.Am., Miami, 1994—; gen. counsel Golden Glades Hosp., Miami, 1992-93; cons. FSLIC, 1988-89, J.E. Robert Cos., Alexandria, Va., 1988-89, Real Estate Recovery, Inc., Boca Raton, Fla., 1991-92, Bank N.Am., Ft. Lauderdale, Fla., 1992; dir. Unitower Mortgage Corp., Miami, Fla.; dir. Unitower Mortgage Corp., Miami; pres. Marquette Realty Corp., Miami. Former mem. Land Devel. Adv. Com. N.Y. State; chmn. student interview com. Georgetown U.; bd. dirs. Lasalle High Sch., Miami; corp. counsel Com. of Dade County, Fla.; trustee Golden Glades Gen. Hosp., Miami, Fla., 1992—, gen. counsel, 1991—, Bank of North Am., Miami, 1992—. Mem. Fla. Bar Assn., Calif. Bar Assn., Md. Bar Assn., D.C. Bar Assn., Fla. State Bar (exec. com. on corp. counsel com.). Democrat. Roman Catholic. Home: 411 Alhambra Cir Miami FL 33134-4901 Office: Bank of North Am Golden Glades Med Plz 8701 SW 137th Ave Ste 301 Miami FL 33183-4498

MUDD, ROGER HARRISON, news broadcaster, educator; b. Washington, Feb. 9, 1928; s. Kostka and Irma Iris (Harrison) M.; m. Emma Jeanne Spears, Oct. 28, 1957; children: Daniel H., Maria M., Jonathan, Matthew M. AB, Washington and Lee U., 1950; MA, U. N.C., 1953. Tchr. Darlington Sch., Rome, Ga., 1951-52; reporter Richmond News Leader, Va., 1953; news dir. Sta. WRNL, Richmond, 1953-56; reporter radio and TV Sta. WTOP, Washington, 1956-61; corr. CBS, 1961-80; chief Washington corr. NBC, 1980-87; Congl. corr. MacNeil/Lehrer News Hour, 1987-92; prof. journalism Princeton U., 1992-94, Washington & Lee U., 1995-96. Host The History Channel, 1995—. Trustee Randolph-Macon Women's Coll., Lynchburg, Va., 1971-78, Robert F. Kennedy Journalism Awards Com., 1971-78, Blue Ridge Sch., Dyke, Va., 1978-84; bd. dirs. Fund for Investigative Journalism, PEN/Faulkner, 1985-92, Va. Found. for Humaniites, Va. Hist. Soc., 1988-94, RIAS Berlin Commn., 1996—, Va. Found. for Ind. Colls., 1997—; mem. adv. com. Mt. Vernon Ladies Assn. With AUS, 1945-47. Mem. Radio-TV Corr. Assn. (chmn. exec. com. 1969-70).

MUDD, SHERYL KAY, secondary school educator, guidance counselor; b. Ft. Thomas, Ky., July 14, 1960; d. Robert Leslie and Marvel Maxine (Youtsey) M.; m. Jackie Elaine Nichols, Lawrence Robert, Gerald Leslie, Randy Kent, Ronald Lee, Rhonda Dee, Michael Todd. BA, Transylvania U., 1982; MEd in Guidance Counseling, Xavier U., Cin., 1988. Cert. elem. tchr., K-12 phys. edn. tchr., Ky. Substitute tchr. Pendleton County Schs., Falmouth, Ky., 1982-84, Campbell County Schs., Alexandria, Ky., 1982-84; tchr. No. Elem. Sch., Butler, Ky., 1984-86; tchr. math. Pendleton Mid. Sch., Falmouth, 1986-88, tchr. reading, 1988-89, tchr. health and phys. edn., 1989-92, 95—; tchr. 7th and 8th grades Risk Youth, 1992-95. Named to Honorable Order of Ky. Colonels, Commonwealth of Ky., 1979, 96, Tchr. of Yr., Pendleton Mid. Sch., 1989, 93, 94, 95, 96. Mem. ASCD, AAHPERD, Assn. for Advancement Health and Phys. Edn., AACD, Ky. Assn. for Gifted Assn., Ky. Mid. Sch. Assn., No. Ky. Assn. Counseling and Devel. Democrat. Roman Catholic. Avocations: basketball, softball, volleyball, bowling, field hockey. Home: Box 166 RR 2 Butler KY 41006-0166 Office: Pendleton County Mid Sch 500 Chapel St Falmouth KY 41040-1410

MUDD, SIDNEY PETER, former beverage company executive; b. St. Louis, Jan. 21, 1917; s. Urban Sidney and Hallie Newell (Perry) M.; m. Ada Marie Herbermann, Oct. 22, 1942; children: Sidney Peter, Ada Marie, Peter, Michael, Mary, Elizabeth, Catherine. A.B. magna cum laude, St. Louis U., 1938; L.H.D., Coll. New Rochelle, N.Y., 1974; LHD, Iona Coll., 1985. Distr. Joyce Seven-Up, Chgo., 1938; sales mgr. Joyce Seven-Up, 1939; coordinator N.Y. ops. Joyce Seven-Up, New Rochelle, 1941; v.p. charge ops. Joyce Seven-Up, 1949-51; exec. v.p. N.Y. Seven-Up Bottling Co., Inc., New Rochelle, 1951-63; pres. N.Y. Seven-Up Bottling Co., Inc., 1963-73, dir., 1952-84, chmn. bd., 1973-84; pres. Joyce Beverages, Inc. (Joyce Advt.), 1973-84; past chmn. bd. Joyce Beverages/N.Y., N.J., Conn., Ill., Wis.; past dir. Joyce Beverages Inc., Joyce Advt., Joyce Beverages/N.Y., N.J., Conn., Chgo., Washington, Wis., Ill., Joyce Assocs.; dir., vice-chmn. Westchester Fed. Savs. Bank; bd. dirs. Marine Midland Bank Regional Bd., chmn. 1987-88. Past pres., bd. trustees St. Joseph's Hosp., N.Y.C., St. Francis Hosp.; chmn. Westchester County Assn.; past bd. lay advisers St. Agnes Hosp., White Plains; past chmn. bd. trustees Coll. of New Rochelle; past bd. dirs. U.S. Cath. Hist. Soc.; former trustee St. Louis U.; bd. dirs., v.p. John M. and Mary A. Joyce Found.; chmn. N.Y. Industry-Labor Com. for Resource Recovery; bd. dirs. Am. Alliance Resource Recovery Interests; pres. New Rochelle Devel. Council; bd. dirs. Keep Am. Beautiful, Inc.; chmn. Westchester 2000, 1984-85. Served with USNR. Decorated Knight of Malta, knight Equestrian Order of Holy Sepulchre; recipient St. Louis U. Alumni award, 1967, Dr. Martin Luther King, Jr. award New Rochelle Community Action Agy., 1978, New Rochelle K.C. Civic award, 1978, Outstanding Citizen award New Rochelle YMCA, 1979, Disting. Service award Westchester region NCCJ, 1980, Medallion award Westchester Community Coll. Found., 1981; honoring resolution N.Y. State Senate, 1982; honoring resolution N.Y. State Assembly, 1982; honoring proclamation County of Westchester, City of Yonkers, City of White Plains, 1982; ARC award of excellence, 1983, Man of Yr. award Beverage Industry, 1974, Disting. Service award Sr. Personnel Employment Council, 1986, Disting. Achievement award Mental Health Assn., 1987, Disting. Citizen award New Rochelle Hosp. Med. Ctr., 1990; named to St. Louis U. Sports Hall of Fame, 1976, Beverage World Hall of Fame, 1984. Mem. Nat. Soft Drink Assn. (dir., pres. 1974-76, Disting. Achievement award 1980), N.Y. State Soft Drink Assn. (pres. 1966-67, Disting. Service award 1985, 86), Theta Kappa Phi, Crown and Anchor Soc. (St. Louis U.). Clubs: Winged Foot Golf (Westchester) (founder, past v.p., dir.); Sales and Mktg. Execs. *A happy life, a successful life is a life lived in love; love of God; love of self, love of others. To love and be loved is life's greatest reward on earth.*

MUDGE, LEWIS SEYMOUR, theologian, educator, university dean; b. Phila., Oct. 22, 1929; s. Lewis Seymour and Anne Evelyn (Bolton) M.; m. Jean Bruce McClure, June 15, 1957; children: Robert Seymour, William McClure, Anne Evelyn. B.A., Princeton, 1951, M. Div., 1955, Ph.D. (Kent fellow), 1961; B.A. with honors in Theology, Oxford (Eng.) U., 1954, M.A. (Rhodes scholar), 1958. Ordained to ministry Presbyn. Ch., 1955. Presbyn. univ. pastor Princeton, 1955-56; sec. dept. theology World Alliance Ref. Chs., Geneva, 1957-62; minister to coll. Amherst Coll., 1962-68, asst. prof. philosophy and religion, 1962-64, assoc. prof., 1964-70, prof. philosophy and religion, 1970-76, chmn. dept. philosophy and religion, 1968-69, 75-76; dean faculty, prof. theology McCormick Theol. Sem., Chgo., 1976-87, San Francisco Theol. Sem., 1987—; prof. Grad. Theol. Union, Berkeley, Calif., 1987-95; dir. Ctr. for Hermeneutical Studies, Grad. Theol. Union/U. Calif., Berkeley, 1990—; Stuart prof. theology Grad. Theol. Union, Berkeley, Calif., 1995—; mem. commn. on faith and order Nat. Council Chs., 1965-70; sec. spl. com. on confession faith United Presbyn Ch., 1965-67, chmn. spl. com. on theology of the call, 1968-71; chmn. theol. commn. U.S. Consultation on Ch. Union, 1977-89; co-chmn. Internat. Ref.-Roman Cath. Dialogue Commn., 1983-90; observer Extraordinary Synod Bishops, 1985. Author: One Church: Catholic and Reformed, 1963, Is God Alive?, 1963, Why is the Church in the World?, 1967, The Crumbling Walls, 1970, The Sense of a People: Toward a Church for the Human Future, 1992; also numerous articles and revs.; editor: Essays on Biblical Interpretation (Paul Ricoeur), 1980, (with James Poling) Formation and Reflection: the Promise of Practical Theology, 1987. Pres. Westminster Found. in New Eng., 1963-67; chmn. bd. Nat. Vocation Agy., 1972-75; mem. com. selection Rhodes Scholars, Wis., 1983-85, Iowa, 1986. Mem. Phi Beta Kappa. Democrat. Home: 2444 Hillside Ave Berkeley CA 94704-2529 Office: San Francisco Theol Sem 2 Kensington Rd San Anselmo CA 94960-2905

MUDRY, MICHAEL, pension and benefit consultant; b. Lucina, Czechoslovakia, Dec. 5, 1926; (parents Am. citizens); s. John Zaleta and Helen (Molchan) M.; m. Kendall Archer, June 17, 1960; children: F. Goodrich Archer, Benjamin Kendall. BA, U. Conn., 1951. Sr. v.p. Hay/Huggins Co. Inc., Phila., 1956-93; self-employed pension and benefit cons. Wayne, Pa., 1994—; former actuary Ch. Pensions Conf. Contbr. articles to profl. jours. Bd. mem., actuary Am. Coun. on Gift Annuities, Dallas, 1978—. Served with U.S. Army, 1945-46. Fellow Soc. Actuaries, Conf. Cons. Actuaries; mem. Am. Acad. Actuaries, Internat. Actuarial Assn., Internat. Assn. Cons. Actuaries. Democrat. Home: 749 Mancill Rd Wayne PA 19087-2004

MUECKE, CHARLES ANDREW (CARL MUECKE), federal judge; b. N.Y.C., Feb. 20, 1918; s. Charles and Wally (Roeder) M.; m. Claire E. Vasse; children by previous marriage: Carl Marshall, Alfred Jackson, Catherine Calvert. B.A., Coll. William and Mary, 1941; LL.B., U. Ariz., 1953. Bar: Ariz. 1953. Rep. AFL, 1947-50; reporter Ariz. Times, Phoenix, 1947-48; since practiced in Phoenix; with firm Parker & Muecke, 1953-59, Muecke, Dushoff & Sacks, 1960-61; U.S. atty. Dist. Ariz., 1961-64, U.S. dist. judge, 1964—, now sr. judge.; mem. 9th cir. Jud. Coun. com. review local dist. Ct. Rules. Mem. Phoenix Planning Commn., 1955-61, chmn., 1960; chmn. Maricopa County Dem. Party, 1961-62; trustee U. San Diego Coll. Law. Maj. USMC, 1942-45, USMCR, 1945-60. Mem. Fed. Bar Assn., Ariz. Bar Assn., Maricopa Bar Assn., Am. Trial Lawyers Assn., Dist. Judges Assn. Ninth Circuit, Phi Beta Kappa, Phi Alpha Delta, Omicron Delta Kappa. Office: US Dist Ct US Courthouse & Fed Bldg 230 N 1st Ave Ste 7009 Phoenix AZ 85025-0007*

MUEDEKING, GEORGE HERBERT, editor; b. Arcadia, Wis., Aug. 19, 1915; s. George Fredrick and Rosalie Carolina (Brodt) M.; m. Harriet Laura Rollwagen, June 26, 1941; children—Miriam Harriet (Mrs. W. Ron Heyer), George David. B.A., Capital U., 1936, D.D. (hon.), 1955; M.A., Ind. U., 1938; B.D., Evang. Lutheran Theol. Sem., 1941; Ph.D., U. Calif., Berkeley, 1961. Ordained to ministry Luth. Ch., 1941; pastor Luth. Ch. of Holy Trinity, Long Beach, Calif., 1941-47, First Luth. Ch., Fullerton, Calif., 1947-51, Christ Luth. Ch., El Cerrito, Calif., 1951-59; instr. Pacific Luth. Theol. Sem., Berkeley, 1953-55, asst. prof., 1956-59, asso. prof., 1960-64, prof., 1965-66; editor Luth. Standard, Mpls., 1967-78, roving editor, 1978-80; lectr. Australian Luth. Tchrs. Coll., 1981-82; sr. mentor Calif. Luth. U., 1984, 87; resident faculty Luth. Bible Inst. Calif., 1993; v.p. Calif. dist. Am. Luth. Ch.; mem. com. on interpretation Am. sect. World Coun. Chs.; pres. Luth Editors Assn.; bd. dirs. Assn. ch. Press, Luths. for Life. Author: Emotional Problems and the Bible, 1956; editor FOCL-Point, 1991—; contbr. articles to religious publs. Mem. Assn. for Profl. Edn. for Ministry, Nat. Council on Family Relations, Minn. Press Club, Am. Acad. Religion and Mental Health, Am. Acad. Polit. and Social Sci., Phi Beta Kappa. Republican. Home and Office: 4414 Springwood Dr Napa CA 94558-1724

MUEHLBAUER, JAMES HERMAN, manufacturing executive; b. Evansville, Ind., Nov. 13, 1940; s. Herman Joseph and Anna Louise (Overfield) M.; m. Mary Kay Koch, June 26, 1965; children: Stacey, Brad, Glen, Beth, Katy. BSME, Purdue U., 1963, MS Indsl. Adminstrn., 1964. Registered profl. engr., Ind. Engr. George Koch Sons, Inc., Evansville, 1966-67; chief estimator George Koch Sons, Inc., 1968-72, chief engr., 1973-74, v.p., 1975-81, dir., 1978—, exec. v.p., 1982—; v.p., bd. dirs. Brake Supply Co., Evansville, Gibbs Die Casting Corp., Henderson, Ky., Uniseal, Inc., Evansville; bd. dirs. Citizens Nat. Bank, Evansville, Page-Koch (Europe) Ltd., Lichfield, Eng., Red Spot Paint & Varnish Co., Inc., Evansville. Co-author: Tool & Manufacturing Engineering Handbook, 1976; patentee in paint finishing equipment. Bd. dirs., past pres. Evansville Indsl. Found., 1980—; bd. dirs., past pres., past campaign chmn. United Way S.W. Ind., Evansville, 1983—; bd. dirs., past vice-chmn. Univ. So. Ind. Found., Evansville, 1988—, Deaconess Hosp., Evansville, 1986—, treas., 1991-96. Named Engr. of Yr. S.W. chpt. Ind. Soc. Profl. Engrs., 1983; recipient Tech. Achievement award Tri-State Coun. for Sci. and Engring., Evansville, 1984, Purdue U. Alumni Citizenship award, 1991. Mem. Soc. Mfg. Engrs. (past nat. chmn. finishing and coating tech. divsn.), ASME, NSPE, Evansville Country Club, Evansville Petroleum Club, Evansville Kennel Club. Republican. Roman Catholic. Home: 2300 E Gum St Evansville IN 47714-2338 Office: George Koch Sons Inc 10 S 11th Ave Evansville IN 47744-0001

MUEHLEISEN, GENE SYLVESTER, retired law enforcement officer, state official; b. San Diego, Dec. 28, 1915; s. Adolph and Vesta C. (Gates) M.; m. Elsie Jane Conover, Sept. 14, 1940; 1 son, John Robert. Student, San Diego State Coll., 1935-39, San Diego Jr. Coll., 1957. U.S. park ranger Yosemite Nat. Park, summers 1936-39, 79-84; with San Diego Police Dept., 1940-60, dir. tng., 1957-59, comdg. officer patrol div., capt., 1958-60; exec. dir. Commn. on Peace Officer Standards and Tng., Calif. Dept. Justice, Sacramento, 1960-65, 67-76; assoc. dir. Pres.'s Commn. on Law Enforcement and Adminstrn. of Justice, Nat. Crime Commn., 1965-67; chmn. police sci. adv. com. San Diego Jr. Coll., 1957-60, police sci. faculty, 1957-60; staff instr. San Diego Police Acad., 1954-60; guest instr. police adminstrn. Sacramento State Coll., 1964; grad. FBI Nat. Acad. 51st Session, 1953, pres. of class, guest faculty, 1963-66; cons. Ford Found. Internat. Assn. Chiefs of Police Project, 1964-67; cons. U.S. Nat. Park Svc., 1965-84, spl. asst. to regional dir. Western region, 1977-79; adviser Royal Can. Mounted Police, 1961—; guest lectr., 1960—. Mem. tng. com. Internat. Assn. Chiefs of Police, 1963—; mem. adv. com. on police tng. Ford Found., 1964—; U.S. rep. Interpol Symposium on Police Edn. and Tng., Paris, 1965; chmn. Atty. Gen.'s Com. on Law Enforcement Standards, 1957-59; vice chmn. Calif. Commn. Peace Officer Standards and Tng., 1959-60; chmn. police services task force Calif. Council Criminal Justice, 1968-78; mem. Atty. Gen.'s Commn. Police-Community Relations, 1971—; mem. adv. com. FBI, 1972—; mem. Gov.'s Pub. Safety Planning Council, 1974—; Pres. San Diego Police Officers Assn., San Diego Police and Fire Retirement System; bd. dirs. San Diego Hist. Soc. Served to capt. USNR, World War II. The Gene

Muehleisen Nature Area, Valley Oak Park, Sacramento dedicated, 1992. Mem. Nat. Conf. Police Assns. (com. chmn.), Calif. Peace Officers Assn. (com. chmn.), Peace Officers Research Assn. Calif. (pres. 1959-60, com. chmn.), Am. Soc. Pub. Adminstrn. (dir. San Diego County chpt.), Nat. Assn. State Dirs. Law Enforcement Tng. (pres. 1972-73), Am. Corrections Assn., Calif. Assn. Adminstrn. of Justice Educators, Park Rangers Assn. of Calif., Internat. Police Assn. (life, v.p. region 29 USA), Internat. Assn. Chiefs of Police (life), Calif. Parks and Recreation Soc. (Citizen of Yr. 1992), Sacramento Tree Found. (tech. adv. com. 1983—). Clubs: Kiwanis, San Diego Ski (pres.). Home and Office: 4221 Corona Way Sacramento CA 95864-5301

MUEHLNER, SUANNE WILSON, library director; b. Rochester, Minn., June 29, 1943; d. George T. and Rhoda (Westin) Wilson. Student Smith Coll., 1961-63; A.B., U. Calif.-Berkeley, 1965; M.L.S., Simmons Coll., 1968; M.B.A., Northeastern U., Boston, 1979. Librarian, Technische Univ. Berlin, Germany, 1970-71; earth and planetary scis. librarian MIT Libraries, Cambridge, 1968-70, 1971-73; personnel librarian, 1973-74, asst. dir. personnel services, 1974-76, asst. dir. pub. services, 1976-81; dir. libraries Colby Coll., Waterville, Maine, 1981—. Mem. ALA, New Eng. Assn. Coll. and Research Librarians (sec.-treas. 1983-85, pres. 1986-87), Maine Libr. Assn. (chmn. intellectual freedom com. 1984-88, OCLC Users Coun., 1988-95), Nelinet (bd. dirs. 1985-91, chair 1989-91). Office: Colby Coll Miller Libr Waterville ME 04901

MUELLER, BARBARA STEWART (BOBBIE MUELLER), youth drug use prevention specialist, volunteer; b. Weslaco, Tex., Oct. 5, 1934; d. Roy Wesley Stewart and Marjorie Eleanor (Crossley) Willis; m. Charles Paul Mueller, Sept. 5, 1957 (div. 1985); children: Kathryn Anne, John Stewart. BA, U. Tex., 1957. Owner Kid Puppets and Co., San Antonio; cons. Parent Music Resource Ctr., Washington, 1986; edn. prevention chmn. U.S. Attys. Office, San Antonio, 1989-90; prevention chmn. Mayor's Alcohol and Drug Task Force, San Antonio, 1986-88. Author: (childrens TV): Henry Blue Shoe KONO-TV San Antonio, 1957; contbr. articles to profl. publs. Sec. Alamo Heights (Tex.) Recreation Coun., 1977-78; pres. San Antonio Petroleum Aux., 1978-79; founder, pres. Community Families in Action, 1980-89; trustee Youth Alternatives, Inc., 1983-85; mem. allocation panel United Way, 1988-90; mem. alcolol and drug adv. com. N.E. Ind. Sch. Dist., 1986-91; mem. drug free schs. com. S.W. Ind. Sch. Dist., 1991-92; regional coord. Texans War on Drugs, 1988-92; vol. U.S. Dept. Justice, San Antonio, 1984-88; mem. proclamation com. Stop Tex. Epidemic, 1982; active Trinity Bapt. Ch. Recipient Yr. award Drug Awareness Ctr., San Antonio, 1984, Bexar Co. Med. Soc. Aux., San Antonio, 1984, Gov.'s Cert., Texans War on Drugs, Austin, 1982, Commendation U.S. Pres. Child Safety Partnership, Washington, 1986. Mem. Women in Communications, Inc. (hon.) (Pub. Awareness award 1984), Zeta Tau Alpha (sec., v.p., pres. San Antonio chpt. 1969-77, Nat. Merit award 1980). Avocations: genealogy, puppetry, hand embroidery, sailing, creative writing.

MUELLER, BETTY JEANNE, social work educator; b. Wichita, Kans., July 7, 1925; d. Bert C. and Clara A. (Pelton) Judkins; children—Michael J., Madelynn J. MSSW, U. Wis., Madison, 1964, PhD, 1969. Asst. prof. U. Wis., Madison, 1969-72; vis. asso. prof. Bryn Mawr (Pa.) Coll., 1971-72; asso. prof., dir. social work Cornell U., Ithaca, N.Y., 1972-78, 92-94, prof. human services studies, 1978—; nat. cons. Head Start, Follow Through, Appalachian Regional Commn., N.Y. State Office Planning Services, N.Y. State Dept. Social Services, N.Y. State Div. Mental Hygiene, Nat. Congress PTA, ILO. Author: (with H. Morgan) Social Services in Early Education, 1974, (with R. Reinoehl) Computers in Human Service Education, 1989, Determinants of Human Behavior, 1995; contbr. articles to profl. jours. Grantee HEW, 1974-76, 79-80, State of N.Y., 1975—, Israeli Jewish Agy., 1985-87, Israeli Nat. Council for Research, 1986-87; Fulbright Research award, 1990. Mem. Leadership Am., Chi Omega. Democrat. Unitarian. Home: 412 Highland Rd Ithaca NY 14850 Office: Cornell U Human Services Studies N132MVR Hall Ithaca NY 14853

MUELLER, CARL GUSTAV, JR., lawyer; b. Houston, June 30, 1929; s. Carl G. and Louise (Young) M.; m. Joanne Youngblood, Aug. 2, 1950; children—Carl Clinton, Craig Steven, Robert Loyd. BBA, U. Tex., 1951, JD, 1953. Cert. in estate planning and probate law, comml. real estate law, residential real estate law, farm and ranch real estate law, Tex. Mem., tchr. Hines Baker Bible Class; former chmn. adminstrv. bd., former chmn.bd. trustees St. Luke's Meth. Ch.; dir., sec. Retina Rsch. Found.; bd. dirs. Student Aid Found. Fellow Am. Coll. Trust and Estate Counsel; mem. Tex. Bar Assn., Houston Bar Assn., Am. Coll. Real Estate Lawyers, Tex. Acad. Probate and Trust Lawyers, Tex. Acad. Real Estate Lawyers, Houston Estate and Fin. Forum (past pres.), Houston Real Estate Lawyers Counsel. Avocations: fishing, hunting, walking, travel. Office: 17 S Briar Hollow Ln Ste 204 Houston TX 77027-2810

MUELLER, CARL RICHARD, theater arts educator, author; b. St. Louis, Oct. 7, 1931; s. Anton John and Bonita Blanche (Lacy) M. BS, Northwestern U., 1954; MA, UCLA, 1960, PhD, 1967; cert., Freie U., Berlin, 1961. Prof. theater dept. Sch. Theater, Film and Television UCLA, 1967—; dramaturg New Theatre, Inc., L.A., 1975—; cons. U. Calif. Press., 1972—. Translator plays published include Buechner: Complete Plays and Prose, 1963, Brecht: The Visions of Simone Machard, 1965, Brecht: The Measures Taken, 1977, Hauptmann: The Weavers, 1965, Hebbel: Maria Magdalena, 1962, Strindberg: A Dream Play and The Ghost Sonata, 1966, Schnitzler: La Ronde and Game of Love, 1964, Hofmannsthal: Electra, 1964, Wedekind: The Marquis of Keith, 1964, Wedekind: The Lulu Plays, 1967, Zuckmayer: The Captain of Koepenick, 1972; translator plays produced include Anon: The Puppet Play of Dr. Johannes Faustus, Hauptmann: The Beaver Coat, Schnitzler: Dr. Bernhardi, Schnitzler: Anatol, Sternheim: The Underpants, Brecht: Mother Courage, Brecht: Caucasian Chalk Circle, Brecht: The Trial of Joan of Arc, Brecht: In the Jungle of Cities, Brecht: Man is Man, Brecht: He Who Says Yes, Brecht: He Who Says No, Brecht: The Exception and the Rule, Brecht: Round Heads, Peaked Heads, Brecht: Schweyk in the Second World War, Kleist: The Broken Jug, 1992, Lessing: Nathan the Wise, 1993, Toller, The Blind Goddess, 1993, Sophokles, Elektra, 1994, Zweig, Volpone, 1995, Sternheim, The Snob, 1996; gen. editor Visual Resources, Inc., 1976—; theater editor Mankind mag., 1975-82; editor New Theater/Teatro Nuevo, 1985-87; author catalogue and slides A Visual History of European Theater Arts, 1978, A Visual History of European Experimental Theater, 1983, Greek and Roman Classical Theatre Structures and Performance Iconography, 1991, Medieval Theater and Performance Iconography, 1991, The Theater of Meyerhold, 1992, Stanislavsky and the Moscow Art Theater, 1992, The Commedia dell'Arte, 1992, Russian Scene and Costume Design, vols. 1 and 2, 1993, The Baroque Stage, 1993, 18th and 19th Cen. European Theater Structures, Performance Ionography and Costume Designs, 1994, Renaissance Theater Structures, Performance Ionography and Costume Designs, 1994, The Genius of the Russian Theatre 1900-1990, 1995, 20th Century World Theater, From Appia to Dali, 1900-50, vol. 1, 1996, 20th Century World Theater, From Mother Courage to Hair, 1951-68, vol. 2, 1996, 20th Century World Theater, From Svoboda to Hockney, 1968-91, vol. 3, 1996, The Genius of the Russian Theater, From Meyerhold to the Present, 1996, Contemporary European Experimental Theater, vol. 1, Italy and Germany, 1996, The Classical Experience: The Greek Theater and Its World, 1996, The Classical Experience: The Roman Theater and Its World, 1996; dir.: (plays) Spring's Awakening, Endangered Species, Hedda Gabler, My Body, Frankly Yours, Hamlet, Macbeth. Served with U.S. Army, 1954-56. Recipient Samuel Goldwyn Creative Writing award Goldwyn Found., 1959; Fulbright exchange grantee Berlin, 1960-61. Mem. Internat. Arthur Schnitzler Research Assn., UCLA Center for Medieval and Renaissance Studies (mem. adv. com. 1980-83). Democrat. Office: UCLA Dept Theater Sch Theater Film and TV 102 E Melnitz Box 951622 Los Angeles CA 90095-1622 *Communication has always been the primary goal of my life. The challenge of passing on to generations of new students the life sustaining ideas of human culture is formidable; the joy of searching out new ideas and methods of thought and action is a privilege of which far too few of us take proper advantage.*

MUELLER, CHARLES BARBER, surgeon, educator; b. Carlinville, Ill., Jan. 22, 1917; s. Gustav Henry and Myrtle May (Barber) M.; m. Jean Mahaffey, Sept. 7, 1940; children: Frances Ann, John Barber, Richard Carl, William Gustav. A.B., U. Ill., 1938; M.D., Washington U., St. Louis, 1942; LHD (honoris causa), Blackburn Coll., 1987. Intern, then resident in surgery Barnes Hosp., St. Louis, 1942-43, 46-51; asst. prof. Washington U. Med. Sch., 1951-56; prof. surgery, chmn. dept. State U. N.Y. Med. Sch., Syracuse, 1956-67; prof. surgery McMaster U. Med. Sch., Hamilton, Ont., Can., 1967—; chmn. dept. McMaster U. Med. Sch., 1967-72. Contbr. articles to med. jours. Served with USNR, 1943-46. Decorated Purple Heart with 2 oak leaf clusters, Bronze Star; recipient Favorite Son award So. Ill. Med. Soc., 1996; Jackson Johnson fellow, 1938-42; Rockefeller postwar asst., 1946-49; Markle scholar, 1949-54. Mem. ACS (v.p. 1987-88, Disting. Svc. award 1984), Am. Surg. Assn., Ctrl. Surg. Assn., Soc. Univ. Surgeons, Assn. Acad. Surgery, Royal Coll. Physicians and Surgeons (Duncan Graham Disting. Svc. award 1992), Phi Beta Kappa, Sigma Xi, Alpha Omega Alpha, Phi Kappa Phi. Home: 139 Dalewood Crescent, Hamilton, ON Canada L8S 4B8 Office: McMaster U, 1200 Main St W, Hamilton, ON Canada L8N 3Z5

MUELLER, CHARLES FREDERICK, radiologist, educator; b. Dayton, Ohio, May 26, 1936; s. Susan Elizabeth (Wine) W.; m. Kathe Louise Lutterbei, May 28, 1966; children: Charles Jeffrey, Theodore Martin, Kathryn Suzanne. BA in English, U. Cin., 1958, MD, 1962. Diplomate Am. Bd. Radiology, Am. Bd. Nuclear Medicine. Asst. prof. radiology U. N.Mex., Albuquerque, 1968-72, assoc. prof. radiology, 1972-74; assoc. prof. radiology Ohio State U., Columbus, 1974-79, acting chmn. dept. radiology, 1975, prof. radiology, 1979—, prof. radiology, dir. post grad. program radiology, 1980—; bd. dirs. Univ. Radiologists, Inc., Columbus, v.p., 1980-86; pres., founder Ambulatory Imaging, Inc., Columbus, 1985—; founder Am. Soc. Emergency Radiology, 1988, pres., 1993-94. Author: Emergency Radiology, 1982; contbr. articles to profl. jours. Com. chmn. Boy Scouts of Am., Columbus, 1980-84. Served to capt. USAF, 1966-68. Research grantee Ohio State U. 1975, Gen. Electric Co., 1986-88. Fellow Am. Coll. Radiologists; mem. Assn. Univ. Radiologists, Am. Roentgen Ray Soc., Radiol. Soc. N.Am., AMA, N.Mex. Soc. Radiologists (pres. 1973-74), Ohio State Radiol. Soc. (pres. 1986-87). Republican. Presbyterian. Lodges: Commandery #6, Consistory. Avocations: flying, fly fishing, hiking. Office: Ohio State Univ Hosps Dept Radiology 410 W 10th Ave Columbus OH 43210-1240

MUELLER, CHARLES WILLIAM, electric utility executive; b. Belleville, Ill., Nov. 29, 1938; s. Charles A. and Clara R. (Jorn) M.; m. Janet Therese Vernier, July 9, 1960; children: Charles R., Michael G., Craig J. BSEE, St. Louis U., 1961, MBA, 1966. Registered profl. engr., Mo., Ill. Engr. Union Electric Co., St. Louis, 1961-75, supervisory engr., 1975-77, asst. dir. corp. planning, 1977-78, treas., 1978-83, v.p. fin., 1983-88, sr. v.p. adminstrv. svcs., 1988-93; pres., CEO, 1994—; bd. dirs. Union Electric Devel. Corp., Electric Energy Inc., Regional Commerce and Growth Assn., Edison Electric Inst., Angelica Corp., United Way of Greater St. Louis, BJC Health Sys., Kiel Ctr. Corp.; dir. The Boatmen's Nat. Bank of St. Louis, Assn. of Edison Illuminating Cos., St. Louis Children's Hosp., St. Louis Sci. Ctr., Civic Progress, The Mcpl. Theatre Assn. Trustee Webster U. Mem. IEEE, Mo. Athletic Club, St. Clair Country Club, The Bogey Club, Saint Louis Club. Avocations: tennis, boating, travel. Office: Union Electric Co 1901 Chouteau Ave Saint Louis MO 63103-3003

MUELLER, EDWARD ALBERT, retired transportation engineer executive; b. Madison, Wis., May 12, 1923; s. Edward F. and Lulu (Wittl) M.; m. Margaret Wetzel, Sept. 12, 1953; children: Lynn, Karen. Student, U. Wis., 1941-43; B.C.E., Notre Dame U., 1947; cert. in traffic, Yale U., 1953; postgrad., Fla. State U., 1955-62; M.C.E., Catholic U. Am., 1967. Registered profl. engr., Fla. Project engr. Carl C. Crane, Inc., 1947-50; engr. Ammann & Whitney, Inc., Milw., 1950-52; asst. dir., dir. traffic and planning div. Fla. State Rd. Dept., Tallahassee, 1955-63; engr. traffic and ops. Hwy. Research Bd., Washington, 1963-70; sec. Fla. Dept. Transp., Tallahassee, 1970-72; exec. dir. Jacksonville (Fla.) Transp. Authority, 1972-80; mgr. transp. div. Reynolds, Smith & Hills, 1980-83; v.p. Morales and Shumer Engrs., Inc., 1983-95; occasional lectr. U. Fla., 1971-76, U. N.Fla., 1974-76. Author: Steamboating on the St. Johns, 1979, Ocklawaha River Steamboats, 1983, St. Johns River River Steamboats, 1986, Perilous Journeys, 1990, Upper Mississippi River Ratting Steamboats, 1995, Steamships of the Two Henrys, 1996; contbr. engring. articles to profl. jours. Mem. Fla. Com. of 100, 1970-72; bd. dirs. Luth. Social Svcs., Jacksonville, 1982-94, v.p., 1981-91; regional v.p. Fla.-Ga. dist. Luth. Laymen's League, 1982-92; curator Jacksonville MAritime Mus., 1990—, mem. exec. com., 1989-95, pres., 1993-95, exec. dir., 1995—. Recipient Disting. Service award Coll. Engring., U. Fla., 1975; named one of top 10 pub. works ofcls. in U.S., 1978. Mem. Southeastern Assn. State Hwy. Ofcls. (pres., v.p. 1971-72), Engrs. in Govt. (chmn., vice chmn. sec.), Fla. Engring. Soc. (pres. Northeast chpt. 1982-83, engr. of yr. Tallahassee chpt. 1972, Jacksonville chpt. 1974, award for outstanding tech. achievement 1976, outstanding svc. to engring. profession 1989), Inst. Transp. Engrs. (pres. 1977, disting. svc. award Fla. sect. 1976), Fla. Transit Assn. (pres. 1974, 75), Fla. Engring. Found. (sec. 1986-95). Lutheran. Home: 4734 Empire Ave Jacksonville FL 32207-2136

MUELLER, GERD DIETER, financial and administrative executive; b. Hannover, Germany, Nov. 12, 1936. Student, U. Munich, 1957-59; LLB, U. Cologne, Germany, 1961; LLM, Nordrhein-Westfalen, Duesseldorf, Germany, 1965. Mgr. fin. Bayer AG Leverkusen, Germany, 1965-72; sr. v.p. fin. svcs. Rhinechem Corp., N.Y.C., 1972-74; treas. Mobay Chem. Corp., Pitts., 1974-77; v.p. and treas. Mobay Corp., Pitts., 1977-83; exec. v.p. fin. Miles, Inc., Elkhart, Ind., 1983-86; exec. v.p. adminstrn. and fin. Mobay Corp., Pitts., 1986-88; exec. v.p., CFO Bayer U.S.A. Inc., Pitts., 1988-91; exec. v.p., chief adminstrv. and fin. officer Bayer Corp., Pitts., 1992—; pres. CDS Internat., N.Y.C.; bd. trustees Robert Morris Coll. Mem. Nat. Assn. Mfrs. Office: Bayer Corporation 1 Mellon Ctr 500 Grant St Pittsburgh PA 15219-2507

MUELLER, GERHARD G(OTTLOB), financial accounting standard setter; b. Eineborn, Germany, Dec. 4, 1930; came to U.S., 1952, naturalized, 1957; s. Gottlob Karl and Elisabeth Charlotte (Hossack) M.; m. Coralie George, June 7, 1958; children: Kent, Elisabeth, Jeffrey. AA, Coll. of Sequoias, 1954; BS with honors, U. Calif.-Berkeley, 1956, MBA, 1957, PhD, 1962; D Econs. (hon.), Swedish Sch. Econs. and Bus. Adminstrn., 1994. CPA, Wash. Staff accountant FMC Corp., San Jose, Calif., 1957-58; faculty dept. accounting U. Wash., Seattle, 1960-96, assoc. prof., 1963-67, prof., 1967-96, chmn. dept., 1969-78, dir. grad. profl. acctg. program, 1979-90, sr. assoc. dean, 1990-95, acting dean, 1994, Hughes M. Blake prof. internat. bus. mgmt., 1992-95, Julius A. Roller prof. acctg., 1995-96; dir. U. Wash. Acctg. Devel. Fund, Overlake Hosp. Med. Ctr., Bellevue, 1984-96, chmn. bd. trustees, 1991-93; cons. internat. tax matters U.S. Treasury Dept., 1963-68; cons. Internat. Acctg. Rsch., 1964-96; vis. prof. Cranfield Sch. Mgmt., Eng., 1973-74, U. Zurich, Switzerland, 1973-74; lectr. in field. Author: International Accounting, 1967; co-author: Introductory Financial Accounting, 3d edit., 1991, A Brief Introduction to Managerial and Social Uses of Accounting, 1975, International Accounting, 1978, 2nd edit., 1992, Accounting: An International Perspective, 1987, 3rd edit., 1994, 4th edit., 1997; editor: Readings in International Accounting, 1969, Accounting-A Book of Readings, 2d edit., 1976, A New Introduction to Accounting, 1971, A Bibliography of Internat. Accounting, 3d edit., 1973, Essentials of Multinational Accounting—An Anthology, 1979, Frontiers of International Accounting, 1986, AACSB Curriculum Internationalization Resource Guide, 1988; contbr. numerous articles to profl. jours. Expert legal witness, IRS, 1991-93. Recipient U. Wash. Disting. Teaching award, 1983, Disting. Service award, 1984; Price Waterhouse internat. accounting research fellow, 1962-64; Ford Found. fellow, 1958-59. Fellow Acad. Internat. Bus.; mem. AICPAs (internat. practice exec. com. 1972-75, exec. coun. 1987-89), Am. Acctg. Assn. (pres. 1988-89, acad. v.p. 1970-71, chmn. adv. bd. internat. acctg. sect. 1977-79, Wildman medal 1986, Nat. Outstanding Educator 1981, Disting. Internat. Lectr. in Black Africa 1987, Outstanding Internat. Acctg. Educator 1991), Fin. Execs. Inst., Wash. Soc. CPAs (pres. 1988-89, Outstanding Educator award 1985, Pub. Svc. award 1995), Acctg. Edn. Change Commn. (chmn. 1994-96), Beta Alpha Psi (Acad. Acct. of Yr. 1987), Beta Gamma Sigma (Disting. scholar 1978-79), Alpha Gamma Sigma. Home: 40 Breed's Hill Pl Wilton CT 06897-1538 Office: Fin Acctg Standards Bd 401 Merritt 7 PO Box 5116 Norwalk CT 06856-5116 *It has always been important to me to associate with people and tangible and intangible things of the highest quality. I make it a practice to set clear goals and then pursue them actively. A broad world view on all aspects of life engenders more success and happiness than special interest perspectives. I welcome change in professional matters, but seek constancy in personal and family affairs. Fate has played a role in my successes. I believe in God, Protestant ethics, and the merits of classical academic scholarship.*

MUELLER, JAMES BERNHARD, anesthesiologist, pain managememt consultant; b. Milw., Sept. 5, 1952; s. Bernhard Oscar and Perl Elizabeth (Benda) M.; m. Reba Marie Tisdale, Dec. 18, 1982; children: James Preston, Catherine Elizabeth. BS in Chemistry, Coll. Charleston, 1978; MD, Med. U. S.C., 1983. Diplomate Am. Bd. Anesthesiology, Am. Bd. Pain Medicine; added qualifications in pain mgmt. Commd. lt. USN, 1983, advanced through grades to lt. comdr., 1990; intern Naval Hosp., Portsmouth, Va., 1983-84, resident, 1986-87; fellow Naval Hosp./Med. Coll. Va., Richmond, 1986-87; staff anesthesiologist Naval Hosp., Richmond, 1987-89; resigned USN, 1991; staff anesthesiologist Julius Snyder and Assocs., Norfolk, Va., 1989-92; pvt. practice anesthesiology and pain mgmt. Irving, Tex., 1992-93, Dallas, 1993—; chief anesthesiology Med. City Hosp., Dallas, 1995-97; asst. prof. clin. anesthesiology Med. Coll. Hampton Rds., Norfolk, 1988-92, Med. Coll. Va., Richmond, 1989-92; lectr. Nurse Anesthesia Faculty Assocs., Richmond, 1989-92; med. cons. Janssen Pharmaceutica, N.J., 1989—. Contbr. book chpts. Mem. Operation Smile, The Philippines, 1988, Norfolk, 1989. Mem. Am. Soc. Anesthesiologists, Internat. Assn. for Study Pain, Soc. for Regional Anesthesia, Internat. Anesthesial Rsch. Assn., Va. Soc. Anesthesiologists (bd. dirs. 1990-92), Tex. Soc. Anesthesiologists, Tex. Med. Assn., Dallas County Med. Soc. Episcopalian. Home: 1454 Cottonwood Valley Ct Irving TX 75038 Office: 7777 Forest Ln Ste B 143 Dallas TX 75230-2508

MUELLER, JOHN ERNEST, political science educator, dance critic and historian; b. St. Paul, June 21, 1937; s. Ernst A. and Elsie E. (Schleh) M.; m. Judy A. Reader, Sept. 6, 1960; children—Karl, Karen, Susan. A.B., U. Chgo., 1960; M.A., UCLA, 1963, Ph.D., 1965. Asst. prof. polit. sci. U. Rochester, N.Y., 1965-69, assoc. prof., 1969-72, prof., 1972—, prof. film studies, 1983—, founder, dir. Dance Film Archive, 1973—; lectr. on dance in U.S., Europe, Australia, 1973—; OP-ED columnist Wall St. Jour., 1984—, L.A., Times, 1988—, N.Y. Times, 1990—; mem. dance panel NEA, 1983-85; columnist Dance Mag., 1974-82; dance critic Rochester Dem. and Chronicle, 1974-82; mem. adv. bd. Dance in Am., PBS, 1975. Author: War, Presidents and Public Opinion, 1973 (book selected as one of Fifty Books That Significantly Shaped Public Opinion Rsch. 1946-95 Am. Assn. Pub. Opinion Rsch. 1995), Dance Film Directory, 1979, Astaire Dancing: The Musical Films, 1985 (de la Torre Bueno prize 1983), Retreat From Doomsday: The Obsolescence of Major War, 1989, Policy and Opinion in the Gulf War, 1994, Quiet Cataclysm: Reflections on the Recent Transformation of World Politics, 1995; co-author: Trends in Public Opinion: A Compendium of Survey Data, 1989; editor: Approaches to Measurement, 1969; co-editor: Jour. Policy Analysis and Mgmt., 1985-89; mem. editl. bd. Pub. Opinion Quar., 1988-91; producer 12 dance films/recorded commentator on 2d soundtrack of laser disc edit. Swing Time, 1986. Grantee NSF, 1967-70, 74-75, NEH, 1972-73, 74-75, 77-78, 79-81; Guggenheim fellow, 1988. Mem. Am. Acad. Arts and Scis., Am. Polit. Sci. Assn., Dance Critics Assn. (bd. dirs. 1983-85), Am. Assn. for Public Policy and Mgmt. (editorial bd. 1985-89). Home: 246 Roslyn St Rochester NY 14619-1812 Office: U Rochester Polit Sci Dept Rochester NY 14627

MUELLER, KURT M., hotel executive. Pres. Motels Am., Des Plaines, Ill. Office: Motels America 701 Lee St Ste 1000 Des Plaines IL 60016-4555

MUELLER, LISEL, writer, poet. vis. faculty Goddard Coll., 1977-80, Warren Wilson Coll., 1983, 85-86; vis. lectr. U. Chgo., 1984. Author: Dependencies, 1965, Life of a Queen, 1970, The Private Life, 1976, Voices from the Forest, 1977, The Need to Hold Still, 1980. Recipient Pulitzer Prize for Poetry; named Disting. Writer in Residence, Wichita State U. *

MUELLER, LOIS M., psychologist; b. Milw., Nov. 30, 1943; d. Herman Gregor and Ora Emma (Dettmann) M.; BS, U. Wis.-Milw., 1965; MA, U. Tex., 1966, PhD, 1969. Cert. family mediator. Postdoctoral intern VA Hosp., Wood, Wis., 1969-71; counselor, asst. prof. So. Ill. U. Counseling Center and dept. psychology, Carbondale, 1971-72, coordinator personal counseling, asst. prof., 1972-74, counselor, asst. prof., 1974-76; individual practice clin. psychology, Carbondale, 1972-76, Clearwater, Fla., 1977-90, Port Richey, Fla., 1990—; family mediator, 1995—; mem. profl. adv. com. Mental Health Assn. Pinellas County, 1978, Alt. Human Services, 1979-80; cons. Face Learning Center, Hotline Crisis Phone Service, 1977-87; advice columnist Clearwater Sun newspaper, 1983-90; pub. speaker local TV and radio stas., 1978, 79; talk show host WPLP Radio Sta., Clearwater, 1980-83, WTKN Radio Sta., Tampa Bay, 1988-89, WPSO Radio Sta., New Port Richey, 1991. Campaign worker for Sen. George McGovern presdl. race, 1972. Lic. psychologist, Ill., Fla. Mem. APA,, Fla. Psychol. Assn., Pinellas Psychol. Assn. (founder, pres. 1978), Am. Soc. Clin. Hypnosis, Fla. Soc. Clin. Hypnosis, West Pasco C. of C., Calusa Bus. & Profl. Women. Contbr. articles to profl. jours. Office: 9501 Us Highway 19 Ste 212 Port Richey FL 34668-4641

MUELLER, MARK CHRISTOPHER, lawyer; b. Dallas, June 19, 1945; s. Herman August and Hazel Deane (Hatzenbuehler) M.; m. Linda Jane Reed. BA in Econs., So. Meth. U., 1967, MBA in Acctg., 1969, JD, 1971. Bar: Tex. 1971, U.S. Dist. Ct. (no. dist.) Tex. 1974, U.S. Tax Ct. 1974; CPA, Tex. Acct. Arthur Young & Co., Dallas, 1967-68, A.E. Krutilek, Dallas, 1968-71; pvt. practice law, Dallas, 1971—; assoc. L. Vance Stanton, Dallas, 1971-72; instr. legal writing and rsch. So. Meth. U., Dallas, 1970-71, instr. legal acctg., 1975. Leading articles editor Southwestern Law Jour., 1970-71. Mem. NRA, Tex. Bar Assn., Tex. State Rifle Assn., Tex. Soc. CPA's, Dallas Bar Assn., Sons of Am. Revolution, Sons Republic Tex., Sons of Union Vets. of Civil War, Sons Confederate Vets., Mil. Order Stars and Bars, Order of Coif, Dallas Hist. Soc., Dallas County Pioneer Assn., Beta Alpha Psi, Phi Delta Phi, Sigma Chi. Club: Rock Creek Barbeque. Lodges: Masons, Shriners, Grotto, 32d degree KCCH Scottish Rite. Home: 7310 Brennans Dr Dallas TX 75214-2804 Office: Ste 410 9401 Lyndon B Johnson Fwy Dallas TX 75243-4540

MUELLER, NANCY SCHNEIDER, retired biology educator; b. Wooster, Ohio, Mar. 8, 1933; d. Gilbert Daniel and Winifred (Porter) Schneider; m. Helmut Charles Mueller, Jan. 27, 1959; 1 child, Karl Gilbert. AB in Biology, Coll. of Wooster, 1955; MS in Zoology, U. Wis., 1957, PhD in Zoology, 1962. Instr. zoology U. Wis., Madison, 1966; asst. prof. poultry sci. and zoology N.C. State U., Raleigh, 1968-71; vis. prof. biology N.C. Ctrl. U., Durham, 1971-73, assoc. prof., 1973-79, prof., 1979-93; ret., 1993; vis. scientist U. Vienna, Austria, 1975. Contbr. articles, abstracts to profl. publs. Mem. Am. Soc. Zoologists, Am. Ornithologists Union, Cooper Ornithol. Soc., Wilson Ornithol. Soc., Wis. Acad. Sci., Arts and Letters, N.C. Acad. Sci., LWV (bd. dirs. 1988—, natural resources com. 1988—), Sigma Xi. Avocations: bird migration, conservation and environmental issues. Home: 409 Moonridge Rd Chapel Hill NC 27516-9385

MUELLER, O. THOMAS, molecular geneticist, pediatrics educator; b. Berlin, Germany, Aug. 17, 1950; arrived in U.S., 1955; s. Heinz Carl and Gertrud (Jung) M.; m. Mary Gail Craig, April 24, 1976; children: Cara Lynne, Kyle Thomas, Eric Andreas. BA, Lehigh U., 1972; PhD in biol. chemistry, Pa. State U., 1978. Diplomate: Am. Bd. Med. Genetics in Molecular and Biochemical Genetics. Postdoctoral fellow U. Colo. Med. Ctr., Denver, 1978-80; rsch. asst. Roswell Park Meml. Inst., Buffalo, N.Y., 1980-84, rsch. affiliate, 1984-87; assoc. prof. pediats. U. So. Fla., Tampa, 1987—; dir. molecular genetics All Children's Hosp., St. Petersburg, Fla., 1994—. Contbr. numerous articles to scientific jours. including Human Genetics, Am. Jour. Med. Genetics, Am. Jour. Human Genetics, Jour. Biol. Chemistry, and others. Avocations: triathlons, sailing. Home: 207 Halton Cir Seffner FL 33584-4158 Office: Dept Pathology All Children's Hosp 801 6th St S Saint Petersburg FL 33701-4816

MUELLER, PAUL HENRY, retired banker; b. N.Y.C., June 24, 1917; s. Paul Herbert and Helen (Cantwell) M.; m. Jean Bonnel Vreeland, Sept. 10, 1949; 1 child, Donald Vreeland. BS, NYU, 1940; AB, Princeton U., 1941; LittD (hon.), Heriot-Watt U., Edinburgh, Scotland, 1981; LHD (hon.), Bloomfield Coll., 1991. Page Citibank N.A., 1934; on leave, 1939-46, asst. cashier, 1947-52, asst. v.p., 1952-58, v.p., 1958-65, sr. v.p., 1965-74, chmn. credit policy com., 1974-82; chmn. Saab-Scania Am. Inc., 1982-90, Atlas Copco N.Am. Inc., 1975-93; dir. Atlas Copco AB, Stockholm, 1982-91,

Skandinaviska Enskilda Banken Corp., 1983-93, Ericson N.Am., Inc., 1986-91; entered U.S. Fgn. Svc., served in Panama, Cairo, Washington, 1941-43; asst. adminstrv. sec. UN Montary and Fin. Conf., Bretton Woods, N.H., 1944; divisional asst. Dept. State, 1946; sec. West Indian Conf., 2d session, St. Thomas, V.I., 1946; vis. lectr. U. Va., 1980—; founding chmn., sr. fellow Ctr. Internat. Banking Studies, 1977-91. Contbg. author: Offshore Lending by U.S. Commercial Banks, 1975, 81, Bank Credit, 1981, Classics in Commercial Bank Lending, 1981, Vol. II, 1985, Loan Portfolio Management, 1988, Credit Culture, 1994, Credit Risk Management, 1995; author: (with Leif H. Olsen) Credit and the Business Cycle, 1979, Learning from Lending, 1979, Credit Doctrine for Lending Officers, 1976, 81, 97, Credit Endpapers, 1982, Perspective on Credit Risk, 1988; contbr. articles to profl. jours. Trustee Bloomfield Coll., N.J., 1983-91, vice chmn., 1987-88, chmn., 1988-91, trustee emeritus; treas. Marcus Wallenberg Found. (U.S.), 1984—. Served from 2d lt. to capt. USMCR, 1944-45. Decorated Royal Order Polar Star (Sweden); recipient Alumni award Grad. Sch. Credit and Fin. Mgmt., Dartmouth Coll., Disting. Svc. award Robert Morris Assocs., award for journalistic excellence, 1991. Mem. Bankers Assn. Fgn. Trade (hon., v.p. 1976), Pilgrims, SAR, Swedish-Am. C. of C. U.S. (chmn. 1989-90, hon. dir.), Royal Econ. Soc. (U.K.), Univ. Club (N.Y.C.), Beta Gamma Sigma. Republican. Presbyterian. Home: 75 Rotary Dr Summit NJ 07901-3131

MUELLER, RICHARD WALTER, foreign service officer; b. Washington, Dec. 1, 1944; s. Walter Julius and Eleanor (Maack) M.; m. Claire McCormick, Mar. 15, 1975; children: Jonathan R., Eric R. AB, Coll. William and Mary, 1966. Joined Fgn. Svc., Dept. State, 1966; assigned Am. Embassy, Canberra, Australia, 1967-68; polit. officer Am. Embassy, Saigon, Vietnam, 1969-71; staff officer Office Sec. State, Washington, 1971-74; econ. officer U.S. Liaison Office, Beijing, Peoples Republic China, 1976-78; dep. dir. Office East-West Trade Dept. State, Washington, 1978-81, dep. dir. Office Chinese Affairs, 1981-83; chief econ. sect. Am. Consulate Gen., Hong Kong, 1983-86; dep. exec. sec. Office Sec. of State Dept. State, Washington, 1986-89, dep. asst. sec. Office Legis. Affairs, 1989-92; consul gen. Am. Consulate Gen., Hong Kong, 1993—. Office: Am Consulate General, 26 Garden Rd, Hong Kong Hong Kong

MUELLER, ROBERT KIRK, management consulting company executive; b. St. Louis, July 25, 1913; s. Edward Robert Otto and Lucille M. (Flaugher) M.; m. Jane Elizabeth Konesko, Dec. 27, 1939; children: Lucy Alison, Patricia Kirk, James Arno. BS, Washington U., St. Louis, 1934; MS, U. Mich., 1935; grad., Advanced Mgmt. Program, Harvard U., 1950. Chemist Sinclair Refining Co., East Chicago, Ind., 1935; with Monsanto Co., 1935-68, gen. mgr. plastic div., 1952-61, v.p., dir., exec. com. co., 1963-68; prodn. supt. Shawinigan Resins Corp., Springfield, 1938-40, pres., dir., 1952-61, chmn. bd., dir., 1961-63; supt. Longhorn Ordnance Works, 1942-44, plant mgr., 1944-46; indsl. research, cons., corp. exec. Arthur D. Little, Inc., 1968-88, v.p., 1973-77, chmn. bd., 1977-89; bd. dirs. Decision Resources, Inc., Waltham, Mass., Interneuron Pharms. Inc., Lexington, Mass., Arthur D. Little, Ltd., London, Bus. Ethics Found., Brookline, Mass.; chmn. faculty, lectr. Salzburg (Austria) Seminar in Am. Studies, 1970, bd. dirs., mem. exec. com., 1972-85. Author: Effective Management Through Probability Controls, 1950, Risk, Survival, and Power, 1970, The Innovation Ethnic, 1971, Board Life, Realities of Being a Corporate Director, 1974, Buzzwords: A Guide to the Language of Leadership, 1974, Metadevelopment, Beyond the Bottom Line, 1977, New Directions for Directors, Behind the Bylaws, 1977, Career Conflict, Management's Inelegant Dysfunction, 1978, Board Compass, What a Director Needs to Know in a Changing World, 1979, The Incompleat Board, The Unfolding of Corporate Governance, 1981, Behind the Boardroom Door, 1984, Corporate Networking: Building Channels of Information and Influence, 1986, Directors and Officers Guide to Advisory Boards, 1990, Boardworthiness: From a President's and Director's Perspective, 1992, Building a Power Partnership: The CEO and the Board of Directors, 1993, Anchoring Points for Corporate Directors: Obeying the Unenforceable, 1996. Trustee Cheswick Ctr., 1968-96, Colby Sawyer Coll., N.H., 1972-91, Am. Austrian Found., 1988-94. Recipient Disting. Alumnus Achievement award Washington U., 1963. Fellow AAAS, N.Y. Acad. Scis., Inst. Dirs. (London), Internat. Acad. Mgmt.; mem. AIChE, Am. Chem. Soc., Am. Mgmt. Assn. (life, mem. internat. coun.), Soc. Chem. Industry, Nat. Assn. Corp. Dirs. (bd. dirs.), Algonquin Club (Boston). Office: Arthur D Little Inc 25 Acorn Park Cambridge MA 02140-2301

MUELLER, ROBERT LOUIS, business executive; b. Denver, Aug. 25, 1927; s. George Winchester and Ruth Mabel (Cole) M.; m. Sue McCoy, July 3, 1949; children: Robert, Richard, Edward, Mark; m. Susan Galbraith, June 23, 1985. BSMechE, Yale U., 1948. Chief computer Western Geophys. Co., Mont., Wyo., Colo., Tex., 1949-50; dist. mgr. Armco Steel Corp., Colo., Ohio, N.Y., 1950-63, L.B. Foster Co., N.Y.C., 1963-66; v.p. Wheeeling Pitts. Steel Co., W.Va. and Pa., 1966-75; chmn., pres., chief exec. officer Connors Steel Co., Ala., 1975-82; pres., chief exec. officer Judson Steel Co., Calif., 1982-87; pres., COO Proler Internat., Houston, 1987-94, also bd. dirs., cons., 1994—; dir. Employee Solutions, Inc., 1995—; pres. Nueller Resources, Inc., Sedona, Ariz. Co-author: Handbook of Drainage and Construction Products, 1954. With USN, 1945-46. Mem. ASCE, Assn. Iron and Steel Engrs., Duquesne Club (Pitts.), Houston City Club, Sedona Racquet Club, Sedona 30.

MUELLER, ROBERT WILLIAM, process and instrument engineer; b. Louisville, Aug. 18, 1964; s. Harris Clinton and Elizabeth Anne (Scholz) M.; m. Marilyn Jean Williams, May 22, 1987; children: Christopher, Jaclyn. BSChemE, U. Louisville, 1986, M of Engring. in Chem. Engring., 1987. Registered profl. engr., Ky. Grad. asst. Protein Techs. Internat., Louisville, 1986-87, process engr., sr. process engr., 1989-93; sr. process and controls engr. Ballard Engring. Co., Inc., Louisville, 1993-94; process instrument engr. United Catalysts Inc., Louisville, 1994—. Mem. AICE (past local sect. chair), Instrument Soc. Am. Republican. Home: 9427 Fairground Rd Louisville KY 40291-1472 Office: United Catalysts Inc PO Box 32370 Louisville KY 40232

MUELLER, ULRICH, literature educator; b. Goeppingen, Germany, Dec. 19, 1940; arrived in Austria, 1976; s. Rudolf and Julie (Bayer) M.; m. Ursula Speiser, Oct. 6, 1967; children: Michaela, Felix. PhD, U. Tuebingen, Fed. Republic Germany, 1967; PhD Habil., U. Stuttgart, Fed. Republic Germany, 1971. Asst. U. Tuebingen, 1967-68; asst. U. Stuttgart, 1968-71, lectr., 1972-76; prof. medieval lit. U. Salzburg (Austria), 1976—. Author books on medieval and modern lit. and music; contbr. articles and essays to profl. publs. Recipient Grimm prize, 1984. Mem. Oswald-von-Wolkenstein-Gesellschaft (pres.), Gesellschaft für Interkulturelle Germanistik (pres.). Avocations: photography, performing arts. Home: Niederalm 247, A-5081 Anif Austria Office: U Salzburg, Akademiestrasse 20, A-5020 Salzburg Austria

MUELLER, WERNER HEINRICH, organic chemist, chemical engineering technology administrator; b. Aldersbach, Germany, Apr. 7, 1939; came to U.S., 1984; s. August and Rosina (Schned) M.; m. Janice Williams, Aug. 14, 1968; children: Carolyn, Alexander. BS, Tech. U. Munich, 1963, MS in Organic Chemistry, 1965, PhD in Organic Chemistry, 1967; postgrad., Temple U., 1967-68. Rsch. specialist Monsanto Co., Pensacola, Fla., 1968-72; group leader spl. chemistry Hoechst AG, Frankfurt, Germany, 1972-80, asst. to mem. bd., 1980-83; rsch. specialist div. electronic products Hoechst AG, Wiesbaden, Germany, 1983-84; asst. ops. mgr. Knapsack Works Hoechst AG, 1984-85; mgr. indsl. chemistry Am. Hoechst Corp., Coventry, R.I., 1985-88; assoc. dir. R&D adv. tech. group Hoechst Celanese, Corpus Christi, Tex., 1988-89, tech. dir. chems. group, 1989-93; dir. tech. devel. group engring., spl. chems. group Hoechst Celanese, Charlotte, N.C., 1993—; mem. indsl. vis. com. dept. chemistry and biochem. U. Tex., Austin, 1990-93. Contbr. articles to profl. jours. Mem. AAAS, Am. Chem. Soc., N.Y. Acad. Scis., Indsl. Rsch. Inst., Inc., Coun. for Chem. Rsch. Achievements include 80 patents in field of specialty chemicals, polymers, nylon intermediates, pharmaceuticals and agricultural chemicals. Office: Hoechst Celanese Corp Bldg 5200 77 Center Dr Charlotte NC 28217

MUELLER, WILLARD FRITZ, economics educator; b. Ortonville, Minn., Jan. 23, 1925; s. Fritz and Adele C. (Thormaehlen) M.; m. Shirley I. Liesch, June 26, 1948; children: Keith, Scott, Kay. B.S., U. Wis., 1950, M.S., 1951; Ph.D., Vanderbilt U., 1955. Asst. prof. U. Calif., Davis, 1954-57; prof. U. Wis., 1957-61; chief economist small bus. com. U.S. Ho. of Reps., 1961; chief economist, dir. bur. econs. FTC, 1961-68; exec. dir. President's Cabinet Com. Price Stability, 1968-69; William F. Vilas rsch. prof. agrl. econs./Law Sch. emeritus U. Wis., Madison, 1969—. Bd. editors Rev. Ind. Orgn., Antitrust Law and Econ. Rev., Antitrust Bull., Jour. Reprints for Antitrust Law and Economy. Served with USN, 1943-46. Recipient Distinguished Service award FTC, 1969. Fellow Am. Agrl. Econs. Assn.; mem. AAAS, Am. Econ. Assn., Am. Agr. Assn., Assn. Evolutionary Econs. (pres. 1974-75), Indsl. Orgn. Soc. (pres. 1989-90). Unitarian. Home: 121 Bascom Pl Madison WI 53705-3975 Office: U Wis 427 Lorch St Madison WI 53706-1513

MUELLER, WILLIAM MARTIN, former academic administrator, metallurgical engineering educator; b. Denver, Jan. 14, 1917; s. Charles Franklin M. and Nydia (Hough) Mueller; m. Kathryn C. Connor, Nov. 3, 1942; children: Kathryn Irene Ingram, Joann Elaine Goss. Met.E., Colo. Sch. Mines, 1940, M.S., 1949, D.Sc., 1952. Registered profl. engr., Colo. Metallurgist ALCOA, New Kensington, Pa., 1940-45; engr. Gates Rubber Co., 1945-47; instr. Colo. Sch. Mines, Golden, 1947-52; prof. metall. engring., dept. head Colo. Sch. Mines, 1974-79, v.p., 1979-83; staff metallurgist Dow Chem. Co., Rocky Flats, Colo., 1952-57; div. head Denver Research Inst., 1957-65; dir. edn. Am. Soc. Metals, Metals Park, Ohio, 1965-74; cons. Western Forge Corp., Colorado Springs, Colo., 1975-83; invited lectr. Beijing U., 1980; del. leader for People to People to China, 1984, to S.E. Asia, 1986, to USSR, 1990, to Russia, 1993. Author: (with Blackledge and Libowitz) Metal Hydrides, 1968, (with McCall) Microstructural Analysis, 1973; editor: Energetics in Metallurgical Phenomena, 4 vols., 1965-68, (with McCall) Metallographic Specimen Preparation, 1974; sr. editor: Advances in X-Ray Analysis, 1960-66. Recipient Waltman award Colo. Sch. Mines, 1940, Disting. Achievement award, 1972, Halliburton award, 1983. Fellow Am. Soc. Metals (life, trustee 1964-65); mem. ASTM (dir. 1980-83), AIME (life, com. chmn. 1980-83), Am. Soc. Engring. Edn., Mining and Metall. Soc. Am. Home: 14430 W Ellsworth Ave Golden CO 80401-5322 Office: Colo Sch Mines Hill Hall Golden CO 80401

MUELLER-HEUBACH, EBERHARD AUGUST, obstetrician gynecologist, medical researcher; b. Berlin, Feb. 24, 1942; came to U.S., 1968; s. Heinrich Gustav and Elisabeth (Heubach) M.; m. Cornelia Rosemarie Uffmann, Feb. 6, 1968; 1 child, Oliver Maximilian. MD, U. Cologne, 1966. Diplomate Am. Bd. Ob-Gyn. Intern U. Cologne, Germany, 1967-68, Middlesex Gen. Hosp., New Brunswick, N.J., 1968-69; rsch. fellow reproductive physiology Columbia U., N.Y.C., 1969-71; resident ob-gyn. Columbia-Presbyn. Med. Ctr., N.Y.C., 1971-74, chief resident ob-gyn., 1974-75; asst. prof. ob-gyn. U. Pitts., 1975-81, assoc. prof. ob-gyn., 1981-89; prof., chmn. dept. ob-gyn. Wake Forest U., Winston-Salem, N.C., 1989—; oral examiner Am. Bd. Ob-Gyn., Dallas, 1984—. reviewer Am. Jour. Ob-gyn., Ob-gyn., Biology Reproduction. Fellow Am. Coll. Ob-gyn. (Hoechst award 1972); mem. Soc. Gynecol. Investigation, Am. Gynecol. Obstet. Soc., Perinatal Rsch. Soc., Coun. Univ. Chairs Ob-gyn. (pres.-elect), Soc. Perinatal Obstetricians. Avocations: equestrian sports, travel. Office: Bowman Gray Sch Medicine Med Ctr Blvd Winston Salem NC 27157

MUENCH, KARL H., clinical geneticist; b. St. Louis, May 3, 1934. MD, Wash. U., St. Louis, 1960. Diplomate Am. Bd. Med. Genetics, Am. Bd. Clin. Genetics. Intern Barnes Hosp., St. Louis, 1960-61; fellow in biological chemistry Stanford U. Sch. Medicine, 1961-65; staff mem. Jackson Meml. Hosp., Miami, Fla.; prof. medicine U. Miami Sch. Medicine. Mem. AMA, Am. Chemistry Soc., Am. Coll. Med. Genetics, Am. Coll. Physicians. Office: U Miami Sch Med Div Genetic Med PO Box 16960 Miami FL 33101-6960

MUENCH, ROBERT W., bishop; b. Louisville, Dec. 28, 1942. Student, St. Joseph Sem., New Orleans, Notre Dame Sem., New Orleans, Cath. U. Ordained priest, 1968-90; ordained titular bishop Mactaris, New Orleans, 1990—; aux. bishop New Orleans, 1990—. Office: Chancery Office The Cath Ctr PO Box 18548 Erlanger KY 41018

MUESING ELLWOOD, EDITH ELIZABETH, writer, researcher, publisher, editor; b. N.Y.C., Sept. 18, 1947; d. Carl Earl and Elsbeth (Bushbeck) Muesing; m. William Adonis Ellwood, Sept. 15, 1980; children: Jeanie, Colin, Caroline. BA, Fordham U., 1969; MA, NYU, 1971. Adminstrv. asst. The English Speaking Union, N.Y.C., 1979; freelance writer, researcher The Acad. Rsch. Group, Rutherford, N.J., 1975-78, 80-82; pres. Colin-Press, Bklyn., 1984-88; editor Ellwood Editing Svc., 1990-93; writer, editor Bushkill, Pa., 1993—. Author: U.S. Democracy: Myth vs. Reality, 1985, The Alternative to Technological Culture, 1986; contbr. haiku poems and sketches to mags., newsletters and anthologies, 1979—; contbr. articles to jours., mags., tabloids and newsletters; mem. panel experts Freelance Writers Report, monthly issue. Active Nat. Trust for Hist. Preservation, Washington, 1980—, South St. Seaport Mus., N.Y.C., 1974-83, 90-93; founding mem. Nat. Mus. Women in Arts, Washington, 1985-88; mem. Environ. Def. Fund, 1973-95—, Nature Conservancy, 1986-93, Nat. Chronic Pain Outreach Assn., 1991-94; contbg. mem. Dem. Nat. Com., 1991—; founding patron Katharine Houghton Hepburn Fund, 1992, Planned Parenthood, 1989-93. Mem. Nat. Writers Assn., Internat. Women's Writing Guild, Women in Scholarly Pub. (editor column in newsletter 1990), Am. Acad. Poets (contbr.), Interstitial Cystitis Assn., Nat. Writers Union, Nat. Trust Historic Preservation. Democrat. Roman Catholic. Avocations: water colors, sketching, music, guitar, collecting country furnishing antiques. Home and Office: RR1 PML 178 Bushkill PA 18324

MUETH, JOSEPH EDWARD, lawyer; b. St. Louis, Aug. 8, 1935; s. Joseph and Marie Clare (Reher) M.; m. Ellen Agnes O'Heron, Dec. 24, 1973; children: Erin R., Patricia A. B.Chem. Engring., U. Dayton, 1957; LL.B., Georgetown U., 1960, LL.M., 1961. Bar: Calif. 1964. Practice law L.A.; ptnr. Wills, Green & Mueth, L.A., 1974-83; pvt. practice law Calif., 1983-94; of counsel Sheldon & Mak, Pasadena, Calif., 1994—; adj. prof. law U. Calif. Hastings Coll. Law, San Francisco, 1972-75; lectr. Claremont Grad. Sch., 1982—. Author: Copyrights Patents and Trademarks, 1974. Chmn. bd. Rio Hondo council Camp Fire Girls Inc., 1967-72. Mem. AAAS, Am., Los Angeles County bar assns., State Bar Calif., N.Y. Acad. Scis., L.A. Athletic Club. Home: PO Box 3369 1217 Seal Way Seal Beach CA 90740-6419 Office: 225 S Lake Ave Ste 800 Pasadena CA 91101

MUFFOLETTO, BARRY CHARLES, engineering executive; b. Buffalo, N.Y., Oct. 19, 1950; s. Vincent Hugo and Lucille Elva (Sorge) M.; m. Michelle Louise Pariso, June 16, 1978; children: Daniel, Mark. AS in Elec. Tech., Erie Cmty. Coll., Buffalo, N.Y., 1975; BET in Elec. Engring., SUNY, 1983. Prodn. supr. Wilson Greatbatch Ltd., Clarence, N.Y., 1975-76; asst. prodn. mgr., 1976-77, project engr., 1977-79, process control engr., 1979-81, mgr. Welding Tech., 1981-82, dir. Battery Engring., 1982-94, dir. Capacitor Products, 1994—. Mem. IEEE, Am. Welding Soc., Am. Soc. Metals. Republican. Avocations: golf, fishing. Office: Wilson Greatbatch Ltd 10000 Wehrle Dr Clarence NY 14031-2033

MUFFOLETTO, MARY LU, retired school program director, consultant, editor; b. Chgo., May 25, 1932; d. Anthony Joseph and Lucile (Di Giacomo) M. B in Philosophy, DePaul U., 1959; ME, U. Ill., 1967. Tchr. elem. edn. Community Cons., Palatine, Ill., 1959-65; tchr. gifted children Sch. Dist. 15, Palatine, Ill., 1965-67, curriculum supr., 1967-75; dir. gifted edn. program Sch. Dist. 15, Palatine, Ill., 1972-95; coord. state and fed. programs Sch. Dist. 15, Palatine, 1975-95; asst. prin. Sch. Dist. 15, Palatine, Ill., 1975-95, retired, 1995; assoc. prof. Nat. Coll. Edn., Evanston, Ill., 1979-95; editor Tchg. Ink, Inc., 1995—; chairperson State Bd. of Edn. Adv. Com. on Gifted Edn., Springfield, Ill., 1977-85; pres. No. Ill. Planning Commn. for Gifted, 1978-80. Editor: (tchr. activity books) Teaching Ink, 1995—. Mem. Nat. Coun. for Social Studies, Assn. for Curriculum and Supervision, Coun. for Exceptional Children, U. Ill. Alumni Assn. (pres. Champaign chpt. 1982-85, Loyalty award), Kiwanis, Phi Delta Kappa (sec. 1985-87). Home: 21302 W Brandon Rd Kildeer IL 60047-8618

MUFSON, MAURICE ALBERT, physician, educator; b. N.Y.C., July 7, 1932; s. Max and Faye M.; m. Diane Cecile Weiss, Apr. 1, 1962; children: Michael Jeffrey, Karen Andrea, Pamela Beth. AB, Bucknell U., 1953; MD, NYU, 1957. Intern Bellevue Hosp., N.Y.C., 1957-58; resident Bellevue Hosp., 1958-59; chief resident Cook County Hosp., Chgo., 1965-66; sr. surgeon USPHS Lab. Infectious Diseases, NIH, 1961-65; from asst. prof. medicine to prof. U. Ill., 1965-76; prof., chmn. dept. medicine Marshall U., 1976—; vis. scientist Karolinska Inst., 1984-85. Contbr. articles to profl. jours. Served with U.S. Navy, 1959-61. WHO grantee, 1967; recipient Meet-the-Scholar award Marshall U., 1986, Rschr. of Yr. award Sigmz Xi, Marshall U., 1989, Solomon A. Berson Alumni Achievement award in health sci. NYU Sch Medicine, 1997; co-recipient Louis Weinstein award Jour. Clin. Infectious Diseases, 1994. Fellow ACP (traveling scholar 1987, Laureate award W.Va. chpt.), Infectious Diseases Soc. Am.; mem. AMA, Soc. Exptl. Biology and Medicine, Ctrl. Soc. Clin. Rsch., So. Soc. Clin. Investigation, W.Va. State Med. Assn., Assn. Profs. Medicine (counselor 1992-95, pres.-elect 1995-96, pres. 1996-97), Alpha Omega Alpha. Office: Marshall U Sch Medicine Dept Medicine Huntington WV 25701

MUFTIC, FELICIA ANNE BOILLOT, consumer relations professional; b. Muskogee, Okla., Feb. 27, 1938; d. Lowell Francois and Geneva Margaret (Halstead) Boillot; m. Michael Muftic, Sept. 6, 1961; children: Tanya Muftic-Streicher, Theodore B., Mariana C. BA, Northwestern U., 1960. Exec. dir. Metro Dist. Atty.'s Consumer Office, Denver, 1973-79; talk show host KNUS, Denver, 1981-83; clk., recorder City and County of Denver, Colo., 1984-91; spl. projects dir. Consumer Credit Counseling, Denver, 1991-95; cons. consumer affairs pvt. practice, Denver, 1995—; pres. Muftic and Assocs., Denver, 1980-83; commr. Uniform Consumer Credit Code, Colo., 1991—. Author: Colorado Consumer Handbook, 1982. Candidate for mayor, Denver, 1979. Named Media person of Yr., NASW, Colo., 1982; recipient Outstanding Contbrn. in Consumer Affairs award Denver (Colo.) Fed. Exec. Bd., 1982. Mem. Am. Arbitration Assn. (chmn. regional dispute settlement bd. 1993-96), Inst. Internat. Edn. (bd. mem. 1980—), Rotary Internat. Democrat. Avocation: showing horses in dressage. Home and Office: 3671 S Pontiac Way Denver CO 80237-1326

MUGGERIDGE, DEREK BRIAN, dean, engineering consultant; b. Godalming, Surrey, U.K., Oct. 10, 1943; arrived in Can., 1956; s. Donald William and Vera Elvina (Jackson) M.; m. Hanny Meta Buurman, Dec. 4, 1965; children: Karen Julie, Michael Brent. BS in Aero. Engring., Calif. State Polytech. U., 1965; MASc in Aerospace Engring., U. Toronto, 1966, PhD in Aerospace Engring., 1970. Spl. lectr. U. Toronto, Ont., Can., 1971; indsl. post-doctoral fellow Fleet Mfg. Co., Fort Erie, Ont., 1970-72; from asst. prof. to prof. Meml. U. of Nfld., St. John's, 1972-93, univ. rsch. prof., 1990-93; dir. Ocean Engring. Rsch. Ctr., 1982-93; dean Okanagan U. Coll., Kelowna, B.C., Can., 1993—; pres. Offshore Design Assocs. Ltd., Portugal Cove, Nfld., 1980—; sec., ptnr. Nfld. Ocean Cons., St. John's, 1981-93; ptnr. LNF Joint Venture Ltd., St. John's, 1984-90; vis. prof. U. Victoria, B.C., 1988-89. Co-author: Ice Interaction with Offshore Structures, 1988; contbr. articles to profl. jours.; contbr. conf. articles, reports. U. Toronto Grad. fellow, 1965, Nat. Rsch. Coun. Can. Grad. fellow U. Toronto, 1966-70. Mem. Assn. Profl. Engrs. & Geoscis. of Province of B.C. and Marine Engrs. Avocations: windsurfing, sailing, skiing. Home: 16438 Carr's Landing Rd, Winfield, BC Canada V4V 1C3 Office: Okanagan Univ Coll, 3333 College Way, Kelowna, BC Canada V1V 1V7

MUGNAINI, ENRICO, neuroscience educator; b. Colle Val d'Elsa, Italy, Dec. 10, 1937; came to U.S., 1969; children: Karin E., Emiliano N.G. MD summa cum laude, U. Pisa, Italy, 1962. Microscopy lab. rsch. fellow Dept. Anatomy U. Oslo Med. Sch., 1963, asst. prof., head of electron microscopy lab., 1964-66, assoc. prof., 1967-69; prof. biobehavioral scis. and psychology, head lab. of neuromorphology U. Conn., Storrs, 1969-95; dir. inst. for neurosci. Northwestern U., Chgo., 1995—; vis. prof. Dept. Anatomy Harvard U., Boston, 1969-70; traveling lectr. Grass Found., spring 1986, fall 1990. Mng. editor USA Anatomy and Embryology Jour., 1989—; contbr. more than 150 articles to books and jours. Recipient Decennial Camillo Golgi award Acad. Nat. dei Lincei, 1981, Sen. Javits Neurosci. Rsch. Investigator award NIH, 1985-92. Mem. AAAS, Am. Assn. Anatomists, Am. Soc. Cell Biology, Internat. Brain Rsch. Orgn., Internat. Soc. Developmental Neurosci., N.Y. Acad. Scis., Norwegian Nat. Acad. Scis. and Letters, Soc. Neurosci., Cajal Club (pres. 1987-88). Office: U Northwestern Inst Neurosci 5-474 Searle Bldg 320 E Superior St Chicago IL 60611-3010

MUGRIDGE, DAVID RAYMOND, lawyer; b. Detroit, Aug. 6, 1949; s. Harry Raymond and Elizabeth Lou (Aldrich) M.; m. Sandra Lee Jackson, June 25, 1988; children: James Raymond, Sarah Lorraine. BA, U. of Ams., Puebla, Mex., 1970; MA, Santa Clara U., 1973; JD, San Joaquin Coll. of Law, 1985. Bar: Calif. 1986, U.S. Dist. Ct. (ea. dist.) Calif. 1986, U.S. Ct. Appeals (9th cir.) 1987, U.S. Supreme Ct. 1996. Staff atty. to presiding justice 5th Dist. Ct. Appeals, Fresno, Calif., 1985-87; assoc. Law Office of Nuttall, Berman, Magill, Fresno, 1987-88; pvt. practice Fresno, 1988—; tchr. Fresno City Coll., 1988-96; tchr. Spanish for legal profession, Fresno, 1994; tchr. Fresno Pacific U., 1997; arbitrator Fresno County Bar Assn., 1988-96; judge pro-tem Fresno County Juvenile Ct., 1992-97, Fresno Mcpl. Ct., 1994-97. Contbg. author: Practical Real Estate Law, 1995. Mem. ABA, Calif. Attys. for Criminal Justice, Nat. Assn. Criminal Def. Lawyers, Calif. Trial Lawyers Assn. Republican. Roman Catholic. Avocations: fishing, travel, photography, hiking.

MÜHLANGER, ERICH, ski manufacturing company executive; b. Liezen, Austria, Aug. 26, 1941; came to U.S., 1971, naturalized, 1975; s. Alois and Maria (Stückelschweiger) M.; m. Gilda V. Oliver, July 13, 1973; 1 child, Erich. Assoc. Engring., Murau Berufsschule Spl. Trade, Austria, 1959; student Inst. Tech. and Engring., Weiler Im Allgau, Germany, 1963-65. Salesman, Olin Ski Co. (Olin-Authier), Switzerland, 1965-67, mem. mktg. dept., 1967-69, svc. and mfg., 1969-71, quality control insp., Middletown, Conn., 1971-77, supr., 1977-78, gen. foreman, 1978-83, process control mgr., 1983-88; dir. mfg. Entech Corp., 1988-89; prodn. mgr. Metallizing div. Risden Corp., Thomaston, Conn., 1989-94, quality process engr., 1994—. ; pres. Bus. Consolidating Svcs. Internat., Rocky Hill, Conn., 1989—, quality control technician, 1990—; quality process request divsn., fragrance divsn., 1993—; pres. Consulting Svcs. Internat. Charter mem. Presdl. Task Force, trustee; preferred mem. of U.S. Senatorial Club. Served to cpl. Austrian Air Force, 1959-60. Mem. Screenprinting Assn. Am., Am. Mgmt. Assn., Am. Soc. for Qualtiy Control, Mgmt. Club. Roman Catholic. Home: 13 Clemens Ct Rocky Hill CT 06067-3218 Office: 60 Electric Ave Thomaston CT 06787-1617 also: Bus Cons Svcs Internat Bus Consolidating Svcs Internat Rocky Hill CT 06067

MUHLBACH, ROBERT ARTHUR, lawyer; b. Los Angeles, Apr. 13, 1946; s. Richard and Jeanette (Marcus) M.; m. Kerry Eldene Mahoney, July 26, 1986. BSME, U. Calif., Berkeley, 1967; JD, U. Calif., San Francisco, 1976; MME, Calif. State U., 1969; M in Pub. Adminstrn., U. So. Calif., 1976. Bar: Calif. 1976. Pub. defender County of Los Angeles, 1977-79; assoc. Kirtland & Packard, Los Angeles, 1979-85, ptnr., 1986—. Chmn. Santa Monica Airport Commn., Calif., 1984-87. Served to capt. USAF, 1969-73. Mem. ABA, AIAA, Internat. Assn. Def. Counsel, Am. Bd. Trial Advs. Office: Kirtland & Packard Ste 2600 1900 Avenue Of The Stars Los Angeles CA 90067-4507

MUHLBERGER, RICHARD CHARLES, former museum administrator, writer, educator; b. Engelwood, N.J., Jan. 20, 1938; s. George Albert and Margaret Bertha (Heins) M. A.A., Calif. Concordia Coll., 1958; B.A., Wayne State U., 1964; M.A. in Art History, Johns Hopkins U., 1967. Curator mus. edn. Worcester Art Mus., Mass., 1966-72; chmn. edn. Detroit Inst. Arts, 1972-75; dir. Mus. Fine Arts and George Walter Vincent Smith Art Mus., Springfield, Mass., 1976-87; vice dir. for edn. Met. Mus. Art, N.Y.C., 1987-89; dir. Knoxville (Tenn.) Mus. Art, 1990-91; adj. prof. art history Western New Eng. Coll., Springfield, Mass., 1991—; mem. adv. panel NEH, 1976-78, Mass. Council on Arts and Humanities, 1979-81; mem. policy panel, mus. program Nat. Endowment Arts, 1981-83. Author: The Bible in Art, The New Testament, 1990, The Bible in Art, The Old Testament, 1990, The Christmas Story, 1990, What Makes a Raphael a Raphael, 1993, What Make a Bruegel a Bruegel, 1993, What Makes a Rembrandt a Rembrandt, 1993, What Makes a Monet a Monet, 1993, What Makes a Degas a Degas, 1993, What Make a Van Gogh a Van Gogh, 1993, What Makes a Leonardo a Leonardo, 1994, What Makes a Goya a Goya, 1994, What Makes a Cassatt a Cassatt, 1994, What Make a Picasso a Picasso, 1994;. Woodrow Wilson fellow, 1965-66; recipient Outstanding Young Man award Greater Worcester Jaycees, 1970. Mem. Am. Assn. Museums (chmn. com. on edn. 1974-76, councilor 1988-91), New Eng. Mus. Assn. (pres. 1985-87). Home: 41 Smithfield Ct Springfield MA 01108-3129

MUHLENBRUCH, CARL W., civil engineer; b. Decatur, Ill., Nov. 21, 1915; s. Carl William and Clara (Theobald) M.; m. Agnes M. Kringel, Nov. 22, 1939; children: Phyllis Elaine (Mrs. Richard B. Wallace), Joan Carol (Mrs. Frederick W. Wenk). BCE, U. Ill., 1937, CE, 1945; MCE, Carnegie Inst. Tech., 1943; LLD, Concordia U., River Forest, Ill., 1995. Research engineer Aluminum Research Labs., Pitts., 1937-39; cons. engring., 1939-50; mem. faculty Carnegie Inst. Tech., 1939-48; assoc. prof. civil engring. Northwestern U., 1948-54; pres. TEC-SEARCH, Inc. (formerly Ednl. and Tech. Consultants Inc.), 1954-67, chmn. bd., 1967—; Pres. Profl. Centers Bldg. Corp., 1961-77. Author: Experimental Mechanics and Properties of Materials; Contbr. articles engring. publs. Treas., bd. dirs. Concordia Coll. Found.; dir. Mo. Lutheran Synod, 1965-77, vice chmn. 1977-79. Recipient Stanford E. Thompson award, 1945. Mem. Am. Econ. Devel. Coun. (cert. econ. developer), Am. Soc. Engring. Edn. (editor Ednl. Aids in Engring.), NSPE, ASCE, Sigma Xi, Tau Beta Phi, Omicron Delta Kappa. Club: University (Evanston). Lodge: Rotary (dist. gov. 1980-81, dir. service projects Ghana and the Bahamas). Home and Office: Tec-Search Inc 4071 Fairway Dr Wilmette IL 60091-1005

MUILENBURG, ROBERT HENRY, hospital administrator; b. Orange City, Iowa, Apr. 29, 1941; s. Henry W. and Anna (Vander Zwaag) M.; m. Judith Ann Gebauer, Jan. 1, 1959; children: Ronald, Eric, Matthew. B.A., U. Iowa, 1964, M.A., 1966. Adminstrv. asst. Ill. Masonic Med. Ctr., Chgo., Ill., 1966-67; asst. adminstr. Ill. Masonic Med. Ctr., Chgo, Ill, 1967-68; assoc. adminstr. Ill. Masonic Med. Ctr., Chgo., Ill., 1968-71; assoc. adminstr. U. Utah Hosp., Salt Lake City, 1971-75, adminstr., 1975-78; adminstr. U. Wash. Med. Ctr., Seattle, 1978-84; clin. assoc. prof. health services adminstrn. and planning U. Wash., Seattle, 1978—; exec. dir. U. Wash. Med. Ctr., 1984—. USPHS trainee, 1966. Fellow Am. Coll. Hosp. Adminstrs.; mem. Am. Hosp. Assn. (del. 1984-88, chmn. metro. hosp. sect. 1987, bd. dirs. 1992-94), Wash. State Hosp. Assn. (bd. dirs. 1982-84, 89-94), Seattle Area Hosp. Coun. (pres. 1983), Univ. Health System Consortium (bd. dirs. 1994—), Seattle C. of C. (bd. dirs. 1994—). Home: 10019 49th Ave NE Seattle WA 98125-8131 Office: U Wash Med Ctr RC-35 1959 NE Pacific St Seattle WA 98195-0004

MUIR, HELEN, journalist, author; b. Yonkers, N.Y., Feb. 9, 1911; d. Emmet A. and Helen T. (Flaherty) Lennehan; student public schs.; m. William Whalley Muir, Jan. 23, 1936; children: Mary Muir Burrell, William Torbert. With Yonkers Herald Statesman, 1929-30, 31-33, N.Y. Evening Post, 1930-31, N.Y. Evening Jour., 1933-34, Carl Byoir & Assos., N.Y.C., and Miami, Fla., 1934-35; syndicated columnist Universal Svc., Miami, 1935-38; columnist Miami Herald, 1941-42; children's book editor, 1949-56; women's editor Miami Daily News, 1943-44; freelance mag. writer, numerous nat. mags., 1944—; drama critic Miami News, 1960-65. Trustee Coconut Grove Libr. Assn., Friends U. Miami Libr., Friends Miami-Dade Pub. Libr.; vis. com. U. Miami Librs.; bd. dirs. Miami-Dade County Pub. Libr. System; past chmn., mem. State Libr. Adv. Coun., 1979-91, past chmn. Recipient award Delta Kappa Gamma, 1960; Fla. Libr. Assn. Trustees and Friends award, 1973, Coun. Fla. Librs. award, 1990; trustee citation ALA, 1984, Spirit of Excellence award, 1988; named to Fla. Women's Hall of Fame, 1984, Miami Centennial '96 Women's Hall of Fame. Mem. Women in Communications (Cmty. Headliner award 1973), Soc. Women Geographers (Meritorious Svc. award 1996), Author's Guild. Clubs: Florida Women's Press (award 1963); Cosmopolitan (N.Y.C.); Biscayne Bay Yacht. Author: Miami, U.S.A., 1953, 3d rev. edit., 1990, Biltmore: Beacon for Miami, 1987, 2d rev. edit., 1993, Frost In Florida: A Memoir, 1995. Home: 3855 Stewart Ave Miami FL 33133-6734

MUIR, J. DAPRAY, lawyer; b. Washington, Nov. 9, 1936; s. Brockett and Helen Cassin (Dapray) M.; m. Louise Rutherfurd Pierrepont, July 16, 1966. A.B., Williams Coll., 1958; J.D., U. Va., 1964. Bar: Md., Va., D.C. 1964, U.S. Supreme Ct. 1967. Asst. legal advisor for econ. and bus. affairs U.S. Dept. State, 1971-73; pvt. practice law, 1974—; mem. U.S. del. to Joint U.S./USSR Comml. Commn., 1972; chmn. D.C. Securities Adv. Com., 1981-84, mem. 1985-88; bd. dirs. Internat. Fed. Insts. for Advanced Study. Bd. editors Va. Law Rev, 1963-64; contbr. articles to profl. jours. Mem. bd. adv. G.W. Jour. Internat. Law & Econs., 1976-; bd. dirs. Trust Mus. Exhbns. Lt. (j.g.) USNR, 1958-61. Mem. D.C. Bar (chmn. internat. law div. 1977-78, chmn. environ., energy and natural resources div. 1982-83, Met. Club (Washington), Chevy Chase (Md.) Club. Home: 3104 Q St NW Washington DC 20007-3027 Office: 1025 Connecticut Ave NW Ste 20 Washington DC 20036

MUIR, MALCOLM, federal judge; b. Englewood, N.J., Oct. 20, 1914; s. John Merton and Sarah Elizabeth (Stabler) M.; m. Alma M. Brohard, Sept. 6, 1940 (dec. 1985); children: Malcolm, Thomas, Ann Muir Weinberg, Barbara (dec.), David Clay. B.A., Lehigh U., 1935; LL.B., Harvard U., 1938. Sole practice Williamsport, Pa., 1938-42, 45-49, 68-70; mem. firm Williamsport, 1949-68; judge U.S. Dist. Ct. (mid. dist.) Pa., 1970—. Active charitable orgns., Williamsport, 1939-70. Mem. ABA, Pa. Bar Assn. (pres.-elect 1970). Avocation: reading. Office: US Dist Ct PO Box 608 Williamsport PA 17703-0608

MUIR, PATRICIA ALLEN, educational association administrator; b. Dallas, Nov. 4, 1929; d. Jack Charleton Allen and Anna Patricia (Hovis) Allen Atchison; m. Lester Doyle Rader, Jr., Aug. 4, 1950 (dec. Sept. 1950); 1 child, Lester Doyle III; m. Perren James Muir, June 2, 1956 (div.); children: Edward John, Patricia Jane. Grad., Our Lady of Victory Coll., 1948; student, George Washington U., 1948-49, Washington Sch. for Secs., 1949-50. Traffic mgr. Am. Storage Co., Washington, 1960-69; asst. sec. Ind. Telephone Pioneer Assn., Washington, 1969-76; adminstrv. asst. ALA, Washington, 1977—, staff liaison to Fed. Librs. Round Table, 1991—, staff liaison to Armed Forces Librs. Round Table, 1991—, staff liaison to Govt. Documents Round Table, 1991—. Columnist, contbr. The Ind. Pioneer, 1969-76. V.p. Friendship House Child Devel. Ctr. Parents, Washington, 1978, pres., 1979-83; mem. parish coun. St. Peter's Cath. Ch., 1987-91, mem. edn. and spiritual devel. com., 1986—, chair, 1988-91. Mem. Ladies Ancient Order of Hibernians (state pres. 1991—, nat. budget com. 1996—). Avocations: travel, geneology, reading, writing. Home: 343 11th St SE Washington DC 20003 Office: Am Libr Assn 1301 Pennsylvania Ave NW Washington DC 20004-1701

MUIR, RUTH BROOKS, counselor, substance abuse service coordinator; b. Washington, Nov. 27, 1924; d. Charles and Adelaide Chenery (Masters) B.; m. Robert Mathew Muir, Nov. 26, 1947 (dec. Feb. 20, 1996); children: Robert Brooks, Martha Louise, Heather Sue. BA in Art, Rollins Coll., Winter Park, Fla., 1947; MA in Rehab. Counseling, U. Iowa, 1979. Cert. substance abuse counselor, Iowa. Program advisor Iowa Meml. Union, Iowa City, 1959-66; counselor, coord. Mid Eastern Coun. on Chem. Abuse, Iowa City, 1976-81; patient rep. Univ. Hosp., Iowa City, 1982-85; rsch. project interviewer dept. psychiatry, U. Iowa Coll. Medicine, 1985-88. Art exhibited at Iowa City Sr. Ctr., 1987, 92, Iowa City Art Ctr., 1989, U. Iowa Hosp., 1991, Great Midwestern Ice Cream Co., 1991, Summit St. Gallery, 1995; creator, coord. therapeutic series Taking Control, Iowa City Sr. Ctr., 1986-87. Vol. coord. art exhibits Sr. Ctr., Iowa City, 1992-94, Iowa City Arts exibitn. com., 1996, Arrowmont Sch. of Art, 1996—, Arrowmont Amb., 1996—; treas. bd. dirs. Crisis Ctr., Iowa City, 1975-77; sec. coun. elders Sr. Citizens Ctr., Iowa City, 1976-78; pres. Unitarian-Universalist Iowa City Women's Fedn., 1985; friend of U. of Iowa-Mus. Art; mem. Johnson County Arts Coun., Opera Supers, Iowa City Unitarian U.N. Envoy; fgn. rels. coun., bd. dirs. annual changing family conf. U. Iowa, 1986-92; non-govtl. rep. Earth Summit Global Forum, 1992. Mem. AAUW (state cultural rep. 1990-92, painting presented to young leader 1996), Iowa City Unitarian Soc. (mem. adult program com. 1993-94, mem. unitarian care com. 1993-96), Pi Beta Phi (pres. alumnae club 1995-97), U. Iowa Print and Drawing Study Club. Home and Office: 6 Glendale Ct Iowa City IA 52245-4430

MUIR, WARREN ROGER, chemist, toxic substances specialist; b. N.Y., 1945; s. Ernest Roger and Phyllis (Stirn) M.; m. Jo-Ann McNally; children: Amy, Douglas, Michael, Gregory, Daniel. AB in Chemistry cum laude, Amherst Coll., 1967; MS in Chemistry, Northwestern U., Evanston, Ill., 1968, PhD in Chemistry, 1971; postgrad. in epidemiology, Johns Hopkins U., 1975-77. Sr. staff mem. environ. health Council on Environ. Quality, EPA, Washington, 1971-78; dir. Office of Toxic Substances, EPA, 1978-81; pres. Hampshire Rsch. Assocs., Inc., 1981—, Hampshire Rsch. Inst., 1987—; assoc. environ. health scis. Johns Hopkins U., 1981—; rsch. prof. biology Am. U., 1985; sr. fellow INFORM, 1982-95; mem. Nat. Conf. Lawyers and Scientists, 1987-89; bd. environ. scis. & toxicology Nat. Rsch. Coun. Contbr. articles on environ. quality to profl. jours. Mem., chair several Nat. Rsch. Coun. coms.; locl coord. Children's Friendship Project for No. Ireland, 1993—, bd. dirs. 1995—. Recipient NSF Acad. award, 1966, Howard Waters Doughty prize Amherst Coll., 1967, Forris Jewett Moore fellow, 1967; comdr., 1996, officer brother Most Venerable Order of St. John, 1992; co-recipient Adminstrs.' award U.S. EPA, 1992. Mem. AAAS, Am. Chem. Soc.), Soc. Risk Analysis, Soc. Epideiol. Rsch., Sigma Xi. Home: 9426 Forest Haven Dr Alexandria VA 22309-3151

MUIR, WILLIAM KER, JR., political science educator; b. Detroit, Oct. 30, 1931; s. William Ker and Florence Taylor (Bodman) M.; m. Paulette Irene Wauters, Jan. 16, 1960; children: Kerry Macaire, Harriet Bodman. B.A., Yale U., 1954, Ph.D., 1965; J.D., U. Mich., 1958. Bar: N.Y. 1960, Conn. 1965. Instr. U. Mich. Law Sch., 1958-59; assoc. firm Davis Polk & Wardwell, N.Y.C., 1959-60; lectr. in polit. sci. Yale U., 1960-64, 65-67; from assoc. to ptnr. Tyler Cooper Grant Bowerman & Keefe, New Haven, 1964-68; prof. polit. sci. U. Calif.-Berkeley, 1968—, dept. chmn., 1980-83; speechwriter v.p. U.S., 1983-85; columnist Oakland (Calif.) Tribune, 1992-93; writer Gov. of Calif., Sacramento, 1994; sr. cons. Calif. State Assembly, Sacramento, 1975-76; cons. Oakland (Calif.) Police Dept., 1969-74; vis. prof. polit. sci. Harvard U., summers 1976, 79. Author: Prayer in the Public Schools, 1967, later republished as Law and Attitude Change, 1974, Police: Streetcorner Politicians, 1977, Legislature: California's School for Politics, 1982, The Bully Pulpit: The Presidential Leadership of Ronald Reagan, 1993. Mem. Berkeley (Calif.) Police Rev. Commn., 1981-83; chmn. New Haven Civil Liberties Coun., 1965-68; Rep. candidate Calif. State Assembly, 1996. Recipient Hadley B. Cantril Meml. award, 1979, Disting. teaching award U. Calif., Berkeley, 1974, Phi Beta Kappa No. Calif. Assoc. Excellence In Teaching award, 1994. Mem. Am. Polit. Sci. Assn. (Edward S. Corwin award 1966). Republican. Presbyterian. Home: 59 Parkside Dr Berkeley CA 94705-2409 Office: Dept Polit Sci U Calif Berkeley CA 94720

MUIR, WILLIAM LLOYD, III, academic administrator; b. Norton, Kans., Mar. 20, 1948; s. John Thomas and Rosalie June (Benton) M. BBA, Kans. State U., 1977. Asst. sec. of state State of Kans., Topeka, 1971-72, fin. adminstr. atty. gen. office, 1972-79, comptroller, gov.'s office, 1979-87; dir. econ. devel. Kans. State U., Manhattan, 1987-91, asst. to v.p., 1991—; Faculty rep., senator, Kans. State U. student govt. assn., 1992—. Bd. dirs. United Way of Riley County, 1989—, chair, 1992; mem. task force City of Manhattan/Riley County Blank Page Econ. Devel., 1989-91; trustee Kans. State U. Found., 1993—; mem. Leadership Kans., 1989. Named to Outstanding Young Men in Am., 1983, 84, 85. Mem. Friends of Cedar Crest Assn., Inc., Nat. Geog. Soc., Sierra Club, Masons, Alpha Tau Omega (nat. officer), Alpha Kappa Psi. Episcopalian. Avocations: travel, volunteer work, advising. Home: 2040 Shirley Ln Manhattan KS 66502-2059 Office: Kansas State U 122 Anderson Hall Manhattan KS 66506-0100

MUIRHEAD, VINCENT URIEL, aerospace engineer; b. Dresden, Kans., Feb. 6, 1919; s. John Hadsell and Lily Irene (McKinney) M.; m. Bobby Jo Thompson, Nov. 5, 1943; children: Rosalind, Jean, Juleigh. B.S., U.S. Naval Acad., 1941; B.S. in Aero. Engring, U.S. Naval Postgrad. Sch., 1948; Aero. Engr., Calif. Inst. Tech., 1949; postgrad., U. Ariz., 1962, 64, Okla. State U., 1963. Midshipman U.S. Navy, 1937, commd. ensign, 1941, advanced through grades to comdr., 1951; nav. officer U.S.S. White Plains, 1945-46; comdr. Fleet Aircraft Service Squad, 1951-52; with Bur. Aeros., Ft. Worth, 1953-54; comdr. Helicopter Utility Squadron I, Pacific Fleet, 1955-56; chief staff officer Comdr. Fleet Air, Philippines, 1956-58; exec. officer Naval Air Tng. Center, Memphis, 1958-61; ret., 1961; asst. prof. U. Kans., Lawrence, 1961-63; assoc. prof. aerospace engring. U. Kans., 1964-76, prof., 1976-89, prof. emeritus, 1989—, chmn. dept., 1976-88; cons. Black & Veatch (cons. engrs.), Kansas City, Mo., 1964—. Author: Introduction to Aerospace, 1972, 5th edit., 1994, Thunderstorms, Tornadoes and Building Damage, 1975. Decorated Air medal. Fellow AIAA (assoc.); mem. Am. Acad. Mechanics, Am. Soc. Engring. Edn., Tau Beta Pi, Sigma Gamma Tau. Mem. Ch. of Christ (elder 1972-96). Research on aircraft, tornado vortices, shock tubes and waves. Home: 503 Park Hill Ter Lawrence KS 66046-4841 Office: Dept Aerospace Engring Univ Kans Lawrence KS 66045

MUJICA, MARY BERNADETTE, mechanical engineer; b. Red Bank, N.J., Feb. 2, 1963; d. Patrick Peter and Linda Jean (Mohler) McCall; m. Frank Elias Mujica, Apr. 16, 1988; children: Keith Alan, Shannon Yvette, Angela Andrea, Kasey Alan. BSME summa cum laude, Bucknell U., 1985. Asst. to corp. maintenance mgr. Air Products & Chems., Allentown, Pa., 1985-86; plant maintenance engr. Air Products & Chems., Pasadena, Tex., 1986-87; prodn./quality engr. Air Products & Chems., Pasadena, 1987-88; chem. plant engr., project engr. Shell Oil/Chem., Deer Park, Tex., 1988-90, chem. plant and refinery effluent engr., 1990-92, safety/process safety mgmt. engr., 1992-93, asst. maintenance mgr., reliability engr., 1993—. Asst. leader Jr. Achievement, Allentown, 1985-86; industry sponsor Soc. Women Engrs., Allentown, 1985-86; mem. fin. com. Heritage Park Bapt. Ch., Webster, Tex., 1990-92; firefighter, mem. rescue squad Shell Emergency Response, 1990-94. Kodak scholar, 1982-85. Mem. Tau Beta Pi (sec. 1984). Avocations: cycling, rollerblading. Home: 1001 Glenshannon Ave Friendswood TX 77546-5339 Office: Shell Oil Co PO Box 100 Deer Park TX 77536-0100

MUJICA, MAURO E., architect; b. Antofagasta, Chile, Apr. 20, 1941; came to U.S., 1965, naturalized, 1970; s. Mauro Raul and Graciela (Parodi-Blayfus) M.; m. Barbara Louise Kaminar, Dec. 26, 1966; children: Lillian Louise, Mariana Ximena, Mauro Eduardo Ignacio III. BArch, MArch, Columbia U., 1971. Head designer Columbia U. Office Archtl. Planning, N.Y.C., 1966-71; project mgr. Walker, Sander, Ford & Kerr, Architects, Princeton, N.J., 1971-72; prin. Mauro E. Mujica, Architect, N.Y.C., 1972-74; dir. internat. div. Greenhorne & O'Mara, Inc., Riverdale, Md., 1974-78; ptnr. Mujica & Reddy Architects, Washington, 1978-80; prin. Mauro E. Mujica, Architect, Washington, 1980-81; ptnr. Mujica & Berlin Investment Bankers, Washington, 1982-85, Mujica Keppie Henderson Internat., Washington and Glasgow, Scotland, 1981-83, Mujica-Seifert Architects, Washington and London, 1983-87; pres., chief exec. officer The Pace Group, Washington, 1987-91; ptnr. PACE/WALSHE Internat., London and Washington. Chmn. bd. and CEO U.S. English Found., Washington, 1993—; hon. mem. Emmanuel Coll. Cambridge U., Eng., 1995; mem. adv. bd. U.S.-U.K. Fulbright Commn.

MUJUMDAR, VILAS SITARAM, structural engineer, management executive; b. Indore, India, June 26, 1941; s. Sitaram and Kamala (Kulkarni) M.; m. Ingrid M. Dietrich, Mar. 1, 1969. BScin Civil Engring., Vikram U., India, 1961; MS, U. Roorkee, India, 1962; MBA, U. Santa Clara, Calif., 1980. Registered profl. engr., U.S., Can., U.K.; registered structural engr., Calif. Design engr. U.S.D. & Co., India, 1962-65, Donovan H. Lee & Ptnrs., London, 1965-66; asst. chief engr. Francon & Spancrete Ltd., Montreal, Can., 1966-68; gen. mgr., dir. engring. Modular Constructors, Woburn, Mass., 1968-70; sr. project engr., tech. mgr. LeMessurier Assocs., Cambridge, Mass., 1970-74; v.p. Precast Systems Cons., Woburn, Mass., 1974-77; prin. structural engr. Ecodyne Corp., Santa Rosa, Calif., 1977-79; v.p. Foster Engring., Inc., San Francisco, 1979-81, 3D/Internat. Inc., Houston, 1981-85; pres. VSM Assocs., Santa Rosa, Calif., 1986-88; v.p. BSHA, Inc., San Diego, 1988-90; pres. McNamara, Salvia, Mujumdar, Inc., San Diego, 1990-92; chief of office of regulation svcs. Div. State Architect Dept. Gen. Svcs., Calif., 1992—; tchr. concrete course Calif. State U., Long Beach; mem. steering com. U.S. - Japan Seismic Rsch.; mem. Earthquake Engring. Rsch. Inst., 1994—, Bldg. Seismic Safety Coun., 1995—. Author: Concrete Design Manual, Structural Engineer Review Course; inventor pre-cast concrete bldg. systems; contbr. articles to profl. jours. Merit scholar Govt. India, 1957-62, Gold medal; recipient numerous awards. Fellow ASCE, Inst. Structural Engrs., Am. Concrete Inst.; mem. Prestressed Concrete Inst. (chmn. several Earthquake Engring. coms.), Structural Engrs. Assn. Calif. (chmn. seismology com. 1992-93), Beta Gamma Sigma (hon. bus. soc.). Home: 725 Bell Russell Way Sacramento CA 95831-4245 Office: 1300 I St Ste 800 Sacramento CA 95814-2919

MUKASEY, MICHAEL B., federal judge; b. 1941. AB, Columbia U., 1963; LLB, Yale U., 1967. Assoc. Webster Sheffield Fleishchmann Hitchcock & Brookfield, 1967-72, Patterson, Belknap, Webb & Tyler, 1976-88; asst. U.S. atty. U.S. Dist. Ct. (so. dist.) N.Y., 1972-76, dist. judge, 1988—; lectr. in law Columbia Law Sch. Contbr. articles to profl. jours. Mem. Assn. of Bar of City of N.Y. (fed. cts. com. 1979-82, communications law com. 1983-86). Office: US Dist Ct US Courthouse 500 Pearl St New York NY 10007-1316

MUKAWA, AKIO, pathology educator; b. Kanazawa, Ishikawa, Japan, June 10, 1928; s. Tatsuchiyo and Moto (Ohtsuka) M.; m. Hiroko Matsuo, May 5, 1968; children: Chisui, Yasutake. MD, U. Kanazawa, Japan, 1954, PhD, 1959. Diplomate Am. Bd. Pathology. Resident pathology Queens Hosp. Ctr., N.Y.C., 1959-63; lectr. pathology U. Kanazawa Med. Sch., 1963-67; neuropathology fellow Albert Einstein Coll. Medicine, N.Y.C., 1966-67; dir. pathology Nat. Hosp. Kanazawa, 1967-72; prof. pathology Kanazawa Med. U., Uchinada, Japan, 1972-96, emeritus prof. pathology, 1996—; cons. Mukawa Inst. Pathology, Uchinada, 1996—. Author: Autopsy Technique, 1988. Mem. Japanese Path. Soc. (trustee 1971—), Am. Soc. Clin. Pathologists (fgn. fellow 1989—). Avocation: gardening. Home and Office: Taiseidai 55 Uchinada, Ishikawa 920-02, Japan

MUKERJEE, PASUPATI, chemistry educator; b. Calcutta, India, Feb. 13, 1932; s. Nani Gopal and Probhabati (Ghosal) M.; m. Lalita Sarkar, Feb. 29, 1964. B.Sc., Calcutta U., 1949, M.Sc., 1951; Ph.D., U. So. Calif., 1957. Lectr., vis. asst. prof. U. So. Calif., 1956-57; research assoc. Brookhaven Nat. Lab., L.I., 1957-59; reader in phys. chemistry Indian Assn. Cultivation of Sci., Calcutta, 1959-64; guest scientist U. Utrecht, Holland, 1964; sr. scientist chemistry dept. U. So. Calif., 1964-66; vis. assoc. prof. U. Wis., Madison, 1966-67, prof. Sch. Pharmacy,, 1967-94, emeritus prof., 1994—; vis. prof. Indian Inst. Tech., Kharagpur, 1971-72; mem. commn. on colloid and surface chemistry Internat. Union Pure and Applied Chemistry. Contbr. articles to profl. jours.; editorial bd. Jour. Colloid and Interface Sci., 1978-80, Asian Jour. Pharm. Scis., 1978-85, Colloids and Surfaces, 1980-86. Grantee USPHS, NSF, Nat. Bur. Standards, Petroleum Research Fund. Fellow AAAS, Acad. Pharm. Scis., Am. Inst. Chemistry; mem. Am. Chem. Soc. (editorial bd. Langmuir 1985-86), Am. Pharm. Assn., Acad. Pharm. Scis., Rho Chi. Home: 5526 Varsity Hl Madison WI 53705-4652 Office: 425 N Charter St Madison WI 53706-1508

MUKHERJEE, AMIYA K, metallurgy and materials science educator. PhD, Oxford (Eng.) U., 1962. Prof. U. Calif., Davis. Recipient Alexander von Humboldt award Fed. Republic Germany, 1988, Albert Easton White Disting. Tchr. award Am. Soc. Materials, 1992, Pfeil medal and prize Inst. Materials, 1993, U. Calif. prize and citation, 1993, Anatoly Bochvar medal U. Moscow, 1996. Office: U Calif Davis Dept Chem Engring & Material Sci Davis CA 95616

MUKHERJEE, KALINATH, materials science and engineering educator, researcher; b. Calcutta, India, Feb. 19, 1932; naturalized U.S. citizen, 1966; s. Ramkrisna and Saraju Mukherjee; m. Patricia Stapleton, Aug. 20, 1959; children: Joia S., Maia S., Janam S. BS in Engring., Calcutta U., 1956; MS in Engring., U. Ill., Urbana, 1959, PhD, 1963. Metallurgist Indian Iron and Steel Co., 1956-57; rsch. asst. U. Ill., Urbana, 1957-63, rsch. assoc., instr., 1963-64; asst. prof. SUNY, Stony Brook, 1964-67; assoc. prof. Poly. Inst. Bklyn., 1967-72, prof., 1972-80; head dept. metallurgy Poly. Inst. N.Y., 1974-80; prof. Mich. State U., East Lansing, 1980—, chmn. dept., 1985—, univ. disting. prof., 1997—. Co-editor: Lasers in Metallurgy, 1982, Laser Processing of Materials, 1985, Laser Materials Processing III, 1989, Laser Materials Processing IV, 1994; eidtor: Metall./Materials Sci. Edn. yearbook, 1974—; contbr. numerous articles to profl. jours. Recipient Alumnus award Bengal Engring. Coll., India, 1989. Fellow AAAS, Am. Soc. Metals (Edn. award N.Y. chpt. 1976); mem. AIME, Am. Phys. Soc., Am. Soc. Engring. Edn., Metal Soc. N.Y., Minerals, Metals and Materials Soc. (bd. dirs. 1991-94, dir. structural materials divsn. 1991-94), Sigma Xi, Alpha Sigma Nu. Democrat. Office: Mich State U Dept Materials Sci & Mechs East Lansing MI 48824

MUKOYAMA, JAMES HIDEFUMI, JR., securities executive; b. Chgo., Aug. 3, 1944; s. Hidefumi James and Miye (Maruyama) M.; m. Kyung Ja Woo, June 20, 1971; children: Sumi Martha, Jae Thomas. BA in English, U. Ill., 1965, MA in Social Studies, 1966; honor grad. U.S. Army Inf. Sch., 1966; grad. U.S. Army Command and Gen. Staff Coll., 1979, U.S. Army War Coll., 1984. Registered prin., sr. registered options prin. Nat. Assn. Securities Dealers. Commd. 2nd. lt. U.S. Army, 1965-70; with USAR, 1970—, brig. gen., 1987-90, maj. gen., 1990-95; asst. dept. mgr. Mitsui & Co. (USA), Inc., Chgo., 1971-74; mem. Chgo. Bd. Options Exchange, 1974-75; v.p. 1st Omaha Securities, Chgo., 1975-76, Heartland Securities, Chgo., 1976-90; allied mem. N.Y. Stock Exchange, 1982-84; v.p. Lefta Advt., Chgo., 1976-90; v.p. Fleet Brokerage, Chgo., 1990-95, exec. v.p. and chief op officer Regal Discount Securities, 1995—. Mem. exec. bd. Hillside Free Meth. Ch., Evanston, Ill., 1982-93; dir. chgo. coun. Boy Scouts of America, 1993-95; trustee Nat. Japanese Am. Meml. Found., 1995—. Decorated Silver Star, Legion of Merit, Purple Heart, 3 Bronze Stars; Vietnamese Army Cross of Gallantry; Japanese Army Parachutist badge; recipient cert. of merit Korean Army, others. Mem. U. Ill. Alumni Assn. (life), Assn. U.S. Army, U.S. Army War Coll. Alumni Assn. (life), Vets. of Fgn. Wars (life), Army Res. Assn. (pres., founder 1992—), Mil. Order Purple Heart (life), Am. Legion (life), Res. Officers Assn. (life), Sr. Army Res. Comdrs. Assn. (life). Home: 4009 Tracey Ct Glenview IL 60025-2468 Office: 209 W Jackson Blvd Fl 4 Chicago IL 60606

MULARZ, THEODORE LEONARD, architect; b. Chgo., Nov. 6, 1933; s. Stanley A. and Frances (Baycar) M.; m. Ruth L. Larson, Nov. 9, 1963; children: Anne Catherine, Mark Andrew. BArch, U. Ill., 1959. Registered arch. Colo., Calif., Oreg. Prin. Theodore L. Mularz, AIA Architects, Aspen, 1963-77; v.p. Benedict-Mularz Assocs. Inc., 1978-81; prin. Theodore L. Mularz & Assocs., Aspen, 1981-90; pvt. practice, Ashland, Oreg., 1990—. Designer numerous archtl. projects including comml., indsl., religious, recreational, residential and historic restoration. Vice-chmn. Pitkin County Bd. Appeals, 1972-90, City of Aspen Bd. Appeals, 1985-90; City of Aspen Planning/Building Dept. adv. com., 1988-89; planning dir. search. com. City of Aspen, Pitkin County, 1989; mem. Colo. Bd. Examiners of Archs., 1975-85, pres., 1976-80, v.p., 1978; mem. Oreg. Bd. Examiners of Architects, 1996—; bd. dirs. Rogue Valley Symphony, Ashland, 1990-92, treas., 1991-92, chmn. fin. com., 1991-92. Served with USCGR, 1953-55. Fellow AIA (chair Southern Oreg. program com. 1994-95); mem. Nat. Coun. Archtl. Registration Bds. (profl. conduct com. 1977-78, procedures/documents com. 1978-82, chmn., 1983-84, chmn. edn. com. 1982-83, dir. 1982-84, pres. 1985-86, internat. rels. com. 1984-89, exec. com. 1984-87, mem. interprofl. coun. on registration 1984-85, pres., 1985, internat. oral exam. com. 1984-89), Colo. Soc. Architects (Cmty. Svc. award 1975), Aspen C. of C. (past dir., pres. and v.p.), Aspen Hist. Soc. (com. chmn. 1963-64), Rotary (bull. editor Ashland Lithia Springs 1994-95). Roman Catholic. Home: 793 Elkader St Ashland OR 97520-3307 Office: 585 A St Ste 2 Ashland OR 97520-2093

MULASE, MOTOHICO, mathematics educator; b. Kanazawa, Japan, Oct. 11, 1954; came to U.S., 1982; s. Ken-Ichi and Mieko (Yamamoto) M.; m. Sayuri Kamiya, Sept. 10, 1982; children: Kimihico Chris, Paul Norihico, Yurika. BS, U. Tokyo, 1978; MS, Kyoto U., 1980, DSc, 1985. Rsch. assoc. Nagoya (Japan) U., 1980-85; JMS fellow Harvard U., Cambridge, Mass., 1982-83; vis. asst. prof. SUNY, Stony Brook, 1984-85; Hedrick asst. prof. UCLA, 1985-88; asst. prof. Temple U., Phila., 1988-89; assoc. prof. U. Calif., Davis, 1989-91, prof., 1991—, vice chair dept. math., 1995—; mem. Math. Scis. Rsch. Inst., Berkeley, Calif., 1982-84, Inst. for Advanced Study, Princeton, N.J., 1988-89; vis. prof. Max-Planck Inst. for Math., Bonn, Germany, 1991-92, Kyoto U., 1993, 94, Humboldt U., Berlin, Germany, 1995, 96. Contbr. articles to profl. jours. Treas. Port of Sacramento Japanese Sch., 1990-91. Mem. Math. Soc. Japan, Am. Math. Soc. (com. on internat. affairs 1993-96). Avocation: music. Office: U Calif Dept Math Davis CA 95616

MULCAHY, CHARLES CHAMBERS, lawyer, educator; b. Milw., Oct. 5, 1937; s. Thomas Lawrence and Mary (Chambers) M.; m. Judith Ann Schweiger, June 29, 1963; children: Mary Mulcahy Muth, Meg Mulcahy Ekmark, Beth. BS, Marquette U., 1959, JD, 1962. Bar: Wis. 1962, Fla. 1987. Atty., pres. Mulcahy & Wherry, Milw., 1966-91; atty. Whyte Hirschboeck Dudek S.C., Milw., 1991—; adj. prof. Marquette U. Law Sch., Milw., 1975-90; hon. consul Belgium, Milw., 1985—; pres. Pub. Policy

Forum, 1992-94; bd. dirs. Wis. Mfrs. and Commerce, 1988-95; mem. Wis. Coun. on Mcpl. Collective Bargaining, 1993—; bd. dirs. Med. Coll. Wis., 1980—, Greater Milw. Com., 1976—. Author: Public Employer Managers Manual, 1968; co-editor: Public Employment Law , 1974, 2nd edit., 1979, 3rd. edit., 1988. County supr. Milw. County, 1964-76; pres. Milw. Tennis Classic, 1975—; chmn. War Meml. Corp., 1976-84; pres. Wis. World Trade Ctr., 1987-91 (Meritorious Svc. award 1991). With USAF, 1962-68. Recipient County Achievement award Nat. Assn. Counties, 1976; named Father of Yr. Children's Outing Assn., 1984; named to Marquette U. Athletic Hall of Fame, 1988. Mem. Milw. County Hist. Soc. (pres. 1980-81), Marquette Law Alumni Assn. (pres. 1971-72). Republican. Roman Catholic. Avocations: tennis, history, reading, travel. Home: 1820 E Fox Ln Fox Point WI 53217-2858 Office: Whyte Hirschboeck Dudek SC 111 E Wisconsin Ave Ste 2100 Milwaukee WI 53202-4809

MULCAHY, ROBERT EDWARD, management consultant; b. Cambridge, Mass., Mar. 2, 1932; s. George Frances and Hazel (Douglas) M.; m. Ethel Walworth, Nov. 14, 1953; children: Linda, Scott, Steven, Susan. B.S., Lowell Textile Inst., 1953. With Allied Chem. Corp., Morristown, N.J., 1953—; from engr. to mktg. mgr. Nat. Aniline div. Allied Corp., 1953-63, from dir. indsl. mktg. to v.p.-mktg. Fibers div., 1963-69, asst. to group v.p., corporate office, 1969, v.p. and gen. mgr.-consumer group Fabricated Products div., 1969-71, pres. Fibers div., 1971-74, group v.p., 1974-75, pres., dir., 1975-79, asst. to chmn. and dir., 1979-80; sr. assoc. The Corp. Dir., Inc., N.Y.C., 1981-83; pres. Counselors to Mgmt. Inc., 1984—.

MULCAHY, ROBERT WILLIAM, lawyer; b. Milw., Jan. 11, 1951; s. T. Larry and Mary Margaret (Chambers) M.; m. Mary M. Andrews, Aug. 3, 1974; children: Molly, Kathleen, Margaret, Michael. BS, Marquette U., 1973, JD, 1976. Staff atty. NLRB, Milw., 1976-79; ptnr. Mulcahy & Wherry, S.C., Milw., 1979-90, Michael, Best & Friedrich, Milw., 1990—; bd. dirs. WERC Coun. on Mcpl. Collective Bargaining, 1990-93. Co-author: Comparable Worth: A Negotiator's Guide, Public Sector Labor Relations in Wisconsin, Strike Prevention and Control Handbook. Bd. dirs. Milw. Repertory Theater, 1993-97, Charles Allis/Villa Terrace, 1991—; mem. St. Monica Parish Coun., 1988-96; mem. Whitefish Bay Police Commn.; divsn. chmn. United Performing Arts Fund, 1993-94. Mem. ABA, State Bar Wis. (chair labor sect. 1986-87), Milw. Bar Assn. (co-chair labor sect. 1988-95), Nat. Assn. Counties, Nat. Pub. Employers Labor Rels. Assn., Wis. Counties Assn., Indsl. Rels. Rsch. Assn., Mgmt. Resources Assn., Milw. Area Mcpl. Employers Assn. Office: Michael Best & Friedrich 100 E Wisconsin Ave Milwaukee WI 53202-4107

MULCH, ROBERT F., JR., physician; b. Quincy, Ill., June 21, 1951; s. Robert Franklin and Martha Jo (Nisi) M.; m. Barbara Ann Best, Apr. 5, 1975; children: Matthew, Luke. BS, U. Ill., 1973; MD, Rush Med. Coll., Chgo., 1977. Diplomate Am. Bd. Family Practice; cert. in geriatrics. Intern Riverside Meth. Hosp., Columbus, Ohio, 1977-78; resident in family practice Riverside Meth. Hosp., Columbus, 1978-80; family practice medicine Hillsboro, Ill., 1980—; ptnr. Springfield Clin.; asst. clin. prof. family medicine So. Ill. U., Springfield, 1981—; advisor Montgomery County Counseling Ctr.; reviewer Cen. Ill. Peer Rev. Orgn.; chmn. pharmacy and therapeutics com. Hillsboro Hosp. Sec. Hillsboro Sports Assn. Fellow Am. Acad. Family Practice; mem. Am. Geriatric Soc., Am. Heart Assn., Montgomery County unit Am. Cancer Soc. (pres.). Lutheran. Avocations: computers, boating, coaching youth baseball. Office: Hillsboro Med Ctr SC 1250 E Tremont St Hillsboro IL 62049-1912

MULCKHUYSE, JACOB JOHN, energy conservation and environmental consultant; b. Utrecht, The Netherlands, July 21, 1922; came to U.S., 1982; s. Lambertus D. and Aagje (Van Geyn) M.; m. Cornelia Jacoba Wentink, Jan. 17, 1953; children: Jacobien, Hans, Dieuwke, Linda, Marlies. MSc, U. Amsterdam (the Netherlands), 1952, PhD, 1960. Dir. Chemisch-Farmaceutische Fabriek Hamu, the Netherlands, 1951-57; tech. asst. mgr. Polak & Schwarz (now IFF), the Netherlands, 1957-60; asst. tech. mgr. Albatros Superphosphate Fabrieken, the Netherlands, 1960-61; tech. mgr. for overseas subsidiaries Verenigde Kunstmestfabrieken, the Netherlands, 1961-64, gen. mgr. process engring. dept., 1964-70; dept. head process engring. dept. Unie van Kunstmestfabrieken, the Netherlands, 1970-82; sr. chem. engr. World Bank, Washington, 1982-83, sr. cons. chem. engr., 1983-87; ind. cons. environ. engring. World Bank and several cons. firms, 1987—. Author: (with Heath and Venkataraman) The Potential for Energy Efficiency in the Fertilizer Industry, 1985, (with Gamba and Caplin) Industrial Energy Rationalization in Developing Countries and Constraints in Energy Conservation, 1990, Process Safety Analysis: Incentive for the Identification of Inherent Process Hazards, 1985, Energy Efficiency and Conservation in the Developing World, 1992; editor: Environmental Balance of the Netherlands, 1972. Mem. AIChE, Royal Dutch Chem. Soc., Fertilizer Soc. (pres. 1969-70), Internat. Inst. for Energy Conservation (bd. dirs. 1990-93), N.Y. Acad. Scis., Rotary. Avocations: philosophy, tennis, advising developing countries. Home: Watersedge 5 Broken Island Rd Palmyra VA 22963-2064

MULDAUR, DIANA CHARLTON, actress; b. N.Y.C., Aug. 19, 1938; d. Charles Edward Arrowsmith and Alice Patricia (Jones) M.; m. James Mitchell Vickery, July 26, 1969 (dec. 1979); m. Robert J. Dozier, Oct. 11, 1981. B.A., Sweet Briar Coll., 1960. Actress appearing in: Off-Broadway theatrical prodns., summer stock, Broadway plays including A Very Rich Woman, 1963-68; guest appearances on TV in maj. dramatic shows; appeared on: TV series Survivors, 1970-71, McCloud, 1971-73, Tony Randall Show, 1976, Black Beauty, 1978; star: TV series Born Free, 1974, Hizzoner, 1979, Fitz & Bones, 1980, Star Trek: The Next Generation, 1988-89; NBC miniseries and TV series A Year in the Life, 1986; TV movie Murder in Three Acts, The Return of Sam McCloud, 1989; TV series L.A. Law, 1989-91; motion picture credits include McQ, The Lawyer, The Other, One More Train to Rob, Mati, etc. Bd. dirs. Los Angeles chpt. Asthma and Allergy Found. Am.; bd. advisors Nat. Ctr. Film and Video Preservation, John F. Kennedy Ctr. Performing Arts, 1986. Recipient 13th Ann. Commendation award Am. Women in Radio and TV, 1988, Disting. Alumnae award Sweet Briar Coll., 1988. Mem. Acad. Motion Picture Arts and Scis., Screen Actors Guild (dir. 1978), Acad. TV Arts and Scis. (exec. bd., dir., pres. 1983-85), Conservation Soc. Martha's Vineyard Island. Office: The Artists Group Ltd 1930 Century Park W Ste 403 Los Angeles CA 90067-6803

MULDER, DAVID S., cardiovascular surgeon; b. Eston, Sask., Can., July 28, 1938; s. Peter and Laura (Lovie) M.; m. Norma D. Johnston, Aug. 19, 1961; children—Scott D., Lizabeth J., John C. M.D., U. Sask., 1962; M.Sc., McGill U., 1964. Intern, resident in surgery Montreal Gen. Hosp., McGill U., 1963-67; resident in cardiac surgery U. Iowa, 1967-69; surgeon-in-chief Montreal Gen. Hosp., 1977—; prof. surgery McGill U., 1979—; chmn. dept. surgery, 1993—. Contbr. articles to med. jours. Fellow Royal Coll. Surgeons Can., ACS; mem. Soc. Univ. Surgeons, Am. Assn. Surgery of Trauma, Am. Assn. Thoracic Surgery, Soc. Thoracic Surgeons. Conservative. Home: 76 Sunnyside Ave, Westmount, PQ Canada H34 1C2 Office: Montreal Gen Hosp, Room D-6-136, Montreal, PQ Canada H3G 1A4

MULDER, DONALD WILLIAM, physician, educator; b. Rehoboth, N.Mex., June 30, 1917; s. Jacob D. and Gertrude (Hofstra) M.; m. Gertrude Ellens, Feb. 22, 1943. B.A., Calvin Coll., 1940; M.D., Marquette U., 1943; M.S., U. Mich., 1946. Intern Butterworth Hosp., Grand Rapids, Mich., 1943-44; resident U. Hosp., Ann Arbor, Mich., 1944-46, Denver, 1947-49; asst. prof. medicine in neurology U. Colo., 1949-50; prof. neurology Mayo Found. Faculty, 1964—, Mayo Med. Sch., 1973—; cons. neurology Mayo Clinic, Rochester, Minn., 1950—; gov. Mayo Clinic, 1962-69, chmn. dept. neurology, 1966-71, pres. staff, 1971—, Andersen prof. neurology, 1977-83, prof. emeritus, 1983—; sci. advisor ALS. Contbr. articles on neuromuscular disease to sci. jours. Ret. capt. USNR. Recipient Disting. Alumni award Calvin Coll., 1992. Fellow A.C.P., Am. Acad. Neurology; mem. Am. Neurol. Assn. (hon.). Home: 331 75th St NW Rochester MN 55901-8868 Office: 200 1st St SW Rochester MN 55902-3008

MULDER, EDWIN GEORGE, minister, church official; b. Raymond, Minn., Mar. 25, 1929; s. Gerrit and Etta (Dresselhuis) M.; m. Luella Rozeboom, June 14, 1952; children: Timothy, Mary, Mark, Elizabeth. BA, Cen. Coll., Pella, Iowa, 1951, DD (hon.), 1979; BD, Western Theol. Sem., Holland, Mich., 1954. Ordained to ministry Ref. Ch. in Am., 1954. Pastor Reformed Ch. in Am., 1954-83, v.p. particular N.J. Synod, 1975-76, pres. particular N.J. Synod, 1976-77, v.p., then pres. Gen. Synod, 1978-80, gen. sec., 1983-94; chmn. bd. dirs. Relgion in Am. Life, 1995—; chair U.S. Ch. Leaders, 1989-94; mem. exec. com. World Alliance Reformed Chs., 1990—, Nat. Coun. Chs., 1991; mem. cen. com. World Coun. Chs., 1991-94. Trustee Cen. Coll., 1968-94. Office: Ref Ch in Am 2 Queenston Pl Rm 200 Princeton NJ 08540-3820

MULDER, PATRICIA MARIE, education educator; b. South Bend, Ind., Dec. 28, 1944; d. Ervin James and Carmen Virginia (Sheeley) Anderson; m. James R. Mulder, Dec. 27, 1964; children: Todd Alan, Scott Robert. BA, Western Mich. U., 1967. Freelance writer, photographer Berrien Springs, Mich., 1980—; tchr. Eau Claire (Mich.) Pub. Schs., 1969-70; staff writer, sales rep. Jour. Era, Berrien Springs, 1979-81; sales rep. Berrien County Record, Buchana, Mich., 1981-82; account exec. WHFB Radio Palladium Pub. Co., St. Joseph, Mich., 1982-86; substitute tchr. Berrien County Intermediate Dist., 1986-89; instr. Southwestern Mich. Coll., Dowagiac, 1989-96; cons. Writing Ctr. Southwestern Mich. Coll., 1996—. Editor The Positive Image newsletter, 1980—, The F Stop, 1982-90; author: Poetry Anthologies, 1989—; staff writer Decision Point, 1988-89; newsletter editor Fernwood Nature Photographers, 1980—. Ofcl. photographer Ind. and Internat. Spl. Olympics, Notre Dame, 1986. Named Emerging Artist Ind. Coun. for the Arts, 1989, Honor award Southwestern Coun. of Camera Clubs, 1988, Photographer of the Yr. Berrien County Photographic Artists, 1987, 90. Mem. AAUW, Nat. Authors Registry, Meth. Profl. Women (sec. 1990—), Berrien County Artists (v.p. 1986), Berrien County Photographic Artists (v.p. 1984), Southwestern Mich. Coun. Camera Clubs, Berrien Springs Camrea Club (v.p. 1980—). Methodist. Avocations: writing, photography, oil painting, watercolor painting. Home: 10252 Castner Dr Berrien Springs MI 49103-9602 Office: Southwestern Mich Coll 58900 Cherry Grove Rd # 316L Dowagiac MI 49047-9726

MULDOON, BRIAN, lawyer; b. Phila., Oct. 7, 1947; s. Joseph Patrick and Isabella K. (O'Flynn) M.; m. Andrea K. Bloom, Apr. 1, 1984; 1 child, Lily Bloom. BA, Lafayette Coll., 1969; postgrad., U. Pa., 1969; JD, Temple U., 1978. Bar: Colo. 1978, U.S. Dist. Ct. Colo. 1978, U.S. Ct. Appeals (10th cir.) 1978. Law clk. to justice Colo. Supreme Ct., Denver, 1978-79; assoc. Holland & Hart, Denver, 1979-84, ptnr., 1984—; mem. Colo. Grievance Hearing Bd., 1983—. Contbg. author: Bloom, Lender Liability, Practice and Prevention, 1989. Mem. ABA, Assn. Trial Lawyers Am., Colo. Bar Assn., Colo. Trial Lawyers Assn., Denver Bar Assn. (chmn. subcom. on alternative dispute resolution 1985). Avocations: basketball, cycling, mountain climbing. Home: 337 Emerson St Denver CO 80218-3705 Office: Holland & Hart 555 17th St Ste 2900 Denver CO 80202-5555

MULDOON, FRANCIS CREIGHTON, Canadian federal judge; b. Winnipeg, Manitoba, Canada, Aug. 3, 1930; s. William John and Laura Grace (Meredith) M.; m. M. Lucille Shirtliff, Aug. 6, 1955; 2 children. BA, U. Manitoba, 1952, LLB, 1956. Cert. barrister, solicitor, notary pub. Lawyer Monnin, Grafton, Deniset & Co., Winnipeg, Man., 1956-70; chmn. Manitoba Law Reform Commn., Winnipeg, 1970-77; v.p. Law Reform Commn. Can., Ottawa, 1977-78, pres., 1978-83; judge Fed. Ct. Can., Ottawa, 1983—, Ct. Martial Appeal Ct., Ottawa, 1983—; Bencher Law Soc. Manitoba, Winnipeg, 1968-71. Contbr. articles to profl. jours. President Children Aid Soc. Winnipeg, 1969-70, Manitoba Medico-Legal Soc., Winnipeg, 1973-77. Lt. Can. Army, 1952-60. Disting. Svc. Manitoba Bar Assn., 1987; hon. mem. Bar U.S. Ct. Milit. Appeals, 1991. Mem. Med. Legal Soc. Ottawa-Carleton (co-founder), St. Paul's Coll. (hon.). Roman Catholic. Avocations: reading, bicycling, public speaking. Office: Fed Ct Can, Kent & Wellington Sts, Ottawa, ON Canada K1A 0H9

MULDOON, PAUL, creative writing educator, poet; b. Portadown, No. Ireland, 1951; came to U.S., 1987; BA in English Lang. and Lit., Queen's U., Belfast, No. Ireland, 1973. Prodr. arts programs radio BBC No. Ireland, 1973-78, sr. prodr. arts programs radio, 1978-85, TV prodr., 1985-86; Judith E. Wilson vis. fellow Cambridge U., 1986-87; creative writing fellow U. East Anglia, 1987; writer-in-residence 92d St. Y, N.Y.C., 198; Roberta Holloway lectr. U. Calif., Berkeley, 1989; lectr. Princeton (N.J.) U., 1990—, prof., 1995—, dir. creative writing program, 1993—; part-time tchr. writing divsn. Sch. of Arts, Columbia U., 1987-88; part-time tchr. creative writing program Princeton U., 1987-88; vis. prof. U. Mass., Amherst, 1989-90. Author: (poetry) Knowing My Place, 1971, New Weather, 1973, Spirit of Dawn, 1975, Mules, 1977, Immram, 1980, Why Brownlee Left, 1980, Out of Siberia, 1982, Quoof, 1983, Selected Poems 1968-83, 1986, Meeting the British, 1987, Madoc: A Mystery, 1990, Incantata, 1994, The Prince of the Quotidian, 1994, The Annals of Chile, 1994, others, (opera libretto) Shining Brow, 1993, (TV play) Monkeys, 1989, (translation from Irish) The Astrakhan Cloak, 1993, (children's book) The O-O's Party, 1981; editor: (poetry) The Scrake of Dawn, 1979, The Faber Book of Contemporary Irish Poetry, 1986, The Essential Byron, 1989; contbr. to anthologies. Recipient Eric Gregory award, 1972, Sir Geoffrey Faber Meml. award, 1980, 91, T.S. Eliot prize, 1994, Acad. award in lit. Am. Acad. Arts and Letters, 1996; John Simon Guggenheim Meml. fellow, 1990. Fellow Royal Soc. Lit.; mem. Aosdana. Office: Princeton Univ Creative Writing Program Princeton NJ 08544

MULDOON, ROBERT JOSEPH, JR., lawyer; b. Somerville, Mass., Nov. 16, 1936; s. Robert Joseph and Catherine Eileen (Hurley) M.; m. Barbara Joyce Mooney, Aug. 24, 1968; children: Andrew Robert, Catherine Lane, Timothy John. A.B., Boston Coll., 1960, MA, 1961, LL.B., 1965. Bar: Mass. 1965, U.S. Tax Ct 1966, U.S. Supreme Ct 1970. Law clk. Supreme Jud. Ct. Mass., 1965-66; assoc. Withington, Cross, Park & Groden, Boston, 1966-71; ptnr. Withington, Cross, Park & Groden, 1972-82, Sherin and Lodgen, LLP, Boston, 1982—; mem. Bd. Bar Examiners Mass.; chmn. Nat. Conf. Bar Examiners, 1985-86; prs. Mass. Continuing Legal Edn., Inc., 1992-94. Trustee Boston Coll. H.S., 1990-96, chmn. bd. trustees, 1995-96. Fellow Am. Coll. Trial Lawyers; mem. ABA, Am. Law Inst., Boston Bar Assn., Curtis Club. Office: Sherin and Lodgen LLP 100 Summer St Boston MA 02110-2106

MULDOON, THOMAS LYMAN, writer; b. Sioux Falls, S.D., Apr. 23, 1945; s. Lyman Thomas and Margaret Mary (Wallace) M.; m. Kathryn Lee Harmon, June 30, 1973; m. Kathryn Muldoon. B in Polit. Sci., Merrimack Coll., 1967; MS in Mass. Comm., Fla. State U., 1973, MA in English, 1994. Bur. chief Palm Beach Post, 1970; gen. reporter Daytona Beach News-Jour., 1973; contract editor Frankfurt, Germany, 1973-74; reporter North Dade County bur. Miami Herald, 1977-78; journalist Nat. Enquirer, 1978-89; travel editor Petite Mag., 1992; tchr. journalism, TV journalism, cinema, TV prodn. Fla. State U., 1971-73. Contract writer: Football Little Big Leaguers, 1990, More Baseball Little Big Leaguers, 1991; freelance writer newspapers and mags.; appearances on local TV shows; interviewee nat. programs; producer TV programs for local ednl. TV; scriptwriter Future Shock; screenwriter 4 movie scripts. Polit. press sec. Mayor Kevin White, Boston, 1974-75; pub. affairs dir. Boston Community Schs., 1975; campaign pres sec. State Rep. Joseph Timilty, 1975; pub. affairs dir. Barry U., Miami, 1976-77; sports info. dir. Quantico Marines football and basketball programs, 1968. With USMC, 1968-70, Vietnam.

MULDROW, TRESSIE WRIGHT, psychologist; b. Marietta, Ga., Feb. 1, 1941; d. Festus Blanton and Louise Williams Wright Summers; BA, Bennett Coll., 1962; MS, Howard U., 1965, PhD, 1976; 1 child, DeJuan Denise. Research asst. W.C. Allen Corp., Washington, 1966-68; personnel research psychologist Dept. Navy, Washington, 1968-73, Office Personnel Mgmt., CSC, 1973-79; chief, adv. council on alternative selection procedures Office Personnel Mgmt., Washington, 1979-86, chief consultative services, 1986-91, chief multidimentional assessment br., 1992-94; spl. advisor Office of Diversity, 1994-95; leader Bus. Re-engring. Task Force, 1995-96, acting divsn. dir. Assessment Svcs. Divsn., 1996—; lectr. Howard U., 1979. Mem. Washington Inter-Alumni council United Negro Coll. Fund, 1970—, pres., 1988-92; trustee Bennett Coll., vice chmn., 1985-90; v.p. Family Life Ctr. Br., Boys and Girls Clubs of Washington, 1984-90. Named Alumnae of Yr., United Negro Coll. Fund, 1971, Outstanding Alumnae, Morehouse Coll., 1978, Outstanding Alumnae, Bennett Coll., 1993, Outstanding Woman, Am. Bus. Women Assn., 1994; recipient UNCF Individual Achievement award, 1985, Exemplary Performance award UNCF, 1996. Mem. Bennett Coll. Alumnae Assn. (nat. pres. 1978-85, 93-97, Alumnae of Yr. award 1987), Am. Psychol. Assn., Delta Sigma Theta. Presbyterian. Contbr. articles to profl. publs. Office: 1900 E St NW Washington DC 20415-0001

MULFORD, DAVID CAMPBELL, finance company executive; b. Rockford, Ill., June 27, 1937; s. Robert Lewis Mulford and Theodora Henie Countryman; m. Jeannie Louise Simmons, Oct. 19, 1985; children: Robert Ian, Edward Maitland. BA in Econs. cum laude, Lawrence U., 1959; postgrad., U. Cape Town, South Africa, 1960; MA in Polit. Sci., Boston U., 1962; PhD, Oxford U., 1966; LLD (hon.), Lawrence U., 1984. White House fellow Dept. Treas., Washington, 1965-66, under asst. sec. internat. affairs, 1984-89; dir. White Weld & Co., N.Y.C. and London, 1966-74; sr. investment advisor Saudi Arabian Monetary Agy., Riyadh, 1974-84; asst. sec. internat. affairs Dept. of Treas., 1984-89; under sec. treasury internat. affairs U.S. Treas. Dept., Washington, 1989-92; vice chmn. CS First Boston, N.Y.C., 1992-93; chmn., CEO Credit Suisse First Boston, London, 1993—. Author: Northern Rhodesia General Election, 1962, Zambia: The Politics of Independence, 1967. Trustee Lawrence U., 1986—. Decorated Legion d'Honneur, 1990; recipient Order of May Merit Pres. Argentina, 1993, Officers Cross of the Medal of Merit Pres. Poland, 1995; Rotary Internat. fellow Oxford U., U. Cape Town, 1961-62, Woodrow Wilson fellow Boston U., Oxford U., 1962, Ford Found. fellow St. Anthony's Coll., Oxford, 1963-65; named Disting. Alumni Boston U., 1992; Disting. scholar Ctr. Strategic and Internat. Studies, Washington, 1993—. Mem. Coun. Fgn. Rels., White House Fellows Assn., Metropolian Club (Washington). Republican. Home: 301 S St Asaph St Alexandria VA 22314-3745 Office: Credit Suisse 1st Boston, One Cabot Square, London E14 4QJ, England

MULHOLLAN, DANIEL PATRICK, research director; b. Louisville, July 12, 1944; s. Daniel Paul and Martha Nell (McClain) M.; m. Julianne Finlayson, June 3, 1967; children: Willa Joanna Mulhollan Neale, Erin Finlayson, Julianne Gertrude. BA with honors, Coll. of St. Thomas, St. Paul, 1966; PhD, Georgetown U., 1969. Sr. specialist Am. nat. govt., chief govt. divsn. Congrl. Rsch. Svc., Libr. of Congress, Washington, 1991, dir., 1994—; acting dep. libr. Libr. of Congress, Washington, 1992-94; cons. Georgetown U., Washington, 1990-92; bd. visitors Sch. Info. Scis., U. Pitts., 1995. Contbr. essay to book and articles to profl. jours. GE scholar, 1962; NDEA fellow, 1966. Mem. ALA, Am. Polit. Sci. Assn., Midwest Polit. Sci. Assn. Roman Catholic. Office: Library of Congress Congressional Rsch Svc 1st & Independence Ave SE Washington DC 20540

MULHOLLAN, PAIGE ELLIOTT, academic administrator emeritus; b. Ft. Smith, Ark., Dec. 10, 1934; s. Paige Elwood and Ruth Dickinson (Berry) M.; m. Mary Bess Flack, July 8, 1956; children: Paige E. Jr., Kelly V. BBA, U. Ark., 1956, MA in History, 1962; PhD in History, U. Tex., 1966. From asst. to assoc. prof. history U. Ark., Fayetteville, 1963-70; assoc. dean arts and scis. Kans. State U., Manhattan, 1970-73; dean arts and scis. U. Okla., Norman, 1973-78; provost, v.p. acad. affairs Ariz. State U., Tempe, 1978-81, exec. v.p., 1981-85; pres. Wright State U., Dayton, Ohio, 1985-94; ret., 1994; cons. examiner North Ctrl. Assn., Chgo., 1972-94; chair Interuniv. Coun. Ohio, 1993-94. Mem. Okla. Humanities Com., 1974-77, chmn., 1975-77; bd. dirs. Pub. Sta. WPTD-TV, Dayton Art Inst., Miami Valley Rsch. Found., Coastal Discovery Mus., Hilton Head Island, 1995—; mem. adv. com. Air Force ROTC, 1989-93. 1st lt. U.S. Army, 1956-57. Mem. nat. Assn. State Univs. and Land Grant Colls. (commn. on arts and scis. 1973-78, chmn. 1974-76), Am. Assn. State Colls. and Univs. (bd. dirs. 1991-92), Coun. Colls. Arts and Scis. (bd. dirs. 1976-78, sec.-treas. 1977-78), Dayton Area C. of C., Ohio Coll. Assn. (pres. 1989), Rotary (Hilton Head bd. dirs. 1996—). Avocations: sailing, birdwatching. Home: 24 Big Woods Dr Hilton Head Island SC 29926

MULHOLLAND, BARBARA ANN, school director; b. Pendleton, Oreg., Sept. 27, 1951; d. John Gordon Bensel and D. Lois (Carey) Bohlender; m. James Noel McCann, Aug. 6, 1982 (div. 1987); children: Sage, David; m. Harold Palmer Mulholland, Jan. 1, 1997; stepchildren: Kelli, Hoag, Ryan. Cert., Fla. Inst. Tech., 1969; BA, Western Wash. U., 1974; cert. in manual interpretation, Blue Mountain Coll., 1987; MS in Edn., Lewis and Clark Coll., 1988. Cert. tchr., Wyo.; cert. interpretor, domestic violence counselor, Oreg.; cert. fed. contract specialist, Wash. Housing and employment commr. City of Bellingham, Wash., 1970-74; contract specialist U.S. Forest Svc., Seattle, 1974-76; ind. contract cons. Seattle and Tacoma, 1976-78; loan specialist Island Savs. and Loan, Mt. Vernon, Wash., 1978-80; materials specialist Umatilla County Edn. Svc. Dist., Pendleton, Oreg., 1980-87; specialist for hearing impaired Fremont County Sch. Dist. 1, Lander, Wyo., 1988-91; instr. sign lang. and edn. Cen. Wyo. Coll., Riverton, 1988—; dir. Title VII and V programs and curriculum Wyo. Indian Schs., Ethete, 1991-96; ednl. cons., 1992—; mem. north ctrl. accreditation team Wyo. Indian Schs., 1991-96; English instr. Blue Mountain C.C.; drama dir. Lander Dist. 1. Author, illustrator sign lang. edn. materials. Mem. Fairhaven com. Fairhaven Coll., Bellingham, 1970-71, advocate, 1970-72; mem. Bellingham Landlords' Assn., 1970-74; rep. Pioneer Sq. Assn., Seattle, 1976-78; vol. counselor Domestic Violence Svcs., Pendleton, Oreg., 1982-87; vol. sign lang. interpreter various orgns., Wyo., 1988—. Named Outstanding Vol., Domestic Violence Svcs., Pendleton, 1986; recipient Exceptional Svc. award United Way Umatilla County, 1986, Outstanding Instr. award Ctrl. Wyo. Coll., 1990. Mem. ASCD, NEA, Nat. Indian Edn. Assn., Nat. Assn. Bilingual Edn., Wyo. Speech and Hearing Assn., Conv. Am. Instrs. of Deaf, Ethete Ednl. Assn., Wyo. Edn. Assn. Avocations: singing, guitar, needlework, drawing, cooking. Office: PO Box 1110 Riverton WY 82501-1110

MULHOLLAND, JOHN HENRY, physician, educator; b. Charlottesville, Va., May 24, 1932; s. Henry B. and Elizabeth (Brown) M.; m. Anne P.C., Sept. 1, 1956; children: Anne Randol, David Bearden, Jeffrey Bolton. BA, U. Va., 1955; MD, Johns Hopkins U., 1959. Diplomate Am. Bd. Internal Medicine; lic. physician, N.C., Md. Asst. prof. medicine Johns Hopkins U., Balt., 1966—; co-dir. nurse clin. assoc. program Union Meml. Hosp., Balt., 1972-90, gen. med. attending, 1968—, infections disease cons., 1968—; asst. prof. medicine U. Md., Balt., 1976-85, clin. assoc. prof. medicine, 1985—; assoc. med. dir. BCBS, 1993-96; assoc. head dir., v.p. Doctors Health Sys., Md., 1995—. Author: Bugs and Drugs-Antibiotic Guidelines, 1970; contbr. numerous articles to profl. jours. Fellow ACP (chmn. arrangements com. 1975—, nat. chmn. group ins. programs subcom. 1986-87, membership policy com. 1986-87, postgrad. courses suybcom. 1990, Gov. Md. region 1984-88, Gov. of Yr. award 1988); mem. ASIM, Am. Clin. and Climatological Assn. (v.p. 1990), Md. Soc. Internal Medicine (mem. coun. 1976-78, 82-86), Md. Hosp. Edn. Inst. (mem. steering com. quality assurance/risk mgmt. project 1980—, mem. quality assurance/risk mgmt. tech. adv. com. 1985—), Balt. City Med. Soc. (nominating com. 1984—, chmn. liaison com. 1991—), Infectious Disease Soc. Am. Home: 1317 Walnut Hill Ln Baltimore MD 21204 Office: Doctors Health 10451 Millrun Cir Owings Mills MD 21117

MULHOLLAND, KENNETH LEO, JR., health care facility administrator; b. Chgo., July 16, 1943; s. Kenneth Leo Sr. and Virginia May (Groble) M.; m. Betty Lou Bledsoe, Feb. 18, 1978; children: Arthur G. Pope (dec.), Michelle Rae Pope Nobles. BS, Loyola U., 1969; M in Mgmt., Northwestern U., 1974. RN. Nurse VA Med. Ctr., Chgo., 1970-72, health care adminstr. tng., 1972-74; assoc. dir. tng. VA Med. Ctr., Lexington, Ky., 1976-77; assoc. dir. VA Med. Ctr., Muskogee, Okla., 1977-79; assoc. dir. VA Med. Ctr., Knoxville, Iowa, 1979-81, acting dir., 1981; assoc. dir. VA Med. Ctr., Richmond, Va., 1981-83; dir. VA Med. Ctr., Bronx, N.Y., 1983-85, Memphis, 1985—. Pres. Memphis Area Fed. Exec. Assn., 1988—; bd. dirs. Memphis chpt. ARC, 1985—, Health Sys. Agy., Memphis, 1985-87; mem. citizen's adv. bd. St. Joseph's Hosp., 1993—; mem. dean's adv. bd. Grad. Sch. Bus., Christian Brothers U., 1996—. Recipient Presdl. Rank award for meritorious executive, 1989. Mem. Memphis Area Fed. Exec. Assn. Lodge: Rotary. Home: 2024 Thorncroft Dr Germantown TN 38138-4017 Office: VA Med Ctr 1030 Jefferson Ave Memphis TN 38104-2127

MULHOLLAND, S. GRANT, urologist; b. Springfield, Ohio, Sept. 1, 1936; s. Stanford Wallace and Florence Kathryn (Grant) M.; m. Ruth Fritz, Aug. 21, 1961; children: David, Michael, Mark, John. BS, Dickinson Coll., Carlisle, Pa., 1958; MD, Temple U., 1962; MS, U. Va., 1966. Intern Reading (Pa.) Hosp., 1962-63; resident in surgery Tampa (Fla.) Gen. Hosp., 1963-64; resident in urology U. Va., Charlottesville, 1964-68; urologist U.S. Naval Hosp., St. Albans, N.Y., 1968-70; epidemiologist Grad. Hosp. of U. Pa., Phila., 1971-74, asst. urologist, 1970-77; chief urologist Phila. Gen. Hosp., 1972-77; asst. surgeon Children's Hosp. Phila., 1974-77; urologist Hosp. U. Pa., Phila., 1974-77; chmn. dept. urology Thomas Jefferson U. Hosp., Phila., 1977—; cons. VA Ctr., Phila., 1974-77; cons. urologist Lankenau Hosp.,

Bryn Mawr Hosp., VA Hosp., Wilmington, Del., 1977—. Author: Urinary Tract Infection, 1990, Bladder Infections, 1991, (with others) Prostate Cancer, 1992, Antibiotic Treatment, 1996. Lt. comdr. USN, 1968-70. Grantee NIH, Jefferson U., 1989. Fellow ACS; mem. Am. Urol. Assn. (pres. 1988-89), Phila. Urol. Assn. (pres. 1988-89), Internat. Soc. Urology, AMA, Phila. Country Club (Gladwyne, Pa.). Republican. Avocations: golf, fishing, skiing. Home: 1050 Sentry Ln Gladwyne PA 19035-1009 Office: Jefferson Med Coll 1025 Walnut St # 1112 Philadelphia PA 19107-5001

MULHOLLAND, TERENCE JOHN (TERRY MULHOLLAND), professional baseball player; b. Uniontown, Pa., Mar. 9, 1963. Student, Marietta Coll. Pitcher San Francisco Giants, 1984-89, Phila. Phillies, 1989-94, N.Y. Yankees, 1994-96, Seattle Mariners, 1996, Chgo. Cubs, 1997—; mem. Nat. League All-Star Team, 1993. Pitched no-hit victory, Aug. 15, 1990. Office: Chgo Cubs 1060 W Addison St Chicago IL 60613-4397*

MULICH, STEVE FRANCIS, safety engineer; b. Kansas City, Mo., Apr. 23, 1934; s. Stephen Francis and Mary Margret (Mish) M.; m. m. Apr. 5, 1974 (div.); children: Michael Francis, Mischelle Marie, Merko Mathew, Cherie Regina, Michael Klaus, Gary John, Josette Marie. BS in Gen. Sci., U. Notre Dame, 1956. Phys. chemist high altitude combustion Army Rocket and Guided Missile Agy., Huntsville, Ala., 1957-59; ballistics facility mgr. Aerojet Gen. Corp., Sacramento, 1960-65; chief engr. minute man penetration aids MB Assoc., Bollinger Canyon, Calif., 1968-72; lab mgr. hazardous materials and ballistics Martin Marietta, Waterton, Colo., 1966-75; plant mgr. smog sampler collectors mfg. Gen. Tex. Corp., Santa Clara, Calif., 1976-77; chief engr. auto airbag plant mgr. Talley Industries, Mesa, Ariz., 1978-84; prin. engr., engring. unit mgr. high energy test labs. FMC Corp., Mpls., 1984-95; v.p. ops. NEI Corp., Rock Island, Ill., 1995-96; COO Mulich Marine & Engring., Mpls., 1996—. Author: Solid Rocket Technology, 1967; inventor stun gun, combustion augemented plasma gun, semiconductor initiator. With U.S. Army, 1957-59. Recipient Acad. Achievement award Bausch & Lomb, Kenosha, Wis., 1952. Mem. IEEE, AIAA (assoc.), Am. Def. Preparedness Assn., Navy League. Avocations: skiing, sailing, climbing, camping, hiking. Home: 1325 104th Pl NE Minneapolis MN 55434-3620 Office: Mulich Marine & Engirng 1988 Sheridan Ave S Minneapolis MN 55405-2211

MULKEY, CHARLES ERIC, environmental engineer; b. Sweetwater, Tenn., Jan. 27, 1955; s. Charles Franklin and Margaret Elizabeth (Autry) M. BA in Natural Scis., Johns Hopkins U., 1976; MS in Environ. Engring., U. Del., 1978. Registered profl. engr., Tenn.; cert. hazardous materials mgr.; diplomate Am. Acad. Environ. Engrs. Environ. engr. II TVA Water Quality Dept., Chattanooga, 1978-79, environ. engr. III, 1979-81, environ. engr. IV, 1981-87; environ. engr. IV TVA Watts Bar Nuclear Plant, Spring City, Tenn., 1987-88, sr. environ. engr. Watts Bar Nuclear Plant, 1988-90; sr. environ. engr. PAI Corp., Oak Ridge, Tenn., 1990, Oak Ridge Nat. Lab., 1990—. Author tech. reports in field; contbr. articles to profl. jours. Publicity chmn. Chattanooga Engrs. Week, 1983-87. Maj. USAFR, 1994—. Recipient Davis fellowship U. Del., Newark, 1976-77, state scholarship, State of Md., Annapolis, 1972-76. Fellow ASCE; mem. NSPE (Nat. Publicity award 1984), Tenn. Soc. Profl. Engrs. (state dir. 1990-91, pres. Chattanooga chpt. 1989-90, v.p. 1988-89, sec. 1987-88, treas. 1986-87, young engrs. chmn. 1984-86), Water Environ. Fedn., Am. Acad. Hazardous Materials Mgrs., Res. Officers Assn. (life), Air Force Assn. (life), Chattanooga Engrs. Club, U.S. Triathlon Fedn., U.S. Masters Swimming, Mensa. Republican. Presbyterian. Avocations: triathlons, masters swimming. Office: Oak Ridge Nat Lab MS 6049 Bldg 2001 Oak Ridge TN 37831-6049

MULKEY, JACK CLARENDON, library director; b. Shreveport, La., Oct. 31, 1939; s. Jack Youmans and Hilda Lillian (Beatty) M.; m. Mary Lynn Shepherd, Jan. 30, 1971; 1 child, Mary Clarendon. B.A., Centenary Coll., 1961; postgrad. (Rotary scholar), U. Dijon, France, 1961-62, Duke U. Law Sch., 1962-63; M.S., La. State U., 1969. Jr. exec. Lykes Bros. S.S. Co., 1964-66; asst. dir. admissions Centenary Coll. of La., 1966-67; head reference services and acquisitions Shreveport Pub. Library, 1968-71; dir. Green Gold Library System of N.W. La., 1971-73; mgmt. cons. Miss. Library Commn., 1973-74, asst. dir., 1974-76, dir., 1976-78; dir. Jackson Met. Library System, 1978-85; assoc. dir. Ark. State Library, 1986—; adj. prof. U. So. Miss. Grad. Sch. Library Sci., 1979—; treas., bd. dirs. Southeastern Library Network (SOLINET), 1985-86; cons. in field; mem. White House Conf. Taskforce on Libraries and Info. Services, 1980—. Chmn. Miss. Govs. Conf. on Libraries, 1979; chmn. Miss. delegation White House Conf. on Libraries, 1979; hon. del. White House Conf. on Librs., 1991. Served with USAF, 1963-64. Mem. ALA (chmn. state libr. agy. sect. 1995-97), Southeastern Libr. Assn., Miss. Libr. Assn. (pres. 1981-82), Ark. Libr. Assn. (exec. bd. dirs. 1994-96), Chief Officers of State Libr. Agys., Phi Alpha Delta, Beta Phi Mu, Omicron Delta Kappa, Phi Kappa Phi. Episcopalian. Home: 1805 Martha Dr Little Rock AR 72212-3840 Office: 1 Capitol Mall Little Rock AR 72201-1049

MULKEY, SHARON RENEE, gerontology nurse; b. Miles City, Mont., Apr. 14, 1954; d. Otto and Elvera Marie (Haglof) Neuhardt; m. Monty W. Mulkey, Oct. 9, 1976; children: Levi, Candice, Shane. BS in Nursing, Mont. State U., 1976. RN, Calif. Staff nurse, charge nurse VA Hosp., Miles City, Mont., 1976-77; staff nurse obstetrics labor and delivery Munster (Ind.) Cmty. Hosp., 1982-83; nurse mgr. Thousand Oaks Health Care, 1986-88; unit mgr. rehab. Semi Valley (Calif.) Adventist Hosp., 1988-89, DON TCU, 1989-91; DON Pleasant Valley Hosp. Extended Care Vacility and Neuro Ctr., 1991-93; dir. nurses Victoria Care Ctr., Ventura, Calif., 1993—; clin. supr. Procare Home Health, Oxnard, Calif., 1996-97. Mem. ANA, Nat. Gerontol. Nursing Assn., Internat. Platform Assn., Alpha Tau Delta (pres. 1973-75), Phi Kappa Phi. Home: 3461 Pembridge St Thousand Oaks CA 91360-4565

MULL, GALE W., lawyer; b. Hillsdale, Mich., Sept. 8, 1945; s. Wayne E. and Vivien M. (Bavin) M.; m. Holly Ann Allen, Aug. 2, 1969 (div. Nov. 1983); 1 child, Carter B.; m. Jeanne Anne Haughey, Aug. 18, 1985. BA, Mich. State U., 1967; MA in Sociology, Ind. U., 1969; JD, Emory U., 1972. Bar: Ga. 1972, U.S. Dist. Ct. (no. dist.) Ga. 1972, U.S. Ct. Appeals (5th cir.) 1973, U.S. Ct. Appeals (11th cir.) 1981. Instr. sociology Clemson (S.C.) U., 1968-69, Spelman Coll., Atlanta, 1969-70; pvt. practice, Atlanta, 1972-75; ptnr. Mull & Sweet, Atlanta, 1975-81; pres. Gale W. Mull, P.C., Atlanta, 1981—; bd. dirs. BOND Community Fed. Credit Union, Atlanta, 1975-81; directing atty. Emory Student Legal Services, Atlanta, 1975-91; Sociology instr. Clemson U., Clemson, S.C., 1968-69, Spelman Coll., Atlanta, Ga., 1969-70. Pres. Inman Park Restoration, Inc., Atlanta, 1972-74, BASS Orgn. for Neighborhood Devel., Inc., 1974-78; mem. Housing Appeals Bd., Atlanta, 1982-88; mem. Mayor's Task Force on Prostitution, 1984-86; bd. dirs. ACLU Ga., 1981-92, sec. bd. dirs., 1983-85, cooperating atty., 1972—; vestry St. John's Episcopal Ch., 1992—; bd. dirs. St. John's Episcopal Day Sch., 1992—. Mem. ABA, Ga. Bar Assn., Atlanta Bar Assn., Lawyers Club Atlanta. Clubs: East Lake Country; Quail Unltd. (bd. dirs., sec. 1984-86). Office: 990 Edgewood Ave NE Atlanta GA 30307-2581

MULLALEY, ROBERT CHARLES, manufacturing company executive; b. Marion, Iowa, Dec. 31, 1926; s. Harold C. and Blanche A. (McGuire) M.; m. Josephine E. Fiala, Apr. 23, 1949; children: Maureen, Kathleen, Mary, Daniel, Michael, Susan. BA, U. Iowa, 1949, JD, 1951. Bar: Iowa 1951, Tex. 1976. With Collins Radio Co., Richardson, Tex., 1951-75; v.p. adminstrn. Collins Radio Co., 1970-71, sr. v.p., 1971-75; also adv. dir.; v.p. Avantek, Inc., Santa Clara, Calif., 1976-82; bd. dirs. Celeritek, Inc. Author: History of the Mullaleys: A Twelve Hundred Year Journey from County Galway to Iowa, 1993. With USNR, 1945-46. Mem. Tex. Bar Assn., Phi Kappa Theta. Home: 710 Rose Ln Los Altos CA 94024-4146

MULLALLY, PIERCE HARRY, retired steel company executive; b. Cleve., Oct. 6, 1918; s. Pierce Harry and Laura (Lynch) M.; student U. Western Ont., 1935; B.S., John Carroll U., 1939; M.D., St. Louis U., 1943; m. Mary Eileen Murphy, Feb. 22, 1943; children—Mary Kathleen, Pierce Harry. Intern, St. Vincent Charity Hosp., Cleve., 1943, resident in surgery, 1944, 47-50, staff surgeon, 1951-62, head peripheral vascular surgery, 1963-76, dir. med. edn., 1967-73, dir. dept. surgery, 1968-75, trustee, 1977-86 ; plant physician Republic Steel Corp., Cleve., 1952-68, med. dir., 1968-76, corp. dir. occupational medicine, 1976-84; cons. LTV Steel Co., 1984-86; med. dir., chmn. med. adv. bd. Ohio Health Choice Plan Inc. Vice-chmn. Cleve. Clinic-Charity Hosp. Com. Surg. Residency Tng., 1970-78; health com. Bituminous Coal Operators Assn.; trustee Wood Hudson Cancer Research Labs., Inc., 1984—; bd. dirs. Phoenix Theatre Ensemble, 1982-86. Served to capt. U.S. Army, 1944-46; PTO. Diplomate Am. Bd. Surgery. Fellow ACS, Am. Coll. Angiology; mem. Am. Iron and Steel Inst. (chmn. health com. 1977-79), Am. Acad. Occupational Medicine, Am., Ohio occupational med. assns., Acad. Medicine, Cleve. (dir. 1969-72), Cleve. Surg. Soc., Western Res. Med. Dirs., Soc. Clin. Vascular Surgery. Roman Catholic. Clubs: Cleve. Skating, Cleve. Playhouse, Serra. Home: 2285 Harcourt Dr Cleveland OH 44106-4614

MULLAN, DONALD WILLIAM, bishop; b. Galt, Ont., Apr. 26, 1937; s. William James and Lillian Maude (Sachs) M.; m. Cathy Templeman. P-residing bishop Christ Cath. Ch. Internat.; pastor Cathedral of St. Luke, Niagara Falls, Ont. Editor (mag.) The St. Luke Mag. Trustee Bd. Edn., Preston, Ont., 1962-68, Waterloo County, Ont., 1969-70, Wellington County, Ont., 1971-72. Mem. Order of Noble Companions of the Swan (prelate), Moose. *

MULLAN, FITZHUGH, public health physician; b. Tampa, Fla., July 22, 1942; s. Hugh and Mariquita (Macmanus) M.; m. Judith Wentworth, June 9, 1968; children: Meghan Elizabeth, Jason Michael, Caitlin Patricia. BA, Harvard U., 1964; MD, U. Chgo., 1968; DSc, U. Osteo. Medicine, 1993; LHD, Coll. Osteo. Medicine Pacific, 1993. Intern Jacobi Hosp., Bronx, 1968-70; resident Lincoln Hosp., Bronx, 1970-72; physician Nat. Health Svc. Corps., Santa Fe, N.Mex., 1972-75; dir. Nat. Health Svc. Corps, Rockville, Md., 1977-81; scholar-in-residence Inst. Medicine, Washington, 1981-82; sr. med. officer NIH, Bethesda, Md., 1982-84; sec. for health and environment State of N.Mex., Santa Fe, 1984-85; assoc. prof. Johns Hopkins Sch. Hygiene and Pub. Health, Balt., 1986-88; dir. pub. health history project Office of Surgeon Gen., Rockville, 1988-90; dir. bur. health professions USPHS, Rockville, 1990-96; contbr. editor Health Affairs, Bethesda, 1996—. Author: White Coat, Clenched Fist: The Political Education of an American Physician, 1976, Vital Signs: A Young Doctor's Struggle With Cancer, 1983, Plagues and Politics: The Story of the United States Public Health Service, 1989; contbr. articles to profl. jours. Fellow Am. Acad. Pediatrics; mem. AMA, Am. Pub. Health Assn., Am. Assn. for History of Medicine, Inst. of Medicine of the Nat. Acad. of Sci. Office: Health Affairs 7500 Old Georgetown Rd Ste 600 Bethesda MD 20814-6133

MULLAN, JOHN FRANCIS (SEAN MULLAN), neurosurgeon, educator; b. County Derry, Northern Ireland, May 17, 1925; came to U.S., 1955; naturalized, 1962; s. John and Mary Catharine Ann (Gilmartin) M.; m. Vivian C. Dunn, June 3, 1959; children: Joan Claire, John Charles, Brian Francis. MB, BCh, BAO, Queen's U., Belfast, Northern Ireland, 1947, DSc (hon.), 1976; postgrad., McGill U., 1953-55. Diplomate Am. Bd. Neurol. Surgery. Trainee gen. surgery Royal Victoria Hosp., Belfast, 1947-50, trainee in neurosurgery, 1951-53; trainee gen. surgery Guy's Hosp. and Middlesex Hosp., London, 1950-51, Montreal Neurosurg. Inst., Que., Can., 1955; asst. prof. neurol. surgery U. Chgo., 1955-61, assoc. prof., 1961-63, prof., 1963—, John Harper Seeley prof., chmn. dept., 1967—, dir. Brain Rsch. Inst., 1970-84. Author: Neurosurgery for Students, 1961; contbr. over 150 articles to profl. jours.; mem. editorial bd. Jour. Neurosurgery, 1974-84, Archives of Neurology, 1976-87. Recipient Olivecrona medal Karolinska Inst., 1976, Wilder Penfield medal Can. Neurosurg. Soc., 1979, Jamieson medal Australian and New Zealand Neurosurg. Soc., 1980. Fellow ACS, Royal Coll. Surgeons; mem. Soc. Neurol. Surgeons (past pres.), Acad. Neurol. Surgery, Am. Assn. Neurol. Surgeons, Am. Neurol. Assn., Cen. Neurosurg. Soc., Chgo. Neurol. Soc., World Fedn. of Neurosurg. Socs. (sec. 1989-93, hon. pres. 1993—). Roman Catholic. Conductor of research on vascular diseases of the brain, pain, head injury. Avocations: walnut tree farming, gardening. Office: U Chgo Med Ctr 5841 S Maryland Ave Chicago IL 60637-1463

MULLANAX, MILTON GREG, lawyer; b. Galveston, Tex., Mar. 16, 1962; s. Milton Gayle and Sharon Kay (Sanders) M.; m. Susan Lynn Griebe, Apr. 19, 1986; 1 child, Adrienne Irene. BA in History, U. Tex., Arlington, 1987; JD, U. Pacific, 1991. Bar: Calif., 1991, Nev., 1992, Tex., 1993, Colo., 1993, Minn., 1994, D.C., 1993; U.S. Dist. Ct. (ea. dist.) Calif. 1991, U.S. Dist. Ct. Nev., 1993, U.S. Dist. Ct. (no. dist.) Tex. 1996. Congrl. intern U.S. Rep. Richard K. Armey, Arlington, Tex., 1985; senate aide U.S. Sen. Phil Gramm, Dallas, 1985-86; legis. aide State Rep. Kent Grusendorf, Austin, Tex., 1987; law clk. Criminal Divsn. U.S. Atty.'s, Sacramento, 1989-90; legal researcher Nev. Atty. Gen., Carson City, 1991-92, dep. atty. gen., 1992-94; pvt. practice Fort Worth, Tex., 1995—. Vol. Reagan/Bush 1984, Dallas/Ft. Worth, 1984, Rep. Nat. Conv., Dallas, 1984, Armey for Congress, Arlington, 1984, Vol. Lawyers of Washoe County, Reno, Nev., 1993-94. Mem. ABA, ATLA, Tarrant County Bar Assn. Avocations: sports, politics, reading, shortwave radio. Office: 111 N Houston St Ste 205 Fort Worth TX 76102-2000

MULLANE, DENIS FRANCIS, insurance executive; b. Astoria, N.Y., Aug. 28, 1930; s. Patrick F. and Margaret (O'Neill) M.; m. Kathryn Mullman, June 28, 1952; children: Gerard, Kevin, Denise. BS in Mil. Engring, U.S. Mil. Acad., 1952; LHD (hon.), U. Conn., 1988, St. Joseph's Coll., 1990; LLD (hon.), U. Hartford, 1993, Trinity Coll., Hartford, Conn., 1995; MS in Fin. Svcs., The Am. Coll., Bryn Mawr, Pa., 1995. CLU. With Conn. Mut. Life Ins. Co., Hartford, 1956—, v.p., 1969-72, sr. v.p., 1972-74, exec. v.p., 1974-76, pres., 1977—, chief exec. officer, 1983-85, chmn., chief exec. officer, 1985-90; chief exec. officer, pres. Conn. Mut. Life Ins. Co., 1990-93; chmn. Mullane Enterprises, Inc., Hartford, Conn., 1994—; with Mullane Enterprises, West Hartford, Conn., 1994—; bd. dirs. Conn. Natural Gas Co.; chmn. The Am. Coll., Bryn Mawr, Pa., 1993-96; chmn. joint planning com. Am. Coll. and Am. Soc. CLU/ChFC, 1996—. Dir. U.S. Chamber, 1991-95. 1st lt. C.E., U.S. Army, 1952-56. Recipient John Newton Russell award, 1987, Knight of St. Gregory award. Mem. Am. Soc. Corp. Execs., Nat. Assn. Life Underwriters, Assn. Grads. U.S. Mil. Acad. (pres. 1989-93). Republican. Roman Catholic. Office: Mullane Enterprises Inc 29 S Main St West Hartford CT 06107-2420

MULLANE, JOHN FRANCIS, pharmaceutical company executive; b. N.Y.C., Mar. 10, 1937; s. John Gerard and Rita Ann (Hoben) M.; m. Ruth Ann Cecka, Nov. 17, 1962; children—Rosemarie, Michael, Kathleen, Therese, Thomas. M.D., SUNY, 1963, Ph.D., 1968; J.D., Fordham U., 1977. Bar: N.Y. 1978, D.C. 1979. Assoc. med. dir. Ayerst Labs. div. Am. Home Products Corp., N.Y.C., 1973-75, dir. clin. research, 1975-76, v.p. clin., 1977, v.p. sci., 1978-82, sr. v.p., 1982, exec. v.p., 1983-88; pres. Mullane Health Care Cons., N.Y.C., 1989—; dir. drug devel. DuPont Med. Products, Wilmington, Del., 1990; sr. v.p. DuPont-Merck, Wilmington, 1991-94; exec. v.p. Amylin Pharms., 1994-96. Contbr. articles to profl. jours. Served to lt. col. U.S. Army, 1970-73. Recipient Upjohn Achievement award, 1970; N.Y. Heart Assn. Crawford-Maynard fellow, 1966-68. Fellow Am. Coll. Clin. Pharmacology; mem. ABA, Am. Soc. Clin. Pharmacology and Therapeutics, Am. Assn. Study of Liver Diseases, Lomas Sante Fe Country Club, Tara Golf and Country Club. Roman Catholic. Avocation: golf. Home: 1137 Via Mil Cumbres Solana Beach CA 92075-1724 Office: Amylin Pharms 9373 Towne Centre Dr San Diego CA 92121-3027

MULLANEY, JOSEPH E., lawyer; b. Fall River, Mass., Mar. 22, 1933; s. Joseph E. and Beatrice (Hancock) M.; m. Rosemary Woodman, June 22, 1957; children: Joseph E. III, Brian, Sean, Evan. AB magna cum laude, Coll. Holy Cross, Worcester, Mass., 1955; LLB magna cum laude, Harvard U., 1958. Bar: Ohio bar, D.C. bar, Mass. bar. Ptnr. Jones, Day, Cockley & Reavis, Cleve., 1960-70; gen. counsel Office Spl. Rep. Trade Negotiations, Exec. Office Pres., Washington, 1970-71, Cost of Living Council, 1971-72; assoc. gen. counsel Gillette Co., Boston, 1972-77, sr. v.p., gen. counsel, 1977-90, vice-chmn. bd., 1990—; dir. Park St. Corp., Greater Boston Legal Services Corp.; mem., dir. Boston Mcpl. Research Bur. Bd. dirs. New Eng. Legal Found.; trustee Boston Pub. Libr. Office: Gillette Co Prudential Towers Bldg Boston MA 02199

MULLARE, T(HOMAS) KENWOOD, JR., lawyer; b. Milton, Mass., Jan. 19, 1939; s. Thomas Kenwood and Catherine Marie (Leonard) M.; m. Joan Marie O'Donnell, May 27, 1967; children: Jennifer M., Tracy K., Jill M., Joyce M. AB, Holy Cross Coll., 1961; LLB, Boston Coll., 1964. Bar: Mass. 1964. Atty. New Eng. Electric System, 1964-70; v.p., gen. counsel, sec. AVX Corp., N.Y.C., 1970-73; v.p., gen. counsel, clk. Tyco Labs., Inc., Exeter, N.H., 1973-78; v.p., gen. counsel, sec. SCA Svcs., Inc., Boston, 1978-84; spl. counsel Houghton, Mifflin Co., Boston, 1984-85, v.p., dir. bus. software divsn., 1985-90; pres. North River Capital Co., Inc., Norwell, Mass., 1990—; also bd. dirs. Broadcast Info. Tech., Amherst, N.H.; bd. dirs. North River Capital Co., Inc., PartnerSoft Co. Mem. regional adv. bd. Commonwealth of Mass. Dept. Mental Retardation; bd. dirs. Barque Hill Assn., Norwell, 1980-84, pres., 1981-83; pres. Ch. Hillers, Norwell, 1983-84; bd. dirs., chmn. South Shore Assn. for Retarded Citizens, Weymouth, Mass., 1993—. Mem. ABA, Mass. Bar Assn., Boston Bar Assn. Home: 31 Barque Hill Dr Norwell MA 02061-2815 Office: 6A Grove St Ste 271 Norwell MA 02061

MULLARKEY, MARY J., state supreme court justice; b. New London, Wis., Sept. 28, 1943; d. John Clifford and Isabelle A. (Steffes) M.; m. Thomas E. Korson, July 24, 1971; 1 child, Andrew Steffes Korson. BA, St. Norbert Coll., 1965; LLB, Harvard U., 1968; LLD (hon.), St. Norbert Coll., 1989. Bar: Wis. 1968, Colo. 1974. Atty.-advisor U.S. Dept. Interior, Washington, 1968-73; asst. regional atty. EEOC, Denver, 1973-75; 1st atty. gen. Colo. Dept. Law, Denver, 1975-79, solicitor gen., 1979-82; legal advisor to Gov. Lamm State of Colo., Denver, 1982-85; ptnr. Mullarkey & Seymour, Denver, 1985-87; justice Colo. Supreme Ct., Denver, 1987—. Recipient Alumni award St. Norbert Coll., De Pere, Wis., 1980, Alma Mater award, 1993. Fellow ABA Found., Colo. Bar Found.; mem. ABA, Colo. Bar Assn., Colo. Women's Bar Assn. (recognition award 1986), Denver Bar Assn., Thompson G. Marsh Inn of Ct. (pres. 1993-94). Office: Supreme Ct Colo 2 E 14th Ave Denver CO 80203-2115

MULLE, GEORGE ERNEST, petroleum geologist; b. Collingswood, N.J., Dec. 21, 1919; s. George Melvin and Eleanor (Matilda) (Clevenger) M.; m. Molly Elizabeth Jones, Nov. 17, 1950; children: Alan Russell, David George, William Ernest. Student Rutgers U., 1942-44; A.B. in Earth Scis., U. Pa., 1948. Cert. petroleum geologist, Tex. Geologist, Tide Water Oil Co., Houston and Corpus Christi, 1948-51; dist. geologist La Gloria Oil & Gas Co., Corpus Christi, Tex., 1952-60; ptnr. Santa Rosa Gas Co., 1960-62; pvt. practice geology, Corpus Christi, 1962-73, 75-80, 83—; v.p. Corpus Christi Mgmt. Co., 1973-75; exploration mgr. So. Tex., Mormac Energy Corp., 1980-82. Pres. Palm Harbor Property Owners Assn., Rockport, Tex., 1984, 90, 91, 92, Bahia Log Libr., Corpus Christi, 1980, Santa Fe Log Libr., Corpus Christi, 1981; sec.-treas. The Villas of Harbor Oaks Owners Assn., 1985-88, v.p., 1992-96; del. People-to-People Petroleum Tech., People's Republic China, 1983. Served with USN, 1944-46. Author, spec. editor AAPG symposium natural gases N.Am., 1968. Mem. Corpus Christi Geol. Soc. (author book 1967), Soc. Ind. Profl. Earth Scientists (chmn. Corpus Christi chpt. 1995). Republican. Baptist. Avocation: photography. Home: 121 Ocean Dr Rockport TX 78382-9405

MULLEN, CHARLES FREDERICK, health educator; b. Washington, June 14, 1938; s. DeWitt Cliffton and Annabelle (Fischer) M.; m. Rita Mae Keintz, Oct. 23, 1996; children from a previous marriage: Henry John, Elizabeth Mary. BA, U. Va., 1962; BS, New England Coll. Optometry, 1969, OD, 1970; D of Ocular Sci., So. Coll. Optometry, 1994. Dir. clinics New Eng. Coll. Optometry, Boston, 1970-76; exec. dir. The Eye Inst., Pa. Coll. Optometry, Phila., 1976-90; dir. optometry svc. Dept. VA, Washington, 1990-96; pres. Ill. Coll. Optometry, Chgo., 1996—; adj. clin. prof. SUNY, N.Y.C., 1990—; mem. Dept. VA Spl. Subcom. Eye Care, Washington, 1990-96; observer Eye Coun., Nat. Eye Inst., Bethesda, Md., 1990-96, del. Am. Nat. Stds. Inst., 1990-96. Contbr. articles to profl. jours. Host parent Overbrook Sch. Blind, Phila., 1985-86; vol. Big Bro., West Chester, Pa., 1988-89; bd. dirs. Clavary Schlter, Washington, 1990-92. Lt. (j.g.) USNR. Mem. Am. Acad. Optometry, Am. Pub. Health Assn., Am. Optometric Assn., Nat. Assn. VA Ops., Assn. Mil. Surgeons U.S. (chmn. optometric sect. 1991, 95), Assn. Schs. & Colls. Optometry. Democrat. Episcopalian. Home: 3750 N Lake Shore Dr #3E Chicago IL 60613 Office: Ill Coll Optometry 3241 S Michigan Ave Chicago IL 60616-3816

MULLEN, DANIEL ROBERT, finance executive; b. Swedesboro, N.J., Apr. 17, 1941; s. Harold Legrand and Gladys (DeVault) M.; m. Elizabeth A. Willers, Dec. 17, 1977; children: William H., Jonathan O. BS in Fin., Ariz. State U., 1966, postgrad., 1966-67. Appraiser Ariz. Dept. Revenue, 1966-68; financial analyst Amerco, Inc., Phoenix, 1968-70; treas., CFO Amerco, Inc., 1970-82; pres., dir. Continental Leasing Co., 1980—; v.p. Southwest Pipe and Supply Co., 1982; treas. Talley Industries, Inc., 1982—; v.p. Talley Industries, Inc., Phoenix, 1993—. Del. Ariz. Presdl. Dem. Conv., 1972; bd. dirs. Big Sisters of Ariz., 1975, Found. for Blind Children, 1984-90, Phoenix Little Theatre, 1985-91, Kachina Country Day Sch., 1988-94, New Way Sch., 1994—. With U.S. Army, 1959-62. Ariz. Soc. CPAs grantee, 1964-65. Mem. Fin. Execs. Inst. Home: 3627 E Medlock Dr Phoenix AZ 85018-1505 Office: 2702 N 44th St Phoenix AZ 85008-1583

MULLEN, EDWARD JOHN, JR., Spanish language educator; b. Hackensack, N.J., July 12, 1942; s. Edward J. and Elsie (Powell) M.; m. Helen Cloe Braley, Apr. 2, 1971; children: Kathleen, Julie Ann. B.A., W.Va. Wesleyan Coll., 1964; M.A., Northwestern U., 1965, Ph.D., 1968. Asst. prof. modern langs. Purdue U., West Lafayette, Ind., 1967-71; assoc. prof. Spanish U. Mo., Columbia, 1971-78, prof. Spanish, 1978—. Author: La Revista Contemporáneos, 1972, Carlos Pellicer, 1977, Langston Hughes in the Hispanic World and Haiti, 1977, The Life and Poems of a Cuban Slave: Juan Francisco Manzano 1797-1854, 1981, Critical Essays on Langston Hughes, 1986, Sendas Literarias: Hispanoamerica, 1988, El cuento hispánico, 1994, 96; co-editor Afro-Hispanic Rev., 1987—. Recipient Diploma de Honor Instituto de Cultura Hispánica, 1964; Woodrow Wilson fellow, 1964-65; Northwestern U. fellow, 1965-67; summer research grantee U. Mo., 1972, 76; grantee Am. Council Learned Socs., 1979. Mem. MLA, Am. Assn. Tchrs. Spanish and Portuguese, Assn. of Depts. Fgn. Langs. (pres. 1989-91). Home: 207 Edgewood Ave Columbia MO 65203-3413 Office: U Mo Dept Romance Langs 143 Arts and Sci Bldg Columbia MO 65211

MULLEN, EDWARD K., paper company executive. CEO Newark Group, Cranford, N.J.; also chmn. bd. dirs. Office: Newark Group 20 Jackson Dr Cranford NJ 07016-3609*

MULLEN, EILEEN ANNE, human resources executive; b. Phila., Feb. 14, 1943; d. Joseph Gregory and Helen Rita (Kane) M.; m. William John Raschiatore (dec.). BS in English, St. Joseph U., 1967; MA in English, Villanova U., 1978. Cert. tchr., Pa. Tchr., St. Anastasia Sch., Newtown Square, 1960-67, West Cath. Girls High Sch., 1967-74; mgr. staff tng. and devel. ASTM, Phila., 1974-96, mgr. human resources, 1996—; instr. lit., speech and communications Widener U. Weekend Coll., Chester, Pa. and Wilmington, Del. Author: Speech Command, 1995; contbg. author articles on communications tng. programs; contbr. articles to profl. publs. Mem. ASTD (pres. Phila./Delaware Valley chpt. 1980-81, award for outstanding leadership as pres. 1981), Am. Soc. Assn. Execs. (Delaware Valley chpt.). Democrat. Roman Catholic. Office: ASTM 100 Barr Harbor Dr West Cnshohocken PA 19428-2951

MULLEN, FRANK ALBERT, university official, clergyman; b. Lafayette, Ind., Apr. 7, 1931; s. Albert Edwin and Bernice Elizabeth (Weidlich) M.; m. Ruth Charlotte Ackerman, May 28, 1960 (dec. Oct. 1969). BA, Wabash Coll., Crawfordsville, Ind., 1953; MDiv, Yale U., 1956; DD (hon.), Berkeley Div. Sch., New Haven, 1988. Ordained to ministry Christian Ch. (Disciples of Christ), 1956. Exec. dir. YMCA of Wilmington, Del., 1956-60, YMCA of Greater N.Y., N.Y.C., 1960-74; pastor St. Marks United Ch. of Christ, Ridgewood, N.Y., 1973—; assoc. dir. Campaign for Yale, Yale U., N.Y.C., 1975-79; min. Cmty. Ch. of Elmhurst, 1974—; dir. devel. Bapt. Med. Ctr., N.Y.C., 1980-83; dir. devel. Div. Sch. Yale U., New Haven, 1984—; dir. planned giving Guideposts, Inc., Carmel, N.Y., 1983-84. Trustee Park Avenue Christian Ch., N.Y.C., 1970—. Recipient Liberty Bell award Queens County Bar Assn., 1969, Alumni award of merit Wabash Coll., 1970; Wright fellow Yale U., 1955, fellow Trumbull Coll., 1985—. Mem. Assn. Theol. Schs., Coun. for Advancement in Secondary Edn., Wellness Assn., Travelers' Century Club. Home: 178-33 Croydon Rd Jamaica Estates NY 11432-2203 Office: Yale U 409 Prospect St New Haven CT 06511-2167 *Live for others. It is the only true way to find happiness.*

MULLEN, GRAHAM C., federal judge; b. 1940. BA, Duke U., 1962, JD, 1969. Bar: N.C. 1969. Ptnr. Mullen, Holland, Cooper, Morrow, Wilder & Sumner, 1969-90; judge U.S. Dist. Ct. (we. dist.) N.C., Charlotte, 1990—. Lt. USN, 1962-66. Mem. N.C. Bar Assn. (bd. govs. 1983-88), Mecklenburg

County Bar Assn. Office: US Courthouse 401 W Trade St Charlotte NC 28202-1619

MULLEN, J. THOMAS, lawyer; b. Evanston, Ill., Aug. 27, 1940. BSE, Princeton U., 1963; JD cum laude, U. Mich., 1967. Bar: Ill. 1967. Ptnr. Mayer, Brown & Platt, Chgo.; ptnr.-in-charge London office, 1974-78. Bd. dirs. Legal Assistance Found. Chgo., 1979-85. Mem. ABA, Ill. State Bar Assn., Chgo. Bar Assn., Chgo. Coun. Lawyers. Office: Mayer Brown & Platt 190 S La Salle St Chicago IL 60603-3410

MULLEN, JAMES GENTRY, physics educator; b. St. Louis, Sept. 17, 1933; s. James and Lillian A. (Nelms) M.; children by previous marriage: Anne Lynette, Barbara Gaye, James Gentry, Laura Marie; m. Sara Jane; children: Carol Melissa, Erin Joy, Elizabeth Nancy Jane, Kevin Alexander. B.S., U. Mo., 1955; M.S., U. Ill., 1957, Ph.D., 1960. Asst. physicist Argonne Nat. Lab., 1960-63, assoc. physicist, 1963-64; mem. faculty Purdue U., 1964—, asst. prof., 1964-66, assoc. prof., 1966-75, prof. physics, 1975—; pres. Word Technologies, Inc., West Lafayette, Ind., 1981-85; mem. organizing com., program chmn. Internat. Conf. for Applications of Mössbauer Effect, 1993; appt. mem. of the synchrotron Rsch. Instruments Collaborative Access Team Advanced Photon Source at The Argonne Nat. Lab., 1995. Contbr. to profl. jours. Fundamenteel Onderzoek Materie fellow, 1979-80. Mem. Am. Phys. Soc., Am. Assn. Physics Tchrs., AAUP, Sigma Xi, Phi Kappa Phi, Tau Beta Pi. Home: 3212 Elkhart St West Lafayette IN 47906-1151 Office: Purdue U Dept Physics West Lafayette IN 47907

MULLEN, PETER P., lawyer; b. N.Y.C., Apr. 8, 1928; m. Cecilia Kirby; 5 children. A.B. cum laude, Georgetown U., 1948; LL.B., Columbia U., 1951. Bar: N.Y. 1951. Partner firm Skadden Arps Slate Meagher & Flom, N.Y.C., 1961—, exec. ptnr., 1981-94; co-chmn. Cardinal's Com. Laity Archdiocese N.Y., 1992—; bd. dirs., sec., treas., Eye Surgery, Inc.; bd. dirs. 1st Unum Life Ins. Co. Formerly mem., pres. Bd. Edn. Pub. Schs., Bronxville, N.Y., 1979-81; chmn. Skadden Fellowship Found., 1988—; bd. dirs., vice-chmn. Lawrence Hosp., Bronxville, 1984-89; bd. dirs. Project Orbis, Georgetown U., Washington, 1982—, chmn., 1985-92; bd. dirs. Legal Aid Soc., 1987-93, Vols. Legal Svcs., Inc., 1988—, United Way Bronxville, 1985-93, Practicing Attys. Law Students; trustee Lawyer's Commn. Civil Rights Under Law, 1984—; chmn. Gregorian U. Found., 1989—; bd. dirs., chmn. endowment com. Vatican Obs. Found., 1993. Stone scholar, 1951; named Man Yr. Cath. Big Bros., 1987; recipient John Carroll award Georgetown U., 1984, John Carroll Medal Merit, 1988, Thomas More award Lawyers Com. Cardinal's Com. of the Laity, 1996. Mem. Am. Bar Assn., N.Y. State Bar Assn. (com. securities regulation 1980-83), Assn. Bar City N.Y. (com. corp. law 1964-67, com. admissions 1965-68, com. securities regulation 1970-73), Soc. friendly Sons St. Patrick (N.Y., pres. 1989-90), Knight Malta. Office: Skadden Arps Slate et al 919 3rd Ave New York NY 10022

MULLEN, REGINA MARIE, lawyer; b. Cambridge, Mass., Apr. 22, 1948; d. Robert G. and Elizabeth R. (McHugh) M. BA, Newton Coll. Sacred Heart, 1970; JD, U. Va., 1973. Bar: Pa., Del., U.S. Dist. Ct. Del., U.S. Ct. Appeals (3d cir.), U.S. Supreme Ct. Dep. atty. gen. State Del. Dept. Justice, Wilmington, 1973-79, state solicitor, 1979-83, chief fin. unit, 1983-88; v.p., counsel MBNA Am. Bank, N.A., Newark, Del., 1988-91, 1st v.p., sr. v.p., counsel, 1991—; Mem. bd. Bar Examiners, State Del., 1979-89; bd. dirs. Del. Cmty. Investment Corp., Wilmington, 1994-96, Wilmington Music Festival, 1992—; mem. bd. profl. responsibility State of Del., 1996—. Bd. dirs. Wilmington Music Festival, 1992—; mem. fin. com. Chesapeake Bay Girl Scout coun. Wilmington, 1985-94, bd. dirs., 1988-94, v.p., 1990-94, mem. fund devel. com., 1994-96, chair personnel com., 1996—; bd. dirs. Comty. Legal Aid Soc., 1994—, treas., 1995—. Mem. ABA, Del. State Bar Assn. (chair adminstrv. law sect. 1983-85). Democrat. Roman Catholic. Office: 1100 N King St Wilmington DE 19884-0850

MULLEN, RON, insurance company executive; b. Tex., Aug. 8, 1939; s. Durward Lacy and Blanche V. (Coulson) M.; m. Carole King, Dec, 29, 1959; children: Lacy Lynne Holcomb, Misty Kay. Student, Abilene Christian Coll., 1957-58, San Antonio Coll., 1958-59; BBA, S.W. Tex. State U., 1965. C.L.U., Chartered Fin. Cons. City council mem. City of Austin, 1977-83, mayor, 1983-85; mgr. Prin. Fin. Group, Austin, 1965—; pres., prin. Fin. Group, Ron Mullen & Assocs. Inc., Austin, 1966—; chmn. TML Ins. Trust Fund Com., 1983—; mem. Gov.'s Task Force on State Employees Health Ins. Benefits, Austin, 1984. Chmn. Austin Transp. Study Com., Austin, 1983—, Greater Austin-San Antonio Corridor Coun., 1984—, Social Policy Adv. Com., Austin, 1979-80, March of Dimes campaign, Austin, 1974-75; co-chmn. Consumers United for Rail Equity, Austin, 1983—; v.p. Austin Symphony Orch., 1974-75; mem. exec. com. Capital Area Planning Coun., Austin, 1976—, exec. bd. Tex. Mcpl. League, Austin, 1983—, Gov.'s Task Force on Indigent Health Care, Austin, 1984, Tex. Adv. Commn. on Intergovtl. Rels., Austin, 1981—; chmn. Infant Parent Tng. Ctr., 1985-96; bd. dirs., chmn. South MoPac Transp. Com., 1986-87; life mem. Austin Jaycees, bd. dirs., 1974-75; vice-chmn. mental health Mental Retardation Bd.; vice chmn. South Tex. Audio Reader Svc. Recipient Road Hand award Tex. Dept. Hwys. and Transp., 1985, award for regional statesmanship Greater Austin-San Antonio Corridor Commn.; named Boss of Yr., Treaty Oaks chpt. Am. Bus. Women's Assn., 1978, Nat. Mgr. of Yr., Bankers Life Ins. Co., 1977, 82, 84-85, Alumnus of Yr. Austin Jaycees, 1988-90. Mem. Am. Coll. Life Underwriters (pres.), Tex. Assn. Life Underwriters (v.p. 1995-96, pres. 1997-98), Austin Assn. Life Underwriters (pres. 1974-75), Austin Gen. Agts. and Mgrs. Assn. (pres. 1978-80), Sales and Mktg. Execs. of Austin (pres. 1972-73), Downtown Rotary (pres.). Baptist. Home: 6902 Mesa Dr # B Austin TX 78731-2822

MULLEN, THOMAS EDGAR, real estate consultant; b. Hackensack, N.J., Feb. 10, 1936; s. Luke B. and Jean (Edgar) M.; m. Sarah Lee Huff, Aug. 17, 1984. BS in Engring., Va. Poly. Tech., 1954; grad mgmt. program, Harvard U., 1964. Cons. in field. Mgr. mktg. Eastern Airlines, N.Y.C., 1954-69; pres. Profl. Sprits Mktg., N.Y.C., 1969-72, Shelter Devel. Corp. Am., N.Y.C., 1972-79; supr. ops. Gen. Mills, Orlando, Fla., 1980-86; cons., exec., realtor A.H.M. Graves Co. Inc., Indpls., 1986-92; pres. Pegasus Assocs. Ltd., 1992—. Inventor TV Guider Holder, patent, 1971. Fundraiser Am. Cancer Soc., Miami, 1967-70, Westchester Hosp., N.Y.C., 1967-70; pres. Brighton Found. Mem. Met. Bd. Realtors, Builders Assn. Greater Indpls. (bd. dirs.), Ind. Builders Assn. (bd. dirs.), Nat. Assn. Realtors, Inst. Residential Mktg. (pres. sales & mktg. coun., bd. dirs.). Republican. Roman Catholic. Avocations: tennis, recreational pilot. Home: 6251 Behner Way Indianapolis IN 46250-1494

MULLEN, WILLIAM COCKE, classics educator; b. Houston, Tex., Nov. 4, 1946; s. Joseph and Edith (Donnan) M. BA magna cum laude, Harvard Coll., 1968; PhD, U. Tex., 1972. Asst. prof. classics & comparative lit. U. Calif., Berkeley, Calif., 1971-73; Hodder fellow Princeton U., Princeton, N.J., 1973-74; asst. prof. classics Boston U., Boston, 1974-80; jr. fellow Ctr. for Hellenic Studies Harvard U., Washington, 1977-78; tutor St. John's Coll., Annapolis, Md., 1980-84, Santa Fe, N.Mex., 1985; assoc. prof. Bard Coll., Annandale, N.Y., 1985-93, prof., 1994—; lectr. The Ariz. Homer Inst., Tucson, 1987, 90, Inst. Study of Classical Architecture, N.Y., 1994, jury mem., 1994. Author: Choreia: Pindar and Dance , 1982; video: Songs of Sappho, 1987. Adv. NEH, Washington, 1982. Mem. Internat. Soc. Classical Tradition, Phi Beta Kappa. Avocations: writing poetry, catastrophist research. Home and Office: Bard Coll Annandale On Hudson NY 12504

MULLEN, WILLIAM JOSEPH, III, military analyst, retired army officer; b. Plattsburg, N.Y., Dec. 26, 1937; s. William Joseph Jr. and Georgia (Cook) M.; m. Norma Sturgeon, Aug. 6, 1962; 1 child, William Joseph IV. BS, U.S. Mil. Acad., West Point, N.Y., 1959; MS in Internat. Affairs, George Washington U., 1971. Commd. 2d lt. U.S. Army, 1959, advanced through grades to brig. gen., 1987; various assignments in U.S., Vietnam, Korea, Panama, Germany, Saudi Arabia, 1959-92; mem. staff, faculty U.S. Mil. Acad., West Point, 1967-70; comdr. 1st Brigade, 1st Inf. Div., Ft. Riley, Kans., 1983-86; asst. div. comdr. 5th Inf. Div., Ft. Polk, La., 1986-87; comdg. gen. U.S. Army Combined Arms Tng. Activity, Ft. Leavenworth, Kans., 1987-89, 1st Inf. Div. (Forward), Germany, 1989-91; dep. dir. ops. J3 Forces Command, Ft. McPherson, Ga., 1991-92; dir. mil. tng. sys. BDM Fed., Inc., Monterey, Calif., 1992—. Co-author: Changing an Army, An Oral History of Gen. W.E. DePuy, 1979; contbr. articles, book revs. to Mil. Rev. Decorated D.S.C., D.S.M. Mem. Assn. U.S. Army, Soc. of 1st Div. (chpt. officer 1968, assoc. 1989-93, trustee found. 1989-93, bd. dirs.), Legion of Valor. Avocations: sports, reading. *When in doubt, I have always found direction from the guidance explicit in the 1st Infantry Division's motto, "Duty first!".*

MULLENDER, BARTON, insurance company executive; b. N.Y.C.; s. Franklin and Simone (Gardner) M.; m. Maria Gordon; children: Simon, Jake, Marie. BA, NYU, 1965, MS, 1971. With Prudential Ins. Co. Am., N.Y.C., 1965-71; mgr., dir. Franklin Ins. Assocs., N.Y.C., 1971-86; exec. dir. Werik Ins. Co. Inc., N.Y.C., 1986—. Author: Insurance in America: What's Right, What's Wrong, 1992, Insurance Planning for Home and Home Office, 1995. Revere Ave. block assn. secy., neighborhood kid warch. Office: Werik Ins Co 169 Revere Ave Bronx NY 10465-3322

MULLENDORE, WALTER EDWARD, economist; b. Harrah, Okla., Apr. 22, 1940; s. Newton and Ida Minnie (Lohmann) M.; m. Edra Janell Havenstrite, July 4, 1963; children—Matthew Edward, Karen Kay, Mark Andrew. BS, Okla. State U., 1961, MS, 1963; PhD in Econs, Iowa State U., 1968. Grad. asst. Okla. State U., 1961-63; instr. Iowa State U., 1965-67; mem. faculty dept. econs. U. Tex., Arlington, 1968—, prof., 1975—, dean Coll. of Bus., 1980-93. Contbr. articles to profl. jours. Served with U.S. Army, 1963-65. Mem. Mo. Valley Econ. Assn. (v.p. 1980-81, pres. 1982-83), Atlantic Econ. Soc., Regional Sci. Assn., Western Regional Sci. Assn., Gt. S.W. Rotary (pres. 1989-90), Omicron Delta Epsilon. Methodist. Home: 8003 John T White Rd Fort Worth TX 76120-3611 Office: U Tex Coll Bus Box 19479-UTA Arlington TX 76019

MULLENIX, KATHY ANN, relocation company executive; b. Goodland, Ind., Mar. 8, 1955; d. Boyd Dale and Edith Marie Hoaks; 1 child, Joseph F. Hamburg IV. Diploma, South Newton Jr./Sr. H.S., Goodland, Ind., 1973. Asst. to pres. Planes Moving, Cin., 1981-88; sales mgr. Tru-Pak Moving, Greenville, S.C., 1988-89; account exec. Armstrong Relocation, Atlanta, 1989—. Den leader Cub Scouts, Blue Ash, Ohio, 1982-86; coach's asst. Soccer Assn., Mason, Ohio, 1985-88; treas. PTA Mason Mid. Sch., 1988; tutor Gwinnette Co. Adult Literacy, Lawrenceville, Ga., 1994. Mem. NAFE. Avocations: reading, dance, oil painting, horseback riding, camping. Office: Armstrong Relocation 6950 Business Ct Atlanta GA 30340-1429

MULLENIX, LINDA SUSAN, lawyer, educator; b. N.Y.C., Oct. 16, 1950; d. Andrew Michael and Roslyn Marasco; children: Robert Bartholomew, John Theodore, William Joseph. B.A., CCNY, 1971; M. Philosophy, Columbia U., 1974, Ph.D. (Pres.'s fellow), 1977; J.D., Georgetown U., 1980. Bar: D.C. 1981, Tex. 1991, U.S. Dist Ct. D.C. 1981, U.S. Supreme Ct. 1986. U.S. Ct. Appeals (D.C. cir.) 1981, U.S. Ct. Appeals (5th cir.) 1995. Assoc. prof., lectr. George Washington U., Washington, 1977-80; asst. prof. Am. U., Washington, 1979; clin. prof. Loyola U. Law Sch., Los Angeles, 1981-82, vis. asst. prof., 1982-83; vis. asst. prof. Catholic U. Law Sch., Washington, 1983-84, asst. prof., 1984-86, assoc. prof., 1986-90, prof., 1990; Jud. Fellow U.S. Supreme Ct. and Fed. Jud. Ctr., 1989-90; Bernard J. Ward Centennial prof. U. Tex., 1991—; Vinson & Elkins chair, U. Tex., 1993; vis. prof. Harvard Law Sch., 1994-95, Mich. Law Sch., 1996; assoc. Pierson, Ball & Dowd, Washington, 1980-81; adj. instr. Fordham U., N.Y.C., 1975-76, adj. asst. prof. 1977; adj. asst. prof. CCNY, 1977; adj. instr., adj. asst. prof. Cooper Union Advancement Sci., Art, N.Y.C., 1977; instr. N.Y. Inst. Tech., N.Y.C., 1976, U. Md. European div., Ramstein, Germany, 1974. Author: Mass Tort Litigation: Cases and Materials, 1996; co-author: Federal Courts in the Twenty-First Century, 1996, Moore's Federal Practice and Procedure, 1991, 1997; editor bibliographies Polit. Theory, A Jour. Polit. Philosophy, 1972-74, The Tax Lawyer Jour., 1978-80; contbg. editor Preview of U.S. Supreme Ct. Cases, Pub. Edn. Div. ABA, 1988—; reporter ABA Task Force on Class Actions, 1995-97, co-reporter Report and Plan of Civil Justice Reform Act Adv. Group, S.D., Tex. 1991; assoc. reporter ALI, Restatement of the Law Governing Lawyers; contbr. articles to profl. publs. Alt. del. Va. Democratic State Conv., 1980. Fellow NDEA, 1971-74, Georgetown U. Law Sch., 1978; N.Y. State Regents scholar, 1967-71. Mem. ABA, Am. Law Inst., D.C. Bar Assn. (com. on ethics, CLE and the Model Rules 1987), Am. Assn. Law Schs. (exec. com. sect. on civil proc. 1987-88, exec. com. sec. on conflicts of law 1991-92, chair prof. devel. com. 1991-93), Jour. Legal Edn. (editl. bd. 1997—), Phi Beta Kappa, Phi Alpha Delta. Home: 722 Crystal Creek Dr Austin TX 78746-4730 Office: U Tex Sch Law 727 E 26th St Austin TX 78705-3224

MULLENS, WILLIAM REESE, retired insurance company executive; b. Franklin, Tenn., Sept. 12, 1921; s. William Pope and Elizabeth (Reese) M.; m. Katherine Ann Jones, Nov. 24, 1945; children: Jo Ann Mullens Sanditz, Carol Ann Mullens Slegers. B.A., Vanderbilt U., 1942. With Bus. Men's Assurance Co., Kansas City, Mo., 1947-75; exec. v.p., dir. Bus. Men's Assurance Co., 1969-75; pres., dir. J.C. Penney Life Ins. Co., 1975-82; pres. Gt. Am. Res. Ins. Co., 1975-84, dir., 1975-89; dir. Nat. Fidelity Life Ins. Co., 1986-89. Served to lt. comdr. USNR, 1943-46. Fellow Soc. Actuaries; mem. Phi Beta Kappa, Alpha Tau Omega. Presbyterian. Home: 2502 N Broken Circle Rd Flagstaff AZ 86004

MULLER, ALEXANDRA LIDA, real estate management director; b. N.Y.C., June 9, 1949; d. John William and Elisa (Bianco) M. BA in Math., Western N.E. Coll., 1971; Cert. in Real Estate, NYU, 1982, Cert. as Real Estate Broker, 1991. Lic. notary pub. Ptnr. Raffles, Florence, Italy, 1972-74; bookkeeper Emmeti, Florence, Italy, 1974-76; tchr. English and Italian Berlitz Sch. Langs., Florence, Italy, 1976-77; tchr., interpreter, translator Italy, 1977-84; office mgr. UNICEF, Milan, Italy, 1982-83; dir. Barhite & Holzinger, N.Y.C., 1985-89; dir., office mgr. The Robert-Thomas Co., N.Y.C., 1990-92; assoc. broker The Thomas Campenni Co., N.Y.C., 1992—; ind. real estate broker. Pres. Gallery House Condominium. Avocations: scuba diving, bridge, card collecting, travel. Office: The Thomas F Campenni Co 21 W 46th St New York NY 10036-4119

MULLER, CHARLOTTE FELDMAN, economist, educator; b. N.Y.C., Feb. 19, 1921; d. Louis and Lillian (Drogin) Feldman; m. Jonas N. Muller, 1942 (dec.); m. Carl Schoenberg, 1970; children: Jeremy Lewis Muller, Sara Linda Muller. A.B., Vassar Coll., 1941; A.M., Columbia U., 1942, Ph.D. in Econs., 1946. Instr. econs. Bklyn. Coll., 1943; lectr. Barnard Coll., 1943-46; asst. prof. Occidental Coll., 1947; asst. study dir. Survey Rsch. Ctr., U. Mich., 1948; rsch. assoc. U. Calif., Berkeley, 1948-50; lectr. Yale U. Sch. Pub. Health, 1952-53; asst. prof. Columbia U. Sch. Pub. Health, 1957-67; assoc. dir. Ctr. for Social Rsch. CUNY, 1967-86, prof. econs., 1978-91, prof. emerita, 1991—, prof. sociology, 1982-91, prof. urban studies Ctr. for Social Rsch., 1967-78; v.p. CUNY Acad. for Humanities and Scis., 1985-88; prof. health econs. Mt. Sinai Sch. Medicine, 1986-91, prof. emerita, 1991—, dir. div. health econs., 1988-91, prof. dept. geriatrics, 1990-91, assoc. dir. Internat. Longevity Ctr., 1991—; cons. Health Care Financing Adminstrn., U.S. VA; disting. alumna speaker Vassar Centennial, 1971. Author: Health Care and Gender, 1990; mem. editorial bd. Am. Jour. Pub. Health, 1980-84, Women and Health, Rsch. on Aging; contbr. numerous articles on health econs. to profl. publs. Mem. N.Y.C. Mayor's Com. on Prescription Drug Abuse, 1970-73; bd. dirs. Alan Guttmacher Inst., 1972-81, CUNY Rsch. Found., 1985-91; vice chmn. Med. and Health Rsch. Assn., N.Y.C.; mem. health care tech. study sect. Nat. Ctr. Health Svcs. Rsch., 1976-79; mem. commn. on nat. policy Am. Jewish Congress, 1980-91. Ford/Rockefeller Founds. grantee, 1972-73, 75-76; Russell Sage Found. grantee, 1985-90. Mem. APHA, NOW, Am. Econ. Assn. Jewish. Office: Internat Longevity Ctr 1216 5th Ave Ste 552 New York NY 10029-5202

MULLER, DAVID WEBSTER, architectural designer; b. Norwich, Conn., Aug. 25, 1956; s. Richard Johnson and Barbara Alice (Reading) M.; m. Susan Akers, Dec. 31, 1989; 1 stepchild, Shannon. BA in Polit. Sci., George Washington U., 1978. Rsch. assoc. Rep. Nat. Com., Washington, 1978-80, dep. dir. spl. projects, 1981-83; western field dir. Nat. Rep. Congl. Com., Washington, 1983-85; v.p. Russo Watts & Rollins, Sacramento, Calif., 1985-86; campaign mgr. Chavez for U.S. Senate, Silver Spring, Md., 1986; v.p. Russo Watts & Rollins, Sacramento, 1987-89; cons. Sacramento, 1989, pvt. investor, 1990—; archtl. design and restoration Muller/West, 1990—. Mem. Nat. Coun. for Arts and Scis. George Washington U. Avocations: sailing, photography, writing fiction, international travel. Home and Office: Muller/West 380 Wyndgate Rd Sacramento CA 95864-5945

MULLER, EDWARD ROBERT, lawyer; b. Phila., Mar. 26, 1952; s. Rudolph E. and Elizabeth (Steiner) M.; m. Patricia Eileen Bauer, Sept. 27, 1980; children: Margaret Anne, John Frederick. AB summa cum laude, Dartmouth Coll., 1973; JD, Yale U., 1976. Assoc. Leva, Hawes, Symington, Martin & Oppenheimer, Washington, 1977-83; dir. legal affairs Life Scis. group Whittaker Corp., Arlington, Va., 1983-84; v.p. Whittaker Health Svcs., Arlington, Va., 1984-85; v.p., gen. counsel, sec. Whittaker Corp., L.A., 1985-93, chief adminstrv. officer, 1988-92, CFO, 1992-93, bd. dirs., 1993—; v.p., gen. counsel, sec. BioWhittaker, Inc., Walkersville, Md., 1991-93; pres., CEO, bd. dirs. Edison Mission Energy, Irvine, Calif., 1993—; mem. Brookings Task Force on Civil Justice Reform, 1988-89; bd. dirs. Global Marine, Inc. Trustee Exceptional Children's Found., L.A., 1988-94, treas., 1988-93; bd. dirs. Oasis Resdl., Inc., 1995—; co-chair Internat. Energy Devel. Coun., Washington, 1993—; bd. govs. Jr. Achievement of Orange County and the Inland Empire, 1995—. Office: Edison Mission Energy 18101 Von Karman Ave Ste 1700 Irvine CA 92612-1046

MULLER, ERNEST H., geology educator; b. Tabriz, Iran, Mar. 4, 1923; (parents U.S. citizens); s. Hugo Arthur and Laura Barnett (McComb) M.; m. Wanda Custis, Apr. 7, 1951; children: Ruth Anne, David Stewart, Katherine Lee. BA, Wooster Coll., 1947; MS, U. Ill., 1949, PhD, 1952. Geologist U.S. Geol. Survey, Washington, 1947-54; asst. prof. geology Cornell U., Ithaca, N.Y., 1954-59; assoc. prof. Syracuse U., N.Y., 1959-63, prof., 1963-89, interim chmn. dept. geology, 1970-71, 79-81, prof. emeritus, 1989—; seasonal geologist N.Y. Geol. Survey, 1956-76; geologist Am. Geog. Soc., Chile, 1959; rsch. assoc. Natural History Mus., Rejkjavik, Iceland, 1968-69; vis. prof. Alaska Pacific U., Anchorage, 1979; Erskine vis. prof. U. Canterbury, Christchurch, New Zealand, 1974; mem. Bering Glacier (Alaska) Rsch. Group, 1988—, N.Y. Pleistocene Stratigraphy. Author: Geology of Chautauqua County, New York, 1964, Seaway Trail Rocks and Landscapes, 1987. 1st lt. USAAF, 1943-46. Fellow Geol. Soc. Am. (geomorphology panel 1962-64, 66-68, 75-77), AAAS; mem. Am. Quaternary Assn. (counselor 1982-86), Glaciological Soc., Nat. Assn. Geology Tchrs., Sigma Xi. Home: 874 Livingston Ave Syracuse NY 13210-2936 Office: Syracuse U 204 Heroy Geology Lab Syracuse NY 13244-1070

MULLER, FRANK, mediator, arbitrator; b. Prague, Czechoslovakia, Nov. 24, 1930; m. Louise De Vel, Dec. 14, 1957; children: Robert, William, David. BE in Civil Engring., Yale U., 1952; LLB, Boston Coll., 1959. Bar: N.Y. 1973, Mass. 1959; registered profl. engr., N.Y., N.J., Mass. Field engr., field supt. Raymond Internat., Inc., N.Y.C., 1955-58; project engr. New Eng. Found., Inc., Boston, 1958-59; house counsel, chief project engr. Daniel O'Connell's Sons, Inc., Holyoke, Mass., 1959-64; v.p., dir., sec. Madigan Praeger, Inc., N.Y.C., 1964-76; dir. constrn. mgmt. svcs. and constrn. dept. Parsons Brinckerhoff Quade Douglas, Inc., N.Y.C., 1976-79; sr. v.p. O'Brien-Kreitzberg & Assocs., N.Y.C., 1979-89; pres. Metro Mediation Svcs. Ltd., N.Y.C., 1989—; counsel Goetz, Fitzpatrick & Flynn, N.Y.C., 1989—; bd. dirs. O'Connell's Enterprises Inc., Holyoke, Mass. and Boston; adj. asst. prof. NYU Sch. Continuing Edn.; adj. instr. Polytechnic Inst. N.Y., 1975-77; lectr. profl. assns.; pvt. judge The Pvt. Adjudication Ctr., Inc.; arbitrator N.Y. Small Claims Ct.; mediator Community Dispute Settlement Svc., N.Y. State; arbitrator and mediator panel Am. Arbitration Assn. Co-author: Construction Management: A Professional Approach, 1978; contbr. articles to profl. jours., chpts. to books. Lt. (j.g.) CEC USN, 1952-55. Recipient Constrn. Mgmt. award ASCE. Mem. Nat. Constrn. Industry Arbitration Com. (past chair), Constrn. Mgmt. Assn. Am. (past pres.). Office: Metro Mediation Svcs Ltd 685 3rd Ave Ste 2100 New York NY 10017-4024

MULLER, FRANK B., advertising executive; b. Copenhagen, Nov. 25, 1926; came to U.S., 1927; s. Herman B. and Johanne M. (Ammentorp) M.; m. Judith Hunter, Apr. 14, 1956; children: Mark W., Hunter J., Chip. Student, Harvard U., 1944; BNS in Naval Sci., Tufts Coll., 1946; BS in Mech. Engring., Tufts U., 1948. Account supr. advt. dept. GE, 1948-55; exec. v.p. Muller Jordan Weiss Inc., N.Y.C., 1955-90; pres. MultiMedia Unltd., Inc., N.Y.C., 1990—. Lt. (j.g.) USNR, 1944-47. Mem. ASME. Republican. Congregationalist. Clubs: Saugatuck Harbor Yacht (Westport, Conn.) (bd. govs. 1965-75, 79-80, commodore 1970-71). Home: 46 Marion Rd Westport CT 06880-2923 Office: MultiMedia Unltd Inc 46 Marion Rd Westport CT 06880-2923

MULLER, FREDERICA DANIELA, psychology educator; d. Leopold and Elena; m. Dr. L. Muller; children: Daniela, Adrian. Grad., Med. Inst. Radiology, Romania, 1962, PsyD in Clin. Psychology, 1965, M in Internat. Law and Bus., 1966; specialization courses in Psychodrama, Moreno Inst., Vienna, 1969; grad., Inst. Rsch. in Aging, Rome, 1970, Miami Inst. Psychology, 1987. Diplomate Am. Bd. Forensic Medicine, Am. Bd. Forensic Examiners; lic. psychologist, Pa.; lic. psychotherapist, Fla.; cert. family mediator, Fla. Supreme Ct. continuing edn. units provider psych. Prof. Sch. Continuing Edn. Barry U., North Miami, Fla.; instr. advanced courses in psychology, psychodrama, med. ethics, social manners; guest speaker Colloque Internat., Bucharest, Romania, 1989-93; guest lectr. U. Arboga, Sweden 1968-72; founder Internat. Studies for Biopsychosocial Issues, 1991; cons. dept. of marriage, family and child devel. systemic studies, Nova U., 1992; founder Euro Am. Exch. Co., 1980; with Santé Internat., Switzerland, 1982-85; dir. Ctr. Biopsychosocial Medicine, 1995. Conducted rsch. on stress and aging with Dr. Anna Aslan, world renowned author; developed 45 minute stress reduction program for use in the work place. Author: The Management of Occupational Stress and Its Linkage to Social Pressures; contbr. articles to profl. jours. Mem. APA, Medicins du Monde (hon.), Am. Soc. Group Psychotherapy and Psychodrama, Soc. Psychol., Studies Social of Issues, World Fedn. for Mental Health.

MULLER, GREGORY ALAN, health facilities administrator, mayor; b. Newark, Feb. 11, 1947; s. Richard Mapes and Doris J. (Morgan) M.; m. Geraldine A. Bleach, May 1, 1976; children: Laura M., Gregory P. AS in Psychology, Union Coll.; BSBA, S.W. U. La.; MBA, Can. Sch. Mgmt., Toronto, 1994. Sr. br. mgr. fin. divsn. Household Internat., Inc., 1972-84, ops. mgr. retail svcs. divsn., 1984-87, mgr. legal svcs., 1987-89; v.p., chief loan officer Lehigh Savs. Bank, Union Twp., N.J., 1989-91; program dir., bus. mgr., lectr., fin. counselor St. Barnabas Behavioral Health Hosp., Union, N.J., 1991-96, govt., cmty., pub. rels. liaison, 1996—; dir. administrative ops. behavioral health Union (N.J.) Hosp., 1991—; mayor, 1997. Mem. Union Twp. Com., 1987-90, 90-93, mcpl. drug alliance, Union ctr. spl. improvement dist., mayor Union Twp., 1995, 97; Fire and Police Commr., Union Twp., 1996; sec. Union County Planning Bd., 1993—; mem. Union Twp. Bd. Edn., chmn. fin., 1985-87; active Regular Rep. Club Union, bd. dirs.; mem. N.J. Coun. on Affordable Housing. Mem. DAV, VFW, Union County Coll. Alumni, Rutgers Sch. Drug & Alcohol Studies Alumni,Am. Soc. Profl. Appraisers, Union County Assn. Realtors, Am. Soc. Notary Pubs., Vietnam Vets. Am., Am. Legion, Masons, Shriners, Elks, Optimists. Home: 1675 Kenneth Ave Union NJ 07083-5115

MULLER, HENRY JAMES, journalist, magazine editor; b. Garmisch-Partenkirchen, Germany, Feb. 10, 1947; came to U.S., 1953; s. Henri Jacques and Helga (Mensch) M.; m. Maggie McComas, June 19, 1968. BA, Stanford U., 1968. Tchr. U.S. Peace Corps, Ethiopia, 1968-70; chief Vancouver (B.C., Can.) bur. Time mag., 1971-73; European econ. corr. Time mag., Brussels, 1973-77; chief Paris bur. Time mag., 1977-81; world editor Time mag., N.Y.C., 1982-85, chief of corrs., 1986-87, mng. editor, 1987-93; editorial dir. Time Inc., 1993—; faculty mem. profl. pub. course Stanford (Calif.) U., 1989—. Trustee Stanford U., 1991—, Carnegie Corp., 1992—, Overseas Press Club, 1993—. Recipient David Brower Environ. Journalism award Sierra Club, 1990, Gerald Loeb award for disting. bus. and fin. journalism, 1992. Mem. Am. Soc. Mag. Editors (bd. dirs. 1991-95), Coun. of Fgn. Rels. Avocations: hiking, reading, skiing. Office: Time Inc Time & Life Bldg 1271 Avenue Of The Americas New York NY 10020-1300*

MULLER, HENRY JOHN, real estate developer; b. N.Y.C., July 27, 1919; s. Henry and Anne (Wulf) M.; m. Cecelia M. Ziffer, May 19, 1943; children: Richard, Robert, Ceil Anne, Roger. BS, Bklyn. Poly. Inst., 1949. Engr. GE Co., Bloomfield, N.J., 1948-49, Prudential Ins. Co., Newark, 1949-56; dep. dir. Harvard U., 1956-64; sr. v.p. 1st Nat. City Bank, N.Y.C., 1964-71; chmn. Citicorp. Realty, N.Y.C., 1971-72; sr. v.p. Allied Maintenance Corp., N.Y.C., 1972-74; exec. v.p. Moorings Devel. Co., Vero Beach, Fla., 1974-77; pres. Muller & Assocs. Inc., Vero Beach, 1977-89, Criterion Svcs. Corp., Vero Beach, 1988—. With AUS, 1941-46. Mem. Tau Beta Pi, Lambda Chi

Alpha. Home: 5954 River Run Dr Sebastian FL 32958-4709 Office: Criterion Svcs Corp 9025 N Us Highway 1 Sebastian FL 32958-7515

MULLER, H(ENRY) NICHOLAS, III, foundation executive; b. Pitts., Nov. 18, 1938; s. Henry N. Jr. and Harriet (Kerschner) M.; m. Nancy Clagett, June 20, 1959 (div. 1985); children: Charles T., Brook W.; m. Carol A. Cook, Jan. 4, 1986. BA, Dartmouth Coll., 1960; PhD, U. Rochester, 1968. Instr. Dartmouth Coll., Hanover, N.H., 1964; lectr. Mt. Allison U., Sackville, N.B., Can., 1964-66; asst. prof. history U. Vt., Burlington, 1966-69; assoc. prof. history, 1970-73; prof. history U. Vt., Burlington, 1974-78, asst. dean Coll. Arts and Scis., 1969-70, assoc. dean Coll. Arts and Scis., 1970-73, dir. Living/Learning Ctr., 1973-78; pres. Colby-Sawayer Coll., New London, N.H., 1978-85; dir. State His. Soc. Wis., Madison, 1985-96; pres., CEO Frank Lloyd Wright Found., Spring Green, Scottsdale, Wis. Ariz., 1996—; chmn. State Hist. Records Adv. Bd., 1985-96, Wis. Burial Sites Bd., 1988-96, Wis. Submerged Cultural Resources, 1993-96, Standex Internat. Corp., Salem, N.H., 1984—, Nat. Trust for Hist. Preservation, 1989—; mem. Gov. Coun. on Tourism, 1987-96. Co-author: An Anxious Democracy, 1982; co-editor: Science, Technology and Culture, 1974, In a State of Nature, 1982; sr. editor Vt. Life mag., 1975-87; editor Vt. History, 1977-85. Chmn. Bicentennial Com., Burlington, 1976, Vt. Coun. Hist. Preservation, 1975-78; fin. chmn. Vt. Bicentennial Commn., 1970-77; mem. Wis. Sesquicentennial Commn., 1995—; mem. N.H. Postsecondary Edn. Commn., 1983-85; trustee Vt. Hist. Soc., 1972-85, v.p., 1975-82; bd. dirs. USS Wisconsin, 1989-93, Wis. Preservation Fund Inc., 1989—; trustee, vice chmn., sec. Taliesin Preservation Commn., 1990—. Fellow Ctr. for Rsch. on Vt.; mem. Nat. Coun. on Pub. History (bd. dirs. 1988-90), Am. Assn. State and Local History (councillor 1988-91), Vt. Archeol. Soc. (pres. 1971-74), Madison Club. Office: Frank Lloyd Wright Found Taliesin-West Scottsdale AZ 85261-4430 Other Office: Frank Lloyd Wright Found Spring Green WI

MULLER, JENNIFER, choreographer, dancer; b. Yonkers, N.Y., Oct. 16, 1944; d. Don Medford and Lynette (Heldman) Muller. BS, Juilliard Sch. Music, 1967. instr. in dance H.S. Performing Arts, 1967-72, Sarah Lawrence Coll., 1968-72, The Juilliard Sch., 1969-70, Nederlands Dans Theater, 1971-76, Utah rep., 1973-74; commns.: Alvin Ailey Am. Dance Theatre, N.Y.C., 1977, 85, Festival d'Avignon, France, 1980, Lyon Opera Ballet, France, 1984, Aterballetto, 1988, Ballet Stagium, 1991, Dansgroep Krisztina de Chatel, 1992, Tanz-Forum Staatsoper Koln, Sachsische Staatopera-Dresden, ARTSCAPE-Balt., 1991, 95, Aterballetto, Italy, 1993, Les Ballet Jazz de Montreal, 1994, Ballet du Nord, France, 1995, White Wave Rising, 1996, Bat Dor Dance Co., Israel, Nederlands Dans Theatre III, Ballet Contemporaneo, Argentina; cons. Met. Mus. Art, 1971-72. Mem. Pearl Lang Dance Co., N.Y.C, 1959-63, prin. dance, Jose Limon Dance Co., N.Y.C., 1963-71, assoc. dir., choreographer, prin. dancer, Louis Falco Dance Co., N.Y.C., 1968-74; founder, dir. choreographer: Jennifer Muller/The Works, N.Y.C., 1974—; choreographic works include: Nostalgia, 1971, Rust, 1971, Cantata, 1972, Tub, 1973, An American Beauty Rose, 1974, Biography, 1974, Speeds, 1974, Winter Pieces, 1974, Clown, 1974, Four Chairs, 1974, Wyeth, 1974, White, 1975, Strangers, 1975, Beach, 1976, Crossword, 1977, Predicaments for Five, 1977, Mondriaan, 1977, Lovers, 1978, Solo, 1979, Conversations, 1979, Chant, 1980, Terrain, 1981, Shed, 1982, Kite, 1983, Souls, 1984, The Enigma, 1986, Fields, 1986, Couches, 1986, Life/Times, 1986, Darkness and Light, 1986, Interrupted River, 1987, Occasional Encounters, 1988, City, 1988, The Flight of a Predatory Bird, 1989, Refracted Light, 1990, RIGHTeous About Passing (on the LEFT), 1990, Woman with Visitors at 3am, 1991, Regards, 1991, arm in arm in arm..., 1991, Thesaurus, 1991, Glass Houses, 1991, 2-1=1/Attic, 1992, Momentary Gathering, 1992, The Waiting Room, 1993, The Politician/Peeling the Onion, 1993, Orbs, Spheres and Other Circular Bodies, 1993, HUMAN/NATURE-A Response to the Longhouse Gardens, 1993, Pierrot, 1993, Desire-That DNA Urge, 1994, Point of View (A Case of Persimmons and Picasso), 1994, The Spotted Owl, 1995, Some Days are Like That, 1995, Promontory, 1996, Fruit, 1996, The Dinner Party, 1996, A Broken Wing, 1996; choreographer for theatrical prodns.: Frimbo, 1980, The Death of von Richthofen..., 1982, Fame, The Musical, 1988, Up Against It, 1989, The Seven Deadly Sins, 1990, Signature, 1990, Esther, 1993. Recipient Best Performance award Berlin Festival, 1977, Acad. award Juilliard Sch. Music, 1967, Carbonell award, 1989; grantee Nat. Endowment for Arts, 1971-77, 80-85, 86-87, 87-88, Creative Artists Pub. Svc., 1976-77, N.Y. State Coun. on Arts, 1976-77, 78-79, 85-93, N.Y.C. Dept. Cultural Affairs, 1978-79, 94-97. Mem. Am. Guild Mus. Artists, Soc. Stage Dirs. and Choreographers. Home and Office: The Muller/Works Found Inc 131 W 24th St New York NY 10011-1942

MULLER, JEROME KENNETH, photographer, art director, editor; b. Amityville, N.Y., July 18, 1934; s. Alphons and Helen (Haberl) M.; m. Nora Marie Nestor, Dec. 21, 1974. BS, Marquette U., 1961; postgrad., Calif. State U., Fullerton, 1985-86; MA, Nat. U., San Diego, 1988; postgrad., Newport Psychoanalytic Inst., 1988-90. Comml. and editorial photographer N.Y.C., 1952-55; mng. editor Country Beautiful mag., Milw., 1961-62, Reprodns. Rev. mag., N.Y.C., 1967-68; editor, art dir. Orange County (Calif.) Illustrated, Newport Beach, 1962-67, art editor, 1970-79, exec. editor, art dir., 1968-69; owner, CEO Creative Svcs. Advt. Agy., Newport Beach, 1969-79; founder, CEO Mus. Graphics, Costa Mesa, Calif., 1978—; tchr. photography Lindenhurst (N.Y.) High Sch., 1952-54; tchr. comic art U. Calif., Irvine, 1979; guest curator 50th Anniversary Exhbn. Mickey Mouse, 1928-78, The Bowers Mus., Santa Ana, Calif., 1978; organized Moving Image Exhbn. Mus. Sci. and Industry, Chgo., Cooper-Hewitt Mus., N.Y.C., William Rockhill Nelson Gallery, Kansas City, 1981; collector original works outstanding Am. cartoonists at major mus. One-man shows include Souk Gallery, Newport Beach, 1970, Gallery 2, Santa Ana, Calif., 1972, Cannery Gallery, Newport Beach, 1974, Mus. Graphics Gallery, 1993, White Gallery Portland State U., 1996, U. Calif., Irvine, 1997; author: Rex Brandt, 1972; contbr. photographs and articles to mags. Served with USAF, 1956-57. Recipient two silver medals 20th Ann. Exhbn. Advt. and Editorial Art in West, 1965. Mem. APA, Mus. Modern Art (N.Y.C.), Met. Mus. Art, Art Mus. Assn. Am., L.A. Press Club, Newport Beach Tennis Club, Orange County Mus. Art, Alpha Sigma Nu. Home: 2438 Bowdoin Pl Costa Mesa CA 92626-6304 Office: PO Box 10743 Costa Mesa CA 92627-0234

MULLER, JOHN BARTLETT, university president; b. Port Jefferson, N.Y., Nov. 8, 1940; s. Frederick Henry and Estelle May (Reeve) M.; m. Barbara Ann Schmidt, May 30, 1964 (dec. 1972); m. Lynn Anne Spongberg, Oct. 10, 1987. AB in Polit. Sci., U. Rochester, 1962; postgrad. in apologetics, Westminster Sem., Phila., 1962-63; MS in Psychology, Purdue U., 1968, PhD in Psychology, 1975. Asst. prof. psychology Roberts Wesleyan Coll., Rochester, N.Y., 1964-66, acting chmn. div. behavioral sci., dir. instl. research, 1967-70; vis. asst. prof. psychology Wabash Coll., Crawfordsville, Ind., 1970-71; research assoc. Ind. U.-Purdue U., Indpls., 1971-72; prof. psychology, v.p. for acad. affairs Hillsdale (Mich.) Coll., 1972-85; pres. BMW Assocs., Osseo, Mich., 1984-85, Bellevue (Nebr.) U., 1985—; bd. dirs. Nebr. Ind. Coll. Found., Omaha, Assn. Ind. Colls. Nebr., Lincoln; bd. advisors Norwest Bank of Bellevue, Applied Information Mgmt. Inst. Contbr. articles to profl. jours. and textbooks. Bd. dirs. Midlands Community Hosp., 1989—, Boys Club of Omaha. Nat. Inst. Mental Health fellowship Purdue U., 1963, Nat. Tchg. fellowship Fed. Govt., 1967, Townsend fellowship U. Rochester, 1962. Mem. APA, Bellevue C. of C. (bd. dirs. 1989-95), Phi Beta Kappa, Phi Kappa Phi. Republican. Home: 404 Ridgewood Dr Bellevue NE 68005-4745 Office: Bellevue U Office of the Pres 1000 Galvin Rd S Bellevue NE 68005-3058

MULLER, LYLE DEAN, religious organization administrator; b. Owatonna, Minn., Mar. 9, 1935; s. Robert John and Esther Ida (Eaker) M.; m. Marlene K. Kliemek, Sept. 7, 1957; children: Mark, Susan. BA, Valparaiso U., 1956; MDiv, Concordia Sem., 1961. Ordained to ministry Luth. Ch.- Mo. Synod. Pastor Emmanuel Luth. Ch., Ft. Wayne, Ind., 1961-63, Trinity Luth. Ch., Danville, Ill., 1963-69, St. Luke Luth. Ch., Itasca, Ill., 1969-79; exec. evangelism and missions no. Ill. Dist. Luth. Ch.-Mo. Synod, Hillsdale, 1979-90; exec. dir. evangelism svcs. Luth. Ch.-Mo. Synod, St. Louis, 1990-94, exec. dir. congl. svcs., 1994—. Author: (manuals) Good News Day, 1982, Witness Workshop, 1983, Ministry to Inactives, 1987, Assimilation, 1988. Office: Luth Ch Mo Synod 1333 S Kirkwood Rd Saint Louis MO 63122-7226

MULLER, MARCEL W(ETTSTEIN), electrical engineering educator; b. Vienna, Austria, Nov. 1, 1922; came to U.S., 1940; s. Georg and Josephine (David) M.; m. Esther Ruth Hagler, Feb. 2, 1947; children: Susan, George, Janet. BSEE, Columbia U., 1949, AM in Physics, 1952; PhD, Stanford U., 1957. Sr. scientist Varian Assocs., Palo Alto, Calif., 1952-66; prof. elec. engring. Washington U., St. Louis, 1966-91, prof. emeritus, rsch. prof., 1991—; vis. lectr. U. Zurich, Switzerland, 1962-63; vis. prof. U. Colo., Boulder, summer 1969; vis. scientist Max Planck Inst., Stuttgart, Fed. Republic of Germany, 1976-77; cons. Hewlett-Packard Labs., Palo Alto, 1985-89, SRI Internat., Menlo Park, Calif., 1986—. Sgt. U.S. Army, 1943-46. Recipient Humboldt prize Alexander von Humboldt Soc., 1976; Fulbright grantee, 1977, grantee NSF, 1967—. Fellow IEEE, Am. Physical Soc. Achievements include development of Maser quantum noise theory; developments in micromagnetism; contributions to magnetic information storage; invention Magneprint security system. Home: 4954 Lindell Blvd Saint Louis MO 63108-1500 Office: Washington Univ Campus Box 1127 1 Brookings Dr Saint Louis MO 63130-4862

MULLER, MARGIE HELLMAN, financial services consultant; b. L.A., Nov. 30, 1927; d. S. Jack and Marjorie (Ullman) Hellman; m. Steven Muller, June 19, 1951; children: Julie, Elizabeth. BA, UCLA, 1949. Sales promotion asst. Joyce (Calif.) Ltd., London, 1950-51; copywriter Hamrick Advt., Ithaca, N.Y., 1951-54; sr. assoc. Conant and Co., N.Y.C., 1954-57; mgr. advt. and pub. relations Theodore Presser Co., Bryn Mawr, Pa., 1957-58; acct. exec. Laux Advt., Ithaca, 1959-60; asst. v.p. mktg. Tompkins County Trust Co., Ithaca, 1960-71; v.p. Md. Nat. Bank, Balt., 1971-77; sr. v.p. Union Trust Bancorp., Balt., 1977-83; state bank commr. Balt., 1983-96. Contbr. articles to profl. jours. Bd. dirs. The Leadership Balt., 1985-87; pres. Balt. Promotion Coun., 1974-75, Health and Welfare Coun., Ctrl. Md., 1982-85; mem. adv. commn. Md. Dept. Econ. and Cmty. Devel., 1975-83; mem. adv. coun. Credit Rsch. Ctr., Krannert Grad. Sch. Mgmt., Purdue U., vice chmn., 1993-94, chmn., 1994-95. Mem. Bank Mktg. Assn. (bd. dirs. 1974-78, exec. com. 1977-78, nat. conv. chmn. 1977), Nat. Assn. State Credit Union Suprs. (bd. dirs. 1984-88), Conf. State Bank Suprs. (bd. dirs. 1988-94, vice chmn. 1990-91, chmn. 1991-93), Fed. Fin. Instns. Exam. Coun. (state liaison com. 1991-94, chmn. 1993-94), mem. adv. coun. cmty.Resource Bank (chmn., 1990-95).

MULLER, MERVIN EDGAR, information systems educator, consultant; b. Hollywood, Calif., June 1, 1928; s. Emanuel and Bertha (Zimmerman) M.; m. Barbara McAdam, July 13, 1963; children: Jeffrey McAdam, Stephen McAdam, Todd McAdam. AB, UCLA, 1949, MA, 1951, PhD, 1954. Instr. in math. Cornell U., 1954-56; rsch. assoc. in math. Princeton U., 1956-59; sr. statistician, dept. mgr. IBM, N.Y.C., White Plains, 1956-64; sr. scientist statis. and elec. engring. Princeton U., 1968-69; prof. computer sci. and stats. U. Wis., 1964-71; prof. computer sci. George Mason U., 1985; dept. dir. World Bank, Washington, 1971-81, sr. advisor, 1981-85; Robert M. Critchfield prof. computer info. sci. Ohio State U., 1985—, dept. chair, 1985-94; chair sci. and tech. info. bd. NRC, NAS; bd. dirs. Advanced Info. Tech. Ctr., Columbus, Ohio. Contbr. numerous articles to profl. jours. Bd. trustees First Unitarian Ch., Bethesda, Md., 1975-79. Rsch. grantee AT&T, Columbus, Ohio, 1987. Fellow Am. Statis. Assn.; mem. Internat. Statis. Inst. (steering com. Internat. Rsch. Ctr., 1987-89), Internat. Assn. for Statis. Computing (sci. sec. 1979-83, pres. 1977-79). Avocations: reading, jogging, walking. Home: 4171 Clairmont Rd Columbus OH 43220-4501 Office: Ohio State U Dept Computer Info Sci 2015 Neil Ave Columbus OH 43210-1210

MULLER, NICHOLAS GUTHRIE, lawyer, business executive; b. Porterville, Calif., Nov. 27, 1942; s. Francis J. and Jane Ellen (Guthrie) M.; m. Sally Anne Diggles, June 10, 1964; children: Thomas, Amy. A.B. in English, U. Notre Dame, 1964; J.D., U. Calif., Berkeley, 1967. Bar: Colo. 1968; Lic. real estate broker, Colo. Summer intern Solicitor's Office, Dept. Interior, Washington, 1966; assoc. Gorsuch, Kirgis, Campbell, Walker & Grover, Denver, 1967-69; legal counsel Gates Aviation Corp., Denver, 1970-71; corp. sec., gen. counsel Gates Learjet Corp., Denver, 1971-72; legal counsel Samsonite Corp., Denver, 1972-75, gen. counsel, 1975-85, v.p., 1978-85; gen. counsel Gates Corp. and Gates Rubber Co., 1985-87; mem. mgmt. com., gen. counsel Colo. Power Ptnrs., Denver, 1987—; exec. dir. Colo. Ind. Energy Assn., Denver. Formerly bd. dirs. Presbyn./St. Luke's Med. Ctr.; bd. dirs. Mt. Med. Affiliates, Leadership Denver. Mem. ABA, Colo. Bar Assn. (bd. dirs., bd. govs.), Denver Bar Assn., Am. Corp. Counsel (dir. nat. assn. and Colo. chpt.), U.S. C. of C., Denver C. of C., Notre Dame Club of Denver, Rotary. Home: 25931 Village Cir Golden CO 80401-7228 Office: Colorado Power Ptnrs 475 17th St Ste 940 Denver CO 80202-4019

MULLER, PETER, lawyer, entertainment company executive, retail company executive, consultant; b. Teplitz-Sanov, Czechoslovakia, Mar. 4, 1947; came to U.S., 1949; s. Alexander and Elizabeth Rudolpha (Weingarten) M.; m. Irene Smolarski, Nov. 18, 1971 (div. 1973); children: Chloe, Aurora; m. Esther Unterman Meisler, Jan. 4, 1987 (div. 1995). BA, NYU, 1968, JD cum laude. Entertainment editor Ambience mag., N.Y.C., 1978-79, Women's Life mag., N.Y.C., 1980-81; sole practice N.Y.C., 1984—; entertainment writer Jewish Press; chief exec. officer Producers Releasing Corp., N.Y. and Nev., 1987-88, pres. entertainment div., 1987-88; pres., founder Muller Entertainment Group, N.Y.C. and Calif., 1988—; pres., chief oper. officer ACA Joe, Inc., San Francisco and N.Y.C.; also bd. dirs. ACA Joe Inc., San Francisco and N.Y.C.; expert tech. adv. svc. for attys., Pa., 1987—; lectr. entertainment and comm. bus. to various orgns.; adj. prof. NYU, UCLA. Author: Show Business Law, 1991, The Music Business: A Legal Perspective, 1994. Mem. Vol. Lawyers for the Arts, N.Y.C., 1987—. Mem. ABA (forum on entertainment and sports industries, forum on copyright, trademark and patent law), N.Y. State Bar Assn., NYU Alumni Assn. (bd. dirs. 1987—, v.p. bd. dirs., coun.), NYU Alumni Coun., Assn. of Am. Mgmt. Assn. (pres.). Avocations: sports, swimming, car enthusiast, writing, travel.

MULLER, PRISCILLA ELKOW, art historian; b. N.Y.C., Feb. 15, 1930; d. John and Katherine (Bulka) Elkow; m. C. Robert Muller, Feb. 15, 1950. BA, Bklyn. Coll., 1951; MA, NYU, 1959, PhD, 1963. Asst. curator Hispanic Soc. Am., N.Y.C., 1964-68, curator, 1968-94, curator emeritus, 1994—; lectr. Bklyn. Coll., 1966; cons. in field. Author: The Drawings of Antonio del Castillo y Saavedra, 1964, Jewels in Spain, 1972, Goya's Black Paintings, 1984, Sorolla: An 80th Anniversary Exhibition; contbr. articles to profl. jours. NEA fellow, 1977. Mem. Author's Guild, Coll. Art Assn. Am., Internat. Coun. Mus. (internat. com. fine arts), Am. Soc. Hispanic Art Hist. Studies, Internat. Found. Art Rsch. (adv. coun.), The Soc. for Jewelry Historians. Avocation: distance running. Office: Hispanic Soc Am 155th St 613 W Broadway New York NY 10032

MULLER, RICHARD AUGUST, physicist, author; b. N.Y.C., Jan. 6, 1944; s. August Joseph and Catherine (Harabin) M.; m. Rosemary Findley, Sept. 3, 1966; children: Betsy, Melinda. AB, Columbia U., N.Y.C., 1964; PhD, U. Calif., Berkeley, 1969; LHD, Am. U. Switzerland, Leysin, 1989. Rsch. physicist U. Calif., Berkeley, 1969-78, assoc. prof. physics, 1978-80, prof. physics, sr. faculty scientist, 1980—; Jason cons. U.S. Dept. Def., Washington, 1974—; mem. arms control com. U.S. Nat. Acad. Scis., Washington, 1984-87; mem. adv. bd. Inst. Theoretical Physics, Santa Barbara, Calif., 1982-86; fellow Com. for Sci. Investigation Claims of Paranormal. Author: Nemesis, 1988, The Three Big Bangs, 1996. Recipient Founder's prize Tex. Instruments Found., 1977, Alan T. Waterman award NSF, 1978; MacArthur Found. fellow, 1982. Fellow AAAS, Am. Phys. Soc.; mem. Am. Geophys. Union, Fedn. Am. Scientists (trustee), Bohemian Club. Avocations: skiing, backpacking. Home: 2831 Garber St Berkeley CA 94705-1314 Office: Lawrence Berkeley Lab 50-232 Lbl Berkeley CA 94720 *Learning is the second greatest joy in life.*

MULLER, RICHARD STEPHEN, electrical engineer, educator; b. Weehawken, N.J., May 5, 1933; s. Irving Ernest and Marie Victoria Muller; m. Joyce E. Regal, June 29, 1957; children: Paul Stephen, Thomas Richard. ME, Stevens Inst. Tech., Hoboken, N.J., 1955; MSEE, Calif. Inst. Tech., 1957, PhD in Elect. Engring. and Physics, 1962. Engr.-in-tng., 1955. Test engr. Wright Aero/Curtiss Wright, Woodridge, N.J., 1953-54; mem. tech. staff Hughes Aircraft Co., Culver City, Calif., 1955-61; instr. U. So. Calif., L.A., 1960-61; asst. prof., then assoc. prof. U. Calif., Berkeley, 1962-72, prof., 1973—; guest prof. Swiss Fed. Inst. Tech., 1993; founder, dir. Berkeley Sensor and Actuator Ctr., 1985—. Co-author: Device Electronics for Integrated Circuits, 1977, 2d rev. edit., 1986, Microsensors, 1990; contbr. more than 200 articles to profl. jours. Pres. Kensington (Calif.) Mcpl. Adv. Coun.; trustee Stevens Inst. of Technology, 1996—. Fellow Hughes Aircraft Co., 1955-57, NSF, 1959-62, NATO postdoctoral fellow, 1968-69, Fulbright fellow, 1982-83, Alexander von Humboldt prize, 1993, Tech. U. Berlin, 1994; Berkeley citation, 1994, Stevens Renaissance award, 1995. Fellow IEEE; mem. IEEE Press Bd., NAE, Nat. Materials (adv. bd. 1994—), Electron Devices Soc. (adv. com. 1984—), Internat. Sensor and Actuator Meeting (chmn. steering com.). Achievements include 18 U.S. and foreign patents; construction of first operating micromotor. Office: U Calif Dept EECS 401 Cory Hall Berkeley CA 94720-1770

MULLER, ROBERT JOSEPH, gynecologist; b. New Orleans, Dec. 5, 1946; s. Robert Harry and Camille (Eckert) M.; m. Susan Philipsen, Aug. 22, 1974; children: Ryan, Matt. BS, St. Louis U., 1968; BS, MSc, Emory U., 1976; MD, La. State U., New Orleans, 1981. Intern Charity Hosp., New Orleans, 1981-82; resident La. State U. Affiliate Hosp., 1982-85; resident staff physician La. State U. Med. Ctr., New Orleans, 1981-85; pvt. practice Camellia Women's Ctr., Slidell, La., 1985—; staff physician Tulane Med. Ctr., New Orleans, 1986—; med. dir. Northshore Regional Med. Ctr., Slidell, 1987—, New Orleans Police Dept., 1981-95, S.W. La. Search and Rescue, Covington, La., 1986—, St. Tammany Parish Sheriff Dept., Covington, 1989—, commdr., 1990—, Camellia City Classic, Slidell, 1989—, Crawfishman Triathalon, Mandeville, La., 1988—, Res-Q-Med Laser Team, 1984—. Contbr. articles to profl. jours. Recipient Commendation Medal New Orleans Police Dept., 1986, 87, 89, Medal Valor St. Tammany Parish Sheriff Office, Covington, 1990, Cert. Valor S.E. La. Search and Rescue, Mandeville, 1990; named one of Outstanding Young Men of Am., 1984. Mem. Am. Coll. Ob-Gyn., La. State Med. Soc., Profl. Assn. Diving Instrs. (divemaster 1991, asst. instr. 1995), So. Offshore Racing Assn. (med. dir. 1982—), Offshore Profl. Racing Tour (med. dir. staff 1990—), Am. Power Boat Assn. (med. staff 1984-89). Roman Catholic. Avocations: scuba diving, boating, shooting. Home: 128 Golden Pheasant Dr Slidell LA 70461-3007 Office: Camellia Womens Ctr 105 Smart Pl Slidell LA 70458-2039

MULLER, SIGFRID AUGUSTINE, dermatologist, educator; b. Panama City, Panama, Feb. 20, 1930; came to U.S., 1932, naturalized, 1967; s. Louis and Marciana (Espino) M.; m. Jane Barbara Zierden, Dec. 28, 1964; children—Sigfrid Augustine, Stephen, Scott, Maria. A.B., Pepperdine U., 1949; M.D., St. Louis U., 1953; M.S., Mayo Grad. Sch. Medicine, 1958. Intern Gorgas Hosp., C.Z., 1953-54; resident Indpls. Hosp., 1954-55, Mayo Grad. Sch. Medicine, 1955-58; practice medicine specializing dermatology Rochester, Minn., 1961—; cons. dermatology Mayo Clinic, 1961—; asst. prof. dermatology U. Panama, 1958-60; prof. dermatology Mayo Clinic, 1972-95, Robert H. Kieckhefer prof. dermatology, 1983-95, chmn. dept., 1983-94, dir. dermatology residency tng., 1983-94, dir. dermatopathology lab., 1983-94; prof. emeritus dermatology Mayo Med. Sch., 1995; chair dept. dermatology, prof. med. U. Nev. Sch. Med., 1995—; dir. task force for genetics Nat. Program for Genetics, 1969; bd. dirs., treas. Found. for Internat. Dermatol. Edn., 1976-85, pres., 1985—. Contbr. articles to profl. jours. Asst. chief editor: Archives of Dermatology, 1974—, Medicins Cutanea, 1968—, Internat. Bull. Psoriasis, 1973—. Recipient Pres.'s award Pepperdine U., 1973, condecoracion Order of Vasco Nunez de Balboa, Panama, 1994. Fellow ACP; mem. AAAS, AMA, Am. Dermatol. Assn., Am. Acad. Dermatology, Soc. Investigative Dermatology, Am. Soc. Dermatopathology, Am. Fedn. Clin. Rsch., Minn. Dermatol. Soc. (pres. 1972-73), Soc. Dermatol. Genetics (pres. 1972-73), Noah Worcester Dermatol. Soc. (pres. 1972-73), Internat. Soc. Dermatology (v.p., sec.-gen. 1979-89, pres. 1989-94, hon. pres. 1994—), Found. for Internat. Dermatol. Edn. (sec./treas. 1975-84, pres. 1985—). Office: 630 S Rancho Dr Ste E Las Vegas NV 89106-4849 *I have never felt like a foreigner in this wonderful land of opportunity. Rather, I perceived at an early age that achievement is within almost everyone's abilities. Ultimately, my success will not be determined by honors or recognition but by love: love of God, love of family, and love of my fellow man.*

MULLER, WILLARD C(HESTER), writer; b. Havre, Mont., May 7, 1916; s. Chester Rudolph and Clara (Hansen) M.; m. Carolyn Elfrid Bue, Jan. 27, 1945; children: Marolyn Jean, Barbara Anne, Nancy Eleanor. BA, Stanford U., 1941; MPA, Maxwell Grad. Sch. Govt. Adminstrn., 1943; student, Nat. War Coll., 1961-62. Newspaper reporter, short story writer Bremerton (Wash.) Daily Searchlight, 1934-36; White House corr. Bremerton Daily Searchlight and Port Angeles Evening News, Washington, 1941; mgmt. analyst USDA, 1942, 46-47; mem. staff for food, agr. and forestry U.S. Dept. Army and U.S. High Commr. for Germany, Munich and Frankfurt, Fed. Republic Germany, 1948-50; dist. adminstr., Am. consul U.S. Trust Territory of Pacific Islands, Truk, Caroline Islands, 1951-55; dep. dir. ICA, U.S. Ops. Mission to Nepal, Kathmandu, 1956-58; dir. U.S. Ops. to Somali Republic, 1958-61, Office East and Southern African Affairs, AID, Dept. State, Washington, 1962-65, AID, Kampala, Uganda, 1965-70; assoc. dir. for land reform AID, Saigon, Republic of Vietnam, 1970-73; ret. AID, 1973, cons., 1974-81; free lance writer, 1973—. Author various short stories; contbr. articles to profl. jours. Chmn. steering com. 4-state program dialogue on peace Pacific NW dist. Am. Luth. Ch., Seattle, 1983-85; mem. Clallam br. Wash. State Centennial Commn., 1986-89; mem. Food Bank Bd., Port Angeles, Wash., 1986-90. Lt. USNR, 1943-45, PTO. Mem. Am. Soc. Pub. Adminstrn., Am. Forestry Assn., Am. Fgn. Service Assn., Pacific N.W. Morgan Horse Assn. Lodge: Kiwanis. Avocations: horseback riding, backpacking, world travel. Home and Office: 3624 S Mount Angeles Rd Port Angeles WA 98362-8910

MULLER, WILLIAM ALBERT, III, library director; b. Savannah, Ga., Jan. 1, 1943; s. William Albert Jr. and Julia Catherine (Cleary) M.; m. Claudya Barbara Burkett, Dec. 12, 1965 (div. 1986); 1 child, Martha Genevieve; m. Pamala Qualls, Apr. 9, 1988; 1 child, Tabitha Wade. BA, Ga. So. Coll., 1966; MLS, Emory U., 1969. Dir. War Woman Regional Libr., Elberton, Ga., 1969-73; rsch. libr. City of Savannah, 1973-75; dir. Mason County Pub. Libr., Point Pleasant, W.Va., 1976-78; pub. rels. cons. Eastern Shore Regional Libr., Salisbury, Md., 1978-81; dir. Brooke County Pub. Libr., Wellsburg, W.Va., 1982-84, McDowell Pub. Libr., Welch, W.Va., 1984-88, Bristol (Va.) Pub. Libr., 1988—; sec. So. W.Va. Libr. Automation Corp., Beckley, 1984-87, pres. 1987-88, S.W. Info. Network Group, Abindgdon, Va., 1990-91, treas. (swing) 1993—. Fundraiser Paramount Found., Bristol, 1989; acct. exec. United Way Fund of Bristol, 1991; bd. dirs. Mid-Atlantic Chamber Orch., Bristol, 1988-92, treas., 1992; bd. dirs. Bristol Preservation Soc., 1988—, Nat. Ctr. for Quality, 1992, Main St. Bristol, 1991-95, treas., 1994. Mem. ALA, Southeastern Libr. Assn., Va. Libr. Assn., Rotary Internat. (club pres. 1980-81). Democrat. Avocations: gardening, cabinetry, photography, traveling, model railroads. Home: 706 Piedmont Ave Bristol VA 24201-3446 Office: Bristol Pub Libr 701 Goode St Bristol VA 24201-4155

MULLER, WILLIAM HENRY, JR., surgeon, educator; b. Dillon, S.C., Aug. 19, 1919; s. William Henry and Octavia Elizabeth (Bethea) M.; m. Hildwin Clare Headly, Mar. 23, 1946; children: William Henry III, Marietta John Lewis. BS, The Citadel, 1940, DS (hon.), 1972; MD, Duke U., 1943; DHL (hon.), Med. U. S.C., 1977. Diplomate Am. Bd. Thoracic Surgery, Am. Bd. Surgery (rep. conf. com. grad. tng. in surgery). Intern Johns Hopkins Hosp., Balt., 1944, asst. surgery, asst. resident, 1944-46, resident gen. surgery, instr. surgery, 1948-49, resident cardiovascular surgery, 1949; practice gen. surgery Dillon, 1947-48; asst. prof. surgery UCLA, 1949-53, assoc. prof. Sch. Medicine, 1953-54; attending specialist thoracic surgery Wadsworth VA Hosp., Los Angeles; chief sect. cardiovascular surgery Los Angeles County-Harbor Gen. Hosp., Torrance, Calif.; cons. surgery St. Johns's, Santa Monica Hosps., 1949-54; cons. cardiovascular surgery U.S. Naval Hosp., San Diego, 1953-54; Stephen H. Watts prof. surgery, chmn. dept. U. Va. Sch. Medicine, 1954-82, v.p. health affairs, 1976-88, univ. prof. surgery and health policy, 1988-90, S. Hurt Watts prof. surgery emeritus, 1990—, v.p. for health affairs emeritus; surgeon-in-chief U. Va. Hosp., 1954-82; chmn. S.E. Surg. Congress; mem. Pres.'s Panel on Heart Disease, 1972; past chmn. surgery study sect. NIH; mem. exec. com., div. med. scis. NRC. Mem. editorial bd.: Am. Jour Surgery, Annals of Surgery, Am. Surgeon; contbr. articles to med jours. Trustee, mem. exec. com. Duke U. Served as capt. M.C. AUS, 1946-47. Named One of 10 Outstanding Young Men of Yr. U.S. Jr. C. of C., Calif. Jr. C. of C., 1952; recipient Disting. Alumni award (1st award) Duke U. Med. Ctr., 1969; Thomas Jefferson award U. Va., 1982; McCallie Sch. Alumni Achievement award, 1986; Paul Harris fellow Nat. Rotary Found., 1988. Fellow ACS (past chmn., forum com. fundamental surg. problems, regent 1971—, chmn. bd. regents 1976-78, pres.-elect 1979); mem. Internat. Soc. Surgery, Internat. Cardiovascular Soc. (past v.p.), AMA, Am. Surg. Assn. (pres. 1974-75), So. Surg. Assn. (pres. 1975), Pacific Coast Surg. Assn., Am. Assn. Thoracic Surgery, Soc. Univ. Surgeons (past pres.), Soc. Surgery Alimentary Tract, Assn. Acad. Surgeons, James IV Assn. Surgeons (v.p. U.S.), Med. Soc. Va., Albemarle County Med. Soc., Soc. Vascular Surgery (past pres.), Am. Heart Assn. (chmn. surgery research study com., mem. central research com.), Va. Surg. Soc, Halsted Soc., Johns Hopkins Soc. Scholars, Raven Soc., Sigma Xi, Alpha Omega Alpha, Phi Chi. Office: U Va Health Sci Ctr PO Box 470 Charlottesville VA 22902-0470

MÜLLER-EBERHARD, HANS JOACHIM, medical research scientist, administrator; b. Magdeburg, Germany, May 5, 1927; came to U.S., 1959, naturalized, 1973; s. G. Adolf and Emma (Jenrich) Müller-E.; m. Irma Gigli, June 29, 1985. M.D., U. Göttingen, Fed. Republic Germany, 1953; M.D.Sc., U. Uppsala, Sweden, 1961; D. Medicinae h.c., Ruhr U., Bochum, W.Ger., 1982. Asst. physician dept. medicine U. Göttingen, 1953-54; asst., also asst. physician hosp. Rockefeller Inst., 1954-57; fellow Swedish Med. Research Council, 1957-59; asst. prof., then assoc. prof., also hosp. physician Rockefeller U., 1959-63; mem. dept. exptl. pathology Scripps Clinic and Research Found., La Jolla, Calif., 1963-74, chmn. dept. molecular immunology, 1974-82, chmn. dept. immunology, 1982-85, head div. molecular immunology, 1985-87; assoc. dir. Scripps Clinic and Research Found. (Research Inst.), 1978-86; dir. Bernhard Nocht Inst. for Tropical Medicine, Hamburg, Fed. Republic Germany, 1988-95; Cecil H. and Ida M. Green investigator med. rsch., 1972-86; lectr. immunochemistry U. Uppsala, 1961—; Harvey lectr., 1970; adj. prof. pathology U. Calif. Med. Sch., La Jolla, 1968-94; prof. U. Hamburg, 1990—; prof. internal medicine, prof. molecular medicine, dir. inst. molecular medicine for the prevention of human diseases U. Tex. Med. Sch., Houston, 1995—, Cullen chair in molecular medicine, 1996—. Co-editor: Textbook of Immunopathology, 1976, Springer Seminars in Immunopathology, 1978-87; author numerous sci. articles; adv. editor: Jour. Exptl. Medicine, 1963—; mem. jour. editorial bds. Recipient Squibb award Infectious Diseases Soc. Am., 1970; T. Duckett Jones Meml. award Helen Hay Whitney Found., 1971; Distinguished Achievement award Modern Medicine mag., 1974; Karl Landsteiner Meml. award Am. Assn. Blood Banks, 1974; ann. Internat. award Gairdner Found., Can., 1974; Mayo H. Soley award Western Soc. Clin. Research, 1975; Emil von Behring prize Philipps U., Marburg, Ger., 1977; Caballero de la Orden de San Carlos (Colombia), 1984, Robert Koch Medal in Gold, 1987, Rous-Whipple award Am. Assn. Pathologists, 1988, Philip Levine award Am. Soc. of Clin. Pathologists, 1988. Fellow AAAS; mem. NAS, Am. Soc. Exptl. Pathology (Parke, Davis award 1966), Assn. Am. Physicians, Western Assn. Physicians, Am. Soc. Clin. Investigation, Am. Assn. Immunologists, Am. Acad. Allergy, Am. Soc. Biochemistry and Molecular Biology, German Soc. Immunology (hon.), Sigma Xi. Office: Inst Molecular Medicine 2121 W Holcombe Blvd Houston TX 77030-3303

MULLIGAN, DAVID KEITH, consulting company executive; b. Detroit, Jan. 25, 1951; s. Robert Keith and Yvonne Bette (Yankosky) M. Student, Oakland Coll., 1973-78. Cert. data processor, quality technician, quality auditor, software quality engr.; NASD gen. securities registered rep. Pres. Atlas Prodns., N.Y.C., 1973—; cons. info. systems, human factors, tech. and mktg. comm. Author: Human Factors in Document Design, 1982, Computer Aids to Software Engineering, 1984, Document Design and Production for the '90s, 1989, Documentation and System Maintenance, 1989, Avoiding Outsourcing and Its Demoralizing Consequences, 1990, Programmer-Analyst: Dinosaur of the '90s, 1990, Information Management: New Thinking for the '90s, 1991, Product Documentation: Key to Internat. Marketing Success, 1993, Joint Application Design Critical Success Factors, 1994, Successful Worldwide Interactive Marketing, 1995, Management Information: Lifeblood of Business, 1996, Executive Ego: Most Powerful Force in Business, 1997, Investigation Techniques in the Healthcare Industry, 1997; co-author: Structured Analysis and Design for the Case User, 1993. Mem. ASCAP, Am. Soc. Quality Control, Am. Fedn. of Musicians, Inst. Certification Computer Profls., Data Processing Mgmt. Assn., Am. Soc. for Automation in Pharmacy, The Authors Guild, Am. Mensa. Avocations: musical composition, music, photography. Office: Atlas Prodns 109 E 36th St Ste 3F New York NY 10016-3447

MULLIGAN, ELINOR PATTERSON, lawyer; b. Bay City, Mich., Apr. 20, 1929; d. Frank Clark and Agnes (Murphy) P.; m. John C. O'Connor, Oct. 28, 1950; children: Christine Fulena, Valerie Clark, Amy O'Connor, Christopher Criffan O'Connor; m. William G. Mulligan, Dec. 6, 1975. BA, U. Mich. 1950; JD, Seton Hall U., 1970. Bar: N.J., 1970. Assoc. Springfield and Newark, 1970-72; pvt. practice, Hackettstown, N.J., 1972; ptnr. Mulligan & Jacobson, N.Y.C., 1973-91, Mulligan & Mulligan, Hackettstown, 1976—; atty. Hackettstown Planning Bd., 1973-86, Blairstown Bd. Adjustment, 1973-95; sec. Warren County Ethics Com., 1976-78, sec. Dist. X and XIII Fee Arbitration Com., 1979-87, mem. and chair., 1987-91, mem. dist. ethics com. XIII, 1992—; mem. spl. com. on atty. disciplinary structure N.J. Supreme Ct., 1981—. lectr. Nat. Assn. Women Judges, 1979, N.J. Inst. Continuing Legal Edn., 1988—. Contbr. articles to profl. jours. Named Vol. of Yr. Attys. Vols. in Parole Program, 1978. Fellow Am. Acad. Matrimonial Lawyers (pres. N.J. chpt. 1995—); mem. ABA, Warren County Bar Assn. (pres. 1987-88), N.J. State Bar Assn., N.J. Women Lawyers Assn. (v.p. 1985—), Am. Mensa Soc., Kappa Alpha Theta, Union League Club (N.Y.C.), Baltusrol Golf Club (Springfield, N.J.), Panther Valley Golf and Country Club (Allamuchy, N.J.). Republican. Home: 12 Goldfinch Way Hackettstown NJ 07840-3007 Office: 480 Hwy 517 PO Box 211 Hackettstown NJ 07840-0211

MULLIGAN, HUGH AUGUSTINE, journalist; b. N.Y.C., Mar. 23, 1925; s. John Joseph and Jeanette (Wilton) M.; m. Brigid Mary Murphy, Jan. 14, 1948. B.A. summa cum laude, Marlboro Coll., 1948, L.H.D. (hon.), 1973; M.A. in English Lit, Harvard U., 1951; M.S. in Journalism, Boston U., 1951. With AP, 1952—; feature writer AP, N.Y.C., 1956-65; fgn. corr. AP, Vietnam, 1965-68; fgn. corr. Biafra, Middle East, Paris Peace Talks, 1968-69, Cambodia, Laos, 1971, No. Ireland, Nigeria, Mid. East, China, Russia, Persian Gulf, Iceland, 1971-75, The Sahel, Angola, Ulster, Svalbard, Iran, 1975-77; as fgn. corr. covered wars in Vietnam, Middle East, Oman, Biafra-Nigeria, Cambodia, Upper Volta-Mali, No. Ireland, Vietnam, Middle East, Biafra-Nigeria, Oman, Upper Volta-Mali, No. Irel; as spl corr. covered papal journeys (Pope John Paul II) Mex., Poland, Ireland, U.S., Africa, Cen. Am., Brit. Isles, Can., 1979-87; columnist Mulligan's Stew, 1977-86. Author: The Torch is Passed, 1963, No Place to Die, The Agony of Vietnam, 1967, (with Sid Moody, John Barbour) Lightning Out of Israel, 1967, anthologies How I Got That Story, 1967, Reporting, Writing from Front Row Seats, 1971, Best Sports Stories, 1980, 82, The Family Book of Humor, The Best of Irish Wit an Wisdom, 1987, The Annotated Night Before Christmas, 1991, (with Sid Moody) The 50th Anniversary: Pearl Harbor, 1991; editor: anthologies The World in 1964, 1965; now A.P. sr. feature writer and roving reporter. Served with U.S. Army, 1944-46. Recipient Gold medal Am. Newspaper Pubs. Assn., 1951, award for feature writing Nat. Headliners, 1963, award for fgn. coverage, 1967, award for internat. reporting Overseas Press Club, 1967, award for fgn. corr. Sigma Delta Chi, 1970, Mng. Editor's award for top reportial performance AP, 1972, 78, Disting. Alumni award Boston U. Sch. Pub. Communication, 1983, Yankee Quill award Acad. New Eng. Journalists, 1993; Eugene Pulliam lectureship Ball State U., 1985. Mem. Overseas Press Club, Silurians Club, Soc. 1st Divsn. 9th Air Force Assn., Nat. Soc. Newspaper Columnists. Roman Catholic. Home: 50 Crest Rd Ridgefield CT 06877-2115 Office: 50 Rockefeller Plz New York NY 10020-1605 *"Life is too short to read good books—read the best." This advice from a high school English teacher has given a golden glow to my leisure hours that TV's dreadful dross can never outsparkle.*

MULLIGAN, JAMES FRANCIS, retired business executive, lawyer; b. Attleboro, Mass., Aug. 27, 1925; s. Henry D. and Eleanor R. (Carey) M.; m. Mary Alice Mangels, Aug. 28, 1948; 1 child, Christopher. AB, Tufts U., 1947; JD, Columbia U., 1950. Bar: N.Y. 1950, Pa. 1968, U.S. Supreme Ct. 1986. Gen. atty. Erie-Lackawanna R.R., Cleve. and N.Y.C., 1950-61; gen. counsel Monroe Internat. div. Litton Industries, Orange, N.J., 1961-67; v.p., sec., gen. counsel Lukens Steel Co., Coatesville, Pa., 1967-83; v.p. law and corp. affairs, sec. Lukens, Inc., Coatesville, Pa., 1983-88; ret. Lukens, Inc., Coatesville, 1988. Pres. United Way Chester County, West Chester, Pa., 1980-81. Lt. (j.g.) USNR, 1943-46. Mem. Radley Run Country Club, Springhaven Country Club, Mariner Sands Country Club. Avocations: running, golf. Home: PO Box 213 Pocopson PA 19366-0213 Home (winter): 5623 Foxcross Pl Stuart FL 34997

MULLIGAN, JAMES KENNETH, government official; b. Pawtucket, R.I., Aug. 31, 1911; s. James Alexander and Margaret (Fitzsimmons) M.; m. Louise Wring Lane, June 3, 1932; children—Kathryn Lane, Martha Louise, Jean Margaret. Ph.B., U. Chgo., 1934, M.A., 1937. Personnel adminstr. Chgo. Park Dist., 1938-40; dir. youth personnel Chgo. Nat. Youth Adminstrn., 1941-42; manpower analyst HEW, 1942-43; chief wage classification New Eng., Atlantic and Mediterranean area Dept. Navy, Boston, 1946-56; with U.S. CSC, Washington, 1956-71; exec. vice chmn. inter-agy. adv. group U.S. CSC, 1957-58; dir. Bur. Tng., 1959-71; cons. AID, State Dept., Nat. Civil Service League, WHO, 1971-79, Fed. Energy Adminstrn., UN, 1974-76; chmn. task force Presdl. Commn. on Exec., Legis. and Jud. Salaries, July-Dec. 1976; adj. instr. Boston U., 1955, Dept. Agr. Grad. Sch., 1958. Chmn. Personnel Bd. Wakefield, Mass., 1954-56; mem. adv. bd. Washington Tech. Inst., 1969-70, George Washington U., 1970—; mem. governing bd. Washington Interns in Edn., 1966-68. Served to lt. USNR, 1944-46. Recipient Commr.'s award CSC, 1968, founder's award Federal Exec. Inst., 1993. Address: 4615 Hunt Ave Chevy Chase MD 20815-5424

MULLIGAN, JEREMIAH T., lawyer; b. Rochester, N.Y., 1944. BA, St. Bernard's Seminary and Coll., 1966; JD, Fordham U., 1970. Mem. Curtis, Mallet-Prevost, Colt & Mosle, N.Y. Office: Curtis Mallet-Prevost Colt & Mosle 101 Park Ave New York NY 10178

MULLIGAN, JOSEPH FRANCIS, physicist, educator; b. N.Y.C., Dec. 12, 1920; s. Joseph Lawrence and Mary (Collins) M.; m. Eleanor L. Wells 1984. Student, Fordham Coll., 1938-39, 41-43; A.B., Boston Coll., 1945, M.A., 1946; Ph.D. in Physics, Cath. U. Am., 1951. Instr. physics St. Peter's Coll., Jersey City, 1946-47; faculty Fordham U., 1955-68, assoc. prof. physics, 1963-68, chmn. dept., 1956-64, dean Grad. Sch. Arts and Scis., dean liberal arts faculty, 1964-67; prof. physics U. Md., Baltimore County, 1968-89, prof. emeritus, 1989—, dean for grad. studies and rsch., 1968-82; Mem. adv. com. grad. fellowship program NDEA, 1960-63. Author: Practical Physics: The Production and Conservation of Energy, 1980, Introductory College Physics, 2d edit., 1990, translated into 3-vol. Italian edit., Fisica, 1993; editor: Heinrich Rudolf Hertz (1857-1894); A Collection of Articles and Addresses, 1994; contbr. articles to profl. jours. NSF fellow U. Calif. at La Jolla, 1961-62. Mem. Am. Phys. Soc., Am. Assn. Physics Tchrs., History of Sci. Soc., AAAS, Sigma Xi. Home: 228 Canal Park Dr Salisbury MD 21804-7249 Office: U Md 1000 Hilltop Cir Baltimore MD 21228-5329

MULLIGAN, MARTIN FREDERICK, clothing executive, professional tennis player; b. Sydney, Australia, Oct. 18, 1940; s. Frederick William and Marie Louise (Tome) M.; m. Rossella Rita Labella, Sept. 19, 1969 (div. Mar. 1980); children: Monica, Martin Thomas. Winner Tennis Singles Championships of Australia, 1952, 53, 55, 56, 57, 58; mem. Davis Cup team Australia, 1959, 60; winner Australian Hard Court Singles and Doubles tournaments, 1960, 64; finalist Wimbledon Singles tournaments, 1962; winner Italian Open Singles tournaments, 1963, 65, 67, German Open Singles tournament, 1963; winner singles and doubles titles Monte Carlo Championships, 1964; coach Italian Davis Cup team, 1966-76; winner, Davis Cup tournament, 1976; winner Spanish Open tournament, 1966, 67, Swedish Open tournament, 1966, 67, Austrian Open tournament, 1966, 67, Champion Cup tournament, 1966, 67; promotional cons. Alpina Australian Mfg. Co., 1973-74; cons. and internat. promotion mgr. Diadora Co., 1973-78; internat. promotion mgr. FILA U.S.A. Inc. subs. FILA-Italy Sportswear, Hunt Valley, Md., 1979-90, v.p. internat. promotion and pub. rels., 1979—; co-promotor, tournament dir. Italian Open Tennis Championships, 1972, 73; negotiator contracts between FILA and various sports profls. and celebrities. Ranked Number 3 in World in Tennis, 1967, ranked 5 times in world's top 10 tennis players. Avocation: stamp collecting. Office: FILA USA Inc 145 Park Ln Brisbane CA 94005-1311

MULLIGAN, MICHAEL DENNIS, lawyer; b. St. Louis, Mar. 9, 1947; s. Leo Virgil and Elizabeth (Leyse) M.; m. Theresa Baker, Aug. 7, 1971; children—Brennan, Colin. B.A. in Biology, Amherst Coll., 1968; J.D., Columbia U., 1971. Bar: Mo. 1971, U.S. Dist. Ct. (ea. dist.) Mo. 1972, U.S. Ct. Appeals (8th cir.) 1982, U.S. Tax Ct. 1985. Law clk. to judge U.S. Dist. Ct. (ea. dist.) Mo., 1971-72; assoc. Lewis, Rice & Fingersh, L.C., St. Louis, 1972-80, ptnr., 1980—. Served as cpl. USMC, 1968-70. Fellow Am. Coll. Trust and Estate Counsel; mem. ABA (mem. real property, probate and trust, and taxation sects.), Mo. Bar Assn. (mem. probate and trust, taxation sects.). Contbr. numerous articles to profl. jours. Mem. editorial bd. Estate Planning Mag., 1985—. Office: Lewis Rice & Fingersh LC 500 N Broadway Ste 2000 Saint Louis MO 63102-2130

MULLIGAN, RICHARD M., actor, writer; b. Bronx, N.Y., Nov. 13, 1932; s. Robert Edward and Ann-Elizabeth (Gingell) M.; m. Lenore Mulligan, June 25, 1978 (div.); 1 son, James. Regular on TV series The Hero, 1966-67, Diana, 1973-74, Soap, 1977-80 (Emmy award 1980), Reggie, 1983, Empty Nest, NBC, 1988-95 (Emmy award 1989, Golden Globe award); numerous other TV appearances include Kate McShane, Charlie's Angels, Medical Story, Dog & Cat, Doctor's Hospital, Knowledge, Little House on the Prairie, Love Boat, Switch, Kingston, Mike Douglas Show, Merv Griffin Show, Dinah Shore Show, Hollywood Squares; TV movies include Jealousy, Malibu, Harvey, The Pueblo Incident, Having Babies III, Guess Who's Coming for Christmas, 1992, London Suite, 1996, Dog's Best Friend, 1996; films include One Potato, Two Potato, 1964, The Group, 1966, Little Big Man, 1970, A Change in the Wind, 1972, The Big Bus, 1976, S.O.B, 1981, Trail of the Pink Panther, 1982, Summertime, 1983, Mickey and Maude, 1984, Meatballs II, 1984, Teachers, 1984, The Heavenly Kid, 1985, A Fine Mess, 1986, Quicksilver, 1986, (voice) Oliver and Company, 1988; Broadway debut in All the Way Home, 1960; other Broadway plays include Special Occasions; other stage appearances include Mating Dance (Theatre World award), The Crucible, Luv, Other People, Pound on Demand, Nobody Loves an Albatross, Hogan's Goat (Theatre World award), Beyond the Horizon, Glass Menagerie, The Great God Brown; playwright: Never Too Late. Recipient star on Hollywood Walk of Fame. Mem. Actors Equity Assn., AFTRA, Screen Actor's Guild. Office: Innovative Artists 1999 Ave of the Stars Ste 2850 Los Angeles CA 90067-6082 *Que sais-je? (Montaigne).**

MULLIGAN, ROBERT PATRICK, film director, producer; b. N.Y.C., Aug. 23, 1925; s. Robert Edward and Elizabeth (Gingell) M. Grad., Fordham U. Dir.: TV prodns. including Philco Playhouse, Suspense, Playhouse 90; film prodr./dir.: films The Jimmy Piersall Story, Come September, The Spiral Road, To Kill a Mockingbird, Love with the Proper Stranger, Inside Daisy Clover, Summer of '42, Bloodbrothers, Same Time Next Year, The Other, Kiss Me Goodbye, Nickel Ride, Stalking Moon, Baby the Rain Must Fall, Pursuit of Happiness, Up the Down Staircase, Clara's Heart, The Man in the Moon. Office: Boardwalk Prodns 5150 Wilshire Blvd Ste # 505 Los Angeles CA 90036*

MULLIGAN, ROBERT WILLIAM, university official, clergyman; b. Chgo., Oct. 11, 1916; s. John Sexton and Esther Mary (Cordesman) M. A.B., Loyola U., 1937; M.A., U. Detroit, 1946; Ph.D., Louvain U., Belgium, 1953; LL.D., U. Cin., 1976. Ordained priest Roman Cath. Ch., 1949; chmn. dept. philosophy Loyola U., 1953-59, trustee, 1958-71, v.p., dean faculties, 1959-69; provost Xavier U., Cin., 1971-72; pres. Xavier U., 1972-82; sec. St. Louis U., 1982-89; acad. v.p. St. Joseph's U., Phila., 1989—; cons. Grolier Soc., 1959-65; mem. vis. faculty Oxford U., Eng., 1970-71. Mem. adv. com. Bd. Higher Edn., Luth. Ch. Mo. Synod, 1966-67; chmn. bd. Greater Cin. Consortium Colls. and Univs., 1973; bd. dirs. Cin. chpt. ARC, Campion Hall, Oxford U., 1976—. Decorated chevalier Legion of Honor France; recipient Blue Key award, 1959; key City Cin., 1972. Mem. Am. Ednl. Assn., Am. Philos. Assn., Am. Cath. Philos. Assn. (chmn. Midwest chpt. 1956), Ill. Philos. Assn, No. Ill. Philos. Assn., Metaphys. Soc., Phi Sigma Tau (nat. pres. 1962—). Home: Loyola U Jesuit Residence 6525 N Sheridan Rd Chicago IL 60626-5385

MULLIGAN, ROSEMARY ELIZABETH, paralegal; b. Chgo., July 8, 1941; d. Stephen Edward and Rose Anne (Sannasardo) Granzyk; children: Daniel R. Bonaguidi, Matthew S. Bonaguidi. AAS, Harper Coll., Palatine, Ill., 1982; student, Ill. State U., 1959-60. Paralegal Miller, Forest & Downing Ltd., Glenview, Ill., 1982-91; ind. contractor mcpl. law, 1991—; paralegal seminar educator Harper Coll. Program chair White House Women's Econ. Leadership Summit, 1997. Pro-choice activist and mem. Ill. Ho. of Reps., 1993—, chmn. human svcs. appropriations com.; gov.'s work-group on early childhood. Recipient Disting. Alumnus award Ill. C.C. Trustee Assn., 1993, Legislator of Yr. award Ill. Assn. Cmty. Mental Health Agys., 1996, Heart Start award Nat. Ctr. Clin. Infant Programs, Legis. Leadership award Ill. Alcoholism and Drug dependence Assn., 1996, Cert. Appreciation Ill. Libr. Assn.; Flemming fellow Ctr. for Policy Alts., 1995. Mem. LWV, Nat. Women's Polit. Caucus, Ill. Fedn. Bus. and Profl. Women, Ill. Women in Govt., Chgo. Women in Govt. Rels., Ill. Fedn. Bus. and Profl. Women (nat. legis. platform rep. 1991-92, chair Outstanding Working Women of Ill. 1991-92, recipient Ida B. Wells-Barnett award, 1996, state membership chair 1989-90, state legis. co-chair, nat. platform rep. 1988-89, state legis. chair, nat. platform rep. 1987-88). Roman Catholic. Avocations: politics, tennis, reading. Home: 856 E Grant Dr Des Plaines IL 60016-6260 Office: Ill Ho of Reps State Capitol Springfield IL 62706 also: 932 Lee St Ste 204 Des Plaines IL 60016-6546

MULLIKIN, HARRY COPELAND, mathematics educator; b. Flintville, Tenn., July 10, 1940; s. Houston Yost and Daisy (Copeland) M.; m. Gary W. Parker. Student, U. Paris, France, 1960-61; BA, U. the South, Sewanee, Tenn., 1963; MA, U. Wis., Madison, 1964, PhD, 1968. Asst. prof. math. Pomona Coll., Claremont, Calif., 1968-74, assoc. prof. math., 1974-82, prof. math., 1982—, chmn. dept. math., 1979-85, William Polk Russell prof. math., 1984—, acting assoc. dean of students, 1982. Bd. dirs. Calif. br. Humane Soc. U.S., Long Beach, 1974-78; bd. dirs. Golden State Humane Soc., Garden Grove, Calif., 1974-82, sec., 1978-82. Woodrow Wilson fellow, 1963-64; recipient Disting. Prof. award Pomona Coll., 1972, 76, 80, 90, 96. Mem. Am. Math. Soc., Math. Soc. Am., Assn. Computing Machinery, So. Calif. Phi Beta Kappa Alumni Assn. (treas. 1990-94), Phi Beta Kappa (chpt. pres. 1973-74, sec.-treas. 1979-80, 82-83). Democrat. Home: 4433 N Glen Way Claremont CA 91711-2122 Office: Dept Math Pomona Coll Claremont CA 91711

MULLIKIN, THOMAS WILSON, mathematics educator; b. Flintville, Tenn., Jan. 9, 1928; s. Houston Yost and Daisy (Copeland) M.; m. Mildred Virginia Sugg, June 14, 1952; children—Sarah Virginia, Thomas Wilson, James Copeland. Student, U. South, 1946-47; A.B., U. Tenn., 1950; post-grad., Iowa State U., 1952-53; A.M., Harvard, 1954, Ph.D., 1958. Mathematician Rand Corp., Santa Monica, Calif., 1957-64; prof. math. Purdue U., 1964-93, interim v.p., dean grad. sch., 1991-93, dean grad. sch., prof. math emeritus, 1993—. Served with USNR, 1950-52. Mem. Am. Math. Soc., AAAS, Sigma Xi. Home: 104 Club Ct Cape Carteret NC 28584

MULLIKIN, VERNON EUGENE, aerospace executive; b. Windsor, Ill., July 16, 1935; s. Charles Austin and Oma Leah (Gilbreath) M.; m. Mary Lou Walker (div.); children: Michael, Mark; m. Joan Marie Boes, Aug. 1, 1986. BS in Aero. Engring., U. Ill., 1957; MBA, So. Ill. U., Edwardsville, 1977. Aero. engr. Northrup Aircraft Co., Hawthorne, Calif., 1957-60; group engr. Douglas Missile & Space Systems, Santa Monica, Calif., 1960-63; chief engr. McDonnell Douglas Astronautics Co., St. Louis, 1963-87; program dir. Convair div. Gen. Dynamics Corp., San Diego, 1987-92; mgr. adv. programs and tech. Hughes Missile Systems Co., Tucson, 1992—. Mem. AIAA (cert. recognition 1987), Phi Eta Sigma, Sigma Gamma Tau, Tau Beta Pi, Beta Gamma Sigma. Office: GM Hughes Missile Systems PO Box 11337 Mail Zone 807-05 Tucson AZ 85734

MULLIN, CHRIS(TOPHER) PAUL, professional basketball player; b. N.Y.C., July 30, 1963. Student, St. John's U., 1981-85. Basketball player Golden State Warriors, 1985—; mem. U.S. Olympic Team (received Gold medal), 1984, 92. Recipient Wooden award, 1985; named to Sporting News All-Am. First Team, 1985, NBA All-Star team, 1989-93, NBA First Team, 1992.. Office: Golden State Warriors San Jose Arena 1221 Broadway Fl 20 Oakland CA 94612-1822*

MULLIN, GERARD EMMANUEL, physician, educator, researcher; b. Pequannock, N.J., Nov. 5, 1959; s. Gerard Vincent Jr. and Frances Rita (Magnanti) M. BS in Biology and Chemistry, William Patterson Coll., 1981; MD, U. Medicine and Dentistry N.J., 1985; MS in Nutrition, U. Bridgeport, 1994. Diplomate Am. Bd. Internal Medicine, Am. Bd. Gastroenterology, Am. Bd. Med. Examiners. Intern Mt. Sinai Hosp., N.Y.C., 1985-86, resident, 1986-88; fellow in gastroenterology Johns Hopkins Hosp., Balt., 1988-91; fellow NIH, Bethesda, Md., 1989-91; instr., scientist Cornell U. Med. Coll., N.Y., 1991-93, asst. prof., 1993—. Cotbr. articles to med. and sci. jours. Bd. dirs. Our Lady of Fatima Chapel. Grantee Nat. Found. Ileitis and Colitis, 1990, 92-94, 95-97, North Shore U. Hosp., 1991. Fellow ACP; mem. AMA, Crohn's and Colitis Found. Am. (Young Investigator of Yr. 1991, 93, grantee 1991, 96), N.J. Med. Sch. Alumni Assn. (bd. dirs.), Fieri No. N.J. (bd. dirs.), Alpha Omega Alpha, Phi Beta Sigma. Roman Catholic. Achievements include discovery that suppressor cell function is elevated in AIDS, lymphomas are increased in inflamatory bowel disease, helicobacter pylori gastritis causes increased gastric acid secretion and hypergastrinemia, intestinal T cells are activated and make IL2 in Crohn's disease but not ulcerative colitis, Crohn's Disease mucosa has a T-helper-1 profile of lymphokine gene expression, inflamatory bowel disease intestine has increased oxygen free radical production and decreased antioxidant content, inflammatory bowel disease has abnormal levels of chemokines, interleukin-10 and interleukin-13 heliobacter pylori has increased nitric oxide synthase gene expression, increased Rantes RNA levels and increased production of tumor necrosis factor and interleukin-6. Also discovered that intestines of patients with colon cancer and adenomatous polyps have increased iron content and elevated oxygen free radical production. Office: Cornell U Med Coll N Shore U Hosp 300 Community Dr Manhasset NY 11030-3801

MULLIN, LEO FRANCIS, utility executive; b. Concord, Mass., Jan. 26, 1943; s. Leo F. and Alice L. (Fearns) M.; m. Leah J. Malmberg, Sept. 10, 1966; children: Jessica, Matthew. AB, Harvard U., 1964, MS, 1965, MBA, 1967. Assoc. McKinsey & Co., Washington, 1967-73, prin., 1973-76; sr. v.p. strategic planning Consol. Rail Corp., Phila., 1976-78; sr. v.p. 1st Chgo. Corp., 1981-84, exec. v.p., 1984-91; chmn. Am. Nat. Bank and Trust Co. Chgo. subs. 1st Chgo., Chgo., 1991-93; pres., COO 1st Chgo. Corp., Chgo., 1993-95; vice chmn. Unicom/Commonwealth Edison, Chgo., 1995—; bd. dirs. Pittway Corp., Inland Steel Industries, Inc. Vice chmn. Chgo. Urban League, 1993—; chmn. bd. trustees Field Mus. Natural History, 1994—; bd. dirs. Chgo. chpt. Juvenile Diabetes Found., 1985—, Met. Planning Coun., 1983—, Children's Meml. Hosp., Chgo., 1989—, Chgo. Coun. Fgn. Rels., 1994—; mem. Chgo. Econ. Devel. Commn., 1992-95; trustee Northwestern U., 1992—. Mem. Chgo. Club, Harvard Club of Chgo., Econ. Club of Chgo. Office: Commonwealth Edison Co PO Box 767 Chicago IL 60690-0767

MULLIN, MARY ANN, career counselor; b. Passaic, N.J., Feb. 9, 1943; d. M. Joseph and Rose M. (Rienzi) DeVita; m. John G. Mullin Jr.; children: Kathleen, John, Robert. BA in Comms., William Paterson Coll., 1991, MA in Urban Studies, 1994; postgrad., Jersey City State U., 1995—. Office mgr. Joseph DeVita, Inc., Paterson, N.J., 1978-94; grad. rsch. asst. William Paterson Coll., Wayne, N.J., 1992-94; ednl. broker/counselor Bergen County Tech. Inst., Hackensack, N.J., 1994-95; grad. admissions counselor Sch. Arch. N.J. Inst. Tech., Newark, 1995—. Pres., bd. dirs. Lenni Lenape Girl Scout Coun., Bulter, N.J., 1989-96; pastoral care/eucharistic min. St. Anthony's Ch., Hawthorne, N.J., 1978—; eucharistic min. Wayne (N.J.) Gen. Hosp., 1978—. Recipient Thanks badge Girl Scouts Am., 1996, Honor pin Lenni Lenape Girl Scout Coun., 1991, Outstanding Vol. Svc. award Paterson Task Force, 1994; named Vol. of Week, The Record, 1993. Mem. Pi Lambda Theta (dir. rsch. projects Beta Chi chpt. 1994-96, Outstanding Svc. award 1995, regional chair N.E. conf. Beta Chi chpt. 1996). Democrat. Roman Catholic. Avocations: Girl Scout activities, travel. Home: 519 Goffle Hill Rd Hawthorne NJ 07506-3056 Office: N J Inst Tech Sch Arch Martin L King Blvd Newark NJ 07102

MULLIN, MICHAEL MAHLON, Biology and oceanography educator; b. Galveston, Tex., Nov. 17, 1937; m. Constance Hammond; children: Stephen J., Keith A., Laura A. AB, Shimer Coll., 1957, Harvard U., 1959; MA,

Harvard U., 1960, PhD in Biology, 1964. Asst. prof., asst. rsch. biologist Inst. Marine Resources U. Calif., San Diego, 1965-71, assoc. prof. oceanography, assoc. rsch. biologist, 1971-77, chmn. grad. dept., 1977-80, assoc. dir., 1980-87; prof. oceanography Scripps Inst. Oceanography, 1977—, dir. marine life rsch. group, 1987—; assoc. dean Scripps Inst. Oceanography, San Diego, 1993-96. Editor-in-chief Fisheries Oceanography, 1997—. Mem. Ocean Sci. Bd., Nat. Rsch. Coun., 1979-81; sr. Queen;s fellow marine sci., Australia, 1981-82. Office: Univ CA San Diego Scripps Inst Oceanography Marine Life Rsch Group La Jolla CA 92093-0227

MULLINAX, OTTO B., retired lawyer; b. Clearwater, Tex., June 28, 1912; s. Claxton Napoleon and Essie Ruth (Shelby) M.; m. Ernestine Maxey, July 20, 1941; 1 child, Michael Lewis. B.A., U. Tex., 1937, LL.B., 1937. Bar: Tex. 1937, U.S. Ct. Mil. Appeals 1957, U.S. Supreme Ct. 1958. Assoc. firm Mandell & Combs, Houston, 1938-40; sr. ptnr. Mullinax, Wells, Morris & Mauzy (named changed to Mullinax, Wells, Baab & Cloutman, 1980); ret., 1995. Author: Some Mullinax Roots: South Carolina to Texas, 1982, Thus Spake Idion, 1983, Sam Adams: Freedom Fighter, 1991, Gods, Prophets and Slaves, 1994, The Historical Jesus: A Socialist Revolutionary of the Common Table and Communal Code, 1996. Pres. Dallas UN Assn., 1971-72; bd. dirs. Ams. for Dem. Action, 1952-71; active 1st Unitarian Ch. Dallas, 1990. Fellow Am. Law-Sci. Acad.; mem. Dallas Trial Lawyers Assn. (pres. 1956), Tex. Trial Lawyers Assn. (dir.), Nat. Assn. Compensation Claimants Attys. (asso. editor jour. 1952-65). Home: 11806 Cheswick St Dallas TX 75218-1803 *The history of the ancient Mediterranian world, which I have studied since my retirement, is the best of all the histories I've tried to master. Those Moses books, the most ancient written histories of this planet, are vastly mind expanding.*

MULLINAX, PERRY FRANKLIN, rheumatologist, allergist, immunologist; b. Quebec City, Que., Can., June 7, 1931. MD, Med. Coll. Va., 1955. Diplomate Am. Bd. Allergy and Immunology, Am. Bd. Diagnostic Lab. Immunology, Am. Bd. Internal Medicine, Am. Bd. Rheumatology. Intern Yale Med. Ctr., New Haven, 1955-56, resident in medicine, 1958-59; fellow in medicine Mass. Gen. Hosp., Boston, 1959-61; fellow in microbiology immunology Washington U., St. Louis; fellow in biology MIT, Boston, 1962-63; mem. faculty dept. internal medicine Med. Coll. Va./Va. Commonwealth U., 1963—, prof. internal medicine, 1977—. Mem. AAAS, Am. Coll. Rheumatology, Am. Fedn. Clin. Rsch. Office: Med Coll Va PO Box 980263 Richmond VA 23298-0263

MULLINEAUX, DONAL RAY, geologist; b. Weed, Calif., Feb. 16, 1925; s. Lester Ray and Mary Lorene (Drew) M.; m. Diana Suzanne Charais, Nov. 21, 1951; children: Peter, Lauren, Keith. Student, U. Wash., 1942, BS in Math, 1947, BS in Geology, 1949, MS in Geology, 1950, PhD in Geology, 1961. Drilling insp. U.S. Army C.E., 1948; geologist U.S. Geol. Survey, 1950-86; contracting geologist, 1987-90; scientist emeritus U.S. Geol. Survey, 1990—. Author articles on volcanic activity and hazards, Mt. St. Helens, other Cascade Range volcanoes, stratigraphy and engring. geology of Puget Sound lowland, Wash. With USNR, 1943-54, active duty, 1943-46, 51-53. Rsch. fellow Engring. Expt. Sta. U. Wash., 1949-50. Fellow Geol. Soc. Am. (E.B. Burwell Jr. award 1983); mem. Colo. Sci. Soc. Unitarian. Home: 14155 W 54th Ave Arvada CO 80002-1513 Office: PO Box 25046 Denver CO 80225-0046

MULLINIX, EDWARD WINGATE, lawyer; b. Balt., Feb. 25, 1924; s. Howard Earl and Elsie (Wingate) M.; m. Virginia Lee McGinnes, July 28, 1944; children: Marcia Lee Ladd, Edward Wingate. Student, St. John's Coll., 1941-43; JD summa cum laude, U. Pa., 1949. Bar: Pa. 1950, U.S. Supreme Ct. 1955. Assoc. Schnader, Harrison, Segal & Lewis, Phila., 1950-55, ptnr., 1956-92, now sr. coun.; mem. adv. bds. Antitrust Bull., 1970-81, BNA Antitrust and Trade Regulation Report, 1981-94; mem. Civil Justice Reform Act of 1990 adv. group U.S. Dist. Ct. (ea. dist.) Pa., 1991—; co-chmn. Joint U.S. Dist. Ct./Phila. Bar Assn. Alternative Dispute Resolution Com., 1990—; cons. on revision of local civil rules U.S. Dist. Ct. (ea. dist.) Pa., 1995—; mem. adv. com. U. Pa. Law Sch. Ctr. on Professionalism, 1988-92; judge pro tem Ct. Common Pleas of Phila. County Day Forward program; faculty participant Pa. Bar Inst., Phila. Bar Edn. Ctr., others. Trustee Sta. KYW-TV Project Homeless Fund, 1985-86. Served with USMCR, 1943-44; to lt. (j.g.) USNR, 1944-46. Fellow Am. Bar Found. (life), Am. Coll. Trial Lawyers (emeritus, mem. complex litigation com. 1980-91, vice-chmn. com. 1981-83); mem. ABA (spl. com. complex and multidist. litigation 1969-73, co-chmn. com. 1971-73, coun. litigation sect. 1976-80), Phila. Bar Assn., Juristic Soc., Hist. Soc. U.S. Dist. Ct. (ea. dist.) Pa. (bd. dirs. 1984—, pres. 1991-94), Hist. Soc. U.S. Ct. Appeals for Third Cir. (bd. dirs. 1991-94), Order of Coif, Union League (Phila.), Socialegal Club (Phila.), Aronimink Golf Club (Newtown Sq., Pa.). Republican. Presbyterian. Home: 251 Chamounix Rd Saint Davids PA 19087-3605 Office: 1600 Market St Ste 3600 Philadelphia PA 19103-7286

MULLINS, BETTY JOHNSON, realtor; b. Killen, Ala., Dec. 29, 1925; d. James E. and Vernie (Muse) Johnson; m. Charles Harvey Mullins, Nov. 18, 1944; children: Charles Harvey Jr., Susan. BS, U. North Ala., 1945. Tchr. Biloxi (Miss.) City Schs., 1945-46, Elizabeth City County Schs., Buckroe Beach, Va., 1946-47, Sheffield (Ala.) City Schs., 1949-58; with family automobile bus., 1958-86; real estate assoc. Neese Real Estate, Inc., Florence, Ala., 1986—. Pres. Project Courtview, Florence, 1980, Heritage Found., Florence, 1994—, Concert Guild, Florence; mem. Tenn. Valley Art Guild, Tuscumbia, Tenn. Valley Art Ctr., Tuscumbia, Friends of Kennedy Douglas Art Ctr., Florence; v.p. Salvation Army Aux., 1991-92; mem., past pres. United Meth. Women, First Meth. Ch., Florence, mem. adminstrv. bds.; bd. dirs. Friends of Libr., Florence, 1993—, Downtown Florence Unltd., Florence Main St., Bd. Rape Response; mem., past pres. Lauderdale-Colbert-Franklin Foster Grandparent Adv. Bd., Russellville, Ala., Ret. Sr. Vol. Program Adv. Bd.; pres. cabinet U. North Ala., mem. found. bd., 1994, 95, 96; trustee United Way, Shoals, 1992—; family built and maintains garden at First Meth. Ch., Florence in memory of Charles Mullins, Jr. Recipient Shoals Area Citizen of Yr., 1984, Shoals Area Top Prodr. Muscle Shoals Area Bd. Realtors, 1991, 92, 93, 94, Realtor of the Yr., 1996-97, Cmty. Svc. award U. North Ala., 1994; named Woman of Yr. Bus. and Profl. Women, 1980. Mem. LWV, Shoals-AAUW (pres. 1990-91), Nat. Bd. Realtors, U. North Ala. Alumni Assn. (past pres., bd. dirs., Alumni of Yr. award 1985, Cmty. Svc. award 1994, Found. Bd. 1994, 95, 96), Internat. Fertilizer Devel. Ctr. Century Club (past pres. Muscle Shoals, Ala. chpt.), Shoals C. of C. (past bd. dirs.), Tenn. Valley Hist. Assn., U. North Ala. Sportsman Club, Muscle Shoals Bd. Realtors, Ala. Bd. Realtors. Republican. Methodist. Avocation: family. Home and Office: PO Box 70 Florence AL 35631-0070

MULLINS, CHARLES BROWN, physician, academic administrator; b. Rochester, Ind., July 29, 1934; s. Charles E. and Mary Ruth B. (Bamberger) M.; B.A., N. Tex. State U., 1954; M.D., U. Tex., 1958; m. Stella Churchill, Dec. 27, 1955; children—Holly, David. Intern, U. Colo. Med. Center, Denver, 1958-59; resident medicine Parkland Meml. Hosp., Dallas, 1962-64; USPHS rsch. fellow U. Tex. Southwestern Med. Sch., Dallas, 1964-65; chief resident medicine Parkland Meml. Hosp., 1965-66; USPHS spl. rsch. fellow cardiology br. Nat. Heart Inst., Bethesda, Md., 1967-68; practice medicine specializing in cardiology, Dallas, 1966—; mem. sr. attending staff Parkland Meml. Hosp., dir. med. affairs, 1977-79; mem. cons. staff Presbyn. Hosp., VA Hosp.; asst. prof. medicine U. Tex. Southwestern Med. Sch., Dallas, 1968-71, asso. prof., 1971-75, dir. clin. cardiology, 1971-77, prof., 1975-79, clin. prof. medicine, 1979-81, prof., 1981—; prof. medicine U. Tex. Health Sci. Center, Dallas, 1979-81; exec. vice-chancellor health affairs U. Tex. System, 1981—; chief exec. officer Dallas County Hosp. Dist., 1979-81. Served with M.C., USAF, 1959-62. Diplomate Am. Bd. Internal Medicine. Fellow ACP, Am. Coll. Cardiology (Tex. gov. 1974-77, chmn. bd. govs. 1976), Am. Heart Assn. Council on Clin. Cardiology; mem. Am. Fedn. Clin. Rsch., Assn. Acad. Health Ctrs., Assn. Univ. Cardiologists, Laennec Soc., AMA, Alpha Omega Alpha. Contbr. articles on cardiology to med. jours. Office: 601 Colorado St Austin TX 78701-2904

MULLINS, JAMES LEE, library director; b. Perry, Iowa, Nov. 29, 1949; s. Kenneth Wiley and Lorene (Gift) M.; m. Kathleen Stiso, May 10, 1986; 1 stepchild, Michael Stiso. BA, U. Iowa, 1972, MA, 1973; PhD, Ind. U., 1984. Instr. Ga. So. U., Statesboro, 1973-74; assoc. law librarian Ind. U., Bloomington, 1974-78; dir. library Ind. U., South Bend, 1978-96; dir. Falvey Meml. Libr., Villanova U., 1996—. Contbr. articles to profl. publs. Mem. exec. com. South Bend Art Ctr., 1984-89; mem. Mayor's Task Force Redevel., South Bend, 1986; pres. Fischoff Nat. Chamber Music Assn., 1989-91, Gov. Conf. on Libr. Planning Com., 1989-91, Mich. Freenet bd., 1993-96; pres. Ind. Coop. Libr. Svcs. Authority, 1993-94; mem. ACRL Standards Com., 1994—. Mem. ALA, Ind. Libr. Assn., Assn. Coll. and Rsch. Libis., Ind. Liv. Endowment Bd. (pres. 1988-91), Rotary. Avocations: reading, gardening, cross-country skiing, historic preservation. Office: Falvey Meml Libr Villanova Univ 800 E Lancaster Ave Villanova PA 19085-1603

MULLINS, RICHARD AUSTIN, chemical engineer; b. Seelyville, Ind., Apr. 22, 1918; s. Fred A. and Ethel (Zenor) M.; B.S. in Chem. Engring., Rose Poly. Inst., 1940; postgrad. Yale, 1942-43; m. Margaret Ann Dellacca, Nov. 27, 1946 (dec. Nov. 1982); children—Scott Alan, Mark Earl. Chemist, Ayrshire Collieries Corp., Brazil, Ind., 1940-49; chief chemist Fairview Collieries Corp., Danville, Ill., 1949-54; preparations mgr. Enos Coal Mining Co., Oakland City, Ind., 1954-72, Enoco Collieries, Inc., Bruceville, Ind., 1954-62; mining engr. Kings Station Coal Corp.; mgr. analytical procedures Old Ben Coal Corp., 1973-84; ret., 1984. Am. Mining Congress cons. to Am. Standards Assn. and Internat. Orgn. for Standards, 1960-74; mem. indsl. cons. com. Ind. Geol. Survey, 1958-72; mem. organizing com. 5th Internat. Coal Preparation Congress, Pittsburgh, 1966. Mem. exec. bd. Buffalo Trace council Boy Scouts Am., also mem. speakers bur. Bd. dirs. Princeton Boys Club. Served with AUS, 1942-46; ETO. Decorated Medaille de la France Liberee (France); recipient Eagle Scout award, Boy Scouts Am., 1935, Silver Beaver award, 1962, Wood Badge Beads award, 1960; Outstanding Community Svc. award Princeton Civitan Club, 1964; Engr. of Year award S.W. chpt. Ind. Soc. Profl. Engrs., 1965; Prince of Princeton award Princeton C. of C., 1981, Sagamore of the Wabash award Ind. gov. R.D. Orr, 1984. Registered profl. engr., Ind., Ill., registered profl. land surveyor. Mem. AIME (life mem.), ASTM (sr. mem., R.A. Glenn award 1985), Am. Chem. Soc., Nat. Soc. Profl. Engrs. (life mem.), Ind., Ill. mining insts., Ind. Coal Soc. (pres. 1958-59), Am. Mining Congress (chmn. com. coal preparation 1964-68), Am. Legion (life, past county comdr.), VFW (life), 40 & 8 (life), Ind. Soc. Profl. Land Surveyors, Rose Tech. Alumni Assn. (pres. 1976-77, Honor Alumnus 1980), Order of Ring, Sigma Nu. Methodist (lay speaker). Mason, Elk. hon. founder, Elks Nat. Found. Contbr. articles to profl. jours. Home: RR 4 Box 310 Princeton IN 47670-9412

MULLINS, RUTH GLADYS, nurse; b. Westville, N.S., Can., Aug. 25, 1943; d. William G. and Gladys H.; came to U.S., 1949, naturalized, 1955; student Tex. Womans U., 1961-64; BS in Nursing, Calif. State U.-Long Beach, 1966; MNursing, UCLA, 1973; m. Leonard E. Mullins, Aug. 27, 1963; children: Deborah R., Catherine M., Leonard III. Pub. health nurse, L.A. County Health Dept., 1967-68; nurse Meml. Hosp. Med. Center, Long Beach, 1968-72; dir. pediatric nurse practitioner program Calif. State U., Long Beach, 1973—, asst. prof., 1975-80, assoc. prof., 1980-85, prof., 1985—; health svc. credential coord. Sch. Nursing Calif. State U., Long Beach, Calif., chmn., 1979-81, coord. grad. programs, 1985-92; mem. Calif. Maternal, Child and Adolescent Health Bd., 1977-84; vice chair Long Beach/Orange County Health Consortium, 1984-85, chair 1985-86. Tng. grantee HHS, Divsn. Nursing Calif. Dept. Health; cert. pediatric nurse practitioner. Fellow Nat. Assn. Pediatric Nurse Assocs. and Practitioners (exec. bd., pres. 1990-91), Nat. Fedn. Nursing Specialty Orgns. (sec. 1991-93); mem. Am. Pub. Health Assn., Nat. Alliance Nurse Practitioners (governing body 1990-92), Assn. Faculties Pediatric Nurse Practitioner Programs, L.A. and Orange County Assn. Pediatric Nurse Practitioners and Assocs., Am. Assn. U. Faculty, Ambulatory Pediatric Assn. Democrat. Methodist. Author: (with B. Nelms) Growth and Development: A Primary Health Care Approach; contbg. author: Quick Reference to Pediatric Nursing, 1984; asst. editor Jour. Pediatric Health Care. Home: 6382 Heil Ave Huntington Beach CA 92647-4232 Office: Calif State U Dept Nursing 1250 N Bellflower Blvd Long Beach CA 90840-0006

MULLIS, KARY BANKS, biochemist; b. Lenoir, N.C., Dec. 28, 1944; s. Cecil Banks Mullis and Bernice Alberta (Barker) Fredericks; children: Christopher, Jeremy, Louise. BS in Chemistry, Ga. Inst. Tech, 1966; PhD in Biochemistry, U. Calif., Berkeley, 1973; DSc (hon.), U. S.C., 1994. Lectr. biochemistry U. Calif., Berkeley, 1972; postdoctoral fellow U. Calif., San Francisco, 1977-79, U. Kans. Med. Sch., Kansas City, 1973-76; scientist Cetus Corp., Emeryville, Calif., 1979-86; dir. molecular biology Xytronyx, Inc., San Diego, 1986-88; cons. Specialty Labs, Inc., Amersham, Inc., Chiron Inc. and various others, Calif., 1988-96; chmn. StarGene, Inc., San Rafael, Calif.; v.p. Histotec, Inc., Cedar Rapids, Iowa; v.p. molecular biology chemistry Vyrex Inc., La Jolla, Calif.; Disting. vis. prof. U. S.C. Coll. of Sci. and Math. Contbr. articles to profl. jours.; patentee in field. Recipient Preis Biochemische Analytik award German Soc. Clin. Chem., 1990, Allan award Am. Soc. of Human Genetics, 1990, award Gairdner Found. Internat., 1991, Nat. Biotech. award, 1991, Robert Koch award, 1992, Chiron Corp. Biotechnology Rsch. award Am. Soc. Microbiology, 1992, Japan prize Sci. and Tech. Found. Japan, 1993, Nobel Prize in Chemistry, Nobel Foundation, 1993; named Calif. Scientist of Yr., 1992, Scientist of Yr., R&D Mag., 1991. Mem. Am. Chem. Soc., Am. Acad. Achievement, Inst. Further Study (dir. 1983—). Achievements include invention of Polymerase Chain Reaction (PCR). Office: Vyrex Inc 6767 Neptune Pl Apt 5 La Jolla CA 92037-5924*

MULLIS, MADELINE GAIL HERMAN, music educator, choir director; b. Lenoir, N.C., Oct. 26, 1936; d. William Richard and Madeline Edythe (Harris) Herman; m. Thad McCoy Mullis Jr., Dec. 18, 1960 (div. Oct. 1978); children: Thad McCoy III, Myra Lynn, Martin Harper. MusB, U. N.C., Greensboro, 1958; MA, Appalachian State U., 1963; level I Orff cert., Memphis State U. Cert. elem., secondary instrumental and choir music tchr. N.C. Jr. choir dir. St. Stephens Luth. Ch., Lenoir, 1970-80, sr. choir dir., 1960—, handbell choir dir., 1970—, deacon, 1980-82, 84-86;, 88-90; Sunday sch. tchr. St. Stephens Luth. Ch., Lenoir, 1983-86; tchr. classroom music, chorus, band Caldwell County Schs., Lenoir, 1958-65, 77—; chair St. Stephens Worship and Music, Lenoir, 1988-93; rep. N.C. Synod Conv., Hickory, N.C., 1990; del. Women of Evang. Luth. Ch. in Am. Spring Gathering; pres. Agape Women's Cir., Lenoir, 1991-92. Chairperson Sesquicentennial Children's Chorus, Caldwell County, 1991; coord. 1st Caldwell County Children's Choral Festival, 1993. Recipient 25 Superior Ratings at Jr. H.S. Choral Festivals. Mem. NEA, N.C. Ctr. for Advancement of Tchg. (hon.), Assn. Luth. Musicians, N.C. Assn. Educators, Music Educators Nat. Conf., N.C. Music Educators Assn., Am. Orff-Schulwerk Assn., Cmty. Music Club (pres. 1993-95), Caldwell County Hist. Soc., Alpha Delta Kappa (hon.). Republican. Home: 119 Ellison Pl NE Lenoir NC 28645-3716 Office: 1406 Harper Ave NW Lenoir NC 28645-5089 also: Happy Valley Sch PO Box 130 Patterson NC 28661

MULLMAN, MICHAEL S., lawyer; b. N.Y.C., Sept. 17, 1946; s. Herbert and Harriet (Weissman) M.; m. Ellen Mullman, 1975; children: Jeremy, Cassie. BA in Polit. Sci. cum laude, Union Coll., Schenectady, N.Y., 1968; JD, Columbia U., 1971. Bar: N.Y. 1972, U.S. Ct. Appeals (2d cir.), U.S. Dist. Ct., 1975. Atty. Paskus, Gordon & Hyman, N.Y.C., 1976-80; ptnr. Schonwald, Schaffzin & Mullman, N.Y.C., 1980-89, Tenzer Greenblatt LLP, N.Y.C., 1989—. Bd. editors Columbia Jour. Law and Soc. Problems, articles edition, 1970-71. Nott scholar Union Coll., 1967, Harlan Fiske Stone scholar Sch. Law Columbia U., 1971. Mem. Bar Assn. N.Y.C., Phi Beta Kappa. Avocations: tennis, skiing, reading, gardening. Office: Tenzer Greenblatt LLP 405 Lexington Ave New York NY 10174-0002

MULLONEY, PETER BLACK, steel, oil and gas executive; b. Boston, Oct. 24, 1932; s. Daniel Clifford and Mabel (Black) M.; m. Marie Weprich. BA, Yale U., 1954. V.p. mktg. U.S. Steel Corp., Pitts., 1978-81; v.p., asst. to chmn. USX Corp., Pitts., 1981—; bd. dirs. Pitts. Vintage Grand Prix. Mem. adv. bd., sec. Salvation Army, Pitts.; vice chmn. World Affairs Coun. Pitts.; mem. bd. trustees La Roche Coll. Mem. Am. Iron and Steel Inst. (active com. on internat. trade, Washington, chmn. com. 1983-85), Internat. Iron and Steel Inst. (active com. on econ. studies, Brussels, chmn. com. 1983-85). Roman Catholic. Clubs: Duquesne (Pitts.), Harvard-Yale-Princeton, Pitts., Army and Navy (Washington), Pitts. Athletic Assn. Avocations: reading, walking. Home: 213 Grandview Ave Pittsburgh PA 15211-1525 Office: USX Corp 600 Grant St Pittsburgh PA 15219-2702

MULREANY, ROBERT HENRY, retired lawyer; b. Bklyn., Aug. 5, 1915; s. John Robert and Elfriede (Hartman) M.; m. Dorothy E. Muens, Sept. 7, 1940; children: Doreen Elizabeth Mulreany O'Brien, Carol Ann Mulreany Henwood. LLB, NYU, 1940. Bar: N.Y. 1940. Law clk. DeForest, Cullom & Elder, N.Y.C., 1933-39; mng. clk., atty. Neil P. Cullom, N.Y.C., 1939-42; since practiced in N.Y.C.; mem. DeForest & Elder, 1942-47, ptnr., 1947-49; ptnr. DeForest, Elder & Mulreany, 1949-69, sr. ptnr., 1954-69; ptnr. DeForest & Duer, 1969-87, of counsel, 1988-91; pres. Provident Loan Soc. N.Y., 1955-89, trustee, 1989—. Mem. adv. coun. Sch. Social Work, Columbia, 1960-64; mayor, Westfield, N.J., 1965-68; pres. Bd. Edn. Westfield, 1959-62; chmn. N.Y.C. Adv. Com. Pub. Welfare, 1963-67; chmn. bd. trustees Comty. Svc. Soc. of N.Y., 1959-72; trustee Overlook Hosp., 1970-78, chmn., 1976-78; trustee John A. Hartford Found.; trustee Smith Richardson Found., 1975—, Found. Ctr., Inc., 1975—; former trustee Westfield YMCA, Westfield Found., Tuskegee Inst.; trustee, pres. Overlook Hosp. Found., 1978-84, trustee, 1993—; trustee Smith Richardson Found. Lt. (j.g.) USNR, 1944-46. Mem. ABA, Bar Assn. City N.Y. Presbyterian. Clubs: Downtown Assn. (N.Y.C.), Echo Lake Country (Westfield, N.J.), Bay Head Yacht (N.J.). Home: 11 Euclid Ave Apt 4B Summit NJ 07901-2166

MULRONEY, (MARTIN) BRIAN, former prime minister of Canada; b. Mar. 20, 1939; s. Benedict and Irene (O'Shea) M.; m. Mila Pivnicki, 1973; 4 children. BA, St. Francis Xavier U., LLD, 1979; LLL, U. Laval, Que.; LLD, Meml. U. Nfld., Nfld., 1980, U. W.I., 1993, Tel Aviv U., 1994, Ctrl. Conn. State U., 1994, Barry U., 1995. Ptnr. Ogilvy Renault, Montreal, 1965-76; exec. v.p. Iron Ore Co. Can., Montreal, 1977-83, Iron Ore Co. of Can., Montreal, Que., 1976-77; mem. Parliament Can. from Ctrl. N.S., Ottawa, Ont., 1983-84; mem. Parliament Can. from Manicouagan, 1984-88, mem. Parliament Can. from Charlevoix, 1988-93, leader of Her Majesty's Loyal Opposition, 1983-84; prime minister Can., 1984-93; royal commr. Cliche Commn. investigating violence in Que. constrn. industry, 1974; sr. ptnr. Ogilvy Renault, Montreal, 1993—; chmn. internat. adv. bd. Barrick Gold Corp., The Chase Manhattan Corp.; mem. internat. adv. coun. Power Corp. Can.; mem. adv. bd. The China Internat. Trust and Investment Corp.; mem. Bombadier/Aerospace Group N.Am.; trustee Freedom Forum; mem. internat. adv. coun. Inst. Internat. Studies; bd. dirs. Archer Daniels Midland Co., Barrick Gold Corp., Chase Manhattan Corp. N.Y., The Trizec Hahn Corp., Petrofina, S.A., Power Corp., Quebecon. Author: Where I Stand, 1983. Office: Ogilvy Renault, 1981 McGill College Ave Ste 1100, Montreal, PQ Canada H3A 3C1

MULRONEY, MICHAEL, lawyer, law educator, graduate program director; b. Chgo., Feb. 26, 1932; s. Alphonsus James and Genevieve (Moran) M.; m. Ellen Goen Mulroney, Dec. 28, 1959; children: Sean, Conor, Dermot, Kieran, Moira. BSC in Econ., State U. Iowa, 1954; JD, Harvard Law Sch., 1959. Bar: Iowa 1959, D.C. 1960, U.S. Supreme Ct., U.S. Ct. Appeals (2nd, 3rd, 4th, 5th, 6th, 7th, 8th, 9th, 10th and D.C. cirs.), U.S. Tax Ct., U.S. Dist. Ct. D.C., D.C. Ct. Appeals, D.C. Superior Ct. Atty. adv. U.S. Tax Ct., Washington, 1959-61; appellate atty. Tax Div. U.S. Dept. Justice, Washington, 1961-65; assoc. Lee, Toomey & Kent, Washington, 1965-68, ptnr., 1969-87, counsel, 1987-88; prof., dir. Grad. Tax Program Villanova (Pa.) Law Sch., 1988—; adjunct prof. Grad. Tax Program Georgetown Law Sch., Washington, 1986—. Author: Federal Tax Examinations Manual, 1988, Foreign Taxation, 1992; mng. editor: The Tax Lawyer, 1989-96; reporter Invitational Conf. on Professionalism in Tax Practice, 1993, 96; contbr. articles to profl. jours. With U.S. Army, 1954-56. Fellow Am. Coll. of Tax Counsel; mem. ABA (taxation sect., chmn. important devels. com., mem. govt. submissions com., ct. procedure com., stds. of practice com., tchg. taxation com.; legal edn. and admissions to the bar sect.), D.C. Bar (tax sect.), Fed. Bar Assn. (tax sect.), Iowa Bar Assn. (tax sect.), J. Edgar Murdock Am. Inn. of Ct. (founding master), Internat. Fiscal Assn. (U.S. br. coun. mem.), Internat. Fiscal Rsch. Inst. (mem. coun. experts), Wash. Tax Lawyers' Study Group, Phila. Tax Conf. (mem. exec. coun.), Am. Assn. Law Schs. (tax sect.). Roman Catholic. Avocation: sports car racing. Office: Villanova Law Sch Villanova PA 19085

MULROW, PATRICK JOSEPH, medical educator; s. Patrick J. and Delia (O'Keefe) M.; m. Jacquelyn Pinover, Aug. 8, 1953; children: Deborah, Nancy, Robert, Catherine. AB, Colgate U., 1947; MD, Cornell U., 1951; MSc (hon.), Yale U., 1969. Intern N.Y. Hosp., 1951-52, resident, 1952-54; instr. physiology Med. Coll. Cornell U., 1954-55; research fellow Stanford U., 1955-57; instr. medicine Yale U., 1957-60, asst. prof., 1960-66, assoc. prof., 1966-69, prof. medicine, 1969-75; chmn. dept. medicine Med. Coll. Ohio, Toledo, 1975-95, prof. medicine, 1975—; chmn. ednl. com. Council for high blood pressure rsch. Am. Heart Assn., 1968-70, mem. exec. com., 1986-96, vice-chmn. of coun., 1990-92, chmn. 1992-94, past chmn., 1995-96; mem. study sect. NIH, 1970-74. Editorial bd. Jour. Clin. Endocrinology and Metabolism, 1966-70, 75-79, Endocrine Rsch., 1974—, Jour. Exptl. Biology and Medicine, Hypertension, 1994—; contbr. articles to profl. jours. With USNR, 1944-46. Mem. ACP, Am. Soc. Clin. Investigation, Assn. Am. Physicians, Am. Physiol. Soc., Endocrine Soc., Am. Fedn. Clin. Rsch., Am. Clin. and Climatol. Assn., Am. Heart Assn. (nat. rsch. com., chmn. cardiovasc. regulation rsch. study com. 1986-91), Assn. Profs. Medicine, Assn. Program Dirs. in Internal Medicine, Cen. Soc. Clin. Rsch. (pres. 1988-89), Internat. Soc. Hypertension, World Hypertension League (sec.-gen. 1995—), Inter-Am. Soc. Hypertension, Sigma Xi (pres. Yale chpt. 1965-66), Alpha Omega Alpha. Home: 9526 Carnoustie Rd Perrysburg OH 43551-3501 Office: Med Coll of Ohio Dept of Medicine PO Box 10008 Toledo OH 43699-0008

MULROY, RICHARD E., JR., lawyer. Sr. v.p., gen. counsel Mutual Life Ins. Co. of N.Y. Office: Mutual Life Ins Co of NY 1740 Broadway New York NY 10019-4315

MULRYAN, HENRY TRIST, mineral company executive, consultant; b. Palo Alto, Calif., Jan. 6, 1927; s. Henry and Marian Abigail (Trist) M.; m. Lenore Hoag, Aug. 25, 1948; children: James W., Carol. Student, Yale U., 1945-46; AB in Econs., Stanford U., 1948; postgrad., Am. Grad. Sch. Internat. Bus., 1949, Columbia U., 1983. V.p. mktg. Sierra Talc Co., South Pasadena, Calif., 1955-65; v.p. mktg. United Sierra, Trenton, N.J., 1965-67, v.p., gen. mgr., 1967-70, pres., 1970-77; v.p. Cyprus Mines Corp., Los Angeles, 1978-80; sr. v.p. ops. Cyprus indsl. minerals div. Amoco Minerals Co., Englewood, Colo., 1980-85; pres. Cyprus Indls. Minerals Co., Englewood, 1985-87; v.p. Cyprus Minerals Co., Englewood, 1985-87, sr. v.p. mktg., corp. adminstr., 1987-89; pres. Mineral Econs. Internat., 1989—. Served with U.S. Army, 1944-46. Clubs: Jonathan (Los Angeles). Lodge: Rotary (pres. South Pasadena club 1964-65) (bd. dirs. Princeton, N.J. club 1969-75). Office: 15237 W Sunset Blvd # 72 Pacific Palisades CA 90272-3690

MULTHAUP, MERREL KEYES, artist; b. Cedar Rapids, Iowa, Sept. 27, 1922; d. Stephen Dows and Edna Gertrude (Gard) Keyes; m. Robert Hansen Multhaup, Apr. 7, 1944; children: Eric Stephen, Robert Bruce. Student fine art, State U. of Iowa, 1942-43; student color theory, Rice U., 1971. Mem. teaching faculty Summit (N.J.) Art Assn., 1956-60; art instr. studio classes Springfield, N.J., 1954-55, Bloomfield (N.J.) Art Group, 1955-56, Westport, Conn., 1962-63; mem. teaching faculty Hunterdon Art Ctr., Clinton, N.J., 1985-92. One woman exhbns. include Coriell Gallery, 1995; exhibited in group shows at Nat. Assn. Women Artists, N.Y.C., 1957-97 (awards in figure painting), Hartford (Conn.) Athanaeum Mus., 1961 (1st prize), Highgate Gallery, N.Y.C., Waverly Gallery, N.Y.C., Leicester Gallery, London, Silvermine Gallery, Conn., Pendut Gallery, Tex., Benedict Gallery, Sidney Rothman Gallery, N.J., Stamford (Conn.) Mus., Bridgeport (Conn.) Mus., Montclair (N.J.) Mus., Newark Mus., Coriell Gallery, Albuquerque; included in traveling exhibit Nat. Assn. Women Artists, 1996—, Gallery Art 54, N.Y.C., 1997. Bd. dirs., exhbn. chmn. Summit Art Assn., 1950-60, Silvermine Guild of Art, New Canaan, Conn., 1960-64; bd. dirs. Artist's Equity of N.J., 1977-84, chmn. state-wide event, 1983, 86; artist's adv. coun. Hunterdon Art Ctr., Clinton, 1988-92. Recipient awards in juried exhbns. in Iowa, Pa., N.J., Conn., N.Y.C. Mem. Nat. Mus. for Women in Arts (charter mem.), Nat. Assn. Women Artists Inc. (awards for figure painting 1957, 80, 89), Albuquerque United Artists. Avocations: entertaining, sewing, singing, playing the piano and reading, dancing. Home and Studio: 1321 Stagecoach Rd SE Albuquerque NM 87123-4320

MULVANEY, JAMES FRANCIS, lawyer; b. Chgo., Nov. 2, 1922; m. Mary Ruth Rinderer, 1945; 7 children. BS, Loyola U., Chgo., 1942, JD, 1948. Atty. Chgo., 1948-55, San Diego, Calif., 1956-62; exec. v.p. U.S. Nat.

Bank, 1963-72, pres., CEO, 1972-73; pres. San Diego Baseball Co., 1955-68; v.p., gen. counsel San Diego Padres Nat. League, 1968-73; sr. ptnr. Mulvaney, Kahan & Barry, San Diego, 1974—; chmn., CEO Chela Fin., San Francisco, 1983—. Bd. vis. U. San Diego Sch. Law, 1971-88; chmn. United Way Internat., 1991-94, mem. exec. com., United Way Am., 1987-93, various officers; co-chmn. San Diego Organizing Project, 1983—; bd. dirs. World SHARE, Inc., 1986-92, Old Globe Theatre London, Del Mar Charities, 1985-95; numerous other civic activities. Officer USN, WWII; lt. comdr. USNR, Korea. Recipient Mr. San Diego award, 1991, First Annual Spirit of Charity award Cath. Community Svcs., 1984, Brotherhood award Nat. Conf. Christians and Jews, Inc., 1983, Citizen of Yr. award Jr. C. of C. and The City Club, 1983, numerous others. Mem. San Diego County Bar Found. (treas., Outstanding Svc. award 1988), ABA, Calif. State Bar Assn., Ill. State Bar Assn., San Diego C. of C., San Diego Coun. on World Affairs, The City Club of San Diego, Navy League. Office: Mulvaney Kahan & Barry 401 W A St Fl 17 San Diego CA 92101-7901

MULVANEY, MARY JEAN, physical education educator; b. Omaha, Jan. 6, 1927; d. Marion Fowler and Blanche Gibons (McKee) M. BS, U. Nebr., 1948; MS, Wellesley Coll., 1951; LHD (hon.), U. Nebr., 1986. Instr. Kans. State U., Manhattan, 1948-50; instr. U. Nebr., Lincoln, 1951-57, asst. prof., 1957-62; asst. prof. U. Kans., Lawrence, 1962-66; assoc. prof. U. Chgo., 1966-76, prof., 1976-90, prof. emeritus, 1990—, chmn. women's divsn., 1966-76, chmn. dept. phys. edn. and athletics, 1976-90; mem. vis. com. on athletics MIT, 1978-81, Wellesley Coll., 1978-79. Recipient Honor award Nebr. Assn. Health, Phys. Edn. and Recreation, 1962. Mem. AAHPERD, Nat. Collegiate Athletic Assn. (mem. coun. 1983-87), Collegiate Coun. Women Athletic Adminstrs., Midwest Assn. Intercollegiate Athletics for Women (chmn. 1979-81), Nat. Assn. Collegiate Dirs. of Athletics (mem. exec. com. 1976-80, Hall of Fame 1990), Ill. Assn. Intercollegiate Athletics for Women (chmn. 1978-80), Univ. Athletic Assn. (sec. 1986-90, mem. exec. com. 1986-90, mem. dels. com. 1986-90, chmn. athletic adminstr.'s com. 1986-88), Mortar Bd., Alpha Chi Omega. Home: 12 Skyline Dr Ogden Dunes IN 46368-1017

MULVEE, ROBERT EDWARD, bishop; b. Boston, Feb. 15, 1930; s. John F. and Jennie T. (Bath) M. BA, U. Sem. Ottawa, 1953, PhB, 1953; MRE, Am. Coll., Louvain, Belgium, 1957; D Canon Law, Lateran U., Rome, 1964; DD (hon.), Rivier Coll., Nashua, N.H., 1979. Ordained priest Roman Catholic Ch., 1957; asst. chancellor of diocese, 1964-72, named monsignor, 1966, elevated to domestic prelate, 1970, named chancellor, 1972; aux. bishop Roman Catholic Diocese of Manchester, N.H., 1977-85; bishop of Wilmington, 1985-95; coadjutor bishop Roman Cath. Diocese of Providence, 1995—. Trustee Nat. Shrine Imaculate Conception, Washington D.C, 1987. Mem. Nat. Conf. Cath. Bishops (campaign for human devel. com. 1985, joint com. Orthodox and Roman Cath. Bishops 1986, chmn. bd. bishops Am. Coll. of Louvain, Belgium, 1986, Cath. Relief Services bd., 1987); Nat. Conf. Cath. Bishops/ U.S. Cath. Conf. (adminstrv. com. and bd. dirs. 1986, com. on personnel and adminstrv. services 1987). Office: One Cathedral Sq Providence RI 02903-3695*

MULVEY, HELEN FRANCES, emeritus history educator; b. Providence, Feb. 22, 1913; d. William James and Anna (Nelson) M. A.B., Pembroke Coll., 1933; A.M., Columbia U., 1934; A.M., Radcliffe Coll., 1942; Ph.D., Harvard U., 1949. Instr. history Russell Sage Coll., Troy, N.Y., 1944-46; asst. prof. to prof. history, Conn. Coll., New London, 1946-83, prof. emeritus, 1983—, Brigida Pacchiana Ardenghi chair, 1975-78; vis. prof. Brit. history, U. Wis., Madison, 1971-72; vis. lectr. Yale U., 1974-83; lectr. Irish history, Pfizer Adult Edn., Groton, Conn., 1983-84; vis. scholar Phi Beta Kappa, Washington, 1982-83. Author articles, essays Irish and Brit. history; co-editor bibliog. vol. in A New History of Ireland, 9 vols. Anne Crosby Emery fellow, Brown U., 1933. Mem. AAUP (chpt. pres. 1962-64), Am. Hist. Assn., Am. Conf. for Irish Studies, North Am. Conf. on Brit. Studies, New Eng. Hist. Assn. (pres. 1971-72), Phi Beta Kappa. Clubs: Harvard. Office: Conn Coll PO Box 5508 New London CT 06320

MULVEY, JOHN THOMAS, JR., financial consultant; b. N.Y.C., Mar. 13, 1941; s. John T. and Jeanette (Fox) M.; m. Ruth I. Dieicks, May 5, 1962 (div. June 1982); m. Elaine R. Anderson, Oct. 6, 1984; children: Deborah, Karen, Laura. BA, Westminster Coll., Fulton, Mo., 1972. Corp. trust rsch. clk. Chem. Bank N.Y. Trust Co., 1959-60; asst. dir. personnel Fedn. Bank and Trust Co., 1960-62; personnel rep. Meadow Brook Nat. Bank, 1962-65; controller Reevesound Co., 1965-69; cost control mgr. Veco Instruments, Inc., 1972-74; supr. corp. income tax Mo. Dept. Revenue, 1974-80; asst. treas., controller Sangamon Co., 1980-82; mgr. Ford and Co. CPA, 1982-84; asst. controller Meml. Hosp., 1984-88; fin. cons. Pompano Beach, Fla.; pres. Ardus Real Estate, Inc., Pompano Beach, Fla., Ardus, Inc., Pompano Beach; pres., CEO Atlantic Mgmt. Svcs., Inc., Pompano Beach, Fla. Republican. Episcopalian. Home: 1800 S Ocean Blvd Apt 107 Pompano Beach FL 33062-7915 also: Ardus Inc PO Box 1178 Pompano Beach FL 33061-1178

MULVEY, MARY C., retired adult education director, gerontologist, senior citizen association administrator; b. Bangor, Maine, Aug. 17, 1909; d. Michael J. and Ann Loretta (Higgins) Crowley; m. Gordon F. Mulvey, Jan. 25, 1940. BA, U. Maine, 1930; MA, Brown U., 1953; EdD, Harvard U., 1961; LHD (hon.), U. Maine, 1991. Chmn. R.I. Com. on Aging, 1953-65; Dir. adminstrn. on aging State of R.I., 1960-63; co-founder Nat. Coun. Sr. Citizens, 1961; pres. Nat. Sr. Citizens Edn. and Rsch. Ctr., Washington, 1963—; 1st v.p. Nat. Coun. Sr. Citizens, 1976—; guidance counselor Providence Sch. Dept., 1963-65; dir. adult edn. City of Providence Sch. Dept., 1965-79; reg. prog. rep. Title V, Older Ams. Act, Nat. Coun. Sr. Citizens, Washington, 1980-94; major role in enactment of Medicare and Older Americans Act, 1950-65; del., adv. com. White House Conf. on Aging, 1961, 71, 81, 95; cons. Fed. Housing for the Aging, Washington, 1963-65, mem. tech. rev. com. Older Ams. Act Title IV, 1966-70; instr. preparing retirement, developer women's program U. R.I., 1963-80; appt. by Pres. Carter to Fed. Coun. Aging, 1979, pres. R.I. State Coun. Sr. Citizens, 1982—; charter mem. adv. bd. Coll. Arts, Humanities, U. Maine, 1992—; mem. various coms. state and nat. level. Publs. and contbr. articles to profl. jours. Recipient Soroptomists fellow award in rsch. in gerontology Harvard U., 1955, 57, 59, Cert. of award as Project Dir. of Sr. AIDES Employment Program, 1968-79, Medicare award R.I. State Coun. Sr. Citizens and Nat. Coun. Sr. Citizens, 1985, Disting. Achievement award U. Maine, 1980, Disting. Achievement award Berwick Acad., 1981, Justice for All award R.I. Bar Assn., 1981, Woman of Yr. award Nat. Sr. Pageant, 1982, R.I. Women 1st R.I. Sec. of State, 1991, citation Syracuse U., 1991, R.I. Dept. Elderly Affairs, 1993, 25th Anniversary Title V Sr. Employment award Nat. Coun. Sr. Citizens, 1993, Lifetime Achievement award Nat. Coun. Sr. Citizens, 1994, Co-Founder and Continuing Bd. Mem. award Nat. Coun. Sr. Citizens, 1995, Svcs. for St. Citizens award, 1995; inducted into R.I. Heritage Hall of Fame, 1993; Citation by Gov. Lincoln Almond for contbns. to R.I. Fellow Gerontol. Soc. Am.; mem. ACA, AAUW, Am. Assn. Adult and Continuing Edn., Harvard U. Alumni Assn. (Alumni award R.I. chpt. 1986), U Maine Alumni Assn., Brown U. Alumni Assn., Pi Lambda Theta, Delta Delta Delta. Home: 117 Evergreen Ln Windham ME 04062

MULVIHILL, DAVID BRIAN, lawyer; b. Pitts., Jan. 21, 1956; s. Mead J. Jr. and Margaret (O'Brien) M.; m. Elizabeth Miles, May 21, 1988; stepchildren: Jennifer A. Miles, Heath A. Miles. BA, U. Pitts., 1977; JD, Duquesne U., 1981. Bar: U.S. Dist. Ct. (we. dist.) Pa. 1981, U.S. Ct. Appeals (3d cir.) 1985. Assoc. Mansmann, Cindrich & Titus, Pitts., 1981-86; ptnr. Cindrich & Titus, Pitts., 1986-94, Titus & McConomy, Pitts., 1994—. Bd. dirs. Make-A-Wish Found. Am., 1992—; bd. dirs. Make-A-Wish Found. Western Pa., 1986-93, v.p., 1989-90, pres. 1990-92. Recipient Jefferson medal Am. Inst. for Pub. Svc., 1991, Outstanding Citizen award Pitts. Post-Gazette, 1991. Mem. ABA, Pa. Bar Assn., Allegheny County Bar Assn., Acad. Trial Lawyers of Allegheny County, Nat. Order of Barristers. Avocations: reading, tennis, classic cars. Office: Titus & McConomy 4 Gateway Ctr Pittsburgh PA 15222-1207

MULVIHILL, JAMES EDWARD, periodontist; b. Cleve., Sept. 24, 1940; s. John F. and Teresa J. (Carlos) M.; m. May Jane Forino, 1963; children—Karen, Kristen, Jason. B.A., Coll. of Holy Cross, 1962; D.M.D., Harvard U., 1966. Asst. dean for student affairs, coordinator Harvard-VA continuing edn. program Harvard Sch. Dental Medicine, Boston, 1970-71; dean clin. campus L.I. Jewish-Hillside Med. Ctr., Queens Hosp. Ctr. Affiliation, Jewish Inst. for Geriatric Care, Health Scis. Ctr. SUNY-Stony Brook, 1971-80; v.p. for edn. and research L.I. Jewish-Hillside Med. Ctr., New Hyde Park, N.Y., 1975-80; v.p., provost for health affairs, exec. dir. Health Ctr., prof. periodontics U. Conn., Farmington, 1980-92; attending periodontist John Dempsey Hosp., U. Conn. Health Ctr., Farmington, 1982-92; pres. John Dempsey Fin. Corp., Farmington, 1988-92; sr. v.p. for health policy The Travelers Corp., Hartford, Conn., 1992-94; chmn. bd. The Travelers Health Co., Hartford, 1992-93; sr. fellow in health policy Assn. of Acad. Health Ctrs., 1994; pres., CEO Managed Health, Inc., 1994, Comty. Health Plan of Queens/Nassau, New Hyde Park, N.Y., 1994-95, Forsyth Dental Ctr., Boston, 1995-96, Juvenile Diabetes Found. Internat., 1996—; cons. in field. Author: (with others) Guide to Foreign Medical Schools, 1975, Editorial Instructions for Dental Authors, 1979-80, 1979, Human Subjects Research: The Operational Handbook for IRB's, 1982, 2d edit., 1984, Japanese edit., 1987; also articles, chpt. in book. Bd. dirs. and chair Nat. Fund for Med. Edn. Recipient Disting. Alumnus award Harvard Sch. Dental Medicine, 1982, Disting. alumnus award Holy Cross Coll., 1991. Fellow AAAS, Am. Coll. Dentistry, Internat. Coll. Dentistry; mem. ADA, Am. Acad. Periodontology, Harvard Dental Alumni Assn., Internat. Assn. for Dental Rsch., Alpha Sigma Nu, Sigma Psi. Avocations: golf; gardening. Home: 2 Muls Hill Dr Farmington CT 06032-1638 Office: Juvenile Diabetes Found Internat 120 Wall St New York NY 10005-3904

MULVIHILL, JOHN GARY, information services administrator; b. Mpls., Mar. 3, 1933; s. Jack Albert and Aurelia Dolores (Voelker) M.; m. Anna Marie Stubenrauch, Aug. 24, 1959; children: Lawrence, Daniel. BA, U. St. Thomas, Houston, 1955; MA, Rice U., 1958; MLS, U. Tex., 1959. Assoc. libr. St. Benedicts Coll., Atchison, Kans., 1960-62; libr. Astra Pharm. Products, Worcester, Mass., 1962-64; indexer, asst. to mgr. Am. Petroleum Inst., N.Y.C., 1964-74; dir. GeoRef Information System, Am. Geol. Inst., Alexandria, Va., 1974—. Mem. Geoscience Info. Soc. (pres. 1977), Spl. Librs. Assn. Democrat. Roman Catholic. Avocation: woodworking. Home: 9516 Rockport Rd Vienna VA 22180-3446 Office: Am Geol Inst 4220 King St Alexandria VA 22302-1507

MULVIHILL, JOHN JOSEPH, medical geneticist; b. Washington, Aug. 20, 1943; s. John F. and Teresa J. (Carlos) M.; m. Charlotte K. Graeber, Aug. 20, 1966; children: Katherine R., J. Peter, William P. BS, Coll. Holy Cross, 1965; B in Med. Scis., Dartmouth Coll., 1967; MD, U. Washington, 1969. Chief clin. genetics sect. Nat. Cancer Inst., Bethesda, Md., 1974-90; prof., chmn. human genetics U. Pitts., Pa., 1990-94; dir. interninst. med. genetics program NIH, Bethesda, 1983-89; co-dir. Pitts. Genetics Inst., 1990—; acting dir. dept. reproductive genetics Magee Womens Hosp., Pitts., 1990-93; instr. dept. pediatrics Johns Hopkins U., Balt., 1982-91. Editor: Genetics of Human Cancer, 1975, Neurofibromatosis, 1982; mem. editorial bd. Jour. Nat. Cancer Inst., 1974-80, Teratology, 1980-88, Cancer Investigations; mem. editorial bd. Genetic Epidemiology, 1984—, editor-in-chief, 1993—; contbr. 230 articles to profl. jours. Sec.-gen. 8th Internat. Congress on Human Genetics, 1987-91, sec.-gen. permanent com., 1991—. Capt. USPHS, 1970-90. Fellow Am. Bd. Med. Genetics, Am. Acad. Pediatrics, Am. Coll. Epidemiology; mem. Commd. Officers Assn., Nat. Neurofibromatosis Found. (editor rsch. newsletter 1986-93). Democrat. Roman Catholic. Office: U Pitts Dept Human Genetics A-300 Crabtree Hall 130 Desoto St Pittsburgh PA 15213-2535

MULVIHILL, MAUREEN ESTHER, writer, educator, scholar; b. Detroit; d. Charles James and Esther (Byrne) M.; m. Daniel R. Harris, June 18, 1983. BPhil, Wayne State U., 1966, MA, 1968; PhD, U. Wis., 1982; post-grad., Columbia U., Yale U. Instr. U. Detroit, 1968-70, Wayne State U., Detroit, 1969-70, Penn Valley C.C., Kansas City, Mo., 1970-71; project writer Office of Gov., State of Wis., Madison, 1972-82; assoc. fellow Inst. for Rsch. in History, N.Y.C., 1984-89; vis. asst. prof. Hunter Coll. CUNY, 1983-85; vis. asst. prof. Touro Coll., N.Y.C., N.Y., 1983-85; corp. comm. dir. Gruntal & Co., N.Y.C., 1983-85; mem. Princeton (N.J.) Rsch. Forum, 1983—; proposal evaluator NEH, Washington, 1989—; juror Clifford com. Am. Soc. for 18th Century Studies, 1991; vis. faculty NYU, 1983-85, 93, Marymount-Manhattan Coll., 1993-94; assoc. prof. Fordham U.-Lincoln Ctr., 1994-96, St. Joseph Coll., Bklyn., 1997; guest spkr. Bklyn. Mus., NYU, Princeton U., Utah State U.; corp. liaison Irish Art Exhbn., U.S., U.K. Editor: (book) Poems by Ephelia (ca. 1679), 1992, 93; contbr. to profl. publs. Recipient scholarships Wayne State U., 1966, 67-68, U. Wis., 1971-81; NEH fellow, 1990-91, Princeton Rsch. Forum, N.J. Democrat. Roman Catholic. Avocation: rare book collecting (17th Century British & continental lit.). Home: 1 Plaza St W Brooklyn NY 11217-3952

MULVIHILL, PETER JAMES, fire protection engineer; b. Honolulu, Jan. 24, 1956; s. James H. and Jane A. (Norton) M. BSCE, Worcester (Mass.) Poly. Inst., 1978. Registered profl. engr. Fire Protection, Nev. Sr. engr. Indsl. Risk Insurers, San Francisco, 1978-84; fire protection engr. Aerojet Gen. Corp., Sacramento, 1984-87, Reno Fire Dept., 1987-93; bn. chief Boise (Idaho) Fire Dept., 1993-95; cons. Rolf Jensen & Assocs., Inc., Lehi, Utah, 1995-96; fire protection engr. Rolf Jensen & Assocs., Inc., Las Vegas, Nev., 1996—; part-time instr. univ. extension U. Calif., Davis, 1993-95, Truckee Meadows Community Coll., Reno, 1988-93. Commr. Gov.'s Blue Ribbon Commn. to Study Adequacy of State Regulations Concerning Highly Combustible Materials, Carson City, Nev., 1988. Mem. Soc. Fire Protection Engrs., No. Nev. Fire Marshal's Assn. (pres. 1992-93), Nat. Fire Protection Assn., Internat. Assn. Fire Chiefs, Calif. Fire Chiefs' Assn. (fire prevention officers sect. No. divsn.), Fire M arshals' Assn. N. Am.

MULVIHILL, TERENCE JOSEPH, investment banking executive; b. Omaha, Feb. 4, 1931; children: Mary Louise, Patricia, Kathleen (dec.), Joan, Carol, Nancy. BS in Econs., Georgetown U., 1952. Sec., treas. Mulvihill Co., Streator, Ill., 1955-64; instl. salesman Goldman, Sachs & Co., Chgo., 1964-71, v.p., 1971-80, asst. regional mgr., 1972-74, regional sales mgr., 1974-92, ptnr., 1980-92, COO, 1988-92, limited ptnr., 1992—; dir. Gen. Rental Fin. Co. Pres. St. Francis Xavier Sch. Bd., Wilmette, Ill., 1971, Regina Dominican H.S. Parents Assn., 1973; bd. dirs. Glenkirk Assn. for Retarded, Glenview, Ill., 1980-82, St. Joseph's Carondelet Child Ctr., Chgo., 1980-86; trustee Univ. of Chgo. Coun. Grad. Sch. of Bus., 1980—, Regina Dominican H.S. Charitable Trust, Wilmette, 1992, Marmion Military Acad., 1990—, Children's Meml. Hosp., Chgo., 1992—; mem. adv. com. Treas.'s Office of City of Chgo., 1990—; mem. Govs. Task Force Human Svcs. Reform, 1992—; governing mem. Orchestral Assn. Chgo. Symphony Orch., 1992—. 1st lt. U.S Army, 1952-54. Mem. Chgo. Coun. Fgn. Rels., Met. Club, Carlton Club, Bond Club of Chgo. (dir. 1981-82). Office: Goldman Sachs & Co 4900 Sears Tower Chicago IL 60606-6324

MUMAW, JAMES WEBSTER, lawyer; b. Youngstown, Ohio, Apr. 11, 1920; s. Daniel W. and Helen (James) M.; m. Lois M. Baird, May 28, 1948; children: Thomas, Daniel, William. A.B., Coll. of Wooster, 1941; J.D., U. Cin., 1948. Bar: Ohio 1949. Since practiced in Youngstown; partner Luckhart, Mumaw, Morrisroe & Zellers and predecessor firm, 1959-66; mem. firm Luckhart, Mumaw, Zellers & Robinson, 1966—; Dir. Ohio Bar Title Ins. Co., 1955-91, Western Res. Bank of Ohio, 1963-95. Mem. Youngstown City Bd. Edn., 1972-75; pres. Christ Mission Kindergarten Assn., Goodwill Industries, 1967-69; trustee Ohio Land Title Assn., 1975-78, v.p., 1981, pres., 1982-83, Penn Ohio Coll., 1989-96. Served with AUS, 1943-46. Mem. Ohio State Bar Found. (life), ABA, Ohio State Bar (exec. com. 1978-81), Mahoning County Bar Assn. (pres. 1963-64), Am. Judicature Soc., Phi Alpha Delta. Presbyterian (elder, trustee). Club: Kiwanian. Home: 845 Wildwood Dr Youngstown OH 44512-3244 Office: Legal Arts Ctr Youngstown OH 44503-1701

MUMFORD, CHRISTOPHER GREENE, corporate financial executive; b. Washington, Oct. 21, 1945; s. Milton C. and Dorothea L. (Greene) M.; B.A., Stanford U., 1968, M.B.A., 1975. Cons., Internat. Tech. Resources Inc., 1974; asst. v.p. Wells Fargo Bank, San Francisco, 1975-78; v.p., treas. Arcata Corp., San Francisco, 1978-82, v.p. fin., 1982-87, exec. v.p. fin., 1987-94. gen. ptnr. Scarff, Sears & Assocs., San Francisco, 1986-95, mng. dir. Questor Ptnrs. Fund, L.P., San Francisco, 1995—; v.p. bd. dirs. Triangle Pacific Corp., Dallas, 1986-88, Norton Enterprises Inc., Salt Lake City, 1988-90; bd. dirs. Community Home Med. Enterprises, Inc., Grass Valley, Calif., Crown Pacific Ltd., Portland, Oreg., Ryder TRS, Inc., Miami, Fla., Ockham Personal Ins. Agy., PLC, London, Union Security Mortgage, Inc., Santa Ana, Calif., 1993-94. Office: 601 California St Ste 1800 San Francisco CA 94108-2823

MUMFORD, DAVID BRYANT, mathematics educator; b. Worth, Sussex, Eng., June 11, 1937; came to U.S., 1940; s. William Bryant and Grace (Schiott) M.; m. Erika Jentsch, June 27, 1959 (dec. July 30, 1988); children: Stephen, Peter, Jeremy, Suchitra; m. Jenifer Moore, Dec. 29, 1989. B.A., Harvard U., 1957, Ph.D., 1961; D.Sc. (hon.), U. Warwick, 1983. Jr. fellow Harvard U., 1958-61, assoc. prof., 1962-66, prof. math., 1966-77, Higgins prof., 1977-97, chmn. dept. math, 1981-84; prof. Brown U., 1996—; v.p. Internat. Math. Union, 1991-94, pres., 1995—. Author: Geometric Invariant Theory, 1965, Abelian Varieties, 1970, Introduction to Algebraic Geometry, 1976. Recipient Fields medal Internat. Congress Mathematicians, 1974; MacArthur Found. fellow, 1987-92. Fellow Tata Inst. (hon.); mem. Accad. Nazionale dei Lincei, Nat. Acad. Scis., Am. Acad. Arts and Scis. Home: 26 Gray St Cambridge MA 02138-1510 Office: Brown U 182 George St Providence RI 02912-9056

MUMFORD, GEORGE SALTONSTALL, JR., former university dean, astronomy educator; b. Milton, Mass., Nov. 13, 1928; s. George S. and Alice (Herrick) M.; m. Nancy Carey, Dec. 22, 1949; children: Barbara, Elizabeth, Robert, George. A.B., Harvard U., 1950; M.A., Ind. U., 1952; Ph.D., U. Va., 1955. Mem. faculty Randolph-Macon Woman's Coll., 1952-53; mem. faculty Tufts U., Medford, Mass., 1955—, prof. astronomy, 1968-97, dean Coll. Liberal Arts, 1969-79, dean research and instl. programs, dean Grad. Sch. Arts and Scis., 1979-84, prof. emeritus, 1997—; acting dir. Dudley Wright Ctr. for Innovation in Sci. Teaching, 1991-92; vis. astronomer Kitt Peak Nat. Obs., Tucson, 1962-82; cons. NSF, 1967-68; vis. astronomer Cerro Tololo Inter-Am. Obs., La Serena, Chile, 1969-72; dir. Wyman-Gordon Inc., Worcester, Mass., 1968-96; bd. dirs. Coun. of Grad. Schs. in U.S., 1979-83; mem. space sci. rev. panel NAS, 1989-95; mem. planetarium adv. com. Mus. Sci., Boston; bd. dirs. Miramichi Salmon Assoc., Charles River Watershed Assoc.; chmn. class com. Harvard U.; corp. mem. The Trustees of Reservations. Mem. AAAS, Am. Astron. Soc., Astron. Soc. Pacific, Am. Phys. Soc., Internat. Astron. Union, Am. Assn. Physics Tchrs., Royal Astron. Soc. Can., Royal Astron. Soc., N.E. Assn. Grad. Schs. (pres. 1981-82), Sigma Xi. Research in photometric studies of cataclysmic variables and related objects, early Am. astronomy, software for astronomy education. Home: Pegan Ln Dover MA 02030 Office: Tufts U Dept Physics And Astro Medford MA 02155

MUMFORD, MANLY WHITMAN, lawyer; b. Evanston, Ill., Feb. 25, 1925; s. Manly Stearns and Helen (Whitman) M.; m. Luigi Thorne Horne, July 1, 1961; children—Shaw, Dodge. A.B., Harvard U., 1947; J.D., Northwestern U, Chgo., 1950. Bar: Ill. 1950, U.S. Supreme Ct. 1969. Assoc. Chapman and Cutler, Chgo., 1950-62, ptnr., 1963-90. Contbr. articles to profl. jours. Served with USNR, 1942-46. Mem. Nat. Assn. Bond Lawyers (Bernard P. Friel medal 1987). Democrat. Clubs: Cliff Dwellers, University, Chgo. Literary. Avocation: computers. Home: 399 W Fullerton Pky Chicago IL 60614-2810 Office: 22 W Monroe St Ste 1503 Chicago IL 60603-2505

MUMFORD, STEPHEN DOUGLAS, population growth control research scientist; b. Louisville, Aug. 28, 1942; s. Adrian Leroy and Mildred Margaret (Cardwell) M.; m. Judy Sheng-Ju Lee, Dec. 26, 1966; children: Christopher Lee, Sonia Lea. BS in Agr., U. Ky., 1966; MPH in Internat. Health/Population Study, U. Tex., Houston, 1971, DrPH in Health Svcs. Adminstrn., 1975. Indsl. hygienist Ky. State Dept. Health, Frankfort, 1966-67; rsch. asst. dept. ob.-gyn. Baylor Coll. Medicine, Houston, 1973-75; rsch. statis. aide population studies U. Tex., Houston, 1971-75, rsch. asst. dept. reproductive biology/endocrinology, 1971-76; dir. rsch., sr. vasectomy counselor Planned Parenthood of Houston, 1972-76; adminstr. Nat. Swine Flu Immunization Program/Houston/Harris County, Tex., 1976-77; from sect. leader design/analysis divsn. to scientist Internat. Fertility Rsch. Program, Research Triangle Park, N.C., 1977-83; pres. Ctr. for Rsch. on Population and Security, Research Triangle Park, N.C., 1984—; bd. dirs. The Churchman Assocs., Inc., St. Petersburg, Fla. Author: The Pope and the New Apocalypse: The Holy War Against Family Planning, 1986, American Democracy and the Vatican: Population Growth and National Security, 1984, Population Growth Control: The Next Move is America's, 1977, The Decision-Making Process that Leads to Vasectomy: A Guide for Promoters, 1977, Vasectomy Counseling, 1977, The Life and Death of NSSM 200: How the Destruction of Political Will Doomed a U.S. Population Policy, 1996; contbr. numerous articles to profl. jours., chpts. to books; contbr. editor The Churchman, 1991—. Mem. Alan Guttmacher Inst., Assn. for Vol. Sterilization, Environ. Def. Fund, Fund for Feminist Majority, Nat. Abortion Rights Action League, Population Inst., Population Ref. Bur., Ams. United for Separation of Ch. and State, Religious Coalition for Abortion Rights. Capt. U.S. Army, 1966-70. Recipient Cert. of Appreciation for Outstanding Contbns. to Advancing the Cause of Reproductive Rights, Feminist Caucus of Am. Humanist Assn., 1986, Humanist Disting. Svc. award, 1981, Margaret Mead Leadership prize in population and ecology, 1981, Award for Outstanding Single Project in Area of Human Rels., U.S. Jaycees, 1974-75, Award for Outstanding Chmn. of a Single Project in Area of Human Rels., 1974-75. Mem. Am. Humanist Assn., Am. Pub. Health Assn. (population sect.), Ams. for Immigration Control, Ams. for Religious Liberty, Fedn. for Am. Immigration Reform, Internat. Epidemiol. Assn., Negative Population Growth, Carrying Capacity Network, Soc. for Epidemiologic Rsch., World Future Soc., Zero Population Growth, NOW. Avocations: gardening, fruit growing, woodworking, fishing, running. Home: 322 Azalea Dr Chapel Hill NC 27514-9120 Office: Ctr Rsch Population PO Box 13067 Research Triangle Park NC 27709-3067

MUMFORD, WILLIAM PORTER, II, lawyer; b. Kewanee, Ill., July 13, 1920; s. Harold E. and Mary K. (Harry) M.; m. Jean N. Hagemann, Nov. 22, 1951; children—William Porter III, James F., Michael E. B.S. in Accounting, U. Ill., 1943, J.D., 1949. Bar: Ill. bar 1949, Oreg. bar 1955; C.P.A., Ill., Oreg. Jr. accountant Price Waterhouse & Co., Chgo., 1949-51; practiced in Chgo., 1951-54, Grants Pass, Ore., 1955-57, Eugene, Oreg., 1957—; mem. firm McAdams & Kirby, 1951-55; sr. accountant B.K. Herndon & Co., 1955-57; partner Thompson, Mumford, Anderson & Fisher, 1957-86, ret., 1986. Eugene campaign mgr. Hatfield for Gov., 1960-62; Chmn. bd. trustees Oreg. State Library. Served to capt., inf. AUS, 1943-46. Mem. Am. Legion, Pi Kappa Alpha, Phi Alpha Delta. Republican. Club: Elk. Home: 1960 Alder St Eugene OR 97405-2938

MUMMA, ALBERT G., retired naval officer, manufacturing company executive, management consultant; b. Findlay, Ohio, June 2, 1906; grad. U.S. Naval Acad., 1926; D.Eng. (hon.) N.J. Inst. Tech.; m. Carmen Braley, 1927; children—Albert G. Jr., John S., David B. Commd. ensign USN, 1926, advanced through grades to rear adm.; head tech. intelligence div. Naval Forces Europe, World War II; comdr. David Taylor Model Basin, Mare Island Naval Shipyard, also chief Bur. Ships, U.S. Navy, 1955-59; builder nuclear high speed submarines, U.S.S. Enterprise, Long Beach, Bainbridge and Polaris submarines; ret., 1959; v.p., group exec. Worthington Corp., 1964, exec. v.p., dir. in charge all domestic ops., 1967, pres., chief operating officer, 1967, chmn. bd., 1967-71; chmn. Am. Shipbldg. Commn., 1971-73. Trustee emeritus Drew U., Madison, N.J. Recipient Adm. Jerry Land Gold medal; awarded Knight Grand Officer of Orange Nassau by the Queen of the Netherlands. Fellow Soc. Naval Architects and Marine Engrs. (hon.; past pres.); mem. Am. Soc. Naval Engrs. (hon.; past pres.), Nat. Acad. Scis. (past mem. research council; past chmn. numerous coms.), Nat. Acad. Engring. (life). Clubs: Army and Navy, Army and Navy Country (Washington), Baltusrol Golf (Springfield, N.J.); Mountain Lake (Lake Wales, Fla.). Home: 69 Mountain Lk Lake Wales FL 33859 summer: 1400 Waverly Rd # 25 Gladwyne PA 19035-1254

MUMMA, ALBERT GIRARD, JR., architect; b. Long Beach, Calif., July 2, 1928; s. Albert Girard and Carmen (Braley) M.; m. Janeal Thomas Woolf, Dec. 24, 1973; children: Eugenia M. Villagra, Albert Girard III, Peter Brenaman. B.Arch., U. Va., 1951. Designer McLeod & Ferrara, Architects, Washington, 1951-56; assoc. Deigert & Yerkes, Architects, 1956-62; prin. Mumma & Assocs., Washington, 1962—; archtl. designer hotel div. Marriott Corp., 1980-82. Prin. archtl. works include Nat. Arboretum Hdqrs. Bldg, 1961, Finnmark Sq., Silver Spring, Md., 1964, Inverness townhouses, Potomac, Md., 1971, Post Office and Fed. Bldg., Elkins, W.Va., 1971, U.S.

Trade Fairs in Spain, Finland, Japan, El Salvador, Poland 1963-72, Fallswood housing project, Falls Church, Va., 1972, Bristow Village townhouses, Annandale, Va., 1972-73, Marriott Hotel, Dayton, Ohio, 1982, Plaza Venetia, Biscayne Bay, Miami, Fla., 1983, Houston Med. Ctr. Hotel, Newark Airport Hotel, 1984, pvt. residences, No. Neck, Rappahanock River, Lancaster County, Va., 1993-96, subdivision and townhouse projects, Washington, Md., Va., Pa., 1962—. Served with USMC, 1945-47. Recipient Design award Washington Bd. Trade, 1964; winner Newark Airport Hotel Competition, 1981. Mem. AIA (medal 1951), Rappahannock River Yacht Club.

MUMMA, GORDON, composer, educator, author; b. Framingham, Mass., Mar. 30, 1935; s. Colgan Thomas and Adamae (McCoy) M.; children: Christopher, Jonathan. Student, U. Mich., 1952-53. Guest lectr. Brandeis U., 1966, 67; composer, musician Merce Cunningham Dance Co., 1966-74, Sonic Arts Union, from 1966; guest lectr. U. Ill., 1969-70, Ferienkurse für Neue Musik, Darmstadt, Fed. Republic Germany, 1974; mem. faculty Cursos Latinoamericanos de Música Contemporánea, Montevideo, 1975, Buenos Aires, 1977, Dominican Republic, 1981; prof. music U. Calif., Santa Cruz, 1975-94; prof. emeritus U. Calif., 1994—; Darius Milhaud prof. Mills Coll., 1981; co-founder ONCE Festivals of Contemporary Music, Ann Arbor, Mich., 1961-66, Cybersonics, Ann Arbor, 1963; electronic designer Pepsi Pavilion, Expo 70, Osaka, Japan; tech. dir. Intermedia Inst., N.Y.C., 1970; founder Tao Chem. Co., performance-arts prodn. co., N.Y.C., 1976; vis. prof. U. Calif.-San Diego, 1985, 87; vis. disting. composer Mills Coll., 1989. Commd. works, recs. and performances include music for Venezia Space Theatre, Venice, Italy, 1963, Megaton for William Burroughs, Ann Arbor, 1964, Mesa, St. Paul de Vence, France, 1966, Hornpipe, Boston, 1967, Beam, Tokyo, 1969, Cybersonic Cantilevers, Syracuse, 1973, Some Voltage Drop, Paris, 1974, Passenger Pigeon, Albany, N.Y., 1976, (with David Cotter, Jann McCauley, Tom Robbins), Ear Heart, Portland, Oreg., 1977, (with Jann McCauley, Henk Pander, Peter West), Echo, Portland, 1978, Pontpoint, 1980, (with William Winant) Than Particle, 1985, (with Tandy Beal Dance Co.), Orait, 1988, (with Abel-Steinberg-Winant Trio) Ménages à Deux, 1990; author: (with James Klosty) Merce Cunningham, 1975, (with Jon Appleton) Development and Practice of Electronic Music, 1975. N.Y. State Council on Arts grantee; Nat. Endowment Arts grantee, 1977-78; Oreg. Arts Council grantee, 1977-78. Mem. Broadcast Music Inc., Internat. Horn Soc., Soc. Ethnomusicology. Office: Univ Calif Dept Music Santa Cruz CA 95064*

MUMMA, MICHAEL JON, physicist; b. Lancaster, Pa., Dec. 3, 1941; s. John Henry and Violet Lyndell (Baxter) M.; m. Sage Bailey Tower, Aug. 20, 1966; children: Peter Robb, Amy Elizabeth. A.B. in Physics with honors, Franklin and Marshall Coll., 1963; Ph.D. in Physics, U. Pitts., 1970. Grad. research asst. U. Pitts., 1963-70; astrophysicist NASA Goddard Space Flight Center, Greenbelt, Md., 1970-76; head br. Infrared and Radio Astronomy NASA Goddard Space Flight Center, 1976-84, assoc. chief Lab. Extraterrestrial Physics, 1984-85, head Planetary Systems br., 1985-90, chief scientist Lab. Extraterrestrial Physics, 1990—; adj. research assoc. in physics Pa. State U., 1978-81, prof. physics, 1981-88; mem. numerous working groups and adv. coms. NASA, Nat. Bur. Standards, NSF, Nat. Acad. Scis., 1973—; lectr. in field. Contbr. numerous articles to profl. publs., 1970—; editor: The Study of Comets, Vols. 1, 2, 1976, Vibrational-Rotational Spectroscopy for Planetary Atmospheres, vols. 1, 2, 1982, Astrophysics from the Moon, 1990. Recipient NASA medal for Exceptional Sci. Achievement, 1986; Kershner award for physics, 1962; Coll. Trustee's scholar Franklin and Marshall Coll., 1963. Fellow Am. Phys. Soc., Washington Acad. Sci.; mem. AAAS, Am. Astron. Soc., Am. Geophys. Union, Internat. Astron. Union, Sigma Pi Sigma. Achievements include discovery of natural lasers in atmospheres of Mars, Venus, and Jupiter; first detection of water vapor in comets, discovery of formaldehyde, methanol, methane, and ethane in comets; discovery of x-rays in comets; first definitive measurements of deuterium and hydrogen on Mars and Venus; first absolute wind measurements on Venus and Mars; invention of tunable diode laser heterodyne spectrometer and other advanced instruments; development of Doppler-limited infrared spectroscopy for laboratory and astrophysical applications, of absolute calibration procedures in vacuum ultraviolet, of molecular branching ratio technique for intensity calibration in vacuum ultraviolet; measurement of many absolute cross sections in vacuum ultraviolet; research on atomic and molecular physics and chemistry, on comets, on planetary atmospheres, on infrared astronomy, on high-resolution spectroscopy, and in the field of dissociative excitation of molecules. Office: Code 690 Goddard Space Flight Ctr Greenbelt MD 20771

MUNCH, DOUGLAS FRANCIS, pharmaceutical and health industry consultant; b. Bronx, N.Y., Mar. 15, 1947; s. Robert Joseph and Isabel (Fiordelisi) M.; m. Janice Ann Davis, Apr. 3, 1976: children: Sarah Christine, Eric Christopher. BSChemE, Villanova U., 1969; MS, U. Calif., Santa Barbara, 1974; PhD, Johns Hopkins U., 1978. Project engr. Grumman Aerospace Corp., Bethpage, N.Y., 1969-73; postdoctoral fellow U. South Ala., 1978-80; program mgr. Travenol Labs., Round Lake, Ill., 1980-82; dir. Kimberly Clark Corp., Atlanta, 1982-86; pres. Biomed. Products Group Inc., Roswell, Ga., 1986-87; cons., pres. D.F. Munch & Assocs., Roswell, 1986-88; pres., dir. Sphinx Pharmaceuticals, Inc., Durham, N.C., 1988-89; v.p., dir. Orthopharm Corp.-Advanced Care Products, Johnson & Johnson, Raritan, N.J., 1989-92; pres. D.F. Munch, Ltd., Basking Ridge, N.J., 1992—. Author: Cardiovascular Pharmacology, 1981; contbr. articles to profl. jours. Pres. Hollyberry Civic Assn., Roswell, 1980-87, Roswell Neighborhood Network, 1987, Basking Ridge (N.J.) Little League, 1992—; elder Basking Ridge Presbyn. Ch., 1992-95; mem. BME bd. dirs. Johns Hopkins Med. Sch., Balt., 1997—. Recipient Apollo Achievement award NASA, 1969; Profl. Achievement award Villanova U., 1987; NIH fellow, 1974-78. Fellow Royal Soc. Medicine; mem. Am. Physiol. Soc., Biomed. Engring. Soc., Johns Hopkins Med. and Surg. Assn. Avocations: woodworking, music, camping, cycling, swimming. Home: 41 Fieldstone Dr Basking Ridge NJ 07920-1605

MUNCK, ALLAN ULF, physiologist, educator; b. Buenos Aires, Argentina, July 4, 1925; came to U.S., 1945, naturalized, 1959; s. Carl and Elisabeth (Schmidt) M.; m. Claire Brosi, Oct. 5, 1957; children—Alexander Charles, Ingrid Claire, Kirsten Tanya. B.S. in Chem. Engring, Mass. Inst. Tech., 1948, M.S., 1949, Ph.D. in Biophysics, 1956. Chem. engr. Ducilo, Buenos Aires, 1949-50; mem. staff Huntington Lab. Mass. Gen. Hosp., Boston, 1956-57, Worcester Found. Exptl. Biology, Shrewsbury, Mass., 1957-59; mem. med. sch. faculty Dartmouth Coll., 1959—; prof. physiology Dartmouth Med. Sch., 1967—. Assoc. editor: Jour. Steroid Biochemistry; editorial bd.: Jour. Biol. Chemistry. Served with Argentine Army, 1949. Mem. Physiol. Soc., Endocrine Soc., Am. Soc. Biochemistry and Molecular Biology. Home: PO Box 114 Norwich VT 05055-0114 Office: Dartmouth Med Sch Dept Physiology Lebanon NH 03756

MUNCY, ESTLE PERSHING, physician; b. Tazewell, Tenn., Apr. 9, 1918; s. William Loyd and Flora Media (Monday) M.; m. Dorothy Davis, Dec. 31, 1946 (div. Apr. 1980); children: Robert H., Teresa A., Dorothy J., Estle II, James; m. Jean Marie Hayter, Mar. 19, 1985. AB, Lincoln Meml. U., 1939; MD, U. Tenn., 1943. Resident Dallas Meth. Hosp., 1948; tchg. resident Tufts Med. Sch., Boston, 1949-50; physician Jefferson City, Tenn., 1950-96. Author: The Muncys in the New World, 1988, People and Places in Jefferson County, Tennessee, 1994. Alderman Jefferson City, 1974-77; chmn. Jefferson City Planning Commn., 1976-79. Capt. M.C., U.S. Army, 1944-46. Mem. Tenn. Heart Assn. (pres. 1966-67), Hamblen County Med. Soc. (pres. 1960-61), Jefferson County Hist. Soc. (pres. 1993-94, historian 1995—). Republican. Baptist. Avocations: photography, gardening. Home: 1428 Russell Ave Jefferson City TN 37760-2529

MUND, GERALDINE, bankruptcy judge; b. L.A., July 7, 1943; d. Charles J. and Pearl (London) M. BA, Brandeis U., 1965; MS, Smith Coll., 1967; JD, Loyola U., 1977. Bar: Calif. 1977. Bankruptcy judge U.S. Ctrl. Dist. Calif., 1984—, bankruptcy chief judge, 1997—. Past pres. Temple Israel, Hollywood, Calif.; mem. bd. Jewish Fedn. Coun. of Greater L.A. Mem. ABA, L.A. County Bar Assn. Office: 21041 Burbank Blvd Woodland Hills CA 91367-6603

MUND, RICHARD GORDON, foundation executive; b. Balt., Feb. 11, 1942; s. Allan Winfield and Irma Louetta (Kaufman) M.; m. Joan Ann Dennis, June 24, 1967; children: Mary Jean, John Winfield, Elizabeth Anne. Student, Johns Hopkins U., 1960-63; BA, Ill. Wesleyan U., 1965; M.A., U. Denver, 1967, Ph.D., 1970. Asst. dir. admissions Marshall U., Huntington, W.Va., 1970, dir. fin. aid, 1971, v.p. student affairs, 1971-77; coll. rels. coord. Mobil Oil Corp., N.Y.C., 1977-79; asst. sec. Mobil Found., Inc., N.Y.C., 1979, sec., exec. dir., 1980—; mem. contbns. coun. Conf. Bd., N.Y.C., 1980—, chmn., 1985. Trustee Huntington (W.Va.) Galleries, 1975-77, Coun. for Advancement and Support of Edn., 1987-89, Fairfax County Pub. Schs. Edn. Found., 1991—, Soc. of Yeager Scholars, Marshall U., 1995—; adv. coun. mem. ARC, BBB, Nat. Ctr. Non-Profit Bds., United Way Am. Mem. Kappa Delta Pi, Kappa Alpha Order, Phi Delta Kappa. Office: Mobil Found Inc 3325 Gallows Rd Fairfax VA 22037

MUNDELL, ROBERT ALEXANDER, economics educator; b. Kingston, Ont., Can., Oct. 24, 1932; s. William C. and Lila (Knifton) M.; m. Barbara Sheff, Oct. 14, 1957 (div. 1972); children: Paul Alexander, William Andrew, Robyn Leslie. BA, U. B.C., Can., 1953; postgrad., U. Wash., 1953-54, London Sch. Econs. and Polit. Sci., 1955-56; PhD, MIT, 1956; postdoc., U. Chgo., 1956-57; PhD (hon.), Renmin U. China, 1985, U. Paris, 1992. Instr. econs. U. B.C., Vancouver, Can., 1957-58; acting asst. prof. econs. Stanford U., Calif., 1958-59; vis. prof. econs. Sch. Advanced Internat. Studies, Johns Hopkins U. Ctr., Bologna, Italy, 1959-61; sr. economist research dept. IMF, Washington, 1961-63; vis. prof. econs. McGill U., Montreal, Que., Can., 1963-64; Rockefeller vis. research prof. internat. econs. Brookings Instn., Washington, 1964-65; prof. Grad. Inst. Internat. Studies, Geneva, summers 1965-75; Ford Found. vis. research prof. econs. U. Chgo., 1965-66, prof., 1966-71; prof. econs., chmn. dept. U. Waterloo, Ont., Can., 1972-74; prof. econs. Columbia U., N.Y.C., 1974—; economist Can. Royal Commn. on Price Spreads on Food Products, summer 1957; mem. joint fiscal mission to Peru OAS and Inter-Am. Devel. Bank, summer 1964; cons. FRS, IBRD, 1966—, U.S. Treasury Dept., 1969-74, EEC, 1970-73, UN, Govt. Panama; organizer, participant internat. confs., lectr. numerous univs. and profl. orgn. meetings; hon. prof. Renmin U. China, Beijing. Author: The International Monetary System--Conflict and Reform, 1965, Man and Economics, 1968, International Economics, 1968, Monetary Theory--Interest, Inflation and Growth in the World Economy, 1971; contbr. sects. to books, encys., U.S. Congl. Hearings, numerous articles to profl. jours.; co-editor, contbr.: Monetary Problems of the International Economy, 1969, Trade, Balance of Payments and Growth, 1971; co-editor: The New International Monetary System, 1977; editor: Jour. Polit. Economy, 1966-70, Global Disequilibrium in the World Economy, 1989, 92, Building the New Europe, 1991, Debt, Deficit and Economic Importance, 1990, Inflation and Growth in China, 1996. Recipient Jacques Rueff Prize medal, 1983; NSF rsch. grantee, 1967-70; Guggenheim fellow, 1970-71; Marshall lectr. Cambridge U., 1974. Mem. Am. Econ. Assn. (Disting. fellow 1997). Office: Dept Econs Columbia U 1031 Internat Affairs 118th St & Amsterdam Ave New York NY 10027

MUNDEN, ROBIN GHEZZI, lawyer; b. Rome, May 22, 1947; (parents Am. citizens); s. Kenneth White and Lia (Ghezzi) M.; m. Gail J. Schoch, June 2, 1973. BA in Polit. Sci., U. Denver, 1970; JD cum laude, Northwestern U., 1973. Bar: Ill. 1973, U.S. Dist. Ct. (no. dist.) Ill. 1973. Litigation assoc. McDermott, Will & Emery, Chgo., 1973-79; gen. counsel King-Seeley Thermos Co., Prospect Heights, Ill., 1979-82; v.p., gen. counsel, sec. Household Mfg. Inc., Prospect Heights, Ill., 1982-89; ptnr. Trizna, Lepri & Munden, Chgo., 1990-93; v.p., gen. counsel DSC Logistics, Inc., Des Plaines, Ill., 1993—. Mem. editorial bd. Northwestern Univ. Law Review, 1971-73. Mem. Sheffield Neighbors, Chgo. Mem. ABA, Ill. Bar Assn., Chgo. Bar Assn., Burnham Pk. Yacht Club (Chgo.), Royal Ocean Racing Club (U.K.). Democrat. Avocation: sailing. Home: 2140 N Bissell St Chicago IL 60614-4202 Office: DSC Logistics Inc 1750 S Wolf Rd Des Plaines IL 60018-1924

MUNDHEIM, ROBERT HARRY, law educator; b. Hamburg, Germany, Feb. 24, 1933; m. Guna Smitchens; children: Susan, Peter. BA, Harvard U., 1954, LLB, 1957; MA (hon.), U. Pa., 1971. Bar: N.Y. 1958, Pa. 1979. Assoc. Shearman & Sterling, N.Y.C., 1958-61; spl. counsel to SEC, Washington, 1962-63; vis. prof. Duke Law Sch., Durham, N.C., 1964; prof. law U. Pa., Phila., 1965—, Univ. prof. law and fin., 1980-93, dean, 1982-89, Bernard G. Segal prof. law, 1987-89; co-chmn. Fried, Frank, Harris, Shriver & Jacobson, N.Y.C., 1990-92; v.p., gen. counsel Salomon Inc.; gen. counsel U.S. Dept. Treasury, Washington, 1977-80; dir. Ctr. for Study of Fin. Instns., U. Pa.; dir. Corestates Bank N.A., 1980-92, Commerce Clearing House, 1980-96, Appleseed Found., The Kitchen; gen. counsel Chrysler Loan Guarantee Bd., 1980; exec. v.p., gen. counsel Salomon, Inc., 1992—; mng. dir., mem. mgmt. bd. Salomon Bros. Inc., N.Y.C., 1992—. Served with USAF, 1961-62. Recipient Alexander Hamilton award U.S. Dept. Treasury, 1980, Harold P. Seligson award Practicing Law Inst., 1988, Francis J. Rawle award, ABA-ALI, 1992. Mem. Am. Law Inst. (council, mem. exec. com.), Nat. Assn. Securities Dealers (gov.-at-large, vice-chmn.), San Diego Securities Regulation Inst. (chmn.). Author: Outside Director of the Publicly Held Corporation, 1976; American Attitudes Toward Foreign Direct Investment in the United States, 1979; Conflict of Interest and the Former Government Employee: Re-thinking the Revolving Door, 1981; chmn. adv. bd. Jour. of Internat. Econ. Law, 1996—. Office: Salomon Brothers Inc 7 World Trade Ctr New York NY 10048-1102

MUNDINGER, DONALD CHARLES, college president retired; b. Chgo., Sept. 2, 1929; s. George Edward and Bertha (Trelkenberg) M.; m. June Myrtle Grubbe, June 17, 1951; children: Debra Sue, Donald William, Mary Ruth (dec.). Student, U. Ill., 1947-48; BA, Concordia Coll., River Forest, Ill., 1951, LLD (hon.), 1982; MA, Northwestern U., 1952; PhD, Washington U., St. Louis, 1956; DH (hon.), MacMurray Coll., Jacksonville, Ill., 1984, Ritsumeikan U., Kyoto, Japan, 1992; LLD (hon.), Ill. Coll., Jacksonville, 1993; postdoctoral study, Cambridge U. (Eng.), 1967-68. Asst. prof. polit. sci., chmn. dept. Augustana Coll., Sioux Falls, S.D., 1956-58; asst. prof. govt. Valparaiso (Ind.) U., 1958-61, assoc. prof., 1961-65, prof., 1965-73; dean Valparaiso (Ind.) U. (Coll. Arts and Scis.), 1965-67; dir. Overseas Center, Cambridge, Eng., 1967-68; v.p. acad. affairs Overseas Center, 1968-73; pres. Ill. Coll., Jacksonville, 1973-93; chmn. Fedn. Ind. Ill. Colls. and Univs., 1975-78; chmn. non-public adv. com. Ill. Bd. Higher Edn., 1988-91; postdoctoral fellow Center Study Higher Edn., U. Mich., 1964-65; chmn. bd. Council Ind. Colls., 1988-90. Contbr. articles to profl. jours. Mem. Ill. State Bar Assn. (com. on fed. judicial and related appointments 1983-89), Nat. Assn. Ind. Colls. and Univs. (commn. on new initiatives, 1988-90), Pi Sigma Alpha, Phi Eta Sigma. Home: 3803 Pheasant Walk Dr Valparaiso IN 46383-2205

MUNDORF, NANCY KNOX, early childhood educator; b. Columbus, Ohio, Jan. 19, 1947; d. John William and Cecilia Catherine (Callaghan) Knox; m. Michael John Mundorf, June 15, 1968; children: Colleen Ann, Mark John. BS in Home Econs., Ohio State U., 1968; MS, U. Nebr., 1982. Tchr. presch. Greenhills (Ohio) Coop. NurserySch., 1978-79; home economist Am Distbr., Omaha, 1979-83; parent educator Urban Program Boys Town, Omaha, 1983-85; health educator Omaha Children's Mus., U. Nebr. Med. Ctr., Omaha, 1986; ext. agt. U. Nebr., Omaha, 1986-88; gender equity specialist Lehigh County C.C., Schnecksville, Pa., 1988-90; ext. agt. Pa. State U., Reading, 1990-91; supervising tchr. Lipman Sch. U. Memphis, 1992-95; cons. for 3 internat. preschs. Guangzhou, China, 1995—; destination svcs. counselor Bennett & Assocs., Guangzhou, China, 1996—; mem. adv. com. Omaha Pub. Sch. Supt.'s Vocat. Edn. Adv. Commn., 1986-88; rsch. in China, 1996—. Mem. Tenn. Assn. Edn. of Young Children, Nebr. Home Econs. Assn. (bd. dirs. 1981-86), Nat. Assn. for Edn. of Young Children, Am. Home Econs. Assn., Assn. Childhood Edn. Internat., Mid-South Ednl. Rsch. Assn., AAUW, Assn. Ext. 4-H Agts., Guangzhou Women's Internat. Club (v.p., pres. 1997-98), Guangzhou Wine & Food (v.p. 1996-98). Avocations: reading, needlework, music, travel. Office: China Hotel, # 1827 Liu Hua Lu, Guangzhou 50015, China

MUNDT, BARRY MAYNARD, management consultant; b. San Francisco, June 28, 1936; s. Kenneth Francis and Janet (Doughty) M.; m. Sally Hanscom, June 13, 1960; children: Kevin Warren, Trevor Stevens, Stacey Corbin. BS in Indsl. Engring., Stanford U., 1959; MBA, U. Santa Clara, 1964. Registered indsl. engr., Calif. Statistician Aerojet-Gen., Sacramento, 1957-58; reliability engr. Lockheed Missiles, Sunnyvale, Calif., 1959-61; mgmt. engr. C-E-I-R, Inc., Los Altos, Calif., 1961-65; sr. cons. Peat, Marwick, Livington & Co., Los Angeles, 1965-68; mgr., prin. Peat, Marwick, Mitchell & Co., Atlanta, 1968-84; ptnr.-in-charge, ops. mgmt. cons. KPMG Peat Marwick Main & Co., N.Y.C., 1984-88; internat. mgmt. cons. ptnr. KPMG Internat., N.Y.C. and Amsterdam, The Netherlands, 1988-92; mgmt. cons., ptnr. KPMG Peat Marwick U.S., Montvale, N.J., 1992-95; prin. The Strategy Facilitation Group, Darien, Conn., 1995—. Author-editor: Managing Public Resources, 1982; co-author Il Manager Pubblico (Italy), 1986; contbr. articles to profl. jours. Mem. ann. campaign Atlanta Symphony Orch., 1974-82, Atlanta Arts Alliance, 1976-81; del. to assembly United Way of Met. Atlanta, 1974-84; bd. chmn., mem. Brandon Hall Sch., Atlanta, 1980—. Fellow Inst. Indsl. Engrs. (treas. 1976-81, prse. 1982-83, asst. treas. 1985-92). Episcopalian. Avocations: golf; residential remodeling. Home and Office: 26 Searles Rd Darien CT 06820-6222

MUNDY, JOHN HINE, history educator; b. London, Dec. 29, 1917; s. John and Clytie; m. Charlotte Fisher Williams, Sept. 3, 1942; children—Martha W., John W. B.A., Columbia, 1940, M.A., 1941, Ph.D., 1950. Mem. faculty Columbia U., N.Y.C., 1947-88, prof. history, 1962-88, prof. emeritus, 1988—, chmn. dept., 1967-70; vis. prof. Brown U., Providence, 1990-91; mem. Inst. Advanced Study, Princeton, 1963-64, 70-71. Author: Liberty and Political Power in Toulouse, 1954, The Medieval Town, 1958, Europe in the High Middle Ages, 1150-1309, 2d edit., 1990, The Repression of Catharism at Toulouse, the Royal Diploma of 1279, 1985, Men and Women at Toulouse in the Age of the Cathars, 1990, Society and Government at Toulouse in The Age of the Authors, 1997; contbr. articles to profl. jours. Served with AUS, 1943-46. Fulbright fellow, 1958-59; Am. Council Learned Socs. fellow, 1958-59; Guggenheim fellow, 1965, 77-78; Nat. Endowment Humanities fellow, 1970-71. Fellow Medieval Acad. Am. (2d v.p. 1986, 1st v.p. 1987, pres. 1988), Am. Acad. Arts and Scis. Home: 29 Claremont Ave New York NY 10027-6822

MUNECHIKA, KEN KENJI, research center administrator; b. Waimea, Kauai, Hawaii, June 18, 1935; s. Masako (Yasutake) Kitamura; m. Grace Shizue Wakayama, June 10, 1958; children: Curtis K., Stacy M., Kenny K. BS, U. Hawaii, 1958; MS, U. So. Calif., 1976, PhD, 1979. Commd. 2d lt. USAF, 1958, advanced through grades to col., 1980, ret., 1989; exec. dir. State of Hawaii, Honolulu, 1992-93; dir. Ames Rsch. Ctr. NASA, Mountain View, Calif., 1994-96; dir. Moffett Fed. Airfield NASA, Calif., 1996—. Mem. AIAA, Air Force Assn. Baptist. Avocations: golf, jogging, fishing. Home: 318 Casitas Bulevar Los Gatos CA 95030-1120 Office: Moffett Fed Airfield Mail Stop 19-20 Moffett Field CA 94035

MUNEIO, PATRICIA ANNE, public health nurse; b. Detroit, Oct. 7, 1949; d. Charles Eli and Mary Jane (Voletti) M. BSN, Wayne State U., 1973; MS, Calif. Coll. for Health Scis., San Diego, 1994. RN, Mich. Staff nurse to head nurse Detroit Osteo. Hosp., Highland Park, Mich., 1974-75; nurse emergency rm. Grace Hosp., Detroit, 1975-77; pub. health nurse, team leader Detroit VNA, Detroit, 1977-83; staff nurse, head nurse Comprehensive Health Svcs. of Detroit, 1983-85; pvt. duty nurse AbCare, Inc., Detroit, 1985; pub. health nurse, supr. Cmty. Home Care, Sterling Heights, Mich., 1985-88; home care supr. Med. Personnel Pool, Southfield, Mich., 1988-89; pub. health nurse III Macomb County Health Dept., Mt. Clemens, Mich., 1989-96; health care surveyor spl. svcs. sect. Mich. Dept. Consumer and Industry Svc., Lansing, 1996—. Mem. ANA, Mich. Nurses Assn. (rep. 1992, Blue Water Dist. v.p. 1990-92, pres. 1992-96), Macomb County Health Dept. Staff Coun. (pres. 1990-94). Democrat. Roman Catholic. Avocations: knitting, embroidery, painting, travel, sports. Home: 8669 Crestview Dr Sterling Heights MI 48312-6028 Office: Mich Dept Consumer and Industry Svc Spl Svcs Section 1808 W Saginaw St Lansing MI 48915-1359

MUNERA, GERARD EMMANUEL, manufacturing company executive; b. Algiers, Algeria, Dec. 2, 1935; s. Gabriel and Laure (Labrousse) M.; m. Paule A. Ramos, July 28, 1959; children: Catherine, Philippe, Emmanuelle, Jean-Marie. M in Math., M in Physics, M in Chemistry, Ecole Polytechnique, Paris, 1956; CE, Ecole des Ponts et Chaussees, Paris, 1959. Chief county engr. Dept. Rds. and Bridges, South Algiers, 1959-62; cons. French Ministry Fgn. Affairs, Argentina, 1962-66; sr. v.p. fin. Camea Group Pechiney Ugine Kuhlmann, Buenos Aires, 1966-70, chmn. bd., chief exec. officer, 1976-77; exec. v.p. Howmet Aluminum Corp., Greenwich, Conn., 1976-77, pres., chief operating officer, 1977-79, pres., chief exec. officer, 1980-83; corporate v.p. nuclear fuels Pechiney, Brussels, 1983-85; vice chmn., chief exec. officer Union Minière, Brussels, 1985-89; head corp. planning and devel. RTZ, London, 1989-90; pres., CEO Minorco USA, Englewood, Colo., 1990-94, also bd. dirs.; chmn. and CEO Latin Am. Gold, Inc., N.Y.C., 1994-96, Synergex Inc., 1996—; bd. dirs. Arcadia Inc., Scaltech, Inc., Nevsun Resources, Inc.; chmn., CEO Synergex, Inc. Patentee low-income housing system. Served with French Air Force, 1956-57. Decorated Legion of Honor. Roman Catholic.

MUNGER, BENSON SCOTT, professional society administrator; b. St. Johns, Mich., Jan. 21, 1942; s. Kenneth L. and Doris (Benson) M.; m. Bette Louise Johnson, June 15, 1963; children: Heidi Lynn, Chad Benson. BA, Mich. State U., 1965, PhD, 1969. Tchr. Grand Ledge Pub. Schs., Mich., 1965-66; mem. staff Southwest Regional Lab, Los Angeles, 1969-70; dir. negotiations Mich. Edn. Assn., East Lansing, 1970-75; vis. asst.prof. Indsl. Relations Ctr., U. Minn., Mpls., 1975-76; dep. exec. dir. Am. Coll. Emergency Physicians, 1976-80; exec. dir. Am. Bd. Emergency Medicine, East Lansing, Mich., 1980—, chmn. com. bd. execs., 1991—; commr. City of Johns, 1983—; bd. dirs. Old Kent Bank, St. Johns; cons. in field; chmn. com. bd. reps. and execs. Am. Bd. Med. Specialties, 1995—. Contbr. articles in field. Mich. State U. fellow, 1966-69. Mem. Am. Soc. Assn. Execs., Am. Assn. Med. Soc. Execs. Office: Am Bd Emergency Med 3000 Coolidge Rd East Lansing MI 48823-6319

MUNGER, BRYCE L., physician, educator; b. Everett, Wash., May 20, 1933; s. Leon C. and Lina (Eaton) M.; m. Donna Grace Bingham, July 20, 1957; children: Ailene, D'Arcy, Gareth Torrey, Bryce Kirtley. Student, U. Wash., 1951-54; MD magna cum laude, Wash. U., 1958. Intern in pathology Johns Hopkins U., 1958-59; asst. prof. anatomy Washington U., St. Louis, 1961-65; assoc. prof. U. Chgo., 1965-66; prof. Milton S. Hershey Med. Ctr., Pa. State U., 1966-91, chmn. dept. anatomy, 1966-87; prof., head dept. anatomy U. Tasmania, Hobart, 1992-96. Bd. dirs. Pa. Spl. Olympics Inc. With M.C., USAF, 1959-61. Mem. AAAS, Am. Assn. Anatomists, Am. Soc. Cell Biology, Phi Beta Kappa, Sigma Xi, Alpha Omega Alpha.

MUNGER, CHARLES T., diversified company executive; b. 1924; married. Ptnr. Wheeler Munger & Co., 1961-76; chmn., chief exec. officer Blue Chip Stamps, 1976-78; vice chmn. Berkshire Hathaway, Inc., Omaha, Nebr., 1978—. Office: Berkshire Hathaway Inc 1440 Kiewit Plz Omaha NE 68131-3302

MUNGER, EDWIN STANTON, political geography educator; b. LaGrange, Ill., Nov. 19, 1921; s. Royal Freeman and Mia (Stanton) M.; m. Ann Boyer, May 2, 1970; 1 child, Elizabeth Stanton Gibson. B.Sc., U. Chgo., 1948, M.Sc., 1949, Ph.D., 1951. Fulbright fellow Makerere U., 1949-50; research fellow U. Chgo.; field assoc. Am. Univs. Field Staff, 1950-60; faculty Calif. Inst. Tech., Pasadena, 1961—; prof. polit. geography Calif. Inst. Tech., 1960—; research fellow Stellenbosch U., 1955-56; vis. prof. U. Warsaw, 1973. Author books including Afrikaner and African Nationalsim, 1968, The Afrikaners, 1979, Touched by Africa: An Autobiography, 1983, Cultures, Chess and Art: A Collector's Odyssey Across Seven Continents, Vol. 1 Sub Saharan Africa, 1996, VO12 Americas, 1997; editor books including Munger Africana Library Notes, 1969-82; contbr. chpts. to books and numerous articles to profl. jours. Evaluator Peace Corps, Uganda, 1966, Botswana, 1967; chmn. State Dept. Evaluation Team South Africa, 1971; trustee African-Am. Inst., 1956-62; acting pres. Pasadena Playhouse, 1966; chmn. bd. trustees Crane Rogers Found., 1979-82, fellow, 1950-54; mem. exec. com. NAACP, Pasadena, 1979—, nat. del., 1984, 85; trustee Leakey Found., 1968—, pres., 1971-84; pres. Cape of Good Hope Found., 1985—; pres. Internat. Vis. Coun., L.A., 1991-93, bd. dirs., 1979-93. Recipient Alumni Citation award for pub. svc. U. Chgo., 1993. Fellow South African Royal Soc., Royal Soc. Arts, African Studies Assn. (founding bd. dirs. 1963-66); mem. PEN USA West (v.p.), Coun. Fgn. Rels., Cosmos Club, Athenaeum Club, Twilight Club. Office: Calif Inst Tech Div Humanities and Social Scis 1201 E California Blvd Pasadena CA 91125-0001

MUNGER, ELMER LEWIS, civil engineer, educator; b. Manhattan, Kans., Jan. 4, 1915; s. Harold Hawley and Jane (Green) M.; m. Vivian Marie Bloomfield, Dec. 28, 1939; children: John Thomas, Harold Hawley II, Jane Marie. B.S., Kans. State U., 1936, M.S., 1938; Ph.D., Iowa State U., 1957.

Registered profl. engr., Nebr., Kans., Iowa, Vt.; registered pvt. land surveyor Republic of The Philippines. Rodman St. Louis-Southwestern Ry., Ark., Mo., 1937-38; engr. U.S. Engr. Dept., Ohio, Nebr., 1938-46; missionary engr. Philippine Episcopal Ch., 1946-48; engr. Wilson & Co., Salina, Kans., 1948; tchr. Iowa State U., 1948-51, 54-58; engr. C.E., U.S. Army, Alaska, 1951-54; from tchr. to dean Norwich U., Northfield, Vt., 1958-69; prof. gen. engring. U. P.R., Mayagüez, 1969-75; prof. civil engring. Mich. Tech. U., 1975-80; ret.; mem. spl. com. on engring. Inter-Am. Devel. Bank, U. W.I., 1971. Author: (with Clarence J. Douglas) Construction Management, 1970. Fellow ASCE; mem. NSPE, Vt. Soc. Profl. Engrs., Am. Soc. Engring. Edn., Phi Kappa Phi, Sigma Tau, Tau Beta Pi, Chi Epsilon. Episcopalian. Clubs: Masons, Shriners. Home: 21260 Brinson Ave Apt 311 Pt Charlotte FL 33952-5005

MUNGER, JANET ANNE, education administrator; b. N.J., Feb. 27, 1947; d. Victor J. and Ann L. Ferri Munger. BA, Fairleigh Dickinson U., 1968, MA, 1971; EdD, Seton Hall U., 1985. Cert. sch. adminstr., prin., supr. Tchr. Meml. Sch. No. 11, Passaic, N.J., 1968-70; dir., tchr. Morristown Head Start Program, N.J., 1970-71 (summers); curriculum devel. specialist N.J. State Coun. Arts Grant Program, 1973 (summer); tchr. Ctrl. Sch., Montville, N.J., 1970-73, William Mason Sch., Montville, 1973-81; tchr. gifted and talented William Mason, Valley View and Woodmont Schs., Montville, 1981-82; coord. of curriculum instr. South Plainfield (N.J.) Bd. Edn., 1986-91, supr. fed. and state projects, 1989-92, supr. ednl. programs, 1992-94, prin., 1994—; presenter in field profl. assns.; researcher, writer, cons., 1982—. Mem. ASCD, NEA, Am. Assn. Sch. Adminstrs., N.J. Assn. Sch. Adminstrs., N.J. Edn. Assn., Assn. Secondary Sch. Prins., Prins. and Suprs. Assn., New Eng. Coalition Ednl. Leaders, N.J. Assn. Fed. Program Adminstrs., Phi Delta Kappa, Kappa Delta Pi. Office: S Plainfield Bd Edn Cromwell Pl South Plainfield NJ 07080

MUNGER, PAUL DAVID, educational administrator; b. Selma, Ala., Oct. 12, 1945; s. Paul Francis and Arlene Lorraine (McFillen) M.; m. Paula Jean Dominici, May 30, 1969; children: Kimberley Beth, Christopher David. AB in Philosophy, Kenyon Coll., 1967; MA in Govt., Ind. U., 1969. Commd. 2d lt. USAF, 1969, advanced through grades to capt., resigned, 1972; asst. dir. faculty devel. Ind. U., Bloomington, 1974-77; from asst. dean to dean continuing studies Am. U., Washington, 1980-83, asst. provost acad. devel., 1983-84; dir. Commn. on Future Acad. Leadership, Washington, 1984-86; v.p. Acad. Strategies, Washington, 1986-88; pres. Strategic Edn. Svcs. Inc., Sterling, Va., 1988—. Bd. advisors Madeira Sch., McLean, Va., 1993-96; treas. Bus.-Higher Edn. Fedn., Washington, 1992—; asst. scoutmaster Boy Scouts Am., 1991-93, scoutmaster, 1994—; dir. Czech-am. LaCrosse Found., 1996—. Mem. Am. Soc. Tng. & Devel. (chmn. strategic planning com. 1993-95, continuing profl. edn. electronic forum coord. 1995—), Assn. Continuing Higher Edn., Am. Soc. Curriculum Devel. Office: Strategic Education Services Inc 624 W Church Rd Sterling VA 20164-4608

MUNGER, PAUL R., civil engineering educator; b. Hannibal, Mo., Jan. 14, 1932; s. Paul Oettle and Anne Lucille (Williams) M.; m. Frieda Ann Mette, Nov. 26, 1954; children: Amelia Ann Munger Fortmeyer, Paul David, Mark James, Martha Jane Munger Cox. BSCE, Mo. Sch. Mines and Metallurgy, 1958, MSCE, 1961; PhD in Engring. Sci., U. Ark., 1972. Registered profl. engr., Mo., Ill., Ark. Minn. Instr. civil engring Mo. Sch. Mines and Metallurgy, Rolla, 1958-61, asst. prof., 1961-65; assoc. prof. U. Mo., Rolla, 1965-73, prof., 1973—; dir. Inst. River Studies, U. Mo., Rolla, 1976-93; exec. dir. Internat. Inst. River and Lake Systems, U. Mo., Rolla, 1984-93. Mem. NSPE, Mo. Soc. Profl. Engrs., Am. Soc. Engring. Edn., ASCE, Nat. Coun. Engring. Examiners (pres. 1983-84), Mo. Bd. Architects, Profl. Engrs. and Land Surveyors (chmn. 1978-84, 95—). Office: U Mo 110 Civil Engring Rolla MO 65409

MUNHALL, EDGAR, curator, art history educator; b. Pitts., Mar. 14, 1933; s. Walter and Anna (Burns) M.; life ptnr. Richard Barsam. BA, Yale U., 1955, PhD, 1959; MA, NYU, 1957. Instr. art history Yale U., New Haven, 1959-64, asst. prof., 1964-65; curator The Frick Collection, N.Y.C., 1965—; adj. prof. Columbia U., 1979, 81—. Decorated chevalier Ordre des Arts et des Lettres. Office: The Frick Collection 1 E 70th St New York NY 10021-4907

MUNIAIN, JAVIER P., computer company executive, physicist, researcher; b. Madrid, Apr. 4, 1966; came to U.S., 1989.; s. Luis Perez De Muniain y Leal and Crescencia Mohedano Hernandez. BSc, U. Complutense of Madrid, 1990; M. in Physics, U. Calif., Riverside, 1992, PhD in Theoretical Physics, 1996. Rsch., teaching asst. U. Calif., Riverside, 1992-96; pres., CEO Surfernet, San Diego, 1996—. Author: Gauge Fields, Knots and Gravity, 1994; contbr. articles to profl. jours. Mem. Am. Phys. Soc., Riverside Wine Tasing Soc. (co-founder 1994). Avocations: classic car restoration, playing and studying chess, surfing, antiques. Home: C/Alcala 236, Madrid Spain 28027 Office: Surfernet PO Box 1836 La Jolla CA 92038

MUNIC, RACHELLE ETHEL, health services administrator; b. Hartford, Conn., Apr. 15, 1953; d. Abe and Sara (Levenberg) M. BS in Med. Tech. summa cum laude, U. Bridgeport, 1975; physician asst. cert., Yale U., 1979; MBA in Health & Med. Svcs. Adminstrn., Widener U., 1991. Med. technologist St. Francis Hosp., Hartford, 1975-77; physician asst. Fox Chase Cancer Ctr., Phila., 1979-85; clin. dir. Fox Chase Network, Phila., 1986-92; adminstrv. dir., oncology Cooper Hosp., U. Med. Ctr., Camden, N.J., 1992-96, healthcare cons., 1996—; corp. mgr. cancer svcs. Grad. Health Sys., Phila., 1996—; cancer svc. line adminstr. Albert Einstein Med. Ctr., Phila., 1996—; mem. Cancer Prevention and Control Adv. Group to N.J. Commn. on Cancer Rsch., New Brunswick, N.J., 1993-96; mem. program com. Greater Phila. Health Assembly, 1996; presenter in field. Dana scholar U. Bridgeport, 1972; recipient Foster G. McGaw Scholarship award Assn. Univ. Programs in Health Adminstrn., 1990, Student award Hosp. Assn. Pa., 1992; Breast Cancer project grantee The Susan G. Komen Breast Cancer Found., Dallas, 1995. Mem. Am. Hosp. Assn., Am. Cancer Soc. (Camden County), Assn. Cancer Execs., Soc. Radiation Oncology Adminstrs., Assn. Cmty. Cancer Ctrs. (del.), Widener Alumni Assn. (pres. 1995), U. Bridgeport Asteria Honor Soc. Avocations: softball, golf, swimming, cross-country skiing, reading.

MUNIER, WILLIAM BOSS, medical service executive; b. Corning, N.Y., Dec. 8, 1942; s. John Hammond and Marguerite (Boss) M.; m. Sandra Lorraine Koerber, 1965 (div. 1976); m. Ann Elizabeth Wessel, 1980; children: Michael, Andrew, Laura. BA, U. Pa., 1964; MD, Columbia U., 1968; MBA, Harvard U., 1973. Diplomate Nat. Bd. Med. Examiners; lic. physician, surgeon, N.Y. Surg. intern Roosevelt Hosp., N.Y.C., 1968-69; profl. staff HEW, Washington, 1969-71, 73-75, dir. Office Quality Standards, 1975-77, dir. Office Health Practice Assessment, 1977-79; exec. v.p. Mass. Med. Soc., Boston, 1979-84; prin. Ernst & Whinney, Boston, 1984-85; pvt. practice mgmt. cons. Wellesley, Mass., 1985-86; dir. program for civilian peer rev. Dept. Def., 1986-87; pres. Quality Standards in Medicine, Inc., Boston, 1986—; v.p., med. dir. Health Care Microsystems, Inc., 1996—; vis. prof. Harvard Sch. Pub. Health, Boston, 1980-90. Contbr. articles to profl. jours. Mem. human services com. Town of Wellesley, 1984-85. Served with USPHS, 1969-79. Mem. AMA, Mass. Med. Soc., St. Botolph Club, Capitol Hill Club. Republican. Episcopalian. Avocations: golf, skiing, squash, music.

MUNISTERI, JOSEPH GEORGE, construction executive; b. Rome, Sept. 24, 1930; s. Peter P. and Inez Gertrude (Ziniti) M.; m. Theresa Grasso, June 7, 1952; children: Joanne, Robert, Laura, Stephen, James, Richard. BE, Yale U., 1952. With Bechtel Corp., San Francisco, 1952-59; with The Lummus Co., N.Y.C., London and Houston, 1959-67, gen. mgr., 1964-67; sr. v.p. sales Brown & Root, Inc., Houston, 1967-75, group v.p. power div., 1975-80, group v.p. corp. devel., 1980-81, also bd. dirs.; pres. Enserch Engrs. & Constructors, Inc., Houston, 1981-85; exec. v.p. Ford, Bacon & Davis, Inc., Dallas, 1985-87; chmn., pres., CEO Comstock Group, Inc., Danbury, Conn., 1987-88; pres. Joseph G. Munisteri Co., Houston, 1989—; former chmn. bd. Pine-O-Pine. Former mem. Bd. dirs. Atomic Indsl. Forum; Bd. dirs. Am. Nuclear Energy Council. Mem. Atomic Indsl. Forum, Am. Inst. Chem. Engrs., Am. Nuclear Soc., Atomic Indsl. Forum, ASTM, Council Engring. Law, ASCE, Assn. Iron and Steel Engring., Assoc. Builders and Contractors (dir.). Clubs: Yale of N.Y, Yale S.E.T, Houston. Office: 4265 San Felipe St Ste 1100 Houston TX 77027-2913

MUNITZ, BARRY, university administrator, English literature educator, business consultant; b. Bklyn., July 26, 1941; s. Raymond J. and Vivian L. (LeVoff) M.; m. Anne Tomfohrde, Dec. 15, 1987. BA, Bklyn. Coll., 1963; MA, Princeton U., 1965, PhD, 1968; cert., U. Leiden, Netherlands, 1962. Asst. prof. lit. and drama U. Calif., Berkeley, 1966-68; staff assoc. Carnegie Commn. Higher Edn., 1968-70; mem. presdl. staff, then assoc. provost U. Ill. System, 1970-72, acad. v.p., 1972-76; v.p., dean faculties Central campus U. Houston, 1976-77, chancellor, 1977-82, chmn. coordinating bd. faculty workload, 1976-80; chmn. Tex. Long Range Planning, 1980-82; pres., COO Federated Devel. Co., 1982-91; vice chmn. Maxxam Inc., L.A., 1982-91; chancellor Calif. State U. System, Long Beach, Calif., 1991—; prof. English lit. Calif. State U., L.A., 1991—; bd. dirs. Sta. KCET-TV, Am. Coun. on Edn., Nat. Bus. Higher Edn. Forum, SunAmerica Inc.; cons. in presdl. evaluation and univ. goverance. Author: The Assessment of Institutional Leadership, 1977, also articles, monographs. Mem. task force NSF. Recipient Disting. Alumnus award Bklyn. Coll., 1979, U. Houston Alumni Pres.'s medal, 1981; Woodrow Wilson fellow, 1963. Mem. Young Pres. Orgn., Heritage Club, Phi Beta Kappa. Office: Calif State U System Office of Chancellor 400 Golden Shore St Long Beach CA 90802-4209

MUNK, PETER, mining executive; b. Budapest, Hungary, Nov. 8, 1927; arrived in Can., 1948; s. Louis L. and Katherine (Adler) M.; m. Linda Gutterson; children: Anthony, Nina; m. Melanie Jane Bosanquet, 1973; children: Natalie, Cheyne, Marc David. BASc in Elec. Engring., U. Toronto, Ont., Can., 1953, LLD, 1995; LLD, Upsala Coll., N.J., 1991, U. Toronto, Que., Can., 1995, Bishops Coll., Quebec, 1995. Chmn., chief exec. officer So. Pacific Hotel Corp., Sydney, Australia, 1969-81; chmn. Barrick Resources, Toronto, 1981-83, Am. Barrick Resources Corp. (now Barrick Gold Corp.), Toronto, 1983—, The Horsham Corp., Toronto, 1987-96; chmn., bd. dirs. Clark Oil & Refining Corp., St. Louis, Trizec Hahn Corp. Ltd.; bd. dirs. World Gold Coun., Geneva. Trustee Toronto Hosp.; bd. dirs. U. Toronto Found. Decorated officer Order of Can. Office: Barrick Gold Corp, 200 Bay St 27th Fl S Tower, Toronto, ON Canada M5J 2J3

MUNK, WALTER HEINRICH, geophysics educator; b. Vienna, Austria, Oct. 19, 1917; came to U.S., 1933; m. Edith Kendall Horton, June 20, 1953; children: Edith, Kendall. BS, Calif. Inst. Tech., 1939, MS, 1940; PhD in Oceanography, U. Calif., 1947; PhD (hon.), U. Bergen, Norway, 1975, Cambridge (Eng.) U., 1986, U. Crete, 1996. Asst. prof. geophysics Scripps Inst. Oceanography, U. Calif., San Diego, 1947-54, prof., 1954—; dir. Inst. Geophysics and Planetary Physics, U. Calif., La Jolla, 1960-82; prof. geophysics, dir. heard island expt. Scripps Inst., U. Calif. Author: (with Mac Donald) The Rotation of the Earth: A Geophysical Discussion, 1960, (with Worcester & Wunsch) Ocean Acoustic Tomography, 1995; contbr. over 200 articles to profl. jours. Recipient Albatross award Am. Misc. Soc., 1959, gold medal Royal Astron. Soc., 1968, Nat. Medal Sci., 1985, award Marine Tech. Soc., 1969, Capt. Robert Dexter Conrad award Dept. Navy, 1978, G. Unger VVetlesen prize Columbia U., 1993, Presdl. award N.Y. Acad. Scis., 1993, Rolex Lifetime Achievement award, 1997; named Calif. Scientist of Yr., Calif. Mus. Sci. and Industry, 1969; fellow Guggenheim Found., 1948, 55, 62, Overseas Found., 1962, 81-82, Fulbright Found., 1981-82, sr. Queen's fellow, 1978. Fellow Am. Geophys. Union (Maurice Ewing medal 1976, William Bowie medal 1989), AAAS, Am. Meteorol. Soc. (Sverdrup Gold medal 1966), Acoustical Soc. Am., Marine Tech. Soc. (Compass award 1991); mem. Nat. Acad. Scis. (Agassiz medal 1976, chmn. ocean studies bd. 1985-88), Am. Philos. Soc., Royal Soc. London (fgn. mem.), Russian Acad. of Sci., Deutsche Akademie der Naturforscher Leopoldina, Am. Acad. Arts and Scis. (Arthur L. Day medal 1965), Am. Geol. Soc., NY Acad. of Scis. (Presidl. Awd., 1994). Office: U Calif San Diego Scripps Inst Oceanography 0225 La Jolla CA 92093

MUNK, ZEV MOSHE, allergist, researcher; b. Stockholm, July 14, 1950; m. Susan Deitcher; 4 children. BS, McGill U., 1972; MD, C.M., 1974. Licentiate Med. Council Can.; diplomate Am. Bd. Internal Medicine, Am. Bd. Allergy and Clin. Immunology. Intern Royal Victoria Hosp., Montreal, 1974-75, resident, 1975-76; resident in clin. immunology and allergy Montreal Gen. Hosp., 1976-78; practice medicine specializing in allergy and clin. immunology, Houston, 1978—; mem. staff Meml. City Med. Ctr., Meml S.W., Meth., Spring Branch Meml., West Houston Med. Ctr, Cy-Fair hosps. (all Houston); clin. instr. allergy and clin. immunology Baylor Coll. Medicine, 1979—, U. Tex.-Houston, 1979—; pres. Breco Rsch., Pharm-Olam Internat. Clin. Rsch. Orgn., 1994—. Pres. Young Israel Synagogue of Houston, 1994-96; founder Allergy Ctr., Inc., Houston, Clin. Rsch. Ctr., Houston. McGill U. scholar, 1968-74. Fellow Am. Acad. Allergy, Am. Coll. Allergy and Immunology, Royal Coll. Physicians (Can.); mem. ACP, Tex. Med. Assn., Que. Med. Assn., Am. Fedn. Clin. Research, Am. Acad. Allergy, Tex. Allergy Soc., Harris County Med. Soc., Houston Allergy Soc. Contbr. articles to med. jours. Office: 902 Frostwood Dr Ste 222 Houston TX 77024-2402

MUNN, CECIL EDWIN, lawyer; b. Enid, Okla., Aug. 8, 1923; s. Cecil Edwin and Margaret (Kittrell) M.; m. Carolyn Taylor Culver, May 8, 1948; children: Franklin Culver, Charlotte Munn Forswall. BA, U. Okla., 1945; JD cum laude, Harvard U., 1947. Bar: Okla. 1947, Tex. 1955. Practice in Enid, 1947-54, Ft. Worth, 1954—; partner firm Cantey & Hanger, Ft. Worth, 1960-91, of counsel, 1992—; with Champlin Petroleum Co., 1954-60, v.p., atty., 1958-60, dir., 1962-75. Fellow Am. Coll. Trial Lawyers, Am. Bar Found.; mem. ABA (chmn. natural resources law sect. 1970-71), Southwestern Legal Found. (past dir.), Tex. Bar Found., Phi Delta Theta, Phi Delta Phi. Presbyterian. Home: 42 Valley Ridge Rd Fort Worth TX 76107-3108 Office: 2100 Burnett Plz 801 Cherry St Fort Worth TX 76102-6803 *Some things in life are better decided wrong than left undecided. It is amazing how much one can accomplish if unconcerned with who gets the credit.*

MUNN, JANET TERESA, lawyer; b. De Funiak Springs, Fla., Nov. 7, 1952; d. Willard Ernest and Olive Pauline (Wilkinson) M.; m. Michael E. Fass, Sept. 27, 1975. BA in Anthropology, Fla. State U., 1975, MA in Social Scis., 1977; JD with high honors, Nova U., 1985. Bar: Fla. 1985, U.S. Dist. Ct. (so. dist.) Fla. 1986, U.S. Dist. Ct. (mid. dist.) Fla. 1988, U.S. Ct. Appeals (11th cir.) 1989, U.S. Supreme Ct. 1990. Jud. clerk for Judge Jose A. Gonzalez Jr. U.S. Dist. Ct. (so. dist.) Fla., Ft. Lauderdale, 1985-87; litigation assoc. Steel Hector & Davis, Miami, Fla., 1987-91, litigation ptnr., 1992—. Editor: Southern District Digest, 1987-88. Leo S. Goodwin fellow Nova U., 1983-84. Mem. ABA (co-chmn. intellectual properties litigation com. litigation sect. 1991-92, chmn. trade regulation/intellectual property com. gen. practice sect. 1990-91, vice chmn. 1989-90), Fed. Bar Assn., Fla. Bar (Pro Bono award 1988), Phi Kappa Phi. Office: 200 S Biscayne Blvd Ste 4000 Miami FL 33131-2310

MUNN, WILLIAM CHARLES, II, psychiatrist; b. Flint, Mich., Aug. 9, 1938; s. Elton Albert and Rita May (Coykendall) M.; student Flint Jr. Coll., 1958-59, U. Detroit, 1959-61; M.D., Wayne State U., 1965; children by previous marriage—Jude Michael, Rachel Marie, Alexander Winston. Intern David Grant USAF Med. Center, Travis AFB, Calif., 1965-66; resident in psychiatry Letterman Army Hosp., San Francisco, 1967-70; practice medicine, specializing in psychiatry, Fairfield, Calif., 1972—; chief in-patient psychiatry David Grant Med. Center, 1970-71, chmn. dept. mental health, 1971-72; psychiat. cons. Fairfield-Suisun Unified Sch. Dist., 1971—, Fairfield Hosp. and Clinic, 1971, N. Bay Med. Ctr.(formerly Intercommunity Hosp.), Fairfield, 1971—, Casey Family Program, 1980—, Solano County Coroner's Office, 1981; asst. clin. prof. psychiatry U. Calif., San Francisco, 1976—; cons. Vaca Valley Hosp., Vacaville, Calif., 1988—, VA Hosp., San Francisco, 1976, David Grant USAF Hosp., 1976. Served to maj., M.C., USAF, 1964-72, flight surgeon, chief public health, chief phys. exam. center McGuire AFB, N.J., 1966-67. Diplomate Am. Bd. Psychiatry and Neurology (examiner). Mem. Am. Psychiat. Assn., No. Calif. Psychiat. Soc., E. Bay Psychiat. Assn. Office: 1245 Travis Blvd Ste E Fairfield CA 94533-4842

MUNNEKE, GARY ARTHUR, law educator, consultant; b. Cedar Rapids, Iowa, Dec. 29, 1947; s. Leslie Earl and Margaret Frances (Fortsch) M.; children—Richard Arthur, Matthew Frederick. B.A. in Psychology, U. Tex. 1970; J.D., 1973. Bar: Tex. 1973. Asst. dean, dir. placement U. Tex., Austin, 1978-80; asst. prof., asst. dean Del. Law Sch., Widener U., Wilmington, 1980-84, assoc. prof., 1984-87; pres. Legal Info. Systems, 1987-92; assoc. dean, assoc. prof. Sch. Law Pace U., 1988—. Contbr. articles to profl. jours. Mem. ABA (chmn. standing com. on profl. utilization and career devel. 1981—, chmn. law practice mgmt. sect. pub. bd., articles editor Legal Econs. mag. 1984—), State Bar Tex. Presbyterian. Office: Pace U Sch Law 78 N Broadway White Plains NY 10603-3710

MUÑOZ, CARLOS RAMÓN, bank executive; b. N.Y.C., Dec. 8, 1935; s. Alejandro and Gladys Helena (Judah) M.; m. Wilhelmina Elaine North, June 8, 1957 (div. 1993); children: Carla Christine, Kyle Alexander. BA, Columbia U., 1957, MA, 1961. Insp., ofcl. asst. Citibank, N.A., N.Y.C., 1959-64, asst. mgr., then mgr. in Dominican Republic and P.R., 1965-70, asst. v.p., N.Y.C., 1971-72, v.p., dept. head, 1972-78, sr. v.p., regional mgr. and dir. Citicorp. USA, San Francisco, 1978-81, sr. v.p., mem. Credit Policy Com., 1982-95; exec. v.p., chief credit officer Dime Savings Bank, N.Y.C., 1995—; adv. coun. Credit Rsch. Ctr., 1994—; bd. dirs. Credit Depot Corp. Bd. dirs. Episcopal Mission Soc., N.Y.C., 1974—, chmn. exec. com., 1990-93, v.p., 1995—; bd. dirs. Inner City Scholarship Fund, 1984-95, Corp. for Relief Widows and Orphans of Protestant Episcopal Clergymen in State N.Y., 1974-79, Credit Depot Cor., 1996—; trustee Episcopal Diocese of N.Y., 1994—. Served as 1st lt. USAR, 1958-64. Recipient Productivity award State Senator Diane Watson, Los Angeles, 1981; named Fairfield County Alumnus of Yr., 1989-90. Mem. Columbia Coll. Alumni Assn. (bd. dirs. 1983—, treas. 1988-92, v.p. 1992-93, 1st v.p. 1994-96, pres. 1996—), Univ. Club (N.Y.C.). Republican.

MUNOZ, GEORGE, federal agency administrator. BBA with high honors, U. Tex., 1974; M in Pub. Policy, Harvard U., 1978, JD, 1978; LLM, DePaul U., 1984. CPA. Assoc. Gary, Thomasson, Hall & Marks, Corpus Christi, Tex., 1978-80; assoc., ptnr. Mayer, Brown & Platt, Chgo., 1980-89; mng. ptnr. GM&A Internat. Attys. & Bus. Counselors, p.c., Chgo., 1989-93; CFO, asst. sec. mgmt. U.S. Dept. Treasury, Washington, 1993—. Pres. Chgo. Bd. Edn., 1984-86; trustee Chgo. Symphony Orch., Northwestern Meml. Hosp., DePaul U., Chgo. Coun. on Fgn. Rels., Ill. Internat. Port Authority, Chgo. Econ. Devel. Commn. Office: Dept of Treasury Management 15th & Pennsylvania Ave NW Washington DC 20220*

MUNOZ, JOHN JOAQUIN, research microbiologist; b. Guatemala City, Guatemala, Dec. 23, 1918; came to U.S., 1938, naturalized, 1954; s. Juan Muñoz and Carmen Valdés; m. Margaret Allen, June 21, 1947; children: William Allen, Maureen Carmen, John Richard, Michael Raymond. Grad., Escuela Preparatoria, Guatemala City, 1938; B.S., La. State U., 1942; M.S., U. Ky., 1945; Ph.D., U. Wis., 1947. Asst. prof. U. Ill. Med. Sch., 1947-51; rsch. assoc. Merck-Sharp & Dohme Rsch. Labs., 1951-57; prof. bacteriology, dir. Stella Duncan Meml. Fund rsch. U. Mont., 1957-61, staff affiliate, 1968—; rsch. microbiologist Inst. Allergy and Infectious Diseases, NIH, Rocky Mountain Lab., 1961—, head allergy-immunology sect., 1968-79, head pertussis sect., 1979-82, acting head immunopathology sect., 1985-88, scientist emeritus, 1989—; spl. assignment Pasteur Inst., Paris, 1966-67, Walter and Eliza Hall Inst. Med. Rsch., Melbourne, Australia, 1982-83. Author: (with R.K. Bergman) Bordetella pertussis—immunological and other biological activities, 1977; Contbr. articles to profl. jours. Fellow Am. Acad. Microbiology (emeritus); mem. Am. Soc. Microbiology, Am. Assn. Immunologists, Soc. Exptl. Biology and Medicine, Reticuloendothelial Soc., Internat. Endotoxin Soc., Sigma Xi, Phi Sigma. Home: 199 Meadowlark Ln Hamilton MT 59840-9111 Office: NIH Rocky Mountain Lab 903 S 4th St Hamilton MT 59840-2932

MUÑOZ, MARGARET ELLEN, reading specialist; b. Jacksonville, Ill., Jan. 30, 1947; d. George William and Lois Lottie (Ankrom) Greene; m. Juan James Muñoz, Mar. 31, 1972; children: Aaron Joseph, Lauri Elizabeth. BA, Culver-Stockton Coll., 1969; MA, Western Ill. U., 1971. Cert. tchr. reading K-12 and English 7-12, Mo. Tchr. lang. arts 10-12 Quincy (Ill.) Sr. H.S., 1970-72; tchr. lang. arts 7-12 Sch. Dist. R-S, New Raymer, Colo., 1972-73; tchr. lang. arts 9-12 Kansas City (Mo.) Sch. Dist., 1973-78; tchr. lang. arts 10-12 Ft. Osage Sch. Dist., Independence, Mo., 1978-80; Tchr. Title I Reading 7-8 Independence Pub. Schs., 1980-81, 89—, tchr. ESL and Am. Indian K-12, 1985-89; chairperson Profl. Devel.-Palmer, Independence, 1993—; sponsor Sharing Stories With Children, Independence, 1993—; presenter reading strategies Ottawa U., Overland Park, Kans., 1994, Chpt. I State Conf., 1994, Ann. Assessment & Authentic Performance Conf., Olathe, Kans., 1996, Assessment Conf., Olathe, 1996; mem. Dist. Profl. Devel., Independence, 1994—; mem. adv. bd. Kansas City Regional Profl. Devel. Ctr., 1995-96. Active Blue Ridge Blvd. United Meth. Ch., Kansas City, 1982—; officer Mothers' Coun., Boy Scouts Am., Kansas City, 1993—; mem. Kansas City Regional Profl. Devel. Coun. Mem. ASCD, Mo. Nat. Edn. Assn., Independence/Ft. Osage Internat. Reading Assn. (com. chair 1984—), PTA (life). Avocations: reading, sewing, walking, time with family. Office: Palmer Jr HS 218 N Pleasant St Independence MO 64050-2655

MUNOZ, MARIO ALEJANDRO, civil engineer, consultant; b. Havana, Cuba, Feb. 27, 1928; s. Ramón and Concepción (Bermudo) M.; came to U.S., 1961, naturalized, 1968; M.Arch., U. Havana, 1954; postgrad. City Colls. Chgo., 1974, U. Wis., 1974; m. Julia Josephine Garrofe, Jan. 17, 1970. *Wife Julia chose exile in 1960 while attending the Catholic University of Villanova in Havana, Cuba and completed her education at the University of Barcelona, Spain. In Chicago, she served on the Board of the Cardinal's Committee for the Spanish Speaking in the mid-1960s, working with the Cuban exodus. She is a Docent at the Art Institute of Chicago and serves on the Board of the Women's Association of the Chicago Symphony. She and her husband are Patrons of the St. James Steeplechase held annually for the benefit of Marianjoy Rehabilitation Hospital of Wheaton, Illinois .* Owner, Muñoz Bermudo-Construcciones, Havana, 1954-61; designer various cos., Chgo., 1961-65; designer Chgo. Transit Authority, Mdse. Mart, Chgo., 1965-69; civil engr. Dept. Water and Sewers, City of Chgo., 1969-79, supervising engr. Dept. of Sewers, 1979-85, coordinating engr., 1985-88, asst. chief engr., 1988-93; mem. ctrl. area subway sys. utilities com. City of Chgo., 1974-93 , mem. computer graphics com., 1977-78. Mem. Am. Pub. Works Assn., Western Soc. Engrs., Chgo. Architecture Found., Theodore Thomas Soc. Chgo. Symphony, Chgo. Coun. Fgn. Rels., Am. Mgmt. Assn., Ground Hog Club, Execs. Club (speaker's table com.), Polo and Equestrian Club of Oak Brook. Roman Catholic. Home: 5455 N Sheridan Rd Apt 1912 Chicago IL 60640-1933

MUNOZ, STEVEN MICHAEL, physician associate; b. Dallas, Aug. 7, 1952; s. Joseph Paul and Connie Rae (Coffman) M.; m. Paula Lou Marchant, Dec. 12, 1974 (div. 1983); 1 child, Kimberly Rene; m. Maureen Geneva Flowers, Aug. 12, 1984; children: Danielle Geneva, Sean Michael. B Med. Sci., Emory U., 1977. Physician assoc. Med. Ctr. Cen. Ga., Macon, 1977-79, William B. Martin M.D., P.C., Loganville, Ga., 1979-80, Howell Indsl. Clinic, Atlanta, 1980-81, Stanley Fineman M.D., P.C., Marietta, Ga., 1981-82; physician assoc., dir. sales and adminstrn. Family Practice Ctr./Atlanta Occupational Medicine, 1982-85; physician assoc., dir. mktg. Gwinnette Ctr. med. Clinic, Norcross, Ga., 1985-89; physician assoc. So. Orthopedic Clinic, Atlanta, 1989-90, North Fulton Health Care Assoc., Roswell, Ga., 1990-96; physician assoc. adult & pediatric care Kaiser Permanente Internal Medicine Clinic, Atlanta, 1996—; asst. clin. prof. Emory U. Sch. Medicine, Atlanta, 1981—; dir. patient edn. com. Ga. Lung Assn., 1981-82; med. adviser ARC, Atlanta, 1980-83, Ga. Statewide Hypertension Task Force, 1981-82. With U.S. Army, 1972-75, Res., 1975-94. Mem. Am. Acad. Physician Assts., Ga. Assn. Physician Assts. (bd. dirs., pub. edn. com. chair 1984), Soc. Army Physician Assts. Republican. Avocations: backpacking, camping, water sports, jogging. Home: 5785 Stonehaven Dr Kennesaw GA 30152 Office: Kaiser Permanente 750 Townpark Ln Kennesaw GA 30144-5579

MUÑOZ DONES CARRASCAL, ELOISA, hospital administrator, pediatrician, consultant, educator; b. San Lorenzo, P.R., Oct. 25, 1922; d. Pedro and Maria (Dones) Muñoz; m. José D. Carrascal, Dec. 7, 1962; children: Lilia, Maria. BA in Edn. cum laude, BS in Chemistry cum laude, U. P.R., Rio Piedras, 1943; MD, Tulane U., 1948. Diplomate Am. Bd. Pediatrics. Intern Arecibo Charity Dist. Hosp., 1948-49; resident in pediatrics San Juan (P.R.) City Hosp., 1949-51, chief newborn svc., attending pediatrician, 1951—, dir. neonatal-perinatal medicine, 1965—, dir. fellowship tng. program, 1972—; from instr. to assoc. prof. clin. pediatrics sch. medicine U. P.R., 1951-89, prof., 1989—; courtesy pediatrician neonatologist Tchrs. Hosp., Hato Rey, P.R., 1951-76, Ashford Presbyn. Drs. Hosp., Santurce, P.R., 1951-76, San Jorge H. H. Pavia Fernandez, Santurce, 1951-76; cons. pediatrician neonatologist Tchrs. H. Auxilio Mutuo H., Hato Rey, 1976—,

Drs. H. San Jorge H. Ashford, San Juan, 1976—; mem. exec. com. San Juan City Hosp., 1976—, pres. med. faculty, 1976-77, 87-89, mem. instl. rev. bd., mem. ednl. rev. bd., mem. various coms.; lectr. in field. Contbr. articles to profl. jours. U.S. del. Care Orgn. Latin Am., 1962-63. Recipient Bronze medal Brazilian Acad. Human Scis., 1975, Hon. Cert. Internat. Yr. Women, City Mayor Lodo Carlos Romero Barceló, 1975, Hon. Cert. Disting. Svc. to Cmty., Julio Sellés Solá Elem. Sch., 1976, Pioneer Pediatrician award P.R. Pediat. Sect. Convention, 1993, Pioneer in Neonatology award P.R. Pediat. Sect. Convention, 1995, Pioneer Pidiat. Critical Care award Pediat. Critical Care Assn., 1996; grantee NIH, 1962. Fellow Am. Acad. Pediatrics (neonatal perinatal sect., mem. com. fetus and newborn P.R. chpt. 1956—, sec.-treas. 1962-64, mem. com. history perinatal sect. 1992—, Plaque in Recognition Disting. Pediatrician and Tchr. 1985), Pan Am. Pediatrics; mem. Am. Med. Women Assn., P.R. Med. Assn. (pediat. sect., mem. chamber of dels. 1962-63, Bronze plaque 1967, 91, Gold Pin 1980), P.R. Med. Women Assn. (sec.-treas. 1957-60, pres. 1960-64), Pan Am. Med. Women Assn. (pres. P.R. chpt. 1960-64, P.R. del. VIII Congress Manizales Colombia 1962), Pan Am. Med. Women Alliance (vis. lectr. 1962), Tulane Med. Alumni, London Royal Soc. Health, Colegio de Químicos, Soc. Dominicana de Pediatría (hon., vis. lectr. 1971), Dominican Rep. Soc. (hon.). Avocation: poetry. Home: Duke C 12 Esq Tulane Santa Ana Rio Piedras San Juan PR 00927 Office: Las Americas Profl Ctr Domenech 400 Ste 309 Hato Rey San Juan PR 00918

MUÑOZ-SOLÁ, HAYDEÉ SOCORRO, library administrator; b. Caguas, P.R., Dec. 27, 1943; d. Gilberto Muñoz and Carmen Haydeé (Solá) de Muñoz; m. Juan M. Masini-Soler, Jan. 8, 1966 (div. 1979); children: Juan Martín Masini-Muñoz, Haydeé Milagros Masini-Muñoz. BA in Psychology, U. P.R., Río Piedras, 1965, MLS, 1970; D in Libr. Sci., Columbia U., 1985. Asst. libr. U. P.R., Río Piedras, 1964-67; dir. libr. Interam. U., Aguadilla, P.R., 1974-75; head svcs. to pub. U. P.R., Aguadilla, 1975-76; cataloguer Cath. U., Ponce, P.R., 1976-79; cataloguer U. P.R., Río Piedras, 1982-84, head libr. and info. sci. libr., 1984-85, prof. grad. libr. sch., 1986, dir. libr. sys., 1986-93; coord. external resources libr. sys. U. P.R.; dir. P.R. Newspaper Project, Río Piedras, 1986-90; mem. Adv. Com. on Pub. Librs., San Juan, 1987-93; proposal reviewer NEH, 1990—; chmn. Puerto Rican Del. to Nat. White House Conf. on Libr. and Info. Svcs., 1991. Author: La Información y la Documentación Educativa/Informe Sobre la Situación Actual en Puerto Rico, 1991, Memorias: Sequnda Pre-Conferencia de Casa Blanca Sobre Bibliotecas y Servicios de Información en Puerto Rico, 1991, Lineamientos para Colecciones Bibliograficas Nacionales, 1997; contbr. articles to profl. jours. Mem. Ponce Sport Club, 1976-83, ARC, Ponce, 1978. Recipient plaque White House Pre-Conf. on Libr. and Info. Scis., 1990, others; French Alps Study Tour scholar Assn. Caribbean Univ. Rsch. and Instl. Librs., 1989, Germany Study Tour scholar Fgn. Rels. Office, Germany, 1991. Mem. ALA, Am. Mgmt. Assn., Grad. Sch. Libr. and Info. Sci. Alumni Assn. (pres. 1988-90), Seminar for Acquisitions L.Am. Libr. Materials, Iberoamerican Nat. Librs. Assn. (pres. 1992-93), Puerto Rican Librs. Soc. (coord. So. area 1974, Lauro award 1989), Assn. Caribbean U. Rsch. and Instnl. Librs. (Parchment award 1988), Asoc. para las Comunicaciones y Tecnología Educativa, Mid. States Assn. Colls. and Schs. (collaborator), Am. Women Assn., Phi Delta Kappa (chair P.R. com. 1988-90, Kappan of Yr. 1990), Eta Gamma Delta. Roman Catholic. Avocations: reading, crewel work, embroidery, knitting, movies. Office: U of PR Library System PO Box 23302 University Sta San Juan PR 00931-3302

MUNRO, ALICE, author; b. Wingham, Ont., Can., July 10, 1931; d. Robert Eric and Anne Clarke (Chamney) Laidlaw; m. James Armstrong Munro, 1951 (div. 1976); children: Sheila, Jenny, Andrea; m. Gerald Fremlin, 1976. BA, U. Western Ont., 1952, DLitt (hon.), 1976. Author: (short stories) Dance of the Happy Shades, 1968 (Gov.-Gen.'s Lit. award 1969), A Place for Everything, 1970, Lives of Girls and Women, 1971 (Can. Booksellers award, 1972), (short stories) Something I've Been Meaning To Tell You, 1974, Who Do You Think You Are?, 1979 (pub. in U.S. as Beggar Maid: Stories of Flo and Rose, 1984, Gov.-Gen.'s Lit. award 1978), The Moons of Jupiter, 1982, The Progress of Love, 1986 (Gov. Gens. Lit. award 1987), Friend of My Youth, 1990, (short stories) Open Secrets, 1994, A Wilderness Station, 1994, Selected Stories, 1996; TV scripts: A Trip to the Coast, 1973, Thanks For The Ride, 1973, How I Met My Husband, 1974, 1847: The Irish, 1978. Recipient Can.-Australia Lit. Prize 1994, Marian Engel award, 1986. Home: PO Box 1133, Clinton, ON Canada N0M 1L0 Office: care Alfred A Knopf Inc 201 E 50th St New York NY 10022-7703*

MUNRO, BARBARA HAZARD, nursing educator, college dean, researcher; b. Wakefield, R.I., Nov. 28, 1938; d. Robert J. and Honore (Egan) Hazard; m. Bruce Munro, June 1, 1961; children: Karen Aimee, Craig Michael, Stephanie Anne. BS, MS, U. R.I., Kingston; PhD, U. Conn. RN, Conn. Asst. prof. U. of R.I. Coll. of Nursing, Kingston; assoc. prof., chmn. program in nursing rsch. Yale U., New Haven, Conn.; assoc. prof., asst. dir. Ctr. for Nursing Rsch. U. Pa., Phila.; dean, prof. Boston Coll. Sch. Nursing, 1991—; presenter and workshop leader various nursing confs. and seminars in U.S. Contbr. articles and rsch. to profl. pubs. Trustee St. Elizabeth's Med. Ctr. Boston, 1994—. Recipient Nat. Rsch. Svc. award. Fellow Am. Acad. Nursing; mem. ANA, Nat. League for Nursing, Golden Key, Sigma Theta Tau, Pi Lambda Theta, Phi Kappa Phi. Office: Boston Coll Sch Nursing Cushing Hall Chestnut Hill MA 02167-3812

MUNRO, DONALD JACQUES, philosopher, educator; b. New Brunswick, N.J., Mar. 5, 1931; s. Thomas B. and Lucile (Nadler) M.; m. Ann Maples Patterson, Mar. 3, 1956; 1 child, Sarah de la Roche. A.B., Harvard U., 1953; Ph.D. (Ford Found. fellow), Columbia U., 1964. Asst. prof. philosophy U. Mich., 1964-68, asso. prof., 1968-73, prof. philosophy, 1973-96, prof. philosophy and Asian langs., 1990-96; prof. emeritus philosophy and Chinese, 1996—; chmn. dept. Asian langs. and cultures U. Mich., 1993-95; vis. research philosopher Center for Chinese Studies, U. Calif., Berkeley, 1969-70; asso. Center for Chinese Studies, U. Mich., 1964—; chmn. com. on studies of Chinese civilization Am. Council Learned Socs., 1979-81; mem. Com. on Scholarly Communication with People's Republic China, 1978-82, China Council of Asia Soc., 1977-80, Com. on Advanced Study in China, 1978-82, Nat. Com. on U.S.-China Rels., Nat. Faculty of Humanities, Arts and Scis., 1986—; Evans-Wentz lectr. Stanford U., 1970; Fritz lectr. U. Wash., 1980; Gilbert Ryle lectr. Trent U., Ont., 1983; John Dewey lectr. U. Vermont, 1989; vis. rsch.scholar Chinese Acad. Social Scis. Inst. Philosophy, Beijing, 1983, dept. philosophy Beijing U., 1990. Author: The Concept of Man in Early China, 1969, the Concept of Man in Contemporary China, 1977;, editor: Individualism and Holism, 1985, Images of Human Nature: A Sung Portrait, 1988, The Imperial Style of Inquiry in Twentieth Century China, 1996. Mem. exec. com. Coll. Literature, Sci. and The Arts U. Mich., 1986-89. Served to lt. (j.g.) USNR, 1953-57. Recipient letter of commendation Chief Naval Ops.; Disting. Svc. award U. Mich., 1968, Excellence in Edn. award, 1992; Rice Humanities award, 1993-94; Nat. Humanities faculty fellow, 1971-72; John Simon Guggenheim Found. fellow, 1978-79; grantee Social Sci. Rsch. Coun., 1965-66, Am. Coun. Learned Socs., 1982-83, China com. grantee NAS, 1990. Mem. Assn. for Asian Studies (China and Inner Asia Council 1970-72), Soc. for Asian and Comparative Philosophy. Club: Ann Arbor Racquet. Home: 14 Ridgeway St Ann Arbor MI 48104-1739 Office: Dept Philosophy U Mich Ann Arbor MI 48104 *I believe that much knowledge is interrelated and that academic disciplinary boundaries are transitory conveniences. The human significance of any research task I undertake should be obvious to those inside and outside my professional group (a goal I seek but do not always achieve).*

MUNRO, JANET ANDREA, artist; b. Woburn, Mass., Dec. 8, 1949; d. John Lehne, Jr. and Celina (Herbert) Baehr; m. Charles Eldon Munro, II, May 16, 1968; children—Jacquelyn, David, Chad. Represented by Jay Johnson Gallery, N.Y.C., 1979-89, Frank Miele Gallery, N.Y.C., 1990—, Sternberg Galleries, Chgo., 1990—, Gallery 53 Artworks, Cooperstown, N.Y., 1990—, Toad Hall Gallery, N.Y.C., 1990—. Exhbns. include: Soutyby's Galleries, N.Y.C., 1986, 89, Christies Auction Galleries, N.Y.C., 1988, Bloomingdales Dept. Store, N.Y.C., The MacArthur Found., West Palm Beach, Fla., 1987, Squibb Gallery, Princeton, N.J., 1983, Marshall Fields Dept. Store, Chgo., 1983, Jay Johnsons America's Folk Heritage Gallery, N.Y.C., 1982-84, Galerie Pro Arte Kasper, Morges, Switzerland, 1983-84, Occidental Oil Corp., San Francisco, 1980, Nassau County Mus. Fine Arts, Roslyn, N.Y., Silver Guild Ctr. Arts, New Canaan, Conn., John Judkyn Meml. Am. Mus. in Britain, Bath, Eng., Central Sch. Art and Design, London, Haworth Gallery, London, numerous others; featured in numerous publs.; represented in permanent collections: The White House, Smithsonian Inst., The Wallace House Mus., Somerset County, N.J., Fenimore House, N.Y. State Hist. Assn., Cooperstown, N.Y.; represented in numerous pub. and pvt. collections; featured in numerous newspapers and mags. Recipient Diploma award Internat. Naive Art Exhibit, Morges, Switzerland, 1983, 84. Active Cooperstown PTA, N.Y., 1985. Home: PO Box 303 Portlandville NY 13834-0303 also: 212 Coolidge Dr Sarasota FL 34236-2021

MUNRO, JOHN HENRY ALEXANDER, economics educator, writer; b. Vancouver, B.C., Can., Mar. 14, 1938; s. Hector Gordon and Blanche (Almond) M.; m. Jeanette Roberta James, May 25, 1968; children: Robert Ryder, Valerie Marlene. B.A. with honors, U. B.C., Vancouver, 1960; M.A. in History, Yale U., 1961, Ph.D. in History, 1965. Instr. in history U. B.C., 1964-65, asst. prof. history and econs., 1965-68; assoc. prof. econs. U. Toronto, 1968-73, prof., 1973—; assoc. dir. Centre for Medieval Studies, U. Toronto, 1975-78; cons. on coinage to pub. U. Toronto Press, 1973—. Author: Wool, Cloth, and Gold, 1973, Bullion Flows and Monetary Policies in England and the Low Countries, 1350-1500, 1992, Textiles, Towns and Trade: Essays in the Economic History of Late-Medieval England and the Low Countries, 1994; contbr. articles to profl. jours., essays to books; mem. editorial bd. Textile History, 1980—; Medieval area editor Oxford Ency. of Econ. History, 1996—. Can. Coun. leave fellow, Belgium, 1970-71, Social Scis. and Humanities Rsch. Coun. Can. fellow, Engl. and Holland, 1979-80, Belgium, 1986-87, Eng. and Belgium, 1992-96, 96—, Connaught Rsch. fellow, 1993-94. Mem. Can. Econ. Assn., Econ. History Assn. (U.S.), Econ. History Soc. (U.K.), Medieval Acad. Am. (councillor 1990-93). Presbyterian. Home: 9 Woodmere Ct, Islington, ON Canada M9A 3J1 Office: Dept Econs U Toronto, 150 Saint George St, Toronto, ON Canada M5S 3G7

MUNRO, MEREDITH VANCE, lawyer; b. Natick, Mass., Aug. 4, 1938; s. George Lawrence and Florence Estella (Murphy) M.; m. Gail Wittekind, June 10, 1960 (div. 1974); children: Susan Heidi, Elizabeth Holly, Meredith Heather. AB, Princeton U., 1960; JD, Harvard U., 1963. Bar: Mass. 1963. Assoc. atty. Gaston Snow & Ely Barlett, Boston, 1963-71, ptnr., 1971—; bd. dirs. Heath Cons. Inc., Stoughton, Mass., 1974—. Trustee The Tabor Acad., Marion, Mass., 1975—. Mem. Mass. Bar Assn., Boston Bar Assn. Avocations: antiques, gardening, cooking. Home: 5 Patricia Rd Framingham MA 01701-3931

MUNRO, MICHAEL DONALD, hotel industry executive, retired military officer; b. Kindley AFB, Bermuda, May 6, 1953; (parents Am. citizens); s. Donald M. and Marilyn Barbara (Ravenelle) M. AAS in Criminology, U. Md., 1978; BA in Sociology, SUNY, Plattsburg, 1981; MA in Mgmt., Embry-Riddle U., 1986. Commd. 2d lt. USAF, 1976, advanced through grades to capt., 1985; chief security adminstr. Plattsburg AFB, N.Y., 1979-81; ICBM launch officer Grands Forks AFB, Grand Forks AFB, N.D., 1981-83; ICBM flight comdr. Grands Forks AFB, N.D., 1984-86; satellite officer Colorado Springs, Colo., 1986-87; chief satellite officer U.S. Space Command, Colorado Springs, 1987; chief U.S. Space Def. Ops. Ctr., Colorado Springs, 1988-91; ret., 1991, profl. voice talent, broadcaster, 1991—; gen. mgr. Entertainment Concepts, Colorado Springs, 1991-94; mgr. corp. ops. The Gambler Nightclubs and Restaurants, 1994-95; food and beverage exec. The Westin Hotel, Denver, 1995-96; beverage dir. Sheraton/CAPSTAR Hotels, 1996-97, Adam's Mark Hotels, 1997—; cons. 1980 Winter Olympics, Lake Placid, N.Y., 1979-80; dir. Grand Forks City Govt., 1986. Contbr. articles to profl. jours. Mem. Pike's Peak Rodeo Com., Colorado Springs, 1987. Recipient Scholastic Achievement award Boeing Aerospace, 1988; named Outstanding Young Man Grand Forks County, 1985. Mem. Profl. Rodeo Cowboys Assn. (judge 1987-88, announcer, broadcaster 1988—), Assn. Govt. Execs., Crewmembers Assn. (pres. 1985-86), Grand Forks C. of C., Wild Horse Futurity Assn. (bd. dirs. 1992-94). Republican. Roman Catholic. Avocations: profl. rodeo, hunting, fishing, horseback riding. Home: PO Box 49266 Colorado Springs CO 80949

MUNRO, RALPH DAVIES, state government official; b. Bainbridge Island, Wash., June 25, 1943; s. George Alexander and Elizabeth (Troll) M.; m. Karen Hansen, Feb. 17, 1973; 1 son, George Alexander. BA in History and Edn. (scholar), Western Wash. U. Successively indsl. engr. Boeing Co.; sales mgr. Continental Host, Inc.; asst. dep. dir. ACTION Agy.; spl. asst. to gov. of Wash.; gen. mgr. Tillicum Enterprises & Food Services Co.; dir. Found. for Handicapped; pres. Northwest Highlands Tree Farm; now sec. of state State of Wash. Chmn. community service com. Seattle Rotary Club 4; founder 1st pres. Rotary Youth Job Employment Center, Seattle. Named Man of Yr. Assn. Retarded Citizens, Seattle, 1970. Mem. Nat. Assn. Secs. State (pres.), Nat. Assn. Retarded Children, Wash. Historic Mus. (dir.), Wash. Trust Historic Preservation (founder), Nature Conservancy. Republican. Lutheran. Office: Sec of State Legislative Bldg PO Box 40220 Olympia WA 98504-0220

MUNROE, GEORGE BARBER, former metals company executive; b. Joliet, Ill., Jan. 5, 1922; s. George Muller and Ruth (Barber) M.; m. Elinor Bunin, May 30, 1968; children by previous marriage: George Taylor, Ralph W. Taylor. AB, Dartmouth Coll., 1943; LLB, Harvard U., 1949; BA (Rhodes scholar), Christ Church, Oxford (Eng.) U., 1951, MA, 1956; DHL (hon.), No. Ariz. U., 1981; LLD (hon.), Dartmouth Coll., 1993. Bar: N.Y. 1949. Assoc. Cravath, Swaine & Moore, N.Y.C., 1949; atty. Office Gen. Counsel U.S. High Commn. Germany, Frankfurt and Bonn, 1951-53; justice U.S. Ct. Restitution Appeals Allied High Commn. Germany, Nuremberg, 1953-54; assoc. Debevoise, Plimpton & McLean, N.Y.C., 1954-58; with Phelps Dodge Corp., 1958-90, v.p., 1962-66; also bd. dirs., 1966-94; pres. Phelps Dodge Corp., 1966-75, 80-82, chief exec. officer, 1969-87, chmn. bd., 1975-87, chmn. fin. com., cons., 1987-90; bd. dirs. N.Y. Times Co., Santa Fe Pacific Gold Corp. Trustee, chmn. fin. com. Met. Mus. Art; chmn. bd. dirs. Acad. Polit. Sci. Lt. (j.g.) USNR, 1943-46. Mem. Mining and Metall. Soc. Am., Coun. Fgn. Rels., Century Assn., River Club, Univ. Club (N.Y.C.), Bridgehampton Club. Office: 866 3rd Ave Fl 26 New York NY 10022-6221

MUNROE, PAT, retired newsman; b. Quincy, Fla., Nov. 3, 1916; s. Mark Welch and Mary Frances (Gray) M.; m. Mary Johnson Norris, Dec. 6, 1952; children: Anne Logan, Katherine Gray. B.S. in Indsl. Mgmt., Ga. Inst. Tech., 1939; M.S., Columbia Sch. Journalism, 1941. Reporter Atlanta Jour., 1939-40, Washington Post, 1946-47; former propr. Munroe News Bur., Washington, rep. book pubs. and newspapers, 1947-83; covered maj. polit. convs., presdl. campaigns, 1948—, (Vice Pres. Nixon's trip to Russia), 1959; chmn. standing com. corrs. U.S. Senate-House Press Galleries, 1955-56; bd. govs. Nat. Press Club, 1955-56. Bd. govs. Nat. Cathedral Sch., Washington; trustee Webb Sch., Bell Buckle, Tenn.; former trustee James Monroe Meml. Found., Fredericksburg, Va. Served to lt. comdr. USNR, 1941-45. Recipient Raymond Clapper Meml. award and cert. Columbia Sch. Journalism, 1957. Mem. White House Corrs. Assn., Chevy Chase Club, Univ. Club (N.Y.C.), Met. Club, Nat. Press Club, Sigma Delta Chi (pres. Washington 1964-65). Republican. Episcopalian. Home: 9025 Bronson Dr Potomac MD 20854-4607

MUNSAT, STANLEY MORRIS, philosopher, educator; b. Rutland, Vt., Apr. 12, 1939; s. Leo and Ethel (Geron) M.; m. Rosemary S.; children—Steven, Tobin. A.B., Cornell U., 1960; M.A., U. Mich., 1962, Ph.D., 1965. Asst. prof. U. Calgary, Alta., Can., 1963-66; asst. prof. philosophy U. Calif., Irvine, 1966-68; asso. prof. U. Calif., 1968-71, prof., 1971-72; prof. philosophy U. N.C., Chapel Hill, 1972—. Author: The Concept of Memory, 1967; Editor: The Analytic Synthetic Distinction, 1971; gen. editor: (with A.I. Melden) Wadsworth Basic Problems in Philosophy Series; contbr. articles to profl. jours. Mem. Am. Philos. Assn. Home: 837 Shadylawn Rd Chapel Hill NC 27514-2007 Office: Univ NC Dept Philosophy Chapel Hill NC 27514

MUNSELL, ELSIE LOUISE, lawyer; b. N.Y.C., Feb. 15, 1939; d. Elmer Stanley and Eleanor Harriet (Dickinson) M.; m. George P. Williams, July 14, 1979. AB, Marietta Coll., 1960; JD, Marshall-Wythe Coll. William and Mary, 1972. Bar: Va. 1972, U.S. Dist. Ct. (ea. dist.) Va. 1974, U.S. Ct. Appeals (4th cir.) 1976, U.S. Supreme Ct. 1980. Tchr. Norview High Sch., Norfolk, Va., 1964-69; asst. Commonwealth atty. Commonwealth Atty.'s Office, Alexandria, Va., 1972-73; asst. U.S. atty. Alexandria, 1974-79; U.S. magistrate U.S. Dist. Ct. (ea. dist.) Va., Alexandria, 1979-81; U.S. atty. Dept. Justice, Alexandria, 1981-86; sr. trial atty. Office of Gen. Counsel, Dept. Navy, Washington, 1986-89, asst. gen. counsel installations and environ. law, 1989-91; dep. asst. environ. and safety Sec. Navy, 1991—. Active Va. Commn. on Status of Women, 1966-74; bd. vistors Coll. William and Mary, 1972-76; active Atty. Gen.'s Adv. Com. U.S. Attys., 1981-83; bd. dirs. Carpenter's Shelter, Inc., 1990-93; vestry St. Alban's, Annandale, Va., 1996—. Mem. Environ. Law Inst. (assoc.), Sr. Execs. Assn. Episcopalian. Office: Dept Navy 1000 Navy Pentagon Washington DC 20350-1000

MUNSEY, VIRDELL EVERARD, JR., retired utility executive; b. Washington, Sept. 25, 1933; s. Virdell Everard and Mildred Lovenia (Wood) M.; m. Bernice Ann Wilson, Sept. 20, 1956; children: Wanda Louise, Allan Coll, Andrew Everard, Carolyn Jane. B.A. magna cum laude, Yale U., 1955; M.P.A., Harvard U., 1967. Reporter Washington Post, 1957-63; legis. asst. Rep. Henry S. Reuss, Washington, 1963-68; info. dir. United Democrats for Humphrey, Washington, 1968; asst. dir. public affairs Dem. Nat. Com., 1968; with Nat. Planning Assn., Washington, 1969-77; exec. v.p. Nat. Planning Assn., 1974-76; dep. asst. sec. for public affairs Dept. Treasury, Washington, 1977-81; cons. World Bank, 1981; with Va. Electric and Power Co., 1981-86, mgr. corp. communications, 1982-83, exec. dir. pub. policy, 1983-86, v.p. pub. policy, 1986; v.p. pub. policy Dominion Resources Inc., 1986-96; cons., 1996—; mem. Va. Coal and Energy Commn., 1983-95. Chmn. Arlington County Dem. Party, 1967-69; mem. Arlington County Bd., 1972-75, chmn., 1973; vice chmn. No. Va. Transp. Commn., 1973, chmn., 1974; bd. dirs. Washington Met. Area Transit Authority, 1975; mem. transp. planning bd. Met. Washington Coun. Govts., 1973-75; treas. Competitive Power Policy Forum, 1990-96. Served with U.S. Army, 1955-57. Am. Polit. Sci. Assn. fellow, 1966-67. Mem. United Ch. Christ.

MUNSON, ALEX ROBERT, judge; b. L.A., Sept. 25, 1941; s. Robert Alexander and Lillian Agnus (Hamel) M.; m. Kathleen Rae Abernathey, June 29, 1968. BA, Long Beach (Calif.) State Coll., 1964, MA, 1965; EdD, U. So. Calif., L.A., 1974; JD, Loyola U., L.A., 1975. Atty. Kirtland and Packard, L.A., 1978-82; chief justice High Ct. of The Trust Terr. of The Pacific Islands, Saipan, Commonwealth of the No. Mariana Islands, 1982-88; chief judge U.S. Dist. Ct. of No. Mariana Islands, Saipan, Commonwealth of the No. Mariana Islands, 1988—. Mem. ABA, Calif. Bar Assn. Republican. Home: Box 5356 CHRB, Saipan MP Office: US Dist Ct PO Box 687 Saipan MP 96950-0687

MUNSON, HAROLD LEWIS, education educator; b. Windham, N.Y., Aug. 2, 1923; s. Esmond Lewis and Gladys (Disbrow) M.; m. Evelyn Claire Moore, Sept. 8, 1946; children: Michael Lewis, Jeffrey Charles. A.B., Hobart Coll., 1947; M.A., SUNY, Albany, 1948; Ed.D., NYU, 1961. Tchr. social studies, counselor Cairo (N.Y.) Central Sch., 1948-50; dir. guidance Williamson (N.Y.) Central Sch., 1950-54; supr. guidance N.Y. State Edn. Dept., Albany, 1954-59; prof. edn., chmn. Center for Counseling, Family and Worklife Studies, U. Rochester, N.Y., 1959-85; prof. emeritus Center for Counseling, Family and Worklife Studies, U. Rochester, 1985—; prof. edn. Overseas Program, Boston U., 1985-87; pres. Munson Assocs., 1988—; vocat. cons. Social Security Adminstrn., HEW, 1962-79. Author: (with H.W. Houghton) Organizing Orientation Activities, 1956, My Educational Plans, 1959, 70, Guidance Activities for Teachers of English, Social Studies, Science, Mathematics and Foreign Languages, 1965, (with Gilbert Gockley) Career Insights and Self Awareness Games, 1973; contbg. author: Ency. of Careers, 1967, Elementary School Guidance: Concepts, Dimensions and Practice, 1970, The Foundations of Developmental Guidance, 1971, Career Education for Deaf Students: An Inservice Leader's Guide, 1975. Served with USNR, 1944-46. Mem. Am. Counseling Assn., Nat. Career Devel. Assn., Am. Sch. Counselor Assn., Phi Delta Kappa. Home: 745 Thayer Rd Fairport NY 14450-9514 Office: U Rochester Warner Grad Sch Edn and Human Devel Rochester NY 14627 *Success is whatever you want it to be. By defining it in such personal terms, everyone should be able to experience some degree of success. For me, it has been being able to feel a measure of personal fulfillment through my accomplishments in helping others to define and examine their own existence.*

MUNSON, HOWARD G., federal judge; b. Claremont, N.H., July 26, 1924; s. Walter N. and Helena (O'Halloran) M.; m. Ruth Jaynes, Sept. 17, 1949; children: Walter N., Richard J., Pamela A. B.S. in Economics, U. Pa., 1948; LL.B., Syracuse U., 1952. Bar: N.Y. With Employers' Assurance Corp., Ltd., White Plains, N.Y., 1949-50; mem. firm Hiscock, Lee, Rogers, Henley & Barclay, Syracuse, N.Y., 1952-76; judge U.S. Dist. Ct. No. Dist. N.Y., Syracuse, 1976—. Mem., pres. Syracuse Bd. Edn.; bd. dirs. Sta. WCNY-TV; chmn. ethics com. Onondaga County Legislature. Served with U.S. Army, 1943-45, ETO. Decorated Bronze Star, Purple Heart. Mem. Am. Coll. Trial Lawyers, Nat. Assn. R.R. Trial Counsel, Am. Arbitration Assn., Justinian Soc., Alpha Tau Omega, Phi Delta Phi. Office: US Dist Ct US Courthouse P O Box 7376 Syracuse NY 13261-7376

MUNSON, JOHN BACKUS, computer systems consultant, retired engineering company executive; b. Chgo., May 1, 1933; s. Mark Frame and Catherine Louise (Cherry) M.; m. Anne Lorraine Cooper, July 6, 1957; children: David B., Sharon A. BA, Knox Coll., 1955. With Unisys Corp., McLean, Va., 1957-93, v.p. corp. software engring., 1977-81, v.p. tech. ops., 1981-84, v.p., gen. mgr. space transp. systems, 1984-89, 89-93; v.p., gen. mgr. Space Systems div., 1989-94, retired, 1994; mem. sci. adv. bd. USAF, 1981-86, mem. USN panel on F14D issues, 1987-88. Recipient Exceptional Civilian Service award USAF, 1986, Superior Pub. Svc. award USN, 1988, cert. of appreciation NATO, 1984. Mem. bd. advisors U. Houston, Clear Lake, 1988-93, chmn. 1990-92; bd. dirs. Bay Area YMCA, 1988-93, chmn. 1992, Clear Lake Am. Heart Assn., 1989-93; co-chmn. Bay Area United Way, 1988—, chmn., 1992; Disting. visitor IEEE Computer Soc., 1981-94. Capt. U.S. Army, 1955-57. Named to Nat. Mgmt. Assn. Hall of Fame, 1994. Fellow IEEE (editor Trans. on Software Engring. 1982-84, bd. dirs. tech com. software engring. 1982—); mem. AIAA, Am. Astronautical Soc. (bd. dirs. Southwest sect. 1989-94), Aerospace Industries Assn. (space com. 1989-94), U.S. Army Assn., Nat. Security Indsl. Assn., Armed Forces Communication Electronics Assn. (pres. Houston chpt. 1987-90), S.W. Regional Coun. Corp. CEOs. Home and Office: 1018 Westcreek Ln Westlake Vlg CA 91362-5462

MUNSON, JOHN CHRISTIAN, acoustician; b. Clinton, Iowa, Oct. 9, 1926; s. Arthur J. and Frances (Christian) M.; m. Elaine Hendershot, Sept. 2, 1950; children: John Christian, Holly Elizabeth. BS, Iowa State Coll., 1949; MS, U. Md., 1952, PhD, 1962; Navy Dept. scholar, MIT, 1956. Electronic scientist Naval Ordnance Lab., Washington, 1949-66; tech. dir. navy portion Practice Nine, Naval Air Systems Command, 1967; supt. acoustics divsn. Naval Rsch. Lab., 1968-85; v.p. Engring. & Sci. Assocs., 1983-94; chmn. bd. dirs., 1994; ret.; asst. extension prof. elec. engring. U. Md., 1964-66; mem. Underwater Sound Adv. Group, 1969-75, U.S. Sonar Team, 1971-85, Mobile Sonar Tech. Com., 1972-85; cons., 1985—. Editor U.S. Navy Jour. Underwater Acoustics, 1983-91; patentee in field. Mem. exec. bd. D.C. Bapt. Conv., 1973—, chmn. fin. com., 1973, v.p., 1996-97; trustee Midwestern Bapt. Theol. Sem., 1970-80; trustee Bapt. Sr. Adult Ministries of Washington Met. Area, 1976-91, 92—, pres., 1981-88, CEO, 1991-92; mem. Gen. Bd. Am. Bapt. Chs. U.S.A., 1994—; dir., pres. Allied Silver Spring Interfaith Svcs. to Srs. Today, 1994—; bd. mgrs. Am. Bapt. Hist. Soc., 1996—. Fellow IEEE, Signal Processing Soc. (mem. adminstrv. com. 1974-76, chmn. underwater acoustics com. 1973-76), Acoustical Soc. Am.; mem. Sigma Xi. Home: 119 Marine Ter Silver Spring MD 20905-5925 *I have a positive joy for life, and I am an incurable optimist: my basic attitude is that things will work out for the best—but only if we do our very best. Each of us has a responsibility to grow to our maximum capacity and to be of reasonable service to mankind. The proper balance among family, job, service to God, service to others, and attention to yourself is essential. Whatever you are doing, do it from the right motivation and with enthusiasm.*

MUNSON, LAWRENCE SHIPLEY, management consultant; b. N.Y.C., Jan. 10, 1920; s. Lawrence J. and Anna (Lee) M.; m. Gretchen Thannhauser, May 24, 1947; children: Catherine Anne, Shipley John. A.B., Harvard U., 1942, JD, 1948. Bar: N.Y. 1948. Assoc. Willkie, Owen, Farr, Gallagher & Walton, N.Y.C., 1948-51; assoc., then partner McKinsey & Co., Inc., N.Y.C., 1953-67; pres. Loral Corp., Scarsdale, N.Y., 1967-69; v.p. Allegheny Power System, Inc., N.Y.C., 1969-72; v.p., mng. prin. Louis Allen Assocs., Inc., 1972—. Author: How To Conduct Training Seminars, 1984, 2d edit.,

1992. Chmn. bd. Planned Parenthood N.Y.C., 1966-70; mem. bd. Planned Parenthood Manhattan and Bronx, 1960-66, Planned Parenthood World Population, 1967-70; bd. dirs. Greater N.Y. Fund, 1966-88, chmn. mgmt. assistance com., 1970-75; pres. East Hampton Village Preservation Soc., 1982-87, trustee, 1982—, chmn., 1993—; bd. dirs. United Way N.Y.C., 1988-89. Served to maj. USAAF, 1942-46; with USAF, 1951-53. Mem. Am. Soc. Tng. and Devel. (pres. N.Y. met. chpt. 1988-89, chmn. bd. dirs. 1990-93), Maidstone Club (East Hampton), Harvard Club (N.Y.C.). Home: 25 Dayton Ln East Hampton NY 11937-2415

MUNSON, LUCILLE MARGUERITE (MRS. ARTHUR E. MUNSON), real estate broker; b. Norwood, Ohio, Mar. 26, 1914; d. Frank and Fairy (Wicks) Wirick; R.N., Lafayette (Ind.) Home Hosp., 1937; A.B., San Diego State U., 1963, student Purdue U., Kans. Wesleyan U.; m. Arthur E. Munson, Dec. 24, 1937; children—Barbara Munson Papke, Judith Munson Andrews, Edmund Arthur. Staff and pvt. nurse Lafayette Home Hosp., 1937-41; indsl. nurse Lakey Foundry & Machine Co., Muskegon, Mich., 1950-51, Continental Motors Corp., Muskegon, 1951-52; nurse Girl Scout Camp, Grand Haven, Mich., 1948-49; owner Munson Realty, San Diego, 1964—. Mem. San Diego County Grand Jury, 1975-76, 80-81, Calif. Grand Jurors Assn. (charter). Office: 2999 Mission Blvd Ste 102 San Diego CA 92109-8070

MUNSON, NANCY KAY, lawyer; b. Huntington, N.Y., June 22, 1936; d. Howard H. and Edna M. (Keenan) Munson. Student, Hofstra U., 1959-62; JD, Bklyn. Law Sch., 1965. Bar: N.Y. 1966, U.S. Supreme Ct. 1970, U.S. Ct. Appeals (2d cir.) 1971, U.S. Dist. Ct. (ea. and so. dists.) N.Y. 1968. Law clk. to E. Merritt Weidner Huntington, 1959-66, sole practice, 1966—; mem. legal adv. bd. Chgo. Title Ins. Co., Riverhead, N.Y., 1981—; bd. dirs., legal officer Thomas Munson Found. Trustee Huntington Fire Dept. Death Benefit Fund; pres., trustee, chmn. bd. Bklyn. Home Aged Men Found.; bd. dirs. Elderly Day Svcs. on the Sound. Mem. ABA, N.Y. State Bar Assn., Suffolk County Bar Assn., Bklyn. Bar Assn., NRA, DAR, Soroptimists (past pres.). Republican. Christian Scientist. Office: 197 New York Ave Huntington NY 11743-2711

MUNSON, PAUL LEWIS, pharmacologist; b. Washta, Iowa, Aug. 21, 1910; s. Lewis Sylvester and Alice E. (Orser) M.; m. Aileen Geisinger, Mar. 7, 1931 (div. 1948); 1 dau., Abigail (Mrs. Mark Krumel); m. Mary Ellen Jones, Aug. 15, 1948 (div. 1971); children: Ethan Vincent, Catherine Laura; m. Yu Chen, Feb. 27, 1987; 1 stepchild, Ming An Chen. B.A., Antioch Coll., 1933; M.A., U. Wis., 1937; Ph.D., U. Chgo., 1942; M.A. (hon.), Harvard, 1955. Fellow, asst. biochemistry U. Chgo., 1939-42; research biochemist William S. Merrell Co., Cin., 1942-43; research biochemist, head endocrinology research Armour Labs., Chgo., 1943-48; research asst., then research asso. Yale Sch. Medicine, 1948-50; asst. prof., asso. prof. pharmacology, then prof. Harvard Sch. Dental Medicine, 1950-65; prof. pharmacology, chmn. dept. U. N.C. Sch. Medicine, 1965-77, Sarah Graham Kenan prof., 1970—; Mem. U.S. Pharmacopeia Panel on Corticotropin, 1951-55; mem. pharmacology test com. Nat. Bd. Med. Examiners, 1966-71; mem. gen. medicine B study section NIH, 1966-70, chmn., 1969-70, mem. pharmacology-toxicology rev. com., 1972-76. Author numerous articles on hormones; co-editor: Vitamins and Hormones, 1968-82; editl. bd. Endocrinology, 1957-63, Jour. Pharmacology and Exptl. Therapeutics, 1959-65, Jour. Dental Rsch., 1962-64, Biochem. Medicine, 1967-84, Am. Jour. Chinese Medicine, 1973-79, Pharmacol. Revs., 1967-70, editor-in-chief, 1977-81; editor-in-chief: Principles of Pharmacology, 1981-94. Fellow AAAS, Am. Acad. Arts and Scis.; mem. Am. Soc. Pharmacology and Exptl. Therapeutics (council 1970-73, sec.-treas. 1971-72), Am. Soc. Biol. Chemists, Endocrine Soc. (council 1963-65, Fred Conrad Koch award 1976), Am. Soc. Bone and Mineral Research (William F. Neuman award 1982), Am. Chem. Soc., Biometrics Soc., Internat. Assn. Dental Research (councillor 1957-59), AAUP, ACLU (mem. internat. confs. on calcium regulating hormones, Elsevier Sci. Pubs. award 1989), Assn. Med. Sch. Pharmacology (council 1971-73, sec. 1972-73, pres. 1974-76), Am. Thyroid Assn. (nominating com. 1973), Sigma Xi. Dem. Socialist. Unitarian. Home and Office: 1520 Taylor Ave Parkville MD 21234-5241

MUNSON, RICHARD HOWARD, horticulturist; b. Toledo, Dec. 20, 1948; s. Stanley Warren and Margaret Rose (Winter) M.; m. Joy Ellen Smith, July 8, 1972; children: Sarah Joy, David Remington. BS, Ohio State U., 1971; MS, Cornell U., 1973, PhD, 1981. Plant propagator The Holden Arboretum, Mentor, Ohio, 1973-76; asst. prof. Agrl. Tech. Inst., Wooster, Ohio, 1976-78, Tex. Tech U., Lubbock, 1981-84; dir. botanic garden Smith Coll., Northampton, Mass., 1984-95; exec. dir. The Holden Arboretum, Kirtland, Ohio, 1995—; v.p. Childs Park Found., Northampton, Mass., 1985-95. Lt. col. USAR. Mem. Internat. Plant Propagators Soc., Am. Soc. for Hort. Sci., Am. Assn. Bot. Gardens and Arboreta (com. chmn. 1987-92), Am. Assn. Nurserymen, Internat. Soc. Arboriculture, Sigma Xi, Pi Alpha Xi, Gamma Sigma Delta. Republican. Methodist. Avocations: fishing, golf, woodworking, gardening. Office: Holden Arboretum 9500 Sperry Rd Kirtland OH 44094-5149

MUNSON, RICHARD JAY, congressional policy analyst; b. Hollywood, Calif., Aug. 10, 1950; s. Jay S. and Grace P. (Palmer) M.; m. Diane MacEachern; children: Daniel, Dana. BA, U. Calif., Santa Barbara, 1971; MA, U. Mich., 1973. Instr. U. Mich., Ann Arbor, 1973-75; coord. Environ. Action Found., Washington, 1975-77; exec. dir. Solar Lobby, Washington, 1977-83, N.E.-Midwest Inst., Washington, 1986—. Author: The Power Makers, 1985, Cousteau, 1988, The Cardinals of Capitol Hill, 1993. Office: NE Midwest Inst 218 D St SE Washington DC 20003-1900

MUNSON, WILLIAM LESLIE, insurance company executive; b. Chgo., Apr. 28, 1941; s. David Curtiss and Leona Ruth (Anderson) M.; m. Marian Lee Blanton, July 16, 1966; children: Katherine, Sandra, Deborah. Student, U. Md., 1959-62; BBA cum laude, Coll. of Ins., 1968. CPCU, 1967. Asst. mgr. N.Y. Fire Ins. Rating Orgn., N.Y.C., 1959-69; br. mgr. CNA Ins. Co., N.Y.C., 1969-75; pres., dir. Commerce & Industry Ins. Co., N.Y.C., 1975-83; pres. Commerce & Industry of Can., 1980-83; sr. v.p., chief underwriting officer Am. Internat. Underwriters, 1983-87; exec. v.p. Home Ins. Co., 1987-93; pres., chief exec. officer Home Indemnity Ins. Co., 1987-93, also bd. dirs.; chmn. City Internat. Ins. Co. Ltd., 1991-93; pres., COO Merc. and Gen. Reins. Co. Am., 1993—; chmn., pres., CEO Toa-Re-Ins. Co. Am., 1993—; trustee Coll. of Ins., 1985—; bd. dirs. Nat. Coun. Compensation Ins., 1989-92, ISO Comml. Risk Svcs., 1993; mem. comml. lines com. Ins. Svcs. Office, 1989-92; trustee Am. Inst. for Charter Property Casualty Underwriters, 1996—. Pres. Wyckoff (N.J.) Bd. Edn., 1979-82; chmn. bd. lay leaders Grace United Meth. Ch., Wyckoff, 1989-92. Mem. Soc. CPCUs (bd. dirs. N.Y. chpt.), Conf. Spl. Risk Underwriters, Reinsurance Assn. Am. (bd. dirs.). Republican. Club: John St. (N.Y.C.). Home: 762 Albemarle St Wyckoff NJ 07481-1005 Office: Merc and Gen Reins 177 Madison Ave Morristown NJ 07960-6016

MUNSTER, ANDREW MICHAEL, medical educator, surgeon; b. Budapest, Hungary, Dec. 10, 1935; came to U.S., 1965; s. Leopold S. and Marianne (Barcza) M.; m. Joy O'Sullivan, Dec. 7, 1963; children: Andrea, Tara, Alexandra. MD, U. Sydney (Australia), 1959. Diplomate Am. Bd. Surgery. Research fellow Harvard U. Med. Sch., Boston, 1966-67; asst. prof. surgery U. Tex.-San Antonio, 1968-71, assoc. prof. surgery Med. U. S.C., Charleston, 1971-76; assoc. prof. Johns Hopkins U., Balt., 1976-85, prof. surgery, 1985—; dir. burn ctr. Balt. City Hosp., 1976—; v.p. Chesapeake Physicians, Balt., 1978-84. Author: Surgical Anatomy, 1971; Surgical Immunology, 1976; Burn Care for House Officers, 1980; contbr. numerous articles to med. jours. Pres., Chesapeake Ednl. Research Trust, Balt., 1980-84, Charleston Symphony, 1974-75, Charleston TriCounty Arts Council, 1975-76. Served to lt. col. U.S. Army, 1968-71. Recipient John Hunter prize U. Sydney, 1959; named Hunterian prof. Royal Coll. Surgeons, 1974. Fellow Royal Coll. Surgeons of Eng., Royal Coll. Surgeons of Edinburgh (Scotland), Am. Assn. Surgeons of Trauma, Colombian Coll. Surgeons (hon.); mem. Am. Burn Assn. (sec. 1990-93, 1st v.p. 1993-94, pres.-elect 1994-95, pres. 1995), Soc. Surg. Assn., Soc. Univ. Surgeons, Am. Surg. Assn. Office: Balt Reg Burn Ctr 4940 Eastern Ave Baltimore MD 21224-2735

MUNTZ, ERIC PHILLIP, aerospace engineering and radiology educator, consultant; b. Hamilton, Ont., Can., May 18, 1934; came to U.S., 1961, naturalized, 1985; s. Eric Percival and Marjorie Louise (Weller) M.; m. Janice Margaret Furey, Oct. 21, 1964; children: Sabrina Weller, Eric Phillip. B.A.Sc., U. Toronto, 1956, M.A.Sc., 1957, Ph.D., 1961. Halfback Toronto Argonauts, 1957-60; group leader Gen. Electric, Valley Forge, Pa., 1961-69; assoc. prof. aerospace engring. and radiology U. So. Calif., Los Angeles, 1969-71, prof., 1971-87, chmn. aerospace engring., 1987—; cons. to aerospace and med. device cos., 1967—; mem. rev. of physics (plasma and fluids) panel NRC, Washington, 1983-85. Contbr. numerous articles in gas dynamics and med. diagnostics to profl. publs., 1961—; patentee med. imaging, isotope separation, nondestructive testing, net shape mfg., transient energy release micromachine. Mem. Citizens Environ. Avc. Coun., Pasadena, Calif., 1972-76. Pilot RCAF, 1955-60. U.S. Air Force grantee, 1961-74, 82—; NSF grantee, 1970-76, 87—; FDA grantee, 1980-86. Fellow AIAA (aerospace Contbn. to Soc. award 1987), Am. Phys. Soc.; mem. NAE. Episcopalian. Home: 1560 E California Blvd Pasadena CA 91106-4104 Office: U So Calif Univ Pk Los Angeles CA 90089-1191

MUNTZ, ERNEST GORDON, historian, educator; b. Buffalo, Nov. 15, 1923; s. J. Palmer and Laura Estelle (Wedekindt) M.; m. Marjorie Corinne Wilson, June 29, 1948; children—Carolyn Odell, Deborah Lynn, Howard Gordon. A.B., Wheaton (Ill.) Coll., 1948; Ph.D., U. Rochester, N.Y., 1960. Asst. prof. social sci. Blue Mountain (Miss.) Coll., 1954-56; from asst. prof. to prof. history Union U., Jackson, Tenn., 1956-61; assoc. faculty U. Cin., 1961-91, prof. history, 1969-91, prof. emeritus, 1991—; dean Raymond Walters Coll., Cin., 1969-90, dean emeritus, 1991—; cons.-evaluator North Central Assn. Colls. and Schs., 1974-91, mem. Commn. on Instns. of Higher Edn., 1983-87. Served as officer USAAF, 1943-46. So. Fellowships Fund fellow, 1955. Mem. Am. Hist. Assn., Am. Assn. Community and Jr. Colls. (bd. dirs. coun. 2 yr. colls. of 4 yr. instns. 1988-90), Cincinnatus Assn., Phi Alpha Theta, Pi Gamma Mu. Presbyterian. Clubs: Cin. Literary, University. Home: 7950 Indian Hill Rd Cincinnati OH 45243-3906

MUNTZING, L(EWIS) MANNING, lawyer; b. Harrisonburg, Va., June 24, 1934; s. H. Gus and Virginia (Manning) M.; m. Nancy Snyder, June 20, 1959; children: Catherine Muntzing Boyden, Elizabeth Muntzing McKaig, Nancy Muntzing Seward, Kimberly Stuart. AB, U. N.C., 1956; postgrad., Woodrow Wilson Sch. Public and Internat. Affairs, Princeton U., 1956-57; LLB, Harvard U., 1960. Bar: D.C. 1960, Md. 1960, W.Va. 1960. Atty. Chesapeake & Potomac Telephone Cos., Washington, 1960-71; dir. of regulation Atomic Energy Commn., Washington, 1971-75; pvt. practice Washington, 1975-79; ptnr. Doub & Muntzing, Chartered, Washington, 1979-88, Doub, Muntzing & Glasgow, Washington, 1988-91, Newman & Holtzinger, Washington, 1991-94; spl. counsel Morgan, Lewis & Bockius, Washington, 1994—; co-chmn. Pacific Basin Nuclear Cooperation Com., 1985-89. Editor: International Instruments for Nuclear Technology Transfer, 1978. Trustee Bridgewater Coll., 1984—. Recipient Arthur S. Fleming Disting. Service award Atomic Energy Commn., 1974, Disting. Service award U.S. Atomic Energy Commn., 1974. Mem. Coun. of Sci. Soc. Pres. (exec. com. 1984-88, chmn. 1987, legal advisor 1988—), Am. Nuclear Soc. (pres. 1982-83, v.p. 1981-82, bd. dirs. 1977-80), Am. Assn. of Engring. Socs. (sec./treas. 1985), Am. Stds. of Testing Materials (chmn. rsch. and tech. planning com.), Internat. Nuclear Socs. Coun. (vice chmn. 1991-92, chmn. 1993-94), Internat. Nuclear Energy Acad. (chmn. 1975-77, exec. com. 1975—), D.C. Bar Assn., Md. Bar Assn., W.Va. Bar Assn., Internat. Nuclear Law Assn. (vice chmn. 1995-97), Knights of Malta, Phi Beta Kappa. Republican. Presbyterian. Clubs: Harvard, Princeton. Home: 10805 Pleasant Hill Dr Rockville MD 20854-1512 Office: Morgan Lewis & Bockius 1800 M St NW Washington DC 20036-5802

MUNYER, EDWARD A., zoologist, museum administrator; b. Chgo., May 8, 1936; s. G. and M. (Carlson) M.; m. Marianna J. Munyer, Dec. 12, 1981; children: Robert, William, Richard, Laura, Cheryl. BS, Ill. State U., 1958, MS, 1962. Biology tchr. MDR High Sch., Minonk, Ill., 1961-63; instr. Ill. State U., Normal, 1963-64; curator zoology Ill. State Mus., Springfield, 1964-67, asst. dir., 1981—; assoc. prof. Vincennes (Ind.) U., 1967-70; dir. Vincennes U. Mus., 1968-70; assoc. curator Fla. Mus. Natural History, Gainesville, 1970-81; mem. Mus. Accreditation Vis. Com. Roster, 1976—. Contbr. articles to profl. jours. Mem. Am. Assn. Mus. (bd. dirs. 1990-95), Midwest Mus. Conf. (pres. 1990-92), Ill. Assn. Mus. (bd. dirs. 1981-86), Wilson Ornithol. Soc. (life). Office: Ill State Mus Spring & Edward Sts Springfield IL 62706

MUNZER, CYNTHIA BROWN, mezzo-soprano; b. Clarksburg, W.Va., Sept. 30, 1948; d. Ralph Emerson and Doris Marguerite (Dixon) Brown; 1 dau., Christina Marie. Student, U. Kans., 1965-69. Adj. prof. voice U. So. Calif., 1994—. Debut. Oxford (Eng.) Opera, 1969, Met. Opera debut, N.Y.C., 1973; performed 1973-96 with: Met. Opera, Phila. Opera, Wolftrap Festival, Washington Opera, Goldovsky Opera, Washington Civic Opera, St. Petersburg Opera, Dallas Opera, Metropolitan Opera-Japan, Boston Concert Opera, Dayton Opera, Chgo. Opera Theatre, Mich. Opera, Kansas City Opera, New Orleans Opera, Houston Grand Opera, Ft. Worth Opera, Florentine Opera-Milw., Minn. Opera, Central City Opera, Aspen Festival, Opera Colo., Boston Festival Orch., Ontario Opera, Salt Lake City Opera, Nev. Opera, Cleve. Opera, Opera Pacific, Des Moines Opera, Ky. Opera, Mobile Opera, Internat. Artist Series in Kuala Lumpur, Penang, Jakarta, Hong Kong Philharm., Shanghai Symphony, Singapore Symphony, Philippine Philharm., N.Y.C. Ballet, Am. Symphony, Nat. Symphany, Charleston Symphony, Phila. Orch., New Haven Symphony, Houston Symphony, Ft. Wayne Symphony, El Paso Symphony, San Antonio Symphony, Amarillo Symphany, Wichita Symphony, Milw. Symphony, Minn. Orch., L.A. Chamber Orch., Ventura Chamber Orch., Denver Symphony, Phoenix Symphony, Oreg. Bach. Festival, San Francisco Symphony, L.A. Philharm., Louisville Symphony, Rochester Philharm., Binghamton Symphony, Rode Island Symphony, Carmel Bach Festival, Anchorage Symphony, L'Opera De Montreal, Colo. Opera Festival, N.Y. Mozart Bicentennial Festival, Brattleboro Festival, Knoxville Opera, Gold Coast Opera, Hawaii Opera, Augusta Opera, Berkshire Opera, Madison Opera, Chattanooga Symphony, Shreveport Opera, New York City Opera. Recipient Frederick K. Weyerhaeuser award, Gramma Fisher Found. award, Goeran Gentele award, Sullivan Found. award, Geraldine Farrar award, Joseph Schland Opera Presentations award; Nat. Opera Inst. grantee; winner Met. Opera Nat. auditions. Office: Wolf Artists Mgmt 788 Columbus Ave 15A New York NY 10025

MUNZER, STEPHEN IRA, lawyer; b. N.Y.C., Mar. 15, 1939; s. Harry and Edith (Isacowitz) M.; m. Patricia Eve Munzer, Aug. 10, 1965; children: John, Margaret. AB, Brown U., 1960; JD, Cornell U., 1963. Bar: N.Y. 1964, U.S. Supreme Ct. 1974, U.S. Dist. Ct. (so. and ea. dists.) N.Y., U.S. Ct. Appeals (3rd cir.). Formerly ptnr. Pincus Munzer Bizar & D'Alessandro, 1978-83; atty. and real estate investor Stephen I. Munzer & Assocs. P.C., 1984—; pres. Simcor Mgmt. Corp., N.Y.C., 1984—. Served to lt., USNR, 1965-75. Mem. Assn. of Bar of City of N.Y., N.Y. State Bar Assn., City Athletic Club, Washington Club. Jewish. Avocations: golf, skiing. Home: 429 Greenwich St New York NY 10013 also: 170 Shearer Rd Washington CT 06793-1013 Office: 777 3rd Ave New York NY 10017

MUNZER, STEPHEN R., law educator; b. 1944. BA, U. Kans., 1966; BPhil, Oxford U., Eng., 1969; JD, Yale U., 1972. Assoc. Covington & Burling, Washington, 1972-73; staff atty. Columbia U., N.Y.C., 1973-74; asst. prof. philosophy Rutgers U., New Brunswick, N.J., 1974-77; assoc. prof. U. Minn., Mpls., 1977-80, prof., 1980-81; prof. UCLA, 1982—. NEH fellow, 1991. Office: UCLA Sch Law 405 Hilgard Ave Los Angeles CA 90095-9000

MURAD, FERID, physician; b. Whiting, Ind., Sept. 14, 1936; s. John and Josephine (Bowman) M.; m. Carol Ann Leopold, June 21, 1958; children: Christine, Marianne, Carrie, Julie, Joseph. BA, DePauw U., 1958; MD, Case Western Res. U., 1965, PhD, 1965. Diplomate Nat. Bd. Med. Examiners. Intern and resident Mass. Gen. Hosp., Boston, 1965-67; clin. assoc. NIH, Bethesda, Md., 1967-70; from assoc. prof. to prof. U. Va., Charlottesville, 1970-81, dir. clin. research ctr., 1971-81, dir. clin. pharmacology, 1973-81; prof. Stanford (Calif.) U., 1981-88, assoc. chmn. dept. medicine, 1984-88; chief of medicine VA Med. Ctr., Palo Alto, Calif., 1981-88; v.p. pharm. div. Abbott Labs., 1988-92, CEO, pres. molecular geriatrics, 1993-95. Co-editor The Pharmacological Basis of Therapeutics, 7th edit., 1985; patentee in field; contbr articles to profl. jours. Recipient numerous awards for accomplishments in field. Mem. Am. Fedn. Clin. Research, Am. Soc. for Pharmacology and Exptl. Therapeutics, Endocrine Soc., Am. Soc. Biol. Chemi st s, Am. Soc. Clin. Investigation, Assn. Am. Physicians, Western Assn. Physicians (Ciba award 1988, Lasker award 1996). Home: 1421 Lake Rd Lake Forest IL 60045-1425

MURAD, JOHN LOUIS, clinical microbiology educator; b. Tyler, Tex., Dec. 15, 1932; s. Louis George and Ruby (Sawyer) M.; m. Sameera Hamra; children: John Nichols, Philip Louis, David Clay, Richard Andrew. BA, Austin Coll., 1956; MS, North Tex. State U., 1958; PhD, Tex. A&M U., 1965. Instr. biology Stephen F. Austin State U., Nacogdoches, 1959-61, Tex. A&M U., College Station, 1961-65; mem. faculty La. Tech. U., Ruston, 1965-88, asso. prof. zoology, 1967-70, prof., 1970-88, dir. rsch. and grad. studies, Coll. Life Scis., 1971-88, ret., 1988; prof. med. lab. scis. U. Tex. Southwestern Med. Ctr., Dallas, 1991—; safety mgmt. cons. Author: Laboratory Exercises in Zoology, 1967, The Laboratory in Biology, 1968, Zoology, 1971, Workbook in Zoology, 1975, Explorations in Zoology, 1980, 2d edit., 1984, Adventures in Zoology, 1989; contbr. articles to profl. jours. Served with M.C. AUS, 1953-55, Korea. U. Tex. Med. Br. rsch. fellow Galveston, 1958-59; NSF travel grantee, 1972; NATO regional sci. participant Germany, 1972; Sci. Info. Exch. fellow Gt. Britain, 1974. Mem. ASCP, AAAS, ASTM, AAUP, Am. Inst. Biol. Scis., Am. Soc. Microbiology, Southwestern Soc. Microbiology, La. Acad. Sci., Tex. Acad. Sci., N.Y. Acad. Sci., Helminthol. Soc. Washington, Soc. Nematologists, European Soc. Nematology, Masons, Shriners, Kiwanis, Sigma Xi. Presbyterian (elder). Home: 5724 Melshire Dr Dallas TX 75230-2116

MURAI, RENE VICENTE, lawyer; b. Havana, Cuba, Mar. 11, 1945; came to the U.S., 1960; s. Andres and Silvia (Muñiz) M.; m. Luisa Botifoll, June 12, 1970; 1 child, Elisa. BA, Brown U., 1966; JD cum laude, Columbia U., 1969. Bar: Fla. 1970, N.Y. 1972, U.S. Supreme Ct. 1977. Atty. Reginald Heber Smith Fellow Legal Svcs. Greater Miami, Fla., 1969-71; assoc. Willkie, Farr & Gallagher, N.Y.C., 1971-73; ptnr. Paul, Landy & Beiley, Miami, 1973-79; shareholder Murai, Wald, Biondo & Moreno, Miami, 1979—; bd. dirs. PanAm. Bank, Miami; dir. Cuban Am. Bar Assn., 1982-96, pres., 1985; vice chmn., lectr. Internat. Conf. for Lawyers of the Ams., 1982, chmn. and lectr., 1984; mem. panel grievance com. Fla. Bar, 1983-86. Mng. editor Columbia Law Rev., 1967-69. Bd. dirs., sec. Archtl. Club of Miami, 1978-86; bd. dirs. Dade Heritage Trust, 1979-82, Facts About Cuban Exiles, Inc., 1982—, pres., 1989, Legal Svcs. of Greater Miami, Inc., 1980-90, pres. 1986-88, ARC, 1984-90, exec. com., 1988-90, Mercy Hosp. Found., 1985-91, United Way, 1986-89, chmn. voluntary sector trust, Dade Cmty. Found., 1988-93, chair grants com., 1991-93; chmn. adminstrn. of justice com. Fla. Bar Found., 1996—, bd. dirs., 1991—, chmn. audit and fin. com., 1993—; mem. task force leadership Dade County Ptnrs. for Safe Neighborhoods, 1994-95, Code Enforcement Bd. City of Coral Gables, 1982-86, Bd. Adjustment, 1987-89, city mgr. selection com., 1987, charter rev. commn., 1980; trustee U. Miami, 1994-96. Mem. ABA, Cuban-Am. Bar Assn., Dade County Bar Assn. (dir. 1987-88), Greater Miami C. of C., Spain-U.S. C. of C. Democrat. Roman Catholic. Avocation: sports. Home: 3833 Alhambra Ct Coral Gables FL 33134 Office: Murai Wald Biondo & Moreno PA 25 SE 2nd Ave Ste 900 Miami FL 33131-1600

MURANAKA, HIDEO, artist, educator; b. Mitaka, Tokyo, Japan, Feb. 4, 1946; s. Nobukichi and Hisae M. BFA, Tokyo Nat. U. of Fine Arts, 1970, MFA, 1972. Calif. Community Coll.- Instr. Cred. Drawing accepted for The Pacific Coast States Collection from the v.p. house, Washington, 1980, Nat. Mus. Art, Bklyn. Mus., Achenbach Found., Calif. Palace of Legion of Hon., Yergeau-Musee Internat. d'Art (Can.). Mem. Democratic Nat. Comm., Wash., 1985—. Recipient second prize Iternat. Art Exhbn. Museo Hosio, Italy, 1984, V.J.'s Artist award Palm Springs Desert Mus., 1995; named to Hist. Preservation Am. Hall of Fame. Mem. Oakland Mus. Assn., The Fine Arts Mus. San Francisco, Lepidopterist's Soc. Avocations: collecting butterflies, music. Home: 179 Oak St #W San Francisco CA 94102

MURANE, WILLIAM EDWARD, lawyer; b. Denver, Mar. 4, 1933; s. Edward E. and Theodora (Wilson) M.; m. Rosemarie Palmerone, Mar. 26, 1960; children: Edward Wheelock, Peter Davenport, Alexander Phelps. AB, Dartmouth Coll., 1954; LLB, Stanford U., 1957. Bar: Wyo. 1957, Colo. 1958, Calif. 1958, D.C. 1978, U.S. Supreme Ct. 1977. Assoc. then ptnr. Holland & Hart, Denver, 1961-69; dep. gen. counsel U.S. Dept. Commerce, Washington, 1969-71; gen. counsel FDIC, Washington, 1971-72; ptnr. Holland & Hart, Denver, 1972—, chmn. litigation dept., 1986-90; pub. mem. Adminstrv. Conf. of the U.S., Washington, 1978-81. Bd. dirs. Ctr. for Law and Rsch., Denver, 1973-76, Acad. in the Wilderness, Denver, 1986—; trustee Colo. Symphony Orch., 1994—; mem. bd. visitors Stanford U. Law Sch. Capt. USAF, 1958-61. Fellow Am. Coll. Trial Lawyers; mem. ABA (ho of dels. 1991-96), U. Club, Cactus Club. Republican. Avocations: fishing, classical music. Office: Holland & Hart 555 17th St Ste 3200 Denver CO 80202-5555

MURASE, JIRO, lawyer; b. N.Y.C., May 16, 1928. B.B.A., CCNY, 1955; J.D., Georgetown U., 1958, LL.D. (hon.), 1982. Bar: D.C. 1958, N.Y. 1959. Sr. ptnr. Marks & Murase L.L.P., N.Y.C., 1971—; legal counsel Consulate Gen. of Japan; mem. Pres.'s Adv. Com. Trade Negotiations, 1980-82; mem. Trilateral Commn., 1985—; apptd. mem. World Trade Coun., 1984-94; adv. com. internat. investment, tech. and devel. Dept. State, 1975. Editorial bd.: Law and Policy in Internat. Bus. Trustee Asia Found., 1979-83, Japan Ctr. Internat. Exchange, Japanese Ednl. Inst. N.Y.; bd. dirs. Japan Soc., Japanese C. of C. in N.Y., Inc.; bd. regents Georgetown U.; adv. coun. Pace U., Internat. House Japan; pres. Japanese-Am. Assn. N.Y., Inc., 1996—. Recipient N.Y. Gov.'s citation for contbns. to internat. trade, 1982; named to Second Order of Sacred Treasure (Japan), 1989. Mem. ABA, Assn. of Bar of City of N.Y., N.Y. State Bar Assn., N.Y. County Lawyers Assn., Maritime Law Assn., Consular Law Soc., Fed. Bar Council, Am. Soc. Internat. Law, World Assn. Lawyers, Japanese-Am. Soc. Legal Studies, Am. Arbitration Assn., Lic. Execs. Soc., U.S. C. of C. Clubs: Nippon (dir.); Ardsley Country; N.Y. Athletic; Mid-Ocean (Bermuda). Office: Marks & Murase LLP 399 Park Ave New York NY 10022

MURASHIGE, ALLEN, defense analysis executive; b. Lihue, Hawaii, Mar. 20, 1946; s. Fred A. and Evelyn Y.T. M.; m. Rae Ann Sears, June 7, 1981; children: Lance, Danielle. BS in Aero. Engring., U. Washington, 1968; MS in Statistics/Ops. Rsch., U. Denver, 1973; postgrad. Program for Execs. in Nat. Security, Harvard U., 1989; postgrad., Fed. Exec. Inst., 1993, Brookings Inst. Leadership, 2000, 1996. Aero. engr. Air Force Western Test Range, Vandenberg AFB, Calif., 1968-70; aero. engr. Space & Missile Test Ctr., Vandenberg AFB, 1970-73, ops. analyst, 1973-77; ops. analyst Hdqrs. USAF in Europe, Ramstein AFB, Germany, 1977-84; chief current ops. div. Hdqrs. USAF in Europe, Ramstein AFB, 1985-87; sci., tech. advisor Air Force Studies and Analysis, Washington, 1987-95; U.S. rep. and com. chmn. NATO Adv. Group for Aero Rsch. & Devel., Paris, 1987—; mem. NATO Sci. and Tech. Coordinating Commn., 1994—; chief scientist air force modeling, simulation and analysis, 1995-96; chief scientist Air Force Command and Control, 1997—; mem. Joint Tech. Coord. Group Sr. Adv. Bd., 1989—; mem. Dept. of Def. Simulation Validation Sr. Steering Com., 1990—, Joint Test & Evaluation Tech. Adv. Bd., 1993—; bd. dirs. Air Force Incentive Awards Bd., Pentagon, Washington, 1987—; rep. Dept. of Def. C3I Test and Evaluation Steering Com., Pentagon, 1989-91, Dept. of Def. Modeling and Simulation Policy Group, 1990-94, Dept. of Def. Exec. Coun. for Modeling and Simulation, 1995—; sr. civilian rep. Air Force Sci. Adv. Bd., 1992-94, Def. Sci. Bd., 1996—; chmn. Air Force AOA Tech. Rev. Group, 1997—. Author tech. reports in field. Fellow Grad. Study in Ops. Rsch., 1972. Mem. AIAA, Mil. Ops. Rsch. Soc., Air Force Assn., Am. Def. Preparedness Assn., Internat. Platform Assn., Porsche Club of Am. Avocations: pvt. pilot, tennis, skiing. Office: USAF Modelling Simulation & Analysis Pentagon Washington DC 20330

MURASUGI, KUNIO, mathematician, educator; b. Tokyo, Mar. 25, 1929; s. Kiyoshi and Torae (Nakatani) M.; m. Yasue Kuwahara, Oct. 30, 1955; children—Chieko, Kumiko, Sachiho. B.Sc., Tokyo U. Edn., 1952, D.Sc., 1961. Research asso. Princeton (N.J.) U., 1962-64; asst. prof. U. Toronto, Ont., Can., 1964-66; asso. prof. U. Toronto, 1966-69, prof. dept. math., 1969-94; prof. emeritus, 1994—. Editor: Can. Jour. Math, 1969-71; assoc. editor: Jour. Knot Theory and its Ramification, 1992—; contbr. articles to profl. jours. Fellow Royal Soc. Can.; mem. Am. Math. Soc., Japanese Math. Soc. (Fall prize 1993). Anglican. Home: 611 Cummer Ave, Willowdale, ON

Canada M2K 2M5 Office: 100 Saint George St, Toronto, ON Canada M5S 1A1

MURATA, TADAO, engineering and computer science educator; b. Takayama, Gifu, Japan, June 26, 1938; came to U.S., 1962; s. Yonosuke and Ryu (Aomame) M.; m. Nellie Kit-Ha Shin, 1964; children: Patricia Emi, Theresa Terumi. B.S.E.E., Tokai U., 1962; M.S.E.E., U. Ill., 1964, Ph.D. in Elec. Engring., 1966. Research asst. U. Ill., Urbana, 1962-66; asst. prof. U. Ill. at Chgo., 1966-68, assoc. prof., 1970-76, prof., 1977—; assoc. prof. Tokai U., Tokyo, Japan, 1968-70; vis. prof. U. Calif., Berkeley, 1976-77; cons. Nat. Bur. Stds., Gaithersburg, Md., 9184-85; panel mem. NAS, Washington, 1981-82, 83-85; vis. scientist Nat. Ctr. For Sci. Rsch., France, 1981; guest rschr. Gesellschaft für Mathematik und Datenverarbeitung, Germany, 1979; Hitachi-Endowed prof. Osaka (Japan) U., 1993-94. Editor IEEE Trans. on Software Engring., 1986-92; assoc. editor Jour. of Cirs., Sysems and Computers, 1990—; contbr. articles to sci. and engring. jours. Recipient Sr. Univ. Scholar award U. Ill., 1990; dNSF grantee, 1978—, U.S.-Spain coop. research grantee, 1985-87. Fellow IEEE (golden core charter mem. IEEE Computer Soc., Donald G. Fink Prize award 1991); mem. Assn. Computing Machinery, Info. Processing Soc. Japan, European Assn. for Theoretical Computer Sci., Upsilon Pi Epsilon (hon.). Avocations: golf; travel. Office: U Ill Dept Elec Engring & Comp Sci 851 S Morgan St Chicago IL 60607-7042

MURAYAMA, MAKIO, biochemist; b. San Francisco, Aug. 10, 1912; s. Hakuyo and Namiye (Miyasaka) M.; children: Gibbs Soga, Alice Myra. B.A., U. Calif., Berkeley, 1938, M.A., 1940; Ph.D. (NIH fellow), U. Mich., 1953; ScD honoris causa, Open Internat. U., Sri Lanka, 1994. Rsch. biochemist Children's Hosp. of Mich., Detroit, 1943, 45-48, Bellevue Hosp., N.Y.C., 1943-45; Research biochemist Harper Hosp., Detroit, 1949-54; research fellow in chemistry Calif. Inst. Tech., Pasadena, 1954-56; research asso. in biochemistry Grad. Sch. Medicine, U. Pa., Phila., 1956-58; spl. research fellow Nat. Cancer Inst. at Cavendish Lab., Cambridge, Eng., 1958; sr. research biochemist NIH, Bethesda, Md., 1958-93. Author: (with Robert M. Nalbandian) Sickle Cell Hemoglobin, 1973; discovered DIPA (decompression-inducible platelet aggregation), 1975; discovered DIPA causes vascular occlusion in both acute mountain sickness and diver's syndrome. Fellow Am. Inst. Chemists; mem. AAAS, Am. Chem. Soc., Am. Soc. Biol. Chemists, Assn. Clin. Scientists, Undersea and Hyperbaric Med. Soc., Aerospace Med. Assn., Internat. Platform Assn., West African Soc. Pharmacology (hon.), N.Y. Acad. Sci., Sigma Xi. Achievements include patent for automatic amperometric titration apparatus; development of molecular mechanism of human red cell sickling and prevention of sickle cell crisis by oral prophylactic carbamide; discovery of decompression inducible platelet aggregation by means of simulation of decompression-inducible platelet aggregation of diving in frogs and mice that diver's disease and acute mountain sickness could be alleviated by piracetam and thymol, antiplatelet agents. Home: 5010 Benton Ave Bethesda MD 20814-2804

MURCH, WALTER SCOTT, director, writer, film editor, sound designer; b. N.Y.C., July 12, 1943; s. Walter Tandy and Katherine (Scott) M.; m. Muriel Ann Slater, Aug. 6, 1965; children: Walter, Beatrice, Carrie, Connie. BA, Johns Hopkins U., 1965. Ind. film editor, sound designer, 1969—. Sound recorder, supr. re-rec., film editor: (films) The Rainpeople, 1969, THX-1138, 1971, The Godfather, 1971, American Graffiti, 1973, The Conversation, 1974 (Best Sound award Brit. Acad. 1974, Best Editing award Brit. Acad. 1974, Acad. award nomination 1974), The Godfather Part II, 1974, Julia, 1977 (Acad. award nomination 1977), Apocalypse Now, 1979 (Acad. award 1979, Brit. Acad. award nomination), Dragonslayer, 1981, The Right Stuff, 1984, (writer, dir.) Return to Oz, 1985, Captain Eo, 1986, The Unbearable Lightness of Being, 1988, Ghost (Acad. award nomination), 1990, The Godfather Part III (Acad. award nomination), 1990, The Godfather Trilogy, 1991, House of Cards, 1993, Romeo is Bleeding, 1994, I Love Trouble, 1994, Crumb, 1995, First Knight, 1995, The English Patient, 1996; writer Black Stallion, THX 1138, Return to Oz, 1985. Mem. Writers Guild Am., Dirs. Guild Am., Acad. Motion Picture Arts and Scis. Home: 77 Bolinas Rd Bolinas CA 94924

MURCHAKE, JOHN, publishing executive; b. Washington, July 30, 1922; s. John Sr. and Mary Ann (Keretzman) M.; m. Mary Evelyn Graninger, June 15, 1946 (dec. Sept. 1989); children: Evelyn Ann, Stephen John. BA, George Washington U., 1961, MA, 1964. CPA, Md. Office mgr. Army Times Pub. Co., Washington, 1940-43, 46-47; subscription mgr. Kiplinger Washington Editors Inc., Washington, 1947-82; pres., CEO Co-Op New Issue Svc., Stuart, Fla., 1966—; pres. Jonev Orchids, Stuart, Fla., 1980—, J.M. and Assocs., Stuart, Fla., 1982—; pres., CEO Nat. Postal Forum, Washington, 1990-93; mem. adv. bd. Smithsonian Postal History Mus., 1993—; chmn. founder Met. Washington Postal Customer Coun., 1972-74, Treasure Coast Fla. Postal Customers Coun., 1994; industry chmn. Mailers Tech. Adv. Com., 1978-80. Editor, founder: (newsletter) The Postal Counselor, 1974, Information, 1981. Pres. Martin County Orchid Soc., Stuart, 1985-86, Port St. Lucie Orchid Soc., 1997—. 1st lt. USAF, 1943-46, ETO. Decorated Air medal with 4 clusters; recipient of 2 Disting. Service awards U.S. Postal Service, Washington, 1980. Mem. Dir. Mktg. Assn. (pres., founder 1979, Profl. of Yr. 1980, Disting. Svc. award 1980, chmn. Max Sackheim awards com. Fla. chpt. 1987), Fulfillment Mgmt. Assn. (Lee C. Williams award 1980, pres., founder Washington chpt. 1977-78, founder Fla. chpt. 1987, Hall of Fame award 1989). Republican. Methodist. Avocations: stamp collecting, raising orchids, public speaking. Home: 974 NW Pine Lake Dr Stuart FL 34994-9427 Office: JM & Assocs PO Box 83 Stuart FL 34995-0083

MURCHIE, EDWARD MICHAEL, accountant; b. N.Y.C., Apr. 21, 1947; s. Edward Thomas and Dorothy (Busk) M.; m. Karen M. Raftery, Aug. 26, 1967; children: David, Maureen, Carolyn. BS, Fordham U., Bronx, N.Y., 1968. CPA, N.Y. Staff acct. Price Waterhouse, N.Y.C., 1968-75; asst. contr. Eltra Corp., N.Y.C., 1975-78; v.p. fin. Eltra Corp., Morristown, N.J., 1981, Converse Rubber, Wilmington, Mass., 1979-80, Allied Corp: Allied Electronic Components Co., Morristown, 1982-84; sr. v.p., CFO Emery Air Freight Corp., Wilton, Conn., 1984-87; from sr. v.p., CFO to pres., COO Fairchild Industries, Inc., Chantilly, Va., 1987-89; pres., COO Vernitron Corp., N.Y.C., 1989-95; pres. Caledonia Capital Corp., Great Falls, Va., 1995-96; pres., COO EIT, Inc., Sterling, Va., 1997—. Chmn., South Brunswick Rank Levelling Bd., N.J., 1977-78; bd. dirs. Norwalk/Wilton chpt. ARC, 1985. Mem. AICPA. Republican. Roman Catholic. Office: EIT Inc 108 Carpenter Dr Sterling VA 20164-4422

MURCHISON, DAVID CLAUDIUS, lawyer; b. N.Y.C., Aug. 19, 1923; s. Claudius Temple and Constance (Waterman) M.; m. June Margaret Guilfoyle, Dec. 19, 1946; children: David Roderick, Brian, Courtney, Bradley, Stacy. A.A., George Washington U., 1947, J.D. with honors, 1949. Bar: D.C. 1949, Supreme Ct. 1955. Assoc. Dorr, Hand & Dawson, N.Y.C., 1949-50; founding ptnr. Howrey & Simon, Washington, 1956-90; of counsel Howrey & Simon, 1990—; legal asst. under sec. army, 1949-51; counsel motor vehicle, textile, aircraft, ordinance and shipbldg. divsns. Nat. Prodn. Authority, 1951-52; assoc. gen. counsel Small Def. Plants Adminstrn., 1952-53; legal adv. and asst. to chmn. FTC, 1953-55. Chmn. So. Africa Wildlife Trust. With AUS, 1943-45, ETO. Mem. ABA (chmn. com. internat. restrictive bus. practices sect. antitrust law 1954-55, sect. adminstrv. law, sect. litigation), FBA, D.C. Bar Assn., N.Y. State Bar Assn., Met. Club, Chevy Chase Club, Talbot Country Club, Order of Coif. Republican. Office: 1299 Pennsylvania Ave NW Washington DC 20004-2402

MURCHISON, DAVID RODERICK, lawyer; b. Washington, May 28, 1948; s. David Claudius and June Margaret (Guilfoyle) M.; m. Kathy Ann Kohn, Mar. 15, 1981; children: David Christopher, Benjamin Michael. BA cum laude, Princeton U., 1970; JD, Georgetown U., 1975. Bar: D.C. 1975, Fla. 1993. Legal asst. to vice chmn. CAB, Washington, 1975-76, enforcement atty., 1976-77; sr. atty. Air Transport Assn., Washington, 1977-80, asst. v.p., sec., 1981-85; sr. assoc. Zuckert, Scoutt and Rasenberger, Washington, 1980-81; v.p., asst. gen. counsel Piedmont Aviation, Inc., Winston-Salem, N.C., 1985-88; v.p., gen. counsel, sec. Braniff, Inc., Dallas, 1988-89; chief exec. officer Braniff, Inc., Orlando, 1990-94; fed. adminstrv. law judge Office of Hearings and Appeals, Charleston, W.Va., 1994-96; chief adminstrv. law judge Office of Hearings and Appeals, Mobile, Ala., 1996—; lectr. continuing legal edn. program Wake Forest U., Winston-Salem, 1988. Contbr. articles to legal jours. Lt. USNR, 1970-72. Mem. ABA, Met. Club Washington. Republican. Roman Catholic. Office: Office Hearings and Appeals 3605 Springhill Bus Park Mobile AL 36608

MURDOCH, BERNARD CONSTANTINE, psychology educator; b. Greensboro, N.C., Dec. 5, 1917; s. Homer Odell and Hilma Caroline (Lang) M.; m. Martha Grace Hood, June 29, 1946; children: Norma, Constance, Joyce, Diana. B.S., Appalachian State Tchrs. Coll., 1938; Ed.M., U. of Cincinnati, 1939; Ph.D., Duke, 1942; postgrad., N.Y. U., 1942-43. Licensed applied psychologist, Ga. Math. critic tchr. Appalachian State Tchrs. Coll. demonstration sch., 1938; math. and sci. tchr. Lexington (N.C.) High Sch., 1939-40; sci. tchr. Harding High Sch., Charlotte, N.C., 1945-46; also dir. Guidance and Testing Bur., Vets. Info. Center, Charlotte; prof. edn. and psychology Presbyn. Coll., Clinton, S.C., 1946-48; acad. dean Presbyn. Coll., 1947-48; also extension prof. edn. U. S.C., 1946-48; mem. research staff Am. Council on Edn., Office of Naval Rsch., Washington, 1948-50; dean Muskingum Coll., New Concord, Ohio, 1950-54; prof., head psychology dept. Wesleyan Coll., Macon, Ga., 1954-82, prof. emeritus, 1982—; chmn. dept. behavioral scis. Wesleyan Coll., 1973-82, also dir. testing.; pres. Fore(In)Sight Found., 1991—. Author: Consistency of Test Responses, 1942, Love and Problems of Living, 1992; co-author: The Production of Doctorates in the Sciences, 1936-48; contbr. to sci., ednl. and religious publs. Served to capt. USAAF, 1942-45. Fellow AAAS; mem. APA (life), Southeastern Psychol. Assn., Ga. Psychol. Assn. (dir., pres. 1969-70), Ga. Mental Health Assn. (dir.), NEA, Ga. Mental Health Council (psychology rep. 1973-74), Ga. State Bd. Examiners Psychologists (pres. 1974-75), Am. Ednl. Rsch. Assn., Masons,. Presbyterian. Home: 4966 Zebulon Rd Macon GA 31210-4405 *Opportunities vary widely, and the necessary perception to capitalize on such also is a distinct variable. Those of us who have achieved a measure of "success" in vocational or other ways must feel very humble as we recognize our good fortune. We have not only had opportunities come before us, but we were able to perceive them in such a way as to accomplish whatever recognition has been ours. Millions have not been so fortunate.*

MURDOCH, DAVID ARMOR, lawyer; b. Pitts., May 30, 1942; s. Armor M. and N. Edna (Jones) M.; m. Joan Wilkie, Mar. 9, 1974; children: Christina, Timothy, Deborah. AB magna cum laude, Harvard U., 1964, LLB, 1967. Bar: Pa. 1967, U.S. Dist. Ct. (we. dist.) Pa. 1967, U.S. Ct. Mil. Appeals 1968, U.S. Supreme Ct. 1990, U.S. Ct. Appeals (3d cir.) 1991. Assoc. Kirkpatrick & Lockhart, LLP, Pitts., 1971-78, ptnr., 1978—. Co-author: Business Workouts Manual. Vice pres., bd. dirs. Avonworth Sch. Dist., 1977-83; chmn. bd. dirs. Pitts. Expt., 1980-82, mem. 1988-93, chmn., 1989-90; mem. Pa. Housing Fin. Agy., 1981-88, vice chmn., 1983-87; alt. del. Rep. Nat. Conv., 1980; elder The Presbyn. Ch. of Sewickley, 1986-92; past pres. Harvard Law Sch. Assn. W. Pa.; bd. advisors Geneva Coll., 1993-94, trustee, 1994-97; trustee Sewickley Pub. Libr., 1994—, World Learning, Inc., 1995—; dir. Allegheny County Libr. Assn., 1994-96; chair Czech Working Group, Presbyn. Ch. USA, 1995—; bd. visitors U. Ctr. for Internat. Studies, U. Pitts., 1996—; bd. advisors The Ctr. for Bus., Religion, and Professions, Pitts. Theol. Sem., 1997—. Capt. U.S. Army, 1968-71. Fellow Am. Coll. Bankruptcy, Am. Bar Found.; mem. ABA (mem. bus. bankruptcy com., chmn. subcom. on bankruptcy coms., trust indentures and claims trading 1991-96 Office: Kirkpatrick & Lockhart LLP 1500 Oliver Bldg Pittsburgh PA 15222-2404

MURDOCH, LAWRENCE CORLIES, JR., retired banker, economist; b. Phila., June 3, 1926; s. Lawrence C. and Barbara (Boyd) M.; children: Lawrence C. III, Anne G.; m. 2d Eleanor M. Egan, June 16, 1970. B.S. Wharton Sch., U. Pa. in Econs., 1948; M.B.A., Wharton Sch., U. Pa., 1956. With Fed. Res. Bank Phila., 1954-92; ret., 1992; bd. dirs. Cliveden Inc., 1981, Fort Mifflin, 1990. Contbr. articles to consumer and monetary publs.; producer documentary films; spokesman (radio and TV). Lt. (j.g.) USN, 1948-54. Mem. Soc. Cin. (pres. 1990-93), Little Egg Harbor Yacht Club (Beach Haven, N.J.), Beta Gamma Sigma, Zeta Psi. Home: 115 Hilltop Rd Philadelphia PA 19118-3737

MURDOCH, (KEITH) RUPERT, publisher; b. Melbourne, Australia, Mar. 11, 1931; came to U.S., 1974, naturalized, 1985; s. Keith and Elisabeth Joy (Greene) M.; m. Anna Maria Torv, Apr. 28, 1967; children: Prudence, Elisabeth, Lachlan, James. M.A., Worcester Coll., Oxford, Eng., 1953. Chmn. News Am. Pub. Inc. (pub. London Times), 1974—, News Internat., Ltd. Group, London; mng. dir. News Ltd. Group & Associated Cos., Australia; chmn. 20th Century Fox Prodns., 1985—, William Collins PLC, Glasgow, 1989—; owner, pub. numerous newspapers, mags. and TV stas. in U.S.A., Australia, U.K., Asia, 1983—; Chmn., CEO, News Corp. Ltd., Sydney, Australia, 1991—. Office: The News Corp Limited, 2 Holt St, Surry Hills Sydney NSW 2010, Australia*

MURDOCK, CHARLES WILLIAM, lawyer, educator; b. Chgo., Feb. 10, 1935; s. Charles C. and Lucille Marie (Tracy) M.; m. Mary Margaret Hennessy, May 25, 1963; children: Kathleen, Michael, Kevin, Sean. BSChemE, Ill. Inst. Tech., 1956; JD cum laude, Loyola U., Chgo., 1963. Bar: Ill. 1963, Ind. 1971. Asst. prof. law DePaul U., 1968-69; assoc. prof. law U. Notre Dame, 1969-75; prof., dean Law Sch. Loyola U., Chgo., 1975-83, 86—; dep. atty. gen. State of Ill., Chgo., 1983-86; of counsel Chadwell & Kayser, Ltd., 1986-89; vis. prof. U. Calif., 1974; cons. Pay Bd., summer 1972, SEC, summer 1973; co-founder Loyola U. Family Bus. Program; arbitrator Chgo. Bd. Options Exch., Nat. Assn. Securities Dealers, N.Y. Stock Exch., Am. Arbitration Assn.; co-founder, mem. exec. com. Loyola Family Bus. Ctr., 1990—. Author: Business Organizations, 2 vols., 1996; editor: Illinois Business Corporation Act Annotated, 2 vols., 1975; tech. editor The Business Lawyer, 1989-90. Chmn. St. Joseph County (Ind.) Air Pollution Control Bd., 1971; bd. dirs. Nat. Center for Law and the Handicapped, 1973-75, Minority Venture Capital Inc., 1973-75. Capt. USMCR. Mem. ABA, Ill. Bar Assn. (cert. of award for continuing legal edn.), Chgo. Bar Assn. (cert. of award for continuing legal edn., bd. mgrs. 1976-78), Ill. Inst. Continuing Legal Edn. (adv. com). Roman Catholic. Home: 2126 Thornwood Ave Wilmette IL 60091-1452 Office: Loyola U Sch Law 1 E Pearson St Chicago IL 60611-2055

MURDOCK, DAVID H., diversified company executive; b. Kansas City, Apr. 10, 1923; m. Maria Ferrer, Apr., 1992. LLD (hon.), Pepperdine U., 1978; LHD (hon.), U. Nebr., 1984, Hawaii Loa Coll., 1989. Sole proprietor, chmn., chief exec. officer Pacific Holding Co., L.A.; chmn., chief exec. officer Dole Food Co. (formerly Castle & Cooke, Inc.), L.A., 1985—, also bd. dirs. Trustee Asia Soc., N.Y.C., L.A.; founder, bd. dirs. Found. for Advanced Brain Studies, L.A.; bd. visitors UCLA Grad. Sch. Mgmt.;bd. govs. Performing Arts Coun. of Music Ctr., L.A.; bd. govs. East-West Ctr., L.A.; patron Met. Opera, N.Y.C. With USAAC, 1943-45. Mem. Regency Club (founder, pres.) Bel-Air Bay Country Club, Sherwood Country Club (founder, pres.), Met. Club (N.Y.C.). Office: Dole Food Co Inc 31355 Oak Crest Dr Westlake Vlg CA 91361-4633 also: Pacific Holding Co 10900 Wilshire Blvd Ste 1600 Los Angeles CA 90024-6535*

MURDOCK, MARY-ELIZABETH, history educator; b. Boston, Jan. 4, 1930; d. Lester Joseph and Elizabeth Rowe (Collingwood) M. A.B., Tufts U., 1952; A.M., Boston U., 1958; Ph.D., Brown U., 1962; S.M., Simmons Coll., 1970; cert. mgmt. inst. women in higher edn., Wellesley Coll., 1985; cert. master gardener, U. Mass., 1988. Tchr. Nat. Cathedral Sch., Washington, 1954-57; assoc. prof. Trenton State Coll, N.J., 1962-66, U. R.I., Kingston, 1966-69; archivist, dir. Sophia Smith collection Smith Coll., Northampton, Mass., 1970-84, lectr. history, 1973-86, instr. Southeast Asian ESL program, 1986-88; guest lectr. colls. and univs., 1986—; cons. N.Y.C. YWCA, 1974-75, HEN, 1976-86, Greenfield Cmty. Coll., Mass., 1983-86, Ednl. Testing Svc., Princeton, N.J., 1985—; faculty cons. Nat. Evaluation Sys., Amherst, Mass., 1984-92; bd. reviewers Hist. Jour. Mass., 1985-88; adv. bd. Ctr. Am. Studies, Concord, Mass., 1985-88; indexer Liberty Party newspaper (1845-48). Author articles, monographs, analytical catalogs. Mem. Am. Studies Assn., New Eng. Am. Studies Assn., Orgn. Am. Historians (state membership chmn. 1980-88), Am. Assn. State and Local History, Hist. Deerfield Inc., Hist. Northampton, Nat. Trust for Hist. Preservation, Phi Alpha Theta. Avocations: choral singing, piano, painting, photography, gardening.

MURDOCK, PAMELA ERVILLA, travel and advertising company executive, b. Los Angeles, Dec. 3, 1940; d. John James and Chloe Conger (Keefe) M.; children: Cheryl, Kim. BA, U. Colo., 1962. Pres., Dolphin Travel, Denver, 1972-87; owner, pres. Mile Hi Tours, Denver, 1973—, MH Internat., 1987—, Mile-Hi Advt. Agy., 1986—. Bd. dirs. Rocky Mountain chpt. Juvenile Diabetes Found. Internat. Named Wholesaler of Yr., Las Vegas Conv. and Visitors Authority, 1984. Recipient Leadership award Nat. Multiple Sclerosis Soc., 1996. Mem. NAFE, Am. Soc. Travel Agts., Nat. Fedn. Independent Businessmen. Republican. Home: 5565 E Vassar Ave Denver CO 80222-6239 Office: Mile Hi Tours Inc 2160 S Clermont St Denver CO 80222-5007

MURDOCK, ROBERT MCCLELLAN, military officer; b. Montclair, N.J., Sept. 27, 1947; s. George Rutherford and Mary (Newell) M.; m. Ann Marie Wingo, Aug. 20, 1977; 1 child, Kristen. BA, Davis and Elkins Coll., 1969; MA, Ctrl. Mich. U., 1979; postgrad., Armed Forces Staff Coll., 1983, U.S. Army War Coll., 1988. Lic. command pilot, USAF. Aide, chief of staff The Pentagon, Washington, 1980-82; ops. officer 22 Airlift Squadron, Travis AFB, Calif., 1984, comdr., 1985-87; dep. inspector gen. Hdqs. European Command, Stuttgart, Germany, 1988-90; vice comdr. 436 Airlift Wing, Dover AFB, Del., 1990-92; nat. def. fellow The Atlantic Coun., Washington, 1992-93; comdr. Air Force Inspection Agy., Kirtland AFB, N.Mex., 1993-96; dep. U.S. Mil. Rep. to NATO Brussels, Belgium, 1996—. Decorated D.F.C., Air medal, Legion of Merit. Mem. Air Force Assn., The Airlift and Tanker Assn., Order of Daedalians. Methodist. Avocations: skiing, golf, travel. Address: US Mil/Del PSC 80 Box 200 APO AE 09724 Office: HQ NATO, Brussels Belgium

MURDOCK, ROBERT MEAD, art consultant, curator; b. N.Y.C., Dec. 18, 1941; s. Robert Davidson and Elizabeth Brundage (Mead) M.; m. Ellen Rebecca Olson, Apr. 22, 1967 (div.); children: Alison Mead, Anne Davidson; m. Deborah C. Ryan, Apr. 28, 1995. B.A., Trinity Coll., Conn., 1963; M.A., Yale U., 1965; student, Mus. Mgmt. Inst., U. Calif., Berkeley, 1980. Ford Found. intern Walker Art Center, Mpls., 1965-67; curator Albright-Knox Art Gallery, Buffalo, 1967-70; curator contemporary art Dallas Mus. Fine Arts, 1970-78; dir. Grand Rapids (Mich.) Art Mus., 1978-83; chief curator Walker Art Ctr., Mpls., 1983-85; program dir. IBM Gallery of Sci. and Art, N.Y.C., 1985-87, 90-93; dir. exhbns. Am. Fedn. Arts, N.Y.C., 1987-88; panelist, cons. Nat. Endowment for Arts, 1974-90. Author: (with others) Tyler Graphics: The Extended Image, 1987, A Gallery of Modern Art, 1994, Paris Modern, The Swedish Ballet 1920-1925, 1995; contbr. articles on David Novros, William Conlon, 1985, Bill Freeland, 1989, Nassos Daphnis, 1990; exhbn. catalogues Early 20th Century Art from Midwestern Muesums, 1981, Berlin/Hanover: The 1920's, 1977. Nat. Endowment for Arts fellow, 1973. Home: 202 1st Ave #14 New York NY 10009-3726

MURDOCK, STUART LAIRD, banker, investment adviser; b. Hackensack, N.J., July 18, 1926; s. Charles Watson and Mary-Evelyn (Mehrhof) M.; m. Lois Maura Anderson, Aug. 12, 1950; 1 dau., Susan Lynn. AB, Yale U., 1949; MBA, STanford U., 1951. Security analyst Bank of N.Y., 1952-53; portfolio mgr. Brown Bros. Harriman & Co., N.Y.C., 1954-56; trust investment officer United Mo. Bank Kansas City N/A, 1957-62, v.p., 1963-66, sr. v.p., sr. trust investment officer, 1967-70, exec. v.p., sr. trust investment officer, 1971-94. Retired marshal City of Countryside, Kans., 1968-93; past mem. fin. adv. com. to bd. trustees Pub. Sch. Retirement Sys. Kansas City; trustee Kans. Pub. Employees Retirement Sys.; adv. dir., past pres. Friends of the Zoo; bd. dirs. Youth Symphony of Kansas City. With U.S. Army, 1945-46. Mem. Kansas City Soc. Fin. Analysts (past pres.), Inst. Chartered Fin. Analysts, Fin. Analysts Fedn., C. of C., Yale Club (past pres.), Saddle and Sirloin Club (past pres.), Mercury Club, Desert Caballeros, Shriners. Home: 4613 W 113th Ter Leawood KS 66211-1728 Office: care United Mo Bank Kans 7109 W 80th St Overland Park KS 66204-3716

MURDOLO, FRANK JOSEPH, pharmaceutical company executive; b. Summit, N.J., Nov. 21, 1946; s. Joseph and Rose Murdolo; m. Nancy Lynn Vinci, Jan. 25, 1970; children: Kimberly L., Tracy L., Christy L. BS in Econs./Fin., Fairleigh Dickinson U., Madison, N.J., 1977, postgrad., 1978-79. Mgr. fin. planning Monroe Bus. Sys., Morris Plains, N.J., 1970-77; sr. fin. analyst Schering-Plough Rsch., Kenilworth, N.J., 1977-79; mgr. budgets & analysis Schering-Plough Corp., Madison, N.J., 1979-83, dir. fin. reporting, 1987-91, dir. investor rels., 1991-97; mgr. capital planning Schering-Plough Internat., Kenilworth, N.J., 1983-87; dir. fin. reporting Schering-Plough Corp., Madison, N.J., 1987-91; v.p., dir. investor rels. Glaxo Wellcome, plc, 1997—, Gloxo Wellcome, PLC, London, England, 1997—; lectr. MBA program for investor rels. Fairleigh Dickinson U., Madison, N.J., 1993—; exec. advisor exec. scholars program Fairleigh Dickinson U., Madison, N.J., 1993-97. Mem. Nat. Investor Rels. Inst. (v.p. and treas. N.Y.C. chpt.), Inst. Mgmt. Accts., Mfg. Alliance Investor Rels. Coun. II. Avocation: bicycling. Office: Glaxo Wellcome plc 499 Park Ave New York NY 10022-1240

MUREN, DENNIS E., visual effects director; b. Glendale, Calif., Nov. 1, 1946; s. Elmer Ernest and Charline Louise (Clayton) M.; m. Zara Pinfold, Aug. 29, 1981; children: Gregory, Gwendolen. AA, Pasadena (Calif.) City Coll., 1966; student, Calif. State U., L.A. Freelance spl. effects expert, 1968-75; camera operator Cascade of Calif., Hollywood, 1975-76; visual effects dir. photography Indsl. Light & Magic, San Rafael, Calif., 1976-80, visual effects dir., 1980—; guest speaker Berlin Film Festival, UCLA, Film Dept., U. Calif. Berkeley Film Series, Liverpool (Eng.) U. Film Program, Mill Valley Film Festival Program, Siggraph '86, Siggraph '87, Am. Film Inst., Portland Creative Conf. '89. Cameraman, photographer various films including Star Wars, 1977, Close Encounters of the Third Kind, 1977, Battlestar Galactica, 1978, The Empire Strikes Back, 1980 (Oscar award); visual effects supr. films include Dragonslayer, 1981 (Oscar nomination), ET: The Extraterrestrial, 1982 (Oscar award), Return of the Jedi, 1983 (Oscar award, Brit. Acad. of Film and TV award), Indiana Jones and the Temple of Doom, 1984 (Oscar award, Brit. Acad. of Film and TV award), Young Sherlock Holmes, 1985 (Oscar nomination), Captain Eo, 1986, Star Tours, 1986, Innerspace, 1987 (Oscar award), Empire of the Sun, 1987, Willow, 1988 (Oscar nomination), Ghostbusters II, 1989, The Abyss, 1989 (Oscar award), Terminator 2, 1991 (Oscar award, Brit. Film and TV award), Jurassic Park, 1993 (Oscar award, Brit. Film and TV award), Casper, 1995; effects supr. Jurassic Park-The Lost World, 1997; creative advisor Twister, 1996, Mission Impossible, 1996; visual effects supr. (TV program) Caravan of Courage (Emmy award); creative advisor Twister, 1995, Mission Impossible, 1995, Jurassic Park: The Lost World, 1997. Academy Scientific/Technical Award for the development of a Motion Picture Figure Mover for animation photography, 1981. Mem. Am. Soc. Cinematographers, Acad. Motion Picture Arts and Scis.

MURIAN, RICHARD MILLER, book company executive; b. East St. Louis, Ill., Sept. 17, 1937; s. Richard Miller Jr. and Margaret Keyes (Gregory) M.; m. Judith Lee, Aug. 11, 1961 (dec. Apr. 1992); 1 child, Jennifer Ann. BA, U. Calif., Davis, 1969; MLS, U. Calif., Berkeley, 1972; MA, Calif. State U., Sacramento, 1975; MDiv, Trinity Evang., 1977. Cert. history instr., libr. sci. instr., Calif. History reader Calif. State U., Sacramento, 1965-66; history reader U. Calif., Davis, 1966-68, philosophy rschr., 1968-69; bibliographer Argus Books, Sacramento, 1970-71; rsch. dir. Nat. Judicial Coll., Reno, 1971-72; libr. Calif. State U., Sacramento, 1972-76; tv talk show host Richard Murian Show, L.A., 1979-80; pres. Alcuin Books, Ltd., Phoenix, 1981—; bd. dirs. Guild of Ariz. Antiquarian Books; pres. East Valley Assn. Evangs., Mesa, Ariz., 1984-86; cons. Ariz. Hist. Soc., 1993—. Contbr. articles to profl. jours. Active U. Calif. Riverside Libr., 1981-83, KAET (PBS), 1988—, Ariz. State U., 1989—. Recipient Sidney B. Mitchell fellowship U. Calif., Berkeley, 1971. Mem. Am. Assn. Mus., Ariz. Preservation Found., Grand Canyon Nature Assn., Internat. Platform Assn., Ariz. Publ. Book Assn. (awards com.), Phi Kappa Phi. Democrat. Presbyterian. Avocations: fgn. films, jazz. Office: Alcuin Books Ltd 115 W Camelback Rd Phoenix AZ 85013-2519

MURILLO, VELDA JEAN, social worker, counselor; b. Miller, S.D., Dec. 8, 1943; d. Royal Gerald and Marion Elizabeth (Porter) Matson; m. Daniel John Murillo, June 25, 1967 (div. Dec. 1987); 1 child, Damon Michael. BS, S.D. State U., 1965; MA, Calif. State U., Bakersfield, 1980. Cert. marriage, family and child counselor. Social worker adult svcs. Kern County Dept. Welfare, Bakersfield, 1965-78, social worker child protective svcs., 1978-84; asst. coord. sexual abuse program Kern County Dist. Atty., Bakersfield, 1985-91, coord. sexual abuse program, 1991—; Mem. Calif. Sexual Assault Investigators, 1982-84, Kern Child Abuse Prevention Coun., Bakersfield,

1982-84; co-developer, presenter Children's Self Help Project, Bakersfield, 1982-87; cons. mem. Sexual Assault Adv. Com., Bakersfield, 1991-96. Democrat. Avocations: spiritual healing, travel, metaphysical pursuits, Reiki (master). Office: Kern County Dist Atty 1215 Truxtun Ave Bakersfield CA 93301-4619

MURILLO-ROHDE, ILDAURA MARIA, marriage and family therapist, consultant, educator, dean; b. Garachine, Panama; came to U.S., 1945; d. Amalio Murillo and Ana E. (Diaz) de Murillo; m. Erling Rohde, Sept. 19, 1959. BS, Columbia U., 1951, MA, 1953, MEd, 1969; PhD, NYU, 1971; hon. diploma, Escuela Nat. de Enfermeria, Guatemala, 1964; diploma naturopatia, Centro Estudios Naturista, Barcelona, Spain, 1992. RN; lic. marriage and family therapist, N.J.; cert. mental health-psychiat. nursing, ANA; lic. sex. therapist, N.J. Instr., supr. Bellevue Psychiat. Hosp., N.Y.C., 1950-54; asst. dir., dir. psychiat. div. Wayne County Gen. Hosp., Eloise, Mich., 1954-56; chief nurse psychiat. div. Elmhurst Gen. Hosp., Queens, N.Y., 1956-58, Met. Hosp. Med. Ctr., N.Y.C., 1961-63; psychiat. cons. to govt. of Guatemala WHO, UN, Guatemala, 1963-64; assoc. prof., chmn. psychiat. dept. N.Y. Med. Coll. Grad. Sch. Nursing, N.Y.C., 1964-69; dir. mental health-psychiatry, asst. prof NYU, N.Y.C., 1970-72; assoc. prof. Hostos Coll., CUNY, N.Y.C., 1972-76; assoc. dean. acad. affairs U. Wash., Seattle, 1976-81; prof., dean Coll. of Nursing SUNY, Downstate Med. Ctr., Bklyn., 1981-85; dean and prof. emeritus SUNY, Bklyn., 1985—; bd. dirs. Puerto Rican Family Inst., N.Y.C., 1983—; dir. Latin Am. Oncological Nurses Fuld Fellowships, 1989-90; psychiat. cons. Sch. Nursing, U. Antioquia, Medellin, Colombia, 1972-73, WHO; psychiat./rsch. cons. for master program Sch. Nursing, U. Panama, Project Hope, 1986. Editor: National Directory of Hispanic Nurses, 1981, 2d edit., 1986, 3d edit., 1994; contbr. numerous articles to profl. nat. and internat. jours., chpts. to books in field. Mem. Wash. State adv. com. U.S. Commn. on Civil Rights, Seattle, 1971-81; nat. adv. com. White House Conf. on Families, Washington, 1979-81; pres. King County Health Planning Council, Seattle, 1979-81; exec. com. Puget Sound Health Systems Agy., Seattle, 1979-81; mem. Mosby Consumer Health's Hispanic adv. bd. 1996. Univ. Honors scholar NYU, 1972; named Citizen of the Day, Radio Sta. KIXI and N.W. Airlines, Seattle, 1979, Disting. lectr. Sigma Theta Tau, 1988-89, Woman of Yr., N.Y. Gotham Club Bus. and Profl. Women, 1989; recipient 1st Nat. Intercultural Nursing award Coun. of Intercultural Nursing, ANA, New Orleans, 1984, Women's Honors in Pub. Svc. award Minority Fellowship Programs and Cabinet Human Rights, ANA, 1986, Disting. Alumna award Divsn. Nursing, NYU Alumni Assn., 1989, 1st Nat. Dr. Hildegard Peplau award for outstanding svcs. in mental health, psychiat. nursing, edn., rsch. and practice, Las Vegas conv. ANA, 1992, Practice award Tchrs. Coll., Columbia U. Nursing Edn. Alumni, 1994; designated Living Legend for leadership in practice, edn. and rsch. Am. Acad. Nursing, 1994. Fellow Am. Assn. Marriage and Family Therapy; mem. ANA (affirmative action task force 1974-84, commn. human rights, cabinet human rights, rep. ANA at ICN Cong. Tokyo 1977, spokesperson Nat. Health Ins., conceived and designed Coun. Intercultural Nursing), Am. Orthopsychiat. Assn. (bd. dirs. 1976-79, treas. 1986-89, Presdl. nominee 1980, 93), N.Y. Ass. Marriage and Family Therapy (pres. 1973-76), Nat. Assn. Hispanic Nurses (founder, 1st pres. 1976-80), Internat. Fedn. Bus. and Profl. Women (UN rep. to UNICEF London 1987—, del. to World UN Summit for Children N.Y.C. 1990, UN N.Y. Com. for Internat. Yr. of Family 1994), Am. Rsch. Inst. (dep. govt. 1987), NYU Club, Gotham Bus. and Profl. Women's Club. Democrat. Avocations: travel, reading, music, stamp collecting, skiing. Home: 300 W 108th St Apt 12A New York NY 10025-2704 Office: SUNY Bklyn Coll Nursing Box 22 450 Clarkson Ave Brooklyn NY 11203-2012

MURIS, TIMOTHY JOSEPH, law educator; b. Massillon, Ohio, Nov. 18, 1949; s. George William and Louise (Hood) M.; m. Susan Sexton, Aug. 10, 1974; children—Matthew Allen, Paul Austin. B.A., San Diego State U., 1971; J.D., UCLA, 1974. Bar: Calif. 1974, U.S. Supreme Ct. 1983. Asst. to dir. policy planning and evaluation FTC, Washington, 1974-76, dir. Bur. Consumer Protection, 1981-83, dir. Bur. Competition, 1983-85; exec. assoc. dir. Office Mgmt. and Budget, Washington, 1985-88, cons., 1988-89; law and econs. fellow U. Chgo. Law Sch., 1979-80; asst. prof. antitrust and consumer law U. Miami Law Sch. and Law Econs. Ctr., Fla., 1976-79, assoc. prof., 1979-81, prof., 1981-83; Found. prof. law George Mason U., Va., 1988—; dep. counsel Presdl. Task Force on Regulatory Relief, Washington, 1981; cons. Coun. on Wage and Price Stability, Washington, 1981; mem. Nat. Issues Forum, Brookings Inst., 1986-88; mem. adv. bd. Anti-Trust and Trade Regulation Report, 1990—. Editor: The Federal Trade Commission Since 1970: Regulation and Bureaucratic Behavior, 1981. Mem. Reagan-Bush transition team for FTC, Washington, 1980; sr. advisor Bush-Quayle transition team, 1988-89. Am. Bar Found. affiliated scholar, 1979. Mem. ABA (antitrust law spl. com. to study role of FTC 1988-89), Calif. Bar Assn., Order of Coif. Office: George Mason U Sch Law 3401 Fairfax Dr Arlington VA 22201-4411

MURKISON, EUGENE COX, business educator; b. Donalsonville, Ga., July 2, 1936; s. Jeff and Ollie Mae (Shores) M.; m. Marilyn Louise Adams, July 3, 1965; children: James, David, Jennifer. Grad., U.S. Army JFK Spl. Warfare Sc., 1967, U.S. Naval War Coll., 1972, U.S. Army Command/Staff Coll., 1974; BSA, U. Ga., 1959; MBA, U. Rochester, 1970; PhD, U. Mo., 1986. Surveyor USDA, Donalsonville, Ga., 1956-59; commd. 2d lt. U.S. Army, 1959, advanced through grades to lt. col., 1974; inf. bn. leader U.S. Army, Vietnam, 1967-68; mechanized comdr. (G-3), ops. officer Brigade Exec. Officer, Korea, Europe and U.S., 1968-70; prof. leadership & psychology West Point, N.Y., 1970-73; ops. officer (J-3) Office of Chmn. Joint Chiefs of Staff, Washington, 1974-77; prof. mil. sci. and leadership Kemper Mil. Coll., 1977-81; ret. U.S. Army, 1981; instr. U. Mo., Columbia, 1981-84; asst. prof. Ga. So. U., Stateboro, 1984-89, assoc. prof., 1989-94, prof., 1995—; vis. prof. mgmt. and bus. U. Tirgoviste, Romania, 1994, 95, 96; vis. prof. human resource mgmt. Tech. U. Romania, Cluj-Napoca, 1995, 96. Contbr. numerous articles to profl. jours., chpts. to books in field. V.p. Optimist Club, 1993-94, dir., 1993, 96-97, v.p., 1994-95; trustee Pittman Pk. Meth. Ch., Statesboro, 1992—, chmn., trustee, 1995-96. Recipient Bronze Star medal with oak leaf cluster, Devel. award Ga. So. U., 1990, Teaching award U. Mo., 1983, Albert Burke Rsch. award, 1992; grantee IREX, 1994, SOROS, 1995, 96. Mem. VFW, Inst. Mgmt. Sci., So. Mgmt. Assn., Inst. for Info. and Mgmt. Sci., Internat. Acad. Bus. (program chair 1994, 95), Acad. Mgmt., Bus. History Conf., Newcomen Soc., Blue Key, Scabbard & Blade, Beta Gamma Sigma, Alpha Zeta. Republican. Avocations: bus. history, mil history, tomato prodn., hiking, boating. Office: Ga So U Coll Bus Adminstrn Statesboro GA 30460-8152

MURKOWSKI, FRANK HUGHES, senator; b. Seattle, Mar. 28, 1933; s. Frank Michael and Helen (Hughes) M.; m. Nancy R. Gore, Aug. 28, 1954; children: Carol Victoria Murkowski Sturgulewski, Lisa Ann Murkowski Martell, Frank Michael, Eileen Marie Murkowski Van Wyhe, Mary Catherine Murkowski Judson, Brian Patrick. Student, Santa Clara U., 1952-53; BA in Econs, Seattle U., 1955. With Pacific Nat. Bank of Seattle, 1957-58, Nat. Bank of Alaska, Anchorage, 1959-67; asst. v.p., mgr. Nat. Bank of Alaska (Wrangell br.), 1963-66; v.p. charge bus. devel. Nat. Bank of Alaska, Anchorage, 1966-67; commr. dept. econ. devel. State of Alaska, Juneau, 1967-70; pres. Alaska Nat. Bank, Fairbanks, 1971-80; mem. U.S. Senate from Alaska, Washington, D.C., 1981—; chmn. Com. on Energy and Natural Resources; mem. Com. on Fin., Vets Affairs Com., Indian Affairs Com., Japan-US Friendship Com.; Rep. nominee for U.S. Congress from Alaska, 1970. Former v.p. B.C. and Alaska Bd. Trade; mem. U.S. Holocaust Mus. Coun. Served with U.S. Coast Guard, 1955-57. Mem. AAA, AMVETS, NRA, Am. Legion, Polish Legion Am. Vets., Ducks Unltd., Res. Officer's Assn., Alaska Geog. Soc., Alaska World Affairs Coun., Fairbanks Hist. Preservation Found., Coalition Am. Vets., Alaska Native Brotherhood, Naval Athletic Assn., Am. Bankers Assn., Alaska Bankers Assn. (pres. 1973), Young Pres.'s Orgn., Alaska C. of C. (pres. 1977), Anchorage C. of C. (bd. dirs. 1966), B.C. C. of C., Fairbanks C. of C. (bd. dirs. 1973-78), Pioneers of Alaska, Internat. Alaska Nippon Kai, Capital Hill Club, Shilla Club, Army Athletic Club, Congl. Staff Club, Diamond Athletic Club, Washington Athletic Club, Elks, Lions. Office: US Senate 322 Hart Senate Bldg Washington DC 20510

MURNAGHAN, FRANCIS DOMINIC, JR., federal judge; b. Baltimore, Md., June 20, 1920; m. Diana Edwards; children: Sheila H., George A., Janet E. B.A., Johns Hopkins U., 1941; LL.B., Harvard U., 1948. Bar: Md. 1949. Asso. firm Barnes Dechert Price Smith & Clark, Phila., 1948-50; staff atty. Office of Gen. Counsel, U.S. High Commr. for Ger., 1950-52; asst. atty. gen. State of Md., 1952-54; asso. firm Venable Baetjer & Howard, Balt., 1952-57; partner Venable Baetjer & Howard, 1957-79; judge U.S. Ct. Appeals for 4th Circuit Balt., 1979—. Chmn. Balt. Charter Rev. Commn., 1963-64; trustee Walters Art Gallery, 1961, v.p. 1961-63, pres. 1963-80, chmn. 1980-85, chmn. emeritus, 1985—; pres. Balt. Sch. Bd., 1967-70; trustee Johns Hopkins U., 1976—. Lt. USNR, 1942-46. Mem. ABA, Am. Coll. Trial Lawyers. Office: US Ct Appeals 4th Cir 101 W Lombard St Baltimore MD 21201-2626

MURNICK, DANIEL ELY, physicist, educator; b. N.Y.C., May 5, 1941; s. Jacob Michael and Lena (Tishman) M.; m. Janet Barbara George, Oct. 26, 1969; children: Jonathan, Carolyn. AB in Physics and Math., Hofstra U., 1962; PhD, MIT, 1966. Physics instr. MIT, Cambridge, 1966-67; mem. tech. staff Bell Labs, Murray Hill, N.J., 1967-88; prof. physics Rutgers U., Newark, 1988—, chmn. dept. physics, 1988-95; cons. High Voltage Engrng., Burlington, Mass., 1965-67, Diagnostics and Devices, Morristown, N.J., 1985—, Am. Standard, Piscataway, 1990—, Alimenterics Inc., Morris Plains, N.J., 1992—; mem. sci. adv. bd. Surgilase, Warwick, R.I., 1984-94; Donald H. Jacobs chair in applied physics Rutgers U., 1996. Contbr. more than 100 articles to profl. jours.; inventor method and apparatus for stable isotope analysis and for localized surface glazing. Recipient Humboldt award, Rep. of Germany, 1984, Thomas Alva Edison Patent award R&D Coun. of N.J., 1996. Fellow Am. Phys. Soc.; mem. IEEE, Am. Assn. Physics Tchrs., Sigma Xi. Office: Rutgers U Dept Physics 101 Warren St Newark NJ 07102-1811

MURO, ROY ALFRED, retired media service corporation executive; b. N.Y.C., Sept. 22, 1942; s. Angelo Dominick and Virginia (Guangi) M.; m. Lorraine D. Friedman, July 5, 1966; children: Bradley, Jessica. BS, Bklyn. Coll., 1964; MBA, N.Y. Grad. Sch. Bus., 1966. CPA, N.Y. Sr. acct. Price Waterhouse & Co., N.Y.C., 1966-71; comptr. Vitt Media Internat. Inc., N.Y.C., 1971-82, chmn., COO, 1982-91, chmn., 1991-94, CEO, 1991-95; ret., 1995; lectr. in field. Mem. AICPA, N.Y. State Soc. CPA's, Advt. Agy. Fin. Mgmt. Group, Nat. Agrimktg. Assn., Internat. Radio and TV Soc., N.Y. Credit and Fin. Mgmt. Assn. (lectr.),Am. Travel Mktg. Execs. Home: 8 Irene Ct East Brunswick NJ 08816-2223

MUROFF, LAWRENCE ROSS, nuclear medicine physician; b. Phila., Dec. 26, 1942; s. John M. and Carolyn (Kramer) M.; m. Carol R. Savoy, July 12, 1969; children: Michael Bruce, Julie Anne. AB cum laude, Dartmouth Coll., 1964, B of Med. Sci., 1965; MD cum laude, Harvard U., 1967. Diplomate Am. Bd. Radiology, Am. Bd. Nuclear Medicine. Intern Boston City Hosp., Harvard, 1968; resident in radiology Columbia Presbyn. Med. Ctr., N.Y.C., 1970-73, chief resident, 1973; instr. dept. radiology, asst. radiologist Columbia U. Med. Ctr., N.Y.C., 1973-74; dir. dept. nuc. medicine, computed tomography and MRI Univ. Cmty. Hosp., Tampa, Fla., 1974-94, H. Lee Moffitt Cancer Hosp., Tampa, 1994—; pres. Imaging Cons. Inc., Tampa, 1994—; clin. asst. prof. radiology U. South Fla., 1974-78, clin. assoc. prof., 1978-82, clin. prof., 1982—; clin. prof. U. Fla., 1988—. Contbr. articles to profl. jours. Pres. Ednl. Symposia, Inc., 1975—. Lt. comdr. USPHS, 1968-70. Fellow Am. Coll. Nuclear Medicine (disting. fellow., Fla. del.), Am. Coll. Nuclear Physicians (regents 1976-78, pres.-elect 1978, pres. 1979, fellow 1980), Am. Coll. Radiology (councilor 1979-80, 91-96, chancellor 1981-87, chmn. commn. on nuclear medicine 1981-87, fellow 1981); mem. Am. Assn. Acad. Chief Residents Radiology (chmn. 1973), AMA, Boylston Soc., Fla. Assn. Nuclear Physician (pres. 1976), Fla. Med. Assn., Hillsborough County Med. Assn., Radiol. Soc. N.Am., Soc. Nuclear Medicine (coun. 1975-90, trustee 1980-84, 86-89, pres. Southeastern chpt. 1983, vice chmn. correlative imaging coun. 1983), Fla. Radiol. Soc. (exec. com. 1976-91, treas. 1984, sec. 1985, v.p. 1986, pres. elect 1987, pres. 1988-89, gold medal 1995), West Coast Radiol. Soc., Soc. Mag. resonance Imaging (bd. dirs. 1988-91, chmn. ednl. program 1989, chmn. membership com. 1989-93), Clinical Magnetic Resonance Soc. (pres. elect 1995-97, pres. 1997—), Phi Beta Kappa, Alpha Omega Alpha. Office: 1527 S Dale Mabry Hwy Tampa FL 33629-5808

MURPHEY, ARTHUR GAGE, JR., law educator; b. Macon, Miss., June 16, 1927; s. Arthur Gage and Elizabeth (Crutcher) M.; m. Linda Chaney, May 17, 1975; children by previous marriage—Mason Alexander, Arthur Nesbit; 1 stepchild, Leslie Jo (Mrs. Thomas) Pafford. Student, Vanderbilt U., 1947-48; AB, U. N.C., 1951; JD, U. Miss., 1953; postgrad., London Sch. Econs., U. London, 1953-54; LLM, Yale U., 1962. Assoc. Satterfield, Ewing Williams and Shell, Jackson, Miss., 1953; asst. prof. U. Ga., Athens, 1956-58, Emory U., Atlanta, 1958-61; asst. prof. U. Akron, 1962-63, assoc. prof., 1963-67; prof. U. Ark., Little Rock, 1967-96, asst. dean Sch. Law, 1970-73; prof. Ark. Bar Found., 1996—; vis. lectr. Case Western Res. U., Cleve., 1966; vis. prof. U. Miss., 1977. Faculty editor: Jour. Public Law, 1958-61; faculty adv.: Ga. Bar Jour., 1958-61; contbr. articles to profl. jours. Served with USAAF, 1945-47. Fulbright scholar, 1953-54; Sterling fellow, 1961-62; Ford Found. grantee, 1964. Mem. ABA, Ark. Bar. Assn, Phi Delta Phi, Beta Theta Pi, Phi Beta Kappa. Mem. Anglican Ch. Home: 1918 Old Forge Dr Little Rock AR 72227-5515 Office: U Ark Sch Law 1201 Mcalmont St Little Rock AR 72202-5142

MURPHEY, MARGARET JANICE, marriage and family therapist; b. Taft, Calif., July 24, 1939; d. Glen Roosevelt Wurster and Lucile Mildred (Holt) Lopez; m. Russell Warren Murphey, June 20, 1959; children: Lucinda Kalbfleisch, Rochelle Murphey, Janice Sorenson. BA in Social Sci., Calif. State U., Chico, 1986, MA in Psychology, 1989; postgrad., La Salle U. Sec. Folson State Prison, Calif., 1963-66; tchr. Desert Sands Unified Schs., Indio, Calif., 1969-72; claims determiner Employment Development Dept., Redding, Calif., 1976-78; sec. Shasta County Pers., Redding, 1978-79; welfare worker Shasta County Welfare Office, Redding, 1979-85; therapy intern Counseling Ctr. Calif. State U., Chico, 1989-90; therapist Family Svc. Assn., Chico, 1987-90, Butte County Drug and Alcohol Abuse Ctr., Chico, 1989-90; mental halth counselor Cibecue (Ariz.) Indian Health Clinic, 1990—; mem. Kinisba Child Abuse Com., 1994—. Vol. Pacheco Sch., Redding, 1972-76; Sunday sch. tchr., dir. vacation Bible sch. Nazarene Ch., Sacramento, Indio and Redding, 1958-85. Recipient Sch. Bell award Pacheco Sch. Mem. APA, ACA, Am. Assn. Christian Counselors, Am. Assn. Multi-Cultural Counselors, Internat. Assn. Trauma Counselors. Avocations: study of American Indian history, sewing, crafts, travel, canoeing. Home: PO Box 1114 Show Low AZ 85901-1114 Office: Cibecue Health Ctr Apache Behavioral Health PO Box 1089 Whiteriver AZ 85941-1089

MURPHEY, MICHAEL MARTIN, country western singer, songwriter; b. Tex., Mar. 14, 1945; married; children: Ryan, Brennan, Laura Lynn. Attended, UCLA. Profl. musician, 1962—; with Lewis & Clark Expedition, 1966-70. Songwriter for Monkees, Kenny Rogers, Nitty Gritty Dirt Band; pop hit Wildfire, 1975, What's Forever For, Carolina in the Pines, Love Affairs, Still Taking Chances; founder Westfest Annual celebration; albums: Geronimo's Cadillac, 1971, Blue Sky Night Thunder, 1981, The Best of Michael Martin Murphey, 1981, The Heart Never Lies, 1986, Tonight We Ride, 1986, Americana, 1987, River of Time, 1988, Land of Enchantment, 1989, Best of County Michael Martin Murphey, 1990, Cowboy Songs, 1990, Cowboy Christmas: Cowboy Songs II, 1991, Cowboy Songs III, 1993, Americas Horses Sagebrush Symphony. Named Best New Artist, County Music Assn., Acad. County Music; recipient Grammy nomination for a Face in the Crowd, Nat. Am. Video award for She Wants, award Cowboy Hall of Fame (3), 1990-92, 95, 96. Office: PO Box Fff Taos NM 87571-2550

MURPHEY, MURRAY GRIFFIN, history educator; b. Colorado Springs, Colo., Feb. 22, 1928; s. Bradford James and Margaret Winifred (Griffin) M.; children—Kathleen Rachel, Christopher Bradford, Jessica Lenoir. A.B., Harvard U., 1949; Ph.D., Yale U., 1954. Asst. prof. U. Pa., Phila., 1956-61, assoc. prof., 1961-66, prof., 1966—, chmn. dept. Am. civilization, 1969-81, 87-94. Author: Development of Peirce's Philosophy, 1961, Our Knowledge of the Historical Past, 1973, (with E. Flower) A History of Philosophy in America, 1977, Philosophical Foundations of Historical Knowledge, 1994. Democrat. Home: 200 Rhyle Ln Bala Cynwyd PA 19004-2324 Office: U Pa 323A 3401 Walnut St Philadelphia PA 19104-3337

MURPHEY, RHOADS, history educator; b. Phila., Aug. 13, 1919; s. William Rhoads and Emily (Hawkins) M.; m. Katherine Elizabeth Quinn, Nov. 26, 1942 (dec. July 1950); children: Katherine Ann, Rhoads; m. Eleanor Taylor Albertson, Jan. 12, 1952; children: David, Ellen. A.B., Harvard U., 1941, M.A., 1942, Ph.D., 1950. Asst. prof. geography Ohio State U., 1950-51; from asst. prof. geography to prof. U. Wash., also Far Eastern Inst., 1952-64; prof. Asian studies and history U. Mich., Ann Arbor, 1964—; dir. Center Chinese Studies U. Mich., 1969-76, dir. Asian studies, 1975—, dir. South and S.E. Asian studies, 1987-90. Author: Shanghai-Key to Modern China, 1953, An Introduction to Geography, 4th edit., 1978 (with others) A New China Policy, 1965, The Scope of Geography, 1969, 1973, 3d rev. edit., 1982, The Treaty Ports and China's Modernization, 1970, China Meets the West, 1975 (with others) The Mozartian Historian, 1976, The Outsiders, 1977, The Fading of the Maoist Vision, 1980, (with others) Civilizations of the World, 1990, 3d edit., 1996, A History of Asia, 1992, 2d edit., 1996, East Asia: A New History, 1996; co-editor (with others) Approaches to Modern Chinese nese History, 1967; asst. editor, the editor Jour. Asian Studies, 1959-65; regional editor Asia: (with others) Ency. Brit., 1953-61; editor Mich. Papers in Chinese Studies, 1967-77, Assn. Asian Studies Monographs, 1992—; contbr. articles to profl. jours. Social Sci. Research Council fellow, 1948-50; Ford Found. fellow, 1955-56; Guggenheim fellow, 1966-67; Nat. Endowment Humanities fellow, 1972-73, JSPS fellow, 1978-79. Mem. Assn. Am. Geographers (council 1963-66, Honors award 1980), Assn. Asian Studies (dir., exec. sec. 1976-83, v.p. 1985, pres. 1987-88). Home: 2012 Washtenaw Ave Ann Arbor MI 48104-3639

MURPHEY, ROBERT STAFFORD, pharmaceutical company executive; b. Littleton, N.C., Oct. 29, 1921; married; 2 children. B.S., U. Richmond, 1942; M.S., U. Va., 1947, Ph.D. in Organic Chemistry, 1949. Research chemist in medicinal chemistry A.H. Robins & Co. Inc., Richmond, Va., 1948-53, dir. chemistry research, 1953-55, assoc. dir., 1955-57, dir. research, 1957-60, dir. internat. research, 1960-66, dir. sci. devel., 1966-82, asst. v.p., 1967-73, dir. sci. devel., v.p., 1973-82, v.p. sci. affairs and corp. devel., 1982-83, sr. v.p. sci. affairs and corp. devel., 1983-87, sr. v.p., dir. new bus. devel., 1983-90; sr. v.p., dir. bus. devel. E.C. Robins Internat., Inc., Glen Allen, Va., 1990—. Mem. AAAS, Am. Chem. Soc. Office: E C Robins Internat Inc 11064 Staples Mill Rd Glen Allen VA 23060-2404

MURPHEY, SHEILA ANN, infectious diseases physician, educator, researcher; b. Phila., July 10, 1943; d. William Joseph and Sara Esther (Mallon) M. AB, Chestnut Hill Coll., 1965; MD, Women's Med. Coll. of Pa., 1969. Diplomate Am. Bd. Internal Medicine, Am. Bd. Infectious Diseases. Intern in internal medicine Mt. Sinai Hosp. of N.Y., 1969-70, resident in internal medicine, 1970-72, instr. internal medicine, 1971-72; fellow infectious diseases U. Pa. Sch. Medicine, Phila., 1972-74, instr. dept. medicine, 1974-75, asst. prof. dept. medicine, 1975-77; chief infectious diseases sect. Phila. Gen. Hosp., 1974-77; attending physician Hosp. U. Pa., Phila. Gen. Hosp., 1974-77; dir. divsn. infectious diseases, asst. prof. medicine Jefferson Med. Coll., Phila., 1977-80, clin. assoc. prof. medicine, 1980—; dir. divsn. infectious diseases Thomas Jefferson U., Phila., 1977-88; infection control officer, attending physician Thomas Jefferson U. Hosp., Phila., 1977—. Contbr. articles to profl. jours. Fellow Coll. Physicians Phila.; mem. Am. Soc. Microbiology, Am. Coll. Physicians, Am. Fedn. Clin. Rsch., Soc. Healthcare Epidemiology of Am., Infectious Diseases Soc. Am., Alpha Omega Alpha. Democrat. Roman Catholic. Office: Jefferson Med Coll 1015 Chestnut St Ste 1020 Philadelphia PA 19107-4382

MURPHREE, HENRY BERNARD SCOTT, psychiatry and pharmacology educator, consultant; b. Decatur, Ala., Aug. 11, 1927; s. Henry Bernard and Nancy Mae (Burrus) M.; m. Dorothy Elaine Simmons, Nov. 14, 1953 (dec.); children: Julie Elizabeth, Susan Louise, Jefferson Van; m. Dorothy Elizabeth Olson, Sept. 23, 1993. Student, MIT, 1944-45; BA, Yale U., 1950; MD, Emory U., 1959. Intern internal medicine, fellow clin. pharmacology, instr. Emory U., 1959-61; resident psychiatry Med. Sch. Rutgers U., 1972-76, mem. grad. faculty psychology, 1972—; rsch. asst. Johns Hopkins U., Balt., 1950; asst. chief neuropharmacology Bur. Rsch., Princeton, N.J., 1961-68; from assoc prof. to prof. Univ. of Medicine and Dentistry Robert Wood Johnson Med. Sch., Piscataway, N.J., 1968—, assoc. dean acad. affairs Univ. Medicine and Dentistry, 1977-81, chmn. psychiatry Univ. Medicine and Dentistry, 1977-91; cons. medicinal chemistry and pharmacology FMC Chem. R&D Ctr., Princeton, N.J., 1962-68, Hoffman-LaRoche, Nutley and Verona, N.J., 1968-77. Contbr. articles to profl. jours. Founding mem. Somerset Coun. Alcoholism, Somerville, N.J., 1974-77; mem. Sci. Adv. Com., State of N.J., 1981—; bd. trustees Carrier Found., Belle Mead, N.J., 1981-95, vice chmn. bd., chmn. exec. com., 1989-95. Lt. MSC USN, 1951-55. Mem. Am. Soc. for Pharmacology and Exptl. Therapeutics, Am. Psychiat. Assn., Soc. Biol. Psychiatry, Am. Coll. Neuropsychopharmacology, Sigma Xi, Alpha Omega Alpha. Avocations: music, electronics. Home: 757 Route 518 Skillman NJ 08558-2513 Office: U Med & Dentistry NJ Robert Wood Johnson Med Sch 675 Hoes Ln Piscataway NJ 08854-5627 *Early on, in this sorry world, I pondered the concept of the "perfectibility of humankind". I concluded the best approach is education and devoted my career to teaching and consultation, a variant of teaching.*

MURPHY, ALVIN LEO, educational administrator; b. New Orleans, July 19, 1934; s. James J. and Marie Adele (Perret) M.; m. Celeste Marie Ferry, Nov. 24, 1956; children: Angelle, Alice, Emily, Claire. BS in Secondary Edn., Loyola U., New Orleans, 1956; MEd, Loyola U., 1967. Tchr. De La Salle High Sch., New Orleans, 1958-67; asst. prin. De La Salle High Sch., 1967-72; asst. supt. Archdiocese of New Orleans, 1972-74, assoc. supt., 1974-83; prin. Archbishop Chapelle High Sch., Metairie, La., 1983-89; pres. Archbishop Chapelle High Sch., 1989—. Contbr. articles to profl. jours. Mem. Kenner Bus. Assn., 1989—, Metairie chpt. Am. Heart Assn., 1990—. 1st lt. U.S. Army, 1956-58. Recipient Blue Ribbon Sch. Excellence award U.S. Dept. Edn., 1987, 91, 95, One to Watch in '79 award New Orleans Mag., 1979, Presdl. award Nat. Cath. Ednl. Assn., 1984, St. Louis medal Archdiocese of New Orleans, 1983; named Outstanding Educator La., La. Libr. ASsn., 1994. Mem. Nat. Cath. Edn. Assn. (Nat. Outstanding Contbn. award 1980, reg. assoc. 1988—), Cath. Secondary Prin. Assn. (treas. 1985-87), Nat. Chief Adminstrs. of Cath. Edn., Am. Mgmt. Assn., Nat. Assn. Secondary Sch. Prins. Roman Catholic. Avocations: reading, sports, computers, photography. Office: Archbishop Chapelle High 8800 Veterans Memorial Blvd Metairie LA 70003-5235

MURPHY, ANDREW J., managing news editor. Now mng. editor, news editor Columbus (Ohio) Dispatch. Office: Columbus Dispatch 34 S 3rd St Columbus OH 43215-4201*

MURPHY, ANN PLESHETTE, magazine editor-in-chief. Editor-in-chief Parents mag., N.Y.C. Office: Parents Magazine 685 3rd Ave New York NY 10017-4024*

MURPHY, ARTHUR JOHN, JR., lawyer; b. Aug. 13, 1950; s. Arthur John, Sr. and Joan Marie (von Albade) M.; m. Joanne Therese Blak, Dec. 18, 1976; children—Arthur John III, Matthew Newsom, Ryan. B.A., U. San Diego, 1972, J.D., 1975. Bar: Calif. 1975. Atty., SEC, Washington, 1975-78; assoc. Bronson, Bronson & McKinnon, San Francisco, 1979-82, ptnr., 1983—; lectr.; arbitrator Nat. Assn. Securities Dealers, 1982—. Contbr. securities law articles to profl. jours. Recipient Franklin award for Outstanding Grad., U. San Diego, 1972. Mem. ABA, Calif. Bar Assn. (exec. com. bus. law sect. 1986-90, chmn. 1989-90), San Francisco Bar Assn. Roman Catholic. Club: Olympic, Bankers Club of San Francisco. Home: 1116 Butterfield Rd San Anselmo CA 94960-1157 Office: Bronson Bronson & McKinnon 505 Montgomery St San Francisco CA 94111-2552

MURPHY, ARTHUR THOMAS, systems engineer; b. Hartford, Conn., Feb. 15, 1929; s. Arthur T. and Mary (Beakey) M.; m. Jane M. Gamble, Aug. 16, 1952; children: Thomas, Patricia, Mary, John, Sheila, Jane, Joseph. BEE, Syracuse U., 1951; MS, Carnegie-Mellon U., 1952, PhD, 1957. Registered profl. engr., Kans. Instr. Carnegie-Mellon U., Pitts., 1952-56; asst., assoc. prof., head. elec. engring. Wichita State U., Kans., 1956-61; vis. assoc. prof. mech. engring. MIT, Cambridge, Mass., 1961-62; prof., dean engring. Widener U., Chester, Pa., 1962-71, v.p., acad. dean, 1971-75; Brown prof., head mech. engring. dept. Carnegie-Mellon U., Pitts., 1975-79; prof. industry, mgr. computer and automated systems, sr. research fellow Du Pont de Nemours Co., Camp Hill, Pa., 1979-87; Du Pont fellow Du Pont de Nemours Co., Wilmington, Del., 1987—; vis. rsch. fellow Sony Corp. Rsch. Ctr., Yokohama, Japan, 1991-92, Internat. Superconductivity Tech. Ctr., Tokyo, 1993; vis. prof. control engring. U. Manchester, Eng., 1968-69; cons. Boeing Co., Wichita and Morton, Pa., 1957-68; bd. dirs. Rumford Pub. Co., Chgo., 1975-90; lectr. Pa. State U., 1983-87; Dupont rep. Chem. Rsch. Coun.

Author: Introduction to System Dynamics, 1967; contbr. articles to profl. jours.; editor: Pergamon Press, 1966-75; patentee thick film filter connector, ceramic land grid array, superconducting active antenna array. Former mem. adv. coun. Tex. A&M U., Swarthmore Coll. DuPont fellow, 1987—; recipient DuPont Spl Accomplishment award, 1988, Mktg. Excellence award DuPont Co., 1990. Fellow AAAS, IEEE (exec. com., treas. computer packaging), Am. Soc. Engring. Edn. (chmn. grad. studies, instrumentation, awards com., DuPont rep., Western Electric Fund award 1966); mem. ASME (exec. com. control divsn.), Sigma Xi, Tau Beta Pi, Eta Kappa Nu, Sigma Pi Sigma, Pi Mu Epsilon, Phi Kappa Phi. Avocations: hiking, photography. Home: 388 Spring Mill Rd Chadds Ford PA 19317 Office: Du Pont Co Exptl Sta PO Box 80357 Wilmington DE 19880-0357

MURPHY, ARTHUR WILLIAM, lawyer, educator; b. Boston, Jan. 25, 1922; s. Arthur W. and Rose (Spillane) M.; m. Jane Marks, Dec. 21, 1948 (dec. Sept. 1951); 1 dau., Lois; m. Jean C. Marks, Sept. 30, 1954; children—Rachel, Paul. A.B. cum laude, Harvard, 1943; LL.B., Columbia, 1948. Bar: N.Y. State bar 1949. Asso. in law Columbia Sch. Law, N.Y.C., 1948-49; asso. dir. Legislative Drafting Research Fund, 1956, prof. law, 1963—; trial atty. U.S. Dept. Justice, 1950-52; asso. firm Hughes, Hubbard, Blair & Reed, N.Y.C., 1953-56, 57-58; partner firm Baer, Marks, Friedman & Berliner, N.Y.C., 1959-63; mem. safety and licensing panel AEC, 1962-73; mem. spl. commn. on weather modification NSF, 1964-66; mem. Presdl. Commn. on Catastrophic Nuclear Accidents, 1988-90. Author: Financial Protection against Atomic Hazards, 1957, (with others) Cases on Gratuitous Transfers, 1968, 3d edit., 1985, The Nuclear Power Controversy, 1976. Served with AUS, 1943-46. Decorated Purple Heart. Mem. ABA, Assn. of Bar of City of N.Y. (spl. com. on sci. and law). Office: Columbia Sch of Law 435 W 116th St New York NY 10027-7201

MURPHY, AUSTIN DE LA SALLE, economist, educator, banker; b. N.Y.C., Nov. 20, 1917; s. Daniel Joseph and Marie Cornelia (Austin) M.; m. Mary Patricia Halpin, June 12, 1948 (dec. May 1974); children: Austin Joseph, Owen Gerard; m. Lee Chilton Romero, Dec. 14, 1974; stepchildren: Thomas Romero, Robert Romero. AB, St. Francis Coll., Bklyn., 1938; AM (Hayden fellow 1938-40), Fordham U., 1940, PhD, 1949. Instr. econs. Fordham U., 1938-41; Instr. econs. Georgetown U., 1941-42; asst. statistician, statis. controls Bd. Econ. Warfare, 1942; sr. econs. research editor N.Y. State Dept. Labor, 1947-50; lectr. econs. Fordham U. Sch. Edn., 1946-55; instr. N.Y. U. Sch. Commerce, 1949-51; dean sch. bus. adminstrn. Seton Hall U., South Orange, N.J., 1950-55; Albert O'Neill prof. Am. enterprise, dean sch. bus. adminstrn. Canisius Coll., Buffalo, 1955-62; dir. edn. dept. NAM, 1962-63; exec. v.p. Savs. Banks Assn. N.Y. State, 1963-70; chmn., pres. River Bank Am. (formerly East River Savs. Bank), 1970-89, vice chmn., dir., 1989-96, chmn. adv. bd., 1996—; charter trustee Savs. Bank Rockland County, 1965-70; dir. Bank of Charleston (S.C.), 1989-91; chmn. bd., trustee Savs. Bank Life Ins. Fund, 1983-87; chmn. dist. I, mem. adv. coun. Conf. State Bank Suprs., 1986-93; bd. dirs. MSB Fund, Inc. Author: (with Fleming Frasca, and Mannion) Social Studies Review Book, 1946, Leading Problems of New Jersey Manufacturing Industries, (with Bullock and Doerflinger), 1953, Reasons for Relocation, 1955, Forecast of Industrial Expansion in Buffalo and the Niagara Frontier, 1956, Metropolitan Buffalo Perspective, 1958; editor Handbook of New York Labor Statistics, 1950. Mem. Livingston (N.J.) Charter Commn., 1954-55; mem. capital expenditures com., City of Buffalo, 1957-63; trustee Fordham U., 1973-79, N.Y. Med. Coll., 1978-81; bd. dirs. N.Y. council Boy Scouts Am., 1974—, Jr. Achievement of Buffalo, 1958-63, Invest-in-Am. 1st lt. U.S. Army, 1942-46. Named Knight of Malta, 1971. Mem. NAM (chmn. ednl. aids com. 1958-63), Am. Fin. Assn., Def. Transp. Assn. (life), Nat. Assn. Mut. Savs. Banks (bd. dirs., treas. 1976-81), Friendly Sons. St. Patrick (1st v.p.), DownTown Lower Manhattan Assn. (dir., vice chmn. 1982-93), Union League Club (pres. 1991-93), World Trade Club, Larchmont Yacht Club, KC, Alpha Kappa Psi, Pi Gamma Mu. Home: 1060 Bayhead Dr Mamaroneck NY 10543-4701 Office: River Bank Am 645 5th Ave New York NY 10022-5910 *Through the various happy events and the difficult and sorrowful, loss of loved ones as well as the vagaries of business life, I have found that an ongoing prayerful relationship to God brings a certain detachment and peace that overcomes life's passing problems.*

MURPHY, BARBARA ANN, protective services official; b. Union City, N.J., Oct. 4, 1922; d. Thomas Henry and Charlotte Ruth (Ticer) Murphy. BS, Jersey City State Coll., 1944; MA, Columbia U., 1949. Ret. educator; chair child placement rev. bd., Hudson County Superior Court of N.J., Chancery Divsn. Family, 1992—. Pres. bd. trustees Weehawken (N.J.) Libr., 1994—. Recipient Gov.'s Tchr. Recognition Program award, Princeton, N.J., 1989; named to Weehawken H.S. Hall of Fame, Weehawken Bd. Edn., 1992. Mem. AAUW (pres. 1988-91), N.J. Schoolwomen's Club (v.p. 1980), Weehawken Hist. Soc. (life mem.), Weehawken Adult Club (charter), Palisade Gen. Hosp. Vols. Avocations: travel, reading, gardening, piano. Home: 107 Hauxhurst Ave Weehawken NJ 07087-6838

MURPHY, BARBARA ANNE, emergency physician, surgery educator; b. Cin., Oct. 20, 1937; d. Harold August and Lorna Louise (Gabbard) Tiemeyer; m. D. Michael Murphy, Feb. 5, 1960; children: Michael Patrick, Douglas Andrew. BS cum laude, Ohio State U., 1959; MD magna cum laude, Med. Coll. Pa., 1975. Diplomate Am. Bd. Emergency Medicine. Resident in emergency medicine Geisinger Med. Ctr., Danville, Pa., 1978; staff physician Albemarle Hosp., Elizabeth City, N.C., 1978-79, Durham County Hosp., Durham, N.C., 1979-87; asst. prof. emergency medicine East Carolina U., Greenville, N.C., 1987-90; asst. prof. surgery-emergency medicine Duke U., Durham, 1990—; dir. propsed residency emergency medicine Duke U., Durham, 1994—. Author: (book chpt.) Pediatric Emergency Medicine, rev. edit., 1992; editor: Micromedia Emergency Med. Abstracts, 1988—; book reviewer: Annals of Emergency Medicine, 1995—; contbr. articles to profl. jours. Fellow Am. Coll. Emergency Physicians (mem. clin. policies com. 1991—); mem. Soc. for Acad. Emergency Medicine, Alpha Omega Alpha, Phi Beta Kappa. Avocations: antique rose propagation, 18th-century American furniture collection, herbalism, needlework reproductions. Home: PO Box 837 Hillsborough NC 27278 Office: Duke U Med Ctr Box 3096 Durham NC 27710

MURPHY, BARRY AMES, lawyer; b. Summit, N.J., Mar. 3, 1938; s. Robert Joseph and Florence C. (Ames) M.; m. Leslie Lynn Smith, June 9, 1962; children—Karen Irene, Sean Patrick, Conor Brendan, Ilana Taraleigh. B.A. in English, Stanford U., 1960; M.B.A., Harvard U., 1963; J.D., U. So. Calif., 1972. Bar: Calif. bar 1973, U.S. Supreme Ct 1976, U.S. Tax Ct 1976. Fin. analyst Office of Sec. Def., 1963-65; pres. Tech. Industries Inc., Los Angeles, 1966-72; invididual practice law San Mateo, Calif., 1972-74; corp. counsel Falstaff Brewing Co., San Francisco, 1974-77; sr. partner firm Levine & Murphy, San Francisco, 1978-81; v.p. Microvertics, Mountain View, Calif., 1981-86; pres. Murphy Law Corp., San Anselmo, 1987—. Mem. Am., Calif. bar assns., Calif. Trial Lawyers. Address: 28 Fern Ln San Anselmo CA 94960-1807

MURPHY, BENJAMIN EDWARD, actor; b. Jonesboro, Ark., Mar. 6, 1942; s. Patrick Henry and Nadine (Steele) M. Student, Loras Coll., 1960-61, Loyola U., New Orleans, 1961-62, U. Americas, 1962-63, 64-65; B.A. in Polit. Sci, U. Ill., 1964; student, Pasadena Playhouse, 1965-67; B.A. in Theatre Arts, U. So. Cal., 1968. Appeared in: TV series Name of the Game, NBC, 1968-70, Alias Smith and Jones, ABC, 1971-73, Griff, 1973-74, Gemini Man, NBC, 1976, The Chisholms, CBS, 1979-80, The Winds of War, 1983, Lottery, 1983-84, Berrenger's, NBC, 1985, The Dirty Dozen, Fox Network, 1988.

MURPHY, BETTY JANE SOUTHARD (MRS. CORNELIUS F. MURPHY), lawyer; b. East Orange, N.J.; d. Floyd Theodore and Thelma (Casto) Southard; m. Cornelius F. Murphy, May 1, 1965; children: Ann Southard, Cornelius Francis Jr. AB, Ohio State U.; student, Alliance Française and U. Sorbonne, Paris; JD, Am. U.; LLD (hon.), Eastern Mich. U., 1975, Capital U., 1976, U. Puget Sound, 1986; LHD, Tusculum coll., 1987. Bar: D.C. 1958. Corr., free lance journalist Europe and Asia, UPI, Washington; pub. relations counsellor Capital Properties, Inc. of Columbus (Ohio), Washington; practiced in Washington, 1959-74; mem. firm McInnis, Wilson, Munson & Woods (and predecessor firm); dep. asst. sec., adminstr. Wage and Hour Divsn. Wage and Hour div. Dept. Labor, 1974-75; chmn. and mem. NLRB, 1975-79; ptnr. firm Baker & Hostetler, 1980—; adj. prof. law Am. U., 1972-80; mem. adv. com. on rights and responsibilities of women to Sec. HEW; mem. panel conciliators Internat. Ctr. Settlement Investment Disputes, 1974-85; mem. Adminstrv. Conf. U.S., 1976-80, Pub. Svc. Adv. Bd., 1976-79; mem. human resouces com. Nat. Ctr. for Productivity and Quality of Working Life, 1976-80; mem. Presdl. Commn. on Exec. Exch., 1981-85. Trustee Mary Baldwin Coll., 1977-85, Am. U., 1980—, George Mason U. Found., Inc., 1990—, George Mason U. Edn. Found., 1993—; nat. bd. dirs. Med. Coll. Pa., bd. corporators, 1976-85; bd. dirs. Ctr. for Women in Medicine, 1980-86; bd. govs. St. Agnes Sch., 1981-87; mem. exec. com. Commn. on Bicentennial of U.S. Constn., chmn. internat. adv. com., 1985-92; vice chmn. James Madison Meml. Fellowship Found., 1989-96; bd. dirs. Meridian Internat. Ctr., 1992-96, Friends of Congl. Law Libr., 1992—, Friends of Dept. of Labor; bd. dirs. Union Internationale des Advocats, 1996—; mediator World Intellectual Property Orgn., 1996—. Recipient Ohio Gov.'s award, 1980, fellow award, 1981, Outstanding Pub. Service award U.S. Info. Service, 1987; named Disting. Fellow John Sherman Myers Soc., 1986. Mem. ABA (adminstrv. law sect., chmn. labor law com. 1980-83, chmn. internat. and comparative law adminstrv. law sect. 1983-88, chmn. customs, tariff and trade com. 1988-90, employment law sect. 1990, chmn. internat. com. dispute resolution sect. 1995—), FBA, Inter-Am. Bar Assn. (editor newsletter, Silver medal 1967, co-chmn. labor law com. 1975-83), Bar Assn. D.C., World Peace Through Law Ctr., Am. Arbitration Assn. (bd. dirs. 1985—, mem. editl. bd. 1992, mem. exec. com. 1995—, mem. internat. arbitration com. 1995—), Rep. Nat. Lawyers Assn. (nat. v.p. 1990-95, nat. vice chmn. 1996—), Supreme Ct. Hist. Soc., Am. U. Alumni Assn. (bd. dirs.), Mortar Bd., Kappa Beta Pi. Republican. Office: Baker & Hostetler 1050 Connecticut Ave NW Washington DC 20036

MURPHY, BEVERLEY ELAINE PEARSON, scientist, physician, educator; b. Toronto, Ont., Can., Mar. 15, 1929; d. Ernest Wallace and Edith (Johnson) Pearson; m. David Raymond Murphy, June 15, 1958; children: Madeleine, Catherine. B.A., U. Toronto, 1952, M.D., 1956; M.Sc., McGill U., Can., 1960, Ph.D., 1964. Cert. Med. Biochemistry, Endocrinology. Rotating interne Toronto Gen. Hosp., 1956-57; rsch. fellow Royal Victoria Hosp., Montreal, Que., Can., 1957-59, resident in medicine, 1959-61; rsch. fellow Queen Mary Vets. Hosp., Montreal, 1961-64, dir. endocrinology lab., 1964-78, cons. in endocrinology, 1970-73; asst., assoc. obstetrician & gynecologist Montreal Gen. Hosp., 1972-79; dir. reproductive physiology unit Montreal Gen. Hosp. Rsch. Inst., 1972—; sr. physician, sr. obstetrician and gynecologist Montreal Gen. Hosp., 1979—; med. scientist Royal Victoria Hosp., Montreal, 1981—; lectr., asst., assoc. prof. medicine McGill U., Montreal, 1964-74, prof., 1975—, prof. obstetrics and gynecology, 1979—, assoc. mem. dept. physiology, 1981—, prof. psychiatry, 1985—; lectr. in U.S., Fed. Republic of Germany, Eng., France, Mex., India, Italy, Switzerland, New Zealand, Can.; organizer Satellite Symposium, Internat. Congress Endocrinology, McGill U., 1982, Symposium on Psychoendocrinology, McGill U., 1989; reviewer grant applications for Med. Rsch. Coun. Can., Fonds de la recherche en Santé du Qué, March of Dimes, Ont. Mental Health Found., Can. Heart Found., Can. Liver Found., NSF, B.C. Health Scis; career investigator Med. Rsch. Coun. Can., 1968-94. Mem. editorial bd. Jour. Clin. Endocrinology Metabolism, 1975-79, Jour. Steroid Biochemistry, 1976-94, Jour. Immunoassay, 1979—; contbr. articles, abstracts to profl. jours.; patentee in field. Fellow Royal Soc. Can.; mem. ACP, Am. Soc. Clin. Investigation, Endocrine Soc., Can. Assn. Med. Biochemists, Can. Soc. Clin. Investigation, Can. Soc. Endocrinology and Metabolism (sec.-treas. 1984-89), Can. Investigators in Reproduction, Can. Biochem. Soc., Montreal Physiol. Soc. (pres. 1972-73, 73-74), Que. Assn. Lab. Physicians, Soc. Obstetricians and Gynecologists Can., Syndicat Professionel des Médecins Endocrinologues du Québec, Assn. Women in Sci. Avocations: art, music, jogging, skiing. Office: Montreal Gen Hosp, 1650 Cedar Ave, Montreal, PQ Canada H3G 1A4

MURPHY, BOB, professional golfer; b. Bklyn., Feb. 14, 1943; m. Gail Murphy. Profl. golfer, 1967—, Sr. PGA Tour, 1993—. Named Rookie of Yr., PGA Tour, 1968; winner in Phila. Classic, 1968, Thunderbird Classic, 1968, Greater Hartford Open, 1970, Jackie Gleason-Inverray Classic, 1975, Can. Open, 1986; PGA Sr. Tour wins include Bruno's Meml. Classic, 1993, GTE North Classic, 1993, Raley's Sr. Gold Rush, 1994, Hyatt Regency Maui Kaanapali Classic, 1994, IntelliNet Challenge, 1995, Paine Webber Invitational, 1995, nationwide Championship, 1995, VFW Sr. Championship, 1995, Royal Caribbean Classic, 1996, Cadillac NFL Classic, 1996. Office: care Eddie Elias Enterprise PO Box 5118 1720 Merriman Rd Akron OH 44334-0118*

MURPHY, CALVIN JEROME, professional sports team executive; b. Norwalk, Conn., May 9, 1948. Student, Niagara Coll. With San Diego Clippers, 1970-71, Houston Rockets, 1971-83. Named to Basketball Hall of Fame, 1992. All-time assists leader Houston Rockets, 1970-83; holds single-season record for highest free-throw percentage, 1981; mem. NBA All-Rookie Team, 1971. Office: c/o Houston Rockets Two Greenway Plaza Ste 400 Houston TX 77046

MURPHY, CHARLES HAYWOOD, JR., retired petroleum company executive; b. El Dorado, Ark., Mar. 6, 1920; s. Charles Haywood and Bertie (Wilson) M.; m. Johnie Walker, Oct. 14, 1939; children: Michael Walker, Martha, Charles Haywood, III, Robert Madison. Ed. pub. schs., Ark.; LLD (hon.), U. Ark., 1966. Ind. oil producer, 1939-50; ret. chmn., also bd. dirs. Murphy Oil Corp., El Dorado, Ark., 1972—; chmn. exec. com. 1st Comml. Corp., Little Rock. Bd. govs. Oschner Med. Found.; bd. adminstrs. Tulane U.; mem. nat. adv. bd. Smithsonian Instn.; past mem. Ark. Bd. Higher Edn. Served as infantryman World War II. Recipient citation for outstanding individual service in natural resource mgmt. Nat. Wildlife Fedn. Mem. Am. Petroleum Inst. (past exec. com., hon. bd. dirs.), Nat. Petroleum Council (past chmn.), 25 Yr. Club Petroleum Industry (past pres.).

MURPHY, CHARLES JOSEPH, investment banker; b. N.Y.C., Sept. 18, 1947; s. Charles Joseph and Mary V. (Vaughan) M.; m. Karen Lyn Canevari, Aug. 18, 1973; 4 children. BEE, Manhattan Coll., 1969; MBA, NYU, 1974, APC, 1975. Chartered fin. analyst. Avionics engr. Sikorsky Aircraft, Stratford, Conn., 1969-70; engr., rate/fin. analyst Am. Electric Power Co., N.Y.C., 1970-76; equity analyst First Boston Corp., N.Y.C., 1976-78, v.p. capital markets, 1982-84, mng. dir. utilities and telecommunications fin., 1984-87, head investment banking group, 1988-92, head investment banking dept., 1992-94, co-head worldwide investment banking, 1994-95, head global equities, 1995-96; mng. dir. Sextant Group Inc., N.Y.C., 1996—; mem. CS First Boston operating com., 1993—, exec. bd., 1995—, co-chmn. investment banking operating com., 1994-95. Mem. N.Y. Soc. Security Analysts (sr.). Roman Catholic. Avocations: golf, field shooting, winter sports. Office: Sextant Group Inc 630 5th Ave New York NY 10111-0100

MURPHY, CHRISTOPHER JOSEPH, III, financial executive; b. Washington, Apr. 24, 1946; s. Christopher Joseph Murphy Jr. and Jean Murphy Vos; m. Carmen Morris Carmichael, Feb. 1, 1969; children: Christopher IV, Sean, Kelly, Kevin, Conor, Dillon. BA, U. Notre Dame, 1968; JD, U. Va., 1971; MBA with distinction, Harvard U., 1973. Bar: Va. 1971, U.S. Dist. Ct. D.C. 1971. Officer, pres. 1st Source Corp., South Bend, Ind., 1977—; bd. dirs. Weldun Internat., Bridgman, Mich., 1981-89, Meml. Health Systems, South Bend, 1981-90, chmn., 1990-92, Omega Health Group, Inc., South Bend, 1984-90, Comair Inc., Cin., 1989—, Discover Re Insurance Inc., 1991-95, Trust Corp. Mortgage Inc., 1991—, Quality Dining, 1994—, Titan Holdings, 1995—; adv. council Notre Dame Coll. Arts and Letters, 1981—, chmn., 1985-89; bd. dirs. South Bend C. of C., 1984-95; bd. dirs. Meml. Hosp., South Bend, 1980-86, South Bend Symphony, 1981-83, chmn. Med. Edn. Found., South Bend, 1982—; chmn. United Way Campaign, St. Joseph County, Ind., 1980. Mem. ABA, Young Pres.'s Orgn. (internat. bd. dirs. 1993-95, exec. com.), Ind. Bar Assn., Va. Bar Assn., St. Joseph County Bar Assn., Nat. Assn. Bus. Economists (chpt. pres. 1980), Robert Morris Assocs., Nat. Assn. Publically Traded Cos. (bd. dirs. 1983—, chmn. 1986-87, 1990-95), Nat. Assn. Security Dealers (corp. adv. bd. 1988-92), Am. Bankers Assn. (chmn. payment systems policy bd. 1984-85). Roman Catholic. Office: 1st Source Corp 100 N Michigan St PO Box 1602 South Bend IN 46634

MURPHY, DIANA E., federal judge; b. Faribault, Minn., Jan. 4, 1934; d. Albert W. and Adleyne (Heiker) Kuske; m. Joseph Murphy, July 24, 1958; children: Michael, John E. BA magna cum laude, U. Minn., 1954, JD magna cum laude, 1974; postgrad., Johannes Gutenberg U., Mainz, Germany, 1954-55, U. Minn., 1955-58. Bar: Minn. 1974, U.S. Supreme Ct. 1980. Assoc. Lindquist & Vennum, 1974-76; mcpl. judge Hennepin County, 1976-78, Minn. State dist. judge, 1978-80; judge U.S. Dist. Ct. for Minn., Mpls., 1980-94, chief judge, 1992-94; judge U.S. Ct. of Appeals (8th cir.), Minneapolis, 1994—. Bd. editors: Minn. Law Rev., Georgetown U. Jour. on Cts., Health Scis. and the Law, 1989-92. Bd. dirs. Spring Hill conf. Ctr., 1978-84, Mpls. United Way, 1985—, treas., 1990-94, vice chair, 1996-97, chmn. bd. dirs., 1997—; bd. dirs. Bush Found., 1982—, chmn. bd. dirs., 1986-91; bd. dirs. Amicus, 1976-80, also organizer, 1st chmn. adv. coun.; mem. Mpls. Charter Commn., 1973-76, chmn., 1974-76; bd. dirs. Ops. De Novo, 1971-76, chmn. bd. dirs., 1974-75; mem. Minn. Constl. Study Commn., chmn. bill of rights com., 1971-73; regent St. Johns U., 1978-87, 88—, vice chmn. bd., 1985-87, chmn. bd. 1995—; mem. Minn. Bicentennial Commn., 1987-88; trustee Twin Cities Pub. TV, 1985-94, chmn. bd., 1990-92; trustee U. Minn. Found., 1990—, treas., 1992—; bd. dirs. Sci. Mus. Minn., 1988-94, vice chmn., 1991-94; trustee U. St. Thomas, 1991—; dir. Nat. Assn. Pub. Interest Law Fellowships for Equal Justice, 1992-95. Fulbright scholar; recipient Amicus Founders' award, 1980, Outstanding Achievement award U. Minn., 1983, Outstanding Achievement award YWCA, 1981, Disting. Citizen award Alpha Gamma Delta, 1985. Fellow Am. Bar Found.; mem. ABA (mem. ethics and profl. responsibility judges adv. com. 1981-88, standing com. on jud. selection, tenure and compensation 1991-94, mem. standing com. on fed. jud. improvements, 1994—, Appelate Judges conf. exec. com. 1996—), Minn. Bar Assn. (bd. govs. 1977-81), Hennepin County Bar Assn. (gov. coun. 1976-81), Am. Law Inst., Am. Judicature Soc. (bd. dirs. 1982-93, v.p. 1985-88, treas. 1988-89, chmn. bd. 1989-91), Nat. Assn. Women Judges, Minn. Women Lawyers (Myra Bradwell award 1996), U. Minn. Alumni Assn. (bd. dirs. 1975-83, nat. pres. 1981-82), Fed. Judges Assn. (bd. dirs. 1982—, v.p. 1984-89, pres. 1989-91), Hist. Soc. for 8th Cir. (bd. dirs. 1988-91), Fed. Jud. Ctr. (bd. dirs. 1990-94, 8th cir. jud. coun. 1992-94, mem. U.S. jud. conf. com. on ct. adminstrn. and case mgmt. 1994—), Order of Coif, Phi Beta Kappa. Office: US Dist Ct 684 US Courthouse 110 S 4th St Minneapolis MN 55401-2244

MURPHY, DONN BRIAN, theater educator; b. San Antonio, July 21, 1930; s. Arthur Morton and Claire Frances (McCarthy) M. BA, Benedictine Coll., 1954; MFA, Catholic U., 1956; PhD, U. Wis., 1964. Prof. Georgetown U., Washington, 1954—; exec. dir. Nat. Theatre Corp., Washington, 1985—; tech. theater liaison The White House, Washington, 1961-65. Author: A Director's Guide to Good Theatre, 1968, Stage for a Nation, 1985, Helen Hayes: A Bio-Bibliography, 1993; (plays) Creation of the World, 1970, Something of a Sorceress, 1971, Tyger/Tyger, 1977; (with others) Eleanor: First Lady of the World, 1984. Cpl. U.S. Army, 1950-52. Recipient Outstanding Svc. award Am. Theatre Assn., 1984, Forrest Roberts award No. Mich. U., 1977; Ford Found. fellow, 1963; inducted Coll. Fellows of Am. Theatre, 1994. Democrat. Roman Catholic. Avocations: travel, motorcycling. Home: 2401 N Kenmore St Arlington VA 22207-4938

MURPHY, DONNA JEANNE, actress; b. Corona, N.Y., Mar. 7, 1959. Student, NYU Sch. of the Arts. Stage appearances include: (regional theater) Miss Julie, Pal Joey, (off-Broadway) Song of Singapore, Hey Love: The Songs of Mary Rodgers, Privates on Parade, Showing Off, Birds of Paradise, Little Shop of Horrors, A...My Name Is Alice,, Twelve Dreams, Hello Again, 1995, (Broadway) The King and I, 1996 (Best Leading Actress Tony award 1996), Passion (Leading Actress in Mus. Tony award 1994), The Mystery of Edwin Drood, They're Playing Our Song, The Human Comedy; appeared in film Jade, 1995; TV appearances include Law & Order, All My Children, Another World, Murder One, 1995-96, HBO Lifestories, 1996 (Cable Ace award, Emmy award), Passion, 1996. Office: William Morris Agy 1325 Avenue Of The Americas New York NY 10019-6026

MURPHY, EDDIE, comedian, actor; b. Bklyn., Apr. 3, 1961; s. Vernon and Lillian Murphy Lynch; m. Nicole Mitchell, March 18, 1993; children: Bria, Myles. Student pub. schs., Bklyn. Began performing Richard M. Dixon's White House, L.I., N.Y.; performed at various N.Y.C. clubs, including The Comic Strip; with Saturday Night Live, N.Y.C., 1980-84; host 35th Ann. Emmy Awards, 1983. Starring roles in motion pictures include 48 Hours, 1982, Trading Places, 1983, Best Defense, 1984, Beverly Hills Cop, 1984, The Golden Child, 1986, Beverly Hills Cop II, 1987, Eddie Murphy Raw, 1987, Coming to America, 1988, Harlem Nights,1989, Another 48 Hours, 1990, Boomerang, 1992, The Distinguished Gentleman, 1992, Beverly Hills Cop III, 1994, The Vampire of Brooklyn, 1995, The Nutty Professor, 1996; one-man HBO spl., 1983; albums include Eddie Murphy, 1982, Eddie Murphy Comedian, 1983, How Could it Be, 1984, So Happy, 1989, Distinguished Gentleman, 1992, Love's Alright, 1993, Metro, 1997. Office: ICM 8942 Wilshire Blvd Beverly Hills CA 90211*

MURPHY, EDMUND MICHAEL, federal agency administrator, demographer; b. Steubenville, Ohio, Apr. 7, 1936; s. Edmund Bernard and Catherine Margaret (Allen) M.; m. Mary Elizabeth Jeske, Dec. 15, 1962; 1 child, Maureen Cecilia. BA, Miami U., Oxford, Ohio, 1959; MA, U. Chgo., 1963, PhD, 1965. Asst. prof. U. Chgo., 1965-68, U. Pa., Phila., 1968-70; statistician Statistics Can., Ottawa, Ont., 1970-73; dir. rsch. Manpower and Immigration Dept. Can., Ottawa, 1973-77; dir. gen. Dept. Health and Welfare Can., Ottawa, 1977-78, asst. dep. min. policy and planning, 1978-82, asst. dep. min. social svcs. programs, 1982-86, asst. dep. min., sec. rev. of demography and its implications for social and econ. policy, 1986-92; sr. demographer Statistics Canada, Ottawa, 1992-94; pres., CEO Global Demographics Inc., Ottawa, 1994-96; cons., 1996—. Contbr. numerous articles to profl. jours. With Carleton Condominium Corp. # 43, Ottawa, 1983-93, pres., 1994-96. With U.S. Army, 1960-62. NSF fellow, 1962-65. Mem. Population Assn. Am., Population Assn. Can. Roman Catholic. Home and Office: Chemin de la Dole, Les Grands Champs, 1274 Signy Vaud, Switzerland

MURPHY, EDWARD FRANCIS, sales executive; b. Chgo., July 30, 1947; s. Edward F. and Marjorie (Mooney) M.; m. Kay A. Worcester, Apr. 17, 1970; 1 child, Dean D. BA in Mktg., No. Ill. U., 1976. Dist. mgr. Midas Internat. Corp., Chgo., 1977-85; sales mgr. Raybestos, McHenry, Ill., 1985-89, Wagner Brakes, St. Louis, 1989—. Author: Vietnam Medal of Honor Heroes, 1987, Heroes of World War II, 1990, Korea's Heroes, 1990, Dak To, 1993, Semper Fi-Vietnam, 1996; hist. cons. (book) Above and Beyond, 1985. Sgt. U.S. Army, 1965-68. Recipient Dist. Svc. award Congl. Medal of Honor Soc., 1989. Mem. Medal of Honor Hist. Soc. (founder, pres. 1975—). Republican. Avocations: writing, flying. Home: 2659 E Kael St Mesa AZ 85213

MURPHY, ELLIS, association management executive; b. Lincoln, Nebr.; s. Ellis F. and Virgie (Olson) M.; m. Judy Neel, 1975; children by previous marriage: Sharon, Michael, Edward, Randall; stepchildren: Mary, Janet, Susan. BS in Agr, Purdue U., 1947; MBA, Northwestern U., 1957; postgrad., Ill. Inst. Tech., 1969-81, U. Wash., 1950-51, Mexico City Coll., 1947, U. Chgo., 1964. Assoc. editor Pacific Builder & Engr., Seattle, 1948-51; tech. editor Portland Cement Assn., 1953-55; dir. public relations Chgo. chpt. AIA, 1955-56; account exec. Carrier & Jobson, Inc., Chgo., 1956-57; pres. Ellis Murphy, Inc., Chgo., 1957-73, Murphy, Tashjian & Assocs., Chgo., 1973-78; v.p. Lurie/Murphy Assocs., Inc., Chgo., 1979-83; pres. Murphy & Murphy Inc., Chgo., 1984—; cons. mktg. communication to various bus. firms, 1970—; instr. (part-time) mktg. Ill. Inst. Tech., Chgo., 1977-79; instr. (part-time) assn. mgmt. DePaul U., Chgo., 1985—; cons. to various trade assns., 1970—. Mem. Bd. Edn. Thornton Fractional Dist., Ill., 1961-67; trustee First Meth. Ch., Lansing, Ill., 1959-65; chmn. dirs. funds Purdue Club, Chgo. Major USMCR, 1943-46, 50-52. Mem. Public Relations Soc. Am. (citation 1963), Am. Mktg. Assn., Am. Soc. Assn. Execs., Chgo. Soc. Assn. Execs. (Disting. Service award 1986), Knights Templar, St. Bernard Commndery (past comdr.), Sigma Delta Chi. Club: Plaza. Home: 3100 N Sheridan Rd Chicago IL 60657-4954 Office: Murphy & Murphy Inc 325 W Huron St Ste 403 Chicago IL 60610-3689

MURPHY, EUGENE F., aerospace, communications and electronics executive; b. Flushing, N.Y., Feb. 24, 1936; s. Eugene P. and Delia M.; m. Mary Margaret Cullen, Feb. 20, 1960. BA, Queens Coll., 1956; JD, Fordham U., 1959; LLM, Georgetown U., 1964. Bar: N.Y. With RCA Global Communications Inc., N.Y.C., 1964-81, v.p. and gen. counsel, 1969-71, exec. v.p. ops., 1972-75, pres., chief operating officer, 1975-76, pres., chief exec. officer, 1976-81; chmn., chief exec. officer RCA Communications Inc., N.Y.C., 1981-

86; sr. v.p. communications and info. svcs. GE, N.Y.C., 1986-91; pres., chief exec. officer GE Aerospace, King of Prussia, Pa., 1992-93; pres., CEO GE Aircraft Engines, Cin., 1993—; bd. dirs. Lockheed Martin Corp.; mem. Pres. Reagan's Nat. Sec. Telecommunications Adv. Com.; bd. govs. Aerospace Industries Assn. Bd. Served with USMCR, 1959-60. Mem. Armed Forces Comm. and Electronics Assn. (past nat. chmn.). Clubs: Marco Polo, Plandome Country, Plandome Field and Marine. Office: GE Aircraft Engines Maildrop 101 1 Neumann Way Cincinnati OH 45215-1915

MURPHY, EUGENE FRANCIS, retired government official, consultant; b. Syracuse, N.Y., May 31, 1913; s. Eugene Francis and Mary Grace (Thompson) M.; m. Helene M. Murphy, Dec. 31, 1955; children: Anne F., Thomas E. BSME, Cornell U., 1935; MME, Syracuse U., 1937; PhD, Ill. Inst. Tech., 1948. Tchg. asst. Syracuse U., 1935-36; engr. Ingersoll-Rand Co., Painted Post, N.Y., 1936-39; instr. Ill. Inst. Tech., 1939-41; from instr. to asst. prof. U. Calif., Berkeley, 1941-48; staff engr. NAS, Washington, 1945-48; adv. fellow Mellon Inst., Pitts., 1947-48; with VA, N.Y.C., 1948-83, chief R & D divsn. Prosthetic and Sensory Aids Svc., 1948-73, dir. Rsch. Ctr. for Prosthetics, 1973-78, dir. Office of Tech. Transfer, 1978-83, sci. advisor Office of Tech. Transfer, 1983-85; mem. coun. Alliance for Engring. in Medicine and Biology, 1970-90; mem. adv. com. U. Wis., 1978-82, Case Western Res. U., 1981, Am. Found. for Blind, 1981-83; cons. disability and rehab. rsch., 1983—. Contbg. author: Human Limbs and their Substitutes, 1954, Orthopaedic Appliances Atlas, vol. 1, 1952, vol. 2, 1960, Human Factors in Technology, 1963, Biomedical Engineering Systems, 1970, Critical Revs. in Bioengring, 1971, CRC Handbook of Materials, Vol. III, 1975, Atlas of Orthotics, 1975, 2d edit., 1985, Therapeutic Medical Devices: Application and Design, 1982, McGraw-Hill Ency. Sci. and Tech. Yearbook, 1985; contbr. to Wiley Ency. of Medical Devices and Instrumentation, 1988; editor Bull. Prosthetics Rsch., 1978-82; contbr. articles to profl. jours. Recipient Silver medal Paris, 1961; Meritorious Svc. award VA, 1971; Disting. Career award VA, 1983; Biomedical Engring. Leadership award Alliance for Engring. in Medicine and Biology, 1983; citation Outstanding Handicapped Fed. Employee, 1971; Profl. Achievement award Ill. Inst. Technology, 1983; Fulbright lectr. Soc. and Home for Cripples, Denmark, 1957-58. Fellow AAAS, ASME, Rehab. Engring. Soc. N.Am. (now RESNA), Internat. Soc. for Prosthetics and Orthotics, N.Y. Acad. Medicine; mem. NAE, ASTM, Soc. for Urology and Engring. (hon.), N.Y. Acad. Scis., Acoustical Soc. Am., Optical Soc. Am., Sigma Xi, Tau Beta Pi, Phi Kappa Phi. Home: 111 Savage Farm Dr Ithaca NY 14850-6500

MURPHY, EVELYN FRANCES, healthcare administrator, former lieutenant governor; b. Panama Canal Zone, Panama Canal Zone, May 14, 1940; d. Clement Bernard and Dorothy Eloise (Jackson) M. AB, Duke U., 1961, PhD, 1965; MA, Columbia U., 1963; hon. degrees, Regis Coll., 1978, Curry Coll., Northeastern U., Simmons Coll., Wheaton Coll., Anna Maria Coll., Bridgewater State Coll., Salem State Coll., Emmanuel Coll.; hon. degree, Suffolk U. Pres. Ancon Assocs., Boston, 1971-72; ptnr. Llewelyn-Davies, Weeks, Forrester-Walker & Bor, London, 1973-74; sec. environ. affairs Commonwealth of Mass., Boston, 1975-79, sec. econ. affairs, 1983-86, lt. gov., 1987-91; mng. dir. Brown Rudnick Freed and Gesmer, Boston, 1991-93; exec. v.p. Blue Cross/Blue Shield of Mass., Boston, 1994—; also bd. dirs. Blue Cross Blue Shield Mass., Boston; pres. Health Care and Policy Inst., Boston, 1997—; vis. pub. policy scholar Radcliffe Coll., 1991; vice chmn./chmn. Nat. Adv. Com. on Oceans and Atmosphere (Presdl. apptd.), 1979-80; bd. dirs. Fleet Bank of Mass., Fleet Bank of Conn., Fleet Bank R.I.; pres. Health Care and Policy Inst., 1997—. Recipient Dist. Svc. award New Eng. Coun., 1996, Nat. Seirra Club, 1978, Nat. Bd. Govs. Assn., 1978, Outstanding Citizen award Mass. Audobon Soc., 1978; Harvard U. fellow, 1979-80. Mem. Women Execs. in State Govt. (chair 1987). Democrat. Avocation: jogging. Office: Blue Cross Blue Shield Mass 100 Summer St Boston MA 02110-2106

MURPHY, EWELL EDWARD, JR., lawyer; b. Washington, Feb. 21, 1928; s. Ewell Edward and Lou (Phillips) M.; m. Patricia Bredell Purnell, June 26, 1954 (dec. 1964); children: Michaela, Megan Patricia, Harlan Ewell. B.A., U. Tex., 1946, LL.B., 1948; D.Phil., Oxford U., Eng., 1951. Bar: Tex. 1948. Assoc. Baker & Botts, Houston, 1954-63, ptnr., 1964-93, head internat. dept., 1972-89; pres. Houston World Trade Assn., 1972-74; trustee Southwestern Legal Found., 1978—; chmn. Houston Com. on Fgn. Rels., 1984-85, Inst. Transnat. Arbitration, 1985-89, Internat. and Comparative Law Ctr., 1986-87; mem. J. William Fulbright Fgn. Scholarship Bd., 1991-96, vice chmn., 1992-93, chmn., 1993-95; vis. prof. U. Tex. Law Sch., 1993—; Disting. lectr., U. Houston Law Ctr., 1996—. Contbr. articles to profl. jours. Served to lt. USAF, 1952-54. Recipient Carl H. Fulda award U. Tex. Internat. Law Jour., 1980; Rhodes scholar, 1948-51. Mem. ABA (chmn. sect. internat. law 1970-71), Houston Bar Assn. (chmn. internat. law com. 1963-64, 70-71), Houston C. of C. (chmn. internat. bus. com. 1964, 65), Philos. Soc. Tex., Internat. Law Inst. (bd. dirs. 1994—). Home: 17 W Oak Dr Houston TX 77056-2117 Office: Baker & Botts 3000 One Shell Plz Houston TX 77002-4995

MURPHY, FRANCES LOUISE, II, newspaper publisher; b. Balt.; d. Carl James and L. Vashti (Turley) M.; m. James E. Wood (div.); children: Frances Murphy Wood Draper, James E. Jr., Susan Wood Barnes. BA, U. Wis., 1944; BS, Coppin State Coll., Balt., 1958; MEd, Johns Hopkins U., 1963. City editor Balt. Afro-Am., 1956-57; dir. News Bur., Morgan State Coll., Balt., 1964-71; chmn. bd. dirs. Afro-Am. Newspapers, Balt., 1971-74; assoc. prof. journalism State Univ. Coll., Buffalo, 1975-85, Howard U., Washington, 1985-91; editor Washington Afro-Am., 1951-56, pub., 1987—; bd. dirs. Afro-Am. Newspapers, Balt., 1985-87; mem. adv. bd. Partnership Inst., Washington, 1985-91; treas. African Am. Civil War Meml. Freedom Found., African Am. Leadership Summit. Trustee State Colls. Md., 1971-76, U. D.C., 1994—; bd. dirs. Delta Rsch. and Ednl. Found., 1993-95; nat. bd. dirs. NACCP, 1971-76. Named One of 100 Most Influential Black Ams., Ebony mag., 1973, 74, Disting. Marylander, Gov. State of Md., 1975; recipient Ida B. Wells award Congl. Black Caucus, 1989, Public Svc. award African Methodist Episcopal Ch., 1991, Invaluable Svc. award Martin L. King Jr. Found., 1992, Black Women of Courage award Nat. Fedn. Black Women Bus. Owners, 1993, Black Awareness Ach. award Holy Redeemer Catholic Ch., 1993, Bus. of the Yr. award Bus. and Profl. Women's League, 1993, Oustanding Svc. award Capital Press Club, 1993, Black Conscious Commitment trophy Unity Nation, 1993, Dedicated Cmty. Svc. award Ward I Cmty. and D.C. Pub. Schs., 1994, Women of Strength award Nat. Black Media Coalition, 1994, 95, Outstanding Woman of Yr. award Alpha Gamma chpt. Iota Phi Lambda, 1994, Art Carter Excellence award Capital Press Club, 1994, Excellence in Comm. award Washington Inter-Alumni Coun. United Negro Coll. Fund, 1994, 95, Disting. Cmty. Svc. award The Questers, Inc., 1995, Outstanding Journalist award Masons, 1995, Outstanding Achievement award Beta Zeta chpt. Zeta Phi Beta, 1996, award in recognition of outstanding contbns. made to youth The Soc., 1996, Disting. Black Women award BISA, 1996. Mem. Nat. Newspaper Pubs. Assn. (editl. com. 1987—, Merit award 1987, 89-93), Soc. Profl. Journalists (Disting. Svc. in local journalism award Washington chpt. 1994), Links, Capital Press Club (exec. bd. 1987—, Outstanding Svc. award 1993, Art Carter award of excellence 1994), Delta Sigma Theta (Frances L. Murphy II Comm. award Fed. City Alumnae chpt. 1993, Fortitude Image award Prince George's County chpt. 1994, Ethel L. Payne award 1996), Kiwanis Club (first woman hon., 1995). Democrat. Episcopalian. Avocation: bridge. Home: 5709 1st St NW Washington DC 20011-2319 Office: Washington Afro-Am 1612 14th St NW Washington DC 20009-4307

MURPHY, FRANCIS, English language educator; b. Springfield, Mass., Mar. 13, 1932; s. Frank Edward and Sarah (O'Connor) M. B.A., Am. Internat. Coll., 1953; M.A., U. Conn., 1955; Ph.D., Harvard U., 1960; LittD (hon.), Am. Internat. Coll., 1986. Mem. faculty English lang. and lit. Smith Coll., 1959—, assoc. prof., 1966-69, prof., 1970—; vis. curator Springfield Mus. Fine Arts, 1975-76, Hudson River Mus., 1983-84. Editor: The Diary of Edward Taylor, 1964, Major Am. Poets, 1967, Form and Structure in Poetry, 1964, Edwin Arlington Robinson, 1970, Walt Whitman, 1969, The Uncollected Essays of Yvor Winters, 1973, The Complete Poems of Walt Whitman, 1975, Of Plymouth Plantation (William Bradford), 1981; author: Willard Leroy Metcalf, 1976, (with Dean Flower) A Catalogue of American Paintings, Water Colors and Drawings (to 1923) in the G.W.V. Smith Museum, 1976, The Landscape Within: J. Francis Murphy, 1982, The Book of Nature: American Painters and the Natural Sublime, 1983; co-editor: Norton Anthology of American Literature, 1979—, Mass. Rev., 1966-67.

MURPHY, FRANCIS SEWARD, journalist; b. Portland, Oreg., Sept. 9, 1914; s. Francis H. and Blanche (Livesay) M.; BA, Reed Coll., 1936; m. Clare Eastham Cooke, Sept. 20, 1974. With The Oregonian, Portland, 1936-79, TV editor, Behind the Mike columnist, 1952-79. Archeol. explorer Mayan ruins, Yucatan, Mex., 1950—, mem. Am. Quintana Roo Expdn., 1965, 66, 68. With U.S. Army, 1942-46. Author: Dragon Mask Temples in Central Yucatan, 1988. Mem. Am. Philatelic Soc. (life), Royal Asiatic Soc., City Club (bd. govs. 1950, 64-66), Explorers Club, Am. Club of Hong Kong, Oreg. Hist. Soc., Soc. Am. Archeaology, Am. Philatelic Soc., Hong Kong Philatelic Soc., World Wide Fund Nature, Royal Hong Kong Jockey Club. Democrat. Congregationalist. Home: 4213 NE 32nd Ave Portland OR 97211-7149

MURPHY, GEORGE, special effects expert. Computer graphics artist, effects supr. Indsl. Light & Magic, San Rafael, Calif. Films include: Hook, 1991, Death Becomes Her, 1992, Jurassic Park, 1993, Forrest Gump, 1994 (Acad. award best visual effects, Brit. Acad. Film and TV award for best visual effects 1994), Mission Impossible, 1995, Congo, 1995, Star Trek: First Contact, 1996. Mem. Acad. Motion Picture Arts and Scis. (visual effects br.). Office: care ILM PO Box 2459 3160 Kerner Blvd San Rafael CA 94912

MURPHY, GEORGE AUSTIN, justice; b. Bklyn., Mar. 16, 1923; s. Frank V. and Catherine L. (Milroy) M.; m. Teresa Marie Short, July 3, 1952; children: Michael, Timothy, Terence, Mary, James, Maureen, Christopher, Marjorie, Paul. LLB, St. John's U., N.Y.C., 1949; BS, Fordham U., 1951. Bar: N.Y. 1949, U.S. Dist. Ct. (so. and ea. dists.) N.Y. 1951, U.S. Supreme Ct. 1956. Sole practice, Freeport, N.Y., 1949-52, Seaford, N.Y., 1956-69; mem. Kelly, McDonald, Deeley & Murphy, Freeport, 1953-55, Sullivan, Rowley & Murphy, 1970-78; justice N.Y. State Supreme Ct. 10th Jud. Dist., Mineola, 1979—. Councilman, Town of Hempstead (N.Y.), 1963-71; mem. N.Y. State Senate, 1971-72, N.Y. State Assembly, 1973-78. Served to lt. U.S. Army, 1943-46, ETO, CBI; maj. Res. ret. Mem. Nassau County Bar Assn., Nassau Lawyers Assn., Catholic Lawyers Assn., Am. Legion. Roman Catholic. Lodges: K.C., Elks. Office: Supreme Court Supreme Court Building Mineola NY 11501

MURPHY, GEORGE EARL, psychiatrist, educator; b. Portland, Oreg., Oct. 17, 1922; s. George Earl and Mary Ella M.; m. Amanda Daniel, Mar. 24, 1976; children: Paul Douglas, Bruce Kevin. Student, U. Wash., 1940-42, U. Portland, 1946-47; BS, Oreg. State U., 1949; MD, Washington U., St. Louis, 1952. Diplomate Am. Bd. Psychiatry and Neurology. Intern Alameda County Hosp., Oakland, Calif., 1952-53, asst. resident in medicine, 1953-54; fellow in psychosomatic medicine Washington U., St. Louis, 1954-55; asst. resident in psychiatry Mass. Gen. Hosp., Boston, 1955-56, Washington U., St. Louis, 1956-57; instr. sch. of medicine Washington U., 1957-59, asst. prof. sch. of medicine, 1959-66, assoc. prof. sch. of medicine, 1966-69, prof. sch. of medicine, 1969-90, prof. emeritus psychiatry, 1990—; dir. psychiatry clinic Washington U., 1976-90, psychiat. student health, 1978-83, coursemaster human sexuality, 1978-90. Author: Suicide in Alcoholism, 1992; contbr. articles to profl. jours. Recipient Rsch. award for Advances in Suicide Prevention Am. Suicide Found. (now Am. Found. Suicide Prevention), 1994; Louis I. Dublin award for rsch. in suicide Am. Assn. Suicidology, 1995; NIMH grantee, 1963-83, 85-88. Fellow Am. Psychiat. Assn. (life); mem. Internat. Assn. for Suicide Prevention, Am. Psychopathological assn., Sigma Xi. Avocation: archaeology of the bronze age. Office: Washington U Sch Medicine Dept Psychiatry 4940 Childrens Pl Saint Louis MO 63110-1002

MURPHY, GERALD, government official; b. Washington, Aug. 25, 1938; s. Jeremiah T. and Jean (Curley) M.; m. Kathryn Beckman, Sept. 24, 1988; children by previous marriage: William Michael, Janet Marie, Kathleen Anne. B.C.S. with honors, Benjamin Franklin U., Washington, 1960, M.C.S., 1963. C.P.A., D.C. Dep. div. dir. Dept. Treasury, Washington, 1970-71, div. dir., 1971-74, asst. commr., 1974-75, dep. commr., 1975-79, dep. fiscal asst. sec., 1979-86; fiscal asst. sec. Dept. Treasury, 1986—; lectr. in acctg. Southeastern U., Washington, 1965-70, Dept. Agr. Grad. Sch., Washington, 1970-76; mem. Govt. Acctg. Standards Adv. Council, 1984-89; mem. Fed. Acctg. Standards Adv. Bd., 1991—. Served with U.S. Army, 1956. Recipient Meritorious Svc. award Dept. Treasury, 1972, Treasury Honor award, 1983, Pres.'s Rank award, 1992, Disting. Alumni award Benjamin Franklin U., Washington, 1976. Mem. Am. Inst. C.P.A.s, Assn. Govt. Accts. (nat. pres. 1977-78, Robert W. King award 1983), Sr. Execs. Assn., Fed. Exec. Inst. Alumni Assn. Roman Catholic. Office: Dept Treasury 15th & Pennsylvania Ave NW Washington DC 20220

MURPHY, GERARD NORRIS, trade association executive; b. Washington, July 10, 1950; s. Maurice J. and Marguerite (Norris) M.; m. Jacqueline F., May 26, 1973; children: Anne Marie, Michael Jonathan, Kathleen Elizabeth. BA, U. Md., 1972, MA, 1975; JD, George Mason U., 1980. Mgmt. trainee Washington Area New Automobile Dealers Assn., Rockville, Md., 1972-74, asst. CEO, 1974-82, pres., CEO, 1982—; bd. dirs. Internat. Credit Assn. Greater Washington, Silver Spring, Md., 1991-96; bd. dirs., chmn. Met. Washington Better Bus. Bur., 1992—; chmn. Nat. Capital Area Transp. Fedn., Washington, 1990—. Co-founder, past chmn. Washington Regional Alcohol Program, Vienna, Va., 1983-86; trustee Nat. Automobile Dealers Assn. Sales Rep. Cert. Commn., 1995—; sec. Boys & Girls Clubs Greater Washington, Silver Spring, 1987—; co-founder Montgomery Students Automotive Trades Found., Montgomery Pub. Schs., 1978, sec., 1990—. Recipient Govs. citation, Gov. William Donald Schaefer, 1990, Silver medallion Boys & Girls Clubs of Am., 1997. Fellow Am. Soc. Assn. Execs. (cert., com. chmn. 1989-90, 96-97); mem. ABA, Assn. Healthcare Coalition (sec. 1995, v.p. 1996—), Automotive Trade Assn. Execs. (bd. dirs. 1987-88, sec., treas. 1996, v.p. 1997), D.C. Bar Assn., Greater Washington Soc. Assn. Execs. (com. chmn. 1993-94, chmn. award 1994, found. bd. dirs. 1997—), Leadership Washington (8th class 1993-94), Rotary (Paul Harris fellow 1990), Delta Theta Phi, Delta Tau Delta. Democrat. Roman Catholic. Office: Washington Area New Auto Dealers Assn 15873 Crabbs Branch Way Rockville MD 20855-2635

MURPHY, GLORIA WALTER, novelist, screenwriter; b. Hartford, Conn., Feb. 22, 1940; d. Frank and Elizabeth (Lemkin) Walter; m. Joseph S. Murphy; children: William Gitelman, Laurie Gitelman, Daniel Gitelman, Julie Gitelman, Caitlin Fleck. Student, No. Essex Community Coll., Haverhill, Mass., 1979-81, Boston U., 1981-82. Columnist Pandora's Box The Peabody (Mass.) Times, 1975; columnist Murphy's Law The Methuen (Mass.) News, 1979. Author: Nightshade, 1986, Bloodties, 1987, Nightmare, 1987, The Playroom, 1987, Cry of the Mouse, 1991, Down Will Come Baby, 1991, A Whisper in the Attic, 1992, A Shadow on the Stair, 1993, Simon Says, 1994 (also movie 1996), A Stranger in the House, 1995, Til Death Do Us Part, 1997. Mem. Mystery Writers Am., Authors Guild. Office: PO Box 365 Ringwood NJ 07456-0365

MURPHY, GORDON JOHN, engineering educator; b. Milw., Feb. 16, 1927; s. Gordon M. and Cecelia A. (Knerr) M.; m. Dorothy F. Brautigam, June 26, 1948; children—Lynne, Craig. B.S., Milw. Sch. Engring., 1949; M.S., U. Wis., 1952; Ph.D., U. Minn., 1956. Asst. prof. elec. engring. Milw. Sch. Engring., 1949-51; systems engr. A C Spark Plug div. Gen. Motors Corp., 1951-52, cons., 1959-62; instr. U. Minn., 1952-56, asst. prof. elec. engring., 1956-57; faculty Northwestern U., Evanston, Ill., 1957—; prof. Northwestern U., 1960—, head dept. elec. engring., 1960-69, dir. Lab. for Design of Electronic Systems, 1987—; cons. numerous corps., 1959—; founder, 1st chmn. Mpls. chpt. Inst. Radio Engrs. Profl. Group on Automatic Control, 1956-57, Chgo. chpt., 1959-61. Author: Basic Automatic Control Theory, 1957, 2d edit., 1966, Control Engineering, 1959; contbr. articles, papers to profl. jours.; patentee TV, electronic timers, periodontal instruments and motion control systems. Mem. indsl. adv. com. Milw. Sch. Engring., 1971—. Served with USNR, 1945-46. Recipient ECE Centennial medal U. Wis., Outstanding Alumnus award Milw. Sch. Engring. Alumni Assn.; named One of Chgo.'s Ten Outstanding Young Men Chgo. Jr. C. of C. Fellow IEEE (for edn. and rsch. in automatic control); mem. feedback control systems com. 1960-68, discrete systems com. 1962-68, adminstrv. com. profl. group on automatic control 1966-69, chmn. membership and nominating coms. 1966-67); mem. Am. Automatic Control Coun. (edn. com. 1967-69), Engr.'s Coun. for Profl. Devel. (guidance com. 1967-69), Nat. Electronic Conf. (bd. dirs. 1983-85), Am. Electronics Assn. (exec. com. M.W. coun. 1990-93), Sigma Xi, Eta Kappa Nu, Tau Beta Pi. Home: 638 Garden Ct Glenview IL 60025-4105 Office: Northwestern U Elec Engring Dept Evanston IL 60208

MURPHY, GREGORY GERARD, lawyer; b. Helena, Mont., Feb. 3, 1954; s. Michael Anthony and Elizabeth (Cooney) M.; m. Katherine Joan Koch, Dec. 30, 1977; children: Megan, Brian, Allison. BA, U. Mont., 1976; JD, U. Notre Dame, 1979. Bar: Oreg. 1979, U.S. Dist. Ct. Oreg. 1979, U.S. Ct. Appeals (9th cir.) 1979, Mont. 1980, U.S. Dist. Ct. Mont. 1980. Clk. to judge U.S. Ct. Appeals (9th cir.), Portland, 1979-80; assoc. Moulton, Bellingham, Longo & Mather P.C., Billings, Mont., 1980-84; shareholder Moulton, Bellingham, Longo & Mather, P.C., Billings, Mont., 1984—; trustee Mont. dist. U.S. Bankruptcy Ct., 1982-85; examiner Mont. Bd. Bar Examiners, 1990-95, chmn. 1995—; trustee Nat. Conf. Bar Examiners, 1990—, mem. multistate bar exam. com., 1986-94, chmn. 1994—; vice chmn. commn. on rules of admission to the bar Mont. Superior Ct., 1996-97. Assoc. editor Notre Dame Law Rev., 1978-79. Bd. dirs. Billings Symphony Soc., 1982-91, French hornist, 1981—. Thomas and Alberta White scholar U. Notre Dame, 1978-79. Mem. Mont. Bar Assn., Oreg. Bar Assn., Am. Law Inst., Yellowstone County Bar Assn., Rotary. Roman Catholic. Avocations: french horn, golf, camping. Home: 5533 Gene Sarazen Dr Billings MT 59106-1121 Office: Moulton Bellingham et al PO Box 2559 Billings MT 59103-2559

MURPHY, GRETA WERWATH, retired college official; b. Milw., Aug. 24, 1910; d. Oscar and Johanna (Seelhorst) Werwath; m. John Heery Murphy, Sept. 18, 1941. Ed. Ohio State U., 1943-45; PhD in Comms. (hon.) Milw. Sch. Engring., 1993 . With Milw. Sch. Engring., 1928—, head admissions dept., 1931-42, dir. pub. rels, 1945-66, v.p. pub. rels. and devel., 1966-77, v.p., cons., 1978—, regent emeritus, 1985—. Mem. Milw. County Planning Commn., 1966—, vice chmn., 1974-75, chmn., 1976-77. Fellow Pub. Rels. Soc. Am. (founder, past pres. Wis. chpt.); mem. Am. Coll. Pub. Rels. Assn. (past dir., sec., trustee), Women's Advt. Club (pres.). Club: Womans of Wis. Home: 1032 Malaga Ave Miami FL 33134-6319 also: 5562 Cedar Beach S Belgium WI 53004-9646

MURPHY, HAROLD LOYD, federal judge; b. Haralson County, Ga., Mar. 31, 1927; s. James Loyd and Georgia Gladys (McBrayer) M.; m. Jacqueline Marie Ferri, Dec. 20, 1958; children: Mark Harold, Paul Bailey. Student, West Ga. Coll., 1944-45, U. Miss., 1945-46; LL.B., U. Ga., 1949. Bar: Ga. 1949. Pvt. practice Buchanan, Ga., from 1949; ptnr. Howe & Murphy, Buchanan and Tallapoosa, Ga., 1958-71; judge Superior Cts., Tallapoosa Circuit, 1971-77; U.S. dist. judge No. Dist. of Ga., Rome, 1977—; rep. Gen. Assembly of Ga., 1951-61; asst. solicitor gen. Tallapoosa Jud. Circuit, 1956; mem. Jud. Qualifications Commn., State of Ga., 1977. With USNR, 1945-46. Fellow Am. Bar Found.; mem. ABA, Ga. Bar Assn., Dist. Judges Assn. for 11th Cir. Bar Assn., Am. Judicature Soc., Tallapoosa Cir. Bar Assn., Old War Horse Lawyers Club, Am. Inns Ct. (past pres. Joseph Henry Lumpkin sect.), Fed. Judges Assn. (exec. com.). Methodist. Home: 321 Georgia Highway 120 Tallapoosa GA 30176-3114 Office: US Dist Ct PO Box 53 Rome GA 30162-0053

MURPHY, HELEN, recording industry executive; b. Glasgow, Scotland, Oct. 2, 1962; came to U.S., 1990; d. Francis and Kathleen (Gallagher) M.; m. Michael Christopher Luksha, Apr. 1, 1989. BA in Econs. with honors, U. Guelph, Can., 1982; MBA, U. Western Ontario, Can., 1984. CFA. Asst. mgr. securities rsch. Confederation Life, Toronto, Can., 1984-86; sr. analyst entertainment & merchandising Prudential Bache Securities, Toronto, Can., 1986-89; v.p. rsch. Richardson Greenshields Can., Toronto, 1989-90; v.p. investor rels. Polygram Holding, Inc., N.Y.C., 1990-91; v.p., treas. Polygram Records Inc., N.Y.C., 1991-92, sr. v.p. corp. fin., treas., 1992-95; sr. v.p. investor rels. PolyGram Internat. Ltd., N.Y.C., 1995—; sr. v.p. mergers and acquisitions PolyGram Holding, Inc., N.Y.C., 1995—; lectr. U. Guelph, 1982-90. Fellow Nat. Investor Rels. Inst., N.Y. Soc. Security Analysts, N.Y. Treas. Group. Office: Polygram Holding Inc 825 8th Ave New York NY 10019-7416

MURPHY, JAMES E., public relations and marketing executive. Degree in Journalism, U. Ill. Sr. corp. comms. officer Owens-Corning Fiberglas, Beatrice, Merrill Lynch; exec. v.p. Burson-Marsteller, vice chmn., 1990, chmn., CEO Burson-Marsteller, N.Y., 1991-93; pres. Murphy & Co., 1993—; mng. dir. worldwide mktg. and comm. Andersen Cons., 1993—. Mem. bd. advisors Medill Sch. Journalism, Northwestern U.; mem. adv. bd. Coll. Bus. and Commerce, U. Ill., also mem. devel. bd. Coll. Comm.; mem. exec. com., trustee N.Y. March of Dimes. Mem. Inst. Pub. Rels. Rsch. (trustee), Sky Club, Union League Club, Belle Haven Club, Woodway Country Club, Palmetto Golf Club, Preston Mountain Club. Office: Andersen Cons c/o Andersen Cons. 1345 Avenue Of The Americas New York NY 10105-0302

MURPHY, JAMES GILMARTIN, lawyer; b. N.Y.C., June 13, 1959; s. Maurice Joseph and Irene Abigail (Fay) M.; m. Patricia Ann O'Malley, Jan. 26, 1991. BBA, U. Notre Dame, 1981; JD, Wake Forest U., 1984. Bar: Ga. 1984, N.C. 1986, N.Y. 1989. Law clk. to Hon. Daniel A. Manion U.S. Ct. Appeals 7th Cir., South Bend, Ind., 1986-88; ptnr. McMillan, Constabile, Maker, Murphy & Raymond, LLP, Larchmont, N.Y., 1993—. Mem. editorial staff Wake Forest U. Law Review, 1982-84. Republican. Roman Catholic. Avocations: golf, reading. Office: 2180 Boston Post Rd Larchmont NY 10538-3616

MURPHY, JAMES LEE, college dean, economics educator; b. Detroit, Feb. 14, 1939; s. Philip E. and Julie T. M.; m. Linda J. Masson, July 31, 1965; children—Janel K., John R. B.S., Spring Hill Coll., 1961; M.S., Purdue U., 1963, Ph.D., 1964. Asst. prof. econs. U. N.C., Chapel Hill, 1964-67, assoc. prof., 1967-72, prof., 1972—, chmn. dept., 1975-85, dir. summer session, 1987-88, dean summer sch., 1988—; vis. prof. Thammasat U., Bangkok, Thailand, 1968-69, Econs. Inst., U. Colo., Boulder, 1979, U. New South Wales, Sydney, Australia, 1980, overseas program U. Utah, 1974; cons. in field, 1968—. Author: Introductory Econometrics, 1973, Introductory Statistical Analysis, 1975, 2d edit., 1980, Spanish lang. edit., 1987, Statistical Analysis for Business and Economics, 1985, Statistical Analysis, 1993. NDEA fellow, 1961-64; NSF grantee, 1969-71. Mem. Am. Econ. Assn., So. Econ. Assn., Assn. Univ. Summer Sessions, N.Am. Assn. Summer Sessions. Republican. Roman Catholic. Office: U NC Dept Econs Gardner Hall Campus Box 3305 Chapel Hill NC 27599-3305

MURPHY, JAMES PAUL, lawyer; b. Jackson, Tenn., Apr. 29, 1944; s. Paul Joseph and Marjorie Mary (Smyth) M.; m. Marcia Mae Gaughan, Sept. 5, 1975. B.A., U. Notre Dame, 1966; J.D., U. Mich., 1969. Bar: Ohio 1969, D.C. 1984, Md. 1984, U.S. Dist. Ct. (no. dist.) Ohio 1970, U.S. Ct. Appeals (6th cir.) 1972, U.S. Supreme Ct. 1976, U.S. Dist. Ct. Md., 1984, U.S. Dist. Ct. D.C., 1984, U.S. Dist. Ct. of Appeals (4th cir., D.C. cir.) 1984. Vol. VISTA, 1969-70; assoc. Squire, Sanders & Dempsey, LLP, Cleve., 1970-79, ptnr., 1979—. Mem. Cleve. Bar Assn. (fed. ct. com.), Md. Bar Assn., D.C. Bar Assn., Ohio State Bar Assn. (antitrust sect.). Clubs: Westwood Country (Rocky River, Ohio), City (Washington). Home: 4512 Wetherill Rd Bethesda MD 20816-1837 Office: Squire Sanders & Dempsey LLP PO Box 407 1201 Pennsylvania Ave NW Washington DC 20004-2401

MURPHY, JANET GORMAN, college president; b. Holyoke, Mass., Jan. 10, 1937; d. Edwin Daniel and Catherine Gertrude (Hennessey) Gorman. B.A., U. Mass., 1958, postgrad. 1960-61, Ed.D., 1974, LL.D. (hon.) 1984; M.Ed., Boston U., 1961. Tchr. English and history John J. Lynch Jr. High Sch., Holyoke, 1958-60; tchr. English, Chestnut Jr. High Sch., Springfield, Mass., 1961-63; instr. English and journalism Our Lady of Elms Coll., Chicopee, 1963-64; mem. staff Mass. State Coll., Lyndonville, Vt., 1977-83; pres. Mo. Western State Coll., St. Joseph, 1983—. Mem. campaign staff Robert F Kennedy Presdl. Campaign, 1967. Recipient John Gunther Tchr. award NEA, 1961, award Women's Opportunity Com., Boston Fed. Exec. Bd., 1963, Phi Delta Kappa Educator of Yr. award NAACP, 1992; named one of 10 Outstanding Young Leaders of Greater Boston Area, Boston Jr. C. of C., 1973. Office: Mo Western State Coll Office of the President 4525 Downs Dr Saint Joseph MO 64507-2246*

MURPHY, JEANNE ANN, parochial school educator; b. Chgo., Aug. 28, 1949; d. Harold Barrett and Emma Jean (Rozantz) Harper; m. James Stanley Murphy, June 5, 1976; children: Annathea, Elyse, Brenton, Breauna. BS,

Pa. State U., 1971. Cert. tchr., Pa. Tchr. St. John's Elem. Sch., Uniontown, Pa., 1971-72, Rosemont Elem. Sch., Martinsburg, W.Va., 1972-76, Worthington Elem. Sch., Fairmont, W.Va., 1976-77; substitute tchr. Doddridge County Schs., West Union, W.Va., 1977-88, tchr. adult basic edn., 1981-88; tchr. kindergarten and early childhood edn. St. Mary's Cath. Sch., Clarksburg, W.Va., 1988—. Co-composer songs. Mem. W.Va. Gov.'s Adv. Bd. on Alcohol and Drug Abuse, Charleston, 1975-76; attended Space Camp, Huntsvillve, Ala., 1990; team mem. Space Camp Program Harrison County, W. Va., 1991. Republican. Roman Catholic. Avocations: musician (piano, guitar, recorder), art work, cake decorating, computers. Home: RR 2 Box 211-a Jane Lew WV 26378-9427 Office: FBI CJIS WVa Br Fl D1 1000 Custer Hollow Rd Clarksburg WV 26306

MURPHY, JENNY LEWIS, special education educator; b. Trenton, Mo., Sept. 6, 1947; d. Homer Lewis and Betty Jo (Jennings) Kidd; mm. Larry D. Murphy, July 2, 1971; children: Daniel Joe, Jaclyn Kate. BS in Elem. Edn., Cen. Mo. State U., 1969. Cert. elem. tchr., severe devel. delayed edn., Mo. Tchr. severely handicapped Mo. State Sch., Chillicothe, 1981-84; dir., tchr. Grundy County Learning Ctr., Trenton, 1984-86; tchr., dir. spl. svcs. Livingston County R-III schs., Chula, Mo., 1986—; curriculum developer for ind. living State Schs. Mo. Mem. com. Trenton Handicap Bd., 1984-86; v.p. adv. bd. Ret. Sr. Vol. Program, Trenton, 1984-86. Mem. Coun. for Exceptional Children (children-mental retardation divsn. 1986—, profl. devel. com. 1991-94), Mo. Tchrs. Assn., N.E. Mo. Local Adminstrs. Spl. Edn., Classroom Tchrs. Assn. (v.p. 1988-89, sec. 1994—). Democrat. Methodist. Home: 127 SE Olive Ln Trenton MO 64683-9517 Office: Livingston County R-III Sch PO Box 40 Chula MO 64635-0040

MURPHY, JOHN ARTHUR, tobacco, food and brewing company executive; b. N.Y.C., Dec. 15, 1929; s. John A. and Mary J. (Touhy) M.; m. Carole Ann Paul, June 28, 1952; children: John A., Kevin P., Timothy M., Kellyann, Robert B., Kathleen. B.S., Villanova U., 1951; J.D., Columbia U., 1954. Bar: N.Y. 1954. Since practiced in N.Y.C.; ptnr. firm Conboy Hewitt O'Brien & Boardman, 1954-62; asst. gen. counsel Philip Morris Co. Inc., N.Y.C., 1962-66, v.p., 1967-76, exec. v.p., 1976-78, group exec. v.p., 1978-84, pres., 1984-91, vice chmn., 1991-92, also bd. dirs.; asst. to pres. Philip Morris Internat., 1966-67, exec. v.p., 1967-71; pres., chief exec. officer Miller Brewing Co., Milw., 1971-78, chmn. bd., chief exec. officer, 1978-84. Trustee North Shore Univ. Hosp., Marquette U., 1973-91; mem. exec. com. Keep Am. Beautiful, Inc.; mem. bd. consultors Sch. Law Villanova U.; mem. bus. com. Met. Mus. Art. Decorated Knight of Malta. Mem. ABA, N.Y. State Bar Assn. Office: Philip Morris Cos Inc 100 Park Ave New York NY 10017-5516

MURPHY, JOHN CARTER, economics educator; b. Ft. Worth, July 17, 1921; s. Joe Preston and Rachel Elsie (Carter) M.; m. Dorothy Elise Haldi, May 1, 1949; children: Douglas C., Barbara E. Student, Tex. Christian U., 1939-41; BA, North Tex. State U., 1943, BS, 1946; AM, U. Chgo., 1949, PhD, 1955; postgrad., U. Copenhagen, 1952-53. Instr. Ill. Inst. Tech., 1947-50; instr. to assoc. prof. Washington U., St. Louis, 1950-62; vis. prof. So. Meth. U., Dallas, 1961, prof., 1962-90, prof. emeritus, 1990—, dir. grad. studies in econs., 1963-68, chmn. dept., 1968-71, faculty summer program in Oxford, 1982-91, dir., 1991, pres. faculty senate, 1988-89, co-dir. Insts. on Internat. Fin., 1982-87; vis. prof. Bologna (Italy) Ctr., Sch. Advanced Internat. Studies, Johns Hopkins U., 1961-62; UN tech. assistance expert, Egypt, 1964; vis. prof., spl. field staff Rockefeller Found., Thammasat U., Bangkok, 1966-67; sr. staff economist Coun. Econ. Advisers, 1971-72, U.S. dels. econ. policy com. and working party III OECD, 1971-72, U.S. del. 8th meeting Joint U.S.-Japan Econ. Com., 1971; cons. Washington U. Internat. Econs. Rsch. Project, 1950-53, U.S. Treasury, 1972, Fed. Res. Bank Dallas, 1994—; referee NSF; witness and referee congl. coms.; lectr. USIA Program, Germany, 1961-62, 84, Philippines, South Viet Nam, Thailand, 1972, France, Belgium, 1984; lectr. Southwestern and Midwestern Grad. Sch. Banking; adj. scholar Am. Enterprise Inst. for Pub. Policy Rsch., 1976—. Author: The International Monetary System: Beyond the First Stage of Reform, 1979; (with R.R. Rubottom) Spain and the U.S.: Since World War II, 1984; editor: Money in the International Order, 1964; contbr. articles to profl. books and jours. Chmn. rsch. com. on internat. conflict and peace Washington U., 1959-61; lectr. mgmt. tng. programs Southwestern Bell Telephone Co., 1961-66, St. Louis Coun. on Econ. Edn., 1958-61; mem. regional selection com. H.S. Truman Fellowships, 1976-89; pres. Dallas Economists, 1981, Town and Gown of Dallas, 1980-81; mem. Dallas Com. on Fgn. Rels. Lt. USNR, 1943-46. Decorated Silver Star; Fulbright scholar to Denmark, 1952-53; Ford Found. Faculty Research fellow, 1957-58; U.S.-Spanish Joint Com. for Cultural Affairs fellow, 1981; Sr. Fulbright lectr. Italy, 1961-62. Mem. Am. Econ. Assn., So. Econ. Assn. (bd. editors Jour. 1969-71), Midwest Econ. Assn., Am. Fin. Assn., Soc. Internat. Devel., Peace Rsch. Soc., Southwestern Social Sci. Assn. (pres. econs. sect. 1971-72), AAUP (chpt. pres. 1964-65). Home: 10530 Somerton Dr Dallas TX 75229-5323 Office: So Meth Univ Dept Econs Dallas TX 75275

MURPHY, JOHN CONDRON, JR., lawyer; b. Mpls., May 26, 1945; s. John Condron and Elaine Anne (Wentink) M.; m. Marie Antoinette Calcara, Aug. 17, 1968; children: Justin Peter, Jonathan Patrick. AB cum laude, Georgetown U., Washington, 1967; JD cum laude, U. Pa., 1972. Bar: Calif. 1972, D.C. 1978. Assoc. O'Melveny & Myers, L.A., 1972-75; spl. counsel U.S Securities & Exch. Commn., Washington, 1975-77; assoc. Cleary, Gottlieb, Steen & Hamilton, Washington, 1977-81, ptnr., 1982-84, 87—; gen. counsel Fed. Deposit Ins. Corp., Washington, 1984-87. Mem. bd. editors Banking Expansion Reporter, 1988—. editorial adv. bd. Bank Atty., 1988—; contbr. articles to profl. jours. Lt. j.g. USN, 1968-69. Mem. ABA (subcom. chmn. banking law com., chmn. acquisitions and dispositions subcom. 1992-95), Fed. Bar Assn. (chmn. banking law com. 1992-94), Columbia Country Club (Chevy Chase, Md.). Republican. Roman Catholic. Home: 6 Newlands St Chevy Chase MD 20815-4202 Office: Cleary Gottlieb et al 1752 N St NW Washington DC 20036-2907

MURPHY, JOHN CULLEN, illustrator; b. N.Y.C., May 3, 1919; s. Robert Francis and Jane (Finn) M.; m. Katherine Joan Byrne, July 14, 1951; children: John Cullen, Mary Cullene, Katherine Siobhan, Joan Byrne, Robert Finn, Brendan Woods, Cait Naughton, Mairead Walsh. Student, Phoenix Art Inst., Chgo. Art Inst., Art Students League, N.Y.C. Illustrator: numerous mags. including Colliers, 1946-51; illustrator: comic strip King Features Syndicate, 1950-69, Prince Valiant, King Features Syndicate, 1970—; Illustrator numerous books. Co-founder of The Wild Geese (an Irish-Am. Cultural Assn.). Maj. U.S. Army, 1941-46. Decorated Bronze star. Recipient 6 Best Story Strip Artist awards Nat. Cartoonists Soc., 1988. Mem. Nat. Cartoonists Soc. (pres., Best Story Strip Cartoonist award (6), Segar award 1983), Soc. Illustrators, Artists and Writers Assn. Roman Catholic. Club: Dutch Treat. Office: care King Features Syndicate Inc 235 E 45th St New York NY 10017-3305

MURPHY, JOHN JOSEPH, manufacturing company executive; b. Olean, N.Y., Nov. 24, 1931; s. John Joseph and Mary M.; m. Louise John; children: Kathleen A. Murphy Bell, Karen L. Murphy Rochelli, Patricia L. Murphy Smith, Michael J. AAS in Mech. Engring., Rochester Inst. Tech., 1952; MBA, So. Meth. U. Engr. Clark div. Dresser Industries, Olean, 1952-67; gen. mgr. roots blower div. Dresser Industries, Connersville, Ind., 1967-69; pres. crane, hoist and tower div. Dresser Industries, Muskegon, Mich., 1969-70; pres. machinery group Dresser Industries, Houston, 1970-75; sr. v.p. ops. Dresser Industries, Dallas, 1980, exec. v.p., 1982, pres., 1982-92, CEO, 1983-96, chmn. bd., 1983-96; with Mfg. Investment Group, Dallas, 1996—; bd. dirs. PepsiCo, Inc., NationsBank Corp., Kerr-McGee Corp., W.R. Grace & Co., CARBO Ceramics, Inc.; mem. Bus. Coun. Active Citizens Democracy Crops. With U.S. Army, 1954-56. Office: Mfg Investment Group 5956 Sherry Ln Ste 710 Dallas TX 75225

MURPHY, JOHN JOSEPH, city official, retail executive; b. St. John's, Nfld., Can., Sept. 24, 1922; s. John and Gertrude (Wadden) M. Student, St. Bonaventure's Coll., 1929-40. Pres. Halley and Co. Ltd., St. Johns, Nfld., 1956—; Pres. John J. Murphy Ltd., St. Johns, Nfld., 1966—; mayor City of St. John's, 1981-90, 93—; chmn. bd. Cabot Celebrations (1997) Corp., 1992-93; worked in advt. and ins. investigation, 1943; freelance broadcaster, 1948; adv. bd. Royal trust. Former pres., senator Jaycees; pres. Nfld. Bd. of Trade, Nfld. Cancer Soc.; campaign chmn., life mem. Can. Cancer Soc.; chmn. new bldg. fund Can. Nat. Inst. for Blind; mem. Royal Commn. on Edn., 1968-71; campaign chmn. new bldg. fund Salvation Army, St. John Ambulance; bd. regents Meml. U. Nfld. Recipient Order of Can., 1985, Can. medal. 1992, Order of St. John, 1994. Mem. Royal Nfld. Yacht Club. Avocations: sailing, archives. Home: 36 Smithville Crescent, Saint Johns, NF Canada A1B 2V2 Office: City of St John's, PO Box 908, Saint John's, NF Canada A1C 5M2

MURPHY, JOHN NOLAN, mining executive, researcher, electrical engineer; b. Pitts., July 14, 1939; s. Maurice J. and Elizabeth (McVey) M.; m. Catherine V. Schneider, Nov. 24, 1962; 1 child, Michael J. BSEE, U. Pitts., 1961; MBA, Duquesne U., 1967. With Nat. Inst. of Occupational Safety and Health (NIOSH), Pitts., 1961—, rsch. supr., 1971-78, rsch. dir., 1978—. Contbr. numerous articles to profl. jours. Asst. scoutmaster Boy Scouts Am., Bethel Park, Pa., 1987—. Recipient Brian Morgans Meml. Lecture award U.K., 1983, Disting. Svc. award, Gold medal Dept. Interior, 1985. Mem. IEEE (sr.), Soc. Mining, Metallurgy and Exptl. Engring. (past chmn., bd. dirs. Pitts. chpt.), Nat. Mine Rescue Assn. (pres. 1990-91, bd. dirs. 1991—), Pitts. Coal Mine Inst. Am. (bd. dirs. 1989—). Avocation: golf. Office: Nat Inst of Occ Safety & Health Pitts Rsch Ctr Cochrans Mill Rd PO Box 18070 Pittsburgh PA 15236-0070

MURPHY, JOSEPH EDWARD, JR., broadcast executive; b. Mpls., Mar. 13, 1930; s. Joseph Edward Murphy and Ann Hynes; m. Diana Kuske, July 24, 1958; children: Michael, John. BA, Princeton U., 1952; postgrad., U. Minn., 1956-60. Chartered fin. analyst. Teaching asst. dept. history U. Minn., Mpls., 1957-59; dir. investment rsch. and fin. analysis, corp. sec. Woodward-Elwood & Co., Mpls., 1961-67; lectr. fin. grad. bus. sch. U. Minn., Mpls., 1968; v.p. Northwestern Nat. Bank, Mpls., 1967-83; chmn. Midwest Communications, Inc., Mpls., 1990-92; ret.; dir. Midwest Communications, Inc., 1956-89, vice chmn., 1985-89, sec.; bd. dirs., v.p. Northwest Advisers, Inc., 1982-83. Author: Adventure Beyond the Clouds: How We Climbed China's Highest Mountain and Survived, 1986 (Friends Am. Writers award 1986), With Interest: How to Profit From Interest Rate Fluctuations, 1987, Stock Market Probability, 1988, revised edit., 1994, South to the Pole by Ski, 1990, The Random Character of Interest Rates, 1990. Vice chmn., rep. 5th cong. dist. Minn. Coun. on Quality Edn., 1971-77; trustee, vice chmn. fin. com. Mpls. Soc. Fine Arts, 1977-78; bd. dirs., chmn. fin. com., mem. exec. bd. Childrens Theater Co., 1975-80; trustee, chmn. various coms. Macalester Coll., St. Paul, 1973-87. 2d lt. U.S. Army, 1952-55. Mem. Explorers Club, Am. Alpine Club (life, v.p. and bd. dirs. 1975-81), Himalayan Club (life), Mpls. Club. Avocations: mountaineering, exploration. Home: 2116 W Lake Isles Blvd Minneapolis MN 55405-2425

MURPHY, JOSEPH JAMES, chiropractic physician; b. Newark, N.J., July 30, 1956; s. Joseph P. and Roberta (Nittolo) M.; m. Rebecca Lynn Swanson, June 21, 1986; children: Joseph Raymond, Alexandra Renee. BA in Biology, Rider Coll., 1978; D in Chiropractic Medicine, Palmer Coll., 1984. Diplomate Nat. Bd. Chiropractic Examiners; cert. N.J. State Bd. Med. Examiners. Rsch. chemist Mallinckrodt, Inc., Englewood, N.J., 1979-81; staff physician Mid-Island Chiropractic, Levittown, N.Y., 1984; dir., chief exec. officer Suburban Chiropractic Ctr., Chatham, N.J., 1984—. Advisor Chatham High Sch. Key Club, 1986-87. D. D. Palmer scholar, 1981, 82, 83. Mem. APHA, AAAS, Am. Assn. Cereal Chemists, Am. Chiropractic Assn., N.J. Chiropractic Soc. (bd. dirs. 1987—, chmn. inter profl. rels. com. 1989—, 1st v.p. 1992-95, pres. 1995—, editor-in-chief Jersey Jour. 1986—, Meritorious Svc. award 1986, Disting. Svc. award 1987-97), N.Y. Acad. Sci., Internat. Soc. Food Technologists, Morris County Chiropractic Soc. (pres. 1987—), Chatham C. of C. (chmn. profl. rels. com. 1988-92, pres. 1989-92, Dist. Mem. Svc. award 1996), Kiwanis (bd. dirs. Chatham club 1986-89, Disting. Svc. award 1995), Kiwanis (bd. dirs. Chatham club 1986-89), Tri Beta. Republican. Presbyterian. Avocations: skiing, photography, model building, automobiles, bicycling. Home: 139 Woods End Dr Basking Ridge NJ 07920-1970 Office: Suburban Chiropractic Ctr 301 Main St Chatham NJ 07928-2410

MURPHY, JOSEPH SAMSON, political science educator; b. Newark, Nov. 15, 1933; m. Susan Crile, 1984; children from previous marriage: Lisa, Susanne, Peter. Student, U. Colo., 1951-53; AB, Olivet Coll., Mich., 1955; Graham Kenan fellow, Woodrow Wilson fellow, U. N.C., 1955-56; MA, Brandeis U., 1959, PhD, 1961, DHL (hon.), 1988; LLD (hon.), U. Wis., 1989. Tchg. fellow, instr., asst. prof. Brandeis U., 1957-65; dir. V.I. Peace Corps Tng. Ctr., St. Croix, 1965-66; asst. Office Sec. HEW, Washington, 1966-67; assoc. dir. Job Corps, OEO, Washington, 1967-68; dir. U.S. Peace Corps, Ethiopia, 1968-70; vice chancellor for higher edn. State of N.J., 1970-71; pres. Queens Coll., prof. polit. sci. Grad. Faculty, CUNY, 1971-77; pres. Bennington (Vt.) Coll., 1977-82; chancellor CUNY, 1982-90; prof. CUNY Grad. Sch., N.Y.C., 1990—; cons. Constl. Commn., Addis Ababa, Ethiopia, 1993; bd. dirs. Yivo Inst. for Jewish Rsch., 1993—, UNESCO Global Project, 1992—; election observer The African Inst., Ethiopia, 1992. Author: The Theory of Universals in Eighteenth Century British Empiricism, 1961, Political Theory: A Conceptual Analysis, 1968; contbr. articles to profl. jours. Recipient Merit award U.S. Fgn. Service, 1965. Mem. AAAS, AAUP, Am. Philos. Assn., Am. Polit. Sci. Assn. Office: CUNY 450 W 41st St New York NY 10036-6807

MURPHY, JOSEPH TIMOTHY, army officer; b. Brookings, SD, Jan. 29, 1942; s. Charles Ray and Alice Mae (Bork) M.; m. Carol Lea Jenison, Nov. 29, 1963; 1 child, Paula Renee. Student, S.D. State Coll.; BS, Liberty U. Commd. 2d lt. S.D. Army Nat. Guard, 1965, advanced through grades to brig. gen., 1996; technician, staff adminstrv. officer HHD, 139th Transp. Bn., Brookings, 1965-71; recruiting and retention mgr. S.D. Nat. Guard, 1971; comdr. 129th Pub. Affairs Detachment S.D. State Area Command; U.S. property and fiscal officer S.D. Nat. Guard, 1989-91, chief staff, 1991-96, asst. adj. gen., 1996—; pres. bd. dirs. Army Guard Fed. Credit Union. Bd. dirs. Rapid City Regional Airport. Decorated Meritorious Svc. medal with four oak leaf clusters, Army Commendation medal with two oak leaf clusters, Air Force Commendation medal, Achievement medal with three oak leaf clusters, others. Mem. Am. Legion, Rapid City C. of C. (mil. affairs com.), Elks. Office: SD Nat Guard Dept Mil & Vet Affairs 2823 W Main Pub Affairs Off Rapid City SD 57702-8186

MURPHY, JUDITH CHISHOLM, trust company executive; b. Chippewa Falls, Wis., Jan. 26, 1942; d. John David and Bernice A. (Hartman) Chisholm. BA, Manhattanville Coll., 1964; postgrad., New Sch. for Social Research, 1965-68, Nat. Grad. Trust Sch., 1975. Asst. portfolio mgr. Chase Manhattan Bank, N.A., N.Y.C., 1964-68; trust investment officer Marshall & Ilsley Bank, Milw., 1968-72; asst. v.p. Marshall & Ilsley Bank, 1972-74, v.p., 1974-75; v.p., treas. Marshall & Ilsley Invesmtent Mgmt. Corp., Milw., 1975-94; v.p. Marshall & Ilsley Trust Co., Phoenix, 1982—, Marshall & Ilsley Trust Co. Fla., Naples, 1985—; v.p., dir. instnl. sales Marshall & Ilsley Trust Co., Milw., 1994—; coun. mem. Am. Bankers Assn., Washington, 1984-86; govt. relations com. Wis. Bankers Assn., Madison, 1982-88. Contbr. articles to Trusts & Estates Mag., 1980, ABA Banking Jour., 1981, Maricopa Lawyer, 1983. Chmn. Milw. City Plan Commn., 1986-97; commr. Milw. County Commn. on Handicapped, 1988-90; bd. dirs. Cardinal Stritch Coll., Milw., 1980-89, Children's Hosp. Wis., Milw., 1989—, Milw. Ballet Co., 1996—. Recipient Outstanding Achievement award YWCA Greater Milw., 1985, Sacajawea award Profl. Dimensions, Milw., 1988, Pro Urbe award Mt. Mary Coll., 1988, Vol. award Milw. Found., 1992; named Disting. Woman in Banking, Comml. West Mag., 1988. Mem. Milw. Analysts Soc. (sec. 1974-77, bd. dirs. 1977-80), Fin. Women Internat. (bd. dirs., v.p. 1976-80), Am. Inst. Banking (instr. 1975-78), TEMPO (charter), Profl. Dimensions (hon.), University Club, Woman's Club Wis., Rotary. Democrat. Roman Catholic. Home: 1139 N Edison St Milwaukee WI 53202-3147 Office: Marshall & Ilsley Trust Co 1000 N Water St Milwaukee WI 53202-3197

MURPHY, KATHLEEN ANNE FOLEY, advertising agency executive; b. Fresh Meadows, N.Y., Oct. 15, 1952; d. Thomas J. and Audrey L. (Finn) F.; m. Timothy Sean Murphy, Sept. 26, 1992. BA, Marymount Coll., 1974; postgrad., Smith Coll., 1985. V.p. acct. supr., sr. v.p. mgmt. supr., sr. v.p. group dir. Ogilvy & Mather Inc., N.Y.C., 1974-90; sr. v.p., worldwide account dir. Young & Rubicam, San Francisco, 1990-92, sr. v.p., dir. account svcs., 1992-95, exec. v.p., dir. acct. svcs., 1995-97, exec. v.p., gen. mgr., 1997—. Mem. San Francisco Advt. Club, Advt. Edn. Fedn. Roman Catholic. Home: One Brookside Ave Berkeley CA 94705 Office: Young & Rubicam 100 1st St San Francisco CA 94105-2634

MURPHY, KATHRYN MARGUERITE, archivist; b. Brockton, Mass.; d. Thomas Francis and Helena (Fortier) M. AB in History, George Washington U., 1935, MA, 1939; MLS, Cath. U., 1950; postgrad. Am. U., 1961. With Nat. Archives and Records Svc., Washington, 1940-89, ret., supervisory archivist Ctrl. Rsch. br., 1958-62, archivist, 1962—, mem. fed. women's com. Nat. Archives, 1974, rep. to fed. women's com. GSA, 1975; docent, 1989—; lectr. colls., socs. in U.S., 1950—; lectr. Am. ethnic history, 1978-79; free lance author and lectr. in field. Founder, pres. Nat. Archives lodge Am. Fedn. Govt. Employees, 1965—, del. conv., 1976, 78, 80, recipient award for outstanding achievement in archives, 1980. Recipient commendation Okla. Civil War Centennial Commn., 1965; named hon. citizen Oklahoma City, Mayor, 1963. Mem. ALA, Soc. Am. Archivists (joint com. hosp. librs. 1965-70), Nat. League Am. Pen Women (corr. sec. Washington 1975-78, pres. chpt. 1978-80), Bus. and Profl. Womens' Club Washington, Phi Alpha Theta (hon.). Contbr. articles on Am. ethnic history to profl. pubis. Home: 1500 Massachusetts Ave NW Washington DC 20005-1821

MURPHY, KENNETH RAY, non-governmental organization executive; b. Lebanon, Ohio, Sept. 8, 1946; s. Raymond C. and Gloria J. (Machemehl) M.; m. Jennifer Pope, Aug. 15, 1969; children: Nicholas R., Samuel W. BA, Mich. State U., 1968; MA, Johns Hopkins U., 1971. Exec. dir. Environ. Resources Inc., Washington, 1970-72; reporter Bur. Nat. Affairs, Washington, 1973-75; editor Environ. Study Conf., U.S. Congress, Washington, 1975-79, staff dir., 1979-84; exec. Environ. and Energy Study Inst., Washington, 1984—. Mem. Sycamore Island Club. Office: Environ and Energy Study Inst 122 C St NW Ste 700 Washington DC 20001-2109

MURPHY, LEWIS CURTIS, lawyer, former mayor; b. N.Y.C., Nov. 2, 1933; s. Henry Waldo and Elizabeth Wilcox (Curtis) M.; m. Carol Carney, Mar. 10, 1957; children—Grey, Timothy, Elizabeth. B.S. in Bus. Adminstrn, U. Ariz., 1955, LL.B., 1961. Bar: Ariz. bar 1961. Individual practice law Tucson, 1961-66; trust officer So. Ariz. Bank & Trust Co., 1966-70; atty. City of Tucson, 1970-71; mayor, 1971-87, ret.; mem. law firm Schroeder & Murphy, Tucson, 1978-88; trustee U.S. Conf. Mayors, 1978-87, chmn. transp. com., 1984-87; mem. pub. safety steering com. Nat. League Cities, 1973-87, mem. transp. steering com., 1973-87; v.p. Ctrl. Ariz. Project Assn., 1978-87; bd. dirs. Ariz. Bank, Community Food Bank. Mem. adv. bd. Ariz. Cancer Ctr., 1988—; bd. dirs. United Way Greater Tucson, 1988-92. Served with USAF, 1955-58. Mem. Ariz. Bar Assn., Pima County Bar Assn., Ariz. Acad. Republican. Presbyterian.

MURPHY, MARGARET HACKETT, federal bankruptcy judge; b. Salisbury, N.C., 1948. BA, Goucher Coll., Charlotte, N.C., 1970; JD, U. N.C., Chapel Hill, 1973. Bar: Ga. 1973, U. S. Dist. Ct. (no. dist. 1973) Ga., U.S. Ct. Appeals (11th cir. 1981), U.S. Ct. Appeals (5th cir. 1974). Assoc. Smith, Cohen, Ringel, Kohler and Martin, Atlanta, 1973-79; ptnr. Smith, Gambrell & Russell (formerly Smith, Cohen, Ringel, Kohler and Martin), Atlanta, 1980-87; U.S. bankruptcy judge U.S. Dist. Ct. (no. dist.) Ga., Atlanta, 1987—. Office: 1290 US Courthouse 75 Spring St SW Atlanta GA 30303-3309

MURPHY, MARY KATHLEEN, nursing educator; b. Elkins, W.Va., Jan. 27, 1953; d. Wyatt W. and Emma Loretta (Bohan) M.; children: Bridget Allyn, Kelley M. Poling. Diploma, Upshur County Sch. Nursing, Buckhannon, W.Va., 1982; ADN, Davis and Elkins Coll., 1984, BSN magna cum laude, 1986; MSN, W.Va. U. Cert. correctional health profl., substitute vocat. tchr. practical nursing, W.Va. Nurse, asst head nurse in ob-gyn. Meml. Gen. Hosp., Elkins, W.Va.; staff nurse, resource pool in ob-gyn. W.Va. U., Morgantown; DON Correctional Med. Systems, Huttonsville, W.Va.; asst. prof. in nursing Davis and Elkins Coll.; nurse mgr. Elkins Mountain Sch. Randolph County Bd. Edn. Reviewer nursing texts Lippincott-Raven Pub. Mem. ANA, W.Va. Nursing Assn. (reviewer approval unit com. edn., dist. 7 v.p., chairperson legislative com.), Inst. Noetic Scis., So. States Correctional Assn., Alpha Chi, Sigma Theta Tau.

MURPHY, MARY MARGUERITE, artist; b. S.I., N.Y., Mar. 29, 1958; d. Vincent Joseph and Teresa Marie (O'Connell) M.; m. James Thomas Primosch, Apr. 5, 1986. Student, Tyler Sch. Art, 1989-91; BA cum laude, Barnard Coll., 1981; MFA in Painting, Tyler Sch. Art, 1991; student, Skowhegan Sch. Painting/Sculp., 1990. tchg. fellow Tyler Sch. Art, Phila., 1989-91, instr., 1995; instr. Fleisher Art Meml., Phila., 1992—; vis. artist Ohio State U., Columbus, 1993, 97; reader Ednl. Testing Svc., Princeton, N.J., 1994; tchg. artist Inst. for Arts in Edn., Phila., 1994; vis. artist lectr. Ohio State U., Columbus, 1993, Tyler Sch. Art, Phila., 1994; panel mem. Coll. New Rochelle, N.Y., 1985; panel moderator Beaver Coll., Glenside, Pa., 1995, Nat. Mus. Jewish History, 1997; sr. lectr. U. of Arts, Phila., 1996. One person shows include S.P.A.C.E.S., Cleve., 1994, Fleisher Art Meml., Phila., 1995, Larry Becker Contemporary Art, Phila., 1995; exhibited in group shows 80 Washington Sq. East Galleries, N.Y.C., 1985, Va. Ctr. for Creative Arts, Sweet Briar, Va., 1986, The Drawing Ctr., N.Y.C., 1989, Larry Becker Gallery, Phila., 1991, 95, Temple Univ. Gallery, Phila., 1991, State Theatre Ctr. for the Arts. Easton, Pa., 1991, Momenta Art Alternatives, Phila, 1991, Beaver Coll., Glenside,Pa., 1992, White Columns, N.Y.C., 1992, Moore Coll. of Art and Design, Phila., Pa., 1992, 1708 E Main St. Gallery, Richmond, Va., 1993, Ohio State U., Columbus, 1993, 55 Mercer St., N.Y.C., 1994, Vox Populi, Phila., 1994, 558 Broome St., N.Y.C., 1994, Tyler Sch. Art, Phila., 1994, Larry Becker Contemporary Art, Phila., 1995, Del. ARt Mus., Wilmington, 1996, Beaver Coll., 1996, Borowsky Gallery, Phila., 1996, Ohio State U., Columbus, 1997; works included in publs. Richmond Times Dispatch, Phila. City Paper, New Art Examiner, The Phila. Inquirer, The Plain Dealer, Artnews, Eyelevel; contbr. to The New Art Examiner. Mem. alumni bd. Tyler Sch. Art, Elkins Park, Pa., 1994—. Resident Va. Ctr. for Creative Arts, 1985, 86; fellow Skowhegan Sch. Painting and Sculpture, 1990, Nat. Endowment for Arts fellow in painting, 1993-94; Fleisher Challenge grantee Phila. Mus. Art, 1994. Mem. Coll. Art Assn. Roman Catholic. Home: 231 N 3d St # 220 Philadelphia PA 19106

MURPHY, MARY PATRICIA, elementary education educator; b. Buffalo, Mar. 5, 1950; d. Anthony Ralph and Lena (Tirone) Scime; m. Dennis Patrick Murphy, May 4, 1973; children: Gregory Raymond, Daniel Anthony. BS, Damien Coll., 1972; MS in Elem. Edn., SUNY, Buffalo, 1975. Cert. elem. and secondary tchr., N.Y. Tchr. grade 4 North Tonawanda (N.Y.) Sch. Dist., 1972-75; tchr. grades 1 and 2 Shenendehowa Ctrl. Sch. Dist., Clifton Park, N.Y., 1984-92, tchr. grade 2, 1992—; mem. Assistance Tchr./Mentor Program, Shenendehowa Sch. Dist., 1993—; presenter in field. Mem. PTA, Am. Diabetes Assn., Juvenile Diabetes Found. Shenendehowa Ctrl. Sch. Dist. grantee, 1988, 89, 90. Mem. ASCD, Am. Fedn. Tchrs., N.Y. United Tchrs., N.Y. Coun. Tchrs. English, Intergenerational Writers' Conf. Avocations: reading, cross-country skiing. Home: 250 Moe Rd Clifton Park NY 12065-6700 Office: Shenendehowa Ctrl Sch Dist Karigon Sch 970 Route 146 Clifton Park NY 12065-3600

MURPHY, MICHAEL EMMETT, food company executive; b. Winchester, Mass., Oct. 16, 1936; s. Michael Cornelius and Bridie (Curran) M.; m. Adele Anne Kasupski, Sept. 12, 1959; children: Leslie Maura, Glenn Stephen, Christopher McNeil. B.S. in Bus. Adminstrn, Boston Coll., 1958; M.B.A., Harvard, 1962. Financial analyst Maxwell House div. Gen. Foods Corp., White Plains, N.Y., 1962-64; cost mgr. Maxwell House div. Gen. Foods Corp., San Leandro, Calif., 1964-65; controller Maxwell House div. Gen. Foods Corp., Jacksonville, Fla., 1965-67; controller Maxwell House div. Gen. Foods Corp., Hoboken, N.J., 1967-68, mgr. fin. planning and analysis, 1968-69; mgr. planning Hanes Corp., Winston-Salem, N.C., 1969-70, corp. controller, 1970—; v.p. adminstrn. Hanes Corp. (Hanes Knitwear), Winston-Salem, N.C., 1972-74; v.p. fin. Ryder System Inc., Miami, Fla., 1974-75, exec. v.p., 1975-79; exec. v.p., dir. Sara Lee Corp., Chgo., 1979-93, vice chmn., 1993—; bd. dirs. GATX Corp., Payless Shoe Source, Inc., True North Comms., Inc. Mgmt. adviser Jr. Achievement, 1965-66; mem. exec. com. Hudson County Tax Rsch. Coun., 1967-68; trustee Boston Coll., 1980-88; chmn. Civic Fedn. Chgo., 1984-86; bd. dirs. Jobs for Youth, Chgo., 1983-86, Lyric Opera, 1986—; bd. dirs. Northwestern Meml. Hosp., Chgo., Big Shoulders Fund, Chgo. Ctrl. Area Com., 1995—, Chgo. Cultural Ctr. Found., 1995—; prin. Chgo. United, 1995—. Mem. NAM (bd. dirs. 1989—, dir. Big Shoulders Fund 1995—), Fin. Execs. Inst., Hoboken C. of C.,

Winson-Salem C. of C., Miami C. of C., Internat. Platform Assn., UN Assn., Ouimet Scholar Alumni Group, Beta Gamma Sigma. Roman Catholic. Home: 1242 N Lake Shore Dr Chicago IL 60610-2361 Office: Sara Lee Corp 3 First National Plz Chicago IL 60602

MURPHY, MICHAEL R., federal judge; b. Denver, Aug. 6, 1947; s. Roland and Mary Cecilia (Maloney) M.; m. Maureen Elizabeth Donnelly, Aug. 22, 1970; children: Amy Christina, Michael Donnelly. BA in History, Creighton U., 1969; JD, U. Wyo., 1972. Bar: Wyo. 1972, U.S. Ct. Appeals (10th cir.) 1972, Utah 1973, U.S. Dist. Ct. Utah 1974, U.S. Dist. Ct. Wyo. 1976, U.S. Ct. Appeals (5th cir.) 1976, U.S. Tax Ct. 1980, U.S. Ct. Appeals (9th cir.) 1981, U.S. Ct. Appeals (fed. cir.) 1984. Law clk. to chief judge U.S. Ct. Appeals (10th cir.), Salt Lake City, 1972-73; with Jones, Waldo, Holbrook & McDonough, Salt Lake City, 1973-86; judge 3d Dist. Ct., Salt Lake City, 1986-95, pres. judge, 1990-95; judge U.S. Ct. Appeals (10th cir.), Salt Lake City, 1995—; mem. adv. com. on rules of civil procedure Utah Supreme Ct., Salt Lake City, 1985-95, mem. bd. dist. ct. judges, 1989-90; mem. Utah State Sentencing Commn., 1993-95, Utah Adv. Com. on Child Support Guidelines, 1989-95, chair 1993-95; mem. Utah Child Sexual Abuse Task Force, 1989-93. Recipient Freedom of Info. award Soc. Profl. Journalists, 1995, Utah Minority Bar Assn. award, 1995; named Judge of Yr., Utah State Bar, 1992; recipient Alumni Achievement citation Creighton U., 1997. Fellow Am. Bar Found.; mem. ABA, Utah Bar Assn. (chmn. alternative dispute resolution com. 1985-88), Salt Lake County Bar Assn., Sutherland Inn of Ct. II (past pres.). Roman Catholic. Office: 5438 Federal Bldg 125 S State St Salt Lake City UT 84138

MURPHY, MILLENE FREEMAN, psychiatric rehabilitation nurse, business executive; b. Idaho Falls, Idaho, Feb. 3, 1941; d. Eson Milton and Maurine (Dustin) Freeman; m. Stanley Dee Murphy, Aug. 24, 1962; children: Madison Dee, D'Lene, Eric Daniel, Aaron Milton, William Stanley, Sarah Anne, Nona Reen. BSN, Brigham Young U., 1963; MS in Psychiatric Nursing, U. Utah, 1970; PhD in Neuropsychology, Brigham Young U., 1982. Advanced practice RN. Nurses aid LDS Hosp., Idaho Falls, Idaho, 1959-63; pub. health nurse Salt Lake City Health Dept., 1963-64; staff nurse LDS Hosp., Salt Lake City, 1964-68; instr. nursing Brigham Young U., Provo, 1965-67, asst. prof., 1970-83; assoc. prof., dir. nursing SEMO U., Cape Girardeau, Mo., 1983-85; assoc. prof. Brigham Young U., 1985-96; founder, pres. Wellness Consultation and Edn. Inc., Richfield, Utah, 1992—; pres. Psychiat. Rehab. Nurses Inc., Nine Mile Falls, Wash.; co-founder Three R's Wellness Program for psychiatric rehab.; founder, adminstr. Adelaide's House, Richfield. Author: (with others) How to Enter the World of Psychosis, 1994, Recovering from Psychosis; A Wellness Approach, 1996, My Symptom Management Workbook: A Wellness Expedition, 1996. Coach Payson Youth Soccer Program, 1990-93; mem. Sevier County Planning Com. Mem. ANA, Am. Psychiatric Nurses Assn., Soc. Edn. and Rsch. Psychiatric Nursing, Utah Psycho-Social Nursing Orgn. (pres., chair 1988-92), Utah Coun. Psychiatric Nurses, Phi Kappa Phi, Sigma Theta Tau, Sigma Xi. Mem. LDS Ch. Avocations: family history, genealogy, travel. Home: PO Box 13 Richfield UT 84701

MURPHY, NEWTON JEROME, steel company executive; b. Spencer, Iowa, Nov. 22, 1928; s. Newton Hawley and Marian Rebecca (Livingston) M.; m. Shirley Anne Howard; children: Kathleen, Sarah (dec.), Michael Howard, Laura. BA, U. Iowa, 1952. Trainee Studebaker Corp., South Bend, Ind., 1952-53; car distbr. Studebaker Corp., Buffalo, 1953-54; trainee, sales rep. U.S. Steel Corp., Pitts., 1954-60; asst. to mgr. sales U.S. Steel Corp., Balt., 1960-65; v.p., gen. mgr. Feralloy Corp., Balt., 1965-68; v.p., gen. mgr. Feralloy Corp., Chgo., 1968-71, pres., CEO, dir., 1971-94; pres., CEO Salzgitter Indsl. Corp., Chgo., 1975-94; ret., 1994; pres., CEO Chicago Cold Rolling, Portage, Ind., 1995—. With USN, 1946-48, PTO. Republican. Congregationalist. Club: Northshore Country (Glenview, Ill.). Avocations: golf, tennis. Office: Chicago Cold Rolling 6600 Us Highway 12 Portage IN 46368-1281

MURPHY, PATRICK GREGORY, real estate executive; b. Salina, Kans., May 21, 1947; s. Jorel Edward and Geneva Gail (Jordan) M. Student, Tulsa U., 1971-72; cert. grad. realtors inst., Okla. State U., 1977. Lic. real estate broker. V.p. Profl. Home Finder, Tulsa, 1972-77, Sunshine Properties, Tulsa, 1977-81, Robert A. McNeil Corp., Phoenix, 1981-85, Resources Property Mgmt. div. Integrated Resources, Houston, 1985-88; sr. asset mgr. M.I.G. Cos., West Palm Beach, Fla., 1988-91, G.A.C. Cons., Atlanta, 1991—. Co-author: Todays Real Estate, 1979. Mem. real estate com. Tulsa Jr. Coll., 1977-81; bd. dirs. Trinity Episcopal Ch., Tulsa, 1972-81. Served with USN, 1965-70. Mem. Nat. Assn. Realtors (cert. residential specialist and broker), Inst. Real Estate Mgmt. (cert. property mgr., edn. com. Houston chpt. 1987, bd. dirs. Fla. chpt. 1989-91, pres. Fla. chpt. 1992), Nat. Apt. Assn. (cert. apt. property supr.), Tex. Apt. Assn., Houston Apt. Assn. (steering com. 1986-87), Internat. Real Estate Inst. (registered property mgr.). Democrat. Episcopalian. Avocations: travel, bridge, reading. Office: GAC Cons 1403 S Ponce De Leon Ave NE Atlanta GA 30307-1665

MURPHY, PATRICK JOSEPH, state representative; b. Dubuque, Iowa, Aug. 24, 1959; s. Lawrence John and Eileen (Heitz) M.; m. Therese Ann Gulick, Dec. 27, 1980; children: Jacob, John, Joey, Natalie. BA, Loras Coll., 1980. Transporter, security and safety officer, mental health technician Mercy Health Ctr., Dubuque, Iowa, 1975-88; documentation specialist software systems Cycare Systems Inc., Dubuque, 1988-90; state representative State of Iowa, Des Moines, 1989—. Adv. com. Iowa Birth Defects, 1995. Recipient Robert Tyson award Cmty. Action Assn., 1993, Pub. Svc. award Coalition for Family and Children's Svcs., 1994; Henry Toll fellow, 1996. Mem. NAACP, YMCA, Dubuque Mental Health Assn. (bd. dirs., Legis. of Yr.), Loras Club, FDR Club. Democrat. Roman Catholic. Avocations: weightlifting, jogging. Home: 1770 Hale St Dubuque IA 52001-6049 Office: Ho of Reps Des Moines IA 50319

MURPHY, PHILIP EDWARD, broadcast executive; b. Chgo., May 11, 1945; s. Edward Curtis and Mary Francis (D'Incecco) M.; m. Carol Jean Sefton, Mar. 11, 1967 (div. 1985); children: Mandy Jean, Patrick Jeffrey. BS, Ind. U., 1967. Prodn. mgr. Sta. WFIU-FM, Bloomington, Ind., 1968; news reporter, photographer, editor Sta. WTHR-TV, Indpls., 1969, sr. account exec., 1970-80; acct. exec. Blair TV, L.A., 1980-81; pres. Am. Spot Cable Corp., Hollywood, Calif., 1981-82; sr. v.p. TV group ops. Paramount Pictures, Hollywood, 1982—, overseer asset protection program worldwide, 1982—; responsible for tech. preparation and distbn. material provided to worldwide electronic ancillary markets United Paramount Network Ops.; spkr. film preservation, in field; advisor Libr. of Congress, Washington, Nat. Archives, Washington. Lighting designer Civic Theatre, Indpls., 1979; tech. dir. Footlite Mus., Indpls., 1970-78; bd. dirs. Cathedral Arts, Indpls., 1978-80. Mem. Assn. Moving Image Archivists, Human Rights Campaign (Washington), Gay and Lesbian Alliance Against Defamation L.A., Hollywood Supports Assn., Soc. Motion Picture and TV Engrs. Avocations: photography, videography, audio, theatre. Office: Paramount Pictures TV Stage 3/212 5555 Melrose Ave Los Angeles CA 90038-3112

MURPHY, PHILIP FRANCIS, bishop; b. Cumberland, Md., Mar. 25, 1933; s. Philip A.M. and Kathleen (Huth) M. Ed. St. Mary Sem., Balt., N.Am. Coll., Rome. Ordained priest Roman Catholic Ch., 1958; asst. pastor St. Bernardine Ch., Balt., 1959-61; asst. vice rector N.Am. Coll., Rome, 1961-65; sec. to Cardinal Archbishop, Balt., 1965-74, chancellor, 1975; ordained titular bishop of Tacarata and aux. of Balt., 1976—. Office: Archdiocese of Balt 320 Cathedral St Baltimore MD 21201-4421*

MURPHY, RAMON J.C., physician, pediatrician; b. N.Y.C., Feb. 12, 1944; s. William J. and Angelines (Castroviejo) M.; m. Lila J. Kalinich, Sept. 2, 1971; children: Jessica, David. BA, U. Notre Dame, 1965; MD, Northwestern U., 1969; MPH, Columbia U., 1974. Diplomate Am. Bd. Pediats. Intern in medicine Cook County Hosp., Chgo., 1969-70; resident in pediats. Children's Meml. Hosp., Chgo., 1970-71, Babies Hosp.-Columbia-Presbyn. Med. Ctr., N.Y.C., 1971-73; resident in cmty. medicine Mt. Sinai Hosp., N.Y.C., 1973-74, clin. asst. pediatrician, 1974-75, asst. attending pediatrician, 1975-83, assoc. attending pediatrician, 1983—, assoc. instr. cmty. medicine, 1974-75, asst. prof. clin. pediats., asst. prof. cmty. medicine, 1975-83, assoc. prof. clin. pediats., 1983—; pediatrician Uptown Pediats., P.C., N.Y.C., 1976—; vis. clin. fellow pediats. Columbia U., Coll. Physicians and Surgeons, N.Y.C., 1971-73; pediats. cons. Oxford Health Plan, 1990-94. Contbr. articles to profl. jours. Co-med. dir. Benito Juarez People's Health Ctr., Chgo., 1970-71; dep. co-dir. Wagner Child Health Project, N.Y.C., 1973-75; sch. physician The Day Sch., 1984—, The Trinity Sch., 1992—, trustee, 1993—. Fellow Am. Acad. Pediats; mem. N.Y. Pediat. Soc. (program chmn. 1986-89, pres. 1989-90), Soc. for Adolescent Medicine, Mt. Sinai Alumni Assn. Office: 1175 Park Ave New York NY 10128-1211

MURPHY, RANDALL KENT, training consultant; b. Laramie, Wyo., Nov. 8, 1943; s. Robert Joseph and Sally (McConnell) M.; student U. Wyo., 1961-65; MBA, So. Meth. U., 1983; m. Cynthia Laura Hillhouse, Dec. 29, 1978; children: Caroline, Scott, Emily. Dir. mktg. Wycoa, Inc., Denver, 1967-70; dir. Communications Resource Inst., Dallas, 1971-72; account exec. Xerox Learning Systems, Dallas, 1973-74; regional mgr. Systema Corp., Dallas, 1975; pres. Performance Assocs.; pres., dir. Acclivus Corp., Dallas, 1976—; founder, chmn. Acclivus Inst., 1982—. Active, Dallas Mus. Fine Arts, Dallas Hist. Soc., Dallas Symphony Assn.; vice chmn. bd. trustees The Winston Sch., 1994—; mem. adv. bd. The Women's Ctr. of Dallas, 1995—. Served with AUS, 1966. Mem. Am. Soc. Tng. and Devel., Sales and Mktg. Execs. Internat., Inst. Mgmt. Scis., Soc. Applied Learning Tech., Nat. Soc. Performance and Instrn., , Assn. Mgmt. Cons., Am. Assn. Higher Edn., World Future Soc., Soc. for Intercultural Edn., Tng. and Rsch., Internat. Fedn. Tng. and Devel. Orgns., Inst. Noetic Scis., Nat. Peace Inst., Amnesty Internat. The Acad. Pol. Sci., The Nature Conservancy, Children's Arts & Ideas Found., So. Meth. U. Alumni Assn. U. Wyo. Alumni Assn. Roman Catholic. Author: Performance Management of the Selling Process, 1979; Coaching and Counseling for Performance, 1980; Managing Development and Performance, 1982; Acclivus Performance Planning System, 1983; (with others) BASE for Sales Performance, 1983, Acclivus Coaching, 1984, Acclivus Sales Negotiation, 1985; BASE for Effective Presentations, 1987, BASE for Strategic Sales Presentations, 1988, The New BASE for Sales Excellence, 1988, Major Account Planning and Strategy, 1989, Strategic Management of the Selling Process, 1989, Building on the BASE, 1992, Negotiation Mastery, 1995; co-inventor The Randy-Band, multi-purpose apparel accessory, 1968. Home: 6540 Crestpoint Dr Dallas TX 75240-8615

MURPHY, REG, publishing executive; b. 1934. Reporter Macon (Ga.) Telegraph and News, 1953-60; polit. editor, editorial page editor Atlanta Constitution, 1961-74; pub., editor San Francisco Examiner, 1975-81; pub., pres. Balt. Sun, 1981-90, chmn., 1990-92; exec. v.p. Nat. Geog. Soc., Washington, 1993-96, pres., 1996-97; pres., CEO, 1996—. Office: Nat Geographic Soc 1145 17th St NW Washington DC 20036-4701

MURPHY, RICHARD PATRICK, lawyer; b. Elizabeth, N.J., Dec. 13, 1954; s. Richard Francis and Marie (Conlon) M.; m. Ana Alvarez. AB with distinction, Cornell U., 1976; JD cum laude, AM, U. Mich., 1980. Bar: D.C. 1980, U.S. Dist. Ct. (D.C.) 1981, U.S. Ct. Appeals (D.C. cir.) 1981, U.S. Supreme Ct. 1984, Calif. 1987, U.S. Dist. Ct. (so. dist.) Calif. 1987, U.S. Dist. Ct. (cen. dist.) Calif. 1992, Ga. 1993, U.S. Dist. Ct. (no. dist.) Ga. 1993, U.S. Ct. Appeals (11th cir.) 1993. Assoc. Bergson, Borkland, Margolis & Adler, Washington, 1980-82; atty. enforcement div. SEC, Washington, 1982-84, br. chief enforcement div., 1984-87; assoc. Gray, Cary, Ames & Frye, San Diego, 1987-92; sr. trial counsel SEC, Atlanta, 1993—. Mem. ABA, D.C. Bar Assn., Calif. Bar Assn., Ga. Bar Assn. Office: SEC 3475 Lenox Rd NE Ste 1000 Atlanta GA 30326-1232

MURPHY, RICHARD WILLIAM, retired foreign service officer, Middle East specialist, consultant; b. Boston, July 29, 1929; s. John Deneen Murphy and Jane (Diehl) Bonner; m. Anne Herrick Cook, Aug. 25, 1955; children: Katherine Anne, Elizabeth Drew, Richard McGill. Grad., Phillips Exeter Acad., 1947; AB, Harvard U., 1951, Cambridge (Eng.) U., 1953; postgrad. Arabic studies, U.S. Fgn. Service Inst., Beirut, 1959-60; LLD (hon.), New Eng. Coll., 1989, Balt. Hebrew U., 1992. Vice consul U.S. Consulate Gen., Salisbury, So. Rhodesia, 1955-58; consul Aleppo, Syria, 1960-63; polit. officer Am. Embassy, Jidda, Saudi Arabia, 1963-66, Amman, Jordan, 1966-68; pers. officer U.S. State Dept., Washington, 1968-69, dir. Office Arabian Peninsula Affairs, 1969-71, asst. sec. state for Near Ea. and South Asian affairs, 1983-89; U.S. amb. to Mauritania, 1971-74, Syria, 1974-78, The Philippines, 1978-81, Saudi Arabia, 1981-83; sr. fellow for Middle East Coun. Fgn. Rels., N.Y.C., 1989—; cons. Richard Murphy Assocs., N.Y.C., 1993—; chmn. Fgn. Students Svc. Coun., Washington, 1989-93, Mid. East Inst., Washington, 1993—, Chatham House Found., 1993—; mem. bd. advisors Naval War Coll., 1991-94; bd. dirs. MAXUS Energy, 1990-95, Harvard Med. Internat., 1995—. Trustee Am. U. of Beirut, 1995—. Served with U.S. Army, 1953-55. Recipient Superior Honor award, U.S. Dept. State, 1969, Pres.'s Disting. Svc. award, 1986, 88, 89. Mem. Coun. Fgn. Rels., Fgn. Svc. Assn., Century Club. Republican. Episcopalian. Avocations: tennis, scuba diving. Home: 16 Sutton Pl # 9A New York NY 10022-3057

MURPHY, ROBERT BLAIR, management consulting company executive; b. Phila., Jan. 19, 1931; s. William Beverly and Helen Marie (Brennan) M.; B.S., Yale, 1953; children: Stephen, Emily, Julia, David, Catherine. Indsl. engr. DuPont Corp., Aiken, S.C., 1953-55; mgr. sales can div. Reynolds Metals Co., Richmond, Va., 1955-69; gen. mgr. corrugated div. Continental Can Co., N.Y.C., 1969-73; v.p. and gen. mgr. beverage div. Am. Can Co., Greenwich, Conn., 1973-75; assoc. Heidrick & Struggles, Inc., N.Y.C., 1976-78, v.p., 1978; v.p., mng. dir. Stamford office Spencer Stuart & Assocs., 1978-84, ptnr., 1982-84; co-founder Sullivan-Murphy Assocs., 1984—. Clubs: Riverside Yacht (Greenwich); Yale (N.Y.C.); Merion Cricket (Haverford, Pa.). Home: 11 Indian Mill Rd Cos Cob CT 06807-1315 Office: 6 Landmark Sq Stamford CT 06901-2704

MURPHY, ROBERT BRADY LAWRENCE, lawyer; b. Madison, Wis., Dec. 5, 1905; s. Lawrence B. Murphy and Elizabeth M. Brady; m. Arabel Zenobia Alcott, Oct. 11, 1947. AB, U. Wis., 1929, AM, 1930, LLB, 1932, LLD (hon.), 1994; DHL (hon.), Edgewood Coll., 1996. Bar: Wis. 1932. Mem. Murphy & Desmond, S.C. and predecessors, Madison, 1932—; lectr. U. Wis. Law Sch.; mem. Supreme Ct. Wis. Bd. Bar Examiners, 1981-86. Mem. Madison Police and Fire Commn., 1947-52; curator State Hist. Soc. Wis., 1948-90, pres., 1958-61; bd. dirs. Wis. History Found., 1958—, pres., 1960-90; bd. advisors Nat. Trust Hist. Preservation, 1967-73; bd. dirs. or advisor several founds.; bd. visitors U. Wis. Law Sch., 1975-81. Lt. USNR, 1943-46. Fellow Am. Bar Found.; mem. ABA, State Bar Wis., Am. Law Inst., Selden Soc. (Eng.), Bascom Hill Soc. (Wis.), Phi Beta Kappa Assocs., Phi Kappa Phi, Chi Phi, Phi Delta Phi. Republican. Roman Catholic. Clubs: Madison, Blackhawk Country. Home: 3423 Valley Creek Cir Middleton WI 53562-1991 Office: Murphy & Desmond S C 2 E Mifflin St Madison WI 53703-2860

MURPHY, ROBIN ROBERSON, computer science educator; b. Mobile, Ala., Aug. 25, 1957; d. Fred Blakely and Ada Lee (Wills) Roberson; m. Kevin Eddy Murphy, Aug., 27, 1982; children: Kathleen Freebern, Allan Roberson. B in Mech. Engring., Ga. Inst. Tech., 1980, MS in Computer Sci., 1989, PhD in Computer Sci., 1992. Project engr. Dow Chem. USA, Plaquemine, La., 1980-84; software project engr. Turbitrol Co., Atlanta, 1984-86; asst. prof. dept. math. and comp. sci. Colo. Sch. Mines, Golden, 1992—, assoc. dir. Ctr. Robotics and Intelligent Systems, 1994—; mem. NSF vis. com. on computer sci. curriculum U. Va., Charlottesville, 1992-95. Author: (with others) The Handbook of Brain Theory and Neural Networks, 1995; spl. column editor Robotics and Autonomous Systems, 1997—; contbr. articles to profl. jours. Rsch. grantee NSF, 1994—, Advanced Rsch. Projects Agy., 1994—, NASA, 1994—; Rockwell Internat. Doctoral fellow. Mem. AAAI, IEEE, AIAA, Assn. Computing Machinery. Office: Colo Sch Mines Dept Math and Computer Sci Golden CO 80401-1887

MURPHY, ROSEMARY, actress; b. Munich, Germany; came to U.S., 1939; d. Robert D. and Mildred (Taylor) M. Ed. in, Paris, France and Kansas City, Mo. Broadway appearances include Look Homeward Angel, 1958, Night of the Iguana, World premier at Spoleto (Italy) Festival of Two Worlds, 1959, Period of Adjustment, 1961, King Lear, 1963, Any Wednesday, 1964-66, Delicate Balance, 1966, Weekend, 1968, Butterflies are Free, 1970, Lady Macbeth, Stratford, Conn., 1973, Ladies of the Alamo, 1977, John Gabriel Borkman, 1980, Learned Ladies, 1982, Coastal Disturbances, 1987, The Devil's Disciple, 1988, A Delicate Balance, 1996; motion picture appearances include To Kill a Mockingbird, 1962, Any Wednesday, 1966, Ben, 1972, Walking Tall, 1972, You'll Like My Mother, 1972, Forty Carats, 1973, Julia, 1976, September, 1987, For the Boys, 1991, And The Band Played On, 1993, The Tuskegee Airmen, 1995; TV appearance Eleanor and Franklin, 1975 (Emmy award for best supporting actress 1976), George Washington, 1983 (Tony award nominations 1961, 64, 67, award Motion Picture Arts Club 1966), E-Z Streets, 1996. Recipient Variety Poll award, 1961, 67. Address: 220 E 73rd St New York NY 10021-4319

MURPHY, RUSSELL STEPHEN, theater company executive; b. North Canton, Ohio, Aug. 24, 1957; s. Allen Forest and Gene Selma (Russell) M. BA in Dance, Point Park Coll., 1984. Mem. stage crew, set constrn. Shenandoah Coll. & Conservatory of Music, Winchester, Va., 1977-78; student libr. Point Park Coll., Pitts., 1978-80; dancer, actor, costume constrn. and maintenance Fayette Heritage, Inc., Farmington, Pa., 1980; dancer, bookkeeper and tchr. Alloy Dance Ctr., asst. to dir. Pitts. Dance Alloy, 1981-84; asst. sales mgr., group leader, sponsor, host/cashier Macy's, Stamford, Conn., 1984-87; mgr., sales supr. Trans-Pacific Stores, Ltd. (Russell's), N.Y.C., 1987-88; box office mgr. Music Theatre Group, N.Y.C., 1987-89; gen. and bus. mgr., bus. assoc., office and box office mgr. Pan Asian Repertory Theatre, N.Y.C., 1987—. Deacon Met. Community Ch. of N.Y.C., 1989—; merchandise chmn. Heritage of Pride, N.Y.C., 1993-94. Democrat. Avocations: beach combing, fighting for civil and Gay-Lesbian rights. Home: 3528 34th St Apt 1C Long Island City NY 11106-1966 Office: Pan Asian Repertory Theatre 47 Great Jones St New York NY 10012-1118

MURPHY, SANDRA ROBISON, lawyer; b. Detroit, July 28, 1949; m. Richard Robin. BA, Northwestern U., 1971; JD, Loyola U., Chgo., 1976. Bar: U.S. Dist. Ct. (no. dist.) Ill. 1976. Assoc. Notz, Craven, Mead, Maloney & Price, Chgo., 1976-78; ptnr. McDermott, Will & Emery, Chgo., 1978—. Mem. ABA (family law sect.), Ill. Bar Assn. (chair sect. family law coun. 1987-88), Chgo. Bar Assn. (chair matrimonial law com. 1985-86), Am. Acad. Matrimonial Lawyers (sec. 1990-91, v.p. 1991-92, pres. Ill. chpt. 1992-93, pres.-elect 1994-95, pres. 1995-96), Legal Club Chgo.

MURPHY, SHARON MARGARET, university official, educator; b. Milw., Aug. 2, 1940; d. Adolph Leonard and Margaret Ann (Hirtz) Feyen; m. James Emmett Murphy, June 28, 1969 (dec. May 1983); children: Shannon Lynn, Erin Ann. BA, Marquette U., 1965; MA, U. Iowa, 1970, PhD, 1973. Cert. K-14 tchr., Iowa. Tchr. elem. and secondary schs., Wis., 1959-69; dir. publs. Kirkwood C.C., Cedar Rapids, Iowa, 1969-71; instr. journalism U. Iowa, Iowa City, 1971-73; asst. prof. U. Wis., Milw., 1973-79; assoc. prof. So. Ill. U., Carbondale, 1979-84; dean/prof. Marquette U., Milw., 1984-94; provost, v.p. acad. affairs, prof. Bradley U., Peoria, Ill., 1994—; pub. rels. dir., editor Worldwide mag., Milw., 1965-68; reporter Milw. Sentinel, 1967; Fulbright sr. lectr. U. Nigeria, Nsukka, 1977-78. Author: Other Voices: Black, Chicano & American Indian Press, 1971; (with Wigal) Screen Experience: An Approach to Film, 1968, (with Murphy) Let My People Know: American Indian Journalism, 1981, (with Schilpp) Great Women of the Press, 1983; editor: (book, with others) International Perspectives on News, 1982. Bd. dirs. Dirksen Congl. Leadership Ctr., Dow Jones Newspaper Fund, N.Y., 1986-95, Peoria Symphony; v.p. women's fund Peoria Cmty. Found.; mem. Peoria Riverfront Commn. Recipient Medal of Merit, Journalism Edn. Assn., 1976, Amoco Award for Teaching Excellence, 1977, Outstanding Achievement award Greater Milw. YWCA, 1989; named Knight of Golden Quill, Milw. Press Club, 1977; Nat. headliner Women in Communication, Inc., 1985. Mem. Assn. Edn. in Journalism and Mass Comm. (pres. 1986-87), Internat. Comm. Assn., Peoria C. of C. (bd. dirs.), Soc. Profl. Journalists, Nat. Press Club. Democrat. Roman Catholic. Office: Bradley U Office of Provost Peoria IL 61625

MURPHY, SHAUN EDWARD, bank executive; b. London, June 3, 1961; came to U.S., 1962; s. John Joseph and Annie (Coyle) M.; m. Angela Mary Murphy, July 19, 1986. BSBA, Villanova U., 1983; MSc, London Sch. Econs., 1984. Rating analyst Fireman's Fund Ins. Co., N.Y.C., 1978-83; corp. officer Marine Midland Bank, N.A., N.Y.C., 1985-88; v.p., mgr. Nat. Bank Washington, 1988-89; sr. v.p., divsn. mgr. Riggs Nat. Bank, Washington, 1989-96; chief credit officer Riggs AP Bank, London, 1991; sr. v.p., mgr. First Nat. Bank Md., Washington, 1996—. Senate mem. U. London Convocation, 1984—; exec. Cath. Charities Washington, 1988—. Mem. Am. Friends of London Sch. Econs., Treasury Mgmt. Assn., Greater Washington Ceili Club (cir.), Wolf Trap Found. (corp. com.). Republican. Roman Catholic. Avocations: golf, scuba, cross-country track, traditional Irish music, marathons. Home: 1045 31st St NW Washington DC 20007-4407 Office: First Nat Bank Md 601 13th St NW Washington DC 20005-3807

MURPHY, STEPHAN DAVID, electrical engineer; b. Cin., July 12, 1948; s. James Martin and Oswalda (Magalli) M.; m. Nancy Elizabeth Benton, Apr. 20, 1979; children: Colleen B., Brian B. BSEE, Case Western Res. U., 1971. Design engr. Gould Ocean Systems, Cleve., 1971-74; project engr. Victoreen Inst. div. Sheller-Globe, Cleve., 1974-78, TRW, Inc., Euclid, Ohio, 1978-85; engring. mgr. Textron, Inc., Danville, Pa., 1985-96; prin. staff mem. Concurrent Techs. Corp., West Chester, Pa., 1997—. Author, editor: In-Process Measurement of Control, 1990; contbr. tech. articles to profl. publs. Community chmn. Cleve. unit Am. Heart Assn., 1984; coach Am. Youth Soccer Orgn., Danville, Pa., 1992, Danville Little League, 1992. Mem. AAAS, IEEE, Soc. Mfg. Engrs. (sr.). Republican. Presbyterian. Achievements include patent in area of non-contact gaging and ultrasonic defect detection, pioneering in development of non-contact gaging. Office: Concurrent Techs Corp 211 Carter Dr West Chester PA 19382-4501

MURPHY, TERENCE MARTIN, biology educator; b. Seattle, July 1, 1942; s. Norman Walter and Dorothy Louise (Smith) M.; m Judith Baron, July 12, 1969; 1 child, Shannon Elaine. BS, Calif. Inst. Tech., 1964; PhD, U. Calif. San Diego, La Jolla, 1968. Sr. fellow dept. biochemistry U. Wash., Seattle, 1969-70; asst. prof. botany U. Calif., Davis, 1971-76, assoc. prof., 1976-82, prof. biology, 1982—, chmn. dept. botany, 1986-90. Author: Plant Molecular Development, 1988; N.Am. exec. editor, N.Am. office, Physiologia Plantarum, 1988—; contbr. articles to profl. jours. Mem. AAAS, Am. Soc. Plant Physiologists, Am. Soc. Photobiology, Scandinavian Soc. Plant Physiology. Home: 725 N Campus Way Davis CA 95616-3518 Office: U Calif Sect Plant Biology Davis CA 95616

MURPHY, TERENCE ROCHE, lawyer; b. Laurium, Mich., Oct. 20, 1937; s. M. Leonard and Alice Lenore (Roche) M.; m. Suzanne Kathryn Dupré, Oct. 14, 1967 (div. Apr. 1980); children: Braden Mathias, Fiona Elizabeth Dupré; m. Patricia Ann Sherman, May 21, 1983. A.B., Harvard Coll., 1959; J.D. cum laude, U. Mich., 1966. Bar: D.C. 1967, U.S. Supreme Ct. 1971. Trial atty. Dept. Justice, Washington, 1966-68; assoc. Wald, Harkrader & Ross, Washington, 1968-72, ptnr., 1972-83; ptnr. McDermott, Will & Emery, Washington, 1983-84, Adams, Duque & Hazeltine, Washington, 1984-86; founding ptnr. Murphy & Weber (formerly Murphy & Malone), 1986—; bd. dirs. internat. bus. assns.; author, lectr. on internat. trade, antitrust and administrv. law; founding chmn. Brit.-Am. Bus. Coun., 1989-90, legal counsel, 1993-96; officer, bd. dirs. Industry Coalition of Tech. Transfer. Co-editor: Coping With U.S. Export Controls, ann. edits., 1986, 87, 88; bd. advisors The European Inst., 1993—; contbr. articles to European and Am. legal publs. Mem. com. visitors U. Mich. Law Sch., 1975—; trustee Lawyer's Com. for Civil Rights Under Law, 1975-89. Lt. USN, 1959-63. Decorated U.S. Navy Commendation, Cuban Missle Crisis, 1962, Hon. Officer, Order Brit. Empire, 1993. Fellow Royal Soc. of Arts; mem. ABA (coun. administrv. law sect. 1980-83, co-chmn. com. on internat. and comparative administrv. law 1994-97), Am. Law Inst., Am. Assn. Exporters and Importers (bd. dirs.), Internat. Bar Assn. (sec. antitrust and monopolies com. 1981-83), Am. Soc. Internat. Law, Brit.-Am. Bus. Assn. (Washington, founding dir. 1987—, chmn. 1989—, legal advisor 1992-95), Royal Inst. Internat. Affairs (London), Am. Coun. on Germany, Deutsch-Amerikanische Juristen-Vereinigung (Bonn), Met. Club (Washington), Harvard Club (N.Y.C.), Miscowaubik Club (Calument, Mich.). Home: 2710 Cathedral Ave NW Washington DC 20008-4120 also: Ave de l'Esplanade 17, 1970 Wezembeek-Oppem Brussels Belgium Office: Murphy & Weber 818 Connecticut Ave NW Washington DC 20006-2702

MURPHY, THOMAS AQUINAS, former automobile manufacturing company executive; b. Hornell, N.Y., Dec. 10, 1915; s. John Joseph and Alma (O'Grady) M.; m. Catherine Rita Maquire, June 7, 1941; children: Catherine, Maureen, Thomas Aquinas. B.S., U. Ill., 1938. With Gen. Motors Corp.,

1938-88; asst. treas. Gen. Motors Corp., N.Y.C., 1959; comptroller Gen. Motors Corp., Detroit, 1967; treas. Gen. Motors Corp., 1968, v.p. in charge car and truck group, 1970-72, vice chmn., 1972-74, chmn., chief exec. officer, 1974-80, dir., 1980-88. Bd. dirs. U. Ill. Found. Served with USNR, 1943-46. Mem. Fin. Execs. Inst., Bus. Coun., Bloomfield Hills (Mich.) Country Club, Delray Dunes (Fla.) Golf Club, Ocean Club (Fla.). Office: 3044 W Grand Blvd Detroit MI 48202-3037

MURPHY, THOMAS BAILEY, state legislator; b. Bremen, Ga., Mar. 10, 1924; s. W.H. and Leita (Jones) M.; m. Agnes Bennett, July 22, 1946; children: Michael L., Martha L., Marjorie Lynn, Mary June. Grad., North Ga. Coll., 1943; LLB, U. Ga., 1949. Bar: Ga. 1949. Ptnr. Murphy & Murphy, Bremen, 1949—; mem. Ga. Ho. of Reps., Atlanta, 1961—, adminstrv. floor leader for gov., 1969-70, spkr. pro tem, 1971-74, spkr., 1974—. Mem. Ga. Bar Assn., Am. Legion, VFW, Ga. Peace Officers Assn. (hon. life), Ga. Fraternal Order Police (hon.), Ga. Sheriffs Assn., Moose, Gridiron. Democrat. Baptist. Club: Moose. Office: Ho of Reps State Capitol SW Rm 332 Atlanta GA 30334-1160

MURPHY, THOMAS J., JR., mayor; m. Mona McMahon. BS in Biology and Chemistry, John Carroll U., 1967; MS in Urban Affairs/Planning summa cum laude, Hunter Coll., 1973. Vol. Peace Corps., Paraguay, 1970-72; exec. dir. Perry Hilltop Citizen's Coun., 1973-76; chem. sales rep. Alcoa, 1967-70; exec. dir. North Side Civic Devel. Coun., 1976-78; state rep. 20th Legis. Dist., 1979-94; mayor City of Pitts., 1994—. Democrat. Office: Office of the Mayor 512 City County Bldg 414 Grant St Pittsburgh PA 15219-2404*

MURPHY, THOMAS JOHN, publishing executive; b. Lockport, N.Y., Mar. 29, 1931; s. Matthew J. and Mary Frances (Tracy) M.; m. Maryann Elizabeth Stadnicki, Dec. 29, 1956; children: Kevin, Janine, Peter, Thomas. B.S., SUNY-Brockport, 1952; postgrad., Boston U., 1955-57, Northwestern U., 1976. Sales rep., asst. dir. advt., mgr. sales services, dir. tng., asst. dir. mktg., dir. mktg. McGraw-Hill Co., St. Louis, N.Y.C., 1954-73; v.p., gen. mgr. sch. dept. Holt, Rinehart & Winston pub. CBS, Inc., N.Y.C., 1973-78; sr. v.p. CBS Sch. Pub., 1978-80, pres., 1980-82; v.p. AICPA, 1982-88; ptnr. Profl. Pub. Svcs. Co., Westport, Conn., 1988—; pres. World Book Pubs., 1991. Contbr. articles to profl. jours. Bd. dirs. Brockport Found., 1977-83, Rec. for the Blind, 1980-89, Inter-Faith Housing Assn., 1991-94. Named to Heritage Hall of Fame, SUNY. Democrat. Roman Catholic. Home and Office: 4 Ivanhoe Ln Westport CT 06880-5038

MURPHY, THOMAS JOSEPH, archbishop; b. Chgo., Oct. 3, 1932; s. Barthomew Thomas and Nellie M. AB, St. Mary of the Lake Sem., 1954, STB, 1956, MA, 1957, STL, 1958, STD, 1960. Ordained priest Roman Cath. Ch., 1958. Various positions with Archdiocese of Chgo.; bishop of Great Falls-Billings Mont., 1978-87; coadjutor archbishop of Seattle, 1987-91, archbishop of Seattle, 1991—. Office: Archdiocese of Seattle 910 Marion St Seattle WA 98104-1274*

MURPHY, THOMAS JOSEPH, strategic communications consultant; b. Jersey City, Sept. 26, 1945; m. Carol Elizabeth Murphy, Sept. 10, 1988. BS in Econs., Siena Coll., 1967; postgrad., SUNY, Albany, 1968-71. Sr. budget analyst N.Y. State Ways & Means Com., Albany, 1972-76; dir. program devel. N.Y. State Assembly, Albany, 1977-79, dir. ops., 1980-82; ptnr. Policy Econs. Group, Washington, 1983-86; owner Thomas J. Murphy Assocs., Albany, 1987-91; ptnr. Decision Strategies Group, Albany, 1991—; chmn. Dormitory Authority of N.Y. State, 1995—, mem. N.Y. State Facilities Devel. Corp., 1995, N.Y. State Med. Care Facilities Agy., 1995; co-exec. dir. Med. Waste Policy Com., 1988-89; mem. rev. panel Office of Tech. Assessment, Washington, 1990. Exec. dir. Rep. Assembly Campaign Com., Albany, 1982. Roman Catholic. Home: 1 Fox Run Latham NY 12110-5035 Office: Decision Strategies Group 99 Washington Ave Albany NY 12210

MURPHY, THOMAS MILES, pediatrician; b. Sioux City, Iowa, Dec. 5, 1945; s. Charles Thomas and Madeline Elizabeth (McGovern) M.; m. Priscilla Rollin Coit, Oct. 4, 1969; 1 child, Nicholas Charles. AB in Math., Harvard Coll., 1969; MD, U. Rochester, 1973. Diplomate Am. Bd. Med. Examiners, Am. Bd. Internal Medicine, Am. Bd. Pediatrics, subbd. pulmonology; lic. physician, Va., D.C., Md., Ill., N.C. Intern Georgetown U. Med. Divsn., D.C. Gen. Hosp., Washington, 1973-74; resident in internal medicine Georgetown U. Med. Ctr., Washington, 1974-76, fellow pediat. pulmonary medicine, 1976-78; asst. prof. pediat. Georgetown U. Sch. Medicine, Washington, 1979-80, asst. prof. clin. pediat., 1980-85; asst. prof. clin. pediat. U. Chgo., 1985-87, asst. prof. pediat. and medicine, 1990-93; asst. prof. pediat. U. Chgo. Pritzker Sch. Medicine, 1987-90, chief sect. pulmonary medicine dept. pediat., 1992-93; chief divsn. pediat. pulmonary diseases Duke U., Durham, N.C., 1993—; assoc. dir. Pediatric Pulmonary and Cystic Fibrosis Ctr., Georgetown U., 1978-80; asst. prof. child health and devel. George Washington U. Sch. Medicine and Health Scis., Washington, 1980-85; assoc. chmn. dept. pulmonary medicine, co-dir. Cystic Fibrosis Ctr. for Care, Teaching and Rsch., Children's Hosp. Nat. Med. Ctr., Washington, 1980-85; dir. pediatric pulmonary fellowship tng. program U. Chgo., 1990-93, dir. Cystic Fibrosis Ctr., 1991-93, assoc. chief sect. allergy, immunology and pulmonology, dept. pediatrics, 1991-92. Contbr. articles to profl. jours., chpts. to books; cons. referee editor New Eng. Jour. Medicine, 1989, Am. Rev. Respiratory Disease, 1989—, Am. Jour. Physiology: Lung Cellular and Molecular Physiology, 1990—, Pediatric Rsch., 1991—, Jour. Applied Physiology, 1991—, Pediat. Pulmonology, 1993—, mem. editl. bd., 1996—; contbg. editor The Hudson Monitor. Mem. ctr. com. Cystic Fibrosis Found., 1992—; chmn. childhood lung disease com. D.C. Lung Assn., 1980-83, lung disease com., 1984; mem. adv. coun. D.C. Sudden Infant Death Syndrome, 1981-83, chmn. med. adv. com., 1982-83. Recipient Cmty. Svc. award So. Md. Lung Assn., 1980, Media award Am. Acad. Pediatrics, 1980, Svc. award homicide br. Met. Police Dept. D.C., 1983, Svc. award Met. D.C. chpt. Cystic Fibrosis Foun., Washington, 1985, Nat. Cystic Fibrosis Found., 1997; Rsch. grantee Am. Lung Assn., N.Y.C., 1992, NIH, Bethesda, Md., 1993. Mem. AAAS, Soc. Pediatric Rsch., Am. Physiol. Soc., N.Y. Acad. Scis., Am. Thoracic Soc. (program com. assembly on respiratory structure and function 1993—). Avocations: refereeing soccer, jazz. Office: Duke U Med Ctr PO Box 2994 Durham NC 27715-2994

MURPHY, THOMAS PATRICK, lawyer; b. Syracuse, N.Y., Feb. 12, 1952; s. George Edward and Sara Eileen (Murphy) M.; m. Susan Hollis Francher, Oct. 19, 1976 (div. Oct. 1992); m. Lise M. Adkins, Aug. 6, 1994; children: Casey Marie, Matthew Thomas. BS, Clarkson U., 1974; JD, Vermont Law Sch., 1978. Bar: N.Y. 1978, D.C. 1981, Md. 1988, Va. 1989. Asst. U.S. atty. U.S. Atty.'s Office, Washington, 1982-85; assoc. Highsaw & Mahoney, Washington, 1985-87, McGuire, Woods, Battle & Boothe, Washington, 1987-90; ptnr. Reed Smith Shaw & McClay, McLean, Va., 1990—. Contbr. articles to profl. jours. Chmn. bd. profl. responsibility D.C. Ct. Appeals. With USN, 1978-82, USNR, 1978-90. Recipient Spl. Achievement Award U.S. Dept. Justice, 1984; named one of Best Lawyers in Am. for employment law. Mem. ABA, Fed. Bar Assn., N.Y. State Bar Assn., D.C. Bar Assn. (chmn. pro se litigants com.), Md. Bar Assn., Asst. U.S. Attys., Bd. Profl. Responsibility D.C. Ct. Appeals (hearing com.). Office: Reed Smith Shaw & McClay 8251 Greensboro Dr Ste 1100 Mc Lean VA 22102-3809

MURPHY, WILLIAM ALEXANDER, JR., diagnostic radiologist, educator; b. Pitts., Apr. 26, 1945; s. William Alexander and LaRue (Eshbaugh); m. Judy Marie Lang, June 18, 1977; children: Abigail Norris, William Lawrence, Joseph Ryan. BS, U. Pitts., 1967; MD, Pa. State U., 1971. Diplomate Am. Bd. Radiology. Medicine intern Barnes Hosp., St. Louis, 1971-72, staff radiologist, 1975-93; radiology resident Washington U., St. Louis, 1972-75, prof. radiology, 1983-93; sect. chief Mallinckrodt Inst. Radiology, St. Louis, 1975-93; cons. Office Med. Examiner City and County St. Louis, 1977—; radiologist, prof. radiology, head divsn. diagnostic imaging, chmn. diagnostic radiology, John S. Dunn Sr. prof. MD Anderson Cancer Ctr. U. Tex., 1993—, v.p. hosp. and clinics, 1996—. Contbr. numerous articles to profl. jours. and books. Fellow Am. Acad. Forensic Scis., Am. Coll. Radiology; mem. Radiol. Soc. N.Am. (1st v.p. 1997—), Am. Roentgen Ray Soc., Am. Soc. Bone and Mineral Research, Internat. Skeletal Soc., Assn. Univ. Radiologists. Methodist. Home: 4808 Bellview St Bellaire TX 77401-5306 Office: U Texas Anderson Cancer Ctr Div Dx Imaging 057 1515 Holcombe Blvd Houston TX 77030-4009

MURPHY, WILLIAM HOST, sales executive; b. South Bend, Ind., June 7, 1926; s. Joseph Patrick and Edna Emma (Host) M.; m. Dorothy A. Dubala, Jan. 29, 1949 (div. 1968); m. Barbara Joan Mellinger, Sept. 11, 1987; children: Kent Alan, Thomas Aquinas, Catherine Ann, Molly Teresa. BS in Commerce, U. Notre Dame. Lic. English and Math tchr. Salesman Lyon Metal Products, Inc., Aurora, Ill., 1954; sales tng. dir. Lyon Metal Products, Aurora, 1987—. With US Navy, 1944-46. Mem. Mensa, South Bend Press Club. Christian. Avocation: science. Home and Office: 1913 Stonehedge Ln South Bend IN 46614-6367

MURPHY, WILLIAM MICHAEL, literature educator, biographer; b. N.Y.C., Aug. 6, 1916; s. Timothy Francis and Florence Catherine (McDonald) M.; m. E. Harriet Doane, Sept. 2, 1939; children: David Timothy Michael, Susan Doane, Christopher Ten Broeck. B.A. magna cum laude, Harvard U., 1938, M.A., 1941, Ph.D., 1947. Instr. English Harvard U., 1938-40, 42-43, sec. univ. com. ednl. relations, 1940-42; asst. prof. English Union Coll., Schenectady, 1946-48, assoc. prof., 1948-60, prof., 1960-78, Thomas Lamont prof. ancient and modern lit., 1978-83, rsch. prof., 1983-94, prof. emeritus, 1995—; mem. adv. bd. Cornell Yeats Series, Ithaca, N.Y., 1978—; resident fellow Rockefeller Found. Study and Conf. Ctr., Bellagio, Italy, 1991. Author: David Worcester (1907-1947): A Memorial, 1953, The Yeats Family and the Pollexfens of Sligo, 1971, Prodigal Father: The Life of John Butler Yeats (1839-1922), 1978, Family Secrets: William Butler Yeats and His Relatives, 1995. Mem. N.Y. State com. U.S. Commn. on Civil Rights, 1962-74. Served to lt. USNR, 1943-46. Recipient Meritorious Service award United Negro Coll. Fund, 1967; fellow Am. Council Learned Soc., 1968; grantee Am. Philos. Soc., 1968, 75. Mem. MLA, AAUP, Am. Com. on Irish Studies, Can. Assn. Irish Studies, N.S. Bird Soc., Phi Beta Kappa (pres. Alpha chpt. 1954-56). Clubs: Harvard of Eastern N.Y. (pres. 1960-62); Fortnightly (Schenectady) (pres. 1966-67). Office: Humanities Bldg Union Coll Schenectady NY 12308

MURPHY, WILLIAM ROBERT, lawyer; b. New Haven, Oct. 6, 1927; s. Michael David and Loretta Dorothy (Murphy) M.; m. Virginia Anne Selfors, July 23, 1960; children: David M., Christopher W. B.A., Yale U., 1950, LL.B., 1953. Bar: Conn. 1953, U.S. Dist. Ct. Conn. 1957, U.S. Ct. Appeals (2d cir.) 1966, U.S Supreme Ct. 1956, U.S. Ct. Appeals (Fed. cir.) 1986. Assoc. Tyler Cooper & Alcorn, New Haven, 1957-60, ptnr., 1960—. Exec. editor: Yale Law Jour., 1952-53. Sec. John Brown Cook Found., 1971—; mem. Woodbridge Bd. Edn., Conn., 1969-75, Woodbridge Planning and Zoning Commn., 1967-69.Served to lt (j.g.) USNR, 1945-46, 53-56. James Cooper fellow Conn. Bar Found. Fellow Am. Coll. Trial Lawyers, Am. Bar Found.; mem. ABA, Conn. Bar Assn., New Haven County Bar Assn., Quinnipiack Club, Mory's Assn. Home: 15 Ledge Rd Woodbridge CT 06525-1801 Office: Tyler Cooper & Alcorn 205 Church St New Haven CT 06510-1805

MURPHY, WILLIAM SCHAEFER, cardiologist; b. Portland, Oreg., Dec. 9, 1951; s. John Joseph Murphy and Elizabeth (Schaefer) Wheeler; m. Mary Collins, June 18, 1976; children: Jennifer, Melissa. BS, Oreg. State U., 1973; MD, U. Oreg. Health Scis., 1977. Resident and fellow Loma Linda (Calif.) U. Med. Ctr., 1977-82; pres. Inland Cardiology Assocs., Spokane, Wash., 1982—. Fellow Am. Coll. Cardiology, Am. Coll. Chest Physicians; mem. Spokane Heart Inst., Momentum, Spokane C. of C. Republican. Avocations: downhill skiing, golf. Home: 733 E Plateau Rd Spokane WA 99203-3309 Office: Inland Cardiology Assocs 122 W 7th Ave Spokane WA 99204-2349

MURPHY-BARSTOW, HOLLY ANN, financial consultant; b. St. Joseph, Mo., Jan. 16, 1960; d. Roy Edward and Kathryn Louise (Bachle) Murphy; m. Bruce William Barstow, Oct. 1, 1983; children: Brett Murphy, Taylor Lin. Student, U. Mo., 1978-79; BS, N.W. Mo. State U., 1981. Acct. exec. S.C. Johnson, Omaha, Nebr., 1982-83; dir. mktg. YMCA, Omaha, Nebr., 1983-85; fin. cons. Merrill Lynch, Omaha, Nebr., 1985-89, Smith Barney, Omaha, Nebr., 1989—; instr. fin. seminar Creighton U., Omaha, 1993—, Dana Coll., Blair, Nebr., 1993—; fin. corres. KMTV-3, KETV-7, WOWT-6, Omaha, 1993—. Pres. Am. Lung Assn. Nebr., Omaha, 1992-96; vice chair bd. trustees First Presbyn. Ch., Omaha, 1989-93; membership chair bd. mgrs. West YMCA, Omaha, 1991—; mem Columbian Sch. PTA; campaign chair Toys for Tots, 1994—; founding mem. Omaha Women's Fund. Named one of Ten Outstanding Young Omahans, Omaha Jaycees, 1994. Mem. Omaha Panhellenic Assn., Leadership Omaha (grad.), River City Roundup (trail boss 1989), Sigma Sigma Sigma. Avocations: reading, sewing, travel, golf. Office: Smith Barney 9394 W Dodge Rd # 250 Omaha NE 68114-3319

MURPHY-LIND, KAREN MARIE, health educator, dermatology nurse; b. Boston, Oct. 7, 1953; d. William Joseph and Mary Catherine (Mulcahy) Murphy; m. Gary W. Lind, Feb. 28, 1976; 1 child, Nicholas. RN, AS, Laboure Coll., Dorchester, Mass., 1993. Health edn./cmty. outreach coord. Mass. Gen. Hosp., Charlestown Health Care Ctr., 1993-96, dermatology nurse, 1993—, Dept. Pub. Health breast cancer initiative outreach worker, 1992-96, advisor cmty. adv. bd., 1992—, substance abuse initiative dir. cmty. health, 1996—. Mem. Health Charlestown Coalition, 1993—; bd. dirs. Am. Cancer Soc. Cen. Boston Breast, 1995-96, co-chair cancer control core team, 1995-96. Recipient Lifesaver pub. edn. award Am. Cancer Soc., Metro North, Mass., 1994, Make A Difference award, 1995. Mem. Am. Cancer Soc. (Ctrl. Boston bd. dirs. 1995-96, co-chair Boston breast cancer control team 1995-96), Mass. Nurses Assn., Dermatology Nurses Assn., Soc. Pub. Health Edn. Home: 387 Central Ave Milton MA 02186-2803 Office: MGH Bunker Hill Health Ctr 73 High St Charlestown MA 02129-3037

MURR, JAMES COLEMAN, federal government official; b. Lake Charles, La., Oct. 29, 1944; m. Connie Paige Chadwell, Sept. 21, 1968; children: Christopher David, Richard Reno. BA, Tex. Tech U., 1966; MPA, Am. U., 1974. With Sears, Roebuck & Co., Tex., 1971-72, Dept. Labor, Washington, 1972-74, U.S. Customs Svc., Treasury, Washington, 1975-76; legis. analyst Office Mgmt. and Budget, Washington, 1977-81, br. chief, 1982-89, assoc. dir. administrn., 1990-93, asst. dir. legis. reference, 1994—. Capt. USAF, 1967-70. Roman Catholic.

MURRAY, ALAN STEWART, publishing executive; b. Akron, Ohio, Nov. 16, 1954; s. John and Catherine (Case) M.; m. Lori Esposito, Sept. 8, 1984; children: Lucy Ann, Amanda. BA in English, U. N.C.; MS in Econs., London Sch. Econs. Editor bus. and econs. Chattanooga Times, 1977-79; reporter Congrl. Quarterly, Washington, 1980-81, 82-83, Nihon Keizai Shimbun, Tokyo, 1981-82; reporter econs. Wall Street Jour., Washington, 1983-92, dep. bur. chief, 1992-93, bur. chief, 1993—. Co-author: Showdown At Gucci Gulch, 1987 (Carey McWilliams award 1988); panelist Sta. PBS, Washington in Rev.; commentary Sta. NBC, News at Sunrise. Bd. dirs., exec. com. Small Enterprise Assistance Fund, Washington, 1992—. Recipient Overseas Press Club award, 1991, Gerald Loeb award, 1992, Excellence in Bus./Fin. Journalsim award John Hancock Fin. Svcs., 1992; John Motley Morehead scholar; Luce fellow, Tokyo, 1981-82. Mem. U. N.C. Gen. Alumnus Assn. (bd. dirs. 1993—, Disting. Young Alumnus award), Gridiron Club, Phi Beta Kappa. Office: Wall St Jour 1025 Connecticut Ave NW Washington DC 20036*

MURRAY, ALBERT L., writer, educator; b. Nokomis, Ala., May 12, 1916; s. John Lee and Sudie (Graham) Young; m. Mozelle Menefee, May 31, 1941; 1 child, Michele. B.S. in Edn., Tuskegee Inst., 1939; M.A. in English, NYU, 1948; postgrad., U. Mich., 1940, Northwestern U., 1941, U. Paris, 1950; Litt. D. (hon.), Colgate U., 1975; DLitt (hon.), Hampton Coll., 1997. Tchr. undergrad. composition and lit. Tuskegee Inst., 1940-43, 46-51, also dir. Coll. Little Theatre, cons. on jazz; lectr. Grad. Sch. Journalism, Columbia U., N.Y.C., 1968; O'Connor prof. lit. Colgate U., 1970, O'Connor lectr., 1973, prof. humanities, 1982; vis. prof. lit. U. Mass., Boston, 1971; Paul Anthony Brick lectr. U. Mo., 1972; writer-in-residence Emory U., 1978; adj. assoc. prof. creative writing Barnard Coll., N.Y.C., 1981-83; lectr., participant symposia in field; duPont vis. scholar Washington and Lee U., 1993. Author: The Omni Americans, 1970, South to a Very Old Place, 1972, The Hero and the Blues, 1973, Train Whistle Guitar, 1974 (Lillian Smith award for fiction), Stomping the Blues, 1976 (ASCAP Deems Taylor award for music criticism), Good Morning Blues: The Autobiography of Count Basie as told to Albert Murray, 1985, The Spyglass Tree, 1991, The Seven League Boots, 1996, The Blue Devils of Nada, 1996; also numerous articles. Served to maj. USAAF, World War II; ret. USAAF. Woodrow Wilson fellow Drew U., 1983, Lincoln Ctr. Dirs. Emeriti award, 1991, Nat. Book Critic's Cir. Lifetime Achievement award, 1996, Doctor of Humane Letters Spring Hill Coll., 1996, Doctor Letters Hamilton Coll., 1997. Mem. Am. Acad. Arts and Letters.

MURRAY, ALLEN EDWARD, retired oil company executive; b. N.Y.C., Mar. 5, 1929; s. Allen and Carla (Jones) M.; m. Patricia Ryan, July 28, 1951; children: Allen, Marilyn, Ellen, Eileen, Allison. B.S. in Bus. Adminstrn, NYU, 1956. Trainee Pub. Nat. Bank & Trust Co., N.Y.C., 1948-49; acct. Gulf Oil Corp., 1949-52; various fin. positions Socony-Vacuum Overseas Supply Co. (Mobil), 1952-56; with Mobil Oil Corp. (subs. Mobil Corp.), 1956-94, v.p. planning N.Am. div., 1968-69, v.p. planning, supply and transp. N.Am. div., 1969-74, exec. v.p. N.Am. div., 1974, pres. U.S. mktg. and refining div., exec. v.p., 1975-82, pres. worldwide mktg. and refining, 1979-82, corp. pres., 1983-84, COO, 1984-86, CEO, COO, chmn. exec. com., 1986—, chmn. bd., 1986—, also dir., 1976—; pres., chief operating officer Mobil Corp., N.Y.C., 1984-86, chmn., pres., chief exec. officer, 1986—, dir., 1977—; dir. Met. Life Ins. Co., 3M Co., Lockheed Martin Corp., Morgan Stanley Group Inc., St. Francis Hosp. Trustee NYU. Served with USNR, 1946-48. Mem. Am. Petroleum Inst. (hon. dir.), Coun. Fgn. Rels., Bus. Coun., Bus. Roundtable, Tri Lateral Commn. Club: Huntington Country. Office: Mobil Corp PO Box 2072 New York NY 10163-2072

MURRAY, ANNE, singer; b. Springhill, N.S., Can., June 20, 1945; d. Carson and Marion (Burke) M.; m. William M. Langstroth, June 20, 1975; children: William Stewart, Dawn Joanne. B.Phys. Edn., U. N.B., 1966, D.Litt. (hon.), 1978; D.Litt. (hon.), St. Mary's U., 1982. Rec. artist for, Arc Records, Can., 1968, Capitol/EMI Records, 1969—; appeared on series of TV spls., CBC, 1970-81, 88-93; star CBS spls., 1981-85; toured N. Am., Japan, England, Germany, Holland, Ireland, Sweden, Australia and New Zealand, 1977-82, Australia, 1997; released 31 albums including: A Little Good News, 1984, As I Am, 1988, Greatest Hits, vols. I, 1981, vol. II, 1989, Harmony, 1987, You Will, 1990, Yes I Do, 1991, Croonin', 1993, The Best So Far, 1994, Now and Forever, Anne Murray, 1996, others. Hon. chmn. Can. Save the Children Fund, 1978-80. Recipient Juno awards as Can.'s top female vocalist, 1970-81; Can.'s Top Country Female Vocalist, 1970-86; Grammy award as top female vocalist-country, 1974; Grammy award as top female vocalist-pop, 1978; Grammy award as top female vocalist-country, 1980, 83; Country Music Assn. awards, 1983-84; named Female Rec. Artist of Decade, Can. Rec. Industry Assn., 1980, Top Female Vocalist 1970-86; star inserted in Hollywood Walkway of Stars, 1980; Country Music Hall of Fame Nashville; decorated companion Order of Can.; inducted Juno Hall of Fame, 1993. Mem. AFTRA, Assn. Canadian TV and Radio Artists, Am. Fedn. Musicians. Office: Bruce Allen Talent, 406-68 Water St, Vancouver, BC Canada V6B 1A4 also: EMI Music Distbn # 700 21700 Oxnard St Woodland Hills CA 91367

MURRAY, ARCHIBALD R., lawyer; b. Barbados, Aug. 25, 1933; came to U.S., 1950; m. Kay Crawford, July 29, 1961. BA, Howard U., 1954; LLB, Fordham U., 1960; LittD (hon.), Coll. New Rochelle, 1983; LLD (hon.), N.Y. Law Sch., 1988, John Jay Coll. CUNY, 1990, Fordham U., 1992. Bar: N.Y. 1960, U.S. Dist. Ct. (so. dist.) N.Y. 1967, U.S. Ct. Appeals (2d cir.) 1982, U.S. Supreme Ct. 1984. Asst. dist. atty. N.Y. County Dist. Atty., N.Y.C., 1960-62; asst. counsel Gov., Albany, N.Y., 1962-65; pvt. practice N.Y.C., 1965-68; counsel Crime Control Coun. N.Y.S., N.Y.C., 1968-71, adminstr. div. Criminal Justice, 1971-72, commr. div. Criminal Justice Svcs., 1972-74; atty. in chief, exec. dir. Legal Aid Soc., N.Y.C., 1975-94, chair of the bd., 1994—; trustee Columbia U., N.Y.C., 1981-92, Fordham U., N.Y.C., 1992—. Vestry mem. St. Philip's Ch., N.Y.C., 1970-93; mem. City Charter Revision Commn., N.Y.C., 1982-83, 86-89, mem. City/State Commn. on Integrity in Govt., N.Y.C., 1986. Recipient Cromwell award N.Y. County Lawyers Assn., 1977, Ruth Whitehead Whaley award Fordham U., Black Am. Law Students Assn., 1982, Alumni award Fordham Law Alumni Assn., 1985, Leadership award Associated Black Charities, 1987, Emory Buckner award Fed. Bar Coun., 1989, Sp. Merit award Metro. Black Bar Assn., 1991. Mem. ABA (ho. of dels. 1985—), N.Y. State Bar Assn. (pres. 1993, Defender award 1986), Assn. Bar of City of N.Y. (chmn. exec. com. 1981-82). Episcopalian. Office: Legal Aid Soc 90 Church St New York NY 10007-2919

MURRAY, ARTHUR JOSEPH, engineering executive, lecturer; b. Portsmouth, Va., Jan. 12, 1954; s. Arthur Patrick and Regina Agneta (Lescavage) M.; m. Deborah Marie Moyer, Sept. 6, 1975; children: Arthur III, Andrew. BSEE, Lehigh U., 1975; MEA, George Washington U., 1982, DSc, 1989. Electronics engr. USN Ordnance Sta., Indian Head, Md., 1975-81; rsch. engr. Inst. for Artificial Intelligence, Washington, 1985-87; sr. tech. staff The Titan Corp., Vienna, Va., 1982-89; professorial lectr. Sch. Engring. and Applied Sci., The George Washington U., Washington, 1985—; mgr. advanced technology McDonnell Douglas Electronic Sys. Co., McLean, Va., 1989-91; sr. tech. cons. Gemini Industries, Inc., Vienna, Va., 1991-93; pres. Telart Techs., Arlington, Va., 1993—; conf. com. Artificil Intelligence Sys. in Govt. Conf., Washington, 1986, 90, Am. Soc. Info. Sci., Atlanta, 1988; referee Interfaces, 1993—; founder, bd. dirs. BCN Group, Inc. Named First Titan fellow Titan Sys., Inc., 1985. Mem. IEEE, Am. Assn. for Artificial Intelligence, Nat. Bus. Incubation Assn., Agility Forum, Am. Soc. for Performance Improvement (bd. dirs. 1978-79), Lambda Chi Alpha. Republican. Roman Catholic. Achievements include development of a knowledge management system for global virtual enterprises. Home: 203 S Fillmore St Arlington VA 22204-2079 Office: Telart Techs 203 S Fillmore St Arlington VA 22204-2079

MURRAY, BARBARA ANN, bank officer; b. Mitchell, S.D., Apr. 17, 1953; d. John Richard and Shirley Ann (Larson) McNary; m. Wayne Allan Murray, Jan. 25, 1975; children: Corissa Ann, Rebecca Lea, Jeffrey Wayne, Katie Aileen. BS in Edn., Dakota State Coll., 1975. Substitute tchr. Sioux Falls Pub. Schs., S.D., 1975; assoc. Murray Constrn., Sioux Falls, 1975-82; tel. rep. Citibank S.D. NA, Sioux Falls, 1982-83, sr. svc. rep., 1983-84, unit mgr. customer svc., 1984-88, unit mgr. image processing, 1988-89, mgr. corr. svcs., 1989-90, unit mgr., chargeback specialist, 1990-91, unit mgr. cardmem. acctg., 1991-92, unit mgr. nat. accounts payable, 1992-94, mem. gen. ledger implementation mgmt. team, 1994; owner-operator Hartford Café & Catering, 1994—; mng. officer customer svc. First Premier Bank, 1996—. Supr. Sunday sch., 1988—, confirmation tchr., 1992-94; mem. bd. edn. First Luth. Ch. Mem. NAFE, Customer Svc. Assn. Democrat. Lutheran. Clubs: Mothers (pres. 1977-78), Christian Women's (prayer adviser 1980-82). Lodge: Order Eastern Star. Avocations: sewing, camping, hiking, sports. Home: Country Villa Estates 46466 267th St Hartford SD 57033-6917

MURRAY, BARBARA OLIVIA, psychologist; b. Summit, N.J., July 8, 1947; d. Archibald and Anna Cutler (Mattison) M.; student Inst. d'Etudes Francaises Pour Etrangers, France, 1965, Universite de Grenoble, France, 1968; BA in Psychology, Lake Erie Coll., 1969; MA in Clin. Psychology, Cleve. State U., 1971; postgrad. Gestalt Inst. Cleve., 1971-73; PhD in Clin. Psychology, Calif. Sch. Profl. Psychology, Fresno, 1976. Mental health worker Cleve. Clinic Hosp., 1970-71, assoc. psychologist, 1971-73; psychiat. intake worker Cleve. Free Clinic, 1971, group leader, 1972; cons. St. John's Coll., Cleve., 1972-73; psychology intern Fresno County Dept. Health, 1973-75, student profl. worker, 1974; mem. faculty Calif. Sch. Profl. Psychology, Fresno, 1974; psychology intern Calif. State U., Fresno, 1975, lectr., 1976-77; treatment program dir. E. Ross Clark Home for Children, Inc., Modesto, Calif., 1976-77; clin. psychologist Santa Cruz County (Calif.) Community Mental Health Svcs., 1977-79, dir. psychol. svcs., 1979-83; pvt. practice psychotherapy, Soquel, Calif., 1979—; oral commr. Calif. State Psychology Licensing Exam, 1988— (designated expert for med. bd. Calif., 1991—); mem. Dominican Hosp. med. staff, 1983-93, vice-chmn. dept. psychiatry/psychology, 1985-87; acting chair, 1987-88, Citizens Involvement Assocs., 1984-87; adj. faculty Pacific Grad. Sch. Psychology, 1984-89; mem. faculty San Francisco State U., 1987; cons. NOW, 1973-76, Community Hosp., Fresno, 1974; expert witness Santa Cruz, Monterey, Santa Clara and San Francisco counties, 1979—, law and ethics workshop, 1984, CPI-MMPI workshop, 1986, child sexual assault asst. workshop, 1986, The Role of the Profl. in Complex Custody Disputes, 1993. Mem. Women's Studies Adv. Bd., Fresno, 1975-76. Recipient Disting. Psychologist award Calif. State Psychol. Assn., 1982, recognition for Contbns. to the fields of Psychology and MCPA, 1996. Hill scholar, 1968, Smith scholar, 1969, Fritz Perls scholar, 1970; lic. psychologist, Calif. Mem. Am. Psychol. Assn., Calif. Psychol. Assn. (bd. dirs. Observer 1981-83), Mid-Coast Psychol. Assn. (pres. 1981, forensic chmn. 1983-96), Psychol. Inst., Forensic Mental Health Assn., No. Calif. Psychologists for Social Responsibility, Laurel Soc., Psi Chi (v.p. 1968-69), Kappa Alpha Sigma. Club: Cotuit Mosquito Yacht Contbr. articles to jours. in psychology. Home and Office: 4595 Fairway Dr Soquel CA 95073-3010

MURRAY, BILLY DWAYNE, SR., church administrator; b. Nash County, N.C., Apr. 8, 1930; m. Oma Lee Hensley; children: B. Dwayne, Jr., Susan Murray Duncan, Beth Murray Aukerman. Student, Kings Bus. Coll., Raleigh, N.C. Ordained to ministry, Ch. of God of Prophecy, 1950. Pastor Ch. God of Prophecy, Waynesville, N.C., 1950-51, Biltmore and Elk Mountain, N.C., 1951, Selma, N.C., 1954-58, Leaksville, N.C., 1958-61, Bethany, N.C., 1961-65, Greenville, S.C., 1965-66; served at N.C. state hdqs. Ch. God of Prophecy, 1951-54; gen. Sunday sch. sec. world hdqs. Ch. God of Prophecy, Cleveland, Tenn., 1966-72; state overseer Tenn. Ch. God of Prophecy, 1972-77; asst. editor White Wing Messenger, 1977-89; overseer Ill. Ch. God of Prophecy, 1989-90, gen. overseer, 1990—; chief usher Gen. Assembly, 1967-72; mem. questions and subjects com., mem. editorial com. ch. history, policy and doctrine, gen. properties com. Office: Church of God of Prophecy PO Box 2910 Cleveland TN 37320-2910*

MURRAY, BRIAN WILLIAM, lawyer; b. Newton, Mass., Jan. 20, 1960; s. William Andrew and Arleen Veronica (Dagnese) M.; m. Emily Gottschling, Aug. 22, 1987; children: Alexandra Leland, John William, Leah Jane. BA, Stonehill Coll., Newton, Mass., 1981; JD, New Eng. Sch. Law, Boston, 1984. Bar: Mass. 1985, R.I. 1985, U.S. Dist. Ct. Mass. 1985. Assoc. William A. Murray Law Office, Milford, Mass., 1985—; conveyancing atty. Milford Fed. Savs. & Loan, 1992—; mem. hearing com. Bd. Bar Overseers, Boston, 1993—. Mem., chmn. War Meml. Com., Milford, 1986-93, Milford Sch. Com., 1989—; mem. Milford Sch. Bldg. Com., 1991—; pres. Friends Milford Sr. Ctr., 1990—; pro bono atty. Vol. Lawyers Svc., Worcester, Mass., 1993—. Recipient Fenn award for leadership John F. Kennedy Libr., Boston, 1992, citation Milford Bd. Selectmen, 1993, citations State Senate and Ho. of Reps., 1993. Mem. Mass. Bar Assn., R.I. Bar Assn., Worcester County Bar Assn., Mass. Acad. Trial Lawyers. Democrat. Avocations: bicycling, skiing, home. Home: 23 Congress Ter Milford MA 01757-4021 Office: 260 Main St Milford MA 01757-2504

MURRAY, BRYAN CLARENCE, professional sports team executive; b. Shawville, Que., Can., Dec. 5, 1942; came to U.S., 1980; s. Clarence Herbert and Rhoda (Schwartz) M.; m. Geraldine Frances Sutton, July 8, 1967; 1 dau., Heide Alicia. Grad., McGill U., 1964. Former athletic dir., hockey coach McGill U.; athletic dir. MacDonald Coll., Ste. Anne de Bellevue, Que., 1968-72; coach, tchr. Rockland Nat.-Pontiac High Sch., Rockland, Ont., 1974-76; coach Pembroke-Kings, Pembroke, Ont., 1976-79, Regina Pats, Sask., 1979-80, Hershey (Pa.) Bears, 1980-81; former coach Washington Capitals, Landover, Md., from 1981; coach, gen. mgr. Detroit Red Wings, 1990-94; gen. manager Florida Panthers, Fort Lauderdale, Flor., 1994—. Recipient Jack Adams award as NHL Coach of Yr., 1983-84. Office: Florida Panthers 100 NE 3rd Ave Fl 10 Fort Lauderdale FL 33301-1155*

MURRAY, CAROLINE FISH, psychologist; b. Buenos Aires, Argentina, Mar. 28, 1920; came to U.S., 1924; d. Alfred Dupont and Caroline Johnston (Ramsay) Chandler; m. Henry A. Murray, May 17, 1969; children by previous marriages: Caroline D. Janover, Alexander M. Davis, Ann Kelso D. MacLaughlin, Quita D. Palmer, Maude I. Fish. AB magna cum laude, Smith Coll., 1942; MEd, U. N.H., 1962; EdD, Boston U., 1967. Exec. sec. to dir. Alfred I. duPont Inst., Wilmington, Del., 1953-55; tchr. Kingston (N.H.) Pub. Schs., 1962-63; instr. Boston U., 1966-67, asst. prof. psychology, 1967-71, co-dir. psycho-educational clinic, 1966-70, coord. headstart evaluation and rsch. ctr., 1966-69, cons., 1969-83; mem. clin. staff Mass. Mental Health Ctr., Boston, 1983-90; lectr. psychology dept. psychiatry Harvard Med. Sch., 1983-91; mem. profl. adv. com. Mass. Dept. Mental Health, 1983-85; cons. Indochinese Psychiatry Clinic, Brighton, Mass., 1987—, sch. consultation and treatment team Mass. Mental Health Ctr., 1987-90; mem. profl. adv. com. Mass. Dept. Mental Health, 1983-85, adolescent planning subcom., 1990—. Corporator Nantucket Cottage Hosp., 1993—; bd. dirs. Friends Nantucket Pub. Schs., 1993—, Wediko Children's Svcs., 1975-85, Shaker Village, Hancock, Mass., Douglas A. Thom Clinic, Boston, 1974-77, pres., 1977; chmn. bd. Ariel Chamber Music, Cambridge, 1979, Mass. Children's Lobby, 1978-82, pres., 1979-81, Nantucket Edn. Trust, 1990—, Friends of Nantucket Atheneum, 1990—; chmn. statewide adv. council Office for Children, 1980-82. Mem. APA, Am. Assn. Advancement Psychology, Mass. Psychol. Assn., Eastern Psychol. Assn., N.Y. Acad. Scis., Fedn. Am. Sci., Jean Piaget Soc., Pi Lambda Theta. Democrat. Home: 11 Lincoln Ave Nantucket MA 02554-3412

MURRAY, CHERRY ANN, physicist, researcher; b. Ft. Riley, Kans., Feb. 6, 1952; d. John Lewis and Cherry Mary (Roberts) M.; m. Dirk Joachim Muehlner, Feb. 18, 1977; children: James Joachim, Sara Hester. BS in Physics, MIT, 1973, PhD in Physics, 1978. Rsch. asst. physics dept. MIT, Cambridge, 1969-78; rsch. assoc. Bell Labs., Murray Hill, N.J., 1976-77; mem. tech. staff AT&T Bell Labs., Murray Hill, 1978-85, disting. mem. tech. staff, 1985-87, dept. head low-temperature and solid-state physics rsch., 1987-90, dept. head condensed matter physics rsch., 1990-93, dept. head semicond. physics rsch., 1993—; co-chair Gordon Rsch., Wolfeboro, N.H., 1982, chair, 1984. Contbr. numerous articles to profl. jours. and chpts. to books. NSF fellow, 1969; IBM fellow MIT, 1974-76. Fellow Am. Phys. Soc. (Maria Goeppart-Mayer award 1989), Sigma Xi. Office: Bell Labs Lucent Techs 700 Mountain Ave Rm Id-334 New Providence NJ 07974-1208

MURRAY, CHRISTOPHER CHARLES, III, architect; b. Bklyn., July 6, 1950; s. Christopher Charles and Gertrude Rose (Marr) M.; m. Ann Herring, Nov. 16, 1974. BArch, U. Notre Dame, 1973. Registered architect, N.Y., Md., D.C., Va., Ga. Project architect Hibner Architects, Garden City, N.Y., 1973-76; project mgr. BBM Architects, N.Y.C., 1976-79; project dir. Gensler & Assocs., N.Y.C., 1979-84, office dir., v.p., mem. nat. mgmt. com., 1984—. Prin. works include interior design Sidley & Austin Worldwide, Hewlett-Packard Regional HQ, Dept. Edn., First Am. Bankshares. Asst. scoutmaster Boy Scouts Am., also cubmaster, NCAC unit commr.; active Greater Washington Bd. Trade, 1986. Mem. AIA, N.Y. Soc. Architects, Md. Soc. Architects, Notre Dame Club, Club at Franklin Sq (bd. dirs.). Roman Catholic. Home: 12517 Knightsbridge Ct Rockville MD 20850-3732 Office: Gensler & Assocs 1101 17th St NW Washington DC 20036

MURRAY, COLETTE MORGAN, healthcare executive, fundraising consultant; b. San Francisco, July 28, 1935; d. Thomas Ralph and Althea L. (Bail) Morgan; m. J. Roger Samuelsen, Sept. 14, 1959 (div. 1969); 1 child, Thea S. Kano; m. Richard Arlan Murray, Nov. 4, 1983. AB, U. Calif., Berkeley, 1959; JD, U. San Francisco, 1964; cert. in mgmt., U. Calif., Davis, 1975, U. Tex., 1989. Cert. fund raising exec. Pvt. practice law Walnut Creek, Calif., 1965-73; exec. dir. Calif. Alumni Assn., Berkeley, 1973-78; asst. chancellor univ. rels. U. Calif., Santa Cruz, 1978-85; v.p. for devel. and alumni U. Louisville, Ky., 1985-88; v.p. for devel. and univ. rels. Tex. Tech. U., Lubboch, 1988-90; corp. v.p. for philanthropy and community devel. Henry Ford Health System, Detroit, 1990-95; CEO Sharp Healthcare Found., San Diego, 1995—; cons. Coun. for the Advancement and Support of Edn., Washington, 1980—, bd. dirs. NSFRE, Wash., Leadership Detroit, Leadership Calif.; pres. Leadership Am. Assn., Washington, 1993-94. Bd. dirs. CATCH, Detroit, 1990-95, bd. dirs., Ladership, Calif., 1996-98. Mem. LEAD San Diego, Class of 1996-97. Recipient Dorothy Shaw award Alpha Delta Pi, 1958; named Citizen of Yr., Santa Cruz C. of C., 1981. Mem. NSFRE (chpt. pres. 1994, sec. nat. bd. 1997), Coun. for Advancement and Support of Edn. (chair bd. 1981-82, Hesburgh award 1984), Univ. Club, San Diego Country Club. Avocations: art and teddy bear collecting, music, travel, golf, cooking. Office: Sharp Healthcare Found 8525 Gibbs Dr Ste 302 San Diego CA 92123-1700

MURRAY, DANIEL RICHARD, lawyer; b. Mar. 23, 1946; s. Alfred W. and Gloria D. Murray. AB, U. Notre Dame, 1967; JD, Harvard U., 1970. Bar: Ill. 1970, U.S. Dist. Ct. (no. dist.) Ill. 1970, U.S. Ct. Appeals (7th cir.) 1971, U.S. Supreme Ct. 1974. Ptnr. Jenner & Block, Chgo., 1970—; trustee Chgo. Mo. and Western Rlwy. Co., 1988—; adj. prof. U. Notre Dame, 1997—. Co-author: Illinois Code Comments, 1976, Secured Transactions, 1978. Bd. dirs. Big Shoulders Fund, Archdiocese of Chgo., Cath. Lawyers Guild, Bernadin Ctr. Mem. Am. Bankruptcy Inst., Am. Law Inst., Am. Coll. Comml. Fin. Lawyers, Transp. Lawyers Assn., Assn. of Transp. Practitioners, Law Club, Legal Club. Roman Catholic. Home: 1307 N Sutton Pl Chicago IL 60610-2007 Office: Jenner & Block One IBM Plz Chicago IL 60611

MURRAY, DAVID, journalist, author; b. Boston, July 2, 1925; s. David and Jane (Davies) M.; m. Leda Feldman Hanson, July 12, 1990. A.B., Harvard, 1947; student, Sorbonne, Paris, 1948. With Boston Herald-Traveler, 1946-48; European staff corr. U.P.I., 1948-52; asso. editor Newsweek mag., 1952-59; editor Fgn. News Service, N.Y.C., 1960-63; polit. reporter N.Y. Post, 1963-65, N.Y. Herald-Tribune, 1965-66; nat. polit. corr. Chgo. Sun-Times, 1966-77; press sec. to Gov. of N.Y. State, 1977-78; freelance writer in field. Author: Charles Percy of Illinois, 1968; Contbr. articles to newspapers and periodicals. Home: 206 Francis Ave Pittsfield MA 01201

MURRAY, DAVID GEORGE, architect; b. Tulsa, Nov. 9, 1919; s. Lee Cloyd and Marion (Bennett) M.; m. Margaret Elizabeth Oldham, Sept. 23, 1944; children: Michael Allen, Lucy Margaret (Mrs. Norman Scheer), Patrick David. BArch, Okla. State U., 1942. Registered architect, Okla. Ptnr. Atkinson & Murray, Tulsa, 1949-52; prin. David G. Murray & Assocs., Tulsa, 1952-56; pres. Murray, Jones, Murray, Inc., Tulsa, 1957-85, chmn., 1986-89; chmn., bd. govs. Licensed Architects, Oklahoma City, 1964-74. Prin. works include Cities Service Technology Ctr., Broken Arrow, Okla., Terminal Bldg. Tulsa Internat. Airport, St. Patrick's Ch., Oklahoma City, Coll. of Osteopathic Medicine and Surgery, Tulsa, First Nat. Tower, Tulsa, Hillcrest Med. Ctr., Tulsa, Thomas Gilcrease Mus., Tulsa, Tulsa Civic Ctr. Bldgs. Chmn., dir. Goodwill Industries of Tulsa, 1966-87; chmn., exec. com. Downtown Tulsa Unltd., 1975-87; v.p., exec. com., dir. Met. Tulsa C. of C., 1979-85. Served to 1st lt. USAF, 1942-45. Named to Hall of Fame Coll. Engring. Okla. State U., 1969. Fellow AIA (pres. Tulsa chpt. 1964, mem. com. office practice 1983-87); mem. Southern Hills Country Club (dir. 1977-80). Republican. Methodist. Avocations: travel, golf.

MURRAY, DAVID GEORGE, orthopedic surgeon, educator; b. Ames, Iowa, July 1, 1930; s. William Gordon and Mildred (Furniss) M.; m. Lee McFarland, Dec. 27, 1952 (div. 1984); children: Christopher, Bruce, James; m. Judith M. Sayles, Aug. 4, 1984. Student, Cornell U., 1948-51; M.D., Washington U., St. Louis, 1955. Diplomate: Am. Bd. Orthopaedic Surgery. Intern Vancouver (B.C., Can.) Gen. Hosp., 1955-56; asst. resident in surgery Upstate Med. Center, Syracuse, N.Y., 1958-59; resident in orthopedics State U. Iowa, Iowa City, 1959-62; asst. prof. orthopaedic surgery Upstate Med. Center, Syracuse, 1962-66; asso. prof. Upstate Med. Center, 1966-69, prof., 1969—, Disting. prof., 1990—, chmn. dept., 1966-86, 91—, acting chmn. dept., 1990-91; mem. staff State Univ. Hosp., Syracuse, 1962—, Crouse-Irving Meml. Hosp., Syracuse, 1962—, Syracuse VA Hosp., 1962—; cons. Community Gen. Hosp., Syracuse, 1965—; hon. staff Charles A. Wilson Meml. Hosp., Johnson City, N.Y., 1972—; med. dir. Muscular Dystrophy Assn. Clinic, 1962-67; mem. Task Force for Oral Exams., Nat. Bd. Med. Examiners; examiner Am. Bd. Orthopaedic Surgery. Bd. asso. editors: Jour. Bone and Joint Surgery, 1969-78, Clin. Orthopaedics, 1968-78, Jour. Surg. Research, 1972-82, Orthopaedic Surgery, 1978-79; contbr. articles to profl. jours.; trustee Am. Jour. Bone and Joint Surgery, 1984-90, treas., 1986-90. Bd. dirs. Planned Parenthood Ctr. of Syracuse; chmn. affiliate med. com. Planned parenthood Ctr. of Syracuse, 1976-82; trustee Orthopaedic Rsch. Edn. Found., 1986-92, pres., 1988-91, Martin Momoriac Found., 1988-92, chmn., 1990-92; mem. med. adv. com. Shirners Hosps., 1989-93. Served to lt., M.C. USNR, 1956-57. Mem. AMA, ACS (bd. regents 1985-94, vice chmn. 1992-93, chmn. 1993-94, pres.-elect 1995-96, pres. 1996-97), AAAS, Am. Orthopaedic Assn. (exec. com., chmn. program com. 1982), Am. Acad. Orthopaedic Surgeons (bd. dirs. 1980-86, pres. 1982-83), Assn. Acad. Surgery (sec.-treas., chmn. com. constn. and bylaws), N.Y. State Med. Soc., Onondaga County Med. Soc. (v.p. 1989-90, pres. 1992-93), Am. Rheumatism Assn., Orthopaedic Rsch. Soc., Assn. Bone and Joint Surgeons, Continental Orthopaedic Soc., Knee Soc. (pres. 1989), N.Y. State Soc. Orthopaedic Surgeons, Assn. Orthopaedic Chmn., Phi Beta Kappa, Sigma Xi, Alpha Omega Alpha. Home: 5 Quaker Hill Rd Syracuse NY 13224-2011 Office: 750 E Adams St Syracuse NY 13210-2306

MURRAY, DAVINA ANN, financial analyst, accounting officer; b. Sabetha, Kans., Nov. 12, 1951; d. Jim R. and Shirley A. (Ellington) Murphy; m. Brian C. Murray, July 2, 1981; 1 child, Bria Lynne. AS in Bus., Point Park Coll., 1992, BS in Acctg. (cum luade), 1992; postgrad., Robert Morris Coll., 1996—. With Integra Fin. Corp., Pitts., 1978-96, past acctg. clk., 1978-79, adminstrv. asst., 1980-86, fin. analyst, 1986-96; fixed asset supr. Pitts. Nat. Corp, 1996—. Mem. com. Pitts. City Sch. Redistricting, 1993. Mem. Inst. Mgmt. Accts., Alpha Sigma Lambda. Avocations: reading, sewing, music. Office: Pitts Nat Corp 2 Pnc Plz Pittsburgh PA 15222-2705

MURRAY, DIANE ELIZABETH, librarian; b. Detroit, Oct. 15, 1942; d. Gordon Lisle and Dorothy Anne (Steketee) LaBoueff; m. Donald Edgar Murray, Apr. 22, 1968. AB, Hope Coll., 1964; MLS, Western Mich. U., 1968; MM, Aquinas Coll., 1982; postgrad., Mich. State U., East Lansing, 1964-66. Catalog libr., asst. head acquisitions sect. Mich. State U. Librs., East Lansing, 1968-77; libr. tech. and automated svcs. Hope Coll., Holland, Mich., 1977-88; dir. librs. DePauw U., Greencastle, Ind., 1988-91; acquisitions libr. Grand Valley State U., Allendale, Mich., 1991—; sec., vice chair, chairperson bd. trustees Mich. Libr. Consortium, Lansing, 1981-85. Vice pres. Humane Soc. of Putnam County, Greencastle, 1990-91. Mem. ALA. Methodist. Avocations: dog breeding and showing. Office: Grand Valley State U Zumberge Libr Allendale MI 49401

MURRAY, EDDIE CLARENCE, professional baseball player; b. L.A., Feb. 24, 1956. Student, Calif. State U., L.A. Player minor league teams Bluefield, Miami, Asheville, Charlotte, Rochester, 1973-76; player Balt. Orioles, 1973-88, 96, L.A. Dodgers, 1988-91, N.Y. Mets, 1991-93, Cleveland Indians, 1993-96, Anaheim Angels, 1997—. Named to All-Star Team, 1978, 81-86, 91; named Appalachian League Player of Yr., 1973, Am. League Rookie of Yr., Baseball Writers Assn. Am., 1977, First Baseman, Sporting News Am. League All-Star Team, 1983, 90, ; recipient Gold Glove award, 1982-84, Silver Slugger award, 1983-84, 90. Office: Anaheim Angels 2000 Gene Autry Way Anaheim CA 92806*

MURRAY, EDWARD ROCK, insurance broker; b. Bklyn., Jan. 31, 1947; s. Garrett Francis and Anne M. (Rock) M.; m. Barbara Marie Robotti; children: Pamela Jean, Stephanie Elise. BA in Bus. Adminstrn., St. Bonaventure U., 1968. Claims examiner N.Y.C., 1970-72; agt. and mgr. John Hancock Life Ins., Albany, N.Y., 1972-76; regional dir. Colonial Life Insur, Albany, 1976-80; ptnr. Murray & Zuckerman, Inc., Schenectady, N.Y., 1980—; bd. dirs. Am. Med. Ins., Hicksville, N.Y., 1988—, Northeast Mgmt. Forum, 1990—; mem. adv. bd. William Penn Life Ins. Co. 1st lt. U.S. Army, 1968-70, Vietnam. Mem. Mohawk Club (pres.). Roman Catholic. Avocation: golf. Office: Murray & Zuckerman Inc 128 Erie Blvd Schenectady NY 12305-2203

MURRAY, ELIZABETH DAVIS REID, riter, lecturer; b. Wadesboro, N.C., June 10, 1925; d. James Matheson and Mary Kennedy (Little) Davis; A.B. cum laude, Meredith Coll., Raleigh, N.C., 1946; postgrad. N.C. State U., 1967-68, 74-75; m. James William Reid, Feb. 7, 1948 (dec. June 1972); children: Michael Ernest, Nancy Kennedy Reid Baker, James William; m. Raymond L. Murray, May 12, 1979; stepchildren: Stephen, Ilah Murray Garton, Marshall. Continuity writer Sta. WPTF, Raleigh, 1946-47; program mgr., women's commentator Sta. WADE, Wadesboro, 1947-48; dir. news bur. Meredith Coll., 1948-51; state woman's news editor, columnist Raleigh News and Observer, 1951-52; exec. sec. Gov.'s Coordinating Com. on Aging, 1959-61; rsch. asst. to Dr. Clarence Poe, Raleigh, 1963-64; contbg. editor Raleigh Mag., 1969-72, contbr. articles Hnadbook of North Carolina HISTORY, 1996; local history corr. Raleigh Times, News and Observer, Spectator of Raleigh; lectr. art and local history; tchr. Wake history Wake Tech. Coll., Wake pub. schs. and librs.; rsch. cons. Wake County Pub. Libraries, Mordecai Historic Park, State Visitor Ctr., Exec. Mansion; resource person Wake Public Schs.; dir. Capital County Pub. Co.; writer; books include: From Raleigh's Past (cert. of commendation Am. Assn. State and Local History), 1965; Wake: Capital County of North Carolina, vol. 1, 1983 (W.P. Peace award for best book on N.C. history 1983); editor, compiler: North Carolina's Older Population: Opportunities and Challenges, 1960; editor, contbr. Wake County Hist. Soc. newsletter, 1965-69; History of Raleigh Fire Dept., 1970; guest editor Raleigh Mag. Wake County Bicentennial Issue, 1971; author, photographer filmstrip for Wake Pub. Schs., 1971; author sect. Windows of the Way, 1964; Am. arts slide lectures for pub. library; author instructional materials State Exec. Mansion and Mordecai Hist. Park docents; author monthly history page Raleigh Mag., 1969-72; contbr. biog. sketches Dictionary of North Carolina Biography, 1979; contbr. to newspapers and mags. Mem. Raleigh City Council, 1973; com. mem. Meredith Coll. History and Archives, 1995—; pres. Jr. Woman's Club, 1956-57; organizing pres. Arts Council Raleigh, 1965; contbr. segments Handbook of North Carolina History, 1996; exec. com. N.C. Humanities Found., 1974-76; dir., officer North Carolinians for Better Libraries, 1965-69; mem. Meredith Bd. Assos., 1976-79, Meredith Heritage Soc.; trustee Pub. Libraries, 1956-67, Meredith Coll., 1966-69; pres. Wake Meml. Hosp. Aux., 1962-63; mem. Raleigh Hist. Sites Commn., 1969-73; trustee Pullen Meml. Bapt. Ch., 1975-78, chmn., 1977-78, also deacon; chmn. Mayor's Com. to Preserve Hist. Objects, 1965—; mem. Tryon Palace Commn., 1967-78; adv. council WUNC-FM, 1976-80, N.C. Art Soc.; vis. lectr. N.C. Mus. History Assos., 1980; docent, lectr. N.C. Exec. Mansion, Mordecai Hist. Park, N.C. Mus. Art; bd. dirs. Raleigh-Wake County Symphony Orch. Devel. Assn., 1979-83, Estey Hall Found., 1980—, Friends of Meredith Library, 1980-83; mem. adv. bd. Raleigh City Mus., mem. task force on local history; bldg. adv. com. local history Wake County Pub. Libr.; com. 1000 to establish Children's Mus. About World. Recipient Outstanding Community Service award, 1952, best all-round Jr. Woman's Club mem., 1955, Disting. Alumna award Meredith Coll., 1970, recognition for service award Raleigh Hist. Sites Commn., 1973, Raleigh City Council, 1973; Community Service award Raleigh Bd. Realtors, 1983, Phi Beta Kappa award Wake County, 1985, Silver Bowl award N.C. Mus. of Art, 1987, Anthemion award Capital Area Preservation Inc., 1994. Mem. N. Caroliniana Soc., N.C. Soc. County and Local Historians (life), N.C. Lit. and Hist. Assn., Apex Hist. Soc. (charter), Yates Mill Assocs., Inc. (charter), N.C. Art Soc. (Disting. Service citation 1979), Docents N.C. Mus. Art (pres. 1980-81), Friends of N.C. State U. Library, Friends of Carlyle Campbell Library (charter, life), Wake County Hist. Soc. (Pres.'s Cup 1994), Wake County Genealogical Soc., N.C. African-Am. Genealogical and Hist. Soc., Friends of N.C. Archives (life), Kappa Nu Sigma. Democrat. Clubs: Carolina Country, Capital City (charter mem.). Home: 8701 Murray Hill Dr Raleigh NC 27615-2531

MURRAY, ERNEST DON, artist, educator; b. Asheville, N.C., Apr. 21, 1930; s. Ernest Burgin and Daisy Ann (Bishop) M. Student, Asheville-Biltmore Jr. Coll., 1950; A.A., B.A., U. Tenn., 1952; student, Art Students League, 1953; M.F.A., U. Fla., 1957, M.Ed., 1958. Instr. art Chipola Jr. Coll., Marianna, Fla., 1958; head div. humanities Chipola Jr. Coll., 1964-68; instr. humanities U. Fla., Gainesville, 1969-72; prof. humanities, asso. chmn. dept. humanities U. Fla., 1974-78, prof. fine art and humanities dept. fine art, 1978—; cons. Holt, Rinehart & Winston, Inc., N.Y.C., 1963-76, Harcourt Brace, Jovanovich, Inc., N.Y.C., 1964-76. One-man shows in Knoxville, Tex., 1952, N.Y.C., 1953, Gainesville, 1968, 71, 72, 75, 90, 93, Pub. Sculpture Commns., 1989, 90, 91, 93, 95, Fla. Mus. Natural History, Fla. State Fire Coll., Mathieson Hist. Ctr.; exhibited in group shows Asheville, 1949, Knoxville, 1951, 65, N.Y.C., 1953, 61, 67, Gainesville, Miami, Tallahassee, 1979—; represented in pvt. collections. With C.E. U.S. Army, 1954-56, USNR, 1949-54. Mem. So. Highlands Craftsman's Guild, Fla. Artists Assn., Phi Theta Kappa, Phi Kappa Phi, Phi Beta Kappa. Unitarian. Office: Univ of Florida 302C Architecture Bldg Gainesville FL 32611-2004

MURRAY, FLORENCE KERINS, retired state supreme court justice; b. Newport, R.I., Oct. 21, 1916; d. John X. and Florence (MacDonald) Kerins; m. Paul F. Murray, Oct. 21, 1943 (dec. June 2, 1995); 1 child, Paul F. AB, Syracuse U., 1938; LLB, Boston U., 1942; EdD, R.I. Coll. Edn., 1956; grad., Nat. Coll. State Trial Judges, 1966; LLD (hon.), Bryant Coll., 1956, U. R.I., 1963, Mt. St. Joseph Coll., 1972, Providence Coll., 1974, Roger Williams Coll., 1976, Salve Regina Coll., 1977, Johnson and Wales Coll., 1977, Suffolk U., 1981, So. New Eng. Law Sch., 1995. Bar: Mass. 1942, R.I. 1947, U.S. Dist. Ct. 1948, U.S. Tax Ct. 1948, U.S. Supreme Ct. 1948. Sole practice Newport, 1947-52; mem. firm Murray & Murray, Newport, 1952-56; assoc. judge R.I. Superior Ct., 1956-78; presiding justice Superior Ct. R.I., 1978-79; assoc. justice R.I. Supreme Ct., 1979-96, 1979-96; staff, faculty adv. Nat. Jud. Coll., Reno, Nev., 1971-72, dir., 1975-77, chmn., 1979-87, chair emeritus, 1990—; mem. com. Legal Edn. and Practice and Economy of New Eng., 1975—; former instr. Prudence Island Sch.; legal adv. R.I. Girl Scouts; sec. Commn. Jud. Tenure and Discipline, 1975-79; apptd. by Pres. Clinton to bd. dirs. State Justice Inst., 1994—; participant, leader various legal seminars. Mem. R.I. Senate, 1948-56; chmn. spl. legis. com.; mem. Newport Sch. Com., 1948-57, chmn., 1951-57; mem. Gov.'s Jud. Coun., 1950-60, White House Conf. Youth and Children, 1950, Ann. Essay Commn., 1952, Nat. Def. Adv. Com. on Women in Service, 1952-58, Gov.'s Adv. Com. Mental Health, 1954, R.I. Alcoholic Adv. Com., 1955-58, R.I. Com. Youth and Children, Gov.'s Adv. Com. on Revision Election Laws, Gov.'s Adv. Com. Social Welfare, Army Adv. Com. for 1st Army Area; mem. civil and polit. rights com. Pres.'s Commn. on Status of Women, 1960-63; mem. R.I. Com. Humanities, 1972—, chmn., 1972-77; mem. Family Ct. Study Com., R.I. com. Nat. Endowment Humanities; bd. dirs. Newport YMCA; sec. Bd. Physicians Service; bd. visitors Law Sch., Boston U.; bd. dirs. NCCJ; mem. edn. policy and devel. com. Roger Williams Jr. Coll.; trustee Syracuse U.; pres. Newport Girls Club, 1974-75, R.I. Supreme Ct. Hist. Soc., 1988—; chair Supreme Ct. Mandatory Continuing Legal Edn. Com., 1993—. Served to lt. col. WAC, World War II. Decorated Legion of Merit; recipient Arents Alumni award Syracuse U., 1956, Carroll award R.I. Inst. Instn., 1956, Brotherhood award NCCJ, 1983, Herbert Harley award Am. Judicature Soc., 1988, Melvin Eggers Sr. Alumni award Syracuse U., 1992, Merit award R.I. Bar Assn., 1994; named Judge of Yr. Nat. Assn. Women Judges, 1984, Outstanding Woman, Bus. and Profl. Women, 1972, Citizen of Yr. R.I. Trial Lawyers Assn.; Newport courthouse renamed in her honor, 1990. Mem. ABA (chmn. credentials com. nat. conf. state trial judges 1971-73, chair judges adv. com. on standing com. on ethics and profl. responsibility 1991—, joint com. on jud. discipline of standing com. on profl. discipline 1991-94), AAUW (chmn. state edn. com. 1954-56), Am. Arbitration Assn., Nat. Trial Judges Conf. (state chmn. membershiup com., sec. exec. com.), New Eng. Trial Judges Conf. (com. chmn. 1967), Boston U. Alumni Coun., Am. Legion (judge adv. post 7, mem. nat. exec. com.), Bus. and Profl. Women's Club (past state v.p., past pres. Newport chpt., past pres. Nat. legis. com.), Auota Club (past gov. internat., past pres. Newport chpt.), Alpha Omega, Kappa Beta Pi.

MURRAY, FRED F., lawyer; b. Corpus Christi, Tex., Aug. 1, 1950; s. Marvin Frank and Suzanne Louise Murray. BA, Rice U., 1972; JD, U. Tex., 1974. Bar: Tex. 1975, U.S. Dist. Ct. (so. dist.) Tex. 1976, U.S. Ct. Claims 1976, U.S. Tax Ct. 1976, U.S. Ct. Appeals (5th, D.C. and fed. cirs.) 1976, U.S. Supreme Ct. 1978, U.S. Ct. Internat. Trade 1985, N.Y. 1987, D.C. 1987, U.S. Dist. Ct. (ea. dist.) Tex. 1987; CPA, Tex. Ptnr. Chamberlain, Hrdlicka, White, Williams & Martin, P.C., Houston, 1985-92; spl. counsel (legislation) U.S. Dept. Treasury, IRS, Washington, 1992-96; v.p. tax policy Nat. Fgn. Trade Coun., 1996—; mem. Tax Law Adv. Commn., Tex. Bd. Legal Specialization, 1984—, vice chmn., 1987-92; mem. Commn. Tax Law Examiners, 1984—, vice chmn., 1987-92; adj. prof. U. Houston Law Ctr., 1984-92, U. Tex. Sch. Law, 1987; faculty lectr. Rice U. Jones Grad. Sch. Adminstrn., 1987-92; spkr. various assns. and univs.; mem. bd. advisors Houston Jour. Internat. Law, 1986—, chmn., 1987-91; v.p. for tax policy Nat. Fgn. Trade Coun., Inc., 1996—. Author various publs. Del. Bishop's Diocesan Pastoral Coun., 1979-80; chmn. parish coun. Sacred Heart Cathedral, Cath. Diocese Galveston-Houston, 1979-81, 89, mem. Red Mass steering com., 1986-92; mem. exec. com., bd. dirs., 1987-91, chmn. deferred giving com. Houston Symphony Soc., 1987-88, chmn. govt. and pub. affairs com., 1988-91; co-trustee Houston Symphony Soc. Endowment Fund, 1987-91; mem. fund coun. Rice U., 1987—, exec. com. 1988-92, chmn. Major Gifts Com., 1988-92; gen. counsel, bd. dirs., com. on fin. and adminstrn. S.E. Tex. chpt. Nat. Multiple Sclerosis Soc.; mem. Red Mass com. Archdiocese Washington, 1993—; bd. dirs. John Carroll Soc., Archdiocese of Washington, 1996—. Fellow Am. Coll. Tax Counsel; mem. ABA (officer various coms.), FBA (mem. steering com. tax sect. 1995—), AICPA, Am. Arbitration Assn. (panels comml. and internat. arbitrators 1980—), Internat. Bar Assn., Houston Bar Assn., State Bar of Tex. (various coms.), N.Y. State Bar Assn., D.C. Bar Assn., Tex. Soc. CPAs, Internat. Tax Forum of Houston (sec. 1981-84, pres. 1984-92), Internat. Fiscal Assn., Am. Soc. Internat. Law, Am. Fgn. Law Assn., Am. Law Inst. (tax adv. group 1990—).

MURRAY, GROVER ELMER, geologist, educator; b. Maiden, N.C., Oct. 26, 1916; s. Grover Elmer and Lucy (Lore) M.; m. Nancy Beatrice Setzer, June 21, 1941 (dec. Sept. 1985); children: Martha Murray Poag, Barbara Elizabeth Murray Baca; m. Sally Marie Sowell Williams, Oct. 26, 1986. BS, U. N.C., 1937; MS, La. State U., 1939, PhD, 1942. Rsch. geologist La. Geol. Survey, 1938-41; geologist Magnolia Petroleum Co., Jackson, Miss., 1941-48; prof. dept. geology La. State U., 1948-55, chmn. dept., 1950-53, Boyd prof. geology, 1955-66, cons. prof. geology, 1966—, v.p., dean acad. affairs, 1963-65; v.p. acad. affairs La. State U. System, 1965-66; pres., prof. geosci. Tex. Tech U., Lubbock, 1966-76; pres. Tex. Tech U. Sch. Medicine, 1969-76; designee Grover E. Murray Disting. prof., 1996; Univ. prof., prof. geosci. Tex. Tech U. Complex, 1976-87; Univ. prof. emeritus and pres. emeritus Tex. Tech U. and Tex. Tech U. Health Scis. Ctr., 1988—; founder Ranching Heritage Ctr. Tex. Tech U., dir. Niger Agrl. Project, 1976-78; prof. La. State U. geology camp, Colo., 1949, 51, La., 1961; dir. U. Tex. geology camp, East Tex., 1949, 51; vis. lectr. U. Tex., 1958; dir. Global Exploration Inc., now pres.; bd. govs. Icasals, Inc., 1967-76; mem. Internat. Sub commn. on Stratigraphic Classification, 1955—; cons. geologist, 1988—; chmn. U.S. Nat. Com. on Geology, 1964-68; dir. NSF project for basic geologic studies in, Northeastern Mex., 1956-66; mem. Nat. Sci. Bd., 1968-80, vice chmn., 1978-80; mem. Tex. Natural Fibers and Food Protein Commn., 1966-76; U.S. del. Internat. Geol. Congresses, Mex., 1956, Scandinavia, 1960, India, 1964, Czechoslovakia, 1968, Can., 1972, U.S.A., 1989, hon. mem.; bd. dirs. Ashland Oil Inc., 1977-87, dir. emeritus, 1987—. Author: Geology of Atlantic and Gulf Coastal Province of North America, 1961; Contbr. articles to ednl., sci. jours. Bd. dirs. Africare, Inc., 1975-86, Tex. Ptnrs. with Peru. Recipient Disting. Alumnus award U. N.C., 1971, La. State U., 1988, Hollis D. Hedberg award in energy La. State U.-Inst. for Study of Earth and Man, So. Meth. U., 1986. Fellow Geol. Soc. Am. (chmn. symposium on sedimentary vols. in Coastal Plain, U.S. and Mex. 1952, commr. Am. Stratigraphic Commn. 1951-54, program chmn. New Orleans Meeting 1955, councilor 1961-64, gen. chmn. New Orleans meeting 1967, chmn. Southeastern sect. 1960); mem. Am. Assn. Petroleum Geologists (chmn. com. geol. names and nomenclature 1952-54, disting. lectr. com., Disting. lectr. 1954, editor 1959-63, pres. 1964-65, mem. Am. Stratigraphic Commn. 1957-63, hon. mem. 1972, Sidney Powers Meml. medal 1983), Soc. Econ. Paleontologists and Mineralogists (editor Jour. Paleontology 1952-54, chmn. rsch. com. 1958-59, pres. 1963-64, hon. mem. Gulf Coast sect. 1973, hon. mem. Permian Basin sect. 1992, hon. mem. nat. soc. 1981, mem. assn. found. 1986-89, W.H. Twenhofel medal 1996), Am. Inst. Profl. Geologists (hon. mem., pres. 1978-79, exec. com. 1979-80, inst. found. 1989-92, Ben H. Parker Meml. medal 1990), Am. Geol. Inst. (vis. geosci. lectr. 1959-60, v.p. 1979, pres. 1980, exec. com. 1981, Ian Campbell Meml. medal 1989, William B. Heroy, Jr. award, 1992), Orgn. for Tropical Studies (dir., exec. com.), Gulf Univs. Research Corp. (pres. 1965-66, chmn. bd. dirs. 1967), Tex. Acad. Scis. (Disting. Tex. Scientist 1986), Soc. Exploration Geophysicists, Paleontol. Research Inst. (dir. 1978-81), Geol. and Mining Soc., Norsk Geologisk Forening (life), Asociación Mexicana de Geólogos Petroleros, Sociedad Geológica Mexicana, AAAS, Am. Geophys. Union, Golden Key, Sigma Xi, Sigma Gamma Epsilon, Omicron Delta Kappa (designee Grover E. Murray chpt. Tex. Tech U.), Phi Kappa Phi. Home: 4609 10th St Lubbock TX 79416-4827

MURRAY, HAYDN HERBERT, geology educator; b. Kewanee, Ill., Aug. 31, 1924; s. Herbert A. and Ardis M. (Adams) M.; m. Juanita A. Appenheimer, Dec. 16, 1944; children: Steven, Marilyn, Lisa. B.S., U. Ill., 1948, M.S., 1950, Ph.D., 1951. Asst. prof. geology Ind. U., 1951-53, assoc. prof., 1953-57, prof., chmn. dept. geology, 1973-84, prof. geology, 1984-94, prof. emeritus, 1994—; dir. research Georgia Kaolin Co., Elizabeth, N.J., 1957-60; mgr. ops. Georgia Kaolin Co., 1960-62, v.p. ops., 1962-64, exec. v.p., 1964-73; dir. Oil-Dri Corp. Am. Contbr. numerous articles to profl. jours.; patentee in field. Trustee Union Found., E.J. Grassmann Trust. Served with AUS, 1943-46. Recipient Disting. Svc. award Ind. U., 1993. Fellow Geol. Soc. Am., Mineral Soc. Am., Am. Ceramic Soc. (v.p. 1974-75), Tech. Assn. Pulp and Paper Industry; mem. Clay Minerals Soc. (pres. 1965-66, Disting. mem. 1980), Soc. Mining Metallurgy and Exploration (dist. mem., pres. elect 1987, pres. 1988, Hal Williams Hardinge award 1976, found. bd. trustees 1993-96), Internat. Clay Minerals Soc. (pres. 1993—), Am. Assn. Petroleum Geologists, Am. Inst. Profl. Geologists (pres.-elect 1990, pres. 1991), Am. Geol. Inst. Found. (dir. 1990-96), Geol. Soc. Am. Fdn. (trustee 1992—). Home: 3790 S Inverness Farm Rd Bloomington IN 47401-9141

MURRAY, HERBERT FRAZIER, retired federal judge; b. Waltham, Mass., Dec. 29, 1923; s. Arnold Howatt and Hilda (Frazier) M.; m. Jane Ward, Sept. 4, 1948; 1 child, Douglas Frazier. B.A., Yale U., 1947; postgrad., Harvard U., 1947-48; LL.B., U. Md., 1951. Bar: Md. 1951. Law clk. to presiding judge U.S. Dist. Ct., 1951-52; assoc. Ober, Grimes & Stinson, Balt., 1952-54; asst. U.S. atty. for Md., 1954-56; from assoc. to ptnr. Smith, Somerville & Case, Balt., 1956-71; judge U.S. Dist. Ct. Md., 1971-94. Past bd. dirs. Union Meml. Hosp., Legal Aid Bur., Inc. of Balt. Capt. USAAF, World War II, MTO. Decorated Air medal with 3 oak leaf clusters, D.F.C. Mem. ABA, Md. Bar Assn., Balt. Bar Assn., Fed Bar Assn. (hon.), Wednesday Law Club Balt., Nat. Lawyers Club of Washington (hon.).

MURRAY, J. P. R., Canadian protective services official. Commr. Royal Can. Mounted Police, Ottawa, Ont., Can., 1994—. Office: Royal Canadian Mounted Police, 1200 Vanier Pkwy, Ottawa, ON Canada K1A 0R2

MURRAY, JAMES DICKSON, mathematical biology educator; b. Moffat, Scotland, Jan. 2, 1931; s. Peter and Sarah Jane (Black) M.; m. Sheila Todd Campbell, Oct. 1959; children: Mark Woodeaton, Sarah Corinne. BSc in Math. with 1st class honors, U. St. Andrews, Scotland, 1953, PhD in Applied Math., 1956; MA, U. Oxford, Eng., 1961, DSc in Math., 1968; DSc (hon.), U. St. Andrews, 1994. Lectr. applied math. King's Coll. Durham U., Newcastle, Eng., 1955-56; Gordon McKay lectr. and rsch. fellow Harvard U., Cambridge, Mass., 1956-59, rsch. assoc. engring., applied physics, 1963-64; prof. engring. mechanics U. Mich., Ann Arbor, 1965-67; prof. math. NYU, N.Y.C., 1967-70; lectr. Univ. Coll., London, 1959-61; fellow in math. Hertford Coll. U. Oxford, 1961-63, reader, 1972-86, prof. math. biology, 1986-92, fellow Corpus Christi Coll., 1970-92, dir. Ctr. Math. Biology, 1983-92, emeritus prof., 1992—; vis. prof. applied math. MIT, 1979, U. Utah, Salt Lake City, 1979, 85, Calif. Tech. U., 1983; vis. rsch. prof. Nat. Tsing Hua U., Republic of China, 1975, U. Florence, Italy, 1976, Winegard Guelph U., 1980; guest prof. U. Heidelberg, Fed. Republic Germany, 1980; disting. vis. prof., Scott Hawkins lectr. So. Meth. U., Dallas, 1984; adj. prof. zoology U. Wash., 1988—, prof. applied math., 1988—, Robert F. Philip prof., 1988-94, Boeing prof., 1997—; ULAM scholar Los Alamos Nat. Lab., 1985; Lansdowne lectr. U. Victoria, 1990, Ostram lectr. Wash. State U. Author: Asymptotic Analysis, 1974, Nonlinear Differential Equation Models in Biology, 1977, Russian translation, 1983, Mathematical Biology, 1989; co-author: (with L. Wolpert and S. Brenner) Theories of Biological Pattern Formation, 1981, (with W. Jäger) Modelling Patterns in Space and Time, 1983, (with H.G. Othmer and P.K. Maini) Experimental and Theoretical Advances in Biological Pattern Formation, 1993; contbr. numerous articles to learned jours. Recipient Naylor prize for applied math. London Math. Soc., 1989; vis. fellow St. Catherine's Coll., U. Oxford, 1967, Guggenheim fellow, 1967-68; La Chaire Europénne, U. Paris, 1994, 95, 96. Fellow Royal Soc., Royal Soc. Edinburgh, European Soc. for Math. and Theoretical Biology (pres. 1991-94). Office: U Wash Dept Applied Math Box 352420 Seattle WA 98195-2420

MURRAY, JAMES DOYLE, accountant; b. Rochester, N.Y., July 24, 1938; s. William Herbert and Mildred Frances (Becker) M.; m. Mary Louise Goodyear, June 22, 1962; children: William Doyle, Robert Goodyear. B.S., U. Rochester, 1961. CPA, N.Y. With Ernst & Whinney, Rochester, N.Y., 1963—, ptnr., 1977-86; pvt. practice Rochester, 1986—; mem. faculty Found. for Acctg. Edn., N.Y.C., 1979—. Contbr. articles to profl. jours. Treas. William Warfield Scholarship Fund, 1987—, bd. dirs. March of Dimes, Rochester chpt.; active fund raising Boy Scouts Am., Rochester Philharm., Rochester Mus. and Sci. Ctr., bd. dirs., treas. Downstairs Cabaret, 1985; bd. dirs. Rochester chpt. March of Dimes, 1996—; mem. Eagle bd. of rev. Boy Scouts Am.; elder Presbyn. Ch., 1987—; pres. Egypt Vol. Fire Dept., 1975. Lt. USN, 1961-63. Mem. AICPA, N.Y. State Soc. CPAs (pres. Rochester chpt. 1982-83), Nat. Assn. Accts. (bd. dirs. 1978-80). Republican. Presbyterian. Home: 42 Blackwatch Trl Fairport NY 14450-3702 Office: 349 W Commercial St Ste 3000 East Rochester NY 14445-2402

MURRAY, JAMES JOSEPH, III, association executive; b. Boston, Dec. 31, 1933; s. James Joseph Jr. and Anne Louise (Gurvin) M.; children: James Arthur, Paul, Douglas Joseph, Laura Anne. AB, Harvard U., 1955. Regional editor Prentice Hall, Inc., 1957-60, editor, 1960-64, exec. editor, 1964-69; pres. Winthrop Pubs., Inc. subs. Prentice Hall, Cambridge, Mass., 1969-82; also bd. dirs. Winthrop Pubs., Inc. subs. Prentice Hall; spl. mng. cons. Am. Coun. Edn., Washington, 1983-84, dir. external affairs, 1984—; chmn. N.J. Heart Fund; spl. cons. NEH, 1975—. Mem. editorial bd. Capitol Pub., 1992—. Mem. Dem. Nat. Com. from N.J., 1968; del. Dem. Nat. Conv., 1968; mem. gov. bd. Marine Mil. Acad., 1995—. 1st lt. USMCR, 1955-57. Mem. Am. Polit. Sci. Assn., Assn. Physical Plant Adminstrs. (bd. dirs.), Am. Assn. of Higher Edn., Harvard Club, Varsity Club, Pi Eta. Office: One DuPont Circle Ste 800 Washington DC 20036

MURRAY, JAMES MICHAEL, librarian, law librarian, legal educator, lawyer; b. Seattle, Nov. 8, 1944; s. Clarence Nicholas and Della May (Snyder) M.; m. Linda Monthy Murray; MLaw Librarianship, U. Wash., 1978; JD, Gonzaga U., 1971. Bar: Wash., 1974, U.S. Dist. Ct. (we. dist.) Wash. 1975, U.S. Dist. Ct. (ea. dist.) Wash. 1985. Reference/reserve libr. U. Tex. Law Libr. Austin, 1978-81; assoc. law libr. Washington U. Law Libr. St. Louis, 1981-84; law libr., asst. prof. Gonzaga U. Sch. Law, Spokane, 1984-91; libr. East Bonner County Libr., 1991-97; libr. U.S. Cts. Libr., Spokane, 1997—; cons. in field. Author: (with Gasaway and Johnson) Law Library Administration During Fiscal Austerity, 1992. Bd. dirs. ACLU, Spokane chpt., 1987-91; Wash. Vol. Lawyers for the Arts, 1976-78. Mem. ABA, Idaho Libr. Assn., Wash. State Bar Assn (law sch. liaison com., 1986-88, civil rights com. 1996-97). Mem. state adv. bd. National Reporter on Legal Ethics and Professional Responsibility, 1982-91; author: (with Reams and McDermott) American Legal Literature: Bibliography of Selected Legal Resources, 1985; editor Texas Bar Jour. (Books Appraisals Column), 1979-82; contbr. numerous articles and revs. to profl. jours., acknowledgements and bibliographies in field. Home: 921 W 29th Ave Spokane WA 99203-1318 Office: US Cts Libr US Courthouse Rm 650 West 920 Riverside Spokane WA 92201

MURRAY, JEANNE See STAPLETON, JEAN

MURRAY, JEANNE MORRIS, scientist, educator, consultant; b. Fresno, Calif., July 6, 1925; d. Edward W. and Augusta R. (French) Morris; m. Thomas Harold Murray, June 19, 1964; children: Jeanne, Margaret, Barbara, Thomas, William. BS in Math., Morris Harvey Coll., 1957; MS in Info. and Computer Sci., Ga. Inst. Tech., 1966; PhD, in Pub. Adminstrn., Tech. Mgmt., Am. U., 1981, post doctoral student in internat. rels., 1993. Research scientist Ga. Inst. Tech., Atlanta, 1959-68; adj. prof. Am. U., Washington, 1968-73; computer scientist U.S. Dept. Def., Washington, 1968-69; staff scientist Delex Systems, Inc., Arlington, Va., 1969-70; mgmt. analyst GSA, Washington, 1971-74; assoc. prof. No. Va. Community Coll., 1975-76, U. Va., 1976—; guest lecturer, Computers and Soc., U. Md., 1986—, Govtl. Rels., Marymount U. Arlington Va., 1990; cons., TechDyn Systems, ABA Corp., OrKand Corp., 1978-80; pres. Sequoia Assocs., Arlington, Va., 1981—; panelist Inst. Agr., Akadamgorodok, Siberia, 1991, Inst. Nuclear Physics, 1991, M.Ulughbek Inst., Samarkand, Uzbekistan, 1991; chmn. confs. Future on Fin. Structure and Pvt. Industry for Uzbekistan, 1994; rschr., developer cons. large info. warfare project, 1995—; developer indirect personality profiles for spl. internat. persons, 1995—; pres. Sequoia Enterprises, Inc., Arlington, 1995—, R&D Alt. Med. Approaches, 1996; sponsor, mem. team devel. and testing vaccine for specific infectious diseases, 1995; active U.S. Global Strategy Coun., 1993—. Author: Development and Testing of a System of Encoding Visual Information Based on Optimization of Neural Processing in Man--with Application to Pattern Recognition in the Computer, 1966, Cybernetics and the Management of the Research and Development Function in Society, 1971, Cybernetics as a Tool in the Control of Drug Abuse, 1972, Development of a General Computerized Forecasting Model, 1971, Political Humankind and the Future of Governance, 1974, The Doctrine of Management Planning, 1973, Policy Design, 1980, Computer Futures, 1982, A Search for Positive Response Level Indicators (PRLI's) Under Stress, 1987, Strategic Planning: Pathfinder to the Future, Beijing, 1988, Strategic Planning: A Systems Perspective, Shanghai PRC 1988, Electronic Control Systems for Railroads, Wuhan PRC 1988, Technology Forecasting Methodologies for Use on Personal Computers, 1989, Japan's Burgeoning Rates of Economic Expansion in the U.S. and other Western Countries, 1990, Technology Transfer and National Security, 1992, Privatization Mechanism for the Former Soviet Union and Central European Countries, 1992, Curriculum Development for Privatization Training of Entrepreneurs in Siberia, 1993, Development of Training Courses for Automated Acquisition Management Systems, 1994, Presentations on Methods of Achieving More Effective, Less Costly Federal Government, 1994; panel participant in field; co-developer TV program "Cybernetics and You", Fairfax County, Va., 1995. OPSEC and Info. Warfare, 1996—; participant in panels on econ. espionage and its impact upon sci. and engring. competitiveness in the U.S., 1997. Mem. Carter transition team, 1976-77, Arlington (Va.) Civil Def. Com., 1983—, Washington Met. Area Emergency Assistance Com., Arlington County Com. on Sci. and Tech. Mem. IEEE (sr. mem., vice chmn. Washington sect., chmn. panel on internat. mktg. high tech. in the presence of def. tech. controls 1983, nat. com. on a tech. transfer policy for the U.S. 1986, mem. land transp. com. Vehicular Tech. Soc. 1993-94), AAAS, N.Y. Acad. Scis., Assn. Computing Machinery, Washington Evolutionary Systems Soc., Inst. Noetic Scis., Soc. Gen. Rsch., Am. Soc. Pub. Adminstrn., World Future Soc., Better World Soc., Acad. Polit. Sci., Personality Assessment System Found., Soc. for the Advance of Socio-Econs.; Episcopalian. Home and Office: 2915 27th St N Arlington VA 22207-4922

MURRAY, JOHN DANIEL, lawyer; b. Cleve., Feb. 13, 1944; s. Clarence Daniel and Mary Anne (Bormann) M.; m. Pamela Mary Seese, Aug. 20, 1966 (div. Sept. 1978); children: Laura Jane, Joshua Daniel, Katherine Anne; m. Marilyn Nohren, June 15, 1979. BA, Marquette U., 1965, JD, 1968. Bar: Wis. 1968, Ill. 1968, U.S. Dist. Ct. (ea. and we. dist.) Wis. 1968, U.S. Supreme Ct. 1971, U.S. Ct. Appeals (7th cir.) 1979. Assoc. Law Offices of Elmo Koos, Peoria, Ill., 1968-70; ptnr. Coffey, Lerner & Murray, Milw., 1970-72, Coffey, Murray & Coffey, Milw., 1972-76, Murray & Burke, S.C., Milw., 1983-85; pvt. practice Milw., 1976-83; shareholder Habush, Habush, Davis & Rottier, S.C., Appleton, Wis., 1985—; adj. prof. law Marquette U., Milw., 1993—; lectr. Law Sch. U. Wis., Madison, 1976-80. Mem. ABA, ATLA, Nat. Bd. Trial Advocacy (cert.), Am. Soc. Law and Medicine, Wis. State Bar (chmn. criminal law sect. 1977-78, tort law com. 1990—, bd. dirs. litigation sect. 1995—), Wis. Acad. Trial Lawyers (bd. dirs. 1990—), Woolsack Soc. Roman Catholic. Avocations: golf, travel. Home: 3095 Fox Run Appleton WI 54914-8735 Office: Habush Habush Davis Rottier PO Box 1915 Appleton WI 54913-1915

MURRAY, JOHN EDWARD, JR., lawyer, educator, university president; b. Phila., Dec. 20, 1932; s. John Edward and Mary Catherine (Small) M.; m. Isabelle A. Bogusevich, Apr. 11, 1955; children: Bruce, Susan, Timothy, Jacqueline. BS, LaSalle U., 1955; JD scholar, Cath. U., 1958; SJD fellow, U. Wis., 1959. Bar: Wis. 1959, Pa. 1986. Assoc. prof. Duquesne U. Sch. Law, Pitts., 1963-64, prof., 1965-67; prof. Villanova U. Sch. Law, 1964-65; prof. U. Pitts. Sch. Law, 1967-84, dean, 1977-84; dean Sch. Law Villanova U., 1984-86; disting. svc. prof. U. Pitts., 1986-88; pres. Duquesne U., Pitts., 1988—; cons. to law firms; chmn. Pa. Chief Justice's com. on comprehensive jud. and lawyer edn. Author: Murray on Contracts, 1974, 90, Murray, Commercial Transactions, 1975, Murray, Cases & Materials on Contracts, 1969, 76, 83, 91, Purchasing and the Law, 1978, Problems & Materials on Sales, 1982, Murray, Problems & Materials on Secured Transactions, 1987, Sales & Leases: Problems and Materials in National/International Transactions, 1993. Mayor Borough of Pleasant Hills, Pa., 1970-74. Mem. Assn. Am. Law Schs. (life, editor Jour. Legal Edn.), mem. Am. Law Inst. Democrat. Roman Catholic. Office: Duquesne U Pres Office Adminstrn Bldg Pittsburgh PA 15282

MURRAY, JOHN EINAR, lawyer, retired army officer, federal official; b. Clifton, N.J., Nov. 22, 1918; s. Joseph Michael and Maru Elizabeth (Liljeros) M.; m. Elaine Claire Riehlmann (dec. 1970); 1 dau., Valerie Anne; m. Phyllis Irene Harris (div. 1989). Student, St. Johns U., 1938-41; LLB, N.Y. Law Sch., 1949, LLD, 1975; MA, George Washington U., 1961. lectr. U.S. Marine Corps Nat. Def. U.; mem. sci. panel of White House Agent Orange Working Group, Def. Intelligence Agy. Task Force on POWS and MIAS; participant Georgetown U. Panel on Crisis Mgmt. Drafted pvt. U.S. Army, 1941, advanced through grades to maj. gen., 1972; comdr. truck group Europe Mil. Ports, Vietnam and maj. logistic units, 1968; dir. Army Transp., 1969-70; chief logistics Pacific Command, 1970-72, Mil. Assistance Command, Vietnam, 1972-73; def. attache Vietnam, 1973-74; ret., 1974; v.p. Assn. Am. Railroads, Washington, 1974-84; spl. counsel Am. Internat. Underwriters, 1985; prin. dep. asst. sec. of def. for spl. ops. and low intensity conflict, 1988-89; with Am. Internat. Group Cos., Washington, 1989; spl. counsel Snavely, King & Assocs., Inc. (econ. cons.), Washington, 1990—; adv. bd. U.S. Army Transp. Mus.; lectr. Nat. Def. U.; mem. sci. panel of White House Agent Orange Working Group, Def. Intelligence Agy. Task Force on POWs and MIAs; participant Georgetown U. Panel on Crisis Mgmt. Author: (with A.M. Chester) Orders and Directive, 1952, (with V.F. Caputo) Quick on the Vigor, 1966, The Myths of Business and the Business of Myths, 1975, The Third Curse of Moses, 1975, The Military Mind and the New Mindlessness, 1976, Lawyers, Computers and Power, 1977, Pothole Plague and Knothole Outlook, 1978, Railroads, Terrorism and the Pinkerton Legacy, 1978, Raising Corn and Beans and Hell, 1979, Remembering Who You Are, 1979, Running A Muck—The Folly of Coal Slurry, 1979, The Railroads and the Energy Crisis, 1980, U.S. Security Assistance—The Vietnam Experience, 1980, Hopeless Cause or Cause of Hope, 1980, War, Transport and Show Biz, 1981, Forget Everything You Ever Knew About the Japanese Railroads, 1981, Sweet Adversity: The U.S. Army-How It Motivates, 1982, Random Danger: The Railroad Response, 1983, Vietnam Logistics: An American Debacle, 1984, Dead Headheads and Warheads, 1987 ; Operation Desert Shield: The Smart Way to War, 1991; He Was There, 1992, The Logistics of Limited Wars, 1992, The United Nations: Sizing Up Consultant Prospects, 1992, How to Win a Lost War, 1997; contbr.: book revs. to Nat. Def. Transp. Mag., Time-Life books, Vietnam mag. Decorated D.S.M., Legion of Merit with 4 oak leaf clusters, Bronze Star medal, Joint Services Commendation medal with oak leaf cluster, Army Commendation medal with 2 oak leaf clusters, Sec. of Def. medal for Outstanding Pub. Svc., Italian Cross of War, Knight Order of Crown of Italy, Korean Chung Mu with gold star, Vietnamese Kim Khanh medal 1st class, Vietnamese Army Distinguished Service Order 1st class, Vietnamese Navy Distinguished Service Order 1st class, Vietnamese Air Force Distinguished Service Order 1st class, Vietnamese Gallantry Cross with palm. Mem. Spl. Forces Assn., Nat. Def. Transp. Assn., Army War Coll. Grad. Assn., Army and Navy Club. Home: 3823 Bosworth Ct Fairfax VA 22031-3807 Office: Mullenholz & Brimsek 1150 Connecticut Ave NW Washington DC 20036

MURRAY, JOHN PATRICK, psychologist, educator, researcher; b. Cleve., Sept. 14, 1943; s. John Augustine and Helen Marie (Lynch) M.; m. Ann Coke Dennison, Apr. 17, 1971; children: Jonathan Coke, Ian Patrick. PhD, Cath. U. Am., 1970. Rsch. dir. Office U.S. Surgeon Gen. NIMH, Bethesda, Md., 1969-72; assoc. prof. psychology Macquarie U., Sydney, Australia, 1973-79, U. Mich., Ann Arbor, 1979-80; dir. youth and family policy Boys Town Ctr., Boys Town, Nebr., 1980-85; prof., dir. Sch. Family Studies and Human Svcs. Kans. State U., Manhattan, 1985—; scholar-in-residence Mind Sci. Found., San Antonio, 1996-97; mem. children's TV com. CBS, 1996—. Author: Television and Youth: 25 Years of Research and Controversy, 1980, The Future of Children's TV, 1984, (with H.T. Rubin) Status Offenders: A Sourcebook, 1983, (with E.A. Rubenstein, G.A. Comstock) Television and Social Behavior, 3 vols., 1972, (with A. Huston and others) Big World, Small Screen: The Role of Television in American Society, 1992; contbr. articles to profl. jours. Mem. Nebr. Foster Care Rev. Bd., 1982-84; mem. Advocacy Office for Children and Youth, 1980-85; mem. Nat. Coun. Children and TV, 1982-87; trustee The Villages Children's Homes, 1986—, Menninger Found., 1996—. Fellow Am. Psychol. Assn. (pres. div. child youth and family svcs. 1990); mem. Am. Sociol. Assn., Soc. Rsch. in Child Devel., Royal Commonwealth Soc. (London), Manhattan Country Club. Home: 1731 Humboldt St Manhattan KS 66502-4140 Office: Kans State U Sch Family Studies & Human Svcs Manhattan KS 66506-1403

MURRAY, JOHN RALPH, former college president; b. Alva, Okla., Apr. 17, 1916; s. John and Euna Vista (Young) M.; m. Fern Berniece Brauch, July 26, 1936; children: John Ralph III, Ann Elaine. A.B., Northwestern State U., 1937; A.M., U. So. Calif., 1939; Ph.D., U. Fla., 1952; L.H.D. (hon.), Elmira Coll., 1976. Prin., tchr. English Carrier and Gore high schs., Okla., 1936-38; teaching asst. U. So. Calif., 1939-41; instr. English U. Miami, Coral Gables, Fla., 1941; exec. asst. to pres. U. Miami, 1942, asst. prof. English, adminstrv. asst. dean, 1945, acting dean, dir. south campus, 1946-50, asst. to pres., assoc. prof. English, 1948-51; lectr., instr. English Ohio U., 1942-44; pres. Greenbrier Coll., Lewisburg, W.Va., 1952-54; pres. Elmira (N.Y.) Coll., 1954-72, chancellor, 1972-76, cons. to bd. trustees, 1976—; dir. Hardinge Bros.; Mem. N.Y. State Senate Adv. Com. on Higher Edn. Author: Secretary's Handbook, 1941; Editorial bd.: Learning Today; mem. pub. com.: The College and World Affairs; chmn. com. pub.: Non-Western Studies in Liberal Arts Colleges. Trustee Robert Packer Hosp., Coll. Center of Finger Lakes, Am. Center for Students and Artists, Paris; bd. mgrs. Arnot Ogden Hosp.; bd. regents Council on Tchr. Edn.; bd. dirs. Library Coll. Assocs.; mem. Pres.'s Task Force on Internat. Edn.; chmn. long range planning com. Friends of Weymouth; chmn. bd. dirs. Council on Internat. Ednl. Exchange; v.p. Given Meml. Library Bd.; chmn. dirs. Empire State Found., 1963-65, dir., mem. exec. com.; trustee Internat. Coll.; pres. World Golf Hall of Fame. Served as ensign USNR, 1944-45. Mem. Internat. Assn. U. Presidents, Assn. Am. Colls. (past chmn. com. on internat. understanding), Phi Sigma Pi, Kappa Delta Pi, Phi Kappa Phi, Epsilon Phi. Lodge: Rotary. Home: 6152 N Verde Trl Apt D 123 Boca Raton FL 33433-2419

MURRAY, JOHN WILLIAM, JR., writer, legal investigator; b. Apr. 8, 1934; s. John William and Frances (Bryan) M.; m. Norma Sousa, Oct. 30, 1959 (div. Apr. 1989); children: John William III, James Patrick, Jeffrey Dean, Jerome Bryan, Jay Joseph. BS, U. Hartford, 1968; MBA, U. Conn., 1971. Legal investigator Dallas, 1974—. Author: Accident Investigation in the Private Sector, 1994 (Best New Investigative Book of Yr.), vol. 2, 1997, Forensic Photography in the Private Sector, 1995, Sex Crimes, 1995. 1st lt. USMC, 1957-60. Mem. Nat. Assn. Legal Investigators (cert., chmn. nat. cert. 1987-89, nat. chmn. editor-pub. awards com. 1992-96, Editor-Pub. award Legal Investigator mag. 1989, 91), Evidence Photographers Internat. Coun., Nat. Assn. Investigative Specialists (cert. expert in investigative photography, expert in accident investigation, Outstanding Spkr. of Yr. award 1995, Lifetime Achievement award 1996), Nat. Acad. for Continuing Edn. (co-founder). Avocations: photography, stamp collecting. Office: 3942 Rochelle Dr Dallas TX 75220-1814

MURRAY, JOSEPH JAMES, JR., zoologist; b. Lexington, Va., Mar. 13, 1930; s. Joseph James and Jane Dickson (Vardell) M.; m. Elizabeth Hickson, Aug. 24, 1957; children—Joseph James III, Alison Joan, William Lister. B.S., Davidson Coll., 1951; B.A., Oxford U., Eng., 1954, M.A., 1957, D.Phil., 1962. Instr. biology Washington & Lee U., Lexington, Va., 1956-58; asst. prof. biology U. Va., Charlottesville, 1962-67, assoc. prof., 1967-73, prof., 1973-77, Samuel Miller prof. biology, 1977—, chmn. dept. biology, 1984-87; co-dir. Mountain Lake Biol. Sta., Pembroke, Va., 1963-91. Author: Genetic Diversity and Natural Selection, 1972; contbr. articles to profl. jours. Served with U.S. Army, 1955-56. Rhodes scholar, 1951-54. Fellow AAAS, Va. Acad. Sci.; mem. Am. Soc. Naturalists, Genetics Soc. Am., Soc. Study Evolution, Am. Soc. Ichthyologists and Herpetologists, Va. Acad. Sci. (pres. 1986-87), Va. Soc. Ornithology (pres. 1976-79). Avocations: walking; mountaineering; shooting. Office: U Va Dept Biology Gilmer Hall Charlottesville VA 22901

MURRAY, JOSEPH WILLIAM, banker; b. Alamosa, Colo., July 20, 1944; s. Joseph A. and Virginia (Wood) M.; m. Helen Hoberg, Jan. 20, 1970; children: Brian, Beth, Meghan. BS in Bus. with hon., U. Colo., 1966; MBA with hon., Northwestern U., 1967. Various positions with Continental Ill. Nat. Bank, Chgo., 1967-82; sr. v.p. First Nat. Bank Md., Balt., 1982—; faculty mem. U. N.C. Exec. Programs on Cash Mgmt., Chapel Hill, 1982—; lectr. cash mgmt.; mem. corp. svcs. commn. Bank Adminstrn. Inst., 1992-94. Assoc. editor: Essentials of Cash Management, 4th edit., 1992, 5th edit., 1995. Pres. Wakefield Improvement Assn., Timonium, Md., 1987, 96, bd. dirs., 1996—; pres. Glen Ellyn (Ill.) Libr., 1978-82, trustee; pres. Glen Ellyn Tennis Assn., 1981, bd. dirs.; bd. trustees, sec. Ctr. Stage, 1987—. Mem.

Treasury Mgmt. Assn., L'Hirondelle Club (Ruxton, Md.), Beta Gamma Sigma. Avocations: tennis, jazz piano, reading, racewalking. Office: 1st Nat Bank Md PO Box 1596 Baltimore MD 21203-1596

MURRAY, JULIA KAORU (MRS. JOSEPH E. MURRAY), occupational therapist; b. Wahiawa, Oahu, Hawaii, 1934; d. Gijun and Edna Tsuruko (Taba) Funakoshi; m. Joseph Edward Murray, 1961; children: Michael, Susan, Leslie. BA, U. Hawaii, 1956; cert. occupational therapy U. Puget Sound, 1958. Therapist, Inst. Logopedics, Wichita, Kans., 1958; sr. therapist Hawaii State Hosp., Kaneohe, 1959; part-time therapist Centre County Ctr. for Crippled Children and Adults, State College, Pa., 1963; vice chmn. adv. bd. Hosp. Improvement Program, East Oreg. State Hosp., Pendleton, 1974; v.p. Ind. Living, Inc., 1976-79; job search instr.; mem. adv. com. Oreg. Ednl. Coordinating Commn., 1979-82; mem. Oreg. Bd. Engring. Examiners, 1979-87; supr., occupational therapist Fairview Tng. Ctr., Salem, Oreg., 1984-94; occupational therapist U.S. Naval Hosp., Okinawa, Japan, 1994—. Rep. from Umatilla County Commrs. to Blue Mountain Econ. Devel. Council, 1976-78; mem. Ashland Park and Recreation Bd., 1972-73; vice chmn. adv. bd. LINC, 1978; mem. exec. bd. Liberty-Boone Neighborhood Assn., 1979-83. Mem. Am. Occupational Therapy Assn., Oreg. Occupational Therapy Assn., Hawaii Occupational Therapy Assn. (sec. 1960) Occupational Therapy Assn., LWV (bd. dirs. Pendleton 1974, 77-78, pres. 1975-77; bd. dirs. Oreg. 1979-81, Ashland, Wis., 1967-71, Wis. v.p. 1970). Office: Medically Related Svcs US Naval Hosp Okinawa Japan Psc 482 FPO AP 96362

MURRAY, LARRY, Canadian Forces officer; b. Stratford, Ont., Can., June 6, 1949; s. William Alexander and Ethel May (Mulholland) M.; m. Susan Ann Maclean, Jan.6, 1968; children: Wendi, Kimberly, Jeffrey, Sean. BA in History, Carleton U., Ottawa, 1968; Cert., Casn. Forces Staff Coll., 1980. Commd. Can. Forces, advanced through grades to vice admiral., 1993; comdr. can. Destroyer Squadron Maritime Command, Halifax, N.S., 1987-88; dir. gen. maritime doctrine and ops. Nat. Defence Hdqs., Ottawa, 1989-91, assoc. asst. dep. min. policy and comm., 1991-93, dep. chie def. staff, 1993-94, vice chief def. staff, 1995—; comdr. Maritime Command, Halifax, 1994-95; acting chief def. staff Nat. Defence Hdqrs., Ottawa, 1997—. Decorated Can. 125 medal, NATO Spl. Svc. medal, Order of Mil. Merit. Office: Nat Defence Hdqs, M Gen George R Pearkes Bldg, Ottawa, ON Canada K1A OK2

MURRAY, LEONARD HUGH, railroad executive; b. Evanston, Ill., Sept. 26, 1913; s. Albert L. and Estelle A. (Matthews) M.; m. Virginia P. Dutcher, Aug. 23, 1940; children: Carole J., Linda P., John L. J.D., U. Minn., 1938. Bar: Minn. 1938. Law clk. to assoc. justice Minn. Supreme Ct., 1938-40; pvt. practice law Mpls., 1940-42; chief price atty. dist. office OPA, Minn., 1942-44; pvt. practice law, specializing r.r. re-orgn. Mpls., 1944-54; asst. to pres. Duluth, S. Shore & Atlantic R.R., 1949-52, v.p., 1952-58, pres., dir., 1958-60; v.p., dir. Wis. Central R.R., 1954-60, v.p., gen. counsel, dir., 1958-60; counsel C.P. Ry. Co., 1958-60; pres., chief exec. officer, dir. Soo Line R.R. Co., 1961-78, chmn. bd., chief exec. officer, 1978-79, chmn. exec. com., 1980-83; former dir. First Bank System, Inc.; dir. Gt. No. Ins. Co., 1963-84; dir. emeritus First Bank Mpls. Pres. Jr. Achievement Mpls., 1964-66; former trustee Dunwoody Indsl. Inst., pres., 1966-67; bd. dirs. Minn. Council on Crime and Justice; pres. Correctional Service of Minn., 1976-79. Recipient Outstanding Achievement award U. Minn., 1971. Mem. Greater Mpls. C. of C. (pres. 1977-78), Beta Gamma Sigma. Republican. Episcopalian.

MURRAY, LOWELL, Canadian senator; b. New Waterford, N.S., Can., Sept. 26, 1936; s. Daniel and Evelyn (Young) M.; m. Colleen Elaine MacDonald; children: William, Colin. BA, St. Francis Xavier U., Antigonish, N.S., Can.; MA in Pub. Adminstrn., Queen's U., Kingston, Ont., Can. Chief of staff Minister of Justice and Minister of Pub. Works Can., Ottawa, Ont., Senator M. Wallace McCutcheon, Ottawa, Ont.; leader of opposition Can., Ottawa, Ont.; dep. minister Premier N.B. (Can.); mem. Senate of Can., Ottawa, Ont., 1979—, co-chmn. joint Senate-House of Commons com. ofcl. langs., 1980-84, chmn. standing Senate com. on banking, trade and commerce, 1984-86, chmn. standing senate com. on nat. fin., 1995; bd. dirs. SONY Can. Inc.; trustee Inst. Rsch. Pub. Policy, 1984-86, mem. Trilateral Commn., 1985-86. Nat. campaign chmn. gen. election Progressive Conservative Party Can., 1977-79, 81-83; sworn of the privy coun., appointed Leader of the Govt. in the Senate, 1986-94; Min. of the State Fed.-Provincial Rels., 1986-91; Min. Responsible for the Atlantic Can. Opportunities Agy., 1987-88. Roman Catholic. Office: The Senate, Ottawa, ON Canada K1A 0A4

MURRAY, LYNDA BERAN, counselor; b. Richmond, Va., Feb. 29, 1944; d. Lynn Carlyle and Clelia (Crawford) Beran; m. Frank Stephen Murray, Feb. 3, 1968 (dec. 1990); children: Stephanie, Frank Stephen Jr., Rebecca, Jeremy, Anthony, Nicholas. BA, U. Richmond, 1965; MA, U. Ky., 1968; MEd, Lynchburg Coll., 1988; CAGS, Va. Poly. Inst. and State U., 1993, PhD, 1995. Cert. elem. and secondary counselor, Va. Instr. psychology Randolph-Macon Woman's Coll., Lynchburg, Va., 1970-72; contractural sch. psychologist Lynchburg City Schs., 1975-91, elem. sch. counselor, 1989-91; supr. counselor edn. dept. Va. Poly. Inst. and State U., Blacksburg, 1991-93; emergency svcs. clinician New Rivery Valley Community Svcs. Bd., 1993-94; elem. sch. counselor Montgomery County Pub. Schs., Elliston, Va., 1994—; emergency mental health cons. Lynchburg Gen. Hosp., 1986-90. Mem. ACA, Va. Counselors Assn., New River Valley Counselors Assn. (pres. 1996—), Chi Sigma Iota (sec. 1990-91, pres. 1992-93). Home: 310 Cherokee Dr Blacksburg VA 24060-1822 Office: Elliston-Lafayette Elem Sch Dept Counselor Edn 9812 Roanoke Rd Elliston VA 24087-2314

MURRAY, MARY, early childhood, elementary and secondary educator; b. Beverly, Mass.; d. Edward James and Anne (Dowd) M. AS in Nursing, Endicott Coll.; AB, Boston Coll., 1985; MSEd in Early Childhood & Elem. Edn., Wheelock Coll., 1993. Cert. tchr., Mass. Tchr. Glen Urquhart Sch., Beverly Farms, Mass., 1982-87, kindergarten asst., 1982-83; kindergarten tchr., 1983-85, first grade tchr., 1985-87; dir. extended day program Glen Urquhart Sch., Beverly Farms, Mass., 1982-85, coord. summer camp program, 1984-86; lower sch. assoc. Shady Hill Sch., Cambridge, Mass., 1987-88; rsch. asst. Wheelock Coll., Boston, 1987-91; tchr. kindergarten, curriculum coord. Prospect Hill Parents' and Childrens' Ctr., Waltham, Mass., 1988-91; substitute tchr. Marblehead (Mass.) Mid. Sch., 1993—; ednl. cons. Beverly Farms, Mass., 1992—; substitute tchr. Shore Country Day Sch., Beverly, Mass., 1992—; mentor, tchr., faculty summer compass program Lesley Coll. Grad. Sch. of Edn., Cambridge, Mass., 1994—; substitute tchr. Beverly Pub. Schools, 1996—; founder, dir. Summer Enrichment at Lanesville, Mass., 1987-89; certification cons., adv. bd. Power Industries, Wellesley Hills, Mass., 1989—; cons. Activities Club, Inc., Waltham, 1986-91; mem. Early Childhood Adv. Coun., Medford, Mass., 1990-93; lifeguard supr. West Beach Corp., 1980-86; mem. cert. team Nat. Assn. Educators Young Children, 1989-91, Ind. Sch. Assn. Mass., 1983-88; presenter workshops. Author curriculum materials, activity kits for children. Tchr. religious edn. program St. Margaret Parish, Beverly Farms, 1970—, dir., coord., 1989—; synod group leader Archdiocese of Boston, 1987; water safety instr. ARC; coach Christian Youth Orgn. Girls Basketball, St. Joseph Parish, Medford, Mass., 1991-93; active Mass. Spl. Olympics; mem. Youth Activities Coord., Farms/Prides Cmty. Orgn., Feed the Hungry Project, Beverly, Mass., Good Friday Walk Orgnl. Com.; adv. bd. Wenham (Mass.) Mus.; friends-of-com. Fitz Meml. Libr. Endicott Coll., Beverly, Mass. Wheelock Coll. grad. grantee, 1993. Mem. ASCD, Nat. Assn. Edn. Young Childen, Assn. Childhood Edn. Internat., Young Alumni Club Boston Coll. (program coord./spl. events 1988-90), Ste. Chretienne Acad. Alumnae Assn., Wheelock Coll. Alumni Assn. Democrat. Roman Catholic. Avocations: reading, photography, travel, seasonal sports, children's literature. Home: 650 Hale St Beverly Farms Beverly MA 01915-2117

MURRAY, MICHAEL PETER, economist, educator; b. N.Y.C., Sept. 15, 1946; s. Thomas John and Marie Fitzgerald; m. Rosanne Ducey, June 21, 1969; children: Sarah, Anna, Adam, Ben, Seth, Peter. BA, U. Santa Clara, 1968; MS, Iowa State U., 1971, PhD, 1974. Acting asst. prof. U. Calif., San Diego, 1972-73; asst. prof. U. Va., Charlottesville, 1973-77; vis. asst. prof. U. Calif., Berkeley, 1977-78; assoc. prof. Duke U., Durham, N.C., 1978-80; prof. Claremont (Calif.) Grad. Sch., 1980-86; sr. economist The RAND Corp., Santa Monica, Calif., 1980-86; Charles Franklin Phillips prof. econs. Bates Coll., Lewiston, Maine, 1986—; cons. HUD, Washington, 1973, The World Bank, Washington, 1981—. Author: Subsidizing Industrial Location, 1988, Building Organizational Decision Support Systems, 1992; contbr. articles to profl. jours. NDEA fellow U. Calif., San Diego, 1971; vis. scholar HUD, Washington, 1979. Mem. Am. Econ. Assn., Western Econ. Assn., Order of Silver Spade. Democrat. Roman Catholic. Avocations: soccer, bridge, theater. Home: 342 College St Lewiston ME 04240-6001 Office: Bates Coll Dept Econs Lewiston ME 04240

MURRAY, NEIL VINCENT, computer science educator; b. Schenectady, N.Y., July 14, 1948; s. Robert Emslie and Eileen Marie (Milano) M. BS in Engring. Physics, Cornell U., 1970; MS in Computer and Info. Sci., Syracuse U., 1974, PhD in Computer and Info. Sci., 1979. Rsch. asst. Syracuse (N.Y.) U., 1977-78; instr. computer sci. dept. LeMoyne Coll., Syracuse, 1978-79, asst. prof., 1979-82; asst. prof. computer sci. SUNY, Albany, 1982-87, assoc. prof. computer sci., 1987—; Sec.-treas. CADE, Inc., Assn. Automated Reasoning; presenter in field. Contbr. articles to profl. jours. Mem. IEEE Computer Soc., Am. Assn. Artificial Intelligence, Assn. Automated Reasoning, Assn. Computing Machinery. Home: 1125 Glenmeadow Ct Niskayuna NY 12309 Office: SUNY Dept Computer Sci L1 # 67A Albany NY 12222

MURRAY, PATTY, senator; b. Seattle, Wash., Oct. 11, 1950; d. David L. and Beverly A. (McLaughlin) Johns; m. Robert R. Murray, June 2, 1972; children: Randy P., Sara A. BA, Wash. State U., 1972. Sec. various cos., Seattle, 1972-76; citizen lobbyist various ednl. groups, Seattle, 1983-88; legis. lobbyist Orgn. for Parent Edn., Seattle, 1977-84; instr. Shoreline Community Coll., Seattle, 1984—; mem. Wash. State Senate, Seattle, 1989-92, U.S. Senate, Washington, 1993—; ranking minority mem. Appropriations Legis Br.; vice chmn. Senate Dem. Policy Com.; mem. Com. on Banking, Housing and Urban Affairs, Budget Com., Senate Dem. Tech. and Comms. Com., Com. on Vets. Affairs, Select Com. on Ethics. Mem. bd. Shoreline Sch., Seattle, 1985-89; mem. steering com. Demonstration for Edn., Seattle, 1987; founder, chmn. Orgn. for Parent Edn., Wash., 1981-85; lst Congl. rep. Wash. Women United, 1983-85. Recipient Recognition of Svc. to Children award Shoreline PTA Coun., 1986, Golden Acorn Svc. award, 1989; Outstanding Svc. award Wash. Women United, 1986, Outstanding Svc. to Pub. Edn. award Citizens Ednl. Ctr. NW, Seattle, 1987. Democrat. Office: US Senate 111 Russell Senate Office Bldg Washington DC 20510-4704*

MURRAY, PETER, metallurgist, manufacturing company executive; b. Rotherham, Yorks, Eng., Mar. 13, 1920; came to U.S., 1967, naturalized, 1974; s. Michael and Ann (Hamstead) M.; m. Frances Josephine Glaisher, Sept. 8, 1947; children: Jane, Paul, Alexander. BSc in Chemistry with honors, Sheffield (Eng.) U., 1941, postgrad., 1946-49; PhD in Metallurgy, Brit. Iron and Steel Research Bursar, Sheffield, 1948. Research chemist Steetley Co., Ltd., Worksop, Notts, Eng., 1941-45; with Atomic Energy Research Establishment, Harwell, Eng., 1949-67; head div. metallurgy Atomic Energy Research Establishment, 1960-64, asst. dir., 1964-67; tech. dir., mgr. fuels and materials, advanced reactors div. Westinghouse Electric Corp., Madison, Pa., 1967-74; dir. research Westinghouse Electric Europe (S.A.), Brussels, 1974-75; chief scientist advanced power systems divs. Westinghouse Electric Corp., Madison, Pa., 1975-81; dir. nuclear programs Westinghouse Electric Corp., Washington, 1981-92; sr. cons. Nuclear Programs, 1992—; mem. divisional rev. coms. Argonne Nat. Lab., 1968-73; Mellor Meml. lectr. Inst. Ceramics, 1963. Contbr. numerous articles to profl. jours.; editorial adv. bd.: Jour. Less Common Metals, 1968—. Recipient Holland Meml. Research prize Sheffield U., 1949. Fellow Royal Inst. Chemistry (Newton Chambers Research prize 1954), Inst. Ceramics, Am. Nuclear Soc.; mem. Brit. Ceramics Soc. (pres. 1965), Am. Ceramic Soc., Nat. Acad. Engring. Roman Catholic. Home: 20308 Canby Ct Gaithersburg MD 20879-4014 Office: Westinghouse Electric Corp One Montrose Metro 11921 Rockville Pike Ste 450 Rockville MD 20852

MURRAY, PETER BRYANT, English language educator; b. N.Y.C., Oct. 6, 1927; s. Frederick James and Florence (Leech) M.; m. Frances N. Pearson, Apr. 24, 1954 (div. Apr. 1970); children: Jean P., Stephen F., Susan C., Christopher J.; m. Karen Louise Olson, Aug. 14, 1970. Student, Va. Mil. Inst., 1945-47; A.B., Swarthmore Coll., 1950; M.A., U. Pa., 1959, Ph.D., 1962. Research chemist Sun Oil Co., Marcus Hook, Pa., 1950-57; instr. English U. Pa., 1961-63, asst. prof., 1963-67; assoc. prof. English U. Del., 1967-68; prof. Macalester Coll., St. Paul, 1968—; chmn. dept. Macalester Coll., 1971-77; Vice pres. Spencer-Murray Corp., Swarthmore, Pa., 1961—. Author: A Study of Cyril Tourneur, 1964, A Study of John Webster, 1969, Thomas Kyd, 1969, Shakespeare's Imagined Persons: The Psychology of Role-Playing and Acting, 1996. Served with AUS, 1946-47. Mem. Modern Lang. Assn. Am., Modern Humanities Research Assn., Am. Assn. U. Profs. (past chpt. pres.), Shakespeare Assn. Am., Nat. Council Tchrs. English. Patentee in petroleum chemistry field, 1953-57, games entertainment field, 1962-66. Office: Macalester Coll Dept English Saint Paul MN 55105

MURRAY, PETER WILLIAM, airline executive, educator, college administrator; b. Boston, Mar. 24, 1942; s. William Andrew Murray and Carlotta Catherine (Cenedella) Catusi; m. Carolyn Pfaff, Feb. 23, 1967; children: Eric, Trevor. AB, U. Notre Dame, South Bend, Ind., 1964; MBA, U. Pa., 1966. Analyst Delta Airlines, Atlanta, 1966-67; mgr. So. Airways, Atlanta, 1969-72; sr. analyst Eastern Airlines, N.Y.C., 1968-69; mgr. Eastern Airlines, Miami, Fla., 1972-89; dir. Discovery Airways, Honolulu, 1989-90; dean sch. bus. Chaminade U. Honolulu, 1990-94, dir. MS in Japanese bus. studies, 1990-93; assoc. prof. mgmt., dir. grad. adminstrn. Winthrop U., Rock Hill, S.C., 1995-96; dir. divsn. of lifelong learning Johnson C. Smith U., Charlotte, N.C., 1996—; adj. prof. U. Miami, Fla. Internat. U., Barry U., U. Hawaii, Pfeiffer U., Montreat Coll., Embry-Riddle Aero. U., 1975—. Mem. Wharton Grad. Alumni Club, Notre Dame Alumni Club, Am. Mktg. Assn. Democrat. Home: 4307 Cantey Pl Charlotte NC 28211-0404 Office: Johnson C Smith U Divsn of Lifelong Learning PO Box 27 Charlotte NC 28216

MURRAY, PHILIP JOSEPH, III, lawyer; b. Pitts., Sept. 20, 1961; s. Philip Joseph Jr. and Dorothy Cecelia (Hollinger) M.; m. Carol Jean Gibson, July 7, 1990; children: Vanessa Lee, Keenan Patrick. BS in Psychology, U. Pitt., 1985; JD, Duquesne U., 1988. Bar: Pa. 1988, U.S. Dist. Ct. (we. dist.) Pa. 1988, U.S. Ct. Appeals (3d cir.) 1992, U.S. Ct. Appeals (8th cir.) 1995. Law clk. to Hon. Barron P. McCune U.S. Dist. Ct. We. Dist., Pitts., 1988-90; assoc. Thorp, Reed & Armstrong, Pitts., 1990—. Exec. dir. William P. Fralic Found., Pitts., 1992—. Mem. Allegheney County Bar Assn. Republican. Roman Catholic. Avocations: golf, athletics. Office: Thorp Reed and Armstrong One Riverfront Ctr Pittsburgh PA 15222

MURRAY, PHYLLIS CYNTHIA, educator; b. Farmville, Va., Nov. 3, 1938; d. Claude and Frazure Young; m. Robert William Murray, Dec. 14, 1963; 1 child, Sidney Adolphus. BA, Hunter Coll., 1960; MS, U. Pa., 1961; diploma, Cornell U., 1980; cert., Vassar Coll., 1991. Tchr. D.C. Bd. Edn., Washington, 1961-63, N.Y. Bd. Edn., 1963—; TV producer TCI, Mamaroneck, N.Y., 1990—; radio host Sta. WVOX Radio, New Rochell, N.Y., 1994—; founder One Love Tennis, White Plains, 1994—. Author: Huggy Bean Visits Ethiopia, 1985; co-author: Enslaved Africans of the North, Encounters in Living History: Activity based lessons on the Enslaved Africans of the North, 1996; contbr. articles to profl. jours. Mem. Town and Village Civic Club, Scarsdale, N.Y., 1994—; mem. UFT-Unity com., N.Y.C., 1994—. Recipient Edn. award Nat. Coun. Negro Women, 1990, Outstanding Vol. award Mayor of White Plains, 1996; Impact II grantee, 1990, 94, 95. Mem. NAACP (life), United Fedn. of Tchr. (del. unity 1993), Alpha Kappa Alpha (Silver Star 1991). Home: 1181 Post Rd Scarsdale NY 10589-2023 Office: Bd of Edn PS75X 984 Faile St Bronx NY 10459-3703

MURRAY, PIUS CHARLES WILLIAM, priest, educator; b. Worcester, Mass., July 24, 1957; s. Charles William and Ann Frances (Donoghue) M. BA, Coll. Holy Cross, 1979; MLS, U. R.I., 1982; MA, Holy Apostles Coll. & Sem., 1990, MDiv, 1991; postgrad., Hebrew Univ. Jerusalem, 1992-93; Licentiate in Sacred Scripture, Pontifical Biblical Inst., Rome, 1995. Ordained priest Roman Cath. Ch., 1992. Libr. supr. Holy Cross Coll. Libr., Worcester, Mass., 1980-86; libr. dir. Greenfield (Mass.) Pub. Libr., 1982-83; town libr. West Springfield (Mass.) Pub. Libr., 1985-86; instr. sacred scripture, assoc. libr. Holy Apostle Coll. & Sem., Cromwell, Conn., 1995-96; prof. Old Testament, dir. libr. svcs. Pope John XXIII Nat. Sem., Weston, Mass., 1996—; adj. prof. old testament Pope John XXIII Nat. Sem., Weston, Mass., 1995-96; chaplain cruises Princess Lines, 1996—; leader pilgrimages to Holy Land, 1997—; author by-laws Cath. Theol. Libr. Consortium. Book reviewer Cath. Bibl. Quarterly, Medievalia et Humanistica, The Natural Cath. Register, Religion and the Arts; abstractor Old Testament Abstracts, 1996; contbr. articles to profl. jours. Trustee Worcester Pub. Libr., 1983-86; sec. West Springfield Kiwanis Club, 1986; participant Ctr. French-Am. Studies Libr. Sci., Paris, 1986, Cath. Jewish Com. Met. Boston, 1996—; mem. Theology Faculty Pastoral Provision, 1997—/. Mem. ALA, Am. Acad. Religion, Cath. Biblical Assn., Cath. Libr. Assn., Cath. Biblical Assn., Soc. Biblical Lit., Inst. on Religion in an Age of Sci., Equestrial Order of the Holy Secupchre in Jerusalem, Stigmatine Fathers & Bros., Ancient Order Hibernians (divsn. 14), Authors Guild, Phi Beta Kappa, Alpha Sigma Nu, Phi Sigma Iota, Beta Phi Mu. Avocations: autograph collecting, bowling, tennis, movies, theatre. Home: Stigmatine Fathers and Brothers 544 Lexington St Waltham MA 02154

MURRAY, RAYMOND CARL, forensic geologist, educator; b. Fitchburg, Mass., July 2, 1929; s. Henry C. and Hattie (Mindt) M.; children: Robert, Martha; Maureen J. Fleming, Aug. 20, 1988. A.B., Tufts U., 1951; Ph.D., U. Wis., 1955. Head prodn. geol. research Shell Devel. Co., 1955-66; prof. geology U. N.Mex., 1966-67; prof. geology, head dept. Rutgers U., New Brunswick, N.J., 1967-77; v.p. research U. Mont., Missoula, 1977-96; scholar-in-residence Associated Western Univs., 1996—. Contbr. articles to books, profl. jours. Home: 106 Ironwood Pl Missoula MT 59803-2425

MURRAY, RAYMOND HAROLD, physician; b. Cambridge, Mass., Aug. 17, 1925; s. Raymond Harold and Grace May (Dorr) M.; children—Maureen, Robert, Michael, Margaret, David, Elizabeth, Catherine, Anne. B.S., U. Notre Dame, 1946; M.D., Harvard U., 1948. Diplomate: Am. Bd. Internal Medicine, also Sub-bd. Cardiovascular Disease. Practice medicine Grand Rapids, Mich., 1955-62; asst. prof. to prof. medicine Ind. U. Sch. Medicine, 1962-77; prof. dept. medicine Mich. State U. Coll. Human Medicine, 1977-95, chmn. dept. medicine, 1977-89, emeritus, 1995—; chmn. aeromed-bioscis panel Sci. Adv. Bd., USAF, 1977-81. Contbr. numerous articles to profl. publs. Served with USNR, 1942-45; Served with USPHS, 1950-53. Fellow ACP (gov. Mich. chpt. 1994—); mem. Am. Heart Assn. (fellow coun. clin. cardiology), Am. Fedn. Clin. Rsch. Office: Mich State U 210B Clinical Ctr East Lansing MI 48824-1313

MURRAY, RAYMOND LE ROY, nuclear engineering educator; b. Lincoln, Nebr., Feb. 14, 1920; s. Ray Annis and Bertha (Mann) M.; m. Ilah Mae Rengler, June 16, 1941; children: Stephen, Maureen, Marshall; m. Quin Meyer, June 3, 1967; 1 stepdau., Tucker; m. Elizabeth Reid, May 12, 1979; stepchildren: Michael, Nancy, James. B.S., U. Nebr., 1940, M.S., 1941; Ph.D., U. Tenn., 1950; postgrad., U. Calif., Berkeley, 1941-43. Physicist U. Calif. Radiation Lab., Berkeley, 1942-43; asst. dept. supt. Tenn. Eastman Corp., Oak Ridge, 1943-47; research physicist Carbide & Carbon Chem. Co., Oak Ridge, 1947-50; prof. physics N.C. State U., 1950-57, Burlington prof. physics, 1957-80, prof. emeritus, 1980—, head dept. physics, 1960-63, head dept. nuclear engring., 1963-74; acting dir. Nuclear Reactor Project, 1956-57; cons. Oak Ridge Nat. Lab., 1950-68, Los Alamos Nat. Lab., 1988-92, also to industry and govt. Author: Introduction to Nuclear Engineering, 1954, 2d edit., 1961, Nuclear Reactor Physics, 1957, Physics: Concepts and Consequences, 1970, Nuclear Energy, 1975, 4th edit., 1993, Understanding Radioactive Waste, 1982, 4th edit., 1994; mem. edit. adv. bd., U.S. exec. editor Jour. Nuclear Energy, 1963-73; adv. editor Annals Nuclear Energy, 1973—; contbr. numerous articles to profl. jours. and encys. Mem. adv. com. on radiation N.C. Bd. Health, 1958-59; mem. Gov.'s Tech. Adv. Com. on Low Level Radioactive Waste, 1980-87; mem. N.C. Radiation Protection Commn., 1979-87, chmn., 1980-82; mem., vice chmn., chmn. N.C. Low Level Radioactive Waste Mgm. Authority, 1987-93. Recipient O. Max Gardner award U. N.C., 1965; Arthur H. Compton award, 1970, Donald G. Fink award IEEE, 1988, Eugene P. Wigner Reactor Physicist award, 1994. Fellow Am. Phys. Soc., Am. Nuclear Soc. (chmn. edn. div. 1966-67, chmn. Eastern Carolinas sect. 1976-77, mem. nominating com. 1989); mem. Am. Soc. Engring. Edn. (chmn. com. on relationships with AEC 1967-68, chmn. nuclear engring. div. 1970-71, Glenn Murphy award 1976), N.C. Soc. Engrs. (Outstanding Engring. Achievement award 1975), Atomic Indsl. Forum (edn. coun. 1970-73), Inst. Nuclear Power Ops. (adv. coun. 1985-87, 89-94), Phi Beta Kappa, Sigma Xi, Pi Mu Epsilon, Phi Kappa Phi. Home: 8701 Murray Hill Drive Raleigh NC 27615

MURRAY, REBECCA BRAKE, lawyer; b. Kingsport, Tenn., Jan. 31, 1949; d. Joseph Albert and Marie (Stinnett) Brake; m. David W. Murray III, Sept. 18, 1971; children: Allison Marie, David W. IV. BS, cert. in phys. therapy, U. Mich., 1971; MS in Health Scis., Case Western Res. U., 1978; postgrad., Cleve. State Law Sch., 1981-83; JD, U. Tenn., 1985. Bar: Tenn. 1985, U.S. Dist. Ct. (ea. dist.) Tenn. 1986, U.S. Ct. Appeals (6th cir.) 1988. Assoc. Kennerly Montgomery & Finley, P.C., Knoxville, 1985-90, shareholder, 1991—. Editor: (law rev.) Cleve. State Law Sch., 1983. Mem. ABA, Tenn. Bar Assn., Knoxville Bar Assn., Def. Rsch. Inst., Tenn. Def. Lawyers Assn. Office: Kennerly Montgomery & Finley PC 550 W Main St Knoxville TN 37902-2567

MURRAY, RICHARD BENNETT, physics educator; b. Marietta, Ga., Dec. 5, 1928; s. William Moore and Ruth (Mozley) M.; m. Clella Bay, Apr. 1, 1956; children: Ada, Annette. BA, Emory U., 1947; MS, Ohio State U., 1950; PhD, U. Tenn., 1955. Rsch. asst. Gaseous Diffusion Plant, Oak Ridge, 1947-48; rsch. physicist Oak Ridge Nat. Lab., 1955-66; vis. assoc. prof. physics U. Del., Newark, 1962-63, assoc. prof., 1966-69, prof., 1969—, acting chmn. dept. physics, 1975-76, univ. coord. for grad. studies, 1979-85, assoc. provost for grad. studies, 1986-88, acting provost and v.p. for acad. affairs, 1988-91, provost, 1993-94; lectr. physics U. Tenn., Knoxville, 1963-66; vis. rsch. physicist U.S. Naval Rsch. Lab., 1991-92; vis. scientist Clarendon Lab., Oxford U., 1992; cons. to industry, 1957-93; councillor Oak Ridge Associated Univs., 1979-88, bd. dirs., 1983-94, vice chmn. coun., 1983-85, chmn. coun., 1985-88; sec.-treas. NE Assn. Grad. Schs., 1982-84; dir. U. Del. Press, 1979-82. Contbr. numerous articles on exptl. nuclear and solid state physics to profl. publs., 1948—. Trustee Sanford Sch., Hockessin, Del., 1981-85; chmn. bd dirs. Oak Ridge Associated Univs. Found., 1989-94; bd. dirs. Del. Inst. for Med. Edn. and Rsch., 1989-91. Predoctoral fellow Oak Ridge Inst. Nuclear Studies, 1953-55; grantee AEC, NSF, Dept. Energy, 1967-84. Fellow AAAS, Am. Phys. Soc.; mem. Southeastern Univs. Rsch. Assn. (bd. dirs. 1989—), Phi Beta Kappa, Sigma Xi, Sigma Pi Sigma, Phi Kappa Phi. Home: 4 Bridlebrook Ln Newark DE 19711-2058 Office: U Del Dept Physics & Astronomy Newark DE 19716

MURRAY, RICHARD MAXIMILIAN, insurance executive; b. Vienna, Austria, Nov. 21, 1922; came to U.S., 1955, naturalized, 1961; s. and Elizabeth Helen Peiker. Grad. in world commerce studies, U. Vienna; postgrad., Columbia U. Asst. sec. Sterling Offices Ltd. (reins. intermediaries), London, Toronto, N.Y.C., 1951-59; v.p. Guy Carpenter, Inc. (reins. intermediaries), N.Y.C., 1959-68; v.p. Travelers Ins. Cos., 1968-87, ret., 1987; mng. dir. La Metropole Ins. Co., Brussels, ret., 1987; chmn. bd. Nippon Mgmt. Corp., N.Y.C., ret., 1991; chmn. bd. Travelers Marine Corp., ret., 1987; pres. Travelers Reins Co. Bermuda Ltd., ret., 1987; pres. Travelers of Asia Ltd., Hong Kong, ret., 1987; vice-chmn. bd. La Prov Corp., N.Y.C.; bd. electors Ins. Hall of Fame; bd. dirs. SCOR U.S. Corp., N.Y., SCOR Reins Co., N.Y., Unity Fire and Gen. Ins. Co., N.Y.C., Gen. Security Ins. Corp. N.Y., Rockleigh Mgmt. Corp., N.Y.C., Preferred Life Ins. Co. N.Y., United Am. Inst. Co., United Am. Holdings Co., Inc.; mem. adv. bd. Firemark Global Ins. Fund, L.P.; chair audit com. Davis Internat. Total Return Fund. Contbr. articles to profl. publs. Decorated for promotion of pvt. ins. (Peru); Knight Order of St. John, Knights of Malta (ambassador at large). Mem. Internat. Ins. Coun. (chmn. 1979-81, award 1990), City Midday Club. Home: 60 Remsen St Brooklyn NY 11201-3453 Office: 80 Broad St Fl 35 New York NY 10004-2209

MURRAY, ROBERT FULTON, JR., physician; b. Newburgh, N.Y., Oct. 19, 1931; s. Robert Fulton and Henrietta Frances (Judd) M.; m. Isobel Ann Parks, Aug. 26, 1956; children: Colin Charles (dec.), Robert Fulton III, Suzanne Frances, Dianne Akwe. B.S., Union Coll., Schenectady, 1953; M.D., U. Rochester, N.Y., 1958; M.S., U. Wash., Seattle, 1968. Diplomate Am. Bd. Internal Medicine, Am. Bd. Med. Genetics. Rotating intern Denver Gen. Hosp., 1958-59; resident in internal medicine U. Colo. Med. Center, 1959-62; staff investigator (service with USPHS) Nat. Inst. Arthritis and Metabolic Diseases, NIH, Bethesda, Md., 1962-65; NIH spl. fellow med.

genetics U. Wash., 1965-67; mem. faculty Howard U. Coll. Medicine, Washington, 1967—; prof. pediatrics and medicine Howard U. Coll. Medicine, 1974—, grad. prof., 1976, prof. oncology, 1976, chief div. med. genetics, 1968—, chmn. dept. genetics and human genetics Grad. Sch., 1976—; nat. adv. gen. med. scis. coun. NIH, 1971-75, recombinant DNA adv. com., 1988-92; sci. adv. bd. Nat. Sickle Cell Anemia Found.; ethics adv. bd. to sec. HEW, 1978-80; chmn. Washington Mayor's Adv. Com. on Metabolic Disorders, 1980-89; active Med. Com. Human Rights. Co-author: Genetic Variation and Disorders in Peoples of African Origin, 1990; co-editor: Genetic, Metabolic and Developmental Aspects of Mental Retardation, 1972, Genetic Counseling: Facts, Values and Norms, 1979, The Human Genome Project and the Future of Health Care, 1996; assoc. editor Am. Jour. Clin. Genetics, 1977-93; mem. editl. adv. bd. Ency. Bioethics, 1975-77, 93-95; mem. editl. bd. Jour. Clin. Ethics, 1990. Trustee Union Coll., 1972-80. Rotary Found. fellow, 1955-56; research grantee NIH, 1969-75. Fellow ACP, AAAS, Inst. Medicine (coun. mem. 1983-85), Inst. Soc., Ethics and Life Scis. (bd. dirs.), Am. Coll. Med. Genetics; mem. AAUP, Assn. Acad. Minority Physicians, Am. Soc. Human Genetics, Genetics Soc. Am., Acad. Medicine Washington, Neighbors Inc. D.C., Sigma Xi, Alpha Omega Alpha. Unitarian. Home: 510 Aspen St NW Washington DC 20012-2740 Office: Howard U Coll Medicine Box 75 Washington DC 20059

MURRAY, ROBERT GRAY, sculptor; b. Vancouver, B.C., Can., Mar. 2, 1936; s. John Gray and Vera (Meakin) M.; m. Cintra Wetherill Lofting, Jan. 23, 1971; children: Rebecca and Megan (twins), Claire, Hillary. Student, U. Sask., Can., 1956-58. One man shows Betty Parsons Gallery, N.Y.C., 1965, 66, 68, David Mirvish Gallery, Toronto, 1967, 68, 72, 73, 74, 75, Jewish Mus., N.Y.C., 1967, Hammarskjold Plaza, N.Y.C., 1971, Paula Cooper Gallery, N.Y.C., 1974, Janie Lee Gallery, Houston, 1977, Hamilton Gallery, N.Y.C., 1977, 79, 80, Klonaridis Inc., Toronto, 1979, 81, 82, Rice U., 1978, Dayton Mus., 1979, Columbus Mus., 1979, Lamont Gallery, Phillips Acad., Exeter, N.H., 1983, Art Gallery Greater Victoria, 1983, Gallery One, Toronto, 1985, Culturale Canadese Roma, 1985, Gallery 291, Atlanta, 1986, Richard Greene Gallery, N.Y.C.,1986, L.A., 1987, Del. Art Mus., Wilmington, 1990, Muhlenberg Coll., Allentown, Pa., 1992, Mira Godard Gallery, Toronto, Reading (Pa.) Pub. Mus., 1994, 96, Andre Zarre Gallery, N.Y.C., 1994, spl. showing Hillary Ground for Sculpture, Trenton N.J., 1997; exhibited in group shows at Whitney Mus. 1996— Am., Art, N.Y.C., 1964-66, Tibor de Nagy Gallery, N.Y.C., 1965, Musée cantonal des Beaux Arts, Lausanne, Switzerland, 1966, World House Gallery, N.Y.C., 1966, Betty Parsons Gallery, 1966, Sch. Visual Arts, N.Y.C., 1967, Los Angeles County Mus., 1967, Nat. Gallery Can., Toronto, 1967, Inst. Contemporary Art, Boston, 1967, U. Toronto, 1967, Guggenheim Mus., N.Y.C., 1967, Inst. Torcuato Di Tella, Buenos Aires, 1967, Musée d'Art Moderne, Paris, 1968, Whitney Mus., 1967, Walker Art Gallery, 1969, X Sao Paulo Biennial, Brazil, 1969, Boston City Hall, 1971, Artist and Fabricator, Amherst, Mass., 1975, Met. Mus., N.Y.C., 1983, Del. Art Mus., 1990, GrandRapids (Mich.) Mus., 1994; represented in permanent collections, Montreal Mus. Fine Arts, Nat. Gallery Can., Joseph Hirshhorn Collection, Art Gallery Ont., Larry Aldrich Mus., Ridgefield, Conn., New Brunswick Mus., Whitney Mus. Am. Art, Met. Mus., N.Y.C., Columbus Mus., Dayton Art Inst., Storm King Art Centre, Del. Art. Mus., Wilmington, Muhlenberg Coll., Allentown, Pa., others; major commns. include, Everson Mus., Syracuse, N.Y., Fredonia (N.Y.) State Coll., Canadian Dept. External Affairs, Ottawa, Ont., U. Mass., U. Toronto, Ont., State Ct. Bldg., Juneau, Alaska, Honeywell Corp., Mpls., also others.

MURRAY, ROBERT JOHN, think-tank executive. Grad., Suffolk Coll., Harvard U. Under sec. Navy U.S. Govt., dep. asst. sec. defense, asst. to the sec., dep. sec. defense; pol. mil. attaché Am. Embassy, London; dean Naval War Coll., 1981-83; dir. Ctr. Naval Warfare Studies, 1981-83; mem. faculty, dir. nat. security program John F. Kennedy Sch. Govt. Harvard U., 1983-90; with CNA Corp., 1990—, pres., CEO, also trustee; pres. Ctr. Naval Analyses; mem. bd. advisors Naval War Coll., Nat. War Coll., Washington. Served USMC. Recipient numerous awards for pub. svc. Fellow Nat. Inst. Pub. Affairs; mem. Internat. Inst. Strategic Studies, In and Out Club (London). Office: CNA Corp 4401 Ford Ave Alexandria VA 22302-1432

MURRAY, ROBERT WALLACE, chemistry educator; b. Brockton, Mass., June 20, 1928; s. Wallace James and Rose Elizabeth (Harper) M.; m. Claire K. Murphy, June 10, 1951; children: Kathleen A., Lynn E., Robert Wallace, Elizabeth A., Daniel J., William M., Padraic O'D. AB, Brown U., 1951; MA, Wesleyan U., Middletown, Conn., 1956; PhD, Yale U., 1960. Mem. tech. staff Bell Labs., Murray Hill, N.J., 1959-68; prof. chemistry U. Mo., St. Louis, 1968-81; chmn. dept. U. Mo., 1975-80, curators' prof., 1981—; vis. prof. Engler-Bunte Inst. U. Karlsruhe, Fed. Republic Germany, 1982, dept. chemistry Univ. Coll., Cork, Ireland, 1989; cons. to govt. and industry. Coeditor: Singlet Oxygen, 1979; contbr. articles to profl. jours. Mem. Warren (N.J.) Twp. Com., 1962-63, mayor, 1963; mem. Planning Com. and Bd. Health, 1962-64, Bd. Edn., 1966-68. Served with USN, 1951-54. Grantee EPA, NSF, NIH, Office of Naval Research. Fellow AAAS, Am. Inst. Chemists, N.Y. Acad. Scis.; mem. Am. Soc. Photobiology, Am. Chem. Soc., The Oxygen Soc., Sigma Xi. Home: 1810 Walnutway Dr Saint Louis MO 63146-3659 Office: Univ Mo Dept Chemistry Saint Louis MO 63121

MURRAY, ROGER FRANKLIN, economist, educator; b. N.Y.C., Oct. 11, 1911; s. Walter Fletcher and Mary (Van Horne) M.; m. Agnes M. McDede, Oct. 19, 1934; 1 child, Roger Franklin III. Grad., Phillips Andover, 1928; BA, Yale U., 1932; MBA, NYU, 1938, PhD, 1942; LLD, Hope Coll., Holland, Mich., 1960, Tulane U., 1992. Investment adminstr. Bankers Trust Co., N.Y.C., 1932-43, v.p., 1946-56; assoc. dean Grad. Sch. Bus. Columbia U., N.Y.C., 1956-58, S. Sloan Colt prof. banking and fin., 1958-65, 71-77; v.p. Tchrs. Ins. and Annuity Assn. and Coll. Retirement Equities Fund, 1965-67, exec. v.p., 1967-70; bd. dirs. Alliance Group Mut. Funds, 1966-88, Chgo. Bd. Options Exch., Putnam Group of Mut. Funds; pres. Fund for Mut. Depositors, 1970-77, Investor Responsibility Rsch. Ctr., Inc.; trustee N.Y. Bank for Savs., 1947-77, Common Fund for Nonprofit Orgns., 1969-81. Pres. alumni coun. Phillips Andover Sch., 1973; mem. N.Y. State Coun. Econ. Advisers, 1973-74, Pension Rsch. Coun.; mem. investment policy panel Pension Benefit Guaranty Corp., 1975-84; mem. President's Task Force on Aging, 1969-70; mem. investment adv. com. N.Y. State Tchrs. Retirement Sys., SEC Adv. Com. on Corp. Disclosure; life trustee Collegiate Sch., pres., 1968-72; trustee Smith Coll., 1969-70; trustee Mayhew program Wolfeboro Area Children's Ctr.; selectman Town of Wolfeboro, N.H. Capt. USAAF, 1943-45. Decorated Legion of Merit. Mem. Am. Econ. Assn., Am. Fin. Assn. (pres. 1964), SR, Phi Beta Kappa, Beta Gamma Sigma. Mem. United Ch. Christ. Home: 32 Pleasant Valley Rd PO Box 669 Wolfeboro NH 03894-0669

MURRAY, ROYCE WILTON, chemistry educator; b. Birmingham, Ala., Jan. 9, 1937; s. Royce Leeroy and Justina Louisa (Herd) M.; m. Judith Studinka, 1957 (div.); children: Katherine, Stewart, Debra, Melissa, Marion; m. Mirtha X. Umana, Dec. 11, 1982. BS in Chemistry, Birmingham So. Coll., 1957; PhD in Analytical Chemistry, Northwestern U., 1960. Instr. U. N.C., Chapel Hill, 1960-61, asst. prof., 1961-66, assoc. prof., 1966-69, prof., 1969—, vice chmn., 1970-75, acting chair dept. chemistry, 1970-71, dir. undergrad. studies, 1978-80, dept. chmn., 1980-85, chmn. curriculum applied scis., 1995—, div. chmn., 1987-93, Kenan prof., 1980—. Contbr. articles to jours. in field. Recipient award Japanese Soc. for Promotion Sci., 1978, Electrochem. Group medal Royal Soc. Chemistry, 1989; Alfred P. Sloan fellow, 1969-72, Guggenheim fellow, 1980-82. Fellow AAAS, Am. Inst. Chemists, Am. Acad. Arts and Scis., Electrochem. Soc.; mem. NAS, Soc. for Electroanalytical Chemistry (bd. dirs., co-founder 1982-84, Charles N. Reilley award 1988, pres. 1991-93), Am. Chem. Soc. (Electrochemistry award 1990, Analytical Chemistry award 1991, editor in chief Analytical Chemistry 1991—), Electrochem. Soc. (hon. life, Carl Wagner Meml. award 1987-95). Presbyterian. Office: U NC Dept Chemistry Chapel Hill NC 27599-3290

'IURRAY, RUSSELL, II, aeronautical engineer, defense analyst, con'tant; b. Woodmere, N.Y., Dec. 5, 1925; s. Herman Stump and Susanne izabeth (Warren) M.; m. Sally Tingue Gardiner, May 22, 1954; children: nn Tingue, Prudence Warren, Alexandria Gardiner. BS in Aero. Engring, MIT, 1949, MS, 1950. Guided missile flight test engr. Grumman Aircraft Engring. Corp., Bethpage, N.Y., 1950-53, asst. chief operations analysis, 1953-62; prin. dep. asst. sec. of def. for systems analysis The Pentagon, Washington, 1962-69; dir. long range planning Pfizer Internat., N.Y.C., 1969-73; dir. review Center for Naval Analyses, Arlington, Va., 1973-77; asst. sec. of def. for program analysis and evaluation Dept. of Def., The Pentagon, Washington, 1977-81; prin. Systems Research & Applications Corp., Arlington, Va., 1981-85; spl. counsellor Com. on Armed Services U.S. Ho. of Reps., 1985-89, nat. security cons., 1989—. Served with USAAF, 1944-45. Recipient Sec. of Def. Medal for meritorious civilian service, 1968; Disting. Public Service medal Dept. Def., 1981. Home: 210 Wilkes St Alexandria VA 22314-3839

MURRAY, SANDRA ANN, biology research scientist, educator; b. Chgo., Oct. 7, 1947; d. Charles William and Muggie (Wise) M. BS, U. Ill., 1970; MS, Tex. So. U., 1973; PhD, U. Iowa, 1980. Instr. biology Tex. So. U., Houston, 1972-73; NIH rsch. fellow U. Calif., Riverside, 1980-82; asst. prof. anatomy U. Pitts., 1982-89, assoc. prof. cell biology and physiology, 1989—; prof. Health Officers Inst. Office Def., Addis Ababa, Ethiopia, 1996—; vis. scientist Scripps Rsch. Inst., La Jolla, Calif., 1991-92, INSERM-INRA Hosp. Debrousse, Lyon, France, 1995; cons. NIH, NSF; vis. sci. cons. Fedn. Am. Soc. Exptl. Biology; invited internat. rsch. lectr. at sci. confs. Contbr. articles to Jour. Cell Biology, Anat. Records, Endocrinology, Am. Jour. Anatomy, Molecular and Cellular Endocrinology, Cancer Rsch. Bd. dirs. NAACP, Riverside, 1980-81. Ford Found. fellow, 1978; Rsch. grantee NSF, 1984—, Beta Kappa Chi, Tri Beta Biol. Soc.; recipient Outstanding Achievment award in Sci., Omega Psi Chi; recipient Faculty award Student Nat. Med. Assn. Mem. Am. Soc. Cell Biology (mem. minority affairs com. 1980—, rsch. award to marine biol. lab. 1986, 87, 88, 89, rsch. presentation travel award 1984), Am. Soc. Biol. Chemists (rsch. presentation travel award 1985), Am. Assn. Anatomists, Tissue Culture Assn. (chairperson internat. sci. com. 1982), Endocrine Soc. (student affairs com.). Office: U Pitts Scaife Hall 864A Pittsburgh PA 15261

MURRAY, SONIA YVETTE, newswriter; b. Ft. Ord, Calif., Jan. 23, 1968; d. Oliver Eddie and Mattie (Leggett) M. BA in Print Journalism, Howard U., 1989. Staff writer Intown Extra Atlanta Jour./Constn., 1989-90, staff writer bus., 1990-92, staff writer arts, 1992—. Named Overall Print Journalist by Atlanta Assn. Media Women, 1994; Nev. fellow U. Nev., Reno, 1992. Mem. Alpha Kappa Alpha. Avocations: photography, tennis, music. Home: 1285 Heatherland Dr SW Atlanta GA 30331-7403 Office: Atlanta Journal Constitution Entertainment Desk 72 Marietta St NW Atlanta GA 30303-2804

MURRAY, SUZANNE MARIE, accountant; b. Frankfurt, Germany, Aug. 12, 1970; (parents Am. citizens); d. Peter A. and Suzanne Marie (Falzo) M. BBA in Acctg., Siena Coll., 1992. CPA, N.Y., Tex. Assoc. acct. Bollam Sheedy Torani & Co., LLP, Albany, N.Y., 1992-95, Margolis & Co., PC, Bala Cynwyd, Pa., 1995-96; sr. fin. analyst Morven Ptnrs. LP, Dallas, 1996—. Asst. vol. Arsenal City Run, Watervliet, N.Y., 1992-93. Mem. Inst. Mgmt. Accts. (dir. student activities Albany chpt. 1994-95, mem. pub. rels. com. Phila. chpt. 1995—). Home: 17200 Westgrove Dr Apt 1524 Dallas TX 75248 Office: Morven Ptnrs LP 5151 Belt Line Rd Ste 956 Dallas TX 75240-7030

MURRAY, TERRENCE, banker; b. Woonsocket, R.I., July 11, 1939; s. Joseph W. and Florence (Blackburn) M.; m. Suzanne Young, Jan. 24, 1960; children: Colleen, Paula, Terrence, Christopher, Megan. B.A., Harvard U., 1962. With Fleet Nat. Bank, Providence, 1962—, pres., 1978-86; with Fleet Fin. Group Inc., Providence, 1969—, pres., 1978—, chmn., pres., chief exec. officer, 1982-88, pres., 1988, chmn., pres., chief exec. officer, 1988—, also bd. dirs.; bd. dirs. Fleet Nat. Bank, A.T. Cross Co., State Mut. Assurance Co. Am., Fed. Res. Bank Boston, Stop & Shop Cos. Inc. Trustee R.I. Sch. of Design, Brown U. Recipient Outstanding Bus. Leader award Northwood Inst., 1986, Humanitarian award Nat. Jewish Ctr. for Immunology and Respiratory Medicine, 1988, Never Again award Jewish Fedn., 1989, New Englander of Yr. award New England Coun., 1990, New England Businessperson of Yr. award New England Bus. Mag., 1991, Humanitarian award Fogarty Found., 1991. Mem. Am. Bankers Assn. (bd. dirs.), Assn. of Res. City Bankers (bd. dirs.), Harvard Alumni Assn. (bd. dirs.). Office: Fleet Bank Peter D Liernan Plz Albany NY 12207*

MURRAY, TERRY (TERENCE RODNEY MURRAY), professional hockey team coach; b. Shawville, Que., Can., July 20, 1950; m. Linda Murray; children: Megan, Lindsey. Hockey player Calif. Golden Seals, 1972-75, Phila. Flyers, 1975-77, 78-81, Detroit Red Wings, 1977; hockey player Washington Capitals, 1981-82, asst. coach, 1982-88, head coach, 1990-94; head coach Balt. Skipjacks, 1988-90, Philadelphia Flyers, 1994—. Named to 3 Am. Hockey League all-star teams; named most valuable defenseman Am. Hockey League, 1978, 79. Office: Philadelphia Flyers Core States Spectrum 3601 N Broad St Philadelphia PA 19140-4107*

MURRAY, THOMAS DWIGHT, advertising agency executive; b. Middletown, Ohio, May 1, 1923; s. Charles H. and Rose (Newbrander) M.; m. Barbara Helen Howlett, Oct. 5, 1946; children—Cynthia Helen, Susan Howlett; m. Carol Callaway Muehl, Apr. 13, 1968; children—David Rutherford, Piper Dee. Student, U. Va., 1941-43. Passenger relations agt. United Airlines, N.Y.C., 1946-47; tech. and advt. writer, copy supr. Frigidaire div. Gen. Motors Corp., Dayton, O., 1947-55; with Campbell-Ewald Co., Detroit, 1955-71; sr. v.p., creative dir. Campbell-Ewald Co., 1968-69, dir., mem. exec. com., 1968-71, exec. v.p., creative dir., 1969-71; chmn. bd., creative dir. Thomas Murray & Austin Chaney, Inc., Hudson, Ohio, 1971-80; Lectr. Wayne State U., U. Mich., Mich. State U., U. Ill., Art Center Los Angeles, Kent State U., Cleve. Advt. Sch., others; advt. adv. council Kent State U., 1976. Author: A Child to Change Your Life, 1976, A Look at Tomorrow, 1985, Tire Tracks Back, 1989; sr. editor Car Collector mag.; essayist Wall St. Jour., 1991—; wrote ad on Apollo 11 moonshot which was read into Congl. Record; contbr. articles to profl. jours. Vice pres., pres. local PTA, 1962-64; chmn. advt. com. United Found., 1966; Bd. dirs. Mich. Mental Health Soc., Big Bros. and Sisters of Greater Akron. Served with F.A. AUS, 1943-46, ETO. Recipient numerous advt. awards including Clio, Andy of N.Y., MOTO award, 1984. Mem. Detroit Copy Club (past pres., dir.). Clubs: Recess, Flying, Uptown Athletic Detroit, Birmingham Athletic, Brown's Run Country. Home: 6650 Washington Cir # 18 Franklin OH 45005-5521

MURRAY, THOMAS HENRY, bioethics educator, writer; b. Phila., July 30, 1946; s. Thomas Henry and Colombia Rita (Lucci) M.; m. Sharon Marie Engelkraut, Jan. 1968 (div. Sept. 1975); children: Kathleen Elizabeth, Dominique Maria, Peter Albert; m. Cynthia Sarah Aberle, Apr. 1, 1978; 1 child, Emily Sarah Aberle. BA in Psychology, Temple U., 1968; PhD in Social Psychology, Princeton, 1976. Instr. New Coll., Sarasota, Fla., 1971-75; asst. prof. Interdisciplinary Studies Miami U., Oxford, Ohio, 1975-80, assoc. prof., 1980; assoc. social behavioral studies The Hastings Ctr., Hastings-on Hudson, N.Y., 1980-84; assoc. prof. Inst. Med. Humanities U. Tex Med. Br., Galveston, Tex., 1984-86, prof., 1986-87; prof., dir. Ctr. Biomed. Ethics Case We. Reserve U., Cleve., 1987—; mem. Nat. Bioethics Adv. Commn., ethical, legal and social issues working group Human Project Orgn. NIH/Dept. Energy, 1989-95. Author: The Worth of a Child, 1996; founder, editor Med. Humanities Rev.; mem. editl. bd. Physician and Sportsmedicine, Human Gene Therapy. Mem. U.S. Olympic com., com. sports medicine. Fellow NEH, 1977-78, 1979-80, Aspen Inst., 1989. Fellow Soc. Values in Higher Edn., Hastings Ctr., Environ. Health Inst.; mem. APHA, Assn. Practical and Profl. Ethics (exec. com.), Am. Soc. Law Medicine and Ethics (bd. dirs. 1993—), Assn. Integrative Studies (bd. dirs. 1980-87, pres. 1983), Soc. Health and Human Values (chair program dirs. sect. 1989-90, faculty assn. 1989-90, SHHV program com. 1990, pres.-elect 1992-93, pres. 1993-94), Am. Soc. Human Genetics (social issues com.), Am. Coll. Ob-Gyn. (com. on ethics), Human Genome Orgn. (ethics com.). Office: Case Western Res U Sch Medicine Ctr Biomed Ethics 10900 Euclid Ave Cleveland OH 44106-1712

MURRAY, THOMAS JOHN (JOCK MURRAY), medical humanities educator, medical researcher, neurologist; b. Halifax, N.S., Can., May 30, 1938; m. Janet Kathleen Pottie; children: Shannon, Bruce, Suellen, Brian. Grad. pre-med, St. Francis Xavier U., 1958, LLD (hon.), 1989; MD, Dalhousie U., 1963; DSc (hon.), Acadia U., 1991. Family physician, Nashwaaksis, N.S., 1963-65; chief of medicine Camp Hill Hosp., Halifax, N.S., 1974-79; chief of neurology Dalhousie U., Halifax, 1979-85, dir. multiple sclerosis rsch. unit, 1980—, dean of medicine, 1985-92; prof. med. humanities, 1992—; mem. working group on Diability in U.S. Pres., 1994-96. Co-author: (textbook) Essential Neurology; author over 200 pub. works, including contbns. to 7 textbooks. Bd. dirs. St. Francis Xavier U., Pictou Acad. Found., Robert Pope Found., Nat. Coun. on Bioethics and Health Rsch. Decorated officer Order Can. Fellow Royal Coll. Physicians (Can.), ACP (gov. 1985-90, chmn. bd. govs. 1990-91, bd. regents, chmn. 1995—); mem. Can. Neurol. Soc. (pres. 1982-84), Am. Acad. Neurology (v.p. 1981-83), Can. Med. Forum (chair), Can. Med. Assn., N.S. Med. Soc., Assn. Can. Med. Colls. (pres. 1991-92), Can. Med. Forum (chmn. 1992-95), Consortium of Multiple Sclerosis Ctrs. (pres. 1997—). Avocations: medical history, piano, windsurfing, beer-making. Home: 16 Bobolink St, Halifax, NS Canada B3M 1W3 Office: Dalhousie Med Sch, Clin Rsch Ctr, Halifax, NS Canada B3H 4H7

MURRAY, THOMAS JOSEPH, advertising executive; b. Bridgeport, Conn., Mar. 12, 1924; s. Thomas and Mary (Diskin) M.; m. Mary Elizabeth Cull, Feb. 22, 1945; children: Joshua Francis, Mary Elizabeth, Katherine Diskin. A.B., Dartmouth Coll., 1947. Instr., Dartmouth Coll., 1947-48; with Warwick & Legler, N.Y.C., 1948-68; sr. v.p., mgmt. account supr. Warwick & Legler, 1964-68; sr. v.p. group supr. Gaynor & Ducas, Inc., 1968-74, exec. v.p., 1974—, chief fin. officer and gen. mgr., 1978-87; pres. TJM & Assn., 1987—. Pres., trustee Hillcrest Gen. Hosp., N.Y.C.; Westchester Inst. for tng. in Psychoanalysis and Psychotheraphy, Mt. Kisco, N.Y. Served as 1st lt. USAAF, 1942-45. Decorated D.F.C., Air medal with 4 oak leaf clusters. Mem. Nat. Wholesale Druggists Assn., Propriety Assn., Nat. Assn. Chain Drug Stores, Am. Mktg. Assn. Home and Office: 65 Norfield Rd Weston CT 06883-2213

MURRAY, THOMAS MICHAEL, civil engineering educator, consultant; b. Dubuque, Iowa, May 22, 1944; s. Raymond M. and Laura R. (Juergens) M.; m. Margaret Ann Schrodt, July 13, 1964 (div. 1995); children: Matthew R., Elizabeth A., Nicholas P. BSCE, Iowa State U., 1962; MSCE, Lehigh U., 1966; PhD in Engring. Mechanics, U. Kans., 1970. Registered profl. engr., Iowa, Okla. Engr. trainee Pitts. Des Moines (Iowa) Steel Co., 1962-64; instr. civil engring. U. Omaha, 1966-67, U. Kans., Lawrence, 1967-69; asst. prof., assoc. prof., prof. U. Okla. Sch. Civil Engring., Norman, 1970-86; Disting. vis. prof. USAF Acad., Colorado Springs, Colo., 1986-87; Montague-Betts prof. structural steel design Va. Poly. Inst. and State U., Blacksburg, 1987—; pres. Structural Engrs. Inc., Radford, Va., 1973—. Author: Design Guide for Connections, 1990, Design Guide on Floor Vibrations, 1997; also numerous articles; patentee in field. Recipient various teaching awards U. Okla., 1979, 81, 84. Fellow ASCE (numerous offices 1970—); mem. Am. Inst. Steel Constrn. (T.R. Higgins lectr. 1991), Am. Soc. for Engring. Edn., Structural Stability Rsch. Coun., also others. Republican. Roman Catholic. Avocations: skiing, spectator sports, railroads. Office: Va Poly Inst and State U Dept Civil Engring Blacksburg VA 24061

MURRAY, THOMAS VEATCH, lawyer; b. Phoenix, July 17, 1947; s. Robert Morrison Jr. and Jane Veatch (Murray) Barber; m. Cynthia Ann Burnett, June 2, 1971; children: Anne Caroline, Thomas Veatch Jr. BA, U. Kans., 1969; JD, U. Mich., 1972. Bar: Kans. 1972, U.S. Dist. Ct. Kans. 1972, U.S. Ct. Appeals (10th cir.) 1983, U.S. Supreme Ct. 1976. Assoc. Barber, Emerson, Six, Springer & Zinn, Lawrence, Kans., 1972-76; mem. Barber, Emerson, Springer, Zinn & Murray, L.C., Lawrence, Kans., 1976—; dir. The First Nat. Bank of Lawrence, 1980-91, Hall Ctr. for the Humanities, Lawrence, 1988—. Contbr. articles to profl. jours. Mem. Kans. Bd. Law Examiners, 1995—, Bd. Edn. Unified Sch. Dist. 497, Lawrence, 1991-95; dir. Lawrence C. of C., 1993-95. Mem. Fedn. Ins. and Corp. Counsel (regional v.p. 1994—), Kans. Assn. Def. Counsel (dir. 1993—), Univ. Club (Kansas City). Republican. Presbyterian. Avocations: classical and operatic music. Office: Barber Emerson Springer Zinn & Murray LC 1211 Massachusetts St Lawrence KS 66044-3351

MURRAY, TY (THE KID MURRAY), professional rodeo cowboy; s. Harold "Butch" and Joy M. Student, Odessa (Tex.) Coll. Five-time world all-around world champion Profl. Rodeo Circuit Assn., 1989-93; world champion bull rider, 1993. Named Nat. H.S. Rodeo All-Around Champion, 1987, PRCA Rookie of the Year Profl. Rodeo Cowboy Assn., 1988, Nat. Intercollegiate Rodeo All-Around Champion, 1988. Record for single season earnings, 1991. Office: Profl Rodeo Cowboy Assn 101 Pro Rodeo Dr Colorado Springs CO 80919-2301*

MURRAY, WALLACE SHORDON, publisher, educator; b. Dorchester, Mass., May 9, 1921; s. Wallace Jennings and Ina (Shordon) M.; m. Eleanor Muriel Grandy, Oct. 30, 1948; children: Patricia Ann, William Howard. B.S., MIT, 1942; M.Ed., Boston U., 1949; Litt.D. (hon.), Western New Eng. Coll., 1965. Tchr. Bolles Sch., Jacksonville, Fla., 1945-46; head math. dept., asst. prin. Bolles Sch., 1946-49; headmaster Berwick Acad., South Berwick, Maine, 1949-50; sales rep. D.C. Heath & Co., Boston, 1950-52; editor D.C. Heath & Co., 1952-53, head elementary editorial dept., 1953-55, editor in chief, 1955-66, v.p., 1962-66, dir., 1956-66, sec. of corp., 1957-66; dir. Erica Corp., 1956-66; exec. v.p. Heath de Rochemont Corp., 1960-66, dir., 1960-66; editor-in-chief, pres. subs. Raytheon Edn. Co., 1966-68; v.p., editorial dir. domestic and internat. ops. Grolier Inc., 1968-80, dir., 1969-82, cons., 1980-82; dir. Grolier Edn. Corp., 1968-80, Scarecrow Press Inc., 1969-80; Chmn. elementary and high sch. research com. Am. Ednl. Pubs. Inst., 1966-68, chmn. elem. and high sch. sect., 1968-69. Lay leader Boston dist. Meth. Ch., 1952-56; mem. adv. bd. Boston U. Student Christian Assn., 1954-62, treas., 1957-59, chmn., 1959-61; mem. president's adv. council St. Joseph's Coll., North Windham, Maine, 1973-88; mem. corp. New Eng. Deaconess Assn., 1965-95, exec. com., 1965-68; mem. corp. New Eng. Deaconess Hosp., 1967-93; dir. Japan America Soc. of Maine, 1981-91, pres., 1984-86; merit badge counselor Pine Tree Coun., Boy Scouts Am., 1984—; dir. Children's Mus. of Maine, 1987-89; dir. Leisure Ctr. for the Handicapped, Inc., Portland, Maine, 1987-93, treas. 1988-93; mem. adv. council So. Maine Retired Sr. Vol. Program, 1987-90, chmn. fin. com., 1987-89; mem. Foster Care Case Review Panel Maine Dept. Human Services, 1987-91; dir. Foreside Common Condominium Assn., Falmouth, Maine, 1986-89, 1991-92, pres., 1987-89; vol. staff mem. Vol. Lawyers Project of Maine, 1987-90; vol. math. instr. Adult Basic Learning Exchange, Portland, 1987-91. Served to capt. AUS, 1942-46, to maj. USAR. Mem. Newcomen Soc., World Affairs Council of Maine, Phi Delta Kappa. Republican. Methodist. Lodges: Masons, Shriners. Home: PO Box 17 Sebago Lake ME 04075-0017

MURRAY, WARREN JAMES, philosophy educator; b. St. Paul, Dec. 3, 1936; s. James Bernard and Louise (Robertson) M.; m. Mary Ann McAulay, July 18, 1959; children: Mark, Anne, Kathleen. Student, St. Thomas Coll., 1954-55; B.A. in Chemistry, Wis. State Coll., River Falls, 1962; B.Ph. in Philosophy, Universite Laval, Que., Can., 1964, Ph.L., 1965, scolarite Ph.D., 1966. Analytical chemist 3M Co., St. Paul, 1957-61, research chemist, 1961-63; prof. philos. sci. U. Laval, Sainte-Foy, 1966—, vice dean, 1979—; invited prof. Faculte de philosophie Comparee, Paris, 1969, 72, Universite libre des sciences de l'homme, Paris, 1975—, Ecole des Hautes Etudes, Paris, 1976, Universidad Nacional de Tucuman, Argentina, 1991. fgn. exchange teaching grantee Province Que., 1969. Mem. Soc. Aristotelian Studies (pres.), Can. Soc. History and Philosophy Sci. Office: Faculte De Philosophie, Universite Laval, Sainte Foy, PQ Canada G1K 7P4

MURRAY, WILLIAM JAMES, anesthesiology educator, clinical pharmacologist; b. Janesville, Wis., July 20, 1933; s. James Arthur and Mary Helen (De Porter) M.; m. Therese Rose Dooley, June 25, 1955; children: Michael, James, Anne. BS, U. Wis., 1955, PhD, 1959; MD, U. N.C., 1962. Diplomate Am. Bd. Anesthesiology. Rsch. asst. U. Wis., Madison, 1955-59; instr. pharmacology U. N.C., Chapel Hill, 1959-62, resident and fellow in surgery (anesthesiology), 1962-64, instr., 1964-65, asst. prof., 1965-68; asst. to dir. for drug availability FDA, Washington, 1968-69; assoc. prof. pharmacology, clin. pharmacology and anesthesiology U. Mich., Ann Arbor, 1969-72; assoc. prof. anesthesiology Duke U., Durham, N.C., 1972-81, prof., 1981—; assoc. dir. Upjohn Ctr. for Clin. Pharmacology, Ann Arbor, 1969-72. Mem. AMA, Am. Soc. Anesthesiologists, Internat. Anesthesia Rsch. Soc., Soc. for Ambulatory Anesthesia, Am. Pharm Assn., N.Y. Acad. of Sci., N. C. Soc. Anesthesiologists, Am. Soc. Hosp. Pharmacists, U.S. Pharmacopeial Conv., Am. Coll. Clin. Pharmacology, Am. Soc. for Clin. and Therapeutic Pharmacology, Am. Soc. Pharmacology and Exptl. Therapeutics, N.C. Soc. Hosp. Pharmacists, So. Med. Assn., The Annals of

Pharmacotherapy, Am. Med. Writers Assn. Republican. Roman Catholic. Home: 135 Pinecrest Rd Durham NC 27705 Office: Duke U Med Ctr Dept Anesthesiology DUMC Box 3094 Durham NC 27710

MURRAY, WILLIAM MICHAEL, lawyer; b. Buffalo, Dec. 21, 1953; s. William Joseph and Mary Ann (Lichtenthal) M.; m. Antoinette Ioco, Aug. 12, 1978; children: Colleen Elizabeth, William Michael Jr., Caitlin Anne. BA, U. Notre Dame, 1975; JD, U. Detroit, 1978. Bar: N.Y. 1978, U.S. Dist. Ct. (we. dist.) N.Y. 1980. Asst. county atty. Erie County, Buffalo, 1978-79; ptnr. Stamm & Murray, Williamsville, N.Y., 1979-96, Renaldo Myers & Palumbo, Williamsville, N.Y., 1996—; dep. atty. Town of Amherst, N.Y., 1993-96; gen. counsel Town of Amherst Indsl. Devel. Agy., 1996—. Mem. Amherst (N.Y.) Rep. Com., 1980—; chmn. Amherst Zoning Bd. Appeals, 1986-93. Mem. N.Y. State Bar Assn., Erie County Bar Assn., Williamsville Bus. Assn. (bd. dirs., v.p. 1985—), Rotary (pres. Williamsville 1989). Roman Catholic. Home: 28 Northledge Dr Snyder NY 14226-3946 Office: 5555 Main St Buffalo NY 14221-5430

MURRELL, ESTELLE C., elementary school educator; b. Warren County, Ky., Feb. 13, 1931; d. James B. and Mary Ellen (Johnson) Clark; m. Allen Leslie Murrell, Mar. 14, 1953; children: Leslie Allen, Lisa Ellen. BS, Western Ky. U., 1956. Cert. elem. tchr., Ky. 5th grade tchr. Bowling Green (Ky.) Ind. Bd. Edn.; 6th grade tchr. Warren County Bd. Edn., Bowling Green; 4th grade tchr. Hardin County Bd. Edn., Elizabethtown, Ky.; 4th, 6th and 7th grades tchr. lang. arts Bowling Green Bd. Edn.; tchr. Draughons Jr. Coll., Bowling Green, Ky. Named to Leader of Am. Elem. Edn., 1971, 73. Mem. NEA, Ky. Edn. Assn., Bowling Green Edn. Assn. (membership chair), Nat. Coun. Tchrs. English, Ky. Coun. Tchrs. English Lang. Arts, Ky. Retired Tchrs. Assn. Home: 1404 Woodhurst St Bowling Green KY 42104-3322

MURRELL, SUSAN DEBRECHT, librarian; b. St. Louis, Aug. 10, 1951; d. Edward August and Edith (Keeney) DeB.; m. Harry Thornton Murrell, Oct. 18, 1974; children: Brian, Katherine. BA in History, U. Ky., 1973; MLS, U. Mo., 1976. Children's libr. Louisville Free Pub. Libr., 1974-76, talking book libr. head, 1976-83; lower/mid. sch. libr. Ky. Country Day Sch., Louisville, 1983-84; children's libr. Emmet O'Neal Libr., Mountain Brook, Ala., 1984-86, asst. dir., 1986-89, dir., 1989—. Bd. dirs. Mountain Brook Libr. Found., 1993—; active Jefferson County Pub. Libr., mem. publicity com., 1989-92; mem. allocations com. United Way. Mem. ALA, Ala. Libr. Assn. (mem. publicity com. 1992-93, pub. libr. chair 1995-96), Rotary Internat. Roman Catholic. Office: Emmet O'Neal Libr 50 Oak St Birmingham AL 35213-4219

MURRIAN, ROBERT PHILLIP, magistrate, judge, educator; b. Knoxville, Tenn., Apr. 1, 1945; s. Albert Kinzel and Mary Gilbert (Eppes) M.; m. Jerrilyn Sue Boone, Oct. 29, 1983; children—Kimberley Ann, Jennifer Rebecca, Albert Boone, Samuel Robert. B.S., U.S. Naval Acad., 1967; J.D., U. Tenn., 1974. Bar: Tenn. 1974, U.S. Dist. Ct. (ea. dist.) Tenn. 1975, U.S. Ct. Appeals (6th cir.) 1982. Law clk. to judge U.S. Dist. Ct. (ea. dist.) Tenn., 1974-76; assoc. Butler, Vines, Babb & Threadgill, Knoxville, 1976-78; magistrate, judge U.S. Dist. (ea. dist.) Tenn., Knoxville, 1978—; adj. prof. U. Tenn. Coll. Law, 1990-93, 95-96. Lt. USN, 1967-71. Green Scholar, 1973-74; Nat. Moot Ct. scholar, 1974. Fellow Tenn. Bar Found.; mem. ABA, Knoxville Bar Assn. (bd. govs. 1994), Tenn. Bar Assn., Order of Coif, Am. Inn of Ct. (master of the bench). Presbyterian. Office: US Dist Ct US Court House 800 Market St Knoxville TN 37902-2312

MURRILL, PAUL WHITFIELD, former utility executive, former university administrator; b. St. Louis, July 10, 1934; s. Horace Williams and Grace (Whitfield) M.; m. Nancy Williams, May 17, 1959; children: Paul Whitfield, John Parham, William Britton. BS, U. Miss., 1956; MS, La. State U., 1962, PhD, 1963. Registered profl. engr., La. Instr. chem. engring. La. State U., 1961-62, spl. lectr. chem., mech., indsl. and aerospace engring., 1962-63, asst. prof., 1963-65, assoc. prof., 1965-67, assoc. prof., head dept. chem. engring., 1967-68, prof., head dept. chem. engring., 1968-69, prof., 1968-80, vice chancellor, dean acad. affairs, 1969-70, provost, 1970-74, chancellor, 1974-80; sr. v.p. Ethyl Corp., Richmond, Va., 1980-82; chmn. bd., chief exec. officer Gulf States Utilities Co., Beaumont, Tex., 1982-87, spl. advisor to chmn., 1987-90; pres. Monarch Internat. Corp., 1978—; chmn. FMOL Health System Inc., 1991-94; chmn. bd. dirs. Burden Found., 1992—, Piccadilly Cafeterias, 1994—; cons. in field; project mgr. Dept. Def. project THEMIS, 1967-72; bd. dirs. Tidewater Inc., New Orleans, Gulf State Utilities Co., Howell Corp. Piccadilly Cafeterias, Zygo, Inc., Entergy Corp., Pavilion Techs., Inc. Author: Automatic Control of Processes, 1967; co-author: Fortran IV Programming for Engineers and Scientists, 1968, The Development and Utilization of Mathematical Models, 1970, An Introduction to Fortran IV Programming: A General Approach, 1970, COBOL Programming, 1970, Basic Programming, 1970, PL/I Programming, 1973, Introduction to Computer Science, 1973, Fundamentals of Process Control, 1980, 2d edit., 1991, Application Concepts in Process Control, 1988; cons. editor: Chemical Engineering series, Internat. Textbook Co., 1966-72, Instrument Soc. Am., 1981—. Bd. dirs. local Boy Scouts Am., United Way; deacon Bapt. ch. Served to lt. comdr USNR, 1956-59. Recipient Faculty Service award Nat. U. Extension Assn., 1968, Halliburton Found. award for excellence in engring. teaching, 1966. Mem. La. Engring. Soc. (Tech. Accomplishment medal 1970, Andrew Lockett medal 1978), Am. Soc. Engring. Edn., Am. Inst. Chem. Engrs., Instrument Soc. Am. (Donald Eckman Nat. award 1976), Sigma Xi, Omicron Delta Kappa, Tau Beta Pi, Pi Kappa Pi, Phi Kappa Phi (Disting. Nat. medal 1976), Phi Eta Sigma, Phi Lambda Epsilon. Lodge: Rotary.

MURRIN, REGIS DOUBET, lawyer; b. Erie, Pa., June 2, 1930; s. John III and Gabrielle (Doubet) M.; m. Evelyn L. Alessio, Aug. 22, 1959; children: Catherine Shaw Murrin Hargenrader, Mary Murrin Smith, Elizabeth Murrin Talotta, Rebecca Fielding Lamanna. BA, U. Notre Dame, 1952; JD, Harvard U., 1959; LLM, Temple U., 1968. Bar: Pa. 1959, U.S. Supreme Ct. 1971. Assoc. Murrin & Murrin, Butler, Pa., 1959-62; atty. Housing & Home Fin. Agy., Phila., 1962-64; ptnr. Baskin & Sears, Pitts., 1964-84; ptnr. Reed Smith Shaw & McClay, Pitts., 1985-95, of counsel, 1995—. Trustee Pitts. Oratory, 1976-93; chmn. Zoning Bd. Adjustment, City of Pitts., 1994—; bd. dirs. Ellis Sch., 1991—. Served as lt. USNR, 1952-55, Korea, Vietnam. Mem. Pa. Bar Assn. (real estate and common interest ownership coms.), Edwin Sorin Soc. Democrat. Roman Catholic. Office: Reed Smith Shaw & McClay 435 6th Ave Pittsburgh PA 15219-1809

MURRIN, THOMAS EDWARD, insurance company executive; b. Bklyn., Sept. 12, 1923; s. Maurice Joseph and Agnes (O'Brien) M.; m. Marguerite Judge, Aug. 23, 1947; children—Maureen, Thomas, Rosemary, Ann, Patricia, Elizabeth, James, Marguerite. B.S. magna cum laude, St. John's U., 1944. Actuary Nat. Bur. Casualty Underwriters, N.Y.C., 1946-61; v.p., actuary Am. Ins. Group, Newark, 1961-63, Fireman's Fund Am. Ins. Cos., San Francisco, 1963-68; sr. v.p., actuary Fireman's Fund Am. Ins. Cos., 1968-76, exec. v.p. ins. services office, 1976-83; exec. cons. Coopers and Lybrand, San Francisco, 1984—. Served to lt. (j.g.) USNR, 1944-46. Fellow Casualty Actuarial Soc. (past pres.); mem. Am. Acad. Actuaries (past pres.), Internat. Congress Actuaries. Home: 275 Calle de la Selva Novato CA 94949-6084 Office: 333 Market St San Francisco CA 94105-2102

MURRISH, CHARLES HOWARD, oil and gas exploration company executive, geologist; b. Rochester, Mich., Dec. 27, 1940; s. Richard John and Emily Louise (Marsh) M.; m. Brigitte Marie Furlotte, Oct. 23, 1965; children: Stephanie, Stephen, Brian. Student Mexico City Coll., 1962; BS, Mich. State U., 1963, MS, 1966. Exploration geologist and geophysicist Chevron, New Orleans, 1966-71; mgr. exploration Odeco, New Orleans, 1971-77; v.p. McMoRan Offshore Exploration Co., Metairie, La., 1977-79, sr. v.p., 1979-81; pres. McMoRan-Freeport Oil Co., New Orleans, 1981-83; pres. McMoRan Exploration Co., Metairie, 1983-86 ; exec. v.p. McMoran Oil & Gas Co., 1986; sr. exec. v.p. McMoRan Oil & Gas Co., 1986-90; sr. exec. v.p. Freeport-McMoran Oil & Gas Co., 1990-92, also bd. dirs.; ptnr. CLK Co., 1992-94; pres., COO McMoRan Oil & Gas Co., 1994—. Chmn. bd. Hysell Ballet Arts, Inc., New Orleans, 1982-83; chmn. petroleum majors campaign United Way, 1996; bd. dirs. Lenpac, Metairie, 1983. Mem. New Orleans Geol. Soc., Geol. Soc. Am., Am. Assn. Petroleum Geologists, Petroleum Club of New Orleans (bd. dirs. 1988, 89, 90), Houston Geol. Soc., La. Assn. Ind. Producers, Mid-Continent Oil and Gas Assn. Office: McMoRan Oil & Gas Co 1615 Poydras St New Orleans LA 70112-1254 also: PO Box 60004 New Orleans LA 70160-0004

MURRY, CHARLES EMERSON, lawyer, official; b. Hope, N.D., June 23, 1924; s. Raymond Henry and Estelle Margarete (Skeim) M.; m. Donna Deane Kleve, June 20, 1948; children: Barbara, Karla, Susan, Bruce, Charles. B.S., U. N.D., 1948, J.D., 1950. Bar: N.D. 1950. Mem. firm Nelson and Heringer, Rugby, N.D., 1950-51; dir. N.D. Legis. Council, 1951-75; adj. gen. with rank of maj. gen. State of N.D., Bismarck, 1975-84; mgr. Garrison Diversion Conservancy Dist., 1985-93; cons. Council State Govts.; mem. res. forces policy bd. Sec. of Def. Vice-pres. Mo. Slope Luth. Home of Bismarck, 1965-66. Served with AUS, 1942-45. Decorated D.S.M., Legion of Merit, Meritorious Service medal, Bronze Star, Army Commendation medal; Fourragere Belgium; Orange Lanyard Netherlands; recipient Sioux award U. N.D., 1970; Gov.'s award of excellence, 1971; Nat. Leadership award Bismarck C. of C., 1971. Mem. Adjs. Gen. Assn. (exec. com., sec. 1983-84), Nat. Legis. Conf. (past chmn.), N.G. Assn., Am. Bar Assn., N.D. Bar Assn., Commrs. Uniform State Laws. Lutheran. Lodges: Elks, Masons. Office: HC 9 5505 Ponderosa Ave Bismarck ND 58501-9159

MURRY, FRANCIE ROBERTA, special education educator; b. Waukegan, Ill.. BA, Ctrl. Wash. U., 1980, MEd, 1988; PhD, U. Va., 1991. Cert. tchr., Wash. Spl. edn. tchr. Adna (Wash.) Sch. Dist., 1980-81; itinerant spl. edn. tchr. Ellensburg Sch. Dist., Kittitas, Wash., 1981-85; dist. cons., spl. edn. tchr. Ellensburg (Wash.) Sch. Dist., 1985-86, at-risk project cons./coord., 1987-88; dist. cons., spl. edn. tchr. Yelm (Wash.) Sch. Dist., 1986-87; grad. asst. Commonwealth Ctr. Edn. of Tchrs., Va. Behavior Disorders, Charlottesville, Va., 1988-89; grad. instr. U. Va., Charlottesville, 1990, grad. intern, 1990; asst. prof. U. Wyo., Laramie, 1991-93; asst. prof. U. No. Colo., Greeley, 1993-96, assoc. prof., 1996—; adj. instr. Ctrl. Wash. U., Ellensburg, 1987-91; cons. Ellensburg Sch. Dist., 1987, Yelm Sch. Dist., 1989, Hampton (Va.) City Schs., 1989, U. Va., Behavior Disorders Project, 1990, Auburn (Ala.) U., 1991, Niobrara Sch. Dist., 1991, 92, 93; in-svc. presenter; nat. and internat. conf. speaker. Contbr. articles to profl. jours. Mem. North Ctrl. Evaluation Team, Wyoming Indian High Sch., 1992. Grantee N.W. Spl. Edn., 1980, Vocat. Edn. Spl. Project, 1982, Title VI-B, 1982, Wash. Edn. Rsch. Assn., 1988, Wash. Mental Health, 1988, Region 10, Va. Commonwealth Div., 1989; Dean's fellow, Curry Sch. Edn., U. Va., 1990, U. Va. Deptl. fellow, 1989; recipient Outstanding scholarship Assn. Colls. and Schs. Edn. in State Univs. and Land Grant Colls., 1992. Mem. ASCD, Am. Ednl. Rsch. Assn., Coun. for Exceptional Children (Va. chpt. v.p. 1990), Coun. for Exceptional Children with Behavior Disorders (pres., Wyo. rep. 1992, 93), Coun. for Exceptional Children with Devel. Delays, Tchr. Educators of Children with Behavior Disorders (pres. 1992, v.p. 1993), Colo. Fedn. for Exceptional Children (child advocacy networker 1996—), Ea. Ednl. Rsch. Assn., Phi Delta Kappa. Office: 310 McKee Hall U of No Colo Greeley CO 80639

MURRY, HAROLD DAVID, JR., lawyer; b. Holdenville, Okla., June 30, 1943; s. Harold David Sr. and Willie Elizabeth (Dees) M.; m. Ann Moore Earnhardt, Nov. 1, 1975; children: Elizabeth Ann, Sarah Bryant. BA, Okla. U., 1965, JD, 1968. Bar: Okla. 1968, D.C. 1974. Asst. to v.p. U. Okla., Norman, 1968-71, legal counsel Research Inst., 1969-71; atty. U.S. Dept. Justice, Washington, 1971-74; spl. asst. U.S. Atty., Washington, 1972; assoc. Clifford & Warnke, Washington, 1974-78, ptnr., 1978-91; ptnr. Howrey & Simon, Washington, 1991—. Mem. ABA, Okla. Bar Assn., D.C. Bar Assn., Fed. Bar Assn., Met. Club (Washington), Chevy Chase Club (Md.), Phi Alpha Delta. Democrat. Home: 8931 Bel Air Pl Potomac MD 20854-1606 Office: Howrey & Simon 1299 Pennsylvania Ave NW Washington DC 20004-2400

MURTAGH, FREDERICK REED, neuroradiologist, educator; b. Phila., Nov. 20, 1944; s. Frederick and Mary (Shaner) M.; (div.); children: Ryan David, Kevin Reed; m. Dorothy Rossi. BA, William and Mary Coll., 1966; MD, Temple U., 1971. Prof., dir. neuroradiology U. S. Fla., Tampa, 1978—. Author: Imaging Anatomy of Head & Spine, 1991. Lt. USNR, 1972-74. Mem. Am. Coll. Radiology (cert. added qualification in neuroradiology 1995), Assn. Univ. Radiologists, Am. Soc. Neuroradiology (sr. mem.), Radiol. Soc. N.Am., Southeastern Neuroradiology Soc. Office: U South Fla 3301 Alumni Dr Tampa FL 33612-9413

MURTAGH, JOHN EDWARD, alcohol production consultant; b. Wallington, Surrey, Eng., Sept. 12, 1936; came to U.S., 1982; s. Thomas Henry and Elsie (Kershaw Paterson) M.; m. Eithne Anne Fawsitt, July 18, 1959; children: Catherine, Rhoda, Sean, Aidan, Doreen. BSc, U. Wales, 1959, MSc, 1970, PhD, 1972. Rsch. coord. House of Seagram, Long Pond, Jamaica, 1959-63; whisky distillery mgr. House of Seagram, Beaupre, Que., Can., 1963-65; rum distillery mgr. House of Seagram, Richibucto, N.B., Can., 1965-68; rsch. mgr. House of Seagram, Montreal, Que., 1968-70; alcohol prodn. cons. Murtagh & Assocs., Buttevant, Ireland, 1972-77, 79-82, Winchester, Va., 1982—; vodka distillery mgr. Iran Beverages, Tehran, 1977-79; ethanol tech. cons., adv. bd. Info. Resources, Inc., Washington, 1988—; lectr. Alltech Ann. Alcohol Sch., Lexington, Ky., 1982—. Author: Glossary of Fuel-Ethanol Terms, 1990; co-author, editor: The Alcohol Textbook, 1995; editor: Worldwide Directory of Distilleries, 1996; contbr. articles to profl. jours. Adv. bd. Byrd Sch. Bus., Shenandoah U., Winchester, Va., 1989-95. Recipient Millers Mutual prize, U. Wales, 1959. Fellow Am. Inst. Chemists, Inst. Chemistry of Ireland, Inst. Food Sci. and Tech. of Ireland; mem. Royal Soc. Chemistry (chartered), Am. Arbitration Assn. (arbitrator nat. comml. panel 1990—). Achievements include development of proprietary process for production of ethanol from cheese whey and the design of whey-ethanol production plants. Home and Office: 160 Bay Ct Winchester VA 22602-4700

MURTAUGH, CHRISTOPHER DAVID, lawyer; b. Darby, Pa., Oct. 25, 1945; s. John Michael and Rita (Sullivan) M.; m. Nancy R. Hanauer, Nov. 30, 1968; children: Jason C., Colin M., Alison M. AB, U. Ill., 1967, JD, 1970. Bar: Ill. 1970, Fla. 1973, U.S. Dist. Ct. (no. dist.) Ill. 1975. Ptnr. Winston & Strawn, Chgo., 1974—, capital ptnr., 1987—, real estate dept. chmn., 1994—. Mem. Glen Ellyn (Ill.) Capital Improvements Com., 1985-89, Glen Ellyn Plan Com., 1989-96, Met. Planning Coun., 1995—. Lt. USNR, 1971-74. Mem. ABA, Am. Coll. Real Estate Lawyers, Fla. Bar Assn., Ill. State Bar Assn., Chgo. Bar Assn., Order of Coif. Office: Winston & Strawn 35 W Wacker Dr Chicago IL 60601-1614

MURTHA, JOHN PATRICK, congressman; b. New Martinsville, W.Va., June 17, 1932; s. John Patrick and Mary Edna (Ray) M.; m. Joyce Bell; three children. B.A. in Econs., U. Pitts., 1961; postgrad., Indiana U. of Pa., 1962-65; H.H.D. (hon.), Mt. Aloysius Jr. Coll. Mem. Pa. Ho. of Reps., 1969-73, 93rd-105th Congresses from 12th Pa. dist., Washington, D.C., 1974—; mem. appropriations com. Served to lt. USMC, 1952-55, as maj. 1966-67, Vietnam; ret. col. Res. Decorated Bronze Star, Purple Heart (2); Cross of Gallantry Vietnam; Pa. Disting. Svc. award, 1978, Pa. Meritorious Svc. medal, numerous service awards for work during Johnstown flood, 1977, Iron Mike award Marine Corps League, 1988, Disting. Am. award Nation's Capital chpt. Air Force Assn., 1989, Outstanding Veteran award Vets. Caucus of Am. Acad. Physician Assts., 1989, Man of Steel award Cold Finished Steel Bar Inst., 1989; named Man of Yr. Johnstown Jaycees, 1978. Office: US Ho of Reps 2423 Rayburn Ho Office Bldg Washington DC 20515-3812*

MURTHA, JOHN STEPHEN, lawyer; b. Hartford, Conn., Apr. 30, 1913; s. John J. and Agnes E. (Hennessey) M.; m. Winifred Garvan, July 7, 1939; children—John Garvan, Leslie A., Brenda A. B.A., Yale, 1935, LL.B., 1938. Bar: Conn. bar 1938. Ptnr. Murtha, Cullina, Richter & Pinney, Hartford, 1946-88, of counsel, 1989—; asst. states atty., Hartford County, 1946-51; dir. Kaman Corp. Pres. Greater Hartford Cmty. Chest, 1968-70, Oxford Sch., Hartford, 1960-62; chmn. distbn. com. Hartford Found. for Pub. Giving, 1983-86; bd. dirs. emeritus Blue Cross and Blue Shield Conn., Boys Clubs Hartford; trustee emeritus St. Joseph Coll., West Hartford, Conn., St. Thomas More Corp., New Haven, pres., 1962-64. Served to lt. (j.g.) USNR, 1943-46. Fellow Am. Coll. Trial Lawyers; mem. ABA, Greater Hartford C. of C., Conn. Bus. and Industry Assn., Hartford Golf Club (pres. 1961-63). Republican. Roman Catholic. Home: 6 Shibah Way Bloomfield CT 06002-1527 Office: City Place Hartford CT 06103

MURTHY, SRINIVASA K., engineering corporation executive; b. Bangalore, Karnataka, India, June 12, 1949; came to U.S., 1979; s. Ramaswamy and Gowramma Kadur. BS in Physics, Bangalore U., India, 1967; MS in Physics, Bangalore U., 1969; MSEE, Mysore U., India, 1971. Mgr. project engrng. Indian Space Rsch. Orgn., Bangalore, 1971-79; asst. prof. Calif. State U., Pomona, 1979-80, Fullerton, 1981-82; mgr. project Systems and Applied Scis. Corp., Anaheim, Calif., 1980-83; dir. div. IMR Systems Corp., Arlington, Va., 1983-84; mgr. systems engrng. GE, Portsmouth, Va., 1984-85; bus. and program mgr. govt. rsch. programs AT&T Bell Labs, Homdel, N.J., 1985-94, Murray Hill, N.J., 1994—; area mgr. AT&T Bus. Comms. Svcs., Pleasaton, Calif., 1996—; bd. advisors IMR Sys. Corp., Roslyn, Va., 1988—; mem. editl. adv. bd. R&D Mag., Cahners Publs.; judge R&D 100 awards. Editorial adv. bd. Rsch. and Devel. Mag. Calvert Publs., Reed Publs. Group; contbr. articles to profl. jours. Recipient Disting. Achievement award Dept. Space, Indian Govt., 1975. Mem. IEEE (sr. mem., bd. govs. 1986—, standards bd. 1986—, bd. dirs. Electronics and Aerospace Systems conf. 1983-84, editorial bd. dirs. Network Jour. 1986—, area activities bd. and tech. activities bd. 1988, Computer Soc. 1987—, lectr. India, Singapore, Australia 1989, South Am. 1990, inducted into Nat. Rsch. Coun., Advt. Rsch. Found. and Engring. Consortium, numerous other coms.), Engring. Mgmt. Soc. of IEEE (bd. govs. 1986—, v.p.). Home: 13 Willow Ave Somerset NJ 08873-1426 Office: AT&T Bus Comms Svcs 4460 Rosewood Dr Rm 6276 Pleasanton CA 94588-3085

MUSA, JOHN DAVIS, computer and infosystems executive, software reliability engineering researcher and expert, independent consultant; b. Amityville, N.Y., June 11, 1933; s. Khan Hussein and Ione Geraldine (Ryan) M.; m. Marilyn Laurene Allred, June 24, 1959. BA, Dartmouth Coll., 1954, MSEE, 1955. With AT&T Bell Labs., Murray Hill, N.J., 1958-96, mem. tech. staff, 1958-63, supr. guidance program devel., 1963-68, supr. command and control program devel., 1968-69, supr. mgmt. control and new software tech., 1969-72, supr. human factors test, 1972-74, supr. computer graphics, 1974-80, supr. computer measurements, 1980-85, supr. software quality, 1985-90, tech. mgr. software reliability engring., 1991-96; mem. N.J. Coun. R&D; lectr., spkr. in field. Author: Software Reliability: Measurement, Prediction, Application, 1987; contbr. more than 90 articles to prof. jours. and books.more than 175 major talks. Lt. USN, 1955-58. Fellow IEEE; mem. IEEE Computer Soc. (2d v.p. 1986, v.p. publs. 1984-85, v.p. tech. activities 1986, chair tech com. software engring. 1982-84, founding mem. editl. bd. IEEE Software Mag., Disting. lectr. 1980-83, Meritorious Svc. award 1984, 85, 87, founding officer com. on software reliability engring., mem. editl. bds. Spectrum mag., 1984-86, Proc. of the IEEE 1983-90, Technique et Science Informatiques jour., sr. editor Software Engring. Inst. book series, chair steering com. Internat. Conf. on Software Engring.), IEEE Reliability Soc., Assn. for Computing Machinery. Internat. leader in software engring. and in creation new tech. software reliability engring.; created two software reliability models; developed concepts and practice of operational profile software-reliability engineered testing; reduced operation software (ROS), and operational development. Office: 39 Hamilton Rd Morristown NJ 07960-5341

MUSA, MAHMOUD NIMIR, psychiatry educator; b. Arraba, Jenin, Palestine, Mar. 22, 1943; came to U.S., 1964; s. Nimir A. and Zarifa (Haseeb) M.; m. Wafaa M. Arafat, Mar. 24, 1991. BS, Am. U. Beirut, 1964; MS, U. Wis., 1966, PhD, 1972; MD, Med. Coll. Wis., 1979. Diplomate Am. Bd. Psychiatry. Rsch. assoc. U. Wis., Madison, 1972-75; asst. prof. Idaho State U., Pocatello, 1975-76; resident Ill. State Psychiat. Inst., Chgo., 1979-83; assoc. prof. psychiatry Chgo. Med. Sch., North Chicago, Ill., 1987-90; prof. psychiatry Loyola U., Maywood, Ill., 1990—; cons. Mus. Sci. & Industry, Chgo., 1985-90; editl. bd. Jour. Clin. Pharmacology. Editor: Pharmacikinetics and Monitoring Psychiatry Drugs, 1992; mem. editl. bd. Jour. Clin. Pharmacology. Cons. Kovler Ctr. for Treatment of Survivors of Torture, CHgo., 1989-92. Recipient Scientific Achievement award Ill. Psychiat. Soc., Chgo., 1982. Fellow Am. Coll. Clin. Pharmacology, Great Lakes Soc. Clin. Pharmacology (pres. 1991-92); mem. AAAS, Am. Psychiat. Assn. Avocations: reading, photography, theater. Home: PO Box 487 Lockport IL 60441-0487

MUSA, SAMUEL ALBERT, technology and manufacturing executive director; m. Judith Friedman; children: Gregory, Jeffrey. BA, Rutgers U., 1961, BSEE, 1961; MS in Applied Physics, Harvard U., 1962, PhD in Applied Physics, 1965. Rsch. scientist Gen. Precision Inc., Little Falls, N.J., 1965-66; asst. prof. elec. engring. U. Pa., Phila., 1966-71; project leader Inst. for Def. Analyses, Arlington, Va., 1971-78; dep. dir. Office of Under Sec. Def., Washington, 1978-83; dir. rsch. and advanced tech. E-Systems, Inc., Dallas, 1983-86, v.p. rsch. and advanced tech., 1986-95; exec. dir. Ctr. Display Tech. and Mfg. U. Mich., 1995—; cons. sci. adv. bd. USAF, 1987-91; mem. adv. bd. Def. Intelligence Agy. Contbr. articles to profl. jours. Fellow IEEE; mem. AIA (tech. and ops. coun. 1986-95, vice chmn. 1993, chmn. 1994), Sigma Xi, Tau Beta Pi, Pi Mu Epsilon. Office: 2360 Bonisteel Blvd Ann Arbor MI 48109-2108

MUSACCHIA, X(AVIER) J(OSEPH), physiology and biophysics educator; b. Bklyn., Feb. 11, 1923; s. Castrense and Orsolina (Mazzola) M.; m. Betty Cook, Nov. 23, 1950; children: Joseph, Mary, Thomas, Laura Ann. BS, St. Francis Coll., Bklyn., 1944; MS, Fordham U., 1947, PhD, 1949. Instr. biology Marymount (N.Y.) Coll., 1948-49; from instr. to prof. biology St. Louis U., 1949-65; prof. physiology U. Mo., Columbia, 1965-78; prof. physiology and biophysics U. Louisville, 1978-91, prof. emeritus, 1991—, dean Grad. Sch., 1978-89, assoc. provost for rsch., 1985-89; bd. dirs. Coun. Grad. Schs., 1986-89. Author: Depressed Metabolism, 1969, Regulation of Depressed Metabolism and Thermogenesis, 1976, Survival in Cold, 1981; also articles. Bd. govs. J. Graham Brown Cancer Ctr., Louisville, 1978-83; bd. dirs. Oak Ridge Associated Univs. Served with AUS, 1943-45. Research grantee NIH; Research grantee NASA. Fellow AAAS; mem. Am. Physiol. Soc., Am. Soc. Zoologists, Am. Soc. for Space and Gravitational Biology (v.p. 1988-89, pres. 1989-90), Soc. Exptl. Biology and Medicine, Corp. Marine Biol. Lab., Sigma Xi. (past chpt. pres.). Address: PO Box 5054 Bella Vista AR 72714-0054

MUSACCHIO, MARILYN JEAN, nurse midwife, educator; b. Louisville, Dec. 7, 1938; d. Robert William and Loretta C. (Liebert) Poulter; m. David Edward Musacchio, May 13, 1961; children: Richard Peter, Michelle Marie. BSN cum laude, Spalding Coll., 1968; MSN, U. Ky., 1972, degree in Nurse-Midwifery, 1976; PhD, Case Western Res U., 1993. RN; cert. nurse-midwife; advanced registered nurse practitioner; registered nurse-midwife. Staff nurse gynecol. unit St. Joseph Infirmary, Louisville, 1959-60, staff nurse male gen. surgery unit, 1960; instr. St. Joseph Infirmary Sch. Nursing, Louisville, 1960-71; from asst. prof. to assoc. prof., dir. dept. nursing edn. Ky. State U., Frankfort, 1972-75; asst. prof. U. Ky. Coll. Nursing, Lexington, 1976-79, assoc. prof., coord., 1979-92, acting coordinator nurse-midwifery, 1982-84, coordinator for nurse-midwifery, 1987-92; assoc. prof., dir. nurse-midwifery U. Ala., Birmingham, 1992-96, assoc. prof., 1997—; cons. in field. Mem. editorial bd. Jour. Obstet., Gynecol. and Neonatal Nursing, 1976-82; author pamphlet; contbr. articles to profl. jours. Active St. James Parish Coun., chmn., 1980-81; mem. Louisville Fire Prevention Coun., 1973-80, Louisville Safety Coun., 1973-80. Brig. Gen. Army Nurse Corps, USAR, 1992-95. Recipient Disting. Citizen award City of Louisville, 1977, Jefferson Cup award Jefferson County, Ky., 1991; named Outstanding Alumna, Mercy Acad., 1993; named to Hall of Disting. Alumni, U. Ky., 1995; recipient scholarships and fellowships, other awards. Fellow Am. Acad. Nursing; mem. AWHONN, NAFE, Am. Nurses Assn. (nurse rschr. coun. 1985—, maternal child coun. 1985—), Nurse Assn. Am. Coll. Ob-Gyn (charter; nat. sec. 1970-72, chmn. dist. V 1969), Am. Coll. Nurse-Midwives, Internat. Childbirth Edn. Assn., Am. Soc. Psychoprophylaxis in Obstetrics, Nat. Assn. Parents and Profls. for Safe Alternatives in Childbirth, Res. Officers Assn., Assn. Mil. Surgeons U.S., Sr. Army Res. Commdr. Assn., Assn. U.S. Army, Retired Army Nurse Corps. Assn., Army War Coll. Alumni Assn. Roman Catholic. Avocations: reading, candy making, cake decorating, cooking, sewing. Home: 1318 Springs Ave Birmingham AL 35242-4862

MUSAH, AL-HASSAN ISSAH, reproductive physiologist; b. Pong-Tamale, Ghana, Aug. 3, 1954; came to U.S., 1980; s. Issah and Mariama (Adam) M.; m. Hadiyatu Seidu Al-Hassan, July 16, 1981 (div. Nov. 1989); children: Abdul-Razak, Ayisha, Abdul-Faruk. BSc with honors, U. Ghana, 1978;

MS, Iowa State U., 1983, PhD in Physiology of Reprodn., 1980. Rsch. asst. U. Ghana, Legon, 1978-79; tng. officer IFCAT-URADEP, Narrongo, Ghana, 1979-80; postdoctoral rsch. assoc. Iowa State U., Ames, 1986-89; asst. prof. St. Cloud (Minn.) State U., 1990-94, assoc. prof. reproductive physiology, 1994-96, dir. applied rsch., prof. reproductive physiology, 1996—, interim dean coll. sci. and engring., 1997—; pres. Allbest Enterprises, Inc., Takoradi, Ghana, 1989—. Contbr. articles to profl. jours. Recipient Excellence award Iowa State U., 1986, Holco award Holco Agrl. Products, Inc., 1986. Mem. Endocrine Soc., Soc. for Study of Reprodn., Soc. for Exptl. Biology and Medicine, Sigma Xi. Achievements include research on elucidating the role of relaxin and ANP in ovarian luteal function. Home: 1823 15th Ave SE Saint Cloud MN 56304-2385 Office: St Cloud State Univ 720 4th Ave S Saint Cloud MN 56301-4442

MUSANTE, TONY (ANTHONY PETER MUSANTE, JR.), actor; b. Bridgeport, Conn.; s. Anthony Peter and Natalie Anne (Salerno) M.; m. Jane Ashley Sparkes, June 2, 1962. B.A. (Baker scholar), Oberlin Coll., 1958; postgrad., Northwestern U., 1957; student, HB Studios, N.Y.C., 1961-65. Appearances include: (off Broadway prodns.) Borak, 1960, Zoo Story, Night of the Dunce, The Collection, Match-Play, Kiss Mama, L'Histoire du Soldat, A Gun Play, Falling Man, Cassatt, Grand Magic, The Big Knife, The Taming of the Shrew, Two Brothers, The Archbishop's Ceiling, Souvenir, A Streetcar Named Desire, Double Play, Dancing in the End Zone, Snow Orchid, Wait until Dark, Widows, Anthony Rose, Mount Allegro, Frankie and Johnny in the Clair de Lune, Breaking Legs, The Flip Side, Love Letters, The Sisters, Italian Funerals and Other Festive Occasions (Broadway prodns.) PS Your Cat is Dead, 1975 (N.Y. Drama Desk nomination), Memory of Two Mondays, 27 Wagons Full of Cotton, The Lady from Dubuque; films: Once a Thief, 1964, The Incident (Best Actor award Mar del Plata Internat. Film Festival), 1967, The Detective, The Mercenary, One Night at Dinner, Bird with the Crystal Plumage, Grissom Gang, Anonymous Venetian, The Last Run, Pisciotta Case, Goodbye and Amen, Break-Up, Collector's Item, The Repenter, Devil's Hill, Appointment in Trieste, Nocturne, The Pope of Greenwich Village; TV appearances include Ride with Terror, 1963, star series Toma, 1973-74 (Photoplay Gold medal award 1974), scriptwriter several episodes; star HBO series Oz; also starred in TV miniseries and movies: Deep Family Secrets, High Ice, Breaking Up is Hard to Do, The Baron, Legend of the Black Hand, The Story of Esther, My Husband is Missing, Nowhere to Hide, The Quality of Mercy (Emmy nominee 1975), Court Martial of Lt. William Calley, Night Heat, Rearview Mirror, Nutcracker: Money, Madness and Murder, Acapulco HEAT, American Playhouse: Weekend, Last Waltz on a Tightrope; daytime TV (guest star): Loving, ABC, 1993. Mem. SAG, AFTRA, ATAS, Actors Equity Assn., Writers Guild Am. West, Acad. Motion Picture Arts and Scis.

MUSCATINE, CHARLES, English educator, author; b. Bklyn., Nov. 28, 1920; m. Doris Corn, July 21, 1945; children: Jeffrey, Alison. B.A., Yale U., 1941, M.A., 1942, Ph.D., 1948; L.H.D. (hon.), New Sch. for Social Research, 1982; Litt.D., SUNY, 1989, Rosary Coll., 1991. Mem. faculty dept. English U. Calif., Berkeley, 1948—; prof. U. Calif., 1960-91, prof. emeritus, 1991—, dir. Collegiate Seminar Program, 1974-80; vis. prof. Wesleyan U., 1951-53; Ward Phillips lectr. U. Notre Dame, 1969; mem. com. of selection J.S. Guggenheim Found., 1969-89, chmn. 1985-89. Author: Chaucer and the French Tradition, 1957, The Book of Geoffrey Chaucer, 1963, Poetry and Crisis in the Age of Chaucer, 1972, The Old French Fabliaux, 1986. Co-author, editor: Education at Berkeley, 1966, (with M. Griffith) The Borzoi College Reader, 1966, 7th edit., 1992, First Person Singular, 1973; co-editor Integrity in the Coll. Curriculum, 1985. Bd. dirs. No. Calif. chpt. ACLU, 1959-62, 63-66, Assn. Am. Colls., 1979-82, Ctr. for the Common Good, 1994—; bd. dirs. Fedn. State Humanities Couns., 1989-94, chair, 1991-93; mem. Commn. on Humanities, Rockefeller Found., 1978-79, Calif. Coun. Humanities, 1986-94. With USNR, 1942-45. Recipient Navy Commendation ribbon, 1945, Berkeley citation, 1991; Fulbright fellow, 1958, 62, ACLS Rsch. fellow, 1958, Guggenheim fellow, 1962, NEH Sr. fellow, 1968. Fellow Am. Acad. Arts and Scis., Medieval Acad. of Am.; mem. MLA, New Chaucer Soc. (pres. 1980-81), Aircraft Owners and Pilots Assn., Phi Beta Kappa. Club: Arts (Berkeley). Home: 2812 Buena Vista Way Berkeley CA 94708-2016

MUSCATO, ANDREW, lawyer; b. Newark, Aug. 28, 1953; s. Salvatore and Bertha (Kubilus) M.; m. Ann Marie Hughes, Aug. 19, 1978; children: Amy, Andrew Joseph, Amanda. AB magna cum laude, Brown U., 1975; JD, Seton Hall U., 1978. Bar: N.J. 1978, U.S. Dist. Ct. N.J. 1978, U.S. Ct. Appeals (3d cir.) 1981, N.Y. 1984, U.S. Dist. Ct. (so. and ea. dists.) N.Y. 1984. Law clk. to presiding judge, appellate div. N.J. Superior Ct., Somerville, 1978-79; staff atty. Adminstrv. Office of Cts., Trenton, N.J., 1979-80; assoc. Simon & Allen, Newark, 1980-86; ptnr. Kirsten & Simon, Newark, 1987-89, Whitman & Ransom, Newark, 1989-93, Whitman Breed Abbott & Morgan, Newark, 1993—; atty. Irvington (N.J.) Rent Leveling Bd., 1980—. Author: Executing on a Debtor's Interest in a Tenancy by the Entirety, 1986. Mem. ABA, Essex County Bar Assn., Trial Attys. N.J., N.J. Inst. Mcpl. Attys. Republican. Roman Catholic. Home: 66 Addison Dr Basking Ridge NJ 07920-2202 Office: Whitman Breed Abbott Et Al 1 Gateway Ctr Newark NJ 07102-5311

MUSCHEL, LOUIS HENRY, immunologist, educator; b. N.Y.C., July 4, 1916; s. Maurice and Betty (Tobey) M.; m. Anne Orzel, Oct. 22, 1946; 1 child, Ruth Josephine. B.S., NYU, 1936; M.S., Yale U., 1951, Ph.D., 1953. Joined U.S. Army, 1941, advanced through grades to lt. col., 1961; chief dept. serology (Walter Reed Army Inst. Research), Washington, 1958-62; faculty U. Minn., Mpls., 1962-70; prof. microbiology U. Minn., 1964-70; prof. bacteriology U. Calif., Berkeley, 1965, 67; with research dept. Am. Cancer Soc., 1970-88; adj. prof. microbiology Columbia U., 1977-83; adj. prof. pathology NYU, 1983—. Mem. Am. Assn. Immunologists, Brit. Soc. Immunology, N.Y. Acad. Scis., Am. Soc. Microbiology, Soc. Exptl. Biology and Medicine, Am. Assn. for Cancer Research, Phi Beta Kappa, Sigma Xi, Phi Lambda Upsilon. Research, publs. on bactericidal action of serum and its role in host defs., natural bactericidal and viral neutralizing antibodies, applications of complement fixation technique. Home: 3333 Henry Hudson Pky W Apt 8A Bronx NY 10463-3255

MUSCHENHEIM, FREDERICK, pathologist; b. N.Y.C., July 9, 1932; s. Carl and Haroldine (Humphreys) M.; m. Linda Alexander, Mar. 29, 1958; children: Alexandra Lydia, Carl William, David Henry. AB, Harvard U., 1953; MDCM, McGill U., Montreal, Can., 1963. Intern Santa Clara County Hosp., San Jose, Calif., 1963-64; resident in pathology U. Colo. Med. Ctr., Denver, 1964-68, chief resident in clin. pathology, 1968-69; pathologist Freeman, Hanske, Munkittrick & Foley PA, Mpls., 1969-77; clin. pathologist Union-Truesdale Hosp., Fall River, Mass., 1977-78; chief pathologist St. Clare's Hosp., Denville, N.J., 1978-83, Oneida Healthcare Ctr., 1984—; clin. asst. prof. SUNY Health Sci. Ctr., Syracuse, 1984-90, clin. assoc. prof., 1990—; chief med. staff Oneida City Hosps., 1991; pres. Sunderman Fund, Bermuda Biol. Sta. for Rsch., v.p. Madison County (N.Y.) bd. health, 1995-96, pres., 1997—. Choir 1st Presbyn. Ch. of Cazenovia, N.Y., 1984—, trustee, 1985-89. Mem. Assn. Clin. Scientists (v.p. 1989, pres. 1990, rec. sec. 1995—, Diploma of Honor 1991), Coll. Am. Pathologists (mem. govt. affairs com. 1994—, nominating com. 1995), Med. Soc. State of N.Y. (mem. legis. com. 1991—), Med. Soc. Madison County (v.p. 1990-91, pres. 1991-93), N.Y. State Assn. Pub. Health Labs. (v.p. 1992-93, pres. 1993-94, edn. chmn. 1994-95), N.Y. Soc. State Pathologists (councilor 2nd dist. 1991—, chmn. legis. com. 1991—), ARC Blood Svcs. (chmn. med. adv. coun. 1995—). Home: 5257 Owera Point Rd Cazenovia NY 13035-9340 Office: Oneida Healthcare Ctr 321 Genesee St Oneida NY 13421-2611

MUSE, WILLIAM VAN, academic administrator; b. Marks, Miss., Apr. 7, 1939; s. Mose Lee and Mary Elizabeth (Hisaw) M.; m. Anna Marlene Munden, Aug. 22, 1964; children: Amy Marlene, Ellen Elizabeth, William Van. B.S. (T.H. Harris scholar), Northwestern La. State U., 1960; M.B.A. (Nat. Def. Grad. fellow), U. Ark., 1961, Ph.D. (Nat. Def. Grad. fellow), 1966. Instr. U. Ark., 1962-63; field supr. Tau Kappa Epsilon Fraternity, 1963-64; asst. prof. Ga. Tech., 1964-65; assoc. prof., chmn., dir. rsch. Ohio U., 1965-70; dean Coll. Bus. Appalachian State U., Boone, N.C., 1970-73; dean Coll. Bus. Adminstrn. U. Nebr., Omaha, 1973-79; dean Coll. Bus. Adminstrn. Tex. A&M U., College Station, 1979-82, vice chancellor, 1983-84; former pres. U. Akron, Ohio, 1984-92; now pres. Auburn U., Ala., 1992—. Author: Business and Economic Problems in Appalachia, 1969, Management Practices in Fraternities, 1965; Contbr. articles to profl. jours. Found. for Econ. Edn. fellow, 1967. Mem. Blue Key, Omicron Delta Kappa, Phi Kappa Phi, Delta Sigma Pi, Beta Gamma Sigma, Pi Omega Pi, Tau Kappa Epsilon. Club: Rotarian. Office: Auburn U Office of Pres 107 Sanford Hall Auburn AL 36849*

MUSFELT, DUANE CLARK, lawyer; b. Stockton, Calif., Sept. 14, 1951; s. Robert H. and Doris E. (Roth) M.; m. Linh T. To, Sept. 6, 1980. Student, U. Calif., Davis, 1969-71; BA in Econs., U. Calif., Berkeley, 1973; JD, UCLA, 1976. Bar: Calif. 1976, U.S. Dist. Ct. (cen. dist.) Calif. 1977, U.S. Ct. Appeals (9th cir.) 1980, U.S. Dist. Ct. (no. dist.) Calif. 1982, U.S. Dist. Ct. (ea. and so. dists.) Calif. 1983, U.S. Supreme Ct. 1987. Assoc. Haight, Dickson, Brown & Bonesteel, L.A., 1976-77, Mori & Ota, L.A., 1977-79, Lewis, D'Amato, Brisbois & Bisgaard, L.A., 1979-82; ptnr. Lewis, D'Amato, Brisbois & Bisgaard, San Francisco, 1982—. Mem. State Bar Calif., No. Calif. Assn. Defense Counsel, Bar Assn. San Francisco, Defense Rsch. Inst. Democrat. Presbyterian. Avocations: tennis, skiing, bridge. Office: Lewis D'Amato Brisbois & Bisgaard 601 California St Ste 1900 San Francisco CA 94108-2824

MUSGRAVE, CHARLES EDWARD, retired music director, correctional official; b. Alton, Ill., Nov. 17, 1932; s. Clay Everett and Fannie Adeline (Peek) M.; m. Barbara Jean Robertson, Aug. 11, 1952 (div. Feb. 1971); children: Michael David, Debra Ann; m. Toby Elaine Riley, Aug. 18, 1973. B in Mus. Edn., Shurtleff Coll., 1954; MS, U. Ill., 1957; postgrad., U. No. Colo., 1970. Cert. tchr., Ill., Ind. Tchr. music Alton (Ill.) Pub. Schs., 1953-67; v.p. Monticello Coll., Godfrey, Ill., 1967-69; asst. to v.p. U. No. Colo., Greeley, 1970; chmn. dept. music Duneland Sch. Corp., Chesterton, Ind., 1970-72; dir. devel. Interlochen (Mich.) Arts Acad., 1972-73; v.p. Musart Corp., Chgo., 1973-74; dir. music and coll. coord. Ind. State Prison, Michigan City, 1974-95; ret., 1995; assoc. dir. music Willowbrook Meth. Ch., Sun City, Ariz., 1996—; vice chmn. La Porter Fed. Credit Union, Michigan City, 1975-96; facility coordinator adult continuing edn. Ind. U. Author: Fussell's Individual Technique Guide, 1973, (music) Why Only on Christmas, 1981. Rep. committeeman, Chesterton, 1976-95, del. to state conv., Ind., 1978-89; mem. Porter County (Ind.) Planning Commn., 1984-85; chmn. govt. workers sect. United Way, Michigan City, 1981-90; mem. Ind. Gov.'s Adv. Com., 1983; minister of music 1st United Meth. Ch., Chesterton, 1978-91; bd. dirs. Five Lakes Conservation Club, Wolcottville, Ind., 1983-95; bd. dirs., v.p. Valparaiso Cmty. Concerts Assn., 1986-95. Grantee Systems Mgmt. U. W. Va., U. Chgo., 1979. Mem. Correctional Edn. Assn. (Internat. Tchr. of Yr. 1981), Ind. Soc. Chgo., LaGrange Country Club, Masons, Shriners, Scottish Rite, Phi Delta Kappa. Avocations: sailing, golf, photography, computers. Home: 9815 Evergreen Dr Sun City AZ 85373-2169 also: 7230 S 175 E Wolcottville IN 46795

MUSGRAVE, R. KENTON, federal judge; b. 1927. Student, Ga. Inst. Tech., 1945-46, U. Fla., 1946-47; BA, U. Wash., 1948; JD with distinction, Emory U., 1953. Asst. gen. counsel Lockheed Internat., 1953-62; v.p., gen. counsel Mattel, Inc., 1963-71; mem. firm Musgrave, Welbourn and Fertman, 1972-75; asst. gen. counsel Pacific Enterprises, 1975-81; v.p., gen. counsel Vivitar Corp, 1981-85; v.p., dir. Santa Barbara Applied Rsch., 1982-87; judge U.S. Ct. Internat. Trade, N.Y.C., 1987—. Trustee Morris Animal Found., The Dian Fossey Gorilla Fund, Dolphins of Sharks Bay (Australia); hon. trustee Pet Protection Soc.; mem. United Way, South Bay-Centinela Svc. Orgn., Save the Redwoods League; active LWV, Legal Aid, Palos Verdes Community Assn. Mem. ABA, Internat. Bar Assn., Pan Am. Bar Assn., State Bar Calif. (chmn. corp. law sect. 1965-66, del. 1966-67), L.A. County Bar Assn., State Bar Ga., Fng. Trade Assn. So. Calif. (bd. dirs.), Sierra Club. Office: US Ct Internat Trade 1 Federal Plz New York NY 10278-0001

MUSGRAVE, STORY, astronaut, surgeon, pilot, physiologist, educator; b. Boston, Aug. 19, 1935; children: Lorelei Lisa, Bradley Scott, Holly Kay, Christopher Todd, Jeffrey Paul, Lane Linwood. BS in Math. and Statis., Syracuse U., 1958; MBA, UCLA, 1959; BA in Chemistry, Marietta Coll., 1960; MD, Columbia U., 1964; MS in Biophysics, U. Ky., 1966; MA in Lit., U. Houston, 1987, MA in Humanities, 1989. Surg. intern U. Ky. Med. Ctr., Lexington, 1964-65; scientist-astronaut NASA, Houston, 1967—, backup sci.-pilot 1st Skylab mission, 1973, flew on first Challenger flight, STS-6, 1983, flew on Spacelab 2, 1985, flew on space shuttle mission STS-33, 1989, flew on STS-44, 1991; flew as payload comdr. STS61 Hubble Telescope Repair Mission STS61 Hubble Telescope Repair Mission, 1993; flew on STS-80, 1996. Contbr. articles to profl. jours. With USMC, 1953-56. Recipient Reese AFB Comdr.'s trophy, 1969, NASA exceptional svc. medal, 1974, 83, 90, NASA disting. svc. medal, 1992, 94, 97, NASA spaceflight medal, 1983, 85, 89, 91, 93, 96; USAF postdoctoral fellow, 1965-66, Nat. Heart Inst. postdoctoral fellow, 1966-67. Mem. AAAS, AAS, AIAA, Flying Physicians Assn. (Airman of Yr. award 1974, 83), Civil Aviation Med. Assn., N.Y. Acad. Sci., Nat. Geog. Soc., Soaring Soc. Am., U.S. Parachute Assn., Marine Corps Assn., Alpha Kappa Psi, Phi Delta Theta, Omicron Delta Kappa, Beta Gamma Sigma. Address: 16011 Diana Ln Houston TX 77062-4406 *From subatomic particles, to the stardust from which I was created, from the forming galaxies, to the universes beyond our own, I live to participate physically and spiritually in every aspect of this cosmic creation and evolution.*

MUSGRAVE, THEA, composer, conductor; b. Edinburgh, Scotland, May 27, 1928; m. Peter Mark, 1971. Ed., Edinburgh U., Paris Conservatory; Mus.D. (hon.). Composer: (opera) The Abbot of Drimock, 1955, The Decision, 1964-65, The Voice of Ariadne, 1972-73, Mary, Queen of Scots, 1975-77, (first performed Scottish Opera) A Christmas Carol, 1978-79 (first performed Va. Opera Assn., 1979), An Occurence at Owl Creek Bridge, 1981, Harriet, The Woman Called Moses, 1981-84 (first performed Va. Opera 1985), Simon Bolivar, (ballet) Beauty and the Beast, 1969, (symphony and orchestral music) Obliques, 1958, Nocturnes and Arias, 1966, Concerto for Orch., 1967, Clarinet Concerto, 1968, Night Music, 1969, Scottish Dance Suite, 1969, Memento Vitae, 1969-70, Orfeo II, 1975, Soliloquy II and III, 1980, From One to Another, 1980, Peripeteia, 1981, The Seasons, 1988, (marimba concerto) Journey through a Japanese Landscape, (bass-clarinet concerto) Autumn Sonata, (oboe concerto) Helios, (chamber and instrumental music) String Quartet, 1958, Trio for flute, oboe and piano, 1960, Monologue, 1960, Serenade, 1961, Chamber concerto No. 1, 1962, Chamber Concerto No. 2, 1966, Chamber Concerto No. 3, 1966, Music for horn and piano, 1967, Impromptu No. 1, 1967, Soliloquy I, 1969, Elegy, 1970, Impromptu No. 2, 1970, Space Play, 1974, Orfeo I, 1975, Fanfare, 1982, Pierrot, 1985, Narcissus, 1987, Niobe, 1987, (vocal and choral music) Two Songs, 1951, Four Madrigals, 1953, Six Songs: Two Early English Poems, 1953, A Suite O'Bairnsangs, 1953, Cantata for a Summer's Day, 1954, Song of the Burn, 1954, Five Love Songs, 1955, Four Portraits, 1956, A Song for Christmas, 1958, Triptych, 1959, Sir Patrick Spens, 1961, Make Ye Merry for Him That Is to Come, 1962, Two Christmas Carols in Traditional Style, 1963, John Cook, 1963, Five Ages of Man, 1963-64, Memento Creatoris, 1967, Primavera, 1971, Rorate Coeli, 1973, Monologues of Mary, Queen of Scots, 1977-86, O Caro M'e Il Sonno, 1978, The Last Twilight, 1980, Black Tambourine, 1985, For the Time Being, 1986, Echoes Through Time, 1988, Wild Winter for Viols & Voices, 1993, On the Underground Sets 1, 2 & 3, 1994, 95, (Robert Burns' poems for soprano & orch.) Songs for a Winter's Evening, 1995. Office: VA Opera Assn PO Box 2580 Norfolk VA 23501-2580

MUSGROVE, RONNIE, state official; b. July 29, 1956; m. Melanie Ballard; children: Jordan, Carmen Rae. Grad., Northwest Miss. Jr. Coll., U. Miss.; JD, U. Miss. Ptnr. Smith, Musgrove & McCord, Batesville, Miss.; lt. gov. State of Miss., Jackson, 1996—. Sec.-treas. Nat. Conf. Lt. Govs. Fellow Miss. Bar Found.; mem. Am. Inns Ct., Miss. State Bar (bd. bar commrs. 1990), Miss. Bar Assn., Miss. Young Lawyers Assn. (bd. dirs.), Panola County Bar Assn. (v.p., pres.), Tri-County Bar Assn. (pres.), Phi Beta Lambda. Office: Office of Lt Governor PO Box 1018 Jackson MS 39215

MUSHER, DANIEL MICHAEL, physician; b. N.Y.C., Feb. 27, 1938; s. Sidney and Hadassah (Kaplan) M.; m. Karol Sue Katz, June 17, 1967; children: Rebecca Leah, Benjamin Leon, Deborah Ann. AB magna cum laude, Harvard Coll., 1959; MD, Columbia U., 1963; postgrad., MIT, 1969-70. Diplomate Am. Bd. Internal Medicine, specialty infectious diseases. Intern, jr. med. resident first med. divsn. Bellevue Hosp., 1963-65; sr. med. resident Tufts-New Eng. Med. Ctr. Hosps., 1967-68; NIH trainee in infectious diseases New Eng. Med. Ctr. Hosps., 1968-71; instr. medicine Tufts U. Sch. Medicine, 1970-71; asst. prof. medicine, asst. prof. microbiology & immunology Baylor Coll. Medicine, Houston, 1971-73, assoc. prof., 1974-78, prof. microbiology and immunology, 1979—, prof. medicine, 1979—, chief infectious diseases, 1994—; chief infectious disease sect. VA Med. Ctr., Houston, 1971—; mem. Baylor House Staff Selection Com., 1973—; mem. infection control com. VA Med. Ctr., 1971—, chmn., 1971, mem. AIDS task force, 1987—; mem. Baylor Dept. Medicine Task Force, 1987—; mem. Baylor Dept. Medicine Exec. Faculty, 1992—. Mem. editl. bd.: Sexually Trasmitted Diseases, 1979-83, Infection and Immunity, 1996—; assoc. editor Jour. Infectious Diseases, 1983-88; contbr. numerous articles to profl. jours. Chmn. edn. William Malev Schs. of Congregation Beth Yeshurun, Houston, 1993—; bd. mem., past pres. I. Weiner Jewish Secondary Sch., Houston, 1979—; bd. mem. Congregation Beth Yeshurun, Houston, 1975—; bd. mem., v.p., pres. Houston Friends of Music, 1975—. With USAF, 1965-67. Recipient Physician's Recognition award AMA, 1991—, Dir.'s award for profl. leadership VA Med. Ctr., Houston, 1991. Fellow ACP; mem. AAAS, Am. Assn. Immunologists, Am. Fedn. Clin. Rsch., Am. Soc. Clin. Investigation, Am. Soc. Microbiology, So. Soc. Clin. Investigation, Soc. Exptl. Biology and Medicine, Sigma Xi, Phi Beta Kappa, Alpha Omega Alpha. Avocations: music (string quartet playing), reading. Office: VA Hosp 2002 Holcombe Blvd Houston TX 77030-4211

MUSIAL, STAN(LEY) (FRANK MUSIAL), hotel and restaurant executive, former baseball team executive, former baseball player; b. Donora, Pa., Nov. 21, 1920; s. Lukasz M.; m. Lillian Labash, 1939; children: Richard, Geraldine, Janet, Jean. Ed. high sch., Donora. Baseball player St. Louis Cardinals Farm Team, 1938-41; 1st baseman, outfielder St. Louis Cardinals, Nat. League, 1941-63; sr. v.p. St. Louis Cardinals, 1963-91; pres. Stan Musial & Biggies, Inc., St. Louis. Author: Stan Musial: The Man's Own Story, 1964. Served with USNR, World War II. Voted Nat. League Rookie of Yr., 1943; named most valuable player Nat. League, 1943, 46, 48; mem. Nat. League All-Star Team, 1943-44, 46-63; voted most valuable player Baseball Writers Com., 1946; Maj. League Player of Year Sporting News, 1946, 51; Sid Mercer award N.Y. Baseball Writers, 1947; Kenesaw Mountain Landis Meml. plaque, 1948; Sports Illus. Sportsman of Yr., 1957; recipient Freedom Leadership medal, 1968; named to Baseball Hall of Fame, 1969; holder .331 lifetime batting average. Office: care St Louis Cardinals 250 Stadium Plz Saint Louis MO 63102-1722

MUSICK, GERALD JOE, entomology educator; b. Ponca City, Okla., May 24, 1940; s. Arlie A. and Leona (Beier) M.; m. Florene Ione Thompson, May 11, 1962; children: Linda Kaye, Mary Louise. BS, Okla. State U., 1962; MS, Iowa State U., 1964; PhD, U. Mo., 1969. Grad. asst. Iowa State U., 1962-64; instr. U. Mo., 1964-69; asst. prof. Ohio State U., Wooster, 1969-71, assoc. prof., 1971-76; dept. head U. Ga., Tifton, 1976-79; prof., dept. head U. Ark., 1979-86, interium dir. agrl. exptl. sta., 1986-87, dean, assoc. v.p. agrl. rsch., 1987-93, univ. prof. entomology, 1993—. Author and co-author numerous publs. Vice-chairperson com. Coop. States Rsch. Svc., 1993, So. Expt. Sta.; chairperson steering com. Midwest Food Safety Consortium, 1991-93. Mem. Entomol. Soc. Am. (pres. S.E. br. 1983-84), Ark. Acad. Sci., Ctrl. States Entomol. Soc. (pres. 1996—), Sigma Xi, Gamma Sigma Delta. Lutheran. Avocation: golf. Office: University of Arkansas AG-321 Dept Entomology Fayetteville AR 72701

MUSICK, ROBERT LAWRENCE, JR., lawyer; b. Richlands, Va., Oct. 3, 1947; s. Robert Lawrence and Virginia (Brooks) M.; m. Robbie Shreve (div. 1983); children: Elizabeth, Robert. BA in History with honors, U. Richmond, 1969; JD, U. Va., 1972, MA in Legal History, 1972; LLM, Coll. William and Mary, 1986. Bar: Va. 1972, U.S. Ct. Appeals (4th cir.) 1974. Law clk. Supreme Ct. Va., Richmond, 1972-73; assoc. Williams, Mullen & Christian, Richmond, 1973-78; ptnr. Williams, Mullen, Christian & Dobbins, Richmond, 1978—; bd. govs. estates and property sect. Va. State Bar, 1977-80, chmn., 1980. Author: RIA Non Qualified Deferred Compensation, 1997, (with others) CCH Federal Tax Service, 1989; contbr. articles to profl. jours. Trustee U. Richmond, 1991—; mem. Estate Planning Coun. Richmond, 1981—, U. Richmond Estate Planning Coun., 1984—; bd. dirs. Barksdale Theatre, 1994—. Lt. col. USAR. Mem. ABA, Va. Bar Assn., Richmond Bar Assn., So. Pension Conf., Va. Assn. Professions (pres. 1980-81), Commonwealth Club, Willow Oaks Country Club. Baptist. Avocations: tennis, golf, scuba, soccer. Office: Williams Mullen Christian & Dobbins 2 James Center 1021 E Cary St PO Box 1320 Richmond VA 23210-1320

MUSKY, JANE MICHELLE, film production designer; b. N.J., May 27, 1954; d. John and Olga (Badaukus) M.; m. Anthony Howard Goldwyn, Apr. 18, 1987. BFA, Boston U., 1976. Asst. designer: (theatre) Barnum, 1980; set designer: (theatre) Marathon 1984, 1984; designer: (theatre) The News, 1985; art dir.: (short film) Split Cherry Tree, 1983 (Academy award nomination best short film 1983), (TV movies) Johnny Bull, 1986, Murrow, 1986; prodn. designer: (films) Blood Simple, 1984, Raising Arizona, 1987, Young Guns, 1988, Patty Hearst, 1988, When Harry Met Sally..., 1989, Ghost, 1990, Glengarry Glen Ross, 1992, Boomerang, 1992, City Hall, 1995, (TV movies) Rockabye, 1986, LBJ: The Early Years, 1987, (TV spls.) Alfred G. Graebner Memorial High School Handbook of Rules and Regulations, 1983 (Emmy award nomination outstanding art direction 1984). Recipient gold medal Nat. Women's Crew Championship, 1976, silver medal, 1978. Democrat. Office: care Gersh Agency 232 N Canon Dr Beverly Hills CA 90210-5302*

MUSOLF, LLOYD DARYL, political science educator, institute administrator; b. Yale, S.D., Oct. 14, 1919; s. William Ferdinand and Emma Marie (Pautz) M.; m. Berdyne Peet, June 30, 1944; children—Stephanie, Michael, Laura. B.A., Huron Coll., 1941; M.A., U. S.D., 1946; Ph.D., Johns Hopkins U., 1950. Mem. faculty Vassar Coll., Poughkeepsie, N.Y., 1949-59, assoc. prof. polit. sci., 1955-59; chief of party adv. group Mich. State U., Republic South Vietnam, 1959-61; prof. polit. sci. Mich. State U., East Lansing, 1961-63; prof. polit. sci. U. Calif.-Davis, 1963-87, dir. Inst. Govtl. Affairs, 1963-84, prof. emeritus, 1988—; vis. prof. Johns Hopkins U., Balt., 1953, U. Del., 1954, U. Mich., 1955-56; U.S. Nat. rapporteur for Internat. Congress Adminstrv. Scis., Berlin, 1983; cons. and lectr. in field. Author: Federal Examiners and the Conflict of Law and Administration, 1953, Public Ownership and Accountability: The Canadian Experience, 1959, Promoting the General Welfare, Government and the Economy, 1965, (with others) American National Government-Policies and Politics, 1971, Mixed Enterprise-A Developmental Perspective, 1972, (with Springer) Malaysia's Parliamentary System-Representative Politics and Policymaking in a Divided Society, 1979, Uncle Sam's Private Profitseeking Corporations-Comsat, Fannie Mae, Amtrak and Conrail, 1983; editor: (with Krislov) The Politics of Regulation, 1964, Communications Satellites in Political Orbit, 1968, (with Kornberg) Legislatures in Developmental Perspective, 1970, (with Joel Smith) Legislatures in Development-Dynamics of Change in New and Old States, 1979; contbr. monographs, chpts. to books, articles to profl. jours. Served to lt. USNR, 1942-45. Johnston scholar Johns Hopkins U., 1946-48; Faculty fellow Vassar Coll., 1954-55; sr. assoc. East-West Ctr., Honolulu, 1968-69; vis. scholar Brookings Instn., Washington, 1980. Mem. Am. Soc. Pub. Adminstrn. (exec. council 1967-70), Nat. Assn. Schs. Pub. Affairs and Adminstrn. (exec. council 1972-75), Western Govtl. Research Assn. (exec. bd. 1966-68), Am. Polit. Sci. Assn., Nat. Assn. State Univs. and Land Grant Colls. (rsch. com. fdiv. urban affairs 1980-81). Home: 844 Lake Blvd Davis CA 95616-2611 Office: U Calif Dept Polit Sci Davis CA 95616

MUSON, HOWARD HENRY, writer, editor; b. Mt. Vernon, N.Y., Mar. 19, 1935; s. Joseph Ernest and Beatrice (Hakmaier) M.; m. Dorothy Regina Tyor, May 21, 1967; children: Eve, Stephanie, Nickolas, Alice. A.B. magna cum laude, Harvard U., Cambridge, Mass., 1956; cert., Johns Hopkins Sch. Advanced Internat. Studies, Bologna, Italy, 1956-57; postgrad., U. Calif., Berkeley, 1957-58. Dir. program research CARE Inc., N.Y.C., 1960-62; bur. chief Hartford Courant, Conn., 1962; newsman, columnist AP, Boston, 1963-66; contbg. editor Time mag., N.Y.C., 1966-70; articles editor N.Y. Times mag., N.Y.C., 1970-77; exec. editor Psychology Today mag., N.Y.C., 1977-82; editor Across The Board, N.Y.C., 1983-89; editor, pub. Family Bus. mag., Phila., 1992—; vis. lectr. in residential colls. Yale U., New Haven, 1982-83; instr. in sci. & environ. reporting program NYU, 1992. Author: Media Violence, 1972, Triumph of the American Spirit: Johnstown, Pennsylvania, 1989; contbr. articles to profl. jours., popular mags. Dir. Project

Concern/No. Westchester Walk for Mankind, Mt. Kisco, N.Y., 1985-86. Mem. Nat. Assn. Sci. Writers.

MUSS, HYMAN BERNARD, oncologist, educator; b. Bklyn., Apr. 18, 1943; m. Loretta Anne Lassam; children: Sarah, Jonathan, Daniel. BA in Chemistry cum laude, Lafayette Coll., 1964; MD summa cum laude, SUNY, 1968. Diplomate Am. Bd. Internal Medicine, sub-splty. med. oncology, Am. Bd. Hematology, Am. Bd. Oncology. Intern Peter Bent Brigham Hosp., Boston, 1969-69, jr. asst. resident, 1969-70, rsch. fellow in medicine, 1972-73, rsch. fellow in hematology, 1973-74; rsch. fellow in hematology Children's Hosp. Med. Ctr., Boston, 1972-73; fellow in oncology Dana Farber Cancer Inst., Boston, 1973-74; asst. prof. medicine, hematology/oncology Wake Forest U., Winston-Salem, N.C., 1974-78, assoc. prof., 1978-85, assoc. dir. clin. rsch. Comprehensive Cancer Ctr., 1979-96, prof. medicine, 1985-96; prof. medicine U. Vt., 1996—; assoc. dir. Vt. Cancer Ctr., 1996—; peer review com. Health Scis. Consortium, Inc., 1978-80; sci. adv. com. black/white survival study, 1985-96; com.consulting staff Forsyth Meml. Hosp., Winston-Salem, N.C., N.C. Bapt. Hosp., Winston Salem. Mem. editl. bd. Am. Jour. Med. Sci., 1986—, Jour. Clin. Oncology, 1994, Nat. Cancer Insts. Computerized, 1986-91, Contemporary Oncology, 1990—; reviewer New Eng. Jour. Medicine, Jour. Clin. Oncology, Archives of Internal Medicine, Breast Cancer Rsch. & Treatment, Cancer, Gynecologic Oncology, Surg. Neurology, Jour. Nat. Cancer Inst., Jour. Immunotherapy, Clin. Chemistry; contbr. articles, abstracts to profl. jours., chpts. to books. Active Am. Cancer Soc., 1978—, bd. dirs., 1985-87; trustee Blumenthal Jewish Home, 1992-93, chair med. ethics com., chair HIV/infectious disease com. Maj. U.S. Army, 1970-72, Vietnam. Decorated Bronze Star U.S. Army; recipient Cooper Meml. award Wake County, 1979; Jr. Faculty fellow Am. Cancer Soc., 1975-79. Fellow ACP; mem. AMA, Am. coll. Obstetricians and Gynecologists (com. human rsch.), Am. Soc. Hematology, Am. Fedn. Clin. Rsch., Am. Soc. Clin. Oncology, Am. Assn. Cancer Rsch., Internat. Gynecologic Cancer Soc., Internat. Assn. Breast Cancer Rsch., So. Assn. Oncology (edn. com. 1988—)So. Med. Assn., So. Soc. Clin. Rsch., N.C. Med. Soc. (cancer com.), Forsyth County Med. Soc. (chmn. cancer com. 1977-80, med. adv. com. 1977-79), Cancer and Acute Leukemia Group B, Gynecologic Oncology Group (sarcoma com. 1977-79, endometrial com. 1978-90, quality control com. 1978-90, chemotherapy com. 1977—, chmn., 1980—, protocol com. 1980-90, new drug liaison com. 1980—, exec. com. 1991—, quality of life com. 1993—, cervix com. 1993—), Piedmont Oncology Assn. (chmn. 1991—), Phi Beta Kappa, Alpha Omega Alpha. Home: 76 Overlook Dr Burlington VT 05403 Office: Fletcher Allen Health Care MCHV Patrick 534 111 Colchester Ave Burlington VT 05401-1473

MUSSEHL, ROBERT CLARENCE, lawyer; b. Washington, May 1, 1936; s. Chester Carl and Clara Cecelia (Greenwalt) Mussehl; children: Debra Lee, David Lee, Omar Chung; spouse: Misook Chung, Mar. 22, 1987. BA, Am. U., 1964, JD, 1966. Bar: Wash. 1967, U.S. Dist. Ct. (we. dist.) Wash. 1967, U.S. Ct. Appeals (9th cir.) 1968, U.S Supreme Ct. 1971. Sr. ptnr. Thom, Mussehl, Navoni, Hoff, Pierson & Ryder, Seattle, 1967-78, Neubauer & Mussehl, Seattle, 1978-80, Mussehl & Rosenberg, Seattle, 1980—; speaker law convs. and other profl. orgns.; moot ct. judge Nat. Appelate Advocacy Competition, San Francisco, 1987; panel mem. ABA Symposium on Compulsory Jurisdiction of World Ct., San Francisco, 1987; chmn. bd., chief exec. officer The Seattle Smashers profl. volleyball club, 1976-80. Contbr. numerous articles to legal publs. Mem. Wash. Vol. Lawyers for Arts, 1976-80; statewide chair Lawyers for Durning for Gov., 1976; mem. task force on the single adult and ch. Ch. Coun. Greater Seattle, 1976-78; bd. dirs. Wash. State Pub. Interest Law Ctr., 1976-81; founder, chair Wash. State Lawyers Campaign for Hunger Relief, 1991—. Recipient Jefferson award for pub. svc. State of Wash., 1997. Fellow Am. Bar Found., Am. Acad. Matrimonial Lawyers; mem. ABA (ho. of dels. 1979-91, spl. adv. com. on internat. activities 1989-91, chair marriage and family counseling and conciliation com. family law sect. 1981-83, mem. world order under law standing com. 1983-89, chair, 1986-89, chair ad hoc com. on the assembly 1986-89, mem. assembly resolutions com. 1979-91, mem. blue ribbon com. for world ct. 1987-88, mem. standing com. on dispute resolution, 1992-93; exec. coun. sect. dispute resolution 1993-95, asst. budget officer, 1995—, others, Achievement award), Wash. State Bar Assn. (exec. com. family law sect. 1973-75, chmn. internat. law com. 1974-76, sec.-treas., exec. com. world peace through law sect. 1980—, chair 1981-82, mem. edit. bd. Family Law Deskbook 1987-89), Wash. State Trial Lawyers Assn., Seattle-King County Bar Assn. (family law sect. 1971-90, other coms. 1970—, chmn. young lawyers sect. 1971-72, sec. 1972-73, trustee), Am. Arbitration Assn. (panel arbitrators), World Assn. Lawyers of World Peace Through Law Ctr. (founding mem.), Heritage Club YMCA Greater Seattle (charter 1977—), UN Assn. U.S.A. (bd. dirs. Seattle chpt. 1989-91). Avocations: biking, tennis, weight training, painting, religious studies. Home: One Pacific Tower 2000 1st Ave Apt 902 Seattle WA 98121-2167 Office: 1111 3rd Ave Ste 2626 Seattle WA 98101-3219

MUSSELMAN, FRANCIS HAAS, lawyer; b. Utica, N.Y., Aug. 3, 1925; s. John Joseph and Kathryn Agnes (Haas) M.; m. Marjorie Louise Balme, June 22, 1948; children: Martha Christina Musselman Sheridan, Kathryn Ann Musselman Bourbonniere, Carol Elizabeth Musselman Kuntz, John Francis. AB, Hamilton Coll., Clinton, N.Y., 1950; JD, Columbia U., 1953; LHD (hon.), Wadhams Hall Seminary/Coll., 1994. Bar: N.Y. 1954, D.C. 1980; U.S. Dist. Ct. (so. dist.) N.Y. 1956, U.S. Ct. Appeals (D.C. cir.) 1981, U.S. Supreme Ct. 1981. Assoc. firm Milbank, Tweed, Hadley & McCloy, N.Y.C., 1953-60; ptnr. Milbank, Tweed, Hadley & McCloy, 1960-90, ret., 1990—; pres., dir. Panfield Corp., N.Y.C., 1961-82; dir. Panfield Nurseries, N.Y.C., 1961-82; law firm mgmt. cons., 1991—; Bankruptcy trustee Finley, Kumble et al, 1988-93. Bd. dirs. Milbank Meml. Fund, 1960-94, chmn., 1985-90; bd. dirs. Memton Fund, 1958-90; trustee Kirkland Coll., Clinton, 1971-78, chmn., 1972-78, Nat. Ctr. for Automated Info. Retrieval, 1979-80, Hamilton Coll., 1978-91, life, 1991, Barnard Coll., 1979-81, Mater Dei Coll., 1991—; chmn. Mater Dei Coll. Found., 1993-95; trustee emeritus Wadhams Hall Sem. Coll., vice chmn., 1979-90. With USN, 1943-46. Fellow Am. Bar Found., N.Y. State Bar Found., Am. Coll. Law Practice Mgmt.; mem. Am. Judicature Soc., Am. Law Inst., Internat. Am., Fed. Bar Assn., N.Y. State Bar Assn., D.C. Bar Assn., Assn. of Bar of City of N.Y., St. Lawrence County Bar Assn., World Trade Club (N.Y.C.), Union League (N.Y.C.), Capitol Hill Club (Washington), Coram Nobis (N.Y.C.), Phi Delta Phi, Lambda Chi Alpha. Roman Catholic. Clubs: World Trade (N.Y.C.), Union League (N.Y.C.); Capitol Hill (Washington), Coram Nobis (N.Y.C.). Home: Oak Point Hammond NY 13646 Office: PO Box 289 Hammond NY 13646-0289

MUSSELMAN, NORMAN BURKEY, retired editor; b. Arkansas City, Kans., Mar. 21, 1929; s. Norman Beachy and E. Ruth (Burkey) M.; m. Elizabeth Temple Henry, Oct. 26, 1957; children: Elizabeth Temple Whitson, Norman Henry, Robert Beachy. BA, U. Okla., 1951, MA, 1954. Columnist McGraw Hill Pub. Co., Washington, 1954-67; editor Nat. Assn. Electric Cos., Washington, 1967-80; dir. govt. com. Edison Electric Inst., Washington, 1980-94; retired, 1994. Pres. Okla. U. Alumni Club, Washington, 1957-58; pres. men of ch. Presbyn. Meeting House, Alexandria, Va., 1962-63, clk. of session, 1980-82; elder 1st Presbyn. Ch., Glenwood Springs; precinct capt. Rep. Party, Fairfax County, Va., 1968-69; cubmaster, pack chmn., scout com. Boy Scouts, Alexandria, 1970-73, 78-82. 1st lt. U.S. Army, 1951-53. Mem. Soc. for the Preservation and Encouragement of Barber Shop Singing in Am. (v.p. Garfield Colo. chpt. 1997), Colo. Archeol. Soc. (Roaring Fork chpt.), Nat. Press Club, Sigma Delta Chi (pres. Okla. U. chpt. 1953-54). Home: 700 Silver Oak Dr Glenwood Springs CO 81601-2804

MUSSENDEN, GERALD, psychologist; b. N.Y.C., June 1, 1941; s. Geraldo and Adele (Gimenez) M.; m. Iris Manuela Prado, Aug. 11, 1967; children: Gerald, Ricardo-Antonio, Gina. BA, Tarkio Coll., 1968; MS, Brigham Young U., 1971, PhD, 1974. Diplomate Am. Bd. Profl. Disability Cons., Am. Bd. Forensic Examiners. Dir. child program Albert Einstein Coll. Medicine, N.Y.C., 1974-76; psychologist Mental Health Ctr., Bartow, Fla., 1976-77, Norside Community Mentala Health Ctr., Tampa, Fla., 1977-80; pvt. practice Brandon (Fla.) Counseling Ctr., 1980—; criminal ct. psychologist Fla. Cts., Hillsborough, Fla., 1978—; with children's svcs. State Rehab., Hillsborough, 1977—; rehab. psychologist Vocat. Rehab., Hillsborough; psychologist Div. Blind Svcs., Hillsborough. Fellow Ford Found., 1972-73. Mem. APA, Fla. Psychol. Assn., Bay Area Psychol. Assn., Soc. Personality Assessment. Home: 317 Cactus Rd Seffner FL 33584-6105 Office: Brandon Counseling Ctr 134 N Moon Ave Brandon FL 33510-4420

MUSSER, SANDRA G., lawyer; b. Hollywood, Calif., July 23, 1944; d. Donald Godfrey Gumpertz and Gloria G. (Rosenblatt) King; m. Michael R.V. Whitman, Feb. 19, 1980. BA, UCLA, 1965; JD, Hastings Coll. of Law, 1970. Bar: Calif. 1971, U.S. Dist. Ct. (no. dist.) Calif. 1971, U.S. Ct. Appeals (9th cir.) 1971. Clk. 9th Cir. Ct. of Appeals, 1971-72; lawyer pvt. practice of family law, 1972-86; ptnr. Musser & Ryan, San Francisco, 1986—; judge pro tem San Francisco County Superior Ct., 1988—. Contbr. articles to profl. jours. Fellow Acad. Matrimonial Lawyers; mem. ABA (chair litig. sect. domestic rels. and family law com. 1993-94), State Bar Calif. (state bar family law sect. 1977—, chair 1982-83, advisor 1983-84), Bar Assn. San Francisco. Office: Musser & Ryan 361 Oak St San Francisco CA 94102-5615

MUSSER, THARON, theatrical lighting designer, theatre consultant; b. Roanoke, Va., Jan. 8, 1925; s. George C. and Hazel (Riddle) M. B.A., Berea Coll., 1946; H.H.D., 1979; M.F.A., Yale U., 1950; H.H.D., Emerson Coll., 1980. Lighting designer over 100 Broadway prodns.; lighting designer for repertory theatre including, Jose Limon Dance Co., 1953-56, Group 20 Players of Mass., 1954-56, Phoenix Theatre Co., 1957-60, Am. Theatre Festival, Boston, 1961, Boston Arts Festival, 1962, Empire State Music Festival, 1959, Nat. Repertory Theatre Co., 1961-68, Am. Shakespeare Festival Theatre and Acad., 1963-68, Lincoln Center Repertory Theatre, 1968, Dallas Civic Opera, 1969-77, New Phoenix Repertory Co., 1972, Miami Opera Guild, 1975-78, Wolf Trap Found., Filene Center for Performing Arts, 1977; staff designer, Mark Taper Forum, Los Angeles Center Theatre Group, 1970-86; lighting designer internat. prodns. including, Jose Limon Dance Co. State Dept. Tour, S. Am., 1953; London prodns. Golden Boy, 1968, Mame, 1969, Applause, 1972, A Little Night Music, 1975, They're Playing Our Song, 1979, London Ballet Festival Romeo and Juliet, 1977; London prodn. Ziegfeld, 1988; internat. prodn. A Chorus Line, 1976; lighting designer and cons. internat. prodn., Ford's Theatre Restoration and TV prodn., Washington, 1968, Man and the Universe at, Hemisfair, San Antonio, 1968, Chgo. Auditorium, 1968, Los Angeles Shubert Theatre, 1971, Dallas Music Hall, Berea Coll. Dramatic Arts Center, 1976-80; London prodn. Children of a Lesser God, 1981, 15 Neil Simon shows including, Broadway Bound, Rumors and Lost in Yonkers. Recipient Los Angeles Drama Critics' Circle award for Dream on Monkey Mountain, 1970, for Follies, 1972, for Pacific Overtures, a Chorus Line, 1976-77, for Terra Nova, 1979; Antoinette Perry award for Follies, 1971-72, for A Chorus Line, 1975-76, for Dreamgirls, 1981-82; Yale arts award, 1985; Theatre Hall of Fame award, 1985. Mem. United Scenic Artists, Soc. Brit. Theatrical Lighting Designers, U.S. Inst. Theatre Tech. Address: 21 Cornelia St New York NY 10014-4121

MUSSER, WILLIAM WESLEY, JR., lawyer; b. Enid, Okla., July 17, 1918; s. William Wesley Sr. and Ethel Rice (McElroy) M.; m. Estelle Bee Wiedeman, Jan. 19, 1947; children: James William, Mary Bee Clark. BA, U. Okla., 1939, LLB, 1941. Bar: Okla. 1941. Ptnr. Elam, Crowley & Musser, Enid, 1946-47; probate judge Garfield County, Okla., 1949-51; ptnr. Otjen, Carter & Musser, Enid, 1952-54; asst. county atty. Garfield County, 1955-56; sole practice Enid, 1957—; chmn. bd. dirs. Tax Roll Corrections, Garfield County, 1950-51; 6th congrl. dist. rep. Okla. Jud. Nominating Com., Enid, 1967-74; judge Okla. Ct. Appeals, Enid, 1982. Pres. Great Salt Plains council Boy Scouts Am., 1955; gen. chmn. St. Mary's Hosp. Bldg. Fund, 1949; bd. dirs. Enid Community Chest, 1950-51, N.W. Okla. Pastoral Care Assn., 1978; v.p. Phillips U., Enid, 1955-74, mem. exec. com., 1955-78, trustee, 1978-82; bd. dirs. Enid Estate Planning Council, 1971-74, sec., 1972, pres., 1973-74. Served to maj. AUS, 1941-45, ETO. Decorated Bronze Star. Fellow Okla. Bar Found.; mem. ABA, Okla. Bar Assn. (v.p. bd. govs. 1957), Garfield County Bar Assn. (pres. 1962), Am. Judicature Soc., U. Okla. Alumni Assn. (exec. bd. 1959-61), Sons and Daus. of Cherokee Strip Pioneers Assn. (exec. bd. dirs. 1967-70), Greater Enid C. of C. (bd. dirs. 1969-71), VFW, Am. Legion, Phi Delta Phi, Alpha Tau Omega. Republican. Mem. Christian Ch. (Disciples of Christ). Clubs: Am. Bus. (pres. 1947), Oakwood Country (Enid). Home: 1301 Indian Dr Enid OK 73703-7012 Office: Broadway Tower 3d Fl 114 E Broadway Ave Enid OK 73701-4126

MUSSINA, MICHAEL COLE, professional baseball player; b. Williamsport, Pa., Dec. 8, 1968. BA Econs., Stanford U., 1990. Pitcher Balt. Orioles, 1990—; player Am. League All-Star Team, 1992-94. Named Internat. League Most Valuable Pitcher, 1991, recipient Am. League Gold Glove, 1996. Office: Balt Orioles 333 W Camden St Baltimore MD 21201-2435*

MUSTACCHI, PIERO, physician, educator; b. Cairo, May 29, 1920; came to U.S., 1947; naturalized, 1962; s. Gino and Gilda (Rieti) M.; m. Dora Lisa Ancona, Sept. 26, 1948; children: Roberto, Michael. BS in Humanities, U. Florence, Italy, 1938; postgrad. in anatomy, Eleve Interne, U. Lausanne, Switzerland, 1938-39; MB, ChB, Fouad I U., Cairo, Egypt, 1944, grad. in Arabic lang. and lit., 1946; D Medicine and Surgery, U. Pisa, 1986; D Honoris Causa, U. Aix-Marseilles, France, 1988; hon. degree, U. Alexandria, Egypt, 1985. Qualified med. examiner, Calif. Indsl. Accident Commn., 1994. House officer English Hosp., Ch. Missionary Soc., Cairo, Egypt, 1945-47; clin. affiliate U. Calif., San Francisco, 1947-48; intern Franklin Hosp., San Francisco, 1948-49; resident in pathology U. Calif., San Francisco, 1949-51; resident in medicine Meml. Ctr. Cancer and Allied Diseases, N.Y.C., 1951-53; rsch. epidemiologist Dept. HEW, Nat. Cancer Inst., Bethesda, Md., 1955-57; cons. allergy clinic U. Calif., San Francisco, 1957-70, clin. prof. medicine and preventive medicine, 1970-90, clin. prof. medicine and epidemiology, 1990-96, head occupl. epidemiology, 1975-90, head divsn. internat. health edn. dept. epidemiology and internat. health, 1985-90; médecin agréé, official physician Consulate Gen. of France, San Fransisco, 1995—; med. cons., vis. prof. numerous edn. and profl. instns., including U. Marseilles, 1981, 82, U. Pisa, Italy, 1983, U. Gabon, 1984, U. Siena, Italy, 1985, work clinic U. Calif., 1975-84, Ctr for Rehab. and Occupl. Health U. Calif., San Francisco, 1984-93; cons. numerous worldwide govtl. agys.; ofcl. physician French Consulate Gen., San Francisco, 1995. Contbr. chpts. to books, articles to profl. jours. Editorial bd. Medecine d'Afrique Noire, Ospedali d'Italia. Served with USN, USPHS, 1953-55. Decorated Order of Merit (Commander) (Italy), Ordre de la Legion d'Honneur (France), Medal of St. John of Jerusalem, Sovereign Order of Malta, Order of the Republic (Egypt); Scroll, Leonardo da Vinci Soc., San Francisco, 1965; award Internat. Inst. Oakland, 1964; Hon. Vice Consul. Italy, 1971-90. Fellow ACP, Am. Soc. Environ. and Occupational Health; mem. AAAS, Am. Assn. Cancer Rsch., Calif. Soc. Allergy and Immunology, Calif. Med. Assn., San Francisco Med. Soc., West Coast Allergy Soc. (founding), Mex. Congress on Hypertension (corr.), Internat. Assn. Med. Rsch. and Continuing Edn. (U.S. rep.), Acad. Italiana della Cucina. Democrat. Avocations: mathematics, music, languages. Home: 3344 Laguna St San Francisco CA 94123-2208 Office: U Calif Parnassus Ave San Francisco CA 94143

MUSTALISH, ANTHONY CHARLES, physician, educator; b. Newark, Oct. 28, 1940; s. Anthony William and Wanda Helen (Macknowski) M.; m. Elayne Harriet Klarsfeld, June 11, 1967; children: Rachel, David, Peter. BA, NYU, 1962, MD, 1966, MPH, Harvard U., 1971. Diplomate Am. Bd. Preventive Medicine, Am. Bd. Emergency Medicine, Nat. Bd. Med. Examiners. Health officer N.Y.C. Dept. Health, 1971-74, dep. commr., 1974-77; chief emergency services Brookdale Hosp., Bklyn., 1977-78, Lenox Hill Hosp., N.Y.C., 1978-90, COO, 1988-90; attending emergency physician N.Y. Hosp., 1990—; asst. prof. emergency medicine and pub. health Cornell U. Med. Coll., 1990—; med. dir. occupl. health svcs. Rockefeller Group, Inc., 1990-95; instr. Mt. Sinai Sch. Med., N.Y.C., 1971-74; assoc. prof. med. N.Y. Med. Coll., N.Y.C., 1971 74, 81-88; adj. prof. Hunter Coll., N.Y.C., 1972-82; lectr. Columbia U. Sch. Pub. Health, N.Y.C., 1971—. Contbr. articles to profl. jours., chpts. to books. Served to capt. U.S. Army, 1968-70, Vietnam. Fellow Am. Coll. Preventive Medicine, N.Y. Acad. Medicine; mem. Am. Coll. Emergency Physicians, ACP, Am. Pub. Health Assn., Am. Bd. Occupl. Medicine and Environ. Health. Home: 170 E 83rd St New York NY 10028-1920 Office: 292 Madison Ave New York NY 10017-6307

MUSTAPHA, TAMTON, gastroenterologist; b. Calicut, Kerala, India, Oct. 17, 1941; s. Mahamood and Asmabi (Tamton) Thoosikannan; student Malabar Christian Coll., India, 1958; M.D., Calicut Med. Coll., 1963; m. Rahma Marikar, June 15, 1969; children: Monisha, Mumtaz, Nigel. Diplomate Am. Bd. Internal Medicine, Am. Bd. Gastroenterology. Resident in internal medicine VA Hosp., Bklyn., 1967-68, Grasslands Hosp., Valhalla, N.Y., 1968-70; resident in gastroenterology Montefiore Hosp., Bronx, 1970-72; practice medicine, specializing in gastroenterology, Hudson, N.Y., 1972—; attending physician Columbia Meml. Hosp., Hudson, 1972—; chief dept. medicine Columbia Greene Med. Ctr., 1989-91; instr. medicine Albany Med. Center, 1972—; bd. dirs., chmn. auditing assurance Hudson Valley PSRO; pres. No. Columbia Assocs., Columbia Greene Med. Assocs., Corro Med. Realty, Prime Med. Assocs., Hudson, 1997—; chmn. bd. Greene Health Care Assocs.; bd. dirs. Regional Heart Assn. Mem. town planning bd. Kinderhook, 1987-96; chmn. bd. trustees Columbia Green C.C. Fellow Am. Coll. Gastroenterologists; mem. AMA, Am. Coll. Physicians, Columbia County Med. Soc., N.Y. State Med. Soc., Am. Gastroent. Assn., Am. Soc. Internal Medicine, Acad. Scis., Am. Heart Assn. (bd. dirs.), Am. Coll. Physician Execs., Columbia and Dutches Lung Assn., Assn. for Mentally Retarded, Am. Assn. Physicians and Dentists of India (pres. Capital dist. 1986). Republican. Lodge: Rotary (dir. 1976-78, pres.-elect 1986-87, pres. 1987—, Paul Harris fellow), Mason (master), Shriners, Cypres Temple. Home: Brindhaven Rd # 1 Valatie NY 12184 Office: 848 Columbia St Hudson NY 12534-2339

MUSTARD, JAMES FRASER, research institute executive; b. Toronto, Oct. 16, 1927; s. Allan Alexander and Jean Anne (Oldham) M.; m. Christine Elizabeth Sifton, June 4, 1952; children: Cameron, Ann, Jim, Duncan, John, Christine. MD, U. Toronto, 1953; PhD, Cambridge U., 1956. Asst., then assoc. prof pathology U. Toronto, 1963-66, asst. prof. medicine, 1965-66, hon. prof. pathology, 1990—; prof. pathology McMaster U., Hamilton, Ont., Can., 1966-88, prof. emeritus, 1988—, chmn. pathology, 1966-72, dean faculty health. scis., 1972-80, v.p. faculty health scis., 1980-82; bd. dirs., pres. Can. Inst. Advanced Rsch., Toronto, 1982-96, founding pres., 1996—; mem. Ont. Coun. Health, 1966-72; chmn. Task Force Health Planning for Ont., Ministry Health and Govt. Ont., 1973-74; mem. Ont. Coun. Univ Affairs, 1975-81; chmn. Adv. Coun. Occupl. Health and Safety, 1977-83; mem. Royal Commn. Matters Health and Safety Arising Use of Asbestos in Ont., 1980-83; mem. Bovey Commn. Study Future Devel. Univ. in Ont., 1984-85; mem. Premier's Coun. Ont., 1986-95, Premier's Coun. Health Strategy, 1988-91; chmn. ctrs. excellence com. Govt. Ont., 1987-91; mem. Prime Minister's Nat. Adv. Bd. on Sci. and Tech., 1987-91, Ottawa, vice chmn., 1988-91; chmn. bd. dirs. Inst. Work & Health, 1990—; mem. adv. bd. Man. Ctr. for Health Policy and Evaluation, 1991—; vice chmn. Internat. Ctr. Health and Soc., 1994—; bd. dirs. Steel Co. Can., Hamilton, Atomic Energy Can. Ltd., 1990-95, Ballard Powers Sys., Inc., 1995—. Bd. dirs. Heart and Stroke Found. Can., 1971-82, Heart and Stroke Found. Ont., 1982-87; bd. govs. McMaster U., 1978-82; bd. dirs. McMaster U. Med. Centre, 1972-82; trustee Advanced Systems Inst. Found., Vancouver, 1986—, Aga Khan U., Karachi, Pakistan, 1985—; mem. chancellor's commn. Aga Khan U., 1992-95. Decorated Order of Ont., 1992, Companion Order of Can., 1994; recipient Disting. Svc. award Can. Soc. Clin. Investigation, J. Allyn Taylor Internat. prize, 1988, Internat. award Gairdner Found., 1967, James F. Mitchell award, 1972, Izaak Walton Killam prize in health sci. Can. Coun., 1987, Robert P. Grant award for contbns. to progress Internat. Congress on Thrombosis and Haemostasis, 1987, Disting. Career award for contbns. Internat. Soc. Thrombosis and Haemostasis, 1989. Home: 422 Sumach St, Toronto, ON Canada M4X 1B5 Office: Can Inst Advanced Rsch Founders Network, 401 Richmond St W Ste 281, Toronto, ON Canada M5V 3A8

MUSTARD, MARY CAROLYN, financial executive; b. North Bend, Nebr., Sept. 21, 1948; d. Joseph Louis and Rosalie Margaret (Emanuel) Smaus; m. Ronald L. Mustard, Apr. 19, 1969 (div. 1988); children: Joel Jonathan, Dana Marie. Student, Creighton U., 1966-67, C.E. Sch. Commerce, 1967-68, Coll. of St. Mary, 1983-84, Met. C.C., Omaha, 1988-90, Bellevue U., 1991-92. With Platte County Dept. Pub. Welfare, Columbus, Nebr., 1968-69; sec. to plant mgr. B.L. Montague Steel Co., Sumter, S.C., 1969-70; property disposal technician Property Disposal Office, Shaw AFB, S.C., 1970-71; libr. technician Hdqs. Strategic Air Command Libr., Offutt AFB, Nebr., 1971-76; sec.-steno Hdqs. Strategic Air Command Comm./Frequency Mgmt., Offutt AFB, 1976-79; security specialist/program analyst Hdqs. Strategic Air Command Security Police, Offutt AFB, 1979-88; budget analyst Hdqs. Strategic Air Command Fin. Mgmt., Offutt AFB, 1988-92; funds control analyst Hdqs. Air Mobility Command, Scott AFB, Ill., 1992-93, chief hdqs. and comm. account, 1993-94, chief hdqs. relocation, transition assistance/comm. programs, 1994-95; chief base realignment and closure program Air Mobility Command, Scott AFB, 1995-96; sys. adminstr. Def. Fin. and Acctg. Svc., Kansas City, Mo., 1996—. Mem. Am. Soc. Mil. Comptrollers (SAC Budget Analyst of Yr. 1990). Democrat. Roman Catholic. Avocations: walking, reading, biking. Office: DFAS-KC/ALS 1500 E Bannister Rd Kansas City MO 64131-3009

MUSTERIC, PETER, engineering manager; b. Bronx, Apr. 28, 1960; s. Matthew Peter and Norma Agnus (White) M.; m. Annette M. Natuzzi, July 1, 1989. B of Elec. Engring., SUNY, Stony Brook, 1982; MSEE, SUNY, 1985; MBA with distinction, Hofstra U., 1991. Design engr. Hazeltine Corp., Greenlawn, N.Y., 1982-86, Grumman Aerospace, Bethpage, N.Y., 1986-89; sr. mgr. Symbol Techs., Bohemia, N.Y., 1989—. Inventor in field. Mem. IEEE, Beta Gamma Sigma, Eta Kappa Knu. Roman Catholic. Avocations: music, computers, travel. Home: 134 S Plaisted Ave Hauppauge NY 11788 Office: Symbol Techs Inc 1 Symbol Plz Holtsville NY 11742-1300

MUSTIAN, MIDDLETON TRUETT, hospital administrator; b. Texarkana, Tex., Mar. 27, 1921; s. Thomas William and Hattie (Cornelius) M.; m. Jackie Cain, Dec. 3, 1955; children—Mark Thomas, John Perry, Janet Louise. B.B.A., Baylor U., 1949. Asst. adminstr. Bapt. Hosp., Alexandria, La., 1950-54; asst. adminstr. Miss. Bapt. Hosp., Jackson, 1954-55; adminstr. Meml. Hosp., Panama City, Fla., 1955-60, Alachua Gen. Hosp., Gainesville, Fla., 1960-64, Cen. Unit Meml. Bapt. Hosp., Houston, 1964; asst. dir. Meml. Bapt. Hosp. System, Houston, 1964; pres., chief exec. officer Tallahassee Meml. Regional Med. Center Hosp., 1964-89, pres. emeritus, 1990—; pres., CEO TMH Reg. Med. Ctr. Found., Inc., 1976-89; clin. instr. dept. health adminstrn. U. Gainesville; mem. Hosp. Cost Containment Bd., State of Fla. Contbr. articles to hosp. jours. Bd. dirs. Blue Cross of Fla.; mem. Fla. Statewide Health Coordinating Council. Served to capt. Med. Adminstrv. Corps U.S. Army, 1940-45. Decorated Purple Heart. Fellow Am. Coll. Hosp. Adminstrs. (regent); mem. Am. Hosp. Assn., Fla. Hosp. Assn. (past pres.). Democrat. Baptist. Clubs: Kiwanis, Masons. Home: 6325 Velda Dairy Rd Tallahassee FL 32308-6308

MUSTO, DAVID FRANKLIN, physician, educator, historian, consultant; b. Tacoma, Jan. 8, 1936; s. Charles Hiram and Hilda Marie (Hanson) Mustoe; m. Emma Jean Baudendistel, June 2, 1961; children: Jeanne Marie, David Kyle, John Baird, Christopher Edward. BA, U. Wash., 1956, MD, 1963; MA, Yale U., 1961. Lic. physician, Conn., Pa. Clerk Nat. Hosp. for Nervous Disease, London, 1961; intern Pa. Hosp., Phila., 1963-64; resident Yale U. Med. Ctr., New Haven, 1964-67; spl. asst. to dir. NIMH, Bethesda, Md., 1967-69; vis. asst. prof. Johns Hopkins U., 1968-69; asst. prof. Yale U., 1969-73, assoc. prof., 1973-78, sr. rsch. scientist, 1978-81, prof., 1981—, exec. fellow Davenport Coll., 1983-88; mem. adv. editorial com. Yale Edits. Private Papers James Boswell, 1975—; cons. Exec. Office of Pres., 1973-75; mem. White House Strategy Coun., 1978-81; mem. panel on alcohol policy NAS, Washington, 1978-82; cons. White House Conf. on Families, 1979-80; vis. fellow Clare Coll., Cambridge U., 1994; mem. alcohol adv. com. Nat. Assn. Broadcasters, 1994—; DuMez lectr. U. Md.; Walter Reed meml. lectr. Richmond Acad. Medicine. Author: The American Disease: Origins of Narcotic Control, 1973, expanded edit., 1987. Historian Pres.'s Commn. on Mental Health, 1977-78; adv. U.S. Del. to UN Commn. Narcotic Drugs, Geneva, 1978-79; mem. nat. coun. Smithsonian Instn., Washington, 1981-90, hon. mem., 1991—; hist. cons. Presdl. Commn. Human Immuno-deficiency Virus Epidemic, 1988; mem. nat. adv. com. on anti-drug program Robert Wood Johnson Found., 1989—; mem. nat. adv. com. on internat. narcotic policy UN Assn. of U.S.A., 1991; mem. adv. com. causes drug abuse Office Tech. Assessment, Congress U.S., 1992-94; commr. Conn. Alcohol and Drug Abuse Commn., 1992-93; bd. dirs. Coll. on Problems of Drug Dependence, 1990-94; trustee Assocs. of Cushing-Whitney Med. Libr., 1994—. With USPHS, 1967-69. Fellow Am. Psychiat. Assn., Coll. Problems of Drug Dependence; mem. New Haven County Med. Assn. (chmn. bicentennial com. 1983), Am. Inst. History of Pharmacy (Kraemers award), Am. Hist. Assn., Am. Assn. History of Medicine (William Osler medal), English-Speaking Union (pres. New Haven br. 1995—, nat. bd. 1996—), Soc. of Cin. in the State of Conn., Beaumont Med. Club (pres. 1985-87), Acorn Club of Conn., Cosmos Club, Yale Club (N.Y.C.), Athenaeum Club (London). Office: Yale U PO Box 207900 New Haven CT 06520-7900

MUSTO, JOSEPH JOHN, lawyer; b. Pittston, Pa., Nov. 22, 1943; s. James and Rose (Frushon) M.; m. Fortunata Giudice, July 5, 1969; children: Laura, Joseph Robert. BA, King's Coll., Wilkes-Barre, Pa., 1965; JD, Dickinson Sch. Law, Carlisle, Pa., 1968. Bar: Pa. 1968, U.S. Ct. Appeals (3d cir.) 1968, U.S. Dist. Ct. (mid. dist.) Pa. 1971. Asst. dist. atty. City of Phila., 1968-69; assoc. Bedford, Waller, Griffith, Darling & Mitchell, Wilkes-Barre, 1969-73; ptnr. Griffith, Darling, Mitchell, Aponick & Musto, Wilkes-Barre, 1973-75; prin. Griffith, Aponick & Musto, Wilkes-Barre, 1975-90; ptnr. Rosenn, Jenkins & Greeenwald, Wilkes-Barre, 1990-93; judge Ct. Common Pleas of Luzerne County, 1993-94; mem. Hourigan, Kluger, Spohrer & Quinn, Wilkes-Barre, Pa., 1994-97; prin. Musto & Saunders, P.C., Wilkes-Barre, Pa., 1997—; solicitor Yatesville (Pa.) Borough, 1973-80, Duryea (Pa.) Borough, 1975-80, Pittston Area Sch. Dist., 1973-93. Mem. Luzerne County Gov. Study Com., Wilkes-Barre, 1973-74; mem., chmn. No. Luzerne Health Adv. Coun., Wilkes-Barre, 1976-80; pres., mem. Health Sys. Agy. of N.E. Pa., Avoca, 1980-86; pres. Pa. Health Planning Assn., Harrisburg, 1985-86; mem. civil justice reform act adv. com. Fed. Dist. Ct. Pa. Ct., 1991-95. Mem. Fed. Bar Assn. (past pres. Ctrl. Pa. chpt.), Pa. Bar Assn., Wilkes-Barre Law and Libr. Assn. Democrat. Roman Catholic. Home: 7 Prospect Pl Pittston PA 18640-2627 Office: Musto & Saunders 133 Oxford St Wilkes Barre PA 18702-3338

MUSTOE, THOMAS ANTHONY, physician, plastic surgeon; b. Columbia, Mo., June 29, 1951; s. Robert Moore and Carolyn (Swett) M.; m. Kathryn Claire Stallcup, Aug. 13, 1977; children: Anthony, Lisa. BA cum laude in biology, Harvard Coll., 1973, MD cum laude, 1978. Diplomate Am. Bd. Otolaryngology, Am. Bd. Plastic Surgery. Rsch. assoc. dept. microbiology Harvard Med. Sch., Cambridge, Mass., 1976-77; intern in medicine Mass. Gen. Hosp., Boston, 1978-79; resident in surgery Peter Bent Brigham Hosp., Boston, 1979-80; resident in otolaryngology Mass. Eye and Ear Infirmary, Boston, 1980-82, chief resident, 1982-83; resident in plastic surgery Brigham and Women;s Hosp., Children's Hosp., Boston, 1983-84, chief resident, 1984-85; asst. prof. in surgery Wash. U. Sch. Medicine, St. Louis, 1985-89, assoc. prof., 1989-91; prof., chief divsn. plastic surgery Northwestern U. Med. Sch., Chgo., 1991—; plastic surgeon Northwestern Meml. Hosp., 1991—, Evanston Hosp., 1991—, Children's Meml. Hosp., 1992—, Shriner's Hosp. Chgo., 1994—; co-chmn. Gorden Rsch. Conf., 1995; spl. cons. Fed. Drug Adminstrn., 1994-95. Editl. bd. Archives of Surgery, 1992—, Plastic and Reconstructive Surgery, 1993—, Wound Repair and Regeneration, 1992—; contbr. articles to profl. jours., more than 125 publs., book chpts.; book reviewer. Harvard Nat. scholar, 1969-73; Rhodes scholar candidate, Harvard Coll., 1973. Fellow Am. Coll. Surgeons (surg. biology club III); mem. AMA, Am. Soc. Plastic and Reconstructive Surgery (rsch. fund proposal com. 1987-92, sci. program com. 1993-95, co-chmn. gen. reconstruction subcom. 1995, plastic surgery device com. 1989-93, resource book for plastic surgery residents com. 1991-93, chmn. resource book com., socioecon., 1992-94, chmn. device and technique assessment com. 1994, domestic clin. symposia com. 1992-95, ednl. tech. com. 1994—, adv. implant group 1994-96, task force for outcomes and guidelines 1995-96, ultrasonic lipectomy task force 1995-96), Am. Assn. Plastic Surgery (rsch. and edn. com. 1994-96), Midwest Assn. Plastic Surgeons, Plastic Surgery Rsch. Coun. (com. indsl. rels. 1992, judge Snyder and Crikelair awards 1991, rep. Coun. Acad. Surgeons 1991-94, program com. 1992-94, 95), Soc. Head and Neck Surgeons (membership com. 1993-95), Soc. Univ. Surgeons, Assn. Acad. Chmn. Plastic Surgery (matching program and ctrl. application svc. com. 1994), Wound Healing Soc. (audit com. 1992, program com. 1990, 92, 94, 97, bd. dirs. 1993-96, fin. com. 1994-96), Chgo. Plastic Surg. Soc., Chgo. Surg. Soc., Double Boarded Soc. (pres. 1995—), Sigma Xi, Aesculapian Club. Avocations: reading, golf, gardening, sports. Home: 144 Greenwood St Evanston IL 60201-4712 Office: Northwestern U Med Sch 707 N Fairbanks Ct Ste 811 Chicago IL 60611-4807*

MUTAFOVA-YAMBOLIEVA, VIOLETA NIKOLOVA, pharmacologist; b. Svishtov, Bulgaria, Apr. 18, 1954; d. Nikola Anastassov Mutafov and Bogdanka Ivanova (Boteva) Mutafova; m. Ilia Angelov Yamboliev, Mar. 24, 1984; children: Irena, Kalina. MD, Med. Acad., Sofia, Bulgaria, 1978, splty. Pharmacology, 1985, PhD, 1987. Physician Dept. Internal Medicine Dist. Hosp., Svishtov, Bulgaria, 1979-82; rsch. asst. prof. pharmacology Med. Acad., Sofia, 1982-87, Bulgarian Acad. Scis., Sofia, 1987-93; Fogarty Internat. fellow Sch. Medicine Univ. Nev. Reno, 1993-95. Co-author: Trends in Pharmacology and Pharmacotherapy; contbr. articles to profl. jours. Mem. AAAS, Bulgarian Pharmacol. Soc. (exec. com., Best Young Pharmacologist award 1988), Soc. Bulgarian Physicians, N.Y. Acad. Scis. Avocations: skiing, theater, opera, books, playing bridge.

MUTH, ERIC PETER, ophthalmic optician; b. Munich, Germany, July 25, 1940; s. Erich Walter and Anna Lisa (Pentenrieder) M.; came to U.S., 1948, naturalized, 1955; BS, Charter Oak Coll., 1978; MBA, PhD in Mgmt., Columbia Pacific U., 1983; degree (hon.) Anoka-Hannipen Tech. Coll., 1995; m. Rachel Hubbard, Apr. 4, 1971; children: Eric Van, Karl George, Ellen Anna. Lic. optician, Conn. Pres. Park Lane Opticians, Inc., Milford, Conn., 1968—; cons. Nat. Acad. Ophthalmology Found. Mus., San Francisco, 1982-88, Nat. Mus. Hist., Smithsonian Inst., 1983-94, Gesell Inst. Human Devel., 1984, 89; mem. adv. com. South Cen. Community Coll., Seattle, 1984; mem. adv. bd. Internat. Scientific Inst., P.R., 1989, adv. bd. Middlesex C.C., 1989 (vice chmn.). Mem. editorial rev. bd. (U.S.A.) Dispensing Optician mag., 1984—; author: Management for Opticians, Butterworths Textbook, 1983; contbr. The Social History of Eyeglasses in Japan, 1991, die Brille, Leipzig, 1989, Thinking on the Edge, Agamennon, 1993; pub. over 200 papers in 6 langs.; contbg. editor Optical Mgmt., 1979-80, OpticScan Canada, 1981-82, Indian Optician, 1982, Prism Mag., Can., 1988; tech. editor Optical Index, 1980-82; reviewer optical books. Presdl. appointment U.S. Selective Svc. Sys., 1991-92; Scoutmaster Boy Scouts Am., 1960-62; bd. dirs. ARC, Conn. chpt., 1988; advisor Tri Hi-Y YMCA, 1964; chmn. Korea-Vietnam Meml. com., Milford, 1985-86; organizer WWII Monument Com. 1991; trustee Conn. Visual Health Ctr., 1982-84; mem. Soc. 3d U.S. INf. Div., 1987. Served with AUS, 1957-59, Conn. Army N.G., 1960-69. Recipient Eng. Nelson/Wingate prize, 1983, Service Above Self award Rotary, 1986, Optician of the Yr. Guild of Prescription Opticians Am., 1991. Fellow Nat. Acad. Opticianry (regional membership chmn., faculty speakers bur., citation 1988), Internat. Acad. Opticianry, Opticians Assn. Am. (historian citation 1993, diploma in refractometry 1995); mem. Conn. Opticians Assn. (pres. 1974, chmn. membership and ethics coms., Optician of Yr 1975), Conn. Guild Prescription Opticians (pres. 1980, Man of Yr 1981), Assn. Dispensing Opticians Eng., Nat. Commn. on Opticianry Accreditation (commr. 1989-93), Brit. Guild Dispensing Opticians, Ednl. Found. in Ophamalic Optics, Calif. Soc. Dispensing Opticians (hon.), Ariz. Soc. Dispensing Opticians (hon.), Am. Legion (citation 1986, life mem. Post 34), Milford C. of C. (chmn. law and safety com. 1975, Community Service award 1986), Internat. Platform Assn., Am. Bd. of Opticianry and Nat. Contact Lens Examiners (cert.), Am. Bd. of Opticianry Master of Ophthalmic Optics, Charter Oak Coll. Alumni Assn. (bd. dirs. 1987, alumni citation 1995). Recipient Senate Citation State of Conn., 1993, German-Am. Friendship award, Germany, 1995, State of Conn. Justice of the Peace, 1995, NRA Legion of Honor, 1996; sr. rsch. fellow Internat. Soc. for Philosophical Inquiry, 1991—, pers. cons., 1996. Lodges: Lions, Rotary. Avocations: skydiving, ballooning, motorcycling, Tae Kwan Do (presdl. sports award, 1973). Home: 25 Parkland Pl Milford CT 06460-7723 Office: Park Lane Opticians Inc 50 Broad St Milford CT 06460-3358

MUTH, JOHN FRANCIS, newspaper editor, columnist; b. N.Y.C., Sept. 18, 1918; s. Ernest and Mary (Bijot) M.; m. Helen Scanlan, Sept. 26, 1948. Student, Fordham Coll., evenings 1939-40. With King Features Syndicate, 1941—; now asso. editor; editor Nat. Press Photographer mag., 1963-67; syndicated columnist, science writer, 1967—. Served with the USAAF, 1942-45, ETO. Mem. Bellerose Civic Assn., VFW (John F. Prince post). Democrat. Roman Catholic. Club: Caterpillar. Home: 81-33 243rd St Bellerose NY 11426-1319 Office: 235 E 45th St New York NY 10017-3305

MUTH, JOHN FRASER, economics educator; b. Chgo., Sept. 27, 1930; s. Merlin Arthur and Margaret Fraser (Ferris) M. B.S.I.E., Washington U., St. Louis, 1952; M.S., Carnegie-Mellon U., 1954, Ph.D., 1962. Research fellow Carnegie-Mellon U., 1956-59, asst. prof. econs., 1959-62, assoc. prof., 1962-64; prof. Mich. State U., 1964-69, Ind. U., 1969-94; ret., 1994. Author: (with others) Planning Production, Inventories, and Work Force, 1960, (with G. K. Groff) Operations Management: Analysis for Decision, 1972; editor: (with G. L. Thompson) Industrial Scheduling, 1963, (with G. K. Groff) Operations Management: Selected Readings, 1969. Fellow Econometric Soc. Home: 21028 4th Ave Summerland Key FL 33042

MUTH, RICHARD FERRIS, economics educator; b. Chgo., May 14, 1927; s. Merlin Arthur and Margaret Ferris M.; m. Helene Louise Martin, Dec. 23, 1955; children: Lisa Helene, Laurianne Martin Love. Student, USCG Acad., 1945-47; A.B., Washington U., St. Louis, 1949, M.A., 1950; Ph.D., U. Chgo., 1958; M of Theol. Studies, Emory U., 1995. Lectr. polit. economy Johns Hopkins U., Balt., 1955-56; economist Resources for Future, Washington, 1956-58; assoc. prof. urban econs. U. Chgo., 1959-64; economist Inst. Def. Analyses, Arlington, Va., 1964-66, cons., 1966-69; prof. econs. Washington U., St. Louis, 1966-70, Stanford U., (Calif.), 1970-83; Callaway prof. econs. Emory U., Atlanta, 1983—, chmn. dept., 1983-90; vis. assoc. prof. econs. Vanderbilt U., 1958-59; vis. sr. fellow Urban Inst., Washington, 1976-77; vis. prof. Sch. Bus., U. Calif. Berkeley, 1991. Author: (with others) Regions, Resources and Economic Growth, 1960, Cities and Housing, 1969, Public Housing, 1974, Urban Economic Problems, 1975; (with Allen C. Goodman) The Economics of Housing Markets, 1989. Mem. Presdl. Task Force on Urban Renewal, 1969; mem. Presdl. Task Forces on Urban Affairs and on Housing, 1980-81, Presdl. Commn. on Housing, 1981-82. Served with USCG, 1951-52. Mem. Am. Econ. Assn., Am. Real Estate and Urban Econs. Assn., Regional Sci. Assn. (v.p. 1975-76), So. Econ. Assn. Libertarian. Methodist. Office: Emory U Dept Econs Atlanta GA 30322

MUTH, ROBERT JAMES, metal company executive, lawyer; b. Phila., May 13, 1933; s. James H. and Ruth M. (Will) M.; m. Shirley M. Carnes, Jan. 31, 1959; children: Christopher James, Jennifer Augusta. BA, Lafayette Coll., 1954; postgrad., Yale Div. Sch., 1954-55; LLB, Columbia U., 1960. Bar: D.C. 1961, N.Y. 1969. Atty. Covington & Burling, Washington, 1960-68; asst. gen. counsel Asarco, Inc., N.Y.C., 1969-71, asso. gen. counsel, 1971-77, v.p., 1977—; chmn. Lead Industries Assn., N.Y.C., 1986-89, 93-97; pres. Silver Inst., Washington, 1987-89; vice chmn. Nat. Legal Ctr. for Pub. Interest, Washington, 1986-90; bd. dirs. So. Peru Copper Corp. Mem. George Sch. Com., Newton, Pa., 1985-95; bd. dirs. No. Lights Inst., Missoula, Mont. Lt. inf. U.S. Army, 1955-57, Korea. Mem. ABA, Met. Club (Washington). Home: 1062 Washington Crossing Rd Newtown PA 18940-9999

MUTHUSWAMY, PETHAM PADAYATCHI, pulmonary medicine and critical care specialist; b. Salem, Tamil Nadu, India, June 12, 1945; came to U.S., 1970; s. Petham Padayatchi and Anjalam M.; m. Rajeswari Muthuswamy, Nov. 11, 1975; children: Sudha, Sathya, Senthil. MB, BS, Stanley Med. Sch., Madras, India, 1969. Diplomate Am. Bd. Internal Medicine, Am. Bd. Pulmonary Disease, Am. Bd. Critical Care Medicine, Can. Bd. Respiratory Medicine. Attending physician Cook County Hosp., Chgo., 1976-79; dir. respiratory therapy Hyde Park Hosp., Chgo., 1977-80; co-dir. ICU Jackson Park Hosp., Chgo., 1978-80; chmn. pulmonary medicine Cook County Hosp., Chgo., 1980—, program dir. pulmonary medicine/critical care, 1980—; assoc. prof. medicine U. Ill. Coll. Medicine, Chgo., 1989-94; dir. cardiopulmonary dept. Jackson Park Hosp., 1994—; consulting physician Mercy Hosp., Chgo., 1978—, Trinity Hosp., 1978—, Jackson Park Hosp., 1978—, Drs. Hosp. of Hyde Park, 1978—. Contbr. numerous articles to profl. jours. Life mem. Tamil Nadu Found., Balt., 1980—; mem. fin. com. Indo Am. Dem. Orgn., Chgo., 1984-86. Recipient Recognition award Statue of Liberty Ellis Island Centennial Commn., N.Y., 1986. Fellow ACP, Am. Coll. Chest Physicians, Royal Coll. Physicians and Surgeons of Can.; mem. AMA (Physician Recognition award 1980—), AAAS, Am. Sleep Disorders Assn., Am. Thoracic Soc., Soc. Critical Care Medicine, Am. Coll. Physician Execs., Am. Assn. Bronchology, European Respiratory Soc., Assn. Am. Physicians of Indian Origin, India Med. Assn. of Ill. (life), World Assn. Bronchology, The World Assn. Sarcoidosis and Other Granulomatous Disorders, Internat. Union Against Tuberculosis and Lung Disease, Chgo. Coun. Fgn. Rels., Nat. Assn. for Med. Direction of Respiratory Care, N.Y. Acad. Scis., Assn. Pulmonary and Critical Care Medicine Program Dirs. Avocations: jogging, tennis, swimming, computers, photo videos. Office: Cook County Hosp Div Pulmonary Medicine 1835 W Harrison St Chicago IL 60612-3701

MUTO, SUSAN ANNETTE, religion educator, academic administrator; b. Pitts., Dec. 11, 1942; d. Frank and Helen (Scardamalia) M. BA in Journalism and English, Duquesne U., 1964; MA, U. Pitts., 1967, PhD in English Lit., 1970. Asst. dir. Inst. of Formative Spirituality, Duquesne U., Pitts., 1965-80, dir., 1980-88, faculty coordinator grad. programs in foundational formation, 1979-88, prof., 1981—; guest lectr. formative reading various colls. and community orgns., 1970—. Author: (with Adrian van Kaam) The Emergent Self, 1968, (with Adrian van Kaam) The Participant Self, 1969, Approaching the Sacred: An Introduction to Spiritual Reading, 1973, Steps Along the Way, 1975, A Practical Guide to Spiritual Reading, 1976, The Journey Homeward: On the Road of Spiritual Reading, 1977, Tell Me Who I Am, 1977, Celebrating the Single Life, 1982, Blessings That Make Us Be, 1982, Pathways of Spiritual Living, 1984, 89, Mediation in Motion, 1986, (with Adrian van Kaam and Richard Byrne) Songs for Every Season, 1989, (with van Kaam) Commitment: Key to Christian Maturity, 1989, Commitment: Key to Christian Maturity, A Workbook and Guide, 1990, John of the Cross for Today: The Ascent, 1990, Womanspirit, 1991, (with Adrian van Kaam) The Power of Appreciation: A New Approach to Personal and Relational Healing, 1992, John of the Cross for Today: The Dark Night, 1994, Stess and the Search for Happiness: A New Challenge for Christian Spirituality, 1993, Harnessing Stress: A Spiritual Quest, 1993, Healthy and Holy Under Stress: A Royal Road to Wise Living, 1994, Divine Guidance: A Basic Directory to the God-Guided Life for All Believers, 1994, A Practical Guide to Spiritual Reading, 1994, Late Have I Loved Thee: The Recovery of Intimacy, 1995, The Commandments: Ten Ways to a Happy Life and a Healthy Soul, 1996, Words of Wisdom for our World: The Precautions and Counsels of St. John of the Cross, 1996; contbr. articles to religious and secular publs. Mem. Edith Stein Guild, Epiphany Assn. (exec. dir. 1988—), Phi Kappa Phi. Home: 2223 Wenzell Ave Pittsburgh PA 15216-3159 Office: Epiphany Assn 948 Tropical Ave Pittsburgh PA 15216-3032

MUTOMBO, DIKEMBE (DIKEMBE MUTOMBO MPOLONDO MUKAMBA JEAN JACQUE WAMUTOMBO), professional basketball player; b. Kinshasa, Zaire, June 25, 1966. Student, Georgetown U. Ctr. Denver Nuggets, 1991-96, Atlanta Hawks, 1996—. NBA All-Star, 1992; NBA All-Rookie Team, 1992; NBA Defensive Player of Year, 1995, 97. *

MUTSCHLER, HERBERT FREDERICK, retired librarian; b. Eureka, S.D., Nov. 28, 1919; s. Frederick and Helena (Oster) M.; m. Lucille I. Gross, Aug. 18, 1945; 1 dau., Linda M. B.A., Jamestown Coll., 1947; M.A., Western Res. U., 1949, M.S., 1952. Tchr. history high sch. Lemmon, S.D., 1947-48; asst. librarian Royal Oak (Mich.) Libr., 1952-55; head librarian Hamtramck (Mich.) Libr., 1955-56; head public svcs. Wayne County Libr. System, Wayne, Mich., 1956-59; asst. county librarian Wayne County Libr. System, 1960-62; dir. King County Libr. System, Seattle, 1963-89; library bldg. cons. Wayne County Libr., 1956-62, Wash. State Libr., 1966—; cons. Salt Lake County Libr., Pierce County Libr., North Olympic Libr.; lectr. U. Wash. Sch. Librarianship, 1970-71; bldg. cons. Hoquiam (Wash.) Libr., Olympic (Wash.) Regional Libr., Camas (Wash.) Pub. Libr., N. Cen. (Wash.) Regional Libr., Spokane (Wash.) County Libr., Enumclaw (Wash.) Libr., Puyallup (Wash.) Pub. Libr., Kennewick (Wash.) Pub. Libr., Lopez Island (Wash.) Libr. Contbr. articles profl. jours. Mem. Foss Home and Village Bd. Trustees, 1989—; bd. dirs. King County Libr. Sys. Found. With AUS, 1941-45; to capt. 1950-52. Decorated Silver Star, Bronze Star with cluster, Purple Heart, Presdl. Unit Citation. Mem. ALA (councilor at large 1965-69, chpt. councilor 1971-75, pres. library adminstrv. div. 1974-75), Pacific N.W. Library Assn., Wash. Library Assn. (exec. bd. 1964-65, 69-71, pres. 1967-69). Republican. Lutheran. Club: City, Municipal League. Lodge: Kiwanis. Home: 5300 128th Ave SE Bellevue WA 98006-2952

MUTTI, ALBERT FREDERICK, minister; b. Hopkins, Mo., Feb. 13, 1938; s. Albert Frederick and Phyllis Margaret (Turner) M.; m. Etta Mae McClurg, June 7, 1959; children: Timothy Allen, John Frederick, Martin Kent. AB, Cen. Meth. Coll., 1960; MDiv., Garrett Theol. Sem., 1963; DMin., St. Paul Sch. Theology, 1975; DD, Baker U., 1993. Sr. pastor Union Star Charge, Mo., 1963-65, Crossroads Parish, Savannah, Mo., 1965-74; assoc. coun. dir. Mo. West Conf. UMC, Kansas City, 1974-80, coun. dir., 1980-82; sr. pastor First United Meth. Ch., Blue Springs, Mo., 1982-87; dist. supt. Cen. Dist. UMC, Mo., 1987-89; dist. supr. Kansas City N. Dist., 1989-92; bishop Kans. Area United Meth. Ch., Topeka, 1992—. Chair Savannah Cmty. Betterment, 1971; bd. mem. St. Mary's Hosp., Blue Springs, 1986; dir. ARC, Savannah, 1968; bd. Discipleship, Nashville, bd. Global Ministries, N.Y.; pres. Mo. Coun. Chs., Jefferson City, Dean Mo. Area Ministers Sch., Ctrl. Meth. Coll.; trustee St. Paul Sch. Theology; organizer Rural, Religion and labor Coun. Kans. Named Disting. Alumni Ctrl. Meth. Coll.; recipient Grad. award St. Paul Sch. Theology. Home: 6841 SW Dunstan Ct Topeka KS 66610-1406 Office: 4201 SW 15th St Topeka KS 66604-2412

MUTZ, OSCAR ULYSSES, manufacturing and distribution executive; b. Edinburg, Ind., Feb. 12, 1928; s. Harold Winterberg and Laura Belle (Sawin) M.; m. Jean Greiling, Aug. 22, 1948; children: Marcia, H. William. B.S., Ind. U., 1949. Vice pres. Peerless Corp., Indpls., 1954-63; v.p., gen. mgr. Space Conditioning, Inc., Harrisonburg, Va., 1964-66; v.p., treas. Cosco, Inc., Columbus, Ind., 1966-67; exec. v.p., 1967-69, pres., 1969-71; chmn. bd. Court Manor Corp., Columbus, 1971-73; pres. Jenn Air Corp., Indpls., 1973-75; pres., CEO Mutz Corp., 1975-81; pres. Forum Group, Inc. (merger Mutz Corp. and Excepticon, Inc.), Indpls., 1981-91; chmn., chief exec. officer Capital Industries, Inc., Indpls., 1991-96, also bd. dirs.; chmn. Lakeland Auto Mall, 1996—; bd. dirs. Ct. Manor Corp., Sargent & Greenleaf; pres. Sovereign Group, Inc., 1991—, also bd. dirs. Nat. trustee Fellowship Christian Athletes, 1985-91, chmn. nat. conf. ctr., 1994-96; mem. pres. coun. and dean's adv. coun. Ind. U. Mem. Ind. Mfrs. Assn. (chmn. 1980), Acad. Alumnae Fellows Ind. U. Sch. Bus. Republican. Baptist. Office: Lakeland Auto Mall 625 Admiralty Parade Naples FL 34102-7802

MUTZ, STEVEN HERBERT, lawyer; b. Rockville Centre, N.Y., July 9, 1958; s. Herbert Edward and Theresa A. (McGowan) M.; m. Bernadette Jane Shaw, Aug. 8, 1987. BA in Econs., St. John's U., 1979, JD summa cum laude, 1982. Bar: N.Y. 1983, U.S. Dist. Ct. (ea. and so. dists.) N.Y. 1983. Law intern to presiding justice N.Y. Supreme Ct., Mineola, 1982; assoc. Sandback & Birnbaum, Mineola, 1982-84, Salvatore R. Gerbasi, Mineola, 1984, Schiavetti, DeVito, Begos & Nicholson, N.Y.C., 1984—; mng. atty. Schiavetti, Geisler, Corgan, Soscia, DeVito, Gabriele & Nicholson, White Plains, N.Y., 1989—, ptnr., 1991—; counsel to Senator Dean G. Skelos, Rockville Centre, 1986. Mem. ABA, N.Y. State Bar Assn., Omicron Delta Epsilon. Avocations: swimming, tennis, travel. Office: Schiavetti Geisler et al 709 Westchester Ave Ste 205 White Plains NY 10604-3103

MUUSS, JOHN, public safety and emergency management director; b. Bklyn., Mar. 8, 1940; s. Leona (Schwanzer; divorced; children: John. Lance, Diana. Student, C.W. Post Coll., Suffolk (N.Y.) C.C., N.Y.C. (N.Y.) Police Acad. Lab. technician Royaltone Photo Finishers, N.Y.C., 1958-59; comml. photographer A. Studley Inc., N.Y.C., 1962-64; police officer N.Y.C. (N.Y.) Police Dept., 1966-70, detective, 1970-78; dir. pub. safety Town of Islip, N.Y., 1978—; dir. emergency mgmt. Town of Islip, 1981—; pvt. practice security cons. East Islip, N.Y., 1986—. Pres., mem. Lakeland Civic Assn., Ronkonkoma, N.Y., 1970-79, Connetquot Bd. Edn., Bohemia, N.Y., 1975-78; campaign chmn. various local and state polit. seats, Islip, 1970—; chmn., mem. MacArthur Airport Adv. Com., Ronkonkoma, 1975-78; vestry mem. St. Marks Episcopal Ch., Islip, 1982-89. With U.S. Army, 1959-62. Mem. Am. Soc. for Indsl. Security, Fire Island Law Enforcement Coun., Internat. Assn. Chiefs of Police, N.Y. State Assn. Chiefs Police, Kiwanis Club of the Islips (charter pres. 1986). Republican. Episcopalian. Avocation: golf. Office: Islip Twp Dept Pub Safety/Emergency 401 Main St Islip NY 11751-3533

MUUSS, ROLF EDUARD, retired psychologist, educator; b. Tating, Germany, Sept. 26, 1924; came to U.S., 1953, naturalized, 1992.; s. Rudolf A. and Else (Osterwald) M.; m. Gertrude Louise Kremser, Dec. 22, 1953; children: Michael John, Gretchen Elise. Diploma, Tchr. Coll., Flensburg, Germany, 1951; student, U. Hamburg, Germany, 1951, Ctrl. Mo. State Coll., 1951-52, Columbia Tchrs. Coll., 1952; MEd, Western Md. Coll., 1954; PhD, U. Ill., 1957. Tchr. pub. sch. Germany, 1945-46, 51, 52-53, substitute prin., 1952-53; tchr. trainee U.S. Office Edn., 1951-52; houseparent Child Study Ctr., Balt., 1953; grad. asst. U. Ill., 1954-57; rsch. assoc. prof. Iowa Child Welfare Rsch. Sta., State U. Iowa, 1957-59; rsch. cons., 1960, 61; mem. faculty Goucher Coll., 1959-95, prof. edn., 1964-95, chmn. dept., 1972-75, dir. spl. edn., 1977-92, Elizabeth C. Todd disting. prof., 1980-85, chmn. dept. sociology and anthropology, 1983-85, prof. emeritus, 1995—; rsch. assoc. edn. Johns Hopkins, 1962-63; part-time or summer tchr. U. B.C., 1962, Johns Hopkins U., 1962, 65, U. Del., 1965, Towson U., 1967, U. Ill., 1967; tchg. assoc. Sheppard and Enoch Pratt Hosp., 1969-80; guest lectr. Tchrs. Coll., Kiel, Fed. Republic Germany, 1977-78; hearing officer spl. edn. cases State of Md., 1980-96. Author: First-Aid for Classroom Discipline Problems, 1962, Theories of Adolescence, 1962, 5th edit., 1988, 6th edit., 1996, Grundlagen der Jugendpsychologie, 1982; also numerous articles; editor: Adolescent Behavior and Society: A Book of Readings, 1971, 4th edit., 1990. Served with German Air Force, 1942-45. Recipient award for disting. scholarship Goucher Coll., 1979; grantee Andrew W. Mellon Found., 1976-77. Fellow Am. Psychol. Soc., Am. Psychol. Assn., Md. Psychol. Assn. (pres. 1971-73); mem. Balt. Psychol. Assn. (chmn. membership com. 1966, v.p. 1970-71), Soc. Rsch. Child Devel., Soc. Rsch. on Adolescence, Kappa Delta Pi (v.p. Alpha chpt. 1956-57), Phi Delta Kappa. Home: 1540 Pickett Rd Lutherville Timonium MD 21093-5822

MUZYCZKA, KATHLEEN ANN, home economics educator; b. Meriden, Conn., Jan. 5, 1952; d. Henry Theodore and Bernice Mary (Jedziniak) Kulesza; mm. Thomas Albin Muzyczka, July 26, 1975. BA in Home Econs. Edn., St. Joseph Coll., West Hartford, Conn., 1973; MS in Early Childhood Edn., Ctrl. Conn. State U., 1979. Cert. profl. educator, Conn. Home econs. tchr. Dodd Middle Sch., Cheshire, Conn., 1973—; unified arts team leader Dodd Middle Sch., Cheshire, 1994—. Instr. St. Stanislaus Ch., Meriden, 1973-75, lecor, 1973-90, facilitator Renew, 1984-86; worker Cheshire Food Drive, 1986, 87; participant Adopt A Hwy, Cheshire Environ. Commn., 1990; tchr. Cheshire Celebrates the Creative Spirit, 1994, Quilts for Kids Dodd Middle Sch., Cheshire, 1993—, Am. Cancer Soc. Relay for Life, 1997. Mem. Nat. Edn. Assn., Conn. Edn. Assn., Edn. Assn. Cheshire, Am. Assn. Family Consumer Scis. Republican. Roman Catholic. Avocations: sewing, cooking, aerobics, flower arranging. Home: 163 Stephen Dr Meriden CT 06450-7315

MUZYKA, DONALD RICHARD, specialty metals executive, metallurgist; b. Northampton, Mass., Aug. 23, 1938; s. Stephen S. and Mary (Paul) M.; m. Eileen J. Hannigan, June 10, 1961; children: Steven Richard, James Paul, David Joseph. Supr. high temperature alloy research Carpenter Tech. Corp., Reading, Pa., 1966-73, mgr. alloy research and devel., 1973-76, mgr. high temperature alloys research, 1975-76, gen. mgr. research and devel. labs., 1976-77, gen. mgr. distbn., 1977-79, v.p. tech. div., 1979-82; dir. tech. Cabot Corp., Boston, 1982-85; gen. mgr. refractory metals Cabot Corp., Boyertown, Pa., 1985-87, gen. mgr. elec. and refractory metals, 1987-88; v.p., gen. mgr. Cabot Corp., Boyertown, 1988-89; v.p. rsch. and devel. Cabot Corp., 1989; pres. Spl. Metals Corp., New Hartford, N.Y., 1990-96; pres., CEO Spl. Metals Corp., New Hartford, 1996—; bd. dirs. Aviall, Inc., CSM Holdings, Inc. Contbr. articles to profl. jours.; patentee in field. Bd. dirs. Wilson Sch. Bd., West Lawn, Pa., 1960-63, Montessori Country Day Sch., Wyomissing, Pa., 1960-63. Recipient Engring. Alumni award U. Mass., 1984. Fellow Am. Soc. Metals (trustee 1982-84, Bradley Stoughton award 1981); mem. The Metall. Soc., Indsl. Research Inst., Am. Ceramic Soc., Am. Soc. Quality Control. Republican. Roman Catholic. Avocation: antique clock collector. Home: 6824 Reservoir Rd Clinton NY 13323-4816 Office: Spl Metals Corp Middle Settlement Rd New Hartford NY 13413

MUZYKA-MCGUIRE, AMY, marketing professional, nutrition consultant; b. Chgo., Sept. 24, 1953; d. Basil Bohdan and Amelia (Rand) Muzyka; m. Patrick J. McGuire, June 3, 1977; children: Jonathan, Elizabeth. BS, Iowa State U., 1975, postgrad., 1978—; registered dietitian, St. Louis U., 1980. Cert. dietitian. Home economist Nat. Livestock and Meat Bd., Chgo., 1975-77; dietary cons. various hosps. and nursing homes, Iowa, 1978-79; supr. foodsvc. Am. Egg Bd., Park Ridge, Ill., 1980-83; assoc. dir., mgr. foodsvc. Cole & Weber Advt., Seattle, 1984-85; prin., owner Food and Nutrition Comms., Federal Way, Wash., 1986—. Co-author: Turkey Foodservice Manual, 1987; editor: (newsletter) Home Economists in Business, 1975-77, Dietitians in Business and Industry, 1982-85; Food Net on Internet, 1995—;

contbr. articles to profl. jours. Active Federal Way Women's Network, 1986-87. Named Outstanding Dietitian of Yr. North Suburban Dietetic Assn., 1983. Mem. Am. Dietetic Assn., Internat. Foodsvc. Editorial Coun., Consulting Nutritionists, Vegetarian Nutrition, Home Economists in Bus. Avocations: gardening, travel, music, food and beverage tastings. Home: 5340 SW 315th St Federal Way WA 98023-2034

MUZYKANTOV, VLADIMIR RURICK, immunochemist, researcher; b. Moscow, Nov. 23, 1957; came to U.S., 1993; s. Rurick Vladimir and Olga Victor Muzykantov; m. Irina Vladimirovna Gorokhovskaia, Feb. 13, 1991. MD, First Med. Sch., Moscow, 1980; PhD, Nat. Cardiology Rsch. Ctr., Moscow, 1985. Lab. asst. Cardiology Rsch. Ctr., Moscow, 1980-84, jr. rsch. assoc., 1984-87, rsch. assoc., 1987-90, sr. rsch. assoc., 1990-92; sr. rsch. assoc. U. Pa., Phila., 1993—; mem. internat. adv. com. 2d Conf. on Eicosanoid, Berlin, 1991; mem. young scientist com. Inst. Exptl. Cardiology, Moscow, 1984-86, chmn., 1986-90. Contbr. articles to profl. jours. including Blood, Jour. Nuclear Medicine, Laboratory Investigations; author: Dances on the Flame, 1992. Named Internat. Young Investigator, 16th Gray Conf., Manchester, Eng., 1991, World Congress Angiology, Rome, 1989, Wood/Whelan award Internat. Biochemistry Union, 1992. Fellow Will Rogers Pulmonology Fellowship; mem. Russian Immunology Soc., Russian Biochemistry Soc., Inflammation Rsch. Assn., N.Y. Acad. Sci. Avocations: writing poetry and songs, audiocassettes. Office: Univ of Pa Med Ctr IFEM 1 John Morgan 36th St Philadelphia PA 19104

MYATT, CLIFFORD E., federal official; b. Boston, Sept. 3, 1929; s. George Myatt and Viola Ryan; m. Graciela de Courceuil, June 28, 1959. BA in Econs., Boston Coll., 1950; Advanced Degree in Acctg., Bentley Coll., 1952. CPA. With Ernst & Ernst, Boston, 1952-59; contr. Internat. Shoe Corp., 1960-62, Caribe Nitrogen Corp., 1962-68; audit mgr. Ernst & Ernst, San Juan, P.R., 1968-69, ptnr., 1969-89; office mng. ptnr. Ernst & Whinney, San Juan, P.R., 1974-89; adminstr. econ. devel. adminstr. Econ. Devel. Adminstrn., Hato Rey, P.R., 1993-94; chief devel. officer for global markets P.R. Dept. Econ. Devel. and Commerce, San Juan, 1995—; bd. dirs. GDB, San Juan, P.R., Ports Authority, San Juan; chmn. bd. dirs. PRIDCO, Hato Rey; vice chmn. bd. dirs., EDB, Hato Rey, 1993-94. Chmn., pres. United Way, P.R., 1972, 73. Mem. Fin. Analyst Club (pres. 1975), Jaycees Internat. (internat. pres. 1967), San Juan Exch. and Rotary (pres. 1969, 82).

MYCIELSKI, JAN, mathematician, educator; b. Wisniowa, Poland, Feb. 7, 1932; s. Jan and Helena (Bal) M.; m. Emilia Przezdziecka, Apr. 25, 1959. MS, U. Wroclaw, Poland, 1955, PhD, 1957. With Inst. Math., Polish Acad. Scis., Wroclaw, 1956-68; prof. math. U. Colo., Boulder, 1969—; vis. prof. Case Western Res. U., Cleve., 1967, U. Colo., 1967, Inst. des Hautes Etudes Scientifiques, Bures-sur-Yvette, 1978-79, dept. math. U. Hawaii, 1987; attache de recherche Centre National de la Recherche Scientifique, Paris, 1957-58; asst. prof. U. Calif., Berkeley, 1961-62, 70; long-term vis. staff mem. Los Alamos Nat. Lab., 1989-90. Author over 140 rsch. papers. Recipient Stefan Banach prize, 1965, Alfred Jurzykowski award, 1977, Waclaw Sierpinski medal, 1990. Mem. Am. Math. Soc., Polish Math. Soc., Assn. for Symbolic Logic. Office: U Colo Dept Math Boulder CO 80309-0395

MYCKANIUK, MARIA ANNA, elementary and special education educator; b. Denver, July 1, 1955; d. Mykola and Stafania (Iwachiw) M. BA, U. No. Colo., 1977; MEd, The Citadel, 1990. Cert. tchr., S.C., Fla. Tchr. kindergarten, 3rd grade St. Catherine's Sch., Denver, 1977-81; remedial tchr. St. Vincent's Home and Sch., Denver, 1978-80; tchr. kindergarten, coord. day camp La Petite Learning Ctr. and Little People's Landing Ctr., Littleton, Colo., 1982-83; tchr. exceptional children Randall-Moore Accelerated Sch., Denver, 1982-83; tchr. 1st grade Bonner Elem. Sch., Macedonia, S.C., 1983-84; tchr. 2nd grade Westview Elem. Sch. Berkeley County Sch. Dist., Goose Creek, S.C., 1984-90; tchr. primary edn. learning disabled Old Kings Elem. Sch. Flagler County Sch. Dist., Palm Coast, Fla., 1990—; mem. adv. com. spl. edn. dept. The Citadel, Charleston, S.C., 1989-90; ednl. cons. Child Find Study Team, 1990—. Active Nat. Wildlife Fedn., 1980—, Gibbs Art Mus., Charleston, 1987-90; tutor Adult Literacy Program, Charleston, 1988-90; co-coord. children's program Piccolo/Spoleto Festival, Charleston, 1989; bd. dirs. Palm Coast Taxpayers Assn., 1991—; active Spl. Olympics, Odessey of the Mind. Recipient Critical Need Tchr. award State of Fla., 1990-91. Mem. Coun. for Exceptional Children, Alpha Delta Kappa, Phi Delta Kappa. Avocations: professional clown and storyteller, theater, travel, music, foreign languages. Home: 8 Prince Michael Ln Palm Coast FL 32164-7154

MYDLAND, GORDON JAMES, judge; b. nr. Hetland, S.D., May 12, 1922; s. Jacob and Anna (Hetl) M.; m. Lorrie Grange, May 29, 1958; 1 child, Gabriel. BS, S.D. State U., 1947; JD, U. S.D., 1956. Bar: S.D. 1956. Pvt. practice law Brookings, S.D., 1956-69, Lake Preston, S.D., 1973; S.D. circuit judge, 1973-87; presiding judge (3d Jud. Circuit), 1975, 79-80; S.D. state's atty. Brookings County, 1959-62; mem. S.D. State Senate, 1963-68; atty. gen. S.D., 1968-72; ret., 1987; part-time instr. constl. and bus. law S.D. State U., 1956-65. Mem. S.D. Code Compilation Commn., 1964-68; mem. S.D. Planning and Adv. Commn. Crime and Juvenile Delinquency, 1970-72; adv. com. S.D. Alcohol Safety Action Project, 1971-72. Served with USNR, 1943-46. Mem. Am. Legion. Lutheran.

MYDLO, JACK HENRY, surgeon, researcher; b. Phila., June 12, 1956; s. Morris and Helen (Finkelstein) M.; m. Jolie Lynn Kanter, June 15, 1986; 1 child, Ariel. BA, SUNY, Buffalo, 1977; MD, SUNY, Bklyn., 1981. Diplomate Am. Bd. Urology. Intern in surgery Montefiore/Einstein, Bronx, 1981-82, resident in surgery, 1982-83, resident in urology, 1983-86; fellow in urology Meml. Sloan-Kettering, N.Y.C., 1986-89; asst. prof. urology SUNY Health Sci. Ctr., Bklyn., 1989—; head uro-oncology Kings County Hosp., Bklyn., 1989—; chief urology divsn. Woodhull Med. Ctr., Bklyn., 1994—; mem. operating room com. Kings County Hosp., Bklyn., 1990-93; mem. urology selection com. SUNY Health Sci. Ctr., Bklyn., 1990—, med. sch. interview com., 1994—, med. student mentor program, 1994—. Contbr. articles to profl. jours. Recipient 2nd prize for rsch. Valentine Competition, N.Y.C., 1985; Urology fellow F.C. Valentine Assn., 1986-88. Fellow ACS (1st prize for rsch. 1985), Internat. Coll. Surgeons; mem. Am. Assn. Cancer Rsch., Am. Urological Assn. (scholar 1986-88), Am. Assn. Clin. Urologists, Soc. Univ. Urologists. Avocations: photography, cycling, audiophile, drums. Office: SUNY Health Sci Ctr Box 79 450 Clarkson Ave Brooklyn NY 11203

MYER, WARREN HITESH, mortgage broker, internet advertising executive; b. New Delhi, India, Sept. 8, 1961; s. Hana N.S. and Veena Myer; m. Suki Myer, Aug. 15, 1991. MS, U. Del., 1986; MBA, U. Chgo., 1990. Instr. U. Del., Newark, 1984-86; mem. tech. staff Lachman Assoc., Naperville, Ill., 1986-88; sys. mgr. Pyramid Tech., San Jose, Calif., 1988-91; pres. Myers Equity Express, San Jose, Calif., 1991—, Myers Fin. Group, Inc., Colorado Springs, 1994—, Myers Internet Svcs., San Jose, Calif., 1995—. Inventor in field. Avocation: windsurfing. Home: 1421 Old Piedmont Rd San Jose CA 95132-2417 Office: Myers Equity Express 1590 Oakland Rd Ste B-207 San Jose CA 95131-2443

MYERBERG, MARCIA, investment banker; b. Boston, Mar. 25, 1945; d. George and Evelyn (Lewis) Katz; m. Jonathan Gene Myerberg, June 4, 1967 (div. Mar. 1994); 1 child, Gillian Michelle. BS, U. Wis., 1966. Corp. trust adminstr. Chase Manhattan Bank, N.Y.C., 1966-67; asst. cashier Glore Forgan, Wm. R. Staats, Phoenix, 1967-68; bond portfolio analyst Trust Co. of Ga., Atlanta, 1969-72; asst. v.p. 1st Union Nat. Bank, Charlotte, N.C., 1973-78; dir. cash mgmt. Carolina Power & Light Co., Raleigh, N.C., 1978-79; sr. v.p., treas. Fed Home Loan Mortgage Corp., Washington, 1979-85; dir. Salomon Bros. Inc., N.Y.C., 1985-89; sr. mng. dir. Bear, Stearns & Co. Inc., N.Y.C., 1989-93; mng. dir. Bear, Stearns Home Loans, London, 1989-93; chief exec. Myerberg & Co., L.P., N.Y.C., 1994—. Home: 201 E 87th St Apt 16R New York NY 10128-1101 Office: 780 3rd Ave New York NY 10017-2024

MYERHOLTZ, RALPH W., JR., retired chemical company executive, research chemist; b. Bucyrus, Ohio, July 29, 1926; s. Ralph W.E. and Vera (Kirkland) M.; m. Lois Ellen Congram, June 24, 1951; children: Carl Alan, Lynne Elaine Myerholtz Patterson. BS, Purdue U., 1950; PhD in Organic Chemistry, Northwestern U., 1954. Project chemist Standard Oil Co. (Ind.), Whiting, Ind., 1954-58; group leader Amoco Chem. Corp., Whiting, 1958-66, rsch. assoc., 1966-69; dir. polymer physics divsn. Amoco Chem. Corp., Naperville, Ill., 1969-86. Contbr. articles to profl. jours.; holder 7 patents. Trustee Greenfield (Ind.) Pub. Libr., 1995—; radio officer CD, Naperville, 1971-81; scoutmaster Boy Scouts Am., Hammond, Ind., 1955-59. Sgt. U.S. Army, 1944-46, PTO. Mem. Am. Chem. Soc., Sigma Xi, Pi Kappa Phi, Phi Lambda Upsilon. Avocations: photography, electronics, woodcarving, nature/environment. Home: 1125 Cricket Reel Greenfield IN 46140-2805

MYEROWITZ, P. DAVID, cardiologist, surgeon, educator; b. Balt., Jan. 18, 1947; s. Joseph Robert and Merry (Brown) M.; B.S., U. Md., 1966, M.D., 1970; M.S., U. Minn., 1977; m. Susan Karen Macks, June 18, 1967 (div.); children—Morris Brown, Elissa Suzanne, Ian Matthew. Intern in surgery U. Minn., Mpls., 1970-71, resident in surgery, 1971-72, 74-77; resident in cardiothoracic surgery U. Chgo., 1977-79; practice medicine, specializing in cardiovascular surgery, Madison, Wis., 1979—; asst. prof. thoracic and cardiovascular surgery U. Wis., Madison, 1979-85, assoc. prof., 1985, chief sect. cardiac transplantation, 1984-85, Karl P. Klassen prof., chief thoracic and cardiovascular surgeon Ohio State Univ. and Hosps., Columbus, 1985-96, Karl P. Klassen prof., 1985—. Served with USPHS, 1972-74. Mem. ACS, Am. Coll. Cardiology, Assn. for Acad. Surgery, Soc. Univ. Surgeons, Soc. Thoracic Surgeons, Am. Soc. Artificial Internal Organs, Am. Coll. Chest Physicians, Am. Heart Assn., Internat. Soc. Heart Transplantation, Internat. Soc. Cardiovascular Surgery, Am. Assn. Thoracic Surgeons. Jewish. Author: Heart Transplantation; contbr. articles to profl. jours. Office: Ohio State Univ Hosps Doan N # 825 Columbus OH 43210

MYERS, A. MAURICE, transportation executive; b. Long Beach, Calif., May 20, 1940; s. H. Priscilla (Larsen) M.; m. Elizabeth Jean Ashburn, July 16, 1960; children: Michele, Tracy, Leanne. BA, Calif. State U., Fullerton, 1964; MBA, Calif. State U., Long Beach, 1972. Fin. mgr. Ford Motor Co., Newport Beach, Calif., 1964-72; fin. cons. Merrill Lynch, Newport Beach, 1972-75; mktg. dir. Continental Airlines, L.A., 1975-82; v.p. ops. On TV, L.A., 1982-83; pres., CEO Aloha Airgroup, Honolulu, 1983-93, Am. West Airlines, Phoenix, 1993-95; chmn., pres., CEO, bd. dirs. Yellow Corp., Overland Park, Kans., 1996—; bd. dirs. Hawaiian Elec. Industries, Honolulu, Pleasant Holidays, West Lake Village, Calif. Bd. dirs. Greater Phoenix Econ. Coun., 1994-95; mem. Greater Phoenix Leadership, 1994-95. Mem. Am. Trucking Assn. (bd. dirs. 1996—), Waialea Country Club (Honolulu). Avocations: reading, golf, travel. Office: Yellow Corp 10990 Roe Ave Overland Park KS 66211-1213

MYERS, ALBERT G., JR., textile manufacturer; b. Charlotte, N.C., Feb. 15, 1917; s. Albert Gallatin and Elfreida (Nail) M.; m. Kittie Brownlee, Feb. 7, 1942; children—Albert Gallatin III, Barbara Brownlee Melvin. Student, Davidson Coll.; B.S., Erskine Coll., 1940; grad., Exec. Program U. N.C., 1959; LLD (hon.), Belmont Abby Coll., 1995. With Textiles-Inc. (name changed to Ti-Caro Inc., 1978), Gastonia, N.C., 1939-82; successively mfg. dept., asst. v.p., sec.-treas., v.p., treas. Textiles-Inc. (name changed to Ti-Caro Inc., 1978), 1939-61, pres., 1961-70, chmn. bd., 1971-82, also dir.; ret., 1982; with Threads-Inc. (now Threads USA), 1946-82, successively purchasing agt., sec., asst. treas., v.p. and sec., v.p. and treas., 1946-61, pres., 1961-70, chmn. bd., 1971-82, also dir.; ret., 1982; past chmn. bd. Carolina Motor Club. Past pres. Piedmont council Boy Scouts Am., regional chmn.; past mem. adv. bd. Red Shield Boys Club; past pres. Gaston County YMCA; past pres. N.C. Textile Found., Inc., 1967-69; past chmn. bd. First Gaston Found.; past treas., dir. Schiele Mus. Natural History; past trustee Gaston Coll.; trustee Brevard Coll.; past mem. bd. advisers Belmont Abbey Coll.; past chmn. bd. trustees Gaston Meml. Hosp.; trustee Crossnore (N.C.) Sch. Served with USAAF, 1942-46. Mem. Gastonia C. of C. (past pres.), Combed Yarn Spinners Assn. (past pres.), N.C. Textile Mfgrs. Assn. (past dir., 1st v.p. 1970-71), Am. Textile Mfrs. Inst. (dir. 1964-68), Am. Legion, Gaston Country Club, Grandfather Golf and Country Club (Linville, N.C.), Linville Golf Club, Key Largo (Fla.) Anglers Club. Methodist (ofcl. bd.).

MYERS, ALFRED FRANTZ, state education official; b. Crooked Creek State Park, Pa., Feb. 19, 1936; s. Jacob Alfred Jr. and Ida Gertrude (Schaeffer) M. BA, Lehigh U., 1958, MA, 1966; postgrad. George Peabody Coll., 1971-72. Instr., Grand River Acad., Austinburg, Ohio, 1966, Culver (Ind.) Mil. Acad., 1966-68, Kiskiminetas Springs Sch., Saltsburg, Pa., 1968-71; asst. prof. social studies Ind. State U., Terre Haute, 1972-73; div. trainer Ency. Britannica, Rochester, N.Y., 1973-75; mgr. Rupp's, Kittanning, Pa., 1976-77; criminal justice system planner Pa. Commn. on Crime and Delinquency, Harrisburg, 1977-80; rsch. assoc. Pa. Dept. Edn., Harrisburg, Pa., 1980-89, basic edn. assoc., 1989—. Social work Dominican Rep., 1958. 1st lt. USAF, 1958-63, 1st. lt., capt. USAFR, 1963-71. Mem. AAUP, ACLU, ASCD, Acad. Polit. Sci., Am. Acad. Polit. and Social Sci., Am. Ednl. Rsch. Assn., Am. Evaluation Assn., Am. Hist. Assn., Conf. Latin Americanist Geographers, Gay Lesbian and Straight Tchrs. Network, Lambda Legal Def. and Edn. Fund, Mid. States Coun. for Social Studies (pres. 1987-88), Nat. Braille Assn., Nat. Coun. Social Studies, Orgn. Am. Historians, Pa. Assn. Adult Continuing Edn., People for Am. Way, Phi Beta Kappa, Phi Delta Kappa. Home: 849 Melissa Ct Enola PA 17025-1551

MYERS, ALLEN RICHARD, rheumatologist; b. Balt., Jan. 14, 1935; s. Ellis Benjamin and Rosina (Blumberg) M.; m. Ellen Patz, Nov. 26, 1960; children: David Joseph, Robert Todd, Scott Patz. BA, U. Pa., 1956; MD, U. Md., 1960. Diplomate Am. Bd. Internal Medicine, Am. Bd. Rheumatology. Intern Univ. Hosp., Balt., 1960-61; resident in medicine Univ. Hosp., Ann Arbor, Mich., 1961-64; fellow in rheumatology Mass. Gen. Hosp. and Harvard Med. Sch., Boston, 1966-69; dir. clin. tng. rheumatology U. Pa. Sch. Medicine, Phila., 1969-72, chief rheumatology sect., 1972-78; dep. chair medicine Temple U. Sch. Medicine, Phila., 1978-84, acting chmn. medicine, 1984-86, dean, 1991-95, prof. medicine, 1978—, assoc. v.p. Health Scis. Ctr., 1988-95; vis. prof. Cardiothoracic Inst., U. London, 1988; mem. med. adv. bd. Scleroderma Rsch. Found., Santa Barbara, Calif., 1986. Mem. editl. bd. Arthritis & Rheumatism, 1985-90, Brit. Jour. Rheumatology, 1989-94; editor: Systemic Scleroderma, 1985, Medicine, 1986, 93, 96. Pres. Phila. Health Care Congress, 1994—; mem. adv. com. Pa. Lupus Found., 1976—. With USPHS, 1964-66. Recipient Margaret Whitaker prize U. Md. Sch. Medicine, 1960, Lindback Found. award Temple, 1981; named Physician of Yr. Temple U. Hosp., 1986. Fellow Phila. Coll. Physicians (councillor 1994—), ACP, Am. Coll. Rheumatology; mem. Phila. Rheumatism Soc., Am. Fedn. Clin. Rsch., N.Y. Acad. Scis., Brit. Soc. Rheumatology. Avocations: walking, classical music, reading. Office: Temple U Sch Medicine 3400 N Broad St Philadelphia PA 19140-5104

MYERS, ANN MARGARET, state agency supervisor; b. Meshoppen, Pa., Mar. 9, 1953; d. Jack William and Sara Elizabeth (Walsh) Morgan; m. Randy Cloyd Myers, Oct. 13, 1984 (div. Nov. 25, 1991). AS in Liberal Arts, Keystone Jr. Coll., LaPlume, Pa., 1993; BA cum laude in Sociology, Psychology, Wilkes U., Wilkes Barre, Pa., 1996. Asst. retail mgr. Rite Aid Corp., Tunkhannock, Pa., 1971-78; prodn. technician Procter & Gamble Corp., Mehoopany, Pa., 1978-85; restaurant mgr. Shaffer's Pink Apple, Tunkhannock, 1991-92; secretarial supr. Pa. Dept. Agr., Tunkhannock, 1992—; N.E. Pa. Tri-County rural devel. com. sec., Tunkhannock, 1992—. Mem. Wyoming County Dem. Women's Soc., 1995—, Wyoming County Emergency Mgmt., 1992-95. Mem. Am. Fedn. State, County, Mcpl. Employees Coun. 87 (sec. local 2370, congl. liaison 1995—), Wyoming County Hillary Rodham Clinton Fan Club (coord. 1995—). Roman Catholic. Avocations: writing, photography, reading, trivial pursuit.

MYERS, ANNE M., church administrator. Sec., pub. rels. adminstr. Ch. of the Brethren. Office: Church of Brethren 1451 Dundee Ave Elgin IL 60120-1674*

MYERS, ARTHUR B., journalist, author; b. Buffalo, Oct. 24, 1917; s. Edward A. and Isabelle (Baker) M.; m. Irma H. Ashley, 1972. BA, Hobart Coll., 1939. Journalist Rochester (N.Y.) Times Union, 1948-52, Washington Post, 1956-57, Berkshire (Mass.) Eagle, 1957-64; contbg. editor Coronet mag., 1965-68; columnist Bergen Record, Hackensack, N.J., 1969-71; exec. editor Berkshire Sampler, Pittsfield, Mass., 1971-77; tchr. writing Mass. U. extension program and Berkshire Community Coll., Pittsfield, 1958-62, Fairleigh Dickinson U., Teaneck, N.J., 1970, Cambridge (Mass.) Coll., 1989. Author: (with J. O'Connell) Safety Last: An Indictment of Auto Industry, 1966, Journalism Careers for the 70's, 1971, Analysis: The Short Story, 1975, Analysis: The Personal Profile Magazine Article, 1976, Kids Do Amazing Things, 1980, The Ghost Hunters, 1980, Sea Creatures Do Amazing Things, 1981; (with Irma Myers) Why You Feel Down and What You Can Do About It, 1982, The Ghostly Register, 1986, Ghosts of the Rich and Famous, 1988, The Ghostly Gazetteer, 1990, Ghost Hunter's Guide, 1993, The Cheyenne, 1992, The Pawnee, 1993, The First Movies, 1993, The First Baseball Game, 1993, The First Football Game, 1993, Drugs and Peer Pressure, 1995, Communicating with Animals, 1997; also short stories, articles. Mem. PEN, Nat. Writers Union, Mensa. Home: 60 Grove St Apt 6202 Wellesley MA 02181-7716

MYERS, BARTON, architect; b. Norfolk, Va., Nov. 6, 1934; s. Barton and Meeta Hamilton (Burrage) M.; m. Victoria George, Mar. 7, 1959; 1 child, Suzanne Lewis. BS, U.S. Naval Acad., 1956; MArch with honors, U. Pa., 1964. Commd. 2d lt. USAF, 1956, resigned, 1961; architect Louis I. Kahn, Phila., 1964-65, Bower, Fradley, Phila., 1967-68; architect, prin. A.J. Diamond & Barton Myers, Toronto, Ont., Can., 1968-75; architect, prin. Barton Myers Assocs., Toronto, 1975-96, Los Angeles, 1981—; disting. vis. prof. Ariz. State U., Tempe, 1986; sr. prof. UCLA, 1981—; Thomas Jefferson Prof. U. Va., Charlottesville, 1982; vis. prof., lectr., Harvard U., U. Pa., other univs. U.S. and Can., 1968—. Prin. works include Myers Residence, Toronto (Ont. Assn. Architects Toronto Chpt. Annual Design award, 1971, Can. Housing Design Coun. award, 1971), Wolf Residence, Toronto (Archtl. Record: Record Houses of 1977, Twenty-five Yrs. of Record Houses, 1981), Housing Union Bldg., Edmonton (Can. Housing Design Coun. award, 1974, Design in Steel award, 1975), Citadel Theatre, Edmonton (City of Edmonton Design award, 1978, Stelco Design award, 1978), Seagram Mus., Waterloo, Ont. (Gov. Gen.'s Medal for Architecture, 1986), Howard Hughes Ctr. Master Plan and Wang Tower, L.A., 1986, Phoenix Mcpl. Govt. Ctr. (Winning Competition Entry, 1985), Portland Ctr. for the Performing Arts, Portland (Progressive Architecture Design award, 1984, USITT Merit award, 1994), Art Gallery Ont. expansion (Winning Competition Entry, 1987), Film and Drama Facility York U., Toronto, 1987, Cerritos (Calif.) Ctr. Performing Arts, 1987 (USITT Honor Award, 1994), N.J. Performing Arts Ctr., Newark, 1991, Ivan Reitman Prodn. Studio, 1994, Scripps Ocean Atmosphere Rsch. Facility, 1995; others. Recipient Gov. Gen.'s award for Architecture Woodsworth Coll., 1992, RAIC Gold Medal, 1994, Royal Archtl. Inst. Canada. Fellow AIA, Royal Archtl. Inst. Can.; mem. Soc. Archtl. Historians, Royal Can. Acad. Art, Tau Sigma Delta. Avocations: travel, reading. Office: Barton Myers Assocs Inc 9348 Civic Center Dr Ste 450 Beverly Hills CA 90210-3615

MYERS, CHARLOTTE WILL, biology educator; b. Harbor Beach, Mich., Jan. 5, 1930; d. Louis John and Ruth (Sageman) Wills; m. John Jay Myers, Dec. 27, 1958; children: Sandra, Andrew, Susan Ruth. BA in Biology, U. Mich., 1951, MS in Edn., 1952. Tchr. biology Birmingham (Mich.) Pub. Schs., 1952-59; tchr. art pvt. practice, Birmingham, 1962-78, Santa Fe, 1979—; instr. Oakland U., Pontiac, Mich., 1975-77; demonstrator, coord. Internat. Porcelain Art Teaching, Birmingham and Santa Fe, 1972—. V.p. PTA, Birmingham, 1957; founder Future Tchrs., Birmingham, 1956; area chmn. Muscular Dystrophy, Birmingham, 1963-64; leader Girl Scouts Am., Birmingham, 1969-71. Mem. N.Mex. State Fedn. Porcelain Artists (sec. 1986—), Mich. China Painting Tchrs. Orgn. (pres. 1973-77), Rocky Mountain Outdoor Writers & Photographers (bd. dirs. 1995—), Internat. Porcelain Arts Tchrs., Artists Equity (treas. 1981-83), Porcelain Arts Club (pres. 1979-81, treas. 1987-89). Democrat. Presbyterian. Avocations: gardening, needlework, travel. Home and Office: 9 Cibola Cir Santa Fe NM 87505

MYERS, CHRIS, network host; b. Mar. 28, 1959. Student, Fla. Internat. U., Miami Dade C.C. Host sports talk show Sta. WKAT-Radio; sportscaster Sta. WCIX-TV and WIOD-Radio, Miami, 1978-80, Sta. WTVJ-TV, Miami, 1980-82; weekend sports anchor, feature reporter Sta. WWL-TV, New Orleans, 1982-88; West Coast corr. ESPN, 1988-90, anchor/reporter SportsCenter, 1990—, host Baseball Tonight, 1992—, host Edge NFL Match-Up, 1994—, host Up Close, 1995—, reporter ESPN Sports Radio and ESPNET (online svcs.). Stories covered for ESPN include the Pete Rose baseball trial, the death of Loyola Marymount forward Hank Gathers, the San Francisco 49ers back-to-back Super Bowl wins, the Detroit Pistons two consecutive world championships, the World Series, including the 1989 San Francisco earthquake, the Major League Baseball All-Star Game, the racial strife surrounding the PGA Championship in Shoal Creek, Ala., 1990, Major League Baseball spring tng. and winter meetings, 1990—, and the NFL draft, 1990—. Recipient Features award Sports Emmy, 1990. Office: care ESPN ESPN Pla Bristol CT 06010

MYERS, CLARK EVERETT, retired business administration educator; b. Rossville, Kans., Oct. 19, 1915; s. Thad James and Rose I (Page) M.; m. Cora Henley Hepworth, May 7, 1942; children—Clark Everett, Richard G. Hepworth. B.S., U. Kans., 1939, M.B.A., 1946; D.C.S., Harvard, 1956. Tchr. Auburn (Kans.) Sch., 1932-34, prin., 1934-36; instr. U. Kans., 1939-41; asst. prof. U. Tex., 1947-49, asso. prof., 1949-53, chmn. dept. mgmt., 1950-53; lectr. Harvard Grad. Sch. Bus. Adminstrn., 1953-54; dean Coll. of Commerce, prof. bus. adminstrn. Ohio U., 1954-57; dir. mgmt. devel. inst. Lausanne, Switzerland, 1957-60; lectr. Harvard Grad. Sch. Bus., 1960-61; dean Sch. Bus. Adminstrn., prof. mgmt. U. Miami, Coral Gables, Fla., 1961-68; dean Grad. Sch. Bus. Adminstrn., Emory U., Atlanta, 1968-75; prof. bus. adminstrn. Grad. Sch. Bus. Adminstrn., Emory U., 1975-85, prof. emeritus, 1985—. Editor: (with William R. Spriegel) The Writings of the Gilbreths, 1953. Served as lt. USNR, 1942-45. Fellow Acad. Mgmt.; mem. Am. Assn. Collegiate Schs. Bus. (exec. com. 1965-68, 1969-70, pres. 1970-71), Phi Kappa Phi, Sigma Iota Epsilon, Delta Sigma Pi, Beta Gamma Sigma, Phi Gamma Delta, Beta Alpha Psi. Home: 1082 Vistavia Cir Decatur GA 30033-3413

MYERS, CLAY, retired investment management company executive; b. Portland, Oreg., May 27, 1927; s. Henry Clay and Helen (Mackey) M.; m. Elizabeth Lex Arndt, Oct. 1, 1955; children: Richard Clay (dec.), Carolyn Elizabeth, David Hobson. B.S., U. Oreg., 1949; postgrad., Northwestern Coll. Law, 1950-52; LHD (hon.), Ch. Div. Sch. of the Pacific, 1992. With 1st. Nat. Bank, Portland, 1949-53; with Conn. Gen. Life Ins. Co., Hartford and Portland, 1953-62; state mgr. Conn. Gen. Life Ins. Co., 1960-62; v.p. Ins. Co. Oreg., Portland, 1962-65; asst. sec. state State of Oreg., Salem, 1965-67; sec. state State of Oreg., 1967-77, state treas., 1977-84; v.p. J.P. Morgan Investment Mgmt. Co., N.Y.C., 1984-89, Capital Cons. Inc., Portland, Oreg., 1989-92; chmn. Oreg. House Adv. Com. Legis. Reapportionment, 1961; chmn. Oreg. Gov.'s Commn. on Youth, 1969-74. Author: (with others) Population Reapportionment Initiative Constitutional Amendment, 1952. Bd. dirs., treas. Ch. Divinity Sch. of Pacific, 1977-83; trustee Pacific U., 1989-92; vestryman Trinity Parish, Wall St., 1986-93; pres. Nat. Interfrat. Conf., 1986-87; mem. social responsibility in investing com. Nat. Episcopal Ch., 1983-87; trustee Ch. Pension Fund; bd. dirs. Ch. Life Ins. Co. Mem. Nat. Assn. State Treas. (past pres.), Multnomah Athletic Club (Portland), DeMolay Club (Legion of Honor), Lambda Chi Alpha (nat. pres. 1974-78), Sigma Nu Phi. Republican. Episcopalian. Home: 10456 NW 2d St Portland OR 97231-1072

MYERS, DANIEL LEE, manufacturing engineer; b. South Bend, Ind., Nov. 15, 1961; s. Harold Lee and Gerda Martha (Schulz) M.; m. Vanessa Rea Burkhart, Aug. 27, 1986; children: Wayne Anthony, Amberli Rea, Jessica Elixis. BS in Indsl. Engring., Purdue U., 1984, MS in Indsl. Engring., 1997. Indsl. engr. Anderson-Bolling Mfg. Co., Goshen, Ind., 1985; mfg. engr. Johnson Controls Inc., Goshen, 1985-88, Siemens Energy and Automation Inc., Bellefontaine, Ohio, 1988-96; with Hill-Rom, Batesville, Ind., 1996—. Mem. NSPE, Inst. Indsl. Engrs., Ind. Soc. Profl. Engrs., Toastmasters. Republican. Home: 4221 N Hamburg Rd Oldenburg IN 47036 Office: Hill-Rom St Rte 46 E Batesville IN 47006-9265

MYERS, DANIEL N., lawyer, association executive; b. Independence, Kans., Sept. 17, 1942; s. James Kenneth and Evalyn Clair Petty (Feather) M.; m. Eileen Carruthers, Dec. 14, 1966; children: Yvette Christine, John Joseph. AA, Coffeyville Coll., 1961; BA, U. Okla., 1963; JD, Georgetown U., 1975. Bar: Va. 1976, U.S. Ct. Customs and Patent Appeals 1977, Ill. 1991. Asst. to pres. J.V. Hurson Assoc., Inc., Washington, 1968-74; mgr. fed. legis. affairs AICPA, Washington, 1974-77; dir. legis. svcs., assoc. counsel Nat. LP-Gas Assn., Arlington, Va., 1977-79; gen. counsel, v.p. govt. relations Nat. Propane Gas Assn., Arlington, Va., 1979-88; exec. v.p. Nat.

Propane Gas Assn., Lisle, Ill., 1989—. Contbr. articles on good samaritan laws and genealogy to various publs. Bd. dirs. Washington Area State Rels. Group, 1980-82, mem. energy task force White House Conf. on Small Bus., 1980; chmn. good samaritan coaliton hazardous materials Adv. Coun., Washington, 1982-88; mem. motor carrier adv. com. Fed. Hwy. Adminstrn., Washington, 1982-88. Sgt. U.S. Army, 1964-68. Mem. Am. Soc. Assn. Execs. (legal sect. coun. 1980—, chmn. legal sect. 1991-92, bd. dirs. 1991-92), Spl. Indsl. Radio Svc. Assn. (bd. dirs. 1979-88), Indsl. Telecomm. Assn. (bd. dirs. 1995—), Chgo. Soc. Assn. Execs., Nat. Vol. Firefighters Coun. Found. (bd. dirs. 1995—). Avocations: golf, genealogy, racquetball. Office: 1600 Eisenhower Ln Lisle IL 60532-2167

MYERS, DANIEL WILLIAM, II, lawyer; b. Camden, N.J., Mar. 21, 1931; s. Charles Rudolph II and Myrtle Henrietta (Kress) M.; m. Eileen Ethel Kohn, Nov. 22, 1959; children: Susan Leigh, Meredith Ann Myers Winner, Kathryn Kress. BS in Commerce, U. Va., 1952, LLB, 1957. Bar: Va. 1957, N.J. 1958, U.S. Dist. Ct. N.J. 1958, U.S. Supreme Ct. 1980. Assoc. Lewis & Hutchinson, Camden, 1958-60; ptnr. Myers, Matteo, Rabii, Norcross & Landgraf, predecessors, Camden, 1960—, Cherry Hill, N.J., 1960-89; ptnr. Montgomery, McCracken, Walker & Rhoads, 1989-94, of counsel, 1994—. 1st lt. U.S. Army, 1952-54. Mem. ABA, N.J. Bar Assn., Va. Bar Assn., Camden County Bar Assn., Am. Arbitration Assn., Exch. Club (pres. Cherry Hill chpt. 1969). Republican. Lutheran. Home: 325 Rhoads Ave Haddonfield NJ 08033-1468 Office: Montgomery McCracken Walker & Rhoads 457 Haddonfield Rd Ste 600 Cherry Hill NJ 08002

MYERS, DAVID N., construction executive; b. June 22, 1900; s. Robert H. and Annie May (Gosberg) M.; m. Inez Pink, Mar. 27, 1929; children: Hal, Dieter. MBA, Dyke Coll., 1922, LHD (hon.), 1981; LHD (hon.), Cleve. State U. Pres. Byerlyte Corp., Cleve., 1931-1965; chmn. bd. Consol. Coatings Corp., 1965-89, Hastings Pavement Co., N.Y.C., 1965—. Life trustee Mt. Sinai Hosp., 1946—; pres. emeritus Menorah Home for Aged; pres. Jewish comty. Fedn., 1964-69; mem. internat. adv. coun. World Jewish Congress, 1966—; chmn. exec. com. Asphalt Inst., 1953-55; hon. life trustee ARC; chmn. Ohio State Commn. on Aging, 1983-87; founder Hebrew U. in Jerusalem, Albert Einstein Coll. Medicine, N.Y.C., David N. Myers Coll. Recipient United Appeal Disting. Svc. award Eleanor Roosevelt Humanities award, Charles Eisenman award of Jewish Community Fedn., Philos. award ARC, Ollie A. Randall award Nat. Coun. on Aging, 1992; mem. Ohio Sr. Hall of Fame, 1985. Mem. ASTM, Mus. of Art (life), Mus. Natural History, Assn. Asphalt Technologists (life), Am. Ordnance Assn. (life), Oakwood Club, Masons (32 degree). Home: 16900 S Park Blvd Cleveland OH 44120-1643 Office: Investment Plz 1801 E 9th St Cleveland OH 44114-3103 *Retirement at 60 or 65 is folly. Older men are blessed with a perception which allows them, through a recollection of decisions in their past years, to judge things well, whether they be in business or in a profession; or in daily life.*

MYERS, DEBRA TAYLOR, elementary school educator, writer; b. Balt., Feb. 5, 1953; d. James Zachary and Gene Elizabeth (Blubaugh) Taylor; m. Kenneth Lee Myers Jr., June 18, 1977; children: Kenneth Andrew, Katherine Elizabeth. BS in Elem. Edn., Towson State U., 1975, MEd, 1983. Cert. tchr., Md. 5th grade tchr. N.W. Mid. Sch., Taneytown, Md., 1975-80; home and hosp. sch. tchr. Balt. County Schs., 1992-93; tchr. educator in elem. edn. dept. Towson (Md.) State U., 1993-94; 2d grade tchr. Balt. County Pub. Schs., 1994—; workshop leader, guest lectr. Harford (Md.) County Schs., Balt. County Schs., United Meth. Commn. on the Young Child, Balt. Editor Kid's View; contbr. articles to children's mags. and jours. Mem. Renew, A Randallstown Cmty. Group Assn., Balt., 1993—; bd. dirs. Child Devel. Ctr., Milford Mill United Meth. Ch., 1992—; coord. Jr. Fieldstone Garden Club. Recipient Outstanding Vol. award Balt. County PTA, 1992, 93, 94. Mem. Kappa Delta Pi. Avocations: travel, reading, writing for children, volunteering, spending time with family. Home: 3607 Blackstone Rd Randallstown MD 21133-4213 Office: Randallstown Elem Sch 9103 Liberty Rd Randallstown MD 21133-3521

MYERS, DEE DEE See MYERS, MARGARET JANE

MYERS, DENYS PETER, JR., architectural historian; b. Boston, Apr. 23, 1916; s. Denys Peter and Ethel May (Johnston) M.; m. Anne Buchonis, Aug. 24, 1940. S.B., Harvard U., 1940; grad. studies, Fogg Art Mus., 1949-50; M.A., Columbia U., 1948. Asst. reference dept. N.Y. Public Library, 1941-42, charge exbhns., 1942-43; instr. Hunter Coll., N.Y.C., 1947; dir. Art Inst., Zanesville, Ohio, 1947-55, Philbrook Art Center, Tulsa, 1955-58, Des Moines Art Center, 1958-59; asst. dir. Balt. Mus. Art, 1959-64; dir. No. Va. Fine Arts Assn., 1964-66; vis. lectr. Johns Hopkins U., 1962-64; historian Nat. Park Service, U.S. Dept. Interior, 1966-68; prin. archtl. historian Historic Am. Bldgs. Survey, Office of Archaeology and Historic Preservation, Washington, 1968-73; pvt. practice cons. archtl. historian Washington, 1973-78; cons. Faulkner, Fryer and Vanderpool (Architects), Washington, 1975-83; archtl. historian Historic Am. Bldgs. Survey, Nat. Park Service, Dept. Interior, Washington, 1978-85; lectr. Smithsonian Instn., 1974-78, 91, Cath. U. Am., 1966-67. Co-author: A Preservation Index for the Federal Hill Historic District, 1973, Nashville, A Short History and Selected Buildings, 1974, Maine Forms of American Architecture, 1976, Alexandria - A Towne in Transition 1800-1900, 1977, Historic America, 1983; author: Maine Catalog: The Historic Architecture of Maine, 1974, American Gas Lighting: A Guide for Historic Preservation, 1978; introduction to Minard Lafever's Beauties of Modern Architecture, (1835), 1968, Introduction to 1876 Mitchell, Vance & Co. catalog reprint; contbr. articles to MacMillan Ency. Arch., 1982, Dictionary of Art, American National Biography and profl. jours. Ordained perpetual deacon Episcopal Ch., 1954. Served with AUS, 1943-46. Mem. Am. Archtl. Found. (mem. adv. com.), Soc. Archtl. Historians (founding mem., dir. 1962-65, pres. Latrobe chpt. 1975-77), Alexandria Assn. (pres. 1968-69), Victorian Soc. in Am. (dir. 1970-72), Alexandria Library Co. (pres. 1982-83), Alexandria Hist. Soc., Steamship Hist. Soc., Preservation Round Table, Soc. for Preservation New Eng. Antiquities, Hist. Alexandria Found. Club: Cosmos (Washington). Home and Office: 201 N Columbus St Alexandria VA 22314-2411

MYERS, DONALD ALLEN, university dean; b. Nebraska City, Nebr., Dec. 17, 1932; s. Merle D. and Ruth Irene (Potter) M.; m. Dixie Lois Ashton, Aug. 10, 1957; 1 son, Eric; m. Lilian Rose Bautista, Apr. 18, 1966; children: Sherri, Johnny, David; m. Alice L. Twining, July 15. 1990; 1 child, Aaron. B.A., Mcpl. U. Omaha, 1956; M.A., U. Chgo., 1957, Ph.D., 1962. Asst. supt. Sch. Dist. Riverview Gardens, Mo., 1962-65; research assoc. NEA, Washington, 1965-66; curriculum and research specialist Inst. for Devel. of Ednl. Activities, Los Angeles, 1966-70; assoc. prof. SUNY, Albany, 1970-73; head dept. curriculum and instrn. Olka. State U., Stillwater, 1973-79; dean Coll. Edn., U. Nebr., Omaha, 1979-85; dean Sch. Edn. Old Dominion U., Norfolk, Va., 1985—. Author: Teacher Power, 1973, Open Education Reexamined, 1973; contbr. articles, chpts. to profl. jours., books. Washington intern in edn. Ford Found., 1965-66. Democrat. Home: 1272 Belvoir Ln Virginia Beach VA 23464-6746 Office: Coll Edn Old Dominion Univ Norfolk VA 23508-1506

MYERS, DOUGLAS GEORGE, zoological society administrator; b. L.A., Aug. 30, 1949; s. George Walter and Daydeen (Schroeder) M.; m. Barbara Firestone Myers, Nov. 30, 1980; children: Amy, Andrew. BA, Christopher Newport Coll., 1981. Tour and show supr. Annheuser-Busch (Bird Sanctuary), Van Nuys, Calif., 1970-74, mgr. zool. ops., 1974-75, asst. mgr. ops., 1975-77, mgr. ops., 1977-78; gen. services mgr. Annheuser-Busch (Old Country), Williamsburg, Va., 1978-80, park ops. dir., 1980-81; gen. mgr. wild animal park Zool. Soc. San Diego, 1981-83, dep. dir. ops., 1983-85, exec. dir., 1985—; cons. in field. Bd. dirs. San Diego Conv. and Visitors Bur.; mem. adv. com. of pres.' assn. Am. Mgmt. Assn. Fellow Am. Assn. Zool. Parks and Aquariums (profl.), Internat. Union Dirs. Zool. Gardens; mem. Internat. Assn. Amusement Parks and Attractions, Calif. Assn. Zoos and Aquariums, Mus. Trustee Assn. Lodge: Rotary. Office: San Diego Zoo PO Box 551 San Diego CA 92112-0551

MYERS, ELISSA MATULIS, publisher, association executive; b. Munich, Aug. 4, 1950; (parents Am. citizens); d. Raymond George and Anne Constance (Moley) Matulis; m. John Wake Myers, Sept. 13, 1967 (div. 1972); 1 child, Jennifer Anne Myers Bick. BA in English Lit., George Mason U., 1972, MA in English Lit., 1982. Dir. rsch. and info. Am. Soc. Assn. Execs., Washington, 1972-80, dir. mem. svcs., 1980-88, v.p., pub. Assn. Mgmt. mag., 1988—. Pub. Principles of Association Management, 1976, 3d edit., 1996; columnist Footnotes, 1988—. Bd. dirs. Ethics Resource Ctr., Washington, 1982-86. Mem. Am. Soc. Assn. Execs. (cert.), Assn. Conv. Mktg. Execs. (bd. dirs. 1994—), Nat. Coalition Black Mktg. Planners, Greater Washington Soc. Assn. Execs. Roman Catholic. Avocations: running, scuba diving. Home: 5315 Moultrie Rd Springfield VA 22151 Office: Am Soc Assn Execs 1575 I St NW Washington DC 20005-1105

MYERS, EUGENE EKANDER, art consultant; b. Grand Forks, N.D., May 5, 1914; s. John Q. and Hattye Jane (Ekander) M.; m. Florence Hutchinson Ritchie, Sept. 9, 1974. BS in Edn., U. N.D., 1936, MS in Edn., 1938; postgrad., U. Oreg., 1937; MA, Northwestern U., 1940, Columbia U., 1947; grad., Advanced Mgmt. Program, Harvard U., 1953; cert., Cambridge (Eng.) U., 1958; postgrad., U. Md., 1958-61, Oxford (Eng.) U., 1964; diploma, various mil. schs. Student asst. U. N.D., 1935-36, instr. summer sessions, 1936, 37, asst., 1936-37; prof., head dept. N.D. Tchrs. Coll., 1938-40; instr. Columbia U. Tchrs. Coll., 1940-41; vis. prof. U. Vt., summers, 1941, 42; commd. 1st lt. USAAF, 1942, advanced through grades to col., 1951; dir. personnel plans and tng. Hdqrs. Air Force Systems Command Washington, 1959-60; dir. personnel research and long-range plans Hdqrs. Air Force Systems Command, 1960-62; head dept. internat. relations Air War Coll., Air U. Maxwell AFB, Ala., 1962-63; dir. curriculum, dean (Air War Coll., Air U.), 1963-65; dir. res. affairs Hdqrs. Air Res. Personnel Center Denver, 1965-66; ret., 1966; dean Corcoran Sch. Art, Washington, 1966-70; founder Corcoran Sch. Art Abroad, Leeds, Eng., 1967; v.p. mgmt. Corcoran Gallery Art, Washington, 1970-72; vis. art dir. Washington, also Palm Beach, Fla.; art cons., 1972—; adv. Washington chpt. Nat. Soc. Arts and Letters.; bd. assos. Artists Equity. Author: (with Paul E. Barr) Creative Lettering, 1938, (with others) The Subject Fields in General Education, 1939, Applied Psychology, 1940; contbr. articles, reports to mags. and profl. publs. bd. dirs. Columbia (Md.) Inst. Art, World Arts Found., N.Y., Court Art Center, Montgomery, Ala. and Palm Beach, Fla., Order of Lafayette, Boston, English-Speaking Union, Palm Beach; mem. Hamilton St. Vol. Fire Dept. and Lit. Soc., Balt., Pundits, Palm Beach. Recipient Sioux award U. N.D., 1978. Mem. Internat. Communication Assn. (hon.), U. N.D. Alumni Assn. (pres. Washington chpt. 1959), Mil. Classics Soc., Titanic Soc., Mil. Order Carabao, Order of St. John of Jerusalem, Knightly Assn. St. George the Martyr, Co. Mil. Historians, Mil. Order World Wars, Ancient Order United Workmen, Saint Andrews Soc., Clan Donnachaidh (Perthshire, Scotland), Soc. Friends St. Andrews (Scotland) U., Delta Omicron Epsilon, Lambda Chi Alpha, Delta Phi Delta, Phi Delta Kappa, Phi Alpha Theta. Republican. Presbyterian. Clubs: Union (Manchester, Eng.) (hon.); Royal Scottish Automobile (Glasgow, Scotland); Royal Overseas (London); New (Edinburgh, Scotland) (assoc.); Army and Navy (Washington), Nat. Aviation (Washington), City Tavern (Washington), Harvard Business School (Washington); Army and Navy Country (Arlington, Va.); Metropolitan (N.Y.C.), Wings (N.Y.C.), Explorers (N.Y.C.) (fellow), Harvard (N.Y.C.); Minneapolis; Everglades (Palm Beach, Fla.), Beach (Palm Beach, Fla.), Sailfish of Fla. (Palm Beach, Fla.); Liitle (Gulf Stream, Fla.); Fairmont (W.Va.) Field Country, Lions. Home: 1 Royal Palm Way Palm Beach FL 33480 also: 3320 Volta Pl NW Washington DC 20007-2733 also: 721 Mount Vernon Ave Fairmont WV 26554-2522

MYERS, EUGENE NICHOLAS, otolaryngologist, otolaryngology educator; b. Phila., Nov. 27, 1933; s. David and Rosalind (Nicholas) M.; m. Barbara Labov, June 10, 1956; children: Marjorie Rose, Jeffrey N. BS in Econs., U. Pa., 1954; MD, Temple U., 1960. Diplomate Am. Bd. Otolaryngology. Intern Mt. Sinai Hosp., N.Y.C., 1960-61; resident Mass. Eye and Ear Infirmary, Boston, 1963-65; asst. prof. clin. otolaryngology U. Pa., 1968-72; prof. clin. oncology dept. oral pathology U. Pitts. Sch. Dental Medicine, Pitts., 1975-82, prof. dept. diagnostic services, 1982—; prof., chmn. dept. otolaryngology U. Pitts. Sch. Medicine, 1972—; chief dept. otolaryngology U. Pitts. Med. Ctr., 1972—; cons. VA Med. Ctr., Pitts., 1972—, Children's Hosp., Pitts., 1972—. Editor: Cancer of the Head and Neck, 1981, 2d edit., 1989, 3d edit., 1996, Tracheotomy, 1985; mem. editorial bd. Laryngoscope, 1973—, Jour. Head and Neck Surgery, 1978-92, AMA Archives of Otolaryngology, 1983-91, Annals of Otology Rhinology and Laryngology, 1984—, Oncology, 1986—, European Archives of Oto-Rhino-Laryngology, 1990—; editor-in-chief Advances in Orolaryngology, Yr. Book Med. Pubs., 1985—; co-editor Butterworth's Intern Med. Revs., Eng., 1981; internat. editor: Otolaryngology - Head and Neck Surgery, 1996—. Mem. adv. bd. Pa. Lion Hearing Research Found., Pitts., 1983—. Served to capt. M.C., U.S. Army, 1965-67. Recipient Cert of Merit Com. Research, Am. Acad. Otolaryngology-Salicylate Otoxicity, 1965; recipient Award of Merit Am. Acad. Otolaryngology-Head and Neck Surgery Inc., 1978, Robert E. Shoemaker Research award Pa. Acad. Ophthalmology and Otolaryngology, 1979. Fellow ACS (mem. bd. govs. 1981-87, mem. adv. coun. 1985-87), Am. Laryngol. Assn. (sec. 1982-88, pres. 1989-90, mem. coun. 1990-93, James Newcomb award 1993), Am. Acad. Otolaryngology (chmn. com. on head and neck surgery 1981-83, bd. dirs. 1985-88, 90—, pres. 1994-95, internat. coord. 1996—); mem. Am. Bd. Otolaryngology (bd. dirs 1981—, pres.-elect 1994-96, pres. 1996—), Assn. Acad. Depts. Otolaryngology (mem. coun. 1978-80), Nat. Cancer Inst. (chmn. upper aerodigestive tract working group 1986-89), am. Soc. Head and Neck Surgery (mem. coun. 1977-93, pres. 1988-90), Triological Soc. (mem. coun. 1989-92, v.p. E. sect. 1994-95), Pitts. Athletic Assn. Republican. Jewish. Office: U Pitts Sch Med Eye & Ear Inst Ste 500 200 Lothrop St Pittsburgh PA 15213-2546

MYERS, EVELYN STEPHENSON, editor, writer; b. N.Y.C.; d. William and Gertrude Maud (Pickett) Stephenson; m. Charles Bogart Myers, June 1, 1946 (dec. Nov. 1990); children—Cynthia Myers Marquardt, Meredith Myers Ballard. Student Simmons Coll., 1940-42; B.A., Barnard Coll., 1943-45; MA in Liberal Studies, Georgetown U., 1976; postgrad. New Sch. Soc. Research, 1945-49, George Washington U., 1977-78. Mng. editor Advance, N.Y.C., 1947-50; editor, Pres.'s Water Resources Policy Commn., Washington, 1950-51; editorial cons. Viet Nam Press, Saigon, 1958-60; chief joint info. service Am. Psychiat. Assn., Nat. Assn. Mental Health, Washington, 1961-63; writer, editor NIMH, Bethesda, Md., 1963-65; mng. editor Am. Jour. Psychiatry, Washington, 1965-87; editor, Eco-Facts, Washington, 1987-91; editorial cons. Am. Psychiat. Assn., Washington, 1993—. Author: (with others) Facing Facts: A Handbook for Reporters in Viet Nam, 1959, Health Insurance and Psychiatric Care: Utilization and Cost, 1972, Health Insurance and Psychiatric Care: Update and Appraisal, 1984, Ethics and Policy in Scientific Publication, 1990. NEH Summer Seminar fellow, 1981. Mem. Council Biology Editors (bd. dirs. 1981-84, editorial policy com. 1984-91), Soc. Scholarly Pub. (program com. 1983-84), LWV, Woman's Nat. Dem. Club, Barnard Club (Washington). Unitarian Universalist. Home: 15107 Interlachen Dr Apt 512 Silver Spring MD 20906-5630

MYERS, FRANCES, artist; b. Racine, Wis., Apr. 16, 1938; d. Stephen George and Bernadette Marie (Gales) M.; m. Warrington Colescott, Mar. 15, 1971. MFA, U. Wis., 1965. lectr. St. Martin's Sch. Art, London, 1967; disting. prof. printmaking Mills Coll., Oakland, Calif., 1979; vis. lectr. U. Calif., Berkeley, 1982; currently prof. art U. Wis., Madison. One-woman shows include Horwich Gallery, Chgo., 1977, 81, Haslem Gallery, Washington, 1981, 88, Madison Art Center, 1981, Carnegie Inst., Pitts., 1982, Wis. Acad. Arts, 1985, Perimeter Gallery, Chgo., 1986, 88, 91, 93, Natasha Nicholson Works of Art, 1989, Dittmar Gallery, Northwestern U., Evanston, Ill., 1989, Peltz Gallery, Milw., 1990, 91, 94; group shows include U.S. Pavilion, World's Fair, Osaka, Japan, 1970, Biennale of Prints Musée d'Art Moderne, Paris, 1970, Bklyn. Mus. 20th Biennale Exhbns. of Prints, 1976, 23d Biennale, 1982, 14th and 16th Internat. Biennial Graphic Arts, Ljubljana, Yugoslavia, 1981, 85, Am. Biennial Graphic Arts, Cali, Colombia, 1981, Brit. Internat. Print Biennale, Bradford, Eng., 1984, Bklyn. Mus. 25th Print Biennale, 1986, prints displayed in Am. Consulate, Leningrad, USSR, 1987, USIA, Yugoslavia, 1989-90, Pace Gallery, N.Y.C., 1990, Figurative Graphics, Amerikahaus, Cologne, Fed. Rep. Germany, 1991, Portland (Oreg.) Art Mus., 1992, Milw. Mus. Art, 1990, Nat. Mus. Am. Art, Washington, 1991, Duke U. Mus. Art, Durham, N.C., 1993, Internat. Biennial of Prints, Bhopal, India, 1995; represented in permanent collections Met. Mus. of Art, Victoria and Albert Mus., London, Chgo. Art Inst., Library of Congress, Phila. Mus. Art, Mus. Fine Arts, Boston. Nat. Endowment for the Arts fellow, 1974-75, 85-86, H.I. Romnes fellow U. Wis., 1991. Mem. Nat. Acad. Design, Am. Print Alliance, Nat. Womens Forum, Phila. Print Club. Home: 8788 County Road A Hollandale WI 53544-9423

MYERS, FRANKLIN, lawyer, oil service company executive; b. Pensacola, Fla., Nov. 2, 1952; s. T.F. Sr. and D. Bernice (Brewer) M.; m. Melinda Munson, Aug. 9, 1974; children: Amanda C., Adam F., Anne Marie M. BS, Miss. State U., 1974; JD, U. Miss., 1977. Bar: Miss. 1977, Tex. 1978. Ptnr. Fulbright and Jaworski, Houston, 1978-88; sr. v.p., gen. counsel Baker Hughes Inc., Houston, 1988-95; sr. v.p., gen. counsel, corp. sec. Cooper Cameron Corp., Houston, 1995—; adj. prof. U. Tex. Sch. Law, 1990—; bd. dirs. Convest Energy, Reunion Industries, Inc. Bd. dirs. U. St. Thomas, Houston. Fellow Houston Bar Found., Tex. Bar Assn., Miss. Bar Assn., Houston Bar Assn. Baptist. Office: Cooper Cameron Corp 515 Post Oak Blvd Ste 1200 Houston TX 77027-9409

MYERS, GEORGE CARLETON, sociology and demographics educator; b. Bklyn., Apr. 8, 1931; s. Francis Murdock and Ruth Emily (Hassinger) M.; m. Pauline Dorothy Kraebel, Apr. 24, 1954; children: George C., Marie E., Peter D., Kathleen A. BA, Yale U., 1953; postgrad., dipl., U. Stockholm, 1956; MA, U. Wash., Seattle, 1960; PhD, U. Wash., 1963. Instr. U. Wash., 1957-59, UCLA, 1960-62; asst. prof. Cornell U., Ithaca, N.Y., 1962-66; assoc. prof. Cornell U., 1966-68; sr. scientist WHO, Geneva, Switzerland, 1968-70; prof. sociology Duke U., Durham, N.C., 1968-96, prof. emeritus, 1996—; dir. Ctr. for Demographic Studies, 1972-96; mem. Nat. Com. on Vital and Health Stats., Washington, 1985-88; mem. com. on aging Nat. Acad. Sci., Washington, 1982-85; mem. Census Adv. Com., 1977-83, WHO Program on Aging, 1988—, NIH Nat. Adv. Com. on Aging, 1991-95; vis. lectr. UN China Nat. Demographic Tng. Ctr., Beijing, 1991; advisor ECE Population Act. Unit, 1992—; vis. prof. U. Geneva Med. Sch., 1994, Flinders U. Med. Sch., 1994. Editor: Jour. of Gerontology, 1986-89; contbr. articles to profl. jours. With U.S. Army, 1953-55. NIH grantee, 1969—; sr. vis. fellow Australian Nat. U., 1984; vis. scholar Can. Soc. Human Coun., 1982; sr. internat. fellow Fogarty Ctr., NIH, London, 1978-79. Fellow Gerontol. Soc. Am.; mem. Population Assn. Am. (bd. dirs. 1977-79), So. Demographic Assn. (pres. 1974-76), Triangle Area Population Soc. (pres. 1988-89), Duke Faculty Club (pres. 1972-74). Avocations: sailing, skiing, golf. Home: 12 Scott Pl Durham NC 27705-5719 Office: Duke U Ctr for Demographic Studies 2117 Campus Dr Box 90408 Durham NC 27708-0408

MYERS, GERALD E., humanities educator; b. Central City, Nebr., June 19, 1923; s. Harold W. and Mary (Ferguson) M.; m. Martha Coleman, Aug. 7, 1948; 1 son, Curt. B.A., Haverford Coll., 1947; M.A., Brown U., 1949, Ph.D., 1954. Instr. Smith Coll., 1950-52; asst. prof. Williams Coll., 1952-61; assoc. prof. Kenyon Coll., 1961-65; prof. C.W. Post Coll., L.I. U., 1965-67, Queens Coll. and Grad. Center, City U. N.Y., 1967—; also dep. exec. officer Ph.D. program Queens Coll. and Grad. Center, City U. N.Y. (Grad. Center); dir. intro. philosophy into N.Y.C. High Schs. project.; dir. humanities-and-dance projects Am. Dance Festival, Durham, N.C., 1979; project dir. African-Am. Perspectives in Am. Moslem Dance, Am. Dance Festival/NEH. Author: Self, Religion and Metaphysics, 1961, Self: An Introduction to Philosophical Psychology, 1969, The Spirit of American Philosophy, 1970, William James: His Life and Thoughts, 1986; editor: The Aesthetic and Cultural Signigicance of Modern Dance, 1984, The Black Tradition in American Modern Dance, 1988, African American Genius in Modern Dance, 1992; co-editor: Emotion Philos. Studies, 1983, Echoes from the Holocaust, 1988; contbr. articles to profl. jours. NEH fellow, 1981-82. Mem. Am. Philos. Assn. (past sec.-treas. Western div.), Metaphys. Soc. Am., Soc. Phenomenology and Existential Philosophy, Phi Beta Kapa. Home: 36 Gardner Ave New London CT 06320-4313 Office: 33 W 42nd St New York NY 10036-8003

MYERS, GLORIA J., elementary education educator; b. Atlantic, Iowa, Feb. 14, 1949; d. Louis E. Sr. and Jean M. (Horacek) M. BA in Elem. Edn., U. No. Iowa, 1971, MA in Spl. Edn., 1978. Cert. tchr., K-14 endorsements in behavioral disorders and mental disabilities, Iowa. Title I remedial reading tchr. Council Bluffs (Iowa) Pub. Schs., 1971-75; K-12 multicategorical resource tchr. Walnut (Iowa) Community Sch., 1975—. Mem. planning com. for annual transition fair for S.W. Iowa, Pottawattamie County, 1987—. Recipient Outstanding Achievement award Loess Hills Area Edn. Agy., 1989, Excellence in Edn. award, 1992, named Profl. Person of the Yr., 1997. Mem. NEA, Iowa Edn. Assn. (local chpt. pres., v.p., sec., treas.), Walnut Edn. Assn. (pres. local chpt., co-chmn.), Delta Kappa Gamma Soc. Internat. Home: PO Box 301 Walnut IA 51577-0301 Office: PO Box 528 Walnut IA 51577-0528

MYERS, HAROLD MATHEWS, academic administrator; b. Doylestown, Pa., Apr. 13, 1915; s. Carl and Alice W. Myers; m. Margaret F. Smith, July 19, 1946 (dec. Sept. 1963); children: Donald Smith, Dean Chappell, Deborah Kay; m. L. Marjorie Bellau, Nov. 28, 1964. BS in Commerce, Drexel Inst. Tech., 1938, DSc in Commerce (hon.), 1983; postgrad., Temple U., 1940-41, U. Omaha, summer 1957. Instr. coop. edn., dir. grad. placement Drexel U., Phila., 1938-46, asst. dean men, dir. student bldgs., adj. instr. labor econs., 1946-52, dean of men, 1952-55, treas., 1955-57, v.p., treas., 1957-80, sr. v.p., 1980-82, sr. v.p. emeritus, 1982-87, interim pres., 1987-88, pres. emeritus, 1988—, life trustee, 1986—; regional dir. First Pa. Banking and Trust Co., 1959-76; dir. Sadtler Rsch. Labs., Inc., 1963-69, Almo Indsl. Elecs., Inc., 1966-68; dir., treas. Uni-Coll Corp., 1974-81; bd. dirs. Beulah Cemetary Assn., asst. treas., 1984-89, treas., 1989-90, v.p and treas., 1990—; bd. dirs., mem. exec. com. Univ. City Sci. Ctr., 1974-90, dir. emeritus, 1991—, chmn. fin. com., 1976-88, vice chmn., 1988-90. Contbr. articles to profl. jours. Bd. dirs. Internat. House of Phila. Inc., 1954-81, exec. com., 1972-81; active Phila. coun. Boy Scouts Am., 1953—, hon. chmn., 1985-97, pres., 1982, 83; mem. citizens fire prevention com. Phila. Fire Dept., 1970-86; bd. dirs. United Fund Greater Phila., 1983-87, Luth. Ch. of Am. Common Investing Fund, 1976-82, NCCJ, Inc., Phila. and S. Jersey region NCCJ, 1959-65; dir. Phila. Coun. of Chs., 1954-61; bd. dirs., pres. Ea. Assn. Coll. and Univ. Bus. Officers, 1971-72; treas. Lambda Chi Alpha Found., 1970-84, dir. emeritus, 1984—; pres. Broadmoor Pines Home Owners Assn., 1993-94. Served to comdr. USNR, ret. Recipient Silver Beaver award Boy Scouts Am., 1963, Mary M. Hart award Phila. coun. Boy Scouts Am., 1986, Drexel Alumni Varsity Club award, 1966, Drexel U. Evening Coll. Alumni Assn. award, 1973, Drexel U. Anthony J. Drexel Paul award, 1988, Dept. of Army Cert. of Appreciation for Patriotic Civilian Svc., 1979, Disting. Bus. Officer award Nat. Assn. Coll. and Bus. Officers, 1989, Disting. Svc. in Trusteeship award Assn. Governing Bd. Univs. and Colls., 1989; named Educator of Yr., Phila. coun. Boy Scouts Am., 1989; named to Legion of Honor, Chapel of Four Chaplins; Drexel U. student dormitory named Myers Hall in his honor, 1984; 1 of 100 alumni honored Centennial of Drexel U., 1992. Mem. AARP, Am. Legion, Mil. Order World Wars (perpetual, comdr. Phila. chpt. 1958-59), Ret. Officers Assn. (life), Swedish Colonial Soc. Phila. (sec. 1968), Welsh Soc. Phila. (life), Internat. Frat. Lambda Chi Alpha (pres. 1966-70), Vet. Corps 1st Regiment Infantry, N.G.P. (hon.), Penn Club, Union League Phila. (pres. 1980-81), Sarasota Yacht Club, Masons, Rotary (Paul Harris fellow), Gulf Coast Corvair Club.

MYERS, HARRY J., JR., retired publisher; b. Denver, Aug. 7, 1931; s. Harry J. and Edith M. (Reed) M.; m. Mary Kay Racine, June 21, 1958; children: Harry J., Hans R. (dec.), Peter C. BA, Colo. U., 1957; postgrad., U. Mo., 1959-60. Pub., or pub. dir. Meredith Corp., 1962-82, Geo, Archtl. Digest, Bon Appetit, Home, Sci. Am., Cowles Mag, 1982-95. Served with USMC, 1953-56. Mem. Kappa Tau Alpha, Phi Gamma Delta. Home: 46 W Ranch Trl Morrison CO 80465-9504

MYERS, HOWARD MILTON, pharmacologist, educator; b. Bklyn., Dec. 12, 1923; s. Charles and Rose (Nassberg) M.; m. Louise Perry, Mar. 14, 1972; children by previous marriage: Clifford Raymond, Nancy Rose, Stephen Andrew. D.D.S., Western Res. U., 1949; Ph.D., U. Rochester, 1958; M.A. (hon.), U. Pa., 1974; M.A., San Francisco State U., 1964. Prof. oral biology U. Calif., San Francisco, 1965-71; prof. biochemistry U. Pacific Sch. Dentistry, San Francisco, 1971-74; dir. Center for Oral Health Research, U. Pa., Phila., 1974-78; prof. pharmacology Sch. of Dental Medicine, 1974-86; dir. research/tchr. tng. grant U. Calif., San Francisco, 1965-71; prof. emeritus pharmacology U. Pa.; adj. prof. pharmacology U. Calif.-San Francisco Sch. Medicine, Calif. Coll. Podiatric Medicine; adj. prof. oral biology U. Calif.-San Francisco Sch. Dentistry, 1987-95; pharmacology cons. Nat. Bd. Podiatric Examiners, 1992-95; reviewer U.S.-Israel Binat. Sci. Found., 1982-95. Contbr. articles to profl. jours.; editor: Monographs in Oral Science, 1972-95. Served with U.S. Army, 1942-45. NIH fellow Karolinska Inst., Stockholm, 1964-65; Fogarty Sr. Internat. Research fellow

U. Geneva, 1980-81. Mem. AAAS (chmn. sect. dentistry 1974), Am. Assn. Dental Research (pres. 1973-75), Council Biology Editors., Am. Chem. Soc. Home and Office: 3649 Market St Apt 601 San Francisco CA 94131-1307 *Intellectual maturity is the realization that there is more misinformation in the world than there is information.*

MYERS, HOWARD SAM, lawyer; b. Bremerhaven, Germany, Sept. 23, 1947. BA, U. N.D., 1969; JD, U. Va., 1972. Bar: Va. 1972, Minn. 1976. Ptnr. Meyers Thompson P.A., Mpls.; adj. prof. law William Mitchell Coll. Law, 1983-90. Mem. Am. Immigration Lawyers Assn. (pres. 1990-91, 92). Office: Meyers Thompson PA 123 3rd Ave N Ste 603 Minneapolis MN 55401-1407

MYERS, IONA RAYMER, real estate and property manager; b. Guymon, Okla., Sept. 18, 1931; m. Harold Rudolph Myers, Mar. 28, 1953; children: Richard Galen, Sandra Dawn, Paula Colleen. BS magna cum laude, So. Nazarene U., 1952; MEd, U. Okla., 1959; postgrad., McNeese State U., 1970. Tchr. home econs. Can. County Pub. Schs., Mustang, Okla., 1952-53; tchr. elem. Oklahoma City Pub. Schs., 1955-61, Transylvania County Pub. Schs., Brevard, N.C., 1961-67; elem. tchr., student tchr. supr. Allen Parish Pub. Schs., Oakdale, La., 1967-71; mgr. DeRidder Tracts and Comml. Property, Metairie, 1968-94; tchr. elem. and jr. high history Lafourche Parish Pub. Schs., Raceland and Lockport, La., 1974-76; tchr. elem. sci. Jefferson Parish Pub. Schs., Metairie, 1976-80; treas. Harold R. Myers Engring. (divsn. Harold R. Myers, Inc.), Metairie, 1993—; mgr. Harion Properties, L.L.C., Metairie, 1980—; vol. founding bd. dirs. Jefferson Performing Arts Soc., Metairie, 1977-83; vol. founding mem. community adv. coun. East Jefferson Gen. Hosp., Metairie, 1980-87. Vol. scout leader S.E. La. Girl Scouts U.S. coun., Metairie, 1977-89, fund raising com., 1992-93; vol. tchr. music Harold Keller Elem. Sch., Metairie, 1981-83; life mem. Rep. Nat. Com., Washington, 1980-91, mem. fin. com., 1988; jubilee chmn., fundraiser Jefferson Performing Arts Soc., Metairie, 1987; candidate La. Ho. of Reps. Dist. 88, Baton Rouge, 1991; com. YWCA New Orleans Role Model Luncheon, 1994-95; financier BPW USA Found., 1990-95. New Orleans Mus. of Art fellow, 1984-94, So. Nazarene U. fellow, 1985-94; recipient Rice in the Ear award S.E. La. Girl Scouts U.S., 1982, Great Lady/Great Gentleman award Ladies Aux. East Jefferson Gen. Hosp., 1987, Commendation award Jefferson Performing Arts Soc., 1988, Women as Winners award YWCA New Orleans, 1993. Mem. AAUW (pres. 1988-90, vol. coord. Metairie chpt. 1990-91, del. 4 nat. and 4 regional convs. 1987-94, corr. sec. La. chpt. 1989-91, scholar and grantee 1989, Magnolia editor 1991-96, Magnolia co-editor 1996-97, chair nominating com. 1992-93, grant honoree La. 1994), Jefferson Hist. Soc. (life), La. Landmarks Soc. (life), Nat. Assn. Parliamentarians (pres. Metairie unit 1996-97), La. Fedn. Bus. Profl. Women's Clubs, Inc. (pres. 1995-96), La. Bus. and Profl. Women (auditor, legis. chmn. 1990-91, rec. sec. 1991-92, membership v.p. 1992-93, pres. Jefferson Parish chpt. 1980-82, 1st v.p. 1993-94, pres.-elect 1994-95, pres. 1995-96, program v.p. 1993-94, Vision editor 1993-96, Jefferson Parish Voice editor 1993—, Outstanding Dist. Dir. award 1985, Nike award 1991, Highest Mem. honor 1992-93, Best Membership Recruiter 1993-94), Metairie Woman's Club (corr. sec. 1994-96); New Orleans Mus. Art (fellow 1984-94). Methodist. Avocations: plate collector, gardening, lobbyist. Home: 4701 Chastant St Metairie LA 70006-2059

MYERS, IRA LEE, physician; b. Monrovia, Ala., Feb. 9, 1924; s. Ira W. and Azelea Juanita (Cobbs) M.; m. Dorothy Will Foust, Sept. 4, 1943; children: Martha Crystal, Ira Grady, Stephen Allen, Joanna Lynn. B.S., Howard Coll., Birmingham, Ala., 1945; M.D., U. Ala., 1949; postgrad., Harvard U. Sch. Public Health, 1953. Diplomate: Am. Bd. Preventive Medicine. Commd. officer USPHS, 1949-55; intern USPHS Marine Hosp., Seattle, 1949-50; epidemic intelligence officer Charleston, W.Va., 1950-52, Erie County Health Dept., Buffalo, 1952, Center Communicable Disease, Atlanta, 1952-55; resigned, 1955; adminstrv. health officer Ala. Dept. Health, Montgomery, 1955-63; state health officer Ala. Dept. Health, 1963-86; sec. Ala. Bd. Med. Examiners, 1962-73; chmn. Ala. Bd. Registration Sanitarians, 1964-81, Ala. Air Pollution Control Commn., 1969-82; v.p. Ala. Pollution Control Fin. Authority, 1971-81; assoc. clin. prof. preventive medicine and pub. health U. Ala. Med. Sch.; mem. Ala. vol. med. adv. com. SSS, 1968-86. Pres. Ala. div. Am. Cancer Soc., 1991-93; chmn. bd. dirs. Dalraida Health Ctr., 1992—. Recipient Ala. Sr. Citizens Hall of Fame Golden Eagle award, 1986, St. George medal Nat. Divisional award Am. Cancer Soc., 1989, 1st Ann. Vol. award Montgomery Bapt. Assn., 1993. Mem. AMA, Med. Assn. Ala. (William Henry Saunders award 1968, 1st annual Ira L. Myers Service award, 1986), Montgomery County Med. Soc., Ala. Pub. Health Assn. (D.G. Gill award 1967, established Ira L. Myers Scholarship Endowment), Am. Assn. Pub. Health Physicians, Assn. State and Territorial Health Officers (Arthur N. McCormick award 1976), Ala. Hosp. Assn. (hon.), State. Ala. Acad. Honor. Republican. Baptist. Lodge: Montgomery Kiwanis. Initiated state narcotic control program, 1967, state hosp. service for indigent, 1958. Home and Office: 925 Green Forest Dr Montgomery AL 36109-1515

MYERS, JACK DUANE, physician; b. New Brighton, Pa., May 24, 1913; s. Louis Albert and Esther Fern (McCabe) M.; m. Jessica Helen Lewis, Aug. 31, 1946; children: Judith (dec.), John, Jessica, Elizabeth, Margaret. AB, Stanford, 1933, MD, 1937. Residency tng. medicine Stanford U. Hosps., Peter Bent Brigham Hosp., Boston, 1937-42; asst. prof. medicine Emory U., 1946-47; from instr. to asso. prof. medicine Duke, 1947-55; prof. medicine, chmn. dept. U. Pitts., 1955-70, univ. prof., 1970-85, univ. prof. emeritus, 1985—; Sec.-treas. Am. Bd. Internal Medicine, 1964-67, chmn., 1967-70; chmn. Nat. Bd. Med. Examiners, 1971-75; chmn. gen. medicine study sect. Nat. Inst. Arthritis and Metabolic Diseases, 1963-65, research career program com., 1966-69, mem. nat. adv. council, 1970-74. Served from capt. to lt. col. M.C. AUS, 1942-46. Mem. Assn. Am. Physicians, Am. Physiol. Soc., Am. Soc. Clin. Investigation (sec. 1954-57), A.C.P. (regent 1971-78, pres. 1976-77), Inst. Medicine of Nat. Acad. Scis. Home: 220 N Dithridge St #900 Pittsburgh PA 15213-1424

MYERS, JACK EDGAR, biologist, educator; b. Boyds Mills, Pa., July 10, 1913; s. Garry Cleveland and Caroline (Clark) M.; m. Evelyn DeTurck, June 19, 1937; children: Shirley Ann, Jacqueline, Linda Caroline, Kathleen. BS, Juniata Coll., 1934, DSc, 1966; MS, Mont. State Coll., 1935; PhD, U. Minn., 1939. NRC fellow Smithsonian Instn., Washington, 1940-41; asst. prof. zoology U. Tex., 1941-45, assoc. prof., 1945-48, prof., 1948—, prof. botany, 1955—, prof. emeritus, 1980—. Author: (with F.A. Matsen and N.H. Hackerman) Premedical Physical Chemistry, 1947; sci. editor Highlights for Children, 1960—; contbg. author: Algal Culture: from Laboratory to Pilot Plant, 1953, proc. of the World Symposium on Applied Solar Energy, 1956; contbr. articles to profl. jours. Guggenheim fellow, 1959. Mem. Soc. Gen. Physiologists, Am. Soc. Plant Physiologists, Phycol. Soc., AAAS, Nat. Acad. Sci., Tex. Acad. Sci., Am. Soc. Photobiology (pres. 1975), Sigma Xi.

MYERS, JAMES CLARK, advertising and public relations executive; b. Chgo., Aug. 26, 1941; s. Herbert George Myers and Lenore (Goldberg) Levi; m. Judy Anne Schnitzer, Feb. 9, 1964; children: Jeffrey Stephan, Jeremy H. BA, Washington U., St. Louis, 1964. Acct. exec. Nahas, Blumberg, Zelikow, Houston, 1967-69; mgr. spl. events Houston Post, 1969-73; pres., creative dir. Motivators, Inc., Houston, 1973—; vice-chmn. Internat. Sci. and Engring. Fair Coun., Washington, 1972-73; bd. dirs. Sci. Engring. Fair of Houston, 1969-73; spl. corrs. Navy Times Newspaper. Contbr. articles to newspapers. Chmn. Boy Scouts Am., Houston Chpt. Served to capt. USNR, 1964-96. Recipient Wood Badge award, Boy Scouts Am., 1979, Shofar award, 1981. Mem. Pub. Relations Soc. Am. (Silver Anvil award 1983, 87). Jewish. Avocations: model railroading, square dancing, photography. Home: 8006 Duffield Ln Houston TX 77071-2017 Office: Motivators Inc 7171 Harwin Dr Ste 206 Houston TX 77036-2119

MYERS, JAMES DAVID, municipal government official; b. Salt Lake City, Sept. 16, 1944; s. James William and Pauline (Winsor) M.; m. Carmen Kay Forsland, Mar. 28, 1979 (div.); stepchildren: James Christopher, Jesse Robin; m. Cleo Ester Evitt, Sept. 20, 1986; stepchild: Jennifer Michelle. Student, U. Calif., Berkeley, 1965; BSBA, Calif. State U., Chico, 1968; MPA, Golden Gate U., 1979. Mgr. Unishops, Inc. (Monte Mart), Del Rey Oaks, Calif., 1968-69; acct.-adminstrv. asst. City of Pacific Grove, 1969-79; gen. mgr. Monterey Regional Waste Mgmt. Dist., Marina, Calif., 1979—; dir., sec. Monterey Fed. Credit Union, 1979-91, vice chmn., 1986-87, chmn. supervisory com., 1976-87. Mem. Monterey County Integrated Waste Mgmt. Task Force, Salinas, Calif., 1979—, vice chair, 1995-97, chair 1997—, chmn. tech. com.; dir. Ecology Action of Monterey Peninsula, 1979-82, Milne Home, Residential Treatment Facility for Boys, Carmel Valley, Calif., 1985-87. Staff sgt. USAFR, 1966-72. Mem. Nat. Solid Waste Mgmt. Assn., Calif. Resource Recovery Assn., Solid Waste Assn. N.Am. (dir. No. Calif. chpt. 1988—, internat. landfill gas steering com. 1984-91, internat. conf. chmn. 1989, chpt. pres. 1992-93, legis. task force, Profl. Achievement award 1996), Calif. Integrated Waste Mgmt. Bd. (local govt. adv. com. 1992—, chmn. 1996—), Commonwealth Club (San Francisco), Marines Meml. Club (San Francisco). Democrat. Avocations: bicycling, tennis, record collecting, numismatics. Office: Monterey Regional Waste PO Box 609 Marina CA 93933-0609

MYERS, JAMES R., lawyer; b. Valdosta, Ga., Aug. 29, 1952; s. J. Walter Jr. and Mary (Gallion) M.; m. Monica Faeth Myers, Sept. 19, 1992. BA cum laude, Harvard U., 1972, JD, 1975. Bar: Mass. 1975, U.S. Dist. Ct. (D.C. dist.) 1976, D.C. 1977, U.S. Ct. Appeals (D.C. cir.) 1977, U.S. Supreme Ct. 1983, U.S. Ct. Appeals (fed. cir.) 1991, Va. 1992, U.S. Ct. Appeals (4th cir.) 1992. Assoc. Wald, Harkrader & Ross, Washington, 1976-77; assoc. solicitor U.S. Dept. Energy, Washington, 1977-79; assoc. Andrews & Kurth, Washington, 1980-85; ptnr. Steele, Simmons & Fornaciari, Washington, 1985-86, Robbins & Laramie, Washington, 1986-89, Venable, Baetjer, Howard & Civiletti, Washington, 1990—. Author Jour. Space Law, 1984, Space Mfg., 1983. Office: Venable Baetjer Howard & Civiletti 1201 New York Ave NW Ste 1000 Washington DC 20005-3917

MYERS, JESSE JEROME, lawyer; b. Anthony, Kans., Sept. 30, 1940; s. Claud Lewis and Lucille S. (Robertson) M.; m. Claire H. Conni, Nov., 1966; children: Timothy Todd, Jessica Joy. B.S., McPherson Coll., 1963; J.D., Washburn U., 1970. Bar: Kans. 1970, Mo.1996, U.S. Dist. Ct. Kans. 1970. Law clk. U.S. Dist. Ct. Judge Frank Theis, Wichita, KS, 1970-72; individual practice law Wichita, KS, 1972-74, 95—; lawyer Cessna Aircraft Co., Wichita, KS, 1974-75; v.p., dir., gen. counsel Martin K. Eby Constrn. Co., Wichita, Kans., 1975-95. Served with USN, 1963-67. Mem. Am. Bar Assn., Kans. Bar Assn.

MYERS, JOHN HERMAN, investment management executive; b. Queens, N.Y., July 2, 1945; s. John Howard and Edna May (Strodthoff) M.; m. JoAnn Barbara Eikamp, Sept. 29, 1973; children: Jennifer Ann, David John, Christina Marie, Kimberly Grace. BS in Math., Wagner Coll., 1967. With GE, 1970—; fin. program trainee GE Internat. GE, N.Y.C. and Frankfurt, Fed. Republic Germany, 1970-74; fin. mgr. Compagnia Generale di Elettricita GE, Milan, 1974-77; fin. mgr. GE, Fairfield, Conn., 1977-81, dep. treas., 1981-84; group fin. mgr. GE, N.Y.C., 1984-86; exec. v.p. GE Investments GE, Stamford, Conn., 1986-96; chmn., pres. GE Investments, Stamford, Conn., 1997—; bd. dirs. Doubletree Hotel Corp., Phoenix Grimes Aerospace Co., Columbus. Bd. trustees Wagner Coll., 1993—. Lt. (j.g.) USN, 1967-70, Vietnam. Mem. Aspetuck Valley Country Club. Republican. Lutheran. Avocations: tennis, basketball, golf.

MYERS, JOHN JOSEPH, bishop; b. Ottawa, Ill., July 26, 1941; s. M.W. and Margaret Louise (Donahue) M. BA maxima cum laude, Loras Coll., 1963; Licentiate in Sacred Theology, Gregorian U., Rome, 1967; Doctor of Canon Law, Cath. U. Am., 1977; DD (hon.), Apostolic See, Vatican City, 1987. Ordained priest Roman Cath. Ch., 1966, bishop, 1987. Asst. pastor Holy Family Parish, Peoria, Ill., 1967-70; asst. dept. internat. affairs U.S. Cath. Conf., Washington, 1970-71; asst. pastor St. Matthew Parish, Champaign, Ill., 1971-74; vice chancellor Cath. Diocese Peoria, 1977-78, vocation dir., 1977-87, chancellor, 1978-87, vicar gen., 1982-90, co-adjutor bishop, 1987-90; bishop of Peoria, 1990—; bd. govs. Canon Law Soc. Am., Washington, 1985-87; bd. dirs. Pope John XXIII Ctr. for Med.-Moral Rsch. and Edn., Boston; mem. sem. com. Mt. St. Mary's Sem., Md., 1989—. Author: (commentary) Book V of the Code of Canon Law, 1983; contbr. numerous articles to religious publs. Mem. Canon Law Soc. Am., Nat. Conf. Cath. Bishops. Roman Catholic. Office: Cath Diocese Peoria PO Box 1406 607 NE Madison Ave Peoria IL 61603-3832*

MYERS, JOHN LYTLE, historian; b. Findlay, Ohio, June 13, 1929; s. Robert James and Doris Lucille (Lytle) M.; m. Ardene Harriet Muller, June 30, 1957; children: John Lytle II, Jennifer Lucile Myers Hathaway, Jeffrey Lawrence. BS in Edn., Bowling Green U., 1951; MA, U. Mich., 1954, PhD, 1961. Asst. to assoc. prof. Southeast Mo. State Coll., Cape Girardeau, 1957-64; assoc. prof., prof. SUNY, Plattsburgh, 1964—; chmn. faculty senate SUNY, Plattsburgh, 1968-70, 77, 86-88, dean social scis., 1970, acting asst. to pres., 1972, chmn. self-study reaccreditation com., 1990-92. Pres. Clinton-Essex-Franklin Libr. System, Plattsburgh, 1981-84, bd. dirs., 1977-94; bd. dirs. Clinton County Hist. Assn., 1986—, pres., 1988-89; session Presbyn. Ch., Plattsburgh, 1966-69, 82-85, 87-89, 91-95, 97—, clk., 1983-85, 92-95. With U.S. Army, 1951-53. Rackham fellow U. Mich., 1956; SUNY fellow, 1965, 67; Penrose fellow Am. Philos. Soc., 1979. Mem. Orgn. Am. Historians, United Univ. Profls. (local pres. 1970), AAUP (local pres. 1963), Soc. Historians of Early Am. Reps. Home: 17 Newell Ave Plattsburgh NY 12901-6418 Office: SUNY Dept History Plattsburgh NY 12901

MYERS, JOHN THOMAS, retired congressman; b. Covington, Ind., Feb. 8, 1927; m. Carol Carruthers; children: Carol Ann, Lori Jan. B.S., Ind. State U., 1951. Cashier, trust officer Fountain Trust Co.; owner, operator farm; mem. 90th-104th Congresses from 7th Dist. Ind., 1967-96; chmn. subcom. on energy & water, appropriations com. Served with AUS, World War II, ETO. Mem. Am. Legion, VFW, Wabash Valley Assn., Res. Officers Assn., C. of C., Sigma Pi. Republican. Episcopalian. Clubs: Mason, Elk, Lion.

MYERS, JOHN WESCOTT, aviation executive; b. L.A., June 13, 1911; s. Louis Wescott and Blanche (Brown) M.; m. Lucia Raymond, Mar. 21, 1941; children: Louis W., Lucia E. A.B., Stanford U., 1933; J.D., Harvard U., 1936. Bar: Calif. 1936. Ptnr. law firm O'Melveny & Myers, L.A., 1936-42; from test pilot to sr. v.p., dir. Northrop Corp., 1942-54, 1954-79; chmn. bd. Pacific Airmotive Corp., 1954-79, Airflite, Long Beach, Calif., 1970-89, Flying M Assocs., Long Beach, 1989—; owner Flying M Ranches, Merced, Calif., 1959—. Mem. Calif. Bar Assn., Los Angeles Bar Assn., Soc. Exptl. Test Pilots, Inst. Aerospace Scis. Republican. Clubs: Bohemian, California, Los Angeles Country, Los Angeles Yacht, Sunset, Aviation Country, Conquistadores del Cielo. Home: 718 N Rodeo Dr Beverly Hills CA 90210-3210 Office: 3200 Airflite Way Long Beach CA 90807-5312

MYERS, JOHN WILLIAM, minister, poet, editor, publisher; b. Huntington, W.Va., Dec. 1, 1919; s. Condon William and Mary Olive (Fox) M.; m. Nancy Hortense Paxton, July 6, 1942 (div. Feb. 22, 1961); children: Martha Ann, Lenora Ellen, Nancy Louise, John Charles; m. Helen Donna File, Nov. 28, 1981. BA, Ohio Wesleyan U., 1951; MA, Bowling Green State U., 1952; STD (hon.), Kletzing Coll. (name now Vennard Coll.), 1951. Ordained to ministry Meth. Ch., 1948, transferred to Unitarian Universalist Ch., 1954. Min. Meth. Ch., Stockport, Ohio, 1944-46, Bradner, Ohio, 1946-50; gen. evangelist Ohio Conf., Toledo, 1954-74; min. First Universalist Ch., Pataskala, Ohio, 1974-78, First Unitarian Universalist, Lyons, Ohio, 1978-81, Horton (Mich.) Universalist Ch., 1981-91; editor, pub. Humanist Edn. Press, Toledo, 1957—; ed.-at-large Dasein, the Quar. Rev., 1962-93. Author: (poetry) Evening Exercises, 1956, These Mown Dandelions, 1959, My Mind's Poor Birds, 1963, Alley to An Island, 1963, Green Are My Words, 1964 (nominated for a Pulitzer prize 1964), Sun Bands and Other Poems, 1964, Anatomy of a Feeling, 1966, Variations on a Nightingale, 1968, A Greene County Ballad, 1979, Annotations, 1951, 82, The Sky is Forever, 1986, Something Will Be Mine, 1991, Hard in a Window, 1996, Amphion in Appalachia, 1997, Windows of Me (A Child's Sheaf of Poems), 1997; editor Ohio Poetry Soc. Bull., 1957-59, Ohio Poetry Rev., 1957-59, Poetry Dial, 1959; poetry editor The Humanist, 1958-59. Promoter Fulton County Dem. Com., Wauseon, Ohio, 1978—, Lyons-Royanton United Fund. Recipient London Lit. Cir. citation for Achievement in Poetry, Ohio Ho. of Reps., 1993. Mem. Am. Acad. Poets, Poetry Soc. Am., Ohio Poetry Soc. (editor 1958-93), Masons (32 degree, lodge edn. officer 1979-93, chaplain Lyons chpt. 1980-91), Beta Theta Pi. Avocations: cooking, walking, reading philosophy. Home: 105 Fulton St #0105 Lyons OH 43533-9600 Office: Humanist Edn Press Inc 109 N Adrian St Lyons OH 43533

MYERS, KATHERINE DONNA, writer, publisher; b. L.A., Nov. 10, 1925; d. John Allen Myers and Eulah Caldwell (Myers) Harris; m. Thomas Miller, Feb. 2, 1944 (div. 1963); children: Kathleen JoAnn Content, David Thomas. Teaching credential in bus. edn., U. So. Calif., L.A., 1975; postgrad., Loyola U., Paris, 1980. Cert. pub. adminstr. Dep. field assessor L.A. County Tax Assessor, L.A., 1944-60; sec. L.A. Unified Sch. Dist., 1960-70; br. sec. bank Crocker Nat. Bank, L.A., 1970-78; instr. legal sec. Southland Coll., L.A., 1975-78; exec. sec. ABC, L.A., 1978-89; v.p. spl. projects Glendale (Calif.) TV Studios, 1990-92; writer, publisher Eagles Wings Publishing Co., L.A., 1992—; owner, pres. Success Secretarial Seminar, L.A., 1980-84; pub., author Eagle's Wings Pub. Co., L.A., 1992—; wedding cons., counselor Crenshaw United Meth. Ch., L.A., 1993—. Author, pub.: Wedding Bells, A New Peal, 1994; (instrnl. book) Productivity Guide, Bilingual Special Education, 1980; (biography) The Eagle Flies on Friday, 1988, (hist. newsletter) Eagle Reader's Newsletter, 1993; author: (tech. booklet) Ronnie Knows about Sickle Cell, 1973 (Founder's award 1973). Troop leader, adminstr. Girl Scouts Am., L.A., 1956; chmn. sickle cell com. MLK Hosp. Guild, L.A., 1974; den mother Boy Scouts Am., 1960; lifetime mem. PTA, L.A., 1960. Recipient THANKS badge Girl Scouts Am., 1959, Founder's award MLK Jr. Hosp. Guild, 1974. Mem. Photo Friends Ctrl. Libr., Wilshire C. of C. (bd. dirs. 1980). Democrat. United Methodist. Avocations: health walking, supporting illiteracy programs, short story writing. Home: 3939 Marlton Ave # 401 Los Angeles CA 90008 Office: Eagles Wings Publishing Co PO Box 361263 5350 Wilshire Blvd Los Angeles CA 90036

MYERS, KENNETH ELLIS, hospital administrator; b. Battle Creek, Mich., Jan. 1, 1932; s. Orlow J. and Kathryn (Brown) M.; m. Nancy Lee Lindgren, June 9, 1956; children—Cynthia Lynn, Anne Lisa, Thomas Scot, Susan Elaine. BBA, U. Mich., 1956, MBA, 1957. Research analyst Bur. Bus. Research, U. Mich., 1956-57; in financial mgmt. Burroughs Corp., Detroit, 1957-66; controller William Beaumont Hosp., Royal Oak, Mich., 1966-68; asso. dir. William Beaumont Hosp., 1968-69, hosp. dir., 1969-80, exec. v.p., 1976-80, pres., 1981-97; retired; pres. Trinity Loss Prevention Systems, 1980-81; bd. dirs. Chateau Properties, Inc. Elder Bloomfield Hills Christian Ch., 1979-82, Grace Chapel, 1988-92, 95—; bd. visitors Oakland Sch. Bus. Adminstrn., 1978-92; adv. bd. Salvation Army, 1985—; bd. dirs. William Tyndale Coll., 1992—, West Bloomfield Bldg. Authority, 1978—; trustee St. Mary's Hosp., 1992-97. Mem. Mich. Hosp. Assn. (past chmn.), Vol. Hosps. Am. Enterprises (bd. dirs. 1984-87), Full Gospel Businessmen's Fellowship, Bloomfield Hills Country Club, Old Club, Phi Delta Theta, Beta Gamma Sigma. Home: 5085 Lakebluff Rd West Bloomfield MI 48323-2430

MYERS, KENNETH L(EROY), secondary education educator; b. Auburn, Nebr., Oct. 5, 1954; s. Kenneth E. and Erma F. (Hardwick) M.; m. Willo Kay Dykstra, July 1, 1995. BS in Edn., Peru State Coll., 1985, mid. sch. endorsement, 1990, MS in Edn., 1992. Cert. tchr., Nebr., Mo., S.D. Tchr. math., coach Nodaway-Holt High Sch., Graham, Mo., 1985-87, Nebraska City (Nebr.) Lourdes High Sch., 1987-89; tchr. math., social studies, coach Newcastle (Nebr.) High Sch., 1989—; chair Newcastle Math. Curriculum Team, 1991—; master tchr. N.E. Nebr. Masters Tchrs. Project, 1991—; mem. N.E. Nebr. Math. Cadre. Mem. NEA, ASCD, Nat. Coun. Tchrs. Math., Nebr. Assn. Tchrs. Math., Nebr. Coaches Assn., Nebr. State Edn. Assn., Newcastle Faculty Orgn. (pres. 1992-95). Office: Newcastle Pub Schs PO Box 187 Newcastle NE 68757-0187

MYERS, KENNETH M., lawyer; b. Miami, Fla., Mar. 11, 1933; s. Stanley C. and Martha (Scheinberg) M.; div. 1973. AB, U. N.C., 1954; JD, U. Fla., 1957. Bar: Sept. 1957, Colo. 1986, N.Y. 1987. Ptnr. Myers, Kenin Levinson & Richards, Miami, 1957-87, Shea & Gould, N.Y.C., 1987-88, Squire, Sanders & Dempsey, Miami, 1988—; mem. Fla. Ho. Reps., 1965-69, mem. Fla. Senate, 1969-80. Trustee U. Miami, 1985—. Mem. ABA, Fla. Bar Assn., Colo. Bar Assn., N.Y. State Bar Assn., Am. Law Inst., Nat. Assn. Bond Lawyers, Dade County Bar Assn., Greater Miami C. of C. (bd. govs.). Democrat. Jewish. Office: Squire Sanders & Dempsey 2900 Miami Ctr 201 S Biscayne Blvd Miami FL 33131-4332

MYERS, LAWRENCE STANLEY, JR., radiation biologist; b. Memphis, Apr. 29, 1919; s. Lawrence Stanley and Jane Myers; m. Janet Vanderwalker, June 13, 1942; children: David Lee, Frederick Lawrence, Lee Scott. BS, U. Chgo., 1941, PhD, 1949. Jr. chemist Metall. Lab. of Manhattan Engring. Dist., U. Chgo., 1942-44; asst. chemist Clinton Labs. of Manhattan Engring. Dist., Oak Ridge, Tenn., 1944-46; chemist Inst. for Nuclear Studies, U. Chgo., 1947-48; assoc. chemist Argonne (Ill.) Nat. Lab., 1948-52; asst. prof. radiology UCLA, 1953-70, assoc. rsch. phys. chemist Atomic Energy project, 1952-59, lectr. in radiol. scis., 1970-76, adj. prof. radiol. scis., 1976-82; rsch. radiobiologist, chief radiobiology div. UCLA Lab. Nuclear Medicine and Radiation Biology, 1959-76; prof. radiology and nuclear medicine Uniformed Svcs. Univ. of Health Scis., 1982-88; sci. advisor Armed Forces Radiobiology Rsch. Inst., 1982-87; cons. Oak Ridge Assoc. Univs., 1987-94; vis. scientist AFRRI, 1987-93; adj. biophysicist Radiation Biology Br. Nat. Cancer Inst. NIH, 1993—; co-organizer UCLA Internat. Conf. on Radiation Biology, 1957, 59; participant in three major Fed. Govt. planning exercises related to energy rsch. and devel. in U.S., 1973-74; mem. adv. com. Ctr. for Fast Kinetic Rsch. U. Tex., Austin, 1975-81, chmn., 1977-81; mem. adv. bd. Radiation Chemistry Data Ctr., U. Notre Dame, 1976-84, sec. 1979-81, chmn. 1981-83; chmn. Long Range Planning Com., Radiation Rsch. Soc., 1976-78; dir. Issues and Requirements Workshop for Analysis of the 1976 "Inventory of Fed. Energy Related Environ. and Safety Rsch.", 1977. Contbr. more than 100 sci. articles and abstracts to profl. jours. Com. mem. Boy Scouts of Am., Pacific Palisades and Malibu, Calif., 1956-67. Fellow AAAS; mem. Radiation Rsch. Soc., Biophys. Soc., N.Y. Acad. Sci., Am. Inst. Biol. Scis., Am. Soc. for Photobiology, Soc. for Free Radical Rsch., European Soc. for Photobiology, Sigma Xi. Home: 11810 Coldstream Dr Potomac MD 20854-3612 Office: NIH Nat Cancer Inst Radiation Biology Br Bethesda MD 20892-1002

MYERS, LONN WILLIAM, lawyer; b. Rockford, Ill., Nov. 14, 1946; s. William H. and Leona V. (Janvrin) M.; m. Janet L. Forbes, May 14, 1968; children: Andrew, Hillary, Corwin. BA, Mich. State U., 1968; MBA, Ind. U., 1973; JD, Harvard U., 1976. Bar: Ill. 1976, U.S. Ct. of Fed. Claims 1977, U.S. Tax Ct. ,1977, U.S. Ct. Appeals (7th cir.) 1977. Ptnr. McDermott, Will & Emery, Chgo., 1976—. Served to maj. USAR, 1968-80. Mem. ABA (capital recovery and leasing com. tax sect. 1994—). Episcopalian. Home: 1711 Highland Ter Glenview IL 60025-2284 Office: McDermott Will & Emery 227 W Monroe St Chicago IL 60606-5016

MYERS, MALCOLM HAYNIE, artist, art educator; b. Lucerne, Mo., June 19, 1917; s. Clyde Emmet and Kathleen M.; m. Roberta Bernice King, May 6. B.F.A., Wichita State U., 1940; M.A., U. Iowa, 1941, M.F.A., 1946. Instr. U. Iowa, 1946-48; prof. art U. Minn., Mpls., 1948—; chmn. dept. art U. Minn., 1957-61. Retrospective print exhbns. include Mr. Possum and Friends, Univ. Art Mus., U. Minn., 1983; traveling exhbn. Worcester (Mass.) Art Mus., 1990-91, The Katherine Nash Gallery, U. Minn., 1996; paintings also exhibited at Amon Carter Mus., Fort Worth and Nelson-Atkins Mus. Art, Kansas City, Mo.; one-man shows include Dolly Fiterman Gallery, Mpls., 1983, 85, 87, Katherine Nash Gallery, Mpls., 1996, Beauxmage Fine Art, St. Paul, 1996; represented in permanent collections Bibliotheque Nationale, Paris, Libr of Congress, Washington, L.A. County Art Mus., Mpls. Inst. Art, St. Louis Art Mus., Seattle Art Mus., Walker Art Ctr., Mpls., Phoenix Art Mus., Am. Embassy, Bonn, Germany, Mus. Am. Art, Smithsonian Instn., Ulrich Art Mus., Wichita, Wichita Art Mus., Fredrick Weiseman Mus., Mpls., Mpls. Art Inst.; contbr. art and articles to book, Am. Prints and Printmakers (Una Johnson). Served with U.S. Mcht. Marines, 1943-45. Recipient Alumni Achievement award Wichita State U., 1973; John Simon Guggenheim fellow Paris, 1950; Guggenheim fellow Mexico City, 1954; trustee Minn. Mus. Art, St. Paul, 1975-78. Mem. Alumni Club U. Minn., Artist Equity (past pres.), Mid-Am. Coll. Art Assn. (past pres.). Presbyterian. Home: 1715 James Ave S Minneapolis MN 55403-2826 Office: U Minn Studio Arts Dept Minneapolis MN 55455

MYERS, MARGARET JANE (DEE DEE MYERS), television personality, editor; b. Quonset Pt., R.I., Sept. 1, 1961; d. Stephen George and Judith Ann (Burleigh) M. BS, U. Santa Clara, 1983. Press asst. Mondale for Pres., L.A., 1984; deputy Senator Art Torres, L.A., 1985; dep. press sec. to press sec. Mayor Tom Bradley, L.A., 1985-87; deputy press sec. Tom Bradley For Gov., L.A., 1986; Calif. press sec. Dukakis for Pres., L.A., 1988; press sec.

Feinstein for Gov., L.A. and San Francisco, 1989-90; campaign dir. Jordan for Mayor, San Francisco, 1991; comm. cons. DeeDee Myers Assocs., Valencia, Calif., 1991; press sec. Clinton for Pres., Little Rock, 1991-92, White House, Washington, 1993-94; co-host Equal Time, CNBC, Washington, 1995—; mag. editor Vanity Fair, Washington, 1995—. Recipient Robert F. Kennedy award Emerson Coll., Boston, 1993. Democrat. Roman Catholic. Avocations: running, cycling, music, major league baseball. Office: CNBC 1233 20th St NW Ste 302 Washington DC 20036-2363*

MYERS, MARILYN GLADYS, pediatric hematologist and oncologist; b. Lyons, Nebr., July 17, 1930; d. Leonard Clarence and Marian N. (Manning) M.; m. Paul Frederick Motzkus, July 24, 1957 (dec. Aug. 1982). BA cum laude, U. Omaha, 1954; MD, U. Nebr., 1959. Diplomate Am. Bd. Pediatrics. Intern Orange County Gen. Hosp., Orange, Calif., 1959-60, resident, 1960-62; fellow in hematology/oncology Orange County Gen. Hosp./Children's Hosp. L.A., 1962-64; assoc. in rsch., chief dept. hematology/oncology Children's Hosp., Orange, 1964-80, dir. outpatient dept., 1964-73, assoc. dir. leukapheresis unit, 1971-80; clin. practice hematology, oncology, rheumatology Orange, 1964-80; instr. Coll. Medicine U. Calif., Irvine, 1968-71, asst. clin. prof. pediatrics, 1971—; pvt. practice hematology, oncology, rheumatology Santa Ana, Calif., 1980—; clin. rschr. exptl. drugs. Contbr. articles to med. jours. Mem. med. adv. com. Orange County Blood Bank Hemophiliac Found. Grantee Am. Leukemia Soc., 1963, Am. Heart Assn., 1964. Fellow Am. Acad. Pediatrics; mem. AMA, Calif. Med. Assn., L.A. County Med. Assn., Orange County Med. Assn., Orange County Pediatric Soc., Southwestern Pediatric Soc., L.A. Pediatric Soc., Internat. Coll. Pediatrics, Orange County Oncologic Soc., Am. Heart Assn. (Cardiopulmonary Coun.). Republican. Methodist. Avocation: reading. Office: 2220 E Fruit St Ste 217 Santa Ana CA 92701-4459

MYERS, MARJORIE LORA, elementary school principal; b. Waco, Tex., Jan. 12, 1950; d. Duncan Clark and Dorothy (Love) M.; m. Larry Lee Brannon, Dec. 19, 1975 (div. 1979). BA in Edn. and Spanish, U. Fla., 1972; MA in Bilingual and Multicultural Edn., George Mason U., 1985; postgrad., Georgetown U., 1986-88. Cert. bilingual tchr., pub. sch. adminstrn., D.C. Lead ESL tchr. Rock Springs Multicultural Adult Edn. Ctr., Atlanta, 1977-81; composite K-12 tchr., adminstr. Bechtel Corp., Andes Mountains, Uribante-Caparo, Venezuela, 1981-83; rsch. asst. NSF, Washington, 1983-84; bilingual and ESL tchr. Lincoln Jr. H.S., Washington, 1984-88; bilingual counselor Deal Jr. H.S., Washington, 1988-89; Leadership in Ednl. Adminstrn. Devel. participant Francis Jr. H.S., Washington, 1989-90; coord. programs and instrn. lang. minority affairs D.C. Pub. Schs., Washington, 1990-93; asst. prin. Cardozo Sr. H.S., Washington, 1993-94; prin. H.D. Cooke Elem. Sch., Washington, 1994-95; prin. Key Spanish Immersion Sch., Arlington (Va.) Pub. Schs., 1995—; mem. adv. bd. Ctr. for Immigration Policy & Refugee Assistance, Georgetown U., Washington, 1986-88; adj. prof. George Washington U., 1991, George Mason U., 1992-94, Marymount U., summer 1995. Mem. ASCD, TESOL, Nat. Assn. Bilingual Educators. Republican. Episcopalian. Avocations: tennis, hunting, biking, horseback riding, skiing, racketball, swimming. Home: 1840 California St NW Washington DC 20009 Iffuce: Francis Scott Spanish Immersion Sch 2300 Key Blvd Arlington VA 22201

MYERS, MARY KATHLEEN, publishing executive; b. Cedar Rapids, Iowa, Aug. 19, 1945; d. Joseph Bernard and Marjorie Helen (Huntsman) Weaver; m. David F. Myers, Dec. 30, 1967; children: Mindy, James. BA in English and Psychology, U. Iowa, 1967. Tchr. Lincoln H.S., Des Moines, 1967-80; editor Perfection Learning Corp., Des Moines, 1980-87, v.p., editor-in-chief, 1987-93; pres., founding ptnr. orgn. to promote Edward de Bono Advanced Practical Thinking Tng., Des Moines, 1992—. Editor: Retold Classics, 1988-91, (ednl. program) Six Thinking Hats, 1991, Lateral Thinking, 1993, Direct Attention Thinking Tools, 1997, Total Creativity, 1997; originator numerous other ednl. products and programs. Mem. Gov.'s Commn. to Enhance Ednl. Leadership Iowa, Dept. of Edn., 1991-93. Mem. ASTD, Am. Soc. Quality Control, Assn. for Quality and Participation, Am. Creativity Assn. (bd. dirs. 1997—). Home: 4315 Urbandale Ave Des Moines IA 50310-3460 Office: APTT 10520 New York Ave Des Moines IA 50322-3775

MYERS, MICHAEL CHARLES, marketing executive; b. Chgo., Oct. 15, 1949; s. Allen Jerome and Helen Emma (Schreiner) M.; m. Diana Jane Usalis, June 23, 1972; children: James Brandon, William Grant. BS in Biology, Northeastern Ill. U., 1974; MBA, Depaul U., 1982. Sales rep. Ortho Pharm., Raritan, N.J., 1974-76; midwest regional mgr. Gambro, Inc., Chgo., 1976-80, IDX Corp., Burlington, Vt., 1985-88, Candela Laser Corp., Wayland, Mass., 1988-90; mktg. mgr. Technicare, Inc., Solon, Ohio, 1980-82; mktg. exec. HBO & Co., Atlanta, 1982-85; v.p. Comdisco, Inc., Rosemont, Ill., 1990—; adj. asst. prof. Kellstadt Grad. Sch. Bus. Depaul U., 1983—; bd. dirs. Prism Data Systems, Inc, Lebanon, Ind., Check Six, Inc., Chgo. With USAF, 1969-72. Avocations: aviation, football. Home: 5176 N Tamarack Dr Barrington IL 60010-5868 Office: Comdisco Inc 6111 N River Rd Rosemont IL 60018-5158

MYERS, MICHELE TOLELA, university president; b. Rabat, Morocco, Sept. 25, 1941; came to U.S., 1964; d. Albert and Lilie (Abecassis) Tolela; m. Pierre Vajda, Sept. 12, 1962 (div. Jan. 1965); m. Gail E. Myers, Dec. 20, 1968; children: Erika, David. Diploma, Inst. Polit. Studies, U. Paris, 1962; MA, U. Denver, 1966, PhD, 1967; MA, Trinity U., 1977; LHD, Wittenberg U., 1994. Asst. prof. speech Manchester Coll., North Manchester, Ind., 1967-68; asst. prof. speech and sociology Monticello Coll., Godfrey, Ill., 1968-71; asst. prof. communication Trinity U., San Antonio, 1975-80, assoc. prof., 1980-86, asst. v.p. for acad. affairs, 1982-85, assoc. v.p., 1985-86; assoc. prof. sociology, dean Undergrad. Coll. Bryn Mawr (Pa.) Coll., 1986-89; pres. Denison U., Granville, Ohio, 1989—; comm. analyst Psychology and Commn., San Antonio, 1974-83; bd. dirs. Am. Coun. on Edn., Sherman Fairchild Found., Nat. Assn. Ind. Colls. and Univs., chmn., 1997—; mem. Fed. Res. Bank of Cleve., 1995—; pres.'s commn. Na. Collegiate Athletic Assn., 1993-97. Author: (with Gail Myers) The Dynamics of Human Communication, 1973, 6th and internat. edits., 1992, transl. into French, 1984, Communicating When We Speak, 1975, 2d edit., 1978, Communication for the Urban Professional, 1977, Managing by Communication: An Organizational Approach, 1982, transl. into Spanish, 1983, internat. edit., 1982. Trustee Phila. Child Guidance Clinic, 1988-89; trustee assoc. The Bryn Mawr Sch., Balt., 1987-89; v.p., bd. dirs. San Antonio Cmty. Guidance Ctr., 1979-83. Am. Coun. Edn. fellow in acad. adminstrn., 1981-82, Bank One Columbus, 1990-94. Mem. Am. Coun. Edn. (commn. on women in higher edn. 1990-92, bd. dirs. 1993—, chmn. 1996-97). Home: 204 Broadway W Granville OH 43023-1120 Office: Denison U Office of the President Granville OH 43023

MYERS, MILES A., educational association administrator; b. Newton, Kans., Feb. 4, 1931; s. Alvin F. and Katheryn P. (Miles) M.; m. Celeste Myers; children: Royce, Brant, Roslyn. BA in Rhetoric, U. Calif., Berkeley, 1953, MAT in English, 1979, MA in English, 1982, PhD in Lang. and Literacy, 1982. Cert. secondary tchr. English, vocat. tchr., supt. Tchr. English Washington Union High Sch., Fremont, Calif., 1957-59, Oakland (Calif.) High Sch., 1959-74, 69-73, Concord High Sch., Mt. Diablo, Calif., 1967-69; sec. Alpha Plus Corp. Preschs., Piedmont, Calif., 1968—; dir. All City High, 1973-74; tchr. English Castlemont High Sch., Oakland, 1974-75; mem. faculty U. Calif., Berkeley, 1975-85; pres., CEO Calif. Fedn. Tchrs., 1985-90; exec. dir. Nat. Coun. Tchrs. of English, Urbana, Ill., 1990-97; co-dir. Nat. Standards Project for English Language Arts, 1992-96, Bay Area writing project Sch. of Edn., Berkeley, 1976-85; adminstrv. dir. nat. writing project sch. edn. U. Calif., Berkeley, 1979-85; adj. prof. English U. Ill., Champaign-Urbana, 1991-94; Co-dir. Literacy Unit of the New Standards Project, 1991-96; vis. lectr. at numerous colleges and Univs.; rschr. in field. Author: The Meaning of Literature, 1973; co-author: Writing: Unit Lessons in Composition, Book III, 1965, The English Book-Composition Skills, 1980; author (with others) Men and Societies, 1968, Teacher as Learner, 1985, The Teaching of Writing, 1986, A Procedure for Holistic Scoring, 1980, Changing our Minds, 1996; co-author: Exemplars of Standards for English Language Arts, 3 vols.; editor Calif. Tchr., 1966-81; contbr. articles to profl. jours.; pub. monographs. Sgt. U.S. Army, 1953-56. Recipient cert. of Merit, Ctrl. Calif. Coun. Tchrs. of English, 1969, Commendation award Oakland Fedn. Tchrs., 1970, First Place award Internat. Labor Assn., 1971, Disting. Svc. award Calif. Coun. Classified Employees, 1991, Svc. award Nat. Writing Project, 1996. Fellow Nat. Conf. Rsch. in English; mem. Nat. Coun. Tchrs. of English, Nat. Conf. on Rsch. in English, Am. Fedn. of Tchrs. (legis. dir. Calif. Fedn. of Tchrs. 1971-72, Union Tchr. Press awards 1969-75, 86-89, 91, Ben Rust award Calif. Fedn. of Tchrs. 1994), Am. Edn. Rsch. Assn., Calif. Assn. Tchrs. of English (Disting. Svc. award 86), Calif. Reading Assn., Internat. Reading Assn., English 300 Soc., U. Calif./Berkeley Alumni Assn., Phi Delta Kappa. Home: 137 Lake Rd Seymour IL 61875-9600 Office: Nat Coun Tchrs English 1111 W Kenyon Rd Urbana IL 61801-1010

MYERS, MINOR, JR., academic administrator, political science educator; b. Akron, Ohio, Aug. 13, 1942; s. Minor and Ruth (Libby) M.; m. Ellen Achin, Mar. 21, 1970; children—Minor III, Joffre V.A. B.A., Carleton Coll., Northfield, Minn., 1964; M.A., Princeton U., 1967, Ph.D., 1972. From instr. to assoc. prof. Conn. Coll., New London, 1968-81, prof. govt., 1981-84; provost, dean of faculty, prof. polit. sci. Hobart and William Smith Colls., Geneva, N.Y., 1984-89; pres., prof. polit. sci. Ill. Wesleyan U., Bloomington, 1989—; adv. Numismatic Collection Yale U., 1975-84; chmn. adv. coun. Lyman Allyn Mus., 1976-81, 82-84, pres., 1982-84. Author: Liberty Without Anarchy: A History of the Society of the Cincinnati, 1983; (with others) New London County Furniture, 1974, (with others) The Princeton Graduate School: A History, 1978, (with others) American Interiors: A Documentary History from the Colonial Era to 1915, 1980. Asst. sec. gen. Soc. of the Cin., 1983-86, sec.-gen., 1986-89; trustee Inst. for European Study, 1992—. Mem. Princeton Club (N.Y.C.), University (Chgo.). Office: Ill Wesleyan U PO Box 2900 Bloomington IL 61702-2900

MYERS, MOREY MAYER, lawyer; b. Scranton, Pa., Aug. 5, 1927; s. Samuel Z. and Libbye (Kaplan) M.; m. Sondra Gelb, Nov. 25, 1956; children: Jonathan S., David N. AB, Syracuse U., 1949; LLB, Yale U., 1952. Bar: Pa. 1953, U.S. Dist.Ct. (mid. dist.) Pa. 1953, U.S. Ct. Appeals (3rd cir.) 1958, U.S. Supreme Ct. 1960, U.S. Dist. Ct. (ea. dist.) Pa. 1981, U.S. Dist. Ct. (we. dist.) Pa. 1988. Asst. solicitor City of Scranton, Pa., 1957-61; asst. atty. gen. Commonwealth of Pa., Harrisburg, 1962-63, chief coun. milk control comm., 1962-63; mng. ptnr. Gelb, Myers, Bishop & Warren, Scranton, 1982-85; sr. ptnr. Hourigan, Kluger, Spohrer, Quinn & Myers, 1985-87; chief coun. Commonwealth of Pa., Harrisburg, 1987-89; ptnr. Schnader, Harrison, Segal & Lewis, Scranton, 1990-95, Myers, Brier & Kelly, Scranton, 1995—; vis. lectr. Hamilton Coll., Clinton, N.Y., 1982-84, Yale U., 1986, 89, 91, 95, Haverford (Pa.) Coll., 1990; chief counsel Gov. of Pa., Harrisburg, 1987-89. Contbr. articles to profl. jours. with USN, 1945-46. Fellow Am. Bar Found.; mem. Nat. Conf. Commrs. Uniform State Laws (commr.). Office: Myers Brier & Kelly 108 N Washington Ave Scranton PA 18503-1818

MYERS, NORMAN ALLAN, marketing professional; b. Beeville, Tex., Dec. 10, 1935; s. Floyd Charles and Ruby (Lee) Myers; m. Suzanne Carlile, Oct. 11, 1935; children: Lisa Leigh Myers Nowlin, Matthew Scott. BS in Banking and Fin., Okla. State U., 1958. Salesman Jones and Laughlin Steel Corp., Houston, 1958-64; agt. Acacia Mutual Life Ins., Houston, 1964-69; from staff to exec v.p. Browning-Ferris Industries, Houston, 1969-81, vice-chmn., chief mktg. officer, 1982-97, exec. v.p., chief devel. officer, 1997—; also bd. dirs. Bd. dirs. My Friends-A Neuenschwander Found. for Children in Crisis. 2d lt. U.S. Army, 1958-59. Named to Okla. State Univ. Coll. of Bus. Adminstrn. Hall of Fame, 1996. Mem. Lakeside Country Club, Hills of Lakeway Club, Barton Creek Lakeside Country Club, Shriners, Holland. Republican. Avocation: golf. Office: Browning-Ferris Ind Inc 757 N Eldridge Pky Houston TX 77079-4435

MYERS, ORIE EUGENE, JR., university official; b. Hagan, Ga., Oct. 14, 1920; s. Orie Eugene and Betty (Shuman) M.; m. Margaret Elizabeth Nesbit, June 7, 1941; children: Orie Eugene III, Curtis Alan, Adrian Marvyn. Student, Ga. Inst. Tech., 1937-38; A.B., Emory U., 1941, M.A., 1957. Personnel asst. Atlanta Personnel Bd., 1940-41; personnel officer Nat. Youth Adminstrn., 1941-43, Office Emergency Mgmt., 1943-44, VA, 1946-48; dir. personnel Emory U., 1948-61, bus. mgr., 1961, dean adminstrn., dir. health services, 1961-64, v.p. bus., 1973-89, sr. bus. analyst, 1989-91; v.p. bus., dir. Woodruff Med. Center, 1964-73; past chmn. bd. Prime Bancshares, Inc., Prime Bank FSB. Trustee, chmn. med. com. Wesley Homes; bd. dirs., past chmn. DeKalb County unit Am. Cancer Soc. Served to 1st lt. USAAF, 1944-46. Mem. Coll. and Univ. Personnel Assn. (past pres.), Nat. Assn. Coll. and Univ. Bus. Officers (past pres.), So. Assn. Coll. and Univ. Bus. Officers (past pres.), DeKalb C. of C. (past pres.), Sigma Nu. Democrat. Baptist. Home: 236 Mt Vernon Dr Decatur GA 30030-1607

MYERS, PHILLIP FENTON, financial services and technology company executive; b. Cleve., June 24, 1935; s. Max I. and Rebecca (Rosenblum) M.; m. Hope Gail Strum, Aug. 13, 1961. B in Indsl. Engring., Ohio State U., 1958, MBA, 1960; D in Bus. Adminstrn., Harvard U., 1966. Staff indsl. engr. Procter & Gamble Co., Cin., 1958; sr. cons. Cresap, McCormack & Paget, N.Y.C., 1960-61; staff assoc. Mitre Corp., Bedford, Mass., 1961; cons. Sys. Devel. Corp., Santa Monica, Calif., 1963-64; dir. long range planning Electronic Specialty Co., Los Angeles, 1966-68; chmn. Atek Industries, 1968-72; pres. Myers Fin. Corp., 1973-82; chmn. Amvid Comm. Svcs., Inc., 1975-79, Omni Resources Devel. Corp., 1979-83; chmn., pres. Am. Internat. Mining Co., Inc., 1979-83; pres. Advent Internat. Mgmt. Co., Inc., 1982—; chmn. Global Bond Mktg. Svcs., Inc., 1987-90; pres., CEO Whitehall Container Mfg. Corp., 1988-91; pres. Whitehall Motors Co., 1989—, Allied Metamatter Tech. Corp., 1994—; chmn. U.S. Water Resources, Inc., 1994-96; pres. Am. Tech. Venture Fund Mgmt., Inc., Advent Internat. Realty Corp., 1996—, First Internat. Capital Corp., 1996—; pres. Turbogen, Inc., 1995—; founding dir. Warner Ctr. Bank, 1980-83; lectr. bus. adminstrn. U. So. Calif., L.A., 1967-74; prof. Grad. Sch. Bus. Adminstrn. Pepperdine U., 1974-81. Trustee, treas. Chamber Symphony Soc. Calif., 1971-78; mem. campaign issues com. Reagan for Pres., 1976, 80; pub. safety commr. City of Hidden Hills, Calif., 1976-83, chmn., 1982-83; co-chmn. budget adv. com. Las Virgenes Sch. Dist., 1983-86; mem. Mayor's Blue Ribbon Fin. Com., 1981-82; mem. dean's select adv. com. Coll. Engring., Ohio State U., 1984-94; mem. state exec. com. Calif. Libertarian Party, chmn. region 61, 1989-90, chmn. strategic planning com.; dep. chmn. Los Angeles County Libertarian Party, 1991-92; chairperson campaign issues com. Marrou for Pres., 1991-92; chmn. bd. trustees WWII Hist. Soc., 1992—; pres. Harvard Bus. Club Columbus, 1996—; dir. Ohio State Alumni Club, Franklin County, 1996—, pres. elect, 1996. Capt. USAF, 1958-60. Ford Found. fellow, 1961-64. Mem. Harvard Bus. Sch. Assn., Ohio State Alumni Assn., Harvard Club (bd. dirs. 1970-74, treas. 1971-73). *Personal philosophy: All out all the time. I stand for the creation of a new system of global governance which stresses individual liberty, freedom and responsibility, and which leads to a world that works for everyone with no one left out. In business, I stand for exceptional vision, creativity, innovation, and success.*

MYERS, PHILLIP SAMUEL, mechanical engineering educator; b. Webber, Kans., May 8, 1916; s. Earl Rufus and Sarah Katharine (Breon) M.; m. Jean Frances Alford, May 26, 1943; children: Katharine Myers Muirhead, Elizabeth Myers Baird, Phyllis Myers Rathbone, John, Mark. BS in Math. and Commerce, McPherson Coll., 1940; BSME, Kans. State Coll., 1942; PhDME, U. Wis., 1947. Registered profl. engr., Wis. Instr. mech. engring. Ind. Tech. Coll., Ft. Wayne, summer 1942; instr. U. Wis., Madison, 1942-47, asst. prof., 1947-50, assoc. prof., 1950-55, prof., 1955-86, emeritus prof., 1986—, chmn. dept. mech. engring., 1979-83; cons. Diesel Engine Mfrs. Assn., U.S. Army, various oil and ins. cos.; bd. dirs. Nelson Industries, Echlin Mfg. Corp., Digisonix, Inc. Contbr. articles to profl. jours. Chmn. Pine Lake com. W. Wis. Conf. Meth. Ch., 1955-60; Mem. Village Bd., Shorewood Hills, 1962-67. Recipient B.S. Reynolds Teaching award, 1964, McPherson Coll. Alumni citation of merit, 1971; Dugald Clerk award, 1971. Fellow ASME (Diesel Gas Power award 1971, Soichiro Honda award 1993), Soc. Automotive Engrs. (Colwell award 1966, 79, Horning award 1968, nat. pres. 1969, hon. mem.); mem. AAAS, NAE, Am. Soc. for Engring. Edn., Blue Key, Sigma Xi, Phi Kappa Phi, Sigma Tau, Pi Tau Sigma (Gold medal 1949), Tau Beta Pi (Ragnar Onstad Svc. to Soc. award 1978). Mem. Brethren Ch. Achievements include patents in field.

MYERS, PHILLIP WARD, otolaryngologist; b. Evanston, Ill., Nov. 11, 1939; s. R. Maurice and Vivian (Ward) M.; m. Lynetta Sargent, Dec. 22, 1963; children: Andrea, Ward, Alycia, Amanda, Andrew. B.S., Western Ill. U., 1961; M.D., U. Ill., 1965. Diplomate: Am. Bd. Otolaryngology. Intern St. Paul-Ramsey Hosp., 1965-66; resident in otolaryngology U. Louisville, 1966-68; resident Northwestern U., 1968-70, fellow, 1970-71; practice medicine specializing in otolaryngology Springfield, Ill., 1973—; clin. assoc. prof. otolaryngology So. Ill. U., Springfield, 1973—. Served to maj. M.C. AUS, 1971-73. Fellow Am. Soc. for Head and Neck Surgery, Am. Acad. Facial Plastic and Reconstructive Surgery; ACS, Am. Acad. Otolaryngology-Head and Neck Surgery. Research perilymphatic fistulas. Home: 3423 N Oak Hill Rochester IL 62563-9229 Office: 331 W Carpenter St Springfield IL 62702-4901

MYERS, R. DAVID, library director, dean; b. Hutchinson, Kans., Mar. 27, 1949; s. William Raymond and Elizabeth (Haas) M.; m. Barbara Jean Burridge, Sept. 15, 1973; 1 child, John David. BA, U. No. Colo., 1972, MA, 1974; ABD, U. Mich., 1976; MA, U. Denver, 1979. Manuscript curator Western History Collection, Denver, 1976-79; rsch. assoc. Colo. Legis. Coun., Denver, 1979-81; reference specialist Libr. of Congress, Washington, 1981-84, reference supr., 1984-88; libr. dir. State Hist. Soc. of Wis., Madison, 1988-94; assoc. dean univ. libr. N.Mex. State U., Las Cruces, 1994—; editor Am. history Macmillan Pub., N.Y.C., 1991-94; cons. history of medicine dept. U. Wis., Madison, 1993-94. Author bibliographies for Libr. of Congress, 1987, 88. Mem. ALA, Am. Hist. Assn., Orgn. Am. Historians, Wis. Libr. Assn. Avocations: research, writing, baseball, mysteries. Office: N Mex State U Dept 3475 PO Box 3006 Las Cruces NM 88003-3006

MYERS, R(ALPH) CHANDLER, lawyer; b. Los Angeles, Jan. 9, 1933; s. Ralph Cather and Winifred (Chandler) M.; m. Rebecca Blythe Borkgren, Jan. 11, 1963. BA, Stanford U., 1954, JD, 1958; LLD (hon.), Whittier Coll., 1988. Bar: Calif. 1959, U.S. Dist. Ct. (cen. dist.) Calif. 1959, U.S. Supreme Ct. 1971. Law clk., then assoc. Parker, Stanbury, Reese & McGee, Los Angeles, 1958-63; assoc. Nicholas, Kolliner & Van Tassel, Los Angeles, 1963-65; ptnr. Myers & D'Angelo and predecessors, Los Angeles and Pasadena, Calif., 1965—; nat. panelist Am. Arbitration Assn., Los Angeles, 1964—; bd. visitors Stanford U. Law Sch., Calif., 1970-73; mem. judge pro tem panel Los Angeles Mcpl. Ct., 1971-81; mem. Los Angeles County Dist. Atty.'s Adv. Council, Calif., 1976-83. Bd. dirs. Opera Guild So. Calif., Los Angeles, 1971-83, pres., 1980-82,. Guild Opera Co. Los Angeles, 1974-83, pres., 1975-77, Western Justice Ctr. Found., 1993—, treas. 1996—; pres. Los Angeles Child Guidance Clinic, 1977-79, bd. dirs., 1972-83; nat. vice chmn. Keystone Gifts, Stanford Centennial Campaign, 1987-92; trustee Whittier Coll., Calif., 1973—, chmn. bd. trustees, 1981-87; bd. dirs. Opera Assocs. of the Music Ctr., Los Angeles, 1976-78; trustee Flintridge Prep. Sch., La Canada Flintridge, Calif., 1981-88, chmn. bd. trustees, 1985-88; co-founder Whittier Coll. Sch. Law, 1975, trustee, 1975—, chmn. bd. trustees, 1981-87, bd. vis., 1988—. Recipient Stanford Assocs. award, 1984, Centennial Medallion award, 1991, Gold Spike award Stanford U., 1989, Disting. Svc. award Whittier Law Sch., 1993, Outstanding Achievement award Stanford Assocs., 1995. Mem. Wilshire Bar Assn. (bd. govs. 1972-81, pres. 1979-80), L.A. County Bar Assn. (trustee 1979-81), Stanford Law Soc. So. Calif. (bd. dirs. 1967-72, pres. 1970-71), Stanford Assocs. (bd. govs. 1992—, treas. 1995—), Jonathan Club, University Club (Pasadena), Stanford Club of L.A. (bd. dirs. 1963-70, pres. 1968-69). Home: La Canada 5623 Burning Tree Dr La Canada Flintridge CA 91011-2861 Office: Myers & D'Angelo 301 N Lake Ave Ste 800 Pasadena CA 91101-4108

MYERS, RANDALL KIRK (RANDY MYERS), professional baseball player; b. Vancouver, Washington, Sept. 19, 1962. Student, Clark C.C., Washington. Baseball player N.Y. Mets, 1982-89, Cin. Reds, 1989-91, San Diego Padres, 1991-92, Chicago Cubs, 1992-95, Baltimore Orioles, 1996—. Named Calif. League Pitcher of the Yr., 1984, Nat. League Fireman of Yr., Sporting News, 1993, 95. All-Star, 1990, 94; 2d in Nat. League in Saves, 1992. Office: Baltimore Orioles 333 W Camden St Baltimore MD 21201*

MYERS, RAYMOND IRVIN, optometrist, researcher; b. Mishawaka, Ind., Nov. 19, 1943; s. Raymond E. Myers and Adeline S. (Hiler) M.; m. Paulette K. Emerine, July 9, 1966; 1 child, Christopher Raymond. BS, U. Notre Dame, 1966, Ind. U., 1968; OD, Ind. U., 1970. Dir. edn. and manpower div. Am. Optometric Assn., St. Louis, 1970-73; mgr. internat. prof. services Bausch & Lomb, Inc., Rochester, N.Y., 1973-77; research fellow Moorfields Eye Hosp., London, 1977-78; pvt. practice optometry St. Louis, 1979—; mem. faculty U. Mo., St. Louis, 1986—; mem. faculty, dir. dept. contact lenses La. State U., New Orleans, 1992-93; adj. faculty La. State U. and U. Houston; rsch. cons. various contact lens and laser mfrs. Patentee in field; contbr. more than 35 articles to profl. jours. Fellow Am. Acad. Optometry; mem. Am. Optometric Assn., Mo. Optometric Assn., Assn. for Rsch. on Vision and Ophthalmology, St. Louis Optometric Soc. (pres. 1985-86), Internat. Soc. for Contact Lens Rsch. (co-founder, v.p. 1980-93), Am. Optometric Student Assn. (co-founder, pres. 1967). Office: U Mo Sch Optometry 8001 Natural Bridge Rd Saint Louis MO 63121-4401

MYERS, REX CHARLES, history educator, retired college dean; b. Cleve., July 1, 1945; s. Charles F. and Merial W. (Jones) M.; m. Susan L. Richards, Jan. 10, 1987; children: Gary W., Laura M. BA, Western State Coll., 1967; MA, U. Mont., 1970, PhD, 1972; postgrad., U. Wash., 1983; Mgmt. Devel. Program, Harvard U., 1990. Instr. Palo Verde Coll., Blythe, Calif., 1972-75; reference librarian Mont. Hist. Soc., Helena, 1975-78; prof., div. chmn., dean Western Mont. Coll., Dillon, 1979-86; dean S.D. State U., Brookings, 1986-91; acad. dean Lyndon State Coll., Lyndonville, Vt., 1991-95; lectr. Western State Coll., Gunnison, Colo., 1995—. Author: Montana Symbols, 1976, Montana Trolleys, 1970, Lizzie, 1989; co-author: Marble Colorado, 1970, Montana: Our Land and People, 1978, Montana and the West, 1984; contbr. articles to profl. jours. Bd. dirs. Ctr. for Western Studies, Sioux Falls, S.D., 1990—, Gunnison Arts Ctr., Gunnison County Libr. Summer stipend NEH, 1973; fellow James J. Hill Library, 1985. Mem. AAUW, Western History Assn. (chmn. membership com. 1980-83), Am. Conf. Acad. Deans, Mont. Oral History Assn. (chmn. 1980-83), N.E. Kingdom C. of C. (bd. dirs.), Phi Kappa Phi. Lutheran. Lodges: Kiwanis (pres. Dillon 1983, lt. gov. 1984), Masons (master 1984). Home: PO Box 931 Gunnison CO 81230-0931

MYERS, ROBERT DAVID, judge; b. Springfield, Mass., Nov. 20, 1937; s. William and Pearl (Weiss) M.; m. Judith G. Dickenman, July 1, 1962; children—Mandy Susan, Jay Brandt, Seth William. A.B., U. Mass., 1959; J.D., Boston U., 1962. Bar: Ariz. 1963. Practice in Phoenix, 1963-89; presiding judge civil dept. Superior Ct. of Arizona in Maricopa County, 1991-92; presiding judge probate and mental health dept. Superior Ct. of Ariz., Maricopa County, Ariz., 1992-95; presiding judge Superior Ct. of Ariz., Maricopa County, 1995—; pro tem judge Ariz. Ct. Appeals; judge Ariz. Superior Ct., 1989—; adj. prof. Ariz. State U. Sch. Law, 1997—; chmn. com. on exams and admissions Ariz. Supreme Ct., 1974-75, chmn. com. on character and fitness, 1975-76, mem. multi-state bar exam. com., 1976-85. Pres. Valley of Sun chpt. City of Hope, 1965-66, Cmty. Orgn. for Drug Abuse Control, 1972-73, Valley Big Bros., 1975; chmn. Mayors Ad Hoc Com. on Drug Abuse, 1974-75; bd. dirs. Maricopa County Legal Aid Soc., 1978, Phoenix Jewish Cmty. Ctr. Mem. ATLA (nat. chmn. gov.), Ariz. Bar Assn. (gov., com. chmn., sect. pres.), Maricopa County Bar Assn. (dir., pres. 1979-80), Ariz. Trial Lawyers Assn. (pres., dir., co-editor newsletter), Phoenix Trial Lawyers Assn. (pres., dir.), Western Trial Lawyers Assn. (pres. 1977), Am. Judicature Soc. (spl. merit citation outstanding svc. improvement of adminstrn. justice 1986), Am. Bd. Trial Advocates, Sandra Day O'Connor Inn of Ct. (pres. 1991-92). Office: Justice Ctr 201 W Jefferson St Phoenix AZ 85003-2205

MYERS, ROBERT DURANT, biologist, research director, medical educator; b. Phila., Oct. 25, 1931; s. Clarence Norman and Martha Louise (Fox) M.; m. Marjorie Anne Fretz, Dec. 20, 1953; children: Robert, James, Elizabeth, Anne. B.S., Ursinus Coll., 1953; M.S., Purdue U., 1954, Ph.D., 1956; D.h.c., U. Granada, 1984. Asst. prof., assoc. prof. Colgate U., 1956-63; fellow neurol. scis. Johns Hopkins U. Sch. Medicine, 1960-61; research scientist Nat. Inst. for Med. Research, Eng., 1963-65; vis. prof. neuropharmacology Nat. Inst. for Med. Research, 1969; prof. psychol. and biol. scis. Purdue U., West Lafayette, Ind., 1965-78, co-dir. neurobiology program, 1969-78; prof. psychiatry and pharmacology U. N.C. Sch. Medicine, Chapel Hill, 1978-87; dir. Bowles Biomed. Research Labs., 1980-87; prof. pharmacology and psychiatric medicine East Carolina U. Sch. Medicine, Greenville, N.C., 1988-96; disting. rsch. prof. pharmacology and psychiatry Ea. Carolina U. Sch. Medicine, Greenville, N.C., 1996—; vis. prof. Latrobe U., Australia, 1975, 82; mem. psychobiology-neurobiology adv. panels NSF; mem. alcohol adv. panel, also neurosci. neurobiol. tng. and rec.

com. NIMH; mem. neurology panel and fellowship rev. panel Nat. Inst. Neurol. and Communicative Disorders and Stroke; cons. Canadian Med. Research Council, Australian Research Grants Council, U.S. VA; mem. peer rev. panel Nat. Council Alcoholism; mem. AIDS related rev. panel NIH; mem. panel Nat. Inst. Environ. Health Scis. Author: Methods in Psychobiology, Vol.I, 1971, Vol.II, 1972, Vol.III, 1977, Neurohumoral Coding of Brain Function, 1974, Handbook Drug and Chemical Stimulation of the Brain, 1974, Neurochemical Analysis of the Conscious Brain, 1986; mem. editorial bd.: Physiol. Behavior, 1967—, Pharmacol. Biochem. Behavior, 1973—, Brain Research Bull, 1976—, Neurosci. and Biobehavioral Rev., 1977—, Prog. Neuropsychopharmacology, 1977—; editor: Alcohol-Biomed. Research Jour., 1984—; contbr. sci. articles to profl. jours. Recipient Alumni award Ursinus Coll., 1967, Sigma Xi research award, 1971, 96, Vol. Service awards Nat. Council Alcoholism, 1974-77; medal Belgrade U., Yugoslavia, 1985, medal Granada U., Spain; NSF grantee, 1960—; NIH grantee, 1980—; Office Naval Research grantee, 1965-81; NIMH grantee, 1969-76. Fellow AAAS, Am. Coll. Neuropsychopharmacology; mem. Collegium Internat. Neuro-Psychopharmacologium, Soc. for Neurosci., Am. Physiol. Soc., Am. Soc. Pharmacology and Exptl. Therapeutics, Rsch. Soc. for Alcoholism, Internat. Soc. Biomed. Rsch., Internat. Behavioral Neurosci. Soc. (pres. 1994-95), N.Y. Acad. Scis., Sigma Xi. Episcopalian. Home: 4006 Sterling Trace Dr Winterville NC 28590-9320

MYERS, ROBERT JAY, retired aerospace company executive; b. Bklyn., Oct. 15, 1934; s. John J. and Clara S. (Martinsen) M.; m. Carolyn Erland, Aug. 10, 1963; children—Susan, Kenneth. BCE, NYU, 1955, postgrad., 1957-65; P.M.D., Harvard U., 1972. With Grumman Corp., Bethpage, N.Y., 1964-94, v.p. resources, 1980-83, sr. v.p. bus. and resource mgmt., 1983-85, sr. v.p. corp. svcs., 1985-86; pres. Grumman Data Systems Corp., Bethpage, 1986-90; pres., chief operating officer, bd. dirs. Grumman Corp., 1991-94, ret., 1994; dir. Burdeshaw Assocs. Ltd., 1994—; mem. sci. adv. coun. Ala. Space and Rocket Ctr., 1986-91. Mem. adv. panel on econ. devel. N.Y. State Project 2000, 1985-86; mem. L.I. Project 2000; mem. adv. bd. L.I. Youth Guidance, 1986-91; chmn., bd. dirs. Poly. U., 1991—, North Shore Health System, 1994—, L.I. Mus. of Sci. and Technology, 1994—, Huntington Hosp., 1997—. 1st lt. U.S. Army, 1955-57. Fellow Poly. U., 1987, Disting. Alumni award, 1989. Mem. Am. Def. Preparedness Assn. (dir. 1992—), Navy League, Industry Exec. Bd., Nat. Space Club (bd. govs. 1986-89), Huntington Country Club. Lutheran. Home: 7 Heather Ln Huntington NY 11743-1011

MYERS, ROBERT MANSON, English educator, author; b. Charlottesville, Va., May 29, 1921; s. Horwood Prettyman and Matilda Manson (Wynn) M. B.A. summa cum laude, Vanderbilt U., 1941; M.A., Columbia, 1942, Harvard, 1943; Ph.D., Columbia, 1948. Instr. English Yale, 1945-47; asst. prof. Coll. William and Mary, 1947-48, Tulane U., 1948-54; tchr. English Brearley Sch., N.Y.C., 1954-56; chmn. dept. English Osbourn High Sch., Manassas, Va., 1956-59; mem. faculty U. Md., College Park, 1959—; prof. English U. Md., 1968-86, prof. emeritus, 1986—. Author: Handel's Messiah, 1948, From Beowulf to Virginia Woolf, 1952, rev., 1984, Handel, Dryden, and Milton, 1956, Restoration Comedy, 1961, The Children of Pride, 1972, abridged edit., 1984 (Nat. Book award 1973), A Georgian at Princeton, 1976, Quintet: Five Plays, 1991. Fulbright Postdoctoral Research fellow U. London, 1953-54; Fulbright lectr. Rotterdam, Netherlands, 1958-59. Mem. Modern Lang. Assn. Am., Am. Soc. 18th Century Studies, Jane Austen Soc. N.Am., Phi Beta Kappa. Home: 3900 Connecticut Ave NW Washington DC 20008-2412

MYERS, RONALD EUGENE, chemist, consultant, educator; b. Hanover, Pa., Aug. 12, 1947; s. Ivan Elmer and Betty Jane (Gibbons) M.; m. Ewha Chun, June 18, 1972; children: Michele, Jennifer. BA in Chemistry, Gettysburg (Pa.) Coll., 1969; PhD in Inorganic Chemistry, Purdue U., 1977. Advanced R & D chemist B.F. Goodrich Co., Brecksville, Ohio, 1977-80, sr. R & D chemist, 1980-83, R & D assoc., 1983-88, sr. R & D assoc., 1988-94; pres. Myers Consulting, Cleve., 1994—; chemistry lectr. John Carroll U., Cleveland, 1995—; vis. scholar Ohio Acad. Sci., Brecksville, 1990-92. Instr. sci. Strongsville (Ohio) Assn. for Gifted and Talented Students, 1987-91. Sgt. U.S. Army, 1970-72, Korea. Fellow Am. Inst. Chemists; mem. AAAS, Am. Chem. Soc., Am. Ceramic Soc. (presdl. com. on pre-coll. edn. 1990—), Phi Lambda Upsilon, Sigma Xi. Achievements include 10 U.S. and foreign patents; inventor electrically conducting polymers, flame retardants, preceramic polymers; current research and development in area of high temperature polymers and composites. Office: Myers Consulting 18436 Rustic Hollow Cleveland OH 44136-7154

MYERS, SHARON DIANE, auditor; b. Lawrence, Kans., Sept. 18, 1955; d. Richard Paul and Helen Carol (Overbey) M. AA, Mt. San Antonio Coll., Walnut, Calif., 1981; BSBA, Calif. State U., Pomona, 1983, MBA, 1986. Cert. fraud examiner; cert. govt. fin. mgr. Revenue agt. IRS, Glendale, Calif., 1984-85; auditor Def. Contract Audit Agy., L.A., 1985-92; auditor Office Inspector Gen. FDIC, Newport Beach, Calif., 1992—; instr. Azusa (Calif.) Pacific U., 1987, 88, West Coast U., San Diego, 1992. Musician, Sunday sch. supt. Covina (Calif.) Bapt. Temple, 1975-95, Liberty Bapt. Ch., Irvine, Calif., 1995—. Mem. Assn. Govt. Accts. Republican. Avocations: piano, traveling. Home: 2702 44th Ave NW Olympia WA 98502

MYERS, SHIRLEY DIANA, art book editor; b. N.Y.C., Jan. 6, 1916; d. Samuel Archibald and Regina (Edelstein) Levene; m. Bernard Samuel Myers, Aug. 11, 1938 (dec. Feb. 1993); children: Peter Lewis, Lucie Ellen. BA, NYU, 1936, MA, 1938. Editorial asst. Am. Dancer mag., N.Y.C., 1936-38; asst. to dir. Nat. Art Soc., N.Y.C., 1938-42; freelance, art book editor N.Y.C. and Austin, Tex., 1947—. Editor: Modern Art in the Making, 1950, 59, Mexican Painting in Our Time, 1956, The German Expressionists, 1957, 63, Understanding the Arts, 1958, 63, Bruegel, 1976, Manet, 1977, (with B.S. Myers) Dictionary of 20th Century Art, 1974; asst. editor Ency. of Painting, 1955, 70, 79; asst. editor, contbr. McGraw-Hill Dictionary of Art, 5 vols., 1960-69; contbg. editor: Art and Civilization, 1956, 67; coord., picture editor Ency. World Art: Supplement, Vol. XVI, 1982, 83. Vol. archives New Sch. for Social Rsch. Libr., 1993-95. Mem. NOW, Older Women's League (rec. sec. Greater N.Y. chpt. 1993-95, v.p. 1995-97), Quest (coord. archaeology 1995-97, the city in history 1996-97).

MYERS, STEPHANIE E., publishing company executive; b. L.A., Mar. 7, 1950; d. Robert Wilson and Estella Elizabeth (Halle) Lee; m. Roy J. Myers, July 13, 1991. BA, Calif. State U.-Dominguez Hills, 1971; MA, Occidental Coll., 1975. Cons. Coro Found., Los Angeles, 1973-77; fundraiser Legal Def. Fund NAACP, Los Angeles, 1978-79; owner, mgr. Contact Calif., Beverly Hills, 1979-81; spl. asst. Dept. Commerce, Washington, 1981-83; asst. sec. pub. affairs HHS, Washington, 1983-89; dir. Office Comml. Space Transp. Dept. Transportation, Washington, 1989-95; v.p. R.J.Myers Pub. Co., Washington, 1995—; mem. U.S. del. to Internat. Women's Conf., Nairobi, Kenya, 1985, UN Commn. on Status of Women, 1987. Co-author: The Rescue of Robby Robo, Can Do Kids (kits). Named Woman of Yr. Women's Transp. Seminar, 1990. Mem. Nat. Links, Inc., Delta Sigma Theta (Outstanding Leader in Govt. 1994). Office: RJ Myers Pub Co PO Box 70427 SW Washington DC 20024

MYERS, STEPHEN HAWLEY, lawyer; b. Washington, Mar. 28, 1953; s. Robert Holt and Antoinette (Hawley) M.; children: Stephen, Hampton, Brielle; m. Laura Lee Fuller, Dec. 1, 1989. BA in Polit. Sci. with honors, Union Coll., 1976; JD, Loyola U., 1979. Bar: D.C. 1979, La. 1979, U.S. Dist. Ct. D.C. 1980, U.S. Tax Ct. 1980, U.S. Ct. Claims 1980, U.S. Ct. Appeals (fed. and D.C. cirs.) 1980, U.S. Ct. Appeals (5th cir.) 1985, U.S. Dist. Ct. (we. and ea. dists.) La. 1985, U.S. Supreme Ct. 1989. Atty. advisor to hon. judge Edward S. Smith U.S. Ct. Appeals (Fed. cir.), Washington, 1979-80; assoc. Duncan Allen & Mitchell, Washington, 1980-82; atty. advisor to Judge Jules G. Körner U.S. Tax Ct., Washington, 1982-84; assoc. Davidson Meaux Sonnier & McElligott, Lafayette, La., 1984-85; ptnr. Roy Forrest, Lopresto, DeCourt & Myers and predecessor firms, Lafayette, 1985-97; pvt. practice Stephen Hawley Myers, LLC, Chevy Chase, Md., 1997—; lectr. for continuing legal edn. seminars on corp., sales tax and personal injury litigation. Vice chmn., bd. dirs. La. Coun. for Fiscal Reform, New Orleans, 1986—; bd. dirs., treas. Acadiana Youth, Inc., Lafayette, 1986-94. Mem. ABA, Am. Platform Assn., Lafayette Bar Assn., La. Counsel Def. Attys., La. Trial Lawyer's Assn., Phi Delta Phi. Avocations: writing, photography. Home: 100 Old Settlement Rd Lafayette LA 70508-7030 Office: Stephen Hawley Myers LLC 15 W Lenox St Lafayette LA 20815 also: 301 French St New Iberia LA 70560-4465

MYERS, SUE BARTLEY, artist; b. Norfolk, Va., Aug. 22, 1930; d. Louis and Rena M. Bartley; m. Bertram J. Myers, Nov. 24, 1949; children: Beth R., Mark F., Alyson S. Student, Stephens Coll., Va. Wesleyan. V.p. Jamson Realty Inc., Myers Realty Inc.; ltd. ptnr. Downtown Plaza Shopping Ctr., Warwick Village Shopping Ctr., Suburban Park Assocs. Solo shows at Village Gallery, Newport News, 1988, Artist at Work Gallery, Virginia Beach, Va., 1991, Va. Wesleyan U., Virginia Beach, 1991, 92, Will Richardson Gallery, Norfolk, Va., 1993, 94, Ctrl. Fidelity Bank, Norfolk, Va., 1995. Pres. adv. coun. Va. Wesleyan U., 1982-94; mayor's del. Sister Cities, Norwich, Eng., 1984, Kidikushu, Japan, 1982, Edinburgh, Scotland, 1991, Toulon, France, 1992; mem. entertainment com. Azalea Festival Norfolk, 1984; founder art scholarship Va. Wesleyan; bd. dirs. corp. campaign Va. Zool. Soc., 1996. Mem. Tidewater Artists Assn., Art Odyssey. Jewish. Avocations: travel, physical fitness, reading, golf. Home: 7338 Barberry Ln Norfolk VA 23505-3001

MYERS, TERRY LEWIS, clinical geneticist, educator; b. Jackson, Miss., Apr. 14, 1941; s. Gordon Harry and Leta Wanda (Smith) M.; m. Marian Kathryn Solowy; children: Wesley, Terry Jr. BS, Mich. State U., 1963; PhD, Fla. State U., 1969; MD, U. Va., 1973. Diplomate Am. Bd. Med. Genetics. Instr. pediats. U. Va., Charlottesville, 1970-73; assoc. prof. pediats. Creighton U., Omaha, Neb., 1973-78; prof. pediats. East Tenn. State U., Johnson City, Tenn., 1978-88, Tex. Tech U., Lubbock, 1988—; assoc. dean Sch. Medicine Tex. Tech U., Amarillo, 1995—; bd. dirs. Texgene. Fellow Am. Coll. Med. Genetics, Am. Acad. Pediats. Avocations: stamp collecting, internat. travel. Home: 6 Cloister Pkwy Amarillo TX 79121 Office: Tex Tech U Health Sci Ctr 1400 Wallace Blvd Amarillo TX 79106-1708

MYERS, VIRGINIA LOU, education educator; b. Indpls., July 18, 1940; d. John Rentschler and Bonnie Mae (Powell) Jones; m. James W. Rose Jr., Aug. 2, 1966 (div. Nov. 1986); m. Byron P. Myers, Sept. 11, 1987. BS in Edn., U. Indpls., 1966; MS in Edn., Butler U., 1971; PhD in Edn. Psychology, U. South Fla., 1991. Cert. elem. tchr., reading specialist and prin., Ind. Tchr. Indpls. Pub. Schs., 1966-72; pvt. tutor Self, Indpls., 1972-74; tchr.'s tchr. Urban/Rural Sch. Devel. Project, Indpls, 1974-77; reading techr. Mid. sch. dist. Pike Twp., Indpls., 1977-80; curriculum specialist Mid. sch. Dist. Washington Twp., Indpls., 1980-82; tchr. chpt. I Noblesville (Ind.) Pub. Schs., 1982-83; instr. social scis. Manatee C.C., Venice, Fla., 1983-87; asst. prof. edn. Mo. So. State Coll., Joplin, 1990-91, East Carolina U., Greenville, N.C., 1992-96; ednl. cons. Cath. Diocese of Venice, Fla., 1996—; cons. Bertie County Schs. (Windsor) N.C., 1994—. Treas. Smart Start Initiative, Greenville, 1993—; chair Birth Through Kindergarten Higher Edn. Consortium, 1994-96. Mem. ASCD, Interat. Reading Assn., Nat. Coun. Tchrs. English, Nat. Assn. for Edn. Young Children, Orton Dyslexia Soc. Presbyterian. Avocations: needle work, reading. Home: Unit D 215 Rubens Dr Nokomis FL 34275

MYERS, WALTER DEAN, young adult book author; b. Martinsburg, W.Va., Aug. 12, 1937; foster s. Herbert Dean and Florence Brown; children from previous marriage: Karen, Michael Dean; m. Constance Brendel, June 19, 1973; 1 child, Christopher. BA, Empire State Coll., 1984. Employment supr. N.Y. State Dept. Labor, Bklyn., 1966-69; sr. trade book editor Bobbs-Merrill Co., Inc., N.Y.C., 1970-77. Author: (for children) Where Does the Day Go?, 1969 (Coun. Interracial Books for Children award 1968), The Dragon Takes a Wife, 1972, The Dancers, 1972, Fly, Jimy, Fly!, 1974, The World of Work: A Guide to Choosing a Career, 1975, Fast Sam, Cool Clyde, and Stuff, 1975 (Woodward Park Sch. Ann. Book award 1976), Social Welfare, 1976, Brainstorm, 1977, Mojo and the Russians, 1977, Victory for Jamie, 1977, It Ain't All for Nothin', 1978 (ALA Best Books for Young Adults citation 1978), The Young Landlords, 1979 (ALA Best Books for Young Adults citation 1979, Coretta Scott King award 1980), The Black Pearl and the Ghost; or, One Mystery After Another, 1980, The Golden Serpent, 1980, Hoops, 1981 (ALA Best Books for Young Adults citation 1982), The Legend of Tarik, 1981 (Notable Children's Trade Book in Social Studies citation 1982), Won't Know Till I Get There, 1982, The Nicholas Factor, 1983, Tales of a Dead King, 1983, Mr. Monkey and the Gotcha Bird, 1984, Motown and Didi: A Love Story, 1984 (Coretta Scott King award 1984), The Outside Shot, 1984, Adventure in Granada, 1985, The Hidden Shrine, 1985, Duel in the Desert, 1986, Ambush in the Amazon, 1986, Sweet Illusions, 1986, Crystal, 1987, Shadow of the Red Moon, Fallen Angels, 1988, Scorpions, 1988 (Newbery Honor Book 1989), Me, Mop and the Moondance Kid, 1988, The Mouse Rap, 1990, Now Is Your Time!: The African American Struggle for Freedom, 1991 (Coretta Scott King award 1991), Somewhere in the Darkness, 1992 (Newbery Honor book 1993), A Place Called Heartbreak: A Story of Vietnam, 1992, The Righteous Revenge of Artemis Bonner, 1992, Mop, Moondance and the Nagasaki Knights, 1992, Young Martin's Promise, 1992, Malcolm X: By Any Means Necessary, 1993, The Test, 1993, Intensive Care, 1993, Fashion by Tasha, 1993, Dangerous Games, 1993, Brown Angels: An Album of Pictures and Verse, 1993, The Glory Field, 1994, Darnell Rock Reporting, 1994, The Story of the Three Kingdoms, 1995, One More River to Cross, 1995, How Mr. Monkey Saw the Whole World, 1996. Recipient Margaret A. Edwards award ALA's Young Adult Library Services Assn., 1994. *

MYERS, WARREN POWERS LAIRD, physician, educator; b. Phila., May 2, 1921; s. John Dashiell and Mary Hall (Laird) M.; m. Katharine Van Vechten, July 1, 1944; children: Warren Powers Laird, Jr., Anne Van Vechten Myers Evans, Duncan McNeir, Sara Myers Gormley. Grad., Episcopal Acad., 1939; B.S., Yale U., 1943; M.D., Columbia U., 1945; M.S. in Medicine, U. Minn., 1952; postgrad. (Eleanor Roosevelt Found. fellow), U. Cambridge, Eng., 1962-63. Diplomate: Am. Bd. Internal Medicine. Rotating intern Phila. Gen. Hosp., 1945-46; intern medicine Maimonides Hosp., N.Y.C., 1948-49; resident fellow in medicine Mayo Clinic, Rochester, Minn., 1949-52; clin. asst. Meml. Hosp., N.Y.C., 1952-54; asst. attending physician Meml. Hosp., 1954-58, assoc. attending physician, 1959, attending physician, 1959-90; instr. Cornell U. Med. Coll., 1955-56, asst. prof., 1956-59, asso. prof., 1959-68, prof. medicine, 1968-86, prof. emeritus, 1986—, assoc. dean, 1977-86; chmn. dept. medicine Meml. Sloan-Kettering Cancer Ctr., N.Y.C., 1967-77; v.p. for ednl. affairs Meml. Hosp., 1977-81, Eugene W. Kettering prof., 1979-86; attending physician N.Y. Hosp., N.Y.C., 1968-86; mem. Sloan-Kettering Inst. Cancer Rsch., N.Y.C., 1969-90; mem. emeritus Meml. Sloan-Kettering Cancer Ctr., N.Y.C., 1990—; cons. Rockefeller U. Hosp., N.Y.C., 1977-86; Mem. clin. cancer tng. com. Nat. Cancer Inst., 1970-73, chmn., 1971-73, chmn. clin. cancer edn. com., 1975-78; adj. prof. medicine Dartmouth Med. Sch., 1987-96, prof. medicine emeritus, 1996—; cons. staff Mary Hitchcock Meml. Hosp., Hanover, N.H., 1987-96. Contbr. articles on cancer, bone metabolism, internal medicine, and med. edn. to med. jours. Bd. dirs. Rye (N.Y.) United Fund, 1969-72, chmn. budget com., 1968-69; bd. dirs. Damon Runyon-Walter Winchell Cancer Fund, 1976-86, pres., 1985-86; trustee Hitchcock Clinic, Hanover, N.H., 1983-96, Dartmouth-Hitchcock Med. Ctr., Hanover, 1983-95, chmn. exec. com., 1992-95, tchr.'s coll. Columbia U., 1980-86. With M.C., USNR, 1946-47. Recipient Alumni award for research Mayo Clinic, 1952, Margaret Hay Edwards Achievement medal Am. Assn. Cancer Edn., 1993. Fellow ACP, N.Y. Acad. Medicine (v.p. 1983-85); mem. Am. Clin. and Climatological Assn., Am. Assn. Cancer Research, Endocrine Soc., Harvey Soc., Am. Fedn. Clin. Research, Practioners' Soc. of N.Y., AMA, Am. Assn. Cancer Edn. (pres. 1984-85), Am. Soc. Clin. Oncology, Founders and Patriots Pa., Alpha Omega Alpha. Presbyterian (elder 1969—). Clubs: Yale, Charaka, Century Assn. (N.Y.C.). Address: 376 Jericho St White River Junction VT 05001-2233

MYERS, WAYNE ALAN, psychiatrist, educator; b. N.Y.C., Dec. 13, 1931; s. Harry and Eve Myers; m. Joanne Jackson, Mar. 23, 1969; children: Tracy Victoria, Blake Andrew. BS with high honors, U. Ark., 1952; MD, Columbia U., 1956. Cert. in psychiatry and psychoanalysis. Intern Bellevue Hosp., N.Y.C., 1956-57; resident Payne Whitney Clinic, N.Y. Hosp., N.Y.C., 1957-59, 61-62; instr. psychiatry Cornell U. Med. Ctr., N.Y.C., 1962-72; clin. asst. prof. psychiatry Cornell U. Med. Ctr., 1972-77, clin. assoc. prof. psychiatry, 1977-84, clin. prof. psychiatry, 1984—; tng. and supervising admitting psychoanalyst Columbia U. Ctr. for Psychoanalytic Tng. & Research, N.Y.C., 1983—; sec. Assn. for Psychoanalytic Medicine, N.Y.C., 1987-89. Author: Dynamic Therapy of the Older Patient, 1984, Shrink Dreams, 1992; editor: New Concepts in Psychoanalytic Psychotherapy, 1987, New Techniques in the Psychotherapy of Older Patients, 1991, The Perverse and the Near Perverse in Clinical Practice, 1991, contbr. articles to profl. jours. Capt. U.S. Army, 1959-61. Fellow Am. Psychiat. Assn. (life), Am. Psychoanalytic Assn.; mem. Assn. for Psychoanalytic Medicine (sec.), N.Y. State Med. Soc., N.Y. County Med. Soc., PEN, Author's Guild. Avocations: skiing, squash, creative writing. Office: 60 Sutton Pl S Ste Icn New York NY 10022-4168

MYERS, WILLIAM GERRY, III, advocate, lawyer; b. Roanoke, Va., July 13, 1955; s. William Gerry and Ruby Grey (Pollard) M.; m. Susan Louise Benzer, Aug. 27, 1988; children: Katherine Coulter, Molly Benzer. AB, Coll. of William and Mary, 1977; JD, U. Denver, 1981. Bar: Colo. 1981, Wyo. 1982, D.C. 1987, U.S. Supreme Ct. 1990. Assoc. Davis & Cannon, Sheridan, Wyo., 1981-85; legis. counsel U.S. Sen. Alan K. Simpson, Wyo., 1985-89; asst. to atty. gen. U.S. dept. Justice, Washington, 1989-92; dep. gen. counsel for programs U.S. Dept. Energy, Washington, 1992-93; corp. counsel The Cattlemen Advocating Through Litigation Fund, 1993—; dir. fed. lands Nat. Cattlemen's Assn., 1993—; exec. dir. Pub. Lands Coun., Washington, 1993—; guest lectr. Yale U., Georgetown U. Sch. Law, Am. U., U. Colo. Sch. Law, Nat. Park Svc. Tng. Ctr., Nat. Acad. Scis., Grazing Lands Forum, Wyo. State Bar. Editl. staff Denver Law Jour., Denver Jour. Internat. Law and Policy; contbr. articles to profl. jours. Office: Public Lands Council 1301 Pennsylvania Ave NW Washington DC 20004-1701

MYERS, WILLIAM HARDY, attorney general; b. Electric Mills, Miss., Oct. 25, 1939; m. Mary Ann Thalhofer, 1962; children: Hardy III, Christopher, Jonathan. AB with distinction, U. Miss., 1961; LLB, U. Oreg., 1964. Bar: U. S. Dist. Ct. Oreg., U.S. Ct. Appeals (9th cir.). Law clk to Hon. William G. East U.S. Dist. Ct., 1964-65; pvt. practice, 1965-96; atty. gen. State of Oreg., Salem, 1997—. Mem. editl. bd. Oreg. Law Rev. Pres. Portland City Planning Commn., 1973-74; com. mem. Commn. on the Judicial Br., 1983-85; chmn. Citizens Task Force on Mass Transit Policy, 1985-86, Oreg. Jail Project, 1984-86, Oreg. Criminal Justice Coun., 1987-91, Portland Future Focus, 1990-91, Metro Charter Com., 1991-92, Govs. Task Force on State Employee Benefits, 1994; co-chmn. Govs. Task Force on State Employee Compensation, 1995. Mem. Oreg. State Bar Assn., Multnomah County Bar Assn., Phi Eta Sigma, Phi Kappi Phi, Omicron Delta Kappa. Office: 1162 Court St NE Salem OR 97310-1320

MYERS, WOODROW AUGUSTUS, JR., physician, health care management director; b. Indpls., Feb. 14, 1954; s. Woodrow Augustus Sr. and Charlotte T. (Tyler) M.; m. Debra Jackson, June 23, 1973; children: Kimberly Leilani, Zachary Augustus. BS, Stanford (Calif.) U., 1973, MBA, 1982; MD, Harvard U., 1977. Intern in internal medicine Stanford U. Med. Ctr., 1977-78, resident in internal medicine, 1978-80, fellow, critical care medicine, 1980-81; asst. prof. critical care medicine San Francisco Gen. Hosp., 1982-84; physician health advisor com. on labor and human resources U.S. Senate, Washington, 1984; commr. Ind. Dept. of Health, Indpls., 1985-90; health commr. N.Y.C. Dept. of Health, 1990-91; corp. med. dir. Assoc. Group, Indpls., 1991-95; dir. health care mgmt. Ford Motor Co., Dearborn, Mich., 1996—; asst. prof. medicine Cornell Med. Coll., N.Y.C., 1990-91; bd. trustees Stanford U., 1987-92; assoc. prof. medicine Ind. U. Sch. Medicine, 1992-95. Bd. dirs. Stanford Health Systems, 1994—. Robert Wood Johnson clin. scholar, Stanford U., 1980-82. Fellow ACP; mem. AMA, Nat. Med. Assn., Soc. Critical Care Medicine. Office: Ford Motor Co The American Rd WHQ-1148 Dearborn MI 48121-1899

MYERSON, ALAN, director, film and television writer; b. Cleve., Aug. 8, 1936; s. Seymour A. and Vivien I. (Caplin) M.; m. Irene Ryan, June 2, 1962; 1 son, Lincoln; m. Leigh French, Apr. 15, 1977; children: Sierra Jasmine French-Myerson, Darcy Anna French-Myerson. Student, Pepperdine Coll., 1956-57, UCLA, 1957. mem. drama faculty U. Calif., Berkeley, 1966, San Francisco State U., 1967. Dir. Broadway and Off Broadway Prodns., 1958-64, including This Music Crept By Me Upon the Waters, The Committee; dir.: Second City, N.Y.C. and Chgo., 1961, 62; founder, producer, dir. The Committee, San Francisco, L.A. and N.Y., 1963-74; dir.: (films) Steelyard Blues, 1972, Private Lessons, 1981, Police Academy 5, 1988, It's Showtime, 1976; numerous TV shows, 1975—, including Laverne and Shirley, Rhoda, Bob Newhart Show, Welcome Back, Kotter, Fame, Crime Story, Dynasty, Miami Vice, Hunter, Sisters, Picket Fences, The Larry Sanders Show, Frazier, Friends; TV films The Love Boat, 1976, Hi, Honey, I'm Dead, 1991, Bad Attitudes, 1991, Holiday Affair, 1996. Active in civil rights, anti-war, anti-nuclear power movements, 1957—. Mem. Acad. Motion Picture Arts and Scis., Acad. TV Arts and Scis., Dirs. Guild Am., Writers Guild Am. West.

MYERSON, ALBERT LEON, physical chemist; b. N.Y.C., Nov. 14, 1919; s. Myer and Dora (Weiner) M.; m. Arline Harriet Rosenfield, May 10, 1953; children: Aimee Lenore, Lorraine Patrice, Paul Andrew. BS, Pa. State U., 1941; postgrad., Columbia U., 1942-45; PhD, U. Wis., 1948. Rsch. asst. Manhattan Project Columbia U., N.Y.C., 1941-45; sr. rsch. chemist Franklin Inst. Labs., Phila., 1948-56; mgr. phys. chemistry Gen. Electric Co., Phila., 1956-60; prin. phys. chemist Aero. Lab. Cornell U., Buffalo, 1960-68; rsch. assoc. Exxon Rsch. and Engring. Co., Linden, N.J., 1969-79; head phys. chemistry sect. Mote Marine Lab., Sarasota, Fla., 1979-85; sr. scientist Princeton (N.J.) Sci. Enterprises, Inc., 1985—; cons. in field. Co-editor: Physical Chemistry in Aerodynamics and Space Flight, 1961; contbr. articles in field to profl. jours.; patentee in field; profl. violinist. Fellow Am. Phys. Soc.; mem. Am. Chem. Soc., Combustion Inst., Pa. State U. Alumni Assn., Sigma Xi, Phi Lambda Upsilon. Home and Office: 4147 Rosas Ave Sarasota FL 34233-1614 *It has always seemed to me that one's satisfacion with life can be expessed as an integral of the intensity of his or her pursuit of contributions to the world as a function of time, throughout one's life.*

MYERSON, JACOB MYER, former foreign service officer; b. Rock Hill, S.C., June 11, 1926; s. Solomon and Lena (Clein) M.; m. Nicole Neuray, June 10, 1965 (dec. Oct. 1968); 1 child, Sylvie Anne; m. Helen Hayashi, Mar. 9, 1974 (dec. Jan. 1995). Student, Pa. State Coll., 1944; B.A. with distinction, George Washington U., 1949, M.A., 1950; grad., Fgn. Service Inst., 1953. Joined U.S. Fgn. Service, 1950; 3d sec. (Office U.S. High Commr. Germany), Berlin, 1950-52; 2d sec. (U.S. Mission to NATO and European Regional Orgn.), Paris, France, 1953-55; also mem. U.S. permanent del. to coordinating com. InterGovtl. Consultative Group on EastWest Trade; internat. economist, internat. relations officer State Dept., 1956-60; adviser U.S. del. GATT session, Geneva, Switzerland, 1958; ministerial session OEEC, Paris, 1958; 1st sec., chief polit. section U.S. Mission to European Communities, Brussels, Belgium, 1960-65; spl. asst. to under sec. state, 1965-66; officer-in-charge NATO Polit. Affairs, Dept. State, 1966-68; adviser U.S. delegation ministerial sessions North Atlantic Council, 1966-67; dep. polit. adviser, counselor U.S. Mission to NATO, Brussels, Belgium, 1968-70; counselor econ. affairs U.S. Mission to European Communities, Brussels, 1970-74; minister counselor U.S. Mission to European Communities, from 1974; U.S. rep. to UN Econ. and Social Council with rank of ambassador, 1975-77; alt. U.S. del. 30th and 31st sessions UN Gen. Assembly, 1975, 76; alt. U.S. rep. 4th session UN Conf. on Trade and Devel., 1976; minister-counselor for econ. and comml. affairs Am. Embassy, Paris, 1977-80; ret., 1980; dep. sec. gen. OECD, Paris, 1980-88. Served with inf. AUS, 1944-46, ETO. Decorated Bronze Star; Order of the Sacred Treasure Gold and Silver medal (Japan). Recipient Meritorious Service award State Dept., 1960. Mem. Fgn. Service Assn. (Rivkin award 1969), Phi Beta Kappa, Artus, Pi Gamma Mu, Phi Eta Sigma. Address: 2 rue Lucien Gaulard, 75018 Paris France

MYERSON, JOEL ARTHUR, English language educator, researcher; b. Boston, Sept. 9, 1945; s. Edward Yale and Gwenne (Rubenstein) M. AB, Tulane U., 1967; MA, Northwestern U., 1968, PhD, 1971. Asst. prof. English U. S.C., Columbia, 1971-76, assoc. prof., 1976-80, prof., 1980-90, Carolina Rsch. prof. Am. lit., 1990-96, chmn. English dept., 1987-90, Carolina Disting. prof. Am. lit., 1996—. Author: Margaret Fuller: An Annotated Secondary Bibliography, 1977, Brook Farm: An Annotated Bibliography and Resources Guide, 1978, Margaret Fuller: A Descriptive Bibliography, 1978, The New England Transcendentalists and the Dial: A History of Magazine and Its Contributors, 1980, Theodore Parker: A Descriptive Bibliography, 1980, Ralph Waldo Emerson: A Descriptive Bibliography, 1982, Emily Dickinson: A Descriptive Bibliography, 1984, Walt Whitman: A

Descriptive Bibliography, 1993; co-author: Melville Dissertations: An Annotated Directory, 1972, Emerson: An Annotated Secondary Bibliography, 1985, Ralph Waldo Emerson: An Annotated Bibliography of Criticism, 1980-91, 1994; editor: The American Renaissance in New England, 1978, Margaret Fuller: Esssays on American Life and Letters, 1978, Antebellum Writers in New York and the South, 1979, Critical Essays on Margaret Fuller, 1980, Margaret Fuller, Woman in the Nineteenth Century, 1980, Emerson Centenary Essays, 1982, The Transcendentalists: A Review of Research and Criticism, 1984, The Brook Farm Book: A Collection of First-Hand Accounts of the Community, 1987, The American Transcendentalists, 1988, Critical Essays on Henry David Thoreau's Walden, 1988, Whitman in His Time, 1991, Emerson and Thoreau: The Contemporary Reviews, 1992, The Walt Whitman Archive, 1993, The Cambridge Companion to Henry David Thoreau, 1995, Studies in the American Renaissance, 1977-96; co-editor: Critical Essays on American Transcendentalism, 1982, Critical Essays on Ralph Waldo Emerson, 1983, The Selected Letters of Louisa May Alcott, 1987, A Double Life: Newly Discovered Thrillers of Louisa May Alcott, 1988, The Journals of Louisa May Alcott, 1989, Louisa May Alcott: Selected Fiction, 1990, Freaks of Genius: Unknown Thrillers of Louisa May Alcott, 1991, Three Children's Novels by Christopher Pearse Cranch, 1993, Emerson's Antislavery Writings, 1995. Mem. Mass. Hist. Soc., Am. Antiquarian Soc. Woodrow Wilson Dissertation Yr. fellow, 1970, summer fellow NEH, 1976, rsch. grantee, 1978-81, 88-91, 94-97; Guggenheim Found. fellow, 1981; rsch. grantee Am. Philos. Soc., 1982, 84. Mem. MLA (del. assembly 1978-80), Assn. for Documentary Editing (pres. 1989-90, Disting. Svc. award 1986, Lyman H. Butterfield award 1996), Philol. Assn. of Carolinas (pres. 1987-88), Thoreau Soc. (pres. 1992-96), Emerson Soc. (pres. 1994-95). Democrat. Home: 6310 Goldbranch Rd Columbia SC 29206-3340 Office: U of SC Dept of English Columbia SC 29208

MYERSON, ROBERT J., radiation oncologist, educator; b. Boston, May 12, 1947; s. Richard Louis and Rosemarie (Farkas) M.; m. Carla Wheatley, Aug. 8, 1970; 1 child, Jacob Wheatley. BA, Princeton U., 1969; PhD, U. Calif., Berkeley, 1974; MD, U. Miami, 1980. Diplomate Am. Bd. Radiology. Asst. prof. dept. physics Pa. State U., State Coll., 1974-76; fellow Inst. Advanced Studies, Princeton, N.J., 1976-78; resident U. Pa. Hosp., Phila., 1981-84; assoc. prof. radiology Washington U. Sch. Medicine, St. Louis, 1984-97, assoc. dir. residency tng. radiation oncology, 1990—, prof. radiology, 1997—. Contbr. articles to profl. jours. Recipient Career Devel. award Am. Cancer Soc., 1985. Mem. Am. Coll. Radiation, Am. Soc. Therapeutic Radiologists, Am. Phys. Soc. Democrat. Jewish. Avocation: bicycling. Office: Washington U Radiation Oncology Ctr Box 8224 4939 Childrens Pl Ste 5500 Saint Louis MO 63110-1001

MYERSON, ROGER BRUCE, economist, game theorist, educator; b. Boston, Mar. 29, 1951; s. Richard L. and Rosemarie (Farkas) M.; m. Regina M. Weber, Aug. 29, 1982; children: Daniel, Rebecca. AB summa cum laude, Harvard U., 1973, SM, 1973, PhD, 1976. Asst. prof. decision scis. Northwestern U., Evanston, Ill., 1976-78, assoc. prof., 1979-82, prof., 1982—, Harold Stuart prof. decision scis., 1986—, prof. econs., 1987—; guest researcher U. Bielefeld, Federal Republic of Germany, 1978-79; vis. prof. econs. U. Chgo., 1985-86. Author: Game Theory: Analysis of Conflict, 1991; mem. editorial bd. Internat. Jour. Game Theory, 1982-92, Games and Econ. Behavior, 1988—; assoc. editor Jour. Econ. Theory, 1983-93; also articles. Guggenheim fellow, 1983-84; Sloan rsch. fellow, 1984-86. Fellow Econometric Soc., Am. Acad. Arts and Scis. Office: Northwestern U Kellogg Grad Sch Mgmt 2001 Sheridan Rd Evanston IL 60208-0814

MYERSON, TOBY SALTER, lawyer; b. Chgo., July 20, 1949; s. Raymond King and Natalie Anita (Salter) M. BA, Yale U., 1971; JD, Harvard U., 1975. Bar: N.Y. 1977, Calif. 1977. Assoc. Coudert Bros., N.Y.C., 1975-77, 81, San Francisco, 1977-81; assoc. Paul, Weiss, Rifkind, Wharton & Garrison, N.Y.C., 1981-83, ptnr., 1983-89; mng. dir. Wasserstein Perella & Co., Inc., N.Y.C., 1989-90; ptnr. Paul, Weiss, Rifkind, Wharton & Garrison, N.Y.C., 1990—; lectr. U. Calif. Berkeley, 1979-81, Harvard U., Cambridge, Mass., 1982-83; visiting lectr. Yale U., New Haven, 1983-84; bd. dirs. Myerson, Van Den Berg & Co., Santa Barbara, Calif. Contbg. editor: Doing Business in Japan, 1983, Council on Foreign Rels., 1993—, Foreign Policy Assn., 1995—. Sec. Japan Soc., Inc., N.Y.C., 1985-89; bd. dirs. 1056 Fifth Ave. Corp., N.Y.C., 1985-88. Mem. ABA (subcom. internat. banking, corp. and bus. law sect.), Internat. Bar Assn., N.Y. State Bar Assn., Assn. Bar City N.Y. (com. on fgn. and comparative law, chmn. 1988-89), Calif. Bar Assn. Avocations: art, music, literature, tennis, golf. Home: 1056 Fifth Ave New York NY 10028-0112 Office: Paul Weiss Rifkind Wharton & Garrison 1285 Avenue Of The Americas New York NY 10019-6028

MYGATT, SUSAN HALL, lawyer; b. Stamford, Conn., Sept. 29, 1947; d. Eben Clarke and Jane Elizabeth (Terhune) Hall; m. Samuel G. Mygatt, June 11, 1977; children: Elizabeth, Jenny, Catherine. BA, Smith Coll., 1969; JD, Boston U., 1977. Bar: Mass. 1977. Adminstrv. asst. HUD, Washington, 1969-73; exec. asst. Urban Devel. Corp., N.Y.C., 1973-74; ptnr. Goodwin, Procter & Hoar, Boston, 1977—. Mem. ABA, Mass. Bar Assn., New Eng. Women in Real Estate. Office: Goodwin Procter & Hoar Exchange Pl Boston MA 02109

MYHAND, WANDA RESHEL, paralegal, legal assistant; b. Detroit, Aug. 15, 1963; d. Ralph and Geraldine (Leavell) M. Office mgr./adminstrv. asst. Gregory Terrell & Co., CPA, Detroit, 1987-90; legal sec. Ford Motor Co., Detroit, 1990-91; office mgr. M.G. Christian Builders, Inc., Detroit, 1991; paralegal, legal asst. Law Office of Karri Mitchell, Detroit, 1991—. Vol. UNCF Telethon Detroit, 1988. Mem. NAFE. Avocations: jigsaw puzzles, crossword puzzles, travel.

MYHRE, BYRON ARNOLD, pathologist, educator; b. Fargo, N.D., Oct. 22, 1928; s. Ben Arnold and Amy Lillian (Gilbertson) M.; m. Eileen Marguerite Scherling, June 16, 1953; children: Patricia Ann, Bruce Allen. B.S., U. Ill., 1950; M.S., Northwestern U., 1952, M.D., 1953; Ph.D., U. Wis., 1962. Intern Evanston (Ill.) Hosp., 1953-54; resident Children's Meml. Hosp., Chgo., 1956-57, U. Wis. Hosp., Madison, 1957-60; assoc. med. dir. Milw. Blood Center, 1962-66; sci. dir. Los Angeles Red Cross Blood Center, 1966-72; dir. Blood Bank Harbor-UCLA Med. Center, Torrance, 1972-85; chief clin. pathology Harbor-UCLA Med. Center, 1985—; prof. pathology UCLA, 1972—. Author: Quality Control on Blood Banking, 1974, (with others) Textbook of Clinical Pathology, 1972, Paternity Testing, 1975; editor seminar procs.; contbr. articles to med. jours., chpts. to books. Served with USAF, 1954-56. Mem. AMA, Am. Soc. Clin. Pathology (dep. commr. commn. on continuing edn.), Am. Assn. Blood Banks (pres. 1978-79), Coll. Am. Pathologists (chmn. blood bank survey com.), Assn. Clin. Scientists (pres. 1993), Calif. Med. Assn., Calif. Blood Bank Systems (past pres.), Wis. Blood Bank Assn. (past pres.), L.A. Acad. Medicine (past pres.), Harbor-UCLA Faculty Soc. (past pres.), Palos Verdes Breadfast Club (v.p. 1995, pres. 1996). Home: 4004 Via Larga Vis Palos Verdes Estates CA 90274-1122 Office: Harbor-UCLA Med Center 1000 W Carson St Torrance CA 90502-2004

MYHRE, KATHLEEN RANDI, nurse; b. Everett, Wash., Apr. 18, 1952; d. Richard Alvin and Beverley Jeanette (Nesbit) M. LPN, Bellingham (Wash.) Tech. Sch., 1970; ADN, Lane C.C., Eugene, Oreg., 1988. RN, Oreg. LPN night charge nurse Island's Convalescent Ctr., Friday Harbor, Wash., 1970-75; LPN float Sacred Heart Gen. Hosp., Eugene, Oreg., 1975-87; charge nurse urgent care unit Eugene Clinic, 1987—. Democrat. Avocations: fishing, hiking, stained glass, gardening. Home: 80687 Lost Creek Rd Dexter OR 97431-9742

MYHREN, TRYGVE EDWARD, communications company executive; b. Palmerton, Pa., Jan. 3, 1937; s. Arne Johannes and Anita (Blatz) M.; m. Carol Jane Enman, Aug. 8, 1964; children: Erik, Kirsten, Tor; m. 2d Victoria Hamilton, Nov. 14, 1981; 1 stepchild, Paige. BA in Philosophy and Polit. Sci., Dartmouth Coll., 1958, MBA, 1959. Sales mgr., unit mgr. Procter and Gamble, Cin., 1963-65; sr. cons. Glendinning Cos., Westport, Conn., 1965-69; pres. Auberge Vintners, 1970-73; exec. v.p. Mktg. Continental, Westport, 1969-73; v.p., gen. mgr. CRM, Inc., Del Mar, Calif., 1973-75; v.p. mktg. Am. TV and Communications Corp., Englewood, Colo., 1975-78, sr. v.p. mktg. and programming, 1978-79, exec. v.p., 1980, pres., 1980, chmn. bd., chief exec. officer, 1981-88; v.p., then exec. v.p. Time Inc., N.Y.C., 1981-88; mem. exec. com., treas., vice chmn., then chmn. bd. dirs. Nat. Cable TV Assn., Washington, 1982-91; mem. adv. com. on HDTV, FCC, 1987-89; bd. dirs. Advanced Mktg. Sys., Inc., La Jolla, Calif., Providence (R.I.) Jour. Co., pres., 1990-96; bd. dirs. Founders Funds, Inc., J. D. Edwards, Inc., Verio, Inc., Denver; pres. Myhren Media, 1989—, Greenwood Cable Mgmt., 1989-91; pres., CEO King Broadcast Co., 1991-96. Vice chmn. Pub. Edn. Coalition; mem. Colo. Forum, 1984-91, chmn. higher edn. com., 1986; bd. dirs., co-founder Colo. Bus. Com. for the Arts, 1985-91; mem. exec. coun. Found. for Commemoration U.S. Constn., 1987-90; mem. Nat. GED Task Force, 1987-90, Colo. Baseball Commn., 1989-91, Colo. Film Commn., 1989-91; trustee Nat. Jewish Hosp., 1989— (Humanitarian award 1996), R.I. Hosp., 1991-95, Lifespan Health Sys., 1994-97, U. Denver, 1996—; chmn. Local Organizing Commn. 1995 NCAA Hockey Championship. Lt. (j.g.) USNR, 1959-63. Recipient Disting. Leader award Nat. Cable TV Assn., 1988, ann. humanitarian award Nat. Jewish Hosp., 1996. Mem. Cable TV Adminstrn. and Mktg. Soc. (pres. 1978-79, Grand Tam award 1985, One of A Kind award 1994), Cable Adv. Bur. (co-founder 1978), Cable TV Pioneers, Cróhns and Colitis Found. Am. (trustee Rocky Mountain chpt.). Episcopalian.

MYLES, KEVIN MICHAEL, metallurgical engineer; b. Chgo., July 18, 1934; s. Michael J. and Ursula (May) M.; m. Joan Christine Ganczewski, Dec. 16, 1967; children: Kathleen, Gary, Jennifer. BS in Metallurgical Engring., U. Ill., 1956, PhD in Phys. Metall. Engring., 1963. Asst. mgr. nuclear fuel repprossing program Argonne (Ill.) Nat. Lab., 1977-79, dep. dir. fossil energy program, 1982-87, dir. fuel cell program, 1987-88, dir. electrochem. tech. program, 1988—, assoc. dir. chem. tech. div., 1992—; adj. prof. materials sci. U. Ill., Chgo., 1967-69; prof. materials sci. Midwest Coll. Engring., Lombard, Ill., 1969-81. Contbr. articles to Jour. Phys. Chemistry, Chem. Engring. Sci., Jour. Electrochem. Soc., Jour. Fusion Energy, Jour. Power Sources. Mem. Sch. Bd. Dist. #58, Downers Grove, Ill., 1964-70. Capt. USAR, 1956-68. Mem. Am. Soc. for Metals, AIME, Alpha Sigma Mu. Achievements include 10 patents in field. Office: Argonne Nat Lab 9700 Cass Ave Argonne IL 60439-4803

MYLNECHUK, LARRY HERBERT, financial executive; b. Littlefork, Minn., Mar. 9, 1948; s. William and Marjorie (Raco) M.; m. Sandy L. Henderson, Mar. 14, 1970; children: Kendra Elizabeth, Scott William. BA, Lewis & Clark Coll., Portland, 1970; JD, Lewis & Clark Coll., 1974. Legal specialist Oreg. Dept. Edn., Salem, 1976-82; sr. v.p., dir. Morley Capital Mgmt. Inc., Portland, 1982-89; founder, pres. Integra Assocs., Inc., Lake Oswego, Oreg., 1989—; exec. dir. The Stable Value Assn., Inc., Lake Oswego, 1990-96; cons. Hueler Analytics, Inc., Mpls., 1989—; conf. chmn. GIC Nat. Forum Conf., Washington, 1993-95; guest lectr. Portland State U., 1978, U. Oreg., 1980. Contbr. articles to profl. jours. Founder Woodstock Neighborhood Assn., 1975; mem. Multnomah County (Oreg.) Charter Rev. Commn., 1978, Tualatin (Oreg.) City Coun., 1980-84, Portland Com. on Fgn. Rels., 1976—, bd. dirs., 1993—; mem. Gov.'s Commn. on Adminstrv. Hearings, State of Oreg., 1988-89; trustee St. Francis of Assisi Endowment Fund, 1993; vestry mem., lay eucharistic min., del. State Episcopal Conv., 1996; mem. Diocesan Coun., 1996—; chmn. corp. fundraising Lake Oswego Children's Choir. Fellow NEH, 1979, ednl. policy fellow George Washington U., 1980. Mem. SAR (pres. Lewis and Clark chpt.), Western Pension Conf., Assn. Soc. Execs., World Affairs Coun. Oreg., Citizen Amb. Program to Western Europe, Gen. Soc. The War of 1812, Soc. Colonial Wars, Sons and Daus. of Pilgrims, Oreg. Soc. Sons of the Revolution (co-founder, treas. 1996), Internat. Bus. Forum (mem. adv. bd. 1996), Sons of the Bench and Bar (charter), SAR (pres. Oreg. State Soc. 1997). Democrat. Episcopalian. Avocations: hiking, diving. Office: Integra Assocs Inc PO Box 1594 Lake Oswego OR 97035-0013

MYLROIE, WILLA WILCOX, transportation engineer, regional planner; b. Seattle, May 30, 1917; d. Elgin Roscoe and Ruth B. (Begg) Wilcox; m. John Ellis Mylroie (dec. 1947); children: Steven Wilcox Mylroie, Jo Mylroie Sohneronne; m. Donald Gile Fassett, Dec. 30, 1966. BS in Civil Engring., U. Wash., 1940, MS in Regional Planning, 1953. Lic. profl. civil engr. Civil engr. U.S. Engring. Dept. C.E., Seattle, 1941-46; affiliate prof. civil engring. U. Wash., Seattle, 1948-51, research asst. prof. civil engring., 1951-56; assoc. prof. civil engring. Purdue U., Lafayette, Ind., 1956-58; research engr. and planner Wash. State Dept. Hwys., Olympia, 1958-69, head research and spl. assignment div., 1969-81; adv. cons. civil engring. and regional planning Thurston County, Wash., 1981-97; cons. King County Design Commn., Seattle, 1981-89; advisor Coll. Engring. U. Wash., 1978-86, affiliate prof. civil engring., 1981-84; advisor Wash. State U. Coll. Engring., Pullman, 1977-85. Active Girls Scouts U.S. coun., Boy Scouts Am., Olympia, Renton, 1950-60; pres. high sch. PTA, Olympia; commr. Thurston County Planning Commn., Olympia; U.S. Coast Guard Auxilliary, 1982-89, U.S. Power Squadron, 1967—; citizen amb. People to People Trip, Moscow, St. Petersburg, Russia and Muensk, Bolarus. Recipient Profl. Recognition award Women's Transp., Spokane, Spl. Svc. award Transp. Rsch. Bd. Coun., Washington, U. Wash. Coll. Engring. Alumni Achievement award, 1993. Fellow ASCE (ad hoc vis. com. engring. coun. for profl. devel., Edmund Friedman Profl. Recognition award 1978), Inst. Transp. Engrs. (hon. mem., internat. bd. dirs., Tech. Coun. award 1982); mem. Planning Assn. Wash. (bd. dirs.), Sigma Xi. Avocations: sailing, gardening, travel, music, vol. community activities. Home and Office: 7501 Boston Harbor Rd NE Olympia WA 98506-9720

MYNATT, CECIL FERRELL, psychiatrist; b. Knoxville, Tenn., May 10, 1995; s. Cecil Ferrell and Ethel (May) Mynatt; m. Minnie Lee Rouser, Dec. 8, 1945 (div. Nov. 1988); children: Matthew, Cecilia, Melissa, Martha, Richard; m. Yong Cha Lee, Oct. 10, 1990; children: Katherine, John. BS, U. Tenn., 1950, MD, 1951. Pvt. practice in gen. medicine Morristown, Tenn., 1952-61; resident Menninger Sch. Psychiatry, 1961-65; suprt. Ea. State Hosp., Knoxville, 1965-67; pvt. practice Wright Ferry Hosp., Knoxville, 1967-68; pvt. practice, co-owner Pvt. Hosp., Knoxville, 1968-73, Las Vegas, 1973-84; dir. Taliferro Mental Health Ctr., Lawton, Okla., 1984-89; supt. Western State Hosp., Woodword, Okla., 1989-91; med. dir. Rolling Hills Psychiat. Hosp., Ada, Okla., 1991-96; med. dir. behavioral medicine Mercy Meml. Hosp., Ardmore, Okla., 1996—; CEO Sun Enterprises, Inc., Ada, 1987—; cons. Pononotoc County Mental Health Assn., Ada, 1992-96, Valley View Meml. Hosp., Ada, 1992-96. Editor, pub. Voice of Experience, 1993—; contbr. articles to profl. jours. Maj. OSS, 1941-45. Decorated Silver star, Bronze star, (2) Purple Hearts. Mem. VFW, AMA, Okla. Med. Assn., Ponontoc County Med. Assn. Republican. Baptist. Avocations: motocycling, bowling, walking with wife. Home: 126 Kings Rd Ada OK 74820 Office: 1908 12th Ave NW Ardmore OK 73401-1255

MYRA, HAROLD LAWRENCE, publisher; b. Camden, N.J., July 19, 1939; s. John Samuel and Esther (Christensen) M.; m. Jeanette Austin, May 7, 1966; children: Michelle, Todd, Gregory, Ricky, Joshua, Lindsey. B.S., East Stroudsburg State Coll., 1961; Litt.D., John Wesley Coll., 1976; D.Lit., Biola U., 1984; DLitt, Gordon Coll., 1992. Tchr. Pocono Mountain Jointure, Cresco, Pa., 1961; editorial asst. Youth for Christ Internat., Wheaton, Ill., 1961-62; asso. editor Youth for Christ Internat., 1962-64, mng. editor, 1964-65, dir. of lit., 1965-66; v.p. lit. div., pub. Campus Life, Wheaton, 1966-75; pres., chief exec. officer Christianity Today, Inc., Carol Stream, Ill., 1975—. Author: No Man in Eden, 1969, Michelle, You Scallawag, I Love You, 1972, The New You, 1972, The Carpenter, 1972, Elsbeth, 1975, Is There a Place I Can Scream?, 1976, Santa, Are You For Real?, 1979, Love Notes to Jeanette, 1979, The Choice, 1980, Halloween, 1982, Your Super-Terrific Birthday, 1985, Living By God's Surprises, 1988, Children in the Night, 1991, The Shining Face, 1993, Morning Child, 1994. Presbyterian. Home: 1737 Marion Ct Wheaton IL 60187-3319 Office: Christianity Today 465 Gundersen Dr Carol Stream IL 60188-[illegible]

MYRBERG, ARTHUR AUGUST, JR., marine biological sciences educator; b. Chicago Heights, Ill., June 28, 1933; s. Arthur August and Helen Katherine (Stelle) M.; divorced; children—Arthur August III, Beverly Priscilla. A.B., Ripon Coll., 1954; M.S., U. Ill., 1958; Ph.D. (NIH fellow), UCLA, 1961. Research asst. Ill. Natural History Survey, Champaign-Urbana, 1957; mem. faculty U. Miami, Fla., 1964—; assoc. prof. Sch. Marine and Atmospheric Sci., 1967-72, prof., 1972—; chmn. div. marine biology and fisheries U. Miami, Fla., 1991, academic chmn. div. marine biology and fisheries, 1991-93. Contbr. articles to profl. jours., chpts. to books; assoc. editor Bull. Marine Sci, 1964-73. Mem. Khoury League, 1967-75. Served to 1st lt., inf. U.S. Army, 1954-57. Recipient Disting. Alumni award Ripon Coll., 1991; NIH postdoctoral fellow Max Planck Inst. Behavioral Physiology, Seewiesen, Germany, 1961-64. Fellow Animal Behavior Soc. (Disting. Fellow Lecture award 1993), Am. Inst. Fishery Rsch. Biologists; mem. Am. Soc. Ichthyologists and Herpetologists, Am. Soc. Zoologists, Ecol. Soc. Am., Am. Inst. Biol. Scis., N.Y. Acad. Scis., Internat. Assn. Fish Ethologists, Am. Elasmobranch Soc. (gov. 1985-90), Sigma Xi (nat. lectr. 1980-81), Phi Sigma, Omicron Delta Kappa. Achievements include demonstration of the importance of sound production for survival and reproduction in fishes, that sharks are attracted to specific types of underwater sound; reported on the social behavior of sharks. Home: 6001 SW 65th Ave Miami FL 33143-2031

MYRDAL, ROSEMARIE CARYLE, state official, former state legislator; b. Minot, N.D., May 20, 1929; d. Harry Dirk and Olga Jean (Dragge) Lohse; m. B. John Myrdal, June 21, 1952; children: Jan, Mark, Harold, Paul, Amy. BS, N.D. State U., 1951. Registered profl. first grade tchr., N.D. Tchr. N.D., 1951-71; bus. mgr. Edinburg Sch. Dist., 1974-81; mem. N.D. Ho. of Reps., Bismarck, 1984-92, mem. appropriations com., 1991-92; lt. gov., State of N.D., Bismarck, 1992—; sch. evaluator Walsh County Sch. Bds. Assn., Grafton, N.D., 1983-84; evaluator, work presenter N.D. Sch. Bds. Assn., Bismarck, 1983-84; mem. sch. bd. Edinburg Sch. Dist., 1981-90; adv. com. Red River Trade Corridor, Inc., 1989—. Co-editor: Heritage '76, 1976, Heritage '89, 1989. Precinct committeewoman Gardar Twp. Rep. Com., 1980-86; leader Hummingbirds 4-H Club, Edinburg, 1980-83; bd. dirs. Camp Sioux Diabetic Children, Grand Forks, N.D., 1980-90, N.D. affiliate Am. Diabetes Assn., Families First-Child Welfare Reform Initiative, Region IV, 1989-92; dir. N.D. Diabetes Assn., 1989-91; chmn. N.D. Ednl. TelecommunicationsCoun., 1989-90; vice chmn. N.D. Legis. Interim Jobs Devel. Commn., 1989-90. Mem. AAUW (pres. 1982-84 Pembina County area), Pembina County Hist. Soc. (historian 1976-84), Northeastern N.D. Heritage Assn. (pres. 1986-92), Red River Valley Heritage Soc. (bd. dirs. 1985-92). Lutheran. Club: Agassiz Garden (Park River) (pres. 1968-69). Avocations: gardening, architectural history, ethnic foods, historic/cultural preservation. Home: 121 E Arikara Ave Apt 302 Bismarck ND 58501-2638 Office: 600 E Boulevard Ave Bismarck ND 58505-0660

MYREN, RICHARD ALBERT, criminal justice consultant; b. Madison, Wis., Aug. 9, 1924; s. Andrew Olaus and Olyanna (Olson) M.; m. Patricia Ross Hubin, June 12, 1948; children: Nina Ross Schroepfer, Tania Ellis Zobel, Kristina Albee Myren Sheldon, Andrew James. BS, U. Wis., 1948; LLB, Harvard U., 1952; LLD (hon.), U. New Haven, 1976. Bar: N.C. 1954. Research chemist U.S. Dept. Agr., No. Regional Research Lab., Peoria, Ill., 1948-49; asst. to assoc. research prof. pub. law and govt. Inst. Govt., Chapel Hill, N.C., 1952-56; asst. to assoc. prof. Ind. U., 1956-66; dean, prof. Sch. Criminal Justice, State U. N.Y., Albany, 1966-76; dean, prof. Sch. Justice, Am. U., Washington, 1976-86, prof. emeritus, 1986—; cons. Washington, 1987—; vis. prof. Inst. Criminology, Cambridge (Eng.) U., 1973-74, East China Inst. for Politics and Law, Shanghai, People's Republic of China, 1988; cons. law enforcement programs for children and youth Children's Bur., HEW, Washington, 1960-62; cons. Pres.'s. Com. on Juvenile Delinquency and Youth Crime, 1962-64, Pres.'s Commn. on Law Enforcement and Adminstrn. Criminal Justice, 1966, U.S. Law Enforcement Assistance Adminstrn., 1968-82, N.Y. State Temp. Commn. on Constl. Conv., 1967, N.Y. State Dept. Edn., 1967, 69, Calif. Coordinating Council for Higher Edn., 1969-70, Nat. Adv. Commn. on Criminal Justice Standards and Goals, 1971-72, Tenn. Higher Edn. Commn., 1976, Ky. Dept. Justice, 1977-78, NSF, 1978—, U.S. Civil Rights Commn., 1978, others. Author: Coroners in North Carolina: A Discussion of Their Problems, 1953, Indiana Sheriffs' Manual of Law and Practice, rev. edit, 1959, Indiana Conservation Officers' Manual of Law and Practice, 1961; (with Lynn D. Swanson) Police Work With Children, 1962; (with Carroll L. Christenson) The Walsh-Healey Public Contracts Act: A Critical Review of Prevailing Minimum Wage Determinations, 1966, Education in Criminal Justice, 1970, Law and Justice: An Introduction, 1988, Investigation for Determination of Fact: A Primer on Proof, 1989; contbr. to: Bases for Justice Systems: Law and the Social Sciences (Gordon E. Misner), 1980, Five Year Outlook: Problems, Opportunities and Constraints in Science and Technology, 1980; assoc. editor: Jour. Criminal Justice; contbr. articles to profl. jours. Bd. dirs. Sex Info. and Edn. Council U.S., 1972-75. Served with inf. AUS, 1943-46, ETO; with USNR, 1954-68. Fulbright research scholar to Argentina Cordoba, 1964-65. Mem. N.C. Bar Assn., Sociedad Argentina de Sociologia. Home: 1051 S Highland St Apt 6D Mount Dora FL 32757-6323

MYRICK, BISMARCK, diplomat; b. Portsmouth, Va., Dec. 23, 1940; children: Bismarck, Jr., Wesley Todd, Allison Elizabeth. BA, U. Tampa, 1972; MA, Syracuse U., 1973, postgrad., 1979-80. Enlisted U.S. Army, 1959, advanced through grades to fgn. area officer; desk officer U.S. Dept. of State, Somalia, 1980-82; polit. officer U.S. Dept. of State, Monrovia, 1982-84; action officer office strategic nuclear policy bur. politico-milit. affairs U.S. Dept. of State, 1985-87, dep. dir. policy plans and coordination bur. inter-Am. affairs, 1987-89, Una Chapman Cox fellow US-African Policy, 1988-90; consul gen. U.S. Dept. of State, Durban, South Africa, 1990-93, Capetown, South Africa, 1993-95; amb. to Kingdom of Lesotho U.S. Dept. of State, Maseru, 1995—. Author: Three Aspects of Crisis in Colonial Kenya, 1975. Decorated Silver Star, Purple Heart, 4 Bronze Stars. Office: Lesotho Dept of State Washington DC 20521-2340

MYRICK, SUE, congresswoman, former mayor; b. Tiffin, Ohio, Aug. 1, 1941; d. William Henry and Margaret Ellen (Roby) Wilkins; m. Jim Forest (div.); children: Greg, Dan; m. Wilbur Edward Myrick Jr., Sept. 11, 1977. Student, Heidelberg Coll., 1959-60, HHD (hon.), 1995. Exec. sec. to mayor and city mgr. City of Alliance, Ohio, 1962-63; dir. br. office Stark County Ct. of Juvenile and Domestic Rels., Alliance, 1963-65; pres. Myrick Agy., Charlotte, N.C., 1971-95; mayor of Charlotte, 1987-91; mem. 104th Congress from 9th N.C. District, Washington, D.C., 1995—; candidate for U.S. Senate from N.C., 1992; active Heart Fund, Multiple Sclerosis, March of Dimes, Arts and Scis. Coun. Fund Dr.; past mem. adv. bd. Uptown Shelter, Uptown Homeless Task Force, bd. dirs. N.C. Inst. Politics; v.p. Sister Cities Internat.; mem. Pres. Bush's Affordable Housing Commn.; founder, coord. Charlotte vol. tornado relief effort; former bd. dirs. Learning How; former mem. adv. bd. U.S. Conf. Mayors; mem.-at-large Charlotte City Coun., 1983-85, Strengthening Am. Commn.; lay leader, Sunday sch. tchr. 1st United Meth. Ch.; treas. Mecklenburg Ministries; former trustee U.S. Conf. of Mayors. Recipient Woman of Yr. award Harrisonburg, Va., 1968; named one of Outstanding Young Women of Am., 1968. Mem. Women's Polit. Caucus, Beta Sigma Phi. Republican. Home: 310 W 8th St Charlotte NC 28202-1704 Office: US House Reps 230 Cannon HOB Washington DC 20515-3309 also: Myrick Enterprises 505 N Poplar St Charlotte NC 28202-1729

MYRLAND, DOUG, broadcast executive. BS in Bus. Adminstrn., St. Mary's Coll. Program dir., ops. mgr. KJZZ-FM, Phoenix; dir. broadcast and affiliate svcs., dir. mktg. Am. Pub. Radio, Mpls.; mktg. and comm. mgr. KPBS, San Diego, 1991-93, gen. mgr., sta. mgr., 1993—. Chmn. Chandler (Ariz.) Salvation Army Adv. Bd. Mem. Pub. Radio Program Dirs. Assn., Queen Creek, Ariz. Kiwanis, San Diego Rotary. Office: KPBS San Diego State U 5164 College Ave San Diego CA 92115-2412

MYSAK, LAWRENCE ALEXANDER, oceanographer, climatologist, mathematician, educator; b. Saskatoon, Sask., Can., Jan. 22, 1940; s. Stephen and Nettie (Trojan) M.; m. Diane Mary Eeles, Aug. 15, 1974; children: Paul Alexander, Claire Anastasia. BSc, U. Alta., Can., 1961; MSc, U. Adelaide, Australia, 1963; AM, Harvard U., 1964, PhD, 1967. Rsch. fellow Harvard U., 1966-67; mem. faculty U. B.C., Vancouver, 1967-86, prof. math. and oceanography, 1976-86; Atmospheric Environ. Svc./Natural Scis. Engring. Rsch. Coun.; sr. indsl. rsch. prof. climatology McGill U., Montreal, Que., Can., 1986-96, dir. Climate Rsch Group, 1986-90, Can. Steamship Lines prof. meteorology, 1989—, founding dir. Ctr. for Climate and Global Change Rsch., 1990-96; vis. rsch. assoc. Oreg. State U., summer 1968; sr. visitor Cambridge (Eng.) U., 1971-72; vis. scientist Inst. Ocean Sci., Sidney, B.C., fall 1976, Nat. Ctr. Atmospheric Rsch., Boulder, Colo., 1977; vis. prof. U.S. Naval Postgrad. Sch., Monterey, Calif., summer 1981, Swiss Fed. inst., Tech., Zurich, 1982-83; George's Lemaître vis. prof. Cath. U. Louvain, Belgium, 1995; invitation fellowship for rsch. in Japan, Japan Soc. for Promotion of Scis., 1997. Co-author: Waves in the Ocean, 1978; also articles in profl. jours.; assoc. editor Jour. Phys. Oceanography, 1977-92, Atmospheric-Ocean, 1988-91, Climatol. Bull., 1992-93; contbg. editor Am. Geophys. Union books on coastal and esturaine studies, 1987—; mem. editl.

bd. Geophys. and Astrophys. Fluid Dynamics, 1983-96. Appt. Order of Can., 1997. Fellow Acad. of Sci. of Royal Soc. Can. (v.p. Acad. of Sci. 1991-93, pres. 1993-96); mem. Can. Applied Math. Soc., Can. Meteorol. and Oceanog. Soc. (co-recipient Pres.'s prize 1980), Royal Soc. Can. (life), Am. Meteorol. Soc., Am. Geophys. Union, Oceanography Soc., European Geophys. Soc. Office: McGill U, 805 Sherbrooke St W, Montreal, PQ Canada H3A 2K6

MYSEL, RANDY HOWARD, publishing company executive; b. Bronx, N.Y., July 26, 1954; s. Sam and Esther (Sinsheimer) M.; m. Rosemary Eileen Vaccari, July 25, 1987; children: Steven, Samantha, Sophie, Lillie. AA, Queensboro C.C., Queens, N.Y., 1975; BA in Acctg., Queens Coll., 1977; MBA, Adelphi U., 1986; grad., Warwick Sch. Bus., London. Mktg./acctg. profl. CBS, Inc., N.Y.C., 1981-86; mktg. analyst Reed Reference Pub., N.Y.C., 1986, bus. mgr., 1987; v.p., planning, in-house sales Reed Reference Pub., New Providence, N.J., 1988—; creator in-house sales dept. Reed Reference Pub., creator all advt. revenue 1997—, in-house sales Martindale-Hubbell. Home: Reed Reference Publishing 63 Lawrence Dr Berkeley Heights NJ 07922 Office: Reed Reference Pub 121 Chanlon Rd New Providence NJ 07974-1541

MYSKO, WILLIAM KEIFER, emergency physician, educator; b. Orange, N.J., Nov. 7, 1943; s. William J. and June O. (Kiefer) M.; m. Madeleine R. Seipp, June 16, 1969; children: Claire, Joseph, Luke, Martha. BS, Rutgers U., 1966; DO, Phila. Coll. Osteo. Medicine, 1975. Bd. cert. diplomate Am. Bd. Emergency Medicine. Intern Walter Reed Army Med. Ctr., Washington, 1975-76; gen. med. officer U.S. Army Health Clinic, Ft. Monroe, Va., 1976-78; emergency physician St. Joseph Hosp., Towson, Md., 1979-83; dir. emergency medicine Mercy Hosp., Balt., 1983-89, Church Hosp., Balt., 1989-90; emergency physician John Hopkins Bayview Med. Ctr., Balt., 1990-91; asst. prof., clin. dir. Johns Hopkins Hosp., Balt., 1991—. Contbr. articles to profl. jours. Capt. U.S. Army, 1975-78. Fellow Am. Coll. Emergency Physicians. Avocations: sports, music, travel, art. Office: Johns Hopkins Hosp Dept Emergency Medicine Baltimore MD 21287-2080

NABATOFF, ROBERT ALLAN, vascular surgeon, educator; b. N.Y.C., Nov. 19, 1918; s. Abraham Louis and Emma (Goldin) N.; m. Joan Herman, Sept. 11, 1955; children: Diane, Richard, Ross. BA, U. Mich., 1939; MD, SUNY, N.Y.C., 1943. Intern Mt. Sinai Hosp., N.Y.C., 1943-44, resident in surgery, 1945-46, Dazian Found. pathology fellow, 1944-45; Rosenstock Found. fellow in cardiovascular surgery Presbyn. Hosp., N.Y.C., 1948-49; asst. clin. prof. in vascular surgery Mt. Sinai Hosp., N.Y.C., 1972-74, assoc. clin. prof. in vascular surgery, 1974-79, clin. prof. vascular surgery, 1978—, attending vascular surgeon, 1979—, dir. ambulatory surg. svc., 1982-96; ret. Mt. Sinai Hosp., 1996; cons. vascular surgeon Jewish Hosp. and Home for Aged, N.Y.C., 1978—. Author 3 book chpts.; contbr. over 60 articles to profl. jours.; inventor 6 surg. devices. Recipient Hon. Medallion, Keio Sch. Medicine, Japan, 1962, Medallion of Honor, Mt. Sinai Alumni Assn., 1965. Fellow AMA, ACS, N.Y. Acad. Medicine; mem. N.Y. State Med. Soc., N.Y. County Med. Soc., N.Y. Soc. for Cardiovascular Surgery, N.Y. Surg. Soc., Pan Am. Med. Assn. (pres. vascular surgery sect.). Avocations: jogging, tennis, walking, theatre, ballet. Office: Medical Office 1020 Park Ave New York NY 10028-0913

NABHOLZ, JOSEPH VINCENT, biologist, ecologist; b. Memphis, Nov. 3, 1945; s. Martin Peter and Helen Kathleen (Garbacz) N.; m. Sue Ann Winterburn, Aug. 12, 1972; children: Karen Stacey, Pamela Michelle. BS, Christian Bros. U., Memphis, 1968; MS, U. Ga., 1973, PHD, 1978. Sr. biologist U.S. EPA, Washington, 1979—; reviewer NSF and profl. jours., 1973—, Standards Methods Com., Am. Water Works Assn., Denver 18th through 20th edits.; evaluator Office Exptl. Learning U. Md., College Park, Md., 1984-86. Co-author: Methods of Ecological Toxicology, 1981, Testing for Effects of Chemicals on Ecosystems, 1981; author: Estimating Toxicity of Industrial Chemicals to Aquatic Organisms Using Structure Activity Relationships, 1988, 94; contbr. numerous articles to profl. jours. Bd. dirs. Community Assn. Rollingwood Village (4th sect.), Woodbridge, Va., 1981-90, v.p. 1981-82, pres. 1983-90, maintainence chmn. 1990—. Decorated Army Commendation medal with oak leaf cluster, U.S. Army, Vietnam, 1969, '70. Mem. AAAS, Am. Inst. Biol. Scis., Assn. Southeastern Biologists, Internat. Assn. Ecology, Ecol. Soc. Am. (life), SETAC, Phi Kappa Phi (life). Roman Catholic. Achievements include pragmatic application of theory of chemical structure activity relationships for routine risk assessment of industrial chemicals for environmental toxicity. Home: 13627 Bentley Cir Woodbridge VA 22192-4340 Office: US EPA 7403 ET 427 401 M St SW Washington DC 20460-0001

NABHOLZ, MARY VAUGHAN, rehabilitation nurse; b. Memphis, July 4, 1938; d. George E. Jr. and Anna Marie (Hannifin) Vaughan; m. William James Nabholz, Jr., May 30, 1959; children: Kathleen Marie, William James III, Michael Vaughan. Diploma, St. Joseph Hosp., Memphis, 1959; BA, Webster U., 1978. Cert. CIRS, CCM. Staff nurse St. Joseph Hosp., St. Charles, Mo., 1965-77; supr. Always Care Nursing Svc., St. Louis, 1977-78; home care nurse Jewish Hosp., St. Louis, 1979-81; regional med. mgr. Md. Casualty Co., St. Louis, 1981-88; case mgr. Am. Health Network, St. Louis, 1988-91; regional mgr., 1990; cons., owner Nabholz & Assocs., Bridgeton, Mo., 1991—; bd. dirs. Ctr. Head Injury Svcs. Bd. dirs. Ctr. Head Injury Svcs. Mem. Nat. Head Injury Assn., Nat. Spinal Cord Assn., Assn. Rehab. Nurses, Nat. Rehab. Assn.

NABI, STANLEY ANDREW, investment executive; b. Baghdad, Iraq, Sept. 17, 1930; came to U.S., 1947; s. Moshi S. and Victoria T. (Mukamal) N.; m. Bette E. Miller, Mar. 31, 1968; children: Deborah Susan, Lisa Meryl. B.A., Columbia U., 1952; postgrad., NYU, 1954-58. Gen. ptnr. Schweickart & Co., N.Y.C., 1954-72; gen. ptnr., chief investment officer Lazard Freres & Co., N.Y.C., 1973-84; exec. v.p. Bessemer Trust Co., N.A., 1985-95; pres., CEO, Bessemer Investors Svcs., 1985-95; vice chmn., chmn. investment policy com. Wood, Struthers & Winthrop, N.Y.C., 1995—; chief investment officer DLJ Investment Mgmt. Corp.; lectr. New Sch. Social Research, N.Y.C., 1963-68; investment cons. U.S. Steel and Carnegie Pension Fund, N.Y.C., 1979—; dir. Bargain Town U.S.A., N.Y.C., 1962-69; mem. Pres.'s Coun. New Sch. Social Rsch., N.Y.C., 1989—; adj. prof. fin. Grad. Sch. Bus. Fordham U., N.Y., 1992—. Editor: weekly jour. The Analyst, 1957-72; assoc. editor: jour. The Fin. Analysts Jour., 1971-83. Trustee NABI Found., 1964—. Served with U.S. Army, 1952-54. Mem. N.Y. Soc. Security Analysts (pres. 1971-72), Inst. Chartered Fin. Analysts, AIMR. Home: 83 Beach Rd Great Neck NY 11023-1019 Office: 630 5th Ave New York NY 10111-0100

NABRIT, SAMUEL MILTON, retired embryologist; b. Macon, Ga., Feb. 21, 1905. BS, Morehouse Coll., 1925; MS, Brown U., 1928; 13 hon. degrees, various U.S. univs. Instr. zoology Morehouse Coll., 1925-27, prof., 1928-31; prof. Atlanta U., 1932-55; pres. Tex. So. U., 1955-66; commr. US AEC, 1966-67; exec. dir. So. Fellows Fund, 1967-81; exch. prof. Atlanta U., 1930, dean Grad. Sch.; gen. edn. bd. fellow Columbia U., 1943; rsch. fellow U. Brussels, 1950; coord. Carnegie Exp. Grant-in-Aid Rsch. Program; mem. sci. bd. NSF, 1956-60; mem. corp. Marine Biol. Lab., Woods Hole; mem. Marine Biol. Labs., AEC, 1966-67; exec. dir. Nat. Fellows Fund, 1967-81; interim dir. Atlanta U. Ctr., 1989-91. Fellow AAAS; mem. Inst. Medicine-NAS, Soc. Devel. Biology, Nat. Assn. Rsch. Sci. Tchg., Nat. Inst. Sci. (pres. 1945), Am. Soc. Zoology, Societé d'honneur Francaise, Phi Beta Kappa, Pi Delta Phi, Sigma Xi.

NACE, BARRY JOHN, lawyer; b. York, Pa., Nov. 28, 1944; s. John Harrison and Mildred Louise (Orwig) N.; m. Andrea Marcia Giardini. Apr. 28, 1973; children: Christopher Thomas, Jonathan Barry, Matthew Andrew. BS, Dickinson Coll., 1965, JD, 1969, DL, 1994. Bar: Md. 1970, D.C. 1971, Pa. 1972, U.S. Ct. Appeals (3d, 4th and D.C. cirs.), U.S. Supreme Ct. Ptnr. Davis & Nace, Washington, 1972-78, Paulson & Nace, Bethesda, Md., 1978-85; sr. ptnr. Paulson, Nace & Norwind, Washington, 1986—. Fellow Roscoe Pound Found. (trustee); mem. Am. Law Inst., D.C. Bar Assn., Montgomery County Bar Assn., Assn. Trial Lawyers Am. (gov. 1976-87, pres. 1993-94), Met. D.C. Trial Attys. (pres. 1977, 87, Atty. of Yr. 1976), Trial Lawyers for Pub. Justice, Civil Justice Found. (trustee), Internat. Acad. Trial Lawyers, Lambert Soc., Am. Inns of Ct., Am. Law Inst. Am. Bd. of Profl. Liability Attorneys. Avocations: golf, tennis, reading, racquetball. Home: 6208 Garnett Dr Bethesda MD 20815-6618 Office: Paulson Nace & Norwind 1814 N St NW Washington DC 20036-2404

NACH, JAMES PETER, foreign service officer; b. Yonkers, N.Y., Aug. 28, 1941; s. Irving Peter and Grace (Sansiper) N.; m. Thuy Duong, Dec. 22, 1978; 1 child, Elizabeth K. BA, St. John's Coll., Annapolis, Md., 1964; Master of Interant. Affairs, Columbia U., 1966; postgrad., Cornell U., 1979-80. Joined fgn. svc. Dept. State, Washington, 1966; with U.S. Consulate, Calcutta, India, 1967-69; with Am. Embassy, Saigon, Vietnam, 1970-74, Manila, 1982-86; various positions U.S. Dept. State, Washington, 1974-82, office dir., 1989-91, with Bur. Pers., 1991-93; polit. counselor Am. Embassy, Kingston, Jamaica, 1986-89; dep. chief mission Am. Embassy, Dhaka, Bangaldesh, 1993—; sr. fgn. svc. officer U.S. Dept. State, 1988—. Author 10 Visual Geography texts, 1962-66. Mem. Am. Fgn. Svc. Assn., Sierra Club. Avocations: bicycling, hiking, philately. Home: 7404 Venice St Falls Church VA 22043-3215

NACHMAN, FREDERICK J., public relations executive; b. Chgo., Mar. 22, 1949; s. Marvin N. and Harriet (Bloomfield) D.; m. Janet M. Neuschatz, Jan. 20, 1973; 1 child, Marisa H. BA in Am. Civilization, Boston U., 1971. Sr.v.p., dir. investor rels. Golin/Harris Comms., Inc., Chgo.; formerly ptnr. Fin. Rels. Bd., Chgo. Office: Golin/Harris Comm Inc 500 N Michigan Ave Chicago IL 60611-3764

NACHMAN, GERALD WEIL, columnist, critic, author, lecturer; b. Oakland, Calif., Jan. 13, 1938; s. Leonard Calvert and Isabel (Weil) N.; m. Mary Campbell McGeachy, Sept. 3, 1966 (div. 1979). Student, Merritt Coll., 1955-57; BA in Journalism, San Jose State U., 1960. TV and humor columnist San Jose (Calif.) Mercury, 1960-63; feature writer N.Y. Post, N.Y.C., 1963-66; drama critic Oakland (Calif.) Tribune, 1966-71; syndicated humor columnist N.Y. Daily News, 1973-79; critic and columnist San Francisco Chronicle, 1979-93; humor columnist N.Y. Times Syndicate, 1997—; juror Pulitzer Prize Com. to choose best play, 1991. Author: The Portable Nachman, 1960, Playing House, 1978, Out on a Whim, 1983, The Fragile Bachelor, 1989; contbr. to (book) Snooze, 1986; contbr. articles to newspapers, mags.; author, co-lyricist (revues) Quirks, 1979, Aftershocks, 1992. Recipient Page One award N.Y. Newspaper Guild, 1965, Deems Taylor award ASCAP, 1989. Home: 281 Juanita Way San Francisco CA 94127-1744

NACHMAN, MERTON ROLAND, JR., lawyer; b. Montgomery, Ala., Dec. 21, 1923; s. Merton Roland and Maxine (Mayer) N.; children: Nancy Nachman Yardley, Linda Nachman Connelly, Betsy Wild, Amy N. DeRoche, Karen Vann; m. Martha Street, June 8, 1968. AB cum laude, Harvard U., 1943, JD, 1948. Bar: Ala. 1949, U.S. Supreme Ct. 1953, U.S. Ct. Appeals (5th and 11th cirs.), U.S. Ct. Claims, U.S. Tax Ct. Asst. atty. gen. State of Ala., 1949-54; ptnr. Knabe & Nachman, Montgomery, 1954-59; adminstrv. asst. to Senator John Sparkman of Ala., 1956; ptnr. Steiner, Crum & Baker, Montgomery, 1959-86; ptnr. Balch & Bingham, 1986-94, coun. 1994—. Chmn. human rights com. Ala. Prison System, 1976-78. With USN, 1943-46. Recipient award of merit Ala. State Bar, 1974; cert. of appreciation Supreme Ct. Ala., 1974. Fellow Am. Coll. Trial Lawyers; mem. ABA (com. on fed. judiciary 1982-88, bd. govs. 1978-81), Ala. State Bar (pres. 1973-74), Am. Judicature Soc. (dir. 1976-80, Herbert Lincoln Harley award 1974), Am. Law Inst., Ala. Law Inst., Unity Club (Montgomery), Am. Acad. Appellate Lawyers. Episcopalian. Office: 2 Dexter Ave PO Box 78 Montgomery AL 36101

NACHMAN, NORMAN HARRY, lawyer; b. Chgo.; s. Harry and Mary (Leibowitz) N.; m. Anne Lev, June 19, 1932; children: Nancy Nachman Laskow, James Lev, Susan Lev. PhB, U. Chgo., 1930, JD, 1932. Bar: Ill. 1932, U.S. Dist. Ct. (no. dist.) Ill. 1932, U.S. Dist. Ct. (we. dist.) Tex. 1978, U.S. Ct. Appeals (7th cir.) 1942, U.S. Ct. Appeals (4th cir.) 1978, U.S. Ct. Appeals (8th cir.) 1994, U.S. Supreme Ct. 1942. Assoc. Michael Gesas, Chgo., 1932-35; assoc. Schwartz & Cooper, Chgo., 1936-40, ptnr., 1940-46; pvt. practice, Chgo., 1947-67; founder, sr. ptnr. Nachman, Munitz & Sweig, Ltd., Chgo., 1967-87; ptnr. Winston & Strawn, 1987-94; counsel McDermott, Will & Emery, 1994—; mem. adv. com. bankruptcy rules Jud. Conf. U.S., 1960-76, 78-88; mem. Nat. Bankruptcy Conf., 1952—, mem. com. bankruptcy reorganization plans and securities problems, 1977-85; mem. faculty numerous bankruptcy seminars throughout U.S. Contbg. editor: Collier on Bankruptcy, 1981, 84. Chmn. appeals bd. Chgo. Dept. Environ. Control, 1960-80. Served to lt. USN, 1943-46. Mem. ABA (past chmn. comml. bankruptcy com.), Chgo. Bar Assn. (pres. 1963-64), Ill. Bar Assn., Standard Club, Law Club. Jewish. Office: McDermott Will & Emery 227 W Monroe St Chicago IL 60606-5016

NACHMAN, RALPH LOUIS, physician, educator; b. Bayonne, N.J., June 29, 1931; s. Samuel Nachman and Ethel Nelson; m. Nancy Rubin; children: Susan, Steve. BA, Vanderbilt U., 1953, MD, 1956. Lic. physician N.Y.; diplomate Am. Bd. Internal Medicine; subsplty. hematology, med. oncology. Intern in medicine Vanderbilt U. Hosp., 1956-57; asst. resident in medicine Montefiore Hosp., 1960-62; asst. resident in pathology N.Y. Hosp.-Cornell U. Med. Ctr., N.Y.C., 1957-58, rsch. fellow in medicine, 1962-63; dir. labs. for clin. pathology N.Y. Hosp., 1963-69, assoc. attending physician, 1968-72, attending physician, 1972—; from instr. to asst. prof. to assoc. prof. medicine Cornell Med. Ctr., 1963-72, chief divns. hematology, 1968-93, prof. medicine, 1972—; vice chmn. dept. medicine Cornell U. Med. Coll., 1974-78, acting chmn. dept. medicine, 1974-75, dir. Specialized Ctr. Rsch. in Thrombosis, 1976—, acting co-chmn. dept. medicine, 1980-81, bd. overseers, 1987-89, chmn. Dept. of Med., 1990; physician-in-chief New York Hospital, 1990; guest investigator Rockefeller U., 1969-70; Wiessberg lectr. Case Western Res. U., 1978; Aggeler lectr. U. Calif., San Francisco, 1981; Patek lectr. Boston U., 1981; Rosenthal lectr. Mt. Sinai, 1982; Beaumont lectr. Wash. U., 1983; Wiener lectr. N.Y. Blood Ctr., 1983; chmn. Gordon Conf. on Hemostasis, 1984; Alpha Omega Alpha lectr. N.Y. Med. Coll., 1985; Sharp lectr. Wayne State U., 1986; Roon lectr. Scripps Rsch. Inst., 1987; Johnson lectr. Internat. Soc. on Thrombosis, 1987; Merck lectr. Cleve. Clinic, 1987; vis. prof. Harvard U., 1991; E. Stanley Emery Jr. Meml. lectr, physician-in-chief pro tempore, 1991; chief resident's vis. prof. Baylor Coll. Medicine, 1991; Samuel S. Riven vis. prof. Vanderbilt U., 1992; Hymie Nossel Meml. lectr. Columbia U., 1992; Pfizer vis. prof. Royal Soc. Medicine, 1992; disting. lectr. Am. Heart Assn., 1994; Seckler lectr. Mt. Sinai Med. Ctr., 1994; Runme Shaw Meml. lectr. Acad. Medicine, Singapore, 1994; chmn. hematology study panel Health Rsch. Coun., N.Y.C., 1973-75; mem. NIH-Program Project Com., Heart and Lung Inst., 1975-79; bd. govs. Am. Bd. Internal Medicine, 1985-88; cons. Manhattan VA Hosp.; vis. physician Rockefeller U. Hosp. Author: Genetics of Coronary Heart Disease, 1992, Systemic Lupus Erythematosus, 1993, (jours.) Blood, 1994, Ann. Internal Medicine, 1993; assoc. editor: Beeson McDermott Textbook of Medicine, XIV edit., 1975, XV edit., 1979, Blood, 1976-82, Am. Jour. Medicine, 1978; adv. editor: Jour. Exptl. Medicine, 1976; editl. bd. Arteriosclerosis, 1983; contbr. articles to med. jours. With USN, 1958-60. Fellow ACP; mem. AAAS, Assn. Am. Physicians, Am. Soc. Clin. Investigation, Am. Fedn. Clin. Rsch., Am. Clin. and Climatol. Assn., N.Y. Acad. Sci., N.Y. Soc. for Study of Blood (pres. 1975), Am. Soc. Hematology (exec. coun. 1978-79), Harvey Soc. (coun. 1980), Am. Physiol. Assn., Internat. Soc. Thrombosis and Hemostasis (coun. 1986-92), Soc. Exptl. Biology and Medicine, Am. Soc. Biol. Chemists, Inst. Medicine of NAS, N.Y. Acad. Medicine, Cornell Med. Alumni (hon.), Nat. Blood Club (pres. 1981-82), Peripatetic Club, Alpha Omega Alpha, Phi Beta Kappa. Home: 657 Floyd St Englewood Cliffs NJ 07632-2049 Office: NY Hosp-Cornell Med Ctr 525 E 68th St # F-433 New York NY 10021-4873*

NACHMAN, RONALD JAMES, research chemist; b. Takoma Park, Md., Feb. 1, 1954; s. Joseph Frank and Rosemary (Anderson) N.; m. Lita Rose Wilson, Dec. 18, 1976 (div. 1987); m. Isidora Austria Panis, May 6, 1989. BS in Chemistry, U. Calif., San Diego, 1976; PhD in Organic Chemistry, Stanford U., 1981. Rsch. asst. Scripps Inst. Oceanography, La Jolla, Calif., 1974-76; chemist Western Regional Rsch. Ctr., USDA, Berkeley, Calif., 1981-89, Vet. Toxicology and Entomology Rsch. Lab., College Station, Tex., 1989—; vis. scientist dept. molecular biology The Salk Inst., La Jolla, 1985, Scripps Rsch. Inst., La Jolla, 1988-89. Contbr. sci. articles to profl. jours. Recipient USDA Cert. of Merit, 1988, 91, Arthur S. Flemming award for sci. achievement, 1994. Fellow Sci. and Humanities Symposia; mem. AAAS, Am. Chem. Soc., N.Y. Acad. Scis., Sigma Xi. Avocations: travel, photography, jogging, racketball. Home: 14891 Pollux Willis TX 77378-0014 Office: USDA Vet Toxicology Entomology Rsch Lab 2881 F And B Rd College Station TX 77845-4988

NACHT, DANIEL JOSEPH, architect; b. Chgo., Sept. 22, 1915; s. George Carl and Hattie (Zaylor) N.; m. Mary Alice Belcher, Nov. 19, 1960; 1 dau., Pamela Jean. B.S., U. Ill., 1940. Mem. faculty U. Ill., 1940-42; with Skidmore, Owings & Merrill, Chgo., 1946-53; designer Rogers Engring. Co., San Francisco, 1953-55; architect Starks, Jozens & Nacht, Sacramento, 1956-70, Nacht & Lewis, 1970. Prin. works include Consumnes River Coll, Sacramento County Courthouse. Mem. Capitol Bldg. and Planning Commn., 1959-67; mem. Core Area Com., 1962-64; mem. adv. bd. Salvation Army Sacramento area. With USNR, 1942-46. Fellow A.I.A.; mem. Crocker Art Gallery, Alpha Chi Rho. Club: Mason (Shriner). Home: 7604 Pineridge Ln Fair Oaks CA 95628-4855 Office: 7300 Folsom Blvd Sacramento CA 95826-2622

NACHT, SERGIO, biochemist; b. Buenos Aires, Apr. 13, 1934; came to U.S., 1965; s. Oscar and Carmen (Scheiner) N.; m. Beatriz Kahan, Dec. 21, 1958; children: Marcelo H., Gabriel A., Mariana S., Sandra M. BA in Chemistry, U. Buenos Aires, 1958, MS in Biochemistry, 1960, PhD in Biochemistry, 1964. Asst. prof. biochemistry U. Buenos Aires, 1960-64; asst. prof. medicine U. Utah, Salt Lake City, 1965-70; rsch. scientist Alza Corp., Palo Alto, Calif., 1970-73; sr. investigator Richardson-Vicks Inc., Mt. Vernon, N.Y., 1973-76; asst. dir., dir. rsch. Richardson-Vicks Inc., Mt. Vernon, 1976-83; dir. biomed. rsch. Richardson-Vicks Inc., Shelton, Conn., 1983-87; sr. v.p. rsch. and devel. Advanced Polymer Systems, Redwood City, Calif., 1987-93, sr. v.p. sci. and tech., 1993—; lectr. dermatology dept. SUNY Downstate Med. Ctr., Blkyn., 1977-87. Contbr. articles to profl. jours.; patentee in field. Mem. Soc. Investigative Dermatology, Soc. Cosmetic Chemists (award 1981), Dermatology Found., Am. Physiological Soc., Am. Acad. Dermatology. Democrat. Jewish. Home: 409 Wembley Ct Redwood City CA 94061-4308

NACHTIGAL, PATRICIA, equipment manufacturing company executive, general counsel; b. 1946. BA, Montclair State U.; JD, Rutgers U.; LLM, NYU. Tax atty. Ingersoll-Rand Co., Woodcliff Lake, N.J., 1979-83, dir. taxes and legal, 1983-88, sec., mng. atty., 1988-91, v.p., gen. counsel, 1991—. Office: Ingersoll-Rand Co 200 Chestnut Ridge Rd Westwood NJ 07675-7703

NACHTWEY, JAMES ALAN, photojournalist; b. Syracuse, N.Y., Mar. 14, 1948; s. James Vincent and Jean (Stockton) N. BA cum laude, Dartmouth Coll., 1970. Contract photographer Time mag., N.Y.C., 1984—; mem. Magnum Photos, N.Y.C., 1986—; tchr. Internat. Ctr. Photography, N.Y.C., 1993, 94, 95, 96, Santa Fe Workshop, 1994, Photography at the Summit, Jackson Hole, Wyo., 1994, 96. Author, photographer: Deeds of War, 1989 (Leica award 1989), The Inferno, 1995; contbg. photographer (books) War Torn, El Salvador, In Our Time-40 Years of Magnum, The Indelible Image, Odyssey-Photography at the National Geographic, National Geographic, The Photographs, (mags.) Time, Life, Nat. Geographic, N.Y. Times mag., GEO, L'Express, Stern; one-man shows Internat. Ctr. Photography, 1989, Hassezblad Ctr., Goteborg, Sweden, 1992, Canon Gallery, Amsterdam, The Netherlands, 1992, Carolinum, Prague, Czech republic, 1994, Nieuwe Kerk, Amsterdam, 1995, Hood Mus., Dartmouth Coll., 1995, Internat. Forum, Tokyo, 1997, Fleethof, Hamburg, Germany, 1997, Japanese Palace, Dresden, Germany, 1997, Mass. Coll. Art, Boston, 1997. Recipient Robert Capa gold medal Overseas Press Club, 1983, 84, 86, 94, Olivier Rebbot award, 1992, 93; photography award World Press Photo Found., 1992, 94, Mag. Photographer of Yr. award Nat. Press Photographers Assn., 1983, 86, 88, 90, 92, 94, Canon Photog. essayist award, 1992; Infinity award Internat. Ctr. Photography, 1991, 93, Leica award New Sch. for Social Rsch., 1989, 90, award Budapest Photgraphic Festival, 1985, Nikon award Maine Workshop, 1985, Nikon World Image award New Sch.-Parsons Sch. Design, 1991, Bayeaux award for war correspondents, 1995; Eugene Smith Meml. grantee, 1994. Avocations: fly fishing, skiing. Office: Magnum Photos 151 W 25th St New York NY 10001-7204

NACHWALTER, MICHAEL, lawyer; b. N.Y.C., Aug. 31, 1940; s. Samuel J. Nachwalter; m. Irene, Aug. 15, 1965; children: Helynn, Robert. BS, Bucknell U., 1962; MS, L.I. U., 1967; JD cum laude, U. Miami, 1967; LLM, Yale U., 1968. Bar: Fla. 1967, D.C. 1979, U.S. Dist. Ct. (so. dist.) Fla. 1967, U.S. Dist. Ct. (mid. dist.) Fla. 1982, U.S. Ct. Appeals (5th and 11th cirs.) 1967, U.S. Supreme Ct. 1975. Law clk. to judge U.S. Dist. Ct. (so. dist.) Fla.; shareholder Kelly, Black, Black & Kenny; now shareholder Kenny Nachwalter Seymour Arnold Critchlow & Spector, P.A., Miami; lectr. Law Sch. U. Miami. Fellow Am. Coll. Trial Lawyers; mem. Judicial Qualifications Commn. (vice chmn. hearing panel); mem. ABA, Am. Bd. Trial Advocates, Fla. Bar Assn. (bd. govs. 1982-90), Fed. Bar Assn., Internat. Soc. Barristers, Dade County Bar Assn., Omicron Delta Kappa, Phi Kappa Phi, Phi Delta Phi, Iron Arrow, Soc. Wig and Robe. Editor-in-chief U. Miami Law Rev., 1966-67. Office: Kenny Nachwalter Seymour Arnold Critchlow & Spector PA 201 S Biscayne Blvd Ste 1100 Miami FL 33131-4327

NACK, CLAIRE DURANI, artist, author; b. N.Y.C.; d. Myron Irving and Rachel Rita Adele (Feldman) N. Student, NYU, 1975, Sculpture Ctr., N.Y.C., 1975; Arts Student League. Pres. Claire Durani Nack Corp. subs. Princess Enterprs./Durani Co., N.Y.C., 1993—, Books of Poetry by Claire Durani Nack, Mystery Stories by Claire Durani Nack, Books of Science Fiction by Claire Durani Nack, Works of Art by Claire Durani Nack, C.D.N. Co.; lectr. N.Y. State Mus., Albany, 1992, Hudson Valley C.C., 1986-92, Schenectady (N.Y.) Mus., Troy Arts League, 1989. Artist sketchbooks; author/artist: Something Happened in the Kitchen, 1981, European Journey, Book II, 1981, Cat Book, 1994, Diary, 2, 1980, Diary, Vol. 4, 1994, Vol. 5, 1994, The Journal of Claire Durani Nack, 1994, Art Book 1, 1982, Art Book 2, 1982, My World, 1994, Blue Book, Upwards Bent (books 1-5), 1993-94, Spiders Web Unspun, 1994, An Unfamiliar Place, 1993, The Adventures of Cora, 1994 (books 1-3), Cahiers de Dessins de Paris, 1994, Big City Lights, 1991, Something Happened in the Bathroom, Something Happened in the Living Room, Children's Coloring Book, 1995, Animal Book, 1995, Liz Muller (play), Sports Products for Sale (catalogue), 1995, The Adventures of Cora (allegorical book), 1993; artist painting series: The Americans, 1987-93, Animal Series; author Journals of Claire Durani Nack, art and text, 1984—, Sports Coloring Book. Recipient poetry award Nat. Libr. of Poetry, Calif., 1991; scholar Art Students League, 1985. Mem. Nat. Mus. of Women in the Arts (charter mem.), Art Students League (life), N.Y. State Mus. Avocations: travel, collecting model airplanes, collecting hats, art and art books. Home and Office: 416 East St Rensselaer NY 12144

NACKEL, JOHN GEORGE, health care consulting director; b. Medford, Mass., Nov. 4, 1951; s. Michael and Josephine (Maria) N.; m. Gail Helen Becker, Oct. 30, 1976; children: Melissa Anne, Allison Elizabeth. BS, Tufts U., 1973; MS in Pub. Health and Indsl. Engring., U. Mo., 1975, PhD, 1977. Sr. mgr. Ernst & Young, Chgo., 1977-83; nat. dir. health care cons. Cleve., 1983-87, regional dir. health industry svcs., 1987-91; mng. dir. health care Ernst & Young, Cleve., 1991-93; nat. dir. Health Care Cons., L.A., 1994—; editorial bd. Jour. Med. Systems, 1983—. Author: Cost Management for Hospitals, 1987 (Am. Hosp. Assn. book award 1988); contbr. articles to profl. jours. Grantee Dept. Health Edn. Welfare, Washington, 1973-76. Fellow Am. Coll. Healthcare Execs., Healthcare Info. and Mgmt. Systems Soc. (articles award); mem. Inst. Indsl. Engrs. (sr.), U. Mo. health Svcs. Mgmt. Alumni Assn. (pres.), Canterbury Golf Club (Cleve.), La Canada-Flintridge Country Club, Annandale Golf Club, Jonathan Club. Republican. Avocations: golf, tennis, squash, paddle, photography. Home: 666 Linda Vista Ave Pasadena CA 91105-1145

NACLERIO, ROBERT MICHAEL, otolaryngologist, educator; b. N.Y.C., Mar. 30, 1950; s. Albert Paul and Lee Ann (Rabinowitz) N.; m. Sharon Ann Silhan, Mar. 30, 1983; children: Jessica, Daniel. BA, Cornell U., 1972; MD with honors, Baylor U., 1976. Diplomate Am. Bd. Otolaryngology. Intern in surgery Johns Hopkins Hosp., Balt., 1976-77, resident in surgery, 1977-78; resident in otolaryngology Baylor Coll. Medicine, Houston, 1978-80, chief resident in otolaryngology, 1982-83; fellow in clin. immunology divsn. Johns Hopkins U. Sch. Medicine, Balt., 1980-82, asst. prof. medicine and otolaryngology, 1983-87, asst. prof. pediat., 1986-87, dir. divsn. pediat. otolaryngology, 1986-94, assoc. prof. otolaryngology, medicine and pediat., 1987-92, prof. otolaryngology, medicine and pediat., 1992-94; chief of otolaryngology, head and neck surgery U. Chgo., Chgo., 1994—; cons. Richardson-Vicks Inc., 1986-89, 90, NIH, 1987, Proctor & Gamble, 1987, 94, Sandoz Rsch. Inst., 1988, Schering Rsch., 1988, Wallace Labs., 1989, Joint Rhinologic Conf., 1989, Internat. Congress Rhinology, 1991, Norwich-Eaton Pharm. Inc., 1991-92, Ciba-Geigy Corp., 1991-92, Mktg. Corp. Am., 1993—, others; mem. med. bd. Children's Ctr., 1991-94, other local comms.; reviewer Am. Jour. Rhinology, others; lectr. in field. Editor: Rhinoconjunctivitis: New Perspectives in Topical Treatment, 1988; asst. editor: Am. Jour. Rhinology, 1986—, Rhinology, 1988—; mem. editl. bd. Otolaryngology-Head and Neck Surgery, 1990—, Laryngoscope, 1990—, Jour. Allergy and Clin. Immunology, 1992-97; contbr. numerous chpts. to books, papers and abstracts to profl. jours. and procs. Fellow ACS, Am. Acad. Otolaryngology-Head and Neck Surgery (mem. com. 1985-90, 90-92, subcom. 1987-92), Am. Laryngol., Rhinol. and Otol. Soc., Inc.; mem. Am. Acad. Allergy and Immunology (mem. com. 1983-88, 88-89, 88-95, chmn. com. 1990-91, 91—, Jerome Glazer Meml. lectureship), Am. Fedn. Clin. Rsch., Am. Soc. Pediat. Otolaryngology (mem. rsch. com. 1990-94, chmn. subcom. 1990), Soc. Univ. Otolaryngologists-Head and Neck Surgeons, Pan-Am. Assn. Otorhinolaryngology, Internat. Symposium on Infection and Allergy of the Nose (v.p.). Office: U Chgo Section of O-HNS 5841 S Maryland Ave # 1035 Chicago IL 60637-1463

NACOL, MAE, lawyer; b. Beaumont, Tex., June 15, 1944; d. William Samuel and Ethel (Bowman) N.; children: Shawn Alexander Nacol, Catherine Regina Nacol. BA, Rice U., 1965; postgrad., S. Tex. Coll. Law, 1966-68. Bar: Tex. 1969, U.S. Dist. Ct. (so. dist.) Tex. 1969. Diamond buyer/appraiser Nacol's Jewelry, Houston, 1961—; pvt. practice law, Houston, 1969—. Author, editor ednl. materials on multiple sclerosis, 1981-85. Nat. dir. A.R.M.S. of Am. Ltd., Houston, 1984-85. Recipient Mayor's Recognition award City of Houston, 1972; Ford Found. fellow So. Tex. Coll. Law, Houston, 1964. Mem. Houston Bar Assn. (chmn. candidate com. 1970, chmn. membership com. 1971, chmn. lawyers referral com. 1972), Assn. Trial Lawyers Am., Tex. Trial Lawyers Assn., Am. Judicature Soc. (sustaining), Houston Fin. Coun. Women, Houston Trial Lawyers Assn. Presbyterian. Office: 600 Jefferson St Ste 850 Houston TX 77002-7326

NADAS, ALEXANDER SANDOR, pediatric cardiologist, educator; b. Budapest, Hungary, Nov. 12, 1913; s. Sandor and Margit (Roth) N.; m. Elizabeth McClearen, Nov. 22, 1941; children: Trudi Norman-Murch, Elizabeth Nadas Seamans, John A. M.D., Budapest Med. Sch., 1937, Wayne U., 1945. Diplomate Am. Bd. Pediatrics, Am. Bd. Pediatric Cardiology. Intern Fairview Park Hosp., Cleve., 1939-40, Wilmington Gen. Hosp., 1940-41; resident in pediatrics Mass. Meml. Hosp., Boston, 1941-42; asst. resident Boston Children's Hosp., 1943; chief resident Mich. Children's Hosp., Detroit, 1943-45; practice medicine specializing in pediatrics Greenfield, Mass., 1945-49; asst. physician, asso. chief cardiology Children's Hosp., Boston, 1949-50; asso. physician Children's Hosp., 1950-51, assoc. cardiologist, 1951-52, cardiologist, 1952-66, sr. asso. in medicine, 1962, chief cardiology div., 1966-69, chief cardiology dept., 1969-83, emeritus chief cardiology, 1983—; research fellow in pediatrics Harvard U. Med. Sch., 1949, instr., 1950-52, clin. assoc., 1952-55, asst. clin. prof. pediatrics, 1955-61, assoc. clin. prof., 1961-64, clin. prof., 1964-69, prof., 1969-83, emeritus prof., 1983—; Fulbright prof. pediatrics U. Groningen, Netherlands, 1956-57; cons. in field. Author: Pediatric Cardiology, 1972, NADAS Pediatric Cardiology, 1991; mem. editorial bd.: Yearbook of Cardiovascular Medicine and Surgery, 1961-85, Circulation, 1968-73, Am. Jour. Cardiology, 1973, Pediatric Cardiology, 1979—; contbr. articles to med. jours. Guggenheim fellow, 1970, recipient Gifted Teacher awd., Am. Coll. of Cardiology, 1993. Mem. Mass. Med. Soc., Am. Heart Assn., Am. Acad. Pediatrics, Soc. Pediatric Research, Am. Pediatric Soc. (pres. 1972-73). Home: 865 Central Ave Needham MA 02192-1316 Office: Children's Hosp Dept Cardiology 300 Longwood Ave Boston MA 02115-5724

NADASKAY, RAYMOND, architect; b. Newark, Aug. 26, 1938; s. Charles and Marie (Roncskevitz) N.; m. Nancy Searle, June 29, 1962; 1 child, Cathy. BArch, Washington U., St. Louis, 1962. Registered architect, N.J., Conn., Vt., Mass., Ill., Ohio; registered planner; cert. NCARB. Designer Rotwein and Blake, Architects, Union, N.J., 1962-63, I.M. Pei, N.Y.C., 1963-64; designer, assoc. McDowell Goldstein, Morristown, N.J., 1964-72; pres. Nadaskay Kopelson Architects, P.A., Morristown, 1972—. Mem. Mendham (N.J.) Twp. Hist. Preservation Commn., Mendham Twp. Roadscape Commn. Recipient numerous spl. commendations, awards of merit for variety of works. Mem. N.J. Soc. Archs. (conv. chmn. 1985-86, past pres. Newark Suburban chpt. 1984, recipient of 30 awards for architecture from 1979-95), Porsche Club (No., N.J.). Avocations: woodworking, sailing, auto rally events, swimming. Office: Nadaskay Kopelson Architects 95 Washington St Morristown NJ 07960-6816*

NADEAU, BERTIN F., diversified company executive; b. May 26, 1940; s. J.-D. and Irene (Daigle) N.; m. Juliette Angell, July 24, 1971; children: Eric, Shahn, Stephanie. BA, Coll. St-Louis, 1961; grad., Ecole des Hautes Etudes Commerciales de Montreal, 1964; postgrad., Harvard U.; DBA, Ind. U., 1969. Chmn., CEO Unigesco Inc., 1982-94; chmn., CEO, Gescolynx Inc., Montreal, 1994—; bd. dirs. Sun Life Can., Lafarge Corp., The Banff Ctr. Office: GescoLynx Inc, 606 Cathcart Ste 1035, Montreal, PQ Canada H3B 1K9

NADEAU, EARL RAYMOND, electronics executive; b. Conrad, Mont., June 8, 1926; s. Raymond Joseph and Marvel Mae (Hunter) N.; m. Frances Ann Gambale, June 30, 1962; children: Nicole Mary, Christopher Earl. Student, Carroll Coll., 1944, U. Wash., 1945, Mont. State U., 1946-48. Supr. method engring. program, mgr. major subcontracting Boeing Airplane Co., Seattle and Wichita, 1950-55; adminstr. Atlas program Convair div. Gen. Dynamics, San Diego, 1955-57; chief plans and proposals Boeing Co., Seattle, 1958-59; mgmt. planning and applications cons. Waldwick, N.J., 1960-65; mgr. project engring/applications engring. Lockheed Electronics Co. Inc., Plainfield, N.J., 1966-69, dir. engring., 1970-76, dir. advanced devel., 1976-83; gen. ptnr. Nadeau Assocs., Watchung, N.J., 1984-96; ret., 1996. Served with USNR, 1943-46, PTO. Electrd to Mont. State U. Athletes Hall of Fame, 1992. Mem. AIAA, Instrument Soc. Am. (sr.), Marine Tech. Soc. Roman Catholic. Home: 132 Sunbright Rd Watchung NJ 07060-6045

NADEAU, JOSEPH EUGENE, health care management consultant, information systems consultant; b. Portland, Maine, Sept. 23, 1937; s. Edwin Tustin and Beatrice Margaret (Spiller) N.; m. Mary Lou Prendible, Dec. 2, 1961; children: Laura, Keith, Michael. BS in Math., Boston Coll., 1960. Dir. sys. devel. Mass. Hosp. Assn., Burlington, 1967-72; S.E. regional mgr. Automatic Data Processing, Miami, Fla., 1972-73; S.E. regional mktg. mgr. Space Age Computer Sys., Louisville, 1973-74; prin. COMPUTERx Cons., Miami, 1974— . Asst. scoutmaster South Fla. coun. Boy Scouts Am., 1972-81. 1st lt. U.S. Army, 1960-64, Germany. Mem. Am. Hosp. Assn., Soc. Computer Medicine, Data Processing Mgmt. Assn., Hosp. Mgmt Sys. Soc., Assn. Sys. Mgmt. (pres. 1971-72), Hosp. Fin. Mgmt. Assn. (chmn. data processing com. 1967-84), Am. Arbitration Assn. (arbitrator 1980—). Cert. computer profl. Home: 7750 SW 118th St Miami FL 33156-4433 Office: COMPUTERx Consulting 9719 S Dixie Hwy # 1 Miami FL 33156-2806

NADEAU, MICHAEL JOSEPH, college service assistant; b. Glens Falls, N.Y., Dec. 19, 1949; s. John Long and Mary Catherine (Cimo) N. Student of Eli Siegel's Aesthetic Realism, N.Y.C., 1977-81; AA in English with honors, Borough of Manhattan C.C., N.Y.C., 1992. Orderly Glens Falls (N.Y.) Hosp., 1969-72; record storage clk. Continental Ins. Co., Glens Falls, 1972-75; purchasing agt. Maersk Inc., Madison, N.J., 1975-93; coll. svc. asst. Passaic County C.C., Paterson, N.J., 1993—. Author: The Adventures of Prudence Longface, 1993. Actor, singer Elbee Audio Players, N.Y.C., 1979-81. With USN, 1969-70. Mem. Am. Legion. Democrat. Roman Catholic. Avocations: bowling, swimming, boating, woodworking, singing. Home: 15 Overlook Ave Mine Hill NJ 07803-3100

NADEAU, REGINALD ANTOINE, medical educator; b. St. Leonard, N.B., Can., Dec. 18, 1932; married, 1957; 2 children. BA, Loyola Coll., Can., 1952; MD, U. Montreal, 1957. From asst. prof. to assoc. prof. Faculty Medicine, U. Montreal, 1964-70, prof. physiology, 1972-75, prof. medicine, 1975—; career investigator Med. Rsch. Coun. Can., 1965; dir. rsch. Cardiol. Hosp. Sacre Coeur, Montreal. Fellow Royal Coll. Physicians (Can.); mem. Can. Physiol. Soc., Can. Cardiovasc. Assn., Am. Coll. Cardiology. Achievements include research in clinical cardiology. Office: Sacre Coeur Hosp Montreal, 5400 Gouin Blvd W, Montreal, PQ Canada H4J 1C5

NADEAU, ROBERT BERTRAND, JR., lawyer; b. Miami Beach, Fla., July 15, 1950; s. Robert B. and Ernestine Inez (Nicholson) N. BBA, U. Notre Dame, 1972; JD, U. Fla., 1975. Bar: Fla. 1975, U.S. Dist. Ct. (mid. dist.) Fla. 1976, U.S. Dist. Ct. (so. dist.) Fla. 1982, U.S. Ct. Appeals (11th cir.) 1982. Asst. to pres. The Fla. Bar, Tampa, Fla., 1975-76; ptnr. Akerman, Senterfitt & Eidson, P.A., Orlando, Fla., 1976—; arbitrator Am. Arbitration Assn., Orlando, 1987—. Mem. ABA, The Fla. Bar (chmn. student edn. and admission to bar com.), Notre Dame Club Greater Orlando (pres. 1979-80). Avocations: golf, running. Office: Akerman Senterfitt & Eidson PA 255 S Orange Ave Orlando FL 32801-3445

NADEAU, STEVEN C., lawyer; b. Schenectady, N.Y., July 6, 1954. AB magna cum laude, Boston Coll., 1974, JD cum laude, 1977. Bar: Mich. 1977. Mediator Wayne County Cir. Ct., 1983-88; mem. Honigman Miller Schwartz and Cohn, Detroit; mem. Wayne County Cir. Com., 1982-87, ad hoc com. on proposed Mich. ct. rules, 1983-85. Mem. ABA (sect. natural resources), State Bar Mich. (sect. environ. law and real estate law), Detroit Bar Assn. Office: Honigman Miller Schwartz and Cohn 660 Woodward Ave Ste 2290 Detroit MI 48226-3583

NADEL, ELLIOTT, investment firm executive; b. N.Y.C., Nov. 23, 1945; s. Archie and Faye (Braverman) N.; children: Lindsey, Amanda. BBA, Baruch Coll., 1969, MBA, 1971. Portfolio mgr. SwissRe Advisors, N.Y.C., 1973-74; v.p., stockbroker E. F. Hutton, N.Y.C., 1975-84, Shearson Lehman Bros., N.Y.C., 1984-85, Oppenheimer & Co., N.Y.C., 1985, Rooney Pace Inc., N.Y.C., 1986-87, Philips Appel & Walden, N.Y.C., 1987-88; sr. v.p. investments Moore, Schley & Cameron, N.Y.C., 1988-90, Prudential-Securities, N.Y.C., 1990-94; sr. v.p. Gilford Securities, N.Y.C., 1994—. With U.S. Army, 1969-74. Jewish. Avocations: jogging, reading, cars, golf, travel. Office: SFI Investments 88 Pine St New York NY 10005-1801

NADEL, ETHAN RICHARD, epidemiology educator; b. Washington, Sept. 3, 1941. BA, Williams Coll., 1963; MA, U. Calif., Santa Barbara, 1966, PhD in Biology, 1969. From asst. prof. to prof. epidemiology Yale U., New Haven, 1970—; from asst. fellow to assoc. fellow John D. Pierce Found. Lab., 1970—; environ. physiol. commn. Internat. Union Physiol. Sci., 1977—; Hall meml. lectr. U. Louisville, 1979. Fellow NIH, 1969-70; grantee USPHS, 1970—. Fellow Am. Coll. Sports Medicine; mem. AAAS, Am. Physiol. Soc. Office: John B Pierce Lab Inc 290 Congress Ave New Haven CT 06519-1403*

NADEL, NORMAN ALLEN, civil engineer; b. N.Y.C., Apr. 10, 1927; s. Louis and Bertha (Julius) N.; m. Cynthia Esther Jereski, July 6, 1952; children: Nancy Sarah Frank, Lawrence Bruce. B.C.E., CCNY, 1949; postgrad., Columbia U., 1949-50. Registered profl. engr., N.Y., Conn. Engr. Arthur A. Johnson Corp., N.Y.C., 1950-53; engr. Slattery Contracting Corp., N.Y.C., 1953-56; mgr., estimator Hartsdale Constrn. Corp., Hartsdale, N.Y., 1956-59; engr. MacLean Grove & Co., Inc., Greenwich, Conn., 1959-63, project mgr., 1963-66, v.p., 1966-70, pres., 1970-94; chmn. Nadel Assocs., Inc., Brewster, N.Y., 1988—; cons. tunnel and underground constrn.; chmn., bd. dirs. United Am. Energy Corp., mem. com. on tunneling Transp. Rsch. Bd., Washington, 1974-75; mem. U.S. Nat. Com. on Tunneling Tech., Washington, 1976-82, chmn., 1980-81; chmn. adv. com. Superconducting Super Collider Underground Tech., 1992-94. Trustee Tunnel Workers Welfare Fund, N.Y.C., 1976-88; mem. adv bd. CCNY Engring. Sch., 1992—. With USNR, 1945-46. Named Heavy Constrn. Man of Yr., United Jewish Appeal, 1984; Benjamin Wright award Conn. Soc. Civil Engrs., 1984, Townsend Harris medal City Coll. of N.Y. Alumni Assn., 1987. Fellow ASCE (Constrn. Mgmt. award 1986); mem. Nat. Acad. Engring., Conn. Acad. Sci. and Engring., The Moles (pres. 1982-83, Outstanding Achievement in Constrn. award 1985), Am. Arbitration Assn., Tau Beta Pi, Chi Epsilon. Home: Reynwood Manor Greenwich CT 06831

NADELBERG, ERIC PAUL, brokerage house executive; b. Providence, Dec. 14, 1947; s. Arnold and Sandra (Schwartz) N.; m. Evelynne Luberoff, Dec. 12, 1968; children: Amanda, Ariel. BA, Bklyn. Coll., 1973; MA, Sch. of Journalism, N.Y.U., 1994. Registered commodities rep. News analyst The Wall Street Jour., N.Y.C., 1973-76; reporter Reuters Ltd., N.Y.C., 1976-77; sr. analyst E.F. Hutton & Co., Inc., N.Y.C., 1977-79, v.p., 1983-85; v.p. Gill & Duffus Svcs., Inc., N.Y.C., 1979-81, Rudolf Wolff Futures, Inc., N.Y.C., 1981-83; pres. Tropical Trader, Inc., Hoboken, N.J., 1985-90; 1st v.p. Merrill Lynch Inc., N.Y.C., N.J., 1990-96; sr. v.p. ABN-AMRO Chgo. Corp., N.Y.C., 1996—; dir. Futures Rsch. co., 1991—; cons. UNCTAD, 1993—, World Bank, 1993—. Contbr. Barrons Fin. Mag., 1976-79; contbg. editor Commodity Rsch. Bur., 1986-93; columnist Cotton Mag., Memphis, 1977-88. With U.S. Army, 1968-71. Democrat. Avocations: fishing, racquetball, walking, writing. Office: ABN-AMRO Chgo Corp 335 Madison Ave New York NY 10017

NADELSON, CAROL COOPERMAN, psychiatrist, educator; b. Bklyn., Oct. 13, 1936; m. Theodore Nadelson, July 16, 1965; children: Robert, Jennifer. B.A. magna cum laude, Bklyn. Coll., 1957; M.D. with honors, U. Rochester, N.Y., 1961. Dir. med. student edn. Beth Israel Hosp., Boston, 1974-79, psychiatrist, 1977; assoc. prof. psychiatry Harvard U. Med. Sch., Boston, 1976-79; research scholar Radcliffe Coll., Cambridge, Mass., 1979-80; prof. psychiatry Tufts Med. Sch., Boston, 1979-95; vice chmn., dir. tng. and edn. dept. psychiatry Tufts-New Eng. Med. Ctr., Boston, 1979-93; clin. prof. psychiatry Harvard Med. Sch., Boston, 1995—. Editor: The Woman Patient, Vols. 1, 2 and 3, 1978, 82; Treatment Interventions in Human Sexuality, 1983; Marriage and Divorce: A Contemporary Perspective, 1984, Women Physicians in Leadership Roles, 1986, Training Psychiatrists for the '90s, 1987, Treating Chronically Mentally Ill Women, 1988, Family Violence, 1988, Women and Men: New Perspectives on Gender Differences, 1990, International Review of Psychiatry Vols. 1 & 2, 1993, 96, Major Psychiatric Disorders, 1982, The Challenge of Change: Perspectives on Family, Work and Education, 1983; editor-in-chief Am. Psychiatric Press, Inc., 1986—, pres., CEO, 1995—; contbr. over 210 articles to profl. jours. Trustee Menninger Found., 1988—. Recipient Gold Medal award Mt. Airy Psychiat. Ctr., 1981, award Case Western Res. U., 1983, Elizabeth Blackwell award Am. Med. Women's Assn., 1985; Picker Found. grantee, 1982-83. Fellow Ctr. for Advanced Study in the Behavioral Scis., Am. Psychiat. Assn. (pres. 1985-86, Seymour D. Vestermark award 1992, Disting. Svc. award 1995); mem. Am. Coll. Psychiatrists (bd. regents 1991-94, Disting. Svc. award 1989), AMA (impaired physicians com. 1984, Sidney Cohen award 1988), Group for Advancement of Psychiatry (bd. dirs. 1984). Avocation: travel. Office: 30 Amory St Brookline MA 02146-3909

NADER, RALPH, consumer advocate, lawyer, author; b. Winsted, Conn., Feb. 27, 1934; s. Nadra and Rose (Bouziane) N. AB magna cum laude, Princeton U., 1955; LLB with distinction, Harvard U., 1958. Bar: Conn. 1958, Mass. 1959, U.S. Supreme Ct. 1959. Practiced law in Hartford, Conn., from 1959; lectr. history and govt. U. Hartford, 1961-63; founder Center for Responsive Law, Pub. Interest Research Group, Center for Auto Safety, Pub. Citizen, Clean Water Action Project, Disability Rights Ctr., Pension Rights Ctr., Project for Corporate Responsibility; lectr. to colls. and univs.; lectr. Princeton U., 1967-68; co-founder Princeton Project 55, 1989. Author: Unsafe at Any Speed, 1965, rev., 1972; sponsor: Working on the System: A Manual for Citizen's Access to Federal Agencies, 1972; co-author: Action for a Change, 1972, You and Your Pension, 1973, Taming the Giant Corporation, 1976, Menace of Atomic Energy, 1977, The Lemon Book, 1980, The Big Boys, 1986, Winning The Insurance Game, 1990; editor: Whistle Blowing: The Report on the Conference on Professional Responsibility, 1972, The Consumer and Corporate Accountability, 1973; co-editor: Corporate Power in America, 1973, Verdicts on Lawyers, 1976, Who's Poisoning America, 1981; contbg. editor: Ladies Home Jour., 1973—, also articles. With U.S. Army, 1959. Recipient Nieman Fellows award, 1965-66; named One of 10 Outstanding Young Men of Year U.S. Jr. C. of C., 1967. Mem. ABA, AAAS, Phi Beta Kappa. Address: Consumer Advocate Ctr PO Box 19367 Washington DC 20036-9367*

NADER, ROBERT ALEXANDER, judge, lawyer; b. Warren, Ohio, Mar. 31, 1928; s. Nassef J. and Emily (Nader) N.; m. Nancy M. Veauthier. B.A., Western Res. U., 1950, LL.B., 1953. Bar: Ohio 1953. Ptnr. Paul G. Nader, Warren, 1953-83. Pres. Warren City Police and Fire Pension Bds., 1960-66; trustee Office Econ. Opportunity, 1970-72; mem. Warren City Coun., 1960-66, pres. pro tem, 1964-66; mem. Ohio Ho. of Reps., 1971-83, chmn. reference com., 1977-81, chmn. judiciary com., 1981-83; presiding judge Trumbull County Ct. Common Pleas, 1983-91; judge Ohio 11th Dist. Ct. Appeals, 1991—; trustee Family Svc. Assn., 1959-65. With AUS, 1946-48. Recipient Outstanding Young Man of Yr. award, 1964, award Am. Arbitration Assn., 1965, Community Action award Warren Area Bd. Realtors, 1967, Outstanding Svc. award Kent State U., Trumbull campus. 1978, Outstanding Svc. award Children's Rehab. Ctr., 1980; named to Warren High Sch. Disting. Alumni Hall of Fame, 1993. Mem. Trumbull County Bar Assn. (past pres.), Ct. Appeals Judges Assn. (chmn. legis. com.), Trumbull County Law Libr. Assn. (trustee 1958-72), Trumbull New Theatre (past pres.), KC, Elks, Lambda Chi Alpha. Roman Catholic. Home: 798 Wildwood Dr NE Warren OH 44483-4458 Office: 11th Dist Ct # Appeals Warren OH 44481 *My parents provided me with a strong moral background and the inspiration to improve. I will never feel that I have achieved success and thus may continue to improve.*

NADICH, JUDAH, rabbi; b. Balt., May 13, 1912; s. Isaac and Lena (Nathanson) N.; m. Martha Hadassah Ribalow, Jan. 26, 1947; children: Leah N. (Mrs. Aryeh Meir), Shira A. (Mrs. James L. Levin), Nahma M. Nadich (Mrs. David Belcourt). B.A., CCNY, 1932; M.A., Columbia U., 1936; rabbi, M.H.L., Jewish Theol. Sem. Am., 1936, D.H.L., 1953, D.D. (hon), 1966. Rabbi Temple Beth David, Buffalo, 1936-40; co-rabbi Anshe Emet Synagogue, Chgo., 1940-42; lecture tour U.S., South Africa and Rhodesia, 1946-47; rabbi Kehillath Israel Congregation, Brookline, Mass., 1947-57; rabbi Park Ave. Synagogue, N.Y.C., 1957-87, rabbi emeritus, 1987—; conducted first Bat Mitzvah in People's Republic of China, 1990. Author: Eisenhower and the Jews, 1953, Jewish Legends of the Second Commonwealth, 1983, Legends of the Rabbis, 2 vols., 1994, Rabbi Akiba and His Contemporaries, 1997; editor, translator: (Menachem Ribalow) The Flowering of Modern Hebrew Literature, 1959; editor: (Louis Ginzberg) Al Halakha v'Aggada, 1960. Pres. Rabbinical Assembly, 1972-74; pres. Jewish Book Coun. Am., 1968-72; bd. dirs., hon. exec. com. Jewish Theol. Sem. Am.; past bd. dirs., mem. exec. com. Nat. Jewish Welfre Bd., Fedn. Jewish Philanthropies N.Y.; mem. hospice com. Beth Israel Med. Ctr.; mem. N.Y.C. Holocaust Meml.; hon. v.p. bd. dirs. Jewish Braille Inst.; bd. dirs. Friends of Jewish Hist. Mus., Warsaw; past pres. Assn. Jewish Chaplains Armed Forces; adv. to Gen. Eisenhower on Jewish affairs, ETO, 1945; com. 50th anniversary World War II U.S. Dept. Defense. Lt. col., chaplain AUS, 1942-46, ETO. Assimilated rank of Maj. Gen. South Vietnam, 1971. Decorated Order Brit. Empire, Croix de Guerre (France); Ittur Lohamai Hamdinah (Israel), ETO medal with Battle Star, Occupation of Germany medal, Victory medal; fellow Herbert Lehman Inst. Talmudic Ethics, 1958. Mem. Mil. Chaplains Assn., Phi Beta Kappa. Lodge: Masons. Home: 1040 Park Ave New York NY 10028-1032 Office: Park Ave Synagogue 50 E 87th St New York NY 10128-1002 *Live so that your life will make a difference for the better in the lives of other people.*

NADIG, GERALD GEORGE, manufacturing executive; b. Astoria, N.Y., May 9, 1945; s. Charles Edwin and Louise (Hahn) N.; m. Nancy Hanford Stewart, June 20, 1970; children: Sara Hanford, Jennifer Stewart. AB cum laude, Harvard Coll., 1967, MBA, 1974. Fin. mgr. Rockwell Internat., Hopedale, Mass., 1974-76; materials mgr. Rockwell Internat., Oshkosh, Wis., 1976-78, Marysville, Ohio, 1978-79; ops. mgr. Rockwell Internat., Marysville, 1979-80, plant mgr., 1980-82; regional mgr. Rockwell Internat., Atlanta, 1984-85; mng. dir. Rockwell Maudslay Ltd., Great Alne, Eng., 1982-84; dir. mfg. Toyoda Machinery USA, Arlington Heights, Ill., 1985-87; v.p., gen. mgr. Toyoda Machinery USA, Arlington Heights, 1987-88; v.p., gen. mgr. Littell div. Allied Products Corp., Chgo., 1988-89; exec. v.p. pre finish metals Material Scis. Corp., 1989-90; pres. Pre Finish Metals Materials Scis. Corp., 1990-91; pres., chief oper. officer Material Scis. Corp., Chgo., 1991-96, pres., CEO, 1997—, bd. dirs. Trustee Village of Lake Barrington, 1989-91. With U.S. Army, 1966-70. Mem. Soc. Mfg. Engrs. (sr.), Biltmore Country Club. Avocations: golf, tennis, game theory. Home: 24354 N Grandview Dr Barrington IL 60010-6218 Office: Material Scis Corp 2200 Pratt Blvd Elk Grove Village IL 60007-5917

NADIRI, M. ISHAQ, economics educator, researcher, lecturer, consultant; b. Kabul, Afghanistan, Oct. 16, 1936; s. M. Alam and Gul-Nasa N.; m. Tahira Homayun, Sept. 9, 1978; children: Youssof, Khalid. B.S. with highest distinction, U. Nebr., 1958; M.A., U. Calif.-Berkeley, 1960, Ph.D., 1965; postgrad., Yale U., 1962-63. Asst. prof. Northwestern U., Evanston, Ill., 1964-66, U. Chgo. Bus. Sch., 1966-67; research fellow Nat. Bur. Econ. Research, N.Y.C., 1968-70; research assoc. Nat. Bur. Econ. Research, 1969—; full prof. econs. NYU, 1970—, Jay Gould prof. econs., 1975—, chmn. dept. econs., 1972-78; Disting. vis. prof. Am. U. Cairo, 1993; cons. in field; participant seminars NSF Ctr Strategic Studies, UN Assn. Author: books, including A Disequilibrium Model of Demand for Factors of Production, 1974; research, numerous publs. in field; editor books including The Importance of Technology and the Permanence of Structure in Industrial Growth, 1978, Commodity Markets and Latin American Development: A Modeling Approach, 1980; editorial bd.: Annals of Econs. and Social Measurement. Mem. Com. to Upgrade Central Park, N.Y.C.; mem. com. to Help Afghan Refugees in the U.S. C. Miller fellow, 1958-59; U. Calif. fellow, 1959-60; Earnhart fellow, 1962-63, 63-64; grantee NSF, Ford Found., IBM Corp., AT&T. Mem. Am. Econs. Assn., Econometrica Soc., Univs.-Nat. Bur. Econ. Research, Internat. Assn. Research in Income and Wealth; mem. AAAS, Am. Statis. Assn., Council Fgn. Relations, Phi Beta Kappa, Pi Sigma Alpha, Beta Gamma Sigma. Office: NYU Dept Econs 269 Mercer St 7th Fl New York NY 10003

NADLER, ALLAN LAWRENCE, institute director; b. Montreal, May 8, 1954; came to U.S., 1976; s. Joseph Y. and Doris (Joseflevsky) N. BA, McGill U., 1976; MA, Harvard U., 1980, PhD, 1988. Ordained rabbi, 1978. Rabbi Charles River Park Synagogue, Boston, 1980-84; asst. prof. McGill U., Montreal, 1982-90; rabbi Congregation Shaar Hashomayim, Montreal, 1984-90; dir. rsch. Yivo Inst. for Jewish Rsch., N.Y.C., 1991—; vis. prof. Cornell U., Ithaca, N.Y., 1993—; adj. prof. NYU. Author: A Religion of Limits, 1995; contbr. articles to profl. jours. Lady Davis fellow Hebrew U., Jerusalem, 1987. Mem. Assn. Jewish Studies. Office: Yivo Inst 555 W 57th St New York NY 10019-2925

NADLER, GEORGE L., orthodontist; b. Bklyn., Jan. 13, 1939; s. Rudolph M. and Hannah (Helfman) N.; m. Essie Rubinstein, June 4, 1961; children: Rudolph M., Eric Marc. Student, Bkly. Coll., 1956-59; DDS, NYU Coll. of Dentistry, 1963, postgrad., 1966-70. Diplomate Am. Bd. Orthodontia, 1979. Intern L.I. Coll. Hosp., Bklyn., 1963-64; pvt. practice Bklyn., 1966-70, Tucson, Ariz., 1970—; cons. El Rio Health Ctr., Tucson, 1973—. Contbr. articles to profl. jours. Cons. Ariz. Crippled Children Svc., Tucson, 1973—; exec. bd. Congregation Anshei Israel, 1988—. With USPHS, 1964-66. Fellow NIH, 1961, 62. Mem. ADA, Ariz. Dental Assn., So. Ariz. Dental Assn., Am. Assn. Orthodontists, Pacific Coast Orthodontic Assn., Ariz. Orthodontic Study Club, Tucson Orthodontic Study Club, Tucson Orthodontic Soc. (pres. 1980-81), Ariz. State Orthodontic Soc. (pres. 1988-90), Angle Orthodontic Soc., Golden Key, Skyline Country Club, Omicron Kappa Upsilon. Avocations: tennis, golf, gardening. Home: 6822 N Longfellow Dr Tucson AZ 85718-2422 Office: 5610 E Grant Rd Tucson AZ 85712-2239

NADLER, GERALD, engineering educator, management consultant; b. Cin., Mar. 12, 1924; s. Samuel and Minnie (Krumbein) N.; m. Elaine Muriel Dubin, June 22, 1947; children: Burton Alan, Janice Susan, Robert Daniel. Student, U. Cin., 1942-43; BSME, Purdue U., 1945, MS in Indsl. Engring, 1946, PhD, 1949. Instr. Purdue U., 1948-49; asst. prof. indsl. engring. Washington U., St. Louis, 1949-52, assoc. prof., 1952-55, prof., head dept. indsl. engring., 1955-64; prof. U. Wis., Madison, 1964-83, chmn. dept. indsl. engring., 1964-67, 71-75; prof., chmn. dept. indsl. and systems engring. U. So. Calif., L.A., 1983-93, IBM chair engring. mgmt., 1986-93, IBM chair emeritus, prof. emeritus, 1993—; v.p. Artcraft Mfg. Co., St. Louis, 1956-57; dir. Intertherm Inc., St. Louis, 1969-85; pres. Ctr. for Breakthrough Thinking Inc., L.A., 1989—; vis. prof. U. Birmingham, Eng., 1959, Waseda U., Tokyo, 1963, Ind. U., 1964, U. Louvain, Belgium, 1975, Technion-Israel Inst. Tech., Haifa, 1976; speaker in field. Author: The Planning and Design Approach,

1981; (with S. Hibino) Breakthrough Thinking, 1990, 2d edit., 1994, Creative Solution Finding, 1995; (with G. Hoffherr, J. Moran) Breakthrough Thinking in Total Quality Management, 1994; contbr. articles to profl. jours.; reviewer books, papers, proposals. Mem. Ladue Bd. Edn., St. Louis County, 1960-63; acting exec. dir. Higher Edn. Coordinating Coun. Met. St. Louis, 1962-63; chmn. planning com. Wis. Regional Med. Program, 1966-69, mem. steering com., 1969-73. Served with USN, 1943-45. Recipient Gilbreth medal Soc. Advancement Mgmt., 1961, Editorial award Hosp. Mgmt. Mag., 1966, Disting. Engring. Alumnus award Purdue U., 1975, Outstanding Indsl. Engr. award, 1997; Book of Yr. award Inst. Indsl. Engrs., 1983, Frank and Lillian Gilbreth award, 1992; Phi Kappa Phi Faculty Recognition award U. So. Calif., 1990. Fellow AAAS, Inst. Indsl. Engrs. (pres. 1989-90), Inst. for Advancement Engrs., Am. Soc. Engring. Edn.; mem. NAE, Inst. Operations Rsch. and Mgmt. Scis., Japan Work Design Soc. (hon. adv. 1968—), World Futurs Soc. Acad. Mgmt. Strategic Leadership forum Engring. Mgmt. Soc., Sigma Xi, Alpha Pi Mu (nat. officer), Pi Tau Sigma, Omega Rho, Tau Beta Pi. Office: Univ Park GER 240 Dept of I&SE Los Angeles CA 90089-0193

NADLER, HENRY LOUIS, pediatrician, geneticist, medical educator; b. N.Y.C., Apr. 15, 1936; s. Herbert and Mary (Kartiganer) N.; m. Benita Weinhard, June 16, 1957; children: Karen, Gary, Debra, Amy. A.B., Colgate U., 1957; M.D., Northwestern U., 1961; M.S., U. Wis., 1965. Diplomate: Am. Bd. Pediatrics, Am. Bd. Med. Genetics. Intern NYU Med. Ctr., 1961-62, sr. resident pediatrics, 1962-63, chief resident, 1963-64; teaching asst. NYU Sch. Medicine, 1962-63, clin. instr., 1963-64; clin. instr. U. Wis. Sch. Medicine, 1964-65; practice medicine specializing in pediatrics Chgo., 1965—; fellow Children's Meml. Hosp. dept. pediatrics Northwestern U., 1964-65; assoc. in pediatrics Northwestern U. Med. Sch., 1965-66, asst. prof., 1967-68, assoc. prof., 1968-70, prof., 1970-81, chmn. dept. pediatrics, 1970-81; prof. Northwestern U. Med. Sch. (Grad. Sch.), 1971-80; mem. staff Children's Meml. Hosp., 1965-81, head div. genetics, 1969-81, chief of staff, 1970-81; dean, prof. pediatrics, ob-gyn Wayne State U. Med. Sch., Detroit, 1981-88; prof. U. Chgo., 1988-89, U. Ill., 1989—; pres. Michael Reese Hosp. and Med. Ctr., Chgo., 1988-91; market med. dir. Aetna Health Plans, Phoenix, 1993-94, mktg. v.p., CEO, 1994-95; v.p. managed care/physician integration, med. dir. Am. Healthcare Sys., San Diego, 1995; mem. vis. staff, div. medicine Northwestern Meml. Hosp., 1972-81; staff Children's Hosp. of Mich., 1981-88. Mem. editorial bd. Comprehensive Therapy, 1973-84, Am. Jour. Human Genetics, 1979-83, Pediatrics in Rev., 1980-83, Am. Jour. Diseases of Children, 1983-91; contbr. articles to profl. jours. Recipient E. Mead Johnson award for pediatric rsch., 1973, Meyer O. Cantor award for Disting. Svc. Internat. Coll. Surgeons, 1987; Irene Heinz Given and John La Porte Given rsch. prof. pediatrics, 1970-81. Fellow Am. Acad. Pediatrics; mem. Am. Soc. for Clin. Investigation, Am. Soc. Human Genetics, Am. Pediatric Soc., Soc. for Pediatric Rsch., Midwest Soc. for Pediatric Rsch., Pan Am. Med. Assn., Alpha Omega Alpha. Home & Office: 25150 N Windy Walk Dr # 23 Scottsdale AZ 85255

NADLER, JERROLD LEWIS, congressman, lawyer; b. Brooklyn, N.Y., June 13, 1947; s. Emanuel and Miriam (Schreiber) N.; m. Joyce L. Miller, 1976; 1 child, Michael. JD, Fordham U., 1978; AB, Columbia Coll., 1969. Mem. Community Planning Bd. No. 7, Manhattan, 1967-71; Dem. leader 67th Assembly Dist. Part C, 1969-71; exec. dir. Community Free Dem., 1972; law clerk Morgan, Finnegan, Pine, Foley & Lee, 1976; Dem. dist. leader 69th Assembly dist. Part A, 1973-77; assemblyman N.Y. State 69th dist., 1977-82, 67th dist., 1983-92; mem. 102d Congress from 17th N.Y. dist., Washington, 1992; mem. 103d, 104th and 105th Congress 8th N.Y. Dist., Washington, 1993—; subcoms. comml./adminstrv. law, cts. intellectual property U.S. Ho. Reps., 1995-96, ranking Dem. subcom. on comml./adminstrv. law, 1997—, mem. subcom. on constn., 1997—, mem. subcoms. on surface transp., water resources, environ., 1993-94, mem. subcoms. on railroads/aviation, 1995—, mem. subcoms. on surface transp. and railroads, 1997—; mem. coms. on judiciary and pub. works and transp. U.S. Ho. Reps., 1995—, subcom. on constitutional law and immigration, 1993-94, chmn. Assembly Com. on Corps, Authorities and Commn., 1991-92, Assembly Consumer Affairs and Protection Com., 1987-90, Assembly Com. on Ethics and Guidance, 1985-86, Assembly Subcom. on Mass Transit and Rail Freight, 1979-86, mem. Assembly Com. on Judiciary, Gov. Ops., Legis. Tax Study Commn.; mem. Assembly Com. Ways and Means, Housing, Real Property Tax, Health, Election Law, Ins. Founder, chmn. West Side Peace Com., 1969-71; former mem. exec. coun. N.Y. State New Dem. Coalition; pres. Zionist Orgn. Am. dist. 7A; active Common Cause, Met. Coun. on Housing, West Side Tenants Union, Community Free Dems.; mem. nat. governing coun. Am. Jewish Congress; former bd. dirs. N.Y. State Nat. Abortion Rights Action League, Women's InterArts Ctr. Recipient hon. recognition award N.Y. State Nurses Assn., 1982, Disting. Svc. award Coalition on Domestic Violence, 1989; named Assembly Mem. of Yr. N.Y. chpt. NOW, 1980; Pulitzer scholar Columbia U. Mem. NOW, NAACP, N.Y. Bar Assn., N.Y. Civil Liberties Union (honor roll), Citizens Union, League Conservation Voters, New Dem. Coalition, Ams. for Dem. Action (bd. dirs., nat. v.p.). Office: US Ho of Reps Washington DC 20515

NADLER, MYRON JAY, lawyer; b. Youngstown, Ohio, July 22, 1923; s. Murray A. and Jean (Davis) N.; m. Alice Blue, Nov. 4, 1951; children: Jed M., Wendy D., John M.S. Student, N.Mex. State Coll., 1943-44; B.S. in Econs, U. Pa., 1947; J.D. with distinction, U. Mich., 1949. Bar: Ohio 1950. Pres., shareholder Nadler, Nadler & Burdman Co., L.P.A., Youngstown, 1950-95, pres., 1950-95; ret., 1996; asst. editor Mich. Law Rev., 1949; instr. Youngstown U. Law Sch., 1952-59. Author: (with Saul Nadler) Nadler on Bankruptcy, 1965, April's Bankruptcy Forms and Practice, 1964; contbr. articles profl. jours. Chmn. exec. budget com. United Appeal, Youngstown, 1964-66, v.p., 1967-70; co-chmn. Mayor's Commn. Human Rights, 1957; mem. Mahoning County Planning Commn., 1965-71, Nat. Budget and Consultation Com., 1967-70; trustee Community Corp., Youngstown, v.p., 1977-82, chmn. pers. com., 1974-92; bd. dirs. Ctr. for Learning, Villa Maria, Pa., 1969-95, pres., 1981-89, chmn. bd., 1989-94, chmn. emeritus, 1994—. With AUS, 1943-45. Decorated Purple Heart with oak leaf cluster. Mem. Fellows of Ohio Bar Assn. Found., Am., Ohio, Mahoning County bar assns., Scribes Assn. Legal Writers, Comml. Law League Am. Clubs: Youngstown, Squaw Creek Country (pres. 1966-68); Hamlet Country. Home: 601 Pine Lake Dr Delray Beach FL 33445 Home: 1313 Virginia Trl Youngstown OH 44505-1641 Office: 20 Federal Plz W Ste 600 Youngstown OH 44503-1423

NADLER, SIGMOND HAROLD, physician, surgeon; b. Bklyn., May 16, 1932; s. Morris and Rose (Levine) N.; m. Beverly Melcher, June 20, 1954; children: Geoffrey, Shail, Tamara, Kimberly. B.A., State U. Iowa, 1955, M.D., 1957. Intern Menorah Med. Center, Kansas City, Mo., 1957-58; surg. resident Menorah Med. Center, 1958-61; surg. resident Roswell Park Meml. Inst., 1961-63, mem. staff, 1962-68, clin. coordinator Eastern region clin. drug evaluation program, 1966-68, project dir. nat. adj. studies, 1966-68, asso. chief cancer research surgery, 1966-68; asso. prof. surgery Jefferson Med. Coll., Phila., 1968-70; also dir. clin. cancer tng.; asst. clin. prof. surgery SUNY-Buffalo, 1970—. Mem. Am. Soc. Clin. Oncology. Research in human tumor immunotherapy. Home: 9513 Preston Trl W Ponte Vedra Beach FL 32082-3311

NADLEY, HARRIS JEROME, accountant, educator, author; b. Phila., July 6, 1926; s. Michael and Celia (Millman) N.; BS, U. Pa., 1950; MA, PhD, Harvard U., 1952; m. Barbara A. Malone, June 28, 1953; children—Jennifer Beth, Amy Jane, Adam Christopher. Asst. trust officer Provident Trust Co., Phila., 1949; exec. trainee Merrill, Lynch, Pierce, Fenner & Smith, N.Y.C., 1950; ptnr. Michael Nadley Co., CPAs, Phila., 1952—. Teaching fellow Harvard, 1952; instr. fin. Wharton Sch., Phila., 1953-54; adj. prof. bus. adminstrn. St. Joseph's Coll., Phila., Acad. Food Mktg., Pa. Inst. CPAs, N.J. Soc. CPAs, AICPA; cons. Control Data Corp., 1971; participant Current Strategy Forum, Naval War Coll., 1978, Naval War Coll. Found., 1979. Gen. chmn. Marine Corps Birthday Ball, Phila., 1973. Bd. dirs. Montgomery County Assn. for Retarded Children, Cruiser Olympia Assn., ea. Pa. chpt. Arthritis Found.; trustee Lesley Coll., Cambridge, Mass.; pres. adv. council Wharton Sch., U. Pa., 1950; del. White House Conf. on Small Bus., 1986, 95; mem. pres.'s council Chestnut Hill Coll., St. Joseph's Coll.; mem. Benjamin Franklin Assocs., U. Pa.; chmn. bd. advisors USMC Tun's Tavern Commn., 1991. Served with USMCR, 1944-46; PTO. Mem. Am. Radio Relay League, Fraternal Order Police (hon.), Econometric Soc., Am. Econ. Soc., Mil. Order Fgn. Wars, Brit. Officers' Club, Preservation Soc. Newport County, St. Joseph's Coll. Acad. Food Mktg. (founder), Quarter Century Wireless Assn., World Affairs Coun. of Phila., The Libr. Co. of Phila., Marine Corps Res. Officers Assn., Sixth Marine Div. Assn., Marine Raiders Assn., Navy League, Pa. Soc., Beta Gamma Sigma, Pi Gamma Mu, Beta Sigma Rho. Clubs: Masons, Union League, Harvard, Harvard Faculty, Mercedes-Benz, Urban (Phila.). Author: A Covey of Peacocks, 1969. Contbr. articles to profl. jours.; fin. columnist Phila. mag., Welcomat Newspaper, Phila. Bus. Jour.; cons. Fin. News Network, Phila. Home and Office: 325 S 3rd St Philadelphia PA 19106-4304

NADZICK, JUDITH ANN, accountant; b. Paterson, N.J., Mar. 6, 1948; d. John and Ethel (McDonald) N. BBA in Acctg., U. Miami (Fla.), 1971. CPA, N.J. Staff acct., mgr. Ernst & Whinney, C.P.A.s, N.Y.C., 1971-78; asst. treas. Gulf & Western Industries, Inc., N.Y.C., 1979-83, asst. v.p., 1980-82, v.p., 1982-83; v.p., corp. contr. United Mchts. and Mfrs. Inc., N.Y.C., 1983-85, sr. v.p., 1985-86, exec. v.p., CFO, 1986—, also bd. dirs. 1987—. Mem. AICPAs, Nat. Assn. Accts., N.Y. State Soc. CPAs, U. Miami Alumni Assn., Delta Delta Delta. Roman Catholic. Home: 280 Lincoln Ave Elmwood Park NJ 07407-2824

NAEF, WESTON JOHN, museum curator; b. Gallup, N.Mex., Jan. 8, 1942; s. Weston John and Kathleen Winifred (Skerry) N.; m. Mary Dawes Meghan, Apr. 4, 1964; children: Edward Weston, Ella Dawes. B.A., Claremont Men's Coll., 1964; M.A., Ohio State U., 1966; postgrad., Brown U., 1966-69. Vis. scholar Boston Pub. Library, 1968; dir. art gallery Wheaton Coll., Mass., 1969; staff dept. prints and photographs Met. Mus. Art, N.Y.C., 1970-84; asst. curator Met. Mus. Art, 1971-81, curator, 1981-84; curator photographs J. Paul Getty Mus., Malibu, Calif., 1984—; cons. in field. Author, exhbn. dir. Behind the Great Wall of China, 1971, The Painterly Photograph, 1973, The Truthful Lens: A Survey of Victorian Books Illustrated with Photographs, 1974, Era of Exploration, The Rise of Landscape Photography in the American West 1860-1885, 1975, Pioneer Photographers of Brazil 1939-1914, 1976, The Collection of Alfred Stieglitz, 1978, Georgia O'Keeffe by Alfred Stieglitz, 1978, Eliot Porter, The Intimate Landscapes, 1979, After Daguerre: Masterworks of 19th Century French Photography from the Bibliotheque Nationale, Paris, 1980, Counterparts: Form and Emotion in Photographs, 1982, Whisper of the Muse: Photographs by Julia Margaret Cameron, 1986, Edward Weston in Los Angeles: The Home Spirit and Beyond, 1986, Rare States and Unusual Subjects: Photographs by Paul Strand, Andre Kertesz and Man Ray, 1987, Capturing Shadows: Notable Acquisitions, 1985-1990, 1990; August Sander: Faces of the German People, 1991; Atget's Magical Analysis; Photographs, 1915-27, 91, Two Lives: O'Keeffe by Stieglitz, 1917-23, 1992, Being and Becoming: Photographs by Edmund Teske, 1993, André Kentesz: A Centennial Tribute, 1994, Palette of Light: Handcrafted Photographs, 1898-1914, 1994, Frederick Sommer: Poetry and Logic, 1994, Hidden Witness: African Americans in Early Photography, 1995, Carrie Mae Weems Reacts to Hidden Witness, 1995, Alfred Stieglitz: Seen and Unseen, 1995, The J. Paul Getty Museum Handbook of the Photographs Collection, 1995, In Focus: Andre Kertesz, 1994, In Focus: Alfred Stieglitz, 1995, The Eye of Sam Wagstaff, 1997, Time Not in Motion, 1997. Kress fellow, 1968. Club: Grolier (N.Y.C.). Office: J Paul Getty Mus Dept Photographs 1000 Getty Ctr Dr Los Angeles CA 90049

NAEGELE, CARL JOSEPH, university academic administrator, educator; b. Newark, Jan. 1, 1939; s. Carl Joseph Sr. and Mabel (Flood) N.; m. Elizabeth C. McVey, June 19, 1971; children: Jennifer, Erin. BS, Kean Coll., 1965; MS, Syracuse U., 1969; PhD, Cornell U., 1974. Tchr. physics Summit (N.J.) High Sch., 1965-68; instr. physics Kean Coll., Union, N.J., 1968-70; physics instr. Cornell U., Ithaca, N.Y., 1973-75; prof. Mich. State U., East Lansing, 1975-79; program dir. NSF, Washington, 1979-81, 91-92; dean coll. arts and scis. U. San Francisco, 1981-91; dir. Sci. Inst., 1984—; prof. physics and computer sci. U. San Francisco, 1981—; computer cons. San Rafael, Calif., 1981—. Author: Physics for the Life and Health Sciences, 1974, Laboratory Experiment in General Physics, 1976, Electronic Mail and Communications Networks, 1984, Computer Systems and Applications, 1989, Experiments in Physical Science, 1995; contbr. articles to profl. jours. Served with U.S. Army, 1959-61, Korea. Recipient Outstanding Tchg. award Mich. State U., 1978, Leadership award U. San Francisco, 1985; grantee NSF, 1968, 78, 94, 95, 96, Coun. for Basic Edn., 1984-89. Mem. Am. Phys. Soc., Am. Assn. Physics Tchrs., Am. Assn. Univ. Adminstrs., Assn. for Computing Machinery. Avocations: flying, boating, skiing, tennis, running. Office: U San Francisco Coll Arts and Scis Ignatian Heights San Francisco CA 94117-1080

NAEGELE, PHILIPP OTTO, violinist, violist, music educator; b. Stuttgart, Fed. Republic Germany, Jan. 22, 1928; came to U.S., 1940; s. Reinhold and Alice (Nordlinger) N.; m. Susanne Russin (div. 1980); 1 child, Matthias Dominic; m. Barbara Wright, Mar. 1992. BA, Queens Coll., 1949; MFA, Princeton U., 1950, PhD, 1955. Violinist, violist Marlboro (Vt.) Music Festival, 1950—; violinist Cleve. Orch., 1956-64; from asst. prof. to assoc. prof. to prof. violin dept. music Smith Coll., Northampton, Mass., 1964-78; William R. Kenan Jr. prof. music Smith Coll., 1978—; violist Cantilena Piano Quartet, 1980—; mem. Boccherini Ensemble, 1980-84; mem. resident string quartet Kent (Ohio) State U., 1960-64; mem. violin faculty Cleve. Inst. Music, 1961-64, Vegh String Quartet, 1977-79; rec. artist Columbia Mus. Heritage Soc., Pro Arte, Nonesuch Records, Bis Records, Marlboro Rec. Soc., Arabesque Records, Da Camera, Spectrum Records, Bayer Records, Sony Classical, Philomusica, Qualitone Records. Contbr. to New Groves Dictionary of Music, also articles to profl. jours. With U.S. Army, 1955-56. Fellow Am. Council Learned Socs., 1949-50, Proctor fellow, 1952-53, Fulbright fellow, 1953-54. Home: 57 Prospect St Northampton MA 01060-2130 Office: Smith Coll Dept Music Northampton MA 01060

NAESER, MARGARET ANN, linguist, medical researcher; b. Washington, June 22, 1944; d. Charles Rudolph and Elma Mathilda (Meyer) N. BA in German, Smith Coll., 1966; PhD in Linguistics, U. Wis., 1970. Chief speech pathology sect. Martinez (Calif.) VA Med. Ctr., 1972-74, Palo Alta (Calif.) VA Med. Ctr., 1974-77; rsch. linguist Boston VA Med. Ctr., 1977—; dir. CT scan/MRI scan Aphasia Rsch. Lab. Boston U. Aphasia Rsch. Sect., Boston U. Sch. Medicine, asst. rsch. prof. neurology, 1978-84, assoc. rsch. prof., 1984-97, rsch. prof., 1997—; mem. adv. bd. CT scan/aphasia VA Nat. Task Force, Washington, 1990-91; panel mem. Office Alternative Medicine NIH, 1994. Contbr. articles to Neurology, Archives of Neurology, Brain; author: Outline Guide to Chinese Herbal Patent Medicines in Pill Form, 1990, Laser Acupuncture: An Introductory Textbook, 1994, Naeser Laser Home Treatment Program for the Hand- An Alternative Treatment for Carpal Tunnel Syndrome and Repetitive Strain Injury, 1996. NDEA fellow, 1967, AAUW fellow, 1970. Mem. Acoustical Soc. Am., Am. Speech, Lang., Hearing Assn., Acad. Aphasia, AAAS, Am. Assn. Acupuncture and Oriental Medicine, Am. Assn. Oriental Medicine. Office: Boston VA Med Ctr 150 S Huntington Ave Boston MA 02130-4817

NAESER, NANCY DEARIEN, geologist, researcher; b. Morgantown, W.Va., Apr. 15, 1944; d. William Harold and Katherine Elizabeth (Dearien) Cozad; m. Charles Wilbur Naeser, Feb. 6, 1982. BS, U. Ariz., 1966; PhD, Victoria U., Wellington, New Zealand, 1973. Geol. field asst. U.S. Geol. Survey, Flagstaff, Ariz., 1966; sci. editor, New Zealand Jour. Geology and Geophysics, New Zealand Dept Sci. and Indsl. Research, Wellington, 1974-76; postdoctoral rsch. assoc., U. Toronto, Ont., Can., 1976-79; postdoctoral rsch. assoc. U.S. Geol. Survey, Denver, 1979-81, geologist, 1981—; adj. prof. Dartmouth Coll., Hanover, N.H., 1985—, U. Wyo., Laramie, 1984—. Editor: Thermal History of Sedimentary Basins - Methods and Case Histories, 1989; contbr. articles on fission-track dating to profl. jours., 1977—. Docent Denver Zoo. Fulbright fellow New Zealand, 1967-68. Fellow Geol. Soc. Am.; mem. Am. Assn. Petroleum Geologists, Geol. Soc. New Zealand, Mortar Bd., Phi Kappa Phi. Methodist. Office: US Geol Survey Mail Stop 926 A 12201 Sunrise Valley Dr Reston VA 20191-3401

NAEVE, MILO MERLE, museum curator and trustee; b. nr. Arnold, Kans., Oct. 9, 1931; s. Bernhardt and Fern (Yasmer) N.; m. Nancy Jammer, July 18, 1954. B.F.A., U. Colo., 1953; M.A., U. Del., 1955. Curatorial asst. Henry Francis duPont Winterthur Mus., 1957, asst. curator, 1958, sec. of mus., 1959-63, registrar, 1963-65; editor Winterthur Portfolio, 1965-66; asst. dir. dept. collections Colonial Williamsburg, Va., 1967-69, curator, dir. dept. collections, 1970; dir. Colorado Springs (Colo.) Fine Arts Center, 1971-74; curator Am. arts Art Inst. Chgo., 1975-91; ret. Am. Arts, Art Inst. Chgo., 1991; curator emeritus Field McCormick. Author: The Classical Presence in American Art, 1978, Identifying American Furniture: A Pictorial Guide to Styles and Terms, Colonial to Contemporary, 1981, 3d edit., 1997, John Lewis Krimmel: An Artist in Federal America, 1987; mem. editorial bd. Am. Art Jour.; contbr. articles to profl. jours. Trustee Sewell C. Biggs Mus., Skowhegan Sch. Painting and Sculpture, Nat. Coun. of the Fine Arts Mus. of San Francisco, Calif. Fellow Royal Soc. Arts; mem. Coll. Art Assn. Am., Nat. Trust Historic Preservation, Am. Assn. Museums, Museums Assn. (Eng.), Ill. Acad. Fine Arts (Lifetime Achievement award 1991). Home: 24 Ingleton Cir Kennett Square PA 19348-2000

NAEYE, RICHARD L., pathologist, educator; b. Rochester, N.Y., Nov. 27, 1929; s. Peter John and Gertrude Ellen (Lookup) N.; m. Patricia Ann Dahl, June 4, 1955; children: Nancy Ellen, Susan Amy, Robert Peter. A.B., Colgate U., 1951; M.D., Columbia U., 1955. Diplomate: Am. Bd. Pathology. Intern N.Y. Hosp., N.Y.C., 1955-56; resident Columbia-Presbyn. Med. Center, 1956-58, Mary Fletcher Hosp., Burlington, Vt., 1958-60; practice medicine, specializing in pathology Burlington, 1960-67, Hershey, Pa., 1967—; asst. attending pathologist Mary Fletcher Hosp., 1960-63; assoc. prof. U. Vt., 1963-67, prof. pathology, 1967; prof., chmn. dept. pathology M.S. Hershey Med. Center, Pa. State U. Coll. Medicine, 1967—; mem. NIH study sect. USPHS, 1968-72. Editorial bd. Human Pathology, 1982—, Pediatric Pathology, 1983—, Pediatric and Perinatal Epidemiology, 1987-94, Modern Pathology, 1993—; contbr. articles to med. jours. Markle scholar in acad. medicine, 1960-65. Mem. Am. Soc. Exptl. Pathology, U.S. Can. Acad. Pathology, Am. Soc. Pathologists, Am. Soc. Clin. Pathologists, Coll. Am. Pathologists, Pediatric Pathology Soc., Pa. Soc. Clin. Pathologists, Investigative Pathology. Home: 50 Laurel Ridge Rd Hershey PA 17033-2513 Office: Pa State U Coll Medicine Dept Pathology 500 University Dr Hershey PA 17033

NAFIE, LAURENCE ALLEN, chemistry educator; b. Detroit, Aug. 9, 1945; s. Marvin Daniel and Edith Allman (Fletcher) N.; m. Dorothy Bondurant Butler, Dec. 28, 1968; children: Bree Lauren, Jordan Wright. B in Chemistry, U. Minn., 1967; MS, U. Oreg., 1969, PhD, 1973. Postdoctoral assoc. U. So. Calif., L.A., 1973-75; asst. prof. chemistry Syracuse (N.Y.) U., 1975-79, assoc. prof., 1979-82, prof., 1982—, chmn. dept., 1984—, assoc. dean Coll. Arts and Scis., 1993-94. Editor BioSpectroscopy; contbr. chpts. to books. With U.S. Army, 1969-71. Alfred P. Sloan Found. fellow, 1978. Mem. Am. Chem. Soc., Am. Phys. Soc., Soc. for Applied Spectroscopy, Biophys. Soc., Coblentz Soc. (pres. 1993-95, Coblentz award 1981). Avocations: running; golf; biking. Home: 208 Crawford Ave Syracuse NY 13224-1712 Office: Syracuse U Dept Chemistry 1-014 CST Syracuse NY 13244-4100

NAFTALIS, GARY PHILIP, lawyer, educator; b. Newark, Nov. 23, 1941; s. Gilbert and Bertha Beatrice (Gruber) N.; m. Donna Arditi, June 30, 1974; children: Benjamin, Joshua, Daniel, Sarah. AB, Rutgers U., 1963; AM, Brown U., 1965; LLB, Columbia U., 1967. Bar: N.Y. 1967, U.S. Dist. Ct. (so. dist.) N.Y. 1969, U.S. Ct. Appeals (2d cir.) 1968, U.S. Ct. Appeals (3d cir.) 1973, U.S. Ct. Appeals (D.C. cir.) 1993, U.S. Supreme Ct. 1974. Law clk. to judge U.S. Dist. Ct. So. Dist. N.Y., 1967-68; asst. U.S. atty. So. Dist. N.Y., 1968-74, asst. chief criminal div., 1972-74; spl. asst. U.S. atty. for V.I., 1972-73; spl. counsel U.S. Senate Subcom. on Long Term Care, 1975, N.Y. State Temp. Commn. on Living Costs and the Economy, 1975; ptnr. Orans, Elsen, Polstein & Naftalis, N.Y.C., 1974-81, Kramer, Levin, Naftalis & Frankel, N.Y.C., 1981—; lectr. in law Law Sch. Columbia U., 1976-88; vis. lectr. Law Sch. Harvard U., 1979; mem. deptl. disciplinary com. Appellate div. 1st Dept., 1980-86. Author: (with Marvin E. Frankel) The Grand Jury: An Institution on Trial, 1977, Considerations in Representing Attorneys in Civil and Criminal Enforcement Proceedings, 1981, Sentencing: Helping Judges Do Their Jobs, 1986, SEC Actions Seeking to Bar Securities Professionals, 1995; editor: White Collar Crimes, 1980. Trustee Boys Brotherhood Rep., 1978—, Blueberry Treatment Ctr., 1981-91, Joseph Haggerty Children's Fund, 1991—. Fellow Am. Coll. Trial Lawyers; mem. ABA (white collar crime com. criminal justice sect. 1985—), Assn. of Bar of City of N.Y. (com. criminal cts. 1980-83, com. judiciary 1984-87, com. on criminal law 1987-90, coun. criminal justice 1985-88), Fed. Bar Coun. (com. cts. 2d cir. 1974-77), N.Y. Bar Assn. (com. state legis. 1974-76, exec. com. comml. and fed. litigation sect.), Internat. Bar Assn. (bus. crimes com. 1988—). Home: 1125 Park Ave Apt 7B New York NY 10128-1243 Office: Kramer Levin Naftalis & Frankel 919 3rd Ave New York NY 10022

NAFTOLIN, FREDERICK, physician, reproductive biologist educator; b. Bronx, N.Y., Apr. 7, 1936; s. Nathan and Jean (Pesacov) N.; children: Michael Eugene, Joshua Joseph; m. Marcie Myerson, Nov. 1, 1987. A.A., UCLA, 1957; B.A. with honors, U. Calif., Berkeley, 1958; M.D. with honors, U. Calif., San Francisco, 1961; D.Phil., U. Oxford, 1970. Intern King County Hosp., Seattle, 1961-62; resident in ob-gyn UCLA, 1962-66; asst. chief gynecology, endocrine fellow USPHS, Seattle, 1966-68; NIH fellow Oxford (Eng.) U., 1968-70; asst. prof. ob-gyn U. Calif., San Diego Sch. Medicine, 1970-73; asso. prof. ob-gyn Harvard Med. Sch., 1973-75; prof., chmn. ob-gyn dept. McGill Faculty Medicine, Montreal, 1975-78; prof., chmn. dept. ob-gyn Yale Med. Sch., New Haven, Conn., 1978—, prof. dept. biology, 1983—; dir. Yale U. Ctr. for Research in Reproductive Biology, 1986—; vis. prof. U. Geneva, 1982-83, Weizmann Inst., 1991-92. Author 15 books including: Subcellular Mechanisms in Reproductive Neuroendocrinology, 1976, Abnormal Fetal Growth, 1978, Clinical Neuroendocrinology, 1979, Dilatation of the Uterine Cervix, 1980; 2-vol. series Basic Reproductive Medicine, Vol. I, Basis of Normal Reproduction, Vol. II, 1981, Male Reproduction, Vol. III, Metabolism of Steroids by Neuroendocrine Tissues, Follicle Stimulation and Ovulation Induction, 1986; mem. editorial bd. Jour. Soc. Gynecologic Investigation, Menopause, Endocrine Revs.; contbr. over 400 papers, articles to med. jours. Fogarty Internat. fellow, 1982, John Simon Guggenheim fellow, 1983; Berlex Internat. scholar, 1991. Mem. Am. Gynecol. and Obstet. Soc., Soc. Gynecol. Investigation (pres. 1991-92), Endocrine Soc., Internat. Soc. Neuroendocrinology, New Haven Ob-Gyn. Soc., Can. Fertility Soc., Soc. for Neurosci., N.Am. Menopause Soc., Pituitary Soc. Office: Yale Med Sch Dept Ob-Gyn 333 Cedar St New Haven CT 06510-3206

NAFZIGER, ESTEL WAYNE, economics educator; b. Bloomington, Ill., Aug. 14, 1938; s. Orrin and Beatrice Mae (Slabaugh) N.; m. Elfrieda Nettie Toews, Aug. 20, 1966; children: Brian Wayne, Kevin Jon. B.A., Goshen Coll., 1960; M.A., U. Mich., 1962; Ph.D., U. Ill., 1967. Rsch. assoc. Econ. Devel. Inst., Enugu, Nigeria, 1964-65; asst. prof. Kans. State U., Manhattan, 1966-73, assoc. prof., 1973-78, prof., 1978—; Fulbright prof. Andhra U., Waltair, India, 1970-71; fellow East West Ctr., Honolulu, 1972-73; vis. scholar Cambridge U., 1976; vis. prof. Internat. U. Japan, Yamato-machi, 1983; external rsch. fellow World Acad. Devel. and Coop., College Park, Md., 1984-85; Indo-Am. Found. scholar Andura U., Waltair, India, 1993; World Inst. for Devel. Econ. Rsch., UN Univ., Helsinki, Finland, 1996. Author: African Capitalism, 1977, Class, Caste and Entrepreneurship, 1978, (with others) Development Theory, 1979, Economics of Political Instability, 1983, Economics of Developing Countries, 1984, 2d edit., 1990, 3d edit., 1997, Entrepreneurship Equity and Economic Development, 1986, Inequality in Africa, 1988 (named one of Outstanding Acad. Books, Choice 1989-90), The Debt Crisis in Africa, 1993, Poverty and Wealth, 1994, Learning From the Japanese, 1995. Sec. bd. overseers Hesston Coll., Kans., 1980-85; chmn. Lou Douglas Lecture Series, 1984-91, 92-93; pres. faculty senate Kans. State U., 1990-92. Recipient Honor Lectr. award Mid Am. State U.'s Assn., 1984-85; grantee Social Sci. Found., 1969. Mem. Am. Econ. Assn., AAUP (pres. chpt. 1981-82), African Studies Assn., Soc. Internat. Devel., Assn. Comparative Econ. Studies, Omicron Delta Epsilon (hon.), Phi Kappa Phi (hon.). Democrat. Avocations: reading; running. Home: 1919 Bluestem Ter Manhattan KS 66502-4155 Office: Kans State U Dept Econs Waters Hall Manhattan KS 66506-4001

NAGA, TAREK A., architect, educator; b. Cairo, June 24, 1953; came to U.S., 1979; s. Samy A. and Aida M. (Cherbini) N.; m. Erika Vagenius, Mar. 1985 (div.). BS in Architecture, Ain Sams U., Cairo, 1975, diploma grad. studies in urban planning, 1977; MArch, U. Minn., 1982; postgrad., U. Pa., 1982-85. Prin. Tarek A. Naga Assocs., Cairo, 1976-79, Sodeco Internat., Phila., 1983-85, Naga Studio Architecture, Venice, Calif., 1991—; cons. Douglas Trones Moser, Inc., Mpls., 1980-81; sr. project architect Architects Collaborative, Inc., Cambridge, Mass., 1985-88; prin. designer Tobishima Assocs., Ltd., Cambridge, 1988-89; sr. architect Rossetti Assocs., Santa

Monica, Calif., 1989-90; asst. prof. architecture Ain Shams U., 1975-79; mem. faculty Sch. Architecture U. Minn., Mpls., 1979-81, Boston Archtl. Ctr., 1987-89, Art Ctr. Coll. Design, Pasadena, Calif., 1991—. Prin. works include Centrum Tower, Worcester, Mass., Oceanside (Calif.) Amphitheatre, Berwind Office Tower, Phila., Calif. State U.-San Bernardino Libr., New Horizon Sch., Pasadena, Calif., Hurghada (Egypt) Tourist Village, U.S. Embassy, Cairo, Va. Poly. Inst. and State U. Performing Arts Ctr. and Student Union, Blacksburg; contbr. articles to profl. publs. Rsch. fellow U. Pa. Grad. Sch. Architecture, 1982-84; recipient Nat. award Soc. Egyptian Architects and Engrs., 1975; Nat. Endowment for Arts fellow, 1981. Mem. Egyptian Syndicate of Engrs., Soc. Egyptian Architects, Soc. Preservation of Archtl. Resources of Egypt, Union Internat. Architects (tourism and heritage work group), Nat. Coun. of Archl. Registration Bds., So. Calif. Inst. Architecture (dir. 1997—). Home: 1508 Abbot Kinney Blvd Venice CA 90291-3743 Office: Naga Studio Architecture 1508 Abbot Kinney Blvd Venice CA 90291-3743

NAGAN, PETER SEYMOUR, publisher; b. N.Y.C., Dec. 18, 1920; s. Arthur and Anna (Janis) N.; m. Gloria Mesinoff, Dec. 23, 1951; children: Laura Evelyn Brown, Michael Jay. BA, Columbia Coll., 1942; MS in Journalism, Columbia U., 1943, MA in Econs., 1948. Wire editor AP, Newark, N.J., 1943-44; staff writer Sunday dept. New York Times, 1944-45; staff writer Fortune Mag., N.Y.C., 1946-47; corr. Bus. Week Mag., Washington, 1948-52; mng. editor newsletters Bur. Nat. Affairs, Washington, 1952-60; editor, pub. Bond and Money Market Letter, 1960—; bd. chmn. Newsletter Svcs., Inc., Lanham, Md., 1972—. Author: Medical Alamanac, 1961, Fail-Safe Investing, 1981. Recipient Loeb award for Bus. Journalism U. Conn., 1965. Office: Newsletter Svcs Inc 9700 Philadelphia Ct Lanham Seabrook MD 20706-4405

NAGANO, KENT GEORGE, conductor; b. Morro Bay, Calif.. B.A. Sociology & Music (high honors), U of Calif., Santa Cruz; MA in Composition, San Francisco State U.; studied with, Laszlo Varga. Former asst. Opera Co. Boston; former prin. guest condr. Ensemble InterContemporain & the Dutch Radio Orch.; mus. dir. & condr. Berkeley Symphony, 1978—; mus. dir. Opéra de Lyon, 1989—; assoc. prin. & guest condr. LSO, London, England, 1990; mus. dir., prin. condr. designate Hallé Orch., England, 1991-94; mus. dir., prin. condr. Hallé Orch., 1994—. has performed with numerous orchestras around the world; recordings include: Songs of the Auvergne, Peter and the Wolf, Turandot and Arlecchino (Grammy nom.), La Boheme, Dialogues of the Carelites, The Death of Klinghoffer (Grammy nom.), Love for Three Oranges (Grammy nom.), Susannah (Grammy award), La damnation de Faust, The Rite of Spring, Rodrgue et chimene. Recipient Seaver/NEA Conducting award, 1985; Record of Yr. award Gramophone; named "officer" of France's Order of Arts and Letters, 1993. Office: care Vincent & Farrell Asso 157 W 57th St Ste 502 New York NY 10019-2210*

NAGAO, MIKE AKIRA, horticulturist, county administrator; b. Hilo, Hawaii, Oct. 23, 1947. BA, U. Hawaii, 1969, MS, 1971; PhD, U. Mass., 1975. From asst. to assoc. prof. U. Hawaii, Hilo, 1975-81; from asst. to horticulturist U. Hawaii, Honolulu, 1981—, county adminstr., 1991—. Contbr. articles to profl. jours. Mem. Am. Soc. Hort. Sci. Office: Univ of Hawaii Beaumont Rsch Sta 461 W Lanikaula St Hilo HI 96720-4037

NAGAO, NORRIS SADATO, political science educator, consultant; b. Sacramento, June 9, 1954; s. Sadao and Misao (Iwahashi) N. AA, Sacramento City Coll., 1973; AB, U. Calif., Berkeley, 1975; MA, Columbia U., 1979, cert. East Asian Inst., 1979, EdM, 1980, MA, 1983. Legis. aide Calif. State Assembly, Sacramento, 1976-77; exec. dir. N.Y.-Tokyo-Beijing Nanshiki Baseball Friendship Series, N.Y.C., 1981-84; exec. sec. N.Am.-Japan Promotions, Inc., N.Y.C., 1986-89; pres. Mediagenesis Inc., L.A., 1988-91; prof. polit. sci. and ethnic studies/history Southwestern Coll., Chula Vista, Calif., 1991—. Columnist Update So. Calif.'s Gay and Lesbian Newspaper, 1997—. Treas. San Diego County Log Cabin Club, 1993, v.p., 1993-94; polit. action chair Calif. Republican League of San Diego County, 1994; selection chair The Harvey Milk/Tom Homann Scholarship Fund-The Imperial Ct. de San Diego, 1993-96; pub. comms. chair The Lesbian and Gay Men's Cmty. Ctr., 1994-96; mem. Mayor Susan Golding's Gay and Lesbian adv. bd. City of San Diego, 1994—; bd. libr. commrs. City of San Diego, 1994—; active Citizens in Action for Local Librs., Friends of Sacramento Pub. Libr.-Belle Cooledge Cmty. Libr., Friends of San Diego Pub. Libr.-Ctrl. Libr., Gay and Lesbian Alliance Against Defamation, Human Rights Campaign, Japanese Am. Republicans, Southwestern Coll. Fine Arts Contbrs., Southwestern Coll. Friends of Libr.-Learning Resource Ctr. Mem. NEA, Am. Polit. Sci. Assn., Alumni Fedn. of Columbia U., Asian Pacific Ams. in Higher Edn., Assn. Asian Am. Studies, Calif. Alumni Assn., Calif. Libr. Assn., Calif. Tchrs. Assn., C.C. Assn., Japan Soc. San Diego and Tijuana, Japanese Am. Citizens League (Asian Pacific Islander Lambda chpt.), Japanese Am. Hist. Soc. San Diego, Media Action Network for Asian Ams., Popular Culture Assn., Sacramento City Coll. Alumni Assn., San Diego-Yokohama Sister City Soc., Southwestern Coll Edn. Assn., Uptown Dist. Owners' Assn., U.S. Postal Svc. Commemorative Stamp Club, Kappa Delta Pi. Office: PO Box 3643 San Diego CA 92163-1643

NAGATA, AKIRA, publishing executive; b. Tokyo, Aug. 8, 1929; s. Koichi and Mikiko (Minami) N.; m. Tomoko Iida, Apr. 21, 1958; children: Junko, Hidehiko, Kazuhiko. BS in Econs., Jiyu-Gakuen Coll., Tokyo, 1953. Gen. mgr. for N.Am. Nihon Keizai Shimbun, Inc., Tokyo, 1973-77, spl. asst. to pres., 1977-80; dir. Nikkei-McGraw-Hill, Inc., Tokyo, 1980-88; sr. exec. dir. Nikkei Bus. Publs., Inc., Tokyo, 1988-90, pres., CEO, 1990-94, chmn., 1994—; pres., CEO Nikkei Nat. Geog. Inc., 1994-96; pres./CEO Nikkei Nat. Geographic Inc., 1994-96; vice chmn. Internat. Fedn. Periodical Press, London, 1995—; chmn. Postal Coop. Assn. of Shin-Tokyo, 1992—; chmn. Postal Coop. Assn. of Harumi, Tokyo, 1983-90. Co-author: Japanese Agriculturl Industry Off for a New Start, 1961, Revaluation of the Japanese Yen, 1971, Business Culture in the U.S., 1978, The Nine Years in New Delhi, London and New York, 1980. Mem. Japan Mag. Pubs. Assn. (exec. dir. 1993—), Rotary (Tokyo Club). Avocations: golf, tennis, opera. Office: Nikkei Bus Publs Inc, 2 7 6 Hirakawa cho, Chiyoda-ku, Tokyo 102, Japan

NAGATANI, PATRICK ALLAN RYOICHI, artist, art educator; b. Chgo., Aug. 19, 1945; s. John Lee and Diane Yoshiye (Yoshimura) N.; m. Rae Jeanean Bodwell, June 17, 1979; children: Methuen, Hart Gen, Louis-Thomas. BA, Calif. State U., L.A., 1967; MFA, UCLA, 1980. Cert. tchr. K-12, Calif. Instr. Alexander Hamilton High Sch., L.A., 1968-80, West. L.A. C.C., 1980-83; artist in residency Calif. Arts Coun., Juvenile Ct. and Cmty. Schs., L.A., 1986-87; instr. Otis Art Inst. Parson Sch. of Design, L.A., 1987; asst. prof. dept. art/art history Loyola Marymount U., L.A., 1980-87; prof. dept. art & art history U. N.Mex., Albuquerque, 1987—; instr. Fairfax Cmty. Adult Sch., L.A., 1976-79; vis. artist/instr. The Sch. of the Art Inst., Chgo., 1983; conductor numerous seminars and workshops; lectr. in field. One man shows include Pal Gallery, Evergreen State U., Olympia, Wash., 1976, BC Space, Laguna Beach, Calif., 1978, Cityscape Gallery, Pasadena, Calif., 1978, Exploratorium Gallery, Calif. State U., L.A., 1979, Orange Coast Coll., Costa Mesa, Calif., 1980, Susan Spiritus Gallery, Newport Beach, Calif., 1981, 83, 85, Canon Photo Gallery, Amsterdam, The Netherlands, 1982, John Michael Kohler Arts Ctr., Sheboygan, Wis., 1983, 86, Arco Ctr. Visual Arts, L.A., 1983, Clarence Kennedy Gallery, Boston, 1984, Colo. Mountain Coll., Breckenridge, 1984, Jayne H. Baum Gallery, N.Y.C., 1985, 87, 89, 91, 94, Torch Gallery, Amsterdam, 1985, 87, Fotografie Forum Frankfurt, Fed. Rep. Germany, 1986, Frederick S. Wight Art Gallery, U. Calif., L.A., 1987, San Francisco Cameraworks, 1988, Koplin Gallery, L.A., 1988, 90, 92, 95, Shadai Gallery, Tokyo Inst. Polytech., 1989, Lubbock (Tex.) Fine Arts Ctr., 1990, Haggerty Mus. Art, Marquette U., Milw., 1991, Richard Levy Gallery, Albuquerque, 1992, Stanford (Calif.) Mus. Art, 1993, numerous others; exhibited in group shows at Friends of Photography, Carmel, Calif., 1976, 81, 85, Ctrl. Wash. State Coll., Ellensburg, 1977, Humboldt State U., Arcata, Calif., 1977, Soho/Cameraworks Gallery, L.A., 1978, Libra Gallery, Claremont (Calif.) Grad. Sch., 1978, Cirrus Gallery, L.A., 1979, Skidmore Coll. Art Gallery, Saratoga, N.Y., 1980, Tortue Gallery, Santa Monica, Calif., 1981, Palos Verdes (Calif.) Cmty. Art Ctr., 1982, Fine Arts Gallery, Cypress (Calif.) Coll., 1982, Fay Gold Gallery, Atlanta, 1982, Mus. Photographic Arts, San Diego, 1983, 84, Jayne H. Baum Gallery, N.Y.C., 1983, 87, Arco Ctr. Visual Art, L.A., 1984, Alt. Mus., N.Y.C., 1984, 88, Black Gallery, L.A., 1985, Mus. N.Mex., Santa Fe, 1986, Whitney Mus. Am. Art, Stamford, Conn., 1986, Balt. Mus. Art, 1987, Ctr. Photography, Woodstock, N.Y., 1988, Oakland Mus., Calif., 1989, Alinder Gallery, Gualala, Calif., 1990, 92, Coll. Santa Fe, 1990, Art Ctr., Waco, Tex., 1991, Lintas Worldwide, N.Y.C., 1991, Dirs. Guild of Am., L.A., 1992, Burden Gallery, N.Y.C., 1992, Nat. Arts Club, N.Y.C., 1992, Knoxville (Tenn.) Art Mus., 1993, G. Ray Hawkins Gallery, L.A., 1994, Houston FotoFest, 1994, Riverside (Calif.) Art Mus., 1994, Mass. Coll. Art, Boston, 1994, numerous others; represented in permanent collections Albuquerque Mus., Balt. Art Mus., Continental Ins., N.Y.C., Chrysler Mus. Art, Norfolk, Va., Denver Art Mus., Ga. Power Co., Atlanta, Honolulu Advertiser, L.A. County Mus. Art, Loyola Marymount U., L.A., Mass. Coll. Art, Boston, Met. Mus. Art, N.Y.C., Mus. Fine Arts, Houston, Mus. N.Mex., Santa Fe, Nev. Mus. Art, Reno, Oakland (Calif.) Mus., Prudential Ins. Co. Am., Newark, Roswell (N.Mex.) Mus., St. Louis Art Mus., Shearson/Am. Express, N.Y.C., Tampa (Fla.) Mus. Art, Tokyo Inst. Polytech., numerous others. Travel grantee Ford Found., 1979; Faculty Rsch. grantee Loyola Marymount U., L.A., 1981, 83, U. N.Mex., 1988, 90; Artist-In-Residence grantee Calif. Arts Coun., 1982-83; Visual Artist fellow Nat. Endowment for the Arts, 1984-85, 92-93; Brody Arts Fund fellow, 1986; Polaroid fellow, 1983-90; named Art Waves competition and exhbn. finalist Cmty. Redevel. Agy. L.A., 1987; recipient Calif. Disting. Artist award Nat. Art Edn. Assn. Conv., Mus. Contemporary Art, L.A., 1988, Kraszna-Krausz award and Photographic Book Innovation award Kraszna-Krausz Found., 1992. Avocations: gardening, gambling. Office: U NMex Dept Art & Art History Albuquerque NM 87131*

NAGATOSHI, KONRAD R., anthropology educator, information systems specialist; b. Chgo., Jan. 18, 1951; s. Paul A. and Dorothea E. (Przybilla) N. BS in Anthropology with honors, Loyola U., 1973; MA in Anthropology, U. Chgo., 1976, PhD in Anthropology, 1984; cert. in data processing-tech., Harper Coll., 1990. Lic. realtor, Ill. Instr. anthropology Loyola U., Chgo., 1979-81; sr. rsch. specialist Ctr. for Craniofacial Anomalies U. Ill., Chgo., 1985-86, clin. asst. prof. biomed. visualization dept., 1987-88, adj. prof. anthropology dept., 1988; comml. real estate sales Samuel Spiro & Assocs., Chgo., 1989; computer micro-asst. Harper Coll., Palatine, Ill., 1990-91, instr. anthropology, 1991—; instr. anthropology Northeastern U., Chgo., 1991; computer programmer and analyst Ill. Dept. Employment Security, Chgo., 1992—, Kemper Nat. Ins., Long Grove, Ill., 1994—. Abstract reviewer Internat. Jour. Primatology, N.Y.C., 1990, Am. Jour. Physical Anthropology, N.Y.C., 1987; abstract reviewer, organizer U. Ill. Rsch. Forum, 1988; contbr. articles to profl. jours. Organist, song leader Our Lady of Mercy Roman Cath. Ch., Chgo., 1983-88. Found. for Rsch. Into the Origins of Man grantee, 1978-84, NSF Found. grantee, 1978-79, Sigma Xi grantee, 1978-79. Fellow Am. Anthropol. Assn.; mem. AAAS, Am. Assn. Phys. Anthropologists. Avocations: piano, art history, fishing, hiking, bicycling. Office: Harper Coll Div Bus/Social Sci 1200 W Algonquin Rd Palatine IL 60067-7373

NAGEL, DARYL DAVID, retail executive; b. Arlington, Minn., Apr. 13, 1939; s. Paul Charles and Frieda L. (Oldenburg) N.; m. Joan Clare Dacey, Dec. 23, 1961; children: Kelly, Andrew, Maureen. BME, U. Minn., 1962; diploma in Advanced Mgmt. Program, Harvard U., 1978. Asst. mdse. mgr. Res. Supply Co., Mpls., 1962-65; mdse. mgr. Reserve Supply Co., Mpls., 1965-66, v.p., gen. mgr., 1966-69; v.p. area gen. mgr. United Bldg. Ctrs., Winona, Minn., 1969-78, exec. v.p., chief ops. officer, 1978-84, pres., chief exec. officer, 1984-87; pres., CEO Lanoga Corp., Seattle, 1987—; bd. dirs. Lanoga Corp., Seattle, 1987—, Badger Foundry, Winona, 1984-87. Bd. dirs. United Way, Winona, 1978-84, Home Ctr. Inst., 1996. Mem. Home Ctr. Leadership Coun., C. of C. (bd. dirs. 1964-69, 73, 78), Sahalee Country Club. Republican. Lutheran. Avocations: golf, gardening, skiing. Office: Lanoga Corp PO Box 97040 Redmond WA 98073-9740

NAGEL, EDWARD MCCAUL, lawyer, former utilities executive; b. Geneva, N.Y., Sept. 6, 1926; s. Edward Samuel and Helen Veronica (McCaul) N.; m. Mary Elizabeth Klein, Sept. 11, 1950; children—Christopher, Linda, Michael, Jeffrey, Ellen. A.B., Harvard, 1949; LL.B., U. Pa., 1952; postgrad., Cornell U. Bus. Sch., 1962. Bar: Pa. 1953. Assoc. Simpson, Thacher & Bartlett, N.Y.C., 1953-54; atty. Pa. Power & Light Co., Allentown, 1952, 54-62; asst. counsel Pa. Power & Light Co., 1962-68, asst. gen. counsel, 1968-71, gen. counsel, 1971-85, sec., 1971-89, v.p., 1973-91; prin. Edward M. Nagel Atty. at Law, 1991—; bd. dirs. Exec. Svc. Corps of Lehigh Valley. Chmn. Mayor's Citizens Adv. Com., Allentown, 1968-72; assoc. counsel, bd. dirs. Minsi Trails council Boy Scouts Am. Served with USNR, 1945-46. Mem. Pa. Bar Assn., Lehigh County Bar Assn. Home: 417 N 28th St Allentown PA 18104-4838

NAGEL, JOACHIM HANS, biomedical engineer, educator; b. Haustadt, Saarland, Feb. 22, 1948; came to U.S., 1986; s. Emil and Margarethe Nagel; m. Monika Behrens. MS, U. Saarbruecken, Fed. Republic Germany, 1973; DSc, U. Erlangen, Fed. Republic Germany, 1979. Rsch. assoc., lectr., instr. U. Saarbruecken, 1973-74; rsch. assoc., lectr., instr. Dept. Biomed. Engring., U. Erlangen-Nuernberg, 1974-75, asst. prof., 1975-79, dir. med. electronics and computer div., 1976-85, assoc. prof., 1980-86; assoc. prof. radiology Med. Sch. U. Miami, Coral Gables, Fla., 1990-91, assoc. prof. psychology Sch. Arts and Scis., 1988-91, assoc. prof. biomed. engring. Coll. Engring., 1986-91, prof. biomed. engring. radiology and psychology, 1991-96; chaired prof. and dir. Inst. Biomed. Engring. U. Stuttgart, 1996—; adj. prof. radiology and biomed. engring. U. Miami, 1996—. Editor Annals of Biomedical Engineering, Section Instrumentation, 1989-94, Inst. of Physics Physiological Measurement, 1994—; contbr. articles numerous articles to profl. jours. NIH grantee since 1986. Mem. IEEE (sr.), IEEE/Engring. in Medicine and Biology Soc. (chmn. Internat. Conf. 1991, chmn. Internat. Progr. Com. Conf. 1989, 90, 92), IEEE/Acoustics, Speech, and Signal Processing Soc., Biomed. Engring. Soc. (sr.), N.Y. Acad. Scis., Internat. Soc. Optical Engring., Romanian Soc. for Clin. Engring. and Med. Computing (hon.), Sigma Xi. Roman Catholic. Achievements include numerous U.S., German and European patents; invention and development of procedure for Sub-Nyquist Sampling of signals for statistic signal processing, NMR imaging of electric currents, passive telemetry for analogue signals, ECG detection; invention of Macro programming; portable drug infusion systems; new techniques for impedance cardiography and perinatal monitors; new techniques for medical image registration and U.S. Doppler analysis; neural network classification of Alzheimer's disease. Office: U Stuttgart, Seidenstrasse 36, D-70174 Stuttgart Germany

NAGEL, PAUL CHESTER, historian, writer, lecturer; b. Independence, Mo., Aug. 14, 1926; s. Paul Conrad and Freda (Sabrowsky) N.; m. Joan Peterson, Mar. 19, 1948; children: Eric John, Jefferson, Steven Paul. B.A., U. Minn., 1948, M.A., 1949, Ph.D., 1952. Historian SAC, USAF, Omaha, 1951-53; asst. prof. Augustana Coll., Sioux Falls, S.D., 1953-54; asst. prof., then assoc. prof. Eastern Ky. U., Richmond, 1954-61; mem. faculty U. Ky., 1961-69, prof. history, 1965-69; dean U. Ky. (Coll. Arts and Scis.), 1965-69; spl. asst. to pres. for acad. affairs U. Mo., 1969-71, v.p. acad. affairs, 1971-74, prof. history, 1969-78; prof., head dept. history U. Ga., 1978-80; dir. Va. Hist. Soc., Richmond, 1981-85; Disting. Lee scholar Lee Meml. Found., 1986-90; vis. prof. Amherst Coll., 1957-58, Vanderbilt U., 1959, U. Minn., 1964; vis. scholar, Duke U., 1991-92, U. Minn., 1992—, Carleton Coll., 1993—. Author: One Nation Indivisible, 1964, 2d edit., 1980, This Sacred Trust, American Nationality, 1798-1898, 1971, 2d edit., 1980, Missouri: A History, 1977 (Best Book award 1977), 2d edit., 1988, Descent from Glory, Four Generations of the John Adams Family, 1983 (Book of the Month Club main selection), The Adams Women: Abigail and Louisa Adams, Their Sisters and Daughters, 1987, The Lees of Virginia: Seven Generations of an American Family, 1990, John Quincy Adams: A Public Life, A Private Life, 1997; co-author: Extraordinary Lives, 1986, George Caleb Bingham, 1989, Massachusetts and the New Nation, 1992; contbg. editor American Heritage. Mem. Coun. Colls. Arts and Scis., 1965-69, Ky. Arts Commn., 1966-69; trustee Colonial Williamsburg Found., 1983-95, disting. rsch. assoc., 1995—; vice-chmn. bd. dirs. Ctr. for Rsch. Librs., Chgo., 1973-74. Elected a Laureate of Va., 1988. Fellow Soc. Am. Historians, Pilgrim Soc.; So. Hist. Assn. (pres. 1984-85), Mass. Hist. Soc. Home: 1314 Marquette Ave Apt 2206 Minneapolis MN 55403-4114

NAGEL, SIDNEY ROBERT, physics educator; b. N.Y.C., Sept. 28, 1948; s. Ernest and Edith (Haggstrom) N. BA, Columbia U., 1969; MA, Princeton U., 1972, PhD, 1974. Rsch. assoc. Brown U., Providence, R.I., 1974-76; asst. prof. physics U. Chgo., 1976-81, assoc. prof., 1981-84, prof., 1984—. Dir. U. Chgo. Materials Research Lab., 1987-91. Contbr. articles to profl. jours. Alfred Sloan Found. fellow, 1978-82. Fellow AAAS, Am. Phys. Soc. Home: 4919 S Blackstone Ave Chicago IL 60615-3003 Office: U Chgo 5640 S Ellis Ave Chicago IL 60637-1433

NAGEL, STUART SAMUEL, political science educator, lawyer; b. Chgo., Aug. 29, 1934; s. Leo I. and Florence (Pritikin) N.; m. Joyce Golub, Sept. 1, 1957; children: Brenda Ellen, Robert Franklin. Student, U. Chgo., 1954-55; BS, Northwestern U., 1957, JD, 1958, PhD, 1961. Bar: Ill. 1958. Instr. Pa. State U., 1960-61; asst. prof. U. Ariz., 1961-62; prof. polit. sci. U. Ill., 1962—; law and social sci. vis. fellow Yale Law Sch., 1970-71; vis. fellow Nat. Inst. Law Enforcement and Criminal Justice, 1974-75; Sr. scholar East-West Center, Honolulu, 1965; fellow Behavioral Scis. Center, Palo Alto, Calif., 1964-65; dir. O.E.O. Legal Services Agy. of Champaign, 1966-69; vol. atty. Lawyers Constl. Def. Com., Miss., 1967; asst. counsel U.S. Senate Jud. Com., 1966. Author: The Legal Process from a Behavioral Perspective, 1969, Law and Social Change, 1970, New Trends in Law and Politics Research, 1971, Rights of the Accused, 1972, Comparing Elected and Appointed Judicial Systems, 1973, Minimizing Costs and Maximizing Benefits in Providing Legal Services to the Poor, 1973, Improving the Legal Process: Effects of Alternatives, 1975, Operations Research Methods: As Applied to Political Science and The Legal Process, 1976, The Application of Mixed Strategies: Civil Rights and Other Multiple Activity Policies, 1976, Legal Policy Analysis: Finding an Optimum Level or Mix, 1977, Too Much or Too Little Policy: The Example of Pretrial Release, 1977, The Legal Process: Modeling the System, 1977, Decision Theory and the Legal Process, 1979, Policy Analysis: In Social Science Research, 1979, Policy Studies Handbook, 1980, Policy Evaluation: Making Optimum Decisions, 1982, Public Policy: Goals, Means and Methods, 1984, Contemporary Policy Analysis, 1984, Prediction Causation and Legal Analysis, 1986, Law, Policy and Optimizing Analysis, 1986, Evaluation Analysis with Microcomputers, 1988, Policy Studies: Integration and Evaluation, 1988, Higher Goals for America, 1988, Decision-Aiding Software and Legal Decision-Making, 1988, Introducing Decision-Aiding Software, 1989, Multi-Criteria Dispute Resolution, 1989, Evaluative and Explanatory Reasoning, 1990, Legal Scholarship and Microcomputers, 1990, Decision-Aiding Software: Skills, Obstacles and Applications, 1990, Judicial Decision-Making and Decision-Aiding Software, 1991, Legal Process Controversies and Super-Optimum Solutions, 1991, Public Policy Substance and Super-Optimum Solutions, 1991, Teach Yourself Decision-Aiding Software, 1991, Social Science, Law, and Public Policy, 1991, Policy Analysis Methods and Super-Optimum Solutions, 1992, Professional Developments in Policy Studies, 1992, Developing Nations and Super-Optimum Policy Analysis, 1993, The Policy Process and Super-Optimum Solutions, 1994, Win-Win Policy: Basic Concepts and Principles, 1996, The Super-Optimum Society, 1996, Developmental Policy Studies, 1996, Creativity and Public Policy: Generating Super-Optimum Solutions, 1996, Economic Policy to Promote Prosperity, 1997, Technology Policy to Promote Innovation, 1997, Social Policy to Promote Merit Treatment, 1997, Political Policy to Promote Democracy, 1997, Judicial Policy to Promote Legal Efficiency, 1997, Constitutional Policy to Promote Rights and Obligations, 1997, Developmental Policy Studies: Being More Effective and More Efficient, 1997, Policy Within and Across Developing Nations, 1997, World Regional Development and Super-Optimizing Analysis Across Four Continents, 1997, Public Policy Evaluation: Making Super-Optimum Solutions, 1997, others; editor: Policy Studies Jour., The Policy Studies Directory, 1973, Environmental Politics, 1974, Policy Studies in America and Elsewhere, 1975, Policy Studies and the Social Sciences, 1975, Sage Yearbooks in Politics and Public Policy, 1975—, Lexington-Heath Policy Studies Orgn. Series, 1975—, Political Science Utilization Directory, 1975, Policy Studies Review Annual, 1977, Policy Grants Directory, 1977, Modeling the Criminal Justice System, 1977, Policy Research Centers Directory, 1978, Policy Studies Personnel Directory, 1979, Improving Policy Analysis, 1980, Policy Publishers and Associations Directory, 1980, Encyclopedia of Policy Studies, 1982, The Political Science of Criminal Justice, 1982, Productivity and Public Policy, 1983, The Policy Studies Field: It's Basic Literature, 1983, Public Policy Analysis and Management, 1986, Law and Policy Studies, 1987, Social Science and Computers, 1988, Decision-aiding Software and Decision Analysis, 1990, Decision-aiding Software and Public Administration, 1990, Global Policy Studies, 1990, Law, Decision-making and Microcomputers, 1990, Policy Theory and Policy Studies, 1990, Advances in Developmental Policy Studies, 1991—, Applications of Decision-Aiding Software, 1991, Applications of Super-Optimum Solutions, 1991, Decision-Aiding Software and Decision Analysis, 1991, Law, Decision-Making, and Microcomputers, 1991, Policy Studies and Developing Nations: A Multi-Volume Treatise, 1991, Public Administration, Public Policy, and The People's Republic of China, 1991, Systematic Analysis in Dispute Resolution, 1991, Computer-Aided Decision Analysis, 1992, Resolving International Disputes Through Win-Win or SOS Solutions, 1992, Computer-Aided Judicial Analysis, 1992, Developing Nations and Super-Optimum Policy Analysis, 1992, Evaluative and Explanatory Reasoning, 1992, Developing Nations and Super-Optimum Policy Analysis, 1993, Legal Scholarship, Super-Optimizing, and Microcomputers, 1993, Encyclopedia of Policy Studies, 1993, African Development and Public Policy, 1994, Asian Development and Public Policy, 1994, East European Development and Public Policy, 1994, Latin American Development and Public Policy, 1994, Policy Studies in Developing Nations, 1994—, Political Reform and Developing Nations, 1995, Policy Studies in Developing Nations, 1994, India Development and Public Policy, 1995, Policy Studies Index, 2nd edit., 1995, Applications of Super-Optimizing Analysis, 1996, Resolving International Disputes through Super-Optimum Solutions, 1996, Creativity: Being Usefully Innovative, 1996, others; mem. editorial bd.: Law and Soc. Assn, 1966—, Law and Policy Studies, 1986—, Pub. Policy Analysis and Mgmt., 1986—. Grantee Social Sci. Research Council, 1959-60; Grantee Am. Council Learned Socs., 1964-65; Grantee NSF, 1970-73; Grantee Rockefeller Found., 1976; Grantee Dept. Transp., 1976; Grantee Ford Found., 1975—; Grantee ERDA, 1977; Grantee Dept. Agr., 1977; Grantee NIE, 1976; Grantee HUD, 1978; Grantee ILEC, 1978; Grantee Dept. Labor, 1978; Grantee NIJ, 1979; Grantee Am. Bar Assn., 1980. Fellow AAAS; mem. ABA, Am. Polit. Sci. Assn., Law and Soc. Assn. (trustee), Policy Studies Orgn. (sec.-treas.). Home: 1720 Park Haven Dr Champaign IL 61820-7153 *There is a need for social scientists to show more interest in applying their knowledge and skills to important policy problems. There is also a need for policy-makers and policy-appliers to become more aware of the relevant knowledge and skills that social scientists have developed. I have tried to stimulate closer relations between social science and public policy by such relevant activities as writing articles, authoring books, editing journals, and founding associations. Those activities will hopefully result in promoting more applications of social science to important public policy problems. I am especially interested in developing solutions to public policy problems whereby liberals, conservatives, and other major viewpoints can all come out ahead of their initial best expectations simultaneously. Such solutions are facilitated by decision-aiding software which enables one to systematically process goals to be achieved, alternatives available for achieving them, and relations be*

NAGEL, THOMAS, philosopher, educator; b. Belgrade, Yugoslavia, July 4, 1937; came to U.S., 1939, naturalized, 1944; s. Walter and Carolyn (Baer) N.; m. Doris Blum, June 18, 1958 (div. 1973); m. Anne Hollander, June 26, 1979. B.A., Cornell U., 1958; B.Phil., Oxford (Eng.) U., 1960; Ph.D., Harvard, 1963. Asst. prof. philosophy U. Calif., Berkeley, 1963-66; asst. prof. Princeton U., 1966-69, assoc., 1969-72, prof., 1972-80; prof. N.Y. U., 1980—, prof. philosophy and law, 1986—; vis. prof. Rockefeller U., 1973, U. Mex., 1977, U. Witwatersrand, 1982, UCLA, 1986; Tanner lectr. Stanford U., 1977, Oxford (Eng.) U., 1979, Howison lectr. U. Calif., Berkeley, 1987, Thalheimer lectr. Johns Hopkins U., 1989, John Locke lectr. Oxford U., 1990, Hempel lectr. Princeton U., 1995, Whitehead lectr. Harvard U., 1995, Kant lectr. Stanford U., 1995. Author: The Possibility of Altruism, 1970, Mortal Questions, 1979, The View from Nowhere, 1986, What Does It All Mean?, 1987, Equality and Partiality, 1991, Other Minds, 1995, The Last Word, 1997; assoc. editor: Philosophy and Public Affairs, 1970-82. Guggenheim fellow, 1966, NSF fellow, 1967-69, NEH fellow, 1978, 84-85, vis. fellow All Souls Coll., Oxford, Eng., 1990. Mem. Am. Philos. Assn., Am. Acad. Arts and Scis., Brit. Acad.

NAGERA, HUMBERTO, psychiatrist, psychoanalyst, educator, author; b. Havana, Cuba, May 23, 1927; m. Gloria Maria Hernandez, Sept. 8, 1952; children: Lisette Maria, Humberto Felipe, Daniel. B.Sc., U. Havana, 1945; M.D., Havana Med. Sch., 1952. Intern, resident in psychiatry Havana U.

Hosp., 1950-55; sr. staff, chmn. research Anna Freud's Clinic, London, 1958-68; prof. psychiatry U. Mich., Ann Arbor, 1968-87; chief youth services U. Mich., 1973-79, prof. emeritus, 1987; prof. psychiatry U. South Fla., 1987—, dir. adolescent inpatient unit and children's inpatient unit, 1987—. Author: Early Childhood Disturbances, Problems of Developmental Psychoanalytic Psychology, 1966, Vincent Van Gogh, 1966, Basic Psychoanalytic Concepts on the Libido Theory, 1969, Basic Psychoanalytic Concepts on the Theory of Instincts, 1970, Basic Psychoanalytic Concepts of Metapsychology Conflicts, Anxiety, and Other Subjects, 1970, Female Sexuality and the Oedipus Complex, 1975, Obsessional Neurosis: Developmental Psychopathology, 1977, 2nd edit., 1993, The Developmental Approach in Child Psychopathology, 1981; Contbr. articles to profl. jours. Mem. Am. Psychiat. Assn., Internat. Psychoanalytic Assn., Mich. Psychoanalytic Inst. (pres. 1975-77), Am. Assn. Child Psychoanalysis, Cuba Med. Assn. in Exile, South Fla. Tampa Bay Psychoanalytic Soc. (pres. 1992-93). Home: 5202 Dwire Ct Tampa FL 33647-1016 Office: U South Fla Dept Psychiatry 3515 E Fletcher Ave Tampa FL 33613-4706

NAGEY, DAVID AUGUSTUS, physician, researcher; b. Cleve., Oct. 14, 1950; s. Tibor Franz and Patricia Ann (Griffin) N.; m. Elaine Traicoff, Aug. 7, 1971; children: Stefan Anastas, Nicholas Tibor. Student Cornell U., 1966-67; BS with distinction, Purdue U., 1969; PhD in Bioengring., Duke U., 1974, MD, 1975. Diplomate Am. Bd. Obstetrics and Gynecology, Am. Bd. Maternal-Fetal Medicine; registered profl. engr., Md. Resident in ob/gyn., Duke U. Sch. Medicine, Durham, N.C., 1975-79, fellow in maternal-fetal medicine, 1979-81; asst. prof. U. Md. Sch. Medicine, Balt., 1981-84, assoc. prof., 1984-95, prof., 1995-96, asst. dir., divsn. maternal-fetal medicine, 1981-85, dir. divsn. maternal-fetal medicine, 1985-96, rsch. assoc. prof. Dept. of Epidemiology and Preventive Medicine, 1992-96; adj. assoc. prof. dept. elec. engring. U. Md., 1986-92; assoc. prof., dir. maternal transport program Johns Hopkins Hosp. and Sch. Medicine, 1996—; assoc. prof. dept. maternal and child health Sch. of Hygiene and Pub. Health, Johns Hopkins U., 1986—; rsch. assoc. Nat. Inst. Child Health & Human Devel., 1991-92; assoc. examiner Am. Bd. Obstetrics and Gynecology, 1991-92, examiner, 1993—, mem. editl. bd. 1985—; examiner Am. Bd. Maternal-Fetal Medicine, 1996—. Assoc. editor: Computers in Medicine and Biology, 1984—; mem. editl. bd. Jour. Maternal-Fetal Investigation, 1991—, Ob/Gyn., 1995—, Birth, 1997—; contbr. articles to med. jours. ACOG/Syntex grantee, 1987. Fellow Am. Coll. Obstetricians and Gynecologists (com. sci. program 1988-95, mem. com. edn. Bulletins-Obstetrics, 1994—) vice chmn., 1996-97; mem. AAAS (chmn. 1997—), IEEE (healthcare engring. policy com. 1987-91), So. Perinatal Assn. (pres. 1987), Nat. Perinatal Assn. (bd. dirs. 1986-90), Bayard Carter Assn. Ob-Gyn., Md. Ob-Gyn. Soc. (pres. 1990-91, exec. com. 1987—). Avocation: sailing. Office: Johns Hopkins Hosp Dept Ob/Gyn Divsn Maternal Fetal Medicine 600 N Wolfe St # 204 Baltimore MD 21205-2110

NAGLE, ARTHUR JOSEPH, investment banker; b. Allentown, Pa., Sept. 11, 1938; s. Paul Arthur and Frances Helene (Kline) N.; m. Paige Carlton, Sept. 12, 1970; children: Kathryn Elizabeth, Christopher Paul. BS in Math., Pa. State U., 1961; MBA in Fin., Columbia U., 1967. Systems engr., mktg. rep. IBM, Pitts., 1961-62; trainee to mng. dir. First Boston Corp., N.Y.C., 1967-88; mng. dir. Vestar Capital Ptnrs., Inc., 1988—; bd. dirs. Chart House Restaurant, Solana Beach, Calif., Russell Stanley Corp., Woodbridge, N.J., La Petite Acad., Inc., Overland Park, Kans., Aearo Corp., Boston, Clark Schwebel Inc., Anderson, S.C., Prestone Products Corp., Danbury, Conn., Remington Products Co., L.L.C., Bridgeport, Conn. Active Community Fund, Bronxville, N.Y.; vice chmn., bd. govs. Lawrence Hosp., Bronxville, Nat. Devel. Coun., Pa. State U., Bronxville Sch. Found. Lt. USN, 1962-66, Vietnam. Office: Vestar Capital Ptnrs Inc 245 Park Ave Fl 41 New York NY 10017-2500

NAGLE, JAMES FRANCIS, lawyer; b. Jersey City, Aug. 5, 1948; s. James Francis and Cecile Marie (Dorgan) N.; m. Ann Marie Thomas, Dec. 28, 1974; children: James, John, Stephen. BS, Georgetown U., 1970; JD, Rutgers U., 1973; LLM, George Washington U., 1981, SJD, 1986. Bar: N.J. 1973, U.S. Ct. Mil. Appeals 1979, U.S. Supreme Ct. 1979, U.S. Ct. Appeals (fed. cir.) 1982, U.S. Ct. Appeals (D.C. cir.) 1983. Enlisted U.S. Army, 1970, advanced through grades to lt. col., 1987; chief of criminal law Presidio of San Francisco, 1974-75; command judge adv. U.S. 8th Army, Korea, 1975-76; chief of administrv. law U.S. Army Electronics Command, Ft. Monmouth, N.J., 1976-79; br. chief Army Def. Appellate Div., Falls Church, Va., 1982-85; team chief Army Chief Trial Atty.'s Office, Falls Church, 1982-85; contracts atty. U.S. Army Forces Command, Ft. McPherson, Ga., 1985-88; chief adminstrv. law U.S. Third Army, Ft. McPherson, 1986-88; chief logistic and contract law dept. U.S. Army, Washington, 1988-90; ret. U.S. Army, 1990; ptnr. Oles, Morrison & Rinker, Seattle, 1990—. Author: Procurement Regulations, 1987, A History of Government Contracting, 1992, How to Review Federal Contracts, 1990, Federal Construction Contracting, 1992; contbr. articles to profl. jours. Mem. Fed. Bar Assn., Wash. State Bar Assn., D.C. Bar Assn. Roman Catholic. Avocations: gardening, karate. Home: 5196 Lynwood Center Rd NE Bainbridge Island WA 98110

NAGLEE, ELFRIEDE KURZ, retired medical nurse; b. Phila., Mar. 13, 1932; d. Emil and Frida (Keppler) Kurz; m. David I. Naglee, Sept. 6, 1952; children: Joy, Miriam, Deborah, Joanna, David. Grad., Phila. Gen. Hosp., 1952. RN, Ga. Dir. nursing City County Hosp., LaGrange, Ga.; house supr. West Ga. Med. Ctr., LaGrange, from 1967; staff nurse med. fl. West Ga. Med. Ctr., LaGange, to 1995; ret., 1995. Mem. Ga. Nursing Assn. Home: 804 Piney Woods Dr La Grange GA 30240

NAGLER, ARNOLD LEON, pathologist, scientist, educator; b. N.Y.C., 1935; s. Max and Esther (Finkel) N.; m. Rosalie Groden, Feb. 18, 1961; children: Stephen Marc, Melissa Sue. B.S., CCNY, 1953; M.D., NYU, 1958, Ph.D., 1960. Lic. dir. labs., N.Y. Postgrad. tng. NYU-Bellevue Med. Ctr., 1958-61; research assoc. Mt. Sinai Hosp., N.Y.C., 1960-61; mem. faculty Albert Einstein Coll. Medicine, Bronx, N.Y., 1961—, assoc. prof. pathology, surgery, 1975—; cons., prof., chmn. pathology dept., dean pre-clin. medicine N.Y. Coll. Osteo Medicine, 1978—; trustee Robert Chambers Microsurgery Research Labs., 1978—; founder, trustee Esther Nagler Dystrophy Research Fund, N.Y. Coll. Osteo. Medicine. Mem. editorial bd.: Circulatory Shock; contbr. articles to profl. jours. Chmn. Jericho council Boy Scouts Am., 1971-73; mem. Pres.'s Task Force, 1981—, Nat. Republican Congressional Com., U.S. Senatorial Club; trustee Liberal Jewish Day Sch., N.Y.C.; corp. mem. Nassau-Suffolk Health Systems Agy., mem. Primary Care Task Force. Served with U.S. Army, 1953-55. NIH grantee, 1961—. Fellow Am. Soc. Clin. Pathologists; mem. N.Y. Acad. Sci., N.Y. Acad. Medicine, AAAS, Am. Trauma Soc. (founder), Sigma Xi. Jewish. Home: 72 Hazelwood Dr Jericho NY 11753-1704 Office: Albert Einstein Coll Medicine 1300 Morris Park Ave Bronx NY 10461-1926 *I was guided by my parents when they were alive and directed by their teachings and precepts after their death to strive to do the best that I possibly may, in any and every endeavor that I undertake. They provided the armoury: Do no harm to anyone—achieve by dedicating yourself to excellence/performance. Do not rally in relegating someone to a lesser state; this is only relative success and is neither satisfying nor worthwhile to the soul, nor is it real.*

NAGLER, LEON GREGORY, management consultant, business executive; b. Buenos Aires, Argentina, Jan. 29, 1932 (parents Am. citizens); s. Morris and Jennie (Golden) N.; BS cum laude, Boston U., 1953, MBA, 1954; J.D., Cleve. State U., 1961; m. F. Elise Charness, Dec. 20, 1953; children: Jeri Lynn, Sandra Michelle. Bar: Ohio 1961. Tchr. psychology Cameron State Agrl. Jr. Coll., Lawton, Okla., 1956-57; supr. employment and tng. Jones & Laughlin Steel Corp., Cleve., 1957-65; exec. dir. indsl. relations Charles Corp., Cleve., 1965-67; dir. personnel ITT Service Industries Corp., Cleve., 1967-72; v.p. personnel Builder Services Corp., Clearwater, Fla., 1972-73; v.p. adminstrn. Damon Corp., Needham Heights, Mass., 1973-77; pres. Nagler & Co., Inc., Wellesley Hills, Mass., 1977-95; pres. Nagler, Robins & Poe, Inc., 1995—. Mem. Mayfield Heights (Ohio) Planning and Zoning Commn., 1965-67; sec. Mayfield Heights Zoning Bd. Appeals, 1963-65; chmn. Combined Health Fund, Mayfield Heights, 1963; pres. N.E. Ohio region, mem. nat. gov. coun. Am. Jewish Congress, 1972-73; bd. dirs. New Eng. region Anti-Defamation League, 1977-80; bd. dirs. Jewish Vocat. Svc., Boston, 1977—, sec., 1980-83, v.p., 1983-88; bd. dirs. Jewish Community Ctr. Greater Boston, 1988—, Am. Friends Wingate Inst., 1987—, v.p. fin., 1987—; trustee Temple Beth Avodah, Newton, 1978—, v.p., 1979-83, pres., 1983-85; trustee Combined Jewish Philanthropies, Boston, 1985-92; bd. overseers Combined Jewish Philanthropies, 1992—. Served with AUS, 1955-57. Mem. Ohio, Cleve. bar assns., Soc. for Human Resource Mgmt., Internat. Assn. Corp. and Exec. Recruiters, Boston U. Alumni Assn. (pres. N.E. Ohio 1969-73, nat. council 1973—). Democrat. Lodge: Masons. Office: Nagler Robins & Poe Inc 65 William St Wellesley MA 02181-3802

NAGLER, STEWART GORDON, insurance company executive; b. Bklyn., Jan. 30, 1943; s. Henry and Mary N.; m. Bonnie Lawrence, Aug. 9, 1964; children: David, Ellen. B.S. summa cum laude, Poly. U., 1963. With Met. Life Ins. Co., N.Y.C., 1963—, exec. v.p., 1978-85, sr. exec. v.p., 1985—. Fellow Soc. Actuaries, Acad. Actuaries. Office: Met Life Ins Co 1 Madison Ave New York NY 10010-3603

NAGLESTAD, FREDERIC ALLEN, legislative advocate; b. Sioux City, Iowa, Jan. 13, 1929; s. Ole T. and Evelyn Elizabeth (Erschen) N.; student (scholar) U. Chgo., 1947-49; m. Beverly Minnette Shellberg, Feb. 14, 1958; children—Patricia Minnette, Catherine Janette. Pub. affairs, pub. relations, newscaster, announcer KSCJ-radio, Sioux City, Iowa, 1949-51; producer, dir., newscaster, announcer WOW-TV, Omaha, 1953-57; program mgr. WCPO-TV, Cin., 1957-58; mgr. KNTV-TV, San Jose, Calif., 1958-61; owner Results Employment Agy., San Jose, 1961-75; legis. advocate Naglestad Assocs., Calif Assn. Employers, Calif. Automotive Wholesalers Assn., Air Quality Products, Calif. Assn. Wholesalers-Distbrs., State Alliance Bd. Equalization Reform, Quakemaster, many others, 1969—. Pres. Calif. Employment Assn., 1970-72. Asst. concertmaster Sioux City Symphony Orch., 1945-47. Sgt. AUS, 1951-53. Recognized for outstanding contbn. to better employment law, Resolution State Calif. Legislature, 1971. Office: 3991 Fair Oaks Blvd Sacramento CA 95864-7254 *Personal philosophy: Tell the truth, perservere and follow through.*

NAGORSKI, ZYGMUNT, political scientist; b. Warsaw, Poland, Sept. 27, 1912; came to U.S., 1948, naturalized, 1953; s. Zygmunt Julian and Maria Nagorski; m. Marie Bogdaszewski, Nov. 22, 1938; children—Maria, Andrew, Teresa. M.A., U. Cracow (Poland), 1935; postgrad. U. Geneva, 1937-38, Internat. Inst. Trade and Patents, Berne, Switzerland, 1937-38, Reporter, Chattanooga Times, 1948; editor-in-chief Fgn. News Service, Inc., N.Y.C., 1949-56; chief Internat. Br. Office Research, USIA, Washington, 1956-59; fgn. service officer, Cairo, 1959-61, Seoul, 1961-64, Paris, 1964-66; spl. asst. to pres. Fgn. Policy Assn., Inc., N.Y.C., 1966-68; mem. profl. staff Hudson Inst., Inc., 1968-69; dir. Members Meetings Program, Council on Fgn. Relations, N.Y.C., 1969-78; v.p. Lehrman Inst., 1978-80; spl. adv. Aspen Inst.; adj. asst. prof. polit. sci. dept. Queens Coll., 1974-75; v.p. Human Resource Services, Inc., 1980-81; guest lectr. Wilton Park, Sussex, Eng., Fgn. Service Inst., Center for Study Human Values, Tanglewood, N.C., Experiment in Internat. Living (Vt.), also numerous univs.; v.p., dir. exec. seminars programs Aspen Inst. Humanistic Studies, 1981- 85; pres. Ctr. for Internat. Leadership, N.Y.C., 1986—. Pres., Am. Friends of Wilton Park, 1967-70, 94-96, Mid-Atlantic Club of New York, 1972—; bd. dirs. Scarsdale Adult Sch., 1968-72, Internat. U. Found. Served with Polish Army, 1939-45 under French and British Command. Decorated Brit. War medal, officer's cross Order of Merit (W. Ger.); comdr. Order of Leopold II (Belgium); recipient Meritorious Svc. award USIA, 1965, Outstanding Fgn. Born Am. award Internat. Ctr. of N.Y., 1988. Mem. Coun. on Fgn. Relations, Am. Polit. Sci. Assn., Internat. Studies Assn., Polish Inst. Arts and Scis., Am. Fgn. Service Assn. Democrat. Roman Catholic. Club: Fgn. Svc., Nat. Press (Washington). Author: Armed Unemployment, 1945; The Psychology of East-West Trade, 1975; co-author: U.S.- Japan Economic Relations, 1979. Contbr. articles to newspapers and mags. Home: 5208 MacArthur Terrace NW Washington DC 20016 Office: Ctr for Internat Leadership 5208 Macarthur Ter NW Washington DC 20016-2617

NAGOURNEY, HERBERT, publishing company executive; b. N.Y.C., Jan. 30, 1926; s. Isidor and Tillie (Burstein) N.; children: Adam, Beth, Eric, Sam. BS, Columbia U., 1946, MS, 1947. Pres. Profl. and Tech. Programs, N.Y.C., 1951-65; v.p. Macmillan Co., N.Y.C., 1965-69; pres. Quadrangle/New York Times Book Co., N.Y.C., 1969-76, New York Times Book Co., N.Y.C., 1971-76, Quartet Books, Inc., N.Y.C. and London, 1976-81, Knowledge Tree Group Inc., 1979-89; v.p., dir. Sci. DataLink, 1981-88, Comtex Sci., 1981-90; pres. Profl. and Tech. Pub. Inc., 1989—, Sci. Datalink, 1990—. Served with AUS, 1944. Home: 320 Joshuatown Rd Lyme CT 06371-3000 Office: 45 Christopher St New York NY 10014-3533

NAGRIN, DANIEL, dancer, educator, choreographer, lecturer, writer; b. N.Y.C., May 22, 1917; s. Harry Samuel and Clara (Wexler) N.; m. Helen Tamiris, 1946 (dec. 1966); m. Phyllis A. Steele, Jan. 24, 1992. BS in Edn., CCNY, 1940; DFA, SUNY, Brockport, 1991; LHD, Ariz. State U., 1992; studied dance with Martha Graham, Anna Sokolow, Helen Tamiris, Mme. Anderson-Ivantzova, Nenette Charisse and Edward Caton, 1936-56, studied acting with Miriam Goldina, Sanford Meisner and Stella Adler, 1936-56. Tchr. Silvermine Guild Art, New Canaan, Conn., 1957-66, SUNY, Brockport, 1967-71, U. Md., College Park, 1970, Davis Ctr. Performing Arts, CCNY, 1973-75, Nat. Theatre Inst., Eugene O'Neill Found., Waterford, Conn., 1974, Hartmann Theatre Conservatory, Stamford, Conn., 1975-77; long-term resident tchr., Nat. Endowment for Arts sponsorship U. Hawaii, 1978-80, tchr., 1981; tchr. Bill Evans Dance Workshop, Seattle, 1981; prof. dance dept. Ariz. State U., Tempe, 1982-92; tchr. grad. liberal studies program Wesleyan U., Middletown, Conn., 1984, Dance Workshop for Movement Rsch., N.Y.C., 1984, Improvisation Workshop, Seattle, 1985, Improvisation, Choreography and Acting Technique for Dancers, Seattle, 1985, Dance Workshop, Glenwood Springs, Colo., 1990; prof. emeritus dance Ariz. State U., 1992; tchr. summer sessions Conn. Coll., New London, 1959, 74; Am. Dance Festival at Conn. Coll., 1960, 77, Duke U., Durham, N.C., 1978, 80, 82, 87, 88, 92, Balasaraswati/Joy Ann Dewey Beinecke Chair Dising. Tchg., 1992; summer dance program Conn. Coll., 1979, E. La Tour Dance Workshop, Sedgewick, 1982, 83; dance workshop U. Minn. at Mpls., 1984, Stanford U., 1990; co-dir. Tamiris-Nagrin Summer Dance Workshop, Sedgewick, 1960-61, (with Tamiris) summer dance session C. W. Post Coll., Greenville, N.Y., 1962-63; dir. summer dance workshop Johnson (Vt.) State Coll., 1972, 73, 75, 76. Featured dance soloist on Broadway: Annie Get Your Gun, Lend an Ear, Touch and Go, Plain and Fancy (Billboard Donaldson award 1954-55), 1940-56; appearance in film, Just for You; adapted and performed one-man theatre piece The Fall, from novel by Albert Camus, 1977-79, choreographer (solo works) Spanish Dance, 1948, Man of Action, 1948, Strange Hero, 1948, Indeterminate Figure, 1957, With My Eye and With My Hand, 1968, Jazz: Three Ways, 1958, 66, Path-Silence, 1965, Not Me, But Him, 1965, The Peloponesian War, 1967-68, Untitled, 1974, Ruminations, 1976, Getting Well, 1978, Poems Off the Wall, 1981, Apartment 18C, 1993, Croissent, 1997, others; (for groups) Faces from Walt Whitman, 1950, An American Journey, 1962; asst. choreographer original Broadway prodns.: Up in Central Park, Stovepipe Hat, Show Boat, Annie Get Your Gun, By the Beautiful Sea, others; dir. off-Broadway: Volpone, 1957, The Firebugs, 1960, The Umbrella, 1961, Emperor Jones, (Boston), 1963, others; film choreography: His Majesty O'Keefe: acted in video The Art of Memory, 1985, play, Three Stories High, others; extensive touring U.S., Europe, The Pacific, and Japan, 1957-84; conceived and directed videos: Steps, 1972, The Edge is Also a Circle, 1973, Nagrin Videotape Library of Dances, 1985; author: How to Dance Forever: Surviving Against the Odds, 1988, Dance and the Specific Image: Improvisation, 1993, The Six Questions: Acting Technique for Dance Performance, 1997. With spl. svcs. Army Airforce, 1942-43. Grantee Rebekah Harkness Found., 1962, Logan Found., 1965, N.Y. State Coun. on Arts and Nat. Found. for Arts and Humanities, 1967-68, N.Y. State Coun. on Arts, 1971-72, 73-74, 75-76, 76-77, 78-79, 80-81, Anne S. Richardson Fund, 1971, 73, 74, 75, 76, 78, Nat. Endowment for Arts, 1975, 79, 81, 83, Ariz. State U., 1983, 84, 85, 86, 88; CAPS fellow N.Y. State Coun. on Arts, 1977-78; fellow NEA, 1977-78, 80, 82, 83, 90, 91, Minn. McKnight Nat. fellow, 1996-97; commd. ballet Rebekah Harkness Ballet Found., 1986. Mem. Actors' Equity, Phi Kappa Phi (hon.). Avocation: reading. Home and Office: 208 E 14th St Tempe AZ 85281-6707

NAGTALON-MILLER, HELEN ROSETE, humanities educator; b. Honolulu, June 27, 1928; d. Dionicio Reyes and Fausta Dumbrigue (Rosete) N.; m. Robert Lee Ruley Miller, June 15, 1952. BEd, U. Hawaii, 1951; Diplôme, The Sorbonne, Paris, 1962; MA, U. Hawaii, 1967; PhD, Ohio State U., 1972. Cert. secondary education educator. Tchr. humanities Hawaii State Dept. Edn., Honolulu, 1951-63; supr. student tchrs. French lab. sch. Coll. of Edn. U. Hawaii, Honolulu, 1963-66, instr. French, coord. French courses Coll. Arts and Scis., 1966-69; teaching asst. Coll. Edn. Ohio State U., Columbus, 1970-72; instr. French lab. sch. Coll. Edn. U. Hawaii, Honolulu, 1974-76; adminstr. bilingual-bicultural edn. project Hawaii State Dept. Edn., Honolulu, 1976-77; coord. disadvantaged minority recruitment program Sch. Social Work, U. Hawaii, Honolulu, 1977-84; coord. tutor tng. program U. Hawaii, Honolulu, 1984-86; program dir. Multicultural Multifunctional Resource Ctr., Honolulu, 1986-87; vis. prof. Sch. Pub. Health, ret. U. Hawaii, Honolulu, 1987-92; bd. dirs. Hawaii Assn. Lang. Tchrs., Honolulu, 1963-66, Hawaii Com. for the Humanities, 1977-83; mem. statewide adv. coun. State Mental Health Adv. Com., Honolulu, 1977-82; task force mem. Underrepresentation of Filipinos in Higher Edn., Honolulu, 1984-86. Author: (with others) Notable Women in Hawaii, 1984; contbr. articles to profl. jours. Chairperson edn. and counseling subcom. First Gov.'s Commn. on Status of Women, Honolulu, 1964; vice chairperson Honolulu County Com. on the Status of Women, 1975-76, Hawaii State Dr. Martin Luther King Jr. Commn., Honolulu, 1982-85; pres. Filipino Hist. Soc. of Hawaii, 1980—; mem. Hawaii State Adv. Com. to U.S. Commn. on Civil Rights, 1981—, chairperson, 1982-85; bd. dirs. Japanese Am. Citizens League Honolulu chpt., 1990—, mem. Hawaiian Sovereignty com., 1994—. Women of Distinction, Honolulu County Com. on Status of Women; 1982; recipient Nat. Edn. Assn. award for Leadership in Asian and Pacific Island Affairs, NEA, 1985, Alan F. Saunders award ACLU in Hawaii, 1986, Disting. Alumni award U. Hawaii Alumni Affairs Office, 1994. Mem. Filipino Am. Nat. Hist. Soc., Filipino Coalition for Solidarity, Gabriela Network (Hawaii chpt.), Filipino Cmty. Ctr., NOW, Alliance Française of Hawaii. Democrat. Avocations: social-political advocacy, reading, classical music, theater, literary presentations. Home and Office: 3201 Beaumont Woods Pl Honolulu HI 96822-1423

NAGY, ANDREW FRANCIS, engineering educator; b. Budapest, Hungary, May 2, 1932; came to U.S., 1957, naturalized, 1968; s. Bela and Lilly (Dekany) N.; children: Robert Bela, Susan Elizabeth. BE, U. New South Wales, 1957; MSc, U. Nebr., 1959; MS, U. Mich., 1960, PhD, 1963. Design engr. Electric Control and Engring. Co., Ltd., Sydney, Australia, 1956-57; instr. elec. engring. U. Nebr., 1957-59; research engr. U. Mich., Ann Arbor, 1959-63; asst. prof. elec. engring. U. Mich., 1963-67, assoc. prof., 1967-71, prof. space sci., prof. elec. engring., 1971—, assoc. v.p. for rsch., 1987-90; vis. assoc. prof. engring. U. Calif. at San Diego, 1969-70; vis. prof. physics Utah State U., 1976-77. Past editor: Revs. of Geophysics and Space Physics, Geophys. Rsch. Letters. Fulbright scholar, 1957. Fellow Am. Geophys. Union (past pres. SPA sect.); mem. IAA, IEEE (sr.), Internat. Radio Sci. Union (commns. 3 and 4), Hungarian Acad. Scis., Sigma Xi, Eta Kappa Nu. Home: 338 Rock Creek Dr Ann Arbor MI 48104-1860

NAGY, CHRISTA FIEDLER, biochemist; b. Marienbad, Czech Republic, July 8, 1943; d. Herbert A. Fiedler and Anna C. (Gluth) Rathmann; m. Bela Imre Nagy, Aug. 22, 1969; 1 child, Byron. BS in Biology, Fairleigh Dickinson U., 1967, MS in Biochemistry, 1974; PhD in Biochemistry, Rutgers U., 1981. Sr. scientist Hoffmann-La Roche Inc., Nutley, N.J., 1981-88, assoc. rsch. investigator, 1988-95; contract med. writer, 1996-97; assoc. dir. preclin. rsch. Eisai Inc., Teaneck, N.J., 1997—. Mem. AAAS, N.Y. Acad. Scis., Am. Soc. Biol. Chemists, Am. Med. Writers Assn. Roman Catholic. Avocations: traveling, skiing, tennis, hiking. Office: Eisai Inc Glenpointe Ctr E 300 Franklin Burr Blvd Teaneck NJ 07666-6741

NAGY, JOANNE ELIZABETH BERG, associate dean university; b. Green Bay, Wis., Jan. 28, 1956; d. Hubert Frederick and Dolores Elizabeth (Busch) Berg; m. Casey Abraham Nagy, Sept. 20, 1980; children: Erin Elizabeth, Nathan Abraham. BS, U. Wis., LaCrosse, 1978; student, Wash. State U., 1978-80. Admissions counselor U. Puget Sound, Tacoma, 1981-82, asst. dir. admissions, 1982-83, dir. admissions, 1983-87; student svc. coord. U. Wis., Madison, 1987-88, asst. dean admissions, 1988-89, asst. dean admissions and student svcs., 1989-94, assoc. dean admissions and student svcs., 1994—; admissions cons. coun. of grad. schs. U. North Tex., Denton, 1995. Contbr. articles to profl. jours. Recipient USA Today and Rochester Inst. Tech. Quality Crystal award, 1993. Mem. Am. Assn. Coll. Registrars and Admissions Officers, Nat. Assn. Grad. Admissions Prof. (rsch. chair 1994-96, conf. chair 1997), Midwest Assn. Coun. Grad. Schs., Coun. Grad. Schs. Avocations: reading, walking, writing poetry. Office: U Wis Grad Sch 500 Lincoln Dr Madison WI 53706-1314

NAGY, JOE HOWARD, lawyer; b. Pearsall, Tex., Dec. 17, 1928; s. Joe H. and Pauline (Howard) N.; m. Dorothy Fay Shelton, May 6, 1951; children: Margaret Nagy Dobbs, Joe Howard Jr. BS, Tex. A&M U., 1950; JD, U. Tex., 1958. Bar: Tex. 1958, U.S. Dist. Ct. (no. and we. dists.) Tex. 1958, U.S. Supreme Ct. 1975. Ptnr. Crenshaw, Dupree & Milam, Lubbock, Tex., 1958-65, 1965—. 1st lt. U.S. Army, 1951-53, Korea. Fellow Tex. Bar Found., Tex. Assn. Def. Counsel; mem. State Bar Tex. (bd. dirs. 1975-78, pres.-elect 1986-87, pres. 1987-88), Lubbock County Bar Assn. (pres. elect 1971-72, pres. 1972-73, bd. dirs.), Am. Coll. Trial Lawyers, Tex. Assn. Mediators, Tex. Assn. Dispute Resolution Profls. Republican. Methodist. Avocation: hunting. Office: Crenshaw Dupree & Milam 1500 Broadway St Ste 9000 Lubbock TX 79401-3116

NAGY, LOUIS LEONARD, engineering executive, researcher; b. Detroit, Jan. 15, 1942; s. Alex and Helen (Marth) N.; m. Dianna M. Skarjune, Aug. 5, 1961; children: Tammy, Kimberly, Kristine, Amanda. BSEE, U. Mich., Dearborn, 1965; MSEE, U. Mich., Ann Arbor, 1969, PhDEE, 1974. Rsch. engr. U. Mich., Ann Arbor, 1962-69; staff rsch. engr. GM R & D Ctr., Warren, Mich., 1969—. Contbr. articles to profl. jours.; patentee in field. Bd. dirs. Convergence Ednl. Found., Birmingham, Mich., 1990—, Convergence Transp. Electronics Assn., Birmingham, 1990—. Fellow IEEE; mem. Convergence Fellowship (bd. dirs. 1988—), Vehicular Tech. Soc. (Spl. Recognition award 1979, Avant Garde award 1986, Paper of Yr. 1975), Soc. Automotive Engrs., Tau Beta Pi, Eta Kappa Nu. Avocations: electronics, antennas, radar, automotive radar, microwaves. Office: GM R & D Ctr MC 480-106-104 30500 Mound Rd Warren MI 48092-2031

NAGY, ROBERT DAVID, tenor; b. Lorain, Ohio, Mar. 3, 1929; s. John Robert and Helen Elizabeth (Polesko) N.; m. Vincenza Rose Ianni, May 1, 1954; children—Robert John, Helena Jean, Gina Kati. Student, Cleve. Inst. Music, 1952-55. tchr., cons. to young opera students. Soloist Met. Opera, 1957-88, ret.; appeared in opera houses throughout U.S., World. Served with U.S. Army, 1950-52, Korea. Weyer Hauser scholar, 1957; Ford Found. scholar, 1959. Winner Met. Opera audition, 1956. Home: 5996 Case Rd North Ridgeville OH 44039

NAGY, STEVEN, biochemist; b. Fords, N.J., Apr. 7, 1936; s. Steven and Martha (Moberg) N.; m. Suzanne Nagy; children: Lacey, Nicolette, Steven. BS in Chemistry, La. State U., 1960; MS in Physiology and Biochemistry, Rutgers U., 1962, PhD in Biochemistry, 1965; MEngring. in Indsl. Engring., U. South Fla., 1977. Analytical chemist USPHS, Metuchen, N.J., 1962-65; rsch. assoc. Lever Bros., Edgewater, N.J., 1965-67; rsch. chemist Dept. Agr., Winter Haven, Fla., 1968-79; rsch. scientist Fla. Dept. Citrus, Lake Alfred, 1979—; adj. prof. U. Fla., 1979—; treas. AgScience Inc. Mem. Am. Chem. Soc. (chmn. divsn. agrl. and food chemistry, Disting. Svc. award 1988, fellow, 1990), Phytochem. Soc. N. Am. (chmn.), Inst. Food Technologists (chmn. citrus products divsn., Citrus Products Rsch. and Devel. award 1996), Am. Soc. for Hort. Sci., Internat. Soc. Citriculture, Fla. Hort. Soc. (v.p.), Sigma Xi. Republican. Author: Citrus Science and Technology, 2 vols., 1977; Tropical and Subtropical Fruits, 1980; Citrus Nutrition and Quality, 1980; Fresh Citrus Fruits, 1986, Adulteration of Fruit Juice Beverages, 1988, Fruits of Tropical and Subtropical Origin, 1990, Fruit Juice Processing Technology, 1993, Methods To Detect Adulteration of Fruit Juice Beverages, 1995, Hypernutritious Foods, 1996; editorial bd. Food Chemistry, Jour. Agrl. and Food Chemistry; contbr. articles to profl. jours. Home: 103 Arietta Shores Dr Auburndale FL 33823-9336 Office: 700 Experiment Station Rd Lake Alfred FL 33850-2243

NAHAS, GABRIEL GEORGES, pharmacologist, educator; b. Alexandria, Egypt, Mar. 4, 1920; came to U.S., 1947, naturalized, 1962; s. Bishara and Gabrielle (Wolff) N.; m. Marilyn Cashman, Feb. 13, 1954; children: Michele, Anthony, Christiane. BA, U. Toulouse, France, 1937, MD, 1944; MS, U. Rochester, 1949; PhD, U. Minn., 1953; DSc (hon.), U. Uppsala, 1988.

Rockefeller Found. fellow U. Rochester, 1947-48; Mayo Found. fellow Mayo Clinic, 1949-50; rsch. fellow U. Minn., 1950-53, mem. faculty, 1955-57; mem. staff Walter Reed Army Inst. Rsch., 1957-59; faculty George Washington U. Med. Sch., 1957-59; mem. faculty Columbia U. Coll. Physicians and Surgeons, N.Y.C., 1959-92, prof. anesthesiology, 1962-92; rsch. prof. anesthesiology NYU Med. Sch., N.Y.C., 1992—; disting. vis. scientist Addiction Rsch. Ctr., NIDA, 1987; adj. rsch. prof. anesthesiology U. Paris, 1968-71; fellow Coun. Circulation and Basic Sci., Am. Heart Assn., 1961—; mem. com. on trauma NRC, 1964-66; mem. adv. bd. Cousteau Soc.; cons. commn. on narcotics, drug control program UN. Author 700 sci. publs. and 30 books and monographs in English and French. Decorated Presdl. Medal of Freedom with gold palm Govt. of U.S.; comdr. Legion of Honor, Croix de Guerre with 3 palms (France), Order Brit. Empire, Order Orange Nassau Netherlands, Silver medal City of Paris; recipient Medal of Honor, Statue of Liberty Centennial, 1986; Fulbright scholar, 1966. Fellow AAAS, N.Y. Acad. Sci.; mem. Am. Physiol. Soc., Harvey Soc., Am. Soc. Pharmacology and Exptl. Therapeutics, Am. Soc. Clin. Pharmacology, Soc. Physiol. Langue Française, French Acad. Medicine (laureate 1995, 96), Brit. Pharm. Soc., Sigma Xi. Research on med. instrumentation, pharmacology Tham, acid-base regulation, pharmacology of cannabis and cocaine, drug dependence, consciousness. Home: 40 E 74th St New York City NY 10021-2732 Office: NYU Med Ctr Dept Anesthesiology 550 1st Ave New York NY 10016-6481 *Courage is to stand by one's own conviction unheeding the trends of fashion or pressure groups. It is to suffer alone and be scorned for a lifetime. But, in the end, one will hear "he was right!".*

NAHAT, DENNIS F., artistic director, choreographer; b. Detroit, Feb. 20, 1946; s. Fred H. and Linda M. (Haddad) N. Hon. degree, Juilliard Sch. Music, 1965. Prin. dancer Joffrey Ballet, N.Y.C., 1965-66; prin. dancer Am. Ballet Theatre, N.Y.C., 1968-79; founder, artistic dir. Cleve. Ballet, 1976—; co-chair Artists Round Table Dance USA, 1991; trustee Cecchetti Coun. Am., 1991; mem. adv. bd. Ohio Dance Regional Dance Am.; founder new Sch. of San Jose Cleveland Ballet, 1996—. Pin. performer Broadway show Sweet Charity, 1966-67; choreographer Two Gentlemen of Verona (Tony award 1972), 1969-70; (ballet) Celebrations and Ode (resolution award 1985), 1985, Green Table, Three Virgins and a Devil (Isadora Duncan award 1985); co-founder Sch. of Cleve. Ballet, 1972, Cleve. Ballet, 1976; founder, artistic dir. San Jose Cleve. Ballet; choreographer, dir. Blue Suede Shoes, 1996. Founder San Jose Cleveland Sch., 1996—. Grantee Nat. Endowment Arts, 1978, Andrew Mellow Found., 1985; recipient Outstanding Achievement award Am. Dance Guild, 1995. Avocation: master chef. Office: Cleve Ballet 1375 Euclid Ave Cleveland OH 44115-1808 also: Cleve San Jose Ballet PO Box 1666 San Jose CA 95109-1666

NAHAVANDI, AMIR NEZAMEDDIN, retired engineering firm executive; b. Tehran, Iran, Apr. 6, 1924; came to U.S., 1956, naturalized, 1970; s. Ahmad and Fatima (Razaghi) N. Electromech. Engring. degree, Tehran U., 1947; M.S. in Mech. Engring, Carnegie Inst. Tech., 1957, Ph.D., 1960. Registered profl. engr., Pa. Engr. Tehran U., 1948-50; head design group Nat. Iranian Oil Co., Tehran, 1950-56; adv. engr. Westinghouse Electric Corp., Pitts., 1957-66; prof., chmn. dept. mech. engring. U. Vt., 1967-68; research prof. N.J. Inst. Tech., 1969-77; prof. engring. and applied Sci. Columbia U., N.Y.C., 1977-81; chief scientist Electronic Assocs., Inc., West Long Branch, N.J., 1981-82; pres. Mazen, Inc., Long Branch, N.J., 1982-92. Decorated Sci. medal 1st degree Iran). Fellow ASME; mem. N.Y. Acad. Scis., Phi Kappa Phi, Sigma Xi, Tau Beta Pi. Research and devel. in dynamics of steam generators and boiling systems, dynamic and accident analysis of conventional and nuclear power plants, vibration of reactor structures, thermal pollution of lakes and rivers, solid-fluid interaction. Home: 168 Seabreeze Cir Jupiter FL 33477

NAHIGIAN, ALMA LOUISE, technical documentation administrator; b. Peabody, Mass., Sept. 17, 1936; d. Walter Daniel and Alma Edith (Knowles) Higgins; m. Franklin Roosevelt Nahigian, April 30, 1961; daus.: Ellen Elise, Dana Leigh, Catherine Elizabeth. AA, Boston U., 1956, BS, 1958, MS in Journalism, 1963. Editor nat. and spl. projects Boston U. News Bur., 1959-61, 63-64; writer, editor Nutrition Found., N.Y.C., 1961-63; writer, editor, cons. Cambridge (Mass.) Communicators, Tech. Edn. Research Ctr., Harvard U., Cambridge, Smart Software, Inc., Belmont, Mass., 1970-82; tech. editor Digital Equipment Corp., Bedford, Mass., 1979-84; prin. tech. writer, editor Wang Labs, Inc., Lowell, Mass., 1984—, documentation sect. mgr. editorial, 1984-93; sr. adv. tech. editor Dun & Bradstreet Software, Westborough, Mass., 1993-95; prin. tech. editor Info. Resources, Inc., Waltham, Mass., 1995—; instr. Harvard U., Cambridge, 1987-88, Radcliffe Coll., Cambridge, 1979; mem. adj. faculty Northeastern U., Boston, 1989—, guest lectr., 1979, 88. Contbr. numerous articles to profl. pubs. Active LWV, Arlington, Mass., 1963-73. Fellow Soc. Tech. Communication (assoc., bd. dirs., Boston chpt. pres. 1992-93, co-mgr. soc.-level com. 1993-95, mem. 1995—, judge internat. level competitions 1993-95, judge trainer local chpt. competitions, Tech. Pubs. Competition Excellence award 1989, 93, 95, Art Competitions Excellence award 1992, co-presenter). Democrat. Roman Catholic. Home: 30 Venner Rd Arlington MA 02174-8028 Office: Info Resources Inc 200 5th Ave Waltham MA 02154-8704

NAHMAN, NORRIS STANLEY, electrical engineer; b. San Francisco, Nov. 9, 1925; s. Hyman Cohen and Rae (Levin) N.; m. Shirley D. Maxwell, July 20, 1968; children: Norris Stanley, Vicki L., Vance W., Scott T. B.S. in Electronics Engring, Calif. Poly. State U., 1951; M.S.E.E., Stanford U., 1952; Ph.D. in Elec. Engring, U. Kans., 1961. Registered profl. engr., Colo. Electronic scientist Nat. Security Agy., Washington, 1952-55; prof. elec. engring., dir. electronics rsch. lab. U. Kans., Lawrence, 1955-66; sci. cons., chief pulse and time domain sect. Nat. Bur. Standards, Boulder, Colo., 1966-73; chief time domain metrology, sr. scientist Nat. Bur. Standards, 1975-83, group leader field characterization group, 1984-85; v.p. Picosecond Pulse Labs, Inc., Boulder, 1986-90; cons. elec. engr., 1990—; prof., chmn. dept. elec. engring. U. Toledo, 1973-75;; prof. elec. engring. U. Colo., Boulder, 1966—; Disting. lectr., prin. prof. Ctr. Nat. d' Etude des Telecomm. Summer Sch., Lannion France, 1978; disting. lectr. Harbin Inst. Tech., Peoples Republic China, summer 1982; mem. faculty NATO Advanced Study Inst., Castelvecchio, Italy, 1983, Internat. Radio Sci. Union/NRC; chmn. Internat. Intercomm. Group Waveform Measurements, 1981-90, chmn. Commn. A, 1985-86; affiliate Los Alamos Nat. Lab., 1990—. Contbr. rsch. articles profl. jours.; patentee in field. Asst. scoutmaster Longs Peak coun. Boy Scouts Am., 1970-73, 75-89. With U.S. Mcht. Marine, 1943-46, U.S. Army, 1952-55. Ford Found. faculty fellow MIT, 1962; Nat. Bur. Standards sr. staff fellow, 1978-79; recipient Disting. Alumnus award Calif. Poly. State U., 1972, Order of Arrow Boy Scouts Am., 1976. Fellow IEEE (life), Internat. Sci. Radio Union; mem. Instrumentation and Measurement Soc. of IEEE (admstrv. com. 1982-84, editorial bd. Trans., 1982-86, Andrew H. chi Best Tech. Paper award 1984, Tech. Leadership and Achievement award 1987), Am. Assn. Engring. Edn., U.S. Mcht. Marine Veterans World War II, Am. Legion, Calif. Poly. State U. Alumni Assn. (life), Stanford U. (life), U. Kans. (life), Am. Radio Relay League Club (life), Sigma Pi Sigma, Tau Beta Pi, Eta Kappa Nu, Sigma Tau, Sigma Xi.

NAHRWOLD, DAVID LANGE, surgeon, educator; b. St. Louis, Dec. 21, 1935; s. Elmer William and Magdalen Louise (Lange) N.; m. Carolyn Louise Hoffman, June 14, 1958; children: Stephen Michael, Susan Alane, Thomas James, Anne Elizabeth. AB, Ind. U., 1957, MD, 1960. Diplomate Am. Bd. Surgery, Am. Bd. Thoracic Surgery. Intern, then resident in surgery Ind. U. Med. Ctr., Indpls., 1960-65; postdoctoral scholar in gastrointestinal physiology VA Ctr., UCLA, 1965; asst. prof. surgery Med. Sch. Ind. U., 1968-70; assoc. prof. Coll. Medicine Pa. State U., 1970-73; vice chmn. dept. surgery Pa. STate U., 1971-82, assoc. provost, dean health affairs, 1981-82, prof., chief divsn. gen. surgery, 1974-82; Loyal and Edith Davis prof., chmn. dept. surgery Med. Sch. Northwestern U., Chgo., 1982—; surgeon-in-chief Northwestern Meml. Hosp., Chgo., 1982—; pres., CEO Northwestern Med. Faculty Found., Inc., 1996—; mem. Nat. Digestive Disease Adv. Bd., 1985-89; bd. dirs. Am. Bd. Surgery; vice chmn. 1994-95, chmn. 1995-96. Editor-in-chief Jour. Laparoendoscopic Surgery, 1993—; mem. editl. bd. Surgery, 1981-94, Archives of Surgery, 1983-93, Digestive Surgery, 1986—, Am. Jour. Surgery, 1994—, Current Opinion in Gen. Surgery, Jour. Lithotripsy and Stone Disease, 1988-92; contbr. articles to profl. jours. With M.C., U.S. Army, 1966-68. Fellow ACS (bd. govs. 1992—, vice-chmn. 1994-96, chmn. bd. govs. exec. com. 1996—); mem. AMA, Am. Bd. Med. Specialties (exec. com. 1997—), Accreditation Coun. for Grad. Med. Edn., Am. Phys. Soc., Am. Surg. Assn. (2d v.p. 1993-94), Assn. Acad. Surgery, Assn. for Surg. Edn., Ctrl. Surg. Assn. (sec. 1994-97, pres.-elect 1997—), Chgo. Med. Soc., Chgo. Surg. Soc. (pres. 1993-94), Collegium Internat. Chirurgiae Digestive (pres. U.S. chpt. 1988-90), Gastroenterology Rsch. Group, Ill. State Med. Soc., Ill. Surg. Soc., Internat. Biliary Assn., Soc. Clin. Surgery (sec. 1984-88), Soc. Surgery Alimentary Tract (pres. 1989-90, trustee), Soc. Univ. Surgeons, Soc. Surg. Chairmen, We. Surg. Assn., Sigma Xi, Alpha Omega Alpha. Office: Northwestern U Med Sch Dept Surgery 250 E Superior St Ste 201 Chicago IL 60611-2914

NAIDORF, LOUIS MURRAY, architect; b. Los Angeles, Aug. 15, 1928; s. Jack and Meriam (Abbott) N.; m. Dorise D. Roberts, June 1948 (div.); children: Victoria Beth Naidorf-Slifer; m. Patricia Ann Shea, June 1, 1968 (div.); m. Patricia Ruth Allen, Dec. 6, 1992. BA, U. Calif., Berkeley, 1949, MA, 1950. Registered architect, Calif. Designer Welton Becket Assocs., L.A., 1950-51, Pereira and Luckman, L.A., 1951-52; project designer Welton Becket Assocs., L.A., 1952-55, sr. project designer, 1955-59, v.p. asst., dir. design, 1959-70, sr. v.p., dir. rsch., 1970-73; sr. v.p., design prin. Ellerbe Becket Assocs., L.A., 1973-95; dean Sch. Architecture and Design Woodbury U., L.A., 1990—; mem. peer rev. panel Nat. Endowment Arts, 1995—; vis. lectr. Calif. Poly. Sch. Architecture, San Luis Obispo, 1975-82; instr. UCLA Sch. Architecture, 1985, UCLA Landscape Archtl. Program, 1980-85, Otis-Parsons, L.A., 1986-92. Prin. works include Capitol Records Bldg., Century City, Los Angeles, Hyatt Regency, Dallas, Restoration Calif. State Capitol Bldg. Bd. dirs. Inst. for Garden Studies, L.A., 1986—. Recipient Honor award Nat. Trust for Hist. Preservation, 1985. Fellow AIA (bd. dirs. Los Angeles chpt. 1977-79, Silver Medal 1950, Nat. Honor award 1985). Office: Woodbury Univ 7500 N Glenoaks Blvd Burbank CA 91504-1052 *Leadership often requires decisions based on limited information. Course corrections can be made but only after action is taken because you can't steer a car that isn't moving.*

NAIFEH, STEVEN WOODWARD, writer; b. Tehran, Iran, June 19, 1952; s. George Amel and Marion (Lamphear) N. AB, Princeton U., 1974; JD, Harvard U., 1977, MA, 1978. Staff lectr. Nat. Gallery Art, Washington, 1976; assoc. Milbank, Tweed, Hadley & McCloy, N.Y.C., 1976; v.p. Sabbagh, Naifeh and Assocs., Washington, 1980—. Author: Culture Making: Money, Success and the New York Art World, 1976; (with Gregory White Smith) Moving Up in Style, 1980, Gene Davis, 1981, How to Make Love to a Woman, 1982, What Every Client Needs to Know About Using a Lawyer, 1982, The Bargain Hunter's Guide to Art Collecting, 1982, Why Can't Men Open Up?: Overcoming Men's Fear of Intimacy, 1984, The Mormon Murders: A True Story of Greed, Forgery, Deceit, and Death, 1988, Jackson Pollack: An American Saga, 1989 (Nat. Book award nomination for nonfiction 1990, Pulitzer Prize for biography 1991), Final Justice: The True Story of the Richest Man Ever Tried for Murder, 1993, A Stranger in the Family: A True Story of Murder, Madness, and Unconditional Love, 1995; editor: (with Smith) The Best Lawyers in America, The Best Doctors in America. Office: 129 1st Ave Aiken SC 29801-4862

NAIMARK, ARNOLD, medical educator, physiologist, educator; b. Winnipeg, Man., Can., Aug. 24, 1933; s. Harvey and Lisa N.; m. Barbara Jean Alder, Feb. 28, 1960; children: David, Mila. MD, U. Man., Winnipeg, 1957, BSc in Medicine, 1957, MSc, 1960; postgrad., U. London, 1962-63, U. Calif., 1960-62; LLD (hon.), Mt. Allison U., 1986, U. Toronto, 1997. Registrar in medicine Hammersmith Hosp., London, 1962-63; asst. prof. physiology U. Man., 1963-64, assoc. prof., 1965-66, prof., 1967-71, acting head dept. physiology, 1966-67, head dept., 1967-71, dean Faculty of Medicine, 1971-81, pres. and vice chancellor, 1981-96; prof. medicine, physiology U. Manitoba, Winnipeg, Man., Can., 1996—; bd. govs. Health Scis. Ctr.,; cons. to govt. agys. and founds.; chmn. North Portage Devel. Commerce, Urban Idea Ctr., North Portage Theater Corp., Inspiraplex Ltd.; mem. adv. coun. Order of Can., 1988-89; v.p., Can., Inter-Am. Orgn. for Higher Edn., 1993-95. Contbr. articles to profl. jours. Mem. nat. hon. bd. dirs. Juvenile Diabetes Fedn. Internat. Can.; trustee Alcoholic Beverage Med. Rsch. Found., 1994—. Lt. Royal Can. Arty., 1950-53. Decorated officer Order of Can.; recipient Queen Elizabeth Silver Jubilee medal; medal in physiology U. Man., 1955; Stefansson Meml. prize, 1957; Prowse prize in clin. rsch., 1959; Isbister scholar, 1950-53, 54-56. Fellow Royal Coll. Physicians, AAAS, Roayal Soc. Can. (G. Malcolm Brown award 1987, com. univ. rsch. 1989-91); mem. Can. Med. Assn., Can. Physiol. Soc., Am. Physiol. Soc., Can. Soc. Clin. Investigation, Med. Rsch. Soc. Gt. BRit., Assn. Chairmen Depts. Physiology, Can. Tb and Respiratory Disease Assn., Can. Assn. Univ. Tchrs., Assn. Commonwealth Univs. (coun. 1985-91), Assn. Univs. and Colls. Am. (pres. 1986-88), Am. Heart Assn., Assn. Commonwealth Univs. (chmn. 1988), Can. Soc. for Acad. Medicine, Nat. Inst. Nutrition (bd. dirs. 1990—). Office: U Manitoba Ctr Advancement of Med, 730 William Ave Ste 230, Winnipeg, MB Canada R3E 3J7

NAIMARK, GEORGE MODELL, marketing and management consultant; b. N.Y.C., Feb. 5, 1925; s. Myron S. and Mary (Modell) N. BS, Bucknell U., 1947, MS, 1948; PhD, U. Del., 1951; m. Helen Anne Wythes, June 24, 1946; children: Ann, Richard, Jane. Rsch. biochemist Brush Devel. Co., Cleve., 1951; dir. quality control Strong, Cobb & Co., Inc., Cleve., 1951-54; dir. sci. svcs. White Labs., Inc., Kenilworth, N.J., 1954-60; v.p. Burdick Assocs., Inc., N.Y.C., 1960-66; pres. Rajah Press, Summit, N.J., 1963—; pres. Naimark and Barba, Inc., Florham Park, N.J., 1966—; pres. Naimark & Assocs., Inc., Florham Park, N.J., 1994—. With USNR, 1944-46. Fellow AAAS, Am. Inst. Chemists; mem. Am. Chem. Soc., N.Y. Acad. Scis., Am. Mktg. Assn. Author: A Patent Manual for Scientists and Engineers, 1961, Communications on Communication, 1971, 3d edit., 1987, A Man Called Skeeter, 1996; patentee in field; contbr. articles in profl. jours. Home: 87 Canoe Brook Pky Summit NJ 07901-1404 Office: Naimark & Barba Inc 248 Columbia Tpke Florham Park NJ 07932-1210

NAIMARK, NORMAN M., academic administrator; b. N.Y.C. BA, Stanford U., 1966, PhD, 1972. Prof. History Boston U.; fellow Russian Rsch. Ctr. Harvard U.; vis. Catherine Wasserman Davis chair of Slavic Studies Wellesley Coll.; Robert and Florence McDonnell chair in East European Studies Stanford U.; chmn. dept. History, sr. fellow Hoover Instn.; dir. Stanford's Ctr. Russian and East European Studies; joint com. Am. Coun. Learned Soc.; program com. Internat. Rsch. and Exchange Corp.; exec. com. Am. Assn. Advancement Slavic Studies. lectr., author, co-editor in field. Grantee IREX, ACLS, Alexander von Humbolt Found, Fulbright-Hays, Nat. Coun. Soviet and East European Studies, Hist. Commn. in Berlin. Office: Hoover Instn on War Revolution and Peace Stanford U Stanford CA 94305*

NAIMI, SHAPUR, cardiologist; b. Tehran, Iran, Mar. 28, 1928; s. Mohsen and Mahbuba (Naim) N.; came to U.S., 1959; MB, ChB, Birmingham (Eng.) U., 1953; m. Amy Cabot Simonds, May 11, 1963; children: Timothy Simonds, Susan Lyman, Cameron Lowell. House physician Royal Postgrad Med. Sch. London, 1955; sr. house officer Inst. Diseases of the Chest, London, 1956; fellow in grad. tng. New Eng. Med. Center and Mass. Inst. Tech., 1961-64; cardiologist Tufts New Eng. Med. Center, Boston, 1966—, dir. intensive cardiac care unit, 1973—, assoc. prof. 1970-93, prof. 1993—. Recipient Distinguished Instr. award, 1972, Teaching citation, 1976, Excellence in Teaching award, 1982 (all Tufts Med. Sch.); diplomate Royal Coll. Physicians London, Royal Coll. Physicians Edinburgh, Am. Bd. Internal Medicine (subsplty. bd. cardiovascular disease). Fellow Royal Coll. Physicians (Edinburgh), A.C.P., Am. Coll. Cardiology; mem. Am. Soc. Exptl. Biology and Medicine, Am. Heart Assn., Mass. Med. Soc. Clubs: Country Brookline; Cohasset Yacht. Contbr. to profl. jours. Home: 265 Woodland Rd Chestnut Hill MA 02167-2204 also: 55 Lothrop Ln Cohasset MA 02025-1425 Office: 750 Washington St Boston MA 02111-1526

NAIMOLI, RAYMOND ANTHONY, infosystems specialist, financial consultant; b. Paterson, N.J., Apr. 16, 1942; s. Ralph A. and Margaret Rita (Calabrese) N.; children: Lisa Marie, Dianne, Dolors, Raymond . B.B.A., U. Notre Dame, 1963; M.S., Columbia U., 1976. C.P.A., N.J. Sr. auditor Arthur Young & Co., Newark, 1963-68; asst. controller Universal Mfg. Co., Paterson, 1968-70; corp. controller Scholastic Mags., Inc., N.Y.C., 1970-80; v.p. fin., treas. U.S. News & World Report, Washington, 1980-84; also dir. U.S. News & World Report; exec. v.p. EBM Systems, Inc., Greenbelt, Md., 1986-90; pres. Naimoli & Assocs., Arlington, Va., 1984—; pres. MedLine, Inc., 1991-93, also bd. dirs.; chief fin. officer Ladish Co., Inc., Milw., 1993-94; sr. v.p., CFO Tampa Bay Devil Rays, 1995—; dir. Parkway Communications Corp., Publishers Service Internat., Madana Realty Co., U.S. News Investment Co.; adj. prof. Grad. Sch., Fairleigh Dickinson U., Rutherford, N.J., 1976-80. Mem. Am. Inst. C.P.A.s, Planning Execs. Inst., N.J. Soc. C.P.A.s. Roman Catholic. Office: Thunderdome 1 Stadium Dr Saint Petersburg FL 33705-1703

NAIMOLI, VINCENT JOSEPH, diversified operating and holding company executive; b. Paterson, N.J., Sept. 16, 1937; s. Ralph A. and Margaret R. (Calabrese) N.; children—Christine, Tory Ann, Alyson, Lindsey. B.S.M.E., U. Notre Dame, 1959; M.S.M.E., N.J. Inst. Tech., 1962; M.B.A., Fairleigh Dickinson U., 1964; grad. Advanced Mgmt. Program, Harvard Bus. Sch., 1974. With Continental Group, 1965-77, v.p., gen. mgr. ops., 1975-77; pres., chief oper. officer Allegheny Beverage Corp., Balt., 1977-78; sr. v.p., group exec. Jim Walter Corp., Tampa, Fla., 1978-81; group v.p. packaging Anchor Hocking Corp., Lancaster, Ohio, 1981-83; chmn. bd., pres., chief exec. officer Anchor Glass Container Corp., Lancaster, 1983-89; chmn., pres., CEO Anchor Industries Internat., Tampa, Fla., 1990—; chmn., chief exec. officer Electrolux Corp., Atlanta, 1990-91; chmn., CEO Doehler Jarvis Corp., Toledo, 1991-95; mng. gen. ptnr., CEO Tampa Bay Devil Rays, 1992—; chmn., CEO Ladish, Inc., Milw., 1992-95; chmn., pres., CEO Harvard Industries, 1993-97; bd. dirs. Simplicity Pattern, Russell-Stanley Corp., Fla. Progress. Roman Catholic. Office: Anchor Industries Internat 2502 N Rocky Point Dr Ste 960 Tampa FL 33607-1448

NAIPAUL, VIDIADHAR SURAJPRASAD, author; b. Trinidad, Aug. 17, 1932. Student, Queen's Royal Coll., Trinidad, 1943-48; B.A., University Coll., Oxford, Eng., 1953; D.Litt. (hon.), St. Andrews Coll., Scotland, 1979, Columbia U., 1981, Cambridge U., 1983, London U., 1988; DLitt (hon.), Oxford U., 1992. Author: Miguel Street, 1959, A House for Mr. Biswas, 1961, An Area of Darkness, 1964, In a Free State, 1971, Guerrillas, 1975, India: A Wounded Civilization, 1977, A Bend in the River, 1979, Among the Believers, 1981, The Enigma of Arrival, 1987, A Turn in the South, 1989, India: A Million Mutinies Now, 1990, A Way in the World, 1994. Office: Aitken & Stone Ltd, 29 Fernshaw Rd, London SW10 0TG, England

NAIR, RAGHAVAN D., accountant, educator; b. Dehradun, United Provinces, India, Oct. 23, 1951; came to U.S., 1973; s. Keshavan R. and Parvati Nair; m. Ruth Marie Nair, 1976; 1 child, Andrea. BA, U. Madras, India, 1970, MA, 1972; MBA, U. Mich., 1974, PhD, 1977. CPA, Wis. Prof. U. Wis., Madison, 1978—, sr. assoc. dean acad. affairs Sch. Bus., 1994—, dir. internat. programs, 1996—; faculty fellow Fin. Acctg. Standards Bd., Norwalk, Conn., 1984-86; faculty resident Arthur Andersen & Co., Chgo., 1991—, dir. PhD Program, 1987-90, chmn. dept. acctg., 1991-94; dir. Arthur Andersen Ctr. Fin. Reporting, 1992-93; prof. acctg. and info. systems Price Waterhouse, 1993—; invited speaker various corps., pub. acctg. firms, mgmt. and exec. edn. groups, 1982—. Contbr. articles to profl. jours. Pres. John Muir PTO, Madison, Wis., 1988-89. Recipient Excellence in Teaching award Lawrence J. Larson Sch. Bus., 1992. Mem. AICPA, Parkwood Hills Community Assn. (treas. 1987-89), Am. Acctg. Assn., Wis. Inst. CPAs (Outstanding Educator award 1989), Bascom Hill Soc., Blackhawk Country Club (bd. dirs. 1994-96). Avocation: golf.

NAIR, VASU, chemist, educator. BSc in Chemistry with high honors, U. Otago, Dunedin, New Zealand, 1963; PhD, U. Adelaide, Australia, 1966, DSc (hon.), 1991. Rsch. assoc. U. Ill., Urbana, 1967-68; rsch, fellow Harvard U., Cambridge, Mass., 1968-69; from asst. prof. chemistry to assoc. prof. U. Iowa, Iowa City, 1969-79, prof., 1980—, U. Iowa Found. Disting. prof. chemistry, 1993—; cons. Miles Lab., West Haven, Conn., 1987, Burroughs Wellcome Co., Rsch. Triangle Park, N.C., 1984-96, Nucleotide Chemistry, Integrated DNA Techs., Inc., Iowa City, 1988-93, Nucleoside Chemistry, San Diego, 1988-94, NIH, 1989—, Lipitek Internat., San Antonio, Tex.; dir. U. Iowa HIgh-Field NMR Facility, 1982-86; assoc. chair dept. chemistry U. Iowa, 1991-93, mem. U. Iowa Biosci. Com., 1995—, Faculty Senate, 1996—. Contbr. 200 articles and abstracts to profl. jours.; speaker in field; patentee: 3 U.S. patents, 2 on antiviral chemicals, 1 on a potential anti-AIDS agent. Recipient Disting. Vis. Scholar award U. Adelaide, Australia, 1987, Sci. medal, Iowa Acad. Scis., numerous rsch. grants and awards. Mem. AAAS, Internat. Soc. Antiviral Rsch., Internat. Soc. Nucleic Acid Chemistry, Am. Soc. Microbiology, Am. Chem. Soc. Office: Univ Iowa Chemistry Dept Iowa City IA 52242

NAIR, VELAYUDHAN, pharmacologist, medical educator; b. India, Dec. 29, 1928; came to U.S., 1956, naturalized, 1963; s. Parameswaran and Ammini N.; m. Jo Ann Burke, Nov. 30, 1957; children: David, Larry, Sharon. Ph.D. in Medicine, U. London, 1956, D.Sc., 1976. Research assoc. U. Ill. Coll. Medicine, 1956-58; asst. prof. U. Chgo. Sch. Medicine, 1958-63; dir. lab. neuropharmacology and biochemistry Michael Reese Hosp. and Med. Center, Chgo., 1963-68; dir. therapeutic research Michael Reese Hosp. and Med. Center, 1968-71; vis. assoc. prof. pharmacology FUHS/Chgo. Med. Sch., 1963-68, vis. prof., 1968-71, prof. pharmacology, 1971—, vice chmn. dept. pharmacology and therapeutics, 1971-76, dean Sch. Grad. and Postdoctoral Studies, 1976—. Contbr. articles to profl. publs. Recipient Morris Parker award U. Health Scis./Chgo. Med. Sch., 1972. Fellow AAAS, N.Y. Acad. Scis., Am. Coll. Clin. Pharmacology; mem. AAUP, Internat. Brain Rsch. Orgn., Internat. Soc. Biochem. Pharmacology, Am. Soc. Pharmacology & Exptl. Therapeutics, Am. Soc. Clin. Pharmacology & Therapeutics, Radiation Rsch. Soc., Soc. Toxicology, Am. Chem. Soc., Brit. Chem. Soc., Royal Inst. Chemistry (London), Pan Am. Med. Assn. (council on toxicology), Soc. Exptl. Biology & Medicine, Soc. Neurosci., Internat. Soc. Chronobiology, Am. Coll. Toxicology, Internat. Soc. Developmental Neurosci., Sigma Xi, Alpha Omega Alpha. Club: Cosmos (Washington). Office: FUHS/Chgo Med Sch 3333 Green Bay Rd North Chicago IL 60064-3037 *Success like happiness is relative and can only be gauged by one's own standards and ideals. There is probably no universal formula for either of them, but I have been guided by the following tenets: Dedication and commitment to one's responsibilities and in the conduct of everyday life, honesty and sincerity in personal relations. One must have tolerance for those in less fortunate situations. As one grows older, one recognizes that no one makes it alone. As for me, I have received help from many; some of whom I can never repay except by passing on the gift which I was privileged to share. Above all, a faith that looks beyond the immediate helps to bear the inevitable ups and downs in life.*

NAIR, VELUPILLAI KRISHNAN, cardiologist; b. Kerala, India, Dec. 30, 1941; came to U.S., 1973; s. Veupillai and Bharathy Nair; m. Sathy C. Nair, Apr. 22, 1971; children: Parvathy, Pradeep. BSc, Kerala U., Trivandum, India, 1961, MB BS, 1965, MD, 1971. Diplomate Am. Bd. Internal Medicine, Am. Bd. Cardiology. Intern, resident, fellow in cardiology Bergen Pines County Hosp., Paramus, N.J.; asst. prof. N.Y. Med. Coll. Lincoln Hosp., Bronx, 1979-80; cardiologist, dir. cardiology svc. Somerset (Pa.) Hosp., 1980—, chief of med. dental staff, 1990-93; v.p., bd. dirs. Somerset Hosp.; clin. asst. prof. Allegheny U. Health Scis., 1996—. Former pres. Somerset County divsn. Am. Heart Assn. Fellow ACP, Am. Coll. Cardiology; mem. AMA, Pa. Med. Soc., Somerset County Med. Soc. (former pres.), Soc. Hypertension, Soc. Echocardiography, Cardiac Club (advisor). Avocations: reading, tennis, travel. Office: 223 S Pleasant Ave Somerset PA 15501-2188

NAITOH, YUTAKA, biology educator; b. Tokyo, Japan, Mar. 23, 1931; s. Hisao and Emiko (Gotoh) N.; 1 child, Takuya. BS, U. Tokyo, Japan, 1955, MS, 1957, DSc, 1960. Rsch. assoc. U. Tokyo, Faculty of Sci., Japan, 1960-71; rsch. assoc. prof. biology UCLA, 1972, adj. assoc. prof., 1972-75; prof. Tsukuba (Japan) U., 1975-94, prof. emeritus, 1994—; guest prof. U. Hawaii, Japan, 1994-95. Author: Behavior of Unicellular Animal, 1990; contbr. sci. articles to profl. jours. Recipient Fulbright grant U.S.-Japan Exch. Progamme, 1966-69, Mitsubishi Rsch. grant, 1976, The Zool. Soc. prize, 1973. Mem. Am. Soc. Cell Biology, Zool. Soc. Japan, AAAS, Soc. Gen. Physiologist. Avocations: butterfly collection, radio amateur. Office: Univ Hawaii at Manoa Pacific Biomed Rsch Ctr 2538 The Mall Honolulu HI 96822-2233

NAJAR, LEO MICHAEL, conductor, arranger, educator; b. Grand Rapids, Mich., Jan. 29, 1953; s. Ammiel George and Claire Elizabeth (Grant) N.; m. Tamara Sinkevich, Aug. 24, 1974; m. Jean Anne Van Winkle, May 10, 1986; children: John Andrew, Erik. MusB in Viola Performance, U. Mich., 1976, MusM in Viola Performance, 1977. Asst. condr. Flint (Mich.) Symphony

Orch., 1975-80; dir. Flint Community Music Sch., 1976-80; music dir. Saginaw (Mich.) Symphony Orch., 1980—; conductor The Gazebo Orch., 1993—; lectr. music Wayne State U., Detroit, 1983-86; guest asst. prof. music U. Mich., Ann Arbor, 1986-87; artistic adviser Dearborn (Mich.) Symphony Orch., 1987-89, Traverse Symphony Orch., 1988-90; spl. artistic adviser Flint Inst. Music, 1991-92; asoc. prof. Ctrl. Mich. U., 1995—; artistic dir. Midland Symphony Orch., 1996—. Prodr., host radio program Preludio: The String Thing, 1978-80; co-prodr. After Glow, 1994-96; prodr.: Prelodio, 1996—. Mem. adv. panel Mich. Coun. for Arts, 1989-91; rev. panel Mich. Coun. for Arts & Cultural Affairs, 1996—. Mem. Am. Symphony Orch. League (various coms. 1980—, Helen M. Thompson award 1982), Mich. Orch. Assn. (pres. 1985-88), Condrs. Guild Am. (bd. dirs. 1991-93), Asn. Can. Orchs. Home: 973 S Linwood Beach Rd Linwood MI 48634-9433 Office: Saginaw Symphony Orch 420 Symphony Ln # 415 Saginaw MI 48607-1211

NAJARIAN, JOHN SARKIS, surgeon, educator; b. Oakland, Calif., Dec. 22, 1927; s. Garabed L. and Siranoush T. (Demirjian) N.; m. Arlys Viola Mignette Anderson, Apr. 27, 1952; children: Jon, David, Paul, Peter. AB with honors, U. Calif., Berkeley, 1948; MD, U. Calif., San Francisco, 1952; LHD (hon.), Univ. Athens, 1980; DSc (hon.), Gustavus Adolphus Coll., 1981; LHD (hon.), Calif. Luth. Coll., 1983. Diplomate Am. Bd. Surgery. Surg. intern U. Calif., San Francisco, 1952-53, surg. resident, 1955-60, asst. prof. surgery, dir. surg. research labs., chief transplant service dept. surgery, 1963-66, prof., vice chmn., 1966-67; spl. research fellow in immunopathology U. Pitts. Med. Sch., 1960-61; NIH sr. fellow and assoc. in tissue transplantation immunology Scripps Clinic and Research Found., La Jolla, Calif., 1961-63; Markle scholar Acad. Medicine, 1964-69; prof., chmn. dept. surgery U. Minn. Hosp., Mpls., 1967-93; med. dir. Transplant Ctr., clin. chief surgery Univ. Hosp., 1967-94; chief hosp. staff U. Minn. Hosp., Mpls., 1970-71, Regents' prof., 1985-95, Jay Phillips Disting. Chair in Surgery, 1986-95; prof. emeritus, clin. prof. surgery, 1995—; spl. cons. USPHS, NIH Clin. Rsch. Tng. Com., Inst. Gen. Med. Scis., 1965-69; cons. U.S. Bur. Budget, 1966-68; mem. sci. adv. bd. Nat. Kidney Found., 1968; mem. surg. study sect. A div. rsch. grants NIH, 1970; chmn. renal transplant adv. group VA Hosps., 1971; mem. bd. sci. cons. Sloan-Kettering Inst. Cancer Rsch., 1971-78; mem. screening com. Dernham Postdoctoral Fellowships in Oncology, Calif. div. Am. Cancer Soc. Editor: (with Richard L. Simmons) Transplantation, 1972; co-editor: Manual of Vascular Access, Organ Donation, and Transplantation, 1984; mem. editorial bd. Jour. Surg. Rsch., 1968—, Minn. Medicine, 1968—, Jour. Surg. Oncology, 1968—, Am. Jour. Surgery, 1967—, assoc. editor, 1982—; mem. editorial bd. Year Book of Surgery, 1970-85, Transplantation, 1970—, Transplantation Procs, 1970—, Bd. Clin. Editors, 1981-84, Annals of Surgery, 1972—, World Jour. Surgery, 1976—, Hippocrates, 1986—, Jour. Transplant Coordination, 1990—; assoc. editor: Surgery, 1971; editor-in-chief: Clin. Transplantation, 1986—. Bd. dirs., v.p. Variety Club Heart Hosp., U. Minn.; trustee, v.p. Minn. Med. Found. Served with USAF, 1953-55. Hon. fellow Royal Coll. Surgeons of Eng., 1987; hon. prof. U. Madrid, 1990; named Alumnus of Yr., U. Calif. Med. Sch., San Francisco, 1977; recipient award Calif. Trudeau Soc., 1962, Ann. Brotherhood award NCCJ, 1978, Disting. Achievement award Modern Medicine, 1978, Internat. Gt. Am. award B'nai B'rith Found., 1982, Uncommon Citizen award, 1985, Sir James Carreras award Variety Clubs Internat., 1987, Silver medal IXth Centenary, U. Bologna, 1988, Humanitarian of Yr. award, U. Minn., 1992, Najarian Festschrift award Am. Jour. Surgery, 1993, Jubilee medal Swedish Soc. Medicine, 1994. Fellow ACS; mem. Soc. Univ. Surgeons, Soc. Exptl. Biology and Medicine, AAAS, Am. Soc. Exptl. Pathology, Am. Surg. Assn. (pres. 1988-89), Am. Assn. Immunologists, AMA, Transplantation Soc. (v.p. western hemisphere 1984-86, pres. 1994-96), Am. Soc. Nephrology, Internat. Soc. Nephrology, Am. Assn. Lab. Animal Sci., Assn. Acad. Surgery (pres. 1969), Internat Soc. Surgery, Soc. Surg. Chairmen, Soc. Clin. Surgery, Central Surg. Assn., Minn., Hennepin County med. socs., Mpls., St. Paul, Minn., Howard C. Naffziger, Portland, Halsted surg. socs., Am. Heart Assn., Am. Soc. Transplant Surgeons (pres. 1977-78), Council on Kidney in Cardiovascular Disease, Hagfish Soc., Italian Research Soc., Minn. Acad. Medicine, Minn. Med. Assn., Minn. Med. Found., Surg. Biology Club, Sigma Xi, Alpha Omega Alpha, others. Office: U Minn Surgery Dept Mayo Meml Bldg Box 195 420 Delaware St SE Minneapolis MN 55455-0374

NAJITA, TETSUO, history educator; b. Honokaa, Hawaii, Mar. 30, 1936; s. Niichi and Kikuno (Bamboku) N.; m. Elinor Moon, Aug. 2, 1958; children: Mie Kim, Kiyoshi Young. BA, Grinnell Coll., 1958; MA, Harvard U., 1960, PhD, 1965; LLD, Grinnell Coll., 1989. Asst. prof. Carleton Coll., Northfield, Minn., 1964-66, Wash. Univ., St. Louis, 1966-68; assoc. prof. U. Wis., Madison, 1968-69; Robert S. Ingersoll Disting. Svc. prof. Japanese studies U. Chgo., 1969—, dir. Ctr. for East Asian Studies, 1974-80, assoc. dean, 1983-87, master collegiate div. social scis., 1983-87; John A. Burns disting. visiting chair U. Hawaii, Manoa, 1994; chair dept. history U. Chgo., 1994—; Ena H. Thompson lectr. Pomona Coll., 1996. Author: Hara Kei in the Politics of Compromise, 1969 (J.K. Fairbank prize Am. Hist. Assn.), Intellectual Foundations of Modern Japanese Politics, 1974, Visions of Virtue in Tokugawa Japan, 1987. Recipient Yamagata Banto prize Prefecture of Osaka, 1989; grantee NEH 1973-74, 1980-81; Fulbright fellow 1961-63, 68, Guggenheim fellow 1980-81. Fellow Am. Acad. Arts and Scis.; mem. Am. Hist. Assn., Assn. for Asian Studies (v.p., pres. 1991-93), Phi Beta Kappa. Office: U Chgo Dept History 1126 E 59th St Chicago IL 60637-1539

NAKAGAKI, MASAYUKI, chemist; b. Tokyo, Apr. 19, 1923; s. Sengoro and Shizue N.; m. Hisako Yoshitake, May 3, 1951. BSc, Imperial U., Tokyo, 1945; DSc, U. Tokyo, 1950. Instr. Imperial U., Tokyo, 1945-51; lectr. U. Tokyo, 1951-54; prof. Osaka (Japan) City U., 1954-60; prof. Kyoto (Japan) U., 1960-87, emeritus prof., 1987—; vis. prof. Wayne State U., Detroit, 1955-57, 68-69; dean faculty pharm. sci. Kyoto U., 1978-80; prof. Hoshi U., Tokyo, 1987-92; dir. Tokyo Inst. Colloid Sci., 1992—. Regional editor: Colloid and Polymer Sci., Darmstadt, Germany, 1982—. Recipient rsch. award Takeda Found. 1971. Mem. Membrane Soc. Japan (inspector 1988—, prse. 1978-88), Pharm. Soc. Japan (Rsch. award 1970, merit mem. 1990—). Home: 354 Kotokujicho Teramachi, Kamigoryo, Kyoto 602, Japan Office: Tokyo Inst Colloid Sci, 502 Higashi-Nakano 4-4-3, Tokyo 164, Japan

NAKAGAWA, ALLEN DONALD, radiologic technologist; b. N.Y.C., Mar. 14, 1955; s. Walter Tsunehiko and Alyce Tsuneko (Kinoshita) N. BS in Environ. Studies, St. John's U., Jamaica, N.Y., 1977; MS in Marine Biology, C.W. Post Coll., 1980. Cert. radiologic technologist, in fluoroscopy, Calif.; cert. Am. Registry Radiol. Technologists. Research asst. environ. studies St. John's U., 1976-78; lab. asst. Bur. Water Surveillance, Nassau Co. of Health Dept., Wantaugh, N.Y., 1978; clin. endocrinology asst. U. Calif. VA Hosp., San Francisco, 1981-83; student technologist St. Mary's Hosp., San Francisco, 1985-86; radiologic technologist Mt. Zion Hosp., San Francisco, 1986-88; sr. radiologic technologist U. Calif., San Francisco, 1989—, urosurg. radiologic technologists, 1988-89; attendee U. Calif. San Francisco Trauma and Emergency Radiology Conf., 1995, U. Calif. San Francisco Musculoskeletal MRI Conf., 1996. Mem. AAAS, ACLU, Calif. Soc. Radiologic Technologists, Marine Mammal Ctr., Calif. Acad. Scis., Japanese-Am. Nat. Mus., World Affairs Coun., San Francisco, Sigma Xi. Democrat. Methodist. Avocations: assisting handicapped, photography, music, computer illustration, studying advanced technology. *If you know, believe and have faith in yourself first, only then can you endeavor to assist someone else. Otherwise, you have wasted your efforts and may have even caused a loss of life.*

NAKAGAWA, KOJI, endocrinologist, educator; b. Sapporo, Hokkaido, Japan, June 5, 1932; s. Satosu and Michi (Yokoyama) N.; m. Keiko Hirato, Oct. 20, 1962; children: Shin, Tamao Yamaguchi. MD, Hokkaido U., 1957, PhD, 1962. Lic. endocrinologist, Japan. Staff scientist Worcester Found. for Experimental Biology, Shrewsbury, Mass., 1964-65; rsch. staff Syntex Rsch. Ctr., Palo Alto, Calif., 1965; rsch. fellow U. Utah Med. Ctr., Salt Lake City, 1965-66; rsch. assoc. 2d dept. medicine Hokkaido U. Sch. Medicine, Sapporo, 1967-83, asst. prof., 1983-89; prof. Health Adminstrn. Ctr., Hokkaido U. Edn., Sapporo, 1989-96, dir. Health Adminstrn. Ctr., 1990-96; retired; lectr. Hokkaido U. Sch. of Medicine, Sapporo, 1989—. Contbr. articles to profl. jours., including Jour. Clin. Endocrinology and Metabolism, Endocrinology, Acta Endocrinologica. Fellow Japan Endocrine Soc.; mem. Endocrine Soc., Japanese Soc. Internal Medicine, Japan Diabetes Soc. Home: 2-8 4-chome Yamanote 1-jo, Nishi-ku, Sapporo 063, Japan

NAKAJIMA, YASUKO, medical educator; b. Osaka, Japan, Jan. 8, 1932; came to U.S., 1962, 69; d. Isao and Taeko Nakagawa; m. Shigehiro Nakajima; children: Hikeko H., Gene A. MD, U. Tokyo, 1955, PhD, 1962. Intern U. Tokyo Sch. Medicine, 1955-56, resident, 1956-57, instr., 1962-67; assoc. prof. Purdue U., West Lafayette, Ind., 1969-76, prof., 1976-88; prof. anatomy and cell biology U. Ill. Coll. Medicine, Chgo., 1988—; vis. rsch. fellow Coll. Physicians and Surgeons, Columbia U., N.Y.C., 1962-64; asst. rsch. anatomist UCLA Sch. Medicine, 1964-65; vis. rsch. fellow Cambridge U., 1967-69; mem. study sect. NIH, 1996—. Contbr. articles to sci. jours. Fulbright travel grantee, 1962-65. Mem. AAAS, Am. Physiol. Soc., Soc. Neurosci., Am. Soc. Cell Biology, Am. Assn. Anatomists, Biophys. Soc., Marine Biol. Lab. Corp. Office: U Ill Coll Medicine Dept Anatomy m/c 512 808 S Wood St Chicago IL 60612-7300

NAKAKUKI, MASAFUMI, physician, psychiatry educator; b. Shimotsuma, Ibaragi, Japan, Mar. 1, 1930; came to U.S., 1969, naturalized 1975; s. Keisuke and Toi (Saito) N.; m. Ritsuko Oka, May 25, 1957; children: Mari, Emma; m. Michael McAndrewes, Sept. 1988. MS, U. Ibaragi, 1949; MD, U. Tokyo, 1953. Diplomate Am. Bd. Psychiatry and Neurology. Intern U. Tokyo Hosp., 1953-54, dir. psychiat. inpatient service, 1966-69; resident in psychiatry U. Tokyo, 1954-60, U. Colo.-Denver, 1962-66; asst. prof. psychiatry U. Colo. Med. Ctr., Denver, 1969-73; staff psychiatrist Ft. Logan Mental Health Ctr., Denver, 1973-74, Arapahoe Mental Health Ctr., Englewood, Colo., 1974-76; med. dir. Park East Mental Health Ctr. Denver, 1977-83; pres. Masafumi Nakakuki, M.D., P.C., Denver, 1977—; pres. med. staff Bethesda Hosp., Denver, 1982-83; psychiat. cons. Asian Pacific Devel. Ctr., Denver, 1983—; vis. prof. psychiatry St. Mariana U., Tokyo, 1995—. Author: Textbook of Psychiatry for the General Practitioner, 1968; New Parenting and Culture, 1982. Recipient Letter of Appreciation for Mental Health Svcs. and Leadership from Gov. Romer, 1995. Bd. dirs. Asian Human Service Assn., Denver, 1982. Fulbright scholar, 1961. Fellow Am. Psychiat. Assn.; mem. AAAS, Am. Group Psychotherapy Assn., Japanese Psychiat. Assn., Japanese Psychoanalytic Assn., Japanese Group Psychotherapy Assn. Office: 4770 E Iliff Ave Denver CO 80222-6061 also: 2-1-15-705 Takanawa, Minato-ku Tokyo 108, Japan

NAKAMOTO, FAY, public health officer. Asst. to dir. Dept. of Health State of Hawaii, Honolulu; pub. health rschr. U. Hawaii. Active Nat. 4-H Found. Mem. Am. Pub. Health Assn., Hawaii Pub. Health Assn. Office: Health Dept State of Hawaii 1250 Punchbowl St Honolulu HI 96813-2416

NAKAMURA, HIDEO, law educator; b. Tokyo, Mar. 2, 1926; s. Muneo and Fumiko (Mitani) N.; m. Mitsuko Terai, Feb. 25, 1958; children: Eri, Akiyoshi. LLB, Waseda U., Tokyo, 1947, LLD, 1980; Dr. honoris causa, Athens U., 1995. Assoc. prof. Faculty of Law Waseda U., tokyo, 1955-60, prof., 1960, dean Grad. Sch. Law, 1980-82, dir. Inst. Comparative Law, 1984-88, pres. Law Assn., 1990-94; dir. Inst. Comparative Civil Law, tokyo, 1975—; ret. hon prof. Waseda U., 1996. Author: (in German) The Japanese Criminal Procedure Code, 1970, Japan and German Civil Procedure, 1995, (in Japanese) Collected Works on Civil Procedure, Vols., 1-5, 1975-86; Civil Procedure, 1987; co-author: (in German) The Japanese Civil Procedure Code, 1978; editor: Family Law Litigation, 1984. Mem. Japanese Assn. of Law of Civil Procedure (exec. com. 1960-80), Japanese Assn. of Law of Pub. Notary (coun. 1978—), Japan Fedn. of Bar Assn. (commr. disciplinary com. 1984-87), Acad. Assn. of Law of Internat. Procedure. Avocation: photography. Home: 2-6-6 Kamitakata Nakano-ku, Tokyo 164, Japan Office: Inst Comparative Civil Law, 43 Waseda-Minamicho, Shinjuku Tokyo 162, Japan

NAKAMURA, HIROSHI, urology educator; b. Tokyo, Mar. 22, 1933; s. Yataroh and Hideko (Tanaka) N.; m. Miyoko Kodachi, Aug. 13, 1966. MD, Keio U., Tokyo, 1960; PhD, Grad. Sch. Medicine, Keio U., 1966. Med. diplomate. Asst. resident Mt. Sinai Hosp., N.Y.C., 1962-63; rsch. fellow Cornell U. Med. Coll., N.Y.C., 1966-68; asst. Sch. Medicine Keio U., Tokyo, 1968-70; chmn. urology dept. Tokyo Elec. Power Hosp., 1970-73; vis. asst. prof. surgery Cornell U. Med. Coll., N.Y.C., 1973; chmn. urology Kitasato Inst. Hosp., Tokyo, 1973-77; chmn. dept., prof. urology Nat. Def. Med. Coll., Tokorozawa, Saitama, Japan, 1977—, dir. dept. acad. affairs, 1994-96. Author: New Clin. Urology, 1982, Practice of Renal Transplantation, 1985, Bedside Urology, 1991; editor: Up-to-date Urology, 1983. Recipient Tamura award Keio U. Sch. Medicine, 1967, All-around Med. award, Igaku-Shoin, Ltd., Tokyo, 1967. Buddhist. Avocations: jazz, audiophile, travel, fishing, baseball. Home: 4-403 Boei Idai 3-2 Namiki, Tokorozawa 359 Saitama, Japan Office: Nat Def Med Coll Dept Urol, 3-2 Namiki, Tokorozawa 359 Saitama, Japan

NAKAMURA, JAMES I., economics educator; b. Toppenish, Wash., Mar. 16, 1919; s. Ichihei and Suya (Hirayama) N.; m. Tetsuko Fujii; children—Richard Ken, Leonard Isamu. A.A., Santa Maria Jr. Coll., 1939; B.S., Columbia U., 1952, Ph.D., 1964. Asst. prof. Columbia U., N.Y.C., 1964-68, assoc. prof., 1968-80, prof. econs., 1980-89, prof. emeritus, 1989—; vis. research scholar Kobe U., Japan, 1971-72; co-founder, co-dir., sec.-treas. Japan Econ. Seminar (supported by Columbia U., Harvard U.,, George Washington U.), 1965—. Author: Agricultural Production and Economic Development of Japan, 1966, Nihon no Keizai Hatten to Nogyo, 1968; mem. editorial bd. Japan Econ. Studies, 1972—; contbr. numerous articles to profl. jours. Editor newspaper War Relocation Ctr., Gila River, Ariz., 1943-44; legal researcher Shanks Village Com. to Fight Closure, Orangeburg, N.Y., 1952. Served to lt. U.S. Army, 1945-48, PTO. Ford Found. fellow 1952-55, 62-63; Fulbright-Hays fellow, 1967. Mem. Econ. History Assn., Am. Econ. Assn., Assn. for Asian Studies, Japan Econ. Research Ctr., Phi Beta Kappa. Buddhist. Home: 35 Claremont Ave New York NY 10027-6823 Office: Columbia U Dept Econ 935 IAB New York NY 10027

NAKAMURA, KAZUO, artist; b. Vancouver, Can., Oct. 13, 1926; s. Toichi and Yoshiyo (Uyemoto) N.; m. Lillian Yuriko Kobayakawa, Sept. 15, 1967; children—Elaine Yukae, Bryan Kazuto. Student, Central Tech. Sch., Toronto, 1948-51. Exhibited in one man shows at, Picture Loan Soc., 1952, Hart House, U. Toronto, 1953, Gallery of Contemporary Art, Toronto, 1956, 58, Jerrold Morris Gallery, Toronto, 1962, 65, 67-70, R. McLaughlin Gallery, Oshawa and Can. Tour, 1974-75, Christopher Cutts Gallery, Toronto, 1991; exhibited in group shows at, Fifth Internat. Hallmark Art Award Exhbn., N.Y.C., 1960, Canadian Prints, Drawings and Watercolor, Am. Fedn. Arts Tour, 1960, Seconde Biennale, Musee d'Art Moderne, Paris, France, 1961, Canadian Painting, Polish Tour, 1962, Canadian Painting, Central Africa, 1962, Nineteen Canadian Painters, Louisville, 1962, Commonwealth Painting, London, Eng., 1962, Recent Acquisitions, Mus. Modern Art, N.Y.C., 1963, Canadian Painting, London, 1963, Member's Loan Gallery Acquisitions, Albright-Knox Gallery, Buffalo, 1963, World Show, Washington Sq. Gallery, N.Y.C., 1964, Cardiff Commonwealth Exhbn. of Drawings, Wales, 1965, Centennial Exhbn. of Canadian Prints and Drawings, Australian Tour, 1967, Painters Eleven in Retrospect, Can. tour, 1979-81, Ont. Heritage Found. Firestone Collection, European tour, 1983-84, Nat. Gallery Can., Ottawa, 1989, Nat. Gallery Can., Ottawa, Can. tour, 1993, Mead Mus., Amherst Coll., 1994; others; represented in permanent collections at Nat. Gallery Can., Mus. Modern Art, N.Y.C., Art Gallery of Ont., Toronto, Musée d'Art contemporain, Montreal, R. McLaughlin Gallery, Oshawa, Hirshhorn Mus., Washington, British Mus., London, Art Gallery of Hamilton, Winnipeg Art Gallery, Beaverbrook Art Gallery, Fredericton, N.B., Windsor (Ont.) Art Gallery, Lugano Collection, Hart House, U. Toronto, Victoria Coll., U. Toronto, U. Western Ont., U. Guelph, Concordia U., Univ. Club Montreal, commd. 2 sculptures, Toronto Internat. Airport. (Recipient prize 4th Internat. Exhbn. Drawings and Engravings, Lugano, Switzerland 1956, Purchase award 5th Internat. Hallmark Art Award Exhbn., N.Y.C. 1960).

NAKAMURA, MITSURU JAMES, microbiologist, educator; b. L.A., Dec. 17, 1926; s. Jingo and Michie (Inadomi) N.; m. Judith Ann Frohreich; children: Monica Suzan, Nancy Midori, Mark James. Student, Drake U., 1944-45; AB, UCLA, 1949, postgrad., 1950-52; MS, U. So. Calif., 1950; PhD, Boston U., 1956; ScD (hon.), Albert Szent-Gyorgyi Med. U., 1991. Diplomate: Am. Bd. Microbiology. Research asst. U. Calif., San Francisco, 1950-52; asst. prof. Northeastern U., 1952-54, assoc. prof., 1954-56; assoc. prof. U. Mont., Missoula, 1956-62; prof. U. Mont., 1962-86, prof. emeritus, 1986—, chmn. dept., 1963-85; assoc. prof. rsch. Wash. State U., summers 1957, 58; internat. vis. prof. Med. U. Pecs, Hungary, 1987; vis. prof. Yang Ming Med. Coll., Taipei, Taiwan, 1988, Albert Szent Gyorgyi Med. U., Szeged, Hungary, 1989, U. West Indies, Trinidad, 1990, Barbados, 1990, Jozsef Attila U. Scis., Szeged, 1991, Inst. Microbiol. Bulgarian Acad. Scis., 1992; rsch. fellow La. State U. Sch. Medicine, 1959, 60. Contbr. articles profl. jours. With AUS, 1945-47, capt. USPHS, 1959—. U.S. Army rsch. grantee 1959-62, NSF grantee, 1959-67, HEW grantee, 1960-67, Dept. Interior grantee 1964-67; Nat. Acad. Sci. awardee Poland, 1976, Yugoslavia, 1978, Hungary, 1982, 84, 89, Bulgaria, 1985, Czechoslovakia, 1987, ProCultura grantee, Hungary, 1991, 93. Fellow AAAS, APHA, Royal Soc. Tropical Medicine (London), Am. Acad. Microbiology, Bulgarian Acad. Scis., Elks. Home: PO Box 2068 Missoula MT 59806-2068

NAKAMURA, ROBERT MOTOHARU, pathologist; b. Montebello, Calif., June 10, 1927; s. Mosaburo and Haru (Suematsu) N.; m. Shigeyo Jane Hayashi, July 29, 1957; children: Mary, Nancy. AB, Whittier Coll., 1949; MD, Temple U., 1954. Cert. of spl. qualification in pathologic anatomy, clin pathology, immunopathology, Am. Bd. Pathology. Prof. pathology U. Calif., Irvine, 1971-74, adj. prof. pathology, 1974-75; chmn. dept. pathology Scripps Clinic and Rsch. Found., La Jolla, Calif., 1974-92; sr. cons., 1992—; pres. Scripps Clinic Med. Group, La Jolla, 1981-91; adj. prof. pathology U. Calif., San Diego, 1975-93. Author, editor profl. publs.; co-editor Jr. Clin. Lab. Analysis, 1989—. Fellow: Coll. Am. Pathologists, Am. Soc. Clin. Pathologists, Assn. Clin. Scientists, Am. Coll. Nutrition; mem. Internat. Acad. Pathology. Avocation: reading. Home: 8841 Nottingham Pl La Jolla CA 92037-2131

NAKANISHI, DON TOSHIAKI, Asian American studies educator, writer; b. L.A., Aug. 14, 1949; m. Marsha Hirano; 1 child, Thomas. BA in Polit Sci. cum laude, Yale U., 1971; PhD in Polit. Sci., Harvard U., 1978. Prof., dir. Asian Am. Studies Ctr. UCLA; researcher Social Sci. Rsch. Coun. of N.Y. and the Japan Soc. for the Promotion of Sci. of Tokyo Joint-Project on Am.-Japanese Mut. Images, 1971-73; mem. Asian Am. task force for social studies guideline evaluation, Calif. State Dept. Edn., 1973; guest spkr. Ctr. for the Study of Ednl. Policy, Grad. Sch. Edn., Harvard U., 1974, Metropathways, Ethni-City Sch. Desegregation Program, Boston, 1974; researcher, co-project chair Hispanic Urban Ctr., Project Sch. Desegregation, L.A., 1974. Author: (with others) Mutual Images: Essays in American-Japan Relations, 1975, Eliminating Racism, 1988, Racial and Ethnic Politics in California, 1991; author: In Search of a New Paradigm: Minorities in the Context of International Politics, 1975, The Education of Asian and Pacific Americans: Historical Perspectives and Prescriptions for the Future, 1983, The UCLA Asian Pacific American Voter Registration Study, 1986; contbr. articles to profl. jours. Chair Yale U. Alumni Schs. Com. of So. Calif., 1978—; bd. dirs. Altamed and La Clinica Familiar Del Barrio of East L.A., 1982—; commr. Bd. Transp. Commrs., City of L.A., 1984-90; v.p. Friends of the Little Tokyo Pub. Libr., 1986-88; co-chair nat. scholars adv. com. Japanese Am. Nat. Mus., 1987—; mem., bd. govs. Assn. of Yale Alumni, 1988-91; mem. exec. coun. Mayor's LA's Best Aftersch. Program, City of Los Angeles, 1988-90. Rsch. fellow Japan Soc. for the Promotion of Sci., 1978; recipient Nat. Scholars awrd for Outstanding Rsch. Article on Asian Pacific Am. Edn., Nat. Assn. for Asian and Pacific Am. Edn., 1985, Civil Rights Impace award Asian Am. Legal Ctr. of So. Calif., 1989; grantee Chancellors' Challenge in the Arts and Humanities, 1991, Calif. Policy Seminar, 1992, U. Calif. Pacific Rim Studies, 1992. Mem. Nat. Assn. for Interdisciplinary Ethnic Studies (bd. dirs. 1976-79), Assn. Asian Am. Studies (nat. pres. 1983-85), Nat. Assn. for Asian and Pacific Am. Edn. (exec. bd. dirs., v.p. 1983—). Office: UCLA Asian Am Studies Ctr Los Angeles CA 90024

NAKANISHI, KOJI, chemistry educator, research institute administrator; b. Hong Kong, May 11, 1925; came to U.S., 1969; s. Yuzo and Yoshiko (Sakata) N.; m. Yasuko Abe, Oct. 25, 1947; children: Keiko, Jun. B.Sc., Nagoya U., Japan, 1947; Ph.D., Nagoya U., 1954; DSc (hon.), Williams Coll., 1987, Georgetown U., 1992. Asst. prof. Nagoya U., 1955-58; prof. Tokyo Kyoiku U., 1958-63, Tohoku U., Sendai, Japan, 1963-69; prof. chemistry Columbia U., N.Y.C., 1969-80; Centennial prof. chemistry Columbia U., 1980—; dir. research Internat. Ctr. Insect Physiology and Ecology, Nairobi, Kenya, 1969-77; dir. Suntory Inst. for Bioorganic Research, Osaka, Japan, 1979-91; hon. prof. Shanghai Inst. Materia Medica, 1995. Author: Infrared Spectroscopy-Practical, 1962, rev. edit., 1977, Circular Dichroic Spectroscopy-Exciton Coupling in Organic Stereochemistry, 1983, A Wandering Natural Products Chemist, 1991. Recipient Asahi cultural prize, 1968, Sci. Workers Union medal, Bulgaria, 1978, E.E. Smissman medal U. Kan., 1979, H.C. Urey award Columbia U., 1980, Alcon ophthalmology award, 1986, Paul Karrer gold medal U. Zurich, 1986, E. Havinga medal Havinga Found., Leiden, 1989, Imperial prize Japan Acad., 1990, Japan Acad. prize, 1990, R.T. Major medal U. Conn., 1991, L.E. Harris award U. Nebr., 1991, award in chem. scis. NAS, 1994, J. Heyrovsky hon. gold medal Czech Acad. Scis., 1995, Robert A. Welch award in chemistry, 1996; Nakanishi prize established in his honor, 1996. Fellow N.Y. Acad. Scis., Nat. Acad. Sci. Italy (fgn.); mem. Chem. Soc. Japan (award in pure chemistry 1954, award 1979, Nakanishi prize established 1996), Am. Chem. Soc. (E. Guenther award 1978, Remsen award Md. sect. 1981, A.C. Cope award 1990, Nichols medal N.Y. sect. 1992, Mosher award Santa Clara Valley sect. 1995, internat. award in agrochems. 1995, Nakanishi prize established 1996), Brit. Chem. Soc. (Centenary medal 1979), Swedish Acad. Pharm. Scis. (Scheele award 1992), Am. Acad. Arts and Scis., Am. Soc. Pharmacognosy (rsch. achievement award 1985), Internat. Chirality Symposium (Chirality gold medal 1995), Pharm. Sc. Japan (hon.). Home: 560 Riverside Dr New York NY 10027-3202 Office: Columbia U Dept Chemistry Mail Code 3114 3000 Broadway New York NY 10027

NAKANO, TATSUHIKO, chemist, educator; b. Osaka, Japan, Feb. 4, 1925; s. Denichi and Shie (Kubo) N.; m. Toshiko Kitagawa, Apr. 23, 1965. BA, Kyoto U., 1950, PhD, 1955. Rsch. fellow Kyoto (Japan) U., 1950-55, assoc. prof., 1960-65; rsch. assoc. Wayne State U., Detroit, 1956-59, Stanford (Calif.) U., 1959-60; prof. Inst. Venezolano de Investigaciones Cientificas, Caracas, Venezuela, 1965-94, investigador emerito, 1994; prof. U. Ctrl. de Venezuela, Caracas, 1979—; disting. prof. Inst. de Tecnologia y Estudios Superiores, Monterrey, Mex., 1979; vis. prof. U. N.C., Chapel Hill, 1990, 91, 93, 95; regional editor Revista Latinoamericana de Quimica, Mexico City, 1970—. Contbr. 200 articles to Jour. Chem. Soc., Jour. Chem. Rsch., Tetrahedron, Tetrahedra Letters, etc.; author: Studies in Natural Products Chemistry, 1989, 90. Recipient Spl. Rsch. fellowship IKUEIKAI, 1950, Fulbright Vis. Scientist Travel award, 1956, Rsch. award Rockefeller Found., 1961, NIH, 1962, Fundación José Maria Vargas, 1969, 80, ABI Twentieth Century Achievement award 1995; decorated Order Andrés Bello, 3rd class, 1979, 2nd class 1989, 1st class 1996; investigador emérito, 1994, Miembro Emérito, PPI Consejo Nacional de Investigaciones Científicas y Technológicas, 1994. Mem. AAAS, Am. Chem. Soc., Royal Soc. Chemistry, N.Y. Acad. Scis., L.Am. Acad. Scis. (acad. mem., diploma outstanding scientific investigation 1995), Japan Fulbright Alumni Assn. Office: Centro de Quimica IVIC, Apartado 21827, Caracas 1020-A, Venezuela

NAKARAI, CHARLES FREDERICK TOYOZO, music educator, adjudicator; b. Indpls., Apr. 25, 1936; s. Toyozo Wada and Frances Aileen N.; B.A. cum laude, Butler U., 1958, Mus.M., 1967; postgrad. U. N.C., 1967-70. Organist, dir. choirs Northwood Christian ch., Indpls., 1954-57; minister music Allisonville Christian Ch., Indpls., 1957-58; asst. prof. music Milligan Coll., Tenn., 1970-72; pvt. instrn. organ, piano, Durham, 1972—; faculty piano camp U. N.C.-Greensboro, 1996—; adjudicator N.C. Fedn. Music Clubs, Raleigh Music Tchrs. Assn., Charlotte Piano Tchrs. Forum. Served with USAF, 1958-64. Mem. Am. Musicol. Soc., Coll. Music Soc., Am. Guild Organists, Music Tchrs. Nat. Assn., Music Library Assn., N.C. Music Tchrs. Assn. (chair student activities), Organ Hist. Soc., Durham Music Tchrs. Assn. Composer: Three Movements for Chorus, 1971, Bluesy, 1979. Address: 3520 Mayfair St Apt 205 Durham NC 27707-2673

NAKASHIMA, MITSUGI, state agency administrator. Chmn. Edn. divsn., Honolulu. Office: Education Dvsn PO Box 2360 Honolulu HI 96804-2360*

NAKASONE, ROBERT C., retail toy and game company executive; b. 1947; married. BA, Claremont Coll., 1969; MBA, U. Chgo., 1971. Pres. Brighams Ice Cream Parlor & Sandwich Shops, 1979-82; v.p., gen. mgrs. Jewel Food Stores, 1982-84; Midwest stores v.p. Toys R Us Inc., 1985—; pres. Toys R Us, USA, 1985-88; pres., vice chmn. Toys R Us Worldwide Toy Stores, 1989-92; now pres., COO Toys R Us Inc.; also bd. dirs. 1st lt.

U.S. Army, 1971. Office: Toys R US Inc 461 From Rd Paramus NJ 07652-3526

NAKAYAMA, PAULA AIKO, justice; b. Honolulu, Oct. 19, 1953; m. Charles W. Totto; children: Elizabeth Murakami, Alexander Totto. BS, U. Calif., Davis, 1975; JD, U. Calif., 1979. Bar: Hawaii 1979. Dep. pros. atty. City and County of Honolulu, 1979-82; ptnr. Shim, Tam & Kirimitsu, Honolulu, 1982-92; judge 1st Cir. Ct. State of Hawaii, Oahu, 1992-93; justice State of Hawaii Supreme Ct., Honolulu, 1993—. Mem. Am. Judicature Soc., Hawaii Bar Assn., Sons and Daughters of 442. Office: Ali'iolani Hale 417 S King St Honolulu HI 96813-2902 Address: PO Box 2560 Honolulu HI 96804-2560*

NAKAYAMA, WATARU, engineering educator; b. Kamakura, Kanagawa, Japan, Jan. 7, 1936; s. Shiroh and Haru N.; m. Michiko Aoyagi, Jan. 8, 1967. BS, Defense Acad., Yokosuka, Japan, 1958; MS, Tokyo Inst. Tech., 1963, DEng, 1966. Lectr. U. Sherbrooke, Que., 1969-70; rschr. Hitachi, Ltd., Tokyo, 1970-71; chief rschr. Hitachi, Ltd., Tsuchiura, Japan, 1971-78, sr. rschr., 1978-88, sr. chief rschr., 1988-91, hon. engr., 1991-92; Hitachi chair prof. Tokyo Inst. Tech., 1989-92, prof., 1992-96; vis. prof. U. Md.; lectr. in field. Author: (with others) Heat Transfer in Electronic and Microelectronic Equipment, 1990, High Performance Computing in Japan, 1992, Computers and Computing in Heat Transfer Science and Engineering, 1993; contbr. articles to profl. jours. Recipient New Tech. Innovation award Ichimura Found., 1978, Best Paper award Gas Turbine Soc. of Japan, 1984, Electronic Packaging Dir. award, 1996. Fellow ASME (K-16 com. 1981—, chmn. Japanese chpt. 1990-92, Best Paper award 1981, Heat Transfer Meml. award 1992); mem. IEEE (sr.), Japanese Soc. Mech. Engrs. (vice chmn. thermal enging. divsn. 1989-90, chmn. 1990-91, Best Paper award 1965, 80, Tech. award 1978), Heat Transfer Soc. Japan (pres. 1994). Achievements include patents for industrial application of heat transfer enhancement techniques to heat exchangers, rotating machinery, cooling systems of computers. Office: U Md College Park College Park MD 20742

NAKHLA, ATIF MOUNIR, scientist, biochemist; b. Cairo, Oct. 23, 1946; came to the U.S., 1981; s. Mounir and Afifa (Nagib) N.; 1 child, Ashraf. BS (hon.) in Biochemistry, Cairo U., 1967, MS, 1971, PhD, 1975. Instr., lectr. Cairo U., 1967-80, assoc. prof., 1980-85; rsch. scientist Coll. Physicians and Surgeons Columbia U., N.Y.C., 1985—; postdoctoral fellow Aarhus (Denmark) U., 1976-79; fellow in residence Rockefeller U., N.Y.C., 1981-85. Contbr. more than 50 articles to profl. jours. Fellow Danish Internat. Devel. Agy., 1976, World Health Orgn., 1981. Mem. AAAS, Am. Soc. Biochemistry and Molecular Biology, Endorcine Soc. U.S.A., Am. Recorder Soc., Egyptian Biochem. Soc., N.Y. Acad. Scis., Sigma Xi. Avocations: music, drawing, horseback riding, swimming, tennis, chess. Home: PO Box 7917 Jersey City NJ 07307-0917

NAKHLEH, EMILE A., governmental sciences educator; b. Galilee, Palestine, May 25, 1938; came to U.S., 1960; s. Abdullah J. and Labibeh (Shiban) N.; m. Mary Bird, Dec. 25, 1965 (div. Aug. 1993); children: Charles, Richard; m. Ilonka Lessnau, Dec. 30, 1993. BA in Polit. Sci., St. John's U., 1963; MA in Polit. Sci., Georgetown U., 1966; PhD in Internat. Relation, Am. U., 1968. From asst. prof. to prof. Mt. St. Mary's Coll., Emmitsburg, Md., 1967-93, chmn. dept., 1975-89, dir. internat. studies, 1981-93, chmn. dept. govt. and internat. studies, 1989-93, John L. Morrison prof. in internat. studies, 1990-93; exec. dir. Inst. for Internat. and Contemporary Affairs, 1990-93; scholar-in-residence, sr. analyst U.S. Govt., Washington, 1993—; adj. scholar Am. Enterprise Inst., Washington, 1981-90, Ctr. for Strategic and Internat. Studies, Washington, 1986-90. Author: Gulf Cooperation Council: Policies, Problems and Prospects, 1986, Persian Gulf and American Policy, 1982, A Palestinian Agenda for West Bank and Gaza, 1980, Bahrain: Political Development in a Modernizing Society, 1976. Founding mem. Cumberland Valley Fgn. Policy Study Group, Waynesboro, Pa., 1981-93, Soc. for Gulf Arab Studies, 1989-93; commr. Town of Emmitsburg Coun., 1977; chmn. City Bd. Commrs., Emmitsburg, 1978-79. Fulbright Sr. Rsch. fellow, Bahrain, 1972-73, Jerusalem, Israel, 1987, Sr. Rsch. fellow NEH, Washington, 1979-80; resident scholar Woodrow Wilson, Washington, 1979, U.S. Govt., Washington, 1990-91, 93-94. Mem. Md. Assn. for Higher Edn. (Outstanding Educator award 1989), Coun. for Advancement and Support of Edn., Soc. for Gulf Arab Studies (founding mem., pres. 1992-93), Am. Polit. Sci. Assn. Roman Catholic. Avocations: reading, traveling, gardening. Home: 11415 Bedfordshire Ave Potomac MD 20854-2009 Office: US Govt Washington DC 20505

NAKONECZNY, MICHAEL MARTIN, artist; b. Detroit, Oct. 30, 1952; s. Michael and Edithe (Pheil) N.; 1 child, Alysha. Student, Kent State U., 1972-74; BA, Cleve. State U., 1979; MFA, Univ. Cin., 1981. Artist in residence Pub. Sch. 1, Long Island City, N.Y., 1986; instr. Cuyahoga C.C., Cleve., 1987, Cleve. Inst. of Art, 1988; vis. artist Herron Sch. of Art Ind. U., Indpls., 1990, Kansas City (Mo.) Art Inst., 1991; artist in residence Bemis Found., Omaha, Nebr., 1992; vis. artist Tamarind Inst., Albuquerque, N. Mex., 1995, Ill. State U., 1997. Artist: solo exhibitions include: Graham Modern Gallery, N.Y.C., 1988, Cleve. Ctr. for Contemporary Art, 1993, Zolla Lieberman Gallery, Chgo. 1991, 92, 93, 96, 97, Horwitch LewAllen Gallery, Santa Fe, N. Mex., 1995, Purdue U., West Lafayette, Ind., 1995; exhibited in group shows at Corcoran Gallery of Art, Washington, 1985, The Alternative Mus., N.Y., 1986, LA County Mus. of Art, 1987 (travelling exhibition), Graham Modern Gallery, N.Y.C., 1989, Machida City Mus. of Graphic Arts, Tokyo, 1993, Galleria De Arte, Sao Paulo, Brazil, 1994, Weatherspoon Art Gallery, U. N.C., 1995 (travelling exhibition), Chgo. Ctr. Book & Paper Arts, Columbia Coll., 1996, Banco Ctrl., Cuenca, Ecuador, 1996, Calif. Mus. Art, Santa Rosa, 1997. Recipient fellowship U. Cin., 1979-81, Ohio Arts Coun., 1990, Arts Midwest NEA Regional fellowship, 1994-95, Ill. Arts Coun., 1995, Summerfair Aid to Artists award, Cin., 1984, Visual Arts 7 in Conjunction with Travelling Exhibition, 1987. Home: 2010 Wesley Ave Evanston IL 60201

NALCIOGLU, ORHAN, physics educator, radiological science educator; b. Istanbul, Feb. 2, 1944; U.S., 1966, naturalized, 1974; s. Mustafa and Meliha N. BS, Robert Coll., Istanbul, 1966; MS, Case Western Res. U., 1968; PhD, U. Ore., 1970. Postdoctoral fellow dept. physics U. Calif.-Davis, 1970-71; Rsch. assoc. dept. physics U. Rochester, N.Y., 1971-74, U. Wis., Madison, 1974-76; sr. physicist EMI Med. Inc., Northbrook, Ill., 1976-77; prof. depts. radiol. scis., elec. engring., medicine and physics U. Calif.-Irvine, 1977—, head divsn. physics and engring., 1985—; dir. Biomedical Magnetic Resonance Rsch., 1987—, dir. Rsch. Imaging Ctr., 1992—; cons. UN, 1980-86. Editor several books; contbr. articles to profl. jours. Mobil scholar, 1961-66. Fellow IEEE (pres. Nuclear and Plasma Scis. Soc., 1993-94), Am. Assn. Physicists in Medicine; mem. Internat. Soc. Magnetic Resonance, IEEE Nuclear Sci. Symposium and Med. Imaging (conf. 1996). Republican. Subspecialty: med. physics. Office: U Calif Irvine Coll Medicine Dept Radiol Sci Irvine CA 92697-5020

NALDER, ERIC CHRISTOPHER, investigative reporter; b. Coulee Dam, Wash., Mar. 2, 1946; s. Philip Richard and Mibs Dorothy (Aurdal) N.; m. Jan Christiansen, Dec. 20, 1968; 1 child, Britt Hillary. BA in Communications, U. Wash., 1968. News editor Whidbey News-Times, Oak Harbor, Wash., 1971; reporter Lynnwood (Wash.) Enterprise, 1972, Everett Herald, Lynnwood, 1972-75; gen. assignment reporter Seattle Post-Intelligencer, 1975-78, edn. writer, 1977-78, investigative reporter, 1978-83; chief investigative reporter Seattle Times, 1983—. Author: Tankers Full of Trouble, 1994. Recipient Edn. Writers Assn. award Charles Stewart Mott Found., 1978, Hearst Comty. Svc. award, 1978, C.B. Blethen awards (13), Outstanding Govt. Reporting award Seattle Mcpl. League, Pub. Svc. in Journalism award Sigma Delta Chi, 1987, Edward J. Meeman award Scripps Howard Found., 1987, Thomas Stokes award, Washington Journalism Ctr., 1990, Pulitzer prize for nat. reporting, 1990, Nat. Headline award, 1991, AP Sports Editors' Investigative Reporting award, 1992, Pub. Svc. award AP Mags. Editors Assn., 1992, Goldsmith prize for investigative reporting, 1992, Worth Bingham prize for investigative reporting, 1992, Headliner award, 1992, Investigative Reporters and Editors award, 1992, 95, Silver Gavel award ABA, 1995, Pulitzer prize for investigative reporting, 1997. Mem. Investigative Reporters and Editors, Pacific N.W. Newspaper Guild. Avocation: downhill skiing. Office: Seattle Times Fairview Avenue St N Seattle WA 98109

NALDRETT, ANTHONY JAMES, geology educator; b. London, June 23, 1933; emigrated to Can., 1957; s. Anthony George and Violet Ethel (Latham) N.; m. Sylvia Robb Clark, Apr. 23, 1960 (div.); children: Anne, Jennifer, Penelope; m. Galina Stanislavovna Rylkova, July 6, 1991. B.A., U. Cambridge, 1956, M.A., 1962; M.Sc., Queens U., Can., 1961, Ph.D., 1964. Geologist Falconbridge Nickel Mines, Ltd., Sudbury, 1957-59; fellow Carnegie Inst. Washington, Geophys. Lab., 1964-67; asst. prof. U. Toronto, Ont., 1967-68; assoc. prof. U. Toronto, 1968-72, prof. mineral deposits geology, 1972-84, univ. prof., 1984—; mine geologist Falconbridge Nickel, 1957-59, exploration geologist, summers 1959-63, sr. prin. rsch. officer CSIRO, Australia, 1972-73; vis. prof. U. Pretoria, South Africa, 1979-80; chercheur associé CNRS, Orleans, France, 1986-87; stagière BRGM, Orleans, France, 1993-94. Contbr. articles to profl. jours.; editor: Jour. Petrology, 1974-82. Served with Royal Air Force, 1951-53. Recipient Barlow medal Can. Inst. Mining/Metallurgy, 1974, Duncan Derry medal Geol. Assn. Can., 1980, Logan medal Geol. Assn. Can., 1994, Bownocker gold medal Ohio State U., 1986. Fellow Royal Soc. Can., Mineral. Soc. Am., European Union Geoscientists (hon. fgn.), Geol. Assn. Can., Soc. Econ. Geologists (v.p. 1982, pres. 1991-92, medal 1982, Disting. lectr. 1996), Geol. Soc. Am., Mineral. Assn. Can. (pres. 1982, 83, Past Pres.'s medal 1991), Societè de Mineralogie et Crystallographie (v.p. 1987), Internat. Mineral. Assn. (1st v.p. 1994—). Avocations: sailing, skiing, carpentry. Home: 33 Harbour Sq Ste 1210, Toronto, ON Canada M5J 2G2 Office: Dept Geology, University of Toronto, Toronto, ON Canada M5S 1A1

NALE, JULIA ANN, nursing educator; b. Chgo., Oct. 27, 1948; d. Anthony John and Mary Elizabeth (Magrady) Doheny; m. Robert Douglas Nale, Feb. 27, 1971; children: Daniel, Kerry. Diploma, St. Francis Sch. Nursing, Evanston, Ill., 1969; BS, U. S.C. Coastal Carolina Coll., Conway, 1989. Staff nurse St. Francis Hosp., 1969-71; charge nurse McDonough Dist. Hosp., Macomb, ill., 1971-72; supr. surg. ICU Victory Meml. Hosp., Waukegan, ill., 1973-78; charge nurse St. Mary's Hosp., Galesburg, ill., 1978-79; assoc. dir. nursing Community Meml. Hosp., Monmouth, Ill., 1979-85; staff nurse Loris (S.C.) Community Hosp., 1987-91; instr. health occupations Horry County Sch. Dist., Conway, S.C., 1985-89, instr. LPNs, 1989—; staff nurse Conway Hosp., 1992—; mem. S.C. Textbook Selection Com., 1988-90. Lectr., tchr. Tommy Trauma Program for Pub. Sch. Children, Monmouth, 1982-84; charter mem. Com. to Combat Alcohol/Drug Abuse, Monmouth, 1985. Named Tchr. of the Yr. Finklea (S.C.) Career Ctr., 1989, Aynor-Conway Career Ctr., 1991, other awards. Mem. AACN, NEA, S.C. Ednl. Assn., Horry County Vocat. Assn., S.C. Vocat. Assn. (pres. health occupations div. 1990-91), Am. Vocat. Assn. Roman Catholic. Avocations: swimming, cross-stitch, reading. Office: Aynor-Conway Career Ctr Four Mile Rd Conway SC 29526

NALEN, CRAIG ANTHONY, government official; b. Montclair, N.J., Apr. 17, 1930; s. Paul Anthony and Mildred A. (Tucker) N.; m. Katherine Andrews, Dec. 30, 1953; children: Katherine M., David A., Peter H. BA, Princeton U., 1952; MBA, Stanford U., 1957. Mktg. exec. Procter & Gamble, Cin., 1957-62, Foremost-McKesson, San Francisco, 1962-64; divisional gen. mgr., corp. v.p. Gen. Mills Inc., Mpls., 1964-72; pres., also bd. dirs. Am. Photograph Corp., Great Neck, N.Y., 1972-75; pres., chmn. bd. dirs. STP Corp., Ft. Lauderdale, Fla., 1975-80; pres., chief exec. officer Overseas Pvt. Investment Corp. (govt. agy.), Washington, 1981-89, also bd. dirs.; chmn. AES Transpower, Washington, 1989—; bd. dirs. Firan Corp., Ont., Can., Sonex Corp. Bd. dirs., founder Children's World, Denver; bd. dirs. Washington Tennis Found. Lt. USNR, 1952-55. Mem. Woodhill Country Club (Wayzata, Minn.), Chevy Chase (Md.) Club, Gulf Stream Golf Club (Fla.), Gulf Stream Bath & Tennis Club (Delray Beach, Fla.), Valley Golf Club (Sun Valley, Idaho). Republican. Home: 532 Banyan Rd Gulf Stream FL 33483 also: 4419 Chalfont Pl Bethesda MD 20816-1812 also: PO Box 2439 Ketchum ID 83340-2439 Office: AES Transpower 1001 19th St N Arlington VA 22209-1722

NALEWAKO, MARY ANNE, corporate secretary; b. Johnstown, Pa., Aug. 15, 1934; d. Charles and Margaret (Timothy) Rooney; m. Michael S. Nalewako, Apr. 8, 1961; 1 child, Michael. BSBA, Coll. St. Elizabeth, Convent Station, N.J., 1987. Adminstrv. asst. to chmn. Gen. Pub. Utilities, Parsippany, N.J., 1975-88, corp. sec., 1988—. Recipient Twin award Central (N.J.) YWCA, 1989, award Exec. Women of N.J., 1992. Mem. Am. Soc. Corp. Secs., Seraphic Soc., Spring Brook Country Club. Office: Gen Pub Utilities Corp 100 Interpace Pky Parsippany NJ 07054-1149

NALLE, PETER DEVEREUX, publishing company executive; b. N.Y.C., July 26, 1947; s. Peter Borie and Margaret Graham (Josephs) N.; m. Eleanor Jo Graham, June 14, 1969; 1 child, Graham Devereux. B.A., Brown U., 1969. Salesman and mem. sales mgmt. dept. McGraw-Hill Book Co., N.Y.C., 1970-76, editor, mem. editorial mgmt. dept., 1976-81, mktg. dir., 1981-82, gen. mgr., 1982-84, group v.p., 1984-87; pres., chief exec. officer J.B. Lippincott Co., Phila., 1987-90; pres. Simon and Schuster Profl. Info. Group, Englewood Cliffs, N.J., 1990-93; COO Grolier, Inc., Danbury, Conn., 1994—. Bd. dirs. Schuylkill River Devel. Coun. Mem. Assn. Am. Pubs. (exec. council profl. and scholarly div. 1985-87, bd. dirs. 1995-96), Soc. Scholarly Pub., Washington Square Assn. (bd. dirs.), Am. Med. Pubs. Assn. (bd. dirs.), Info. Industry Assn., Friends of Schuylkill River Park (v.p.), Athenaeum of Phila. Home: 2113 Delancey St Philadelphia PA 19103-6511

NALLS, GAYIL LYNN, artist; b. Washington, July 17, 1953; d. Hampton Roberts and Doris Winifred (Fields) N.; m. Winfred Overholser III, Feb. 17, 1979 (dec. Oct. 1983); m. John William Steele, Aug. 15, 1992; 1 child, Morgan Nalls. Student, Va. Commonwealth U., 1971-72, Parsons Sch. Design, 1972-74, Am. U., Washington, 1974, Corcoran Sch. Art, 1975-76. Tchr. Parsons Sch. Design, N.Y.C., 1986—; ptnr. Election Satellite Network, Tribeca Film Ctr., N.Y.C., 1991-94; co-founder Digital Network TV, N.Y.C., 1993—. One-person shows include Susan Caldwell Gallery, N.Y.C., 1983, U. Richmond, Va., 1988, Baumgartner Galleries, Washington, 1990, Phillipe Staib Gallery, N.Y.C., 1992, Downtown Cmty. TV Ctr., N.Y.C., 1992; exhibited in group shows at Indpls. Mus. Art, 1984, Corcoran Gallery Art, Washington, 1988, U.S. Mission, Berlin, West Germany, 1988, Bruce Mus., Greenwich, Conn., 1988, Southeastern Ctr. Contemporary Art, Winston-Salem, 1989, Monastery of Santa Clara, Seville, Spain, 1992, Pretoria Art Mus., South Africa, 1994, Hand Workshop, Richmond, 1995, NGO Forum on Women '95 Film Festival, Huairou, China, 1995, (Internet exhibition) Inst. Studies in the Arts Ariz. State U., 1995, Internat. Ctr. N.Y., 1996; represented in permanent collections at Met. Mus.Art, Nat. Mus. Am. Art, Corocoran Gallery; author: The Laments, 1990, (screenplay) X-tips, 1994; author, producer: Permutatude, 1988-94, Gal Gaia/Mother Right, 1990; producer, dir. The Laments, 1994; dir., prodr. (documentary) A Common Destiny: Thomas Banyacya, The Hopi Prophecy, Jewell Praying Wolfe James, Walking in Both Worlds, 1989, Tom Dostou Speaking for Traditional Chief William Commanda: Message from the Elders of the Seven Fires Prophecy, 1995; choreographer (video) Wheels Over Indian Trails, 1993. Conceiver, designer, constructor Commn. Fine Arts and Landmark, Winfred Overholser III Meml. Sculpture Garden, Georgetown U. Hosp., Washington, 1983-85; conceier The Lab Sch. Portfolio for Lab. Sch. Washington, 1986; bd. dirs., curator 10thAnniversary Exhbn. Washington Project for the Arts, 1985-88. Recipient award EarthPeace Internat. Film Festival, Burlington, Vt., 1991, award of merit 20th Biennial Exhbn., U. Del., Newark, 1982, Purchase award Richard B. Russell Bldg. and U.S. Ct. House, Atlanta, 1982, Bay Bank Valley Trust Co. award 66th Nat. Exhbn. George Walter Vincent Smith Art Mus., Springfield, Mass., 1985; D.C. Commn. Arts. and Humanities fellow, Washington, 1987.

NAM, CHARLES BENJAMIN, sociologist, demographer, educator; b. Lynbrook, N.Y., Mar. 25, 1926; s. Samuel and Yetta (Huff) N.; m. Marjorie Lee Tallant, Jan. 1, 1956; children: David Wallace, Rebecca Jane. BA, NYU, 1950; MA, U. N.C., 1957, PhD, 1959. Statistician U.S. Bur. Census, Washington, 1950-53; chief edn. and social stratification br. U.S. Bur. Census, 1957-64; statistician USAF, Montgomery, Ala., 1953-54; rsch. asst. U. N.C., Chapel Hill, 1954-57; prof. sociology Fla. State U., Tallahassee, 1964-96; chmn. dept. sociology Fla. State U., 1968-71; dir. Center for Study of Population, 1967-82; disting. rsch. prof. Fla. State U., Tallahassee, 1994-96, disting. rsch. prof. emeritus, 1996—; mem. population adv. com. U.S. Bur. Census, 1978-81; cons. population divsn. Orgn. for Econ. Coop. and Devel., 1968-70, UNESCO, 1978-83, Indonesian Ministry of Population and Environment, Jakarta, 1988-90; Social Sci. Rsch. Coun., 1981-88. Author: (with John K. Folger) Education of the American Population, 1967, (with Susan Gustavus) Population: The Dynamics of Demographic Change, 1976, Nationality Groups and Social Stratification, 1981, (with Susan Philliber) Population: A Basic Orientation, 1983, (with Mary Powers) The Socioeconomic Approach to Status Measurement, 1983, Our Population: The Face of America, 1988, Understanding Population Change, 1994; editor: Demography, 1972-75; co-editor: (with David Sly, William Serow) International Handbook of Internal Migration, 1990, Handbook of International Migration, 1990; assoc. editor jour. Population Research and Policy Review, 1993-94. Mem. Am. Sociol. Assn. (chmn. sect. on population 1976-78), Population Assn. Am. (pres. 1979), Internat. Union for Sci. Study Population, Am. Statis. Assn. (chmn. social statistics sect. 1974), So. Sociol. Soc. (pres. 1981-82), So. Regional Demographic Group (vice chmn. 1974-75), Soc. Study Social Biology (bd. dirs. 1996—). Home: 820 Live Oak Plantation Rd Tallahassee FL 32312-2413

NAMBA, TATSUJI, physician, medical researcher; b. Changchun, China, Jan. 29, 1927; came to U.S., 1959, naturalized, 1968; s. Yosuke and Michino (Hinata) N. MD, Okayama U., Japan, 1950, PhD, 1955. Asst., lectr. medicine Okayama U. Med. Sch. and Hosp., 1955-62; rsch. assoc. Maimonides Med. Ctr., Bklyn., 1959-66; dir. neuromuscular labs. Maimonides Med. Ctr., 1966-70, dir. neuromuscular disease div., head electromyography clinic, 1966—; instr., asst. prof., assoc. prof. medicine SUNY, Bklyn., 1959-76, prof., 1976—; mem. med. adv. bd. Myasthenia Gravis Found., 1968—. Recipient commendation for rsch. and clin. activities on insecticide poisoning Minister Health and Welfare, Japanese Govt., 1958; Fulbright scholar, 1959-62. Fellow ACP, Royal Soc. Medicine; mem. AMA, Am. Acad. Neurology, Am. Soc. Pharmacology and Exptl. Therapeutics, Am. Soc. Clin. Pharmacology and Therapeutics, Am. Assn. Electrodiagnostic Medicine. Home: 4114 9th Ave Brooklyn NY 11232 Office: 4802 10th Ave Brooklyn NY 11219-2916

NAMBOODIRI, KRISHNAN, sociology educator; b. Valavoor, Ind., Nov. 13, 1929; s. Narayanan and Parvathy (Kutty) N.; m. Kadambari Kumari, Sept. 7, 1954; children: Unni (dec.), Sally. B.Sc., U. Kerala, 1950, M.Sc., 1953; M.A., U. Mich., 1962, Ph.D., 1963. Lectr. U. Kerala, India, 1953-55, 58-59; tech. asst. Indian Statis. Inst., Calcutta, 1955-58; reader demography U. Kerala, 1963-66; asst. prof. sociology U. N.C., Chapel Hill, 1966-67; asso. prof. U. N.C., 1967-73, prof., 1973-84, chmn. dept., 1975-80; Robert Lazarus prof. population studies Ohio State U., Columbus, 1984—, chmn. dept. sociology, 1989-93. Author: (with L.F. Carter and H.M. Blalock) Applied Multivariate Analysis and Experimental Designs, 1975; editor: Demography, 1975-78, Survey Sampling and Measurement, 1978, Auth. Matrix Algebra: An Introduction, 1984, (with C.M. Suchindran) Life Table Techniques and Their Applications, 1987, (with R.G. Corwin) Research in Sociology of Education and Socialization: Selected Methodological Issues, 1989, Demographic Analysis: A Stochastic Approach, 1991, (with R.G. Corwin) The Logic and Method of Macrosociology, 1993, Methods for Macrosociological Research, 1994, A Primer of Population Dynamics, 1996; contbr. articles to profl. jours. Fellow Am. Statis. Assn.; mem. Population Assn. Am. (dir. 1975-76), Internat. Union Sci. Study Population, Am. Sociol. Assn., Indian Sociol. Assn., Am. Statis. Assn., Sociol. Research Assn. Home: 3107 N Star Rd Columbus OH 43221-2366

NAMBU, YOICHIRO, physics educator; b. Toyko, Jan. 18, 1921; came to U.S., 1952; m. Chieko Hida, Nov. 3, 1945; 1 child, Jun-ichi. Research asst. U. Tokyo, 1945-49; prof. physics Osaka City U., Japan, 1950-56; mem. Inst. Advanced Study, 1952-54; research assoc. U. Chgo., 1954-56, mem. faculty, 1956—, prof. physics, 1958, Disting. prof., 1971—; emeritus, 1991—. Contbr. articles to profl. jours. Recipient J.J. Sakurai prize Am. Physical Soc., 1994, Wolf Prize in Physics, 1994. Mem. Nat. Acad. Scis., Am. Acad. Arts and Scis., Am. Phys. Soc. Office: Univ of Chicago Dept of Physics 5720 S Ellis Ave Chicago IL 60637-1434

NAMDARI, BAHRAM, surgeon; b. Oct. 26, 1939; s. Rostam and Sarvar Namdari; M.D., 1966; m. Kathleen Diane Wilmore, Jan. 5, 1976. Resident in gen. surgery St. John's Mercy Med. Ctr., St. Louis, 1969-73; fellow in cardiovascular surgery with Michael DeBakey, Baylor Coll. Medicine, Houston, 1974-75; practice medicine specializing in gen. and vascular surgery and surg. treatment of obesity, Milw., 1976—; mem. staff St. Mary's, St. Luke's, St. Michael, St. Francis hosps. (all Milw.); founder, pres. Famous Mealwaukee Foods Enterprises. Diplomate Am. Bd. Surgery. Fellow ACS, Internat. Coll. Surgeons; mem. Med. Soc. Milw. County, Milw. Acad. Surgery, Wis. Med. Soc., Wis. Surg. Soc., Royal Soc. Medicine Eng. (affiliate), Am. Soc. for Bariatric Surgery, AMA, World Med. Assn., Internat. Acad. Bariatric Medicine (founding mem.), Michael DeBakey Internat. Cardiovascular Soc. Contbr. articles to med. jours.; patentee med. instruments and other devices. Office: Great Lakes Med and Surg Ctr 6000 S 27th St Milwaukee WI 53221-4805

NAMORATO, CONO R., lawyer; b. Bklyn., July 2, 1942. BBA summa cum laude, Iona Coll., 1963; JD, Bklyn. Law Sch., 1968. Bar: N.Y. 1968, D.C. 1969. Atty. Tax Divsn., U.S. Dept. Justice, 1968-75, chief crim. sect., 1975-77, dep. asst. atty. gen., 1977-78; now ptnr. Caplin & Drysdale, Washington. Mem. ABA (numerous offices and coms.), D.C. Bar. Office: Caplin & Drysdale One Thomas Cir NW Washington DC 20005

NANAGAS, MARIA TERESITA CRUZ, pediatrician, educator; b. Manila, Jan. 21, 1946; came to U.S., 1971; d. Ambrosio and Maria (Pasamonte) Cruz; m. Victor N. Nanagas, Jr.; children: Victor III, Valerie, Vivian. BS, U. of the Philippines, 1965, MD, 1970. Diplomate Am. Bd. Pediat. Intern, resident St. Elizabeth's Hosp., Boston, 1971-74; fellow in ambulatory pediat. North Shore Children's Hosp., Salem, Mass., 1974-75; active staff medicine Children's Med. Ctr., Dayton, Ohio, 1976—, head divsn. gen. pediat., 1988-90, 95—, co-interim head ambulatory pediat., 1989-90, med. dir. ambulatory pediat., dir. ambulatory svcs., 1990—; clin. asst. prof. pediat. Wright State U., Dayton, 1977-83, clin. assoc. prof. pediat., 1983—, head divsn. gen. pediat., 1993—, selective dir., 1989—; dir., preceptor Wright State U. resident's family clinic Children's Med. Ctr., 1989—, attending physician family practice programs, 1978—. Active Miami Valley Lead Poisoning Prevention Coalition, 19926. Fellow Am. Acad. Pediat.; mem. Western Ohio Pediat. Soc. Office: Children's Med Ctr Health Clinic 1 Childrens Plz Dayton OH 45404-1898

NANAVATI, GRACE LUTTRELL, dancer, choreographer, instructor; b. Springfield, Ill., Oct. 2, 1951; d. Curtis Loren and Mary Grace (Leaverton) Luttrell; m. P.J. Nanavati, May 11, 1985; 1 child, William P. BA, Butler U., 1973; MA, Sangamon State U., 1978. Owner, dir. Dance Arts Studio, Inc., Springfield, 1975-76; artistic dir. Springfield (Ill.) Ballet Co., 1975-96, artistic dir. emeritus, 1997—; compulsory arts programming com. Sch. Dist. 186, Springfield, 1990—; dance panel Ill. Arts Coun., 1990-92, 94-97. Vol. Meml. Med. Ctr., Springfield, 1980-88. Named Women of Yr., YMCA, Springfield, 1982; recipient Mayor award for Arts, City of Springfield, 1985, Best of Springfield award Ill. Times, Springfield, 1990, Humanitarian award Sangamon County Med. Soc. Alliance, 1996, Chamber-Bus. award, 1996. Home: 1501 Williams Blvd Springfield IL 62704-2346 Office: Dance Arts Studio Inc 2820 Macarthur Blvd Springfield IL 62704-5017

NANCE, ALLAN TAYLOR, lawyer; b. Dallas, Jan. 31, 1933; s. A.Q. and Lois Rebecca (Taylor) N. BA, So. Meth. U., 1954, LLB, 1957; LLM, NYU, 1978. Bar: Tex. 1957, N.Y. 1961. With Simpson Thacher & Bartlett, N.Y.C., 1960-65; asst. counsel J.P. Stevens & Co., Inc., N.Y.C., 1965-70, sec., 1970-78, asst. gen. counsel, 1970-89; gen. counsel J.P. Stevens & Co. Inc. and WestPoint-Pepperell Inc., 1989-93; asst. gen. counsel WestPoint Stevens Inc., N.Y.C., 1993—. With USNR, 1957-59. Woodrow Wilson fellow Columbia U., 1959-60. Mem. Phi Beta Kappa. Home: 201 E 66th St New York NY 10021-6451 Office: WestPoint Stevens Inc 1185 Ave of the Americas New York NY 10036-2601

NANCE, BETTY LOVE, librarian; b. Nashville, Oct. 29, 1923; d. Granville Scott and Clara (Mills) Nance. BA in English magna cum laude, Trinity U., 1957; AM in Library Sci., U. Mich., 1958. Head dept. acquisitions Stephen F. Austin U. Library, Nacogdoches, Tex., 1958-59; librarian 1st Nat. Bank, Fort Worth, 1959-61; head catalog dept. Trinity U., San Antonio, 1961-63; head tech. processes U. Tex. Law Library, Austin, 1963-66; head catalog dept. Tex. A&M U. Library, College Station, 1966-69; chief bibliographic services Washington U. Library, St. Louis, 1970; head dept. acquisitions Va. Commonwealth U. Library, Richmond, 1971-73; head tech. processes Howard Payne U. Library, Brownwood, Tex., 1974-79; library dir. Edinburg (Tex.) Pub. Library, 1980-91; pres. Edinburg Com. for Salvation Army. Mem. ALA, Pub. Library Assn., Tex. Library Assn., Hidalgo County Library Assn. (v.p. 1980-81, pres. 1981-82), Pan Am. Round Table of Edinburg (corr. sec. 1986-88, assoc. dir. 1989-90), Edinburg Bus. and Profl. Womens Club (founding bd. dirs., pres. 1986-87, bd. dirs. 1987-88), Alpha Lambda Delta, Alpha Chi. Methodist. Club: Zonta Club of San Antonio (bd. dirs. 1996-97). Home: 5359 Fredericksburg Rd Apt 806 San Antonio TX 78229-3549

NANCE, CECIL BOONE, JR., lawyer; b. Marion, Ark., Feb. 14, 1925; s. Cecil Boone and Virginia (Essary) N.; m. Harriet Jane McGee, Aug. 7, 1948; children: Janet E., Cecil Boone III. J.D., U. Ark., 1951. Bar: Ark. 1951. Since practiced in West Memphis; mem. firm Nance, Nance & Fleming (named changed to Nance & Nance P.A.), 1951—; Chmn. bd. Fidelity Nat. Bank West Memphis, 1966-71; dir., gen. counsel E. Ark. Savs. & Loan Assn., 1970-83; spl. asso. justice Ark. Supreme Ct. Contbr. articles to profl. jours. Mem. Ark. Ho. of Reps., 1957-68; v.p. Ark. Constl. Conv., 1969. Served with AUS, 1943-46, 52-53. Decorated Bronze Star. Mem. Am. Bar Assn., Ark. Bar Assn. (chmn. jr. bar sect. 1957-58, dir. Ark. Law Rev. and Bar Assn. Jour. 1975). Methodist. Club: Rotarian (West Memphis) (pres. 1970-71). Home: 506 Roosevelt Ave West Memphis AR 72301-2961 Office: 203 W Broadway St West Memphis AR 72301-3903

NANCE, JAMES CLIFTON, business consulting company executive; b. Bryan, Tex., Sept. 2, 1957; s. Joseph Milton and Eleanor Glenn (Hanover) N.; m. Eileen Bonner, June 14, 1980; children: Jordan Eleanor, Robert Clifton, Kira Liane, Sarina Jenet. BS, U.S. Naval Acad., 1980. Registered quality sys. lead auditor Registrar Accreditation Bd. U.S.; cert. lead assessor Internat. Register of Cert. Auditors U.K. Quality assurance engr. Tex. Instruments, Inc., Dallas, 1985-86; people and asset effectiveness coord. Tex. Instruments, Inc., Plano, Tex., 1986-87; mgmt. cons. KPMG, Newport, R.I., 1987-88; sr. compliance auditor Litton Corp. Office, Beverly Hills, Calif., 1989; dir. continuous process improvement Litton Aero Products, Moorpark, Calif., 1989-93; v.p. P-E Handley-Walker, Inc., Independence, Ohio, 1993-97; mng. ptnr. Innovative Solutions Internat., Westfield Center, Ohio, 1997—; pres. Innovative Compliance Solutions, Westfield Center, 1997—; mem. Malcolm Baldridge Nat. Quality Award Bd. Examiners, 1993, 94. Troop com. chmn. Boy Scouts Am., Orlando, 1980-81, unit commr., Vallejo, Calif., 1984-85, varsity coach, McKinney, Tex., 1985-87, scouting coord., Newport, R.I., 1988, chmn. advancement com., Thousand Oaks, Calif., 1989-93, Medina, Ohio, 1994, asst. blazer leader, Medina, 1995, chmn. scout troop com., Wadsworth, Ohio, 1996—. Recipient Adult Varsity Letter, Boy Scouts Am., Circle Ten Coun., 1986, Scouter's Tng. award, 1987. Mem. Assn. for Quality and Participation (chpt. pres. 1992-93), Am. Soc. Quality Control (sr.), U.S. Naval Acad. Alumni Assn. (life), Sons of the Republic of Tex. (life). Avocations: golf, squash, running, genealogy, photography. Home: PO Box 259 9103 Westfield Rd Westfield Center OH 44251-0259 Office: Innovative Solutions Intl PO Box 279 Westfield Center OH 44251-0279

NANCE, JOHN JOSEPH, lawyer, writer, air safety analyst, broadcaster, consultant; b. Dallas, July 5, 1946; s. Joseph Turner and Margrette (Grubbs) N.; m. Benita Ann Priest, July 26, 1968; children: Dawn Michelle, Bridgitte Cathleen, Christopher Sean. BA, So. Meth. U., 1968, JD, 1969; grad., USAF Undergrad. Pilot Tng., Williams AFB, Ariz., 1971. Bar: Tex. 1970, U.S. Ct. Appeals (fed. cir.), 1994. News reporter, broadcaster, newsman various papers and stas. Honolulu and Dallas, 1957-66; radio news anchorman Sta. WFAA-AM, Dallas, 1966-70; newsman including on camera Sta. WFAA-TV, Dallas; pvt. practice law Dallas, 1970—; news dir. Newscom Network, Dallas, 1970; airline pilot Braniff Internat. Airways, Dallas, 1975-82, Alaska Airlines, Inc., Seattle, 1985—; chmn., pres. Exec. Transport, Inc., Tacoma, 1979-85; chmn., chief exec. officer EMEX Corp., Kent, Wash., 1987—; mng. ptnr. Phoenix Ptnrs., Ltd., Tacoma, Wash., 1995—; project devel. assoc. Columbia Tristar TV, 1997—; profl. speaker Human Mgmt., 1984—, Teamwork and Comms. in the Med. Profession; airline safety, advocate Ind. Cons., Broadcast Analyst, nationwide, 1986—, earthquake preparedness spokesman Ind. Cons., Broadcast Analyst, nationwide, 1987-94; dir. steering com. Found. for Issues Resolution in Sci. Tech., Seattle, 1987-89; speaker Northwestern Transp. Ctr. Deregulation and Safety Conf., 1987; cons. NOVA Why Planes Crash, PBS, 1987, ABC World News Tonight, 1994; aviation analyst ABC-TV, 1995—; spkr. in field. Author: Splash of Colors, 1984, Blind Trust, 1986 (Wash. Gov.'s award 1987), On Shaky Ground, 1988, Final Approach, 1990, What Goes Up, 1991, Scorpion Strike, 1982, Operating Handbook USAF Air Carrier Safety and Inspection Office, 1991, Phoenix Rising, 1994, Pandora's Clock, 1995, Medusa's Child, 1997; contbr. to Transportation Deregulation in the U.S., 1988; aviation editor: ABC Good Morning Am., 1995—; appeared in Sheep on the Runway Tacoma Little Theater, 1975; tech. advisor, appeared in Pandora's Clock NBC mini-series, 1996; prodr., writer, dir. USAF Video Prodns.: ANG Introduction to CRM, 1992, USAF SOC CRM Program, 1992, Test and Evaluation CRM, 1993, The Teamwork Connection, 1996; aviation analyst ABC Radio and TV Network, 1994—. Prs. Fox Glen Homeowners Assn., Tacoma, 1974-77; cons. Congl. Office Tech. Assessment, Tacoma, 1987; witness numerous air safety hearings U.S. Congress, Washington, 1986-88; bd. dirs. St. Charles Borromeo Sch., Tacoma, 1975-78; mem. Mayor's Vets. Task Force, Tacoma, 1991; bd. advisors Jour. Air Law and Commerce So. Meth. Sch. Law, 1995—, Pacific Northwest Writer's Conf., 1994—. Lt. col. USAF, 1970-75; lt. col. USAFR, 1975—, Persian Gulf. Decorated Merit Svc. medal; named Airline Safety Man of Year Wash. State Div. of Aeronautics, 1987. Fellow Chartered Inst. Transport (Canberra, Australia); mem. ABA, SAG, Tex. Bar Assn., Author's Guild Am., Res. Officers Assn. (life), Aircraft Owners' and Pilots' Assn., Phi Alpha Delta, Delta Chi. Home and Office: Phoenix Ptnrs Ltd 4512 87th Ave W Tacoma WA 98466-1920 Office: Phoenix Ptnrs Ltd PO Box 5476 Kent WA 98064-5476

NANCE, JOSEPH MILTON, history educator; b. Kyle, Tex., Sept. 18, 1913; s. Jeremiah Milton and Mary Louise (Hutchison) N.; m. Eleanor Glenn Hanover, Mar. 19, 1944; children: Jeremiah Milton, Joseph Hanover, James Clifton. B.A., U. Tex., 1935, M.A., 1936, Ph.D., 1941; cert. in naval communications, Harvard U., 1944. Tex. supr. Am. imprints, manuscripts and newspaper inventories U.S. Hist. Records Survey, 1938-40; instr. history Tex. A&M U., 1941-42, 46-47, asst. prof., 1947-51, assoc. prof., 1951-57, prof., 1957-58, prof., head dept. history and govt., 1958-68, head dept. history, 1968-73, prof., 1973—; instr. U.S. Naval Tng. Sch., College Station, 1942-43; vis. prof. history SW Tex. State Coll., San Marcos, summers 1956, 58. Author: Checklist of Texas Newspapers, 1813-1939, 1941, 3d edit., 1963, The Early History of Bryan and the Surrounding Area, 1962, After San Jacinto: The Texas-Mexican Frontier, 1836-1841, 1963, Attack and Counter-Attack, The Texas Mexican Frontier, 1842, 1964; co-author: Heroes of Texas, 1964; student guide to accompany A History of the American People (Graebner, Fite, White), 1971; also instr.'s man.; editor: Some Reflections upon Modern America, 1969, A Mier Expedition Diary: A Texan Prisoner's Account (Joseph D. McCutchan), 1978, Dare-Devils All: The Texas Mier Expedition, 1842-1844; mem. editl. bd.: Ariz. and the West, 1980-83; sr. editor: Handbook of Texas, 1983—; co-editor: The Handbook of Texas, 6 vols., 1996. Mem. Hood's Brigade-Bryan Centennial Com., 1960-62; panel participant Tex. Legis. Assembly, 1967; mem. Ann. Faculty seminar Standard Oil Co. Calif., summer 1959, Brazos County Hist. Commn., Tex., 1972—. Served to lt. (j.g.) USNR, 1943-46. Recipient 15th Ann. Writers Roundup award Theta Sigma Phi, 1963, Tex. Inst. Letters award, 1964, Walter Prescott Webb award in history U. Tex., 1967, AMOCO Disting. Research award Tex. A&M U., 1979, History award and medal DAR, 1985; 3 ann. scholarships established in his name at Baylor U. Coll. Law, 1979—; ann. lectureship established in his honor Tex. A&M U., 1980—; named Knight of San Jacinto Sons of Republic, 1983. Fellow Tex. State Hist. Assn. (exec. coun.), East Hist. Assn., East Tex. Hist. Assn. (dir. 1980-83); mem. Tex. Inst. Letters, Am. Hist. Assn., So. Hist. Assn., W. Tex. Hist. Assn. (exec. coun., book rev. editor 1975-81, v.p. 1978-81, pres. 1981-82), Orgn. Am. Historians, Western History Assn., Am. Heritage Soc., Am. Studies Assn. Tex. (pres. 1969), Southwestern Social Sci. Assn., Central Tex. Area Writers Conf., Nat. Geog. Soc., Phi Beta Kappa, Phi Kappa Phi, Phi Alpha Theta. Home: 1403 Post Oak Cir College Station TX 77840-2322

NANCE, MARTHA MCGHEE, rehabilitation nurse; b. Huntington, W.Va., Jan. 24, 1944; d. Orme Winford and Sadie Mae (Dudley) McGhee; m. John Edgar Nance, Mar. 17, 1990; children: Laura Beckner, Suzie Brickey. RN, St. Mary's Sch. Nursing, Huntington, W.Va., 1980; student, Marshall U., Huntington, W.Va., 1978-88. Cert. rehab. nurse, cert. case mgr. Surg. head nurse Huntington Hosp. Inc., nursing supr.; quality assurance dir. Am. Hosp. for Rehab., Huntington, 1988-89, DON, 1989-90; rehab. charge nurse Am. Putnam Nursing and Rehab. Ctr., Hurricane, W.Va., 1990—; mgr. health svcs. Mountain State Blue Cross/Blue Shield, Charleston, W.Va., 1995—, mgr. precert., case mgmt. and med. rev., 1995—. Mem. Assn. for Practitioners in Infection Control. Home: RR 4 Box 100 Hurricane WV 25526-9351

NANCE, MARY JOE, secondary education educator; b. Carthage, Tex., Aug. 7, 1921; d. F. F. and Mary Elizabeth (Knight) Born; m. Earl C. Nance, July 12, 1946; 1 child, David Earl. BBA, North Tex. State U., 1953; postgrad., Northwestern State U. La., 1974; ME, Antioch U., 1978. Tchr., Port Isabel (Tex.) Ind. Sch. Dist., 1953-79; tchr. English, Tex., 1965, Splendora (Tex.) High Sch., 1979-80, McLeod, Tex., 1980-81, Bremond, Tex., 1981-84. Vol. tchr. for Indian students, 1964-65, 79. Served with WAAC, 1942-43, WAC 1945. Recipient Image Maker award Carthage C. of C., 1984; cert. bus. educator. Mem. ASCD, NEA, Nat. Bus. Edn. Assn., Tex. Tchrs. Assn., Tex. Bus. Tchrs. Assn. (cert. of appreciation 1978), Nat. Women's Army Corps Vets. Assn., Air Force Assn. (life), Gwinnett Hist. Soc., Hist. Soc. Panola County, Panola County Hist. & Geneal. Assn., Coun. for Basic Edn., Nat. Hist. Soc., Tex. Coun. English Tchrs. Baptist.

NANCE, RETHA HARDISON, reading specialist; b. Athens, Ala., July 18, 1952; d. Roy King and Bertie Mae (Pettus) McLemore; m. Amos Wayne Hardison, July 23, 1971 (dec. Mar. 1983); children: Genoa, Karol, Nancy; m. Robert Arthur Nance, May 30, 1984. BS in Edn., U. Ctrl. Okla., 1987, MEd summa cum laude, 1988; postgrad., U. Va., Charlottesville, 1994. Cert. tchr. reading, Okla. Reading specialist Moore (Okla.) Pub. Schs., 1987—; officer Moore Sch. Dist. Profl. Devel. Com., 1990—, chair 1997; mem. Moo Pub. Schs. Supts. Adv. Com., 1996—; participant Ann. Monticello-Stratford Hall Summer Seminar for Tchrs., U. Va., Charlottesville, 1994, Colonial Williamsburg Summer Tchg. Inst., 1995. Co-founder We the People Living Memls., Oklahoma City, 1987—. Recipient Liberty award Downtown Oklahoma City, 1990. Mem. Internat. Reading Assn., Okla. Reading Assn., Ctrl. Okla. Reading Coun. (pres. 1992), Christian Educators Assn. Internat. Avocations: reading, cross stitching, traveling. Home: PO Box 405 Wheatland OK 73097-0405

NANCE, ROBERT LEWIS, oil company executive; b. Dallas, July 10, 1936; s. Melvin Renfro Nance and Ruth Natlie (Seibert) Nowlin; m. Penni Jane Warfel; children: Robert Scott, Amy Louise, Catherine Leslie. BS, So. Meth. U., 1959; LLD (hon.), Rocky Mountain Coll., 1989. V.p. geology Oliver & West Cons., Dallas, 1960-66; ptnr. Nance & Larue Cons., Dallas, 1966-69; pres., CEO Nance Petroleum Corp., Billings, Mont., 1969—; bd. dirs. First Interstate Bank Commerce, MDU Resources, Rocky Mountain Coll., Billings, chmn., 1986-91; mem. Nat. Petroleum Coun., 1992-94; chmn. Petroleum Technology Transfer Coun. Coun. pres. Am. Luth. Ch., Billings, 1980; trustee, chmn. Deaconess Med. Ctr., Billings; chmn. Deaconess Billings Clinic Healty Sys. Recipient Hall of Fame award Rocky Mountain Coll. Alumni, 1987, Disting. Svc. Trusteeship, Assn. Governing Bds. Univs. Colls., 1988. Mem. Am. Assn. Petroleum Geologists, Ind. Petroleum Assn. Am. (exec. com., nat. bd. govs.), Ind. Petroleum Assn. Mountain States (v.p. Mont. 1977-79), Mont. Petroleum Assn., Hilands Golf Club, Billings Petroleum Club. Avocations: fly fishing, scuba diving, skiing. Office: Nance Petroleum Corp PO Box 7168 550 N 31st St Billings MT 59103

NANCE, TONY MAX-PERRY, designer, illustrator; b. Montclair, N.J., Feb. 25, 1955; s. Perry Hedgeman and Ida Delea (King) N.; m. June Anne Percival, Oct. 31, 1986 (div. May 1994); children: Jack Anthony, Jacqlene Angela, Jihad Conan. Student, U. Denver, 1975; BA, N.Y. Sch. Visual Arts, 1976, postgrad., 1980-81; postgrad., N.J. Inst. Tech., 1977-78, Rutgers U., 1980-82. Design engr. Automation Controls, Montclair, 1975-77; artist, designer Greg Copeland, Inc., Fairfield, N.J., 1976-79; owner, designer Stalhaus, Inc., Montclair, 1976-80; editor contemporary ads Graphics Mag., N.Y.C., 1977-79; illustrator, artist L.C. Graphics, Inc., Clifton, N.J., 1979-80; carrier supr. Montclair Post Office, 1980-93; owner, design engr. Decotech Alternations, Orange, N.J., 1984—, Electronics Tech-Atlas Soundolier, 1993—, Machine Tech-Atlas Soudolier, 1995—. Editor Graphis mag.; artist, art dir. (album covers) Bhang, 1984 Ron Smyth I, 1986; artist, illustrator (album cover, tour and advt. promotion) Passport Greatest Hits/Doldinger, 1977 (album cover, internat. poster) Zap and the Wires-The Saga of the Black Silk Jetmen; producer, illustrator (album cover) The Little Things by Dogs Eating Glass with Loren Tindall; one man shows include Discovery Galleries, Montclair, 1978, The Gallery, Fairfield, 1979, Broghton Galleries, Bloomfield, N.J., 1983, Scotland Galleries, Laurinburg, N.C., 1993; contbr. artist mags. Verotika, 1996, Hard Core, 1996; various musical and graphic copyrights; mem. Southern Ambition band, 1993-97, Southern Fried Dogs band, 1996-97; creator comic strip Appliances, 1995-97. Art dir. Montclair Coalition for Performing Arts, Montclair, 1982. Mem. Soc. for Creative Anachronism (founding assoc.), Local Musicians Union, Nat. Rifle Assn., Mensa, Scotland County Art Guild, Scotland County Chamber Music Soc., Porsche Club Am., N.C. SCCA. Avocations: music, prop and special effect design, collecting plastic toys, computer software design, collecting guitars. Office: NANCEart NANCEtech 1209 N Main St Laurinburg NC 28352-2715

NANCE, WILLIAM BENNETT, economic development specialist; b. Garland, N.C., Nov. 18, 1944; s. Lemon Francis Nance and Hattie McCoy Jones; m. Mildred Elaine McKiever, Dec. 26, 1971; children: William Bennett, David Christopher. BA in Polit. Sci., N.C. Ctrl. U., Durham, 1966; postgrad., Swarthmore Coll., 1966-67; MA in Internat. Affairs, George Washington U., 1979; MA in Pub. Adminstrn., Harvard U., 1989. Asst. program officer, Turkey AID, Ankara, 1971-75; asst. desk officer, Syria AID, Washington, 1975-77, officer-in-charge, Lebanon, 1977-79; chief Office of Program/Planning AID, Kathmandu, Nepal, 1979-83; officer-in-charge, Thailand AID, Washington, 1983-86, officer-in-charge, Philippines, 1986-88, officer-in-charge, Bangladesh, 1989-90; chief Office of Program AID, Rabat, Morocco, 1990-92; rep. to Mongolia AID, Ulaanbaatar, 1992-94; pres. The AMIDA Group, Inc., Chevy Chase, Md., 1994—. Recipient Presdl. award Pres. of U.S., 1993. Avocations: reading, chess, tennis. Home: 4105 Oliver St Chevy Chase MD 20815

NANDA, VED PRAKASH, law educator, university official; b. Gujranwala, India, Nov. 20, 1934; came to U.S., 1960; s. Jagan Nath and Attar (Kaur) N.; m. Katharine Kunz, Dec. 18, 1982; 1 child, Anjali. MA, Punjab U., 1952; LLB, U. Delhi, 1955, LLM, 1958; LLM, Northwestern U., 1962; postgrad., Yale U., 1962-65. Asst. prof. law U. Denver, 1965-68, assoc. prof., 1968-70, prof. law, dir. Internat. Legal Studies Program, 1970—, Thompson G. Marsh prof. law, 1987—, Evans Univ. prof., 1992—, asst. provost, 1993-94, vice provost, 1994—; vis. prof. Coll. Law, U. Iowa, Iowa City, 1974-75, Fla. State U., 1973, U. San Diego, 1979, U. Colo., 1992; disting. vis. prof. internat. law Chgo. Kent Coll. Law, 1981, Calif. We. Sch. Law, San Diego, 1983-84; disting. vis. scholar Sch. Law, U. Hawaii, Honolulu, 1986-87; cons. Solar Energy Rsch. Inst., 1978-81, Dept. Energy, 1980-81. Author: (with David Pansius) Litigation of International Disputes in U.S. Courts, 1987; editor: (with M. Cherif Bassiouni) A Treatise on International Criminal Law, 2 vols., 1973, Water Needs for the Future, 1977; (with George Shepherd) Human Rights and Third World Development, 1985; (with others) Global Human Rights, 1981, The Law of Transnational Business Transactions, 1981, World Climate Change, 1983, Breach and Adaption of International Contracts, 1992, World Debt and Human Conditions, 1993, Europe Community Law After 1992, 1993, International Environmental Law and Policy, 1995; (with William M. Evan) Nuclear Proliferation and the Legality of Nuclear Weapons, 1995, (with others) European Union Law After Maastricht, 1996, (with S.P. Sinha) Hindu Law and Legal Theory, 1996; editor, contbr.: Refugee Law and Policy, 1989; editl. bd. Jour. Am. Comparative Law, Indian Jour. Internat. Law. Co-chmn. Colo. Pub. Broadcasting Fedn., 1977-78; mem. Gov.'s Commn. on Pub. Telecommunications, 1980-82. Mem. World Jurist Assn. (v.p. 1991—, pres. World Assn. Law Profs. 1987-93), UN Assn. (v.p. Colo. divsn. 1973-76, pres. 1986-88, 93—, nat. coun. UNA-USA 1990—, mem. governing bd. UNA-USA 1995—), World Fedn. UN Assns. (vice-chmn. 1995—), Am. Assn. Comparative Study Law (bd. dirs. 1980—), Am. Soc. Internat. Law (v.p. 1987-88, exec. coun. 1969-72, 81-84, bd. rev. and devel. 1988-91, hon. v.p. 1995—), Assn. Am. Law Schs., U.S. Inst. Human Rights, Internat. Law Assn. (mem. exec. com. 1986—), Colo. Coun. Internat. Orgns. (pres. 1988-90), Assn. U.S. Mems. Internat. Inst. Space Law (bd. dirs., mem. exec. com. 1980-88), Internat. Acad. Comparative Law (assoc.), Order St. Ives (pres.), Rotary, Cactus. Office: U Denver Coll Law 1900 Olive St Denver CO 80220-1857

NANGLE, CAROLE FOLZ, counselor; b. Evansville, Ind.; d. Francis Jacob Jr. and Mary Josephine (Metzger) Folz; m. James Francis Nangle Jr., Nov. 21, 1953; children: Cynthia Nangle Bitting, Mary Nangle Boughton, Catherine Nangle Howland. BS, Maryville Coll. Sacred Heart, 1953; MA in Counseling, Webster U., 1985. Substitute tchr. All Saints Cath. Parish, 1962-66; counselor, tchr. Cath. Women's League Day Care Ctr., 1965-74; asst. tchr. art St. Joseph Inst. for Deaf, 1980-81; tutor, counselor St. Vincent German Home, 1979-82; counselor Cath. Family Svcs., 1985—; project Rachel Archdiocese of St. Louis, 1989—. Fundraiser Cath. Women's LEague, 1965-68, fundraiser chmn., 1966, bd. dirs., 1965-71; bd. dirs. Washington U. St. Louis-Newman Club, 1969-74; mem. aux. bd. St. Louis Hosp., 1981-83; mem. alumnae bd. Villa Duchesne Acad. of Sacred Heart, 1963-70, 80-86; weekly fin. accts. Christ the King Parish, 1958-60; bd. govs. Lake Forest Subdivsn., 1982-84, directory, 1982; alumnae class rep. Maryville Coll., 1960-69; bd. dirs. Scholar Program St. Louis, 1966-68, co-chmn., 1967. Mem. Am. Counseling Assn., Assn. Adult Devel. and Aging, Mensa (nat. scholar program 1981-82, chmn. nat. scholar program 1981). Roman Catholic. Avocations: bridge, interior decoration, child care.

NANGLE, JOHN FRANCIS, federal judge; b. St. Louis, June 8, 1922; s. Sylvester Austin and Thelma (Bank) N.; m. Jane Adams, June 7, 1986; 1 child, John Francis Jr. AA, Harris Tchrs. Coll., 1941; BS, U. Mo., 1943; JD, Washington U., St. Louis, 1948. Bar: Mo. 1948. Pvt. practice law Clayton, 1948-73; judge U.S. Dist. Ct., St. Louis, 1973—, chief judge, 1983-90, sr. judge, 1990—; sr. judge Ga., 1991—. Mem. Mo. Rep. Com., 1958-73; mem. St. Louis County Rep. Cen. Com., 1958-73, chmn., 1960-61; pres. Mo. Assn. Reps., 1961, Reps. Vets. League, 1960; mem. Rep. Nat. Com., 1972-73; bd. dirs. Masonic Home Mo. With AUS, 1943-46. Named Mo. Republican of Year John Marshall Club, 1970, Mo. Republican of Year Mo. Assn. Reps., 1971; recipient Most Disting. Alumnus award Harris-Stowe Coll., Most Disting. Alumnus award Washington U. Sch. Law, 1986. Mem. ABA, Am. Judicature Soc., Legion of Honor DeMolay, Mo. Bar Assn., St. Louis Bar Assn., St. Louis County Bar Assn., 8th Cir. Jud. Coun., Jud. Conf. U.S. (apptd. mem. exec. com.), Jud. Panel on Multidist. Litigation (chmn.). Address: Washington DC Fed Judicial Bldg Washington DC 20002

NANK, LOIS RAE, financial executive; b. Racine, Wis., Jan. 6; d. Walter William August and Lanora Elizabeth (Freymuth) N. BS in Econs., U. Wis., 1962; postgrad. in profl. mgmt., Fla. Inst. Tech., 1977. Contract specialist U.S. Naval Ordnance Sta., Forest Park, Ill., 1963-66, U.S. Army Munitions Command, Joliet, Ill., 1966-72; plans/program specialist U.S. Army Munitions Command, Joliet, 1972-73, U.S. Army Armament Command, Rock Island, Ill., 1973-77; chief budget office U.S. Army Auto Log Mgmt. System Act, St. Louis, 1977-81; sr. budget analyst U.S. Army Materiel Command, Alexandria, Va., 1981-87; sr. fin. mgr. Def. Mapping Agy., Reston, Va., 1987-93; cons. Springfield, Va, 1993-96, Leesburg, Fla., 1996—. Coun. mem. chairperson bldg. com. Bread of Life Luth. Ch., Springfield, Va., 1986-90, Christ Luth. Ch., Fairfax, Va., 1990—; bd. dirs. Cedar Wood Homeowners' Assn., Bettendorf, Iowa, 1975-77, Oak Homeowners' Assn., Chesterfield, Mo., 1980-81. Mem. NAFE, Am. Soc. Mil. Comptrollers, Va. Assn. Female Execs., Order of Ea. Star. Avocations: travel, people, fashion, interior design, architecture.

NANNA, MICHELE, cardiologist, educator; b. Mola di Bari, Puglia, Italy, Mar. 21, 1953; came to U.S., 1981; naturalized, 1985; s. Giovanni and Maria (Francese) N.; m. Barbara Luise McKnight, Aug. 5, 1981 (div. Feb. 1991); children: Michael Giovanni Jr., Anna Maria; m. Nancy J. Konovalov, Nov. 14, 1991; 1 child Giovanni Jacob Michele. MD summa cum laude, U. Bari, Italy, 1978. Lic. physician, Italy, Calif., N.Y. Intern Ospedale Conzorziale, Bari, 1978-81; clin. clerkship U. Soc. Calif. Med. Ctr., L.A., 1982-83; instr. medicine, fellow in cardiovascular disease U. So. Calif., 1983-86; asst. prof. medicine U. Rochester, N.Y., 1986-88, Albert Einstein Coll. Medicine, Bronx, N.Y., 1988-94; assoc. prof. of med., 1994—; dir. care unit Bronx Mcpl. Hosp. Ctr., 1988-92; dir. lab. Montefiore Med. Ctr., Bronx, N.Y., 1988—; cardiology cons. Monroe Community Hosp., Rochester, 1987-88; mem. coms. Bronx Mcpl. Hosp. Ctr., 1988—, chmn. com., 1990-92. Editor jour. Ultrasound in Medicine and Biology, 1986—; editor-in-chief Jour. Cardiovascular Diagnosis and Procedures, 1993—; contbr. chpts. to books and articles to profl. jours. Grantee NIH, 1987, Whitaker Found., Genetech Inc., Bristol-Myers Squibb, Inc. Mem. AMA, Am. Heart Assn., Am. Coll. Cardiology, N.Y. Athletic Club. Republican. Roman Catholic. Avocations: boating, swimming, jogging. Office: Albert Einstein Coll Med Montefiore Med Ctr 111 E 210th St Bronx NY 10467-2401

NANNE, LOUIS VINCENT, professional hockey team executive; b. Sault Ste. Marie, Ont., Can., June 2, 1941; s. Michael and Evelyn N.; m. Francine Yvette Potvin, Aug. 27, 1962; children: Michelle, Michael, Marc, Marty. B.S. in Mktg., U. Minn., 1963. Mem. Minn. North Stars hockey club, 1967-78, v.p., gen. mgr., 1978-88, pres., 1988-91; sr. v.p. Piper Capital Mgmt., Mpls., 1991—; bd. govs. Nat. Hockey League, 1981-91; mem. internat. com. USA Hockey. Bd. dirs. Mpls. Community Coll. Found., 1986-90. Recipient Lester Patrick award NHL, 1989; inducted into U. Minn. Hall of Fame, U.S. Hockey Heritage Hall of Fame award. Mem. Interlachen Country Club (bd. dirs. 1992-95), Spring Hill Golf Club (bd. dirs. 1996—). Roman Catholic. Office: Voyageur Asset Mgmt 90 S 7th St Minneapolis MN 55402-3903

NANNEY, DAVID LEDBETTER, genetics educator; b. Abingdon, Va., Oct. 10, 1925; s. Thomas Grady and Pearl (Ledbetter) N.; m. Jean Kelly, June 15, 1951; children: Douglas Paul, Ruth Elizabeth Beshears. A.B., Okla. Bapt. U., 1946; Ph.D., Ind. U., 1951; Laurea honoris causa, U. Pisa, Italy, 1994. Asst. prof. zoology U. Mich., Ann Arbor, 1951-56; asso. prof. U. Mich., 1956-58; prof. zoology U. Ill., Urbana-Champaign, 1959-76; prof. genetics and devel. U. Ill., 1976-86, prof. ecology, ethology and evolution, 1987-91, prof. emeritus, 1991—; sr. postdoctoral fellow Calif. Inst. Tech., 1958-59; predoctoral fellow NIH, Ind. U., 1949-51. Author: (with Herbert Stern) The Biology of Cells, 1965, Experimental Ciliatology, 1980. Recipient Disting. Alumnus award Okla. Bapt. U., 1972; named Disting. Lectr. Sch. Life Scis., U. Ill., 1981; Preisträger, Alexander von Humboldt Stiftung, Fed. Republic Germany, 1984. Fellow AAAS, Am. Acad. Arts and Scis.; mem. Genetics Soc. Am., Am. Genetic Assn. (pres. 1982), Soc. Protozoologists. Home: 703 W Indiana Ave Urbana IL 61801-4835 Office: U Ill Dept Ecology Ethology and Evolution 505 S Gregory St Urbana IL 61801

NANTO, ROXANNA LYNN, marketing professional, management consultant; b. Hanford, Calif., Dec. 17, 1952; d. Lawson Gene Brooks and Bernice (Page) Jackson; m. Harvey Ken Nanto, Mar. 23, 1970; 1 child, Shea Kiyoshi. AA, Chemeketa Community Coll., 1976; BSBA, Idaho State U., 1978. PBX operator Telephone Answer Bus. Svc., Moses Lake, Wash., 1965-75; edn. coord. MimiCassia Community Edn., Rupert, Idaho, 1976-77; office mgr. Lockwood Corp., Rupert, Idaho, 1977-78; cost acct. Keyes Fibre Co., Wenatchee, Wash., 1978-80; acctg. office mgr. Armstrong & Armstrong, Wenatchee, Wash., 1980-81; office mgr. Cascade Cable Constrn. Inc., East Wenatchee, Wash., 1981-83; interviewer, counselor Wash. Employment Security, Wenatchee, 1983-84; pres. chief exec. officer Regional Health Care Plus, East Wenatchee, 1986-88; dist. career coord. Eastmont Sch. Dist., East Wenatchee, 1984-90; prin. Career Cons., 1988-90; exec. dir. Wenatchee Valley Coll. Found., 1990-91; ednl. cons. Sunbelt Consortium, East Wenatchee, 1991-93; cons. CC Cons. Assocs., 1993—; ptnr. Cmty. Devel. Mktg. and Mgmt. Resource Group, Wenatchee, Wash., 1994—; also bd. dirs. Cmty. Devel. Mktg. and Mgmt. Resource Group, Wenatchee; speaker North Cen. Washington Profl. Women, Wenatchee, 1987, Wen Career Women's Network, Wenatchee, 1990, Wenatchee Valley Rotary, 1990, Meeting the Challenge of Workforce 2000, Seattle, 1993; cons., speaker Wash. State Sch. Dirs., Seattle, 1987; speaker Wenatchee C. of C., 1989; sec. Constrn. Coun. of North Cen. Washington, Wenatchee, 1981-83; bd. dirs.

Gen. Vocat. Adv. Bd., Wenatchee, 1986-88, Washington Family Ind. Program, Olympia, 1989—; mem. econ. devel. coun. Grant County, 1992—; ptnr. low income housing devel. Bus. Cons. & Rsch., Wenatchee, 1996—. Mem. at large career Women's Network, 1984—, mem. Econ. Devel. Coun. of No. Cen. Washington; mem. Steering Com. to Retain Judge Small. Recipient Nat. Paragon award, 1991; grantee Nat. Career Devel. Guidelines Wash. State, 1989; named Wenatchee Valley Coll. Vocat. Contbr. of Yr., 1991. Fellow Dem. Women's Club; mem. Nat. Assn. Career Counselors, Nat. Assn. Pvt. Career Counselors, Nat. Coun. Resource Devel., NCW Estate Planning Coun. Avocations: self improvement books, staff and organizational development, motivational audio tapes. Home and Office: 2961 Riviera Blvd Malaga WA 98828-9733

NANTS, BRUCE ARLINGTON, lawyer; b. Orlando, Fla., Oct. 26, 1953; s. Jack Arlington and Louise (Hulme) N. BA, U. Fla., 1974, JD, 1977. Bar: Fla. 1977. Asst. state's atty. State Atty.'s Office, Orlando, 1977-78; pvt. practice, Orlando, 1979—. Columnist The Law and You, 1979-80. Auctioneer pub. TV sta., 1979; campaign coord. cen. Fla. steering com. Bob Dole for Pres., 1988; bd. dirs. Cystic Fibrosis Found. Mem. Acad. Fla. Trial Lawyers, Am. Arbitration Assn., Fellowship Christian Athletes (past bd. dirs. Cen. Fla.), Tiger Bay Club Cen. Fla., Orlando Touchdown Club, Fla. Blue Key, Omicron Delta Kappa, Phi Beta Kappa, Phi Delta Theta. Democrat. Baptist. Avocations: tennis, golf, swimming, scuba diving. Home: 1112 Country Ln Orlando FL 32804-6934 Office: PO Box 547871 Orlando FL 32854-7871

NANZ, ROBERT AUGUSTUS, biochemist; b. Balt., Apr. 3, 1915; s. Theodore and Viola (Wolff) N.; 1 child from previous marriage: Richard K. (dec.); m. Paula M. Olsen, June 14, 1986. BS, Rutgers U., 1937; MS, Columbia U., 1939. Asst. rsch. coord. The Borden Co., N.Y.C., 1946-47; dir. food tech. dept. Foster D. Snell Inc., N.Y.C., 1947-50; food technologist Fla. Citrus Canners Coop., Lake Wales, 1950-53, Crown Can Co., Orlando, Fla., 1952-53; pres., gen. mgr. Fla. Chemists & Engrs., Orlando, 1953-62; aerospace technologist NASA Manned Spacecraft Ctr., Houston, 1962-68; project asst. U.S. Dept. Interior, Bur. Comml. Fisheries, Washington, 1968-69; dir. tech. devel. Aquatic Scis. Inc., Boca Raton, Fla., 1969-71; instr. Lynn U., 1971-75, Palm Beach Community Coll., Lake Worth, Fla., 1975-78; cons. in foods Boca Raton, 1979—. 2d lt. U.S. Army, 1943-46. Mem. Inst. Food Technologists, Kiwanis (pres. 1975-76). Republican. Presbyterian. Avocations: travel, writing, reading, walking. Home: 23371 Blue Water Cir C206 Boca Raton FL 33433

NANZ, ROBERT HAMILTON, petroleum consultant; b. Shelbyville, Ky., Sept. 14, 1923; s. Robert Hamilton and Willie Virginia (O'Brien) N.; m. Norma Lee Peters, Dec. 21, 1944; children—Robert H., Loren P. B.A. in Geology, Miami U., Oxford, Ohio, 1944; Ph.D., U. Chgo., 1952. With Shell Oil Co., 1947-83; exploration mgr. Shell Oil Co., Denver, 1964-66; exploration mgr. Pacific Coast area Shell Oil Co., Los Angeles, 1966-67; dir. exploration research Shell Oil Co., Houston, 1959-64, v.p. exploration and prodn. research center, 1967-70; v.p. exploration Shell Oil Co., N.Y.C., Houston, 1970-75; v.p. Western exploration and prodn. ops. Shell Oil Co., Houston, 1975-81, v.p. tech., 1982-83. Fellow Geol. Soc. Am.; mem. Am. Petroleum Inst. (past chmn. gen. com. exploration affairs, chmn. public lands task force), Am. Assn. Petroleum Geologists (select com. on OCS). Presbyterian. Clubs: Lakeside Country (Houston); Dearborn Country (Ind.). Home: 10102 Briar Dr Houston TX 77042-1209

NAPADENSKY, HYLA SARANE, engineering consultant; b. Chgo., Nov. 12, 1929; d. Morris and Minnie (Litz) Siegel; m. Arnaldo I. Napadensky; children: Lita, Yafa. BS in Math., U. Chgo., MS in Math. Design analysis engineer Internat. Harvester Co., Chgo., 1952-57; dir. rsch. Ill. Inst. Tech. Rsch. Inst., Chgo., 1957-88; v.p. Napadensky Energetics Inc., Evanston, Ill., 1988-94; engring. cons., Lutsen, Minn., 1994—. Contbr. numerous articles to profl. jours. Bd. overseers Armour Coll. Engring. Ill. Inst. Tech., 1988-93. Mem. NAE, Combustion Inst., Sigma Xi. Home and Office: 3284 W Highway 61 Lutsen MN 55612-9537

NAPIER, CAMERON MAYSON FREEMAN, historic preservationist; b. Shanghai, China, Dec. 5, 1931; d. Hamner Garland and Cameron Middleton (Brame) Freeman; m. John Hawkins Napier III, Sept. 11, 1964. Student, L'Ecole des Artes Municipale, Paris, 1950-51; BA, U. Ala., 1955. Photographer's asst. Scott, Demott & Perry, Montgomery, Ala., 1951; art dir. WCOV-TV, Montgomery, 1955; self-employed graphic designer Dallas, 1956-64; self-employed designer Alexandria, Va., 1965-71; restoration chmn. White House Assn. Ala., Montgomery, 1973-76, 1st vice regent, 1976-80, regent, 1980—; co-founder Friends of Stratford Hall for No. Va., Alexandria, late 1960s; docent chmn. Lee's Boyhood Home, Alexandria, late 1960s; bd. dirs. Landmarks Found., Montgomery, 1971-75; advisor Conde Charlotte House, Mobile, Ala., 1994-95. Author, designer booklet: The First White House of the Confederacy, 1978 (nat. printers award 1979). Bd. dirs. English Speaking Union, Montgomery, 1980-83. Recipient awards of excellence Advt. Artists Assn., Dallas, 1960, 61, 62, disting. svc. award Ala. Hist. Commn., Montgomery, 1977, cert. commendation Gov. Ala., 1986; named hon. first lady the Gov.'s wife, Montgomery, 1985. Mem. Nat. Soc. Colonial Dames in Am. (hist. properties com. 1994-95), Antiquarian Soc. (pres. 1981-82), Sojourners Lit. Club (past pres.), United Daus. of the Confederacy (Jefferson Davis award, Winnie Davis award), Am. Soc. Most venerable Order of the Hosp. of St. John of Jerusalem (assoc. officer sister 1995), Sovereign Mil. Order Temple of Jerusalem (aumoniere 1995, dame comdr. 1996), Militi Templi Scotia (dame 1993), Daus. of Barons Runnymede, Nat. Soc. Magna Carta Dames, Soc. descendants of Colonial Clergy, Kappa Delta. Episcopalian. Avocations: crossword puzzles, afternoon tea. Office: First White House Confed 644 Washington St Montgomery AL 36104-4347

NAPIER, JOHN LIGHT, lawyer; b. Blenheim, S.C., May 16, 1947; s. John Light and Miriam (Keys) N.; m. Pamela Ann Caughman, June 12, 1971; 1 child, Page. A.B., Davidson (N.C.) Coll., 1969; J.D., U. S.C., 1972. Bar: S.C. 1972, U.S. Dist. Ct. 1972, U.S. Ct. Appeals 1975, U.S. Tax Ct. 1975, U.S. Supreme Ct. 1978, D.C. 1983, U.S. Ct. Fed. Claims 1987. U.S. senatorial counsel and asst., 1972-78; atty. Goldberg, Cottingham Easterling & Napier, P.A., Bennettsville, S.C., 1978-80, 83-84; mem. 97th Congress 6th Dist. S.C., mem. agr. com., asst. whip, mem. vets. affairs com., 1981-83; ptnr. Napier & Jennings, Bennettsville, S.C., 1984-86; judge U.S. Ct. Fed. Claims, Washington, 1986-89; ptnr. McNair Law Firm, P.A., Washington and Columbia, S.C., 1989-95; of counsel Winston & Strawn, Washington, 1995—; mem. Commn. on Grievance and Discipline, S.C. Supreme Ct., 1984-86; chmn. fee dispute panel 4th Jud. Cir. S.C., 1984-86; nat. adv. coun. U.S. Ct. Fed. Claims, 1989—; pvt. judge The Pvt. Adjudication Ctr., Inc., Duke U., 1992; outside spl. counsel U.S. House Reps. House Adminstrn. Com., 1992. Active local United Way, Boy Scouts Am.; pres. Marlborough Hist. Soc., 1978-80. Served as officer USAR, 1969-77. Recipient Disting. Service award Marlboro County Jaycees, 1980. Mem. ABA, S.C. Bar Assn., Marlboro County Bar Assn., D.C. Bar Assn. Republican. Presbyterian. Office: Winston & Strawn Madison Office Bldg 1400 L St NW Washington DC 20005-3509

NAPIER, WILLIAM JAMES, JR., marine oil and gas construction consultant; b. Dallas, July 19, 1952; s. William James and Frankie (Hanchey) N.; m. Christine Ann Douget, June 18, 1977; children: Jay, Stephanie, George, Catherine. BS in Marine Biology, U. So. Miss., 1974; BS in Civil Engring., La. Tech. U., 1976. Project engr., field engr. inland svcs. divsn. McDermott Internat. Inc., Harvey, La., 1976-80; project coord. McDermott Internat. Inc., New Orleans and Houston, 1982-86; sr. project coord./project coord. worldwide bus. devel. McDermott Internat. Inc., New Orleans, 1986-89; project engr. McDermott Nigeria, Ltd., Warri, 1980-82; mgr. marine sales/dir. marine sales, nat. accounts mgr. Bailey Controls Co., New Orleans, 1989-92; pres. COO Balehi Marine, Inc., Lacombe, La., 1992-94; pres., owner Fairwinds Internat. Inc., Mandeville, La., 1994—. Elder Lakeview Christian Ctr., New Orleans, 1985-92. Mem. Soc. Naval Architects and Marine Engrs., Franco's Athletic Club. Republican. Presbyterian. Avocations: weight lifting, racquetball, bicycling. Home and Office: Fairwinds Internat Inc 913 Beau Chene Dr Mandeville LA 70471-1505

NAPLES, CAESAR JOSEPH, public policy educator, lawyer, consultant; b. Buffalo, Sept. 4, 1938; s. Caesar M. and Fannie A. (Occhipinti) N.; children: Jennifer, Caesar; m. Sandra L. Harrison, July 16, 1983. AB, Yale U., 1960; JD, SUNY, 1963. Bar: N.Y. 1963, Fla. 1977, Calif. 1988, U.S. Supreme Ct. 1965. Assoc. Moot & Sprague, Buffalo, 1965-69; asst. dir., employee rels. N.Y. Gov. Office, Albany, 1969-71; asst. v. chancellor SUNY, Albany, 1971-75; vice chancellor and gen. counsel Fla. State U. System, 1975-82; v. chancellor Calif. State U. System, 1983-92; vice chancellor emeritus Calif. State U., 1992—; prof. law and fin. Calif. State U. System, Long Beach, 1983—; gen. counsel Walden U., Mpls. and Naples, Fla., 1993—; cons. Govt. of Australia, U. Nev. Sys., Assn. Can. Colls. and Univs., Que., also other univs. and colls. Contbr. articles to profl. jours.; co-author: Romanov Succession, 1989 with J.Victor Baldridge. Mem. Metlife Resources Adv. Bd., 1986—, chmn., 1992—; mem. heart bd. Long Beach Meml. Hosp., 1993—; bd. dirs. Calif. Acad. Math. and Scis., 1995—. Capt. U.S. Army, 1963-65. Mem. Acad Pers. Adminstrn. (founder), Nat. Ctr. for Study Collective Bargaining Higher Edn. (bd. dirs.). Avocations: opera, tennis. Office: 816 N Juanita Ave Ste B Redondo Beach CA 90277-2200

NAPLES, RONALD JAMES, manufacturing company executive; b. Passaic, N.J., Sept. 10, 1945; s. James V. and Lee A. N.; B.S., U.S. Mil. Acad., 1967; M.A., Fletcher Sch. Law and Diplomacy, 1972; M.B.A. with distinction (Walter Heller fellow), Harvard U., 1974; m. Suzanne Lorraine Shoudy, June 17, 1967; children—Regen Jeffrey, Marcus Jamison, Tiffany Marie. Assoc. in corp. fin. Loeb Rhoades Co., 1974; White House fellow, asst. to counselor to Pres., 1974-75; spl. asst. to adminstr. Fed. Energy Adminstrn., 1975; exec. dir. Presdl. Task Force on Energy, Washington, 1975-76; v.p. internat. Hunt Mfg. Co., Phila., 1976, exec. v.p., 1980-81, vice chmn., pres., chief exec. officer, 1981-86, chmn., chief exec. officer, 1987-95, also dir.; pres. Hunt Internat. Co., 1977-82; pres., chief exec. Quaker Chem. Corp., 1995-97, chmn., pres., chief exec., 1997—; dir. Advanta Corp. Mem. regional commn. Pres.'s Com. on White House Fellows, 1980—, Fletcher Sch. Law and Diplomacy Adv. Bd., 1982—; chmn.; chmn. Phila. Award, Liberty Medal; vice chmn. Greater Phila. 1st Corp., Free Libr. of Phila. Found.; bd. dirs. Univ. of the Arts, Rock Sch. Pa. Ballet, Free Library Phila., Fgn. Policy Research Inst., Childrens Hosp., Phila., Phila. Mus. of Art, Friends Ctrl. Sch. Served with U.S. Army, 1967-71. Decorated Bronze Star with oak leaf cluster, Army Commendation medal with oak leaf cluster, Air medal (U.S.); Cross of Gallantry (Vietnam); recipient Mil. Order World Wars award U.S. Mil. Acad., 1967, Phila. Inc. Community Leadership award, 1990, Human Rels. Civic Achievement award Am. Jewish Com., 1989; named Outstanding Young Man Am., U.S. Jaycees, 1977, Chief Exec. Officer of decade bus. equipment Fin. World mag., 1990, 91, Stephen Girard award Phila. Fin. Assn., 1992, Touching a Life award Boys and Girls Clubs of Am., 1994, others. Mem. White House Fellows Assn., World Pres.' Orgn., Chief Execs.' Orgn., Assn. Grad. U.S. Mil. Acad., Harvard Bus. Sch. Alumni Assn. Club: Racquet, Pyramid Club, Harvard Bus. Sch. (Phila.). Office: Quaker Chem Corp Elm & Lee Sts Conshohocken PA 19428

NAPODANO, RUDOLPH JOSEPH, internist, medical educator; b. Rochester, N.Y., Oct. 16, 1933. B.A., U. Buffalo, 1955; M.D., SUNY-HSC, Syracuse, 1959. Diplomate Am. Bd. Internal Medicine, Am. Bd. Cardiovascular Diseases. Intern, asst. resident Highland Hosp., Rochester, 1959-61; fellow in cardiology SUNY-Upstate, Syracuse, 1961-62; chief resident in medicine Highland Hosp., 1962-63; spl. trainee in cardiology U. Rochester, 1968, clin. asst. prof. medicine, 1969-70, asst. prof. medicine, 1970-72, assoc. prof., 1972-79, prof., 1979-93, prof. emeritus, 1993—; with U. Rochester Sch. Medicine and Dentistry, 1970-93; retired 1993; prof. medicine SUNY, Syracuse, N.Y., 1994—. Fellow ACP, Am. Coll. Cardiology; mem. AAAS, Soc. Gen. Internal Medicine, Rochester Acad. Medicine (trustee 1976—, pres. 1980-81), Alpha Omega Alpha.

NAPOLES, VERONICA KLEEMAN, graphic designer, consultant; b. N.Y.C., July 9, 1951; d. Florencio Andres and Elena (Colomar) N.; m. Michael Jeffrey Kleeman, May 5, 1985; 1 child, Samuel Andres. BA, U. Miami, 1972; BArch, U. Calif., Berkeley, 1979. Account supr. Marsh & McLennan, Miami, Fla., 1974-76; designer Mus. of Anthropology, San Francisco, 1977-79; project dir. Landor & Assocs., San Francisco, 1979-81; prin. Communications Planning, Kentfield, Calif., 1981—; bd. dirs. Mind Fitness, Mill Valley, Calif., Main Arts Coun., Mykytyn Cons. Group; instr. U. Calif.-Berkeley, San Francisco, 1983—, Sonoma State U., Santa Rosa, Calif., 1983-84; tchr. Dynamic Graphics Ednl. Found., San Francisco. Author: Corporate Identity Design, 1987; exhibited at San Francisco Airport, 1992. Bd. dirs. Marin Arts Coun. Recipient Bay Area Hispanic Bus. Achiever award, 1988, Design award PRINT, 1988, Excellence award Am. Corp. Identity, 1989, 90, 91, 92, 93, 94, 95, 96, Excellence award N.Y. Art Dirs. Show, 1989; finalist Sundance Inst., 1991. Mem. Am. Inst. Graphic Arts, Women in Communications. Avocations: painting, writing. Office: Napoles Design 189 Madrone Ave Larkspur CA 94939-2113

NAPOLIELLO, MICHAEL JOHN, psychiatrist; b. Feb. 14, 1942; s. Frank J. and Anne M. (Palazzo) N. BS, Fordham U., 1962; MD, NYU, 1966; MBA, Xavier U. Grad. Sch. of Bus., 1980. Diplomate Am. Bd. Psychiatry and Neurology. Attending psychiatrist Bernalillo County Med. Ctr., Albuquerque, 1973-74; dir. behavioral medicine U. N.Mex. Sch. of Medicine, Albuquerque, 1973-74; attending psychiatrist Mary Hitchcock Meml. Hosp., Hanover, N.H., 1974-76; assoc. group dir. Merrell Nat. Labs., Cin., 1976-79; assoc. group dir. clin. pharm. Merrell-Nat. Labs., Cin., 1979-84; dir. clin. investigation Merrell-Dow Research Inst., Cin., 1979-84; sci. dir. Bristol-Myers Internat. Group, N.Y.C., 1984-85, dir. med. & sci. affairs, 1986, v.p. med. & sci. affairs, 1986-90; v.p., cen. nervous system clin. planning Bristol-Myers Squibb, Princeton, N.J., 1990-91; sr. dir. clin. rsch. and prodn. devel. Bristol-Myers Squibb, Tokyo, Japan, 1991-93; exec. dir. internat. clin. devel. Bristol-Myers Squibb, Tokyo, 1993-94, exec. dir. worldwide med. affairs, 1994—; clin. asst. prof. psychiatry Cornell U. Med. Coll., N.Y.C., 1985—; asst. clin. prof. U. Cin. Coll. Medicine, 1976-80, assoc. prof., 1980-84; lectr. in field. Contbr. 30 articles to profl. med. jours. Maj. U.S. Army, 1970-73. Recipient Physicians Recognition award AMA, 1969, 72, 76, 79, 82, 85, 88, 91, 94. Mem. Am. Psychiat. Assn., Am. Coll. Neuropsychopharmacology. Roman Catholic. Avocations: foreign languages, creative writing, basketball. Home: 27 Richard Ct Princeton NJ 08540-3802 Office: Bristol-Myers Squibb 27 Richard Ct Princeton NJ 08540-4000

NAPOLITANO, GRACE F., state legislator; b. Brownsville, Tex., Dec. 4, 1936; d. Miguel and Maria Alicia Ledezma Flores; m. Frank Napolitano, 1982; 1 child, Yolando M., Fred Musquiz Jr., Edward M., Michael M., Cynthia M. Student, Cerritos Coll., L.A. Trade Tech, Tec Southwest Coll. Mem. Calif. Assembly, 1993—. Councilwoman City of Norwalk, Calif., 1986-92, mayor, 1989-90; active Cmty. Family Guidance. Mem. Cerritos Coll. Found., Lions Club. Democrat. Roman Catholic. Home: 12009 Firestone Blvd Norwalk CA 90650-3328 Office: Calif Assembly State Capitol Rm 4005 Sacramento CA 95814-4906 also: PO Box 942849 Sacramento CA 94249-0001*

NAPOLITANO, JANET ANN, prosecutor; b. N.Y.C., Nov. 29, 1957; d. Leonard Michael and Jane Marie (Winer) N. BS, U. Santa Clara, Calif., 1979; JD, U. Va., 1983. Bar: Ariz. 1984, U.S. Dist. Ct. Ariz. 1984, Ct. Appeals (9th cir.) 1984, U.S. Ct. Appeals (10th cir.) 1988. Law clk. to hon. Mary Schroeder U.S Ct. Appeals (9th Cir.), 1983-84; assoc. Lewis & Roca, Phoenix, 1984-89, ptnr., 1989-93; U.S. atty. Dist. Ariz., Phoenix, 1993—; mem. Atty. Gen.'s Adv. Com., 1993—, chair, 1995-96. Vice-chair Ariz. Dem. Party, 1991-92; mem. Dem. Nat. Com., 1991-92; State Bd. Tech. Registration, 1989-92; Phoenix Design Standards Rev. Com., 1989-91; bd. dirs. Ariz. Cmty. Legal Svcs. Corp., 1987-92; bd. regents Santa Clara U., 1992—. Truman Scholarship Found. scholar, 1977. Mem. ABA, Am. Law Inst., Ariz. Bar Assn., Maricopa County Bar Assn., Am. Judicature Soc., Ariz. State Bar (chmn. civil practice and procedure com. 1991-92), Phi Beta Kappa, Alpha Sigma Nu. Avocations: hiking, trekking, travel, reading, film. Office: US Attys Office 4000 US Courthouse 230 N 1st Ave Phoenix AZ 85025-0230

NAPOLITANO, LEONARD MICHAEL, anatomist, university administrator; b. Oakland, Calif., Jan. 8, 1930; s. Filippo Michael and Angela (De Fiore) N.; m. Jane M. Winer, July 9, 1955; children—Leonard M., Janet Ann, Nancy Angela. B.S., Santa Clara U., 1951; M.S., St. Louis U., 1954, Ph.D., 1956. Instr. anatomy Cornell Med. Coll., N.Y.C., 1956-58; instr. U. Pitts. Sch. Med., 1958-59, asst. prof., 1959-64; asso. prof. U. N.Mex., 1964-68; prof. anatomy U. N.Mex. (Sch. Medicine), 1968—, acting chmn. dept., 1971-72, dean pro tem, 1972-73, dean, 1973—, interim v.p. for health scis., 1976—; dir. U. N.Mex. (Med. Center); dean U. N.Mex. (Sch. Medicine), 1977—; Mem. NIH Rsch. Resource Coun., 1988-91, ret. cons., 1994. Contbr. articles on lipid research and ultra structure of cholesterol to profl. jours.; Asso. editor: Anatomical Record, 1968-74. Mem. Am. Assn. Anatomists, Am. Soc. Cell Biology, Electron Microscope Soc. Am., Albuquerque, Bernalillo county Med. Assn. (hon.), Assn. Am. Med. Colls. Council of Deans. Home: 2308 Calle De Panza NW Albuquerque NM 87104-3070 Office: Dean Sch of Medicine U of N Mex Health Sci Center Albuquerque NM 87131

NAPSKY, MARTIN BEN, insurance executive; b. Miami, Fla., June 17, 1938; s. Samuel Ben and Dorothy May N.; m. Carol Ann Rella, Sept. 26, 1978; children: David, Kimberly, Victoria, Bradley, Jason, Keith. BA, Houston (Tex.) U., 1957-61; LLB, Atlanta (Ga.) Law Sch., 1971-74. Ins. agent Continental Casualty Co., Chgo., 1961-70; v.p. Eastern Reg Brokerage, Miami, 1974-88, Western Reg Brokerage, San Diego, 1988—; pres. Fla. Bldg. Contractors, Miami, 1978—. Contbg. editor Wings mag., 1984. Chancellor Nu Beta Epsilon, Atlanta, 1973; mem. George Bush Inner Circle, Washington, 1992, Naders Raiders, Atlanta, 1973-74. Mem. Nat. Assn. Health Underwriters (Health Ins. Quality award 1983), Miami Assn. Health Underwriters, Millionaires Club, Presidents Inner Circle (pres. 1983-84). Republican. Jewish. Avocations: hunting, fishing. Home: 1060 Papaya St Hollywood FL 33019

NAQUIN, PATRICIA ELIZABETH, employee assistance consultant; b. Houston, Jan. 28, 1943; d. Louie Dee and Etha Beatrice (English) Price; m. Hollis James Naquin, Mar. 23, 1961; children: Price Naquin, Holli Campbell. BS, U. Houston, 1969, MS, 1982; PhD, Tex. Woman's U., 1988. Lic. profl. counselor; lic. chem. dependency counselor; nat. cert. counselor; cert. chem. dependency specialist; cert. employee assistance profl. Purchasing agt. Internat. Affairs U. Houston, 1966-68; elem. sch. tchr. Pasadena (Tex.) Ind. Sch. Dist., 1969-82; spl. edn. counselor Alvin (Tex.) Ind. Sch. Dist., 1982-85, drug-free schs. coord., 1988-92; marriage and family therapist Lifespan Counseling, Pasadena, 1985-92; employee assistance cons. DuPont, LaPorte, Tex., 1992—; adv. com. mem. Sam Houston U., Huntsville, Tex., 1983; trainer and instr. Bay Area Coun. on Drugs and Alcohol, Houston, 1988-92; cons. Alvin Ind. Sch. Dist., 1989-92, DuPont Valuing People Core Team, 1993—; supr. State Bd. of Profl. Counselors, Houston, 1988—. Co-author: Life is for Everyone Manual, 1990. Com. co-chair Alvin S.A.P. Task Force, 1988-92; com. mem. Tri-Dist. Task Force, Alvin, 1990-91; com. chmn. Alvin Bus./Edn. Partnership, 1992; bd. dirs. Brazoria (Tex.) County Coun. Drugs and Alcohol, 1991. Mem. Am. Assn. Marriage and Family Therapists, Tex. Assn. Counselors of Alcohol and Drug Abuse, Am. Counseling Assn., Employee Assistance Program Assn., Nat. Disting. Svc. Registry/Libr. of Congress, Phi Delta Kappa. Republican. Methodist. Avocations: quilting, playing piano, playing with grandchildren, computer games.

NAQVI, SHEHLA HASNAIN, pediatric infectious disease specialist, pediatrician; b. Karachi, Pakistan, July 21, 1950; came to U.S., 1974; d. Syed Zulfiqar and Akhtar Fatima (Khwaja) Hasnain; m. Nazar H. Naqvi, Dec. 15, 1973 (div. Jan. 1986); children: Erum, Yusuf. MB, BS, U. Karachi, 1973. Diplomate Am. Bd. Pediatrics, Am. Bd. Pediat. Infectious Disease. Asst. prof. pediat. St. Louis U., 1980-86; assoc. prof. pediat. Aga Khan U., Karachi, 1986-90; assoc. prof., acting dir. pediat. infectious diseases St. Louis U., 1990-92; physican-in-charge pediat. infectious diseases Brookdale Hosp. Med. Ctr., Bklyn., 1992—; assoc. prof. SUNY, Bklyn., 1992—; cons. N.Y.C. D.O.H. Bur. TB Control, 1994—. Mem. editl. bd. Jour. Islamic Med. Assn., 1994—. Mem. Am. Soc. for Microbiology. Islam. Avocation: poetry. Home: 52 Hickory Ln Roslyn NY 11577 Office: Brookdale Univ Hosp Med Ctr 1 Brookdale Plz Brooklyn NY 11212-3139

NARA, BONNIE A., psychologist; b. Connellsville, Pa., Jan. 29, 1949; d. Edward G. and Edith R. (Fasson) N.; m. James V. Morley, Oct. 28, 1989. BA with honors, Seton Hill Coll., 1970; MEd, Calif. U. Pa., 1971, MS with highest honors, 1980; PhD, U. W.Va., 1981. Cert. sch. psychologist, Pa. Counselor Uniontown (Pa.) Area Sch. Dist., 1974-86; psychologist Ctr. for Motivation and Achievement, Pitts., 1986—. Chair pers. com. Twin Trees, Inc., Connellsville, 1979-85, chair, 1982-83; mem. Westmoreland County Prevention of Child Abuse, Greensburg, Pa., 1983-86; mem. Immaculate conception Ch., Connellsville. Mem. NEA, AAUW, Am. Counseling and Psychology Assn., Pa. Edn. Assn., Pa. Psychol. Assn., Greater Uniontown Area C. of C. (edn. coun.), Our Lady of Mt. Carmel Club (Connellsville), Lionness Lodge. Republican. Roman Catholic. Avocations: aerobics, tennis, reading, nordic track training, walking, dancing.

NARAHASHI, TOSHIO, pharmacology educator; b. Fukuoka, Japan, Jan. 30, 1927; came to U.S., 1961; s. Asahachi and Itoko (Yamasaki) Ishii; m. Kyoko Narahashi, Apr. 21, 1956; children: Keiko, Taro. BS, U. Tokyo, 1948, PhD, 1960. Instr. U. Tokyo, 1951-65; research assoc. U. Chgo., 1961, asst. prof., 1962; asst. prof. Duke U., Durham, N.C., 1962-63, 65-67, assoc. prof., 1967-69, prof., 1969-77, head pharmacology div., 1970-73, vice chmn. dept. physiology and pharmacology, 1973-75; prof., chmn. dept. pharmacology Northwestern U. Med. Sch., Chgo., 1977-94; Alfred Newton Richards prof. Med. Sch. Northwestern U., Chgo., Ill., 1983—; John Evans prof. Northwestern U., Evanston, Ill., 1986—; mem. pharmacology study sect. NIH, 1976-80; mem. rsch. rev. com. Chgo. Heart Assn., 1977-82, vice chmn. rsch. coun., 1986-87, chmn., 1988-90; mem. Nat. Environ. Health Scis. Coun., 1982-86; rev. com. Nat. Inst. Environ. Health Scis., 1991-95. Editor: Cellular Pharmacology of Insecticides and Pheromones, 1979, Cellular and Molecular Neurotoxicology, 1984, Insecticide Action: From Molecule to Organism, 1989, Ion Channels, 1988—; specific field editor Jour. Pharmacology and Exptl. Therapeutics, 1972—; assoc. editor Neurotoxicology, 1994—; contbr. articles to profl. jours. Recipient Javits Neurosci. Investigator award NIH, 1986. Fellow AAAS; mem. Am. Soc. for Pharmacology and Exptl. Therapeutics, Am. Physiol. Soc., Soc. for Neurosci., Biophys. Soc. (Cole award 1981), Soc. Toxicology (DuBois award 1988, Merit award 1991), Agrochem. Div. Am. Chem. Soc. (Burdick L. Jackson Internat. award 1989). Home: 175 E Delaware Pl Apt 7911 Chicago IL 60611-1732 Office: Northwestern U Med Sch Dept Mol Pharmaco Biol Chem 303 E Chicago Ave Chicago IL 60611-3008

NARAMORE, JAMES JOSEPH, family practice physician, educator; b. Gillette, Wyo., Nov. 29, 1949; s. Kenneth Chester and Joan (Biggerstaff) N.; m. Karen Rae Buttermore, July 9, 1972; children: Lindsay, Marissa, Jessica, Marcus. BA with highest achievement in Biology, John Brown U., Siloam Springs, Ark., 1972; MD with family practice honors, U. Utah, 1977. Diplomate Am. Bd. Family Practice. Resident in family practice U. Nebr., Omaha, 1977-80, chief resident; pvt. practice, Gillette, 1981—; mem. staff Campbell County Meml. Hosp., Gillette, 1980—, chief staff, 1986, chief dept. family practice, 1990-91; instr. dept. human medicine U. Wyo., 1983-86, clin. assoc. prof. family practice, 1986—; ptnr., co-founder Med. Arts Lab., Gillette, 1981—; med. dir. Campbell County Detention Ctr., 1988—; med. dir. Pioneer Manor Nursing Home, Gillette, 1989—; aviation med. examiner FAA, Oklahoma City, 1986—; cons. on occupational medicine to numerous industries, Campbell County, 1986—. Charter mem. Gillette Area Leadership Inst., 1986-87; chmn. missions com. Grace Bible Ch., Gillette, 1983—, chmn. bd. elders, 1989—. Mem. Am. Acad. Family Physicians, Wyo. Med. Soc., Campbell County Med. Soc. (pres. 1983-84), Gillette C. of C. (bd. dirs. 1987-90), Toastmasters (pres. Gillette 1992, Competent Toastmaster award 1986—). Republican. Avocations: snow skiing, bicycling, photography, reading, travel. Home: 1214 Hilltop Ct Gillette WY 82716-5207 Office: Family Health 407 S Medical Arts Ct Ste D Gillette WY 82716-3372

NARASIMHAN, PADMA MANDYAM, physician; b. Bangalore, India; came to U.S., 1976; d. Alasingracher Mandyam and Alamela Mandyam Narasimhan; m. Mandyam N. Venkatesh, Mar. 28, 1981 (div.) 1 child, Ravi. Student, Delhi U., New Delhi, 1964, MBBS, 1969; MD, Maulana Azad Med. Coll., New Delhi, 1970. Diplomate Am. Bd. Internal Medicine. Intern in internal medicine Flushing Hosp., N.Y.C., 1976-77; resident in internal medicine Luth. Med. Ctr., N.Y.C., 1977-79; fellow hematology, oncology Beth-Israel Med. Ctr., N.Y.C., 1979-81; asst. prof. King Drew Med. Ctr., L.A., 1983-87, Harbor UCLA, Torrance, 1987—. Mem. editorial bd. Jour. Internal Medicine, 1986—. Mem. ACP, Am. Soc. Clin. Oncology, So. Calif. Acad. Clin. Oncology. Hindu. Avocations: travel, reading, meeting people, music, walking. Home: 6604 Madeline Cove Dr Palos

Verdes Peninsula CA 90275-4608 Office: Harbor UCLA 100 W Carson St Torrance CA 90509

NARATH, ALBERT, laboratory administrator; b. Berlin, Mar. 5, 1933; came to U.S., 1947; s. Albert Narath and Johanna Agnes Anne (Bruggeman) Bruckmann; m. Worth Haines Scattergood (div. 1976); children: Tanya, Lise, Yvette; m. Barbara Dean Camp (div. 1983); 1 child, Albert; m. Shanna S. Lindeman. BS in Chemistry, U. Cin., 1955; PhD in Phys. Chemistry, U. Calif., Berkeley, 1959. Mem. tech. staff, mgr. phys. sci. Sandia Nat. Labs., Albuquerque, 1959-68, dir. solid state sci., 1968-71, mng. dir. phys. sci., 1971-73, v.p. rsch., 1973-82, exec. v.p. rsch. and adv. weapons sys., 1982-84, pres., 1989-95; pres. energy and environ. sect. Lockheed Martin Corp., Albuquerque, 1995—. Contbr. sci. articles to profl. jours. Fellow AAAS, Am. Phys. Soc. (George E. Pake prize 1991); mem. NAE. Office: Lockheed Martin Corp 1155 University Blvd SE Albuquerque NM 87106-4320

NARAYAN, BEVERLY ELAINE, lawyer; b. Berkeley, Calif., June 19, 1961; d. Jagjiwan and Alexandra (Mataras) N.; m. James Dean Schmidt, Jan. 7, 1989; children: Sasha Karan, Kaiya Maria. Student, San Francisco State U., 1979-80; BA, U. Calif., Berkeley, 1983; JD, U. Calif., San Francisco, 1987. Bar: Calif. 1987, U.S. Dist. Ct. (no. dist.) Calif. 1987, U.S. Dist. Ct. (ctrl. dist.) 1988. Atty. Daniels Barratta & Fine, L.A., 1988-89, Kornblum Ferry & Frye, L.A., 1990-91, Clapp Moroney Bellagamba Davis & Vucinich, Menlo Park, Calif., 1991-93, pvt. practice, Burlingame, Calif., 1993—; arbitrator Nat. Assn. Securities Dealers, San Francisco, 1987—, Pacific Stock Exch., San Francisco, 1994—; mediator Peninsula Conflict Resolution Ctr., San Mateo, Calif., 1995—; judge pro tem San Mateo Superior Ct., Redwood City, Calif., 1994—. Candidate Sch. Bd. San Mateo (Calif.) Unified Sch. Dist., 1993. Recipient U. Calif. Hastings Coll. Law Achievement award, 1986; named Barrister of Yr., San Mateo County, 1996. Mem. ABA, San Mateo County Bar Assn. (co-chair women lawyers 1995, bd. dirs. 1994-96), Nat. Women's Polit. Caucus (bd. dirs., diversity chair 1993—), San Mateo County Barristers Club (bd. dirs. 1993—, child watch chair 1995—). Avocations: baking, cooking, reading, travel, motorcycles, family. Office: 1508 Howard Ave Burlingame CA 94010-5216

NARAYAN, K(RISHNAMURTHI) ANANTH, biochemist; b. Secunderabad, India, Oct. 1, 1930; came to U.S., 1954, naturalized, 1970; s. Ananthnarayan and Rukmani (Sreenivasan) Krishnamurthi; m. Suhasini Naik, Sept. 3, 1961; children—Krishnamuthi, Sheila. B.S. in Chemistry, Christian Coll., India, 1949; M.S. in Chem.Tech., Osmania U., India, 1951; Ph.D. in Food Tech., U. Ill., 1957. Research assoc. Wash. State U., Pullman, 1957-61; asst. prof. U. Ill., Urbana, 1962-71; research biochemist U.S. Army Natick Research and Devel. Ctr., Mass., 1971—. Contbr. chpts. to books. Grantee NIH, 1966-70, Am. Cancer Soc., 1968-70, Am. Heart Assn., 1967-71. Mem. Am. Oil Chemists Soc., Am. Inst. Nutrition, Inst. Food Tech. Hindu. Avocations: photography; woodworking. Home: 84 Indian Head Rd Framingham MA 01701-7920 Office: US Army R and D Ctr SusD/RSD/AFB Natick MA 01760-5018

NARAYAN, RAMESH, astronomy educator; b. Bombay, Sept. 25, 1950; came to U.S., 1983; s. G.N. and Rajalakshmi (Sankaran) Ramachandran; m. G.V. Vani, June 6, 1977. BS in Physics, Madras U., 1971; MS in Physics, Bangalore U., 1973, PhD in Physics, 1979. Rsch. scientist Raman Rsch. Inst., Bangalore, India, 1978-83; postdoctoral fellow Calif. Inst. Tech., 1983-84, sr. rsch. fellow, 1984-85; assoc. prof. U. Ariz., Tucson, 1985-90, prof. astronomy, 1990-91; prof. astronomy Harvard U., Cambridge, Mass., 1991—, chmn. dept. astronomy, 1997—; assoc. dir. Harvard-Smithsonian Ctr. for Astrophysics, 1996-97. Contbr. articles to profl. jours. Named NSF Presdl. Young Investigator, 1989. Mem. AAAS, Am. Astron. Soc., Internat. Astron. Union, Astron. Soc. India. Achievements include research in the general area of theoretical astrophysics, specializing in accretion disks, black holes, gravitational lenses, hydrodynamics, gamma-ray bursts, image processing and scintillation. Office: Harvard-Smithsonian Ctr Astrophysics 60 Garden St # 51 Cambridge MA 02138-1516

NARAYANAMURTI, VENKATESH, research administrator; b. Bangalore, Karnataka, India, Sept. 9, 1939; came to U.S., 1961; s. Duraiswami and Janaki (Subramaniam) N.; m. Jayalakshmi Krishnayya, Aug. 23, 1961; children: Arjun, Ranjini, Krishna. BSc, MSc, St. Stephen's Coll., Delhi, India, 1958; PhD, Cornell U., 1965. Instr., rsch. assoc. Cornell U., Ithaca, N.Y., 1965-68; mem. tech. staff AT&T Bell Labs., Murray Hill, N.J., 1968-76, dept.head, 1976-81, dir., 1981-87; v.p. rsch. Sandia Nat. Labs., Albuquerque, 1987-92; dean engring. U. Calif., Santa Barbara, 1992—; chmn. microelectric bd. Jet Propulsion Lab., Pasadena, Calif., 1988—; chmn. condensed matter and materials phys. panel NRC, 1996; mem. U. Calif. Pres.' Coun. for Nat. Labs., 1995—; bd. dirs. Serpal Interface, Inc., Santa Clara, Calif., 1997—; mem. NAE Pub. Info. Adv. Bd., 1993—, NSF Dir.'s Strategic Planning Bd., 1994—, Los Alamos Nat. Lab. Adv. Bd. for Materials and Indsl. Partnerships, 1994—. Author more than 130 publs.; patentee in field. Fellow IEEE, AAAS, Am. Phys. Soc., Indian Acad. Scis.; mem. NAE, Royal Swedish Acad. Engring. Scis. (fgn.). Avocations: long distance running, squash. Office: U Calif Dept Engring Santa Barbara CA 93106

NARBER, GREGG ROSS, lawyer; b. Iowa City, Sept. 4, 1946; s. James R. and Marguerite Maxine (Lasher) N.; m. Margaret Ann Christiansen, Apr. 22, 1995; children: Joshua Ross, Zachary Edward; stepchildren: John, Peter, Jeffrey Christiansen. BA, Grinnell Coll., 1968; MA, JD, Washington U., St. Louis, 1971. Bar: Iowa 1971, U.S. Dist. Ct. (so. dist.) Iowa 1971, U.S. Ct. Mil. Appeals 1974, U.S. Supreme Ct. 1974. Atty. The Principal Fin. Group, Des Moines, 1975-76, asst. counsel, 1976-80, assoc. counsel, 1980-85, counsel, 1985-89, v.p., gen. counsel, 1989-92, sr. v.p., gen. counsel, 1993—; bd. dirs. Sargasso Mut. Ins. Co., Bermuda, Ban Rueta Seguros de Vida, Chile, Principal Internat., Espãna S.A. de Seguros de Vida, Spain, Principal Internacional, S.A. Compañia de Seguros de Vida,Mex.; lectr. Iowa Humanities Bd., 1981-82, Ats Midwest, 1987. Co-author: New Deal Mural Projects in Iowa, 1982; also articles; artist various works. Pres. intercultural program Am. Fiedl Svc. Internat., West Des Moines, 1990-94; mem. acquistions Des Moines Art Ctr., 1989—; bd. dirs. Des Moines Symphony, 1989-94, Metro Arts Coun. Greater Des Moines, 1990-94, Edmundson Art Found., 1992—. Mem. Iowa Bar Assn., Polk County Bar Assn., Prairie Club (sec. 1982-84, 86-87, pres. 1991-92), West Des Moines Soccer Club (coach 1982-89, referee 1984-89). Democrat. Mem. Congregational Ch. Avocations: art history and collecting, soccer. Home: 4800 Pommel Pl West Des Moines IA 50265-2937 Office: The Prin Fin Group 711 High St Des Moines IA 50392-0001

NARDELLI-OLKOWSKA, KRYSTYNA MARIA, ophthalmologist, educator; b. Myslowice, Poland, June 23, 1939; d. Walerian and Stefania (Jasinska) Nardelli; m. Zbigniew L. Olkowski, Apr. 15, 1963. M.D., Silesian U. Med. Sch., 1964. Diplomate: Am. Bd. Ophthalmology; 1983. Intern, resident ophthalmology Emory U. Med. Sch., Atlanta, 1977-80; fellow in glaucoma Emory U. Med. Sch., 1980-81; asst. prof. dept. ophthalmology Emory U. Med. Sch., Atlanta, 1972—; pvt. practice ophthalmology, 1982—. Postdoctoral fellow Fight for Sight, 1974-75. Mem. Am. Soc. Research in Ophthalmology, Royal Micros. Soc. (Eng.). Home: Villa Sadyba 1018 Mcconnell Dr Decatur GA 30033-3402 Office: 724 Holcomb Bridge Rd Bldg 4 Norcross GA 30071-1325

NARDI, THEODORA P., former state legislator; b. Warwick, R.I., Aug. 28, 1922; widow; 4 children. Attended, Manhattanville Coll. Mem. N.H. Ho. of Reps., 1973-83, mem. appropriations com., 1989-94, ret., 1994. Chmn. Hills County Dem. Com., 1977-78; pres. N.H. Owl, 1979-80; chmn. Manchester (N.H.) Legis. Del., 1979-82; bd. dirs. N.H. Soup Kitchen, 1985-90, New Horizons Soup Kitchen, 1989-93; active N.H. Cath. Charities, 1986—, Manchester Housing Coun., 1986-92. Democrat. Roman Catholic. Avocation: helping needy. Home: 776 Chestnut St Manchester NH 03104-3012

NARDI RIDDLE, CLARINE, association administrator, judge; b. Clinton, Ind., Apr. 23, 1949; d. Frank Jr. and Alice (Mattioda) Nardi; m. Mark Alan Riddle, Aug. 15, 1971; children: Carl Nardi, Julia Nardi. AB, Ind. U., 1971, JD, 1974; LHD (hon.), St. Joseph Coll., 1991. Bar: Ind. 1974, Conn. 1979, U.S. Dist. Ct. Ind. 1974, Fed. Dist. Ct. Conn. 1980, U.S. Ct. Appeals (2d cir.) 1986, U.S. Ct. Appeals (D.C. cir.) 1994, U.S. Supreme Ct. 1980. Staff atty. Ind. Legis. Svc. Agy., Indpls., 1974-78, legal counsel, 1978-79; dep. corp. counsel City of New Haven, 1980-83; counsel to atty. gen. State of Conn., Hartford, 1983-86, dep. atty. gen., 1986-89, acting atty. gen., 1989, atty. gen., 1989-91; judge Superior Ct. State of Conn., 1991-93; sr. v.p. for govtl. affairs, gen. counsel Nat. Multi-Housing Coun., Nat. Apartment Assn., 1995—; asst. counsel state majority Conn. Gen. Assembly, Hartford, 1979, legal rsch. asst. to prof. Yale U., New Haven, 1979; legal counsel com. on law revision Indpls. State Bar Assn., 1979; mem. Chief Justice's Task Force on Gender Bias, Hartford, 1988-90; mem. ethics and values com. Ind. Sector, Washington, 1988-90. Bd. visitors Ind. U., Bloomington, 1974-92; mem. Gov.'s Missing Children Com., Hartford, Conn. Child Support Guidelines Com., Gov.'s Task Force on Justice for Abused Children, Hartford, 1988-90. Named Conn. History Maker Women's Bur. & Permanent Commn. on Status of Women, U.S. Dept. Labor, 1989; recipient Citizen award Nat. Task Force on Children's Constl. Rights. Mem. ABA, Conn. Bar Assn. (chair com. on gender bias, Citation of Merit women and law sect. 1989), Nat. assn. Attys. Gen. (chair charitable trusts and solicitation 1988-90), New Haven Neighborhood Music Sch. (bd. dirs.), Am. Arbitration Assn. (arbitration panel 1994). Democrat. Presbyterian.

NARDULLI, PETER F., political science educator; b. Chgo., May 20, 1947; s. Peter F. and Catherine Rose N.; m. Ann Marie Wannemacher, Oct. 24, 1943. BA, No. Ill. U., 1969; MA, Northwestern U., 1972, JD, 1973, PhD, 1975. Asst. prof. Inst. Pub. Affairs and Dept. Political Sci. U. Ill., Urbana, 1975-80, assoc. prof. Inst. Pub. Affairs and Dept. Political Sci., 1980-85, vis. prof. Coll. of Law, 1985-86, acting dir. Inst. Govt. and Pub. Affairs, 1985-86, prof. Inst. Govt. Pub. Affairs and Dept. Political Sci., 1985—, dir. grad. studies Dept. Political Sci., 1987-91, dept. head and prof. Dept. Political Sci., 1992—. Co-author: (books) The Contours of Justice: Communities and Their Courts, 1987, The Tenor of Justice: Felony Courts & The Guilty Plea Process, 1988, The Constitution and American Political Development: An Institutional Perspective, 1991, The Craft of Justice, 1992. Office: U Ill-Dept Political Sci 361 Lincoln Hall 702 S Wright St Urbana IL 61801-3631

NARIN, STEPHEN B., lawyer; b. Phila., Nov. 23, 1929; s. Bernard E. and Anne (Lipsius) N.; m. Sandra C. Goldberg, Sept. 29, 1963; children: Howard Glen, Brenda Teri. B.S., Temple U., 1951, LL.B., 1953; LL.M. in Taxation, NYU, 1960. Bar: Pa. 1954, U.S. Supreme Ct. 1958; CPA, Pa. Dep. atty. gen. Commonwealth of Pa., Harrisburg, 1955-57; instr. acctg. Temple U., Phila., 1954-55; lectr. in law grad. legal studies div. Temple U. Sch. Law, Phila., 1976-85; lectr. Practicing Law Inst., 1967-69; ptnr. Narin & Chait, Phila., 1970-89, Predecessor Ptnrships., Phila., 1955-70; v.p., gen. counsel Travelco Assocs., Phila., 1989-90; of counsel Krekstein, Wolfson & Krekstein, Phila., 1989-92; v.p., gen. counsel Eagle Nat. Bank, 1990-91; counsel Schachtel, Gerstley, Levine & Koplin, Phila., 1993—; mem. Phila. County Bd. Law Examiners, 1961-65. Mem. nat. governing council Am. Jewish Congress, 1963-84, nat. exec. com., 1978-84, pres. Greater Phila. council, 1965-67; mem. Nat. Commn. on Law and Social Action, 1964-84. Mem. ABA, Am. Judicature Soc., Am. Inst. CPA's, Pa. Inst. CPA's, Pa. Bar Assn., Phila. Bar Assn., Phi Alpha Delta. Office: Schachtel Gerstley et al 4 Penn Center Plz Philadelphia PA 19103-2514

NARITA, HIRO, cinematographer; b. Seoul, Republic of Korea, June 26, 1941; came to Japan, 1945, came to U.S., 1957; s. Masao Morikawa and Masako (Kojima) Morikawa ; m. Barbara Parker, Sept. 9, 1971. BFA in Design, San Francisco Art Inst., 1964. lectr. Mill Valley Film Festival, 1984, Hawaii Internat. Film Festival, 1984. Dir. photography for films: Farewell to Manzanar, 1976 (Emmy nomination 1976), Never Cry Wolf, 1983 (Best Cinematography award 1983), Solomon Northrup's Odyssey, 1984, Go Tell It on the Mountain, 1985, Amerika, 1987, Honey, I Shrunk the Kids, 1989, The Rocketeer, 1991, Star Trek VI, 1992, Hocus Pocus, 1993, White Fang II, 1994, James & The Giant Peach, 1995, The Arrival, 1995, Sub Down, 1996, Stones & Paper, 1997. Served with U.S Army, 1964-66. Mem. Internat. Photographers Guild, Am. Soc. Cinematographers, Acad. Motion Picture Arts and Scis.

NARMONT, JOHN STEPHEN, lawyer; b. Auburn, Ill., June 24, 1942; s. Stephen and Luriel (Welle) N.; m. Sondra J. Nicholls, Feb. 12, 1978. BBA magna cum laude, U. Notre Dame, 1964; JD, U. Ill., Champaign, 1967. Bar: Ill. 1967, U.S. Dist. Ct. (so. dist.) Ill. 1967, U.S. Ct. Appeals (7th cir.) 1967, U.S. Tax Ct. 1978, U.S. Supreme Ct. 1973. Pvt. practice Springfield, Ill.; founder, pres., owner Richland Ranch, Inc., Auburn; originator, pres. The Solid Gold Futurity, Ltd. Mem. ABA, Sangamon County Bar Assn., Ill. State Bar Assn., Assn. Trial Lawyer Am., Am. Agrl. Law Assn., Ill. Inst. for Continuing Legal Edn., Internat. Livestock Exposition (pres., founder). Office: 209 N Bruns Ln Springfield IL 62702-4612

NARSAVAGE, GEORGIA ROBERTS, nursing educator, researcher; b. Pittston, Pa., Jan. 1, 1948; d. George H. Roberts and Betty (Smith) Lanphear; m. Peter P. Narsavage, Oct. 26, 1969; children: Peter A., Paul J., Marea L. BSN, U. Md., Washington DC, 1969; MSN, Coll. Misericordia, 1984; PhD in Nursing, U. Pa., Phila., 1990. RN, Pa.; cert. CPR instr. Staff nurse Mercy Hosp., Scranton, Pa., 1970-72; pvt. duty nursing Pa., 1972-79; pvt. duty nurse Community Med. Ctr., Scranton, Pa., 1979; clinical instr. Lackawanna County Vo-Tech Practical Nursing Program, Dunmore, Pa., 1979-82; clinical and theoretical instr. Mercy Hosp. Sch. of Nursing, Scranton, Pa., 1982-84; asst. prof. nursing Dept. of Nursing, U. Scranton, Pa., 1984-93; assoc. prof. U. Scranton, Pa., 1993—, chmn. dept., 1991-94; dir. RN program Dept. of Nursing U. Scranton, Pa., 1990-92; postdoctoral fellow U. Pa., Phila., 1995-97; cons. in field. Contbr. articles to profl. jours. Gifted program mentor Scranton Sch. Dist.; active in ch. and civic choirs. U. Scranton grantee, 1989, 91, 94-97; Ea. Nursing Rsch. Soc. Am. Nurses Found. rsch. grantee, 1994, NIH NRSA grantee, 1995-97; recipient awards for excellence in nursing rsch. Theta Phi Sigma Theta Tau, 1994, Pa. Nurses Assn., 1996. Mem. ANA, APHA, Am. Thoracic Soc./Am. Lung Assn., Pa. Nurses Assn. (bd. dirs., chmn. com., conv. del.), Lackawanna Nurses Assn. (bd. dirs., com. chmn., dist. pres.), Nat. League for Nursing, Coun. Nursing Informatics (chair nominating com. 1993-95), Pa. League for Nursing (chair nominating com.), U. Md. Nurses Alumnae Assn., Ea. Nursing Rsch. Soc. (mem.-at-large bd. dirs.). Lutheran. Office: U Scranton O'Hara Hall 118 Scranton PA 18510-4595

NARVER, JOHN COLIN, business administration educator; b. Portland, Oreg., Aug. 5, 1935; s. Ursel Colin and Merle (Wells) N.; children: Gregory, Allison Ann, Colin. B.S., Oreg. State U., 1957; M.B.A., U. Calif.-Berkeley, 1960; Ph.D., 1965. With Boise Cascade Corp., Portland, 1960-61; asst. prof. U. B.C., Can., 1964-66; asst. prof. dept. mktg. and internat. bus. U. Wash., Seattle, 1966-68; assoc. prof. U. Wash., 1968-71, prof., 1971—, chmn. dept., 1974-78; vis. prof. Norwegian Sch. Econs., 1973, Bogazici U., Istanbul, Turkey, 1974, U. Helsinki, 1995; cons. in field. Author: Conglomerate Mergers and Market Competition, 1967, (with R. Savitt) The Marketing Economy: An Analytical Approach, 1971, (with S. Slater) The Effect of a Market Orientation on Business Profitability, 1990. Served to lt. U.S. Army, 1957-59. Mem. Am. Mktg. Assn., Phi Delta Theta. Democrat. Episcopalian. Home: 2015 Federal Ave E Seattle WA 98102-4141 Office: U Wash Sch Bus Adminstrn Seattle WA 98195

NARWOLD, LEWIS LAMMERS, paper products manufacturer; b. Cleve., Sept. 4, 1921; s. Lewis Lammers and Dorothy Marie (Andrus) N.; m. Marilyn Ebner, Oct. 26, 1944; 1 dau., Christine. BBA, Western Res. U., 1942; MBA, Harvard, 1947. Salesman Hoerner Boxes, Inc., 1950-54, gen. sales mgr., 1954-57, v.p., gen. mgr., 1957-62; v.p. So. div. Hoerner Waldorf Corp., St. Paul, 1962-70; sr. v.p., container div. Hoerner Waldorf Corp., 1970-72; CEO, founder, pres. SouthWest Packaging Inc., Tulsa, 1972—; dir. UNCA Bankshares, Utica Nat. Bank & Trust, Thermo Chem. Corp., Sooner Box Corp., Hoerner Boxes, Inc., So. Mo. Container Corp.; organizer 1st Bank & Trust Co. of Okla. Chmn. United Fund of Sand Springs, Okla.; pres., trustee Tulsa Charity Horse Show.; Trustee Children's Med. Center of Tulsa, Tulsa Psychiat. Clinic, U. of the Ozarks. Capt. USMC, 1943-45. Decorated Purple Hearts; recipient Presdl. Citation. Mem. Sand Springs C. of C. (dir.), Tulsa C. of C. (dir.), N.A.M., Tulsa Mfg. Club, Mason Club, Summit Club (dir.), So. Hills Country Club, Union League Club (Chgo.), Coves Golf Club. Home: 7116 S College Ave Tulsa OK 74136-5601 Office: 6106 W 68th St Tulsa OK 74131-2429

NARY, JOHN HENRY, interior designer; b. Rochester, N.Y., Oct. 14, 1948; s. Robert John and Edna Gertrude (Gessner) N.; A.A., Erie County Community Coll., 1974; m. Jacqueline Marie Steiger, Jan. 13, 1970. Staff artist, regional mgr. The Birge Co., Buffalo, 1969-71; v.p. Heinzelman Interiors, Inc., Buffalo, 1971-72; dir. design McMullen Dental, Buffalo, 1972-80; v.p. design and sales William H. Prentice, Inc., Buffalo, 1980-91; pres. Corning (N.Y.) Office Interiors, Inc., 1991—; guest lectr. Sch. Dentistry SUNY, Buffalo. Bd. dirs. S.E. Steuben County Habitat for Humanity, 1993-94, v.p., 1995, pres. 1997; mem. Community Services Pilot Program, 1982. Cert., Nat. Council Interior Design Qualification. Mem. Am. Soc. Interior Designers (past pres. N.Y. Upstate/Can. East chpt., bd. dirs., nat. ethics com. 1987, 88, assessment task force 1990, nominating com. 1994, dealer adv. team 1997—), Corning Country Club, Corning Rotary Club. Author: Dental Office Design, 1974. Home: 109 W Hill Ter Painted Post NY 14870-1001 Office: 19 Denison Pky Ste 100 Corning NY 14830

NASAR, SYED ABU, electrical engineering educator; b. Gorakhpur, Uttar Pradesh, India, Dec. 25, 1932; came to U.S., 1956; s. Syed M. and Syeda (Begum) Y.; m. Sara Samad, Sept. 3, 1961; children—Naheed, Sajida. BSc, Agra U., 1951; BSEE, Dacca U., 1955; MSEE, Tex. A&M U., 1957; PhD, U. Calif., Berkeley, 1963. Chartered elec. engr., U.K. Assoc. prof. U. Ky., Lexington, 1968-70, prof. elec. engring., 1970—, Univ. Rsch. prof., 1989—, chmn., 1980-87, dir. grad. studies, 1980-87; visitor Brit. Council, London, 1964. Author or co-author 33 books on elec. engring., 1970-93; editor Elec. Machines and Power Systems Jour., 1976—; contbr. articles to profl. jours. Recipient Aurel Vlaicu award Romanian Nat. Acad., 1978; NSF rsch. grantee, 1966-87, 92—,. Fellow IEEE (life), Instn. Elec. Engrs. London. Office: U Ky 453 Anderson Hall Lexington KY 40506

NASGAARD, ROALD, museum curator; b. Denmark, Oct. 14, 1941; s. Jens Larsen and Petra (Guldbaek) N.; m. Susan Ursula Watterson, Sept. 8, 1967 (divorced). B.A., U. B.C., 1965, M.A., 1967; Ph.D., Inst. Fine Arts, N.Y. U., 1973. Lectr., asst. prof. U. Guelph, 1971-75; curator contemporary art Art Gallery of Ont., Toronto, 1975-78, chief curator, 1978-89, deputy dir., chief curator, 1989-93, sr. curator rsch., 1993; chair dept. art Fla. State U., Tallahassee, 1995—; co-dir. programming Inst. of Modern and Contemporary Art, Calgary, Alta., Can.; vis. lectr. U. Guelph, York U., U. Toronto; adj. prof. U. Toronto. Author: Ron Martin: World Paintings, 1976, Structures for Behavior, 1977, Garry Neill Kennedy: Recent Work, 1978, Ten Canadian Artists in the 1970's, 1980, Yves Gaucher: A Fifteen Year Perspective, 1978, The Mystic North: Symbolist Landscape Painting in Northern Europe and North America, 1890-1940, 1984, Gerhard Richter: Paintings, 1988, Individualites: 14 Contemporary Artists from France, 1991, Free Worlds: Metaphors and Realities in Contemporary Hungarian Art, 1991, Free Worlds: Metaphors and Realities in Contemporary Hungarian Art, 1991; co-organizer The European Iceberg: Creativity in Germany and Italy Today, 1985. Mem. Toronto Pub. Art Commn., Gershon Iskowitz Found. Can. Council fellow, 1967-68, 70-71. Mem. Coll. Art Assn., Univ. Art Assn. Can., Internat. Art Critics Assn.

NASH, ALANNA KAY, critic, writer; b. Louisville, Aug. 16, 1950; d. Allan and Emily Kay (Derrick) N. BA, Stephens Coll., 1972; MS, Columbia U., 1974. Music critic Louisville Courier Jour., 1977; writer, producer Sta. WHAS, Louisville, 1980; pres. Alandale Prodns., Louisville, 1981—; freelance writer specializing in the arts Stereo Rev., Esquire, N.Y. Times, Entertainment Weekly, TV Guide, Ms., Glamour, Working Woman, Good Housekeeping, Saturday Evening Post, Video, 1964—. Author: Dolly, 1978, rev. edit. Dolly Parton: The Early Years, 1994, Behind Closed Doors: Talking with the Legends of Country Music, 1988, Golden Girl: The Story of Jessica Savitch, 1988, 96 (became feature film Up Close and Personal 1996), Elvis Aaron Presley: Revelations from The Memphis Mafia, 1995; (ghostwriter) Elvis: From Memphis to Hollywood, 1992; co-producer: (TV documentary) The Deaners: Cause without a Rebel; primary on-camera sourse Lifetime Cable documentary Intimate Portrait: Jessica Savitch, 1995; writer, producer: network and syndicated specials; contbr. to books. Recipient Nat. Prodn. awards Alpha Epsilon Rho, 1971. Mem. Soc. Profl. Journalists (bd. dirs. Louisville chpt. 1987—, v.p. 1992-93, pres. 1993-94, Nat. Mem. of Yr. award 1994, Howard Dubin award 1994), Authors Guild, Am. Soc. Journalists and Authors, Country Music Assn. Republican. Methodist. Home and Office: 649 Breckenridge Ln Louisville KY 40207-4556

NASH, BOB J. (BOB NASH), federal agency administrator; b. Texarkana, Ark., 1947. ABA Sociology, U. Ark., 1969; MA Urban Studies, Howard U., 1972. Asst. to dep. mayor Washington, 1970-71; asst. to city mgr. Fairfax, Va., 1971-72; adminstrv. officer Nat. Tng. and Devel. Svc., Washington, 1972-74; dir. community and regional affairs Ark. Dept. Planning, 1974-75; v.p. Winthrop Rockefeller Found., Little Rock, 1975-83; sr. exec. asst. econ. devel. Office Ark. gov., 1983-89; pres. Ark. Devel. Fin. Authority, Little Rock, 1989-92; assoc. dir. personnel White House; dep. dir. personnel Clinton Adminstrn. Transition; under sec. agriculture small community and rural devel. with USDA, Rural Devel. Adminstrn., Farmers Home Adminstrn., Alternative Rsch. & Commercialization Ctr., Rural Electrification Adminstrn., Washington, 1993-1995. Office: Dept of Agriculture Small Cmty & Rural Devel 14th & Independence Ave SW Washington DC 20250 Office: The White House Office Presidential Personnel Old Executive Office Bldg Washington DC 20503*

NASH, CHARLES PRESLEY, chemistry educator; b. Sacramento, Calif., Mar. 15, 1932; s. Clarence and Mildred Vida (Johnson) N.; m. Lois Olive Brown, May 29, 1955; children: Nancy Caroline, Sandra Lee, James Roy. BS, U. Calif., Berkeley, 1952; PhD, UCLA, 1958. Instr. chemistry UCLA, 1956-57; from instr. to assoc. prof. U. Calif., Davis, 1957-70, prof., 1970-93; prof. emeritus, 1993—; chmn. acad. senate U. Calif., Davis, 1987-90, chmn. faculty assn., 1993-97; vis. sr. lectr. Imperial Coll., London, 1968-69; disting. vis. prof. USAF Acad., Colorado Springs, 1979-80. Contbr. numerous articles to profl. jours. Bd. pres. Explorit Sci. Ctr., 1995-97. Recipient Disting. Teaching award U. Calif. Davis, 1978. Mem. Am. Chem. Soc., Sigma Xi, Phi Lambda Upsilon. Office: U Calif at Davis Dept Chemistry Davis CA 95616

NASH, CYNTHIA JEANNE, journalist; b. Detroit, Dec. 24, 1947; d. Frederick Copp and Carolyn (Coffin) N.; 1 child, Lydia Anne Maza; m. Richard Zahler, July 22, 1994. BA, U. Mich., 1969. Reporter, Detroit News, 1970-75, sports columnist, 1975-77, Life Style columnist, 1977-79, Life Style editor, 1979-82; news features editor Seattle Times, 1983, asst. mng. editor Sunday Seattle Times, 1983-86, assoc. mng. editor, 1986—. Mem. Harbor Sq. Club. Office: Seattle Times PO Box 70 Fairview Ave N & John St Seattle WA 98111-0070

NASH, DONALD GENE, commodities specialist; b. Paris, Ill., July 20, 1945; s. Lelan and Mildred (Washburn) N.; m. Jo Ann Bellew, Aug. 29, 1964; children—Stacey Alan, Ryan Christopher, Shaun Christian. B.S., So. Ill. U., 1967, M.S., 1969; postgrad., DePaul U., 1970-71. Farm mgr., test farms So. Ill. U., Carbondale, 1968-69; economist Commodity Futures Trading Commn., Chgo., 1969-77; v.p.-ops. Mid. Am. Commodity Exchange, Chgo., 1977-86, Div. Enforcement, Commodity Futures Trading Commn., Chgo., 1986—. With Ill. Army N.G., 1968-74. Recipient Outstanding Mktg. award Wall St. Jour., 1966, award of merit Am. Farm Econ. Assn., 1967, cert. of merit Commodity Exch. Authority, merit award Naperville Art League, 1994, Honorable Mention award Danada Nature Show, 1995. Methodist. Avocations: photography; woodworking; sketching. Home: 923 Bainbridge Dr Naperville IL 60563-2002 Office: Commodity Futures Trading Commn 300 S Riverside Plz Ste 1600N Chicago IL 60606-6615

NASH, EDWARD L., advertising agency executive; b. N.Y.C., Nov. 8, 1936; s. Irving and Mina (Koppel) N.; m. Diana R. Kithcart, June 2, 1968; 1 child, Amelia. B.A., CCNY, 1953. Dir. advt. Crowell, Collier, Macmillan, Inc., N.Y.C., 1961-62; v.p. mktg. LaSalle Extension U., Chgo., 1962-64; pres. Capitol Record Club, Inc., Los Angeles, 1964-69; founder, pres. Nash Pub., Los Angeles, 1969-74; exec. v.p. Rapp & Collins, N.Y.C., 1975-82; pres., chief exec. officer BBDO Direct, N.Y.C., 1982-86; owner, pres. Nash Direct Inc., N.Y.C., 1986-91; chmn. Nash, Wakeman & de Forrest, Inc., 1991-92; exec. v.p. Bozell, Jacobs, Kenyon & Eckhardt, N.Y.C., 1992-95; CEO, mng. ptnr. Team Nash, Inc., N.Y.C., 1996—; lectr. in field; chmn. Direct Mktg. Day, N.Y.C., 1985, Internat. Direct Mktg. Conf., 1996. Author: Direct Marketing: Strategy/Planning/Execution, 1982, 2d edit., 1986, 3d edit., 1995; editor: The Direct Marketing Handbook, 1984, 2d edit., 1991,

Database Marketing, 1993. Mem. Direct Mktg. Assn. (chmn. mktg. coun. 1980-82). Office: Team Nash Inc 162 5th Ave New York NY 10010-5902

NASH, FRANK ERWIN, lawyer; b. Pendleton, Oreg., Feb. 27, 1916; s. Frank Lee and Gertrude (Walbridge) N.; m. Elizabeth Ann Kibbe, Apr. 20, 1943; children: Thomas K., Robert L., Carl F., Frances L. B.S., U. Oreg., 1937, J.D., 1939. Bar: Oreg. 1939. Since practiced in Portland; with firm Miller, Nash, Wiener, Hager & Carlsen (and predecessors), 1939-91, ptnr., 1948-91, ret., 1991. Bd. dirs. Tri-County United Good Neighbors, 1961-66, pres., 1963-64; pres. U. Oreg. Found., 1979-81; bd. dirs. Med. Research Found., pres., 1980-81; bd. dirs. Library Assn. Portland, pres., 1978-81; bd. visitors U. Oreg. Law Sch. Served to lt. col., inf. AUS, 1941-46, PTO. Recipient Pioneer award U. Oreg., 1980, Meritorious Svc. award., 1992. Fellow Am. Bar Found.; mem. ABA, Multnomah Bar Assn. (pres. 1964-65), Oreg. State Bar, Order of Coif, Phi Delta Phi, Phi Delta Theta. Republican. Methodist (past chmn. ofcl. bd.). Clubs: Arlington (Portland) (dir. 1963-65), Multnomah Amateur Athletic (Portland) (dir. 1963-65, pres. 1965-66), Waverley (Portland) (pres. 1979-80). Home: 1885 NW Ramsey Dr Portland OR 97229-4240 Office: 111 SW 5th Ave Fl 35 Portland OR 97204-3604

NASH, GARY BARING, historian, educator; b. Phila., July 27, 1933; s. Ralph C. and Edith (Baring) N.; m. Mary Workum, Dec. 20, 1955 (div.); children—Brooke, Robin, Jennifer, David; m. Cynthia Shelton, Oct. 24, 1981. B.A., Princeton U., 1955, Ph.D., 1964. Asst. to dean Grad. Sch., Princeton (N.J.) U., 1959-61, instr., 1964-65, asst. prof. history, 1965-66; asst. prof. history UCLA, 1966-68, assoc. prof., 1969-72, prof., 1972—, dean undergrad. curriculum devel., 1984-91; assoc. dir. Nat. Ctr. for History in the Schs., 1988-94, dir. 1994—; co-chair Nat. Hist. Stds. Project, 1992-95. Author: Quakers and Politics: Pennsylvania, 1681-1726, 1968, rev. edit., 1993, Class and Society in Early America, 1970, The Great Fear: Race in the Mind of America, 1970, Red, White, and Black: The Peoples of Early America, 1974, 2d edit., 1982, 3d edit., 1991, The Urban Crucible, 1979, Struggle and Survival in Colonial America, 1981, Race, Class and Politics: Essays on American Colonial and Revolutionary Society, 1986, (with others) The American People: Creating a Nation and a Society, 1986, 3d edit., 1994, Forging Freedom: The Formation of Philadelphia's Black Community, 1720-1840, 1988, Race and Revolution, 1990, (with Jean R. Soderlund) Freedom by Degrees: Emancipation and Its Aftermath in Pennsylvania, 1991, American Odyssey: The United States in the 20th Century, 1991, rev. edit., 1996, (with Charlotte Crabtree and Ross Dunn) History in Trial: Culture War and the Teaching of the Past, 1997; mem. editorial bd. William and Mary Quar., 1974-77, Jour. of Black Studies, 1971-73, Am. Indian Culture and Rsch. Jour., 1978—, Am. Quar., 1980-84, Pa. Mag. History and Biography, 1987—, Social History/Histoire Sociale, 1990—. Served with USN, 1955-58. Guggenheim fellow, 1969-70, Am. Council Learned Socs. fellow, 1973-74. Mem. Am. Hist. Assn., Inst. Early Am. History and Culture, Orgn. Am. Historians (exec. com. 1988-91, pres. 1994-95), Soc. Am. Historians, Am. Antiquarian Soc. Home: 16174 Alcima Ave Pacific Palisades CA 90272-2408

NASH, GERALD DAVID, historian; b. Berlin, July 16, 1928; came to U.S., 1938, naturalized, 1944; s. Alfred and Alice (Kantorowicz) N.; m. Marie L. Norris, Aug. 19, 1967; 1 dau., Stephanie Ann. B.A., NYU, 1950; M.A., Columbia U., 1952; Ph.D., U. Calif., Berkeley, 1957. Instr. history Stanford U., 1957-58, vis. asst. prof., 1959-60; asst. prof. No. Ill. U., DeKalb, 1958-59; postdoctoral fellow Harvard U., 1960-61; mem. faculty U. N.Mex., Albuquerque, 1961—; prof. history U. N.Mex., 1968—, chmn. dept., 1974-80, Presdl. prof., 1985-90, Disting. prof., 1990—; faculty rsch. lectr., 1970; vis. assoc. prof. NYU, 1965-66; George Bancroft prof. Am. History U. Goettingen, Fed. Republic Germany, 1990-91. Author: State Government and Economic Development, 1964, U.S. Oil Policy, 1968, Perspectives on Administration, 1969, The Great Transition, 1971, American West in 20th Century, 1973, Great Depression and World War II, 1979, The American West Transformed: The Impact of World War II, 1985, World War II and the West: Reshaping the Economy, 1990; editor: Issues in American Economic History, 3d edit., 1980, F.D. Roosevelt, 1967, Urban West, 1979 (with Noel Pugach and Richard Tomasson) Social Security in the U.S.-The First Half Century, 1988, (with Richard Etulain) Perspectives on the 20th Century West, 1989, Creating the West: Historical Interpretations, 1991, A.P. Giannini and the Bank of America, 1992, The Crucial Era, 1992; editor: (with Richard Etulain) Research Opportunities in 20th Century Western History, 1996; editor The Historian, 1974-84. Fellow Newberry Library, 1959, Huntington Library, 1979; sr. fellow NEH, 1981; Project 87 fellow, 1982-83. Mem. Am. Hist. Assn., Orgn. Am. Historians, Bus. History Soc., Agrl. History Soc., Western History Assn., Phi Beta Kappa. Club: Commonwealth. Office: U NMex Dept History Albuquerque NM 87131 *Anyone reflecting on major trends in the 20th century must conclude that the greatest challenge is to preserve freedom and democratic processes in the effort to achieve greater economic and social equality in America.*

NASH, GRAHAM WILLIAM, singer, composer; b. Blackpool, Lancashire, Eng., 1942. Mem.: Brit. group The Hollies, 1963-68; joined David Crosby and Stephen Stills to form group Brit. group, Crosby, Stills & Nash, 1969, then with Neil Young, to 1971, now soloist and duo (with David Crosby), then regrouped (with Stephen Stills), 1977; (with Hollies) albums include Bus Stop, 1966, Stop, Stop, Stop, 1967, Hollies' Greatest Hits, 1967, Evolution, 1967, Dear Eloise/King Midas in Reverse, 1967, (with Crosby and Stills) Crosby, Stills & Nash, 1969, CSN, 1977, (with Crosby, Stills and Young) Deja Vu, 1970, 4 Way Street, 1971, (with Crosby) Graham Nash and David Crosby, 1972, Wind on the Water, 1975, Whistling Down the Wire, 1976, Crosby/Nash Live, 1977, After The Storm, 1994, Crosby, Stills & Nash, 1994; solo albums Songs for Beginners, 1971, Wild Tales, 1974, Earth & Sky, Innocent Eyes, 1986; appeared in film Woodstock, 1970. Recipient Grammy award (with Crosby and Stills) for Best New Artist of Year, 1969. Office: Atlantic Records 75 Rockefeller Plz New York NY 10019-6908*

NASH, HENRY WARREN, marketing educator; b. Tampa, Fla., Sept. 19, 1927; s. Leslie Dikeman and Mildred (Johnson) N.; m. Frances Lora Venters, Aug. 20, 1950; children: Warren Leslie, Richard Dale. B.S. in Bus. Adminstrn, U. Fla., 1950, M.B.A., 1951; postgrad., Ind. U., 1951-53; Ph.D., U. Ala., 1965. Student asst. U. Fla., 1948-50, grad. asst., 1950-51; grad. asst. Ind. U., 1951-53; salesman Field Enterprises, Inc., Chgo., 1953; assoc. prof. bus. and econs. Miss. Coll., 1953-57; assoc. prof. marketing Miss. State U., 1957-66, prof., head dept., 1966-96; emeritus prof. mktg., emeritus head dept. mktg., quantitative analysis, bus. law, dir. Coll. Bus. and Industry Acad. Advising Ctr., 1995—; ptnr. Southland Cons. Assos., 1968-84; bd. dirs. Govt. Employees Credit Union, 1969-92, v.p., 1969-73, pres., 1973-78. Author: (with others) Principles of Marketing, 1961. Served with USNR, 1945-46. Loveman's Merchandising fellow U. Ala., 1961-62. Mem. Am. Mktg. Assn., Am. Acad. Advt., Acad. Internat. Bus., So. Econ. Assn., So. Mktg. Assn. (sec. 1974-75, pres. 1976-77), Sales and Mktg. Execs. (internat. chmn. educators com. 1967-70), Miss. Retail Mchts. Assn. (bd. dirs.), Pi Sigma Epsilon (Nat. educator, v.p. 1967-69, nat. pres. 1967-71), Kiwanis (treas. Starkville club 1969-70, v.p. 1973-74, pres. 1974-75, lt. gov. 1977-78, gov. 1982-83), Blue Key, Beta Gamma Sigma, Omicron Delta Kappa, Mu Kappa Tau (nat. v.p. 1977-79, 86-88, pres. 1979-81, 88-90), Alpha Kappa Psi, Phi Kappa Phi (v.p. Miss. State U. 1990-91, pres. 1991-92). Baptist (tchr., deacon). Home: 114 Forest Hill Dr Starkville MS 39759-3127 Office: Miss State U COBI Acad Advising Ctr Mississippi State MS 39762

NASH, HOWARD ALLEN, biochemist, researcher; b. N.Y.C., Nov. 5, 1937; s. Harvey and Harriet (Ratner) N.; m. Dominie Maria Shortino, Aug. 31, 1963; children: Janet Elisabeth, Emily Julia. BS, Tufts U., 1957; MD, U. Chgo., 1961, PhD, 1963. Intern U. Chgo. Clinics, 1963-64; rsch. assoc. NIMH, Bethesda, Md., 1964-68, med. officer (res), 1968-84, chief, sec. molecular genetics, 1984—; chmn. Gordon Conf. on Nucleic Acids, 1988; vice-chair FASEB Conf. on Genetic Recombination, 1993, chair, 1995. Assoc. editor: Cell Jour., 1985-91; editl. bd.: Current Biology Jour., 1993—, Genes to Cells, 1996—. Lt. comdr. USPHS, 1964-68. Recipient Superior Svc. award USPHS, 1985, Disting. Svc. award HHS, 1990, Alumni award for Disting. Svc., U. Chgo., 1994. Fellow Am. Acad. Arts and Sci.; mem. NAS. Office: Lab Molecular Biology NIMH 36 Convent Dr Bethesda MD 20892-4034

NASH, JOHN ARTHUR, bank executive; b. Indpls., Mar. 12, 1938; s. Basil and Harriet Nash; m. Susan Moss; children: John, Bill, Stacia. BS, Ind. U., 1960, MBA, 1961. Account officer Nat. City Bank, Cleve., 1961-66; v.p. Irwin Union Bank, Columbus, Ind., 1966-71, exec. v.p., 1971-75, pres., 1975-79; pres. Irwin Fin. Corp., Columbus, 1979—; also bd. dirs. Irwin Fin. Corp., Columbus, Ind.; bd. dirs. Irwin Union Bank, Inland Mortgage Corp., Affiliated Capital Corp., Irwin Home Equity Corp. Bd. dirs., chmn. bd. trustees Columbus Regional Hosp., Columbus Econ. Devel. Bd.; past chmn. Heritage Fund Bartholomew County, Columbus; mem. steering com. Columbus 2000; mem. adv. bd. Ind. U.-Purdue U., Indpls. 2d lt. U.S. Army, 1961-63. Recipient Sagamore of Wabash award Gov. of Ind., 1991. Mem. Am. Bankers Assn. (mem. bank leadership coun.), Ind. Bankers Assn. (bd. dirs., past chmn., chmn. govt. rels. com.), Ind. U. Alumni Assn. (pres. 1991-92). Office: Irwin Fin Corp 500 Washington St Columbus IN 47201-6230

NASH, JOHN FORBES, JR., research mathematician; b. Bluefield, W.Va., 1928. BS in Math., Carnegie-Mellon U., 1945, MS, 1948; PhD, Princeton U., 1950. Rsch. asst., instr. Princeton (N.J.) U., 1950-51; Moore instr. MIT, 1951-53, asst. prof., 1953-57, assoc. prof., 1957-59; sr. rsch. mathematician Princeton U.; cons. RAND Corp., summers 1950, 52, 54; vis. mem. Inst. Advanced Study, Princeton, 1956-57, 61-62, 63-64; rsch. assoc. math. MIT, 1966-67. Co-recipient Nobel Prize in Econ. Scis., 1994; recipient von Neumann Theory prize Ops. Rsch. Soc. Am.; Sloan fellow, NSF fellow; Westinghouse scholar. Fellow Econometric Soc., Am. Acad. of Arts and Scis.; mem. NAS. Office: Princeton U Dept Math Fine Hall Princeton NJ 08544

NASH, JOHN JOSEPH, secondary education educator, real estate manager; b. Des Moines, Aug. 25, 1970; s. Donald Harry and Dortha Darlene (Underwood) N. BA, Iowa State U., 1992. Cert. secondary tchr., Iowa. Office mgr. JDJ Investments, Ankeny, Iowa, 1988-94, real estate mgr., 1994—; tchr. sci. Hubbard (Iowa) Cmty. Sch. Dist., 1992-93, Urbandale (Iowa) Cmty. Sch. Dist., 1994-95, Twin Cedars Cmty. Sch. Dist., Bussey, Iowa, 1995-96. Author: (textbook) Simply Chemistry, 1993. Mem. U.S. Chess Fedn. (life; cert. local tournament dir. 1990—), Iowa State Chess Assn. (bd. dirs. 1994—, Svc. award 1990, editor 1996—). Democrat. Methodist. Avocations: wood carving, computers. Office: 2107 W 1st St Apt 5 Ankeny IA 50021-2419

NASH, JOHN N., professional basketball team executive; b. Phila., Nov. 28, 1946; s. John N. and Rosemary K. (Noon) N.; m. Anne Kelly (div.); children: Andrea, Carolyn; m. Ann Raley, Oct. 27, 1978; children: Brian, Barbara. Dir. group sales Phila. 76ers, 1969-71, asst. gen. mgr., 1981-86, gen. mgr., 1986-90; ticket mgr. athletic dept. U. Pa., Phila., 1971-72, Phila. Blazers, 1972-73, Phila. Flyers, 1973-75; exec. sec. Big 5 Basketball, 1975-81; asst. gen. mgr., bus. mgr. Phila. 76ers, 1981-86, gen. mgr., 1986-90; v.p. and gen. mgr. Washington Bullets, 1990-96; gen. mgr. N.J. Nets, 1996—. Office: NJ Nets 405 Murray Hill Pkwy East Rutherford NJ 07073*

NASH, JONATHON MICHAEL, program manager, mechanical engineer; b. Little Rock, Aug. 10, 1942; s. Bertram B. and Nora B. (Shed) N.; m. Meta W. Smith, Aug. 12, 1972; children: Lillian Kendrick, Caroline Michael. BS in Mech. Engring., U. Miss., 1966, MS in Engring. Sci., 1970, PhD in Engring. Sci., 1973. Registered profl. engr., Ala., Miss., Md. Jr. engr. IBM Fed. Systems div., Huntsville, Ala., 1967-68, Saturn/Apollo manned spacecraft programs sr. assoc. engr., 1973-74, staff engr., 1975-77, solar energy programs project engr., 1977-78, devel. engr., Gaithersburg, Md., 1978-80, adv. engr. synthetic fuels program, 1980-81, tech. planning mgr., 1981-83, sr. engr. FAA programs, Rockville, Md., 1983-88, sr. engr., program mgr. internat. air traffic control programs, 1988-94; program mgr. air traffic control LORAL Fed. Systems, Rockville, Md., 1994-96; program mgr. Lockheed Martin Air Traffic Mgmt., Rockville, 1996—; rsch. assoc. U. Miss., 1970-72, adj. assoc. prof. mech. engring., 1983—; aerospace engr., sci. intern NASA Manned Space Craft Center, summers 1970, 71; instr. U. Ala., Huntsville, 1977-78. Bd. dirs. Arts Council of Frederick City and County, Md., 1981-84, v.p., 1982-83; mem. Lafayette County (Miss.) Rep. Exec. Com., 1972-73. With C.E., U.S. Army, 1968-70, Vietnam; maj. USAR. Decorated Bronze Star; recipient NASA New Tech. award, 1979; NASA Apollo Achievement award 1971; Ala. Young Engr. of Yr. award, Nat. Soc. Profl. Engrs., 1978; Tudor medal for engring. contbns. Soc. Am. Mil. Engrs., 1978; Engring. Achievement award, Huntsville chpt. Soc. Am. Mil. Engrs., 1977; Outstanding Young Engr. of Yr. award Huntsville chpt. Ala. Soc. Profl. Engrs., 1976, others; U. Miss. fellow, 1970-73. Fellow AIAA (assoc.), ASME (exec. com. solar energy div. 1981-86, sec./treas. 1982-83, vice chmn. 1983-84, chmn. 1984-85, mem. coun. engring. 1992—, mem. operating bd. energy resources group 1984—, Cert. of Appreciation, solar energy div. 1982, 85, chpt. chmn., 1978, vice chmn. 1977-78, treas. 1976-77, mem. nat. bur. standards interaction com., chmn. nat. com. tech. planning 1992—, nat. nominating com. 1988-90, nat. sattelite programs com.. 1990-92); mem. NSPE, VFW, ASHRAE (nat. tech. com. on solar energy utilization 1977-80), Am. Inst. Chem. Engrs., Soc. Am. Mil. Engrs. (chpt. pres. 1976-77, bd. dir. 1977-78), Md. Engring. Soc., Ala. Soc. Profl. Engrs. (chpt. dir. 1978), Internat. Solar Energy Soc., Ala. Solar Energy Assn. (chpt. dir. 1978), Am. Def. Preparedness Assn., Sigma Xi (chpt. pres. 1977-78), Omicron Delta Kappa, Alpha Tau Omega (pres. Huntsville alumni 1976-77), Res. Officers Assn. Editor: (with Smok, Thomas and Jenkins) Modeling, Simulation, Testing and Measurements for Solar Energy Systems, 1978; assoc. editor: (jour.) Applied Mechanics Revs., 1985-87, Mfg. Rev., 1987—; contbr. articles to profl. jours.; inventor in field. Home: 300 Rockwell Ter Frederick MD 21701-4912 Office: 9211 Corporate Blvd Rockville MD 20850-3245

NASH, LEE J., banker; b. Elgin, Ill., Aug. 17, 1939; s. Richard Lee and Pearl Kepler (June) N.; m. Ruth Ann Ebeling, June 16, 1963; children—Joanne Elizabeth, J.R.; m. Sandra Gail Clegg, Feb. 16, 1980; children—Jason Lee, Jessica Gail. A.B. with honors, Harvard Coll., 1961; M.B.A., Columbia U., 1963. Mgmt. trainee Bankers Trust Co., N.Y.C., 1963-64; v.p. Pitts. Nat. Bank, 1964-70, Crocker Nat. Bank, San Francisco, 1970-75; sr. v.p. Shawmut Corp., Boston, 1975-79; exec. v.p., treas. Mfrs. Hanover Trust Co., N.Y.C., 1979-87; pres., chief exec. officer Mfrs. Hanover Securities Corp., N.Y.C., 1988-90; exec. v.p. Fed. Farm Credit Banks Funding Corp., 1990—. Mem. Am. Bankers Assn. (chmn. fund mgmt. and fin. markets divsn. 1985-87), Pub. Securities Assn. (bd. dirs. 1982-84), Treas. Securities Luncheon Club, Harvard Club (N.Y.C.), Beta Gamma Sigma. Office: Fed Farm Credit Banks Funding Corp 10 Exchange Pl Jersey City NJ 07302

NASH, LEONARD KOLLENDER, chemistry educator; b. N.Y.C., Oct. 27, 1918; s. Adolph and Carol (Kollender) N.; m. Ava Byer, Mar. 3, 1945; children—Vivian C., David B. B.S., Harvard, 1939, M.A., 1941, Ph.D., 1944. Rsch. asst. Harvard U., Cambridge, Mass., 1943-44, instr., 1946-48, asst. prof., 1948-53, assoc. prof., 1953-59, prof. chemistry, 1959-86, chmn. dept., 1971-74; rsch. assoc. Columbia U., 1944-45; instr. U. Ill., 1945-46; ret.; staff Manhattan Project, 1944-45. Author: Elements of Chemical Thermodynamics, 1962, The Nature of the Natural Sciences, 1963, Stoichiometry, 1966, Elements of Statistical Thermodynamics, 1968, ChemThermo, 1972. Recipient Mfg. Chemists' award, 1966; James Flack Norris award, 1975. Home: 11 Field Rd Lexington MA 02173-8014

NASH, MARY ALICE, nursing educator; b. Erie, Pa., Nov. 13, 1957; d. Robert Stuart and Jean Marie (Clark) N. BSN, Duquesne U., 1979; postgrad., Edinboro U., 1988-95. RN, Pa.; cert. CPR instr. Clin. educator St. Vincent Health Ctr., Erie, 1984, asst. nurse educator, 1988—. Mem. ANA, AACCN, Nat. League Nursing, Pa. Nurses Assn., Sigma Theta Tau. Home: 917 W 30th St Erie PA 16508-1645 Office: St Vincent Health Ctr 232 W 25th St Erie PA 16544-0002

NASH, NICHOLAS DAVID, retailing executive; b. Mpls., June 11, 1939; s. Edgar Vanderhoef and Nancy (Van Slyke) N. A.B., Harvard U., 1962; M.Ed., Bowling Green State U., 1970; Ph.D., U. Minn., 1975. Head lower sch. Maumee Valley (Ohio) Country Day Sch., 1965-71; assoc. dir. Univ. Council for Ednl. Adminstrn.; adj. asst. prof. Ohio State U., 1975-78; v.p. programming Minn. Public Radio, St. Paul, 1978-82, Am. Pub. Radio, St. Paul, 1982-85; pres. The Nash Co., 1985—; bd. dirs. Sta. WCAL-FM. Author works in field. Bd. dirs. Schubert Club, Sigurd Olson Environ. Inst., 1992—, Nash Found., 1975—. Mem. University Club St. Paul. Episcopalian. Home: 1340 N Birch Lake Blvd Saint Paul MN 55110-6716 Office: 2179 4th St # 2-h Saint Paul MN 55110-3028

NASH, PAUL LENOIR, lawyer; b. Poughkeepsie, N.Y., Jan. 29, 1931; s. George Matthew and Winifred (LeNoir) N.; m. Nancy Allyn Thouron, Dec. 30, 1961; children—Andrew Gray, Laurie LeNoir, Daphne Thouron. B.A., Yale U., 1953; LL.B., Harvard U., 1958. Bar: N.Y. 1959. Assoc., Dewey, Ballantine, Bushby, Palmer & Wood, N.Y.C., 1958-66, ptnr., 1966—. Pres. bd. trustees Peck Sch., Morristown, N.J., 1978-82. Served to capt. USMC, 1953-55; Japan. Mem. ABA, N.Y. State Bar Assn., Assn. Bar City of N.Y. Republican. Home: 4 Westminster Pl Morristown NJ 07960-5810 Office: Dewey Ballantine 1301 Avenue Of The Americas New York NY 10019-6022

NASH, PETER HUGH JOHN, geographer, educator, planner; b. Frankfurt-on-Main, Germany, Sept. 18, 1921; came to U.S., 1938, naturalized, 1943; s. John Hans Joseph and Alice (Heuman) N.; m. Inez Mae Frost, July 30, 1955 (dec. Apr. 1988); children: Carina Frost Nash Lawrence, Peter Hugh John Jr. A.A. in Earth Scis, Los Angeles City Coll., 1941; B.A. (Gruen Fellow), UCLA, 1942, M.A. in Geography, 1946; Certificat D'Etudes, U. Grenoble, France, 1945; postgrad., U. Wis., 1946-47; M. City Planning (Holtzer fellow), Harvard U., 1949, M.Pub. Adminstrn., 1956, Ph.D. in Archtl. Scis, 1958; postgrad., U. Cin. Law Sch., 1961-63; hon. degree, Aligarh Muslim U., India, 1968. Prin. planning asst. Boston Planning Bd., 1949-50; sr. planner City of Worcester, Mass., 1950-51; asst. chief urban redevel. div. Boston Housing Authority, 1951-52; dir. planning dept. City of Medford, Mass., 1952-56; vis. critic Harvard Grad. Sch. Design, 1955-57, 66-68; assoc. prof. city and regional planning U. N.C., 1957-59; prof., head dept. geography and regional planning U. Cin., 1959-63; dean Grad. Sch., U. R.I. Kingston, 1963-68, prof. geography and regional planning, dir. grad. curriculum in community planning and area devel., 1963-70; dean faculty of environ. studies U. Waterloo, Ont., Can., 1970-75; prof. architecture, geography and planning U. Waterloo, 1970-93, disting. prof. emeritus, 1993—; instr. Center for Adult Edn., Cambridge, Mass., 1949-57; lectr. Northeastern U., Boston, 1954-56; lectr., acting asst. prof. Boston U., 1956-57; vis. prof. summers U. So. Calif., 1959, 62, Aroostook State Coll., Maine, 1961, Grad. School Ekistics, Athens, Greece, 1967, 70, Inst. Human Scis. Boston Coll., 1969-70; cons. Brookings Inst., 1960-61, ACTION, Inc., 1959-61, Battelle Meml. Inst., Columbus, Ohio and Cleve., 1967-73; corr. Ekistics, 1960-73; Western hemisphere rep. commn. applied geography Internat. Geog. Union, 1964-76. Author 3 books; contbr. over 200 articles, chpts. and revs. in profl. and scholarly jours.; pub. in his honor Peter Nash Festschrift- Abstract Thoughts: Concrete Solutions: Essays, 1987. Participant Delos Symposion, Greece, 1967, 70, 74; mem. alumni council Harvard Sch. Design, pres., 1967-70; mem. exec. coun., sec.-treas. Kennedy Sch. govt., Harvard U., 1982-87; chmn. bd. dirs. K/W Philharm. Choir, 1976-80. Served with AUS, 1942-45. Decorated Purple Heart with oak leaf cluster, Bronze Star; Croix de Guerre (France); recipient Sci. Achievement medal U. Liege, Belgium, 1967; Social Sci. Rsch. Coun. grantee, 1960; NSF grantee, 1960; Am. Council of Learned Socs. grantee, 1968; Can. Coun. grantee, 1974, 80, 82; Can. Social Scis. and Humanities Rsch. Coun. fellow U. Grenoble, France, 1984-85, Yokohama, Japan, rsch. grantee, Athens, Greece, 1985, Barcelona, Spain, 1986, rsch. fellowship grantee, 1986-88. Fellow Am. Geog. Soc. (life), Assn. Am. Geographers (life); mem. Inst. Alpine Geography, Grenoble (hon.), Am. Inst. Planners, Internat. City Mgmt. Assn., AAAS, Am. Soc. Pub. Adminstrn., Can. Assn. Geographers, Can. Inst. Planners, Regional Sci. Assn., World Future Soc. (life), New Eng. Conf. on Grad. Edn. (sec.-treas. 1966-68), Assn. Collegiate Schs. Planning (treas. 1968-70), World Soc. Ekistics (v.p. 1994-96), Sigma Xi, Sigma Nu, Kappa Delta Pi. Clubs: Mason (Boston and Toronto) (K.T.), Harvard (Boston and Toronto); Rotary Internat. (Kitchener, Ont., Paul Harris fellow). Home: 588 Sugarbush Dr, Waterloo, ON Canada N2K 1Z8 *I have never felt constrained by boundaries, whether geographical, intellectual, disciplinary, or any other type. One has to follow those avenues where one's intellectual curiosity points the way, even if these paths lead to entirely different territories. The world of reflective thinkers is inhabited primarily by splitters and drillers, but the lumpers and spreaders are increasing rapidly in this era of knowledge explosion, and I am a standard bearer of this salient group as I help to create better futures.*

NASH, RONALD HERMAN, philosophy educator; b. Cleve., May 27, 1936; s. Herman Nash and Viola McAlpin; m. Betty Jane Perry, June 8, 1957; children: Jeffrey A., Jennifer A. BA, Barrington (R.I.) Coll., 1958; MA, Brown U., 1960; PhD, Syracuse U., 1964. Instr. philosophy Barrington Coll., 1958-60, Houghton (N.Y.) Coll., 1960-62; prof. philosophy Western Ky. U., Bowling Green, 1964-91; prof. philosophy religion Ref. Theol. Sem., Orlando, Fla., 1991—; dept. head Western Ky. U., Bowling Green, 1964-84; mem. adv. bd. CEBA, Lynchburg, Va., 1989—. Author: 30 books, including: Poverty and Wealth, 1986, Faith and Reason, 1988, The Closing of the American Heart, 1990, The Gospel and the Greeks, 1992, Beyond Liberation Theology, 1992, World Views in Conflict, 1992, Great Divides, 1992; contbg. editor: The Freeman, 1993—, Christian Rsch. Jour., 1993—; mem. bd. editors Durell Jour. Money and Banking, 1988-91. Advisor U.S. Civil Rights Commn., Washington, 1988-91. Fellow NEH, 1969. Office: Ref Theol Sem PO Box 945120 Maitland FL 32794-5120

NASH, SHEENA ANN HARGIS, flight nurse; b. Taipei, Taiwan, China, July 11, 1966; came to U.S., 1968; d. Joseph Scott and Julia Ann (Barnes) Hill; m. Earnest Harold Hargis, Jr., July 20, 1985 (div. Mar. 1990); 1 child, Sheena Marie; m. Shannon T. Nash, May 10, 1996. BSN, Tenn. Tech. U., 1990. Cert. emergency med. technician, Tenn. Emergency med. technician Putnam County Ambulance Svc., Cookeville, Tenn., 1985—; staff nurse transplant unit St. Thomas Hosp., Nashville, 1990-92; staff nurse, supr., educator critical care Cookeville Gen. Hosp., 1992—; flight nurse Erlanger Med. Ctr.-Life Force Air Med., Chattanooga, 1995—; preceptor for nursing student Tenn. Tech. U., Cookeville, 1992—; BLS instr., ACLS instr., pediat. advanced life support instr., prehosp. trauma life support instr., 1990—. Mem. PTO Parkview, Cookeville, 1992-96; mem. Cookeville Women's Bowling Assn., team capt., 1992-94, pres., 1994-95; mem. Putnam County Vol. Fire Fighter; asst. coach Boxter T-Ball Assn., 1992-94. Mem. AACN (CCRN), ANA, Emergency Nurses Assn., Nat. Flight Nurses Assn., Tenn. Nurses Assn. (bd. dirs. 1990-92, sec. 1994—), Nat. Wildlife Assn. Avocations: karate, bowling, riflery, camping and hiking, boating. Home: 4049 Ditty Rd Cookeville TN 38506-7663

NASH, STELLA B., government nutrition administrator; b. Gould, Ark., Nov. 3, 1942; d. Virgil and Lessie B. (Bonner) Riley; m. Solomon Nash, Mar. 31, 1973; children: Chad, Jereme. BS, U. Ark., 1964; MA, NYU, 1970; postgrad., Pa. State U., 1973-74, U. Mo., 1974-75. Nutritionist/spl. asst. to the dir. Ark. Office on Aging, Little Rock, 1975-76; supr. child nutrition Ark. State Dept. Edn., Little Rock, 1976-79; supr. Coop. Extension Svc. USDA, Denver, 1979-85; regional nutrition dir. Mountain Plains region USDA Food and Nutrition Svc., Denver, 1985—; home mgmt. specialist U. Ark. Coop. Extension, Pine Bluff, 1972-73; nutritionist N.J. Coll. Medicine and Dentistry, Newark, 1970-72; dietitian King County Hosp., Bklyn., 1964-66. Contbr. (poetry) Windows of the Soul, 1995; co-author: (coloring book) Nutrition Education, 1972; contbr. newspaper articles to Rocky Mountain News, 1992; author (jour.) Ill. Tchr., 1974. State v.p., dist. pres. New Home Makers Am., Ark., 1958-59; mem. Montbello Optimist Club, Denver, 1987-89, Far NE Neighbors Assn., Denver, 1985—; chairperson worship United Ch. of Montbello, Denver, 1989—. Recipient Nutrition Edn. award Western Dairy Coun., 1986; named Outstanding Educator of Am., Outstanding Educators of Am., 1973, Outstanding Young Woman of Am., Outstanding Young Women of Am., 1976. Mem. Am. Dietetic Assn. (registered dietitian), Colo. Dietetic Assn. (scholarship chairperson 1990-91, 95-96, pub. rels. 1983-84, award) Soc. Nutrition Edn., Ark. Gerontol. Soc. (charter), Delta Sigma Theta (undergrad. chpt. sponsor 1972-73). Avocations: reading, sewing, visiting museums and art galleries, piano, public speaking. Home: 3300 S. Tamarac Dr Ste M205 Denver CO 80231

NASH, WILLIAM ARTHUR, civil engineer, educator; b. Chgo., Sept. 15, 1922; s. William A. and Rose (Keck) N.; m. Verna Lucile Baer, Aug. 8, 1953; children: Rebecca Ann, Phillip Arthur. B.S. in Civil Engring, Ill. Inst. Tech., 1944, M.S., 1946; Ph.D., U. Mich., 1949. Research engr. David W. Taylor Model Basin, Navy Dept., Washington, 1949-54; mem. faculty U. Fla., Gainesville, 1954-67; head dept. engring. mechanics U. Fla., 1964-67; prof. civil engring. U. Mass., Amherst, 1967—; cons. to govt. and industry; hon. prof. Shanghai Inst. Tech., 1985; pres. Cons. Engring., Amherst, 1992—. Author: Theory and Outline of Strength of Materials, 2d edit., 1973, 3d edit., 1994, Statics and Mechanics of Materials, 1991, Hydrostatically Loaded Structures, 1995; contbr. 105 rsch. articles to profl. jours.; editor Internat. Jour. Nonlinear Mechanics. Recipient Humboldt U.S. Sr.

Scientist award to Fed. Republic Germany, 1986; named Outstanding Sr. Faculty Mem. in Engring., U. Mass., 1987. Fellow ASME; mem. Internat. Assn. Shell and Spatial Structures, Am. Soc. Engring. Edn. (Curtis W. McGraw Research award 1961), AIAA, Earthquake Engring. Research Inst. Congregationalist. Office: 235 Marston Hall U Mass Amherst MA 01003

NASHE, CAROL, association executive, public relations consultant; b. Boston; d. Max and Sarah Ida (Litcofsky) Naselsky; m. Russell Weinberg (dec. Aug. 1980); children: Richard Dana, Harold Mark (dec.). Student, Mass. Sch. of Art, Boston, 1949. Asst. fashion editor Boston Herald Traveler, 1951; pres., founder Carol Nashe Sch. & Model Agy., Boston, 1951-74; dir. pub. rels. Sheraton Boston Hotel & Tower, 1974-84; cons. Blue Cross and Blue Shield of Mass., Boston, 1984-93; pres. Carol Nashe Group, Boston, 1993—; pub. rels. dir. O'Connor Golf Promotions, 1996—; state chmn. U.S. Olympic Com., Mass., 1986-92; bd. dirs. World Trade Ctr., 1987-97; exec. dir., exec. v.p. Nat. Assn. Radio Talk Show Hosts. Bd. dirs. Morgan Meml. Goodwill Industries, Boston, 1986-93, Wang Ctr., Mass. Spl. Olympics, Pub. Action for Arts, Boys and Girls Clubs, Friends of John F. Kennedy Libr.; chmn. bd. Nat. Kidney Found.; advisor Boston organizing com., Mayors Drug Rally; chmn., founder Harold Weinberg Meml. Found., Friends of Mateo's Ballet Theatre of Boston. Named Woman of Yr., Nat. Kidney Found., 1983, Woman of Achievement, Big Sisters, 1986, Nat. Humanitarian of Yr., Heaven's Children, 1989; recipient Matrix award Women in Communications, Inc., 1988. Mem. Publicity Club, New Eng. Broadcasters Assn. (bd. dirs. 1985-90), Mass. Women's Polit. Caucus, Internat. Inst. Women's Polit. Leaders, Greater Boston C. of C. (bd. dirs. 1986-93), Exec. Club Boston (pres. 1991-92), Boston Club (pub. rels. com. 1987-95). Avocations: travel, photography, reading, golf, collectables. Home and Office: 134 Saint Botolph St Boston MA 02115-4819

NASHMAN, ALVIN ELI, computer company executive; b. N.Y.C., Dec. 16, 1926; s. Joseph and Fay (Portnoy) N.; m. Honey Weinstein, May 29, 1960; children—Jessica Rachel, Pamela Wynne, Stephanie Paige. B.E.E., CUNY, 1948; M.E.E., NYU, 1951; Sc.D. (hon.), Pacific U., 1968, George Washington U., 1986. With Ketay Mfg. Corp., N.Y.C., 1951-52; dir. missile systems lab, dir. rsch. and devel. programs ITT Fed. Labs., Nutley, N.J., 1952-62; dir. ops., systems engring. and tech. advisor Defense Comms. Agency ITT Intelcom, Inc., Falls Church, Va., 1962-65; pres. Computer Scis. Corp., Falls Church, 1965-67, bd. dir., 1968-95, v.p., 1969-92, cons., 1996—; chmn. bd. dirs. Miltope Corp. Patentee in field; contbr. articles to profl. jours. Trustee Fairfax Hosp. System Found. With USN, 1944-46. Fellow IEEE; mem. Armed Forces Communications and Electronics Assn. (dir., internat. v.p. 1976-79, chpt. pres. 1979-80, exec. com. 1980-84, chmn. bd. 1984-86), AIAA, Nat. Space Club, Nat. Security Indsl. Assn., Tau Beta Pi, Eta Kappa Nu. Republican. Jewish. Home: 3609 Ridgeway Ter Falls Church VA 22044 also: Computer Scis Corp 3170 Fairview Park Dr Falls Church VA 22042

NASO, VALERIE JOAN, automobile dealership executive, travel company operator, artist, photographer, writer; b. Stockton, Calif., Aug. 19, 1941; d. Alan Robert and Natalie Grace (Gardner) McKittrick Naso; m. Peter Joralemon, May 31, 1971 (div.). Student pub. schs., Piedmont, Calif. Cert. graphoanalyst. Pres., Naso Motor Co. (formerly Broadway Cadillacs, Oakland, Calif.) Bishop, Calif., 1964—; freelance artist, 1965—; owner, operator Wooden Horse Antiques, Bishop, 1970-82; editor, writer, photographer Sierra Life Mag., Bishop, 1980-83; freelance writer, photographer, 1972—; owner, operator Boredom Tours, Bishop, 1981—; owner, sole photographer, Renaissance Photography, N.Y.C. and Bishop, Calif., 1982—, Keyboard Colors, 1986; cons. graphoanalyst, 1976—. Fiction, non-fiction work pub. in Horse and Horseman, Am. Horseman, Horse & Rider Mag., Cameo Mag., Desert Mag., Sierra Life Mag. Mem. Nat. Assn. Female Execs., Authors Guild, Inc., Authors League Am., Am. Film Inst., Archives of Am. Art, Lalique Soc. Am., Musical Box Soc. Internat., Alliance Francaise (N.Y. chpt.), Bishop C. of C., Victorian Soc. Am., Nat. Trust for Hist. Preservation, Am. Craft Coun., Nat. Rifle Assn. Clubs: Cadillac LaSalle (nat. and so. calif. chpts.); Wagner Soc. (N.Y.C.). Office: 783 N Main St Bishop CA 93514-2427 Office: PO Box 1625 Bishop CA 93515

NASON, CHARLES TUCKEY, financial services executive; b. Pitts., Apr. 22, 1946; s. Raymond W. and Helen (Tuckey) N.; m. Marlane L. Mulac, Nov. 20, 1967; children—Rebecca Ann, Jill Nicole. B.A., Washington and Jefferson Coll., 1968; M.B.A., U. Pitts., 1969. Cert. fin. planner; chartered fin. cons.; CLU. Dist. sales mgr. Met. Life Ins. Co., Pitts., 1971-77; mng. dir. Acacia Group Cos., Pitts., 1977-88; chmn., pres., chief exec. officer Acacia Mut. Life Ins. Co. , Washington, 1988—; founder, pres. Coordinated Capital Ltd., Pitts., 1982-85. Chmn. exec. com. Washington and Jefferson Coll. Devel. Coun., 1982-85; bd. trustees Washington and Jefferson Coll., 1988—; chmn. Nat. Annual Giving Fund Washington and Jefferson Coll., 1992-96; trustee Washington Federal City Coun., 1988—; bd. dirs. Greater Washington Bd. Trade, 1990—, chmn.-elect, 1993, chmn. 1994; bd. dirs. Blue Cross Blue Shield of Washington, 1991-93, Greater Washington Boys and Girls Clubs, 1991—, Am. Coun. of Life Ins., 1993-97, Medlantic Healthcare Group, 1997—. Lt. USAF. 1970-71, Korea. Mem. Gen. Agts. and Mgrs. Assn. (pres. 1984-85), Am. Soc. CLUSs (pres. 1981-82), Estate Planning Coun. (bd. dirs.), Nat. Assn. Securities Dealers, Inst. Cert. Fin. Planners (bd. dirs.), Burning Tree Club, Congl. Country Club, Met. Club (Washington), Melrose Club. Republican. Roman Catholic. Avocations: reading, golf, guitar. Home: 18 Beman Woods Ct Potomac MD 20854-5481 Office: Acacia Group 51 Louisiana Ave NW Washington DC 20001-2105

NASON, JOHN WILLIAM, retired college president, educational consultant; b. St. Paul, Feb. 9, 1905; s. Albert John and Mary Ethel (Eaton) N.; m. Bertha Deane White, June 15, 1935 (dec. Dec. 1955); children: Charles Kirby, Robert White; m. Elizabeth Mercer Knapp, June 29, 1957; stepchildren: Whitman E. Knapp, Caroline Knapp Hines, Marion E. Knapp. BA, Carleton Coll., 1926, LLD, 1948; postgrad., Yale U., 1926-27; MA, Harvard U., 1928; BA, Oxford (Eng.) U., 1931; LLD, U. Pa., 1941; LittD, Muhlenberg Coll., 1943, Hahnemann Med. Coll. and Hosp., 1943; LHD, Dropsie Coll., 1952, Coll. of Wooster, 1961, St. Olaf Coll., 1970, SUNY, 1992; LLD, Swarthmore Coll., 1953, Hamilton Coll., 1955, Brandeis U., 1958, Johns Hopkins U., 1960. Instr. philosophy Swarthmore Coll., 1931-34, asst. prof., 1934-40, asst. to pres., 1937-38, 39-40, acting chmn. dept. philosophy, 1938-39, pres., 1940-53; asst. to Am. sec. Rhodes Trustees, 1934-40; pres. Fgn. Policy Assn., 1953-62, Carleton Coll., Northfield, Minn., 1962-70; dir. studies Assn. Governing Bds., 1973-75, dir. study presdl. selection and assessment, 1977-79; dir. study on found. trustees Coun. on Founds., 1975-77; ednl. cons., 1979—. Author: American Higher Education in 1980—Some Basic Issues, 1965, Crises in the University, 1970, The Future of Trusteeship: The Role and Responsibilities of College and University Boards, 1975, Trustees & the Future of Foundations, 1977, Presidential Search: A Guide to the Process of Selecting and Appointing College and University Presidents, 1979, Presidential Assessment: Challenge to College and University Leadership, 1980, The Nature of Trusteeship, 1982, Foundation Trusteeship: Service in the Public Interest, 1989; various articles, revs. Chmn. Nat. Japanese-Am. Student Relocation Coun., 1942-45; pres. UN Coun. Phila., 1942-45, World Affairs Coun. Phila., 1949-51, 52-53; mem. Fulbright-Hays Com. Internat. Exchange Persons, 1963-66; mem. educators adv. com. Esso Edn. Found., 1964-68; trustee Edward W. Hazen Found., 1945-67, 68-78; Trustee Phillips Exeter Acad., 1946-50, 52-62, Vassar Coll., 1954-62, Danforth Found., 1961-68, United Negro Coll. Fund, 1966-70, Adirondack Conservancy, 1977-90, N.Y. State Conservancy, 1983-90; bd. govs. Bruce L. Crary Found., 1979-93; bd. dirs. Eisenhower Exchange Fellowship, 1953-65, Fgn. Policy Assn., 1953-62, 71-80 ; mem. adv. coun. Inst. Ednl. Mgmt., Harvard U., 1975-76; mem. vis. com. Harvard Grad. Sch. Edn., 1977-82. Rhodes scholar Oxford U., 1931. Fellow Nat. Coun. Religion in Higher Edn. (pres. 1943-49); mem. Soc. Values in Higher Edn., Phi Beta Kappa (senator united chpts. 1967-73), Delta Sigma Rho. Mem. Soc. of Friends. Home: 12 Crosslands Dr Kennett Square PA 19348-2039

NASON, ROBERT E., accountant; b. Sioux Falls, S.D., July 29, 1936; s. Earl V. and Eileen P. (Henegar) N.; m. Carol Ann Nason, Oct. 6, 1962; children: Steven, Jill. BS, U. S.D., 1958. Staff acct., mgr. Grant Thornton, Mpls., 1958-69, audit ptnr., 1969-71; mng. ptnr. Grant Thornton, Cleve., 1971-76; mng. ptnr. Grant Thornton, Chgo., 1976-88, midwest regional mng. ptnr., 1980-90, exec. ptnr., chief exec. officer, 1990—. Governing mem. Chgo. Symphony Orchestral Assn., 1985—. Mem. AICPA, Ill. CPA Soc. (bd. dirs.), Chgo. Assn. Commerce & Industry, Exmoor Country Club (pres. 1988-90), Mid-Am. Club (bd. dirs. 1988-90), The Plaza Club, Econ. Club Chgo. Avocation: golf. Office: Grant Thorton LLP 130 E Randolph Dr Chicago IL 60601

NASON, ROCHELLE, conservation organization administrator; b. Oakland, Calif., May 21, 1959; d. Milton and Ann Frances (Reed) N. BA, U. Calif., Berkeley, 1984; JD, U. Calif., San Francisco, 1987. Bar: Calif. 1987. Law clk. to Chief Justice Malcolm Lucas Supreme Ct. of Calif., San Francisco, 1987-88; litigation assoc. Morrison & Foerster, San Francisco, 1988-92; staff lawyer League to Save Lake Tahoe, South Lake Tahoe, Calif., 1992-93, exec. dir., 1993—; adj. instr. Sierra Nev. Coll., Incline Village, 1992-94, Lake Tahoe C.C., 1992-96. Editor: The Traynor Reader, 1987; sr. rev. editor Hastings Law Jour., 1986-87; editor jour. Keep Tahoe Blue, 1992—; columnist (newspaper) Tahoe Daily Tribune; contbr. articles to profl. jours. V.p., bd. dirs. Jewish Cmty. South Lake Tahoe/Temple Bat Yam, 1992—; mem. leadership coun. Tahoe-Truckee Regional Econ. Coalition, Stateline, Nev., 1992-94; bd. dirs. Tahoe Ctr. for Sustainable Future, Glenbrook, Nev., 1995—. Mem. AAUW, Thurston Soc., Order of Coif. Jewish. Avocations: back-packing, skiing. Office: League to Save Lake Tahoe 955 Emerald Bay Rd South Lake Tahoe CA 96150-6410

NASR, SUHAYL JOSEPH, psychiatrist; m. Norma Nasr; children: Joseph, Carla, Talia. BSc, Am. U., Beirut, Lebanon, 1970, MD, 1974. Diplomate Am. Bd. Psychiatry and Neurology. Intern U. Rochester (N.Y.), 1974-77, fellowship, 1977; from v.p. med. staff to med. dir. Kingwood Hosp., Michigan City, Ind., 1987-95; pvt. practice Michigan City, Ind., 1986—; v.p., dept. medicine, staff physician St. Anthony's Hosp., Michigan City, 1986—, chmn. dept. medicine, 1997—; staff physician Meml. Hosp., Michigan City, 1986—, dir. behavioral medicine, 1995—, v.p. med. staff, 1997—; staff physician LaPorte Hosp., 1986-95; cons. Notre Dame (Ind.) U. Counseling Ctr., 1987—; cons. Valparaiso (Ind.) U., 1992—. Contbr. articles to profl. jours. Mem. AMA, Am. Psychiat. Assn., Soc. Biol. Psychiatry, Am. Acad. Clin. Psychiatrists, Internat. Psychogeriat. Assn., Obsessive Compulsive Found., Anxiety Disorders Assn. Am. Office: Nasr Psychiat Svcs 2814 Franklin St Michigan City IN 46360-6140

NASRALLAH, HENRY ATA, psychiatry researcher, educator; b. Apr. 30, 1947; came to U.S., 1972; s. Ata George and Rose G. (Yameen) N.; m. Amelia C. Tebsherani, June 9, 1972; children: Ramzy George, Rima Alice. BS in Biology, Am. U. of Beirut, 1967; MD, Am. U. Coll Medicine, Beirut-Lebanon, 1971. Intern Am. U. Med. Ctr., Beirut, Lebanon, 1972; resident in psychiatry U. Rochester, N.Y., 1972-75; rsch. assoc. NIMH, Washington, 1975-77; asst. prof. psychiatry U. Calif., San Diego, 1977-79; from assoc. prof. to prof. psychiatry U. Iowa, Iowa City, 1979-85; prof., chmn. dept. psychiatry Ohio State U., Columbus, 1985—; staff psychiatrist VA Med. Ctr., La Jolla, Calif., 1977-79; chief psychiatry svc. VA Med. Ctr., Iowa City, 1979-85. Editor: (5 vol. book series) Handbook of Schizophrenia, 1986-90; co-editor: NMR Spectroscopy in Psychiatric Brain Disorders, 1995; editor-in-chief Schizophrenia Rsch., 1987—, Jour. Psychiatry Disorders, 1996—; author and co-author over 200 published articles, 1976—. Pres. Psychiat. Rsch. Found. of Columbus, 1985—; mem. Alliance for the Mentally Ill, Columbus, 1987—. Recipient VA grants, 1979-84, NIMH, 1983—. Fellow Am. Psychiat. Assn. (coun. on rsch.), Am. Coll. Neuropsychopharmacology (chmn. pubs. com. 1992-95), Am. Coll. Psychiatrists (Deans Award com. 1996—), Am. Acad. Clin. Psychiatrists (pres. 1989-90), Soc. Biol. Psychiatry (awards com. 1988-90). Avocations: photography, tennis, poetry. Office: Ohio State U Dept Psychiatry 1670 Upham Dr Columbus OH 43210-1250

NASSAR, AHMED HASSAN, engineering educator, department head; b. Cairo, May 1, 1948; s. Hassan Ahmed Nassar and Wajiha Amin Ezzelarab N.; m. Rebecca Mylin Leffler, May 15, 1979; 1 child, Aly Ahmed. BSEE, BS in Computer Engring., Alexandria (Egypt) U., 1971; MSEE, N.C. State U., 1976, PhD in Agrl. Engring./Elec. Engring., 1987. Elec. engring. trainee LK-NES Co., Copenhagen, 1968-70; lectr. sch. engring. Alexandria U., 1971-74; instr., tchg. and rsch. asst. N.C. State U., Raleigh, 1974-79; sys. engr. Automata Electronics, Reston, Va., 1979-80; group leader control engring. Raychem Corp., Menlo Pk., Calif., 1980-83; mgr. engring. Raychem Corp., 1983-85, product mgr., 1985-87, internat. project mgr., 1987-91, mgr. internat. sales and mktg. support, 1991-96; chmn. dept. engring. tech. Mo. Western State Coll., St. Joseph, 1996—; instr. Ohlone Coll., Fremont (Calif.)/Newark C.C. Dist., 1992-96. Contbr. articles to profl. jours. Mem. IEEE, Am. Soc. Engring. Edn., Am. Soc. Agrl. Engrs., Mo. Vocat. Assn. Republican. Moslem. Avocations: coaching youth baseball, swimming, racquetball. Home: 1902 Buckingham St Saint Joseph MO 64506 Office: Mo Western State Coll 4525 Downs Dr Saint Joseph MO 64507-2246

NASSAR-MCMILLAN, SYLVIA C., educator; b. Detroit, Aug. 29, 1963; d. Albert S. Nassar and Erika L. Strunk; m. Ian Johnson McMillan, July 17, 1994. BA, Oakland U., 1984; MA, Ea. Mich. U., 1986; PhD, U. N.C., Greensboro, 1994. Grad. asst. Ea. Mich. U., Ypsilanti, 1985-86; bi-lingual officer mgr. Motion Mfg., Detroit, 1986-87; counselor UAW/GM Human Resource Ctr., Pontiac, Mich., 1987-88; program coord. women's ctr. We. Mich. U., Kalamazoo, 1988-89, coord. career planning, 1989-90; career counselor, intern Loyola U., Chgo., 1990; counselor, site supr. Charlevoix Publ Schs., Beaver Island, Mich., 1991; asst. prof., counseling coord. Austin Peay State U., Clarksville, Tenn., 1994-96; asst. prof. counselor edn. U. N.C., Charlotte, 1996—; mem. sexism com. Austin Peay State U., 1995-96, mem. critical incident stress mgmt., 1994-96, mem. univ. hearing bd., 1994-96. Workcamp leader Vols. for Peace, Baxter State Park, Mich., 1990, Girl Scouts Am., Kalamazoo, 1990; group counselor/cmty. edn./vol. tng. HAVEN-Domestic Violence Shelter, Oakland County Mich., 1986-88. Doctoral fellow Residence Life U. N.C., Greensboro, 1991-94; recipient Profl. Devel. award Mich. Coll. Personnel Assn., 1989-90. Mem. Am. Counseling Assn. (editl. bd. Jour. of Counseling and Devel. 1996—, professionalism com. 1995—), Am. Psychol. Assn., So. Assn. counselor Edn. & Supervision, Assn. Counselor Edn. & Supervision, Chi Sigma Iota. Office: Dept Counselor Edn Spl Edn & Child Devel U NC Charlotte NC 28223

NASSAU, MICHAEL JAY, lawyer; b. N.Y.C., June 3, 1935; s. Benjamin and Belle (Nassau) N.; m. Roberta Bluma Herzlich, June 26, 1971; children: Stephanie Ellen, William Michael. BA summa cum laude, Yale U., 1956, LLB cum laude, 1960. Bar: N.Y. 1960, D.C. 1992, U.S. Dist. Ct. (so. dist.) N.Y. 1978, U.S. Tax Ct. 1963, U.S. Ct. Appeals (2d cir.) 1963, U.S. Supreme Ct. 1965. Asst. instr. in constl. law Yale U., 1959-60; law clk. to judge U.S. Ct. Appeals 2d. Cir., 1960-61; assoc. tax dept. Paul, Weiss, Rifkind, Wharton & Garrison, N.Y.C., 1961-73; ptnr. Kramer, Levin, Naftalis & Frankel, and predecessor, N.Y.C., 1974—; mem. adv. bd. Matthew Bender Fed. Pension Law Service, 1975-76; mem. adv. com. NYU Ann. Inst. Employee Plans and Exec. Compensation, 1976-79; mem. steering com. Am. Pension Conf., 1981-83; lectr. in field; panelist various seminars on employee benefits. Mem. ABA (sect. taxation, employee benefits com. 1993—), N.Y. State Bar Assn. (co-chmn. employee benefits sect. taxation 1976-78, mem. exec. com. sect. taxation 1976-79), Assn. of Bar of City of N.Y. (chmn. subcom. pension legis. of com. taxation 1975-76, employee benefits com. 1987-92), WEB (N.Y. chpt. bd. dirs. 1990—, pres. 1993-94), Phi Beta Kappa. Mem. editorial bd. Bank and Corp. Governance Law Reporter, 1989—; contbr. chpts., articles to law publs.; panelist Pension Video Seminar, 1983. Office: Kramer Levin Naftalis & Frankel 919 3rd Ave New York NY 10022

NASSBERG, RICHARD T., lawyer; b. N.Y.C., Mar. 30, 1942; s. Jules and Rhea (Steinglass) N.; m. Kathryn S. Lynn, May 2, 1981; children: Schuyler M. L., Kathryn Cupp. BS in Econs., Wharton Sch., U. Pa., 1963; JD, U. Pa., 1968. Bar: N.Y. 1969, U.S. Ct. Appeals (2d cir.) 1970, Pa. 1972, Tex. 1983. With Milbank, Tweed, Hadley & McCloy, N.Y.C., 1968-70; with Schnader, Harrison, Segal & Lewis, Phila., 1971-78, ptnr., 1978-82; ptnr. Mayor, Day & Caldwell, Houston, 1982-90; pvt. practice law, 1990-92; of counsel Mannino & Griffith, Phila., 1992-95; planning chmn. coreporter study on banking and comml. lending law Am. Law Inst.-ABA, 1979—, mem. adv. com. to subcom. on continuing legal edn., 1982-90 . Served with Army N.G., 1963-65, USAR, 1965-66, USAFR, 1966-69. Mem. NYCOC (standing com. on Nat. Security 1968-71), Am. Law Inst. (advisor comml. law 1985—), ABA, Tex. Bar Assn., Houston Bar Assn. Clubs: Franklin Inn (Phila.). Author: The Lender's Handbook. 1986; editor resource books on banking law; contbr. articles on banking law to profl. publs.; editor U. Pa. Law Rev., 1967-68, assoc. editor, 1966-67. Office: PO Box 5055 Jersey Shore PA 17740-5055

NASSIF, THOMAS ANTHONY, business executive, former ambassador; b. Cedar Rapids, Iowa, July 22, 1941; s. George Joseph and Clara Christine (Nofal) N.; m. Zinetta Marie Meherg, Sept. 14, 1968; children—Jaisa Diane, Matthew Christian. BS, Calif. State U.-Los Angeles, 1965; JD, Calif. Western Sch. Law, 1969, LLD (hon.), 1988. Ptnr. Gray, Cary, Ames & Frye, El Centro, Calif., 1980-81; dep. and acting chief of protocol Dept. State, Washington, 1981-83; dep. asst. sec. Bur. Near Eastern and South Asian Affairs, Dept State, Washington, 1983-85; U.S. ambassador to Morocco, 1985-88; chmn. bd. Gulf Interstate Internat. Corp., San Diego, 1988-95; chmn. of bd. Gulf Intern. Inc., Houston, 1988-95, Gulf Internat. Consulting Inc., San Diego, 1992—; chmn. Am. Task Force for Lebanon, Washington, 1991—; pres. Los Alamos Internat., Inc., San Diego, 1988—. Active campaign Reagan for Pres., 1980; mem. Calif. State Rep. Cen. Com. Served with U.S. Army and USNG, 1960-67. Recipient Disting. Profl. Achievement award Attiyeh Benevolent Soc., Ellis Island Congl. Medal of Honor, 1993. Office: Gulf Internat Consulting Inc Ste 1025 4660 La Jolla Village Dr San Diego CA 92122-4606

NASSIKAS, JOHN NICHOLAS, lawyer; b. Manchester, N.H., Apr. 29, 1917; s. Nicholas John and Constantina (Gagalis) N.; m. Constantina Andreson, Feb. 21, 1943; children: Kira Hohenadel, Marcy (Mrs. Wade B. C. Weathers, Jr.), Elizabeth (Mrs. Watson Lowery), John Nicholas III. A.B., Dartmouth Coll., 1938; M.B.A., Harvard U., 1940, J.D., 1948; LL.D. (hon.), Notre Dame Coll., Manchester, N.H., 1972. Bar: N.H. and Mass. 1948, D.C. 1968, U.S. Supreme Ct. 1953, Va. 1986. Asst., dep. atty. gen. N.H., 1950-53; sr. partner firm Wiggin, Nourie, Sundeen, Nassikas & Pingree, Manchester, 1953-69; chmn. Fed. Power Commn., 1969-75; partner firm Squire, Sanders & Dempsey, Washington, 1975-86; spl. commr., presiding chmn. N.H. Pub. Utilities Commn., 1984-86; spl. commr., presiding chmn. procs. for reorgn. of Pub. Svc. Co. N.H., N.H. Pub. Utilities Commn., 1989-92; arbitrator Duke Power Co., NCEMC and SALVDA River Elect. Coops., 1992-94. Mem. Adminstrv. Conf. U.S., 1969-75; bd. dirs. U.S. Nat. Com. of World Energy Conf., 1970-74, 77-87; mem. Water Resources Council, 1969-75; mem. exec. com. NARUC, 1970-75; mem. Pres.'s Cabinet Task Force on Oil Import Control, 1969-70; mem. energy subcom. domestic council, 1969-73; mem. Pres.'s Joint Bd. on Fuel Supply and Transport, 1970-73, Pres.'s Energy Resources Council, 1974-75, Nat. Petroleum Council, 1975-79; bd. dirs. Ams. for Energy Independence, 1975-84; trustee Pathfinder Mines Corp., 1976-82; mem. adv. council Gas Research Inst., 1977-87; bd. dirs. corp. Madeira Sch., 1972-80. Served to lt. USNR, 1942-46. Mem. ABA, N.H. Bar Assn., Mass. Bar Assn. (spl. commr. Seabrook Nuclear Fin. Hearings), D.C. Bar Assn., Fed. Bar Assn., Va. Bar Assn., Fed. Energy Bar Assn., Cosmos Club, Met. Club, Farmington Country Club, Ahepa, Kappa Kappa Kappa. Republican. Home and Office: 1131 Litton Ln Mc Lean VA 22101-1823

NAST, DIANNE MARTHA, lawyer; b. Mount Holly, N.J., Jan. 30, 1946; d. Henry Daniel and Anastasia (Lovenduski) N.; m. Joseph Francis Roda, Aug. 23, 1980; children: Michael, Daniel, Joseph, Joshua, Anastasia. BA, Pa. State U., 1965; JD, Rutgers U., 1976. Bar: Pa. 1976, U.S. Dist. Ct. Pa. 1976, N.J. 1976, U.S. Dist. Ct. N.J. 1976, U.S. Ct. Appeals (3d, 5th, 6th, 7th, 8th and 11th cirs.) 1976, U.S. Supreme Ct. 1982, U.S. Dist. Ct. Ariz. 1985. Dir., v.p. Kohn, Nast & Graf, P.C., Phila., 1976-95, Roda & Nast, P.C., Lancaster, Pa., 1995—; mem. lawyers adv. com. U.S. Ct. Appeals (3d cir.), 1982-84, chmn., 1983-84, mem. com. on revision jud. conf. conduct rules, 1982-84; mem. U.S. Ct. Appeals for the 3d Cir. Jud. Conf. Permanent Planning Com., 1983-90; bd. dirs. 3d Cir. Hist. Soc., 1993—; bd. dirs. Phila. Pub. Def., 1980-89; dir. U.S. Fed. Judicial Ctr. Found., 1991—; chmn. lawyers adv. com. U.S. Dist. Ct. (ea. dist.) Pa., 1982-90, pres. Hist. Soc., 1988-91. Fellow ABA (coun. litigation sect. 1986-89, co-chmn. anti-trust com. litigation sect. 1984-86, div. dir. 1990-91, practical litigation editorial bd. 1989—, ho. of dels. 1992—, mem. task force state justice initiatives, mem. task force state of justice system 1993, mem. task force long range planning com. 1994), Am. Law Inst. (chair internat. professionalism com. 1991-94, civil justice task force 1993-95), Am. Arbitration Assn. (bd. dirs., mem. alt. dispute resolution and mass torts task force), Am. Judicature Soc., Pa. Bar Assn. (ho. of dels. 1983-95), N.J. Bar Assn., Pa. Trial Lawyers Assn., Phila. Bar Assn. (bd. govs. 1985-87, chmn., bicentennial com. 1986-87, chmn. bench bar conf. 1988-89), Lancaster Bar Assn. (co-chair civil litigation and rules com. trial law sect.), Rutgers Law Sch. Alumni Assn., Pa. Acad. Fine Arts. Home: 1059 Sylvan Rd Lancaster PA 17601-1923 Office: Roda & Nast PC 801 Estelle Dr Lancaster PA 17601-2130

NAST, EDWARD PAUL, cardiac surgeon; b. Balt., Dec. 13, 1958; s. Richard Cecil and Lenora (Heilig) N.; m. Sandye Hammerman, June 3, 1984; 1 child, Bennett Ross. BS, Emory U., 1979; MD, U. Md., 1984. Diplomate Am. Bd. Thoracic Surgery, Am. Bd. Surgery. Intern Georgetown U. Med. Ctr., Washington, 1984-85, resident in gen. surgery, 1985-86, 88-91; resident in thoracic and cardiovascular surgery U. Md. Med. Sys., Balt., 1991-93; fellow in cardiac surgery NIH, Bethesda, Md., 1986-88; cardiac surgeon St. Joseph's Cardiac Surgery Assocs., P.C., Syracuse, N.Y., 1993—. Contbr. articles to profl. jours. Fellow ACS, Am. Coll. Cardiology, Am. Coll. Chest Physicians; mem. AMA, Med. Soc. State N.Y., Soc. Thoracic Surgeons, Phi Beta Kappa. Office: St Josephs Cardiac Surgery 101 Union Ave # 813 Syracuse NY 13203-1743

NASTA, MARILYN JEAN, speech and language pathologist, consultant; b. Newark, July 17, 1947; d. Julian Alexander and Helen Dorothy (Chencharik) Bobrowicz; m. Raymond A. Nasta, Aug. 22, 1970; children: Alexa Jean, Jessica Jean. BS, William Paterson Coll., 1969, MS, 1970; postgrad., NYU, 1971—; sch. supr.'s cert., Montclair State U., 1997. Speech-lang. specialist, tchr. Fairlawn (N.J.) Bd. Edn., 1970-78, Cerebral Palsy of Essex and West Hudson, Belleville, N.J., 1991-92, Edison (N.J.) Bd. Edn., 1992-93, Cranford (N.J.) Bd. Edn., 1993—. Editor, advisor Cougar Cubs News, 1995—. Active Jr. League, Montclair, N.J., 1981—; libr. vol. Montclair-Kimberly Acad., 1984-87; vol. The Chapin Sch., N.Y.C., 1987-93; mem. Lakeland Hills YMCA, Mountain Lakes, N.J., 1993—; lector, mem. St. Cassian's Ch., 1993—. Recipient grad. assistantship Syracuse U., 1970. Mem. AAUW, N.J. Speech, Lang. and Hearing Assn. Roman Catholic. Avocations: running, aerobics, tennis, reading, needlepoint. Office: Walnut Ave Sch Walnut Ave Cranford NJ 07016

NASTASI, KATHLEEN PATRICIA, systems analyst; b. Rochester, N.Y., July 13, 1960; d. Donald P. and Nancy K. (Kleinhans) N. BA in Math., Nazareth Coll., Rochester, N.Y., 1982, BA, 1982; postgrad., St. John Fisher Coll., Rochester, N.Y., 1994—. Cert. notary pub., N.Y.; Microsoft cert. Title exam, book-keeper Pub. Abstract Corp., Rochester, 1982-83; v.p., office mgr. Colon Abstract Corp., Rochester, 1983-86; systems adminstr. First Fed. S & L, Rochester, 1986-95; analyst, cons. Ciber, Inc., Rochester, 1995—; facilitator devel. team meetings Xerox Corp., Rochester, 1995—; mentor SUNY Empire State U. Musician in field. Recipient Achievement in Maths. award Bishop Kearney, 1978; faculty scholar Nazareth Coll., Kodak Co. scholar, 1978-82. Mem. NAFE, Nat. Honor Soc. Avocations: musican, gardening, crafts. Home: 153 Lake Rd Webster NY 14580 Office: Ciber Inc 345 Woodcliff Dr Fairport NY 14450-4210

NATALE, LAUREL A., nursing case manager; b. N.Y.C., Apr. 25, 1945; d. Laurence C. and Grace O. (McIntyre) Armitage; m. Carmen J. Natale, Feb. 13, 1964; children: Julia Ann Gerson, Christine Cartwright, Kathryn Natale. Diploma, Charity Hosp. Sch. Nursing, New Orleans, 1978; BSN, U. Tex., Galveston, 1984; MSN, U. Tex., Houston, 1990. RN, Tex. Staff nurse SICU trauma Hermann Hosp., Houston, asst. head nurse renal transpant intensive care unit; patient care supr. hospice Vis. Nurse Assn., Houston; instr. clin. nursing U. Tex. Health Sci. Ctr.-Houston Sch. Nursing, Houston; staff nurse emergency dept. Meml. Hosp. System, Houston; case mgr. Worklink, 1994-95; supr. case mgmt., 1996—; divsn. case mgr. Nat. Convenience Stores, 1995-96.

NATALICIO, DIANA SIEDHOFF, academic administrator; b. St. Louis, Aug. 25, 1939; d. William and Eleanor J. (Biermann) Siedhoff. BS in Spanish summa cum laude, St. Louis U., 1961; MA in Portuguese lang., U. Tex., 1964, PhD in Linguistics, 1969. Chmn. dept. modern langs. U. Tex., El Paso, 1973-77, assoc. dean liberal arts, 1977-79; acting dean liberal arts,

1979-80; dean Coll. Liberal Arts U. Tex., El Paso, 1980-84, v.p. acad. affairs, 1984-88, pres., 1988—; bd. dirs. El Paso br. Fed. Res. Bd. Dallas, chmn., 1989; mem. Presdl. Adv. Commn. on Ednl. Excellence for Hispanic Ams., 1991; bd. dirs. Sandia Corp., Enserch Corp.; bd. dirs. Nat. Action Coun. for Minorities in Engring., 1993-96; mem. Nat. Sci. Bd. 1994-2000; mem. NASA Adv. Coun., 1994-96; bd. mem. Fund for Improvement of Post-Secondary Edn., 1993-97; bd. dirs. Fogarty Internat. Ctr. of NIH, 1993-96; bd. chair Am. Assn. Higher Edn., 1995-96; bd. dirs. U.S.-Mexico Commn. for Ednl. and Cultural Exch., 1994-96. Co-author: Sounds of Children, 1977; contbr. articles to profl. jours. Bd. dirs. United Way El Paso, 1990-93, chmn. needs survey com., 1990-91, chmn. edn. divsn., 1989; chmn. Quality Edn. for Minorities Network in Math. Sci. and Engring., 1991-92; chairperson Leadership El Paso, Class 12, 1989-90, mem. adv. coun., 1987-90, participant, 1980-81; mem. Historically Black Colls. and Univs./Minority Instns. Consortium on Environ. Tech. chairperson, 1991-93. Recipient Torch of Liberty award Anti-Defamation League B'nai B'rith, 1991, Conquistador award City of El Paso, 1990, Humanitarian award Nat. Coun. Christians and Jews, El Paso chpt., 1990; mem. El Paso Women's Hall of Fame, 1990. Mem. Philos. Soc. Tex. Avocations: hiking, bicycling, skiing, skating. Home: 711 Cincinnati Ave El Paso TX 79902-2616 Office: U Tex at El Paso Office of the President El Paso TX 79968-0500

NATALIE, RONALD BRUCE, lawyer; b. Lynn, Mass., Nov. 29, 1935; s. John Richard and Cecelia Lucy (Fish) N.; m. Betty Ann McEnteggart, Aug. 22, 1958; children: Ronald Bruce Jr., Karen Lorraine, Donna Leslie, John Francis. AB, Tufts Coll., 1957; JD with highest honors, George Washington U., 1962. Bar: D.C. 1962, U.S. Ct. Appeals (D.C. cir.) 1964, U.S. Ct. Appeals (2d cir.) 1970, U.S. Ct. Appeals (5th cir.), 1991, U.S. Ct. Appeals (3d cir.) 1992. Atty. Office of Gen. Counsel, U.S. Commn. on Civil Rights, Washington, 1962-64; assoc. Verner, Liipfert, Bernhard, McPherson and Hand, Washington, 1964-68, ptnr., 1968-81; shareholder Verner Liipfert, Bernarhd, McPherson & Hand, Washington, 1981—; chief counsel Pres.'s Commn. to Investigate the Accident at Three Mil Island, Washington, 1979; vice chmn. Close Up Found., Alexandria, Va., 1971—. Lt. USN, 1957-62. Mem. ABA, D.C. Bar Assn., Ba Assn. of D.C., Assn. for Transp., Law, Logistics and Policy, Phi Alpha Delta. Democrat. Home: 3307 39th St NW Washington DC 20016-3711 Office: Verner Liipfert Bernarhd McPherson & Hand 901 15th St NW Washington DC 20005-2327

NATCHER, STEPHEN DARLINGTON, lawyer, business executive; b. San Francisco, Nov. 19, 1940; s. Stanlus Zoch and Robena Lenore Collie (Goldring) N.; m. Carolyn Anne Bowman, Aug. 23, 1969; children: Tanya Michelle, Stephanie Elizabeth. A.B. in Polit. Sci., Stanford U., 1962; J.D., U. Calif., San Francisco, 1965. Bar: Calif. 1966. Assoc. firm Pillsbury, Madison & Sutro, San Francisco, 1966-68; counsel Douglas Aircraft div. McDonnell Douglas Corp., Long Beach, Calif., 1968-70; v.p., sec. Security Pacific Nat. Bank, 1971-79; asst. gen. counsel Security Pacific Corp., 1979-80; v.p., sec., gen. counsel Lear Siegler, Inc., Santa Monica, Calif., 1980-87; v.p., gen. counsel Computer Scis. Corp., El Segundo, Calif., 1987-88; exec. v.p., gen. counsel, sec. CalFed Inc., 1989-90; sr. v.p. adminstrn., gen. counsel, sec. Wyle Electronics, Irvine, Calif., 1991—. With USCG, 1965-71. Mem. St. Francis Yacht Club (San Francisco), The Pacific Club (Newport Beach). Republican.

NATELSON, STEPHEN ELLIS, neurosurgeon; b. N.Y.C., Dec. 23, 1937; s. Samuel R. and Ethel D. (Nathan) N.; B.A. magna cum laude, Carleton Coll., 1958; Fulbright scholar in Math., Westfälische-Wilhelms U., Germany, 1958-59; M.D., U. Rochester, 1963; m. Laurie Lou Acred, 1990; children from previous marriage: Lea Jane, Jamie Ann, Jessica Ilana, Benjamin Henry, Marissa Claire. Intern, USAF Hosp., Wright-Patterson AFB, 1963-64; resident in neurosurgery Ohio State U., 1967-71; chief resident in neurology U. N.Mex., 1971-72; pvt. practice specializing in neurosurgery, Knoxville, Tenn., 1972—; clin. assoc. prof. U. Tenn. Served with USAF, 1962-67. Decorated Air Force Commendation medal; diplomate Am. Bd. Neurol. Surgery. Fellow ACS; mem. Am. Assn. Neurol. Surgeons, Congress Neurol. Surgeons, AMA, Knoxville Acad. Medicine, Tenn. Neurosurg. Soc. (past press.), Am. Physicians Fellowship, Undersea Med. Soc., Phi Beta Kappa, Sigma Xi, Alpha Omega Alpha. Republican. Jewish. Contbr. articles to profl. jours. Office: 103 Newland Profl Bldg Knoxville TN 37916

NATH, JOGINDER, genetics and biology educator, researcher; b. Joginder Nagar, Panjab, India, May 12, 1932; came to U.S. 1957; s. Moti Ram and Vira Wali (Khorana) N.; m. Charlotte Lynn Reese, Apr. 5, 1969; children—Pravene, Brian. B.S. with honors, Panjab U, Amritsar, India, 1953, M.S. with honors, 1955; Ph.D., U. Wis., 1960. Research assoc. Am. Inst. Biol. Research, Madison, Wis., 1960-63; asst. prof. So. Ill. U., Carbondale, Ill., 1964-66; from asst. to assoc. prof. W.Va. U., Morgantown, 1966-72, prof., chmn. dept. genetics and devel. biology, 1972—. Contbr. articles on cytogenetics, mutagenesis, biochem. genetics and cryobiology to profl. jours. Chmn. bd. Morgantown Day Sch., 1977-79. Recipient Alexander Hollaender award Environ. Mutagen Soc., 1997; grantee NSF, 1967-68, DOE, 1992-95, Nat. Inst. Occupational Safety & Health, 1985-95; recipient Hollaender award Environ. Mutagen Soc., 1997. Mem. Soc. Cryobiology, Environ. Mutagen Soc., Electron Microscopy Soc., Sigma Xi. Office: WVa U Coll Agr Dept Genetics & Devel Biology Morgantown WV 26506

NATHAN, ANDREW JAMES, political science educator; b. N.Y.C., Apr. 3, 1943; s. Paul S. and Dorothy (Goldeen) N.; 1 child, Chloe; 1 stepchild Alexandra Witke. B.A. summa cum laude, Harvard U., 1963, M.A. in East Asian Regional Studies, 1965, Ph.D. in Polit. Sci., 1971. Lectr. U. Mich., Ann Arbor, 1971; research assoc. Ctr. for Chinese Studies, 1970; asst. prof. polit. sci. Columbia U., N.Y.C., 1971-75, assoc. prof., 1975-82, prof., 1982—; dir. East Asian Inst. Columbia U., N.Y.C., 1991-95; mem. steering com. China Internat. Bus. Project, 1978—; mem. nat. com. on U.S.-China rels., 1987—; chair adv. com. Human Rights Watch/Asia, 1995—; cons. Ambrica Prodns., Nat. Endowment for Democracy, others; lectr. in field; external examiner City U. Hong Kong, 1996. Author: A History of the China International Famine Relief Commission, 1965, Modern China, 1840-1972, An Introduction to Sources and Research Aids, 1973, Peking Politics, 1918-1923: Factionalism and the Failure of Constitutionalism, 1976, Chinese Democracy, 1985 (Levenson prize 1987), China's Transition, 1997, (with others) Human Rights in Contemporary China, 1986, China's Crisis, 1990; co-editor Popular Culture in Late Imperial China, 1985, The Great Wall & the Empty Fortress: China's Search for Security, 1997; contbr. book revs. to publs.; manuscript reviewer U. Calif. Press., Columbia U. Press, Harvard U. Press, others; contbr. numerous articles to profl. jours. and current popular publs. Guggenheim fellow, 1973-74; fellow Am. Coun. Learned Soc.-Social Sci. Rsch. Coun., 1977-78, NEH fellow 1986-87, 1992-93; grantee Luce Found., 1979-82, 91-93, 92-95, Chiang Ching-Kuo Found., 1992, 1995-96, 1995-97, NSF, 1993-96 and others. Mem. Am. Polit. Sci. Assn., Assn. for Asian Studies, Coun. Fgn. Rels. Home: 35 Claremont Ave Apt 6N New York NY 10027-6823 Office: East Asian Inst Columbia U 420 W 118th St New York NY 10027-7213

NATHAN, DAVID GORDON, physician, educator; b. Boston, May 25, 1929; s. E. Geoffrey and Ruth (Gordon) N.; m. Jean Louise Friedman, Sept. 1, 1951; children: Deborah, Linda, Geoffrey. BA, Harvard U., 1951; MD, Harvard Med. Sch., 1955. Diplomate Am. Bd. Internal Medicine, Am. Bd. Pediatrics. Intern dept. medicine Peter Bent Brigham Hosp., Boston, 1955-56, sr. resident, 1958-59; jr. assoc. in medicine Brigham and Women's Hosp., Boston, 1961-67, sr. assoc. in medicine, 1967—; assoc. in medicine, hematology Childrens Hosp., Boston, 1963-68, chief, div. hematology, 1968-73, chief div. hematology and oncology, 1974-84; pediatrician-in-chief Dana Farber Cancer Inst., Boston, 1974-85; Robert A. Stranahan prof. pediatrics Harvard Med. Sch., Boston, 1977-95; physician-in-chief Childrens Hosp., Boston, 1985-95; pres. Dana-Farber Cancer Inst., Boston, 1995—; Richard and Susan Smith prof. medicine Harvard Med. Sch., Boston, 1996—, prof. of pediatrics, 1996—. Author: Genes, Blood and Courage, 1994; editor: Hematology in Infancy and Childhood, 4th edit., 1993, 5th edit., 1997. With USMC, 1948-49. Recipient Nat. Medal Sci. NSF, 1990. Fellow AAAS; mem. Inst. of Medicine of NAS, Am. Acad. Arts & Scis., Am. Pediatric Soc., Soc. Pediatric Rsch., Assn. Am. Physicians, Am. Soc. Clin. Investigators, Am. Soc. Hematology (pres. 1986), Phi Beta Kappa (hon.). Avocations: tennis, hiking. Office: Dana-Farber Cancer Inst 44 Binney St Boston MA 02115-6013

NATHAN, EDWARD SINGER, lawyer; b. Newark, Aug. 14, 1954; s. Emanuel and Evelyn (Lachter) N.; m. Merridith Elaine Cramer, Feb. 23, 1995. BA, U. Rochester, 1976; JD, Rutgers U., 1986. Bar: N.J. 1986. Assoc. McCarter & English, Newark, 1986—. V.p. The Children's Inst., Livingston, N.J., 1993-96, pres., 1996—; life mem. South Orange (N.J.) Rescue Squad, 1976—. Mem. N.J. Bar Assn., Vanderbilt Inn of Ct. Avocations: bicycling, fitness. Home: 768 Springfield Ave # B-8 Summit NJ 07901-2340 Office: 100 Mulberry St Newark NJ 07102

NATHAN, FREDERIC SOLIS, lawyer; b. N.Y.C., June 24, 1922; s. Edgar Joshua and Mabel (Unterberg) N.; m. Frances E., Oct. 28, 1956; children: JEan E., Frederic S. Jr., William E. BA, Williams Coll., Williamstown, Mass., 1943; LLD, Yale U., 1948. Bar: N.Y. 1948, U.S. Dist. Ct. (so. and ea. dists) N.Y. 1948, U.S. Ct. Appeals (2d cir.) 1953, U.S. Supreme Ct. 1968. Instr. Williams Coll., Williamstown, 1948; assoc. Rathbone Perry Kelley & Drye, N.Y.C., 1948-53; asst. U.S. atty. U.S. Attys.' Office (so. dist.), N.Y.C., 1953-56; assoc. Greenbaum, Wolff & Ernst, N.Y.C., 1956-58, ptnr., 1959-65, 70-82; 1st asst. corp. counsel N.Y.C. Law Dept., N.Y.C., 1966-69; ptnr. Kelley, Drye & Warren, N.Y.C., 1982—. Mem. N.Y. Rep. County Com., N.Y.C., 1948-66; trustee Mt. Sinai Hosp. and Med. Sch., N.Y.C., 1970—; chmn. bd. FOJP Svc. Corp., N.Y.C., 1977-85, bd. dirs., 1979—; bd. dirs., v.p. Am. Jewish Soc. for Svc., N.Y.C., 1950—. With U.S. Army, 1943-45, ETO. Fellow Am. Coll. Trial Lawyers; mem. ABA, Assn. of Bar of City of N.Y. (exec. com. 1979-81), Fed. Bar Council (pres. 1975-76), N.Y. State Bar Assn. Republican. Jewish. Clubs: Century Assn., Yale of N.Y.C.; Sunningdale Country. Home: 180 East End Ave New York NY 10128-7763 Office: Kelley Drye & Warren 101 Park Ave New York NY 10178

NATHAN, IRWIN, business systems company executive; b. N.Y.C., June 24, 1932; s. Albert Y. and Sarah Nathan; m. Sandra Alpert, June 18, 1955 (dec. June 1989); children: Alan Bradley, Mitchell Jordan; m. Phyllis Davis, Feb. 16, 1992. BSME, Stevens Inst. Tech., Hoboken, N.J., 1953; MSEE, N.Y.U., 1955, MS in Indsl. Engring., 1960; PhD, Poly. U., Bklyn., 1984. Registered profl. engr., N.Y. Rsch. and devel. engr. Dynamics Corp. of Am., Garden City, N.Y., 1953-56; sr. systems engr. Am. Bosch ARMA, Inc., Garden City, N.Y., 1956-63; prin. engr. Gen. Precision, Inc., Totowa, N.J., 1963-66; from section mgr. to mgr. svc. maintenance strategy Xerox Corp., Stamford, Conn., 1967-94; ret., 1994, cons. in reliability and svc., 1994—; guest lectr. George Washington U., 1969, UCLA, 1971, The Wharton Sch., 1985. Mem. IEEE, Ops. Rsch. Soc. Am. Avocations: boating, fishing, woodworking. Home: 12 Linda Ln Westport CT 06880-3945

NATHAN, J(AY) ANDREW, lawyer; b. St. Louis, Aug. 25, 1947; s. Ira L. Nathan and Babette Gross Simon; m. Linda L. Berenbeim, July 27, 1969; children: Joshua, Marni. BA, U. Mo., 1969; JD, U. Colo., 1972. Bar: Colo. 1972, U.S. Dist. Ct. Colo. 1972, U. S. Ct. Appeals (10th cir.) 1972. Assoc. atty. Burnette, Watson, Horan & Hilgers, Denver, 1972-73; shareholder, pres. Watson, Nathan & Bremer, P.C., Denver, 1973—. Mem Colo. Def. Lawyers Assn., Am. Bd. Trial Advocates (pres. Colo. chpt. 1990, nat. bd. dirs. 1990-96). Avocations: scuba diving, golf, oenology. Office: Watson Nathan & Bremer PC 3900 E Mexico Ave Ste 1000 Denver CO 80210-3945

NATHAN, JERRY E., lawyer; b. Bluefield, W.Va., Aug. 15, 1948. BS summa cum laude, Ohio State U., 1970; JD, Yale U., 1973. Bar: Ohio 1973. Ptnr. Bricker & Eckler, Columbus. Mem. ABA, Ohio State Bar Assn., Ohio Coun. Sch. Bd. Attys. (exec. com. 1986—, chmn. 1992), Columbus Bar Assn., Beta Gamma Sigma, Phi Eta Sigma. Address: Bricker & Eckler 100 S 3rd St Columbus OH 43215-4236

NATHAN, LEONARD EDWARD, writer, educator; b. Los Angeles, Nov. 8, 1924; s. Israel and Florence (Rosenberg) N.; m. Carol Gretchen Nash, June 27, 1949; children: Andrew Peter, Julia Irene, Miriam Abigail. Student, Ga. Tech., 1943-44, UCLA, 1946-47; BA summa cum laude, U. Calif.-Berkeley, 1950, MA, 1952, PhD, 1961. Instr. Modesto (Calif.) Jr. Coll., 1954-60; prof. dept. rhetoric U. Calif., Berkeley, 1960-91, ret., 1991, chmn. dept., 1968-72. Author: Western Reaches, 1958, The Glad and Sorry Seasons, 1963, The Matchmaker's Lament, 1967, The Day The Perfect Speakers Left, 1969, The Tragic Drama of William Butler Yeats, 1963, Flight Plan, 1971, Without Wishing, 1973, The Likeness, 1975, Coup, 1975, Returning Your Call, 1975, The Transport of Love: The Meghaduta by Kalidasa, 1976, Teachings of Grandfather Fox, 1977, Lost Distance, 1978, Dear Blood, 1980, Holding Patterns, 1982, Carrying On: New and Selected Poems, 1985, Diary of a Left-Handed Bird Watcher, 1996; also record: Confessions of a Matchmaker, 1973, De Meester van Het WinterLandschap, Selected Poems in Dutch transl. by Cees Nooteboom, Uitgeverij de Arbiedspers, Amsterdam, 1990; translator: Songs of Something Else, 1982, Grace and Mercy in Her Wild Hair, 1982; (with Czeslaw Milosz) Happy As a Dog's Tail: Poems by Anna Swir, 1985, With the Skin: Poems of Aleksander Wat, 1989, Talking to My Body, Poems of Anna Swir, 1996; (with Arthur Quinn) The Poet's Work: Study of Czeslaw Milosz, 1991; (with Milosz) Talking To My Body: Poems by Anna Swir, 1996. With U.S. Army, 1943-45, ETO. Recipient Phelan award, 1955; Longview prize, 1961; award in lit. Nat. Inst. Arts and Letters, 1971; Poetry medal Commonwealth Club, 1976, 81; U. Calif. Creative Arts fellow, 1961-62, 73-74; U. Calif. Humanities research fellow, 1983-84; Am. Inst. Indian Studies fellow, 1966-67; Guggenheim fellow, 1976-77. Mem. Assn. of Lit. Scholars and Critics. Avocation: birdwatching. Home: 40 Beverly Rd Kensington CA 94707-1304

NATHAN, MARTIN, publishing company executive. Pres. Reed Travel Pub., Secaucus, N.J. Office: Reed Travel Pub 500 Plaza Dr Secaucus NJ 07094-3619*

NATHAN, PAUL S., editor, writer; b. Oakland, Calif., Apr. 2, 1913; s. Alfred Jacobs and Frances (Strause) N.; m. Dorothy Goldeen, July 14, 1935 (dec. Dec. 1966); children: Andrew J., Carl F., Janet D.; m. Ruth Wilk Notkins, May 26, 1972. BA, U. Calif., Berkeley, 1934. Reporter Oakland Post-Enquirer, 1929-36; asst. play editor Paramount Pictures, N.Y.C., 1937-48; hosp. pub. relations Will, Folsom & Smith, N.Y.C., 1948-61; sci. editor Nat. Cystic Fibrosis Research Found., N.Y.C., Atlanta, 1963-73; contbg. editor column Rights and Permissions (now Rights), Pubs. Weekly, N.Y.C., 1946—; U.S. liaison Jerusalem Internat. Book Fair, 1976-77. Author: (play) Ricochet, 1980 (Edgar Allan Poe award of Mystery Writers Am. for best play of 1980), Texas Collects: Fine Arts, Furniture, Windmills & Whimseys, 1988; co-editor: (anthology) View: Parade of the Avant-Garde, 1991; author: (novels) Protocol for Murder, 1994, No Good Deed, 1995, Count Your Enemies, 1997; contbr. fiction and articles to Story, N.Y. Times mag., Saturday Evening Post, Saturday Rev., others. Mem. P.E.N., Dramatists Guild, Authors Guild, Authors League, Mystery Writers Am., Phi Beta Kappa. Office: care Pubs Weekly 249 W 17th St New York NY 10011-5300

NATHAN, PETER E., psychologist, educator; b. St. Louis, Apr. 18, 1935; s. Emil and Kathryn (Kline) N.; m. Florence I. Baker, Nov. 26, 1959; children: David Edward, Anne Miller, Laura Carol, Mark Andrew. A.B., Harvard U., 1957; Ph.D., Washington U., 1962. Research fellow psychology Harvard U., 1962-64, research asso., 1964-68, asst. prof. psychology, 1968-69; research psychologist Boston City Hosp., 1964-68, dir. alcohol study unit, 1967-70; prof. Rutgers U., New Brunswick, N.J., 1969-89; dir. clin. psychology tng. Rutgers U., 1969-87, dir. Alcohol Behavior Research Lab., 1970-87, chmn. dept. clin. psychology, 1976-87, dir. Ctr. Alcohol Studies, 1983-89, Henry and Anna Starr prof. psychology, 1983-89; sr. program officer, health program MacArthur Found., 1987-89; v.p. acad. affairs, found. disting. prof. psychology U. Iowa, 1990—, dean faculties, 1990-93, provost, 1993-95, acting pres., 1995; mem. advisory council VA, 1972-76; chmn. alcoholism com. Nat. Inst. on Alcohol Abuse and Alcoholism, 1973-76, co-chmn. spl. rev. com., 1985, mem. nat. adv. coun., 1990-94; mem. psychol. scis. fellowship rev. com. NIMH, 1977-79; chmn. N.J. State Community Mental Health Bd., 1981-84; mem. working group substance use disorders, DSM-IV. Author: Cues, Decisions, and Diagnoses, 1967, Psychopathology and Society, 1975, 2d edit., 1980, Experimental and Behavioral Approaches to Alcoholism, 1978, Alcoholism: New Directions in Behavioral Treatment and Research, 1978, Clinical Case Studies in the Behavioral Treatment of Alcoholism, 1982, Professionals in Distress, 1987, Neuropsychological Deficits in Alcoholism, 1987, Introduction to Psychology, 1987, 2d edit., 1990, Abnormal Psychology, 1992, 2d edit., 1996; exec. editor Jour. Studies Alcohol, 1983-90; assoc. editor Am. Psychologist, 1977-85, Contemporary Psychology, 1991—; mem. numerous editl. bds. including Jour. Clin. Psychology, 1969—, Jour. Cons. Clin. Psychology, 1973—, Profl. Psychology, 1976-89. Fellow Am. Psychol. Assn. (chmn. sect. 3 div. 12 1976-77, rep. to council 1976-79, 82-85, pres. div. 12 1984-85). Democrat. Jewish. Home: 248 Black Springs Cir Iowa City IA 52246-3800 Office: Univ Iowa E119 Seashore Hall Iowa City IA 52242-1316

NATHAN, RICHARD ARNOLD, technology company executive; b. N.Y.C., Sept. 25, 1944; s. Joseph and Mildred (Heller) N.; m. Shelly Ann Michaels, Sept. 5, 1966 (div. Mar. 1992); children: Wendy Beth, Daniel Scott; m. Onalee Louise Bodi, Apr. 27, 1994. BS in Chemistry, MIT, 1965; PhD in Chemistry, Poly. U., Bklyn., 1969. Researcher Polaroid Corp., Cambridge, Mass., 1969; chemist Battelle Meml. Inst., Columbus, Ohio, 1970-74, project mgr., 1974-76, mgr. environ. chem. sect., 1976-79, dir. programs, 1979-80, mgr. nuclear tech. dept., 1980-85, dir. tech. mgmt., 1985-86, div. gen. mgr., 1986-87, corp. v.p., div. pres., 1987-89, group v.p., gen. mgr., 1989-92; sr. v.p., dir. Mason & Hanger Corp., Lexington, Ky., 1993—; bd. dirs. VersaTech Engring., Inc., Mason & Hanger Nat., Inc., Ensycon Internat., Inc. Editor: Fuels from Sugar Crops, 1976; contbr. articles to profl. publs.; patentee in field. Bd. dirs. Ctrl. Ohio coun. Boy Scouts Am., 1981-90, Ctrl. Sci. and Industry, Columbus, 1988—; chmn. Ohio Sci. Tech. and Industry Hall of Fame, 1989-93. Recipient award Indsl. Rsch. Mag., 1976. Mem. Am. Soc. Macro-Engring. (bd. dirs. 1986-92), Am. Nuclear Soc., Am. Mgmt. Assn., Ohio Acad. Sci., Sigma Xi, Phi Lambda Upsilon. Avocations: golf, reading. Office: Mason & Hanger Corp 2355 Harrodsburg Rd Lexington KY 40504-3307

NATHAN, RICHARD P(ERLE), political scientist, educator; b. Schenectady, N.Y., Nov. 24, 1935; s. Sidney Robert and Betty (Green) N.; m. Mary McNamara, June 5, 1957; children: Robert Joseph, Carol Hewit. AB, Brown U., 1957; M in Pub. Adminstrn., Harvard U., 1959, PhD, 1966. Legis. asst. U.S. Senator Kenneth B. Keating, Washington, 1959-62; dir. domestic policy rsch. for Nelson A. Rockefeller, 1963-64; rsch. assoc. The Brookings Instn., Washington, 1966-69, sr. fellow, project dir. monitoring studies gen. revenue sharing, community devel. block grant and pub. svc. employment programs, 1972-79; associated staff The Brookings Inst., Washington, 1980-85; asst. dir. U.S. Office of Mgmt. and Budget, Washington, 1969-71; dep. undersec. U.S Dept. Health, Edn. and Welfare, Washington, 1971-72; prof. pub. and internat. affairs Woodrow Wilson Sch. Pub. and Internat. Affairs Princeton (N.J.) U., 1979-89, also dir. Princeton Urban and Regional Rsch. Ctr., 1979-89; Disting. prof. polit. sci. and pub. policy SUNY, Albany, 1989—, provost Rockefeller Coll. Pub. Affairs and Policy, dir. Rockefeller Inst. Govt., 1989—; assoc. dir. Nat. Adv. Commn. on Civil Disorders, 1967-68; vis. prof. govt. and fgn. affairs U. Va., 1972-77; chmn. Nixon Adminstrn. Transition Task Forces on Poverty and Intergovtl. Fiscal Rels., 1968, Domestic Coun. Com. on Welfare Reform Planning, 1969-70; mem. Commn. on Orgn. Govt. of D.C., 1970-72; bd. overseers New Sch. for Social Rsch., 1982-88; mem. working seminar on family and welfare Marquette U., 1986-87; mem. selection com. Rockefeller Pub. Svc. Awards Program, 1976-78; mem. income maintenance task force Nat. Urban Coalition, 1975-78; treas. Manpower Demonstration Rsch. Corp., 1974-81, chmn., 1981—; mem. coun. scholars U.S. Libr. of Congress, 1989—; mem. N.Y. State Temp. Commn. Constl. Revision, 1993-94; mem. U.S. Adv. Commn. on Intergovtl. Rels., 1994—; bd. dirs. Fleet Bank N.Y. Author: Jobs and Civil Rights, The Role of the Federal Government in Promoting Equal Opportunity in Employment and Training, 1969, The Plot That Failed: Nixon and the Administrative Presidency, 1975, Monitoring Revenue Sharing, 1975, Revenue Sharing, The Second Round., 1977, Monitoring the Public Service Employment Program, 1978, America's Government: A Fact Book of Census Data on the Organization, Finances, and Employment of Federal, State, and Local Governments, 1979, Public Service Employment: A Field Evaluation, 1981, The Administrative Presidency, 1983, Reagan and the States, 1987, Social Sciences in Government Uses and Abuses, 1988, A New Agenda for Cities, 1992, Turning Promises into Performance: The Management Challenge of Implementing Workfare, 1993; contbr. chpts. to books; editor: (with Harvey S. Perloff) Revenue Sharing and the City, 1968, (with John D. DiJulio, Jr.) The View From the States, Making Health Reform Work, Brookings Instn., 1994; mem. editl. bd. Urban Affairs Quar., 1978-85. Eisenhower fellow European Econ. Commn., 1977. Mem. ASPA (intergovtl. mgmt. award 1985), Na.t Acad. Social Inst., Nat. Acad. Pub. Adminstrn. (James E. Webb award 1986), Am. Polit. Sci. Assn. (Charles E. Merriam award 1987), Assn. for Pub. Policy Analysis and Mgmt., Princeton Club (N.Y.C.), Phi Beta Kappa, Theta Delta Chi. Republican. Jewish. Avocations: reading, travel, movies. Home: 9 Pasture Gate Ln Delmar NY 12054-4329 Office: SUNY Rockefeller Coll Provost Office 135 Western Ave Albany NY 12203-1011

NATHANIEL, bishop; b. Aurora, Ill., June 12, 1940; s. Joseph and Vera (Boytor) P. BA, St. Propcopius Coll., 1962; MDiv, Pontifical Gregorian U., Vatican City, 1966. Ordained priest Romanian Greek Cath. Ch., 1966; consecrated bishop Romanian Orthodox Episcopate of Am., 1980. Asst. pastor St. Michael Byz Ch., Aurora, 1967; parish priest Holy Cross Romanian Orthodox Ch., Hermitage, Pa., 1975-80; aux. bishop Romanian Orthodox Episcopate of Am., Orthodox Ch. in Am., Jackson, Mich., 1980-84; ruling bishop Romanian Orthodox Episcopate of Am., Orthodox Ch. in Am., Detroit, 1984—; mem. Holy Snyod Orthodox Ch. in Am., Syosset, N.Y., 1980—; tchr. summer youth programs Romanian Diocese; confessor to sisterhood Holy Transfiguration Monastery; rep. Conf. on Monasticism, Cairo, 1978; mem. participant Monastic Consultation, Cairo, 1979, Seventh Assembly, Vancouver, Can., 1983; active mem. diocesan liturgical commn.; speaker, lectr. in field. Author: Holy Icons, 1969; editor newspaper Solia; contbr. numerous articles to profl. jours. Chmn. Romanian-Am. Heritage Ctr., Grass Lake, Mich.; organizer, chmn. Help for Romania Nat. Relief Fund and Help the Children of Romania Relief Fund. Home and Office: Romanian Orthodox Episcopate Am 2522 Grey Tower Rd Jackson MI 49201-9120

NATHANS, DANIEL, molecular biology and genetics educator; b. Wilmington, Del., Oct. 30, 1928; s. Samuel and Sarah (Levitan) N.; m. Joanne E. Gomberg, Mar. 4, 1956; children: Eli, Jeremy, Benjamin. B.S., U. Del., 1950, M.D., Washington U., 1954. Intern Presbyn. Hosp., N.Y.C., 1954-55, resident in medicine, 1957-59; clin. assoc. Nat. Cancer Inst., 1955-57; guest investigator Rockefeller U., N.Y.C., 1959-62; prof. microbiology Sch. Medicine Johns Hopkins, 1962-72, prof., dir. dept. microbiology, 1972-82, Univ. prof. molecular biology and genetics, 1982—; mem. Pres. Coun. Advisers on Sci. & Tech., 1990-93; sr. investigator Howard Hughes Med. Inst., 1982—. Recipient Nobel prize in physiology or medicine, 1978, Nat. Medal of Sci., 1993. Fellow Am. Acad. Arts and Scis.; mem. NAS. Office: Johns Hopkins U-Sch Med Dept Molecular Biology & Genetics 725 N Wolfe St Baltimore MD 21205-2105

NATHANSON, HARVEY CHARLES, electrical engineer; b. Pitts., Oct. 22, 1936; s. David Benjamin and Ella (Sachs) N.; m. Esther Janet Mishelevich, Oct. 13, 1963; children: Marc Elliot, Elinor Sharon. BSEE, Carnegie Inst. Tech., 1958, MSEE, 1959, PhD, 1962. Sr. engr. Junction Device Physics, Westinghouse, Research/Devel. Center, Pitts., 1962-67; fellow engr. Junction Device Physics, Westinghouse, Research/Devel. Center, 1968-72, mgr. silicon junction physics, 1972-77, mgr. microelectronics dept., 1978-90, chief scientist electronic div., 1990-95; chief scientist Northrop Grumman Sci. Tech. Ctr., Pitts., 1996—; instr. Carnegie Inst. Tech., Pitts., 1959-60; chmn. Westinghouse Sat. Sci. Honors Inst. for High Sch. Students, 1970-76; mem. adv. group on electron devices Dept. Def., 1976-86; adviser to Nat. Materials Bd., 1986-87. Contbr. articles to profl. jours.; mem. editorial bd. Solid State Electronics, 1985—. Bd. dirs. Temple Sinai, 1981-83, 95—; pres. Brotherhood, 1993-95. Recipient IR100 award, 1965, hon. mention Outstanding Young Engr. award Eta Kappa Nu, 1967, Best Display Paper award Soc. Info. Display, 1972, Carnegie-Mellon Alumni award, 1982, Westinghouse Top Corp. Patent award, 1990; named to Westinghouse Order of Merit, Westinghouse Electric Corp., 1987. Fellow IEEE (mem. editorial bd. Spectrum mag. 1989-91); mem. IEEE Electron Device Soc. (pres. 1978-80), Fedn. Materials Socs. (bd. dirs. 1987-90), Sigma Xi, Eta Kappa Nu. Democrat. Jewish. Patentee in field. Home: 5635 Marlborough Rd Pittsburgh PA 15217-1404 Office: Northrop Grumman Sci & Tech Ctr 1310 Beulah Rd Pittsburgh PA 15235-5068

NATHANSON, LEONARD MARK, lawyer; b. Detroit, Nov. 2, 1929; s. Murray and Anna (Brockman) N.; m. Rebecca Stockman, Aug. 6, 1960; children: Keith Murray, Shelley Anose, Wendy Beth. BSEE, Detroit Inst. Tech., 1957; LLB, Detroit Coll. Law, 1961, JD, 1965. Bar: Mich. 1962, U.S. Dist. Ct. (ea. dist.) MIch. 1962, U.S. Ct. Appeals (6th cir.) 1976, U.S. Supreme Ct. 1972. Pvt. practice Detroit, 1962—. Cpl. U.S. Army, 1952-54. Mem. Am. Radio Relay League (v.p. 1984-88, dir. 1980-90). Jewish. Avocation: amateur radio. Home: 29203 Lake Park Dr Farmington MI 48331-2661 Office: Nathanson and Nathanson PC 31700 Wildmile Ste 219 Farmington Hills MI 48331

NATHANSON, MELVYN BERNARD, university provost, mathematician; b. Phila., Oct. 10, 1944; s. Israel and Sophia (Manstein) N.; m. Marjorie Jane Frankel, Jan. 29, 1978; children: Alexander Philip, Rebecca Anne. BA, U. Pa., 1965; postgrad., Harvard U., 1965-66; MA, U. Rochester, 1968, PhD, 1972. Prof. So. Ill. U., Carbondale, 1971-81; dean Rutgers U., Newark, N.J., 1981-86; provost, v.p. acad. affairs Lehman Coll. CUNY, Bronx, 1986-91; prof. math. Grad. Sch. Lehman Coll. CUNY, 1986—; vis. prof. Moscow State U., USSR, 1972-73, Inst. for Advanced Study, Princeton U., N.J., 1974-75, 76, 90-91, Harvard U., Cambridge, Mass., 1977-78, Rockefeller U., 1982-85, Rutgers U., 1991-93. Author, editor fifteen books; contbr. articles to profl. jours. Fellow N.Y. Acad. Sci.; mem. AAAS, Am. Math. Soc., Math. Assn. Am., Assn. Mems. Inst. for Advanced Study (v.p.). Office: CUNY Lehman Coll Dept Math Bronx NY 10468

NATHANSON, MICHAEL, film company executive. Pres. world wide prodn. Columbia Pictures Entertainment Inc., N.Y.C., from 1989, former exec. v.p. prodn.; pres. worldwide prodn. Columbia Pictures Entertainment Inc., Culver City, Calif., to 1993; now pres. MGM. Office: MGM 2500 Broadway St Santa Monica CA 90404*

NATHANSON, NEAL, virologist, epidemiologist, educator; b. Boston, Sept. 1, 1927; s. Robert B. and Leah (Rabinowitch) N.; m. Constance Allen, June 8, 1954; children—Katherine L., John A., Daniel R.; m. Phoebe Starfield, Oct. 7, 1984. B.A., Harvard, 1949, M.D., 1953. Chief polio surveillance unit USPHS, 1955-57; research asso., asst. prof. anatomy Johns Hopkins, Balt., 1957-63; asso. prof. epidemiology Johns Hopkins, 1963-68, prof., 1968-79; chmn. dept. microbiology U. Pa., Phila., 1979-93, vice dean rsch., 1993-95. Editor-in-chief: Am. Jour. Epidemiology, 1964-79, Microbial Pathogenesis, 1985-88. Research, publs. pathogenesis, immunology, and epidemiology of viral infections. Home: 1600 Hagys Ford Rd Apt 9W Narberth PA 19072-1049

NATHWANI, BHARAT NAROTTAM, pathologist, consultant; b. Bombay, Jan. 20, 1945; came to U.S., 1972; s. Narottam Pragji and Bharati N. (Lakhani) N. MBBS, Grant Med. Coll., Bombay, 1969, MD in Pathology, 1972. Intern Grant Med. Coll., Bombay U., 1968-69; asst. prof. pathology Grant Med. Coll., 1972; fellow in hematology Cook County Hosp., Chgo., 1972-73; resident in pathology Rush U., Chgo., 1973-74; fellow in hematopathology City of Hope Med. Ctr., Duarte, Calif., 1975-76, pathologist, 1977-84; prof. pathology, chief hematopathology U. So. Calif., L.A., 1984—. Contbr. numerous articles to profl. jours. Recipient Grant awards Nat. Libr. Medicine, Bethesda, Md., Nat. Cancer Inst., 1991. Mem. AAAS, Internat. Acad. Pathology, Am. Soc. Clin. Pathology, Am. Soc. Hematology, Am. Soc. Oncology. Office: U So Calif Sch Medicine HMR 209 2011 Zonal Ave Los Angeles CA 90033-1034

NATION, EARL F., retired urologist, educator; b. Zephyr, Tex., Jan. 16, 1910; s. Joseph Madison and Alma Emily (Johnson) N.; m. Evelyn Stapp Poynter, Aug. 11, 1936; children: William Earl, Robert Joseph. BA, San Diego State U., 1931; MD, Western Res. U., 1935. Lic. urologist, Calif.; diplomate Am. Bd. Urology. Internship, resident in urology Los Angeles County Gen. Hosp., 1935-39; pvt. practice Pasadena, Calif., 1941-90, ret., 1990; instr., assoc. prof. urology U. So. Calif., L.A., 1941-55; sr. attending staff Huntington Meml. Hosp., Pasadena, 1941—, St. Luke Hosp., Pasadena, 1941—, also past pres.; pres. Pasadena Dispensary, 1946; lectr. Coll. Med. Evangelists (now Loma Linda U.), 1941-48. Mem. editorial bd. Jour. of Urology, 1958-66, Calif. Medicine, 1965-69, Forum on Medicine; contbr. articles to profl. jours., contbg. author to numerous books. Sec.-treas. Pasadena Breakfast Forum, 1970-73, pres. 1974-75. Crile rsch. scholar Western Res. U., 1931. Mem. ACS, AMA, Am. Urological Assn. (past pres.), Am. Osler Soc. (past pres.), L.A. County Med. Assn., Calif. Med. Assn., Pasadena Hist. Soc., So. Calif. Hist. Soc., Am. Soc. Clin. Urologists, Pasadena U. Club, Zamorano Club (v.p. L.A. chpt. 1991), Alpha Omega Alpha. Republican. Avocations: book collecting, reading, writing, gardening, fishing. Home: 311 E Sierra Madre Blvd Sierra Madre CA 91024-2675

NATION, FLOYD REUBEN, lawyer; b. Winder, Ga., Oct. 21, 1946; s. L.R. Nation; divorced; children: Natalie, Allison. BME, Ga. Tech., 1968; JD with honors, U. Tex., 1974. Bar: Tex. 1974, La. 1975, U.S. Patent and Trademark Office 1975, U.S. Supreme Ct. 1986, U.S. Ct. Appeals (5th, 11th, and fed. cirs.). Engr. Exxon U.S.A., Houston, 1968-71; ptnr. Arnold, White & Durkee, Austin, Tex., 1974—; lectr. patent law U. Tex. Sch. Law, 1978-79, 95—. Mem. ABA (chmn. ann. publs. 1988-90, chmn. div. 9 1990-91), State Bar Tex. (chmn. intellectual property law sect. 1992-93), Austin Intellectual Property Law Assn. (pres. 1991-92), Am. Intellectual Property Law Assn. Office: Arnold White & Durkee 600 Congress Ave Ste 1900 Austin TX 78701-3236

NATION, JAMES EDWARD, retired speech pathologist; b. Springfield, Ill., Aug. 22, 1933; s. John Herbert and Margaret Josephine (Weiss) N. B.S., Ill. State U., 1959; M.S., U. Wis., 1960, Ph.D., 1964. Asst. prof. U. Ga., 1964-66; asst. prof., assoc. prof., prof. Case Western Res. U., Cleve., 1966-86; prof., chmn. dept. communication scis. Case Western Res. U., 1979-85; dir. speech pathology Cleve. Hearing and Speech Center, 1970-74; sr. clin. instr. dept. pediatrics Case Western Res. Sch. Medicine, 1979-86; speech-lang. pathologist Tucson Unified Sch. Dist. #1, 1985-95; ret., 1995; chief speech-lang. pathologist craniofacial defects team Rainbow Babies and Childrens Hosp., Univ. Hosps., Case Western Res. U., 1978-85; exec. bd. Nat. Council Grad. Programs in Speech-Lang. Pathology and Audiology; cons. in field. Author: Diagnosis of Speech and Language Disorders, 1977, Child Language Disorders, 1982, 2d rev. edit., 1984; editorial cons.: Cleft Palate Jour.; contbr. chpts. to books; editor: Ohio Speech and Hearing Jour., 1969-73; contbr. articles to profl. jours. Served with U.S. Army, 1953-55. Recipient Wittke award for disting. undergrad. teaching, 1977, Outstanding Service award Ill. State U. Alumni Assn., 1982. Fellow Am. Speech-Lang. and Hearing Assn. (cert. speech-lang. pathologist); mem. Am. Cleft Palate Assn., Ohio Speech and Hearing Assn., Aphasiology Assn. Ohio, Nat. Council Grad. Programs in Speech-Lang. Pathology and Audiology. (Disting. Service award 1982). Home: Apt 19 2600 E Skyline Dr Unit 19 Tucson AZ 85718-3065

NATION, JOHN ARTHUR, electrical engineering educator, researcher; b. Bridgwater, Eng., Aug. 8, 1935; came to U.S., 1965; naturalized, 1991.; s. Arthur John and Doris Edith (Rides) N.; m. Sally Gillian Leeds, May 31, 1961; children—Philip David, Robert James. B.Sc., Imperial Coll., London, 1957; Ph.D., Imperial Coll., 1960. Cons. Comitato Nazionale per L'Energia Nucleare, Frascati, Italy, 1960-61; staff physicist Central Electricity Generating Bd., Leatherhead, Eng., 1962-65; elec. engring. faculty Cornell U., Ithaca, N.Y., 1965—; prof. Cornell U., 1978—, dir. Sch. Elec. Engring., 1984-89; cons. miscellaneous cos., 1965—. Contbr. articles to profl. jours. Fellow Am. Phys. Soc., IEEE (plasma scis. exec. com. 1985-89, chair com. 1987-88, Centennial medal 1984). Avocation: golf, tennis. Home: 1041 Hanshaw Rd Ithaca NY 14850-2741 Office: Cornell U 325 Engring Theory Ctr Ithaca NY 14853

NATIONS, HOWARD LYNN, lawyer; b. Dalton, Ga., Jan. 9, 1938; s. Howard Lynn and Eva Earline (Armstrong) Lamb; m. Ella Lois Johnson, June 4, 1960 (div. Nov. 1976); 1 child, Cynthia Lynn Nations Garcia. BA, Florida State U., 1963; JD, Fla. State U., 1966. Bar: Tex. 1966. Assoc. Butler, Rice Cook & Knapp, Houston, 1966-71; pres. Nations & Cross, Houston, 1971—; v.p., dir./co-founder Ins. Corp. Am., Houston, 1972—; pres. Caplinger & Nations Galleries, Houston, 1973—, Nations Investment Corp., Houston, 1975—, NCM Trade Corp., Houston, 1975; v.p. Delher Am. Inc., Houston, 1975—; pres. Howard L. Nations, P.C., Houston, 1971—; adj. prof. So. Tex. Coll. Law, Houston, 1967—; speaker in field. Author: Structuring Settlements, 1987; co-author: Texas Workers' Compensation, 1988, (with others) The Anatomy of a Personal Injury Lawsuit, 3rd rev. edit. 1991; editor: Maximizing Damages in Wrongful Death and Personal Injury Litigation, 1985; contbr. articles to profl. jours. Chair, trustee Nat. Coll. Advocacy, Washington, 1985-92. With M.I. Corps, U.S. Army, 1957-60. Fellow Tex. Bar Found., Houston Bar Found. (life); mem. ATLA (exec. com. 1991-95), Nat. Bd. Trial Advocacy (diplomate civil trial advocacy), So. Trial Lawyers Assn. (pres. 1994-95), Tex. Trial Lawyers Assn. (pres. 1992-93), Tex. Assn. Cert. Trial Lawyers (past pres.). Office: 3000 Post Oak Blvd Ste 1400 Houston TX 77056-6598

NATKIN, ALVIN MARTIN, environmental company executive; b. Bklyn., Feb. 4, 1928; s. Max Harvey and Rebecca (Rubenstein) N.; m. Lorraine Rothchild, Aug. 26, 1950; children: Jeff Warren, Stacy Ellen, Marcy Caren. B in Chem. Engring., Poly. Inst. Bkyln., 1952; MBA, Rutgers U., 1954. Engr. Standard Oil Devel. Co., Linden, N.J., 1952-57; mgr. exploratory mktg. Esso Standard Oil Co., N.Y.C., 1957-60, mgr. mktg. rsch., 1960-63; gen. mgr. Esso East Africa, Inc., Nairobi, Kenya, 1963-66; v.p. Esso Philippines, Inc., Manila, 1966-68; mgr. mktg. Esso East, Inc., Houston, 1968-77; environ. mgr. Exxon Corp., N.Y.C., 1977-84; Disting. fellow World Resources Inst., Washington, 1984-86; pres. Continental Environment Co., Summit, N.J., 1986—; internat. chmn. Petroleum Environment Inst., London, 1980-84; dir. World Industry Environment Conf., N.Y.C., 1982-86; cons. Environment & Safety Audit Corp., Midland, Mich., 1986-90. Author: Guidelines for Growth, 1984, Improving Environmental Cooperation, 1985; contbr. articles to profl. jours.; patentee in field, 1958. Served as cpl. U.S. Army, 1946-48. Recipient Disting. Service award U. Tex., 1985; named Hunter of Yr. Profl. Hunters Assn., 1965. Mem. AIChE, Am. Assn. Radon Scientists, Am. Chem. Soc., Air Pollution Control Assn., Nat. Assn. Environ. Profls., Explorers Club, Masons, Shriners. Republican. Jewish. Avocations: golf, fishing, hunting. Home: 21567 Villanova Dr Boca Raton FL 33433 Office: 2800 S Ocean Blvd Boca Raton FL 33432

NATOLI, JOE, newspaper publishing executive. Pres. The Miami Herald, Fla. Office: The Miami Herald 1 Herald Plz Miami FL 33132-1609*

NATORI, JEFFREY KAZUO, lawyer; b. Honolulu, Aug. 15, 1958; s. Shigeo and Gertrude Keiko (Miyamoto) N.; m. Eriko Sudo, June 24, 1989; children: Gemma Reina, Justin Kirika. BA, Am. U., 1980; JD, Del. Law Sch., 1983; MBA, Drexel U., 1986; cert. completion, Japan-Am. Inst. Mgmt. Sci., Honolulu and Tokyo, 1986-87. Bar: Pa. 1983, U.S. Dist. Ct. (ea. dist) Pa. 1983, Hawaii, 1987. Pvt. practice law Jeffrey K. Natori, Esquire, Phila., 1983-86; intern Seiko Instruments Inc., Tokyo, 1987; in-house counsel Chiyoda Corp., Yokohama, Japan, 1988-92; assoc. Cades Schutte Fleming & Wright, Honolulu, 1993-96; in-house counsel Chiyoda Corp., Tokyo, 1996—. Mem. ABA (speaker, Hawaii state chair, regions divsn., Fidelity and Surety law com., tort and ins. practice sect. 1994-96), Internat. Bar Assn. (speaker), Japanese Soc. Internat. Transactions, Inter-Pacific Bar Assn. (vice chair com. on internat. constrn. projects 1991-93, chair, 1993-95, com. coord. 1995-97), Internat. Forum Drexel U., Lawasia (spkr.). Office: Chiyoda Corp Legal Dept, 31-19 Shiba 2-Chome Minato-ku, Tokyo 105, Japan

NATORI, JOSIE CRUZ, apparel executive; b. Manila, May 9, 1947; came to U.S., 1964; d. Felipe F. and Angelita A. (Almeda) Cruz; m. Kenneth R. Natori, May 20, 1972; 1 child, Kenneth E.F. BA in Econs., Manhattanville Coll., 1968. V.p. Merrill-Lynch Co., N.Y.C., 1971-77; pres. The Natori Co., N.Y.C., 1977—; bd. dirs. The Alltel Corp., Calyx and Corolla. Bd. dirs. Philippine Am. Found., Jr. Achievement, Inc., 1992, Ednl. Found. for Fashion Industries; trustee Manhattanville Coll., Asia Soc., Asian Cultural Coun. Recipient Human Relations award Am. Jewish Com., N.Y.C., 1986, Harriet Alger award Working Woman, N.Y., 1987, Castle award Manhattanville Coll., Purchase, 1988, Galleon award Pres. Philippines, N.Y.C. Asian-Am. award, Friendship award Philippine-Am. Found., Hall of Fame award Mega Mags., Salute to Am. Fashion Designers award Dept. of Commerce. Mem. CFDA, Young Pres.'s Orgn., Fashion Group, Com. of 200. Avocations: pianist, tennis player. Home: 45 E 62nd St New York NY 10021-8025 Office: Natori Co 40 E 34th St Fl 18 New York NY 10016-4501

NATOW, ANNETTE BAUM, nutritionist, author, consultant; b. N.Y.C., Jan. 30, 1933; d. Edward and Gertrude (Jackerson) Baum; m. Harry Natow, Nov. 30, 1955; children: Allen, Laura, Steven. BS, CUNY Bklyn. Coll., 1955; MS, SUNY Coll. Plattsburg, 1960; PhD, Tex. Women's U., 1963. Registered dietitian, N.Y. Asst. prof. SUNY Coll. Plattsburg, 1967-69, CUNY Coll. Lehman, N.Y.C., 1969-70; assoc. prof., chmn. dept. SUNY Downstate Med. Ctr., Bklyn., 1970-76; prof., dir. nutrition programs Adelphi U., Garden City, N.Y., 1976-90, prof. emerita, 1991—; intern Montreal Diet Dispensary, March of Dimes, 1980; pres., writer, cons. NRH Nutrition Cons., Inc., Valley Stream, N.Y., 1980—. Author: No-Nonsense Nutrition, 1978, Geriatric Nutrition, 1980, Nutrition for the Prime of Your Life, 1983, No-Nonsense Nutrition for Kids, 1985, Megadoses: Vitamins as Drugs, 1985, Nutritional Care of the Older Adult, 1986, Pocket Encyclopedia of Nutrition, 1986, The Cholesterol Counter, 1989, 1988, 2d edit., 1989, The Fat Counter, 1989, The Fat Attack Plan, 1990, The Diabetes Carbohydrate and Calorie Counter, 1991, The Pregnancy Counter, 1992, The Iron Counter, 1993, The Sodium Counter, 1993, The Antioxidant Vitamin Counter, 1994, The Fast Food Counter, 1994, The Supermarket Nutrition Counter, 1995, The Protein Counter, 1997; editor Jour. Nutrition for Elderly, 1983—; mem. editorial bd. Environ. Nutrition Newsletter, 1985—; mem. editorial adv. bd. Prevention, 1984-86; contbr. numerous articles to profl. jours. United Hosp. Fund grantee, 1978. Mem. Am. Dietetic Assn., N.Y. State Dietetic Assn., N.Y. State Nutrition Coun. (sec. 1973-74). Avocations: square dancing, music. Home and Office: NRH Nutrition Cons Inc 187 Cherry St Woodmere NY 11598

NATOWITZ, JOSEPH B., chemistry educator, research administrator; b. Saranac Lake, N.Y., Dec. 24, 1936. BS in Chemistry, U. Fla., 1958; Cert. in Meteorology, UCLA, 1959; PhD in Nuclear Chemistry, U. Pitts., 1965. Staff meteorologist, 1st lt. USAF, 1958-61; grad. teaching asst. U. Pitts., 1961-62, grad. rsch. asst., 1962-65; postdoctoral rsch. assoc. SUNY, Stony Brook, 1965-67; rsch. collaborator Brookhaven Nat. Lab., 1965-67; asst. prof. Tex. A&M U., College Station, 1967-72, assoc. prof., 1972-76, prof., 1976—, head dept. chemistry, 1981-85, dir. Cyclotron Inst., 1991—; part-time instr. SUNY-Stony Brook, 1966-67; rsch. collaborator Lawrence Radiation Lab., Berkeley, Calif., 1966, Los Alamos (N.Mex.) Nat. Lab., 1973-74; Alexander Von Humboldt sr. scientist Max Planck Inst. für Kernphysik, Heidelberg, Germany, 1978; vis. prof. Inst. for Nuclear Studies, U. Tokyo, 1979, U. Claude Bernard, Inst. de Physique Nucleaire, 1983, U. de Caen, 1985, Ctr. des Etudes Nucleaires de Saclay, 1986, U. Cath. de Louvain, 1987; former mem. accelerator review com. TASCC, Chalk River, Can.; former mem. adv. com. LBL Superhilac, ORNL Cyclotron, Nat. Superconducting Cyclotron Lab. Contbr. over 150 articles to profl. jours., also to approx. 40 books and procs. Chmn. Cub Scout Pack 802, 1973-75; v.p. College Hills PTO, 1974-75; mem. A&M Consol. Sch. Bd., 1975-78, pres., 1977-78; pres. A&M Consol. Band Boosters, 1980-81. NSF summer fellow, 1962; NASA predoctoral fellow, 1964-65; recipient Disting. Achievment award-rsch. Tex. A&M U., 1988, Am. Chem Soc. award for Nuc. Chemistry, 1995. Fellow Am. Phys. Soc.; mem. Am. Chem. Soc. (vice chmn. div. nuclear chemistry and tech. 1993, chmn. 1994, award in nuclear chemistry 1995), Sigma Xi, Phi Lambda Upsilon. Office: Tex A&M U Cyclotron Inst College Station TX 77843

NATSIOS, NICHOLAS ANDREW, retired foreign service officer; b. Lowell, Mass., July 31, 1920; s. Andrew and Fanny (Papageorgiou) N.; m. Mitzi Peterson, Sept. 2, 1951; children: Christine Daphne, Deborah Diane, Valerie Sophia, Alexandra Roxanne. Student, Lowell Technol. Inst., 1939-40; B.A. cum laude, Ohio State U., 1948; M.A.L.D., Fletcher Sch. Law and Diplomacy, 1983. Civilian spl. adviser polit. problems U.S. Mil. Mission, Salonika, Greece, 1948-50; polit. adviser mil. secretariat U.S. Mil. Mission, Athens, Greece, 1951-56; polit. officer, 1st sec. embassy, spl. asst. to ambassador Am. embassy, Saigon, Viet Nam, 1956-60; attache Am. embassy, Paris, 1960-62; spl. asst. to ambassador Am. embassy, Seoul, Korea, 1962-65; 1st sec. American embassy, Buenos Aires, Argentina, 1965-69; spl. asst. to ambassador Am. embassy, The Hague, The Netherlands, 1969-72; regional affairs officer. Am. embassy, Tehran, Iran, 1972-74; mgmt. cons., 1977—. Served to capt. AUS, 1942-47; comdg. officer Italian Frontier Control Detachment, U.S. Occupation Forces, 1945-47, Milan, Italy. Decorated Medal of Merit; decorated Bronze Star U.S.; knight comdr. of Italy; Knight comdr. Order of St. George; medal of Mil. Valor Italy; D.S.C. 1st class Knights of Malta; Order of Eagle Yugoslavia; Distinguished Service medal Greece; Order of Service Merit Korea). Mem. Phi Beta Kappa, Phi Eta Sigma. Address: 77 Lincoln Pky Lowell MA 01851-3405

NATSUYAMA, HARRIET HATSUNE, mathematician; b. Honolulu, Sept. 2, 1937; d. Kenjiro and Yakue Natsuyama; children: Julia, Conan. BA, U. Hawaii, 1959, MS, 1960; PhD, Kyoto U., 1965. Math. Rand Corp., Santa Monica, Calif., 1961-68, cons., 1968-77; adj. assoc. prof. U. So. Calif., L.A., 1974-79; sr. scientist Hughes Aircraft Co., El Segundo, 1979-87; chief engr. Infotec Devel. Inc., Camarillo, 1987-89; prof. systems engring. Calif. State U., Fullerton, 1990—; v.p. Advanced Indsl. Materials, 1996—; fgn. spl. vis. prof. Oita U., 1995. Author: Invariant Imbedding and Time-Dependent Transport Processes, 1963, System Identification: Methods and Applications, 1974, Integral Equations via Imbedding Methods, 1974, Multiple Scattering Processes: Inverse and Direct, 1975, Numerical Derivatives and Nonlinear Analysis, 1986. Mem. IEEE, AAAS, Am. Math. Soc., Inst. Advanced Engrng., Grad. Women in Sci. (pres. 1990-91), Phi Beta Kappa, Phi Kappa Phi. Office: Systems Engineering Dept Calif State U Fullerton CA 92634

NATTEL, STANLEY, cardiologist, research scientist; b. Haifa, Israel, Jan. 28, 1951; arrived in Can., 1952; s. William and Julie (Zwirek) N.; m. Celia Anne Reich, Sept. 25, 1973; children: Jonathan, Ilana, Daniel, Sarah. BSc magna cum laude, McGill U., 1972, MD, 1974. Diplomate Am. Bd. Internal Medicine, Am. Bd. Cardiology. Intern in medicine Royal Victoria Hosp., 1974-75, resident in internal medicine, 1975-76; resident in clin. pharmacology Montreal (Que., Can.) Gen. Hosp., 1976-78, cardiologist, clin. pharmacologist, 1981-87, dir. coronary care unit, 1983-87; fellow in cardiology Ind. U., 1978-80; fellow in physiology U. Pa., 1980-81; asst. prof. pharmacology, medicine McGill U., Montreal, 1981-87, assoc. prof., 1987—; cardiologist Montreal Heart Inst., 1987—, dir. rsch. ctr., 1990—; prof. Dept. Medicine, U. Montreal, 1995—; external reviewer Med. Rsch. Coun., 1981—, Ont. Health Ministry, 1983-84, NSF, 1992, others; chmn. libr. com. dept. pharmacology McGill U., 1982-86, mem. grad. com., 1984-89, chmn. grad. tng. com., 1986-89, departmental rep. grad. faculty coun., 1989-91, coord. grad. teaching pharmacology, 1989-91; mem. oper. grants com. Can. Heart Found., 1983-86; chmn. clin. trials com. Montreal Gen. Hosp., 1983-87, chmn. pharmacy and therapeutics com., 1984-87, sec. clin. chemistry rev. com., 1984, course dir. drug therapy, 1984-87, acting dir. divsn. clin. pharmacology, 1984-85, mem. various coms., 1985-87; mem. fellowship awards com. FRSQ, 1988-90, mem. ctr. grants pharmacology/pharmacy com., 1989-90; chmn. pharmacology com. Montreal Heart Inst., 1988-90, mem. search com. pharmacist-in-chief, 1989-90, mem. ethics com., 1991—, chmn. internal rsch. com., 1991—, mem. consultative com. exec. dir., 1991—, chmn. consultative com. rsch. ctr., 1991—; consulting coun. pharmacology Province of Quebec, 1989-90; mem. safety monitoring com. CAMIAT Study, 1990—; assoc. prof. medicine U. Montreal, 1991-95, prof. 1995—, chmn. search com. dir. rsch. Sacré-Coeur Hosp., 1991, mem. rsch. com. Cormes faculty medicine, 1991—, mem. rsch. com. dept. medicine, 1991—; chmn. search com., dir. rsch. Maisonneuve Rosemont Hosp., 1996—; mem. site visit team program project grant NIH, 1991, cons. program project grant, 1993, spl. reviewer cardiovascular study sect., 1993, 95; mem. oper. grants com. Med. Rsch. Coun. Can., 1988-93; mem. sr. personnel awards com. Can. Heart Found., 1994—; lectr. in field. Assoc. editor Can. Jour. Physiology and Pharmacology, 1990—; mem. editl. bd. Jour. Cardiovasc. Electrophysiology, 1991—, Drugs, 1993—, Cardiovasc. Drugs and Therapy, 1993—, Circulation Rsch., 1995—, JACC, 1995—; manuscript reviewer Am. Jour. Cardiology, Can. Med. Assn. Jour., European Jour. Pharmacology, New Eng. Jour. Medicine, others; contbr. chpts. to books and articles to profl. jours. Chmn. edn. com. Hebrew Acad. Sch., Montreal, 1991-92. Grantee Que. Heart Found., 1981—, Nordic Pharms., 1985-87, Knoll Pharms., 1991-93, others; fellow Med. Rsch. Coun. Can., 1979-81; McGill U. scholar, 1967-74, Sir Edward Beatty scholar McGill U., 1967-70, Rsch. scholar Med. Rsch. Coun., 1982-87, Sr. Rsch. scholar Fonds de la Recherche en Santé du Québec, 1990-93. Fellow Am. Coll. Cardiology, Royal Coll. Physicians Can. (cert. medicine, cardiology); mem. Am. Heart Assn. (coun. basic sci.), Am. Soc. Pharmacology and Exptl. Therapeutics, Can. Cardiovasc. Soc. (councilor 1992-95), Can. Soc. Clin. Pharmacology (Kenneth M. Piafsky Young Investigator award 1985), Pharm. Soc. Can. Biophys. Soc. Avocations: studying Jewish religious works, sports. Home: 5609 Alpine Ave, Côte Saint Luc, PQ Canada H4V 2X6 Office: Montreal Heart Inst, 5000 Belanger St E, Montreal, PQ Canada H1T 1C8

NATTRAS, RUTH A(NN), school nurse; b. Wilkes-Barre, Pa., June 30, 1946; d. George James and Jean Harriet (LeGault) Willis; m. John D. Nattras, Aug. 23, 1969; children: John R., Laura R. Diploma, Nesbitt Meml. Hosp., Kingston, Pa., 1967. RN, Pa., N.Y. Operating room staff nurse Morristown (N.J.) Meml. Hosp., 1967-69, Horton Meml. Hosp., Middletown, N.Y., 1969-70; sch. nurse Middletown City Sch. Dist., 1986—; substitute sch. nurse, 1982-86; summer sch. nurse Pine Bush (N.Y.) Cen. Sch. Dist., 1984,86. Vol. Am. Heart Assn., Am. Cancer Soc.; den leader Boy Scouts Am., 1978-80, den leader coach, 1981, awards chmn., 1981, com. mem., 1976-84; mem. planning com. Lienhard Sch. Nursing Pace U., 1994—. Mem. N.Y. State United Tchrs. (bldg. rep. 1993—), Nat. Assn. Sch. Nurses (cert. sch. nurse), N.Y. State Assn. Sch. Nurses, Orange County Sch. Nurses, Middletown Sch. Nurses Assn., Nesbitt Meml. Hosp. Alumni Assn. (life), Order Ea. Star (matron 1991).

NATZLER, OTTO, ceramic artist; b. Vienna, Austria, Jan. 31, 1908; came to U.S., 1938, naturalized, 1944; s. Sigmund and Frieda (Loewy) N.; m. Gertrud Amon, June 1938; m. Gail Reynolds, Sept. 7, 1973. Author: (with others) Form and Fire—Natzler Ceramics 1939-72, 1973; one man exhbns. include, Fine Art Gallery, San Diego, 1940, 42, San Francisco Mus. Art, 1943, 63, Los Angeles County Mus. Art, 1944, 66, Art Inst. Chgo., 1946, 63, La Jolla Mus. Art, Calif., 1953, Cin. Art Mus., 1954, 60, Joslyn Art Mus., Omaha, 1955, Springfield Mus., Mo., 1955, Jewish Mus., N.Y.C., 1958, Bezalel Nat. Mus., Jerusalem, 1959, Mus. Modern Art, Haifa, Israel, 1959, Kunstgewerbemuseum, Zurich, Switzerland, 1959, Stedelijk Mus., Amsterdam, Holland, 1959, Tulane U., 1961, St. Paul Art Center, 1963, Mus. Contemporary Crafts, N.Y.C., 1963, Birger Sandzen Meml. Gallery, Lindsborg, Kans., 1964, Palm Springs Mus., Calif., 1968, George Walter Vincent Smith Art Mus., Springfield Mass., 1970, Carleton Coll., Northfield, Minn., 1970, retrospective, M.W. deYoung Meml. Mus., San Francisco, 1971, Renwick Gallery, Smithsonian Instn., Washington, 1973, Contemporary Crafts Gallery, Portland, 1975, Craft and Folk Art Mus., Los Angeles, 1977, Scottsdale Center for Arts, Ariz., 1977, No. Ariz. U., Flagstaff, 1978, Los Angeles County Mus. Art, 1980; retrospective show Am. Craft Mus, 1993, Juedisches Museum der Stadt, Wien, 1994; works represented in permanent collections, Renwick Gallery, Smithsonian Inst., Am. Craft Mus., N.Y.C., Cooper-Hewitt Mus., N.Y.C., Fine Arts Gallery, San Diego, Everson Mus. Art, Syracuse, N.Y., Cin. Art Mus., Los Angeles County Mus. Art, Walker Art Center, Mpls., Art Inst. Chgo., Dallas Mus. Fine Arts, Tucson Art Mus., Joselyn Art Mus., Met. Mus. Art, U. Nebr., San Francisco Mus. Art, Kantonales Gewerbemuseum, Bern, Switzerland, Phoenix Art Mus., Nat. Mus. Design, Smithsonian Instn., E.B. Crocker Art Gallery, Sacramento, Balt. Mus. Art, Detroit Inst. Art, Fort Worth Mus. Art, U. Minn., Cranbrook Acad. Art, Bloomfield Hills, Mich., Kunstgewerbemuseum, Zurich, Calif. State Fair, Sacramento, Springfield Art Mus., St. Paul Art Center, Phila. Mus. Art, Seattle Art Mus., Slater Meml. Mus., Norwich, Conn., Museo Internazionale delle Ceramiche, Faenza, Italy, Portland Mus. Art, Oreg., U. Wis., UCLA, Ariz. State Coll., Houston Mus. Fine Art, Krannert Art Mus. at U. Ill., Northwestern U., Oakland Art Mus., Calif., La Crosse State Coll., Ind., Birger Sandzen Meml. Gallery, Mus. Modern Art, N.Y.C., Mills Coll., Oakland, Palm Springs Desert Mus., Newark Mus. Art, George Walter Vincent Smith Mus., Springfield, Mass., U. Oreg., Eugene, Victoria and Albert Mus., London, Minn. Mus. Art, St. Paul, Nat. Mus. Am. History, Smithsonian Instn., Washington, Des Moines Art Center, Santa Barbara Mus. Art, Calif., Maurice Spertus Mus. Judaica, Chgo., Staatliche Museen Preussischer Kulturbesitz, Kunstgewerbemuseum, Berlin, Utah Mus., U. Utah, Salt Lake City, Jewish Mus., N.Y.C., Contemporary Crafts Gallery, Portland, Honolulu Acad. Art, Oesterreichisches Mus fuer Angewandte Kunst, Vienna, Austria, Mus. Bellerive, Zurich Switzerland, Bklyn. Mus., Nelson-Atkins Mus. Art, Kansas City, Mo., Skirball Mus., Los

Angeles, Mus. Fine Arts, Boston, Va. Mus. Fine Arts, Richmond, others. Fellow Am. Craft Coun., Internat. Inst. Arts and Letters. Address: 7837 Woodrow Wilson Dr Los Angeles CA 90046-1213*

NAU, CHARLES JOHN, government affairs director, lawyer; b. Chgo., Mar. 12, 1947; s. Charles J. and Roma (Murphy) N. BA maxima cum laude, U. Notre Dame, 1969, LLD cum laude, 1974. Bar: N.Y. 1975, Calif. 1983, France, 1979. Gen. counsel Syntex Labs., Inc., Palo Alto, Calif., 1983-94; dir. govt. affairs ALZA Corp., Palo Alto, Calif., 1995—; cons. Nat. Inst. Drug Abuse CDC, Washington, 1990, legal advisor Nat. Leadership Coalition on AIDS, Washington, 1990—; del. EEC-UNESCO Internat. Conf. AIDS in the Workplace, Paris, 1992. Chair SYNPAC, Palo Alto, 1986-94; del. Dem. Nat. Convention, N.Y., 1980; exec. dir. Dems. Abroad, 1984. Mem. Nat. Health Care Attorneys. Office: ALZA Corp 950 Page Mill Rd Box 10950 Palo Alto CA 94303-0802

NAU, DOUGLAS SCOTT, psychotherapist; b. Perth Amboy, N.J., Aug. 18, 1952; s. Charles Mathiasen and Ruth June (Agesen) N.; m. Jane Elizabeth Zimmerman; 1 child, Adam Henry. BA, Thiel Coll., 1974; MDiv, Princeton (N.J.) Theol. Sem., 1977; PhD, Nova Southeastern U., 1996. Cert. med. hypnotherapist. Chaplain The Peddie Sch., Hightstown, N.J., 1977-81; dir. guidance Roland Park County Sch., Balt., 1981-82; assoc. pastor Second Presbyn. Ch., Balt., 1981-89; dir. pastoral svcs. Charter Glade Hosp., Ft. Myers, Fla., 1989-92; pvt. practice Ft. Myers, Fla., 1989-92; staff therapist Family Therapy Assocs., Ft. Lauderdale, 1993; mental health therapist MCC Behavioral Care, Ft. Lauderdale, 1993-95, West Palm Beach, Fla., 1993-95; therapist All Care Wellness and Rehab., Ft. Lauderdale, 1996; pres. Springdale Behavioral Health, Inc., York, Pa., 1996—; adj. faculty Bradley Acad. for Visual Arts, 1996—, York Coll. Pa., 1997—. Author: The New CR.I.S. Case Studies, 1982, C.R.I.S. Case Studies for the 90's, 1994; contbr. articles to profl. jours. Pres. bd. dirs. Chesapeake Habitat for Humanity, Balt., 1987-88. Recipient Bravo award MCC Behavioral Care, 1994, Doris B. Harold award Nova Southeastern U., 1996. Mem. Am. Assn. for Marriage and Family Therapy (clin. mem.), Fla. Assn. for Marriage and Family Therapy, Scientific Hypnosis Soc., Pa. Assn. for Marriage and Family Therapy, Peace River Presbytery. Avocation: advanced open water diver. Home: 930 Arlington Rd York PA 17403

NAUERT, ROGER CHARLES, healthcare executive; b. St. Louis, Jan. 6, 1943; s. Charles Henry and Vilma Amelia (Schneider) N.; B.S., Mich. State U., 1965; J.D., Northwestern U., 1969; M.B.A., U. Chgo., 1979; m. Elaine Louise Harrison, Feb. 18, 1967; children: Paul, Christina. Bar: Ill. 1969. Asst. atty. gen. State of Ill., 1969-71; chief counsel Ill. Legis. Investigating Commn., 1971-73; asst. state comptroller State of Ill., 1973-75; dir. adminstrn. and fin. Health and Hosps. Governing Commn. Cook County, Chgo., 1975-79; nat. dir. health care services Grant Thornton, Chgo., 1979-88; exec. v.p. Detroit Med. Ctr., 1988-91; exec. v.p. Columbia-Presbyn. Med. Ctr., N.Y.C., 1991-93; sr. v.p. Mt. Sinai Med. Ctr., N.Y.C., 1993-96; pres., CEO Radius Health Sys., Garden City, N.Y., 1996—; vis. lectr. healthcare mgmt. & fin. Columbia U., Vanderbilt U., U. Chgo., 1978—; preceptor Wharton Sch., U. Pa. Ford Found. grantee, 1968-69. Mem. Am. Hosp. Assn., Am. Public Health Assn., Am. Coll. Healthcare Execs., Nat. Health Lawyers Assn., Health Care Fin. Mgmt. Assn. (faculty mem.), Alpha Phi Sigma, Phi Delta Phi, Delta Upsilon. Clubs: N.Y. Athletic, Mt. Kisco Country. Author: A Sociology of Health, 1977; The Demography of Illness, 1978; Proposal for a National Health Policy, 1979; Health Care Feasibility Studies, 1980; Health Care Planning Guide, 1981; Health Care Strategic Planning, 1982; Overcoming the Obstacles to Planning, 1983; Principles of Hospital Cash Management, 1984; Healthcare Networking Arrangements, 1985; Strategic Planning for Physicians, 1986; HMO's: A Once and Future Strategy, 1987, Mergers, Acquisitions and Divestitures, 1988, Tax Exempt Status Under Seige, 1989, Governance in Multi-Hospital Systems, 1990, Planning Alternative Delivery Systems, 1991, Direct Contracting: The Future is Now, 1992, The Rise and Fall of the U.S. Healthcare System, 1993, A Proposal for National Healthcare Reform, 1994, Academic Medical Centers and the New Age of Managed Care, 1995, The Quest For Value in Healthcare, 1996, Managed Behavioral Health Care, 1997. Home: 461 Haines Rd Bedford Corners NY 10549 Office: RCN Assocs 70 W Red Oak Ln White Plains NY 10604-3602

NAUGHTON, JAMES, actor; b. Middletown, Conn., Dec. 6, 1945; s. James Joseph and Rosemary (Walsh) N.; m. Pamela Parsons, Oct. 1968; children: Gregory J., Keira P. BA, Brown U., 1967; MFA, Yale U., 1970. Broadway appearances include Edmund in Long Day's Journey Into Night, 1971 (Theatre World award, N.Y. Drama Critics award, Vernon Rice award 1971), Stone in City of Angels (Tony award 1990, Drama Desk award), I Love My Wife, 1977, Whose Life Is It Anyway, 1980. Feature films include Paper Chase, 1972, Second Wind, 1975, A Stranger is Watching, 1981, Cat's Eye, 1982, The Glass Menagerie, 1987, The Good Mother, 1988, Chicago, 1996 (Tony award, 1997); TV appearances include: (series) Faraday and Company, 1973-74, Planet of the Apes, 1974, Making the Grade, 1982, Trauma Center, 1983; (movies) F. Scott Fitzgerald and "The Last of the Belles", 1974, The Last 36 Hours of Dr. Durant, 1975, The Bunker, 1981, My Body, My Child, 1982, Parole, 1982, The Last of the Great Survivors, 1984, Between Darkness and the Dawn, 1985, Sin of Innocence, 1986, Necessity, 1988, The Cosby Mysteries, 1994. Recipient Tony award Leading Actor in a Musical, 1997. *

NAUGHTON, JAMES LEE, internist; b. 1946. AB, Dartmouth Coll., 1968; MD, Harvard U., 1972. Intern U. Calif. Moffitt Hosp., San Francisco, 1972-73; resident in medicine U. Calif. Affiliated Hosps., San Francisco, 1973-75, San Francisco Gen. Hosp., 1975-76; fellow in nephrology U. Calif., San Francisco, 1976-77, assoc. clin. prof. medicine, 1982—; pvt. practice, ptnr. Pinole Med. Group, Pinole, Calif. Office: Pinole Med Group 2160 Appian Way Pinole CA 94564-2524

NAUGHTON, JAMES MARTIN, journalist; b. Pitts., Aug. 13, 1938; s. Francis Patrick and Martha Ann (Clear) N.; m. Diana Marie Thomas, Sept. 5, 1964; children: Jenifer Mary, Lara Marie, Michael Thomas, Kerry Marie. B.A. cum laude, U. Notre Dame, 1960. Reporter, photographer Painesville (Ohio) Telegraph, summer, 1955-60; reporter Cleve. Plain Dealer, 1962-69; Washington corr. N.Y. Times, 1969-77; nat. editor Phila. Inquirer, 1977-79, met. editor, 1979-83, assoc. mng. editor, 1980-86, dep. mng. editor, 1986-90, mng. editor, 1990-91, exec. editor, 1991-96; pres. The Poynter Inst. for Media Studies, St. Petersburg, Fla., 1996—; Marsh prof. U. Mich., 1977. Served with USMC, 1960-62. Recipient Disting. Service award Sigma Delta Chi, 1973. Roman Catholic. Home: 2500 Coffee Pot Blvd NE Saint Petersburg FL 33704-3466 Office: 801 3rd St S Saint Petersburg FL 33701-4920

NAUGHTON, JOHN PATRICK, cardiologist; b. West Nanticoke, Pa., May 20, 1933; s. John Patrick and Anne Frances (McCormick) N.; children: Bruce, Marcia, Lisa, George, Michael, Thomas. AA, Cameron State Coll., Lawton, Okla., 1952; BS, St. Louis U., 1954; MD, Okla. U., 1958; MD (hon.), Kosin U., 1995. Intern George Washington U. Hosp., Washington, 1958-59; resident U. Okla. Med. Center, 1959-64; asst. prof. medicine U. Okla., 1966-68; assoc. prof. medicine U. Ill., 1968-70; prof. medicine George Washington U., 1970-75, dean acad. affairs, 1973-75, dir. div. rehab. medicine and Regional Rehab. Research and Tng. Center, 1970-75; dean Sch. Medicine, SUNY, Buffalo, 1975-96; prof. medicine, physiology, social and preventive medicine Sch. Medicine, SUNY, 1975—, lectr. in rehab. medicine, 1975—; acting v.p. for health scis. SUNY, 1983-84, v.p. clin. affairs, 1984-96; dir. Nat. Exercise and Heart Disease Project, 1972—; chmn. policy adv. bd. Beta-blocker Heart Attack Trial Nat. Heart, Lung and Blood Inst., 1977-82; pres. Western N.Y. chpt. Am. Heart Assn., 1983-85, v.p. N.Y. State affiliate, 1985, pres. N.Y. State affiliate, 1988-90; chmn. clin. applications and preventions adv. com. Nat. Heart, Lung and Blood Inst., 1984; mem. Fed. COGME working group on consortia, 1996-97, N.Y. Gov.'s Commn. on Grad. Med. Edn., 1985, N.Y. State Coun. on Grad. Med. Edn., 1988-90, chmn. 1996—; pres. Assoc. Med. Schs. N.Y., 1982-84, mem. adminstrv. com. Coun. of Deans, 1983-89; mem. N.Y. State Dept. of Health Adv. Com. on Physician Recredentialing; mem. exec. coun. Nat. Inst. on Disability and Rehab. Rsch. 1991-92. Author: Exercise Testing and Exercise Training in Coronary Heart Disease, 1973, Exercise Testing: Physiological, Biomechanical, and Clinical Principles, 1988. Career devel. awardee Nat. Heart Inst., 1966-71; recipient Brotherhood-Sisterhood award in medicine NCCJ, N.E. Minority Educators award, 1990, Acad. Alumnus of Yr. award Okla. U., 1990, award for svc. to minorities in med. edn., 1991, Honorary Doctor of Medicine award, Kosin U., 1995, Frank Sindelar award N.Y. State Am. Heart Assn., 1995, James Platt White Soc. award, 1995, Outstanding Contbns. in the field of Health Care award Sheehan Meml. Hosp., 1995, Chancellor Charles P. Norton medal, SUNY, Buffalo, 1997. Fellow ACP, Am. Coll. Cardiology, Am. Coll. Sports Medicine (pres. 1970-71), Am. Coll. Chest Physicians; mem. N.Y. State Heart Assn. (pres.), Am. Coll. Cardiology (coun. N.Y. chpt.). Office: SUNY Buffalo Sch Medicine Biomed Scis 3435 Main St Buffalo NY 14214-3001

NAUGHTON, PATRICIA J., gerontological nurse, administrator, consultant; b. Blair, Nebr., Aug. 31, 1938; d. J. Merton and Emily J. (Spanggaard) Kuhr; children: Jeff Kloster, Tara Schnack, Anne LaBrie, Neal Kloster. Diploma Nebr. Meth. Hosp., Sch. Nursing, Omaha, 1974. Cert. gerontology ANCC. DON Bapt. Meml. Home, Harlan, Iowa, Sunny View Care Ctr., Ankeny, Iowa, Quality Health Care Ctr., Des Moines, Regency Care Ctr., Norwalk, Iowa, 1990-91; nurse cons. The Britwill Co., Dallas, 1991-92; DON Good Shepherd Luth. Home, 1992-97; nurse cons. Vetter Health Svcs., Omaha, 1997—. Mem. Nebr. Commn. for Hearing Impaired; sec. Network for the Elderly; mem. Iowa Tri-Coun. Nursing Summit. Mem. Iowa Coun. Gerontol. DONs (sec., pres.), Nebr. Health Care Assn., Omaha Dist. Nursing Soc. (pres.), Liaison Group Nebr. Nurses Orgn., Lions (v.p.), Beta Sigma Phi (past pres., Woman of Yr. 1984, 91, 95).

NAUGLE, ROBERT PAUL, dentist; b. Cleve., May 3, 1951; s. Paul Franklin Albert and Olga (Bigadza) N.; m. Nancy Elaine Baker, June 14, 1975; 1 child, Jennifer Elaine. BS, Heidelberg Coll., Tiffin, Ohio, 1973; DDS, Case Western Res. U., 1977. Pvt. practice Uniontown, Ohio, 1980—. Capt. USAF, 1977-80. Mem. ADA, Am. Soc. Dentistry for Children, Ohio Dental Assn., Acad. Gen. Dentistry, Acad. Sports Dentistry, Stark County Dental Soc., Akron Dental Soc., Air Force Assn., Rotary (past program chmn. Uniontown, Student of Month chmn., past pres., past v.p., past treas., Paul Harris fellow, past sgt.-at-arms). Republican. Mem. United Church of Christ. Office: 13027 Cleveland Ave NW Uniontown OH 44685-8430

NAUHEIM, STEPHEN ALAN, lawyer; b. Washington, Nov. 17, 1942; s. Ferdinand Alan and Beatrice Lillian (Strasburger) N.; children: Terry Beth, David Alan. BS in Acctg., U. N.C., 1964; JD, Georgetown U., 1967; LLM, George Washington U., 1970. Bar: D.C. 1968, U.S. Ct. Claims 1968, U.S. Tax Ct. 1971. Atty. adviser office chief counsel IRS, Washington, 1967-71, asst. br. chief, 1970-71; assoc. Surrey & Morse, Washington, 1971-75, ptnr., 1975-81; prin. Anderson, Hibey, Nauheim & Blair, Washington, 1981-91, Schall, Boudreau & Gore, Washington, 1991-93; pres., gen. counsel CMW Group, Ltd., Washington, 1994-96; dir. Price Waterhouse LLP, 1996—; mem. adv. bd. World Trade Inst., N.Y.C., 1978—, Tax Mgmt. Adv. Bd., Washington, 1980—. Mem. editl. bd. Internat. Tax Jour., N.Y.C., 1982—; contbr. to profl. publs. Mem. ABA (former com. chmn. taxation sect.), Internat. Fiscal Assn., D.C. Bar Assn. (mem. steering com. tax sect. 1987-92, chmn. tax sect. 1990-92), Am. Coll. of Tax Counsel. Avocations: travelling, sailing. Office: Price Waterhouse, No 1 Bridge London, London Bridge England SE1 9QL

NAULT, FERNAND, choreographer; b. Montreal, Dec. 27, 1921. Leading character dancer, ballet master Am. Ballet Theatre, N.Y.C., 1944-65; dir. ABT's Sch. of Classical Ballet, N.Y.C., 1960-64; co-artistic dir., resident choreographer Les Grands Ballets Canadiens, 1965-73, resident choreographer, 1973-90, artistic advisor, 1987-90, choreographer emeritus, 1990—; adv. dir. L'École Supérieure de Danse du Québec, 1973-90; guest choreographer Colorado Ballet, 1978-81, artistic dir., 1981-82. Choreographer works, Am. Ballet Theatre, Joffrey Ballet Co., Harkness Co., Colo. Concert Ballet Co., Md. Ballet Co., Atlanta Ballet, Ballet Fedn. Phillipines; works choreographed include Claytonia, 1960, The Lonely Ones, 1960, Iskushenye, 1960, Giosco, 1961, Latin American Symphoniette, 1961, Cyclic, 1962, Roundabout, 1962, The Sleeping Beauty, 1963, Carmina Burana, 1966, Pas d'Été, 1966, La Lettre, 1966, Hip and Straight, 1970, Tommy, 1970, Coppelia, 1971, Cantique des cantiques, 1974, Liberté Temperée, 1976, La Scouine, 1977. Other choreographed works include Aurki, Ceremonie, Casse-Noisette/The Nutcracker, Chants de douleur chants d'allégresse/Songs of Joy and Sorrow, Gehenne, Incohérence, L'Oiseau de feu, La fille mal gardée, Les sept péchés capitaux/The Seven Deadly Sins, Les sylphides, Miribilia, Mobiles, Paquita (Pas de deux), Pas d'époque, Pas rompu, Quintan, Quintessence, Symphonie de psaumes, Ti-Jean, Try, Ready, Go, Visages. Recipient Silver medal for choreography 7th Internat. Ballet Competition Varna, Bulgaria, 1976; Order of Canada, 1977, Prix Denise-Pelletier, Quebec, 1985, Chevalier de l'ordre national du Quebec, 1990. Office: Les Grands Ballets Canadiens, 4816 rue Rivard, Montreal, PQ Canada H2J 2N6

NAULT, WILLIAM HENRY, publishing executive; b. Ishpeming, Mich., June 9, 1926; s. Henry J. and Eva (Perrault) N.; m. Helen E. Matthews, Nov. 28, 1946; children: William Henry, Rebecca Nault Marks, Ronald, George, Peter, Julia Nault Doyle, Robert, David. AB, No. Mich. U., 1948, LittD (hon.), 1988; MA, U. Mich., 1949; EdD, Columbia U., 1953, LHD (hon.), 1980, LLD (hon.), 1986, LittD (hon.), 1988. Dir. adult edn. Battle Creek, Mich., 1948-49; guidance counselor, 1949-50; prin. W.K. Kellogg High Sch., Battle Creek, 1950-53; research assoc. Columbia U., 1953-54; asst. supt. Ridgewood, N.J., 1954-55; adj. prof. Patterson State Coll., N.J., 1954-55; dir. research World Book, Inc. (formerly Field Enterprises Edn. Corp.), Chgo., 1955-63; v.p. World Book, Inc. (formerly Field Enterprises Edn. Corp.), 1963-66, sr. v.p., editorial dir., 1966-68, exec. v.p. and editorial dir., 1968-83; pres., pub., chief operating officer World Book, Inc., 1983-84, gen. chmn. editorial adv. bds., 1968—, pub., 1983—; past vice chmn. Govt. Adv. Com. on Internat. Library and Book Programs, U.S. Dept. State; past mem. nat. adv. bd. Ctr. on Ednl. Media and Materials for Handicapped; past mem. exec. bd. Commn. Instns. Higher Edn., North Central Assn. Colls. and Secondary Schs.; mem. dean's adv. council Coll. Bus. and Pub. Adminstrn., U. Mo., Columbia; mem. nat. council Inst. Internat. Edn. Author material on courses of study. Mem. alumni com. Columbia Tchrs. Coll. Capital Campaign; mem. White House Conf. on Youth; pres. Oak Park (Ill.) Bd. Edn., 1960-63; bd. regents Lincoln Acad., Ill.; past trustee Adler Planetarium, De Paul U., Chgo. Geol. Soc.; trustee No. Mich. U. Devel. Fund; bd. dirs. H.V. Phalin Found. Grad. Study; mem. adv. bd. Rosary Coll.; liberal arts and scis. adv. council De Paul U. Served with F.A., AUS, 1944-45. Recipient Columbia U. Tchrs. Coll. medal for disting. svc. in edn.; named Disting. Alumnus No. Mich. U., U. Mich. Fellow AAAS; mem. ALA, Chgo. Planetarium Soc. (trustee), Chgo. Geog. Soc. (dir.), Am. Acad. Polit. and Social Sci., Am. Edn. Research Assn., Am. Assn. Sch. Adminstrs., Assn. Supervision and Curriculum Devel., Chgo. Pubs. Assn. (past pres.), Ill. Assn. Sch. Adminstrs., Ill. Acad. Sci., Nat. Sci. Tchr. Assn., Nat. Council Tchrs. English, Assn. Am. Geographers, Assn. Childhood Edn. Internat., Nat. Assn. Elementary Sch. Prins., Nat. Assn. Secondary Sch. Prins., Council for Advancement Sci. Writing, Internat. Platform Assn., Nat. Council Social Studies, Nat. Soc. Study Edn. Roman Catholic. Clubs: Mid-Am, Mchts. and Mfrs. Office: World Book Inc 525 W Monroe St Chicago IL 60661-3629

NAULTY, SUSAN LOUISE, archivist; b. Abington, Pa., May 28, 1944; d. Charles J. and Ruth E. (Schick) N. BA, Whittier Coll., 1967; MA, Loyola U., L.A., 1972. Tchr. history and English, Whittier (Calif.) H.S., 1968-70; from libr. asst. to asst. curator Huntington Libr., San Marino, Calif., 1972-91; archivist Richard Nixon Libr. and Birthplace, Yorba Linda, Calif., 1991—. Republican. Roman Catholic. Office: Richard Nixon Libr & Birthplace 18001 Yorba Linda Blvd Yorba Linda CA 92886-3903

NAUM, CHRISTOPHER JOHN, fire protection management and training consultant, educator; b. Syracuse, N.Y., Feb. 8, 1957; s. John and Florence (Karafile) N.; m. Ann M. McCabe, July 21, 1984 (div.); children: lauren K., Emily N., Ashley C.; m. Lori A. Drosi, Sept. 13, 1997. BA, Syracuse U., 1981; student, SUNY-Onondaga C.C., 1980-86, Nat. Fire Acad., Emmitsburg, Md., 1982-92, U. Md., 1982-84. Cert. fire instr., hazardous materials technician, fire prevention and bldg. code enforcement officer and instr. From fire explorer to fire lt. Moyers Corners Fire Dept., Town of Clay, N.Y., 1975-81; fire capt. Moyers Corners Fire Dept. Moyers Corners Fire Dept., Onondaga County Fire System, Town of Clay, N.Y., 1981-91; project architect Maniktala Assocs., P.C., Syracuse, N.Y., 1981-91; pres., exec. cons. Americana Fire Cons., Inc., Syracuse, 1988-91; fire protection engr. James A. FitzPatrick Nuclear Power Plant, Lycoming, N.Y., 1992-93; pres. L.A. Emergency Mgmt. and Tng. Cons., Syracuse, 1992—; coord. dept. fire protection tech. Onondaga C.C., SUNY, Syracuse, 1984-89; co-dir. Onondaga County Fire Rescue Inst., 1987-89. Contbg. editor Firehouse Mag., 1988—, On-Call Mag., 1995-96, Nat. Fire Protection Assn. Handbook, 18th edit., 1997; contbr. articles to profl. jours. Mem. FEMA US&R Task Force Working Group, 1989-92. Recipient Kodak/KINSA internat. medallion for excellence in photography, 1977, FEMA cert. of appreciation, 1991; others. Mem. AIA, Internat. Soc. Fire Svc. Instrs. (George D. Post award 1987, Nat. Fire Instr. of Yr. award 1987), World Safety Orgn., Internat. Assn. Fire Chiefs (nat. com. on urban rescue and structural collapse 1988—, Cert. of Appreciation 1993), Internat. Fire Photographers Assn., Nat. Fire Protection Assn. (nat. com. 1988—, chair tech. rescue com., trench rescue working group), Nat. Assn. for Search and Rescue, N.Y. State Assn. Fire Chiefs, Alliance for Fire and Emergency Mgmt. (steering com. for Nat. Search and Rescue Assn. 1996-97, Internat. Fire Instr. Exch. fellow 1996). Greek Orthodox. Avocations: downhill skiing, drawing and painting, photography. Office: LA Emergency Mgmt & Tng Cons PO Box 3726 Syracuse NY 13220-3726

NAUMANN, HANS JUERGEN, manufacturing company executive; b. Fed. Republic Germany, May 5, 1935; came to U.S., 1960; s. Herbert and Elfriede (Heydenreich) N.; m. Edith Huempel; children: Irene, Michelle, Jacqueline, John. MME, U. Hamburg, Fed. Rep. Germany, 1960; MBA, Rochester (N.Y.) U., 1965. Registered profl. engr., N.Y. Mgr. engring. Farrell Corp., Rochester, 1961-66; exec. v.p. Hegenscheidt Corp., Troy, Mich., 1966-70; pres., chief exec. officer, stockholder Hegenscheidt GmbH, Erkelenz, Fed. Republic Germany, 1970-82; chmn., chief exec. officer Internat. Knife Corp., Erlanger, Ky., 1982-84; chmn. bd., chief exec. officer, stockholder Simmons Machine Tool Corp., Albany, N.Y., 1984—; chmn., CEO, stockholder Niles-Simmons Industrieanlagen, GmbH, Chemnitz, Germany, 1992—; chmn. bd. dirs., CEO Constant Velocity Systems, Inc., Ballston Spa, N.Y., 1993—. Author: Tool and Manufacturing Engineering Handbook, 1976; patentee roller finishing and deep rolling. Bd. dirs. U. Albany Fund, Inc., 1986—. Mem. ASME, SAE, Am. Inst. Mgmt. (pres.'s coun.), Am. Mgmt. Assn., Am. Pub. Transit Assn., Verein Deutscher Ingenieure, Soc. Mech. Engrs., Capital Region Tech. Devel. Coun., Capital Region World Trade Coun., Assn. for Mfg. Tech. (formerly Nat. Machine Tool Builders Assn.), Albany Colonie Regional C. of C., Rwy. Supply Assn., N.Y. R.R. Club Inc., Lions (past pres.). Avocations: sailing, tennis, golf, skiing. Home: 26 Folmsbee Dr Albany NY 12204-1206 Office: Simmons Machine Tool Corp 1700 Broadway Albany NY 12204-2701 also: Niles-Simmons Industrieanlagen, Zwickauer Str 355, 09117 Chemnitz Germany

NAUMANN, MICHAEL, publishing executive; b. East Germany, 1941. Student, Queen's Coll., Oxford, Eng., Ruhr U. Corr. Die Zeit, Washington; sr. fgn. editor Der Spiegel; pres. Rowohlt Verlag, 1985-95; founder Rowohlt Berlin Verlag, Germany, Metropolitan Books, N.Y.C., 1995—; pres., CEO Henry Holt & Co., Inc., N.Y.C., 1996—. Chmn. Ledig-Rowohlt Found.; bd. dirs. Hamburg Staatsoper. Office: Henry Holt & Co Inc 115 W 18th St New York NY 10011-4113

NAUMANN, ROBERT BRUNO ALEXANDER, chemistry and physics educator; b. Dresden, Germany, June 7, 1929; came to U.S., 1932, naturalized, 1951; s. Eberhard Bruno and Elsa Henriette (Haege) N.; m. Marina Grot Turkevich, Sept. 16, 1961; children: Kristin Ragnhild Naumann Juros, Andrew John Bruno. BS, U. Calif., Berkeley, 1949; MA, Princeton U., 1951, PhD, 1953. Faculty Princeton U., 1953—, prof. chemistry and physics, 1973-92, prof. emeritus, 1992—; mem. vis. staff Los Alamos Nat. Lab., 1970-86; rsch. collaborator Brookhaven Nat. Lab., 1984-87; sci. assoc. CERN, Geneva, 1985-96; vis. prof. physics dept. Tech. U. Munich, 1988; vis. scholar physics Dartmouth Coll., 1992-96, adj. prof. physics and astronomy, 1996—. Author articles electromagnetic isotope separation, nuclear structure via radioactive and charged particle nuclear spectroscopy, implantation radioactive isotopes into solids, formation and properties of muonic atoms. Recipient Alexander von Humboldt Stiftung Sr. U.S. Scientist award, 1978, 83; Allied Chem. and Dye Corp. fellow, 1951-52, Procter and Gamble faculty fellow, 1959-60; Deutsche Forschungsgemeinschaft grantee, 1988. Fellow Am. Phys. Soc., AAAS; mem. Am. Chem. Soc. (chmn. Princeton U. sect. 1975, Chmn. Div. Nuclear Chemistry and Technology 1984), Sierra Club, Phi Beta Kappa, Sigma Xi (chmn. Princeton, N.J. sect. 1986-87). Episcopalian. Home: 387 Hawk Pine Hills Norwich VT 05055-9631

NAUMANN, WILLIAM CARL, consumer products company executive; b. Peoria, Ill., Mar. 25, 1938; s. William Louis and Emma (Bottin) N.; m. Polly Roby, May 20, 1962 (div. 1980); children: Jeff, Heather, Derek; m. Patricia Gallagher, Sept. 9, 1993. BSCE, Purdue U., 1960; MBA, U. Chgo., 1975. With Inland Steel Products Co., Chgo., 1960-74, N.Y. dist. mgr., 1968-70, div. gen. mgr., 1971-74; group v.p., bd. dirs. Inryco, Melrose Park, Ill., 1974-81; asst. chief engr. Inland Steel Co., Chgo., 1981-82, asst. gen. mgr. corp. planning, 1982-83, asst. gen. mgr. sales, 1983-85, gen. mgr. sales and mktg., 1985-87; exec. v.p. internat. ops. Hussmann Corp., Bridgeton, Mo., 1987; exec. v.p. sales and mktg. Hussmann Corp., Bridgeton, 1987; pres. Hussmann Food Svc. Co., Bridgeton, 1987-89; corp. v.p., chief quality officer Whitman Corp., Chgo., 1989-91; CEO Ranger Industries, 1992; sr. v.p., COO Pexco Holdings, Inc., Tulsa, 1993-96; chmn. bd. dirs. Sports Holdings Corp., Montreal, Can., 1997—. Mem. U. Chgo. Exec. Program Club (past pres.), Cedar Ridge Country Club (Tulsa), U. Chgo. Alumni Assn. (past pres., bd. govs. 1986-95), Beta Gamma Sigma. Avocations: sailing, travel, tennis. Home: 5146 E 107th Pl Tulsa OK 74137 Office: 7130 S Lewis Ave Ste 850 Tulsa OK 74136-5490

NAUMOFF, PHILIP, physician; b. Pitts., Feb. 16, 1914; s. Louis and Celia (Rubenstein) N.; m. Esther Zuckerman, Aug. 21, 1937; children—Carolyn Naumoff Lerner, Susan Naumoff Southern, Lawrence Jay, Elizabeth Anne Naumoff McCarthy, Deborah Jane Naumoff Flynn. B.S., U. Pitts., 1934; M.D., Duke U., 1937. Intern U. Pitts. Hosps., 1937-38; resident Bradford (Pa.) Hosp., 1938-39; gen. practice medicine Charlotte, N.C., 1946—; chmn. dept. family practice Meml. Hosp., 1964-79; Asst. clin. prof. community health scis. Duke Med. Center, Durham, N.C., 1973-79. Served to maj. M.C. AUS, 1942-46. Mem. AMA, Am. Acad. Family Physicians, N.C. Acad. Family Physicians (past pres.), Mecklenburg County Med. Soc. (past pres.), Heart Assn. Mecklenburg County (past pres.), B'nai B'rith (past pres. N.C.). Home: 4214 Woodglen Ln Charlotte NC 28226-7247

NAUNTON, RALPH FREDERICK, surgeon, educator; b. London, Sept. 26, 1921; came to U.S., 1954, naturalized, 1962; s. Frederick and Violet (Leader) N.; m. Mary Beatrice Ball, Aug. 25, 1945 (div.); children—Phillip, David; m. Natasha Tjonamon Cofield, Aug. 3, 1978. M.B., B.S., U. Coll., U. London, 1945. Intern U. Coll. Hosp., London, 1945-46; resident in otolaryngology U. Coll. Hosp., 1946-49; mem. Med. Research Council Eng., 1949-54; mem. faculty U. Chgo. Med. Sch., 1954—, prof. surgery, 1964-80, chmn. otolaryngology sect., 1966-79; dir. div. communicative disorders Nat. Inst. Neurol., Communicative Disorders and Stroke, NIH, 1980—. Contbr. articles on physiology and pathology, also treatment hearing and hearing disorders to profl. jours. Fellow ACS, Royal Soc. Medicine; mem. Royal Coll. Surgeons, Am. Otol. Soc., Collegium Oto-Rhino-Laryngol. Soc., Sigma Psi. Home: 3303 Pauline Dr Bethesda MD 20815-3919 Office: NIH Nat Inst Deafness & Comm Disorder 6120 Executive Blvd # 400 C Rockville MD 20852-4909

NAVA, CYNTHIA D., state legislator. BS, Western Ill. U.; MA, Ea. Ill. U. Dep. supt. Gadsden Schools; mem. N.Mex. Senate, mem. rules com., fin. com., chair legis. edn. study com., excellence in higher edn. com., health & human svcs. com., 1997—. Home: 3002 Broadmoor Dr Las Cruces NM 88001-7501 Office: N Mex Senate State Capitol Santa Fe NM 87503*

NAVA, ELOY LUIS, financial consultant; b. N.Y.C., May 19, 1942; s. Eloy and Dolores Nava; m. Diane Margret Binder, Dec. 21, 1968; children: Alyson Beth, David Eloy. BMgmt Engring., Rensselaer Poly. Inst., 1964, BMech. Engring., 1965, MSMgmt., 1970. Cert. fund specialist. Indsl. engr. Johnson & Johnson Inc., Troy, N.Y., 1965-66; nuclear project engr. and chief nuclear test engr. to ops. analysis project mgr. Electric Boat Div., Gen. Dynamics Corp., Groton, Conn., 1966-78; pres., chief fin. officer Collado Ozamiz Co., N.Y.C., 1978-88; pres., chmn. bd. JB Apparel Corp., N.Y.C., 1984-93; v.p., sr. fin. cons. Cruice Investment Advisors, Ltd., 1994-97; sr. assoc. Fleming, Relyea & Cox, Inc., Stamford, Conn., 1996—; bd. dirs. Jose

Blanco Inc., Santo Domingo, Dominican Republic; mgmt., fin. cons. various orgns. in Dominican Republic. Chmn. water, sewer com. City of Waterford, Conn., 1975-77; mem. Rep. Nat. Com.; swimming ofcl. YMCA, USS. Mem. NRA, Am. Philatelic Soc., Internat. Assn. Fin. Planners, Inst. CFPs, Midwest Decoy Collectors Assn., Country Club Darien (Conn.). Roman Catholic. Avocations: fishing, golf, skiing, stamp and antique decoy collecting. Home: 15 Pasture Ln Darien CT 06820-5618

NAVA, GREGORY, film director; b. San Diego, Calif., Apr. 10, 1949. Dir. films The Confessions of Amans, 1976, El Norte, 1984, A Time of Destiny, 1988, My Family, Mi Familia, 1995, Selena, 1997. Office: ICM 8942 Wilshire Blvd Beverly Hills CA 90211*

NAVAB, FARHAD, medical educator; b. Tehran, Iran, Sept. 12, 1938; came to U.S., 1980; s. Hossein and Nahid (Pirnia) N.; m. Nilou Navab, July 22, 1977; children: Sara, June, Linda. BA, Cambridge (Eng.) U., 1960, MD, 1976; MA, MB, B.Chir., Guy's Hosp., London, 1963; MRCP, Westminster Hosp., 1967. Diplomate Am. Bd. Internal Medicine, Am. Bd. Gastroenterology. Asst. prof. U. Tehran, 1972-76, assoc. prof., 1976-79; cons. physician Brook Gen. Hosp., London, 1979-80; assoc. prof. medicine U. Ark. Med. Scis., Little Rock, 1980-87, assoc. prof. physiology, 1985-87, chmn. evaluation com. for gastroenterology, 1986-87; staff physician VA Med. Ctr., Little Rock, 1986-87; chief gastroenterology Baystate Med. Ctr., Springfield, Mass., 1987—; prof. medicine Med. Sch., Tufts U., Boston, 1991—; cons. staff Mcpl. Hosp., Springfield, Mass., 1989—, Mercy Hosp., Springfield, 1989—; assoc. staff Cooley Dickinson Hosp., Northampton, Mass., 1990—; courtesy staff Mary Lane Hosp., Ware, Mass., 1994—. Fellow ACP, Am. Coll. Gastroenterology, Royal Coll. Physicians; mem. Am. Physiol. Soc., Am. Gastroenterol. Assn., Am. Soc. for Gastrointestinal Endoscopy, Am. Assn. for Study Liver Disease, Mass. Med. Soc., So. Soc. for Clin. Investigation, New. Eng. Endoscopic Soc., Am. Soc. for Parenteral and Enteral Nutrition, Crohn's and Colitis Found. of Am. Avocation: photography. Home: 18 Bittersweet Ln Wilbraham MA 01095-2234 Office: Baystate Med Ctr 759 Chestnut St Springfield MA 01199-1001

NAVALKAR, RAMCHANDRA GOVINDRAO, microbiologist, immunologist; b. Bombay, May 7, 1924; s. Govindrao Narayan and Shantabai Navalkar; m. Shubhangi Navalkar, Dec. 27, 1966; children: Sushant, Sudevi. BS, Bombay U., 1946, STC, 1952, PhD, 1956. Research asst. Acworth Leprosy Hosp., Bombay, 1952-56, field and research officer, 1959-60; biologist Stanford Research Inst., Menlo Park, Calif., 1956-58; vis. fellow sch. pub. health Harvard U., Cambridge, Mass., 1958; postdoctoral fellow dept. med. microbiology Stanford (Calif.) U., 1956-58; project assoc. dept. med. microbiology U. Wis., Madison, 1960-63, 66-67; research engr. assoc. Inst. Med. Microbiology, U. Gothenburg, Sweden, 1964-65; asst. prof. microbiology Meharry Med. Coll., Nashville, 1967-72, assoc. prof. microbiology, 1972-76, prof. microbiology, 1976-80; prof., chmn. dept. microbiology and immunology Morehouse Sch. Medicine, Atlanta, 1980—; mem. site visit com. NIH for tuberculosis rsch. programs, India, 1975; prin. co-ord. Immunology of Leprosy Project, Al-Azhar U., Cairo, 1977; mem. ad hoc rev. com. NIH, 1978, 1979, Internat. Leprosy Assn. Workshop on Microbiology, Mexico City, 1978; mem. project site visit com. NIH, Atlanta, 1978, exec. com. Sci. Rsch. Inst., Atlanta Univ. Ctr.; cons. MARC program Tenn. State U., Nashville, 1981; disting. guest and cons. to Inst. Dermatology, People's Republic of China, 1982; chmn., mem. NIH spl. study sect. on AIDS-related infectins, 1990, on tuberculosis present in lung, 1993; mem. AIDS and related-rsch. study sect., DRG, NIH, 1995—. Guest reviewer Internat. Jour. Leprosy, 1984; contbr. numerous articles and rsch. papers to profl. jours. Recipient Golden Apple award Meharry chpt. Student Am. Med. Assn., 1972, Maj. Gen. Sahib Singh Sokhey Outstanding Researcher award, 1976; grantee NIH, 1966-82, 83-87, 89-92, 92-97, PI WHO, 1983-84. Fellow Am. Acad. Microbiology; mem. Am. Soc. Microbiology, The Soc. for Exptl. Biology and Medicine, Internat. Leprosy Assn., Indian Assn. of Leprologists, Acworth Leprosy Hosp. Soc. for Research and Rehab. (life mem.), Assn. Med. Sch. Microbiology Chairmen. Avocations: reading, cooking. Office: Morehouse Sch of Medicine Dept of Microbiology and Immunology Atlanta GA 30310-1495

NAVAR, LUIS GABRIEL, physiology educator, researcher; b. El Paso, Tex., Mar. 24, 1941; s. Luis and Concepcion (Najera) N.; m. Randa Ann Bumgarner, Oct. 15, 1965; children: Tonia, Tess, Gabriel, Daniel. BS, Tex. A&M U., 1962; PhD, U. Miss., 1966, postdoctoral study, 1966-69. Instr. dept. physiology/biophysics U. Miss., Jackson, 1966-67, asst. prof., 1967-71, assoc. prof., 1971-74; assoc. prof. U. Ala., Birmingham, 1974-76, prof., 1976-88, assoc. prof. Nephrology Rsch. and Tng. Ctr., 1979-83, prof., 1983-88; prof., chmn. dept. physiology Tulane U. Med. Sch., New Orleans, 1988—; vis. scientist Duke U. Med. Ctr., Durham, N.C., 1972-73. Assoc. editor: News in Physiol. Scis., 1994—, Am. Jour. Physiology, 1983-89, mem. editl. bd., 1982-83, 97—; mem. editl. bd. Kidney Internat., 1976-87, Hypertension, 1980-83, assoc. editor, 1993—; editl. bd. Kidney, 1992—, Clinical Science, 1994—; contbr. sci. papers, book chpts., slides and tapes to profl. publs. Chmn. cardiorenal rsch. study com. Am. Heart Assn., 1994-95, mem. nat. rsch. com. 1994-99. Recipient Rsch. Career Devel. award Nat. Heart, Lung and Blood Inst., 1974-79, Merit award, 1988. Fellow AAAS; mem. Am. Physiol. Soc. (coun. 1991-94, pres.-elect 1997—), Am. heart Assn. (kidney, high blood pressure couns., nat. rsch. com. 1994—), N.Y. Acad. Sci., Am. Soc. Nephrology, Internat. Soc. Nephrology, Am. Soc. Hypertension (coun. 1992-94), Internat. Soc. Hypertension, Assn. Chmn. Depts. Physiology (councillor 1993-95, pres.-elect 1995-96, pres. 1996-97, Gottschalk Disting. Lectr. Renal Physiology 1997). Democrat. Roman Catholic. Home: 10020 Hyde Pl River Ridge LA 70123-1522 Office: Tulane U Med Sch Dept Physiology 1430 Tulane Ave New Orleans LA 70112-2699

NAVARRO, ANTONIO (LUIS), public relations executive; b. Havana, Cuba, Sept. 26, 1922; came to U.S., 1940; s. Antero Navarro and Aurora (Pérez-Zuazo) Todd; m. Avis Hedges, Dec. 28, 1954; children: Antonio, Avis, Alexander. B.S. in Chem. Engring., Ga. Tech., 1944. With Shell Chem. Corp., Calif., 1944-50, Lobo Sugar Trading, Cuba, 1950-54, Textilera Ariguanabo (Hedges Family Textile Bus.), Cuba, 1954-61; mgr. Peruvian ops. W.R. Grace & Co., Lima, Peru, 1961-73; v.p. corp. adminstrn. group, mgr. corp. communications W.R. Grace & Co., N.Y.C., 1973-78, corp. v.p., 1978-82, sr. v.p., 1982-87, group exec., corp. relations group, corp. communications, govt. relations, investor relations, 1986-87; vice chmn. Jack Hilton Inc., 1987-88; dir. Office of Cuba Broadcasting (Radio Marti and TV Marti) USIA, Washington, 1990-93; pub. rels. cons., 1994—; bd. dirs. Radio Free Europe/Radio Liberty Fund, 1986. Author: (memoir of Cuban revolution) Tocayo, 1981 (Conservative Club Selection award 1981). Bd. dirs. Accion, N.Y.C., 1973-91; mem. Coun. of Ams. (now Ams. Soc.), 1976-86; bd. dirs. Radio Broadcasting to Cuba (Radio Marti), 1985-90; mem. Blue Ribbon panel on minority affairs and indsl. rels. Am. Chem. Soc., 1993—. Recipient Liberty medal N.Y.C., 1986, USIA Superior Honor award, Dir.'s award for superior achievment, 1993, Cuban-Am. Engr. of Yr. award, Fla., 1994; named to Ga. Tech. Engring. Hall of Fame, 1994. Democrat. Roman Catholic. Avocations: tennis, classical music, writing. Home: 151 Crandon Blvd Key Biscayne FL 33149-1573

NAVARRO, BRUCE CHARLES, lawyer; b. West Lafayette, Ind., Oct. 30, 1954; s. Joseph Anthony and Dorothy Gloria (Gnazzo) N.; m. Nancy Elizabeth Pryor; children: Philip Joseph, Joanna Christina, Kelly Finnegan, Ian Chandler Cameron Finnegan. BA, Duke U., 1976; JD, Ind. U., 1980. Bar: D.C. 1980. Asst. counsel U.S. Senate Labor Subcom., Washington, 1981-84; acting dep. undersec. for legis. affairs Dept. Labor, Washington, 1984-85; atty. advisor EEOC, Washington, 1985-86; dir. Office of Congl. Rels. Office of Pers. Mgmt., Washington, 1986-89; prin. dep. asst. atty. gen. for legis. U.S. Dept. of Justice, Washington, 1989-91; spl. asst. to gen. counsel U.S. Dept. HHS, Washington, 1991; expert cons. U.S. Dept. Def., Washington, 1992; counsel to the vice chmn. U.S. Consumer Product Safety Commn., Bethesda, Md., 1992-95; prin. Bruce C. Navarro Regulatory and Legis. Affairs, Washington, 1995—. Mem. Arlington County Republican Com. (Va.), 1983. Mem. D.C. Bar Assn. Roman Catholic. Avocation: music, golf. Home: 4277 Berwick Pl Woodbridge VA 22192-5119 Office: 1742 N St NW Washington DC 20036-2907

NAVARRO, JOSEPH ANTHONY, statistician, consultant; b. New Britain, Conn., July 6, 1927; s. Charles C. and Josephine V. (Bianco) N.; m. Dorothy G. Gnazzo, Feb. 6, 1929; children: Kenneth M., Bruce C., Joseph S. BS, Cen. Conn. State U., 1950; MS, Purdue U., 1952, PhD, 1955. Rsch. staff, cons. GE, 1955-59; rsch. staff, mgmt. IBM, 1962-64; sr. staff mem., asst. dir. Inst. Def. Analyses, Alexandria, Va., 1964-72; pres., chief oper. officer System Planning Corp., Arlington, Va., 1972-86; dep. undersec. test and evaluation Dept. Defense, Washington, 1986-87; now pvt. practice cons., 1987—; pres. Wackenhut Applied Technologies Ctr., Fairfax, Va., 1989-90. Contbr. articles to profl. jours. Mem. Bd. Trade, Washington, 1983-85. Mem. Internat. Test and Evaluation Assn. Republican. Roman Catholic. Club: COSMOS (Washington). Office: JAN Assocs Inc 7825 Fulbright Ct Bethesda MD 20817-3119

NAVAS, WILLIAM ANTONIO, JR., military officer, civil engineer; b. Mayaguez, P.R., Dec. 15, 1942; s. William Antonio Sr. and Ethel Ines (Marin) N.; m. Wilda Margarita Cordova Navas, Aug. 7, 1965; children: William Antonio III, Gretchen Maria. BSCE, U. P.R., 1965; MS in Engring. Mgmt., U. Bridgeport, 1979. Registered profl. engr., P.R. Commd. 2d. lt. U.S. Army, 1966, advanced through grades to maj. gen., 1990; served in U.S. Army Corps of Engrs., 1966-70; project engr. Empresas Navas, Inc., Mayaguez, P.R., 1970-72; ptnr., prin. W.A. Navas Jr. & Assocs., Mayaguez, 1972-80; dir. Navas & Moreda, Inc., Mayaguez, 1973-81; with Interamerican Def. Coll., Washington, 1981-82; dir. ops. P.R. Army Nat. Guard, San Juan, 1982-84, 84-87; comdr. Engr. Task Force, Panama, 1984; dep. dir. Army Nat. Guard Bur., Washington, 1987—; vice chief Nat. Guard Bur., 1990; mil. exec. res. forces policy bd. Office of Sec. of Def., 1992-94, dep. asst. sec. of def., 1994-95; dir. Army Nat. Guard, 1995—; chmn. Dept. of Army Hispanic Employment Commn., Washington, 1988. Decorated Knight Eq. Order of Holy Sepulchre. Mem. Nat. Guard Assn. of the U.S. (del. 1980-86), Nat. Guard Assn. of P.R., Soc. of Am. Mil. Engrs. Roman Catholic. Avocations: militaria collection, reading, running, travel. Home: Qtrs # 16A Fort Myer VA 22211 Office: Army Nat Guard 2500 Army Pentagon Washington DC 20310-2500*

NAVASKY, VICTOR SAUL, magazine editor, publisher; b. N.Y.C., July 5, 1932; s. Macy and Esther Blanche (Goldberg) N.; m. Anne Landey Strongin, Mar. 27, 1966; children: Bruno, Miri, Jenny. A.B., Swarthmore Coll., 1954; LL.B., Yale U., 1959. Spl. asst. to Gov. G. Mennen Williams, Mich., 1959-60; editor, pub. Monocle Mag., 1961-65; editor N.Y. Times mag., 1970-72, The Nation mag., N.Y.C., 1978-94; editl. dir. and pub., 1995—; vis. scholar Russell Sage Found., 1975-76; Ferris prof. journalism Princeton U., 1976-77. Author: Kennedy Justice, 1971 (Nat. Book Award nominee), Naming Names, 1980 (Am. Book award 1981), rev. edit., 1991; editor: (with C. Cerf) The Experts Speak, 1984. Mem. bd. mgrs. Swarthmore Coll., 1991-94. Served with U.S. Army, 1954-56. Guggenheim fellow, 1974-75; fellow Inst. of Politics, Harvard U., 1994; Sr. fellow Freedom Forum, 1994. Mem. Author's Guild (coun.), Com. To Protect Journalists (exec. com.), Phi Beta Kappa. Democrat. Jewish. Home: 33 W 67th St New York NY 10023-6224 Office: The Nation 72 Fifth Ave New York NY 10011-8004

NAVIA, JUAN MARCELO, biologist, educator; b. Havana, Jan. 16, 1927; came to U.S., 1961; s. Juan and Hortensia (DeLaCampa) N.; m. Josefina Blanca Bonich, Aug. 20, 1950; children: Juan, Carlos, Ana, Beatriz. BS, MIT, 1950, MS, 1951, PhD, 1965; DDSc (hon.), Chiang Mai U., Thailand, 1996. Sr. scientist Inst. Dental Rsch. U. Ala., Birmingham, 1969-88; dir. nutrition and oral health tng. program U. Ala., Birmingham, 1968-88, dir. rsch. tng. Sch. Dentistry, 1971-81, dir. clin. rsch. tng. program - MD, PhD, 1972-75, dir Sparkman Ctr., 1981-94, prof. comparative medicine, 1973-94, prof. biochemistry, 1976-86, prof. nutrition scis., 1977-94; ret., prof. emeritus, 1994—; adv. bd. mem. Fogarty Internat. Ctr., Bethesda, Md., 1985-88, Princeton (N.J.) Dental Resource Ctr., 1987-90; dean U. Ala. Sch. Pub. Health, 1989-92. Author: Animal Models in Dental Research, 1977; editor: The Biologic Basis of Dental Caries, 1980; contbr. Encyclopedia Americana, 1968. Am. Inst. Nutrition fellow, 1995, Sr. Internat. Fogarty fellow, 1979, AAAS fellow, 1982; recipient H. Trendley Dean Meml. award Internat. Assn. Dental Rsch., 1990, U. Ala. Birmingham's Pres.'s medal, 1992. Mem. Internat. Assn. Dental Rsch. (pres. cariology 1983-84), Am. Assn. Dental Rsch., Am. Chem. Soc., European Orgn. Caries Rsch., Inst. Food Technologists, Sociedad Latinoamericana de Nutricion, N.Y. Acad. Scis., Internat. Serra Club, Sigma Xi, Sigma Delta Pi. Republican. Roman Catholic. Avocations: walking, writing. Office: U Ala at Birmingham Dept Comparative Medicine Volker Hall 403 Birmingham AL 35294

NAVRATILOVA, MARTINA, former professional tennis player; b. Prague, Czechoslovakia, Oct. 18, 1956; came to U.S., 1975, naturalized, 1981; d. Miroslav Navratil and Jana Navratilova. Student, schs. in Czechoslovakia; Hon. doctorate, George Washington U., 1996. Profl. tennis player, 1975-94; tennis commentator/broadcaster HBO Sports, 1995. Author: (with George Vecsey) Martina, 1985, (with Liz Nickels) The Total Zone, 1995, (with Liz Nickels) The Breaking Point, 1996. Vol. Rainbow Found. Winner Czechoslovak Nat. singles, 1972-74, U.S. Open singles, 1983, 84, 86, 87, U.S. Open doubles, 1977, 78, 80, 83, 84, 87, 90, U.S. Open mixed doubles, 1987, Va. Slims Tournament, 1978, 83, 84, 85, 86, Va. Slims doubles, 1991, Wimbledon singles, 1978, 79, 82, 83, 84, 85, 86, 87, 90, Wimbledon women's doubles, 1976, 79, 81, 82, 83, 84, 86, Wimbledon mixed doubles, 1985, 94, 95, French Open singles, 1982, 84, Australian Open singles, 1981, 83, 85, Australian Doubles (with Nagelsen) 1980, (with Shriver), 1982, 84, 85, 87, 88, 89, Grand Slam of Women's Tennis, 1984, Roland Garros (with Shriver), 1985, 87, 89, Italian Open doubles (with Sabatini), 1987, (with Shriver) COREL WTA Tour doubles team of yr., 1981-89, triple Crown at U.S. Open, 1987; recipient Women's Sports Found. Flo Hyman award, 1987; named Female Athlete of the Decade (1980s) The Nat. Sports Review, UPI, and AP, WTA Player of Yr., 1978-79, 82-86, Women's Sports Found. Sportswoman of Yr., 1982-84, Hon. Citizen of Dallas, AP Female Athlete of Yr., 1983, Chgo. Hall of Fame, 1994; Martina Navratilova Day proclaimed in Chgo., 1992. Mem. Women's Tennis Assn. (dir., exec. com., pres.). Holder of 167 singles titles and 165 doubles titles; holder of record of singles-match wins which is 1,309, 1991. Address: IMG 1 Erieview Plz Cleveland OH 44114-1715*

NAWY, EDWARD GEORGE, civil engineer, educator; b. Baghdad, Iraq, Dec. 21, 1926; came to U.S., 1957, naturalized, 1966; s. George M. and Ava (Marshall) N.; m. Rachel E. Shebbath, Mar. 23, 1949; children: Ava Margaret, Robert M. DIC, Imperial Coll. Sci. and Tech., London, 1951; CE, MIT, 1959; D of Engring., U. Pisa, Italy, 1967. Registered profl. engr. (P.E.), N.J., N.Y., Pa., Calif., Fla. Head structures Israel Water Planning Authority, Tel-Aviv, 1952-57; mem. faculty Rutgers U., New Brunswick, N.J., 1959—; mem. grad. faculty Rutgers U., 1961—, prof. civil engring., 1966-72, Distinguished prof. (prof. II), 1972—, chmn. dept. civil and environ. engring., dir. grad. programs, 1980-86; chmn. Coll. Engring. Del. Assembly, 1969-72; mem. Univ. Senate, 1973-80, exec. com., faculty rep., bd. govs., trustee; guest prof. Nat. U. Tucaman, Argentina, summer 1963, Imperial Coll. Sci. and Tech., summer 1964; vis. prof. Stevens Inst. Tech., Hoboken, N.J., 1968-72; hon. prof. Nanjing Inst. Tech., China, 1987; mem. N.J. Chancellor Higher Edn. for Higher Edn. Master Plan; mem. Rutgers U. rep. Transp. Rsch. Bd. Bridge Com., chmn. com. on concrete materials; cons. to industry; U.S. mem. commn. on cracking Comité EuroInternat. du Beton; mem. Civil Engring. Tech. Adv. Coun. N.J., 1966-72; concrete sys. cons. FAA, Washington; cons. energy divsn. U.S. Gen. Acctg. Office, Washington; gen. chmn. Internat. Symposium on Slabs and Plates, 1971; hon. presidium internat. conf. Reunion Internationale des Laboratories d'Essais et de Recherches sur Les Materiaux et les Constructions, Budapest, 1977; mem. Accreditation Bd. Engring. and Tech. Author: Reinforced Concrete, 1985, 3d edit., 1996, Simplified Reinforced Concrete, 1986, Prestressed Concrete, 2d edit., 1996, High Strength High Performance Concrete, 1996; contbr. more than 140 articles to profl. jours. Vice pres. Berkeley Twp. Taxpayers Assn., Ocean City, N.J., 1966-70. Recipient merit citation and award N.J. Concrete Assn., 1966; C. Gulbenkian Found. fellow, 1972. Fellow ASCE (mem. joint com. on slabs), Instn. Civil Engrs. (London), Am. Concrete Inst. (pres. N.J. chpt. 1966, 77-78, chmn. nat. com. on cracking 1966-73, bd. com. chpts. 1969-72, ACI rep. internat. commn. fractures, H.L. Kenneday award 1972, award of recognition N.J. chpt. 1972, chpt. activities award 1978, chmn. nat. com. on deflection 1989—); mem. NSPE, AAUP (chmn. budget and priorities com. Rutgers U. chpt. 1972), Am. Soc. Engring. Edn., Prestressed Concrete Inst. (Bridge Competition award 1971, mem. tech. activities com.), N.Y. Acad. Scis., Tall Bldgs. Coun., N.J. Contractors Assn. (cons. ednl. com., tall bldgs. coun.), Rotary, Sigma Xi, Tau Beta Pi, Chi Epsilon (hon.). Office: Rutgers State U of NJ Civil Engring Dept New Brunswick NJ 08855 *Success is normally the result of honesty and continuous setting and updating of high goals which have to be perseverely pursued.*

NAYAR, BALDEV RAJ, political science educator; b. Gujrat Dist., India, Oct. 26, 1931; emigrated to Can., 1964; s. Jamna Das and Durga Devi (Marwah) N.; m. Nancy Ann Skinner, Aug. 27, 1961; children—Sheila Jane, Kamala Elizabeth, Sunita Maria. B.A., Punjab U., 1953; M.A., 1956, U. Chgo., 1959; Ph.D., U. Chgo., 1963. Asst. prof. Calif. State Coll., Hayward, 1963-64; mem. faculty dept. polit. sci. McGill U., 1964-94, assoc. prof., 1966-71, prof., 1971-94, prof. emeritus, 1996—, assoc. chmn., 1990-93; research assoc. Internat. Devel. Research Centre, 1978. Author: Minority Politics in the Punjab, 1966, National Communication and Language Policy, 1969, The Modernization Imperative and Indian Planning, 1972, American Geopolitics and India, 1976, India's Quest for Technological Independence, 1983, India's Mixed Economy, 1989, The Political Economy of India's Public Sector, 1990, Superpower Dominance and Military Aid, 1991, The State and International Aviation in India, 1994, The State and Market in India's Shipping, 1996. Bd. dirs. Shastri Indo-Canadian Inst., 1970-72, sr. fellow, 1978, 86. Recipient Watumull prize Am. Hist. Assn., 1966; Charles E. Merriam fellow, 1957; Carnegie Study New Nations fellow, 1962; Can. Council sr. fellow, 1967, 74; SSHRC leave fellow, 1982. Mem. Can. Polit. Sci. Assn., Assn. Asian Studies, Assn., Can. Asian Studies Assn. Office: McGill Univ, Dept Polit Sci, Montreal, PQ Canada H3A 2T7

NAYLON, MICHAEL EDWARD, military officer; b. Rochester, N.Y., Jan. 15, 1943; s. Edward M. and Patricia (Brennan) N.; m. Beverly Marzano, Mar. 27, 1965; children: Michelle A., Colleen M. BA, John Carroll U., 1965; MBA, Marymount U., 1986; grad., U.S. Army War Coll., 1989. Indsl. rels. specialist Gen. Railway Signal Co., Rochester, N.Y., Farrell Co., Rochester; manpower adminstr. City of Rochester; employment mgr. U. Rochester; personnel dir. Interstate Brands Corp., Rochester; office mgr., dir. adminstrn., regional tng. coord. Nat. Machine Tool Builders Assn., McLean, Va.; chief U.S Army Res. Hdqs. Dept. of Army, Washington; staff officer Joint Chiefs of Staff, col., sr. res. advisor Dept. Def., Washington; with U.S. Southern Command, Panama City, Panama; dir. ops. Nat. Assn. Retired Fed. Employees; nat. exec. dir. Am. Vets. WWII, Korea, Vietnam, AMVETS. Mem. Am. Soc. Assn. Execs., Am. Soc. Pers. Adminstrn., U.S. Army War Coll. Alumni Assn., John Carroll U. Alumni Assn., Res. Officers Assn. USA. Home: 1434 Aldenham Ln Reston VA 22090-3901 Office: AMVETS Nat Hq 4647 Forbes Blvd Lanham Seabrook MD 20706-4356

NAYLOR, AUBREY WILLARD, botany educator; b. Union City, Tenn., Feb. 5, 1915; s. Harry Joseph and Clara Mae (Isbell) N.; m. Frances Valentine Lloyd, Dec. 26, 1940; children: Virginia Dawson Naylor Kirby, Edith-Margaret Naylor Eastman DeWitt. BS, U. Chgo., 1937, MS, 1938, PhD, 1940. Mem. staff, bur. plant industry U.S. Dept. Agr., Chgo., 1938-40; instr. botany U. Chgo., 1940-44, Northwestern U., Evanston, Ill., 1944-45; asst. prof. U. Wash., Seattle, 1946-47, Yale U., 1947-52; assoc. prof. Duke U., 1952-59, prof., 1959-72, James B. Duke prof., 1972-85, James B. Duke prof. emeritus, 1985—; program dir. for metabolic biology NSF, Washington, 1961-62, cons., 1960-63; chmn. com. examiners for Grad. (Sch.) Record Examination on Biology, Edn. Testing Svc., Princeton, N.J., 1966-72; cons. Oak Ridge Nat. Lab., 1957-58, Rsch. Triangle Inst., N.C., 1968—, TVA, 1969-75, Schaper and Brümmer Pharm. Co., Salzgitter, Fed. Republic of Germany, 1986-92, Akzo Salt Co., 1991-96; mem. summer faculties U. N.C., Chapel Hill, 1960-61, Greensboro, 1964-65; mem. summer faculties Bennett Coll., Greensboro, N.C.; vis. prof. U. Bristol, Eng., 1958-59, U. Tex., Austin, 1977. Contbr. chpts. to books, articles and book revs. to profl. jours. NRC fellow Boyce Thompson Inst. for Plant Rsch., Yonkers, N.Y., 1945-46, Guggenheim fellow, 1958-59; NSF sr. fellow, 1958-59; grantee, 1956-86, Am. Cancer Soc. grantee, 1953-57, Herman Frasch Found. grantee, 1957-72. Fellow AAAS (life mem.); mem. Am. Soc. Plant Physiologists (life, chmn. bd. trustees 1962-74, pres. 1961, exec. com. 1959-60, 62-74, 81-82, Disting. Svc. award So. sect. 1981, Charles Reid Barnes life membership 1981, archivist 1987—), Am. Inst. Biol. Scis., Am. Soc. Cell Biologists, Bot. Soc. Am. (life, cert. of merit 1988), Scandinavian Soc. Plant Physiologists, Japanese Soc. Plant Physiologists, Australian Soc. Plant Physiologists, Cosmos Club (Washington), Sigma Xi (life, pres. chpt. 1968-69). Home: 2430 Wrightwood Ave Durham NC 27705-5802 *Almost everything interests me. For this reason, I am seldom bored. Channeling my curiosity has been best achieved through a burning desire to learn how living things grow from a single cell, differentiate into a distinct multicellular organism and reproduce. The joy of discovery feeds upon itself and motivates me to work, work, and work some more.*

NAYLOR, BRIAN, news correspondent; b. Mt. Kisco, N.Y., Aug. 7, 1955. BA in Broadcasting/Film, U. Maine, 1978. Gen. assignment reporter, anchor, announcer Sta. WLBZ, Bangor, Maine, 1976-78; statehouse reporter Capital News Svc., Augusta, Maine, 1978; gen. assignment reporter, anchor Sta. WLAM, Lewiston, Maine, 1978-79; statehouse reporter, host Sta. WOSU Radio, Columbus, Ohio, 1979-82; prodr., co-host Sta. WOSU-TV, Columbus, 1979-82; newscaster, gen. assignment reporter, White House reporter Nat. Pub. Radio, Washington, 1982-92, Congl. corr., 1992—; adj. prof. Am. U., Washington, 1991. Named Winner Silver Baton, DuPont-Columbia awards, 1996.; Jefferson fellow, 1990. Office: Nat Pub Radio 635 Massachusetts Ave NW Washington DC 20001-3752

NAYLOR, BRUCE GORDON, museum director; b. Midale, Sask., Can., Aug. 19, 1950; s. John Raymond Naylor and Mary Lynn (Frisby) Redeberg; m. Marlene Johnstone, Dec. 19, 1981 (dec. July 1992); m. Judith Jeune, June 11, 1994; 1 child: John Raymond. BS with high honors, U. Sask., 1972; PhD, U. Alta., 1978. Postdoctoral fellow U. Toronto, Ont., 1978-80; lectr. U. Calif., Berkeley, 1979; asst. prof. U. Alta., Edmonton, 1980-82; curator Tyrrell Mus., Drumheller, Alta., 1982-86; asst. dir. Royal Tyrrell Mus., Drumheller, 1986-92, dir., 1992—; adj. prof. U. Alta., 1983—; sen. U. Calgary, Alta., 1989-90; bd. dirs. Yoho-Burgess Shale Rsch. Found. Contbr. articles to sci. publs. Operating grantee Nat. Sci. & Engring. Rsch. Coun., Ottawa, 1981-82. Fellow Geol. Assn. Can.; mem. Soc. Vertebrate Paleontology, Rotary Club Drumheller. Avocations: horseback riding, gardening. Office: Royal Tyrrell Mus, Box 7500, Drumheller, AB Canada T0J 0Y0

NAYLOR, FRANKLIN LLEWELLYN, JR., financial advisor; b. Arlington, N.J., July 17, 1910; s. Franklin Llewellyn Sr. and Mary H. (Fliedner) N.; m. Edna Anabel Woglom, Sept. 7, 1932 (dec. 1978); children: Marjorie Evelyn Glidden, Franklin III, Virginia Irene Hubacek. Registered profl. engr., gen. bldg. contractor, real estate broker, Calif.; lic. ins. agt., Ariz.; registered fin. adviser SEC. Engaged in various engring. capacities, 1928—; cons. indsl. engr., 1946—; formerly with Indsl. div. S.S. White Dental Mfg. Co., Breeze Corp., Inc., Walker-Turner Corp., Aluminum Co. Am., also U.S. Spring and Bumper Co., Lockhead Aircraft Corp., Pacific div. Bendix Aviation Corp., Grand Central Aircraft Co.; v.p. Baker and Weikel engrs., after 1948; pres. Naylor Engring. & Research Corp., Los Angeles; mng. gen. agt. Nat. Old Line Ins. Co.; pres. Am. Pacific Life Ins. Co., Honolulu, after 1964; owner, operator Ariz. Chem. & Engring. Co., Tucson and Phoenix, Naylor & Assocs., estate and bus. cons., Tucson and Phoenix; lectr. estate preservation and tax planning, also investment planning for retirement; instr. Tucson and Phoenix secondary schs., Burbank and Glendale Unified Sch. Dists., Calif., 1939—, Ariz. Jr. Colls., Ariz. State Colls., Calif. State Colls. Author: Aluminum and Its Alloys; co-author several books on supervisory devel. Contbr. articles to maj. trade jours. Pres. Glendale-Burbank Joint Carpentry Apprentice Com., 1948; mem. War Prodn. Bd., World War II; chmn. trade adv. com. for sheet metal workers Nat. Def. Com., 1943-45, employer rep. trade com. for drafting, lofting and pattern makers, 1943-45.; chmn. SCORE, Phoenix, 1966-86, mem. Hattiesburg, Miss., 1987—; vice chmn. Small Bus. Execs. Clearing House; mem. Internat. Exec. Service Corps.; pres. Greater Phoenix Republican Club, 1962; active Rep. Senatorial Inner Circle, 1963—. Mem. AMSE (life, bd. dirs. profl. mgmt. div.), Am. Ordnance Assn., Bldg. Contractors Assn. Calif., Soc. Advancement Mgmt., Glendale C. of C., Am. Arbitration Assn. (nat. panel arbitrators), Hammond Organ Soc. (pres. Tucson 1955), AIM, Hawaii C. of C. (aero affairs com., vocat. edn. and manpower com., indsl. devel. com.), NSPE, Navy League U.S. Nat. Travel Club, Presidents Club, Phoenix Execs. Club, Statesman's Club. Office: F Naylor & Assocs 1334 W Mulberry Dr Phoenix AZ 85013-4029

NAYLOR, HARRY BROOKS, microbiologist; b. Hewitt, Minn., Mar. 30, 1914; s. George Brooks and Anna Elmira (Larsen) N.; m. Ellen Florence Haanela, Sept. 8, 1940; children—Lynn Brooks, Roy Allen, Gail Ann. B.S., U. Minn., 1938; Ph.D., Cornell U., 1943. Mem. tech. dept. Sheffield Farms Dairy, Inc., N.Y.C., 1946-47; mem. faculty dept. microbiology Cornell U., Ithaca, N.Y., 1947—; prof. emeritus Cornell U., 1977—; cons. Pasco Labs., Inc., Wheat Ridge, Colo., 1978-86; mem. grant review bd. USPHS, 1967-70; OAS lectr., Brazil, 1972, 73; teaching fellow Fed. U. of Rio de Janeiro, 1978. Contbr. articles to profl. jours. Served with USNR, 1943-46. Fulbright-Hayes fellow, 1966-67. Mem. Am. Soc. Microbiology, Am. Acad. Microbiology. Home: 61 Whitetail Dr Ithaca NY 14850

NAYLOR, JAMES CHARLES, psychologist, educator; b. Chgo., Feb. 8, 1932; s. Joseph Sewell and Berniece (Berg) N.; m. Georgia Lou Mason, Feb. 14, 1953; children—Mary Denise, Diana Darice, Shari Dalice. B.S., Purdue U., 1957, M.S., 1958, Ph.D., 1960. Asst. prof. Ohio State U., 1960-63, asso. prof., 1963-67, prof. vice chmn. dept. psychology, 1967-68; prof. Purdue U., Lafayette, Ind., 1968-86, head dept. psychol. scis., 1968-79; prof., chmn. dept. psychology Ohio State U., Columbus, 1986—; Fulbright rsch. scholar, Umea, Sweden, 1976; Disting. scholar, vis. scientist Flinders U., South Australia, 1982-83, UNESCO ednl. cons. to Hangzhou U., Peoples Republic of China, 1984; chmn. Coun. Grad. Depts. Psychology, 1993-94; lead reviewer Psychology Program Rev., State U. Sys. Fla., 1996. Author: Industrial Psychology, 1968, A Theory of Behavior in Organizations, 1980; founder, editor: Organizational Behavior and Human Decision Processes; mem. editorial bd.: Prof. Psychology; Contbr. articles to profl. jours. Served with USN, 1950-54. Fellow AAAS, Am. Psychol. Soc., Am. Psychol. Assn.; mem. Psychonomic Soc., Psychmetric Soc., Internat. Assn. Applied Psychology, Soc. Organizational Behavior (founder), Midwestern Psychol. Assn. (coun. 1994-97), Phi Beta Kappa, Sigma Xi. Home: 176 Tucker Dr Columbus OH 43085-3064 Office: Ohio State U Dept Psychology Columbus OH 43210

NAYLOR, JOHN THOMAS, telephone company executive; b. Orillia, Ont., Can., Jan. 30, 1913; s. Fred Addison and Ethel (Thompson) N.; m. Ruth Louisa Tissot, Dec. 21, 1934; children: Joan Crosby, Carol Manka. BSEE, Oreg. State U., 1934. Registered profl. engr., Calif., Oreg., Wash. Chief accountant McKesson & Robbins, Inc., Portland, Oreg., 1934-38; engr. Pub. Service Commn. Oreg., 1938-41; v.p. Gen. Telephone Co. Calif., 1941-50; v.p., gen. mgr. Philippine Long Distance Telephone Co., Manila, 1950-56; also dir.; v.p. United Utilities, Inc., 1956-59; pres., dir. United Telephone Co.; v.p. Internat. Tel. & Tel. Corp., N.Y.C., 1959-61; pres., dir. Telectronic Systems, Inc., Manila, Philippines, 1962-73; cons., 1973—. Author articles on engring., finance, mgmt., pub. service. Active Boy Scouts Am., YMCA; pres. Am. Sch., Manila; mem. coun. regents Oreg. State U., 1981—. Mem. IEEE, NSPE, Philippine Assn. Mech. and Elec. Engrs., Phi Kappa Phi, Tau Beta Pi, Eta Kappa Nu. Club: Army and Navy. Address: 1451 NE Meier Dr Grants Pass OR 97526-3805

NAYLOR, KENNETH GLEN, federal agency administrator; b. Corpus Christi, Tex., May 23, 1952; s. Glen Rafe and Jeannine May (Withington) N. BBA cum laude, Tex. Agrl. and Indsl. U., 1974; postgrad., Tex. Christian U., 1975-76, Comml. Coll., Dallas, 1983-85. Claims rep. Social Security Adminstrn., Ft. Worth, 1974-79; quality rev. specialist Social Security Adminstrn., Dallas, 1979-89; realtor Jean Hall Realtors, Dallas, 1984-88; program analyst Dept. Health and Human Svcs., Washington, 1990-92; compliance rev. specialist USDA, Washington, 1992—; savs. bond coord. Social Security Adminstrn./Dept. Health and Human Svcs./USDA, Dallas, 1985, 87, Washington, 1991, 92; mem. Globe, USDA; treas. J. Naylor-Cope Cos., 1994. Active Log Cabin Reps. Episcopalian. Avocations: bridge, aerobics, travel, organ. Home: 7532 M Coxton Ct Alexandria VA 22306

NAYLOR, PAUL DONALD, lawyer; b. St. Bernard, Ohio, May 28, 1925; s. David Frederick and Erna Helen (Miller) N.; m. Geraldine L. Lacy, Jan. 20, 1945; children: Linda S., Paul Scott, Todd L. JD, U. Cin., 1948. Bar: Ohio 1948. Ptnr. Pulse & Naylor, Cin., 1949-65; pvt. practice Cin., 1965—. Mem. Nat. Rep. Com. Lt. (j.g.) USN, 1943-46. Recipient Svc. to Mankind award Sertoma Internat. Mem. Cin. Bar Assn. (real property com. 1966-86), Ohio Bar Assn., Cin. Lawyers Club (pres. 1955), Order of the Coif. Office: 30 E Central Pky Ste 210 Cincinnati OH 45202-1118

NAYLOR, PHYLLIS REYNOLDS, author; b. Anderson, Ind., Jan. 4, 1933; d. Eugene Spencer and Lura Mae (Schield) Reynolds; m. Thomas A. Tedesco, Jr., Sept. 9, 1951 (div. 1960); m. Rex V. Naylor, May 26, 1960; children: Jeffrey, Michael. Diploma, Joliet Jr. Coll., 1953; BA, Am. U., 1963. Author: 90 books including Crazy Love: An Autobiographical Account of Marriage and Madness, 1977, Revelations, 1979, A String of Chances, 1982 (ALA notable book), The Agony of Alice, 1985 (ALA notable book), The Keeper, 1986 (ALA notable book), Unexpected Pleasures, 1986, Send No Blessings, 1990 (YASD best book for young adults), Shiloh, 1991 (ALA notable book, John Newbery medal 1992). Recipient Golden Kite award Soc. Children's Book Writers Am., 1985, Child Study award Bank St. Coll., 1983, Edgar Allan Poe award Mystery Writers Am., 1985, Internat. book award Soc. Sch. Librs., 1988, Christopher award, 1989, Newbery award ALA, 1992, Nat. Endowment of Arts Creative Writing fellow, 1987. Mem. Children's Book Guild of Washington (pres. 1974-75, 83-84), Soc. Children's Book Writers, Authors Guild, PEN, Council for a Livable World, SANE, Physicians for Social Responsibility, Amnesty Internat. Unitarian. Avocations: theater, swimming. Home and Office: 9910 Holmhurst Rd Bethesda MD 20817-1618

NAYLOR, THOMAS HERBERT, economist, educator, consultant; b. Jackson, Miss., May 30, 1936; s. Thomas Hector and Martha (Watkins) N.; m. Magdalena Raczkowska, Dec. 14, 1985; children: Susanne, Alexander. B.S. in Math., Millsaps Coll., 1958; B.S. in Indsl. Engring., Columbia U., 1959; M.B.A. in Quantitative Bus. Analysis, Ind. U., 1961; Ph.D. in Econs., Tulane U., 1964. Instr. Sch. Bus. Adminstrn. Tulane U., 1961-63; asst. prof. econs. Duke U., 1964-66, assoc. prof. econs., 1966-68, prof. econs., 1968-93, prof. emeritus econs., 1994—; vis. prof. U. Wis., 1969-70, Middlebury Coll., 1993-94, U. Vt., 1994-96; pres. Social Systems, Inc., 1971-80; mng. dir. Naylor Group, 1980; cons., lectr. worldwide. Co-author: (with Eugene Byrne) Linear Programming, 1963, (with Joseph L. Balintfy, Donald S. Burdick and King Chu) Computer Simulation Techniques, 1966, translated into Japanese, Portuguese, and Spanish, (with John Vernon) Microeconomics and Decision Models of the Firm, 1969, translated into Spanish, (with James Clotfelter) Strategies for Change in the South, 1975, (with John M. Vernon and Kenneth Wertz) Managerial Economics: Corporate Economics and Strategy, 1983, (with William H. Willimon) The Abandoned Generation: Rethinking Higher Education, 1995, Downsizing the U.S.A., 1997, (with Rolf Österberg and William H. Willimon) The Search for Meaning in the Workplace, 1996, others; author of 28 books including: Computer Simulation Experiments with Models of Economic Systems, 1971, translated into Spanish, Polish, and Russian, Corporate Planning Models, 1979, Strategic Planning Management, 1980, The Corporate Strategy Matrix, 1986, translated into Hungarian, The Gorbachev Strategy, 1988, The Cold War Legacy, 1991, The Search for Meaning, 1994; editor: The Impact of the Computer on Society, 1967, The Design of Computer Simulation Experiments, 1969, The Politics of Corporate Planning and Modeling, 1978, Simulation Models in Corporate Planning, 1979, Simulation in Business Planning and Decision Making, 1981, others; co-editor: (with H. Brandt Ayers) You Can't Eat Magnolias, 1972, (with Michele H. Mann) Portfolio Planning and Corporate Strategy, 1983, (with Celia Thomas) Optimization Models for Strategic Planning, 1984, others; contbr. numerous articles to profl. publs.; mem. editl. bd. jours. Exec. dir., founder. L.Q.C. Lamar Soc., Washington, 1969-73; active Charlotte Cong. Ch., Vt. Bus. for Social Responsibility. Named to Lambda Chi Alpha Alumni Hall of Fame, 1996. Mem. Beta Gamma Sigma, Lambda Chi, Omicron Delta Kappa.

NAYLOR-JACKSON, JERRY, public relations consultant, retired, entertainer, broadcaster; b. Chalk Mountain, Tex., Mar. 6, 1939; s. William Guy and Mary Bernice (Lummus) Jackson; m. Pamela Ann Robinson, Jan. 30, 1966; children: Geoffrey K. Naylor, Kelli A. Naylor-Dobrzynski, Gregory K. Naylor. Grad., Elkins Electronics Inst., Dallas, 1957; student, U. Md., Fed. Republic of Germany, 1957-58. Life first class radio/TV engring. lic. FCC. Broadcaster various local TV and AM radio stas., San Angelo, Texas, 1955-57; lead singer Buddy Holly and the Crickets, 1960-65; solo entertainer, performer, recording artist and producer, 1965-87; sr. v.p. corp. devel. Newslink Internat. Satellite Broadcast Comms. Co., Inc., Washington, 1986-88; pres. Internat. Syndications, Inc. subs. Newslink, Inc., Washington, 1986-88; pres., CEO, owner The Jerry Naylor Co., McMinnville, Oreg., 1984—; v.p. capital programs, sr. cons. Calif. Luth. Univ., Thousand Oaks, 1990-92; sr. cons., dir. ann. fund Calif. Luth. U., 1989-90; polit./media cons. various Rep. candidates and orgns., 1968-93; spl. cons. to Violeta Barrios de Chamarro, Pres. of Republic of Nicaragua, 1990-92; disc jockey Sta. KHEY-AM, Sta. KINT-AM, El Paso, Tex., 1959; on-air personality Sta. KRLA-AM, Sta. KDAY-AM, L.A., 1960; on-air disc jockey, air personality, celebrity host KLAC-AM, L.A., 1974-83; on-camera and voice-over spokesman for Safeway Stores, Inc., Avis Rent-a-Car, Mut. of Omaha, Wrigley Co., 1968-83; U.S. presdl. appointee, chmn. Job Tng. Partnership Act work group/youth at risk subcom. Nat. Commn. for Employment Policy, 1985-91; nat. dir. spl. events Reagan for Pres., 1979-81; apptd. mem. commn. for employment policy Pres. Ronald Reagan, 1985-91. Recording artist maj. labels including CBS Records, Motown Records, Warner Bros. Records, EMI Records, 1965-84; host weekly nat. and internat. radio program Continental Country (Number 1 syndicated country music radio show in Am., Billboard Mag., Country Music Assn., 1974), (weekly variety show) Music City, USA, 1966-67. Nat. dir. spl. events Reagan for Pres., 1975-76, 79-80; sr. cons. to White House, 1981-88, 89-92. With U.S. Army, 1957-58, Germany. Named to Top 40 Male Vocalists of Yr., Billboard Mag., 1970, named #1 Rock Group (Crickets), Billboard Mag./New Musical Express Mag., 1958, 62. Mem. NARAS, Country Music Assn., Acad. Country Music (Telly award for TV documentary 1991, 92), Phi Kappa Phi (alumni). Avocation: writing prose and poetry. Home and Office: Jerry Naylor Co 1279 SW Russ Ln Mcminnville OR 97128 *Know no boundaries. Experience the world and become enriched from its varied inhabitants.*

NAYMARK, SHERMAN, consulting nuclear engineer; b. Duluth, Minn., May 12, 1920; s. David N. and Lena (Naymark); children by previous marriage: Ronald L., Janet Naymark Stone. B.S. in Engring., U.S. Naval Acad., 1941; M.S. in Engring. and Constrn., MIT, 1946. Sr. scientist Argonne Nat. Lab., (Ill.), 1948-52; dir. reactor div. project, engring. mgr. Schenectady office AEC, 1952-56; with Gen. Electric Co., 1956-70; engring. mgr. nuclear turnkey plants San Jose, 1967-69; pres. Quadrex Corp., Campbell, Calif., 1970-86; chmn. Quadrex Corp., 1986; lectr. U. Va., MIT, U.S. Naval Res. Officer tng. Schs.; adviser to U.S. del. 3d Internat. Conf. on Peaceful Uses of Atomic Energy, Geneva, 1964; sr. examiner Profl. Engrs. State of Calif., 1960-70; mem. fusion power coordinating com. Dept. Energy. Contbr. numerous articles on nuclear research, devel., engring. to profl. jours. Served to capt. USN, 1941-54. Fellow Am. Nuclear Soc. (gen. chmn. ann. meeting, nat. treas. 1978-80), nat. treas. (mem. governing bd. Nuclear Tech. 1979-81); mem. AAAS, Am. Pub. Power Assn. (assoc.), U.S. Naval Inst. (hon. life). Democrat. Jewish. Home: 218 Forrester Rd Los Gatos CA 95032-6509

NAYOR, CHARLES FRANCIS, lawyer; b. Boston, Dec. 28, 1913; s. Harry H. and Rose (Rofelsohn) N.; m. Phyllis Joyce Ponn, June 28, 1959; 1 child, Nancy. AB, Dartmouth Coll., 1935; LLB, Harvard U., 1938, JD, 1964. Bar: Mass. 1938, N.Y. 1946. counsel Mass. Speech & Hearing Found., Boston, 1960-92; atty. Les Dames d'Escoffier, Boston, 1970-91. Chmn. Mass. Outdoor Advt. Authority, Boston, 1975. Lt. (j.g.) USCG, 1942-46. Republican. Jewish. Home: 205 Gardner Rd Brookline MA 02146-4562

NAYYAR, MOHINDER LAL, mechanical engineer; b. Jullundur, Punjab, India, Dec. 16, 1943; came to U.S., 1971; s. Dina Nath and Lila (Wati) N.; m. Surendra Prabha Suri, May 23, 1970; children: Mukta Mohi, Manav Mohi, Mahak Mohi. BS in Physics, Chemistry and Math., Agra (Ind.) U., 1963, MA in History, 1969; BE, U. Roorkee, India, 1966. Registered profl. engr., Va.; lic. boiler installer, Mich. Lectr. mech. engring., cons. engr. Tech. Coll., Agra, 1966-71; jr. engr. Charles Besseler Co., Florham Park, N.J., 1971-72; dir. engring. Internat. Inventors, Inc., Alexandria, Va., 1973-74; prin. engr. Bechtel Corp., Gaithersburg, Md., 1974—. Author: (collections of poems) Ghatayen, 1983, Ehsas, 1995, (engring. manual) BPC ISI Manual, 1986, 89; editor-in-chief, author: (engring. handbook) Piping Handbook, 1992; editor mags. Recipient Outstanding Participation award Nat. Engrs. Week, 1990-91. Mem. ASME (sect. XI task force 1980-81, power piping code com. 1991—, B16 subcom. C 1993—, subcom. B16 N valves 1996—, main com. B16, standardization of valves, flanges, fittings and gaskets), Engring. Assn. (sr. pres. 1966-71), UN Club (founding mem.), Internat. Hindi Assn. (founding mem.), Metrication Task Force for Am. Nat. Stds. Inst./ B16.10. Avocations: reading, writing, music, social work. Home: 19405 Prospect Point Ct Brookeville MD 20833-2608 Office: Bechtel Corp 9801 Washingtonian Blvd Gaithersburg MD 20878-5355

NAZAIRE, MICHEL HARRY, physician; b. Jérémie, Haiti, Sept. 29, 1939; s. Joseph and Hermance N.; m. Nicole N., Dec. 28, 1968 (div.); children: Hanick and Carline (twins). *Daughters Carline and Hanick, born in 1970, are living in New York: Carline is currently employed as administrative assistant by Rheinbraun Thyssen Inc.; Hanick is a student at City College, studying education-early childhood.* Grad., Coll. St. Louis de Gonzague, 1959; MD Faculty of Medicine and Pharmacology, State U. Haiti, 1966. Intern, State U. Hosp., Port-Au-Prince, Haiti, 1965-66; resident physician Sanitarium, Port-Au-Prince, Haiti, 1966-68; practice medicine specializing in pneumology, 1966-68; practice medicine specializing in pneumo-physiology, Port-Au-Prince, 1966—; physician fellow Klinik Havelhohe, West Berlin, 1969-70, 89-91; attending physician Sanitarium, Port-Au-Prince, 1976-91. Dep. mem. Internat. Parliament for Safety and Peace; envoy-at-large Internat. State Parliament; mem. global environ. technol. network Who. Contbr. articles to Jour. Indsl. Hygiene, Pneumology and Respiratory Protection. Fellow Internat. Soc. for Respiratory Protection, Am. Coll. Chest Physicians (assoc.); mem. Am. Pub. Health Assn., Am. Conf. Govtl. Indsl. Hygienists, Internat. Union Against Tuberculosis, Internat. Platform Assn. Address: 6407 S 12th St Apt 1711 Tacoma WA 98465 also: 1115-25 Dorchester Rd #3C Brooklyn NY 11218

NAZARIAN, JOHN, academic administrator, mathematics educator; b. Pawtucket, R.I., Sept. 6, 1932; s. Zakie and Amenia (Nahas) N. EdB, R.I. Coll., 1954; AM, Brown U., 1956; MA, U. Ill., 1961; PhD, NYU, 1967. Instr. math. R.I. Coll., Providence, 1954-58, asst. prof., 1958-67, assoc. prof., 1967-71, prof., 1971—, assoc. dean Arts and Scis., 1970-72, spl. asst. to pres., 1971-77, v.p. adminstrn. and fin., 1977-90, pres., 1990—. Chmn., vice-chmn. Arabic Ednl. Found., Pawtucket, 1966-72; chmn. Sargeant Rehab. Ctr, Providence, 1983-86, Diocesan Pastoral Coun., West Newton, Mass., 1974-78. Recipient Cross of Jerusalem, Patriarch of Melkite Ch., 1976. Avocations: music, golf, reading. Office: RI Coll 600 Mount Pleasant Ave Providence RI 02908-1924*

NAZARIAN, LAWRENCE FRED, pediatrician; b. N.Y.C., May 17, 1940; s. Samuel George and Winifred Lucia (Zotian) N.; m. Sharon Louise Carlson, June 22, 1963; children: Douglas, Stephen, Sarah. BA, Yale U., 1960; MD, U. Rochester, 1964. Pediatrician Panorama Pediatric Group, Rochester, N.Y., 1969—; clin. prof. pediatrics U. Rochester (N.Y.) Sch. Medicine and Dentistry, 1969—; bd. dirs. James P. Wilmot Fedn., Rochester. Contbr. articles to profl. jours.; assoc. editor PEdiatrics in Rev. Jour., 1990—. Mem. troop com. Boy Scouts Am., Penfield, N.Y., 1978-88; mem. coun. com. Luth. Ch. of Reformation, Rochester, 1969—. Maj. USAR, 1967-69. Fellow Am. Acad. Pediatrics; mem. Med. Soc. State of N.Y., Ctrl. N.Y. Pediatric Club, Monroe County Med. Soc., Rochester Acad. Medicine, Rochester Pediatric Soc. Avocations: hiking, camping, canoeing, gardening, cross-country skiing. Office: Panorama Pediatric Group 220 Linden Oaks Rochester NY 14625-2839

NAZEM, FEREYDOUN F., venture capitalist, financier; b. Tehran, Iran, Dec. 29, 1940; came to U.S., 1960, naturalized, 1976; s. Hassan and Afsar N.; m. Susie Gharib, Jan. 20, 1973; children: Alexander, Taraneh. BSc, Ohio State U., 1964; MSc, U. Cin., 1967; MBA, Columbia U., 1971. Sr. rsch. chemist Matheson Coleman & Bell, Norwood, Ohio, 1967-68; asst. v.p., investment analyst Irving Trust Co., N.Y.C., 1969-74; v.p., venture capital officer Charter N.Y., N.Y.C., 1974-75; mng. dir. Collier Enterprises, N.Y.C., 1976-81; mng. ptnr. Nazem & Co., N.Y.C., 1981—; bd. dir. Tegal Corp., Petaluma Calif., Svc. Corp., Wallingford, Conn., Genesis Health Venture Inc., Kennott Square, Pa., Spatial Tech. Inc., Boulder, Colo., Oxford Health, Darien, Conn., Genetix Corp., Boston. Author: The Chemical Industry and Energy Shortage, 1973; contbr. articles to profl. jours. Mem. N.Y. Soc. Security Analysts, N.Y. Venture Capital Forum. Office: Nazem & Co 645 Madison Ave New York NY 10022-1010 *Don't take activity for progress or comfort for civility. Set aside a peaceful hour a day to get in touch with the divinity within you.*

NAZETTE, RICHARD FOLLETT, lawyer; b. Eldora, Iowa, July 27, 1919; s. Hilmer H. and Genevieve A. (Follett) N.; m. Joan Chehak, June 20, 1942; children—Ronald D., Randall A. B.A., U. Iowa, 1942, J.D. with distinction, 1946. Bar: Iowa bar 1946. Practiced in Cedar Rapids, 1946—; partner firm Nazette, Marner, Good, Wendt & Knoll, 1968—; asst. atty. Linn County, Iowa, 1951-56; county atty., 1957-63; dir. United States Bank, Cedar Rapids, 1968-91, State Surety Co., Des Moines, 1966-78. Bd. dirs. Linn County Health Center, 1968-73, chmn., 1968-69; mem. Iowa Bd. Parole, 1981-84. Served with AUS, 1942-44. Fellow Am. Bar Found., Iowa Bar Assn. (bd. govs. 1972-76), Iowa State Bar Found.; mem. Linn County Bar Assn. (pres. 1963), Iowa County Attys. Assn. (pres. 1959), Iowa Acad. Trial Lawyers (pres. 1964), Sigma Phi Epsilon. Republican. Presbyterian. Clubs: Masons, Shriners, Jesters, Elks, Optimists (internat. v.p. 1955). Home: 2224 Country Club Pky SE Cedar Rapids IA 52403-1639 Office: 100 1st St SW Cedar Rapids IA 52404-5701

NDOUR, YOUSSOU, musician; b. Dakar, Senegal, Oct. 1, 1959; s. Elimane Ndour and Ndeye Sokhana Mboup; m. Mamy; 3 children. Student, Ecole des Arts, Dakar. Singer Star Band, Etoile de Dakar, Super Etoile de Dakar (formerly Etoile de Dakar); participant Human Rights Now! tour Amnesty Internat., 1988, First Internat. Fest. Arts, N.Y.C.; represented by Virgin Records, Columbia Records, 1990-93, Chaos, 1994—; founder Soc. Africaine Prodn. Musicales, Studio Xippi. Singer (album) Xalis, 1979, So, 1986, Nelson Mandela, 1986, Immigres, 1988, The Lion/Gaiende, 1989, Set, 1990, Eyes Open, 1992, The Guide (Wommat), 1994; drummer (album) Graceland, 1986. Office: c/o Verna Gillis 799 Greenwich St New York NY 10014-1843

NEACSU, MARIA, artist; b. Manoleasa, Romania, Aug. 15, 1948; d. Ioan and Valeria (Busuioc) Grosu; m. Marius C. Neacsu, Aug. 15, 1970; 1 child, George Mircea. BSBA, Acad. Econ. Study, Bucharest, 1973; BS in Art, U. Calif., Berkeley, 1993; MFA, U. Calif., 1995. Econ. Iprochim, Bucharest, 1973-81; sr. acct. Bechtel, Inc., San Francisco, 1981-83; acctg. mgr. West Mgmt. Co., Oakland, Calif., 1983-86; sr. acct. Kaiser Engring. Inc., Oakland, 1986-89; artist Walnut Creek, Calif., 1989—. Jack K. and Gertrude Murphy fine arts fellow San Francisco Found., 1994. Republican. Avocations: travel, ballet, political study. Home: 505 Pimlico Ct Walnut Creek CA 94596-3677

NEAD, KAREN L., university professor; b. Grayville, Ill., Sept. 25, 1944; d. Vernon M. and Imogene (Hamilton) Green; m. Morris James Nead, Dec. 22, 1960; children: Martin, Bryan, Morris James II, Serenity Dawn. AS, Wabash Valley Coll., Mt. Carmel, 1976; BA in English, Eastern Ill. U., Charleston, 1978, MA in English, 1979; PhD in higher edn., So. Ill. U., Carbondale, 1994. Prof. English Vincennes U., Vincennes, Ind., 1979—. Recipient Higher Edn. Adminstrn. Acad. Scholarship So. Ill. U., 1994. Mem. Am. Assn. of Univ. Prof. Republican. Methodist. Home: 1209 Old Orchard Rd Vincennes IN 47591 Office: Vincennes Univ 1002 N 2nd St Vincennes IN 47591-1503

NEAGLE, DENNIS EDWARD (DENNY NEAGLE), professional baseball player; b. Gambrills, Md., Oct. 13, 1968. Grad. high sch., Gambrills, Md.; student, U. Minn. With Minn. Twins, 1991; pitcher Pitts. Pirates, 1992-96, Atlanta Braves, 1996—. Selected to N.L. All-Star Team, 1995. Mem. Pitts. Pirates N.L. East Champions, 1992. Office: Atlanta Braves PO Box 4064 Atlanta GA 30302*

NEAL, A. CURTIS, retired lawyer; b. Nacogdoches, Tex., Nov. 25, 1922; s. Berry W. and Mattie E. (Shepherd) N.; m. Martha E. Bishop, Apr. 16, 1942; children: Curtis Jr., Patricia Ann, Dick (dec. 1968). BBA, U. Tex. 1948, LLB 1952. Bar: Tex. 1951; CPA., Tex.; soc. lic., Tex.; lic. E.M.T., Tex., 1983. With Office of Tex. Sec. of State 1948-52; pvt. practice, Amarillo, Tex., 1952-90; ret., 1990. Counsel, exec. com., advancement chmn. Boy Scouts Am., 1957-67; mem. Kids, Inc. (bd. dirs. 1954-68, pres. 1960), Western Merchandisers (bd. dirs. 1970-90), Hastings Books, Music, Video (bd. dirs.1971-93); mem. Key Presdl. Legion of Merit (Rep. Presdl. award 1994); formerly active Amarillo Jaycees, Amarillo C. of C., Amarillo Symphony, United Fund, Nat. Com. Rep. Presdl. Task Force, Barber Shop Quartett Singing in Am., Inc.; deacon, bd. mem. and vol. Paramount Ter. Christian Ch.; vol. High Plains Bapt. Hosp., Amarillo Garden Club, Hospice and ch. work. With USN, 1942-45. Decorated with 11 Combat Stars USN, South Pacific. Fellow Tex. Bar Found. (life); mem. ABA, DRV, Am. Inst. Accts., State Bar Tex. Assn. (com. assistance to local bar assns. 1979-84, chmn. 1982-83, com. on coordination with accts. 1977-79, spl. services to membership div. 1982, state bar coll. law 1981-90), Tex. Soc. CPAs, Amarillo Bar Assn. (pres. 1981-82), Amarillo Jaycees, Amarillo C. of C., Disabled Am. Vets., Masons, York Rite (comdr. 1961) Scottsh Rite Masons, Amarillo Club, Starlighters Dance Club, Amarillo Knife & Fork Club (dir. 1995-97), Tex. Shrine Assn. (all-state dir. gen. 1962, Khiva Temple potentate 1970), Cabiri (pres. 1974), Khiva Stage Band (pres. 1978), Downtown Lions Club, Delta Theta Phi, Beta Alpha Psi. Republican. Home: 6205 Jameson Rd Amarillo TX 79106-3518

NEAL, ANN PARKER See PARKER, ANN

NEAL, AVON, artist, author; b. Morgantown, Ind., July 16, 1922; s. Orval Francis and Goldie Agnes (Prather) N.; m. Ann Russell Parker, Oct. 31, 1964. Student, Long Beach Coll., Calif.; M.F.A., Escuela de Bellas Artes, Mex., 1949. Artist-in-residence Altos de Chavon, Dominican Republic, 1983, 84; mem. advisory bd. Mus. Am. Folk Art, 1968-71, Dublin Seminar for New Eng. Folklife, 1976-78; pres. Thistle Hill Press; lectr., radio and TV appearances. Exhibited stone rubbings in one and two man shows, Am. embassy, London, 1965, Hallmark Gallery, N.Y.C., 1968, Amon Carter Mus., Ft. Worth, 1968, 71, Mus. Am. Folk Art, 1970, Mus. Fine Arts, Springfield, Mass., 1972, Altos de Chavon, 1984, Princeton U. Library, N.J., 1986, others; represented in permanent collections at Met. Mus. Art, N.Y.C., Library of Congress, Smithsonian Instn., Washington, Abby Aldrich Rockefeller Mus. Am. Folk Art, Williamsburg, Va., Winterthur Mus., Wilmington, Del.; author: Rubbings From Early American Stone Sculpture, 1963, Ephemeral Folk Figures, 1969, Molas: Folk Art of the Cuna Indians, 1977, Pigs and Eagles, 1978, Scarecrows, 1978, Early American Stone Sculpture Found in the Burying Grounds of New England, 1981, Los Ambulantes, 1982, Hajj Paintins, Folk Art of the Great Pilgrimage, 1995; contbr. articles to profl. jours. Served with USN, World War II. Ford Found. grantee, 1962-64; fiction writing fellow Mass. Artists Found., 1979; recipient Mass. Arts Coun. award, 1996. Home: 126 School St North Brookfield MA 01535

NEAL, DARWINA LEE, government official; b. Mansfield, Pa., Mar. 31, 1942; d. Darwin Leonard and Ina Belle (Cooke) N. BS, Pa. State U., 1965; postgrad., Cath. U, 1968-70. Registered landscape architect. Landscape architect nat. capital region Nat. Pk. Svc., 1965-69, office of White House liaison, 1969-71, office of profl. services, 1971-74, div. design svcs., 1974-89, chief design svcs., 1989-95; mem. office of stewardship and partnership Nat. Pk. Svc., Washington, 1996—; judge numerous award juries. Contbr. articles to profl. jours.; co-author sects. of profl. bull., mag.; author introduction to book Women, Design and the Cambridge School; columnist: Land monthly, 1975-79. Mem. Women's Coun. on Energy in Environment. Recipient Merit award Landscape Contractors Met. Washington; recipient hon. mention Les Floralies Internationales de Montreal, 1980 Alumni Achievement award Pa. State U. Arts and Architecture Alumni Soc., 1981. Fellow Am. Soc. Landscape Architects (v.p. 1979-81, pres. elect 1982-83, pres. 1983-84, trustee 1976-77, nat. treas. 1977-79, legis. coordinator 1975-79, sec. Coun. Fellows 1988-90, (del. to Internat. Fedn. Landscape Architects, del. 1989—, ex-officio rep. to U.S./internat. com. on monuments and sites, liaison to historically black coll. and univ. program Dept. Interior, recipient Pres.' medal 1987); mem. Landscape Archtl. Accreditation Bd. (roster vis. evaluators), Nat. Recreation and Parks Assn., Nat. Soc. Park Resources (bd. dirs. 1978-80), Nat. Trust Hist. Preservation, Pa. State U. Alumni Assn. (Washington met. chpt. trustee 1972-74), Am. Arbitration Assn. (nat. panel arbitrators), Com. 100 for the Fed. City, Preservation

Action, Nat. Assn. Olmsted Parks, Beekman Pl. Condominium Assn. (bd. dirs. 1985-91, archtl. control com.), Nat. Parks and Conservation Assn., Alliance for Historic Preservation, World Watch, Worldwide, Garden Conservancy. Office: Nat Park Svc/Nat Capital Region Off Stewardship & Ptnrships 1100 Ohio Dr SW Washington DC 20242-0001

NEAL, DENNIS MELTON, middle school educator; b. Lakeland, Fla., Feb. 7, 1966; s. M. H. and Alice Marie (Twiddy) N.; m. Christine Anne Rufo, Oct. 21, 1989; children: Lauren Elizabeth, Waverly Rose. AA, Polk C.C., Winter Haven, Fla., 1987; BS, Fla. So. Coll., 1991; MEd, Stetson U., 1995. Cert. elem. tchr., Fla. Guest svcs. Cypress gardens, Winter Haven, 1985-86; entertainer Boardwalk and Baseball, Baseball City, Fla., 1986-88; guest svcs. Hilton Walt Disney World, Orlando, Fla., 1988-91; tchr. Deltona (Fla.) Middle Sch., 1991-95, asst. prin., 1995—; chair correlate com., team leader Deltona Middle Sch., also mem. sch. adv. coun. Tchr. Emmaus Luth. Ch., Orange City, Fla., 1992-93; active Parent, Tchr., Student Assn. Named One of Top 100 Beginning Tchrs. in Nation, Sallie Mae Student Loan Assn., 1992. Avocations: soccer, racquetball, drawing, painting. Home: 2939 Owen Ct Deltona FL 32738-1846 Office: Deltona Mid Sch 250 Enterprise Rd Deltona FL 32725-8053

NEAL, HOMER ALFRED, physics educator, researcher, university administrator; b. Franklin, Ky., June 13, 1942; s. Homer and Margaret Elizabeth (Holl) N.; m. Donna Jean Daniels, June 16, 1962; children: Sharon Denise, Homer Alfred. BS in Physics with honors, Ind. U., 1961; MS in Physics (John Hay Whitney fellow), U. Mich., 1963, PhD in Physics, 1966. Asst. prof. physics Ind. U., 1967-70, assoc. prof., 1970-72, prof., 1972-81, dean research and grad. devel., 1976-81; prof. physics SUNY, Stony Brook, 1981-87, provost, 1981-86; prof. physics, chmn. U. Mich., Ann Arbor, 1987-93, v.p. rsch., 1993—, interim pres., 1996-97; mem. Nat. Sci. Bd., 1980-86; chmn. Argonne Zero Gradient Synchrotron Users Group, 1970-72; trustee Argonne Univs. Assn., 1971-74, 77-80; NSF physics adv. panel , 1976-79, chmn. NSF physics adv. panel, 1987-89; high energy physics adv. panel U.S. Dept. Energy, 1977-81; bd. dirs. Ogden Corp. Contbr. articles to profl. jours. Bd. dirs. N.Y. Sea Grant Inst., 1982-86; mem. bd. overseers Superconducting Super Collider, 1989-93; mem. bd. regents Smithsonian Instn., 1989—; trustee Ctr. for Strategic and Internat. Studies, 1990—; trustee Environ. Rsch. Inst. of Mich., 1994-96; mem. adv. bd. Oak Ridge (Tenn.) Nat. Lab., 1993—. NSF fellow, 1966-67; Sloan fellow, 1968; Guggenheim fellow, 1980-81. Fellow Am. Phys. Soc., AAAS, Am. Acad. Arts and Scis.; mem. Univs. Research Assn. (trustee 1983-87), Sigma Xi. Office: Office of VP for Rsch 2074 Fleming Adminstrn Bldg 4060 Fleming Admin Bldg Ann Arbor MI 48109-1340

NEAL, IRENE COLLINS, artist, educator; b. Greensburg, Pa., May 14, 1936; d. Oliver Shupe and Betsey Cowap (Mann) Collins; m. Paul Whitaker Neal, Nov. 24, 1960; children: Paul Collins Gordon, Betsey Whitaker. BA, Wilson Coll., 1958; student, Sch. Visual Arts, Rio de Janeiro, 1976-77, Memphis Sate U., 1979-80, U. Bridgeport, 1982-83; participant, Triangle Art Workshop, Pine Planes, N.Y., 1985. guest spkr. Coll. Santa Fe, Albuquerque, N.Mex., 1994. One-woman shows include Allied Chem. Corp., Morristown, N.J., 1975, Planetarium Rio de Janeiro, 1977, Pat Ackerman Gallery, Memphis, 1980, Westmoreland Mus. Art, Greensburg, 1986, Wilson Coll., 1993; group exhbns. include Jersey City Mus., 1975, N.J. State Mus., 1975, Somerset (N.J.) Tri-State Mus., 1975, Nat. Arts Club, N.Y.C., 1975, Garden State Watercolor Soc., 1975, Salao de Marinhas, Rio de Janeiro, 1977, Stamford (Conn.) Mus., 1984, 85, 89, Branchville Soho Gallery, Ridgefield, Conn., 1984, Silvermine Guild, New Canaan, Conn., 1984, Stamford Libr., 1985, Shippee Gallery, N.Y.C., 1986, 110 Greene St., N.Y.C., 1986, Wilton (Conn.) Libr., 1986, Aldrich Mus. Contemporary Art, Ridgefield, 1987, Ariel Gallery, N.Y.C., 1988, 89, Visual Arts Festival, Edmonton, Alta., Can., 1989, Mus. Art., Ft. Lauderdale, Fla., 1991-92, Salander-o'Reilly Galleries, Inc., N.Y., 1994, Vanderleelie Gallery, Edmonton, 1996, Galerie Piltzer, Paris, 1996, Fine Art 2000 Gallery, Stamford, 1996, 97, York Coll., Queens, N.Y., 1997, Ctr. for Perfoming Arts, Stamford, 1997; represented in collections Planetarium Rio de Janeiro, Internat. Paper, N.Y.C., Westmoreland Mus. Art, Greensburg, Pepperdine U., Malibu, Calif., Newport Harbor Art Mus., Newport Beach, Calif., Hoover Instn. Stanford (Calif.) U., St. Matthew's Episcopal Ch., Wilton, Columbia U., N.Y.C., Ctr. Arts, Vero Beach, Fla., Mus. Art, Ft. Lauderdale, Alamo Rent A Car, Ft. Lauderdale, Denver Ctr. Performing Arts, Louis P. Cabot, Boston; pub., contbr. art to book New New Painting, 1996. Republican. Episcopalian. Avocations: ocean diving, tennis, golf, gardening. Home and Studio: 700 River Rd Cos Cob CT 06807-1907

NEAL, JAMES AUSTIN, architect; b. Greenville, S.C., Nov. 23, 1935; s. Charles Albert Neal and Jane (Anderson) Cole; m. Leonette Dedmond, Apr. 13, 1963; 1 child, Heather Anderson. B. Arch., Clemson U., 1959. Registered arch., S.C. Designer McMillan Architects, Greenville, S.C., 1960-62; project mgr. W.E. Freeman Architects, Greenville, 1963-64; project architect J.E. Sirrine Co., Greenville, 1964-68; pres., prin. Neal, Prince & Browning, Greenville, 1969—; vis. prof. Clemson U. Coll. Architecture, 1974-75; mem. bd. advisors Wachovia Nat. Bank. Pres. Leslie Meyer Devel. Ctr., Greenville, 1980-82. Recipient Leadership award Greenville C. of C., 1983. Fellow AIA (Merit Design award 1978, pres. S.C. chpt. 1991, regional dir. S.C., Ga., N.C., mem. nat. bd. 1994-96, co-recipient Twenty-five Yr. award 1997); mem. Greenville Coun. Architects (past pres.), Interfaith Forum of Religious Art and Architecture (mem. nat. bd.). Baptist. Club: Poinsett (pres. 1985-86). Avocations: jogging; flying. Office: Neal Prince & Ptnrs 110 W North St Greenville SC 29601-2741

NEAL, JAMES MADISON, JR., retired editor and educator; b. Oklahoma City, Aug. 6, 1925; s. James Madison and Tillie Belle (Milliken) N.; m. Caroline Dorothy Becker (dec. Dec. 1974); children: Charles, James W., Jody, Carolyn. BA, U. Colo., 1949; MA, S.D. State U., 1970. Editor various newspapers, Colo., Nebr. and Okla., 1949-59; wire editor Rapid City Journal, Rapid City, S.D., 1959-67; instr. S.D. State U., Brookings, S.D., 1967-71; asst. prof. U. Nebr., Lincoln, 1971-73, assoc. prof., 1973-90; S.D. chmn. AP Mng. Editors Assn., 1962-64. Mem. ACLU (bd. dirs. Nebr. affiliate 1979-82, Ariz. affiliate 1994), VFW, Soc. Profl. Journalists, Investigative Reporters and Editors. Unitarian. Avocations: painting, travel. Home: 4700 N Kolb Rd Apt 4113 Tucson AZ 85750-6187

NEAL, JAMES PRESTON, state senator, project engineer; b. Cin., July 1, 1935; s. James Preston and Desha Frank (Thompson) N.; m. Nancy Joan Tyner, June 11, 1961; children: Leslie Neal Driscoll, Karen Desha, James P. BSME, U. Ill., 1960. Registered profl. engr., Del. Tech. svc. engr. DuPont Co., Parlin, N.J., 1960-62; engr DuPont Co., Waynesboro, Va., 1962-64; instrument engr. DuPont Co., Newburgh, N.Y., 1964-68, Newark, 1966-78; project engr. DuPont Co., 1978-92; dir. Tetra Tech Inc., Christiana, Del., 1992—; pres. Tech. Mgmt., 1994—; mem. Del. Ho. of Reps., 1978-80; mem. Del. Senate, 1980-94. Patentee in field. Councilman City of Newark, 1973-78. With U.S. Army, 1954-56. Recipient Disting. Svc. award Forum to Advance Minorities in Engring., 1989, Disting. Svc. citation Del. Libr. Assn., 1994. Fellow Am. Legis. Exch. Coun. (sr. fellow, nat. officer 1991-94, Outstanding Leader 1989, Outstanding Legis. mem. 1994), Conf. World Regions (sr. fellow); mem. IEEE (sr.), Del. Engring. Soc. (Engr. of Yr. 1989), Instrument Soc. Am. Republican. Presbyterian. Avocations: photography, reading. Home: 50 Bridlebrook Ln Newark DE 19711-2061 Office: Tetra Tech Inc 56 W Main St Newark DE 19702-1505

NEAL, JON C(HARLES), accountant, consultant; b. Milw., Oct. 21, 1955; s. C. Conger and Marcella A. (Wichtowski) N.; m. Ann M. Christensen, Feb. 14, 1979; children: Elizabeth, Katherine, David, Michael. BBA in Acctg. and Mgmt. Info. Systems, U. Wis., Milw., 1977, MS in Taxation, 1987. CPA, Wis. Staff acct. Norman J. Smaglik CPA, Wauwatosa, Wis., 1977-78, sr. acct., 1979-81; sr. acct. Conley, McDonald and Co., Brookfield, Wis., 1978-79; ptnr. Smaglik & Neal, Wauwatosa, 1981-83, Mueller & Sebena, Brookfield, 1983-84; pvt. practice Greenfield, Wis., 1984—; advisor to bd. Milw. Hospice, 1979—; cons. Dr. Bob's, Inc., Milw., 1991—. Editor: Multistate Tax Almanac, 1987. Bd. dirs. The Marion Ctr., Milw. Mem. AICPA, Wis. Inst. CPAs (com. mem., seminar leader 1980—), Nat. Soc. Tax Practitioners, Hales Corners (Wis.) Jaycees (treas., charter mem. 1991). Avocations: soccer, basketball, scouting. Office: 7001 W Edgerton Ave Ste 101 Greenfield WI 53220-4480

NEAL, JOSEPH C., JR., church administrator. Sec. of fin. Christian Methodist Episcopal Church, L.A. Address: Christian Methodist Espiscopal Ch PO Box 75085 Los Angeles CA 90075-0058*

NEAL, JOSEPH LEE, vocational school educator; b. Memphis, Feb. 17, 1948; s. James Henry and Minnie Rue (Waldrop) N.; m. Judy Anne Westmoreland, Apr. 26, 1969; children: Janice Celeste Neal, Mary Joanne. AAS, N.W. C.C., Senatobia, Miss., 1979, AS in Bus., 1980; BS, U. S. Miss., 1984, MS, 1986. Cert. tchr. Miss. Police officer City of W. Memphis, Ark., 1970-72; customer svc. rep. Biomed. Labs., Little Rock, Ark., 1972-75; sales, svc. rep Moore Ford Co., N. Little Rock, 1975-77; electronics technician N.W. Miss. C.C., Senatobia, 1979-82, electronics inst., 1982-83; electronics engr. U. So. Miss., Hattiesburg, 1983-85; electronics instr. Tex. State Tech. Inst., Sweetwater, 1985-87, De Soto County Vo-Tech. Ctr., Southaven, Miss., 1988-97, South Panola H.S., Batesville, Miss., 1997—; cons. engr. various radio ops., Hattiesburg, 1982-85; mem. curriculum com. De Soto County Schs., 1990-95; steering com. N.W. Miss. Tech. Prep., Senatobia, 1992-95. Bd. dirs. Optimist Club, Sweetwater, Tex., 1987. Named Outstanding Tchr., Horn Lake So. C. of C., 1992. Mem. Am. Vocat. Assn., Miss. Trade and Tech. Assn. (v.p. 1994-95, pres. 1995-96), Miss. Assn. Vocat. Educators (pres. dist. 1 1991-92, 95-96, bd. dirs. 1991-92, 95-96, sec. dist. 1 1993-94, v.p. 1994-95), Vocat.-Indsl. Clubs of Am. (100% Advisor 1990, 91, 92, VICA state advisor of yr. 1993), N.Am. Hunting Club (life). Baptist. Avocations: hunting, fishing, pub. speaking. Home: 1607 Pierce Avenue Ext Oxford MS 38655-4459 Office: South Panola HS Batesville MS 38606

NEAL, LEORA LOUISE HASKETT, social services administrator; b. N.Y.C., Feb. 23, 1943; d. Melvin Elias and Miriam Emily (Johnson) Haskett; m. Robert A. Neal, Apr. 23, 1966; children: Marla Patrice, Johnathan Robert. BA in Psychology and Sociology, City Coll. N.Y., 1965; MS in Social Work, Columbia U., 1970, cert. adoption specialist, 1977; IBM cert. community exec. tng. program, N.Y., 1982. Cert. social worker N.Y. state. Caseworker N.Y.C. Dept. Social Service, 1965-67, Windham Child Care, N.Y.C., 1967-73; exec. dir., founder Assn. Black Social Workers Child Adoption Counseling and Referral Service, N.Y.C., 1975-96; adoption specialist trainer Ctr. Devel. Human Svcs. N.Y. State Dept. Social Svc., New York, NY, 1996—; cons. adoption, adoption tng. N.Y. State Dept. Social Svc., Columbia U. Sch. Social Work, N.Y.C. Human Resources Adminstrn., U. La., New Orleans; founder Haskett-Neal Pubs., Bronx, N.Y., 1993. Coauthor: Transracial Adoptive Parenting: A Black/White Community Issue, 1993; contbr. articles in field to profl. jours. Child Welfare League Am. fellow, 1976; recipient cert. No Time to Lose cert. N.Y. State Dept. Social Svcs., 1989. Mem. NAFE, Columbia U. Alumni Assn., CCNY Alumni Assn., Missionary Com. Revival Team (outreach chairperson 1982-88). Democrat. Avocations: writing, history and religious studies, traveling, cultural activities. Office: care NY State Dept of Soc Svcs SUNY Ctr Devel Human Svcs 80 Maiden Ln New York NY 10038

NEAL, LOUISE KATHLEEN, life insurance company executive, accountant; b. Seattle, Nov. 25, 1951; d. Paul Bradford and Ruth Catherine (Park) Johnson; m. William Steven Neal, Oct. 25, 1974. B.A. in Bus. Adminstrn. and Acctg., U. Wash., 1974. Sr. acct. Touche Ross & Co., Seattle, 1974-77; internal auditor No. Life Ins. Co., Seattle, 1977-83; auditor Northwestern Nat. Life Ins. Co., Mpls., 1983-84, 2d v.p., auditor, 1984-88; sr. v.p., gen. auditor Transam. Occidental Life Ins. Co., L.A., 1988-89, sr. v.p., 1990-92, sr. v.p., chief adminstrv. officer, 1992-95; pres. USA Admin. Svcs. Inc. sub. Transam. Occidental Life Ins. Co., Overland Park, Kans., 1995—. Fellow Life Mgmt. Inst.; mem. AICPA. Office: USA Admin Svcs Inc PO Box 2948 Overland Park KS 66201-1348

NEAL, MARCUS PINSON, JR., radiologist, medical educator; b. Columbia, Mo., Apr. 22, 1927; s. M. Pinson and Mathilda (Evers) N.; m. Gail S. Fallon, May 27, 1961; children: Sandra G., M. Pinson III, Ruth-Catherine E. AB, U. Mo., 1949, BS, 1951; MD, U. Tenn., 1953. Intern Med. Coll. Va., Richmond, 1953-54; resident U. Wis. Hosp., Madison, 1954-57; instr. dept. radiology Sch. Medicine U. Wis., Madison, 1957-59; mem. staff U. Wis. Hosps., Madison, 1957-63; asst. prof. radiology, dir. dept. radiology Cen. Wis. Colony, Madison, 1959-63; radiologist Wis. Diagnostic Ctr., Madison, 1962-63; mem. staff Med. Coll. Va. Hosps., Va. Commonwealth U., 1963—; assoc. prof. radiology Med. Coll. Va., Va. Commonwealth U., 1963-66, prof. radiology, 1966—, dir. postgrad. edn. dept. radiology, 1964-73, chmn. divsn. diagnostic radiology, 1965-68, asst. dean Sch. Medicine, dir. grad. med. edn., dir. regional med. program, 1968-71, dir. continuing edn. Sch. Medicine,, 1969-72, interim dean Sch. Medicine,, 1971, asst. v.p. for health scis., 1971-73, provost Health Scis. campus, 1973-78, assoc. dean for continuing med. edn. and quality assurance Sch. Medicine,, 1978-79, dir. housestaff edn. Dept. Radiology,, 1979-93, dir. section genitourinary radiology, Dept. Radiology,, 1981-92; bd. dirs. Common Wealth Bank, Richmond; cons., radiologist Va. Hosp., Madison, 1962-63, USAF Hosp., Truax Field, Madison, 1962-63, McGuire VA Hosp., Richmond, 1963—; bd. forestry Commonwealth of Va., 1990-94, chmn. bd. forestry, 1993-94. Editor: Emergency Interventional Radiology: Practical Aspects, 1988; contbr. articles to profl. jours. Pres. Oxford Civic Assn., Richmond, 1965-67, Three Ridges Condominium Assn., Wintergreen, Va., 1979-84. Served as pharmacist mate USNR, 1945-47. Fellow Oak Ridge Inst. Nuclear Studies, Am. Coll. Radiology (councilor Va. chpt. 1977-83, 85-91, 93—); mem. AMA, Radiol. Soc. N.Am., Am. Roentgen Ray Soc., Med. Soc. Va., So. Med. Assn. (pres. 1982-83, Disting. Svc. award 1994), Richmond Acad. Medicine, Capital Club (bd. dirs.), Commonwealth Club, Bull and Bear Club, Willow Oaks Country Club, Sigma Xi. Avocations: hunting, fishing, gardening, skiing. Home: 4607 Stratford Rd Richmond VA 23225-1066 Office: Med Coll Va PO Box 980295 Richmond VA 23298-0295

NEAL, MARGARET SHERRILL, writer, editor; b. Memphis, Apr. 13, 1950; d. Wilburn Franklin and Merle Aileen (Willis) N. BA, Memphis State U., 1972, postgrad., 1973; MS, Columbia Pacific U., 1984. Air traffic contr. FAA, Memphis, 1974-76, New Bern, N.C., 1976-81, Vero Beach, Fla., 1981-83; detection sys. specialist U.S. Customs Svc., Miami, 1983-87, intelligence rsch. specialist, 1987-89; ret., 1989. Mem. NOW, Smithsonian Instn., Mensa, Nat. Trust Hist. Preservation, Greenpeace, Clan Macneil Soc., Nature Conservancy, Lighthouse Point Writers' Workshops, Save the Manatee Club. Republican. Presbyterian. Avocations: genealogy, needlework, traveling, sketching, growing orchids.

NEAL, PHIL HUDSON, JR., manufacturing company executive; b. Birmingham, Ala., Nov. 17, 1926; s. Phil Hudson and Amy (Gross) N.; m. Sarah Swift Britton, Sept. 19, 1959; children: Amy Neal Ager, Phil Hudson, III, Samuel Abney Britton. A.B., Duke U., 1950; M.B.A., Harvard U., 1952. Investment analyst First Nat. Bank, Birmingham, 1952-55; procedures analyst Gen. Electric Co., Hendersonville, N.C., 1955-58; with Ala. By-Products Corp., Birmingham, 1958-79; asst. treas. Ala. By-Products Corp., 1964-68, treas., 1968-79; dir., v.p. Utility Tool Co., Birmingham, 1979-86; dir., pres. Nucor Metal Finishing Inc., Birmingham, 1986-92, chmn., 1992—. Trustee Advent Episcopal Day Sch., 1967—, pres., 1968-89, trustee charitable endowment trust, 1981—; treas. Cathedral Ch. of Advent, 1981-82, mem. chpt., 1983-85, 86-89; bd. dirs. Greater Birmingham Ministries, 1975-77, Advent Episcopal Assn. for Edn., 1968-89, Jefferson County chpt. Ala. Soc. Crippled Children and Adults, Inc., 1977-79; trustee Ala. Found. for Hearing and Speech, 1967-74, v.p., 1968-69, pres., 1969-71. Served with USNR, 1945-46. Mem. Newcomen Soc. N.Am., Phi Beta Kappa, Sigma Nu, Phi Eta Sigma. Episcopalian (vestryman, sr. warden). Clubs: Birmingham Country, The Club. Home: 3336 Hermitage Rd Birmingham AL 35223-2004 also: 81 Old Duck Hole Rd East Orleans MA 02643 Office: 3669 Indsl Pkwy PO Box 170746 Birmingham AL 35217-0746

NEAL, PHILIP, dancer. Grad. magna cum laude, St. Paul's Sch., 1986; trained, Sch. Royal Danish Ballet, Copenhagen, Denmark. With corps. de ballet N.Y.C. Ballet, 1987-91, soloist, 1991-92, prin. dancer, 1992—. Featured in ballets (Balanchine) Divertimento No. 15, Walpurgisnacht, Slaughter on Tenth Avenue, Western Symphony, Swan Lake, Coppelia; (Robbins) Interplay, The Four Seasons, The Goldberg Variations, Glass Pieces, Mother Goose; (Martins) Les Gentilhommes, Ecstatic Orange, Black & White, Fearful Symmetries, The Sleeping Beauty; also appeared in N.Y.C. Ballet's Balanchine Celebration, 1993. Recipient silver medal Internat. Prix de Lausanne ballet competition; summer scholar N.Y.C . Sch. Am. Ballet; named Presdl. scholar of the Arts Nat Found. Advancement of the Arts. Office: New York City Ballet NY State Theater 20 Lincoln Center Plz New York NY 10023-6913*

NEAL, PHILIP MARK, diversified manufacturing executive; b. San Diego, Aug. 28, 1940; s. Philip Mark and Florence Elizabeth (Anderson) N.; children: Brian, Kevin. B.A., Pomona Coll., 1962; M.B.A., Stanford U., 1964. Mgr. financial planning and analysis CBS, Hollywood, 1964-66; cons. McKinsey & Co., Los Angeles, 1966-73; v.p., controller Avery Internat. Corp., Los Angeles, 1974-78; sr. v.p. fin. Avery Internat. Corp., Pasadena, 1979-88, group v.p. materials group, 1988-90; exec. pres. Avery Internat. Corp., 1990, pres., chief operating officer, 1990—; bd. dirs. Ind. Colls. of So. Calif. Trustee Pomona Coll; gov. Town Hall of Calif. Bd. Govs. Mem. Fin. Execs. Inst. Republican. Episcopalian. Office: Avery Dennison Corp PO Box 7090 150 N Orange Grove Blvd Pasadena CA 91103

NEAL, RICHARD EDMUND, congressman, former mayor; b. Worcester, Mass., Feb. 14, 1949; s. Edmund J. and Mary H. (Garvey) N.; m. Maureen Conway, Dec. 20, 1975; children—Rory, Brendan, Maura, Sean. B.S., Am. Internat. Coll., Springfield, Mass., 1972; M.P.A., U. Hartford, Conn., 1976; postgrad., U. Mass., Amherst, 1982. Adminstrv. aide to Mayor City of Springfield, Mass., 1973-78, mem. city council, 1978-83, mayor, 1984-88; mem. 101st-105th Congresses from 2nd. Mass. dist., Washington, DC, 1989—; mem. ways and means com.; lectr. history and politics Springfield Tech. Community Coll., Mass., 1973-83; lectr. bus. and govt. Western New Eng. Coll., Springfield, 1979-82; project dir. Springfield Tech. Community Coll., 1979-82. Trustee ARC, YMCA, Springfield. Named to Outstanding Young Men in Am., U.S. Jr. C. of C., Springfield. Mem. Am. Internat. Coll. Alumni Assn. (pres. 1980, Alumni Achievement award 1985). Springfield Library and Mus. Assn. (trustee). Democrat. Roman Catholic. Clubs: Valley Press. John Boyle O'Reilly (Springfield). Office: US House of Reps 2236 Rayburn Bldg Washington DC 20515-2102*

NEAL, STEVEN GEORGE, journalist; b. Coos Bay, Oreg., July 3, 1949; s. Ernest L. and Ellen Louise (Williams) N.; m. Susan Christine Simmons, May 8, 1971; children: Erin, Shannon. BS in Journalism, U. Oreg., 1971; MS in Journalism, Columbia U., 1972. Reporter Oreg. Jour., Portland, 1971, Phila. Inquirer, 1972-78; gen. assignment reporter, White House corr., polit. writer Chgo. Tribune, 1979-87; polit. editor Chgo. Sun-Times, 1987-92, polit. columnist, 1987—; bd. govs. White House Corrs. Assn., Washington, 1981-83. Co-author: Tom McCall: Maverick, 1977; author: The Eisenhowers, 1978, Dark Horse: A Biography of Wendell Willkie, 1984, McNary of Oregon, 1985; editor: They Never Go Back to Pocatello: The Essays of Richard Neuberger, 1988; contbr. to Am. Heritage, The Nation, The N.Y. Times Books Rev., Dictionary of Am. Biography. Recipient William H. Jones award Chgo. Tribune, 1984; Robert W. Ruhl lectr. U. Oreg., Eugene, 1984; Col. Robert R. McCormick fellow, McCormick Found., Chgo., 1989; Hoover Libr. Assn. scholar, West Branch, Iowa, 1989. Roman Catholic. Home: 411 N Elm St Hinsdale IL 60521-3709 Office: Chgo Sun-Times Inc 401 N Wabash Ave Rm 110 Chicago IL 60611-3532*

NEALE, E(RNEST) R(ICHARD) WARD, retired university official, consultant; b. Montreal, Que., Can., July 3, 1923; s. Ernest John and Mabel Elizabeth (McNamee) N.; m. Roxie Eveline Anderson, June 3, 1950; children—Richard Ward, Owen Curtis. B.Sc., McGill U., Montreal, 1949; M.S., Yale U., 1950, Ph.D., 1952; LL.D. (hon.), Calgary U., Alta., Can., 1977; DSc (hon.), Meml. U., Nfld., Can., 1989. Asst. prof. geology U. Rochester, N.Y., 1952-54; sect. chief Geol. Survey Can., Ottawa, Ont., 1954-63; div. chief Geol. Survey Can., 1965-68, Calgary, 1976-81; commonwealth geol. liaison officer London, 1963-65; prof., head geology Meml. U., St. John's, Nfld., Can., 1986-76; v.p. Meml. U., 1982-87; cons., Calgary, Alta., Can., 1987—; chmn. nat. adv. bd. on sci. publs. NRC-Natural Scis. and Engring. Rsch. Coun., Ottawa, 1982-88. Author: Geology and Geophysics in Canadian Universities, 1980. Editor: Some Guides to Mineral Exploration, 1967, Geology in the Atlantic Region, 1968, The Geosciences in Canada, 1968; Editor: Can. Jour. of Earth Science, 1974-79, Science and the Public, 1988. Bd. dirs. Unitarian Ch. Calgary, 1993—, pres., 1995-96. Petty officer Royal Can. Navy, 1943-45. Decorated officer Order of Can., 1990; recipient Queen's Jubilee medal Govt. of Can., 1977, Can. 125 medal, 1992. Fellow Royal Soc. Can. (coun. 1972-75, chmn. com. pub. awareness of sci. 1987-91, Bancroft medal 1975), Geol. Assn. Can. (pres. 1973-74, Ambrose medal 1986, 1st E.R. Ward Neale medal 1995), Can. Geosci. Coun. (pres. 1975-76, R.T. Bell medal Can. Mining Jour. 1977), Geol. Soc. Am.; mem. Assn. Earth Sci. Editors, Nat. Def. (chmn. biol. and chem. def. rev. com. 1990-93), Univ. Club Calgary, Chancellor's Club, Crows Nest Club, Calgary Sci. Network (pres. 1989), Sigma Xi (nat. lectr. New Haven 1976, chmn. Avalon chpt. 1986). Avocations: golf, cross-country skiing, hiking, canoeing. Home and Office: 5108 Carney Rd NW, Calgary, AB Canada T2L 1G2

NEALE, HENRY WHITEHEAD, plastic surgery educator; b. Richmond, Va., July 18, 1940; s. Richard C. and Eva W. Neale; m. Margaret C. Neale, June 20, 1964; children: Leigh, Jennifer, Henry Whitehead Jr., William. BS, Davidson Coll., 1960; MD, Med. Coll. Va., 1964. Diplomate Am. Bd. Surgery, Am. Bd. Plastic Surgery (guest examiner 1986-90, dir. 1990-96, mem. com. on plans and qualifying exam. com. 1993-96, exec. com. 1993—, chmn. certifying examing com. 1993-95, mem. ethics com. 1993, liaison to Am. Bd. Surgery 1993-96, chmn.-elect 1995-96). Rotating intern Mercy Med. Ctr., Springfield, Ohio, 1964-65; resident in gen. surgery U. Cin. Med. Ctr., 1965-71, dir. div. plastic, reconstructive and hand surgery, 1974—; resident in plastic surgery Duke U. Med. Ctr., Durham, N.C., 1971-74; fellow in hand surgery, Christine Kleinert hand fellow U. Louisville, 1973; asst. prof. surgery U. Cin. Coll. Medicine, 1974-77, assoc. prof., 1977-82, prof., 1982—; active staff, dir. hand surgery and plastic surgery clinics U. Cin. Med. Ctr. Hosp. Group, 1974—; dir. burn reconstructive and plastic surgery, co-dir. hand surgery svc. Shriners Burns Inst., Cin., 1983—; dir. div. plastic, reconstructive and hand surgery and plastic surgery clinic Childrens Hosp. Med. Ctr., Cin., 1983—; assoc. attending staff Good Samaritan Hosp.; courtesy staff Christ Hosp., Jewish Hosp.; numerous presentations in field. Mem. editl. bd. Jour. Plastic and Reconstructive Surgery, 1989—; contbr. numerous articles to med. jours. Capt. M.C., USAF, 1965-70. Rsch. grantee Eli Lilly Co., 1979-91. Fellow ACS; mem. AMA, Am. Assn. Plastic Surgeons, Am. Burn Assn., Am. Cleft Palate Assn., Am. Soc. for Aesthetic Plastic Surgery, Am. Soc. Plastic and Reconstructive Surgeons, Am. Soc. for Surgery of Hand, Acad. Medicine Cin., Assn. Acad. Chairmen in Plastic Surgery, Cin. Surg. Soc., Grad. Surg. Soc. Cin., Greater Cin. Soc. Plastic and Reconstructive Surgeons (pres. 1988-89), Ohio Med. Assn., Ohio Valley Soc. Plaastic and Reconstructive Surgery (pres. 1985-86), Plastic Surgery Rsch. Coun. Home: 2970 Alpine Ter Cincinnati OH 45208-3408 Office: U Cin Coll Medicine Div Pl Reconst Hand Surgery 231 Bethesda Ave Cincinnati OH 45229-2827

NEALE, TRACEY D., news anchor; b. Balboa, Panama, Feb. 16, 1967; d. Larry W. and Ruby S. Neale. Student, Old Dominian U., 1985-87; BS in Journalism, James Madison U., 1989. Reporter, anchor WVEC-TV (ABC), Fort Myers, Fla., 1989-91, WSOC-TV (ABC), Charlotte, N.C., 1991-94; anchor WTTG-TV (FOX), Washington, 1994—. Vol. with handicapped adults and children Muscular Dystrophy Assn., Ft. Myers and Charlotte, 1989-94; vol. United Way Big Bros./Big Sisters, Washington, 1996. Recipient Associated Press Honors for reporting, 1992, Emmy nomination for reporting, 1992, Nat. Unity award for journalism, 1993-94. Mem. Nat. Assn. Black Journalists, U.S. Congress Radio and TV Corr. Avocations: photography/darkroom development, martial arts, windsurfing, snow skiing, cycling. Office: WTTG-TV News Dept 5151 Wisconsin Ave NW Washington DC 20016-4124

NEALON, WILLIAM JOSEPH, JR., federal judge; b. Scranton, Pa., July 31, 1923; s. William Joseph and Ann Cannon (McNally) N.; m. Jean Sullivan, Nov. 15, 1947; children: Ann, Robert, William, John, Jean, Patricia, Kathleen, Terrence, Thomas, Timothy. Student, U. Miami, Fla., 1942-43; B.S. in Econs, Villanova U., 1947; LL.B., Cath. U. Am., 1950; LL.D. (hon.), U. Scranton, 1975. Bar: Pa. 1951. With firm Kennedy, O'Brien & O'Brien (and predecessor), Scranton, 1951-60; mem. Lackawanna County Ct. Common Pleas, 1960-62; U.S. dist. judge Middle Dist. Pa., 1962—, chief judge, 1976-88, sr. status, 1989—; mem. com. on adminstrn. of criminal law Jud. Conf. U.S., 1979—; lectr. bus. law and labor law U. Scranton, 1951-59; mem. jud. council 3d Cir. Ct. Appeals, 1984—; dist. judge rep. from 3d Cir.

Jud. Conf. of U.S., 1987—. Mem. Scranton Registration Commn., 1953-55; hearing examiner Pa. Liquor Control Bd., 1955-59; campaign dir. Lackawanna County chpt. Nat. Found., 1961-63; mem. Scranton-Lackawanna Health and Welfare Authority, 1963—; assoc. bd. Marywood Coll., Scranton; pres. bd. dirs. Cath. Youth Center; pres. Father's Club Scranton Prep. Sch., 1966; chmn. bd. dirs. Mercy Hosp., 1991—; chmn. bd. trustees U. Scranton; vice chmn. bd. trustees Lackawanna Jr. Coll., Scranton; bd. dirs. St. Joseph's Children's and Maternity Hosp., 1963-66, Lackawanna County unit Am. Cancer Soc., Lackawanna County Heart Assn., Lackawanna County chpt. Pa. Assn. Retarded Children, Scranton chpt. ARC, Lackawanna United Fund, Mercy Hosp., Scranton, 1975—; trustee St. Michael's Sch. Boys, Hoban Heights; adv. com. Hosp. Service Assn. Northeastern Pa. Served to 1st lt. USMCR, 1942-45. Recipient Americanism award Amos Lodge B'nai B'rith, 1975; Cyrano award U. Scranton Grad. Sch., 1977; Disting. Service award Pa. Trial Lawyers Assn., 1979; named one of 50 Disting. Pennsylvanians Greater Phila. C. of C., 1980, Outstanding Fed. Trial Judge Assn. Trial Lawyers Am., 1983. Mem. Pa. Bar Assn., Lackawanna County Bar Assn. (Chief Justice Michael J. Eagen award 1987), Friendly Sons St. Patrick (pres. Lackawanna County 1963-64), Pi Sigma Alpha. Club: Scranton Country (Clarks Summit, Pa.) (bd. dirs.). Lodge: K.C. Office: US Courthouse PO Box 1146 Scranton PA 18501-1146

NEAL-PARKER, SHIRLEY ANITA, obstetrician and gynecologist; b. Washington, Aug. 28, 1949; d. Leon Walker and Pearl Anita (Shelton) Neal; m. Andre Cowan Dasent, June 21, 1971 (div. Feb. 1978); 1 child, Erika Michelle Dasent; m. James Carl Parker, Feb. 11, 1979; 1 child, Amirah Nabeehah. BS in Biology, Am. U., 1971; MD, Hahnemann U., 1979. Med. lic. Md., W.Va., Calif., Wash. Intern Howard U. Hosp., 1979-80, resident, 1980-84; physician Nat. Health Svc. Corp., Charleston, W. Va., 1984-86; clin. instr. W. Va. U., Charleston, 1985-86; pvt. practice ob./gyn. Sacramento, 1986-95; pvt. practice Chehalis, Wash., 1995—. Mem. bd. Ruth Rosenberg Dance Ensemble, Sacramento, 1992-95, S.W. Washington Ballet Ctr., 1995—, Human Response Network, Chehalis, 1995-97. Mem. Am. Assn. Gynecologic Laparoscopists, Am. Productive Health Profls., Nat. Med. Assn., Am. Med. Women's Assn. (comty. svc. award Mother Hale br. 1994), Nat. Assn. Gynecol. Laparoscopists, Nat. Assn. Reproductive Profls., Wash. State Med. Assn., Lewis County Med. Soc., Soroptomist Internat. Avocations: traveling, reading, crocheting, collecting ethnic dolls, magnets. Home: 221 Vista Rd Chehalis WA 98532-8766 Office: 171 S Market Blvd Chehalis WA 98532-3037

NEAL-VITTIGLIO, CYNTHIA KAREN, clinical psychologist; b. Detroit, Dec. 30, 1952; d. Gaston O. and Evelyn Jewel (Dunn) N.; m. Thomas Anthony Vittiglio, July 10, 1988; 1 child, Anthony. BA, Wayne State U., 1975, MA, 1977, PhD, 1983. Licensed psychologist. Clin. researcher Sinai Hosp., Detroit, 1977-78; clin. asst. Dept. Neuropsychology Lafayette Clinic, 1974-75; faculty mem. Inst. for Sex Rsch., Bloomington, Ind., 1975, 80; sch. psychologist Lakeshore Pub. Schs., St. Clair Shores, Mich., 1979-80; staff psychologist Evergreen Counseling Ctr., St. Clair Shores, 1979—; consulting psychologist St. John Hosp., Detroit, 1983—. Mem. Jr. Coun., Founders Soc., Detroit, 1985—, Cranbrook Women's Soc., Bloomfield Hills, Mich., 1987—, Am. Ballet Soc., N.Y.C., 1980—. Recipient Grad. Fellowship Wayne State U., 1988. Mem. APA, DAR (Louise St. Clair chpt.). Republican. Avocations: exercise, boating, downhill skiing. Office: Evergreen Counseling Svcs 19900 E 10 Mile Rd Saint Clair Shores MI 48080-4412

NEAME, RONALD, director, producer; b. Hendon, Middlesex, Eng., Apr. 23, 1911; s. Stuart Elwin and Ivy Lillian (Close) N.; m. Beryl Yolanda Heanly, Oct. 15, 1933; 1 son, Christopher Elwyn; m. Dona Friedberg, Sept. 12, 1993. Student pvt. schs., London and Sussex, Eng. Asst. cameraman Brit. Internat. Pictures, Estree, Eng., 1928-35; chief cameraman Brit. Internat. Pictures, 1935-45. Dir.: photography, prodn. supr. various films, including In Which We Serve, 1942, This Happy Breed, 1943, Blithe Spirit, 1944; co-writer, producer: films Brief Encounter, 1945, Great Expectations, 1946; producer: film Oliver Twist, 1947; dir.: films Take My Life, 1948, Golden Salamander, 1949, The Promoter, 1952, Man with a Million, 1953, The Man Who Never Was, 1954, Windom's Way, 1957, The Horse's Mouth, 1958, Tunes of Glory, 1960, I Could Go On Singing, 1962, The Chalk Garden, 1963, Mr. Moses, 1964, Gambit, 1966, The Prime of Miss Jean Brodie, 1968, Scrooge, 1970, The Poseidon Adventure, 1972, The Odessa File, 1974, Meteor, 1978, Hopscotch, 1979, First Monday in October, 1980-81, Foreign Body, 1985, The Magic Baloon, 1989; co-founder film co. Cineguild Co., Denham, Eng., 1943-44. Mem. Dirs. Guild Am., Am. Film Inst., Acad. Motion Picture Arts and Scis. (gov. 1977-79), Brit. Acad. Film and TV Arts (London and Los Angeles), Savile Club (London). *When I am asked which film I consider to be my best, I reply, "I haven't made it yet. Perhaps next time."*

NEARINE, ROBERT JAMES, educational psychologist; b. Fitchburg, Mass., May 15, 1930; s. Raymond Johns and Beatrice Aileen (Strickland) N.; children: Luke, Martha, Amy. BS, Fitchburg State Coll., 1951; EdM, Tufts Coll., 1952; cert. advanced grad. specialization, Boston U., 1961; MA, U. Conn., 1965, profl. diploma, 1996; EdD, Boston U., 1972. Tchr. pub. schs., Holbrook, Mass., 1952-54, Groton, Mass., 1954-55, Winchester, Mass., 1955-59; supr. pub. schs., Inverness, Mont., 1959-60; guidance counselor pub. schs., Manchester, Conn., 1961-66, supr. of evaluation, 1966-73, adminstr. for funding and evaluation, 1973-76; spl. asst. for funding pub. schs., Hartford, Conn., 1976-78; spl. asst. for evaluation rsch. and testing Bd. Edn., Hartford, 1978-93; ednl. cons. Glastonbury, Conn., 1993—; mem. practitioners com. Chpt. I, Com. of N. Sch. Dist. Reporting, State of Conn., 1988-92, mem. requirements adv. com., 1991-92. Contbr. articles to profl. jours. Col., USAR, 1947-86. NDEA fellow Boston U., 1960-61, GE fellow Syracuse U., 1971, Ednl. Policy Inst. fellow for ednl. leadership, 1979-80. Mem. APA, Am. Evaluation Assn., Res. Officers Assn. (nat. councilman 1994—), Gov.'s Foot Guard, Phi Delta Kappa. Avocations: military history, travel.

NEARY, PATRICIA ELINOR, ballet director; b. Miami, Fla.; d. James Elliott and Elinor (Mitsitz) N. Corps de ballet Nat. Ballet of Can., Toronto, Ont., 1957-60; prin. dancer N.Y.C. Ballet, 1960-68; ballerina Geneva Ballet (Switzerland), 1968-70, ballet dir., 1973-78; guest artist Stuttgart Ballet, Germany, 1968-70; asst. ballet dir., ballerina West Berlin Ballet, 1970-73; ballet dir. Zurich Ballet (Switzerland), 1978-86, La Scala di Milano ballet co., Italy, 1986-88; tchr., Balanchine ballets, Balanchine Trust, 1987—.

NEAS, JOHN THEODORE, petroleum company executive; b. Tulsa, May 1, 1940; s. George and Lillian J. (Kaspar) N.; BS, Okla. State U., 1967, MS, 1968; m. Sally Jane McPherson, June 10, 1966; children: Stephen, Gregory, Matthew. CPA, Okla. With acctg. dept. Rockwell Internat., 1965; with controller's dept. Amoco Prodn. Co., 1966-67; mem. audit and tax staff Deloitte, Haskins & Sells, 1968-75; pres. Nat. Petroleum Sales, Inc., Tulsa, 1975—, John Neas Tank Lines, Inc., 1986—; pres. McPherson Fuels & Asphalts, Inc., 1981-88, sec., 1989—; mem. NPS/Hallmark LLC, 1994—; mem. Bailey Ranch Estates LLC, 1994—; asst. instr. U. Tulsa, 1974; former mem., bd. dirs. Waterways Bd. Okla. Dept. Transp., 1989-96. Mem. AICPA, Inst. Mgmt. Accts. (v.p. membership 1976-77), Okla. Soc. CPAs, McClellan-Kerr Arkansas River Navigation System Hist. Soc., Okla. Heritage Assn., Okla. State U. Pres.'s Club, Okla. State U. Coll. Bus. Adminstrn. Assocs. (v.p. memberships 1989-91, Hall of Fame 1991, Acctg. Dept. Hall of Fame, 1993), Oaks Country Club, The Golf Club Okla. Republican. Lutheran. Home: 2943 E 69th St Tulsa OK 74136-4541 Office: Nat Petroleum Sales Inc 5401 S Harvard Ave Ste 200 Tulsa OK 74135-3861

NEASE, STEPHEN WESLEY, college president; b. Everett, Mass., Jan. 15, 1925; s. Floyd William and Madeline Anzelette (Nostrand) N.; m. Dorothy Christine Hardy, June 17, 1946; children: Linda Carol Nease Scott, Floyd William II, Stephen Wesley Jr., David Wayne, Melissa Jo Nease Wallace. A.B., Brown U., 1946; Th.B., Eastern Nazarene Coll., 1947, D.D., 1966; Ed.M., Boston U., 1956; postgrad., Harvard Div. Sch., 1946-48. Ordained to ministry Ch. of the Nazarene, 1951; pastor East Side Ch. of the Nazarene, Newark, Ohio, 1948-50; dean men, instr. religion Ea. Nazarene Coll., Wollaston, Mass., 1950-53, dir. devel., 1953-66, pres. emeritus; founding pres. Mt. Vernon (Ohio) Nazarene Coll., 1966-72, pres. emeritus; pres. Bethany (Okla.) Nazarene Coll., 1973-76, Nazarene Theol. Sem., Kansas City, Mo., 1976-80, Eastern Nazarene Coll., Wollaston, Mass., 1981-89; edn. commr. Ch. of the Nazarene, 1989-94; exec. dir. Capital and Endowment Devel., Mt. Vernon, Ohio, 1994—. Served with USNR, 1943-46. Office: Capital and Endowment Devel 17012 Glen Rd Mount Vernon OH 43050-9501

NEAVOLL, GEORGE FRANKLIN, newspaper editor; b. Lebanon, Oreg., Aug. 20, 1938; s. Jesse Hunter and Mazie Maude (Meyer) N.; m. Laney Lila Hunter Hough, June 21, 1969. BS, U. Oreg., 1965. Reporter, photographer Lebanon Express, 1969-70; state editor Idaho State Jour., Pocatello, 1970-72; editorial writer The Jour.-Gazette, Ft. Wayne, Ind., 1972-75, Detroit Free Press, 1975-78; editorial page editor The Wichita (Kans.) Eagle, 1978-91, Portland (Maine) Press Herald, Maine Sunday Telegram, 1991—. Vol. Peace Corps, India, 1967-69; bd. councilors Save-the-Redwoods League, 1980—. Recipient Edward J. Meeman award Scripps-Howard Found., 1973, Honor Roll award, Izaak Walton League Am., 1974, Global Media award, The Population Inst.,1996; named Hon. Pk. Ranger, Nat. Pk. Svc., 1988. Mem. Inter Am. Press Assn. (bd. dirs. 1985—, Jamaica Daily Gleaner award 1985), Am. Soc. Newspaper Editors, Nat. Conf. Editorial Writers, Soc. Profl. Journalists, Nat. Press Club, Cumberland Club. Home: 410 Chandler's Wharf Portland ME 04101-4653 Office: The Portland Newspapers 390 Congress St Portland ME 04101-3514

NEBEKER, FRANK QUILL, federal judge; b. Salt Lake City, Apr. 23, 1930; s. J. Quill and Minnie (Holmgren) N.; m. Louana M. Visintainer, July 11, 1953; children: Caramaria, Melia, William Mark. Student, Weber Coll., 1948-50; B.S. in Polit. Sci, U. Utah, 1953; J.D., Am. U., 1955. Bar: D.C. 1956. Corr. sec. The White House, 1953-56; trial atty. Internal Security div. Justice Dept., Washington, 1956-58; asst. U.S. atty., 1958-69; assoc. judge D.C. Ct. Appeals, 1969-87; dir. Office Govt. Ethics, Washington, 1987-89; chief judge U.S. Ct. of Vets. Appeals, Washington, 1989—; cons. Nat. Commn. on Reform of Fed. Criminal Laws, 1967-68; adj. prof. Am. U. Washington Coll. Law, 1967-85. Mem. Am., D.C. Bar Assn., Am. Law Inst. Office: US Court of Veterans Appeals 625 Indiana Ave NW Ste 900 Washington DC 20004-2901

NEBEL, HENRY MARTIN, JR., literature historian, educator; b. N.Y.C., Sept. 29, 1921; s. Henry Martin and Margaret (Naumann) N.; m. Sylvia Sue Fuller, July 13, 1967; children—Althea, Keith, Grant, Blake. B.A., Columbia U., 1943, M.A., 1950, Ph.D., 1960. Researcher analyst Nat. Security Agy., Arlington, Va., 1949-50, U.S. Mcht. Marine Acad., Kings Point, N.Y., 1955-56, Duke U., Durham, N.C., 1956-57; mem. faculty Northwestern U., Evanston, Ill., 1957—, prof. Russian lit., 1960-86, prof. emeritus, 1986—. Author: N.M. Karamzin, A Russian Sentimentalist, 1966, Selected Prose of N.M. Karamzin, 1967, Selected Aesthetic Works of Sumarokov and Karamzin, 1981, others; author articles and translations of Russian topics; editor, contbg. editor various jours. Served with USAF, 1943-45. Mem. Am. Assn. Tchrs. Slavic and East European Langs., Soc. for Eighteenth-Century Lit., AAUP.

NEBELKOPF, ETHAN, psychologist; b. N.Y.C., June 13, 1946; s. Jacob and Fannie (Carver) N.; m. Karen Horrocks, July 27, 1976; children: Demian David, Sarah Dawn. BA, CCNY, 1966; MA, U. Mich., 1969; PhD, Summit U., 1989. Social worker Project Headstart, N.Y.C., 1965; coord. Project Outreach, Ann Arbor, 1968-69; program dir. White Bird Clinic, Eugene, Oreg., 1971-75; counseling supr. Teledyne Econ. Devel. Corp., San Diego, 1976-79; dir. planning and edn. Walden House, San Francisco, 1979-89, dir. tng., 1990-93; program evaluator United Indian Nations, Oakland, Calif., 1994-96; clin. dir. Indian Health Ctr. Santa Clara Valley, San Jose, Calif., 1997—; adj. prof. dept. social work San Francisco State U., 1982-87; cons. Berkeley (Calif.) Holistic Health Ctr., 1979-84, Medicine Wheel Healing Co-op, San Diego, 1976-79; alternate del. Nat. Free Clinic Coun., Eugene, 1972-74. Author: White Bird Flies to Phoenix, 1973, The New Herbalism, 1980, The Herbal Connection, 1981, Hope Not Dope, 1990. Mem. Mayor's Task Force on Drugs, San Francisco, 1988; mem. treatment com. Gov.'s Policy Coun. on Drugs, Sacramento, 1989; task force Human Svcs. Tng., Salem, Oreg., 1972; organizer West Eugene Bozo Assn., 1973; founder Green Psychology, 1993. Named Outstanding Young Man of Am., U.S. Jaycees, 1980; recipient Silver Key, House Plan Assn., 1966. Fellow Am. Orthopsychiat. Assn.; mem. Calif. Assn. Family Therapists, World Fedn. of Therapeutic Communities, Nat. Writer's Club, N.Y. Acad. Scis., Internat. Assn. for Human Rels. Lab. Tng., Calif. Assn. of Drug Programs and Profls. (pres. 1988-90), Phi Beta Kappa. Avocations: herbs, rocks, cactus, yoga, baseball cards. Office: 6641 Simson St Oakland CA 94605-2220

NEBENZAHL, KENNETH, rare book and map dealer, author; b. Far Rockaway, N.Y., Sept. 16, 1927; s. Meyer and Ethel (Levin) N.; m. Jocelyn Hart Spitz, Feb. 7, 1953; children: Kenneth (dec.), Patricia Suzanne Nebenzahl Frish, Margaret Spitz Nebenzahl Quintong, Suzanne Spitz Nebenzahl Nichol. Student, Columbia U., 1947-48; L.H.D. (hon.), Coll. William and Mary, 1983. Solicitor new bus. United Factors Corp., N.Y.C., 1947-50; sales rep. Fromm & Sichel, Inc., N.Y.C., 1950-52; v.p. Cricketeer, Inc., Chgo., 1953-58; pres. Kenneth Nebenzahl, Inc., Chgo., 1957—; bd. dirs. Imago Mundi, Ltd., London, 1976—; cons. Rand McNally and Co., 1966—. Author: Atlas of the American Revolution, 1974, Bibliography of Printed Battle Plans of the American Revolution, 1975, Maps of the Holy Land, 1986, Atlas of Columbus and the Great Discoveries, 1990, also edits. in Spanish, German, Italian, Portugese and French langs.; contbr. articles to profl. jours. and monographs. Trustee Glencoe Pub. Libr., 1963-69, pres., 1966-69; bd. dirs. North Suburban Libr. System, 1966-69, Beverly Farm Found., Godfrey, Ill., 1961-67, Nature Conservancy of Ill., 1980-88; trustee Adler Planetarium, 1969—, chmn., 1977-81; mem. exec. com. Northwestern U. Libr. Coun., 1973-75; sponsor Kenneth Nebenzahl Jr. lectures history cartography Newberry Libr., Chgo., 1965—; mem. assoc. coun. John Crear Libr., Chgo., 1972—, trustee, 1976-84; trustee U. Chgo., 1982—, mem. vis. com. to libr., 1978—, chmn., 1987-95; co-chair Phillips Soc.-Libr. of Congress, Washington, 1995—; bd. dirs. Evanston Hosp. Corp., 1978-85, Am. Himalayan Found., 1994—; mem. U.S. nat. adv. coun. World Wildlife Fund, 1993—. With USMCR, 1945-46. Recipient IMCoS-Tooley award (London), 1984. Fellow Royal Geog. Soc., Am. Geog. Soc.; mem. Manuscript Soc. (dir. 1965-71), Am. Library Trustees Assn. (nat. chmn. com. intellectual freedom 1967-68), Bibliog. Soc. Am., Newberry Library Assocs. (bd. govs. 1965-78, chmn. 1976-78), Newberry Library (trustee 1978—, vice chmn. 1994—), Antiquarian Booksellers Assn. Am. (bd. govs. 1965-67, v.p. 1975-77), Am. Antiquarian Soc. (gov. 1981-85), Soc. History Discoveries (dir. 1974-76), Chgo. Map Soc. (dir. 1976-86), Ill. Ctr. for the Book (pres. 1986-88). Clubs: Caxton (Chgo.) (bd. govs. 1961-68, 74-80, pres. 1964-66), Wayfarers (Chgo.) (pres. 1979-80); Lake Shore Country (Glencoe); Century (N.Y.C.), Grolier (N.Y.C.). Office: PO Box 370 Glencoe IL 60022-0370

NEBENZAHL, PAUL, broadcast executive; b. Chgo., Nov. 1, 1954; s. Irving Arthur and Norma (Waggett) N.; m. Christina Marie Senese, Sept. 17, 1982; children: Ian, Aria. B of Philosophy, Thomas Jefferson Coll., 1979. Dir. Channing-Murray Found., Urbana, Ill., 1981-82; dir. devel. The Peace Mus., Chgo., 1982-83, The Acad. - Art, Music, Dance, Theatre, Chgo., 1983-84; co-dir. Chgo. Filmmakers Inc., Chgo., 1984-85; asst. dir. Gateway Found. Inc., Chgo., 1985-87; dir. corp./found. rels Field Mus. Nat. History, Chgo., 1987-89; asst. exec. dir. Boys and Girls Clubs of Chgo., 1989-90; assoc. dir. WTTW/Chgo., 1990-91, dir. devel., 1991-92, v.p. devel., 1992—; bd. com. Donors Forum Chgo., 1991-92. Composer, performer with Joseph Jarman, Leroy Jenkins, Carei Thomas, Big Walter Horton, Homesick James, Fred Simon, Ella Jenkins, Corky Siegal; composer soundtrack Chicago Matters, Dread (nomination Emmy), A Man and His School, 1994; composer, recorder (soundtrack) Journey of Rememberance, 1996. Bd. dirs. Circle Pines Ctr., Delton, Mich., 1987-90, chair 60th Anniversary Celebration com., 1996—; bd. dirs. Joseph Holmes Dance Theatre, Chgo., 1990-91; mem. fundraising com. Greater Chgo. Food Depository, 1990; mem. com. bd. Issues Com. Donors Forum, Chgo., 1993—, Arts and Bus. Coun., 1993—. Mem. Nat. Soc. Fund Raising Execs. (mem. Chgo. chpt. ethics com./membership com. 1990-92, long range planning com., co-chair support com. 1993—, faculty 1st course in fundraising 1993, faculty midwestern conf. 1996), 410 Club. Avocation: musician. Home: 550 Barton Ave Evanston IL 60202-2109 Office: WTTW/Chgo 5400 N Saint Louis Ave Chicago IL 60625-4623

NEBERGALL, DONALD CHARLES, investment consultant; b. Davenport, Iowa, Aug. 12, 1928; s. Ellis W. and Hilda (Bruhn) N.; m. Shirley Elaine Williams, Apr. 12, 1952; children: Robert W., Nancy L. Nebergall Bosma. BS, Iowa State U., 1951. With Poweshiek County Nat. Bank, 1958-72, sr. v.p., to 1972; founding pres., CEO Brenton Bank and Trust Co., Cedar Rapids, Iowa, 1972-82, chmn. bd., 1982-86; v.p. Chapman Co., 1986-88; bd. dirs. Telephone & Data Systems, Inc.; bd. dirs. Guaranty Bank and Trust, Barlow Investment Co.; former vice chmn. bd. Iowa Transfer Svc. V.p., bd. dirs. Iowa 4-H Found., 1972-76; div. campaign chmn. United Way; former bd. dirs., past pres. Methwick Retirement Community; founding trustee Cedar Rapids Community Sch. Dist. Found.; past pres. Cedar Rapids Greater Downtown Assn. With AUS, 1946-48. Recipient Ptnr. in 4-H award Iowa 4-H, 1983, charter 4-H Found. Ct. of Honor, 1989. Mem. Rotary, Alpha Zeta, Gamma Sigma Delta, Delta Upsilon. Republican. Methodist. Office: 2919 Applewood Pl NE Cedar Rapids IA 52402-3323

NEBERGALL, ROBERT WILLIAM, orthopedic surgeon, educator; b. Des Moines, Dec. 31, 1954; s. Donald Charles and Shirley (Williams) N.; children: Nathaniel Robert Baird, Bartholomew William Campbell. BS in Biology, Luther Coll., 1977; DO, U. Osteo. Health Scis., 1981. Intern Des Moines Gen. Hosp., 1981-82; resident orthopedic surgery Tulsa Regional Med. Ctr., 1982-86; trauma fellow Assn. Osteosynthesis/Assn. Study of Internal Fixation Fellowship Program, Stuttgart and Mainz, West Germany, 1986; sports medicine fellow U. Oreg. Orthopedic and Fracture Clinic, Eugene, 1986; orthopedic surgeon Tulsa Orthopedic Surgeons, 1987—; team physician Tulsa Ballet Theatre, 1987—, Internat. Pro Rodeo Assn., Oklahoma City, 1987-96, Nathan Hale H.S. Football, 1992—, Ctrl. H.S., 1993—, Tulsa Roughnecks Soccer, 1993-96, Okla. All State Games, 1994—; clin. asst. prof. surgery Okla. State U. Coll. Osteo. Medicine; chmn. dept. orthopedic surgery Columbia Tulsa Regional Med. Ctr., 1994—; exec. med. com. Columbia Surg. Care Tulsa, 1996—; clin. asst. prof. surgery Kirksville Coll. Osteo. Medicine; mem. pro tempore Okla. Bd. Osteo. Examiners. Contbr. chpt. to Epidemiology of Sports Injuries. Mem. Okla. Found. for Peer Rev., Oklahoma City, 1988—; past pres. Culver (Ind.) Summer Sch. Alumni Assn., 1991; trustee Culver Ednl. Found. of Culver Mil. Acad., 1991-93. Recipient Vol. award Tulsa Ballet Theatre, 1990, Physicians Recognition award AMA, 1990; named Outstanding Young Man in Am., U.S. Jaycees, 1983. Mem. Am. Osteo. Acad. Orthopedics, Am. Coll. Sports Medicine, Am. Osteo. Orthopedic Soc. Sports Medicine (past pres.), N.Y. Acad. Scis., Assn. Osteosynthesis Fellowship Alumni Orgn., Green Country Ind. Practice Assn. (pres. 1994—), Tulsa Orthop. Soc., Sigma Sigma Phi. Methodist. Avocations: strength tng., bicycling, hunting. Office: Tulsa Orthopedic Surgeons 2116 S Detroit Ave Tulsa OK 74114-1208

NEBERT, DANIEL WALTER, molecular geneticist, research administrator; b. Portland, Oreg., Sept. 26, 1938; s. Walter Francis Nebert and Marie Sophie (Schick) Kirk; m. Myrna Sisk, Mar. 12, 1960 (div. 1975); children: Douglas Daniel, Dietrich Andrew; m. Kathleen Dixon, Aug. 15, 1981; children: Rosemarie Dixon, Rebecca Frances, David Porter, Lucas Daniel. BA, Wesleyan U., 1959; BS and MS in Biochemistry, U. Oreg., MD, 1964. Lic. physician, Calif., Ohio; bd. qualified in pediats. and human genetics; Am. Bd. Pediat. and Human Genetics. Pediat. intern UCLA Hosps., 1964-65, resident in pediat., 1965-66; postdoctoral fellow Nat. Cancer Inst., NIH, Bethesda, Md., 1966-68; sr. investigator Nat. Inst. Child Health and Human Devel., Bethesda, 1968-71, sect. head, 1971-74, lab. chief, 1974-89; prof. dept. environ. health U. Cin. Med. Ctr., 1989—, prof. dept. pediatrics, 1991—; dir. Ctr. Environ. Genetics, 1992—; mem. faculty bd. cert. in human genetics NIH, 1981-89; coord. med. genetics program U.S.-China Coop. Med. Health Protocol, 1982-89; Pfizer lectr. U. Vt., Burlington, 1978, Stanford U., 1979; Wellcome vis. prof. biochemistry and molecular biology U. S.D., Vermillion, 1991; assoc. dir. physician scientist tng. program MD/PhD, U. Cin. Med. Ctr., 1994—; joint nomenclature com. Internat. Union Pure and Molecular Biology, Marseilles, France, 1995—. Mem. editl. bd.: Archives Biochemistry and Biophysics, 1973-76, Archieves Internationales de Pharmacodynamie et de Therapie, 1975-81, Jour. Environ. Scis. and Health, 1976-81, Teratogenesis, Carcinogenesis and Mutagenesis, 1980-86, Anticancer Research, 1981-83, Chemico-Biol. Interactions, 1977-83, Molecular Pharmacology and Therapeutics, 1979-87, Biochem. Pharmacology, 1972—, Jour. Exptl. Pathology, 1986-94, DNA and Cell Biology, 1986—, Molecular Endocrinology, 1988-91, Endocrinology, 1989—, Pharmacogenetics, 1991—, N.Am. Assoc. Ed. for Biochem. Pharmacology, 1994—, assoc. editor DNA Cell Biology, 1994—; contbr. more than 420 articles to profl. jours. Capt. USPHS, 1966-89. Recipient Meritorious Svc. medal USPHS, 1978, Frank Ayrey fellow award in clin. pharmacology, U.K., 1984, Bernard B. Brodie award, 1986, Ernst A. Sommer Meml. award, 1988; GM scholar, 1956-59, Lawrence Selling scholar, 1961, 63. Fellow AAAS; mem. Am. Soc. Pharmacology and Exptl. Therapeutics, Am. Soc. Biochemistry and Molecular Biology, Am. Soc. Clin. Investigation, Soc. Pediatric Rsch., Am. Soc. Microbiology, Genetics Soc. Am., Endocrine Soc., Soc. Toxicology, Sigma Xi. Republican. Unitarian. Avocations: gardening, golf, piano, skiing, squash, art. Home: 65 Oliver Rd Cincinnati OH 45215-2630 Office: U Cin Med Ctr Dept Environ Health PO Box 670056 Cincinnati OH 45267-0056

NEBGEN, STEPHEN WADE, stage producer; b. Austin, Tex., Dec. 13, 1955; s. Andrew Paul and Jane (Wade) N.; m. Jill Annette Alpert, June 28, 1991; children: Austin Wade, Lindsay Emily. BA summa cum laude, Fordham U., 1996. Artistic dir. Quicksilver Co., Phoenix, 1977-84; founder, artistic dir. Astoria Arts Ctr., N.Y.C., 1984-88; producer, gen. mgr. Fortune & Men's Eyes, N.Y.C., 1987-88; gen. mgr. The Lamb's Theatre Co., N.Y.C., 1988-89; co. mgr. Lettic & Lovage, N.Y.C., 1989-90; pub. rels./mktg. cons. Strategic Mktg./Atlas Pub., N.Y.C., 1990-91; producer, gen. mgr. Bert Sees the Light, N.Y.C., 1991-92; producer, bookwriter/lyricist The Hunchback of Notre Dame, 1992-94. Contbr. articles to profl. publs. Avocations: golf, tennis. Address: 8035 E Avalon Dr Scottsdale AZ 85251-6610

NEBLETT, CAROL, soprano; b. Modesto, Calif., Feb. 1, 1946; m. Philip R. Akre; 3 children. Studies with, William Vennard, Roger Wagner, Esther Andreas, Ernest St. John Metz, Lotte Lehmann, Pierre Bernac, Rosa Ponselle, George London, Jascha Heifetz. Soloist with Roger Wagner Chorale; performed in U.S. and abroad with various symphonies; debut with Carnegie Hall, 1966, N.Y.C. Opera, 1969, Met. Opera, 1979; sung with maj. opera cos. including Met. Opera, N.Y.C., Lyric Opera Chgo., Balt. Opera, Pitts. Opera, Houston Grand Opera, San Francisco Opera, Boston Opera Co., Milw. Florentine Opera, Washington Opera Soc., Covent Garden, Cologne Opera, Vienna (Austria) Staatsoper, Paris Opera, Teatro Regio, Turin, Italy, Teatro San Carlo, Naples, Italy, Teatro Massimo, Palermo, Italy, Gran Teatro del Liceo, Barcelona, Spain, Kirov Opera Theatre, Leningrad, USSR, Dubrovnik (Yugoslavia) Summer Festival, Salzberg Festival, others; rec. artist RCA, DGG, EMI; appearances with symphony orchs., also solo recitals, (film) La Clemenza di Tito; filmed and recorded live performance with Placido Domingo, La Fanciulla del West; numerous TV appearances. Office: DA CAPO PO Box 180-369 Coronado CA 92178

NECARSULMER, HENRY, investment banker; b. N.Y.C., Mar. 6, 1914; s. Edward and Manuela Fortlouis (Maas) N.; m. Elizabeth Louise Borden, Mar. 21, 1946; children: Susan N. Dallin, John B., Peter B. A.B., Dartmouth Coll., 1934. With Kuhn, Loeb & Co., N.Y.C., 1935-77; gen. partner Kuhn, Loeb & Co., 1956-77, mng. partner, 1969-77; vice chmn. Kuhn, Loeb & Co., Inc., 1977; mng. dir. Lehman Bros. Kuhn Loeb Inc., 1977-81, adv. dir., 1981-84; adv. dir. Shearson Lehman Bros. Inc., 1984-85, mng. dir., 1986-88, adv. dir., 1988-90, cons., 1990-93; cons. Lehman Bros., Inc., 1993-96; dir. Polaroid Corp.; past dir. various corps.;. Mem. Am. Stock Exchange, 1973-78; mem. governing council Securities Industry Assn., 1972-75; mem. State of N.Y. Judiciary Relations Com., Appellate Div., 1st Jud. Dept., 1973-77; Trustee Jewish Child Care Assn. N.Y. Served to capt. AUS, 1942-46. Office: 450 Park Ave Ste 1203 New York NY 10022-2605

NECCO, ALEXANDER DAVID, lawyer, educator; b. Gary, Ind., Jan. 31, 1936; s. Alesandro Necco and Mary Millonovich; m. Caroline Chappel, Apr. 20, 1958 (dec. Mar. 1978); 1 child, Laurie Ann Necco Stansbury; m. Edna Joanne Painter, July 1, 1989. BA in Philosophy, U. Nev., 1958; JD, Oklahoma City U., 1965. Bar: Okla. 1965, U.S. Dist. Ct. (we. dist.) Okla. 1965, U.S. Ct. Appeals (10th cir.) 1987), U.S. Ct. Claims 1989, U.S. Ct. Vets. Appeals 1994. Assoc. Robert Jordan, Oklahoma City, 1965-66, Stuckey & Witcher, Oklahoma City, 1968-69; atty. Okla. Hwy. Dept., Oklahoma City, 1966, Oklahoma City Urban Renewal, 1966-67; ptnr. Stuckey & Necco,

Oklahoma City, 1969-71, Necco & Dyer, Oklahoma City, 1978-82, Dyer, Necco & Byrd, Oklahoma City, 1982-88; pvt. practice Oklahoma City, 1965—; ptnr. Necco & Byrd, Oklahoma City, 1988—; adj. prof. Oklahoma City U. Sch. Bus., 1965—, Webster U., 1995—. Cubmaster Boy Scouts Am., Oklahoma City. With USMC, 1953-82, lt. col. Res. ret. Mem. Assn. Trial Lawyers Assn., Okla. Trial Lawyers Assn., Marine Corps Res. Officers Assn. (pres. Oklahoma City 1984-85), Phi Delta Phi, Sigma Nu. Republican. Roman Catholic. Avocations: golf, swimming, tennis. Office: Necco & Byrd PC 5700 N Portland Ave Ste 121 Oklahoma City OK 73112-1662

NECCO, E(DNA) JOANNE, school psychologist; b. Klamath Falls, Oreg., June 23, 1941; d. Joseph Rogers and Lillian Laura (Owings) Painter; m. Jon F. Puryear, Aug. 25, 1963 (div. Oct. 1987); children: Laura L., Douglas F.; m. A. David Necco, July 1, 1989. BS, Cen. State U., 1978, MEd, 1985; PhD in Applied Behavioral Studies, Okla. State U., 1993. Med.-surg. asst. Oklahoma City Clinic, 1961-68; spl. edn. tchr. Oklahoma City Pub. Schs., 1978-79, Edmond (Okla.) Pub. Schs., 1979-83; co-founder, owner Learning Devel. Clinic, Edmond, 1983-93; asst. prof. profl. tchr. edn. U. Ctrl. Okla., Edmond, 1993—; adj. instr. Ctrl. State U., Edmond, 1989-93, Oklahoma City U., 1991-93; mem. rsch. group Okla. State U., Stillwater, 1991-93; presenter in field. Contbr. articles to profl. jours. Com. mem. Boy Scouts Am., SCUBA Post 604, Oklahoma City, 1981-86; mem. Edmon TAsk Force for Youth, 1983-87, Edmond C. of C., 1984-87; presenter internat. conf. Okla. Ctr. for Neurosci., 1996; evaluator for Even Start Literacy Program, 1994-96, reviewer Okla. Even Start applicants, 1997, presenter internat. conf., Singapore, 1996, Alta., Can., 1996. Mem. ASCD, Nat. Assn. for Sch. Psychologists, Am. Bus Women's Assn., Coun. for Exceptional Children, Learning Disabilities Assn., Am. Assn. for Gifted Underachieving Students, Am. Tchr. Educators, Okla. Learning Disabilities Assn., Okla. Ctr. Neurosci., Okla. Assn. for Counseling and Devel., Okla. Psychol. Soc., Golden Key Nat. Honor Soc., Internat. Soc. for Scientific Study of Subjectivity, Am. Coun. on Rural Spl. Edn., Ctrl State U. (Okla., life), Phi Delta Kappa. Republican. Avocations: scuba diving, underwater photography, water skiing, travel. Home: 17509 Woodsorrel Rd Edmond OK 73003-6951 Office: U Ctrl Okla Coll Edn 100 N University Dr Edmond OK 73034-5207

NECHEMIAS, STEPHEN MURRAY, lawyer; b. St. Louis, July 27, 1944; s. Herbert Bernard and Toby Helen (Wax) N.; m. Marcia Rosentein, June 19, 1966, (div. Dec. 1981); children: Daniel Jay, Scott Michael; m. Linda Adams, Aug. 20, 1983. BS, Ohio State U., 1966; JD, U. Cin., 1969. Bar: Ohio 1969. Ptnr., Taft, Stettinius & Hollister, Cin., 1969— ; adj. prof. law No. Ky. U., Chase Coll. Law. Tax comment author: Couse's Ohio Form Book, 6th edit., 1984. Mem. Ohio State Bar Assn. (chmn. taxation com.), Cin. Bar Assn. (chmn. taxation sect. 1985), Legal Aid Soc. Cin. (pres., trustee). Democrat. Jewish. Home: 777 Cedar Point Dr Cincinnati OH 45230-3755 Office: 1800 Star Bank Ctr 425 Walnut St Cincinnati OH 45202

NECHIN, HERBERT BENJAMIN, lawyer; b. Chgo., Oct. 25, 1935; s. Abraham and Zelda (Benjamin) N.; m. Susan Zimmerman (div.); 1 child, Jill Rebecca; m. Roberta Fishman, Oct. 24, 1976; 1 child, Stefan. BA with distinction, honors in History, Northwestern U., 1956; JD, Harvard U., 1959. Bar: Ill. 1960. From assoc. to ptnr. Brown Fox & Blumberg, Chgo., 1960-75; ptnr. Taussig Wexler & Shaw, Chgo., 1975-79, Fink Coff Stern, Chgo., 1979-81, Holleb & Coff, Chgo., 1981—. Contbr. articles to profl. jours. Pres. Emanuel Congregation, Chgo., 1994—. Staff sgt. USAR, 1960-66. Mem. ABA, Ill. Bar Assn., Chgo. Bar Assn. (chmn. trust law com. 1990-91), Am. Coll. Trust and Estate Counsel, Univ. Club, Cliff Dwellers Club, Phi Beta Kappa. Office: Holleb & Coff 55 E Monroe St Ste 4100 Chicago IL 60603-5803

NECKERMANN, PETER JOSEF, insurance company executive; b. Wuertzburg, Fed. Republic Germany, Oct. 26, 1935; came to U.S., 1977; s. Josef and Annemarie (Brueckner) N.; m. Jutta Voelk, Feb. 10, 1960; children: Susanne, Christian. Grad., J.W. Goethe U., Frankfurt, Fed. Republic Germany, MA, 1962; PhD, Ohio State U., 1990. Pres. Neckermann Versand KGaA, Frankfurt, 1962-77; dir. econ. analysis and systems Nationwide Ins. Cos., Columbus, Ohio, 1977-79, v.p. econ. and investment services, 1979—. CIV. Mem. Columbus Assn. Bus. Economists, Columbus Coun. on World Affairs (bd. dirs.), Rotary Club of Columbus. Avocations: tennis, skiing. Home: 1261 Fountaine Dr Columbus OH 43221-1519 Office: Nationwide Ins Cos 1 Nationwide Plz Columbus OH 43215-2220

NEDELMAN, DOROTHY O'FLAHERTY, primary care nurse; b. N.Y.C., Nov. 9, 1945; d. John Joseph Sr. and Dorothy Mary (Walsh) O'Flaherty; m. Philip B. Nedelman, Aug. 27, 1977; 1 child, Kathryn Hannah. Diploma, St. Elizabeth's Hosp., Boston, 1966; BS, St. Joseph's Coll., North Windham, Maine, 1979. Cert. adult nurse practitioner. DON Franvale Extended Care Facility, Braintree, Mass.; adult nurse practitioner, researcher Braintree Family Physician, Inc. Active Braintree Sch. Com., 1993, vice chair, 1994, chair, 1995; selectman Town of Braintree, 1996—. Mem. ANA (coun. primary health care nurse practitioners), Soc. Tchrs. Family Medicine.

NEDERHOOD, JOEL H., church organization executive, minister, retired; b. Grand Rapids, Mich., Dec. 22, 1930; s. Arthur William and Dena (Homan) N.; m. Mary Lou Nederhood, July 1, 1954; children: Maria, Carol, David. AB, Calvin Coll., 1952; MDiv, Calvin Sem., Grand Rapids, 1957; ThD, Free U. Amsterdam, The Netherlands, 1959. Ordained to ministry Christian Ref. Ch. Broadcast min. Back to God Hour, Christian Ref. Ch., Chgo., 1960-66, dir. Back to God Hour, 1966-81, dir. ministries Back to God Hour, 1981-95; retired, 1995; host Faith 20 TV, 1980-97; vis. prof. Trinity Evang. Div. Sch. Author: God Is Too Much, 1969, The Holy Triangle, 1975, Promises, Promises, Promises, 1980; editor monthly devotional Today, 1965-95. With U.S. Army, 1952-54. Fulbright scholar, 1957. Office: Back to God Hour 6555 W College Dr Palos Heights IL 60463-1770

NEDERLANDER, JAMES LAURENCE, theater owner, producer; b. Detroit, Jan. 23, 1960; s. James Morton and Barbara (Smith) N. Student, Cranbrook Prep, Boston U. Asst. mgr. Pinechob, Clarkston, Mich.; producer Pineknob, N.Y.C.; v.p. Nederlander, N.Y.C. Assoc. producer plays including The Tragedy of Carmen, 1984 (Tony award 1984), Starlight Express, 1989, Cafe Crown, 1989; assoc. producer musicals On Your Toes, 1987, Legs Diamond, 1988, Barry Manilow on Broadway, 1989; producer show Mort Sahl on Broadway, 1988, Kenny Loggins on Broadway, 1988; co-producer Billy Joel at Yankee Stadium, 1990, Harry Connick Jr. on Broadway, 1990, Yanni on Broadway, 1993, Pink Floyd at Yankee Stadium, 1994, Basia on Broadway, 1994, Shari Lewis and Lambchop on Broadway, 1994, Laurie Anderson on Broadway, 1995, How to Succeed.., 1995, A Midsummer Night's Dream, 1996, The King and I, 1996, Ray Davies-20th Century Man, 1996, The Capeman, 1997. Mem. Com. Am. Candlelite Vigil, 1990, Nat. Hyptertension Benefit, N.Y.C., 1988; bd. trustees Entrepid Museum, 1990. Mem. League N.Y. Theatres, Roundabout Theatre Group, City Athletic Club, LaCosta Country Club. *

NEDERLANDER, JAMES MORTON, theater executive; b. Detroit, Mar. 31, 1922; s. David T. and Sarah L. (Applebaum) N.; m. Charlene Saunders, Feb. 12, 1969; children: James Laurence, Sharon, Kristina. Student, Detroit Inst. Tech. Chmn., former pres. Nederlander Orgn., Inc. (formerly Nederlander Producing Co. Am., Inc., N.Y.C., 1966—. Owner and operator of numerous theaters including Palace Theatre, Lunt-Fontanne Theatre, Nederlander Theatre, Brooks Atkinson Theatre, Gershwin Theatre, Neil Simon Theatre, Marquis Theatre, Minskoff Theatre, Richard Rodgers Theatre, N.Y.C., Greek Theatre, Pantages Theatre, Henry Fonda Theatre, L.A., Shubert Theatre, Chgo., Fisher Theatre, Masonic Temple, Detroit, Poplar Creek, Hoffman Estates, Ill., Merriweather Post Pavilion, Columbia, Md., Aldwych Theatre, Adelphi Theatre, Dominion Theatre, London; producer numerous shows for Broadway including She Loves Me, Will Rogers Follies, Me and My Girl, Orpheus Descending, Les Liaisons Dangereuses, Nicholas Nickleby, Annie, La Cage aux Folles, Nine, Applause, Not Now Darling, See Saw, Oliver, Abelard and Heloise, Sherlock Holmes, Treemonisha, Habeus Corpus, Otherwise Engaged, Whose Life is it Anyway?, Betrayal, Woman of the Year, Lena Horne: The Lady and Her Music, The Dresser, Noises Off, Merlin, Night and Day, My Fat Friend, Shirley MacLaine on Broadway, Sweet Charity, Benefactors, Breaking the Code; numerous road show prodns.; revivals: Peter Pan, She Loves Me, Hello Dolly, Porgy and Bess, The Music Man, I Do! I Do!, Oklahoma, On a Clear Day You Can See Forever, Fiddler on the Roof. Office: Nederlander Orgn Inc 810 7th Ave New York NY 10019-5818

NEDERLANDER, ROBERT E., entertainment and television executive, lawyer; b. Detroit, Apr. 10, 1933; s. David T. and Sarah (Applebaum) N.; m. Caren Berman (div.); children: Robert E. Jr., Eric; Gladys Rackmil, Jan. 1, 1988. BA in Econs., U. Mich., 1955, JD, 1958, LLD (hon.), 1990. Ptnr. Nederlander, Dodge & Rollins, Detroit, 1960-90; pres. Nederlander Orgn., Inc., N.Y.C., 1981—, Nederlander TV & Film Prodns., N.Y.C., 1985—; mng. gen. ptnr. N.Y. Yankees, 1990-91. Regent U. Mich., Ann Arbor, 1969-84; trustee Am. Health Found., 1989—; chmn. Gateway Am., 1991—. Recipient Disting. Alumni Svc. award U. Mich., 1985; named Man of Yr. by Gov.'s Com. on Scholastic Achievement, N.Y.C., 1991. Fellow ABA, Mich. Bar Assn. Avocations: tennis, baseball. Office: Nederlander Orgn 810 7th Ave New York NY 10019-5818*

NEDOM, H. ARTHUR, petroleum consultant; b. Lincoln, Nebr., Aug. 19, 1925; s. Henry Arthur and Pearle Bertrick (Swan) N.; m. Patricia Margaret Rankin, July 4, 1974; children: Richard A., Robert L., Nicole C. B.S., U. Tulsa, 1949, M.S., 1950; postgrad. in bus. adminstrn., Northwestern U., Evanston, Ill., 1968. Chief engr. Amerada Petroleum Corp., Tulsa, 1961-65; v.p. Amerada Petroleum Corp., 1965-70, Natomas Co., San Francisco, 1971-74; also dir.; pres. Norwegian Oil Co., Houston, 1974-75; pres., mng. dir. Weeks Petroleum Ltd., Westport, Conn., 1975-82; cons., 1982—; chmn. bd. arbitration Prudhoe Bay Unit, 1983-85; chmn. Offshore Tech. Conf., 1971; bd. dirs. Engrs. Joint Council, 1978. Contbr. articles to profl. jours. Served with inf. U.S. Army, 1943-45, ETO. Decorated Bronze Star; named Disting. Alumnus U. Tulsa, 1972. Mem. Soc. Petroleum Engrs. (dir. 1965-68, pres. 1967, Disting. Lectr. 1973, Disting Svc. award 1978, DeGolyer Disting. Svc. medal 1981, Disting. mem. 1983, Disting. lectr. emeritus 1989, v.p. SPE Found. 1988-89), AIME (dir. 1966-69, 76-79, pres. 1977, hon. mem. 1982, Disting. Svc. award 1993), Am. Assn. Engring. Soc. (dir. 1980-82, chmn. 1981, Spl. award 1979, Engring. Svc. award 1980). Episcopalian. Home: 21 Deerwood Ln Westport CT 06880-2648

NEE, D. Y. BOB, think tank executive, engineering consultant; b. Shanghai, Dec. 13, 1935; came to U.S., 1953; m. Flora Hsu, Sept. 19, 1959; children: Winifred, Vivian, William. BS, Purdue U., 1957; MS, U. Mo., Rolla, 1959. Sr. engr. Westinghouse Electric, Pitts., 1967-83; project mgr. U.S. Govt., San Francisco Bay, 1984-91; founder, pres. Inst. for Sys. Monitor, Tiburon, Calif., 1992—; pres. W.I.S.E., Honolulu, 1995—; sci. and tech. cons. ASTM, 1994. Author: Radicalizing the World Through Social Engineering, 1993. Mem. adv. bd. Reagan for Pres., Washington, 1980. Mem. ASME. Office: Inst for Sys Monitor PO Box 26723 San Francisco CA 94126

NEE, LINDA ELIZABETH, health facility professional; b. Boston, Dec. 29, 1938; d. Thomas Markham and Ellen Thomas (Jamieson) Nee. BA, Russell Sage Coll., 1961; MS in Social Work, Va. Commonwealth U., 1968. Social worker, social svc. dept., N.Y. Neurol. Inst., Columbia Presbyn. Med. Ctr., N.Y.C., 1961-66; med. social worker Tb San., Med. Coll. Va., Richmond, summer 1967; clin. social worker social work dept. Clin. Center, NIH, Bethesda, Md., 1968-74, clin. rsch. social worker sect. exptl. therapeutics, lab. clin. sci., NIMH, Bethesda, 1974-84, clin. genetics rsch. assoc. Nat. Inst. Neurol. Disorders and Stroke, 1984, social sci. analyst, 1984—; mem. ethics com. Md. State Bd. Social Work Examiners, 1979—. Adv., organizer, bd. dirs. Met. D.C. chpt. Alzheimer's and Related Diseases Assn., 1979-88, pres., 1982-86; mem. sci. bd. Familial Alzheimer's Disease Rsch. Found., Tulsa, 1987—; bd. dirs. Friends of Clin. Ctr., Bethesda, 1989—, pres., 1992; trustes The Sage Colls., Troy, N.Y., 1993—. Mem. NASW (chmn. ethics and grievances 1977-79; pres. Met. Washington 1975-77). Editor: Jour. Social Work Met. Washington, 1975-77; columnist: The Bulletin newsletter Nat. Assn. Social Workers, 1975-77; contbr. articles to profl. jours. Office: Clin Ctr NINDS Bethesda MD 20892

NEE, SISTER MARY COLEMAN, college president emeritus; b. Taylor, Pa., Nov. 14, 1917; d. Coleman James and Nora Ann (Hopkins) N. AB, Marywood Coll., 1939, MA, 1943; MS, Notre Dame U., 1959. Joined Order of Sisters, Servants of Immaculate Heart of Mary, 1941; assoc. prof. math. Marywood Coll., Scranton, Pa., 1959-68; pres. Marywood Coll., 1970-88, pres. emerita, 1988—; apostolic coord. Sisters, Servants Immaculate Heart of Mary, Scranton, Pa., 1968-70. Home and Office: Cathedral Convent 333 Wyoming Ave Scranton PA 18503-1223

NEEDELS, CHRISTOPHER JAMES, sports association administrator; b. Martinez, Calif., 1942. BS in Engring., U.S. Mil. Acad.; MS in Ops. Rsch., Navy Postgrad. Sch.; M Mil. Arts and Scis., U.S. Command & Gen. Staff Coll. Commd. 2d lt. U.S. Army, 1965, advanced through grades to col., 1988, dir. internat. programs Nat. Security Coun., ret., 1992; mgmt., pub. rels. and land use cons., 1992—; v.p. Piedmont Environ. Coun.; v.p., chair fin. and budget com. U.S. Parachute Assn., 1974-80, exec. dir., 1980—; sr. fellow Ctr. for Strategic and Internat. Studies Georgetown U. Recipient Silver Star, DFC, Bronze Star, Purple Heart. Mem. Nat. Aero. Assn. (bd. dirs.). Office: US Parachute Assn 1440 Duke St Alexandria VA 22314-3403

NEEDHAM, GEORGE AUSTIN, investment banker; b. Beverly, Mass., Jan. 27, 1943; s. Everett Austin and Edith Strode (Walton) N.; m. Ellen Ann Levin, July 9, 1978; children—Michael Austin, Sarah Elisabeth, Paul Everett. B.S. in Bus. Adminstrn., Bucknell U., 1965; M.B.A., Stanford U., 1971. Portfolio mgr. Bankers Trust Co., N.Y.C., 1967-69; mng. dir. First Boston Corp., N.Y.C., 1971-84; chmn., CEO Needham & Co. Inc., N.Y.C., 1985—. Trustee Stanford Bus. Sch. Trust, Palo Alto, Calif., 1983-89. Served to 1st lt. U.S. Army, 1965-67. Mem. Fin. Analysts Fedn., Bond Club N.Y., The Links, Univ. Club, Sleepy Hollow Country Club, Coral Beach Club. Republican. Home: 79 E 79th St New York NY 10021-0202 Office: Needham & Co Inc 445 Park Ave New York NY 10022-2606

NEEDHAM, GLEN RAY, entology and acarology educator; b. Lamar, Colo., Dec. 25, 1951; s. Robert Lee and Evor Elaine (Kern) N.; m. Karla Marie Lohr, May 28, 1983; children: Kathleen Marie, John Harrison, Elizabeth Anne. BS, S.W. Okla. State U., 1973; MS, Okla. State U., 1975, PhD, 1978. Grad. rsch. asst. Okla. State U., Stillwater, 1974-78; asst. prof. Ohio State U., Columbus, 1978-84, assoc. prof., 1984—, co-organizer and coord. acarology summer program. Co-editor: Africanized Honey Bees and Bee Mites, 1988, Acarology IX: Proceedings and Symposia. Donor ARC, Columbus. Recipient Dist. Alumnus award Okla. State U., 1992. Mem. Acarology Soc. Am. (pres. 1994), Entomol. Soc. Am., Ohio State Beekeepers Assn., Soc. Vector Ecology, Gamma Sigma Delta, Sigma Xi. Methodist. Office: Ohio State U 484 W 12th Ave Columbus OH 43210-1214

NEEDHAM, HAL, director, writer; b. Memphis, Mar. 6, 1931; s. Howard and Edith May (Robinson) N.; m. Dani Janssen, June 28, 1981 (separated); children: Debra Jean, Daniel Albert, David Allyn. Student pub. schs. Founder Stunts Unltd., Los Angeles, 1956; stuntman Stunts Unltd., 1956-68, dir. and stunt coordinator second unit, 1968-76, dir., writer, 1976—; chmn bd. Camera Platforms Internat., Inc., 1986—. Dir., writer films Smokey and The Bandit, 1977, Hooper, 1978, The Villain, 1979, Smokey and The Bandit, II, 1980, The Cannonball Run, 1981, Mega Force, 1982, Stroker Ace, 1983, Cannonball Run Part 2, 1984, Rad, 1986, Body Slam, 1987, TV films Bandit: Beauty and the Bandit, 1994, Bandit Bandit, 1994, Bandit Goes Country, 1994; dir., writer, exec. prodr. Bandit, 1993; dir. pilot TV series Stunts Unltd.; movie of the week Death Car on the Freeway, B.L. Stryker, 1989. Served with Paratroopers U.S. Army, 1951-54. Mem. Screen Actors Guild, Dirs. Guild Am., Writers Guild Am., AFTRA. Owner Budweiser Rocket Car (fastest car in the world) displayed at Smithsonian Inst. Office: c/o Laura Lizer & Assocs 12711 Ventura Blvd Ste 440 Studio City CA 91604-2431 *I feel that if I can become successful with less than ten years of education, anyone in this country is capable of the same goals with positive thinking and total dedication.**

NEEDHAM, JAMES JOSEPH, retired financial services executive; b. Woodhaven, N.Y., Aug. 18, 1926; s. James Joseph and Amelia (Pasta) N.; m. Dolores A. Habick, July 1, 1950 (dec. Feb. 1993); children: James, Robert, Ravenna, Michael, Catherine; m. Patricia Henry Campo, May 24, 1995. Student, Cornell U., 1946; BBA, St. John's U., 1951, LLD (hon.), 1972. CPA, N.Y. Acct. Price Waterhouse & Co., N.Y.C, 1947-54; ptnr. R. T. Hyer & Co., Port Washington, N.Y., 1954-57; ptnr., mem. exec. com. A. M. Pullen & Co., N.Y.C., 1957-69; commr. SEC, Washington, 1969-72; chmn., chief exec. officer N.Y. Stock Exch., 1972-76; v.p. Internat. Fedn. Stock Exchs., 1973-75; pres. Internat. Fedn. Stock Exchanges, 1976-90; councilman Town of Southampton, N.Y., 1986—; Disting. prof., grad. div. Coll. Bus. Adminstrn., St. John's U., Jamaica, N.Y.; U.S. amb. to Japan Expo '85, 1982—; bd. dirs. Mut. of Am. Mut. Funds. Treas. Central Sch. Dist. 4, 1951-52, mem. budget and finance com., 1951, 63, chmn. high sch. planning com., 1947; active local Boy Scouts Am., 1962-65; mem. bishop's com. of laity Catholic Charities, Rockville Center, N.Y., 1960-68; mem. lay adv. bd. Cath. Youth Orgn., 1964-67; bd. advs. Coll. Bus. Adminstrn., St. John's U.; mem. hon. com. Am. Cancer Soc.; N.Y. State co-chmn. fin. Reagan for Pres. Campaign, 1980; Past dir., auditor Plainview (N.Y.) Republican Club.; Bd. govs. Fed. Hall Meml. Assos.; trustee N.Y. Foundling Hosp. Served with USNR, 1944-46. Recipient Disting. Citizen award N.Y. U. Law Sch., Disting. Service award in investment edn. Nat. Assn. Investment Clubs; named Bus. Person of Year Bus. Adminstrn. Soc. St. John's U., 1975; fellow Aspen Inst. for Humanistic Studies. Mem. N.Y. Soc. CPA's (past dir., treas., past pres. Nassau-Suffolk chpt., recognition award), Am. Inst. CPA's (past mem. council), L.I. Assn., N.Y. Chamber Commerce and Industry, Internat. C. of C. (U.S. council), Downtown-Lower Manhattan Assn. (dir., mem. exec. com.), N.Y. Credit and Fin. Mgmt. Assn. (Laurel award), Cath. Accountants Guild (past pres.), Accountants Club Am. Clubs: Serra (Nassau) (past pres.); Cornell of Nassau County, Wheatley Hills Golf (past treas.), Siwanoy Country; Burning Tree. Home: PO Box 1229 Bridgehampton NY 11932-1229

NEEDHAM, JUDY LEN, artist, art educator; b. Big Spring, Tex., Dec. 1, 1941; d. Carl Granvil and Mary Louise (Grilliette) Hill; m. Andrew James Needham III, Jan. 1, 1960; children: Andy, Jack, Johnny, Joshua. Grad. high sch., Tuscola, Tex., 1960. workshop dir., coord. Fine Arts League Coleman (Tex.) County, 1990-96, art exhbn. dir. 1992-96, pres., 1992, 93. Exhibited in group shows Citizens Nat. Bank, Brownwood, Tex., 1992, 1st Coleman (Tex.) Nat. Bank, 1992-95, Coleman County State Bank, 1992-96, Security State Bank, Abilene, Tex., 1995, John Selmon Gallery, Stamford, Tex., 1995, Gage Hotel Emporium, Marathon, Tex., 1994-95, West Tex. Art Gallery, San Angelo, 1994-95, Kendall Art Gallery, San Angelo, 1995, Breckenridge (Tex.) Fine Arts Gallery, 199.4. troop leader Heart of Tex. coun. Girl Scouts Am., Brownwood, 1965-70; den mother, asst. camp dir. Chisholm Tr. coun. Boy Scouts Am., Abilene, 1972-79; pres. Band Boosters Coleman H.S., 1990, 91, 92. Recipient Dist. Award of Merit Boy Scouts Am. Chisholm Trail Coun., 1979, Best of Show Cross Plains (Tex.) Paint and Palett, 1993, Best of Show Coleman County Fine Arts League, 1994, Best of Show Comanche County Art Assn., 1995. Avocations: crochet, photography, reading. Home: 427 Sunrise Ln Coleman TX 76834

NEEDHAM, KATHLEEN ANN, gerontology educator, consultant; b. Saginaw, Mich., Aug. 30, 1944; d. George Whitcomb and Ann (Drensky) N.; m. Kenneth Edward Cassady, June 19, 1982. BA, Olivet (Mich.) Coll., 1967; MA, Mich. State U., 1970, postgrad., 1972-76, 90—; cert., U. Mich., 1977. Cert. tchr., Mich. High sch. tchr. Pontiac (Mich.) schs., 1968-72; grad. asst. Mich. State U., East Lansing, 1972-76; asst. prof., chmn. dept. gerontology Madonna U., Livonia, Mich., 1981-90; mem. faculty Madonna Coll., Livonia, Mich, 1991—; grant project dir. Adminstrn. on Aging, Washington, 1977-83, Mich. Dept. Labor, Lansing, 1985-86; grant project supr. NIMH, Washington, 1981-83; cons. in field. Producer tapes in field. Del. Mich. White House Conf. on Aging, Dearborn, 1981; mem. com. Mich. Office Svcs. to Aging, Lansing, 1983-92; bd. dirs. United Cmty. Svcs., 1985-94, mem. health svcs. com., 1991—; chmn. Mich. Minimum Stds. for Aging, 1987; vol. Focus Hope, Detroit, Mich. Lupus Found.; mem. Mich. Task Force on Older Worker, Lansing, 1987, Mich. Exec. Commn. on Older Learner Summit, 1990-93; chair Mich. Gov.'s Conf. on Aging, 1991; cons. to bd. Mich. Assoc. Svc. Orgns., 1991-93; Mich. regional facilitator and del. White House Conf., 1994; mem. ann. conf. planning com. Mich. Soc. Gerontology, 1994, 95, 96. Recipient Svc. award Internat. Healthcare Assn., 1988, 89, 90. Mem. Gerontol. Soc. Am., Detroit Women's Econ. Club, Mich. Soc. Gerontology (bd. dirs. 1987), Assn. Gerontology in Higher Edn. (membership com. 1982, pub. policy com. 1988, pub. rels. and fund raising 1992, 93), Am. Soc. Aging. Presbyterian. Home: 22760 Clear Lake Dr Farmington MI 48335-3834 Office: Madonna Univ 36600 Schoolcraft Rd Livonia MI 48150-1176

NEEDHAM, LUCIEN ARTHUR, musician, educator; b. Hull, Yorkshire, Eng., Apr. 5, 1929; s. Arthur and A. Nita (Sims) N.; m. Louise Chapman, Aug. 16, 1974 (dec. Oct. 1988). Student, Guildhall Sch. Music, London, 1952-56. Condr. Winnipeg (Man., Can.) Philharm. Choir, 1956-60, Winnipeg Male Voice Choir, 1957-60; vis. instr. voice and theoretical subjects Brandon (Man.) U. Sch. Music, 1959-62, asst. prof. voice, organ and theoretical subjects, 1962-64, asso. prof., 1964-67; founding condr., mus. dir. Western Man. Philharm. Choir, 1965-67; assoc. prof. voice and theoretical subjects U. Lethbridge, Alta., 1967-69, prof. voice and theoretical subjects, 1970-87, chmn. dept. music, 1967-71, condr. U. Lethbridge Choir, 1968-74; condr. Lethbridge Symphony Orch., 1970-76; lectr., speaker, condr. master classes, 1956-87; examiner Western Bd. Music, 1957-87; adjudicator regional, interstate, provincial and local music festivals, scholarship competitions, 1957-87; mem. Alta. Registered Music Tchrs. Assn., 1967-87, pres., 1980-81. Tchr. singing, pianist, accompanist, condr. public concerts and on radio and TV, 1952-87; composer: Christmas Gradual, 1963, The Fields Abroad, 1967; contbr. articles, monographs to music jours. Served with RAF, 1948-50. Fellow Guildhall Sch. Music, 1965; grantee Nuffield Found., 1965; grantee Can. Council, 1966, 71; grantee U. Lethbridge, 1974, 85.

NEEDHAM, MAUREEN, dance educator, writer; b. Washington, June 11, 1938; d. Maurice d'Arlan and Thyria (Hughart) Needham; children: Terri, Jon, Sarah. BA, Harvard U., 1960; MA, U. Ill., 1972; PhD, NYU, 1989. Dancer New Orleans Opera Assn., 1952-56; choreographer, tchr. Harand Theatre Arts, Lake Elkhart, Wis., 1957-59; choreographer Hasty Pudding Theatricals, Cambridge, Mass., 1959; tchr. Jewish Found. Sch., Staten Island, 1961-62, Dwight Sch. for Girls, Englewood, N.J., 1962-63, Tenafly (N.J.) Pub. Schs., 1963-65; dance therapist Adler Zone Ctr., Champaign, Ill., 1971-75; asst. prof. U. Ill., Champaign, 1975-77; assoc. prof. Vanderbilt U., Nashville, 1984—; cons. day care ctrs. for handicapped, Ill., 1974; advisor U.S. Rsch. Internat. Music, 1987—. Editor: Therapy in Motion, 1978; contbr. articles to profl. jours., chpts. to books and encys.; editor Channels newsletter, Am. World Dance Alliance; dance reviewer Champaign-Vebana Courier, 1976-78, Nashville Scene, 1996—. Sen. Vanderbilt Faculty Senate, 1985-89, 96-97; bd. dirs. Nashville City Ballet, 1986-88; active Mayor's Task Force on Arts, Nashville, 1988-90, 94; bd. dirs. Coun. Cmty. Svcs., Nashville, 1995—, Ctr. Health Coalition, Nashville, 1995—; mem. grants allocations com. Metro Arts Coun., 1980, 94; chair faculty adv. coun., Blair Sch. Music, 1991—. Edmund James scholar U. Ill., 1972; Tenn. Endowment for Humanities grantee, 1987; NEH summer rsch. fellow, 1993. Mem. Soc. Dance History Scholars (bd. dirs. 1991-95), World Dance Alliance (North/South Am. rep. 1990—, co-editor calendar 1990-93), Woman's Faculty Orgn. (chair 1991-92, mem. bd. dirs. 1996—). Office: Vanderbilt U Blair Sch Music 3400 Blakemore Ave Nashville TN 37212-3499

NEEDHAM, NANCY JEAN, management consultant; b. Chgo., July 21, 1941; d. Robert Leonard and Grace Irene (Bennett) N.; children: Thomas, Charles, Catharine, Jessica. BA, Wellesley Coll., 1964; MBA, Harvard U., 1972, DBA, 1977. Pubs. specialist MIT, Cambridge, Mass., 1964-65; editor SRA, Chgo., 1966; sr. editor Ency. Britannica, Chgo., 1967; cons. ABT Assocs., Cambridge, 1968; program mgr. Am. Sci. & Engring., Boston, 1969; faculty Harvard Bus. Sch., Cambridge, 1973-75; cons. CRI, Cambridge, 1977-78; prof. mgmt. Poly. U. N.Y., N.Y.C., 1986-96; assoc. dir. Ctr. for Advanced Tech. in Telecommunications, N.Y.C., 1986-96; pres. ICGS Inc., N.Y.C., 1978—. Contbr. articles to profl. jours. Mem. Am. Soc. Macro Engring. (bd. dirs. 1984-92), C.G. Jung Found. (bd. dirs. 1988-94), Phi Beta Kappa. Presbyterian. Home: RR 2 Box 191 B Delhi NY 13753-9643

NEEDHAM, RICHARD LEE, magazine editor; b. Cleve., Jan. 16, 1939; s. Lester Hayes and Helen (Bender) N.; m. Irene Juechter, Aug. 7, 1965; children: Margaret, Richard, Trevor. BA, Denison U., 1961; MA, U. Mo., 1967. Copy editor Sat. Rev., N.Y.C., 1967-68; editor-in-chief Preview Internat., N.Y.C., 1968-69; financial and N.Y. editor Instns. mag.; also editor Service World Internat., N.Y.C., 1969-70; copy dir. American Home mag.,

N.Y.C., 1970-71; exec. editor Ski Mag., N.Y.C., 1971-74, editor, 1974-92, editor-in-chief, 1992-94, sr. contbg. editor, 1994—; contbg. editor Yachting Mag., N.Y.C., 1996; editor Ency. of Skiing, 1978, Ski Fever, 1995; editl. dir. Times Mirror Mags. Conservation, 1994-96; editor-in-chief Inside Tracks, 1996—. Broadcaster: Ski Spot, CBS Radio, N.Y.C., 1978-83, On the Slopes, Audio Features Syndicate, 1984-87; author: Ski--50 Years in North America, 1992, Ski Fever!, 1995. Served to lt. USNR, 1961-65. Recipient Lowell Thomas award, 1985. Mem. N.Am. Ski Journalists Assn., Ea. Ski Writers Assn., Internat. Assn. Ski Journalists, Internat. Motor Press Assn. Home and Office: 115 Old Post Rd Croton On Hudson NY 10520

NEEDLEMAN, ALAN, mechanical engineering educator; b. Phila., Sept. 2, 1944; s. Herman and Hannah (Goodman) N.; m. Wanda Sapolsky, Apr. 12, 1970; children—Deborah, Daniel. B.S., U. Pa., 1966; M.S., Harvard U., 1967, Ph.D., 1970. Instr. applied math. MIT, Cambridge, 1970-72, asst. prof., 1972-75; asst. prof. engrng. Brown U., Providence, 1975-78, assoc. prof., 1978-81, prof., 1981—, dean engrng., 1988-91; Florence Pirce Grant Univ. prof.; vis. asst. prof. Tech. U. Denmark, Lyngby, 1973; vis. fellow Clare Hall, U. Cambridge, Eng., 1978; vis. prof. MIT, Cambridge, 1991. Contbr. articles to profl. jours. Guggenheim fellow, 1977. Fellow ASME, Am. Acad. Mechanics, Danish Ctr. for Applied Math. and Mechanics (fgn.), Groupe Francais de Macanique des Materiaux (hon.). Home: 24 Elton St Providence RI 02906-4106 Office: Brown U Div Engring Providence RI 02912

NEEDLEMAN, HARRY, lawyer; b. N.Y.C., Oct. 13, 1949; s. Jack and Sarah (Friar) N.; m. Roseann Marie Eppolito, Jan. 15, 1971. BA, Bklyn. Coll., 1970; JD, St. John's U., Queens, N.Y., 1975. Bar: N.Y. 1976, U.S. Dist. Ct. (so. dist.) N.Y. 1979, U.S. Supreme Ct. 1980. Staff atty. Merrill Lynch, N.Y.C., 1975-80; gen. counsel Cantor Fitzgerald, L.P., N.Y.C., 1980-93; counsel Furman Selz, N.Y.C., 1995—. Address: 13 Crestview Dr Pleasantville NY 10570-1426

NEEDLEMAN, HERBERT LEROY, psychiatrist, pediatrician; b. Phila., Dec. 13, 1927; s. J. Joseph and Sonia Rita (Shupak) N.; m. Shirley Weinstein, Sept. 12, 1948 (div. 1957); 1 child, Samuel; m. Roberta Pizor, June 2, 1963; children Joshua, Sara. BS, Muhlenberg Coll., Allentown, Pa., 1948; MD, U. Pa., 1952. Intern Phila. Gen. Hosp., 1952-54; resident in pediatrics Children's Hosp. of Phila., 1957-58, chief resident in pediatrics, 1958-59; resident in psychiatry Temple U. Med. Ctr., Phila., 1962-65, asst. prof. psychiatry, 1967-71; spl. fellow in psychiatry NIMH, Bethesda, Md., 1965-67; assoc. prof. psychiatry Harvard Med. Sch., Boston, 1971-81; prof. psychiatry and pediatrics U. Pitts. Sch. Medicine, 1981—; cons. air lead criteria document EPA, Washington, 1977; editor Ctrs. for Disease Control, Atlanta, 1978; mem. adv. com. on childhood lead poisoning prevention, 1990; chmn. devel. toxicology subpanel NAS, 1986. Editor: Low Level Lead Exposure: The Clinical Implications of Current Research, 1980, contbr. articles to profl. jours. Chmn. Com. of Responsibility, Boston, 1966-75, Alliance to End Childhood Lead Poisoning, Washington, 1991-92; bd. dirs. Mass. Advocacy Ctr., Boston, 1972-80. Capt. U.S. Army, 1955-57. Recipient Sarah L. Poiley Meml. award N.Y. Acad. Scis., 1985, The Charles A. Dana award, 1989; NAS IOM, 1990, H. John Heinz award, 1995, Edward Barsby award Physicians' Forum, 1997, Vernon Houk award Soc. Occupl. Environ. Health. Fellow Am. Acad. Pediatrics; mem. Soc. of Toxicology, Am. Pediatric Soc., Am. Acad. of Child and Adolescent Psychiatry, Am. Acad. of Pediatrics Com. on Environ. Hazards, Phi Beta Kappa, Sigma Xi. Democrat. Jewish. Avocations: trout fishing, carpentry. Home: 5734 Aylesboro Ave Pittsburgh PA 15217-1412 Office: Univ Pitts Sch Medicine Bellefield Tower 100 N Bellefield Ave Pittsburgh PA 15213-2600

NEEDLEMAN, JACOB, philosophy educator, writer; b. Phila., Oct. 6, 1934; s. Benjamin and Ida (Seltzer) N.; m. Carla Satzman, Aug. 30, 1959 (div. 1989); children: Raphael, Eve; m. Gail Anderson, Dec. 1990. BA, Harvard U., 1956; grad., U. Freiburg, 1957-58; PhD, Yale U., 1961. Clin. psychology trainee West Haven (Conn.) Veterans Hosp. Adminstrn., 1960-61; rsch. assoc. Rockefeller Inst., N.Y., 1961-62; from asst. prof. to assoc. prof. philosophy San Francisco State U., 1962-66, prof philosophy, 1967—, chair dept. philosophy, 1968-69; vis. scholar Union Theol. Seminary, 1967-68; dir. Ctr. Study New Religions, 1977-83; lectr. psychiatry, cons. med. ethics U. Calif., 1981-84. Author: Being-in-the-World, 1963, The New Religions, 1970, Religion for a New Generation, 1973, A Sense of the Cosmos, 1975, On the Way to Self-Knowledge: Sacred Tradition and Psychotherapy, 1976, Lost Christianity, 1980, Consciousness and Tradition, 1982, The Heart of Philosophy, 1982, Sorcerers, 1986, Sin and Scientism, 1986, Lost Christianity: A Journey of Rediscovery to the Centre of Christian Experience, 1990, Money and the Meaning of Life, 1991, Modern Esoteric Spirituality, 1992, The Way of the Physician, 1993, The Indestructible Question, 1994, A Little Book on Love, 1996; (trans.) The Primary World of Senses, 1963, Essays on Ego Psychology, 1964; editor Care of Patients with Fatal Illness, 1969, The Sword of Gnosis, 1973, Sacred Tradition and Present Need, 1974, Understanding the New Religions, 1978, Speaking of My Life: The Art of Living in the Cultural Revolution, 1979, Real Philosophy: An Anthology of the Universal Search for Meaning, 1991; contbr. Death and Bereavement, 1969, To Live Within, 1971, My Life with a Brahmin Family, 1972, The New Man, 1972, The Universal Meaning of the Kabbalah, 1973, The Phenomenon of Death. Grantee Religion in Higher Edn., 1967-68, Marsden Found., Ella Lyman Cabot Trust, 1969, Marsda Found, Far West Inst., 1975; Fulbright scholar Germany, 1957-58; Fels Found. fellow Munich, 1959; fellow Rockefeller Found. Humanities, 1977-78. Office: San Francisco State U Dept Philosophy 1600 Holloway Ave San Francisco CA 94132-1722

NEEDLEMAN, PHILIP, cardiologist, pharmacologist; b. Bklyn., Feb. 10, 1939. BS, Phila. Coll. Pharm. & Sci., 1960; MS, U. Md. Med. Sch., 1962, PhD in Pharmacology, 1964. Fellow Sch. Medicine Washington U., St. Louis, 1965-67, from asst. prof. to prof. Sch. Medicine, 1967-75, prof. Sch. Medicine, 1975—, with dept. pharmacology, 1976—, sr. v.p. R&D, chief scientist, pres. Searle, 1991—. Contbr. numerous articles to profl. jours. Recipient Rsch. Career Devel. award NIH, 1974, 76, Wellcome Creesy award in clin. pharmacology, 1977, 78, 80, 87, Cochems Thrombosis Rsch. prize, 1980. *

NEEDLES, BELVERD EARL, JR., accounting educator; b. Lubbock, Tex., Sept. 16, 1942; s. Belverd Earl and Billie (Anderson) N.; BBA, Tex. Tech U., 1964, MBA, 1965; PhD, U. Ill., 1969; m. Marian Powers, May 23, 1976; children: Jennifer Helen, Jeffrey Scott, Annabelle Marian, Abigail Marian. CPA, Ill.; cert. mgmt. acct. Asst. prof., assoc. prof. acctg. Tex. Tech U., Lubbock, 1968-72; dean Coll. Bus. and Adminstrn., Chgo. State U., 1972-76; prof. acctg. U. Ill., Urbana, 1976-78; dir. Sch. Accountancy, DePaul U., Chgo., 1978-86, prof. acctg., 1976-88, Arthur Andersen & Co. Alumni Disting. prof. acctg., 1988—. Author: Accounting and Organizational Control, 1973, Modern Business, 2d edit., 1977, Principles of Accounting, 1980, 6th edit., 1996, Financial Accounting, 1982, 6th edit., 1995, The CPA Examination: A Complete Review, 7th edit., 1986, Comparative International Auditing Standards, 1985, Financial and Managerial Accounting, 4th edit., 1996, Managerial Accounting, 4th edit, 1996; editor Accounting Instructor's Report, 1981—, The Accounting Profession and the Middle Market, 1986, Creating and Enhancing The Value of Post-Baccalareate Accounting Education, 1988, A Profession in Transition: The Ethical and Responsibilities of Accountants, 1989, Comparative International Accounting Educational Standards, 1990, Accounting Education for the 21st Century: The Global Challenges, 1994. Treas., bd. dirs. CPAs for Pub. Interest, 1978-86. Gen. Electric fellow, 1965-66; Deloitte Haskins and Sells fellow, 1966-68; named Disting. Alumnus Tex. Tech U., 1986; recipient Award of Merit DePaul U., 1986, Faculty Award of Merit Fedn. of Schs. of Accountancy, 1990. Fellow Am. Acctg. Assn. (sec. internat. sect. 1984-86, vice chmn. 1986-87, chmn. 1987-88, named outstanding internat. acctg. educator 1996); mem. AICPA (named Outstanding Educator 1992), Fedn. Schs. Accountancy (bd. dirs. 1980-87, pres. 1986), Acad. Internat. Bus., Ill. CPA Soc. (bd. dirs. 1994-96, Outstanding Acctg. Educator 1990), European Acctg. Assn. (exec. com. 1986-89), Fin. Execs. Inst., Nat. Assn. Accts., Internat. Assn. for Edn. & Rsch. in Acctg. (v.p. 1989-92, sec.-treas. 1992—), Phi Delta Kappa, Phi Kappa Phi, Beta Alpha Psi (named Acct. of Yr. for Edn. 1992), Beta Gamma Sigma.

NEEL, HARRY BRYAN, III, surgeon, scientist, educator; b. Rochester, Minn., Oct. 28, 1939; s. Harry Bryan and May Birgitta (Bjornsson) N.; m. Ingrid Helene Vaga, Aug. 29, 1964; children: Carlton Bryan, Harry Bryan IV, Roger Clifton. BS, Cornell U., 1962; MD, SUNY-Bklyn., 1966; PhD, U. Minn., 1976. Diplomate Am. Bd. Otolaryngology. Intern Kings County Hosp., Bklyn., 1966-67; resident in gen. surgery U. Minn. Hosps., Mpls., 1967-68; resident in otolaryngology Mayo Grad. Sch. Medicine Mayo Clinic, Rochester, Minn., 1970-74, cons. in otohinolaryngology, 1974—, cons. in cell biology, 1981—, assoc. prof. otolaryngology and microbiology Med. Sch., 1979-84, prof., 1984—, also chmn. dept. otolaryngology. Author: Cryosurgery for Cancer, 1976; contbr. chpts. to books, articles to profl. jours. V.p. bd. dirs. Minn. Orch. in Rochester, Inc., 1982, pres., chmn., 1983-84; mem. devel. com. Minn. Orchestral Assn., 1983, Mayo Found. bd. devel., 1983-86; bd. dirs. Mayo Health Plan, 1986-92, chmn., 1990-92; mem. bd. Mayo Mgmt. Svcs., Inc., 1992—; mem. bd. regents U. Minn., 1991—, chair faculty staff, student affairs com., 1993-95, vice chmn. bd., 1995—; bd. dirs. Greater Rochester Area Univ. Ctr., 1993—. With USPHS, 1968-70. Recipient travel award Soc. Acad. Chmn. Otolaryngology, 1974, Ira J. Tresley rsch. award Am. Acad. Facial and Reconstructive Surgery, 1982, Notable award Nat. Assn. Collegiate Women Athletic Adminstrs., 1992, The Best Doctors in Am. award Woodward/White, 1992-93, 94-95. Mem. AMA, ACS (bd. govs. 1985-90, devel. bd. 1988—, treas. 1990—, sec.-treas. Minn. chpt. 1983-85, pres. 1988-89), Am. Acad. Otolaryngology-Head and Neck Surgery (prize for basic rsch. in otolaryngology 1972, bd. dris. 1988-91, established Neel Disting. Rsch. Lectureship Endowment Fund 1994), Minn. Med. Assn., Zumbro Valley Med. Soc., Am. Broncho-Esophagological Assn. (pres.-elect 1988, pres. 1989-90), Am. Laryngological, Rhinological and Oto. Sco. (Mosher award 1980, pres.-elect 1995-96, centennial pres. 1996-97), Am. Laryngological Assn. (Casselberry award 1985, sec. 1988-93, v.p. 1994, pres. 1994—, Newcomb award 1996), Assn. for Rsch. in Otolaryngology, Assn. Acad. Depts. in Otolaryngology (sec.-treas. 1984-86, pres.-elect 1986, pres. 1988-9), Alumni Assn. Cornell U. (Outstanding Alumni award 1985, Collegium ORL Amicitiae Sacrum 1990—), Am. Bd. Otolaryngology (bd. dirs. 1986—, most admired man of decade 1992). Republican. Presbyterian. Club: Rochester Golf and Country. Home: 828 8th St SW Rochester MN 55902-6310 Office: Mayo Clinic 200 1st St SW Rochester MN 55902-3008

NEEL, JAMES VAN GUNDIA, geneticist, educator; b. Hamilton, Ohio, Mar. 22, 1915; s. Hiram Alexander and Elizabeth (Van Gundia) N.; m. Priscilla Baxter, May 6, 1943; children—Frances, James Van Gundia, Alexander Baxter. A.B., Coll. Wooster, 1935, D.Sc. (hon.), 1959; Ph.D., U. Rochester, 1939, M.D., 1944, D.Sc. (hon.), 1974; D.Sc. (hon.), Med. Coll. Ohio, 1981. Instr. zoology Dartmouth, 1939-41; fellow zoology NRC, 1941-42; intern, asst. resident medicine Strong Meml. Hosp., 1944-46; asso. geneticist lab. vertebrate biology, asst. prof. internal medicine U. Mich. Med. Sch., 1948-51, geneticist Inst. Human Biology, asso. prof. med. genetics, 1951-56, prof. human genetics, chmn. dept., 1956-85, prof. internal medicine, 1957-85, Lee R. Dice U. prof. human genetics, 1966-85, prof. emeritus, 1985—; Galton lectr. U. London,, 1955; Cutter lectr. Harvard U., 1956; Russel lectr. U. Mich., 1966; Wilhemene E. Key lectr. Am. Genetic Assn., 1982; Jacobson lectr. U. Newcastle upon Tyne, 1988; Baker lectr. Pa. State U., 1989; Andros lectr. U. Chgo., 1991; Lederberg lectr. Rockefeller U., 1995; cons. USPHS, AEC, NRC, WHO, EPA, VA; pres. 6th Internat. Congress Human Genetics; chmn. 7th Internat. Symposium Smithsonian Instn., Washington, 1981. Author med. articles; mem. editorial bd.: Blood, 1950-62, Perspectives in Biology and Medicine, 1956—, Human Genetics Abstracts, 1962—, Mutation Research, 1964-75. Served to 1st lt. M.C. AUS, 1943-44, 46-47; acting dir. field studies Atomic Bomb Casualty Commn., 1947-48. Recipient Albert Lasker award, 1960, Allan award Am. Soc. Human Genetics, 1965, Nat. Medal of Sci., 1974, medal Smithsonian Instn., 1981, Conte award Conte Inst. for Environ. Health, 1991, James D. Bruce award ACP, 1995; named Mich. Scientist of Yr., 1984. Fellow Am. Coll. Med. Genetics (hon.), Royal Soc. Medicine; mem. Am. Philos. Assn., Am. Acad. Arts and Scis., Inst. of Medicine, Nat. Acad. Scis. (mem. coun. 1970-72), Genetics Soc. Am., Am. Soc. Human Genetics (v.p. 1952-53, pres. 1953-54), Internat. Genetic Epidemiology Soc. (pres. 1992-93), Am. Fedn. Clin. Rsch., Am. Soc. Naturalists, Assn. Am. Physicians, ACP (Laureate award 1987), Brazilian Soc. Human Genetics, Phi Beta Kappa, Sigma Xi, Alpha Omega Alpha. Avocation: orchid cultivation.

NEEL, JASPER PHILLIP, English educator; b. Florence, Ala., Nov. 14, 1946; s. Jasper Peaster and Jessie Alice (Wright) N.; m. Faye Richardson, July 10, 1982; 1 child, Elizabeth Faye. BA, Miss. Coll., 1968; MA, U. Tenn., Knoxville, 1972, PhD, 1975. Asst. prof. Baylor U., Waco, Tex., 1975-76, NYU, 1976-79; assoc. prof. Francis Marion Coll., Florence, S.C., 1979-84; prof. No. Ill. U., DeKalb, 1984-89, U. Waterloo, Ont., Can., 1989-90, Vanderbilt U., Nashville, 1990—. Author: Plato, Derrida, and Writing, 1988, Aristotle's Voice: Rhetoric, Theory, and Writing in America, 1994. Office: Vanderbilt U English Dept Nashville TN 37235

NEEL, JOHN DODD, memorial park executive; b. McKeesport, Pa., Aug. 7, 1923; s. Harry Campbell and Anna (Dodd) N.; m. Jean Wyatt, Feb. 11, 1948; children: Harry C., John Dodd II, W. Wyatt (dec.), Jeffrey J. BA, Pa. State U., 1946. From salesman to pres. Jefferson Meml. Park, Pitts., 1946-88, chmn. bd. dirs., 1988—. Alternate mem. Zoning Hearing Bd., Pleasant Hills, Pa., 1970—. Mem. adv. bd. Pa. State U., McKeesport; former mem. Pa. State Real Estate Commn. 1st lt. USAAF, 1943-45. Decorated Air medal with 4 clusters, D.F.C. Recipient George Washington cert. Freedom Found., 1974. Mem. Pa. Cemetary Fun. Assn. (pres. 1963-65), Internat. Cemetery and Funeral Assn. (pres. 1973-74), West Jefferson Hills C. of C. (pres. 1984), VFW, Am. Legion, 57th Bomb Wing Assn., South Hills Country Club, Indian Lake Golf Club, Aero Club, OX-5CLUB, Kiwanis (pres. 1959), Masons, Shriners, Tau Kappa Epsilon. Presbyterian. Avocations: golf, travel, reading, hunting. Office: 401 Curry Hollow Rd Pittsburgh PA 15236-4636

NEEL, JUDY MURPHY, association executive; b. Rhome, Tex.; d. James W. and Linna B. (Vess) Neel; m. Ellis F. Murphy, Jr., Dec. 30, 1975; children from previous marriage: Mary B. Schmidt, Janet E. Wescott, Susan E. Salinas. BS, Northwestern U., 1976; MBA, Roosevelt U., 1983. V.p. Murphy, Tashjian & Assocs., Chgo., 1960-73; exec. dir. Automotive Affiliated Rep. Assn., Chgo., 1973-78; mgr. Automotive Svc. Ind. Assn., Chgo., 1978-80; exec. dir. Am. Soc. Safety Engrs., Des Plaines, Ill., 1980—. Mem. Chgo. Soc. Assn. Execs. (bd. dirs. 1979—, pres. 1985—, Shapiro award 1991), Am. Soc. Assn. Execs. (sec.-treas. 1994, found. dir. 1986-90, bd. dirs. 1990-95, Key award 1986). Republican. Office: Am Soc Safety Engrs 1800 E Oakton St Des Plaines IL 60018-2112

NEEL, RICHARD EUGENE, economics educator; b. Bluefield, Va., Jan. 7, 1932; s. Charles Richard and Zell LaVerne (Bowling) N.; m. Binnie Jo LeFever, June 10, 1961; children: Jeffrey Richard, Cynthia Jo. BS, U. Tenn., 1954, MS, 1955; PhD, Ohio State U., 1960. Instr. econs. Ohio State U., 1958-60; asst. prof. econs. Coll. William and Mary, 1960-61; asst. prof. U. South Fla., 1961-63, assoc. prof., 1963-66, chmn. econs. and fin. programs, 1964-66, acting chmn. grad. program Coll. Bus Adminstrn., 1965-66; dir. instl. planning Fla. Tech. U., 1966-68, chmn. dept. econs., prof. econs., 1968-69; assoc. dean Sch. Bus. Adminstrn. Ga. State U., 1969-77, dean grad. studies Sch. Bus. Adminstrn., 1973-77, prof. econs. Sch. Bus. Adminstrn., 1969-78; dean Coll. Bus. Adminstrn. U. N.C., Charlotte, 1978-93, econ. prof., 1993—. Contbg. author: The Case Study of Off-Campus Postsecondary Education on Military Bases, 1980; contbr. numerous articles, monographs to profl. publs.; editor: Readings in Price Theory, 1973. Sec., bd. dirs. Charlotte Fgn. Trade Zone; mem. fin. and adminstrn. com. United Way Ctrl. Carolinas, Inc.. Mem. Charlotte Sales and Mktg. Execs., Phi Kappa Phi, Beta Gamma Sigma. Presbyterian. Office: U NC at Charlotte Economics Dept Charlotte NC 28223

NEEL, SAMUEL ELLISON, lawyer; b. Kansas City, Mo., Feb. 22, 1914; s. Ellison Adger and Serena (Smith) N.; m. Mary Wilson, Oct. 11, 1941; children: James Adger, Amy Bowen, Wilson (dec. 1947), Wendy Busselle, Mary Ellison, Sophia Talbot. BA, Westminster Coll., Mo., 1935, LLD, 1995; LLB, Yale U., 1938. Bar: Mo. 1938, D.C. 1946, Va. 1953. Spl. asst. to atty. gen. anti-trust div. U.S. Dept. Justice, Washington, 1938-40, rep. State-War Dept. Mission on Japanese Combines, 1946; legal staff adv. commn. Coun. Nat. Def., OPM, WPB, 1940-42; pvt. practice Washington and McLean, Va., 1946-93; bd. dirs. emeritus Rouse Co. Mem. Fed. City Coun., Washington, 1954-58; pres. McLean Citizens Assn., 1953-54, Pub. Utilities Commn., Fairfax County, Va., 1956-57, The Squam Lakes Assn., N.H., 1987-89; chmn. Fairfax County Water Authority, 1957-63, Fairfax County Housing Authority, 1970-72; mem. adv. com. mortgage fin. FHA, 1956-66; pres. Neel Found.; trustee Westminster Coll. Lt. comdr. USNR, 1942-46; comdr. air forces Pacific Fleet. Mem. Mortgage Bankers Assn. Am. (exec. v.p. 1965-66, gen. counsel 1946-74), Soc. Cin., Beta Theta Pi, Omicron Delta Kappa. Democrat. Episcopalian (past trustee). Clubs: Lawyers (Washington), Metropolitan (Washington); N.Y. Yacht. Home: 1157 Chain Bridge Rd Mc Lean VA 22101-2215 Office: PO Box 385 Mc Lean VA 22101-0385

NEEL, SPURGEON HART, JR., physician, retired army officer; b. Memphis, Sept. 24, 1919; s. Spurgeon Hart and Pyrle (Womble) N.; m. Alice Glidewell Torti, Nov. 18, 1939; children: Spurgeon Hart III, Alice Leah Neel Zartarian. Student pre-med., Memphis State U., 1939; M.D., U. Tenn., 1942; M.P.H., Harvard U., 1958; M.S.B.A., George Washington U., 1965. Diplomate: Am. Bd. Preventive Medicine. Intern Meth. Hosp., Memphis, 1943; resident x-ray Santa Ana (Calif.) AFB, 1944; resident aviation medicine USAF Sch. Aerospace Medicine, 1960; commd. 2d lt. U.S. Army, 1942, advanced through grades to maj. gen., 1970; various assignments U.S., 1943-44, 47-48, ETO, 1944-47; chief surgeon service Ft. McPherson, Ga., 1949; med. service, 1949; div. surgeon (82d Airborne Div.), Ft. Bragg, N.C., 1949-51; comdr. (30th Med. Group), Korea, 1953-54; dep. dir. div. physiology and pharmacology (WRAIR, WRAMC), 1956; chief aviation br. (OTSG), 1957; chief aviation medicine Ft. Rucker, Ala., 1960; comdg. officer U.S. Army Hosp., post surgeon, 1961-64; stationed in Vietnam, 1965-66, 68-69; dep. surgeon gen. U.S. Army, Washington, 1969-73; comdr. (U.S. Army Health Services Command), 1973-77; clin. assoc. prof. family practice U. Tex. Health Sci. Ctr., San Antoniko, now prof. emeritus occupl. and aerospace medicine U. Tex. Sch. Pub. Health; med. cons. U.S. Automobile Assn., other industries, San Antonio. Contbr. articles med. jours. Decorated D.S.M. with oak leaf cluster, Legion of Merit with 4 clusters, Bronze Star with oak leaf cluster, Air medal with 3 oak leaf clusters, Joint Service Commendation medal, USAF Commendation medal, Purple Heart, others.; Recipient Seaman award Assn. Mil. Surgeons U.S., 1950, Gary Wratten award, 1967; McClelland award Army Aviation Assn. Am., 1962; named to U.S. Army Aviation Hall Fame, 1976; recipient Lyster award Aerospace Med. Assn., 1977. Fellow A.C.P., Am. Coll. Preventive Medicine (past v.p.), Royal Soc. Health, Aerospace Med. Assn. (past pres.), Internat. Acad. Aviation and Space Medicine, Am. Acad. Med. Adminstrs., Am. Coll. Health Care Execs.; mem. AMA (past-sec. sect. mil. medicine), Assn. Mil. Surgeons U.S., Assn. U.S. Army, Army Aviation Assn. Am.; asso. mem. Phi Chi. Home: 1321 Spanish Oaks San Antonio TX 78213-1606

NEELANKAVIL, JAMES PAUL, marketing educator, consultant, researcher; b. Anjoor, India, May 29, 1940; came to U.S., 1973, naturalized, 1985; s. Paul V. and Mary (Velara) N.; m. Salvacion Querol Pena, July 15, 1973; children: Mary Angel, Jacques Prince. BS, St. Thomas Coll., India, 1961; MBA, Asian Inst. Mgmt., Philippines, 1972; PhD, NYU, 1976. Asst. prof. N.Y. Inst., 1976-78; assoc. prof. Montclair State Coll., N.J., 1978-80; asst. prof. NYU, 1980-84; chmn. mktg. and internat. bus. dept. Hofstra U., Hempstead, N.Y., 1984-86, assoc. dean sch. bus., 1986-89, acting dean, 1989-91, prof. mktg. and internat. bus., 1991—; supr. Firestone, Bombay, India, 1961-70; cons. Internat. Advt. Assn., N.Y.C., 1979-88, GTE Inc., Stamford, Conn., 1980-85, Healthchem Inc., N.Y.C., 1980-83. Author: Global Business: Contemporary Issues, Problems and Challenges, Self-Regulation, 1980, Agency Compensation, 1982, Advertising Regulation, 1985, Advertising Regulations in Selected Countries, 1987; co-author Advertising Self-Regulation: A Global Perspective, 1980, Global Business: Contemporary Issues, Problems and Challenges; also articles. Min. Resurrection Ascension Ch., N.Y.C., 1990—. Mem. Internat. Advt. Assn., Am. Mktg. Assn., Acad. Internat. Bus. Avocations: reading, tennis, travel.

NEELD, ELIZABETH HARPER, author; b. Brooks, Ga., Dec. 25, 1940; d. Tommie Frank and Rachel (Leach) Harper; m. Gregory Cowan, Feb. 24, 1975 (dec. 1979); m. Jerele Don Neeld, 1983. BS, U. Chattanooga, 1962, MEd, 1966; PhD, U. Tenn., Knoxville, 1973. Dir. English programs MLA, N.Y.C., 1973-76; prof. English Tex. A&M U., College Station, 1976-83; exec. prof. Coll. Bus. Adminstrn., U. Houston, 1990—. Author: Seven Choices: Taking the Steps to New Life After Losing Someone You Love, 1990, 3d edit., 1997, Sister Bernadette: Cowboy Nun From Texas; author, editor 14 additional books; author: (audiocassette series) Yes! You Can Write; anchor and subject of PBS documentary The Challenge of Grief, 1991. Recipient Disting. Svc. award Mo. State H.S. Activities Assn., 1997. Democrat. Methodist. Avocations: cooking, opera, gardening. Home: 716 Euclid St Houston TX 77009-7229

NEELEY, DELMAR GEORGE, human resources consultant; b. Charleston, Ill., June 4, 1937; s. Glenn Truman and Gladys Bernice (Dittman) N.; m. Yvonne Tamara Penrod, Mar. 2, 1957 (div. Feb. 1969); children: Timothy Del, Kimberly Yvonne, Terry; m. Terry Anne Barbour, Aug. 28, 1971; children: Robert James, Stephen Edward. BA in Philosophy, Olivet Nazarene U., 1965, MA in Lit., 1969; EdD, U. Sarasota, 1996. Cert. mediator and arbitrator, Fla. Mgr. mgmt. devel. Rauland Divsn. Zenith Corp., Chgo., 1967-70; sr. personnel cons. Mid. West Svc. Co., Chgo., 1971-73; dir. human resources Nichols-Homeshield Inc., West Chicago, Ill., 1974-76, Gould Inc./Ind. Battery Divsn., Langhorne, Pa., 1976-81; pres., owner Barbour-Neeley Inc., Sarasota, Fla., 1982-91; Stephen Ministries leader. Recipient Meritorious Svc. award Chgo. Boys Club, 1970, Svc. award Chgo. Jaycees, 1967-71. Mem. ACA, Ctr. for Study of Presidency, Family Mediation Assn. Ga., Coll. of Chaplains, Fla. Acad. Profl. Mediators. Methodist. Avocation: teaching, counseling, mediation. Home: 5161 Cedar Hammock Dr Sarasota FL 34232-2243

NEELY, CAMERON MICHAEL, professional hockey player; b. Comox, B.C., Can., June 6, 1965. Hockey player Vancouver Canucks, 1983-86, Boston Bruins, 1986—; player NHL All-Star Game, 1988-91. Recipient Bill Masterton Meml. trophy, 1993-94; named to Sporting News All-Star Team, 1987-88, 93-94. Office: Boston Bruins 1 Fleet Ctr Ste 250 Boston MA 02114-1303*

NEELY, CHARLES B., JR., lawyer; b. Raleigh, N.C., Dec. 11, 1943. AB with honors, U. N.C., 1965; JD, Duke U., 1970. Bar: N.C. 1970. Lawyer Maupin, Taylor & Ellis P.A., Raleigh; mem. 4th Cir. Jud. Conf. Mem. N.C. Ho. of Reps., 1995—. Capt. USNR, 1965-89. Fellow Am. Bar Found.; mem. ABA (taxation sect.), N.C. Bar Assn. (chmn. law office mgmt. sect. 1986-88, bd. govs. 1995—), Inst. Property Taxation. Address: Maupin Taylor & Ellis PA PO Drawer 19764 Ste 500 3200 Beechleaf Ct Raleigh NC 27619

NEELY, CHARLES LEA, JR., retired physician; b. Memphis, Aug. 3, 1927; s. Charles Lea and Ruby Perry (Mayes) N.; m. Mary Louise Buckingham, Mar. 30, 1957; children: Louise Mayes, Charles Buckingham. A.B., Princeton U., 1950; M.D., Washington U., St. Louis, 1954. Diplomate: Am. Bd. Internal Medicine. Intern Cornell Service, Bellevue Hosp., N.Y.C., 1954-55; resident Barnes Hosp., St. Louis, 1955-57; fellow in hematology Barnes Hosp., 1957-58; dir. U. Tenn. Cancer Clinic, 1979-87; mem. staffs Bapt. Meml. Hosp., Regional Med. Ctr. at Memphis, U. Tenn. Med. Center; prof. medicine and pathology U. Tenn., 1971-87. Served with USNR, 1945-47. Fellow A.C.P.; mem. AMA, Am. Soc. Clin. Oncology, Am. Soc. Hematology, Am. Fedn. Clin. Research, Sigma Xi, Alpha Omega Alpha. Home: 4743 Mint Dr Memphis TN 38117-4010

NEELY, MARK EDWARD, JR., writer; b. Amarillo, Tex., Nov. 10, 1944; s. Mark Edward and Lottie (Wright) N.; m. Sylvia Eakes, June 15, 1966. BA, Yale U., 1966, PhD, 1973; LHD (hon.), Lincoln Coll., 1981. Former dir. Louis A. Warren Lincoln Library and Museum, Ft. Wayne, Ind.; vis. instr. Iowa State U., Ames, 1971-72; editor Lincoln Lore, 1973—; mem. adv. bd. Ind. Historical Bureau, 1980—; mem. editorial adv. com. Ind. Mag. of History, 1981—; mem. editorial bd. Ulysses S. Grant Assn., 1981—. Author: The Abraham Lincoln Encyclopedia, 1981, The Lincoln Family Album: Photographs From The Personal Collection of a Historic American Family, 1990, The Fate of Liberty: Abraham Lincoln and Civil Liberties, 1991 (Pulitzer Prize for history 1992), The Last Best Hope on Earth: Abraham Lincoln and the Promise of America, 1993; (with Harold Holzer and Gabor S. Boritt) The Lincoln Image: Abraham Lincoln and the Popular Print, 1984, The Confederate Image: Prints of the Last Cause, 1987; (with R. Gerald McMurty) The Insanity File: The Case of Mary Todd Lincoln, 1986;

(with Holzer) Mine Eyes Have Seen the Glory: The Civil War in American Art, 1993. Mem. Abraham Lincoln Assn., Soc. Ind. Archivists (pres. 1980-81), Ind. Assn. of Historians (pres. 1987-88). *

NEELY, PAUL, newspaper editor; b. San Francisco, July 30, 1946; s. Ralph and Virginia (Gaylord) N.; m. Linda Borsch, Oct. 6, 1977; children: David King, Michael Paul. BA, Williams Coll., 1968; MS in Journalism, Columbia U., 1970, MBA, 1970. Reporter, editl. writer Press Enterprise, Riverside, Calif., 1970-73; copy editor, asst. mng. editor Courier Jour., Louisville, 1973-79; news features editor St. Petersburg Times (Fla.), 1980-83; mng. editor Chattanooga Times, 1983-91, editor, dep. pub., 1991-92, pub. 1992—; mem. Commn. on Future Tenn. Jud. Sys.; bd. trustees Williams Coll., Tenn. Aquarium, Hunter Mus. Am. Art. Mem. Am. Assn. Sunday and Feature Editors (pres. 1981-82), Am. Soc. Newspaper Editors. Home: 1000 Skillet Gap Chattanooga TN 37419-1048 Office: The Chattanooga Times Po Box 951 100 E 10th St Chattanooga TN 37402-4230

NEELY, RICHARD, lawyer; b. Aug. 2, 1941; s. John Champ and Elinore (Forlani) N.; m. Carolyn Elaine Elmore, 1979; children: John Champ, Charles Whittaker. AB, Dartmouth Coll., 1964; LLB, Yale U., 1967. Bar: W.Va. 1967. Practiced in Fairmont, W.Va., 1969-73; chmn. Marion County Bd. Pub. Health, 1971-72; mem. W.Va. Ho. of Dels., 1971-73; justice, chief justice W.Va. Supreme Ct. of Appeals, Charleston, 1973-95; ptnr. Neely & Hunter, Charleston, 1995—; chmn. bd. Kane & Keyser Co., Belington, W.Va., 1970-88. Author: How Courts Govern America, 1980, Why Courts Don't Work, 1983, The Divorce Decision, 1984, Judicial Jeopardy: When Business Collides with the Courts, 1986, The Product Liability Mess: How Business Can Be Rescued from State Court Politics, 1988, Take Back Your Neighborhood: A Case for Modern-Day Vigilantism, 1990, Tragedies of our Own Making: How Private Choices have Created Public Bankruptcy, 1994; contbr. articles to nat. mags. Capt. U.S. Army, 1967-69. Decorated Bronze Star, Vietnam Honor medal 1st Class. Mem. Am. Econ. Assn., W.Va. Bar Assn., Fourth Cir. Jud. Conf. (life), Internat. Brotherhood Elec. Workers, VFW, Am. Legion, Moose, Phi Delta Phi, Phi Sigma Kappa. Episcopalian. Office: Neely & Hunter 159 Summers St Charleston WV 25301-2134

NEELY, SALLY SCHULTZ, lawyer; b. L.A. BA Stanford U., 1970, JD, 1971. Bar: Ariz. 1972, Calif. 1977. Law clk. to judge U.S. Ct. Appeals (9th cir.), Phoenix, 1971-72; assoc. Lewis and Roca, Phoenix, 1972-75; asst. prof. Harvard U. Law Sch., Cambridge, Mass., 1975-77; assoc. Shutan & Trost, P.C., Los Angeles, 1977-79, ptnr., 1979-80, Sidley & Austin, L.A., 1980—; faculty Am. Law Inst.-ABA Chpt. 11 Bus. Reorgns., 1989-95, 97—, Bankruptcy Law Inst. and Bankruptcy Litigation Inst., 1987-92, Nat. Conf. Bankruptcy Judges, 1988, 90, 95, 96, 97. Fed. Jud. Ctr., 1989, 90, 94-95, Workshop Bankruptcy and Bus. Reorganization NYU, 1992—; rep. 9th cir. jud. conf., 1989-91; mem. Nat. Bankruptcy Conf., 1993—. Chair Stanford Law Sch. Reunion Giving, 1996; bd. visitors Stanford Law Sch., 1990-92. Fellow Am. Coll. Bankruptcy; mem. ABA, Calif. State Bar Assn. (debtor-creditor rels. and bankruptcy subcom. bus. law sect. 1985-87). Office: Sidley & Austin 555 W 5th St Ste 4000 Los Angeles CA 90013-3000

NEELY, THOMAS EMERSON, lawyer; b. Pitts., Oct. 19, 1943; s. William Homer and Frances Elizabeth (Curtis) N.; m. Janice Elaine Fay, July 6, 1968; children: Daniel, Morgan, Benjamin. BA, Williams Coll., 1965; JD, Harvard U., 1968. Bar: Mass. 1968. Assoc. Hale and Dorr, Boston, 1971-80, ptnr., 1980—. With U.S. Army, 1969-71, Vietnam. Office: Hale and Dorr 60 State St Boston MA 02109-1800

NEELY, VICKI ADELE, legal assistant, poet; b. Dallas, Nov. 29, 1962; d. Robert Theodore and Linda Carolyn (Vogtsberger) Kissel; 1 child, Travis Wade. Student, Richland Coll., 1981-82, Austin C.C., 1983, San Antonio Coll., 1983, Am. Coll. Real Estate, 1983. Asst. mgr., leasing cons. Nash Phillips/Copus, Inc., 1983-85; loan processor Univ. Nat. Bank, 1985-87; co-owner Reels on Wheels, 1987; loan sec. Tex. Am. Bank/Richardson, N.A., 1987-88; legal sec., paralegal Clements, Allen & Warren, 1988-89; legal sec. Jackson & Walker, A Profl. Corp., 1989-90, Robins, Kaplan, Miller & Ciresi, 1990-91; freelance litigation sec. Smith & Underwood, 1991-92, legal asst., 1992-94; legal asst. Collins, Norman & Basinger, P.C., Dallas, 1994, Law Offices of Arlen D. (Spider) Bynum, 1995; pvt. practice Richardson, Tex., 1996—. Author: (poems) Animal Love, Believe, 1993; co-author: Texas Rent-A-Bank, 1993. Methodist. Avocations: sailing, reading, dancing, painting. Home and Office: 1911 Eastfield Dr Richardson TX 75081-5435

NEENAN, THOMAS FRANCIS, association executive, consultant; b. Kansas City, Mo., Apr. 3, 1923; s. Emmet Joseph and Mary Helen (Liebst) N.; m. Eileen Margaret Vala, Aug. 4, 1951; children: Nancy, Tom Jr., Pamela, Kathleen, Maureen. BA, Iowa U., 1948; MA, Iowa State U., 1978. Trademark researcher Lampa Christopherson, Chgo., 1948-50; sales mgr. Cedar Rapids (Iowa) Block Co., 1950-53; owner Tywal Co., Center Point, Iowa, 1953-60; mem. sales staff Capp Homes, Center Point, Iowa, 1960-78; property mgr. Center Point, Iowa, 1978-86; exec. dir. Iowa Trails Coun., Center Point, Iowa, 1984—. Editor: (mag.) Trails Advocate, 1986—. Mayor City of Center Point, 1959-61, 65-69; chmn. City Planning an dzoning Com., Center Point, 1970—; active County Dem. Ctrl. Com., Linn County, Iowa, Linn County Conservation Bd., 1972-83; vice chair state legis. com. AARP, Des Moines, 1988-93; active leader Boy Scouts Am. Recipient Silver Beaver award Boy Scouts Am., 1961, St. George award Cath. Archdiocese Dubuque, 1973; named to Iowa's Vol. Hall of Fame, 1995. Mem. Am. Hiking Soc. (bd. dirs., Kern award 1986), Rails to Trails Conservancy, Am. Trails (treas., bd. dirs., award of excellence 1992). Democrat. Roman Catholic. Avocation: trail acquisition, development, and promotion. Home: 1201 Central Ave Center Point IA 52213-9638 Office: Trails Coun Inc PO Box 131 Center Point IA 52213-0131

NEER, CHARLES SUMNER, II, orthopedic surgeon, educator; b. Vinita, Okla., Nov. 10, 1917; s. Charles Sumner and Pearl Victoria (Brooke) N.; m. Eileen Meyer, June 12, 1990; children: Charlotte Marguerite, Sydney Victoria, Charles Henry. BA, Dartmouth Coll., 1939; MD, U. Pa., 1942. Diplomate Am. Bd. Orthopaedic Surgery (bd. dirs. 1970-75). Intern U. Pa. Hosp., Phila., 1942-43; asso. in surgery N.Y. Orthopedic-Columbia-Presbyn. Med. Center, N.Y.C., 1943-44; instr. in surgery Coll. Physicians and Surgeons, Columbia U., N.Y.C., 1946-47; instr. orthopaedic surgery Coll. Physicians and Surgeons, Columbia U., 1947-57, asst. prof. clin. orthopaedic surgery, 1957-64, asso. prof., 1964-68, prof. clin. orthopaedic surgery, 1968-90, prof. clin. orthopaedic surgery emeritus, spl. lectr. orthopaedic surgery, 1990—; attending orthopaedic surgeon Columbia-Presbyn. Med. Ctr., N.Y.C.; chief adult reconstructive svc. N.Y. Orthopaedic Hosp.; chief shoulder and elbow clinic Presbyn. Hosp.; cons. orthopaedic surgeon emeritus N.Y. Orthopaedic-Columbia-Presbyn. Med. Ctr., 1991—; chmn. 4th Internat. Congress Shoulder Surgeons; chmn. Internat. Bd. Shoulder Surgery, 1992—. Founder, chmn. bd. trustees Jour. Shoulder and Elbow Surgery, 1990—; contbr. articles to books, tech. films, sound slides. Served with U.S. Army, 1944-46. Recipient Disting. Svc. award Am. Bd. Orthopaedic Surgeons 1975. Fellow ACS (sr. mem. nat. com. on trauma), Am. Acad. Orthop. Surgeons (com. on upper extremity, shoulder com.); mem. AMA, ACS (mem. com. trauma), Am. Bd. Orthop. Surgeons (bd. dirs. 1970-75, Disting. Svc. award 1975), Am. Shoulder and Elbow Surgeons (inaugural pres.), Am. Assn. Surgery Trauma, Am. Orthop. Assn., Mid-Am. Orthop. Assn. (hon.), N.Y. Acad. Medicine, Allen O. Whipple Surg. Soc., N.Y. State Med. Soc., N.Y. County Med. Soc., Pan Am. Med. Assn., Am. Trauma Soc., Soc. Latino Am. Orthop. y Traumatology, Internat. Soc. Orthop. Surgery and Traumatology, Va. Orthop. Soc. (hon.), Carolina Orthop. Alumni Assn. (hon.), Conn. Orthop. Club (hon.), Houston Orthop. Assn. (hon.), Soc. Française de Chirurgie Orthop. et Traumatology (hon.), Soc. Italiana Orthop. Etravmatologia; patron, Shoulder and Elbow Soc. Australia, South African Shoulder Soc., Giraffe Club, Internat. Bd. Shoulder Surgery (chmn. 1992—), Alpha Omega Alpha, Phi Chi. Home and Office: 231 S Miller St Vinita OK 74301-3625 *Forever grateful I could be a doctor and especially to work in the exciting area of shoulder surgery.*

NEESON, LIAM, actor; b. Ballymena, No. Ireland, June 7, 1952; s. Barney and Kitty N.; m. Natasha Richardson, July 3, 1994; 1 son: Micheál Richard Antonio. Theatrical appearances include (Broadway) Anna Christie, 1993; films include Excalibur, 1981, Krull, 1983, The Bounty, 1984, The Innocent, 1984, Lamb, 1986, Duet for One, 1986, The Mission, 1986, A Prayer for the Dying, 1987, Suspect, 1987, Satisfaction, 1988, The Dead Pool, 1988, High Spirits, 1988, The Good Mother, 1988, Next of Kin, 1989, Darkman, 1990, Crossing the Line, 1990, Ruby Cairo, 1991, Shining Through, 1992, Under Suspicion, 1992, Husbands and Wives, 1992, Leap of Faith, 1992, Ethan Fromme, 1992, Schindler's List, 1993 (Best Actor Acad. award nominee 1994), Nell, 1994, Rob Roy, 1995, Before and After, 1996, Michael Collins, 1996, Les Miserables, 1997. Office: c/o Susan Culley & Assocs 150 S Rodeo Dr Ste 220 Beverly Hills CA 90212-2409*

NEF, EVELYN STEFANSSON, psychotherapist, author, editor, specialist polar regions; b. N.Y.C., July 24, 1913; d. Jeno and Bella (Klein) Schwartz; m. Bil Baird, 1932 (div. 1938); m. Vilhjalmur Stefansson, 1941 (dec. 1962); m. John Ulric Nef, Apr. 21, 1964 (dec. Dec. 1988). Student, Traphagen Art Sch., N.Y.C., summer 1927, Art Student League, 1931, Inst. Study Psychotherapy, N.Y.C., 1974-77, Advanced Psychoanalytic Seminar, 1977-83. Librarian Stefansson Polar Library, N.Y.C., 1941-52; librarian Stefansson collection Baker Library, Dartmouth Coll., 1952-63, also lectr. polar studies program, 1960-61; adminstrv. officer Am. Sociol. Assn., Washington, 1963-64; freelance writer book reviews, newspaper articles N.Y. Times Book Review, also Washington Post, 1942-72; research assoc. dept. dermatology Washington Hosp. Ctr., 1976—, coordinator psoriasis social adjustment study, 1977-80; guest worker Inst. Brain Evolution and Behavior, NIHM; guest on radio and TV programs; mem. vis. com. U. Chgo. Libr., 1973-84, vice chmn., 1977-84; mem. vis. com. on social scis. U. Chgo., 1978-83; bd. dirs. MacDowell Colony, 1992—, fellow, summer 1993. Author: Within the Circle, 1945, Here is the Far North, 1957, Here is Alaska, 4th rev. edit. (with Linda C. Yahn), 1983, also contbg. author other books; editor-in-chief: Beyond the Pillars of Heracles (Rhys Carpenter), 1966, South from the Spanish Main (Earl Hanson), 1967, Silk, Spices and Empire (Owen and Eleanor Lattimore), 1968, West and By North (Louis B. Wright and Elaine Fowler), 1971, The Moving Frontier (Louis B. Wright and Elaine Fowler), 1972; foreward writer for Eleanor Lattimonew's Turkestan Reunion, 1995; editor, contbr.: Polar Notes, 1960-63, Eleanor Holgate Lattimore, 1895-1970, 1970, Jour. of Polar Studies, 1984; contbr. to: A Chronological Bibliography of the Published Works of Vilhjalmur Stefansson, 1978, Vilhjalmur Stefansson and The Development of Arctic Terrestial Science, 1984. Pres. Evelyn S. Nef Found., 1992—; trustee Corcoran Gallery Art, Washington, 1974-89; bd. dirs. Reginald S. Lourie Ctr. for Infants and Young Children, 1989-93, Washington Opera, 1993—, Nat. Symphony, MacDowell Colony, 1991—, Paget Found.; mem. adv. coun. dept. geriatrics Mt. Sinai Hosp., N.Y.C., 1988—. Recipient Vol. Activist award, 1978, recognition award Young Audiences, 1992, Women of Achievement award Washington Irving H.S., 1996, Legend of the Corcoran award Corcoran Gallery, 1996. Mem. Washington Acad. Scis., Smithsonian Assocs. (mem. women's com. 1971-74), Soc. Women Geographers (nat. v.p., chmn. Washington chpt. 1969-71, nat. pres. 1972-75), Explorers Club, Sulgrave Club, Cosmos Club. Research on psychosomatic skin diseases, progressive aging. Home: 2726 N St NW Washington DC 20007-3323

NEFF, A. GUY, lawyer; b. Calcutta, India, Mar. 24, 1951. BA, Vanderbilt U., 1972; JD, U. Fla., 1975. Bar: Fla. 1975. Lawyer Maguire, Voorhis & Wells PA, Orlando, Fla. Mem. ABA, Inter-Am. Bar Assn., Am. Immigration Lawyers Assn. (dir. ctrl. Fla. chpt. 1984-85, 86-87, 90-91), Fla. Bar (internat. law sect.), Orange County Bar Assn., Phi Delta Phi (magister 1975). Office: Maguire Voorhis & Wells 2 S Orange Ave Orlando FL 32801-2606

NEFF, DIANE IRENE, naval officer; b. Cedar Rapids, Iowa, Apr. 26, 1954; d. Robert Mariner and Adeline Emma (Zach) N. BA in Psychology and Home Econs., U. Iowa, 1976; MA in Sociology, U. Mo., 1978; MEd in Ednl. Leadership, U. West Fla., 1990. Contract compliance officer, dir. EEO, City of Cedar Rapids, 1979-81; commd. ensign USN, 1981, advanced through grades to lt. comdr.; asst. legal officer Naval Comm. Area Master Sta., Guam, 1982-83; comm. security plans and requirements officer Comdr.-in-Chief US Naval Forces in Europe, London, 1983-85; dir. standards and evaluation dept. Recruit Tng. Command, Orlando, Fla., 1985-89; rsch. and analysis officer Naval Res. Officers Tng. Corps Office Chief Naval Edn. and Tng., Pensacola, Fla., 1989-91; tech. tng. officer Recruit Tng. Command, Great Lakes, Ill., 1991-92, mil. tng. officer, 1992-93, dir. apprentice tng., 1993-95; coord. ednl. and tng. programs U. Ctrl. Fla., Orlando, 1995—. Founding mem. Unity of Gulf Breeze, Fla., 1990; performer various benefits for chs., mus., others, Orlando, 1988, 91, 95, 96. Fellow Adminstrn. on Aging, 1977. Unitarian. Avocation: piano.

NEFF, DONALD LLOYD, news correspondent, writer; b. York, Pa., Oct. 15, 1930; s. Harry William and Gertrude Marie N.; m. Abigail Trafford; 1 son, Gregory Harry. Student, Trinity Coll., San Antonio, 1949, York Coll., 1950-52, N.Y. U., 1953. Reporter York Dispatch, 1954-56, L.A. Mirror-News, 1956-57, UPI, L.A., 1957-61; with L.A. Times, 1961-64; bur. chief L.A. Times, Tokyo, 1964; with Time mag., 1965-81; corr. Time mag., Vietnam, 1965-66; writer Time mag., N.Y.C., 1966-68; bur. chief Time mag., Houston, 1968-70, L.A., 1970-73, Jerusalem, 1975-78; bur. chief Time mag., N.Y.C., 1978-79, sr. editor, 1973-75; news svcs. editor Washington Star, 1979-80; Washington corr. Middle East Internat., 1989—. Author: Warriors at Suez: Eisenhower Takes America into the Middle East, 1981, Warriors for Jerusalem, The Six Days That Changed the Middle East, 1984; Warriors Against Israel, 1988, Fallen Pillars; U.S. Policy Toward Palestine and Israel since 1945, 1995. Served with AUS, 1948-50. Recipient Theta Sigma Phi Matrix award, 1962, Calif.-Nev. AP Writing Contest best met. spot news story award, 1962, Overseas Press Club award for best fgn. article in a mag., 1979; finalist Am. Book Award History category, 1982. Mem. Fgn. Press Assn. (Israel pres. 1977, v.p. 1978).

NEFF, EDWARD AUGUST, manufacturing company executive; b. Chgo., Feb. 7, 1947; s. Russell Jack and Betty Rae (Heins) N.; m. Janet Irene Picerno; children: Kathleen Rae, David Russell. BA, Ohio Wesleyan U., 1969. Mgmt. trainee Phoenix Trimming Co., Chgo., 1970-73, dir. research and devel., 1973-77; dir. research and devel. Phoenix Trimming Co., Tarboro, N.C., 1977-86, v.p. mfg., 1986-87; v.p. mfg. Murdock Webbing Co., Central Falls, R.I., 1987-95, sr. v.p. ops., 1995—. Deacon, treas. Howard Meml. Presbyn. Ch., Tarboro, N.C., 1984-88; treas. Christ Ch., East Greenwich, R.I., 1994—. Mem. Narrow Fabrics Inst. (pres. 1985-88), Web Sling Assn. (v.p. 1974-76). Republican. Avocations: golf, bridge. Home: 1065 South Rd East Greenwich RI 02818-1435 Office: Murdock Webbing Co 27 Foundry St Pawtucket RI 02863-2317

NEFF, FRANCINE IRVING (MRS. EDWARD JOHN NEFF), former federal government official; b. Albuquerque, Dec. 6, 1925; d. Edward Hackett and Georga (Henderson) Irving; m. Edward John Neff, June 7, 1948; children: Sindle, Edward Vann. AA, Cottey Coll., 1946; BA, U. N.Mex., 1948. Divsn. and precinct chmn. Republican Party, Albuquerque, 1966-71; mem. ctrl. com. Bernalillo County (N.Mex.) Republican Party, 1967-74, mem. exec. bd., 1968-70; mem. N.Mex. State ctrl. com. Republican Party, 1968-74, 77-82, mem. exec. bd., 1970-74, 81-83; Rep. nat. committeewoman State of N.Mex., 1970-74; also mem. exec. com.; Treas. of U.S. U.S. Dept. Treasury, Washington, 1974-77; nat. dir. U.S. Savs. Bonds, 1974-77; mktg. v.p. Rio Grande Valley Bank, Albuquerque, 1977-81; bd. dirs. La.-Pacific Corp., Portland, Oreg., D.R. Horton, Inc., Arlington, Tex. N.Mex. state adviser Teenage Reps., 1967-68; del. Rep. Nat. Conv., Miami, 1968, 72; campaign coord. Congressman Lujan of N.Mex., 1970; pres. Albuquerque Federated Rep. Women's Club, 1977; Leader Camp Fire Girls, Albuquerque, 1957-64; pres. Inez (N.Mex.) PTA, 1961; den mother Cub Scouts Am., Albuquerque, 1964-65; former mem. exec. bd. United Way of Albuquerque; former mem. adv. coun. Mgmt. Devel. Ctr., Robert O. Anderson Grad. Sch. Bus. and Adminstrv. Scis., U. N.Mex.; former mem. Def. Adv. Com. on Women in the Svcs., 1980-83; trustee Cottey Coll., Nevada, Mo., 1982-89. Recipient Exceptional Svc. award U.S. Dept. Treasury, 1976, Horatio Alger award Horatio Alger Assn. Disting. Americans, Inc., 1976. Mem. P.E.O. (pres. Albuquerque chpt. 1958-59, 63-64), Albuquerque City Panhellenic Assn. (pres. 1959-60), Greater Albuquerque C. of C. (bd. dirs. 1978-81), Alpha Delta Pi, Sigma Alpha Iota, Phi Kappa Phi, Pi Lambda Theta, Phi Theta Kappa. Episcopalian.

NEFF, FRED LEONARD, lawyer; b. St. Paul, Nov. 1, 1948; s. Elliott Ira and Mollie (Poboisk) N.; m. Christa Ruth Powell, Sept. 10, 1989. BS with high distinction, U. Minn., 1970; JD, William Mitchell Coll. Law, 1976. Bar: Minn. 1976, N.D. 1994, U.S. Dist. Ct. Minn. 1977, U.S. Ct. Appeals (8th cir.) 1985, U.S. Supreme Ct. 1985, Wis. 1986, U.S. Dist. Ct. (ea. and we. dists.) Wis. 1992. Tchr. Hopkins (Minn.) Pub. Schs., 1970-72; instr. U. Minn., Mpls., 1974-76; pvt. practice law Mpls., 1976-79; asst. county atty. Sibley County, Gaylord, Minn., 1979-80; mng. atty. Hyatt Legal Svcs., St. Paul, 1981-83, regional ptnr., 1983-85, profl. devel. ptnr., 1985-86; pres. Neff Law Firm, P.A., Mpls., 1986—; CEO Profl. Devel. Inst. Inc., Edina, Minn., 1994—, also bd. dirs.; instr. Inver Hills Coll., 1973-77; counsel Am. Tool Supply Co., St. Paul, 1976-78; cons. Nat. Detective Agy., Inc., St. Paul, 1980-83; CEO A Basic Legal Svc., Bloomington, 1990—; CEO, bd. dirs. Profl. Devel. Inst., Inc., Edina, Minn., 1994—; lectr., guest instr. U. Wis., River Falls, 1976-77; spl. instr. Hamline U., St. Paul, 1977; vis. lectr. Coll. St. Scholastica, Duluth, Minn., 1977; program. faculty, cons. Employment Law Seminar for Colo., Fla., La., Oreg., Employment and Labor Law Seminar for Ala., Alaska, Calif., Conn., Ind., N.C., Ohio, Va., N.C. Safety and Health at the Workplace, S.C. Labor Law, Ohio Safety at the Workplace; bd. dirs. Acceptance Ins. Holdings, Inc., Omaha; active Internat. Confederation Jurists, 1993; mem. faculty sem. Ariz. Safety at Workplace, Hawaii Employment & Labor, Miss. Employment & Labor Law, Del. Employment & Labor, Alaska Employment and Labor Law, Ga. Employment & Labor Law, N.J. Employment & Labor, Wash. Employment Law, Mass. Employment & Labor Law, 1995—, Ark. Employment and Labor Law, Mo. Employment and Labor Law, Iowa Employment and Labor Law, Utah Employment and Labor Law. Author: Fred Neff's Self-Defense Library, 1976, Everybody's Self-Defense Book, 1978, Karate Is for Me, 1980, Running Is for Me, 1980, Lessons from the Samurai, 1986, Lessons from the Art of Kempo, 1986, Lessons from the Western Warriors, 1986, Lessons from the Fighting Commandos, 1990, Lessons from the Ancient Japanese Masters of Self-Defense, 1990, Lessons from the Eastern Warrors, 1990, Mysterious Persons of the Past, 1991, Great Mysteries of Crime, 1991; host TV series Great Puzzles In History; co-host TV series Great Unsolved Crimes, Minn.; asst. editor: Hennepic County Lawyer, 1992—. Advisor to bd. Sibley County Commrs., 1979-80; speaker civic groups, 1976-82; mem. Hennepin County Juvenile Justice Panel, 1980-82, Hennepin County (Minn.) Pub. Def. Conflict Panel, 1980-82, 86—, Hennepin County Bar Assn. Advice Panel Law Day, 1987, mem. dist. ethics com., 1990—; mem. Panel Union Privilege Legal Svcs. div. AFL-CIO, 1986—, Montgomery Wards Legal Svcs. Panel, 1986—, Edina Hist. Soc., Decathlon Athletic Club; charter mem. Commn. for the Battle of Normandy Mus.; founding sponsor Civil Justice Found., 1986—; mem. com. for publ. Hennepin County Lawyer, 1992. Recipient Outstanding Tchr. award Inver Hills Coll. Student Body, 1973, St. Paul Citizen of Month award Citizens Group, 1975, Kempo Club award U. Minn., 1975, U. Minn. Student Appreciation award Kempo Club, 1978, Sibley County Atty. Commendation award, 1980, Good Neighbor award WCCO Radio, 1985, Lamp of Knowledge award Twin Cities Lawyers Guild, 1986, N.W. Cmty. TV Commendation award, 1989-91, Presdl. Merit medal Pres. George Bush, 1990, N.W. Cmty. TV award, 1991, HLS Leadership award, 1984, Mng. Attys. Guidance award, 1985, Creative Thinker award Regional Staff, 1986, HLS Justice award, 1986, Honors cert. for Authors, Childrens Reading Round Table of Chgo., 1988. Fellow Roscoe Pound Found., Nat. Dist. Attys. Assn.; mem. ABA, ATLA, Minn. Bar Assn. (com. on ethics, 1994—, com. on alternative dispute resolution, 1994—), Minn. Trial Lawyers Assn., Hennepin County Bar Assn. (dist. ethics com. 1990—), Minn. Bar Assn. (com. on ethics 1994, com. on alternative dispute resolution 1994), Wis. Bar. Assn., Ramsey County Bar Assn., Am. Judicature Soc., Internat. Platform Assn., Am. Arbitration Assn. (panel of arbitrators 1992), Minn. Martial Arts Assn. (pres. 1974-78, Outstanding Instr. award 1973), Nippon Kobudo Rengokai (bd. dirs. North Cen. States 1972-76, regional dir. 1972-76), Internat. Confederation Jurists, Edina C. of C., Southview Country Club, Masons, Kiwanis, Scottish Rite, Sigma Alpha Mu. Avocations: reading, Far Eastern and Oriental studies, civic activities, physical conditioning, gardening. Home: 4515 Andover Rd Minneapolis MN 55435-4031 also: 7250 France Ave S Ste 107 Edina MN 55435-4311 also: 5930 Brooklyn Blvd Ste 206 Brooklyn Center MN 55429-2518 also: 1711 County Road B W Ste 340N Roseville MN 55113-4036

NEFF, GREGORY PALL, manufacturing engineering educator, consultant; b. Detroit, Nov. 23, 1942; s. Jacob John and Bonnie Alice (Pall) N.; m. Bonita Jean Dostal, Apr. 27, 1974; 1 child, Kristiana Dostal Neff. BS in Physics, U. Mich., 1964, MA in Math., 1966, MS in Physics, 1967; MSME, Mich. State U., 1982. Registered profl. engr., Ind.; cert. mfg. engr.; cert. mfg. technologist; cert. sr. indsl. technologist. Rsch. asst. cyclotron lab U. Mich., Ann Arbor, 1968-72, teaching fellow physics dept., 1973; instr. sci. dept. Lansing (Mich.) C.C., 1976-82; guest lectr. Purdue U. Calumet, Hammond, Ind., 1982-83, asst. prof., 1984-91, assoc. prof. mech. engring. tech., 1991—; cons. Inland Steel Co., Indsl. Engring., East Chicago, Ind., 1984-86, Polyurethane divsn. Pinder Industries, East Chicago, 1990-92, Elevated divsn. Pitts. Tank & Tower, Henderson, Ky., 1990-91; program evaluator for tech. accreditation commn. Accreditation Bd. for Engring. and Tech., 1996—. Contbr. articles to profl. jours. County commr. Ingham County Bd. of Commr., Mason, Mich., 1977-80, Tri-County Regional Planning Commn., Lansing, 1978-80, chair, non-motorized adv. coun. Mich. Dept. Transp., Lansing, 1982-83. Mem. ASME, AAUP, Soc. Mfg. Engrs. (chpt. 112 bd. dirs. 1986—, Appreciation award 1990, 92, Outstanding Faculty Advisor award 1991,), Ind. Soc. Profl. Engrs., Am. Soc. for Engring. Edn. (Merl K. Miller award 1994), Nat. Assn. Indsl. Tech., Order of the Engr. Democrat. Roman Catholic. Office: Purdue U Calumet 2200 169th St Hammond IN 46323-2068

NEFF, JACK KENNETH, apparel manufacturing company executive; b. N.Y.C., Feb. 23, 1938; s. William K. and Rose T. N.; m. Barbara Joan Neff, Nov. 4, 1961; 1 son, Craig William. A.A.S., Queens Coll., 1968; postgrad., Stanford Advanced Mgmt. Coll., 1973. Gen. mdse. mgr. youthwear Levi Strauss & Co., 1973-78, v.p. mktg., 1978-80; pres. Salant & Salant Co., N.Y.C., 1980-81; exec. v.p. Salant Corp., N.Y.C., 1981-84; pres., chief exec. officer Thomson Co., N.Y.C., 1984-87; exec. v.p., chief operating officer Stanley Blacker Co., N.Y.C., 1987-90; with Inside Mgmt. Assocs., N.Y.C., 1991-93; v.p. and gen. mgr. Reebok Worldwide Apparel Div., 1993-94; sr. v.p., 1994-96; sr. c.p. Reebok, 1996—; ptnr. The Muller Sports Group, N.Y.C., 1996—. Served in USN, 1956-59.

NEFF, JOHN, recording engineer, producer; b. Birmingham, Mich., Mar. 13, 1951; s. Robert Leslie Joseph and Mary Therese (McElvarr) N.; m. Nancy Louise Boocks, Aug. 29, 1987; children: Jennifer Lyn Neff, Bryan C. Groves, Kenneth John Neff. Student, Oakland Community Coll., Auburn Hills, Mich., 1970-72. Freelance recording artist, session musician Detroit, 1965-73; freelance record producer Toronto, Phoenix, L.A., 1974-79; radio announcer, engr. Stas. KVIB, KHEI, KMVI, KLHI, KAOI, 1981-88; record producer Maui Recorders, Kula, Hawaii, 1986-92; cons. studio design Roadrunner Audio Svcs., Glendale, Ariz., 1993-96; studio engring. cons. TEC:ton, L.A., 1996—; rec. engr. for Walter Becker, Donald Fagen (Steely Dan), Buffy Ste Marie, Willie Nelson, Sagan Lewis; touring musician Detroit, Toronto, Phoenix, L.A., 1969-79; studio monitor design for Kenny "Baby Face" Edmonds, Brian Austin Green; tech. cons. to David Lynch, Fox Scoring Stage. Recipient Grammy award nomination for Kamakiriad, 1994. Mem. ASCAP, Audio Engring Soc. (cert.), Am. Fedn. Musicians. Avocations: photography, hiking, travel. Home and Office: Roadrunner Audio Svcs 23846 N 38th Dr Glendale AZ 85310-4113

NEFF, KENNETH D., realtor; b. Montpelier, Ind., Oct. 19, 1929; s. Clyde A. and Cora I. N.; m. Nancy Stiffler, Dec. 26, 1951 (dec. Oct. 1996); children: David, Susan, Julie, Bradley. BS in Bus., Ball State U. Owner Neff Realty, Montpelier, 1983-95; mayor City of Montpelier, 1983-95. Mem. air pollution bd. Ind. Dept. Environ Mgmt., Indpls., 1991-95; mem. Purdue Hwy. Extension and Rsch. Project, Ind. Counties and Cities Bd., West Lafayette, 1991-95; chmn. adminstrv. coun. Montpelier United Meth. Ch. Lt. col. USAF, 1958-81. Recipient Sagamore of the Wabash award Gov. Bayh's State of Ind. Coun., 1996. Mem. Ind. Dem. Editl. Assn., Ind. Assn. Cities and Towns (exec. bd., legis com. 1988-96), North Ctrl. Mayors' Roundtable (pres. 1991-92), Kiwanis (past state lt. gov.). Democrat. Home: 129 S Washington St Montpelier IN 47359-1331 Office: 109 W Huntington St Montpelier IN 47359-1123

NEFF, P. SHERRILL, health care executive; b. Balt., Dec. 18, 1951; s. Paul Heston and Mary (Poulnot) N.; m. Sarah B. Barrett, June 20, 1976 (div. 1985); 1 child, Jacob Colin; m. Alicia Phyll Felton, May 26, 1988; 1 child, Michael Felton. BA, Wesleyan U., 1974; JD magna cum laude, U. Mich., 1980. Bar: Pa. 1980. Atty. Morgan Lewis & Bockius, Phila., 1980-84;

investment banker Alex Brown & Sons, Inc., Balt., 1984-93, mng. dir., 1992-93; sr. v.p. corp. devel. U.S. Healthcare, Blue Bell, Pa., 1993-94; pres., CFO Neose Techs., Inc., Horsham, Pa., 1994—, also bd. dirs.; bd. dirs. Jeff Banks, Inc., Phila. Trustee Zero Moving Dance Co., Phila., 1984-93. Mem. Pa. Biotech. Assn. (bd. dirs. 1996—). Democrat. Jewish. Home: 619 Revere Rd Merion Station PA 19066-1007 Office: Neose Techs. Inc PO Box 1109 102 Witmer Rd Horsham PA 19044

NEFF, RAY QUINN, electric power educator, consultant; b. Houston, Apr. 29, 1928; s. Noah Grant and Alma Ray (Smith) N.; m. Elizabeth McDougald, Sept. 4, 1982. Degree in Steam Engring., Houston Vocat. Tech., 1957; BSME, Kennedy Western U., 1986. Various positions Houston Lighting & Power Co., 1945-60, plant supr., 1960-70, plant supt. asst., 1970-80, tech. supr., 1980-85, tng. supr., 1985-87; owner, operator Neff Enterprises, Bedias, Tex., 1987—; tng. supr. Tex. A&M U., 1991—; cons. Houston Industries, 1987-89. Author: Power Plant Operation, 1975, Power Operator Training, 1985, Power Foreman Training, 1986. Judge Internat. Sci. and Engring. Fair, Houston, 1982, Sci. Engring. Fair Houston, 1987. Mem. ASME, Assn. Chief Operating Engrs., Masons. Republican. Methodist. Avocations: farming, ranching, classic cars. Home: Hwy 90 Rte 2t Box 193-A Bedias TX 77831 Office: Tex A&M U Power Plant College Station TX 77843

NEFF, ROBERT ARTHUR, business and financial executive; b. Woodbury, N.J., June 20, 1931; s. Arthur Adelbert and Esther Augusta (Fosdick) N.; m. Cristina Archila, Nov. 10, 1961 (div.); children: Robert Arthur, Phillip Adam; m. Julie Ann Ebers, Nov. 23, 1974; 1 child, William Savidge. A.B., Cornell U., 1953, B.P.E., 1954, LL.B., 1956, LL.D., 1969. Bar: N.Y. 1958. Asst. to chmn. bd. Internat. Basic Economy Corp., N.Y.C., 1958-59, v.p. S.Am., 1960-64; v.p. adminstrn., corp. sec. Seaboard World Airlines, Inc., Jamaica, N.Y., 1964-77, sr. v.p., dir., 1977-80; v.p. adminstrn. Flying Tiger Lines, 1980-81; sr. v.p. Vanguard Ventures, Inc., N.Y.C., 1982-85; pres. Icarus, Inc., Lake Success, N.Y., 1985-87; chmn. Greenway Capital Corp., N.Y.C., 1991-94. Mem. coun. Cornell U.; trustee Blair Acad., 1993—. Served to capt. USAF, 1956-58. Mem. Phi Delta Phi, Psi Upsilon. Home: Arreton Rd Princeton NJ 08540 Office: 45 Broadway New York NY 10006-3007

NEFF, ROBERT CLARK, lawyer; b. St. Marys, Ohio, Feb. 11, 1921; s. Homer Armstrong and Irene (McCulloch) N.; m. Betty Baker, July 3, 1954 (dec.); children: Cynthia Lee Neff Schifer, Robert Clark, Abigail Lynn (dec.); m. Helen Picking, July 24, 1975. BA, Coll. Wooster, 1943; postgrad. U. Mich., 1946-47; LLB, Ohio No. U., 1950. Bar: Ohio 1950, U.S. Dist. Ct. (no. dist.) Ohio 1978. pvt. practice law, Bucyrus, Ohio, 1950—; law dir. City of Bucyrus, 1962-95. Chmn. blood program Crawford County (Ohio) unit ARC, 1955-89; life mem. adv. bd. Salvation Army, 1962—; clk. of session 1st Presbyterian Ch., Bucyrus, 1958-96; bd. dirs. Bucyrus Area Cmty. Found, Crawford County Bd. Mental Retardation and Devel. Disabilities, 1977-82. With USNR, World War II; comdr. Res. ret. Recipient "Others" plaque for 30 yrs. adv. bd. svc. Salvation Army, Ohio No. U. Coll. Law Alumni award for cmty. svc., 1996; inducted Ohio Vets. Hall Fame, Columbus, 1996. Mem. Ohio Bar Assn., Crawford County Bar Assn., Naval Res. Assn., Ret. Officers Assn., Am. Legion, Bucyrus Area C. of C. (past bd. dirs., Outstanding Citizen award, 1973, Bucyrus Citizen of Yr., 1981). Republican. Clubs: Kiwanis (life mem., past pres.), Masons. Home: 1085 Mary Ann Ln # 406 Bucyrus OH 44820-3145 Office: 840 S Sandusky Ave Box 406 Bucyrus OH 44820-0406

NEFF, ROBERT MATTHEW, lawyer, investment and insurance executive; b. Huntington, Ind., Mar. 26, 1955; s. Robert Eugene and Ann (Bash) N.; m. Lee Ann Loving, Aug. 23, 1980; children: Alexandra, Graydon, Philip. BA in English, DePauw U., 1977; JD, Ind. U., Indpls., 1980. Bar: Ind. 1980, U.S. Dist. Ct. (so. dist.) Ind. 1980, U.S. Supreme Ct., 1993. Assoc. Krieg, DeVault, Alexander & Capehart, Indpls., 1980-85, ptnr., 1986-88; ptnr. Baker & Daniels, Indpls., 1988-92; of counsel, 1993-96; dept. to chmn. Fed. Housing Fin. Bd., Washington, 1992-93; pres., CEO Circle Investors, Inc., Indpls., 1993—, also bd. dirs.; mem. faculty Grad. Sch. of Banking of South, 1988-90; chmn. Liberty Bankers Life Ins. Co., 1995—, Am. Founders Life Ins. Co., Laurel Life Ins. Co., Aztec Life Assurance Co. Exec. editor Ind. Law Rev., 1979-80. Participant Lacy Exec. Leadership Conf., Indpls., 1985-86; trustee DePauw U., 1977-80. Mem. Ind. Bar Assn. (chmn. corps. banking and bus. law sect. 1987-88), ABA (chmn. bus. law com. young lawyers div. 1988-90, mem. banking law com. 1990-92), DePauw Alumni Assn. (bd. dirs. 1982-88), Phi Kappa Psi, Phi Beta Kappa. Avocations: tae kwon do, golf. Home: 6455 N Olney St Indianapolis IN 46220-4436 Office: Circle Investors Inc 251 N Illinois St Ste 1680 Indianapolis IN 46204-1755

NEFF, ROBERT WILBUR, academic administrator, educator; b. Lancaster, Pa., June 16, 1936; s. Wilbur Hildebr and Hazel Margaret (Martin) N.; m. Dorothy Rosewarne, Aug. 16, 1959; children: Charles Scott, Heather Lynn. BS, Pa. State U., 1958; BD, Yale Div. Sch., 1961, MA, 1963, PhD, 1969; DD, Juniata Coll., 1978, Manchester Coll., 1979; DHL, Bridgewater Coll., 1979. Asst. prof. Bridgewater Coll., 1964-65; mem. faculty dept. Bibl. studies Bethany Theol. Sem., 1965-77, prof., 1973-77; gen. sec. Ch. of the Brethren, Elgin, Ill., 1978-86; pres. Juniata Coll., 1986—; mem. faculty North Park Sem., No. Bapt. Sem., Theol. Coll. No. Nigeria; bd. dirs. Mellon Bank (Ctrl.) Nat. Assn., exec. com., 1989, chair exec. com., 1993, chair CRA com., 1994—; mem. pres.'s com. NCAA, 1996—. Mem. governing bd. Nat. Coun. Chs. of Christ, 1976-86, mem. exec. com., 1979-86; mem. Mid-East panel, 1980, 2d v.p., 1985-86; mem. ctrl. com. World Coun. Chs., 1983-92; rep. Assembly of World Coun. Chs., 1983, mem. exec. com. on interch. rels., 1980-84, mem. del. to China, 1981, chmn. presdl. panel, 1982-84; bd. dirs. Bethany Theol. Sem., 1978-86; campaign chmn. United Way, Huntington County, 1989; chair higher edn. com. Ch. of Brethren, 1993—. Danforth fellow, 1958-69. Mem. Soc. Bibl. Lit., Soc. Old Testament Study, Chgo. Soc. Bibl. Rsch., Soc. Values in Higher Edn., Coun. Ind. Colls. (nat. bd. dirs. 1991-94, treas. 1995—), Pa. Coun. Ind. Colls. and Univs. (exec. com. 1988-90, 92—, chair ann. conf. nominating com. 1993-94), Mid Atlantic Athletic Conf. (sec., mem. exec. com. 1994—). Democrat. Home: 2201 Washington St Huntingdon PA 16652-9762 Office: Juniata Coll 1700 Moore St Huntingdon PA 16652-2119

NEFF, THOMAS JOSEPH, executive search firm executive; b. Easton, Pa., Oct. 2, 1937; s. John Wallace and Elizabeth Ann (Dougherty) N.; m. Susan Culver Paull, Nov. 26, 1971 (dec.); children: David Andrew, Mark Gregory, Scott Dougherty; m. Sarah Brown Hallingby, Jan. 20, 1989; stepchildren: Brooke, Bailey. BS in Indsl. Engring., Lafayette Coll., 1959; MBA, Lehigh U., 1961. Assoc. McKinsey & Co., Inc., N.Y.C. and Australia, 1963-66; dir. mktg. planning Trans-World Airlines, N.Y.C., 1966-69; pres. Hosp. Data Scis., Inc., N.Y.C., 1969-74; prin. Booz, Allen & Hamilton, Inc., N.Y.C., 1974-76; regional ptnr. Spencer Stuart, Inc., N.Y.C., N.Am., 1976-79; bd. dirs. Spencer Stuart & Assocs., N.Y.C., 1976-79, pres., 1979-96, also bd. dirs., chmn. U.S., 1996—; bd. dirs. Lord Abbett & Co. Mut. Funds, Affiliated Fund; chmn. Brunswick Sch., 1991-95. Trustee Lafayette Coll., Greenwich Hosp. 1st lt. U.S. Army, 1961-63. Mem. Links Club, Sky Club, Blind Brook Club, Quogue (N.Y.) Beach Club, Quogue Field Club, Round Hill Club, Mill Reef Club, Coral Beach Club, Quantuck Beach Club. Republican. Roman Catholic. Home: 25 Midwood Rd Greenwich CT 06830-3807 Office: Spencer Stuart & Assocs 277 Park Ave New York NY 10172

NEFF, WALTER PERRY, financial consultant; b. Madison, Wis., Apr. 2, 1927; s. Ezra Eugene and Ruth (Perry) N.; m. Diane Michele Dubois, Mar. 12, 1963; children: Christopher (dec.), Taylor E., Stewart P. (by previous marriage), Michael W.P., Laura D. B.A., Williams Coll., 1950; LL.B., U. Wis., 1954; grad. advanced mgmt. program, Harvard U., 1969. Bar: Wis. 1954. Practiced in Madison, 1954-57; with Chem. Bank N.Y. Trust Co. (now Chem. Bank), N.Y.C., 1957-71; v.p. personal trust dept. Chem. Bank N.Y. Trust Co. (now Chem. Bank), 1965-68, sr. v.p., head fiduciary adminstrn. dept., 1968-71; exec. v.p. Chem. Bank, N.Y.C., 1971-73; sr. operating officer, adminstrv. head trust and investment Chem. Bank, 1973-82; fin. cons., 1983—; bd. dirs. Petroleum & Resources Corp., Balt., Adams Express Corp., Balt.; fin. dir. Manulife, Toronto; dir. Vista Mutual Funds; police justice Village of Centre Island, Oyster Bay, N.Y., 1965-74. Served with USNR, 1945-46. Mem. N.Y. State Bankers Assn. (exec. com. trust div.), Seawanhaka Corinthian Yacht Club (former commodore) (Oyster Bay), Royal Bermuda Yacht Club, Ekwanok Country Club (Manchester, Vt.), Phi Alpha Delta, Psi Upsilon. Home and Office: Holden Hill Rd Weston VT 05161

NEFF, WILLIAM L., lawyer; b. Macon, Mo., June 5, 1947. AB, U. Mo., 1969; JD magna cum laude, Harvard U., 1974. Bar: D.C. 1975, V.I. 1976, Colo. 1976. Law clk. to Hon. Young U.S. Dist. Ct. V.I., 1974-75; mem. Hogan & Hartson, Washington. Mem. Phi Beta Kappa. Office: Hogan & Hartson 555 13th St NW Washington DC 20004-1109

NEFT, DAVID SAMUEL, marketing professional; b. N.Y.C., Jan. 9, 1937; s. Louis and Sue (Horowitz) N.; m. Naomi Silver, May 31, 1964; children: Michael Louis, Deborah Isabel. BA, Columbia U., 1957, MBA, 1959, PhD, 1962. Dir. info. pub. Info. Concepts, Inc., N.Y.C., 1965-68, treas., chief exec. officer, 1968-70; gen. mgr. Sports Illustrated Enterprises, N.Y.C., 1970-73; pres. Sports Products Inc., Ridgefield, Conn., 1973-76; chief statistician Louis Harris and Assocs., N.Y.C., 1963-65, sr. v.p., 1977-78, exec. v.p., chief exec. officer, 1978-85; dir. research Gannett Co., Inc., N.Y.C., 1985-90, v.p. rsch., 1990—; cons. Fed. Energy Adminstrn., Washington, 1973-75. Author: Statistical Analysis for Areal Distributions, 1966; editor: The Baseball Encyclopedia, 1969; author (with others) The World Book of Odds, 1978, The Sports Encyclopedia: Baseball, 1974, 76-77, 81-82, 85, 87-89, 90—, The Sports Encyclopedia: Pro Football, 1974, 76, 78, 83, 87, 88-89, 90—, Pro Football: The Early Years, 1978, 83, 87, The World Series, 1976, 79, 86, The Sports Encyclopedia: Pro Basketball, 1975, 89, 90-91, All-Sports World Record Book, 1974, 75, 76, The Scrapbook History of Pro Football, 1976, 77, 79, The Scrapbook History of Baseball, 1975, The Notre Dame Football Scrapbook, 1977, The Ohio State Football Scrapbook, 1977, The University of Michigan Football Scrapbook, 1978, The Football Encyclopedia, 1991, 94; contbr. articles to profl. and acad. jours. Served with U.S. Army, 1961-63. Mem. Am. Assn. Pub. Opinion Rsch., Profl. Football Rsch. Assn. (v.p. 1985-87), Soc. for Am. Baseball Rsch. Jewish. Home: 525 E 86th St New York NY 10028-7512

NEGELE, JOHN WILLIAM, physics educator, consultant; b. Cleve., Apr. 18, 1944; s. Charles Frederick and Virgil Lea (Wettich) N.; m. Rose Anne Meeks, June 18, 1967; Janette Andrea, Julia Elizabeth. B.S., Purdue U., 1965; Ph.D., Cornell U., 1969. Research fellow Niels Bohr Inst., Copenhagen, 1969-70; vis. asst. prof. MIT, Cambridge, 1970-71, faculty mem., 1971—, prof. physics, 1979—, William A. Coolidge prof., 1991—, assoc. dir. Ctr. for Theoretical Physics, 1988-89, dir. Ctr. for Theoretical Physics, 1989—; cons. Los Alamos Sci. Lab., Brookhaven Nat. Lab., Lawrence Livermore Nat. Lab., Oak Ridge Nat. Lab.; mem. physics div. rev. com. Argonne Nat. Lab., (Ill.), 1977-83; mem. nuclear sci. div. rev. com. Lawrence Berkeley Lab., (Calif.), 1982—; mem. adv. bd., steering com. Inst. for Theoretical Physics, U. Calif.-Santa Barbara, 1982-86; mem. adv. bd. inst. for Nuclear Theory U. Washington, 1990—, chair 1992-94; program adv. com. Tandem Van de Graaff Accelerator, Brookhaven Nat. Lab., 1977-78, Bates Linear Accelerator, 1977-80, Los Alamos Meson Prodn. Facility, 1986-89, Brookhaven Alternating Gradient Synchraton, 1987-90. Author: Quantum Many Particle Systems, 1987; contbr. articles to profl. jours.; editor: Advances in Nuclear Physics, 1977—. Grantee NSF, 1965-69; grantee Danforth Found., 1965-69, Woodrow Wilson Found., 1965, Alfred P. Sloan Found., 1979, Japan Soc. for Promotion Sci., 1981, John Simon Guggenheim Found., 1982. Fellow Am. Phys. Soc. (exec. com. 1982-84, program com. 1980-82, editorial bd. Phys. Rev. 1980-82, exec. com. topical group on computational physics 1992-93, chair divsn. of computational physics 1992-93, exec. com. 1992-94, Bonner prize com. 1984-85), AAAS (nominating com. 1987-91, mem. physics sect. com. 1991—), Fedn. Am. Scientists. Home: 70 Buckman Dr Lexington MA 02173-6000 Office: MIT Dept Physics 6-308 77 Massachusetts Ave Cambridge MA 02139-4301

NEGLIA, JOHN PETER, chemical engineer, environmental scientist; b. Passaic, N.J., Dec. 30, 1957; s. Anthony John and Claire Ann (Graglia) N.; m. Deborah Ann Rean, Apr. 5, 1981; children: Kimberlee Claire, Anthony Richard. BSChemE, N.J. Inst. of Tech., 1981, MS in Environ. Sci., 1992. Cert. hazardous materials mgr. Process engr. Am. Cyanamid Co., Wayne, N.J., 1981-85; mfg./environ. mgr. Powder Tech. Co., Fairfield, N.J., 1985-86; facility/environ. engring. mgr. Curtiss Wright Fligh Systems Inc., Fairfield, 1986-89; plant supt. Dubois Chem. Divsn. of Molson Breweries, East Rutherford, N.J., Toronto, 1989-92; mgr. environ. and safety engring. Becton Dickinson and Co., Franklin Lakes, N.J., 1992—. Author: Encyclopedia of Environmental (vol. 5), 1992, Control Technology (vol. 8), 1992; contbr. articles to profl. jours. Vice chmn. Hazardous Material Control Bd., Clifton, N.J., 1990—; chmn. of edn. subcom. Local Emergency Planning Com., Clifton, 1990—. Mem. AIChe, Am. Soc. of Safety Engrs., Water Pollution Control Fedn. Republican. Roman Catholic. Avocations: music, recreational sports, reading. Home: 9 Glenwood St Clifton NJ 07013-2604 Office: Becton Dickinson & Co 1 Becton Dr Franklin Lakes NJ 07417-1815

NEGRON, CARLOS DANIEL, lawyer; b. Bronx, June 9, 1953; m. Lissette Eileen Lavandeira, Aug. 29, 1992; children: Christine Melissa, Victoria Elizabeth, Catherine Deanna. BBA, Baruch Coll., 1976; JD, N.Y. Law Sch., 1980. Bar: N.Y. 1981, Fla. 1996, U.S. Dist. Ct. (so. and ea. dist.) N.Y. 1981. Legal rsch. assoc. J.C. Penney & Co., Inc., N.Y.C., 1977-79; assoc. atty. Bernstein, Weiss, Coplan, Weinstein & Lake, N.Y.C., 1979-84; sr. assoc. DeOrchis & Ptnrs., N.Y.C., 1984-86; assoc. gen. counsel Through Transport Mutual Svcs. (Americas), Jersey City, N.J., 1987-94, sr. v.p. Latin Am. region, 1994—; exec. dir. Internat. Group Cons., 1996—; exec. dir. Internat. Group, 1995—; lectr. in field. Contbr. articles to profl. jours. Named Disting. Alumnus N.Y. Law Sch., 1994. Roman Catholic. Avocations: travel, tennis, golf.

NEGRON, JAIME, performing arts center sales director; b. San Juan, P.R., Dec. 23, 1939; came to U.S., 1952; s. Rito and Tomasa (Otero) N.; m. Barbara Charlotte Stovall, Nov. 5, 1959; children: Jeannette Michelle, Victoria Frances. BA in Econs., Howard U., 1987. Lic. realtor. Chief receiving & shipping Am. Univ., Washington, 1960-62; book dept. mgr. Am. U., Washington, 1968-71; bookstore mgr. Follett Corp., Chgo., 1962-68, Cath. U., Washington, 1971-74; dir. Howard U. stores Howard Univ., Washington, 1974-87; dir. aux. enterprises Howard U., Washington, 1987-91; real estate agt. Weichert Referral Assocs., Vienna, Va., 1993—; asst. dir. aux. enterprises DeKalb Coll., Atlanta, 1992-96; dir. retail operations J.F. Kennedy Ctr. for Performing Arts, Washington, 1997—; cons. U. Del., Newark, 1988, Wesley Sem., Washington, 1984, R.R. Moton Meml. Inst., N.Y.C., 1974-79. Active Vienna Jaycees, 1970-80. With USN, 1958-60. Mem. Middle Atlantic Coll. Stores (pres. 1984), Nat. Assn. Coll. Stores, Nat. Bd. Realtors, Va. Bd. Realtors. Episcopalian. Avocation: dancing. Office: JFK Ctr Performing Arts 2700 F St NW Washington DC 20566-0002

NEGROPONTE, JOHN DIMITRI, diplomat; b. London, July 21, 1939; s. Dimitri John and Catherine (Coumantaros) N.; m. Diana Mary Villiers, Dec. 14, 1976; children: Marina, Alexandra, John, George, Sophia. BA, Yale U., 1960. Commd. fgn. svc. officer U.S. Dept. of State, 1960; vice consul Hong Kong, 1961-63; 2nd sec. Saigon, 1964-68; mem. U.S. Del. to Paris Peace Talks on Viet-Nam, 1968-69; mem. staff NSC, 1970-73; polit. counselor Quito, Ecuador, 1973-75; consul gen. Thessaloniki, Greece, 1975-77; dep. asst. sec. of state for oceans and fisheries affairs Washington, 1977-79; dep. asst. sec. for East Asian and Pacific affairs U.S. Dept. State, Washington, 1980-81; U.S. amb. to Honduras, 1981-85, asst. sec. for oceans and internat. environ. and sci. affairs, 1985-87; dep. asst. Pres. for Nat. Security Affairs, 1987-89; U.S. amb. to Mexico, 1989-93, U.S. amb. to The Philippines, 1993-96, spl. coord. for post-1999 U.S. presence in Panama, 1996—. Mem. Am. Fgn. Svc. Assn., Coun. on Fgn. Rels. Greek Orthodox. Home: 4936 Lowell St NW Washington DC 20016

NEGUS, LUCY NEWTON BOSWELL, foundation executive; b. Charlottesville, Va., Apr. 27, 1937; d. William Ward and Lucy Tyler (Newton) Boswell; m. Sidney Stevens Negus, Jr., Dec. 23, 1957 (div. Nov. 1971); children: Sidney Stevens III, Lucy Tyler Negus Snidow, Tayloe Newton. Student, Randolph-Macon Woman's Coll., 1955-57; BS in Mass. Comm., Va. Commonwealth U., 1985. Adminstrv. asst. St. Paul's Episcopal Ch., Richmond, Va., 1972-77; coord. comm. Westminster-Canterbury Corp., Richmond, 1977-78; corp. sec. Westminster-Canterbury Found., Richmond, 1980—; dir. cmty. rels. and devel. Westminster-Canterbury Mgmt. Corp., Richmond, 1978-95, dir. devel., 1995—. Writer/editor Coming of Age insert Va. Churchman, 1978-79, The Lamp, 1978-95; contbr. articles, poetry to profl. jours.; writer/rschr. books by other authors including: Christpower, 1974. Mem. Leadership Metro Richmond Class, 1996, Citizens Coalition for Greater Richmond, 1996—; exec. bd. Collegiate Schs. Alumni Assn., Richmond, 1980-83, 91-94; bd. assocs. St. Paul's Coll., Lawrenceville, Va., 1985-88. Mem. Va. Assn. Fundraising Execs. (founding mem., pres. 1983-84, Devel. Recognition award 1993), Va. Planned Giving Study Group (bd. dirs. 1992-95), Estate Planning Coun. of Richmond, Va. Writers Club, The Woman's Club, The Laurels Honor Soc., Phi Kappa Phi, Kappa Tau Alpha. Republican. Episcopalian. Avocations: writing, history, genealogy, travel, local economic development. Home: 5404 Queensbury Rd Richmond VA 23226-2120 Office: Westminster-Canterbury Mgmt 1600 Westbrook Ave Richmond VA 23227-3315

NEHAMAS, ALEXANDER, philosophy educator; b. Athens, Greece, Mar. 22, 1946; came to U.S., 1964; s. Albert and Christine (Yannuli) N.; m. Susan Glimcher, June 22, 1983; 1 child, Nicholas Albert Glimcher. BA, Swarthmore Coll., 1967; PhD, Princeton U., 1971, D in Philosophy (hon.) Athens, 1993. Asst., then assoc. prof. philosophy U. Pitts., 1971-81, prof., 1981-86; prof. philosophy U. Pa., 1986-90; vis. prof. Princeton U., N.J., 1978-79, 89, Edmund Carpenter prof. humanities, prof. philosophy and comparative lit., 1990—, chair humanities coun., 1994—, chmn. program in Hellenic studies, 1994—; Mills vis. prof. U. Calif., Berkeley, 1983, Sather vis. prof., 1993; vis. prof. U. Calif., Santa Cruz, 1988; bd. dir. Princeton Univ. Press; bd. trustees Nat. Humanities Ctr. Author: Nietzsche: Life as Literature, 1985; translator: Plato's Symposium, 1989, Plato's Phaedrus, 1995; co-editor: Aristotle's Rhetoric: Philosophical Essays, 1994; contbr. articles to profl. jours.; mem. editorial bd. Am. Philos. Quar., 1981-86, History of Philosophy Quar., 1983-88, Ancient Philosophy, 1984—, Jour. Modern Greek Studies, 1986—, Arion, 1989—, Philosophy and Lit., 1989—, Philosophy and Phenomenological Rsch., 1990—. Recipient Lindback Found. Teaching award, U. Pa., 1989; Guggenheim fellow 1983; NEH grantee, 1978. Mem. MLA, Am. Philos. Assn. (chmn. program 1982-83, exec. com. 1990-92), Modern Greek Studies Assn. (exec. com. 1983-89), Am. Soc. Aesthetics, North Am. Nietzsche Soc. (exec. com. 1988-91), Phi Beta Kappa (vis. scholar 1995). Office: Princeton U Dept Philosophy Princeton NJ 08544

NEHLS, ROBERT LOUIS, JR., school system administrator; b. Berkeley, Calif., Dec. 27, 1944; s. Robert Louis and Inda May (Kean) N.; m. Diana Jean Smith, June 17, 1967; 1 child, Patrick Robert. AA, Coll. Marin, 1965; BS, San Jose State U., 1967, MA, 1976; EdD, U. San Francisco, 1991. Cert. tchr., sch. adminstr., Calif. Tchr. Diablo Valley Coll., Pleasant Hill, Calif., 1979-86; acct. Kelly and Tama, CPAs, Walnut Creek, Calif., 1978-79; tchr. Pleasanton (Calif.) Unified Sch. Dist., 1970-78, 79-81, dir. fiscal svcs., 1981-83; dep. supt. San Leandro (Calif.) Unified Sch. Dist., 1983-87, 90—; asst. supt. Acalanes Union High Sch. Dist., Lafayette, Calif., 1987-89; supt. Orinda (Calif.) Union Sch. Dist., 1989-90; exec. adv. com. Calif. Found. Improvement of Employee/Employer Relationships, Sacramento, 1992—. Contbr. articles to profl. jours. Mem. Assn. Calif. Sch. Adminstrs. (comptroller 1992-95, pres. 1996), Calif. Assn. Sch. Bus. Ofcls. (bd. dirs. no. sect. 1984-89), No. Calif. Sch. Bus. Ofcls. (past pres.), Acad. of Sci., Phi Kappa Phi. Avocations: fishing, skiing. Home: 1004 Leland Dr Lafayette CA 94549-4130 Office: San Leandro Unified Sch Dist 14735 Juniper St San Leandro CA 94579-1222

NEHMER, STANLEY, economics consultant; b. N.Y.C., Dec. 8, 1920; s. Alexander and Laura (Kessler) N.; m. Phyllis Fleischman, Nov. 30, 1946; children: Sheryl Rae, Jonathan Craig. BSS, CCNY, 1941; MA, Columbia U., 1942; postgrad., George Washington U., 1943-44, Am. U., 1946-47. Faculty CCNY, 1941-42; with OSS, 1942-45; economist Dept. State, 1945-57; dep. dir. Office Internat. Resources, Washington, 1961-64, dir., 1964-65; dep. asst. sec. for resources Dept. Commerce, 1965-73; sr. economist IBRD, 1957-61; prin. and dir. econ. cons. services Wolf & Co., Washington, 1973-78; pres. Econ. Cons. Services Inc., Washington, 1978-88, chmn., 1988-95; chmn. emeritus, 1995—; adj. prof. Am. bus. history Am. U., 1948-63; U.S. rep. commodities com. UN Conf. on Trade and Devel., Geneva, 1965; chmn. Interag. Textile Adminstrv. Com., 1965-72; chmn. U.S. rep. OECD Textiles Com., 1971-73; mem. U.S. Oil Import Appeals Bd., 1965-73; chmn. Com. for Implementation of Textile Agreements, 1972-73; alt. mem. Oil Policy Com., 1970-73; mem. U.S. Govt. Industry Sector Adv. Com. for Trade Negotiations, 1976-88, Treasury Dept. Adv. Com. on Comml. Ops. of Customs Svc., 1988-92. Contbr. to: Ency. Americana, Ency. Brit., U.S. Competiteveness in the World Economy, 1985. Served with AUS, 1943-45. Recipient Commendable Service award Dept. State, 1956, Superior Honor award, 1964; certificate appreciation Sec. Commerce, 1967; Gold medal Dept. Commerce, 1971; N.Y. Bd. Trade Ann. Textile award, 1972; No. Textile Assn. Distinguished Service award, 1973. Fellow Am. Council Learned Socs., mem. Nat. Economists Club, Am. Econ. Assn. Home: 15100 Interlachen Dr Silver Spring MD 20906-5611 also: 2600 S Ocean Blvd Boca Raton FL 33432 Office: 1225 19th St NW Washington DC 20036-2411

NEHRA, GERALD PETER, lawyer; b. Detroit, Mar. 25, 1940; s. Joseph P. and Jeanette M. (Bauer) N.; children: Teresa, Patricia; m. Peggy Jensen, Sept. 12, 1987. B.I.E., Gen. Motors Inst., Flint, Mich., 1962; J.D., Detroit Coll. Law, 1970. Bar: Mich. 1970, U.S. Dist. Ct. (ea. dist.) Mich. 1970, N.Y. 1972, U.S. Dist. Ct. (so. dist.) N.Y. 1972, U.S. Dist. Ct. (no. dist.) N.Y. 1976, U.S. Ct. Appeals (6th cir.) 1978, Colo. 1992. Successively engr., supr., gen. supr. Gen. Motors Corp., 1958-67; mktg. rep., to regional counsel IBM Corp., 1967-79; v.p., gen. counsel Church & Dwight Co., Inc. 1979-82; dep. chief atty-Amway Corp., 1982-83, dep. gen. counsel, 1983-92; dir. legal div., 1989-91, sec. and dir. corp. law, 1991-92; v.p. gen. counsel Fuller Brush, Bolder, Colo., 1991-92; pvt. practice, 1992—; adj. instr. Dale Carnegie Courses, 1983-91. Recipient Outstanding Contbn. award Am. Cancer Soc., 1976. Mem. Mich. Bar Assn., Colo. Bar Assn., N.Y. State Bar Assn., ABA. Contbr. chpt. to book. Home and Office: 1710 Beach St Muskegon MI 49441-1008

NEHRBASS, SETH MARTIN, patent lawyer; b. Lafayette, La., Nov. 10, 1960; s. Neil Martin and Janet (Himbert) N.; m. Isabel Hortelano, July 10, 1982 (div. Feb. 1993); children: Gabriel, Fabian. Student, U. Catholique de l'Ouest, Angers, France, 1980, U. Paul Valéry, Montpellier, France, 1981; BS in Physics summa cum laude, U. Southwe. La., 1982; JD cum laude, Loyola U., 1990. Bar: U.S. Patent & Trademark Office 1984, La. 1990, U.S. Dist. Ct. (ea., mid., and we. dists.) La. 1990, U.S. Ct. Appeals (5th and fed. cirs.) 1990; cert. notary public, La. Patent examiner U.S. Patent & Trademark Office, 1982-84; patent agt. with law firm New Orleans, 1986-87; assoc. Pravel, Hewitt, Kimball & Krieger, New Orleans, 1987-97, shareholder, 1997—; judge practice round moot ct. teams Loyola Law Sch., 1992—; preparer questions patent bar exam PTO Q & A Bd., 1992-93; presenter in field. Contbr. articles to profl. jours. Den leader 2d grade Cub Scouts, Boy Scouts Am., Lusher Sch., Audubon Dist., 1991-92, 3d grade, 1994-95, asst. den leader 3d grade, 1992-93, 4th grade, 1993-94; soccer coach Carrollton Booster Club, New Orleans, 1993-95, Lakeview Soccer Club, New Orleans, 1995-96. Recipient Hornbook award West Pub. Co., 1986-87, 87-88, Corpus Juris Secundum award, 1986-87, Am. Jurisprudence awards (2), 1986; scholar La. State U. Alumni Fedn., 1978, Coun. Devel. French La./French Govt., 1980-81, Loyola Law Sch., 1986. Mem. ABA (sect. law, sci., tech. 1988-91, law student divsn. liaison patent trademark and copyright law 1988-90, intellectual property law sect. 1988—, chmn. law student com. 1996—, chmn. spl. com. drug crisis 1990-93, co-chmn. ann. meeting arrangements com. 1993-94, internat. treaties and laws com. 1994—), Am. Intellectual Property Law Assn. (ADR com., internat. and fgn. law com., patent law com. 1994—), La. State Bar Assn. (internat. law sect. 1992-94, intellectual property law sect. 1996—), New Orleans Bar Assn. (interim chmn. ad hoc com. drug crisis 1991-92, chmn. charter mem. intellectual property law com. 1991-95, chmn. law related edn. com., 1995—), adv. bd. mem. La. Ctr. for Law and Civic Edn., 1996—, Loyola Law Sch. Moot Ct. Alumni Assn., Sigma Pi Sigma, Pi Delta Phi, Alpha Sigma Nu. Democrat. Roman Catholic. Avocations: gardening, dancing, traveling, hunting, fishing. Office: Pravel Hewitt Kimball & Krieger PO Box 24788 New Orleans LA 70184-4788

NEHRT, LEE CHARLES, management educator; b. Baldwin, Ill., Sept. 12, 1926; s. Martin William and Amanda Fredarika (Tillock) N.; m. Ardith Ann Saltzman, Mar. 26, 1952; children: Chadwick Charles, Philip Lee, Dana Ann. BS, USCG Acad., 1949; certificat d'Etudes Politiques, U. Paris, 1955;

MBA, Columbia U., 1956, PhD, 1962. Fgn. ops. supr. Atomics Internat., Canoga Park, Calif., 1956-60; prof. internat. bus. Ind. U., 1962-65, 67-69, 71-74; Ford Found. adv. to minister planning, economy and industry Tunisia, 1965-67; chief adv. group U. Dacca, E. Pakistan, 1969-71; R.P. Clinton prof. internat. mgmt. Wichita (Kans.) State U., 1974-78; pres. World Trade Inst., N.Y.C., 1978-81; Owens-Ill. prof. internat. mgmt. Ohio State U., Columbus, 1981-86; cons. UN, World Bank, advisor Ministry Planning Govt. Indonesia, 1987-89; dir., curator The Blacksmith Mus., 1991-92. Author: Education in International Business, 1963, Foreign Marketing of Nuclear Power Plants, 1965, Financing Capital Equipment Exports, 1966, International Finance for Multinational Business, 1967, 2d rev. edit. 1972, International Business Research: Past, Present and Future, 1969, The Political Climate for Private Investment in North Africa, 1970, Managerial Policy and Strategy for Developing Countries, 1973, Managerial Policy, Strategy and Planning for South-East Asia, 1974, Managerial Policy and Strategy for the Philippines, 1976, 3d rev. edit. 1989, Business and International Education, 1977, The Internationalization of the Business School Curriculum, 1979, Case Studies in the Internationalization of the Business School Curriculum, 1981, The Politico-Economic Analysis of Countries, 1981; also 5 monographs, various articles and reports in field. Chmn. bd. dirs. Monroe County ARC, 1996—. Served to lt. (j.g.) USCG, 1949-53. Mem. Acad. Internat. Bus. (pres. 1972-74, dean fellows 1978-81), Soc. Internat. Devel. (gov. 1968-71).

NEIBERGER, RICHARD EUGENE, pediatrician, nephrologist, educator; b. Onaga, Kans., Nov. 16, 1947; s. Earl Edward and Margaret Bell (Grim) N.; m. Mary June Chamberlin, Oct. 31, 1971; children: Ami, Eric, Chris, Robert. BS in Physics, U. Ctrl. Fla., 1971; PhD, U. Louisville, 1979, MD, 1982. Diplomate Am. Bd. Pediat., Nat. Bd. Med. Examiners. Intern, then resident in pediat. Albert Einstein Coll. Med., Bronx, N.Y., 1982-85; fellow in pediat. nephrology Albert Einstein Coll. Med., Bronx, 1985-88; asst. prof. U. Fla. Coll. Med., Gainesville, 1988-93, assoc. prof., 1993—; assoc. med. dir. Children's Kidney Ctr., Gainesville, 1989—; rsch. peer rev. com. Fla. affiliate Am. Heart Assn., 1993—; physician advisor Fla. Med. Quality Assurance, Tampa, 1994—. Contbr. articles to profl. jours. Sunday Sch. Tchr. Trinity United Meth. Ch., Gainesville, 1992—; Bd. dirs. Children's Home Soc., Gainesville, 1994—; troop com. mem. Boy Scouts Am. Trinity Ch., Gainesville, 1994—. Grantee CoInvest, Bethesda, Md., 1995. Mem. AMA, Fla. Med. Assn., So. Med. Assn., Am. Soc. Nephrology, Internat. Pedait. Nephrology Assn., Am. Soc. Pediat. Nephrology. Republican. Methodist. Avocations: camping, skiing, traveling. Office: Dept Pediat Univ Fla 1600 Archer Rd Gainesville FL 32610-0296

NEIDELL, MARTIN H., lawyer; b. Bklyn., Apr. 5, 1946; s. Sidney B. and Sophie (Goldstein) N.; m. Suzan C. Rucker, June 23, 1968; children: Michael, Sari. BA magna cum laude, Lehigh U., 1968; JD cum laude, NYU, 1971. Bar: N.Y. 1972, U.S. Dist. Ct. (ea. and so. dists.) N.Y. 1973, U.S. Ct. Appeals (2d cir.) 1973. Law clk. to presiding justice U.S. Dist. Ct. (ea. dist.) N.Y., Bklyn., 1971-73; assoc. Stroock & Stroock & Lavan LLP, N.Y.C., 1973-79; ptnr. Stroock & Stroock & Lavan, N.Y.C., 1980—; sec. Page Am. Group, Hackensack, N.J., 1983—. Editor NYU Law Rev., 1971. Trustee North Shore Synagogue, Syosset, N.Y., 1984-90. Mem. ABA. Office: Stroock & Stroock & Lavan LLP 180 Maiden Ln New York NY 10038-4925

NEIDERT, KALO EDWARD, accountant, educator; b. Safe, Mo., Sept. 1, 1918; s. Edward Robert and Margaret Emma (Kinsey) N.; m. Stella Mae Vest, June 22, 1952; children—Edward, Karl, David, Wayne, Margaret. B.S. in Bus. Adminstrn. with honors, Washington U., St. Louis, 1949, M.S. in Bus. Adminstrn, 1950; postgrad., U. Minn., 1950-54. CPA, Nev. Mem. faculty U. Minn., 1950-54; mem. faculty U. Miss., 1954-57, U. Tex., Austin, 1957-61, Gustavus Adolphus Coll., St. Peter, Minn., 1961-62; prof. acctg. and info. systems U. Nev., 1962-90, prof. emeritus, 1990—; auditor Washoe County Employee Fed. Credit Union, 1969-82, dir., treas., 1982-86. Author: Statement on Auditing Procedure in Decision Tree Form, 1974. Asst. scoutmaster local Boy Scouts Am., asst. dist. commr. New Area coun.; bd. dirs. Tahoe Timber Trails, 1980-82, treas., 1981-82, v.p. fin., 1982-84; Bd. dirs. St. Johns Child Care Center, 1982-84; cen. com. mem. Washoe County Rep. Party, Reno, 1986-88, 90—. Mem. AICPA, Assn. System Mgmt. (treas. Reno chpt. 1984—), Am. Acctg. Assn., Am. Econ. Assn., Am. Fin. Assn., Fin. Mgmt. Assn., Nev. Soc. CPAs, Western Fin. Assn., Oddfellows, Beta Alpha Psi, Beta Gamma Sigma. Presbyterian. Office: U Nev Coll Bus Adminstrn Reno NV 89557 *I am the descendent of a second generation American. In addition I was raised on a farm in rural America. Early in life, I learned that achievements come only with hard work and taking advantage of each opportunity that comes along, not waiting to see if there was a better opportunity around the corner. All through life this has been my philosophy; take advantage of each opportunity and work hard to make it succeed.*

NEIDHARDT, FREDERICK CARL, microbiologist; b. Phila., May 12, 1931; s. Adam Fred and Carrie (Fry) N.; m. Elizabeth Robinson, June 9, 1956 (div. Sept. 1977); children: Richard Frederick, Jane Elizabeth; m. Germaine Chipault, Dec. 3, 1977; 1 son, Marc Frederick. BA, Kenyon Coll., 1952, DSc (hon.), 1976; PhD, Harvard U., 1956; DSc (hon.), Purdue U., 1988, Umea U., 1994. Research fellow Pasteur Inst., Paris, 1956-57; H.C. Ernst research fellow Harvard Med. Sch., 1957-58, instr., then assoc., 1958-61; mem. faculty Purdue U., 1961-70, assoc. prof, then prof., assoc. head dept. biol. scis., 1965-70; mem. faculty U. Mich., Ann Arbor, 1970—, chmn. dept. microbiology and immunology, 1970-82, F.G. Novy disting. univ. prof., 1989—, assoc. dean faculty affairs, 1990-93, assoc. v.p. for rsch., 1993-96, acting v.p. for rsch., 1996—; Found. for Microbiology lectr. Am. Soc. Microbiology, 1966-67; cons. Dept. Agr., 1964-65; mem. grant study panel NIH, 1965-69, 88-92; mem. commn. scholars Ill. Bd. Higher Edn., 1973-79; mem. test com. for microbiology Nat. Bd. Med. Examiners, 1975-79, chmn., 1979-83; mem. sci. adv. com. Neogen Corp., 1982-92; mem. basic energy scis. adv. com. U.S. Dept. Energy, 1994—; Wellcome vis. prof. in microbiology U. Ky., 1986. Author books and papers in field; mem. editorial bd. profl. jours. Recipient award bacteriology and immunology Eli Lilly and Co., 1966; Alexander von Humboldt Found. award for U.S. sr. scientist, 1979; NSF sr. fellow U. Copenhagen, 1968-69. Mem. Am. Soc. Microbiology (pres. 1981-82), Am. Acad. Arts and Scis., Am. Soc. Biochemistry and Molecular Biology, Am. Inst. Biol. Scis., Genetics Soc. Am., Soc. Gen. Physiology, Phi Beta Kappa, Sigma Xi. Office: U Mich Med Sch Dept Microbiology and Immunology Ann Arbor MI 48109-0620

NEIDHART, JAMES ALLEN, physician, educator; b. Steubenville, Ohio, Aug. 30, 1940; s. James Leonard and Mary Jane (Daniels) N.; m. Patricia Irene Harpkamp, Aug. 16, 1966 (div. Apr. 1985); children—James, Jeffrey, Jennifer; m. Mary Gagen, Feb. 1986; children: Andrew, Rae Ann. B.S., Union Coll., Alliance, Ohio, 1962; M.D., Ohio State U., 1966. Diplomate Am. Bd. Internal Medicine, Am. Bd. Hematology and Oncology. Intern Bronson Hosp., Kalamazoo, Mich., 1966-67; resident Ohio State U., Columbus, Ohio, 1969-71; postdoctoral fellow Coll. Medicine, Ohio State U., Columbus, 1972-74, asst. prof. medicine, 1974-78, assoc. prof., 1978-84, dir. interdisciplinary oncology unit Comprehensive Cancer Ctr., 1975-80, dep. dir. Comprehensive Cancer Ctr., 1980-84; prof. medicine U. Tex.-Houston-M.D. Anderson Hosp. and Tumor Inst., 1984-86, Hubert L. and Olive Stringer prof. oncology, 1984-86, dep. head div. medicine, 1984-86, chmn. dept. med. oncology, 1984-86; dir. Cancer Rsch. and Treatment Ctr., U. N.Mex., Albuquerque, 1986—, chief hematology and oncology, 1986-91. Contbr. chpts. to Recent Advances in Clinical Therapeutics, Clinical Immunotherapy. Former mem. bd. dirs. Am. Cancer Soc., Columbus; former v.p. Ohio Cancer Research Assocs. Served to lt. USN, 1967-69, Vietnam. Mem. Am. Soc. Hematology, Am. Soc. Clin. Oncology, Am. Assn. Cancer Research, ACP, S.W. Oncology Group, Wilderness Soc., Sierra Club. Home: 21 Rd 3285 Aztec NM 87410 Office: San Juan Regional Cancer Ctr Farmington NM 87401

NEIDICH, GEORGE ARTHUR, lawyer; b. N.Y.C., Feb. 22, 1950; s. Hyman and Rosalyn (Eisenberg) N.; m. Alene Wendrow, Jan. 10, 1982. BA, SUNY, Binghamton, 1971; JD magna cum laude, SUNY, Buffalo, 1974; MLT, Georgetown U., 1981. Bar: N.Y. 1975, D.C. 1979, Va.a 1996, Conn. 1990. Assoc. Runfola & Birzon, Buffalo, 1973-75, Duke, Holzman, Yaeger & Radlin, Buffalo, 1975-77; gen. counsel subcom. on capital, investments and bus. opportunity, com. on small bus. U.S. Ho. of Reps., Washington, 1977-79, subcom on gen. oversight, 1979-80; sr. legal advisor Task Force Product Liability and Accident Compensation, Office of Gen. Counsel, Dept. Commerce, Washington, 1980-81; assoc. Steptoe & Johnson, Washington, 1981-86, of counsel, 1986-89; gen. counsel, sr. v.p. Preferred Health Care, Ltd., Wilton, Conn. (now Value Behavioral Health, Inc.), 1989-93, COO, 1993-95; cons., 1995—; adj. prof. Georgetown U. Law Ctr., 1985-87. Author: Report on Product Liability, 1980. Contbr. articles to profl. jours. Home: 9301 Morison Ln Great Falls VA 22066-4153 Office: PO Box 536 Great Falls VA 22066-0536

NEIER, ARYEH, author, human rights organization administrator; b. Berlin, Apr. 22, 1937; came to U.S., 1947, naturalized, 1955; s. Wolf and Gitla (Bendzinska) N.; m. Yvette Celton, June 22, 1958; 1 son, David. B.S., Cornell U., 1958; LL.D. (hon.), Hofstra U., 1975, Hamilton Coll., 1979, SUNY, Binghamton, 1988. Exec. dir. League Indsl. Democracy, N.Y.C., 1958-60; assoc. editor Current mag., N.Y.C., 1960-63; exec. dir. N.Y. Civil Liberties Union, N.Y.C., 1965-70; field devel. officer ACLU, N.Y.C., 1963-64, exec. dir., 1970-78; adj. prof. law NYU, N.Y.C., 1978—; dir. 20th Century Fund Project on Litigation and Social Policy, 1978-81; exec. dir. Human Rights Watch, N.Y.C., 1981-93; pres. Open Soc. Fund and Inst., N.Y.C., 1993—; lectr. Police Acad., N.Y., 1969-70. Author: Dossier, 1975, Crime and Punishment: A Radical Solution, 1976, Defending My Enemy, 1979, Only Judgment, 1982; co-editor series of handbooks on rights of Americans, 1972-78; mem. editorial bd. The Nation, 1978-86, columnist, 1990—. Commr. juvenile justice standards project Am. Bar Assn.—Inst. for Judicial Adminstrn. Recipient Gavel award Am. Bar Assn., 1974. Club: K.P. (Humanitarian award 1967). Office: 888 7th Ave Fl 31 New York NY 10106-3199*

NEIHARDT, HILDA, foundation administrator, writer, educator; b. Bancroft, Nebr., Dec. 6, 1916; d. John Gneisenau and Mona (Martinsen) N.; m. Albert Joseph Petri, Apr. 18, 1942 (div. Oct. 1963); children; Gail Petri Toedebusch, Robin, Coralie Joyce Hughes. AB, U. Nebr., 1937; postgrad., Letitia Barnum Sch. Theatre, Chgo., 1943-44; JD, U. Mo., 1963. Bar: Mo. 1963. Adminstrv. asst. Consulate of Switzerland, St. Louis, 1937-42; pvt. practice Columbia, Mo., 1963-85, Lake Ozark, Mo., 1985-88; pres. John G. Neihardt Found., Bancroft, 1987—; lectr. in field. Author: Black Elk and Flaming Rainbow, 1995; editor: The Giving Earth, 1991, The End of The Dream, 1991, The Ancient Memory, 1991. Trustee John G. Neihardt Trust, Columbia and Tekamah, Nebr., 1973—. With USN, 1944-45. Mem. AAUW, Westerners, Internat. Avocations: boating, camping, horses. Home: 504 Pennsylvania Ave Bancroft NE 68004 also: PO Box 358 504 Pennsylvania Ave Bancroft NE 68004 Office: John G Neihardt Found Box 344 Bancroft NE 68004

NEIKIRK, WILLIAM ROBERT, journalist; b. Irvine, Ky., Jan. 6, 1938; s. Lewis Byron and Nancy Elizabeth (Green) N.; m. Ruth Ann Clary, Sept. 10, 1960; children: Paul Gregory, John Stuart, Christa Lynn. B.A. in Journalism, U. Ky., 1960. Reporter Lexington (Ky.) Herald, 1959-60; state capital corr. AP, Frankfort, Ky., 1961-66, Baton Rouge, 1966-69; econ. corr. AP (Washington Bur.), 1970-74; nat. econ. writer Chgo. Tribune, Washington, 1974-83, White House corr., 1977, 94—, econ. columnist, 1980—, news editor Washington bur., 1983, fin. editor, 1988-91, sr. writer, 1991—. Author: The Work Revolution, 1983, Volcker: The Money Man, 1987. Recipient Beck award Chgo. Tribune, 1975, Bus. Writing award U. Mo., 1978, 80, Bus. Writing award Amos Tuck Grad. Sch. Bus., Dartmouth Coll., 1980, John Hancock Bus. Writing award Wharton Sch. Fin., U. Pa., 1979, finalist, 1990, 91, John Hancock Bus. Writing award U. Houston, 1980, Loeb Bus. Writing award UCLA Grad. Sch. Mgmt., 1979, Chgo. Headliner Club award, 1979, 84, Raymond Clapper Meml. award, 1981, Barnet Nover award, 1994, Merriman Smith award, 1995, White House Correspondents Assn. Mem. Gridiron Club. Mem. United Ch. of Christ. Home: 5121 38th St N Arlington VA 22207-1827

NEIL, FRED APPLESTEIN, public relations executive; b. Balt., Nov. 26, 1933; s. Frank and Mollie (Schapiro) Applestein; m. Sheila Tilles, Aug. 30, 1959 (div. May 1980); children: Jay Alan, Brian Mark Applestein, Gail Renee Murphy; m. Dawn Francis Fisher, July 6, 1986. BA, U. Md., 1959. News and sports editor Sta. WITH, Balt., 1959-60; dir. news and sports Sta. WCBM, Metromedia, Balt., 1960-69; press officer Mayor William Donald Schaefer, Balt., 1970-71; gen. mgr. Balt. Banners World Team Tennis League, 1971-72; pres. Fred Neil Assocs., Pub. Rels., Balt., 1972—; staff specialist pub. info. Md. Rehab. Ctr., Balt., 1980-91; owner Cruising for Mems., Ellicott City, 1987—, Dir. Office of Comm. and Community Rels., Divsn. Rehab. Svcs., Balt., 1980—; co-owner Carrolltowne Card & Gift Shop. Author: It's a Very Simple Game!, The Life and Times of Charles Eckman II,1995; editor, contbr. Lafayette Sq. Newsletter, 1974-82, Fed. Hill Newsletter, 1974-82, Greater Penn Ave. Newsletter, 1974-82, MPCA News Letter, 1982—, Md. Rehab. Assn. News Letter, 1985—, Front and Center newsletter, 1980-92, Rehab Digest, 1992—; contbr. articles to mags., newspapers, and newsletters. Bd. dirs. Liberty Showcase Theater, 1985-87, Howard County Summer Theatre, 1992—, pres. 1995-96. With U.S. Army, 1956-58. Recipient award for spot reporting Chesapeake AP, 1967, award for in-depth sports reporting, 1967, 69, Media Appreciation award U.S. Intercollegiate Lacrosse Assn., 1970, Humanitarian award Md. Rehab. Assn., 1982, Appreciation award 1986, Profl. Svc. award Md. Rehab. Counseling Assn., 1985, Ams. with Disabilities Act award The Task Force on the Rights and Empowerment of Ams. with Disabilities, 1991, Outstanding Contbns. award, 1994, Md. Gov.'s Com. on Employment of People with Disabilities Print Media award, 1996, Golden Radio Buffs' Golden Mike award, 1996. Mem. Md. Rehab. Assn. (pres. 1985, 87), Md. Press Club (pres. 1988-89, 97-98, bd. dirs. 1990-91), Balt. Sports Reporters Assn. (pres. 1964), Balt. Press Reporters Assn. (pres. 1965), Mid-Atlantic Rehab. Adminstrs. Assn. (pres. 1990). Home: 4029 Pebble Branch Rd Ellicott City MD 21042-5348

NEIL, GARY LAWRENCE, pharmaceutical company research executive, biochemical pharmacologist; b. Regina, Sask., Can., June 13, 1940; came to U.S., 1962; s. Bert Lawrence and Barbara Jessie (Robinson) N.; m. Beverly May Hendry, Apr. 16, 1939; children: Deborah Nadine, Michael Lawrence. BS with honors, Queen's U., Kingston, Ont., Can., 1962; PhD, Calif. Inst. Tech., 1966. Rsch. scientist The Upjohn Co., Kalamazoo, Mich., 1966-73, rsch. head, 1973-79, rsch. mgr., 1979-82, group mgr., 1982-83, exec. dir., 1983-85, v.p., 1985-89; sr. v.p. Wyeth-Ayerst, Radnor, Pa., 1989-90, exec. v.p., 1990-93; pres., CEO Therapeutic Discovery Corp., Palo Alto, Calif., 1993—. Editor Investigational New Drugs, 1983-88; contbr. over 50 articles to profl. jours. Mem. Am. Chem. Soc., Am. Assn. Cancer Rsch., Am. Soc. Clin. Pharmacology and Exptl. Therapeutics. Presbyterian. Avocation: sailing. Office: Therapeutic Discovery Corp PO Box 10051 1454 Page Mill Rd Palo Alto CA 94303-0806

NEILL, DENIS MICHAEL, government relations consulting executive; b. Grand Rapids, Mich., Apr. 27, 1943; s. Thomas Patrick and Agnes Josephine (Weber) N.; m. Mary Kathleen Golden, June 11, 1966; children: Mark, Erin. AB cum laude, St. Louis U., 1964, JD cum laude, 1967. Bar: Mo. 1967, D.C. 1969. Gen. atty. Office of Asst. Regional Counsel IRS, Newark, 1967-68; assoc. Arent, Fox, Kintner, Plotkin & Kahn, Washington, 1969-71, Morgan, Lewis & Bockius, Washington, 1971-72; atty. advisor office gen. counsel AID, Washington, 1972-73, asst. gen. counsel legis. and policy coordination, 1973-75, asst. adminstr. legis. affairs, 1975-77; sr. v.p., gen. counsel Aeromaritime Internat. Corp., Washington, 1977-80; counsel Surrey & Morse, Washington, 1980-81; sr. ptnr. Neill & Shaw, Washington, 1981-92; sr. law ptnr. Dalley, Neill, Assevero, Carroll & Nealer, Washington, 1992-93; pres. Neill & Co., Inc., Washington, 1981—. Bd. dirs. Barker Found., 1981-86, Fed. City Nat. Bank, Washington, 1987. Lt. USCG, 1968-71. Recipient Superior Unit Citation AID, 1976, Disting. Honor award, 1977. Mem. ABA, FBA, D.C. Bar Assn., Mo. Bar Assn., Nat. Security Indsl. Assn. (bd. dirs. 1982-90), Capitol Hill Club, Columbia Country Club (Chevy Chase, Md.), Jefferson Islands Club. Democrat. Home: 5945 Searl Ter Bethesda MD 20816-2022 Office: Neill & Co 5945 Searl Ter Bethesda MD 20816-2022

NEILL, RICHARD ROBERT, retired publishing company executive; b. N.Y.C., June 20, 1925; s. Robert Irving and Mildred Mary (Hall) N.; m. Patricia Mae Robinson, Dec. 27, 1952; 1 son, Robert Kenneth. A.B. summa cum laude, Princeton U., 1948; M.A., N.Y. U., 1953. With Prentice-Hall, Inc., N.Y.C. and Englewood Cliffs, N.J., 1948-85, advt. mgr., 1953-58, v.p. advt., 1958-62; pres. Executive Reports Corporation, 1962-85, ret., 1985; Regional chmn. Princeton Alumni Giving, Yonkers, N.Y., 1960-63, Tarrytown-Irvington, N.Y., 1977-80. Pres. Tarrytown (N.Y.) Jr. High Sch. PTA, 1971-72; bd. dirs. Martling Owners, Tarrytown, 1980-84, 89-93. Lt. (j.g.) USNR, 1943-46, PTO. Mem. USN Meml. Found., Princeton Terrace Club (bd. govs. 1986-92), Great Harbour Cay Club (Bahamas), Phi Beta Kappa. Republican. Mem. Reform Ch. Home: 222 Martling Ave Tarrytown NY 10591-4756 *A thought acquired from one of my first bosses: "Everything happens for the best - or can be made to do so." This has been a lifelong help.*

NEILL, RITA J., elementary school educator; b. Lincolnton, N.C., Oct. 20, 1950; d. George William and Mozelle (Boyles) Jarrett; m. Randy William Neill, Nov. 27, 1970; children: Jennifer Neill Huffman, Julie Neill Foster. AB, Lenoir Rhyne Coll., 1972; MA, Gardner Webb, 1987. Presch. tchr. for developmentally delayed 3- and 4-yr. olds Wayside Elem., Statesville (N.C.)/Iredell County Schs.; kindergarten tchr. Troutman Elem., (N.C.), 1977-96. Mem. ASCD, Assn. Edn. Young Children (treas. Iredell County 1994-96, membership chmn. 1996—), N.C. Assn. Edn. (sec. 1986-88), Iredell County Assn. Edn. Young Children (chmn. 1996-98). Home: 308 Wiggins Rd Mooresville NC 28115-9393

NEILL, ROLFE, newspaper executive; b. Mount Airy, N.C., Dec. 4, 1932; s. Kenneth A. and Carmen (Goforth) N.; m. Rosemary Clifford Boney, July 20, 1952 (div.); children: Clifford Randolph, Sabrina Ashley, Dana Catlin, Jessica Rosemary Ingrid, Quentin Roark Robinson; m. Ann Marshall Snider, Sept. 24, 1988. A.B. in History, U. N.C., 1954. Reporter Franklin (N.C.) Press, 1956-57; reporter Charlotte (N.C.) Observer, 1957-58, bus. editor, 1958-61; editor, pub. Coral Gables (Fla.) Times and The Guide, 1961-63, Miami Beach (Fla.) Daily Sun, 1963-65; asst. to pub. N.Y. Daily News, 1965-67, suburban editor, 1967-68, asst. mng. editor, 1968-70; editor Phila. Daily News, 1970-75; v.p., dir. Phila. Newspapers Inc., 1970-75; chmn., pub. Charlotte (N.C.) Observer, 1975—. Served with AUS, 1954-56. Office: Knight Pub Co 600 S Tryon St PO Box 32188 Charlotte NC 28232

NEILL, SAM, actor; b. Northern Ireland, Sept. 14, 1947; m. Noriko Watanabe; 3 children. Student, U. Canterbury, Eng. Appearances include (film) Land Fall, 1976, Sleeping Dogs, 1977, The Journalist, 1979, Just Out of Reach, 1979, My Brilliant Career, 1980, Attack Force Z, 1981, The Final Conflict, 1981, Possession, 1981, Enigma, 1983, The Country Girls, 1983, Robbery Under Arms, 1984, Plenty, 1985, For Love Alone, 1986, The Good Wife, 1987, A Cry in the Dark, 1988, Dead Calm, 1989, La Révolution Française, 1989, The Hunt for Red October, 1990, Death in Brunswick, 1990, Until the End of the World, 1991, Memoirs of An Invisible Man, 1992, The Piano, 1993, Jurassic Park, 1993, In the Mouth of Madness, 1993, Country Life, 1993, Rudyard Kipling's Jungle Book, 1994, Restoration, 1994, Sirens, 1994, In the Mouth of Madness, 1995, Country Life, 1995, Victory, 1995, Children of the Revolution, 1996, Snow White in the Black Forest, 1996, Revengers Comedy, 1996, Event Horizon, 1997, (TV miniseries) Kane and Abel, 1985, Reilly Ace of Spies, 1986, Amerika, 1987, (TV movies) From a Far Country: Pope John Paul II, 1981, Ivanhoe, 1982, The Blood of Others, 1984, Arthur Hailey's Strong Medicine, 1986, Leap of Faith, 1988, Fever, 1991, One Against the Wind, 1991, The Sinking of the Rainbow Warrior, 1991, Family Pictures, 1993, In Cold Blood, 1996. Recipient O.B.E. award, 1991. Office: Internat Creative Mgmt 8942 Wilshire Blvd Beverly Hills CA 90211-1934

NEILL, VE, make-up artist; b. Riverside, Calif., May 13, 1951; d. Charles and Eileen Anne (Bernasco) Flores. Grad., Louisville H.S., Woodland Hills, Calif. Credits include (TV movies) Cry for Help, 1978, The London Affair, 1978, Sultan and the Rock Star, 1979, Muppets Go to the Movies, 1981, First Lady of the World, 1982, Money on the Side, 1982, Jane Doe, 1986; (TV Spls.) Sold Out-Lily Tomlin, 1981, Lily for President, 1982, Comedy Store 15th Yr. Reunion, 1988; (TV pilots) One Night Band, 1981, T.J. Hooker, 1981, Madeline (Madeline Kahn), 1982, Girls Life, 1982, A-Team, 1982, Rock & Roll Mom, 1987, Kowalski Loves, 1987; (TV show) Pee Wee's Playhouse (Emmy award 1988, Emmy award nominee 1989); (feature films) Star Trek: The Motion Picture (Saturn award 1981), The Incredible Shrinking Woman, 9 to 5, Monty Python at the Hollywood Bowl, Sword and the Sorcerer, The Last Star Fighter, All of Me, The Lost Boys, 1986 (Saturn award 1987), Beetlejuice, 1987 (Acad. award 1987, Saturn award 1988, Brit. Acad. award nominee 1988), Cocoon II, 1988, Big Top Pee Wee, 1988, Dick Tracy, 1989, Flatliners, 1989, Edward Scissorhands, 1990 (Acad. award nominee 1989, Brit. Acad. award nominee 1990), Curly Sue, 1990, Hook, 1991, Batman Returns, 1991 (Saturn award 1992, Acad. award nominee 1992, Brit. Acad. award nominee 1992), Hoffa, 1992 (Acad. award nominee 1992), Rising Sun, 1992, Mrs. Doubtfire, 1993 (Acad. award 1993), Ed Wood, 1993 (Acad. award 1994), Cobb, 1994, Junior, 1994, Batman Forever, 1995. Mem. Acad. Motion Picture Arts and Scis. (mem. exec. bd.), Brit. Acad. Film and TV. Avocations: collecting antiques, beading with antique Am. trade beads, hiking, traveling the U.S. Office: IATSE Local 706 11519 Chandler Blvd North Hollywood CA 91601-2618*

NEILL, WILLIAM HAROLD, JR., biological science educator and researcher; b. Wynne, Ark., Oct. 21, 1943; s. William H., Sr. and Shirley A. (Ellis) N.; m. Charlotte A. Jackson, Dec. 20, 1964; 1 child, Amanda K. BS in Zoology, U. Ark., 1965, MS in Zoology, 1967; PhD in Zoology/Statis., U. Wis., 1971. Rsch. fishery biologist Southwest Fisheries Ctr. Nat. Marine Fisheries Svc., Honolulu, 1971-74; assoc. prof. Tex. A&M U./Tex. Agrl. Expt. Sta., College Station, 1975-83; prof. Tex. A&M U./TAES, College Station, 1983—; interim head Dept. Wildlife and Fisheries Sci., College Station, 1992-93; mem. organizing com. Advanced Rsch. Inst. on Mechanisms Fish Migration, NATO, 1980-82; mem. tech. com. So. Regional Aquaculture Ctr., USDA, 1987-89; mem. sci.-tech. adv. com. Corpus Christi Bay Nat. Estuary Program, 1994-97. Editor Tex. Jour. Sci., 1983-85; mem. editl. adv. bd. Critical Revs. in Aquatic Sci., 1986-90; assoc. editor Transactions of the Am. Fisheries Soc., 1995—; contbr. numerous articles to sci. jours. and books. Grantee numerous orngs., 1975—. Fellow Tex. Acad. Sci.; mem. AAAS, Am. Fisheries Soc. (life, Award of Excellence com. 1987, 89, chair Publ. Awards com. 1993, editl. bd. 1995), Am. Inst. Fishery Rsch. Biologists, Internat. Soc. Ecol. Modelling, World Aquaculture Soc., Phi Beta Kappa, Sigma Xi, Phi Sigma. Office: Texas A&M U Dept Wildlife & Fisheries Sci College Station TX 77843-2258

NEILSON, BENJAMIN REATH, lawyer; b. Phila., July 11, 1938; s. Harry Rosengarten and Alberta (Reath) N.; m. Judith Rawle, June 20, 1959 (div. May 1983); children: Benjamin R. Jr., Theodora C., Johanna K., Alberta R., Marshall R.; m. Meta B. Grace, Dec. 26, 1983. AB magna cum laude, Harvard U., 1960, LLB, 1963. Bar: Pa. 1964. Law clk. to chief justice Pa. Supreme Ct., Phila., 1963-64; assoc. Ballard, Spahr, Andrews & Ingersoll, Phila., 1964-71, ptnr., 1971—. Bd. dirs. WHYY, Inc., Phila; sec.-treas. The Chanticleer Found., Wayne, Pa.; pres. bd. trustees St. Paul's Sch., Concord, N.H. Mem. ABA, Pa. Bar Assn., Phila. Bar Assn., Phi Beta Kappa. Episcopalian.

NEILSON, ELIZABETH ANASTASIA, health sciences educator, association executive, author, editor; b. Medford, Mass., Oct. 13, 1913; d. William H. and Anastasia (Mahony) N. Diploma, Tufts U., 1933; BS in Edn, Boston U., 1934, MEd, 1945, EdD, 1957. Tchr. pub. schs. Medford, 1934-43; instr. health and phys. edn. Boston Coll., 1954-55; mem. faculty State Coll., Lowell, Mass., 1944-72; prof. edn., chmn. dept. health and phys. edn. State Coll., 1966-72; dir. continuing edn. Am. Sch. Health Assn., Kent, Ohio, 1972—; adj. prof. Kent State U., 1971-77; adj. prof. health edn. Boston-Bouvé Coll. Human Devel. Professions, Northeastern U., 1974—; lectr. extension div. Harvard U., 1975—; vis. prof. Boston U., 1960-62, Ind. U., summers 1966-72, Utah State U., summer 1968; del. Internat. Conf. Health and Edn., Madrid, 1965, Pa., 1962, Dusseldorf, Germany, 1959; health edn. cons. to govt. agys., industry, ednl. instns.; del. White House Conf. Children and Youth, 1970; mem. membership com. Am. Nat. Council for Health, 1967-73; chmn. resources council Mass. Sch. Health Council, 1964-69; mem. Nat. Adv. Council on Smoking and Health Edn., 1966-74, Gov.'s Council for Health and Fitness, 1964-69, Gov.'s Council for Nutrition Edn., 1971-74; mem. program evaluation team N.H. State Bd. Edn. Author: Health Living Program, 1977, also school health textbooks; contbg. author: coll. text Personal and Community Health; editor in chief coll. text Journal-Health Values: Achieving High Level Wellness, 1976—; contbr. articles to profl. jours. V.p. bd. dirs. March Against Dental Disease Found.; bd. dirs. Middlesex TB and Health Assn., Mass. Cancer Soc., Lowell MEntal Health

Assn., Lowell Heart Assn., Lowell Diabetes Assn., New Hampshire Lung Assn.; mem. Jackson Sch. Bd.; trustee Jackson Libr.; pres., bd. dirs. Flintlock Village Assn.Inc., Wells, Maine, 1988—; founder Elizabeth A. Neilson-George H. Neilson Advanced Grad. Endowed Scholarship Fund for the Promotion of Health Edn., dept. physiology and health scis., Ball State U., 1992. Recipient William A. Howe award Am. Sch. Health Assn., 1969, Disting. Svc. award 1965, Disting. Svc. award ea. dist. AAHPER, 1967, Profl. Svc. award Mass. chpt. 1965, Svc. award Nat. ARC, 1960, Disting. Alumni award Northeastern U., Boston, 1983, Profl. Svc. award Am. Alliance for Health Edn., 1987; inducted into Mass. Hall of Fame, Medford High, 1990; hon. fellow Ball State U., Muncie, Ind., 1993, named to Fellows Soc. and Pres.'s Cir., 1996. Fellow Am. Sch. Health Assn. (life, pres. 1964-66, chmn. study coms. 1969-72, mem. governing assn. 1960-65, Howe award), Royal Soc. Health; mem. Am. Assn. Higher Edn., Am. Soc. Assn. Execs., Nat. Bus. and Profl. Women's Club, Assn. Supervision and Curriculum Devel., UN Assn. U.S.A., Internat. Union for Health, Smithsonian Assos., Nat. Parks and Conservation Assn., New Eng. Health Assn., Am. Coll. Health Assn. (research council 1954-57), Am. (editorial bd. 1958-60, chmn. coll. health com. Eastern dist. 1948-51, chmn. resolutions com. sch. health div. 1951-53), Mass. assns. health, phys. edn. and recreation, Am. Pub. Health Assn., Soc. Pub. Health Educators, Phi Lambda Theta. Home and Office: PO Box 890 Wells ME 04090-0890 *Since childhood my life has been guided by the concept that it is best to prevent illness by healthful living. On this premise I have devoted my life toward achieving a high level of wellness for myself and my family. As a professor of health education and an exemplar of the concepts associated with the daily application of scientific health information, I have worked toward helping others achieve the level of health their inherited potential would permit.*

NEILSON, ERIC GRANT, physician, educator, health facility administrator; b. Bklyn., Sept. 14, 1949; s. Jack Drew and Lynette Elsie (Lundquist) N.; m. Linda Rae Apolzon, May 27, 1972; children: Tinsley, Sigrid. BS magna cum laude, Denison U., 1971; MD magna cum laude, U. Ala., 1975; MD (hon.), U. Pa., 1987. Asst. prof. U. Pa., Phila., 1980-87, assoc. prof., 1987-91, prof., 1991—, C. Mahlon Kline prof., 1993—, chief renal-electrolyte & hypertension divsn. dept. medicine, 1988—; attending physician Hosp. of U. Pa., 1980—; cons. in field. Med. editorial bds. on sci. jours.; contbr. numerous articles to profl. jours. Chmn. med. adv. bd. Lupus Found. of Phila., 1985-95; chmn. pathology A study sect. NIH, Bethesda, Md., 1990-92; chmn. grant rev. com. Nat. Kidney Found. of Delaware Valley; mem. adv. coun. NIDDK, NIH. Recipient Clin. Scientist award Am. Heart Assn., 1980, Young Investigator award Am. Soc. Nephrology/Am. Heart Assn., 1985, Established Investigator award Am. Heart Assn., President's medal Am. Soc. Nephrology, 1994. Fellow ACP; mem. Am. Soc. Clin. Investigation, Assn. Am. Physicians, Am. Soc. Nephrology, Am. Assn. Immunologists, Am. Fedn. Clin. Rsch., Assn. Subsplty. Profs. (pres. 1994-96). Mem. Soc. of Friends. Office: U Pa Renal Electrolyte Sect 700 Clin Rsch Bldg 415 Curie Blvd Philadelphia PA 19104-4218

NEILSON, WINTHROP CUNNINGHAM, III, communications executive, financial communications consultant; b. N.Y.C., Jan. 7, 1934; s. Winthrop Cunningham, Jr. and Frances Fullerton (Jones) N.; m. Ilse Rossenbeck, Jan. 4, 1957; children: Luise R., Victoria F.; m. Demaris King Hetrick, July 5, 1985; 1 child, Whitney C.; stepchildren: Norman P. Hetrick Jr., D. Page Hetrick. BA, Harvard U., 1956; grad. in security analysis, N.Y. Inst. Finance, 1963. Asst. producer, asst. dir. Rangley Lakes Theater, 1955; gen. assignment reporter Albany (N.Y.) Times-Union, 1959-60; pub. info. writer, speaker Consol. Edison, 1960-61; asst. dir. pub. relations Union Service Corp., 1962; with Georgeson & Co., N.Y.C., 1962-81, prin., 1969-81; sr. v.p. D.F. King & Co. Inc., N.Y.C., 1982-86; founder, mng. dir. Krone Communications, Harrisburg, Pa., 1986-89; pres. Krone Group Inc., Harrisburg, 1987-89; mng. dir. Neilson/Hetrick Group, Montclair, N.J., 1990—, Harrisburg, Pa., 1993—; chmn. Neilson/Hetrick Group, Montclair, N.J., 1993—; mng. dir. Corp. Investor Communications, Carlstadt, N.J., 1991-93; guest lectr. NYU, 1991; bd. dirs. Guardman Products. Author: series Aunt Jane, 1971, 73, The Reluctant Marriage, 1978, Investorism, 1981, Annual Reports, The Agony and the Ecstasy, 1985, Individual Investors, a Counterbalance to Institutional Investors, 1986; writer, assoc. editor: Trends, 1965-81; contbr. articles to profl. jours. Mem. Mountain Lakes (N.J.) Econ. Devel. Council, 1974-79, chmn., 1977-79; pres. Robert A. Taft Republican Club, Queens, N.Y., 1964-65, chmn., 1966-67; treas. 23d Assembly Dist. Rep. Party, 1966-67; county committeeman, 1964-67; del. N.Y. State Nominating Conv., 1966; campaign mgr. for 2 assemblymen and state senator. Served with AUS, 1956-59. Recipient Investor Edn. Disting. Service award Nat. Assn. Investors Clubs, 1986. Mem. Nat. Investor Rels. Inst. (charter dir. 1980-84, v.p. manpower 1980-81, v.p. long-range planning 1981-84), Pub. Rels. Soc. Am. (charter, exec. com. investor rels. 1982-90, chmn. 1987, Pres. award 1987, charter inductee into Hall of Fame for Investor Rels.), Corp. Rels. Soc. Ctrl. Pa. (v.p. 1986-89, pres. 1994-95), Ctrl. Pa. Entrepreneurial Assn. (bd. dirs. 1988-89, adv. bd. tech. coun. Ctrl. Pa. 1994-96), Colonial Country Club, DU Club, Hasty Pudding Club, Ausable Club. Mem. Soc. of Friends. Home: 5778 Nesbit Dr Harrisburg PA 17112-2200 Office: 5778 Nesbit Dr Ste 12 Harrisburg PA 17112-2200

NEIMAN, JOHN HAMMOND, lawyer; b. Des Moines, Jan. 8, 1917; s. Donald Edwin and Bessie A. (White) N.; m. Madeline Clare Flint, July 2, 1941; children—Richard F., Donald F., Nancy J. Student, Grinnell Coll., 1935-37; B.A., Drake U., 1939, J.D., 1941. Bar: Iowa 1941. Ptnr. Neiman, Neiman, Stone & Spellman, Des Moines, 1946-92, Neiman, Stone, McCormick & Wendl, Attys., Des Moines, 1992—; exec. v.p., sec. Nat. Assn. Credit Mgmt., Des Moines, 1956-83; mem. ethics com. Iowa Senate, 1969-73, probate rules com. Iowa Supreme Ct., 1977-81; mem., chmn. Client Security and Atty. Disciplinary Commn., Iowa, 1974-85. Pres. bd. councilors Drake U. Law Sch., 1968; pres. Northwest Community Hosp., Des Moines, 1974-77. Recipient Centennial award Drake U., 1981. Fellow Am. Bar Found., Comml. Law Found., Iowa State Bar Found. (50 Yr. award 1995); mem. ABA (bd. govs. 1984-85, ho. of dels. 1978-87, profl. discipline com. 1979-84, forum com. 1985-89, responsibility for clients protection 1989-90), Iowa Bar Assn. (bd. govs. 1963-67, pres. 1967-68, award of merit 1975), Polk County Bar Assn. (pres. 1960-61), Comml. Law League Am., Iowa State Bar Found. (sec. 1975-78, pres. 1988-92), Wakonda Club (pres. 1973), Met. Club (pres. 1981-82, 84-86). Republican. Methodist. Home: 3514 Wakonda Ct Des Moines IA 50321-2648 Office: Neiman Stone McCormick & Wendl 2910 Westown Pky Ste 104 West Des Moines IA 50266-1308 *There are talkers and doers, it's more important to be a doer. Their accomplishments live long after they are gone.*

NEIMAN, LEROY, artist; b. St. Paul, June 8, 1927; s. Charles and Lydia (Serline) Runquist; m. Janet Byrne, June 22, 1957. Student, Sch. Art Inst., Chgo., 1946-50, U. Ill., 1951, DePaul U., 1951; LittD (hon.), Franklin Pierce Coll., 1976; hon. doctorate, St. John's U., 1980, Iona Coll., 1985, Hofstra U., 1997. Instr. Sch. Art Inst. Chgo., 1950-60, Saugatuck (Mich.) Summer Sch. Painting, 1957-58, 63, Sch. Arts and Crafts, Winston-Salem, N.C., 1963; instr. painting Atlanta Youth Council, 1968-69; printmaker-graphics, 1971—; artist Olympics, ABC-TV, Munich, 1972; ofcl. artist Olympics, ABC-TV, Montreal, 1976, U.S. Olympics, 1980, 84; computer artist CBS-TV (Superbowl), New Orleans, 1978; ofcl. artist Goodwill Games CNN-TV, Moscow, USSR, 1986; 1st ofcl. artist Ky. Derby, Louisville, 1997; mem. adv. com. LeRoy Neiman Ctr. for Print Studies Sch. of the Arts Columbia U., 1995; mem. adv. com. for N.Y.C. Commn. for Cultural Affairs, 1995. Exhibited one-man shows, Oehlshlaeger Gallery, Chgo., 1959, 61, O'Hana Gallery, London, Galerie O. Bosc, Paris, 1962, Hammer Gallery, N.Y.C., 1963, 65, 67, 70, 72, 76, 78, 79, 81-83, 85-87, 89, 92,, 94, 97, Huntington-Hartford Gallery Modern Art, N.Y.C., 1967, Heath Gallery, Atlanta, 1969, Abbey Theatre, Dublin, Ireland, 1970, Museo de Bellas Artes, Caracas, Indpls. Inst. Arts, 1972, Hermitage Mus., Leningrad, Tobu Gallery, Tokyo, 1974, Springfield (Mass.) Mus. Fine Arts, 1974, 84, Knoedler Gallery, London, 1976, Casa gratica, Helsinki, 1977, Renée Victor, Stockholm, 1977, Okla. Art Ctr., Oklahoma City, 1981, Harrod's, London, 1982; retrospective show, Minn. Mus. Art, St. Paul, 1975, Meredith Long Galleries, Houston, 1978, Hanae Mori Gallery, Tokyo, 1988, New State Tretyakov Mus., 1988, Butler Inst., Youngstown, Ohio, 1990, Galerie Marcel Bernheim, Paris, 1993, Ky. Derby Mus., Louisville, 1995, 1997; two-man show, Neiman-Warhol, Los Angeles Inst. Contemporary Art, 1981; exhibited in group shows, Art Inst. Chgo., 1954-60, Carnegie Internat., 1956, Corcoran Gallery Am., Washington, Walker Art Center, Mpls., 1957, Ringling Mus., Sarasota, Fla., 1959, Salon d'Art Mus., Paris, 1961, Nat. Gallery Portraiture, Smithsonian Instn., Washington, Minn. Mus. Art, 1969, Rotunda Della Basana, Milan, Italy, 1971, Royal Coll. Art, London, 1971, Minn. Mus. Art Nat. Tour, 1976-77, Whitney Mus., 1985 ; Master Prints of 19th and 20th Centuries, Hammer Galls., N.Y., 1987, Salon d'Automne, Paris, 1992, 93; represented in permanent collections, Mpls. Inst. Arts, Ill. State Mus., Springfield, Joslyn Mus., Omaha, Wodham Coll., Oxford, Eng., Nat. Art Mus. Sport, N.Y.C., Museo De Ballas Artes Caracas, Hermitage Mus., Indpls. Inst. Arts, U. Ill., Balt. Mus. Fine Art, The Armand Hammer Collection, Los Angeles, Edwin & Ruth Kennedy Mus. of Am. Art at Ohio U.; executed murals at, Merc. Nat. Bank, Hammond, Ind., Continental Hotel, Chgo., Swedish Lloyd Ship S.S. Patricia, Stockholm, ceramic tile mural, Sportsmans Park, Chgo.; author: LeRoy Neiman—Art and Life Style, 1974, Horses, 1979, LeRoy Neiman. Posters, 1980, LeRoy Neiman. Catalogue Raisonné, 1980, Carnaval, 1981, LeRoy Neiman: Winners, 1983, Japanese translation, 1985, LeRoy Neiman, Monte Carlo Chase, 1988, The Prints of LeRoy Neiman, 1980-90, Big Time Golf, 1992, LeRoy Neiman, An American in Paris, 1994, Leroy Neiman on Safari, 1997; illustrator: 12 paintings deluxe edit. Moby Dick, 1975. Served with AUS, 1942-46. Recipient 1st prize Twin City Show, 1953, 2d prize Minn. State Show, 1954, Clark Meml. prize Chgo. Show, 1957, Hamilton-Graham prize Ball State Coll., 1958, Municipal prize Chgo. Show, 1958, Purchase prize Miss. Valley Show, 1959, Gold medal Salon d'Art Modern Paris, 1961; award of merit as nation's outstanding sports artist AAU, 1976; Olympic Artist of Century award, 1979, Gold Medal award St. John's U., 1985. Address: 1 W 67th St New York NY 10023-6200

NEIMAN, NORMAN, aerospace business and marketing executive; b. Phila., May 23, 1935; s. Harry and Clara (Schuller) N.; m. Sandra Elaine Berk (dec. 1989); children: Nadene Lori Eisaman, Andrea Neiman-Pearce, David Michael; m. Bonnie Gail McCoy, Sept. 5, 1990. BSME, U. Miami, 1957; postgrad., Alexander Hamilton Inst., N.Y.C., 1959; postgrad. real estate law, Brevard C.C., Cocoa, Fla., 1973. Lic. real estate broker, Fla.; lic. fed. firearms dealer. Engr. Sperry Gyroscope Corp., Gt. Neck, N.Y., 1957-59; lead mech. engr. Convair Aerospace Co., Cape Canaveral, Fla., 1959-62; engrng. scientist Douglas Aircraft Corp., Cape Canaveral, 1962-65; chief support engr. Grumman Aerospace Corp., Kennedy Space Center, Fla., 1965-73; mgr. Cocoa Beach (Fla.) ops. Grumman Aerospace Corp., 1973-74, mgr. Orlando (Fla.) ops., 1974-79; pres. Neiman and Co., Inc., Orlando, 1980—; pres. Sunshine State Realty, Inc., Cocoa Beach, 1972-76; v.p. Vitality Workshop, Inc., Orlando, 1978-80, Reconnaissance Techs., Arlington, Va., 1985-89; U.S. Govt. sales agt. Calico Light Weapon Systems, 1989-91; dir. program devel. NYMA Inc., Cocoa Beach, 1990—. Patentee waveguide disconnect. Mem. NRA, AIAA, Tech. Mktg. Soc., Range, Missile and Space Pioneers (life), Am. Meteorol. Soc., Am. Numismatic Assn., Air Force Assn., Mensa, Intertel. Republican. Jewish. Avocations: shooting, model railroading, coin collecting, foreign travel. Office: Neiman and Co Inc PO Box 140094 Orlando FL 32814-0094

NEIMANN, ALBERT ALEXANDER, mathematician, business owner; b. Torrington, Wyo., Nov. 29, 1939; s. Alexander and Lydia (Temple) N.; m. Barbara Jean Maw, May 6, 1962; children: Debbie, Todd, Amy, Kelly,. BA, Willamette U., 1967. Mathematician Keyport (Wash.) Naval Torpedo Sta., 1968-70; math. statistician Concord (Calif.) Naval Weapons Sta., 1970-85, engrng. statistician, 1985-94; bus. owner Antioch Sports Cards and Collectibles, A&T Sports Cards, Calif., 1994—. Mgr. Little League Baseball, Antioch, Calif., 1977-84, Little League Softball, Antioch, 1984-87; Sunday sch. tchr. Grace Bapt. Ch., 1979-90; statistician Antioch H.S., 1985-89. Recipient Performance award Concord Naval Weapons Sta., 1978, 88-94. Mem. Am. Statis. Assn., Math. Assn. Am., Am. Soc. for Quality Control, Nat. Coun. Tchrs. Math. Avocations: jogging, electronics, reading, gardening, basketball. Office: Antioch Sports Cards & Collectibles 2550 Somersville Rd Ste 51 Antioch CA 94509-8704

NEIMARK, PHILIP JOHN, financial consultant, editor; b. Chgo., Sept. 13, 1939; s. Mortimer William and Hortense (Peters) N.; m. Vassa Lynn; children: Tanya Lee, Joshua Daniel, Dashiel Charles, Darq-Amber. Student U. Chgo., 1956-58, Northwestern U., 1958-59; D in Bus. Mgmt. (hon.), Ricker Coll., Houlton, Maine, 1976. Ordained minister Babalawo of IFA Ch. of Nigeria, 1989. Mem. Chgo. Mercantile Exchange, 1968-74; owner Josephson Neimark Trading Co., Chgo., 1972-73; ptnr. Rosenthal & Co., Chgo., 1973-77; owner, prin. Philip J. Neimark Investments, Miami, Fla., 1977-79, Chgo., 1979—; pres. Neimark Fin. Pub. Co., 1985—; pres., Croesus Assocs., 1988-90; prin. TBFB, Inc., 1995—; editor, pub. Philip J. Neimark Viewpoint, N.Y.C., 1976-85, editor Pro Trade, 1984—, Low Priced Stock Edit., 1984-91; fin. editor Money Maker mag., 1979-85; mem. Internat. Monetary Market, 1971-74, N.Y. Mercantile Exchange, 1973-74, Chgo. Bd. of Options Exchange, 1973-75; editor, Low Priced Stock Edition, 1984-91, Pro Trade, 1985—; instr. Omega Inst., 1994, Esalen Inst., 1994. Author: How to Be Lucky, 1975, Way of the Orisa, 1992, The Sacred Ifa Oracle, 1995; syndicated columnist Ask the Shaman, 1994—; contbg. editor Consumers Digest mag., 1977-85. Bd. dirs. Luth. Gen. Med. Found. (emeritus), Principal Vassa Inc.; chmn. IFA Found N.Am., 1989—; pres. TBFB II Inc., 1996—. Mem. Fla. Exec. Planning Assn., South Fla. Fin. Planners Assn., Investment Co. Inst., Nat. Paso Fino Assn. (founder), pres. TBFB II, 1996—.

NEIMARK, SHERIDAN, lawyer; b. Youngstown, Ohio, Apr. 7, 1935; s. David and Anne (Kamisar) N.; m. Dana Ellen Perlzweig, Jan. 5, 1963; children: David, Rebecca, Matthew. B.S. in Chem. Engring, Carnegie-Mellon U., 1957; J.D., George Washington U., 1961. Bar: Va. 1962, D.C. 1962, U.S. Ct. of Customs and Patent Appeals 1963, U.S. Ct. Appeals (Fed. cir.) 1982, U.S. Supreme Ct. 1973. Patent examiner U.S. Patent Office, Washington, 1957-62; practiced in Washington, 1962—; patent atty. firms K. Flocks and A. Browdy, Washington, 1962-68; mem. firm Browdy and Neimark, Washington, 1969—, sr. ptnr., 1989—. Contbr. articles, papers to profl. jours. Charter mem. Gov.'s Planning and Adv. Coun. on Devel. Disabilities, State of Md., 1971-86, vice chmn., 1975-77; mem. Legal and Human Rights Task Force, Montgomery County (Md.) Com. for Employment of Handicapped, 1972-73; bd. dirs., co-founder Cmty. Svcs. for Autistic Adults and Children; past bd. dirs. Tifereth Israel Congregation. Recipient Gov.'s citation State of Md., 1986. Mem. Am. Bar Assn. (mem. adv. bd. developmental disabilities model legis. project 1977-81, mem. adv. bd. mental and phys. disabilities law reporter 1979—), D.C. Bar, Va. State Bar, Am. Intellectual Property Law Assn. (mem. com. patent law 1965-69, chem. practice 1970—), Md. Patent Law Assn., Internat. Assn. Jewish Lawyers and Jurists, Patent Office Soc., Autism Soc. Am. (nat. dir. 1973-77, dir. Montgomery County chpt. 1970-72, nat. Plaque awards 1972, 77), Md. State Soc. for Autistic Children (founder, dir. 1971-73), Am. Jewish Com., Am. Jewish Congress, B'nai Brith. Home: 12908 Ruxton Rd Silver Spring MD 20904-5278 Office: 419 7th St NW Suite 300 Washington DC 20004

NEIMS, ALLEN HOWARD, univeristy dean, medical scientist; b. Chgo., Oct. 24, 1938; s. Irving Morris and Ruth (Geller) N.; m. Myrna Gay Robins, June 18, 1961; children: Daniel Mark, Susan Roberta, Nancy Elizabeth. B.A., B.S., U. Chgo., 1957; M.D., Johns Hopkins U., 1961, Ph.D., 1966. Intern, resident in pediatrics Johns Hopkins Hosp., 1961-62, 66-68; research asso. Lab. Neurochemistry, NIH, 1968-70; asst. prof. physiol. chemistry and pediatrics Johns Hopkins Med. Sch., 70-72; assoc. prof. McGill U., 1972-77, prof. pharmacology and pediatrics, 1977-78; dir. Roche developmental pharmacology unit, 1972-78; prof., chmn. dept. pharmacology and therapeutics, prof. pediatrics U. Fla., Gainesville, 1978-89, dean Coll. Medicine, 1989-96, prof. pharmcology, pediat., 1996—; Fulton Bequest prof. U. Melbourne, Australia, 1974; mem. human embryology and devel. study sect. NIH, 1979-83; sci. cons. Can. Found. for Study of Sudden Infant Death, 1974-77, Nat. Soft Drink Assn., 1976-78, Internat. Life Scis. Inst., 1978-89; bd. sci. counsellors Nat. Inst. Child Health and Human Devel., 1984-89. Contbr. chpts. to books, articles to med. jours. Served to comdr. USPHS, 1968-70. NIH, Can. Med. Research Council grantee. Mem. Can. Assn. Research in Toxicology (pres. 1976-78), Am. Soc. Pharmacology and Exptl. Therapeutics (past mem. exec. coms. clin. pharmacology and drug metabolism), Pediatric Research Soc., Am. Soc. Clin. Pharmacology and Therapeutics, Assn. Am. Med. Colls, Coun. of Deans, Am. Pediatric Soc., Am. Acad. Pediatrics. Office: U Fla Coll Medicine PO Box 100267 Gainesville FL 32610-0215

NEINAS, CHARLES MERRILL, athletic association executive; b. Marshfield, Wis., Jan. 18, 1932; s. Arthur Oscar and Blanche Amelia (Reeder) N.; children: Andrew, Toby. B.S., U. Wis., 1957. Asst. exec. dir. Nat. Collegiate Athletic Assn., Kansas City, Mo., 1961-71; commr. Big Eight Conf., Kansas City, 1971-81; exec. dir. Coll. Football Assn., 1981—; Dr. Patricia L. Pacey prof. econs. U. Colo., Boulder, 1981—, econ. cons., 1981—; adviser Am. Football Coaches Assn., 1997—. Served with USNR, 1952-54. Home: 4977 Idylwild Trl Boulder CO 80301-3651 Office: College Football Assoc 6688 Gunpark Dr Boulder CO 80301-3372

NEIS, ARNOLD HAYWARD, pharmaceutical company executive; b. N.Y.C., Feb. 13, 1938; s. Harry H. and Mary Ruth (Bishop) N.; m. Lucy de Puig, Dec. 8, 1989; children by previous marriage: Nancy R., Robert C. B.S. cum laude, Columbia U., 1959; M.B.A., N.Y.U., 1967. With Scott Chem. Co., 1959-64; v.p. mktg., then v.p. Odell, Inc., N.Y.C., 1964-71, pres. Thayer Knomark div., 1969-71; pres., chief exec. officer E.T. Browne Drug Co., Inc., Englewood Cliffs, N.J., 1971—; dir. Esquire A.B. Stockholm, Knomark Can. Ltd., E.T. Browne Internat. Fellow Royal Soc. Chemists, Royal Geog. Soc., Am. Inst. Chemists, N.Y. Acad. Scis.; mem. AAAS, Am. Chem. Soc., Am. Pharm. Assn., New Eng. Soc. (bd. dirs.), Explorers Club (v.p., bd. dirs., Sweeney medal 1997), Chemists Club, Lotos Club, Soldiers, Sailors and Airmans Club (bd. dirs.), St. Georges Soc. Episcopalian. Home: 898 Park Ave New York NY 10021-0234 Office: PO Box 1613 140 Sylvan Ave Englewood NJ 07632-2502

NEIS, ARTHUR VERAL, healthcare and development company executive; b. Lawrence, Kans., May 30, 1940; s. Veral Herbert and Louise (Schlegel) N.; m. Fleeta Weigel, Apr. 12, 1969; children: Frederick Arthur, Benjamin Jason, Sarah Louise. BS in Bus., U. Kans., 1962, MS in Acctg., 1963. CPA, Kans., Iowa. Mgmt. cons. Arthur Andersen & Co., Kansas City, Mo. and Mpls., 1963-74; chief corp. acctg. Carlson Co., Mpls., 1974-76; contr. The Fullerton Cos., Mpls., 1976-78; asst. treas. Fru-Con Corp., St. Louis, 1978-80, asst. contr., 1981, contr., 1982-86; corp. contr. LCS Holdings, Inc. (Weitz Corp. and Subsidaries), Des Moines, 1986-87, treas., CFO, 1987—; treas., CFO Weitz Co., Des Moines, 1987-93, Life Care Services Corp., Des Moines, 1987—; bd. dirs. LCS Holdings, Inc.; mem. adv. group NAIC, 1990-93. Bd. dirs. Inst. Humane Studies George Mason U., Fairfax, Va., 1973—, exec. com., 1975-83, chmn., 1978-83; bd. dirs. Lake Country Sch., Mpls., 1973-78; treas. Villa de Maria Montessori Sch., St. Louis, 1982-86, bd. dirs.; trustee Crossroads Sch., St. Louis, 1984-86, exec. com. bd., 1984-86; bd. dirs. Alliance for Arts and Understanding, 1993—, co-chair, 1993-96, chair, 1996—; trustee Fin. Execs. Rsch. Found., 1994—, Plymouth Congrl. United Ch. of Christ, 1993-97; bd. dirs. Plymouth Congrl. United Ch. of Christ Found., 1997—, Plymouth Ch. Found., 1997—. Mem. AICPA, Kans. Soc. CPAs, Iowa Soc. CPAs, Fin. Execs. Inst. (bd. dirs. Iowa chpt. 1986, 88-94, sec. 1988-90, v.p. 1990-91, pres. 1991-92). Avocations: bibliophile, Kans. history, orientalia. Home: 1575 NW 106th St Clive IA 50325-6604 Office: Life Care Svcs Corp 800 2nd Ave Des Moines IA 50309-1320

NEISER, BRENT ALLEN, public affairs consultant; b. Cin., Sept. 16, 1954; s. Rodger John and Hazel Jean Neiser; m. Marion Alice Hutton, Apr. 1, 1978; children: Christy Jean, Steven José, April Reneé. BA in Pub. Affairs, George Washington U., 1976; MA in Urban Studies, Occidental Coll., 1978; MBA, U. Louisville, 1979; postgrad. in internat. affairs, U. Denver, 1987-90. Cert. fin. planner, 1985; cert. assn. exec., 1994; chartered mut. fund counselor, 1996. Project mgr., analyst Legis. Research Com., Frankfort, Ky., 1978-84; pres. Moneyminder, Denver and Frankfort, 1983-91; dir. edn., govt. affairs and ethics Inst. Cert. Fin. Planners, Denver, 1985-91, exec. dir., 1991-94; pub. affairs, govt. rels. bus. strategies cons. The Brent Neiser Co., Englewood, Colo., 1994—; dir. Nat. Endowment for Fin. Edn., 1995—; mng. dir. Fin. Products Stds. Bd., Denver, 1985-91; co-creator Personal Econ. Summit '93, Washington. Author: EPCOT/World Showcase External Directions, Walt Disney Imagineering, 1977, Personal Management, 1996; co-inventor: Trivia Express (game) Denver, 1986. Vol., v.p. Big Bros./Big Sisters, Frankfort, 1982; del. Colo. Model Constrnl. Conv., 1987; mem. citizens budget rev. com. Greenwood Village; parent trainer The Adoption Exch., Denver, 1988, mem. long range planning com., 1992-93, bd. dirs., 1993—; polit. action dir. Frankfort NAACP, 1983, legis. chmn. state conf., 1984; troop com. mem., asst. scoutmaster Boy Scouts Am., Englewood, 1993—; bd. dirs. Young Ams. Bank Edn. Found., 1993—, chair edn. coun.; bd. dirs. Leadership Denver, 1993. Lt. (j.g.) USNR, 1985-92. Recipient Outstanding Service award Frankfort NAACP, 1981, Assn. Advance Am. award Excellence, 1996; named Man of Yr., Frankfort NAACP, 1983; Pub. Affairs fellow Coro Found., 1976-77. Mem. Investors Edn. Assn. Colo. (bd. dirs.), Nat. Assns. in Colo., Denver C. of C. (pub. affairs coun.), Adoptive Families of Am., Inst. Cert. Fin. Planners, Assn. for Fin. Counseling and Planning Edn., Am. Soc. Assn. Execs., Inst. Mgmt. Cons., Nat. Coun. La Raza, Internat. Assn. Fin. Planners (bd. dirs. Rocky Mountain chpt. 1990-92), N.Am. Securities Adminstrs. Assn. (investment adviser and fin. planner adv. com.), Nat. Soc. Compliance Profls. (bd. dirs. 1987-89), Am. Film Inst. (writers workshop). Office: 5860 Big Canyon Dr Englewood CO 80111-3516

NEISS, EDGAR, civic organization administrator; b. Amsterdam, The Netherlands, Apr. 13, 1939; came to U.S., 1940; s. Nathan and Renee (Machauf) N.; m. Ruth Pauline Chambers, Feb. 2, 1969 (div. 1974); m. Judith Fay Becker, Nov. 14, 1976; children: Michael Joseph, Matthew Solomon, Jennifer Miriam. BA in Speech and Drama, NYU, 1961; postgrad., UCLA, 1965, U. Judaism, 1968. Asst. mdse. mgr. Dohrmann Hotel Supply Co., L.A., 1963-66; buyer housewares Dohrmann Co., L.A., 1966; stagecraft specialist L.A. County Dept. Praks & Recreation, L.A., 1966-67, theatre arts specialist, 1967-68, supr. theatre arts, 1968-72, cultural arts dir., 1972-77; mng. dir. Madison (Wis.) Civic Ctr., 1977-81; gen. mgr. Atlanta Landmarks/Fox Theatre, 1981—. Trustee Hebrew Acad. Atlanta, 1986-92, Atlanta Gt. Artist Series, 1989-90. With USAR, 1963-68. Mem. Midtown Alliance (bd. dirs. 1986—), Internat. Soc. Performing Arts Found. (trustee Grand Rapids, Mich. 1981—, treas., exec. com. 1991-96), Internat. Assn. Assembly Mgrs., League Am. Theatres and Prodrs., Rotary. Avocation: cantorial music. Office: Fox Theatre 660 Peachtree St NE Atlanta GA 30308-1929

NEISSER, ULRIC, psychology educator; b. Kiel, Germany, Dec. 8, 1928; came to U.S., 1933; s. Hans Philip and Charlotte (Schroeter) N. BA, Harvard U., 1950, PhD, 1956; MA, Swarthmore Coll., 1952; Laurea Honoris Causa, U. Rome, 1988, U. Aarhus, Denmark, 1993, U. Cluj, Romania, 1994. Instr. Swarthmore (Pa.) Coll., 1953-54, Harvard U., Cambridge, Mass., 1956-57; from asst. to assoc. prof. Brandeis U., Waltham, Mass., 1957-66; prof. psychology Cornell U., Ithaca, N.Y., 1967-80, Susan Linn Sage prof. psychology, 1980-83; Robert W. Woodruff prof. psychology Emory U., Atlanta, 1983-96; prof. psychology Cornell U., Ithaca, N.Y., 1996—. Author: Cognitive Psychology, 1967, Cognition and Reality, 1976; editor: Memory Observed, 1982, The School Achievement of Minority Children, 1987, Concepts and Conceptual Development, 1987, Remembering Reconsidered, 1988, The Perceived Self, 1993. Ctr. for Advanced Study in Behavior Scis. fellow, 1973-74, Guggenheim fellow, 1987-88. Fellow APA; mem. NAS, Am. Acad. Arts and Scis., Cognitive Sci. Soc., Internat. Soc. Ecol. Psychology, Psychonomic Soc. Office: Cornell U Dept Psychology Ithaca NY 14853

NEISWANDER, LINDA CAROL, realtor, interior decorator; b. Lansing, Mich., Jan. 1, 1951; d. Gordon Field and Phyllis Blanche (Bedell) Priest; m. Paul Clair Neiswander, Aug. 19, 1972; children: Kristin Anne, Ashley Marie. Student, Ea. Mich. U., 1969-71; grad., Realtors Inst., 1996. Lic. notary pub., S.C. Owner Designs by Linda C. Neiswander, Midland, Mich., 1978-84; tchr. Sawtooth Ctr. for Visual Design, Winston-Salem, N.C., 1986-88; realtor, ptnr. Eulalie Salley & Co., 1988—; cons. Mary Kay Cosmetics, Aiken, 1994—; designer Dogwood Flories, Aiken, 1995-96. Mem. Gathering Choir, St. Mary's Cath. Ch., Aiken, 1989—, food coupon coord., 1990-96; v.p., mem. adv. bd. Nuture Home-Cmty. United for Tomorrow's Future, Aiken, 1992—. Recipient cert. of professsionalism S.C. Assn. Realtors, 1993, 94, cert. of scholastic achievement Nat. Assn. Realtors, 1994. Mem. Aiken Bd. Realtors (chmn. cmty. svc. 1991-93, co-chmn. casino night Habitat for Humanity 1991-94, co-chmn. hospitality, 1992-94, sec. 1994-95, President's Club 1992-94), Lions. Republican. Avocations: gardening, basketweaving, oil painting, decorating. Home: 1017 Water Oak Dr Aiken SC 29803 Office: Eulalie Salley & Co 108 Laurens St NW Aiken SC 29801-3846

NEITER, GERALD IRVING, lawyer; b. L.A., Nov. 11, 1933; s. Harry and Ida Florence (Alperin) N.; m. Margaret P. Rowe, Mar. 5, 1961; children:

David, Karen, Michael. BSL, U. So. Calif., 1957, JD, 1957. Bar: Calif. 1958. Judge pro tem Mcpl. Cts., L.A. and Beverly Hills, 1970-94; judge pro tem and mediator Calif. Superior Ct., L.A. County, 1974-94, family law mediator, 1976—; prin. Gerald I. Neiter, P.C., L.A., 1981—; lectr. State Bar of Calif., 1968, 76, 79, 81; former referee State Bar Ct.; arbitrator Am. Arbitration Assn. Mem. Am., Los Angeles County (arbitrator), Beverly Hills, Century City bar assns., State Bar Calif. Office: 1925 Century Park E Ste 200 Los Angeles CA 90067-2701

NEITZKE, ERIC KARL, lawyer; b. Mobile, Ala., Dec. 10, 1955; s. Howard and Otti S. Neitzke; m. Geri Fabricatore, Nov. 5, 1983; children: Kyle, Blake, Blaire. BA, U. Fla., 1979, JD, 1982. Bar: Fla. 1982, U.S. Dist. Ct. (mid. dist.) Fla. 1987. Asst. state atty. 7th Jud. Cir., State Atty., Daytona Beach, Fla., 1982; atty. Dunn, Smith & Withers, Daytona Beach, 1982-88, Monaco, Smith, Hood and Perkins, Daytona Beach, 1988—; adj. faculty family law and criminal law Daytona Community Coll. Contbr. articles to profl. jours. Mem. Fla. Acad. Trial Lawyers, Assn. Trial Lawyers Am., Volusia Bar Assn., Fla. Assn. Criminal Def. Lawyers, Phi Beta Kappa. Avocations: water sports, shooting, travel. Home: 19 Lost Creek Ln Ormond Beach FL 32174-4840 Office: Eric K Neitzke PA 444 Seabreeze Blvd Ste 900 Daytona Beach FL 32118-3953

NEJELSKI, PAUL ARTHUR, judge; b. Chgo., Feb. 24, 1938; s. Leo Lawrence and Rena Grace (Martin) N.; m. Marilyn Ray Mills, Oct. 2, 1965; children: Nicole Rena, Stephen Downing. BA magna cum laude, Yale U., 1959, LLB, 1962; MPA, Am. U., 1969; cert. of theol. studies, Georgetown U., 1989. Bar: N.J. 1963. Law clk. appellate div. N.J. Superior Ct., 1962-63; asst. U.S. atty. U.S. Dist. Ct. N.J., 1964-65; atty., later chief immigration unit Dept. Justice, Washington, 1965-69; chief cts. desk Nat. Inst. Justice, Washington, 1969-70; asst. dir. Criminal Justice Ctr., Harvard U., 1970-71; dir. planning phase Inst. Jud. Adminstrn.-ABA Juvenile Justice Standards Project, N.Y.C., 1971-73; dir. Inst. Jud. Adminstrn., NYU, 1973-76; dep. ct. adminstrn. Conn. Jud. Dept., Hartford, 1976-77; dep. asst. atty. gen. Office for Improvements in Adminstrn. Justice, Dept. Justice, Washington, 1977-79; dir. Action Commn. to Reduce Ct. Costs and Delay, ABA, Washington, 1979-81; cir. exec. 3rd Cir., Phila., 1981-84; ct. adminstr. U.S. Tax Ct., 1984-89; immigration judge Dept. Justice, Arlington, Va., 1989—; mem. faculty law NYU, 1972-74, U. Conn., 1976-77, U. Md., 1981-82; cons. Author: (with C.O. Philip) Where Do Judges Come From?, 1976; editor: Social Research in Conflict With Law and Ethics, 1976; contbr. articles to profl. jours. With U.S. Army, 1963-64. Office: 901 N Stuart St Ste 1300 Arlington VA 22203-1821

NEKRITZ, LEAH KALISH, dean, college administrator; b. N.Y.C., Apr. 6, 1932; d. Jacob Joseph and Anna (Feldman) Kalish; m. Richard Nekritz. BA, Bklyn. Coll., 1953; MLS, Cath. U. Am., 1963. Libr. Prince George's C.C., Largo, Md., 1961-67, dir. libr. svcs., 1967-71, dir. learning resources, 1971-77, assoc. dean for learning resources, 1977-90, dean of learning resources, 1991-95, ret., 1995; mem. adv. com. State Libr. Resource Ctr., Md., 1976; mem. Met. Washington Coun. of Govts. Libr. Coun., 1976-77, 79-81; mem. bd. advisors Libr. System Coop. in Mid Atlantic, Washington, 1985-88; exec. dir. Md. Congress Acad. Libr. Dirs., 1989-90. mem. adv. com. State Libr. Resource Ctr., Md., 1976; mem. libr. coun. Met. Washington Coun. Govts., 1976-77, 79-81; mem. bd. advisors Libr. Sys. Coop. in Mid Atlantic, Washington, 1985-88; exec. dir. Md. Congress Acad. Libr. Dirs., 1989-90; mem. acad. librs. adv. bd. U. Md. CLIS, 1994. Mem. AAUP, ALA (sec. cmty. and jr. coll. sect. 1974), Md. Libr. Assn., Assn. for Ednl. Comm. and Tech. (treas. 1974, chmn. post-secondary guide 1981). Avocations: painting, travel. Home: 417 N Fairfax St Alexandria VA 22314-2321

NELKIN, DOROTHY, sociology and science policy educator; b. Boston, July 30, 1933; d. Henry and Helen (Fine) Wolfers; m. Mark Nelkin, Aug. 31, 1952; children: Lisa, Laurie. B.A., Cornell U., 1954. Research assoc. Cornell U., Ithaca, N.Y., 1963-69, sr. research assoc., 1970-72, assoc. prof., 1972-76, prof. sci. tech. sociology program, 1976-90, prof. sociology, 1977-90; univ. prof., prof. sociology, affiliate prof. law NYU, 1990—, Clare Boothe Luce vis. prof., 1988-90; cons. OECD, Paris, 1975-76, Inst. Environ., Berlin, 1978-79; maitre de conference U. Paris, 1975-76; maitre de recherche Ecole Polytechnique, Paris, 1980-81. Author: The Atom Besieged, 1981, The Creation Controversy, 1982, Science as Intellectual Property, 1983, Workers at Risk, 1984, Selling Science: How the Press Covers Science and Technology, 1987, 2d edit., 1995, Dangerous Diagnostics: The Social Power of Biological Information, 1989, 2d edit., 1994, A Disease of Society: Cultural Impact ofAIDS, 1991, The Animal Rights Crusade, 1991, Controversy: Politics of Technical Decision, 3d edit., 1992, The DNA Mystique: The Gene as Cultural Icon, 1995. Adviser Office Tech. Assessment, 1977-79, 82-83; expert witness ACLU, Ark., 1982; mem. Nat. Adv. Coun. to NIH Human Genome Project, 1991-95. Vis. scholar Resources for the Futures, 1980-81; vis. scholar Russell Sage Found., N.Y.C., 1983; Guggenheim fellow, 1983-84. Fellow AAAS (bd. dirs.), Hastings Inst. Soc. Ethics and Life Scis.; mem. NAS Inst. of Medicine, Soc. for Social Studies Sci. (pres. 1978-79). Home: 3 Washington Square Vlg New York NY 10012-1836 Office: NYU Dept Sociology 269 Mercer St New York NY 10003-6633

NELL, JANINE MARIE, metallurgical and materials engineer; b. Milw., Jan. 15, 1959; d. Joseph Frank (Gabrhel) and Joyce Cecelia (Jans) Clendening; m. Michael Paul Nell, Aug. 19, 1978. SB in Materials Sci. and Engring., MIT, 1981, PhD in Metallurgy, 1989. Rsch. asst. MIT, Cambridge, 1981-89; sr. engr., asst. to pres. Failure Analysis Assocs., Inc., Menlo Park, Calif., 1989-91, sr. engr. exec. office, 1991-92, mgr. corp. lab. and testing svcs., 1992-94, sr. engr. materials and mechanics group, 1994—; mem. vis. com. for undergrad. edn. and student affairs MIT, 1992—. Author: Progress in Powder Metallurgy, 1986, Superalloys 92, 1992; contbr. articles to profl. jours. Recipient Karl Taylor Compton award MIT, 1986; Cabot Corp. fellow, 1981-85. Mem. ASME, ASM Internat., The Metall. Soc., Am. Inst. Mining, Metall. and Petroleum Engrs., Soc. Plastics Engrs., Am. Welding Soc., The Human Factors and Ergonomics Soc., Sigma Xi, Tau Beta Pi. Achievements include designed, manufactured and tested new high temperature alloys for gas turbine applications based on multiphase strengthening and engineered grain structures. Office: Failure Analysis Assocs Inc 149 Commonwealth Dr Menlo Park CA 94025-1133

NELLERMOE, LESLIE CAROL, lawyer; b. Oakland, Calif., Jan. 26, 1954; d. Carrol Wandell and Nora Ann (Conway) N.; m. Darrell Ray McKissic, Aug. 9, 1986; 1 child, Devin Anne. BS cum laude, Wash. State U., 1975; JD cum laude, Willamette U., 1978. Bar: Wash. 1978, U.S. Dist. Ct. (ea. dist.) Wash. 1979, U.S. Dist. Ct. (we. dist.) Wash. 1983. Staff atty. Wash. Ct. Appeals, Spokane, 1978-79; asst. atty. gen. Wash. Atty. Gen. Office, Spokane, 1979-83, Olympia, 1983-85; assoc. Syrdal, Danelo, Klein, Myre & Woods, Seattle, 1985-88; ptnr. Heller Ehrman White & McAuliffe, Seattle, 1989—. Bd. dirs. N.W. Environ. Bus. Coun., 1996—, Campfire Boys & Girls, Seattle, 1991—. Mem. ABA, Wash. State Bar Assn., King County Bar Assn., Wash. Environ. Industry Assn. (bd. dirs.). Office: Heller Ehrman White & McAuliffe 701 5th Ave 6100 Columbia Ctr Seattle WA 98104

NELLI, D. JAMES, business school executive, accountant; b. Seneca Falls, N.Y., Feb. 19, 1917; s. Thomas and Vita N.; m. Victoria Margaret Serino, Aug. 31, 1941 (dec. May 1980); children: Thomas, Diane, Joseph, John; m. 2d, Carmel L. Dowd, Sept. 19, 1981; BS, Syracuse U., 1948. CPA, N.Y. Staff acct. Seidman & Seidman, N.Y.C., 1948-49, Stover, Butler & Murphy, Syracuse, N.Y., 1949-55; instr. Syracuse U., 1953; instr. acctg. Central City Bus. Inst., Syracuse, 1955-58, pres., 1958—, also pvt. practice acctg., Syracuse. Served with USNR, 1943-46. CPA, N.Y. Mem. Am. Inst. CPAs, N.Y. State Soc. CPAs, Am. Acctg. Assn., AAUP. Roman Catholic. Clubs: Lakeshore Yacht and Country (Clay, N.Y.), Italian Am. Athletic (Syracuse). Home: 7929 Boxford Rd Clay NY 13041-8606 Office: Cen City Bus Inst 224 Harrison St Syracuse NY 13202-3052

NELLIGAN, KATE (PATRICIA COLLEEN NELLIGAN), actress; b. London, Ont., Can., Mar. 16, 1951; d. Patrick Joseph and Alice (Dier) N. Attended, York U., Toronto, Ctrl. Sch. Speech and Drama, London. Appeared in plays in Bristol, London, and New York: Barefoot in the Park, 1972, Misalliance, A Streetcar Named Desire, The Playboy of the Western World, London Assurance, Lulu, Private Lives, Knuckle, 1974, Heartbreak House, 1975, Plenty, 1975, As You Like It, A Moon for the Misbegotten, 1984, Virginia, 1985, Serious Money, 1988, Spoils of War, 1988, BAd Habits; films include: The Count of Monte Cristo, 1979, The Romantic Englishwoman, 1979, Dracula, 1979, Mr. Patman, 1980, Eye of the Needle, 1980, Agent, 1980, Without a Trace, 1983, Eleni, 1985, White Room, 1990, Bethune: The Making of a Hero, 1990, Frankie and Johnnie, 1991, The Prince of Tides, 1991, Shadows and Fog, 1992, Fatal Instinct, 1993, Wolf, 1994, Into the Deep, 1994, How to Make an American Quilt, 1995, Margaret's Museum, 1995, Up Close and Personal, 1996; TV appearances include: The Arcata Promise, 1974, The Onedin Line, The Lady of the Camellias, Licking Hitler, Measure for Measure, Therese Raquin, 1980, Forgive Our Foolish Ways, 1980, Kojak: The Price of Justice, 1987, Control, 1987, Love and Hate: A Marriage Made in Hell, 1990, Terror Strickes the Class Reunion, 1992, The Diamond Fleece, 1992, Liar Liar, 1993, Shattered Trust: The Shari Karney Story, 1993, Spoils of War, 1994, Million Dollar Babies, 1994, A Mother's Prayer, 1995, Captive Heart: The James Mink Story, 1996. Recipient Best Actress award Evening Standard, 1978. Avocations: reading, cooking. Office: Internat Creative Mgmt c/o Joe Funicello 8942 Wilshire Blvd Beverly Hills CA 90211-1934

NELLIGAN, KENNETH EGAN, lawyer; b. Revere, Mass., Mar. 21, 1952; s. Kenneth P. and Lillian M. N.; m. S.C. Nelligan. BS in Math., U. N.H., 1974; JD cum laude, Suffolk U., 1977. Bar: Mass. 1977, D.C. 1979, U.S. Claims Ct. 1981, U.S. Supreme Ct. 1983. Asst. counsel Naval Electronic Sys. Command, Arlington, Va., 1977-81; counsel Naval Rsch. Lab., Washington, 1981-85, Naval Underwater Sys. Ctr., Newport, R.I., 1985-92, Naval Undersea Warfare Ctr. Divsn., Newport, 1992—. Assoc. editor Law Rev., 1977. Recipient Am. Jurisprudence awards The Lawyer's Co-op Pub. Co., 1975. Mem. Mass. Bar Assn., D.C. Bar Assn. Avocations: basketball, tennis. Office: Office of Counsel Code OOOC Bldg 11 Naval Undersea Warfare Ctr Newport RI 02840

NELLIGAN, WILLIAM DAVID, professional association executive; b. Halstead, Kans., Aug. 10, 1926; s. William D. and Katherine (Roberts) N.; m. Dorothy Meyer, Aug. 17, 1952; children: Richard, Arthur, Mark. Student, U. Wichita, 1944-46; BS, U. Kans., 1949. Display advt. salesman Kansas City Star and Times, Mo., 1949-51; mgr. SW Kans. Extension Ctr. U. Kans., Garden City, 1951-55; exec. dir. dept. postgrad. med. edn. Sch. Medicine U. Kans., Kansas City, Kans., 1955-64; asst. to pres. Med. Coll. Ga., Augusta, 1964-65; exec. v.p. Am. Coll. Cardiology, Bethesda, Md., 1965-92; v.p. Marion Merrell DOW, Inc., Kansas City, Mo., 1992-94; exec. dir. Am. Soc. Nuc. Cardiology, Bethesda, 1994—. mem. Nat. Commn. Diabetes, 1975-76, adv. council Nat. Diabetes and Digestive and Kidney Diseases, 1987-88; bd. dirs. Arthur E. Hertzler Research Found., Halstead, Kans., 1961—. Recipient Man with a Heart award N.Y. Cardiol. Soc., 1970, Presdl. citation Am. Coll. Cardiology, 1975, Disting. Service award Am. Coll. Cardiology, 1986, CLC Hall of Leaders award, 1986. Fellow Am. Coll. Cardiology; mem. AMA (citation of layman for disting. svc. 1993), Profl. Conv. Mgmt. Assn. (pres. 1974-75, Disting. Svc. award 1990), Am. Med. Writers Assn. (dir., exec. com., treas. 1970-78, Harold Swanberg Disting. Svc. award), Am. Soc. Assn. Execs. (cert., dir. 1975-78, sec.-treas. 1987-88, Key award 1984), Am. Assn. Med. Soc. Execs. (pres. 1986-87), Brit. Cardiac Soc. (hon.), Alliance for Continuing Med. Edn. (Pres.'s award 1994), Masons. Office: 9111 Old Georgetown Rd Bethesda MD 20814-1616

NELMS, CHARLIE, academic administrator; b. Crawfordsville, Ark., Sept. 11, 1946. BS in Agronomy, U. Ark., Pine Bluff, 1968; MS, Ind. U., 1971, EdD, 1977. Various collegiate positions to lectr. and counselor Lehman Coll./CUNY, Pine Bluff, 1971-73; assoc. dean, asst. prof. edn. Earlham Coll., Richmond, Ind., 1973-77; assoc. dir. Ctr. Human Devel. and Edn. Svcs., asst. prof. U. Ark., Pine Bluff, 1977-78; assoc. dean for acad. affairs Ind. U., Northwest Gary, Ind., 1978-84; v.p. student svcs. Sinclair C.C., Dayton, Ohio, 1984-87; chancellor, prof. edn. Ind. Univ., 1987-94; chancellor and prof. edn., pub. adminstrn. Univ. Mich., Flint, 1994—; cons., evaluator N.Cen. Assn. Schs. & Colls., 1987—, Middle States Assn., 1994—. Contbr. articles to profl. jours. Recipient Outstanding Svc. award NASPA, 1990, I-MAEOPP, 1990, Disting. Svc. award Negro Edn. Review, 1990, Nat. Alliance Bus., 1984, Wall Street Joun. Student Achievement award, 1968, Rockefeller Student Leadership award, 1968. Office: U Mich Office of Chancellor 221 University Pavilion Flint MI 48502-2186 Home: 915 Woodlawn Park Dr Flint MI 48503-2762

NELSEN, HART MICHAEL, sociologist, educator; b. Pipestone, Minn., Aug. 3, 1938; s. Noah I. and Nova (Ziegler) N.; m. Anne Kusener, June 13, 1964; 1 dau., Jennifer. B.A., U. No. Iowa, 1959, M.A., 1963; M.Div., Princeton Theol. Sem., 1963; Ph.D. (NSF faculty fellow), Vanderbilt U., 1972. Asst. prof. sociology Western Ky. U., Bowling Green, 1965-70; assoc. prof. Western Ky. U., 1970-73; assoc. prof. Catholic U. Am., 1973-74, prof., 1974-81, chmn. dept. sociology, 1974-77, mem. Boys Town Ctr. for Study Youth Devel., 1974-81; prof. sociology La. State U., Baton Rouge, 1981-84, chmn. dept. sociology, head dept. rural sociology, 1981-84, coordinator rural sociology research, 1981-84; dean Coll. Liberal Arts Pa. State U., 1984-90, prof. sociology, 1984—. Author: (with Anne K. Nelsen) Black Church in the Sixties, 1975; co-author: The Religion of Children, 1977, Religion and American Youth, 1976; editor: (with others) The Black Church in America, 1971; adv. editor: Sociol. Quar, 1976-82; assoc. editor: Sociol. Analysis, 1977-80, Rev. Religious Research, 1977-80, 84—, editor, 1980-84; mem. editorial bd.: Social Forces, 1983-86. Co-rec. sec. Capitol Hill Restoration Soc., 1979-80, v.p., 1980-81; mem. exec. bd. Lafitte Hills Assn., 1983-84. Presbyterian Chs. grantee, 1966-69; NIMH co-grantee, 1969-72; Russell Sage Found. co-grantee, 1972-73; La. Gov.'s Commn. on Alcoholism and Drug Abuse grantee, 1982. Mem. Assn. Sociology Religion (exec. council 1974-76, 78-82, v.p. 1978-79, pres. 1980-81), Religious Research Assn. (dir. 1977-80, pres.-elect 1985-86, pres. 1987-88), Soc. Sci. Study Religion (council 1981-83, exec. sec. 1984-87), Am. Sociol. Assn., So. Sociol. Soc. (chmn. membership com. 1983-85), AAAS (rep. 1984—). Presbyterian. Office: Pa State U Oswald 306 Dept Sociology University Park PA 16802

NELSEN, WILLIAM CAMERON, foundation president, former college president; b. Omaha, Oct. 18, 1941; s. William Peter and Ellen Lucella (Cameron) N.; m. Margaret Leone Rossow, May 30, 1981; children by previous marriage: William Norris, Shawna Lynn; 1 adopted dau., Sarah Ruth. B.A., Midland Lutheran Coll., Fremont, Nebr., 1963; M.A. (Danforth Grad. fellow 1963, Woodrow Wilson fellow 1963), Columbia U., 1966; Ph.D., U. Pa., 1971; Fulbright scholar, U. Erlangen, W. Ger., 1964; D (hon.), Midland Luth. Coll., 1995. Program exec. Danforth Found., St. Louis, 1970-73; asst. dean, then v.p., dean coll. St. Olaf Coll., Northfield, Minn., 1973-80; dir. Project on Faculty Devel. Assn. of Am. Colls., 1979; pres. Augustana Coll., Sioux Falls, S.D., 1980-86, Citizens' Scholarship Found. of Am., St. Peter, Minn., 1986—; bd. dirs. 1st Nat. Bank and Bancommunity Svc. Corp., St. Peter, Minn. Author: Effective Approaches to Faculty Development, 1980, Renewal of the Teacher Scholar, 1981, also articles. Bd. dirs. S.D. Symphony, 1980-85, Sioux Falls YMCA, 1980-86, Luth. Ednl. Conf. N.Am., 1982-86, Sioux Falls United Way, 1983-86. Mem. Am. Assn. Higher Edn., Assn. Am. Colls. (bd. dirs. 1984-86, dir. project faculty devel. 1979), Shoreland Country Club (pres. 1996—), Consortium for Advancement of Pvt. Higher Edn., Coun. of Ind. Colls., Nat. Dollars for Scholars, Rotary Club. Republican. Lutheran. Home: 804 Spruce Pl Saint Peter MN 56082-1598 Office: Citizens' Scholarship Found Am PO Box 297 Saint Peter MN 56082-0297

NELSON, ALAN CURTIS, government official, lawyer; b. Oakland, Calif., Oct. 18, 1933; s. Albert C. and Martha (Peters) N.; m. JoAnn Wallen, Jan. 31, 1960; children: Kristine Ann, Kathryn Donna, Karin Martha. BS, U. Calif., Berkeley, 1955, JD, 1958. Bar: Calif. 1959, U.S. Dist. Cts. Calif. 1959, U.S. Supreme Ct. 1984. Atty. Rogers, Clark & Jordan, San Francisco, 1959-64; dep. dist. atty. Alameda County (Calif.), 1964-69; asst. dir. State of Calif. Human Resource Dept., Sacramento, 1969-72; dir. State of Calif. Dept. Rehab., Sacramento, 1972-75; gen. atty. Pacific Telephone & Telegraph, San Francisco, 1975-81; dep. commr. Immigration and Naturalization Service, Washington, 1981-82, commr., 1982-89; cons. fed. Am. immigration reform U.S. Dept. Justice, Washington, 1989-90; gen. counsel Employment Devel. Dept. State of Calif., 1990-91; atty. and cons. on immigration Sacramento, 1994—; adj. prof. McGeorge Sch. Law, U. Pacific. Chmn. Calif. Gov. Com. for Employment of Handicapped, 1981-82. Recipient Alumnus of Yr. award Tau Kappa Epsilon, 1987; Border Patrol Sta., Imperial Beach, Calif. dedicated to Commr. Nelson, 1988. Mem. State Bar Calif., Assn. Calif. Tort Reform (dir.), Bar Assn. San Francisco, Legal Aid Soc. San Francisco (dir.), Assn. Fed. Investigators (pres. 1987). Republican. Club: Commonwealth. Office: Law Offices of Alan Nelson 835 Shoreside Dr Sacramento CA 95831-1422 *Four Key Personal and Management Concepts: Pride, Integrity, Innovation and Persistence. Pride: pride in ones country, family and traditions are a foundation for all meaningful personal actions. Integrity: most individuals have an innate sense of integrity; this plus integrity which is learned in one's life experience must also form the foundation for all actions. Innovation: constantly pursue new challenges and approaches; innovation, which makes our system so effective, is essential in all business and government. Persistence: in any bureaucratic setting a lack of persistence can often equate to failure because most obstacles must be overcome with some difficulty.*

NELSON, ALAN RAY, internist, medical assocation executive; b. Logan, Utah, June 11, 1933; s. Ray J. and Leah B. (Olson) N.; m. Gwen L. Sparrow, Jan. 2, 1959; children: John R., Shannon, Alan L. Student, Utah State U., 1951-54; MD, Northwestern U., 1958. Diplomate Am. Bd. Internal Medicine, Am. Bd. Endocrinology and Metabolism. Intern Highland Alameda County Hosp., Oakland, Calif., 1958-59; resident in internal medicine U. Utah, Salt Lake City, 1959-62, assoc. clin. prof., 1964-89; clin. prof. U. Utah, 1989-92; practice medicine specializing in internal medicine and endocrinology Salt Lake City, 1964-91; assoc. Meml. Med. Ctr., Salt Lake City, 1964-91; exec. v.p. Am. Soc. Internal Medicine, Washington, 1992—; mem. Nat. Profl. Standard Rev. Coun., 1973-77; pres. Utah Profl. Rev. Orgn., 1971-75; mem. AMA Coun. on Legis., 1977-80, trustee 1980—, chmn. 1986-88, pres.-elect 1988-89, pres. 1989-90; commr. Joint Commn. on Accreditation of Hosps., 1982-86, sec.-treas., 1985-86. Chair Health Care Quality Alliance, 1992-96. With M.C. USAF, 1962-64. Recipient Spl. Recognition award Am. Soc. Internal Medicine, 1973, Disting. Internist award, 1989. Fellow ACP; mem. Utah Med. Assn. (pres. from 1976, award 1973, 79), Inst. Medicine of NAS, (governing coun. 1984-87), World Med. Assn. (pres.-elect 1990-91, pres. 1992-92). Home: 11905 Parkside Dr Fairfax VA 22033-2648 Office: ASIM 2011 Pennsylvania Ave NW Washington DC 20006-1813

NELSON, ALFRED JOHN, retired pharmaceutical company executive; b. Dalmuir, Scotland, Jan. 24, 1922; came to U.S., 1972; s. John and Mary Catherine (Duncan) N.; m. Frances C. Hillier, Dec. 5, 1952; children: J. Stuart, Andrew D. MBChB, U. Glasgow, Scotland, 1945, MD with commendation, 1957; DPH, Royal Inst. Pub. Health and Hygiene, London, 1948. Resident Ayr County Hosp., 1945, Belvidere Fever Hosp., Glasgow, Scotland, 1948; cons. N.Y. State Dept. Health, Albany, 1950-51; dir. venereal disease control B.C. Dept. Health and Welfare, Vancouver, Can., 1952-54, cons. epidemiology, 1954-55; asst. dean medicine U. B.C., Can., 1955-57, clin. assoc. prof. pub. health, 1952-70; dir. health services B.C. Hydro and Power Authority, Vancouver, Can., 1957-70; v.p. Hoechst-Roussel Pharm., Inc., Somerville, N.J., 1972-81, sr. v.p., med. dir., 1981-87, ret., 1987; hon. mem. staff Vancouver Gen. Hosp. Served with RCAF, 1953-56. Recipient John J. Sippy Meml. award APHA, 1959, Spl. award, Order St. John of Jerusalem, 1960; named officer brother Order St. John of Jerusalem, 1966. Fellow ACP, Royal Coll. Physicians and Surgeons Can., Am. Coll. Preventive Medicine, N.Y. Acad. Medicine; mem. Can. Med. Assn. (sec. com. 1954-57). Presbyterian. Home: 29436 Port Royal Way Laguna Niguel CA 92677-7947

NELSON, ANNA MASTERTON, writer; b. West Covina, Calif., July 16; d. Richard Frederick and Mary Winifred (Denk) N. BA in Psychology, U. So. Calif., L.A., 1994. Writer, libr. Fox Broadcasting Corp.; writer's asst., sr. v.p. devel. Dick Clark Prodns., Inc.; asst. dir. admissions Calif. Internat. U.; asst. to dir. Gettysburg; adminstrv. asst. Acuity Entertainment; rsch. session supr. Columbia Broadcasting Sys.; radio promotions asst. Rocky & Laurie Show WPOC FM, Balt.; lectr. dept. anthropology U. So. Calif., L.A., 1994—. Editor (newsletter) Trojan Cailleach, 1995, 96; creator The Star List. Active Malibu (Calif.) Rep. Womens Club, 1993—, Project AIDS, L.A., 1993-95, Project Angel Food, 1997—. Office: 2265 Westwood Blvd # 153 Los Angeles CA 90064-2016

NELSON, ARTHUR HUNT, real estate management development company executive; b. Kansas City, Mo., May 21, 1923; s. Carl Ferdinand and Hearty (Brown) N.; m. Eleanor Thomas, Dec. 27, 1954; children: Carl F., Frances, Pamela. AB, U. Kans., 1943; JD, Harvard U., 1949. Bar: Mass. 1949. Staff radiation lab. MIT, 1943-44; sr. engr., cons. Raytheon Mfg. Co., Boston, 1948-52; pvt. practice Boston, 1949; v.p., treas., dir. Gen. Electronic Labs., Inc., Cambridge, Mass., 1951-64, chmn. bd., 1959-63; treas., dir. Sci. Electronics, Inc., Cambridge, 1955-64; treas., dir. Assocs. for Internat. Rsch., Inc., Cambridge, 1954—, pres., 1968—; treas., dir. Victor Realty Devel., Inc., Cambridge, 1959-76, pres., 1972-76, gen. ptnr., 1976—; gen. ptnr. Prospect Hill Exec. Office Park, Waltham, Mass., 1977—; chmn. Nelson Cos., 1990—, Cambridge Devel. Lab., 1994—; Bd. dirs. Internat. Data Group, Inc., Sterling Bank; chmn. Cambridge Devel. Lab., Inc., 1994—. Pres., trustee Tech. Edn. Rsch. Ctrs., Inc., 1965—; trustee Winsor Sch., Boston, 1978-88, treas., 1978-82; bd. dirs. Charles River Mus. Industry, Waltham, 1986—, pres. 1994. Lt. USRN, 1944-46. Mem. ABA, Mass. Bar Assn., Boston Bar Assn., Boston Computer Soc. (bd. dirs. 1985—, chmn. 1994), Greater Boston C. of C., Harvard Club Boston, Beta Theta Pi, Phi Beta Kappa, Sigma Xi. Home: 75 Robin Rd Weston MA 02193-2436 Office: care The Nelson Cos Prospect Place 230 3rd Ave Waltham MA 02154-7525

NELSON, BARBARA SECREST, educational developer; b. Reidsville, N.C., Jan. 7, 1949; d. Edgar B. and Mary Elizabeth (Slate) Trent; m. Michael William Nelson, Dec. 31, 1985. BA in Edn., U. N.C., 1971, MA in Curriculum and Instrn., 1975. Cert. K-3 tchr., N.C. Kindergarten and primary tchr. Wake County Schs., Raleigh, N.C., 1971-74; rsch. and evaluation cons. N.C. Dept. Pub. Instrn., Raleigh, 1974-84; mktg. and sales mgr. edn. div. Computer South, Charlotte, N.C., 1984-85; mktg. support rep. Apple Computer, Inc., Charlotte, 1985-87; K-8 solutions mgr. Apple Computer, Inc., Cupertino, Calif., 1987-89; account exec. Apple Computer, Inc., Culver City, Calif., 1989-92, ednl. devel., 1990—; S.E. mktg./solutions mgr. Apple Computer, Inc., Charlotte, N.C., 1994—; com. mem. N.C. Effective Teaching Com., Raleigh, 1984; program chmn. N.C. Instrnl. Microcomputing Conf., Greensboro, 1985. Co-author Apple Learning Series for K-2, 1986. Mem. ASCD. Home and Office: 4908 Carmel Club Dr Charlotte NC 28226-8020

NELSON, BEN, JR., retired air force officer; b. Ft. Lewis, Wash., Jan. 31, 1942; s. Ben and Marie (Warn) N.; m. Suzanne Wiseman, Dec. 22, 1963; 1 child, William Bryant. BBA, U. Tex., 1964; MPA, Golden Gate U., 1976. Commd. 2d lt. USAF, 1964, advanced through grades to brig. gen., 1988; instr. pilot 3525th Fighter Tng. Squadron, Williams AFB, Ariz., 1965-70; flight comdr. 390th Tactical Fighter Squadron, DaNang, Vietnam, 1970-71, Sheppard AFB, Tex., 1971-74; chief pers. tng. br. Office Dep. Chief of Staff for Pers., Hdqrs. Tactical Air Command, Langley AFB, Va., 1974-77; ops. officer, comdr. 428th Tactical Fighter Squadron, Nellis AFB, Nev., 1977-81; student Naval War Coll., Newport, R.I., 1981-82; chief fighter plans br. Office Dep. Chief of Staff Plans, Hdqrs. USAF, Washington, 1982-84; vice comdr. 32d Tactical Fighter Group, Soesterberg Air Base, The Netherlands, 1984-85; vice comdr., then comdr. 50th Tactical Fighter Wing, Hahn Air Base, Fed. Republic Germany, 1985-88; asst. dep. chief of staff for plans Hdqrs. Tactical Air Command, Langley AFB, 1988-89; comdr. 56th Fighter Wing, MacDill AFB, Fla., 1989-92; dep. comdr. 5th Allied Tactical Air Forces (NATO), Vicenza, Italy, 1992-94; CEO regional office ARC, Tampa Bay, Fla., 1994—. Recipient Phoenix award Dept. Def., 1987, O'Malley award Dept. Air Force. Mem. Air Force Assn., Tampa C. of C. (bd. dirs. 1989-92), Order of Daedalians. Episcopalian. Avocation: golf.

NELSON, BERNARD EDWARD, lawyer; b. Miles City, Mont., May 9, 1950; s. Theodore M. and Lucille K. Nelson; m. Jane Walker, Sept. 8, 1978; children: Iain, Colin, Stuart. BA, Yale U., 1972; JD, Harvard U., 1975. Bar: N.Y. 1976. Assoc. White & Case, N.Y.C., 1975-84; ptnr. White & Case, N.Y.C. and London, 1984—, London, 1988—. Mem. Union Internationale Des Avocats (U.S. rep. permanent tax commn.). Democrat. Avocations: antique map collecting, antiquarian books. Office: White & Case, 7 Moorgate, London EC2R 6HH, England

NELSON, BERNARD WILLIAM, foundation executive, educator, physician; b. San Diego, Sept. 15, 1935; s. Arnold B. and Helene Christina (Falck) N.; m. Frances Davison, Aug. 9, 1958; children—Harry, Kate, Anne, Daniel. A.B., Stanford U., 1957, M.D., 1961. Asst. prof., asst. dean medicine Stanford U., Palo Alto, Calif., 1965-67, assoc. dean medicine, 1968-71, cons. assoc. prof., 1980-86; assoc. dean U. Wis., Madison, 1974-77, acting vice chancellor, 1978-79; exec. v.p. Kaiser Family Found., Menlo Park, Calif., 1979-81, 1981-86; chancellor U. Colo. Health Sci. Ctr., Denver, 1986—; mem., v.p., pres. Nat. Med. Fellowships, 1969-77. Trustee Morehouse Med. Sch., 1981-83. Fellow Inst. Medicine; mem. Calif. Acad. Sci., Alpha Omega Alpha (bd. dirs. 1978—). Avocations: fishing; photography; gardening; carpentry. Office: U Colo Health Sci Ctr Box 6245 4200 E 9th Ave Denver CO 80262

NELSON, BRIAN JAMES, broadcast journalist; b. Montreal, Que., Can., Oct. 11, 1948; s. Charles Gordon and Mary (Timlin) N.; m. Joan Lynn Osborne, July 31, 1971 (div.); m. Louise Antoinetta Zambon, June 28, 1985. BA cum laude in Comm. Arts, Loyola of Montreal, 1970. News and sports announcer Sta. CJAD Radio, Montreal, 1969-70; news announcer Sta. CFRA Radio, Ottawa, Ont., Can., 1970-71; parliamentary bur. chief, corr. Std. Broadcast News, Ottawa, 1971-77; sr. polit. reporter CFCF-TV, Montreal, 1977-81; corr. CTV Network, Montreal and Ottawa, 1981-83; comm. dir. Don Johnston Liberal Party Leadership Campaign, Ottawa, 1984; news anchor, exec. prodr., corr. CNN, Atlanta, Miami, Fla., and Tokyo, 1984—. Host, exec. prodr. news mag. show This Week in Japan, 1989-90, East Meets West, 1990; host, prodr. news documentary The Everglades, 1994; host, corr. news mag. show The CNN Computer Connection, 1995—. Mem. Atlanta Press Club, Can. Am. Assn. Southeastern U.S. (bd. dirs., comm. dir.). Avocations: tennis, fishing, travel, fitness, reading. Office: CNN Box 105366 One CNN Ctr Atlanta GA 30348-5366

NELSON, BRUCE SHERMAN, advertising agency executive; b. Lansing, Mich., Nov. 3, 1951; s. Max and Blanche (Sherman) N.; m. Minette Raskin. AB, UCLA, 1973. Sr. copywriter Ogilvy & Mather, Los Angeles, 1977-78, Young & Rubicam, N.Y.C., 1978-79; assoc. creative dir. McCann Erickson, Inc., N.Y.C., 1979-80, v.p., 1980-81, sr. v.p., 1981-83, exec. v.p., creative dir., 1983-86, exec. v.p., worldwide dir. strategic creative devel., 1987-93; exec. v.p., worldwide dir. worldwide accounts, 1993-94, exec. v.p., creative dir. worldwide accts., 1994-95; dir. worldwide accounts McCann Erickson, Inc., N.Y.C., 1995—; founder, chief exec. officer Ira Madris, Bruce Nelson & Colleagues, 1986-87; lectr. Columbia Bus. Sch. Exec. Programs, N.Y.C., 1993—; dir. strategy worldwide accts. McCann-Erickson, Inc., N.Y.C., 1997—. Mgmt. fellow Sch. orgn. and Mgmt. Yale U., 1993—. Office: McCann-Erickson Worldwide 750 3rd Ave New York NY 10017-2703

NELSON, CANDICE JEAN, political science educator; b. New Bedford, Mass.; d. Richard Theodore and Jean (Roscow) N.; m. Richard Lee Jacobson, June 30, 1973; children: David, Peter, Michael. BA, Wheaton Coll., 1971; MA, UCLA, 1974; PhD, U. Calif., Berkeley, 1982. Asst. prof. dept. govt. Georgetown U., Washington, 1980-86; congl. fellow Office of Senator Alan Cranston, Washington, 1986-87, spl. asst., 1987-88; vis. fellow The Brookings Instn., Washington, 1988-90; asst. prof. dept. govt. Am. U., Washington, 1990-96, assoc. prof., 1996—; mem. adv. com. money & politics project League of Women Voters Ednl. Fund, Washington, 1995-97. Co-author: The Money Chase, 1990, The Myth of the Independent Voter, 1992; co-editor: Campaigns and Elections American Style, 1995. Mem. nat. governing bd. Common Cause, Washington, 1994-97. Mem. Nat. Capital Area Polit. Sci. Assn. (exec. coun. 1992-93, 2d v.p. 1993-94, 1st v.p. 1994-95, pres. 1995-96), Am. Polit. Sci. Assn. Democrat. Episcopalian. Avocations: tennis, skiing. Office: Am U Dept Govt 4400 Massachusetts Ave NW Washington DC 20016-8001

NELSON, CAREY BOONE, sculptor; b. Lexington, Mass.; d. William M. and Carey (Butler) Boone; m. Kenneth Warwick Nelson; children: Caren, Kenneth Warwick II, Kimberley, Keith, Kyle, Craig. Student, U. Mo.; BA, Wellesley Coll.; MS in Edn., Wagner Coll. Cert. tchr., N.Y.C., N.Y. State. Tchr. N.Y.C. Pub. Schs.; instr. sculpture Snug Harbor Cultural Ctr., N.Y.C., 1982-84; pre dism col., artist USAF, 1974—; artist USCG, 1974—. One-women shows Pietrantonio Galleries, N.Y.C., St. Bartholomew's, N.Y.C., Salmagundi Club, N.Y.C., Poly. Prep. Country Day Sch., Bklyn., Epiphany Libr., N.Y.C.; exhibited in group shows Internat. Art Exchange, Monte Carlo, Paris, Cannes, Athens, Victoria Mus. Libr., Melbourne, Australia, numerous others; represented in permanent collections Victoria Libr. Mus., Australia, Sheldon Swope Mus., Terre Haute, Ind., Esperanza, Antartica, 1988, Durban (Republic South Africa) Mus., also others; sculptures commd. for Am.-Israel Friendship House, Mildred McAffee Horton, Wellesley Coll., Chuck Yeager for USAF, Daniel Boone for Rotunda of Mo. State Capitol, Jimmie Doolittle for USAF, Franklin (N.J.) Mineral Mus., 1980, Munro Monument USCG, 1989, Zinc Miner Monument, Col. Vaughn, Coll. Aeronautics, LaGuardia Airport, N.Y.C., 1991, James Madison Monument, Montpelier, Va., 1992, Subway Riders, Internat. Mus. Cartoon Art, 1996. Bd. dirs. Cerebral Palsy Assn., S.I., N.Y., Vis. Nurse Assn., S.I. Named Woman of Achievement Wagner Coll., 1978, Hon. Life Artist Catharine Lorillard Wolfe Art Club, 1990; recipient awards Salmagundi, 1995, 96, Anna Hyatt Huntington award, Coun. Am. Artists award Hudson Valley, 1996. Fellow Am. Artists Profl. League, Nat. Arts Club, Royal Soc. Arts (London); mem. Composers, Authors and Artists Am. (nat. bd. dirs. 1981-90, 1st pl. award 1982, 84, 86), Soc. Illustrators, Burr Artists (bd. dirs. 1978—), Catharine Lorillard Wolfe Art Club (pres. 1978-81, bd. dirs. 1981—, sculpture chmn., Creative Hands award 1987, Artist of Yr. 1985, tour U.S. Mus., Colls., 1996—), Nat. League Am. Pen Women (pres. N.Y.C. br. 1981-84, Manhattan br. 1990-92, pres. 1996—, Woman of Achievement award 1988), Wellesley Coll. Club (pres. S.I.), Kappa Kappa Gamma (Woman of Achievement award 1978). Episcopalian. Avocations: jewelry design, snorkeling, travel. Home: 282 Douglas Rd Staten Island NY 10304-1526

NELSON, CARL ROGER, retired lawyer; b. Gowrie, Ia., Dec. 26, 1915; s. Carl Helge and Inez Olivia (West) N.; m. Elizabeth Boswell Campbell, Apr. 27, 1946; children: Thomas C., Nancy L. AB, Grinnell Coll., 1937; MA, Columbia, 1938, LLB, 1941. Bar: N.Y. 1941, D.C. 1947, U.S. Supreme Ct. 1947. Law clk. to Chief Justice Stone, 1941-42; Washington asso. firm Root, Ballantine, Harlan, Bushby & Palmer, 1946-51; mem. firm Purcell & Nelson, Washington, 1951-80, Reavis & McGrath, 1980-83, Nelson Thurston Jones & Blouch, 1984-86; Mem. Adminstrv. Conf. U.S., 1967-73. Served to capt. AUS, 1942-46. Fellow Am. Bar Found.; mem. ABA (mem. ho. dels. 1964-66, mem. coun. 1960-66, chmn. sect. adminstrv. law 1963-64), D.C. Bar Assn. (chmn. corp. law, com. 1954-55, 58-60), Mediation Panel U.S. Ct. Appeals (D.C. cir.), Chevy Chase (Md.) Club, Lawyers Club (Washington), Met. Club (Washington), Phi Beta Kappa. Mem. United Ch. of Christ.

NELSON, CARLON JUSTINE, engineering and operations executive; b. Siloam Springs, Ark., May 26, 1960; d. Robert F. and Jean (Caroom) Toenges. BS in Indsl. Engring., U. Ark., 1982; MBA, Houston Bapt. U., 1988. Registered profl. engr., Tex. Supr. codes and regulatory compliance Tex. Ea., Houston, 1982-85, supr. ops. spl. projects, 1985-87, mgr. project devel., 1987-90; dir. spl. projects, tech. asst. to pres. Enron, Houston, 1990-91, dir. throughput engring., 1991-92, project dir., 1992-95; v.p. engring. So. Union Gas Co., Austin, Tex., 1995-96; v.p. ops. Mo. Gas Energy, Kansas City, Mo., 1996—. Mem. NSPE, Tex. Soc. Profl. Engrs. Home: 5601 NE Northgate Xing Lees Summit MO 64064-1240 Office: Mo Gas Energy 3420 Broadway St Kansas City MO 64111-2404

NELSON, CHARLES ARTHUR, publisher, consultant; b. Berwyn, Ill., Dec. 21, 1922; s. Arthur A.R. and Florence Dorothy (Lagergren) N.; m. Anne Ballou Higgins, July 1946; children: Christopher, Janet, Colin, Edward. BA, St. John's Coll., Annapolis, Md., 1947. Dir. liberal arts program, humanities lectr. U. Chgo., 1947-52; exec. dir. Am. Found. For Polit. Edn., Chgo., 1947-56; sr. cons. Cresap, McCormick & Paget, N.Y.C., 1956-58; pres. Nelson Assocs., N.Y.C., 1958-68; prin. Peat Marwick Mitchell & co., N.Y.C., 1968-83; pub. Croton-Cortlandt Gazette, Croton-on-Hudson, 1986—. Author: Developing Responsible Public Leaders, 1963; co-author: The University, The Citizen, & World Affairs, 1956, Financial Management for the Arts, 1975, Ratio Analysis in Higher Education, 1980, Ethics, Leadership and the Bottom Line, 1991, Scott Buchanan: A Centennial Appreciation of His Life and Work, 1995, Stringfellow Bar: A Centennial Appreciation of His Life and Work, 1997; contbr. articles to jours. Chmn. bd. Exec. Council on Fgn. Diplomats, N.Y.C.; trustee St. John's Coll., Annapolis, Md., Santa Fe, 1952-91, chmn. bd., 1978-83. Mem. N.Y. Press Assn. Democrat. Home and Office: PO Box 247 Croton On Hudson NY 10520-0247

NELSON, CHARLES J., university administrator, international consultant, diplomat, consultant; b. Mich., Mar. 5, 1920; m. Maureen Tinsley. A.B., Lincoln U., 1942; M.P.A., NYU, 1948. Research assoc. state govt., 1949-52; program asst. MSA Manila, 1952-53; pub. adminstrn. analyst FOA, 1953-54, pub. adminstrn. specialist, 1954-55; dep. spl. asst. for community devel. ICA, 1955-57; chief community devel. adviser Tehran, 1958; community devel. adviser Dept. State, 1960, chief Africa-Latin Am. br., 1960-61, detailed African br., 1961; assoc. dir. Office Program Devel. and Coordination PC, Washington, 1961-63; dir. Office Devel. Resources, AID, 1963-64, dir. North African affairs, 1964-66; dep. mission dir. Addis Ababa, 1966-68; mission dir. Dar es Salaam, 1968-71; ambassador to Botswana, Lesotho and Swaziland, 1971-74; mission dir. counsellor internat. devel. AID, Nairobi, Kenya, 1974-78; adminstr. program in internat. studies Sch. Human Ecology, Howard U., 1978-81. Mem. Overseas Devel. Coun.; chair Mayor's Internat. Adv. Council; bd. dirs. Nations Capital council Girl Scouts U.S.A., 1981-87, also mem. retention extension outreach com.; bd. dirs. D.C. Council Internat. Programs, 1981-87; v.p. nat. bd. dirs. Sister Cities Internat.; mem. U.S. D.C.-Beijing Friendship Council; mem. Thai-Am. Assn. Coun. Am. Ambassadors, U.S.-Dakar Capital Cities Friendship Council; co-chmn. Soc. for Internat. Devel., Africa Roundtable. Served to capt. AUS, 1942-47. Mem. Georgetown Citizens Assn., Voice of Informed Cmty. Expression, Smithsonian Instn., Overseas Devel. Coun., The Atlantic Coun., Am. Polit. Sci. Assn., UN Assn., Diplomatic and Counselor Officers Ret., Friends of Ethiopia, Univ. Club (Washington). Address: 1401 35th St NW Washington DC 20007-2806

NELSON, CHARLOTTE BOWERS, public administrator; b. Bristol, Va., June 28, 1931; d. Thaddeus Ray and Ruth Nelson (Moore) Bowers; m. Gustav Carl Nelson, June 1, 1957; children: Ruth Elizabeth, David Carl, Thomas Gustav. BA summa cum laude, Duke U., 1954; MA, Columbia U., 1961; MPA, Drake U., 1983. Instr. Beaver Coll., 1957-58, Drake U., Des Moines, 1975-82; office mgr. LWV of Iowa, Des Moines, 1975-82; exec. asst. Iowa Dept. Human Svcs., Des Moines, 1983-85; exec. dir. Iowa Commn. on Status of Women, Des Moines, 1985—. Bd. dirs., pres. LWV, Beloit, Wis., 1960-74; bd. dirs. LWV, Des Moines, 1974-82, Westminster House, Des Moines, 1988—, pres. 1996. Named Visionary Woman, Young Women's Resource Ctr., 1994. Mem. Am. Soc. Pub. Adminstrn. (pres. exec. coun. 1984-86, past pres., Mem. of Yr. 1993), Phi Beta Kappa. Home: 1141 Cummins Cir Des Moines IA 50311-2113 Office: Human Rights Dept Lucas State Office Bldg 321 E 12th St Des Moines IA 50309-5636

NELSON, CRAIG ALAN, management consultant; b. San Rafael, Calif., July 11, 1961; s. Kenneth Alfred and Anne Catherine (Laurie) N. BS in Fin., San Diego State U., 1984. Loan assoc. Union Bank, San Diego, 1984-85, comml. loan officer, 1985-86, corp. banking officer, 1986-87, asst. v.p., 1987-89, v.p. corp. banking, 1989-93; v.p. Alexander & Alexander, San Diego, 1993-95; sr. assoc. Goreham-Moore & Assocs., San Diego, 1995—. Corp. recruiter United Way, San Diego, 1988; community group chair San Diego chpt. Am. Cancer Soc., 1989; mem. com. Juvenile Diabetes Assn.; bd. dirs. San Diego State Found., 1989—. Mem. San Diego State U. Young Alumni Assn. (pres. 1988-89, bd. dirs. emeritus 1989). Home: 1233 San Dieguito Dr Encinitas CA 92024-5116 Office: Goreham-Moore & Assocs 1331 Morena Blvd San Diego CA 92110-1550

NELSON, CRAIG WAYNE, academy administrator; b. Mpls., Mar. 8, 1932; s. Clarence August and Blanche Adeline (Nordell) N.; m. Betty Ann McLouth, Oct. 27, 1956; children: Cynthia Ann, Jon Craig. AA, North Pk. Coll., 1951; student, Trinity Coll., Hartford, Conn., 1951-52; BA, Northwestern U., 1955, MA in History, 1959; BD, North Pk. Theol. Sem., 1956; postgrad., Ea. Mich. U., 1970-71. Ordained clergyperson Covenant Ch. Am. Intern pastor Queen St. Congl. Ch., Bristol, Conn., 1952-53; pastor Evang. Covenant Ch., Villa Park, Ill., 1956-61, 1st Covenant Ch., Red Wing, Minn., 1961-66, Dearborn (Mich.) Evang. Covenant Ch, 1966-71, Bloomington (Minn.) Covenant Ch., 1971-77; pres. Minnehaha Acad., Mpls., 1977-94; ednl. cons., 1995—; tchr. North Park Coll., 1958-59, Minnehaha Acad., 1979-90; chaplain Mpls. Police Dept., 1972-77, Bloomington Police Dept., 1973-77; area co-dir. Evangelism N.W. conf., mem. exec. bd.; sec. N.W. Covenant Ministerium; active Covenant Bd. Ministry, Covenant Stewardship Commn.; dir. Lake Minnetonka Conservation Dist., 1995—, treas., 1997—; ednl. cons., 1994—. Active Bloomington Bd. Health, 1975-77; trustee Minn. Ind. Sch. Fund, 1979-91, v.p., 1980-81, 92-93, treas., 1991-92, chair, 1993-95. Named Disting. Alumni, North Pk. Coll., 1985. Mem. Coun. for Advancement and Support of Edn., North Ctrl. Assn., Bloomington Ministerial Assn. (chmn. 1974-75), Mpls. Ministerial Assn. (chmn. 1976-77), Minn.Ind. Sch. Fund. Avocations: fishing, hunting, boating, reading. Home and Office: 3888 Park Ln Spring Park MN 55384-9605

NELSON, DARRELL WAYNE, university administrator, scientist; b. Aledo, Ill., Nov. 28, 1939; s. Wayne Edward and Olive Elvina (Peterson) N.; m. Nancyann Hyer, Aug. 27, 1961; children: Christina Lynne, Craig Douglas. BS in Agriculture, U. Ill., 1961, MS in Agronomy, 1963; PhD in Agronomy, Iowa State U., 1967. Cert. profl. soil scientist. Div. chief U.S. Army Chem. Corps., Denver, 1967-68; asst. prof. Purdue U., West Lafayette, Ind., 1968-73, assoc. prof., 1973-77, prof. agronomy, 1977-84; dept. head U. Nebr., Lincoln, 1984-88, dean for agr. rsch. and dir. Nebr. Agrl. Experiment Sta., 1988—; cons. U.S. EPA, Washington, 1977-79, Ind. Bd. of Health, Indpls., 1977-83, Eli Lilly Co., Indpls., 1976. Editor: Chemical Mobility and Reactivity in Soils, 1983. Served to capt. U.S. Army, 1967-68. Fellow AAAS, Am. Soc. Agronomy (bd. dirs., CIBA-Geigy award 1975, Agronomic Achievement award 1983, Environ. Quality Rsch. award 1985), Soil Sci. Soc. Am. (bd. dirs., pres. elect 1992, pres. 1993, past. pres. 1994); mem. Internat. Soil Sci. Soc., Lions Lodge (treas. 1980-83, Lafayette, Ind. chpt.). Presbyterian. Avocations: fishing, skiing, jogging. Office: Univ of Nebr Agrl Rsch Div Lincoln NE 68583-0704

NELSON, DAVID ALDRICH, federal judge; b. Watertown, N.Y., Aug. 14, 1932; s. Carlton Low and Irene Demetria (Aldrich) N.; m. Mary Dickson, Aug. 25, 1956; 3 children. A.B., Hamilton Coll., 1954; postgrad., Cambridge U., Eng., 1954-55; LL.B., Harvard U., 1958. Bar: Ohio 1958, N.Y. 1982. Atty.-advisor Office of the Gen. Counsel, Dept. of the Air Force, 1959-62; assoc. Squire, Sanders & Dempsey, Cleve., 1958-67, ptnr., 1967-69, 72-85; cir. judge U.S. Ct. Appeals (6th cir.), Cin., 1985—; gen. counsel U.S. Post Office Dept., Washington, 1969-71; sr. asst. postmaster gen., gen. counsel U.S. Postal Svc., Washington, 1971; mem. nat. coun. Coll. Law, Ohio State U., 1988—. Trustee Hamilton Coll., 1984-88. Served to maj. USAFR, 1959-69. Fulbright scholar, 1954-55; recipient Benjamin Franklin award U.S. Post Office Dept., 1969. Fellow Am. Coll. Trial Lawyers; mem. Fed. Bar Assn., Ohio Bar Assn., Cleve. Bar Assn., Cin. Bar Assn., Emerson Lit. Soc., Ct. of Nisi Prius (sgt. emeritus), Phi Beta Kappa. Office: US Ct Appeals 6th Cir Potter Stewart US Ct House 5th and Walnut St Cincinnati OH 45202-3988

NELSON, DAVID LEONARD, process management systems company executive; b. Omaha, May 8, 1930; s. Leonard A. and Cecelia (Steinert) N.; m. Jacqueline J. Zerbe, Dec. 26, 1952; 1 child, Nancy Jo. BS, Iowa State U., 1952. Mktg. adminstr. Ingersoll Rand, Chgo., 1954-56; with Accuray Corp., Columbus, Ohio, 1956-87, exec. v.p., gen. mgr., 1967, pres., 1967-87, chief exec. officer, 1970-87; pres. process automation bus. unit Combustion Engring., Inc., Columbus, 1987-90; pres. bus. area process automation Asea Brown Boveri, Stamford, Conn., 1990-91, v.p. customer satisfaction Ams. region, 1991-93, v.p. customer support Ams. region, 1994-95; chmn. bd. dirs. Herman Miller Inc., Zeeland, Mich., 1995—. Patentee in field. Bd. dirs. Cardinal Govt. Obligations Fund, Columbus, Cardinal Govt. Securities Trust, Columbus, Cardinal Tax Exempt Money Trust, Columbus, Cardinal Govt. Guaranteed Fund, Columbus, Cardinal Aggressive Growth Fund, Columbus, Cardinal Balanced Fund, Columbus. Served to capt. USMCR, 1952-54. Mem. IEEE, Instrument Soc. Am., Newcomen Soc. N.Am., Tau Beta Pi, Phi Kappa Phi, Phi Eta Sigma, Delta Upsilon. Home: 295 Whispering Way Holland MI 49424-6635

NELSON, DAVID LOREN, geneticist, educator; b. Washington, June 25, 1956; s. Erling Walter and Marlys Joan (Jorgenson) N.; m. Claudia Jane Hackbarth, July 31, 1982; children: Jorgen William, Erik Alexander. BA, U. Va., 1978; PhD, MIT, 1984. Staff fellow NIH, Bethesda, Md., 1985-86; sr. assoc. Baylor Coll. Medicine, Houston, 1986-89, instr., 1989-90, asst. prof., 1990-94, assoc. prof., 1994—; dir. Human Genome Ctr., 1995-96. Editor: Genome Data Base, 1992—; assoc. editor Genomics, 1994—. Achievements include development of Alu PCR; discovery of fragile X syndrome gene (FMR-1), new form of genetic mutation (simple repeat expansion). Office: Baylor Coll Med Dept Molecular & Human Genetics 1 Baylor Plz Houston TX 77030-3411

NELSON, DAWN MARIE, middle school science and math educator; b. Norristown, Pa., Mar. 29, 1960; m. Peirce Watson Nelson, Aug. 12, 1978; children: Adam Christopher, Joshua Peirce. Student, Montgomery County C.C., Blubell, Pa., 1977-78, Temple U., 1979-80, Ursinus Coll.; BS in Edn. summa cum laude, Cabrini Coll., Radnor, Pa., 1992, postgrad., 1996—; postgrad., St. Joseph's U., 1995. Cert. elem. tchr., Pa.; cert. ASCI. Tchr. Penn Christian Acad., Norristown, 1992—; asst. curriculum and program developer; accreditation steering com.; supr. Math. Olympics, co-chmn.; mentor, student tchr. supr. Vol. pub. and pvt. schs., ch. orgns. Mem. ASCD, ACSI, Alpha Sigma Lambda. Avocations: reading, travel, quilting, writing. Office: Penn Christian Acad 50 W Germantown Pike Norristown PA 19401-1565

NELSON, DENNIS GEORGE ANTHONY, dental researcher, life scientist; b. New Plymouth, New Zealand, Dec. 25, 1954; came to U.S., 1983; s. Hugo and Johanna Katherina (Dekker) N.; m. Joanne Elizabeth Dick; children: Kathryn Sarah, John Clifford. BS with honors, Victoria U., Wellington, New Zealand, 1977, PhD, 1981. Postdoctoral fellow Med. Rsch. Coun. of New Zealand, Wellington, 1981-82; rsch. assoc. Materia Technica Rijksuniversiteit, Groningen, Netherlands, 1982-83; Fogarty Internat. fellow Eastman Dental Ctr., Rochester, N.Y., 1983-85; sr. fellow Med. Rsch. Coun. of New Zealand, Wellington, 1985-88; staff scientist Procter & Gamble Co., Cin., 1988-94; mgr. rsch. and devel. Pfizer Inc., 1994—; rev. cons. NIH, Washington, 1991—; sci. reviewer for various jours., 1983—. Contbr. articles to profl. jours. Recipient Colgate-Palmolive Travel award Internat. Assn. for Dental Rsch., 1980, Colgate-Palmolive prize Internat. Assn. for Dental Rsch., 1980, Edward H. Hatton award, 1981, Hamilton Meml. prize Royal Soc. of New Zealand, 1983. Mem. AAAS, Internat. Assn. for Dental Rsch., European Orgn. for Caries Rsch. Achievements include patents in field and patents pending; rsch. in high resolution TEM of hydroxyapatites; rsch. in interaction of laser radiation with dental enamel; rsch. in elucidation of fluoridation mechanisms of dental enamel and apatites.

NELSON, DEWEY ALLEN, neurologist, educator; b. Eldrado, Ark., Dec. 2, 1927; s. Herman Eugene and Pearl Estelle (Shirley) N.; m. E. Jem Nolt, Oct. 7, 1951; children: Allen, Stephen, Jean, John, Daniel. BS, Cornell U., 1948, MD, 1951. Diplomate Am. Bd. Psychiatry and Neurology, Am. Bd. Neurophysiology. Resident Bellevue Hosp., N.Y.C., 1951-52, 54-57; chief neurology Med. Ctr. Del., Wilmington, 1957-83, sr. neurology, 1983-88, hon. sr. neurology, 1988—; chief neurology St. Francis Hosp., Wilmington, 1957-83; founder, neurologist Neurology Assocs., Wilmington, 1957-85; assoc. clin. prof. neurology Thomas Jefferson U. Med. Ctr., Phila., 1971-75, prof. neurology, 1975-96; med. expert, advisor to ct. Social Security Adminstrn., 1982-96; ret., 1996; cons. neurologist, 1996—. Contbr. 70 articles to profl. jours., poetry to periodicals. 1st lt. U.S. Army, 1952-54, Korea. Decorated Bronze Star, United Nations Svc. medal with 2 battle stars, Nat. Def. Svc. medal; recipient Bronze Hope Chest award Nat. Multiple Sclerosis Soc., 1960, Plaque award Multiple Sclerosis Clinic, 1979; Teagle Found. scholar, 1954-51. Republican. Presbyterian (ruling elder). Avocations: metal work cast iron, antique cars, choir. Home: 206 N Spring Valley Rd Wilmington DE 19807-2427

NELSON, DON HARRIS, gas and oil industry executive; b. Phila., Mar. 18, 1932; s. Morris Daniel and Catherine (Kaplan) N.; m. Ruth Kaiser Nelson, Aug. 31, 1959 (div. 1981); children: Michael Stewart, Pamela Blair, Randolph Miles, Timothy Blake; m. Karen Fulton, Feb. 12, 1982. BA, Yale U., 1953; MBA, U. Pa., 1957. Project engr. GE, Phila., 1957-60; mgr. exploration Kaiser Francis Oil Co., Tulsa, 1960-77; CEO Sanguine, Ltd., Greenwich, Conn., 1977—; mem. Yale Devel. Bd., 1988—; chmn. Mus. African Art, N.Y.C., 1991-94. Pres. Family and Childrens Svc. Agy., Tulsa, 1975. Capt. USMC, Korea. Mem. Stanwich Club, Yale Club (N.Y.C.), Tulsa Tennis Club. Avocations: post-impressionistic and African art, tennis, skiing, scuba diving, golf. Home: 1121 Lake Ave Greenwich CT 06831-2748 Office: Sanguine Ltd 3 Pickwick Plz Greenwich CT 06830-5538

NELSON, DON JEROME, electrical engineering and computer science educator; b. Nebr., Aug. 17, 1930; s. Irvin Andrew and Agnes Emelia (Nissen) N. BSc, U. Nebr., 1953, MSc, 1958; PhD, Stanford U., 1962. Registered profl. engr., Nebr. Mem. tech. staff AT&T Bell Labs., Manhattan, N.Y., 1953, 55; instr. U. Nebr., Lincoln, 1955-58, from asst. to assoc. prof., 1960-63, dir. computer ctr., 1963-72, prof. electrical engring., 1967—, prof. computer sci., 1969—, co-dir. Ctr. Comm. & Info. Sci., 1988-91, dir. rsch. computing group, 1993—; cons. Union Life Ins., Lincoln, 1973, Nebr. Pub. Power Dist., Columbus, 1972-83, Taiwan Power Co., Taipei, 1974. 1st lt. USAF, 1953-55. Mem. IEEE (sr., Outstanding Faculty award 1989), Assn. Computing Machinery. Republican. Home: 4911 Concord Rd Lincoln NE 68516-3330 Office: U Nebr Dept Elec Engring 209N WSEC Lincoln NE 68588-0511

NELSON, DOROTHY WRIGHT (MRS. JAMES F. NELSON), federal judge; b. San Pedro, Calif., Sept. 30, 1928; d. Harry Earl and Lorna Amy Wright; m. James Frank Nelson, Dec. 27, 1950; children: Franklin Wright, Lorna Jean. B.A., UCLA, 1950, J.D., 1953; LL.M., U. So. Calif., 1956; LLD honoris causa, Western State U., 1980, U. So. Calif., 1983, Georgetown U., 1988, Whittier U., 1989, U. Santa Clara, 1990; LLD (honoris causa), Whittier U., 1989. Bar: Calif. 1954. Research assoc. fellow U. So. Calif., 1953-56; instr., 1957, asst. prof., 1958-61, assoc. prof., 1961-67, prof., 1967, assoc. dean., 1965-67, dean., 1967-80; judge U.S. Ct. Appeals (9th cir.), 1979—; cons. Project STAR, Law Enforcement Assistance Adminstrn.; mem. select com. on internal procedures of Calif. Supreme Ct., 1987—; co-chair Sino-Am. Seminar on Mediation and Arbitration, Beijing, 1992; dir. Dialogue on Transition to a Global Soc., Weinacht, Switzerland, 1992. Author: Judicial Administration and The Administration of Justice, 1973, (with Christopher Goelz and Meredith Watts) Federal Ninth Circuit Civil Appellate Practice, 1995; Contbr. articles to profl. jours. Co-chmn. Confronting Myths in Edn. for Pres. Nixon's White House Conf. on Children, Pres. Carter's Commn. for Pension Policy, 1974-80, Pres. Reagon's Madison Trust; bd. visitors U.S. Air Force Acad., 1978; bd. dirs. Council on Legal Edn. for Profl. Responsibility, 1971-80, Constnl. Right Found., Am. Nat. Inst. for Social Advancement; adv. bd. Nat. Center for State Cts., 1971-73; chmn. bd. Western Justice Ctr., 1986—; mem. adv. com. Nat. Jud. Edn. Program to promote equality for woman and men in cts. Named Law Alumnus of Yr. UCLA, 1967; recipient Profl. Achievement award, 1969; named Times Woman of Yr., 1968; recipient U. Judaism Humanitarian award, 1973; AWARE Internat. award, 1970; Ernestine Stalhut Outstanding Woman Lawyer award, 1972; Pub. Svc. award Coro Found., 1978, Pax Orbis ex Jure medallion World Peace thru Law Ctr., 1975, Hollzer Human Rights award Jewish Fedn. Coun., L.A., 1988, Medal of Honor UCLA, 1993; Lustman fellow Yale U. 1977. Fellow Am. Bar Found., Davenport Coll., Yale U.; mem. Bar Calif. (bd. dirs. continuing edn. bar commn. 1967-74), Am. Judicature Soc. (dir., Justice award 1985), Assn. Am. Law Schs. (chmn. com. edn. in jud. adminstrn.), Am. Bar Assn. (sect. on jud. adminstrn., chmn. com. on edn. in jud. adminstrn. 1973-89), Phi Beta Kappa, Order of Coif (nat. v.p. 1974-76), Jud. Conf. U.S. (com. to consider standards for admission to practice in fed. cts. 1976-79). Office: US Ct Appeals Cir 125 S Grand Ave Ste 303 Pasadena CA 91105-1621

NELSON, DREW VERNON, mechanical engineering educator; b. Elizabeth, N.J., Oct. 11, 1947; s. Andrew K. and Myra G. (Kempson) N. BSME, Stanford U., 1968, MSME, 1970, PhDME, 1978. Research asst. Stanford U., Calif., 1971-74, asst. prof., 1978-83, assoc. prof., 1983-96; prof. Stanford U., 1996—; engr. Gen. Electric Co., Sunnyvale, Calif., 1975-76, sr. engr., 1977-78; cons. in field. Co-editor: Fatigue Design Handbook, 1989; contbr. articles to profl. jours. Recipient Spergel Meml. award for Most

Outstanding Paper, 32d Internat. Wire and Cable Symposium, 1984, Hetenyi award for Best Rsch. Paper Pub in 1994 in the jour. Exptl. Mechanics. Mem. ASTM, Soc. Automotive Engrs., Soc. for Exptl. Mechanics, Sigma Xi, Tau Beta Pi. Home: 840 Cabot Ct San Carlos CA 94070-3464 Office: Stanford U Dept Mech Engring Stanford CA 94305-4021

NELSON, E. BENJAMIN, governor; b. McCook, Nebr., May 17, 1941; s. Benjamin Earl and Birdella Ruby (Henderson) N.; B.A., U. Nebr., 1963, M.A., 1966, J.D., 1970; LLD (hon.) Creighton U., 1992, Peru State Coll., 1993; m. Diane C. Gleason, Feb. 22, 1980; children by previous marriage—Sarah Jane, Patrick James; stepchildren—Kevin Michael Gleason, Christine Marie Gleason. Bar: Nebr. 1970. Instr. dept. philosophy U. Nebr., 1963-65; supr. Dept. Ins., State of Nebr., Lincoln, 1965-72, dir. ins., 1975-76; asst. gen. counsel, gen. counsel, sec., v.p. The Central Nat. Ins. Group of Omaha, 1972-75, exec. v.p., 1976-77, pres., 1978-81, CEO, 1980-81, of counsel, Kennedy, Holland, DeLacy & Svoboda, Omaha, 1985-90; gov. State of Nebr., Lincoln, 1991—. Co-chmn. Carter/Mondale re-election campaign, Nebr., 1980; chair Nat. Edn. Goals Panel, 1992-94; co-founder Gov.'s Ethanol Coalition, chair 1991, 94; pres. Coun. of State Gov's., 1994. Recipient Disting. Eagle award Nat. Eagle Scout Assn., 1994; named Amb. Plenipotentiary, 1993. Mem. Consumer Credit Ins. Assn., Nat. Assn. Ind. Insurers, Nat. Assn. Ins. Commissioners (exec. v.p. 1982-85), Nebr. Bar Assn., Am. Bar Assn., Midwestern Gov's. Assn. (chair 1994), Western Gov.'s Assn. (vice chair 1994, chair 1995), Happy Hollow Club, Omaha Club, Hillcrest Country Club. Democrat. Methodist. Home: 1425 H St Lincoln NE 68508-3759 Office: State Capitol 2nd Floor Lincoln NE 68509*

NELSON, EDITH ELLEN, dietitian; b. Vicksburg, Mich., Sept. 26, 1940; d. Edward Kenneth and Anna (McManus) Rolffs; m. Douglas Keith Nelson; children: Daniel Lee, Jennifer Lynn. BS, Mich. State U., 1962; MEd in Applied Nutrition, U. Cin., 1979. Lic. dietitian, Fla. Clin. dietitian Macon (Ga.) Gen. Hosp., Blodgett Meml. Hosp., Grand Rapids, Mich.; grad. teaching asst. U. Cin., 1978-79; dir. nutrition svcs. Dialysis Clinic, Inc., Cin., 1979-88; cons. dietitian Panama City Devel. Ctr., Ft. Walton Beach Devel. Ctr., Fla., 1988-94; renal dietitian Dialysis Svcs. Fla., Ft. Walton Beach, 1989-92; cons. dietitian N.W. Fla. Community Hosp., Chipley, Fla., 1993-94, Beverly Enterprises, Panama City Beach, 1994-96, pvt. practice, Panama City, Fla., 1996—. Mich. Edn. Assn. scholar, 1958; Nat. Kidney Found. grantee, 1986. Mem. Am. Dietetic Assn., Fla. Dietetic Assn., Panhandle Dist. Dietetic Assn., Nat. Kidney Found. (coun. on renal nutrition, Fla. coun. on renal nutrition), Omicron Nu. Home and Office: 150 Grand Lagoon Shores Dr Panama City FL 32408

NELSON, EDWARD GAGE, merchant banking investment company executive; b. Nashville, May 17, 1931; s. Charles and Polly (Prentiss) N.; m. Carole Olivia Frances Minton, Sept. 17, 1960; children—Carole Gervais, Emily Minton, Ellen Prentiss. B.A. in Polit. Sci., U. of South, Sewanee, 1952. Exec. v.p. Clark, Landstreet & Kirkpatrick, Inc., Nashville, 1955-64; exec. v.p. Commerce Union Bank, Nashville, 1968-72, pres., 1972-82, cons., 1985—, chmn., chief exec. officer, 1982-84; chmn., pres. Nelson Capital Corp., Nashville, 1985—; hon. consul gen. Japan; bd. dirw. Werthan Packaging, SouthCap Corp., Franklin Industries, Osborn Comm., Trans Arabian Investment Bank, ClinTrials, Inc., Berlitz Internat., Inc. Ctrl. Parking Sys., Advocat Inc., Micro Craft, Inc., NAshville Scene; mem. 1st adv. coun. Japan/Tenn. Soc. Trustee Vanderbilt U., Nashville, 1979—, chmn. med. ctr. bd., 1984—; vice chmn. Pub. Edn. Nashville Citizens; mem. De Tocqueville Soc. of United Way. Spl. agt. U.S. Army, 1955, Japan. Mem. Belle Meade Country Club, Cumberland Club, River Club (N.Y.C.). Republican. Episcopalian. Home: 1305 Chickering Rd Nashville TN 37215-4521 Office: Nelson Capital Corp 3401 W End Ave Ste 300 Nashville TN 37203-1069

NELSON, EDWARD HUMPHREY, architect; b. Winchester, Mass., Sept. 2, 1918; s. Richard MacDonald and Evelyn Miller (Humphrey) N.; m. Lois Whitaker Renouf, Sept. 24, 1948 (dec.); children: Susan, David, Sarah; m. Miriam P. Ketcham, Jan. 2, 1988. Grad., Lenox Sch., 1936; B.Arch., Yale, 1950. Pvt. archtl. practice Tucson, 1953-61; sr. v.p. CNWC Architects, Tucson, 1961-88, pres., 1989-94; ret., 1994; cons. CNWC & Steppe Archs.; mem. adv. com. U. Ariz. Coll. Arch., 1984-93. Works include: design for Tucson Community Ctr. Pres. Tucson Cmty. Coun., 1969-71, Tucson Art Ctr., 1960, Tucson Housing Found., 1969-92; bd. dirs. Tucson Trade Bur., 1976-91, pres., 1984; bd. dirs. Tucson Symphony, 1977-84, Tucson United Way, 1980; trustee Green Fields Sch., 1970-74, Tucson Art Mus.; vestry St. Philips Episc. Ch., 1967-69, sr. warden, 1987-90, parish warden, 1993-94; convenor Episcopal Interparish Coun., 1990-92; mem. Episcopal Diocese of Ariz., S.W. Regional Parish; 1st Phila. City Troop, 1940—, horse cavalry, 1940-42. Served to capt. AUS, 1940-41, WWII, ETO. Decorated Bronze Star with oak leaf cluster, Purple Heart; recipient Disting. Citizen award U. Ariz., 1981. Fellow AIA (emeritus, pres. So. Ariz. chpt. 1962, chmn. Ariz. fellows 1986-90); mem. Ariz. Soc. Architects (pres. 1963), Yale Club (pres. Tucson chpt. 1962, 83, dir. 1979—), U. Ariz. Pres.'s Club. Home: 2020 E 4th St Tucson AZ 85719-5114

NELSON, EDWARD SHEFFIELD, lawyer, former utility company executive; b. Keevil, Ark., Feb. 23, 1941; s. Robert Ford and Thelma Jo (Mayberry) N.; m. Mary Lynn McCastlain, Oct. 12, 1962; children: Cynthia, Lynn (dec.), Laura. BS, U. Cen. Ark., 1963; LLB, Ark. Law Sch., 1968; JD, U. Ark., 1969. Mgmt. trainee Ark. La. Gas Co., Little Rock, 1963-64; sales engr. Ark. La. Gas Co., 1964-67, sales coordinator, 1967-69, gen. sales mgr., 1969-71, v.p., gen. sales mgr., 1971-73, pres., dir., 1973-79, pres., chmn., chief exec. officer, 1979-85; ptnr., chmn. bd., chief exec. officer House, Wallace, Nelson & Jewel, Little Rock, 1985-86; pvt. practice law Little Rock, 1986—; of counsel Jack, Lyon & Jones, P.A., 1991—; bd. dirs. Fed. Res. Mem. N.G., 1957-63; bd. dirs. U. Ark., Little Rock, vice chmn. bd. visitors, 1981; bd. dirs. Philander Smith Coll., 1981; chmn. Ark. Indsl. Devel. Commn., 1987, 88; past chmn. Little Rock br. Fed. Res. Bd. St. Louis; chmn. Econ. Expansion Study Commn., 1987—; bd. dirs. Ark. Ednl. TV Found., Ark. Game and Fish Commn. Found.; founder, 1st pres. Jr. Achievement Ark., 1987-88; Rep. nominee for Gov. of Ark., 1990, 94; co-state chmn. Ark. Reps., 1991-92, nat. committeeman Ark. GOP, 1993—. Named Ark.'s Outstanding Young Man Ark. J. C. of C., 1973; One of Am.'s Ten Outstanding Young Men U.S. Jr. C. of C., 1974; Citizen of Yr. Ark. chpt. March of Dimes, 1983; Humanitarian of Yr. NCCJ, 1983; Best Chief Exec. Officer in Natural Gas Industry Wall Street Transcript, 1983; recipient 1st Disting. Alumnus award U. Cen. Ark., 1987. Mem. Am., Ark., Pulaski County bar assns., Ark. C. of C. (dir.), Little Rock C. of C. (dir., pres. 1981), Sales and Mktg. Execs. Assn. (pres. 1975, Top Mgmt. award 1977), U. Ark. Law Sch. Alumni Assn. (pres. 1980). Methodist. Office: 6th and Broadway 3400 Tcby Bldg Little Rock AR 72201

NELSON, EDWIN CLARENCE, academic administrator, emeritus; b. Dallas, S.D., Apr. 19, 1922; s. Clifford and Vera (Usher) N.; m. Avis Hedrix, Nov. 15, 1941; children—Judy, Roger. A.B., Kearney (Nebr.) State Coll., 1950; M.E., West Tex. State U., 1953; Ed.D., U. Nebr., 1959; postgrad., U. Minn., 1959; LHD (hon.), U. Nebr., Kearney, 1993. Tchr. math. and sci. pub. schs. Nebr., 1947-50; supt. schs. Huntley, Nebr., 1950-52, Wilcox, Nebr., 1953-56, Red Cloud, Nebr., 1956-59; tchr. aircraft mechanics Amarillo (Tex.) AFB, 1952-53; asso. prof. edn. Kearney State Tchrs. Coll., 1959-61; dean coll., dir. grad. studies Chadron (Nebr.) State Coll., 1961-67, pres., 1967-73, 75-86, pres. emeritus, Disting. Service prof., 1986—; community devel. specialist, 1988—; pres. Leadership Seminars, 1988—; exec. officer bd. trustees Nebr. State Colls., 1973-75; pres. Nebr. Ednl. TV Council for Higher Edn., 1967, 85. Served with AUS, 1942-45. Recipient Disting. Svc. award Kearney State Coll., 1968, Disting. Svc. award Chadron State Coll., 1989, Nebr. Statewide Citizen's award, 1996, Disting. Svc. award Nebr. Schoolmasters Club, 1996; named Boss of Yr., Chadron Jaycees, 1971, Chadron Citizen of the Yr., 1985, AK-SAR-BEN Ike Friedman Cmty. Leader, 1994; bldg. on Chadron State Coll. Campus named Edwin and Avis Nelson Phys. Activity Ctr., 1996. Mem. Nebr. Edn. Assn. (pres. 1967), Chadron C. of C. (Magic Key award 1988), Phi Delta Kappa. Republican. Methodist. Clubs: Elk, Kiwanian. *I have appreciated my opportunities to serve education at all levels.*

NELSON, EDWIN L., federal judge; b. 1940. Student, U. Ala., 1962-63, Samford U., 1965-66; LLB, Samford U., 1969. Mem. firm French & Nelson, Ft. Payne, Ala., 1969-73; pvt. practice Ft. Payne, Ala., 1974—; magistrate U.S. Dist. Ct. (no. dist.) Ala., Birmingham, 1974-90, judge, 1990—. With USN, 1958-62. Mem. Ala. Bar Assn., Birmingham Bar Assn., 11th Cir. Assn. U.S. Magistrates, Nat. Coun. Magistrates, Phi Alpha Delta. Office: US Dist Ct Hugo L Black Courthouse Rm 786 1729 5th Ave N Fl 7 Birmingham AL 35203-2000*

NELSON, ELMER KINGSHOLM, JR., educator, writer, mediator, consultant; b. Laramie, Wyo., Sept. 14, 1922; s. Elmer Kingsholm and Alice (Downey) N.; m. Jane Beckwith Oliver, Aug. 4, 1945; 1 son, Elmer Kingsholm III (Kirk). BA, U. Wyo., 1943, JD, 1948, MA, 1949; Dr. Pub. Adminstrn., U. So. Calif., 1959. Instr. psychology U. Wyo., 1947-49; psychologist, staff psychologist dept. probation Contra Costa County, Calif., 1949-51; sr. psychologist Cal. State Dept. Corrections, San Quentin and Chino Prisons, 1951-52; asst. prof. criminology U. B.C., Can., 1952-54; assoc. prof. U. B.C., 1954-56, head criminology div., 1953-56; warden Haney Correctional Instn., B.C., 1956-58; assoc. dir. Youth Studies Ctr. U. So. Calif., 1958-59, dir. Youth Studies Ctr., 1959-64, assoc. prof. pub. adminstrn., 1958-61, prof., 1961—, dean Sch. Pub. Adminstrn., 1971-76, prof., co-dir. Sacramento Pub. Affairs Ctr.; head Bay Area Research Center, Berkeley, 1979—; prof. emeritus U. So. Calif.; dep. adminstr. Youth and Adult Corrections Agy., State of Calif., Sacramento, 1964-65; interim exec. dir. Office Criminal Justice Planning, spring 1975; dir. Nat. Study Probation and Parole, 1976-77; chmn. task force on corrections, assoc. dir. Pres.'s Commn. on Law Enforcement and Adminstrn. of Justice, Washington, 1966-67; dir. nat. study of correctional adminstrn. U. So. Calif. for Joint Commn. on Correctional Manpower and Tng., 1967-69. Co-author: Corrections in America, 1975; contbr. articles, monographs, research reports to profl. jours. Advisor on mgmt. Boys Republic, Chino, Calif., 1967—; bd. dirs., v.p. Am. Justice Inst., Sacramento; bd. dirs. Human Interaction Rsch. Inst., L.A. Recipient Disting. Alumnus award U. Wyo., 1975, Exemplary Alumni award U. Wyo. Coll. Arts and Scis., 1994; Ford Found. Travel Study grantee, 1970-71. E. Kim Nelson endowed doctoral fellowship established at U. So. Calif., 1987. Sr. fellow Nat. Acad. Pub. Adminstrn.; mem. Wyo. Bar Assn., Alpha Tau Omega, Phi Beta Kappa, Phi Kappa Phi. Home: 716 Ivinson Ave Laramie WY 82070

NELSON, FREDA NELL HEIN, librarian; b. Trenton, Mo., Dec. 16, 1929; d. Fred Albert and Mable Carman (Doan) Hein; m. Robert John Nelson, Nov. 1, 1957 (div. Apr. 1984); children: Thor, Hope. Nursing diploma, Trinity Luth. Hosp., Kansas City, Mo., 1950; B. Philosophy, Northwestern U., 1961; MS in Info. and Libr. Sci., U. Ill., 1986. RN. Operating rm. nurse Trinity Luth. Hosp., Kansas City, Mo., 1950-52, Johns Hopkins Hosp., Balt., 1952, Wesley Meml. Hosp., Chgo., 1952-58, Tacoma Gen. Hosp., 1958-59, Chgo. Wesley Hosp., 1959-61; libr. asst. Maple Woods Campus Met. Community Colls., Kansas City, 1987-89, libr., libr. mgr. Blue Springs Campus, 1989-96; ret., 1996; co-founder Coll. for Kids, Knox Coll., Galesburg, Ill., 1982. Nurses scholar Edgar Bergen Found., 1947; recipient Award of Merit, Chgo. Bd. Health, 1952. Avocations: swimming, walking, crossword puzzles. Home: 7000 N Elm St Pleasant Valley MO 64068

NELSON, FREDERICK CARL, mechanical engineering educator; b. Braintree, Mass., Aug. 8, 1932; s. Carl Edwin and Marjorie May (Miller) N.; m. Delia Ann Dwaresky; children: Jeffrey, Karen, Richard, Christine. BSME, Tufts U., 1954; MS, Harvard U., 1955, PhD, 1961. Registered profl. engr., Mass. Instr. Tufts U., Medford, Mass., 1955-57, asst. prof. mech. engring., 1957-64; assoc. prof. mech. engring., 1964-71; prof. mech. engring. Tufts U., Medford, 1971—, dean engring., 1980-94. Translator: (book) Mechanical Vibrations for Engineers, 1983. Recipient Career Achievement award Tufts U. Dept. Mech. Engring., 1996. Fellow ASME (centennial medal award 1980), AAAS, ASA, Nat. Inst. Applied Scis. of Lyon (medal 1988), Korea Advanced Inst. Sci. and Tech. (medal 1988), Tufts U. Alumni Assn. (medal 1991). Office: Tufts U Coll Engring Medford MA 02155-5555

NELSON, FREDERICK DICKSON, lawyer; b. Cleve., Oct. 19, 1958; s. David Aldrich and Mary Ellen (Dickson) N. AB, Hamilton Coll., 1980; JD, Harvard U., 1983. Bar: Ohio 1984, D.C. 1985. Majority counsel subcom. on criminal law U.S. Senate Judiciary Com., Washington, 1983-85; spl. asst. to asst. atty. gen., Office of Legal Policy U.S. Dept. Justice, Washington, 1985-86, dep. asst. atty. gen., Office of Legal Policy, 1986-87; assoc. Taft, Stettinius & Hollister, Cin., 1988-89, of counsel, 1991-93; assoc. counsel to Pres. of U.S. The White House, Washington, 1989-90; advisor to govts. of Ukraine and Russia, ABA Ctrl. and East European Law Initiative, 1992-93; adj. prof. constl. law Salmon P. Chase Coll. Law, U. No. Ky., 1994; chief of staff U.S. Rep. Steve Chabot, 1995—. Exec. editor Harvard Jour. of Law and Pub. Policy, 1982-83. Dir. issues and rsch. Nahra for Congress campaign, Cleve., 1980; mem. Hamilton County Rep. Leadership Coun., 1992; cons. Chabot for Congress Campaign, Cin., 1994. Harry S. Truman Found. scholar, 1978-81. Mem. Federalist Soc., Harvard Club of Cin. (bd. dirs. 1989), Phi Beta Kappa. Republican. Home: 7900 Brill Rd Cincinnati OH 45243-3944

NELSON, GARY, county councilman, engineer; b. Spokane, Wash., Apr. 11, 1936; s. Nels Alfred and Laura Marie (Winberg) Nelson; m. JoAnne Laura Knudson, Nov. 27, 1959; children: Grant, Geoffrey, Gregory. BSEE, Wash. State U., 1958; MSEE, U. Wis., 1963. Engr. RCA, Camden, N.J., 1958-59; officer USAF, Madison, Wis., 1959-62; mgr. U.S. West, Seattle, 1963-90; pvt. practice Edmonds, Wash., 1990-94; bd. dirs. Stevens Hosp. Found., Edmonds, Olympic Ballet, Snohomish County Health Dist., 1994—, United Way of Snohomish County, Everett, 1986-92; Wash. State Legislator, 1972-94. planning commn. City of Edmonds, 1964-67, city coun., 1968-74. Capt. USAF, 1959-62. Mem. Sons of Norway, Rotary. Republican. Lutheran. Home: 9710 Wharf St Edmonds WA 98020-2363 Office: Snohomish County Coun 3000 Rockefeller Ave # 609 Everett WA 98201-4060

NELSON, GARY MICHAEL, lawyer; b. Mpls., July 12, 1951; s. Emery Marshel and Henrietta Margaret (Flategraff) N.; divorced; children: Rachel Mary Margell, Amy Margaret. BA, Gustavus Adolphus Coll., St. Peter, Minn., 1973; JD, Harvard U., 1976. Bar: Minn. 1976, U.S. Dist. Ct. Minn. 1976. Ptnr., CEO Oppenheimer Wolff & Donnelly, Mpls., 1976—; chair corp. practice inst. Minn. Inst. Legal Edn., Mpls., 1985—. Sec., v.p. Mpls. Girls' Club, 1978-83. Recipient Significant Contbns. award Am. Girls' Clubs Am., 1982. Mem. ABA. Lutheran. Avocations: fishing, hunting, hiking, reading. Home: 236 Courtland St Excelsior MN 55331-1728 Office: Oppenheimer Wolff & Donnelly 3400 Plaza VII 45 S 7th St Minneapolis MN 55402-1614

NELSON, GAYLORD ANTON, former senator, association executive; b. Clear-Lake, Wis., June 4, 1916; s. Anton and Mary (Bradt) N.; m. Carrie Lee Dotson, Nov. 14, 1947; children—Gaylord, Cynthia, Jeffrey. Grad., San Jose State Coll., Calif., 1939, U. Wis. Law Sch., 1942. Bar: Admitted Wis. bar 1942. Practiced in Madison, 1946-58; mem. Wis. Senate, 1949-58, Democratic leader, 1948-52; gov. Wis., 1958-62, U.S. senator from Wis., 1963-81; mem. finance com., chmn. subcom. on Social Security; chmn. employment, poverty and migratory labor subcom. of human resources com.; chmn. select com. on small bus., chmn. monopoly subcom. Author: Environmental Education Act, 1970, Nat. Environmental Education Act, 1972; co-author: The National Teacher Corps, 1965. Counselor Wilderness Soc., Washington, 1981—; founder Earth Day. 1st lt. AUS, World War II. Recipient Conservationist of the Year Award, Nat. Wildlife Fedn., 1989, Only One Earth Award, Environmental Leadership Award, UN Environment Prog., 1992, Presdl. Freedom medal, 1995. Mem. State Bar Assn. Wis. Home: 3611 Calvend Ln Kensington MD 20895-3154 Office: Wilderness Soc 900 17th St NW Washington DC 20006-2501

NELSON, GEORGE DRIVER, astronomy and education educator, former astronaut; b. Charles City, Iowa, July 13, 1950; s. George Vernon and Evelyn Elenor (Driver) N.; m. Susan Lynn Howard, June 19, 1971; children: Aimee Tess, Marti Ann. BS, Harvey Mudd Coll., 1972; MS, U. Wash., 1974, PhD, 1978. Astronaut NASA, Houston, 1978-89; mission specialist Space Shuttle flight, 1984, 86, 88; assoc. vice provost for rsch., assoc. prof. astronomy U. Wash., Seattle, 1989-96; dep. dir. project 2061 AAAS, Washington, 1996—; adj. assoc. prof. edn. U. Wash., 1989-96. Recipient Haley Space Flight award AIAA, 1989. Unitarian. Avocations: reading; athletics; guitar. Office: AAAS Project 2061 1333 H St NW Washington DC 20005-4707

NELSON, GLEN DAVID, medical products executive, physician; b. Mpls., Mar. 28, 1937; s. Ralph and Edna S. Nelson; m. Marilyn Carlson, June 30, 1961; children: Diana, Curtis, Wendy. AB, Harvard U., 1959; MD, U. Minn., 1963. Diplomate Am. Bd. Surgery, also sub-bd. bariatric and peripheral vascular surgery. Intern Hennepin County Gen. Hosp., Mpls., 1963-64, resident in gen. surgery, 1964-69; staff surgeon Park Nicollet Med. Ctr. (formerly St. Louis Park Med. Ctr.), Mpls., 1969-86, pres., chmn. bd. trustees, 1975-86; chmn., CEO Am. Med Ctrs., Mpls., 1984-86; exec. v.p. Medtronic, Inc., Mpls., 1986-88, vice chmn., 1988—, also bd. dirs.; clin. prof. dept. surgery U. Minn.; bd. dirs. ReliaStar Fin. Corp. (formerly Northwestern Nat. Life Inst. Co.), Mpls., Carlson Holdings, Inc., Mpls., St. Paul Cos., Medtronic, Inc., Mpls. Fellow ACS (del.); mem. AMA, Am. Acad. Med. Dirs., Am. Coll. Physician Execs., Hennepin County Med. Assn., Greater Mpls. C. of C. (chmn. 1987), Jackson Hole Group. Office: Medtronic Inc 7000 Central Ave NE Minneapolis MN 55432-3568

NELSON, GORDON LEIGH, chemist, educator; b. Palo Alto, Calif., May 27, 1943; s. Nels Folke and Alice Virginia (Fredrickson) N. BS in Chemistry, U. Nev., 1965; MS, Yale U., 1967, PhD, 1970; DSc (hon.), William Carey Coll., 1988. Staff research chemist corp. research and devel. Gen. Electric Co., Schenectady, N.Y., 1970-74; mgr. combustibility tech. plastics div. Gen. Electric Co., Pittsfield, Mass., 1974-79, mgr. environ. protection plastics div., 1979-82; v.p. materials sci. and tech. Springborn Labs. Inc., Enfield, Conn., 1982-83; prof., chmn. dept. polymer sci. U. So. Miss., Hattiesburg, 1983-89; dean Coll. Sci. and Liberal Arts, prof. chemistry Fla. Inst. Tech., Melbourne, 1989—, mem. coun. sci., soc. pres., sec., 1989-90, chair-elect, 1991, chair, 1992; cons. in field. Author: Carbon-13 Nuclear Magnetic Resonance for Organic Chemists, 1972, 2d edit., 1980; co-author: Polymeric Materials--Chemistry for the Future, 1989,Carbon Monoxide and Human Lethality, 1993; editor: Fire and Polymers--Hazard Identification and Prevention, 1990; editor: Fire and Polymers II-Materials and Tests for Hazard Prevention, 1995; editor books on coating sci. tech.; contbr. articles to profl. jours. Mem. ASTM (E5 cert. of appreciation 1985), Am. Inst. Chemists (Mems. and Fellows Lectr. award 1989), Soc. Plastics Engrs., Am. Chem. Soc. (pres. 1988, bd. dirs. 1977-85, 87-89, 92-94, Henry Hill award 1986, 1st Nelson award Orlando sect., 1996), Info. Tech. Industry coun. (chmn. plastics task group), Ctr. Sci., Tech. and the Media (bd. dirs. 1991-94), So. Soc. for Coatings Tech., Internat. Electrotech. Commn. (U.S. tech. adv. group on info. processing equipment), Soc. of Plastics Industry (structural plastics divsn., Man of Yr. 1979), Coun. Colls. Arts and Scis., Yale Chemists Assn. (pres. 1981—), Nev. Hist. Soc., Sigma Xi. Republican. Presbyterian. Avocations: travel, western U.S. history. Office: Fla Inst Tech Coll Sci & Liberal Arts 150 W University Blvd Melbourne FL 32901-6982

NELSON, GRANT STEEL, lawyer, educator; b. Mitchell, S.D., Apr. 18, 1939; s. Howard Steel and Clara Marie (Winandy) N.; m. Judith Ann Haugen, Sept. 22, 1962; children: Mary Elizabeth, Rebekah Anne, John Adam. BA magna cum laude, U. Minn., 1960; JD cum laude, 1963. Bar: Minn. 1963, Mo. 1971. Assoc. Faegre & Benson, Mpls., 1963-67; mem. law faculty U. Mo., Columbia, 1967-91, assoc. prof., 1970-72, prof., 1972-91, Enoch H. Crowder prof. law, 1974-91; prof. UCLA, 1991—; mem. bd. legal advisors Gt. Plains Legal Found., 1978-85; vis. asst. prof. U. Mich., Ann Arbor, 1969-70, Brigham Young U., Provo, Utah, summer 1976; vis. prof. U. Minn., Mpls., 1981-82, UCLA, 1989-90; disting. vis. prof. Pepperdine U., 1987-88; vis. endowed Campbell prof. U. Mo., Columbia, 1996-97; commr. Nat. Conf. Commrs. Uniform State Laws, 1983-91; mem. West Pub. Law Sch. Adv. Bd. Author: (with Van Hecke and Leavell) Cases and Materials on Equitable Remedies and Restitution, 1973, (with Whitman) Cases and Materials on Real Estate Finance and Development, 1976, Cases and Materials on Real Estate Transfer, Finance and Development, 1981, (with Osborne and Whitman) Real Estate Finance Law, 1979, (with Leavell and Love) Cases and Materials on Equitable Remedies and Restitution, 1980, (with Whitman) Land Transactions and Finance, 1983, rev. edit., 1988, (with Whitman) Real Estate Finance Law, 1985, rev. edit., 1994, (with Leavell and Love) Cases and Materials on Equitable Remedies, Restitution and Damages, 1986, rev. edit., 1994 (with Whitman) Cases and Materials on Real Estate Transfer, Finance and Development, 1987, (with Browder, Cunningham, Stoebuck and Whitman) Basic Property Law, 1989, (with Stoebuck and Whitman) Contemporary Property, 1996, (with Whitman) Cases and Materials on Real Estate Transfer, Finance and Development, 1992; co-reporter ALI Restatement of Property-Mortgages; contbr. articles to profl. jours. 1st lt. AUS, 1964-65. Recipient award for meritorious service and achievement U. Mo. Law Sch. Found., 1974; recipient Disting. Faculty Service award U. Mo.-Columbia Alumni Assn., 1978, Disting. Faculty award, 1986, Disting. Non-Alumnus award, 1991. Fellow Am. Bar Found.; mem. ABA, Am. Law Inst., Assn. Am. Law Schs. (sect. chmn. 1976-77), Am. Coll. Real Estate Lawyers, Mo. Bar Assn. (vice chmn. property law com. 1974-75, chmn. 1975-77), Order of Coif, Phi Beta Kappa, Phi Delta Phi. Office: UCLA Sch Law Hilgard Ave Box 951476 Los Angeles CA 90095-1476

NELSON, H. H. RED, insurance company executive; b. Herman, Nebr., June 2, 1912; m. Ruth Hansen; children: John, Steve. B.A., U. Nebr., 1934, J.D., 1937. Bar: Iowa, Nebr. 1938; C.L.U., 1948. Asst. mgr. life accident group depts. Travelers Inc. Co., Omaha, 1939-44; chmn. bd. Redlands Ins. Co., 1945—, Ins. Agts. Inc., Council Bluffs, Iowa, 1945—, Am. Agrisurance Co., 1969—, Am. Growers Ins., 1995—, Acceptance Ins., Texas, 1988—; chmn. Redland Group Cos. Pres. United Fund, Western Iowa council Boy Scouts Am.; bd. dirs. Nat. Scout Council; pres. Christian Home Orphanage, Council Bluffs Indsl. Found. Mem. Ind. Ins. Agts. Am. (pres. 1964-65, Woodworth Meml. award 1966), Iowa Assn. Ins. Agts. (nat. dir., pres. 1957-60, Heritage award 1986, named to 1st State of Iowa Ins. Hall of Fame 1997), C. of C. (bd. dirs.). Lodges: Elks (past exalted ruler), Masons, Shriners. Office: Redland Group Inc 535 W Broadway Council Bluffs IA 51503-0812

NELSON, HAROLD BERNHARD, museum director; b. Providence, R.I., May 14, 1947; s. Harold B. and Eleanor (Lavina) N. BA, Bowdoin Coll., 1969; MA, U. Del., 1972. Rsch. fellow NMAA Smithsonian Inst., Washington, 1976-77; curator Am. art Mus. Art & Archeol., U. Mo., Columbia, 1977-79; registrar Solomon R. Guggenheim Mus., N.Y.C., 1979-83; exhibition program dir. Am. Fedn. Arts, N.Y.C., 1983-89; dir. Long Beach (Calif.) Mus. of Art, 1989—; juror Annual Art Exhibition Mus. Art, Sci. & Industry, Bridgeport, Conn., 1988, Annual Art Exhibition, Clark County Dist. Libr., Las Vegas, Nev., 1984; speaker Am. Assn. Mus. Annual Conf., Detroit, 1985, annual meeting Western Mus. Conf., Portland, Oreg., 1987, Grantmakers in Art Symposium, N.Y.C., 1986, annual meeting Western Mus. Conf., Salt Lake City, 1985; mem. adv. com. APA, Assn. Sci. and Tech. Ctrs.; panelist Aid to Spl. Exhibitions, NEA, Washington, 1986; participant Am. Legal Assn., ABA Conf., San Francisco, 1986; observer, respondent Mus. Symposium, NEA, Dallas, 1985. Author: Sounding the Depths: 150 Years of American Seascape, 1989, New Visions: Selina Trieff, 1997. Office: Long Beach Mus Art 2300 E Ocean Blvd Long Beach CA 90803-2442

NELSON, HARRY, journalist, medical writer; b. Interlachen, Fla., Apr. 18, 1923; s. Knut Alfred and Edith Farr (Wilkes) N.; m. Diane Gabriella Meerschaert, Aug. 29, 1948 (div. 1977); children—Tanya Ann, Lawrence Stephen, Ronald Gerard, James Anthony, John Christopher; m. Gita Doris Wheelis, Jan. 29, 1984. B.A., U. So. Calif., 1949. Reporter, photographer Bakersfield Press, Calif., 1949; reporter, photographer Bakersfield Community Chest, Calif., 1949; promotion writer Los Angeles Times, 1949-57, reporter, 1957-58, med. writer, 1958-88, sr. writer, 1977-80; freelance med. writer, 1988—; staff writer Milbank Meml. Fund, 1993—. Charter mem. bd. dirs. Los Angeles County Comprehensive Health Planning Assn., Los Angeles, 1968-69. Served with USAAF, 1941-45. Recipient spl. commendation AMA, 1974, John Hancock award John Hancock Ins. Co., 1978, Journalism award Am. Acad. Pediatrics, 1979, Disting. Svc. by non-physician award Calif. Med. Assn., 1988, Lifetime Achievement in med. writing award AMA, 1988, Peter Lisagor award for exemplary journalism Chgo. Headliners Club, 1988. Mem. Nat. Assn. Sci. Writers (pres. 1966). Avocations: sailing; hiking; ceramics. Address: Med Writers Internat PO Box N 14016 Yellowstone Dr Frazier Park CA 93222

NELSON, H(ARRY) DONALD, communications executive; b. Chgo., Nov. 23, 1933; s. Harry Emmanual and Elsie Ina (Liljedahl) N.; m. Carol Jacqueline Stewart, Mar. 31, 1956; children: Donald S., David S., Sharon Nelson Arnold. BS in Bus., Northwestern U., 1955, MBA with distinction, 1959. Salesperson Procter & Gamble, Chgo., 1955-58; product mgr. Gen. Electric Corp., Syracuse, N.Y., 1959-72; mktg. mgr. Tex. Instruments, Dallas, 1972-74; v.p. mktg. Rockwell Internat., Anaheim, Calif., 1974-75, HMW-Pulsar, Lancaster, Pa., 1975-77; mgr. market and product devel. Gen. Electric Corp., Louisville, 1977-80; v.p. mktg. Genesco, Nashville, 1981-83; v.p. cellular bus. Telephone and Data Systems, Chgo., 1983-85; pres., chief exec. officer U.S. Cellular, Chgo., 1986—; mem. Deans and Alumni adv. bd. dirs. Kellogg Grad. Sch. With U.S. Army. Mem. Cellular Telecomm. Industry Assn. (bd. dirs. 1984—, com. chmn. 1985-89, exec. com. 1991—, treas.). Republican. Baptist. Office: US Cellular 8410 W Bryn Mawr Ave Ste 700 Chicago IL 60631-3463

NELSON, HARVEY FRANS, JR., retired foreign service officer; b. Long Beach, Calif., Jan. 26, 1924; s. Harvey Frans and Marian (Norris) N.; m. Celia Anne Kendrick, June 27, 1947 (dec. June 1985); children—Erik Frans, Kai David, Peter Norris, Annika Di Vittorio; m. Esta Harrie de Fossard, May 31, 1987; children: Granville, Beatrice. B.A., Occidental Coll., 1948; postgrad., Stockholm U., 1948-49; M.A., Fletcher Sch. Internat. Law and Diplomacy, Medford, Mass., 1950. Commd. fgn. service officer Dept. State, 1951; dep. chief of mission Am. embassy, Pretoria, Republic of South Africa, 1976-79; diplomat in residence Ariz. State U., Tempe, 1979-80; dep. commandant U.S. Army War Coll., Carlisle, Pa., 1980-84; ambassador Am. embassy, Mbabane, Swaziland, 1985-88; sr. advisor U.S. Del. to UN, 1988, 90. Served to lt. (j.g.) USN, 1942-46. *

NELSON, HELAINE QUEEN, lawyer; b. Hamtramck, Mich., Mar. 15, 1945; d. Willard Myron and Helen Victoria (Nebraska) Bowers; m. William Michael Nelson, Apr. 19, 1970; 1 child, Lindsey Paige. BS, Western Mich. U., 1969, MSL, 1971; JD, U. Detroit, 1977. Bar: Ohio 1977, U.S. Dist. Ct. (no. and so. dists.) Ohio 1978, Ill. 1985, Mich. 1996. Corp. counsel Beverage Mgmt., Inc., Columbus, Ohio, 1977-79, assoc. gen. counsel, 1979-80, gen. counsel, 1980-84; sr. atty. Abbott Labs., Abbott Park, Ill., 1984-87; divsn. counsel Abbott Labs., Columbus, 1987-95; sr. counsel Abbott Labs., Abbott Park, Ill., 1995-96; pvt. practice Mich., 1996—. Mem. ABA, Mich. Bar Assn. Unitarian. Avocations: freelance writing, tennis, reading. Office: 16940 Riley St Holland MI 49424-6018

NELSON, HELEN MARTHA, retired library director; b. Anaconda, Mont., Dec. 20, 1929; d. Ole Bertin and Caroline Helen (Massey) N. BA with honors, U. Mont., 1951; MLS, U. Wash., 1960. Asst. documents and serials libr. U. Mont., Missoula, 1951-52; tchr. English and history, libr. Laurel H.S., 1952-54; tchr. English, libr. Beaverhead County H.S., 1954-56; tchr. English, journalism Anaconda Sr. H.S., 1956-59; libr., adminstr. U.S. Army, 1960-68; libr. dir. Oceanside (Calif.) Libr., 1968-94; chmn. Serra Coop. Libr., 1973-74, 84-85, 90-91; mem. coun. Serra Coop. Sys., 1969-94. Chmn. Christian Sponsors, Oceanside, 1975; congl. pres. King of Kings Luth. Ch., Oceanside, 1974, 77, 84, mem. coun. 1971-77, 82-84, 92-94; bd. dirs. Oceanside/Carlsbad ARC, 1970-71; del. Calif. Gov.'s Conf. Librs. and Info. Sci. Mem. ALA, AAUW, LWV, Mont. Libr. Assn., Calif. Libr. Assn. (coun. 1978-80, v.p. Palomar chpt. 1978), Pub. Libr. Execs. of So. Calif., Oceanside C. of C., Calif. Inst. Libr. (bd. dirs. 1978-80). Avocations: photography, travel, crewel embroidery.

NELSON, HERBERT LEROY, psychiatrist; b. Eddyville, Iowa, June 15, 1922; s. Albert and Bessie Mae (Durham) N.; m. Carol Lorayne Hofert, Dec. 23, 1943; children—Richard Kent, Vicki Lurae, Thadeus Leroy, Cylda Vermae. B.A., U. Iowa, 1943, M.D., 1946. Diplomate Am. Bd. Psychiatry and Neurology. Intern Univ Hosps. of U. Iowa, Iowa City, 1946-47; resident Brooke Army Med. Ctr, Fort Sam Houston, Tex, 1947-49, U.S. VA Hosp., Knoxville, Iowa, 1949-51; resident Oreg. State Hosp., Salem, 1951-52, clin. dir., 1952-63; asst. prof. psychiatry U. Iowa, Iowa City, 1963-66; assoc. prof. U. Iowa, 1966-73, prof., 1973-84, prof. emeritus, 1984—; dir. Iowa Mental Health Authority, Iowa City, 1968-82; med. dir. Mideast Iowa Community Mental Health Ctr., Iowa City, 1969-84; adj. prof. Tulane U., New Orleans, 1974-77. Co-author 4 monographs; also articles, 1965-83. Served as capt. M.C., U.S. Army, 1947-49. Fellow Am. Psychiat. Assn.; mem. Iowa Psychiat. Soc. (pres. 1970-71, chmn. subcom. on psychiat. care 1973-77), AMA, Johnson County Med. Soc., Am. Assn. Psychiat. Adminstrs., Am. Coll. Mental Health Adminstrs. Republican. Methodist. Avocations: gardening; fishing; woodworking; painting; travel. Home and Office: 1400 Laura Dr Iowa City IA 52245-1539

NELSON, HOWARD JOSEPH, geographer, educator; b. Gowrie, Iowa, Jan. 12, 1919; s. Joseph A. and Hannah (Swanson) N.; m. Betty Marie Garlick, June 18, 1944; children: Linda Ann, James Allan. B.A. with high honors, Iowa State Tchrs. Coll., 1942; M.A., U. Chgo., 1947, Ph.D., 1949. Mem. faculty UCLA, 1949—, prof. geography, 1963-86, prof. emeritus, 1986—, chmn. dept., 1966-71. Author: (with W.A.V. Clark) Los Angeles, The Metropolitan Experience, 1976, The Los Angeles Metropolis, 1983. Served with AUS, 1943-46. Mem. Assn. Am. Geographers (regional councillor 1968-71), Sigma Xi. Home: 6136 Kentland Ave Woodland Hills CA 91367-1719 Office: Univ Calif Dept Geography Los Angeles CA 90024

NELSON, IRIS DOROTHY, retired guidance and rehabilitation counselor; b. N.Y.C., July 5, 1937; d. Simon and Bertha (Rapkine) N.; B.A., Barnard Coll., 1959; M.A., Tchrs. Coll., Columbia U., 1964, Ed.M., 1980, postgrad. Tchrs. Coll., Columbia U., 1983-84; postgrad. Inst. Rehab. Medicine, 1983-84, Sch. Edn., NYU, 1983-84. Cert. tchr., guidance and rehab. counselor, N.Y. Research asst. to chmn. zoology dept. Columbia U., 1959-64; tchr., activity therapist Psychiat. Treatment Ctr., N.Y.C., 1964-67; tchr., guidance counselor gen. and spl. edn. programs, elem. and jr. high, N.Y.C. Pub. Schs., N.Y.C. Bd. Edn., 1967-77; assoc. chmn. com. on handicapped Community Sch. Dist. Div. Spl. Edn. and Pupil Personnel Services, N.Y.C. Bd. Edn., 1977-78, sch. and rehab. counselor Youth Employment and Tng. Program, N.Y.C. Bd. Edn. Office Career Edn., 1978-82, Bronx Ctr. for Career and Occupational Services, Office of Career Edn., 1982-83, sch. and rehab. counselor div. spl. edn. N.Y.C. Bd. Edn. 1984-90; sch. and rehab. counselor citywide programs spl. edn. dist. # 75 P.S. 186, Bronx, N.Y., 1990-95; ret., 1995; vocational rehab. counselor Internat. Ctr. for the Disabled, N.Y.C., 1988-89. Ann. community sponsor West Side Community Conf.; mem. alumnae adv. vocat. com. Barnard Coll., 1974-76. Mem. ACLU, ACA, Jewish Labor Com. (educators chpt.), Women's Am. Orgn. for Rehab. through Tng. (educators chpt.), United Fedn. Tchrs. Guidance Counselors (retiree chpt.), Am. Rehab. Counselors Assn. (div. mem.), Nat. Career Devel. Assn., Assn. for Religious and Value Issues in Counseling (div. mem.), Assn. Adult Devel. and Aging , N.Y. Counseling Assn., N.Y. State Rehab. Counselors Assn. (div. mem.), N.Y. State Mental Health Counselors Assn. (div. mem.), N.Y. State Career Devel. Assn. (div. mem.), N.Y. Assn. Counselor Educators and Supervisors (div. mem.), N.Y. Sch. Counselors Assn. (div. mem.), N.Y. Assn. Multicultural Counseling & Devel. (div. mem.), N.Y.C. Assn. Counseling and Devel. (bd. dirs.), Nat. Rehab. Assn. (div. mem.), Nat. Rehab. Counseling Assn. (div. mem., job placement div., met. chpt. bd. dirs. 1983), Joint Coun. for Mental Health Svcs., Chi Sigma Iota (life), Kappa Delta Pi (bd. dirs. Kappa chpt.). Home: 235 W 102nd St New York NY 10025-8400

NELSON, IVORY VANCE, academic administrator; b. Curtis, La., June 11, 1934; s. Elijah H. and Mattie (White) N.; m. Patricia Robbins, Dec. 27, 1985; children: Cherlyn, Karyn, Eric Beatty, Kim Beatty. BS, Grambling (La.) State U., 1959; PhD, U. Kans., 1963. Assoc. prof. chemistry So. U., Baton Rouge, 1963-67, head div. sci., 1966-68; prof. chemistry Prairie View (Tex.) A&M U., 1968-83, asst. acad. dean, 1968-72, v.p. rsch., 1972-82, acting pres., 1982-83; exec. asst. Tex. A&M U. System, College Station, 1983-86; chancellor Alamo C.C. Dist., San Antonio, 1986-92; pres. Cen. Wash. U., Ellensburg, 1992—; DuPont teaching fellow U. Kans., 1959; rsch. chemist Am. Oil Co., 1962; sr. rsch. chemist Union Carbide Co., 1969; vis. prof. U. Autonomous Guadalajara, Mex., 1966, Loyola U., 1967; Fulbright lectr., 1966; cons. evaluation coms. Oak Ridge (Tenn.) Assoc. Univs., NSF, Nat. Coun. for Accreditation Tchr. Edn., So. Assn. Colls. and Schs.; mem. regional policy coms. on minorities Western Interstate Com. on Higher Edn., 1986-88; mem. exec. com. Nat. Assn. State Univs. and Land Grant Colls., 1980-82. Contbr. articles to profl. jours. Bd. dirs. Target 90, Goals San Antonio, 1987-89, coun. of pres.NAIDA,(1993-96) Commn. on Student Learning, Wash., 1992—, United Way San Antonio, 1987-89, Alamo Area coun. Boy Scouts Am., 1987-89, San Antonio Symphony Soc., 1987-91, Key Bank of Wash.; mem. bd. dirs. assn. Western U., (1995—) mem. com. fir jud. reform State of Tex., 1991; mem. edn. adv. bd. Tex. Rsch. Park, 1987-89; bd. givs. Am. Inst. for character Edn., Inc., 1988-91; mem. adv. com. Tex. Ho. of Reps., 1978; chmn. United Way Campaign Tex. A&M U. System, 1984, others. Staff sgt. USAF, 1951-55, Korea. T.H. Harris scholar Grambling State U., 1959; fellow Nat. Urban League, 1969. Mem. AAAS, Am. Chem. Soc., Tex. Acad. Sci., NAACP, Phi Beta Kappa, Sigma Xi, Phi Lambda Upsilon, Beta Kappa Chi, Alpha Mu Gamma, Kappa Delta Pi, Sigma Pi Sigma, Omega Psi Phi, Sigma Pi Phi, Phi Kappa Phi. Avocations: fishing, photography, sports. Home: 211 E 10th Ave Ellensburg WA 98926-2911 Office: Office of Pres Cen Wash U Ellensburg WA 98926

NELSON, J. GORDON, geography educator. Prof. dept. geography Sch. Planning U. Waterloo, Ont., Can. Recipient Massey medal Royal Can. Geog. Soc., 1993. Office: U Waterloo, Dept Geography, Waterloo, ON Canada N2L 3G1

NELSON, JACK LEE, education educator; b. Cheyenne, Wyo., Nov. 2, 1932; s. Myron Alfred and Mary Elizabeth (Baker) N.; m. Gwen Margret Names, Mar. 13, 1953; children: Barbara Louise Nelson Vollmer, Steven Lee. B.A., U. Denver, 1954; M.A., Calif. State U.-Los Angeles, 1958; Ed.D., U. So. Calif., 1961. Tchr. pub. schs., Riverside, Calif., 1956-58; instr. Calif. State U., Los Angeles, 1958-59, asst. prof., 1959-63; instr. Citrus Community Coll., Glendora, Calif., 1959-63; assoc. prof. SUNY, Buffalo, 1963-68, chmn. dept., 1966-68; prof. edn. Rutgers U., New Brunswick, N.J., 1968—, Disting. prof., 1975; dean, prof. Sch. Edn. San Jose (Calif.) State U., 1986-87; chmn. dept. sci. and humanities edn. Rutgers U., 1972-75; vis. prof. Cambridge U., Eng., 1974, 75, 79, 80, 83, 84, 85; vis. scholar U. Calif., Berkeley, 1975-76, Stanford U., 1982-83, Western Australia Inst. Tech., 1985, U. Colo., 1989, U. Wash., 1993, U. Sydney, Australia, 1994-95, Edith Cowan U., Australia, 1997; cond. editor Random House Inc., McGraw-Hill Inc.; mem. adv. coun. New World Dictionary. Author: (with J. Michaelis) Secondary Social Studies, 1980, (with V. Green) International Human Rights, 1980, (with Frank Besag) Foundations of Education, 1984, (with S. Palonsky and K. Carlson) Critical Issues in Education, 1990, 2d edit., 1993, 3d edit., 1996; contbr. numerous articles to profl. jours.; editor: Social Sci. Rsch., 1964-68, Theory and Rsch. in Social Edn., 1982-85. Mem. exec. bd. ACLU, Middlesex County, N.J., 1968-83; mem. Erie County Dem. Com., 1967-68, N.J. Gov.'s Task Force on Rehab. Edn. for Prisoners, 1970-74; mem. Highland Park Bd. Edn., N.J., 1972-75, pres., 1974-75; mem. Highland Park Hist. Commn., 1980-86; mem. nat. panel Project Censored, 1976—; mem. N.J. Rural Adv. Commn., 1992—. Robert Taft Found. grantee Inst. in Govt., 1970, 86; Inst. for World Order grantee Rutgers U., 1973—; Rutgers U. grantee; SUNY-Buffalo grantee, 1967-68; ACLU of N.J. grantee, 1972-73; U.S. Office Edn. grantee, 1967-68; N.J. Dept. Higher Edn. grantee, 1985-86. Mem. Am. Acad. Polit. and Social Sci., AAUP (editorial bd. 1977-80, rep. nat. council 1982-85, com. on acad. freedom and tenure 1983-86, com. on legis. affairs 1992-95, exec. bd., state confs. 1996—), Am. Ednl. Research Assn., Internat. Studies Assn., Nat. Council for Social Studies, Social Sci. Edn. Consortium (bd. dirs. 1983-85), Phi Delta Kappa. Home: 299 Woodbridge Ave Metuchen NJ 08840-2039 Office: Rutgers U Grad Sch Edn Rutgers U Grad Sch Edn New Brunswick NJ 08903

NELSON, JAMES ALBERT, librarian, state official; b. Grand Junction, Colo., June 13, 1941; s. Gerhardt Melvin and Lettie Louise (Sanders) N.; m. Judith Ann Brown, Sept. 5, 1965 (div. July 1972); children: Colm Corbett, Rebekah Sanders; m. Carol Stern, Aug. 8, 1982 (div. Apt. 1992); 1 child, Michael Leland. B.A. in English, U. Colo., 1965; M.S. in L.S., U. Ky., 1969. Head librarian Hardin County Pub. Library, Elizabethtown, Ky., 1969-70; dir. interlibrary coop. Ky. Dept. Libraries and Archives, Frankfort, 1970-72; state libr., commr. Ky. Dept. Librs. and Archives, Frankfort, 1980—; speech writer Gov. Ky., Frankfort, 1972-73; dir. continuing edn. Coll. Libr. Sci., U. Ky., Lexington, 1973-77; asst. prof. libr. sci. U. Wis., Madison, 1977-80; vol. U.S. Peace Corps, Bulan, Sorsogon, Philippines, 1965-66; mem. Ky. Sci. and Tech. Coun., 1990—, Ky. Task Force on Open Meetings and Open Records, 1990—; chair Ky. Info. Resources Mgmt. Commn., 1996—. Editor column Jour. Edn. for Librarianship, 1976-79, Gateways to Comprehensive State Information Policy, 1990; contbr. articles to jours. Pres. Increase Lapham Community Edn., Madison, 1979; mem. Ky. Gov.'s Commn. on Literacy; mem. exec. bd. Ky. Oral History Commn.; mem. KMSC Comm. Adv. Coun., 1991—; chair Ky. Info. Resources Mgmt. Commn., 1997—. Recipient Outstanding Alumnus award U. Ky. Coll. Library and Info. Sci., 1985. Mem. ALA (chmn. continuing edn. com. 1976-78, pres. 1984-85, chair 1988-89), Assn. Coop. and Specialized Libr. Agys., Ky. Info. Systems Commn. (chair info. policy spl. com. 1991-96), Continuing Libr. Edn. Network and Exch. (pres. 1979-80), Soc. Am. Archivist (task force archives and soc.), Chief Officers State Libr. Agys. (treas. 1989-91, chair legis. com. 1991-92), ALA Office for Info. Tech. Policy Adv. Com., Beta Phi Mu (chpt. pres. 1969). Democrat. Home: 222 Raintree Rd Frankfort KY 40601-4459 Office: Ky Dept Libr and Archives PO Box 537 Frankfort KY 40602-0537

NELSON, JAMES ALONZO, radiologist, educator; b. Cherokee, Iowa, Oct. 20, 1938; s. Joe George and Ruth Geraldine (Jones) N.; m. Katherine Metcalf, July 16, 1966; children: John Metcalf, Julie Heaps. AB, Harvard U., 1961, MD, 1965. Asst. prof. radiology U. Calif., San Francisco, 1972-74; assoc. prof. U. Utah, Salt Lake City, 1974-79, prof., 1979-86; prof. U. Wash., Seattle, 1986—; dir. radiol. rsch. U. Calif./Ft. Miley VA Hosp., 1973-74, U. Utah, 1974-85, U. Wash., 1986—; mem. bd. sci. advisors NeoVision, 1995—, Oreg. Life Scis.; co-founder Circulation, Inc., 1996; mem. adv. panel on non-radioactive diagnostic agts. USP, 1984-96. Contbr. chpts. to books, articles to Am. Jour. Roentgenology, Radiology, Investigative Radiology, others. Capt. USAF, 1967-69. John Harvard scholar, 1957-61, James Picker Found. scholar, 1973-77; recipient Mallinkrodt prize Soc. Body Computerized Tomagraphy, 1990, Roscoe Miller award Soc. Gastrointestinal Radiology, 1991. Fellow Am. Coll. Radiology (diplomate); mem. Radiol. Soc. N.Am., Assn. Univ. Radiology. Achievements include patents (with others) for Non-Surgical Peritoneal Lavage, Recursive Band-Pass Filter for Digital Angiography, for Unsharp Masking for Chest Films, Improved Chest Tube, Oral Hepatobiliary MRI Contrast Agent, non-surgical myocardial revascularization. Office: U Wash Dept Radiology Diagnostic Imaging Sci Ctr Box 357115 Seattle WA 98195

NELSON, JAMES AUGUSTUS, II, real estate executive, architect, banker; b. Damrascotta, Maine, July 26, 1947; s. Robert Maynard and Margret Rebbeca (Harmision) N.; m. Linda Ray, Aug. 15, 1975 (div. 1985); m. Tina Nides, Oct. 22, 1986 (div. 1991); 1 child, Jennifer Alexandria. BArch, Columbia U., 1973, MBA, 1974. Resident v.p. Citibank, N.Y.C., 1974-77; group v.p. Bank of Am., San Francisco, 1977-82; assoc. John Portman and Assocs., Atlanta, 1983-85; pres. J.A. Nelson and Assocs., L.A., 1986-88; dir. real estate planning and devel. MCA Devel. Co., L.A., 1988-94; founder Mother Co., Hollywood, Calif., 1995. Author: Banker's Guide to Construction, 1978, Doing Business in Saudi Arabia, 1979. Chmn. Laurel Canyon Coalition, L.A.; bd. dirs. Laurel Canyon Area Assn., Hollywood Heritage, Hillside Fedn., L.A., Lookout Mountain Assocs., L.A.; founder Universal City Walk Project. Recipient Innovative Design award for Universal City Walk, Internat. Coun. Shopping Ctrs., 1994. Avocations: gardening, architecture. Home: 8306 Grand View Dr Los Angeles CA 90046-1918 Office: Mother Co 200 Burchett St Glendale CA 91203-1222

NELSON, JAMES CARMER, JR., advertising executive, writer; b. Denver, Nov. 10, 1921; s. James Carmer and Helen (McClelland) N.; m. Mary-Armour Ransom, Sept. 9, 1950; children—James Carmer III, Marie-Louise Nelson Masters, Jeffrey Armour, Rebecca McClelland Nelson Sylla. A.B., Yale, 1943. Mktg. editor Bus. Week mag., N.Y.C., 1946-48; illustration editor Bus. Week mag., 1948-52; freelance author Sonoma, Calif., 1952-57; copy chief Hoefer, Dieterich & Brown, Inc., San Francisco, 1957-59; v.p., creative dir. Hoefer, Dieterich & Brown, Inc., 1959-66, exec. v.p., 1966-76, pres., 1976-79, vice chmn., 1979-80; ptnr. John H. Hoefer & Assocs., 1972—; vice chmn. Chiat/Day/Hoefer, 1980; pvt. advt. cons., 1980—; bd. dirs. McKinney, Inc., Phila.; instr. Golden Gate Coll., San Francisco, 1958-59; alternate mem. Nat. Advt. Rev. Bd., 1971-75. Author: The Trouble With Gumballs, 1957, Great Cheap Wines: A Poorperson's Guide, 1977, Great Wines Under $5, 1983; contbr. articles and fiction to popular mags. Mem. Harold Brunn Soc. for Med. Research, Mt. Zion Hosp., San Francisco; bd. assos. Linus Pauling Inst. Sci. and Medicine, Palo Alto, Calif.; mem. Colony Found., New Haven; trustee Coro Found., 1965-75, Marin Art Complex; bd. mgrs. Marin County YMCA. Served with USNR, 1942-46. Mem. ASCAP. Club: Villa Taverna (San Francisco). Home: 649 Idylberry Rd San Rafael CA 94903-1231

NELSON, JAMES SMITH, pathologist, educator; b. St. Louis, Mar. 19, 1933; s. Victor Paul and Dorothy Gertrude (Smith) N.; children: Paul F., Andrew S. BS, St. Louis U., 1950-53, MD, 1957. Pathology intern, resident St. Louis U. Hosps., 1957-59, 60-61; neuropathology fellow Columbia U. Coll. Phys. & Surgery, N.Y.C., 1959-60; neurochemistry fellow Washington U. Med. Sch., St. Louis, 1961-63, instr. in pathology, 1963-64, assoc. prof., prof. pathology & pediatrics, 1973-87; asst. prof., assoc. prof. pathology St. Louis U. Med. Sch., 1964-73; head divsn. neuropathology Henry Ford Hosp., Detroit, 1987-89; clin. prof. neuropathology U. Mich. Med. Sch., Ann Arbor, 1988-89; prof. pathology La. State U. Med. Ctr., New Orleans, 1989—; chmn. dept. neuropathology Armed Forces Inst. Pathology, Washington, 1990-94; ad hoc cons. NIH, Washington, 1973-92; mem. Nat. Cancer Inst. CNS Oncology Working Group, Washington, 1986-89; mem. neuropathology test com. Am. Bd. Pathology, Tampa, Fla., 1984-90; mem. WHO Brain Tumor Working Group, Zurich, Switzerland, 1990—; adv. mem. neuropathology com. Coll. Am. Pathologists, Chgo., 1992—. Author: Medical School Admission: A Systematic Guide, 1974; author, editor: Principles and Practice of Neuropathology, 1993; contbr. over 150 articles to profl. jours. Col. M.C., U.S. Army, 1990-94. Decorated Legion of Merit; recipient U.S. Sr. Scientist award Alexander von Humboldt Found., Free U. Berlin, 1979-80, Cert. of Achievement, U.S. Surgeon Gen., 1985, Res. Components Achievement medal U.S. Army, 1986; NIH spl. rsch. fellow in neurochemistry, 1961-63; NIH grantee, 1966-87, 95—. Mem. AMA, Coll. Am. Pathologists (com. mem.), Am. Soc. Clin. Pathologists, Am. Assn. Neuropathologists, U.S. & Can. Acad. Pathology, Am. Inst. Nutrition. Roman Catholic. Avocations: sailing, fishing, photography, skydiving. Home: 3443 Esplanade Ave Apt 415 New Orleans LA 70119-2956 Office: Dept of Pathology La State Univ Med Ctr 1901 Perdido St New Orleans LA 70112-1328

NELSON, JOHN HOWARD, food company research executive; b. Chgo., May 29, 1930; s. Harold Eugene and Zoe (Peters) N.; m. Jacqueline Raff, Apr. 30, 1952; children: Keith E., Kevin E., Kristen E. BS in Horticulture and Food Tech., Purdue U., 1952, MS in Food Tech. and Microbiology, 1953; PhD in Biochemistry and Microbiology, U. Minn., 1961. From rsch. biochemist to head R&D dept. Gen. Mills., Mpls., 1955-67; dir. R&D to v.p. R&D Peavey Co., Mpls., 1968-76; ptnr. Johnson Powell & Co., Mpls., 1976-78; v.p. R&D, then v.p. mktg. and product devel. Am. Maize Products Co., Hammond, Ind., 1978-82; v.p. corp. devel., then chief oper. officer Roman Meal Co., Tacoma, Wash., 1982-86; corp. dir. R&D, then v.p. R&D McCormick & Co. Inc., Hunt Valley, Md., 1986-88, v.p. sci. and tech., 1988-94; ret., 1994; prof. food sci. dept. Purdue U., West Lafayette, Ind., 1994—; sci. program advisor Charles F. Kettering Rsch. Lab., Dayton, Ohio, 1976-77. Trustee St. Joseph Hosp., Towson, Md., 1989-95; mem. chancellor's adv. com. U. Md., 1989-96; chmn. Ind./Acad. bd. Towson State U., 1990-92. Visking fellow Visking Corp., 1958. Fellow League for Internat. Food Edn. (pres. 1981-82, chmn. Project SUSTAIN 1988-94); mem. Am. Assn. Cereal Chemists (pres. 1974-75, William F. Geddes award 1979, Geddes lectr. 1991), Am. Chem. Soc., Inst. Food Technologists, Elks, Sigma Xi, Gamma Sigma Delta, Alpha Zeta. Republican. Avocations: travel, golf, gardening. Office: Purdue Univ 7217 NE William Rogers Rd Indianola WA 98342-9705

NELSON, JOHN HOWARD (JACK HOWARD NELSON), journalist; b. Talladega, Ala., Oct. 11, 1929; s. Howard Alonzo and Barbara Lena (O'Donnell) N.; m. Virginia Dare Dickinson, Aug. 4, 1951 (div. Nov. 1974); children: Karen Dare, John Michael, Steven Howard; m. Barbara Joan Matusow, Dec. 7, 1974. Student econs., Ga. State Coll., 1953-57; Nieman fellow, Harvard U., 1961-62. Reporter, Biloxi (Miss.) Daily Herald, 1947-51; Reporter Atlanta Constitution, 1952-65; So. bur. chief Los Angeles Times, Atlanta, 1965-70; with Washington bur. Los Angeles Times, 1970—, Washington bur. chief, 1975-96, chief Washington corr., 1996—. Author: (with Gene Roberts, Jr.) The Censors and the Schools, 1963, (with Jack Bass) The Orangeburg Massacre, 1970, (with R.J. Ostrow) The FBI and the Berrigans, 1972, Captive Voices, Shocken Books, 1974, Terror in the Night, 1993. Mem. vis. com. U. Md. Sch. Journalism, U. Miami Sch. Communications. With AUS, 1951-52. Recipient Pulitzer prize for local reporting under deadline pressure, 1960; Drew Pearson award for gen. excellence in investigative reporting, 1974. Mem. Fgn. Policy Coun., The Gridiron Club. Home: 4 Wynkoop Ct Bethesda MD 20817-5936 Office: 1875 I St NW Ste 1100 Washington DC 20006-5421

NELSON, JOHN KEITH, electrical engineering educator; b. Oldham, Lancashire, Eng., July 3, 1943; s. John Collins and Joyce Palfrey (Simmons) N.; m. Christine Anne Baker, Feb. 10, 1968; children: David John, Peter Mark. BS in Engring., U. London, 1965, PhD, 1969. Rsch. fellow U. London, 1966-69, lectr., 1969-78, reader, 1978-79; rsch. mgr. Gen. Electric, Schenectady, 1979-82; prof. elec. power engring. Rensselaer Poly. Inst., Troy, N.Y., 1982—, head dept.; examiner U. Sri Lanka, 1970-85; cons. in field. Contbr. articles to profl. jours. Patentee in field. Recipient Snell Premium, IEE, London, 1972, J.R. Beard award, 1976, Rsch. award, Brit. Council, 1974, 76; Travel award, Royal Soc., London, 1976, Power Engring. Educator award Edison Electric Inst., 1994. Fellow Inst. Elec. Engrs. (U.K.), IEEE (tech. v.p. Dielectrics and Elect. Insulation Soc. 1991-92, administrv. v.p., 1993-94, pres. 1995-96, Meml. lectr. 1993); mem., Council of Engring. Inst. Episcopalian. Avocations: squash, sailing, scuba diving, flying. Office: Rensselaer Poly Inst Dept Elec Power Engring Troy NY 12180-3590

NELSON, JOHN MARSHALL, medical information services company executive; b. Madison, Wis., Oct. 28, 1941; s. Russell Arthur and Dorothea (Smith) N.; m. Linda Taylor, Oct. 13, 1962 (div. June 1968); children: Ann, David; m. Katherine Dianne Hoagland, Sept. 24, 1972; children: James, George. AB, Harvard Coll., 1963; MD, Case Western Reserve U., 1967; MBA, U. Chgo., 1983. Diplomate Am. Bd. Internal Medicine. Staff assoc. NIH, Bethesda, Md., 1968-71; rsch. assoc., asst. prof. medicine Promis Lab. Med. Sch. Univ. Vt., 1973-76; med. dir. Madison Gen. Hosp., 1976-84; assoc. clin. prof. Med. Sch. U. Wis., 1976-84; v.p. corp. med. affairs Gen. Health Mgmt. Co., Madison, 1984-86; dir. med. and ednl. affairs Washington Hosp. Ctr., 1986-87; pres. Nelson Info. Systems, Bethesda, Md., 1987—; cons. Med. Sch. U. Utah, Salt Lake City, 1985-86; med. reviewer FDA, 1990-91. Contbr. articles to profl. jour. Coach youth soccer, 1984-85; merit badge counselor Boy Scouts Am., 1987; mem. Harvard Schs. Com., Md., 1988-91; vestry St. John's Episcopal Ch., Bethesda, 1988-91. Harvard Hon. Nat. Scholar, 1959-62; recipient Steuer Meml. award Case Western Reserve U., Cleve., 1967; grantee Nat. Libr. Medicine, NIH, 1992-97. Fellow ACP, Am. Coll. Physician Execs.; mem. AMA, Univ. Club Chgo., Harvard Club (Washington), Alpha Omega Alpha. Republican. Episcopalian. Avocations: swimming, reading, cycling. Home: 6616 Millwood Rd Bethesda MD 20817-6058 Office: 4740 Chevy Chase Dr Chevy Chase MD 20815-6461

NELSON, JOHN MARTIN, corporate executive; b. N.Y.C., Aug. 9, 1931; s. Martin H. and Margaret (Larkin) N.; m. Linda Crocker Moore, Aug. 30, 1992; children: Murrey E., Christopher L. A.B., Wesleyan U., 1953; M.B.A., Harvard U., 1959. With Norton Co., Worcester, Mass., 1959-90; pres., chief exec. officer Norton Christensen Inc. subs. Norton Co., Salt Lake City, 1978-86; pres., chief operating officer Norton Co., Worcester, 1986-88, chmn., chief exec. officer, 1988-90; chmn., chief exec. officer Wyman-Gordon Co., Worcester, 1991-94; chmn. Wyman-Gordon Co., Worcester, Mass., 1995—, The TJX Cos., Inc., Framingham, Mass., 1995—; bd. dirs. Browne and Sharpe Mfg. Co., Kingstown, R.I., Aquila Pharms., Inc., Worcester, Mass., Stocker & Yale, Inc., Beverly, Mass. Trustee Wesleyan U., 1978-81, Worcester Poly. Inst., 1986—, chmn. 1995—; bd. dirs. Worcester Mcpl. Rsch. Bur., 1989—, Greater Worcester Cmty. Found., 1990—, pres., 1990-94; bd. dirs. Alliance for Edn., 1991—, U. Mass. Med. Ctr. Found., Inc., 1991—, United Way Ctrl. Mass., 1993; trustee Worcester Found. for Biomed. Rsch., 1993—, Worcester Art Mus., 1988—, chmn., 1996—, Worcester Area C. of C., 1992—, Meml. Health Care, 1991—. Mem. Worcester Area C. of C. Home: 7 Massachusetts Ave Worcester MA 01609-1622 Office: Wyman-Gordon Co 244 Worcester St # 8001 North Grafton MA 01536-1260

NELSON, JOHN ROBERT, theology educator, clergyman; b. Winona Lake, Ind., Aug. 21, 1920; s. William John and Agnes Dorothy (Soderborg) N.; m. Dorothy Patricia Mercer, Aug. 18, 1945; children: Eric Mercer, William John. AB, DePauw U., 1941, LHD, 1960; BD, Yale U., 1944; DTheol, U. Zürich, Switzerland, 1951; LLD, Wilberforce U., 1954; DD, Ohio Wesleyan U., 1964; LHD, Loyola U., 1969; DH, Hellenic Coll., 1985. Ordained to ministry Meth. Ch., 1944; dir. Wesley Found., Chapel Hill, N.C., 1946-48; assoc. dir. Wesley Found., Urbana, Ill., 1950-51; study sect. United Student Christian Council, N.Y.C., 1951-53; sec. commn. on faith and order World Council Chs., Geneva, Switzerland, 1953-57, chmn. working com., 1967-75; dean, prof. theology Vanderbilt Div. Sch., 1957-60; vis. prof. ecumenics Princeton Theol. Sem., 1960-61; vis. prof. United Theol. Coll., Bangalore, India, and Leonard Theol. Coll., Jabalpur, India, 1961-62; Fairchild prof. Christian theology Grad. Sch. Theology, Oberlin Coll., Ohio, 1962-65; prof. systematic theology Boston U. Sch. Theology, 1965-84, dean, 1972-74; Peyton lectr. So. Meth. U., 1961; Merrick lectr. Ohio Wesleyan U., 1964; Lowell lectr., 1966; Burke lectr. U. Calif.-San Diego, 1985; Willson lectr. Centenary Coll., 1985; Nobel lectr. Gustavus Adolphus U., 1985; vis. prof. Pontifical Gregorian U., Rome, 1968-69; Mendenhall lectr. DePauw, 1974; Russell lectr. Tufts U., 1976, Wattson lectr., Cath. U., 1989; cons. Pres.'s Commn. for Study Ethical Problems in Biomed. Research, 1980-82; dir. Inst. Religion, Tex. Med. Ctr., Houston, 1985-92, sr. rsch. fellow 1992—; adj. prof. medicine Baylor Coll. Medicine, 1985—, adj. prof. religious studies Rice U., 1987-91; program dir. Genetics, Religion and Ethics, Baylor Coll. Medicine, 1990—. Author: The Realm of Redemption, 1951, One Lord, One Church, 1958, Overcoming Christian Divisions, rev. edit, 1962, Criterion for the Church, 1963, Fifty Years of Faith and Order, (with J. Skoglund), 1963, Crisis in Unity and Witness, 1968, Church Union in Focus, 1968, Science and Our Troubled Conscience, 1980, Human Life: a Biblical Perspective for Bioethics, 1984, On the New Frontiers of Genetics and Religion, 1994; editor: The Christian Student and the World Struggle, 1952, Christian Unity in North America, 1958, No Man Is Alien, 1971, Life as Liberty, Life as Trust, 1992; editor-at-large, The Christian Century, 1958-91; assoc. editor: Jour. Ecumenical Studies; mem. editorial bd. Human Gene Therapy. Del. all 7 assemblies World Coun. Chs., 5th World Conf. on Faith and Order, 1993, United Meth. Gen. Conf., 1968, 72; mem. commn. on faith and order Nat. Coun. Chs.; mem. U.S. Commn. for UNESCO, 1974-80; bd. dirs. Value of Life Com. Fellow Am. Acad. Arts and Scis.; mem. Am. Theol. Soc. (past pres.), N.Am. Acad. Ecumenists (past pres.), Soc. Europeenne de Culture (v.p.), Houston Philosophy Soc., Country Club of Brookline (Mass.), Rotary, Phi Beta Kappa, Beta Theta Pi. Home: 1111 Hermann Dr Apt 19 A Houston TX 77004-6930 Office: Inst of Religion Tex Med Ctr 1129 Wilkins St Houston TX 77030-2805 *The sequence of my persuasions and commitments has been from Christian unity to human unity to basic concern for the value of human life itself; and these are cumulative convictions from which I cannot deviate.*

NELSON, JOHN THILGEN, retired hospital administrator, physician; b. Aurora, Ill., Feb. 11, 1921; s. George William and Margaret Mary (Thilgen) N. Student, Wheaton (Ill.) Coll., 1941-44; M.D., Chgo. Med. Sch., 1949. Intern Macon (Ga.) Hosp., 1948-49; resident anesthesiology U. Ill. Sch. Medicine, 1949-51, clin. instr., 1949-57; attending physician VA Hosp., Hines, Ill., 1951-57; pvt. practice medicine, specializing in anesthesiology Chgo., 1951-52, Elgin, Ill., 1954-69; chief of dept. St. Joseph Hosp., Elgin, 1954-69; sec. med. staff St. Joseph Hosp., 1966, v.p. med. staff, 1967, pres., 1968; supt. Chgo.-Read Mental Health Center, 1969-74; med. dir. Elgin Mental Health Center, 1974-87; coordinator med. services Ill. Dept. Health and Devel. Disabilities, 1976-87; ret., 1985. Served with AUS, 1952-54. Fellow Am. Coll. Anesthesiology; mem. Am., Ill., Chgo., Kane County med. socs., Am., Ill., Chgo. socs. anesthesiology. Home: RR 1 Box 313 11 N 070 Rohrssen Rd Elgin IL 60120-7598

NELSON, JOHN WILTON, symphonic conductor; b. San Jose, Costa Rica, Dec. 6, 1941; came to U.S., 1953; s. Wilton Mons and Thelma (Agnew) N.; m. Anita Christine Johnsen, Sept. 4, 1964; children: Kirsten, Kari. B. Music, Wheaton Coll., 1963; M.M. (Teaching fellow), Juilliard Sch., 1965, postgrad. diploma (teaching fellow), 1967. Conducting faculty Juillard Sch., N.Y.C., 1968-72; dir. Aspen Choral Inst., 1968-73; music dir. Indpls. Symphony Orch., 1976-87; conductor prodns. at Met. Opera and City Opera in N.Y., Santa Fe, Chgo. Lyric Opera, Rome Opera, Lyon Opera, Geneva Opera, The Bastille, la Monnaie in Brussels and Welsh Nat. Opera; recordings include Berlioz' Beatrice and Benedict, 1992, a disc of works by Paul Schoenfield, 1994, and Gorecki's Miserere with Chgo. Symphony and Lyric Opera choruses. Music dir., ProArte Chorale, Ridgewood, N.J., 1965-75; condr., N.Y. Mozart Festival, 1967, Juilliard Opera Theatre, N.Y.C., 1968; music dir., Greenwich Philharmonica Orch., N.Y.C., 1966-74; condr., N.Y.C. Opera, 1973-75, Santa Fe Opera, 1973, Geneva Grand Theatre, 1974, Met. Opera, N.Y.C., 1974—, Lyon Opera, 1991, Geneva Opera, 1992; condr., music dir., Indpls. Symphony Orch., 1976-87; music adviser, Nashville (Tenn.) Symphony, 1975; conducted, Chgo. Symphony, N.Y. Philharm., Boston Symphony, Phila. Orch., Indpls. Symphony Orch., Cin. Orch., L.A. Philharmonic, London Royal Philharmonic, Suiss Romande, Dresden Staatskapelle, Leipzig Lewardhaus, Orch. de Paris; music dir. St. Louis Opera, 1981-91, prin. guest condr., 1991—. Recipient Irving Berlin Conducting award, 1967, Diapason d'Or award recording Beatrice & Benedict, 1993, Best Operatic Rec. Grammy award for Handel's Semele with English Chamber Orch./Kathleen Battle, 1993. Office: care IMG Artists Media House, 3 Burlington Ln, London Chiswick W4 2TH, England

NELSON, JOHN WOOLARD, neurology educator, physician; b. Hagerstown, Ind., Mar. 9, 1928; s. John Hans and Marvel May (Woolard) N.; m. Nancy Louise Elam, July 21, 1966; 1 son, John Hancock. A.B., Earlham Coll., 1950; M.D., Ind. U., 1953. Diplomate: Am. Bd Psychiatry and Neurology (neurology clin. neurophysiology). Instr. neurology U. Tenn. Coll. Medicine, 1959-61; asst. prof. neurology W. Va. U. Sch. Medicine, 1961-63; assoc. prof. neurology U. Tenn., 1963-66; assoc. prof. to prof. Med. Coll. Wis., Milw., 1966-72; clin. prof. neurology U. Minn., Duluth, 1972-73; prof., head dept. neurology U. Okla. Coll. of Medicine, Oklahoma City, 1973-88, prof. emeritus neurology, 1989—. Served with M.C. U.S. Army, 1955-56. Mem. Okla. County Med. Soc., Okla. Med. Soc., AMA, Am. Acad. Neurology, Am. Electroencephalographic Soc., Am. Med. Electroencephalographic Soc. Home: 2608 Greenfield Dr Edmond OK 73003-6528

NELSON, KARIN BECKER, child neurologist; b. Chgo., Aug. 14, 1933; d. George and Sylvia (Demansly) Becker; m. Phillip G. Nelson, Mar. 20, 1955; children: Sarah Nelson Hammack, Rebecca Nelson Miller, Jenny Nelson Walker, Peter. MD, U. Chgo., 1957; Student, U. Minn., 1950-53. Cert. child neurology Am. Bd. Psychiatry and Neurology. Intern rotating Phila. Gen. Hosp., 1957-58; asst. resident neurology U. Md. Sch. Medicine, Balt., 1958-59; resident neurology George Washington U. Sch. Medicine, Washington, 1959-62; cons. in med. neurology St. Elizabeth's Hosp., Washington, 1960-62; registrar to outpatients Nat. Hosp., Queen Sq., London, 1963; med. officer perinatal rsch. br. Nat. Inst. of Neurol. Disorders and Blindness, NIH, 1964-67; asst. prof. neurology George Washington U., Washington, 1970-72; assoc. neurologist Children's Hosp. of D.C., Washington, 1967-71; instr. neurology George Washington U., Washington, 1967-70; attending neurologist Children's Hosp., Washington, 1971-73, 78—; assoc. clin. prof. neurology George Washington U., Washington, 1972—; mem. orphan products devel. initial rev. group FDA, 1983-86, Boston Collaborative Drug Surveillance Group, 1985-86, vaccine Am. Acad. Pediatrics, 1985, 87, Dept. Health, State of Calif. Birth Monitoring Group, 1986—, Ctr. for Disease Control Birth Defects Monitoring Com., 1987; med. officer Nat. Inst. Neurol. Disorders and Blindness, NIH, Bethesda, 1972—; med. staff Children Hosp., Washington, 1962—; mem. adv. bd. Internat. Sch. Neuroscis., Venice, Italy, Little Found./World Fedn. Neurology, 1992—, rev. bd. Nat. Inst. Aging; mem. epidemiology steering com. NIH, 1993—. Editor: Workshop on the Neurobiological Basis of Autism, 1979, (with J.H. Ellenberg) Febrile Seizures, 1981; editorial bd. Pediatric Neurology, 1984-90, Brain and Development, 1984—, Neurology, 1985-88, Paediatric and Perinatal Epidemiology, 1987—, Developmental Medicine and Child Neurology, 1988; field editor Epilepsy Advances; contbr. papers to profl. jours. Recipient Spl. Recognition award USPHS, 1977, Spl. Achievement award 1981, United Cerebral Palsy Weinstein-Goldenson Rsch. award 1990, Dirs. award NIH, 1992. Fellow Am. Acad. Neurology (exec. bd. 1989-91, councillor); mem. Soc. Perinatal Obstetricians (hon.), Child Neurology Soc. (program chmn. 1973, liaison nat. Inst. of Neurol. and Communicative Disorders and Blindness 1975-80, ethics com. 1985-87, by-laws com. 1990—, ad hoc com. for consensus statement of DPT immunications and the cen. nervous system 1990, long range planning com. 1991—, Hower award 1991), Am. Acad. for Cerebral Palsy and Devel. Medicine (program chmn. 1985), Am. Epilepsy Soc. (Disting. Basic Neuroscientist Epilepsy Rsch. award 1992), Am. Neurol. Assn. (membership com. 1994—), Internat. Child Neurology Assn. (sci. selection com. 1993-94), Can. Assn. Child Neurology (hon.), Soc. Perinatal Obstetricians (hon.), Baltic Child Neurology Soc., Dana Alliance Brain Initiatives, Alpha Omega Alpha. Democrat. Jewish. Office: NIH 7550 Wisconsin Ave Rm 700 Bethesda MD 20814-3559

NELSON, KAY ELLEN, speech and language pathologist; b. Milw., Apr. 14, 1947; d. John A. and Margaret B. (Janke) Strobel; m. Kuglitsch Dale, Mar. 2, 1974 (div. Dec. 1981); 1 child, Ashley Lara. BA with distinction, U. Wis., Madison, 1969; MA, U. Wis., Milw., 1972. Speech and lang. pathologist Sch. Dist. 146, Dolton, Ill., 1970-71, Waukesha County Handicapped Children's Edn. Bd., Waukesha, Wis., 1972-77, 79-80, Kettle Moraine Area Schs., Wales, Wis., 1980-94; dir. speech/lang. pathology MJ Care, Inc., Fond du Lac, Wis., 1994-96; speech-lang. pathologist, team leader, clin. specialist NovaCare, Inc., New Berlin, Wis., 1996—; pvt. practice Dousman, Wis., summers 1991-93. Fellow Herb Kohl Found., 1993. Mem. Am. Speech, Lang and Hearing Assn. (cert. of clin. competence, ACE awards 1990, 91, 92, 94, 95, 96), Wis. Speech, Lang. and Hearing Assn. (sch. rep. dist. VII 1991—, chmn. sch. svcs. com. 1992-94, v.p. sch. svcs. 1994-95, rep.-at-large 1995-96), Internat. Soc. for Augumentive and Alternative Comm. (sec. 1990-92, membership chmn. 1990-93, v.p. profl. affairs 1993). Unitarian. Avocations: sewing, computers, nature activities, travel. Office: NovaCare Inc 13700 W National Ave New Berlin WI 53151-4523

NELSON, KAYE LYNN, healthcare consultant; b. Bismarck, N.D., Oct. 5, 1935; d. Charles and Carolyn Phyllis (Thorne) Staiger; m. Roy Franklin, Dec. 29, 1959; children: Dana Lynn, Erik Roy. BS with honors, Mont. State Coll., Bozeman, 1958; MS with honors, Eastern Mont. Coll. Edn., Billings, 1962. Instr. Mont. State U., Bozeman, 1958-60; insvc. educator Deaconess Med. Ctr., Billings, 1975-83, risk mgr., 1983-88, dir. nursing, 1988-93. Mem. Sigma Theta Tau.

NELSON, KEITH ADAM, chemistry educator; b. N.Y.C., Dec. 8, 1953; s. Sidney and Doris Nelson; m. Martha Leticia Cortes, Oct. 5, 1981; children: Hannah, Dylan. BS in Chemistry, Stanford U., 1976, PhD in Phys. Chemistry, 1981. Postdoctoral scholar UCLA, 1981-82; asst. prof. chemistry MIT, Cambridge, 1982-87, assoc. prof., 1987-92, prof., 1992—. Contbr. over 150 articles to profl. jours. Recipient Presdl. Young Investigator award NSF, 1985-90, Coblentz prize Coblentz Soc., 1988; fellow Alfred P. Sloan Found., 1987-89. Fellow Am. Phys. Soc., Japan Soc. Promotion Sci.; mem. Am. Chem. Soc., Optical Soc. Am., Materials Rsch. Soc., Inter-Am. Photochem. Soc. Avocations: chess, soccer, topless coed roller derby. Office: MIT Dept Chemistry 77 Massachusetts Ave Cambridge MA 02139-4301

NELSON, KEITHE EUGENE, lawyer, state court administrator; b. Grand Forks, N.D., Mar. 23, 1935; s. Herman William and Hannah Marie (Anderson) N.; m. Shirley Jeanne Jordahl, June 10, 1955; children: Kirsti Lynn Nelson Hoerauf, Scott David, Kenen Edward, Karen Lee Nelson Strandquist. PhB, U. N.D., 1958, JD, 1959. Bar: N.D. 1959, U.S. Ct. Mil. Appeals 1967., U.S. Supreme Ct. 1967. With Armour & Co., Grand Forks, 1958-59; commd. 2d lt. USAF, 1958, advanced through grades to maj. gen., 1985; judge advocate USAF, N.D. and, Fed. Republic Germany and Eng., 1959-73; chief career mgmt. USAF, Washington, 1973-77; comdt. USAF JAG Sch., Montgomery, Ala., 1977-81; staff judge adv. Tactical Air Command USAF, Hampton, VA., 1981-82, SAC, Omaha, 1984-85; dir. USAF Judiciary, Washington, 1982-84; dep. JAG USAF, Washington, 1985, JAG., 1988-91, JAG, 1988, ret. JAG, 1991; dir. jud. planning Supreme Ct. N.D.; state ct. administr., 1992—. Chmn. editorial bd. USAF Law Rev., 1977-81. Decorated D.S.M., Legion of Merit with two oak leaf clusters. Mem. ABA. Lutheran. Avocations: skeet shooting, hunting, tennis, theater. Home: 800 Munich Dr Bismarck ND 58504-7050

NELSON, KENT C., delivery service executive; b. 1937. BS, Ball State U., 1959. With United Parcel Svc. Am., Inc., 1959-80, exec. v.p. fin., 1980-86, exec. v.p., 1986-88, vice chmn., 1988-89, chmn. bd., CEO, 1989—; chmn. bd., CEO United Parcel Svc. Inc., N.Y., Ohio. Office: United Parcel Svc AM Inc 55 Glenlake Pkwy NE Atlanta GA 30328-3474*

NELSON, LARRY A., statistics educator, consultant; b. Omaha, Oct. 28, 1932; s. Rudolph Lawrence and Elizabeth Coleman (Lewis) N. BS in Agronomy, Iowa State U., 1954; MS in Soil Sci., Tex. A&M U., 1958; PhD in Soil Sci.-Stats., N.C. State U., 1961. Soil scientist Iowa Agrl. Exptl. Sta., Ames, 1954-55; soils instr. Tex. A&I Coll., Kingsville, 1955; rsch. soil scientist Tex. A&M Rsch. Found., College Station, 1956; soils lab. instr. Tex. A&M U., College Station, 1956-58; rsch. asst. N.C. State U., Raleigh, 1959-61, asst. prof. exptl. stats., 1964-66, assoc. prof. exptl. stats., 1966-71, prof. stats., 1971-89, prof. emeritus stats., 1989—; asst. specialist in land classification Land Study Bur., U. Hawaii, Honolulu, 1961-63; lectr., tchr., cons. in field; spl. advisor head dep. stats. Kasetsart U., Bangkok, Thailand, 1973; evaluator quantitative skills IADS, Bangladesh, 1984; mem. rev. team Ctr. for Agrl. Econs. and Ctr. for Data Processing, Winrock Internat., Indonesia, 1985; statis. cons. PROCAFE, El Salvador, 1993-96, ICRAF, Nairobi, Kenya, 1991—; cons. Potash and Phosphate Inst. Can., China and India, 1990, 94, 96; ptnr. Statis. Rsch. Assocs., Honolulu, 1962-63. Assoc. editor Geoderma, 1976-84, Agronomy Jour., 1981-87; contbr. numerous articles to profl. publs. NATO fellow Data Analysis Lab., Lynbgy, Denmark, 1978. Fellow AAAS, Am. Statis. Assn. (mem. biometrics sect. com. 1989-90, mem. com. on internat. rels. in stats. 1996—), Am. Soc. Agronomy, Soil Sci. Soc. Am.; mem. Statis. Assn. Thailand (life), Internat. Biometric Soc. (bus. mgr. and treas. 1969-79, awards com. 1987-94, chmn. 1990-93), Sigma Xi, Gamma Sigma Delta (internat. pres. 1984-86, award of merit 1973-74, rep. to AAAS 1978-86), Phi Kappa Phi. Baptist. Avocations: music, genealogy, diving, bicycling, travel. Home: 1422 Banbury Rd Raleigh NC 27607-3711 Office: NC State U Dept Stats Box 8203 Raleigh NC 27695-8203

NELSON, LARRY DEAN, telecommunications and computer systems company executive, consultant; b. Newton, Kans., Aug. 5, 1937; s. Carl Aaron and Leta V. (Van Eaton) N.; m. Linda Hawkins, June 2, 1972. BA, Phillips U., 1959; MS, Kans. State U., 1962; PhD, Ohio State U., 1965. From rsch. asst. to rsch. assoc. Rsch. Found., Ohio State U., Columbus, 1962-65; mathematician II, Batelle Meml. Inst., Columbus, 1962-65; from mem. tech. staff to supr. math. dept. and data systems devel. Bellcomm, Inc., Washington, 1965-72; supr. mgmt. info. systems dept. Bell Telephone Labs., Murray Hill, N.J., 1972-77; supr. rate and tariff planning div. AT&T, N.Y.C., 1977-79; dep. adminstr. rsch. and spl. programs adminstrn. U.S. Dept. Transp., Washington, 1979-81; pres. MCS, Inc., Washington, 1981—; supr. govt. communications ctr. AT&T Bell Labs., 1985-89; mgr. govt. mktg. AT&T Network Systems, 1989-90; supr. secure info. system engrng. AT&T Bell Labs., 1990-94; disting. mem. tech. staff, secure systems engring., 1995-96; tech. cons. spl. accounts Info. Security Ctr., AT&T, 1996—; cons. Contel Info. Systems, Denver, 1982-85, Martin Marietta Corp., Denver, 1982-85; mem. info. assurance task force Nat. Security Telecomms. Advisory Com. Contbr. articles to profl. jours. Organizer, sponsor Odd Jobs Club, Washington, 1967-72; pres. Mountain County Condominiums Assn., Dillon, Colo., 1975-83, 85—; treas. Chris' Landing Condominium Assn., 1986-90; mem. Am. del. 5th Meeting of U.S.-USSR Joint Commn. on Cooperation in Field of Transp., Moscow, 1979; head Am. del. 5th Meeting of U.S.-USSR Working Group on Transport of Future, Moscow, 1979. Mem. ABA (assoc., info. security com.), Am. Nat. Stds. Inst. (info. tech. security tech. stds. com.), IEEE (sec. D.C. sect. 1982, cert. appreciation 1968), Systems, Man and Cybernetics Soc. (sec. 1981, v.p. 1982-83), Math. Programming Soc., Am. Math. Soc., N.Y. Acad. Scis., Assn. Computing Machinery, Sigma Xi, Phi Kappa Phi, Pi Mu Epsilon. Democrat. Mem. Disciples of Christ. Current work: requirements definition, analysis, design and development of secure information movement and management systems, networks and network management, digital signature, public key infrastructure, and electronic commerce technology. Subspecialties: secure distributed systems and networks; Systems engineering. Office: AT&T 2020 K St NW Ste 550 Washington DC 20006-1806

NELSON, LARRY KEITH, document investigation laboratory executive; b. Frederick, Okla., Feb. 26, 1948; s. Bernard Leroy and Una Lee (Greeson) N.; m. Barbara Sue Stout, Feb. 26, 1972; children: Shawn Keith, Jeffery Ryan. BS in Forestry, Okla. State U., 1972; MSBA, Boston U., 1986. Diplomate Am. Bd. Forensic Document Examiners (bd. dirs.); cert. fraud examiner. Apptd. warrant officer 1 U.S. Army, 1975, advanced through grades to chief warrant officer 4, 1992; criminal investigator U.S. Army Criminal Investigation Divsn., Ft. Riley, Kans., 1975-78; questioned document student U.S. Army Criminal Investigation Lab., Ft. Gordon, Ga., 1978-80, questioned document examiner, 1980-82; questioned document examiner U.S. Army Criminal Investigation Lab., Frankfurt, Germany, 1982-83, chief questioned document divsn., 1983-86; questioned document tng. officer U.S. Army Criminal Investigation Lab., Ft. Gillem, Ga., 1986-91, chief questioned document divsn., 1991-93; v.p. Carney & Nelson Forensic Document Lab. Inc., Norcross, Ga., 1993-94; pres. Nelson Document Investigation Lab., Inc., Stone Mountain, Ga., 1994—. Contbr. articles to profl. jours. Fellow Am. Acad. Forensic Scis.; mem. Southea. Assn. Forensic Document Examiners (charter, treas. 1988-91, sec. 1991-93, pres. 1993-95). Office: Nelson Document Inv Lab Inc 620 Waterview Ct Stone Mountain GA 30088-1721

NELSON, LARS-ERIK, newspaperman; b. N.Y.C., Oct. 15, 1941; s. Arthur and Freda (Rappaport) N.; m. Mary Elizabeth Cantwell, Dec. 28, 1963; children—Peter, Amanda. A.B., Columbia U., 1964. Editorial asst. N.Y. Herald Tribune, N.Y.C., 1959-63; Russian translator Current Digest, N.Y.C., 1963-64; rewriteman The Record, Hackensack, N.J., 1965-66; corr. Reuters, London, Moscow, Prague and Washington, 1966-77, Newsweek, Washington, 1977-79; corr. N.Y. Daily News, Washington, 1979—, bur. chief, 1981-93; columnist Newsday, Washington, 1993-95, N.Y. Daily News, Washington, 1995—. Mem. State Dept. Corrs. Assn. (pres. 1978-79), Overseas Writers, White Ho. Corrs. Assn. (Merriman Smith award 1980), Gridiron Club (Washington). Office: NY Daily News 1615 M St NW Washington DC 20036-3209

NELSON, LAWRENCE EVAN, business consultant; b. Chgo., Dec. 3, 1932; s. Evan Thomas and Elizabeth Marie (Stettka) N.; m. Jean H. Clayton, July 11, 1953; children: Lori Jean, Lawrence Evan. BS with honors, So. Ill. U., 1959; MBA, U. Chgo., 1969. CPA, Ill. Sr. acct. Price Waterhouse & Co., CPA's, Chgo., 1959-65; sec.-treas. Bradner Cen. Co., Chgo., 1965-73; pres. Protectoseal Co., Bensenville, Ill., 1973-84, Plan Ahead Inc., Palos Park, Ill, 1984—. Author: (book) Personal Financial Planning, 1985. Treas. City of Palos Heights, Ill., 1964-68, alderman, 1970-71; trustee Palos Heights FPD, 1977—. Served with USNR, 1952-56. Mem. Am. Inst. CPA's, Ill. Soc. CPA's. Office: Plan Ahead Inc PO Box 164 Palos Park IL 60464-0164

NELSON, LINDA SHEARER, child development and family relations educator; b. New Kensington, Pa., Dec. 8, 1944; d. Walter M. and Jean M. (Black) Shearer; m. Alan Edward Nelson, Dec. 29, 1973; children: Amelia (Amy), Emily. BS in Home Econs. Edn., Pa. State U., 1966; MS in Child Devel. and Family Rels., Cornell U., 1968; PhD in Higher Edn. and Child Devel., U. Pitts., 1982. Head tchr.-lab. nursery sch. Dept. of Psychology, Vassar Coll., Poughkeepsie, N.Y., 1968-69; instr. child devel. dept. home econs. edn. Indiana U. Pa., 1969-72, asst. prof., 1972-77, assoc. prof., 1977-84, prof. child devel. and family rels., 1984—, dept. chair, 1991-93, prof. child devel. and family rels., human devel. and family environ. studies dept., 1993—, mem. values task force, strategic planning com., 1995-96; mem. refocusing II com. Indiana U. Pa., 1994-95, strategic planning com. mem., 1995—, values task force, 1995-96; ind. cons., trainer Head Start Programs, Pa., 1970—, Child Care Programs and Agys., Pa., 1970—; child devel. assoc. rep. Coun. for Early Childhood Profl. Recognition, Washington, 1989-91; field rep. Keyston U. Rsch. Corp., Erie, 1990-91; keynote/guest spkr. child devel./child care and home econs. confs., Pa. and nat., 1985—. Mem. adv. bd. Early Childhood Edn., Annual Edits., 1985—; mem. adv. bd. Interface: Home Economics and Technology Newsletter, 1993-96; contbr. articles to profl. jours. Bd. dirs. Indiana County Child Care Program, 1970-92; guest spkr. Delta Kappa Gamma, Indiana, 1990, Bus. and Profl. Women, Indiana, 1991, IUP's The Marriage Project, 1996. Grantee in field, 1985—. Mem. AAUW (guest spkr. 1996), Nat. Assn. for Edn. Young Children, Pitts. Assn. for Edn. Young Children (conf. co-chair 1983-85, in-svc. tng. spkr. 1995), Assn. Pa. State Coll. and Univ. Faculties, Kappa Omicron Nu. Democrat. Presbyterian. Avocations: photography, reading, Chautauqua Instn. programs. Office: Indiana U of Pa Human Devel and Environ Studies Dept 207 Ackerman Hall Indiana PA 15705

NELSON, LLOYD STEADMAN, statistics consultant; b. Norwich, Conn., Mar. 29, 1922; s. Ronald Richbourg and Marion Shapley (Rogers) N.; m. Almeda Christine Ponder, Feb. 21, 1947; children: Peter Reid, Fay Hulett-Nelson, Barbara Nelson Ramey; m. Frances Betty Pallant, Mar. 13, 1982. BS, U. N.C., 1943; PhD, U. Conn., 1950. Registered profl. engr., Calif. Instr. physics U. Conn., Storrs, 1943-44; instr. chemistry Ill. Inst. Tech., Chgo., 1949-51; research chemist Gen. Electric Co., Waterford, N.Y., 1951-53; research assoc. Gen. Electric Research Lab., Schenectady, N.Y., 1953-56; cons. statistician Gen. Electric Lamp Div., Cleve., 1956-68; lectr. in math. Case Inst. Tech., Cleve., 1963-64; mgr. applied math. lab. Gen. Electric Major Appliance Group, Louisville, 1968-80; dir. statis. methods Nashua (N.H.) Corp., 1980-92; pvt. practice statis. cons., 1992—. Editor: Indsl. Quality Control, 1966-68; founding editor: Jour. Quality Tech., 1969-71; contbr. over 100 articles to sci. jours. Served with USN, 1944-46. Fellow AAAS, Am. Soc. Quality Control (Shewhart medal, 1978, Deming medal 1985), Am. Statis. Assn. (outstanding statistician of yr. award 1983). Home: 17 Jefferson Dr Londonderry NH 03053-3647

NELSON, LYLE MORGAN, communications educator; b. Yamhill, Oreg., Feb. 28, 1918; s. Guy Calvin and Bessie Alzine (Morgan) N.; m. Corrine Marlis Wignes, Oct. 2, 1941; children: Gayle Kathryn, Judith Lee. AB, U. Oreg., 1941; LHD (hon.), Linfield (Oreg.) Coll., 1981; Dr. honoris causa, U. Autónoma de Guadalajara, Mex., 1981. Acting dir. Univ. News Service, U. Oreg., 1941-43, asst. to pres., asso. prof. journalism, 1947-53; with U.S. Army Ordnance Dept., 1943-45; asst. regional info. officer Bur. Reclamation, Boise, Idaho, 1945-47; asst. to pres., sec. bd. dirs. Ednl. TV and Radio Center, Ann Arbor, Mich., 1953-55; asst. to pres., prof. communications San Francisco State Coll., 1955-57; v.p., prof. journalism U. Mich., 1957-60, v.p., 1960-62; dir. univ. relations Stanford, 1962-72, prof. communications, chmn. dept., 1968-78, dir. John S. Knight profl. journalism fellow program, 1972-86, Thomas M. Storke distinguished prof. emeritus, 1986—; hon. prof. journalism Autonomous U. Guadalajara; cons. edn. Ford Found., 1962-63, 65, Meyer Meml. Trust, 1982—; acad. cons. Xiamen U. Author: (with W. Schramm) Financing of Public Television, Bold Experiment: The Impact of Television on American Samoa; Editor: (with Dan Lerner) Communication Research: A Half Century Appraisal. Exec. dir. White House Conf. Edn., 1965; spl. cons. U.S. Commr. Edn., 1963, 67-70; cons. USIA, 1966-69; cons. higher edn. master plans, Ohio, N.Y., Kans.; mem. Greenbrier Conf. Higher Edn., 1958, U.S. ednl. del. to USSR, 1959; UNESCO ednl. TV Study Team; chmn. UNDP/UNESCO team to Evaluate TV Tng. in India, 1973; 1st vice chmn., bd. govs. Nature Conservancy, 1972-74; chmn. bd. fgn. scholarships State Dept., 1973-76; chmn. bd. trustees Alliance for Devel. of Latin Am. Higher Edn., 1974-79; trustee Hewlett Found., 1975-94. Recipient award for disting. svc. to higher edn. Am. Coll. Pub. Rels. Assn., 1953, 66, award for exceptional svc. to Stanford U., 1984, Disting. Svc. award U. Oreg., 1994; sr. Fulbright scholar, Australia, New Zealand, 1978. Mem. Am. Coll. Pub. Rels. Assn. (bd. dirs. 1956-65, pres. 1959-60), Bohemian Club (San Francisco), Lamplighters Club, Phi Kappa Phi, Sigma Delta Chi, Sigma Chi. Clubs: Bohemian (San Francisco); Lamplighters. Home: 732 San Rafael Pl Stanford CA 94305-1007

NELSON, MARGUERITE HANSEN, special education educator; b. S.I., N.Y., June 23, 1947; d. Arthur Clayton and Marguerite Mary (Hansen) Nelson. AB magna cum laude, Boston Coll., 1969; MS in Edn., SUNY, Plattsburgh, 1973; post master's cert. in gerontology, Yeshiva U., 1982; PhD, Fordham U., N.Y.C., 1995. Cert. elem. and spl. edn. tchr., N.Y. Preprimary tchr. Pub. Sch. 22R S.I., N.Y.C. Bd. Edn., 1969-70; primary tchr. Oak Street Sch., Plattsburgh, N.Y., 1971-73, Laurel Plains Sch., Clarkstown Cen. Schs., New City, N.Y., 1973-78, Resource Rm. Lakewood Sch., Congers, N.Y., 1978—; mem. adj. faculty St. Thomas Aquinas Coll., Sparkill, N.Y., 1985-89, 95—, Fordham U., Lincoln Ctr., N.Y.C., 1990; presenter in field internat. and nat. confs., seminars. Author: Teacher Stories, 1993,

Research on Teacher Thinking, 1993; contbr. articles to profl. jours. and textbooks. Recipient Impact II Tchr. Recognition award, 1984; grantee Chpt. II, 1983-84, Clarkstown Ctrl. Schs., 1986-91, Office of Spl. Edn., 1992, 95. Mem. AAUW, Am. Ednl. Rsch. Assn., Assn. for Children with Learning Disabilities, N.Y. State Congress of Parents and Tchrs. (hon. life), Assn. for Retarded Citizens. Avocations: reading, poetry, ballet, gardening, flower arranging. Home: PO Box 395 Valley Cottage NY 10989 Office: Lakewood Elem Sch 77 Lakeland Ave Congers NY 10920-1733

NELSON, MARK BRUCE, interior designer; b. Los Angeles, Dec. 8, 1921; s. Mark Bruce and Rubie (Henrionnet) N. B.A. in Art, U. Calif., Los Angeles, 1943, postgrad., 1949-50; postgrad., Art Center Sch., Los Angeles, 1946-49. Tchr. Pasadena (Calif.) City Coll., 1950-54; propr. Mark Nelson Interiors, Los Angeles, 1954—; designer DuPont Corp. exhibit N.Y. World's Fair, 1964; co-chmn. Los Angeles show com. Am. Inst. Interior Designers, 1960-67, Living with Famous Paintings, 1964-65; Mem. Los Angeles adv. council Am. Arbitration Assn., 1971-72; chmn. Los Angeles N.C.I.D.Q., 1973-80, Design House West, 1978. Mem. Los Angeles Beautiful Com., 1966. Served as officer USNR, 1942-46, 52-53, ETO, Korea. Fellow Am. Soc. Interior Designers (life mem., exam. chmn. 1972—, chmn. nat. by-laws com. 1973, pres. Los Angeles 1969-71, Calif. regional v.p. 1970-73, pres. Los Angeles found. 1980, Presdl. citation 1973); mem. Phi Kappa Sigma. Home and Office: 554 Lillian Way Los Angeles CA 90004-1106 *During my thirty years as a interior designer, I have enjoyed many successes, while watching the profession grow and improve. Designing the homes of rich and famous Americans has not altered my concept that it is the middle class American consumer who needs and can afford the services of professional designers.*

NELSON, MARLOW GENE, agricultural studies educator; b. Powers Lake, N.D., Aug. 16, 1946; s. Elmer Richard and Beulah Joanne (Johnson) N.; m. Joyce Marlys Dilland, June 14, 1970; children: Paul Richard, Mark Jerrod, Aaron Brent. BS in Agrl. Edn., N.D. State U., 1968. Cert. tchr., N.D. Tchr. Tioga (N.D.) High Sch., 1968-72, 1990—, Carrington (N.D) High Sch., 1972-74; owner farm Battleview, N.D., 1974—; tchr. Stanley (N.D.) High Sch., 1974-87; pres. Burke County Weed Control, Bowbells, N.D., 1988-90. Leader 4-H Burke County, N.D., 1986-90; deacon Bethel Baptist Ch., Powers Lake, N.D., tchr. Sunday sch. Mem. N.D. Vocat. Agrl. Tchrs. Assn. (dist. v.p. 1971-72), N.D. Stockmen's Assn., N.D. Charolais Assn., N.D. Farmers Union (bd. dirs. 1989—), Burke County Farmers Union (pres. 1992—), Burke County Agrl. Improvement Assn. (bd. dirs. 1985-89, Outstanding Agriculturist award 1990, Burke County Soil Conservationist of Yr. 1993). Democrat. Avocation: hunting. Home: HC 1 Box 122 Powers Lake ND 58773-9439 Office: Tioga High Sch 303 N Linda St Tioga ND 58852

NELSON, MARTHA JANE, magazine editor; b. Pierre, S.D., Aug. 13, 1952; d. Bernard Anton and Pauline Isabel (Noren) N. BA, Barnard Coll., 1976. Mng. editor Signs: Jour. of Women in Culture, N.Y.C., 1976-80; staff editor Ms. Mag., N.Y.C., 1980-85; editor-in-chief Women's Sports and Fitness Mag., Palo Alto, Calif., 1985-87; exec. editor Savvy, N.Y.C., 1988-89, editor-in-chief, 1989-91; asst. mng. editor People, 1993; editor In Style Mag., N.Y.C., 1993-97; exec. prodr. TV program Celebrity Weddin In Style, 1997—. Editor: Women in the American City, 1980; cons. editor Who Weekly, Sydney, 1992; contbr. articles to profl. publs. Bd. dirs. Painting Space 122, N.Y.C., 1982-85, 95-96, Urban Athletic Assn. Mem. Am. Soc. Mag. Editors, Women in Film.

NELSON, MARVIN BERNARD, financial executive; b. N.Y.C., Jan. 2, 1931; s. Nathan and Bessie Nelson; m. Reasha Mary Kagan, Mar. 21, 1959; children: Alyson, Bradley. BS in Acctg., Long Island U., 1954, MBA, 1958. Cert. fin. planner. Contr. New Am. Libr., Inc., N.Y.C., 1960-65; treas. Ziff Davis Pub. Co., Inc., Teaneck, N.J., 1965-68; dir acquisitions and planning New Eng. Industries, Inc., N.Y.C., 1968-69; v.p. Babbage Systems, Inc., N.Y.C., 1969-75; v.p. adminstrn. Action Computer, Inc., N.Y.C., 1978-82; pres. Global, Inc., N.Y.C., 1976-83; exec. v.p., CFO Alliance for Health, Inc., N.Y.C., 1983—; bd. dirs. Vis. Home Health Svc., Hackensack, N.J. Sgt. U.S. Army, 1951-53, Europe. Mem. Inst. Cert. Fin. Planners, Nat. Assn. Accts., Am. Mgmt. Assn. Avocations: golf, hiking, travel. Office: 6143 Jericho Tpke Commack NY 11725-2809

NELSON, MARVIN RAY, retired life insurance company executive; b. Thornton, Iowa, Aug. 29, 1926; s. Clarence Anton and Rose Bessie (Nicolet) N.; m. Juanita Mae Brown, May 26, 1951; children: Nancy, Kenneth. BS, Drake U, 1951. Actuary Security Mut. Life Ins. Co., Lincoln, Nebr., 1951-58; assoc. actuary Life Ins. Co. N.Am., Phila., 1958-59; group actuary Bankers Life of Nebr., Lincoln, 1959-66; actuary Mut. Service Life Ins. Co., St. Paul, 1966-68; sr. v.p. Horace Mann Educators Corp., Springfield, Ill., 1968-77; sr. v.p. Security Life of Denver, 1977-83, exec. v.p., 1988-91; pres., chief oper. officer, dir., mem. investment com. Midwestern United Life Ins. Co., Ft. Wayne, Ind., 1983-89; ret., 1991. Bd. dirs., treas. Ft. Wayne Urban League, 1983-87; bd. dirs. Taxpayers Research Assn., Ft. Wayne, 1984-88. Served with U.S. Army, 1946-47. Fellow Soc. Actuaries; mem. Am. Acad. Actuaries, Pi Kappa Phi. Home: 7636 E Windford St Parker CO 80134-5927

NELSON, MARY BERTHA, public relations executive; b. Mpls., Aug. 26, 1921; d. Charles and Edna Eva (Wrabek) Ring; m. Roger Anton Nelson, Jan. 4, 1941 (dec. 1981); children: Barbara Leigh, Judith Ann, Ward Anton. BA in Pub. Rels. and Journalism, Columbia Pacific U., 1983, MA, 1984. Reporter East Mpls. Argus, 1949-57, Southtown Economist, Oak Lawn, Ill., 1958-59; columnist-reporter S.W. Messenger Press, Midlothian, Ill., 1959-68; pub. info. dir. Moraine Valley Coll., Palos Hills, Ill., 1968-82; pub. rels. officer Oak Lawn Pub. Libr., 1982-91; owner, pres. Promoplans, Evergreen Park, Ill., 1991—. Contbr. articles to profl. jours. Bd. dirs. Family/Mental Health Svcs., Worth, Ill., 1968-80, Children's Craniofacial Assn., Dallas, 1994-96; exec. dir. Ch. Coun., Chgo., 1982-92; trustee Ednl. Found., Oak Lawn, 1993—, Cmty. Libr. Found., Oak Lawn, 1993—. Mem. South Suburban Programmers, Publicity Club Chgo., Cmty. Coll. Annuitants, Oak Lawn C. of C. (bd. dirs. 1984—). Lutheran. Avocations: reading, overseas travel, crocheting, power walking. Office: Promoplans 9940 S Spaulding Ave Evergreen Park IL 60805-3441

NELSON, MERLIN EDWARD, international business consultant, company director; b. Fargo, N.D., Jan. 30, 1922; s. Theodore G. and Eva C. (Hultgren) N.; m. Nancy Ellen Craig, June 1952 (div. June 1962); children: Craig Edward, Brian Anthony; m. Janet April Pope, Aug. 30, 1963; children: Claudia Jane, Rolf Merlin. BS in Polit. Sci., U. Oreg., 1943; postgrad., Fordham U., 1943-44; JD, Yale U., 1948. Bar: Oreg. 1948, N.Y. 1954, U.S. Dist. Ct. D.C. 1954. Atty. Office Gen. Counsel, ECA, Washington and Paris, 1949-52; assoc. Davis, Polk, Wardwell, Sunderland & Kiendl, 1952-59; exec. asst. to v.p. AMF, Inc., N.Y.C., 1960-62; chmn., mng. dir. AMF Internat., Ltd., London, 1962-63; v.p., group exec. AMF, Inc., 1963-70, exec. v.p., vice chmn., dir., 1970-84, now cons., 1984—; ret., 1984; bd. dirs. Indsl. Bank Japan Trust Co., Derby Internat. Corp., S.A., Exeter Internat. Corp., S.A., Mitsui Found.; chmn. IBJ Found.; chmn. nat. adv. coun. Trust for Pub. Land; chmn. Econ. Literacy Project, Ltd. Mem. Coun. Fgn. Rels., Overseas Devel. Coun., Avon Internat. Adv. Coun. Decorated Purple Heart. Mem. Phi Beta Kappa. Home and Office: 16 W 77th St # 12E New York NY 10024-5126

NELSON, MICHAEL UNDERHILL, association executive; b. Balt., May 5, 1932; s. Cyril Arthur and Elise (Macy) N.; m. Barbara Gail Hutchins, June 25, 1960; children: Kevin Underhill, Bronwyn Hastings, Gayle Hutchins, Corey Williams. AB, Rutgers U., 1957, EdM, 1968. Salesman J & N Distbg. Co., New Brunswick, N.J., 1957-59; extension assoc. Univ. Coll., Rutgers U., New Brunswick, 1959-61; asst. dir. summer session Rutgers U., 1961-68; asst. dean sch. continuing edn., dir. summer sch. Washington U., St. Louis, 1969-81, dir. div. of profl. and community programs sch. continuing edn., 1975-78; exec. sec. N.Am. Assn. Summer Sessions, 1979—; account exec. Trio Printing Co., 1982-84; sr. procedures analyst McDonnell Douglas Corp, St. Louis, 1984-96. Bd. dirs. Adult Edn. Council of Greater St. Louis, 1975-78. Served with USMC, 1951-54. Mem. North Ctrl. Conf. Summer Schs. (pres. 1974-75), Am. Assn. Univ. Adminstrs., Assn. Univ. Summer Sessions, Am. Summer Sessions Senate, N.Am. Assn. Summer Sessions (pres. 1978), Alpha Sigma Lambda, Phi Delta Kappa. Episcopalian. Home and Office: 43 Belanger Dr Dover NH 03820

NELSON, NANCY ELEANOR, pediatrician, educator; b. El Paso, Apr. 4, 1933; d. Harry Hamilton and Helen Maude (Murphy) N. BA magna cum laude, U. Colo., 1955, MD, 1959. Intern, Case Western Res. U. Hosp., 1959-60, resident, 1960-63; pvt. practice medicine specializing in pediats., Denver, 1963-70; clin. prof. U. Colo. Sch. Medicine, Denver, 1988—, assoc. dean, 1988—. Mem. Am. Acad. Pediats., AMA (sect. med. schs. governing coun. 1994-96), Denver Med. Soc. (pres. 1983-84), Colo. Med. Soc. (bd. dirs. 1985-88, mem. jud. coun. 1992—, mem. liason com. med. edn. 1995—). Home: 1140 Columbine St # 406 Denver CO 80206 Office: 4200 E 9th Ave Denver CO 80220-3706

NELSON, NEVIN MARY, interior designer; b. Cleve., Nov. 5, 1941; d. Arthur George Reinker and Barbara Phyllis (Gunn) Parks; m. Wayne Nelson (div. 1969); children: Doug, Brian. BA in Interior Design, U. Colo., 1964. Prin. Nevin Nelson Design, Boulder, Colo., 1966-70, Vail, Colo., 1970—; program chmn. Questers Antique Study Group, Boulder, 1969. Coord. Bob Kirscht for Gov. campaign, Eagle County, Colo., 1986; state del. Rep. Nat. Conv., 1986-88; county coord. George Bush for U.S. Pres. campaign, 1988, 92; chmn. Eagle County Reps., 1989-93; v.p. bd. dirs. Park Lane Condo Assn., Denver, 1995-96. Mem. Am. Soc. Interior Designers. Episcopalian. Avocations: party planning, cooking, reading, travel, skiing. Home: PO Box 1212 Vail CO 81658-1212 Office: 2498 Arosa Dr Vail CO 81657-4276

NELSON, NORMA RANDY DEKADT, psychotherapist, consultant; b. Irvington, N.J., Nov. 10, 1930; d. Ralph Joseph and Irma Marie (Richardson) Miele; m. Pieter Pim deKadt, Sept. 15, 1956 (div. 1984); children: Sharon, David, John; m. Ronald Prescott Nelson, July 27, 1985. BS, Northwestern U., Evanston, Ill., 1953; MS, Bridgeport U., 1974; cert. therapist, Found. Religion & Mental Heath, 1980; M in Neuro Linguistics, U. Calif., Santa Cruz, 1996. Pers. trainer B. Altman & Co., N.Y.C., 1953-54, asst. to merchandise mgr., 1954-55; dir. promotion Operation Home Improvement U.S. C of C and Time Inc., N.Y.C., 1955-57; counselor Stamford Counseling Ctr., Conn., 1975-80; trainer cons. N.Y.C., 1980-95; psychotherapist, cons. Stamford (Conn.) Counseling Ctr., 1976-82; pvt. practice Old Greenwich, Conn., 1980—; condr. positive parenting programs; keynote spkr. on raising self-esteem, development of motiviation, personal and spirit in the work place; seminar leader personality profile styles and teamwork, work and family life, motivation and mental attitude, Open to Spirit seminars; founder, pres. Positive Parenting Program, Ctr. Well-Being, 1995; founder Family Re-entry Fathers Helping Fathers Program, 1995. Author: Magic of Attitude, 1995; contbr. articles to profl. jours. Pres. Old Greenwich (Conn.) Riverside Community Ctr., 1960; bd. dirs. YWCA, Greenwich, 1968-76, Greenwich Women's Club, Parents Together, Greenwich, 1980-86; chmn. Women Together, Christ Ch., Greenwich, 1989-90; speaker PTAs, Greenwich, 1980-95; vol. Jr. League, 1956-75. Recipient Environ. Beautification award Old Greenwich, Conn., 1975. Mem. Assn. Carlton Learning Systems, Capr. Assn. Bus. Orgn. Colls., Transactional Analysis Assn., Trains Values Realization Inst., Kripalu Cons. Collaborative. Episcopalian. Avocations: teaching meditation and yoga, skiing, art, painting, tennis. Home and Office: 8 Middle Way Old Greenwich CT 06870-2405

NELSON, NORMAN DANIEL, government official; b. Dec. 30, 1968. BSBA, U. Fla., 1991; MBA, U. Miami, 1997. Intern internat. trade and commerce dept. ctrl. Europe office Fla. Dept. Commerce, Frankfurt, Germany, 1992; intern corp. fin. divsn. mergers and acquisitions Commerzbank AG, Frankfurt, 1992; intern corp. fin. divsn. internat. leasing and new stock issues Deutsche Bank AG, Frankfurt, 1992; commd. 2d lt. disting. mil. grad. USAR, 1991; advanced through grades to capt. U.S. Army, 1995; platoon leader 44th engr. bn., 2d inf. divsn. U.S. Army, Republic of South Korea, 1993-94; exec. officer 497th Port Constrn. Engr. Co., Ft. Eustis, Va., 1994-95; intel/ security officer 841st engr. bn. USAR, 1996-97; grad. asst. Toppel Career Planning and Placement Ctr., 1996-97—; plans & program officer U.S. Dept. of State, 1997—. Decorated 2 Army Commendation medals, Army Achievement medal; scholar Army ROTC, 1987-91, Acad. scholar State Fla., 1987-91, Fed. Chancellor scholar Alexander-von-Humboldt Found., 1991-92. Mem. Masons, Phi Kappa Phi, Sigma Chi.

NELSON, OLIVER EVANS, JR., geneticist, educator; b. Seattle, Aug. 16, 1920; s. Oliver Evans and Mary Isabella (Grant) N.; m. Gerda Kjer Hansen, Mar. 28, 1963. A.B., Colgate U., 1941; M.S., Yale, 1943, Ph.D., 1947. Asst. prof. genetics Purdue U., 1947-49, assoc. prof., 1949-54, prof., 1954-69; prof. genetics U. Wis., Madison, 1969—, Brink prof. genetics, 1982-91, Brink prof. emeritus, 1991—, chmn. Lab. of Genetics, 1986-89; vis. investigator Biochem. Inst., U. Stockholm and Nat. Forest Research Inst., Stockholm, 1954-55; NSF, sr. postdoctoral fellow Calif. Inst. Tech., Pasadena, 1961-62. Contbr. articles on controlling elements, genes affecting starch synthesis and genes affecting storage protein synthesis to profl. publs. Recipient John Scott medal City of Phila., 1967; Hoblitzelle award Tex. Research Found., 1968; Browning award Am. Soc. Agronomy, 1974; Donald F. Jones medal Conn. Agrl. Exptl. Sta., 1976. Mem. NAS, AAAS, Am. Acad. Arts and Scis., Genetics Soc. Am., Am. Soc. Plant Physiologists (Stephen Hales award, 1988). Home: Apt 325 325 S Yellowstone Dr Madison WI 53705-4355 Office: U Wis Lab Genetics Madison WI 53706

NELSON, PAUL DOUGLAS, lawyer; b. Silverton, Oreg., Dec. 22, 1948; s. Robert Thorsen and Elene N.; m. Mary Linda Hilligoss, Feb. 28, 1981; children: Christopher R., Matthew D., Patrick D. BA cum laude, Lewis and Clark Coll., 1971; JD, U. Oreg., 1974. Bar: Calif. 1974, Oreg. 1975, U.S. Dist. (no., ca. and cen. dists.) 1975. Law clk. U.S. atty.'s office U.S. Dist. Ct. Oreg., Portland, 1973; assoc. Hoge, Fenton, Jones & Appel, San Jose, 1974-75; ptnr. Hancock, Rothert & Bunshoft, San Francisco and London, 1975—. Nat. Presbyn. scholar Lewis and Clark Coll., Portland, 1967, Oreg. Trial Lawyers scholar U. Oreg., 1973. Mem. ABA, San Francisco Bar Assn., San Francisco Lawyers Club, Am. Law Firm Assn., Assn. Ski Def. Attys., Internat. Amusement and Leisure Def. Assn., Assn. Internat. de Droit des Assurance, Lewis & Clark Coll. Alumni Assn. (bd. dirs.). Avocations: skiing, sailing. Office: Hancock Rothert & Bunshoft 4 Embarcadero Ctr San Francisco CA 94111-4106

NELSON, PAUL WILLIAM, real estate broker; b. Mpls., Mar. 7, 1952; s. William H. and Jean (Darrington) N.; m. Jill Brownson, Oct. 18, 1986 (dec. Nov. 1990); 1 child, Emily J.; m. Robin K. Carpenter, Aug. 14, 1993. BS, U. Colo., 1974. Lic. real estate broker, Colo. Advt. dir. Denver Beechcraft, 1976-77; real estate broker Coldwell Banker, Grand Junction, Colo., 1977—; bd. dirs. Colo. Assn. Realtors, Denver, 1981-83. Mem. Grand Junction City Coun., 1985-93, also mayor pro tem; mem. Downtown Devel. Authority, Grand Junction, 1985-91; bd. dirs. Mesa County Planning Commn., Grand Junction, 1980-85, Colo. Nat. Monument Assn., 1989-91, Grand Junction Visitors and Conv. Bur., 1993-96; Lobbying Group; mem. Mesa County Uranium Mill Tailings Removal Citizens Com.; mem. co-chmn. Mesa County Riverfront Commn.; mem. dist. resource adv. coun. Bur. Land Mgmt., 1990-92, Grand Junction Visitors and Conv. Bur. bd. dirs., 1992-96. Recipient Citizen Svc. award Mesa County, 1985. Mem. Mesa County Assn. Realtors (bd. dirs. 1981-83), Rotary, Club 20 (bd. dirs. 1994-96). Republican. Avocations: pvt. pilot, skiing. Office: Coldwell Banker PO Box 3117 Grand Junction CO 81502-3117

NELSON, PHILIP EDWIN, food scientist, educator; b. Shelbyville, Ind., Nov. 12, 1934; s. Brainard R. and Alta E. (Pitts) N.; m. Sue Bayless, Dec. 27, 1955; children: Jennifer, Andrew, Bradley. BS, Purdue U., 1956, PhD, 1976. Plant mgr. Blue River Packing Co., Morristown, Ind., 1956-60; instr. Purdue U., West Lafayette, Ind., 1961-76, head dept. food sci., 1984—; cons. PEN Cons., West Lafayette, 1974; chair Food Processors Inst., Washington, 1990-93. Editor: Fruit Vegetable Juice Technology, 1980, Principles of Aseptic Processing and Packaging, 1992. Fellow Inst. Food Techs. (Indsl. Achievement award 1976, Nicholas Appert award 1995, 49'er Svc. award 1995); mem. AAAS, Sigma Xi, Phi Tau Sigma (pres. 1976-77). Achievements include 11 U.S. and foreign patents. Office: Purdue U Dept Food Sci 1160 Smith Hall West Lafayette IN 47907-1160

NELSON, PHILIP FRANCIS, musicology educator, consultant, choral conductor; b. Waseca, Minn., Feb. 17, 1928; s. Elmer Philip and Frances (Bretzke) N.; m. Georgia Ann Yelland, June 5, 1950; children: Curtis Ann, Philip Francis Jr. AB, Grinnell Coll., 1950; AM, U. N.C., 1956, PhD, 1958; Diplome (Fulbright scholar), U. Paris, 1957; student, Conservatoire Nat. de Paris, 1956-57; MA (hon.), Yale U., 1971; LHD (hon.), Grinnell Coll., 1981. Asst. prof. Ariz. State U., 1958-62, assoc. prof., 1962-63; prof., chmn. dept. music SUNY, Binghamton, 1963-70; prof., dean Sch. Music, Yale U., 1970-81; prof., provost, dean U. Calif., Santa Cruz, 1981-83; chmn. trustee com. Curtis Inst., 1982-83; sr. v.p. AED, N.Y.C., 1984-87; v.p. Aspen Inst. for Humanistic Studies, 1987-89; interim chancellor Sch. Arts, U. N.C., 1989-90; assoc. fellow Nat. Humanities Ctr., 1990-91; interim vice chancellor U. N.C., Chapel Hill, 1991; cons. edn., arts, 1992-93; chmn. grad. sch. adv. coun. U. N.C., Chapel Hill, 1993-96, cons. arts and humanities, 1996—; music critic Phoenix Gazette, 1959-62; music cons. Taliesin West, 1959-63; chmn. Nat. Screening Com. for Fulbright Awards in Musicology, 1965-68; cons. Nat. Endowment for Arts, 1984—. Contbg. editor: College and Adult Reading List, 1962, Nicolas Bernier, Principles of Composition, 1964, Recherches sur la musique Française classique, 1979, 80; contbr. to Groves Dictionary of Music, 6th edit.; editor publs. in the arts for The Aspen Inst. for the Humanities, 1987-89. Bd. dirs. various symphonies, chamber music socs., arts groups; trustee Curtis Inst. Music, Phila., 1980-83; mem. exec. com. Conn. State Golf Assn., 1975-81; founder Seven Springs Soc., 1975; bd. dirs. Conn. Hospice, 1983-87, Nat. Soc. to Prevent Blindness, 1987-93; bd. dirs., v.p., 1987-93; mem. Chapel Hill Arts Ctr., 1992—; mem. Triangle J. Coun. Govt., 1992-95. Served from ensign to lt. comdr. USCGR, 1952-72. Found. grantee. Mem. Am., Internat. musicol. socs., Coll. Music Soc. (nat. council, editor jour. 1966-69), Société Française de Musicologie, Soc. Ethnomusicology, U.S. Srs. Golf Assn. Clubs: Mory's (New Haven); Yale (N.Y.C.); Elizabethan Grads., New Haven Country, Yale Golf, Finley Golf, Chapel Hill Country. Home: 621 Greenwood Rd Chapel Hill NC 27514-5921 *Keep casting bread on the waters-it may come back as French toast.*

NELSON, PRINCE ROGERS See PRINCE

NELSON, RALPH ALFRED, physician; b. Mpls., June 19, 1927; s. Alfred W. and Lydia (Johnson) N.; m. Rosemary Pokela, Aug. 7, 1954; children—Edward Ancher, Audrey Anne, Elizabeth Marie, Andrew William, Evan Robert. B.A., U. Minn., 1949, M.D., 1953, Ph.D., 1961. Diplomate Am. Bd. Internal Medicine. Intern Cook County (Ill.) Hosp., 1953-54; resident U. Minn. Hosps., Mpls., 1954-55, U. Minn., Mpls., 1955-56; fellow in physiology Mayo Grad. Sch., Rochester, Minn., 1957-60, resident in internal medicine, 1976-78; practice medicine specializing in internal medicine and clin. nutrition Sioux Falls, S.D., 1978-79, Urbana, Ill., 1979—; bd. dirs. Scott Research Lab., Fairview Park Hosp., Cleve., 1962-67; assoc. in physiology Western Res. U., Cleve., 1962-67; asst. prof. physiology Mayo Grad. Sch., 1967-73, Mayo Med. Sch., 1973, assoc. prof. nutrition, 1974; cons. in nutrition Mayo Clinic, 1967-76; assoc. prof. medicine U. S.D. Sch. Medicine, Sioux Falls, 1978-79; prof. nutrition U. Ill. Coll. Medicine, Urbana-Champaign, 1979—, chmn. dept. medicine prof. nutritional sci., physiology, biophysics dept. food sci. Sch. Agr., 1979—, also prof. medicine, exec. head dept. internal medicine , 1989—; dir. research Carle Found. Hosp., Urbana, 1979—; cons. nutritional support service Danville (Ill.) VA Hosp., 1980—. Co-author: The Mayo Clinic Renal Diet Cookbook, 1974; contbr. articles on nutrition, physiology, and hibernation to sci. jours.; editor: Geriatrics, 1980—, The Physician and Sportsmedicine, 1980-88, Am. Jour. Clin. Nutrition, 1980-83. Cons. in nutrition Nat. Cancer Inst., 1976; cons. in nutrition HEW, 1976, 79, 89, Nat. Heart and Lung Inst., 1976. Served with USAF, 1945-47. Fulbright scholar, Morocco, 1988. Mem. Am. Physiol. Soc., Am. Inst. Nutrition, Am. Soc. Clin. Nutrition, Central Soc. Clin. Research, Am. Gastroent. Assn. Lutheran. Home: 2 Illini Cir Urbana IL 61801-5813 Office: Carle Foundation Hospital 611 W Park St Urbana IL 61801-2529

NELSON, RALPH STANLEY, lawyer; b. Mpls., Mar. 15, 1943; s. Stanley L. and Louise M. Nelson; m. Judy E. Nelson, July 8, 1867; children: Sara C., Amy E., David A. BS in Bus. Adminstrn., U. Minn., 1966; JD with honors, Drake U., 1972. Bar: Minn. 1973, Wash. 1982, Tex. 1985, Ind. 1993. Assoc. Wiese and Cox, Ltd., Mpls., 1973-76; atty. Burlington No. R.R., St. Paul, Minn., 1976-81; sr. corp. counsel Burlington No. Inc., Seattle, 1981-85; v.p. law and adminstrn. Burlington Motor Carriers Inc., Ft. Worth, Tex., 1985-88; exec. v.p. and gen. counsel Burlington Motor Carriers Inc., Ft. Worth, 1988-93; sr. v.p., gen. counsel Burlington Motor Carriers Inc., Daleville (Indpls.), Ind., 1992-96, Trism Inc., Kennesaw, Ga., 1992-96. Mem. law rev. Drake U. Capt. USMC, 1966-70. Mem. Order of the Coif.

NELSON, RANDY J., psychology educator; b. Detroit, Mich., Jan. 13, 1954; s. Ralph Edward and Ada B. Nelson; m. Anne Courtney DeVries. AB in Psychology wit honors, U. Calif., Berkeley, 1978, MA in Psychology, 1980, PhD in Psychology, 1983, PhD in Endocrinology, 1984. Rsch. asst. Dr. F.A. Beach U. Calif., Berkeley, 1978, Dr. I Zucker U. Calif., Berkeley, 1978-84; post doctoral fellow U. Tex., Austin, 1984-86; asst. prof. psychology The Johns Hopkins Univ., Balt., 1986-91, assoc. prof. psychology, 1991-96, assoc. prof. population dynamics, 1991-96, prof. psychology, neurosci., population dynamics, 1996—; grant application reviewer NIH, 1986-87, 95—, NSF, 1986—, NSF program officer, 1995-96; jour. reviewer Animal Behavior, Brain Rsch., Biology of Reproduction, Jour. Biol. Rhythms, Jour. Comparative Neurology, Jour. Comparative Psychology, Jour. Mammology, Jour. of Reproduction & Fertility, Jour. Exptl. Psychology, Jour. Reproduction, Fertility & Devel., Jour. Pineal Rsch., Neuroendocrine Letters, Nature, Neurobehavioral Toxicology and Teratology, Neuroendocrinology, Physiology and Behavior, Sci., Procs. of NAS. Author: An Introduction to Behavioral Endocrinology, 1995; contbr. numerous articles to profl. jours. including Nature, Jour. of Nervous and Mental Disease, Jour. Comparative Psychology, Jour. Exptl. Zoology, Biology of Reproduction, Jour. of Urology, Physiology and Behavior, Am. Jour. Physiology, Physiological Zoology, Behavioral and Brain Scis., Can. Jour. Zoology, others. Recipient post-doctoral fellowship NIH, 1984-86, James A. Shannon award Nat. Cancer Inst., 1992-94. Mem. Soc. for Neurosci., Am. Soc. Mammalogists, Animal Behavior Soc., Soc. for Study of Biolog. Rhythyms, Soc. for the Study of Reproduction (mem. edn. com. 1982-83, 85-86, chairperson edn. com. 1986-87, editor newsletter 1986-88, membership com. 1990-94), Phi Beta Kappa, Sigma Chi, Psi Chi. Office: Johns Hopkins Univ Dept Psychology Behavioral Neuroendo Group Baltimore MD 21218

NELSON, RAYMOND JOHN, English literature educator, university dean, author; b. Waterbury, Conn., Sept. 5, 1938; s. Raymond John and Eileen (McGrath) N.; m. Claudine Eva Ligot, Aug. 20, 1972; children: Sylvie, Christopher. BA, U. Conn., 1965; MA, Stanford U., 1967, PhD, 1969. Prof. English U. Va., Charlottesville, 1969—, dean faculty arts and scis., 1989—. Author: Van Wyck Brooks: A Writer's Life, 1981, Kenneth Patchen and American Mysticism, 1984 (Melville Cane award Poetry Soc. Am. 1984); also articles. With USCG, 1958-62. Woodrow Wilson fellow, 1965-66, fellow NEH, 1971-72. Mem. Colonnade Club (U. Va.), Phi Beta Kappa. Avocation: photography. Home: RR 3 Box 14 Earlysville VA 22936-9756 Office: U Va Dean of Faculty Office 419 Cabell Hall Charlottesville VA 22903*

NELSON, RICHARD ARTHUR, lawyer; b. Fosston, Minn., Apr. 8, 1947; s. Arthur Joseph and Thelma Lillian Nelson; m. Kathryn Louise Sims, Sept. 25, 1976; children: Jennifer Kathryn, Kristen Elizabeth. BS in Math., U. Minn., 1969, JD, 1974. Bar: Minn. 1974, U.S. Ct. Appeals (D.C. cir.) 1975, U.S. Dist. Ct. Minn. 1975. Law clk. U.S. Ct. Appeals (D.C. cir.), Washington, 1974-75; ptnr. Faegre and Benson, Mpls., 1975—; seminar lectr. in employee benefits and labor laws, 1983—. Note and articles editor Minn. Law Rev., 1973-74. Active Dem.-Farmer-Labor State Cen. Com., Minn., 1976—, del. dist. and local coms. and convs., 1970—, state exec. com., 1990—; student rep. bd. regents U. Minn., Mpls., 1973-74; v.p. Minn. Student Assn., 1968-69. Served with U.S. Army, 1970-72. Mem. ABA, Minn. Bar Assn., Order of Coif, Tau Beta Pi. Lutheran. Office: Faegre and Benson 2200 Norwest Ctr 90 S 7th St Minneapolis MN 55402-3903

NELSON, RICHARD BURTON, physicist, former patent consultant; b. Powell, Wyo., Dec. 10, 1911; s. Severt A. and Sedona Lenora (Fesenbeck) N.; m. Maxine Caroline George, Feb. 25, 1950 (div. June 1963); 1 child, Anna Afton Ghandour; m. Pauline Wright, Dec. 29, 1969. Student, San Diego State Coll., 1930-32; BS in Physics with honors, Calif. Inst. Tech., 1935; PhD, MIT, 1938. Registered patent agt. Physicist R.C.A. Mfg. Co., Harrison, N.J., 1938-41, NRC, Ottawa, Ont., Can., 1941-42; rsch. assoc. GE Rsch. Lab., Schenectady, 1942-50; div. mgr. Varian Assocs., Palo Alto, Calif., 1960-63, chief engr., 1963-74, patent agt., 1974-77, cons., 1977-91; bd.

dirs. 1st Nat. Bank, Powell (Wyo.), 1st Co., Powell. Author of numerous tech. papers; patentee in field. Fellow IEEE; mem. N.W. Wyo. Coll. Found. Home and Office: Villa 28 23350 Sereno Ct Cupertino CA 95014-6507

NELSON, RICHARD DAVID, lawyer; b. Chgo., Jan. 29, 1940; s. Irving E. and Dorothy (Apolsky) N.; m. Davida Distenfield, Dec. 17, 1960; children: Cheryl, Laurel. BS in Acctg., U. Ill., 1961, LLB, 1964. Bar: Ill. 1964. Ptnr. Defrees & Fiske Law Offices, Chgo., 1964-81; ptnr., counsel, CFO, chief adminstrv. officer Heidrick & Struggles, Inc., Chgo., 1981—; bd. dirs., exec. com. Heidrick & Struggles, Inc., Chgo., 1981—. Pres. Jewish Cmty. Ctrs. of Chgo., 1987-89; chmn. Sign Graphics Task Force, Highland Park, Ill., 1986-88, Bus. and Econ. Devel. Commn., Highland Park; chmn. Econ. Devel. Commn. Highland Park, 1993-96. Mem. ABA, Ill. State Bar Assn., Chgo. Bar Assn., Standard Club, Northmoor Country Club. Office: Heidrick & Struggles Inc 233 S Wacker Dr Ste 4200 Chicago IL 60606-6310

NELSON, RICHARD HENRY, manufacturing company executive; b. Norfolk, Va., May 24, 1939; s. Irvin Joseph and Ethel Blair (Levy) N.; m. Carole Ellen Rosen, Mar. 12, 1966; children: Christopher, Karin. BA, Princeton U., 1961; postgrad., Georgetown U., 1962-63. Spl. asst. to dir. Peace Corps, Washington, 1961-62; mil. aide to U.S. v.p. Office of the V.P., Washington, 1962-63; asst. to U.S. Pres. Office of the Pres., Washington, 1963-66; spl. asst. to sec. HUD, Washington, 1966-68; v.p. Am. Internat. Bank, N.Y.C., 1968-70, Studebaker-Worthington, N.Y.C., 1970-73; pres. Sartex Corp., N.Y.C., 1973-80; pres., CEO Cogenic Energy Systems, Inc., N.Y.C., 1981-91; CEO U.S. Energy Systems, Inc., West Palm Beach, Fla., 1992—; bd. dirs. Nelco Corp., Laurel, Md.; chmn. bd. Powersave, Inc., N.Y.C., 1984-92. Bd. dirs. Nat. Hypertension Assn., N.Y.C., 1982-90; exec. com. Southampton Assn., N.Y., 1983—. 1st lt. U.S. Army, 1962-64. Recipient Presdl. Medal Office of Pres. of U.S., 1965. Mem. Internat. Cogeneration Assn., Am. Gas Assn., Am. Cogeneration Coalition, Ind. Power Producers, Princeton Club, Southampton Hunt and Polo Club (chmn. bd.), Palm Beach Polo and Country Club, U.S. Polo Assn., Meadow Club, Palm Beach Yacht Club, Amateur Trap Assn. Democrat. Avocations: horseback riding, trap and skeet shooting. Home: 12012 Longwood Green Dr West Palm Beach FL 33414-7070 Office: US Energy Systems Inc 515 N Flagler Dr Ste 202 West Palm Beach FL 33401-4322

NELSON, RICHARD JOHN, playwright; b. Chgo., Oct. 17, 1950; s. Richard Finis and Viola (Garbriel) N.; m. Cynthia Blair Bacon, May 21, 1972; children: Zoe Elizabeth, Jocelyn Anne. BA, Hamilton Coll., 1972. Literary mgr. Bklyn. Acad. Music Theater Co., 1979-81; assoc. dir. Goodman Theatre, Chgo., 1980-83; dramaturg Tyrone Guthrie Theater, Mpls., 1981-82. Author: (plays) The Killing of Yablonski, 1975, Conjuring an Event, 1976, Scooping, 1977, Jungle Coup, 1978, The Vienna Notes, 1978 (Obie award for disting. playwriting 1979), Bal, 1980, Rip Van Winkle or 'The Works', 1981, The Return of Pinocchio, 1983, Between East and West, 1985 (HBO Playwrights USA award 1986), Principia Scriptoriae, 1985 (ABC-TV Playwriting award 1985, Timeout London Theatre award 1987), An American Comedy, 1986, Roots in the Water, 1989, Some Americans Abroad, 1989, Sensibility and Sense, 1989, Two Shakespearean Actors, 1990, Columbus and the Discovery of Japan, 1992, (with Alexander Gelman) Misha's Party, 1993, Life Sentences, 1993, New England, 1994, The General From America, 1996, The American Wife, 1996; (radio plays) Languages Spoken Here, 1987 (Giles Cooper award 1988), Eating Words, 1989 (Giles Cooper award 1990), Advice to Eastern Europe, 1990; (book of musical) Chess, 1988; (teleplays) The End of a Sentence, 1991; (screenplay) Ethan Frome, 1993; contbr., editor: Strictly Dishonorable and Other Lost American Plays, 1986; translator: Don Juan (Moliere) 1979, The Wedding (Brecht) 1980, The Suicide (Erdman) 1980, Il Campiello (Goldoni) 1980, Jungle of Cities (Brecht) 1981, The Marriage of Figaro (Beaumarchais) 1982, Three Sisters (Chekhov) 1984, Accidental Death of an Anarchist (Dario Fo) 1984, Jitterbugging, 1989, The Father (Strindberg) 1995, The School (Molieve), 1995, The Imaginary Cuckoid (Molieve), 1995. Thomas J. Watson Traveling fellow, 1972, Creative Writing fellow NEA, 1979, Guggenheim fellow, 1983, Playwriting fellow NEA, 1986-87; Office of Advanced Drama Rsch. grantee, 1976, Rockefeller grantee, 1979, 88; recipient Obie award for innovative programming, 1980, Lila Wallace Writers award Readers Digest Fund, 1991-93. Office: care William Morris Agy 1350 Avenue Of The Americas New York NY 10019-4702*

NELSON, RICHARD LAWRENCE, public relations executive; b. Chgo., Nov. 13, 1953; s. Stanley Eric and Joan Carol (Greif) N. BS in Speech, Northwestern U., 1975. Dep. dir. radio/TV Dem. Nat. Com., Washington, 1975-76; press sec. U.S. Ho. of Reps., Washington, 1976-78; spl. asst. office of media liasion The White House, Washington, 1978-80, asst. press sec. office of media liasion, 1980-81; acct. supr. Hill & Knowlton, Inc., Chgo., Ill., 1981-82; dir. corp. pub. rels. Playboy Enterprises, Inc., Chgo., 1982-84; v.p. pub. rels. First Chgo. Corp., Chgo., 1984-87; prin. Richard Nelson Pub. Rels., Chgo., 1987-89; v.p. pub. rels. The NutraSweet Co., Deerfield, Ill., 1989-94, v.p. integrated mktg. comm., 1994-95; v.p. pub. affairs The NutraSweet Kelco Co., Deerfield, Ill., 1996—; mem. exec. com. Internat. Food Info. Coun., Washington, 1991—; dir. Calorie Control Coun., Atlanta, 1990—. Dir., past pres. Nat. Runaway Switchboard, Chgo., 1987-96; dir. AIDS Found. Chgo., 1993—, treas., 1995—, pres. 1996—. Recipient Silver Trumpet award Publicity Club Chgo., 1991, 94. Trustee Arthur W. Page Soc.; mem. Chgo. Pub. Rels. Forum. Democrat. Avocations: piano, bicycling. Home: 1220 Noyes St Evanston IL 60201-2636 Office: The NutraSweet Co 1751 Lake Cook Rd Deerfield IL 60015-5615

NELSON, RICHARD PHILIP, medical educator, dean; b. Bloomington, Ill., Dec. 28, 1946; s. Edward Philip and Dorothy Emma (Bergquist) N.; m. Phyllis Nelson, June 22, 1969; children: Elyse, Emily. BA, Northwestern U., Evanston, Ill., 1968; MD, Northwestern U., Chgo., 1972. Diplomate Am. Bd. Pediatrics. Resident pediat. Children's Meml. Hosp., Chgo., 1972-75, chief resident, 1975-76; clin. fellow pediatrics Harvard U., Boston, 1976-78; dir. Minn. Svcs. for Children with Handicaps/Minn. Dept. Health, Mpls., 1978-82; asst. prof. U. Minn. Med. Sch., Mpls., 1982-87; dir. developmental disabilities Gillette Children's Hosp., St. Paul, 1982-87; assoc. prof. pediatrics U. Iowa, Iowa City, 1987-94, prof. pediatrics, 1994—, dir. Child Health Specialty Clinics, 1987—, assoc. dean, 1992—. Editor: Maternal and Child Health Practices, 1994; co-author chpts. in books. Mem. Iowa Health Care Reform Coun., 1993; bd. dirs. Health Policy Corp. of Iowa, 1993; mem. Inst. of Medicine, Nat. Forum on Future of Children and Families, MCH Health Care Reform, 1991. James Patton scholar Northwestern U. Med. Sch., 1968-72. Mem. Am. Acad. Pediatrics (com. on child health care financing 1992—), Beta Beta Beta. Office: Child Health Specialty Clin Hospital Sch 100 Hawkins Dr Rm 247 Iowa City IA 52242-1011*

NELSON, RICKY EUGENE, financial executive; b. Newman Grove, Nebr., Jan. 26, 1956; s. Eugene Theodore and Lorraine Doris (Osterloh) N.; m. Roxanne Sich, Sept. 16, 1978. BS in Agrl. Econs./Fin., U. Nebr., 1977; MS in Wealth Mgmt., Coll. Fin. Planning, Denver, 1996. Cert. fin. planner; registered investment advisor. Br. mgr./loan officer Fed. Land Bank, Beatrice, Nebr., 1976-82; reg. rep. Edward D. Jones & Co., Atlantic, Iowa, 1982-84; dir. investments Darryl D. Smith Co., Atlantic, 1984-87; reg. rep. Investment Mgmt. & Rsch. Inc., Atlantic, 1984-87; br. mgr. Investment Mgmt. & Rsch. Inc., Hastings, Nebr., 1987—; pres. Nelson Capital Mgmt. Inc., Hastings, 1989—. Mem. Rotary, Masons (32 deg.), Shriners. Avocations: fishing, securities analysis. Office: Nelson Capital Mgmt Inc PO Box 1385 747 N Burlington Ste 307 Hastings NE 68902-1385

NELSON, ROBERT CHARLES, newspaper executive; b. Phila., Dec. 10, 1924; s. Charles Emil and Florence E. (Kelly) N.; m. Jeanne H. Wallace, Mar. 10, 1945; children—John R., Barbara J., Nancy A. Student, The Citadel, 1942-43; M.E., Stevens Inst. Tech., 1949. Asst. mech. supt. N.Y. News, N.Y.C., 1949-52; with Detroit News, 1952—, prodn. mgr., 1952-69, ops. mgr., 1969-75, v.p., 1973-79, gen. mgr., 1975-81, pres., 1981-87, pres., pub., 1982-87, spl. asst. to chmn., 1987—; exec. v.p. newspaper div. Evening News Assn., Detroit, 1978-87; dir. Evening News Assn., 1985-87, ret., pub. emeritus, 1990—; Bd. dirs., sec. Greater Detroit Safety Council, 1973—; bd. dirs. Engring. Sci. Fair, Detroit, 1975—; bd. dirs., mem. exec. com. Better Bus. Bur., Detroit, 1976—. Trustee New Detroit, 1980—. Served with USNR, 1943-46, PTO. Mem. Engring. Soc. Detroit, Greater Detroit C. of C. (bd. dirs. 1980—, vice chmn. 1985—), Acad. Sr. Profls. at Eckerd Coll., Detroit Club, Orchard Lake Country Club, Adcraft Club of Detroit, Econ. Club, St. Petersburg Yacht Club, St. Anthony's Hosp. Aux., Brookwood, SCORE.

NELSON, ROBERT E., public relations executive, political consultant; b. Jefferson, Wis., Oct. 25, 1951; s. Clifford H. and Mary Ann (Lundquist) N.; m. Heidi Nelson. Fiscal svcs. officer Orange (Calif.) County Med. Ctr., 1968-73; exec. asst. Orange County Bd. Suprs., Santa Ana, 1973-75; sr. assoc. Butcher-Forde Cons., Newport Beach, Calif., 1976-77; CEO, chmn. Nelson Comm. Group, Irvine, Calif., 1979-96; chmn. Nelson Comm. Group, Driggs, Idaho, 1979—. dep. asst. dir. pub. outreach presdl. transition, Little Rock, 1993; presdl. appointee U.S. Competitiveness Policy Coun., Washington, 1994-96. Recipient Rocky Mountain regional Emmy award TV. advt., 1986. Mem. Internat. Assn. Polit. Cons. (bd. dirs. 1992-95), Young Pres. Orgn. (bd. dir.s 1994—), Pacific Club. Avocations: fly fishing, scuba, horses, skiing. Home: Driggs ID 83422 Office: Nelson Comm Group PO Box 800 Driggs ID 83422

NELSON, ROBERT EARL, JR., financial services company executive; b. Mobile, Ala., May 15, 1938; s. Robert Earl Sr. and Frances Lucille (Till) N.; m. Sandra Anne Berry, Aug. 3, 1964; children: Robin Lynne, Robert Earl III, Patricia Anne. BS in Indsl. Mgmt., Ga. Inst. Tech., 1960; MBA, U. Ala., 1963. CPA, Ga., N.Y. Prodn. mgr. Borg Warner Corp., Chgo., 1963-65; mgr., mgmt. cons. Peat, Marwick, & Mitchell, Atlanta, 1965-71; corp. controller VF Corp., Reading, Pa., 1971-73; ptnr., mgmt. services Arthur Young & Co., N.Y.C., 1973-81; sr. v.p., CFO Cable Am. Inc., Atlanta, 1981-84; exec. v.p., chief ops. officer Kroh Bros. Devel. Co., Kansas City, Mo., 1984-87; chief exec. officer Nelson & Co., Atlanta, 1987—. Contbr. articles to profl. jours. Served to 1st lt. USMC, 1960-62. Mem. AICPA, Am. Inst. Indsl. Engrs., Fin. Execs. Inst., Bus. and Tech. Alliance, Venture Forum, Union League Club (N.Y.C.), Cherokee Town and Country Club (Atlanta). Republican. Episcopalian. Avocations: golf, tennis, biking, scuba diving. Home: 5100 Jett Forest Trl NW Atlanta GA 30327-4560 Office: Nelson & Co 1100 Circle 75 Pky NW Ste 800 Atlanta GA 30339-3097

NELSON, ROBERT LOUIS, lawyer; b. Dover, N.H., Aug. 10, 1931; s. Albert Louis and Alice (Rogers) N.; m. Rita Jean Hutchins, June 11, 1955; children: Karen, Robin Andrea. B.A., Bates Coll., Lewiston, Maine, 1956; LL.B., Georgetown U., 1959. Bar: D.C. 1960. With U.S. Commn. Civil Rights, 1958-63, AID, 1963-66; program sec. U.S. Mission to Brazil, 1965-66; exec. dir. Lawyers Com. Civil Rights Under Law, 1966-70; dep. campaign mgr. Muskie for Pres., 1970-72; v.p. Perpetual Corp., Houston, 1972-74; sr. v.p., gen. counsel Washington Star, 1974-76; pres. broadcast div. Washington Star Communications, Inc., 1976-77; asst. sec. of army U.S. Dept. Def., 1977-79; spl. advisor to chief N.G. Bur., Dept. Def., 1980-85; pres., dir. Mid-Md. Communications Corp., 1981-85; ptnr. Verner, Liipfert, Bernhard, McPherson and Hand,, 1979-87; gen. counsel Paralyzed Vets. Am., 1988—. Vice chmn. D.C. Redevel. Land Agy., 1976-77; bd. dirs. Community Found. Greater Washington, 1977-78 ; bd. dirs. Friends of Nat. Zoo, 1975—, pres., 1982-84; bd. dirs. Downtown Progress, 1976-77, Fed. City Council, 1976-77, 83-87, Pennsylvania Ave. Devel. Corp., 1976-77. Served with AUS, 1953-54. Mem. ABA, D.C. Bar Assn., Army Navy Club (Washington). Democrat. Episcopalian. Home: 1001-E 4201 Mass Ave NW Washington DC 20016 Home (summer): Robins Nest Orrs Island ME 04066 Office: 801 18th St NW Washington DC 20006-3517

NELSON, ROGER HUGH, management educator, business executive; b. Spring City, Utah, Mar. 7, 1931; s. Hugh Devere and Maudella Sarah (Larsen) N.; m. DeEtte Munk, Aug. 26, 1955; children—Steven R., Deanne, Mark L. B.S., U. Utah, 53, M.S., 1953; Ed.D., Columbia U., 1958. Mem. faculty U. Utah Coll. Bus., 1953-97, prof. mgmt., 1970-97; pres. faculty David Eccles Sch. Bus., 1995-96; dir. programs in emerging bus. U. Utah Coll. Bus., 1989-97, chmn. mgmt. dept., 1976-82, asst. dean, 1969-74; dir. MBA integrative field studies, 1993-96; pres. David Eccles Sch. of Bus. Faculty, 1995-96; mem. faculty Utah Mgmt. Inst., 1968-75; v.p. Computer Logic Corp., 1970-73; pres. Am. Leisure & Sports Investment Corp., 1973-75, Oil Resources, Inc., 1980-88, Puma Energy Corp., 1981-88, The Ultimate Choice Catalog Co., 1986—; fin. and mgmt. cons., 1965—; founder Utah Small Bus. Devel. Center, U. Utah, 1979; bd. dirs. Omni Data Int.; chmn. Am. Recreation and Sports, Inc., 1996—. Author: Personal Money Management, 1973, The Utah Entrepreneur's Guide, 1995, also articles, reports, manuals. Active local Am. Heart Assn., Am. Cancer Soc. campaigns; mem. exec. bd. Utah Opera Co., 1981-85, gen. bd., 1985-89. Danforth Teaching fellow, 1957. Mem. Acad. Mgmt., Adminstrv. Mgmt. Soc., NEA, AAUP, Phi Kappa Phi, Beta Gamma Sigma, Phi Delta Kappa, Delta Phi Epsilon. Inventor comml. color separation camera and related dye-transfer processes. Home: 2662 Skyline Dr Salt Lake City UT 84108-2855 Office: U Utah David Eccles Sch Bus Salt Lake City UT 84112

NELSON, RON, composer, conductor, educator; b. Joliet, Ill., Dec. 14, 1929; s. Walter E. and Lois (Fulton) N.; m. Helen Mitchell, 1954 (dec. 1967); children: Marc W., Kristen R. Mus.B., Eastman Sch. Music, 1952, Mus.M., 1953, Mus.D., 1956; postgrad., L'École Normale, Normale, Paris, 1954-55; M.A., Brown U., 1959. Prof. Brown U., Providence, chmn. dept. music, 1963-73, Acuff chair of excellence in creative arts, 1991; prof. emeritus Brown U., 1993—. film composer, HEW, Eastman Kodak, ARC, Columbia Pictures, commns. from, Cin. Symphony, Lima Symphony, Rochester Philharmonic, R.I. Philharm., Am. Bapt. Soc., U. Minn., Dartmouth Coll., Brown U., New Music Ensemble, LaSalle Coll., Western Mich. U., Classic Chorale, U.S. Air Force Band, Nat. Symphony Orch.; composer (for orch.) Savannah River Holiday, 1954, Sarabande: For Katherine in April, 1954, (opera) The Birthday of the Infanta, 1956; (cantata) The Christmas Story, 1958: (for orch.) Tocatta for Orchestra, 1963; (oratorio) What is Man?, 1964; (orch./wind ensemble) Rocky Point Holiday, 1968-69; This is the Orchestra; (orch. and tape trilogy) Trilogy: JFK-MLK-RFK, 1969; (choral) Prayer of Emperor of China, 1973; (choral) Thy Truth is Great, 1973; (choral) Psalm 95, 1974; (orch.) Five Pieces for Orchestra after Paintings by Andrew Wyeth, 1975; (choral) Prayer of St. Francis of Assisi, 1976; (orch.) Meditation and Dance for Orch., 1976; (choral) Six Pieces for Chamber Ensemble, 1977, Four Choral Pieces After the Seasons, 1978, Three Autumnal Sketches, 1979, Here We Come As in The Beginning, 1979, Mass in Honor of St. LaSalle, 1981, Three Nocturnal Pieces, 1982, Three Seasonal Reflections, 1982; composer: Fanfare for a Celebration, 1982; (choral) On Christmas Night, 1982; Medieval Suite, 1983; (choral) Dreams, 1982; (band) Fanfare for a Celebration, 1983; (cello-piano) And the Moon Rose Golden, 1983; (band) Medieval Suite, 1983; composer: Aspen Jubilee, 1984; (organ-brass) Pebble Beach Sojourn, 1984; (chorus-band) Te Deum Laudamus, 1985; (choral) Lost and Found, 1985, Light Years, 1985, Three Settings of the Moon, 1985, (strings-trumpet) Elegy, 1986, (brass) Brevard Fanfare, 1986, (chorus/band) Prime: The Hour of Sunrise, 1987, (choral) White, 1987, (choral) Another Spring, 1987, (choral) Miniatures from a Bestiary Parts I and II, 1988, (saxophone-band) Danza Capriccio, 1988, (choral) Three Pieces after Tennyson (1988), (choral) Three Mountain Ballads, 1989, (brass-winds-percussion) Fanfare for the Hour of Sunrise, 1989, (band) Morning Alleluias for the Winter Solstice, 1989, (band) Resonances, 1990; (chorus) And This Shall Be for Music, 1990, Invoking the Powers, 1991, Songs of Praise and Reconciliation, 1991, The Meadow, 1991, (band) Lauds: Praise High Day, 1992, To the Airborne, 1991, Passacaglia (Homage on B-A-C-H), 1992, Chaconne (In Memoriam), 1994, Sonoran Desert Holiday, 1994, (band), Epiphanies (Fanfares and Chorales bands), 1995, Courtly Airs and Dances, 1995, (orch.) Resonances II, 1996, (orch., band) Resonances III, 1996,(orch.) Panels (Epiphanies II), 1996, The Music of Ron Nelson, 1996. Recipient ASCAP awards, 1962-97, Found. award for World tour, 1965-66, Nat. Band Assn. award, 1992, John Philip Sousa medal of merit, 1994; Fulbright fellow, 1954; Ford Found. commn., 1962, NEA grantee, 1973, 76, 79; awarded Acuff Chair of Excellence on the Creative Arts, 1991; winner Am. Bandmasters Assn. Ostwald Contest, 1993, Am. Band Assn. contest, 1992, Sudler Internat. Wind Band Competition, 1993. Office: Brown U Dept Music Providence RI 02912

NELSON, RONALD HARVEY, animal science educator, researcher; b. Union Grove, Wis., Aug. 10, 1918; s. Harvey August and Myra Frances (Sheen) N.; m. Elizabeth Jane Lappley, Apr. 13, 1940; children: David Peter, Marjorie Jean, Linda Louise, Ronda Elizabeth. BS, U. Wis., 1939; MS, Okla. A&M U., 1941; PhD, Iowa State U., 1943. Mem. faculty Mich. State U., 1946-85, prof., head, animal sci. dept., 1950-84, prof. emeritus, 1985—; chief of party Mich. State U. tech. assistance project Balcarce, Pcia, Buenos Aires, 1966-68. Recipient Grad. Distinction award Okla State U., 1987, Nat. Saddle and Sirloin Portrait award, 1990. Fellow Am. Soc. Animal Sci. (Internat. Animal Agr. award 1978, Animal Industry award 1984); mem. Am. Angus Assn. (chmn. research advisory com. 1956-60), Mich. Angus Assn. (pres. 1977-78), Animal Sci. Assn., Sigma Xi, Phi Kappa Phi, Alpha Zeta. Home: 1545 N Harrison Rd East Lansing MI 48823-1801

NELSON, ROY LESLIE, cardiac surgeon, researcher, educator; b. N.Y.C., May 3, 1941; s. Sam and Anna (Kaminetsky) N.; m. Anne Judith Sachs, Jan. 6, 1973; children: Samuel Phillip, Amy Joy, Jill Heather. BS, Lafayette Coll., Easton, Pa., 1963; MD magna cum laude, Free U. Brussels, Belgium, 1971. Cert. MD Am. Bd. Surgery, Am. Bd. Thoracic Surgery; cert. in laser surgery. Intern surgery Bronx Mcpl. Hosp./Albert Einstein Coll. Medicine, 1971-72; resident surgery NYU Med. Ctr. Bellevue Hosp., N.Y.C., 1972-74; thoracic rschr. UCLA Med. Ctr., L.A., Calif., 1974-76; resident surgery NYU Med. Ctr. Bellevue Hosp., 1976-78, fellow cardiothoracic surgery NYU Med. Ctr., 1978-80; asst. attending cardiothoracic surgeon dept. surgery North Shore U. Hosp., Manhasset, N.Y., 1984-90, assoc. attending cardiothoracic surgeon, 1984-90, attending cardiothoracic surgeon, 1991—, asst. dir. dept. surgery, 1990—; rschr. Bureau Biological Rsch., New Brunswick, N.J., 1963-64, Surg. Rsch. Lab., St. Pierre Hosp., Free U. Brussels, 1969-71, Divsn. Thoracic Sugery, UCLA, 1974-76; physician-in-charge Cardiovascular Rsch. Lab., North Shore U. Hosp., 1980—; teaching asst. Dept. Surgery, Albert Einstein Coll. Medicine, 1971-72, NYU Med. Ctr., 1972-74, 76-77; clin. instr. surgery NYU Med. Ctr., 1977-80; asst. prof. surgery Cornell U. Med. Coll., 1980—. Author: (with others) Plasmapheresis, 1982, Pathophysiology and Techniques of Cardiopulmonary Bypass II, 1983; contbr. articles to profl. jours. Recipient Barnett Meml. prize NYU, 1974, Physician's Recognition award AMA, 1986. Fellow ACS, Am. Coll. Angiology, Am. Coll. Cardiology, Am. Coll. Chest Physicians (coun. critical care 1990—), Am. Soc. for Laser Medicine and Surgery, N.Y. Cardiological Soc.; mem. AAAS, Am. Heart Assn. (rsch com. 1982—, coun. cardiovascular surgery 1984—), Am. Soc. Artificial Internal Organs, Am. Soc. Extra-Corporeal Tech., Internat. Soc. for Artificial Organs (reviewer artificial organs 1984—), Internat. Soc. for Heart Transplantation, Med. Soc. State N.Y., Nassau County Med. Soc., N.Y. Acad Scis., N.Y. Soc. for Thoracic Surgery, N.Am. Society for Pacing and Electrophysiology, Soc. Critical Care Medicine, Soc. Thoracic Surgeons, Spencer Surg. Soc., Undersea Med. Soc. Achievements include research in radical transplantation of the lungs studying different experimental procedures, the importance of alkalosis in maintenance of "ideal" blood pH during hypothermia, the effects of profound topical cardiac hypothermia on myocardial blood flow, metabolism, compliance and function, myocardial preservation during cardiopulmonary bypass, citrate reperfusion of ischemic hearts on cardiopulmonary bypass, improved myocardial performance after aortic cross clamping by combining pharmacologic arrest with topical hypothermia, the effects of hypothermia on regional myocardial blood flow and metabolism during cardiopulmonary bypass, optimizing myocardial supply/demand balance with adrenergic drugs during cardiopulmonary resuscitation, hemoconcentration by ultrafiltration, following cardiopulmonary bypass, intra-aortic balloon rupture, cocaine induced acute aortic dissection, the role of cardioplegia oxygen concentration in limiting myocardial reperfusion injury, the role of morbid obesity and diabetes in the outcome of coronary bypass surgery, isolated intra-thoracic trauma following deployment of an air bag. Office: North Shore U Hosp 300 Community Dr Manhasset NY 11030-3801

NELSON, RUSSELL MARION, surgeon, educator; b. Salt Lake City, Sept. 9, 1924; s. Marion C. and Edna (Anderson) N.; m. Dantzel White, Aug. 31, 1945; children: Marsha Nelson McKellar, Wendy Nelson Maxfield, Gloria Nelson Irion, Brenda Nelson Miles, Sylvia Nelson Webster, Emily Nelson Wittwer (dec.), Laurie Nelson Marsh, Rosalie Nelson Ringwood, Marjorie Nelson Helsten, Russell Marion Jr. BA, U. Utah, 1945, MD, 1947; PhD in Surgery, U. Minn., 1954; ScD (hon.), Brigham Young U., 1970; DMS (hon.), Utah State U., 1989; LHD (hon.), Snow Coll., 1994. Diplomate: Am. Bd. Surgery, Am. Bd. Thoracic Surgery (dir. 1972-78). Intern U. Minn. Hosps., Mpls., 1947; asst. resident surgery U. Minn. Hosps., 1948-51; first asst. resident surgery Mass. Gen. Hosp., Boston, 1953-54; sr. resident surgery U. Minn. Hosps., Mpls., 1954-55; practice medicine (specializing in cardiovascular and thoracic surgery), Salt Lake City, 1959-84; staff surgeon Latter-day Saints Hosp., Salt Lake City, 1959-84; dir. surg. research lab. Latter-day Saints Hosp., 1959-72, chief cardiovascular-thoracic surg. div., 1967-72, also bd. govs., 1970-90, vice chmn., 1979-89; staff surgeon Primary Children's Hosp., Salt Lake City, 1960; attending in surgery VA Hosp., Salt Lake City, 1955-84, Univ. Hosp., Salt Lake City, 1955-84; asst. prof. surgery Med. Sch. U. Utah, Salt Lake City, 1955-59, asst. clin. prof. surgery, 1959-66, asso. clin. prof. surgery, clin. prof., 1966-69, research prof. surgery, 1970-84, clin. prof. emeritus, 1984—; staff services Utah Biomed. Test Lab., 1970-84; dir. tng. program cardiovascular and thoracic surgery at Univ. Utah affiliated hosps., 1967-84; mem. policyholders adv. com. New Eng. Mut. Life Ins. Co., Boston, 1976-80. Contbr. articles to profl. jours. Mem. White House Conf. on Youth and Children, 1960; bd. dirs. Internat. Cardiol. Found.; bd. govs. LDS Hosp., 1970-90, Deseret Gymnasium, 1971-75, Promised Valley Playhouse, 1970-79; mem. adv. com. U.S. Sec. of State on Religious Freedom Abroad, 1996—. 1st lt. to capt. M.C., AUS, 1951-53. Markle scholar in med. scis., 1957-59; Fellowship of Medici Publici U. Utah Coll., 1967; Gold Medal of Merit, Argentina, 1974; named Hon. Prof. Shandong Med. U., Jinan, People's Republic of China, 1985; Old People's U., Jinan, 1986; Xi-an (People's Republic of China) Med. Coll., 1986, Legacy of Life award, 1993. Fellow A.C.S. (chmn. adv. council on thoracic surgery 1973-75), Am. Coll. Cardiology, Am. Coll. Chest Physicians; mem. Am. Assn. Thoracic Surgery, Am. Soc. Artificial Internal Organs, AMA, Dirs. Thoracic Residencies (pres. 1971-72), Utah Med. Assn. (pres. 1970-71), Salt Lake County Med. Soc., Am. Heart Assn. (exec. com. cardiovascular surgery 1972, dir. 1976-78, chmn. council cardiovascular surgery 1976-78), Utah Heart Assn. (pres. 1964-65), Soc. Thoracic Surgeons, Soc. Vascular Surgery (sec. 1968-72, pres. 1974), Utah Thoracic Soc., Salt Lake Surg. Soc., Samson Thoracic Surg. Soc., Western Soc. for Clin. Research, Soc. U. Surgeons, Am., Western, Pan-Pacific surg. assns., Inter. Am. Soc. Cardiology (bd. mgrs.), Phi Beta Kappa, Sigma Xi, Alpha Omega Alpha, Phi Kappa Phi, Sigma Chi. Mem. Ch. of Jesus Christ of Latter-day Saints (pres. Bonneville Stake 1964-71, gen. pres. Sunday sch. 1971-79, regional rep. 1979-84, Quorum of the Twelve Apostles 1984—). Home: 1347 Normandie Cir Salt Lake City UT 84105-1919 Office: 47 E South Temple Salt Lake City UT 84150-1005

NELSON, SANDRA KAY, foundation administrator; b. Hicksville, Ohio, July 12, 1961; d. Deloy LaVerl and B. Lucille (Wonderly) Osmun; m. Gregory Lynn Thompson, May 22, 1982 (div. Aug. 1988); 1 child, Andrew Braden; m. Dean Marshall Nelson, July 17, 1993; 1 child, Tanner Marshall. Student, Internat. Bus. Coll., Ft. Wayne, Ind., 1979-80, N.W. State C.C., 1990-93. Supr. Ohio Art Co., Bryan, 1984-87; nat. devel. dir. Nat. Reye's Syndrome Found., Bryan, 1987-93, acting exec. dir., 1993-94, exec. dir., 1994—. Editor (newsletter) In The News, 1989—. Den leader Cub Scout Pack 3186, Fremont, Ind., 1993-95. Mem. Nat. Voluntary Health Agys. (chairperson 1994-95, trustee 1993-96, nat. com. rep. 1989—), Clear Lake Yacht Club (social chair 1993-94), Steuben County Bus. and Profl. Women's Orgn. Lutheran. Avocations: sailing races, bike treks. Office: Reyes Syndrome Found 426 N Lewis PO Box 829 Bryan OH 43506

NELSON, SARAH MILLEDGE, archaeology educator; b. Miami, Fla., Nov. 29, 1931; d. Stanley and Sarah Woodman (Franklin) M.; m. Harold Stanley Nelson, July 25, 1953; children: Erik Harold, Mark Milledge, Stanley Franklin. BA, Wellesley Coll., 1953; MA, U. Mich., 1969, PhD, 1973. Instr. archaeology U. Md. extension, Seoul, Republic Korea, 1970-71; asst. prof. U. Denver, 1974-79, assoc. prof., 1979-85, prof. archaeology, 1985—, chair dept. anthropology, 1985-95, dir. women's studies program, 1985-87, John Evans prof., dir. Asian studies, 1996; vis. asst. prof. U. Colo., Boulder, 1974; resident Rockefeller Ctr. in Bellagio, Italy, 1996. Co-editor: Powers of Observation, 1990, Equity Issues for Women in Archaeology, 1994; author: Archaeology of Korea, 1993, Gender in Archaeology: Analyzing Power and Prestige, 1997; editor: The Archaeology of Northeast China, 1995. Active Earthwatch, 1989. Recipient Outstanding Scholar award U. Denver, 1989; grantee S.W. Inst. Rsch. on Women, 1981, Acad. Korean Studies, Seoul, 1983, Internat. Cultural Soc. Korea, 1986, Colo. Hist. Fund, 1995-97, Rockefeller Found. Residency, Bellagio, Italy. Fellow Am. Anthrop. Assn.; mem. Soc. Am. Archaeology, Assn. Asian Studies, Royal Asiatic Soc., Sigma Xi (sec.-treas. 1978-79), Phi Beta Kappa. Democrat. Avocations: skiing, gardening. Home: 5878 S Dry Creek Ct Littleton CO 80121-1709 Office: U Denver Dept Anthropology Denver CO 80208

NELSON, STEVEN CRAIG, lawyer; b. Oakland, Calif., May 11, 1944; s. Eskil Manfred and Florence Lucille (Boatman) N.; m. Kathryn Cassel Stoltz, Nov. 30, 1974 (div. Apr. 1997); children: Carleton Philip, Whitney Cassel. BA in Econs. with exceptional distinction, Yale U., 1966, LLB, 1969. Bar: DC 1969, Minn. Supreme Ct. 1975, U.S. Supreme Ct. 1973. From atty. adviser to asst. legal adviser U.S. Dept. State, Washington, 1969-74; from assoc. to ptnr. Oppenheimer, Wolff, Foster, Shepard & Donnelly, St. Paul and Mpls., 1975-85; ptnr. Dorsey & Whitney, Mpls., 1985—; mem. bd. appeals NATO, Brussels. 1977—; adj. prof. law U. Minn, 1980-86; speaker in field. Contbr. articles to profl. jours. Mem. ABA (chmn. internat. law and practice 1988-89), Minn. Bar Assn., Am. Fgn. Law Assn., Am. Soc. Internat. Law, Internat. Bar Assn. (mem. coun. 1996—), Union Internat. des Avocats (1st v.p. 1991-94), Minikahda Club. Presbyterian. Avocations: golf, tennis, skiing, sailing. Office: Dorsey & Whitney 220 S 6th St Minneapolis MN 55402-4502

NELSON, STEVEN DOUGLAS, construction company executive; b. Houston, Oct. 13, 1950; s. Stewart L. and Jean (Boyd) N.; m. Elizabeth (Betsy) Lane Brown, Mar. 25, 1972; children: Elizabeth K., D. Andrew, Allison L., Amanda J. BA in Econs., So. Meth. U., 1972, JD, 1976. Bar: Tex. 1976, U.S. Dist. Ct. (no. dist.) Tex. 1980, U.S. Ct. Claims 1980, U.S. Ct. Appeals (5th cir.) 1979, U.S. Ct. Appeals (fed. cir.) 1982, U.S. Supreme Ct. 1980; fellow Am. Coll. Constrn. Lawyers. Shareholder, chmn. constrn. law practice group Winstead, Sechrest & Minick, P.C., Dallas, 1976-95; ptnr. Ford & Nelson, P.C., 1995; gen. counsel Capital Adminstrv. Svcs., Austin, 1995-96; CEO Faulkner Constrn. Co., Austin, 1996—; mem. AIA/AGC liaison com. Dallas chpt. Associated Gen. Contractors, 1984-88, legis. com. Dallas bldg. br., 1988-90, bd. dirs. 1991-95. Author: Bonds and Liens in Texas, 1991; co-author: Texas Lien Law Digest, 1984; contbg. editor: Design and Construction Market Strategist, 1993, Mexican Business Review, 1993, Dallas Construction Industry Practices, 1986-89; author: (audiovisual presentations) Insurable Risks, 1985. Mem. adv. com. magnet ctr. pub. svcs., govt. and law Dallas Ind. Sch. Dist., 1989-94, adv. coun. Ctr. Non-Profit Mgmt., 1992-93, Pub. Safety Com., City University Park, Tex., 1992-93; bd. dirs. Greater Dallas Crime Commn., 1990-94, chmn. legis. com., 1990, v.p. crime stoppers, 1990-91, pres., 1992, gen. counsel, 1993; bd. dirs. and v.p. The City Club, Dallas, 1992-95; asst. scoutmaster Boy Scout Troop # 72, Dallas, 1992-95. Staff sgt. USAR, 1971-77. Mem. ABA (fidelity and surety subcommittee tort and ins. practice sect., pub. contract law sect., forum com. construction law), Am. Surety Assn. (vice-chmn. claims com. 1981-82, chmn. 1982-83, dir. 1983-84, 86-90, v.p. 1988-90), Am. Arbitration Assn. (nat. panel arbitrators), U.S. Arbitration and Mediation, Inc. (nat. constrn. panel), State Bar Tex. (co-founder constrn. law sect., various offices, editor Constrn. Law Newsletter 1992-93), Def. Rsch. Inst., Dallas Bar Assn., Travis County Bar Assn. (chmn. constrn. law sect. 1997—). Republican. Presbyterian. Avocations: backpacking, genealogy, computers. Home: 3701 Moon Lark Ct Austin TX 78746 Office: Faulkner Constrn Co 3901 S Lamar Blvd Austin TX 78704-7989

NELSON, STUART JAMES, internist, medical informatician; b. Santa Monica, Calif., Apr. 25, 1947; s. Clair Edmund and Ruth (Gibson) N.; m. Linda K. F. Mui, June 18, 1978; children: Victoria, Mark, Elizabeth. AB in Math., U. Calif., Berkeley, 1970; MD, SUNY, Bklyn., 1975. Diplomate Nat. Bd. Med. Examiners, Am. Bd. Internal Medicine. Intern Phila. Gen. Hosp., 1975-76; resident Met. Hosp., N.Y.C., 1976-78; instr. medicine SUNY, Stony Brook, 1978-82, asst. prof. clin. medicine, 1982-86, clin. assoc. prof. medicine, preventive medicine, 1986-91; assoc. prof. medicine Med. Coll. Ga., Augusta, 1991-96; head med. subject headings Nat. Libr. Medicine, Bethesda, Md., 1996—; assoc. head divsn. gen. internal medicine SUNY, Stony Brook, 1985-90; reviewer for profl. jours. Contbr. articles to profl. jours. Fellow Am. Coll. Physicians; mem. AAAS, Am. Med. Informatics Assn., Soc. Gen. Internal Medicine, Med. Libr. Assn. Presbyterian. Office: Nat Libr Medicine Bldg 38A Rm B 2 E17 Bethesda MD 20894

NELSON, STUART OWEN, agricultural engineer, researcher, educator; b. Pilger, Nebr., Jan. 23, 1927; s. Irvin Andrew and Agnes Emilie (Nissen) N.; m. Carolyn Joye Fricke, Dec. 27, 1953 (dec. Nov. 1975); children: Richard Lynn, Jana Sue; m. Martha Ellen White Fuller, Apr. 8, 1979. BS in Agrl. Engring., U. Nebr., 1950, MSc in Agrl. Engring., 1952, MA in Physics, 1954; PhD in Engring., Iowa State U., 1972, hon. DSc U. Nebr., 1989. Grad. asst. U. Nebr., Lincoln, 1952-54, rsch. assoc., 1954-60, assoc. prof., 1960-72, prof., 1972-76; project leader Farm Electrification Rsch., Agrl. Rsch. Svc., USDA, Lincoln, 1954-59, rsch. investigations leader, 1959-72, rsch. leader, 1972-76, rsch. agrl. engr. Russell Rsch. Ctr., Athens, Ga., 1976—; adj. prof. U. Ga., 1976—; sci. adv. council Am. Seed Rsch. Found.; mem. CAST Task Force on Irradiation for Food Preservation and Pest Control; adv. com. grain moisture measurement Nat. Council Weights and Measures; mem. sci. bd. 4th Internat. Conf. on Phys. Properties Agrl. Materials, Prague, 1985. Served with USN, 1946-48. Recipient HM Crops and Soils award Am. Soc. Agronomy, 1966; recipient Founders Gold medal, Fed. Engr. of Yr., NSPE, 1985; Superior Svc. award USDA., 1986; Profl. Achievement Citation Engring. award Iowa State U., 1987. Fellow Am. Soc. Agrl. Engrs. (Tech. Paper award 1965, 94, Engr. of Yr. award Ga. sect. 1988, chmn. Ga. sect. 1988-89). Fellow Internat. Microwave Power Inst. (Decade award 1981); mem. AAAS, IEEE (sr.), The Electromagnetics Acad., Internat. Soc. Agromaterials Sci. and Engring., Ga. Soc. Profl. Engrs. (Engr. of Yr. in Govt. award 1991), Nat. Acad. Engring., Nat. Soc. Profl. Engrs., Orgn. Profl. Employees of Dept. of Agr. (pres. Athens area chpt. 1984-86, nat. coun. rep. 1988-95, Profl. of Yr. award 1987), Sigma Xi, Sigma Tau, Gamma Sigma Delta, Tau Beta Pi. Methodist. Club: Athens Optimist (pres. 1980-81, lt. gov. Ga. dist. 1983-84, Optimist of Yr. award 1982, disting. and outstanding lt. gov. Ga. dist. 1985), Assoc. editor Jour. Microwave Power, 1975-76; contbr. more than 300 articles to sci. and tech. jours. Home: 270 Idylwood Dr Athens GA 30605-4635 Office: Russell Rsch Ctr USDA ARS PO Box 5677 Athens GA 30604

NELSON, SYDNEY B., lawyer, state senator; b. Mar. 12, 1935; BBA, U. Okla.; JD, La. State U.; m. Gail Anderson. Law clk. U.S. Dist. Ct., 1963-64; pvt. practice law, Shreveport, La., 1964—; Mem. La. Senate, 1980-92. Mem. adminstrv. bd. 1st Meth. Ch., Shreveport; mem. adv. bd. Norwella coun. Boy Scouts Am. Served as officer USN, 1957-60. Assoc. editor La. Law Rev. Mem. ABA, La. Bar Assn., Shreveport Bar Assn. (pres. 1989), Order of Coif. Republican. Office: 705 Milam St Shreveport LA 71101-3507

NELSON, THERESA, writer; b. Beaumont, Tex., Aug. 15, 1948; d. David Rogers Jr. and Alice Carroll (Hunter) N.; m. Kevin Cooney, Sept. 26, 1968; children: Michael Christopher, Brian David, Errol Andrew. BA magna cum laude, U. St. Thomas, 1972. Actor, tchr. creative dramatics Theatre Under The Stars, Houston, 1971-80; dir. glee club St. Mary's Sch., Katonah, N.Y., 1983-90; spkr. in schs., librs., lit. groups, 1983—. Author: The Twenty-Five Cent Miracle, 1986 (Best Book of Yr. citation Sch. Libr. Jour., 1986, Washington Irving Children's Choice award, 1988), Devil Storm, 1987 (Notable Children's Trade Book in the field of social studies citation Nat. Coun. Social Scis. Children's Book Coun. 1987), And One For All, 1989 (Notable Children's Book citation, Best Book for Young Adults citation ALA, Best Book of Yr. citation Sch. Libr. Jour., Editor's Choice citation Booklist, Fanfare citation Horn Book, Pick of the Lists citation Am. Bookseller, Books for Children citation Libr. Congress/Children's Lit. Ctr., others), The Beggar's Ride, 1992 (Notable Children's Book citation, Best Book for Young Adults ALA, Best Book of Yr. citation Sch. Libr. Jour., Fanfare citation Horn Book, others), (short story) Andrew, Honestly, 1993, (novel) Earthshine, 1994 (Child Study award Bank St. Coll., 1995, Boston Globe/Horn Book honor, Notable Children's Book citation, Best Book for Young Adults ALA, Best Book of Yr. citation Sch. Libr. Jour., others). Mem. Authors Guild, Authors League of Am., Soc. Children's Book Writers and Illustrators, Golden Triangle Writers Guild, So. Calif. Coun. Lit. for Children and Young People. Democrat. Roman Catholic. Avocations: singing, dancing, playing piano, movies, plays.

NELSON, THOMAS G., federal judge; b. 1936. Student, Univ. Idaho, 1955-59, LLB, 1962. Ptnr. Parry, Robertson, and Daly, Twin Falls, Idaho, 1965-79, Nelson, Rosholt, Robertson, Tolman and Tucker, Twin Falls, from 1979; judge U.S. Cir. Ct. (9th cir.), Boise, Idaho, 1990—. With Idaho Air N.G., 1962-65, USAR, 1965-68. Mem. ABA (ho. of dels. 1974, 87-89), Am. Bar Found., Am. Coll. Trial Lawyers, Idaho State Bar (pres., bd. commrs.), Idaho Assn. Def. Counsel, Am. Bd. Trial Advocates (pres. Idaho chpt.), Phi Alpha Delta, Idaho Law Found. Office: US Ct Appeals 9th Circuit 304 N Eighth St PO Box 1339 Boise ID 83701-1339*

NELSON, THOMAS WILLIAM, former management consultant, government official; b. Rupert, Idaho, June 9, 1921; s. John Glenn and Jessie Olive (Wise) N.; m. Frances Grace Rotanzi, Oct. 17, 1948; children: Janet, Neal, Eric, Karen. A.B., San Diego State U., 1948; grad., Fed. Exec. Inst., 1968. Personnel technician U.S. Air Force, 1948-61; chief civilian salary and wage adminstrn. Hdqrs. U.S. Air Force, 1961-66; chief mgmt. div. Office of Sec. of Air Force, 1966-69; dep. adminstrv. asst. to Sec. Air Force, 1969-71, adminstrv. asst., 1971-80; pres., mgmt. cons. Thomas W. Nelson & Assoc. Inc., 1981-96; mgmt. cons. ManTech Internat. Corp., 1981-85. With U.S. Army, 1943-45, ETO. Decorated Purple Heart, Bronze Star; recipient Meritorious Service award Dept. Air Force, 1961, Exceptional Civilian Service award, 1971, 73, 75, 77, 79, 80; Disting. Civilian Service medal Dept. Def., 1980. Mem. Sigma Phi Epsilon. Home: 6344 Nicholson St Falls Church VA 22044-1912

NELSON, VIRGINIA SIMSON, pediatrician, physiatrist, educator; b. L.A.; d. Jerome and Virginia (Kuppler) Simson; children: Eric, Paul. AB, Stanford U., 1963, MD, 1970; MPH, U. Mich., 1974. Diplomate Am. Bd. Pediatrics, Am. Bd. Phys. Medicine and Rehab. Pediatrician Inst. Study Mental Retardation and Related Disabilities, U. Mich., Ann Arbor, 1973-80; mem. faculty phys. medicine and rehab. dept. U. Mich. Med. Ctr., Ann Arbor, 1980-83, 85—, resident in phys. medicine and rehab., 1983-85, chief pediatric phys. medicine and rehab. physician, 1985—. Contbr. articles to profl. jours. Office: Univ Mich Med Ctr F7822 Mott Hospital Ann Arbor MI 48109-0230

NELSON, WALDEMAR STANLEY, civil engineer, consultant; b. New Orleans, July 8, 1916; s. Bernard Stanley and Mary Lockett (Hutson) N.; widowed; children: Mary Sue Nelson Roniger, Martha Nelson Frost, Charles W., Virginia Nelson Dodge, Kenneth H. BS in Mech. and Elec. Engring., Tulane U., 1936. Registered civil, elec. and mech. engr., 44 states. Jr. engr. A. M. Lockett & Co., 1936-37; civil engr. Jeff. Lake Sulphur Co., Brazoria, Tex., 1937-38; chief survey party N.O. Pub. Belt. R.R., New Orleans, 1938; resident engr. James M. Todd, Buras, La., 1938-39; pvt. practice New Orleans, 1939-40; asst. chief engr. W. Horace Williams Co., Camp Claiborne, La., 1940-41; sr. engr. U.S. Engr. Dept., Camp Claiborne, 1941-44; prin. Waldemar S. Nelson and Co. Inc., New Orleans, 1945—, chmn. bd. dirs.; past chmn. La. State Bd. Registration Profl. Engrs. and Land Surveyors; founding mem., pres. bd. advisors sch. engring. Tulane U. Chmn. Tulane Alumni Fund, Mems' Coun., 1984; mem. bd. visitors Tulane U.; active The Chamber/New Orleans, Boy Scouts Am.; past chmn. Com. of 50; past pres. bd. commrs. NewOrleans City Pk. Improvement Assn.; mem. exec. bd. Christmas New Orleans, 1988; past sr. warden of vestry St. Andrew's Episcopal Ch.; past chmn. bd. dirs. St. Andrew's Episcopal Sch.; past pres. bd. trustees St. Martin's Protestant Episcopal Sch.; trustee Tulane Engring. Found.; bd. dirs. River Region, MetroVision. Recipient Outstanding Engring. Alumnus award Tulane U., 1976, Honor award Constrn. Industry Assn. New Orleans, Inc., 1982, Role Model of Yr. award Young Leadership Coun., 1987, Vol. of Yr. award Tulane U. Alumni Affairs, 1992. Fellow ASCE (life), ASME (life, past chmn. New Orleans sect.); mem. IEEE, NSPE (past v.p., past chmn. bd. ethical rev.), Am. Pub. Works Assn. (life), Am. Acad. Environ. Engrs. (diplomate), Nat. Coun. Engring. Examiners (past treas., Disting. Svc. award), Soc. Am. Mil. Engrs., Soc. Naval Archs. and Marine Engrs., La. Engring. Soc. (hon., past pres., Charles M. Kerr Pub. Rels. award, Leo M. Odom Profl. Svcs. award, A.B. Paterson medal, Andrew M. Lockett medal), La. Engring. Found. (trustee 1990, treas. 1991, sec. 1994-95, pres. 1995-96), Soc. Tulane Engrs. (past pres.), French-Am. C. of C. (pres. La. chpt. 1992-93, chmn. 1994, pres. 1996-97), Tulane Alumni Assn. (past pres.), Engrs. Club New Orleans (past pres.), Tau Beta Pi, Pi Tau Sigma, Eta Kappa Nu, others. Avocations: fishing, boating, gardening, shop work, photography. Office: Waldemar S Nelson & Co Inc 1200 Saint Charles Ave New Orleans LA 70130-4334

NELSON, WALLACE BOYD, economics and business administration educator; b. Oilton, Okla., Mar. 17, 1923; s. Frank and Notie (Ferguson) N.; m. Merietta Josephine Lair, Sept. 1, 1942; 1 child, Larry Frank. BS, So. Ill. U., 1947; MA, U. Ia., 1948; PhD, U. Iowa, 1950. From asst. to prof. econs. Kans. State U., 1950-61; prof., chmn. dept. bus. adminstrn. Arlington (Tex.) State Coll., 1961-65; prof. econs. and bus. adminstrn., dean U. Tex. Sch. Bus. Adminstrn., Arlington, 1965-73; prof. econs. and bus. adminstrn. U. Tex., Arlington, 1973-93, prof. emeritus, 1993—; pres. Nelson Assocs., 1974—; co-chmn. regional devel. com. N. Tex. Commn., 1972-77, bd. dirs. commn., 1973-77; personal injury litigation cons. Contbr. articles to profl. jours. With USAAF, 1943-46, USAF, 1951-53. Honor guest Brazil at Celebration Brazil's 150th Anniversary, 1972; Ford Motor Co. fellow, 1955, rsch. fellow Claremont Men's Coll., 1957. Mem. Am. Arbitration Assn., Fed. Mediation Conciliation Service, Nat. Acad. Arbitrators, Arlington, Dallas, Ft. Worth C. of C., Am. Econ. Assn., Indsl. Relations Research Assn., Southwestern Social Sci. Assn., Order of Artus (pres. 1948). Presbyn. (trustee). Club: Rotarian. Home: 917 Sherwood Dr Arlington TX 76013-1571

NELSON, WALLACE WARREN, retired superintendent experimental station, agronomy educator; b. Tracy, Minn., Feb. 17, 1928; s. Elmer R. and Mabel K. (Anderson) N.; m. Arlene S. Michelson, June 18, 1949; children: Thomas W., Kathryn J. BS, U. Minn., 1950, PhD, 1956. Asst. supt., agronomist N.E. Exptl. Sta. U. Minn., Duluth, 1953-59; supt., agronomist S.W. Exptl. Sta. U. Minn., Lamberton, 1959-72, supt., prof., 1972-95; ret.; bd. dirs. North Star Ins., Cottonwood, Minn. Bd. dirs. Minn . Pollution Control Agys., 1980-83. Recipient Outstanding Alumni award U. Minn., 1989. Fellow Am. Soc. Agronomists (chmn. A-7 1988). Lutheran.

NELSON, WALTER GERALD, retired insurance company executive; b. Peoria, Ill., Jan. 2, 1930; s. Walter Dennis and Hazel Marie (Tucker) N.; m. Mary Ann Olberding, Jan. 28, 1952 (dec. Nov. 1989); children—Ann (Mrs. Michael Larkin), Michael, Susan (Mrs. Jay Boor), Patrick, Thomas, Timothy, Molly (Mrs. David Edwards); m. Mary Jo Sunderland, Apr. 6, 1991. Student, St. Benedict's Coll., Atchison, Kans., 1947-49, Bradley U., Peoria, Ill., 1949; JD, Creighton U., Omaha, 1952. Bar: Nebr. 1952, Ill. 1955; CLU. Practice in Peoria, 1955-56; with State Farm Life Ins. Co., Bloomington, Ill., 1956—; counsel State Farm Life Ins. Co., 1968—, v.p., 1970-96; adj. prof. Ill. State U., Bloomington, 1996—; past dir. Ill. Life Ins. Coun.; past chmn. legal sect. Am. Coun. Life Ins.; spkr. in field. Contbr. articles to profl. jours. Community bd. dirs. St. Joseph Med. Ctr., Bloomington, Ill., 1994. Mem. ABA, Ill. Bar Assn., Nebr. Bar Assn., Assn. Life Ins. Counsel (bd. govs., past pres.), Nat. Orgn. Life and Health Ins. Guaranty Assns. (past chmn., bd. dirs.), Bloomington Country Club, KC. Republican. Roman Catholic.

NELSON, WALTER WILLIAM, computer programmer, consultant; b. Seattle, May 7, 1954; s. Arne A. and Helen R. (Truitt) N.; m. Paula E. Truax, Dec. 21, 1985. BA in Zoology, U. Wash., 1976, BS in Psychology, 1977; PhC in Psychology, U. Minn., 1982. Systems analyst Dept. of Social and Health Svcs., State of Wash., Seattle, 1986-89; computer info. cons. Dept. of Health, State of Wash., Seattle, 1989-90; pres. Data Dimensions, Inc. (name now Nelson Consulting, Inc.), Seattle, 1990—; pres. Tech. Alliance, Renton, Wash., 1990-91, Nelson Family Homes, Inc., 1996—. Contbr. articles to profl. jours. Mem. Tech Alliance, Berkeley Macintosh Users Group, Seattle Downtown Macintosh Bus. Users Group, 4th Dimension Spl. Interest Group (founder, pres. 1990—). Avocations: tennis, golf, thoroughbred horse racing. Office: Nelson Consulting Inc 6729 20th Ave NW Seattle WA 98117-5707

NELSON, WILLARD GREGORY, veterinarian, mayor; b. Lewiston, Idaho, Nov. 21, 1937; s. Donald William and Eve Mae (Boyer) N.; m. Mary Ann Eklund, Apr. 3, 1965 (div.); children: Elizabeth Ann, John Gregory. BS in Premedicine, Mont. State U., 1959; DVM, Wash. State U., 1961. Lic. veterinarian, Wash., Oreg., Idaho, Mont. Pvt. practice vet. medicine, Kuna, Idaho, 1963-66; asst. to dir. Idaho Dept. Agr., Boise, 1966-78; asst. chief Idaho Bur. Animal Health, 1978-80, chief, 1980-81; adminstr., state veterinarian Idaho Div. Animal Industries, 1981-90; dir. Idaho Dept. Agr., 1990-95; dir. pub. affairs Idaho Farm Bur. Fedn., 1995—; dir. Leadership Idaho Agriculture, 1994—; mayor City of Kuna (Idaho), 1984—; chmn. Idaho Gov.'s Human and Animal Health Consortium, 1983-90. Kuna city councilman, 1964-68, pres. Planning and Zoning Commn., 1968-72; mem. bd. trustees Joint Sch. Dist. 3, 1970-71, pres., 1972-76; mem. adv. bd. Mercy Med. Hosp., Nampa, Idaho, 1986-96; mem. adv. com. Wash., Oreg., Idaho Coll. Vet. Medicine, 1983—; mem. ADA Planning Assn., 1986—, vice chmn., 1991-92, chmn. 1993-94; mem. Western U.S. Trade Assn., 1990-95, treas., 1992, v.p. 1993, pres. 1994; mem. Idaho Emergency Response Commn., 1992-95, Idaho Export Coun., 1992—, Idaho Rural Devel. Coun., 1992—, vice-chair, 1993, chair 1994; bd. dirs S.W. Idaho Rsch. and Devel., 1993—. Served as capt. U.S. Army Vet Corps, 1961-63; lt. col. Idaho Army N.G., 1979-88, col., 1988—. Mem. VFW, Idaho Vet. Med. Assn. (v.p. 1987, pres.-elect 1988, pres. 1989, Idaho Veterinarian of Yr. 1989), S.W. Idaho Vet. Med. Assn., U.S. Animal Health Assn. (chmn. anaplasmosis com. 1987-90), AVMA (mem. coun. on pub. health and regulatory medicine 1988-94, chmn. 1993, pres. nat. assembly 1988), Western States Livestock Assn., USDA (nat. damage control adv. com. 1992-94, nat. dir. animal welfare coalition 1992—), Am. Legion. Lutheran. Club: Lions (Kuna). Home: PO Box 196 793 W 4th St Kuna ID 83634-1941 Office: 2270 Old Penitentiary Rd Boise ID 83712-8266

NELSON, WILLIAM GEORGE, IV, software company executive; b. Phila., May 26, 1934; s. William George III and Eleanor (Boyle) N. BA in Chemistry, Swarthmore Coll., 1956; MBA in Finance, U. Pa., 1958; PhD in Econs., Rice U., 1965. Various positions Du Pont Co., 1957-62, Monsanto Co., St. Louis, 1965-76; vis. asst. prof. Washington U., St. Louis, 1966-75; sr. v.p. Chase Econs./Interactive Data, Waltham, Mass., 1976-83; pres. Pansophic Systems, Lisle, Ill., 1983-90; pres., CEO OnLine Software, Ft. Lee, N.J., 1990-91, bd. dirs.; pres., CEO Pilot Software, Boston, 1992-94; CEO Harris Data Corp., 1990—; pres., CEO Clarendon Capital Corp., Boston, 1995-96; chmn., pres., CEO GEAC Computer Corp. Ltd., Markham, Ont., Can., 1996—; bd. dirs. GEAC, Toronto, Manugistics, Rockville, Md., Harris Data, Waukesha, Wis., HPR, Inc., Boston, Project Software and Devel. Inc., Cambridge, Mass. Bd. dirs. Swarthmore Coll., Hampton U. NFS fellow in econs., 1963-65. Office: GEAC Computer Corp Ltd, 11 Allstate Pkwy Ste 300, Markham, ON Canada L3R 9TB

NELSON, WILLIAM O., pharmaceutical company executive; b. Upland, Calif., Mar. 30, 1941; s. William Orestas and Glenice Irene (Pearson) N.; m. Sue Farmer, Jan. 27, 1962 (div. Jan. 1971); 1 child, Terri Lynn; m. Deborah Marie Goodwin, Oct. 5, 1985. AA, Pima Coll., Tucson, 1976; BS, U. Phoenix, 1980. Sales rep. Sandoz Pharms., Riverside, Calif., 1966-71, Tucson, 1971-79; regional sales mgr. Sandoz Pharms., Phoenix, 1979-87, western area mgr., med. scis. liaison, 1987-94; assoc. dir. oncology bus. ops. Novartis Pharm. Corp., East Hanover, N.J., 1994-97, ret., 1997. With USN, 1959-63. Republican. Avocations: golf, trap shooting, audiophile. Home: 4810 S Rimrock Loop Gold Canyon AZ 85219

NELSON, WILLIAM RANKIN, surgeon, educator; b. Charlottesville, Va., Dec. 12, 1921; s. Hugh Thomas and Edith (Rankin) N.; m. Nancy Laidley, Mar. 17, 1956 (div. 1979); children: Robin Page Nelson Russel, Susan Kimberly Nelson Wright, Anne Rankin Nelson Cron; m. Pamela Morgan Phelps, July 5, 1984. BA, U. Va., 1943, MD, 1945. Diplomate Am. Bd. Surgery. Intern Vanderbilt U. Hosp., Nashille, 1945-46; resident in surgery U. Va. Hosp., Charlottesville, 1949-51; fellow surg. oncology Meml. Sloan Kettering Cancer Ctr., N.Y.C., 1951-55; instr. U. Colo. Sch. Medicine, Denver, 1955-57; asst. clin. prof. U. Colo. Sch. Medicine, 1962-87, clin. prof. surgery, 1987—; asst. prof. Med. Coll. Va., Richmond, 1957-62; mem. exec. com. U. Colo. Cancer Ctr.; mem. nat. bd., nat. exec. com. Am. Cancer Soc. Contbr. articles to profl. jours. and chpts. to textbooks. Capt. USAAF, 1946-48. Recipient Nat. Div. award Am. Cancer Soc., 1979. Fellow Am. Coll. Surgeons (bd. govs. 1984-89); mem. AMA, Internat. Soc. Surgery, Brit. Assn. Surg. Oncology, Royal Soc. Medicine (U.K.), Soc. Surg. Oncology (pres. 1975-76), Soc. Head and Neck Surgeons (pres. 1986-87), Am. Cancer Soc. (pres. Colo. div. 1975-77, exec. com., nat. bd. dirs., del. dir. from Colo. div. 1975—), Am. Soc. Clin. Oncology, Western Surg. Assn. Colo. Med. Soc., Denver Med. Soc., Denver Acad. Surgery, Rocky Mt. Oncology Soc., Univ. Club, Rotary. Republican. Episcopalian. Avocations: skiing, backpacking, travel, bicycling, fly fishing.

NELSON, WILLIE, musician, songwriter; b. Abbott, Tex., Apr. 30, 1933; children: Jacob, Lukas, Paula Carlene, Amy, Lana, Susie, Billy. Student, Baylor U. Worked as salesman; announcer, host country music shows local Tex. stas.; bass player, Ray Price's band; then formed own band, personal appearances at Grand Ole Opry, Nashville, throughout U.S., 1964—; rec. artist, Atlantic, Columbia and RCA records; albums include One for the Road, Here's Willie Nelson, 1963, Country Willie, 1973, Red Headed Stranger, 1975, The Troublemaker, 1976, Willie Nelson and His Friends, 1976, Willie Before His Time, Wanted/The Outlaw, The Willie Way, The Best of Willie Nelson, Stardust, 1978, Family Bible, 1980, Tougher Than Leather, 1983, City of New Orleans, 1984, Me and Paul, 1985, (with Johnny Cash, Kris Kristofferson and Waylon Jennings) Highwayman, 1985, The Promise Land, 1986, Partners, 1986, Island in the Sea, 1987, Seashores of Old Mexico, 1987, What a Wonderful World, 1988, A Horse Called Music, 1989, Highwayman II, 1990, Born for Trouble, 1990, Clean Shirt Waylon and Willie, 1991, Across the Borderline, 1993, Across the Borderline, 1993, Moonlight Becomes You, 1993, Healing Hands of Time, 1994, Super Hits, 1994, Just One Love, 1995, The Road Goes on Forever (The Highwaymen), 1995, Spirit, 1996, ...and then I wrote, 1995, (with Bonnie Nelson, Jody Payne, Johnny Gamble) Spirit, 1996; film appearances include: Electric Horseman, 1979, Honeysuckle Rose, 1980, Thief, 1981, Barbarosa, 1982; star, co-writer mus. score TV film Stagecoach, 1986; theme song performed, film Welcome Home, 1989; TV films include Where the Hell's That Gold, 1988, Once upon a Texas Train, 1989, A Pair of Aces, 1990, Born for Trouble, 1990, Another Pair of Aces: Three of a Kind, 1991, Big Country, 1994, Big Dreams and Broken Hearts: The Dottie West Story, 1995, The Beach Boys: Nashville Sounds, 1996, Starlight, 1996, ; author: (autobiography) I Didn't Come Here and I Ain't Leading, 1988. Served in USAF. Recipient Grammy award for song Blue Eyes Crying in the Rain 1975, for Georgia on My Mind 1978, for Mammas Don't Let Your Babies Grow Up to Be Cowboys (with Waylon Jennings) 1978, Billboard mag. citation for Top Album Artist 1976, Country Music Assn. award for single Good Hearted Woman, for vocal duo with Waylon Jennings and for album Wanted: The Outlaws, Grammy award for Best Album, 1984, Special Humanitarian award Nat. Farmers Orgn., 1986, (with Julio Iglesias) Best Vocal Duo award Country Music Assn., Grammy Lifetime Achievement award, 1989; named to Nashville Songwriters Assn. Hall of Fame, 1973, CMA Entertainer of Yr., 1979, Country Music Hall of Fame, 1993. Office: care Mark Rothbaum & Assocs Inc PO Box 2689 Danbury CT 06813-2689 also: Island Records Inc 5th Fl 400 Lafayette St New York NY 10003

NELSON-HUMPHRIES, TESSA (TESSA UNTHANK), English language educator, writer, lecturer; b. Yorkshire, Eng.; came to U.S., 1955; m. Kenneth Nelson Brown, June 1, 1957 (dec. 1962); m. Cecil H. Unthank, Sept. 26, 1963 (dec. 1979). BA, U. London, 1953; MA, U. N.C., 1965; PhD in English, U. Liverpool (Eng.), 1973. Head English dept. Richard Thomas Girls Sch., Elmore Green Sch., Walsall, Eng., 1956-58, 59-60; dir. English studies Windsor Coll., Buenos Aires, Argentina, 1958-59; prof. English, Cumberland Coll., Williamsburg, Ky., 1964-90; prof. dept. English, N.Mex. State U., 1990-91. Best Actress award Carlsbad (N.Mex.) Little Theatre, 1962, Cumberland Coll., 1979; Fulbright fellow, 1955-56, Danforth fellow, 1971, James Still fellow, 1983; Mellon travel/study grantee, China, 1981, 87; recipient awards for fiction Eng., 1986, 87, 88, Clemence Dane trophy, 1995, Third prize Cairns Poetry Competition, 1995. Fellow AAUW; mem. Soc. Women Writers and Journalists (Short Story prize 1975, 87, Poetry prize 1988, 89, Julia Cairns Silver trophy for Poetry, 1978, article prize, London, 1986, poetry prizes, 1994, Fiction award U.K. 1995), Soc. Women Writers and Journalists Eng., Soc. Children's Book Writers, Vegetarian Soc. (life), Doña Ana County (N.Mex.) Humane Soc. (life), Mensa. Episcopalian. Contbr. articles to Cats Mag., Let's Live, The Lookout, Child Life, Children's Digest, Vegetarian Times, Alive!, The Dalesman, Mich. Quar. Rev., Bull. of Soc. Children's Book Writers, Bull. Soc. Women Writers and Journalists, others; columnist, British Vegetarian mag., 1976-85, Weekly Telegraph (U.K.), King Charles Spaniel Bull.; contbr. poetry to various mags. including Joycean Lit. Arts Guild, Z-Miscellaneous, Blue Unicorn, Appalachian Heritage, Aireings-U.K., ENVOI (HardBack Anthology)-U.K., Negative Capability, McCann's

Alaska Jour. Poetry Philosophy, Array, New Frontiers of N.Mex., Calliope (U.S.).

NELSON-MAYSON, LINDA RUTH, art museum curator; b. Vincennes, Ind., Jan. 9, 1954; d. Robert Arthur and Darleen Marie (Andrews) N.; m. William A. Mayson, June 12, 1982; 1 child, Eric Nelson. BFA, Miami U., Oxford, Ohio, 1976; MFA, Ohio State U., 1981. Co-dir. Artreach Gallery, Columbus, Ohio, 1980-82; art instr., gallery asst. Ohio U., Chillicothe, 1982-83; asst. curator Ross County Mus., Chillicothe, 1982-83; art dir. Aaron Copland Music & Arts Program, White Plains, N.Y., 1982-85; artist-in-edn. Nebr. Arts Council, Omaha, 1983-85; curator Art Mus. South Tex., Corpus Christi, 1985-89; curator collections Columbia (S.C.) Mus. Art, 1989-92, dep. dir. curatorial svcs., 1992-94; curator Minn. Mus. Am. Art, St. Paul, 1994—; juror art exhibits Corpus Christi Arts Found., 1986-88, Hardin Simmons U., 1987, Anderson Coll., 1989, Hilton Head Art League, 1994; mem. pub. art selection panel S.C. Arts Coun., 1990; mem. steering com. South Tex. Regional Arts Conf., 1986-88; adj. lectr. art history U. S.C., 1989-94; chmn. curators com. S.E. Mus. Conf., 1991-93, chmn. local program com., 1992, mem. program com., 1992-93; mem. exhbns. panel Exhibits USA, 1997. Grantee NEA, S.C. Arts Coun., Tex. Coun. on Arts, Kress Found., Inst. Mus. Svcs. Mem. am. Assn. Mus. (co-chmn. exhibits competition 1991-93, chmn. curator's com. 1993-95, chmn. of SPC com. 1994-95, nominating com. 1994-95), Minn. Assn. Mus., Midwest Mus. Assn., Coll. Art Assn. Democrat. Avocations: dogs, gardening, camping. Office: Minn Mus Am Art Landmark Ctr 75 5th St W Saint Paul MN 55102-1431

NELTNER, MICHAEL MARTIN, lawyer; b. Cin., July 31, 1959; s. Harold John and Joyce Ann (Schell) N.; m. Barbara Ann Phair, July 9, 1988; children: Brandon August, Alexandra Nicole. BA, Mercy Coll., 1981; MA, Athenaeum of Ohio, 1987; JD, U. Cin., 1994. Bar: Ohio 1994, U.S. Dist. Ct. (so. dist.) Ohio 1995. Tchr. Elder H.S., Cin., 1985-91; ins. agt. Ky. Ctrl., Cin., 1987-91; mediator City of Cin., 1992-94; tchg. asst. Ohio Gov.'s Inst., Cin., 1992; legal extern to Chief Justice Thomas Moyer Ohio Supreme Ct., 1993; assoc. Cash, Cash, Eagen & Kessel, Cin., 1994—. Editor-in-chief Mercy Coll. Lit. Mag., 1980-81, U. Cin. Law Rev., 1993-94. Campaign coord. Rep. Orgn. Detroit, 1980. Recipient Merit scholarship Cin. Enquirer, 1977-81, Sage scholarship Mercy Coll., 1980, Am. Jurisprudence award Lawyers Coop. Publishing, 1994. Mem ABA, Ohio Bar Assn., Cin. Bar Assn. (mem. acad. medicine com. 1995—, mem. Ct. Appeals com. 1995—). Home: 3317 Felicity Dr Cincinnati OH 45211-5902 Office: Cash Cash Eagen & Kessel 432 Walnut St Cincinnati OH 45202-3909

NEMAN, DANIEL LOUIS, movie critic; b. Cin., May 18, 1960; s. Albert Henry and Beth Maxine (Smilansky) N.; m. Mary Anne Pikrone. BA in English Lang. and Lit., U. Chgo., 1982. Movie critic, entertainment writer Bryan-College Sta. Tex., Eagle, Tex., 1983-86; movie critic, features writer Richmond (Va.) News Leader, 1986-92, Richmond Times-Dispatch, 1992—. Mem. Soc. Profl. Journalists, Va. Press Assn. Office: Richmond Times-Dispatch 333 E Grace St Richmond VA 23293-1000

NEMAN, THOMAS EDWARD, advertising and marketing executive, researcher; b. Milw., Aug. 7, 1940; s. Edward Louis and Helen (Lawler) N.; m. Jo Ann Spahn, Oct. 14, 1967. A.B., Marquette U., 1962; M.A., Ind. U.-Bloomington, 1963, Ph.D., 1967. Sr. economist, Smith Kline and French, Phila., 1967-69; corp. mgr. statis. applications Gen. Foods Corp., White Plains, N.Y., 1969-72; v.p., assoc. research dir. J. Walter Thompson, N.Y.C., 1972-76; v.p., research dir. Leber, Katz Ptnrs., N.Y.C., 1976-79; sr. v.p., dir. planning and research BBDO, Worldwide Inc., N.Y.C., and Detroit, 1979-97, sr. v.p., dir. strategic svcs., Detroit; mem. council Advt. Research Found., N.Y.C., 1972—. Mem. Advt. Research Found., Am. Acad. Advt., Econ. Club Detroit, Am. Mktg. Assn., Am. Statis. Assn. (sec. N.Y. chpt. 1977-78). Republican. Roman Catholic. Home: 21590 E Valley Woods Dr Franklin MI 48025-2633 Office: BBDO Detroit 26261 Evergreen Rd Southfield MI 48076-4447

NEMEC, JOSEF, organic chemist, researcher; b. Ostresany, Czechoslovakia, Sept. 7, 1929; came to U.S., 1969; s. Josef Nemec and Marie (Joskova) Nemcova; m. Anna Pastush, Aug. 29, 1975; 1 child, Marketa. MS, Inst. Chem. Tech., Prague, Czechoslovakia, 1954; PhD, Czechoslovak Acad. Scis., Prague, 1958. Organic chemist Inst. Chem. Tech., Prague, 1954-61; sr. rsch. chemist Czechoslovak Acad. Scis., Prague, 1961-69; rsch. fellow in organic chemistry Wayne State U., Detroit, 1969-70; sr. rsch. scientist Squibb Inst. Med. Rsch., New Brunswick, N.J., 1970-75; staff mem. St. Jude Children's Rsch. Hosp., Memphis, 1975-84; sr. scientist Nat. Cancer Inst.-Program Resources, Inc. Cancer R&D Ctr., Frederick, Md., 1984-95; adj. prof. med. chemistry U. Tenn., Memphis, 1970-91; external examiner U. Zimbabwe, Harare, 1994—; cons. in field. Contbr. articles to scholarly and profl. jours. Grantee Nat. Cancer Inst., 1975-85. Mem. AAAS, Am. Chem. Soc., Royal Soc. Chemistry, Czechoslovak Soc. Arts and Scis. Achievements include patents in fields of anticancer agents, organic chemicals, semimicroequipment in organic chemistry; research in natural products, synthetic anticancer agents, monosaccharides, experimental semimicrotechniques in organic chemistry.

NEMECEK, ALBERT DUNCAN, JR., retail company executive, investment banker, management consultant; b. Helena, Mont., Mar. 10, 1936; s. Albert Duncan and Geneva (Reindle) N.; m. Marilyn Ann Shaughnessy, Sept. 7, 1963 (div.); children: Maureen Ann, Steven Mathew; m. Judith Eileen Swift, Sept. 18, 1981 (div.); 1 child, Jennifer Eileen. B.S., U. Md., 1960, postgrad. in econs., 1961. Agt. IRS, Washington, 1961-65; tax dir. Macke Co., Washington, 1965-69; tax dir., then sec. Garfinckle, Brooks Bros., Miller & Rhoads, Inc., Washington, 1969-76; treas. Garfinckle, Brooks Bros., Miller & Rhoads, Inc., 1976—, v.p., 1979—; mng. ptnr. Nemecek & Falleroni, 1987, Nemecek & Jacknis, investment bankers, mgmt. cons., Falls Church, Va., 1989; founder Nemecek & Co., Inc., Falls Church, 1990; founder Entrepreneurial Growth Fund, Falls Church, 1990. Founder The Leadership Group, 1996. Home: 18724 Walkers Choice Rd Apt 5 Gaithersburg MD 20879-2621 *A man's success is measured by the respect he has gained from his peers, his understanding and compassion, respect for the feelings of others, appreciation of the world's beauty, and his attempts to leave the world better than he found it.*

NEMECEK, GEORGINA MARIE, molecular pharmacologist; b. Mineola, N.Y., Aug. 27, 1946; d. George and Frances Valerie (Masaryk) N. AB, Mt. Holyoke Coll., 1968; PhD, U. Pa., 1972. Rsch. assoc. dept. biochemistry U. Mass. Med. Sch., Worcester, 1972-73, postdoctoral fellow of Am. Heart Assn., dept. biochemistry, 1974, asst. prof., 1974-80, assoc. prof., 1981-83; sr. scientist platelet dept. Sandoz Pharm. Corp., East Hanover, N.J., 1983-85, mem. sr. sci. staff, platelet dept., 1986, fellow, sect. head molecular biology, 1987-91, fellow diabetes, 1991-93; study dir. regulatory toxicology Sandoz Pharm. Corp., East Hanover, 1993-96; internat. project mgr. preclin. safety Novartis Pharm. Corp., East Hanover, 1997—; vis. scientist dept. molecular biology, Princeton (N.J.) U., 1987, Sea Pharm. Inc., 1985, NATO, U. Libre, Brussels, 1979, biotechnology dept. Sandoz AG, Basel, Switzerland, 1988. Contbr. articles to profl. jours. Named Nat. Heart, Lung, and Blood Inst. Young Investigator, NIH, 1977-81. Mem. Am. Soc. Pharmacol. Exptl. Therapeutics, N.Y. Acad. Scis. (chmn. biochem. sect. 1992-94), Tissue Culture Assn., Soc. Toxicology, Soc. Toxicol. Pathologists, Sigma Xi. Avocations: boating, gardening, riding, needlework. Office: Novartis Pharm Corp 59 State Route 10 East Hanover NJ 07936-1005

NEMEROFF, CHARLES BARNET, neurobiology and psychiatry educator; b. Bronx, N.Y., Sept. 7, 1949; s. Philip Peace and Sarah (Greenberg) N.; m. Melissa Ann Pilkington, May 24, 1980; children: Matthew P., Amanda P., Sarah-Frances P. B.S., CCNY, 1970; M.S., Northeastern U., 1973; Ph.D., U. N.C., 1976, M.D., 1981. Diplomate Am. Bd. Psychiatry and Neurology; lic. physician, N.C., Ga. Research asst. ichthyology Am. Mus. Natural History, N.Y.C., 1968-71, neurochemistry lab. McLean Hosp., Belmont, Mass., 1971-72; research assoc. surgery Beth Israel Hosp., Boston, 1972-73; teaching asst. biology Northeastern U., 1972-73; postdoctoral fellow Biol. Scis. Research Ctr., U. N.C., Chapel Hill, 1976-77, research fellow, 1977-83, clin. instr. psychiatry, 1983; resident in psychiatry N.C. Meml. Hosp., Chapel Hill, 1981-83; asst. prof. dept. psychiatry and pharmacology Duke U., Durham, N.C., 1983-85, assoc. prof. psychiatry, 1985-89, assoc. prof. pharmacology, 1986-89, prof. depts. psychiatry and pharmacology, 1989-91; chief div. biological psychiatry, 1988-91, prof., chmn. dept. psychiatry and behavioral scis. Emory U. Sch. Medicine, 1991—, Reunette W. Harris prof. psychiatry and behavioral scis., 1994—; vis. prof. physiology Cath. U., Santiago, Chile, 1978. Predoctoral fellow Schizophrenia Research Found., Soc. Scottish Rite, Lexington, Mass., 1975-76; postdoctoral fellow Nat. Inst. Neurol., Communicative Disorders and Stroke, 1977; recipient Michiko Kuno award U. N.C., 1978, 79, Merck award for acad. excellence, 1981; grantee Nat. Inst. Aging, 1982-83, NIMH, 1983—; Merck award for young investigators Am. Geriatrics Soc., 1985, 2d prize Anna Monica Found. for Research in Endogenous Depression, 1987, Merit award NIMH, 1987; Nanaline Duke fellow Duke U. Med. Ctr., 1985-87; Rsch. prize World Fedn. Societies of Biol. Psychiatry, 1991; recipient Edward J. Sachar award Columbia U., 1993, Edward A. Strecker prize Instl. Pa. Hosp., 1993, Outstanding Alumni award in health scis. Northeastern U., 1995. Fellow Am. Coll. Neuropsychopharmacology (Mead Johnson travel award 1982, coun. 1993—, pres. 1997), Am. Coll. Psychiatrists (chmn. contbns. com. 1991-93, edn. com. 1993-96, 96—, bd. regents 1994-97); mem. Soc. Neurosci. (program com. 1993-95), AAAS, N.Y. Acad. Scis., Internat. Soc. Psychoneuroendocrinology (pres. 1993-96, Curt P. Richter award 1985), Internat. Soc. Neurochemistry, Am. Soc. Neurochemistry (Jordi-Folch-Pi award 1987), Endocrine Soc., Internat. Soc. Neuroendocrinology, Soc. Biol. Psychiatry (A.E. Bennett award 1979, gold medal award 1996), Am. Fedn. Clin. Research, AMA, Am. Pain Soc., Am. Psychiat. Assn. (Kempf award 1989, Samuel Hibbs award 1991, coun. rsch. 1993—, chmn. 1994-95, rsch. prize 1996), Argentine Assn. Psychoneuroendocrinology (sci. council), Sigma Xi. Democrat. Jewish. Editor: (with A.J. Prange, Jr.) Neurotensin, a Brain and Gastrointestinal Peptide, 1982, (with A.J. Dunn) Peptides, Hormones and Behavior, 1984, (with P.T. Loosen) Handbook of Clinical Psychoneuroendocrinology, Neuropeptides in Psychiatric and Neurological Disorders, 1987, Neuropeptides in Psychiatric Disorders, 1991, Neuroendocrinology, 1992, (with P. Kitabgi) The Neurobiology of Neurotensin, 1992, (with A.F. Schatzberg) Textbook of Psychopharmacology, 1995; editor-in-chief: Depression, 1993—; co-editor-in-chief: Critical Revs. in Neurobiology, 1992—; contbr. numerous articles and abstracts to profl. jours., chpts. in books. Office: Emory U Sch Medicine Dept Psychiatry 1639 Pierce Dr Atlanta GA 30322

NEMEROFF, MICHAEL ALAN, lawyer; b. Feb. 16, 1946; s. Bernard Gregor and Frances (Gotleib) N.; m. Sharon Lynn Leininger, Sept. 22, 1974; children: Theodore, Patrick, James. BA, U. Chgo., 1968; JD, Columbia U., 1971. Asst. counsel Subcom. on Juvenile Delinquency of Senate Jud. Com., Washington, 1971-73; assoc. Sidley & Austin, Washington, 1973-78, ptnr., 1978—. Treas. Friends of Jim Sasser, 1978-96, Andy Ireland Campaign Com., 1984-92. Office: Sidley & Austin 1722 I St NW Washington DC 20006-3705

NEMETH, DIAN JEAN, secondary school educator; b. Lakewood, Ohio, Mar. 5, 1949; d. Alex Ray and Doris Jean (Sakach) N.; 1 child, Kymberlee Marie. BS, Kent State U., 1971, MEd, 1994. Cert. home econs. tchr., vocat. consumer-homemaking tchr., Ohio. Tchr. vocat. family and consumer scis. Cleve. Bd. Edn., 1972—; piloted modern design fine arts course Cleve. Bd. Edn., 1989-90; writer course of study for hospitality and facility care svcs. Active Tchrs.-Leader Inst., 1994—, Urban Task Force. Mem. Am. Vocat. Assn., Ohio Vocat. Assn., Greater Cleve. Assn. Family and Consumer Sci. (auditor 1994-95, treas. 1995—), Am. Assn. Family and Consumer Scis., Nat. Assn. Vocat. Edn. Spl. Needs Pers., Ohio Hotel and Motel Assn., Ohio Assn. Family and Consumer Scis. (v.p. membership 1997), Sigma Sigma Sigma (chpt. adv. bd. 1992, chpt. housing coord. 1992), Omicron Tau Theta. Democrat. Roman Catholic. Home: 8061 Greenwood View Dr Apt 1107 Parma OH 44129-5859

NEMETS, BORIS LVOVICH, programmer; b. Moscow, Mar. 21, 1953; came to the U.S., 1991; s. Lev Markovich and Sophia Aronovna (Shifrina) N.; m. Elena Sergeevna Kantorovitch, Dec. 18, 1976 (div.); 1 child, Anna; m. Marina Urievna Chekis, Nov. 10, 1987 (div. Apr. 1991); 1 child. MS in Mech. Engring., Moscow Automech. Inst., 1975; postgrad., Rsch. Inst. Pipelines, Moscow, 1978, 81. Rschr. Ctrl. Engine Toxity Rsch. Lab., Moscow, 1975, 78, Rsch. Inst. Pipelines, Moscow, 1979, 81; project leader Hydromechanic Equipment Design, Moscow, 1981, 91, sys. adminstr., 1986, 91; computer ops. staff PC Help Svc., Clark, N.J., 1993; cons. Tribase Sys., Florham Park, N.J., 1994; sr. programmer Realistic Techs. Inc., Florham Park, 1994-97, Automated Wagering Internat., Inc., Hackensack, N.J., 1997—. Patentee in field. Mem. IEEE. Home: 14 Royal Ave Livingston NJ 07039-3122 Office: Automated Wagering Internat Inc 411 Hackensack Ave Hackensack NJ 07601-6328

NEMFAKOS, CHARLES PANAGIOTIS, federal official; b. Athens, Greece, Oct. 21, 1942; s. Panagiotis Soterios and Mirka (Kyriakakis) N.; children: Mirka Leigh, Charles Jr. BA, Pan Am. U., 1964; MA, Georgetown U., 1982. Cert. in nat. security. Health advisor Dept. Pub. Health, Washington, 1965-66; fed. mgmt. intern Dept. Navy, Washington, 1966-67; budget analyst Naval Ordnance Systems Command, Washington, 1967-71; supervisory budget analyst Naval Ship Systems Command, Washington, 1971-73; sr. budget analyst Office of Sec. of Def., Washington, 1973-75; divsn. dir. Office of Budget and Reports, Dept. of Navy, Washington, 1975-76; assoc.dir. Office of Budgets and Reports, Dept. of Navy, Washington, 1976-93; dep. asst. sec. Dept. of Navy, Washington, 1994-95, dep. under sec., 1995—; lectr. Naval Postgrad. Sch., Monterey, Calif., 1984—, Georgetown U., Washington, 1987—; mem. base structure com. Dept. Navy, Washington, 1990-91, mem. sr. advisors group, 1991-92, vice chmn. base structure com., 1992-95. Contbr. articles to profl. jours. Coach McLean (Va.) Youth Soccer, 1978-93, chmn., 1982-85; bd. dirs. McLean Youth, Inc., 1980-84; registrar Va. Youth Soccer Assn., 1984-86. Recipient Dept. Navy Superior Civilian Svc. award Asst. Sec. of Navy, 1980, Dept. Navy Disting. Civilian Svc. award Sec. of Navy, 1985, 87, 93, Dept. Def. Disting. Civilian Svc. award Sec. of Def., 1990, Dept. Navy Disting. Pub. Svc. award Sec. of Navy, 1995; named to Rank of Disting. Exec. Pres. of U.S., 1986, 95, to Rank of Meritorious Exec., Pres. of U.S., 1981, 91. Mem. Am. Assn. Budget and Program Analysis (dir.-at-large 1980-83), Am. Soc. of Mil. Comptrs. (v.p. 1988-90), Fed. Execs. Inst. Alumni Assn., Tau Kappa Epsilon (chpt. pres. 1964-65). Greek Orthodox. Avocations: golf, tennis, coaching soccer. Office: Under Sec of Navy Pentagon 4E 775 Washington DC 20350-1000

NEMHAUSER, GEORGE L., industrial, systems engineer, operations research educator; b. N.Y.C., July 27, 1937; s. Martin and Rose (Schwartz) N.; m. Ellen Krupsaw, Sept. 14, 1959; children: Wendy, Dennis. B.Chem.Engring., CCNY, 1958; M.S., Northwestern U., 1959, Ph.D., 1961. Prof. ops. research Johns Hopkins U., Balt., 1961-69; prof. Cornell U., Ithaca, N.Y., 1969-84, Leon C. Welch prof. engring., 1984-85, dir. Sch. Ops. Research and Indsl. Engring., 1977-83; Chandler prof. indsl. and systems engring. Ga. Inst. Tech., 1985—, inst. prof., 1992—; vis. prof. U. Leeds, U.K., 1963-64; vis. prof., dir. research Center for Ops. Research and Econometrics, U. Louvain, Belgium, 1975-77; cons. NSF (others.). Author: Introduction to Dynamic Programming, 1966, Integer Programming, 1972, Integer and Combinatorial Optimization, 1988; editor-in-chief: Ops. Research, 1975-78, Ops. Research Letters, 1981—; contbr. articles to profl. jours. NSF faculty fellow, 1969-70. Mem. NAE, Ops. Research Soc. Am. (pres. 1981-82, Lanchester prize 1977, 89, Kimball medal 1988), Inst. Mgmt. Sci., Soc. Indsl. and Applied Math., Am. Inst. Indsl. Engrs., Math. Programming Soc. (chmn. 1989-1992). Home: 1208 Villa Dr NE Atlanta GA 30306-2567

NEMICKAS, RIMGAUDAS, cardiologist, educator; b. Kaunas, Lithuania, Mar. 10, 1938; came to U.S., 1949; s. Romualdas and Elena (Saulyte) N.; m. Joan A. McLee, Feb. 16, 1965; children: Rimas Jonas, Kristina Nemickas Tomlinson, Tomas Edward, Nikolas. Student, Ind. U., 1954-57; MD magna cum laude, Loyola U., 1961; MD (hon.), Kaunas Med. Acad., 1993. Diplomate in internal medicine and cardiovascular diseases Am. Bd. Internal Medicine; lic. physician, Ill., Ind. Intern U. Chgo. Clinics, 1961-62; resident inmedicine U. Ill. Rsch. and Edn. Hosps., 1966-67; fellow in cardiology Cook County Hosp., Chgo., 1962-63, U. Chgo. Hosp., 1967-69; assoc. chief cardiology Loyola U., Maywood, Ill., 1972-77, clin. prof. medicine, 1979—; dir. cardiology Ill. Masonic Med. Ctr., Chgo., 1980—; chmn. Loyola Med. Practice Plan, Maywood, 1972-77; mem. Ill. Med. Soc. Ins. Svcs. Physician Rev. Com., Chgo., 1977-95. Mem. Task Force for Health Care Reform, Ministry of Health, Vilnius, Lithuania, 1994—. Capt. USAF, 1963-66. Fellow ACP, Am. Coll. Cardiology, Am. Coll. Chest Physicians; mem. AMA, Am. Heart Assn., Chgo. Soc. Internal Medicine, Chgo. Cardiology Group (sec.-treas. 1992-93). Republican. Roman Catholic. Avocations: jogging, traveling, fishing, collecting art. Office: Ill Masonic Med Offices 3000 N Halsted St Chicago IL 60657-5188

NEMIR, DONALD PHILIP, lawyer, commodities trader; b. Oakland, Calif., Oct. 31, 1931; s. Philip F. and Mary (Shavor) N. AB, U. Calif., Berkeley, 1957, JD, 1960. Bar: Calif. 1961, U.S. Dist. Ct. (no. dist.) Calif. 1961, U.S. Ct. Appeals (9th cir.) 1961, U.S. Dist. Ct. (ctrl. dist.) Calif. 1975, U.S. Supreme Ct. 1980. Pvt. practice, San Francisco, 1961—; pres. Law Offices of Donald Nemir, A Profl. Corp. Mem. Calif. State Bar Assn. Home: PO Box 1089 Mill Valley CA 94942-1089

NEMIRO, BEVERLY MIRIUM ANDERSON, author, educator; b. St. Paul, May 29, 1925; d. Martin and Anna Mae (Oshanyk) Anderson; m. Jerome Morton Nemiro, Feb. 10, 1951 (div. May 1975); children: Guy Samuel, Lee Anna, Dee Martin. Student Reed Coll., 1943-44; BA, U. Colo., 1947; postgrad., U. Denver. Tchr., Seattle Pub. Schs., 1945-46; fashion coord., dir. Denver Dry Goods Co., 1948-51; fashion dir. Denver Market Week Assn., 1952-53; free-lance writer, Denver, 1958—; moderator TV program Your Preschool Child, Denver, 1955-56; instr. writing and communications U. Colo. Denver Ctr., 1970—, U. Calif., San Diego, 1976-78, Met. State Coll., 1985; dir. pub. relations Fairmont Hotel, Denver, 1979-80; free lance fashion and TV model; author, co-author: The Complete Book of High Altitude Baking, 1961, Colorado a la Carte, 1963, Colorado a la Carte, Series II, 1966, (with Donna Hamilton) The High Altitude Cookbook, 1969, The Busy People's Cookbook, 1971 (Better Homes and Gardens Book Club selection 1971), Where to Eat in Colorado, 1967, Lunch Box Cookbook, 1965, Complete Book of High Altitude Baking, 1961, (under name Beverly Anderson) Single After 50, 1978, The New High Altitude Cookbook, 1980. Co-founder, pres. Jr. Symphony Guild, Denver, 1959-60; active Friends of Denver Libr., Opera Colo. Recipient Top Hand award Colo. Authors' League, 1969, 72, 79-82, 100 Best Best Books of Yr. award N.Y. Times, 1969, 71; named one of Colo.'s Women of Yr., Denver Post, 1964. Mem. Am. Soc. Journalists and Authors, Colo. Authors League (dir. 1969-79), Authors Guild, Authors League Am., Friends Denver Library, Rotary, Kappa Alpha Theta. Address: 23 Polo Club Dr Denver CO 80209-3309

NEMIROW, ARNOLD MYLES, manufacturing executive; b. Hartford, Conn., Mar. 25, 1943; s. Benjamin and Elsie (Nozik) N.; m. Barbro Sandberg, Dec. 22, 1967 (dec. Aug. 1983); children: Matthew, Adam; m. Sharon Green, April 23, 1988. AB cum laude, Harvard U., 1966; JD, U. Mich., 1969. Bar: N.Y. Atty. Carter, Ledyard & Milburn, N.Y.C., 1969-73; asst. gen. counsel Coleco Industries Inc., Hartford, 1973-74; atty., asst. gen. counsel Gt. No. Nekoosa Corp., Stamford, Conn., 1974-80, dir. indsl. rels., 1981-83, v.p., 1984-90; pres. Gt. Southern Paper Co., Cedar Springs, Ga., 1984-87, Nekoosa Papers Inc., Port Edwards, Wis., 1988-90; pres., CEO Wausau Papers, Wausau, Wis., 1990-94; CEO, pres. Bowater Inc., 1995—; chmn. Bowater, 1996—. Office: 55 E Camperdown Way Greenville SC 29601-3511

NEMO, ANTHONY JAMES, lawyer; b. St. Paul, May 18, 1963; s. Joseph Marino Jr. and Dianne Marie (Wegner) N.; m. Mary Rose Mazzitello, July 17, 1987; children: Anne Marie, Katherine Mary, Anthony James Jr. BA in English Lit., U. St. Thomas, 1986; JD, William Mitchell Coll. Law, 1991. Bar: Minn. 1991, U.S. Dist. Ct. Minn., U.S. Dist. Ct. Ariz., U.S. Ct. Appeals (4th cir.), U.S. Supreme Ct. Account exec. div. info. svcs. TRW, Mpls., 1986-90; assoc. atty. Meshbesher & Spence, Ltd., St. Paul, 1990—. Assoc. editor William Mitchell Law Rev., 1988-90; author law rev. note. Recipient R. Ross Quaintance award, Douglas K. Amdahl-Mary O'Malley Lyons Trial Advocacy award. Mem. ABA, Minn. Trial Lawyers Assn., Assn. Trial Lawyers Am., Minn. State Bar Assn., Hennepin County Bar Assn., John P. Sheehy Legal History Soc. Roman Catholic. Home: 2125 Heath Ave N Oakdale MN 55128-5207 Office: Meshbesher & Spence Ltd 1616 Park Ave Minneapolis MN 55404-1631

NEMSER, EARL HAROLD, lawyer; b. N.Y.C., Jan. 17, 1947; s. Harold Summers and Eleanor Patricia (Beckerman) N.; m. Randy Lynn Lehrer, June 17, 1974 (div.); children: Eliza Sarah, Maggie Lehrer. B.A., NYU, 1967; J.D. magna cum laude, Boston U., 1970. Bar: N.Y. 1970, U.S. Supreme Ct. 1975, U.S. Claims Ct. 1979, U.S. Tax Ct. 1985. Law clk. Hon. Collins J. Seitz, Chief Judge U.S. Ct. appeals 3rd Cir., 1970-71; ptnr. Cadwalader, Wickersham & Taft, N.Y.C., 1971-95, Shereff, Friedman, Hoffman & Goodman, L.L.P., N.Y.C., 1996—; mng. dir. Interactive Brokers, Inc., Valhalla, N.Y., 1995—; dir. Timber Hill, Inc., Valhalla, N.Y., 1989—. Mem. ABA, Assn. Bar City of N.Y., Fed. Bar Council, Boston U. Law Sch. Alumni Assn. (pres. 1984). Clubs: Downtown Assn.; Contbr. note to legal rev. Office: Shereff Friedman Hoffman & Goodman 919 3d Ave New York NY 10038

NEN, ROBERT ALLEN (ROBB NEN), professional baseball player; b. San Pedro, Calif., Nov. 28, 1969; s. Dick Nen. Grad. high sch., Los Alamitos, Calif. With Tex. Rangers, 1993; pitcher Fla. Marlins, 1993—. Office: Fla Marlins 2267 NE 199th St Miami FL 33180*

NENNEMAN, RICHARD ARTHUR, retired publishing executive; b. Chgo., Oct. 13, 1929; s. William T. and Fannie (Peterson) N.; m. Katherine Ann LaBrunerie, June 29, 1954; children: Ann Walker, Mary Lisa, Katherine Conley. A.B. magna cum laude, Harvard U., 1951, M.A. in Internat. Affairs, 1953. With No. Trust Co., Chgo., 1957-58; v.p., treas., dir. First Fed. Savs. & Loan Assn., St. Joseph, Mo., 1958-60; with Valley Nat. Bank, Phoenix, 1960-65; asst. v.p., 1963-65; bus. and financial editor Christian Sci. Monitor, Boston, 1965-74; v.p., dir. investment research Girard Bank, Phila., 1974-77; sr. v.p., chmn. trust investment policy com. Girard Bank, 1977-82; mng. editor Christian Sci. Monitor, Boston, 1983-86; editor, exec. prodr., TV broadcasting Christian Sci. Pub. Soc., Boston, 1987; editor-in-chief Christian Science Monitor, 1988-93; ret., 1993; mem. investment com. Gen. Accident Ins. Group., until 1982; dir. DLB Fund Group, 1994—. Contbr. to Understanding Our Century, 1984; editor: (with Earl Foell) How Peace Came to the World, 1986, The New Birth of Christianity, 1992. Trustee Barnes Found., until 1982; selectman Town of Weston, Mass., 1973-74; vice chmn. Boston Com. on Fgn. Rels. Served with AUS, 1954-57. Mem. Coun. on Fgn. Rels., Am. Coun. Ger., Harvard Grad. Coun. Home: PO Box 634 East Orleans MA 02643-0634

NENNER, VICTORIA CORICH, nurse, educator; b. Marshall, Tex., Jan. 17, 1945; d. Bernard Paul and Mary DeLayne (Bowen) Corich; BSN (Regents scholar, Krost-Freeman scholar, Mary Gobbs Jones Nursing scholar), Tex. Women's U., 1966; cert. U. Paris, summer 1966; MSN, U. San Diego, 1984; m. Paul Edwin Nenner, Aug. 12, 1970. Mem. nursing staff St. Thomas Hosp., London, 1966-67, Parkland Meml. Hosp., Dallas, 1967-68; coord. nursing continuing edn. Scripps Meml. Hosp., La Jolla, Calif., 1974-85; owner, pres. Marvik Ednl. Svcs., Inc., 1985—; mem. part-time faculty U. Calif., San Diego; mem. vis. faculty U. B.C.; mem. Inservice Council San Diego and Imperial Counties, 1974-80, pres., 1976-77; mem. San Diego Community Colls. Health Edn. Adv. Bd., 1976-84. Served to capt. Nurse Corps, USAF, 1968-73. Named Tex. Student Nurse of Year, 1966. Mem. ANA, Am. Soc. Health Edn. and Tng., Nat. League Nursing (Leadership award 1995), Calif. League for Nursing (pres. 1993-94), Sigma Theta Tau. Author articles in field; contbg. author in healthcare software; producer oncology nursing ednl. videotapes. Home: 1677 1/2 Los Altos Rd San Diego CA 92109

NENTWICH, MICHAEL ANDREAS ERHART, educator, consultant; b. Prague, Czech Republic, Sept. 6, 1941; came to U.S., 1994; s. Walter Joseph and Charlotte Rosina (Hawle) N. Student, Nuremberg (Germany) U., 1960; PhD, Heidelberg (Germany) U., 1973. English lectr. Mannheim (Germany) U., 1969-75; rsch. scholar in English Tech. U. Berlin, 1980-81; educator, cons. Goethe-Inst., Bremen, Germany, 1982, Madrid, 1983-85, Düsseldorf, Germany, 1985-88, São Paulo, 1988-92; educator, cons. Goethe Inst., Munich, 1992—; vis. lectr. in German, Chinese U. of Hong Kong, 1975-80. Author: Der Schottische Shaw, 1973; contbr. articles to profl. jours. Recipient Sophie Bernsthen scholarship U. Heidelberg, 1968. Avocations: music, painting, travel. Office: Goethe Inst NY 1014 5th Ave New York NY 10028-0104

NEPOMUCENO, CECIL SANTOS, physician; b. The Philippines, Feb. 1, 1936; came to U.S. 1967; s. Dominador and Augustina (Santos) N.; m. Edna Manacsa, Dec. 4, 1963; children: Joy, Regina, Celeste. MD, U. Santo Tomas, Manila, The Philippines, 1962. Diplomate Am. Bd. Physical Medicine and Rehab. Intern St. Francis Hosp., Wichita, Kans., 1963; resident Baylor U. Med. Ctr., Dallas, 1967-70; med. dir. orthopedic svcs. HealthSouth Lakeshore Rehab. Hosp., Birmingham, Ala., 1994—; cons. Social Security Adminstrn.; oral bd. examiner Am. Acad. Physical Medicine and Rehab. Lt. col. USAMR, 1982-94. Mem. So. Soc. Phys. Medicine and Rehab. (past pres.), Ala. Soc. Phys. Medicine and Rehab. (past pres.), Am. Acad. Phys. Medicine and Rehab. (oral bd. examiner), Am. Assn. Electrodiagnostic Medicine, Ala. Med. Assn., Nat. Assn. Disability Evaluating Profls. Catholic. Home: 1070 Country Club Cir Birmingham AL 35244-1478 Office: Lakeshore Hosp. 3800 Ridgeway Dr Birmingham AL 35209-5506

NEPPL, WALTER JOSEPH, retired retail store executive; b. Halbur, Iowa, June 15, 1922; s. Frank and Anna (Halbur) N.; m. Marian Maher, Oct. 15, 1945; children: Eugenie Neppl Kauffman, Marilee Neppl Cumming, Deborah Neppl Johnson, John, Thomas (dec.), Christina Neppl Totino, Nancy Neppl Tripucka. Grad. h.s., Carrol, Iowa. With J.C. Penney Co., Inc., 1940—; mgr. store J.C. Penney Co., Inc., Albuquerque, 1954-55; dist. mgr. J.C. Penney Co., Inc., Pitts., 1955-61; store coordination mgr. J.C. Penney Co., Inc., N.Y.C., 1961-64; asst. to dir. dist. mgmt. dept. J.C. Penney Co., Inc., 1964-65, gen. mdse. mgr. hard lines, 1965-67, v.p., 1967-68, gen. sales and mdse. mgr., 1968-71, dir. merchandising, 1971-72, exec. v.p., 1972-76, pres., chief operating officer, 1976-81, vice-chmn. bd., 1981-82, ret., 1982, dir., 1968-85; bd. dirs. emeritus J.C. Penney Co. Inc. Trustee emeirtus Geraldine R. Dodge Found. Served to capt. USAAF, 1943-45. Decorated D.F.C. Roman Catholic. Home: The Enclave 5345 Annabel Ln Plano TX 75093-3428

NEPPLE, JAMES ANTHONY, lawyer; b. Carroll, Iowa, Jan. 5, 1945; s. Herbert J. and Cecilia T. (Irlmeier) N.; m. Jeannine Ann Jennings, Sept. 9, 1967; children: Jeffrey B., Scott G., Carin J., Andrew J. BA, Creighton U., 1967; JD, U. Iowa, 1970; postgrad. in bus., Tex. Christian U., 1971; LLM in Taxation, NYU, 1982. Bar: Iowa 1970, Ill. 1973, U.S. Dist. Ct. (so. dist.) Iowa 1972, U.S. Dist. Ct. (no. dist.) Iowa 1975, U.S. Ct. Claims 1976, U.S. Tax Ct. 1976, U.S. Ct. Appeals (7th and 8th cirs.) 1975, U.S. Supreme Ct. 1975. Tax acct. Arthur Young & Co., Chgo., 1970; v.p., treas., bd. dirs. Stanley, Rehling, Lande & VanDerKamp, Muscatine, Iowa, 1972-92; pres. Nepple, VanDerKamp & Flynn, P.C., Rock Island, Ill., 1992—. Scoutmaster Boy Scouts Am., Muscatine, 1982-85; trustee State Hist. Soc. Iowa, 1986-92, vice-chmn., 1991-92; bd. dirs. Iowa Hist. Found., 1988-96, pres., 1991-93. Capt. U.S. Army, 1971-72. Recipient Gov.'s Vol. award State of Iowa, 1988, 90. Fellow Am. Coll. Trust and Estate Counsel; mem. ABA (tax sect. 1972—), IA (tax com. 1979-91, chmn. 1988-91), Fed. Bar Assn., Ill. Bar Assn. (mem. fed. tax sect. coun. 1993—, vice chair 1996, chair 1997), Muscatine and Scott County (Iowa) and Rock Island County (Ill.) Bar Assn. (pres. 1982-83), Iowa Assn. Bus. and Industry (chmn. tax com. 1986-88, leadership Iowa award 1985), Quad City Estate Planning Coun. (pres. 1987), Muscatine C. of C. (pres. 1985), Geneva Golf and Coutry Club (pres. 1990-91), Kiwanis (pres. Muscatine chpt. 1978), Elks. Republican. Roman Catholic. Home: 2704 Mulberry Ave Muscatine IA 52761-2746

NEPTUNE, JOHN ADDISON, chemistry educator, consultant; b. Barnesville, Ohio, Nov. 27, 1919; s. George Addison and Lola Mae (Skinner) N.; m. Ruth Elizabeth Dorsey, Aug. 24, 1947; 1 child, Benjamin. BS summa cum laude, Muskingum Coll., 1942; MS, U. Wis., 1949, PhD, 1952. Instr. chemistry Muskingum Coll., New Concord, Ohio, 1943-44, 45-48; foreman Tenn. Eastman Corp., Manhattan Project, 1944-45; asst. prof. chemistry Bowling Green State U., Ohio, 1949-50; instr. pharm. chemistry U. Wis.-Madison, 1952-55; asst. prof. chemistry San Jose State U., Calif., 1955-58, assoc. prof., 1958-61, prof., 1961-90, chmn. dept., 1973-86. Mem. Am. Chem. Soc., AAUP. Methodist. Home: 50 Cherokee Ln San Jose CA 95127-2513 Office: San Jose State U Dept Chemistry San Jose CA 95192

NEPTUNE, RICHARD ALLAN (DICK NEPTUNE), superintendent of schools; b. Lawton, Okla., Oct. 1, 1934; s. Everett and Mary Louise (Green) N.; m. Carol Faye Brewer; stepchildren: Derek Knowles, Larrie Knowles, Ronnie Joe Knowles. BS, Okla. Bapt. U., 1956; MEd, U. Okla., 1962. Cert. standard supt. Photography tchr. Lawton (Okla.) Pub. Schs., 1957-60, dir. activities, 1960-62, asst. prin. behavior, 1962-66, asst. prin. instrn., 1966-69, prin., 1969-77, asst. supt., 1977-79, assoc. supt., 1979-80, dep. supt., 1980-85, supt., 1985—. Bd. dirs. Hotel Lawtonian, Lawton Indsl. Svc., Lawton Pub. Libr., Lawton Jaycees, McMahon Cmty. Auditorium Theatre League, Mus. of the Great Plains, United Way, C. of C., Nat. PTA; pres. USO, v.p. With USAR, 1957-63. Recipient Nat. Pub. Rels. Assn. award, 1987, Exec. Educators 100, 1989, Kennedy Ctr. Sch. Adminstrs. award, 1990, State of Okla. medal, 1990, Disting. Svc. award Cameron U., 1996, Martin Luther King, Jr. Leadership award, 1997, DAR medal of honor, 1997. Mem. Am. Assn. of Sch. Personnel Administrs., Am. Assn. of Sch. Administrs., Am. Mgmt. Assn., Am. Soc. Tng. and Devel., Lawton Assn. of Secondary Sch. Prins. (pres.), Nat. Assn. Secondary Sch. Prins., Nat. Edn. Assn., Nat. Sch. Bds. Assn., Okla. Assn. Secondary Sch. Prins. (bd. dirs., chmn. leadership com.), Okla. Assn. for Supervision and Curriculum Devel., Okla. Curriculum Improvement Commn. (pres. 1988), Okla. Edn. Assn. Secondary Sch. Prins., Kappa Delta Pi, Phi Delta Kappa. Home: 453 NW Chimney Creek Dr Lawton OK 73505-5919 Office: Lawton Pub Sch PO Box 1009 753 NW Ft Sill Blvd Lawton OK 73502

NEQUIST, JOHN LEONARD, retired food company executive; b. Sparta, Mich., July 31, 1929; s. John Ormond and Leola Irene (Fessenden) N.; m. Patricia Ann Kelley, Jan. 7, 1950; children: Eric Martin, Kelley Jo; m. Donna Jean Williams, 1990. B.B.A., U. Mich., 1956. With Kellogg Co., Battle Creek, Mich., 1957-88; chief accountant, then asst. controller Kellogg Co., 1967-75, controller, 1975-79, v.p., controller U.S. Foods Products div., 1979-84, dir. spl. assignments McCanly Sq. div., hotel and retail area, 1984-88. Chmn. planning and budget com. Battle Creek United Fund, 1969-70, Battle Creek Family/Childrens Service, 1973, Battle Creek United Arts Council, 1975; dir. spl. assignments Gov.'s Exec. Corps, 1984-85; bd. dirs. ARC, Battle Creek; chmn. bd. Downtown Bus. Assn., Battle Creek., 1987-88; mem. South Haven (Mich.) City Council. Served with USAF, 1948-52. Mem. Beta Alpha Psi. Home: 36 Lake Shore Dr South Haven MI 49090-1131 Home (winter): 196 Forse Lakes Cir Naples FL 34104-6436

NEREM, ROBERT MICHAEL, engineering educator, consultant; b. Chgo., July 20, 1937; s. Robert and Borghild Guneva (Bakken) N.; m. Jill Ann Thomson, Dec. 21, 1958 (div. 1977); children: Robert Steven, Nancy Ann Nerem Chambers; m. Marilyn Reed, Oct. 7, 1978; stepchildren: Christina Lynn Maser, Carol Marie Maser. BS, U. Okla., 1959; MS, Ohio State U., 1961, PhD, 1964; D (honoris causa), U. Paris, 1990. Asst. prof. Ohio State U., Columbus, 1964-68, assoc. prof., 1968-72, prof., 1972-79, assoc. dean Grad. Sch., 1975-79; prof. mech. engring., chmn. dept. U. Houston, 1979-86; Parker H. Petit prof. Ga. Inst. Tech., Atlanta, 1987—, Inst. prof., 1991—, dir. Inst. for Bioengring. and Biosci., 1995—; mem. Ga. Gov.'s Adv. Coun. on Sci. and Tech. Devel., Atlanta, 1992-95; ALZA disting. lectr. Biomed. Engring. Soc., 1991, ASME Thurston lectr., 1994. Contbr. over 100 articles to profl. jours. Fellow Am. Inst. Med. and Biol. Engring. (founding pres. 1992-94), ASME, AAAS; mem. NAE, Biomed. Engring. Soc., Inst. Medicine, Internat. Union for Phys. and Engring. Scis. in Medicine (pres. 1991-94), Internat. Fedn. for Med. and Biol. Engring. (pres. 1988-91), U.S. Nat. Com. on Biomechanics (1988-91 chmn.), Polish Acad. Scis. Home: 2950 Waverly Ct NW Atlanta GA 30339-4200

NERENBERG, AARON, lawyer; b. Phila., Sept. 22, 1940; s. Jacob and Rose (Solominsky) N.; m. Adrianne Daufman, May 30, 1965; children: Jeffrey, Kimberly. BSME, Pa. State U., 1963; MSME, Villanova U., 1967; JD, Temple U., 1971. Bar: Pa. 1971, U.S. Dist. Ct. (ea. dist.) Pa., 1973, U.S. Ct. Appeals (3d cir.),1973, U.S. Supreme Ct., 1974, U.S. Patent Office, 1972. Devel. engr. Naval Air Engring. Ctr., Phila., 1963-71; sole practice Phila., 1971-72; patent advisor Naval Air Devel. Ctr., Warminster, Pa., 1972-74; patent atty, SPS Techs. Inc., Jenkintown, Pa., 1974-78, patent counsel, 1978-82, assoc. gen. counsel, Newtown, Pa., 1982-86, gen. counsel, 1986—, sec., 1986—, v.p., 1988. Mem. ABA, Phila. Patent Law Assn. (chmn. placement com. 1977-85), Pa. State Alumni Assn. (v.p. 1982-86, Disting. Alumni award 1982). Republican. Jewish. Avocations: golf, swimming. Office: SPS Techs Inc Jenkintown Plz 101 Greenwood Ave Ste 470 Jenkintown PA 19046-2627

NERLINGER, JOHN WILLIAM, trade association administrator; b. Detroit, June 22, 1920; s. John W. and Bessie Prudence (Beith) N.; m. Pearl Pauline Procup, Nov. 4, 1943; children: John Charles, Ruth Marie Nerlinger Blazevich. Grad., Detroit Bus. Inst., 1939; BA, Detroit Inst. Tech., 1950; LLD (hon.), Northwood U., Midland, Mich., 1990. Bus. mgr. Retail Gasoline Dealers Assn. Mich., Detroit, 1939-51; exec. sec. Retail Gasoline Dealers Assn. Mich., 1951-63, Nat. Congress Petroleum Retailers, Detroit, 1951-63; asst. exec. v.p. Automotive Service Industry Assn., Chgo., 1963-73; exec. v.p. Automotive Service Industry Assn., 1973-80, pres., 1981-91; ret., 1991; Vice chmn. Automotive Hall of Fame; advisor Nat. Hwy. Users Fedn. Served with AUS, 1942-45, PTO. Recipient Petroleum Man of Yr. award Gasoline News, 1961, Automotive Replacement Edn. award Northwood U., Midland, Mich., 1975, Disting. Svc. citation Automotive Hall of Fame, 1978, Industry Leadership award Automotive Svc. Industry Assn., 1978. Mem. Am. Soc. Assn. Execs. (mem. edn. com.), Chgo. Soc. Assn. Execs., Automotive Old Timers, Automotive Info. Council (dir.), Automotive Boosters Clubs Internat., Chgo. Assn. Commerce and Industry (mem. govt. relations com.), Nat. Assn. Wholesalers-Distbrs. (exec. com., dir. distbn. research and edn. found), Automotive Acad. Lutheran. Clubs: Mid-America, Inverness Golf. Lodge: Masons (32 deg.), Shriners. Home: 601 E Fairview St Arlington Heights IL 60005-2770

NERLOVE, MARC LEON, economics educator; b. Chgo., Oct. 12, 1933; s. Samuel Henry and Evelyn (Andelman) N.; children: Susan, Miriam. BA, U. Chgo., 1952; MA, Johns Hopkins U., 1955, PhD, 1956. Analytical statistician USDA, Washington, 1956-57; assoc. prof. U. Minn., Mpls., 1959-60; prof. Stanford (Calif.) U., Stanford U., 1960-65, Yale U., 1965-69; prof. econs. U. Chgo., 1969-74; F.W. Taussig rsch. prof. Harvard Coll., Cambridge, Mass., 1967-68; vis. Cook prof. Northwestern U., Evanston, Ill., 1973-74, Cook prof., 1974-82; prof. econs. U. Pa., Phila., 1982-86, Univ. prof., 1986-93; prof. agriculture and resource econs. U. Md., College Park, 1993—. Author: Dynamics of Supply, 1958, Distributed Lags and Demand Analysis, 1958, Estimation and Identification of Cobb-Douglas Production Functions, 1965, Analysis of Economic Time Series: A Synthesis, 1979, Household and Economy: Welfare Economics of Endogenous Fertility, 1987; contbr. numerous articles to profl. jours. 1st lt. AUS, 1957-59. Recipient award Am. Farm Econ. Assn., 1956, 58, 61, 79, P.S. Mahalanobis medal Indian Econ. Soc., 1975. Fellow Am. Statis. Assn., Econometric Soc. (v.p. 1980, pres. 1981), Am. Acad. Arts and Scis., Am. Agrl. Econ. Assn.; mem. NAS, Am. Econ. Assn. (mem. exec. com. 1977-79, John Bates Clark medal 1969), Royal Econ. Soc., Phi Beta Kappa, others. Achievements include research on economics of agriculture with particular reference to developing countries, population and economic growth; analysis of categorical data, particularly business and household surveys. Office: U Md Dept Agri & Rsch Econs College Park MD 20742-5535

NERO, ANTHONY VINCENT, JR., physicist, environmental scientist, writer; b. Salisbury, Md., Apr. 11, 1942; s. Anthony V. Nero and Anna Elizabeth Coladonato. BS summa cum laude, Fordham U., 1964; PhD in Physics, Stanford U., 1971. Rsch. fellow physics dept. Fordham U., summers 1962-63; grad. rsch. asst. Nuclear Physics Lab., Stanford (Calif.) U., 1966-70; postdoctoral rsch. fellow Kellogg Radiation Lab., Calif. Inst. Tech., Pasadena, 1970-72; asst. prof. physics Princeton (N.J.) U., 1972-75; physicist energy and environ. div. Lawrence Berkeley (Calif.) Lab., 1975—, leader indoor radon group, 1980-86, sr. scientist, 1986—, dep. leader indoor environ. program, 1986-94; visitor nuclear power div. Electric Power Rsch. Inst., summers 1974-75; phys. sci. officer Non-Proliferation Bur., ADCA, 1978; lectr. dept. mech. engring. U. Calif., Berkeley, 1979, lectr. energy and resources program, 1980, lectr. Sch. Pub. Health, 1989, mem. environ. health scis. ctr., 1992-94, acad. coord. energy and resources program, 1993-94; mem. adv. com. 3d Internat. Conf. on Indoor Air Quality and Climate, Stockholm, 1984, symposium organizer, rapporteur for radon 4th Conf., Berlin, 1987; mem. various adv. and rev. panels EPA, 1984—; mem. program com. 4th Internat. Symposium on Natural Radiation Environ, Lisbon, 1987, 5th internat. syposium, Salzburg, Austria, 1991. Author: A Guidebook to Nuclear Reactors, 1979; co-author: Instrumentation for Environmental Monitoring, Vol. 1, 1983, Radon and Its Decay Products in Indoor Air, 1988; contbr. articles to profl. and popular publs., chpts. to books. Gen. Motors Corp. nat. scholar, 1960-64; NSF undergrad. summer rsch. fellow, 1962, 63, NSF grad. fellow, 1964-68. Fellow Am. Physics Soc. (panel on pub. affairs 1981-83, Leo Szilard award of Physics in the Pub. Interest 1989, exec. com. forum on physics and soc. 1988-90, vice-chair forum on physics and soc. 1992-93, chair-elect 1993-94, chair 1994-95); mem. AAAS, Health Physics Soc., Fedn. Am. Scientists, Soc. Risk Analysis, Phi Beta Kappa, Sigma Xi. Office: Lawrence Berkeley Lab 1 Cyclotron Rd Rm 3058 Berkeley CA 94720

NERO, PETER, pianist, conductor, composer, arranger; b. N.Y.C., May 22, 1934; s. Julius and Mary (Menasche) N.; m. Marcia Dunner, June 19, 1956; children—Beverly, Jedd; m. Peggy Altman, Aug. 31, 1977. Student, Juilliard Sch., N.Y.C.; doctorate (hon.), Bklyn. Coll. Nat. tour with Paul Whiteman on TV and in concert, 1953-57, appearances concert halls, theatres, colls., TV and supper clubs throughout U.S., Eng., France, Holland, Italy, Scandinavia, 1962—; appeared at Grand Gala du Disque, Amsterdam, The Netherlands, 1964, five TV specials on BBC-TV; arranged, appeared and recorded with Boston Pops Orch.; pops music dir. Tulsa Philharm., 1987—; music dir., Philly Pops Orch., 1979—, Fla. Philharm., 1981—; rec. artist for Arista Records, Pro Arte, Columbia; albums include Peter Nero Now, The Sounds of Love, Anything But Lonely and Peter Nero and Friends, 1993; appeared in film Sunday in New York; composer, condr. more than 150 symphony orchs., 1971—; recordings include (with the Rochester Philharmonic) Classic Connections. Honored by Internat. Soc. Performing Arts Adminstrs., 1986; recipient 8 Grammy nominations, 2 Grammy awards; named #1 Instrumentalist Cashbox Mag. Office: Tulsa Philharm 2901 S Harvard Ave Tulsa OK 74114-6119 also: care Gurtman & Murtha Assoc 450 7th Ave # 603 New York NY 10123-0101 also: Pro Arte 90 Intersound Internat Inc P O Box 1724 Roswell GA 30077*

NERODE, ANIL, mathematician, educator; b. L.A., June 4, 1932; s. Nirad Ranjan and Agnes (Spencer) N.; m. Sondra Raines, Feb. 12, 1955 (div. 1968); children: Christopher Curtis, Gregory Daniel; m. Sally Riedel Sievers, May 16, 1970; 1 child, Nathanael Caldwell. B.A., U. Chgo., 1949, B.S., 1952, M.S., 1953, Ph.D., 1956. Group leader automata and weapons systems Lab. Applied Sci., U. Chgo., 1954-57; mem. Inst. for Advanced Study, Princeton, 1957-58, 62-63; vis. asst. prof. math. U. Calif. at Berkeley, 1958-59; mem. faculty Cornell U., 1959—, prof. math., 1965—, Goldwin Smith prof. math., 1990—, chmn. dept. math., 1982-87, dir. Math. Sci. Inst., 1986—; acting dir. Center for Applied Math., 1965-66; vis. prof. Monash U., Melbourne, Australia, 1970, 74, 78, 79, U. Chgo., 1976, M.I.T., 1980, U. Calif., San Diego, 1981; disting. vis. scientist EPA, 1985-87; prin. investigator numerous grants; CEO Hybrythims Corp., 1995—; mem. sci. adv. bd. EPA, 1988-93, chair tech. adv. panel Global Change, 1990-92; mem. sci. adv. bd. Ctr. for Intelligent Control, Harvard-MIT-Brown U., 1988-94; cons. to govt. and industry. Author: (with John Crossley) Combinatorial Functors, 1974, (with Richard Shore) Logic for Applications, 2d edit., 1996, (with G.A. Metakides) Principles of Logic and Logic Programming, 1996; editor Advances in Mathematics, 1967-70, Jour. Symbolic Logic, 1967-82, Annals of Pure and Applied Logic, 1983-96, Future Generation Computing Systems, 1983—, Jour. Pure & Applied Algebra, 1988—, Annals of Math. and Artificial Intelligence, 1989—, Logical Methods in Computer Sci., 1991-94, Computer Modelling and Simulation, 1991—, Constraints, 1995—. Mem. AIII, IEEE, Assn. Computing Machinery, Am. Math. Soc. (assoc. editor procs. 1962-65, v.p. 1992-95), Soc. Indsl. and Applied Math., Math. Assn. Am., Assn. Symbolic Logic, European Assn. for Theoretical Computer Sci. Home: 406 Cayuga Heights Rd Ithaca NY 14850-1402 Office: Cornell U Math Sci Inst 409 College Ave Ithaca NY 14850-4694

NESBIT, ROBERT CARRINGTON, historian; b. Ellensburg, Wash., July 16, 1917; s. Sidney Shaw and Verna Mildred (Carrington) N.; m. Marie Richert, Nov. 24, 1942. B.A., Central Wash. Coll., 1939; M.A., U. Wash., 1947, Ph.D., 1957. Tchr. Cashmere (Wash.) Pub. Schs., 1939-41; state archivist Wash., 1951-57; adminstrv. asst. Wash. Dept. Gen. Adminstrn., 1958-59, supr. state purchasing, 1959-62; assoc. prof. U. Wis., Madison, 1962-68; prof., assoc. chmn. dept. history U. Wis., 1967-80. Author: He Built Seattle: A Biography of Judge Thomas Burke, 1961, Wisconsin, A History, 1973 (award of merit Am. Assn. State and Local History 1975), rev. edit. (with William F. Thompson Jr.), 1990; The History of Wisconsin, Vol. III, Industrialization and Urbanization, 1873-1893, 1985. Served with USAAF, 1941-46. Named Hon. fellow State Hist. Soc. Wis., 1986. Wis. History Found. grantee, 1971-72; NEH grantee, 1980-82. Home: 2406 Fir St SE Olympia WA 98501-3048

NESBIT, ROBERT GROVER, management consultant; b. Scranton, Pa., Feb. 8, 1932; s. George Archibald and Mildred Maude (Bohl) N.; m. Nancy Elizabeth Wilson, June 17, 1961; children: Robert, Jonathan. B.S., U. Scranton, 1957; M.S., NYU, 1958. Asst. to dean NYU, N.Y.C., 1960-64; mdse. mgr. Associated Merchandising Corp., N.Y.C., 1964-67; dir. corp. mktg. Genesco, Inc., Nashville, 1968-77; v.p., div. gen. mgr. Levi Straus & Co., San Francisco, 1977-79; sr. partner Korn/Ferry Internat., N.Y.C., 1979—. Trustee Rollins Coll., 1992-95, U. Scranton, 1995—. With U.S. Army, 1953-55. Mem. Nat. Retail Mchts. Assn., Am. Apparel Mfrs. Assn., Sigma Nu. Presbyterian. Club: N.Y. Athletic. Home: 71 Bank St New Canaan CT 06840-6203 Office: 237 Park Ave New York NY 10017-3140

NESBITT, ARTHUR WALLACE, mail order and manufacturing executive; b. Enon Valley, Pa., July 29, 1927; s. William and Frances Mildred (Gilmore) N.; m. Donna Saviers Fox, Aug. 19, 1967; children: Warren P., David G.; stepchildren: Marsha, Marilyn, William, Leann, Sandra Fox. B.S., Pa. State U., 1950. Asst. county agt. Pa. State U., Clarion, 1950-51; exec. sec. Pa. Holstein Assn., State College, 1952-59; v.p. sales Nasco, Fort Atkinson, Wis., 1959-71; exec. v.p. Nasco Internat., Inc., 1972-74, pres., CEO, 1974—; bd. dirs., v.p. World Dairy Expo, 1967-90; bd. dirs., treas. Nat. Dairy Shrine, 1969-93; chmn. bd., dir. Gehl Co., Bank Ft. Atkinson, Geneve Corp. Bd. govs. Agrl. Hall of Fame; bd. dirs. Wis. 4-H Found., Blue Cross-Blue Shield United Wis., 1990—, United Wis. Svc., 1991—; trustee Pa. State U., 1987-88; pres.-elect Competitive Wis. Inc., 1996—. With U.S. Army, 1945-46. Recipient Nat. 4-H Alumni award, 1979, Fellow award Pa. State U., Disting. Alumnus award, Pa. State U., 1987; named Hon. County Agt., 1988, Person of Yr. World Dairy Expo. Industry, 1989, Guest of Honor Nat. Dairy Shrine, 1993. Mem. Dairy and Food Industries Supply Assn. (bd. dirs., past pres. 1974—), Wis. Mfg. and Commerce Assn. (bd. dirs. 1980—, chmn. 1990-91), Nat. Speakers Assn., Am. Dairy Sci. Assn., Holstein-Friesian Assn. Am., Pa. State U. Soc. for Disting. Alumni (pres. 1993—), Delta Theta Sigma (past pres.), Gamma Sigma Delta. Mem. United Ch. of Christ. Home: 711 Blackhawk Dr Fort Atkinson WI 53538-1047 Office: Nasco Internat Inc 901 Janesville Ave Fort Atkinson WI 53538-2402

NESBITT, CAROL KELLEY, health services administrator; b. Panama City, Fla., Sept. 27, 1963; d. Bobby G. Kelley and Peggy (Spears) Barnett; m. Curtis R. Nesbitt, Feb. 22, 1992; 1 chld, Jacob Randal. Diploma, St. Vincent Sch. Nursing, Birmingham, Ala., 1984; student, U. Ala., Birmingham, 1981, Wallace State C.C., Hanceville, Ala., 1983-85. RN, Ala.; diplomate Am. Bd. Quality Assurance and Utilization Rev. Physicians. Staff and charge nurse St. Vincent's Hosp., Birmingham, 1984-90, staff nurse, flex pool, 1990-94; instr. St. Vincent's Hosp. Good Health Sch., Birmingham, 1988-91; patient care coord. S.E. HealthPlan, Birmingham, 1988-91, med. rev. analyst, 1990-91; utilization rev. quality assurance mgr. Health Choice, Birmingham, 1993-94; health svcs. dir. Advance HealthLink, Birmingham, 1994-96; dir. med. support svcs. GuideStar Health Systems, Birmingham, Ala., 1996—. Mem. Nat. Assn. Healthcare Quallity, Ala. Assn. Healthcare Quality. Home: 1080 Manuel Hill Rd Cordova AL 35550-4514 Office: GuideStar Health Systems Ste 450 1400 Urban Center Dr Birmingham AL 35242-2515

NESBITT, CHARLES RUDOLPH, lawyer, energy consultant; b. Miami, Okla., Aug. 30, 1921; s. Charles Rudolph and Irma Louise (Wilhelmi) N.; m. Margot Dorothy Lord, June 6, 1948; children: Nancy Margot Nesbitt Nagle, Douglas Charles, Carolyn Jane Nesbitt Gresham. B.A., U. Okla., 1942; LL.B., Yale, 1947. Bar: Okla. 1947, U.S. Supreme Ct. 1957. Pvt. practice Oklahoma City, 1948-62, 67-69;, 75-91, 95—; atty. gen. Okla., 1963-67; mem. Okla. Corp. Commn., 1968-75, chmn., 1969-75; sec. of energy State of Okla., Oklahoma City, 1991-95; pvt. practice Oklahoma City, 1995—; Okla. rep., v.p. Interstate Oil and Gas Compact. Bd. dirs., trustee endowment fund St. Gregory's Coll.; trustee Oklahoma City U.; pres. Hist. Preservation, Inc.; pres. bd. trustees Okla. Mus. Art; v.p., bd. dirs. Western History Collections Assocs., U. Okla. Librs.; mem. panel arbitrators Am. Arbitration Assn., NASD, NYSE; mem. Ecclesiastical Ct., Diocese Okla. With AUS, 1942-46. Mem. Am., Okla. bar assns., Oklahoma City C. of C., Phi Beta Kappa, Phi Delta Phi. Episcopalian. Home: 1703 N Hudson Ave Oklahoma City OK 73103-3428 Office: 1703 N Hudson Ave Oklahoma City OK 73103-3428

NESBITT, LENORE CARRERO, federal judge; m. Joseph Nesbitt; 2 children: Sarah, Thomas. A.A., Stephens Coll., 1952; BS, Northwestern U., 1954; student U. Fla. Law Sch., 1954-55; LLB, U. Miami, 1957. Rsch. asst. Dist. Ct. Appeal, 1957-59, Dade County Cir. Ct., 1963-65; pvt. practice Nesbitt & Nesbitt, 1960-63; spl. asst. attorney gen., 1961-63; with Law Offices of John Robert Terry, 1969-73; counsel, Fla. State Bd. Med. Examiners, 1970-71; with Petersen, McGowan & Feder, 1973-75; judge Fla. Cir. Ct., 1975-82, U.S. Dist. Ct. (so. dist.) Fla., Miami, 1983—. Bd. trustees U. Miami; bd. dirs. Miami Children's Hosp. Mem. FBA, Fla. Bar Assn., U.S. Jud. Conf. Com. on Criminal Law and Probation Adminstrn. Office: US Dist Ct 301 N Miami Ave Miami FL 33128-7702

NESBITT, LLOYD IVAN, podiatrist; b. Toronto, Ont., Can., Sept. 24, 1951; s. Allan Jay and Rose (Shuster) N.; m. Marlene Cindy Wegler, May 13, 1984; children: Hilary Liza, Andrea Eve, Jeffrey Ryan. D in Podiatric Medicine, Calif. Coll. Podiatric Medicine, San Francisco, 1975. Diplomate Internat. Soc. Podiatric Laser Surgery. Residency program Vancouver (B.C.) Gen. Hosp., Can., 1975-76; pvt. practice podiatric medicine Toronto; lectr. numerous colls., fitness ctrs. and sports medicine confs., Ont., 1979—. Contbr. numerous articles to sports medicine books and jours; editor Canadian Podiatrist Jour., 1979-88. Fellow Can. Podiatric Sports Medicine Acad. (pres. 1979-89, editor newsletter 1977-89), Am. Acad. Podiatric Sports Medicine; mem. Internat. Soc. Podiatric Laser Surgery (diplomate), Am. Podiatric Med. Assn., Sierra Club. Avocations: skiing, in-line skating, sailing, cycling, gardening. Home: 122 Argonne Crescent, Willowdale, ON Canada M2K 2K1 Office: Madison Ctr Office Tower, 4950 Yonge St Ste 2414, Toronto, ON Canada M2N 6K1

NESBITT, MARK, management consultant; b. Ottawa, Ont., Can., Dec. 31, 1952; s. William Alonzo and Barbara (Ellis) N.; 1 child, Karen Elizabeth. BSc, Carleton U., Ottawa, 1973, BA, 1974; MBA, Harvard U., 1978. Cert. Mgmt. Cons. Cons. Peat Marwick & Ptnrs., Ottawa, 1978; assoc./ mgr. Veritas Cons. Inc., Toronto, Ont., Can., 1978-86, pres., 1986-93; pres., CEO Vertex Cons. Inc., Toronto, 1993—; IS com. mem. YMCA Metro Toronto, 1992-93; bd. dirs. Inst. Cert. Mgmt. Cons. Can. Mem. Am. Mktg. Assn., Inst. Cert. Mgmt. Cons. Ont., Inst. Cert. Mgmt. Cons. Can. (pres. 1997—), Assn. for Creative Change, Internat. Mgmt. Devel. (1st v.p., sec.-treas.). Anglican. Avocations: bicycling, photography, programming. Office: Vertex Cons Inc, 14 Dundonald St, Toronto, ON Canada M4Y 1K2

NESBITT, PAUL EDWARD, historian, author, educator; b. Balt., Dec. 25, 1943; s. William Ervin and Margaret Caroline (Shaw) N.; m. Donna Jean Coppock, Aug. 15, 1966 (dec. 1972); children: Erik-Paul A., Janelle M., m. Pamela Jean Lichty, May 25, 1974 (div. 1983); m. Anita Louise Wood, Dec. 8, 1984 (div. 1989); m. Paula Jane Sawyer, May 7, 1994. AB, U. Wash., 1965; MA, Wash. State U., 1968, PhD (hon.), 1970; PhD, U. Calgary, 1972. Reader in Anthropology, U. Wash., 1965, grad. research-tchr. Wash. State U., 1966-68, instr., Tacoma Community Coll., Wash., 1968-69; grad. research-tchr. U. Calgary, Alta., Can., 1969-71; exec. Hudson's Bay Co., Calgary, 1971; prof. Western Oreg. U., Monmouth, 1971-74; state historian State of Calif., Sacramento, 1974—; dir. Am. Sch. of Interior Design, San Francisco, 1974, HBC Bow Fort Rsch., Morley, Alta., 1970-71; instr. Am. River Coll., Sacramento, 1980-86; exec. mgr. Calif. State Govt. United Way Campaign, 1986, 87, also bd. dirs., mem. fiscal and communication coms., El Dorado County and Sacramento chpts., 1988—; designer, cultural rsch. cons. pvt. contracts western states, 1960—; exec. dir. Heritage Areas Assn., 1993—, pres. bd. dir., 1994—. Contbr. articles to prof. jours. Fellow Am.

Anthropl. Assn.; mem. Calif. Hist. Soc., Am. Inst. of Interior Designers (profl. 1974-77, bd. dirs. energy planning and devel. cos. 1986-88), AIA (Cen. Valley chpt. 1975-77), Rotary. Home: 3177 Clark St Placerville CA 95667-6405 Office: PO Box 942896 Sacramento CA 94296-0001

NESBITT, ROBERT EDWARD LEE, JR., physician, educator, scientific researcher, writer; b. Albany, Ga., Aug. 21, 1924; s. Robert E.L. and Anne Louise (Hill) N.; m. Ellen Therese Morrissey. B.A., Vanderbilt U., 1944, M.D., 1947. Diplomate: Am. Bd. Ob-Gyn (asso. examiner). Asst. prof. Johns Hopkins U., 1954-56, chief obstetric pathology lab., acting chief obstetrics, 1955-56; prof., chmn. dept. ob-gyn Albany (N.Y.) Med. Coll., Union U., 1956-61; prof., chmn. dept. ob-gyn SUNY Health Sci. Ctr., Syracuse, 1961-81, dir. gen. gynecology service, 1982-84, prof. and chmn. emeritus dept. ob-gyn; obstetrician-gynecologist-in-chief Albany Hosp., 1956-61; obstetrician, gynecologist-in-chief Syracuse Meml. Hosp., 1961-65; obstetrician-gynecologist-in-chief Crouse-Irving Hosp., 1963-70, attending staff, 1970-84; prof. surgery U. South Fla., Tampa, 1988-92, prof. ob.-gyn., 1988-92; chief ob-gyn State U. Hosp., 1964-81, chmn. med. staff and med. bd., 1964-66; attending staff St. Joseph's Hosp.; cons., chief gynecology sect. surg. service Syracuse VA Hosp., 1984-88; chief gynecology sect., asst. chief surgery, dir. uro-gynecology VA Med. Ctr., Bay Pines, Fla., 1988-92, acting chief of staff, 1990, interim chief surgery, 1991-92, chmn. O.R. com. surg. svc., 1988-92, chmn. patient care evaluation com., 1989-90, chmn. clin. exec. bd., 1990, chmn. drug usage evaluation com., 1990-91, chmn. profl. standards bd., 1990; cons. Syracuse Psychiat. Inst.; mem. cancer tng. grants and edn. com. Nat. Cancer Insts.; mem. adv. com. Bur. Maternal and Child Health, N.Y. State Dept. Health, 1957-61; nat. adviser to Children, publ. of Children's Bur., HEW, 1959-63; cons. Children's Bur., 1959-62; mem. prenatal care guide subcom. Am. Pub. Health Assn., 1962-64; cons. to regional adviser in maternal and child health Pan Am. San. Bur., WHO, 1963-65; numerous guest professorships including univs. in Mex., Chile, Uruguay, Colombia, St. Vincent (W.I.), Venezuela, People's Republic of China; numerous guest professorships including univs. in others. Author: Perinatal Loss in Modern Obstetrics, 1957; sect. on ob-gyn in Rypin's Med. Licensure Exams; also chpts. in numerous anthologies; co-author: Infant, Perinatal, Maternal and Childhood Mortality in U.S, 1968; editor: sect. on obstetrics and gynecology Stedman's Medical Dictionary, 1958-64; sect. on fetus Funk and Wagnalls Universal Standard Ency, 1959; 1st guest editor: sect. on fetus Clinics in Perinatology, 1974; 1st editor: sect. on fetus Clinical Diagnosis Quiz for Obstetrics and Gynecology, 1976, Clini-Pearls in Obstetrics and Gynecology, 1977; contbr. to: sect. on fetus Attorneys' Textbook of Medicine. Capt. M.C., U.S. Army, 1952-54. Named One of Ten Outstanding Young Men in Am., U.S. Jr. C. of C., 1957; Robert E.L. Nesbitt Jr. scholarship, Sr. Resident in Ob-Gyn, and Robert E.L. Nesbitt Jr. student scholarship established in his honor, SUNY Health Sci. Ctr. at Syracuse, 1987. Fellow Am. Assn. Maternal and Child Health, Am. Coll. Obstetricians and Gynecologists (chmn. com. mental retardation and perinatal health 1966), A.C.S. (com. forum fundamental surg. problems 1962-67), Venezuelan Obstetrics-Gynecol. Soc. (hon.), N.Y. Acad. Scis.; mem. AMA, Soc. for Gynecol. Investigations (council), Pan Am. Med. Assn. (med. ambassador goodwill, life mem. sect. on cancer), Med. Soc. N.Y. State (regional obstetrics chmn., subcom. Maternal and Child Welfare), Onondaga County Med. Soc., Am. Soc. Cytology, Pub. Health Council N.Y. State, Alpha Omega Alpha; hon. mem. Southwest, Fla. obstet. and gynecol. socs., others. Research and 230 publs. on cytologic, cytochem. and histochem. study of early cervical cancer, perinatal and placental pathology, cytologic and hormonal studies in normal and high-risk obstet. patiens, exptl. prodn. of abruptio placentae, reproductive endocrinology, animal experimentation, induced endocrine insults upon pregnant and nonpregnant ewes and hormonal influence on placentation, invitro placenta perfusion, fetal growth and devel., female urology, new surgical technique for restoration of female pelvic floor integrity while preserving the uterus (published 1989); creation science. Home: 11639 Grove St North Seminole FL 33772-7137

NESBITT, ROSEMARY SINNETT, theatre educator; b. Syracuse, N.Y., Oct. 12, 1924; d. Matthew A. and Mary Louise (Kane) Sinnett; m. George R. Nesbitt, June 18, 1955 (dec. Nov. 1971); children: Mary, Anne, George R., Elizabeth. BS magna cum laude, Syracuse U., 1947, MS, 1952. Instr. in speech Wells Coll., Aurora, N.Y., 1949-52, Syracuse U., 1952-57; asst. prof. SUNY, Oswego, 1965-68, assoc. prof., 1968-72, prof. theatre, 1972-77, Disting. teaching prof., 1977—, dir. children's theatre, 1969—; cons., lectr. pub. schs., N.Y. and New Eng., 1965—; lectr. in field. Author: The Great Rope, 1968, Colonel Meacham's Giant Cheese, 1971; (play) The Great Rope, 1975 (George Washington medal Freedom Found. 1975); plays for children. Founding mem. Oswego Heritage Found., 1963; historian City of Oswego, 1973-80, 88—; founder, bd. dirs. H. Lee White Marine Mus., Oswego, 1983—; chmn. bd. dirs. Port of Oswego Authority, 1986-88, bd. dirs., 1978-88. Recipient George R. Arents Disting. Alumnus award Syracuse U., 1975, Jefferson award Jefferson Award Com., 1984, Svc. to Arts award Cultural Resources Coun. Onondaga County, 1985, Franklin award for Disting. Svc. in Transp. Syracuse U. Sch. mgmt., 1989, Amelia Earhart Woman of the Yr. award Zonta Club of Oswego; named Woman of Yr. in Cultural Devel., Syracuse Post Standard, 1971, Citizen of Yr., City of Oswego, 1974. Mem. AAUW, Alpha Psi Omega. Democrat. Roman Catholic. Avocations: history, reading, travel. Home: 119 W 4th St Oswego NY 13126-2002 Office: SUNY Theatre Dept Oswego NY 13126

NESBITT, VANCE GORDON, computer software company executive; b. Apr. 27, 1959. Student in computer sci., U. Tex., 1977-82. Operator Seismic Data Ctr. Tex. Instruments, Austin, 1983-84; facilities and tech. svcs. assoc. Microelectronics & Computer Tech. Corp., Austin, 1984-85; v.p. product devel. Kent * Marsh Ltd., Houston, 1985-90; chmn., CEO Kent & Marsh Ltd., Houston, 1990—. Author: (comml software) MacSafe, 1990, FolderBolt, 1992, Cryptomatic, 1993, WinShield, 1995. Mem. IEEE Computer Soc., Computer Security Inst., Nat. Computer Security Assn., Assn. Computing Machinery, Electronic Frontier Found., Computer Profls. for Social Responsibility, Info. Systems Security Assn., South Tex. Info. Systems Security, Houston Area Apple Users Group, Houston Area League of PC Users, Boston Computer Soc., Apple Programmers and Developers Assn., Assn. Corp. Computing Tech. Profls., Data Processing Mgmt. Assn., Optimist Club, Alpha Phi Omega. Office: Kent & Marsh Ltd 2109 Driscoll St Houston TX 77019-6824

NESHEIM, DENNIS WARREN, art educator, artist, writer, instructional materials producer; b. Decorah, Iowa, Nov. 24, 1948; s. Kenneth H. and Adelle T. (Amundson) N.; m. Lavonne Selene Jones, Mar. 29, 1968. AA, Rochester State Jr. Coll., Minn., 1970; BS in Art/Art Edn., Winona (Minn.) State U., 1972. cert. art tchr. K-12, Minn., Wis., Ark., Colo. Dept. Def. Dependent Schs. Tchr. art Cassville (Wis.) Pub. Schs., 1972-74, Franklin Mid. Sch., Shawano, Wis., 1974-76; substitute tchr., tchr. 4th grade Dept. Def. Dependent Schs., Neu Ulm, Germany, 1977-78; tchr. art Ulm. Am. Sch. Dept. Def. Dependent Schs., Neu Ulm, 1978-80, tchr. art and video arts, 1980-87; tchr., artist art ctrs., Fla., 1987-89; owner, producer Nesheim Arts & Video, Lakeland Fla., Lakewood, Colo., 1989—; tchr. art, tchr. aide Synergy Sch., Denver, Colo.; presenter workshops and seminars, 1980-86; video tng., cons., Lakeland, 1988-93. Author, illustrator: (workbook) Making Waves, An Imagination Starter, 1994; creator, producer: (instrnl. video/handbook kits) Look and Draw series, 1990—; editor lit. quar. Onionhead, 1989-93, others; cons. writer, editor Frugal Times, 1992; part-time writer, editor Free Shopping News, 1985-87, S&N Advertising, 1985-87; prodr. (videos) Fantastic Realism, The Video, 1989, Epic Silence, 1989, Verbal Science, 1989, October 26, 1970, 1990, See in the Dark, 1990, Look and Draw, 1990, Head in the Clouds, 1990, Look and Draw Faces and Figures, 1991, Look and Draw Space In Perspective, 1992; prodr. (with David Lee Jr.) Produce Better Video, 1989; one-man shows include Donau Casino, Neu Ulm, Germany, 1977, Maas Brothers Gallery, Lakeland, 1990; exhibited in group shows Wurzburg (Germany) Milcom, 1979, Oberstube Gallery, Ulm, Germany, 1985, 86, Ridge Art, Winter Haven, Fla. (Merit award), 1988, Arts on the Park, Lakeland, (Honorable Mention award) 1988, 89, 90, 91, Arts Ctr., St. Petersburg, Fla. 1989, Art League Manatee, Bradenton, Fla., 1989, Ridge Art Assn., Winter Haven, Fla., 1990, Mt. Dora (Fla.) Ctr. for the Arts, 1990, Imperial Artists Gallery, Lakeland, 1990, 1991; contbr. articles to profl. jours. Mem. Arts on Park, Lakeland Ctr. for Creative Arts, 1987-95, bd. dirs., 1991-93; mem. Green Mountain Park Vols. Recipient various commendations and appreciation awards from schs. and cmty. orgns. Mem. Nat. Art Edn. Assn., Fine Art Forum, Compuserve. Avocations: hiking, reading, creative cooking. Office: Synergy Sch 4123 S Julian Way Denver CO 80236-3101

NESHEIM, MALDEN C., academic administrator, nutrition educator. Provost emeritus Cornell U., Ithaca, N.Y., prof. nutrition, 1997—. Office: Cornell U 376 Uris Hall Ithaca NY 14853-7601

NESHEIM, ROBERT OLAF, food products executive; b. Monroe Center, Ill., Sept. 13, 1921; s. Olaf M. and Sena M. (Willms) N.; m. Emogene P. Sullivan, July 13, 1946 (divorced); children: Barbara Mowry, Susan Yost (dec.), Sandra Rankin; m. doris Howes Calloway, July 4, 1981. BS, U. Ill., 1943, MS, 1950, PhD, 1951; postgrad. in advanced mgmt. program, Harvard U., 1971. Farm mgr. Halderman Farm Mgmt. Svc., Wabash, Ind., 1946-48; instr. U. Ill., 1951; mgr. feed rsch. The Quaker Oats Co., Barrington, Ill., 1952-64; prof., head of dept. animal sci. U. Ill., 1964-67; dir. nutrition rsch. The Quaker Oats Co., Barrington, Ill., 1967-69, v.p. R & D, 1969-78; v.p. sci. & tech. The Quaker Oats Co., Chgo., 1978-83; sr. v.p. sci. & tech. Avadyne, Inc., Monterey, Calif., 1983-85; pres. Advanced Healthcare, Monterey, 1985-91; ret., 1991. Capt. U.S. Army, 1943-46, South Pacific. Fellow Am. Inst. Nutrition (treas. 1983-86), AAAS; mem. Inst. Food Technologists, Fed. Socs. Exptl. Biologists (treas. 1973-79), APHA, Corral de Tierra Club (Salinas, Calif.). Avocations: gardening, golf.

NESHYBA, VICTOR PETER, retired aerophysics engineer; b. New Ulm, Tex., Oct. 8, 1922; s. Peter and Anna (Zietz) N.; m. Mary Cecilia Gwazdacz, Jan. 6, 1945; children: Victor Jr., Ronald, Janice, Mary Lee, Valiant, Michele, Dolores, Keith, David. BSEE, U. Calif., 1949; diploma, Mass. Inst. Tech., 1968, Naval Intelligence Sch., 1950. Registered profl. engr., Tex. Commd. 2d lt. USMC, 1942-47, advance through grades to col., 1970; Aerophysics engr. Gen. Dynamics, Ft. Worth, Tex., 1957-62; mgr., project off NASA, Houston, 1962-73; pres. Ener-G-Eco, Inc., Dickinson, Tex., 1974-80; owner, gen. mgr. Star Square Ranches, Wilson, Galveston, Colorado counties, Tex., 1980—; dir. Rabbit Hill Sch. Charity Found. Precinct chmn. Rep. Party, Galveston, Tex., 1974-76; sch. bd. Cath. Diocesan Schs., 1968. Decorated Medal of Honor by Shah of Iran, 1952; recipient Mgmt. award U.S. pres., 1970. Mem. Profl. Engrs. of Tex., Marine Corps. Res. Officers Assn., Rep. Senatorial Club, VFW, Knights of Columbus (4th degree), Min. of the Word, Shrine of True Cross. Roman Catholic. Avocations: reading, research.

NESIN, JEFFREY D., academic administrator; b. N.Y.C.; m. Diane Garvey, 1968; children: Kate Dillon, Sarah Grace. BA in Eng. Lit., Hobart Coll., 1966; MA in Eng. Lit, SUNY, Buffalo, 1971, MA in Am. Studies, 1973. Faculty dept. humanities & scis. Sch. Visual Arts, N.Y.C., 1974-91; pres. Memphis Coll. Art, 1991—; adj. lectr. CCNY, Hunter Coll.; advisor dept. fine arts Sch. Visual Arts, 1975-82, dir. spl. programs, 1978-91, asst. to pres., 1982-91; cons. Smithsonian Instn., IBM, 1st Tenn. Bank; panelist, speaker in field. Contbg. editor: High Fidelity, Creem; contbr. reviews, interviews, essays to mags.; adv. editor Jour. Popular Music and Society. Mem. Am. Studies Assn., Met. Am. Studies Assn. (past pres.), Assn. Ind. Colls. Art & Design (bd. dirs. 1991—), Memphis Rotary, Nat. Assn. Schs. Art & Design (commn. accreditation 1993—). Avocations: mystery novels, barbecue, baseball. Office: Memphis Coll Art Office of President 1930 Poplar Ave Memphis TN 38104-2756 Home: 1545 Vinton Ave Memphis TN 38104-4923

NESMITH, AUDREY MARIE, military housing manager (retired), writer; b. Washington, Apr. 6, 1937; d. John Wallace and Elsie Mae (Welsh) Cullins; m. Adolfo Mier Delhierro, May 11, 1960; (dec. Mar., 1978), children: Alicia Marie Delhierro Carver, Julia Mae Delhierro Crawford; m. Benjamin Rea Nesmith, Jan. 9, 1985. Student, U. Md., 1982-86. Chief bachelor officers qtrs. U.S. Army White Sands Missile Range, WSMR, N. Mex., 1978-80; chief housing referral office U.S. Army, Ft. Sam Houston, Tex., 1980-82; chief housing divsn. U.S. Army-U.S. Army Mil. Command, Garmsich, Fed. Republic Germany, 1982-85; dep. dir. housing divsn. U.S. Navy Washington Naval Dist., 1985-89; Equal Employment Opportunity officer, Garmisch, Fed. Republic Germany, 1984-85; v.p. Profl. Housing Mgmt. Assn., Garmisch, 1983-84. Author: (book) Loved into Life, 1985. Treas. First Ch. Christian and Missionary Alliance, 1994-96. Republican. Avocations: writing, reading, theatre, films, opera. Home: 1533 Merion Way # 26-e Seal Beach CA 90740-4979

NESMITH, MICHAEL, film producer, video specialist; b. Houston, Dec. 30, 1942; s. Warren and Bette Nesmith; m. Phyliss Nesmith; children: Christian, Jonathan, Jessica; m. 2d, Kathryn Nesmith. Chmn., chief exec. officer Pacific Arts Corp. (div. Nesmith Enterprises), L.A., 1987—. Author, producer, performer various records, 1968-77; mem. (rock group) The Monkees; co-author, exec. producer: (films) including Timerider; actor: (films) Head, 1968, Burglar, 1987, (TV series) The Monkees; exec. producer: (films) Repo Man, 1984, Square Dance, 1986, Tapeheads, 1988; exec. producer, actor: (video) Dr. Duck's Super Secret All-Purpose Sauce; producer: (series) Television Parts, 1985; co-author, producer: (pilot) for TV Pop Clips, original concept for MTV.; creator PBS Home Video. Trustee Gihon Found., 1970—, McMurray Found., 1970—. Recipient 1st Video Grammy for Elephant Paris. Christian Scientist. Office: William Morris Agy 151 S El Camino Dr Beverly Hills CA 90212-2704*

NESMITH, RICHARD DUEY, clergyman, theology educator; b. Belleville, Kans., Jan. 9, 1929; s. Eugene Gordon and Edith Mae (Duey) N.; m. Patricia N. Nichols, Aug. 24, 1985; children: Leslie Ann, Lisa Lorraine, Laurel Sue, Lana Louise, Christopher Toscano. B.A., Nebr. Wesleyan U., 1950; M.Div., Garrett Evang. Sem., 1953; Ph.D., Boston U., 1957. Ordained to ministry United Methodist Ch., 1953; dean students MacMurray Coll., Jacksonville, Ill., 1957-61; prof. sociology of religion St. Paul's Sch. Theology, Kansas City, 1961-67; dir. planning Nat. div. Methodist Bd. of Global Ministries, N.Y.C., 1967-73; pastor Trinity Ch., Lincoln, Nebr., 1973-77; dean Sch. Theology Boston U., 1977-88, prof., 1988—; bd. dirs. State Line Farms, Inc.; pres. Nesmith Inc. Producer religious TV program, Perspectives. Office: Boston U Sch Theology 745 Commonwealth Ave Rm 438 Boston MA 02215-1401

NESPECHAL, SUSAN MARY, community college administrator; b. Ann Arbor, Mich., Apr. 3, 1947; d. Robert Francis and Patricia May (Hodges) Browning; m. Robert John Nespechal, Dec. 30, 1971; children: Kristina Marie, Katherine Susan. BS in Psychology, U. Ill., 1969; MS in Adult Edn., No. Ill. U., 1987. Tchr. 8th grade St. Therese Mission Sch., Chgo., 1969-71; part-time faculty Triton Coll. and Waubonsee C.C., Aurora and River Grove, Ill., 1987-88, coord. ESL, 1988-89, mgr. adult edn., 1989-90, dir. adult edn., 1990-92, assoc. dean adult edn., 1992—; chair Dist. 516 Area Planning Coun.,Aurora, 1989—; cons. tng. Caterpillar, Aurora, 1990; mem. adv. bd. Family Focus, Aurora, 1990—; presenter in field. Vol. Literacy Vols. Am., Aurora, 1990—; v.p. Aurora Cmty. Resource Team, 1992, pres., 1996-97; commodore Abbey Yacht Club, Lake Geneva, Wis., 1992-93. Mem. Am. Assn. Adult Continuing Edn., Hispanic C. of C., Aurora Cmty. Resource Team (pres.), Family Focus, State Bd. Edn. Area Planning Coun. (chair). Avocations: photography, power boating, mysteries. Home: 4458 Burgundy Pl Lisle IL 60532-1047 Office: Waubonsee Community College Adult Basic Education 5 E Galena Blvd Aurora IL 60506-4128

NESS, ALBERT KENNETH, artist; b. St. Ignace, Mich., June 21, 1903; s. Albert Klingberg and Violet Matilda (Sutherland); m. Lenore Consuelo Chrisman, Aug. 4, 1926; children: Peter, James Kenneth, Jane Lenore. Student U. Detroit, 1923-24, Detroit Sch. of Applied Art, 1924-26, Wicker Sch. of Fine Art, 1926-28; Diploma, Sch. of Art Inst., 1932. Show-card writer, window display man S.S. Kresge Co., Detroit, 1923-24; artist poster and advt. Cunningham Drugs, Detroit, 1924-26; artist layout lettering and design W.L. Flemming Studios, Detroit, 1926-28, McAleer Displays, Chgo., 1929-32; artist, design asst. Layman-Whitney Assocs., 1933 World's Fair, Chgo.; layout artist, poster designer Elevated Advt. Co., Chgo., 1934-37; instr., art dir. Sch. of Applied Art, Chgo., 1938-40; Carnegie resident artist U. N.C., Chapel Hill, 1941-43, dir. War Art Ctr., 1942-43, resident artist, assoc. prof. art, 1943-49, acting head, dept. art, acting dir. Person Hall Art Gallery, 1944-45, resident artist, prof. art, 1949-73, acting head dept. of art, acting dir. Person Hall Art Gallery, 1955, 57-58, resident artist, prof. emeritus, 1973—. One man shows include: Chester Johnson Galleries, Chgo., 1932, Evanston Art Ctr., Ill., 1940, Person Hall Art Gallery, 1941, N.C. Art Soc. Gallery, Raleigh, 1942, Duke U. Art Gallery, Durham, N.C., 1955, Louisburg Coll. Gallery, N.C., 1964, Ackland Art Mus., U.N.C. Chapel Hill, 1973; Internat. Water Color Exhbn. Chgo. Art Inst., 1934-39; Golden Gate Internat. Exposition, San Francisco, 1939, exhibited in group shows: Whitney Mus., N.Y.C., 1933, U. Chattanooga, Tenn., 1946, Centennial Exhbn. U. Fla., Gainesville, 1953, Jacksonville Art Mus, Fla., 1960; exhibited nationally Am. Artists' Anns., Chgo. Art Inst., 1935-37, Butler Art Inst., Youngstown, Ohio, 1951, Pa. Acad. Am. Annuals, Phila., 1953-54, Optique Gallery, Lambertville, N.J., 1991—, Ross-Constantine Gallery, N.Y.C., 1991—, Marita Gilliam Gallery, Raleigh, N.C., 1993—, others; works in pub. collections include: N.C. Mus., Raleigh, Ackland Art Mus., Reynolds Found., Winston Salem, Duke U. Art Mus., Durham. Contbr. to local and state newspapers. Editor, designer, photographer: A brochure on art study, 1964. Recipient Jenkins Meml. prize 38th Ann. Chgo. Artists' Exhbn., 1934, Purchase award N.C. Artists' Ann., Raleigh, 1953; 2-Star award Movie Maker Competition, London, 1970, N.C. award in Fine Arts, 1973, Purchase award Reynolds Competition, Winston Salem, 1977. Home: PO Box 14 Chapel Hill NC 27514-0014

NESS, ANDREW DAVID, lawyer; b. San Francisco, Oct. 29, 1952; s. Orville Arne and Muriel Ruth (Trendt) N.; m. Rita M. Kobylenski, May 25, 1980; children: Katherine, Austin, Emily. BS, Stanford U., 1974; JD, Harvard U., 1977. Bar: Calif. 1977, D.C. 1979, Va. 1986, U.S. Dist. Ct. (no. dist.) Calif. 1977, U.S. Dist. Ct. D.C. 1983, U.S. Dist. Ct. (ea. dist.) Va. 1988, U.S. Ct. Appeals (4th cir.) 1989. Law clk. U.S. Dist. Ct., San Francisco, 1977-78; assoc. Lewis, Mitchell & Moore, Vienna, Va., 1979-82, ptnr., 1982-87; ptnr. Morgan, Lewis & Bockius LLP, Washington, 1987—; instr. U. Md., College Park, 1987-90; mem. faculty constrn. exec. program Stanford (Calif.) U., 1984-87. Contbr. chpt. to book, 1990, also articles to profl. jours. Mem. ABA (forum on constrn. industry, chair environ. restoration com., pub. contract law sect.). Avocations: hiking, bicycling. Office: Morgan Lewis & Bockius LLP 1800 M St NW Washington DC 20036-5802

NESS, FREDERIC WILLIAM, former academic administrator, educator, consultant; b. York, Pa., Feb. 2, 1914; s. Harry and Rosalyn Barbara (Eichelberger) N.; m. Dore Roberts, June 30, 1943 (dec. May 1959); children: Lynne, Diane, Merryl Joan, Melanie Barbara; m. Eleanor H. Hedge, Sept. 1, 1962 (dec. May 1994); 1 child, Brook H. A.B., Dickinson Coll., 1933, LL.D., 1973; student, Cin. Conservatory Music, 1930, 31, 33-35; A.M., U. Cin., 1935; Ph.D., Yale U., 1940; Litt.D., Ursinus Coll., 1971, Coll. Idaho, 1972, Monmouth Coll., 1976; L.H.D., Beaver Coll., 1972, Millikin U., 1972, Coll. St. Scholastica, 1972, Ottawa U., 1976, York Coll., 1978, Moravian Coll., 1984; Ped. D., Hofstra U., 1975; H.H.D., Rider Coll., 1975, Bridgewater Coll., 1977; LL.D., Elizabethtown Coll., 1976, New Eng. Coll., 1982. Instr. English, dean men Cin. Conservatory Music, 1938-39; instr. English U. Cin., 1939, Yale U., 1939-42; fellow Berkeley Coll., Yale U., 1940-42; asst. to vice chancellor/sec. NYU, 1945-52; dean, prof. English Dickinson Coll., 1952-60, acad. v.p., 1955-60, chmn. dept. English, 1956-58, William W. Edel prof. humanities, 1959-60; v.p., provost, dean Grad. Sch. L.I. U., 1960-62; v.p. Hofstra U., 1962-64; pres. Fresno (Calif.) State Coll., 1964-69, pres. emeritus, 1975—; pres. Assn. Am. Colls., Washington, 1969-78, pres. emeritus, 1978—; founding dir. Presdl. Search Consultation Svc., 1979-86, sr. cons., 1986-94; vis. prof. Poly. Inst., San German, P.R., 1955; mem. Pa. Gov.'s Com. Edn., 1958-60; pres. Western Colls. Assn., 1967-69. Author: The Use of Rhyme in Shakespeare's Plays, 1941; co-author: Graduate Study in the Liberal Arts College, 1961; editor, author: The Role of the College in the Recruitment of Teachers, 1958, A Guide to Graduate Study, 1957, 61, A Regional Faculty Orientation Program, 1961, An Uncertain Glory, 1970, Mostly Academic, 1996. Chmn. bd. dirs. Cmty. Chest, Carlisle, Pa., 1960; bd. dirs. Bklyn. Acad., 1960-62, Fresno Philharmonic Orch., 1965-69, Am. Coun. Edn., 1968-69, Change, 1970-72, Common Fund, 1970-76, Catalyst, 1974-78, Ind. Coll. Fund Am., 1976-86, Moravian Coll., 1976-84, Am. U., 1980-88, Annapolis Life Care, 1994—, Md. Hall for Creative Arts, 1990-95; bd. dirs., pres. Tchg. Film Custodians, 1970-73; mem. acad. adv. bd. U.S. Naval Acad., 1978-86. Lt. commdr. USNR, 1942-46. Mem. Elizabethan Club, Cosmos Club, Annapolis Yacht Club, Phi Beta Kappa, Beta Gamma Sigma, Omicron Delta Kappa, Phi Mu Alpha, Beta Theta Pi. Presbyterian. Office: 3105 River Crescent Dr Annapolis MD 21401-7719

NESS, NORMAN FREDERICK, astrophysicist, educator, administrator; b. Springfield, Mass., Apr. 15, 1933; s. Herman Hugo and Eva (Carlson) N.; children: Elizabeth Ann, Stephen Andrew. B.S., Mass. Inst. Tech., 1955, Ph.D., 1959. Space physicist, asst. prof. geophysics UCLA, 1959-61; Nat. Acad. Sci.-NRC post doctoral research assoc. NASA, 1960-61; research physicist in space scis. Goddard Space Flight Center, Greenbelt, Md., 1961-86; head extraterrestrial physics br. Goddard Space Flight Center, 1968-69; chief Lab. for Extraterrestrial Physics, 1969-86; pres., prof. Bartol Research Inst., U. Del., 1987—; lectr. math. U. Md., 1962-64, assoc. research prof., 1965-67. Contbr. articles profl. jours. Recipient Exceptional Sci. Achievement award NASA, 1966, 81, 86, Arthur S. Flemming award, 1968, Space Sci. award AIAA, 1971, Disting. Svc. medal NASA, 1986, Nat. Space Club Sci. award, 1993, Emil Wiechert medal German Geophys. Soc., 1993, Space Sci. award COSPAR, 1996. Fellow Am. Geophys. Union (John Adam Fleming award 1965), Royal Astron. Soc.; mem. NAS, Academia Nazionale dei Lincei, Royal Ocean Racing Club. Achievements include research, experimental studies of interplanetary and planetary magnetic fields by satellites and space probes. Home: 9 Wilkinson Dr Landenberg PA 19350-9359 Office: U Del Bartol Research Inst Newark DE 19716-4793

NESS, OWEN MCGREGOR, retired aluminum company executive; b. Howick, Que., Can., Apr. 3, 1930; s. John Earle and Jane Ella (McGregor) N.; m. Carolyn Mary Graham, Sept. 12, 1953; children: David Graham (dec.), Peter Earle, William Bruce (dec.), Richard Andrew. BSc in Agr., McGill U., Montreal, Que., 1952; postgrad., Ctr. Indsl. Studies, Geneva, 1961. Various positions including works pers. mgr. Alcan Smelters & Chems., Arvida, Que., 1954-71; various positions in compensation Alcan Can., Montreal, 1971-76, dir. pers., 1985-89; pers. dir. Alcan Aluminium (UK) Ltd., 1979-84; mgr. R & D, Alcan Internat. Ltd., Montreal, 1984-85; regional pers. mgr. Alcan Aluminium Ltd., Montreal, 1976-79, v.p. pers., 1989-93; mem. internat. human resource mgmt. coun. Conf. Bd., 1990-93. Mem. agrl. and environ. scis. adv. bd. Macdonald Coll., McGill U., 1988-93. Mem. Montreal Amateur Athletic Assn., Ormstown Golf Club (Que.). Avocations: farming, golf, badminton, aerobics. Home: 1595 Rte 202, Athelstan, PQ Canada J0S 1A0

NESSEL, EDWARD HARRY, swimming coach; b. Roselle, N.J., 1945; s. Irving Meyer Nessel and Ruth Eliott; m. Eileen Robin Berstein, 1973; children: Lee Allyson, Jason Eric, Matthew Scott (dec.). BS in Chemistry, Rutgers U., 1967, degree in pharmacy chemistry, 1968, postgrad., 1971; postgrad., Jersey City State, 1970; MS in Bacteriology, Wagner Coll., 1978, MPH, 1978. Registered pharmacist, Calif., N.J., Fla.; cert. U.S. Swimming Coach. Researcher, product developer Mennen Cos., Morrisplains, N.J., 1967; pharmacist supr. Pathmark Pharmacies, N.J., 1968-79; pharmacist, mgr. Roxy Drug Co., Inc., Irvington, N.J., 1979-90; diet and nutrition cons. Fanwood Scotch Plaines YMCA, 1985—, masters swim coach, 1984—, swimming and racing cons., head age group coach, asst. sr. coach, 1989-91; head swim coach Jewish Cmty. Ctr. Metrowest, West Orange, 1991—, Maccabi, 1990-91, 92, 93, 94; coach N.J. Masters Swimming, 1985—; physiology and sports medicine cons. Nat. Health and Fitness; health and fitness chmn. N.J. Masters Swimming; nat. masters swimming coaches com. Nat. Com. for Sports Medicine; nat. libr. U.S. Masters Swimming; chair N.J. Masters Swimming; pres. Jersey Masters Swimming Inc.; sports chair age group and masters swimming Garden State Games; summer coord. long-course 50 meter swim season Rayway YMCA, 1987—. Contbr. articles on swimming, self def. and physiology to profl. jours. Athletic and swimming cons. N.J. Spl. Olympics, 1986; cons. Essex County Narcotic Strike Force, Garden State Games ofcl.; chairperson govs. coun. phys. fitness for swimming events Garden State Games, 1989, 90. Recipient Presdl. Series award 1986; winner N.J. State Pentathlon champion Masters Swimming, 1986, 87, YMCA Masters Nat. Swim champion, 1988, 91, 95; apptd. head swim coach U.S. Jr. Nat. Swim Team, World Maccabi Games, Israel, 1997. Mem. NRA (disting. expert rating in pistol shooting), Am. Assn. Microbiologists, N.J. Pharm. Assn., N.J. Guild Pharmacists, Internat. Practical Shooters Confedn. (N.J. State Champion 1982, 83), Am. Swimming Coaches Assn. (master level), U.S. Swimming Coaches Assn. (cert. level 5), Master Swim Coaches Assn. Am., Rutgers Coll. Alumni Assn., Am. Med. Athletic Assn. (life, contbg.

editor quar. 1993—), Willow Grove Swim Club (bd. dirs. 1986-90), South River Pistol Club. Avocations: playing clarinet, saxophone and flute, museum quality ship builder. Home: 10 Irene Ct Edison NJ 08820-1024 Office: JCC Metrowest 760 Northfield Ave West Orange NJ 07052-1102

NESSEN, RONALD HAROLD, broadcast executive; b. Washington, May 25, 1934; s. Frederick E. and Ida Edith (Kaufman) N.; m. Johanna Neuman, Feb. 14, 1988; children: Caren Jayne, Edward Song. B.A., Am. U., 1959; LL.D. (hon.), Heidelberg Coll., 1975, Ursinus Coll., 1977. News announcer Sta. WEPM, Martinsburg, W.Va., 1952-54, Sta. WARL, Arlington, Va., 1954-55; writer Montgomery County (Md.) Sentinel, Rockville, 1955-56; editor UPI, Washington, 1956-62; news corr. NBC News, Washington, 1962-74; press sec. to Pres. Gerald R. Ford, 1974-77; freelance writer, lectr., 1977-80; exec. v.p. Marston & Rothenberg Public Affairs, Inc., Washington, 1980-84; sr. asso. Robert Marston & Assos., N.Y.C., 1980-84; moderator Pro-Con TV series Pa. Pub. Broadcasting System, 1983-84; v.p. MBS, Arlington, Va., 1984-92; sr. v.p. pub. affairs comm. Cellular Telecom. Industry Assn., 1992-96; host Issues and Answers Nostalgia TV, Washington, 1995—. Author: It Sure Looks Different from the Inside, 1978, The First Lady, 1979, The Hour, 1984, (with J. Neuman) Knight and Day, 1995, Press Corpse, 1996; contbr. articles to popular publs. Bd. trustees Peabody Awards. Recipient George Foster Peabody Broadcasting award, 1964, George Polk Meml. award Overseas Press Club, 1967, Edward R. Murrow Brotherhood award, 1988, 1989, Grand award Internat. Radio Festival, 1988, Nat. Headliner award, 1989. Mem. Nat. Press Club. Home: 6409 Walhonding Rd Bethesda MD 20816-2264

NESSEN, WARD HENRY, typographer, lawyer; b. Empire, Mich., Nov. 29, 1909; s. Henry L. and Louise (Stecher) N.; m. Jane Randall, Apr. 4, 1959. AB, U. Mich., 1931; JD, John Marshall Law Sch., Chgo., 1937; course in acctg. Northwestern U. Grad. Sch., 1946. Bar: Ill. 1937. With trust dept. No. Trust Co., Chgo., 1934-41; sales planning Am. Home Products, 1946-51; sales exec. Permacel Tape Corp., 1951-55; pres. The Highton Co., Newark, 1955-75; sr. v.p. Arrow Typographers, Newark, 1975-84; chmn. Coll. Communications Seminar, 1973. Mem. Civic Clubs Council Greater Newark Area, 1957-59, Bd. Comml. Arbitration N.Y.C., 1982-86; pres. Dale Carnegie course, 1964; chmn. selection com. Advt. Hall of Fame of N.J., 1983. Lt. col. AUS, 1941-46, ETO, assigned ETOUSA. Decorated Bronze Star with oak leaf cluster, Army Commendation medal; recipient Svc. to Industry award Printing Industries, N.J., 1973, recipient award of Excellence for Exhbn. Insides Am. Inst. Graphic Arts, 1974, Elmer G. Voigt award, 1975; named to Advt. Hall of Fame N.J., 1990. Mem. Internat. Platform Assn., Typographers Internat. Assn. (pres. 1970-71), N.J. Typographers Assn. (pres. 1957-59), Print/N.J. (pres. 1967-69), Assn. Graphic Arts N.Y. (bd. govs. 1967-69), Advt. Club N.J. (chmn. com. Constnl. bylaws 1980-81), John Monteith Soc., Pres.'s Club of U. Mich., Order of John Marshall, Sigma Phi. Republican. Episcopalian. Clubs: Type Dirs.; Advt. N.J. (bd. govs 1972-84). Home: 11 Euclid Ave Summit NJ 07901-2143

NESSLER, BRAD RAY, sports commentator; b. June 3, 1956. BA in Broadcasting, Mankato State U., 1977. Radio play-by-play for Ga. Tech basketball, 1980-85; sports anchor, talk show host Sta. WGST-Radio, Atlanta, 1980; radio play-by-play commentator Atlanta Falcons Sta. WGST-Radio, 1982-85; sports dir. Sta. WSB-Radio, Atlanta, 1985; radio play-by-play Sta. WSB-Radio, 1985-88; radio play-by-play commentator Minn. Vikings Sta. WCCO, 1988-89; radio play-by-play commentator ACC football and basketball Raycom/Jefferson Pilot telecasts, 1988; commentator Sta. WLAF games USA Network, 1991-92; commentator coll. and NFL football, men's and women's basketball CBS, 1989-92; network host for speed skating coverage Olympic Games CBS, Albertville, France, 1992; play-by-commentator Big Ten coll. football, NCAA basketball ESPN, 1992—, play-by-play commentator Miami Dolphins pre-season telecasts, 1992—; coll. football play-by-play ABC Sports, 1997—. Office: c/o ESPN ESPN Pla Bristol CT 06010

NESSMITH, H(ERBERT) ALVA, dentist; b. Miami, Fla., Nov. 27, 1935; s. William Boyd and Florence Editha (Lowe) N.; m. Paula Ann Fox, Oct. 1, 1960 (div. 1984); children: Amy Susan, Lynn Margaret, Mark Alva. Student, U. Miami, Fla., 1953-56; DDS, Northwestern U., 1960. Gen. practice dentistry Tequesta, Fla., 1963—; dental cons. Palm Beach-Martin County Med. Ctr., Jupiter, Fla., 1970—; rsch. assoc. Colgate Palmolive Co., 1997—; examiner, cons. Colgate Dental Rsch., 1997—. Mem. advmnistrv. bd. United Meth. Ch. Tequesta, Jupiter, 1970—, chmn., 1988-90; pres. Meth. Men, 1982; chmn. Coun. on Ministries, 1992-94; pres. Jupiter Elem. PTO, 1972; clarinetist Symphonic Band of Palm Beaches, Fla. Concert Band; pianist and clarinetist United Meth. Ch.; active Village of Tequesta Hist. Commn., 1992-96, Jupiter (Fla.) Cmty. Resource Ctr., 1994—; mem. adminstrv. bd., v.p. Christian Dental Soc., 1994—, v.p., 1995—. Mem. ADA, North Palm Beach County Dental Soc., Fla. Dental Assn., Jupiter-Tequesta-Juno Beach C. of C. Democrat. Lodge: Kiwanis (pres. Jupiter/Tequesta chpt. 1980-81). Avocations: sailing, gardening, music, travel. Home: 196 River Dr Tequesta FL 33469-1934 Office: Inlet Profl Bldg 175 Tequesta Dr Jupiter FL 33469

NESTER, WILLIAM RAYMOND, JR., retired academic administrator and educator; b. Cin., Feb. 19, 1928; s. William Raymond and Evelyn (Blettner) N.; m. Mary Jane Grossman; children: William Raymond, Mark Patrick, Brian Philip, Stephen Christopher. BS, U. Cin., 1950, EdM, 1953, EdD, 1965. Dir. student union U. Cin., 1952-53, asst. dean of men, 1953-60, dean of men, 1960-67, assoc. prof. edn., 1965-70, dean of students, 1967-69, vice provost student and univ. affairs, 1969-76, prof. edn., 1970-78, assoc. sr. v.p., assoc. provost, 1976-78; v.p. student svcs. Ohio State U., Columbus, 1978-83, prof. edn., 1978-83; pres. Kearney State Coll., Nebr., 1983-91, prof. edn., 1983-93; chancellor U. Nebr., Kearney, 1991-93, prof. emeritus, chancellor emeritus, 1993—; pres. emeritus Mus. Nebr. Art, 1991—; cons. on edn., 1993—. Pres. Metro-Six Athletic Conf., 1975-76, Ctrl. States Intercollegiate Conf., 1986-89. Mem. AAUP, Am. Assn. State Colls. and Univs. (bd. dirs.), Nat. Assn. Intercollegiate Athletics, Nat. Assn. Student Pers. Adminstrs. (past regional v.p., mem. exec. com.), Am. Assn. Higher Edn., Ohio Assn. Student Pers. Adminstrs. (past pres.), Nat. Intrafrat. Conf. (pres. 1991-92), Frat. Scholarship Officers Assn. (past pres.), Mortar Bd., Pi Kappa Alpha (nat. pres. 1978-80, past pres. ednl. found.), Omicron Delta Kappa, Phi Delta Kappa, Phi Alpha Theta, Phi Eta Sigma, Sigma Sigma. Episcopalian. Home: 7674 Coldstream Dr Cincinnati OH 45255-3932

NESTOR CASTELLANO, BRENDA DIANA, real estate executive; b. Palm Beach, Fla., Nov. 10, 1955; d. John Joseph and Marion O'Connor Nestor; m. Robert Castellano. Student, U. Miami, Fla., 1978. Lic. real estate broker, Fla. Salesman Oscar E Dooley, Inc., Miami, Fla., 1978-80; prin. Brenda Nestor Assocs, Inc., Miami Beach, Fla., 1980—; exec. v.p., bd. dirs. D.W.G. Corp., N.V.F. Corp., Salem Corp., Southeastern Pub. Svc., Graniteville Corp., Essex Ins., Chesapeake Ins.; exec. v.p., dir. Security Mgmt. Named Ms. Charity, City of Miami, 1985. Mem. Miami Beach Bd. Realtors (bd. dirs. 1984—), Real Estate Securities and Exch. Com., Le Club (N.Y.C.), La Gorce Country Club, Fisher Island Club, Bath Club, Surf Club. Roman Catholic. Avocations: golf, tennis, boating, skiing. Home and Office: 6917 Collins Ave Miami FL 33141-3263

NESTVOLD, ELWOOD OLAF, oil and gas industry executive; b. Minot, N.D., Mar. 19, 1932; came to Netherlands 1979; s. Ole Enevold and Ragnhilda (Quanbeck) N.; m. Simone Chriqui, Dec. 6, 1955 (dec. Jan. 1990); children: Rebecca Lynn, Paul Stephen; m. Jeannette Garvin, Mar. 23, 1991; stepchildren: Michele Marie, Jennifer Ann, Michael Dennis. BA, Augsburg Coll., Mpls., 1952; postgrad., U. Wash., 1952-53; MS, U. Minn., 1959, PhD, 1962. Physics instr. U. Minn., Mpls., 1956-61; physicist and section leader Shell EP Rsch. Lab., Houston, 1962-68, mgr. geophysics rsch., 1968-71; mgr. geophysics Shell Western Div., Denver, Houston, 1971-74, Pecten Internat., Houston, 1974-77; chief geophysicist Woodside Petroleum, Perth, Australia, 1977-78; mgr. EP processing ctr. Shell EP Rsch. Lab., Rijswijk, Netherlands, 1979-81; chief geophysicist Shell Internat. Petroleum, The Hague, 1981-86, dir. geophysics and topography, 1986-92; chief geophysicist Geco-Prakla div. Schlumberger Ltd., Paris, 1992-94, v.p. mktg. Geco-Prakla div., 1993-94; sr. geophysics cons. Schlumberger Oilfield Svcs., Houston, 1994-95; exploration and prodn. sector exec. IBM Corp., Houston, 1995-97; prin. Nestvold Cons. Internat. Inc., Houston, 1997—; cons. Lighting and Transients Rsch. Inst., Mpls., 1957-61; lectr. Australian Petroleum Exploration Assn, 1991, Internat. Assn. Geophysical Contractors, 1992, European Assn. Exploration Geophysicists, 1994 and others. Presenter keynote addresses; contbr. articles to profl. and trade jours. 1st lt. USAF, 1952-56. Recipient award of appreciation Internat. Assn. Geophys. Contractors, 1992. Mem. IEEE, Am. Assn. Petroleum Geologists (Disting. lectr. 1993-94), Am. Assn. Physics Tchrs., European Assn. Petroleum Geoscientists, European Assn. Exploration Geophysicists, Soc. Exploration Geophysicists, N.Y. Acad. Scis., Soc. Petroleum Engrs. (Disting. lectr. 1994-95), Sigma Xi. Avocations: hiking, museums. Home & Office: 9059 Briar Forest Houston TX 77024

NETER, JOHN, statistician; b. Germany, Feb. 8, 1923; m. Dorothy Rachman, June 24, 1951; children: Ronald J., David L. B.S., U. Buffalo, 1943; M.B.A., U. Pa., 1947; Ph.D., Columbia U., 1952. Asst. prof. Syracuse (N.Y.) U., 1949-55, chmn. dept. bus. stats., 1952-55; prof. U. Minn., Mpls., 1955-75; chmn. dept. quantitative analysis U. Minn., 1961-65; C. Herman and Mary Virginia Terry prof. mgmt. sci., stats. U. Ga., Athens, 1975-89, prof. emeritus, 1990—; supervisory math. statistician U.S. Bur. Census, 1959-60; chmn. panel on quality control of fed. assistance programs Nat. Acad. Scis., 1986-87; cons. in field. Co-author: Statistical Sampling for Auditors and Accountants, 1956, Fundamental Statistics for Business and Economics, 4th edit., 1973, Applied Linear Statistical Models, 1974, 4th edit., 1996, Applied Statistics, 1978, 4th edit., 1993, Applied Linear Regression Models, 1983, 3d edit., 1996; editor: Am. Statistician, 1976-80; assoc. editor: Decision Scis., 1973-74; contbr. articles to profl. jours. Chmn. citizens adv. com., City of St. Louis Park, Minn., 1972, mem. planning commn., 1974-75. Served with AUS, 1943-45. Ford Found. faculty research fellow, 1957-58. Fellow Am. Statis. Assn. (council 1963-64, 67-70, dir. 1975-80, pres. 1985), AAAS (chmn., sec. on statistics 1991), Decision Scis. Inst. (pres. 1978-79); mem. AAUP (chpt. pres. 1969-70), Inst. Math. Stats., Internat. Statis. Inst. Home: 310 St George Dr Athens GA 30606-3910 Office: Terry Coll Bus Univ Ga Athens GA 30602-6255

NETH, JERRY, publishing company executive. Exec. v.p. pub. ops. Cahners Pub. Co., Newton, Mass. Office: Cahners Pub Co 275 Washington St Newton MA 02158-1646

NETHERCUT, PHILIP EDWIN, honorary consul, retired; b. Indpls., Apr. 3, 1921; s. William Richard and Ruth Salome (Habbe) N.; m. Leah Teresa Diehl, Apr. 9, 1949; children: Bruce Philip, Gail Ellen, Anne Louise. B.S., Beloit Coll., 1942; M.S., Lawrence Coll., 1944, Ph.D., 1949. With Watervliet Paper Co., Mich., 1949-50; research mgr. Scott Paper Co., 1951-56; with TAPPI, N.Y.C., now Atlanta, 1957-86; sec.-treas. TAPPI, 1959-60, exec. sec., 1960-75, treas., 1964-75, exec. dir., 1975-82, vice. chmn. bd., 1983-86; hon. consul for Finland in Ga., 1976-96; trustee Inst. Paper Chemistry, 1979-83, TAPPI Found., 1990-96. Bd. dirs. Met. Atlanta Boys' and Girls' Club, 1979—. Served to lt. (j.g.) USNR, 1944-46. Recipient Distinguished Service citation Beloit Coll., 1967; Clarke award Ga. Soc. Assn. Execs., 1979; decorated Knight Finnish Order of White Rose, 1987. Fellow TAPPI; mem. Am. Soc. Assn. Execs. (CAE award 1968, Key award 1981), Inst. Paper Chemistry Alumni Assn. (chmn. 1960), Council Engring. and Sci. Soc. Execs. (pres. 1968), Finnish-Am. C. of C. S.E., Phi Beta Kappa, Beta Theta Pi. Club: Mountain View. Home: 9240 Huntcliff Trce Atlanta GA 30350-1603

NETHERCUTT, GEORGE RECTOR, JR., congressman, lawyer; b. Spokane, Wash., Oct. 4, 1944; s. George Rector and Nancy N.; m. Mary Beth Socha Nethercutt, Apr. 2, 1977; children: Meredith, Elliott. BA in English, Wash. State U., 1967; JD, Gonzaga U., 1971. Bar: D.C. 1972. Law clk. to Hon. Raymond Plummer U.S. Dist. Ct. Alaska, Anchorage, 1971; staff counsel to U.S. Senator Ted Stevens Washington, 1972, chief of staff to U.S. Senator Ted Stevens, 1972-76; pvt. practice Spokane, Wash., 1977-94; mem. 104th Congress from 5th Wash. dist., Washington, 1994—; mem. agriculture, interior, nat. security comms. Chmn. Spokane County Rep. Party, 1990-94, co-founder Vanessa Behan Crisis Nursery, pres. Spokane Juvenile Diabetes Found., 1993-94. Mem. Masons (lodge #34), Lions Club (Spokane Ctrl.), Sigma Nu. Republican. Presbyterian. Avocations: running, handball, squash. Office: US House Reps 1527 Longworth Bldg Ofc Bldg Washington DC 20515-4705

NETHERY, JOHN JAY, government official; b. Mpls., June 4, 1941; s. Ronald Jay and Mary Vesta (McVeety) N.; m. Sonya Elisabeth Magin, July 27, 1968; children: William Jay, Mary Elisabeth (dec.), Sarah Ann. BA, U. Denver, 1963, MPA, 1968. Mgmt. intern USAF Logistics Command, San Antonio, 1969-71; budget analyst USAF Logistics Command, Dayton, Ohio, 1971-72; chief, fiscal analysis USAF Hdqrs., Washington, 1973-80, chief, investment div., 1980-81, chief budget mgmt., 1981-85; dep. asst. sec. Dept. of USAF, Washington, 1986-88, asst. to undersecretary, 1988-89, dep. asst. sec., 1989—; mem. Air Force bd. for the correction of mil. records, Washington, 1980—. Recipient Gov.'s Scholastic award Gov. of Colo., 1968, Presdl. Rank award, 1988. Mem. Sr. Execs. Assn., Air Force Assn. Presbyterian. Avocations: history, military minatures. Home: 12349 Coleraine Ct Reston VA 20191 Office: Dept USAF SAF/FM The Pentagon Washington DC 20330-1130

NETI, SUDHAKAR, mechanical engineering educator; b. Bapatla, India, Sept. 27, 1947; came to U.S., 1968, naturalized, 1977; s. Chiranjeeva Rao and Meenakshi Neti; BME, Osmania U., 1968; MS, U. Ky., 1970, PhD, 1977; m. Kathy Gibson, Jan. 11, 1974. Research asst. U. Ky., 1968-77; asst. prof. mech. engring. Lehigh U., Bethlehem, Pa., 1978-83, assoc. prof., 1983-92, prof., 1992—; vis. fellow Wolfson Coll., Oxford U., Eng.; vis. rsch. assoc. U.K. Atomic Energy Rsch. Establishment, Harwell, Eng.; fallout shelter analyst Fed. Emergency Mgmt. Adminstrn.; chair Mech. Engring. Thermo-Fluids Divsn., 1996—, mem. Lehigh Valley Joint Planning Commn., 1996—; bd. dirs. ANS, PANE; cons. to industry. Summer faculty fellow NASA-Am. Soc. Engring. Edn., 1978; grantee Electric Power Research Inst., 1979, NSF, 1980, NRC, 1981. Mem. ASME, AAAS, Sigma Xi. Contbr. articles to profl. jours. Office: Lehigh U Mech Engring Dept 19 Memorial Dr W Bethlehem PA 18015-3006

NETT, LOUISE MARY, nursing educator, consultant; b. Sept. 25, 1938. Diploma, St. Cloud Sch. Nursing, 1959; cert. in therapy program, Gen. Rose Hosp., Denver, 1967. Staff nurse med. unit Mt. Sinai Hosp., Mpls., 1959-60; staff nurse nursing registry San Francisco, 1960-61; emergency rm. staff nurse Colo. Gen. Hosp., Denver, 1961-62; head nurse Outpatient Clinic Charity Hosp., New Orleans, 1962-64; dir. respiratory care U. Colo. Health Scis. Ctr., Denver, 1965-85, pulmonary program specialist Webb-Waring Lung Inst., 1985-89; rsch. assoc. Presbyn./St. Luke's Ctr. for Health Scis. Edn., Denver, 1989—; clins. assoc. prof. nursing U. Colo. Sch. Nursing, Denver; adj. asst. prof. U. Kans. Sch. Allied Health; instr. medicine pulmonary divsn. U. Colo. Sch. Medicine, Denver, 1980-89; mem. Nat. Heart, Lung, and Blood Inst. adv. coun., NIH, 1979-82, mem. safety and data monitoring bd. for early intervention for chronic obstructive pulmonary disease, lung divsn., 1985-91; mem. clin. practice guidelines for smoking cessation and presentation panel Agy. for Health Care Policy and Rsch., 1994; dir. numerous courses, confs. in field; worldwide lectr. assns., symposia, confs., TV, convs., meetings, workshops; internat. cons. hosps., health depts., 1975—; local, regional lectr. through med. programs Am. Lung Assn., Am. Cancer Soc. Colo., cmty. hosps., businesses. Author: (with T.L. Petty) For Those Who Live and Breathe with Emphysema and Chronic Bronchitis, 1967, 2d edit., 1971, Enjoying Life with Emphysema, 1984, 2d edit., 1987 (Am. Jour. Nursing Book of Yr. award 1987), Rational Respiratory Therapy, 1988; mem. editl. bd. Heart and Lung Jour., 1972-87, Respiratory Times Newsletter, 1986-88, Jour. Home Health Care Practice, 1988; contbr. articles to profl. jours., chpts. to books. Mem. subcom. on nursing Am. Lung Assn., 1975-76; mem. exec. bd. dirs. Colo. divsn. Am. Cancer Soc., 1984—, chairperson pub. edn. com., 1985-86; mem. exec. com. Am. Stop Smoking Intervention Study, 1991-94, mem. alliance bd. Recipient Rocky Mountain Tobacco Free Challenge Regional award for treatment of nicotine addiction program, 1989, award for ednl. seminars, 1989, award in profl. end., 1992, award for outstanding work in developing and promoting smoking cessation, 1992, profl. educator award, 1993, award for nicotine treatment network, 1993. Mem. ANA, Am. Assn. for Respiratory Care (health promotion com. 1987—, internat. liaison com. 1987-90, Charles H. Hudson Pub. Respiratory Health award 1991), Am. Assn. of Cardio Vascular and Pulmonary Rehab., Am. Thoracic Soc. (ad hoc com. role of non-physician in respiratory care 1972, respiratory therapy com. 1972-74, program planning com. 1989), Behavioral Medicine Soc., Colo. Trudeau Soc. (v.p. 1981, pres.-elect 1982, pres. 1983), Colo. Pub. Health Assn., Internat. Oxygen Club, Internat. Soc. for Humor Studies, Soc. of European Pnemonology. Office: Presbyn/St Lukes Ctr Health Clin Rsch Divsn 1719 E 19th Ave Denver CO 80218-1235

NETTELS, ELSA, English language educator; b. Madison, Wis., May 25, 1931; d. Curtis Putnam and Elsie (Patterson) N. BA, Cornell U., 1953; MA, U. Wis., 1955, PhD, 1960. From instr. to asst. prof. English Mt. Holyoke Coll., South Hadley, Mass., 1959-67; asst. prof. to prof. English Coll. William and Mary, Williamsburg, Va., 1967—. Author: James and Conrad, 1977 (South Atlantic Modern Lang. Assn. award 1975), Language, Race and Social Class in Howells' America, 1988, Language and Gender in American Fiction: Howells, James, Wharton, and Cather, 1997; contbr. articles to profl. jours. NEH fellow, 1984-85. Mem. Modern Lang. Assn., South Atlantic Modern Lang. Assn. (edit. bd. 1977-83), Henry James Soc. (edit. bd. 1983—), Am. Studies Assn. Home: 211 Indian Springs Rd Williamsburg VA 23185-3940 Office: Coll William and Mary Dept English Williamsburg VA 23185

NETTELS, GEORGE EDWARD, JR., mining executive; b. Pittsburg, Kans., Oct. 20, 1927; s. George Edward and Mathilde A. (Wulke) N.; m. Mary Joanne Myers, July 19, 1952; children: Christopher Bryan, Margaret Anne, Katherine Anne, Rebecca Jane. B.S. in Civil Engring, U. Kans., Lawrence, 1950. With Black & Veatch Engrs., Kansas City, Mo., 1950-51, Spencer Chem. Co., Kansas City, Mo., 1951-55, Freeto Constrn. Co., Pittsburg, 1955-57; pres. Midwest Minerals, Inc., Pittsburg, 1957—; chmn. bd. McNally Pittsburg Mfg. Corp., 1970-76, pres., chief exec. officer, 1976-87; ret. McNally Pitts. Inc., 1987; bd. dirs. Bank IV, Pitts., Kansas City Power & Light Co.; past chmn. bd. Nat. Limestone Inst.; bd. dirs. Pitts. Indsl. Devel. Com. Bd. advisers Kans. U. Endowment Assn.; mem. Kans. U. Chancellor's Club, Kans., Inc.; past pres. Bd. Edn. 250, Pittsburg; past chmn. bd. trustees Mt. Carmel Hosp.; past mem. Kans. Commn. Civil Rights; chmn. Kans. Republican Com., 1966-68; Kans. del. Rep. Nat. Conv., 1968, Kans. Bus. and Industry Com. for Re-election of the President, 1972. Served with AUS, 1946-47. Recipient Disting. Service citation U. Kans., 1980, Disting. Engring. citation U. Kans., 1985; named Kansan of Yr., 1986. Mem. ASCE, NAM (past. dir.), Kans. C. of C. and Industry (dir., chmn. 1983-84), Kans. Right to Work (dir.), Pittsburg C. of C. (past dir.), Kans. U. Alumni Assn. (pres. 1977), Kans. Leadership Com., Tau Beta Pi, Omicron Delta Kappa, Beta Theta Pi. Presbyterian. Clubs: Crestwood Country (Pittsburg); Wolf Creek Golf (Olathe). Office: Midwest Minerals Inc 509 W Quincy St Pittsburg KS 66762-5689

NETTER, KURT FRED, retired building products company executive; b. Mannheim, Fed. Republic Germany, Dec. 3, 1919; came to U.S., 1941, naturalized, 1944; s. Arthur and Kate (Gruenfeld) N.; m. Alice Dreyfus, May 26, 1942; children: Nadine, Ronald, Alfred. Student, Swiss Inst. Tech., 1938-39, U. Toronto, 1939-41; BS, Columbia U., 1942. Ptnr. Interstate Engring. and Machinery Co., N.Y.C., 1942-44; officer, dir. Supradur Cos., Inc., 1946-95, pres., CEO, 1953-93; chmn., 1986-95. Bd. dirs. Selfhelp Community Svcs., Inc., treas., 1970-85, pres., 1985-90, chmn., 1990—. With AUS, 1944-46. Home: 203 Griffen Ave Scarsdale NY 10583-7905

NETTER, VIRGINIA THOMPSON, produce company owner; b. Hardyville, Ky., Nov. 2, 1931; d. Duluth Sydnor and Vera (Asbury) Thompson; m. S. Mitchell Netter, Oct. 4, 1947; children: Ronald Lee, Candace Netter Harrison. BA, U. Louisville, 1982; MA in Counseling/Clin. Psychology, Spalding U., 1989. Owner, Netter Produce Co., Louisville, 1954—, Big Four Farms, Belmont, Ky., 1959—. Named to Hon. Order Ky. Cols., 1982. Mem. AAUW, Woodcock Soc., Psi Chi, Phi Kappa Phi. Avocations: ballroom dancing, riding, golf, travel. Home: 1029 Alta Vista Rd Louisville KY 40205-1727 Office: Netter Produce Co 331 Produce Plz Louisville KY 40202-1227

NETTL, BRUNO, anthropology and musicology educator; b. Prague, Czechoslovakia, Mar. 14, 1930; s. Paul and Gertrud (Hutter) N.; m. Wanda Maria White, Sept. 15, 1952; children: Rebecca, Gloria. A.B., Ind. U., 1950, Ph.D., 1953; M.A. in L.S., U. Mich., 1960; LHD (hon.), U. Chgo., 1993, U. Ill., 1996. Mem. faculty Wayne State U., Detroit, 1953-64; asst. prof. Wayne State U., 1954-64, music librarian, 1958-64; mem. faculty U. Ill., Urbana, 1964—; prof. music and anthropology U. Ill., 1967—, chmn. div. musicology, 1967-72, 75-77, 82-85; vis. lectr., Fulbright grantee U. Kiel, Fed. Republic of Germany, 1956-58; cons. Ency. Britannica, 1969—, also on ethomusicology to various univs.; vis. prof. Williams Coll., 1971, Wash. U., 1978, U. Louisville, 1983, U. Wash., 1985, 88, 89, 93, 95, Fla. State U., 1988, Harvard U., 1989, U. Alta., 1991, Colo. Coll., 1992, Northwestern U., 1993, U. Minn., 1994, U. Chgo., 1996, Carleton Coll., 1996. Author: Theory and Method in Ethnomusicology, 1964, Music in Primitive Culture, 1956, Folk and Traditional Music of the Western Continents, 1965, 2d edit., 1973, Eight Urban Musical Cultures, 1978, The Study of Ethnomusicology, 1983, The Western Impact on World Music, 1985, The Radif of Persian Music, 1987, rev. edit., 1992, Blackfoot Musical Thought, 1989, Comparative Musicology and Anthropology of Music, 1991, Heartland Excursions, 1995; co-author Excursions in World Music, 1992, 2d edit., 1996; editor Ethnomusicology, 1961-65, Yearbook of the International Folk Music Council, 1975-77; contbr. articles to profl. jours. Recipient Koizumi prize in ethnomusicology, Tokyo, 1994. Fellow Am. Acad. of Arts and Scis.; mem. Soc. Ethnomusicology (pres. 1969-71), Am., Internat. musicol. socs., Internat. Coun. for Traditional Music. Home: 1423 Cambridge Dr Champaign IL 61821-4958 Office: Sch Music U Ill Urbana IL 61801

NETTLES, JOHN BARNWELL, obstetrics and gynecology educator; b. Dover, N.C., May 19, 1922; s. Stephen A. and Estelle (Hendrix) N.; m. Eunice Anita Saugstad, Apr. 28, 1956; children: Eric, Robert, John Barnwell; m. 2d, Sandra Williams, Sept. 14, 1991; stepchildren: Steven Williams, Clayton Williams. B.S., U. S.C., 1941; M.D., Med. Coll. S.C., 1944. Diplomate: Am. Bd. Obstetrics and Gynecology. Intern Garfield Meml. Hosp., Washington, 1944-45; research fellow in pathology Med. Coll. Ga., Augusta, 1946-47; resident in ob-gyn. U. Ill. Rsch. and Ednl. Hosps., Chgo., 1947-51; instr. to asst. prof. ob-gyn. U. Ill. Coll. Medicine, Chgo., 1951-57; asst. prof., assoc. prof., prof. ob-gyn. U. Ark. Med. Ctr., Little Rock, 1957-69; dir. grad. edn. Hillcrest Med. Ctr., Tulsa, 1969-73; prof. ob-gyn Coll. Medicine, U. Okla., Oklahoma City, 1969—; chmn. dept. ob-gyn. U. Okla.-Tulsa Med. Coll., 1975-80, prof., 1980—, mem. coun. on residency edn. in ob-gyn., 1974-79; dir. Tulsa Obstet. and Gynecol. Edn. Found., 1969-80; Coordinator med. edn. Nat. Def., Ark., 1961-69; mem. S.W. regional med. adv. com. Planned Parenthood Fedn. Am., 1974-78; mem. adv. com. Health Policy Agenda Am. People, 1982-, rev. com. Accrediation Council for Continuing Med. Edn., 1987-92. Contbr. articles on uterine malignancy, kidney biopsy in pregnancy, perinatal morbidity and mortality, human sexuality sch. age pregnancy to profl. jours. Served as lt. (j.g.) M.C. USNR, 1945-46; as lt. 1953-54. Fellow Am. Coll. Obstetricians and Gynecologists (dist. sec.-treas. 1964-70, dist. chmn. exec. bd. 1970-73, v.p. 1977-78), A.C.S. (bd. govs. 1969-71, program com. 1970-71, Surg. forum 1977-84, adv. com. gyn/ob 1985—), Royal Soc. Health, Royal Soc. Medicine; mem. Ark. Obstet. and Gynecol. Soc. (exec. sec. 1959-69), Central Assn. Obstetrics and Gynecology (exec. com. 1966-69, pres. 1978-79), Internat. Soc. Advancement Humanistic Studies in Gynecology, Assn. Mil. Surgeons U.S., AMA (sect. council on obstetrics and gynecology 1975—, chmn. 1982—, del. from Am. Coll. Obstetricians and Gynecologists 1987—, Young at Heart award Young Physicians sect. 1994), Nurses Assn. Am. Coll. Obstetricians and Gynecologists (exec. bd. 1970-73, assoc. 1980—), So. Med. Assn. (chmn. obstetrics 1973-74), Okla. Med. Soc., Tulsa County Med. Soc., Chgo. Med. Soc., Am. Assn. for Maternal and Infant Health, Assn. Am. Med. Colls., Am. Public Health Assn., Am. Assn. Sex Edn. Counselors and Therapists (S.W. regional bd. 1976-79), Soc. for Gynecol. Investigation, AAAS, Am. Soc. for Study Fertility and Sterility, Internat. Soc. Gen. Semantics, So. Gynecol. and Obstet. Soc. (pres. 1981-82), Am. Cancer Soc. (pres. Okla. div. 1979-83, St. George's medal 1991), Com. on In-Tng. Exam. in Obstetrics and Gynecology, Am. Coll. Nurse Midwives (governing bd. examiners 1979-83), Sigma Xi (pres. Tulsa chpt. 1992-93), Phi Rho Sigma. Lutheran. Office: U Okla Tulsa Med Coll 2808 S Sheridan Rd Tulsa OK 74129-1014 *To live life fully, with faith and trust in God and his people, working with others to make our world a little better, and willing to fill the gaps wherever they are.*

NETTLES, TONI OLESCO, non-commissioned officer; b. Ensley, Ala., Sept. 14, 1961; d. Willie Edward and Rosie Lee (Cooke) Pace; m. Jonathan Paul Nettles, Dec. 25, 1980 (div. Dec. 1991); 1 child, Ashley. AS in Applied Sci., Cmty. Coll. of the Air Force, 1988; AA, U. Md., 1990, BS, 1996. Computer operator 2162CS USAF, Buckley, Colo., 1979-84; COMSEC acct. USAF, Lowry AFB, Colo., 1984-85; facility chief 3d Combat Comm. Group USAF, Tinker AFB, Okla., 1985-88; non-commd. officer in charge 603rd Aerial Port Squadron USAF, Kadena, Japan, 1988-92; non-commd. officer in charge 305th CS USAF, Grissom AFB, Ind., 1992-94; supt. ops. 55th Computer Sys. Squadron USAF, Offutt AFB, Nebr., 1994—, master sgt. 55th computer sys. squadron, 1995-96; base Comsec mgr. 55 Comm. Squadron, 1996—; instr. total quality mgmt., 1992-94. Leader troop Girl Scouts Am., West Pacific, 1990; mem. PTA, Omaha, 1994—; vol. Nebr. Spl. Olympics, Omaha, 1995, United Way/CHAD, Omaha, 1994-95. Recipient Letter of appreciation MADD Nat. Pres., 1995, 96, Letter of Appreciation regional commr. Girl Scouts U.S., West Pacific, 1990. Mem. Vis. Nurse Assn. (vol. 1994-95), Black Heritage Com. (citation, letter of appreciation, 1989). Home: 2802 Lynnwood Dr Omaha NE 68123-1955 Office: Base COMSEC Mgr 55 Communications Sq #206 201 Lincoln Hwy Omaha NE 68113-2040

NETZEL, PAUL ARTHUR, fund raising management executive, consultant; b. Tacoma, Sept. 11, 1941; s. Marden Arthur and Audrey Rose (Jones) N.; BS in Group Work Edn., George Williams Coll., 1963; m. Diane Viscount, Mar. 21, 1963; children: Paul M., Shari Ann. Program dir. S. Pasadena-San Marino (Calif.) YMCA, 1963-66; exec. dir. camp and youth programs Wenatchee (Wash.) YMCA, 1966-67; exec. dir. Culver-Palms Family YMCA, Culver City, Calif., 1967-73; v.p. met. fin. devel. YMCA Met. Los Angeles, 1973-78, exec. v.p. devel., 1979-85; pres. bd. dirs. YMCA Employees Credit Union, 1977-80; chmn. N.Am. Fellowship of YMCA Devel. Officers, 1980-83; adj. faculty U. So. Calif. Coll. Continuing Edn., 1983-86, Loyola Marymount U., L.A., 1986-90, Calif. State U., L.A., 1991-92, UCLA Extension, 1991—; chmn., CEO Netzel Assocs., Inc., 1985—; pvt. practice cons., fund raiser. Chmn. Culver-Palms YMCA, Culver City, 1991-93, chmn. 1989-91, bd. mgrs. 1985—; pres. bd. Culver City Guidance Clinic, 1971-74; mem. Culver City Bd. Edn., 1975-79, pres., 1977-78; mem. Culver City Edn. Found., 1982-91; bd. dirs. Los Angeles Psychiat. Svc., 1971-74, Goodwill Industries of So. Calif., 1993—; mem. Culver City Council, 1980-88, vice-mayor, 1980-82, 84-85, mayor, 1982-83, 86-87; mem. Culver City Redevel. Agy., 1980-88, chmn., 1983-84, 87-88, vice chmn, 1985-86; bd. dirs. Los Angeles County Sanitation Dists., 1982-83, 85-87, Western Region United Way, 1986-93, vice chmn, 1991-92; chmn. bd. dirs. Calif. Youth Model Legislature, 1987-92; mem. World Affairs Coun., 1989—; mem. adv. bd. Automobile Club of So. Calif., 1996—. Recipient Man of Yr. award Culver City C. of C., 1972. Mem. Nat. Soc. Fund Raising Execs. (nat. bd. dirs. 1989-91, vice chmn. 1994, v.p. bd. dirs. Greater L.A. chpt. 1986-88, pres. bd. dirs. 1989-90, Profl. of Yr. 1983), Calif. Club, Rotary (L.A. # 5, pres. 1992-93, treas. L.A. found. 1995-96), Rotary Internat. (gov. dist. 5280 1997—), Mountain Gate Country. Address: Netzel Assocs Inc 9696 Culver Blvd Ste 204 Culver City CA 90232-2753

NETZER, DICK, economics educator; b. N.Y.C., May 14, 1928; s. Solomon and Sue (Dick) N.; m. Carol Risika, Dec. 30, 1945; children: Jenny, Katherine. B.A., U. Wis., 1946; M.A., M.P.A., Harvard U., 1948, Ph.D., 1952. Successively economist, sr. economist, asst. v.p. Fed. Res. Bank Chgo., 1948-60; econ. cons. Regional Plan Assn., N.Y.C., 1960-80; assoc. prof. N.Y. U., 1961-64, prof. econs., 1964—, dean Grad. Sch. Pub. Adminstrn., 1969-82, dir. Urban Research Center, 1981-86; cons. in field, 1960—. Author: Economics of the Property Tax, 1966, The Economics of Public Finance, 1974, The Subsidized Muse, 1978, Urban Politics New York Style, 1990; editor: N.Y. Affairs, 1973-88. Mem. Mayor N.Y.C. Fiscal Adv. com., 1969-73; treas. Colony-South Bklyn. Houses, 1968-73; mem. Mcpl. Securities Rulemaking Bd., 1978-81, vice chmn., 1980-81; bd. dirs. Mcpl. Assistance Corp., N.Y.C., 1975—, Citizens Union Found., 1981—; bd. dirs., treas. Adolph and Esther Gottlieb Found., 1975—, v.p., 1979-88, pres. 1989—. Mem. Am. Econs. Assn., Regional Sci. Assn., Nat. Tax Assn., Am. Inst. Cert. Planners, Assn. Cultural Econs. Internat. (pres. 1993-94). Home: 227 Clinton St Brooklyn NY 11201-6144 Office: 4 Washington Sq N New York NY 10003-6671

NETZER, LANORE A(GNES), retired educational administration educator; b. Laona, Wis., Aug. 27, 1916; d. Henry N. and Julia M. (Niquette) Netzer; m. Glen G. Eye, 1979. Diploma, Oconto County Normal Sch., 1935; BS, State Tchrs. Coll., Oshkosh, Wis., 1943; MS, U. Wis., 1948, PhD, 1951. Tchr. Goldhorn Rural Sch., Pound, Wis., 1935-36; tchr. Goldfield Sch., Pound, 1936-37, tchr., acting prin., 1937-39; tchr., prin. Spruce (Wis.) Grade Sch., 1939-41; tchr. pub. schs. Neenah, Wis., 1943-46; demonstration and critic tchr. Campus Sch. State Tchrs. Coll., Oshkosh, 1946-48; supr. student tchrs.' coll. instrn. State Tchrs. Coll., Milw., 1950-55; teaching asst. U. Wis., Madison, 1948-50; assoc. prof. edn. U. Wis., Milw., 1955-63; prof. ednl. adminstrn. U. Wis., Madison, 1963-77, emeritus prof., 1977—; rsch. assoc. U.S. Office Edn., 1963-66; supr. student tchrs. coll. instrn. State Tchrs. Coll., Milw., 1950-55; mem. curriculum adminstrn. com. Wis. Coop. Curriculum Planning Program, 1945-52; mem. Wis. Joint Com. on Edn., 1957-59, E.B. Fred Fellowship Com., U. Wis., 1966—; ednl. cons. Educators Progress Svc., 1970—. Author: The Use of Industry Aids in Schools, 1952, (with Glen G. Eye) Supervision of Instruction: A Phase of Administration, 1965, 2d. edit., 1971, (with others) Interdisciplinary Foundations of Supervision, 1969, (with G. Eye) School Administrators and Instruction, 1969, (with others) Education Administration and Change, 1970, (with others) Supervision of Instruction, 1971, Strategies for Instructional Management, 1977; contbr. articles to profl. jours. Rsch. grantee Hill & Knowlton, Inc., N.Y.C., 1949; grantee Wis. Mfrs. Assn., 1954; recipient award of Distinction Nat. Coun. of Adminstrv. Women in Edn., 1975. Mem. AAUP, Wis. Edn. Assn. (life), So. Wis. Edn. Assn., Nat. Assn. Supervision and Curriculum Devel., Wis. Assn. Supervision and Curriculum Devel., Southwestern Assn. Supervision and Curriculum Devel., Wis. Elem. Sch. Prins. Assn., Am. Assn. Sch. Adminstrs., Wis. Assn. Sch. Dist. Adminstrs., Am. Edn. Rsch. Assn., Wis. Edn. Rsch. Assn., Univ. Coun. Ednl. Adminstrn., U. Wis. Alumni Assn. (life), U. Wis. Meml. Union (life), Phi Beta Sigma, Kappa Delta Pi, Pi Lambda Theta, Phi Delta Kappa. Home: 110 S Henry St Apt 1506 Madison WI 53703-3168 Office: U Wis Dept Ednl Adminstrn 1025 W Johnson St Madison WI 53706-1706 *My life achieves meaning as I help people to appreciate, reinforce, and serve each other. Kindness may be a goal, a process of living, or a product of effort, but to me it is the main road to self-realization.*

NETZLOFF, MICHAEL LAWRENCE, pediatric educator, endocrinologist, geneticist; b. Madison, Wis., Sept. 11, 1942; s. Harold Harvey Netzloff and Garnet Lucille (Wilson) MacFarlane; m. Cheryl Lynne Crandall, July 20, 1963; children: Michelle Lynne, Rochelle Anne, Cherie Lucille. BS with high honors, Eckert Coll., 1964; MS, U. Fla., 1968, MD, 1969. Diplomate Am. Bd. Pediatrics, Am. Bd. Pediatric Endocrinology, Am. Bd. Med. Genetics. Rsch. fellow, rsch. trainee dept. of anat. scis. U. Fla. Coll. Medicine, Gainesville, 1965-69, intern and resident in pediatrics, 1969-71, clin. and rsch. fellow div. genetics, endocrinology and metabolism, dept. pediatrics, 1971-73, instr. in pediatrics, 1973-74, asst. prof. of pediatrics, 1974-79; assoc. prof. of pediatrics and human devel. Mich. State U. Coll. of Human Medicine, East Lansing, 1979-85, dir. of pediatric endocrinology, pediatrics and human devel., 1981-89, dir. div. of human genetics, genetic toxicology, endocrinology and oncology, pediatrics and human devel., 1982-89, prof. dept. pediatrics and human devel., 1985—, chmn. dept., 1987-91; vis. prof. dept. pediatrics U. Mich., 1992-93; cons. Juvenile Diabetes Found., Lansing, 1981—; mem. diabetes adv. coun. Mich. State Dept. Pub. Health and Chronic Disease Control, Lansing, 1980-90. Recipient Carithers award for Child Health and Human Dev., U. Fla. Coll. Medicine, 1969, Edward Bogen fellowship U. Fla. Coll. Med., 1972, Basil O'Connor rsch. grant Nat. Found. March of Dimes, 1973, pediatric residency teaching award, Grad. Med. Edn., Inc., Mich. State U. Affiliated Residency program, 1982, 86. Fellow Am. Acad. Pediatrics; mem. Assn. Clin. Scis. Inst. (sci. com. 1979—), Am. Diabetes Assn. (coun. on diabetes in youth 1979—), Am. Pediatric Soc., Lawson-Wilkins Pediatric Endocrine Soc., Mich State Med. Soc., Ingham County Med. Soc., Soc. for Pediatric Rsch., Sigma Xi. Democrat. Lutheran. Home: 4432 Greenwood Dr Okemos MI 48864-3044 Office: Mich State U Dept Pediatrics B240 Life Scis East Lansing MI 48824-1317

NEU, CARL HERBERT, JR., management consultant; b. Miami Beach, Fla., Sept. 4, 1937; s. Carl Herbert and Catherine Mary (Miller) N.; BS, MIT, 1959; MBA, Harvard U., 1961; m. Carmen Mercedes Smith, Feb. 8, 1964; children—Carl Bartley, David Conrad. Cert. profl. mgmt. cons. Indsl. liaison officer MIT, Cambridge, 1967-69; coord. forward planning Gates Rubber Co., Denver, 1969-71; pres., co-founder Dyna-Com Resources, Lakewood, Colo., 1971-77; pres., founder Neu & Co., Lakewood, 1977—; mng. dir. Pro-Med Mgmt. Systems, Lakewood, 1981—; lectr. Grad. Sch. Pub. Affairs, U. Colo. Denver, 1982-84. Mem. exec. coun. Episcopal Diocese Colo., 1974; mem. Lakewood City Coun., 1975-80, pres., 1976; chmn. Lakewood City Charter Commn., 1982, Lakewood Civic Found., Inc., 1986—; pres. Lakewood on Parade, 1978, bd. dirs., 1978-80; pres. Classic Chorale, Denver, 1979, bd. dirs., 1978-83; pres. Lakewood Pub. Bldg. Authority, 1983—; bd. dirs. Metro State Coll. of Denver Found., 1990—, treas., 1994—; bd. dirs. Kaiser Permanente Health Adv. Com., 1990—, chair, 1997. With U.S. Army, 1961-67. Decorated Bronze Star medal, Army Commendation medal; recipient Arthur Page award AT&T, 1979; Kettering Found. grantee, 1979-80. Mem. World Future Soc., Internat. City Mgrs. Assn., Lakewood-So. Jefferson County C. of C. (bd. dirs. 1983-89, chmn. 1988, chmn. 1987-88), Jefferson County C. of C. (chmn. 1988). Republican. Episcopalian. Contbr. articles to profl. jours. Home: 8169 W Baker Ave Denver CO 80227-3129

NEU, CHARLES ERIC, historian, educator; b. Carroll, Iowa, Apr. 10, 1936; s. Arthur Nicholas and Martha Margaret (Frandsen) N.; m. Deborah Dunning, Sept. 2, 1961 (div. 1978); children: Hilary Adams, Douglas Bancroft.; m. Susan Jennifer Kane, May 14, 1983 (div. 1991). B.A., Northwestern U., 1958; Ph.D., Harvard U., 1964. Instr. history Rice U., 1963-64, asst. prof., 1964-67, asso. prof., 1968-70; asso. prof. history Brown U., Providence, 1970-76; prof. Brown U., 1976—, chmn. dept. history, 1995—; fellow Charles Warren Center for Studies in Am. History, 1971-72; dir. summer seminar NEH, 1979, 86-87, 89, 92. Author: An Uncertain Friendship: Theodore Roosevelt and Japan, 1906-1909, 1967, The Troubled Encounter: The United States and Japan, 1975; co-editor: The Wilson Era: Essays in Honor of Arthur S. Link, 1991. Woodrow Wilson fellow, 1958-59; NEH younger scholar, 1968-69; Am. Council Learned Socs. fellow, 1975-76; Howard Found. fellow, 1976-77; Guggenheim fellow, 1981-82; guest scholar Woodrow Wilson Ctr., summer 1988. Mem. Am. Hist. Assn., Orgn. Am. Historians, Soc. Historians of Am. Fgn. Policy, Phi Beta Kappa. Democrat. Club: Agawam Hunt (Providence). Home: 346 Rochambeau Ave Providence RI 02906-3516 Office: Brown U Dept History Providence RI 02912

NEUBAUER, CHARLES FREDERICK, investigative reporter; b. Berkeley, Ill., Feb. 13, 1950; s. Fred Charles and Dolores Jeanne (Pries) N.; m. Sandra Carol Bergo, Oct. 4, 1975; 1 child, Michael Frederick. B.S.J., Northwestern U., 1972, M.S.J., 1973. Investigator Better Govt. Assn., Chgo., 1971-73; investigative reporter Chgo. Today, 1973-74, Chgo. Tribune, 1974-83, Chgo. Sun Times, 1983—. Recipient Pulitzer prize local reporting, 1976; Edward Scott Beck award for domestic reporting Chgo. Tribune, 1980. Office: 401 N Wabash Ave Chicago IL 60611-5642

NEUBAUER, HUGO DUANE, JR., software engineer; b. Mankato, Minn., Oct. 31, 1959; s. Hugo Duane and Joan Marie (Habinger) N.; m. Susan A. May, July 7, 1990. Student, U. Miami, 1978-80; AA, U. Fla., 1981; AS, Santa Fe C.C., 1984; student, U. Fla., 1984—. Aquaculture specialist, technician Aqualife Rsch. Inc., 1979-80; automotive dept. K-Mart, 1981-82; electronic technician Synergetics, Inc., 1983-84; water resources equipment technician Environ. Sci. and Engring., Inc., Gainesville, Fla., 1984-89; tech. ops. equipment mgr. Environ. Sci. and Engring., Inc., Gainesville, 1990-91, geosciences divsn. equipment mgr., 1992-93, Ctr. 3 equipment mgr., 1994-95; office mgr. Keck South Office/Keck Instruments, Inc., 1996—; founder, owner ICIS, 1996—; ind. cons. in field; owner, founder Innovative Computer and Instrument Svcs., Dances with Hooves Horse Farm. Mem. IEEE, IEEE Computer Soc., Assn. for Computing Machinery. Avocations: computer programming and Internet, horses, gun collecting and shooting, videography and photography (including underwater), scuba diving (cert. Profl. Assn. Diving Instrs.). Home: PO Box 1270 14108 NW 195th St Alachua FL 32615 Office: ICIS PO Box 1270 Alachua FL 32616-1270 also: Kech Instruments Inc Kech South 404 SW 140th Terr Ste A Newberry FL 32669

NEUBAUER, JOSEPH, food services company executive; b. Oct. 19, 1941; s. Max and Herta (Kahn) N.; children: Lawrence, Melissa. B.S. in Chem. Engring, Tufts U., 1963; M.B.A. in Fin, U. Chgo., 1965. Asst. treas. Chase Manhattan Bank, 1965-68, asst. v.p., 1968-70, v.p., 1970-71; asst. treas. Pepsico Inc., Purchase, N.Y., 1971-72; treas. Pepsico Inc., 1972-73, v.p., 1973-76; v.p. fin. and control Wilson Sporting Goods Co., River Grove, Ill., 1976-77, sr. v.p., gen. mgr. team sports div., 1977-79; exec. v.p. fin. and devel., chief fin. officer, dir. ARA Svcs., Inc., Phila., 1979-81; pres., chief operating officer, dir. ARA Services, Inc., Phila., 1981-83, pres., chief exec. officer, 1983-84; chmn., CEO ARA Svcs., Inc. (in 1994, name changed to Aramark Corp.), Phila., 1984—; bd. dirs. 1st Fidelity Bancorp, Bell Atlantic, Federated Dept. Stores; trustee Penn Mut. Life Ins. Co. Chmn., CEO Phila. Orch. Assn., Mann Music Ctr., Inroads/Phila., Inc.; trustee Hahnemann U., Tufts U., Mus. Am. Jewish History, Greater Phila. First Corp., Com. for Econ. Devel., U. Chgo.; bd. govs. Joseph H. Lauder Inst. Mgmt. and Internat. Studies, U. Pa. Mem. Phila. C. of C., Union League Club, Locust Club, Phila. Club, Bus. Coun., Bus. Roundtable. Office: ARAMARK Corp ARAMARK Tower 1101 Market St Philadelphia PA 19107-2934*

NEUBAUER, PETER BELA, psychoanalyst; b. Krems, Austria, July 5, 1913; came to U.S., 1941, naturalized, 1946; s. Samuel and Rose (Blau) N.; m. Susan Rachlin, Nov. 25, 1953 (dec.); children—Joshua Rachlin, Alexander Lewis. M.D., U. Berne, 1938. Intern Lawrence Meml. Hosp., New London, Conn., 1941, Beth-El Hosp., Bklyn., 1942; resident in psychiatry Bellevue Hosp., N.Y.C., 1943-45; dir. Child Devel. Ctr., Jewish Bd. Family and Children's Services, N.Y.C., 1951-83; clin. prof. psychiatry Psychoanalytic Inst., N.Y. U., 1979—; lectr. child psychoanalysis Psychoanalytic Inst. for Tng. and Research Columbia U., 1973. Author: Children in Collectives: Child Rearing Aims and Practices in Kibbutzim, 1965, Early Child Day Car, 1974, Process of Child Development, 1976, (with Alexander Neubauer) Nature's Thumbprint, 1990; contbg. author: Fathers and Their Families, 1989; mem. editorial bd. Psychoanalytic Study of the Child, 1978. Recipient Hulse award N.Y. Council Child Psychiatry, 1975, Heinz Hartmann award N.Y. Psychoanalytic Soc., 1981, Mary S. Sigourney award, 1994. Mem. Am. Psychoanalytic Assn., Am. Acad. Child Psychiatry, Assn. Child Psychoanalysis, Internat. Assn. Child and Adolescent Psychiatry, Assn. for Child Psychoanalysis (pres. 1974-76). Office: 33 E 70th St New York NY 10021-4941

NEUBAUER, RICHARD A., library science educator, consultant; b. Meadville, Pa., Oct. 9, 1933; s. Carl Gustave and Velma Winston (Watson) N.; m. Janice Ernest; children: David, Lynda, Karl, Jennifer; m. Carol Barton. BS, Clarion U., 1955; MLS, SUNY, Geneseo, 1966; attended, Kent St. U., 1966-68, Simmons Coll., 1970-72. Cert. profl. libr., sch. libr., tchr. Tchr. geography Franklin (Pa.) Sch. Dept., 1957-58, N. Bedford County Schs., Woodbury, Mass., 1958-60; tchr. history Hornell (N.Y.) Jr. High Sch., 1960-62, sch. libr., 1962-65; prof. libr. sci. Edinboro (Pa.) U., 1965-68, assoc. libr. Hamilton Libr., 1965-68; dir. sch. librs. Duxbury (Mass.) Sch. Dept., 1968-69; dir., cons. Pub. Libr., Lincoln, Mass., 1969-70; prof. libr. sci. Bridgewater (Mass.) State Coll., 1969-78, chair dept. libr. sci., 1978-80, prof. libr. sci., 1980-91, coord. libr. media program, 1991-95; prof. emeritus libr. sci., 1996—; adj. prof. libr. sci. U. R.I., Kingston, 1975-88; cons. Tabor Acad., Marion, Mass., 1970-71, Abington (Mass.) Pub. Libr. Trustees, 1973-76, Duxbury Free Libr., 1968-72. Author: Planning the Elementary School Library, 1968; author, editor Exploring the U.S.-Northeast, 1994. Chmn. Mass. Dept. Edn. Cert., Quincy, 1989-90; resource cons. Project Contemporary Competitiveness, Bridgewater, Mass., 1973-83. 1st It. USMC, 1955-57. Inst. grantee HEA of 1965 Edinboro U., 1968. Mem. NEA, Am. Libr. Assn., Intellectual Freedom Found., Mass. Assn. of Edn. Media, Mass. Sch. Libr. Media Assn., Mass. Tchrs. Assn. Democrat. Avocations: gardening, woodworking, reading. Home: 22 Pleasant St Carver MA 02330-1013

NEUBERGER, EGON, economics educator; b. Zagreb, Croatia, Yugoslavia, Feb. 27, 1925; came to U.S., 1940; s. Paul and Ann (Freund) N.; m. Florence Perlmutter, Dec. 22, 1949; children: Leah Ruth, Marc Joseph. BA, Cornell U., 1947; MA, Harvard U., 1949, PhD, 1958. Econ. analyst State Dept., Washington, 1949-54; asst. prof. econ. Amherst (Mass.) Coll., 1957-60; economist RAND Corp., Santa Monica, Calif., 1960-67; prof. econ. SUNY, Stony Brook, 1967-81, leading prof. econs., 1982—, dean social and behavioral scis., 1982-88; vice provost for undergraduate studies SUNY, 1989-90; econ. officer Am. Embassy, Moscow, 1952-53; vis. prof. U. Mich., Ann Arbor, 1965-66, U. Konstanz, Germany, 1995, U. Tuebingen, Germany, 1996. Served with U.S. Army, 1943-46, ETO. Mem. Assn. Comparative Econ. Studies (mem. exec. com. 1974-76, pres. 1990-91), Am. Econ. Assn., Assn. Study of Grants Economy (adv. bd.), Omicron Delta Epsilon (pres. 1979-81, exec. bd., Disting. Ser. award 1981). Democrat. Jewish. Home: 5 Somerset Ct East Setauket NY 11733-1831 Office: SUNY Dept Econs Stony Brook NY 11794

NEUBERGER, ROY R., investment counselor; b. Bridgeport, Conn., July 21, 1903; s. Louis and Bertha (Rothschild) N.; m. Marie Salant, June 29, 1932; children—Ann Marie Neuberger Aceves, Roy S., James A. Ed., NYU, U. Sorbonne; DFA (hon.), SUNY, Purchase, 1982; LHD (hon.), Parsons Sch. Design, New Sch. for Social Research, N.Y.C., 1985; DHL (hon.), Bar-Ilan U., Israel, 1987. Buyer B. Altman & Co., 1922-25; art student Paris, 1925-29; broker Halle & Stieglitz, N.Y.C., 1929-40; sr. partner Neuberger & Berman, N.Y.C., 1940—; pres. Guardian Mut. Fund, Inc., 1950-79, chmn. bd., 1979-91, chmn. emeritus, 1991—; chmn. bd. Genesis Fund, Inc., 1988-91; chmn. emeritus, 1991—; chmn. bd., dir. Neuberger & Berman Asset Mgmt., Inc. (formerly Neuberger & Berman Pension Mgmt. Inc.), 1976-87, chmn. emeritus, 1991—; chmn. bd., dir. Neuberger & Berman Mgmt. Inc. (formerly Cedar St. Cons.), 1970—. Art collector, collection exhibited museums throughout, U.S. and abroad, 1936—. Bd. dirs. Bard Coll. Ctr., 1979-91, City Ctr. Music and Drama, N.Y.C., 1957-74, trustee, 1974—, fin. chmn., 1971-74; chmn. adv. coun. on arts N.Y.C. Housing Authority, 1960-70; trustee Whitney Mus. Am. Art, 1961-69, trustee emeritus, 1969-94, hon. trustee, 1994—; collectors com. Nat. Gallery Art, Washington, 1975—; trustee, exec. com. New Sch. Social Rsch., 1967-75; hon. trustee Met. Mus. Art, N.Y.C., 1968—; coun. friends Inst. Fine Arts/NYU, 1961—; pres. coun. Mus. City N.Y.; trustee Purchase Coll. Found., 1971-85, chmn., 1974-85; donor Neuberger Mus. Art/SUNY, Purchase, 1969—. Recipient award Artists Equity Assn., 1972; Gari Melchers medal Artists Fellowship, Inc., N.Y.C., 1984, Arts award Council for Arts in Westchester, 1985, Art in Am. award, 1959, North Shore Com. Arts Ctr. award, 1971; Benjamin Franklin fellow Royal Soc. Arts, 1969—; fellow R.I. Sch. Design, 1981. Fellow in perpetuity NAD; mem. Am. Fedn. Arts (pres. 1955-67, hon. pres. 1968—), N.Y. Soc. Security Analysts, Soc. Ethical Culture N.Y.C. (treas. 1956-64, pres. 1965-68), Century Assn. Club, City Athletic Club, Harmonie Club. Home: 795 5th Ave New York NY 10021-8401 Office: Neuberger & Berman 605 3rd Ave New York NY 10158

NEUDECK, GEROLD WALTER, electrical engineering educator; b. Beach, N.D., Sept. 25, 1936; s. Adolph John and Helen Annette (Kramer) N.; m. Mariellen Kristine MacDonald, Sept. 1, 1962; children: Philip Gerold, Alexander John. BSEE, U. N.D., 1959, MSEE, 1960; PhD in Elec. Engring., Purdue U., 1969. Asst. prof. U. N.D., Grand Forks, 1960-64; grad. instr. Purdue U., West Lafayette, Ind., 1964-68; asst. prof. Purdue U., 1968-71, assoc. prof., 1971-77, prof. elec. engring., 1977—; asst. dean engring. Purdue U., West Lafayette, 1988-90, assoc. dir. NSF/ERC Engring., 1988-94, dir. Optoelectronics Rsch. Ctr., 1993-96; cons. in field. Author: Electric Circuit Analysis and Design, 1976, 2d edit., 1987, Junction Diode/Bipolar Transisters, 1983, 2d edit., 1989; author, editor: Modular Series on Solid State Devices, 1983; contbr. over 220 articles to profl. jours.; inventor/holder 13 U.S. patents in field. Bd. dirs. W. Lafayette Devel. Commn., 1990—, Greater Lafayette Pub. Transp., 1975-80; pres. Lafayette Tennis, 1976-78. Recipient Dow Outstanding Faculty award Am. Soc. Engring. Edn., 1972, Western Elec. Fund award, 1974-75, D.D. Ewing award Purdue U., 1973, A.A. Potter award, 1973, Honeywell Teaching award, 1995. Fellow IEEE (Harry S. Nyquist award 1992, editor Transactions on Electron Devices 1994—); mem. Am. Vacuum Soc., Sigma Xi, Eta Kappa Nu, Sigma Tau, Sigma Pi Sigma. Avocations: tennis, backpacking, fishing, woodworking, bread baking. Office: Purdue U Elec Engring Bldg West Lafayette IN 47907

NEUEFEIND, WILHELM, economics educator, university administrator; b. Viersen, Germany, Mar. 6, 1939; came to U.S., 1977; m. Ingrid Leuchtenberg, Mar. 30, 1966; children: Nicole, Bettina. MBA, U. Cologne, Germany, 1962, MA in Math., 1969; PhD in Econs., U. Bonn, 1972. Lectr. econs. U. Bonn, 1973-77; prof. Washington U., St. Louis, 1977—; chmn. dept. econs. Wash. U., St. Louis, 1983—; Contbr. articles to profl. jours. Mem. Econometric Soc., Am. Econ. Assn., Assn. for Advancement Econ. Theory. Office: Washington U Dept Econs 1 Brookings Dr # 1208 Saint Louis MO 63130-4862

NEUENSCHWANDER, PIERRE FERNAND, medical educator. BS in Chemistry, 1985; PhD in Biochemistry & Molecular Biology, SUNY, Stony Brook, 1990. Lab. tchg. asst. SUNY, Stony Brook, 1985-86, lecture tchg. asst. in biochemistry, 1986, 87; assoc. rsch. scientist Cardiovascular Biology Rsch. Program Okla. Med. Rsch. Found., Oklahoma City, 1990-93, sr. rsch. scientist, 1993-94, found. rsch. scientist, 1994-95, asst. mem., 1995—. Co-editor Trigger newsletter; rev. Jour. Biol. Chemistry; contbr. articles to profl. jours. Recipient Am. Heart Assn. Travel stipend, 1994, Internat. Soc. Haematology Travel award, 1992, Am. Soc. Hematology Travel award, 1989, 90. Mem. Am. Heart Assn. (coun. on thrombosis), Am. Chem Soc. (divsn. biol. chemistry), Internat. Soc. Thrombosis and Haemostasis, Sigma Xi, Alpha Chi Sigma. Office: Okla Med Rsch Found 825 NE 13th St Oklahoma City OK 73104-5005

NEUER, PHILIP DAVID, lawyer, real estate consultant; b. Bklyn., May 31, 1946; s. Murray and Adele (Jacobs) N.; m. Rena Donna Levine, July 30, 1972 (div. 1987); children: Jeremy Evan, Linzy Michelle, Sari Faith. BBA, CCNY, 1968; postgrad., Boston U., 1968-69; JD, Seton Hall U., 1976. Bar: N.J. 1976, U.S. Dist. Ct. N.J. 1977, U.S. Supreme Ct. 1980. Asst. town atty. Town of West Orange (N.J.), 1976-77; assoc. Margolis and Bergstein, Verona, N.J., 1979-80; ptnr. Slavitt and Slavitt, West Orange, 1980-81; assoc. Mandelbaum and Targan, West Orange, 1981-83; ptnr. Margolis Neuer, Verona, 1984-91; of counsel Slavitt Simon & Neuer, Parsippany, 1991—; exec. v.p., gen. counsel Safer Prints Inc., Safer Devel. and Mgmt. Co., Newark, 1993—. With USN, 1969-73. Mem. ABA, N.J. State Bar Assn., Essex County Bar Assn., Internat. Assn. Corp. Real Estate Execs. (pres., bd. dirs., gen. counsel N.J. chpt., designated internat. assoc., Mem. of Yr. 1993, N.J. Corp. Real Exec. of Yr. 1993, internat. bd. dirs.), Inst. Corporate Real Estate (bd. dirs.), Internat. Real Estate Inst. (registered internat. mem.), Urban Land Inst., Mensa. Office: 1875 Mccarter Hwy Newark NJ 07104-4211

NEUFELD, ELIZABETH FONDAL, biochemist, educator; b. Paris, Sept. 27, 1928; US citizen; m. 1951. PhD, U. Calif., Berkeley, 1956; DHC (hon.), U. Rene Descartes, Paris, 1978; DSc (hon.), Russell Sage Coll., Troy, N.Y., 1981, Hahnemann U. Sch. Medicine, 1984, Queens Coll., 1996. Asst. research biochemist U. Calif., Berkeley, 1957-63; with Nat. Inst. Arthritis, Metabolism and Digestive Diseases, Bethesda, Md., 1963-84, research biochemist, 1963-73, chief sect. human biochem. genetics, 1973-79, chief genetics and biochem. br., 1979-84; prof., chmn. dept. biol. chemistry UCLA Sch. Medicine, 1984—. Passano Found. sr. laureate, 1982; named Calif. Scientist of Yr., 1990; recipient Dickson prize U. Pitts., 1974, Hillenbrand award, 1975, Gairdner Found. award, 1981, Albert Lasker Clin. Med. Rsch. award, 1982, William Allan award, 1982, Elliott Cresson medal, 1984, Wolf Found. prize, 1988, Christopher Columbus Discovery award for biomed. rsch., 1992, Nat. Medal of Sci., 1994. Fellow AAAS; mem. NAS, Inst. Medicine of NAS, Am. Acad. Arts and Scis., Am. Soc. Human Genetics, Am. Chem. Soc., Am. Soc. Biochemistry and Molecular Biology (pres. 1992-93), Am. Soc. Cell Biology, Am. Soc. Clin. Investigation. Office: UCLA Sch Medicine Dept Biol Chemistry Los Angeles CA 90095-1737

NEUFELD, MACE, film company executive; b. N.Y.C., July 13, 1928; s. Philip M. and Margaret Ruth (Braun) N.; Feb. 28, 1954; children: Bradley David, Glenn Jeremy, Nancy Ann. BA, Yale U., 1948; postgrad., NYU, 1958-60. Photographer various N.Y. pubs., 1943-45; prodn. asst. Raymond E. Nelson, 1949-50; founder, owner Ray Bloch Assos., Inc., N.Y.C., 1951-59; ptnr. BNB Prodns., N.Y.C., 1959-70, Neufeld-Davis Prodns., Inc., Beverly Hills, Calif., 1981—; Trustee Am. Film Inst., 1978—; chmn. life achievement award nominating com. and scholarship fund. Producer in assn.

with Harvey Bernhard The Omen, 1976, Damien - Omen II, 1977, Omen III - The Final Conflict, 1980; producer: The Frisco Kid, 1979, Angel on My Shoulder, 1980, The American Dream, 1980; ABC-TV mini-series East of Eden, 1981; CBS-TV series Cagney and Lacey, 1984; MGM film The Aviator, 1984, ABC-TV A Death in California, 1985; producer films Transylvania 6-5000, 1985, No Way Out, 1987, The Hunt for Red October, 1989, Flight of the Intruder, 1990, Necessary Roughness, 1991, Patriot Games, 1992, Clear and Present Danger, 1994, Gettysburg, 1994, Beverly Hills Cop 3, 1994, The Saint, 1996. Photograph entitled Sammy's Home voted Picture of Yr. N.Y. World Telegram-Sun, 1955; recipient Grand prize Eastman Kodak's First Nat. Salon of Photography, 1945; named N.A.T.O./Showest Producer of the Yr., 1993. Mem. Acad. TV Arts and Scis., Acad. Motion Picture Arts and Scis., ASCAP, Am. Film Inst. Democrat. Clubs: Friars, Yale of N.Y. Home: 624 N Arden Dr Beverly Hills CA 90210-3510 Office: Paramount Pictures 5555 Melrose Ave Los Angeles CA 90038-3112

NEUFELD, MICHAEL JOHN, curator, historian; b. Edmonton, Alta., Can., July 7, 1951; s. Henry John and Isabel Grace (Mitchell) N.; m. Sheila Faith Weiss, May 29, 1983 (div. Dec. 1992); m. Karen Lee Levenback, June 14, 1994. BA with 1st class honors, U. Calgary, Alta., 1974; MA, U. B.C., Vancouver, Can., 1976, Johns Hopkins U., 1980; PhD in History, Johns Hopkins U., 1984. Hist. rschr. Dept. Supply and Svcs., Ottawa, Ont., Can., summer 1973, 74; teaching asst. Johns Hopkins U., Balt., 1979-80; instr. Clarkson U., Potsdam, N.Y., 1983-84, from part-time instr. to part-time asst. prof., 1983-85; vis. asst. prof. SUNY, Oswego, 1985-86, Colgate U., Hamilton, N.Y., 1986-88; Verville fellow Nat. Air and Space Mus., Washington, 1988-89, Smithsonian postdoctoral fellow, 1989-90, curator dept. aeronautics, 1990—; curator Air Power in WWII series, 1991-94. Author: The Skilled Metalworkers of Nuremberg, 1989, The Rocket and the Reich, 1995; editor: Planet Dora, 1997; contbr. articles and book revs. to profl. jours. Recipient History Manuscript award AIAA, 1995, NSF Scholar's award History of Sci. and Tech. Program, 1989-90. Mem. Am. Hist. Assn., Conf. Group on Ctrl. European History, Soc. Mil. History, Soc. for History in Tech., History of Sci. Soc. Avocation: amateur astronomy. Office: Nat Air & Space Mus Divsn Aeronautics (MRC312) Smithsonian Instn Washington DC 20560

NEUFELD, NAOMI DAS, pediatric endocrinologist; b. Butte, Mont., June 13, 1947; d. Dilip Kumar and Maya (Chaliha) Das; m. Timothy Lee Neufeld, Nov. 27, 1971; children: Pamela Anne, Katherine Louise. AB, Pembroke Coll., 1969; M. in Med. Sci., Brown U., 1971; MD, Tufts U., 1973. Diplomate Am. Bd. Pediatrics, Am. Bd. Endocrinology. Intern R.I. Hosp., Providence, 1973-74, resident in pediatrics, 1974-75; fellow in pediatric endocrinology UCLA, 1975-78; staff endocrinologist Cedars-Sinai Med. Ctr., Los Angeles, 1978-79, chief pediatric endocrinology sect., 1979-85, dir. pediatric endocrinology, 1985—; asst. research pediatrician UCLA, 1978-79, asst. prof.-in-residence pediatrics, 1979-85, assoc. prof.-in-residence, 1985—; med. dir. Kidshape Program Children's Weight Control, 1986—; pres. Neufeld Med. Group, Inc., 1996—; consulting physician Ventura County Med. Ctr., 1989—; attending physician Ceders Sinai Med. Ctr., 1995—; clin. prof. pediatrics Sch. Med. UCCA, 1995—; med. dir., owner Kidshape. Contbr. articles to profl. jours. Mem. bd. deacons Pacific Palisades Presbyn. ch. 1988—. Named Clin. Investigator, NIH, 1978; grantee United Cerebral Palsy Soc., 1979, March of Dimes, 1981, NIH, 1983-88. Mem. Am. Diabetes Assn., Soc. Pediatric Research, Endocrine Soc., Juvenile Diabetes Found. (research grantee 1980). Presbyterian. Avocations: sailing, reading, sewing, cooking. Home: 16821 Charmel Ln Pacific Palisades CA 90272-2218 Office: 8635 W 3rd St Ste 295 Los Angeles CA 90048-6101

NEUGEBAUER, MARCIA, physicist, administrator; b. N.Y.C., Sept. 27, 1932; d. Howard Graeme MacDonald and Frances (Townsend) Marshall; m. Gerry Neugebauer, Aug. 25, 1956; children: Carol, Lee. B.S., Cornell U., 1954; M.S., U. Ill., 1956. Grad. asst. U. Ill., Urbana, 1954-56; vis. fellow Clare Hall Coll., Cambridge, Eng., 1975; sr. research scientist Jet Propulsion Lab. Calif. Inst. Tech., Pasadena, 1956-96, disting. vis. scientist Jet Propulsion Lab., 1996—, vis. prof. planetary sci., 1986-87; mem. com. NASA, Washington, 1960-96, NAS, Washington, 1981-94; Regents lectr. UCLA, 1990-91. Contbr. numerous articles on physics to profl. jours. Named Calif. Woman Scientist of Yr. Calif. Mus. Sci. and Industry, 1967; recipient Exceptional Sci. Achievement medal NASA, 1970, Outstanding Leadership medal NASA, 1993, Disting. Svc. medal, 1997. Fellow Am. Geophys. Union (sec., pres. solar planetary relationships sect. 1979-84, editor-in-chief Rev. Geophysics 1988-92, pres.-elect 1992-94, pres. 1994-96)mem. governing bd. Amer. Inst. Physics, 1995-97. Democrat. Home: 1720 Braeburn Rd Altadena CA 91001-2708 Office: Calif Inst Tech Jet Propulsion Lab/MS 169-506 4800 Oak Grove Dr Pasadena CA 91109-8001

NEUGROSCHEL, ARNOST, electrical engineering educator; b. Prešov, Czechoslovakia, June 18, 1942; came to U.S., 1973; s. Ludovit and Irene (Gottfried) Neugröschl; m. Susan M. Pertz, June 20, 1982. Diploma in engrng., Slovak Tech. U., Bratislava, Czechoslovakia, 1965; PhD, Technion-Israel Inst. Tech., Haifa, 1973. Engr. Tesla, Inc., Piešťany, Czechoslovakia, 1966-67; instr. Technion-Israel Inst. Tech., 1969-73; postdoctoral rsch. assot. dept. elec. engrng. U. Ill., Urbana, 1973-75; asst. prof. U. Fla., Gainesville, 1975-79, assoc. prof., 1979-83, prof., 1983—; on leave Interuniv. Microelectronic Ctr., Leuven, Belgium, 1986; mem. summer faculty IBM T.J. Watson Rsch. Ctr., Yorktown Heights, N.Y., 1982. Contbr. over 75 articles to profl. jours.; patentee in field. Fellow IEEE. Avocations: tennis, travel. Office: U Fla Dept Elec Engring Gainesville FL 32611

NEUHARTH, ALLEN HAROLD, newspaper publisher; b. Eureka, S.D., Mar. 22, 1924; s. Daniel J. and Christina (Neuharth) N.; m. Loretta Fay Helgeland, June 16, 1946 (div. 1972), m. Lori Wilson, Dec. 31, 1973 (div. 1982), m. Rachel Fornes, March 21, 1993; children: Daniel J. II, Jan, Alexis Rae Fornes-Neuharth; . BA cum laude, U. S.D., 1950. Reporter Rapid City (S.D.) Jour., 1948; sports writer Mitchell (S.D.) Daily Republic, 1949; staff writer AP, Sioux Falls, S.D., 1950-52; editor, pub. SoDak Sports, Sioux Falls, 1952-54; with Miami (Fla.) Herald, 1954-60, asst. mng. editor, 1958-60; asst. exec. editor Detroit Free Press, 1960-63; gen. mgr. Times-Union and Democrat and Chronicle, Rochester, N.Y., 1963-66; exec. v.p. Gannett Co., Inc., Washington, 1966-70, pres., chief operating officer, 1970-73, pres., chief exec. officer, 1973-79, chmn., chief exec. officer, 1979-86; founder, chmn. USA Today, 1982; chmn. Gannett Co., Inc., Washington, 1986-89, Gannett Found., Arlington, Va., 1989-91, Freedom Forum, 1991—. Author: Confessions of an S.O.B., 1989. Trustee, chmn. Gannett Found. Served with inf. AUS, 1943-46, ETO, PTO. Decorated Bronze Star; recipient Horatio Alger award, 1975; named Outstanding Chief Exec. of Yr. in Pub. and Printing Industry for 3 consecutive yrs. Mem. Am. Newspaper Pubs. Assn. (bd. dirs. 1968-82, chmn., pres. 1979-80), Jockey Club (Miami), Ocean Reef Club (Key Largo, Fla.), Sky Club, Sigma Delta Chi (past nat. region I dir.). Office: Freedom Forum 1101 Wilson Blvd Arlington VA 22209-2248*

NEUHARTH, DANIEL J., II, psychotherapist; b. Sioux Falls, S.D., Nov. 10, 1953; s. Allen Harold and Loretta Faye (Helgeland) N. BA, Duke U., 1975; MS in Journalism, Northwestern U., 1978; MA, John F. Kennedy U., 1988; PhD in Clin. Psychology, Calif. Sch. Profl. Psychology, 1992. Lic. marriage, family and child counselor. Reporter USA Today, Washington, 1982-83; lectr. San Diego State U., 1983-84; talk show host KSDO-AM, San Diego, 1983-84; pres. Dialogues, San Francisco, 1987—; psychotherapist pvt. practice, San Francisco, 1992—; vis. prof. U. Fla., Gainesville, 1980-81, U. Hawaii, Honolulu, 1981-82; adj. faculty U. San Francisco, 1989—. Host, producer radio talk show Saturday Night People, 1984; contbg. author: Confessions of an S.O.B., 1989. Office: Dialogues PO Box 1022 Fairfax CA 94978-1022

NEUHAUS, OTTO WILHELM, biochemistry educator; b. Zweibrucken, Germany, Nov. 18, 1922; came to U.S., 1927, naturalized, 1931; s. Clemens Jakob and Johanna Amalie (Schnorr) N.; m. Dorothy Ellen Rehn, Aug. 30, 1947; children: Thomas William, Carol Alida, Joanne Marie. B.S., U. Wis., 1944; M.S., U. Mich., 1947, Ph.D., 1953. Research chemist Huron Milling Co., 1951-54; mem. faculty Wayne State U., Detroit, 1954-66; asso. prof. Wayne State U., 1965-66; prof., chmn. dept. biochemistry U. S.D., Vermillion, 1966-76, acting chmn. dept. physiology and pharmacology, 1975-76, 82-83, prof., chmn. div. biochemistry, physiology and pharmacology, 1976-82, prof., 1982-88, chmn. dept. biochemistry, 1982-86; prof. emeritus U. S.D., 1988—. Author: (with John Halver) Fish in Research, 1969, (with James Orten) Human Biochemistry, 1982; also research articles. NATO Research fellow, 1961-62. Fellow AAAS; mem. Am. Chem. Soc., Am. Soc. Biol. Chemists, Sigma Xi, Phi Sigma, Alpha Chi Sigma, Phi Lambda Upsilon. Lutheran. Home: 1090 Valley View Dr Vermillion SD 57069-3587

NEUHAUS, PHILIP ROSS, investment banker; b. Houston, Dec. 25, 1919; s. Hugo Victor and Kate Padgitt (Rice) N.; m. Elizabeth Lacey Thompson, Oct. 31, 1942 (div. 1967); children: Philip Ross (dec.), Lacey Neuhaus Dorn, Elizabeth Neuhaus Armstrong, Joan Thompson Neuhaus; m. Barbara R. Haden, Aug. 14, 1968; 5 stepchildren. Grad., St. Mark's Sch., Southborough, Mass., 1938; BA, Yale, 1942. With Nat. City Bank of Cleve., 1946-47, McDonald & Co., Cleve., 1947; with Neuhaus & Co., 1947; chmn. Underwood, Neuhaus & Co., Inc., Houston, 1948-89; hon. chmn. Lovett Underwood Neuhaus & Webb, Houston, 1989-92; sr. v.p. Kemper Securities Inc., Houston, 1992-95, Everen Securities, Inc., Houston, 1995—; chmn. bd. Voss-Woodway, Inc., 1994—. Trustee Tex. Childrens Hosp.; assoc. Rice U.; advisory bd. Salvation Army, Houston, 1969-91. Served to capt., cav. AUS, 1942-45. Mem. Securities Industry Assn. Am. (bd. govs., chmn. Tex. dist. 1973, exec. com. 1975), Houston Soc. Financial Analysts (pres. 1959), Stock and Bond Club Houston (past pres.), Nat. Fedn. Financial Analysts (v.p. 1963, dir.). Clubs: Bayou, Houston Country, Houston, Eagle Lake Rod and Gun. Home: 407 Thamer Ln Houston TX 77024-6939 Office: Everen Securities Inc 909 Fannin St Houston TX 77010

NEUHAUS, RICHARD JOHN, priest, research institute president; b. Pembroke, Ont., Can., May 14, 1936; Came to U.S., 1950; s. Clemens Henry and Ella Carolina (Prange) N. M Div., Concordia Sem., 1960; DD (hon.), Benedictine Coll., 1985, Gonzaga U., 1985, Valparaiso U., 1986, Nichols Coll., 1986, Boston U., 1988. Ordained to ministry Luth. Ch., 1960; ordained priest Roman Cath. Ch., 1991. Pastor St. John The Evangelist, Bklyn., 1961-78; sr. editor Worldview Mag., N.Y.C., 1972-82; dir. Rockford Inst. Ctr. on Religion and Soc., N.Y.C., 1984-89, Inst. on Religion and Pub. Life, N.Y.C., 1989—. Author: Freedom for Ministry, 1979, The Naked Public Square, 1984, The Catholic Moment, 1987, America Against Itself, 1992; editor-in-chief First Things Mag., N.Y.C., 1990—. Office: Inst Religion & Pub Life 156 Fifth Ave Ste 400 New York NY 10010

NEUHAUS, WILLIAM OSCAR, III, architect; b. Houston, Mar. 16, 1944; s. W. Oscar and Betty Palmer (Bosworth) N.; m. Kay Ficklen; children: Kimberly Sautelle, Sara Palmer. BArch, Ga. Inst. Tech., 1967. Registered architect, Tex., N.Mex. Intern architect Caudill Rowlett Scott, Houston, 1967-69; assoc. Charles Tapley Assocs., Houston, 1969-72; prin. W.O. Neuhaus Architecture/Planning, Houston, 1972-83; owner, mgr. W.O. Neuhaus Assocs., Houston, 1984—. Co-author trading Toilets: The Subterranean Zoning of Houston, 1982; author Foreward, 1992. Pres. Rice Design Alliance, Houston, 1982-83, bd. dirs. 1978-84; pres. Armand Bayou Nature Ctr. Found., 1986-90, Stages Repertory Theatre, Houston, 1988-89; mem. Mayor's Land Use Strategy com., Houston, 1990, Arts Task Force, Houston, 1992; exec. com. Cultural Arts Coun. Houston/Harris City, 1997—. Fellow Am. Leadership Forum, AIA (pres. 1990-91, chair design com. 1988-89); mem. Tex. Soc. Architects (mem. design com. 1989-90). Office: WO Neuhaus Assocs 4100 Montrose Blvd Ste D Houston TX 77006-4938

NEUHAUSEN, BENJAMIN SIMON, auditor, accountant; b. Urbana, Ill., Apr. 23, 1950; s. Stanley Edward and Dolores Renee (Epstein) N.; m. Madeline Cohen, Sept. 6, 1987; 3 children. BA, Mich. State U., 1971; MBA, NYU, 1973. CPA, Ill. Staff auditor Arthur Andersen & Co., N.Y.C., 1973-75, sr. auditor, 1975-78, audit mgr., 1978-79, 81-85; audit ptnr. Arthur Andersen LLP, Chgo., 1985—; practice fellow Fin. Acctg. Standards Bd., Stamford, Conn., 1979-81. Contbr. articles to profl. jours. Bd. dirs. The Renaissance Soc., Chgo., 1987-90. Recipient Charles W. Haskins medal N.Y. Soc. CPAs, 1974. Mem. AICPA, Ill. Soc. CPAs, Chgo. Athletic Assn. Jewish. Office: Arthur Andersen LLP 33 W Monroe St Chicago IL 60603-5300

NEUHAUSER, DUNCAN VON BRIESEN, health services educator; b. Phila., June 20, 1939; s. Edward Blaine Duncan and Gernda (von Briesen) N.; m. Elinor Toaz, Mar. 6, 1965; children: Steven, Ann. B.A., Harvard U., 1961; M.H.A., U. Mich., 1963; M.B.A., U. Chgo., 1966, Ph.D., 1971. Research assoc. U. Chgo., 1965-70; asst. prof. Sch. Pub. Health, Harvard U., Boston, 1970-74; assoc. prof. Sch. Pub. Health, Harvard U., 1974-79; cons. in medicine Mass. Gen. Hosp., Boston, 1975-80; assoc. dir. Health Systems Mgmt. Ctr. Case Western Res. U., Cleve., 1979-85, prof. epidemiology, biostats. and orgnl. behavior, 1979—, prof. medicine, 1981—, prof. family medicine, 1990—, Charles Elton Blanchard prof. health mgmt., 1995—, co-dir. Health Systems Mgmt. Ctr., 1985—; cons. in medicine Cleve. Met. Gen. Hosp., 1981—; adj. mem. med. staff Cleve. Clinic Found., 1984—. Author numerous books, sci. papers; editor: jours. Health Matrix, 1982-90, Med. Care, 1983-97. Vice chmn. bd. dirs. Vis. Nurse Assn. Greater Cleve., 1983-84, chmn., 1984-85; bd. dirs. New Eng. Grenfell Assn., Boston, 1972—, Braintree (Mass.) Hosp., 1975-86; trustee Internat. Grenfell Assn., St. Anthony, Nfld., Can., 1975-83, Blue Hill (Maine) Hosp., 1983-89; trustee Hough Norwood Health Ctr., 1983-94, chmn., 1993-94. Recipient E.F. Meyers Trustee award Cleve. Hosp. Assn., 1987, Hope award Nat. Multiple Sclerosis Soc., 1992; Kellogg fellow, 1963-65; Keck Found. scholar, 1982—; Neuhauser lectr. Soc. Pediatric Radiology, 1982; Freedlander lectr. Ohio Permanente Med. Group, 1986. Mem. Inst. Medicine of NAS, Soc. for Clin. Decision Making, Cleve. Skating Club, St. Botolph Club (Boston), Kollegewidgwok Yacht Club (Blue Hill, Maine, commodore 1991-93), Beta Gamma Sigma. Home: 2655 N Park Blvd Cleveland Heights OH 44106-3622 Office: Case Western Reserve U Med Sch 10900 Euclid Ave Cleveland OH 44106-1712

NEUMAIER, GERHARD JOHN, environment consulting company executive; b. Covington, Ky., July 27, 1937; s. John Edward and Elli Anna (Raudies) N.; m. Ellen Elaine Klepper, Oct. 24, 1959; children: Kevin Scott, Kirsten Lynn. BME, Gen. Motors Inst., 1960; MA in Biophysics, U. Buffalo, 1963. Research ecologist, project mgr. Cornell Aero. Lab., Buffalo, 1963-70; pres., chief exec., chmn. bd. Ecology and Environment Inc., Buffalo, 1970—. Recipient Theodore Roosevelt Citizen of Yr. award City of Buffalo, 1990. Mem. APHA, Air Pollution Control Assn., Internat. Assn. Gt. Lakes Research, Inst. Environ. Scis., Ecol. Soc. Am., Am. Inst. Biol. Scis., Urban Land Inst., Arctic Inst. N.Am., Nat. Parks and Conservation Assn., Defenders of Wildlife, Nat. Wildlife Fedn., Wilderness Soc., Am. Hort. Soc., Smithsonian Assocs., Nat. Audubon Soc. Home: 284 Mill Rd East Aurora NY 14052-2805 Office: Ecology & Environment Inc 368 Pleasant View Dr Lancaster NY 14086-1316

NEUMAN, CHARLES P., electrical and computer engineering educator; b. Pitts., July 26, 1940; s. Daniel and Frances G. Neuman; m. Susan G. Neuman, Sept. 4, 1967. B.S. in Elec. Engring. with honors, Carnegie Inst. Tech., 1962; S.M., Harvard U., 1963, Ph.D. in Applied Math., 1968. Tchg. fellow Harvard U., Cambridge, Mass., 1962-64, rsch. asst., 1964-67; mem. tech. staff Bell Telephone Labs., Whippany, N.J., 1967-69; asst. prof. elec. engring. Carnegie-Mellon U., Pitts., 1969-71, assoc. prof., 1971-78, prof. elec. engring., 1978-83, prof. elec. and computer engring., 1983—, undergrad. advisor, 1994—. Mem. editorial bd. Internat. Jour. Modelling and Simulation, Control and Computers; contbr. numerous articles to profl. jours. Mem. IEEE (sr., assoc. editor Trans. on Systems, Man and Cybernetics), Inst. Mgmt. Scis., AAAS, Instrument Soc. Am. (sr.), Soc. Harvard Engrs. and Scientists, Soc. Indsl. and Applied Math., Sigma Xi, Phi Kappa Phi, Tau Beta Pi, Eta Kappa Nu. Office: Carnegie-Mellon U Dept Elec & Computer Engring Pittsburgh PA 15213

NEUMAN, CURTIS WILLIAM, computer systems company executive; b. Pitts., July 22, 1942; s. Joel McKee and Margaret Lucille (Baer) N.; m. Susan Marie Naderer, Feb. 5, 1980 (div. July 1985); children: Brett Jerris Nadan, Tal Devery Nadan. BS, Case Western Res. U., 1971. Cert. in prodn. and inventory control. Systems analyst, mgr. White Motor Corp., Eastlake, Ohio, 1972-80; mgr. prodn. and systems True Temper Corp., Cleve., 1980-83; cons. Avon Co., Rye, N.Y., 1983-85; sr. cons. Coopers & Lybrand, N.Y.C., 1985-90; pres. Nadan Neuman Assocs., Norwalk, Conn., 1990—. Team leader Clinton Campaign, Washington, 1992. Capt. U.S. Army, 1967-70, Viet Nam. Mem. Am. Prodn. and Inventory Control Soc., Conn. PC Users Group. Democrat. Avocations: personal computers, golf, arts, movies, literature. Home: 50 Aiken St Apt 412 Norwalk CT 06851-2034 Office: Nadan Neuman Assocs 50 Aiken St Apt 412 Norwalk CT 06851-2034

NEUMAN, NANCY ADAMS MOSSHAMMER, civic leader; b. Greenwich, Conn., July 24, 1936; d. Alden Smith and Margaret (Mevis) Mosshammer; BA, Pomona Coll., 1957, LLD, 1983; MA, U. Calif. at Berkeley, 1961; LHD, Westminster Coll., 1987; m. Mark Donald Neuman, Dec. 23, 1958; children: Deborah Neuman Metzler, Jennifer Fuller, Jeffrey Abbott. William A. Johnson Disting. lectr. Am. govt. Pomona Coll., 1990; disting. vis. prof. Washington and Jefferson Coll., 1991, 94, Bucknell U., 1992. Pres., Lewisburg (Pa.) area League Women Voters, 1967-70; bd. dirs. LWV Pa., 1970-77, pres., 1975-77; bd. dirs. LWV U.S., 1977-90, 2d v.p., 1978-80, 1st v.p., 1982-84, pres., 1986-90; bd. dirs. Pathmakers, Inc., 1993—, pres. 1993-95; mem. Pa. Gov.'s Commn. on Mortgage and Interest Rates, 1973, Pa. Commonwealth Child Devel. Com., 1974-75, Nat. Commn. on Pub. Svc., 1987-90; bd. dirs. Housing Assistance Council, Inc., Washington, 1974—, pres., 1978-80; bd. dirs. Nat. Council on Agrl. Life and Labor, 1974-79, Nat. Rural Housing Coalition, 1975-95, Pa. Housing Fin. Agy., 1975-80, Jud. Inquiry and Rev. Bd. Pa., 1989-93; Disciplinary Bd. Supreme Ct. Pa., 1980-85; mem. Pa. Gov.'s Task Force on Voter Registration, 1975-76, Nat. Task Force for Implementation Equal Rights Amendment, 1975-77; mem. adv. com. Pa. Gov.'s Interdepartmental Council on Seasonal Farmworkers, 1975-77; mem. Appellate Ct. Nominating Commn. Pa., 1976-79; mem. Fed. Jud. Nominating Commn. Pa., 1977-85, chmn., 1978-81, 82-83; mem. Pa. Gov.'s Study Commn. on Pub. Employee Relations, 1976-78; del. Internat. Women's Yr. Conf., 1977; bd. dirs. ERAmerica, Inc., 1st v.p., 1977-79, Nat. Low Income Housing Coalition, 1979-82; Rural Am., 1979-81, Fed. Home Loan Bank Pitts., 1979-82; mem. Nat. Adv. Com. for Women, 1978-79; mem. nat. adv. com. Pa. Neighborhood Preservation Support System, 1976-77; bd. dirs. Pa. Women's Campaign Fund, 1984-86, 92—, pres., 1992-96, Rural Coalition, Washington, 1984-90, Com. on the Constitutional System, 1988-90, Am. Judicature Soc., 1989-93; exec. com. Leadership Conf. Civil Rights, 1986-90; bd. dirs. Pennsylvanians for Modern Cts., 1986— trustee Citizen's Rsch. Found., 1989—; mem. mid. dist. Pa. adv. com. judicial and U.S. atty nominations, 1993-94. Editor: A Voice Of Our Own: Leading American Women Celebrate the Right to Vote, 1996. Virginia Travis lectureship Bucknell U., 1982. Recipient Disting. Alumna award MacDuffie Sch. for Girls, 1979, Liberty Bell award Pa. Bar Assn., 1983, Barrows Alumni award Pomona Coll., 1987, Thomas P. O'Neill Jr. award for exemplary pub. svc., 1989; named Disting. Daughter of Pa., 1987 Woodrow Wilson vis. fellow, 1993—. Mem. ABA (com. election law and voter participation, 1986-90, accreditation com. 1990-96). Home: 132 Verna Rd Lewisburg PA 17837-8747

NEUMAN, ROBERT HENRY, lawyer; b. N.Y.C., Oct. 14, 1936; s. Sydney A. and Ethel (Pekelner) N.; m. Emily Mann, Dec. 30, 1960 (div. 1975); children: David Marshall, Anthony Howard, Amanda Sarah; m. Joyce Thompson, May 5, 1975; 1 child, Nicole Sydney. AB magna cum laude, Harvard U., 1958, JD, 1961. Bar: N.Y. 1962, D.C. 1962. Ford Found. fellow West Africa, 1961-62; assoc. Meyers & Batzell, Washington, 1962-64; asst. legal adviser U.S. Dept. of State, Washington, 1964-70; ptnr. Arent, Fox, Kintner, Plotkin & Kahn, Washington, 1970-93, Baker & Hostetler, Washington, 1993—. U.S. rep. to UN Conf. on Marine Pollution, 1969. Recipient Superior Honor award Dept. State, 1965. Mem. ABA, FBA, Am. Soc. Internat. Law, Internat. Bar Assn., Phi Beta Kappa. Avocation: sailing. Home: 7915 Sandalfoot Dr Potomac MD 20854 Office: Baker & Hostetler 1050 Connecticut Ave NW Washington DC 20036

NEUMAN, ROBERT STERLING, art educator, artist; b. Kellogg, Idaho, Sept. 9, 1926; s. Oscar C. and Katherine (Samuelson) N.; m. Helen Patricia Feddersen, Apr. 6, 1947 (div. 1971); children—Ingrid Alexandra, Elizabeth Catherine; m. Sunne Savage, June 3, 1979; 1 dau., Christina Mary. Student, U. Idaho, 1944-46; B.A.A., M.F.A., Calif. Coll. Arts and Crafts, 1947-51; student, San Francisco Sch. Fine Arts, 1950-51, Mills Coll., 1951. Assoc. prof. art Brown U., 1962-63; lectr. drawing Carpenter Center for Visual Arts, Harvard, 1963-72; prof. art, chmn. dept. Keene (N.H.) State Coll., 1972-90. Exhbns. include, Mus. Modern Art, Whitney Mus. Am. Art, Carnegie Internat., San Francisco Mus. Art, Boston Mus. Fine Arts, Worcester (Mass.) Art Mus., also, Japan and Europe. Served with AUS and USAAF, 1945-46. Recipient Howard Found. award for painting, 1967; Fulbright grantee, 1953-54; Guggenheim fellow, 1956-57; Bender grantee San Francisco Art Assn., 1952. Home: 135 Cambridge St Winchester MA 01890-2411

NEUMAN, SHLOMO P., hydrology educator; b. Zilina, Czechoslovakia, Oct. 26, 1938; came to U.S., 1963, naturalized, 1970; s. Alexander Neumann and Klara (Pikler) Lesny; m. Yael B. Boritzer, Jan. 30, 1965; children: Gil, Michal, Ariel. BSc in Geology, Hebrew U., Jerusalem, 1963; MS in Engring. Sci., U. Calif., Berkeley, 1966, PhD in Engring. Sci., 1968. Cert. profl. hydrogeologist. Acting asst. prof., asst. rsch. engr. dept. civil engring. U. Calif., Berkeley, 1968-70, vis. assoc. prof. dept. civil engring., 1974-75; sr. scientist, assoc. rsch. prof. Inst. Soil and Water Agrl. Rsch. Orgn., Bet-Dagan, Israel, 1970-74; prof. hydrology dept. hydrology and water resources U. Ariz., Tucson, 1975-88, Regents' prof. dept. hydrology and water resources, 1988—; vis. scientist dept. isotope Weizmann Inst. Sci., Rehovot, Israel, 1976; maître de rsch. Ctr. d'Informatique Geologique, Ecole Mines Paris, Fontainebleau, France, 1978, dir. rsch., 1981; vis. prof. dept. fluid mechanics and heat transfer Tel-Aviv U., 1981; hon. appointment concurrent prof. Nanjing U., China; disting. lectr. in field. Mem. editorial adv. bd. Jour. Hydrology, 1977-84, Water Sci. and Tech. Libr. (The Netherlands), 1983-86, Stochastic Hydrology and Hydraulics, 1992—; assoc. editor Water Resources Rsch. Jour., 1987-93; contbr. articles to profl. jours. Hebrew U. scholar, 1962-63, Edwin Letts Oliver scholar, 1965-66; Jane Lewis fellow, 1966-68; recipient Cert. of Appreciation award USDA, 1975, C.V. Theis award Am. Inst. Hydrology, 1990. Fellow Geol. Soc. Am. (O.E. Meinzer award 1976, Birdsal Disting. Lectr. 1987), Am. Geophys. Union (4th Walter B. Langbein lectr. hydrology 1996, Robert E. Horton award 1969); mem. Soc. Petroleum Engrs. of AIME, U.S. Nat. Acad. Engring., Assn. Groundwater Scientists and Engrs. of Nat. Well Water Assn. (Sci. award 1989), Ariz. Hydrol. Soc., Internat. Assn. Hydrogeologists, Sigma Xi. Jewish. Office: U Ariz Dept Hydrology & Water Resources Tucson AZ 85721

NEUMAN, SUSAN CATHERINE, public relations and marketing consultant; b. Detroit, Jan. 29, 1942; d. Paul Edmund and Elsie (Goetz) N.; AB, U. Miami (Fla.), 1964; MBA, Barry U., Miami Shores, Fla., 1985. APR (PRSA), 1973. Journalist, writer The Miami Herald (Fla.), 1962-65; editor Miamian Mag., 1965-69; pres. Susan Neuman Inc., Miami, 1969—. Mem. Fla. Gov.'s Pub. Relations Adv. Council, 1978-86. Mem. Pub. Relations Soc. Am. (accredited, past officer, bd. dirs. Miami chpt.), Econ. Soc. South Fla. (past officer, bd. dirs.), Miami C. of C., Counselor's Acad. Democrat. Roman Catholic. Clubs: Miami City (founder), Miami Internat. Press (charter, founder, pres. 1985-86) (Miami), Com. of One Hundred. Home: 13540 NE Miami Ct Miami FL 33161-2739 Office: Susan Neuman Inc Pla Venetia 25th Fl 555 NE 15th St Ste 25K Miami FL 33132-1404

NEUMAN, TED R., principal. Prin. Duluth (Ga.) High Sch. Recipient Blue Ribbon award U.S. Dept. Edn., 1990-91. Office: Duluth High Sch 3737 Brock Rd Duluth GA 30096-2724*

NEUMAN, TOM S., emergency medical physician, educator; b. N.Y.C., July 23, 1946; s. Otto and Susan Ann (Baltaxe) N.; m. Doris Rubin, Aug. 24, 1969; children: Allison Rachel, Russell Solomon. AB, Cornell U., 1967; MD, NYU, 1971. Diplomate Nat. Bd. Med. Examiners, Am. Bd. Internal Medicine, Am. Bd. Preventative Medicine, Am. Bd. Emergency Medicine. Intern Bellevue Hosp., N.Y.C., 1971-72, resident, 1972-73; commd. med. officer USN, 1973; advanced through grades to capt. USNR, 1990; instr. Naval Undersea Med. Inst., New London, Conn., 1973-74; staff med. officer Submarine Devel. Group One, San Diego, 1974-76, 78-80; emergency room physician Chula Vista (Calif.) Community Hosp., 1975-80; attending physician VA Med. Ctr., La Jolla, Calif., 1976-78; fellow in pulmonary medicine and physiology U. Calif. Sch. Medicine at San Diego, 1976-78, clin. instr., 1978-80, asst. clin. prof., 1980-84, flight physician Life Flight Aeromed. Program, 1980-86, asst. dir. dept. emergency medicine, 1980-94; assoc. dir. dept. emergency medicine, 1994—; attending physician pulmonary divsn. U. Calif. Sch. Medicine at San Diego, 1980—, assoc. clin. prof. medicine and surgery, 1984-87, base hosp. physician, 1984—, dir. Hyperbaric Med. Ctr.,

1984—; med. officer UDT/SEAL Res. Unit 119, San Diego, 1980-84, Mobile Diving and Salvage Unit One, USNR, San Diego, 1984-86, PRIMUS Unit 1942-A, U. Calif. at San Diego, 1988-90; sr. med. officer Seal Teams 1/3/5, USNR, Coronado, Calif., 1986-87; asst. officer in charge Med. Unit 1942-A U. Calif. Sch. Medicine, San Diego, 1990-95, prof. clin. medicine, 1996—; mem. med. adv. bd. western regional underwater lab. program U. So. Calif. Marine Sci. Ctr., Catalina, 1982-85; assoc. adj. prof. medicine and surgery U. Calif. Sch. Medicine at San Diego, 1987-90, adj. prof. medicine and surgery, 1990-96, prof. clin. medicine and adj. prof. surgery, 1996—; mem. San Diego Coroner's com. for investigation of diving fatalities, 1974—; mem. diving cons. Vocat. Diver Tng. Facility, Calif. Inst. Med., Chino, Calif., 1967; mem. task force City Mgr. on Carbon Monoxide Poisoning, San Diego, 1991; active Am. Nat. Stds. Inst. com. for minimal course content for recreational scuba instr. cert., 1992-94; chmn. emergency med. physician quality improvement com., 1992-94; spkr. in field. Author book chpts.; contbr. articles to profl. jours. Fellow ACP, Am. Coll. Preventive Medicine; mem. Am. Thoracic Soc., Am. Lung Assn., Undersea and Huperbaric Med. Soc. (program com. 1981-82, nominations com. 1982-83, chmn. 1988-89, mem. edn. com. 1982-87, chmn. awards com. 1983-84, v.p. exec. com. 1983-84, co-chmn. credentials com. 1984-85, editor-in-chief Undersea and Hyperbaric Medicine 1995—), Profl. Assn. Diving Instrs. (emeritus). Avocations: scuba diving, fishing, photography. Office: Dept Emergency Medicine UCSD Med Ctr 200 W Arbor Dr Dept 8676 San Diego CA 92103-8676

NEUMANN, ANDREW CONRAD, geological oceanography educator; b. Oak Bluffs, Mass., Dec. 21, 1933; s. Andrew Conrad Neumann and Faye Watson (Gilmore) Gilmour; m. Jane Spaeth, July 7, 1962; children: Jennifer, Christopher, Jonathan. BS in Geology, Bklyn. Coll., 1955; MS in Oceanography, Tex. A&M U., 1958; PhD in Geology, Lehigh U., 1963. Asst. prof. marine geology Lehigh U., Bethlehem, Pa., 1963-65; asst. prof. marine sci. U. Miami, Fla., 1965-69, assoc. prof. marine sci., 1969-72; prof. marine sci. U. N.C., Chapel Hill, 1972-85, Bowman and Gordon Gray prof. geol. oceanography, 1985—; program dir. NSF, Washington, 1969-70; Kenan prof. U. Edinburgh, Scotland, 1978; summer vis. investigator U.S. Geol. Survey, Woods Hole, Mass., 1981—, Woods Hole Oceanographic Inst., 1981—; vis. prof. U. Naples, Italy, 1984, 92, 95, Eötvös U., Budapest, Hungary, 1991. Contbr. articles to profl. jours. Trustee Bermuda Biol. Sta. for Research Inc., 1972-76. Recipient Disting. Alumni award Bklyn. Coll., 1987. Fellow Geol. Soc. Am.; mem. Soc. Econ. Paleontologists and Mineralogists, N.C. Acad. Sci. Avocations: fishing, gardening, sailing. Office: U NC Dept Marine Scis 1205 Venable Hall 045a Chapel Hill NC 27599-3300

NEUMANN, CHARLES HENRY, mathematics educator; b. Washington, Jan. 30, 1943; s. Bernhardt Walter and Emma (Habitz) N.; m. Cheryl Elaine Girard, June 18, 1965; children: Matthew Roy, Kristen Elizabeth. AS, Alpena (Mich.) C.C., 1962; BS in Math., Mich. State U., 1964, M.A.T. in Math., 1965. Sci. tchr. Alpena Pub. Schs., 1965-66; instr. math. Alpena C.C., 1966-84, math. sci. dept. chair, 1969-84; instr. math. Oakland C.C., Bloomfield Hills, Mich., 1984—; mem. fin. com. Luth. Social Svcs. of Mich. Scoutmaster troop 92 Boy Scouts Am., Alpena, 1981-84; bd. dirs. Mich. Vision Svc. Assn., Columbus, 1985-89, Ohio Vision Svc. Assn., 1988-89, Blue Cross Blue Shield of Mich., 1986-94; mem. exec. com. Oakland County (Mich.) Dem. Com., 1995-96; mem. fin. com. Luth. Social Svcs. Mich., 1995—; bd. dirs., 1996—; trustee, bd. dirs. Blue Cross/Blue Shield of Mich., 1986-94. Mem. NEA (del. 1974-80, adv. com. on membership 1993-96), Math. Assn. Am., Am. Math. Assn. of Two-Yr. Colls., Mich. Edn. Assn. (bd. dirs. 1974-80), Mich. Edn. Spl. Svcs. (trustee 1975-93, pres. 1976-93), Mich. Math. Assn. of Two-Yr. Colls., Mich. Assn. Higher Edn. (v.p. two-yr. colls. 1970-96), Oakland C.C. Faculty Assn. (v.p. 1994-95, pres. 1995—), Phi Kappa Phi. Lutheran. Avocations: collecting antique books, racquetball, cross country skiing. Home: 5871 Warbler Clarkston MI 48346-2973 Office: Oakland CC 2900 Featherstone Rd Auburn Hills MI 48326-2817

NEUMANN, FORREST KARL, retired hospital administrator; b. St. Louis, Oct. 7, 1930; s. Metz Earl and Ruth (McGhee) N.; m. Erika Stefanie Turkl, Feb. 11, 1955; children: Tracey Neumann Liberson, Karen Neumann Kruger, Scott, Lisa. B.S., Roosevelt U., 1953; M.S. in Hosp. Adminstrn., Northwestern U., 1955. Adminstrv. resident Louis A. Weiss Hosp., Chgo., 1954-55; mem. staff Sparrow Hosp., Lansing, Mich., 1958-90; CEO, dir. Edward W. Sparrow Hosp., Lansing, 1962-90; pres., chief exec. officer, dir. Mason Gen. Hosp., Mich., 1973-85; chmn. bd. Caymich Ins. Co. Ltd., Cayman Islands, 1979-91; emeritus dir. Caymich Ins. Co. Ltd., Cayman Islands, 1991—; chmn. bd. Caymich Ins. Co. (Barbados) Ltd., 1986-91; pres., CEO, Mich. Hosp. Assn. Ins. Co., 1990-96; dir. Mich. Hosp. Assocs. Ins. Co., 1976—; pres., CEO, Sparrow, Inc., 1984-90; chmn. bd. Mich. Hosp. Assn. Ins. Co., 1979-90; dir. 1st Am. Bank Corp., 1980-95, Auto Owners Ins. Co., 1980-90. Chmn. hosp. div. United Community Chest, 1965-68, chmn. budget steering com., 1970-71, bd. dirs., mem. exec. com., 1969-75; mem. adv. com. Capitol Area Comprehensive Health Planning Assn., 1969, bd. dirs., 1971-75, treas., 1974-75; mem., vice chmn. Mich. Arbitration Adv. Com., 1975-80; bd. dirs. Grad. Med. Edn., Inc., 1971-80, pres., 1972-73, treas. 1973. Fellow Am. Coll. Hosp. Adminstrs. (life); mem. Southwestern Mich. Hosp. Council (trustee 1968-73, pres. 1970-71), Am. Hosp. Assn. (del. 1979-87), Mich. Hosp. Assn. (1st v.p. 1972-73, bd. dirs., exec. com., treas. 1974-75, chmn. 1976-77, Meritorious Key award 1979). Lodge: Rotary (Lansing).

NEUMANN, FREDERICK LOOMIS, accounting educator, academic administrator, consultant; b. New Britain, Conn., Nov. 16, 1930; s. Carl Samuel and Rachel Louise (Clark) N.; m. Elizabeth Ann Robinson, Sept. 10, 1960; children: Bradford E., Carla C., Marshall G. A.B. magna cum laude, Dartmouth Coll., 1952; M.B.A. with highest distinction, Amos Tuck Sch. Bus. Administrn., 1953; M.B.A., U. Chgo., 1965, Ph.D., 1967. CPA, Ill., Conn.; cert. internal auditor. Sr. acct. Arthur Andersen & Co., N.Y.C., 1956-62; mem. faculty U. Ill., Urbana-Champaign, 1965—, asst. prof. accountancy, 1965-70, assoc. prof., 1970-75, prof., 1975—, Price Waterhouse prof. auditing, 1979—, head dept. accountancy, 1981-86, assoc. dean acad. affairs, 1992—; cons. in field; pres. Fedn. Schs. of Accountancy, 1987—; sec. Adminstrs. of Accountancy Programs, 1986. Author: Case Studies in Computer Control and Auditing, 1975, Questions and Problems in Auditing, 11th edit., 1995; editor: Issues in Accounting Education, 1991-95; contbr. numerous articles to profl. jours., chpts. to books. Cons. Champaign County Headstart and Child Devel. Corp., 1970-87; treas. Weslye Meth. Ch., 1987—; chmn. com. Champaign County Regional Blood Ctr., 1982—; bd. govs. Univ. YMCA, 1990-96, chmn., 1992-95; mem. Univ. Senate. Lt. (j.g.) USNR, 1953-56, comdr. Res. Ford Found. fellow, 1962-65, Ernst & Whinney fellow, 1972-73. Mem. Inst. Decision Scis., Am. Acctg. Assn. (chmn. auditing sect. 1976-77, chmn. tchg. and curriculum sect. 1991-92, named Outstanding Audit Educator 1991, named for Disting. Svc. in Auditing 1994, dir. pubs. 1995-97, exec. com. 1995-97), Ill. CPA Soc. (bd. dirs. 1983-85), AICPAs, Inst. Internal Auditors (Leon Radde Outstanding Educator award 1986), Info. Systems Audit and Control Assn., Acctg. Historians, Inst. Mgmt. Accts., Fin. Execs. Inst., Phi Beta Kappa (treas. local chpt. 1981-96, v.p. 1996—), Beta Gamma Sigma, Beta Alpha Psi. Home: 2211 S Cottage Grove Ave Urbana IL 61801-6815 Office: U Ill 1206 S 6th St Champaign IL 61820-6915

NEUMANN, GERHARD, mechanical engineer. Recipient Ordre Nationale de la Legion d'Honour award Govt. France, 1977, Elder Statesman of Aviation award NAA, 1984, R. Tom Sawyer award ASME, 1991, Wright Bros. Meml. award, 1993. Home: 53 Ocean View Rd Swampscott MA 01907-2242

NEUMANN, HARRY, philosophy educator; b. Dormoschel, Germany, Oct. 10, 1930; came to U.S., 1937, naturalized, 1948; s. Siegfried and Frieda (Lion) N.; m. Christina Sopher, Sept. 25, 1959. B.A., St. John's Coll., 1952; M.A., U. Chgo., 1954; Ph.D., Johns Hopkins U., 1962; postgrad., U. Heidelberg, Germany, 1956-58. Mem. faculty Mich. State U., 1962-63, Lake Forest Coll., 1963-65; prof. philosophy, and govt. Claremont Grad. Sch. Scripps Coll., Claremont (Calif.) Grad. Sch., 1966—; research assoc. Rockefeller Inst., N.Y.C., 1963. Author: Liberalism, 1991; contbr. articles profl. jours. With AUS, 1954-56. Classical Philosophy fellow Ctr. Hellenic Studies, Dumbarton Oaks, Washington, 1965-66, rsch. fellow Salvatori Ctr. for Study of Individual Freedom in the Modern World, 1970; rsch. fellow Earhart Found., 1973-74, 78, 82, 86, 90, 94. Mem. AAUP, Univ. Ctrs. Rational Alternatives, Univ. Profs. for Acad. Order, John Brown Cook Assn. for Freedom (advisor). Office: Scripps Coll Claremont CA 91711

NEUMANN, HERSCHEL, physics educator; b. San Bernardino, Calif., Feb. 3, 1930; s. Arthur and Dorothy (Greenhood) N.; m. Julia Black, June 15, 1951; 1 child, Keith. BA, U. Calif., Berkeley, 1951; MS, U. Oreg., 1959; PhD, U. Nebr., 1965. Theoretical physicist Gen. Electric Co., Richland, Wash., 1951-57; instr. physics U. Nebr., Lincoln, 1964-65; asst. prof. physics U. Denver, 1965-71, assoc. prof. physics, 1971-85, prof. physics, 1985—, chmn. physics and astronomy, 1985-97. Contbr. over 20 articles to profl. jours. Dir. numerous pub. outreach programs in physics. Mem. Am. Phys. Soc., Am. Assn. Physics Tchrs. Home: 2425 S St Paul St Denver CO 80210-5516 Office: U Denver Dept Physics and Astronomy Denver CO 80208-2238

NEUMANN, LISELOTTE, professional golfer; b. Finspang, Sweden, May 20, 1966. With LPGA, 1987—; mem. European Solheim Cup Team, 1992. Named Golf Digest Rolex Rookie of Year, 1988, Swedish Golfer of Year, 1994, GolfWorld's Most Improved Golfer, 1994. LPGA victories include: U.S. Women's Open, 1988, Mazda Japan Classic, 1991, Minn. LPGA Classic, 1994, Weetabix Women's Brit. Open, 1994, GHP Heartland Classic, 1994, Chrysler-Plymouth Tournament of Champions, 1996, PING/Welch's Championship, 1996, First Bank-Edina Realty Classic, 1996; other victories include: European Open, 1985, German Open, 1986-88, French Open, 1987. Office: LPGA 100 Internat Golf Dr Daytona Beach FL 32124*

NEUMANN, MARK W., congressman; b. Waukesha, Wis., Feb. 27, 1954; m. Sue; 3 children. BS, U. Wis., Whtiewater, 1975; MS, U. Wis., River Falls, 1977. Real estate developer Neumann Devels., 1980—; mem. 104th and 105th Congresses from 1st Wis. dist., 1994—; mem. appropriations, nat. security, vets. affairs, HUD & ind. agys., budget coms. Office: US House Reps 415 Cannon Bldg Washington DC 20515-4901

NEUMANN, PETER GABRIEL, computer scientist; b. N.Y.C., Sept. 21, 1932; s. J.B. and Elsa (Schmid) N.; 1 child, Helen K. AB, Harvard U., 1954, SM, 1955; Dr rerum naturarum, Technisch Hochschule, Darmstadt, Fed. Republic Germany, 1960; PhD, Harvard U., 1961. Mem. tech. staff Bell Labs, Murray Hill, N.J., 1960-70; Mackay lectr. Stanford U., 1964, U. Calif., Berkeley, 1970-71; computer scientist SRI Internat., Menlo Park, Calif., 1971—. Author: Computer-Related Risks, 1995. Fulbright fellow, 1958-60. Fellow AAAS, IEEE, Assn. for Computing Machinery (editor jour. 1976-93, chmn. com. on computers and pub. policy 1985—). Avocations: music, tai chi, holistic health. Office: SRI Internat EL-243 333 Ravenswood Ave Menlo Park CA 94025-3453

NEUMANN, ROBERT GERHARD, ambassador, consultant; b. Vienna, Austria, Jan. 2, 1916; s. Hugo and Stephanie (Taussky) N.; m. Marlen Eldredge, July 27, 1941; children: Ronald E., Gregory W. Diplome superieur, U. Rennes, France, 1936; diploma Consular Acad. Vienna, Geneva Sch. Internat. Studies, 1937; student, U. Vienna, 1938; M.A., Amherst Coll., 1940; Ph.D. (Shevlin fellow 1940-41), U. Minn., 1946. Instr. State Tchrs. Coll., Oshkosh, Wis., 1941-42; lectr. U. Wis., 1946-47; asst. prof. UCLA, 1947-52, asso. prof., 1952-58, prof., 1958-70, dir. Inst. Internat. and Fgn. Studies, 1959-65, chmn. Atlantic and West European Program, 1965-66; U.S. ambassador to Afghanistan Kabul, 1966-73; to Morocco Rabat, 1973-76; dir. transition team Dept. State, 1980-81; to Saudi Arabia Jidda, 1981; sr. staff assoc. Center for Strategic and Internat. Studies, 1976-80; vice chmn., 1980-81, cons., 1980-81, sr. advisor, 1982—, cons. to bus. and govt., 1983—. Author: The Government of the German Federal Republic, 1966, European and Comparative Government, 4th edit, 1968, Toward a More Effective Executive-Legislative Relationship in the Conduct of America's Foreign Policy, 1977; contbr.: The Austrian Solution, 1982; Contbr. articles to jours.; Editorial writer: Los Angeles Times, 1952-59. Chmn. internat. relations sect. Town Hall, 1956-62; mem. Calif. Rep. Cen. Com., 1954-60; bd. dirs. Coun. Am. Ambs., 1982—; vice chmn., trustee Moroccan-Am. Found., 1982-90; vice chmn. Am.-Saudi Bus. Roundtable, 1982-83, chmn., 1984-91; mem. exec. com. Islam and the West, 1984-88; v.p. Am. Friends of Afghanistan, 1985-93; hon. dir. Afghanistan Relief Com., 1985-93; mem. regional task force Am.-Russian Rels., 1984—; mem. adv. bd. Nat. Coun. U.S.-Arab Rels., 1989—; founding mem. Reps. Abroad. Served from pvt. to 1st lt. AUS, 1942-46. Haynes Found. fellow, 1950-51; Social Sci. Research Council fellow, 1950-51; Fulbright fellow France, 1954-55; Nat. Woodrow Wilson Found. fellow, 1984-93; recipient hon. medal U. Brussels, 1955; decorated Legion of Honor (France), 1957; officers cross Order of Merit (Fed. Republic of Germany), 1963; Comdr.'s Cross, 1974; Order of the Star (Afghanistan), 1973; grand officer Order and Star of Ouissam Alaoui (Morocco), 1976; Knight Comdr.'s Cross and Star (Austria), 1991. Mem. Atlantic Coun. U.S. (sponsor), Am. Polit. Sci. Assn., Internat. Polit. Sci. Assn., Internat. Law Assn., Univ. Club (Washington). Roman Catholic. Home: 4986 Sentinel Dr Apt 301 Bethesda MD 20816-3580 *The following thoughts and principles, forged on the ladder to success, took their roots earlier when I was a prisoner in Nazi concentration camps and then a penniless immigrant to America: 1. When in doubt, choose the road of courage. The dynamics of action will carry others with you and confound your opponents. 2. While action must be carefully considered, it is generally better to act than not to act. It is easier to correct the course of action than to move from inaction to action. 3. Dream big and without restraint. There will always be time afterwards to reduce the scope of your action in the light of confining realities. But if you start dreaming small, you shackle your imagination from the outset. 4. Have some reasonable and constant ideas as to what you will not put up with and examine your conscience from time to time to check the possible corrosion success might have wrought. It might keep you honest, or, at least—humble.*

NEUMANN, RONALD DANIEL, nuclear medicine physician, educator; b. Watertown, Wis., Oct. 10, 1947. BS summa cum laude, Carroll Coll., 1970; MD with highest honors, Yale U., 1974. Diplomate Nat. Bd. Med. Examiners, Am. Bd. Nuclear Medicine; lic. physician, Md., D.C. Resident in pathology Yale-New Haven Hosp., 1974-77, resident in nuclear medicine, 1977-79, chief resident in nuclear medicine, 1978-79, attending physician, 1979-85; asst. prof. diagnostic radiology Sch. Medicine Yale U., 1979-83, assoc. prof. diagnostic radiology and pathology, 1983-86; dep. chief dept. nuclear medicine NIH, Bethesda, Md., 1985-88, chief. dept. nuclear medicine, 1988—, dir. nuclear medicine residency tng. program, 1986-92; clin. prof. diagnostic radiology and nuclear medicine Sch. Medicine George Washington U., Washington, 1986—; chmn. med. isotopes and radiation safety com. West Haven VA Med. Ctr., 1979-85; mem. clin. rsch. panel Nat. Inst. Diabetes and Digestive and Kidney Diseases, 1987-88; mem. radiation safety com. Nat. Ctr. for Health Stats., 1987-89. Patentee Antigen-specific composition and in-vivo methods for detecting and localizing and antigenic site and for radiotherapy; contbr. over 160 articles and abstracts to med. and sci. jours., 24 chpts. to books and conf. proceedings. Nat. Merit scholar; NASA fellow. Fellow Am. Coll. Chest Physicians; mem. AAAS, Am. Coll. Nuclear Physicians, Am. Soc. for Investigative Pathology, Soc. Nuclear Medicine (greater N.Y. chpt. 1979-85, co-chmn. sci. program com. 1979, Mid.-Atlantic chpt. 1985—, acad. coun. 1987—), Metastasis Rsch. Soc., Soc. for Chmn. Acad. Nuclear Medicine Depts., Internat. Acad. Pathology (U.S. and Can. divsns.), European Assn. Nuclear Medicine, Sigma Xi., Delta Sigma Nu. Office: NIH Dept Nuclear Medicine CC 9000 Rockville Pike # 453 Bethesda MD 20814-1436

NEUMANN, RONALD ELDREDGE, diplomat; b. Washington, Sept. 30, 1944; s. Robert G. N. and Marlen Eldredge; m. Margaret Elaine Grimm, Jan 23, 1966; children: Helen, Brian. BA, U. Calif., Riverside, 1966, MA, 1967; student, Nat. War Coll., 1991. Joined Fgn. Svc., 1970; vice consul Am. Embassy, Dakar, Senegal, 1971-73, Am. Consulate, Tabriz, Iran, 1973-76; desk officer office of so. European affairs Dept. State, Washington, 1976-77, aide to asst. sec. Near East and South Asian Affairs, 1977-78, dep. dir. Arabian Peninsula Affairs, 1983-86, dir. No. Gulf affairs, 1991-94; desk officer Jordanian Affairs Dept. State, Jordan, 1978-81; dep. chief mission Am. Embassy, Sanaa, North Yemen, 1981-83; with Arabic Lang. Tng., Washington, 1986-87; dep. chief mission Am. Embassy, Abu Dhabi, United Arab Emirates, 1987-90; amb. to Algeria, 1994—. 1st. lt. US Army, 1969-70, Vietnam. Decorated Bronze star, Combat Infantry Badge, US Army, 1967-70. Mem. Am. Fgn. Svc. Assn., U. Calif. Riverside Alumni Assn., Assn. of 5th Divsn. Nat. War Coll. Alumni, Phi Beta Kappa. Avocations: reading, backpacking, hiking. Office: Am Emb Algiers Dept of State Washington DC 20521-6030

NEUMANN, ROY COVERT, architect; b. Columbus, Nebr., Mar. 1, 1921; s. LeRoy Franklin and Clara Louise (Covert) N.; m. Hedy Charlotte Schultz, Aug. 28, 1948; children: Tali, Scott. Student, Midland Coll., 1939-40, U. Calif.-Berkeley Armed Forces Inst., overseas, 1942-43; AB, U. Nebr., 1948, BArch, 1949; MA, Harvard U., 1952; postgrad., U. Wis., Iowa State U. Registered profl. architect, Iowa, Nebr., Kans., Minn., S.D., N.Y., N.J., Mass., Ohio, Pa., Tenn., Ky., Va., W.Va., Ga., Mich., Mo., Ill., Wis., Tex., Colo. Ptnr., architect R. Neumann Assocs., Lincoln, Nebr., 1952-55; officer mgr. Sargent, Webster, Crenshaw & Folley, Schenectady, N.Y., 1955-59; dir. architecture, ptnr. A.M. Kinney Assocs., Cin., 1959-65; officer mgr. Hunter, Campbell & Rea, Johnstown, Pa., 1965-66; dir. architecture, ptnr. Stanley Cons., Muscatine, Iowa, 1966-76; pres., chmn. bd. Neumann Monson P.C., Iowa City, 1976—; ptnr. Clinton St. Ptnrs., Iowa City, 1983—, Iris City Devel. Co. Mt. Pleasant, Iowa, 1986. Prin. works include Harbour Facilities, Antigua, W.I., S.C. Johnson Office Bldg., Racine, Wis., Iowa City Transit Facility Bldg., addition to Davenport Ctrl. High Sch., V.A. Adminstrv. Office Bldg., Iowa City, Johnson County Office Bldg., Iowa City Mercer Park Aquatic Ctr., Iowa City, Coll. Bus. U. Iowa, Iowa City, renovation Lawrence County Courthouse, Deadwood, S.D. Mem. bd. edn. Muscatine Community Sch. Dist., 1974-76. Served with USN, 1942-46, PTO. Recipient Honor award Portland Cement Assn., 1949. Mem. AIA (Honor award 1975), Constrn. Specifications Inst. (pres. 1974-76, Honor award 1983, 84, 85, 86), Soc. Archtl. Historians, Archtl. Assn. London, U. Nebr. Alumni Assn., Harvard U. Alumni Assn., Iowa City C. of C., Phi Kappa Psi, Univ. Athletic Club (Iowa City), Masons, Ea. Star, Elks. Republican. Presbyterian. Avocations: golf, fishing, medieval history, big band music. Home: 2014 Burnside Dr Muscatine IA 52761-3510 Office: Neumann Monson Architects 111 E College St Iowa City IA 52240-4002

NEUMANN, THOMAS WILLIAM, archaeologist; b. Cin., Aug. 30, 1951; s. William Henry and Virginia Marie (Walz) N.; m. Mary Louise Spink, Sept. 3, 1988. BA in Anthropology, U. Ky., 1973; PhD in Anthropology, U. Minn., 1979. Instr. U. Minn., Mpls., 1977-79; asst. prof. Syracuse U., 1979-86, dir. archaeology field program, 1979-86; sr. ptnr. Neumann & Sanford Cultural Resource Assessments, Syracuse, 1985-87; sr. scientist R. Christopher Goodwin & Assocs., Inc., Frederick, Md., 1987-92; rsch. assoc. Terrestrial Environ. Specialists, Phoenix, N.Y., 1980-83, SUNY Rsch. Found., Potsdam, 1985-87; external reviewer NSF, Washington, 1982-85; dir. Ctr. for Archaeol. Rsch. and Edn., Houston, Minn., 1982-84; vis. assoc. prof. Emory U., 1991-93, 96; ind. cons., 1991—. Author, co-author more than 70 monographs including 2 winners of the Anne Arundell County Hist. Preservation award; asst. editor Amanuensis, 1972-73; contbr. more than 30 articles to profl. jours. Nat. Trust Historic Preservation honor award. Grantee, Am. Philos. Soc., 1981, Appleby-Mosher Found., 1983, Landmarks Assn. Cen. N.Y., 1984; recipient Oswald award, U. Ky., 1973. Mem. AAAS, N.Y. Acad. Sci., Soc. for Am. Archaeology, Ea. States Archaeol. Fedn., Mid. Atlantic Archaeol. Conf., Phi Beta Kappa. Roman Catholic. Achievements include development of use of vegetation successional stages for cultural resource assessments; identification of cause of passenger pigeon extinctions, microlithic compound tool industry in the eastern prehistoric U.S., contingency planning budget system for Archdiocese of Atlanta. Home: 3859 Wentworth Ln SW Lilburn GA 30247-2260 Office: Ind Archeol Cons 3859 Wentworth Ln SW Lilburn GA 30047-2260

NEUMANN, WILLIAM ALLEN, judge; b. Minot, N.D., Feb. 11, 1944; s. Albert W. and Opal Olive (Whitlock) N.; m. Jaqueline Denise Buechler, Aug. 9, 1980; children: Andrew, Emily. BSBA, U. N.D., 1965; JD, Stanford U., 1968. Bar: N.D. 1969, U.S. Dist. Ct. N.D. 1969. Pvt. practice law Williston, N.D., 1969-70, Bottineau, N.D., 1970-79; former judge N.D. Judicial Dist. Ct., N.E. Judicial Dist., Rugby, 1979-92; justice N.D. Supreme Ct., Bismarck, 1993—; chmn. exec. com. N.D. Jud. Conf., 1985-87, chmn. 1987-89. Mem. ABA, State Bar Assn. N.D., Am. Judicature Soc. Lutheran. Office: ND Supreme Ct Judicial Wing 1st Fl 600 E Boulevard Ave Bismarck ND 58505-0660

NEUMARK, GERTRUDE FANNY, materials science educator; b. Nuremberg, Germany, Apr. 29, 1927; came to U.S., 1939; d. Siegmund and Bertha (Forchheimer) N.; m. Henry Rothschild, Mar. 18, 1950. BA, Barnard Coll., 1948; MA, Radcliffe Coll., 1949; PhD, Columbia U., 1951. Advanced rsch. physicist Sylvania Rsch. Labs., Bayside, N.Y., 1952-60; sr. mem. tech. staff Philips Labs., Briarcliff Manor, N.Y., 1960-85; prof. materials sci. Columbia U., N.Y.C., 1985—; cons. Am. Inst. Physics, N.Y.C., 1968-69; NSF vis. prof., 1982; panelist NRC; panelist, reviewer NSF. Contbr. Encyclopedia of Advanced Materials, numerous articles to sci. jours., chpt. to books; patentee in field. Rice fellow, 1948, Dana fellow, 1948, AAUW Anderson fellow, 1951. Fellow Am. Phys. Soc. (Goeppert-Meyer award com. 1987-89); mem. Materials Rsch. Soc., Electrochem. Soc. (sr.), Soc. Women Engrs. (sr.), Am. Chem. Soc.

NEUMARK, MICHAEL HARRY, lawyer; b. Cin., Oct. 28, 1945; s. Jacob H. and Bertha (Zubor) N.; m. Sue Daly, June 5, 1971; children: Julie Rebecca, John Adam. BS in Bus., Ind. U., 1967; JD, U. Cin., 1970. Bar: Ohio 1970, D.C. 1972. Atty. chief counsel's office IRS, Washington, 1970-74; acting br. chief IRS, 1974-75; sr. atty. regional counsel's office IRS, Cin., 1975-77; assoc. Paxton & Seasongood Legal Profl. Assn., Cin., 1977-80; ptnr. Thompson, Hine & Flory, 1980—, mem. mgmt. com., 1993—; chmn. So. Ohio Tax Inst., 1987; mem. IRS and Bar Liaison Com.; speaker at profl. confs. Contbr. articles to profl. jours. Bd. dirs. 1987 World Figure Skating Chamionship, Cin., 1986-89; precinct exec. Hamilton County Rep. Orgn., 1980-86; vol. referee Hamilton County Juvenile Ct., 1980-86; adv. bd. Cin. Entrepreneurship Inst.; trustee St. Rita Sch. for Deaf, 1991—. Recipient Commendation Resolution Sycamore Twp., 1987. Mem. ABA (tax sect. S corp. subcom. chmn. 1981-88), Ohio State Bar Assn., Cin. Bar Assn. (pres. 1996—, recognition award 1985, treas., bd. trustees 1988-91, trustee 1992—, chair tax sect., 1990-91), Leadership Cin., Kenwood Country Club, Indian Hill Club. Republican. Avocations: golf, travel. Office: Thompson Hine & Flory 312 Walnut St Cincinnati OH 45202-4024

NEUMEIER, JOHN, choreographer, ballet company director; b. Milw., Feb. 24, 1942; s. Albert and Lucille N. BA, Marquette U., 1961, DFA (hon.), 1987; student, Stone-Camryn Ballet Sch., Chgo., 1957-62, Royal Ballet Sch., London, 1962-63; student of Vera Volkova, Copenhagen, 1962-63. Dancer Sybil Shearer Co., Chgo., 1960-62, Stuttgart (Fed. Republic Germany) Ballet, 1963-69; artistic dir. Frankfurt (Fed. Republic Germany) Opera Ballet, 1969-73, Hamburg (Fed. Republic Germany) State Opera Ballet, 1973—; prof. City of Hamburg, 1987; dir. Hamburg Ballet, 1996; found. ballet sch. Hamburg State Opera, 1978; found. ballet ctr. John Neumeier, ballet sch., Hamburg State Opera co. tng. under one roof., 1989. Guest choreographer for various cos. including Am. Ballet Theatre, Royal Ballet London, Royal Danish Ballet, Nat. Ballet Can., Royal Winnipeg Ballet, Stuttgart Ballet, Munich Opera, Vienna Opera, Ballet du XX siecle, Brussels, Opera de Paris, Opera of Stockholm; guest opera dir.: Otello, Munich Opera, Hamburg State Opera, ballet dir.: films Rondo, 1971 (Prix Italia 1972), Third Symphony of Gustav Mahler (Golden Camera award 1978), Legend of Joseph, Wendung (String Quintet in C major by Schubert), 1979, Scenes of Childhood, The Lady of the Camellias, 1986, Othello, 1987. Decorated knight's cross Danebrog Order (Denmark); recipient Dance mag. award, 1983, Fed. German Cross of Merit, 1987, German Dance prize, 1988; title of Prof. conferred by City of Hamburg, 1987, Deutscher Tanzpreis, Fed. Republic of Germany, 1988; recipient Prix Diaghilev award, France, 1988, Order Des Arts et des Lettres award French Minister Culture, 1991, Carina Ari award, Stockholm, 1994, Nijinsky medal Polish Minister Culture, 1996. Mem. Acad. der Kuenste Hamburg, Acad. der Kuenste Berlin. Roman Catholic. Office: Ballettzentrum Hamburg, Caspar-Voght-Strasse 54, D-20535 Hamburg Germany

NEUMEIER, MATTHEW MICHAEL, lawyer; b. Racine, Wis., Sept. 13, 1954; s. Frank Edward and Ruth Irene (Effenberger) N.; m. Annmarie Prine, Jan. 31, 1987; children: Ruthann Marie, Emilie Irene. B in Gen. Studies with distinction, U. Mich., 1981; JD magna cum laude, Harvard U., 1984. Bar: N.Y. 1987, Mich. 1988, Ill. and Trial1991, U.S. Dist. Ct. (ea. dist.) Mich. 1988, U.S. Dist. Ct. (ea. and no. dists.) Ill. 1991, U.S. Ct. Appeals (7th cir.) 1992, U.S. Supreme Ct. 1991. Sec.-treas. Ind. Roofing & Siding Co., Escanaba, Mich., 1973-78; mng. ptnr. Ind. Roofing Co., Menominee, Mich., 1977-78; law clk. to presiding justice U.S. Ct. Appeals (9th cir.), San Diego, 1984-85; law clk. to chief justice Warren E. Burger U.S. Supreme Ct., Washington, 1985-86; spl. asst. to chmn. U.S. Constn. Bicentennial Comm., Washington, 1986; assoc. Cravath, Swaine & Moore, N.Y.C., 1986-88; spl.

counsel Burnham & Ritchie, Ann Arbor, Mich., 1988; assoc. Schlussel, Lifton, Simon, Rands, Galvin & Jackier, P.C., Ann Arbor, 1988-90, Skadden, Arps, Slate, Meagher & Flom, Chgo., 1990-96; ptnr. Jenner & Block, Chgo., 1996—. Editor Harvard Law Rev., 1982-84. Pres., bd. dirs. Univ. Cellar Inc., Ann Arbor, 1979-81; bd. dirs. Econ. Devel. Corp., Menominee, 1978-79, Midwestern divsn. Am. Suicide Foun., sec. 1992—; mem. vestry Ch. Our Savior. Mem. ABA, State Bar Mich., Assn. of Bar of City of N.Y., Ill. State Bar Assn., Chgo. Bar Assn. Republican. Avocations: classic automobiles, piano, choir. Office: Jenner & Block Ste 4200 One IBM Plz Chicago IL 60611

NEUMEIER, RICHARD L., lawyer; b. Boston, Nov. 22, 1946; s. Victor L. and Crystal Gladys (Mueller) N.; m. Mary Edna Malcolm, Mar. 15, 1975; children: Hannah Catherine, Edmund Malcolm, Thomas Richard. AB, U. Chgo., 1968, AM, 1968; JD, Columbia U., 1971. Bar: N.Y. 1972, U.S. Dist. Ct. (so. dist.) N.Y. 1972, Mass. 1973, U.S. Dist. Ct. Mass. 1973, U.S. Ct. Appeals (1st cir.) 1974, R.I. 1979, U.S. Supreme Ct. 1985. Assoc. Hart & Hume, N.Y.C., 1971-73; assoc. to ptnr. Parker, Coulter, Daley & White, Boston, 1973-95; ptnr. McDonough, Hacking & Neumeier, Boston, 1995—. Me. bd. editors Def. Counsel Jour., Chgo., 1989-92, editor, chmn. bd. editors, 1992—; mem. bd. editors Boston Bar Jour., 1988-94; contbr. articlesto profl. jours. Bd. dirs. Common Cause/Mass., Boston, 1980-91, chmn., 1990-91, 94-96; mem. Town Meeting, Lexington, Mass., 1989—. Fellow Am. Bar Found.; mem. ABA, Fed. Bar Assn. (pres. Mass. chpt. 1989-90), Mass. Bar Assn., Boston Bar Assn. (chmn. ethics com. 1991-94, chmn. torts com. 1994—), Internat. Assn. Def. Counsel (exec. com. 1992—). Democrat. Home: 2 Pitcairn Pl Lexington MA 02173-7134 Office: McDonough Hacking & Neumeier 73 Tremont St Boston MA 02108-3916

NEUMEYER, JOHN LEOPOLD, research company administrator, chemistry educator; b. Munich, Germany, July 19, 1930; came to U.S., 1945, naturalized, 1950; s. Albert and Martha (Stern) N.; m. Evelyn Friedman, June 24, 1956; children: Ann Martha, David Alexander, Elizabeth Jean. BS, Columbia U., 1952; PhD, U. Wis., 1961. Rsch. chemist Ethicon Inc., New Brunswick, N.J., 1952-57, FMC Corp., Princeton, N.J., 1961-63; sr. staff chemist Arthur D. Little Inc., Cambridge, Mass., 1963-69; prof. medicinal chemistry, chemistry Northeastern U., Boston, 1969-91, dir. grad. sch., 1978-85, disting. emeritus prof., 1992—; chmn. bd., chief sci. officer, co-founder Rsch. Biochem. Internat., Natick, Mass., 1981-97; mem. com. of revision U.S. Pharmacopeia, 1970-85; lectr. in psychiatry dept. psychiatry Harvard Med. Sch., 1996—; dir. medicinal chemistry program Alcohol and Drug Abuse Rsch. Ctr. McLean Hosp., Belmont, Mass., 1996—; cons. in field. Patentee in field. Contbr. articles to profl. jours., also chpts. to books in field. Mem. Bd. Health, Wayland, Mass., 1968-75, Pesticide Bd., Mass., 1972-75; mem. panel to sec. HEW Commn. on Pesticides and their Relationship to Environ. Health, 1969; mem. Mass. Tech. Collaborative, 1996—. Served to cpl. U.S. Army, 1953-55. Recipient Lunsford Richardson award, 1961, Marie Curie award in Nuclear Medicine, 1992; Sr. Hayes Fulbright fellow, 1975-76. Fellow AAAS (mem. at large 1983-87, chmn. pharm. sci. sect. 1992-93), Am. Assn. Pharm. Scis., Acad. Pharm Scis. (rsch. achievement award in medicinal chemistry 1982, Northeastern U. faculty lectr. award 1978, U. disting. prof. 1982—); mem. Am. Soc. Neurosci., Am. Soc. Exptl. Pharm. & Eptl. Therapeutics, Am. Chem. Soc. (councilor 1985—, trustee 1989-93, bd. editors Jour. Medicinal Chemistry 1974-88, chmn. div. med. chem. 1982). Office: 1 Holiday Rd Wayland MA 01778-1905 Also: Harvard Med Sch/McLean Hosp ADARC 115 Mill St Belmont MA 02178

NEUMEYER, ZACHARY T., hotel executive. Pres. Sage Hospitality Resources LP, Denver. Office: Sage Hospitality Resources LP 1512 Larimer St Ste 800 Denver CO 80202-1610

NEUNZIG, CAROLYN MILLER, elementary, middle and high school educator; b. L.I., May 5, 1930; kd. Stanley and Grace (Walsh) Miller; m. Herbert Neunzig, May 28, 1955; children: Kurt Miller, Keith Weidler. BA, Beaver Coll., Glen Side, Pa., 1953; MSSc, Syracuse U., 1989; postgrad., Adelphi U.; Cert., N.C. State U., Raleigh. Cert. in elem. edn., reading, history and English, N.C. Reading tchr. grades K-6 St. Timothy's Sch., Raleigh, N.C., 1971-83, 5th grade tchr., 1983-88, 5th grade lead tchr., 1986-88; tchr. English and geography 7th grade St. Timothy's Mid. Sch., Raleigh, 1991—; tchr Am. govt. 12th grade St. Timothy's Mid. Sch./Hale H.S., Raleigh, 1991-93; instr. continuing edn. program history Meredith Coll., Raleigh, 1990-91, spl. high sch. registration commr., 1991-93, instr. continuing edn. program in history, 1995-96; mem. Ctr. for Study of the Presidency, 1996-97. Mem. Am. Acad. Polit. and Social Sci., Acad. Polit. Sci., Nat. Coun. Social Studies, Nat. Coun. Tchrs. English, Ctr. for Study of the Presidency.

NEUSCHEL, ROBERT PERCY, management consultant, educator; b. Hamburg, N.Y., Mar. 13, 1919; s. Percy J. and Anna (Becker) N.; m. Dorothy Virginia Maxwell, Oct. 20, 1944; children—Kerr Anne Ziprick, Carla Becker Neuschel Wyckoff, Robert Friedrich (Fritz). B.A., Denison U., 1941; M.B.A., Harvard U., 1947. Indsl. engr. Sylvania Elec. Products Co., Inc., 1947-49; with McKinsey & Co., Inc., 1950-79, sr. partner, dir., 1967-79; prof. corp. governance, assoc. dean J. L. Kellogg Grad. Sch. Mgmt.; former dir. Northwestern U., assoc. dean J.L. Kellogg Sch. Mgmt.; mem. exec. coun. Internat. Air Cargo Forum, 1988—; mem. com. study air passenger svc. and safety NRC, 1989—; bd. dirs. Butler Mfg. Co., Combined Ins. Co. Am., Templeton, Kenley & Co., U.S. Freightways Co.; lectr. in field; mem. McKinsey Found. Mgmt. Rsch., Inc.; transp. task force Reagan transition team; chmn. bd. dirs. Internat. Intermodal Expn. Atlanta. Contbr. to profl. jours. Pres. Bd. Edn., Lake Forest, Ill., 1965-70; rep. Nat. council Boy Scouts Am., 1970—, mem. N.E. exec. coun., 1969—; chmn. bd. Lake Forest Symphony, 1973; bd. dirs. Loyola U., Chgo., Chgo. Boys' Club, Nat. Ctr. Voluntary Action, Inst. Mgmt. Consultants; trustee N. Suburban Mass Transit, 1972-73, Loyola Med. Ctr.; mem. adv. coun. Kellogg Grad. Sch. Mgmt., Northwestern U., White House conferee Drug Free Am.; mem. Nat. Petroleum Coun. Transp. and Supply Com. Served to capt. USAAF, World War II. Named Transporation Man of Yr. Chitransp. Assoc., 1994. Fellow Acad. Advancement Corp. Governance; mem. Transp. Assn. Am., Nat. Def. Transp. Assn. (subcom. transp. tech. agenda 1990—), Intermodal Assn. N.Am. (chmn. bd. dirs.). Presbyterian (ruling elder). Clubs: Harvard Bus. Sch. (pres. 1964-65), Economic, Executive, Chicago, Mid America, Mid-Day (Chgo.); Onwentsia (Lake Forest). Home: 101 Sunset Pl Lake Forest IL 60045-1834 Office: 1936 Sheridan Rd Evanston IL 60208-0849 *My observations and experiences with corporate executives convince me that leadership is based less on sheer intelligence and more on fundamental qualities of character. By traits of character I would suggest such things as trust, staying power, guts, fairness, maturity, and the capacity to be 'big'. And the primary task of the individual leader is, above all else, to manage himself—his time, talents, emotions, sense of values, and priorities, as a living example to those who follow his leadership.*

NEUSNER, JACOB, humanities and religious studies educator; b. Hartford, Conn., July 28, 1932; m. Suzanne Richter, Mar. 15, 1964; children: Samuel Aaron, Eli Ephraim, Noam Mordecai Menahem, Margalit Leah Berakhah. AB in History magna cum laude, Harvard U., 1953; postgrad. (Henry fellow), Lincoln Coll., Oxford, Eng., 1953-54; postgrad. (Fulbright scholar), Hebrew U., 1957-58; M.H.L., Jewish Theol. Sem. Am., 1960; Ph.D. in Religion (Univ. scholar), Columbia U., 1960; A.M. ad eudem, Brown U., 1969; L.H.D., U. Chgo., 1978; D.Phil. (hon.), U. Cologne, 1979; Hon. Doctorate, U. Bologna, Tulane U., St. Louis U., U. Rochester. Instr. religion Columbia U., 1960-61; asst. prof. Hebrew U. Wis.-Milw., 1961-62; research asso. Brandeis U., 1962-64; asst. prof. religion Dartmouth Coll., 1964-66; assoc. prof. Dartmouth Coll., Providence, 1966-68; prof. religious studies Brown U., Providence, 1968-75, prof. religious studies, Ungerleider Disting. scholar Judaic studies, 1975-82, Univ. prof., Ungerleider Disting. scholar, 1982-90; Disting. Rsch. prof. religious studies U. S. Fla., Tampa, 1990—; vis. prof. Jewish Theol. Sem. Am., summer 1977, Iliff Sch. Theology, Denver, summer 1978, U. Frankfurt, 1991, Cambridge (Eng.) U., 1992, Abo Akademi U., 1993, U. Canterbury, Eng., 1994, U. Goettingen, Germany, 1995; Hill vis. prof. U. Minn., 1978; pres. Max Richter Found., 1969—; mem. Nat. Coun. for Humanities; governing bd. Nat. Endowment Humanities, 1978-84, Nat. Coun. for the Arts, 1984-90; lectr. in field. Author 650 books including: A Life of Yohanan ben Zakkai, 1962 (Abraham Berliner prize in Jewish History), A History of the Jews in Babylonia, 1965-70, Development of a Legend: Studies on the Traditions Concerning Yohanan ben Zakkai, 1970, Aphrahat and Judaism: The Christian-Jewish Argument in Fourth Century Iran, 1971, The Rabbinic Traditions about the Pharisees before 70, 1971, Eliezer ben Hyrcanus: The Tradition and the Man, 1973, The Idea of Purity in Ancient Judaism, 1973, A History of the Mishnaic Law of Purities, 1974-80, Judaism: The Evidence of the Mishnah, 1981, others; author numerous textbooks including American Judaism, Adventure in Modernity, 1972, From Politics to Piety: The Emergence of Pharisaic Judaism, 1973, 78, Invitation to the Talmud: A Teaching Book, 1974, Between Time and Eternity: The Essentials of Judaism, 1976, Form-Analysis and Exegeis: A Fresh Approach to the Interpretation of Mishnah, 1980; editor numerous books including Studies in Judaism in Late Antiquity, 1973—, Studies in Judaism in Modern Times, 1975—, Library of Judaic Learning, 1975—, Brown Judaic Studies, 1976-90, Chicago Studies in the History of Judaism, 1980-90; founder, editor-in-chief Brown Studies on Jews and Their Societies, 1985-90. Kent fellow Nat. Council for Religion in Higher Edn., 1957-60; Lown fellow, 1962-64; Guggenheim Found. fellow, 1973-74, 79-80; Am. Council Learned Socs. fellow, 1966-67, 70-71; research grantee Am. Philos. Soc., 1965, 67; recipient Univ. Medal for Excellence Columbia U., 1974, Von Humboldt prize Von Humboldt Found., 1981, Disting. Humanitarian award Ohio State U., 1983. Fellow Royal Asiatic Soc.; mem. Am. Acad. Religion (v.p., program chmn. 1967-68, pres. 1968-69, chmn. sect. on history of Judaism 1979-81, dir. 1981—), Soc. Bibl. Lit., Phi Beta Kappa. Home: 735 14th Ave NE Saint Petersburg FL 33701-1413 Office: U South Fla Dept Religious Studies Tampa FL 33620

NEUSTADT, BARBARA MAE, artist, illustrator, etcher; b. Davenport, Iowa, June 21, 1922; d. David and Cora (Wollensky) N.; children: Diane Elizabeth Walbridge Wheeler, Laurie Barbara Meyer Hall. B.A., Smith Coll., 1944; postgrad., U. Chgo., 1945-46; Art Student's League scholar, Ohio U. Sch. Fine Arts, 1952. Art dir., designer Shepherd Cards, Inc., N.Y.C., 1956-63; dir., instr. Studio Graphics Workshop, Woodstock, N.Y., 1970—; lectr. on printmaking; participant artist in schs. program N.Y. State Schs., 1972-74; Bd. dirs., editor bull. LWV of Woodstock, 1969-70. Illustrator: The First Christmas, 1960, A Dream of Love (by Joseph Langland), 1986 (exhibited in Sarasota, Fla., 1986, Ga. So. Coll., Statesboro, 1987), Nat. Mus. Women in the Arts, Washington, 1993-94, The Works of B. Neustadt from 1939-93, 1995; commd. etching edits to Collectors Am. Art, N.Y.C., 1956, 58, 61, Internat. Graphic Arts Soc., N.Y.C., 1960, N.Y. Hilton Art Collection, N.Y.C., 1961; one-man shows include Ruth White Gallery, N.Y.C., 1958, Phila. Art Alliance, 1959, Portland (Maine) Mus. Art, 1965, L.I. U., Bklyn., 1973, Smith Coll., Northampton, Mass., 1974, Manatee Art League, Bradenton, Fla., 1980, 91, Sarasota, Fla., 1985, 86, Unity Gallery, Sarasota, 1994; group shows include Mus. Modern Art, N.Y.C., 1958-59, Yale U. Art Gallery, New Haven, 1960, Soc. Am. Graphic Artists nat. and internat. exhbns., 1954, 55, 57, 59, 60, 61, 73, 75, 76, 78, L'Antipoete Galerie Librairie, Paris, 1961, Quito, Ecuador, S.Am., 1987, Fla. Printmakers, 1987, 88, So. Printmakers, U. of S. Ala., 1988, Springfest '89, Bradenton, Fla., 1989, Invitational Manatee Art League, Bradenton, 1992, 93, 94, Soc. Exptl. Artists, Longboat Key, juried 1992, juried Shreveport, La., 1993, Nat. Mus. Women Arts, Washington, 1993-94, Longboat Key Art Ctr., 1994; represented in permanent collections including Met. Mus. Art, N.Y.C., Library of Congress, Nat. Gallery Art, Washington, Phila. Mus. Art, USIA, Bonn, Germany, N.Y. Public Library N.Y.C., Rare Book Rm., William A. Neilson Libr., Smith Coll., Henderson Libr., Ga. So. Coll. Found., Statesboro, Ga., McFarlin Libr., Spl. Collections, U. of Tulsa, 1990, Ward Meml. Collection, Gilkey Ctr. for Graphic Arts, Portland (Oreg.) Art Mus., 1992, Nat. Mus. Women Arts, others. Recipient prize Boston Printmakers, 1957, Joseph Pennell Meml. medal Phila. Watercolor Club, 1972; Yasuo Kuniyoshi Meml. award, 1978; Am. the Beautiful Fund of N.Y. of Natural Area Council grantee, 1973. Mem. Soc. Am. Graphic Artists (prize 1954, 78), Phila. Water Color Club (prize 1972), Fla. Printmakers, The So. Graphics Coun., Art Uptown Inc. Gallery (Sarasota, Fla.), Gallery Two (Rockville, Md.). Studio: Pleiades Press/Studio Graphics 3014 Avenue C Holmes Beach FL 34217-2166

NEUSTADT, DAVID HAROLD, physician; b. Evansville, Ind., Dec. 2, 1925; s. Mose and Leah (Epstein) N.; m. Carolyn Jacobson, June 15, 1952; children: Susan Miriam, Jeffrey Bruce, Robert Alan. Student, DePauw U., 1943-44, 46-47; M.D., U. Louisville, 1950. Intern Morrisania City Hosp., N.Y.C., 1950-51; resident in internal medicine Lenox Hill Hosp., N.Y.C., 1951-52; NIH trainee in rheumatic diseases Lenox Hill Hosp., 1952-53, resident in gastroenterology, 1953-54; practice medicine specializing in rheumatic diseases Louisville, 1954—; chief arthritis clinic Louisville Gen. Hosp., 1960-76; asst. prof. medicine Sch. Medicine, U. Louisville, 1963-67, asso. prof. clin. medicine, 1967-75, clin. prof. medicine, 1974—, head sect. rheumatic diseases, 1960-76; chief dept. medicine Jewish Hosp., Louisville, 1965-67; pres. med. staff Jewish Hosp., 1967-69; cons. in rheumatology VA, 1970—; advisor Network for Continuing Med. Edn., 1983—. Author: The Chemistry and Therapy of Collagen Diseases, 1963, (with other) Aspiration and Injection Therapy in Arthritis and Musculoskeletal Disorders, 1972; editor: (with other) Arthritis Abstracts, References Indexes, 1970-75; contbr. articles to profl. jours. Former pres., chmn. bd. med. sci. com. Ky. chpt. Arthritis Found. Served with AUS, 1944-46. Master Am. Coll. Rheumatology (formerly Am. Rheumatism Assn.; mem. editl. bd. 1989-94, exec. com., pres. ctrl. region 1982-84); fellow Am. Med. Writers Assn., ACP; mem. AMA, N.Y. Acad. Sci., N.Y. Rheumatism Soc., Ky. Rheumatism Assn. (pres. 1956-57), Internat. Soc. Internal Medicine, So. Med. Assn. (edn. com., sect. rheumatology), Am. Physicians Fellowship (nat. trustee 1984—), Spondylitis Assn. (adv. bd. 1986—, contbg. editor 1989—, mem. editl. bd. Arthritis Care and Rsch. Newsletter 1989—), Mason, Shriner. Jewish. Home: 216 Smithfield Rd Louisville KY 40207-1267 Office: Med Towers Louisville KY 40202 *I believe the qualities necessary to achieve success include a combination of ability, commitment to hard work, enthusiasm or enjoyment of your work, plus a liberal chunk of optimism, faith, luck, and a supporting family and co-workers.*

NEUSTADT, RICHARD ELLIOTT, political scientist, educator; b. Phila., June 26, 1919; s. Richard Mitchells and Elizabeth (Neufeld) N.; m. Bertha Frances Cummings, Dec. 21, 1945 (Dec. 1984); children: Richard Mitchells (Dec. 1995), Elizabeth Ann; m. Shirley Williams, Dec. 19, 1987. AB, U. Calif., Berkeley, 1939; MA, Harvard U., 1941, PhD, 1951. Economist OPA, 1942; mem. staff Bur. Budget, 1946-50, White House, 1950-53; prof. pub. adminstrn. Cornell U., 1953-54; prof. govt. Columbia U., 1954-64; prof. govt. Harvard U., 1965-78, Lucius N. Littauer prof. pub. adminstrn., 1978-87, Douglas Dillon prof., 1987-89, assoc. dean John Fitzgerald Kennedy Sch. Govt., 1965-75, dir. Inst. Politics, 1966-71, prof. emeritus, 1989—; spl. cons. subcom. on nat. policy machinery U.S. Senate, 1959-61; mem. adv. bd. Commn. Money and Credit, 1960-61; spl. cons. to Pres. elect Kennedy, 1960-61; to subcom. on nat. security staffing and ops. U.S. Senate, 1962-68; cons. to Pres. Kennedy, 1961-63, Pres. Johnson, 1964-66, Dept. State, 1962-69, Bur. Budget, 1961-70, AEC, 1962-68, Rand Corp., 1964-79, Pres.'s Reorgn. Project, Office Mgmt. and Budget, 1977-79; chmn. adv. com. candidate selection Commn. Presdl. Debates, 1988, 92, 96; vis. lectr. Nuffield Coll., Oxford, Eng., 1961-62, assoc. mem., 1965-67, 90-92; vis. prof., Princeton U., 1957, U. Calif., Berkeley, 1986, Cornell U., 1992, U. Essex, UK, 1994-96. Author: Presidential Power, 1960, rev., 1990, Alliance Politics, 1970; (with Harvey V. Fineberg) The Swine Flu Affair, 1978, reissued as The Epidemic That Never Was, 1983; (with Ernest R. May) Thinking in Time, 1986; contbr. articles to mags., revs. Mem. staff Dem. Platform Com., 1952, 56, chmn., 1972; trustee Radcliffe Coll., 1976-80; mem. exec. bd. Coll. Letters & Scis., U. Calif., Berkeley, 1994-97. With USNR, 1942-46. Fellow Ctr. Advanced Study in the Behavioral Scis., 1978-79. Fellow Am. Acad. Arts Scis; mem. Am. Polit. Sci. Assn., Nat. Acad. Pub. Adminstrn., Council Fgn. Rels., Inst. Strategic Studies, Am. Philos. Soc., Cosmos Club. Office: Harvard U Kennedy Sch Govt 79 Jfk St Cambridge MA 02138-5801

NEUTRA, DION, architect; b. Los Angeles, Oct. 8, 1926; s. Richard Joseph and Dione (Niedermann) N.; children: Gregory, Wendy, Haig, Nicholas. Student, Swiss Inst. Tech., 1947-48; B.Arch. cum laude, U. So. Calif., 1950. With Richard J. Neutra (architect), Los Angeles, 1942-55; assoc. Neutra & Alexander, Los Angeles, 1955-60; asso. Robert E. Alexander, Los Angeles, 1960-62; prin. Richard & Dion Neutra, Architects and Assos., Los Angeles, 1962—; pres. Richard J. Neutra, Inc., 1970—; exec. con. Inst. for Survival Through Design, L.A.; lectr. Calif. State U., L.A., Sacramento City Coll., Mira Costa State U., Cabrillo State U., Soka U., Tokyo, San Diego City Coll., Germany, Switzerland, Eng., Austria; vis. prof. Calif. State U.-Pomona, 1970, 85-86; vis. lectr. U. So. Calif. prin. works include various residential, ednl., religious and instnl. facilities including Am. Embassy Karachi, Pakistan, Gettysburg Meml., Simpson Coll. Libr., Adelphi Coll. Libr., Libr. and Resource Ctr. for City of Huntington Beach, Calif., Treetops Townhouses, 1980; exhbns. "View from Inside", 1984, 86, 92, "Visions & Exiles", Vienna, 1995. Mem. Silver Lake-Echo Park Dist. Plan Adv. Com., Master Plan City of Los Angeles, 1970-71; mem. Citizens to Save Silver Lake, 1973-76; dir. Child Care and Devel. Services, 1970-71, Preservation and Maintenance of Existing Neutra Projects. Served with USNR, 1944-46. Street named Neutra Pl. in firm's honor, Silverlake, 1992; Neutra Centennial, 1992. Mem. AIA, Nat. Council Archtl. Registration Bds., Alpha Rho Chi. Studio: Richard & Dion Neutra 2440 Neutra Pl Los Angeles CA 90039-3141

NEUWIRTH, ALAN JAMES, lawyer; b. N.Y.C., July 4, 1943; s. Bernard and Audrey (Hattenbach) N.; m. Patricia E. Neuwirth, Sept. 4, 1966; children: John A., Daniel P. BA, Lehigh U., 1965; JD, NYU, 1969. Bar: N.Y. 1970, U.S. Dist. Ct. (so. and ea. dists.) N.Y. 1972, U.S. Ct. Appeals (2d cir.) 1972, U.S. Ct. Internat. Trade 1983, U.S. Ct. Appeals (Fed. cir.) 1984, U.S. Supreme Ct. 1988. Assoc. Miller & Summit, N.Y.C., 1970-72, Ratheim, Hoffman, Kassel & Silverman, N.Y.C., 1973-75; ptnr. Kassel, Neuwirth & Geiger, N.Y.C., 1976-86, Webster & Sheffield, N.Y.C., 1987-90; sr. ptnr. Morgan, Lewis & Bockius, N.Y.C., 1990—; bd. dirs. various cos. With U.S. Army, 1969-74, USAR. Mem. ABA, Assn. of Bar of City of N.Y., N.Y. County Lawyers Assn., Internat. Trade Commn., Trial Lawyers Assn. Office: Morgan Lewis & Bockius 101 Park Ave New York NY 10178

NEUWIRTH, ALLAN CHARLES, designer, director, screenwriter; b. N.Y.C., Jan. 21; s. David Osias and Bella Jenta (Gajzt) N. BFA, Pratt Inst., 1977. Designer, dir. Studios of Diamond & Diaferia, N.Y.C., 1979-84; producer Klassy Prodns., N.Y.C., 1984-92, Neuwirth Design, N.Y.C., 1992—; freelance comedy writer N.Y.C., 1984—; ptnr. Two Idioms, 1995—; poster designer, The Phoenix Theater, N.Y.C., 1983-84; dir. various stage prodns., N.Y.C., 1985. TV logo and title designer World Series, 1979, ABC News Nightline, 1980, ABC News This Week, 1982, ABC News Closeup, 1983; art dir. (TV shows) Mother's Day, 1983-88, Mother's Minutes, 1984-89; animator (home video) Your Newborn Baby, 1985; effects animator: (films) Sgt. Kabukiman, NYPD, 1990, King's Ransom, 1991; illustrator: (book) Where in America is Carmen Sandiego, 1992; co-author: (screen story) Haunted Hacienda, 1995, (TV series) The Wubbulous World of Dr. Seuss, 1996-97, (cartoon series) Koki, 1996—; co-developer: (TV series) Big Bag, 1996, assoc. animation prodr., story editor, 1997—. Avocations: collecting vintage animation and cartoon art.

NEUWIRTH, BEBE, dancer, actress; b. Newark, Dec. 31; d. Lee Paul and Sydney Anne Neuwirth. Student, Juilliard Sch., 1976-77. Appeared on Broadway and internationally as Sheila in A Chorus Line, 1978-81; other stage appearances include West Side Story, 1981, (on Broadway) Little Me, 1982, Upstairs at O'Neal's, 1982-83, The Road to Hollywood, 1984, Just So, 1985, (on Broadway) Sweet Charity, 1985-87 (Tony award for Best Supporting Actress in a Musical 1985-86), Waiting in the Wings: The Night the Understudies Take the Stage, 1986, Showing Off, 1989, Chicago, 1992 (L.A. Drama Critics Circle award), Kiss of the Spider Woman (London), 1993, (on Broadway) Damn Yankees, 1994, Pal Joey, 1995, Chicago, 1996 (Tony award for Best Leading Actress in a Musical, 1997); prin. dancer on Broadway Dancin', 1982; leading dance role Kicks, 1984; TV series Cheers, 1984-93 (Emmy award for Best Supporting Actress in a Comedy Series 1990, 91); TV guest appearances Frasier, 1994, Aladdin, 1994; TV movies Without Her Consent, 1990, Unspeakable Acts, 1990, Wild Palms, 1993; films Say Anything, 1989, Green Card, 1990, Bugsy, 1991, Painted Heart, 1992, Malice, 1993, Jumanji, 1994, Pinocchio, 1995. Vol. performances for March of Dimes Telethon, 1986, Cystic Fibrosis Benefit Children's Ball, 1986, Ensemble Studio Theater Benefit, 1986, Circle Repertory Co. Benefit, 1986, all in N.Y.C. Recipient Tony award Leading Actress in a Musical, 1997. Democrat. Office: Internat Creative Mgmt 8942 Wilshire Blvd Beverly Hills CA 90211-1934 Also: Internat Creative Mgmt 40 W 57th St New York NY 10019-4001*

NEUWIRTH, JESSICA ANNE, lawyer; b. N.Y.C., Dec. 10, 1961; d. Robert Samuel and Gloria (Salob) N. BA, Yale U., 1982; JD, Harvard U., 1985. Bar: Mass. 1986, N.Y. 1987. Policy advisor Amnesty Internat., N.Y.C., 1985-90; assoc. Cleary, Gottlieb, Steen & Hamilton, N.Y.C., 1990-93, Kridel & Neuwirth, N.Y.C., 1993-94; exec. dir., pres. Equality Now, N.Y.C., 1992-94; legal officer UN, 1994-96. Mem. nat. adv. com. Physicians for Human Rights, Boston, 1986—. Mem. Assn. Bar City N.Y. (mem. com. on sex and law 1992-95, mem. com. on internat. human rights 1988-91).

NEUWIRTH, ROBERT SAMUEL, obstetrician, gynecologist; b. N.Y.C., July 11, 1933; s. Abraham Alexander and Phyllis Neuwirth; children from previous marriage: Susan, Jessica, Laura, Michael, Alexander. BS, Yale U., 1954, MD, 1958. Intern Presbyn. Hosp., N.Y.C., 1958-59, resident, 1959-64; asst. prof. ob-gyn. Columbia U., 1964-68, assoc. prof., 1968-71, prof., 1972—, Babcock prof., 1977—; dir. ob-gyn. Bronx Lebanon Hosp., N.Y.C., 1967-72, Woman's Hosp., N.Y.C., St. Luke's Hosp. Ctr., 1974—; prof. Albert Einstein Coll. Medicine, 1971-72; cons. WHO, NIH, AID, FDA. Author: Hysteroscopy, 1975; contbr. articles to profl. jours. Mem. Am. Coll. Obstetricians and Gynecologists, Soc. Gynecologic Investigation, N.Y. Obstet. Soc., Am. Assn. Profs. Ob-Gyn., Assn. Vol. Sterilization (chmn. biomed. com. 1971—). Office: 425 W 59th St Fl 5 New York NY 10019-1128

NEVA, FRANKLIN ALLEN, physician, educator; b. Cloquet, Minn., June 8, 1922; s. Lauri Albin and Anna (Lahti) N.; m. Alice Hanson, July 5, 1947; children: Karen, Kristin, Erik. SB, U. Minn., 1944, MD, 1946; AM (hon.), Harvard U., 1964. Diplomate Am. Bd. Internal Medicine. Intern Harvard Med. Services, Boston City Hosp., 1946-47, resident, 1949-50; research fellow Harvard Med. Sch., 1950-53; asst. prof. U. Pitts. Med. Sch., 1953-55; mem. faculty Harvard Sch. Pub. Health, 1955-69, John LaPorte Given prof. tropical pub. health, 1964-69; chief Lab. Parasitic Diseases Inst. Allergy and Infectious Diseases, NIH, 1969-95, acting sci. dir., 1994-95; mem. commn. parasitic diseases, assoc. mem. commn. virus infections Armed Forces Epidemiol. Bd., 1963-68; mem. Latin Am. sci. bd. Nat. Acad. Scis.-NRC, 1963-68; bd. sci. counselors Inst. Allergy and Infectious Diseases, NIH, 1966-69. Served to lt. (j.G.) USNR, 1947-49. Mem. Soc. Exptl. Biology and Medicine, Infectious Diseases Soc. Am. (Joseph Smadel lectr. 1985), Am. Soc. Tropical Medicine and Hygiene (Bailey K. Ashford award 1965, Craig lectr. 1986, Ben Kean award 1995), Assn. Am. Physicians (Presdl. Meritorious Exec. Rank award 1985). Achievements include special research infectious diseases especially tropical, parasitic and virus infections. Home: 10851 Glen Rd Potomac MD 20854-1401 Office: NIH Inst Allergy & Infectious Diseases Bethesda MD 20892

NEVANS-PALMER, LAUREL SUZANNE, rehabilitation counselor; b. N.Y.C., Aug. 1, 1964; d. Roy N. and Virginia (Place) Nevans; m. Russell Baird Palmer III, Oct. 12, 1991. BA in English, Secondary Edn. cum laude, U. Richmond, 1986, postgrad., 1989-92; MA in Edn. and Human Devel., George Washington U., 1991, cert. in job devel. and placement, 1992. Group leader S.E. Consortium for Spl. Svcs., Larchmont, N.Y., 1980-85; vocat. instr. Assn. for Retarded Citizens Montgomery County, Rockville, Md., 1986-89; edn. specialist George Washington U. Out of Sch. Work Experience Program, Washington, 1989-90; rsch. asst. George Washington U. Dept. Tchr. Prep. & Spl. Edn., Washington, 1989-91; employability skills tchr., rsch. intern Nat. Rehab. Hosp. Rehab. Engring. Dept., Washington, 1991; vocat./ind. living skills specialist The Independence Ctr., Rockville, Md., 1991-93; leadership team mgr. Career Choice project The Endependence Ctr. of No. Va., Arlington, 1993-94; program dir. United Cerebral Palsy of D.C. and No. Va., Washington, 1994-97; sr. assistive tech. specialist Tech., Automation & Mgmt., Inc., Greenbelt, Md., 1997—; teaching asst. Rehab. Counseling Program, George Washington U., 1991. Recipient traineeship GWU Counseling Dept., 1990, 91. Mem. Nat. Rehab. Assn., Nat. Rehab. Counselors Assn., D.C. Met. Area Assn. Person's in Supported Employment (editor newsletter 1995—), Nat. Career Devel. Assn., Nat. Employment Counseling Assn., Nat. Assn. Ind. Living, Am. Assn. Counseling and Devel., Am. Rehab. Counseling Assn. Democrat. Avocations: writing, photography, music, travel, jewelry making. Home: 611 Woodside Pky Silver Spring MD 20910 Office: TEAM Inc 6411 Ivy Ln Ste 502 Greenbelt MD 20770-1405

NEVELOFF, JAY A., lawyer; b. Bklyn., Oct. 11, 1950; s. Cydelle (Weber) Elrich; m. Arlene Sillman, Aug. 26, 1972; children: David, Kevin. BA, Bklyn. Coll., 1971; JD, NYU, 1974. Bar: N.Y. 1975, D.C. 1992, U.S. Dist. Ct. (so. and ea. dists.) N.Y. 1975, U.S. Ct. Appeals (2d cir.) 1975, U.S. Supreme Ct. 1982. Assoc. Marshall, Bratter, Greene, Allison & Tucker, N.Y.C., 1974-82; assoc. Rosenman, Colin, Freund, Lewis & Cohen, N.Y.C., 1982-83, ptnr., 1983-88; ptnr. Kramer, Levin, Naftalis, Nessen, Kamin & Frankel, N.Y.C., 1988—. Editor N.Y. Real Property Service. Mem. planning bd. Briarcliff Manor, 1995—. Mem. ABA (vice chmn. com. partnerships, joint ventures and other investment vehicles 1988-95), Am. Law Inst., Am. Coll. Real Estate Attys., N.Y. State Bar Assn. (financing com.), Practising Law Inst. (lectr. 1988—, mem. adv. bd. 1991—), N.Y. County Lawyers Assn. (lectr. 1984—), Assn. of Bar of City of N.Y. (real property law com., chmn. condominium resale contract com., lectr. 1984-88), Cmty. Assns. Inst. (lectr. 1986), Law Jours. Seminars (lectr. 1987—), Strategic Resources Inst. (lectr. 1994—), Internat. Health Network Soc. (vice chmn. 1995—). Home: 134 Alder Dr Briarcliff Manor NY 10510-2218 Office: Kramer Levin Naftalis & Frankel 919 3rd Ave New York NY 10022

NEVES, KERRY LANE, lawyer; b. San Angelo, Tex., Dec. 19, 1950; s. Herman Walter and Geraldine (Ball) N.; m. Sharon Lynn Briggs, July 28, 1973; 1 child, Erin Lesli. BBA, U. Tex., 1975, JD, 1978. Bar: Tex. 1978, U.S. Dist. Ct. (so. and ea. dists.) Tex. 1979, U.S. Ct. Appeals (5th cir.) 1979, U.S. Dist. Ct. (we. dist.) 1980; cert. personal injury trial law, Tex. Bd. Legal Specialization, 1994. Ptnr. Mills, Shirley, Eckel & Bassett, Galveston, Tex., 1978-93, Neves & Crowther, Galveston, Tex., 1993—. Vice-chmn. Bldg. Stnds. Commn., Dickinson, Tex., 1991—. Sgt. USMC, 1969-72. Fellow Tex. Bar Found. (life); mem. ABA, State Bar Tex. (grievance com. 1989-92, disciplinary rules profl. conduct com. 1990-92, dir. dist. 5 1997—), Galveston County Bar Assn. (pres. 1989-90), U. Tex. Law Alumni Assn. (pres. 1991-92). Avocations: gardening, bicycling, wine, books. Home: RR 2 Box 95 Dickinson TX 77539-9204 Office: Neves & Crowther 1802 Broadway St Ste 206 Galveston TX 77550-4953

NEVEU, JEAN, printing company executive. Chmn., CEO, Quebecor Printing Inc., Montreal, Que., Can. Office: Quebecor Printing Inc, 612 Saint-Jacques St, Montreal, PQ Canada H3C 4M8

NEVIASER, ROBERT JON, orthopaedic surgeon, educator; b. Washington, Nov. 21, 1936; s. Julius Salem and Jane Frances (Gibbons) N.; m. Anne Maclean Shedden, Dec. 3, 1966; children: Jeanne Nicole, Robert Jon Jr., Ian Maclean, Andrew Shedden. Grad., Phillips Acad., Andover, Mass., 1954; AB, Princeton U., 1958; MD, Jefferson Med. Coll., 1962. Diplomate Am. Bd. Orthop. Surgery with cert. of added qualification in surgery of hand. Intern N.Y. Hosp., Cornell Med. Ctr., N.Y.C., 1962-63, asst. resident, 1963-64; asst. resident in orthopaedic surgery N.Y. Orthop. Hosp., Columbia-Presbyn. Med. Ctr., N.Y.C., 1964-66, jr. Annie C. Kane fellow, resident, 1966-67; fellow in surgery of the hand Orthop. Hosp., L.A., 1969-70; asst. prof. divsn. orthop. and hand surgery, chmn. dept. U. Conn., Hartford, 1970-71; assoc. prof. orthop. surgery George Washington U., Washington, 1971-76, prof., 1976—, dir. orthop. edn., assoc. chmn. dept. orthop. surgery, 1984-87, chmn. dept. orthop. surgery, 1987—; chmn. governing bd. Med. Faculty Assocs. George Washington U. Med. Ctr., 1995—. Contbr. articles in field to profl. jours. Lt. comdr. USNR, 1967-69. Fellow Am. Soc. Surgery of the Hand, Am. Acad. Orthop. Surgeons, Ea. Orthop. Assn., Am. Shoulder and Elbow Surgeons, Am. Orthop. Assn.; mem. Alpha Kappa Kappa. Republican. Clubs: Princeton (N.Y. and Washington); Darnestown Swim and Racquet, Cosmos. Office: 2150 Pennsylvania Ave NW Washington DC 20037-3201

NEVILL, WILLIAM ALBERT, chemistry educator; b. Indpls., Jan. 1, 1929; s. Irwin Lowell and Mary Marie (Barker) N.; m. Nancy Neiman Roll, May 19, 1979; children: Paul David, John Michael, Steven Joseph, Anne Marie, Deborah Ruth. BS magna cum laude, Butler U., 1951; PhD, Calif. Inst. Tech., 1954. Research chemist Proctor-Gamble, Cin., 1954; prof. chemistry, chmn. dept. Grinnell Coll., 1956-67; prof. chemistry Ind. U.-Purdue U., Indpls., 1967-83, chmn. dept., 1967-72; dean Sch. Sci. Ind. U.-Purdue U., 1972-79, dir. grad. studies, 1979-83; pres. B&N Cons. Co., 1972-93; vice chancellor acad. affairs La. State U., Shreveport, 1983-85; prof. La. State U., 1983-94; pres. Catoctin Assocs., 1993—; arbitrator, mediator Ind. Employment Rels. Bd., 1975-83. Author: General Chemistry, 1967, Experiments in General Chemistry, 1968. Bd. dirs. Indpls. Sci. and Engring. Found., 1972-75, 79-82, Westminster Found., Lafayette, Ind., 1972-74, Am. Chem. Soc., 1986-92. With U.S. Army, 1954-56; col. USAR, 1956-84. Grantee NSF, 1959-74; Grantee NIH, 1963-70; Grantee Office Naval Research, 1953. Mem. Ind. Acad. Sci., Am. Chem. Soc. (chmn. sect. 1972, counselor 1973-92). Presbyterian. Home: 2229 Greenpark Dr Richardson TX 75082-4219

NEVILLE, AARON, musician; m. Joel; 1 d., Ernestine; 3 s., Aaron, Jr., Ivan, Jason. Singer (singles): Over You, 1959, Tell It Like It Is, 1966, 91; (albums): Orchid in the Storm, 1990, The Classic: My Greatest Gift, 1990, Warm Your Heart, 1991, The Grand Tour, 1993, Aaron Neville's Soulful Christmas, 1993; singles (with Linda Ronstadt) Don't Know Much, 1990 (Grammy award), All My Life, 1990, albums (with Neville Brothers) The Neville Brothers, 1978, Fiyo On the Bayou, 1980, Neville-ization, 1984, Uptown, 1987, Treacherous: A History of the Neville Brothers, 1987, Yellow Moon, 1989, Brother's Keeper, 1990, Treacherous Too, 1991, Family Groove, 1992, Live on Planet Earth, 1994. Recipient Down Beat Blues, Soul, R&B Group award, 1990; 2 Grammy nominations, 1994. Office: care A&M Records Inc 1416 N La Brea Ave Los Angeles CA 90028-7506*

NEVILLE, ART, musician. Albums include: Mardi Gras Rock 'N' Roll, 1987, (with Neville Brothers) The Neville Brothers, 1979, Treacherous: A History of the Neville Brothers, 1987, Brother's Keeper, 1990, Fiyo On the Bayou, 1980, Neville-ization, 1984, Uptown, 1987, Yellow Moon, 1989, Treacherous Too, 1991, Family Groove, 1992, Live on Planet Earth, 1994; (with The Meters) Sophisticated Sissy, 1968, Sissy Strut, Look-Ka Py Py, Chicken Strut, Cabbage Alley, also backup for many groups until 1980's. Recipient Down Beat Blues, Soul, R&B Group award, 1990. Office: care A & M Records Inc 1416 N La Brea Ave Los Angeles CA 90028-7506*

NEVILLE, CHARLES, musician. Albums include: (with Neville Brothers) The Neville Brothers, 1979, Fiyo on the Bayou, 1980, Neville-ization, 1984, Uptown, 1987, Treacherous: A History of the Neville Brothers, 1987, Yellow Moon, 1989, Brother's Keeper, 1990, Treacherous Too, 1991, Family Groove, 1992, Live on Planet Earth, 1994. Recipient Down Beat Blues, Soul, R&B Group award, 1990. Office: care A & M Records Inc 1416 N La Brea Ave Los Angeles CA 90028-7506*

NEVILLE, CYRIL, musician. Albums include: (with Neville Brothers) The Neville Brothers, 1979, Fiyo on the Bayou, 1980, Neville-ization, 1984, Uptown, 1987, Treacherous: A History of the Neville Brothers, 1987, Yellow Moon, 1989, Brother's Keeper, 1990, Treacherous Too, 1991, Family Groove, 1992, Live on Planet Earth, 1994. Recipient Down Beat Blues, Soul, R&B Group award, 1990. Office: care A & M Records Inc 1416 N La Brea Ave Los Angeles CA 90028-7506*

NEVILLE, ELISABETH, computer applications specialist; b. Winchester, Mass., Dec. 5, 1967; d. Joseph and Elinor (Lindsey) N. BA in Graphic Design, Northeastern U., 1993. Adminstr. art room Mercer Photography, Danvers, Mass., 1985-92; photograph restorer Take Two, Arlington, Mass., 1991-94; prodn. artist Ligature Inc., Boston, 1993-94; computer applications specialist Scitex Am. Corp., Bedford, Mass., 1994-96; editl. installations specialist Atex Media Solutions, Bedford, Mass., 1996—. Active Big Sister Assn., 1993-94. Mem. NAFE, Northeastern U. Alumni Assn., Shore Country Day Sch. Alumni Assn., Lawrence Acad. Alumni Assn. Mem. United Ch. of Christ. Avocations: painting, mountain biking, weights, reading. Home: 6 Stafford Rd Danvers MA 01923

NEVILLE, EMILY CHENEY, author; b. Manchester, Conn., Dec. 28, 1919; d. Howell and Anne (Bunce) Cheney; m. Glenn Neville; children—Emily Tam, Glenn H.H., Dessie, Marcy, Alec. A.B., Bryn Mawr Coll., 1940; J.D., Albany Law Sch., 1976. Bar: N.Y. bar 1977. Feature writer N.Y. Mirror, 1941-42. Author books including: Seventeen Street Gang, 1966, Traveler from a Small Kingdom, 1968, Fogarty, 1969, Garden of Broken Glass, 1975, The Bridge, 1988, The China Year, 1991. Recipient Newbery award for It's Like This Cat 1964, Jane Addams award for Berries Goodman 1966. Address: PO 22 Market St Keene Valley NY 12943

NEVILLE, GWEN KENNEDY, anthropology educator; b. Taylor, Tex., Mar. 23, 1938; d. Matthew Ranken and Gwendolyn (Harrison) Kennedy; m. William Gordon Neville (div.); children: Katherine, Mary Grace, William Kennedy; m. Jack Gregory Hunnicutt, Jr., 1975. BA, Mary Baldwin Coll., Staunton, Va., 1959; MA, U. Fla., 1968, PhD, 1971. Asst. prof. Emory U., Atlanta, 1971-78, assoc. prof., 1978-79; assoc. prof. Southwestern U., Georgetown, Tex., 1979-84, prof. anthropology, 1984—, Elizabeth Root Paden chairholder, 1979—; cons. Wenner-Gren Conf., Mt. Kisco, N.Y., 1983; grant holder NEH, Washington, 1972, 89; researcher, writer Lilly Endowment, Indpls., 1988—; bd. dirs. Soc. for Anthropology of Europe, 1988—. Author: Kinship and Pilgrimage, 1987, The Mother Town, 1995; co-author: Generation to Generation, 1973, Learning Through Liturgy, 1978; contbr. articles to profl. jours. Fellow Am. Anthropol. Assn.; mem. Am. Ethnological Soc., Am. Folklore Soc., Soc. for Anthropology of Europe (bd. dirs. 1989-92), Assn. for Scottish Ethnography, Coun. on Anthropology and Edn. (bd. dirs. 1971-74), So. Anthropol. Soc. (editor 1974-77). Methodist. Office: Southwestern Univ University Ave at Maple St Dept Anthropolgy Georgetown TX 78626

NEVILLE, JAMES MORTON, food company executive, lawyer; b. Mpls., May 28, 1939; s. Philip and Maurene (Morton) N.; m. Judie Martha Proctor, Sept. 9, 1961; children: Stephen Warren, Martha Maurene. BA, U. Minn., JD magna cum laude, 1964. Bar: Minn. 1964, Mo. 1984. Assoc. firm Neville, Johnson & Thompson, Mpls., 1964-69, ptnr., 1969-70; assoc. counsel Gen. Mills, Inc., Mpls., 1970-77, sr. assoc. counsel, 1977-83, corp. sec., 1976-83; v.p., sec., asst. gen. counsel Ralston Purina Co., St. Louis, 1983-84, v.p., gen. counsel, sec., 1984—; lectr. bus. law. U. Minn., 1967-71. Named Man of Yr. Edina Jaycees, 1967. Mem. ABA, Minn., Mo. Bar Assns., U.S. Supreme Ct. Bar Assn., Hennepin County Bar Assn., St. Louis Bar Assn., U. Minn. Law Sch. Alumni Assn., Am. Soc. Corp. Secs., Old Warson Country Club, Ladue Racquet Club, Noonday Club, Order of Coif, Phi Delta Phi, Psi Upsilon. Episcopalian. Home: 9810 Log Cabin Ct Saint Louis MO 63124-1133 Office: Ralston Purina Co Checkerboard Sq Saint Louis MO 63164-0002

NEVILLE, MARGARET COBB, physiologist, educator; b. Greenville, S.C., Nov. 4, 1934; d. Henry Van Zandt and Florence Ruth (Crozier) Cobb; m. Hans E. Neville, Dec. 27, 1957; children: Michel Paul, Brian Douglas. BA, Pomona Coll., 1956; PhD, U. Pa., 1962. Asst. prof. physiology U. Colo. Med. Sch., Denver, 1968-75, assoc. prof., 1975-82, prof., 1982—, dir. med. scientist tng. program, 1985-94. Editor: Lactation: Physiology, Nutrition, Breast Feeding, 1983 (Am. Pubs. award 1984), Human Lactation I, 1985, The Mammary Gland, 1987, Jour. Mammary Gland Biology and Neoplasia, 1995—; contbr. numerous articles to profl. jours. Recipient Rsch. Career Devel. award NIH, 1975, NIH merit award, 1993. Mem. AAAS, Am. Physiol. Soc., Am. Soc. Cell Biology, Internat. Soc. Rsch. in Human Milk and Lactation, Phi Beta Kappa. Office: U Colo Dept Physiology PO Box C240 Denver CO 80262

NEVILLE, PHOEBE, choreographer, dancer, educator; b. Swarthmore, Pa., Sept. 28, 1941; d. Kennith R. and Marion (Eberbach) Balsley; m. Philip Corner, Nov. 3, 1996. Student, Wilson Coll., 1959-61. Cert. practitioner body-mind centering; registered movement therapist. Instr. Bennington (Vt.) Coll., 1981-84, 87-88; vis. lectr. UCLA, 1984-86. Dancer, choreographer Judson Meml. Ch., N.Y.C., 1966-70, Dance Uptown Series, N.Y.C., 1969, Cubiculo Theatre, N.Y.C., 1972-75, Delacorte Dance Festival, N.Y.C., 1976, Dance Umbrella Series, N.Y.C., 1977, Riverside Dance Festival, N.Y.C., 1976, 78, N.Y. Seasons, 1979—; dancer, artistic dir. Phoebe Neville Dance Co., N.Y.C., 1975—, Jacob's Pillow Splash! Festival, 1988, Dance Theater Workshop Winter Events, 1988; performances with Philip Corner: Venice, Genoa, San Michele and Adige, 1996, BBB Festival, Thailand, Genoa, Salso and Maggiore Terme. Recipient Creative Artist Public Svc. award, 1975; Nat. Endowment for Arts fellow, 1975, 79, 80, 85-87, 92-94, Choreographic fellow N.Y. Found. for Arts, 1989. Mem. Laban Inst. Movement Studies, Dance Theater Workshop, Body-Mind Centering Assn. (cert. practitioner and tchr.), Internat. Movement Therapy Assn. (registered), Internat. Assn. Healthcare Practitioners. Buddhist. Club: Recluse.

NEVILLE, ROY GERALD, scientist, chemical management and environmental consultant; b. Bournemouth, Dorsetshire, Eng., Oct. 15, 1926; came to U.S., 1951, naturalized, 1957; s. Percy Herbert and Georgina Lallie (Jenkins) N.; m. Jeanne Frances Russ, July 26, 1952; children: Laura Jean, Janet Marilyn. BSc with honors, U. London, 1951; MSc, U. Oreg., 1952, PhD, 1954; FRIC, Royal Inst. Chemistry, London, 1963, DSc (hon.), 1973. Research chemist Monsanto Chem. co., Seattle, 1955-57; sr. chem. engr. Boeing Co., Seattle, 1957-58; sr. research scientist Lockheed Missiles & Space Co., Palo Alto, Calif., 1958-61; sr. staff scientist Aerospace Corp., El Segundo, Calif., 1961-63; prin. scientist Rockwell Internat. Corp., Los Angeles, 1963-67; head dept. materials Scis. Lab., Boeing Sci. Research Labs. Boeing Co., Seattle, 1967-69; sr. environ. engring. specialist Bechtel Corp., San Francisco, 1969-73; pres. Engring. & Tech. Cons., Inc., Redwood City, Calif., 1973—. Contbr. numerous sci. articles on inorganic and organic synthesis, thermally stable polymers, pollution control processes to profl. jours. and books; many U.S. and fgn. patents in field. Fulbright scholar to U.S., 1951; USPHS fellowship, 1951-52, Research Corp. fellow, 1952-54; chartered chemist, London. Fellow Royal Soc. Chemistry (London), Am. Inst. Chemists, AAAS; mem. Am. Chem. Soc., Am. Inst. Chem. Engrs., History Sci. Soc., Soc. Study Early Chemistry, Royal Instn. Great Britain, Research Soc. Am., Soc. Mining Engrs. of AIME, Calif. Mining Assn., Sigma Xi. Office: ETC Inc 1068 Eden Bower Ln Redwood City CA 94061-1806

NEVILLE, THOMAS LEE, food service company executive; b. Columbus, Ind., Jan. 1, 1947; s. Frank Thomas and Esquline Coons (Davis) N.; m. Shavona Rose Lagneau, Aug. 10, 1966; children: Timothy David, Sherry Lynn. AAS, Austin Peay State U., Clarksville, Tenn., 1994. Cert. exec. chef. Enlisted U.S. Army, 1966, apptd. WO1, 1976, commd. CW3, 1986; food advisor Army Food Rsch., Devel. and Engring. Ctr., Natick, Mass.; ret. U.S. Army, 1990; regional mgr. KCA Corp., Hopkinsville, Ky., 1990—; mem. Warrant Officers Assn., 1976-90. Mem. Ret. Officers Assn., Am. Soc. Quality Control, Am. Culinary Fedn., Am. Mgmt. Assn., Masons. Home: 1728 Clara Ct Clarksville TN 37040-7823 Office: KCA Corp PO Box 641 Hopkinsville KY 42241-0641

NEVIN, CROCKER, investment banker; b. Tulsa, Mar. 14, 1923; s. Ethelbert Paul and Jennie Crocker (Fassett) N.; m. Mary Elizabeth Sherwin, Apr. 24, 1952 (div. 1984); children: Anne, Paul, Elizabeth, Crocker; m. Marilyn Elizabeth English, Nov. 3, 1984; 1 child, Jennie Fassett. Grad. with high honors, St. Paul's Sch., 1942; A.B. with high honors, Princeton U., 1946. With Vick Chem. Co., 1949-50, John Roberts Powers Cosmetic Co., 1950-52; with Marine Midland Grace Trust Co. of N.Y., 1952—, exec. v.p., 1964-66, pres., 1966-70, chmn. bd., chief exec. officer, 1968-73; also dir.; vice chmn. bd. Evans Products Co., N.Y.C., 1974-76, Drexel Burnam Lambert Co., investment bankers, N.Y.C., 1976-88; chmn. bd., chief exec. officer CF & I Steel Corp., Pueblo, Colo., 1985-93; dir. Magnatek, Inc. Chmn. exec. com. ACCION Internat. Lt. (j.g.) AC USN, 1942-46. Mem. Riverside Yacht Club, N.Y. Yacht Club (N.Y.C.), Blind Brook Club. Home: 20 Hope Farm Rd Greenwich CT 06830-3331

NEVIN, JOHN ROBERT, business educator, consultant; b. Joliet, Ill., Jan. 27, 1943; s. Robert Charles and Rita Alice (Roder) N.; m. Jeanne M. Conroy, June 10, 1967; children: Erin, Michael. BS, So. Ill. U., 1965; MS, U. Ill., 1968, PhD, 1972. Asst. prof. bus. U. Wis., Madison, 1970-77, assoc. prof. bus., 1977-83, prof. bus., 1983—, Wis. disting. prof. bus., 1988-89, Grainger Wis. disting. prof. bus., 1989—, dir. Grainger Ctr. for Distbn. Mgmt., 1992—; mem. editorial bd. Jour. of Mktg. Channels, The Haworth Press, Inc., 1991—; mem. investment adv. com. Venture Investors of Wis., Inc., Madison, 1986—. Author: International Marketing: An Annotated Bibliography, 1983; contbr. articles to profl. jours. Bd. dirs. Madison Civic Ctr., 1983—. Mem. Am. Mktg. Assn. (bd. dirs. PhD consortium 1979, editorial bd. Jour. of Mktg. Chgo. chpt. 1983—), Am. Coun. on Consumer Interests, Assn. for Consumer Rsch. Avocations: golf, skiing, running. Home: 7514 Red Fox Trl Madison WI 53717-1860 Office: U Wis 975 University Ave Madison WI 53706-1324

NEVIN, JOSEPH FRANCIS, computer systems engineer; b. Washington, Mar. 20, 1947; s. John Joseph and Mary Frances (O'Donnell) N.; m. Kathleen Cecelia Ridgell, Mar. 16, 1991; children: Christopher, Andrew, Amy, Megan. BA, Georgetown U., 1969; MS, Am. U., 1977. Chief of systems devel. USPHS, Bethesda, Md., 1980—; historian Smithsonian Assocs., Washington, 1982—. Pres. Balt. and Ohio RR Hist. Soc., 1982-83, 94—, v.p., 1984-94. Recipient Adminstrs. award Health Resources and Svcs., 1983; Pub. Health Spl. Recognition award USPHS, 1984. Avocations: railroad and transportation history. Office: Balt and Ohio RR Hist Soc 5600 Fishers Ln Rockville MD 20857-0001

NEVIN, ROBERT CHARLES, information systems executive; b. Dayton, Ohio, Nov. 4, 1940; s. Robert Steely and Virginia (Boehme) N.; m. Linda Sharon Fox, Apr. 16, 1966; children: Heather, Andrew. B.A., Williams Coll., 1962; M.B.A., U. Pa., 1970. Fin. planning mgr. Huffy Corp., Dayton, Ohio, 1971-72, asst. treas., 1972-73, treas., 1973-75, v.p. fin., 1975-79, exec. v.p., 1982-85; pres., gen. mgr. Frabill Sporting Good, Milw., 1979-82; exec. v.p. Reynolds & Reynolds, Dayton, Ohio, 1985-88, pres. bus. forms divsn., 1988-97; pres. automotive divsn., 1997—; bd. dirs. Reynolds & Reynolds, Olympic Title Ins. Co. Bd. dirs., pres. Camp Fire Girls, Dayton, 1975; bd. dirs. ARC, 1977; participant, then trustee Leadership Dayton, 1986-95; vice chmn. Med. Am. Corp.; trustee, treas. Victory Theater Assn., 1985-91, Dayton Mus. Natural History, 1982-96; trustee, chmn. Alliance for Edn., Dayton Art Inst. 1st lt. USN, 1962-70. Mem. Beta Gamma Sigma, Racquet (Dayton), Dayton Country, Country Club of the North. Republican. Episcopalian. Office: Reynolds & Reynolds 800 Germantown St Dayton OH 45407-3311

NEVINS, ALBERT J., publisher, editor, author; b. Yonkers, N.Y., Sept. 11, 1915; s. Albert J. and Bessie (Corcoran) N. Ed., Venard Coll., Clarks Summit, Pa., 1936, Maryknoll (N.Y.) Sem., 1942; LHD (hon.), St. Benedict's Coll., Atchison, Kans., 1963, Universidad Catolica de Puerto Rico, 1978. Ordained priest Roman Catholic Ch., 1942. Dir. social communications Cath. Fgn. Mission Soc. Am., 1960-69; v.p., pub., editor-in-chief Our Sunday Visitor, Inc., 1969-80; editor The Pope Speaks, 1980—, Diaconate Mag., 1985-91, Nova, 1989—; editor Maryknoll mag., 1955-69, World Campus mag., 1958-67; dir. World Horizon Films, 1945-68; cons. internat. visitors office U.S. Cath. Conf.; treas. Inter-Am. Tech. Ctr., 1972-88. Author: The Catholic Year, 1949, Adventures of Wu Han of Korea, 1951, Adventures of Kenji of Japan, 1952, Adventures of Pancho of Peru, 1953, Adventures of Ramon of Bolivia, 1954, St. Francis of the Seven Seas, 1955, The Adventures of Duc of Indochina, 1955, The Meaning of Maryknoll, 1956, Adventures of Men of Maryknoll, 1957, The Maryknoll Golden Book, 1956, The Making of a Priest, 1958, Away to Africa, 1959, The Maryknoll Book of Peoples, 1959, The Young Conquistador, 1960, Aways to the Lands of the Andes, 1962, Maryknoll Catholic Dictionary, 1964, Church in the Modern World, 1964, Away to Mexico, 1966, Away to Central America, 1967, Maryknoll Book of Treasures, 1968, Away to Venezuela, 1969, The Prayer of the Faithful, 1970, Our American Catholic Heritage, 1972, General Intercessions, 1977, A Saint for Your Name, 1980, Life After Death, 1983, The Sunday Readings, 1984, Builders of Catholic America, 1985, The Life of Jesus Christ, 1987, American Martyrs, 1987, Strangers at Your Door, 1988, Ask Me a Question, 1989, Answering a Fundamentalist, 1990, Scriptures of Faith, 1991, Catholicism, 1994, Indulgences, 1995; prodr., author, photographer numerous films, from 1946, including The Story of Juan Mateo (Film Festival award), 1957, A Problem of People (Film Festival award), 1961, The Gods of Todos Santos (Film Festival awards 1966, 67). Comdr. Westchester group Civil Air Patrol; pres. Cath. Journalism Scholarship Fund; bd. dirs. Cath. League for Religious and Civil Rights, 1975—. Recipient Nat. Brotherhood award NCCJ, 1958, Maria Moors Cabot prize Columbia, 1961, St. Augustine award Villanova U., 1962, Benemerenti gold medal Holy See, 1980. Mem. Inter-Am. Press Assn. (treas. tech. ctr., bd. dirs. 1965-94), Cath. Press Assn. (pres. 1959-61, bd. dirs., award 1961), Cath. Inst. Press (co-founder, mem. exec. bd. 1945-60), U.S. Cath. Hist. Soc., Latin Am. Studies Assn., Cath. Assn. Internat. Peace, Fellowship of Cath. Scholars, Overseas Press Club. Address: 4606 W Loughman St Tampa FL 33616-1826

NEVINS, JOHN J., bishop; b. New Rochelle, N.Y., Jan. 19, 1932. Student, Iona Coll. (N.Y.), Cath. U. Washington. Ordained priest, Roman Catholic Ch., 1959. Ordained titular bishop of Rusticana and aux. bishop Diocese of Miami, Fla., 1979-84; first bishop Diocese of Venice, Fla., 1984—. Office: PO Box 2006 1000 Pinebrook Rd Venice FL 34292-1426*

NEVINS, JOSEPH ROY, medical educator; b. June 21, 1947. BS, U. Okla., 1970, MS, 1972; PhD, Duke U., 1976. Asst. prof. molecular cell biology Rockefeller U., 1979-82, assoc. prof., 1982-87, investigator Howard Highes Med. Inst., 1986-87; prof. microbiology Duke U. Med. Ctr., 1987—, investigator Howard Hughes Med. Inst., 1987—, prof. genetics and head, sect. genetics, 1990-94, chmn. dept. genetics, 1994—; lectr. in field. Dept. Microbiology and Immunology fellow Duke U. Med. Ctr., 1972-76, Postdoctoral fellow Rockefeller U., 1976-79; guest scholar Inst. Virus Rsch., Kyoto U., 1986. Mem. Am. Soc. Microbiology, Am. Soc. Virology, Am. Assn. Cancer Rsch. Office: Howard Hughes Med Inst Duke U Med Ctr Dept Genetics Durham NC 27710

NEVINS, LYN (CAROLYN A. NEVINS), educational supervisor, trainer, consultant; b. Chelsea, Mass., June 9, 1948; d. Samuel Joseph and Stella Theresa (Maronski) N.; m. John Edward Herbert, Jr., May 1, 1979; children: Chrissy, Johnny. BA in Sociology/Edn., U. Mass., 1970; MA in Women's Studies, George Washington U., 1975. Cert. tchr., trainer. Tchr. social studies Greenwich (Conn.) Pub. Schs., 1970-74; rschr. career/vocat. edn. Conn. State Dept. Edn., Hartford, 1975-76; rschr., career/vocat. edn. Area Coop. Edn. Svcs., Hamden, Conn., 1976-77; program mgr., trainer career edn. and gender equity Coop. Ednl. Svcs., Norwalk, Conn., 1977-83; trainer, mgr., devel., Beginning Educator Support and Tng. program Coop. Ednl. Svcs., Fairfield, Conn., 1987—; state coord. career edn. Conn. State Dept. Edn., Hartford, 1982-83; supr. Sacred Heart U., Fairfield, 1992—; mem. bias com. Conn. State Dept. Edn., Hartford, 1981—; mem. vision com. Middlesex Mid. Sch., Darien, Conn., 1993-95; mem. ednl. quality and diversity com. Town of Darien, 1993-95; cons., trainer career devel./pre-retirement planning Cohen and Assocs., Fairfield, 1981—, Farren Assocs., Annandale, Va., 1992—, Tracey Robert Assocs., Fairfield, 1994—; freelance cons., trainer, Darien, 1983-87; presenter Nat. Conf. GE, 1980, Career Edn., 1983, Am. Edn. Rsch. Assn., 1991; lectr. in field. Coach Spl. Olympics, 1993—, Darien (Conn.) Girls' Softball League, 1992—. Mem. NOW (founder, state coord. edn. 1972-74), ASCD. Avocations: tennis, running, walking, golf, travel. Home: 4 Hollister Ln Darien CT 06820-5404 Office: Coop Ednl Svcs 25 Oakview Dr Trumbull CT 06611-4723

NEVINS, SHEILA, television programmer and producer; b. N.Y.C.; d. Benjamin and Stella N.; B.A., Barnard Coll.M.F.A. (Three Arts fellow), Yale U.; m. Sidney Koch; 1 son, David Andrew. TV producer Great Am. Dream Machine, NET, 1971-73, The Reasoner Report, ABC, 1973, Feeling Good, Children's TV Workshop, 1975-76, Who's Who, CBS, 1977-78; dir. documentary and family programming HBO, N.Y.C., 1978-82, v.p. documentary programming Home Box Office, N.Y.C., 1986-95, sr. v.p. documentary and family programming, 1995—. Bd. dirs. Women's Action Alliance. Recipient Peabody award, 1986, 92, 95, 96, 97, Acad. Award Documentary, 1993, 96, Emmy award, 1994, 1995, 96, Glaad Media award, 1996; named Woman of Achievement YWCA, 1991, Top 25 Women in TV Emmy mag., 1996. Mem. Writers Guild Am., Women in Film.

NEVOLA, ROGER PAUL, lawyer; b. N.Y.C., Apr. 30, 1947; s. Frank S. and Kathryn N.; m. Molly Cagle; children: Adrienne L., Jake F. Student, U. Notre Dame, 1964-66; BSME, Stanford U., 1968; JD, U. Tex., 1974. Bar: Tex. 1974. Assoc. Vinson & Elkins, Houston, 1974-79; assoc. Vinson & Elkins, Austin, 1979-81, ptnr., 1981-95; pvt. practice Austin, 1995—; Tex. reporter Mineral Law Newsletter/Rocky Mountain Mineral Law Found., 1984—. Fellow Tex. Bar Found.; mem. Tex. Water Conservation Assn. (dir. 1978—). Avocations: golf, hiking, travel. Home: 4304 Bennedict Ln Austin TX 78746-1940 Office: 2050 Franklin Plz 111 Congress Ave Austin TX 78701-4043

NEW, ANNE LATROBE, public relations, fund raising executive; b. Evanston, Ill., May 10, 1910; d. Charles Edward and Agnes (Bateman) N.; m. John C. Timmerman, Sept. 30, 1933; 1 child, Jan LaTrobe. AB, U. S.C., 1930; postgrad., Hunter Coll., 1930-31, NYU, 1932-33. APR (Accredited Pub. Relations Practitioner). Editorial asst. Pictorial Review Mag., N.Y.C., 1930-32; copy asst. J. Walter Thompson Co., N.Y.C., 1932-33; sub editor Cosmopolitan Mag., N.Y.C., 1933-37; with Girl Scouts of the U.S., N.Y.C., 1937-57, chief pub. rels. officer, 1945-57; dir. pub. info. edn. Nat. Recreation and Park Assn., 1957-66; special asst. gen. dir. Internat. Social Svc. Am. Branch, N.Y.C., 1966-68; dir. devel. Nat. Accreditation Coun. for Agys. Serving Blind and Visual Handicapped, N.Y.C., 1969-78; pres. Timmerman & New Inc., Mamaroneck, N.Y., 1980—; cons. dept. pub. adminstrn. Baruch Coll., CUNY, 1987-94, Sch. Pub. Affairs, 1994—. Author: Service For Givers, The Story of the National Information Bureau, 1983, Raise More Money for Your Nonprofit Organization, 1991; contbr. articles to profl. jours. Mem. Westchester Dem. Com. Westchester County, 1963-67, 89—; bd. dirs. Mamaroneck (N.Y.) United Fund, 1963-64; chmn. nominating com. LWV, Mamaroneck, 1988, chmn. by-law com., 1989; warden emerita, mem. fin. com. St. Thomas' Episc. Ch., Mamaroneck. Recipient Marzella Garland award for outstanding achievement in promotion of improved housing conditions in Mamaroneck Village, 1995. Mem. Pub. Rels. Soc. Am. (bd. dirs. N.Y. chpt. 1958-72), Women Execs. Pub. Rels. (sec. 1962--63), Nat. Soc. Fund Raising Execs. (bd. dirs. greater N.Y. chpt. 1978-84), Phi Beta Kappa (Scarsdale/Westchester Phi Beta Kappa Assn.). Democrat. Avocations: tennis, dancing, swimming. Office: Timmerman & New Inc 235 S Barry Ave Mamaroneck NY 10543-4104

NEW, MARIA IANDOLO, physician, educator; b. N.Y.C.; d. Loris J. and Esther B. (Giglio) Iandolo; m. Bertrand L. New, 1949 (dec. 1990); children: Erica, Daniel, Antonia. B.A., Cornell U., 1950; M.D., U. Pa., 1954. Diplomate: Am. Bd. Pediatrics. Med. intern Bellevue Hosp., N.Y.C., 1954-55; resident pediatrics N.Y. Hosp., 1955-57; fellow NIH, 1957-58, 61-64; practice medicine specializing in pediatrics N.Y.C., 1955—; mem. staff N.Y. Hosp., N.Y.C.; dir. Pediatric Endocrine and Metabolism Clinic, N.Y. Hosp., 1964—, attending pediatrician, 1971-80, pediatrician-in-chief, 1980—; asst. prof. dept. pediat. Cornell U. Med. Coll., N.Y.C., 1963-68, assoc. prof., 1968-71, prof., 1971—, Harold and Percy Uris prof. pediatric endocrinology, 1978—, prof., chmn. dept. pediat., 1980—; program dir. Childrens Clin. Rsch. Ctr., 1996—; assoc. dir. Pediatric Clin. Rsch. Ctr., 1980-88; adj. faculty prof. Rockefeller U., 1981—; career scientist N.Y.C. Health Rsch. Coun., 1966-75; adj. attending pedatrician dept. pediat. Meml. Sloan-Kettering Cancer Ctr., 1979-93; cons. United Hosp., Port Chester, N.Y., 1977—, North Shore Univ. Hosp., 1982—, dept. pediat. Cath. Med. Ctr. Bklyn. and Queens, N.Y., 1987; vis. physician Rockefeller U. Hosp., N.Y.C., 1973-87; mem. endocrine study sect. NIH, 1977-80, Gen. Clin. Rsch. Ctrs. Adv. Com.; chmn. Divsn. Rsch. Resources Gen. Clin. Rsch. Ctrs. Com. NIH, 1987-88; bd. dirs. Robert Wood Johnson Clin. Scholars Program; mem. N.Y. State Gov.'s Task Force on Life and Law, 1985—; mem. NIH Reviewers Res.; mem. FDA endocrinology and metabolism drug adv. com., 1994—; panelist ACGME bd. appeals, 1994—; cons. Meml. Sloan-Kettering Cancer Ctr., 1993—, Meml. Hosp. for the Cancer and Allied Diseases, 1993—; hon. mem. pediat. dept. Blythedale Children's Hosp., Valhalla, N.Y., 1992—; mem. rsch. adv. com. Population Coun. Ctr. for Biomed. Rsch., 1991-97. Editor-in-chief Jour. Clin. Endocrinology and Metabolism, 1994—; mem. editorial adv. coun. Jour. Endocrinol. Investigation, 1995—; mem. editorial bd. Jour. Women's Health, 1993; corr. editor Jour. Steroid Biochemistry, 1985; mem. adv. bd. pediatric anns., assoc. editor Metabolism. Trustee Irma T. Hirschl Trust. Recipient Mary Jane Kugel award Juvenile Diabetes Found., 1977, Katharine D. McCormick Disting. Lectureship, 1981, Robert H. Williams Disting. Leadership award, 1988, Albion O. Bernstein award Med. Soc. State N.Y., 1988, medal N.Y. Acad. Medicine, 1991, Disting. Grad. award U. Pa. Sch. Medicine, 1991, Optimate Recognition award Assn. Student-Profl. Italian-Ams., 1991, Outstanding Woman Scientist award N.Y. chpt. Am. Women in Sci., 1986, Maurice R. Greenberg Disting. Svc. award, 1994, Humanitarian award Juvenile Diabetes Found., 1994, Rhône Poulenc Rorer Clinical Investigator Lecture award, 1994, Dale medal Brit. Endocrine Soc., 1996; grantee. Fellow Italian Soc. Endocrinology (hon.); mem. NAS, AAAS, Am. Soc. Human Genetics, Am. Acad. Pediatrics, Soc. for Pediatric Research, Harvey Soc., Endocrine Soc. (mem. coun. 1981-84, pres. 1991-92), Lawson Wilkins Pediatric Endocrine Soc. (pres. 1985-86), Am. Soc. Nephrology, Am. Soc. Pediatric Nephrology, Am. Pediatric Soc., Am. Fedn. Clin. Research, Am. Diabetes Assn., European Soc. Pediatric Endocrinology, Soc. for the Advancement of Women's Health Rsch. (basic sci. award 1996), Am. Coll. Clin. Pharmacology, Am. Clin. & Climatol. Assn., N.Y. Acad. Scis., Pan Am. Med. Assn., Assn. Am. Physicians, Am. Fertility Soc., U.S. Pharmacopeial Conv. (elected), Am. Acad. of Arts and Scis. (elected 1992), Alpha Omega Alpha. Office: New York Hosp-Cornell Med Ctr Dept Pediatrics 525 E 68th St New York NY 10021-4873

NEW, PAMELA ZYMAN, neurologist; b. Chgo., Jan. 24, 1953; d. HIllard Anthony and Virginia Lillian (Drechsler) Zyman; m. Joseph Keith New, Sept. 12, 1982; children: Matthew, Anneliese, Theresa. BS in Medicine, Northwestern U., 1973, MD, 1976. Resident in internal medicine Baylor Affiliated Hosps., Houston, 1977-80, resident in neurology, 1983-85; mem. staff dept. medicine VA Hosp., Houston, 1980-81; resident in gen. surgery N.Y. Hosp., Cornell Med. Ctr., N.Y.C., 1981, resident in neurosurgery, 1981-83; fellow neuro-oncology M.D. Anderson Hosp. and Tumor Inst., Houston, 1985-87; asst. prof. divsn. neurology dept. medicine U. Tex. Health Sci. Ctr., San Antonio, 1987—; staff physician Audie L. Murphy Meml. VA Hosp., San Antonio, 1987—; lectr., researcher in field. Contbr. articles to profl. publs., chpts. to books. Mem. ACP, S.W. Oncology Group, Assn. VA Investigators and Rsch. Adminstrs., Am. Acad. Neurology, Am. Parkinson's Disease Assn. (co-dir. Parkinson's Disease Info. Referral Ctr.), Movement Disorders Soc., Soc. of Neuro-Oncology. Roman Catholic. Avocation: cooking. Office: U Tex Health Sci Ctr 7703 Floyd Curl Dr San Antonio TX 78284-6200

NEW, ROSETTA HOLBROCK, home economics educator, nutrition consultant; b. Hamilton, Ohio, Aug. 26, 1921; d. Edward F. and Mabel (Kohler) Holbrock; m. John Lorton New, Sept. 3, 1943; 1 child, John Lorton Jr. BS, Miami U., Oxford, Ohio, 1943; MA, U. No. Colo., 1971; PhD, The Ohio State U., 1974; student Kantcentrum, Brugge, Belgium, 1992, Lesage Sch. Embroidery, Paris, 1995. Cert. tchr., Colo. Tchr. English and sci. Monahans (Tex.) H.S., 1943-45; emergency war food asst. U.S. Dept. Agr., College Station, Tex., 1945-46; dept. chmn. home econs., adult edn. Hamilton (Ohio) Pub. Schs., 1946-47; tchr., dept. chmn. home econs. East H.S., Denver, 1948-59, Thomas Jefferson H.S., Denver, 1959-83; mem. exec. bd. Denver Pub. Schs.; also lectr.; exec. dir. Ctr. Nutrition Info. U.S. Office of Edn. grantee Ohio State U., 1971-73. Mem. Cin. Art Mus., Nat. Trust for Historic Preservation. Mem. Am. Home Econs. Assn., Am. Vocat. Assn., Embroiders Guild Am., Hamilton Hist. Soc., Internat. Old Lacers, Ohio State U. Assn., Ohio State Home Econs. Alumni Assn., Fairfield (Ohio) Hist. Soc., Republican Club of Denver, Internat. Platform Assn., Phi Upsilon Omicron. Presbyterian. Lodges: Masons, Daughters of the Nile, Order of Eastern Star, Order White Shrine of Jerusalem. Home and Office: 615 Crescent Rd Hamilton OH 45013-3432

NEW, WILLIAM NEIL, physician, retired naval officer; b. Atoka, Okla., Oct. 24, 1908; s. Robert Calvin and Nommar Bell (Willmore) N.; m. Ruth Anderson Pride, Mar. 30, 1940. B.A., Central State Tchrs. Coll., Edmond, Okla., 1931; B.S. in Medicine, U. Okla., 1932, M.D., 1934; postgrad., Northwestern U. Med. Sch., 1947-48. Diplomate: Am. Bd. Dermatology and Syphilology. Intern So. Pacific R.R. Hosp., San Francisco, 1934-35; commd. lt. (j.g.), M.C. U.S. Navy, 1935, advanced through grades to rear adm., 1963; resident dermatology and syphilology Naval Hosp., Phila., 1946-47; med. officer on gunboat and USMC Hosp., Shanghai, 1937-39; regtl. surgeon 7th Marines in Guadalcanal; later div. surgeon 5th Marine Div. (Japanese occupation), 1945; established Naval Med. Field Research Lab., Camp Lejeune, 1943; chief dermatology services naval hosps. Great Lakes, Ill., 1948-51, Phila., 1951-53, San Diego, 1956-59; force surgeon Fleet Marine Force, Pacific, 1954-56; comdg. officer U.S. Naval Hosp., Yokusuka, Japan, 1959-62; dir. staff Office Dep. Asst. Sec. Def. for Health and Med., 1962-66; pvt. practice dermatology Dallas Med. and Surg. clinic, 1968-91; ret., 1991; clin. assoc. prof. dermatology Southwestern Med. Sch., U. Tex., Dallas, 1966-92. Mem. ACP (life), Am. Acad. Dermatology (life), Pacific Dermatol. Assn. (life), Assn. Mil. Dermatologists (past pres.), N.Am. Clin. Dermatol. Soc. (co-founder, life), Space Dermatol. Found. (co-founder), Cutaneous Therapy Soc. (co-founder, life). Home: 3310 Fairmount St Apt 17C Dallas TX 75201-1241 *Love and live today as we plan a rewarding tomorrow.*

NEWACHECK, DAVID JOHN, lawyer; b. San Francisco, Dec. 8, 1953; s. John Elmer and Estere Ruth Sybil (Nelson) N.; m. Dorothea Quandt, June 2, 1990. AB in English, U. Calif., Berkeley, 1976; JD, Pepperdine U., 1979; MBA, Calif. State U., Hayward, 1982; LLM in Tax, Golden Gate U., 1987. Bar: Calif. 1979, U.S. Dist. Ct. (no. dist.) Calif. 1979, U.S. Ct. Appeals (9th cir.) 1979, U.S. Supreme Ct. 1984, Washington D.C. 1985. Tax cons. Pannell, Kerr and Forster, San Francisco, 1982-83; lawyer, writer, editor Matthew Bender and Co., San Francisco, 1983—; instr. taxation Oakland (Calif.) Coll. of Law, 1993—; lawyer, tax cons., fin. planner San Leandro, Calif., 1983—; bd. dirs. Aztec Custom Co., Orinda, Calif., 1983—; cons. software Collier Bankruptcy Filing Sys., 1984. Author/editor: (treatises) Ill. Tax Service, 1985, Ohio State Taxation, 1985, N.J. Tax Service, 1986, Pa. Tax Service, 1986, Calif. Closely Held Corps., 1987, Texas Tax Service, 1988; author: (software) Tax Source 1040 Tax Preparation, 1987, Texas Tax Service 1988, California Taxation, 1989, 2d edit., 1990, Bender's Federal Tax Service, 1989, Texas Litigation Guide, 1993, Family Law: Texas Practice & Procedure, 1993, Texas Transaction Guide, 1994, Ohio Corporation Law, 1994, Michigan Corporation Law, 1994, Massachusetts Corporation Law, 1994. Mem. youth com. Shepherd of the Valley Luth. Ch., Orinda, 1980-85, ch. coun., 1980-82. Mem. ABA, Internat. Platform Assn., State Bar Assn. Calif., Alameda County Bar Assn., U. Calif. Alumni Assn., U. Calif. Band Alumni Assn., Mensa. Republican. Club: Commonwealth (San Francisco). Avocations: music, competitive running, sports. Home: 5141 Vannoy Ave Castro Valley CA 94546-2558 Office: 438 Estudillo Ave San Leandro CA 94577-4908

NEWBAUER, JOHN ARTHUR, editor; b. Newport, R.I., Apr. 24, 1928; s. John Arthur and Theo Caroline (Trewhella) N.; m. Marilyn Mahler, Oct. 14, 1956; children: April, Dana, Miranda. B.A., U. Calif.-Berkeley, 1951. Sr. editor and writer sci. and engring., rocket devel. dept. U.S. Naval Ordnance Test Sta., China Lake, Calif., 1951-56; editor in chief Astronautics and Aeronautics jour., N.Y.C., 1963-83; adminstr. sci. publs. AIAA, 1983-91, cons. editor, 1991—; editor in chief Aerospace Am., 1983-87, aquisitions editor, 1987-89. Fellow AIAA (assoc.), Brit. Interplanetary Soc. Home: 356 Bay Ridge Ave Brooklyn NY 11220-5315

NEWBERG, DOROTHY BECK (MRS. WILLIAM C. NEWBERG), portrait artist; b. Detroit, May 30, 1919; d. Charles William and Mary (Labedz) Beck; student Detroit Conservatory Music, 1938; m. William C. Newberg, Nov. 3, 1939; children: Judith Bookwalter Bracken, Robert Charles, James William, William Charles. Trustee Detroit Adventure, 1967-71, originator A Drop in Bucket Program for artistically talented inner-city children. Cmty. outreach coord. Reno Police Dept.; bd. dirs. Bloomfield Art Assn., 1960-62, trustee 1965-67; bd. dirs. Your Heritage House, 1972-75, Franklin Wright Settlement, 1972-75, Meadowbrook Art Gallery, Oakland U., 1973-75, Sierra Nevada Mus. Art, 1978-80, NCCJ; mem. adv. bd. Gang Alternatives Partnership Adv. Bd. Recipient Heart of Gold award, 1969; Mich. vol. leadership award, 1969, Outstanding Vol. award City of Reno, 1989-90. Mem. Nevada Mus. Art, No. Nev. Black Cultural Awareness Soc. (bd. dirs.), Hispanic 500 C. of C. No. Nev. Roman Catholic. Home: 2000 Dant Blvd Reno NV 89509-5193

NEWBERN, WILLIAM DAVID, state supreme court justice; b. Oklahoma City, May 28, 1937; s. Charles Banks and Mary Frances (Harding) N.; m. Barbara Lee Rigsby, Aug. 19, 1961 (div. 1968); 1 child, Laura Harding; m. Carolyn Lewis, July 30, 1970; 1 child, Alistair Elizabeth. B.A., U. Ark., 1959, J.D., 1961; LL.M., George Washington U., 1963; M.A., Tufts U., 1967. Bar: Ark. 1961, U.S. Dist. Ct. (we. dist.) Ark. 1961, U.S. Supreme Ct. 1968, U.S. Ct. Appeals (8th cir.) 1983. Commd. 1st lt. advanced to maj. U.S. Army JAGC, 1961-70; Prof. law U. Ark., Fayetteville, 1970-84; adminstr. Ozark Folk Ctr., Mountain View, Ark., 1973; judge Ark. Ct. Appeals, Little Rock, 1979-80; assoc. justice Ark. Supreme Ct., Little Rock, 1985—; mem. faculty sr. appellate judges seminar NYU, 1987-91. Editor Ark. Law Rev., 1961; author: Arkansas Civil Practice and Procedure, 1985, 2d edit., 1993. Mem. Fayetteville Bd. Adjustment, 1972-79; bd. dirs. decision Point, INc., Springdale, Ark., 1980-85, Little Rock Wind Symphony, 1993, pres. 1993-95. Fellow Ark. Bar Found.; mem. Am. Judicature Soc. (bd. dirs. 1985-89), Washington County Bar Assn., Inst. Jud. Adminstrn., Ark. IOLTA Found. (bd. dirs. 1985-87). Democrat. Avocation: string band-guitar, mandolin, banjo and brass quintet-tuba. Office: Ark Supreme Ct 625 Marshall St Little Rock AR 72201-1054

NEWBERRY, CONRAD FLOYDE, aerospace engineering educator; b. Neodesha, Kans., Nov. 10, 1931; s. Ragan McGregor and Audra Anitia (Newmaster) N.; m. Sarah Louise Thonn, Jan. 26, 1958; children: Conrad Floyde Jr., Thomas Edwin, Susan Louise. AA, Independence Jr. Coll., 1951; BEME in Aero. Sequence, U. So. Calif., 1957; MSME, Calif. State U., Los Angeles, 1971, MA in Edn., 1974; D.Environ. Sci. and Engring., UCLA, 1985. Registered profl. engr., Calif., Kans., N.C., Tex. Mathematician L.A. divsn. N.Am. Aviation Inc., 1951-53, jr. engr., 1953-54, engr., 1954-57, sr. engr., 1957-64; asst. prof. aerospace engring. Calif. State Poly. U., Pomona, 1964-70, assoc. prof. aerospace engring., 1970-75, prof. aerospace engring., 1975-90, prof. emeritus, 1990—; staff engr. EPA, 1980-82; engring. specialist space transp. systems div. Rockwell Internat. Corp., 1984-90; prof. aeronautics and astronautics Naval Postgrad. Sch., Monterey, Calif., 1990—, acad. assoc. space systems engring., 1992-94. Recipient John Leland Atwood award as outstanding aerospace engring. educator AIAA/Am. Soc. Engring. Edn., 1986. Fellow AIAA (dep. dir. edn. region VI 1976-79, dep. dir. career enhancement 1982-91, chmn. L.A. sect. 1989-90, chmn. Point Lobos sect. 1990-91, chmn. acad. affairs com. 1990-93, dir. tech.-aircraft sys. 1990-93), Inst. Advancement Engring., Brit. Interplanetary Soc.; mem. IEEE, AAAS, ASME, NSPE, Royal Aero. Soc., Calif. Soc. Profl. Engrs., Am. Acad. Environ. Engrs. (cert. air pollution control engr.), Am. Soc. Engring. Edn. (chmn. aerospace divsn. 1979-80, divsn. exec. com. 1976-80, 89-94, exec. com. ocean and marine engring. divsn. 1982-85, 90-97, program chmn. 1991-93, chmn. 1993-95, chmn. PIC II 1995-97), Am. Soc. Pub. Adminstrn., Am. Meteorol. Soc., U.S. Naval Inst., Am. Helicopter Soc., Soc. Naval Architects and Marine Engrs., Air and Waste Mgmt. Assn., Inst. Environ. Scis., Exptl. Aircraft Assn., Water Environ. Fedn., Soc. Automotive Engr., Soc. Allied Weight Engrs., Assn. Unmanned Vehicle Sys., Calif. Water Pollution Control Assn., Nat. Assn. Environ. Profls., Am. Soc. Naval Engrs., SAFE, SID, Planetary Soc., Tau Beta Pi, Sigma Gamma Tau, Kappa Delta Pi. Democrat. Mem. Christian Ch. (Disciples of Christ). Achievements include research on aircraft, space craft, missiles, and engine design, wavierders, aircrew centered system design and related impacts on exergy, quality, concurrent engineering, cost and environmental controls. Home: 9463 Willow Oak Rd Salinas CA 93907-1037 Office: Naval Postgrad Sch Dept Aeronautics and Astronautics AA/Ne 699 Dyer Rd Monterey CA 93943-5195

NEWBERRY, ROBERT CURTIS, SR., communications executive, newspaper editor; b. Port Arthur, Tex., Feb. 20, 1945; s. Ira and Nona (Houston) N.; m. Carolyn Annette Ponder, Dec. 21, 1968; children: Renita, Renona, Robert Jr.; m. Jackolyn Cone, Oct. 8, 1994. BA, U. Houston, 1967. Sports editor The Houston Informer, 1964-65, Sports World, Houston, 1965; asst. news editor, columnist The Houston Post, 1967-87, columnist, 1987-95; exec. editor The Houston Reader, 1995; columnist, editorial writer, asst. news editor The Houston Daily News, 1996—; owner, pres. Newberry Comm.; editor, pub. newsletter Stress-Less. Bd. dirs. I Have a Dream, Houston, Citizens for Better Health, Houston Child Guidance Ctr., 1988-92, tutor and mentor, 1991—. Recipient Life Svc. award Tex. So. U., Houston, 1972, Print Media award Mental Health Assn., 1987, Print Media award Tex. Mental Health Assn., 1988, Julia C. Hester Achievement award Trailblazer, 1988, Awards of Excellence Dallas Press Club, 1989, Houston Press Club, 1990, 1st Pl. award UPI Regional Awards, 1990, 2d Pl. award commentary newspapers over 100,000 circulation, 1995, Disting. Alumnus award U. Houston, 1990. Fellow Am. Leadership Forum (sr., bd. dirs. 1990-92); mem. Nat. Assn. Black Journalists, Soc. Profl. Journalists (bd. dirs. 1968), Houston Assn. Black Journalists, U. Houston Alumni Orgn. (bd. dirs. 1991—). Democrat. Avocations: writing, fishing, boating. Office: Newberry Communications Box 44 3700 Wakeforest Houston TX 77098

NEWBILL, KAREN MARGARET, elementary school educator, education educator; b. East Orange, N.J., Oct. 6, 1945; d. Richard Oliver and Edna Mae (Crook) Jacobson; m. Gary C. Newbill, Aug. 18, 1965; children: Kari L., Erick D. BA, Seattle Pacific U., 1968; MEd, City U., Bellevue, Wash., 1993. Cert. tchr., Wash. Tchr. Shoreline Pub. Schs., Seattle, 1969-71, Northshore Sch. Dist., Bothell, Wash., 1971-74; tutor, substitute tchr. Issaquah (Wash.) Sch. Dist., 1980-89, tchr., 1989—, tech. and curriculum integration cons., 1991—; adj. prof. N.W. Coll., Kirkland, Wash., 1994—, mem. profl. edn. adv. bd., 1994—; adj. prof. Seattle Pacific U., 1994—; student tchr. supr. U. Wash., Seattle, 1991—. Children's choir dir. Westminster Chapel, Bellevue, Wash., 1980-88; children's worship leader Evergreen Christian Fellowship, Issaquah, 1993-94. Mem. ASCD, NEA, Wash. Edn. Assn., Nat. Coun. Tchrs. Math., Internat. Reading Assn. Avocations: decorative painting, reading, traveling, music. Home: 420 Kalmia Pl NW Issaquah WA 98027-2619 Office: Issaquah Sch Dist. 565 NW Holly St Issaquah WA 98027-2834

NEWBLATT, STEWART ALBERT, federal judge; b. Detroit, Dec. 23, 1927; s. Robert Abraham and Fanny Ida (Grinberg) N.; m. Flora Irene Sandweiss, Mar. 5, 1965; children: David Jacob, Robert Abraham, Joshua Isaac. B.A. with distinction, U. Mich., 1950, J.D. with distinction, 1952. Bar: Mich. bar 1953. Ptnr. firm White & Newblatt, Flint, Mich., 1953-62; judge 7th Jud. Cir. Mich., 1962-70; ptnr. firm Newblatt & Grossman (and predecessor), Flint, 1970-79; judge U.S. Dist. Ct. (ea. dist.) Mich., Flint, 1979—; adj. instr. U. Mich.-Flint, 1977-78, 86. Mem. Internat. Bridge Authority Mich., 1960-62. Served with AUS, 1946-47. Mem. Fed. Bar Assn., State Bar Mich., Dist. Judges Assn. 6th Circuit. Jewish. Office: US Dist Ct 140 Federal Bldg 600 Church St Flint MI 48502-1214

NEWBOLD, BENJAMIN MILLARD, JR., library manager, education consultant; b. La Grange, Ga., June 20, 1941; s. Benjamin Millard and Zeppa (Dasher) N.; married, 1968 (div. 1977); 2 children. BA in Sociology, Roger Williams Coll., 1970; MEd in Spl. Edn., Mid. Tenn. State U., 1975; MLS, U. So. Fla., 1985. Cert. tchr., Tenn., Fla., Ga., S.C., La. Tchr. psychotic, emotionally disturbed, mentally retarded Montanari Clin. Sch., Hialeah, Fla., 1970-72, 76-77; tchr. educatable mentally retarded Colleton County Bd. Edn., Walterboro, S.C., 1972-73, John Coleman Sch., Smyrna, Tenn., 1973-76, Hahnville H.S., Boutte, La., 1978-79, Gulf Comprehensive H.S., New Port Richie, Fla., 1979-80; tchr. severely mentally retarded, psychology supr. Sunniland Tng. Ctr., Ft. Myers, Fla., 1983-84; grad. asst. U. So. Fla., Tampa, 1984-85; adult reference libr. Houston Pub. Libr., 1986-89, libr. br. mgr., 1989-94, collection devel. mgr. Scenic Woods Regional Cluster, 1994; geneal. researcher Clayton Libr./Ctr. for Geneal. Rsch., 1994—; pilot project tchr. Garrison Environ. Model, Rutherford County Bd. Edn., Murfreesboro, 1973-76; county coord. Spl. Edn. Grad. Credit, Murfreesboro, 1973-76; supr., adminstr., cons. pub. schs., pub. and pvt. facilities, librs.; active community pub. rels. P.T.A., sch. dists., librs.; ind. distbr. Enviro-tech Internat., Family of Eagles; ptnr. Bus. Leadership Inst. Vol. tchr. ESL Houston Pub. Libr., 1996—; active CONNECTEXAS, Austin, Fonwood P.T.A., Houston, Fontaine-Scenic Woods Civic Club, Houston, positive interaction program Houston Police Dept.; past mem. exec. bd. Houston Pub. Libr. Staff Assn. Recipient Spirit award Wall St.-The Club, 1991. Republican. Avocations: education, art, writing, politics, acting. Home: 401 S Bender Ave Apt 1109 Humble TX 77338-7706 Office: Clayton Libr Ctr Gen Rsch 5300 Caroline St Houston TX 77004-6803

NEWBORG, GERALD GORDON, historical agency administrator; b. Ada, Minn., Dec. 13, 1942; s. George Harold and Olea (Halstad) N.; m. Jean Annette Gruhl, Aug. 14, 1964; children: Erica, Annette. BA, Concordia Coll., Moorhead, Minn., 1964; MA, U. N.D., 1969; MBA, Ohio State U., 1978. Cert. archivist. Tutor, preceptor Parsons Coll., Fairfield, Iowa, 1964-67; state archivist Ohio Hist. Soc., Columbus, 1968-76; v.p. Archival Systems Inc., Columbus, 1978-81; state archivist State Hist. Soc. of N.D., Bismarck, 1981—; instr. Franklin U., Columbus, 1974; adj. prof. Bismarck State Coll., 1985-86. Co-author: North Dakota: A Pictorial History, 1988. Recipient Resolution of Commendation Ohio Ho. of Reps., Columbus, 1976. Mem. Soc. Am. Archivists, Nat. Assn. Govt. Archives & Records Adminstrs. (bd. dirs. 1984-86, sec. 1994—), Midwest Archives Conf., N.D. Libr. Assn. (exec. bd. 1985-86). Home: 1327 N 18th St Bismarck ND 58501-2827 Office: State Hist Soc 612 E Boulevard Ave Bismarck ND 58505-0660

NEWBORN, IRA, composer. Scores include (films) The Blues Brothers, 1980, All Night Long, 1981, Sixteen Candles, 1984, Into the Night, 1985, Weird Science, 1985, Ferris Bueller's Day Off, 1986, Wise Guys, 1986, Dragnet, 1987, Amazon Women on the Moon, 1987, Planes, Trains and Automobiles, 1987, Caddyshack II, 1988, The Naked Gun, 1988, Uncle Buck, 1989, Short Time, 1990, My Blue Heaven, 1990, The Naked Gun 2 1/2: The Smell of Fear, 1991, Brain Donors, 1992, Innocent Blood, 1992, The Opposite Sex and How to Live with Them, 1993, Naked Gun 33 1/3: The Final Insult, 1994, Ace Ventura, Pet Detective, 1994, The Jerky Boys, 1995, Mall Rats, 1995 (TV movies) Cast the First Stone, 1989, (Cable TV Films) The Late Shift, 1996. Office: Vangelos Mgmt 16030 Ventura Blvd Ste 550 Van Nuys CA 91436*

NEWBORN, JUD, anthropologist, writer, lyricist; b. N.Y.C., Nov. 8, 1952; s. Solomon and Rita (Cohen) N. BA magna cum laude in Anthropology and English, NYU, 1974; postgrad., Clare Hall, Cambridge U., 1974-75; MA in Anthropology, U. Chgo., 1977, PhD with distinction, 1994. Free-lance writer N.Y.C., Munich, Chgo., 1974—; publicist Oxford U. Press, N.Y.C., 1975-76; mus. historian, curatorial cons. Mus. Jewish Heritage (N.Y. Holocaust Meml. Commn.), N.Y.C., 1986-92, 96—; cons. Sci. Inst. for Pub. Info., N.Y.C., 1987-90; cons., spkr., lectr. in field. Author: Shattering the German Night: The Story of the White Rose Anti-Nazi Resistance, 1986; freelance writer, lyricist. Fulbright fellow, 1980-82; Newcombe fellow, 1984-85. Mem. ASCAP, Am. Anthrop. Assn., The Am. Hist. Assn., Authors Guild, Phi Beta Kappa.

NEWBRAND, CHARLES MICHAEL, advertising firm executive; b. Staten Island, N.Y., May 2, 1944; s. Charles Henry and Edith (Kotte) N.; m. Clare Ann Holmes, Aug. 26, 1967; 1 child, Alexis Christina. BA, U. Notre Dame, 1965; JD, U. Pa., Phila., 1968. Bar: N.J. 1968. Media planner Ogilvy & Mather, N.Y.C., 1968-71, account exec., 1971-74, account supr., 1974-77, v.p. mgmt. supr., 1977-82, sr. v.p. mgmt. supr., 1982-85, sr. v.p., group dir., 1985-89; mem. N.Y. oper. bd. Ogilvy & Mather, 1987-89; sr. v.p., group acct. dir., mem. exec. com. Foote, Cone & Belding, Inc., Chgo., 1990; sr. v.p. The Martin Agy., Richmond, Va., 1991—. Recipient Stephen E. Kelly award Mag. Pubs. Assn., 1981, Golden Effie Am. Mktg. Assn., N.Y. chpt., 1982, 87. Office: The Martin Agy One Shockoe Plz Richmond VA 23219-4132

NEWBRANDER, WILLIAM CARL, health economist, management consultant; b. Irumagawa, Japan, Sept. 14, 1951; parents Am. citizens; s. Virgil Ray and Ella Jeannette (Rae) N.; m. Nancy Sharon Wilson, June 15, 1974; children: Sharon, Billy, Andrew, Jonathan, Daniel. BA, Wheaton Coll., 1973; M of Hosp. Adminstrn., 1975; M of Applied Econs., U. Mich., 1981, PhD, 1983. Teaching/rsch. asst. U. Mich., Ann Arbor, 1979-83; mgmt. specialist V-HSR&D, Ann Arbor, 1980-83; hosp. adminstr. Whittaker Corp., Tabuk, Saudi Arabia, 1983-85; health economist WHO, Geneva, Switzerland, 1985-92; dir. health financing program Mgmt. Scis. for Health, Boston, 1992—. Author: Health Policy and Planning, 1988, 89, 90, 91, 94, Health Planning and Mgmt., 1988, 90, 91, 96, Decentralization in a Developing Country, 1991, Hospital Economics and Financing in Developing Countries, 1992, World Health Forum, 1994, Health Sector Reform in Asia: Issues and Experiences Related to Private Sector Growth, 1997, Private Health Sector Growth in Asia: Issues and Implications, 1997. Eagle Scout advisor, scout troop com. chmn. Boy Scouts Am., Geneva and Hopkinton, Mass., 1990—; mgr. Little League baseball team, Geneva and Hopkinton, 1990—; elder First Congl. Ch., Hopkinton, 1995—. Capt. U.S. Army, 1975-79. VA Rsch. fellow, 1981-83. Fellow Am. Coll. Healthcare Execs. Office: Health Fin Program Mgt Sciences Health 165 Allandale St Boston MA 02130-3443

NEWBROUGH, EDGAR TRUETT, retired management consultant; b. Madison, Ill., June 22, 1917; s. Edgar M. and Iris M. (Webb) N.; m. Muriel E. Amos, Nov. 26, 1936; children—Sherrill (Mrs. T.D. McIntyre), Sandra (Mrs. D. S. Cole), Arthur T. B.A., San Diego State U., 1938. Registered profl. engr., Pa., Mo., Ill., Mich. cert. mgmt. cons. With Solar Aircraft Co.,

San Diego, 1937-43; supt. Des Moines plant, 1942-43; mem. staff Albert Ramond & Assos., Chgo., 1943-72, v.p., 1956-61, pres., 1962-72; spl. cons. Theodore Barry & Assocs., L.A., 1977-82, ind. mgmt. cons., 1982-89, cons. fellow; ret. Author: Effective Maintenance Management; also articles. Mem. Inst. Indsl. Engrs., Assn. Cons. Mgmt. Engrs. (dir. 1964-66), Am. Inst. Plant Engrs., Inst. Mgmt. Cons.'s (charter), St. Joe Valley Golf Club, Masons, Shriners. Presbyterian. (elder). Home: 24664 Ridgewood Dr Sturgis MI 49091

NEWBRUN, ERNEST, oral biology and periodontology educator; b. Vienna, Austria, Dec. 1, 1932; came to U.S., 1955; s. Victor and Elizabeth (Reichl) N; m. Eva Miriam, June 17, 1956; children: Deborah Anne, Daniel Eric, Karen Ruth. BDS, U. Sydney (New South Wales), 1954; MS, U. Rochester, 1957; DMD, U. Ala., 1959; PhD, U. Calif., San Francisco, 1965; Odont. Dr. (hon.), U. Lund, Sweden, 1988. Cert. periodontology, 1983. Rsch. assoc. Eastern Dental Ctr., Rochester, N.Y., 1955-57, U. Ala. Med. Ctr., Birmingham, 1957-59; rsch. fellow Inst. Dental Rsch., Sydney, Australia, 1960-61; rsch. tchr. trainee U. Calif., San Francisco, 1961-63, postdoctoral fellow, 1963-65, assoc. prof., prof., 1965-70, prof. oral biology, 1970-83, prof. oral biology and periodontology, 1983-94, prof. emeritus, 1994—; cons. FDA, 1983—. Author: Cariology, 1989, Pharmacology and Therapeutic Dentistry, 1989, (with others) Pediatrics, 1991; editor: Fluorides and Dental Caries, 1986; mem. editorial bd. Jour. Periodontal Rsch., 1985-90, Jour. Peridontology, 1990—. Bd. dirs. Raoul Wallenberg Dem. Club, San Francisco, 1987-92. Mem. AAAS (chmn. dental section, 1988-89), Internat. Assn. Dental Rsch. (pres. 1989-90), Dental Health Foun. (chmn. bd. dirs., 1985-92). Jewish.

NEWBURGER, BETH WEINSTEIN, medical telecommunications company executive; b. Schenectady, July 8, 1937; d. H. Edward and Shirley (Diamond) Weinstein; m. Alan C. Newburger, Jan. 23, 1963 (dec. Oct. 1980); children: Mark, Lori, Eric, Jill; m. Richard Schwartz, May 26, 1989. BA, Cornell U., 1959. Dir. advt. New Republic, Washington, 1974-77; mktg. mgr. Washington Post, 1977-84; pres. Owlcat/Digital Rsch., Inc., Monterey, Calif., 1984-86; pres., CEO Corabi Internat. Telemetrics, Inc., Alexandria, Va., 1986-95; chmn. bd. Health Street, Inc., Bethesda, Md., 1985-95, assoc. adminstr. gen. svc. adminstrn., 1996—; bd. dirs. Tyson Nat. Bank, Vienna, Va.; mem. NASA adv. coun. Tech. Commercialization Adv. Com., 1995—. Bd. dirs. Arena Stage, Washington, 1993—, BOAT/U.S., 1990—; chmn. bd. Capital Children's Mus., Washington, 1984—. Named Woman of Yr., Svc. Guild, Washington, 1972, 73. Mem. Women in Advt. and Mktg. (bd. dirs. 1986-89). Home: 1401 N Oak St Arlington VA 22209-3648

NEWBURGER, FRANK L., JR., retired investment broker; b. Phila., Nov. 26, 1908; s. Frank L. and Helen (Langfeld) N.; m. Dorothy Hess, Nov. 7, 1946 (dec.); children: Patricia S. (dec.), Frank L., III; m. Jane Berger, Aug. 19, 1973. AB, Cornell U., 1929. Ptnr. Newburger, Loeb & Co., Phila., 1930-46, Newburger & Co., 1946-70, Advest Co.; mng. partner Newburger & Co. div. Advest, 1970-77; sr. v.p. Newburger & Co. div. Advest, Phila., 1977-84; Bd. govs. N.Y. Stock Exchange, 1959-62; bd. govs. Phila.-Balt. Stock Exchange, 1946-56, pres., 1954-57. Vice chmn. United Fund, 1957-63; dir. Fedn. Jewish Agys., 1950—, pres., 1966, 67; emeritus bd. dirs., past treas., trustee (hon.) Acad. Natural Scis.; emeritus trustee Albert Einstein Med. Center, treas., 1957-60; mem. council Cornell U., 1965-71, 74-77, emeritus, 1978-88, life mem., 1989; mem. Health and Welfare Council, 1965-70. Mem. Bond Club Phila. (pres. 1966). Home: 8302 York Rd Apt B-63 Elkins Park PA 19027 Office: # 807 The Pavilion 261 York Rd Jenkintown PA 19046-3706

NEWBURGER, HOWARD MARTIN, psychoanalyst; b. N.Y.C., May 16, 1924; s. Bernhard and Bertha (Travers) N.; m. Doris Schekter, July 3, 1949; children: Amy, Barry, Cary. B.A., N.Y. U., 1948, M.A., 1950, Ph.D., 1952; tng. in Jungian, Neo-Freudian and Horneyian psychoanalysis. Cert. in group psychotherapy and psychodrama. Rotating intern N.J. Dept. Instns. and Agys., 1948-49; chief psychologist N.J. State Instn., Annandale, 1949-52; dir. psychoanalysis Div. Social Def. UN, 1952; pvt. practice in psychoanalysis and group psychotherapy, 1952—; dir. rsch. HEW, 1958; rsch. assoc. Beth Israel Hosp., 1958-69; staff mem. St. Agnes Hosp., White Plains, 1991—; lectr., adj. assoc. prof. NYU, 1951-60, chmn. dept. exceptional child and youth, 1954-62; chmn. faculty and supr. treatment Inst. Applied Human Dynamics, 1960—; lectr., cons. in field; prelect prof. psychology John Jay Coll. Criminal Justice, 1969-72; chmn. bd. dirs. Inst. Applied Human Dynamics, N.Y.C. and Westchester, N.Y., 1960-81, exec. v.p., 1983-85; cons. Police Dept., Harrison, N.Y., 1970—. Co-author: Winners and Losers. Assoc. editor: Excerpta Medica, 1951-62. Contbr. articles and papers to tech. jours. Trustee Acad. Jewish Religion, 1991—. Served with AUS, World War II, ETO; with AUS, MTO. Recipient Outstanding Service to Humanity award Inst. Applied Human Dynamics for Handicapped, 1970. Mem. Am. Psychol. Assn., Am. Soc. Group Psychotherapy and Psychodrama (sec.-treas. 1954-55). Office: Timber Trail Rye NY 10580-1935 *Our country affords tremendous opportunity. Through the development of our inner resources, and their assertion, we can all have happy and effective lives.*

NEWBY, JOHN ROBERT, metallurgical engineer; b. Kansas City, Mo., Nov. 17, 1923; s. Merritt Owen and Gladys Mary (McCleery) N.; m. Audry Marie Loniker, Sept. 21, 1963 (div. 1980); children: Deborah A., Walter J., William F., Matthew O., Robert J. BA, U. Mo., Kansas City, 1947; BS in Metall. Engring., Colo. Sch. Mines, 1949; MS, U. Cin., 1963. Cert. profl. engr. Chemist Bar Rusto Plating Corp., Kansas City, 1949; supr. United Chromium, Ferndale, Mich., 1949-52; prin. rsch. metallurgist Armco Inc., Middletown, Ohio, 1952-85; prin. John Newby Cons., Middletown, 1985—; cons. Phoenix Cons., Inc., Cin., 1988—. Author, editor: Formability 2000, 1982, Metallic Materials, 1978, Sheet Metal Forming, 1976; editor: Mechanical Testing, Vol. 8, 9th edit., 1985. Scoutmaster Boy Scouts Am., Middletown, 1952-86; chmn. Safety Coun., Middletown, 1978-80. Staff sgt. USAF, 1943-46, PTO. Fellow ASTM (chmn. 1963—, Award of Merit 1984), ASM (chpt. chmn. 1970, Award of Merit 1980); mem. SAE (sect. chmn. 1984). Democrat. Achievements include patent for high strength formable steel sheet; development of interstitial free steel, strain analysis process for metallic sheet formability. Home and Office: 100 Marymont Ct Middletown OH 45042-3735

NEWBY, TIMOTHY JAMES, education educator, researcher; b. Nampa, Idaho, Oct. 9, 1955; s. Neal Arthur and Margy Lou (Hooker) N.; m. Deedra Diane Hays, May 3, 1978; children: Timbre, Landon, Alexis, Brayden. BS, Brigham Young U., 1979, PhD, 1984. Prof. Purdue U., West Lafayette, Ind. Mem. Am. Edn. Rsch. Assn. Home: 216 Berwick Dr Lafayette IN 47905-6904 Office: Purdue U Curriculum and Instruction 1442 LAEB West Lafayette IN 47907

NEWCOM, JENNINGS JAY, lawyer; b. St. Joseph, Mo., Oct. 18, 1941; s. Arden Henderson and Loyal Beatrice (Winans) N.; m. Cherry Ann Phelps, Apr. 4, 1964; children: Shandra Karine, J. Derek Arden. BA, Graceland Coll., Lamoni, Iowa, 1964; JD, Harvard U., 1968. Bar: Ill. 1968, Calif. 1973, Mo. 1979, Kans. 1981. Atty. McDermott, Will & Emery, Chgo., 1968-73; ptnr. Rifkind, Sterling & Lockwood, Beverly Hills, Calif., 1973-79, Shook, Hardy & Bacon L.L.P., Kansas City, Mo., 1979—; chmn. bd. Graceland Coll. Trustee Hubbard Found., Linde Found. Mem. Kansas City Bar Assn., State Bar Assn. Calif., Lawyers Assn. Kansas City. Office: Shook Hardy & Bacon 1200 Main St Ste 3100 Kansas City MO 64105-2100

NEWCOMB, DANFORTH, lawyer; b. Tarrytown, N.Y., Jan. 24, 1943; s. Russell Ladd and Louise Munroe (Blazer) N.; m. Elizabeth W. Newcomb, Nov. 25, 1966; children—Alexander, Thomas. B.A., U. Vt., 1965; LL.B., Columbia U., 1968. Bar: N.Y. 1968, D.C. 1990, U.S. Dist. Ct. (so. and ea. dists.) N.Y. 1971, U.S. Ct. Claims 1971, U.S. Tax Ct. 1971, U.S. Ct. Appeals (2d and 3d cir.) 1971, U.S. Supreme Ct. 1981, U.S. Dist. Ct. (ea. dist.) Mich. 1983, U.S. Ct. Appeals (11th cir.) 1983, U.S. Ct. Appeals (6th cir.) 1986. Assoc., Shearman & Sterling, N.Y.C., 1968-69, 71-78, ptnr., 1979—; mem. panel of mediators U.S. Dist. Ct. (so. dist.) N.Y. Served to capt. U.S. Army, 1969-70. Decorated Bronze Star. Mem. ABA, Fed. Bar Council, Am. Arbitration Assn. (panel of arbitrators). Office: 153 E 53rd St New York NY 10022-4611

NEWCOMB, ELDON HENRY, retired botany educator; b. Columbia, Mo., Jan. 19, 1919; s. Ernest Henry and Ruby Josephine (Anderson) N.; m. Joyce Bright Rieling, June 21, 1949; children—Norman Robert, Barbara Pauline, Cynthia Irma. Student, U. Kansas City, 1936-38; A.B., U. Mo., 1940, A.M., 1942; Ph.D., U. Wis., 1949; DS honoris causa, U. Mo., Columbia, 1993. Asst. prof. botany U. Wis.-Madison, 1949-54, assoc. prof., 1954-58, prof., 1958-90, prof. emeritus, 1990—; dir. Inst. Plant Devel., 1979-88; chmn. dept. botany U. Wis.-Madison, 1982-88, Folke Skoog prof. botany, 1987—; cons. Shell Devel. Co., 1954-59. Sr. author: Plants in Perspective, 1963; mng. editor Protoplasma, 1969-73; mem. editorial bd. Ann. Rev. Plant Physiology, 1965-69, Protoplasma, 1973—, Planta, 1981-90; contbr. articles to profl. jours. Served with AUS, 1942-45. NRC predoctoral fellow U. Wis., 1946-49; Guggenheim Found. fellow U. Calif. at Berkeley, 1951-52; Sci. Faculty fellow Harvard, 1963-64; Fulbright Sr. Research scholar Australian Nat. U., Canberra, 1976. Mem. NAS, Am. Soc. Cell Biologists, Am. Acad. Arts and Scis., Bot. Soc. Am., Am. Soc. Plant Physiologists, Soc. Devel. Biology, Phi Beta Kappa (pres. Wis. Alpha chpt. 1978-79), Sigma Xi. Mem. expdn. to Great Barrier Reef, 1973. Home: 52 Oak Creek Trl Madison WI 53717-1510

NEWCOMB, ROBERT WAYNE, electrical engineering educator; b. Glendale, Calif., June 27, 1933; s. Robert Dobson and Dorothy Opal (Bissinger) N.; m. Sarah Eleanor Fritz, May 22, 1954; children: Gail E., Robert W. BSEE, Purdue U., 1955; MS, Stanford U., 1957, PhD, U. Calif., Berkeley, 1960. Registered profl. engr., Calif. Rsch. intern Stanford Rsch. Inst., Menlo Park, Calif., 1955-57; teaching assoc. U. Calif., Berkeley, 1957-60; asst. and assoc. prof. Stanford U., 1960-70; prof. elec. engring. U. Md., College Park, 1970—; bd. dirs. PARCOR Rsch. program, Universidad Politecnica de Madrid, Spain. Author: Linear Multiport Synthesis, 1966, Active Integrated Circuit Synthesis, 1968, Concepts of Linear Systems and Control, 1968, Network Theory, 1967. Fulbright fellow, 1963; Fulbright-Hays fellow, 1976; Robert Wayne Newcomb Lab. opened U. Politecnica Madrid, 1995. Fellow IEEE; mem. Soc. Indsl. and Applied Math., Math. Assn. Am., Acad. Am. Poets. Avocations: film, literature, poetry. Home: 13120 Two Farm Dr Silver Spring MD 20904-3418 Office: Univ Md Microsystems Lab Elec Engring Dept College Park MD 20742

NEWCOMBE, GEORGE MICHAEL, lawyer; b. Newark, Nov. 11, 1947; s. George Anthony and Mary Hellen Newcombe; m. Joan Sharon Hanlon, May 30, 1969; children: Sean Michael, Scott Ryan, Jennifer Leigh. B-SChemE, N.J. Inst. Tech., 1969; JD, Columbia U., 1975. Bar: N.J. 1975, N.Y. 1976, U.S. Dist. Ct. N.J. 1975, U.S. Ct. Appeals (2d cir.) 1975, U.S. Dist. Ct. (so. dist.) N.Y. 1976, U.S. Dist. Ct. (we. dist.) Tex. 1985, U.S. Ct. Appeals (5th cir.) 1986, U.S. Ct. Appeals (3d cir.) 1992, U.S. Ct. Appeals (fed. cir.) 1995, U.S. Supreme Ct. 1987. Ptnr. Simpson, Thacher & Bartlett, N.Y.C., 1975—; dir. Columbia Law Sch. Assn., Inc., Columbia Jour. Environ. Law; dir., legal sec. Am. Ditchley Found., 1994; bd. visitors Columbia Law Sch., 1997—. Mem. coun. com. law offices vol. divsn. Legal Aid Soc., N.Y.C., 1980-86. Lt. USPHS, 1970-72. James Kent scholar Columbia Law Sch., 1974, Harlan Fiske Stone scholar Columbia Law Sch., 1975. Mem. Am. Law Inst., ABA, AICE, Assn. of Bar of City of N.Y., Tau Beta Epsilon, Omicron Delta Kappa. Office: Simpson Thacher & Bartlett 425 Lexington Ave New York NY 10017-3903

NEWCOMBE, HOWARD BORDEN, biologist, consultant; b. Kentville, N.S., Can., Sept. 19, 1914; s. Edward Borden and Mabel Elsie (Outerbridge) N.; m. Beryl Honor Callaway, Feb. 14, 1942; children—Kenneth Donald, Charles Philip, Richard William. B.Sc., Acadia U., Wolfville, N.S., 1935; Assoc., Imperial Coll. Tropical Agr., Trinidad, 1938; Ph.D., McGill U., Montreal, P.Q., Can., 1939; D.Sc. (hon.), McGill U., 1966, Acadia U., 1970. Sci. officer Brit. Ministry of Supply, London, 1940-41; research assoc. Carnegie Instn. Washington, 1946-47; research sci. Atomic Energy of Can. Ltd., Chalk River, Ont., 1947-79; head biology br. Atomic Energy of Can. Ltd., 1949-70, head population research br., 1970-79; vis. prof. genetics Ind. U., Bloomington, 1963; mem. Internat. Commn. on Radiol. Protection, 1965-77, chmn. com. on biol. effects, 1965-72. Contbr. articles to profl. jours. Served to lt. Brit. Royal Naval Vol. Res., 1941-46. Fellow Royal Soc. Can.; mem. Genetics Soc. Am. (sec. 1956-58), Am. Soc. Human Genetics (pres. 1965), Genetics Soc. Can. (pres. 1964-65). Home: 67 Hillcrest Ave, PO Box 135, Deep River, ON Canada K0J 1P0

NEWELL, BARBARA WARNE, economist, educator; b. Pitts., Aug. 19, 1929; d. Colston E. and Frances (Corbett) Warne; m. George V. Thompson, June 15, 1954 (dec. 1954); m. George S. Newell, June 9, 1956 (dec. 1964); m. Ernest Kolowrat, Mar. 18, 1996; 1 child, Elizabeth Penfield. BA, Vassar Coll., 1951; MA, U. Wis., 1953, PhD, 1958, D. Pub. Svc.; LHD, Trinity Coll., 1973, Lesley Coll., 1978; LLD, Central Mich. U., 1973, Williams Coll., 1974, Rollins Coll., 1981, Butler U., 1983, Monmouth Coll., 1986; DLitt, Northeastern U., 1974, Mt. Vernon Coll., 1975, Lesley Coll., 1978, Denison U., 1978, Eckerd Coll., 1982, Gettysburg Coll., 1982, Dennison U., 1978; D.Adminstrn., Purdue U., 1976; DSc, Fla. Inst. Tech., 1981; LHD, Eckerd Coll., 1982; LLD, Butler U., 1983; D Pub. Service, Alaska Pacific U., 1986; DsPS, U. Md., 1987. Asst. to chancellor U. Wis., 1965-67; research, teaching asst., assoc. U. Ill., 1954-59; asst. prof., then assoc. prof. econs. Purdue U., 1959-65; asst. to pres., assoc. prof. econs. U. Mich., Ann Arbor, 1967-71, acting v.p. student affairs, 1968-70; prof. econs., assoc. provost grad. study and research U. Pitts., 1971; pres. Wellesley (Mass.) Coll., 1972-79; U.S. rep. with rank ambassador to UNESCO, Paris, 1979-81; chancellor State U. System Fla., Tallahassee, 1981-85; Regents prof. Fla. State U., 1985-96; ret., 1996; vis. scholar Harvard U., 1985-86, vis. lectr., 1986-87. Author: Chicago and the Labor Movement, 1961, The Pulse of the Nation, 1961, Our Labour Force, 1962; contbr. articles and revs. to profl. jours. and mags. Trustee Carnegie Endowment for Internat. Peace, 1973—; bd. dirs. Americans for the Universality of UNESCO, 1984—; mem. Fla. Edn. and Employment Coun. for Women and Girls, 1992—. Home: 1214 Clark Ave Tallahassee FL 32301

NEWELL, BYRON BRUCE, JR., retired theological seminary dean, clergyman; b. Long Beach, Calif., July 31, 1932; s. Byron Bruce and Eleanor Whitaker (Davis) N.; m. Ingrid Charlotte Asche, June 11, 1955 (dec. July 1989); children: Thomas, Susan, Robert, Michael; m. Theresa Ann Troncale, Sept. 1, 1990. Student, Wesleyan U., 1950-51; BS, U.S. Naval Acad., 1955; MSEE, U.S. Naval Postgrad. Sch. Monterey, 1962; postgrad. nuclear power tng., 1964-65; MDiv, Va. Theol. Sem., 1987. Ordained priest, Episcopal Ch., 1988. Commd. ensign U.S. Navy, 1955, advanced through grades to rear adm., 1980; weapons officer U.S.S. Lowry, Hull (destroyers), 1955-58; comdg. officer salvage ship, 1962-64, exec., comdg. officer nuclear cruisers, 1968-77, manpower/tng. surface ship personnel, 1977-79; with Nat. Mil. Command Center, Washington, 1979-80, chief navy info., 1980-82, chief navy legis. affairs, 1982-84; assoc. dean Trinity Episcopal Sch. for Ministry, Ambridge, Pa., 1990-96; chmn., trustee Breakthrough, Inc. Decorated Legion of Merit, D.S.M. Mem. Naval Inst., Naval Hist. Soc., Met. Club. Home: 256 Thorn St Sewickley PA 15143-1204

NEWELL, CHARLDEAN, public administration educator; b. Ft. Worth, Oct. 14, 1939; d. Charles Thurlow and Mildren Dean (Looney) N. BA, U. North Tex., 1960, MA, 1962; PhD, U. Tex., 1968; cert., Harvard U., 1988. Instr. U. North Tex., Denton, 1965-68, asst. prof., 1968-72; assoc. prof., dir. Fedn. North Tex. Area Univs., Denton, Dallas, 1972-74; assoc. prof., assoc. v.p. acad. affairs U. North Tex., Denton, 1974-76, assoc. prof., chair dept. polit. sci., 1976-80, prof. polit. sci., 1980-92, assoc. v.p., spl. asst. to chancellor, 1982-92, regents prof. pub. adminstrn., 1992—; cons. Miss. Bd. Trustees State Instns. Higher Learning, Jackson, 1983-84, Ednl. Testing Svc., Princeton, N.J., 1980, 82, 85, Spear, Down & Judin, Dallas, 1994-95, North Tex. Inst. Edn. in Visual Arts, Denton, 1993-94; bd. dirs. Mcpl. Clks. Ednl. Found., San Dimas, Calif.; bd. regents Internat. City/County Mgmt. Assn., Washington. Author: (with others) City Executives: Leadership Roles, Work Characteristics and Time Management, 1989, The Effective Local Government Manager, 1993, Essentials of Texas Politics, 1995, Texas Politics, 1996; contbr. articles to profl. jours. Chmn. Denton Charter Rev. Com., 1978-79; mem. Denton CSC, 1989—, chmn., 1992—; mem. adv. com. Ann's Haven Hospice, Denton, 1981-85; mem. exec. coun. Episcopal Diocese Dallas, 1985-88; mem. Denton Blue Ribbon Capital Improvements Com., 1995-96, Denton Devel. Plan Com., 1996-97. Recipient Elmer Staats Career Pub. Svc. award Nat. Assn. Sch. Pub. Affairs Adminstrn., 1993. Mem. ASPA (sect. chmn. 1982-83, mem. editl. bd. 1985-88), Internat. Pers. Mgmt. Assn. (regional program com. 1982-83), Am. Polit. Sci. Assn., Southwestern Polit. Sci. Assn. (sec., treas. 1975-79), Denton C. of C., Denton Tennis Assn., Pi Sigma Alpha (exec. coun. 1988-92), Pi Alpha Alpha (exec. coun. 1995—). Democrat. Avocations: walking, reading. Home: 709 Mimosa Dr Denton TX 76201-8814 Office: U North Tex PO Box 310617 Denton TX 76203-0617

NEWELL, ERIC JAMES, financial planner, tax consultant, former insurance executive; b. Toronto, Ont., Can., Sept. 24, 1930; came to U.S., 1959, naturalized, 1970; s. James and Anne (Brown) N.; m. Essie Miskelly, Sept. 30, 1950; 1 son, Eric Wayne. Student, U. Toronto, 1951-53. Pub. acct. W.J. Wilcox & Co., Toronto, 1949-53; chief acct. Toronto Mut. Life Ins. Co., 1953-57; asst. sec. Holland Life Ins. Co., Toronto, 1957-59; with Penn Mut. Life Ins. Co., Phila., 1959-86; assoc. controller Penn Mut. Life Ins. Co., 1965-70, 2d v.p., controller, 1970-84, v.p., controller, 1984-86, ret., 1986; fin., tax cons., 1986—; dir. Hotel Brunswick, Lancaster, Pa., 1982-85. Mem. Traffic and Transp. Bd., Cherry Hill, N.J., 1971-73, Zoning Bd., 1975-78; vice chmn. Cherry Hill Econ. Devel. Bd., 1973-75; pres. Greater Kingston Civic Assn., Cherry Hill, 1970-76; Democratic committeeman, Camden County, 1976-79; vice chmn. Dem. Party, Cherry Hill, 1976. Fellow Life Mgmt. Inst., Royal Commonwealth Soc.; mem. Fin. Execs. Inst., Am. Inst. Corp. Contrs., N.Y. Ins. Accts. Club (chmn. 1984), Nat. Soc. Tax Profls., Royal Black Knights of Ireland, Loyal Orange Assn. (past master), Scotch-Irish Soc. of U.S. (mem. coun.), Am. Legion. Presbyterian (deacon 1969—). Home and Office: 137 E Partridge Ln Cherry Hill NJ 08003-4407

NEWELL, FRANK WILLIAM, ophthalmologist, educator; b. St. Paul, Jan. 14, 1916; s. Frank John and Hilda (Turnquist) N.; m. Marian Glennon, Sept. 12, 1942; children: Frank William, Mary Susan Newell O'Connell, Elizabeth Glennon Newell Murphy, David Andrew Newell. M.D., Loyola U., Chgo., 1939; M.Sc., U. Minn., 1942. Diplomate Am. Bd. Ophthalmology (chmn. bd. 1967-69). James and Anna Raymond prof. dept. ophthalmology U. Chgo., 1953—; prof. extraordinario Autonomous U. Barcelona, Spain, 1972—; hon. prof. Tech. U., Japan, 1986—; sci. counselor Nat. Inst. Neurol. Diseases and Blindness, 1959-62, chmn., 1961-62; mem. nat. adv. eye coun. NIH, 1972-75; mem. Internat. Council Ophthalmology, 1977-85; bd. dirs. Heed Ophthalmic Found., 1965-93, chmn., 1975-90; dir. Ophthalmic Pub. Co., 1962—, sec., treas., 1971-95. Author: Ophthalmology: Principles and Concepts, 1965, 8th edit., 1996, The American Ophthalmological Society 1864-89, 1989; also articles; editor in chief Am. Jour. Ophthalmology, 1965-91, pub., 1972-95; editor: Trans Glaucoma Conf., Vols. 1-5, 1955-61, Amblyopia and Strabismus, 1975, Hereditary Diseases of the Eye, 1980, Stedman's Medical Dictionary, 25th edit., 1990, Documenta Ophthalmologica Historia, 1996—. Trustee Loyola U., Chgo., 1977-81. Served from 1st lt. to maj. M.C. AUS, 1942-46. Recipient Alumni Citation award Loyola U., 1962, Stritch medal, 1966, Outstanding Achievement award U. Minn., 1975, 92, Gold Key U. Chgo., 1981, Lang medal Royal Soc. Medicine, London, 1974, medal honor Soc. Eye Surgeons, 1975, Vail medal Internat. Eye Found., 1986, medalla André Bello U. Chile, 1977, medalla de Oro Instituto Barraquer, Barcelona, Spain, 1982; Disting. Svc. award Physicians Edn. Network, 1983; decorated knight Order of St. John. Mem. Nat. Soc. Prevention Blindness (dir., v.p. 1970-81, pres. 1981-83, chmn. bd. 1983-85, Dunnington medal 1976), AMA (chmn. sect. ophthalmology 1964-65, Howe prize 1968), Am. Acad. Ophthalmology and Otolaryngology (pres. 1975), Inst. Barraguer (pres. 1970-88, hon. pres. 1988—), Assn. Univ. Profs. Ophthalmology (trustee 1966-69, pres. 1968-69), Assn. Research Ophthal. (chmn. bd. trustees 1967-68), Pan-Am. Assn. Ophthalmology (dir. 1969—, pres. 1981-83), Am. Ophthal. Soc. (pres. 1986-87, Howe medal 1979), Chgo. Ophthal. Soc. (pres. 1957-58), Oxford (Eng.) Ophthal. Congress (hon. mem., dep. master 1980), Hellenic Ophthal. Soc. (hon.), Royal Soc. Medicine (hon.), Academia Ophthalmologica Internationalis (pres. 1980-84), Columbia Ophthal. Soc. (hon.), Sigma Xi, Alpha Omega Alpha. Roman Catholic. Clubs: Literary (Chgo.), Quadrangle (Chgo.). Home: 4500 N Mozart St Chicago IL 60625-3817 Office: 939 W 57th St Chicago IL 60621-2217

NEWELL, HAROLD JOE, quality assurance engineer; b. Fernbank, Ala., Dec. 31, 1945; s. Homer Isaiah and Beulah Mae (Tomlin) N.; m. Brenda Kay Guin, Sept. 24, 1966 (div. Jan. 1993); m. Kathy Lane Vaughn, Oct. 2, 1995; children: Tyrena Kay, Wesley Joe. Student, E. Miss. Jr. Coll., 1976, Miss. U. for Women, 1984, 86, U. Ala., 1990—. lic. rep. Franklin Life Ins. Co. Lineman Four-County Elec. Power Assn., 1964-65; tool and die apprentice Quality Tooling, Fayette, Ala., 1965-66; quality assurance engr., quality control supr. United Techs. Motor Sys., Columbus, Miss., 1966-95; factory sales rep. Am. Home Sunrooms divsn. Am. Std. Constrn. Co., Birmingham, Ala., 1996-97; sales rep. Ala. Leisure Rooms, Tuscaloosa, 1997—. Pastor S.C. Bapt. Ch., Vernon, Ala., Mt. Olive Bapt. ch., Millport, Ala.; conducts weekly radio program Sta. WVSA, Vernon; mgr. five mem. band, 1968-73. Recipient award of excellence in photography Photographer's Forum Mag., Santa Barbara, Calif., 1984, 87. Mem. Am. Soc. Quality Control (sr. mem., pub. rels. com.). Republican. Avocations: music, photography, collector. Home: 6215 Hwy 18 W Vernon AL 35592

NEWELL, MIYAKO DE LIGE, medical/surgical nurse; b. Tachikawa-shi, Japan, Oct. 4, 1960; d. Harry and Yayako (Kasai) De Lige. BSN, Keuka Coll., Keuka Park, N.Y., 1984. RN, N.Y.; cert. in med-surg. nursing, cert. nephrology nurse. Staff nurse Geneva (N.Y.) Gen. Hosp., 1984-90; hemodialysis nurse Rochester Gen. Hosp., 1990—, nurse clinician II, 1994—. Recipient RN of Yr. award Geneva Gen. Hosp., 1989. Mem. Am. Nephrology Nurses Assn., Gt. Lakes of N.Y. Nephrology Nurses Assn.

NEWELL, NORMAN DENNIS, paleontologist, geologist, museum curator, educator; b. Chgo., Jan. 27, 1909; s. Virgil Bingham and Nellie (Clark) N.; m. Valerie Zirkle, Feb. 25, 1928 (dec. 1972); m. Gillian Wendy Wormall, Apr. 28, 1973. B.S., U. Kans., 1929, M.A., 1931; Ph.D. in Geology, Yale U., 1933. Faculty mem. U. Kans., Lawrence, 1934-37; assoc. prof. geology U. Wis.-Madison, 1937-45; prof. geology Columbia U., N.Y.C., 1945-77, prof. emeritus, 1977—; curator Am. Mus. Nat. History, N.Y.C., 1945-77, curator emeritus, 1977—; geologist Kans. Geol. Survey, Lawrence, 1929-37; cons. on petroleum geology Peruvian Govt., 1942-45. Author: Permian Reef Complex of the Guadalupe Mountains Region, Texas and New Mexico, 1953, Creation and Evolution: Myth or Reality?, 1982, also numerous sci. articles and papers. Recipient Disting. Svc. Alumni award Kans. U., 1961, Hayden award Phila. Acad. Sci., 1965, Verrill medal Yale U., 1966, Gold medal for achievment in sci. Am. Mus. Natural History, 1978, Raymond C. Moore medal Soc. Econ. Paleontologists and Mineralogists, 1980, Scientific Freedom and Responsibility award AAAS, 1987. Mem. Nat. Acad. Scis. (Mary Clark Thompson medal 1960), Am. Philos. Soc., Am. Acad. Arts and Scis., Am. Assn. Petroleum Geologists (spl. award 1996), Geol. Soc. Am. (Penrose medal 1990), Soc. Study Evolution (pres. 1949), Soc. Systematic Zoology (pres. 1972-73), Paleontol. Soc. (pres. 1960-61, medal 1979), Can. Soc. Petroleum Geologists (hon.). Avocations: geologic field expeditions. Home: 135 Knapp Ter Leonia NJ 07605-1216 Office: Am Mus Natural History Central Park W and 79 St New York NY 10024

NEWELL, PAUL HAYNES, JR., engineering educator, former college president; b. Nashville, July 1, 1933; s. Paul Haynes Newell; m. Martha A. Newell; children: Paul Haynes III, Mike, Nan. B.M.E., U. Tenn., 1958, M.M.E., 1961; Mech.E., Mass. Inst. Tech., 1964, Ph.D., 1966. Registered profl. engr., Ala., Tenn., Tex., N.J. Student asst. mech. engring. U. Tenn., 1957, instr. mech. engring., 1958-62; NSF Sci. faculty fellow Mass. Inst. Tech., 1962-65; asso. prof. mech. engring. U. Ala. Coll. Engring., 1966-69; prof. mech. engring. Tex. A. and M. U., 1969-72, assoc. dean engring., 1972; prof. biomed. engring., dept. phys. medicine Baylor Coll. Medicine, 1969-74, prof. biomed. engring., dept. physiology, 1970-74, prof. biomed. engring., dept. community medicine, 1972-74, prof. biomed. engring., dept. rehab., 1972—, mem. grad. faculty, 1970-74; prof., head indsl. engring. dept. Tex. A. & M. U., 1972-74, prof., head combined programs of behavioral engring., bioengring., cybernetic engring., hygiene and safety engring., indsl. engring., 1972-74; pres., prof. Newark Coll. Engring., N.J. Inst. Tech., 1974-78; prof. Adminstrn. Prosthetics Ctr., N.Y., 1973-75, VA Hosp., Houston, 1972-75, Baylor Coll. Medicine, Houston, from 1971; pres. Newell Engring., Greenbrier, Tenn., 1979—; dir. N.J. Bell Telephone Co., Mid Atlantic Nat. Bank, Thomas-Betts Corp. Contbr. articles to profl. jours., chpts. to books. Mem. NSF liaison com., Newark Transp. Council, N.J. Safety Council; sec. exec. com. council Boy Scouts Am., Birmingham, Ala., 1966-68; bd. dirs. N.J. State Opera, United Hosps. Newark. Served with USMCR, Korean Conflict. Recipient NSF Sci. Faculty fellowship. Mem. Am. Soc. Tool and Mfg. Engrs., N.Y., Ala. acads. scis., AAAS, Am. Congress Rehab. Medicine, Am. Heart Assn., Am. Inst. Indsl. Engrs., Am. Soc. Artificial Internal Organs, Am. Soc. Engring. Edn., ASME, Biomed. Engring. Soc., Inst. Engring.

Deans, Internat. Soc. Prosthetics and Orthotics, Nat. Soc. Profl. Engrs., Soc. Advanced Med. Systems, Soc. Engring. Sci., Pres.'s Assn., Am. Fluid Power Soc., N.J. Soc. Engrs., Sigma Xi, Tau Beta Pi, Phi Kappa Phi, Pi Tau Sigma. Club: Rotary. Address: 1855 Lake Rd Greenbrier TN 37073-4619 Office: Newell Engring Greenbrier TN 37073-4619

NEWELL, PETER, retired basketball coach; b. Vancouver, B.C., Can., Aug. 31, 1915. Coach U. San Francisco, 1946-50, Mich. State U., 1950-54, U. Calif., Berkeley, 1954-60. Named Coach of Yr., 1960, Basketball Hall of Fame, 1978. Achievements include coach of Pacific-8 Title Team, 1957-60. Office: c/o Basketball Hall of Fame PO Box 179 Springfield MA 01101-0179

NEWELL, REGINALD EDWARD, physics educator; b. Peterborough, Eng., Apr. 9, 1931; came to U.S., 1954, naturalized, 1969; s. Harold Aubrey and Edith (Swiffin) N.; m. Maireen W. Lees, Sept. 6, 1954; children: Madeleine, Elizabeth, Oliver, Nicholas. B.S. in Physics, U. Birmingham, Eng., 1954; M.S., Mass. Inst. Tech., 1956, Sc.D., 1960. With Brit. Meteorol. Office, 1947-50; successively research staff asst., asst. prof., asso. prof., prof. MIT, Cambridge, 1954—; mem IUGG Internat. Commn. Meteorology Upper Atmosphere, 1967-75; mem. Internat. Commn. Atmospheric Chemistry and Global Pollution, 1971-83; pres. Internat. Commn. on Climate, 1977-83. Joint author: The General Circulation of the Tropical Atmosphere, Vol. I, 1972, Vol. 2, 1974, Global Ocean Surface Temperature Atlas, 1990; contbr. articles to profl. jours. Served with RAF, 1950-51. Fellow Royal Meteorol. Soc., Am. Meteorol. Soc.; mem. Am. Geophys. Union. Home: 45 Jason St Arlington MA 02174-6446 Office: MIT 54-1824 77 Massachusetts Ave # 54-1824 Cambridge MA 02139-4301

NEWELL, ROBERT LINCOLN, retired banker; b. Hartford, Conn., Dec. 2, 1922; s. Robert B. and Helen C. (Lincoln) N.; m. Sally C. Erdman, July 28, 1944; children: Sally Newell Huss, Helen Newell Douglas, Robert Lincoln, Katharine Newell Chiodo, William Henry II. Student, Wesleyan U., Middletown, Conn. With Conn. Nat. Bank, Hartford, 1946-88, exec. v.p., 1967-72, 1st exec. v.p., 1972-75, pres., 1975-78, chmn., 1978-87, ret., 1987; former chmn. Hartford Nat. Corp. Corporator Hartford Hosp., Mt. Sinai Hosp.; bd. dirs. Mustic Seaport Mus. Lt. USNR, 1943-46. Home: 42 Mountain View Dr West Hartford CT 06117-3029

NEWELL, WILLIAM JAMES, sign language educator; b. Port Jefferson, N.Y., Sept. 13, 1947; s. William James and Mary Louise (Pinder) N.; m. Beverly Jo Beller, June 18, 1971; children: Eric James, Christopher Ian. BA, St. Edwards U., Austin, Tex., 1970; MS, St. Cloud State U., 1977; PhD, Greenwich U., 1994. Cert. tchr. Am. Sign Lang.; cert. Coun. on Edn. of the Deaf. Houseparent, tchr. aide Tex. Sch. for the Deaf, Austin, 1969-70; tchr. of the deaf Harris County Pub. Schs., Houston, 1970-72, Dade County Pub. Schs., Miami, Fla., 1972-74; supervising tchr. of the deaf Hennepin Tech. Ctrs., Mpls., 1974-78; instr. Am. Sign Lang. Rochester (N.Y.) Inst. Tech., 1978-81; chairperson sign communication dept. Nat. Tech. Inst. for the Deaf, Rochester, 1981-91, rsch. assoc., 1991-96, assoc. prof. Am. sign lang. and deaf studies, 1996—; proprietor Sign Lang. Consulting Svcs., Ednl. Cons., Adult Edn. Resource. Co-developer: Sign Communication Proficiency Interview, 1981—; author: Basic Sign Communication, 1983. Recipient Outstanding Svc. award Sign Instrs. Guidance Network, Silver Spring, Md. Mem. Am. Sign Lang. Tchrs. Assn. (pres. 1986-90, chairperson evaluation and cert. com. 1990—, Veditz award 1996), Conv. of Am. Instrs. for the Deaf. Avocations: home brewing, walking for fitness, backyard birdfeeding. Home: 5259 Lower Egypt Rd Canandaigua NY 14424-9311 Office: Nat Tech Inst for the Deaf 52 Lomb Memorial Dr Rochester NY 14623-5604

NEWELL, WILLIAM TALMAN, JR., hospital administrator; b. Newport News, Va., Apr. 4, 1932; s. William Talman and Helen Louise (Woolfolk) N.; m. Mary Hill Chilton, Feb. 11, 1956; children—William Talman III, John Chilton, Anne Caroline. B.S. in Hotel Adminstrn., Cornell U., 1954; M.B.A. in Health Care Adminstrn., George Washington U., 1967. Asst. mgr. Dayton (Ohio) Biltmore Hotel, 1956-57; restaurant mgr. Marriott Corp., Washington, 1957-60; food service mgr. The Fairfax Hosp., Falls Church, Va., 1960-63, asst. dir. gen. services div., 1963-64, dir. gen. services div., 1964-66, asst. to the adminstr., 1966-67; asst. dir. Yale-New Haven (Conn.) Hosp., 1967-70, assoc. dir., 1970-75; chief exec. officer U. Miss. Hosp., 1975-83; exec. dir. Univ. Hosp., SUNY, Stony Brook, 1983-94, ret., 1994; lectr. Sch. Epidemiology and Pub. Health, Yale U. Sch. Medicine, 1969-75; dir. Miss. Blue Cross & Blue Shield, 1979-83; mem. Appalachian Council Teaching Hosps., 1979; mem. Miss. Gov.'s Health Care Task Force on Children and Youth, 1982-83. Chmn. bd. Vocat. Rehab. Ctr. for Blind, Jackson, Miss.; adminstrv. bd. Nassau-Suffolk Hosp. Council Bd.; v.p. ops. Suffolk County council Boy Scouts Am.; bd. dirs. U. Hosp. Consortium; pres. bd. dirs. Miss. Blood Services, 1977-83; bd. dirs. Hosp. Assn. N.Y. Served to 1st lt. U.S. Army, 1954-56. Mem. Am. Coll. Health Care Adminstrs. Episcopalian.

NEWEY, PAUL DAVIS, lawyer; b. Mpls., July 4, 1914; s. Paul S. and Mary (Yonan) N.; m. Viola W. Raymond, Dec. 16, 1943 (dec. June 1982); children: Paul S. Newey II, Davis Raymond, Dean Alan, Arthur Tyler. AA, Cen. YMCA, 1935; LLB, JD, John Marshall Law Sch., 1940; AB, Detroit Inst. Tech., 1947; diploma, U.S. Treasury Dept. Law Enforcement Sch., 1943; spl. courses, U.S. Gov. and Mil. Intelligence Schs., 1951-53. Bar: Ill. 1946. Squad leader Bur. Census, Dept. Commerce, 1940; officer Uniformed Force U.S. Secret Svc., 1940-42; agt. Bur. Narcotics, Treasury Dept., 1942-47; pvt. practice law, real estate and ins. broker Chgo., 1948-51; spl. rep. CIA, 1951-57; asst. state's atty.-investigator County of Cook, Ill., 1957-58; asst. state's atty.-chief investigator, chief state's atty.'s police County of Cook, 1958-60; pvt. practice law Chgo., 1961-65, spl. investigator, 1961—; ptnr. Adamowski, Newey & Adamowski, Chgo., 1965-82; spl. atty. Ill. Sec. of State, 1975-80; ptnr. firm Adamowski & Newey, Chgo., 1982-89; ret., 1989; sec., dir. Master Fishing Gear, Inc., 1956-57. Pvt. AUS, 1941; 1st lt. Counter Intelligence Corps. USAR, 1949-54. Recipient Medal of Merit and elected to Hall of Fame Nat. Police Officers Assn. Am., 1960, Disting. Citizen award Assyrian-Am. Welfare Council, 1970, Hammurabi award Assyrian Heritage Orgn., 1985; recipient Outstanding Svc. citation John Marshall Law Sch., 1975, Disting. Alumnus merit citation, 1970; honored by proclamation by Ill. gov., resolution by City of Chgo. aldermen and granted by mayor of Chgo. setting June 8, 1985 as Paul D. Newey Day. Mem. ABA, Fed. Bar Assn., Ill. Bar Assn., Chgo. Bar Assn., Internat. Assn. Investigators and Spl. Police (chmn. bd. dirs.), N. Am. Inst. Police Sci. (bd. dirs.), N.Am. Detective Agy. (bd. dirs.), Spl. Agts. Assn. (3d v.p. and legal counsel 1977—), U.S. Treasury Agts. Assn. (pres. 1970-71), John Marshall Law Sch. Alumni Assn. (treas. 1973-75, bd. dirs. 1966-84), Internat. Assn. Chiefs of Police (life), Spl. Agts. Assn. Chgo. (life), Amvets, Am. Legion, Assn. Former Fed. Narcotic Agents, Fed. Criminal Investigators Assn., Edward T. Lee Found. John Marshall Law Sch. (life), Amvets, Am. Legion, Smithsonian Assocs., Congl. Club (pres. 1963-64, bd. dirs., trustee 1962-65), Masons (32 degree, life), Medina Temple, Shriners (life), Lawyers Shrine Club (life). Mem. United Ch. of Christ. Home: 1034 W Altgeld St Chicago IL 60614-2209 *Life is an interlude in eternity, and material gain, by itself, makes it a nullity. The Master's admonition, "whatsoever ye have done for the least of these thy brethren, ye have done it unto me!" demands pro bono conduct; or perish without paying your debt for existence. I know that "man does not live by bread alone!" and try to shape my sojourn here accordingly.*

NEWHALL, DAVID, III, former federal government official; b. Phila., Dec. 6, 1937; s. David Jr. and Jane Martyn (Dunn) N. AB in Politics, Princeton U., 1961. Mgr. Bell Tel. Co. of Pa., Norristown, 1961-63; adminstrv. asst. to U.S. Rep. R.S. Schweiker Washington, 1963-69, chief of staff to U.S. Senator R.S. Schweiker, 1969-81; chief of staff HHS, Washington, 1981-83; pres. Marmion Plantation Co., King George, VA., 1983-91; prin. dep. asst. sec. def.(health affairs) U.S. Dept. Def., Washington, 1985-90, acting asst. sec. def. (health affairs), 1989-90; gen. ptnr. Marmion Partnership Restorations, 1990—; bd. dirs. Western Healthcare Alliance, Phoenix, Trail Blazer Ins. Co., Dallas; mem. nat. adv. bd. Am. Compliance Inst., Alexandria, Va. Republican. Episcopalian. Club: Princeton Tower. Avocation: beef cow-calf operation. Home and Office: 7382M Marmion Ln King George VA 22485-7300

NEWHALL, DAVID SOWLE, history educator; b. Burlington, Vt., July 26, 1929; s. Chester Albert and Nella Perry (Tillotson) N.; m. Edna Irene Newton, Mar. 25, 1952; children: Rebecca, John Newton, Jesslyn, Melissa, David Chester. BA, U. Vt., 1951; postgrad., Boston U., 1951; AM, Harvard U., 1956, PhD, 1963. Instr., asst. prof. U. Vt., Burlington, 1959-66; asst. prof., assoc. prof. history Centre Coll., Danville, Ky., 1966, prof., 1970, disting. prof. humanities, 1987, Pottinger disting. prof. history, 1994-95; Pottinger disting. prof. history emeritus, 1995—; mem. adv. com. Danville High Sch., 1980-81; cons. dept. history Berea (Ky.) Coll., 1983; rep. Ky. Coun. on Internat. Edn., Lexington, 1984-85. Author: Clemenceau: A Life at War, 1991; contbr. to Historical Dictionary of the Third French Republic, 1988, Kentucky Ency., 1992, Historic World Leaders, 1994. Elder Presbyn. Ch., U.S.A., Danville, 1969—; officer Danville H.S. Band Parents Assn., 1968-82; bd. dirs. Project Opportunity, Lee and Breathitt Counties, Ky., 1968-74; mem. Citizens Com. on Coal-Hauling Traffic, Boyle County, Ky., 1982—; mem. adv. bd. Ky. Elderhostel, 1996—. With U.S. Army, 1951-53, Korea. Recipient Acorn award Ky. Advocates for Higher Edn., 1994; Nat. Meth. scholar Boston U., 1953-55. Mem. Soc. for French Hist. Studies, World History Assn., Phi Beta Kappa (officer Centre Coll. 1971-95), Omicron Delta Kappa, Phi Alpha Theta. Avocations: church choir, railroading. Home: 634 N 3rd St Danville KY 40422-1125 Office: Dept of History Centre Coll Danville KY 40422

NEWHALL, JEFFREY ROBERT, religious organization administrator; b. Washington, July 14, 1946; s. Robert Moody and Shirley Emily (Raw) N.; m. Sarah Elisabeth Studenmund, Sept. 25, 1971; children: Sarah E., Jeremiah R. BA, George Washington U., 1969; MA, Hartford Seminary, 1972, MDiv, 1972; DMin, Andover/Newton, 1975. Assoc. pastor Ctrl. Bapt., Hartford, Conn., 1972-73, First Calvary, Lawrence, Mass., 1974-78; sr. pastor Palisades Cmty. Ch., Washington, 1978-85; pastor Orchard Park (N.Y.) Cmty. Ch., 1985-91; exec. dir. Internat. Coun. Cmty. Chs., Mokena, Ill., 1991—; therapist Samaritan Counseling Ctr., Buffalo, 1985-91; exec. com. Nat. Coun. Chs., N.Y., 1991—, Consultation on Ch. Union, Princeton, N.J., 1991—; del. U.S. chpt. World Coun. Chs., N.Y. Editor, writer newsletter Christian Cmty., 1991-97. Mem. Am. Assn. Pastoral Counselors. Democrat. Avocations: reading, writing, hiking, gardening.

NEWHALL, JOHN HARRISON, management consultant; b. Phila., Sept. 29, 1933; s. Blackwell and Mary Large (Harrison) N.; m. Jane Carol Ward, July 15, 1961; children: Carol Newhall Neilson, Thomas Blackwell, Daniel Ward. BA, Williams Coll., 1955; MBA, Harvard U., 1960. Dir. corp. planning, gen. mgr. Europe H.J. Heinz Co., Pitts., 1970-77; v.p. mktg. Sun Co., Phila., 1977-81; chmn., chief exec. officer Aitkin-Kynett Co. (subs. Foote Cone & Belding), Phila., 1981-84; mng. dir., exec. v.p. Campbell-Ewald Co., N.Y.C., 1984-86; prin. mgmt. cons. SRI Internat., Menlo Park, Calif., 1987-90; mng. dir. Strategic Directions, Narberth, Pa., 1990—; pres. Advanced Promotion Techs., Deerfield Beach, Fla., 1992-93. Mem. devel. council Williams Coll., Williamstown, Mass., 1977-87, Reg. v. chmn. Capital Campaign, 1991-93; mem. Com. of 70, Phila., 1981-84; bd. dirs. Bryn Mawr (Pa.) Hosp., 1982-88, The Haverford (Pa.) Sch., 1980-86, Headmaster sel. comm., 1992, Strategic Planning Comm., 1994, World Affairs Council, Phila., 1982-86, Found. for Vascular Hypertension Research, Phila., 1982—, chmn., 1987, Jr. Achievement, Phila., 1977-81, vice chmn., 1981, SE chpt. ARC, Phila., 1981-84, Pa. Economy League, 1981-84; vestryman, lay reader Episcopal Ch., 1964-70, chmn. ann. campaign, 1992, vice chmn. capital campaign, 1994. Lt. USN, 1955-58. Recipient Cert. of Merit Chapel of Four Chaplains, 1983, 85. Mem. Assn. Nat. Advertisers (exec. com. 1977-81), Harvard Bus. Sch. Club Phila. (pres. 1994-96, vice chmn. 1996—). Republican. Episcopalian. Clubs: Union League (Phila.); Merion Cricket (Haverford); Gulph Mills (Pa.) Golf; Harbor (Seal Harbor, Maine). Avocations: skiing, tennis, sailing. Home and Office: Strategic Directions 414 Righters Mill Rd Narberth PA 19072-1423

NEWHART, BOB, entertainer; b. Oak Park, Ill., Sept. 29, 1929; m. Virginia Quinn, Jan. 12, 1963; 4 children. BS, Loyola U., Chgo., 1952. Acct. U.S. Gypsum Co.; copywriter Fred Niles Film Co.; appeared on Jack Paar Show, 1960; TV performer numerous guest appearances, 1961—; star TV series Newhart, 1982-90. Rec. artist (album) Button Down Mind on TV; royal command performance, London, 1964, appeared in films Hot Millions, 1968, Catch 22, 1970, Cold Turkey, 1971, First Family, 1980, Little Miss Marker, 1982; TV films include Thursday's Game, 1978, Marathon, 1980. Grand marshall Tournament Roses Parade, 1991. Served with U.S. Army, 1952-54. Recipient Emmy award, 1961, Peabody award, 1961, Sword of Loyola award, 1976, Legend to Legend award, 1993; named to Acad. Hall of Fame, 1993. Office: c/o David Capell 1875 Century Park E Ste 2250 Los Angeles CA 90067-2523

NEWHOUSE, ALAN RUSSELL, retired federal government executive; b. N.Y.C., Feb. 27, 1938; s. Russell Conwell and Clara Lucille (Scovell) N.; m. Margo Stiles Hicks, Feb. 3, 1960; children: Daryl, Jeffrey, William. BEE, Cornell U., 1960. Engr. Bur. of Ships, Washington, 1964-66; nuclear power engr., chief West Milton field office AEC, Schenectady, N.Y., 1966-69; sr. exec. AEC, ERDA, U.S. Dept. Energy, Washington, 1969-92; dep. asst. sec. Space and Def. Power Systems Office Nuclear Energy, Washington, 1992-93; dir. Office Space and Def. Power Systems, 1993-95, retired, 1995, ind. cons., 1995—; cons. Energy Conversion Techs. Composer numerous musical works. Bd. trustees River Road Unitarian Ch., Bethesda, Md., 1973-75; mem. McLean Symphony Orchestra, Washington Men's Camerata, Musica Antiqua, Interamerican Chamber Singers, Continuum Chamber Singers, U. Md. Chorus. Lt. USN, 1960-64. Mem. IEEE, AIAA, Am. Nuclear Soc., Am. Soc. Naval Engrs., Soc. Naval Architects and Marine Engrs., Am. Astronautical Soc. Republican. Unitarian. Home and Office: 11108 Deborah Dr Potomac MD 20854-2721

NEWHOUSE, DONALD E., newspaper publishing executive; b. 1930; s. Samuel N. Student, Syracuse U. With Advance Publs., Staten Island, N.Y., 1951—, now pres.; co-founder Newhouse Newspapers, N.Y.C., 1963, now v.p.; pres. Newark (N.J.) Star-Ledger; v.p. Times Picayune Pub. Corp., New Orleans; treas. Herald Am., Syracuse, 1960—, The Post Standard, Syracuse, 1960—, The Syracuse Herald Journal, 1960—, The Herald Co. Inc., 1960—; co-founder Metro-Suburbia, Inc., N.Y.C., 1963; prin. The Trenton (N.J.) Times, Times of Trenton Pub. Corp. Office: Star-Ledger 1 Star Ledger Plz Newark NJ 07102-1200*

NEWHOUSE, JOSEPH PAUL, economics educator; b. Waterloo, Iowa, Feb. 24, 1942; s. Joseph Alexander and Ruth Linnea (Johnson) N.; m. Margaret Louise Locke, June 22, 1968; children: Eric Joseph, David Locke. BA, Harvard U., 1963, PhD, 1969; postgrad (Fulbright scholar), Goethe U., Frankfort, Germany, 1963-64. Staff economist Rand Corp., Santa Monica, Calif., 1968-72, dep. program mgr., health and biosci. rsch., 1971-88, sr. staff economist, 1972-81, head econs. dept., 1981-85, sr. corp. fellow, 1985—; John D. MacArthur prof. health policy and mgmt., dir. div. Health Policy Rsch. and Edn., Harvard U., 1988—; lectr. UCLA, 1970-83, adj. prof., 1983-88; mem. faculty Rand Grad. Sch., 1972-88; dir. Rand-UCLA Ctr. for Study Health Care Fin. Policy, 1984-88, co-dir., 1988-92; prin. investigator health ins. study grant HHS, 1971-86; chmn. health svcs. rsch. study sect. HHS-Agy. for Health Care Policy and Rsch., 1989-93; mem. Nat. Commn. Cost Med. Care, 1976-77; mem. health svcs. devel. grants study sect. HEW, 1978-82, Inst. Medicine of NAS, 1978—, mem. coun., 1991-97; mem. Physician Payment Rev. Commn., 1993-96, chmn. Prospective Payment Assessment Com., 1996—. Author: The Economics of Medical Care, 1978, The Cost of Poor Health Habits, 1991, A Measure of Malpractice, 1993, Free for All?, 1993; editor Jour. Health Econs., 1981—; assoc. editor Jour. Econ. Perspectives, 1992—; contbr. articles to profl. jours. Recipient David Kershaw award and prize Assn. Pub. Policy and Mgmt., 1983, Baxter Am. Found. prize, 1988, Adminstr.'s citation Health Care Fin. Adminstrn., 1988, Hans Sigrist Found. prize, 1995, Elizur Wright award, 1995. Fellow Am. Acad. Arts and Scis.; mem. Assn. for Health Svcs. Rsch. (Article of Yr. award 1989, bd. dirs. 1991—, pres. 1993-94), Am. Econ. Assn., Royal Econ. soc., Econometric Soc., Phi Beta Kappa. Office: Harvard U Health Policy Rsch and Edn 25 Shattuck St Fl 1 Boston MA 02115-6027

NEWHOUSE, MARK WILLIAM, publishing executive; b. N.Y.C., Oct. 14, 1948; s. Norman Nathan and Alice (Gross) N.; m. Lorry A. Whitehead, June 1, 1974; children: Jesse Louis, Charlotte Ann. BA, Yale U., 1969. V.p., gen. mgr. The Star-Ledger, Newark, N.J., 1980—. Bd. dirs. N.Y.C. Opera, 1992—, pres., 1993—; bd. dirs. Audit Bur. of Circulations, 1995—. Office: Newark Morning Star Ledger Co One Star Ledger Plz Newark NJ 07102-1200

NEWHOUSE, NANCY RILEY, newspaper editor; b. Bellingham, Wash.; d. Fenwick Charles and Elizabeth (Grace) Riley; m. John Newhouse, Sept. 27, 1961 (div. 1970); m. Michael Iovenko, Mar. 6, 1983. BA, Vassar Coll., 1958. Sr. editor N.Y. Mag., N.Y.C., 1970-75, House & Garden Mag., N.Y.C., 1976; successively home editor, style editor and travel editor N.Y. Times, N.Y.C., 1976—. Editor: Hers: Through Women's Eyes, 1985; editor Hers column N.Y. Times, 1976-92; mem. adv. bd. Vassar Quar., Poughkeepsie, N.Y., 1985—. Recipient Penney-Mo. Newspaper award U. Mo. Sch. Journalism, 1982-83. Mem. The Century Assn., Women's Forum N.Y. Office: NY Times Co 229 W 43rd St New York NY 10036-3913

NEWHOUSE, QUENTIN, JR., social psychologist, educator, researcher; b. Washington, Oct. 20, 1949; s. Quentin Sr. and Berlene Delois (Byrd) N.; m. Brenda Joice Washington, Feb. 17, 1973 (div. Mar. 1984); m. Debra Ann Carter, July 7, 1984; 1 child, Alyse Elizabeth Belinda. BA in Psychology, Marietta (Ohio) Coll., 1971; MS in Psychology, Howard U., 1974, PhD in Psychology, 1980. Asst. prof. Antioch U., Balt., 1976-79; pres. Quentin Newhouse Jr. and Assocs., Inc., Washington, 1981-84; computer systems analyst U.S. Army, Washington, 1984, 85; asst. prof. Howard U., Washington, 1982-88; adj. prof. U. D.C., 1984, 91—, Bowie State U., 1982-86, 91—; mentor Prince George's Community Coll., Largo, Md., 1986-89; computer specialist Bur. of the Census, Ctr. for Survey Methods Rsch., Suitland, Md., 1988-91, social sci. statistician, 1991-93; dir. mktg. analyst Safeway Inc., Lanham, Mo., 1994; job developer Prince George's Pvt. Industry Coun., Largo, Md., 1994-95; exec. dir. Nat. Behavioral Scis. Student Network, Inc., 1995—; asst. prof., interim chair dept. behaviour and human svcs. Bowie (Md.) State U., 1995—; v.p. Bureautots, Inc., Largo, 1989-91. Commr. Prince George's County Children and Youth, Upper Marlboro, Md., 1991, Prince George's County Commn. for Children, Youth and Families, 1992-95; bd. dirs. Prepare Our Youth, Inc., Tacoma Park, Md., Shiloh Bapt. Ch. Nursery, Washington, 1988-90; mem. State of Md. Adv. Com. for Children, Youth and Families, 1992-93, regional coun. Prince George's United Way, 1994—; bd. dirs. Met. Boys and Girls Clubs, 1995—, Mental Health Assn. of Prince George's County, 1994-95. Recipient Cmty. Svc. award U. D.C., 1982, 84, Gov.'s cert. of svc. State of Md., 1993, Appreciation cert. Prince George's County, 1995, 96; named Outstanding Young Man of Am., 1982, 86. Mem. APA, Social Sci. Computing Assn., Census SAS Users Group (co-chair 1991-93), Tau Epsilon Phi (life). Democrat. Avocations: walking, reading, working with computers. Office: Bowie State U MLK 201 Dept Behavioral Scis & Human Svcs Bowie MD 20715

NEWHOUSE, SAMUEL I., JR., publishing executive; b. 1928; m. Victoria Newhouse. Chmn. Condé Nast Publs. Inc., N.Y.C.; also chmn. bd. dirs., CEO Advance Publs. Inc., S.I., N.Y. Recipient Henry Johnson Fisher award Mag. Pubs. Assn., 1985. Office: Condé Nast Publs Inc 350 Madison Ave New York NY 10017-3704 also: Advance Pubs Inc 950 Fingerboard Rd Staten Island NY 10305-1453*

NEWHOUSER, HAL, retired baseball player; b. Detroit, May 20, 1921. Baseball player Detroit Tigers, 1939-53; baseball player Cleve. Indians, 1954-55, scout, 1961-64; scout Balt. Orioles, 1956-61. Named to Baseball Hall of Fame, 1992, Most Valuable Player award, 1944-45. Office: c/o Nat Baseball Hall Fame PO Box 590 Cooperstown NY 13326-0590

NEWICK, CRAIG DAVID, architect; b. Orange, N.J., Feb. 14, 1960; s. Russel Forester and Helen (Welch) N.; m. Linda Hammer Lindroth, June 6, 1987; 1 child, Zachary Eran. BA in Architecture, Lehigh U., 1982; MArch, Yale U., 1987. Registered architect, Conn. Designer, draftsman The Archtl. Studio, Easton, Pa., 1983-84; job capt., project designer Svigals & Assocs., New Haven, 1985; designer, draftsman Centerbrook (Conn.) Architects, 1986; job capt., project designer Allan Dehar Assocs., Architects & Planners, New Haven, 1988-90; ptnr. Lindroth & Newick, New Haven, 1991—; designer Cesar Pelli & Assocs., Inc., New Haven, 1992; project arch. Tai Soo Kim Ptnrs., Hartford, Conn., 1995—; vis. faculty Vis. Critics Studio, Lehigh U., 1993; vis. critic Wesleyan U., 1990-93, R.I. Sch. Design, 1988; faculty Creative Arts Workshop, New Haven, 1991, 92. Out Of Bounds (fisrt prize artists books 1994). Recipient 1st place award Am. Visionary Set Design Competition, 1989, 3d place award Astronauts Meml. Design Competition, 1988, ID Mag. Ann. Design Rev. award, 1990, 2d prize African Burial Ground Competition Mcpl. Arts Soc. N.Y., 1994; grantee New Eng. Found. for Arts, 1992, NEA Interarts grantee Rockefeller Found., 1989-90, Found. for Contemporary Performance Art, 1989, 90, Humanities Coun. of Fairfield U., 1995; New Eng. Found. for Arts Regional fellow, 1993, others. Mem. Architecture League N.Y. (young architects forum 1991, emerging voices, 1996). Office: Lindroth & Newick 219 Livingston St New Haven CT 06511-2209

NEWKIRK, JOHN BURT, metallurgical engineer, administrator; b. Mpls., Mar. 24, 1920; s. Burt Leroy and Mary Louise (Leavenworth) N.; m. Carolyn Mae Jordan, Aug. 4, 1951; children: Jeffrey Burt (dec.), John Jordan, Victoria Louise Lierheimer, Christina Brooks. B. Metall. Engring, Rensselaer Poly. Inst., Troy, N.Y., 1941; M.S., Carnegie Inst. Tech., 1947, Sc.D., 1950. Metall. investigator Bethlehem Steel Co., Pa., 1941-42; Fulbright postdoctoral fellow Cambridge (Eng.) U., 1950-51; research metallurgist research lab. Gen. Electric Co., Schenectady, 1951-59; prof. Cornell U., 1959-65; Phillipson prof. U. Denver, 1965-74, prof. phys. chemistry, 1975-84, Phillipson prof. emeritus, 1984—; pres. Colo. Biomed., Inc., 1969—, ret. Editor Rews. on High Temperature Materials, 1973-78; 16 ann. volumes Advances in X-Ray Analysis; contbr. over 75 articles profl. jours. With USNR, 1942-46. Fellow Am. Soc. Metals (life); mem. Sigma Xi, Tau Beta Pi, Phi Kappa Phi, Alpha Sigma Mu (internat. pres. 1950), Alpha Tau Omega. Republican. Presbyterian. Office: Colo Biomed Inc 6851 Highway 73 Evergreen CO 80439-6558

NEWKIRK, RAYMOND LESLIE, management consultant; b. Shreveport, La., July 13, 1944; s. Raymond Clay and Dorothy Emily (Parker) N.; m. Felicisima Guese Calma, Jan. 19, 1985. AA, Dayton Community Coll., 1973; BS in Behavioral Sci., N.Y. Inst. Tech., 1976; MS in Philosophy, Columbia Pacific U., 1980, PhD in Behavioral Sci., 1982; PhD in Human Sci., Saybrook Inst., 1992. Clin. intern Fielding Inst., 1995; chief exec. officer, cons. Newkirk & Assocs., Ft. Lauderdale, Fla., 1980-84; head dept. ADP Royal Saudi Naval Forces, Jeddah, 1984-86; pres., cons. Internat. Assn. Info. Mgmt., Santa Clara, Calif., 1984; cert. quality analyst Quality Assurance Inst., Orlando, Fla., 1986—; prin. cons. Info. Impact Internat., Nashville, 1988—; pres., CEO Sys. Mgmt. Inst., Pleasant Hill, Calif., 1987; pres., COO P.Q. Info. Group, Egmont ann Hoeff, The Netherlands, 1992-94; pres., CEO Systems Mgmt. Inst., 1994—; prin. Forum 2000, 1996—; dep. gov. Am. Biog. Inst., 1995. Author: Chronicles of the Making of A Philosopher, 1983; contbr. articles to profl. jours. Speaker, mem. Union for Concerned Scientists, San Francisco, 1988. Fellow Brit. Inst. Mgmt., Internat. Biog. Assn.; mem. Assn. Systems Mgmt., Assn. Profl. Cons., Planetary Soc., Columbia Pacific Alumni Assn. (pres. Mid-east chpt. 1985), Assn. Computing Machinery, IEEE Computer Soc., Am. Biograph. Inst. (dep. gov. 1995), Phi Theta Kappa (outstanding scholar award 1973), Confedn. of Chivalry (knight). Roman Catholic. Avocations: writing, classical guitar, tennis, weight lifting. Home: 95 Greenock Ln Pleasant Hill CA 94523-2083

NEWLAND, CHESTER ALBERT, public administration educator; b. Kansas City, Kans., June 18, 1930; s. Guy Wesley and Mary Virginia (Yoakum) N. BA, U. N. Tex., Denton, 1954; MA, U. Kans., 1955, PhD, 1958. Social Sci. Rsch. Coun. fellow U. Wis. and U.S. Supreme Ct., 1958-59; instr. polit. sci. Idaho State U., Pocatello, 1959-60; mem. faculty U. North Tex., Denton, 1960-66, prof. govt., 1963-66, dir. dept. govt., 1963-66; prof. polit. sci. U. Houston, 1967-68; dir. Lyndon Baines Johnson Libr., Austin, Tex., 1968-70; prof. pub. adminstrn. U. So. Calif., 1966-67, 68-71, 76-82, 84-92, Duggan disting. prof. pub. adminstrn., 1992—; prof. George Mason U., Fairfax, Va., 1982-84; mem. faculty Fed. Exec. Inst., 1971-76, dir. 1973-76, 80-81; mgr. task force on fed. labor-mgmt. rels. U.S. Pers. Mgmt. Project, Pres.'s Reorgn., Washington, 1977-78. Editor in chief Pub. Adminstrn. Rev., 1984-90; contbr. articles to profl. jours. Chmn. Mcpl. Rsch. Coun., Denton, 1963-64; city councilman, Denton, 1964-66; mem. Pub. Sector Commn. on Productivity and Work Quality, 1974-78; trustee Sacramento (Calif.) Mus. History, Sci. and Tech., 1993-95; mem. UN Devel. Program Moldova, 1994, Kuwait, 1995-96, Kazakstan, 1997; cons. Poland, 1990-91, Hungary, 1991, Czech and Slovak Republics, 1992, Kazakstan, 1997. Mem. Nat. Acad. Pub.

Adminstrn., Southwestern Social Sci. Assn. (chmn. govt. sect. 1964-65), Am. Soc. Pub. Adminstrn. (pres. Dallas-Ft. Worth chpt. 1964-65, nat. coun. 1976, 78-81, editorial bd. jour. 1972-76, chmn. publ. com. 1975-79, program chmn. 1977, nat. pres. 1981-82, Dimock award 1984), Am. Polit. Sci. Assn., Internat. Pers. Mgmt. Assn. (program chmn. 1978, Stockberger award 1979), Am. Acad. Polit. and Social Sci., Internat. City Mgmt. Assn. (hon.), Nat. Assn. Schs Pub. Affairs and Adminstrn. (Staats Pub. Svc. award 1989). Office: Univ Southern California 1201 J St Sacramento CA 95814-2906

NEWLAND, JANE LOU, nursing educator; b. Toledo, July 18, 1931; d. Clarence Charles Meinen and Bernice Isabell (Floyd) Scott; m. Byron Merle Newland, Aug. 4, 1962; children: Jeffrey Bruce, Brian James. Diploma in nursing, Lima (Ohio) Meml. Hosp., 1952; BSN, Ohio State U., 1959; M Vocat. Edn., U. South Fla., 1983, EdS in Vocat. Edn., 1989. RN, Ohio, Fla.; cert. tchr., Fla. Stewardess nurse Balt. & Ohio R.R., Cin., 1953-56; dir. nursing Lima State Hosp., 1960-67, dir. nursing edn., 1967-72; renal nurse children's svc. Health and Rehabilitative Svcs. Fla., Ft. Myers, 1975-78; practical nursing instr. Lee High-Tech. Ctr. Ctrl., Ft. Myers, 1979—; mem. adv. bd. Practical Nurse Assn., Lima, 1966-71. Mem., sec. St. James City Civic Assn., 1973-76; den leader Boy Scouts Am., St. James City, 1970-76; treas. PTA Pine Island Elem. Sch., Pine Island Center, Fla., 1973-75. Recipient Assoc. Master Tchr. award Fla. State Bd. Edn., 1986. Mem. Assn. Practical Nurse Educators Fla., Nat. Assn. health Occupations Tchrs., Lee County Vocat. Assn. (Outstanding Health Occupation Tchr. award 1985, Outstanding Vocat. Edn. Tchr. award 1990), Fla. Vocat. Assn., Health Occupation Educators Assn. Fla., Ladies Aux. VFW, Ladies Oriental Shrine, Order Ea. Star, Niobians of Cape Coral (Fla.), Kappa Delta (v.p. 1983-85, pres. 1993—), Phi Kappa Phi. Lutheran. Avocations: crafts, stamp collecting, history. Home: 2261 Carambola Ln Saint James City FL 33956-2018 Office: Lee County High Tech Ctr 3800 Michigan Ave Fort Myers FL 33916-2204

NEWLAND, LARRY J., orchestra conductor; b. Winfield, Kans., Jan. 24, 1935; s. Roy E. and Frances M. (Hammond) N.; m. Paula Kahn, Feb. 18, 1977; children: Lee Ann, Sara. MusB, Oberlin Conservatory, 1955; MusM, Manhattan Sch. Music, 1957. artistic adminstr. Sr. Concert Orch., N.Y.C., 1987-89. Asst. condr., musician N.Y. Philharm., N.Y.C., 1960-85; music dir., condr. Harrisburg (Pa.) Symphony, 1978-94, Philharm. Chamber Orch. (formerly Diabolus Musicus Chamber Orch.), N.Y.C., 1974—; music dir. Sr. Concert Orch. N.Y., 1987-89; regular guest condr. Seoul (Republic of Korea) Philharm.; prof., dir. ensembles Adelphi U., Garden City, N.Y., 1990—, acting chair music dept., 1993-94, chair music dept., 1994—. Served with U.S. Army, 1957-60. REcipient Harold Bauer Meml. award, 1957, Kousevitzky Conducting prize, 1963, Pa. Gov.'s citation, 1982, Pa. Ho. of Reps. citation, 1988, Disting. Pub. Svc. award City of Harrisburg, 1982, Golden Baton award Harrisburg Symphony, 1994, Pa. State Senate commendation, 1994; Leonard Bernstein conducting fellow, 1964. Mem. Am. Symphony Orch. League, Am. Fedn. Musicians, Condrs. Guild (pres. 1993-95). Avocations: tennis, sailing, mountain climbing, hiking, reading.

NEWLAND, RUTH LAURA, small business owner; b. Ellensburg, Wash., June 4, 1949; d. George J. and Ruth Marjorie (Porter) N. BA, Cen. Wash. State Coll., 1970, MEd, 1972; EdS, Vanderbilt U., 1973; PhD, Columbia Pacific U., 1981. Tchr. Union Gap (Wash.) Sch., 1970-71; ptnr. Newland Ranch Gravel Co., Yakima, Wash., 1970—, Arnold Artificial Limb, Yakima, 1981-86; owner, pres. Arnold Artificial Limb, Yakima and Richland, Wash., 1986—; ptnr. Newland Ranch, Yakima, 1969—. Contbg. mem. Nat. Dem. Com., Irish Nat. Caucus Found.; mem. Pub. Citizen, We The People, Nat. Humane Edn. Soc.; charter mem. Nat. Mus. Am. Indian. George Washington scholar Masons, Yakima, 1967. Mem. NAFE, NOW, Am. Orthotic and Prosthetic Assn., Internat. Platform Assn., Nat. Antivisection Soc. (life), Vanderbilt U. Alumni Assn., Peabody Coll. Alumni Assn., Columbia Pacific U. Alumni Assn., World Wildlife Fund, Nat. Audubon Soc., Greenpeace, Mus. Fine Arts, Humane Soc. U.S., Wilderness Soc., Nature Conservancy, People for Ethical Treatment of Animals, Amnesty Internat., The Windstar Found., Rodale Inst., Sierra Club (life), Emily's List. Democrat. Avocations: reading, gardening, sewing, handcrafts, people. Home: 2004 Riverside Rd Yakima WA 98901-9526 Office: Arnold Artificial Limb 9 S 12th Ave Yakima WA 98902-3106 *Personal philosophy: God first. Then be politically and socially conservative but liberal in your concern for others.*

NEWLIN, CHARLES FREMONT, lawyer; b. Palestine, Ill., Nov. 18, 1953; s. Charles Norris and Regina Helen (Correll) N.; m. Jean Bolt, Jan. 6, 1975; children: Christian N., Charles W., Ethan A. BA in Polit. Sci. summa cum laude, Ill. Wesleyan U., 1975; JD cum laude, Harvard U., 1978. Bar: Ill. 1978, U.S. Dist. Ct. (no. dist.) Ill. 1978, U.S. Tax Ct. 1980. Law clk. Sugarman, Rogers, Barshak & Cohen, Boston, 1976-78; assoc. Mayer, Brown & Platt, Chgo., 1978-84, ptnr., 1985-94; ptnr. Sonnenschein, Nath & Rosenthal, 1994—; adj. prof. law DePaul U., Chgo., 1986-90; lectr. in field. Contbg. author: Am. Law of Property, 1975, Trust Adminstrn. Ill., 1983, 87, 92, Bogert on Trusts, 1986-91, The Lawyer's Guide to Retirement, 1991, 94; contbr. articles to profl. jours. Scouting coord. DuPage area coun. Boy Scouts Am., Woodridge, Ill., 1984-86; bishop's counselor Mormon Ch., Woodridge, 1984-86; mem. planned giving com. Ill. divsn. Am. Cancer Soc., 1988—, Boys and Girls Clubs of Chgo., 1993—; mem. bd. dirs. Suburban Chgo. Planned Giving Coun., 1996—; vol. legal cons. The Tower Chorale, Western Springs, Ill., 1989-91. Fellow Am. Coll. Trust and Estate Counsel; mem. Chgo. Bar Assn., Chgo. Estate Planning Coun. Democrat. Methodist. Office: Sonnenschein Nath & Rosenthal 8000 Sears Tower Chicago IL 60606

NEWLIN, KIMREY DAYTON, international trade consultant, political consultant, personal computer analyst; b. Greensboro, N.C., Jan. 27, 1944; s. Dayton Gilbert and Pearl (Kimrey) N.; m. Beverly Jane Agnew, Mar. 9, 1968; children: Kim, Jr., Stephanie, Laurie. BS in Physics, Guilford Coll., 1966; MS in Agrl. Econs., Clemson U., 1969; MEd in Indls. Engring., Texas A&M U., 1970. Cert. Prof. Logistician, Cost Analyst, Profl. Estimator. Gen. engr., lifetime staff and faculty mem. Army Logistics Mgmt. Ctr./Darcom/Dept. of Def., Ft. Lee, Va., 1968-71; economist Army Procurement Rsch. Office/Army Logistics Mgmt. Ctr./Darcom/Dept. of Def., Ft. Lee, Va., 1971-75, ops. rsch. analyst, 1975-78; statistician, environ. compliance officer fisheries mgmt. S.E. Fisheries Ctr./Nat. Marines Fisheries Svc./Nat. Oceanographic Atmospheric Adminstrn./Dept. Commerce, Miami, 1978—. Author: Treatment of Textile Waste, 1971, How to Run Successful Projects, 1976-90, Handbook for Chapter Plan Guide, 1976-90, DT LCC, Logistics Spectru, 1978, 18 seafood dealer directories, 1996; contbr. numerous articles to profl. jours. Logistics chmn. U.S. JCI Senate, 1992; chief of staff Coconut Grove (Fla.) Jaycees, 1979-90; adminstrv. v.p., treas. Fla. JCI Senate, Lakeland, 1988-90, lifetime mem., 1983—; presdl. advisor Fla. Jaycees Act Team, 1983-89, Fla. Jaycees Lakeland, 1985-86; sec. Friendship JCS, 1990—; v.p. Va. Jaycees, Roanoke, 1978-79, commonity devel., life mem., 1977—; lifetime col. Fla. Gator Corps, 1993—; ctr. rep. SEFSC Miami Fed. Exec. Bd., 1986—. Recipient Outstanding Svc. Plaque as Adminstr. V.P. Fla. JCI Senate, 1990, Coconut Grove Jaycees Palm award for Outstanding Svc. for Last 10 Yrs., 1989, Hommer Shepard Meml. award Fla. JCI Senate, 1989, Presdl. award of Honor Plaque for Outstanding Svc. Cocnut Grove Jaycees, 1981-87, Cert. Appreciation for Inter City Marine Program Performance Dade County Pub. Schs., 1987-88, Henry Colona award Fla. Jaycees, 1986, 82, Expo 87 Career & Job Fair award Greater Miami C. of C., 1987, Logistics Cert. Miami Fed. Volunteerism Cert. Exec. Bd., 1991, Adminstrvt. Spt. Cert., Exec. Bd., 1992, Get Up Off That Thing Plaque, Coconut Grove JCS, 1993, Cert. Resource Com, Roster Update Chmn. Cert., Fla. JCI Senate, 1995. Fellow Soc. Logistics Engrs. (life, corp.), Nat. Estimating Soc. Republican. Presbyterian. Avocations: woodworking, flea markets, personal computers, travel, yard sales. Home: 755 Allendale Rd Miami FL 33149-2402

NEWLIN, LYMAN WILBUR, bookseller, consultant; b. Buda, Ill., May 26, 1910; s. Fred Matheny and Maude Lillian (Potter) N.; m. Evy Ottonia Magnusson, 1966; children: Fred M. II, Erik B.M. Student, Coll. Emporia, Kans., 1928-30, U. Chgo., 1930-32. Buyer, bus. mgr. Follett Book Co., Chgo., 1934-44; mgr. Minn. Book Store and Macalester Coll. Book Store, Mpls. and St. Paul, 1944-48; co-owner Broadwater Lodge, Hackensack, Minn., 1948-65; founder, owner Broadwater Books, Lewiston, N.Y., 1948—; buyer, dept. mgr. Kroch's & Brentano's Book Store, Chgo., 1951-65; regional mgr. Richard Abel and Co., Portland, Oreg. and Zion, Ill.,, 1966-69, asst. to pres., 1969-75; founder, prin. counselor Lyman W. Newlin Book Trade Counsellors, Lewiston, N.Y., 1975—; mdse. mgr. Coutts Library Services, Inc., Lewiston, 1976-90; pub. rels. advisor The Charleston (Coll. Libr.) Conf., 1985—; pub. liaison Book News, Inc., Portland, 1989—; program coord. Acad. of Scholarly Pub. seminar Coll. of Charleston, 1995—; cons. Rutgers U. Press, New Brunswick, N.J., 1975-81; panelist and lectr. to acad. librs. and schs., booksellers. Pub. Rev. Index Quar. Guide to Profl. Revs., 1941-43; pub. rels. advisor, contbr. Quar. Publ. Against the Grain, 1985—; contbr. articles to profl. jours. Founder, 1st pres. Boy River Chain of Lakes Improvement Assn., Cass County, Minn., 1961-65, Concerned Parents Orgn., Freehold, 1976-79; trustee, v.p., sec., chmn. new libr. bldg. com. Lewiston Pub. Libr., 1985—; committeeman Niagara County Dem. Party, 1987—, sec., 1988-90; mem. coun. Luth. Ch. Messiah, Lewiston, 1982-93, deacon, 1992-97; mem. Town of Lewiston Sr. Citizens Adv. Bd., 1992—. Mem. ALA, Assn. Book Travelers (50 Yr. award 1984), Am. Booksellers Assn., Soc. Scholarly Pub. (program com. 1985), Book Industry Study Group, Pi Kappa Delta. Lutheran. Democrat. Avocations: amateur ornithology, Am. folk music, New Orleans jazz, book collecting. Office: PO Box 278 Lewiston NY 14092-0278 *If the Golden Rule is truly one's rule in living, no other rule is needed.*

NEWMAN, ANDREW, physician; b. Phila., Mar. 29, 1938; s. Louis M. and Ruth (Auerbach) N.; m. Sandra S. Mislove, June 18, 1960; children: Kenneth T., Marjorie F., Pamela B. BA summa cum laude, Temple U., 1959, MD, 1963; JD, Rutgers U., 1987. Bar: Pa. 1987, N.J. 1987, D.C. 1988; bd. cert. Am. Bd. Legal Medicine, 1988, bd. cert. Am. Acad. Pain Mgmt., 1989, bd. cert. Am. Bd. Orthopedic Surgery, 1971, recert., 1995. Intern Lower Bucks County Hosp., Bristol, Pa., 1963-64; resident East Orange (N.J.) V.A. Hosp., 1964-65, Phila. (Pa.) Gen. Hosp., 1967-69, Shriners Hosp., Phila., 1969-70; pvt. practice in orthopedic surgery Phila., 1970—; clin. asst. prof. Hahnemann Med. Univ., Dept. Orthopedics, 1970—; attending physician, Dept. Orthopedics Rolling Hill Hosp., Elkins Park, Pa., 1970-84, Parkview Div. of Met. Hosp., 1971—; prof. of medicine Pa. Coll. Podiatric Medicine, Phila.; adj. prof. med. ethics Beaver Coll., Glenridge, Pa., 1996; cons. in orthopedics to Pa. Blue Shield; MD mem. Osteopathic Med. Bd., Pa.; team physician Lower Moreland High Sch. Football Team, Huntingdon Valley, Pa.; cons. Liberty Mutual Ins. Co., Bd. Med. Licensure and Discipline, R.I.; prof. legal medicine Pa. Coll. Podiatric Medicine. Contbg. editor (textbook) Legal Medicine Update, 1988-89; asst. editor Legal Aspects Medical Practice; assoc. editor Bulletin of the Am. Acad. of Orthopedic Surgery; contbr. articles to profl. jours. Lt. col. USAFR. Named Man of Yr., Am. Podiatry Assn., Chgo., 1982; recipient pres.'achievement award Am. Coll. Legal Medicine, Palm Springs, Colo. 1988. Fellow Am. Acad. Orthopedic Surgery, Am. Coll. Legal Medicine; mem. AMA, Internat. Coll. Surgeons, Am. Assn. Hand Surgery (assoc.), Am. Soc. Law and Medicine, Pa. Med. Soc., Phila. County Med. Soc., Am. Orthopedic Foot Soc., Phila. Orthopedic Soc., Soc. Mil. Orthopedic Surgeons, Nat. Bd. Podiatric Med. Examiners. Avocations: gardening, Am. history (civil war). Office: 300 City Ave Bala Cynwyd PA 19004

NEWMAN, ANDREW EDISON, restaurant executive; b. St. Louis, Aug. 14, 1944; s. Eric Pfeiffer and Evelyn Frances (Edison) N.; m. Peggy Gregory, Feb. 14, 1984; children: Daniel Mark, Anthony Edison. BA, Harvard U., 1966, MBA, 1968. With Office of Sec. Def., Washington, 1968-70; with Edison Bros. Stores, Inc., St. Louis, 1970-95, v.p. ops. and adminstrn., 1975-80, dir., 1978-96, exec. v.p., 1980-86, chmn., 1987-95; chmn., CEO Race Rock Internat., St. Louis, 1995—; bd. dirs. Sigma-Aldrich Corp., St. Louis, Lee Enterprises, Davenport, Iowa, Dave and Buster's, Dallas. Trustee Washington U. Office: 501 N Broadway Saint Louis MO 63102-2102

NEWMAN, BARBARA MAE, retired special education educator; b. Rockford, Ill., July 16, 1932; d. Greene Adam and Emma Lorene (Fields) N. BS Edn., No. Ill. U., 1973. Cert. elem. edn. K-8 tchr., spl. edn. (blind and p.s.) K-12 tchr. Exec. sec. Rockford Art Assn., 1961-70; tchr. Title 1 Rockford Pub. Sch. Dist. #205, 1975-76, tchr. vision impaired, 1977-91. Feature editor (Rock Valley Coll. newspaper) The valley Forge, 1970; contbg. writer (Rockford Coll. history) A Retrospective Look, 1980. St. Bernadette adult choir, 1958-95, Cathedral Chorale, 1995—; holder 5 offices Am. Bus. Women's Assn., Forest City chpt., 1963-70; vol. Winnebago Ctr. for the Blind, Rockford, 1965-70; mem. Rockford Diocesan Chorale, 1969—. Named Woman of Yr., Am. Bus. Women's Assn., Forest City chpt., Rockford, 1966; scholar Ill. State Scholarship Commn., No. Ill. U., 1970-73. Mem. Ill. Ret. Tchrs. Assn. Roman Catholic. Avocations: writing, swimming, gardening.

NEWMAN, BARBARA MILLER, psychologist, educator; b. Chgo., Sept. 6, 1944; d. Irving George and Florence (Levy) Miller; student Bryn Mawr Coll.; AB with honors in Psychology, U. Mich., 1966, PhD in Devel. Psychology, 1971; m. Philip R. Newman, June 12, 1966; children: Samuel Asher, Abraham Levy, Rachel Florence. Undergrad. research asst. in psychology U. Mich., 1963-64, research asst. in psychology, 1964-69, teaching fellow, 1965-71, asst. project dir. Inst. for Social Research, 1971-72, univ. lectr. in psychology and research assoc., 1971-72; asst. prof. psychology Russell Sage Coll., 1972-76, assoc. prof., 1977-78; assoc. prof. dept. family relations and human devel., chmn. dept. family relations and human devel. Ohio State U., 1978-83, prof., 1983-86, assoc. provost for faculty recruitment and devel., 1987-92, prof., 1992—. Mem. Eastern Psychol. Assn., Soc. Research in Child Devel., AAAS, Am. Psychol. Assn., Nat. Council Family Relations, Groves Conf. on Marriage and Family, N.Y. Acad. Scis., Midwestern Psychol. Assn., Western Psychol. Assn., Am. Assn. Family and Consumer Scis. Author books including: (with P. Newman) Living: The Process of Adjustment, 1981; Development Through Life, 1995; Understanding Adulthood, 1983; Adolescent Development, 1986; When Kids Go to College, 1992, Childhood and Adolescence, 1997; contbr. chpts., articles to profl. publs. Office: Ohio State U Dept Family Rels & Human Devel 151 Campbell Hall Columbus OH 43210

NEWMAN, BARBARA POLLOCK, journalist, television writer, producer; b. N.Y.C., June 15, 1939; d. Irving G. and Jeanne (Ginsberg) Pollock; div.; 1 child, Penelope. BA, Mount Holyoke Coll., 1960; MA, Columbia U., 1962. Legis. asst. Rep. James Scheuer, Washington, 1964-65, Mayor John Lindsay, N.Y.C., 1965-67; mem. President's Nat. Adv. Commn. on Civil Disorders, Washington, 1967-79; reporter, interviewer Nat. Pub. Radio, N.Y.C., 1971-78; investigative reporter, producer "20/20" ABC News, Washington, 1978-81; exec. producer Jack Anderson Confidential, Washington, 1982-83; pres. Praetorian Prodns., Inc., Washington, 1984—; moderator Nat. Town Meetings, Pub. TV, 1975-78; Hostess McNeill Lehrer Report, Aug. 1977; mem. adv. bd. Washington Journalism Review, 1977-80. Author: The Covenant: Love and Death in Beirut, 1989; contbr. news and editl. articles to newspapers and popular jours.; sr. prodr. Now It Can Be Told, 1991; prodr. documentaries for investigative reports Arts and Entertainment Network; prodr. Channel 4 and Ctrl. TV, London. Recipient Peabody award thorugh Nat. Pub. Radio, 1972, Ohio State award, 1973, 74, 76, Silver Gavel award, ABA, 1974, Cadmus award, Am. Lebanese League, 1981; Emmy nominee, 1981 for investigative reporting. Home: 5336 29th St NW Washington DC 20015-1332

NEWMAN, BARRY INGALLS, retired banker, lawyer; b. N.Y.C., Mar. 19, 1932; s. M.A. and T.C. (Weitman) N.; BA, Alfred U., 1952; JD, NYU, 1955; m. Jean Short, Mar. 6, 1965; children: Suzanne, Cathy, David. Bar: N.Y. 1957, Ohio 1957, U.S. Supreme Ct. 1967, Calif. 1990; practiced in N.Y.C., 1957; assoc., then ptnr. firm Shapiro Persky Marken & Newman, Cleve., 1957-63; asst. v.p. Meinhard & Co. (now Meinhard Comml. Corp.), N.Y.C., 1963-65; v.p. Amsterdam Overseas Corp., N.Y.C., 1966-68; pres. No. Fin. Corp., L.A., 1968-72; sr. v.p. Aetna Bus. Credit, Inc., Hartford, Conn., 1972-78; exec. v.p. Security Pacific Fin. Group, San Diego, 1978-81, chmn., pres., chief exec. officer, 1981-82; sr. exec. v.p. Gt. Am. First Savs. Bank, 1982-88; ret. 1988; chmn. bd. dirs. San Diego County Capital Asset Leasing Corp. With U.S. Army, 1955-57. Recipient Disting. Svc. award Cleve. Jr. C. of C., 1961. Mem. ABA, N.Y. State Bar Assn., Ohio Bar Assn., Calif. Bar Assn., San Diego Bar Assn., Masons. Republican. Home: 3308 Avenida Sierra Escondido CA 92029-7937

NEWMAN, BARRY MARC, pediatric surgeon; b. N.Y.C., Dec. 13, 1951; s. Sheldon and Miriam (Jasphy) N.; m. Jane Post, July 2, 1989; 1 child, Alexander Ross. BA, U. Pa., 1973; MD, SUNY, Stony Brook, 1976. Diplomate Nat. Bd. Med. Examiners, Am. Bd. Surgery, Am. Bd. Pediatric Surgery. Resident in surgery N.Y. Med. Coll., N.Y.C., 1976-78; sr. resident in surgery SUNY, Stony Brook, 1978-81; chief resident pediatric surgery Childrens Hosp. of Buffalo, 1981-83, fellow pediatric surgery and gastroenterology, 1983-84; asst. prof. surgery U. Va., Charlottesville, 1984-88, U. Ill., Chgo., 1988-93; dir. pediatric surgery Luth. Gen. Children's Hosp., Park Ridge, Ill., 1991-96; clin. assoc. prof. surgery U. Chgo., 1993-95; dir. pediatric surg. svcs. Loyola U. Med. Ctr., Maywood, Ill., 1996—, co-dir. surg. laparoscopy lab., 1996—, assoc. prof. surgery and pediatrics, 1996—; instr. Adv. Trauma and Life Support, ACS, Chgo., 1984—. Contbr. articles to profl. jours., chpts. to books. NIH grantee, 1982-83, 87-88. Fellow Am. Acad. Pediatrics, ACS; mem. Am. Gastroenterol. Assn., Am. Pediatric Surg. Assn. Democrat. Jewish. Avocations: wine collecting, scuba diving, underwater photography, personal computing. Office: Loyola U Med Ctr Dept Surgery 2160 S 1st Ave Maywood IL 60153-3304

NEWMAN, BERNARD, federal judge; b. N.Y.C., Oct. 28, 1907; s. Isidor J. and Sarah C. (Berkowitz) N.; m. Kathryn Bereano, Apr. 3, 1932; children: Phyllis Newman Cechini, Helene Newman Bernstein. BS, NYU, 1928, LLB, 1929. Bar: N.Y. 1930. With Newman & Newman, intermittently 1930-65; asst. corp. counsel N.Y.C., 1936-42; law sec. to N.Y. Supreme Ct. Justice Samuel H. Hofstadter, 1942-48; ofcl. referee appellate div. N.Y. Supreme Ct., 1948-62, spl. referee, 1963-65, justice, 1962; judge Family Ct. N.Y., N.Y.C., 1965-68, U.S. Customs Ct., 1968—; now sr. judge U.S. Ct. Internat. Trade; lectr. motion practice N.Y. U. Law Sch., Practicing Law Inst.; speaker colls., univs., civic assns.; mem. spl. panel examiners N.Y. State Labor Relations Bd.; spl. panel arbitrators N.Y. State Mediation Bd.; govt. appeals agt. Selective Service. Pres. PTA High Sch. of Sci., N.Y.C., 1953-56, Bentley High Sch., 1955-56; mem. exec. com. Fedn. Jewish Philanthropies; Rep. dist. leader, 1955-62; counsel N.Y. Rep. County Com., 1957-58, chmn., 1958-62; mem. exec. com. N.Y. Rep. State Com., 1958-62; del. to jud., state, nat. convs.; bd. dirs. Met. adv. bd. Anti-Defamation League, LaGuardia Meml. Assn., Civic Ctr. Synagogue, Community Synagogue Ctr., N.Y.C.; dir. congregations Jewish synagogue, 1950—; patron Met. Opera Assn., 1962—. Served with USCG, World War II. Recipient Silver medal Nat. Essay Contest; named Merit Man for N.Y.C.; cited by Internat. Trade Bd., N.Y. U. Mem. ABA, N.Y. State Bar Assn., Assn. of Bar of City of N.Y., Fed. Bar Coun., Am. Judicature Soc., Nat. Legal Aid Assn., NYU Law Rev. Alumni Assn. (pres. 1958-61, gov. and bd. dirs. 1956—). Office: US Ct Internat Trade 1 Federal Plz New York NY 10278-0001*

NEWMAN, BRUCE MURRAY, antiques dealer; b. N.Y.C., Jan. 27, 1930; s. Meyer and Evelyn (Kantor) N.; m. Judith S. Brandus, June 26, 1965; 1 child, Emily Rachel. BA, Pratt Inst., 1953, BFA (hon.), 1997. Pres. Newel Art Galleries Inc., N.Y.C., 1975—; lectr. mus. and univs.; regional adv. bd. Chase Manhattan Bank. Author: Fantasy Furniture, 1989; featured on numerous TV & radio programs, mags. and other publs.; guest CBS Morning Show, 1988; prime time host PBS Chanel 13, N.Y.C. Bd. dirs. N.Y.C. Ctr., 1988-90; assoc. mem. Mt. Sinai Med. Ctr., 1988-90; trustee Pratt Inst., Bklyn., 1983—; mem. regional adv. bd. Chase Manhattan Bank. Recipient Designer award Art Dirs. Club, 1984, Man of Yr. award Pratt Inst., 1993; featured on Lifestyles of the Rich and Famous, 1991, other TV programs, Cover Connoisseur Mag., 1989, (story) Architectural Digest, 1989, N.Y. Times, 1983, 84, (2) 89, 92, 95, Internat. Herald Tribune, 1992, others. Mem. Am. Soc. Interior Designers (bd. dirs. 1989—), Victorian Soc. Am. Avocations: golfing, reading, jogging, traveling. Office: Newel Art Galleries Inc 425 E 53rd St New York NY 10022-5122

NEWMAN, CAROL L., lawyer; b. Yonkers, N.Y., Aug. 7, 1949; d. Richard J. and Pauline Frances (Stoll) N. AB/MA summa cum laude, Brown U., 1971; postgrad. Harvard U. Law Sch., 1972-73; JD cum laude, George Washington U., 1977. Bar: D.C., 1977, Calif., 1979. With antitrust div. U.S. Dept. Justice, Washington and L.A., 1977-80; assoc. Alschuler, Grossman & Pines, L.A., 1980-82, Costello & Walcher, L.A., 1982-85, Rosen, Wachtell & Gilbert, 1985-88, ptnr., 1988-90; ptnr. Keck, Mahin & Cate, 1990-94; pvt. practice, L.A., 1994—; adj. prof. Sch. Bus., Golden Gate U., spring 1982. Candidate for State Atty. Gen., 1986; L.A. city commr. L.A. Bd. Transp. Commrs., 1993—, v.p., 1995-96; bd. dirs. Women's Progress Alliance, 1996—. Mem. ABA, State Bar Calif., L.A. County Bar Assn., L.A. Lawyers for Human Rights (co. pres. 1991-92), Log Cabin (bd. dirs. 1992—, pres. 1996—), Calif. Women Lawyers (bd. dirs., bd. govs. 1991-94), Women's Progress Alliance (bd. dirs. 1996—), Order of Coif, Phi Beta Kappa.

NEWMAN, CHARLES A., lawyer; b. L.A., Mar. 18, 1949; s. Arthur and Gladys (Barnett) N.; m. Joan Kathleen Meskiel, Aug. 8, 1971; children: Anne R., Elyse S. BA magna cum laude, U. Calif., 1970; JD, Washington U., 1973. Bar: Mo. 1973, D.C. 1981, U.S. Dist. Ct. (ea. dist.) Mo. 1973, U.S. Dist. Ct. (ctrl. dist.) Ill., 1996, U.S. Ct. Appeals (3d, 5th, 7th and 10th cirs.) 1996, (8th cir.) 1975, (9th cir.) 1995, (11th cir.) 1994, U.S. Tax Ct. 1981, U.S. Claims Ct. 1981, U.S. Supreme Ct. 1976. From assoc. to ptnr. Thompson & Mitchell, St. Louis, 1973-96; ptnr. Thompson Coburn, St. Louis, 1996—; lectr. law Washington U., St. Louis, 1976-78. Trustee Mo. Bar Found., 1990-96, mem. Mo. Bar Bd. Govs, 1980-84; bd. dirs. United Israel Appeal, N.Y.C., 1990-93, Coun. Jewish Fedns., N.Y.C., 1992-95, United Jewish Appeal Young Leadership Cabinet, N.Y.C., 1985-88, Ctr. for Study of Dispute Resolution, 1985-88, Legal Svcs. Ea. Mo., 1985-94, St. Louis Community Found., 1992—, vice-chmn. 1997—, St. Louis chpt. Young Audiences 1993-95, Planned Parenthood St. Louis, 1986-89, Jewish Fedn., St. Louis, 1986—, asst. treas., 1989-90, v.p. fin. planning, 1990-93, asst. sec., 1994—; v.p. Repertory Theatre, St. Louis, 1986-89, sr. v.p., 1990-91; pres. St. Louis Opportunity Clearinghouse, 1974-78. Recipient Lon O. Hocker Meml. Trial award Mo. Bar Found., 1984. Mem. Bar Assn. Met. St. Louis (Merit award 1976). Democrat. Avocations: golf, tennis, reading, music. Office: Thompson Coburn 1 Mercantile Ctr Ste 2900 Saint Louis MO 63101-1618

NEWMAN, CLAIRE POE, corporate executive; b. Jacksonville, Fla., Dec. 12, 1926; d. Leslie Ralph and Gertrude (Criswell) Poe; student Fla. State Coll. for Women, 1944-45, Tulane U., 1971-73; m. Robert Jacob Newman, July 3, 1948; children—Leslie Claire, Robert, Christopher David. Co-owner Vineyards in Burgundy, France. Mem. various coms. New Orleans Mus. Art. Mem. Women's com. New Orleans Philharmonic Symphony Assn., 1961—, chmn. orch. rels. com., 1961-63; chmn. New Orleans Easter Seal Drive, 1963; La. trustee Nat. Soc. Crippled Children and Adults, 1963-65. Mem. Women's Aux. C. of C., New Orleans Soc. Archeol. Inst. Am. (v.p. 1972-74), Confrérie des Chevaliers du Tastevin, Sigma Kappa. Club: Metairie Country, Kitzbuehel (Austria) Golf, Golden Skibook (Kitzbuehel), Pass Christian (Miss.) Yacht; Ski (Arlberg). Home: 1111 Falcon Rd Metairie LA 70005-4129 Other: Tiemberg, Kitzbuehel Austria

NEWMAN, CONSTANCE BERRY, museum administrator; b. Chgo., July 8, 1935; d. Joseph Alonzo and Ernestine (Siggers) B.; m. Theodore Roosevelt Newman, July 25, 1959 (div. 1980). AB, Bates Coll., 1956; BSL, U. Minn., 1959; JD (hon.), Bates Coll., 1972, Amherst Coll., 1980; LHD (hon.), Central State U., 1991. Dir. VISTA, Washington, 1971-73; commr. Consumer Product Safety Commn., Washington, 1973-76; asst. sec. U.S. HUD, Washington, 1976-77; pres. The Newman & Hermanson Co., Washington, 1977-82; cons. Govt. of Lesotho, 1987-88; dir. nat. voter coalition Bush-Quayle '88, Washington, 1988; dir. Office Pers. Mgmt., Washington, 1989-92; under sec. Smithsonian Instn., Washington, 1992—; mem. adj. faculty John F. Kennedy Sch. Govt., Harvard U., Cambridge, Mass., 1979-82. Contbr. articles to profl. jours. Mem. Adminstrn. Conf. U.S., Washington, 1973-76, 1989—; commr. M.L. King Fed. Holiday Commn., Washington, 1989; chmn. Def. Adv. Com. on Women in the Svcs., Washington, 1985-86; trustee Community Coll. Balt., 1985-89; adv. to chmn. 1988 Rep. Nat. Conv., New Orleans, 1988; bd. overseers Morehouse Coll. Sch. Medicine, Atlanta, 1976-77; dir. Radio Free Europe, Radio Liberty, Washington, 1979-82. Recipient Pub. Svc. award Ohio State U., 1991. Mem. NAACP, Exec. Women in Govt. (founding mem.), Evaluation Rsch. Soc. (founding mem.). Avocation: photography.

NEWMAN, CORY FRANK, clinical psychologist; b. Phila., Jan. 20, 1960; s. Norman Jerome and Phyllis (Stutman) N.; m. Jane Evans, June 24, 1990; 1 child, Lindsey Diana. BA, U. Pa., 1981; MA, SUNY, Stony Brook, 1983, PhD, 1987. Lic. psychologist, Pa. Postdoctoral fellow Ctr. for Cognitive Therapy, Phila., 1987-88, assoc. dir. edn., 1988-90, clin. dir., 1990—, asst.

prof. psychology, 1991—; lectr. in field. Composer: Rhapsody on a Thematic Mirage, chamber music, 1981; co-author: Cognitive Therapy of Borderline Personality Disorder, 1993, Cognitive Therapy of Substance Abuse, 1993, Choosing To Live: How To Defeat Suicide Through Cognitive Therapy, 1996; contbr. articles to profl. jours. Grad. Coun. fellow SUNY, 1981; rsch. grantee Sigma Xi, 1985. Mem. APA, Assn. for Advancement Behavior Therapy, Soc. for Exploration Psychotherapy Integration, Phi Beta Kappa. Avocations: classical piano, composing, tennis, ice hockey. Office: U Pa Ctr for Cognitive Therapy 3600 Market St Ste 754 Philadelphia PA 19104-2641

NEWMAN, DAVID WHEELER, lawyer; b. Salt Lake City, Apr. 5, 1952; s. Donnell and Vera Mae (Siratt) N.; m. Mahnaz Navai, Mar. 14, 1981; 1 child, Anthony Dara. BA cum laude, Claremont Men's Coll., 1973; JD, UCLA, 1977; LLM in Taxation, NYU, 1979. Bar: Calif. 1978, U.S. Dist. Ct. Calif. 1978, U.S. Tax Ct. 1979. Tax ptnr. Mitchell, Silberberg & Knupp, L.A., 1982—; bd. dirs. Indsl. Bank, Nat. Com. on Planned Giving; mem. exec. com. tax sect. L.A. County Bar, 1991—. Mem. Calif. Club. Avocations: tennis, skiing. Office: Mitchell Silberberg & Knupp 11377 W Olympic Blvd Los Angeles CA 90064-1625

NEWMAN, DENIS, fund executive; b. Short Hills, N.J., June 9, 1930; s. Rockwell and Helen (O'Brien) N.; m. Mary McMorrow, Aug. 4, 1966; children—Stephen, Brian, Kerry. B.A., Yale U., 1952; M.B.A., Harvard U., 1954. Mng. dir. First Boston Corp., N.Y.C., 1954-87; pres. The Dunmore Group, Inc., Morristown, N.J., 1987-89; mng. dir. MidMark Assocs., Inc., Chatham, N.J., 1989—; fin. officer IBRD, Washington, 1960-62; sr. advisor Investment Corp. of Pakistan, Karachi, 1967-68, Devel. and Indsl. Bank of Iran, Teheran, 1975; chmn. bd. Acc Tech., Inc., Nanuet, N.Y.; bd. dirs. First Brands Corp., Danbury, Conn., Charles River Data, Framingham, Mass., Clearview Cinema Group, Inc., Madison, N.J., MRI Flexible Packaging, Inc., Newtown, Pa., SL (Santana) HOlding Corp., East Rutherford, N.J., Spring Broadcasting, Inc., Rockville, Md. Author: (with others) The International Banking Handbook, 1983. Mem. Republican County Com., N.J., 1975-80, Millburn-Short Hills Cable Adv. Com., (N.J.), 1981—. Served with U.S. Army, 1954-56. Mem. Securities Industry Assn. (chmn. internat. com. 1980-82), Fin. Analysts Fedn., N.Y. Soc. Security Analysts, Bond Club, Links Club, Short Hills Club, Morristown Club.

NEWMAN, DENNIS COLLINS, SR., accountant; b. Memphis, Apr. 9, 1932; s. Dennis Garland and Dorothy Elenora (White) N.; m. Debra Marlene Stone, Dec. 10, 1983; children: Denise, Terry, Phyllis, Dennis Jr., John, Paul. BBA, U. Tenn., 1956, MBA, 1958; M Acctg., Stanford U., 1961; PhD in Bus., Harvard U., 1965. Cert. tax profl. V.p. ops. Holiday Inns of Am., Memphis, 1965-72; dir. Popeyes Fried Chicken, New Orleans, 1972-76; v.p. so. div. McDonald's, New Orleans, 1976-84; v.p. tng. Burger King, New Orleans, 1984-88; gen. ptnr. Newman & Hastings P.A., Biloxi, Miss., 1988—. Author: Tax of Small Business, 1978, How to Work Smarter, 1983, Tax Professionals, 1989. Dep. chmn. State Rep. Party, Jackson, Miss., 1991. 1st lt. U.S. Army, 1951-53, Korea. Mem. Nat. Soc. Pub. Accts. (del. at large 1992), Nat. Soc. Mgmt. Cons. (pres. 1992), Nat. Soc. Tax Profls. (bd. mem. 1992), Am. Mgmt. Assn., Nat. Assn. Ind. Paralegals (membership com. 1991), Nat. Paralegal Assn. (rules com. 1991-92), Am. Fedn. Police (bd. mem. 1991-92), Miss. Assn. Pub. Accts. (bd. dirs. 1992), Nat. Fedn. Ind. Bus. (guardian mem.). Republican. Baptist. Avocations: golf, fishing, hunting, boating.

NEWMAN, DIANA S., community foundation executive, consultant; b. Toledo, June 15, 1943; d. Fred Andrew and Thelma Elizabeth (Hewitt) Smith; m. Dennis Ryan Newman, Feb. 15, 1964; children: Barbara Lynn Newman LaBine, John Ryan, Elizabeth Anne. Student, Oberlin Coll., 1961-64. Asst. treas. Marble Cliff Quarries Co., 1964-68; community vol., 1968-83; dir. Ohio Hist. Found., Columbus, 1983-90; v.p. advancement The Columbus (Ohio) Found., 1990-95; pres. Philanthropic Resource Group, Columbus, 1995—. Chair governing com. First Community Ch., 1983-88; bd. dirs. LWV, 1968-72, Ohio Mus. Assn., 1985-90, Nat. Soc. Fundraising Execs. Cen. Ohio chpt., Columbus, 1983—, Crittenton Family Svcs., Columbus, 1992-95; founder Franklin County Com. on Criminal Justice, Columbus, 1972; past pres. Jr. League Columbus. Mem. Ctrl. Ohio Planned Giving Coun. (bd. dirs. 1990—), Columbus Female Benevolent Soc. (bd. dirs. 1984—). Home: 1944 Chatfield Rd Columbus OH 43221-3702 Office: Philanthropic Resource Group 1944 Chatfield Rd Columbus OH 43221-3702

NEWMAN, EDGAR LEON, historian, educator; b. New Orleans, Jan. 21, 1939; s. Isidore and Anna (Pfeifer) N.; children: Jonathan, Suzanne; m. Linda Loeb Clark, Apr. 21, 1989. BA, Yale U., 1962; PhD, U. Chgo., 1969. Asst. prof. N.Mex. State U., Las Cruces, 1969-75, assoc. prof. history, 1975—; lectr. U. Peking, 1985. Fulbright fellow, 1965-66; Am. Philos. Soc. fellow, 1971; Nat. Endowment for Humanities fellow, 1975-76. Mem. Western Soc. for French History (pres. 1977-78, governing coun. 1990-92, 96—), Societe d'histoire de la Revolution de 1848 (comite directeur), Soc. Scis. History Assn., French Hist. Studies Assn., Am. Hist. Assn. (annotator for France bibliographical survey 1815-52). Editor: Historical Dictionary of France from the 1815 Restoration to the Second Empire; contbr. Dictionnaire de Biographie Française, Dictionnaire du Movement Ouvrier Français, Jour. of History of Ideas, Jour. Modern History, Dictionary of Am. Biography, others. Office: NMex State U PO Box 3H Las Cruces NM 88003-0001

NEWMAN, EDWARD HENRY, judge, lawyer; b. Providence, Nov. 21, 1947; m. Dinae J. Newman. BA, Providence Coll., 1969; JD, Suffolk Coll., Boston, 1972. Vis. lectr. Providence Coll., 1975-85; probate judge Richmond, R.I., 1988—; town solicitor, Richmond, 1975-81; mem. ethics adv. panel, Supreme Ct., 1996—. Chmn. Richmond Dem. Town Com., 1984-86; bd. dirs. Olean Ctr., Westerly, R.I., 1983-87; treas. Woodriver Health Ctr., Hopkinton, R.I., 1984-93. Mem. R.I. Trial Lawyers (v.p. 1980-84), Washington County Bar (pres. 1991—). Office: 42 Granite St Westerly RI 02891-2250

NEWMAN, EDWARD MORRIS, engineering executive; b. Bay Shore, N.Y., Jan. 22, 1945; s. Edward and Eleanor Newman; m. Catherine Newman, June 29, 1968; children: Edward, John. BSEE, Rensselaer Poly. Inst., 1967; MSEE, Poly. Inst. Bklyn., 1973; MS in Acctg., L.I. U., 1978. Engr. Sanders Assocs., Nashua, N.H., 1967-69; various engrng. positions Hazeltine Corp., Greenlawn, N.Y., 1969-82, head Wheeler labs., 1982-87, dir. advanced tech., 1987-89, dir. advanced devel., 1989-93, v.p. advanced devel., 1993—. Mem. IEEE. Avocation: sailing. Home: 19 Robinhood Ct Nesconset NY 11767-2036 Office: Hazeltine Corp 450 Pulaski Rd Greenlawn NY 11740-1609

NEWMAN, EDWIN HAROLD, news commentator; b. N.Y.C., Jan. 25, 1919; s. Myron and Rose (Parker) N.; m. Rigel Grell, Aug. 14, 1944; 1 child, Nancy (Mrs. Henry Drucker). BA, U. Wis., 1940; postgrad. (fellow), La. State U., 1940. With Washington bur. Internat. News Svc., 1941, U.P., 1941-42, 45-46, N.Y. Daily PM, 1946-47; ind. Washington news bur., 1947; asst to Eric Sevareid at Washington bur. CBS, 1947-49; freelance writer, broadcaster London, 1949-52; with European Recovery Program, 1951-52, NBC, 1952—; chief news bur. NBC, London, 1956-57, Rome, 1957-58, Paris, 1958-61; news commentator NBC, N.Y.C., 1961-83; columnist King Features Syndicate, 1984-89; moderator 1st Ford-Carter Debate, 1976, 2d Reagan-Mondale debate, 1984; moderator ann. conf. former secs. of state, 1983—, former secs. of def., 1987—. Narrator: TV spls. including Japan: East is West, 1961, Orient Express, 1964, Who Shall Live?, 1965, Pensions-The Broken Promise, 1972, Violence in America, 1977, I Want It All Now, 1978, Spying for Uncle Sam, 1978, Oil and American Power, 1979, The Billionaire Hunts, 1981, Congress: We the People, 1983-84, On Television, 1985-86, Freud, 1987, The Borgias, 1988; host Saturday Night Live, 1984; drama critic WNB C-TV, 1965-71 (Emmy awards 1966, 68, 70, 72, 73, 74, 82, Peabody award 1966); author: Strictly Speaking: Will America Be The Death of English?, 1974, A Civil Tongue, 1976, Sunday Punch, 1979, I Must Say, 1988; contbr. articles and revs. to various periodicals, U.S., Can. and Eng.; chmn. usage panel Am. Heritage Dictionary, 1975-80. Served from ensign to lt. USNR, 1942-45. Decorated chevalier Legion of Honor France; recipient awards Overseas Press Club, 1961, awards U. Wis. Sch. Journalism, 1967, awards U. Mo. Sch. Journalism, 1975. Mem. AFTRA, Authors Guild, Screen Actors Guild. Address: care Richard Fulton Inc 66 Richfield St Plainview NY 11803-1441

NEWMAN, ELIAS, artist; b. Staszow, Poland, Feb. 12, 1903; came to U.S., 1913, naturalized, 1928; s. Simon and Rebecca (Becker) N.; m. Lillian Judith Tesser, Feb. 26, 1945 (dec. June 1990). Student, N.A.D., 1919-20, Edn. Alliance Art Sch., 1920-25, Academie du Chaumiere, Paris, 1929. Art instr. Ednl. Alliance Art Sch., 1946-48; instr. painting YMHA 92nd St. Art Sch., 1949-51, Elias Newman Sch. of Art, Rockport, Mass., 1951-64; art dir. Palestine Pavilion, N.Y. World's Fair, 1939-40; cons. Internat. Exposition, Cleve., 1941; chmn. Conf. Am. Artists, 1971-75; exec. officer Artists Welfare Fund, Inc., 1975-88, prse. emeritus, 1988—; lectr. art of Israel, trends in Am. art. Editor: Improvisations, 1950, 51, 52, Artists' Equity, N.Y.; author: Art in Palestine, 1939; one-man shows, 1927—, including Salon Henri Brendle, Zurich, Switzerland, 1929, High Mus. Art, Atlanta, 1928, Yorke Gallery, Washington, 1929, Balt. Mus. Art, 1928, 30, 34, 41, The Art Ctr., N.Y.C., 1931, Montross Gallery, N.Y.C., 1932, Sears Roebuck & Co. Art Gallery, Washington, 1932, Md. Art Inst., Balt., 1932, 35, 36, Maxwell Galleries, San Francisco, 1945, Modernage Art Gallery, N.Y., 1945, Phila. Art Alliance, 1946, Jewish Mus., N.Y.C., 1949, Babcock Galleries, N.Y.C., 1947, 49, 51, 53, 60, Tel Aviv Mus., (Israel), 1934, 38, 49, 62, Werbe Galleries, Detroit, 1956, Doll & Richards Galleries, Boston, 1947, 50, 60, Rubin Mus. Found., Tel viv, Israel, 1986; participated juried exhbns. including Ohel Group of Modern Artists, Tel Aviv, 1927, The Group of Palestinian Artists, Tel Aviv, 1930, Nat. Acad. of Design, Am. Acad. Arts and Letters, Am. Watercolor Soc., Nat. Soc. Painters in Casein and Acrylics, Audubon Artists, Rockport Art Assn., Am. Soc. Contemporary Artists, Butler Mus. Art, Youngstown, Ohio, The Currier Gallery of Art, Manchester, N.H., Cape Ann Soc. Modern Artists; works in permanent collections Nat. Mus. Am. Art of Smithsonian Instn., Washington, Jewish Mus., N.Y.C., San Francisco Mus. of Art, Balt. Art Mus., John Herron Mus. Art, Indpls., Denver Mus. Art, Tel Aviv Mus. (Israel), Bklyn. Mus. Art, Haifa Mus. Modern Art, Israel, Histadruth House, Tel Aviv, Butler Mus. Am. Art, Youngstown, Ohio, Boston Mus. Fine Arts, Nebr. U. Gallery, Inst. Man and Sci., Rensselaerville, N.Y., Brandeis U., Hillel House, Boston U., Jasper Rand Art Mus., Westfield, Mass., Joslyn Mus., Omaha, Addison Gallery Am. Art, Andover, Mass., George Washington Carver Mus., Tuskegee, Ala., Arnot Art Mus., Elmira, N.Y., Everson Mus. Art, Syracuse, N.Y., Ga. Art Mus., Athens, Slater Meml. Mus., Norwich, Conn., Norfolk (Va.) Mus. Arts and Scis., Phoenix Mus. Art, Met. Ins. Co., Newark, DeCordova Mus., Lexington, Mass., Tel Aviv Municipality, Israel, Mishkan Le'omanut Mus. Art, Ein Harod, Israel, Mus. of the City of N.Y., others. Served with C.A.C. AUS, 1942-43. Recipient Minnie R. Stern Meml. medal and prize Audubon Artists 18th Ann. Exhibit, N.Y., 1960, Pauline Mintz Meml. award 28th Ann. Exhibit, 1970, Stanley Grumbacher Meml. medal and prize 35th Ann. Exhibit, 1977, Elaine and James Hewitt award, 1988, awards Nat. Soc. Painters in Casein and Acrylics, Joseph Meyer Co. prize, 1966, Gramercy prize, 1968, M.J. Kaplan Meml. prize, 1970, Today's Art mag. medal merit, 1971, Shiva award for casein painting, 1980, 91, The Elizabeth Erlanger Meml. award, 1992, Beatrice S. Katz prize Am. Soc. Contemporary Artists, 1971, Morrilla Co. award, 1981, Grumbacher art award, 1983, Philip Reisman Meml. award, 1994, Doris Kreindler Meml. award, 1996, Doris Kreindler Meml. award, 1996, Municipality Tel-Aviv-Jaffo, Israel medal, 1987, Pres.'s Spl. citation of merit 47th Ann. Exhibit, 1989, Audubon Artists, Cert. Achievement for cultural contbn. and the outstanding accomplishments in the field of art award of lifetime achievement, Rubin Mus. Exbn. "The Last of the Firstones", 1996, Tel Aviv. Mem. Palestine Artists and Sculptors Assn. (organizer 1935), Am. Artists for Israel (chmn. 1949), Cape Ann Soc. Modern Artists (pres. 1958-59), Am. Soc. Contemporary Artists (bd. dir. 1970, 87), Artists Equity Assn. (nat. sec. 1954, exec. dir. 1959-60, pres. N.Y. chpt. 1960-62, v.p. 1963-64, 67, 68), N.Y. Artists Equity Assn. (pres. 1970-75, pres. emeritus 1975—), Audubon Artists (bd. dir. 1971-74, treas. 1976-77, bd. dir. 1977-78, v.p. 1978-82), Nat. Soc. Painters in Casein and Acrylics (bd. dir. 1963, chmn. ways and means com. 1966, pres. 1967-71, hon. pres. 1971—), Am. Jewish League for Israel. Club: Overseas Press. Home: 215 Park Row New York NY 10038-1149 *I have tried in the course of my life in art to be guided by the following concepts: Art is a continuum that expresses the time in which we live. I am involved with the phenomenon of nature, the changing scene and the life around me. I believe that each painting should be the result of an experience deeply felt. I try to absorb influences, refine them and recreate them in my own image. I believe great works of art always had affinity with humanity, nature, and the soul of mankind.*

NEWMAN, FRANCES MOODY, foundation executive; b. 1912. With The Moody Found., Galveston, Tex., 1942—, now chairperson. Office: The Moody Found 2302 Post Office St Ste 704 Galveston TX 77550-1936*

NEWMAN, FRANCIS A., medical device company executive; b. 1947. Sr. v.p. merchandising F.W. Woolworth, 1980-84, exec. v.p. household merchandising, 1984-85; pres., CEO, dir. F&M Distributors, Inc., 1986-93; pres., COO Eckerd Fleet, Inc., Largo, Fla., 1993—. Office: Eckerd Fleet Inc 8333 Bryan Dairy Rd Largo FL 33777-1230

NEWMAN, FRANK NEIL, bank executive; b. Quincy, Mass., Apr. 20, 1942; m. Lizabeth Newman. B.A. in Econs. magna cum laude, Harvard U., 1963. Exec. v.p., CFO Wells Fargo & Co. and Wells Fargo Bank, San Francisco, 1980-86; CFO, vice-chmn. bd. dirs. Bank Am. Corp, Bank of Am., San Francisco, 1986-93; under sec. domestic fin. Dept. Treasury, Washington, 1993-94, dep. sec., 1994-95; sr. vice chmn. Bankers Trust, 1995—, pres., 1996—, CEO, chmn., 1996—. Office: Bankers Trust 130 Liberty St New York NY 10006-1105

NEWMAN, FREDRIC ALAN, plastic surgeon, educator; b. Bklyn., Aug. 16, 1948; s. Harold Louis and Isabel (Seltzer) N.; m. Stacey Hope Clarfield, Nov. 27, 1983; children: Benjamin, Marissa, Alexandra. BA, Yale Coll., 1970; MD summa cum laude, SUNY Downstate, Bklyn., 1974. Bd. cert. Am. Bd. Plastic Surgery, Am. Bd. Surgery. Resident gen. surgery Beth Israel Hosp., Boston, 1974-77; resident and chief gen. surgery SUNY Downstate, Bklyn., 1977-79; fellow plastic surgery NYU/Inst. Reconstrv. Plastic Surgery, N.Y.C., 1979-81; fellow facial reconstruction Jackson Meml. Hosp., Miami, Fla., 1981-82; asst. clin. prof. dept. plastic surgery N.Y. Med. Coll., West, 1984-95, Columbia Coll. Physicians and Surgeons, N.Y.C., 1995—; chmn. bd. Cutting Edge Techs., Inc., 1994—. Author: Aesthetic Plastic Surgery, 1984, Plastic Surgery, 1985; contbr. articles to profl. jours. Fellow ACS, Internat. Coll. Surgeons (regent 1990—); mem. Am. Soc. Plastic and Reconstructive Surgeons, Am. Soc. Aesthetic Plastic Surgery, Am. Cleft Palate Assn., N.Y. State Med. Soc. Avocations: sailing, skiing, reading, computers. Office: Two Overhill Rd Scarsdale NY 10583

NEWMAN, FREDRIC SAMUEL, lawyer, business executive; b. York, Pa., June 22, 1945; s. Nat. Howard and Josephine (Farkas) N.; m. Mary E. Kiley, May 19, 1973; children: Lydia Ann, Anne Marie, Pauline. AB cum laude, Harvard U., 1967; JD, Columbia U., 1970; cert. the exec. program, U. Va., 1984. Bar: N.Y. 1971, U.S. Dist. Ct. (so. and ea. dists.) N.Y. 1972, U.S. Ct. Appeals (2d cir.) 1974, U.S. Ct. Claims 1993. Assoc. White & Case, N.Y.C., 1970-80; asst. gen. counsel Philip Morris Cos., N.Y.C., 1981-87; gen. counsel, v.p., sec. Philip Morris, Inc., N.Y.C., 1987-90; chief exec. officer TeamTennis, Inc., 1991; prin. Law Office of Fredric S. Newman, N.Y.C., 1992-95; founding ptnr. Hoguet Newman & Regal, LLP, 1996—; pres., CEO, Pathe Comm. Corp., N.Y.C., 1993—; bd. dirs. Exel Ins. Co., Bermuda. Trustee Calhoun Sch., N.Y.C., 1985-88; bd. dirs. N.Y. Fire Safety Found., N.Y.C., 1985-88. Fellow Am. Bar Found. Office: 10 E 40th St New York NY 10016-0200

NEWMAN, GERALDINE ANNE, advertising executive, inventor; b. Boston, Apr. 1; d. Joseph M. and Clara (Bistry) N. BS, UCLA; postgrad., Alliance Francaise, Paris, Los Angeles Sch. Fine Arts, NYU. Writer Tinker Dodge and Delano, N.Y.C., 1970-72, Ketchum Advt., N.Y.C., 1972-75, Advt. to Women, N.Y.C., 1975-78; v.p., creative supr. Young and Rubicam, N.Y.C., 1978-83; v.p., assoc. creative dir. Backer Spielvogel Bates Worldwide Internat. Div., N.Y.C., 1983-90; pres. Geraldine Newman Comm., Inc., N.Y.C., 1990—. County committeewoman Dem. Party, N.Y.C., 1972; advt. adviser Youth at Risk, Breakthrough Found., Food Bank, Food for All, Gifts that Give Back. Featured in Adweek mag., 1986; winner Andy award 1975, 78, 82, 84, Clio award 1982, numerous others. Mem. Ad-net (bd. dirs. 1984-89, creative dir. 1986-89, Pres.'s award 1988). Avocations: painting, travel. Home and Office: 315 E 72nd St New York NY 10021-4625

NEWMAN, HARRY RUDOLPH, urologist, educator; b. Russia, Sept. 10, 1909; naturalized, 1919, came to U.S., 1935, naturalized, 1944; s. Abraham and Mary (Rudolph) N.; m. Lillian Lear, Aug. 18, 1942; children: Nancy Ellen, Robert Lear, Suzanne Mary. M.D., U. Toronto, 1935; M.S., U. Pa., 1940. Diplomate: Am. Bd. Urology. Resident urology U. Minn. Hosps., 1936-37, All Saints Hosp., London, Eng., 1937-38; sr. resident urology N.Y. Postgrad. Med. Sch. and Hosp., 1939-40, Boston Long Island Hosp., 1941-42; resident surgery N.Y. Postgrad. Hosp., 1942; resident gen. surgery Prince of Wales Hosp., Plymouth, Eng.; asst. clin. prof. urology N.Y. Postgrad. Med. Sch. & Hosp., 1946-54; sr. attending urologist Bellevue Hosp., N.Y.C., 1946-54; attending urologist Yale New-Haven Hosp.; attending univ. service Yale U., asst. clin. prof. urology, 1949—; dir. urology Albert Einstein Coll. Medicine, also clin. prof. surgery, chief urology, 1957—, clin. prof. urology, 1957-62, prof. urology, 1963-65, 66-80, emeritus chmn. and prof. urology, 1980—, chmn. dept., 1966-80; prof. history; chief urology Bronx Mcpl. Hosp., 1966—; chief urology community div. Grace New Haven Hosp., 1965-66; cons. urologist Stamford (Conn.) Hosp., St. Joseph Hosp., Stamford, 1965—; former asst. clin. prof. urology NYU; dir. urology City N.Y. Bronx Mcpl. Med. Center, 1954-65; chief urology Regional Hosp., Hunter Field, Savannah, Ga. Served from capt. to maj. USAAF, 1942-46. Fellow ACS, N.Y. Acad. Medicine, Royal So. of Health (Great Britian); mem. AMA, Physicians and Surgeons of Conn., Soc. Univ. Urologists, Masons (32 deg.), Shriners, Yale Club (N.Y.), Sigma Xi. Home: 95 Broadfield Rd Hamden CT 06517-1543 Office: 2 Church St S New Haven CT 06519-1717

NEWMAN, HOWARD NEAL, lawyer, educator; b. N.Y.C., June 11, 1935; s. Herman and Sarah (Steinsaltz) N.; m. Carol Redstone, Dec. 25, 1960; children: Leslie, Amy. A.B., Dartmouth Coll., 1956, M.B.A., 1957; M.S., Columbia U., 1959; J.D., Temple U., 1970. Trainee to asst. v.p. Roosevelt Hosp., N.Y.C., 1957-65; assoc. adminstr. Pa. Hosp., Phila., 1965-70; commr. Med. Services Adminstrn., Washington, 1970-74; pres. Dartmouth-Hitchcock Med. Center, Hanover, N.H., 1974-80; adminstr. Health Care Financing Adminstr., Dept. Health and Human Services, Washington, 1980-81; ptnr. Memel, Jacobs, Pierno & Gersh, Washington, 1982-86, Powell, Goldstein, Frazer & Murphy, Washington, 1986-88; dean, prof. health policy and mgmt. NYU, 1988-94, prof. health policy and mgmt., 1994—. Served with USAR, 1959-65. White House fellow, 1967-68. Mem. Nat. Inst. for Dispute Resolution, D.C. Bar Assn. Jewish. Office: 4 Washington Sq N New York NY 10003-6671

NEWMAN, J. KEVIN, broadcast journalist; b. Toronto, Ont., Can., June 2, 1959; came to U.S., 1994; s. George Edmund and Sheila Lorraine (Stevenson) N.; m. Catharine Erica Kearns, June 15, 1985; children: John Alexander, Erica Louise. BA, U. Western Ont., 1981. Atlantic bur. chief CTV Nat. News, Halifax, N.S., Can., 1987; parliament reporter CTV Nat. News, Ottawa, Ont., Can., 1987-89, CBC Nat. News, Ottawa, 1990-92; anchor CBC Midday, Toronto, 1992-94, ABC World News This Morning, N.Y.C., 1994-96, Good Morning America-Sunday, N.Y.C., 1996—; corr. ABC World News Tonight, N.Y.C., 1996—; instr. in journalism Ryerson U., Toronto, 1992-94. Avocations: skiing, canoeing, camping. Office: ABC News 47 W 66th St New York NY 07901

NEWMAN, JAMES WILSON, business executive; b. Clemson, S.C., Nov. 3, 1909; s. Charles Carter and Grace (Strode) N.; m. Clara Collier, July 1934; children: Clare Adelaide, Mildred Bledsoe, James Wilson, Charles Carter II. B.S., Clemson U., 1931, also LL.D. (hon.); student, Am. Inst. Banking, 1931-32; J.D., N.Y. U., 1937. Bar: N.Y. bar 1937. Reporter R.G. Dun & Co., 1931-46; v.p. Dun & Bradstreet, Inc., 1946-52, pres., chief exec. officer, 1952-60, chmn., chief exec. officer, 1960-68, chmn. finance com., 1968-80, dir., to 1980; adv. bd. Chem. Bank, Gen. Foods Corp., 1963-81, Internat. Paper Co., until 1982; trustee Atlantic Mut. Ins. Co., Mut. Life Ins. Co. Am., until 1982; chmn. spl. rev. com. Lockheed Corp., 1976-78. Chmn. Pres.'s Task Force on Small Bus., 1969; mem. Commn. on Bankruptcy Laws U.S., 1970-73; chmn. Nat. Bur. Econ. Rsch., 1974-78; trustee Com. Econ. Devel., Va. Mus. Fine Arts, 1978-94; mem. coun. Miller Ctr. Pub. Affairs, U. Va., 1983-94; mem. Price Commn., 1971-72; chmn. Sweet Briar Coll., 1963-69. Mem. ABA, Farmington Country Club (Va.), Commonwealth Club (Richmond, Va.), Army and Navy Club (Washington), Phi Delta Phi. Home: 2401 Old Ivy Rd Apt #2606 Charlottesville VA 22903 Office: 503 Falconer Dr Madison Park Suite 4A Charlottesville VA 22903

NEWMAN, JANET ELAINE, elementary education educator; b. Savannah, Ga., Dec. 4, 1947; d. Oral Kenneth and Mary Gertrude (Flynn) N. AA, R.I. Jr. Coll., Providence, 1967; A in B., R.I. Jr. Coll., 1976; BA, Mt. St. Joseph Coll., 1969. Elem. tchr. Coventry (R.I.) Sch. Dept., 1970-73; supr. elec. soldering Harwood Mfg., Providence, 1973-80; elem. tchr. Providence Sch. Dept., 1980—; mem. Legal/Edn. Partnership, 1990—, Classroom Alternate Programs/Classroom Alternate Strategies of Teaching Team, 1993—; mem. adv. bd. West Broadway Schoolwide Project, 1994—, Sch. Improvement Project, 1994—; Times 2 tchr., 1997. Bd. dirs. Woodland Estates Condominium Assn., 1988—; tchr. CCD, St. Martha's Ch., 1985-87; mem. tech. com. Carl G. Lauro Elem. Sch., 1996—. Fellow R.I. Writing Consortium, 1990, Taft Inst. at R.I. Coll., 1991. Roman Catholic. Home: 1145 Hartford Ave Johnston RI 02919-7128 Office: Providence Sch Dept 797 Westminster St Providence RI 02903-4018

NEWMAN, JAY, broadcast executive. Reporter/documentary & exec. newscast prodr./assignment mgr. various TV stas., 1973-79; news dir. WNEP-TV, Scranton, 1979-80, KOVR-TV, Sacramento, 1980-81, KDKA-TV, Pitts., 1981-83, WBBM-TV, Chgo., 1985-86, WCAU-TV, Phila., 1983-85, 86-88; v.p., sta. mgr. WCIZ-TV, Miami, 1988-90; gen. mgr. WWJ-TV, Detroit, 1990—. Office: WWJ-TV 300 River Place Dr Ste 6200 Detroit MI 48207-4225

NEWMAN, JOAN MESKIEL, lawyer; b. Youngstown, Ohio, Dec. 12, 1947; d. John F. and Rosemary (Scarmuzzi) Meskiel; m. Charles Andrew Newman, Aug. 8, 1971; children: Anne R., Elyse S. BA in Polit. Sci., Case-Western Reserve U., 1969; JD, Washington U., St. Louis, 1972, LLM in Taxation, 1973. Bar: Mo. 1972. Assoc. Lewis & Rice, St. Louis, 1973-80, ptnr., 1981-90; ptnr. Thompson Coburn, St. Louis, 1990—; adj. prof. law Washington U. Sch. Law, St. Louis, 1975-92; past pres., mem. Midwest Pension Conf., St. Louis chpt.; lectr. in field. chmn. bd. dirs. Great St. Louis coun. Girl Scouts U.S.A., 1988-92, officer, 1978-92; mem. bd. dirs. and exec. com. Girl Scouts U.S.A., 1993—; nat. treas. Girl Scouts U.S.A., 1996—; chmn. bd. dirs. Met. Employment and Rehab. Svcs., 1994-96; bd. dirs. Jewish Fedn. St. Louis, 1991-96, Jewish Ctr. Aged, 1990-92; chmn. bd. dirs. Women of Achievement, 1993-96; mem. cmty. wide youth svcs. panel United Way Greater St. Louis, 1992-96; fin. futures task force Kiwanis Camp Wyman, 1992-93; mem. nat. coun. Washington U. Sch. Law, 1988-91; chmn. staff blue ribbon fin. com. Sch. Dist. Clayton, 1986-87; vol. Women's Self Help Ctr. Named Woman of Achievement St. Louis, 1991. Mem. Mo. Bar Assn. (staff pension and benefits com. 1991—), Bar Met. St. Louis (past chmn. taxation sect.), St. Louis Forum, Order of Coif (hon.). Office: Thompson Coburn 1 Mercantile Ctr Ste 3300 Saint Louis MO 63101-1643

NEWMAN, JOHN KEVIN, classics educator; b. Bradford, Yorkshire, Eng., Aug. 17, 1928; came to U.S., 1969, naturalized, 1984; s. Willie and Agnes (Shee) N.; m. Frances M. Stickney, Sept. 8, 1970; children: Alexandra, John, Victoria. B.A. in Lit.-Humaniores, Exeter Coll., Oxford U., 1950, B.A. in Russian, 1952, M.A., 1953; Ph.D., Bristol U., 1967. Classics master St. Francis Xavier Coll., Liverpool, Eng., 1952-54, Downside Sch., Somerset, Eng., 1955-69; mem. faculty U. Ill., Urbana, 1969—, prof. classics, 1980—, chmn. dept., 1981-85. Author: Augustus and the New Poetry, 1967, Latin Compositions, 1976, Pindar's Art, 1984, The Classical Epic Tradition, 1986, Roman Catullus, 1990, Lelio Guidiccioni, Latin Poems, 1992; co-author: (with A.V. Carozzi) Horace-Benedict de Saussure, 1995, Augustan Propertius, 1997; editor: Ill. Classical Studies, 1982-87; contbr. The New Princeton Encyclopedia of Poetry and Poetics, 1993. mem. sr. common room Corpus Christi Coll., Oxford U., 1985-86. Recipient silver medals Vatican, Rome, 1960, 62, 65. Roman Catholic. Home: 703 W Delaware Ave Urbana IL 61801-4806 Office: Dept Classics U Ill 4072 Fgn Lang Bldg 707 S Mathews Ave Urbana IL 61801-3625

NEWMAN, JOHN M., JR., lawyer; b. Youngstown, Ohio, Aug. 15, 1944. BA, Georgetown U., 1966; JD, Harvard U., 1969. BAr: Ill. 1970, Calif. 1972, Ohio 1976. Law clerk ctrl. dist. U.S. Dist. Ct., Calif., 1969-70, asst. U.S. Atty. ctrl. dist., 1970-75; ptnr. Jones, Day, Reavis & Pogue, Cleve. Fellow Am. Coll. Trial Lawyers; mem. Phi Beta Kappa. Office: Jones Day Reavis & Pogue North Point 901 Lakeside Ave E Cleveland OH 44114-1116

NEWMAN, JOHN MERLE, lawyer; b. Cleve., June 25, 1934; s. Emanuel Robert and Theresa Esther (Dreissinger) N.; 1 child, Thomas Edward; m. Thelma Aitken, July 10, 1992; 1 child, Jennifer Ann Newman-Brazil. AB, Miami U., Oxford, Ohio, 1957; LLB, Cornell U., 1957. Bar: N.J. 1971, U.S. Ct. Appeals (3d cir.) 1961, U.S. Dist. Ct. N.J. 1983, U.S. Dist. Ct. (so. and ea. dists.) N.Y. 1983; cert. civil atty. Supreme Ct. of N.J. Assoc. Bertram Polow, Morristown, N.J., 1960-62; ptnr. Porzio Bromberg & Newman P.C., Morristown, 1962-76, 80—; presiding judge chancery/family divsn. Superior Ct. of N.J., Morristown, 1976-80. Trustee, officer Cmty. Med. Ctr., Randolph Libr., Morristown, 1970-74, Hist. Speedwell Mus., Morristown, 1991—, Family Svc., Morristown, 1988-91; trustee Occupational Tng. Ctr., Morristown, 1965-69. Recipient Cert. of Acad. Performance U. Edinburgh, Scotland, 1956, various certs. for bar and cmty. svcs. Mem. ABA (litigation sect., environ. subcom., environ. law sect. corp. counsel subcom., vice chair various coms.), N.J. State Bar Assn., Morris County Bar Assn., Omicron Delta Kappa. Avocations: cycling, tennis. Office: Porzio Bromberg & Newman 163 Madison Ave Morristown NJ 07960-7324

NEWMAN, JOHN NICHOLAS, naval architect educator; b. New Haven, Mar. 10, 1935; s. Richard and Daisy (Neumann) N.; m. Kathleen Smedley Kirk, June 16, 1956; children—James Bartram, Nancy Kirk, Carol Ann. B.S. Mass. Inst. Tech, 1956, M.S., 1957, Sc.D., 1960; postgrad., Cambridge (Eng.) U., 1958-59; D Technicae honoris causa, U. Trondheim, Norway, 1992. Research naval architect David Taylor Model Basin, Navy Dept., Washington, 1959-67; assoc. prof. naval architecture MIT, Cambridge, 1967-70, prof., 1970—; vis. prof. U. New South Wales, Australia, 1973, U. Adelaide, Australia, 1974, Tech. U. Norway, 1981-82; cons. Navy Dept., Dept. Justice, pvt. firms. Author: Marine Hydrodynamics, 1977; Contbr.: articles to profl. jours., including Sci. Am. Recipient prize Am. Bur. Shipping, 1956; Walter Atkinson prize Royal Instn. Naval Architects, 1973, also Bronze medal, 1976; Guggenheim fellow, 1973-74; research grantee Office Naval Research; NSF. Mem. AAAS, NAE, Soc. Naval Architects and Marine Engrs. (Davidson medal 1988), Norwegian Acad. Sci. Home: 60 Campbell Rd Wayland MA 01778-1024 Office: MIT Dept Ocean Engring Cambridge MA 02139

NEWMAN, JOHN SCOTT, chemical engineer, educator; b. Richmond, Va., Nov. 17, 1938; s. Clarence William and Marjorie Lenore (Saucerman) N.; m. Nguyen Thanh Lan, June 30, 1973; children—Natalie Diane, Michael Alexander. B.S., Northwestern U., 1960; M.S., U. Calif., Berkeley, 1962, Ph.D., 1963. Asst. prof. chem. engring. U. Calif., Berkeley, 1963-67, assoc. prof., 1967-70; prof. U. Calif., 1970—; prin. investigator energy & environ. divsn. Lawrence Berkeley Nat. Lab., 1963—; vis. prof. U. Wis., Madison, 1973; summer participant Oak Ridge Nat. Lab., 1965, 66. Author: Electrochemical Systems, 1973, rev. edit. 1991; assoc. editor Jour. Electrochem. Soc., 1990—; contbr. articles to profl. jours. Fellow Electrochem. Soc. (Young Author's prize 1966, 69, David C. Grahame award 1985, Henry B. Linford award 1990, Olin Palladium medal 1991); mem. Am. Inst. Chem. Engrs. Home: 114 York Ave Kensington CA 94708-1045 Office: U Calif Dept Chem Engring Berkeley CA 94720-1462

NEWMAN, JON O., federal judge; b. N.Y.C., N.Y., May 2, 1932; s. Harold W. Jr. and Estelle L. (Ormond) N.; m. Martha G. Silberman, June 19, 1953; children: Leigh, Scott, David. Postgrad., Hotchkiss Sch., 1949; AB magna cum laude, Princeton U., 1953; LLB, Yale U., 1956; LLD (hon.), U. Hartford, 1975, U. Bridgeport, 1980, Bklyn. Law Sch., 1995, N.Y. Law Sch., 1996. Bar: Conn. 1956, D.C. 1956. Law clk. to Hon. George T. Washington U.S. Ct. Appeals, 1956-57; sr. law clk. to chief justice Hon. Earl Warren, U.S. Supreme Ct., 1957-58; ptnr. Ritter, Satter & Newman, Hartford, Conn., 1958-60; counsel to majority Conn. Gen. Assembly, 1959; spl. counsel to gov. Conn., 1959-61; asst. to sec. HEW, 1961-62; adminstrv. asst. to U.S. senator, 1963-64; U.S. atty. Dist. of Conn., 1964-69; pvt. practice law, 1969-71; U.S. dist. judge Dist. of Conn., 1972-79; U.S. cir. judge 2d Cir. Ct. of Appeals, 1979-93, chief judge, 1993-97. Co-author: Politics: The American Way. With USAR, 1954-62. Recipient Learned Hand medal Fed. Bar Coun., 1987. Fellow Am. Bar Found.; mem. ABA, Am. Law Inst., Conn. Bar Assn., Am. Judicature Soc. Democrat. Office: US Ct Appeals 450 Main St Hartford CT 06103-3002

NEWMAN, JOSEPH HERZL, advertising consultant; b. N.Y.C., Dec. 1, 1928; s. Max A. and Tillie C. (Weitzman) N.; m. Ruth Z. Marcus, Dec. 19, 1954 (div. Feb. 1987); children: Deborah Lynn, David Alan, Mark Jonathan; m. Nancy K. Deutschman, Aug. 19, 1990; stepchildren: Pamela Sue Deutschman, Douglas Hayes Deutschman, Cindi Elaine Deutschman. AB, Bethany Coll., W.Va., 1949; MS, Columbia U., 1956. With 20th Century Fox Film Corp., N.Y.C., 1949-53; media supr. Fred Wittner Advt. Agy. (now Hammond Farrell Inc.), N.Y.C., 1953-56; media dir. O.S. Tyson & Co. (now Poppe Tyson, Inc.), N.Y.C., 1956-64; v.p., media dir. Marsteller Inc. (now Lord, Dentsu and Ptnrs.), N.Y.C., 1965-85; v.p., assoc. media dir. HBM/Creamer, N.Y.C., 1985-87, Della Femina, McNamee, Inc., N.Y.C., 1987-89; pres. Newman And Assocs., Cleve., 1989—; mem. faculty Advt. Age Media Workshop, 1972; past chmn. media mgrs. adv. com. Bus. Publs. Audit of Circulation Inc., N.Y.C.; condr. profl. media planning seminars, 1989—. Contbr. articles to profl. jours. Past chmn. bus.-to-bus. media com. Am. Assn. Advt. Agys.; vice chmn. tax incentive rev. coun. City of Mayfield Heights, Ohio, 1994-97, chmn., 1997—. With U.S. Army, 1950-52. Mem. Bus. Mktg. Assn. (past mem. media comparability coun., media data form com. and rsch. resource com., Agy. Exec. of Yr., N.Y. chpt. 1960, 66, 71, 73). Home and Office: 6338 Woodhawk Dr Cleveland OH 44124-4153

NEWMAN, JOYCE KLIGERMAN, sculptor; b. Atlantic City, July 7, 1927; d. Louis and Anne (Levine) Kligerman; m. Melvin Micklin Newman, Sept. 11, 1949; children—Rebecca, Morris Henry. B.A., Cornell U., 1948; Ph.D. in Biochemistry, U. Chgo., 1955; student, Art Students League, N.Y.C., 1962. Research asso. biochemistry U. Colo. Med. Center, Denver, 1963-70; mem. faculty dept. chemistry Met. State Coll., 1976-77. Profl. sculptor, Denver, 1968-84, Pasadena, Calif., 1984—, sculpture installed, Douglas County (Colo.) Pub. Library, 1971; commd. public sculpture, City of Littleton (Colo.), 1979, U. No Colo., Greeley, 1981, City of Chandler, Ariz., 1986; Contbr. numerous articles on biochemistry, also artists' rights to profl. jours. Mem. Artists Equity Assn. (pres. Colo. chpt. 1970-72, nat. pres. 1973-75), U. Chgo. Alumni Assn. (bd. govs. 1995—, pres. Denver club 1967-84, bd. dirs. L.A. club 1985-96, v.p. 1987-91, pres. 1992-94). Address: 1750 E Mountain St Pasadena CA 91104-3937

NEWMAN, KENNETH E., lawyer; b. N.Y.C., Sept. 28, 1946; s. Stanley and Muriel (Orenstein) N.; children: Douglas C., Jason B., Gregory R. BA, Queens Coll., N.Y.C., 1967; JD, St. John's U., N.Y.C., 1971. Bar: N.Y. 1972, U.S. Supreme Ct. 1976, U.S. Ct. Appeals (2nd cir.) 1974, U.S. Ct. Appeals (D.C. cir.) 1974, U.S. Ct. Appeals (3d cir.) 1980, U.S. Ct. Appeals (10th cir.) 1982, (4th cir.) 1988, U.S. Dist. Ct. (so. dist.) N.Y. 1974, (ea. dist.) N.Y.) 1979. Trial atty. U.S. Dept. Justice, Washington, 1971-73; assoc. Donovan Leisure Newton & Irvine, N.Y.C., 1973-80; ptnr. Donovan Leisure Newton & Irvine, 1980-95; v.p., ea. regional counsel Walt Disney Co., N.Y.C., 1995—; trial faculty Practicing Law Inst., N.Y.C., 1983-94. Mem. ABA, Fed. Bar Coun., Assn. Bar City of N.Y. Office: The Walt Disney Co 114 5th Ave New York NY 10011-5604

NEWMAN, LAWRENCE WALKER, lawyer; b. Boston, July 1, 1935; s. Leon Bettoney and Hazel W. (Walker) N.; m. Cecilia Isette Santos, Nov. 29, 1975; children: Reynaldo W., Timothy D., Virginia I.S., Isabel B., Thomas H. A.B., Harvard U., 1957, LL.B., 1960. Bar: D.C. 1961, N.Y. 1965. Atty. U.S. Dept. Justice, 1960-61, Spl. Study of Securities Markets and Office Spl. Counsel on Investment Co. Act Matters, U.S. SEC, 1961-64; asst. U.S. atty. So. Dist. N.Y., 1964-69; assoc. Baker & McKenzie, N.Y.C., 1969-71, ptnr., 1971—; mem. internat. adv. coun. World Arbitration Inst., 1984-87; mem. adv. com. Asia Pacific Ctr. for Resolution of Internat. Trade Disputes, 1987—; mem. adv. bd. Inst. for Transnational Arbitration, 1988—; chmn. U.S. Iranian Claimants Com., 1982—; mem. adv. bd. World Arbitration Mediation Report, 1993—; mem. bd. adv. to Corporate Counselor Internat. Adviser, 1995—. Co-author: The Practice of Internat. Litigation, 1992, 93, Litigating Internat. Commercial Disputes, 1996; columnist N.Y. Law Jour., 1982—; adv. bd. World Arbitration and Mediation Report; contbr. articles to profl. jours. and books on litigation and internat. arbitration. Mem. ABA (internat. litigation com., internat. arbitration com.), Internat. Bar Assn. (com. dispute resolution, com. constrn. litigation), Inter-Am. Bar Assn., Fed. Bar Coun., Am. Fgn. Law Assn., Maritime Law Assn. U.S., Assn. Bar City N.Y. (com. on arbitration & alternative dispute resolution 1991-94), Am. Arbitration Assn. (corp. counsel com. 1987—, panel comml. arbitrators), U.S. Coun. Internat. Bus., Ct. Arbitration of Polish Chamber Fgn. Trade (panel of arbitrators), Brit. Col. Internat. Comml. Abitration Ctr. Home: 1001 Park Ave New York NY 10028-0935 Office: Baker & McKenzie 805 3rd Ave New York NY 10022-7513

NEWMAN, LAWRENCE WILLIAM, financial executive; b. Chgo., Jan. 14, 1939; s. Eskil William and Adele Diane (Lawnicki) N.; m. Christine Harriet Jaronski, Sept. 22, 1962; children: Paul, Scott, Ron. BBS, U. Ill., 1965; MBA, Northwestern U., 1970. CPA, Ill. Controller ECM Corp., Schaumburg, Ill., 1966-70; controller Nachman Corp., Des Plaines, Ill., 1970-76, v.p., treas., controller, 1976-79; v.p. fin. P & S Mgmt. Inc., Schiller Park, Ill., 1979-83; controller Underwriters Labs., Northbrook, Ill., 1983-85, asst. treas., 1985-89; v.p., treas. Underwriters Labs., Northbrook, 1990—. Mem. Fin. Execs. Inst., Am. Inst. CPA's. Club: Exec. of Chgo. Office: Underwriters Labs 333 Pfingsten Rd Northbrook IL 60062-2002

NEWMAN, MALCOLM, civil engineering consultant; b. N.Y.C., June 29, 1931; s. George and Evelyn (Weber) N.; m. Estelle Ruth Glotzer, June 11, 1955; children: Roberta Gail, Leonard Scott, Alisa Gwen. BSCE, CCNY, 1952; MSCE, Columbia U., 1957; D in Engring. Sci., NYU, 1962. Registered profl. engr., N.Y. Chief structural mechanics Republic-Fairchild Hiller Corp., Farmingdale, N.Y., 1962-65, staff cons., 1970-71; dir. structural mechanics Harry Belock Assocs. Inc., Great Neck, N.Y., 1965-69; dir. structural mechanics and design Analytical Mechanics Assn., Jericho, N.Y., 1969-70; prof. mech. engring. Tel Aviv U., 1972-75; pres., tech. dir. Inter-City Testing and Cons., Mineola, N.Y., 1976—; pres. Athletic Safety Products Inc., Mineola, 1985—; adj. prof. engring. Cooper Union. Contbr. over 80 articles to profl. jours.; patentee in field. Bd. dirs. Cinema Arts Ctr., Huntington, N.Y., 1989—. Mem. NSPE, Am. Soc. Safety Engrs., Nat. Assn. Profl. Accident Reconstruction Specialists, Soc. Automotive Engrs., System Safety Soc. (pres. 1983-85). Office: Inter-City Testing & Cons 167 Willis Ave Mineola NY 11501-2621

NEWMAN, MARGARET ANN, nursing educator; b. Memphis, Oct. 10, 1933; d. Ivo Mathias and Mamie Love (Donald) N.; BSHE, Baylor U., 1954; BSN, U. Tenn., Memphis, 1962; MS, U. Calif., San Francisco, 1964; PhD, NYU, 1971. Dir. nursing, asst. prof. nursing Clin. Research Center, U. Tenn., 1964-67; asst. prof. N.Y.U., 1971-75, assoc. prof., 1975-77; prof. in charge grad. program and research dept. nursing Pa. State U., 1977-80, prof. nursing, 1977-84; prof. nursing U. Minn., 1984-96, prof. emeritus 1996—; disting. resident Westminster Coll., Salt Lake City Utah, 1991. Travelling fellow New Zealand Nursing Ednl. & Rsch. Fund, 1985; Am. Jour. Nursing scholar, 1979-80; recipient Outstanding Alumnus award U. Tenn. Coll. Nursing, 1975, Disting. Alumnus award NYU Div. Nursing, 1984; Disting. Scholar in Nursing award NYU Div. Nursing, 1992, Sigma Theta Tau Founders Rsch. award, 1993, Nursing Scholar award St. Xavier U., 1994, E. Louise grant award for nursing excellence U. Minn., 1996, Margaret Newman scholar award Zeta chpt. Sigma Theta Tau, 1996—. Fellow Am. Acad. Nursing. Author: Theory Development in Nursing, 1979, Health as Expanding Consciousness, 1986, 2nd edit., 1994, A Developing Discipline, 1995; editor: (with others) Source Book of Nursing Research, 1973, 2d edit., 1977. Research on patterns of person-environment interaction as indices of health as expanding consciousness; also models of profl. practice. Home: 289 5th St E Saint Paul MN 55101-1995

NEWMAN, MARY THOMAS, communications educator, management consultant; b. Howell, Mo., Oct. 15, 1933; d. Austin Hill and Doris (McQueen) Thomas; m. Grover Travis Newman, Aug. 22, 1952 (div. 1967); 1 child, Leah Newman Lane; m. Rodney Charles Westlund, July 18, 1981. BS, S.F. Austin State U., 1965; MA, U. Houston, 1956; PhD, Pa. State U., 1980. Cert. permanent tchr., Tex. Instr. communications South Tex. Coll., Houston, 1965-70; assoc. prof. communications Burlington County Coll., Pemberton, N.J., 1970-72; teaching asst. in communications Pa. State U., University Park, 1972-73; asst. prof. Ogontz Campus Pa. State U., Abington, 1973-80; lectr. mgmt. and communications U. Md., Europe and Asia, 1980-83; mem. vis. faculty dept. communications U. Tenn., Knoxville, 1984-85; asst. prof. human factors U. So. Calif., L.A., 1985-88; assoc. prof. human factors, dir. profl. devel. U. Denver Coll. Systems Sci., 1988-92; assoc. prof. USC, Berlin, Germany, 1992-93; assoc. prof., assoc. dir. Whitworth Coll., Spokane, Wash., 1993-95; assoc. prof. comms. Houston Baptist U., 1995—; pres. Human Resource Communications Group, Easton, Md., 1984—; lectr. Bus. Rsch. Inst., Toyo U., Tokyo, 1983, Saitama Med. U., Japan, 1983; scholar in residence U.S. Marine Corps., Quantico, Va., 1990-92; mem. final phase faculty USC MSSM Troop Draw Down, Berlin, Germany, 1992-93; team mem. Spokane Inter-Collegiate Rsch. & Tech. Inst., 1993-95; dir. Women's Leadership Conf., Moses Lake, Wash., 1993; mem. world svcs. com. YWCA, Spokane; Lilly fellow 1996. Author: Introduction to Basic Speech Communication, 1969; contbr. articles to profl. jours. Program developer U.S. Army Hdqrs. Sch. Age Latch Key Program, Alexandria, Va., 1987; mem. Govt. of Guam Women's Issues Task Force, 1985. Lilly fellow in humanities and arts, summer 1996. Mem. Human Factors Soc., Speech Communication Assn. (legis. coun. 1970-73, editl. bd. jour. 1970-76), Ea. Communication Assn. (editl. bd. jours. 1975-80), Univ. Film Assn. (publicity dir. 1978-80), Indsl. Comm. Coun., Chesapeake Women's Network, Easton Bus. and Profl. Women, Alpha Chi, Alpha Psi Omega, Pi Kappa Delta, Delta Kappa Gamma. Avocations: military history and women's issues research. Office: Houston Baptist U Dept Comms 7502 Fondren Rd Houston TX 77074-3204

NEWMAN, MICHAEL RODNEY, lawyer; b. N.Y.C., Oct. 2, 1945; s. Morris and Helen Gloria (Hendler) N.; m. Cheryl Jeanne Anker, June 11, 1967; children: Hillary Abra, Nicole Brooke. Student NASA Inst. Space Physics, Columbia U., 1964; BA, U. Denver, 1967; JD, U. Chgo., 1970. Bar: Calif. 1971, U.S. Dist. Ct. (cen. dist.) Calif. 1972, U.S. Ct. Appeals (9th cir.) 1974, U.S. Dist. Ct. (no. dist.) Calif. 1975, U.S. Supreme Ct. 1978, U.S. Dist. Ct. (so. dist.) Calif. 1979, U.S. Tax Ct. 1979, U.S. Dist. Ct. (ea. dist.) Calif. 1983. Assoc. David Daar, 1971-76; ptnr. Daar & Newman, 1976-78, Miller & Daar, 1978-88, Miller, Daar & Newman, 1988-89, Daar & Newman, 1989—; judge pro tem L.A. Mcpl. Ct., 1982—, L.A. Superior Ct., 1988—. Lectr. Ea. Claims Conf., Ea. Life Claims Conf., Nat. Health Care Anti-Fraud Assn., AIA Conf. on Ins. Fraud; mem. L.A. Citizens Organizing Com. for Olympic Summer Games, 1984, mem. govtl. liaison adv. commn. 1984; mem. So. Calif. Com. for Olympic Summer Games, 1984; cert. ofcl. Athletics Congress of U.S., co-chmn. legal com. S.P.A-T.A.C, chief finish judge; trustee Massada lodge B'nai Brith. Recipient NYU Bronze medal in Physics, 1962, Maths. award USN Sci., 1963. Mem. ABA (multi-dist. litigation subcom., com. on class actions), Los Angeles County Bar Assn. (chmn. attys. errors and omissions prevention com., mem. cts. com. litigation sect.), Conf. Ins. Counsel, So. Pacific Assn., TAC (bd. dirs., Disting. Svc. award 1988), Porter Valley Country Club. Office: 865 S Figueroa St Ste 2500 Los Angeles CA 90017-2567

NEWMAN, MONROE, retired economist, educator; b. Bklyn., Jan. 31, 1929; s. David A. and Ida Mary (Leight) N.; m. Ruth Zielinski, Feb. 6, 1951. BA, Antioch Coll., 1950; MA, U. Ill., 1953, PhD, 1954. Mem... staff AFL, 1947-48; examiner NLRB, 1949-50; rsch. analyst ... research analyst Assn. Casualty and Surety Cos., ... State U., University Park, 1955-86; prof. ... emeritus, 1986—, head dept., ... planning, 1971-72, dir. Ctr. ... prof. econs. U. Pitts... Washington... advis...

(pres.), Am. Econ. Assn., Regional Sci. Assn. Home: 4101 Cathedral Ave NW Washington DC 20016-3585

NEWMAN, MORRIS, mathematician; b. N.Y.C., Feb. 25, 1924; s. Isaac and Sarah (Cohen) N.; m. Mary Aileen Lenk, Sept. 18, 1948; children: Sally Ann, Carl Lenk. A.B., N.Y.U., 1945; M.A., Columbia U., 1946; Ph.D., U. Pa., 1952. Mathematician applied math div. Nat. Bur. Standards, Washington, 1951-63, chief numerical analysis sect., 1963-70, sr. rsch. mathematician, 1970-76; prof. math. U. Calif., Santa Barbara, 1976-94, prof. emeritus, 1994—; dir. Inst. Interdisciplinary Applications of Algebra and Combinatorics, 1976-80; lectr. U. B.C., 1960, U. Calif.-Santa Barbara, 1965, Am. U., Cath. U., U. Md. Author: Matrix Representations of Groups, 1968, Integral Matrices, 1972; editor: Jour. Research Nat. Bur. Standards, 1966-76, Math. of Computation, 1975-86; assoc. editor: Jour. Linear and Multilinear Algebra, 1973—, Letters in Linear Algebra, 1979—; contbr. articles to profl. jours. Recipient Gold medal U.S. Dept. Commerce, 1966. Mem. Am. Math. Soc. (council 1980-86), London Math. Soc., Math. Assn. Am., Washington Acad. Scis., AAAS, sigma Xi. Home: 1050 Las Alturas Rd Santa Barbara CA 93103-1608 Office: U Calif Dept Math Santa Barbara CA 93106

NEWMAN, MURIEL KALLIS STEINBERG, art collector; b. Chgo., Feb. 25, 1914; d. Maurice and Ida (Nudelman) Kallis; m. Albert H. Newman, May 14, 1955; 1 son by previous marriage, Glenn D. Steinberg. Student, Art Inst. Chgo., 1932-36, Ill. Inst. Tech., 1947-50, U. Chgo., 1958-65. hon. life trustee, benefactor Met. Mus. Art, N.Y.C., mem. vis. com. dept. 20th Century Art, mem. acquisitions com., 1981—, mem. decorative arts com., 1989; also Costume Inst. Dir., 20th Century Painting and Sculpture Com., Art Inst. Chgo., 1955-80, governing mem. inst., 1955—, major benefactor, 1979—; pioneer collector Am. abstract expressionist art, 1949—, major show of collection, Met. Mus. Art, N.Y.C., 1981, also show of personal collection of costumes and jewelry, 1981. Bd. govs. Landmarks Preservation Council, Chgo., 1966-78; mem. woman's bd. U. Chgo., 1960-81, Art Inst. Chgo., 1953—; trustee Mus. Contemporary Art, 1970—, benefactor, 1970—; trustee Chgo. Sch. of architecture Found., 1971—, Archives Am. Art, 1976—; mem. bd. Bright New City Urban Affairs Lecture Series, 1966—. Recipient Scroll Recognition of Pub. Svc., U.S. Dept. State, 1958. Mem. Antiquarian Soc. of Art Inst. Chgo., Chgo. Hist. Soc. (mem. guild 1958—). Clubs: Arts (Chgo.), Casino (Chgo.). *Searching for truth is a given for a life of value. For me visual art ontologically reveals the truth of the search. Striving for excellence is the spearhead with which to proceed.*

NEWMAN, MURRAY ARTHUR, aquarium administrator; b. Chgo., Mar. 6, 1924; emigrated to Can., 1953, naturalized, 1970; s. Paul Jones and Virginia (Murray) N.; m. Katherine Greene Rose, Aug. 8, 1952; 1 child, Susan. B.Sc., U. Chgo., 1949; postgrad., U. Hawaii, 1950; M.A., U. Calif., Berkeley, 1951; Ph.D., U. B.C. (Can.), Vancouver, 1960. Curator fisheries UCLA, 1951-53, Ichthyology Museum, U. B.C., 1953-56; curator Vancouver Public Aquarium, 1956-66, dir., 1966-93; pres. Mana Aquarium Cons.; fgn. adv. Nat. Mus./Aquarium Project, Taiwan; past chmn. adv. com. Western Can. Univs. Marine Biol. Soc.; co-chmn. Enoshima (Japan) Internat. Aquarium Symposium, 1997. Author: Life in a Fishbowl: Confessions of an Aquarium Director, 1994. Served with USN, 1943-46. Decorated Order of Can.; recipient Man of Yr. award City of Vancouver, 1964; Centennial award Govt. Can., 1967, cert. of merit, 1988; Harold J. Merilees award Vancouver Visitors Bur., 1976, 75 Achievers award, 1987, Silver Bravery medal Royal Soc. Canada, 1992, Canada 125 medal, 1992. Mem. Am. Assn. Zool. Parks and Aquariums, Internat. Union Dirs. Zool. Gardens, Can. Assn. Zool. Parks and Aquariums (pres. 1978-79), Vancouver Club, Round Table Club. Office: Vancouver Pub Aquarium, PO Box 3232, Vancouver, BC Canada V6B 3X8

NEWMAN, NANCY, publishing executive. Pub. PC Mag. Davis Pub. Co., N.Y.C. Office: Davis Pub Co 1 Park Ave New York NY 10016*

NEWMAN, PAULINE, federal judge; b. N.Y.C., N.Y., June 20, 1927; d. Maxwell Henry and Rosella N. B.A., Vassar Coll., 1947; M.A., Columbia U., 1948; Ph.D., Yale U., 1952; LL.B., NYU, 1958. Bar: N.Y. 1958, U.S. Supreme Ct. 1972, U.S. Ct. Customs and Patent Appeals 1978, Pa. 1979, U.S. Ct. Appeals (3d cir.) 1981, U.S. Ct. Appeals (fed. cir.) 1982. Research chemist Am. Cyanamid Co., Bound Brook, N.J., 1951-54; mem. patent staff FMC Corp., N.Y.C., 1954-75; mem. patent staff FMC Corp., Phila., 1975-84, dir. dept. patent and licensing, 1969-84; judge U.S. Ct. Appeals (fed. cir.), Washington, 1984—; bd. dir. Research Corp., 1982-84; program specialist Dept. Natural Scis. UNESCO, Paris, 1961-62; mem. State Dept. Adv. Com. on Internat. Indsl. Property, 1974-84; lectr. in field. Contbr. articles to profl. jours. Bd. dirs. Med. Coll. Pa., 1975-84, Midgard Found., 1973-84; trustee Phila. Coll. Pharmacy and Sci., 1983-84. Mem. ABA (council sect. patent trademark and copyright 1983-84), Am. Patent Law Assn. (bd. dirs. 1981-84), U.S. Trademark Assn. (bd. dirs. 1975-79, v.p. 1978-79), Am. Chem. Soc. (bd. dirs. 1972-81), Am. Inst. Chemists (bd. dirs. 1960-66, 70-76), Pacific Indsl. Property Assn. (pres. 1979-80). Clubs: Vassar, Yale. Office: US Ct Appeals Nat Cts Bldg 717 Madison Pl NW Washington DC 20439-0002*

NEWMAN, RACHEL, magazine editor; b. Malden, Mass., May 1, 1938; d. Maurice and Edythe Brenda (Tichell) N.; m. Herbert Bleiweiss, Apr. 6, 1973 (div. Apr. 1989). BA, Pa. State U., 1960; cert., N.Y. Sch. Interior Design, 1963. Accessories editor Women's Wear Daily, N.Y.C., 1964-65; designer, publicist Grandoe Glove Corp., N.Y.C., 1965-67; assoc. editor McCall's Sportswear and Dress Merchandiser mag., N.Y.C., 1967; mng. editor McCall's You-Do-It Home Decorating, 1968-70, Ladies Home Jour. Needle and Craft mag., N.Y.C., 1970-72; editor-in-chief Am. Home Crafts mag., N.Y.C., 1972-77; fashion dir. Good Housekeeping mag., N.Y.C., 1977-78, home bldg. and decorating dir., 1978-82; editor-in-chief Country Living mag., N.Y.C., 1978—; founding editor Country Cooking mag., 1985—, Dream Homes mag., 1989—, Country Kitchens mag., 1990—, Country Living Gardener Mag., 1993—, Healthy Living mag., 1996—. Pa. State U. Alumni fellow, 1986; recipient Cir. of Excellence award IFDA, 1992, YMCA Hall of Fame, 1992; named Disting. Alumni Pa. State U., 1988. Mem. N.Y. Fashion Group, Nat. Home Fashions League, Am. Soc. Interior Designers, Am. Soc. Mag. Editors. Office: Country Living 224 W 57th St New York NY 10019-3212

NEWMAN, RALPH GEOFFREY, literary scholar historian; b. Chgo., Nov. 3, 1911; s. Henry and Dora (Glickman) N.; m. Estelle Hoffman, 1934 (div.); children: Maxine (Mrs. Richard G. Brandenburg), Carol (Mrs. John Fox); m. Patricia Lyons Simon, 1972. Litt.D., James Milliken U. (Lincoln Coll.), 1950, Knox Coll., Rockford Coll.; LL.D., Iowa Wesleyan Coll.; Litt. D., Meisei U., Tokyo. Founder Abraham Lincoln Book Shop, Inc., Chgo., 1933-84; pres. Americana House, Inc., 1946-89, Lincoln's New Salem Enterprises, Inc., 1952-92, Ralph Geoffrey Newman, Inc., 1967—, Civil War Enterprises, Ltd., 1985-90; cons. Broadcast Music, Inc., 1941-89, Chgo. Sports Hall of Fame, 1989—. Author: (with Otto Eisenschiml) The American Iliad, 1947, Abraham Lincoln: An Autobiographical Narrative, 1970; Editor: The Diary of a Public Man, 1945, The Railsplitter, 1950, (with Otto Eisenschiml, E.B. Long) The Civil War, 1956; radio series The A... Lincoln Story, 1958-59; Lincoln for the Ages, 1960, (with O... Evewitness, 1960, (with E.B. Long) The Civil War... Autobiography of Abraham Lincoln, 196... Funeral, 1965, Abraham Lincoln... Abraham Lincoln's Last... Academy: A History... The General'... Book...

Group of N.Y., 1987. Mem. Civil War Round Table Chgo. (founder 1940, Harry S. Truman award Kansas City chpt. 1966), Royal Arts Soc. (London), Abraham Lincoln Assn. (dir.), Stephen A. Douglas Assn. (chmn., bd. dirs.), Ulysses S. Grant Assn. (pres. 1962-90, pres. emeritus 1990—), Am., Ind., Ill., Iowa, Kans., Chgo. hist. socs., Am. Legion, ALA, Am. Booksellers Assn., Bibliog. Socs. Am., U.S. Info. Agy. (book and library com.), Soc. Am. Historians, Newberry Library Assocs. Chgo., Phi Alpha Theta. Clubs: Arts, Casino, Caxton, Internat. Tavern (Chgo.), Sangamo (Springfield, Ill.), Union League. Address: 175 E Delaware Pl Chicago IL 60611-1756 Office: Fine Arts Bldg 410 S Michigan Ave Chicago IL 60605-1302 *I believe opportunity exists wherever you are if you are willing to work hard enough to achieve it. No goal is impossible. If you are willing to forego dependence on anyone else and realize that your own, and only your own, efforts will bring success, you can be successful.**

NEWMAN, RANDY, singer, songwriter, musician; b. Los Angeles, Calif., Nov. 28, 1943; s. Irving and Adele N.; m. Roswitha Newman; children: Amos, Eric, John. Degree, U. Calif. Arranger, singer, songwriter, musician various record firms; singer-composer: (albums) including Randy Newman, 1968, Twelve Songs, 1969, Live, 1971, Sail Away, 1972, Good Old Boys, 1974, Little Criminals, 1977, Born Again, 1979, Trouble In Paradise, 1983, Land of Dreams, 1988, (with others) Randy Newman's Faust, 1995; appeared in film: Ragtime, 1981; also TV and concert engagements; music composer for films: Performance, 1970, Pursuit of Happiness, 1971, Cold Turkey, 1971, Ragtime, 1981, The Natural, 1984, Three Amigos (also co-wrote screenplay), 1986, Parenthood, 1989, Avalon, 1990, Awakenings, 1990, Toy Story, 1995 (Acad. award nominee for best original score 1996, Acad. award nominee for best original song 1996); composer (films) Michael, 1996, James and the Giant Peach, 1996 (Acad. award nomination), Cat's Don't Dance, 1997, Air Force One, 1997. Recipient Grammy award for best instrumental composition, 1984. Office: Reprise Records 3300 Warner Blvd Burbank CA 91505*

NEWMAN, RICHARD ALAN, publisher, editor and consultant; b. Watertown, N.Y., Mar. 30, 1930; s. Gordon Leon and Belle (Burton) N.; m. Ann Cowan Meredith, 1955 (div. 1960); m. Peggy J. Hoyt, 1964 (div. 1978); stepchildren: David W. Bauer, Paul W. Bauer, Nancy E. Beck; m. Belynda Blair Bady, 1996. B.A., Maryville Coll., 1952; M.Div., Union Theol. Sem., 1955; postgrad., Syracuse U., 1959-61, Harvard U., 1966. Ordained to ministry Presbyn. Ch., 1955, demitted, 1977; minister Westminster Presbyn. Ch., Syracuse, N.Y., 1955-59; instr. religion Vassar Coll., Poughkeepsie, N.Y., 1962-63; prof., chmn. dept. social scis. Boston U., 1964-73; sr. editor G.K. Hall Co., Boston, 1973-79; exec. editor Garland Pub. Co., N.Y.C., 1978-81; mgr. publs. N.Y. Pub. Libr., 1981-92; cons. Columbia U., N.Y.C., 1992-93; publs. officer, mng. editor The Harvard Guide to African-Am. History, W.E.B. DuBois Inst., Harvard U., 1993-95, fellows officer, 1995-97, rsch. officer, 1997—. Author: Black Index, 1981, Bless All Thy Creatures, Lord, 1982, Lemuel Haynes, 1984, Afro-American Education, 1984, Black Access: A Bibliography, 1984, Black Power and Black Religion, 1987, Words Like Freedom, 1989, Black Preacher to White America, 1990; editor: Treasures From the New York Public Library, 1985, This Far By Faith, 1996, Everybody Say Freedom, 1996, Go Down, Moses, 1997, Encyclopedia of African-American Quotations, 1998; contbr. articles to profl. jours. Dem. candidate for N.Y. State Assembly from Onondaga County, 1960. Mem. Friends of Union Sem. Libr., Boston Athenaeum, Studio Mus. in Harlem, Friends of Amistad Rsch. Ctr., Schomburg Commn. for Preservation of Black Culture. Home: 160 Commonwealth Ave Apt 614 Boston MA 02116-2744

NEWMAN, RICHARD AUGUST, psychiatrist, educator; b. Oak Park, Ill., May 27, 1931; s. Henry Adolph and Mildred Kathryn (Haaker) N.; BS, U. Ill., 1953, MD, 1956; m. Nancy Jane Werdelin, Aug. 28, 1954; children: John Henry, Kurt Alan, Richard Steven, Scott David. Intern, Swedish-Am. Hosp., Rockford, Ill., 1956-57; resident in psychiatry Walter Reed Gen. Hosp., Washington, 1958-61; research Walter Reed Army Inst., 1961; chief psychiatric service Valley Forge Gen. Hosp., Phoenixville, Pa., 1962-64, also asst. chief dept. psychiatry and neurology, 1962-64; practice medicine, specializing in psychiatry, Paoli, Pa., 1962-96; dir. milieu therapy Phila. Gen. Hosp., 1968-69; dir. residency tng., dept. mental health scis. Hahnemann Med. Coll., 1969-73, asso. prof., 1970-79; prof. psychiatry Med. Coll. Pa., Phila., 1979—, prof. psychiatry, 1995—, dir. continuing mental health edn., 1983-87, dir. continuing med. edn., 1985-87; regional med. dir. for mental health Intracorp/Cigna, 1989-93; assoc. med. dir. for mental health U.S. Healthcare, 1993-95; prof. psychiat. Hahnemann U., Phila., 1995—; vis. prof. psychiatry U. Alta., 1975; chief cons. psychotherapy Chester County Cmty. Mental Health Clinic, 1967-68; psychiatrist Chester County Commr.'s Bd. for Mental Health/Mental Retardation, 1971-77; instr. Phila. Psychoanalytic Soc. Extension Sch., 1972-90, mem. faculty Inst., of Phila. Psychoanalytic Soc.; chmn. psychiatric sect. Paoli Meml. Hosp., 1974-83, med. dir. psychiatry service, 1977-83; psychiat. cons. St. Judes Hosp., St. Lucia, WI, 1983-89; interim med. dir. Connections CSP, Wilmington, Del., 1995-96; staff psychiatrist Philhaven Hosp., Mt. Gretna, Pa., 1996. Served to maj. M.C., AUS, 1958-64. Diplomate Am. Bd. Psychiatry and Neurology. Fellow APA, Pa. Psychiat. Assn. (chmn. ethics com.); mem. AMA, Phila. Psychoanalytic Soc., Am. Psychoanalytic Assn. (cert. psychoanalyst), Christian Med. Soc., Soc. Med. Coll. Dirs. Continuing Med. Edn., Pa., Chester County Med. Socs., Dirs. of Residency Tng. in Psychiatry of Del. Valley (past pres.). Lutheran. Contbr. articles to profl. jours. Home: PO Box 174 Lionville PA 19353-0174 Office: Philhaven Hosp PO Box 550 Mount Gretna PA 17064

NEWMAN, ROBERT GABRIEL, physician; b. The Netherlands, Oct. 26, 1937; came to U.S., 193[illegible] s. Randolph H. and Eva E. (Feilchenfeld) N.; m. Seiko Kusuba, Oct. 26[illegible] children—Henry Seiji, Hana Marie. B.A., NYU, 1958; M.D. w[illegible] U. Rochester, 1963; M.P.H., U. Calif.-Berkeley, 1969. Inter[illegible] surgery Univ. Hosps., Cleve., 1963-65; dist. health officer [illegible] 1968; dir. Nat. Nutrition Survey of N.Y.C., 1969-70; [illegible] Dept., 1970-74; health cons., 1974-76; assoc. [illegible] N.Y.C., 1976-78; chief exec. officer, pres. Be[illegible] community medicine Mt. Sinai Sch[illegible] epidemiology and social medic[illegible] 1994—; cons. addiction [illegible] in field of methadon[illegible] Univ. of Rochest[illegible] 972. Fellow [illegible] Healt[illegible] N.Y [illegible] Isr[illegible]

95; head dept. project support Fleet Pa. Svcs. Inc., Scranton, Pa., 1995—; past chmn. bd. dirs. S.W.I.F.T. Terminal Svcs.; past chmn. N.Y. Clearing House funds transfer com.; speaker industry confs. Contbr. articles to profl. jours. Advisor Nat. Conf. of Commrs. on Uniform State Laws; former mem. U.S. coun. Internat. Banking Exec. Com., U.S. del. to Uncitral Working Group on Internat. Payments; former chief U.S. del. to tech. com. 168 Internat. Standards Orgn. Mem. Soc. Worldwide Fin. Telecom. (bd. dirs. 1978-92, dep. chmn 1989-92). Avocations: numismatist; collecting Hummel figurines and plates. Office: Fleet Pa Svcs Inc PO Box 5600 Scranton PA 18505-5600

NEWMAN, SHARON ANN, principal; b. Denver, Sept. 25, 1946; d. Paul G. and Agnes J. (Hillesheim) Schneible; m. John G. Newman, June 30, 1973; children: Michael, Lisa. BA in Speech, Coll. Mt. St. Joseph, Cin., 1969; MAT in Liberal Studies, Lewis and Clark Coll., Portland, Oreg., 1992. Textbook editor Nat. Textbook Co., Chgo., 1972; tchr. speech and drama Seton High Sch., Cin., 1968-69; tchr. 6th grade St. Therese Sch., Aurora, Colo., 1979-70; tchr. speech and English Seton High Sch., Pueblo, Colo., 1970-71; tchr., head speech dept. Jefferson County Pub. High Schs., Denver, 1971-74; tchr. grades 7 and 8 Shakopee (Minn.) Cath. Middle Sch., 1983-84; tchr., team leader Regis High Sch., Denver, 1985-87; dir. admissions Jesuit High Sch., Portland, 1988-90; prin. St. Thomas More Sch., Portland, 1992—; speaker, cons. in field. Author newspaper columns, booklets, books for local use. Mem. Cin. Human Rels. Commn., 1967. Recipient Oreg. Disting. Pvt. Sch. Prin. award Oreg. Elem. & Secondary Prins. Assn., 1995. Mem. ASCD, AAUW, Nat. Assn. Elem. and Secondary Prins., Nat. Cath. Edn. Assn., Nat. Middle Level Assn., N.W. Women in Ednl. Adminstrn., Confedn. Oreg. Sch. Adminstrs., Oreg. Middle Level Assn. Avocations: family activities, singing, reading, writing, entertaining. Office: St Thomas More Sch 3521 SW Patton Rd Portland OR 97221-4124

NEWMAN, SHARON LYNN, elementary education educator; b. Lewisburg, Tenn., Jan. 9, 1946; d. Hermit Taft and Martha Elizabeth (Pardue) Simmons; m. George Wynne Newman Sr., June 11, 1967; 1 child, George Wynne Jr. BS in Edn., Athens State Coll., 1979. Substitute tchr. Giles County Bd. Edn., Pulaski, Tenn., 1979-81; chpt. 1 reading tchr. Giles County Bd. Edn., Pulaski, 1981-91, chpt. 1 math. tchr., 1991—; chpt. 1 coord. Elkton (Tenn.) Elem. Sch., 1989—, mem. steering com., 1989—, chair math. dept., 1993-95, chpt. title I com., 1995—, mem. disaster preparedness team. Ch. libr. Elkton (Tenn.) Bapt. Ch., 1992—; vol. Giles County Hist. Soc. Libr. and Mus., 1995—. Mem. NEA, Nat. Coun. Tchrs. Math., Giles County Edn. Assn. (rsch. chairperson 1993-95). Home: 1758 Old Stage Rd Ardmore TN 38449-5308 Office: Elkton Elem Sch Elkton TN 38455

NEWMAN, SHELDON OSCAR, computer company executive; b. N.Y.C., June 25, 1923; s. Morris and Anna (Schlanger) N.; m. Miriam Jasphy, July 30, 1950; children: Barry Marc, Amy Stacy, Andrew Eric. BS in Elec. Engring., CUNY, 1944. Project engr. NASA, Sunnyvale, Calif., 1946-47; gen. mgr. info. and communications div. Sperry Corp., Gt. Neck, N.Y., 1947-67; chmn. bd., chief exec. officer Algorex Corp., Hauppauge, N.Y., 1968-93. Chmn. bd. trustees Hosp. for Joint Diseases, Orthopaedic Inst., N.Y.C.; trustee NYU Med. Ctr.; bd. dirs. HJD Rsch. and Devel. Found., Sjogrens Syndrome Found., Woodbridge Assn., Boca Raton, Fla.; pres. Pine Lake Park Coop. Assn., Peekskill, N.Y. Patentee in field. Lt. (j.g.), USN, 1944-46. Recipient Disting. Trustee award United Hosp. Fund, 1995. Mem. IEEE (sr.), Archaeol. Inst. Am. (pres.), L.I. Soc., Masons, Tau Beta Pi, Eta Kappa Nu.

NEWMAN, SLATER EDMUND, psychologist, educator; b. Boston, Sept. 8, 1924; s. Max and Gertrude (Raphael) N.; m. Corrine Lois Silfen, June 18, 1950 (div. 1968); children—Kurt Douglas, Jonathan Mark, Eric Bruce; m. Patricia Ellen Christopher Thomas, July 2, 1969; 1 stepchild, Arthur C. Thomas III. B.S., U. Pa., 1947; M.A., Boston U., 1948; Ph.D., Northwestern U., 1951. Research psychologist U.S. Air Force, 1951-57; mem. faculty N.C. State U., Raleigh, 1957—; now prof. psychology N.C. State U.; vis. fgn. mem. Exptl. Psychology Soc. U.K., 1973-74, 82-83, 90. Contbr. chpts. to books, articles to profl. publs. Bd. dirs. ACLU, 1992—, mem. biennial conf. com., 1994—, mem. task force internat. human rights, 1994—, mem. spl. nominating com, 1996, mem. constn. com., 1996—, youth affairs com., 1997—; pres. N.C. Civil Liberties Union, 1980-82, exec. com., 1986-87, bd. dirs., 1969-73, 76-82, 84-90, 91—; chmn. Com. on Internat. Human Rights, 1988—; mem. steering com. ACLU-Affiliate Leadership Network, 1991-95; mem. Mayor's Com. UN Week, Raleigh, 1986-95; active Amnesty Internat.; coord. Com. to Reverse Arms Race, 1982—; cofounder, mem. steering com. North Carolinians Against Apartheid, 1985-87; mem. Wake County com. Bicentennial U.S. Constn., 1987-89; co-founder, co-chair N.C. Com. for Celebration of Human Rights, 1989-97. Served to 2nd lt. USAF, 1943-46, 52-53. USPHS spl. rsch. fellow U. Calif.-Berkeley, 1965-66; U. London hon. rsch. fellow, 1973-74, 82-83, 90. Fellow AAAS, APA, Am. Psychol. Soc.; mem. NAACP, Psychonomic Soc., UN Assn. (bd. dirs. Wake County chpt. 1991-95), People for the Am. Way, Southeastern Psychol. Assn., So. Soc. Philosophy and Psychology, Cognitive Sci. Soc., Soc. Rsch. in Child Devel., Southeastern Workers in Memory (founder, N.C. Cognition Group (founder), Ea. Psychol. Assn., AAUP (pres. N.C. State U. chpt. 1968-69), Carolinas Conf. for Undergrad. Rsch. in Psychology (co-founder 1976), Sigma Xi, Psi Chi (v.p. southeastern region 1990-94, nat. pres. elect. 1996—, mem. nat. coun. 1990-94, 96), Internat. Human Rights Coalition (founder, chair 1996-97), Human Rights Coalition N.C. (co-chair 1997—). Home: 315 Shepherd St Raleigh NC 27607-4031 Office: Dept Psychology NC State U Raleigh NC 27695-7801

NEWMAN, STANLEY RAY, oil refining company executive; b. Milo, Idaho, Mar. 5, 1923; s. Franklin Hughes and Ethel Amelda (Crowley) N.; student Tex. A&M U, 1944-45; B.S., U. Utah, 1947, Ph.D., 1952. m. Rosa Klein, May 27, 1961 (div. Mar. 1980); children: Trudy Lynn, Susan Louise, Karen Elizabeth, Paul Daniel, Phillip John; m. Madelyn Wycherly, Jan. 10, 1991; children: Heidi, Heather, Amy. With Texaco Res. Ctr., Beacon, N.Y., 1951-82, technologist, 1973-77, sr. technologist research mfg.-fuels, 1977-82, profl. cons. on fuels and chems., 1983-91. Chmn., Planning Bd., Village of Fishkill, N.Y., 1973- 77; village trustee, 1990-92; mem. Dutchess County Solid Waste Mgmt. Bd., 1974-76. With inf. Signal Corps U.S. Army, 1944-46. Mem. AAAS, N.Y. Acad. Sci., Dutchess County Geneal. Soc. (pres. 1981-87, exec. v.p. 1987-88), N.Y. Fruit Testing Assn., Sigma Xi (pres. Texaco Res. Ctr. br. 1980-81). Republican. Mormon. Patentee in field. Home: 285 Plantation Cir Idaho Falls ID 83404-7990 *I was born of humble parents in Idaho. Life was hard and difficult so early in my life at consider-[illegible]le sacrifice I went the extra distance to go to a good high school to prepare [illegible]llege. By working at night and weekends, I was able to complete [illegible]th a Ph.D. Blessed with an inquiring mind, a strong will to work, [illegible] learn, I moved to the east coast, worked hard both at my job [illegible]unity, always retaining the honesty, integrity and strong [illegible]ht by my humble parents. At retirement, I had [illegible]ations, and had world wide responsibility for fuels*

[illegible] lawyer; b. Buffalo, Jan. 12, 1945; s. [illegible]m. Gayle Mallon, May 24, 1969; [illegible] 1966; JD, U. Mich., 1969. [illegible] Russ, Andrews, Woods & [illegible]ld. Bd. dirs. Leukemia [illegible]reater Buffalo Inc., [illegible] Jewish Com., [illegible]lo and Erie [illegible]personal [illegible] and

1987—; chmn. GCR Holdings, 1993—, Reins. Assn. Am., 1995—; bd. dirs. Capital Corp., 1995—. Fellow Casualty Actuarial Soc. (pres. 1981-82); mem. Am. Acad. Actuaries, Internat. Actuarial Assn.

NEWMAN, STUART, lawyer; b. Hackensack, N.J., June 7, 1947; s. Joseph and Rose (Wilenski) N.; m. Tina Gilson; children: Leslie, Dara, Mindy, Robert. BA, SUNY, Cortland, 1971; JD cum laude, Albany Law Sch., 1974. Bar: N.Y. 1975, Ga. 1978. Assoc. Dewey, Ballantine, Bushby, Palmer & Wood, N.Y.C., 1974-76; from assoc. to ptnr. Jackson, Lewis, Schnitzler & Krupman, Atlanta, 1976—; lectr. U. Ala., Tuscaloosa, 1980-84, Auburn U., 1986—. Dir. Ruth Mitchell Dance Co. of Atlanta, 1986-88. Mem. ABA, Atlanta Bar Assn., Ga. Bar Assn., Shakerag Hounds, Inc., Midlands Fox Hounds, Inc., Live Oak Hounds, Ansley Golf Club. Office: Jackson Lewis Schnitzler & Krupman 2400 Peachtree Ctr Harris Tower 233 Peachtree St NE Atlanta GA 30303-1504

NEWMAN, THEODORE ROOSEVELT, JR., judge; b. Birmingham, Ala., July 5, 1934; s. Theodore R. and Ruth L. (Oliver) N. A.B., Brown U., 1955, LL.D., 1980; J.D., Harvard U., 1958. Bar: D.C. 1958, Ala. 1959. Atty. civil rights div. Dept. Justice, Washington, 1961-62; practiced law in Washington, 1962-70; assoc. judge D.C. Superior Ct., 1970-76; judge D.C. Ct. Appeals, 1976-91, chief judge, 1976-84, sr. judge, 1991—; bd. dirs. Nat. Center for State Cts., v.p., 1980-81, pres., 1981-82. Trustee Brown U. With USAF, 1958-61. Fellow Am. Bar Found.; mem. Nat. Bar Assn. (past pres. jud. coun., C. Francis Stradford award 1984, William H. Hastie award 1988).

NEWMAN, THOMAS, composer. Scores include: (films) Grandview, U.S.A., 1984, Reckless, 1984, Revenge of the Nerds, 1984, Girls Just Want to Have Fun, 1985, Desperately Seeking Susan, 1985, The Man with One Red Shoe, 1985, Real Genius, 1985, Gung Ho, 1986, Jumpin' Jack flash, 1986, Quicksilver, 1986, Light of Day, 1987, The Lost Boys, 1987, Less Than Zero, 1987, The Great Outdoors, 1988, The Prince of Pennsylvania, 1988, Cookie, 1989, Men Don't Leave, 1990, Naked Tango, 1990, Welcome Home, Roxy Carmichael, 1990, Career Opportunities, 1991, Deceived, 1991, The Rapture, 1991, Fried Green Tomatoes, 1991, The Linguini Incident, 1992, The Player, 1992, Whispers in the Dark, 1992, Scent of a Woman, 1992, Flesh and Bone, 1993, Josh and S.A.M., 1993, The Favor, 1994, Threesome, 1994, The Shawshank Redemption, 1994 (Acad. award nominee for best original score 1994), Little Women, 1994 (Acad. award nominee for best original score 1994), Unstrung Heroes, 1995 (Acad. award nominee for best original score 1996); (TV movies) The Seduction of Gina, 1984, Heat Wave, 1991, Those Secrets, 1992, Citizen Cohn, 1992. Office: Gorfaine Schwartz Agency 3301 Barham Blvd Ste 201 Los Angeles CA 90068-1477*

NEWMAN, THOMAS DANIEL, minister, school administrator; b. London, Eng., May 12, 1922; s. Frederick and Margaret (O'Leary) N.; m. Louise Johannah Albertano, Apr. 1, 1963; 1 dau., Susan (Mrs. Alan J. Rennie). Student, Glasgow Sch. Accounting, 1946, Unity Sch. Christianity, 1962-66, Harvard Div. Sch., 1967—; DSc, Alma Coll., 1975. Ordained to ministry Ch. of Christ, 1966. Mng. dir. Thomas Newman (Printers) Ltd., 1945-49; mng. dir. H. & M.J. Pubs. Ltd., 1947-49, Forget-Me-Not Greeting Cards Ltd., 1949-61, Diplomat Greetings Ltd., 1957-61, Nevill's Ltd., 1955-57; pastor Christ's Ch., Springfield, Mo., 1966-67, Longwood, Brookline, Mass., 1967—; adminstrv. dir. Am. Schs. Oriental Research, 1968, treas., 1970—, trustee, 1972—; founder Carthage Research Inst., Khereddine, Tunisia, 1975, Cyprus Archaeol. Research Inst., Nicosia, 1977; cons. Joint Archeol. Expdns. to, Ai, 1969-73, to; Tell-El-Hesi, 1970-73, to, Idalion, 1970-73; mem. Joint Archeol. Expdn. to, Caesarea Maritima, 1971, to; Carthage, 1975; dir. Logistics Survey Qu'Rayyah, Saudi Arabia, 1973; pub. cons. (Dead Sea Scrolls Com.), 1968-73; Trustee Allbright Inst. Archeol. Research, Jerusalem.; Am. Center Oriental Research, Amman, Jordan. Served with RAF, 1940-45. Mem. Archeol. Inst. Am., Soc. Bibl. Lit., Soc. O.T. Studies. Clubs: Mason, Harvard Faculty; University (Boston) (Sarasota). Home: 8 Club Acre Ln Bedford NH 03110-6901 Office: Colchester and Chapel Sts Brookline MA 02146

NEWMAN, WADE DAVIS, trade association executive; b. Chgo., June 23, 1936; s. Clifford and Mary Gwendolyn (Parsons) N.; m. Rita Esmoer, Apr. 30, 1960; children—Erik Parsons, Sherrill Susan. Student, Northwestern U., 1954-57. Sales mgr. Schramm Fiberglass Products, Inc., Chgo., 1958-65; sales promotion mgr. Monogram Models, Inc., Morton Grove, Ill., 1965-68; dir. info. Nat. Sch. Supply & Equipment Assn., Chgo., 1968-72; product mgr. Skillcraft Corp., Chgo., 1972-73; dir. communications and convs. Nat. Bldg. Material Distbrs. Assn., Chgo., 1973-79; exec. dir. Nat. Assn. Floor Covering Distbrs., Chgo., 1979-91, Steel Plate Fabricators Assn., Des Plaines, Ill., 1992-97. Bd. dirs. Edison Park (Ill.) Community Council, 1973—, pres., 1975. Mem. Am. Soc. Assn. Execs. (con. mgmt. cert.), Chgo. Soc. Assn. Execs., Assn. Econ. Coun. Republican. Methodist. Home: 7300 W Ibsen St Chicago IL 60631-1151

NEWMAN, WILLIAM BERNARD, JR., railroad executive; b. Providence, Nov. 16, 1950; s. William Bernard and Virginia (Crosby) N.; m. Karen O'Connor, Jan. 11, 1951. B.A., Ohio Wesleyan U., 1972; J.D., George Mason U., Arlington, Va., 1977; attended advanced mgmt. program, Harvard U., 1987. Bar: Va. 1977, D.C. 1978. Atty. com. energy Ho. of Reps., Washington, 1978-81; v.p., Washington counsel Consol. Rail Corp. Dept. Govt. Affairs, Washington, 1981—. Bd. dirs. Nat. Coun. for Adoption. Mem. ABA, Va. Bar Assn., D.C. Bar Assn. Home: 1009 Priory Pl Mc Lean VA 22101-2134 Office: Consol Rail Corp 990 Lenfant Plz SW Washington DC 20024-2116 also: Consol Rail Corp 6 Penn Center Plz Philadelphia PA 19103-2919

NEWMAN, WILLIAM C., bishop; b. Balt., Aug. 16, 1928. Student, St. Mary Sem., Cath. U., Loyola Coll. Ordained priest Roman Cath. Ch., 1954. Aux. bishop Archdiocese of Balt., 1984—. Address: 5300 N Charles St Baltimore MD 21210-2023 Office: Chancery Office 320 Cathedral St Baltimore MD 21201-4421*

NEWMAN, WILLIAM LOUIS, geologist; b. Rockford, Ill., July 14, 1920; s. Lyle Winfred and Carrie (Waterman) N.; m. Lucille Mary Hagen, Feb. 21, 1946; children: William Dwight, Christopher. BS, Beloit Coll., 1942; postgrad., Mont. Sch. Mines, 1946, U. Mont., 1948-50. Geologist Anaconda Mining Co., Butte, Mont., 1946-48; geologist U.S. Geol. Survey, 1950-80; uranium exploration U.S. Geol. Survey, Colo. Plateau, 1950-57; staff asst. to asso. dir. U.S. Geol. Survey, 1957-59; chief Metallogenic Map Project, 1959-62; staff asst. Office of Chief Geologist, 1962-63, staff geologist, 1963-67, chief nontech. reports, 1967-78; dep. chief Office Sci. Publs., 1978-80; cons., 1981—. Served with AUS, 1942-46. Recipient Superior Performance awards, 1963, 70; Superior Service award, 1972. Fellow AAAS, Geol. Soc. Am., Soc. Econ. Geologists; mem. Am. Assn. Petroleum Geologists (rep. Capital dist. 1966-68), Geochem. Soc., Fed. Editors Assn., Assn. Earth Sci. Editors, Am. Geol. Inst. (sec.-treas., bd. dirs. 1971-72), Geol. Soc. Washington (program chmn. 1963, sec. 1968-69), Geol. Soc. Grand Junction (Colo.) (sec. 1954), SAR, KC, Sigma Chi. Home and Office: 5624 E Wethersfield Rd Scottsdale AZ 85254-4317

NEWMAN, WILLIAM STEIN, music educator, author, pianist, composer; b. Cleve., Apr. 6, 1912; m. Claire Louise Murray, Dec. 20, 1947; 1 son, Craig William (dec. 1983). B.S., Cleve. Inst. Music, 1933, hon. doctorate, 1986; B.S. in Mus. Edn. (Cleve. Pub. Sch. Music scholar), Western Res. U., 1933, M.A. in Musicology (grad. fellow), 1935, Ph.D., 1939; postgrad. in Europe, Columbia U., 1940. Pvt. tchr. piano and theory, 1926—; fed. relief adminstr. Cleve., 1933-34; asst. choral dir. Western Res. U., 1934-36, instr. undergrad., grad. music courses, summer 1942; music tchr. Wilson Jr. High Sch., Cleve., 1935-37, Collinwood High Sch., 1937-42, Cleve. Music Sch. Settlement, 1937-38; vocal coach, accompanist Juilliard Sch. Music, Chautauqua, summer 1937; lectr. recitalist Juilliard Sch. Music, summer 1948; instr. music [illegible]ory Bennington Coll., summer 1940; instr. grad. courses Columbia Tchrs. [illegible]ummer 1941, asst. prof., summers 1946-48; asst. to librarian Cleve. [illegible]y System, 1941-42; asst. prof. U. N.C., 1945-46, mem. grad. [illegible] Carnegie research grantee, 1947, 48, asso. prof. music, chmn. [illegible]-69, prof., 1955-62, Alumni Disting. prof., 1962—, dir. [illegible] 1966—, prof. emeritus, 1977—; prof. music summers [illegible] 1963, U. Oreg., 1965, 69, Harpur Coll., 1966, [illegible]., 1978, U. Alta., 1982; piano recitals, lectrs. [illegible]anists' Problems, rev. edit, 1956 (London

1952), 1974, 84, Understanding Music, rev. edit. 1961, 67, The Sonata in the Baroque Era, rev. edit. 1966, 72, 83, Sonata in the Classic Era, 1963, 72, 83, The Sonata Since Beethoven, (vols. 1, 2, and 3 of a History of the Sonata Idea, 1969, rev. edit., 1972, 83), Performance Practices in Beethoven's Piano Sonatas, 1971; Beethoven on Beethoven-Playing His Piano Music His Way, 1988; editor: Thirteen Keyboard Sonatas of the 18th and 19th Centuries, 1947, Two-Part Inventions of J.S. Bach, 1957, A Chopin Anthology, 1957, Diabelli Variations, 16 Contemporaries of Beethoven on a Waltz Tune, 1958, Six Keyboard Sonatas from the Classic Era, 1965; Contbg. editor: Piano Quar; contbr. numerous articles to profl. jours., reference works. Served with USAAF, 1943-45. Recipient Ann. Composition award Fortnightly Mus. Club, Cleve., 1935, Disting. Alumnus award Cleve. Inst. Music, 1986; scholarship Concord (Mass.) Sch. Music, 1935; Kenan rsch. leave U. N.C., 1956; Ford Found.-U. N.C. Rsch. grantee, 1958; Ford Found. Teaching grantee WUNC-TV, 1959; Guggenheim fellow musicology, 1960-61; Am. Council Learned Socs. grantee-in-aid, 1960, 61, 66-67, 80-81; sr. fellow NEH, 1973; summer seminars, 1975, 79; dir. year-long seminar, 1977-78; fellow Nat. Humanities Ctr., 1983-84. Mem. Music Tchrs. Nat. Assn. (chmn. theory forum 1940, membership chmn. N.C. 1949, chmn. sr. piano com. 1950-53, exec. bd. 1952-56), Am. Musicological Soc. (hon. life, exec. coun. 1955-57, nat. v.p. 1968-69, pres. 1969-70, program chmn. 1958, 66, editor jour. summer 1959), Internat. Musicological Soc. (U.S. rep. on directorium 1971-82), N.C. Music Educators, Music Libr. Assn., Coll. Music Soc. Home: 808 Old Mill Rd Chapel Hill NC 27514-3928

NEWMAN-GORDON, PAULINE, French language and literature educator; b. N.Y.C., Aug. 5, 1925; d. Bernard and Eva Newman; m. Sydney A. Gordon, Sept. 13, 1959 (dec.); m. Richard Yellin, Feb. 9, 1997. BA, Hunter Coll., 1947; MA, Columbia U., 1948; PhD, Sorbonne U., Paris, 1951. Instr. French Wellesley (Mass.) Coll., 1952-53; mem. faculty Stanford (Calif.) U., 1953—, prof. French lit., 1969-93, prof. emerita, 1994—. Author: Marcel Proust, 1953, Eugene Le Roy, 1957, Corbiere, Laforgue and Apollinaire, 1964, Helen of Troy Myth, 1968, (poetry) Mooring to France, (prose poem) Sydney: editor: Dictionary of Ideas in Marcel Proust, 1968, also articles in field; contbr. articles to profl. jours. Scholar Internat. Inst. Edn., 1948-51, MLA, 1956-57, AAUW, 1962-63, Am. Philos. Soc., 1970-71, NEH, 1989; elected to Hall of Fame, Alumni Assn. Hunter Coll. of CUNY, 1990. Mem. MLA, Am. Assn. Tchrs. French, Soc. Friends Marcel Proust. Office: Stanford U Dept French and Italian Stanford CA 94305

NEWMARK, EMANUEL, ophthalmologist; b. Newark, May 25, 1936; s. Charles Meyer and Bella (Yoskowitz) N.; m. Tina Steinberg, Aug. 25, 1957; children: Karen Beth, Heidi Ellen, Stuart Jeffry. BS in Pharmacy, Rutgers U., 1959; postgrad., U. Amsterdam, The Netherlands, 1960-63, Armed Forces Inst. Pathology, Washington, 1971; MD, Duke U., 1966; Lancaster course in ophthalmology, Harvard U., 1967. Diplomate Am. Bd. Ophthalmology. Intern George Washington U. Hosp., Washington, 1966; trainee NIH rsch. Univ. Fla., Gainesville, 1967-70; resident ophthalmology U. Fla. Hosp., 1967-70; instr. dept. ophthalmology Univ. Fla., 1970; cons. ophthalmology Gainesville VA Hosp., 1970; clin. instr. ophthalmology U. Tex. Med. Sch., San Antonio, 1971-72; cons. ophthalmology Kerrville (Tex.) VA Hosp., 1971-72; asst. chief ophthalmology svc. Brooke Army Gen. Hosp., Fort Sam, Tex., 1971-72; clin. prof. Bascom Palmer Eye Inst., Miami, Fla., 1995—; clin. asst. prof. ophthalmology Bexar County Hosp. and Clinics, San Antonio, 1971-72; tchg. faculty Joint Com. Allied Health Pers. Ophthalmology, St. sec., treas. Palm Beach Eye Assocs., Atlantis, 1973—; mem. pharm. adv. com. Agy. for Health Care Adminstrn. Bd. Optometry, 1991—; mem. med. adv. bd. Fla. east coast chpt. Nat. Sjorgren's Syndr. adv. com. Agy. for Health Care Adminstrn. Bd. Optometry, 1991—; mem. med. adv. bd. Fla. east coast chpt. Nat. Sjorgren's Syndrome Assn., 1990—; bd. dirs. Fla. Eye Injury and Disease Registry. Contbr. chpts. to 4 textbooks, over 13 articles to med. jours. Alumni assoc. Rutgers Coll. Pharmacy, 1960—; chmn. reunion 1986 Duke U. Med. Alumni Assn., N.C., 1967—; centurian Davison Club-Duke U. Med. Sch., N.C., 1982—; campaign chmn., nat. vice chmn. Israel Bonds, Palm Beach County, Fla., 1988—; participant charitable orgns.; v.p. Palm Beach Liturgical Culture Found., 1994—ss, treas., trustee, 1987-94. Decorated Lion of Judea State of Israel, 1984; recipient Gates of Jerusalem medal, 1991, Jerusalem 3000 medal, 1996. Fellow ACS, Am. Acad. Ophthalmology (del. coun., Fla. state chmn. ednl. trust), Am. Castroveiejo Cornea Soc.; mem. AMA, Internat. Platform Assn., Assn. for Rsch. in Vision and Ophthalmology, Am. Orgn. for Rehab. Through Tng. Fedn. (nat. exec. com.-campaign cabinet 1987, pres. 1990—, Palm Beach Men's Achievement award 1988, Pres. award 1989), Fla. Med. Assn. (ho. dels. 1993—), Palm Beach County Ophthal. Soc. (pres. 1984-85), Fla. Soc. Ophthalmology (ethics chmn. 1985-90, pres. 1990-91, James W. Clower Jr. Cmty. Svc. award 1995), Founder's Soc. Duke U. Jewish. Avocations: travel, radio broadcasting, teaching. Home: 335 Glenbrook Dr Atlantis FL 33462-1009 Office: Palm Beach Eye Assocs 140 Jfk Dr Lake Worth FL 33462-1159

NEWMARK, HAROLD LEON, biochemist; b. N.Y.C., July 21, 1918; s. Abraham and Mollie W. (Wolf) N.; m. Helen Rosenberg, Mar. 13, 1949 (dec. Aug. 1985); children: Jonathan, Robin L.; m. Phyllis Klein, Sept. 6, 1987. BS, CCNY, 1939; MS, N.Y. Poly. U., 1950. Chemist Chem. Spec. of N.J.-Syntex, Newark, 1939-41, Intramed Co., N.Y.C., 1946-49, Chase Chem. Co., Newark, 1949-50, Vitarine Co., N.Y.C., 1950-59; chemist Hoffmann LaRoche, Inc., Nutley, N.J., 1966-81, dir. food, agrl. products, 1959-81; chemist Ludwig Inst. for Cancer Rsch., Toronto, Ont., Can., 1981-84; biochem. rschr. Sloan-Kettering Inst., N.Y.C., 1984-95; rsch. scientist Strang Cancer Prevention Ctr. Rockefeller U., N.Y.C., 1996—; adj. prof. Coll. Pharmacy, Rutgers U., Pisacataway, N.J., 1987—. Author, editor: Calcium, Vitamin D and Colon Cancer, 1991; contbr. over 100 articles to sci. publs. Cpl. USAAF, 1942-46. Mem. AAAS, Am. Chem. Soc., Am. Assn. Cancer Rsch., N.Y. Acad. Sci., N.J. Cancer Inst. Achievements include more than 20 patents for pharmaceuticals. Home: 11 Claremont Dr Maplewood NJ 07040-2119

NEWMARK, LEONARD DANIEL, linguistics educator; b. Attica, Ind., Apr. 8, 1929; s. Max Jacob and Sophie (Glusker) N.; m. Ruth Broessler, Sept. 16, 1951; children: Katya, Mark. AB, U. Chgo., 1947; MA, Ind. U., 1951, PhD, 1955. Instr. English U. Ill., Urbana, 1951; vis. asst. prof. linguistics U. Mich., Ann Arbor, 1961; assoc. prof. English Ohio State U., 1954-62; assoc. prof. linguistics Ind. U., Bloomington, 1962-63; prof. linguistics U. Calif., San Diego, 1963-91, prof. emeritus, 1992—, chmn. dept., 1963-71, 79-85, head program in Am. lang. and culture, 1979-84, rsch. linguist Ctr. for Rsch. in Lang., 1992—. Author: Linguistic History of English, 1963, Spoken Albanian, 1981, Standard Albanian, 1982, Albanian-English Dictionary, 1997; inventor memory aid device. Mem. Linguistics Soc. Am., Dictionary Soc. N.Am., Phi Beta Kappa. Home: 2643 St Tropez Pl La Jolla CA 92037-3541 Office: U Calif San Diego Dept Linguistics La Jolla CA 92093

NEWMARK, MILTON MAXWELL, lawyer; b. Oakland, Calif., Feb. 24, 1916; s. Milton and Mary (Maxwell) N.; m. Marion Irene Johnson, July 31, 1941 (dec.); children—Mari Newmark Anderson, Lucy Newmark Sammons, Grace Newmark Lucini; m. Aylene Pruett Rosselli, June 21, 1991. A.B., U. Calif.-Berkeley, 1936, J.D., 1947. Bar: Calif. 1940, U.S. Supreme Ct. 1944. Ptnr. Milton Newmark, San Francisco, 1941-56; sole practice, 1956-62; sole practice, Lafayette, Calif., 1962-80, Walnut Creek, Calif., 1980-94; lectr. bankruptcy State Bar of Calif. Continuing Edn. Program. Served with U.S. Army, 1942-46; to lt. col. USAR. Mem. Alameda County Rep. Cen. Com., 1940-41; pres. Alameda County Rep. Assembly, 1950. Mem. Am. Legion, ABA, San Francisco Bar Assn., Contra Costa Bar Assn., Alameda County Bar Assn., Scabbard and Blade. Lodges: Masons, Shriners, Rotary. Home: 609 Terra California Dr Apt 6 Walnut Creek CA 94595-3344

NEWMEYER, FREDERICK JARET, linguist, educator; b. Phila., Jan. 30, 1944; s. Alvin S. and Fritzie B. (Nisenson) N.; m. Carolyn V. Platt, Apr. 28, 1968 (div. 1974); m. Marilyn M. Goebel, Dec. 25, 1993. BA, U. Rochester, 1965, MA, 1967; PhD, U. Ill., 1969. Asst. prof. linguistics U. Wash., Seattle, 1969-75, assoc. prof., 1975-81, prof., 1981—; chair, 1990—; vis. prof. U. London, 1979, Cornell U., 1981, U. Md., 1982, UCLA, 1982-83, La Trobe U., Australia, 1987. Author: English Aspectual Verbs, 1975, Linguistic Theory in America, 1980, Grammatical Theory, 1983, Politics of Linguistics, 1986, Generative Linguistics, 1995; editor: Linguistics: The Cambridge Survey, 1988, Natural Language and Linguistic Theory, 1987—; assoc. editor: Language, 1980-85. NEH fellow, 1973-74. Mem. Linguistic Soc. Am. (sec.-treas. 1989-94). Avocations: gardening. Home: 4621 NE 107th St Seattle WA 98125-6947 Office: Univ of Wash Dept Linguistics Seattle WA 98195

NEWPORT, JOHN PAUL, philosophy of religion educator, former academic administrator; b. Buffalo, Mo., June 16, 1917; s. Marvin Jackson and Mildred (Morrow) N.; m. Eddie Belle Leavell, Nov. 14, 1941; children: Martha Ellen, Frank M., John P. Jr. BA, William Jewell Coll., Liberty, Mo., 1938; ThM, So. Bapt. Theol. Sem., Louisville, 1941, ThD, 1946; PhD, U. Edinburgh, Scotland, 1953; MA, Tex. Christian U., 1968; LittD, William Jewell Coll., 1967. Assoc. prof. Baylor U., 1949-51, New Orleans Bapt. Theol. Sem., 1951-52; prof. Southwestern Bapt. Theol. Sem, Ft. Worth, 1952-76, Rice U., 1976-79; v.p. acad. affairs, provost Southwestern Bapt. Theol. Sem., 1979-90, v.p. emeritus, spl. asst. to pres., 1990—, disting. prof. philosophy of religion, 1990—; vis. prof. Princeton Theol. Sem., 1982. Author: Theology and Contemporary Art Forms, 1971, Demons, Demons, Demons, 1972, Why Christians Fight over the Bible, 1974, Christ and the New Consciousness, 1978, Christianity and Contemporary Art Forms, 1979, Nineteenth Century Devotional Thought, 1981, Paul Tillich, 1984, What Is Christian Doctrine? 1984, The Lion and the Lamb, 1986, Life's Ultimate Questions, 1989; contbr. numerous articles to jours. and mags. Sealantic fellowship Rockefeller Found., Harvard U., 1958-59. Mem. Am. Acad. Religion (pres. S.W. div. 1967-68), Soc. Bibl. Lit. and Exegesis, Southwestern Philos. Assn., N.Am. Paul Tillich Soc. (dir. 1984-86), Southside C. of C. (Ft. Worth), Downtown Rotary Cub (Ft. Worth), Ft. Worth Club. Democrat. Avocations: golf, swimming, tennis. Office: Southwestern Bapt Theol Sem PO Box 22000 Fort Worth TX 76122

NEWPORT, L. JOAN, clinical social worker, psychotherapist; b. Ponca City, Okla., July 5, 1932; d. Crawford Earl and Lillian Pearl (Peden) Irvine; m. Don E. Newport, July 9, 1954 (div. July 1971); children: Alan Keith, Lili Kim. BA cum laude, Wichita State U., 1955; MSW, U. Okla., 1977. Bd. cert. diplomate in clin. social work Acad. Cert. Social Workers; lic. social worker, Okla. Dir. children's work Wesley United Meth. Ch., Oklahoma City, 1969-71; social worker Dept. Human Svcs., Newkirk, Okla., 1972-77; in-sch. suspension counselor Kay County Youth Svcs., Ponca City, Okla., 1977; med. social worker St. Joseph Med. Ctr., Ponca City, 1977-78, dir. social work, 1978-83; pvt. practice Ponca City, 1979—; med. social worker Healthcare Svcs., Ponca City, 1983-84; cons. Blackwell, Perry, Pawhuska, O'Keene Hosps., 1978-85; cons. social work Bass Meml. Hosp., Enid, Okla., 1985; sponsor, organizer Kay County Parents Anonymous, Ponca City, 1976-83; vice chair Okla. State Bd. Lic. Social Workers, Oklahoma City, 1988-90; presentor, lectr. in field; supr. students Okla. U. Sch. Social Work, Okla. State U., No. Okla. Coll., Okla. Christian Coll., 1977-85; supr. for clin. social workers working toward lic. in Okla., 1985—. Mem. Okla. Women's Network, 1989—; mem. adv. bd. Displaced Homemakers, Ponca City, 1985-89; mem. adv. bd. Kay County Home Health, 1979-83, chair, 1979-81. Named Hon. State Life Mem. Burbank PTA, Oklahoma City, 1971; scholar Wichita (Kans.) Press and Radio Women, 1953, Conoco, Inc., Houston, 1951-54. Mem. NASW (Okla. del. Del. Assembly Washington 1987, chmn. vendorship com. 1985-87, pres. Okla. chpt. 1988-90, Social Worker of Yr. 1987), Child Abuse Prevention Task Force (pres. dist. 17 1986-88, mem. grant evaluation com. 1986-96), Zeta Phi Eta. Democrat. Methodist. Home: 109 N Walnut Ave Newkirk OK 74647-2036 Office: 619 E Brookfield Ave Ponca City OK 74601-2804

NEWQUIST, DON, federal agency administrator; b. Stamford, Tex., Aug. 23, 1943. BBA, McMurry U., 1966; postgrad., Tex. Tech U. Farmer Jones County, 1973—; asst. gen. mgr. C. of C., Corpus Christi, Tex., 1969-72; gen. mgr. C. of C., Denver, 1972-74; asst. v.p. Valero Energy Corp., San Antonio, 1974-80, v.p., then sr. v.p., dir. subs. cos., 1980—; commr. U.S. Internat. Trade Commn., Washington, 1988—, chmn., 1991-94. With USN, 1967-69, Vietnam. Mem. South Tex. C. of C. (past pres.). Office: US Intl Trade Commn 500 E St NW Ste 704 Washington DC 20436-0003*

NEWSOM, CAROLYN CARDALL, management consultant; b. South Weymouth, Mass., Feb. 27, 1941; d. Alfred James and Bertha Virginia (Roy) Cardall; m. John Harlan Newsom, Feb. 4, 1967; children: John Cardall, James Harlan. AB, Brown U., 1962; MBA, Wharton Sch., 1978; PhD, U. Pa., 1985. Systems engr. IBM, Seattle, 1964-70, Newsom S.E. Services, Seattle, 1970-76; instr. U. Pa. Wharton Sch., Phila., 1978-81; v.p., prin. sr. cons. PA Cons. Group, Princeton, N.J., 1981-88; pres. Newsom Assocs., Yardley, Pa., 1988; ptnr. Bus. Strategy Implementation, Princeton, N.J., 1989-90; pres. Strategy Implementation Solutions, Yardley, Pa., 1990—; examiner, sr. examiner N.J. Quality Achievement Award, 1993-97. Trustee St. Mary Hosp., Langhorne, Pa., 1986-94; bd. dirs. Chandler Hall. Mem. AAUW, Acad. Mgmt., Am. Mgmt. Assn., Am. Soc. for Quality Control, Am. Bus. Women's Assn., Brown Alumni Assn. (pres.-elect 1993-95, pres. 1995-97), Quality N.J. Office: Strategy Implementation Solutions 1588 Woodside Rd Yardley PA 19067-2611

NEWSOM, DAVID DUNLOP, foreign service officer, educator; b. Richmond, Calif., Jan. 6, 1918; s. Fred Stoddard and Ivy Elizabeth (Dunlop) N.; m. Jean Frances Craig, Nov. 17, 1942; children: John, Daniel, Nancy, David, Catherine. AB, U. Calif., 1938; MS, Columbia U., 1940; LLD, U. Pacific, 1979. Pulitzer traveling scholar, 1940-41; pub. Walnut Creek (Calif.) Courier-Jour., 1946-47; 3d sec., info. officer Am. embassy, Karachi, Pakistan, 1948-50; 2d sec., vice consul Oslo, 1950-51; pub. affairs officer Baghdad, Iraq, 1952-55; officer-in-charge Arabian peninsula affairs Dept. State, Washington, 1955-59; with Nat. War Coll., 1959-60; 1st sec. Am. embassy, London, 1960-62; dep. dir. Office No. African Affairs, Dept. State, Washington, 1962-63; dir. Office No. African Affairs, Dept. State, 1963-65; U.S. ambassador Libya, 1965-69; asst. sec. state for African affairs, 1969-74; U.S. ambassador Indonesia, 1974-77, Philippines, 1977-78; undersec. state of polit. affairs Washington, 1978-81; dir. Inst. Study of Diplomacy, Sch. Fgn. Svc., Georgetown U., 1981-90, Marshall Coyne rsch. prof. diplomacy, 1989-91; interim dean Sch. Fgn. Svc. Goergetown U., 1995-96; Cumming Meml. prof. internat. rels. U. Va., 1991—; spl. adviser U.S. del. UN Gen. Assembly, 1972, 78, 79, 80. Served to lt. USNR, 1942-46. Recipient Commendable Service award USIS, 1955; Dept. State Meritorious Service award, 1958; Nat. Civil Service League award, 1972; Rockefeller Pub. Service award, 1973. Mem. U.S. Fgn. Svc. Assn., Coun. Fgn. Rels., Cosmos Club. Presbyterian. Home: 4990 Sentinel Dr Apt 102 Bethesda MD 20816

NEWSOM, GERALD HIGLEY, astronomy educator; b. Albuquerque, Feb. 11, 1939; s. Carroll Vincent and Frances Jeanne (Higley) N.; m. Ann Catherine Bricker, June 17, 1972; children: Christine Ann, Elizabeth Ann. BA, U. Mich., 1961; MA, Harvard U., 1963, PhD, 1968. Research asst. McMath-Hulbert Obs., Pontiac, Mich., summers 1959, 61; research asst. astronomy dept. U. Mich., Ann Arbor, 1959-61; research asst. Shock Tube Lab. Harvard U., Cambridge, Mass., 1962, 64-68; research asst. dept. physics Imperial Coll., London, 1968-69; asst. prof. astronomy Ohio State U., Columbus, 1969-73, assoc. prof., 1973-82, prof., 1982—, acting chmn. dept. astronomy, 1991-93, vice chmn. dept. astronomy, 1993—, acting asst. dean, 1985-86; sr. post-doctoral research asst. Physikalisches Institut, Bonn, Fed. Republic of Germany, 1978. Author: Astronomy, 1976, Exploring the Universe, 1979; contbr. articles to profl. and scholarly jours. Fellow Woodrow Wilson Found., 1961-62, NSF, 1961-63; grantee Noble Found., 1961-64. Mem. Internat. Astron. Union, Am. Astron. Soc. Home: 46 W Weisheimer Rd Columbus OH 43214-2545 Office: Ohio State U Dept Astronomy 174 W 18th Ave Columbus OH 43210-1106

NEWSOM, JAMES THOMAS, lawyer; b. Carrollton, Mo., Oct. 6, 1944; s. Thomas Edward and Hazel Love (Mitchell) N.; m. Sherry Elaine Retzloff, Aug. 9, 1986; stepchildren: Benjamin A. Bawden, Holly K. Bawden. AB, U. Mo., 1966, JD, 1968. Bar: Mo. 1968, U.S. Supreme Ct. 1971. Assoc. Shook, Hardy & Bacon, London and Kansas City, Mo., 1972, ptnr., 1976—. Mem. Mo. Law Rev., 1966-68. Lt. comdr. JAGC, USNR, 1968-72. Mem. ABA, Internat. Bar Assn., Kansas City Met. Bar Assn., Lawyers Assn. Kansas City, U. Mo. Law Sch. Law Soc., Kansas City Club, U. Mo. Jefferson Club, Order of Coif, Perry (Kans.) Yacht Club, Stone Horse Yacht Club (Harwich Port, Mass.). Avocations: skiing, sailing, car racing. Office: Shook Hardy & Bacon One Kansas City Pl 1200 Main St Ste 3100 Kansas City MO 64105-2100

NEWSOM, MELVIN MAX, retired research company executive; b. El Paso, Tex., Dec. 27, 1931; s. Melvin William and Dorthy Maxine (Kinnison) N.; m. Rose Marie Neill, June 5, 1953; children—Terri Laine, Cherri Leigh, Michael Dirk, Thomas Cody. B.S. in Elec. Engring, Tex. A. and M. U., 1955, M.S. in Elec. Engring. (Tex. Power & Light fellow), 1956. Mem. tech. staff Sandia Lab., Albuquerque, 1956—; sect. supr. Sandia Lab., 1961-64, div. supr., 1964-77, dept. mgr., 1977-92, dir. Ctr. for Applied Def. Tech., 1992-94; cons. Dept. Energy; mem. U.S. group on petroleum tech. Joint U.S./USSR Energy Program; participant several programs Nat. Acad. Engring. Contbr. numerous articles to profl. jours. Dist. chmn. Rep. Party, 1960-61, asst., 1963-64. With USN, 1951-53. Decorated Am. Spirit Honor medal; Dept. Energy grantee. Mem. Am. Inst. Mining Engrs., Am. Rose Soc., Tau Beta Pi, Etta Kappa Nu. Presbyterian. Club: Coronado (chmn. bd. 1965-66, 69-70, 73-74, 76-79, dir.). Research in improved drilling tech. for petroleum, geothermal and sci. drilling, and on high temperature well logging. Home: PO Box 856 3628 Scenic Dr Cibolo TX 78108

NEWSOME, EDWARD BALDWIN, retired real estate broker, retired insurance agent; b. Utica, Miss., Dec. 1, 1920; s. Baldwin Mims and Tommie Effie (Pickett) N.; m. Mary Janet Kirkwood, June 11, 944; children: Janet Therese, Kirk Edward. BS, Miss. State U., 1941. Cert. ins. agent, real estate agent; CPCU, GRI. Ins. agent Jim Newsome Ins., Moscow, Idaho, 1948-88; real estate broker, owner Jim Newsome Real Estate, Moscow, 1988-95; ret., 1995; adj. prof. ins. U. Idaho, Moscow, 1975-87, Wash. State U., 1989-90. Bd. mem. Moscow Cemetary Bd. Lt. USN, 1942-45. Mem. VFW, Am. Legion (dept. state commdr. 1967-68, local commdr.), Elks (bd. trustees chmn. 1948); Moose, Moscow C. of C. (pres., bd. trustees). Republican. Avcoations: hunting, fishing, billiards.

NEWSOME, GEORGE LANE, JR., education educator; b. Bessemer, Ala., Oct. 5, 1923; s. George Lane and Mary Viola (Mobbs) N.; m. Martha Cornelia Merchant, June 8, 1947; children: George Lane III, Mary Virginia, Elizabeth Ann. BS, U. Ala., 1949, MA, 1950; PhD, Yale, 1956. Asst. prof. edn. U. Bridgeport, 1955-57, assoc. prof., 1957-58; assoc. prof. philosophy edn. U. Ga., 1958-63, prof., head dept., 1963-85, prof. emeritus philosophy edn., 1990—, mem. dept. curriculum and supervision, 1985-90; guest prof. Philosophy Inst., No. Ill. U., U. Pacific, 1970; guest lectr. U. Bridgeport, 1954-55. Author: Philosophical Perspectives, 1961; editor: Philosophy of Education Proces., 1968, (with William T. Blackstone) Education and Ethics, 1969; mem. editorial bd. Ga. Rev., 1973-75, Ednl. Theory, 1976-78; co-editor Jour. R & D in Edn., 1982-85, editor, 1985-89, bd. cons., 1991—. Bd. mem. Kingswood Cmty. Assn. With AUS, 1943-46. Mem. Philosophy of Edn. Soc. (sec.-treas. 1964-66, pres. 1981-82), Southeastern Philosophy of Edn. Soc. (sec.-treas. 1961, v.p. 1962, pres. 1963), U. Ga. Ret. Tchrs. Assn. (v.p. 1994-95, pres. 1995-96), Athens Kiwanis Club, Phi Kappa Phi, Kappa Delta Pi. Home: 145 Tuxedo Rd Athens GA 30606-3133

NEWSOME, GEORGE MARVIN, lawyer; b. Phenix City, Ala., June 30, 1919; s. Thomas L. and Mary E. (Spivey) N.; m. Norma Elizabeth Hollomon, Aug. 19, 1941; children—Keith, Glenn, Carol. AA, George Washington U., LLB, 1948. Bar: D.C. Dist. Ct. 1949, Va. 1990. With IBM 1945-83, office adminstrn., Washington, 1945-49, atty., N.Y.C., 1949-51, plant counsel, Poughkeepsie, Kingston, N.Y., 1951-59, div. counsel, White Plains, N.Y., 1959-68, staff counsel, Armonk, N.Y., 1968-79, staff counsel, Washington, 1979-83; pvt. practice law, Washington, 1983-89, Fairfax, Va., 1989—. Pres., United Way No. Westchester, 1974-79, v.p., 1977-79. Sgt. USAF, 1942-45; 1st lt. (JAG) Res., 1951-56. Recipient Marshall award United Way No. Westchester, 1977. Mem. ABA, Fairfax Bar Assn., D.C. Bar Assn., Va. Bar Assn., Nat. Security Indsl. Assn. Home: 10520 Wickens Rd Vienna VA 22181-3032 Office: 10623 Jones St Ste 301-b Fairfax VA 22030-7514

NEWSOME, RANDALL JACKSON, judge; b. Dayton, Ohio, July 13, 1950; s. Harold I. and Sultana S. (Stony) N.; B.A. summa cum laude, Boston U., 1972; J.D., U. Cin., 1975. Bar: Ohio 1975, U.S. Dist. Ct. (so. dist.) Ohio 1977, U.S. Ct. Appeals (6th cir.) 1979, U.S. Supreme Ct. 1981. Law clk. to chief judge U.S. Dist. Ct., So. Dist. Ohio, 1975-77; assoc. Dinsmore & Shohl, Cin., 1978-82; judge U.S. Bankruptcy Ct., So. Dist. Ohio, Cin., 1982-88, No. Dist. Calif., Oakland, 1988—. Faculty mem. Fed. Jud. Ctr., ALI-ABA, 1987—; mem. Nat. Conf. of Bankruptcy Judges, 1983—, mem. bd. govs., 1987-88. Contbg. author: Collier on Bankruptcy. Fellow Am. Coll. Bankruptcy (v.p. elect 1996); mem. Phi Beta Kappa. Democrat. Mem. United Ch. of Christ. Office: US Bankruptcy Ct PO Box 2070 Oakland CA 94604-2070

NEWSOME, SANDRA SINGLETON, secondary education educator, principal; b. Bayboro, N.C., Apr. 4, 1948; d. John Wilson Singleton and Cora Lee (Beasley) Hatchel; m. Edward Newsome Jr., Feb. 14, 1971. BS, Elizabeth City State U., 1970; MS, Bowie State U., 1979; EdD, Pensacola Christian Coll., 1992. Cert. tchr., Washington. Tchr. D.C. Pub. Schs., Washington, 1970-80, reading tchr., 1980-82, reading specialist, 1982—; asst. prin. Calvary Temple Christian Sch., Sterling, Va., 1985-86; prof. Bowie State U., 1994—; adminstrv. intern Roper Mid. Sch. of Math. Sci. and Tech., Washington, 1993-95; cons. Bowie State Spl. Interest Coun., 1991-92, D.C.-Dakar Friendship Coun., 1991-92; mem. adv. bd. Walk In Faith mag., Washington, 1991-92; dir. Acad. Tutorial Program, Temple Hills, Md., 1990-91. Contbr. to profl. publs. Mentor Teen Parenting, Inc., Hyattville, Md., 1989, Valuettes, Washington, 1990-92; dir. Adult Literacy Coun., Temple Hills, 1990; asst. dir. Jr. Toastmasters, Brightwood, 1993; program developer, dir. Visions: A Tour into Values, Washington, 1993; pres. Hellen Lee Dr. Civic Assn., Clinton, 1994-95; dir. Christian Edn., Alexandria (Va.) Christian Ctr., 1994—. Recipient Save Our Youth Am. award Soya, Inc., Washington, 1989, Literacy award Bowie State U., 1991; Teacher-to-Teacher grantee, 1990-92; fellow Cafritz Found., 1991. Mem. ASCD, AFT, AAUW, LEAD Program, Nat. Black Child Devel. Inst., Bowie State Spl. Interest Orgn., Alexandria Christian Ctr., Hellen Lee Dr. Civic Assn. (pres. 1994-95).

Avocations: interpretative poetry reading, travel, African studies, photography. Home: 2319 Parkside Dr Mitchellville MD 20721 Office: Roper Mid Sch Math Sci Tech 4800 Meade St NE Washington DC 20019-3948

NEWSOME, WILLIAM ROY, JR., state official; b. Asheville, N.C., July 8, 1934; s. William R. and Mary (Morgan) N.; m. Mary Grace Daniel, Dec. 22, 1958; children: William Daniel, Bo Nathan. Cert., Tollare Folkhögskola, Stockholm, 1959; BS, U. Tenn., 1960; M in Regional Planning, U. N.C., 1962. Planner Tenn. State Planning Commn., Knoxville, 1959-62; city planner Athens (Tenn.) City Govt., 1962-64; campus planner U. Tenn., Knoxville, 1964-66; regional planner Atlanta Regional Planning Commn., 1966-68; planner Pa. State Planning Bd., Harrisburg, 1968-70; spl. advisor Pa. Dept. Community Affairs, Harrisburg, 1970-77; spl. asst. Fed. Emergency Mgmt. Agy., Washington, 1977-81; ptnr. The GNP Firm, Harrisburg, 1982-87; dir. Gov.'s Policy Office, Harrisburg, 1987-88; spl. asst. Pa. Housing Fin. Agy., Harrisburg, 1988-96; ret., 1996; bd. dirs. Pa. Cmty. Devel. and Fin. Corp., Harrisburg, Tri-County Housing Devel. Corp., Harrisburg, Rural Opportunities, Inc., Harrisburg. Pres., bd. dirs. Ctrl. Pa. Literary Coun., Harrisburg, 1992—; bd. dirs. Cmty. Rsch. and Devel. Group, Burlington, Vt., 1994—; elected voting official Dauphin County, 1990—; mem. planning commn. Lower Paxton Twp., 1994—, sec. 1996. With USMC, 1954-57. Bd. dirs. Cen. Pa. Literary Coun., Harrisburg, 1992—; mem. Gov.'s Bldg. Energy Conservation Com., Harrisburg, 1989—; elected voting official Dauphin County, 1990—; mem. planning commn. Lower Paxton Twp., 1994—, sec. 1996. Served with USMC, 1954-57. Mem. Am. Inst. Cert. Planners (charter). Democrat. Home: 112 Maple Rd Harrisburg PA 17109-2730 Office: Pa Housing Fin Agy 2101 N Front St Harrisburg PA 17110-1036

NEWSTEAD, ROBERT RICHARD, urologist; b. Detroit, Sept. 16, 1935; s. Oran Henry and Agnes Audery (Lewandowski) N.; m. Marie Carmela LiPuma, Aug. 5, 1961; children: Elizabeth Marie, Peter Joseph, Angela Agnes, Paul Michael. Student, Coll. Idaho, 1955-57, Quincy Coll., 1957-58; MD, Loyola U., Chgo., 1963. Intern Walter Reed Gen. Hosp., Washington, 1963-64; resident U. Iowa, Iowa City, 1967-71; urologist Urology Clinic Yakima, Wash., 1971-84, pres., 1984—; chief of staff Yakima Valley Meml. Hosp., 1995—; chief of surgery St. Elizabeth Med. Ctr., Yakima, 1980-81, Yakima Valley Hosp., 1978-79. Bd. dirs. St. Elizabeth Found., Yakima, 1983-93, The Capital Theater, 1987-93, Boy Scouts Am., Yakima, 1982-86.

Capt. U.S. Army, 1962-67. Fellow Am. Cancer Soc., Iowa City, 1969-70, Am. Cancer Soc., 1961; named one of Outstanding Young Men Am., 1968. Fellow Am. Bd. Urology, ACS, Am. Urol. Assn., Wash. State Urol. Bd. (mem. at large exec. com.); mem. AMA, Rubin Flocks Soc. (pres. 1985-86), Yakima Surgical Soc. (pres. 1982-83), Yakima County Med. Soc. (pres. 1989-90), Rotary. Roman Catholic. Avocations: art, skiing, golf. Home: 814 Conestoga Blvd Yakima WA 98908-2419 Office: Urology Clinic Yakima 206 S 11th Ave Yakima WA 98902-3205

NEWTON, CHARLES CHARTIER, architect; b. Albuquerque, Feb. 18, 1933; s. Charles Edward and Aileen (Chartier) N.; m. Patricia Clarke, Sept. 6, 1958; children: Heather Ann, Amy Marie, April Chartier. BArch, Tex. A&M U., 1956; MArch, Cranbrook Acad. of Art, 1957. Lic. architect, Tex. Designer Caudill, Rowlett & Scott, Architects, Bryan, Tex., 1958, Eero Saarinen & Assocs., Birmingham, Mich., 1959-60; head design dept. Harrell & Hamilton, Architects, Dallas, 1960-63; project architect Matthews and Assocs., Bryan, 1963-66; assoc. prof. design, dir. Basic Architecture Program Tex. A&M U., College Station, 1963-68; assoc. prof. Sch. Architecture Rice U., Houston, 1968-70; designer Rapp, Tacket, Fash, Houston, 1968; assoc. Van Ness and Mower, Houston, 1969-70; ptnr. Emerson, Fehr, Newton, Austin, Tex., 1970-74; pres. Chartier Newton & Assocs., Austin, 1975-89; prin., v.p. Jessen, Inc., Austin, 1989-91; prin. Chartier Newton & Assocs., Austin, 1991—. Major projects include Clear Lake Grad. Ctr., 1972 (Houston AIA merit award), additions to Robert Mueller Airport, 1976 (Austin AIA design award), Chartier Newton family residence, 1976 (Austin AIA hon. award), Pecan Sq. Splty. Shopping Ctr. (Austin AIA design citation), restoration Henry Hirshfield House and Cottage, 1980 (Austin AIA design award with others), South Austin Multi-Purpose Ctr., 1980 (Austin AIA design award with others), Cedar St. Ct., 1981 (Austin Heritage Soc. award, Austin AIA design award, Tex. Soc. Architects award 1983, Carl W. Burnett award Austin Devel. Found. 1983), office Moore Trust Group, 1982 (Austin AIA design award), Seay House, 1982 (Austin AIA award), renovation Sutton Hall U. Tex. Austin, 1983 (Tex. Soc. Architects design award with others), Riverbend Bapt. Ch., 1985 (merit award ch. architecture dept. Sun. Sch. Bd. So. Bapt. Conv.), Goldsmith Hall U. Tex. (Tex. Soc. Architects honor award with others 1989), Corps of Cadets Ctr. Tex. A & M U. Pres. Environ. Conservancy Austin and Cen. Tex., 1978-79; vice chmn. Sierra Club Austin, 1973-75; mem. Rollingswood (Tex.) Planning and Zoning Commn., 1980-83; mem. guild bd. Austin History Ctr., 1981-82; sr. warden St. Michael's Episc. Ch., 1990. 1st lt. USAR, 1957-58. Fellow AIA (pres. Austin chpt. 1981, mem. Loop 361 Bridge Task Force 1978); mem. Tex. Soc. Archs. (chmn. educators liaison com. 1989-90), Rotary (bd. dirs. Austin 1982-83, 95-96). Episcopalian. Avocations: backpacking, sketching, fishing. Office: 3001 S Lamar Blvd Ste 301 Austin TX 78704-4794

NEWTON, CHRISTOPHER, artistic director. BA with honors, Univ. Leeds; MA, U. Ill.; LLD (hon.), Brock U., U. Guelph; DLitt, Wilfrid Laurier U. Founding artistic dir. Theatre Calgary, 1968-71; artistic dir. Vancouver Playhouse, 1971-79, Shaw Festival, 1979—. Dir. Hobson's Choice, Cavalcade, Will Any Gentleman, Sherlock Holmes, Hobson's Choice, The Cherry Orchard, Will Any Gentleman?, Busman's Honeymoon, The Silver King, Candida, Pointe Valaine, Lulu, Pygmalion, Misalliance, Man and Superman, Don Juan in Hell, Saint Joan, You Never Can Tell, Caesar and Cleopatra, Heartbreak House, Major Barbara, The Millionairess, (opera) Barber of Seville, Madama Butterfly, Die Fledermaus, Patria I, Porgy and Bess, I Due Foscari, Candida, The Silver King; actor (stage) The Marrying of Ann Leete, Charley's Aunt, Peter Pan, Private Lives, Camille, A Flea in Her Ear, Present Laughter; writer (stage plays) Slow Train to St. Ives, You Stay Here, The Rest Come With Me, Trip, The Sound of Distant Thunder, Where Are You When We Need You Simon Fraser. Recipient Queen's Silver Jubilee medal, 1977, Dora award, 1986, Chalmers award for artistic direction; Royal Conservatory of Music fellow (hon.), 1993, Ryerson Polytechnic U. Mem. Order of Can. Office: Shaw Festival Theatre Found, PO Box 774, Niagara on the Lake, ON Canada L0S 1J0

NEWTON, DAVID GEORGE, diplomat; b. Boston, Nov. 13, 1935; s. Charles Paul and Gladys Emelda (Moore) N.; m. Christa Margarete Rathay, Dec. 16, 1961; children: Mark Andrew, Lesley Christina. BA cum laude, Harvard U., 1957; MA with honors, U. Mich., 1970; diploma, Arabic Lang. Sch., Fgn. Service Inst., Beirut, 1966, Nat. War Coll., Washington, 1978. Vice consul Am. consulate gen., Zurich, Switzerland, 1962-64; econ. officer Am. embassy, Sanaa, Yemen, 1966-67; econ. officer for Arabian Peninsula affairs Dept. State, Washington, 1967-69; polit. officer Am. embassy, Jeddah, Saudi Arabia, 1970-72; dep. chief of mission Sanaa, Yemen, 1972-75; div. chief Near East div. intelligence and research bur. Dept. State, Washington, 1975-77; dep. chief of mission Am. embassy, Damascus, Syria, 1978-81; polit. counselor Am. embassy, Jeddah, 1981-84; prin. officer U.S. Interests Sect., Baghdad, Iraq, 1984; ambassador to Iraq Baghdad, 1985-88; dir. Office for Lebanon, Jordan & Syria Near East Bur. Dept. State, 1988-90; internat. affairs advisor, chmn. Dept. Nat. Security Policy, Nat. War Coll., Washington, 1990-93; sr. inspector, team leader Office of Inspector Gen. Dept. State, Washington, 1993-94; ambassador to Yemen Sanaa, 1994—. Served to 1st lt. U.S. Army, 1958-61. Recipient awards Dept. State, 1967, 75, 83-90, Dept. Army, 1993. Mem. Middle East Inst., Middle East Studies Assn. Mem. United Ch. of Christ. Avocations: philately, book collecting, running. Office: Am Embassy Sanaa Dept of State Washington DC 20521-6330

NEWTON, DON ALLEN, chamber of commerce executive; b. Laurel, Miss., Oct. 19, 1934; s. Wilfred L. and Mary (McMullan) N.; m. Coleta Farrell, Oct. 11, 1958; children: Don Jr., Coleta Midge Rast. AA, Meridian C.C., 1954; BA in Journalism, U. Ala., 1956; postgrad. bus. mgmt., U. N.C.; postgrad., U. Okla. Asst. mgr. Meridian C. of C., Miss., 1956; mgr. Winston County C. of C., Louisville, Miss., 1960-61; asst. dir. Delta Council Indsl. and Community Devel. Bd., Stoneville, Miss., 1961-62; dir. Delta Coun. Indsl. and Cmty. Devel. Bd., Stoneville, Miss., 1963-70; exec. v.p. Met. Devel. Bd., Birmingham, Ala., 1970-74; exec. v.p. Birmingham Area C. of C., 1974-88, pres., 1988—; pres. Birmingham Area C. of C. Found., Inc., 1988—; pub. Birmingham Mag., Birmingham Bus. Mag. Contbr. articles to profl. jours., newspapers. Appointee Ala. Export Coun.; bd. dirs. Birmingham Met. Devel. Bd., Ala. Sports Found., Birmingham Festival Arts. Lt. USNR, 1957-60. Named Ala. Mktg. Man of Yr., 1972. Mem. Ala. C. of C. Execs., Econ. Devel. Assn. Ala., Am. C. of C. Execs., U. Ala. Commerce Execs. Soc., Sigma Chi. Home: 2541 Canterbury Rd Birmingham AL 35223-1909 Office: Birmingham Area C of C PO Box 10127 2027 First Ave N Birmingham AL 35202-0127

NEWTON, FLOYD CHILDS, III, lawyer; b. Griffin, Ga., Feb. 4, 1955; s. Floyd Childs Jr. and Jean (Hunt) N.; m. Katrina Dalton, Aug. 30, 1986; children: Stephanie, Amanda. BA, Princeton (N.J.) U., 1977; JD, U. Ga., 1980. Bar: Ga. 1980, U.S. Dist. Ct. (no. dist.) Ga. 1980, U.S. Ct. Appeals (11th cir.) 1980. Ptnr. King & Spalding, Atlanta, 1980—. Office: King & Spalding 191 Peachtree St NE Atlanta GA 30303-1740

NEWTON, GEORGE ADDISON, investment banker, lawyer; b. Denver, Apr. 2, 1911; s. George Addison and Gertrude (Manderson) N.; m. Mary Virginia Powell, Sept. 18, 1937; children: George Addison IV, Nancy Ella Newton Shafer, Virginia Powell Newton Jacobi. AB, U. Colo., 1933; LLB, Harvard U., 1936. Bar: Ill. 1937, Mo. 1946. Assoc. Scott, MacLeish & Falk, Chgo., 1936-42; ptnr. G.H. Walker & Co., St. Louis, 1946-62, mng. ptnr., 1962-72; chmn. bd. dirs. Stifel Nicolaus & Co., Inc., St. Louis, 1972-82, chmn. emeritus, 1982—, CEO, 1974-78. Mem. bd. govs. Greater St. Louis Cmty. Chest; mem. Coun. on Civic Needs; bd. dirs. Goodwill Industries, 1963—, chmn. bd. dirs., 1980-82; bd. dirs. U. Colo. Improvement Corp., U. Colo. Found., St. Louis Conservatory Music; dir. devel. fund U. Colo., 1954-55, chmn., 1955; trustee Fontbonne Coll., 1972-80, chmn., 1974-77; trustee Govtl. Rsch. Inst.; trustee Whitfield Sch., 1978—, chmn., 1986-88, 89-90. Maj., USAAF, 1942-45. Decorated Order of the Rising Sun, Gold Rays and Rosette, Emperor of Japan, 1991; recipient C. Fobb award U. Colo., 1955, alumni Recognition award, 1958, named to C Club Hall of Fame, 1968, Silver Ann. All Am. award Sports Illustrated, 1957, Norlin award U. Colo., 1968; U. Colo. medal, 1984. Mem. Investment Bankers Assn. Am. (pres. 1961), Nat. Assn. Securities Dealers (gov. 1954-56, vice chmn. 1956), Assn. Stock Exchange Firms (gov. 1969-72), Sales Execs. Assn. (bd. dirs. 1955-60), U. Colo. Assn. Alumni (bd. dirs. 1965-67), Japan-Am. Soc. St. Louis (dir. 1980—, pres. 1982-85), The Robert Burns Club of St. Louis (pres. 1993), Phi Beta Kappa, Phi Gamma Delta. Episcopalian (treas. diocese of Mo., 1958-69; sr. warden; trustee diocesan investment trust). Clubs: Racquet (St. Louis), Noonday (St. Louis), St. Louis (St. Louis), Bellerive Country (St. Louis). Home: 6428 Cecil Ave Saint Louis MO 63105-2225 Office: Stifel Nicolaus & Co Inc 500 N Broadway Saint Louis MO 63102-2110 *A reward of one's own accomplishment is realizing how help of others made it possible.*

NEWTON, HUGH C., public relations executive; b. N.Y.C., Oct. 17, 1930; s. Avery Curtis and Ruth (Juster) N.; m. Charlotte Eloise Wallin, Nov. 3, 1956 (div. 1968); 1 child, Margaret Wren Newton Rosello; m. Joanne Elaine Harding, Dec. 27, 1969; children: Matthew Curtis, Christopher Stuart, Kimberly Kelly. BA, Washington & Lee U., 1956. Reporter Danville (Va.) Bee, 1955; mgr. news Carnegie Inst. Tech., Pitts., 1956-57; staff writer Westinghouse Elec., Pitts., 1957; account exec. Burson Marsteller Assocs., Pitts., 1958-59; asst. dir. pub. rels. Rockwell Mfg., Pitts., 1959-61; mgr. spl. projects Reynolds Metals Co., Richmond, Va., 1961-64; dir. pub. rels. Nat. Right to Work Com., Washington, 1964-67, Air Transport Assn., Washington, 1967-68; pres. Hugh C. Newton & Assocs., Washington, 1968—; mem. Interstate Commn. on Potomac River Basin (ICPRM), Washington, 1982-89. Contbr. to Lesly's Public Relations Handbook, 1991. Bd. dirs. Friends of the Torpedo Factory Art Ctr., Alexandria, Va., 1987-91. Mem. Pub. Rels. Soc. Am. (Silver Anvil 1966, 85), Soc. Profl. Journalists, Nat. Press Club. Episcopalian. Avocations: skiing, boating, stamp collecting. Home: 800 S Lee St Alexandria VA 22314-4334 Office: Hugh C Newton & Assocs 214 Massachusetts Ave NE Washington DC 20002-4958

NEWTON, JAMES QUIGG, JR., lawyer; b. Denver, 1911; s. James Quigg and Nelle (Singleton) N.; m. Virginia Shafroth, June 6, 1942; children: Nancy Grusin, Nelle Grainger, Abby Hornung, Virginia Rice. AB, Yale U., 1933, LLB, 1936, MA (hon.), 1951; DPS (hon.), U. Denver, 1952; LLD, Adams State Coll., 1960, Colo. Coll., 1962, U. Colo., 1975. Bar: Colo. 1938. Legal sec. to W.O. Douglas SEC, 1936-37; practiced in Denver, 1938-42, 46-47; lectr. U. Denver, 1938-41; with Ford Found., N.Y.C., 1955-56; v.p. Ford Found., 1956; pres. U. Colo., 1956-63, Commonwealth Fund, N.Y.C., 1963-75; vice chmn. Commonwealth Fund, 1975-76, dir., 1951-55, 57-78; sr. cons. Henry J. Kaiser Family Found., Menlo Park, Calif., 1978-80; of counsel firm Davis, Graham & Stubbs, 1981—; dir. N.Y. Life Fund, 1972-95, Kaiser Found. Hosps./Health Plan, 1972-80; trustee Dry Dock Savs. Bank; mem. Yale Corp., 1951-55, Western Interstate Com. Higher Edn., 1957-63; mem. nat. adv. mental health coun. NIH, 1964-68; mem. Inst. Medicine, Nat. Acad. Scis., 1972—, VA Spl. Med. Adv. Group, 1968-74; fellow Ctr. for Advanced Study in Behavioral Scis., 1977-78. Mayor, City and County of Denver, 1947-55; Sec. bd. trustees U. Denver, 1938-42, pres., 1946-47; pub. trustee Nutrition Found.; chmn. bd. YMCA Greater N.Y., 1976-77. Served with USNR, 1942-46. Fellow Acad. Arts and Scis.; mem. Am. Municipal Assn. (pres. 1950), Am. Council Edn. (dir. 1959-62), Am. Arbitration Assn. (dir., exec. com.), Fgn. Bondholders Protective Council (dir. 1975—), Phi Delta Phi, Alpha Delta Phi. Home: 2552 E Alameda Ave Denver CO 80209-3320 Office: Davis Graham & Stubbs 370 17th St Denver CO 80202

NEWTON, JOHN MILTON, acadmeic administrator, psychology educator; b. Schenectady, Feb. 25, 1929; s. Harry Hazleton and Bertha A. (Lehmann) N.; m. Elizabeth Ann Slattery, Sept. 11, 1954; children: Patricia, Peter, Christopher. B.S., Union Coll., Schenectady, 1951; M.A., Ohio State U., 1952, Ph.D., 1955. Lic. psychologist, Nebr. Research psychologist Electric Boat div. Gen. Dynamics Corp., Groton, Conn., 1957-60; mem. faculty U. Nebr., Omaha, 1960—; prof. psychology U. Nebr., 1966—, chmn. dept., 1967-74; dean U. Nebr. (Coll. Arts and Scis.), 1974-94; acting vice chancellor academic affairs U. Nebr., Omaha, 1994-95; cons. in field, 1960-72. Author research papers in field. Served to 1st lt. Med. Service Corps, AUS, 1955-57. Mem. Am. Psychol. Assn., Psychonomic Soc., Midwestern Psychol. Assn. Home: 5611 Jones St Omaha NE 68106-1232 Office: Univ of Nebr-Omaha Dept Psychology Omaha NE 68182

NEWTON, LEILANI L., bank executive. BA, U. Wis.; MA, U. Mich. Credit mgr. for Austria and Ea. Europe Dow Chemical, Vienna, 1971-73; computer programmer Export-Import Bank of the U.S., 1973-77, asst. to the treas.-contr., 1977-90; mgr., v.p. Credit Adminstrn., 1990-96; v.p. Process Improvement, 1997—. Mem. Women in Internat. Trade, Profl. Banker's Assn. Office: Export Import Bank of the US 811 Vermont Ave NW Washington DC 20571-0001

NEWTON, LISA HAENLEIN, philosophy educator; b. Orange, N.J., Sept. 17, 1939; d. Wallen Joseph and Carol Bigelow (Cypiot) Haenlein; m. Victor Joseph Newton, June 3, 1972; children: Tracey, Kit, Cynthia Perkins, Daniel Perkins, Laura Perkins. Student, Swarthmore Coll., 1957-59; BS in Philosophy with honors, Columbia U., 1962, PhD, 1967. Asst. prof. philosophy Hofstra U., Hempstead, N.Y., 1967-69; asst. prof. philosophy Fairfield U., Conn., 1969-73, assoc. prof., 1973-78, prof., 1978—, dir. program in applied ethics, 1983—, dir. program in environ. studies, 1986—; lectr. in medicine Yale U., 1984—; lectr., cons. in field. Author: Ethics in America; co-author: Watersheds, 1994, 2d edit., 1997, Wake-Up Calls, 1996; co-editor: Taking Sides: Controversial Issues Business Ethics, 4th edit., 1996; contbr. articles to profl. jours. Mem. exec. bd. Conn. Humanities Council, 1979-83. Mem. Am. Soc. Value Inquiry (past pres.), Am. Philos. Assn., Am. Soc. Polit. and Legal Philosophy, Am. Soc. Law, Medicine and Ethics, Soc. Bus. Ethics (past pres.), Phi Beta Kappa. Home: 4042 Congress St Fairfield CT 06430-2041 Office: Fairfield U Dept Philosophy Fairfield CT 06430-5195

NEWTON, NATE, professional football player; b. Orlando, Fla., Dec. 20, 1961. Student, Fla. A&M U. Guard Tampa (Fla.) Bay Bandits, U.S. Football League, 1984-85, Dallas Cowboys, 1986—. Selected to Pro Bowl, 1992-96; mem. Dallas Cowboys Super Bowl Champions XXVII, 1992, XXVIII, 1993. Office: Dallas Cowboys One Cowboys Pkwy Irving TX 75063*

NEWTON, PYNKERTON DION, chiropractor; b. Marion, Ind., Nov. 9, 1960; s. John Walter Newton and Olivia (Taylor) McNair. BA, Ball State U., 1983, MA, 1986; D of Chiropractic, Logan Coll., 1992. Substitute tchr. Marion (Ind.) Community Schs., 1983-86; group leader Ops. Crossroads Africa, Kenya, 1986; acting asst. dir. admissions Ball State U., Muncie, Ind., 1986; corp. analyst Marine Midland Bank, N.Y.C., 1986-87, ops. mgr., 1987-89; admissions coord. Logan Coll. Chiropractic, St. Louis, 1989-92; chiropractic physician Pynkerton Chiropractic Group, P.C., Indpls., 1992—; cons. Logan Coll. Chiropractic, 1993-95. Grad. fellow Ball State U., 1984, 85, 4 Yr. Football scholar, 1979-83. Mem. NAACP, Am. Chiropractic Assn., Nat. Assn. Med. Minority Educators (cons. 1990-91), Ind. State Chiropractic Assn., Am. Black Chiropractic Assn. (exec. dir. 1995-96), Schomburg Ctr. Rsch. Black Culture, Ball State U. Alumni Assn., Pi Kappa Chi. Democrat. Baptist. Avocations: weight lifting, piano, reading, writing poetry. Office: 2102 E 52nd St Ste E Indianapolis IN 46205-1408

NEWTON, RHONWEN LEONARD, writer, microcomputer consultant; b. Lexington, N.C., Nov. 13, 1940; d. Jacob Calvin and Mary Louise (Moffitt) Leonard; children: Blair Armistead Newton Jones, Allison Page, William Brockenbrough III. AB, Duke U., 1962; MS in Edn., Old Dominion U., 1968. French tchr. Hampton (Va.) Pub. Schs., 1962-65, Va. Beach (Va.) Pub. Schs., 1965-66; instr. foreign lang. various colls. and univs., 1967-75; foreign lang. cons. Portsmouth (Va.) Pub. Schs., 1973-75; dir. The Computer Inst., Inc., Columbia, S.C., 1983; pres., founder The Computer Experience, Inc., Columbia, 1983-88, RN Enterprises, Columbia, 1991—. Author: WordPerfect, 1988, All About Computers, 1989, Microsoft Excel for the Mac, 1989, Introduction to the Mac, 1989, Introduction to DOS, 1989, Introduction to Lotus 1-2-3, 1989, Advanced Lotus 1-2-3, 1989, Introduction to WordPerfect, 1989, Advanced WordPerfect, 1989, Introduction to Display/Write 4, 1989, WordPerfect for the Mac, 1989, Introduction to Microsoft Works for the Mac, 1990, Accountant, Inc for the Mac, 1992, Introduction to Filemaker Pro, 1992, Quicken for the MAC, 1993, Quicken for Windows, 1993, WordPerfect for Windows, 1993, Advanced WordPerfect for Windows, 1993, Lotus 1-2-3 for Windows, 1993, Introduction to Quick Books, 1994, Quick Book for Windows, 1994, Introduction to Word for Windows, 1995. Mem. Columbia Planning Commn., 1980-87; bd. dirs. United Way Midlands, Columbia, 1983-86, Assn. Jr. Leagues, N.Y.C., 1980-82, S.C. Wildlife Fedn., 1997—; trustee Heathwood Hall Episcopal Sch., Columbia, 1979-85. Mem. Investment Club (pres. 1995—). Republican. Episcopalian. Avocations: golf, walking. Home and Office: 1635 Kathwood Dr Columbia SC 29206-4509

NEWTON, ROBERT EUGENE, mechanical engineering educator; b. St. Louis, Oct. 16, 1917; s. H. Melville and Lily C. (Peterson) N.; m. Dorothy M. Fairbank, Jan. 31, 1942; children: Peggy D. (Mrs. Alan L. Rector), Gary Fairbank. B.S. in Mech. Engring, Washington U., St. Louis, 1938, M.S., 1939; Ph.D., U. Mich., 1951. From asst. applied math. to asso. prof. Washington U., 1938-51; head structural methods unit Curtiss-Wright Corp., 1941-45; sr. engr. McDonnell Aircraft Corp., 1945; prof. mech. engring. Naval Postgrad. Sch., Monterey, Calif., 1951-86; prof. emeritus Naval Postgrad. Sch., Monterey, 1986—, chmn. dept., 1953-67; vis. prof. U. Wales, Swansea, 1968-69, Universite de Nantes, 1981-82; cons. to industry, 1938—. Author articles, chpt. in book. Trustee Carmel (Calif.) Unified Sch. Dist., 1961-68, pres., 1962-67; Gov. Cmty. Theatre Monterey Peninsula, 1971-73; dir. Cypress Fire Protection Dist., 1993-96. Recipient Distinguished Service award St. Louis County Jr. C. of C. Fellow ASME (life, Jr. award 1940); mem. Am. Soc. Engring. Edn., Soc. for Exptl. Mechanics, Sigma Xi, Tau Beta Pi, Omicron Delta Kappa. Home: 3810 Whitman Cir Carmel CA 93923-8326 Office: Naval Postgrad Sch Monterey CA 93943

NEWTON, V. MILLER, medical psychotherapist, neuropsychologist, writer; b. Tampa, Fla., Sept. 6, 1938; s. Virgil M. Jr. and Louisa (Verri) N.; m. Ruth Ann Klink, Nov. 9, 1957; children: Johanna, Miller, Mark. BA, U. Fla., 1960; MDiv, Princeton Theol. Sem., 1963; postgrad., U. Geneva, Switzerland, 1962; PhD in Med. Anthropology, The Union Inst., 1981, PhD in Clin. Neuropsychology, 1993. Min. dir. Fletcher Pl. Urban Social Ministry, Indpls., 1963-65; coord. staff tng. and community rels. Breckinridge Job Corps Ctr., Ky., 1965-66; asst. prof., program dir. social scis. Webster Coll., St. Louis, 1966-69; assoc. prof., program dir. edn. U. South Fla., Tampa, 1969-73; clk. of the cir. ct. Pasco County, Fla., 1973-76; exec. dir. Fla. Alcohol Coalition, Inc., 1979-80; program and nat. clin. dir. Straight, Inc., St. Petersburg, Fla., 1980-83; dir. KIDS of North Jersey, Inc., 1983—; mem. Sec. Task Force Confidentiality and Client Info. System, Fla. Dept. of Health and Rehab. Svcs., 1979-80; chmn. pres.'s adv. Coun. Webster Coll., 1968-69; guest lectr. at the Grad. Inst. of Community Devel. So. Ill. U., 1968-69; cons. Tampa Model Cities Program, 1969-70; chmn. planning com. Tchr. Corps. Nat. Conf.; faculty mem. Internat. U. for Pres., Munich; co-chmn. Mayor's com. on Pre-sch. Edn., Indpls., 1964-65; mem. med. staff Meadowlands Hosp. Med. Ctr., Secaucus, N.J., 1996—; speaker in field. Author: Gone Way Done: Teenage Drug-Use is a Disease, 1981, Kids, Drugs, and Sex, 1986, Adolescence: Guiding Youth Through the Perilous Ordeal, 1995; co-author: Not My Kid: A Parent's Guide to Kids and Drugs, 1984; appeared on TV programs NBC Mag., 1982, 1986 NBC, 1986, Drugs: A Plague upon America with Peter Jennings ABC, 1988; contbr. articles to profl. jours. Member drug abuse adv. coun. State of N.J., 1985-91; chmn., bd. dirs. Adjustment Madeira Beach, Fla., 1981—, Alcohol Community Treatment Svcs., Inc., Tampa, 1979; pres. Pasco County Coun. on Aging, 1977-79; chmn. bd. San Antonio Boys Village, 1975-76; chmn. Pasco County Data Ctr. Bd., 1973-75, Cen. Pasco Urban Planning Commn., 1972-73; adult del. White House Conf. on Youth, 1971; chmn. Nat. Tchr. Corps Field Coun., 1970-71; pres. Christian Inner City Assn., Indpls., 1964-65; mem. Gov. Ashew's Adv. Com., Pasco County, 1974-76. Aldersgate fellow, 1962; recipient Honor award Nat. LWV, 1963, Cert. Appreciation Pinellas County Bd. of County Commrs., 1982; named Outstanding Young Man of Yr., Indpls. Jaycees, 1965, Outstanding Govt. Leader, Dade City Jaycees, Fla., 1973-74. Mem. ACA, APHA, APA, Am. Bd. Med. Psychotherapists, Am. Anthrop. Assn., Nat. Acad. Neuropsychology (assoc.), Soc. Med. Anthropology, Psychol. Anthropology, Soc. Behavioral Medicine, Soc. Adolescent Medicine, Phi Delta Theta, Rotary Internat., Order of DeMolay (state master counselor 1957). Democrat. Methodist. Office: KIDS of North Jersey PO Box 2455 Secaucus NJ 07096-2455

NEWTON, VERNE WESTER, library director; b. Long Beach, Calif., Mar. 21, 1944; s. Robert Thomas and Bette (Wester) N. BA, Am. U., Washington, 1967; PhD candidate, Syracuse U., 1967-69. V.p. MPG Capital Corp., N.Y.C., 1975-77; exec. sec. AID, Washington, 1977-80; writer, internat. cons., 1980-91; dir. Franklin D. Roosevelt Presdl. Libr., Hyde Park, N.Y., 1991—; sr. cons. Nat. Dem. Inst., Washington, 1984-92; cons. The Creative Factory, Palm Beach, Fla., 1989-91, Ctr. for Nat. Policy, Washington, 1989-91. Author: Cambridge Spies, 1991; writer, producer documentary film Harry Hopkins: At FDR's Side; contbr. articles to profl. jours. Democrat. Congregationalist. Avocations: tennis, squash, rollerblading. Office: Franklin D Roosevelt Libr 511 Albany Post Rd Hyde Park NY 12538-1927

NEWTON, VIRGINIA, archivist, historian, librarian; b. Walters, Okla., Oct. 5, 1938; d. John Walter and Reba Catherine (Mawdsley) N.; m. Gary J. Mounce, Dec. 27, 1963 (div. 1982). Student, Inst. Tecnológico y de Estudios Superiores de Monterrey, Nuevo Leon, Mex., 1957; AA in Bus. Adminstrn., Stephens Coll., 1958; BA in History, Okla. State U., 1960; M of Librarianship, U. Wash., 1963; cert. in libr. sci., U. Tex., 1968, MA in History Archives and Libr. Sci., 1975, PhD in History, Archives and Libr. Sci., 1983. Libr. Inst. Pub. Affairs U. Tex., Austin, 1963-65, libr. Art Libr., 1965-67; coord. Sr. Community Svcs. Program Econ. Opportunities Devel. Corp., San Antonio, 1968-69; archivist, spl. collections libr. Trinity U., San Antonio, 1969-73; spl. collections and reference libr. Pan Am. U., Edinburg, Tex., 1974-77; archivist, records analyst Alaska State Archives and Records Svc., 1983-84, dep. state archivist, 1984-87; state archivist Alaska State Archives & Records Mgmt. Svcs., 1988-93; dir. Columbus Meml. Libr. OAS, Washington, 1993—; archives cons. Ford Found. for Brazilian Archivists Assn., 1976, Soc. for Ibero-Latin Thought, 1980, Project for a Notarial Archives Computerized Guide, 1980; reviewer grant proposal NEH, 1978—; chair Alaska State Hist. Records Adv. Bd., 1988-93, coords. steering com., 1991-93. Author: An Archivists' Guide to the Catholic Church in Mexico, 1979; contbr. articles to profl. publs. founder jail libr. Bexar County Jail, San Antonio; hon. dep. sheriff Bexar County, 1972-75; mem. Dem. party; chair Dems. Abroad in Mex., 1979-81; mem. Dems. Abroad Del. The Dem. Nat. Conv., N.Y., 1980; vice- chair Bill Egan Forum Greater Juneau Dem. Precinct, 1986-88. Recipient Commendation award Gov. of Alaska William Sheffield, 1985, Masonic Scholarship for internat. rels. George Washington U., 1960-61; univ. fellow U. Tex.-Austin, 1982-83, post masters fellow U.S. Dept. Edn.-U. Tex., Austin, 1967-68; scholar Orgn. Am. States, 1980, 81, Fulbright-Hays scholar, 1979, 80, scholar Nat. Def. Fgn. Lang.-U. Tex., Austin, 1978-79, scholar Calif. State Libr., 1962-63. Mem. AAUW (bd. dirs. 1983-86, scholar 1983), Nat. Assn. Govt. Archives and Records Adminstrs. (bd. dirs. 1989-93, chair membership com. 1989-93), Alaska Hist. Soc. (bd. treas. 1988-94), Alaska Libr. Assn., Acad. Cert. Archivists (cert. 1989), Rotary, Phi Kappa Phi. Democrat. Unitarian. Avocations: skiing, dancing, researching, reading, hiking. Home: 2801 Park Center Dr # A909 Alexandria VA 22302-1431 Office: Columbus Meml Libr OAS 19th & Constitution Ave NW Washington DC 20006-4499

NEWTON, WAYNE, entertainer, actor, recording artist; b. Norfolk, Va., Apr. 3, 1942; s. Patrick and Evelyn (Smith) N.; m. Elaine Okamura, 1968 (div.); 1 child, Erin; m. Kathleen McCrone, April 9, 1994. L.H.D. (hon.), U. Nev.-Las Vegas, 1981. Owner Tamiment Internat. Resort. Appearances include Sands, Caesar's Palace, Desert Inn, Flamingo and Frontier hotels, Las Vegas, Harrah's Club, Reno and Lake Tahoe, I Love N.Y. Concert, Americana Hotel, N.Y.C., Talk of the Town, London, London Paladium, Grand Ole Opry House, Nashville, 4th of July, Washington, Astrodome, Houston, Hollywood (Calif.) Bowl, Melodyland, Anaheim, Calif., Circle Star, San Francisco, Sea World, Orlando, Fla., Sherman House, Chgo., Wis. State, Iowa State fairs, Valley Forge Music, Westbury Music fairs, Deauville and Eden Roc hotels, Miami Beach, Carlton Club, Bloomington, Minn., hotels Atlantic City, N.J., before U.S. troops, Beirut; TV appearances on shows of Red, White & Wow, A Christmas Card, miniseries North and South: Book II, 1986, TV spls. Las Vegas on Ice, 1997, Feed the Children, 1997; film appearance in 80 Steps to Jonah, 1969, The Adventures of Ford Fairlane, 1990; numerous recs. including Moods and Moments, Greatest Hits; author (with Dick Maurice): Once Before I Go, 1989. A supporter St. John's Indian Mission, Levene, Ariz. Recipient citation as distinguished recording artist and humanitarian, 1971; Freedom Lantern award Commonwealth of Mass., 1979; Entertainer of Yr. award Variety Clubs So. Nev., 1973; Gov.'s award Commonwealth of Mass., 1976; cert. of appreciation Gov. of Nev., 1978; Outstanding Indian Entertainer of Yr. Navajo Nation, 1980; Founders award St. Judes Childrens Hosp.; Humanitarian award

AMC Cancer Research Ctr.; Recipient award for Daddy Don't Walk So Fast ASCAP; platinum record for Danke Schoen, also gold album and gold records; also others.; named One of 10 Outstanding Young Men of Am. Nat. Jaycees, 1976, Most Disting. Citizen of Yr. NCCJ. Office: Flying Eagle Inc care WNIFC 290 Akron Rd Lake Worth FL 33467*

NEWTON, WILLIAM ALLEN, JR., pediatric pathologist; b. Traverse City, Mich., May 19, 1923; s. William Allen and Florence Emma (Brown) N.; m. Helen Patricia Goodrich, Apr. 21, 1945; children: Katherine Germain, Elizabeth Gale, William Allen, Nancy Anne. B.Sc. cum laude, Alma (Mich.) Coll., 1943; M.D., U. Mich., 1946. Diplomate: Am. Bd. Pathology, Am. Bd. Pediatrics. Intern Wayne County Gen. Hosp., Detroit, 1947; resident in pediatric pathology/pathology/hematology Children's Hosp. Mich., Detroit, 1948-50; res. in pediatrics Children's Hosp. Phila., 1950; dir. labs. Children's Hosp. Columbus, Ohio, 1952-88, rsch. pathologist, 1989—; mem. faculty Coll. Medicine, Ohio State U., 1952—, prof., 1965—, chief pediatric pathology, 1952-89, chief div. pediatric hematology, 1952-88, prof. emeritus, 1989—; chmn. pathology com. Children's Cancer Study Group, 1965-91; chmn. Pathology Com. Intergroup Rhabdomyosarcoma Study Group; chmn. pathology com. Late Effects Study Group. Contbr. articles to med. jours. Trustee, mem. exec. com. Am. Cancer Soc., Ohio div., 1972-86; mem. adv. com. on childhood cancer Am. Cancer Soc.; chmn. exec. com. Consortium for Cancer Control of Ohio, 1982-86; mem. sci. adv. com. Armed Forces Inst. Pathology. Served to capt. M.C. U.S. Army, 1950-52, brig. gen. Res. ret. Mem. Ohio State Med. Assn. (com. on cancer), Midwest Soc. Pediatric Research (mem. council 1960-63, pres. 1964-65), Soc. Pediatric Research, Am. Pediatric Soc., Pediatric Pathology Club (pres. 1968-69), Am. Soc. Clin. Oncology, Internat. Soc. Pediatric Oncology, Sigma Xi, Phi Sigma Pi. Republican. Baptist. Home: 2500 Harrison Rd Johnstown OH 43031-9540 Office: 700 Childrens Dr Columbus OH 43205-2664

NEWTON-JOHN, OLIVIA, singer, actress; b. Cambridge, Eng., Sept. 26, 1948; d. Brin and Irene (Born) N.-J.; m. Matt Lattanzi; 1 child, Chloe. Student pub. schs. Co-owner Koala Blue, 1982—. Singer, actress in Australia, Eng. and U.S., 1965—; actress: (films) Grease, 1978, Xanadu, 1980, Two of a Kind, 1983; albums include: Let me Be There, 1973, If You Love Me Let Me Know, 1974, Long Live Love, 1974, First Impressions, 1974, Have You Ever Been Mellow, 1975, Clearly Love, 1975, Come on Over, 1976, Don't Stop Believing, 1976, Making a Good Thing Better, 1977, Greatest Hits, 1977, Totally Hot, 1978, Grease, 1978, Xanadu, 1980, Physical, 1981, Greatest Hits, 1982, (with John Travolta) Two of a Kind, 1984, Soul Kiss, 1985, The Rumour, 1988, Warm And Tender, 1989, Back To Basics-The Essential Collection, 1992; TV prodn. In Australia, 1988. Decorated Order Brit. Empire; recipient Acad. Country Music, 1973, Country Music Assn. U.K., 1974-75, Country Music Assn. award, 1974, Grammy award, 1973-74, AGVA award, 1974, Billboard Mag. award, 1974-75, People's Choice award 1974, 76, 79, Record World award, 1974-76, 78, Nat. Assn. Retail Merchandisers/Cashbox, 1974-75, Am. Music award 1974-76, Nat. Juke Box award, 1980. Address: care Bill Sammeth Orgn PO Box 960 Beverly Hills CA 90213-0960 Office: MCA 70 Universal City Plz Universal Cty CA 91608-1011*

NEWTSON, RICHARD EVAN, stockbroker; b. Decatur, Ill., Aug. 17, 1950; s. Raymond Earl and Evelyn Lucille (Johnson) N.; m. Robyn Elaine Bock, Dec. 21, 1974; children: Rachel Elizabeth, Randall Eric. BS, Culver-Stockton Coll., 1973. Registered rep. Investors Diversified Svcs., Springfield, Ill., 1972-74; securities broker Reinholdt & Gardner, Springfield, 1975-78; securities broker A.G. Edwards & Sons, Inc., Springfield, 1978—, v.p. investments, 1981—. Fin. industry appointee Ill. Coal Devel. Bd., 1990—. With USAR, 1971-77. Melvin Jones fellow, 1994. Mem. Lions (pres. Springfield Noon club 1980, zone chmn. dist. 1-L 1981-82). Republican. Presbyterian. Avocations: woodworking, cooking, sports. Home: 2400 Westchester Blvd Springfield IL 62704-5427 Office: AG Edwards & Sons Inc Ste 100 1 W Old State Capitol Plz Springfield IL 62701-1290

NEXSEN, JULIAN JACOBS, lawyer; b. Kingstree, S.C., Apr. 14, 1924; s. William Ivey and Barbara (Jacobs) N.; m. Mary Elizabeth McIntosh, Jan. 28, 1948; children: Louise Ivey (Mrs. Heyward Harles Bouknight, Jr.), Julian Jacobs Jr. Student, The Citadel, 1941-43; BS magna cum laude, U. S.C., 1948, JD magna cum laude, 1950. Bar: S.C. 1950, U.S. Supreme Ct. 1960. Partner firm Nexsen Pruet Jacobs & Pollard, Columbia, S.C., 1950—. Trustee Richland County Pub. Libr., chmn., 1976-77; trustee Providence Hosp., chmn., 1984-86; trustee Providence Found., Sisters of Charity of St. Augustine Health Sys.; past bd. dirs. Columbia Music Festival Assn., ARC Richland-Lexington Counties, Ctrl. Carolina Cmty. Found.; mem. U.S.C. Law Sch. partnership bd.; elder Presbyn. Ch., trustee Congaree Presbytery, 1967-87, Synod, S.C., 1969-74, mem. Trinity Presbytery Coun., 1991-95. Lt. inf. AUS, 1943-46, ETO, capt., 1950-51, Korea. Decorated Bronze Star with oak leaf cluster. Mem. ABA, S.C. Bar (treas., bd. govs. 1974-79, ho. of dels. 1980-92), Richland County Bar Assn. (pres. 1974-75, Disting. Svc. award 1987), Am. Bar Found., S.C. Bar Found. (pres. 1971-72), S.C. Law Inst. (coun., exec. com. 1986—), Am. Law Inst., Am. Coll. Trust and Estate Counsel (regent 1973-82), Am. Judicature Soc., Forest Lake Country Club, Palmetto Club, Kiwanis (bd. dirs. 1972-74, 77-79), Phi Beta Kappa. Home: 2840 Sheffield Rd Columbia SC 29204-2332 Office: Nexsen Pruet Jacobs & Pollard Drawer 2426 1441 Main St Columbia SC 29202-2848

NEY, EDWARD N., ambassador, advertising and public relations company executive; b. St. Paul, May 26, 1925; s. John Joseph and Marie (Noonan) N.; m. Suzanne Hayes, 1950 (div. 1974); children: Nicholas, Hilary, Michelle; m. Judith I. Lasky, May 24, 1974. B.A. (Lord Jeffrey Amherst scholar 1942), Amherst Coll., 1947. With Young & Rubicam, Inc., N.Y.C., 1951-86; chmn., pres. CEO Young & Rubicam, Inc., 1970-86; chmn. Paine Webber/Young & Rubicam Ventures, N.Y.C., 1987-89; vice-chmn. Paine Webber, Inc., N.Y.C., 1987-89; amb. to Can., Am. Embassy, Ottawa, Ont., 1989-92; chmn. bd. advisors Burson-Marsteller, N.Y.C., 1992—; bd. dirs. Barrick Gold Corp., Toronto, Ont., Mattel Corp., L.A., Bar Tech, Johnston, Pa.; chmn. Manteller Advt., 1996—. Trustee Amherst Coll., 1979—, Mus. of Broadcasting, 1982—; mem. adv. bd. Ctr. for Strategic and Internat. Studies, 1986—, Coun. on Fgn. Rels., 1975—. Lt. (j.g.) USNR, 1943-46. Office: Burson-Marsteller 230 Park Ave S New York NY 10003-1513

NEY, JAMES WALTER EDWARD COLBY, English language educator; b. Nakaru, Kenya, July 28, 1932; came to U.S., 1951; s. Reginald Osborne and Elizabeth Grace Colby (Aikins) N.; m. Joan Marie Allen, June 12, 1954; children: Cheryl Lynn, James Allen Colby, Peter Cameron. AB, Wheaton Coll., 1955, AM, 1957; EdD, U. Mich., 1963. Cons. Dade County (Fla.) schs., 1961-62; mem. Faculty U. Ryukyus, Okinawa, 1962-64; asst. prof. Mich. State U., Hunt Valley, 1964-69; prof. English Ariz. State U., Tempe, 1969—; vis. prof. U. Montreal, 1962, George Peabody Coll., Nashville, 1965, U. Hawaii, 1967, Western N.Mex. U., 1971; pres. Ariz. Bilingual Council, 1973-74; appointed to council on practice The Am. Assn. Nurse Anesthetists, 1976-83. Author: Readings on American Society, 1969, Exploring in English, 1972, Discovery in English, 1972, American English for Japanese Students, 1973, Linguistics, Language Teaching and Composition in the Grade, 1975, Semantic Structures for the Syntax of the Modal Auxiliaries and Complements in English, 1982, Transformational Grammar: Essays for the Left Hand, 1988, American College Life in English Communication, 1991, GMAT Study Guide and Time Saver, 1993, English Proficiency through American Culture, 1994, others. Instr. workshop Community Assn. Inst. Tech. Writing, 1988; cons. TESL and bilingual edn. with Sta. KFYI, 1986-88. Recipient Best Pedagogical Article award Am. Assn. Tchrs. of Spanish and Portuguese and Hispania mag., 1976. Mem. Am. Linguistic Assn., Nat. Council Tchrs. English, Can. Linguistic Assn., Nat. Assn. Fgn. Student Affairs. Home: 13375 N 96th Pl Scottsdale AZ 85260-4406 Office: Ariz State U Dept English College and University Sts Tempe AZ 85287-0302

NEY, ROBERT TERRENCE, lawyer; b. Pensacola, Fla., July 18, 1944; s. Robert Jackson and Maybelle (Carriere) N.; m. Ursula Christa Deutsch, Sept. 17, 1983; children: Ashley Chamberlain, Shaler Brooke Lindsay. BA, Harvard U., 1966; JD, U. Tex., 1969. Bar: Va. 1970, U.S. Ct. Appeals (4th cir.) 1971, U.S. Supreme Ct. 1975. Atty. Bauknight, Prichard, McCandlish & Williams, Fairfax, Va., 1969-71; ptnr. Boothe, Prichard & Dudley, Fairfax, McLean, Va., 1971-87, McGuire Woods Battle & Boothe, McLean, Va., 1987—. Editor, chpt. author: Appellate Practice, 1986, 2d edit., 1992. Mem. Va. Bar Assn. (pres. 1995). Home: 36878 Snickersville Tnpk Philomont VA 20131 Office: McGuire Woods Battle & Boothe Ste 900 8280 Greensboro Dr Mc Lean VA 22102-3807

NEY, ROBERT W., congressman; b. Wheeling, W. Va., July 5, 1954; m. Candy (div.); children: Bobby, Kayla Marie. BS in Edn., Ohio State U., 1976. Am. Embassy tchr., supr. affiliate school of Shiraz (Iran), 1978; health and edn. program mgr. Ohio Office of Appalachia, 1979; safety dir. City of Bellaire, Ohio, until 1980; mem. Ohio Ho. of Reps., 1980-84, Ohio Senate, 1984-94, 104th Congress from 18th Ohio dist., 1995—; mem. banking and fin. svc. com., mem. vets. affairs com., mem. house oversight com., dep. whip, mem. subcom. on fin. instns. and consumer credit, mem. subcom. on domestic and internat. monetary policy, mem. subcom. on housing/cmty. opportunity, mem. banking com., trans. com., vice chmn. house oversight com. Mem. Kiwanis, Elks, Lions, Sportsmen clubs, NRA. Office: US House of Reps 1024 Longworth HOB Washington DC 20515-3518 also: 3201 Belmont St Ste 504 Bellaire OH 43906-1547

NEYER, JEROME CHARLES, consulting civil engineer; b. Cin., July 15, 1938; s. Urban Charles and Marie Helen (Hemsteger) N.; m. Judy Ann Drolet, June 17, 1961; children: Janet, Karen. B.C.E., U. Detroit, 1961; M.C.E., U. Wash., 1963. Registered profl. engr. 16 states. Facilities engr. Boeing Co., Seattle, 1961-62; found. engr. Metro Engrs., Seattle, 1962-65; project engr. Hugo N. Helpert Assocs., Detroit, 1965-70; pres. NTH Cons. Ltd., Farmington Hills, Mich., 1970—; adj. prof. U. Detroit, 1973-79. Contbr. articles to profl. jours. Chmn. bldg. appeals bd. City of Farmington Hills, 1983; mem. mineral well adv. bd., Lansing, Mich., 1975, mem. constrn. safety standards bd., 1982. Mem. ASTM, ASCE (br. pres. 1973-74), Engring. Soc. of Detroit, Cons. Engrs. of Mich. (pres. 1981), Mich. Soc. Profl. Engrs. (bd. dirs. 1980), Assn. Engring. Firms Practicing in the Geoscis, (pres. 1991). Roman Catholic. Avocations: golfing; tennis. Home: 37972 Tralee Trail Northville MI 48167-2940 Office: Neyer Tisco & Hindo Ltd 38955 Hills Tech Dr Farmington MI 48331-3434

NEYLON, MARTIN JOSEPH, retired bishop; b. Buffalo, Feb. 13, 1920; s. Martin Francis and Delia (Breen) N. PhL, Woodstock Coll., 1944, ThL, 1951; MA, Fordham U., 1948. Ordained priest Roman Cath. Ch., 1950. Bishop Roman Cath. Ch., 1970; mem. Soc. of Jesus; tchr. Regis High Sch., N.Y.C., 1952-54; master Jesuit novices Poughkeepsie, N.Y., 1955-67; chaplain Kwajalein Missile Range, Marshall Islands, 1967-68; superior Residence for Jesuit Students, Guam, 1968-70; coadjutor bishop Caroline and Marshall Islands, 1970-80; Vicar apostolic, 1971—; residential bishop New Diocese of Carolines-Marshalls, 1980-96, bishop emeritus, 1996—. Address: PO Box 250 Chuuk FM 96942

NG, KWOK-WAI, physics educator; b. Hong Kong, Aug. 15, 1958; came to U.S., 1981; s. Wan-Fu and Kam-Har (Sin) N.; m. Grace Mun Yan, Dec. 28, 1987; 1 child, Nelson Eukai. BSc, U. Hong Kong, 1981; PhD, Iowa State U., 1986. Postdoctoral fellow U. Tex., Austin, 1986-88; asst. prof. physics U. Ky., Lexington, 1988-94, assoc. prof., 1994—. Contbr. articles to Phys. Rev. Letter, Phys. Rev. B, Japanese Jour. Applied Physics. Mem. IEEE, Am. Phys. Soc., Phi Kappa Phi. Achievements include gap anisotropy of high Tc superconductors; superconducting tunneling spectroscopy. Office: Univ Ky Dept Physics Astronomy Lexington KY 40506

NG, LAWRENCE MING-LOY, pediatric cardiologist; b. Hong Kong, Mar. 21, 1940; came to U.S., 1967, naturalized, 1977; s. John Iu-cheung and Mary Wing (Wong) N.; m. Bella May Ha Kan, June 25, 1971; children: Jennifer Wing-yee, Jessica Wing-yee. B in Medicine, U. Hong Kong, 1965, B in Surgery, 1965. House physician Queen Elizabeth Hosp., Hong Kong, 1965-66, med. officer, 1966-67; resident physician Children's Hosp. of Los Angeles, 1967-68; resident physician Children's Hosp. Med. Center, Oakland, Calif., 1968-70, fellow in pediatric cardiology, 1970-72, now mem. teaching staff; practice medicine, specializing in pediatrics and pediatric cardiology, San Leandro, Calif., 1972—, Oakland, Calif., 1982—; mng. ptnr. Pediatric Med. Assocs. of East Bay, 1990—; chief of pediatrics Oakland Hosp., 1974-77; chief of pediatrics Vesper Meml. Hosp., 1977-79, sec. staff, 1984, v.p. staff, 1985; chief pediatrics Meml. Hosp., San Leandro, 1986-88; founder Pediatric Assocs. of East Bay, 1990. Active Republican Party. Diplomate Am. Bd. Pediatrics. Fellow Am. Acad. Pediatrics; mem. AMA, Calif. Med. Assn., Am. Heart Assn., Alameda County Assn. Primary Care Practitioners (membership chmn. 1993—, sec. treas 1994—), Los Angeles Pediatric Soc., East Bay Pediatric Soc., Smithsonian Assocs., Nat. Geog. Soc., Orgn. Chinese Ams. (chpt. pres. 1984), Chinese-Am. Physicians Soc. (co-founder, sec. 1980, pres. 1983), Chinese-Am. Polit. Assn. (life), Oakland Mus. Assns., Oakland Chinatown C. of C. (bd. dirs. 1986-91); Oakland Asian Cultural Ctr. (dir. 1996—, treas. 1996—), Hong Kong U. Alumni Assn. (sec. No. Calif. chpt. 1992-96, pres. 1997—), Stanford U. Alumni Assn. (life), Chancellor's Assocs. U. Calif. at Berkeley, Commonwealth Club, Consumers' Union (life); Chinese Am. Golf Club. Buddhist. Office: 345 9th St Ste 204 Oakland CA 94607-4206 also: 101 Callan Ave Ste 401 San Leandro CA 94577-4519

NGAI, SHIH HSUN, physician; b. Wuchang, China, Sept. 15, 1920; came to U.S., 1946, naturalized, 1953; s. Chih F. and Shen (Shih) N.; m. Hsueh-hwa Wang, Nov. 6, 1948; children: Mae, Janet, John. M.B., Nat. Central U. Sch. Medicine, China, 1944. Mem. staff Presbyn. Hosp., N.Y.C., 1949-88; attending anesthesiologist Presbyn. Hosp., 1965-88; faculty Columbia Coll. Phys. and Surg., 1949—, prof. anesthesiology, 1965-88, prof. pharmacology, 1974-88, prof. emeritus, 1988—, chmn. dept. anesthesiology, 1970-73; mem. com. on anesthesia NRC-Nat. Acad. Scis., 1961-70; cons. NIH, 1963-67, 78-82. Author: Manual of Anesthesiology, 1959, 62, Metabolic Effects of Anesthesia, 1962, Highlights of Clinical Anesthesiology, 1971; contbr. to: Physiol. Pharmacology, 1963, Handbook of Physiology, 1964, Modern Trends in Anesthesia, 1966, Advances in Anesthesiology-Muscle Relaxants, 1967, Handbook of Experimental Pharmacology XXX, Modern Inhalation Anesthetics, 1972, Muscle Relaxants, 1975, Enzymes in Anesthesiology, 1978; editor: Anesthesiology, 1967-77. Mem. Am. Physiol. Soc., Am. Soc. Pharmacology and Exptl. Therapeutics, Assn. Univ. Anesthetists, Am. Soc. Anesthesiologists, Academia Sinica. Home: 281 Edgewood Ave Teaneck NJ 07666-3023

NGO, PAUL Y.L., psychology educator; b. Ames, Iowa, Mar. 21, 1961; s. Peter D.T. and Cecilia T.L. (Pho) N.; m. Stephanie Ngo, June 30, 1996; 1 child, Nicholas T.V. BA with distinction in Psychology, Rutgers U., 1983; MA in Exptl. Psychology, U. Notre Dame, 1986, PhD in Exptl. Psychology, 1988. Tchg. aide Douglass Coll. Rutgers U., New Brunswick, N.J., 1982-83; instr. freshman writing program U. Notre Dame (Ind.), 1984-88, tchg. asst. in psychology, 1987; adj. prof. psychology St. Mary's Coll., City of Notre Dame, 1988, Ind. U., South Bend, 1988-89; asst. prof. psychology U. Wis.-Stout, Menomonie, 1989-93, assoc. prof. psychology, 1993-96; assoc. prof. psychology St. Norbert Coll., De Pere, Wis., 1996—; reviewer Harcourt Brace Coll. Publs., Ft. Worth, 1994-96; instr. ergonomics dept. apparel textiles and design U. Wis.-Stout, 1995; spkr. in field. Author (videotape) Advantages of Campus Diversity, 1991, (book chpts.) Torn Between Two Worlds, 1994, Resiliency in Ethnic Minority Families, 1995. U. Notre Dame fellow, 1983-84, Nakatani Ctr. Curriculum Devel. grantee, 1994; George H. Cook scholar Rutgers U., 1983. Mem. Midwestern Psychol. Assn. (Chgo. moderator 1993-96, local rep. 1993—), Internat. Assn. for Cross-Cultural Psychology, Psi Chi (pres. Douglass Coll. chpt. 1982-88). Roman Catholic. Avocations: outdoor activities, tennis, tropical fish. Home: 900 Liebman Ct Apt 12 Green Bay WI 54302-5083 Office: St Norbert Coll 204 John Minahan Sci Bldg 100 Grant St De Pere WI 54115

NGUYEN, KING XUAN, language educator; b. Hue, Vietnam, Dec. 20, 1930; came to U.S., 1975; s. Duong Xuan Nguyen and Thi Thi Ton-Nu. BA, U. Saigon, 1960, LLB, 1963; MEd, Boise State U., 1980. Tchr. Boise Sch. Dist., 1975-95; lectr. S.E. Asian Studies Summer Inst./U. Wash., 1992, 93, U. Wis., 1994, Ariz. State U., 1996, 97; spl. lectr. Boise State U., 1975-77. Col. Vietnamese Air Force to 1975. Recipient Red Apple Award for Outstanding Svc. to Edn., Boise, 1990. Mem. NEA, Idaho Edn. Assn., Boise Edn. Assn., Consortium Tchrs. Southeast Asian Langs., Assn. of TESOL. Home: 9674 W Pattie Ct Boise ID 83704-2824

NGUYEN, TAI ANH, minister. Supt. Vietnamese Ministry Dist. of the Christian and Missionary Alliance. Office: 2275 W Lincoln Ave Anaheim CA 92801-6551*

NGUYEN, THINH VAN, physician; b. Vietnam, Apr. 16, 1948; came to U.S., 1971; s. Thao Van and Phuong Thi (Tran) N.; m. Phi Thi Ho, Jan. 2, 1973; children: Anh-Quan, Andrew. BS, U. Saigon, 1970; MS, U. Mo., 1973; MD, U. Tex., 1982. Diplomate Am. Bd. Internal Medicine, Am. Acad. Pain Mgmt., Fed. Lic. Examination. Rsch. asst. U. Tex. Med. Sch., Dallas, 1974-78; intern U. Tex. Med. Br., Galveston, 1982-83, resident, 1983-85; internist Family Health Plan, Inc., Long Beach, Calif., 1985-88, internist, area chief, 1988-89; pvt. practice San Jose, Calif., 1990—; chmn. quality assurance/UM com. Premier Care of No. Calif. Med. Group, Inc., 1996—; chmn. interdisciplinary com. Charter Cmty. Hosp., Hawaiian Gardens, Calif., 1988-89, San Jose Med. Ctr., 1993—. Fellow Am. Acad. Otolaryngic Allergy (affiliate); mem. ACP, AMA, Am. Acad. Pain Mgmt., Calif. Assn. Med. Dirs. (bd. dirs. 1988-92), Calif. Med. Assn., Santa Clara County Med. Assn. Office: 2470 Alvin Ave Ste 5 San Jose CA 95121-1664

NGUYEN, TIEN MANH, communications systems engineer; b. Saigon, Vietnam, Apr. 5, 1957; came to the U.S., 1975; s. Hung The and Bi Thi (Luu) N.; m. Thu Hang Thi, Dec. 28 1986. BS in Engring., Calif. State U., Fullerton, 1979, MS in Engring., 1980; MSEE, U. Calif., San Diego, 1982; PhD in Elec. Engring., Columbia Pacific U., 1986; MA in Math., Claremont Grad. Sch., 1993, PhD in Engring. Math., 1995. Cert. electro magnetic compatibility engr., mfg. technologist. Tchg. asst. U. Calif., San Diego, 1982-83; chief automated mfg. dept. ITT Ednl. Svcs., West Covina, Calif., 1983-85; tech. staff Jet Propulsion Lab., Pasadena, Calif., 1985-96; engring. specialist The Aerospace Corp., El Segundo, Calif., 1996—; prin. tech. advisor Internat. Consultative Com. for Space Data Systems (CCSDS), Pasadena, 1985-90, 93-96. Editor: Proceedings of Consultative Com. for Space Data Systems, Radio Frequency & Modulation, 1989, 94, VACET Tech. Jour., 1996—; contbr. over 60 articles to profl. jours. Grad. rep. EECS dept. U. Calif., San Diego, 1982-83; NASA del. to internat. Consultative Com. for Space Data Systems, 1986—. San Diego fellow, 1980-82, Long Beach Found. scholar Calif. State U.; recipient Bendix Mgmt. Club award, 1987, NASA Hon. award, 1988, over 23 NASA monetary awards, 1989-96, 2 NASA Hon. awards, 1993, West Bond prize award for best PhD dissertation, 1995. Mem. IEEE (sr., vice chmn. 1987-94, session chmn. internat. symposium on electro magnetic compatibility 1986, internat. conf. on telecomm. 1995, session organizer and chmn., award 1986, 95, student activities chair Orange County Sect., 1997—), AIAA (sr.), AAAS, Soc. Mfg. Engrs., Am. Math. Soc., Armed Forces Commn. and Electronics Assn., Vietnamese-Am. Sci. and Profl. Engring. Soc. (chmn. bd. dirs. 1995-96, planning chair and tech. program chair conf. 1996, presenter in field, editor VASPES '96 Conf. Proc.), Vietnamese Assn. for Computing, Engring., Tech., and Sci. (gen. co-chmn. Viet-Tech. Internat. Conf. 1996 (editor-in-chief VACETS Tech. Jour. 1996-97, mem. steering com. 1997), N.Y. Acad. Scis., U.S. Naval Inst., Phi Kappa Phi, Sigma Xi. Republican. Buddhist. Achievements include patent for technique to resolve phase ambiguity for QPSK systems; development of new algorithms to design communications systems for space applications; development of future standards for space data systems. Home: 1501 Maxzim Ave Fullerton CA 92833-4511 Office: The Aerospace Corp 2350 El Segundo Blvd El Segundo CA 90245

NGUYEN, TRUC CHINH, analytical chemist; b. Saigon, Vietnam, Apr. 21, 1960; came to the U.S., 1981; s. Duc Huu Nguyen and Cam Thi Doan. BS, U. Tex., 1987. Rsch. asst. Univ. Tex., San Antonio, 1984-87; assoc. scientist Radian Corp., Austin, Tex., 1987-88; scientist Radian Corp., Austin, 1988-90, staff scientist, project dir., 1991—; assistance dir. Southeast Asia Internat. Trade Assocs., Inc., 1992-93; pres. L'Expression Internat., Austin, 1993—. Contbr. articles to profl. jours. Pres. Young Vietnamese-Am. Assn., Tex., 1990-94; bd. dirs. Vietnam TV, Austin, 1988-90. Recipient Minority Biomed. Rsch. Support grant NIH, 1984-87. Mem. Am. Chem. Soc. (analytical chemistry div.), Internat. Platform Assn. Home: 11914 Snow Finch Rd Austin TX 78758-3008 Office: L'Expression Internat 8760-A Rsch Blvd Ste 293 Austin TX 78758

NGUYEN, VUNG DUY, radiologist, educator; b. Nhatrang, Vietnam, Dec. 25, 1938; came to U.S., 1975; s. Con Duy and Duc Thi Nguyen; m. Quy Tran, Nov. 10, 1963; children: Khanh Duy, Phong Duy, Lam Duy, Linhda. MD with honors, Saigon (Vietnam) U., 1964; cert., U. Tex. Health Sci. Ctr., San Antonio, 1979. Lic. radiologist, Tex. Radiologist chief Draftee Ctr., Gia Dinh, Vietnam, 1967-69; staff radiologist Cong Hoa Hosp., Saigon, 1969-74; asst. chief radiology dept. Saigon Med. Sch., Saigon, 1974-75; instr. radiology U. Tex. Health Sci. Ctr., San Antonio, 1977-79, asst. prof. radiology, 1980-84, assoc. prof. radiology, 1985—; cons. skeletal radiology Med. Hosp. Ctr., San Antonio, 1979—; cons., chief of svc. Audie Murphy VA Hosp., San Antonio, 1979—. Contbr. chpts. to books, 30 articles to profl. jours. Advisor Vietnamese med. students, San Antonio, 1980—. maj. South Vietnamese Army Med. Corps, 1958-74. Recipient Am. Physician Recognition award AMA, 1983. Mem. AAAS, U. Radiologists Assn., Radiol. Soc. N.Am., Internat. Skeletal Soc., N.Y. Acad. Scis. Avocations: soccer, swimming, fishing, gardening, traveling. Home: 3511 Hunters Sound San Antonio TX 78284 Office: U Tex Health Scis Ctr 7703 Floyd Curl Dr San Antonio TX 78284-6200 also: Woodward/White Inc 129 1st Ave SW Aiken SC 29801

NGUYEN-TRONG, HOANG, physician, consultant; b. Hue, Republic of Vietnam, Sept. 4, 1936; s. Nguyen-Trong Hiep and Nguyen-Phuoc Ton-nu-Thi Sung. B in Math., Lycée d'Etat Michel Montaigne, Bordeaux, 1956; state diploma of medicine, Sch. Medicine, Paris, 1966, also cert. aeronautical medicine and health and sanitation, 1965, diploma Health and Smoking, 1993; diploma post traumatic stress disorder, crises and disasters, The Am. U. and Centre Internat. de Scis. Criminelles de Paris, Washington, 1995. Resident surgeon Compiegne State Hosp., 1963-64, Meaux State Hosp., 1964-66, Lagny State Hosp., 1966; specialist in health and sanitation Paris Sch. Medicine, 1965—; specialist in family planning French Action of Family Planning, Paris, 1968—; practice medicine, Nanterre, France, 1969—; cons. physician various pharm. labs., Paris, 1987; investigator physician WHO regional office for Europe, 1991. Contbr. articles to profl. jours. Active mem. task force on tobacco dependency Biomed. Saints Pères Rsch. Unit, Paris, 1993, AIDS treatment assn. Le Val de Seine, 1993. Recipient World Decoration of Excellence, 1990, Commemorative Medal of Honor, 1990, Internat. Order of Merit, 1990. Mem. French Soc. Aviation and Space Physiology and Medicine (titulary, specialist in aviation medicine), Assn. Nanterre Physicians, Assn. Vietnamese Practitioners in France, Assn. Le Val de Seine, Chambre Syndicale des Medecins des Hauts de Seine, Ordre des Medecins des Hauts de Seine, Les Ex du XIV Shooting Club. Avocations: painting, poetry, classical and modern jazz music, riflery, martial arts. Home: 3 Rue Gazan, 75014 Paris France Office: Cabinet Med Privé, 38 Rue des Fontenelles, 92000 Nanterre France

NIBLEY, ANDREW MATHEWS, editorial executive; b. Maxwell AFB, Ala., May 25, 1951; s. Owen Smoot and Frances Elizabeth (Browder) N.; m. Mary Elizabeth Michael, Nov. 24, 1984; children: Kevin Mathews, Carlyle Gower, Leath Michael. Attended, Montgomery Coll, Rockville, Md., 1970-72, Univ. Md., 1973. Legis. corr. UPI, Hartford, Conn., 1975-78; bur. chief UPI, Concord, N.H., 1979; Treasury corr. UPI, Washington, 1980; Treasury corr. Reuters N.Am., Washington, 1980-82, editor-in-charge, 1982, news editor, 1982-85; news editor Reuters N.Am., N.Y.C., 1985-87; news editor Europe Reuters Holdings, London, 1987-89; editor, America Reuters America Inc., N.Y.C., 1989-94; sr. v.p., news and TV Reuters America Inc., 1993-94; editor, exec. v.p., bd. dirs. Reuters New Media Inc., N.Y.C., 1994—; mem. Knight-Bagehot editl. panel Columbia U., 1995—; bd. dirs. InGenius Inc., Sportsline USA, Inc.; bd. advisors Red Herring Mag.; exec. mgmt. com. Reuters Am. Holdings, Inc. Mem. Gov.'s Coun. on Alcoholism and Drug Abuse, mem. media subcom., 1991-92; trustee N.J. Ctr. for Family Studies; bd. advisors Grad. Sch. Journalism U. Calif., Berkeley; patron Met. Opera, Birds of Vt. Mus.; mem. bd. dirs. Knight-Bagehot fellow Columbia U. Recipient Meritorious Service award Nat. Press Club. Mem. Am. Soc. Newspaper Editors (editl. bd. 1992-93), Overseas Press Club (program vice chmn. 1990-93, bd. govs. 1993-96, treas. 1996—), Fgn. Press Assn., Internat. Platform Assn., N.Y. New Media Assn., Triathlon Fedn. Am., Montclair Golf Club (Verona, N.J.), Essex Running Club, The Athletic and Swim Club (N.Y.C.). Avocations: golf, tennis, jogging, racquetball, triathlons. Office: Reuters New Media Inc 1700 Broadway New York NY 10019-5905

NIBLEY, ROBERT RICKS, retired lawyer; b. Salt Lake City, Sept. 24, 1913; s. Joel and Teresa (Taylor) N.; m. Lee Allen, Jan. 31, 1945 (dec.);

children—Jane, Annette. A.B., U. Utah, 1934; J.D., Loyola U., Los Angeles, 1942. Bar: Calif. bar 1943. Accountant Nat. Parks Airways, Salt Lake City, 1934-37, Western Air Lines, Los Angeles, 1937-40; asst. mgr. market research dept. Lockheed Aircraft Corp., Burbank, Calif., 1940-43; asso. firm Hill, Farrer and Burrill, Los Angeles, 1946-53; partner Hill, Farrer and Burrill, 1953-70, of counsel, 1971-78. Served from ensign to lt. comdr. USNR, 1943-46. Mem. ABA, L.A. Bar Assn., Calif. Club, Phi Delta Phi, Phi Kappa Phi, Phi Delta Theta. Home: 4860 Ambrose Ave Los Angeles CA 90027-1866

NIBLOCK, WALTER RAYMOND, lawyer; b. Little Rock, Nov. 19, 1927; s. Freeman John and Nellie (Wolfe) N.; m. Marjorie Lee Hammond, Oct. 17, 1953; children: Fred William, George Hammond, Walter Lester, Raymond Lee. Student, Tex. A&M Coll., 1945, Little Rock Jr. Coll., 1947; B.S., U. Ark., 1951, J.D., 1953. Bar: Ark. 1953. Field dir. ARC, 1953-59; asst. gen. mgr., dir. Industria de Pollos (S.A.), Cali, Colombia, 1959-61; practice in Fayetteville, 1961—; now sr. ptnr. Niblock Law Firm; exec. sec. Ark. Judiciary Commn., 1963-65; U.S. commr. Fayetteville div. U.S. Dist. Ct., Western Dist. Ark.; part-time mem. U.S. Magistrate, 1965-79; mem. Jud. Ethics Com. State Ark., 1978-83, Supreme Ct. Com. on Profl. Conduct, 1979-86, chmn., 1981; mem. com. U.S.-Soviet Rels., 1992—. Bd. dirs. Washington County chpt. ARC.; mem. Pub. Employees Retirement Study Commn., 1983-85; trustee Iolta Found., 1989—. Served with AUS, 1945-47. Recipient Meritorious Service award ARC, 1963. Fellow Ark. Bar Found. (sec.-treas. 1973-74, chmn. 1976-77), Roscoe Pound Found.; mem. ABA, ATLA (bd. govs. 1978-90, home office and budget com. 1987-88, chair, key person com. 1987-88, chair ATLA PAC taskforce com. 1988-89, co-chair membership com. 1989-90, co-chair state fund devel. com. 1989-90, mem. exec. com. 1989-90, bd. dirs. ATLA assurance 1991—, PAC trustee 1993—, chair Group Ins. Trust 1994—), Am. Bd. Trial Advocates, So. Trial Lawyers Assn. (gov. 1988—, War Horse award 1992, parliamentarian 1995-96, sec. 1996-97, treas. 1997-98), Ark. Trial Lawyers Assn. (pres. 1974-76), Ark. Bar Assn. (pres. 1977-78), Washington County Bar Assn. (v.p. 1973-74, pres. 1974-75), N.Y. Trial Lawyers Assn., Am. Inns. Ct. (master 1989), William B. Putnam Inn, Delta Theta Phi. Democrat. Home: 265 Holly St Fayetteville AR 72703-1814 Office: Niblock Bldg 20 E Mountain St Fayetteville AR 72701-6050

NIBLOCK, WILLIAM ROBERT, manufacturing executive; b. Phila., Aug. 15, 1928; s. William and Grace Neary (Rennie) N.; m. Barbara Ann Parsons, Sept. 26, 1956; children: Elizabeth Ann, Christopher Parsons. BSChemE, Drexel U., 1951; MBA, U. Chgo., 1956. Dir. corp. devel. and planning Pitts. Coke and Chem. Co., 1956-68, U.S. Chems., Inc., Pitts., 1966-70; v.p. corp. devel. Courtaulds Coatings, Inc., Louisville, 1970-95; v.p. investments Courtaulds Coatings Inc. (Porter Paint Co.), Louisville, 1995—; bd. dirs. Internat. Paint of Am. Inc., v.p., 1988; chmn., bd. dirs. The Hanseatic Group Inc., Louisville, 1990; bd. dirs. Econs. Am. Bd. dirs. Ky. Ednl. Found., Lexington, 1984—; bd. dirs. Jr. Achievement of Kentuckiana; pres., co-dir. Porter Paint Found. Inc; pres., dir. Porter Paint Found., Inc. Lt. USN, 1952-55. Mem. Wynn-Stay Club, Jefferson Club. Republican. Episcopalian. Avocations: sailing, skiing, coins, computers. Home: 2210 Wynnewood Cir Louisville KY 40222-6342 Office: Courtaulds Coatings Inc 400 S 13th St Louisville KY 40203-1714

NICANDROS, CONSTANTINE STAVROS, business consultant, retired oil company executive; b. Port Said, Egypt, Aug. 2, 1933; came to U.S., 1955, naturalized, 1963; s. Stavros Constantine and Helen (Lianakis) N.; m. Tassie Boozalis, May 24, 1959; children: Steve Constantine, Vicky Ellen. Diploma, HEC Ecole des Hautes Etudes Commerciales, 1954; lic. en droit, Law Sch. U. Paris, 1954, doctorate in econ. sci., 1955; MBA, Harvard U., 1957. With planning dept. Conoco Inc., Houston, 1957-61; with planning dept. Conoco Inc., N.Y.C., 1961-64, with land acquisition internat. exploration-prodn. dept., 1964-66, dir. planning ea. hemisphere, 1966-71, gen. mgr., then v.p. supply and transp. ea. hemisphere, 1971-74, exec. v.p. ea. hemisphere refining, mktg., supply, transp., 1974-75; exec. v.p. worldwide supply and transp. Conoco Inc., Stamford, Conn., 1975-78; group exec. v.p. petroleum products Conoco Inc., Houston, 1978-83, pres. petroleum ops., 1983-87, pres., CEO, 1987-96; vice chmn. E.I. duPont deNemours (parent co. of Conoco), 1991-96, bd. dirs., mem. strategic direction co., 1993-96; ret., 1996; chmn. CSN and Co.; bd. dirs. Tex. Commerce Bank, Cooper Industries, Inc., Mitchell Energy and Devel., Keystone Internat.; active mem. adv. bd. Tex. Ctr. for Superconductivity, U. Houston, 1989-91. Bd. dirs., chmn. Houston Symphony; bd. dirs. Greater Houston Partnership, 1989-95; bd. dirs. Tex. Gulf Coast affiliate United Way, 1986-91, campaign chmn., 1988; trustee Mus. Fine Arts, Houston, 1987, 95—, Houston Ballet Found., Baylor Coll. Medicine; trustee, bd. govs. Rice U.; sr. chmn. bd. trustees Houston Grand Opera; chmn. Tex. chpt. Am. Com. on French Revolution Bicentennial, 1989. Mem. Am. Petroleum Inst. (bd. dirs.), Houston Forum (bd. govs.). Greek Orthodox. Office: CSN and Co 10000 Memorial Dr Houston TX 77024-3422

NICASSIO, SUSAN VANDIVER, history and humanities educator; b. Muskogee, Okla., Mar. 25, 1941; d. Clarence Raymond and Sari Frances (Chase) Vandiver; m. Anthony Robert Nicassio, Oct. 7, 1961; 1 child, Alexander Raymond. BA, La. State U., 1981, MA, 1985, PhD, 1989. Asst. prof. history Elon (N.C.) Coll., 1989-91; asst. prof. U. Ala., Birmingham, 1991-96; assoc. prof. history and interdisciplinary humanities U. Southwestern La., Lafayette, 1996—; Am. Soc. for 18th-Century Studies fellow Newberry Libr., Chgo., 1990; fellow Am. Acad. in Rome, 1993-94. Fulbright fellow, 1986-87. Roman Catholic. Avocations: walking tours, choral and solo singing, collecting memorabilia of Puccini's Tosca. Office: Univ SW La Dept History and Geography PO Box 42531 Lafayette LA 70504-2531

NICASTRO, FRANCIS EFISIO, defense electronics and retailing executive; b. N.Y.C., Apr. 21, 1942; s. Louis and Janet Amaloa (Onnis) N.; m. Rosalind Piperno, Nov. 22, 1972 (div. Aug. 1995); 1 child, Jason. BS in Econs., U. Pa., 1964. Audit analyst ops., coordinator audit and procedures S.H. Kress and Co., N.Y.C., 1967-68; mgr. audit and acctg. Singer Co., N.Y.C., 1968-76, dir. acctg. and budgets, 1976-77, dir. cons. acctg., 1977-79; dir. domestic treasury ops. Singer Co., Stamford, Conn., 1979-80, asst. treas., 1980-86, treas., 1986-89; corp. v.p., treas. Grand Union Co., Wayne, N.J., 1989—. Served to 1st lt. U.S. Army, 1964-66. Republican. Home: 11 Moshier St Greenwich CT 06831-4308 Office: The Grand Union Co 201 Willowbrook Blvd Wayne NJ 07470-7025

NICCOLINI, DREW GEORGE, gastroenterologist; b. Rockville Center, N.Y., July 27, 1945; s. George D. and Elaine A. (Augsbury) N.; m. Martha Dodge, Jan. 3, 1971; children: Alyssa, Rachael, Lesley, Matthew, Adam. BA, Johns Hopkins U., 1967; MD, Tufts U., 1971. Diplomate Am. Bd. Internal Medicine, Am. Bd. Gastroenterology. Intern St. Elizabeth Hosp., Boston, 1971-72, resident, 1972-74, gastrointestinal fellow, 1974-75; gastrointestinal fellow Faulkner Hosp., Boston, 1975-76; clinician Pentucket Med. Assocs., Haverhill, Mass., 1976—; staff physician Hale Hosp., Haverhill, 1976—, Lawrence (Mass.) Gen. Hosp., 1976—; cons. Holy Family Hosp., Methuen, Mass., 1976—; chief medicine Hale Hosp., haverhill, Mass., 1987-88. Capt. U.S. Army, 1971-77. Fellow Am. Coll. Gastroenterology; mem. ACP, AMA, New Eng. Endoscopy Soc. (bd. dirs. 1997—), Am. Soc. Gastroent. Endoscopy, Alpha Omega Alpha. Avocations: skiing, tennis. Address: One Parkway Haverhill MA 01830

NICE, CARTER, conductor, music director; b. Jacksonville, Fla., Apr. 5, 1940; s. Clarence Carter and Elizabeth Jane (Hintermister) N.; m. Jennifer Charlotte Smith, Apr. 4, 1983; children: Danielle, Christian, Olivia. MusB, Eastman Sch. Music, 1962; MusM, Manhattan Sch. Music., 1964. Asst. condr., concert master New Orleans Philharm., 1967-79; condr., music dir. Sacramento Symphony, 1979-92; music dir., conductor Bear Valley Music Fest., 1985—. Office: 7729 Rio Barco Way Sacramento CA 95831-4458

NICE, CHARLES MONROE, JR., physician, educator; b. Parsons, Kans., Dec. 21, 1919; s. Charles Monroe and Margaret (McClenahan) N.; m. Mary Ellen Cranmer, Dec. 21, 1940; children: Norma Jane Nice Murphy, Pamela, Deborah, Julianne, Charles Monroe III, Thomas, Mary Ellen, Rebecca. AB, U. Kans., MD, 1943; MSc in Medicine, U. Colo., 1948; PhD, U. Minn., 1956. Intern Grasslands Hosp., 1943-44; resident in radiology U. Minn. Hosp., 1948-50; mem. faculty U. Minn. Hosp., Mpls., 1951-58; prof. radiology Tulane U. Sch. Medicine, New Orlens, 1958—; chmn. dept. Tulane U. Sch. Medicine, 1960-85; mem. staff Charity Hosp., New Orleans, 1958—; mem. tng. com.investigative radiology NIH, 1967-69, mem. subcom. Sickle Cell, heart, lung, blood com., 1982-83; mem. com. on radiology NRC, 1965-67; chmn. tng. adv. com. Bur. Radiol. Health, 1970-72; guest lectr. Congress of Radiology, Japan, Colombian Radiol. Soc.; U.S. counselor Inter Am. Coll. Radiology, 1985-90. Author: Roentgen Diagnosis of Abdominal Tumors in Childhood, 1957, Clinical Roentgenology of Collagen Disease, 1966, Differential Diagnosis of Cardiovascular Disease by X-ray, 1966, Cardiovascular Roentgenology; a validated program, 1967, Cerebral Computed Tomography; contbr. articles to profl. jours. Served with AUS, 1944-46, PTO. Fellow Am. Coll. Chest Physicians (bd. gov's 1975-81), Am. Coll. Radiologists. Home: 508 Millaudon St New Orleans LA 70118-3805 Office: 1415 Tulane Ave New Orleans LA 70112-2605

NICELY, CONSTANCE MARIE, paralegal, physician recruiter, medical consultant; b. St. Louis, Sept. 30, 1955; d. Austin and Gertrude Carol (Hogenmiller) N. AA, St. Louis Community Coll., 1989; BA in Polit. Sci., Webster U., St. Louis, 1991. Cert. paralegal; lic. cosmetologist. Cosmetologist Headquarters, Ltd., St. Louis, 1974-75, Eastside/Westside, St. Louis, 1975-79, Joseph Kemble's, Houston, 1980-84, Bushwackers, Houston, 1979-80, Ta Da Hair Salon, St. Louis, 1984—; paralegal Legal Assistance of St. Louis, 1990-91, Snyder, Weir, Shaller, Bachman, St. Louis, 1991, Dubail Judge, P.C., St. Louis, 1992-93, Brown & Crouppen, P.C., 1992-93, Rosen Law Firm, 1993; fin. planner Mut. of N.Y., Clayton, Mo., 1993-94, Mass. Mut., Chesterfield, Mo., 1995-96; physician recruiter Physician Opportunities Network, Inc., Wildwood, Mo., 1996—. Mem. NAFE, Assn. Trial Lawyers Am., Gateway Paralegal Assn. (dir. bylaws and elections 1991—), NOW, Nat. Abortion Rights Action League, Ct. Appointed Advocate for Abused and Neglected Children. Democrat. Avocations: singing, ballet, theatre, dance. Home and Office: Physician Opportunities 4501 Fox Creek Ln Wildwood MO 63069-1465

NICELY, OLZA M. (TONY), insurance company executive. Pres., CEO GEICO Corp., Washington. Office: GEICO 5260 Western Ave Washington DC 20076-0001

NICELY, ROBERT FRANCIS, JR., education educator, administrator; b. Greensburg, Pa., Jan. 10, 1940; s. Robert Francis and Jean Isabelle (Baird) N.; m. Donna Comnale, Dec. 29, 1962; children: Lisa Ann, Scott Alan. BS, Pa. State U., 1961; MEd, Indiana U. of Pa., 1965; PhD, U. Pitts., 1970. Cert. tchr. math. and sci., Pa. Tchr. math. and chemistry Norwin and Gateway Schs., 1961-67; instructional cons. Pitts. Sch. Dist., 1967-68; lectr., asst. prof., rsch. assoc. U. Pitts., 1968-72; asst. prof. edn. Pa. State U., University Park, 1972-76, assoc. prof., 1976-86, prof., 1986—, also asst. dean, 1987-90, acting dean, 1989, assoc. dean edn., 1990—. Contbr. articles to profl. jours.; speaker in field. Mem. ASCD (bd. dirs. 1981-85, 95-98, chair nominating com. 1986-87, chair conf. com. 1990, assoc. editor, co-editor, mem. editorial bd. Jour. Curriculum and Supervision 1985-92, Outstanding Affiliate Newsletter and Jour. awards 1993, 94, 96), Pa. ASCD (pres. 1982-84, exec. bd. 1978—, editor PASCD Update and Pa. Ednl. Leadership, Outstanding Rsch. and Publ. award 1985, Disting. Svc. award 1986, Spl. Leadership award 1990), Cen. Pa. ASCD, Coun. Profs. Instructional Supervision, Nat. Council Tchrs. Math. (chair instrnl. issues adv. com. 1992-94), Pa. Council Tchrs. Math. (pres. 1988-90, Outstanding Leadership and Service award 1983, Outstanding Contbns. to Math. Edn. award 1991, co-editor 4 PCTM Yearbooks), Pa. Edn. Rsch. Assn. (pres. 1987-88, 94-95, editor Pera-Scope 1985-95), Phi Delta Kappa (pres. Pa. State chpt. 1984-85). Avocations: aerobic conditioning, golf, landscape design and construction, genealogy. Home: 109 Cherry Ridge Rd State College PA 16803-3309 Office: Pa State U 277 Chambers Bldg University Park PA 16802-3206

NICHOL, HENRY FERRIS, former government official, environment consultant; b. Charleston, S.C., Jan. 21, 1911; s. A. Ferris and Ella (Humphrey) N.; m. Elizabeth B. Holmes, Apr. 15, 1944; children: Susan (Mrs. William C. Thompson), Elizabeth H. Nicol, David A., Peter B. AB, Davidson Coll., 1933; postgrad., Georgetown U. Law Sch., 1936-37. Clk. HOLC, 1934-37; adminstrv. asst. FSA, 1937-46; fgn. affairs specialist Dept. State, 1946-63, fgn. service officer, 1955-63; conf. attache Geneva, Switzerland, 1952-58; consul Liverpool, Eng., 1958-63; acting prin. officer, 1958-59; sec. U.S. delegations to numerous confs.; adviser U.S. delegations, exec. com. Internat. Refugee Fund, Geneva, 1956-57; asst. dir., asst. to adminstr. Rural Community Devel. Service, U.S. Dept. Agr., 1963-66; staff rep. to Pres.'s Recreation Adv. Council, 1963-66, vice chmn. staff, 1964-66; mem. staff Pres.'s Council on Recreation and Natural Beauty, 1966-69; asst. to asso. adminstr. Soil Conservation Service, 1966-70; environ. cons., 1970—; Liaison officer Dept. Agr. to White House Conf. Natural Beauty, 1965; sr. warden Am. Ch., Geneva, Switzerland; Eastern rep. Nat. Outdoor Leadership Sch. Chmn. Montgomery County Citizens Adv. Com. on Bikeways and Trails; chmn. Potomac Com. Bikeways and Trails; trustee Potomac Conservation Found., Wilderness Edn. Assn.; v.p. Potomac Appalachian Trail Club; founder Potomac Clean and Green. Served to comdr. USNR, 1942-45. Recipient Pres. Theodore Roosevelt Conservation award Pres. of U.S., 1990, Community Svc. award Potomac Almanac, 1990; named Outstanding Citizen of Yr. Potomac C. of C., 1976. Mem. Explorers Club, Diplomatic and Consular Officers Ret., Am. Fgn. Svc. Assn., Phi Beta Kappa. Presbyterian. Home: Plantation Village 7809 Blue Heron Dr Villa 2 Wilmington NC 28405

NICHOL, NORMAN J., manufacturing executive; b. East Cleveland, Ohio, Feb. 12, 1944; s. Norman George and Irene Josephine (Peters) N.; m. Janice E. Nichol, Oct. 19, 1968; children: Gerard, Katherine. B.B.A., Kent State U. Mktg. trainee A.B. Dick Co., Chgo., 1968, sales rep., supr.-spl. markets mgr., 1971-75, br. mgr. Indpls. and Chgo., 1975-80, dir.-gen. mgr. internat., 1980-82, pres., 1982—; pres. Rycoline Products Co., 1985—, Sun Graphic Inc., Robersol Inc. Served with U.S. Army, 1968-70. Home: 1021 Dover Ct Libertyville IL 60048-3509 Office: Rycoline Products Inc 5540 N Northwest Hwy Chicago IL 60630-1116

NICHOLAS (RICHARD G. SMISKO), bishop; b. Perth Amboy, N.J., Feb. 23, 1936; s. Andrew and Anna (Totin) S. Grad., Christ the Saviour Sem., Johnstown, Pa., 1959; student, Patriarchal Theol. Acad., Istanbul, Turkey; BA, U. Youngstown, 1961; BTh, U. Pitts. Ordained priest Am. Carpatho-Russian Orthodox Greek Cath. Diocese, 1959. Pastor Sts. Peter and Paul Ch., Windber, 1959-62; prefect of discipline, tchr. Christ the Saviour Sem., Johnstown, 1963-65; pastor Sts. Peter and Paul Ch., Homer City, 1965-71, St. Michael's Ch., Clymer, 1971-72, St. Nicholas Ch., N.Y.C., 1972-78; elevated to archimandrite Am. Carpatho-Russian Orthodox Greek Cath. Diocese, 1976; abbot Monastery of Annunciation, Tuxedo Park, N.Y., 1978-82; elected titular bishop of Amissos, aux. bishop Ukrainian Orthodox Diocese of Ecumenical Patriarchate, 1983; consecrated bishop Am. Carpatho-Russian Orthodox Greek Cath. Diocese, 1985, bishop, 1985—; asst. Christ the Saviour Cathedral, 1963-65; chmn. XIV Diocesan Coun., New Brunswick, N.J., 1985, XV Diocesan Coun., Pitts., 1991. Office: 312 Garfield St Johnstown PA 15906-2122

NICHOLAS, ARTHUR SOTERIOS, manufacturing company executive; b. Grand Rapids, Mich., Mar. 6, 1930; s. Samuel D. and Penelope A. (Kalapodes) N.; m. Bessie Zazanis, Aug. 25, 1957; children: Niki Stephanie, Arthur S., Thomas. B.S. in Chem. Engring, U. Mich., 1953; B.A. in Indsl. Mgmt, Wayne State U., 1957. Registered profl. engr., Mich. Project engr. B.F. Goodrich Co., 1953-54; plant mgr. Cadillac Plastics and Chem. Co., 1954-69; pres., chief exec. officer Leon Chem. and Plastics, Inc., Grand Rapids, 1960-69; with U.S. Industries, Inc., 1969-73, pres., chief operating officer, 1973; now pres. The Antech Group; bd. dirs. ERO Industries, Inc. Judge Jr. Achievement, Chgo. Served with USNR, 1948-49. Recipient Distinguished Alumni award Grand Rapids Jr. Coll., 1970. Mem. Young Pres. Orgn., Soc. Plastic Engrs., Mich. Acad. Sci., Arts and Letters, Chgo. Coun. on Fgn. Rels., Pres.' Assn. Mem. Greek Orthodox Ch. Clubs: Chgo. Athletic Assn. (Chgo.), Executives (Chgo.). Patentee in field. Home: 655 Oak Rd Barrington IL 60010-3135 Office: 135 S La Salle St Ste 1140 Chicago IL 60603-4501

NICHOLAS, DAVID ROBERT, minister, college president; b. L.A., May 10, 1941; s. Robert Grant and Pearl Elizabeth (Pickard) N.; m. Donna Lynn Roberts, June 28, 1969; children: Joy Lynn, Faith Elizabeth. AB, Azusa Pacific U., 1963; MS, U. So. Calif., 1967; MDiv., L.A. Bapt. Theol. Sem., 1966; ThM, Talbot Theol. Sem., 1971; ThD, Grace Theol. Seminary, 1982. Ordained to ministry Gen. Assn. Regular Bapt. Chs., 1970. Dir. admissions, mem. faculty L.A. Bapt. Coll., Newhall, Calif., 1966-71; dean, pres. Van Nuys (Calif.) Christian Coll., 1972-76; pastor Tri-Lakes Bapt. Ch., Columbia City, Ind., 1977-78; acad. dean, assoc. prof. Southwestern Coll., Phoenix, 1978-80; sr. pastor, acad. supt. Grace Bapt. Ch., Yuba City, 1980-82; sr. pastor Placerita Bapt. Ch., Newhall, 1982-84; pres., prof. theology Shasta Bible Coll., Redding, Calif., 1985—; chmn. Greater Redding Area Christian Edn. Conv., 1988—; mem. accreditation commn. Transnat. Assn. Christian Colls. and Schs., 1994—; trustee Regular Bapt. Conf. So. Calif., 1983-85, pres., 1963-65; dir. Bapt. Youth Assn., So. Calif., 1969-71. Author: Foundations of Biblical Inerrancy, 1978, What's A Woman to Do ... In the Church?, 1979, Church Discipline: Option or Obligation, 1991; contbr. articles to religious jours.; recordings include Trombone Testimonies, 1990; Bible tchr. broadcast program Truth for Today, 1988—, Bible Answer Man, 1978-80. Trustee Christian Heritage Coll., El Cajon, Calif., 1981-85; mem. steering com. Calif. Activists Network, Los Altos, Calif., 1991; del. Conf. on the Preservation of the Family, 1991; gov. Am. Coalition for Trad. Values, Washington, 1984; chaplain Los Angeles County Bd. Suprs., 1984. Recipient Svc. award Am. Legion, 1955. Mem. Evang. Theol. Soc., Creation Rsch. Soc., Shasta County Evang. Ministerial Assn. (pres. 1992-95), Kappa Tau Epsilon. Republican. Home: 8264 Taylor Ln Redding CA 96001-9530 Office: Shasta Bible Coll 2980 Hartnell Ave Redding CA 96002-2312

NICHOLAS, FREDERICK M., lawyer; b. N.Y.C., May 30, 1920; s. Benjamin L. and Rose F. (Nechols) N.; m. Eleanore Berman, Sept. 2, 1951 (div. 1963); children: Deborah, Jan, Tony; m. Joan Fields, Jan. 2, 1983. AB, U. So. Calif., 1947; postgrad., U. Chgo., 1949-50; JD, U. So. Calif., 1952. Bar: Calif. 1952, U.S. Dist. Ct. Calif. 1952, U.S. Ct. Appeals (9th cir.) 1952. Assoc. Loeb & Loeb, L.A., 1952-56; ptnr. Swerdlow, Glikbarg & Nicholas, Beverly Hills, Calif., 1956-62; pvt. practice Beverly Hills, 1962-80; pres., atty. Hapsmith Co., Beverly Hills, 1980—; bd. dirs. Malibu Grand Prix, L.A., 1982-90; gen. counsel Beverly Hills Realty Bd., 1971-79; founder, pres. Pub. Counsel, L.A., 1970-73. Author: Commercial Real Property Lease Practice, 1976. Chmn. Mus. Contemporary Art, L.A., 1987-93, chmn. com. Walt Disney Concert Hall, L.A., 1987-95; trustee Music Ctr. L.A. County, 1987-95, L.A. Philharm. Assn., 1987-95; chmn. Calif. Pub. Broadcasting Commn., Sacramento, 1972-78; pres. Maple Ctr., 1977-79. Recipient Citizen of Yr. award Beverly Hills Bd. Realtors, 1978, Man of Yr. award Maple Ctr., 1980, Pub. Svc. award Coro Found., 1988, The Medici award L.A. C. of C., 1990, Founders award Pub. Counsel, 1990, Trustees award Calif. Inst. Arts, 1993, City of Angels award L.A. Ctrl. Bus. Assn.; named Outstanding Founder in Philanthropy, Nat. Philanthropy Day Com., 1990. Mem. Beverly Hills Bar Assn. (bd. govs. 1970-76, Disting. Svc. award 1974, 81, Exceptional Svc. award 1986), Beverly Hills C. of C. (Man of Yr. 1983). Home: 1011 Cove Way Beverly Hills CA 90210-2818 Office: Hapsmith Co 9300 Wilshire Blvd Beverly Hills CA 90212

NICHOLAS, LYNN HOLMAN, writer; b. New London, Conn., Nov. 11, 1939; d. William Grizzard Holman and Carol (Ackiss) Wakelin; m. Robert Carter Nicholas III, Dec. 20, 1965; children: William C., R. Carter, Philip H. Student, Radcliffe Coll., 1957-59; diploma, U. Madrid, 1960; BA, Oxford (Eng.) U., 1964. Author: The Rape of Europa, 1994 (Nat. Book Critics Circle award 1995).

NICHOLAS, PETER, medical educator; b. Little Falls, N.Y., June 5, 1942; s. Peter Sr. and Helen K. N.; m. Joan Marie Popadak, 1970. BS magna cum laude, Union Coll., 1964; MD, Yale U., 1968. Intern Mt. Sinai Hosp., N.Y.C., 1968-69, resident, 1969-70, 70-71, chief resident, 1971-72; instr. assoc., asst. prof. medicine, assoc. prof. CCNY, Mt. Sinai Sch. Medicine, 1971—; attending physician City Hosp. Ctr. Mt. Sinai Svcs., 1987—; assoc. dean; Lic. physician N.Y., 1969. Contbr. articles to profl. jours. Fellow Am. Coll. Physicians, N.Y. Acad. Medicine; mem. Am. Soc. Microbiology, AMA, Assn. Asm. Med. Colls., Soc. Hosp. Epidemiologists Am., N.Y. Heart Assn., N.Y. Sco. Tropical Medicine, Soc. Health and Human Values, Assn. Practitioners in Infection Control.

NICHOLAS, RALPH WALLACE, anthropologist, educator; b. Dallas, Nov. 28, 1934; s. Ralph Wendell and Ruth Elizabeth (Oury) N.; m. Marta Ruth Weinstock, June 13, 1963. BA, Wayne U., 1957; MA, U. Chgo., 1958, PhD, 1962. From asst. prof. to prof. Mich. State U., East Lansing, 1964-71; prof. anthropology U. Chgo., 1971—, chmn. dept., 1981-82, dep. provost, 1982-87, dean of coll., 1987-92, dir. Ctr. Internat. Studies, 1984-95, William Rainey Harper prof. of Anthropology and Social Scis., 1992—; pres. Internat. House of Chgo., 1993—; cons. Ford Found., Dhaka, Bangladesh, 1973. Author: (with others) Kinship Bengali Culture, 1977; editor: Jour. Asian Studies, 1975-78. V.p. Am. Inst. Indian Studies, 1974-76, treas., 1993—; trustee Bangladesh Found. Ford Found. fgn. area tng. fellow, India, 1960-61; Sch. Oriental and African Studies research fellow, London, 1962-63; sr. Fulbright fellow, West Bengal, India, 1968-69. Fellow AAAS, Am. Anthrop. Assn., Royal Anthrop. Inst. (Eng.); mem. Assn. Asian Studies, India League of Am. Found. (trustee). Home and Office: Internat House of Chicago 1414 E 59th St Chicago IL 60637-2940

NICHOLAS, ROBERT LEON, foreign language educator; b. Lebanon, Oreg., Dec. 10, 1937; s. Elmer Leon Nicholas and Luella Lillian (Haberling) Haffner; m. Carole Anne Roberts, June 11, 1967; children: Scott Alan, Paul Elliot. BA, U. Oreg., 1959, MA, 1963, PhD, 1967. Instr. U. Wis., Madison, 1965-67, asst. prof., 1967-71, assoc. prof., 1971-76, prof., 1976-96; prof. emeritus, 1996—; chair dept. Spanish and Portuguese U. Wis., Madison, 1979-82, 93-96. Author: (textbooks) En camino, 1977, 81, 85, 89, Adelante, 1977, 81, 85, Motivos de conversación, 1984, 88, 92, 97, Mundo Unido: Lectura y Escritura, 1995, and several books of literary criticism written in Spanish. Mem. Am. Assn. Tchrs. Spanish and Portuguese, Kiwanis Club (pres. 1989). Democrat. Unitarian. Avocations: gardening, singing, piano and guitar, cycling, traveling. Home: 2126 Chadbourne Ave Madison WI 53705-3928

NICHOLAS, THOMAS ANDREW, artist; b. Middletown, Conn., Sept. 26, 1934; s. Michael and Lena (Sequenzia) N.; m. Gloria R. Spencer, Oct. 11, 1958; 1 child, Thomas Michael. Student of Ernst Lohrmann, 1949-53; scholarship student, Sch. Visual Arts, N.Y.C., 1953-55. Instr. Famous Artists Schs., Inc., Westport, Conn., 1958-60; instr. painting, Rockport, Mass., 1963-66. Commd. by Franklin Mint Gallery Am. Art to produce lithographs of Am. coastline, 1977; one-man shows include Grand Cen. Galleries, N.Y.C., 1962, 64, 66, 68, 70, 78, I.F.A. Galleries, Washington, 1964-92, A. Huney Gallery, San Diego, 1980, 82;, Carolyn Hill Gallery, Soho, N.Y.C., 1988-89, 3 person show, 1992; represented in permanent collections Butler Inst. Am. Art, Youngstown, Ohio, Ga. Mus., Athens, New Britain (Conn.) Art Mus., U. Utah, Adelphi U., Greenshields Mus., Montreal, Can., Farnsworth Mus., Rockland, Maine, Springfield (Mo.) Art Mus., Ranger Collection at NAD (2 works), Peabody Mus., Salem, Mass.; author articles; recipient numerous awards 1957—, including, Emile Lowe award for watercolor Am. Watercolor Soc. 1961, watercolor prize 1964, Gold medal honor 1969, Clare Stout award 1971, Mary S. Litt award 1972, medal honor for watercolor Knickerbocker Artists 1962, Purchase award watercolor Butler Inst. Am. Art 1962, Henry Ward Ranger Fund purchase watercolor NAD 1962, 71, Obrig prize watercolor 1964, 66, 79, 87, gold medal honor watercolor Allied Artists Am. 1962, Grumbacher prize 1978, Today Mag. Art medal 1970, 74, gold medal honor watercolor Am. Artists Profl. League 1964, best landscape award 1974, gold medal 1978, Edwin S. Webster award honor watercolor Boston Soc. Watercolor 1964, gold medal honor watercolor Hudson Valley Art Assn. 1964, DuMond Meml. award 1971, Isabel Stinschneider Meml. award 1972, Herman Wick Meml. award Salmagundi Club, N.Y.C. 1966, 2d prize 1966, June Justin J. Impasto award 1972, Arthur T. Hill prize 1973, Arthur T. Hill Meml. prize 1975, Louis Z. Seley prize 1978, Gwynne Lennon prize 1979, Gold medal honor oil Rockport Art Assn. 1966, 69, 76, 86, 96, cash award Wichita Centennial Watercolor 1970, Providence Art Club prize 1972, gold medal Franklin Mint Competition 1974, Gold medal Honor Acad. Assn. 1976, others. Elizabeth Greenshields grantee, 1961, 62; recipient Gold medal of Honor New Eng. Watercolor Soc., Boston, 1985, Acad. Artists Assn., 1985; named Knickerbocker Honoree Artist of Yr., 1989; recipient Grumbacher award watercolor, Acad. Artists Assn., 1990, Grumbacher Gold medal Gouache New Eng. Watercolor Soc., 1992, Gouache Transparent Watercolor, 1995. Mem. NAD (cert. merit watercolor 1992), Am. Watercolor Soc. (ea. v.p. 1994—, Dolphin fellow), Boston Watercolor Soc., Conn. Watercolor Socs., Allied Artists Am., Knickerbocker Artists (dir.'s prize 1971, Gold medal 1989), Boston Guild Artists (Grumbacher Gold medallion award watercolor 1988, No. Shore Arts Assn. award oil 1991), Rockport Art Assn. (Silver medal 1988, 94, Darrand award oil 1992, Cirino award 1st prize Gouache 1992, Clark Polupar award Gouache 1992, Cooley award graphics 1995, Clark Popular award Gouache 1995, Cirino award Gouache 1995, Davis Meml. award watercolor 1996, Mills Meml. award Gouache 1996), Hudson Valley Artists (Gold medal 1974, 85, 94, Huntington Meml. award oil 1995, Bohnert Meml. award oil 1996). Home: 7 Wildon Hts Rockport MA 01966-2007 Office: Tom Nicholas Gallery 71 Main St Rockport MA 01966-1512 *I have been fortunate to have been encouraged by my family at an early age and have a number of people to thank for their support, especially my wife. I feel artists must never compromise their ideals and principles, no matter how high their standards. Originality and professional ethics with one's work make goals achieved meaningful. On the one hand, an artist should inwardly feel that there is little he can't accomplish, and yet he must learn to work within his realized limitations.*

NICHOLAS, THOMAS PETER, library administrator, community television consultant, producer; b. Laramie, Wyo., Dec. 6, 1948; s. Thomas Lloyd Nicholas and Frances (Collins) Chambers; m. Tanya Michelle Villont; 1 child, Ja'el Michelle. AA in Fine Arts, Cabrillo Coll., 1970; BA in English, U. Colo., 1972; MS in Librarianship and Info. Sci., U. Denver, 1982. Real estate salesperson Sun Country, Lakewood, Colo., 1972-74; v.p. Nicholas Properties, Denver, 1971-77; libr. City of Aurora, Colo., 1975-80, system support mgr., 1981-83, dir. libr. and TV svcs., 1984—; dir. Libr., Recreation & TV Svcs. City of Aurora, 1995—; pres. bd. Irving Libr. Network Inc., Denver, 1985—; adv. CL System Inc., Boston, 1985—; acting pers. dir. City of Aurora; Denver Regional Coun. of Govt. award for Cmty. Svc. and Govt. Coop., 1995. Exec. producer TV programs: Election Night 85 (Franny award 1986), Miss Plumjoy's Place, 1988 (Starwards 1988), Aurora's Can't Afford Not To, 1988 (Starwards 1988). Mem. exec. bd., chmn. Arapahoe Pub. Access to Librs., 1984-85; site coordinator Am. Cancer Soc., Aurora, 1988; adv. Youth at Risk, Aurora, 1989; bd. dirs. Cen. Colo. Libr. System, Lakewood, 1985-87; mem. exec. bd. Colo. Libr. Legis. Com., Denver, 1988—; pres. Greater Metro Cable Consortium, 1992—; acting dep. city mgr. City of Aurora, 1993—. Mem. ALA, Colo. Libr. Assn. (advisor 1982-83, Programming award 1982, 1st Colo. Childrens Program award 1983, 88), Nat. Assn. Telecommunications Officers and Advisors (regional pres. 1983-84, T.V. Program award 1986), Rotary (program chmn. 1987-88), Eastgate Lions Club (pres. 1989-90). Democrat. Greek Orthodox. Avocations: fine art, poetry, automobile restoration, martial arts (Black Belt). Office: Aurora Pub Libr 14949 E Alameda Dr Aurora CO 80012-1544*

NICHOLAS, WILLIAM RICHARD, lawyer; b. Pontiac, Mich., June 19, 1934; s. Reginald and Edna Irene (Bartlett) N.; m. Diana Lee Johnson, Aug. 20, 1960; children: Susan Lee, William Richard Jr. BS in Bus., U. Idaho, 1956; JD, U. Mich., 1962. Bar: 1963. Ptnr. Latham & Watkins, Los Angeles, 1962—. Contbr. numerous articles on taxation. Served to lt. (j.g.) USN, 1956-59. Mem. Calif. Bar Assn., Los Angeles County Bar Assn., Am. Coll. Tax Counsel. Home: 1808 Old Ranch Rd Los Angeles CA 90049-2207 Office: Latham & Watkins 633 W 5th St Ste 4000 Los Angeles CA 90071-2005

NICHOLLS, BERNARD IRVINE, hockey player; b. Haliburton, Ont., Can., June 24, 1961. Hockey player L.A. Nat. Hockey League, 1982-90, hockey player N.Y. Rangers, 1990-92, hockey player Edmonton, 1992-93, hockey player N.J., 1993-94, hockey player Chgo. Blackhawks, 1994-96, hockey player San Jose (Calif.) Sharks, 1996—; played in All-Star Game, 1984, 89, 90. Office: San Jose Sharks 525 W Santa Clara St San Jose CA 95113-1520

NICHOLLS, DAVID G., editor, scholar, educator; b. Indpls., Oct. 6, 1965; s. Thomas G. and Natalie A. (Keinonen) N. AB, Bowdoin Coll., 1988; MA, U. Chgo., 1989, PhD, 1995. Nonfiction editor Chgo. Rev., 1989-91, editor, 1991-96; Rockefeller resident postdoctoral fellow Ctr. for Afroamerican and African Studies, U. Mich., Ann Arbor, 1996-97; lectr. U. Chgo., 1992, 95; lectr. Loyola U., 1994. Co-editor: The Penguin New Writing in India, 1994. Javits fellow U.S. Dept. Edn., 1989-93, Mellon fellow U. Chgo., 1993-94; Witter Bynner Found. grantee, 1991; Century scholar, 1988-92, Webb and Mitchell scholar, 1988-95, Fulbright Sr. scholar, 1996—. Mem. MLA, Am. Studies Assn.

NICHOLLS, RICHARD ALLEN, middle school social studies educator; b. Chgo., Sept. 1, 1944; s. Harry Allen and Rita Mae (O'Connell) N.; m. Linda Lee Soderberg, Mar. 27, 1969 (div. 1979). AA, Lincoln Coll., 1964; BA, MacMurray Coll., 1966; postgrad., Loyola U., 1967; MA, Nat. Lewis U., 1991. Cert. volleyball coach. 6th grade tchr. Chgo. Pub. Schs., 1966-67; 7th & 8th grades tchr. Palos Sch. Dist. 118, Palos Park, Ill., 1967—; sponsor student govt. Palos Sch. Dist. 118, 1971-73, sponsor pompon squad, 1971-73, mem. curriculum devel. com., 1970-72; writer (with others) curriculum for devel. of thematic units for transition of Palos South Jr. H.S. to Palos Mid. Sch., summer 1995; volleyball coach Palos South Jr. H.S. (now Palos South Mid. Sch.), 1977-90, Victor J. Andrew H.S., 1981-84, Carl Sandburg H.S., 1985-91; mem. Ill. Goals Assessment Program com. for sch. stds., 1992-93. Mem. NEA, Ill. Edn. Assn., U.S. Volleyball Assn., Palos Edn. Assn., Am. Athletic Union (volleyball coach, nat. champions 1981, 82, finalists 1984, 85, 87 jr. Olympics Nat. Tournament, 5th pl. jr. Nats., 1994) Am. Legion (Citizenship award 1964), Phi Theta Kappa. Avocations: coaching volleyball, sponsoring school trips, personal training for physical fitness. Office: Palos Sch Dist 118 8800 W 119th St Palos Park IL 60464-1004

NICHOLLS, RICHARD H., lawyer; b. Toronto, Ont., Can., Oct. 27, 1938; s. Richard S. and Roberta T.; m. Judy Carter, Apr. 15, 1963; children: Christopher T., Jamie C.; m. Anne Delaney, June 10, 1978. BA cum laude, Amherst Coll., 1960; LLB, Stamford U., 1963; LLM, NYU, 1964. Bar: Calif. 1964, N.Y. 1965, D.C. Assoc. Mudge Rose Guthrie, Alexander & Ferdon and predecessor, N.Y.C., 1964-70, ptnr., 1971-94; of counsel Orrick, Herrington & Sutcliffe, N.Y., 1995—. Mem. ABA, N.Y. State Bar Assn., Nat. Assn. Bond Lawyers, Stamford Yacht Club. Home: 159 Ocean Dr W Stamford CT 06902-8004 Office: Orrick Herrington & Sutcliffe 666 5th Ave New York NY 10103-0001

NICHOLLS, THOMAS MAURICE, business owner; b. Hancock, Mich., June 22, 1960; s. David and Ericka (Weiss) N.; m. Mary Ann Erspamer, Apr. 30, 1983; 1 child, Michael. Owner Northland Svcs., Hurley, Wis., 1983—; gen. mgr. K & L Enterprises, Marquette, Mich., 1985-91; exec. mgr. S & S Inc., Sun Prairie, Wis., 1991-94; owner Northern Venture, Hurley, Wis., 1992—. Mem. Just Say No, Ironwood, Mich., 1992. With USN, 1979-83. Mem. Jaycees (v.p. 1986, Presdl. award of Honor 1986, Jaycee of Yr., Mich. 1986). Avocations: photography, woodworking, hunting. Home and Office: Northern Venture 502 Poplar St Hurley WI 54534-1169

NICHOLS, ALAN, newspaper publishing executive. CFO San Francisco Chronicle, 1993—. Office: San Francisco Chronicle 901 Mission St San Francisco CA 94103-2905*

NICHOLS, ALBERT L., economics consultant; b. Poughkeepsie, N.Y., Feb. 13, 1951; s. Albert and Margaret (Schaefer) N.; m. Eve Kaufman, June 16, 1973; children: Matthew, Elizabeth. AB, Stanford U., 1973; M of Pub. Policy, Harvard U., 1975, PhD, 1981. Assoc. prof. Harvard U., Cambridge, Mass., 1977-83, 85-88, dir. adminstrv. planning, 1988-89; dir. econ. analysis EPA, Washington, 1983-85; v.p. Nat. Econ. Rsch. Assocs., Cambridge, 1989—; cons. various corps., 1976-89. Author: Targeting Economic Incentives for Environmental Protection, 1984; contbr. numerous articles to profl. jours. Nat. Merit scholar, 1969. Mem. Am. Econ. Assn., Soc. for Risk Analysis, Assn. Environ. and Resource Economists, Phi Beta Kappa. Avocation: woodworking. Home: 14 Baskin Rd Lexington MA 02173-6929 Office: Nat Econ Rsch Assocs 1 Main St Cambridge MA 02142-1531

NICHOLS, BUFORD LEE, JR., physiologist; b. Ft. Worth, Dec. 12, 1931; married; 3 children. BA, Baylor U., 1955, MS, 1958; MD, Yale U., 1960. Diplomate Am. Bd. Pediatrics, Am. Bd. Nutrition. Instr. pediatrics Baylor U. Coll. Medicine, Houston, 1956-57, instr. physiology and pediatrics, 1964-66, from asst. prof. to assoc. prof. pediatrics, 1966-67, instr. physiology, 1967-74, chief sect. nutrition and gastroenterology, dept. Pediatrics, 1970-78, assoc. prof. community medicine, 1975—, prof. physiology and pediatrics, 1977—, head sect. nutrition and physiology, 1979—; intern in pediatrics Yale-New Haven Med. Ctr., 1960-61, chief resident in pediatrics, 1963-64; resident in pediatrics Johns Hopkins Hosp., 1961-63; instr. pediatrics Yale U. Sch. Medicine, 1963-64; dir. USDA Children's Nutritional Rsch. Ctr., Houston, 1979—. Recipient award Bristol-Myers, 1984. Mem. Am. Acad. Pediatrics, Am. Soc. Clin. Nutrition, Am. Coll. Nutrition (v.p. 1975-76, pres. 1977-79). Achievements include research in environmental effects upon growth and development in the infant especially alterations in body composition and muscle physiology in malnutrition, chronic diarrhea and malnutrition. Office: Baylor Coll Medicine Childrens Nutrition Rsch Ctr 1100 Bates Ave Houston TX 77030-2600

NICHOLS, C. WALTER, III, retired trust company executive; b. N.Y.C., Aug. 25, 1937; s. Charles Walter and Marjorie (Jones) N.; B.A., U. Va., 1959; m. Anne Sharp, Aug. 8, 1959 (wid. Nov. 1996); children—Blair, Sandra, Walter, Hope. Vice pres. Citibank, N.Y.C., 1962-78, J.P. Morgan & Co., N.Y.C., 1979-93; 1st v.p. Republic Nat. Bank N.Y., N.Y.C., 1994—. Bd. dirs. Nichols Found., Inc., 1969—; bd. dirs. Greenwich House, 1969-94, pres., 1984-90; bd. dirs. Choate Rosemary Hall, 1972-77, 82-89, Westover Sch., 1979-81, Lower Hudson (N.Y.) chpt. Nature Conservancy, 1978-87, hon. trustee, 1988—, John Jay Homestead, 1980—, Nat. Audubon Soc., 1983-87; mem. adv. bd. N.Y. Zool. Soc. (Bronx Zoo), 1987-94; mem. adv. bd. Caramoor Music Festival, 1994—. Served to 1st lt. U.S. Army, 1960-62. Decorated Army Commendation medal. Mem. Naturist Soc., Nat. Assn. Railroad Passengers (bd. dirs. 1996—), Am. Sunbathing Assn. Clubs: Bedford (N.Y.) Golf and Tennis, Pilgrims of U.S.

NICHOLS, CARL MICHAEL, interactive media executive; b. Springfield, Mass., Sept. 19, 1961. BS, Brown U., 1983; MBA, Harvard U., 1987. Mgr. Aarhus Olrefabrik, Aarhus, Denmark, 1983; project mgr. Booz Allen & Hamilton, San Francisco, 1983-85, 87-91; mgr. AT&T Internat., Morristown, N.J., 1986; v.p. strategic bus. mgmt. Scrivner Inc., Oklahoma City, 1991-94; asst. v.p. Pacific Telesis, San Francisco, 1994-96; v.p., CFO Interactive Minds, San Francisco, 1996—; COO Internat Fin. Network Corp., 1996—; v.p. bus. devel. Net Channel, Inc., 1996—. Editor: Technology in Business, 1983 (award 1984). Cons. Jr. Achievement, Edmond, Okla., 1991-93; vol. Okla. Sch. Sci. and Math., Oklahoma City, 1992-94; bd. dirs. San Francisco Edn. Fund, 1996—. Mem. Sigma Xi. Avocations: tennis, skiing, sailing.

NICHOLS, CARL WHEELER, retired advertising agency executive; b. Ottawa, Kans., Oct. 9, 1923; s. Carl Wheeler and Cora Merle (Hanks) N.; children: Christine, Carl Wheeler, Nancy, Matthew; m. Anna Norris, Apr. 18, 1992. Student, Baker U., 1940-41, U. Mo., 1941-43; B.A., U. Mich., 1944. Research analyst Cunningham & Walsh, Inc. (advt. agy.), N.Y.C., 1946-49; copywriter Cunningham & Walsh, Inc. (advt. agy.), 1949-56, co-creative dir., v.p., 1956-59, dir. account mgmt., 1959-61, pres., 1961-69, chmn., chief exec. officer, 1969-85, chmn. emeritus, 1986. Trustee Ctr. for the Arts, Vero Beach, Fla., 1996. Capt. USMCR, 1943-46, 50-52, Korea. Named to Advt. Hall of Fame, 1986. Mem. N.Y. Advt. Coun. (bd. dirs. 1974-85), Am. Advt. Fedn. (dir. 1972-75, chmn. 1975-76), Advt. Ednl. Found. (bd. dirs., sec., treas. 1983-91), Woodway Country Club, John's Island Club, Sigma Xi. Presbyterian (elder). Home: 241 Island Creek Dr Vero Beach FL 32963-3304

NICHOLS, CAROL D., real estate professional, association executive. BA, U. Pitts., 1964; cert. in advanced mgmt., U. Chgo. From mgmt. trainee to buyer May Dept. Stores Co., Pitts., 1964-70; various mgmt. positions, then mng. dir. mortgage and real estate div. Tchrs. Ins. and Annuity Assn. Am., N.Y.C., 1970—; instr. real estate div. continuing edn. Marymount Manhattan Coll., N.Y.C., 1975-76, Woman's Sch. Adult Edn. Ctr., N.Y.C., 1976-77; v.p. instn. owners div. Real Estate Bd. N.Y., past chmn. fin. com., mem. seminar and gen. meetings coms. Trustee, mem. investment com. Nat. Jewish Ctr. for Immunology and Respiratory Medicine. Recipient Nat. Humanitarian award Nat. Jewish Med. and Rsch. Ctr., Nat. Brotherhood award NCCJ. Mem. Assn. Real Estate Women (past pres.), Urban Land Inst. (trustee, past chmn. urban devel. and mixed use coun.). Home: 165 Winfield St East Norwalk CT 06855-1622 Office: Teachers Ins & Annuity Assn 730 3rd Ave New York NY 10017-3206

NICHOLS, DAVID ARTHUR, mediator, retired state justice; b. Lincolnville, Maine, Aug. 6, 1917; s. George E. and Flora E. (Pillsbury) N. A.B. magna cum laude, Bates Coll., 1942; J.D., U. Mich., 1949. Bar: Maine bar 1949, Mass. bar 1949, U.S. Supreme Ct 1954. Pvt. practice Camden, Maine, 1949-75; justice Maine Superior Ct., 1975-77, Maine Supreme Jud. Ct., 1977-88; mediator, 1988—; Mem. Maine Exec. Council, 1955-57; moderator Lincolnville Town Meeting, 1950-74. Mem. editorial bd. Picton Press, 1989—; contbr. to legal and geneal. publs. Chmn. Maine Republican Com., 1960-64; mem. Rep. Nat. Com., 1960-68; chmn. Maine council Young Reps., 1950-54; New Eng. council Young Reps., 1952-54; trustee, past pres. Penobscot Bay Med. Center. Served with USAAF, 1942-45. Fellow Am. Bar Found., Am. Coll. Trial Lawyers; mem. Am. Law Inst., Camden-Rockport C. of C. (past pres.), Maine Hist. Soc., Camden Hist. Soc. (past pres.), Camden Bus. Men's Assn. (past pres.), ABA (bd. govs. 1960-63, ho. dels. 1957-78), Maine Bar Assn., Am. Judicature Soc. (dir. 1960-64), New Eng. Historic Geneal. Soc. (trustee), Bates Coll. Alumni Assn. (past pres.), Maine Trial Lawyers Assn. (past pres.), Phi Beta Kappa, Delta Sigma Rho. Clubs: Odd Fellows, Rotary (past pres.). Home: PO Box 76 Lincolnville ME 04849-0076

NICHOLS, DAVID EARL, pharmacy educator, researcher, consultant; b. Covington, Ky., Dec. 23, 1944; s. Earl and Edythe Lee (Brooker) N.; m. Kathy J. Nichols; children: Charles D., Daniel P. BS, U. Cin., 1969; PhD, U. Iowa, 1973. Asst. prof. medicinal chemistry Purdue U., West Lafayette, Ind., 1974-79, assoc. prof., 1979-85, prof., 1985—; founder, pres. Heffter Rsch. Inst. Contbr. over 200 articles to sci. jours.; patentee in field. Grantee Nat. Inst. on Drug Abuse, 1978—, NIMH, 1978—. Fellow ACNP, Am. Pharm. Assn., Am. Assn. Pharm. Scientists. Office: Purdue U Sch Pharmacy West Lafayette IN 47907

NICHOLS, DAVID HARRY, gynecologic surgeon, obstetrics and gynecology educator, author; b. Utica, N.Y., July 30, 1925; s. Harry Harrison and Katherine Valentine (Belknap) N.; m. Lorraine Elizabeth Landel, June 23, 1948; children: David L., Laurie L., Nancie L., Daniel A., Julie L. MD, U. Buffalo, 1947; MA (hon.), Brown U., 1982. Diplomate Am. Bd. Ob-Gyn. Intern E.J. Meyer Meml. Hosp., Buffalo, 1947-48; resident in ob-gyn Millard Fillmore Hosp., Buffalo, 1948-51; assoc. cancer rsch. gynecologist Roswell Pk. Meml. Inst., Buffalo, 1953-60; asst. clin. prof. ob-gyn. SUNY, Buffalo, 1958-68, clin. prof., 1968-75, prof., 1975-80; prof. Brown U., Providence, 1980-92, chmn. dept. ob-gyn., 1980-91, dir. Ctr. for Women's Surgery, 1990-91; chief of pelvic reconstructive surgery Mass. Gen. Hosp., Boston, 1991—; pres. Erie County unit Am. Cancer Soc., 1962-68, Buffalo Ob/Gyn. Soc., 1975-76; vis. prof. ob-gyn., reproductive biology Harvard U. Sch. Med., 1991—. Author: Atlas of Gynecological Pathology, 1951, Vaginal Surgery, 1976, 4th edit., 1996; author, editor: (med. monograph) Clinical Problems, Injuries, and Complications of GYN Surgery, 1983, 3d edit., 1995, Ambulatory Gynecology, 1985, 2d edit., 1995, Reoperative Gynecologic Surgery, 1991, Gynecologic and Obstetric Surgery, 1993. Maj. M.C., USAF, 1949-53. Fellow ACS, Am. Coll. Ob-Gyn., Internat. Coll. Surgeons, Boston Obstet. Soc.; mem. Soc. Pelvic Surgeons, Soc. Gynecol. Surgeons (nat. pres. 1984-85), N.E. Obstet. Soc., Boston Obstet. Soc., Am. Gyn. Club (pres. 1993-94), Harvard Club. Republican. Roman Catholic. Avocations: travel, music, literature. Office: Mass Gen Hosp Vincent 1 Boston MA 02114 Address: 101 Prospect St Providence RI 02906-1440

NICHOLS, DAVID L., retail executive; b. Toledo, Sept. 1, 1941; s. Lee Roy and Marianne (smith) N.; children: Fredericka, JoLynn, Jennifer, Laurie, Martha, Meredith; m. Lenore Grotke Nichols, Sept. 15, 1990. BA in Bus., U. Toledo, 1990. With The McAlpin Co., Cin., 1963-76; store mgr. McAlpin's Northgate, Cin., 1976-78; gen. mdse. mgr. Mercantile Stores Co., Inc., N.Y.C., 1978-82, v.p., CFO, treas., 1989-91, exec. v.p., CFO, treas., 1991-92, chmn., CEO, 1992—; pres. Lion Store, Toledo, 1982-89. Active Cin. Bus. Com., 1992. Recipient Green Thumb award Am. Apparel Mfr. Assn., 1993. Avocations: golf, gourmet cooking. Office: Mercantile Stores Co Inc 9450 Seward Rd Fairfield OH 45014-5412*

NICHOLS, DONALD ARTHUR, economist, educator; b. Madison, Conn., Dec. 20, 1940; s. Edward Charles and Ruth (Nilson) N.; m. Linda Powley, Aug. 19, 1962 (dec. Oct. 1982); children: Charles Spencer, Elizabeth Clarke.; m. Barbara Jakubowski Noel, May 22, 1983. B.A., Yale U., 1962, M.A., 1963, Ph.D., 1968. Mem. faculty dept. econs. U. Wis., Madison, 1966—, prof., 1977—, chmn. dept. econs., 1983-86, 88-90, mem. exec. com. faculty senate, 1987-90, chmn., 1989-90; lectr. Yale U., 1970-71; sr. economist Senate Budget Com., Washington, 1975-76; dep. asst. sec. for econ. policy and rsch. Dept. Labor, Washington, 1977-79; dir. Ctr. for Rsch. on Wis. Economy; econ. advisor to gov. State of Wis., 1983-86; exec. sec. Gov.'s Coun. Econ. Advisors, 1983-86; mem. Gov.'s Export Strategy Commn., 1994-95; bd. dirs. Thompson, Plumb Funds; bd. dirs. PROFS, 1987-90, treas., 1987-88, pres., 1988-89; cons. in field; mem. LaFollette Inst. Pub. Affairs; dir. Initiative for World Affairs and Global Economy. Author: (with Clark Reynolds) Principles of Economics, 1970, Dollars and Sense, 1994; contbr. articles to profl. jours. Trustee U. Wis. Bookstore, 1990-95; bd. advisors Am. Players Theatre, Spring Green, Wis., 1993—. NSF fellow, 1963-66, 70-72; Nat. Commn. Employment Policy rsch. grantee, 1980-82; recipient William H. Kiekhofer Meml. Teaching prize U. Wis., 1973. Mem. Am. Econ. Assn., Econometric Soc., Royal Econ. Soc. Office: U Wis 1180 Observatory Dr Madison WI 53706-1320

NICHOLS, DONALD RICHARDSON, medical educator; b. Mpls., Feb. 22, 1911; s. Arthur R. and Agusta (Fisher) N.; m. Margery Spicer, Mar. 5, 1942 (dec.); children: Virginia (Mrs. Gregory Blanchfield), John; m. Mary Jean Scholberg, Mar. 2, 1957 (dec.); children: Arthur, Edwin, Mary Jean (Mrs. Vincent Grimaldi), Barbara (Mrs. Todd McCallister). AB, Amherst Coll., 1933; MD, U. Minn., 1938, MS in Medicine, 1942. Diplomate: Am. Bd. Internal Medicine. Intern Milw. County Hosp., 1939; fellow medicine Mayo Found., 1939-42; mem. faculty Mayo Grad. Sch. Medicine, U. Minn., 1948-72, prof. clin. medicine, 1965-72; prof. medicine Mayo Med. Sch., 1972-81; cons. medicine Mayo Clinic, 1942-81, chmn. divsn. infectious diseases, 1963-73, sr. cons. medicine, 1973-81; dir. health svc. Rochester (Minn.) C.C., (Minn.), 1981-86. Treas. Rochester Human Rights Commn., 1983-89. Surgeon U.S. Mcht. Marines, 1941. Fellow Infectious Diseases Soc. Am., ACP; mem. AMA, Minn. State Med. Assn., Central Soc. Clin. Research, Mayo Alumni Assn., Sigma Xi, Nu Sigma Nu, Theta Delta Chi. Methodist. Home: 207 5th Ave SW Rochester MN 55902-3100

NICHOLS, EDIE DIANE, executive recruiter; b. Grahamstown, Eastern Cape Province, Republic of South Africa, Mar. 28, 1939; came to U.S., 1963; d. Cyril Doughtry and Dorothy Ethel (Nottingham) Tyson; m. John F. Nichols, Dec. 16, 1962; 1 child, Ian Tyson. Adminstrv. asst. Am. Acad. Medicine, N.Y.C., 1963-64, Jack Lenor Larsen, Inc., N.Y.C., 1964-70; v.p. John Scott Fones, Inc., N.Y.C., 1971-76, Howard J. Rubenstein Assocs. Inc., N.Y.C., 1976-80; dir. communications Carl Byoir & Assocs., N.Y.C., 1981-83; account supr. Hill and Knowlton, N.Y.C., 1983-85; broker Cross & Brown Co., N.Y.C., 1986-88; v.p. Marc Nichols Assocs., Inc., N.Y.C., 1989-95; mng. ptnr. Nichols Brown Internat., N.Y.C., 1995—. Trustee Cen. Park Hist. Soc., N.Y.C., 1978-80. Mem. NOW, N.Y. Women in Comm. (pub. rels. chair 1980-81, v.p., programs bd. dirs 1985-87), Fin. Women's Assn. of N.Y. Republican. Episcopalian. Club: City of N.Y. (trustee, v.p., fin. and devel. 1987-89). Home: 155 W 20th St Apt 2K New York NY 10011-3612 Office: Nichols Brown Internat 330 Madison Ave Fl 11 New York NY 10017-5001

NICHOLS, ELIZABETH GRACE, nursing educator, administrator; b. Tehran, Iran, Feb. 1, 1943; came to U.S., 1964; d. Terence and Eleanor Denny (Payne) Quilliam; m. Gerald Ray Nichols, Nov. 20, 1965; children: Tina Lynn, Jeffrey David. BSN, San Francisco State U., 1969; MS, U. Calif.-San Francisco, 1970, Dr. Nursing Sci., 1974, MA Idaho State U., 1989. Staff nurse Peninsula Hosp., Burlingame, Calif., 1966-72; asst. prof. U. Calif.-San Francisco Sch. Nursing, 1974-82; chmn. dept. nursing Idaho State U., Pocatello, 1982-85; assoc. dean Coll. Health Scis. Sch. Nursing U. Wyo., Laramie, 1985-91, asst. to pres. for program reviews, 1991-95, dean Coll. Nursing, U. N.D., 1995—; cons. U. Rochester, N.Y., 1979, Carroll Coll., Mont., 1980, div. Nursing Dept. HHS, Washington, 1980, 84, 85, 86, 87, 89, 93, U. Maine, Ft. Kent, 1992, Stanford Hosp. Nursing Service, Calif., 1981-82, Ea. N.Mex. U., 1988. Contbr. articles on nursing to profl. jours. Mem. adv. bd. dirs. Ombudsman Service of Contra Costa Calif., 1979-82, U. Calif. Home Care Service, San Francisco, 1975-82, Free Clinic of Pocatello, 1984. ACE fellow U. Maine system 1990-91. Fellow ACE, Gerontol. Soc. Am., Am. Acad. Nursing; mem. Gerontol. Soc. Am. (chmn. clin. medicine section 1987, sec. 1990-93), Am. Nurses Assn., N.D. Nurses Assn., Idaho Nurses Assn. (dist. 51 adv. bd. dirs. 1982-84), Western Inst. Nursing (chair, 1990-92, bd. govs.), Sigma Theta Tau. Club: Oakland Ski (1st v.p. 1981-82). (Calif.).

NICHOLS, EUGENE DOUGLAS, mathematics educator; b. Rovno, Poland, Feb. 6, 1923; came to U.S., 1946, naturalized, 1951; s. Alex and Anna (Radchuk) Nichiporuk; m. Alice Bissell, Mar. 31, 1951. BS, U. Chgo., 1949, postgrad., 1949-51; MEd, U. Ill., 1953, MA, 1954, PhD, 1956. Instr. math. Roberts Wesleyan Coll., North Chili, N.Y., 1950-51, U. Ill., 1951-56; assoc. prof. math. edn. Fla. State U., 1956-61, prof., head dept., 1961-73; dir. Project for Mathematical Devel. of Children, 1973-77; dir. math program NSF, 1958-61; dir. Math. Inst. Elem. Tchrs., 1961-70; pres. Nichols Schwartz Pub., 1992—; prof. math. edn. Fla. State U., 1974-90; Chmn. U. Ill. Com. on Sch. Math., 1954-55; cons. editor math McGraw-Hill Book Co., summer 1956. Co-author: Modern Elementary Algebra, 1961, Introduction to Sets, 1962, Arithmetic of Directed Numbers, 1962, Introduction to Equations and Inequalities, 1963, Introduction to Coordinate Geometry, 1963, Introduction to Exponents, 1964, Understanding Arithmetic, 1965, Elementary Mathematics Patterns and Structure, 1966, Algebra, 1966, Modern Geometry, 1968, Modern Trigonometry, 1968, Modern Intermediate Algebra, 1969, Analytic Geometry, 1973, Holt Algebra 1, 1974, 78, 82, 86, 92, Holt Algebra 2, 1974, 78, 82, 86, 92, Holt Geometry, 1974, 78, 82, 86, Holt School Mathematics, 1974, 78, 81, Holt Pre-Algebra Mathematics, 1980, 86, Holt Mathematics, 1981, 85, Elementary School Mathematics and How to Teach It, 1982, Geometry, 1991, Holt Pre-Algebra, 1992, Mathematics Dictionary and Handbook, 1993, 95; author: Pre-Algebra Mathematics, 1970, Introductory Algebra for College Students, 1971, Mathematics for the Elementary School Teacher, 1971, College Mathematics, 1975, College Mathematics for General Education, rev. edit., 1975. Named Fla. State U. Disting. Prof., 1968-69; recipient Disting. Alumni award U. Ill. Coll. Edn., 1970. Mem. Am. Math. Soc., Math. Assn. Am., Sch. Sci. and Math. Assn., Nat. Coun. Tchrs. Math., Coun. Basic Edn., Text and Acad. Authors Assn., Pi Mu Epsilon, Phi Delta Kappa. Home: 3386 W Lakeshore Dr Tallahassee FL 32312-1305 *Do not look for a career--look for opportunities to do kind things for others. Be honest with yourself and with those around you.*

NICHOLS, GERRY LYNN, occupational therapist; b. Larned, Kans., Nov. 18, 1951; d. James H. and Dorthea (Griffith) Sooby; m. William P. Hesley, July 1975 (div. July 1981); m. Douglas J. Nichols, Oct. 9, 1987; 1 child, Rebecca. BS in Occupl. Therapy, San Jose State U., 1980; MBA, U. Dallas, Irving, Tex., 1990. Lic. occupl. therapist; cert. case mgr. Mgr. occupl. therapy Meth. Med. Ctr., Dallas, 1985-87; pvt. practice Dallas, 1981-89; occupl. therapist Progressive Rehab. Inst. of Dallas for Ergonomics, Dallas, 1987-88; v.p. bus. devel./strategic planning and devel., dir. rehab., dir. ops., occupl. therapist Am. Rehab. Ctr./Rehab. Sys., Inc., Dallas, 1989-91; pres. GSN Cons., Inc., Carrollton, Tex., 1991—; pres., CEO WorkWell Sys., Inc., Carrollton, 1994-95; dir. therapy svcs. The Co. Dr., Dallas, 1995—. Contbr. articles to profl. jours. Mem. adv. bd. Home Health Svcs., Inc., 1990—. Mem. Am. Occupl. Therapy Assn. (roster of accreditation evaluators 1993—), Tex. Occupl. Therapy Assn. (dist. chairperson, bd. dirs. 1984-88, Cert. of Appreciation 1989), Metrocrest C. of C. Democrat. Avocations: snow skiing, camping, needlework, reading. Home: 2208 Sunrise Ln Carrollton TX 75006-2754

NICHOLS, GREG MARK, systems analyst; b. Elgin, Ill., Nov. 25, 1967; s. Grace (Ipema) N. A in Data Processing, Blackhawk Tech.; student, U. Wis., Whitewater. Cert. assoc. computer profl. Analyst Ameritech Svcs., Milw., 1988—, analyst, LAN adminstr., 1990—; pres. Nichols Consulting, Delavan, Wis., 1991—. Sunday sch. tchr. Delavan Christian Ch., 1990; cadet leader Ch. Boys Club, Delavan, 1990-91; speaker Boy Scouts Am., Milw., 1991—. Avocations: sports, farming. Home: 518 E Washington St Delavan WI 53115-1820

NICHOLS, GUY WARREN, retired institute executive, utilities executive; b. Colchester, Vt., Oct. 27, 1925; s. Guy W. and Gladys (Tomlinson) N.; m. Shirley Hibbard, June 21, 1947; children: Pamela, Gail, Sally. BSCE, U. Vt., 1947; postgrad., Worcester Poly. Inst. Sch. Indsl. Mgmt., 1953-56; MS in Bus. Adminstrn., MIT, 1961. With New. Eng. Electric System, Westborough, Mass., 1947-84, exec. v.p., 1968-70, pres., 1970-84, chief exec. officer, 1972-84, chmn. bd., 1978-84. Chmn., trustee Woods Hole Oceanographic Instn., 1985-95; trustee Worcester Found. Biomed. Rsch. Sloan fellow, MIT, 1961. Fellow Am. Acad. Arts and Scis. Office: 22 Beacon St Boston MA 02108-3703

NICHOLS, HAROLD JAMES, theatre educator; b. Mitchell Field, N.Y., July 27, 1945; s. Harold J. and Ruth (McCain) N.; m. Mary Frances Lutes, Nov. 25, 1967 (div. 1992); children: Ruth, David, Debra; m. Anna Marie Douet, July 4, 1992. BS, Iowa State U., 1967; MA, Ind. U., 1969, PhD, 1971. Assoc. instr. Ind. U., Bloomington, 1970-71; asst. prof. Kans. State U., Manhattan, 1971-75, assoc. prof., 1975-81, prof., 1981-84, prof., head speech dept., 1985-93; dean coll. fine arts and humanities U. Nebr., Kearney, 1993-97; dean Sch. Arts and Scis. Ga. Southwestern State U., Americus, 1997—; guest scholar DePauw U. Undergrad. Honors Conf., Greencastle, Ind., 1988; cons. Commonwealth of Va. Dept. Edn., 1988, Nebr. Wesleyan U., Lincoln, 1989, So. Ill. U., 1989, U. Va., 1992, U. No. Iowa, 1992. Co-editor: Status of Theatre Research-1984, 1986; contbr. articles to profl. jours. Named Outstanding Coll. Tchr., Kans. Speech Communications Assn., 1985. Mem. Assn. Theatre in Higher Edn. (pres. 1987-88), Am. Coll. Theatre Festival (region chair 1987-88, Kennedy Ctr. medallion 1990), Mid-Am. Theatre Conf. (chief regional officer 1978-81). Home: 1923 Rose Ave Americus GA 31709 Office: Ga Southwestern State Univ Sch Arts and Scis Americus GA 31709

NICHOLS, HAROLD NEIL, corporate executive, former pipeline company executive; b. Digby, N.S., Can., June 15, 1937; m. Doris E. Outhouse, 1957. Grad. high sch. Cert. Mgmt. Acct. Various fin. positions TransCan. PipeLines Ltd., Toronto, Ont., from 1956, chief fin. officer, from 1983, exec. v.p., 1988-89; mgmt. cons. Unionville, Ont., 1989-92; chmn. Battery Techs., Inc., 1993-95; bd. dirs. Union Bank Switzerland (Can.); pres. Corrosion Interventions Ltd., Metocean Data Sys. Ltd. Mem. Fin. Execs. Inst. Home: 7 Blackwell Ct, Unionville, ON Canada L3R 0C2

NICHOLS, HENRY ELIOT, lawyer, savings and loan executive; b. N.Y.C.; m. Frances Griffin Morrison, Aug. 12, 1950 (dec. July 1978); children: Clyde Whitney, Diane Spencer; m. Mary Ann Wall, May 31, 1987. BA, Yale U., 1946; JD, U. Va., 1948. Bar: D.C. 1950, U.S. Dist. Ct. 1950, U.S. Ct. Appeals 1952, U.S. Supreme Ct. 1969. Assoc. Frederick W. Berens, Washington, 1950-52; sole practice, Washington, 1952—; real estate columnist Washington Star, 1966-81; pres., gen. counsel Hamilton Fed. Savs. & Loan Assn., 1971-74; vice chmn. bd. Columbia 1st Bank (formerly Columbia 1st Fed. Savs. & Loan Assn.), Washington, 1974-90, bd. dir.; pres. Century Fin. Corp., 1971-90; regional v.p. Preview, Inc., 1972-78; bd. dir., exec. com. Columbia Real Estate Title Ins. Co., Washington, 1968-78; bd. dir. Greater Met. Bd. Trade, 1974-78, Distr. Realty Title Ins. Co., 1978-86. Nat. adv. bd. Harker Prep. Sch., 1975-80; exec. com. Father Walter E. Schmitz Meml. Fund, Cath. U., 1982-83; bd. dirs. Vincent T. Lombardi Cancer Rsch. Ctr., 1979-84; del. Pres. Johnson's Conf. Law and Poverty, 1967; vice chmn. Mayor's Ad Hoc Com. Housing Code Problems, Washington, 1968-71; mem. Commn. Landlord-Tenant Affairs Washington City Coun., 1970-71; vice chmn. Washington Area Realtors Coun., 1970; exec. com., dir. Downtown Progress, 1970; bd. dirs. Washington Mental Health Assn., 1973, Washington Med Ctr., 1975. Capt. USAAF, 1942-46. Mem. Am. Land Devel. Assn., Nat. Assn. Realtors, Nat. Assn. Real Estate Editors, Washington Bd. Realtors (pres. 1970, Realtor of Yr. 1970, Martin Isen award 1981), Greater Met. Washington Bd. Trade (bd. dirs. 1974-80), U.S. League Savs. Assns. (attys. com. 1971-80), Washington Savs. and Loan League, ABA, D.C. Bar Assn., Internat. Real Estate Fedn., Omega Tau Rho. Episcopalian. Clubs: Yale, Cosmos, Rolls Royce, Antique Auto, St. Elmo. Patentee med. inventions; contbr. articles profl. jours. Address: 1 Kittery Ct Bethesda MD 20817-2137 Office: 1112 16th St NW Washington DC 20036-4823

NICHOLS, HENRY LOUIS, lawyer; b. Collin County, Tex., Nov. 7, 1916; s. Jesse Cleveland and Leva (Stiff) N.; m. Elaine Guentherman, May 17, 1949; children: David Michael, Martha Marie. LL.B., So. Meth. U., 1940. Bar: Tex. 1939. Asst. city atty. Dallas, 1946-50, sole practice, 1951—; mem. adv. bd. Ctr. for Legal Mcpl. Studies. Served to lt. col. AUS, 1941-46; col. USAR ret. Rsch. fellow Southwestern Legal Found., 1964. Fellow Am. Bar Found.; mem. ABA, Dallas Bar Assn. (pres. 1963-64), State Bar Tex., Tex. Bar Found. (charter). Club: Lakewood Country. Home: 3131 Maple Ave Apt 13H Dallas TX 75201-1204 Office: 1800 Lincoln St Dallas TX 75226-2248 *As a night-school graduate (Law School), I believe the opportunities in America are unlimited for anyone willing to work. Nowhere in the world are such opportunities available. We who live in the U.S.A. are blessed and the most fortunate of all people. We should strive to maintain that which our fathers preserved for us.*

NICHOLS, HORACE ELMO, state justice; b. Elkmont, Ala., July 16, 1912; s. William Henry and Lou Ella (Bates) N.; m. Edith Bowers, Oct. 20, 1945; children: Nancy (Mrs. Lewis Glenn), Carol (Mrs. Scott Henwood), Horace Elmo Jr. Mus.B., Columbia U., 1933, postgrad. in constnl. law, 1937-38; LL.B., Cumberland Law Sch., 1936. Bar: Ga. 1935. Practice in Canton, Ga., 1938-40, Rome, Ga., 1940-48; judge Superior Ct., Rome, 1948-54; mem. Ct. Appeals Ga., 1954-66; justice Supreme Ct. Ga., Atlanta, 1966-80; chief justice Supreme Ct. Ga., 1975-80. Vocal soloist, World's Fair, Chgo., 1933. Mem. Sigma Alpha Epsilon, Blue Key. Democrat. Presbyterian. Clubs: Coosa Country (Rome); Piedmont Driving (Atlanta), Capitol City (Atlanta), Atlanta City (Atlanta). Lodge: Elks (Rome). Home: 10 Highway 411 E Rome GA 30161-4473 Office: 28 Jud Bldg Atlanta GA 30334*

NICHOLS, IRIS JEAN, illustrator; b. Yakima, Wash., Aug. 2, 1938; d. Charles Frederick and Velma Irene (Hacker) Beisner; (div. June 1963); children: Reid William, Amy Jo; m. David Gary Nichols, Sept. 21, 1966. BFA in Art, U. Wash., 1978. Freelance illustrator, graphic designer Seattle, 1966—; med. illustrator, head dept. illustration Swedish Hosp. Med. Ctr., Seattle, 1981-86; owner, med. and scientific illustrator Art for Medicine, Seattle, 1986—; part-time med. illustrator U. Wash., Seattle, 1966-67; part-time med. illustrator, graphic coord. dept. art The Mason Clinic, 1968-78; instr. advanced illustration Cornish Coll. Arts, Seattle, 1988—. Illustrator various books including Bryophytes of Pacific Northwest, 1966, Microbiology, 1973, 78, 82, 94, Introduction to Human Physiology, 1980, Understanding Human Anatomy and Physiology, 1983, Human Anatomy, 1984 Regional Anesthesia, 1990, and children's books on various subjects; exhibited in group shows at Seattle Pacific Sci. Ctr., summer 1979, 82, Am. Coll. Surgeons (1st prize 1974), N.W. Urology Conf. (1st prize 1974, 76, 2d prize 1975). Pres. ArtsWest (formerly West Seattle Arts Coun.), 1983; active Seattle Art Mus. Named to West Seattle H.S. Alumni Hall of Fame, 1986, Matrix Table, 1986-96. Mem. Assn. Med. Illustrators (Murial McLatchie Fine Arts award 1981), Nat. Mus. Women in the Arts (Wash. state com., bd. dirs. 1987-95, pres. 1993-94), Women Painters of Wash. (pres. 1987-89), U. Wash. Alumni Assn., Lambda Rho (pres. 1995-96). Avocations: artwork, printmaking small books, entering juried art exhibitions.

NICHOLS, J. LARRY, energy company executive, lawyer; b. Oklahoma City, July 6, 1942; s. John Whiteman and Mary (Davis) N.; m. Polly Puckett, Oct. 16, 1971; children: Tyler, Sally. BA in Geology, Princeton U., 1964; JD, U. Mich., 1967. Bar: Okla. 1967. Law clk. to chief justice U.S. Supreme Ct., Washington, 1967-68; spl. asst. to asst. atty. gen. U.S. Dept. Justice, Washington, 1968-70; pres. Devon Energy Corp., Oklahoma City, 1970—. Commr. Urban Renewal Authority Bd., Oklahoma City, 1989; pres. domestic petroleum coun. Okla. Nature Conservancy. Mem. Okla. Bar Assn. (bd. dirs., v.p.), Ind. Petroleum Assn. Am. (bd. dirs.), NAM (bd. dirs.), Oklahoma City C. of C., Econ. Club (pres. 1988-89). Office: Devon Energy Corp 20 N Broadway Ave Oklahoma City OK 73102-8202

NICHOLS, JAMES RAYMOND, JR., civil engineer; b. Holyoke, Mass., Mar. 14, 1966; s. James Raymond and Donna Jean (Riley) N. BSCE, Northeastern U., 1989; MS in Environ. Engring., U. Conn., 1994. Registered profl. engr., Wash. Staff engr. N.L. Jacobson & Assocs., Chester, Conn., 1989-95; project engr. II City of Olympia (Wash.) Pub. Works Dept., 1995—; instr. South Puget Sound C.C., Olympia, 1997—; speaker Am. Filtration & Separations Soc. conf., Nashville, 1995, Impervious Surface Reduction Rsch. Symposium, Olympia, Wash., 1996, Western Regional Urban Streams Conf., Arcata, Calif., 1996. Contbr. articles to profl. jours. Mem. Chester Inland Wetlands Commn., 1993-95. Mem. ASCE. Achievements include research in the area of recirculating sand filters for wastewater treatment. Home: 5500 Park Place Loop SE Lacey WA 98503-4339 Office: City Olympia Pub Works Dept 520 Pear St P O 1967 Olympia WA 98507

NICHOLS, JAMES RICHARD, civil engineer, consultant; b. Amarillo, Tex., June 29, 1923; s. Marvin Curtis and Ethel (Nichols) N.; m. Billie Louise Smith, Dec. 24, 1944; children: Judith Ann, James Richard Jr., John M. B.S. in Civil Engring., Tex. A&M U., 1949, M.S. in Civil Engring., 1950. Registered profl. engr., Tex., Okla., N.Mex. Ptnr. Freese & Nichols, Inc., Cons. Engrs., Fort Worth, 1950-76; pres. Freese & Nichols, Inc., Cons. Engrs., 1977-88, chmn., 1988—; bd. dirs. Cornerstone Investment Group, Kentex Sales, Inc. Chmn. Ft. Worth Conv. and Visitors Bur.; bd. dirs. United Way Tarrant County, Pub. Comm. Found. North Tex., Tex. A&M Rsch. Found., Tex. Wesleyan U. With U.S. Army, 1943-46. Fellow Am. Cons. Engrs. Council; mem. Cons. Engrs. Coun., Nat. Soc. Profl. Engrs., Tex. Water Conservation Assn. (pres.), Exchange Club, Fort Worth Club, Fort Worth C. of C. (bd. dirs., mem. adv. coun.), Newcomen Soc., Mason, Rotary. Methodist. Home: 4821 Overton Woods Dr Fort Worth TX 76109-2429 Office: Freese & Nichols Inc 4055 Internat Plz Ste 200 Fort Worth TX 76109-4895

NICHOLS, JAMES ROBBS, university dean; b. Jackson, Tenn., May 30, 1926; s. William Ed and Buelha (Robbs) N.; m. Johnnie Jones; 1 dau., Tina Jean Nichols Benson. BS, U. Tenn., 1949; MS, U. Minn., 1955, PhD, 1957. Former mem. faculty Pa. State U., U. Tenn.; mem. faculty Va. Poly. Inst. and State U., Blacksburg, 1964-71, 73—; head dairy sci. dept. Va. Poly. Inst. and State U., 1964-69; assoc. dean Va. Poly. Inst. and State U. (Coll. Agr.), 1969-71, 73-75; dean Coll. Agr. & Life Scis., dir. Va. Agr. Exptl. Sta., 1975-91; dean emeritus Va. Poly. Inst. and State U., 1991—; exec. v.p., gen. mgr. Select Sires, Inc., Columbus, Ohio, 1971-73. Served with USAAF, World War II. Named Man of Yr. in Agr. in Va. Progressive Farmer mag., 1975; hon. state farmer Tenn. Mem. AAAS, Am. Dairy Sci. Assn., Sigma Xi, Phi Kappa Phi, Alpha Zeta, Gamma Sigma Delta. Methodist. Clubs: Rotary.

NICHOLS, JOHN DAVID, insurance and financial services broker; b. Walton/Oneonta, N.Y., Mar. 18, 1948; s. Sidney Newton and Emily Matilda (Clark) N.; m. Annemarie Margaret Meinke, June 24, 1978; children: David Sean, Christine Marie, James Edmund. BA, Muskingum Coll., 1971; postgrad., Am. Coll. Lic. ins. broker, CPCU, 1992. Underwriter trainee U.S. Fidelity & Guaranty, Scranton, Pa., 1972-73; underwriter U.S. Fidelity & Guaranty, Balt., 1973-76; supervising underwriter U.S. Fidelity & Guaranty, Toledo, Ohio, 1976-77; sr. casualty underwriter The Hartford Ins. Group, Mt. Kisco, N.Y., 1977-81; assoc. account exec. Murray, Schoen & Homer, Inc., Bronxville, N.Y., 1981-84; sr. casualty underwriter N.Am. mgrs. Am. Internat. Group, N.Y.C., 1984-85; assoc. acct. exec. A. Matarasso & Co., Inc., White Plains, N.Y., 1985-88; acct. exec. Walter Kaye Assocs., Inc., N.Y.C., 1988-90; analyst Interstate Risk Mgmt. Corp., Bedford, N.Y., 1990-92; mgr. dirs. and officers liability ins. dept. Interstate Risk Placements, Inc., Interstate Coverage Corp., Bedford, N.Y., 1990-92; with Prudential Ins. Co., Yorktown Hghts., N.Y., 1992-93; ins. broker Yorktown Heights, 1993—; agt. Gtr. Beneficial Union Pitts., 1994—; comml. underwriter Utica First Ins. Co., Peekskill, N.Y., 1994-96; prin. Bus. Ins. and Risk Mgmt. Svcs., 1994—; underwriter, broker Sieger & Smith, Inc., Scarsdale, N.Y., 1996; ins. broker, 1996—; gen. contractor new house rehab. all trades, 1997. Asst. scoutmaster Boy Scouts Am., Balt., 1974-75, Yorktown, 1990-93, asst. cubmaster, 1990-93, Webelos den leader, 1991-93, mem. coun. 1990-92; advisor Jr. Achievement, Balt., 1975-76; bd. dirs. Coachlight Condominium Assn., Montrose, N.Y., 1982-84; mem. parish vestry, 1989, 90, 91, 94, 95; ch. del. Inter-Parish Coun., 1990-97, vice chmn., 1992-94, chmn., 1994-96; chmn. Brotherhood Fund, 1995-96, treas., 1996-97; ch. del. N.Y. Diocese Conv., 1990, 91; chmn. Parish Outreach, 1991, librarian project, 1997. Life Underwriter Tng. Coun. fellow, 1994. Mem. NRA, NALU, CPCU Soc., Am. Soc. of CLUs and ChFCs (assoc.), Masons. Republican. Episcopalian. Avocations: family activities, outdoor sports, home projects, music, church activities.

NICHOLS, JOHN DOANE, diversified manufacturing corporation executive; b. Shanghai, China, 1930; m. Alexandra M. Curran, Dec. 4, 1971; children: Kendra E., John D. III. BA, Harvard U., 1953, MBA, 1955. Various operating positions Ford Motor Corp., 1958-68; dir. fin. controls ITT Corp., 1968-69; exec. v.p., COO Aerojet-Gen. Corp., 1969-79, Ill. Tool Works Inc., Chgo., 1980-81; CEO, dir. Ill. Tool Works Inc., 1982-95, chmn., 1986-96; bd. dirs. Household Internat., Philip Morris Cos., Inc., Rockwell Internat., Stone Container Corp., Grand Eagle Corp.; overseer Harvard U. Trustee U. Chgo., 1987-93, Lyric Opera Chgo., Mus. Sci. and Industry, Jr. Achievement Chgo., Chgo. Commerce Civic Com.; life trustee Chgo. Symphony Orch.; chmn. bd. dirs. Art Inst. Chgo.; mem. bd. govs. Argonne (Ill.) Nat. Lab., 1988-93; mem. exec. com. Chgo. Cmty. Trust, 1997—. Mem. Harvard Club (N.Y.C., Chgo.), Indian Hill Club (Winnetka, Ill.), Chgo. Club, Comml. Club, Econ. Club Chgo. Home: 900 Mount Pleasant Rd Winnetka IL 60093-3613 Office: Ill Tool Works Inc 3600 W Lake Ave Glenview IL 60025-1215

NICHOLS, JOSEPH J., SR., surgeon; b. Atlanta, July 16, 1929. MD, Med. Coll. Ga., 1958. Diplomate Am. Bd. Surgery, Am. Bd. Colon & Rectal Surgery. Intern Ga. Bapt. Hosp., Atlanta, 1958-59, resident, 1959-61, 65-67; fellow Precept Drs. Boling-Finch, 1967-69; with Piedmont Hosp., Atlanta; asst. clin. prof. surgery Med. Coll. Ga.; clin. asst. prof. surgery Emory U. Sch. Med. Mem. AMA, ACS, Am. Soc. Colon and Rectal Surgery, Southern Med. Assn., Southeastern Surg. Congress. Office: 2001 Peachtree Rd NE Ste 540 Atlanta GA 30309-1476

NICHOLS, KENNETH DAVID, consulting engineer; b. Cleve., Nov. 13, 1907; s. Wilbur Loren and Minnie May (Colbrunn) N.; m. Jacqueline Darrieulat, Dec. 15, 1932; children: Jacqueline Anne Thompson, K. David. BS, U.S. Mil. Acad., 1929; CE, Cornell U., 1932, MCE, 1933; postgrad., Technische Hochschule, Charlottenburg, Fed. Republic Germany, 1934-35; PhD in Hydraulics, U. Iowa, 1937. Commd. 2d lt. C.E. U.S. Army, 1929, advanced through grades to maj. gen., 1948, various mil. positions, 1929-41, dep. and dist. engr., Manhattan Engr. Dist., 1942-46; prof. mechanics U.S. Mil. Acad., West Point, N.Y., 1947-48; chief armed forces spl. weapons project (atomic) Pentagon, Va., 1948-50; dep. dir. guided missiles Office of Sec. of Def., Pentagon, Va., 1951-53; chief R&D Office of Chief of Staff, U.S. Army, Pentagon, Va., 1952-53; ret. U.S. Army, 1953; gen. mgr. U.S. AEC, Washington, 1953-55; cons. engr. Md., 1955-92; with World War II prodn. plants plutonium and uranium U-235, 1942-46; Cold War chief Armed Forces Spl. Weapons Project, 1948-50; cons. Yankee Atomic Power Plant, Conn. Atomic Power Plant, 1955-71. Author: The Road to Trinity, 1987. Trustee Thomas Alva Edison Found., Detroit, 1963-76; bd. dirs., v.p. Army Distaff Found., Washington, 1965-69; mem. at large engring. and indsl. rsch. divsn., NRC, Washington, 1954-58. Decorated DSM, 1945 and DSM with oak leaf cluster, 1954; named to Comdr. Brit. Empire Order, Brit. Amb., 1946, Disting. Grad. U.S. Mil. Acad., Assn. Graduates, 1996; recipient Presdl. Medal of Merit, Pres. of Nicaragua, 1931, Disting. Svc. medal Commn. AEC, 1955, Chiefs of Engrs. award for Outstanding Pub. Svc. Fellow Am. Nuclear Soc.; mem. ASME (hon.), Nat. Acad. Engring., ASCE (Collinwood Prize 1938). Republican. Home: Knollwood 6200 Oregon Ave NW Apt 345 Washington DC 20015-1542

NICHOLS, KYRA, ballerina; b. Berkeley, Calif., July 2, 1958. Studied with Alan Howard, Pacific Ballet, Sch. Am. Ballet, N.Y.C. With N.Y.C. Ballet, 1974—, prin. dancer, 1979—. Created roles in Tricolore, 1978, A Sketch Book, 1978, Jerome Robbins' Four Seasons, 1979, John Taras' Concerto for Piano and Wind Instruments, Stravinsky Centennial Celebration, 1982, Jacques d'Amboise's Celebration, 1983; performed in N.Y.C. Ballet's Balanchine Celebration, 1993. Ford Found. scholar; recipient Dance Mag. award, 1988. Office: Peter S Diggins Assocs 133 W 71st St New York NY 10023 also: NYC Ballet Inc NY State Theater Lincoln Ctr Pla New York NY 10023

NICHOLS, LEE ANN, library media specialist; b. Denver, Apr. 27, 1946; d. Bernard Anthony and Margaret Mary (Pughes) Wilhelm; m. Robert Joseph Nichols, July 12, 1975; children: Rachel, Steven, Sarah. BS in Edn., St. Mary of the Plains, Dodge City, Kans., 1968; MA in Edn., Colo. U., 1978. Cert. type B profl. tchr., Colo. Tchr. So. Tama Sch. Dist. Montour, Iowa, 1968-70, Strasburg (Colo.) Sch. Dist., 1970-73; svc. rep. Montain Bell, Denver, 1973-75; libr., tchr. Simla (Colo). Sch. Dist., 1976-78; dir. Simla Br. Libr., 1978-81; dir. Christian edn. St. Anthony's Ch/, Sterling, Colo., 1983-84; libr. cons. Rel Valley Sch., Iliff, Colo., 1984—, Plateau Sch. Dist., Peetz, Colo., 1986—; mem. Colo. Coun. for Libr. Devel., Denver, 1986-92, chmn. 1991; instr. Northeastern Jr. Coll., Sterling; del. Gov.'s Conf. on Libr. and Info. Scis., 1990. Contbr. articles to profl. jours. Active Sterling Arts Coun., sec., 1982-85, v.p., 1985, pres., 1986-87; chair Northeastern Jr. Coll. Found., Sterling, 1983-87, mem. 1981-91; mem. community adv. coun. Northeastern Jr. Coll., 1991-93, chair, 1993; bd. dirs. Wagon Wheel chpt. Girl Scouts Am., 1975-78. Mem. ALA, Am. Assn. Sch. Librs., Assn. Libr. Svcs. to Children, Colo. Ednl. Media Assn., Colo. Libr. Coun., Internat. Reading Assn. (Colo. Coun.). Avocations: reading, sewing. Home: 12288 County Road 370 Sterling CO 80751-8421 Office: Caliche Jr High Sch RR 1 Iliff CO 80736-9801

NICHOLS, MARCI LYNNE, gifted education coordinator, educator, consultant; b. Cin., July 7, 1948; m. James G. Nichols, June 19, 1970; children: Lisa, Jeannette. B in Arts and Sci., Miami U., Oxford, Ohio, 1970, MEd, 1990, PhD, 1997. Cert. Secondary English, elem. gifted edn., computer edn., Ohio. Secondary English tchr. West Clermont Local Schs., Cin., 1970-71; coord. gifted edn. and tchr. Batavia (Ohio) Local Schs., 1981—; speaker, cons. Local Gifted Orgns., Cin., 1988—; vis. instr. dept. ednl. psychology Miami U., Oxford, Ohio, 1991—; presenter Nat. Rsch. Symposium on Talent Devel., 1991. Author, presenter: (videotape series) Parenting the Gifted Parts I and II, 1992; columnist, contbr. Resources for Everyday Living; contbr. articles to profl. jours. Speaker Christian Women's Club, Ohio, Ind., Ky., W.Va., 1981—; deacon First Presbyn. Ch. of Batavia, Ohio, 1986-88; bd. trustee Super Saturday program gifted edn. com. Miami U., 1995—. Recipient Douglas Miller Rsch. award Miami U., 1991. Mem. ASCD, Am. Ednl. Rsch. Assn. (presenter 1997), Nat. Assn. for Gifted Children, Consortium Ohio Coords. of Gifted, Parents Assn. for Gifted Edn. (trustee 1997), Midwest Ednl. Rsch. Assn. (presenter), Internat. Platform Assn., Phi Kappa Phi. Home: 110 Wood St Batavia OH 45103-2923 Office: Batavia Local Schs 800 Bauer Ave Batavia OH 45103-2837

NICHOLS, MIKE, stage and film director; b. Berlin, Nov. 6, 1931; s. Nicholaievitch and Brigitte (Landauer) Peschowsky; m. Patricia Scott, 1957 (div.); m. Margot Callas, 1974 (div.); m. Annabel Davis-Goff (div.); m. Diane Sawyer, Apr. 29, 1988. Student, U. Chgo., 1950-53; student acting, Lee Strasberg. Ptnr. with Elaine May in comedy act; first appeared at Playwrights Theatre Club, Compass Theatre, Chgo.; N.Y. debut An Evening with Mike Nichols and Elaine May, 1960; acted in A Matter of Position, Phila., 1962; dir.: (plays) Barefoot in the Park, 1963 (Tony award best dir.), The Knack, 1964, Luv, 1964 (Tony award best dir.), The Odd Couple, 1965 (Tony award best dir.), The Apple Tree, 1966, The Little Foxes, 1967, Plaza Suite, 1968 (Tony award best dir.), The Prisoner of 2d Avenue, 1971 (Tony award best dir.), Uncle Vanya (co-adapted), 1973, Streamers, 1976, Comedians, 1976, The Gin Game, 1977, (L.A. Drama Critics award), Drink Before Dinner, 1978, Lunch Hour, 1980, Fools, 1981, The Real Thing, 1984 (Tony award 1984,), Hurlyburly, 1984, Social Security, 1984, Elliot Loves, 1990, Death and the Maiden, 1992; (films) Who's Afraid of Virginia Woolf?, 1966, (Academy award nomination best director 1966), The Graduate, 1967 (Academy award best director 1967), Catch-22, 1970, Carnal Knowledge, 1971, The Day of the Dolphin, 1973, The Fortune, 1975, Silkwood, 1983 (Academy award nomination best director 1983), Heartburn, 1986, Biloxi Blues, 1987, Working Girl, 1988 (Academy award nomination best director 1988), Postcards From the Edge, 1990, Regarding Henry, 1991, Wolf, 1994, The Bird Cage, 1995; producer: (musical) Annie, 1977; performed at N.Y. musical Pres. Johnson's Inaugural Gala, 1965; TV appearances include Today Show. Office: care Bryan Lourd CAA 9830 Wilshire Blvd Beverly Hills CA 90212-1804

NICHOLS, RALPH ARTHUR, lawyer; b. Clinton, N.Y., Jan. 27, 1919; s. Arthur Britcher and Carrie Lena (Pitcher) N.; m. Pamela Crow Bermingham, May 3, 1947 (dec. Feb. 1980); children: Jeremy Nichols Pierce, Ralph A. Jr., Melinda Nichols Mayer; m. Victoria Requa Lalli, Sept. 5, 1981. AB, Hamilton Coll., 1940; LLB, Yale U., 1947. Bar: Conn. 1949, N.Y. 1947, U.S. Dist. Ct. (so. dist.) N.Y. 1949, U.S. Dist. Ct. Conn. 1950, U.S. Supreme Ct. 1959. Assoc. Burke & Burke, N.Y.C., 1947-49, Maguire, Walker & Middleton, Stamford, Ct., 1949-54; assoc., then ptnr. Cummings & Lockwood, Stamford, 1954—. Founder, former bd. dirs. Stamford Land Conservation Trust; former bd. dirs. Conservationists Stamford, Inc., Stamford YMCA; former bd. dirs., sec. Stamford Area Commerce and Industry; trustee Stamford YMCA. Lt. USNR, 1942-46, ETO, PTO. Fellow Am. Coll. Trust and Estate Counsel; mem. ABA, Woodway Country Club (Darien, Conn.), Yale Club (N.Y.C.), Phi Delta Phi. Republican. Episcopalian. Home: 656 Den Rd Stamford CT 06903-3824 Office: Cummings & Lockwood PO Box 120 10 Stamford Forum Stamford CT 06901-3215

NICHOLS, RICHARD DALE, former congressman, banker; b. Ft. Scott, Kans., Apr. 29, 1926; s. Ralph Dale and Olive Marston (Kittell) N.; m. Constance Weinbrenner, Mar. 25, 1951 (dec. June 1994); children: Philip William, Ronald Dale, Anita Jane Nichols Bomberger; m. Linda Hupp, Apr. 21, 1996. BS in Agr. and BS in Journalism, Kans. State U., 1951. Info. counsel Kans. State Bd. Agr., Topeka, 1951-54; assoc. far, dir. Sta. WIBW, WIBW-TV, Topeka, 1954-57; agr. rep. to v.p. Hutchinson (Kans.) Nat. Bank and Trust, 1957-69; pres., CEO Home State Bank, McPherson, Kans., 1969-79, chmn., pres., CEO, 1979-91; chmn. Home State Bank & Trust, McPherson, Kans., 1985-91, 93—; mem. 102d Congress from 5th Kans. dist., 1991-92. Pres. Arts Coun., McPherson, 1979; 5th Dist. chmn. Kans. Rep. Party, 1986-89; bd. dirs. Camp Wood YMCA Camp, Elmdale, Kans., 1995; Meth. Ch. lay spkr., 1994—; bd. trustees Ctrl. Coll., McPherson. Ensign USNR, 1944-47; ATO. Named Hon. Citizen N.Y.C., 1988. Mem. VFW, Kans. Bankers Assn. (pres. 1985-86), Am. Bankers Assn. (advisor 1986-88), Kans. Assn. Banking Ag. Reps. (pres. 1965), Am. Legion, McPherson C. of C. (pres. 1977), Optimist (pres. Hutchinson club 1965), Rotary (pres. McPherson club 1978), Kans. Cavalry (cmdg. gen. 1986-89). Methodist. Home: 404 N Lakeside Dr Mc Pherson KS 67460-3600 Office: Home State Bank and Trust PO Box 1266 Mc Pherson KS 67460-1266

NICHOLS, ROBERT LEIGHTON, civil engineer; b. Amarillo, Tex., June 24, 1926; s. Marvin Curtis and Ethel N.; m. Frances Hardison, June 8, 1948; children—Eileen, William C., Michael L. B.S.C.E., Tex. A&M U., 1947, M.S.C.E., 1948. Grad. asst., instr. Tex. A&M U., 1947-48; assoc. Freese & Nichols (and predecessors), Ft. Worth, 1948-50; partner Freese & Nichols (and predecessors), 1950-77, v.p., 1977-88, pres., 1988-91, vice chmn., 1991-92, pres. emeritus, 1992—; mem. Bldg. Standards Commn., 1956-62. Chmn. Horn Frog dist. Boy Scouts Am., pres. Longhorn coun., 1990-93. Mem. ASCE, NSPE (pres. 1977-78), Tex. Soc. Profl. Engrs. (pres. 1965-66, Engr. of Yr. award Ft. Worth chpt. 1966), Am. Water Works Assn., Tex. Water Conservation Assn., Water Environ. Fedn., Water Environ. Assn. Tex. (pres. 1962-63), Am. Pub. Works Assn., Tex. Water Utilities Assn., Tex. Pub. Works Assn., Nat. Inst. for Engring. Ethics (pres. 1995—), Masons, Tau Beta Pi, Chi Epsilon. Methodist. Office: 1 S Main St Ste 102 Webb City MO 64870-2325

NICHOLS, ROGER SABIN, school counselor; b. Ames, Iowa, Oct. 21, 1938; s. Sabin Alfred and Margaret Pauline (Andrew) N.; m. Glendene Donna Greta, June 12, 1960; children: Margaret Emily, Charles Sabin II. BS, Iowa State U., 1960; MA in Edn., U. No. Iowa, 1965, EdS, 1976. Cert. tchr. sci., social studies, lang. arts, counselor K-12, dir. pupil svcs., Iowa. Tchr., counselor Bridgewater-Fontanelle (Iowa) Cmty. Sch. Dist., 1960-66; counselor, guidance dir. Sioux City (Iowa) Cmty. Sch. Dist., 1966—; human rels. cons. Western Hills Area Edn. Agy., Sioux City, 1979-82, spl. edn. transition adv. com., 1987—, chmn. career devel. unit writing com., 1989-90; mem., chmn. spl. needs adv. com. Western Iowa Tech. Cmty. Coll., Sioux City, 1982-87, area planning coun. for vocat. edn., 1986-90; com. mem. Sioux City Cmty. Sch. Dist., 1967-89; evaluation team N. Ctrl. Assn. Colls. and Schs., 1983; brief counseling rsch. project Iowa State U., 1989-90;

counselor's adv. com. office of admissions U. S.D., 1990-92; state conf. presenter Iowa Assn. Counseling and Devel., 1990, 94; local coord. Counseling for Higher Skills Rsch. Project, Kans. State U., 1994-96. Contbg. author: Critical Incidents in School Counseling, 1973, Simmerman Family Record, 1995; contbr. poetry to Lyrical Iowa, 1965, 67; contbr. articles to profl. jours. On-air friendraiser host Friends of FM-90, Sioux City, 1982—; mem. 4-H subcom. Woodbury County Extension Svc., Sioux City, 1984-96; fair supt. Woodbury County Fair Assn., Moville, Iowa, 1984-89. Named Iowa Counselor of Yr., Iowa Assn. Coll. Admissions Counselors, 1995; recipient Nat. Def. Edn. Act Stipend, U. S.D., 1968. Mem. NEA (life), Iowa State Edn. Assn. (del. assembly 1965), Sioux City Edn. Assn. (chmn. profl. rights and responsibilities com. 1967-68, rep. assembly 1968-69), Am. Counseling Assn., Iowa Counseling Assn., Am. Sch. Counselors Assn., Iowa Sch. Counselors Assn., Nat. Career Devel. Assn. (career info. rev. svc. 1970-73), Iowa Career Devel. Assn. (state membership chmn. 1975-76), Iowa Specialists in Group Work, Iowa State Hist. Soc., Iowa State Geneal. Soc., Conn. Soc. Genealogists, N.E. Historic Geneal. Soc., Derbyshire Family History Soc., Siouxland Master Chorale (pres. 1968-71, v.p. 1977-80, 88-90, treas. 1982-83), Sioux City Chamber Music Assn. (pres. 1980-81), Phi Delta Kappa (pres. Siouxland chpt. 1996-97). Republican. Methodist. Avocations: genealogist, church musician. Home: 3819 Peters Ave Sioux City IA 51106-1813 Office: East High Sch 5011 Mayhew Ave Sioux City IA 51106-4528

NICHOLS, RONALD LEE, surgeon, educator; b. Chgo., June 25, 1941; s. Peter Raymond and Jane Eleanor (Johnson) N.; m. Elsa Elaine Johnson, Dec. 4, 1964; children: Kimberly Jane, Matthew Bennett. MD, U. Ill., 1966, MS, 1970. Diplomate: Am. Bd. Surgery (assoc. cert. examiner, New Orleans, 1991), Nat. Bd. Med. Examiners. Intern U. Ill. Hosp., Chgo., 1966-67, resident in surgery, 1967-72, instr. surgery, 1970-72, asst. prof. surgery, 1972-74; assoc. prof. surgery U. Health Scis. Chgo. Med. Sch., 1975-77, dir. surg. edn., 1975-77; William Henderson prof. surgery Tulane U. Sch. Medicine, New Orleans, 1977—, vice chmn. dept. surgery, 1982-91, staff surgeon, 1977—, prof. microbiology, immunology and surgery, 1979—; cons. surgeon VA Hosp., Alexandria, La., 1978-93, Huey P. Long Hosp., Pineville, La., 1978—, Lallie Kemp Charity Hosp., Independence, La., 1977-85, Touro Infirmary, New Orleans, Monmouth Med. Ctr., Long Branch, N.J., 1979-88; mem. VA Coop. Study Rev. Bd., 1978-81, VA Merit Rev. Bd. in Surgery, 1979-82; mem. sci. program com. 3d Internat. Conf. Nosocomial Infections, Ctr. Disease Control, mem. sci. program and fundraising com. 4th Internat. Conf.; bd. dirs. Nat. Found. Infectious Diseases, 1989—, v.p., 1994-97, pres.-elect., 1997—; hon. fellow faculty Kasr El Aini Cairo U. Sch. Medicine, 1989; mem. adv. com. on infection control Ctrs. for Disease Control, 1991-97; disting. guest, vis. prof. Royal Coll. Surgeons Thailand 14th Ann. Clin. Congress, 1989, 17th Ann. Clin. Congress, 1992; mem. infectious diseases adv. bd. Roche Labs., 1988-95, Abbott Labs., 1990-92, Kimberly Clark Corp., 1990—, SmithKline Beecham Labs., 1990-95, Fujisawa Pharm., chmn., 1990—, Bayer Pharm., 1994—, Merck Sharpe Dohme, 1996, Depotech, 1996, Zeneca Pharm., 1997; mem. study group Prophylaxis Antibiotic Project La. Health Care Rev., Inc., 1995—. Author: (with Gorbach, Bartlett and Nichols) Manual of Surgical Infection, 1984; author, guest editor: (with Nichols, Hyslop Jr. and Bartlett) Decision Mking in Surgical Sepsis, 1991; guest editor, author: Surgical Sepsis and Beyond, 1993; mem. editl. bd. Current Surgery, 1977—, Hosp. Physician, 1980—, Infection Control, 1980-86, Guidelines to Antibiotic Therapy, 1976-81, Am. Jour. Infection Control, 1981—, Internat. Medicine, 1983—, Confronting Infection, 1983-86, Current Concepts in Clin. Surgery, 1984—, Fact Line, 1984-91, Host/Pathogen News, 1984—, Infectious Diseases in Clin. Practice, 1991—, surg. sect. editor, 1992—, Surg. Infections: Index and Revs., 1991—, So. Med. Jour., 1992—, ANAEROBE, 1994—; mem. adv. bd. Physician News Network, 1991-95; patentee (with S.G. schoenberger and W.R. Rank) Helical-Tipped Lesion Localization Needle Device. Elected faculty sponsor graduating class Tulane Med. Sch., 1979-80, 83, 85, 87, 88, 91-92. Served to major USAR, 1972-75. Recipient House Staff teaching award U. Ill. Coll. Medicine, 1973, Rsch. award Bd. Trustees U. Health Scis.-Chgo. Med. Sch., 1977, Owl Club Teaching award, 1980-86, 90; named Clin. Prof. of Yr. U. Health Scis., Chgo. Med. Sch., 1977, Clin. Prof. of Yr., Tulane U. Sch. Medicine, 1979; Douglas Stubbs Lectr. award Surg. Sect. Nat. Med. Assn., 1987, Prix d'Elegance award Men of Fashion, New Orleans, 1993; named Brit. Jour. of Surgery Lectr., 1997. Fellow Infectious Disease Soc. Am. (mem. FDA subcom. to develop guidelines in surg. prophylaxis 1989-93, co-recipient Joseph Susman Meml. award 1990), Am. Acad. Microbiology, Internat. Soc. Univ. Colon and Rectal Surgeons, ACS (mem. operating rm. environ. com. 1978-80, vice chair operating rm. environ. com. 1980-81, chmn. operating rm. environ. com. 1981-83, sr. mem. operating rm. environ. com. 1983-87, mem. internat. rels. com. 1987-93, sr. mem. internat. rels. com. 1993-97); mem. AMA, Nat. Found. for Infectious Diseases (bd. dirs. 1988—, v.p. 1994—), Joint Commn. on Accreditation of Health Care Orgn. (Infection Control adv. group, 1988—, sci. program com. 3d internat. conf. nosocomial infections CDC/Nat. Found. Infectious Diseases 1990, FDA Subcom. to Develop Guidelines in Surg. Prophylaxis, prophylactic antibiotic study group La. Health Care Rev. Inc. 1996—, AIDS commr. State of La. 1992-94), 5th Nat. Forum on AIDS (sci. program com.), U.S. Pharmacopeial Convention Inc. (adv. panelsurg. drugs and devices 1995—), Assn. Practitioners in Infection Control (physician adv. coun. 1991—), Internat. Soc. Anaerobic Bacteria, So. Med. Assn. (vice chmn. sect. surgery 1980-81, chmn. 1982-83), Assn. Acad. Surgery, N.Y. Acad. Sci., Warren H. Cole Soc. (pres.-elect 1988, pres. 1989-90), Assn. VA Surgeons, Soc. Surgery Alimentary Tract, Inst. Medicine Chgo., Midwest Surg. Assn., Cen. Surg. Assn., Ill. Surg. Soc., European Soc. Surg. Rsch., Collegium Internationale Chirugiae Digestivae, Chgo. Surg. Soc. (hon.), New Orleans Surg. Soc. (bd. dirs. 1983-87), Soc. Univ. Surgeons, Surg. Soc. La., Southeastern Surg. Soc., Phoenix Surg. Soc. (hon.), Hellenic Surg. Soc. (hon.), Cen. N.Y. Surg. Soc. (hon.), Tulane Surg. Soc., Alton Ochsner Surg. Soc., Am. Soc. Microbiology, Soc. Internat. de Chirugie, Surg. Infection Soc. (sci. study com. 1982-83, fellowship com. 1985-87, ad hoc sci. liaison com. 1986-89, program com. 1986-87, chmn. ad hoc com. rels. with industry 1990-93, mem. sci. liaison com. 1995-96), Soc. for Intestinal Microbial Ecology and Disease, Soc. Critical Care Medicine, Am. Surg. Assn., Kansas City Surg. Soc., Bay Surg. Soc. (hon.), Cuban Surg. Soc. (hon.), Panhellenic Surg. Soc. (hon.), Tacoma Surg. Club (hon.), Sigma Xi, Alpha Omega Alpha. Episcopalian. Patentee in field. Home: 1521 7th St New Orleans LA 70115-3322 Office: 1430 Tulane Ave New Orleans LA 70112-2699

NICHOLS, RUSSELL JAMES, manufacturing company executive; b. Brockton, Mass., Nov. 12, 1943; s. Clarence Willard and Hattie Matilda (Harlow) N.; m. Patricia Anna Rogers, Aug. 1, 1964; children: James E., Sharon L., Deborah L. Student, Rutgers U., 1966-68, Marion (Ohio) Tech. Coll., 1973-75, Findlay (Ohio) Coll., 1979-80. Registered profl. engr., Ohio; cert. quality engr., cert. quality auditor, cert. reliability engr. Rsch. technician Princeton Rsch. Ctr. Columbian Carbon divsn. Cities Svc. Co., Cranberry, N.J., 1965-68; tech. svc. engr. HPM Corp., Mount Gilead, Ohio, 1969-71, rsch. engr., 1971-73, product engr., 1974, area sales mgr., 1975, product mgr., 1976-77; process engring. mgr. Hancor Inc., Findlay, 1977-80; dir. devel. and tech. dir. Welding Engrs., Inc., Blue Bell, Pa., 1981-88; v.p. engring. Farrel Corp., Ansonia, Conn., 1989-90, v.p. quality, 1991—. Contbr. articles to profl. jours.; patentee in field. With USN, 1961-64. Fellow Soc. Plastics Engrs.; mem. NSPE, Am. Mgmt. Assn., Am. Soc. Quality Control (sr. mem.), Am. Chem. Soc. (Akron Rubber Group divsn.). Avocations: computers, reading. Home: 292 Elmwood Cir Cheshire CT 06410-4211 Office: Farrel Corp 25 Main St Ansonia CT 06401-1605

NICHOLS, SALLY JO, geriatrics nurse; b. Coldwater, Mich., Jan. 28, 1965; d. Leo Arnold and Charlotte (Ferguson) N. LPN, Pasco-Hernando C.C., 1985, AA, 1986, ASN, 1992; student, U. South Fla., 1990-91, 94—. RN, LPN, Fla. LPN All Cmty. Walk-In Clinic, Spring Hill, Fla., 1986; office mgr. Internat. Clerical Labs., Crystal River, Fla., 1986; LPN, charge nurse Eastbrooke Health Care Ctr., Brooksville, Fla., 1987-91; pvt. duty LPN Nursefinders, Inverness, Fla., 1991; med.-surg. LPN Oak Hill Hosp., Spring Hill, 1991; LPN charge nurse, then RN supr. Avante at Inverness, 1991—, resident assessment coord., care plan asst. coord., 1993-95, care plan coord., 1995-96, utilization rev./Medicare rev. coord., 1995-96, nurse mgr., 1996-97, dir. of nurses, 1997—. Relief ch. pianist Grace Tabernacle Ind. Bapt. Ch., Brooksville, 1983-91. Mem. ANA, Fla. Nurses Assn., Golden Key Honor Soc. Democrat. Avocations: piano, reading, travel, education. Home: 1225 W Highland Blvd Inverness FL 34452-4517 Office: Avante of Inverness 304 N Citrus Ave Inverness FL 34450-4157

NICHOLS, SANDRA B., public health service officer; b. Little Rock, Mar. 27, 1958; m. Ronnie A. Nichols, 1985; 1 child, Marquise. BA in Chemistry, Columbia Coll., Mo., 1980; student, Meharry Med. Coll., 1979-80; MS in Biology, Tenn. State U., 1982; MD, U. Ark., 1988. With dept. physiology U. Ark. Med. Scis., Little Rock, 1984-85, with microbiology lab., 1985-88, resident dept. family and community medicine, 1988-91, chief resident dept. family and community medicine, 1990-91, fellow dept. family and community medicine, occupational and environ. medicine, 1991-92; dir. Ark. Dept. of Health, Little Rock, 1994—; physician Mid Delta Health Clinic, 1992-94, interim med. dir., 1993-94; med. educator Delta Area Health Agy., U. Ark. Med. Scis., 1992—. Author: (with others) Family Practice textbook. Officer HHS, FDA; co-chair Pine Bluff Arsenal Citizen's Adv. Com.; mem. Gov.'s Partnership Coun. for Children and Families, Women Execs. in State Govt.; conf. participant Am. Swiss Found. Young Leaders Conf., 1995; mem. Ark. chpt. Internat. Women's Forum; mem. Ark. Arts Ctr.; spkr. Career Day, local schs.; vol. physician high schs. Recipient Nat. FBI Cmty. Leadership award, 1996; named one of Ark. Bus. Top 100 Women in Ark., 1996, 97, Top 10 Women in Ark., 1995, one of Outstanding Young Women in Am., 1981; Nat. Med. fellow, 1984-85; Pub. Health Leadership Inst. scholar, 1996, scholar Columbia Coll., 1976-80. Avocations: tennis, reading, speaking, cycling, traveling. Office: Ark Dept of Health 4815 W Markham St Ste 39 Little Rock AR 72205-3866

NICHOLS, STEPHEN GEORGE, Romance languages educator; b. Cambridge, Mass., Oct. 24, 1936; s. Stephen George and Marjorie (Whitney) N.; m. Mary Winn Jordan, June 22, 1957 (div. 1972); children: Stephen Frost (dec.), Sarah Winn; m. Edith Karetzky, 1972; stepchildren: Laura Natalie Karetzky, Sarah Karetzky Rothman. A.B. cum laude, Dartmouth Coll., 1958; Ph.D., Yale U., 1963; Docteur es lettres honoris causa, Université de Genève, 1992. Asst. prof. French UCLA, 1963-65; assoc. prof. comparative lit. U. Wis.-Madison, 1965-68, chmn. dept., 1967-68; prof. Romance langs. and comparative lit. Dartmouth Coll., 1968-84, chmn. dept. comparative lit., 1969-72, 74, 79-82, chmn. dept. Romance langs., 1974-77, Edward Tuck prof. French, 1984-85, chmn. dept. French and Italian, 1982-85, liaison officer Sch. Criticism and Theory, 1983-85; faculty Dartmouth Inst., 1980-85, faculty dir., 1984-85; prof. Romance langs. U. Pa., 1985-86, Edmund J. Kahn Disting. prof. humanities, 1986-92; James M. Beall prof. French and humanities Johns Hopkins U., Balt., 1992—; grad. group chmn. French and Italian U. Pa., 1986-88, chmn. dept. romance langs., 1987-88, assoc. dean for humanities, 1988-91; acting chair French, 1993-94; dir. grad. studies dept. French The Johns Hopkins U., Balt., 1992-94; R. Champlin and Debbie Sheridan interim dir. Eisenhower Libr., Johns Hopkins U., 1994-95, chair dept of French, 1995—; dir. sch. Criticism and Theory, 1995-2000; vis. prof. U. Tel Aviv, 1977, NYU, 1979-81, Exeter (Eng.) U., 1980, Ariz. State U., 1982, U. Calif., Irvine, 1985, Sch. Criticism and Theory, 1989, 95, Humanities Rsch. Inst. U. Calif., 1990, Ecole Pratique des Hautes Etudes, Paris, 1995, U. Pa., 1995, Dartmouth Coll., 1995-96, Cornell U., 1996—, Ecole Normale Superieure, Paris, 1996; NEH fellow, 1978-79, rev. panelist 1979-81, 84, 91, Guggenheim fellow, 1987-88; Phi Beta Kappa vis. scholar, 1983-84; Lauder fellow Aspen Inst. for Humanistic Study, 1988; mem. adv. bd. Institut d'Etudes Francaises d'Avignon, Bryn Mawr Coll., 1965—; dir. seminar NEH, 1975-79, Mellon summer seminar in humanities Johns Hopkins U., 1993, 94; exec. com. Ea. Comparative Lit. Conf.; mem. adv. coun. dept. comparative lit. Princeton U., 1982-88, chmn., 1984-88; co-dir. Ctr. Cultural Study, U. Pa., 1986-92; co-dir. Louis Marin Ctr. for French Studies, 1992—; advisor Waverly Consort, 1987-95; mem. adv. bd. Soc. Humanities Cornell U., 1993—; reviewer Guggenheim Fellowship applications, medieval sect., 1995—, French, 1996—. Author: Formulaic Diction and Thematic Composition in the Chanson de Roland, 1961, The Songs of Bernard de Ventadorn, 1962, 2d edit., 1968, La Roman de la Rose, 1967, 72, Comparists at Work, 1968, The Meaning of Mannerism, 1972, Mimesis: From Mirror to Method, Augustine to Descartes, 1982, Medieval and Renaissance Theories of Representation/New, 1984, Romanesque Signs: Early Medieval Narrative and Iconography, 1983, 85, Images of Power: History/Text/Discourse, 1986, The Legitimacy of the Middle Ages, 1988, The New Philology, 1990, Boundaries and Transgressions, 1991, The New Medievalism, 1991, Commentary as Cultural Artifact, 1992, Medievalism and the Modernist Temper: On the Discipline of Medieval, 1996, The Whole Book: Miscellany and Order in the Medieval Manuscript, 1996; editor: (book series) Parallax: Revisions of Culture and Society, 1987—; asst. editor French Rev., 1968-88; mem. editl. bd. Olifant, 1974-94, Medievalia et Humanistica, 1974-95, Medievalia, 1975—, Comparative Lit. Studies, 1986, Publ. of the MLA, 1988-89, Recentiores, 1991—, Modern Lang. Notes, 1992; mem. adv. bd. Colleagues Press, 1986—, Exemplaria: A Jour. Medieval Theory, 1987—; mem. adv. com. PMLA, 1980-84; adv. editor Romanic Rev., 1986—, Storia della Storiographia, 1992—. Rotary Found. fellow U. d'Aix Marseilles, France, 1958-59; fellow Inst. Rsch. in Humanities, 1966-67; sr. fellow Sch. of Criticism and Theory, 1988—. Fellow Medieval Acad. Am.; mem. Acad. Lit. Studies (nominating com. 1974-78, sec.-treas. 1978-87), Dante Soc., Internat. Comparative Lit. Assn., New Eng. Medieval Assn. (adv. com. 1981-85), MLA (chmn. com. on careers 1985-86, James Russell Lowell prize com. 1986-88, com. on profl. ethics 1987-88, del. assembly 1994-97), Medieval Acad. Am., Société Rencesvals (sec.-treas. Am. sect. 1964-69). Home: 5 Saint Martins Rd Baltimore MD 21218-1815

NICHOLS, STEVEN PARKS, mechanical engineer, university official; b. Cody, Wyo., July 1, 1950; s. Rufus Parks Nichols and Gwen Sena (Frank) Keyes; m. Mary Ruth Barrow, Aug. 5, 1990; 1 child, Nicholas Barrow Nichols. PhD, U. Tex., Austin, 1975, JD, 1983. Assoc. dir. Tex. Space Grant Consortium, Austin, 1989-91; dep. dir. ctr. for energy studies U. Tex., Austin, 1988-91, dir. ctr. for energy studies, 1991—, acting dir. ctr. for electromechanics, 1994—, assoc. prof., 1996—. Patentee (with others) railgun igniter, inert burner, rail thruster, other patents pending. Mem. NSPE, ASME, ABA, Am. Soc. Engring. Edn., Nat. Inst. Engring. Ethics (bd. govs. 1987-93). Home: 1400 Lorrain St Auston TX 78703 Office: U Tex Ctr for Energy Studies 10100 Burnet Rd Austin TX 78758-4445

NICHOLS, WILLIAM CURTIS, psychologist, family therapist, consultant; b. Fayette, Ala., Apr. 16, 1929; s. William Curtis and Eva (Hargett) N.; m. Alice Louise Mancill, May 29, 1954 (dec. 1990); children: Alice Camille, William Mancill, David Paul; m. Mary Anne Pace, Feb. 29, 1992. AB, U. Ala., 1953; EdD, Columbia U., 1960. Diplomate Am. Bd. Profl. Psychology. Asst. prof. sociology U. Ala., Birmingham, 1960-63; postdoctoral fellow Merrill-Palmer Inst., 1963-64, mem. psychotherapy faculty, 1965-69; prof. sociology Samford U., Birmingham, Ala., 1963-65; pvt. practice clin. psychology and marital and family therapy Grosse Pointe, Mich., 1969-73, 76-87; pvt. practice psychology, marital and family therapy Birmingham, Mich., 1976-87; prof. home and family life, dir. marriage and family counseling Fla. State U., 1973-76; exec. dir. Gov.'s Constituency Children, Fla., 1987-89; pvt. practice marital and family therapy S.E. Family Inst., 1989-90; pres. William Nichols Assocs., Organizational Cons., 1990-91; cons., marital and family therapist Atlanta, 1992—; adj. prof. clin. psychology U. Detroit, 1976-83; adj. prof. family therapy Fla. State U., 1990-91; adj. prof., grad. faculty child and family devel. dept. U. Ga., 1992—, founder, chair adv. com. Family Therapy Archives, 1993—. Author: Treating People in Families: An Integrative Framework, 1997, Marital Therapy: An Integrative Approach, 1988, Treating Adult Survivors of Childhood Sexual Abuse, 1992, The AAMFT: Fifty Years of Marital and Family Therapy, 1992; co-author: Systematic Family Therapy, 1986; editor: The Family Coord., 1970-75, Jour. Marriage and Family Counseling, 1974-76, Contemporary Family Therapy: An Internat. Jour., 1986—, Family Therapy News, 1986-91, The Internat. Connection, 1996—; mem. editl. bd. Internat. Jour. Family Therapy, 1977-85, Jour. Divorce and Remarriage, 1976-83, 85—, Internat. Jour. Family, Sage Family Studies Abstracts, 1977—, Family Systems Medicine, 1982-96, Jour. Marital and Family Therapy, 1984—, Jour. Family Psychotherapy, 1990—, Jour. Family Psychology, 1986-90. Mem. mental health and health coms. Mayor's Commn. on Children and Youth, 1966-69; bd. dirs. Family and Children's Svc., Oakland, Mich., 1977-87, chmn., 1984-86, dir. emeritus, 1987—. With C.E., U.S. Army, 1948-49. Recipient Svc. award Ala. Assn. for Mental Health, 1962, Spl. award for Outstanding Contbns. Fla. Assn. Marriage and Family Therapy, 1977, 82, 90; NSF fellow U. Colo., 1963, Disting. Svc. to families award Southeastern Coun. on Family Rels., 1996. Fellow APA, Am. Psychol. Soc., Am. Assn. Marriage and Family Therapy (dir. 1969-72, 1979-83, chmn. accreditation com. 1976-77, co-chmn. Atlanta Multiregional Conf. 1975, 77, founding editor Jour. Marital and Family Therapy 1974-76, Spl. awards 1976, 78, Disting. Leadership awards 1982, 83, pres.-elect 1979-80, pres. 1981-82, Disting. Leadership award 1991, Orgnl. Contributions award 1992), Acad. of Clin. Psychology; mem. Am. Assn. Marriage and Family Therapy Edn. and Rsch. Found. (trustee 1992-94), Assn. Marital and Family Therapy Regulation Bds. (mem. MFT Examination Adv. bd. 1989-92), Mich. Inter-Profl. Assn. on Marriage, Divorce and Family (Orgnl. Contbn. award 1992, trustee 1977-80, com. chmn. 1968-71, 76—), Mich. Assn. Marriage Counselors (pres. 1969-71, chmn. profl. liaison com. 1972-73), Nat. Coun. on Family Rels. (pres. 1976-77, dir., mem. exec. com. 1969-78), Mich. Bd. Marriage Counselors (chair 1980-87), Ga. Assn. for Marriage and Family Therapy (pres.-elect 1994-95, pres. 1996), Internat. Family Therapy Assn. (charter, editor Internat. Connections 1996—, bd. dirs. ex officio 1996—), Internat. Acad. Family Psychology. Home: 1041 Ferncreek Dr Watkinsville GA 30677-4212 Office: The Family Workshop Atlanta GA 30329-4210

NICHOLS, WILLIAM FORD, JR., foundation executive, business executive; b. Palo Alto, Calif., July 4, 1934; s. William Ford and Elizabeth (Woodyatt) N.; m. Rosemary Peterson, 1988; children: Deborah, John, Andrew. AB, Stanford U., 1956, MBA, 1958. CPA, Calif. With Price Waterhouse, San Francisco, 1958-69, Price Waterhouse & Co., Sydney, Australia, 1966; asst. contr. Saga Corp., Menlo Park, Calif., 1969-72, contr., 1972—, asst. treas., 1981-83; assoc. prof. San Jose State U., 1983-88; treas. William and Flora Hewlett Found., Menlo Park, 1985—; trustee Investment Fund for Founds., 1991—. Mem. AICPA, Calif. Soc. CPA's, Inst. Mgmt. Accts. (nat. v.p. 1974-75, bd. dirs.), Fin. Execs. Inst. (pres. Santa Clara Valley chpt. 1979-80). Home: 330 August Cir Menlo Park CA 94025-5829

NICHOLSON, BRADLEY JAMES, lawyer; b. Montebello, Calif., Sept. 22, 1958; s. Thomas Edwin and Charlotte Elizabeth (Knight) N.; m. Anne Marie Dooley, Oct. 6, 1990. BA, Reed Coll., 1983; JD, U. Pa., 1990. Bar: Calif. 1990, U.S. Ct. Appeals (9th cir.) 1990, U.S. Ct. Appeals (8th cir.) 1993, U.S. Dist. Ct. (no. dist.) Calif. 1990. Atty. Wilson, Sonsini, Goodrich & Rosati, Palo Alto, Calif., 1990-91; law clk. to Hon. Morris S. Arnold U.S. Dist. Ct., Ft. Smith, Ark., 1991-92; atty. Coudert Bros., San Jose, Calif., 1992-94; law clerk to Hon. Morris S. Arnold U.S. Cir. Ct., Little Rock, 1994-96; atty. Brown & Bain, Palo Alto, Calif., 1997—. Contbr. articles to profl. jours. Mem. Federalist Soc.(vice chmn. publications Litigation practice group, 1997—pres. Little Rock lawyers chpt. 1995-96), Am. Soc. for Legal History, Ninth Jud. Cir. Hist. Soc., Phi Beta Kappa (devel. chmn. no. Calif. chpt. 1990). Avocations: golf, fishing, music. Office: Brown & Bain 1755 Embarcadero Rd Ste 200 Palo Alto CA 94303-3309

NICHOLSON, BRUCE, graphics expert, executive. With Ray Mercer & Co., Apogee, Future Gen.; from optical camera asst. to optical supr. Indsl. Light & Magic, San Rafael, Calif., 1976-83, visual effects supr., 1984—. Optical camera asst. (films) Close Encounters of the Third Kind, 1976, Star Wars, 1977; optical supr. (films) The Empire Strikes Back, 1980 (Oscar award), Raiders of the Lost Ark, 1981 (Oscar award), Dragonslayer, 1981, Poltergeist, 1982, Return of the Jedi, 1983, Indiana Jones and the Temple of Doom, 1984; visual effects supr. (films) Starman, 1985, Explorers, 1986, Batteries Not Included, 1987, Field of Dreams, 1989, Always, 1989, Ghost, 1990, Memories of An Invisible Man, 1991, Meteor Man, 1993, In The Mouth of Madness, 1994, (commls.) HDTV, 1988, Panasonic, 1988, Subaru, 1989, Honda, 1990, Choice Hotels, 1994. Office: Indsl Light and Magic PO Box 2459 San Rafael CA 94912-2459*

NICHOLSON, DOUGLAS ROBERT, accountant; b. Avon, N.Y., Dec. 4, 1921; s. Robert William and Ruth (Neff) N.; m. Gertrude Jane Scott, Apr. 24, 1944; children—Laurie, Scott, Susan, Steven. A.B., U. Rochester, 1942, M.S., 1948. Baseball player St. Louis Cardinal Farm Teams, 1942, 46; Staff acct. Oliver & Clapp, 1948-49; sr. acct. Charles L. Clapp & Co., 1949-51; tchr. income taxes U. Rochester, 1950-61; office mgr. Williams, Clapp & Co., 1951-53, ptnr., 1953-56; prin. Haskins & Sells, CPA's, Rochester, N.Y., 1956-59, ptnr., 1959-67, ptnr.-in-charge Rochester office, 1967-82. Pres. Estate Planning Coun. Rochester; team capt. YMCA capital fund dr., 1961, Rochester Inst. Tech. new campus fund dr., 1964; chmn. spl. gifts com. U. Rochester, 1965, group leader 38 million capital fund campaign, 1966; mem. acctg. adv. bd. Syracuse U., 1968; adv. com. M.S. program Rochester Inst. Tech. Bd. Dirs.; treas. Highland Hosp., Rochester; bd. dirs. Hosp. Computer Ctr. Rochester, Rochester Regional Rsch. Libr. Coun.; mem. deferred giving adv. coun. Rochester Inst. Tech.; mem. N.Y. State Bd. Pub. Accountancy, 1977-82. Lt. USNR, 1942-45. Recipient Gannett Newspapers award, 1956. Mem. Am. Inst. C.P.A.'s, N.Y. State Soc. C.P.A.'s (past pres. Rochester), Nat. Assn. Accountants, Am. Accounting Assn., Am. Mgmt. Assn., Rochester C. of C., Beta Alpha Psi. Democrat. Unitarian (trustee). Clubs: Oak Hill Country, University, Genesee Valley. Home and Office: 663 Lake Rd Webster NY 14580-1552

NICHOLSON, GEORGE ALBERT, JR., financial analyst; b. Baldwin City, Kan., May 7, 1908; s. George Albert and Nellie May (Ruthrauff) N.; m. Elizabeth Farnham, Sept. 1, 1933; children: George Albert III, Edwin F., John R., Elizabeth C. (Mrs. David D. Hamm). A.B., U. Mich., 1928; M.B.A., Harvard U., 1930; LL.D., Carthage Coll., 1972. Chartered fin. analyst. With Hudson Motor Co., 1930-31, Union Guardian Trust Co., 1931-33; fin. analyst Whitlock, Smith & Co., Detroit, 1933-37, Am. Industries, Detroit, 1937-41, Inc. Investors, Boston, 1941; civilian renegotiator USAF, 1942-45; fin. analyst Watling, Lerchen & Co., Detroit, 1945-58; rsch. dir. Smith, Hague & Co. Inc., Detroit, 1958-90; columnist Better Investing Mag.; cons. 1st of Mich. Merger, Detroit, 1990—; chmn. Investment Edn. Inst., Internat. Investment Edn. Inst., World Fedn. Investment Clubs. Nicholson awards for best ann. reports for individual investors established by Nat. Assn. Investors, 1978. Mem. Fin. Analyst Soc. Detroit (pres. 1957), Nat. Assn. Investment Clubs (chmn. adv. bd.), Delta Kappa Epsilon. Republican. Episcopalian. Clubs: Country (Detroit), Indian Village (Detroit). Home: 1017 Cadieux Rd Grosse Pointe MI 48230-1511

NICHOLSON, GERALD LEE, medical facilities administrator; b. Belleville, Ill., Dec. 30, 1944; s. Chester Lee and Bette Joan (Tarr) N.; m. Cathy Ann Sammons, May 3, 1975; children: Laura, Brianna. BA in Sociology, So. Ill. U., 1974, BS in Math., 1976, MBA, 1976. Bus. mgr. Northland Orthopedic Group, St. Louis, 1976-78; cons. AMA, Chgo., 1978-80; cons. pvt. practice Evansville, Ind., 1981-85; adminstr. Mo. Eye Inst., St. Louis, 1985-91; regional v.p. Co-Care Eye Cts., St. Louis, 1985-91; adminstr. Orthopaedic Assoc., P.C., Cape Girardeau, Mo., 1992—; tax preparer Nicholson Cons., St. Louis, 1990-92. Mem. Citizen Interaction Com., Chesterfield, Mo., 1989, Leadership Cape, 1992. Capt. USMC, 1966-72, Vietnam. Mem. Marine Corps Res. Officers Assn., Am. Coll. Med. Practice Execs., Med. Group Mgrs. Assn., S.E. Mo. Med. Mgrs. (pres.), Aircraft Owners and Pilots Assn., Rotary Internat. (pres. club). Avocations: running, flying. Home: 3010 Melrose St Cape Girardeau MO 63701-2200 Office: Orthopaedic Assocs of SE Mo PC 48 Doctors Park Cape Girardeau MO 63703-4928

NICHOLSON, HENRY HALE, JR., surgeon; b. Statesville, N.C., June 22, 1922; s. Henry Hale and Haseltine Witherspoon (Miller) N.; m. Freda Hyams, Sept. 24, 1956; children: Henry Hale III, Thomas Dalton Miller, John Christie, Michael Witherspoon, Freda Amanda, W. Stuart, Cooper. BA in Chemistry, Duke U., 1944, MD, 1947. Diplomate Am. Bd. Gen. Surgery, Am. Bd. Colon and Rectal Surgery. Rotating intern U. Wis., Madison, 1948; resident in gen. surgery Med. Coll. Va., Richmond, 1949; resident in gen. surgery Alton Ochsner Hosp. and Clinic, New Orleans, 1949-51, 53-55, inaugural resident in colon and rectal surgery, 1955-56; resident in gen. surgery Tulane U., La. Charity Hosp., New Orleans, 1949-51, 53-55; pvt. practice gen., colon and rectal surgery, aerospace medicine Charlotte, N.C., 1956—; mem. surg. staff Charlotte (N.C.) Presbyn. Hosp.; sr. surg. staff mem. Carolinas Med. Ctr. and Mercy Hosp., Charlotte; sr. active staff Presbyn. Hosp., Charlotte; sr. active teaching staff Carolinas Med. Ctr., 1956-85, cons. staff, 1985—. Mem. adv. authority Charlotte/Douglas Internat. Airport, 1992—; mem. com. of 100 Regional Transp. Study and Recommendations, 1993-94; sr. examiner FAA, 1952—; mem. athletic-med. bd. N.C. Shrine Bowl, 1980. With U.S. Army, 1943-46; flight surgeon USAF, 1951-53, Korea; col. USAFR, 1961-82; 1st air surgeon N.C. Air. NG, 1970-82. Fellow ACS, Am. Soc. Colon and Rectal Surgeons; mem. Mecklenberg County Med. Soc. (pres. 1972), Charlotte Surg. Soc. (pres. 1987), Shriners (Scotish Rite), Masons (32 degree), Jesters, Alton Ochsner Surg. Soc., Hazel Creek Trout Club, Robert Burns Soc., St. Andrews Soc. of Carolina, Hound Ears Club (Blowing Rock, N.C.), Charlotte Country Club, Alpha Tau Omega, Phi Chi, Omicron Delta Kappa. Methodist. Avocations:

golf, snow skiing, fly fishing, travel, painting. Home: 635 Manning Dr Charlotte NC 28209-3441 Office: 1012 S Kings Dr Charlotte NC 28283-0003

NICHOLSON, JACK, actor, director, producer; b. Neptune, N.J., Apr. 28, 1937; s. John and Ethel May N.; m. Sandra Knight, 1961 (div. 1966); children: Jennifer, Lorraine Broussard. Acting debut Hollywood stage prodn. Tea and Sympathy; films include Cry-Baby Killer, 1958, Studs Lonigen, 1960, Little Shop of Horrors, 1960, Ensign Pulver, 1964, The Trip, 1967, Easy Rider, (Acad. award nomination for best supporting actor), 1969, Five Easy Pieces, 1970, Carnal Knowledge, 1971, A Safe Place, 1971, The-Last Detail, 1974 (Cannes Film Festival prize), Chinatown, 1974 (Acad. award nomination, N.Y. Film Critics Circle award), Tommy, The Passenger, 1975, The Fortune, 1975, One Flew Over the Cuckoo's Nest (Golden Globe award, Acad. award for best actor, N.Y. Film Critics Circle award), 1975, The Missouri Breaks, 1976, The Last Tycoon, 1976, The Shining, 1980, The Postman Always Rings Twice, 1981, Reds,1981 (Acad. award nomination for best supporting actor), The Border, 1982, Termsof Endearment (Acad. award for best supporting actor), 1983, Prizzi's Honor,1985 (Acad. award nomination for best actor), Heartburn, 1986, The Witches of Eastwick, 1987, Broadcast News, 1987, Ironweed, 1987 (Acad. award nomination for bestactor), Batman, 1989, Man Trouble, 1991, A Few Good Men, 1992, Hoffa, 1992, Wolf, 1994, The Crossing Guard, 1995, Mars Attacks!, 1996, The Evening Star, 1996, Blood and Wine, 1996; producer films Head, 1968, Ride the Whirlwind, The Shooting; dir. films Drive, He Said, 1971; dir., actor films Goin' South, 1978, The Two Jakes, 1990. Co-recipient (with Bobby McFerrin) Grammy award for best recording for children,1987. Office: Bresler Kelly Kipperman 15760 Ventura Blvd Ste 1730 Encino CA 91436-3028*

NICHOLSON, JOSEPH BRUCE, real estate developer; b. San Jose, Calif., Jan. 21, 1940; s. Wilmot Joseph and Ruth (Russell) N.; m. Susan Knight, Nov. 1963 (div. 1972); children: Kelsey Erin, Craig Wilmot; m. Linda Mirassou, Aug. 1992. BArch, U. Oreg., 1963. Exec. v.p. Nicholson-Brown Inc., Santa Clara, Calif., 1967-80; prin. Nicholson Assocs., Aptos, Calif., 1977—; v.p., gen. mgr. Nicholson-Wilson Co., Santa Clara, 1980-83; prin. The Nicholson Co., Campbell, Calif., 1984—; v.p. Pacific Property Ventures Inc., Campbell, 1988—; pres. Nicholson Constrn. Inc., Campbell, 1989—; v.p. Nicholson Property Mgmt. Inc., Campbell, 1989—; pres. The Nicholson Family Found., 1996—; bd. dirs. Transmetrics Inc., San Jose. Bd. dirs. Triton Mus., Santa Clara, 1979, Hope Rehab. Svc., San Jose, 1979, United Way Cen. Area, San Jose, 1991; pres. adv. bd. de Saisset Mus., Santa Clara U., 1991; trustee Mus. of Art and History, Santa Cruz, 1993. Lt. USN, 1963-67. Mem. Rotary, Commonwealth Club (San Francisco), World Trade Club (San Francisco). Republican. Avocations: travel, reading, art collecting, cooking, tennis. Home: 218 Shoreview Dr Aptos CA 95003-4621 Office: The Nicholson Co 75 Cristich Ln Campbell CA 95008-5403

NICHOLSON, LELAND ROSS, retired utilities company executive, energy consultant; b. Carrington, N.D., Feb. 21, 1924; s. Malcom and Lena May (Kerlin) N.; m. Virginia E. Blair, Mar. 16, 1946; children: Heather Le Nicholson Studebaker, Leland B., Holly Kay. Student, Northwestern U., 1940-41; BSEE, U. N.D., 1949; postgrad. in utility mgmt., U. Minn., 1952. Planning and mktg. engr. Minkota Power Coop., Grand Forks, N.D., 1949-54; dir. new bus. Kans. Power & Light Co., Topeka, 1954-64, v.p. mktg., 1964-76, sr. v.p., 1976-80, exec. v.p., 1980-83, also bd. dirs.; pres. Kans. Power & Light Gas Service, Topeka, 1985-88, ret., 1988; pres., chief operating officer The Gas Service Co., Kansas City, Mo., 1983-85; pres. Indsl. Devel. Corp., Topeka; chmn. Kans. Council on Electricity and Environment; exec. com. Kansas City Labor Mgmt. Council, 1986-89; mem. Mktg. Execs. Conf.; bd. dirs. Gas Service Energy Corp., Kansas City, Merchants Nat. Bank, Topeka. Idea innovator heat pump water heater, photo cell controlled yard light, electric grill. Bd. dirs., area relations com. Kansas City (Mo.) Area Econ. Devel. Council, 1983-89; bd. dirs. Kansas City Pvt. Industry Council, 1986-89, Kansas City Downtown Council; trustee U. Mo., Kansas City, 1984-91; mktg. chmn. Kansas City Full Employment Council; past chmn., mem. Topeka-Shawnee County Planning Commn.; adult adv. com. Sea Scouts. Served to master sgt. USMC, 1942-46. Mem. Am. Gas Assn., Midwest Gas Assn. (bd. dirs. 1985-89), Mo. Valley Electric Assn. (chmn. 1979-81), Edison Electric Inst. (mktg. chmn. 1978-80), Assoc. Industries of Mo., Kans. Assn. Commerce and Industry, Greater Kansas City (Mo.) C. of C. (bd. dirs. 1979-82), Shawnee Yacht Club (Topeka) (commodore 1972-74), Lake Gaston Assn. (pres. 1993—), Kansas City Club, Rotary. Republican. Congregationalist. Avocations: sailing, canoeing, fishing, reading, electronics.

NICHOLSON, MORRIS EMMONS, JR., metallurgist, educator; b. Indpls., Feb. 15, 1916; s. Morris Emmons and Jessie (Cox) N.; m. Norma Story, Aug. 21, 1943; children: Morris Emmons III, Robert A., Richard A. BS, MIT, 1939; ScD, Mass. Inst. Tech., 1947. Registered profl. engr., Minn. Sect. head engring. research dept. Standard Oil Co., Ind., 1947-50; asst. prof. Inst. Study Metals, U. Chgo., 1950-55; prof. metallurgy U. Minn., 1956-85, prof. emeritus, 1985—, head dept., 1956-62, dir. continuing edn. in engring. and sci., 1973-85; mem. Materials Adv. Bd., 1960-62. Active Boy Scouts Am., 1952—, dist. commr., 1961-64, 70-71; trustee Ind. Dist. 623 Sch. Bd., 1959-65, treas., 1965-77; bd. dirs. 916 Area Vocat. Tech. Sch., 1976-83, 916 Found., 1984-95, sec., 1984-90; bd. dirs. Minn. Sch. bd. Assn., 1973-79; amb. N.W. Youth and Family Svcs., 1988-93; mem. Falcon Heights Parks and Recreation Commn., 1992-95. Recipient Silver Beaver, Boy Scouts Am., 1966; named Outstanding Sch. Bd. Mem., Minn. Sch. Bd. Assn., 1981. Mem. Am. Soc. Engring. Edn. (chmn. U. Minn. chpt. 1957-58, CPD divsn. 1962—, archivist 1985-94, Disting. Svc. award 1980), Am. Soc. Metals (chmn. Minn. chpt. 1958, mem. hist. sites com. 1989-92, chmn. 1991-92), Minerals, Metals and Materials Soc. (profl. registration com. 1982-93, chmn. 1986-93, Disting. Svc. award 1994), Assn. for Media-Based Continuing Edn. for Engrs. (bd. dirs. 1976-85), Sigma Xi, Theta Delta Chi, Tau Beta Pi, Alpha Chi Sigma. Mem. United Ch. Christ. Home: 1776 Pascal Ave N Saint Paul MN 55113-6259

NICHOLSON, MYREEN MOORE, artist, researcher; b. Norfolk, Va., June 2, 1940; d. William Chester and Illeen (Fox) Moore; m. Roland Quarles Nicholson, Jan. 9, 1964 (dec. 1986); children: Andrea Joy, Ross (dec. 1965); m. Harold Wellington McKinney II, Jan. 18, 1981; 1 child, Cara Isadora. AA, William and Mary Coll., 1960; BA Old Dominion U., 1962; MLS, U. N.C., 1971; MA in Humanities Old Dominion U. 1997; postgrad. The Citadel, 1968-69, Hastie Sch. Art, 1968, Chrysler Mus. Art Sch., 1964. English tchr., Chesapeake, Va., 1962-63; dept. head, Portsmouth (Va.) Bus. Coll., 1963-64; tech. writer City Planning/Art Commn., Norfolk, 1964-65; art tchr. Norfolk pub. schs., 1965-67; prof. lit., art Palmer Jr. Coll., Charleston, S.C., 1968; tchr. Penn Sch. John's Island, S.C., 1968; librarian Charleston Schs., 1968-69; asst. to asst. dir. City Library Norfolk, 1970-72, art and audio-visual librarian, 1972-75, rsch. librarian, 1975-83, librarian dept. fiction, 1983-90; dir. W. Ghent Arts Alliance, Norfolk, 1978—. Poet-in-schs., Virginia Beach, Va., 1987. Book reviewer Art Book Revs., Library Jour., 1973-76; editor, illustrator Acquisitions Bibliographies, 1970—, (play) Eldorado: The Poes in Norfolk, 1996, West Ghent newsletter, 1995—; juried exhibits various cities including Grand Hyatt, Mayflower, Washington, by Joan Mondale, Nohra Haime, curator of Freer Gallery, by sr. curator Nat. Mus. Am. Art, curator Phillips Collection, asst. curator, White House by curator of White House and by dir. of Nat. Portrait Gallery; group shows include Ctr. Comtemporary Art, Va. Beach, 1993, Yorktown Small Works Show, 1996, Hampton Arts Commn. and Tidewater Artists Assn. Portfolio Show, 1996, Suffolk Artists and Writers Invitational Exhibit, 1996, Artists In Virginia, 1996, Peninsula Ann. Juried Art Exhibit, 1996, Hampton Bay Days Juried Art Exhibit, 1996, Portsmouth Mus., 1997others; contbr. art and poetry to various publs. and anthologies. Mem. Virginia Beach Arts Ctr., 1978-93, Hampton Art League, 1990—, Suffolk Art League, 1990—; bd. dirs. W. Ghent Art/Lit. Festival, 1979; poetry reader Poetry Soc. Va., Va. Ctr. for Creative Arts, Sweetbriar, 1989, Walden Books, 1991, Christopher Newport U., 1994-95, Caberet Voltaire, 1994, J.M. Prince Books and Coffeehouse, 1995—, Statues St. Mark's Cath. Ch., 1991-92, Newport U., 1996, U. Mich., 1996; graphics of hundreds of celebrities from life; curator Va. Winter Show Life Saving Mus., 1991-92; judge Bornstein art scholarship Chrysler Mus., 1992; mem. staff Mid-Atlantic Antiques Mag., 1993—. Recipient awards various art and poetry contests; Coll. William and Mary art scholar, 1958, Tricentenial award for Contbns. to the Arts in Va., 1993; recipient Cert. for Vol. Contbns. to Va. by Gov., 1994. Nat. Endowment Arts grantwriter, 1975; bd. dirs. Tidewater Literacy Coun., 1971-72; bd. dirs. West Ghent League. Mem. ALA (poster sessions rev. com. 1985-96, pub. relations judge, subcom. comm. 1988-90), Pub. Libr. Assn. (com. bylaws and orgns. 1988-90), Va. Libr. Assn. (pub. relations com. 1984-86, grievance and pay equity com. 1986-88, co-designer Paraprofl. Logo for Norfolk Pub. Libr., 1970, co-winner Paraprofl. Logo award 1985, chair Pub. Documents Forum, 1992-93), Southeastern Libr. Assn. (Rothrock award com. 1986-88, com. on coms. 1991-92), Poetry Soc. Va. (v.p. 1986-89, nominating com. 1989-90, state corr. sec., editor newsletter 1990-93, dir. publicity 1993-95, 70th Anniversary plaque for Wren Bldg., mem. commn. 75th anniversary poster and book cover 1997—), Art Librs. Soc. N.Am., Tidewater Artists Assn. (bd. dirs. 1989—, chair grantwriting com. 1990—, pres. 1991-92), Southeastern Coll. Art Assn., Acad. Am. Poets, Irene Leache Soc., Internat. Platform Assn. (artists assn.), Old Dominion U. Alumni Assn. (artistic dir. Silver Reunion), Southeastern Soc. Archtl. Historians, Ikara (pres. 1989—), D'Art Ctr. (Dockside art rev., bd. dirs. 1991-92), Ex Libris Soc. (charter), Va. Writers Club (editor West Ghent newsletter). Home and Office: 1404 Gates Ave Norfolk VA 23507-1131

NICHOLSON, R. STEPHEN, organization administrator; b. Radford, Va., Mar. 4, 1926; s. Roy S. and Ethel Dovie (Macy) N.; m. Carol Peterson, 1987; 1 child, Suzanne Carpenter. A.B., Marion Coll., 1950; M.A., Syracuse U., 1956; Ph.D., Mich. State U., 1971. Prof. Lansing (Mich.) Community Coll., 1963-66, Acad. dean, 1966-69; pres. Daley Coll., Chgo., 1969-71, Clark County Community Coll., 1971-76, Mt. Hood Community Coll. Dist., 1976-85; chancellor Oakland Community Coll., 1985-90; vice chancellor Higher Colls. of Tech., United Arab Emirates, 1990-92; CEO Internat. Christian Leadership, 1992-93; pres. emeritus Mt. Hood Coll., 1993—; CEO Mercy Corps Internat., 1994-95, chmn. bd. dirs., 1997—. Rsch. advisor M.J. Murdock Trust, 1993-95, sr. fellow higher edn., 1996—. Mem. Am. Assn. Community and Jr. Colls. (pres. Pres.'s Acad. 1982, bd. dirs. 1985-87), N.W. Assn. Community and Jr. Colls. (pres. 1976), Am. Sch. Adminstrs. Assn., Am. Sociology Assn., Am. Acad. Polit. and Social Scis., Gresham C. of C. (dir. 1977-79), Japan-Am. Soc., World Affairs Council, Am. Futurist Soc., Phi Delta Kappa. Club: Rotary (pres. 1983, Paul Harris fellow 1986). Home: 3901 SW 22nd Dr Gresham OR 97080-8381

NICHOLSON, RALPH LESTER, botanist, educator; b. Lynn, Mass., Aug. 25, 1942; s. Nathan Aaron and Muriel Spinney (Buxton) N. BA, U. Vt., 1964; MS, U. Maine, 1967; PhD, Purdue U., 1972. Prof. dept. botany and plant pathology Purdue U., West Lafayette, Ind., 1972—; Contbr. chpts. to books, more than 100 articles to profl. jours. Active Big Bros./Big Sisters, Lafayette, Ind., 1974—. Fellow Am. Phytopathol. Soc. Office: Purdue U Botany and Plant Pathology Lafayette IN 47907

NICHOLSON, RICHARD JOSEPH, trust banking executive; b. N.Y.C., Feb. 19, 1932; s. Robert William and Mary Elizabeth (McShane) N.; m. Barbara Helen Malisky, Oct. 15, 1955; 1 child, Richard Jr. BS in Social Sci., Georgetown U., 1952; MBA, NYU, 1957. Asst. cashier Citibank Trust Divsn., N.Y.C., 1952-66; sr. v.p. 1st Fidelity Bank, Newark, 1966-90, ret., 1990; mem. exec. com. N.J. Bankers Assn. Trust Divsn., Princeton, 1983-85. Bd. dirs. Family Svc. Bur. of Newark, 1976—; mem. coun. Newark Mus., 1979-90. Republican. Roman Catholic. Avocations: tennis, travel, history.

NICHOLSON, RICHARD SELINDH, educational association administrator; b. Des Moines, Apr. 5, 1938; s. George Eugene and Margaret (Selindh) N.; m. Mary Lou Weisbrod, Aug. 1, 1958 (div. 1971) 1 child, Jeffrey Richard; m. Lois Ann Karls, Aug. 15, 1976; 1 child, Gregory Michael. BS, Iowa State U., 1960; PhD, U. Wis., 1964; LHD (hon.), CUNY, 1994, CUNY-Mt. Sinai Med. Ctr., 1994. Rsch. assoc. U. Wis., Madison, 1963-64; asst. prof. Mich. State U., East Lansing, 1964-67, assoc. prof., 1967-70; program dir. NSF, Washington, 1970-77, div. dir., 1977-82, chief of staff, 1983-85, asst. dir., 1985-89; exec. dir. Nat. Sci. Bd. Commn., Washington, 1982-83; exec. officer, pub. Science AAAS, Washington, 1989—; cons. on sci. affairs Pres. of U.S., Washington, 1978-79; exec. sec. Pres.' Com. on Nat. Medal Sci., Washington, 1976-84; mem. Pres.' Nat. Commn. on Superconductivity, 1989; vice chair Commn. on Phys. Scis., Math and Resources NRC, 1989—, Edn. Coordinating Coun., 1991—, com. on environ. rsch., 1991-92, co-chair coun. on competitiveness, 1993—; mem. statutory vis. com. Nat. Inst. of Stds. and Tech., 1990-93; vis. com. chemistry dept. Harvard U., 1989—; bd. dirs. Quality Edn. for Minorities Network, 1989—; trustee Gordon Rsch. Conf., 1989—; sci. policy adv. com. com. space, sci. and tech. U.S. Ho. Reps., 1992—; co-chair Coun. on Competitiveness, 1993—, Dept. of Energy Panel on Basic Rsch., 1995—; chmn. edn. adv. com. Genentech, 1993—. Mem. editorial bd. Analytical Chemistry, 1980-82, Chem. and Engring. News, 1985-88; contbr. articles to profl. jours. and chpts. to books. Served as seaman USN, 1956-63. Recipient Presdl. Disitng. Ranking, Pres. Reagan, 1982, Alumni Citation Merit award Iowa State U., 1983. Fellow AAAS; mem. Am. Chem. Soc. (chmn. Mich. State U. sect. 1968-70), Chem. Soc. Washington (nominations com. 1977), Cosmos Club, Nat. Press Club. Avocations: sports, tennis, reading. Home: 1020 Union Church Rd Mc Lean VA 22102-1115 Office: AAAS 1200 New York Ave NW Washington DC 20005-3928

NICHOLSON, ROBERT ARTHUR, college president; b. Pepin, Wis., Oct. 13, 1923; s. Arthur W. and Ethel (Weeden) N.; m. Dorothy Nelis, June 17, 1944; children: Paul, Gary. BS, Anderson U., Ind., 1944; MA, NYU, 1946, Ph.D., 1953. With Anderson U., 1945-90, successively instr., asst. prof., assoc. prof. music, chmn. dept., asst. to dean, 1945-58, dean, 1958-83, v.p., 1964-83, pres., 1983-90, pres. emeritus, 1990—. Author: Handbook to the Hymnal of the Church of God, 1953; Editor: Hymnal of the Church of God, 1953, 71. Mem. pub. bd. Ch. of God, 1955-80, chmn. commn. higher edn., 1963-70, 83-86, vice chmn., 1970-83, cons., 1990-96; cons. Warner Pacific Coll., Oreg., 1990—, N.Ind. United Meth. Found., Inc., 1992-95, Anderson Pub. Libr., 1994-95, United Faith Housing Corp., 1994, Hopewell Ctr., 1996, Alexandria Cmty. Ctr., Inc., 1997, Family Network Agy., Inc., 1997; bd. dirs. Anderson Symphony Orch., 1974-87, 93-94, United Way Madison County, 1985-89, 91-94, Minnetrista Cultural Found., 1988—; bd. dirs., v.p. Anderson Internat., 1990-93; bd. dirs. Cmty. Hosp. Madison County, 1986-95, vice chmn., 1988-94, interim pres., CEO, 1991; pres. Madison County Comty. Found., Inc., 1991—. Mem. Associated Colls. of Ind., Ind. Colls. and Univs. of Ind. (chmn. 1988-89), Anderson Area C. of C. (bd. dirs. 1985-90, vice chmn. and chmn. elect 1988, chmn. 1989). Home: 721 Maplewood Ave Anderson IN 46012-3028

NICHOLSON, WILL FAUST, JR., bank holding company executive; b. Colorado Springs, Colo., Feb. 8, 1929; s. Will Faust and Gladys Olivia (Burns) N.; m. Shirley Ann Baker, Nov. 26, 1955; children: Ann Louise Nicholson Naughton, Will Faust III. S.B., M.I.T., 1950; M.B.A., U. Denver, 1956. V.p. Van Schaack & Co., Denver, 1954-66; pntr. N. G. Petry Constrn. Co., Denver, 1966-70; sr. v.p. Colo. Nat. Bankshares, Inc., Denver, 1970-75; pres. Colo. Nat. Bankshares, Inc., 1975-95, chmn. bd., chief exec. officer, 1985-95; chmn. Rocky Mountain Bankcard Sys., Denver, 1995—; bd. dirs. Pub. Svc. Co., Colo.; bd. dirs., chmn. VISA USA, Inc., VISA Internat. Bd. dirs. Boys and Girls Clubs of Metro Denver; active Downtown Denver, Inc., Colo. Assn. of Commerce and Industry, chmn. 1990-91, Denver Urban Renewal Authority, 1958-59, Denver Bd. Water Commrs., 1959-65, pres. 1964, 65; Nat. Western Stock Show; bd. Health One. With USAF, 1950-53. Mem. Assn. Bank Holding Cos. (bd. dirs. 1979-87, 89-91, exec. com. 1980-85, vice chmn. 1981-82, chmn. 1983-84), U.S. C. of C. (bd. dirs. 1990—), U.S. Golf Assn. (exec. com. 1974-82, v.p. 1978, 79, pres. 1980, 81), Denver Country Club, Univ. Club Colo., Univ. Club N.Y., Castle Pine Golf Club, Royal and Ancient Golf Club (St. Andrews, Scotland), Augusta (Ga.) Nat. Golf Club. Republican. Episcopalian. Home: 37 Polo Club Cir Denver CO 80209-3307 Office: Colo Nat Bankshares PO Box 5168 Denver CO 80217-5168

NICHOLSON, WILLIAM JOSEPH, forest products company executive; b. Tacoma, Aug. 24, 1938; s. Ferris Frank and Athyleen Myrtle (Fesenmaier) N.; m. Carland Elaine Crook, Oct. 10, 1964; children: Courtney, Brian, Kay, Benjamin. SB in ChemE, MIT, 1960, SM in ChemE Practice, 1961; PhD in ChemE, Cornell U., 1965; MBA, Pacific Luth. U., 1969. Registered profl. chem. engr., Wash. Sr. devel. engr. Hooker Chem. Co., Tacoma, 1964-69, Battelle N.W., Richland, Wash., 1969-70; planning assoc. Potlatch Corp., San Francisco, 1970-75, mgr. corp. energy service, 1976-94, dir. corp. energy and environ. svcs., 1994—; chmn. electricity com. Am. Forest and Paper Assn., 1977—, mem. solid waste task force, 1988-91, air quality com., 1989—, mem. environ. policy and oversight com., 1994—, vice-chmn. life cycle analysis work group, 1994—, chmn. wood products environ. task force, 1994—; U.S. expert on environ. labelling to Internat. Stds. Orgn., 1994—; chmn., mem. adv. bd. Forest Products Lab., U. Calif., Richmond, 1992-95; mem. adv. bd. Coll. of Natural Resources, U. Calif., Berkeley, 1993-95. Mem. AAAS, AIChE (assoc.), Am. Chem. Soc., Tech. Assn. Pulp and Paper Industry, Sigma Xi, Commonwealth Club (San Francisco), Cornell Club (N.Y.). Republican. Avocation: industrial history. Home: PO Box 1114 Ross CA 94957-1114 Office: Potlatch Corp 244 California St Ste 610 San Francisco CA 94111-4351

NICHOLSON, WILLIAM MAC, naval architect, marine engineer, consultant; b. Napa, Calif., June 15, 1918; s. William John and Hazel (McIlmoil) N.; m. Lynda Bishop, Feb. 10, 1947 (div. Aug. 1959); children: Lynda Joanne, Samuel Bishop; m. Leslie Marie Earle-Thomas, Apr. 1, 1964; children: Richard Thomas, Glenn Thomas, Ronald Thomas. BS, U.S. Naval Acad., 1941; MS, MIT, 1948. Commd. ensign USN, 1941, advanced through grades to capt., 1960; ret., 1971; design supt. Boston Shipyard, 1951-52; project officer minesweeping, hydrofoils Bur. of Ships, Washington, 1955-59; comptr. Puget Sound Naval Shipyard, Bremerton, Wash., 1959-62; prof. naval constrn. MIT, Cambridge, 1962-65; dir. ship design div. Bur. of Ships, Washington, 1965-66; program mgr. deep submergence Chief of Naval Material, Washington, 1966-71; assoc. dir. Nat. Ocean Survey, NOAA, Washington, 1971-81; retired, 1981. chmn. U.S.-Japan panel on marine facilities under U.S.-Japan Natural Resource Agreement., 1972-81; vice-chmn. marine bd. Acad. Engring., NAS, Washington, 1984-85; pres., 1983, chmn., bd. dirs., 1984, Sea-Space Symposium. Decorated Legion of Merit. Mem. Soc. Naval Architects and Marine Engrs. (sect. chmn. N.E. 1964-65), Soc. Naval Engrs. (coun. 1966-68), Marine Tech. Soc. (sect. chmn. 1974-75), N.Y. Yacht Club, Sigma Xi, Tau Beta Pi. Republican. Home: 1672 Saint Albans Sq Annapolis MD 21401-6431

NICHOLSON-GUTHRIE, CATHERINE S. See GUTHRIE, CATHERINE S. NICHOLSON

NICHOLSON-O'BRIEN, DAWN, government official; b. Halifax, Canada, May 23, 1959; d. Roy MacLean and Shirley (Levy) Nicholson; m. Gregory Keith O'Brien, Aug. 23, 1980; children: Nicholas, Connor, Serena. BA, Dalhousie U., 1980, postgrad., 1980-81. Policy program analyst Canadian Unity Info. Office, 1981-87; from dir. gen. comms. and pub. affairs to dir. gen. comms. Dept. Justice Canada, 1987-96; dir. gen. policy, strategic planning and liaison Dept. Fisheries and Oceans, 1996-97. mem. Assn. Profl. Execs. of Can., Internat. Assn. Pub. Participation Practitioners, Fed. Comms. Coun. Avocations: writing, music, gardening, decorating, swimming. Office: Fed Dept Fisheries and Oceans, 200 Kent St Rm 1109, Ottawa, ON Canada K1A 0E6

NICITA, RICK, agent. Agent Creative Artists Agy.; now chmn. Creative Artists Agy., Beverly Hills, Calif. Office: Creative Artists Agy 9830 Wilshire Blvd Beverly Hills CA 90212-1804*

NICKEL, ALBERT GEORGE, advertising agency executive; b. Pitts., July 12, 1943; s. Frank George and Dorothy (Wiefling) N.; m. Dana Cooper; children: Melissa, Mark. AB, Washington and Jefferson Coll., 1965; MBA, Ind. U., 1967. Mktg. rsch. analyst Pfizer, Inc., N.Y.C., 1967, profl. svc. rep., 1967-68, mktg. rsch. mgr., 1968-69, product mgr., 1969-70; product mgr. USV Internat., Tuckahoe, N.Y., 1970-71; account exec. J. Walter Thompson (Deltakos), N.Y.C., 1971-72, account supr., 1972-73; account supr. Sudler & Hennessey, N.Y.C., 1973-77; sr. v.p. mgmt. group supr. Young and Rubicam, N.Y.C., 1977-79; pres., COO Dorritie Lyons & Nickel, Inc., N.Y.C., 1979-94; pres., COO Lyons, Lavey, Nickel, Swift, Inc., 1994—. Trustee Wilton YMCA, Five Town Found.; bd. dirs., exec. com. Wilton LaCrosse Assn.; bd. dirs. Dominican Coll., Healthcare Businesswoman's Assn., Wilton H.S. Long Range Planning Team, Am. Coun. on Sci. and Health. Capt. USAF, 1969. Mem. Pharm. Rsch. and Mfrs. Assn. (bd. dirs.), Healthcare Mktg. and Comm. Coun. (bd. dirs.), Midwest Healthcare Mktg. Assn., Wilton Riding Club (pres.), Shore and Country Club, Silver Spring Country Club. Home: 65 Keelers Ridge Rd Wilton CT 06897-1608

NICKEL, HENRY V., lawyer; b. Chgo., Aug. 8, 1943. AB, U. Va., 1965; JD, George Washington U., 1968. Bar: D.C. 1968. Mem. Hunton & Williams, Washington. Rsch. editor: George Washington Law Rev., 1967-68. Mem. Order of Coif. Office: Hunton & Williams 1900 K St NW Washington DC 20006-1110

NICKEL, JANET MARLENE MILTON, geriatrics nurse; b. Manitowoc, Wis., June 9, 1940; d. Ashley and Pearl (Kerr) Milton; m. Curtis A. Nickel, July 29, 1961; children: Cassie, Debra, Susan. Diploma, Milw. Inst., 1961; ADN, N.D. State U., 1988. Nurse Milw. VA, Wood, Wis., 1961-62; supervising nurse Park Lawn Convalescent Hosp., Manitowoc, 1964-65; newsletter editor Fargo (N.D.) Model Cities Program, 1970-73; supervising night nurse Rosewood on Broadway, Luth. Hosps. and Homes, Fargo, 1973-92; assoc. dir. nursing Elim Nursing Home, Fargo, 1992-94, night nurse, 1994—. Mem. Phi Eta Sigma. Home: 225 19th Ave N Fargo ND 58102-2352 Office: 3534 S University Dr Fargo ND 58104-6228

NICKEL, MELVIN EDWIN, metallurgical engineer; b. St. Louis, Aug. 24, 1915; s. Jacob William and Mary Anna Nickel; m. Mary Louise Breuer, Sept. 12, 1942; children: Elizabeth Ann Nickel Medve, Mary Patricia Nickel Hepburn, Sheila Breuer Nickel Stojak, William Louis. BS in Metall. Engring., U. Mo., Rolla, 1938, Profl. Degree of Metall. Engring., 1967. Mgmt. trainee Bethlehem (Pa.) Steel Corp., 1938-39; asst. to supt. blast furnaces Wis. Steel div. Internat. Harvester Co., Chgo., 1939-43, gen. foreman furnaces, blast furnaces, 1943-48, asst. supt. blast furnaces, 1948-49, supt. open hearths, 1949-61, supt. basic oxygen furnaces, mgr. steel prodn., 1961-68, mgr. primary ops., 1968-77; mgr. facilities planning and appropriations, works mgr. Envirodyne Industries, Inc., Wis. Steel Corp., 1977-80; pres. Melvin E. Nickel & Assocs., Inc., Chgo., 1980—. Contbr. articles to profl. jours.; developer early practices for prodn. of spl. bar quality and alloy steel in top blown basic oxygen furnace, 1962-64. Bd. trustees Iron and Steel Soc. Found., Warrensdale, Pa., 1980-91. Recipient Disting. Merit award U. Mo., Rolla, 1960; inducted Mo. Sch. Mines/U. Mo.-Rolla Athletic Hall of Fame U. Mo., Rolla, 1993. Mem. AIME (hon., nat. v.p., dir. 1974-76), Iron and Steel Soc. of AIME (nat. pres. 1974-75), Metall. Soc. of AIME (nat. chmn. iron and steel divsn. 1972-74), Assn. of Iron and Steel Engrs., Western States Blast Furnaces and Coke Assn., U. Mo., Rolla Alumni Assn. (pres. 1956-59, bd. dirs.), Triangle Fraternity, Jackson Hole Wildlife Soc., Ridge Country Club of Chgo., Beverly Hills Univ. Club. Republican. Roman Catholic. Avocations: hunting, fishing, carpentry, mineral collecting, boating. Home and Office: 10601 S Hamilton Ave Chicago IL 60643-3127

NICKELSEN, ERIC J., bank executive. With Citizens & Peoples Nat. Bank of Pensacola (Fla.), 1966-93; chmn. Barnett Bank of West Fla., Pensacola, 1993—, pres, CEO, 1994—. Office: Barnett Bank of West Fla 100 W Garden St Pensacola FL 32501-5618

NICKENS, CATHERINE ARLENE, retired nurse, freelance writer; b. Litchfield, Ill., Oct. 30, 1932; d. Harley Lloyd Moore and Ida Mae Reynolds; m. Carl Roland Nickens, Sept. 4, 1954 (div. Apr. 1975); children: Linda Dianne, Carl Roland Jr., Karen Patricia, Eric Moore. Nursing diploma, St. Joseph's Hosp., 1954. RN, Calif. Staff nurse St. Joseph's Hosp., Alton, Ill., 1954-55; staff nurse St. Mary's Hosp., Streator, Ill., 1962-68, supr., acting dir., 1968-70; nursing supr. Illini Hosp., Silvis, Ill., 1970-74; office nurse pediatrician's office Silvis, 1974-75; staff nurse telemetry/drug abuse North Miami Gen. Hosp., Miami, Fla., 1975-80; staff nurse, relief supr. Petaluma (Calif.) Valley Hosp., 1981-97; participant women's health study Brigham and Women's Hosp., Boston, 1994—. Author: (hist. fiction) The Thoroughly Compromised Bride, 1991 (award 1992), The Highwayman, 1993 (award 1994). Mem. ACLU, N.Y.C., 1995, Parents, Families and Friends of Lesbians and Gays, Washington, 1994-97, Nat. Mus. of Am. Indian/Smithsonian Instn., Washington, 1996-97; friend of the quilt NAMES Project Meml. Quilt, San Francisco, 1992-97; mem. friendship cir. Am. Found. for AIDS Rsch., Washington, 1994-97. Mem. Romance Writers of Am. (mentor to unpublished writers 1995-96). Avocations: reading, traveling, needlework, doll-making. Home and office: 105 Olive St Santa Rosa CA 95401-6241

NICKENS, HARRY CARL, academic administrator; b. Monterey, Tenn., June 25, 1944; s. Van B. and Martha (Winningham) N.; m. Alicia Beck, Aug. 26, 1967; children: Kimberly, Cassidee, Brad. BS, Tenn. Tech. U., 1966, MS, 1968; EdD, U. Tenn., 1972. Counselor Va. Western Community Coll., Roanoke, 1972-76, dir. student devel., 1977-78, dean students, 1979-84, exec. dir. community devel. and tng., 1985-89; pres. Coll. Health Scis., Roanoke, 1989—; chair Roanoke Valley Chamber's Sch., originator Grad. Ctr. Pres. Roanoke Valley Career Edn.; bd. dirs. Va. Cares, Adult Care Ctr., Am. Heart Assn., Va. Amateur Sports.; active mem. First Bapt. Ch.; sr. mem. Roanoke County Bd. Suprs. Mem. Kiwanis (pres. Roanoke chpt. 1990—). Avocation: gardening. Home: 4179 Toddsbury Dr Vinton VA 24179-1113 Office: Coll Health Scis PO Box 13186 Roanoke VA 24031-3186

NICKERSON, GARY LEE, secondary education educator; b. Cleve., Nov. 7, 1942; s. Alto Lee and Louise Evelyn (Watson) N.; m. Barbara Marie Butler, Aug. 17, 1968; 1 child, L'Oreal. BS, Ohio U., 1966; MA, Atlanta U., 1971. Cert. secondary tchr., Ohio. With Cleve. Pub. Schs., 1966—; sci. dept. chmn. John F. Kennedy High Sch., Cleve., 1985—; physics instr. Case Western Res. U., Cleve., summer 1988; sci. instr. Std. Oil Elem. Teaching Retraining Program summer 1986; mem. adv. panel Ednl. Devel. Ctr., Inc., Newton, Mass., 1989—; sci. instr. Cleve. Ednl. Found. Elem. Teaching Retraining Program, 1990—, Baldwin Wallace U. Upward Bound Program, 1992; engrng. project instr. MEIOP Summer Program Case Western Res. U., 1991; tchr. trainer Kent State U. Trivet program, 1991—; sci. tchr. Gov.'s Inst. for Gifted and Talented, Cleve. State U., 1992—. Co-author curriculum guides. Recipient Cert. of Excellence in Teaching Rotary, 1990. Mem. NAACP, Urban League, Cleve. Regional Coun. Sci. Tchrs. (bd. dirs. 1986-87), Metrocabse Assn., Nat. Sci. Tcrhrs. Assn., Sci. Edn. Coun. Ohio, Kappa Alpha Psi. Democrat. Baptist. Avocations: ice skating, tennis, swimming, singing, weight lifting. Home: 5871 White Pine Dr Cleveland OH 44146-3075 Office: John F Kennedy High Sch 17100 Harvard Ave Cleveland OH 44128-2214

NICKERSON, GREG, public relations executive; b. Iowa, Nov. 3, 1958. BS in Agrl. Journalism, Iowa State U., 981. Mkt. analyst, exec. editor Brock Assocs., Brookfield, Wis., 1981-85; with pub. rels. dept. Bader Rutter & Assocs., Brookfield, 1985-88, acctg. group supr., 1988-90, v.p., group supr., 1990-92, v.p., dir. pub. rels. group, 1992—. Office: Bader Rutter & Assocs 13555 Bishops Ct Brookfield WI 53005-6224

NICKERSON, GUY ROBERT, lumber company executive; b. Salt Lake City, May 20, 1956; s. Charles Augustus and Florence May (Fogel) N.; m. Maggie Rose McDonnell, May 30, 1992; children: Melissa Marie, Rebecca Rose. B Acctg., U. Utah, 1977, M Profl. Accountancy, 1978. CPA, Utah. Sr. mgr. Deloitte Haskins & Sells, Salt Lake City and N.Y.C., 1978-87; v.p. fin. Anderson Lumber Co., Ogden, Utah, 1987-96, v.p. ops., 1996—. Office: Anderson Lumber Co 4700 Harrison Blvd Ogden UT 84403-4305

NICKERSON, HARDY OTTO, football player; b. Compton, Calif., Sept. 1, 1965; m. Amy Nickerson; children: Ashleigh, Hardy, Haleigh. Degree in sociology, U. Calif. Linebacker Pitts. Steelers, 1987-92, Tampa Bay Buccaneers, 1993—. Named to 1st Team All-Pro by AP and the Sporting News, 1993, Pro Bowl, 1996. Office: care Tampa Bay Buccaneers 1 Bucaneer Pl Tampa FL 33607*

NICKERSON, JAMES FINDLEY, retired educator; b. Gretna, Nebr., Dec. 16, 1910; s. Elmer Samuel and Lulu Perkins (Patterson) N.; m. Juanita M. Bolin, Mar. 3, 1934; children: Ann Rogers Nickerson Lueck, Maria De Miranda. BS, Nebr. Wesleyan U., 1932; MA, Columbia Tchrs. Coll., 1940; PhD, U. Minn., 1948; ScD (hon.), Yankton (S.D.) Coll., 1971. Tchr. pub. schs. Giltner, Nebr., 1932-35; sch. music supr. Gordon, Nebr., 1936-38, Bayshore, L.I., 1939-41, Grand Island, Nebr., 1941-42; instr. Coll. Edn., music supr. high sch. U. Minn., 1942-46, vis. prof. Coll. Edn., summer 1948; asst. prof. music edn. U. Kans., 1946-48, assoc. prof., 1948-53; rsch. assoc. dept. psychology U. So. Calif., assigned human factors div. U.S. Navy Electronics Lab., San Diego, 1953-54; dean edn., dir. summer quar., prof. psychology Mont. State U., 1954-64, head dept. psychology, 1954-56, rsch. assoc. Electronics Rsch. Lab, 1958-64; v.p. acad. affairs N.D. State U., Fargo, 1964-66; pres. Mankato (Minn.) State U., 1966-73, then pres. emeritus, disting. svc. prof., 1973-76; dir. Svc. Mems. Opportunity Colls., Am. Assn. State Colls. and Univs., Washington, 1973-81; dir. Northwestern Nat. Bank, Mankato, 1967-69; cons. publ. edn. Office Gov. Wash., 1964; exec. sec., study dir. interim com. edn. Wash. Legislature, 1959-60; chmn. regional conf. womanpower Nat. Manpower Coun. and Mont. State Coll., 1957; mem. steering com. Pacific N.W. Con. Higher Edn., 1962; mem. nat. adv. com. sci. edn. NSF, 1968-71, chmn., 1970-71; mem. vis. com. Harvard Grad. Sch. Edn., 1970-76, Schola Cantorum, N.Y.C., 1938-39, Choral Arts Soc., Washington, 1969-71. Stringbass Mont. State Coll. Symphonette, 1959-63, Mankato Symphony Orch., 1967-73, 83-93, bd. dirs., 1987-90. Recipient citation interim study Wash. Legislature and Gov., 1960, Outstanding Achievement award Bd. Regents U. Minn., 1968, Alumni award Nebr. Wesleyan U., 1968; Sec. Def. medal for outstanding pub. svc., 1981, citation Am. Coun. Edn., 1981; James F. Nickerson Medal of Merit for outstanding svc. to mil. edn. created by Am. Assn. Sr. Colls. and Univs., 1981; Danforth Found. adminstrn. grantee, 1969. Mem. Nat. Assn. State Univs and Land Grant Colls. (senate, chmn. div. tchr. edn. 1962-65, sec. coun. acad. officers 1965), Am. Assn. State Colls. and State Univs. (bd. dirs. 1966-71), Am. Assn. Colls. Tchr. Edn. (bd. dirs. 1969-71), Am. Assn. Higher Edn. (chmn. resolutions com. 1974), Assn. Minn. Colls. (pres. 1972), Edn. Commn. States (commr. 1967-73, mem. task force on coordination, governance and structure postsecondary edn. 1973), Sigma Xi, Phi Mu Alpha Sinfonia. Home and Office: PO Box 204 Elysian MN 56028-0204

NICKERSON, JERRY EDGAR ALAN, manufacturing executive; b. North Sydney, N.S., Can., Apr. 28, 1936; s. Jeremiah Beldon and Jean Frances (Innes) N.; m. Jean Frances Ritcey, Sept. 20, 1958; children: Mark Alan, Jerry Ross. B.Commerce, Dalhousie U., 1958. Chmn. bd. H.B. Nickerson & Son, Ltd., North Sydney; bd. dirs. Gt. West Life & Annuity, Gt. West Life Assurance Co., Bank of Montreal, Seaside Cable TV Ltd., Great-West Lifeco Inc. Mem. Zeta Psi (CEO). Office: HB Nickerson & Sons Ltd, PO Box 130, North Sydney, NS Canada B2A 3M2

NICKERSON, JOHN MITCHELL, political science educator; b. Lewiston, Maine, July 1, 1937; s. Elmer Winfield and Marion Gertrude (Howard) N. B.A., U. Maine, 1959; M.A., Wash. State U., 1966; Ph.D., U. Idaho, 1971. Commd. 2d lt. U.S. Army, 1959, advanced through grades to capt., resigned, 1967; rsch. assoc. Bur. Pub. Adminstrn. U. Maine, Orono, 1967-68, mem. grad. faculty, 1970-88; assoc. prof. polit. sci. U. Maine, Augusta, 1970-81, prof., 1981—, developer Baccalaureate program in pub. adminstrn.; dir. New Eng. Govtl. Research Inst., Inc., Waterville, Maine, 1971; lectr. Colby Coll., Waterville, Maine, 1979, Maine State Dedimus Justice; cons. in field. Author: The Control of Civil Disturbances, 1968, Municipal Police in Maine - A Study of Selected Personnel Practices with Emphasis on Recruit Selection and Training, 1969, (with others) A Study of Policy-Making: The Dynamics and Adaptability of the U.S. Federal System, 1971; editor, author foreward: Is the Municipality Liable for Insufficiently Trained Police? (James P. Murphy), 1968; contbr. articles to profl. jours. Mem. Maine State Police Planning Adv. Group, Maine State Bd. Assessment Rev., Maine Hwy. Safety Com.; vice chmn. adv. bd. Salvation Army, Augusta; trustee, treas. Lithgow Library; incorporator Kennebec Valley Med. Ctr., Augusta. Dept. Justice grantee, 1967. Mem. AAUP, Am. Polit. Sci. Assn., New Eng. Polit. Sci. Assn., Northeastern Polit. Sci. Assn., Acad. Polit. Sci. (life), Am. Acad. Polit. and Social Sci. (life), Am. Soc. for Pub. Adminstrn., ACLU (life), Kennebec Hist. Soc. (life), Kennebec Valley Humane Soc. (life), Maine Civil Liberties Union (life, legis. com.), Pi Sigma Alpha, Pi Alpha Alpha. Home: 192 Capitol St Augusta ME 04330-6237 Office: U Maine University Heights Augusta ME 04330

NICKERSON, RICHARD GORHAM, research company executive; b. Harwich, Mass., Nov. 20, 1927; s. Ephriam Gorham and Elizabeth (Wardle) N.; m. Eileen Florence Tressler, June 7, 1957; children: Holly Anne, Wendy Elyse, Susan Denise. BS cum laude, U. Mass., 1950; PhD, Northwestern U., 1955; postgrad., Poly. Inst. Bklyn., 1955-57; MBA cum laude, Boston U., 1983. Rsch. chemist DuPont, Cellophane Tech. Sect., Richmond, Va., 1954-55; rsch. chemist Dewey & Almy divsn. Dewey & Almy divsn. W.R. Grace Corp., Cambridge, Mass., 1957-60; v.p. R & D Electronautics Corp., Maynard, Mass., 1960-61; pres. Electronautics Corp., Maynard, 1961-63; project leader Polyco Borden Chem. divsn. Borden, Inc., Leominister, Mass., 1963-65, group leader, 1965-67, devel. mgr., 1967-81, lab. mgr., 1981-87; pres., mng. dir. Boston Profls. Internat., Inc., Hopkinton, Mass., 1987—. Patentee in field; designer, developer of water based polymers to meet specific performance requirement. With Chem. Corps, U.S. Army, 1955-57. Mem. Am. Chem. Soc., Soc. Plastics Engrs., Sigma Xi, Phi Lambda Upsilon, Alpha Chi Sigma. Avocations: sailing, photography, antique autos, classical music, dancing. Home: 9 Lyford Rd Hopkinton MA 01748-1581

NICKERSON, WILLIAM MILNOR, federal judge; b. Balt., Dec. 6, 1933; s. Palmer Rice and Eleanor (Renshaw) N.; m. Virginia Arlen Bourne, Apr. 25, 1954; children: Carol Lee, Deborah, Susan, Wendy, Laura. BA, U. Va., 1955; LLB, U. Md., Balt., 1962. Bar: Md. 1962. Ptnr. Whiteford, Taylor & Preston, Balt., 1962-85; assoc. judge Cir. Ct. Baltimore County, Towson, Md., 1985-90; judge U.S. Dist. Ct. Md., Balt., 1990—. Served to lt. USCGR, 1955-59. Mem. ABA (judicial adminstrn. div.), Am. Judicature Soc., Fed. Judges Assn., Md. State Bar Assn.,. Office: US Dist Ct 101 W Lombard St Baltimore MD 21201-2626

NICKFORD, JUAN, sculptor, educator; b. Havana, Cuba, Aug. 8, 1925; s. Basil and Maria (Hoshko) N.; m. Jene Rashkind, Aug. 16, 1952; children—Dena, Marc. M.F.A., Bellas Artes, Havana, 1945; postgrad., U. Havana, 1944-46. Head welding dept. Sculpture Center of N.Y., 1955-62; vis. artist Vasar Coll., 1962-63, Smith Coll., 1966-67, U. Hartford, 1965-66, Bklyn. Mus. Art Sch., 1968-70, Finch Coll., San Marino, 1975; prof. art CCNY, 1975-91, prof. emeritus, 1991—. One man shows, Leonard Gallery, Woodstock, N.Y., 1981, Emanuel Coll. Gallery, Boston, 1977, Sculpture Center, 1974, Art Glass Gallery, Toronto, Ont., Can., 1985, numerous others; retrospective Hopper House, Nyack, N.Y., 1986; group shows include, Thorpe Intermedia Gallery, Sparkill, N.Y., 1974, Hopper House, Nyack, N.Y., 1978, Sculpture Center, N.Y.C., 1978, Sculpture Gallery, Palo Alto, Calif., 1981, numerous museums; represented in permanent collection, Newberger Coll., N.Y., numerous pvt. collections. Cintas Found. grantee, 1970-71, CUNY Faculty Research Found. grantee, 1982-83; recipient Bronze medal N.Y. State Expn., 1964. Mem. Sculptors Guild. Home: 161 Old Tappan Rd Tappan NY 10983-2311

NICKLAS, ROBERT BRUCE, cell biologist; b. Lakewood, Ohio, May 29, 1932; s. Ford Adelbert and Marthabelle (Beckett) N.; m. Sheila Jean Counce, Sept. 17, 1960. B.A., Bowling Green State U., 1954; M.A. (Eugene Higgins fellow), Columbia U., 1956, Ph.D., 1958. Instr. in zoology Yale U., 1958-61, asst. prof. zoology, 1961-64, asso. prof., 1964-65; asso. prof. Duke U., 1965-71, prof., 1971—, chairperson dept., 1983-86; mem. NSF Postdoctoral Fellowship Panel, 1969-71, Am. Cancer Soc. Sci. Adv. Com. for Virology and Cell Biology, 1975-78; mem. adv. bd. 12th Internat. Chromosome Conf., 1994. Contbr. numerous articles to profl. publs.; mem. editorial bd. Chromosoma, 1966-83, Jour. Exptl. Zoology, 1970-72, Jour. Cell Biology, 1980-81, Jour. Cell Sci., 1984-91, European Jour. Cell Biology, 1985-89. Recipient award of disting. tchg. Duke Alumni, 1975; Yale fellow in scis., 1963-64; John Simon Guggenheim fellow, 1972-73, E.B. Wilson medal Am. Soc. Cell Biology, 1995, Inst. Gen. Med. Scis. USPHS grantee, 1960—. Fellow AAAS; mem. Am. Soc. Cell Biology (exec. com. 1976-78, coun. 1975-78, E.B. Wilson medal 1995), Am. Soc. Naturalists, Genetics Soc. Am., Sigma Xi. Home: 3101 Camelot Ct Durham NC 27705-5405 Office: Duke U Dept Zoology Durham NC 27708-1000

NICKLAUS, JACK WILLIAM, professional golfer; b. Columbus, Ohio, Jan. 21, 1940; s. Louis Charles, Jr. and Helen (Schoener) N.; m. Barbara Bash, July 23, 1960; children: Jack William II, Steven Charles, Nancy Jean, Gary Thomas, Michael Scott. Student, Ohio State U., 1957-62, D of Athletic Arts (hon.), 1972; LLD (hon.), U. St. Andrews, 1984. Chmn., chief exec. officer Golden Bear Internat., Inc. Author: My 55 Ways to Lower Your Golf Score, 1964, Take a Tip From Me, 1968, The Greatest Game of All, 1969, Jack Nicklaus' Lesson Tee, 1972, Golf My Way, 1974, Jack Nicklaus' Playing Lessons, 1976, On and Off the Fairway, 1978, Play Better Golf, Vols. 1-3, 1980, 81, 83, The Full Swing, 1982, My Most Memorable Shots in the Majors, 1988. Chmn. Ohio div. Am. Cancer Soc., 1967; chmn. sports div. Nat. Easter Seal Soc., 1967. Named PGA Player of Year, 1967, 72, 73, 75, 76, Dunlop Profl. Athlete of Yr., 1972, Golfer of Year Profl. Golfers Assn., 1973, Byron Nelson award, 1964, 65, 72, 73, Bob Jones award, 1975; named Sportsman of Year, Sports Illus. mag., 1978; named to World Golf Hall of Fame; named Athlete of the Decade for 1970-79, 1979, Golfer of the '70s, 1979, Golfer of the Century, 1988. Mem. President's Club Ohio State U., Phi Gamma Delta. Over 105 golf courses on 5 continents, 12 ranked in U.S. Top 100; hosted 185 profl. tournaments 1973—; won 71 tournaments including 20 maj. championships; maj. tournaments won include Tournament of Champions, 1963, 64, 71, 73, 77, U.S. Amateur, 1959, 61, U.S. Open, 1962, 67, 72, 80, U.S. Masters, 1963, 65, 66, 72, 75, 86, Brit. Open, 1966, 70, 78, PGA Championship, 1963, 71, 73, 75, 80, Internat. Pro-Amateur, 1973, Atlanta Golf Classic, 1973, Walt Disney World Golf Classic, 1971-73, 75, Hawaiian Open, 1974, Tournament Players Championship, 1974, 76, 78, Hawaiian Open, 1974, Doral-Eastern Open, 1975, Heritage Classic, 1975, Australian Open, 1964, 68, 71, 75, 76, 78, World Series of Golf, 1962, 63, 67, 70, 76, Gleason Inverrary Classic, 1976, 77, 78, Phila. Classic, 1965, 78, Colonial Nat. Invitational, 1982, PGA Seniors Championship, 1991, U.S. Senior Open, 1991, 93, Mercedes Sr. Championship, 1994, others. Office: Golden Bear Internat Inc 11780 US Hwy #1 North Palm Beach FL 33408*

NICKLE, DENNIS EDWIN, electronics engineer, church deacon; b. Sioux City, Iowa, Jan. 30, 1936; s. Harold Bateman and Helen Cecilia (Killackey) N. BS in Math., Fla. State U., 1961. Reliability mathematician Pratt & Whitney Aircraft Co., W. Palm Beach, Fla., 1961-63; br. supr. Melpar Inc., Falls Church, Va., 1963-66; prin. mem. tech. staff Xerox Data Systems, Rockville, Md., 1966-70; sr. tech. officer WHO, Washington, 1970-76; software tech. mgr. Melpar div. E-Systems, Inc., Falls Church, 1976-95; software process improvement mgr. Bell Atlantic, Arlington, Va., 1996—; lectr. in field. Ordained deacon Roman Catholic Ch., 1979. Chief judge for computers Fairfax County Regional Sci. Fair, 1964-88; scoutmaster, commr. Boy Scouts Am., 1957-92; youth custodian Fairfax County Juvenile Ct., 1973-87; chaplain No. Va. Regional Juvenile Detention Home, 1978-88; moderator Nocturnal Adoration Soc.; parochial St. Michael's Ch., Annandale, Va., 1979-89, Christ the Redeemer, Sterling, Va., 1990-93. Served with U.S. Army, 1958-60. Recipient Eagle award, Silver award, Silver Beaver award, other awards Boy Scouts Am.; Ad Altare Dei, St. George Emblem, Diocese of Richmond. Mem. Assn. Computing Machinery, Computer Soc., Am. Soc. For Quality Control, CODSIA (mem., chmn working groups), ORLANDO II (Govt./industry working group), Old Crows Assn., Rolm Mil-Spec Computer Users Group (internat. pres.), San Antonio I (select industry coordination group), Nat. Security Indsl. Assn. (convention com. 1985-96, software quality assurance subcom., regional membership chmn. 1981-89, nat. exec. vice-chmn. 1989-94, chmn. 1994-96), Am. Security Coun., IEEE (sr., mem. standards working group in computers 1983—, Outstanding Vol. award 1993, Golden Core mem. 1996), Defense Software Devel. Standards Avd. Bd. (chmn. 1991-96), Soc. Software Quality, Hewlett Packard Users Group, Smithsonian Assn., Internat. Platform Assn., NRA (endowment), Nat. Eagle Scout Assn. (life), Alpha Phi Omega (life), Sigma Phi Epsilon. Club: KC (4 deg.). Author: Stress in Adolescents, 1986; co-author: Handbook for Handling Non-Productive Stress in Adolescence, Standard For Software Life Cycle Processes, IMPEESA Junior Leader Training Guide, Standard for Software Quality Assurance, 1984-91, Standard for Developing Software Life Cycle Processes, Configuration Management Procedures, Software Quality Assurance Procedures, Software Development Procedures; contbr. to profl. jours. Office: 1320 N Court House Rd Arlington VA 22201-2508

NICKLES, DONALD (DON NICKLES), senator; b. Ponca City, Okla., Dec. 6, 1948; s. Robert C. and Coeweene (Bryan) N.; m. Linda L. Morrison, Sept. 5, 1968; children—Donald Lee II, Jennifer Lynn, Kim Elizabeth, Robyn Leigh. BA in Bus. Adminstrn., Okla. State U., 1971. Owner, operator Don Nickles Profl. Cleaning Svc., Stillwater, Okla., 1968-71; v.p., gen. mgr. Nickles Machine Corp., Ponca City, 1972—; mem. Okla. Senate, 1979-80; mem. U.S. Senate from Okla., 1981—, chmn. Senate Rep. policy com.; chem. Senate Rep. policy com., mem. com. on energy and natural resources,s com. on rules and adminstrn., com. on budget fin. and select com. on Indian affairs, mem. arms control observer group, coal caucus, rail caucus, rural health caucus, world climate conv. observer group, Rep. task force on nat. security and regulatory reform; passed legislation to provide for econ. and employment impact statement for all new laws and regulations. Chmn. platform com. Rep. Nat. Conv., 1992; bd. dirs. Ponca City United Way; bd. advisors Close Up Found.; mem. Kay Coun. for Retarded Children, Ponca City, St. Mary's Roman Cath. Parish Coun.; mem. adv. bd. Salvation Army, Ponca City. With USNG, 1970-76. Named one of Outstanding Young Men of Am., U.S. Jaycees, 1983. Mem. Fellowship Christian Athletes, Ponca City C. of C. Republican. Club: Rotary. Office: US Senate 133 Hart Senate Office Bldg Washington DC 20510*

NICKLES, I. MACARTHUR, librarian; b. Pittsfield, Mass., Feb. 5, 1944; s. Irving J. and Elsie (Hutchinson) N.; m. Rosalie M. Cangialose, Jan. 14, 1978; 1 child, Vincent Charles Nickles. BA, SUNY, Albany, 1965, MA, 1968, MLS, 1971. Asst. libr. SUNY Coll. at Oneonta, 1971-77; jr. libr. Passaic (N.J.) Pub. Libr., 1978; dir. Garfield (N.J.) Pub. Libr., 1979—; pres. Bergen County Coop. Libr. System, Hackensack, N.J., 1993. Gate attendant Tanglewood, Lenox, Mass., 1965—. With U.S. Army, 1969-70. Mem. ALA, N.J. Libr. Assn., Garfield Rotary (pres. 1981-82, Paul Harris fellow 1992), Garfield C. of C. Avocations: reading, classical music. Office: Garfield Pub Libr 500 Midland Ave Garfield NJ 07026-1606

NICKLIN, GEORGE LESLIE, JR., psychoanalyst, educator, physician; b. Franklin, Pa., July 25, 1925; s. George Leslie and Emma (Reed) N.; m. Katherine Mildred Aronson, Sept. 30, 1950. B.A., Haverford Coll., 1949; M.D., Columbia U., 1951; cert. in psychoanalysis, William A. White Inst., N.Y.C., 1962. Diplomate Am. Bd. Psychiatry and Neurology. Resident, then chief resident Bellevue Psychiat. Hosp., N.Y.C., 1953-56; pvt. practice specializing in psychoanalytic psychiatry, 1956—; staff Bellevue Hosp., 1956—; asst. clin. prof. psychiatry NYU Med. Sch., 1962-70, assoc. clin. prof. psychiatry, 1970—, dir. L.I. Inst. Psychoanalysis, 1978-88, dir. emeritus, 1988—; attending psychiatrist Nassau County Med. Center Clin. Campus; assoc. clin. prof. psychiatry SUNY-Stony Brook Health Sci. Ctr., 1976—; mem. Com. to Award Martin Luther King Peace Prize. Founder Friends World Coll., 1958, trustee, 1968-89. Served with AUS, 1943-46, ETO. Decorated Purple Heart with oak leaf cluster, Bronze Star with oak leaf cluster and three battle stars. Fellow Am. Acad. Psychoanalysis, Am. Psychiat. Assn.; mem. AAAS, NAACP, Soc. Med. Psychoanalysts (pres. 1986-87), White Psychoanalytic Soc., Assn. for World Edn. (charter trustee, treas. 1970-78), 9th Inf. Divsn. Assn., Vets. of the Bulge, Mil. Order of the Purple Heart. Mem. Soc. of Friends. Clubs: Gardiner's Bay Country (Shelter Island, N.Y.); Penn (London). Home and Office: 6 Butler Pl Garden City NY 11530-4603 *Education is essential to the future evolution of human society. But education alone is not enough. Integrity, creative thinking and informed action opens the path to the future.*

NICKON, ALEX, chemist, educator; b. Poland, Oct. 6, 1927; came to U.S., 1955, naturalized, 1961; s. Steve and Maria (Nickon); m. Beulah Monica Godby, Aug. 22, 1950; children—Dale Beverly, Linda Cheryl, Leanne Marie. B.Sc., U. Alta., 1949; M.A., Harvard U., 1951, Ph.D., 1953. Vis. lectr. Bryn Mawr Coll., 1953; postdoctoral fellow Birkbeck Coll., U. London, Eng., 1953-54, NRC, Ottawa, Can., 1954-55; NSF sr. fellow, Imperial Coll., London, 1963-64, U. Munich, Germany, 1971-72; mem. faculty Johns Hopkins, 1955—, prof. chemistry, 1964-94, Vernon K. Krieble prof. chemistry, 1975-94, prof. emeritus, 1994—; vis. assoc. Am. Chem. Soc. on Profl. Tng., 1975-95; mem. medicinal chem. panel NIH, 1966-70; postdoctoral panel NRC, 1968-69. Sr. editor Jour. Organic Chemistry, 1965-71; Am. exec. editor: Tetrahedron Reports, 1978-96. Recipient Md. Chemist award, 1990; Sloan Found. fellow, 1957-61. Fellow N.Y. Acad. Scis.; mem. Am. Chem. Soc. (nat. awards com. 1974-76), Brit. Chem. Soc. Home: 1009 Painters Ln Cockeysville Hunt Valley MD 21030-1729 Office: Dept Chemistry Johns Hopkins U Baltimore MD 21218-2685

NICKS, STEVIE (STEPHANIE NICKS), singer, songwriter; b. Calif., May 26, 1948. albums include: (with Lindsey Buckingham) Buckingham Nicks, 1973, (with Fleetwood Mac) Fleetwood Mac, 1975, Rumours, 1977 (co-winner, Billboard award for Album of the Year, Group of Year 1977), Tusk, 1979, Fleetwood Mac Live, 1980, Mirage, 1982, Tango in the Night, 1987, Greatest Hits, 1989, Behind The Mask, 1990, 25 Years-The Chain, 1992; (solo) Bella Donna, 1981, The Wild Heart, 1983, Rock a Little, 1985, The Other Side of the Mirror, 1989, Time Space, 1991, Street Angel, 1994; composer songs Rhiannon, 1975, Landslide, 1975, Leather and Lace, 1975, Dreams, 1977, Sara, 1979, Edge of Seventeen, 1981, If Anyone Falls (with Sandy Stewart), 1982, Stand Back (with Prince Rogers Nelson), 1983, I Can't Wait (with others), 1985, Seven Wonders (with Sandy Stewart). Office: Modern Records care WEA 111 N Hollywood Way Burbank CA 91505-4301*

NICOL, ROBERT DUNCAN, architect; b. La Jolla, Calif., Sept. 16, 1936; s. Duncan and Catherine (Muffly) N.; m. Susann Kay Larson; 1 child, Jennifer E. AA, Principia Coll., 1956; BArch, U. Calif., Berkeley, 1961. Registered arch., Ariz., Calif., Mont., Wash. Designer Kawneer Mfg. Co., Richmond, Calif., 1961-62, Claude Oakland, San Francisco, 1962-64; project arch. David T. Johnson, Oakland, Calif., 1964-68; pvt. practice Oakland, Calif., 1968—. Mem. bd. appeals City of Alameda, 1971-73, vice chair planning commn., 1973-77, founder, chair, vice chair design rev. bd., 1974-80, founder, chair, vice chair hist. adv. bd., 1976—, co-founder, chair, vice chair mayor's com. for handicapped, 1980-86; mem. Calif. State Access Bd., 1995—. Recipient Design award Am. Registered Archs., 1969, Harper Plz. Design award Calif. Bldg. Ofcls. Assn., 1985. Fellow AIA; mem. Soc. Am. Registered Archs., Nat. Coun. Archtl. Registration Bds. (sr.), Alexander Graham Bell Assn. for Deaf (lectr.), Oral Hearing Impaired Sec., San Leandro Hist. Railway Soc. (founder, charter mem., chair, vice-chair), Alameda Jr. C. of C. (project dir. 1969), Alameda Victorian Preservation Soc. Republican. Office: 455 17th St Oakland CA 94612-2101

NICOLA, JAMES B., stage director, composer, playwright, lyricist; b. Worcester, Mass., Oct. 28, 1958; s. George Anthony and Settimia (Palumbo) Balko. BA cum laude, Yale U., 1980; studies with Maury Yeston, Lehman Engel. Script cons. Manhattan Theatre Club, 1980-82; assoc. dir. Am. Stage Festival, 1985; vis. asst. prof., guest dir. U. Mont., Missoula, 1987, 91, Marymount Manhattan Coll., 1996, Whitman Coll., 1990, 95; dir. Ark. Repertory Theatre, 1992, Worcester Foothills Theatre, Mass., 1990, 92, Heritage Repertory, Charlottesville, Va., 1990, Montana Rep, 1996, Telluride (Colo.) Repertory Theatre, 1992, 93, 94, 95, Wayside Theatre, 1992, N.Y. Deaf Theatre, 1994, Seacoast Repertory, 1994, Seven Angels Theatre, 1995, American Globe, 1995, Mont. Repertory Theatre, 1996, Actors Studio, 1997; dir. Indsl. Arts Theater, Denver, 1993, 94, 96; resident dir. Mint Theatre Co., N.Y.C., 1993-96; dir. Nat. Shakespeare Co., 1995-96, The Actors Studio, 1997, Kings County Shakespeare, 1997. Dir. (plays) (with Tony Musante) Italian Funerals and Other Festive Occasions, The Sunshine Boys, Hamlet, Madwoman of Chaillot, Macbeth, Long Day's Journey Into Night, Lady Windermere's Fan, Amadeus (Pierrot award for Best Dir./Best Profn. 1987), Romeo and Juliet, The Attic, Children of a Lesser God, Rapid Transit, The Elephant Man, Measure for Measure, Uncle Vanya, Much Ado About Nothing; (mus.) Kerovac, I Do!, Anything Goes, Kiss Me Kate, A Little Night Music, I Do! I Do!, Working, You're a Good Man Charlie Brown, Kerouac, My Fair Lady, Into the Woods; composer: Round for Four, 1987, The Tempest, Goodbye Columbus Ave.; playwright: Donuts, 1987. Madolin Cervantes grantee, SDC Workshop Found., 1984, 87, Meet the Composers grantee, 1987; semi-finalist Christina Crawford award, U. S.D., 1987. Mem. Soc. Stage Dirs. and Choreographers, Dramatists Guild. Home and Office: 484 W 43rd St Apt 45-0 New York NY 10036-6319

NICOLAI, EUGENE RALPH, public relations consultant, editor, writer; b. Renton, Wash., June 26, 1911; s. Eugene George and Josephine (Heidinger) N.; student U. Wash., 1929, Whitman Coll., 1929-30; B.A., U. Wash., 1934; postgrad. Am. U., 1942; M.A., George Washington U., 1965; m. Helen Margaret Manogue, June 5, 1935; 1 son, Paul Eugene. Editor, U. Wash. Daily, Seattle, 1934; asst. city editor, writer, nat. def. editor Seattle Times, 1934-41; writer Sta. KJR, Seattle, 1937-39; writer, editor, safety edn. officer Bur. Mines, Washington, 1941-45; news dir. Grand Coulee Dam and

Columbia Basin Project, Washington, 1945-50; regional info. dir. Bur. Mines, Denver and Pitts., 1950-55, asst. chief mineral reports, Washington, 1955-61, news dir. office of oil and gas, 1956-57; sr. info. officer, later sr. public info. officer Office Sec. Interior, Washington, 1961-71, staff White House Nat. Conf. on Natural Beauty, spl. detail to White House, 1971, ret.; now public relations cons., tech. editor, writer. Formerly safety policy adviser Interior Dept.; com. mem. Internat. Cooperation Year, State Dept., 1971. With George Washington U. Alumni Found.; founder, mng. dir. Josephine Nature Preserve; pres. Media Assocs. Bd. dirs. Wash. State Council on Alcoholism; adviser Pierce Transit Authority, Pierce County Growth Mgmt., Pierce County Ethics Commn. Named Disting. Alumnus, recipient Penrose award, both Whitman Coll., 1979. Mem. Nature Conservancy, Wash. Environ. Council, Nat. Audubon Soc. (Am. Belgian Tervuren dist. rep.), Crook County (Oreg.) Hist. Soc., Washington State Hist. Soc., Emerald Shores Assn, Sigma Delta Chi, Pi Kappa Alpha. Presbyn. Clubs: George Washington U., Purdy (pres.). Lodge: Masons. Author: The Middle East Emergency Committee; editor: Fed. Conservation Yearbooks. Home: 9809 N Seminole Dr Spokane WA 99208-8608

NICOLAÏ, JUDITHE, international business trade executive; b. Lawrence, Mass., Dec. 15, 1945; d. Victor and Evelyn (Otash) Abisalih. Student in photography, L.A. City Coll., 1967, UCLA, 1971; AA in Fgn. Langs., Coll. of Marin, 1983; hon. degree, Culinary Inst., San Francisco, 1981. Photographer Scott Paper Co., N.Y.C., 1975; owner, operator restaurant The Raincheck Room, West Hollywood, Calif., 1976; prin., pres., chief exec. officer, photographer fashion Photographie sub. Nicolaï Internat. Svcs., Nice, France, 1977—; prin., pres., chief exec. officer, instr. catering and cooking Back to Basics sub. Nicolaï Internat. Svcs., San Francisco, 1980—; chief photographer exhibit and trade show, chief of staff food div. Agri-Bus. U.S.A., Moscow and Washington, 1983; head transp. U.S. Summer Olympics, L.A., 1984, interpreter for Spanish, French, Portuguese, and Italian, 1985; prin., pres., chief exec. officer, interpreter Intertrans subs. (Nicolaï Internat. Svcs.), San Francisco, 1985—; founder, pres. Nicolaï Internat. Svcs., San Francisco, 1985—; pres., CEO Cyprus Personal Care Products, 1994—. Contbr. column on food and nutrition to jour., 1983-84. Mem. NAFE, Alpha Gamma Sigma. Avocations: cooking, fencing, swimming, golf, photography. Office: Nicolai Internat Svcs 1686 Union St Ste 203 San Francisco CA 94123-4509 Mailing Address: 2269 Chestnut St Ste 237 San Francisco CA 94123-2607

NICOLAIDES, MARY, lawyer; b. N.Y.C., June 7, 1927; d. George and Dorothy Nicolaides. BCE, CUNY, 1947; MBA with distinction, DePaul U., 1975, JD, 1981. Bar: Ill. 1982, U.S. Dist. Ct. (no. dist.) Ill. 1982, U.S. Patent Office 1983. Sr. design engr. cement subs. U.S. Steel Corp., N.Y.C., then Pitts., 1948-71; sole practice Chgo., 1982—. Mem. ABA. Republican. Greek Orthodox. Address: 233 E Erie St Apt 1804 Chicago IL 60611-2903

NICOLAS, KENNETH LEE, international financial business executive; b. San Francisco, Feb. 7, 1944; s. Norman L. and Bernice L. (Hameister) N.; m. Anne Vanderwielen, July 5, 1992; children: Juliana M., Camille G. BA in Polit. Sci., Calif. State U., Fullerton, 1968; MA in Legis. Affairs/Econs., George Washington U., 1975. Exec. asst. Congressman Richard T. Hanna, Washington, 1970-72; sr. staff assoc. Nat. Assn. Ednl. Broadcasters, Washington, 1972-74; founder, pres. Nicolas Assocs. Internat., Inc., 1972; exec. dir. Am. Coll. Nuclear Physicians, Washington, 1974-77; aide to the Pres. White House, Washington, 1977-80; v.p. McSweeney & Co. Consulting, Newport Beach, Calif., 1980-83, L.E. Peterson & Co. Investment Banking, Costa Mesa, Calif., 1983-85; pres. Fin. Strategies Group, Inc., Newport Beach, 1985—; CEO Tradex Internat., Inc., Newport Beach, 1988-94; founder, CEO Trade Access Group, Inc., 1994—; bd. dirs. Amtrex Corp., Irvine, Calif.; adj. prof. Orange Coast Coll., Costa Mesa, 1983—, internat. MBA program U. So. Calif., 1989-90, Thunderbird Sch. Internat. Bus., Orange County, 1990-92, U. Calif., Riverside and Irvine, 1996—, internat. bus. edn. U. Calif.-Riverside, 1996—; adj. prof. U. Calif., Riverside and Irvine, 1996—. Author: (article series) Business to Business Mag., 1984-87 (Excellence award 1984-87). 10K race dir. Leukemia Soc. Am., Orange County, Calif., 1982-86, bd. dirs., v.p., 1982-88; chmn. Holiday Project, 1992-94. With U.S. Army, 1968-70, Vietnam. Recipient Outstanding Svc. award Nat. Holiday Project, 1993, Nat. Svc. Appreciation award Pres. Jimmy Carter, 1980, Excellence award Leukemia Soc. Am., 1988. Mem. Internat. Mktg. Assn. (corp. mem., Outstanding Export award 1993), Export Mgrs. Assn. Calif. (bd. dirs. 1990—, Excellence award 1992), World Trade Ctr. Assn. of Orange County (corp. mem., com. chmn. 1983-85, Outstanding Achievement award 1983, 84), Japan Am. Soc. (Orange County chpt. exec. bd. dirs. 1995—), Japan Am. Soc. So. Calif. (exec. bd. 1996—). Avocations: Karate (Shito-Ryu black belt 2d degree), sailing, travel, triathlons, chess.

NICOLAU, ALEXANDRU, educator; b. Bucharest, Romania, June 7, 1957; came to U.S., 1976; s. Frederick and Silvia (Pach) N.; m. Anca Arivei, Oct. 22, 1978; children, Danielle, Rebecca. BA, Brandeis U., 1980; MA, Yale U., 1982, PhD, 1984. Asst. prof. Cornell U., Ithaca, N.Y., 1984-88; assoc. prof. U. Calif., Irvine, 1988-92, prof., 1992—. Editor-in-chief Internat. Jour. Parallel Programming, 1993—; editor: Language and Compilers for Parallel Computing, 1994, Advanced in Languages and Compilers, 1994, Parallel Language and Compiler Research in Japan, 1995; contbr. articles to profl. jours. Mem. IEEE, Assn. for Computing Machinery.

NICOLETTI, PAUL LEE, veterinarian, educator; b. Goodman, Mo., Oct. 26, 1932; s. Felix and Clarice Nicoletti; m. Earlene Blackburn, June 6, 1954; children: Diana, Julie, Nancy. BS in Agr., U. Mo., 1956, DVM, 1956; MS, U. Wis., 1962. Diplomate Am. Coll. Vet. Preventative Medicine. Veterinarian, U.S. Dept. Agr., Mo., Wis., N.Y., 1956-68, UN Food and Agr. Orgn., Tehran, Iran, 1968-72, U.S. Dept. Agr., Jackson, Miss., 1972-75, Gainesville, Fla., 1973-78; prof. veterinarian medicine U. Fla., Gainesville, 1978—. Contbr. numerous articles to profl. jours. Recipient awards from Fla. Cattleman's Assn., 1978, Dairy Farmers, Inc., 1978, Borden award, 1979, Gold Star award Fla. Veterinary Medicine Assoc., 1981, 1986, Universidad Austral de Chile, 1981, Puerto Rico Dairy Assn., 1978, Faculty Alumni award U. Mo., 1987; named Basic Scis. Tchr. of Yr., Nat. Student Am. Veterinary Med. Assn., 1994; Veterinarian of the Yr. award, Fla. Veterinary Med. Assn., 1994, (pres. 1995-96). Mem. Am. Veterinary Medicine Assn. (int. prize 1991), Am. Assn. Bovine Practice, Academia Veterinaria Mexicana. Home: 2552 SW 14th Dr Gainesville FL 32608-2042 Office: Univ of Fla Coll Vet Medicine PO Box 110880 Gainesville FL 32611-0880

NICOLINI, FRANCESCA ANTONIA, health science association administrator; b. Imola, Italy, Jan. 3, 1961; came to U.S., 1989; d. Roberto and Maria Luisa (Barbieri) N. BA, Liceoclassico Statale, 1979; MD, U. Bologna, 1986; PhD, U. Uppsala, 1993. Resident U. Bologna (Italy), 1985-86; dir. exptl. thrombosis program The Cleve. Clinic Found., 1992—; cons. in field. Cardiology fellow U. Bologna, 1987-89. Fellow Am. Coll. Cardiology, European Soc. Cardiology; mem. Am. Heart Assn. (coun. curiculation 1992—, rsch. fellow 1990-92). Avocations: skiing, sailing, travel. Office: The Cleve Clinic Found 9500 Euclid Ave Cleveland OH 44195-0001

NICOTRA, JOSEPH CHARLES, artist; b. Corona, N.Y., Aug. 9, 1931; s. Charles C. and Constanta (Maglienti) N.; m. Mary C. Losquadro, Sept. 9, 1951; children: Therese, Nanette, Marie. Student, Art Students League, N.Y.C., 1955-59, Art Students League, Woodstock, N.Y., 1959-60, Am. Art Sch., N.Y.C., 1960-61; diploma of merit, U. Art, Italy, 1982. Registered artist, N.Y.C., GSA, Met. Transp. Authority N.Y. Freelance easel painter N.Y.C., 1962—; lectr. painting and drawing Queens Mus. One-man shows include Armstrong Mural Gallery, Flushing, N.Y., 1968, La Galerie Mouffe, Paris, 1976, Long Beach Artists Assn. Gallery, N.Y.C., 1978, 79, Long Beach Libr. Art Gallery, 1979, Cam Art Ctr., Bayshore, N.Y., 1982, Pricilla Redford Roe Gallery, Suffork, N.Y., 1982, Queens Mus., 1982, 84, Pla. Del Malfestazione, Italy, 1983, 6th Internat. Biennale, Garbo, Bulgaria, 1983, Flushing Coun. on Culture and Arts, 1986, Atlanta Gallery Generve, 1987 (Primo Milano Gold medal 1988), St. Paul's Ch., Beth Page, N.Y., 1992, "Time Capsule-Schedule Mail Call" from the People of the Borough of Queens, 1992 A.D., for 2292 A.D.; exhibited in group shows at Art Students League 57th St. Gallery, N.Y., 1957, A.S.L. Woodstock N.Y. Gallery, 1961, Roma Gallery, Miami Beach, 1973, Long Beach (N.Y.) Mus., 1976, Flushing Coun. on Culture and Arts, 1986; represented in permanent collections Nat. Archives, Washington, Queens Mus. Art, African Meth. Episcopal Ch., Robert F. Kennedy Libr., 1976; prin. works include mural for Queens Mus. Title Wall for Nat. Travel Show; contbr. Smithsonian Inst. Kennedy Gallery; med. illustrator of cancer surgery for Dr. Weiss, L.I. Jewish Hosp., 1996; (video) Nicotra, 1993 and numerous articles in art and popular publs. concerning his work. Vol. Artist, tchr., docent, lectr. Queens Mus. Art, Flushing, N.Y., 1972-97. With U.S. Army, 1952-54; mem. Queens Coun. Arts, Flushing Coun. Culture and Arts. Recipient Outstanding Svc. award Queens Mus. Art, 1972-91, 1st prize for Oil, Long Beach Mus., 1976; Bernsay scholar, 1958, scholar VA, 1959, 1st prize Long Beach Artists Assn., 1980, Accademia delle Art Gold medal, Italy, 1980, Gold medal for Safety, Peace & Artist Merit, Internat. Parliament, U.S.A., 1983, Accademia D'Europa award, 1983, Statue of Victory, Com. for World Culture, 1984, European Banner of Arts award 1985, Gold Plaque award Italian Academia, 1987. Mem. Art Students League (life), Orgn. Ind. Artists, Internat. Confedn. Order of Artists (hon.), Queens Mus. Art (hon.), DAV (life). Home and Studio: 59-32 156th St Flushing NY 11355-5517

NIDA, JANE BOLSTER (MRS. DOW HUGHES NIDA), retired librarian; b. Chgo., July 19, 1918; d. Chalmer A. and Elsie R. (Sonderman) Bolster; m. Dow Hughes Nida, Sept. 1, 1946; 1 child, Janice Beth (Mrs. Robert M. Michaels). B.A., Aurora (Ill.) U., 1942; B.S. in Library Sci, U. Ill., 1943. Circulation librarian Aurora Pub. Library, 1940-42, 43-44, reference librarian, 1946; program dir. A.R.C., Eng., France, 1944-46; acquisitions librarian Ohio U., Athens, 1947; dir. Falls Church (Va.) Pub. Library, 1951-54; asst. dir. Arlington County Dept. Libraries, Arlington, Va., 1954-57; dir. Arlington County Dept. Libraries, 1957-80; on loan to AID, 1979-80; Mem. Va. Adv. Legis. Council, Com. to Revise State Library Laws, 1968-69, Women's Joint Congl. Com., 1968-80. Vol. Am. Cancer Soc., 1971-84, bd. dirs. Arlington chpt., 1974-84; mem. exec. com. Regional Adv. Group, Va. Regional Med. Program, 1971-76; v.p., founder, dir. Cultural Laureate Found. Recipient Meritorious Service award A.R.C., World War II, Outstanding Alumnus award Aurora U., 1979. Mem. AAUW, ALA, D.C. Libr. Assn., Va. Libr. Assn. (pres. 1969-70), Arlington Hist. Soc. (charter, bd. dirs. 1989-93), Army-Navy Country Club. Baptist. Home: 4907 29th St N Arlington VA 22207-2755 also: 1617 Bayhouse Ct #218 Sarasota FL 34231-6755

NIE, ZENON STANLEY, manufacturing company executive; b. Chgo., Nov. 19, 1950; m. Carol Ann Klockowski, Mar. 27, 1970; 1 child, Andrea Nicole. BS, U Ill., Chgo., 1971; MBA, Loyola U., Chgo., 1974. Mgr. sales stats. Zenith Electronics, Chgo., 1971-74; mktg. mgr. Hollister, Inc., Chgo., 1974-79; dir. market devel. Sealy, Inc., Chgo., 1979-81; sr. v.p. Serta, Inc., Chgo., 1981-89, exec. v.p., 1988-89, pres., 1989-91; pres. The Bibb Co., Macon, Ga., 1991-93; chm. pres. Ceo Simmons Co., 1993—; instr. Coll. of Lake County, Ill., 1978-81. Mem. Internat. Sleep Products Assn. (chmn. stats. com. 1985—), Young Presidents Orgn. Avocations: scuba diving, fishing, skiing, jogging. Office: Simmons One Concourse Pky Atlanta GA 30328

NIED, THOMAS H., publishing company executive; b. Queens, N.Y., May 4, 1942; s. Herman Joseph and Margaret (Jos) N.; m. Carol J. Thomas, June 6, 1964; children: Stacey, Allison. BA, Rutgers U., 1964, LLB, 1967; LLM in Taxation, NYU, 1972. CPA, N.J., Ga. Tax mgr. Ernst & Young, N.Y.C., Atlanta, Newark and Trenton, N.J., 1968-77, N.Y. Times Co., N.Y.C., 1977—; founder Media Tax Group, 1979, mem., 1979-96. Mem. ABA, AICPA, Tax Execs. Inst. (bd. dirs. 1986-96, pres. N.Y. chpt. 1991-92, exec. com. 1992-93), Newspaper Assn. of Am. (chmn. tax com. 1995-97, chmn. ind. contractor task force 1995-97, mem. pub. policy com. 1995-97). Avocations: travel, reading, philately, birding. Home: 31 Vreeland Ct Princeton NJ 08540-6760 Office: NY Times Co 229 W 43rd St New York NY 10036-3913

NIEDEL, JAMES E., pharmaceuticals executive; b. Milw., Mar. 30, 1944; m. Selaine Benaim, Mar. 12, 1969; children: Ian Edward, Felisa Ann, Shira Beth. BS, U. Wis., 1965; MD, U. Miami, 1973, PhD, 1974. Diplomate Am. Bd. Internal Medicine. Scientist Burroughs-Wellcome, Research Triangle Park, N.C., 1977-80; prof. medicine Duke U., Durham, N.C., 1980-89; v.p. rsch. Glaxo Rsch. Inst., Research Triangle Park, 1989-92, sr. v.p. R & D, 1992-95; bd. dirs. Glaxo Wellcome plc, London, 1995—; chmn., CEO Glaxo Wellcome R & D Ltd., Greenford, U.K., 1995—; chmn. Affymax Tech. N.V., 1995—. Bd. overseers Duke Cancer Ctr., Durham, 1990—. Searle scholar, 1981-84; recipient Career Devel. award NIH, 1981-84. Mem. Am. Soc. Clin. Investigation, Am. Soc. Biochemistry and Molecular Biology, Am. Soc. Immunology. Office: Glaxo Wellcome R&D PO Box 13408 5 Moore Dr Research Triangle Park NC 27709

NIEDERAUER, GEORGE H., bishop; b. Los Angeles, CA, June 14, 1936; s. George and Elaine N. B.A. Philosophy, St. John's Seminary, Camarillo, CA, 1959; B.A. Sacred Theology, Catholic U., Washington, DC, 1962; M.A. English Lit., Loyola U., Los Angeles, CA, 1962; Ph.D. English Lit., USC, 1966. ordained priest April 30, 1962; named prelate of honor (monsignor) 1984; named bishop of Diocese of Salt Lake City, Nov. 3, 1994. Asst. pastor Our Lady of the Assumption Parish, Claremont, CA, 1962-63; priest in residence Holy Name of Jesus Parish, Los Angeles, CA, 1963-65; instr. English Lit. St. John's Seminary Coll., Camarillo, CA, 1965-79; instr. of English Lit. Mt. St. Mary's Coll., Los Angeles, CA, 1967-74; English Dept. chmn. St. John's Seminary Coll., Camarillo, CA, 1968-77; spiritual dir. St. John's Seminary Coll., 1972-79; part-time instr. of Spiritual Theology St. John's Seminary Theologate, 1976-79, full-time instr. of Spiritual Theology, 1979-87; part-time instr. of English Lit. St. John's Seminary Coll., 1979-92; rector St. John's Seminary, 1987-92, spiritual dir., 1979—; co-dir. Cardinal Manning House of Prayer for Priests, Los Angeles, CA, 1992—; mem. Nat. Fedn. of Spiritual Dirs. (pres. 1975-77); mem. Alpha Sigma Nu (Jesuit Honor Soc. - LMU Chapter); pres. Western Assn. of Spiritual Dirs., 1973-75; mem. bd. of the Comm. of Priests' Retreat, Archdiocese of Los Angeles; mem. select comm. for the revision of the U.S. Catholic Conf. "Program for Priestly Formation" 3rd edition; mem. Vatican Visitation Team for Theologates; speaker World Vision Internat, Fuller Theological Seminary, Calif. Lutheran Coll.; mem. Camarillo Ministerial Assn. Avocations include: classical music, stamp collecting, reading, film appreciation. Office: Chancery Office 27 C St Salt Lake City UT 84103-2302

NIEDERHUBER, JOHN EDWARD, surgical oncologist and molecular immunologist, university educator and administrator; b. Steubenville, Ohio, June 21, 1938; s. William Henry and Helen (Smittle) N.; m. Tracey J. Williamson; children: Elizabeth Ann, Matthew John. B.S., Bethany Coll., 1960; M.D., Ohio State U., 1964. Diplomate Am. Bd. Surgery. Internship, surgery Ohio State U. Hosp., Columbus, 1964-65; resident, surgery U. Mich. Med. Ctr., Ann Arbor, 1967-69, NIH acad. trainee in surgery, 1969-71, resident, surgery, 1971-72, chief resident surgery, 1972-73, asst. prof. surgery and asst. prof. microbiology, 1973-77, dir. transplantation program, 1975-76, assoc. prof. surgery and assoc. prof. microbiology, 1977-80, chief divsn. surg. oncology and transplantation, sect. gen. surgery, 1979-82, sr. assoc. dean med. sch., 1983-86, assoc. dean research, 1982-86, chief divsn. surg. oncology sect. gen. surgery, 1982-86, prof. surgery, prof. microbiology and immunology, 1980-87; cons. Wayne County Gen. Hosp. Mich., 1973-84; cons. surgery Ann Arbor VA Hosp., 1973-87; prof. surgery, oncology, molecular biology and genetics The Johns Hopkins U. Sch. Med., Baltimore, 1987-91; Emile Holman prof. surgery, chair, dept. surgery, head sect. surgical scis. Stanford (Calif.) U. Sch. Medicine., 1991—, prof. microbiology and immunology, 1991—; chief of surgery Stanford (Calif.) U. Hosp., 1991—; dir. Comp. Cancer Ctr. Stanford (Calif.) Med. Ctr., 1991—; vis. prof. Howard Hughes Med. Inst. Dept. Molecular Biology and Genetics The Johns Hopkins U. Sch. Medicine, Baltimore, 1986-87. Authored books on cancer; mem. editorial bd. Jour. Immunology, 1981-85, Jour. Surg. Res., 1989—, Current Opinion in Oncology, 1989—, Annals of Surgery, 1991—, Surg. Oncology, 1991—, Cancer, 1992—, Jour. Clin. Oncology, 1993, Annals of Surg. Oncology, 1993—, Jour. Am. Coll. Surgeons, 1994—; contbr. articles to profl. jours. Active NCI divsn. Cancer Treatment Bd. Scientific Councilors, 1986-91, chmn., 1987-91, Gen. Motors Cancer Rsch. Found. Awards Assembly, 1988-92. Served to capt. U.S. Army, 1965-67. Recipient USPHS Rsch. Career Devel. award Nat. Inst. Allergy and Infectious Disease, 1974-79, Disting. Faculty Svc. award U. Mich., 1978, Alumni Achievement award Ohio State U. Coll. Medicine, 1989, Alumni Achievement award in Medicine Bethany Coll., 1995; vis. rsch. fellow divsn. immunobiology Karolinska Inst., Stockholm, 1970-71, Am. Cancer Soc. Jr. Faculty Clin. fellow, 1977-79. Fellow ACS; mem. Am. Soc. Transplant Surgeons, Transplantation Soc., Am. Surg. Assn., Am. Assn. Immunologists, Coller Surg. Soc., Soc. Univ. Surgeons, Assn. Acad. Surgeons, Soc. Surg. Oncology, Ctrl. Surg. Soc., Am. Assn. Cancer Rsch., Am. Soc. Clin. Oncology, Soc. Clin. Surgery, Biology Club II, Robert M. Zollinger-Ohio State U. Surg. Soc., Pacific Coast Surg. Assn. Avocations: tennis, golf, gardening. Office: Stanford Univ Sch Medicine Dept of Surgery MSOB X300 Stanford CA 94304-5408

NIEDERMAN, JAMES CORSON, physician, educator; b. Hamilton, Ohio, Nov. 27, 1924; s. Clifford Frederick and Henrietta (Corson) N.; m. Miriam Camp, Dec. 12, 1951; children—Timothy Porter, Derrick Corson, Eliza Orton, Caroline Noble. Student, Kenyon Coll., 1942-45, D.Sc. (hon.), 1981; M.D., Johns Hopkins U., 1949. Intern Johns Hopkins Hosp., Balt., 1949-50; asst. resident in medicine Yale-New Haven Med. Center, 1950-51, assoc. resident, 1953-55; med. ctr. practice specializing in internal medicine, infectious disease and clin. epidemiology New Haven, 1955—; instr. Yale U., 1955-58, asst. prof., 1958-66, assoc. prof., 1966-76, clin. prof. medicine and epidemiology, 1976—; mem. Nat. Coun. for Johns Hopkins Medicine. Trustee Kenyon Coll.; bd. counselors Smith Coll., 1970-77; mem. Alumni Coun. Johns Hopkins U.; mem. Conn. Soc. of Arts and Scis. Served to 1st lt. M.C. U.S. Army, 1951-53. Fellow Silliman Coll., Yale U. Fellow Am. Coll. Epidemiology; mem. Infectious Diseases Soc. Am., Am. Epidemiol. Soc., Johns Hopkins Med. and Surg. Assn.; trustee Assocs. of Chusing Whitney Med. Libr.; mem. The Kenyon Rev. Bd. Trustees. Democrat. Episcopalian. Clubs: Yale (N.Y.C.); New Haven Lawn. Research in clin. epidemiology. Home: 429 Sperry Rd Bethany CT 06524-3544 Office: 60 College St New Haven CT 06510-3210

NIEDERREITER, HARALD GUENTHER, mathematician, researcher; b. Vienna, June 7, 1944; s. Simon and Erna (Emig) N.; m. Gerlinde Hollweger, Aug. 30, 1969. PhD, U. Vienna, 1969. Asst. prof. So. Ill. U., Carbondale, 1969-72, assoc. prof., 1972-73; mem. Inst. Advanced Study, Princeton, N.J., 1973-75; vis. prof. UCLA, 1975-76; prof. U. Ill., Urbana, 1976-78, U. W.I., Kingston, Jamaica, 1978-81; researcher Austrian Acad. Scis., Vienna, 1981-89, dir. Inst. Info. Processing, 1989—; mem. math. & info. scis. panel TMR Tng. Grants EU Commn., Brussels, 1995—, chmn., 1996—, TMR Networks, 1995—. Author: Uniform Distribution of Sequences, 1974, Russian transl., 1985, Finite Fields, 1983, Russian transl., 1988, Introduction to Finite Fields and Their Applications, 1986, rev. edit., 1994, Random Number Generation and Quasi-Monte Carlo Methods, 1992 (Outstanding Simulation Publ. award 1995), Monte Carlo and Quasi-Monte Carlo Methods in Scientific Computing, 1995, Finite Fields and Applications, 1996; contbr. numerous rsch. articles to math. jours.; assoc. editor Maths. of Computation, 1988—, ACM Trans. Modeling and Computer Simulation, 1990—, Fibonacci Quar., 1995—; mem. editl. bd. Caribbean Jour. Math., 1982—, Applicable Algebra, 1990—, Stochastic Optimization and Design, 1991—, Jour. Ramanujan Math. Soc., 1991—, Acta Arithmetica, 1992—, Monatshefte Math., 1993—, Finite Fields and Their Applications, 1993—, Jour. Info. and Optimization Scis., 1995—, Jour. Complexity, 1996—. Named hon. prof. U. Vienna, 1986. Mem. Am. Math. Soc., Austrian Math. Soc., Austrian Acad. Scis., Internat. Assn. Cryptologic Rsch., Austrian Computer Soc., Gesellschaft für Informatik, Soc. Indsl. Applied Math., German Acad. Natural Scientists Leopoldina (elected, 1996), N.Y. Acad. Scis. Home: Sieveringer Str 41, A1190 Vienna Austria Office: Austrian Acad Scis, Sonnenfelsgasse 19, A1010 Vienna Austria

NIEDZIELSKI, HENRI ZYGMUNT, French and English language educator; b. Troyes, France, Mar. 30, 1931; came to U.S., 1956, naturalized, 1963; s. Zygmunt and Anna (Pelik) N.; children: Henri Zygmunt, Daniel Domenic, Robert Nicholas, Anna-Pia Irene. B.A., U. Conn., 1959, M.A., 1963, Ph.D., 1964. Instr. U. Mass., 1962-64, asst. prof., 1965-66; free-lance interpreter, 1960—; asst. prof. U. Laval, Quebec, Can., 1964-65; assoc. prof. U. Hawaii, 1966-72, prof., 1972-90, chmn. div. French, 1968-70, prof. emeritus; linguistic specialist NDEA, Edn. Profl. Devel. Act, 1963-69; Fulbright lectr. linguistics and TESL Krakow, Poland, 1972-74, Bujumbura, Burundi, 1980-81, Poznan, Poland, 1990-92; guest prof. Avignon, France, 1983-84, Bonn, Fed. Republic Germany, 1986-87; Disting. fellow Auckland U., New Zealand, 1989. Author: Le Roman de Helcanus, 1966, Basic French: A Programmed Course, 1968, Handbook of French Structure; A Systematic Review, 1968, Intermediate French: An Individualized Course, 1972, The Silent Language of France, 1975, French Sound Visuals, 1976; Films on Polish Body Language, 1989; editor: Language and Literature in Hawaii, 1968-72, Jean Misrahi Memorial Volume: Studies in Medieval Languages and Literature, 1977, Studies on the Seven Sages of Rome, 1978; assoc. editor: The Phonetician, 1994—. Pres. Family Counseling Center Hawaii, 1968-70; chmn. bd. Family Edn. Centers Hawaii, 1969-72. Served with French Armored Cav., 1951-53. Mem. MLA, Am. Translators Assn., Am. Assn. Tchrs. French (pres. Hawaii chpt. 1981-83), Am. Coun. Tchg. Fgn. Langs. (dir. 1970-72), Internat. Sociol. Assn., Hawaii Assn. Lang. Tchrs. (pres. 1968-69), Chopin Soc. Hawaii (dir. 1990—), Alliance Française Hawaii (pres. 1978-80), Hawaii Assn. Translators (founding pres.s 1982—), Hawaii Second Lang. Articulation Com. (chmn. 1986-89), Rotary, Elks, Phi Beta Kappa, Pi Delta Phi, Phi Kappa Phi, Sigma Delta Pi. *There is more than one way to help people but there is only one way to live: Help people.*

NIEFELD, JAYE SUTTER, advertising executive; b. Mpls., May 27, 1924; s. Julius and Sophia (Rosenfeld) N.; m. Piri Elizabeth Von Zabrana-Szilagy, July 5, 1947; 1 child, Peter Wendell. Cert., London U., 1945; B.A., U. Minn., 1948; B.S., Georgetown U., 1949; Ph.D., U. Vienna, 1951. Project dir. Bur. Social Sci. Research, Washington, 1952-54; research dir. McCann-Erickson, Inc., N.Y.C., 1954-57; v.p., dir. mktg. Keyes, Madden & Jones, Chgo., 1957-60; pres., dir. Niefeld, Paley & Kuhn, Inc., Chgo., 1961-71; exec. v.p. Bozell, Inc., Chgo., 1971-89; pres. The Georgetown Group, Inc., 1991—; cons. U.S. Dept. State, Commerce, HEW, also others; lectr. Columbia U., Northwestern U., U. Chgo., 1989-94; chmn. Ctr. Advanced Comm. Rsch.; pres. Glencoe Angus Farms, J&J Enterprises, The Georgetown Group Inc., 1991; bd. dirs. Mktg. Decisions, Inc., E. Morris Comms., Inc. Author: The Making of an Advertising Campaign, 1989; (with others) Marketing's Role in Scientific Management, 1957, Advertising and Marketing to Young People, 1965, The Ultimate Overseas Business Guide for Growing Companies, 1990; contbr. articles to profl. jours. Mem. adv. bd. Glencoe Family Svc.; bd. dirs. Big Bros. Met. Chgo.; exec. v.p. City of Hope; mem. Theodore Thomas Soc. Chgo. Symphony Orch., Overture Soc. Lyric Opera Chgo. Capt. AUS, 1942-46. Decorated Bronze Star. Mem. Am. Assn. Pub. Opinion Rsch., Am. Film Inst., Am. Mktg. Assn., Am. Sociol. Assn., Smithsonian Instn. Home: 1011 Bluff St Glencoe IL 60022-1120

NIEFORTH, KARL ALLEN, university dean, educator; b. Melrose, Mass., July 7, 1936; s. Reginald Lemuel and Mabel (Zeimetz) N.; children from previous marriage: Scott, Keith, Karla, Kraig; m. Joan Carolyn Whitney, Feb. 14, 1989. BS, Mass. Coll. Pharmacy, 1957; MS in Med. Chemistry, Purdue U., 1959, PhD, 1961. Lic. pharmacist, Conn., Mass. Asst. prof. med. chemistry Sch. Pharmacy, U. Conn., Storrs, 1961-68, assoc. prof., 1968-75, prof., 1975—, asst. dean, 1967-76, assoc. dean, 1976-81, dean, 1981-93; lectr. psychiatry Yale U., 1970-76; mem. evaluation panels NSF, 1974-76, NIH, 1972-75; bd. dirs. Ctr. Drug and Alcohol Studies, Farmington, Conn., 1976-78; mem. pharmacy educators com. Nat. Assn. Chain Drugstores, 1988-93. Mem. adv. com. Conn. Dept. Mental Health, 1972-75; bd. dirs. Ea. Conn. Drug Action Program, 1970-72; mem. pharm. tripartite com. Conn. Dept. Consumer Protection, 1979-82, 89-95. Mem. Am. Found. Pharm. Edn. (Charles Lynn Fellow 1960-61), Am. Chem. Soc., Am. Pharm. Assn., Am. Assn. Colls. Pharmacy, Conn. Pharm. Assn., Conn. Soc. Hosp. Pharmacists, Acad. Pharm. Scis., Sigma Xi, Kappa Psi, Phi Lambda Sigma, Phi Lambda Upsilon, Rho Chi, Phi Kappa Phi. Republican. Home: 83 Brookside Ln Mansfield Center CT 06250-1109 Office: U Conn Sch Pharmacy Storrs CT 06269

NIEHAUS, LENNIE, composer, jazz saxophonist; b. St. Louis, Mo., June 1, 1929. Scores include (films) Tightrope, 1984, City Heat, 1984, Sesame Street: Follow That Bird, 1985, Pale Rider, 1985, Never Too Young to Die, 1986, Ratboy, 1986, Heartbreak Ridge, 1986, Emanon, 1987, Bird, 1988, Hot Men, 1989, White Hunter, Black Heart, 1990, The Rookie, 1990, Unforgiven, 1992, A Perfect World, 1993, The Bridges of Madison County, 1995, (TV movies) The Child Saver, 1988, Lush Life, 1994. Office: The Robert Light Agency 6404 Wilshire Blvd Ste 900 Los Angeles CA 90048-5511*

NIEHAUS, MERLE H., agricultural educator, international agriculture consultant; b. Enid, Okla., Mar. 25, 1933; s. Roy H. and Hazel (Farris) N.; m. Allene Rollier, Aug. 20, 1954; children: Lisa, Mark. BS, Okla. State U., 1955, MS, 1957; PhD, Purdue U., 1964. From asst. prof. to prof. agr. Ohio Agrl. Research and Devel. Ctr., Wooster, 1964-75, assoc. chmn. dept. agr., 1975-78; head dept. agronomy N.Mex. State U., Las Cruces, 1978-83, dir. agrl. exptl. sta., 1983-84; dean Coll. Agrl. Scis. Colo. State U., Ft. Collins, 1984-91, prof., 1991-92, dir. internat. R & D, 1993—; cons. FAO, UN, Rome, 1982. Contbr. articles to profl. jours. Mem. Wooster Sch. Bd., 1976-77. Fellow AAAS, Crop Sci. Soc. Am., Am. Soc. Agronomy. Office: Colo State U Internat R & D Fort Collins CO 80523

NIEHAUS, ROBERT JAMES, investment banking executive; b. Ann Arbor, Mich., Jan. 6, 1930; s. Julius Herman and Mary Johanna (Koch) N.; m. Jacqueline C. Mallier, Aug. 5, 1982. BBA, U. Mich., 1951; MBA, U. Detroit, 1958. Asst. sr. buyer Ford Motor Co., Dearborn, Mich., 1954-58; gen. purchasing agt. Hercules Motors Co., Canton, Ohio, 1959-60; v.p. procurement Schwitzer Corp., Indpls., 1960-66; sr. v.p. Wallace Murray Corp., N.Y.C., 1966-82; v.p. spl. projects Fischbach Corp., N.Y.C., 1983-84, sr. v.p., 1985-87; pres., chief exec. officer, vice chmn. Fischbach & Moore, Inc., Dallas, 1987-90; pres. Fischback Corp., 1989-90, 1st Phila. Corp., Radnor, Pa., 1991-92, Comutone corp., Atlanta, 1993; dir. Computone Corp., Atlanta, Ga., 1993-95; pres. Mile Marker, Inc., Pompano Beach, Fla., 1994-95; bd. dirs. Software Group, Barrie, Ont., Can. Bd. dirs. South Fla. Blood Bank, West Palm Beach. Served to lt. USN, 1951-54. Mem. Am. Mgmt. Assn. (gen. mgmt. council 1982—), Lighthouse Point (Fla.) Yacht and Racket Club. Clubs: Union League (N.Y.C.); Greenwich (Conn.) Country. Avocations: boating, music, tennis, golf, swimming. Home: 5960 NE 28th Ave Fort Lauderdale FL 33308

NIEHM, BERNARD FRANK, mental health center administrator; b. Sandusky, Ohio, Feb. 7, 1923; s. Bernard Frank and Hedwick (Panzer) N.; m. Eunice M. Patterson, Oct. 4, 1924; children—Julie, Patti, Bernie. BA, Ohio State U., 1951, MA, 1955, PhD, 1968. Tchr. pub. schs. Sandusky, 1951-57; chief ednl., vocat. and occupational therapy svcs. Vineland (N.J.) Tng. Sch., 1957-61; exec. dir. Franklin County Coun. Retarded Children, Columbus, Ohio, 1962-64; dir. Ohio Sheltered Workshop Planning Project Mental Retardation, 1964-66; coordinator mental retardation planning Ohio Bur. Planning and Grants, Div. Mental Health and Mental Retardation, 1966-68; project dir. Ohio Gov.'s Citizen Com. on Mental Retardation Planning, 1966-68; adminstr. Franklin County Program for Mentally Retarded, 1968-70; supt. Gallipolis (Ohio) State Inst., 1970-76; tchr. spl. edn. Ohio U., 1975—; dir. consultation and edn. Gallia-Jackson-Meigs Community Mental Health Ctr. (now Woodland Ctrs. Inc.), Gallipolis, 1977-79, dir., 1979-95; mgr. Woodland Farm, Gallipolis, 1995—; pres. Gallco, 1989-90; outreach bd. Woodland Ctr., Inc., Gallipolis, 1995. Contbr. articles to profl. jours. Active Foster Grandparents Adv. Coun., Gallia County, 1974-76, Gallipolis State Inst. Parent Vol. Assn., 1970-76, Franklin County Bd. Mental Retardation, 1967-68; chmn. MGM dist. Tri-State Boy Scout Coun.; chmn. Meigs, Gallia, Mason Counties Boy Scout Dist., 1972-94; pres. Gallipolis Girls Athletic Assn. Booster Club, 1976—, Gallia County Arthritis Unit, 1986—, Galleo Industries Bd. to Serve Handicapped Adults, 1987-94, St. Paul Luth. Ch., 1996-97; bd. dirs. United Cerebral Palsy, Columbus, 1968-70. With U.S. Army, 1943-46. Mem. Am. Assn. Mental Deficiency (past chmn. Ohio chpt., chmn. Great Lakes region), Am. Mental Health Adminstrs. (nat., Ohio chpts.), Nat. Rehab. Assn., Ohio Rehab. Assn., Ohio Assn. Retarded Children (2d v.p. 1974-76, dir.), Vocat. Rehab. Assn., Ohio Coun. Community Mental Health Ctrs., Gallia County Arthritis Assn. (pres. 1991—), Gallipolis Area C. of C., Rotary. Lutheran. Home: 1525 Mill Creek Rd Gallipolis OH 45631-8616 Office: Woodland Ctr Inc 3086 State Route 160 Gallipolis OH 45631-7800

NIEHOFF, KARL RICHARD BESUDEN, financial executive; b. Cin., May 11, 1943; s. Karl George and Jean (Besuden) N.; children: K. Richard B. Jr., Kelly B. BA, U. Cin., 1967. Corp. trust officer 5th-3d Union Trust, Cin., 1968-74; v.p., gen. mgr. Sabina (Ohio) Water Co., 1974-76; v.p., sec. Weil, Roth and Irving, Inc., 1974-76; co-mgr., mcpl. fin. dept. Thomson McKinnon Securities, Cin. and N.Y.C., 1976-79; trustee Cin. Stock Exch., 1974-80, 87-90, chmn. bd. trustees, 1978-79, pres., COO, 1979-90; exch. rep. Consol. Quote, Consol. Tape Oper. Coms., 1979-90, alt., 1991-92; pres. Fin. Instruments Svcs. Corp., Cin., Chgo., London, 1985-90; v.p. Trading Svcs. NASDAQ, Inc., 1991-92, D.E. Shaw & Co., N.Y.C., 1992-94; pres., mng. ptnr. Niehoff and Assocs., N.Y.C., 1994—; mgr. market devel. OTC Project, Warsaw, Poland, 1995-96; voting mem. Inter-Market Trading Com., 1980-90, Stock Exch. Chief Execs. Com., 1988-90; mem. Cin. Stock Exch., 1974-89, P.B.W. Stock Exch., 1975-76; mgr., advisor to Ministry, Mass Privatization for the Republic of Poland, 1995-96. Trustee, sec. Contemporary Arts Ctr., Cin., 1975-83; mem. Young Mens Mercantile Libr. Assn., 1974-90, adv. com., 1974-77; mem. devel. com. Tangeman Gallery of Art, 1981-82. Mem. Securities Traders Assn. N.Y., Univ. Club (Cin.), Miami Club (Miamitown), Keeneland Assn. (Lexington, Ky.), Internat. Ops. Assn. (N.Y.), European Assn. Securities Dealers (Laventem, Belgium), N.Y. Stock Exch. Luncheon Club, N.Y. Athletic Club, NYAC Yacht Club (Pelham Manor, N.Y.), Cin. Stock and Bond Club (trustee and 1st v.p. 1974-90), Queen City Mcpl. Bond Club (trustee 1974-80), India House, Phi Alpha Theta. Office: Niehoff and Assocs 2200 Star Bank Tower 5th and Walnut Sts Cincinnati OH 45202

NIELSEN, ALDON DALE, retired government agency official, economist; b. Mason City, Nebr., Jan. 13, 1922; s. Seren and Sena (Nielsen) N.; m. Vivian Leola Lee, Mar. 26, 1944; children: Carol Ann, Aldon Lynn, Dennis Lee, Brian Paige. Student, Biarittz Am. U., France, 1945; B.Sc., U. Nebr., 1948, postgrad., 1951. With Bur. Reclamation, Dept. Interior, 1948-86; successively economist Bur. Reclamation, Dept. Interior, Grand Island, Nebr., 1948-60; regional agrl. economist Bur. Reclamation, Dept. Interior, Denver, 1960-63; contract and repayment specialist Bur. Reclamation, Dept. Interior, 1963-65; chief economics and program analysis br. Bur. Reclamation, Dept. Interior, Washington, 1965-77; asst. chief div. water and land Bur. Reclamation, Dept. Interior, 1977-78; dir. operation and maintenance policy staff Bur. Reclamation, Dept. Interior, Washington, 1978-83, dir. Office of Water Research, 1983-85; asst. chief div. fgn. activities Dept. Interior, 1985-86; mem. Internat. Commn. on Irrigation and Drainage. Pres. Nebr. Bapt. Men, 1957-59; bd. mgrs. Nebr. Bapt. Conv., 1957-59; mem. Nebr. Bapt. Lay Devel. Com., 1957-58; bd. dirs. Colo. Bapt. Conv., 1960-63; sec. Colo. Bapt. Men, 1961-63; exec. v.p. Am. Bapt. Men, 1962-65, pres., 1965-67; mem. exec. bd. D.C. Bapt. Conv., 1964-72, 76-78, 80-82, 88-97, v.p., 1989-90, pres., 1990-91. Served with AUS, 1944-46, ETO. Decorated Bronze Star; recipient Superior Service award Dept. Interior, 1958, 59, 61, 66, Meritorius Service award, 1973, Spl. Achievement award, 1978, Disting. Service award, 1985. Mem. Internat. Water Resources Assn. Home: 519 S Harrison St Arlington VA 22204-1217

NIELSEN, FORREST HAROLD, research nutritionist; b. Junction City, Wis., Oct. 26, 1941; s. George Adolph and Sylvia Viola (Blood) N.; m. Emily Joanne Currie, June 13, 1964; children: Forrest Erik, Kistin Emily. BS, U. Wis., 1963, MS, 1966, PhD, 1967. NIH grad. fellow, dept. biochemistry U. Wis., Madison, 1963-67; rsch. chemist, Human Nutrition Rsch. Inst. USDA, Beltsville, Md., 1969-70; rsch. chemist Human Nutrition Rsch. Ctr., USDA, Grand Forks, N.D., 1970-86, ctr. dir. and rsch. nutritionist, 1986—; adj. prof. dept. biochemistry, U. N.D., Grand Forks, 1971—, speaker in field. Assoc. editor Magnesium and Trace Elements Jour., 1990-93; mem. editl. bd. Jour. Trace Elements in Exptl. Medicine, 1988—, Biol. Trace Element Rsch. Jour., 1979—, Jour. Nutrition, 1984-88; contbr. articles to profl. jours. Capt. U.S. Army, 1967-69. Recipient Klaus Schwarz Commemorative medal and award Internat. Assn. of Bioinorganic Scientists; named Scientist of Yr. U.S. Dept. Agrl., 1993. Mem. Internat. Soc. Trace Element Rsch. in Humans (gov. bd. 1989—, pres. 1992-95), Internat. Assn. Bioinorganic Scis., Soc. for Exptl. Biology and Medicine, Am. Soc. for Nutritional Scis., N.D. Acad. Sci. (pres. 1988-89), Sigma Xi (pres. U. N.D. chpt. 1976-77). Lutheran. Achievements include patent for use of Boron Supplements to Increase in Vivo Production of Hydroxylated Steroids; discovery of the nutritional essentiality of the trace elements boron and nickel. Office: USDA ARS GFHNRC PO Box 9034 Grand Forks ND 58202-9034

NIELSEN, GEORGE LEE, architect; b. Ames, Iowa, Dec. 12, 1937; s. Verner Henry and Verba Lucile (Smith) N.; m. Karen Wall, Feb. 28, 1959; children: David Stuart, Kristina, Melissa. B.Arch., Iowa State U., 1961; M.Arch., M.I.T., 1962. Registered arch., Mass., Ohio, N.Y., Ill., Ind., Nat. Coun. Archtl. Registration Bds. Designer Perry, Shaw, Hepburn & Dean, Boston, 1961-64, F.A. Stahl & Assos., Cambridge, Mass., 1964-65; project architect Peirce & Pierce, Boston, 1965-70; project mgr. A.M. Kinney Assos., Cin., 1970—, partner, 1978—; sec. A.M. Kinney Assocs., Inc., Ill., 1993—; also dir. A.M. Kinney Assocs., Inc., Cin.; v.p. A.M. Kinney Inc., Cin., 1992-94, pres., 1994—, also dir. Architect assoc. with major projects for Avco Rsch. Lab., Children's Hosp. Med. Ctr., Square D. Corp., Nalco Chem. Co., Olin Corp., Mead Johnson/Bristol Myers Squib, Cin. Gas and Elec. Co., Sandoz Pharm. Corp., Hoechst Celanese, Witco Corp., Sotheby's, Shell Chem. Co., Bayer Corp. Served with U.S. Army, 1962-64. Mem. AIA (design awards 1970-71, 74, 78, 81, 91, 94, 95). Episcopalian. Home: 3419 Ault View Ave Cincinnati OH 45208-2518 Office: A M Kinney Inc 2900 Vernon Pl Cincinnati OH 45219-2436

NIELSEN, GLADE BENJAMIN, mayor, former state senator; b. Hyrum, Utah, Mar. 8, 1926; s. George Benjamin and Katie Ione (Jensen) N.; m. Alpha Fern Strempke, Oct. 15, 1955; children: Karen Lynn, Sharon Kay, Roger Glade, Laura Mae, Lance Eric (dec. 1996). BS, Utah State U., 1949. Supt. various constrn. cos., Wyo., Nev., and Calif., 1949-55; pres. Glade Nielsen Builder, Roy, Utah, 1955-86; mem. Utah State Senate, Salt Lake City, 1987-92; mayor Roy City, 1994—; chmn. Roy Redevel. Agy., 1994—. Pres. Weber Basin Homebuilders Assn., 1967-68, Home Builders Assn. Utah, 1972-73; v.p. Nat. Assn. Home Builders, Washington, 1974-75, mem. exec. com., 1976-79; exec. com. Weber Econ. Devel. Corp.; pres. Roy C. of C., 1980; bd. dirs. Utah Housing Fin. Agy., Salt Lake, 1975-83. With USN, 1944-46, PTO. Recipient Builder of Yr. award Home Builders Assn. Utah, 1988, Svc. award Utah State Com. Consumer Svcs., 1989, Recognition award Utah State Dept. Commerce, 1989, Hon. Commendation award Ogden Air Logistics Command, 1989, Roy City Outstanding Citizen award, 1993. Mem. U.S. Indiana Assn. (pres. 1996), VFW, Am. Legion, Thunderbird Motor Club Utah (pres.), Elks, Ogden/Weber C. of C. (dir.). Republican. Avocations: travel, antique cars.

NIELSEN, GREG ROSS, lawyer; b. Provo, Utah, Sept. 24, 1947; s. Ross T. and Carma (Peterson) N.; m. Jo Rita Beer, Sept. 3, 1971; children: Jennifer, Jerilyn, Eric Michael, Brittany Anne. BA in Polit. Sci. magna cum laude, Brigham Young U., 1971; JD cum laude, Harvard U., 1975. Bar: Ariz. 1975, U.S. Dist. Ct. Ariz. 1975, U.S. Ct. Appeals (9th cir.) 1977, Utah 1990. Assoc. Snell & Wilmer, Phoenix, 1975-80, ptnr., 1981-91; mng. ptnr. Snell & Wilmer, Salt Lake City, 1991—; adminstrv. coord. real estate practice group Snell & Wilmer, Phoenix, 1988-90. Mem. dist. com. Theodore Roosevelt coun. Boy Scouts Am., 1988-90, Valley Partnership, Phoenix, 1989-90. Hinckley scholar Brigham Young U., 1970; fellow Ford Found., 1970. Mem. ABA, State Bar Ariz., Utah Bar Assn. Republican. Mem. LDS Ch. Office: Snell & Wilmer 111 E Broadway Ste 900 Salt Lake City UT 84111-5235

NIELSEN, HARALD CHRISTIAN, retired chemist; b. Chgo., Apr. 18, 1930; s. Svend Aage and Seena (Hansen) N.; m. Eloise Wilma Soule, Dec. 19, 1953; children—Brenda Mae, Paul Erick, Gloria Lynn, Judy Ann. B.A., St. Olaf Coll., 1952; Ph.D., Mich. State U., 1957. Cereal grain protein chemist Nat. Ctr. for Agrl. Utilization Rsch. (formerly No. Regional Research Ctr.), Agrl. Research Service, USDA, Peoria, Ill., 1957-87. Contbr. articles to profl. jours. Pres. local 3247 Am. Fedn. Govt. Employees, AFL-CIO, 1977-86; mem. Peoria Area Combined Fed. Campaign Coordinating Com., 1980-87. Mem. ACLU, Am. Assn. Cereal Chemists, Nat. Assn. Ret. Fed. Employees (officer chpt. 268 1989-92, pres. chpt. 268 1991), Sigma Xi. Democrat. Lutheran. Home: 2318 N Gale Ave Peoria IL 61604-3229 *What useful thing have I accomplished this day? What did I learn today? These two questions I ask myself at the end of each day.*

NIELSEN, KENNETH ANDREW, chemical engineer; b. Berwyn, Ill., Oct. 10, 1949; s. Howard Andrew and La Verne Alma (Wentzer) N.; m. Linda Kay Miller, Aug. 20, 1970; children: Annette Marie, Kirsten Viola. BS in Chem. Engring., Iowa State U., 1971, MS in Chem. Engring., 1974, PhD in Chem. Engring., 1977. Sr. engr. Union Carbide Corp., Charleston, W.Va., 1976-80, project scientist, 1980-87, rsch. scientist, 1987-94, sr. rsch. scientist, 1994—. Contbr. articles to profl. jours. Co-founder Forest Hills Assns., Charleston, 1981; advisor Boy Scout Explorer Post, Charleston, 1992. Recipient Fellowships NDEA Title IV, Procter and Gamble Co., Am. Oil Co., Elias Singer award Troy Chem. Co., 1990, Kirkpatrick Chem. Engring. Achievement award Chem. Engring. mag., 1991, Profl. Progress in Engring. award Coll. Engring. Iowa State U., 1992. Mem. Am. Inst. Chem. Engrs., Soc. Rheology, Inst. Liquid Atomization and Spraying Sys. Achievements include invention of UNICARB system for spray coating, a recognized major new pollution-prevention tech.; co-inventor of SERT process for applying mold release agents in polyurethane foam manufacture; discovery of fundamentally new type of spray atomization, known as a decompressive spray. Holder of 25 U.S. patents and 7 U.S. patents pending, also foreign patents. Home: 108 Stratford Pl Charleston WV 25303-2819 Office: Union Carbide Corp PO Box 8361 South Charleston WV 25303

NIELSEN, LELAND C., federal judge; b. Vesper, Kans., June 14, 1919; s. Carl Christian and Christena (Larson) N.; m. Virginia Garland, Nov. 27, 1958; 1 child, Christena. A.B., Washburn U., 1946; J.D., U. So. Calif., 1946. Bar: Calif. 1947. Practice law Los Angeles, from 1947; dep. city atty. City of Los Angeles, 1947-51; judge Superior Ct. Calif. San Diego County, 1968-71; judge, now sr. judge U.S. Dist. Ct. (so. dist.) Calif., San Diego, 1971—. Served to maj. A.C., U.S. Army 1941-46. Decorated Purple Heart, Disting. Svc. Cross, Air medal with oak leaf clusters. Mem. Am. Coll. Trial Lawyers. Republican. Presbyterian. Office: US Dist Ct Courtroom 10 940 Front St San Diego CA 92101-8994*

NIELSEN, LEONARD MAURICE, physician assistant; b. Bklyn., June 6, 1949; s. Leonard Maurice Nielsen and Alma Dorothy (Weber) Sherman; m. Therese Marie Wright, Aug. 4, 1979; children: Daniel Weber, Carolyn Wright. AA, Allan Hancock Coll., Santa Maria, Calif., 1969; BS in Zoology, U. Ga., 1972; BS in Medicine/Physician Asst. Cert., Emory U., 1977; MPH, U. Ala., Birmingham, 1987. Nat. bd. cert. physician asst. Rsch. asst. and asst. instr. Physiology dept. Emory U., Atlanta, 1972-75; physician asst. Neurology-P.A.C., St. Petersburg, Fla., 1977-79; sr. physician asst. VA, Birmingham, 1979-88; med. regional clin. evaluator Dept. Vets. Affairs, Tuscaloosa, Ala., 1988-90; adminstrv. assoc. to chief staff Dept. Vets. Affairs, Tuskegee, Ala., 1990-91; dir. quality mgmt. and utilization rev. The Children's Hosp. of Ala., Birmingham, 1991-93; physician asst. U. Ala.-Birmingham Hosps., 1993-95, Walker Bapt. Regional Med. Ctr., Jasper, Ala., 1995—, Internal Medicine West, Bessemer, Ala., 1995—; cons. in quality improvement, Birmingham, 1988—; lectr. in field; adj. prof. Tuskegee Inst., 1990. Co-author: Catastrophic State of Catastrophic Health Care (in the United States), 1987; editor newsletter Ala. Soc. Physician Assts., 1990-91. Advisor EPIC Sch. fundraiser, 1985-91; active participant Birmingham Regional Healthcare Execs., 1990-95; co-chair Forest Park Neighborhood Crimefighters, Birmingham, 1980-84, Putnam Middle Sch. fundraiser, Birmingham, 1991-93; founding mem. Ala. Sch. Fine Arts Music Support Group, 1995—. Major USAFR, 1996—. Recipient VA Suggestion award, 1981; Optimist Club scholar, 1967. Fellow Am. Acad. Physician Assts. (del. 1977—), Ala. Soc. Physician Assts. (sec., del. 1979—, bd. dirs. 1982-85); mem. Am. Mensa (award 1980), Nat. Assn. Quality Assurance Professions, Alumni Assn. U. Ala.-Birmingham (bd. dirs. 1992-94). Avocations: bicycle riding, camping, canoeing, skiing, computers. Home: 4736 Vermont Ave Birmingham AL 35210-3232

NIELSEN, LYNN CAROL, lawyer, educational consultant; b. Perth Amboy, N.J., Jan. 11, 1950; d. Hans and Esther (Pucker) N.; m. Russell F. Baldwin, Nov. 22, 1980; 1 child, Blake Nielsen Baldwin. BS, Millersville U., 1972; MA, NYU, 1979; JD, Rutgers U., 1984. Bar: N.J. 1984; cert. tchr. handicapped, reading specialist, learning disability tchr. cons., elem. edn. supr. Instr. Woodbridge (N.J.) Twp. Bd. Edn., 1972-83; legal intern appellate sect. divsn. criminal justice Atty. Gen. State N.J., Trenton, 1983, dep. atty. gen. divsn. civil law, 1985; assoc. Kantor & Kusic, Keyport, N.J., 1984-86, Kantor & Linderoth, Keyport, N.J., 1986-92. Officer Fords (N.J.) Sch. # 14 PTO, 1974-75; elder First Presbyn. Ch. Avenel, N.J., 1985-88; bd. dirs. New Beginnings Nursery Sch., Woodbridge, 1989-90, Flemington (N.J.) Presbyn. Nursery Sch., 1991-93. Mem. ABA, N.J. Bar Assn., Monmouth County Bar Assn., Hunterdon County Bar Assn. Avocations: reading, skiing, sailing. Home and Office: 3 Buchannan Way Flemington NJ 08822-3205

NIELSEN, NIELS CHRISTIAN, JR., theology educator; b. Long Beach, Calif., June 2, 1921; s. Niels Hansen and Frances (Nofziger) N.; m. Erika Kreuth, May 10, 1958; children—Camilla Regina, Niels Albrecht. BA, George Pepperdine Coll., L.A., 1942; BD, Yale U., 1946, PhD, 1951. Ordained to ministry Meth. Ch., 1946. Pastor Woodbury (Conn.) Meth. Ch., 1944-46; instr. religion Yale U., New Haven, 1948-51; faculty Rice U., Houston, 1951—; J. Newton Rayzor prof. religious studies. Rice U., prof. emeritus, 1991—; Amax presdl. prof. humanities Colo. Sch. Mines, Golden, 1982-83; scholar in residence St. Paul's United Meth. Ch., Houston. Author: Philosophy and Religion in Contemporary Japan, 1957, Geistige Landerkunde USA, 1960, A Layman Looks at World Religions, 1962, God in Education, 1966, Solzhenitsyn's Religion (Nelson), 1975, The Religion of Jimmy Carter, 1977, The Crisis of Human Rights, 1978, Religions of the World, 1982, Revolutions in Eastern Europe: The Religious Roots, 1991, Fundamentalism, Mythos and World Religions, 1993; editor: Religion After Communism in Russia, 1994; contbr. articles to profl. jours. Mem. Am. Acad. Religion, Am. Philos. Soc., Am. Soc. Study Religion (sec. 1977-89), Soc. European Culture, Soc. for Values in Higher Edn. Democrat. Home: 2424 Swift Blvd Houston TX 77030-1806

NIELSEN, STEVEN B., medical products executive; b. 1947. BA, Calif. State U., Long Beach, 1973. With Acme United Corp., 1973-76, Bergen Brunswig Med. Surgical Inc., 1976-78, 80-84, Hosp. Pharmacies Inc., 1978-80; exec. v.p. Gen. Med. Corp., Richmond, Va., 1984-88, pres., 1988-89, dir., 1989-93, chm. bd., CEO, 1993—. Office: General Medical Corp 8741 Landmark Rd Richmond VA 23228-2801*

NIELSEN, WILLIAM FREMMING, federal judge; b. 1934. BA, U. Wash., 1956, LLB, 1963. Law clk. to Hon. Charles L. Powell U.S. Dist. Ct. (ea. dist.) Wash., 1963-64; mem. firm Paine, Hamblen, Coffin, Brooke & Miller, 1964-91; judge to chief of judge U.S. Dist. Ct. (ea. dist.) Wash., Spokane, 1991—. Lt. col. USAFR. Fellow Am. Coll. Trial Lawyers; mem. ABA, Wash. State Bar Assn., Spokane County Bar Assn. (pres. 1981-82), Fed. Bar Assn. (pres. 1988), Spokane County Legal Svcs. Corp. (past pres.), Lawyer Pilot Bar Assn., Assn. Trial Lawyers Am., Wash. State Trial Lawyers Assn., Assn. Def. Trial Attys., Am. Inns of Ct., Charles L. Powell Inn (pres. 1987), The Spokane Club, Rotary, Alpha Delta Phi, Phi Delta Phi. Office: US Dist Ct PO Box 2208 920 W Riverside Ave 9th Fl Spokane WA 99210-2208*

NIELSON, HOWARD CURTIS, former congressman, retired educator; b. Richfield, Utah, Sept. 12, 1924; s. Herman Taylor and Zula May (Curtis) N.; m. Julia Adams, June 18, 1948; children: Noreen (Mrs. Stephen Astin), Elaine (Mrs. Stanley Taylor), John, Mary Lee (Mrs. Paul Jackson), James, Jean (Mrs. Clay Cundick), Howard Curtis Jr. BS in Math., U. Utah, 1947; MS in Math., U. Oreg., 1949; MBA, Stanford U., 1956, PhD in Bus. Adminstrn. and Stats., 1958. Statistician C & H Sugar Refining Corp., 1949-51; rsch. economist and statistician Stanford Rsch. Inst., 1951-57; mem. faculty Brigham Young U., Provo, Utah, 1957-82; prof. statistics Brigham Young U., 1961-82, chmn. dept., 1960-63; sr. devel. engr. Hercules, Inc., 1960-66; dir. Ctr. for Bus. and Econ. Rsch., 1971-72; sr. statistician, acting field mgr. C.E.I.R, Inc., 1963-64, mgr., cons., 1964-65; prin. scientist GCA Corp., 1965-67; dir. econ. rsch. Eyring Rsch. Inst., 1974-75; assoc. commr. higher edn. State of Utah, 1976-79; mem. 98th-101st Congresses from 3d dist. Utah; missionary LDS Ch., Australia, 1991-92, Hungary, 1993-94; econ. adviser Kingdom of Jordan, Ford Found., 1970-71; prof. Am. U., Beirut, 1970; adj. prof. U. Utah, 1972-76. Author: The Efficiency of Certain Truncated Order Statistics in Estimating the Mean of Various Distributions, 1949, Population Trends in the United States Through 1975, 1955, The Hows and Whys of Statistics, 1963, Experimental Designs Used in industry, 1965, Membership Growth of the Church of Jesus Christ of Latter-Day Saints, 1957, 67, 71, 75, 78, Evaluation of the Seven Year Plan for Economic Development in Jordan, 1971, Economic Analysis of Fiji, Tonga, Western and Am. Samoa, 1972; co-author: The Newsprint Situation in the Western Region of North America, 1952, America's Demand for Wood, 1954, also reports. Mem. Utah Gov.'s Econ. Rsch. Adv. Coun., 1967-72; dir. bur. ch. studies Ch. of Jesus Christ of Latter-day Saints, 1958-63; rsch. dir. Utah Republican Party, 1967-68; mem. Utah Ho. of Reps, 1967-75, majority leader, 1969-71, speaker, 1973-75, mem. legis. budget-audit com., 1967-73, chmn., 1971-73, chmn. legis. coun., 1973-75; mem. Utah 3d Dist., U.S. Ho. of Reps., 1983-91; chmn. Utah County Rep. Com., 1979-81; mem. Utah Senate, 1997—. Mem. Am. Statis. Assn. (pres. Utah br. 1964-65, mem. nat. coun. 1967-70), Sci. Rsch. Soc. Am., Order of Artus, Phi Beta Kappa, Phi Kappa Phi, Sig,a Xi, Pi Mu Epsilon.

NIELSON, NORMA LEE, business educator; b. Augusta, Ga., Dec. 26, 1953; d. Norman Lyle and Betty Lou (Buckner) Parrott; m. Mark G. Nielson, Nov. 20, 1985 (div. 1988); 1 child, Eric Gordon. BS, Northwest Mo. State U., 1974; MA, U. Pa., 1976, PhD, 1979. CLU. Asst. prof. Iowa State U., Ames, 1977-79, U. So. Calif., L.A., 1979-84; cons. profl. Mercer-Meidinger, L.A., 1984-85; assoc. prof. Oreg. State U., Corvallis, 1985-90; prof. Oreg. State U., 1990-97; bd. examiners Internat. Bd. Stds. and Practice for CFP, 1991-94. Developer software; contbg. author: Handbook for Corporate Directors, 1985; contbr. articles to profl. publs. Vol. Linn-Benton Food Share, Corvallis; bd. dirs. Corvallis Cmty. Dare Care, Inc., 1988-91; candidate for Oreg. Ho. of Reps., 1994; bd. dirs. Boys and Girls Club Corvallis, 1995-97. Andrus Found. rsch. grantee, 1989-91. Mem. Am. Risk and Ins. Assn. (bd. dirs. 1990-97, officer 1993-96), Western Risk and Ins. Assn. (officer 1981-84), Risk and Ins. Mgmt. Soc. Avocations: piano, stained glass, flying. Office: Oreg State U Coll Bus 200 Bexell Hall Corvallis OR 97331-8527

NIELSON, THEO GILBERT, law enforcement official, university official; b. Roosevelt, Utah, June 29, 1938; s. John Gilbert and Mazie (Alexander) N.; m. Martha Perez, May 22, 1961; children: Lucille Marie, Sherry Lou, Mark Andrew, Rex Alexander, Theo Gilbert Jr., Cristal Ina, Gregory Angus, Mazie Leah, Rosanna Alma. Grad., FBI Nat. Acad., 1970; BA, Ariz. State U., 1975, MS, 1977. Officer Univ. Police, Ariz. State U., Tempe, 1963-67, sgt., 1967-70, lt., 1970-79; chief police Douglas (Ariz.) Police Dept., 1979-82; div. adminstr. Ariz. Criminal Intelligence Systems Agy., Tucson, 1982-84; dir. campus safety and security No. Ariz. U., Flagstaff, 1984-92; chief police Ariz. Dept. Adminstrn., 1992—. Mem. Am. Soc. for Indsl. Security (chmn. No. Ariz. chpt. 1987), Internat. Assn. Chiefs Police, Internat. Assn. Campus Law Enforcement Adminstrs., Ariz. Assn. Campus Law Enforcement (pres. 1989-90). Republican. Mormon. Avocations: genealogy, hiking, grandchildren. Home: 3335 E Hampton Ave Mesa AZ 85204-6410 Office: Ariz State Capitol Police 1700 W Washington St Ste B15 Phoenix AZ 85007-2812

NIELSON, WILLIAM BROOKS, clergyman; b. Jeffersonville, Vt., Nov. 26, 1949; s. John Bechtold and Marguerite Helene (Mann) N.; m. Susan Gail Walter, May 2, 1992; children: Anya Helene, Abigail Brooke, Aliece Gwen. AB in Religion, Ea. Nazarene Coll., Quincy, Mass., 1971; MDiv cum laude, Nazarene Theol. Sem., Kansas City, Mo., 1974. Ordained to ministry Ch. of Nazarene, 1979. Min. music St. Paul's Ch. of Nazarene, Kansas City, 1971-74, min. youth and music, 1974-75; min. youth and music Balt. 1st Ch. of Nazarene, Ellicott City, Md., 1975-81; sr. pastor Ch. of Nazarene, Concord, Ohio, 1981—; mem. bi-dist. camp bd. N.E. Camp, mem. program com., youth ministries rep., mem. bd. Christian life, dir. youth ministries, pres. Nazarene Youth Internat., Washington Dist. Ch. of Nazarene; mem. gen. coun. Nazarene Youth Internat., ea. regional rep. Ch. of Nazarene, 1977-80, gen. sec. Nazarene Youth Internat., 1980-85; spkr. team camps, retreats, revivals and Nazarene Youth Internat. convs., 1975—. Author: Unlocking the Bible, 1979, The Distinguishing Mark, 1980; contbr. to religious publs. Mem. alumni coun. bd. dirs. Ea. Nazarene Coll., 1979—; founder Painesville (Ohio) Christian Acad., 1983; bd. dirs., mem. founding bd. Painesville Counseling Ctr., 1985-87, 88-90; chaplain, maj. CAP, 1993—. Republican. Home: 6123 Chestnut St Concord OH 44077-2436 Office: Ch of Nazarene 6235 Chestnut St Concord OH 44077-2438

NIEMANN, BERNARD JOHN, JR., land and geographical system educator, researcher, consultant; b. Highland Park, Ill., July 23, 1937; s. Bernard J.. and Emma (Gaeble) N.; m. Sondra Sue, Dec. 29, 1962; 1 child, Ben. BA,

U. Ill., 1960; MLA, Harvard U., 1964. Site planner Leo A. Daly Co., Omaha, 1960-63, Sasaki-Walker & Assocs., Watertown, Mass., 1963-64; asst. prof. dept. landscape architecture U. Wis., Madison, 1963-68, assoc. prof., 1969-71, chmn. dept., 1971-75, prof. dept. landscape architecture Inst. Environ.. Studies, adj. prof. urban and regional planning, 1976—, dir. land info. and computer graphics facility Sch. Natural Resources, 1988—; cons. resource and land investigations program U.S. Dept. Interior, Reston, Va., 1976-80; mem. com. on integrated land data mapping NRC, Washington, 1981-82, mem. com. mapping sci. NRC, Washington, 1990-94; prin. Landscapes Ltd., Madison, 1964-73; cons. Wis. Dept. Justice, Office Pub. Intervenor, Madison, 1978-84; mem. Lower Wis. Riverway Planning Task Force, Wis. Dept. Natural Resources, Madison, 1983-87; vice chair Wis. Gov.'s Land Records Com., 1985-87; adviser nat. geodetic survey U.S. Dept. Commerce. Author: (with others) Modernization of the Pubic Land Survey System, 1982; editor: Land Records Can and Should Be Improved, 1980, editor Wis. Land Info. Newsletter, 1983—; co-editor Jour. Urban and Regional Systems Assn., 1988—; editl. bd. Jour. Transactions in Wis., 1996—. Bd. dirs. Wis. Land Info. Bd., 1989—, chmn., 1989-90. vice chmn., 1990-94; pres. Wis. Land Info. Assn., 1989-90. Recipient Educator of Yr. award Coun. Educators in Landscape Architecture, 1986, Wis. Idea award in natural resource policy, 1991, award of distinction and svc. Wis. Land Info. Assn., 1990, Pres. award, 1995. Mem. Am. Soc. Landscape Architects (award of achievement 1959, award of merit 1970, 74, 88, award of honor 1982, 84, 89, Horwood Merit award, Horwood Dist. Svc. award 1996), Urban and Regional Info. Assn. (bd. dirs. 1986-88), Gamma Sigma Delta. Home: 2501 Marshall Pky Madison WI 53713-1030 Office: U Wis Land Info/Comp Graph B102 Steenbock Meml Libr 550 Babcock Dr Madison WI 53706-1201

NIEMANN, LEWIS KEITH, lamp manufacturing company executive; b. Alliance, Nebr., Dec. 10, 1930; s. William Grover and Vivian Zelma (Holloway) N. BS in Mktg. with honors (Standard Oil grantee), San Diego State Coll., 1956. Mdse. mgr. Fed Mart Corp., San Diego, 1954-61; store mgr. GEX, Atlanta, 1961-63; mdse. mgr. J. C. Penney Co., Pitts., 1963-67; mgr. sales planning and product devel. RCA Sales Corp., 1967-70; spl. asst. to pres. Magnavox Consumer Electronics Co., 1970-73, v.p. internat. and comml. sales, 1973-74; v.p. mktg., div. mfg. Beatrice Foods Co., Chgo., 1974-75; v.p. mktg., div. luggage Samsonite Corp., Denver, 1975-78; pres. Stiffel Co., Chgo., 1978-80, Westwood Lighting Group, Inc., Paterson, N.J., 1980-87, El Paso, Tex., 1987-90, Sunset-Richards Lighting, City of Commerce, Calif., 1990-91. Bd. dirs. Jr. Achievement, Denver, 1976-78, Pvt. Industry Council, Passiaic County. Served with USMC, 1948-52, Korea. Recipient CLIO award for Best TV Comml. in class, 1978. Republican. Presbyterian.

NIEMETH, CHARLES FREDERICK, lawyer; b. Lorain, Ohio, Nov. 25, 1939; s. Charles Ambrose and Christine Cameron (Mollison) N.; m. Anne Marie Meckes, Oct. 12, 1968. B.A., Harvard U., 1962; J.D., U. Mich., 1965. Bar: Calif. 1966, N.Y. 1984. Assoc. O'Melveny & Myers, Los Angeles, 1965-72, ptnr., 1973—. Mem. nat. com. Mich. Law Sch. Fund; trustee Challengers Boys and Girls Club, 1968-83; mem. bus. adv. coun. UCLA, 1979-83; mem. exec. com. Internat. Student Ctr., 1979-83; bd. dirs. Olympic Tower Condominium, 1986-92; bd. visitors Mich. Law Sch., mem. Tri-Bar Opinion Com. Mem. Riviera Tennis Club, Regency Club, N.Y. Athletic Club, Field Club (Greenwich, Conn.), Bel-Air Bay Club. Democrat. Roman Catholic. Home: 10660 Bellagio Rd Los Angeles CA 90077-3713 also: 70 Oneida Dr Greenwich CT 06830-7131 Office: O'Melveny & Myers 1999 Avenue Of The Stars Los Angeles CA 90067-6022 also: O'Melveny & Myers 153 E 53rd St Fl 54 New York NY 10022-4611

NIEMEYER, GERHART, political science educator; b. Essen, Germany, Feb. 15, 1907; came to U.S., 1937, naturalized, 1943; s. Victor and Kaethe (Ley) N.; m. Lucie Lenzner, Sept. 18, 1931; children: A. Hermann, Lucian L., Paul V., Lisa M., Christian B. Student, Cambridge U., 1925-26, Munich U., 1926-27; J.U.D., Kiel U., 1932. Ordained priest Episcopal Ch. 1980, canon, 1987. Lectr., asst. prof. Princeton U., 1937-44; prof., head div. Oglethorpe U., 1944-50; fgn. affairs officer Dept. State, 1950-53; research analyst Council Fgn. Relations, 1953-55; prof. U. Notre Dame, 1955-76, emeritus, 1976—; mem. Bd. Fgn. Scholarships, 1981-84, chmn., 1982-84; vis. prof. Yale U., 1942, 46, 54-55, Columbia U., 1952, Vanderbilt U., 1962-66; faculty Nat. War Coll., 1958-59, 61; Fulbright prof. U. Munich, 1962-63; Distinguished vis. prof. Hillsdale Coll., 1976-82. Author: Law Without Force, 1941, An Inquiry into Soviet Mentality, 1956, Facts on Communism, vol. 1: The Communist Ideology, 1959, Handbook on Communism, 1962, Between Nothingness and Paradise, 1971, Deceitful Peace, 1971, Aftersight and Foresight, 1988, Within and Above Ourselves, 1996; assoc. editor Modern Age, 1965—. Mem. task force on fgn. policy Republican Nat. Com., 1965-68. Mem. Am. Polit. Sci. Assn. Roman Catholic. Home: 47 Lafayette Pl Apt 5C Greenwich CT 06830-5404

NIEMEYER, GLENN ALAN, academic administrator, history educator; b. Muskegon, Mich., Jan. 14, 1934; s. John T. and Johanna F. (Walhout) N.; m. Betty Sikkenga, July 8, 1955; children: Kristin, Alexis, Sander. BA in History, Calvin Coll., 1955; MA in History, Mich. State U., 1959, PhD in History, 1962. Tchr. soc. sci. Grand Haven Christian Sch., Mich., 1955-58; teaching asst., asst. instr. Mich. State U., East Lansing, 1958-63; asst. prof. history Grand Valley State U., Allendale, Mich., 1963-66, assoc. prof., 1966-70, prof., 1970—, dean Coll. Arts and Scis., 1970-73, v.p. of colls., 1973-76, v.p. acad. affairs, 1976—, provost, 1980—; evaluator commn. on instns. of higher edn. North Ctrl. Assn., Chgo., 1974—, vice chair, 1994, chair, 1995, v.p., 1996, pres., 1997; mem. Acad. Officers, Pres.'s Coun. State Univs. of Mich. Author: The Automotive Career of Ransom E. Olds, 1963; contbr. articles and book revs. to profl. publs. Trustee Calvin Coll., Grand Rapids, Mich., 1974-80; trustee Unity Christian High Sch., Hudsonville, Mich., 1978-80, pres. bd., 1979-80. Mem. Am. Coun. on Edn., Am. Assn. Higher Edn. Mem. Christian Ref. Ch. Office: Grand Valley State U Allendale MI 49401

NIEMEYER, PAUL VICTOR, federal judge; b. Princeton, N.J., Apr. 5, 1941; s. Gerhart and Lucie (Lenzner) N.; m. Susan Kinley, Aug. 24, 1963; children Jonathan K., Peter E., Christopher J. AB, Kenyon Coll., 1962; student, U. Munich, Federal Republic of Germany, 1962-63; JD, U. Notre Dame, 1966. Bars: Md. 1966, U.S. Dist. Ct. Md. 1967, U.S. Ct. Appeals (4th cir.) 1968, U.S. Supreme Ct. 1970, U.S. Dist Ct. (so. dist.) Tex. 1977, U.S. Ct. Appeals (5th cir.) 1978, U.S. Ct. Appeals (3d cir.) 1980. Assoc. Piper & Marbury, Balt., 1966-74, ptnr., 1974-88; U.S. dist. judge U.S. Dist. Ct. Md., Balt., 1988-90; fed. judge U.S. Ct. Appeals (4th cir.), Balt., 1990—; lectr. advanced bus. law Johns Hopkins U., Balt., 1971-75; lectr. Md. Jud. Conf., Md. Ct. Clks. Assn.; sr. lecturing fellow in appellate advocacy Duke U. Sch. of Law, 1994—; mem. standing com. on rules of practice and procedure cts. appeals, 1973-88, atty. grievance com.-hearing panel, 1978-81, select com.-profl. conduct, 1983-85, adv. com. on Fed. Rules of Civil Procedure, 1993—, chmn., 1996—. Co-author: Maryland Rules Commentary, 1984, supplement, 1988, 2d edit., 1992; contbr. articles to profl. jours. Recipient Spl. Merit citation Am. Judicature Soc., 1987. Fellow Am. Coll. Trial Lawyers, Am. Bar Found., Md. Bar Found., Md. Bar Assn. (Disting. Svc. award litigation sect. 1981), Am. Law Inst.; mem. Wednesday Law Club, Lawyers' Round Table. Republican. Episcopalian. Office: US Cir Ct Md 101 W Lombard St Ste 910 Baltimore MD 21201-2611

NIEMI, BEATRICE NEAL, social services professional; b. Fitchburg, Mass., July 23, 1923; d. Albert G. and Florence E. (Copeland) Neal; m. Walter V. Niemi, Oct. 21, 1944 (div. 1970); children: Karen Smith-Gary, Gail Niemi Shaw. AS, Colby-Sawyer Coll., 1942; BS in Psychology, Northeastern U., 1972; MA in Counseling Psychology, Assumption Coll., 1974. Dir. homemaker svcs. Children's Aid and Family Svcs., Inc., Fitchburg, 1965-73; founder, exec. dir. Home Health Aide Svc. of North Cen. Mass., Inc., Fitchburg, 1973-85, Ctr. for Well Being, Inc., Fitchburg, 1985—; instr. Touch for Health Found., Pasadena, Calif., 1977—; tchr., 7th degree master The Radiance Technique Assn. Internat., St. Petersburg, Fla., 1986—; Outreach trainer The Monroe Inst., Faber, Va., 1990—; v.p. Mass. Coun. for Homemaker-Home Health Aide Svcs., Inc., 1973-81. Pres. Children's Aid and Family Svcs., Inc., Fitchburg, 1964-65; bd. dirs. United Way of Greater Fitchburg, Inc., 1964-70, Leominster (Mass.) Vis. Nursing Assn, 1972-78; chmn. adv. bd. Salvation Army, Fitchburg, 1970-72; v.p. Fitchburg Coun. of Girl Scouts. Fellow Acad. Holistic Health Practitioners; mem. ACA, Am. Mental Health Counselors Assn., Am. Holistic Health Assn., Am. Holistic Med. Found., Mass. Assn. Cmty. Health Agys. (bd. dirs. 1970-83), Mass. Mental Health Counselors Assn., Assn. for Transpersonal Psychology, Nat. Guild Hypnotists, N.E. Holistic Counselors Assn., others. Avocations: Yoga, meditation, travel. Office: Ctr for Well Being Inc 70 Bond St Fitchburg MA 01420-2251

NIEMI, JANICE, lawyer, former state legislator; b. Flint, Mich., Sept. 18, 1928; d. Richard Jesse and Norma (Bell) Bailey; m. Preston Niemi, Feb. 4, 1953 (divorced 1987); children—Ries, Patricia. BA, U. Wash., 1950, LL.B., 1967; postgrad. U. Mich., 1950-52; cert. Hague Acad. Internat. Law, Netherlands, 1954. Bar: Wash. 1968. Assoc. firm Powell, Livengood, Dunlap & Silverdale, Kirkland, Wash., 1968; staff atty. Legal Service Ctr., Seattle, 1968-70; judge Seattle Dist. Ct., 1971-72, King County Superior Ct., Seattle, 1973-78; acting gen. counsel, dep. gen. counsel SBA, Washington, 1979-81; mem. Wash. State Ho. of Reps., Olympia, 1983-87, chmn. com. on state govt., 1984; mem. Wash. State Senate, 1987-95; sole practice, Seattle, 1981-94; superior ct. judge King County, 1995—, chief criminal judge, 1997; mem. White House Fellows Regional Selection Panel, Seattle, 1974-77, chmn., 1976, 77; incorporator Sound Savs. & Loan, Seattle, 1975. Bd. dirs. Allied Arts, Seattle, 1971—, Ctr. Contemporary Art, Seattle, 1981-83, Women's Network, Seattle, 1981-84, Pub. Defender Assn., Seattle, 1982-84; bd. visitors dept. psychology U. Wash., Seattle, 1983-87, bd. visitors dept sociology, 1988— . Named Woman of Yr. in Law, Past Pres.'s Assn., Seattle, 1971; Woman of Yr., Matrix Table, Seattle, 1973, Capitol Hill Bus. and Profl. Women, 1975. Mem. Wash. State Bar Assn., Wash. Women Lawyers, Allied Arts of Seattle Bd. Democrat. Home: PO Box 20516 Seattle WA 98102-1516

NIEMI, RICHARD GENE, political science educator; b. Green Bay, Wis., Jan. 10, 1941; s. Eugene H. and Dorothy M. (Stevens) N.; m. Shirley A. Gill, Aug. 4, 1962; children: Nancy, Patricia, Jennifer, Julie. BA, Lawrence Coll., 1962; PhD, U. Mich., 1967. Asst. prof. polit. sci. U. Rochester, N.Y., 1967-71, assoc. prof., 1971-75, prof., 1975—, disting. grad. tchg. prof., 1983-86, chmn. dept. polit. sci., 1979-83, assoc. dean, 1986-89, sr. assoc. dean, 1989-91; vis. prof. U. Lund, Sweden, 1974, 81, U. Iowa, 1985; vis. rschr. Kobe U., Japan, 1991. Author: (with M. Kent Jennings) The Political Character of Adolescence, 1974, Generations and Politics, 1981, How Family Members Perceive Each Other, 1974; (with B. Grofman, L. Handley) Minority Representation and the Quest for Voting Equality, 1992; editor: (with Herbert Weisberg) Controversies in Voting Behavior, 1993; (with Harold Stanley) Vital Statistics in American Politics, 1988, 5th edit., 1995; co-author: Trends in Public Opinion; editor: (with L. LeDuc and P. Norris) Comparing Democracies, 1996. Rsch. grantee NIMH, 1969-70, NSF, 1974-77, 80-86, 94—, Am. Ednl. Rsch. Assn., Ford Found., 1972-73; fellow Guggenheim Found., 1983-84, Ctr. for Advanced Study in Behavioral Sci., 1989. Mem. Am. Polit. Sci. Assn., Phi Beta Kappa. Lutheran. Home: 45 Boniface Dr Rochester NY 14620-3333 Office: U Rochester Dept Polit Sci Rochester NY 14627

NIEMIEC, DAVID WALLACE, investment company executive; b. Midland, Mich., Dec. 17, 1949; s. George G. and Eleanor (Yack) N.; m. Melanie Taveau Mason, Oct. 4, 1975; children—Elizabeth Street, Margaret Johnson. A.B., Harvard U., 1972, M.B.A., 1974. Assoc. Dillon, Read & Co., Inc., N.Y.C., 1974-78, v.p., 1979-81, sr. v.p., chief adminstrv. officer, 1982-83, mng. dir., chief adminstrv. officer, 1984—, vice chmn., 1991—; dir. Nat. Securities Clearing Corp., N.Y.C., 1989-92. Trustee Nightingale-Bamford Sch., N.Y.C., 1993—; bd. govs. The Mannes Coll. of Music, N.Y.C., 1996—. Republican. Unitarian. Clubs: Union, Down Town (N.Y.C.). Office: Dillon Read & Co Inc 535 Madison Ave New York NY 10022-4212

NIEMIEC, EDWARD WALTER, professional association executive; b. Detroit, Nov. 1, 1936; s. Walter A. and Mary N.; m. Nancy M. Bennett, Aug. 25, 1962; children: Lisa, Julie, Brenda. B.S., U. Detroit, 1959, M.B.A., 1961. With Paine Webber Jackson & Curtis, N.Y.C., 1959-80, exec. v.p., dir. adminstrv. div., to 1980; v.p., bd. dirs. Moseley, Hallgarten, Estabrook, Weeden, Inc., 1980-82; also bd. dirs. Moseley, Hallgarten, Estabrook & Weeden Holding Corp.; pres., chief exec. officer, dir., mem. exec. com. Securities Settlement Corp. (subs. The Travelers 1982), N.Y.C., 1980-87; pres., dir. Inc Trading Co. subs. Instinet Corp., 1988-89; chief oper. officer Instinet Corp. subs. Reuters Holdings Plc., 1988-89; group v.p. AICPA, N.Y.C., 1989—. Served with U.S. Army. Roman Catholic. Office: AICPA Harborside Fin Ctr 201 Plaza Three Jersey City NJ 07311-3801

NIEMIEC, PETER JUDE, lawyer; b. Yonkers, N.Y., Mar. 9, 1951; m. Ann Majchrzak. BA, Columbia U., 1973; JD, NYU, 1976. Bar: Calif. 1976, U.S. Dist. Ct. (cen. dist.) Calif. 1976, D.C. 1982, Ind. 1983. Sr. atty. U.S. EPA, Washington, 1980-83; dep. atty. gen. State of Ind., Indpls., 1983-86; sr. counsel Pacific Enterprises, L.A., 1986-89; ptnr. Greenberg, Glusker, Fields, Claman & Machtinger, L.A., 1990—; adj. prof. Ind. U. Sch. of Law, Indpls., 1984. Assoc. editor Ann. Survey of Am. Law, 1975. Mem. ABA (natural resources, energy and environ. law sect.), L.A. County Bar Assn. (exec. com. 1990-91), Nat. Rsch. Coun. (com. review and evaluation Army chem. stockpile disposal program, 1992-98). Office: Greenberg Glusker Fields Claman & Machtinger 1900 Avenue Of The Stars Los Angeles CA 90067-4301

NIENBURG, GEORGE FRANK, photographer; b. N.Y.C., Feb. 14, 1938; s. Carl George and Louise Elizabeth (Baum) N. Grad., Germain Sch. Photography, 1989. Veterinarian asst. Stamen Animal Hosp., New Rochelle, N.Y., 1966-70; trainer guard dogs Paradise Guard Dog Service, N.Y.C., 1970-71; animal care technician Am. Soc. for Prevention Cruelty to Animals, N.Y.C., 1971-82; security guard Cen. Nat. Investigation agy., New Rochelle, 1983-88; mem. rsch. bd. advisors Am. Biographical Inst., 1989—. Mem. Nat. Rep. Com., Washington, 1986—; mem. nat. leadership coalition Campaign Am., Washington, 1987—; mem. Nat. Rep. Sen. Com., 1989—; sustaining sponsor Ronald Reagan Found., 1987—; chartered founder Presdl. Trust Fund, 1992; charter mem., supporter Battle Normandy Mus., 1988—; sponsor Nat. Rep. Congl. Com., 1983; life mem. Rep. Presdl. Task Force, 1988; charter founder Ronald Reagan Ctr., 1988—; mem. Pres.'s Congl. Task Force, 1990, Rep. Campaign Com., 1991; supporter USN Meml. Owner Navy Plank, 1991. Recipient Congl. Order of Liberty award, 1993, Rep. Presdl. Legion of Merit; named in inscription in U.S. Pres. Bush's Spl. Honor Roll, Honor Roll Commemorating the Reagan-Bush Adminstrn., 1991; included in the "Life Mem. Wall of Honor" at Ronald Reagan Rep. Ctr.; inducted to Rep. Nat. Senatorial com.'s full and complete presdl. commn., 1992, The Ronald Reagan Presdl. Libr. Register, 1991; named to Ronald Reagan Freed Flame, 1994, Election Registry, Washington, 1994. Mem. Washington Legal Found. (patron), U.S. Sen. Club, Internat. Freelance Photographer Orgn. (life), Westchester Photographic Soc., Nat. Fedn. Rep. Women, English First, Nat. Wildlife Fedn. (assoc.), Am. Mus. Natural History, Nat. Trust for Hist. Preservation, Am. Space Frontier Com. (sustaining mem.), Nat. Flag Found. (std. bearer 1987—), Internat. Platform Assn., Masons (master 1986—, royal arch and knight templer 1992), Golden Heart Club, Mil. Order Purple Heart Svc. Found., HeartHighlander Club, Oxford Club. Avocations: music, photography. Home: PO Box 511 65 Bayview Ave New Rochelle NY 10802-0511

NIENHUIS, ARTHUR WESLEY, physician, researcher; b. Hudsonville, Mich., Aug. 9, 1941; s. Willard M. and Grace (Prince) N.; m. Sheryl Ann Kalmink Nienhuis, Sept. 20, 1968; children: Carol Elizabeth, Craig Wesley, Kevin Robert, Heather Grace. Student, Cornell Coll., 1959-61; MD, U. Caif., L.A., 1963-68. Am. Bd. Internal Medicine, Am. Bd. Hematology. Intern Mass. Gen. Hosp., Boston, 1968-69, asst. resident, 1969-70; clin. assoc. NHLBI, NIH, Bethesda, Md., 1970-72; clin. fellow hematology Children's Hosp., Boston, 1972-73; chief. clin. svc. Molecular Hematology NIH, Bethesda, Md., 1973-77; dept. clin. dir. NHLBI, NIH, Bethesda, Md., 1976-93, chief clin. Hematology Branch, 1976-93; dir. St. Jude Children's Rsch. Hosp., Memphis, 1993—; editor BLOOD-J Am. Soc. Hematology, Bethesda, Md., 1988-92; chmn. Hematology Bd. Am. Bd. Internat Med., Phila., 1988-92; mem. bd. dirs. Am. Bd. Internat Med., Phila., 1988-92. Editor: Molecular Basis of Blood Diseases, 1986, 93. Mem. Am. Soc. Hematology (pres. 1994), Am. Soc. Clin. Investigation, Assn. Am. Physicians. Office: St Jude Children's Rsch Hosp 332 N Lauderdale St Memphis TN 38105-2729

NIERENBERG, ROGER, symphony conductor; b. N.Y.C., June 14, 1947; s. Gerard I. and Julliet L. N.; BA, Princeton U., 1969; postgrad. diploma Mannes Coll. Music, 1971; Mus.M., Juilliard Sch. Music, 1979. Mus. dir. Pro Arte Chorale, Paramus, N.J., 1976-85, Juilliard Pre-Coll. Orchestra, N.Y.C., 1979-84, Stamford (Conn.) Symphony Orchestra, 1980—, Jacksonville Symphony (Fla.), 1984—, also condr. Office: Stanford Symphony Orch 1 Stamford Plz 263 Tresser Blvd Stamford CT 06901-3236*

NIES, BOYD ARTHUR, hematologist, oncologist; b. Orange, Calif., Jan. 12, 1935; s. Arthur J. and Mary Dora (Sheffer) N.; m. Helen May Salter, July 28, 1957; children: Nancy, Linda, Boyd Jr. AB, Stanford U., 1956, MD, 1959. Diplomate Am. Bd. Internal Medicine, Am. Bd. Internal Medicine: Hematology, Med. Oncology. Intern UCLA, 1959-60, asst. resident, 1960-61; assoc. resident Wadsworth VA Hosp., L.A., 1961-62; clin. assoc. Nat. Cancer Inst., Bethesda, Md., 1962-64; fellow in hematology Stanford U., Palo Alto, Calif., 1964-65; pvt. practice internal medicine and hematology Redlands, Calif., 1965-68; pvt. practice hematology and med. oncology San Bernardino, Calif., 1968—; hematologist, oncologist St. Bernardine Med. Ctr., San Bernardino, 1997—. Contbr. articles to profl. jours. Bd. dirs. First United Meth. Ch., Redlands, 1985-88, St. Bernardine Hosp., San Bernardino, 1975-77, Riverside-San Bernardino Counties Blood Bank, 1984—, pres. 1988-90, bd. dirs. Inland Med. Providers, 1990-93. Fellow ACP; mem. AMA, Am. Soc. Internal Medicine, Am. Soc. Hematology, Am. Soc. Clin. Oncology, Internat. Soc. Hematology, Redlands Country Club, Redlands Swim and Tennis Club. Republican. Methodist. Avocations: tennis, golf, photography, stamp collecting. Home: 645 E Mariposa Dr Redlands CA 92373-7353 Office: Inland Hematology Oncology 401 E Highland Ave San Bernardino CA 92404-3834

NIESEN, JAMES LOUIS, theater director; b. St. Louis, Feb. 15, 1946; s. James Louis and Emily Elise (Brennecke) N. BFA, Ill. Wesleyan U., 1968; MFA, Ohio U., 1974. Actor Stage South, Columbia, S.C., 1974-75, Long Wharf Theatre, New Haven, 1977-78, Geva Theater, Rochester, N.Y., 1978-79; freelance dir., 1980-83; stage mgr. Roundabout Theater, N.Y., 1982-83; artistic dir. Irondale Ensemble Project, N.Y., 1983—; panelist N.Y. Found. on the Arts, N.Y., 1988-89. Author: (book) Game Guide, 1988; contbr. articles to profl. jours.; dir. (play) St. Joan of the Stockyards, 1993, Donton's Death, 1994. Mem. Actor's Equity Assn. Avocations: country music, tennis. Home: 419 Pacific St Brooklyn NY 11217-2204 Office: Irondale Ensemble Project 351 W 18th St New York NY 10011-4402

NIESZ, GEORGE MELVIN, tool and die company executive; b. Norwood, Ohio, Aug. 6, 1926; s. George John and Anita Agnes Lucille (Chialastri) N.; student pub. schs., Norwood and Deer Park; m. Evelyn Catherine Rayburn, Oct. 18, 1946; children—Nancy L., George J., Jr. Profl. baseball player St. Louis Cardinals Orgn., 1944-45; tool and die maker Steelcraft Mfg. Co., Cin., 1946-51; supt., mgr. Abco Tool & Die Co., 1951-70; founder, pres. Niesz Tool & Die Co., Cin., 1970-85; officer, dir. Pvt. Investment Co., 1985—. State dir., v.p. Sycamore-Deer Park Jr. C. of C., 1956-59. Ky. Col. Mem. Am. Soc. Metals, Soc. Mfg. Engring., Cin. C. of C., Anderson Twp. C. of C. Republican. Clubs: Masons (32 deg); Shriners. Patentee portable tool attachment; chess champion. Home: 4171 Winesap Ct Cincinnati OH 45236-1735 Office: DPHS Alumni Assn 8351 Plainfield Rd Cincinnati OH 45236-2445

NIETO, BEATRIZ CHAVEZ, nursing educator; b. Edinburg, Tex., Apr. 14, 1958; d. Ruben and Amelia (Guerra) Chavez; m. Roy Munoz Nieto, June 17, 1983; 1 child, Vincent Michael. BSN, Incarnate Word Coll., 1981; MSN, U. Tex. Health Sci. Ctr., 1993. Cert. clin. nurse specialist in med.-surg. nursing. Charge nurse Santa Rosa Children's Hosp., San Antonio, 1981-82; asst. DON Beverly Enterprises Home Health, McAllen, Tex., 1982-83; staff nurse St. David's Comty. Hosp., Austin, Tex., 1983-84; instr. for nurse asst. program Tex. State Tech. Inst., Harlingen, 1984-87; insvc./infection control dir. Mission (Tex.) Hosp., Inc., 1987-90; specialist nursing dept. U. Tex. Pan Am., Edinburg, 1990-93, asst. prof. nursing, 1993—; adv. bd. nurse asst. program Tex. State Tech. Inst., Harlingen, 1987-88; mem. Am. Heart Assn./CPR Valley task Force, Rio Grande Valley, Tex., 1992-94; peer advisor U. Tex. Health Sci. Ctr., San Antonio, 1992-93; planning com. workshop in field, 1993. Co-author: Healing and the Grief Process, 1996. Instr., instr. trainer Am. Heart Assn., 1992-93. Mem. ANA, Assn. Practitioners in Infection Control (pres. 1987-90), Tex. Nurses Assn., 1984—, Sigma Theta Tau (Delta Alpha chpt. 1993—). Democrat. Avocations: reading, writing, needlepoint, spending time with family. Home: 518 E Fay St Edinburg TX 78539-4738 Office: U Tex Pan Am 1201 W University Dr Edinburg TX 78539-2909

NIETO DEL RIO, JUAN CARLOS, marketing executive; b. Mexico City, Mar. 1, 1962. BA, Tufts U., 1984. Latin Am. sales TELEVISA, Miami, Fla., 1984-86; rsch. assoc. UNIVISION, N.Y.C., 1986-87; asst. to v.p. UNIVISA, L.A., 1987-88; pres. Spanish Comm., A Divsn. of Western Media, L.A., 1989-93; pres. mktg. HES, L.A., 1993-95; founder Entertainment Comms. Mgmt. L.A., 1996—. Vol. Hermandad Mexicana, L.A. Avocations: travel, languages, multimedia computers. Home: 1208 S Chavez St Burbank CA 91506-3316

NIEUWENDORP, JUDY LYNELL, special education educator; b. Sioux Center, Iowa, Jan. 3, 1955; d. Leonard Henry and Jenelda Faith (Van't Hul) N. BA in Religious Edn., Reformed Bible Coll., 1977; BA in Secondary Edn. and Social Scis., Northwestern Coll., 1980; degree edn. of emotional disabilities, Mankato State U., 1984; MEd, Marian Coll., 1989. Tutor, counselor The Other Way, Grand Rapids, Mich., 1976-77; sr. counselor Handicap Village, Sheldon, Iowa, 1978-79; florist Sheldon Greenhouse, 1979-80; K-6 summer sch. tchr. Worthington (Minn.) Sch. Dist., 1982-83; tchr. of emotional/behavioral disabilities class Worthington Sr. H.S., 1981-85, White Bear Lake (Minn.), 1985-89, Northland Pines H.S., Eagle River, Wis., 1989—; negotiator Coop. Edn. Svcs. Agy., Tomahawk, Wis., 1994—; instr. workshop Advanced Learning, Cedar Falls, Iowa, 1991-92; regional rep. for coun. of spl. program devel. Den. Coop. Svc. Unit, 1983-85; basketball/volleyball coach Worthington, White Bear Lake and Three Lakes, Wis., 1981-89. Mem. scholarship com. Profl. Bus. Women Am., Worthington, 1984-85; asst. devel. mem.Hosp. Mental Health Unit, Worthington, 1983-84; founder parent support group for parents of spl. edn. students Worthington Sch. Dist., 1983-84. Mem. Nat. Edn. Coun., Wis. Edn. Assn., Coun. for Exceptional Children, Minn. Educators for Emotionally Disabled, AKF Martial Arts. Avocations: kuy-ky-do, golf, gardening, reading, art. Home: 5148 Hwy G Eagle River WI 54521

NIEVERGELT, JURG, computer science educator; b. Luzern, Switzerland, June 6, 1938; came to U.S., 1962; s. Albert and Hedwig Nievergelt; m. Teresa Quiambao; children: Mark, Derek. Diploma in math., Swiss Fed. Inst. Tech. (ETH), Zurich, Switzerland, 1962; PhD in Math., U. Ill., 1965. Research fellow Dept. Computer Sci. and Math. U. Ill., 1962-65; asst. prof. computer sci. and math. U. Ill., Urbana, 1965-68, assoc. prof. computer sci., 1968-72, prof., 1972-77; prof. Swiss Fed. Inst. Tech. (ETH), Zurich, 1975-85, 89—; Kenan prof., chmn. dept. computer sci. U. N.C., Chapel Hill, 1985-89; rsch. scientist various rsch. labs. and univs., including U. Grenoble, U. Stuttgart, Keio U.; mem. Computing Rsch. Bd., 1987-89. Author: (with E.M. Reingold and N. Deo) Combinational Algorithms: Theory and Practice, 1977, (with A. Ventura and H. Hinterberger) Interactive Computer Programs for Education—Philosophy, Techniques and Examples, 1986, (with K. Hinrichs) Algorithms and Data Structures, with Applications to Graphics and Geometry, 1993; mem. editorial bd. Sci. Computer Programming, Decision Support Systems, Informatik Spektrum; contbr. articles to profl. jours. Grantee NSF, 1972-76, 86-89, Office Naval Rsch., 1986-89. Fellow IEEE, AAAS, Assn. Computing Machinery. Research interests include algorithms and data structures, parallel computation, interactive systems. Office: ETH Informatik, CH-8092 Zurich Switzerland

NIEVES, CARMEN, emergency services coordinator; b. Biddeford, Maine, Aug. 26, 1950; d. Roland E. and Yvette T. (Lessard) Therrien; m. Jose E. Nieves, June 27, 1987. Cert. mgmt., Riverside City Coll., 1996. Cert. emergency mgr. Police svcs. rep. Riverside (Calif.) Police, 1986-91, emer. svc. coord., 1991—. Adv. com. local gov., 1990-97; chair mgmt. adv. group. Mem. Western Riverside Emer. Council (chair. 1993—), Emergency Mgrs. Assn. (chair 1997—), Calif. Emergency Svcs. Assn., Earthquake Survival Program, Mgmt. Adv. Group-Suprs. (chmn. 1997—). Office: Riverside Police 4102 Orange St Riverside CA 92501-3614

NIEWIAROSKI, TRUDI OSMERS (GERTRUDE NIEWIAROSKI), social studies educator; b. Jersey City, Apr. 30, 1935; d. Albert John and

Margaret (Niemeyer) Osmers; m. Donald H. Niewiaroski, June 8, 1957; children: Donald H., Donna, Margaret Anne, Nancy Noel. AB in History and German, Upsala Coll., East Orange, N.J., 1957; MEd, Montgomery County Pub. Schs., Rockville, Md., 1992. Cert. tchr., Md. Tchr. geography Colego Americano, Quito, Ecuador, 1964-66; bd. dirs. Cotopaxi Acad., Quito, 1964-65; tchr. speed reading Escuela Lincoln, Buenos Aires, Argentina, 1966-67; substitute thcr. Montgomery County Pub. Schs., Rockville, 1978-83, tchr. social studies, 1984—; del. Eisenhower People to People Educators' Del. Vietnam, 1993. Author curricula; contbr. chpts. to books, articles to profl. jours.; lectr. at workshops. Bd. dirs. Cotopaxi Acad., Quito, 1964-65; pres. Citizens Assn., Potomac, Md., 1977-81; leader Girl Scouts U.S., 1975-76; adv. coun. Milken Found. Recipient Md. Tchr. of Yr. award State of Md. Edn. Dept., 1993, finalist nat. Tchr. of Yr., 1993, Disting. Alumni award Upsala Coll., 1993, Nat. Educator award Milken Found., 1994; Fulbright fellow, India, 1985, China, 1990, Japan Keizai Koho Ctr. fellow, 1992, Fulbright Meml. Fund Tchr. Program, Japan, 1997; UMBC-U. Mex. Art and Culture scholar, 1995. Mem. AAUW, ASCD, Nat. Coun. Social Studies, Md. Coun. for Social Studies, Asia Soc., Smithsonian Instn., Montgomery County Hist. Soc., Spl. Interest Groups-China, Japan and Korea, Md. Bus. Roundtable for Edn., Nat. Social Studies Suprs. Assn., Kappa Delta Pi. Avocations: cake and cookie decorating, travel. Office: R Montgomery High Sch Rockville MD 20852

NIEWIAROWSKI, STEFAN, physiology educator, biomedical research scientist; b. Warsaw, Poland, Dec. 4, 1926; came to U.S., 1972, naturalized, 1978; s. Marian and Janina (Sledzinska) N.; m. Marta Ciswicka (div. 1974); children: Agata, Tomasz; m. Jeanette P. Nichols, June 1995. MD, Warsaw U., 1952, PhD, 1960, Dozent, 1961; Hon. Doctorate, Bialystok U. Med. Sch., Warsaw, Poland, 1993. Lic. physician, Pa.; cert. Ednl. Coun. Fgn. Med. Grads. Intern, med. resident Inst. Hematology, Warsaw, 1951-54; rsch. fellow, rsch. assoc. dept. physiol. chemistry Warsaw U. Med. Sch., 1948-54; rsch. assoc., sr. rsch. assoc. Lab. Clin. Biochemistry, Inst. Hematology, Warsaw, 1951-61; physician in charge Outpatient Dept. for Hemophiliacs, Warsaw, 1957-61; head dept., prof. physiol. chemistry Med. Sch., Bialystok, Poland, 1961-68; assoc. prof. pahtology dept. pathology McMaster U., Hamilton, Ont., Can., 1970-72; rsch. prof. medicine, head coagulation sect. Specialized Ctr. Thrombosis Rsch., Temple U. Sch. Medicine, Phila., 1972-78; prof. physiology Temple U. Sch. Medicine, Phila., 1975—, prof. physiology Thrombosis Rsch. Ctr., 1978—; cons. dept. infectious diseases Warsaw U. Med. Sch., 1954-60; vis. scientist Centre Nat. de Transfusion Sanguine, Paris, 1959; cons. dept. pediatrics Warsaw U. Med. Sch., 1961-65; vis. scientist Vascular Lab., Lemeul Shattuck Hosp., Boston, 1965, 68-70; vis. prof. medicine Tufts U. Sch. Medicine, Boston, 1968-70; dir. Blood Components Devel. Lab., Hamilton Red Cross and McMaster U., 1971-72; mem. sr. coun. Internat. Com. on Haemostatis and Thrombosis, 1973—; mem. NIH rsch. rev. coms., 1975—. Editor Thrombosis Rsch., 1972-80; mem. editorial com. Procs. of Soc. of Exptl. Biology and Medicine, 1980-82, mem. editorial bd., 1980—; reviewer Jour. Clin. Investigation, Jour. Lab. and Clin. Medicine, Blood, Biochimica et Biophysica Acta, Archives of Biochemistry and Biophysics, Jour. Biol. Chemistry, Am. Jour. Physiology; author, co-author 250 articles in the field of blood coagulation, platelet physiology and cell adhesion; contbr. articles to profl. jours. Ont. Heart Found. fellow, 1970-71; recipient Jurzykowski Found. award, 1990, rsch. awards NIH, 1972—. Mem. Internat. Soc. Hematology, Internat. Soc. Thrombosis and Hemostasis, Am. Physiology Soc., Am. Soc. Hematology, Coun. of Thrombosis of Am. Heart Assn., Soc. Exptl. Biology and Medicine, Polish Inst. Arts and Scis. in Am., Am. Soc. Exptl. Pathology, Polish Am. Med. Soc. (hon.). Achievements include patent for trigramin a platelet aggregation inhibiting polypeptide. Home: 445 S Woodbine Ave Narberth PA 19072-2027 Office: Temple U Sch Medicine 3400 N Broad St Philadelphia PA 19140-5104

NIEWYK, ANTHONY, lawyer; b. Utrecht, The Netherlands, Feb. 28, 1941; arrived in U.S., 1956; s. John and Anthonia B. (Thomassen) N.; m. Ruth Ann Hunderman, Aug. 20, 1965; children: Robert, Deborah. BS, Calvin Coll., 1961; BSEE, U. Mich., 1963, MSEE, 1964; JD, George Washington U., 1972. Engr. Whirlpool Corp., Benton Harbor, Mich., 1965-69; patent agt. Whirlpool Corp., Benton Harbor, 1969-72, patent atty., 1972-78, dir. labor rels., 1978-84; atty. Jeffers, Irish, Hoffman, Wayne, Ind., 1984-86; ptnr. Jeffers, Hoffman, Niewyk, Ft. Wayne, Ind., 1987-91, Baker & Daniels, Ft. Wayne, Ind., 1991—. Avocations: reading, golf, fishing, flying, gardening. Home: 12215 Glen Lake Dr Fort Wayne IN 46804-4572 Office: Baker and Daniels 111 E Wayne St # 800 Fort Wayne IN 46802-2603

NIGAM, BISHAN PERKASH, physics educator; b. Delhi, India, July 14, 1928; came to U.S., 1952; s. Rajeshwar Nath and Durga (Vati) N.; m. Indira Bahadur, Nov. 14, 1956; children—Sanjay, Shobhna, Ajay. B.S., U. Delhi, 1946, M.S., 1948; Ph.D., U. Rochester, N.Y., 1955. Research fellow U. Delhi, 1948-50; lectr. in physics, 1950-52, 55-56; postdoctoral fellow Case Inst. Tech., Cleve., 1954-55; postdoctoral research fellow NRC, Ottawa, Can., 1956-59; research assoc. U. Rochester, 1959-60, asst. prof. physics, part-time 1960-61; prin. scientist Gen. Dynamics/Electronics, Rochester, N.Y., 1960-61; assoc. prof. physics SUNY, Buffalo, 1961-64; prof. physics Ariz. State U., Tempe, 1964—, U. Wis., Milw., 1966-67. Author: (with R.R. Roy) Nuclear Physics, 1967; also articles. Govt. of India scholar U. Rochester, 1952-54. Fellow Am. Phys. Soc. Office: Ariz State U Dept Physics Box 871504 Tempe AZ 85287-1504

NIGG, BENNO MAURUS, biomechanics educator; b. Walenstadt, St. Gallen, Switzerland, Apr. 10, 1938; s. Josef B. Nigg and Edwina Nigg-Widrig; m. Margaretha J. Bolleter, Aug. 28, 1965; children: Andreas, Reto, Claudio, Sandro. Diploma in physics, ETH, Zurich, Switzerland, 1965, Dr. sci. nat., 1975. Instr. Lyceum Alpinum Zuoz, Switzerland, 1965-71; rschr. Biomechs. Lab. Eidgenössische Technische Hochschule (ETH), Zurich, 1971-76, dir., 1976-81; prof. U. Calgary, 1981—, dir. Human Performance Lab., 1981—; cons. Adidas, Germany, 1976—, Nike, 1981-85; mem. steering com. World Congress on Biomechs., 1988—. Recipient Michael Jaeger award Gesellschaft für Orthopaedie und Traumatologie in Sport, Munich, 1986, Wartenweiler Meml. award Internat. Soc. for Biomechs., UCLA, 189, NOVEL award, Vienna, 1991. Mem. Am. Soc. Biomechanics, Can. Soc. Biomechanics, Internat. Soc. Biomechanics (pres. 1983-85). Office: U Calgary, Human Performance Lab, Calgary, AB Canada T2N 1N4

NIGHTINGALE, ELENA OTTOLENGHI, geneticist, physician, administrator; b. Livorno, Italy, Nov. 1, 1932; came to U.S., 1939; d. Mario Lazzaro and Elisa Vittoria (Levi) Ottolenghi; m. Stuart L. Nightingale, July 1, 1965; children—Elizabeth, Marisa. A.B. summa cum laude, Barnard Coll., 1954; Ph.D., Rockefeller U., 1961; M.D., NYU, 1964. Asst. prof. Cornell U. Med. Coll., N.Y.C., 1965-70, Johns Hopkins U., Balt., 1970-73; fellow in clin. genetics and pediatrics Georgetown U. Hosp., Washington, 1973-74; sr. staff officer NAS, Washington, 1975-79, sr. program officer Inst. Medicine, 1979-82, sr. scholar in residence, 1982-83; spl. advisor to pres. Carnegie Corp. N.Y., N.Y.C., 1983-94, sr. program officer, 1989-94; scholar-in-residence Nat. Acad. Scis., Washington, 1995—; vis. assoc. prof. Harvard U. Med. Sch., Boston, 1980-84, vis. lectr., 1984-95; adj. prof. pediatrics Georgetown U. Med. Ctr., 1984—, George Washington U. Med. Ctr., 1994—; mem. recombinant DNA adv. com. NIH, Bethesda, Md., 1979-83. Editor: The Breaking of Bodies and Minds: Torture, Psychiatric Abuse and the Health Professions, 1985, Prenatal Screening, Policies and Values: The Example of Neural Tube Defects, 1987; co-author: Before Birth: Prenatal Screening for Genetic Disease, 1990, Promoting the Health of Adolescents: New Directions for the 21st Century, 1993; contbr. numerous sci. articles to profl. publs. Bd. dirs. Ctr. for Youth Svcs., Washington, 1980-84, Sci. Svc. Inc., Washington, 1985-96, Amnesty Internat., U.S.A., 1989-91. Sloan Found. fellow, 1974-75. Fellow AAAS (chmn. com. on sci. freedom and responsibility 1985-88), N.Y. Acad. Scis., Royal Soc. Medicine; mem. Harvey Soc., Am. Soc. Microbiology, Am. Soc. Human Genetics (social issues com. 1982-85), Genetics Soc. Am., Inst. Medicine of NAS (chmn. com. on health and human rights 1987-90), Phi Beta Kappa, Sigma Xi. Office: Nat Acad Scis 2101 Constitution Ave NW Washington DC 20418-0007

NIGHTINGALE, RETHA LEE, federal agency administrator; b. Wichita, Kans., Dec. 15, 1954; d. L.D. and Barbara Louise (McClain) Figgins; m. William Boyd III, Dec. 30, 1982; children: Theodore Jacob, Katharine Ann. BA, U. Kans., 1977. Hydrologic technician U.S. Geol. Survey, Lawrence, Kans., 1975-78; personnel clk. U.S. Geol. Survey, Denver, 1978-79, position class specialist, 1979-80; personnel mgmt. specialist Office of Personnel Mgmt., Denver, 1980-81; personnel officer USDA Forest Service, Glenwood Springs, Colo., 1981-83; adminstrv. officer USDA Forest Service, Nemo, S.D., 1983-87, Bighorn Nat. Forest, Sheridan, Wyo., 1987-88; acting dist. ranger Ketchikan (Alaska) Ranger Dist., 1990; adminstrv. officer Tongass Nat. Forest, Ketchikan, Alaska, 1989—; mem. human resource investment coun. Ketchikan Gateway Borough, 1996—; chmn. exec. com. Regional Adminstrv. Team, 1987-88. Rep. Pres. Carter's Adv. Com. on the Status of Women, Denver, 1980, Civil Rights Commn., Custer, S.D., 1986-87; bd. dirs. Ketchikan Youth Svcs., 1989-91; chair steering com. Alaska Region Adminstrv. Leadership Team, 1997; mem. strategic improvement team Ketchikan Sch. Dist., 1997. Named one of Outstanding Young Women in Am., Jaycees, 1983, 87, Fed. Employee of Yr. for Ketchikan, Fed. Employee Exec. Assn., 1996. Mem. Am. Soc. Pers. Adminstrn. (treas. 1975-76), Bus. and Profl. Women (dir. young career woman program 1984-85, Young Career Women award for Western Colo. 1983), Fed. Employed Women (sec. 1980-81), Rotary, Epsilon Sigma Alpha (dir. pub. rels. 1982-83), Alpha Delta Pi. Democrat. Presbyterian. Avocations: bicycling, swimming, hiking, reading.

NIGHTINGALE, STUART LESTER, physician, public health officer; b. N.Y.C., Jan. 26, 1938; s. Lester M. Nightingale and Beatrice L. N. (Liebowitz) Helpern; m. Elena Ottolenghi, July 1, 1965; children: Elizabeth S., Marisa O. BA, Yale U., 1959; MD, NYU, 1964. Diplomate Am. Bd. Internal Medicine. Intern in medicine and surgery Montefiore Hosp. and Med. Ctr., Bronx, N.Y., 1964-65, resident in internal medicine, fellow in adolescent medicine, 1965-66, 67-69, asst. attending physician, 1969-70; resident in anatomical pathology NYU Sch. Medicine, 1966-67; med. dir. drug abuse adminstrn. Dept. Health and Mental Hygiene State of Md., Balt., 1971-72; chief treatment and rehab., office of programs, spl. action office for drug abuse prevention Exec. Office of Pres., Washington, 1972-74, chief office treatment and rehab., spl. action office for drug abuse prevention, 1974-75; dir. divsn. resource devel. Nat. Inst. on Drug Abuse, Rockville, Md., 1974-76; asst. to dir. Bur. Drugs, Food and Drug Adminstrn., Rockville, 1976-79; dep. assoc. commr. for health affairs FDA, Rockville, 1979-82, acting assoc. commr. for health affairs, 1979-82, assoc. commr. for health affairs, 1982—; med. dir. The Fort Greene/Bklyn.-Cumberland Narcotic Detoxification Program, Bklyn., 1969-70; vis. physician Balt. City Hosps., 1970-72; clin. instr. dept. medicine Coll. Medicine SUNY, Bklyn., 1970; asst. physician out-patient dept., instr. dept. medicine Johns Hopkins U. Sch. Medicine, Balt., 1970-72, med. dir. drug abuse ctr., 1970-71, instr. dept. med. care and hosps. Sch. Hygiene and Pub. Health, 1971-74, rsch. program mgr. health svcs. rsch. and devel. ctr., 1970-71; chmn. rsch. involving human subjects com. FDA, 1979-84; liaison mem. Commn. on Fed. Drug Approval Process, U.S. Congress, 1980-81; mem.-at-large U.S. Pharmacopeial Conv., Inc., 1985-95; bd. trustees The Milton Helpern Libr. of Legal Medicine, N.Y.C., 1982—; bd. dirs. Nat. Coun. on Patient Info. and Edn., Washington; mem. forum on drug devel. and regulation Inst. Medicine, NAS, Washington, 1986—. Contbg. author Jour. AMA, 1985—, Am. Family Physician, 1986—. Capt. med. corps USAR, 1966-72; with USPHS. Recipient Disting. Svc. Spl. Action Office for Drug Abuse Prevention award Exec. Office of Pres., 1975, Pub. Health Superior Svc. award, 1983, Disting. Contbn. award Nat. Coun. Patient Info. and Edn., 1987, Achievement award Am. Assn. Physicians for Human Rights, 1990, Presdl. Meritorious Exec. Rank award, 1990, Pub. Health Svc. Spl. Recognition award, 1993. Fellow ACP (mem. clin. pharmacology subcom., health and pub. policy com. 1984-87, 87-88); mem. AMA, Sr. Execs. Assn., Cosmos Club, Yale Club of Washington. Office: FDA 5600 Fishers Ln Rockville MD 20857-0001

NIGHTINGALE, WILLIAM JOSLYN, management consultant; b. Mpls., Sept. 16, 1929; s. William Issac and Gladys (Joslyn) N. B.A., Bowdoin Coll., 1951; M.B.A., Harvard U., 1953; children: Paul, Sara, William Joslyn, Margaret. Mktg. mgr. Gen. Mills Inc., Mpls., 1957-66; sr. assoc. Booz, Allen & Hamilton Inc., N.Y.C., 1966-68; v.p. fin. Hanes Corp., Winston-Salem, N.C., 1969; pres. Bali Co. Inc., N.Y.C., 1970-75; sr. advisor Nightingale & Assocs. Inc., Stamford, Conn., 1975—; bd. dirs. Ring's End Lumber Inc., GlassTec Inc., Yale Internat. Inc., Leslie Fay Co., Inc., Sassco Fashion, Ltd.; trustee Naragansett Tax Free Bond Fund, Churchill Cash Reserves Fund, Churchill Tax Free Bd. Fund. Active numerous charitable orgns.; vestryman St. Luke's Episcopal Ch., 1975-78, sr. warden, 1989-91; mem. Darien Representative Town Meeting, 1971-74. Lt. (j.g.) USNR, 1953-57. Republican. Clubs: Wee Burn Country; Harvard (N.Y.C.); Noroton (Conn.) Yacht. Home: 195 Rowayton Ave Norwalk CT 06853-1237 Office: Soundview Plz 1266 E Main St Stamford CT 06902-3546

NIGUIDULA, FAUSTINO NAZARIO, surgeon; b. Pasay City, Philippines, June 27, 1926; s. Aquilino Uriarte and Encarnacion (Nazario) N.; MD, U. of Philippines, 1953; m. Barbara Ann Brooks, Dec. 17, 1977; children: Andrew, Nicole; children by previous marriage—David, Diane, Susan, John, Stephen, Daniel, Nancy, Kathy. Came to U.S., 1953, naturalized, 1970. Intern, Arnot-Ogden Meml. Hosp., Elmira, N.Y., 1953-54; resident surgery Strong Meml. Hosp., Rochester, N.Y., 1954-59; resident in thoracic surgery Buffalo Gen. Hosp., 1959-61; fellow pediatric cardiothoracic surgery Children's Hosp., Buffalo, 1961-62, Hosp. Sick Children, Toronto, Ont., Can., 1963-64; instr. surgery U. Rochester (N.Y.), 1958-59; clin. instr. surgery U. Buffalo, 1965-66; asst. prof. surgery Temple U., Phila., 1967-70, asso. prof. surgery, pediatrics, 1970-75; clin. assoc. prof. Rutgers U., 1979-83; prof. surgery, prof. pediatrics N.Y. Med. Coll., 1983—; dir. pediatric cardio-thoracic surgery Deborah Heart and Lung Center, Browns Mills, N.J., 1975-83; chief pediatric cardiothoracic surgery St. Christopher's Hosp. for Children, Phila., 1967-75, Westchester Med. Ctr., Valhalla, N.Y., 1983—. Mem. ACS, Soc. Thoracic Surgeons, Am. Heart Assn., Assn. Thoracic and Cardiovascular Surgeons Asia, Westchester County Med. Soc., N.Y. State Med. Soc., Westchester Acad. Medicine, AAAS, Soc. Philippine Surgeons in Am., N.Y. Acad. Scis., Cardiology Soc. Poland (hon., 7th commemorative medal 1982). Presbyterian. Home: 2 Pine Hill Ct Briarcliff Manor NY 10510-1742 Office: Westchester County Med Ctr Valhalla NY 10595

NIHART, FRANKLIN BROOKE, marine museum consultant, writer and editor; b. Los Angeles, Mar. 16, 1919; s. Claude Eugene and Vera Howard (Brooke) N.; m. Mary Helen Brosius, Feb. 11, 1945; children: Mary Catherine, Virginia Brooke Nihart-Martinez. BA, Occidental Coll., 1940. Commd. 2d lt. USMC, 1940, advanced through grades to col., 1957; dep. dir. Marine Corps. History and Mus. USMC, Washington, 1973-92; fellow, past gov., pres. Co. Mil. Historians, 1967-71; founder Marine Corps Hist. Found., 1979. Editor Jour. Am. Mil. Past; contbg. editor Almanac of Seapower. Bd. advisors Am. Mil. U. Decorated Navy Cross, Bronze Star with one gold star; named to Order del Mar Oceano; recipient Disting. Svc. award Co. Mil. Historians, 1982, Disting. Svc. award Marine Corps. Hist. Found., 1992. Mem. Am. Assn. Mus., Internat. Coun. Mus., Nat. Firearms Mus. (bd. dirs.), Nat. Hist. Intelligence Mus. (bd. dirs.), Va. Mus. Mil. Vehicles (bd. dirs.), Internat. Assn. Mus. Arms and Mil. History (hon. life), Orgn. Mil. Mus. Can. (hon. life), Washington Naval Corrs. Circle, Army and Navy Club, Mil. Order of Carabao (Disting. Svc. award 1987), Dacor House, Ends of the Earth Club, Masons. Republican. Presbyterian. Avocations: history, politics, travel, shooting, writing.

NIJENHUIS, ALBERT, mathematician, educator; b. Eindhoven, Netherlands, Nov. 21, 1926; came to U.S., 1952, naturalized, 1959; s. Hendrik and Lijdia (Koornneef) N.; m. Marianne Dannhauser, Aug. 14, 1955; children: Erika, Karin, Sabien, Alaine. Candidaat, U. Amsterdam, Netherlands, 1947, Doctorandus, 1950, Doctor cum laude, 1952. Assoc. Math. Ctr., Amsterdam, Netherlands, 1951-52; asst. Inst. Advanced Study, Princeton, N.J., 1955; mem. Inst. Advanced Study, 1953-55, 61-62; instr., rsch. assoc. U. Chgo., 1955-56; faculty U. Wash., Seattle, 1956-63, prof., 1961-63, affiliate prof., 1988—; prof. math. U. Pa., Phila., 1963-87, prof. emeritus, 1987—; Fulbright lectr. U. Amsterdam, 1963-64; vis. prof. U. Geneva, Switzerland, 1967-68, Dartmouth Coll., 1977-78; researcher and author publs. on subjects including differential geometry, deformation theory in algebra, combinatorics, especially tensors, holonomy groups, graded lie algebras, algorithms. Co-author: Combinatorial Algorithms, 1975, 78; editor: Jour. Algorithms. Postdoctoral fellow Princeton, 1952-53; Fulbright grantee, 1952-53, 63-64; Guggenheim fellow, 1961-62. Mem. Am. Math. Soc., Math. Assn. Am., Netherlands Math. Soc., Assn. for Computing Machinery, AAUP, Royal Netherlands Acad. Scis. (corr.). Office: U Wash Dept Math Box 354350 Seattle WA 98195-4350

NIKAIN, REZA, civil engineer; b. Tehran, Iran, Sept. 26, 1962; came to U.S., 1978; s. Heshmatalah and Maryam N.; m. Denise Maroon; children: Cyrus A., Aaron D. BSCE, Rutgers U., 1985, MS, 1988. Registered profl. engr., N.J., Pa., Del., Ky., Fla., Ohio, Kans.; cert. project mgmt. profl. Asst. supt. Lefrak Orgn., New Brunswick, N.J., 1981-86; project mgr. N.J. Transit Corp., Newark, 1986-88; sr. v.p. The Nielsen-Wurster Group, Inc., Princeton, N.J., 1988—. Mem. ASCE, NSPE, Am. Concrete Inst., Soc. Am. Value Engrs. Achievements include development of a computerized program for schedule delays analysis; methods to evaluate construction schedules and delays on construction projects. Office: The Nielsen-Wurster GroupInc 345 Wall St Princeton NJ 08540-1518

NIKIFORUK, PETER N., university dean; b. St. Paul, Alta., Can., Feb. 11, 1930; s. DeMetro N. and Mary (Dowhaniuk) N.; m. Eugenie F. Dyson, Dec. 21, 1957; children: Elizabeth, Adrienne. BSc, Queen's U., Ont., Can., 1952; PhD, Manchester U., Eng., 1955, DSc, 1970. Engr. A.V. Roe Ltd., Toronto, Ont., 1951-52; def. sci. service officer Def. Research Bd., Quebec, Que., Can., 1956-57; systems engr. Canadair Ltd., Montreal, Que., 1957-59; asst. prof. U. Sask., Saskatoon, 1960-61; assoc. prof. U. Sask., 1961-65, prof., 1965—, chmn. div. control engring., 1964-69, head mech. engring., 1966-73, dean engring., 1973-96; mem. coun. NRC, 1973-78; mem. Def. Sci. Adv. Bd., 1993—; mem. coun., exec. and chmn. audit fin. com. Sask. Rsch. Coun., 1978—. Contbr. articles to profl. jours. Bd. dirs. Can. Inst. Indsl. Tech. Fellow Royal Soc. Arts, Inst. Physics, Inst. Elec. Engrs. (Kelvin Premium), Can. Acad. Engring., Engring. Inst. Can. (C. Julian Smith medal, Centennial medal), Can. Soc. Mech. Engr. (past v.p.), RSC; mem. Assn. Profl. Engrs. Sask. (chmn. bd. examiners, Disting. Svc. award, IEEE Centennial medal). Home: 31 Bell Crescent, Saskatoon, SK Canada S7J 2W2

NIKKEL, RONALD WILBERT, social services administrator; b. Lethbridge, Alta., Can., June 8, 1946; came to U.S., 1978; s. Henry Peter and Katharine (Penner) N.; m. Celeste Carisa Friesen, June 11, 1970. BA, U. Winnipeg (Can.), 1970; MPS, Loyola U., Chgo., 1983. Nat. dir. YFC/Youth Guidance, Toronto, Ont., Can., 1973-78, Chgo., 1978-82; field dir. Prison Fellowship Internat., Washington, 1982-84, v.p., 1984-88, pres., 1988—, CEO, 1996—. Editor: Guidelines for Volunteer Programs in Justice, 1988-95. Chmn. Non Govtl. Orgns. Alliance in Crime Prevention and Criminal Justice, N.Y.C., 1988-96; bd. dirs. Love and Action, Annapolis, Md., 1989—, Jericho Rd. Found., Chgo., 1992-96, Advocates Internat., 1993—. Mem. Acad. Criminal Justice Scis. Episcopalian. Avocations: photography, hiking, gardening. Office: Prison Fellowship Internat PO Box 17434 Washington DC 20041-0434

NIKOLAI, LOREN ALFRED, accounting educator, author; b. Northfield, Minn., Dec. 14, 1943; s. Roman Peter and Loyola (Gertrude) N.; m. Anita Carol Baker, Jan. 15, 1966; children: Trishia, Jay. BA, St. Cloud State U., 1966, MBA, 1967; PhD, U. Minn., 1973. CPA, Mo. Asst. prof. U. N.C., Chapel Hill, 1973-76; assoc. prof. U. Mo., Columbia, 1976-80, prof., 1980-82, Ernst & Young Disting. prof. Sch. Accountancy, 1982—. Author: Principles of Accounting, 3d edit., 1990, Financial Accounting: Concepts and Uses, 3d edit., 1995, Intermediate Accounting, 7th edit., 1997. Recipient Faculty award of merit Fedn. Schs. of Accountancy, 1989, Disting. Alumni award St. Cloud U., 1990, Coll. of Bus. Faculty Mem. of Yr. award, 1991, Mo. Outstanding Acctg. Educators award, 1993; Kemper fellow U. Mo., 1992, Alumni award MU Faculty, 1996. Mem. AICPA, Am. Acctg. Assn., Mo. Soc. CPAs, Fedn. Schs. of Acctg. (pres. 1994). Office: U Mo Sch Accountancy 326 Middlebush Columbia MO 65211

NIKOUI, HOSSEIN REZA, quality assurance professional; b. Tehran, Iran, Feb. 4, 1949; came to U.S., 1977; s. Gholam Reza and Monireh (Jahanshahi) N.; m. Niki Forouzi, Oct. 25, 1983; children: Neda Lili, Amir Reza. BS in Chem. Enging., Arya-Mehr Univ., Tehran, 1971; Diploma in Ops. Rsch., U. Toronto, 1981; cert. in quality assurance, Ryerson Univ., Toronto, 1983; cert. sys. approach/quality improvement, Madonna U., Livonia, Mich., 1996. Registered profl. engr.; cert. quality engr., cert. quality auditor, cert. quality systems lead auditor, cert. quality mgr. Quality engr. Gen. Motors, Tehran, 1971-72, supt. supplier quality assurance, 1973-74, mgr. quality assurance, 1975-78; resident materials mgr. Gen. Motors, Oshawa, Ont., Can., 1978-79; mgr. quality control G.S. Woolley, Toronto, 1979-82, mgr. quality assurance, 1982-85; dir. corp. quality assurance The Progressive/Woolley Group, Toronto, 1985-88, Manchester Plastics, Troy, Mich., 1988—; instr. Centenial Coll., Toronto, 1984-88; cons. Can. Post Corp., Toronto, 1985-86. Author numerous manuals, guides and articles in field. Fellow Am. Soc. for Quality Control; mem. ASTM, Soc. Plastic Engrs., Am. Inst. Indsl. Engrs., Soc. Automotive Engrs., Engring. Soc. Detroit, Inst. of Quality Assurance. Avocations: collecting stamps and coins, tennis, reading, classical music. Home: 8275 Fawn Valley Dr Clarkston MI 48348-4545 Office: Manchester Plastics 201 W Big Beaver Rd Ste 1040 Troy MI 48084-4154

NILES, JOHN GILBERT, lawyer; b. Dallas, Oct. 5, 1943; s. Paul Dickerman and Nedra Mary (Arendts) N.; m. Marian Higginbotham, Nov. 21, 1970; children: Paul Breckenridge, Matthew Higginbotham. BA in History, Stanford U., 1965; LLB, U. Tex., 1968. Bar: Tex. 1968, Calif. 1969, U.S. Dist. Ct. (cen. dist.) Calif. 1973, U.S. Ct. Appeals (9th cir.) 1973, U.S. Dist. Ct. (so. dist.) Calif. 1977, U.S. Supreme Ct. 1979, U.S. Dist. Ct. (no. dist.) Calif. 1983. Assoc. O'Melveny & Myers, Los Angeles, 1973-77, ptnr., 1978—; judge pro tem mcpl. ct. L.A.; spkr., panel mem. Practicing Law Inst., Calif. C.E.B. Served to lt. comdr. USNR, 1968-72, Vietnam. Mem. ABA, Los Angeles County Bar Assn., Am. Judicature Soc. Clubs: Bel-Air Bay (Pacific Palisades, Calif.); Calif. (Los Angeles). Avocation: sailing. Home: 1257 Villa Woods Dr Pacific Palisades CA 90272-3953 Office: O'Melveny & Myers 400 S Hope St Los Angeles CA 90071-2801

NILES, NICHOLAS HEMELRIGHT, publisher; b. Carbondale, Pa., Oct. 17, 1938; s. John Southworth and Helen (Hemelright) N.; m. Margaretta Linen Goodbody, Aug. 19, 1961; children: Jennifer Collett, Arthur David. BS, Columbia U., 1965; MBA, Fordham U., 1976. With Time Inc., 1965-75; assoc. pub. New Times mag., N.Y.C., 1975-79, The Runner mag., 1978-79; pub. Changing Times mag., N.Y.C., 1979-88; v.p., pub. Food & Wine mag., N.Y.C., 1988-90; exec. v.p. Sprinhouse (Pa.) Corp., 1990-92; pres., CEO The Sporting News, N.Y.C., 1992-96; sr. v.p. Times Mirror Mags., N.Y.C., 1992-96; pres., CEO Golf Mag. Properties, N.Y.C., 1995-96; sr. v.p. Times Mirror Mags., N.Y.C., 1995; sr. advisor Ad Media Ptnrs., 1996—; bd. dirs. Kiplinger Washington Editors, 1981-88; chmn. bd. Internat. Art of Jazz, Inc., 1985-89; mem. adv. bd. Cornell U. Alumni Mag., 1981-89; mem. exec. com. Times Mirror Mag., 1992-96. Rec. Jazz Piano Player, 1980. Chmn. PTA Hinley Sch., Darien, Conn., 1974-76; bd. dirs., mem. exec. com. Urban League Southwestern Fairfield County, Conn., 1976-82; bd. dirs. Guthrie Clinic Found., Sayre, Pa., 1977, Call for Action, 1984-88, League for Hard of Hearing, 1986—; mem. adv. bd. Sch. Gen. Studies Columbia U., N.Y.C., 1996—. Lt. U.S. Army, 1961-63. Mem. Met. Advt. Golf, Mag. Pub. Assn., Nat. Golf Found. (bd. dirs. 1995), Wee Burn Country Club, Union League, Blooming Grove Hunting and Fishing Club, Bohemian Club (San Francisco), Anglers Club, TPC Sawgrass Golf Club. Office: Ad Media Ptnrs 866 3d Ave New York NY 10022

NILES, THOMAS MICHAEL TOLLIVER, ambassador; b. Lexington, Ky., Sept. 22, 1939; s. John Jacob and Rena (Lipetz) N.; m. Carroll C. Ehringhaus, July 22, 1967; children: John Thomas, Mary Chapman. BA, Harvard U., 1960; MA, U. Ky., 1962. Commd. fgn. service officer Dept. State, Washington, 1962, U.S. ambassador to Can., 1985-1989; then permanent rep. EEC, Brussels; asst. sec. of state Europe and Can., 1991-93; amb. to Greece Athens, 1993—. Recipient Superior Honor award Dept. State, 1982, 85. Mem. Phi Beta Kappa. Office: Greece Psc 108 Box 56 APO AE 09842-0001*

NILLES, JOHN MATHIAS (JACK NILLES), futurist; b. Evanston, Ill., Aug. 25, 1932; s. Elmer Edward and Hazel Evelyn (Wickum) N.; m. Laila Padorr, July 8, 1957. BA magna cum laude, Lawrence Coll., 1954; MS in Engring., UCLA, Los Angeles, 1964. Sr. engr. Raytheon Mfg. Co., Santa Barbara, Calif., 1956-58; section head. Ramo-Woodridge Corp., L.A., 1958-59; project engr. Space Technology Lab., L.A., 1960; dir. The Aerospace Corp., L.A., 1961-67; sr. systems engr. TRW Systems, L.A., 1967-69; assoc. group dir. The Aerospace Corp., L.A., 1969-72; dir. interdisciplinary programs U. So. Calif., L.A., 1972-81, dir. info. technology program, 1981-

89; pres. JALA Internat. Inc., L.A., 1980—; coord. EC Telework Forum, Madrid, 1992—; dir. Telecommuting Adv. Coun., L.A., 1991—, pres., 1993-94; chmn. Telecommuting Rsch. Inst., Inc., L.A., 1990—. Author: The Telecommunications Transportation Tradeoff, 1976, Japanese edit., 1977, Exploring the World of the Personal Computer, 1982, French edit., 1985, Micros and Modems, 1983, French edit., 1986, Making Telecommuting Happen, 1994, Portuguese edit., 1997. Capt. USAF, 1954-56. Recipient Rod Rose award Soc. Rsch. Adminstrs., 1976, Environ. Pride award L.A. Mag., 1993, Environ. Achievement award Renew Am., 1994-96. Mem. IEEE, IEEE Computer Soc., AAAS, Assn. Computing Machinery, Inst. Ops. Rsch. and Mgmt. Scis., World Future Soc., Calif. Yacht Club. Avocations: sailing, photography. Office: JALA Internat Inc 971 Stonehill Ln Los Angeles CA 90049-1400

NILLES, JOHN MICHAEL, lawyer; b. Langdon, N.D., Aug. 20, 1930; s. John Joseph and Isabele Mary (O'Neil) N.; m. Barbara Ann Cook, June 22, 1957; children: Trese M., Daniel J., Marcia L., Thomas M., Margaret J. BA cum laude, St. Johns U., 1955; JD cum laude with distinction, U. N.D., 1958. Bar: N.D. 1958, U.S. Dist. Ct. N.D. 1958, U.S. Ct. Appeals (8th cir.) 1958, Minn. 1991. Shareholder, dir., pres. Nilles, Hansen and Davies, Ltd., Fargo, N.D., 1958-90, of counsel, 1990-95; exec. v.p., gen. counsel Met. Fin. Corp., Mpls., 1990-95, First Bank F.S.B., Mpls., 1995; ret., 1995; pres., bd. dirs. Legal Aid Soc. N.D., Fargo, 1970-76, Red River Estate Planning Coun., 1980-87; vice-chmn. disciplinary bd. Supreme Ct. N.D., 1984-90. Bd. editors N.D. Law Rev., 1957-58. Mem. exec. bd. Red. River Valley coun. Boy Scouts Am., 1959-70; bd. regents U. Mary, Bismarck, N.D., 1967-77; pres., bd. dirs. Cath. Charities, Fargo, 1959-65, Southeast Mental Health Ctr., Fargo, 1972-80. Staff sgt. USAF, 1951-54. Fellow Am. Coll. Trust and Estate Counsel (state dir. 1979-90); mem. ABA, State Bar Assn. N.D., Minn. Bar Assn., Order of Coif. Republican. Roman Catholic. Avocations: tennis, downhill skiing, cross-country skiing, hunting. Home: 10412 Fawns Way Eden Prairie MN 55347-5117

NILSON, GEORGE ALBERT, lawyer; b. N.Y.C., Jan. 15, 1942; s. Howard Seth and Beatrice Ethyl (McCurdy) N.; m. Elizabeth Hughes Logan, July 18, 1942; children: Scott Logan, Douglas George. BA, Yale U., 1963, LLB, 1967, M of Urban Studies, 1967. Bar: Md. 1967, U.S. Dist. Ct. Md., U.S. Ct. Appeals (4th cir.), U.S. Supreme Ct. Assoc. Piper & Marbury, Balt., 1967-73, ptnr., 1982—; asst. atty. gen. Md. State Law Dept., Balt., 1973-76, dep. atty. gen., 1976-82; chmn. Gen. Assembly Compensation Commn., Annapolis, Md., 1984-93, Commn. to Rev. Md. Elections Laws, Annapolis, 1986-87. Pres. Guilford Assn., Balt., 1990-92. Mem. Rule Day Club, The Wranglers, Sergeants Inn. Democrat. Avocations: fishing, golf. Office: Piper & Marbury 36 S Charles St Baltimore MD 21201-3020

NILSON, PATRICIA, clinical psychologist; b. Boulder, Colo., Oct. 22, 1929; d. James William and Vera Maude (Peacock) Broxon; m. Eric Walter Nilson, Dec. 23, 1950; children: Stephen Daniel, Eric Jon, Christopher Lawrence. Registered Phys. Therapist, Med. Coll. Va., 1951; MA in Clin. Psychology, L.I. U., 1972, PhD, 1973. Lic. psychologist, N.Y. Clin. psychologist Court Cons. Unit, Hauppauge, N.Y., 1972-92, Three Village Counseling Svc., Setauket, N.Y., 1974-75, Farmingville (N.Y.) Mental Health Ctr., N.Y., 1992-95; pvt. practice Commack, N.Y., 1975—; adj. asst. prof. C.W. Post Coll., Brookdale, 1974-80; cons., supr. psychologist Wayside Sch. for Girls, Valley Stream, 1975-85; cons. L.I. Lighting Co., 1980; lectr. in field. Author children's therapeutic stories; author therapeutic games: The Road to Problem Mastery; contbr. articles to profl. jours. Mem. APA, Suffolk County Psychol. Assn., Nat. Register Health Svc. Providers in Psychology, Soc. for Clin. and Exptl. Hypnosis (life), Am. Soc. Clin. Hypnosis (cert. and approved cons. in hypnosis). Office: 11 Montrose Dr Commack NY 11725-1312

NILSSON, A. KENNETH, investor; b. L.A., Mar. 16, 1933; s. Arthur V. and Esther (Dean) N.; m. Lesley Swanson, Sept., 1965; children: Kerstin, Keith. BA, U. So. Calif., 1955; MA, U. Calif., 1960; grad., U.S. Defense Language Inst., 1956. Founder Koken, Ltd., Tokyo, 1960-63; mng. dir. Pfizer Internat., Tokyo, 1963-66; pres. Pfizer Inc., Manila, The Philippines, 1966-68, Max Factor & Co. Japan Ltd., Tokyo, 1968-72, Cooper Labs Internat., Inc., Geneva and Brussels, 1972-80, Cooper Labs Inc., N.Y.C. and Palo Alto, Calif., 1980-85, Cooper Lasersonics, Inc., Palo Alto, 1982-85; dir. Monterey County Bank, Monterey, Calif., 1982-86; vice chmn. The Cooper Cos., 1986-89; chmn. Monterey Inst. Internat. Studies, 1983—; dir. U.S. China Indsl. Exch., 1996—. Contbr. articles to profl. jours. Mem. Coun. on Foreign Rels., World Affairs Coun., Pacific Coun. on Internat. Policy. 1st lt. U.S. Army, 1955-58. Fellow Am. Soc. Laser Medicine, Internat. Inst. Stragetic Studies. Avocation: philology.

NILSSON, BIRGIT, soprano; b. Karup, Sweden, May 17, 1918; d. Nils P. and Justina (Paulsson) Svensson; m. Bertil Niklasson, Sept. 10, 1948. Student, Royal Musical Acad., Stockholm; MusD (hon.), Amherst U., Mass., Andover U., Manhattan Sch. Music, 1982, Mich. State U., 1982, Sibelius Acad., Helsinki, Finland, 1982. Tchr. master classes Manhattan Sch. Music, N.Y.C., 1983—. Appeared opera and concert houses in Europe, N.Am., S.Am., Japan and Australia; most famous roles include: Isolde, Brünnhilde, Turandot, Elektra, Dyer's wife, Salome, Fidelio; now ret. Decorated 1st comdr. Order of Vasa (Sweden); comdr. Order of St. Olav 1st class (Norway); comdr. Arts et Lettres (France); recipient Swedish Golden medal Illis Quorum CL.18; Austrian and Bavarian Kammersaengerin; named Swedish Royal Court Singer. Hon. mem. Royal Acad. Music London, Royal Acad. Music Stockholm, Vienna State Opera.

NILSSON, NANCY MITCHELL, playwright; b. Milw., Mar. 16, 1928; d. Roy David and Marie Lucille (Toney) Mitchell; m. John Dexter Nilsson, Oct. 29, 1955; 1 child, David Samuel. BA, Huntingdon Coll., Montgomery, Ala., 1949; MA, Vanderbilt U., 1955. Primary tchr. Madison County Sch. Sys., Huntsville, Ala., 1950-58; h.s. tchr. Madison County Sch. Sys., Huntsville, 1964-66; feature writer Huntsville News, 1964; pub. rels. officer Cmty. Chest (United Way), Huntsville, 1964-65; sr. publs. engr. Vitro Corp., Silver Spring, Md., 1980-90. Playwright: Reunion, 1973, All God's Chillun Got Shoes, 1978, Alvin Was a Mean Old Boy, 1984, Very Truly Yours, Mary Lincoln, 1986, This Lemon is Soft, 1988, Clara Barton, 1991, Faulty Genes, 1993, All I Could See, 1995, Great Scott, 1996, others. Founder Huntsville Little Theatre, 1949, bd. dirs., pres., 1949-66, dir., 1949-66; pres. Ala. Theatre Conf., 1965; bd. dirs., dir., pres. Rockville (Md.) Little Theatre, 1967-85; chmn. City of Rockville Humanities Commn., 1980-81. Recipient numerous awards and commns. for plays. Mem. Playwrights Forum 2 of Washington, Chi Delta Phi. Republican. Roman Catholic. Home: 309 Twinbrook Pkwy Rockville MD 20851

NIMETZ, MATTHEW, lawyer; b. Bklyn., June 17, 1939; s. Joseph L. and Elsie (Botwinik) N.; m. Gloria S. Lorch, June 24, 1975; children: Alexandra Elise, Lloyd. B.A., Williams Coll., 1960, LL.D. (hon.), 1979; B.A. (Rhodes scholar), Balliol Coll., Oxford (Eng.) U., 1962; M.A., Oxford (Eng.) U., 1966; LL.B., Harvard U., 1965. Bar: N.Y. 1966, D.C. 1968. Law clk. to Justice John M. Harlan, U.S. Supreme Ct., 1965-67; staff asst. to Pres. Johnson, 1967-69; asso. firm Simpson Thacher & Bartlett, N.Y.C., 1969-71; partner Simpson Thacher & Bartlett, 1972-77; counselor Dept. of State, Washington, 1977-80; acting coordinator refugee affairs Dept. of State, 1979-80, under sec. of state for security assistance, sci. and tech., 1980; partner firm Paul, Weiss, Rifkind, Wharton & Garrison, N.Y.C., 1981—; commr. Port Authority N.Y. and N.J., 1975-77; dir. World Resources Inst., chmn., 1982-94; dir. Coun. for U.S. and Italy, Inc.; mem. N.Y. State Adv. Coun. on State Productivity, 1990-92; presdl. envoy Greed-Macedonian Negotiations, 1994-95. Trustee William Coll., 1981-96; chmn. UN Devel. Corp., 1986-94; bd. dirs. Charles H. Revson Found., 1990—. Mem. Assn. of Bar of City of N.Y., Coun. on Fgn. Rels. Club: Harvard (N.Y.C.). Office: Paul Weiss Rifkind Wharton & Garrison 1285 Avenue Of The Americas New York NY 10019-6028

NIMITZ, CHESTER WILLIAM, JR., manufacturing company executive; b. Bklyn., Feb. 17, 1915; s. Chester William and Catherine V. (Freeman) N.; m. Joan Leona Labern, June 18, 1938; children: Frances Mary, Elizabeth Joan, Sarah Catherine. BS, U.S. Naval Acad., 1936. Commd. ensign USN, 1936, advanced through grades to rear adm., 1957, principally assigned to submarines and destroyers, ret., 1957; with Tex. Instruments Co., 1957-61; with Perkin-Elmer Corp., Norwalk, Conn., 1961—, pres., chief exec. officer, 1965-73, chmn. bd., 1973—, chief exec. officer, 1973-78, chmn. exec. com., 1980-85. Decorated Navy Cross, Silver Star (3). Home: PO Box 1485 Boca Grande FL 33921-1485

NIMKIN, BERNARD WILLIAM, retired lawyer; b. N.Y.C., Apr. 15, 1923; s. Myron Benjamin and Anabel (Davidow) N.; m. Jean Horowitz, Feb. 9, 1947; children—David Andrew, Margaret Lee, Katherine. B.S. cum laude, Harvard U., 1943, LL.B. cum laude, 1949. Bar: N.Y. State bar 1949. Asso. firm Carter, Ledyard & Milburn, N.Y.C., 1949-58; asso. and partner firm Kaye, Scholer, Fierman, Hays & Handler, LLP, N.Y.C., 1958-91; lectr. Practising Law Inst., Banking Law Inst.; Mem. Am. Law Inst.; vis. com. U. Miami Law Sch.; mem. adv. bd. Rev. of Securities Regulation. Contbr. articles to profl. jours. Mem. Conservation Commn., Town of Mamaroneck, N.Y., 1970-74; bd. dirs., sec. United Way of Tri-State, 1985-91. Served to 1st lt. U.S. Army, 1943-46. Mem. ABA (mem. fed. regulation of securities com. 1975—, corp. laws com. 1984-92, legal opinions com. 1989—), N.Y. State Bar Assn. (chmn. sect. banking corp. and bus. law 1979-81, ho. of dels. 1981-84, chmn. corp. law com. 1976-79), Assn. Bar City of N.Y. (chmn. uniform state laws com. 1962-65), Tribar Opinion Com. Democrat. Jewish. Home: 116 E 63rd St New York NY 10021-7343 Office: Kaye Scholer Fierman Hays & Handler LLP 425 Park Ave New York NY 10022-3506

NIMMONS, PHILLIP RISTA, composer, conductor, clarinetist, educator; b. Kamloops, B.C., Can., June 3, 1923; s. George Rista and Hilda Louise (McCrum) N.; m. Noreen Liese Spencer, July 5, 1950; children: Holly Jayne, Carey Jocelyn, Phillip Rista. BA, U. B.C., 1944; scholar, Juilliard Sch. Music, 1945-47, Royal Conservatory Music, U. Toronto, 1948-50. Performances include CBC radio and TV spls., 1948-79, CBC drama, mus. comedy, variety shows and own jazz program, 1953—; appearances include Royal Alexander Theatre, Crest Theatre, Toronto Symphony Orch., Expo 67, 1976 Olympics; composer numerous jazz works including: The Atlantic Suite, 1974, Transformations, 1975, Invocation, 1976, Contemporary Piano Suite/Jazz Band, 1980; commd. works: Duologue, 1985, PS42JS, 1985, L'Images Entre Nous, 1987, all by Ont. Arts Coun., Plateaux, 1986, by Can. Broadcasting Corp., The Torch, 1988, (Winter Olympics, Calgary); commd. works Trumpet Concerto, 1988, Skyscape, 1988, Bach in My Own Back Yard, 1988, Twosome: Concerto for Piano and Vibraphone, 1988, Of Moods and Contrasts: A Sound Poem, 1994, Riverscape, 1994; rec. artist; co-founder Advanced Sch. Contemporary Music, 1960, dir., 1961-66; on tour of Can. bases with CBC, 1965-72; tour of Atlantic Provinces, 1974, 77; dir. jazz program, prof. U. Toronto, 1970-80, adj. prof., 1980—, dir. emeritus Jazz Faculty, 1991; prof., dir. jazz program U. N.B., summers 1967—, Banff Sch. Fine Arts, 1972, U. Western Ont., 1968—; leader Nimmons 'n Nine Plus Six jazz ensemble, 1953—; pres. Nimmons 'N Music, Ltd., 1975—; lectr. schs., colls. and community groups; dir. Can. Stage Band Festival, 1981—; adjudicator numerous festivals; prodr. double CD featuring Atlantic Suite, Suite P.E.I., St. Pierre et Miquelon and Tributes, 1996. Mem. adv. bd. Humber Coll., Banff Sch. Fine Arts; trustee, then chmn. York Edn. Clinic, 1968-74; mem. parents adv. bd. Thornlea Secondary Sch., 1967-72; bd. dirs. Toronto Arts Award; artistic dir. Courtenay Youth Music Camp, B.C., 1985—, Jazz Camp, Manitouwabing, Ont., Can., 1986—. Decorated officer Order of Can., Order of Ont.; recipient cert. for music contbn. to Expo '67 Govt. of Can., 1967, cert. of honor BMI, Can., 1968, cert. of recognition City of Fredericton, N.B., 1976, Juno award Can. Soc. Rec. Arts and Scis., 1976, Toronto Arts award for excellence, 1986, Best Jazz Clarinetist award Can. Jazz Report, 1994, 95, 96, Clarinetist of Yr. award Jazz Report, 1996. Mem. Am. Fedn. Musicians, Performance Rights Orgn. Can. (award 1980), Can. League Composers (charter), Can. Music Centre, Guild Can. Film Composers (dir. 1981—), Celebrity Club (Toronto), Performing Arts Lodge (adv. bd.). Home and Office: 114 Babcombe Dr, Thornhill, ON Canada L3T 1N1

NIMMONS, RALPH WILSON, JR., federal judge; b. Dallas, Sept. 14, 1938; s. Ralph Wilson and Dorothy (Tucker) N.; m. Doris Penelope Pickels, Jan. 30, 1960; children—Bradley, Paige, Bonnie. BA, U. Fla., 1960, JD, 1963. Bar: Fla. 1963, U.S. Dist. Ct. (mid. dist.) Fla. 1963, U.S. Ct. Appeals (5th cir.) 1969, U.S. Supreme Ct. 1970. Assoc. Ulmer, Murchison, Ashby & Ball, Jacksonville, Fla., 1963-65, ptnr., 1973-77; asst. pub. defender Pub. Defender's Office, Jacksonville, 1965-69; first asst. state atty. State Atty.'s Office, Jacksonville, 1969-71; chief asst. gen. counsel City of Jacksonville, 1971-73; judge 4th Jud. Cir. Ct., Jacksonville, 1977-83, First Dist. Ct. of Appeal Fla., Tallahassee, 1983-91; judge U.S. Dist. Ct. Mid. Dist. Fla., 1991—; mem. faculty Fla. Jud. Coll., Tallahassee, 1985, 86; mem. Fla. Bar Grievance Com., 1973-76, vice chmn., 1975-76; mem. Fla. Conf. Cir. Judges, 1977-83, mem. exec. com., 1980-83; mem. Met. Criminal Justice Adv. Council, 1977-79; mem. Fla. Gov.'s Task Force on Prison Overcrowding, 1983; mem. Trial Ct. Study Commn., 1987-88. Chmn. lay bd. Riverside Baptist Ch., Jacksonville, 1982; chmn. deacons First Bapt. Ch., Tallahassee, 1988—; trustee Jacksonville Wolfson Children's Hosp., 1973-83. Recipient Carroll award for Outstanding Mem. Judiciary Jacksonville Jr. C. of C., 1980, Disting. Svc. award Fla. Council on Crime and Delinquency, 1981; named Outstanding Judge in Duval County, Jacksonville Bar Assn. Young Lawyers Sect., 1981. Mem. Phi Alpha Delta (pres. chpt. 1962-63), Am. Inns of Ct. (master of bench), Delta Tau Delta (pres. chpt. 1959-60). Office: US Dist Ct 611 N Florida Ave Tampa FL 33602-4500*

NIMNI, MARCEL EPHRAIM, biochemistry educator; b. Buenos Aires, Feb. 1, 1931; came to U.S., 1955; s. Sam and Sarah Dora (Freedman) N.; children: Elizabeth, Brian Sam; m. Fabiola Cordoba, Dec. 21, 1996. BS in Pharmacy, U. Buenos Aires, 1954, PhD, 1960; MS, U. So. Calif., 1957. Cert. nutrition specialist. Rsch. fellow U. So. Calif., L.A., 1960-61, asst. prof. biochemistry, 1963-66, assoc. prof., 1966-72, prof., 1972—; dir. biology Don Baxter Labs., Glendale, Calif., 1962; cons. Hancock Labs., Glendale, Calif., 1962; cons. Hancock Labs., Anaheim, Calif., 1970-78, pathobiochemistry study sect. NIH, 1980-85, orthopaedics and biomechanics study sect., 1987-90; dir. biochemistry rsch. Orthopaedic Hosp., L.A., 1980-91; cons. Tillots Pharma Labs., Basle, Switzerland, 1986-94; dir. surg. rsch. Children's Hosp. of L.A., 1991—; mem. adv. bd. Maimonides U., Buenos Aires. Editor: Collagen: Biochemistry, Biotechnology and Molecular Biology, Vols. I-V, 1987-91; editor Matrix, 1980-93, Connective Tissue Rsch., 1973-91, Jour. Orthopaedic Rsch., 1989-94; patentee collagen tech., transderman drug delivery. Recipient Merit award NIH, 1987; rsch. grantee NIH Arthritis Inst., 1966-94, NIH Aging Inst., 1982—. Fellow AAAS, Soc. Biomaterials (Founders award 1986); mem. Am. Inst. Nutrition, Am. Assn. Biochem. and Molecular Biology. Office: Childrens Hosp LA Mailstop # 35 4650 W Sunset Blvd Los Angeles CA 90027-6062

NIMOITYN, PHILIP, cardiologist; b. Phila., Mar. 6, 1951; s. Benjamin Solomon and Edith (Ornstein) N.; m. Hillary Rachel Saul, June 11, 1989. BS in Biology with distinction, Phila. Coll. Pharmacy and Sci., 1972; MD, Thomas Jefferson U., 1976. Cert. Nat. Bd. Med. Examiners, Am. Bd. Internal Medicine, Am. Bd. Cardiovascular Disease. Intern Hahnemann U. Hosp., Phila., 1976-77; resident in internal medicine Thomas Jefferson U. Hosp., Phila., 1977-79, cardiovascular disease fellow, 1979-81, instr. medicine, 1981-90, clin. asst. prof., 1990—; attending physician Pa. Hosp., Phila., 1995—; cons. physician Wills Eye Hosp., Phila., 1981—; attending physician Penn. Hosp., Phila., 1995—. Author: (with others) Artificial Cardiac Pacing, 1984, Quick Reference to Cardiovascular Disease, 1987, Cardiac Emergency Care, 1991; contbr. articles to profl. jours. Recipient Cert. of Merit for Sci. Exhibits AMA, 1974, 2d prize for sci. exhibits Ind. State Med. Assn., 1974. Fellow Am. Coll. Cardiology; mem. AMA, Pa. Med. Soc., Phila. County Med. Soc. Office: 1128 Walnut St Ste 401 Philadelphia PA 19107-5568

NIMS, ARTHUR LEE, III, federal judge; b. Oklahoma City, Jan. 3, 1923; s. Arthur Lee and Edwina (Peckham) N.; m. Nancy Chloe Keyes, July 28, 1950; children: Chloe, Lucy. B.A., Williams Coll., 1945; LL.B., U. Ga., 1949; LL.M. in Taxation, NYU, 1954. Bar: Ga. 1949, N.J. 1955. Practice law Macon, Ga., 1949-51; spl. atty. Office Chief Counsel, IRS, N.Y.C. and Washington, 1951-55; assoc. McCarter & English, Newark, 1955-61; ptnr. McCarter & English, 1961-79; judge U.S. Tax Ct., Washington, 1979-88, chief judge, 1988-92. Mem. standing com. Episcopal Diocese of Newark, 1971-75; pres. Colonial Symphony Soc., Madison, N.J., 1975-78. Served to lt. (j.g.) USNR, 1943-46. Recipient Kellogg award Williams Coll., 1990, Career Achievement award The Tax Soc. NYU, 1990. Fellow Am. Coll. Tax Counsel; mem. ABA (sect. taxation 1977-79), N.J. Bar Assn. (chmn. sect. taxation 1969-71, Am. Law Inst., J. Edgar Murdock Am. Inn of Ct. (pres. 1988-92). Office: US Tax Ct 400 2nd St NW Washington DC 20217-0001

NIMS, JOHN FREDERICK, writer, educator; b. Muskegon, Mich., Nov. 20, 1913; s. Frank McReynolds and Anne (McDonald) N.; m. Bonnie Larkin, Sept. 11, 1947; children—John (dec.), Frank, George (dec.), Sarah Hoyt, Emily Anne. A.B., U. Notre Dame, 1937, M.A., 1939; Ph.D., U. Chgo., 1945. Mem. faculty U. Notre Dame, 1939-45, 46-52, 54-58, U. Toronto, 1945-46, Bocconi U., Milan, Italy, 1952-53, U. Florence, Italy, 1953-54, U. Madrid, 1958-60, Harvard U., 1964, 68-69, summer 1974, U. Ill.-Urbana, 1961-65, U. Ill., at Chgo., 1965-85, Bread Loaf Writers Conf., 1958-71, Bread Loaf Sch. English, 1965-69, U. Fla., fall 1972, 73-77; Margaret Scott Bundy prof. lit. Williams Coll., fall 1975; prof. lit. Coll. of Charleston, spring 1981; mem. editorial bd. Poetry mag., 1945-48, vis. editor, 1960-61, editor, 1978-84; Phi Beta Kappa poet Harvard U., 1978; Cockefair chair U. Mo., Kansas City, spring 1986; Kilby cons. in poetry Wheaton (Ill.) Coll., fall 1988. Author: The Iron Pastoral, 1947, A Fountain in Kentucky, 1950, The Poems of St. John of the Cross, 1959, rev., 1979, Knowledge of the Evening, 1960, Of Flesh and Bone, 1967, Sappho to Valéry: Poems in Translation, 1971, rev. edit., 1990, Western Wind, 1974, rev. edit., 1992, The Kiss: A Jambalaya, 1982, Selected Poems, 1982, A Local Habitation; Essays on Poetry, 1985, The Six Cornered Snowflake, 1990, Zany in Denim, 1990; contbr.: Five Young American Poets, 1944, The Complete Greek Tragedies, 1959; also anthologies, mags.; editor: Ovid's Metamorphoses, 1965, (James Shirley) Love's Cruelty, 1980, Harper Anthology of Poetry, 1981; assoc. editor: The Poem Itself, 1960; editorial adviser, Princeton U. Press, 1975-82. Recipient Harriet Monroe Meml. award Poetry mag., 1942, Guarantors prize, 1943, Levinson prize, 1944, Disting. fellowship Acad. Am. Poets, 1982; Fulbright grantee, 1952, 53; Smith Mundt grantee, 1958, 59; Nat. Found. Arts and Humanities grantee, 1967-68; award for creative writing Am. Acad. Arts and Letters, 1968, Aiken Taylor award, 1991, Melville Cane award 1992, Hardison Poetry prize, 1993; Creative Arts citation in Poetry Brandeis U., 1974; fellow Inst. Humanities U. Ill., 1983-84; Guggenheim fellow, 1986-87. Democrat. Roman Catholic. Address: 3920 N Lake Shore Dr Chicago IL 60613-3447

NING, CUN-ZHENG, physicist; b. Xianyang, Shaanxi, China, Oct. 21, 1958; arrived in Germany, 1988; s. Xi-Wu and Shu-Xian (Cheng) N.; m. Ya-E Zhang, Jan. 1, 1983; children: Feng-Tao, Anna. BS, Northwestern U., 1982, MS, 1985; D in Natural Sci., U. Stuttgart, Fed. Republic of Germany, 1991. Vis. scientist U. Stuttgart, 1986-87, rsch. scientist, 1988-93; lectr. Northwestern U., Xian, 1987-88; rsch. assoc. Ariz. Ctr. Math. Sci. U. Ariz., Tucson, 1994-95, rsch. asst. prof. Ariz. Ctr. for Math. Scis., 1996—. Co-editor: Lectures in Synergetics, 1987; contbr. numerous papers to profl. jours.; referee several internat. profl. jours. Mem. Optical Soc. Am. Home: # 104 3814 E 4th St Apt 104 Tucson AZ 85716-5032 Office: U Ariz Ariz Ctr Math Sci Tucson AZ 85721

NING, JOHN TSE-TSO, urologic surgeon; b. Tso-Ying, Taiwan, Aug. 25, 1951; came to U.S., 1963; s. Joseph Pei-Ying and Yuan-Chen (Chow) N.; m. Linda J. Ching, July 27, 1975; children: Lena, Jonathan. BS in Chemistry, MIT, 1978; MS in Pharmacology, Northeastern U., 1981, MS in Med. Lab. Sci., 1982; PhD Biochemistry & Molecular Biophysics, Med. Coll. of Va., 1988, MD, 1991. Diplomate Nat. Bd. Med. Examiners; lic. M.D., S.C.; cert. clin. chemist Nat. Registry Clin. Chemistry. Postdoctoral fellow dept. biochemistry/molecular biophysics Med. Coll. V., Va. Commonwealth U., Richmond, Va., 1988-91; postdoctoral fellow radiation biology br. Ctr. Devices and Radiol. Health FDA, Rockville, Md., 1991-92; affiliated rsch. assoc. Dept. of Biochemistry & Molecular BioPhysics Med. Coll. Va., Richmond, 1990-92; rsch. assoc. dept. of elect. engring. U. Md., College Park, 1991-92; vis. scholar Quindao (People's Rep. of China) Med. Coll. Affiliated Hosp., 1987-92; vis. scientist Peking (People's Rep. of China) Third Hosp., 1992; gen. surgery intern dept. surgery Med. U. of S.C., Charleston, 1992-93; gen. surgery resident dept. surgery Med. U. of S.C., 1993-94; urologic surgery resident dept. urology Brown U., Providence, R.I., 1994—; surgeon Indian Health Svc. U.S. Public Health Svc., Rockville, Md., 1992—; mem. planning com. prostate disorders and minorities NIH, 1997. Contbr. to Annals of N.Y. Acad. Sci., 1992. Cultural chmn. MIT Chinese Student Club, Cambridge, Mass., 1974; bd. dirs. South CDVC Cmty. Health Ctr., Boston, Mass., 1979. Recipient Commemorative medal of honor Am. Biographical Inst., 1987. Fellow Am. Inst. Chemists; mem. Bioelectromagnetics Soc., Biolect. Repair and Grwth Soc., Am. Med. Assn., Sigma Xi, Rho Chi (life), Phi Lambda Upsilon (life). Republican. Roman Catholic. Achievements include contributions to knowledge of effects of extremely low frequency electromagnetic fields on gene expression; effects of extremely low frequency electromagnetic fields on genitourinary system in rabbits; health effects of electromagnetic field and potential therapeutic applications in medicine and surgery. Avocations: swimming, tennis, playing trumpet and saxophones, bowling. Home: 1 Columbia Ct Middletown RI 02842-4401 also: Health Professions Support Branch Indian Health Svc/USPHS 5600 Fishers Ln Rockville MD 20857

NING, TAK HUNG, physicist, microelectronic technologist; b. Canton, China, Nov. 14, 1943; came to U.S., 1964; s. Hong and Kwai-Chan (Lee) N.; m. Yin Ngao Fan; children: Adrienne, Brenda. BA in Physics, Reed Coll., 1967; MS in Physics, U. Ill., 1968, PhD in Physics, 1971. IBM Rsch. Div., Yorktown Heights, N.Y., 1973-78, mgr. bipolar devices and cirs., 1978-82, mgr. Advanced Silicon Technology Lab., 1982-83, mgr. silicon devices and technology, 1983-90; mgr. VLSI design and tech. IBM Rsch. Div., 1990-91; IBM fellow, 1991—. Patentee in field. Fellow IEEE (assoc. editor Trans. on Electron Devices 1988-90, J.J. Ebers award 1989, Jack a. Morton award 1991); mem. Nat. Acad. Engring. Home: 3085 Weston Ln Yorktown Heights NY 10598-1962 Office: IBM T J Watson Research Ct Yorktown Heights NY 10598

NING, XUE-HAN (HSUEH-HAN NING), physiologist, researcher; b. Peng-Lai, Shandong, People's Republic of China, Apr. 15, 1936; came to U.S., 1984; s. Yi-Xing and Liu Ning; m. Jian-Xin Fan, May 28, 1967; 1 child, Di Fan. MD, Shanghai 1st Med. Coll., People's Republic of China, 1960. Rsch. fellow Shanghai Inst. Physiology, 1960-72, leader cardiovasc. rsch. group, 1973-83, head, assoc. prof. cardiovasc. rsch. unit, 1984-87, prof. and chair hypoxia dept., 1988-90, vice chairperson academic com., 1988-90; NIH internat. rsch. fellow U. Mich., Ann Arbor, 1984-87, vis. prof., hon. prof., rsch. investigator, 1990-95; prof. and dir. Hypoxia Physiology Lab. Academia Sinica, Shanghai, 1989—; acting leader, High Altitude Physiology Group, Chinese mountaineering and sci. expdn. team to Mt. Everest, 1975; leader High Altitude Physiology Group, Dept. Metall. Industry of China and Ry. Engring. Corps, 1979; vis. prof. dept. physiology Mich. State U., East Lansing, 1989-90; vis. prof. dept. pediat. U . Wash., Seattle, 1994—. Author: High Altitude Physiology and Medicine, 1981, Reports on Scientific Expedition to Mt. Qomolungma, High Altitude Physiology, 1980, Environment and Ecology of Qinghai-Xizang (Tibet) Plateau, 1982; mem. editl. bd. Chinese Jour. Applied Physiology, 1984—, Acta Physiologica, 1988—; contbr. articles to profl. jours. Recipient Merit award Shanghai Sci. Congress, 1977, All-China Sci. Congress, Beijing, 1978, Super Class award Academia Sinica, Beijing, 1986, 1st Class award Nat. Natural Scis., Beijing, 1987, # 1 Best Article award Tzu-Chi Med. Jour., Taiwan, 1995. Mem. Am. Physiol. Soc., Internat. Soc. Heart Rsch., Royal Soc. Medicine, Shanghai Assn. Physiol. (bd. dirs. 1988—), Chinese Assn. Physiol. (com. applied physiology 1984—, com. blood, cardiovascular, respiratory and renal physiology 1988—), Chinese Soc. Medicine, Chinese Soc. Biomed. Engring. Achievements include research in predictive evaluation of mountaineering performance, paradox phenomenon of cardiac pump function injury after climbing or giving oxygen, blood flow-metabolism-function relationship of heart during hypoxia and ischemia, effect of medicinal herbs on cardiac performance, cardiovascular adaptation and resistance to hypoxia and ischemia, Hypothermic adaptation to subsequent ischemia and reperfusion; the critical temperature 30 degrees celsius for modulating myocardial metabolism to resist ischemia, first electrocardiograph recording at summit of Mt. Everest. Home: 7033 43rd Ave NE Seattle WA 98115-6015 Office: U Wash Dept Pediatrics Box 356320 1959 NE Pacific St Seattle WA 98195

NINOS, NICHOLAS PETER, retired miliatry officer, physician; b. Chgo., May 11, 1936; s. Peter Spiros and Ann (Lesczynsky) N. BA in Art, Bradley U., 1958, BS in Chemistry, 1959; MD, U. Ill., Chgo., 1963. Diplomate Am. Bd. Internal Med., Am. Bd. Cardiology, Am. Bd. Critical Care Medicne.

Intern Cook County Hosp., Chgo., 1963-64, resident in internal medicine, 1964-67, fellow in cardiology, 1967-68; commd. capt. U.S. Army, 1968, advanced through grades to col., 1979; chief dept. medicine U.S. Army Community Hosp. U.S. Army, Bremerhaven, Fed. Republic Germany, 1968-69, Wurzberg, Fed. Republic Germany, 1969-72; chief critical care Letterman Army Med. Ctr., San Francisco, 1976-91; dep. comdr. San Francisco med. command Letterman Army Med. Ctr./Naval Hosp. of Oakland, San Francisco and Oakland, Calif., 1988-90; ret., 1991; assoc. prof. medicine and surgery Uniformed Svcs. U. Health Scis., Bethesda, Md., 1981-91; critical care medicine cons. to U.S. Army Surgeon Gen., 1981-91; lectr. in field. Author: (jour.) Ethics, 1988; co-editor: Nutrition, 1988, Problems in Critical Care, Nutrition Support; mem. editl. bd. Jour. Critical Care Medicine, 1988-91; illustrator: Medical Decision Making, 1988. 2d v.p. Twin Springs Condominium Homeowners Assn., Palm Springs, Calif., 1993-94, sec., 1994-96; ch. bd. councilman St. George Orthodox Ch. of the Desert, Palm Desert, Calif., 1993-95; active Palm Springs Comm., 1993—; bd. dirs. Mizell Sr. Ctr., Palm Springs, 1996—. Decorated Legion of Merit, Meritorious Svc. medal with oak leaf cluster. Fellow Am. Coll. Critical Care Medicine (mem. bd. regents 1989-94, chmn. 1989-91); mem. AMA, Soc. Critical Care Medicine (pres. uniformed svcs. sect. 1987-90, Shubin/Weil award 1988), Soc. Med. Cons. to Armed Forces (assoc.), Inst. Critical Care Medicine (exec. v.p. 1991-92), Toastmasters Internat. (sec.-treas. Palm Springs chpt. 1993-94, pres. 1994, gov. area D-3 1994-95, divsn. D dist. 12 gov. 1995-96, spkrs. bur. dist. 12 1994-96). Avocations: art, skiing, jogging, traveling, music.

NINTEMANN, TERRI, legislative staff member; b. Rochester, Minn., Mar. 13, 1963; d. John F. and Janice A. (Blair) Nintemann; m. Vincent J. Kiernan, Aug. 27, 1994. BS, U. Minn., 1985. Legis. asst. Farm Credit Svcs., St. Paul, Minn., 1986; intern, receptionist U.S. Senator Rudy Boschwitz, Washington, 1985, legis. corr., 1986-87, legis. asst., 1987-91; legis. dir. U.S. Rep. Dave Camp, Washington, 1991-92; profl. staff mem. Senate Agrl. Com., U.S. Senate, Washington, 1992—. Mem. U. Minn. Alumni, FFA Alumni (life mem.). Republican. Roman Catholic. Avocations: movies, yoga, volunteer work. Office: Senate Agrl Com 328 A Russell Senate Office Bldg Washington DC 20510

NIRENBERG, LOUIS, mathematician, educator; b. Hamilton, Ont., Can., Feb. 28, 1925; came to U.S., 1945, naturalized, 1954; s. Zuzie and Bina (Katz) N.; m. Susan Blank, Jan. 25, 1948; children: Marc, Lisa. BSc, McGill U., Montreal, 1945, DSc (hon.), 1986; MS, NYU, 1947, PhD, 1949; DSc (hon.), U. Pisa, Italy, 1990, U. Paris Dauphine, 1990. Mem. faculty N.Y. U., 1949—, prof. math., 1957—, dir. Courant Inst., 1970-72; visitor Inst. Advanced Study, 1958; hon. prof. Nankai U., Zhejiang U. Author research articles. Recipient Crafoord prize Royal Swedish Acad., 1982, Nat. Medal of Science, 1995; NRC fellow, 1951-52; Sloan Found. fellow, 1958-60; Guggenheim Found. fellow, 1966-67, 75-76; Fulbright fellow, 1965; Leroy P. Steele prizes Am. Mathematical Society, 1994. Mem. NAS, Am. Acad. Arts and Scis., Am. Math. Soc. (v.p. 1976-78, M. Bôcher prize 1959, L. P. Steele prize 1994), Am. Philos. Soc., French Acad. Scis. (fgn. mem.), Accademia dei Lincei (fgn. mem.), Istituto Lombardo, Accad. de Scienze e Lettere (fgn. mem.), Ukrainian Acad. Sci. (fgn. mem.). Home: 221 W 82nd St New York NY 10024-5406 Office: Courant Inst 251 Mercer St New York NY 10012-1110

NIRENBERG, MARSHALL WARREN, biochemist; b. N.Y.C., N.Y., Apr. 10, 1927; s. Harry Edward and Minerva (Bykowsky) N.; m. Perola Zaltzman, July 14, 1961. B.S. in Zoology, U. Fla., 1948, M.S., 1952; Ph.D. in Biochemistry, U. Mich., 1957. Postdoctoral fellow Am. Cancer Soc. at NIH, 1957-59; postdoctoral fellow USPHS at NIH, 1959-60; mem. staff NIH, 1960—; research biochemist, chief lab. biochem. genetics Nat. Heart, Lung and Blood Inst., 1962—; researcher mechanism protein synthesis, genetic code, nucleic acids, regulatory mechanisms in synthesis macromolecules, and neurobiology. Recipient Molecular Biology award Nat. Acad. Scis., 1962, award in biol. scis. Washington Acad. Scis., 1962, medal HEW, 1964, Modern Medicine award, 1963, Harrison Howe award Am. Chem. Soc., 1964, Nat. Medal Sci. Pres. Johnson, 1965, Hildebrand award Am. Chem. Soc., 1966, Research Corp. award, 1966, A.C.P. award, 1967, Gairdner Found. award merit Can., 1967, Prix Charles Leopold Meyer French Acad. Scis., 1967, Franklin medal Franklin Inst., 1968, Albert Lasker Med. Research award, 1968, Priestly award, 1968; co-recipient Louisa Gross Horowitz prize Columbia, 1968, Nobel prize in medicine and physiology, 1968. Fellow AAAS, N.Y. Acad. Scis.; mem. Am. Soc. Biol. Chemists, Am. Chem. Soc. (Paul Lewis award enzyme chemistry 1964), Am. Acad. Arts and Scis., Biophys. Soc., Nat. Acad. Scis., Washington Acad. Scis., Soc. for Study Devel. and Growth, Soc. Devel. Biology, Harvey Soc. (hon.), Leopoldina Deutsche Akademie der Naturforscher, Pontificial Acad. Scis. Office: NIH Lab Biochemical Genetics Bldg 36 Rm 1C06 Bethesda MD 20892*

NISBET, JOHN STIRLING, electrical engineering educator; b. Darval, Scotland, Dec. 10, 1927; s. Robert George Jackson and Kathleen Agnes (Young) N.; m. J. Valerie Payne, Jan. 10, 1953; children: Robert John, Alexander Stevens. B.S., London U., 1950; M.S., Pa. State U., 1957, Ph.D., 1960. Trainee, engr. Nash & Thompson Ltd., Surbiton, Eng., 1944-51; engr. Decca Radar Ltd., Surbiton, 1951-53, Can. Westinghouse, Hamilton, Ont., 1953-55; research assoc. electric engring. dept. Pa. State U., University Park, 1955-60, prof., 1960—; Disting. Alumni prof. elec. engring. Pa. State U., 1985-90, Disting. Alumni prof. elec. engring. emeritus, 1990—, dir. Ionosphere Rsch. Lab., 1971-84, dir. Communications and Space Scis. Lab., 1984-86. Author numerous sci. papers; mem. editorial bd.: Jour. Atmospheric and Terrestrial Physics. NSF sr. postdoctoral fellow Brussels, 1965; Fulbright Hays lectr. Council Internat. Exchange Scholars, USSR, 1979; NRC-Nat. Acad. Sci. fellow Goddard Space Flight Ctr., 1980. Sr. mem. IEEE, Am. Geophys. Union, Sigma Xi, Phi Kappa Phi. Unitarian. Home: 618 Glenn Rd State College PA 16803-3474 Office: Communications & Space Scis Lab 316 Electrical Eng University Park PA 16802

NISBETT, DOROTHEA JO, nursing educator; b. Lodi, Tex., May 16, 1940; d. Cecil Robey and Lola Ruby (Pippin) Lovett; m. Leonce Paul Lanoux Jr., June 10, 1966 (div. July 1984); 1 child, Cecil Lance Lanoux; m. James Harris Nisbett, May 12, 1990. Diploma in nursing, Tex. Ea. Sch. Nursing, 1963; BSN, Tex. Christian U., 1965; MS, Tex. Woman's U., 1977. RN, Tex. Asst. charge nurse med./surg. unit Med. Ctr. Hosp., Tyler, Tex., 1963-64, asst. dir. nursing, 1967; instr. nursing Tex. Ea. Sch. Nursing, Tyler, 1965-66; head nurse med./surg. unit Providence Hosp., Waco, Tex., 1966-67; dir. nursing Laird Meml. Hosp., Kilgore, Tex., 1967-69; instr. nursing Kilgore Coll., 1969-73; instr. nursing McLennan C.C., Waco, 1973-96, ret., 1996; asst. prof. U. Tex. Health Sci. Ctr., San Antonio, 1996—. Charter sec. Am. Heart Assn., Kilgore, 1968-69; bd. dirs. Heart of Tex. Soccer Assn., Waco, 1982-85. Mem. Nat. Orgn. Assoc. Degree Nursing, Tex. Jr. Coll. Tchr. Assn., Assn. Profl. and Staff Devel., Beta Sigma Phi (Outstanding Young Woman of Yr. 1981, Sweetheart 1970, 82, 91, Woman of Yr. 1990, Order of the Rose 1980, Silver Cir. award 1990). Methodist. Avocations: golf, arts and crafts. Office: Univ Tex Health Sci Ctr 7703 Floyd Curl Dr San Antonio TX 78284-6200

NISBETT, RICHARD EUGENE, psychology educator; b. Littlefield, Tex., June 1, 1941; s. R. Wayne and Helen (King) N.; m. Susan Ellen Isaacs, June 29, 1969; children: Matthew, Sarah. A.B. summa cum laude, Tufts U., 1962; Ph.D., Columbia U., 1966. Asst. prof. psychology Yale U., New Haven, 1966-71; assoc. prof. psychology U. Mich., Ann Arbor, 1971-77, prof., 1977—, Theodore M. Newcomb prof. psychology, 1989-92, Theodore M. Newcomb disting. univ. prof. of psychology, 1992—. Author: (with others) Attribution: Perceiving the Causes of Behavior, 1972, Induction: Processes of Inference, Learning and Discovery, 1986, Rules for Reasoning, 1992, (with L. Ross) Human Inference: Strategies and Shortcomings of Social Judgment, 1980, The Person and the Situation, 1991, (with D. Cohen) Culture of Honor, 1996. Recipient Donald T. Campbell award for disting. rsch. in social psychology APA, 1982, Disting. Sci. Contbn. award APA, 1991, Disting. Sr. Scientist award Soc. Exptl. Social Psychology, 1995; fellow Ctr. for Advanced Studies in Behavioral Scis., William James fellow Am. Psychol. Assn., 1995. Office: U Mich 5261 ISR Rsch Ctr Group Dynamics Ann Arbor MI 48106

NISENHOLTZ, MARTIN ABRAM, telecommunications executive, educator; b. Phila., Apr. 1, 1955; s. Louis William and Rhoda Greta (Koenig) N.; m. Anne Ermine Stockler, July 26, 1987; children: Johanna, Marjorie. BA, U. Pa., 1977, MA, 1979. Research scientist NYU, N.Y.C., 1979-83; mgr. Ogilvy & Mather, N.Y.C., 1983-84, v.p., 1984-89, sr. v.p., 1989-94; dir. content strategy Ameritech Corp., Chgo., 1994-95; pres. N.Y. Times Electronic Media Co., 1995—; mem. oper. com. Ogilvy & Mather Direct, 1992-94; adj. assoc. prof. NYU, 1983—. Grantee Nat. Endowment Arts, 1981. Mem. Interactive Svcs. Assn. (dir. 1985-94, chmn. 1991, Disting. Svc. award 1994). Office: The New York Times 229 W 43rd St New York NY 10036-3913

NISHI, OSAMU, law educator; b. Toyama City, Japan, June 2, 1940; m. Masako Hanaoka, June 16, 1943; children: Sachiko, Hideji. B, Waseda (Japan) U., 1964, M, 1966. Lectr. Def. Acad., Yokosuka, 1970-74; assoc. prof. Komazawa U., Tokyo, 1974-80, prof., 1980—, dean faculty law; lectr. Waseda U., 1990—, Keio (Japan) U., 1991-93. Author: The Constitution and the National Defense Law System in Japan, 1987, Ten Days Inside General Headquarters, 1989, Series of Constitutions of the Countries of the World, 1990. Exec. Japan Internat. Rescue Action Com., Tokyo, 1992—; mem. Yomiuri Constn. Study Coun., Tokyo, 1992—. Mem. Japan Comparative Constnl. Assn. (sec. gen. 1988—), Japan Def. Law Soc. (rep. 1996—), Japan Def. Acad. Soc. (exec. 1988—), Yokohama Internat. Soc. (rep. 1991—), Human Rights Advs. Internat. (v.p. 1990—), Phila. Constn. Found. (v.p. 1990—). Avocations: tennis, skiing. Office: Komazawa U, 1 23 1 Komazawa, Setagaya Tokyo 154, Japan

NISHIMURA, JOSEPH YO, retired retail executive, accountant; b. Berkeley, Calif., Nov. 4, 1933; s. Masamoto and Kimiko (Ishihara) N.; m. Joyce Toshiye Mori, Sept. 1, 1956; children: Brenda Joyce, Stephen Lloyd. AB cum laude, Princeton U., 1956; MBA, Stanford U., 1961. CPA, Calif., N.Y.; cert. Employee Benefit Specialist. Audit supr. Touche Ross & Co., San Francisco, 1961-66; contr. Scott Co. of Calif., Oakland, 1966-67, Purity Stores, Inc., Burlingame, Calif., 1967-69; pres. Cubit Systems Corp., Burlingame, 1969-72; sr. v.p. Golden West Fin. Corp., Oakland, 1972-73; exec. v.p. Victory Markets, Inc., Norwich, N.Y., 1973-90, dir., 1976-90; dir. Carl's Drug Co., Rome, N.Y., 1988-90, mem. site devel. com., Wakefern Food Corp., Edison, N.J., 1996—. V.p., bd. dirs. Chenango Meml. Hosp., Norwich, 1981-87; bd. dirs. United Fund, Norwich, 1984-90, N.Y. State Food Mchts. Assn., 1988-90, Binghamton (N.Y.) Philharmonic, 1988—, treas., 1990-93; gen. ptnr. Mori Enterprises, 1994—. Served to lt. (j.g.) USN, 1956-59; Japan. Mem. AICPA, N.Y. State Soc. CPA's, Calif. Soc. CPAs. Democrat. Presbyterian. Club: Princeton (N.Y.C.).

NISHIMURA, PETE HIDEO, oral surgeon; b. Hilo, Hawaii, Aug. 7, 1922; s. Hideichi and Satsuki N.; m. Tomoe Nishimura, June, 1949; children—Dennis Dean, Grant Neil, Dawn Naomi. Student, U. Hawaii, 1940-44; D.D.S., U. Mo., 1947; M.S.D., Northwestern U., 1949. Practice dentistry specializing in oral surgery Honolulu, 1952—; pres. Oral Surgery Group, 1978—; mem. coun. Nat. Bd. Dental Examination; dir. Hawaii Dental Svc., 1962-85, pres., 1970-72, 76-78; pres. State Bd. Dental Examiners, Delta Sigma Delta, Fedn. Dentaire Internat. Served with U.S. Army, 1952-54. Fellow Am. Coll. Dentists, Internat. Coll. Dentists; mem. Hawaii Dental Assn. (past pres.), Delta Dental Plans Assn. (dir.), Honolulu County Dental Soc., ADA, Hawaii Soc. Oral Surgeons, Am. Assn. Oral and Maxillofacial Surgeons, Western Soc. Oral and Maxillofacial Surgeons, Am. Assn. Dental Examiners, Pierre Fauchard Acad. Democrat. Home: 494 Halemaumau St Honolulu HI 96821-2135 Office: 848 S Beretania St Honolulu HI 96813-2551

NISHITANI, MARTHA, dancer; b. Seattle, Feb. 27, 1920; d. Denjiro and Jin (Aoto) N. B.A. in Comparative Arts, U. Wash., 1958; studied with, Eleanor King, Mary Ann Wells, Perry Mansfield, Cornish Sch., Conn. Coll. Sch. Dance, Long Beach State U. Founder, dir. Martha Nishitani Modern Dance Sch. and Co., Seattle, 1950—; dance dir. Helen Bush Sch. and Central YWCA, 1951-54; choreographer U. Wash. Opera Theater, 1955-65, Intiman Theater, 1972—; dance instr. Elementary and Secondary Edn. Act Program, 1966; dance specialist spl. edn. program Shoreline Pub. Schs., 1970-72; condr. workshops and concerts King County Youth Correctional Instns., 1972-73; Dance adv. counsel Wash. Cultural Enrichment Program; dance adv. bd. Seattle Parks and Recreation. Dancer Eleanor King Co., Seattle, 1946-50, dance films, 1946-51, Channel 9, Ednl. TV, 1967-68; lectr. demonstrator numerous colls., festivals, convs., childrens theater.; author articles on dance; one of the subjects: A Celebration of 100 Years of Dance in Washington, 1989. Trustee Allied Arts Seattle, 1967. Recipient Theta Sigma Phi Matrix Table award, 1968, Asian Am. Living Treasure award Northwest Asian Am. Theater, 1984; listed Dance Archives, N.Y.C. Libr., 1991, N.Y.C. Lincoln Ctr. Dance Archives, 1991, U. Wash. Libr. Archives, 1993, exhibit of Japanese Am. Women of Achievement, Burke Mus., 1997, 46th Anniversary of Martha Nishitani Modern Dance Sch. Mem. Am. Dance Guild (exec. com. 1961-63), Com. Research in Dance, Seattle Art Mus., Internat. Dance Alliance (adv. council 1984), Smithsonian Assos., Progressive Animal Welfare Soc. Address: 4205 University Way NE PO Box 45264 Seattle WA 98145-0264 *Until a few years ago a compelling force within me would let nothing interfere with performing, teaching, and directing dance. My belief: "I must be selfish about that which means most to me." This dedication was in constant battle with loneliness, frugality and neglect of loved ones. My first solo dance was Credo in Conflict. I have earned a degree of success, satisfaction, joy and recognition. My thoughts are now that I have learned to pursue a balance in life as I battle. The scars of selfishness persist but the broader view brings validity to my beliefs.*

NISHIYAMA, CHIAKI, economist, educator; b. Fukuoka-ken, Japan, Aug. 9, 1924; s. Michiki and Teruko (Tsuji) N.; m. Shigeko Okabe, June 9, 1957; children: Keita, Mikiko. BA in Econs., Rikkyo U., Tokyo, 1950; MA in Polit. Sci., U. Chgo., 1952, PhD in Social Thought, 1960, postgrad. in econs., 1959-60. Lectr. U. Chgo., 1957-61; assoc. prof. Rikkyo U., 1962-64, prof. econs., 1964-90, prof. emeritus, 1990—; sr. rsch. fellow Hoover Instn., Stanford U., 1977—; prof. econs. Grad. Sch. Internat. Mgmt. Internat. U. Japan, 1994—; lectr. Tng. Inst., Ministry Trade and Industry, Japanese Govt., 1964-66, Gakushuin U., 1970-71, Waseda U., 1972-74; exec. dir. Assembly on U.S.-Japan Econ. Policy, 1972-76; prime minister's spl. envoy to U.S., 1971, 75; specialist counselor Japan Employers' Assn., 1975-85; del. European Assembly, Strasbourg, France, 1982; world travel for Japanese Ministry Fgn. Affairs, Japan External Trade Orgn., 1968-82; lectr. various univs., U.S. and Europe, 1976-94; mem. Am. Citizen to Citizen Econ. and Fin. Mgmt. Del. to the USSR, 1991; spl. envoy of Japan to Germany, Czechoslovakia, Hungary, Bulgaria, Ukraine, Russia, 1991. Author numerous books, including: Lecture on Modern Economics, 1964; Free Economy, Its Policies and Principles, 1974; The Price for Prosperity, 1974; A Monetary History and Analysis of the Japanese Economy, 1868-1970, 1974; Reflection on Japanese Economy, 1976; Monetarism, 1976; The Last Chance for Creativity, Liberty and Prosperity, 1981; Human Capitalims, 1982; The Fourth Philosophy, Vol. I, 1982, Vol. II, 1983; No Limits to Growth, 1984; The Essence of Hayek, 1984, The Japanese Economy, 1987, Panadigm Shift, 1987, Japanese Economy and Life Tomorrow, 1988, A New Economics Under a New Paradigm, 1991, The End of Recession, 1994; editorial bd. Jour. Internat. Money and Fin., 1981—. Hon. fellow Inst. Econ. Affairs, London, 1976—; mem. adv. bd Econ. Inst. Paris, 1984-86, Carl Menger Inst. Wien, 1984; councilor The Daiwa Welfare Found., 1994—. Recipient Japan Econ. Lit. award Japan Econ. Jour., 1974; Earhart fellow, 1957-61; E. C. Nef fellow, 1958-59; fellow Woodrow Wilson Internat. Ctr. for Scholars, 1976-77; grantee Relm, 1964-67, Ford, 1965-66, Lilly, 1966-67, Bank of Japan, Bankers Assn. Japan, other fin. orgns., 1978-83. Mem. Am. Enterprise Inst. (adj. scholar), Am. Econ. Assn., Econometric Soc., Theoretical Econs. Assn., Internat. Econ. Assn., Statis. Soc., Mont Pelerin Soc. (pres. 1980-82, sr. v.p. 1982-85, hon. v.p. 1986-88), Japan Econ. Rsch. Ctr. (spl. mem., 1964). Episcopalian. Home: 5-15-18 Kamiuma, Setagaya-ku, 154 Tokyo Japan Office: Nishiyama-Kenkyushitsu, 5-15-18 Kamiuma Setagaya-ku, 154 Tokyo Japan

NISKANEN, WILLIAM ARTHUR, JR., economist, think tank executive; b. Bend, Oreg., Mar. 13, 1933; s. William Arthur and Nina Elizabeth (McCord) N.; children: Lia, Pamela, Jaime. BA, Harvard U., 1954; MA, U. Chgo., 1955, PhD, 1962. Staff economist RAND Corp., Santa Monica, Calif., 1957-62; staff dir. U.S. Dept. Def., Washington, 1962-64; divsn. dir. Inst. Def. Analyses, Washington, 1964-70; asst. dir. Office of Mgmt. and Budget, Washington, 1970-72; prof. U. Calif., Berkeley, 1972-75; chief economist Ford Motor Co., Dearborn, Mich., 1975-80; prof. UCLA, 1980-81; mem. Coun. Econ. Advisers, Washington, 1981-85; chmn. CATO Inst., Washington, 1985—. Author: Bureaucracy and Representative Government, 1971, Reaganomics, 1988; editor Regulation mag., 1990-96. Founder Nat. Tax Limitation Com. Mem. Am. Econ. Assn., Pub. Choice Soc., Atlantic Econ. Assn. (former pres.). Republican. Office: Cato Inst 1000 Massachusetts Ave NW Washington DC 20001-5400

NISONOFF, ALFRED, biochemist, educator; b. N.Y.C., Jan. 26, 1923; s. Hyman and Lillian (Klein) N.; m. Sarah Weiseman, July 17, 1946; children: Donald Michael, Linda Ann. B.S. (State scholar), Rutgers U., 1942; M.A., Johns Hopkins U., 1948, Ph.D. (AEC fellow), 1951. Postdoctoral fellow Johns Hopkins Med. Sch., 1951-52; research chemist U.S. Rubber Co., Naugatuck, Conn., 1952-54; sr. cancer research scientist Roswell Park Meml. Inst., Buffalo, 1954-57; assoc. cancer research scientist Roswell Park Meml. Inst., 1957-60; assoc. prof. microbiology U. Ill., Urbana, 1960-62; prof. U. Ill., 1962-66; prof. microbiology U. Ill. Coll. Medicine, Chgo., 1966-69; head dept. biol. chemistry U. Ill. Coll. Medicine, 1969-75; prof. biology Rosenstiel Research Center, Brandeis U., Waltham, Mass., 1975-93, prof. emeritus, 1993—; Mem. grant rev. bd. allergy and immunology study sect. NIH, 1965-67, 71-74, chmn., 1984-87; grant rev. bd. Nat. Multiple Sclerosis Soc., 1972-75, 77-80. Author: The Antibody Molecule, 1975, Introduction to Molecular Immunology, 1982; Editorial bd.: Jour. Immunology, 1962-67, 69-74, sect. editor, 1971-74, sr. editor, 1975-79; editorial bd.: Immunochemistry, 1964-70, Bacteriological Revs, 1968-70, Jour. Exptl. Medicine, 1974-78, Critical Reviews in Immunology, 1980—, European Jour. Epidemiology, 1986—; contbr. articles to profl. jours. Served to lt. (j.g.) USNR, 1943-46. Recipient Research Career award NIH, 1962-69; Pasteur Inst. medal, 1970. Fellow Am. Acad. Arts and Scis.; mem. NAS, Am. Assn. Immunologists (coun. 1985-92, pres. 1990-91), Belgian Royal Acad. Medicine (fgn. corr.), Phi Beta Kappa, Phi Lambda Upsilon. Home: 116 Florence St Apt I Chestnut Hill MA 02167-1938 Office: Brandeis Univ Rosenstiel Rsch Ctr Dept Biology Waltham MA 02254

NISONSON, IAN, urologist; b. Montreal, Que., Can., Jan. 10, 1937; came to U.S., 1947; s. Nathan and Rebecca (Etzkovich) N.; m. Myrna J. Goodman, Apr. 9, 1960; children: Evan J., Andrea B., Lauren R., Ronald S. BA, Columbia U., 1958, MD, 1962. Diplomate Am. Bd. Urology. Intern Strong Meml. Hosp.U. Rochester, 1962-64; resident Squire Urol. Clinic Presbyn. Hosp. Columbia U., N.Y.C., 1966-70; NIH fellow in infectious diseases Columbia Presbyn. Hosp., N.Y.C., 1967-68; pvt. practice, Miami, Fla., 1970—; chief surgery Bapt. Hosp., Miami, 1986-87. Editor-in-chief Miami Medicine, 1987-91. Capt. M.C., USAF, 1964-66. Fellow ACS (pres. Greater Miami chpt. 1979-80, bd. govs. Fla. 1990-95), Greater Miami Urol. Soc. (pres. 1986). Office: Urology Ctr South Fla 7800 SW 87th Ave Miami FL 33173-3570

NISSEL, MARTIN, radiologist, consultant; b. N.Y.C., July 29, 1921; s. Samuel David and Etta Rebecca (Ostrie) N.; m. Beatrice Goldberg, Dec. 26, 1943; children: Philippa Lyn, Jeremy Michael. BA, NYU, 1941; MD, N.Y. Med. Coll., 1944. Diplomate Am. Bd. Radiology. Intern Met. Hosp., N.Y.C., 1944-45, Lincoln Hosp., N.Y.C., 1947-48; resident in radiology Bronx Hosp., 1948-50, attending radiologist, 1952-54; resident in radiotherapy Montefiore Hosp., Bronx, 1950-51, attending radiotherapist, 1954-65; attending radiologist Buffalo (N.Y.) VA Hosp., 1951-52; attending radiotherapist Univ. Hosp. Boston City Hosp., 1965-69; asst. prof. radiology Boston U. Sch. of Medicine, 1965-69; chief radiotherapist,dir. radiation ctr. Brookside Hosp., San Pablo, Calif., 1969-77; group leader, radiopharm. drugs FDA, Rockville, Md., 1977-86; pvt. cons. radiopharm. drug devel., 1986—. Contbr. articles to profl. jours. Lectr. Am. Cancer Soc., Contra Costa County, Calif., 1973-76. Capt. MC AUS, 1945-47, Korea. Recipient Contra Costa County Speakers Bur. award Am. Cancer Soc., 1973, 76, Responsible Person for Radiol. Health Program for Radiopharm. Drugs award FDA, 1980-86. Mem. Am. Coll. Radiology, Radiol. Soc. N.Am. Avocations; photography, model train building, travel. Office: PO Box 5537 Eugene OR 97405-0537

NISSEN, WILLIAM JOHN, lawyer; b. Chgo., July 28, 1947; s. William Gordon Jr. and Ruth Carolyn (Banas) N.; m. Patricia Jane Press, Jan. 16, 1971; children: Meredith Warner, Edward William. BA, Northwestern U., 1969; JD magna cum laude, Harvard U., 1976. Bar: Ill. 1976, U.S. Dist. Ct. (no. dist.) Ill. 1976, U.S. Ct. Appeals (7th cir.) 1981. Assoc. Sidley & Austin, Chgo., 1976-83, ptnr., 1983—; gen. counsel Heinold Commodities, Inc., Chgo., 1982-84. Editor Harvard U. Internat. Law Jour., 1974-76. Served to lt. USN, 1969-73. Mem. ABA (co-chmn. futures regulation subcom. on pvt. litigation 1996—), Chgo. Bar Assn. (chmn. futures regulation com. 1985-86), Am. Legion (comdr. union league post 758 1994-95), Union League Club Chgo. Home: 348 Foss Ct Lake Bluff IL 60044-2753 Office: Sidley & Austin 1 First Natl Plz Chicago IL 60603-2003

NISSENBAUM, GERALD, physician, educator; b. Jersey City, Feb. 5, 1932; m. Sylvia Sinakin, Sept. 4, 1957; children: Gary David, Eliot Mark, Robert Samuel. BA, Yeshiva U., 1954; MD, SUNY, 1958. Intern Brookdale Hosp., Bklyn., 1958-59, resident, 1959-60; sr. resident Jersey City Med. Ctr., 1960-61; research fellow in gastroenterology Nat. Cancer Inst., 1962-63; asst. med. dir. Hebrew Hosp., Jersey City, 1962-73; clin. instr. medicine U. Medicine and Dentistry N.J., 1963-72; asst. attending dept. medicine Jersey City Med. Ctr., 1963-68, assoc. attending, 1968-69, attending, 1970—, dir. gastroenterology, 1973-76; clin. asst. prof. medicine U. Medicine and Dentistry N.J., 1972—; pvt. practice internal medicine and gastroenterology, Jersey City. Contbr. articles to profl. jours.; developed classic cytol. reagt. used worldwide in medicine and microbiology, "Nissenbaum's Fixative", 1953; patentee device for localizing gastrointestinal bleeding; inventor various med. devices. Capt. M.C., U.S. Army. Recipient Bernard Revel Meml. award Yeshiva U., 1972. Mem. AMA, Soc. Protozoologists, N.J. Med. Soc., NRA, Phi Lambda Kappa.

NISSINEN, MIKKO PEKKA, dancer; b. Helsinki, Finland, Mar. 4, 1962; came to U.S., 1987; s. Pekka and Pirkko (Pulkkinen) N. Grad., Finnish Nat. Ballet Sch., 1977; postgrad., Leningrad Acad. Ballet Sch., 1979-80. Mem. corps de ballet Finnish Nat. Ballet, Helsinki, 1977-79, soloist, 1980-82; grand sujete Dutch Nat. Ballet, Amsterdam, The Netherlands, 1982-84; soloist Basel (Switzerland) Ballet, 1984-87; soloist San Francisco Ballet, 1987-88, prin. dancer, 1988-96; artistic dir. Marin Ballet, 1996—; guest artist La Bayadere, Nat. Ballet Can., 1989, Oberlin Dance Collective, 1993; advisor to sch. dir. Nat. Ballet Sch., Toronto, Ont., Can., 1992; bd. dirs. Le Don Des Etoiles, 1989—; guest tchr. Royal Acad. of Dancing, 1993, Kennedy Ctr. Ednl. Program, 1994, Nat. Ballet Sch., Toronto, 1994; lectr. on dance history and state of dance today Stanord U., St. Mary's Coll., Christensen Soc. Repertoire as dancer includes (with San Francisco Ballet) The Sleeping Beauty, Swan Lake, Bizet Pas de Deux, Handel-a Celebration, Haffner Symphony, Con Brio, Ballet d'Isoline, Giuliani: Variations on a Theme, Tchaikovsky Pas de Deux, Symphony in C, Theme and Variations, Ballo della Regina, The Nutcracker, Airs de Ballet, Variations de Ballet, Rodin, Rodeo, Maelstrom, Dark Elegies, Harvest Moon, Napoli, Job, The Wanderer Fantasy, In the middle, somewhat elevated, Calcium Light Night, Le Corsaire Pas de Deux, Dreams of Harmony, Pulcinella, The Dream; (with other cos.) Don Quixote, Giselle, A Midsummer Night's Dream, Les Biches, Sleeping Beauty, Pyrrich Dances, Masse, Le Tombeau de Couperin, Symphony in C, The Four Temperaments, The Prodigal Son, Rodin, Pierrot Lunaire, La Fille mal gardée, Swan Lake, Henze, Five Tangos, In and Out, Bits and Pieces, Jeu de Cartes; appeared in the Canadian Internat. Ballet Gala, 1989, 90, 91, 92, 93, 94, 95, Reykjavik Arts Festival, 1990, Internat. Ballet Gala, Kuodio, Finland, 1992, Internat. Ballet Gala, Vail, Colo., 1993, Night of Stars Ballet Gala, Helsinki, 1993; profiled in nat. and internat. radio and TV programs, including CNN Worldwide Report, 1992; featured on cover of Dance Mag., 1992; choreographer Full Evening Nutcracker, 1996. Recipient 1st prize 1st Nat. Dance Competition Kuopio, Finland, 1978.

NISWENDER, GORDON DEAN, physiologist, educator; b. Gillette, Wyo., Apr. 21, 1940; s. Rex Lel and Inez Irene (Dillinger) N.; m. Joy Dean Thayer, June 14, 1964; children: Kevin Dean, Kory Dean. B.S., U. Wyo., 1962; M.S., U. Nebr., 1964; Ph.D., U. Ill., 1967. NIH postdoctoral fellow U. Mich., 1967-68, asst. prof. physiology, 1968-72; mem. faculty Colo. State U., Ft. Collins, 1972—; prof. physiology Colo. State U., 1975—; assoc. dean research Coll. Veterinary Medicine and Biomed. Scis., 1982-95, dir. animal reproduction and biotech. lab., 1986—, disting. prof., 1987—; mem. rev.

panels NIH; cons. FDA. Recipient Merit award NIH, grantee, 1968—. Mem. Am. Assn. Animal Scientists (Outstanding Young Scientist award western sect. 1974, Animal Physiology and Endocrinology award 1983), Soc. for Study Reprodn. (treas. 1972-75, pres. 1981-82, editor-in-chief Biology of Reprodn. 1995—), rsch. award 1988). Office: Colo State U Animal Reprod & Biotech Lab College of Veterinary Med Fort Collins CO 80523-1683

NITECKI, JOSEPH ZBIGNIEW, librarian; b. Dabrowa Górnicza, Poland, Jan. 31, 1922; came to U.S., 1951, naturalized, 1956; s. Henryk W. and Antonina S. N.; m. Sophie V. Zboinski, June 17, 1945; children: Zbigniew H., Danuta A. B.A. in Philosophy, Wayne State U., 1955; M.A., Roosevelt U., 1959; M.A. in L.S., U. Chgo., 1963. Various profl. and adminstrv. positions in libraries U. Chgo., 1961-63, Chgo. City Coll., 1963-66, U. Wis., Milw., 1967-70, Temple U., Phila., 1970-78; prof., exec. dir. libraries U. Wis., Oshkosh, 1978-80; dir. libraries SUNY, Albany, 1980-88, prof. Sch. Info Sci. and Policy, 1988-90, prof. emeritus, 1990—; cons. library issues. Author, editor compiler and reviewer in field; ref. and manuscript reader. Served with Polish Armed Forces under Brit. command, 1939-48. Mem. ALA, Beta Phi Mu. Home: 22 Shetland Dr Delmar NY 12054-3630

NITECKI, ZBIGNIEW HENRY, mathematician, educator; b. Plymouth, UK, May 12, 1946; came to U.S., 1950; s. Joseph Zbigniew and Zofia (Zboinska) N.; m. Alicia Korzeniowska, Mar. 25, 1972; 1 child, Elizabeth Lauren. SB, U. Chgo., 1965; MA, PhD, U. Calif., Berkeley, 1969. Gibbs instr. Yale U., New Haven, 1969-71; asst. prof. CUNY, 1971-72; asst. prof. Tufts U., Medford, Mass., 1972-75, assoc. prof., 1975-80, prof. math., 1980—; program dir. for geometric analysis NSF, Washington, 1982-83. Author: Differentiable Dynamics, 1971; co-author: Differential Equations—A First Course, 1984, Differential Equations with Linear Algebra, 1986; contbr. articles to profl. jours. Mem. Am. Math. Soc., Soc. for Indsl. and Applied Maths. Office: Dept of Mathematics Bromfield-Pearson Bldg Tufts University Medford MA 02155

NITIKMAN, FRANKLIN W., lawyer; b. Davenport, Iowa, Oct. 26, 1940; s. David A. and Janette (Gordon) N.; m. Adrienne C. Drell, Nov. 28, 1972. BA, Northwestern U., 1963; LLB, Yale U., 1966. Bar: Ill. 1966, U.S. Dist. Ct. (no. dist.) Ill. 1967, U.S. Tax Ct. 1972, Fla. 1977, D.C. 1981. Assoc. McDermott, Will & Emery, Chgo., 1966-72, ptnr., 1973—. Co-author: Drafting Wills and Trust Agreements, 1990. Bd. dirs. Owen Coon Found., Glenview, Ill., 1985—, Spertus Inst. Jewish Studies, Chgo., 1991—, Jewish United Fund, Jewish Fedn. Metro. Chgo., 1994—. Fellow Am. Coll. Trust and Estate Coun., Am. Bar Found.; mem. Standard Club, Arts Club (Chgo.). Home: 365 Lakeside Pl Highland Park IL 60035-5371 Office: McDermott Will & Emery 227 W Monroe St Chicago IL 60606-5016

NITOWSKY, HAROLD MARTIN, physician, educator; b. Bklyn., Feb. 12, 1925; s. Max and Fannie (Gershowitz) N.; m. Myra Heller, Nov. 28, 1954; children—Fran Ellen, Daniel Howard. A.B., N.Y. U., 1944, M.D., 1947; M.S., U. Colo., 1952. Intern Mt. Sinai Hosp., N.Y.C., 1947-48; resident pediats. U. Colo. Med. Center, 1948-50; USPHS postdoctoral fellow U. Colo., 1950-51; staff Sinai Hosp., Balt., 1953-67; dir. pediat. rsch. Sinai Hosp., 1960-67; faculty Johns Hopkins Sch. Medicine, 1953-67, assoc. prof. ob-gyn., pediats., molecular genetics, 1962-67; prof. pediats. and genetics Albert Einstein Coll. Medicine, 1967—; cons. Nat. Inst. Child Health and Human Devel., 1966—; Sr. surgeon USPHS, 1951-53. Contbr. articles on nutrition, metabolism, genetics to profl. jours. Mem. Am. Pediat. Soc., Soc. Pediat. Rsch., Am. Soc. Human Genetics. Home: 25 Devonshire Rd New Rochelle NY 10804-3925 Office: Albert Einstein Coll Med Dept Ob-Gyn Divsn Reproductive Genetics 1695 Eastchester Rd Bronx NY 10461-2330

NITSCHE, JOHANNES CARL CHRISTIAN, mathematics educator; b. Olbernhau, Germany, Jan. 22, 1925; came to U.S., 1956; s. Ludwig Johannes and Irma (Raecke) N.; m. Carmen Dolores Mercado Delgado, July 1, 1959; children: Carmen Irma, Johannes Marcos and Ludwig Carlos (twins). Diplom für Mathematik, U. Göttingen, 1950; PhD, U. Leipzig, 1951; Privatdozent, Tech. U. Berlin, 1955. Asst. U. Göttingen, 1948-50; rsch. mathematician Max Planck Institut für Strömungsforschung Göttingen, 1950-52; asst. Privatdozent Tech. U., Berlin, 1952-56; vis. assoc. prof. U. Cin., 1956-57; assoc. prof. U. Minn., Mpls., 1957-60; prof. math. U. Minn., 1960—, head Sch. Math., 1971-78; vis. prof. U. P.R., 1960-61, U. Hamburg, 1965, Tech. Hochschule Vienna, 1968, U. Bonn, 1971, 75, 77, 80, 81, U. Heidelberg, 1979, 82, 83, U. Munich, 1983, U. Florence, 1983, Tech. Hochschule Aachen; keynote speaker Festive Colloquium, U. Ulm, 1986; co-organizer workshop statis. thermodynamics and differential geometry U. Minn., 1991; keynote speaker Meml. Colloquium Tech. U. Berlin, 1991, speaker Internat. Workshop on Geometry and Interfaces, Aussois, France, 1990. Author: Vorlesungen uber Minimalflachen, Springer-Verlag, 1975, Lectures on Minimal Surfaces, 1989; mem. editorial bd. Archive of Rational Mechanics and Analysis, 1967-91; editor: Analysis, 1980—; assoc. editor: Contemporary Math., 1980-88, Zeitschrift für Analysis und ihre Anwendungen, 1993—; contbr. articles to profl. jours. Mem. Am. del. joint Soviet-Am. Symposium on Partial Differential Equations, Novosibirsk, 1963, U.S.-Japan Seminar on Differential Geometry, Tokyo, 1977; speaker 750th Berlin Anniversary Colloquium, Free U. Berlin, 1987. Recipient Lester R. Ford award for outstanding expository writing, 1975, George Taylor Disting. Svc. award U. Minn. Found., 1980, Humboldt prize for sr. U.S. scientists Alexander von Humboldt Found., 1981; Fulbright rsch. fellow Stanford, 1955-56. Fellow AAAS; mem. Am. Math. Soc., Circolo Matematico di Palermo, Deutsche Mathematiker-Vereinigung, Edinburgh Math. Soc., Gesellschaft für Angewandte Mathematik und Mechanik, Math. Assn. Am., N.Y. Acad. Scis., Österreichische Mathematische Gesellschaft, Soc. Natural Philosophy. Home: 2765 Dean Pky Minneapolis MN 55416-4382

NITTOLY, PAUL GERARD, lawyer; b. Bklyn., July 13, 1948; s. Edward Joseph and Philomena (Lorenzo) N.; m. Maryann Racioppi, May 31, 1970; children: Melissa Beth, Matthew Edward. AB, Rutgers U., 1970; JD, N.Y. Law Sch., 1973. Bar: N.J. 1973, U.S. Dist. Ct. N.J. 1973, U.S. Supreme Ct. 1979; cert. trial atty. (civil and criminal) N.J. Supreme Ct. Asst. prosecutor, sr. trial atty. Essex County Prosecutor's Office, Newark, 1974-79; ptnr. Shanley & Fisher, P.C., Morristown, N.J., 1984—; moot trial ct. judge Seton Hall Law Sch., Newark, 1982—; lectr. symposium on perinatal malpractice Am. Coll. Ob-Gyn and Rutgers U. Med. Sch., Morristown, N.J., 1984; mem. practitioner's adv. group to U.S. Sentencing Commn., 1992—. Author: Readings in White Collar Crime, 1991; contbr. chapts to books; mem. editorial adv. bd. Corporate Criminal Liability Reporter; pres. C. Willard Heckel Am. Inn. of Court, master; del advocate Am. Bd. Trial Advocates. Served to capt. U.S. Army, 1972. Mem. ABA, N.J. Bar Assn., Essex County Bar Assn., Morris County Bar Assn., Nat. Assn. Criminal Defense Lawyers, Assn. Criminal Defense Attys. N.J., Trial Attys. N.J., Park Avenue Club (Morristown), Morristown Club, Delta Upsilon. Roman Catholic. Home: 275 Meetinghouse Ln Mountainside NJ 07092-1305 Office: Shanley & Fisher 131 Madison Ave Morristown NJ 07960-6086

NITZE, WILLIAM ALBERT, government official, lawyer; b. N.Y.C., Sept. 27, 1942; s. Paul Henry and Phyllis (Pratt) N.; m. Ann Kendall Richards, June 5, 1971; children: Paul Kendall, Charles Richards. BA, Harvard U., 1964, JD, 1969; BA, Oxford U., 1966. Bar: N.Y. 1970, U.S. Supreme Ct. 1987. Assoc. Sullivan and Cromwell, N.Y.C., 1970-72; v.p. London Arts, Inc., N.Y.C., 1972-73; counsel Mobil South, Inc., N.Y.C., 1974-76; gen. counsel Mobil Oil Japan, Tokyo, 1976-80; asst. gen. counsel exploration and producing divsn. Mobil Oil Corp., N.Y.C., 1980-87; dep asst. sec. for environment, health and natural resources U.S. Dept. State, Washington, 1987-90; pres. Alliance to Save Energy, Washington, 1990-94; asst. adminstr. for internat. activities U.S. EPA, Washington, 1994—; mem. adv. com. Sch. Advanced Internat. Studies, Washington, 1982-95, professorial lectr., 1993-94; vis. scholar Environ. Law Inst., Washington, 1990; dir. Charles A. Lindbergh Fund, Mpls., 1990-94, Nat. Symphony Orch. Assn., Washington, 1990—. Trustee Aspen Inst., Queenstown, Md., 1988—, Krasnow Inst., Fairfax, Va., 1996—. Mem. Assn. of Bar of City of N.Y., Coun. on Fgn. Rels., Met. Club, Links Club. Republican. Episcopalian. Avocations: running, piano, collecting art. Home: 1336 30th St NW Washington DC 20007-3349 Office: US EPA 401 M St SW Washington DC 20460-0001

NITZSCHE, JACK, composer; b. Mich., 1937. music arranger Phil Spector, 1962-66, Specialty Records, Original Sound Records; session musician Rolling Stones, 1965-66, Buffalo Springfield, 1967; keyboardist, prodr. Crazy Horse, 1970-71; keyboardist Stray Gators, 1973; prodr. Lee Hazlewood, Rolling Stones, James Gang, Neil Young, Ringo Starr, Buffy Sainte-Marie, Rick Nelson, Graham Parker, Mink DeVille. Composer, music dir.: (films) Village of the Giants, 1965; composer, music dir., orchestrator: (films) When You Comin' Back, Red Ryder?, 1979; composer: (films) Performance, 1970, Greaser's Palace, 1972, The Exorcist, 1973, One Flew Over the Cuckoo's Nest, 1975 (Academy award nomination best original score 1975), (with Richard Hazard) Heroes, 1977, (with Ry Cooder) Blue Collar, 1978, Hardcore, 1979, Heart Beat, 1979, Melvin and Howard, 1980, Cruising, 1980, Cutter's Way, 1981, An Officer and a Gentleman, 1982 (Academy award nomination best original score 1982), Cannery Row, 1982, Personal Best, 1982, Without a Trace, 1983, Breathless, 1983, The Razor's Edge, 1984, Starman, 1984, Windy City, 1984, The Jewel of the Nile, 1985, (with Michael Hoenig) 9 1/2 Weeks, 1986, Stand By Me, 1986, Streets of Gold, 1986, (with Buffy Sainte-Marie) Stripper, 1986, The Whoopee Boys, 1986, The Seventh Sign, 1988, Next of Kin, 1989, Revenge, 1990, The Hot Spot, 1990, The Last of the Finest, 1990, Mermaids, 1990, The Indian Runner, 1991, (TV movies) Middle Ages, 1992, (TV series) Starman, 1986-86, (songs) (with Sonny Bono) Needles and Pins, 1963, The Lonely Surfer, 1963, Gone Dead Train, 1970, (with Cooder and Paul Schrader) Hard Working Man, 1978, No One Knows Better Than You, 1979, I Love Her Too, 1979, We're Old Enough to Know, 1981, (with Will Jennings and Sainte-Marie) Up Where We Belong, 1982 (Academy award best original song 1983), Hit and Run Lovers, 1984; album: The Lonely Surfer, 1963, St. Giles Cripplegate, 1972. Office: Creative Artists Agency 9830 Wilshire Blvd Beverly Hills CA 90212-1804*

NIVARTHI, RAJU NAGA, anesthesiology educator. BSc with Chemistry, Zoology and Botany, Sri Venkateswara U., Tirupati, India, 1984, MSc in Biochemistry, 1986; postgrad., U. Hyderabad, India, 1987-93. Doctoral fellow Sch. Life Scis., U. Hyderabad, India, 1987-93; rsch. asst. prof. dept. anesthesiology NYU Med. Ctr., N.Y.C., 1993-96, rsch. asst. scientist, 1996—. Contbr. articles to profl. jours. Recipient jr. rsch. fellowship Coun. Sci. and Indls. Rsch., India, 1987, sr. rsch. fellowship, 1990. Mem. AAAS, Acad. Med. Cmty., Am. Chem. Soc., Am. Soc. Anesthesiologists, Am. Soc. Biochemistry and Molecular Biology, Internat. Anesthesia Rsch. Soc., Internat. Soc. for Study of Xenobiotics, Nat. Geographic Soc., N.Y. Acad. Scis. Home: Apt 1-I Woodside 37-06 69th St New York NY 11377 Office: NYU Med Ctr Dept Anesthesiology 550 1st Ave New York NY 10016-6481

NIVISON, DAVID SHEPHERD, Chinese and philosophy educator; b. Farmingdale, Maine, Jan. 17, 1923; s. William and Ruth (Robinson) N.; m. Cornelia Green, Sept. 11, 1944; children—Louise, Helen Thom, David Gregory, James Nicholas. A.B. summa cum laude, Harvard U., 1946, M.A., 1948, Ph.D., 1953. Instr. Chinese Stanford U., 1948-52, Ford Found. faculty fellow, 1952-53, instr. Chinese and philosophy, 1953-54; Fulbright research scholar Kyoto, Japan, 1954-55; lectr. philosophy Stanford U., 1955-58, asst. prof. Chinese and philosophy, 1958-59, assoc. prof., 1959-66, prof., 1966-88, Walter Y. Evans-Wentz prof. Oriental Philosophies, Religions and Ethics, 1983-88, chmn. dept. philosophy, 1969-72, 75-76, acting chmn. dept. Asian langs., 1985-86; emeritus, 1988—. Author: The Life and Thought of Chang Hsüeh-ch'eng, 1738-1801, 1966, The Ways of Confucianism: Investigations in Chinese Philosophy, 1996; co-author: Chinese Language, Thought and Culture: Nivison and His Critics, 1996; editor, co-compiler: Stanford Chinese Concordance Series, 1979; co-editor: Confucianism in Action, 1959; contbr. articles to profl. jours. and encys. Served with AUS, 1943-46. Recipient Prix Stanislas-Julien Inst. de France, 1967; Am. Council Learned Socs. fellow, 1973; John Simon Guggenheim fellow, 1973-74. Mem. Assn. Asian Studies, Am. Philos. Assn. (v.p. Pacific div. 1978-79, pres. 1979-80), Am. Oriental Soc. (Western br. v.p. 1964-65, sec. 1965-70, pres. 1971-72), AAUP (pres. No. Calif. Conf. 1964-66), Internat. Acad. Chinese Culture (Beijing, Peoples Republic of China), Phi Beta Kappa. Home: 1169 Russell Ave Los Altos CA 94024-5066 Office: Stanford U Philosophy Dept Stanford CA 94305

NIX, EDMUND ALFRED, lawyer; b. Eau Claire, Wis., May 24, 1929; s. Sebastian and Kathryn (Keirnan) N.; m. Mary Kathryn Nagle Daley, Apr. 27, 1968; children: Kim, Mary Kay, Norbert, Edmund Alfred, Michael. B.S., Wis. State U., 1951; LL.B., U. Wis., 1954, postgrad. in speech, 1956-57. Bar: Wis. 1954. Practice in Eau Claire, 1954-65; dist. atty. Eau Claire County, 1958-64; U.S. atty. Western Dist. Wis., Eau Claire, 1965-69; U.S. magistrate Western Dist. Wis., 1969-70; dist. atty. La Crosse County, Wis., 1975-77; mcpl. judge City of La Crosse, 1992—. Co-chmn. United Fund, Eau Claire, 1958; Pres. Young Democrats Wis., 1951-53; mem. adminstrv. bd. Wis. Dem. party, 1953-54; chmn. 10th Congl. dist., 1965; sec. Kennedy for Pres. Club Wis., 1959-60. Served with AUS, 1954-56. Mem. Fed. Bar Assn., Wis. Bar Assn. (state chmn. crime prevention and control com.), La Crosse County Bar Assn. (pres.), Nat. Dist. Attys. Assn., KC. Roman Catholic. Office: 123 4th St N La Crosse WI 54601-3235

NIX, JAMES RAYFORD, nuclear physicist, consultant; b. Natchitoches, La., Feb. 18, 1938; s. Joe Ebbin and Edna (Guin) N.; m. Sally Ann Wood, Aug. 19, 1961; children—Patricia Lynne, David Allen. B.S. in Physics, Carnegie Inst. Tech., 1960; Ph.D. in Physics, U. Calif.-Berkeley, 1964. Summer physicist Lawrence Livermore Nat. Lab., Livermore, Calif., 1961; research asst. Lawrence Berkeley Lab., Berkeley, Calif., 1961-64, postdoctoral physicist, 1966-68; NATO postdoctoral fellow Niels Bohr Inst., Copenhagen, Denmark, 1964-65; staff mem. Los Alamos Nat. Lab., 1968-77, 89-94, group leader, 1977-89, fellow, 1994—; vis. prof. Centro Brasileiro de Pesquisas Fisicas, Rio de Janeiro, Brazil, 1974; cons. Calif. Inst. Tech., Pasadena, 1976, 79; chmn. Gordon Research Conf. Nuclear Chemistry, New London, N.H., 1976; chmn. physics div. adv. com. Oak Ridge Nat. Lab., 1976, 77, chmn. nuclear sci. div. vis. com. Lawrence Berkeley Lab., 1979-80. Contbr. articles to numerous publs. Alfred P. Sloan Found. scholar, Pitts., 1956-60; Phi Kappa Phi fellow, Berkeley, Calif., 1960-61; Alexander von Humboldt Sr. U.S. Scientist award Univ. Munich and Max-Planck Inst. for Nuclear Physics, 1980-81. Fellow Am. Phys. Soc. (exec. com. 1973-75); mem. AAAS, Sigma Xi, Phi Kappa Phi. Democrat. Home: 12 Los Pueblos Los Alamos NM 87544-2659 Office: Los Alamos Nat Lab Nuclear Theory T-2 MS B243 Los Alamos NM 87545

NIX, ROBERT LYNN, minister; b. Belleville, Ark., Nov. 24, 1940; s. Huey Watson and Edna Mae (Johnson) N.; m. Patricia Sue Palmer, Aug. 27, 1961; children: Kevin Lynn, Robert Keith, Jonathan Kyle, Kelly Eugene. Diploma, Jackson (Miss.) Coll. Ministries, 1965. Ordained to ministry United Pentecostal Ch. Internat., 1963. Prof. Pentecostal Bible Inst., Tupelo, Miss., 1965-66; missionary to Peru, United Pentecostal Ch. Internat., 1966-69; missionary supt. United Pentecostal Ch., Peru, 1966-85; pres. United Pentecostal Sem., Peru, 1969-85; missionary supt. United Pentecostal Ch., Costa Rica, Cen. Am.; pres. United Pentecostal Sem. United Pentecostal Ch., Costa Rica, Cen. Am., 1983-85; pastor United Pentecostal Spanish Ch., Hilsboro, Oreg., 1985-86, Christian Apostolic Ch., San Antonio, 1987—. Bd. dirs. Tex. Bible Coll., Houston, 1993—. Home and Office: 12016 White Birch St San Antonio TX 78245-3350 *The Apostle Paul said, "For me to live is Christ." (Phil. 1:21). In this age of hedonism and materialism many believe that life consists of worldly goods and human achievements. How mistaken they are! People never really live until they die to self and allow Jesus Christ to become the Supreme Lord of their lives.*

NIX, ROBERT N(ELSON) C(ORNELIUS), JR., state supreme court chief justice; b. Phila., July 13, 1928; s. Robert Nelson Cornelius and Ethel (Lanier) N.; m. Renate Bryant; children from previous marriage: Dorothy Lewis (dec.), Robert Nelson Cornelius III, Michael, Anthony, S. Jude. A.B., Villanova U., LLD (hon.); J.D., U. Pa.; postgrad. bus. adminstrn. and econs., Temple U.; LLD (hon.), St. Charles Sem., Dickinson U. Sch. Law, Scranton U., Delaware Law Sch., Lafayette Coll. Bar: Pa. 1956, U.S. Dist. Ct. (ea. dist.) Pa., U.S. Ct. Appeals (3d cir.). Dep. atty. gen. Commonwealth of Pa., 1956-58; ptnr. Nix, Rhodes & Nix, Phila., 1958-68; judge Common Pleas Ct., Phila., 1968-71; justice Supreme Ct. Pa., Phila., 1972-84, chief justice, 1984-96; chmn. bd. dirs. Nat. Ctr. for State Cts., 1990-91. Bd. dirs. Nat. Ctr. for State Cts., 1985—, Scranton U., Duquesne U., Lincoln U.; life mem. bd. consultors Villanova U., trustee, 1986—; bd. overseers U. Pa. Sch. Law, 1987—; bd. dirs. Archdiocese of Phila. Served with AUS, 1953-55. Recipient First Pa. award, Benjamin Franklin award Poor Richard Club Pa., James Madison award Soc. Profl. Journalists; named Knight Comdr. Order of St. Gregory the Great. Fellow Am. Bar Found.; mem. ABA, Pa. Bar Assn., Phila. Bar Assn., Nat. Bar Assn. (past chmn. jud. coun.), Barristers Club, Am. Law Inst., Conf. of Chief Justices (bd. dirs., pres. 1990-91), The Legal Club, Omega Psi Phi. Lodge: KC. Office: Pa Supreme Ct Ea Dist Office City Hall Rm 468 Philadelphia PA 19107-3292 Office: 1 South Penn Sq Widener Building Rm 500 Philadelphia PA 19107-3519 *America is slowly becoming aware of the vast potential she possesses because of the varied backgrounds and cultures of her citizens. When this fact is fully appreciated and full advantage is taken of this resource, she will reach an unprecedented level of civilization.*

NIX, ROBERT ROYAL, II, lawyer; b. Detroit, Mar. 27, 1947; s. Robert R. and Betty Virginia (Karicofe) N.; m. Suzanne Martha Turner, July 11, 1970; children: Christian Michael, Heather Michele. BS, Ea. Mich. U., 1968; JD cum laude, Wayne State U., 1971. Bar: Mich. 1971, U.S. Dist. Ct. (ea. dist.) Mich. 1971, U.S. Ct. Appeals (6th cir.) 1976. Rsch. atty. Mich. Ct. Appeals, Lansing, 1971-72; law clk. to Hon. Charles L. Levin Mich. Ct. Appeals, 1971; law clk. to Hon. S. Jerome Bronson Mich. Ct. Appeals, Detroit, 1972-73; ptnr. Kerr, Russell and Weber, Detroit, 1973—; lectr. in field. Contrb. articles to Michigan Real Property Law Review. Mem. ABA (partnership com. real property, probate and trust law sect., mortgages and secured financing com. corp., banking and bus. law sect., forum constrn. industry sect.), State Bar Mich. (chmn. real property law sect. 1994-95, coun. vice-chmn. 1992-93, chmn. com. on mortgage related financing devices, 1984-87, mem. sect., 1973—, partnership com. 1982—), Oakland County Bar Assn., Detroit Bar Assn., Am. Coll. Real Estate Lawyers, Am. Coll. Mortgage Attys. Republican. Methodist. Office: Kerr Russell and Weber Detroit Ctr Ste 2500 Detroit MI 48226

NIXON, AGNES ECKHARDT, television writer, producer; m. Robert Nixon; 4 children. Student, Sch. Speech, Northwestern U. Writer for radio and TV; freelance writer for: TV programs Hallmark Hall of Fame, Robert Montgomery Presents, Studio One; creator, packager, head writer: daytime TV series All My Children; creator nightime mini-series The Manions of America; creator, packager daytime TV series One Life to Live; creator, packager: daytime TV series Loving; co-creator: daytime TV series As The World Turns; formerly head writer, The Guiding Light, daytime TV series Another World. Recipient Trustees award Nat. Acad. TV Arts and Sci., 1981, Super Achiever award Jr. Diabetes Found., 1981, Wilmer Eye Inst. award, 1981, Communicator award Am. Women in Radio & TV, 1984, Gold Plate award Am. Acad. Achievement, 1993, Popular Culture Lifetime Achievement award Popular Culture Assn., 1995, Pub. Svc. award Johns Hopkins Hosp., 1995, Humanitarian award Nat. Osteoporosis Found., 1996; inducted into TV Hall of Fame, 1993. Mem. Internat. Radio and TV Soc. Nat. Acad. TV Arts and Scis., Harvard Found. (bd. dirs.), Mus. TV and Radio (bd. dirs.), The Friars Club. Address: 774 Conestoga Rd Rosemont PA 19010-1257

NIXON, ARLIE JAMES, gas and oil company executive; b. Ralston, Okla., May 22, 1914; s. James Gordon and Wella May (Platt) N.; BS, Okla. State U., 1935; m. Wylie Elizabeth Jones, Apr. 21, 1938 (div. May 1950); children: Cole Jay, Kathleen (Mrs. S. Brent Joyce); m. Lisa Marie Grant, Dec. 7, 1981 (div. June 1989). Airline capt. Trans World Airlines, N.Y.C., 1939-74; pres. Crystal Gas Co., Jennings, Okla., 1960—, Blackburn Gas Co., Jennings, 1964—, Blackberry Oil Co., Jennings, 1969—; represented U.S. in several ofcl. dels. to internat. aviation tech. meetings, also represented Internat. Fedn. Air Line Pilots Assns. at internat. confs. Lt. (j.g.) USNR, 1935-63. Mem. Internat. Fedn. Air Line Pilots Assn. (regional v.p. 1972), Internat. Platform Assn., Wings Club. Democrat. Home: RR 2 Jennings OK 74038-9802 Office: PO Box 68 Jennings OK 74038-0068

NIXON, CHARLES WILLIAM, bioacoustician; b. Wellsburg, W.Va., Aug. 15, 1929; s. William E. and Lenora S. (Treiber) N.; m. Barbara Irene Hunter, May 19, 1956; children: Timothy C., Tracy Scott. BS, Ohio State U., 1952, MS, 1953, PhD, 1960. Tchr. spl. edn. Ohio and W.Va. Pub. Schs., Wheeling, 1954-56; rsch. audiologist Aeromed Lab., Wright Patterson AFB, Ohio, 1956-67; supervisory rsch. audiologist Armstrong Lab., Wright Patterson AFB, 1967-96, Sys. Rsch. Labs., Dayton, 1996—; chair W4 Am. Nat. Stds. Inst., N.Y.C., 1968—; U.S. rep. hearing protection Internat. Stds. Orgn., Geneva, 1968—; USAF rep. NRC-NAS Hearing Com., Washington, 1976—; chair robotics panel Joint Dirs. Labs., Washington, 1987-88. Author reports and book chpts. Cpl. U.S. Army, 1953-55. Recipient Meritorious Svc. medal U.S. Dept. Def., Dayton, Ohio, 1986. Fellow Acoustical Soc. Am.; mem. Rsch. Soc. Am. Achievements include research on noise exposure, voice communications, hearing protection, sonic boom, active noise reduction, 3-D audio displays, others. Home: 4316 Sillman Pl Dayton OH 45440-1141

NIXON, DANIEL DAVID., physician; b. L.A., Jan. 7, 1934; s. Irving I. and Sara Ruth (Cohen) N.; m. Tamara Hope Friedman, June 14, 1959; children: Asa Joel, Naomi Devorah, Victoria Eve. BA, Dartmouth Coll., 1955; MD, U. Pitts., 1959. Diplomate in internal medicine and med. oncology Am. Bd. Internal Medicine. Intern Mt. Sinai Hosp., N.Y.C., 1959-60, resident in internal medicine, 1961-62, fellow in hematology; resident in internal medicine U. Pitts., 1960-61; pvt. practice internal medicine Rockville Centre, N.Y., 1963-66; internist, chief gen. med. svc. Valley Forge Gen. Hosp., Phoenixville, Pa., 1967-68; instr. medicine Columbia U. Coll. P&S, N.Y.C., 1968-69; pvt. practice hematology and oncology Miami Beach, Fla., 1969—; clin. assoc. prof. U. Miami Sch. Medicine, 1981—; chief divsn. oncology Mt. Sinai Med. Ctr., Miami Beach, 1969—; med. dir. Dade County Hospice Inc., Miami, 1989-93; mem. sci. adv. bd. Israel Cancer Rsch. Fund, N.Y.C., 1978—; co-dir. Mt. Sinai Comprehensive Cancer Ctr., Miami Beach, 1989—. Capt. M.C., U.S. Army, 1966-68, Vietnam. Alfred B. Stengel traveling fellow ACP, 1972. Fellow ACP; mem. Am. Soc. Hematology, Am. Soc. Oncology, Internat. Soc. Hematology, Alpha Omega Alpha. Avocations: tennis, gardening, fishing. Office: Mt Sinai Med Ctr 4306 Alton Rd Miami Beach FL 33140-2840

NIXON, DAVID, dancer; b. Windsor, Ont., Can.. Student, The Nat. Ballet Sch. With Nat. Ballet of Can., 1978-84, 1st soloist, 1982-84, prin. dancer, 1984-90; prin. dancer Berlin Opera Ballet, 1985-90, Bayerisches Staatsoper Ballet Munich, 1990-91; prin. dancer and 1st Ballet master Deutsche Opera Ballet Berlin, 1994-95; various guest appearances including Alexander Godunov and Stars, summer 1982, Milw. Ballet, 1984, Sydney Ballet Australia, 1984, World Ballet Festival Tokyo, 1985, 88, Hamburg Ballet, 1988, 89, Staatsoper Berlin, 1988-91, Bayerisches Staatsballet, 1988-90, Komische Opera Berlin, 1990-93; prodr. David Nixon's Dance Theatre, Hebbel Theatre, Berlin, 1990, 91; prodr., artistic dir. BalletMet, 1995—; choreographer Butterfly, 1983, La Follia, 1984, Dangerous Liaisons, 1990, 96, African Fantasy, 1990, Celebrate Mozart, 1991, Sudden Impulse, 1994, A Summer's Nights Reflections, 1995, Full-Length Nutcracker, 1995, Butterfly, 1996, Beauty and the Beast, 1997.

NIXON, EUGENE RAY, chemist, educator; b. Mt. Pleasant, Mich., Apr. 14, 1919; s. William S. and Grace (Brookens) N.; m. Phyllis R. Jones, June 10, 1945; children—Cynthia L., Emily E. Sc.B. summa cum laude, Alma Coll., 1941; Ph.D., Brown U., 1947. Research chemist Manhattan Project, 1942-46; instr. chemistry Brown U., 1947-49; mem. faculty U. Pa., Phila., 1949—; prof. chemistry U. Pa., 1965—, vice dean grad. sch., 1958-62, acting chmn. dept. chemistry, 1965-66, dir. materials research lab., 1969-72; vis. prof. U. London, 1963-64; vis. lectr. Bryn Mawr Coll., 1957-58. Mem. Am. Chem. Soc., Am. Phys. Soc., Soc. Applied Spectroscopy (Jour. award 1965, Spectroscopist of Yr. award Del. Valley sect. 1988), Coblentz Soc. (bd. mgrs.), Sigma Xi. Research, publs. on phys. chemistry, molecular structure and molecular spectroscopy, properties of crystals, intermolecular interactions, laser spectroscopy and laser chemistry. Home: 35 Julio Dr Apt 106 Shrewsbury MA 01545-3049 Office: Univ Pa Dept Chemistry Philadelphia PA 19104

NIXON, JAMES GREGORY, economic development consultant; b. Kansas City, Mo., Dec. 7, 1962; s. Gerald Glen and Jane Ardis (Mountain) N.; m. Carol Ann Lake, June 21, 1986; 1 child, Kathryn Grace. BBA, U. Okla., 1985; MBA, Okla. State U., 1992. Cert. econ. developer. Govt. rels. aide Pub. Svc. Okla., Oklahoma City, 1985-86; info. analyst Pub. Svc. Okla., Tulsa, 1986-87, econ. devel. cons., 1987-97; with CSW Energy Svcs., Tulsa, 1997—. Mem. Am. Econ. Devel. Coun., So. Indsl. Devel. Coun. (alt. dir. 1986—), Order of Arrow (Vigil honor mem.). Republican. Mem. Disciples of Christ. Avocations: sailing, golf, water skiing, snow skiing, music. Office: CSW Energy Svcs 2 W 2nd St Tulsa OK 74103

NIXON, JEREMIAH W. (JAY NIXON), state attorney general; b. DeSoto, Mo., Feb. 13, 1956; s. Jeremiah and Betty (Lea) N.; m. Georganne Nixon; children: Jeremiah, Will. BS in Polit. Sci., U. Mo., 1978, JD, 1981. Ptnr. Nixon, Nixon, Breeze & Roberts, Jefferson County, Mo., 1981-86; mem. Mo. State Senate from Dist 22, 1986-93; atty. gen. State of Mo., 1993—; chmn. select com. ins. reform.; created video internat. devel. and edn. opportunity program. Honoree, Conservation Fedn. Mo., 1992; named Outstanding Young Missourian, Mo. Jaycees, 1994, Outstanding Young Lawyer, Barrister's Mag., 1993. Mem. Nat. Assn. Attys. Gen. (antitrust com., chair FTC working group, criminal law com., consumer protection com.), Midwest Assn. Attys. Gen. (chmn.), Mo. Assn. Trial Attys. Democrat. Methodist. Office: Atty Gen Office PO Box 899 Jefferson City MO 65102-0899*

NIXON, JOHN HARMON, economist; b. Mpls., Apr. 7, 1915; s. Justin Wroe and Ida Elisabeth (Wickenden) N. AB, Swarthmore Coll., 1935; AM, Harvard U., 1949, PhD, 1953. Analyst U.S. R.R. Retirement Bd., Washington, 1938-41; economist U.S. Office of Price Adminstrn., Washington, 1941-46; teaching fellow, sr. tutor Harvard Coll., Cambridge, Mass., 1947-50; asst. prof. econs. CCNY, 1953-56; dir. econ. devel. N.Y. State Dept. Commerce, Albany, 1956-59; dir. area devel. Com. for Econ. Devel., N.Y.C., 1959-65; dir. tech. assistance U.S. Econ. Devel. Adminstrn., Washington, 1966-67; urban economist U.S. AID, Saigon, Vietnam, 1967; economist Ralph M. Parsons Co., Washington, 1968-70; chief economist/systems Ralph M. Parsons Co., Pasadena, Calif., 1971-82; mem. adv. bd. U.S. Area Devel. Adminstrn., Washington, 1963-65. Co-author, editor: Community Economic Development Efforts, 1964, Living Without Water (Cairo), 1980. Vice chmn. Mayor's Com. on Econ. Devel., L.A., 1974-75; pres. Pasadena Devel. Corp., 1982-84. Mem. Nat. Economists Club, Nat. Assn. Bus. Economists, Harvard Club N.Y.C., Phi Beta Kappa. Democrat. Presbyterian. Office: PO Box 76267 Los Angeles CA 90076-0267

NIXON, JOHN TRICE, judge; b. New Orleans, La., Jan. 9, 1933; s. H. C. and Anne (Trice) N.; m. Betty Chiles, Aug. 5, 1960 (div. Nov. 1985); children: Mignon Elizabeth, Anne Trice. A.B. cum laude, Harvard Coll., 1955; LL.B., Vanderbilt U., 1960. Bar: Ala. bar 1960, Tenn. bar 1972. Individual practice law Anniston, Ala., 1960-62; city atty. Anniston, 1962-64; trial atty. Civil Rights Div., Dept. Justice, Washington, 1964-69; staff atty., comptroller of Treasury State of Tenn., 1971-76; pvt. practice law Nashville, 1976-77; cir. judge, 1977-78, gen. sessions judge, 1978-80; judge U.S. Dist. Ct. (mid. dist.) Tenn., Nashville, 1980—, now chief judge, 1980. Served with U.S. Army, 1958. Democrat. Methodist. Clubs: D.U. (Cambridge); Harvard-Radcliffe (Nashville). Office: US Dist Ct 825 US Courthouse Nashville TN 37203

NIXON, JUDITH MAY, librarian; b. Gary, Ind., June 14, 1945; d. Louis Robert Sr. and Mable Sophia (Reiner) Vician; m. Cleon Robert Nixon III, Aug. 20, 1967; 1 child, Elizabeth Marie. BS in Edn., Valparaiso U., 1967; MA in LS, U. Iowa, 1974. Tchr. U.S. Peace Corps, Kingdom of Tonga, 1968-69; popular books libr. Lincoln Libr., Springfield, Ill., 1971-73; reference libr. Cedar Rapids (Iowa) Pub. Libr., 1974-76; reference coord. U. Wis., Platteville, 1976-82; bus. libr. U. Ariz., Tucson, 1982-84; consumer and family sci. libr. Purdue U., West Lafayette, La., 1984-93; Krannert mgmt. and econs. libr. Purdue U., West Lafayette, 1993—. Editor: Industry and Company Information, 1991, Organization Charts, 1992, 2d edit., 1996, Hotel and Restaurant Industries, 1993; editor quar. serial Lodging and Restaurant Index, 1985-93. Leader Girl Scouts U.S., Lafayette, 1985—. Recipient John H. Moriarty award Purdue U. Librs., 1989. Mem. ALA (chairperson bus. reference and svcs. sect. 1995-96, GALE Rsch. award for excellence in bus. librarianship 1994). Home: 2375 N 23rd St Lafayette IN 47904-1242 Office: Purdue U Mgmt and Econs Libr Krannert Grad Sch Mgmt West Lafayette IN 47907

NIXON, MARNI, singer; b. Altadena, Calif., Feb. 22, 1930; d. Charles and Margaret (Wittke) McEathron; m. Ernest Gold, May 22, 1950 (div. 1969); children: Andrew Maurice, Martha Alice, Melani Christine; m. Lajos Frederick Fenster, July 23, 1971 (div. July 1975); m. Albert David Block, Apr. 11, 1983. Student opera workshop, Los Angeles City Coll., UCLA, U. So. Calif., Tanglewood, Mass. Dir. vocal faculty Calif. Inst. Arts, Valencia, 1970-72; pvt. tchr., vocal coacn, condr. master classes, 1970—, pvt. voice tchr., coach, condr. master classes, 1970—; head apprentice div. Santa Barbara Music Acad. of West, 1980; formerly dir. opera workshop Cornish Inst. Arts, Seattle.; tchr. in field; judge Met. Opera Internat. Am. Music Awards, Nat. Inst. Music Theatre, 1984, 85-86, 87; panelist New Music, Nat. Assn. Tchrs. Singing, pres. (N.Y. chpt.), 1994—; dialect dir., opera recs. Child actress Pasadena (Calif.) Playhouse, 1940-45, soloist Roger Wagner chorale, 1947-53, appeared with New Eng. Opera Co., Los Angeles Opera Co., also Ford Found. TV Opera, 1948-63, San Francisco Spring Opera, 1966, Seattle Opera, 1971, 72, 73; classical recitals and appearances with symphony orchs. throughout U.S., Can., also Eng., Israel, Ireland; appeared on Broadway as Eliza Doolittle in My Fair Lady, 1964; in motion picture as Sister Sophia in Sound of Music, 1964, Aunt Mabel in I Think I Do, 1996; also in numerous TV shows and night clubs; star children's ednl. TV show Boomerang, ABC-TV, from 1975; off-Broadway show Taking My Turn, from 1983, Opal, from 1992; appeared in (stage plays) Romeo & Juliet, N.Y.C.; taped for Great Performances PBS-TV Role of Edna, 1994; voice dubbed in for musical motion pictures My Fair Lady, The King and I, An Affair to Remember, West Side Story, and others; rec. artist for Columbia, Mus. Heritage Records, Capital, RCA Victor, Ednl.Records, Reference Recs., Varese-Sarabande, Nonesuch; played violin at age 4; studied in youth orch., 10 yrs; studied voice at age 10. Recipient 4 Emmy awards for best actress, 2 Action for Childrens TV awards, 1977; nominee Drama Desk award; recipient Chgo. Film Festival award, 1977, Gold Record for Songs from Mary Poppins, 2 time Grammy award nominee Nat. Acad. Rec. Arts and Scis. (1st rec. Cabaret Songs and Early Songs by Arnold Schoenberg, RCA, 1977 and 1st rec. Emily Dickinson Songs by Aaron Copland, Reference Recs., 1988). Mem. Nat. Assn. Tchrs. Singing (pres. N.Y. chpt. 1994-97).

NIXON, PHILIP ANDREWS, diversified company executive; b. Bklyn., Nov. 23, 1938; s. Philip A. and Hilda (Weidman) N.; m. Brooke Nichols, June 9, 1963; children: Lucia, Rachel, Eliot, Oliver, Preya, Malini, Biplab, Jasmine, Hilda, Rajani. B.A., Yale U., 1960. Vol. Peace Corps, Sierra Leone, Africa, 1965-67; aide to gov. State of Maine, Augusta, 1967-70; asst. to chmn. Dead River Co., Bangor, Maine, 1970-71, v.p., 1971-73, exec. v.p., 1973, pres., chief exec. officer, 1974—; pres., chief exec. officer Dead River Group of Cos., Bangor, Maine, 1974-85; chnm. bd. Dead River Group of Cos., 1985—; dir. Fleet/Norstar Bank Maine, Forster Mfg. Co., Wilton, Maine. Sec. Maine Pulp & Paper Found., 1976-86; bd. dirs. New Eng. Council, 1978-86, Maine Community Found.; trustee Kenduskeag Found., Bangor, 1979—, Portland Sch. Art, 1983—; chmn. Maine Community Found., 1989-94. Served with USN, 1961-65. Mem. C. of C. of U.S., Conf. Bd. Democrat. Clubs: Union (Boston). Home: 71 Federal St Brunswick ME 04011-2114 Office: Dead River Co 1 Dana St Portland ME 04101-4014

NIXON, RALPH ANGUS, psychiatrist, educator, research neuroscientist; b. Somerville, Mass., Jan. 29, 1947; s. Ralph Angus and Eleanor Nixon; m. Katharine Sangree Faulkner, Aug. 20, 1974; children: Abigail, Rebecca. AB, Brandeis U., 1968; PhD in Cell and Devel. Biology, Harvard U., 1974; MD, U. Vt., 1976. Intern Mass. Gen. Hosp., 1976, Salem Hosp., 1977; resident in psychiatry Mass. Gen. Hosp., 1977-79, McLean Hosp., 1979-80; clin. assoc. in psychiatry Mass. Gen. Hosp., Boston, 1980—; assoc. in neurosci. Children's Hosp Med. Ctr., Boston, 1982-88; staff physician Rehab. Ctr. for Aged, Boston, 1984-90; asst. prof. psychiatry Harvard Med. Sch., Boston, 1982-86, assoc. prof., 1986—; assoc. neuropathologist McLean Hosp., Belmont, Mass., 1982-90, assoc. psychiatrist, 1988-93, neuropathologist, 1991; psychiatrist, 1993—; mem. sci. rev. com. Am. Fedn. for Aging Rsch., 1990-92; mem. neurosci., behavior and sociology of aging rev. com., subcom. A, Nat. Inst. on Aging, NIH, 1991-95, chmn., 1994-95; dir. labs. for molecular neurosci. McLean Hosp., 1992. Mem. editl. bd. Jour. Neurochemistry, 1986—, Neurochem. Rsch., 1988—, Harvard Rev. Psychiatry, 1992—, Neurobiology of Aging, 1994—; contbr. numerous biol. articles to Sci. Jour. Cell Biology, Jour. Biol. Chem., Annals N.Y. Acad. Sci., Proc. NAS, chpts. to books; Proteases and protease Inhibitors Banner C Nixon R.A. eds. Annals Acad. Sci. vol. 67, 1992. Hon. bd. dirs. Ch. League for Civic Concerns, Boston, 1987-89. Recipient Merit award NIH, 1990, Leadership and Excellence in Alzheimer Disease award, Nat. Inst. Aging, 1992; Ethel DuPont Warren Fellow, 1979-80, rsch. fellw Med. Found., 1980-82, Alfred P. Sloan Found., 1981-83, Scottish Rite Schizophrenia Rsch. Program, 1983-85. Mem. AAAS, Soc. for Neurosci., Fedn. Am. Scientists, Am. Soc. for Neurochemistry, Internat. Soc. for Neurochemistry, Am. Psychiat. Assn., Am. Soc. for Cell Biology, Am. Assn. for Geriatric Psychiatry, Gerontol. Soc. Am., Am. Assn. Neuropathologists. Achievements include patents (with others) on cupric chloride spot test and neural calcium-activated neutral proteinase inhibitors; four patents pending. Office: McLean Hosp-Harvard Med Sch 115 Mill St Belmont MA 02178-1041

NIXON, ROBERT OBEY, SR., business educator; b. Pitts., Feb. 14, 1922; s. Frank Obey and Margurite (Van Buren) N.; m. Marilyn Cavanagh, Oct. 25, 1944 (dec. 1990); children: Nan Nixon Friend, Robert Obey, Jr., Dwight Cavanagh. BS in bus. adminstrn., U. Pitts., 1948; MS, Ohio State U., 1964; MBA, U. Phoenix, 1984. Commd. 2d lt. USAF, 1943, advanced through grades to col., 1970, master navigator WWII, Korea, Vietnam; sales, adminstrn. U.S. Rubber Corp., Pitts., 1940-41; asst. engr. Am. Bridge Corp., Pitts., 1941-42; underwriter, sales Penn Mutual Life Ins. Corp., Pitts., 1945-50; capt., nav. instr. USAF Reserves, 1945-50; ret. USAF Col., divsn. chief Joint Chiefs of Staff, 1973; educator, cons. U. Ariz., 1973-79; bus. dept. chmn., coord., founder weekend coll. Pima Community Coll., Tucson, 1979-90, prof. mgmt., coord. Weekend Coll. program, 1991—; founder, pres. Multiple Adv. Group ednl. cons., Tucson, 1978—. Author: Source Document: On Accelerated Courses and Programs at Accredited Two- and Four-Year Colleges and Universities, 1996; contbr. articles to profl. jours. Mem. Soc. Logistics Engrs. (sr., charter mem.), Phi Delta Theta. Presbyterian. Avocations: tennis, hiking, swimming. Home: 1824 S Regina Cleri Dr Tucson AZ 85710-8664

NIXON, SCOTT SHERMAN, lawyer; b. Grosse Pointe, Mich., Feb. 7, 1959; s. Floyd Sherman and Marjorie Jane (Quermann) N.; m. Cathryn Lynn Starnes, Aug. 27, 1983; children: Jeffry Sherman, Kelsy Jane, James Robert. BABA, Mich. State U., 1981; JD, U. Denver, 1984. Bar: Colo. 1984, U.S. Dist. Ct. Colo. 1984, U.S. Ct. Appeals (10th cir.) 1984. Assoc. Pryor, Carney & Johnson, P.C., Englewood, Colo., 1984-89, shareholder, 1990-95; shareholder Pryor, Johnson, Montoya, Carney & Karr, P.C., Englewood, 1995—. Officer, bd. dirs. Luth. Brotherhood Br. 8856, Denver, 1993—, Mark K. Ulmer Meml. Native Am. Scholarship Found., Denver, 1994—; officer, mem. coun. Bethan Luth Ch., Englewood, 1993-95. Mem. ABA, Colo. Bar Assn., Denver Bar Assn., Colo. Def. Lawyers Assn. Avocations: music performance, physical fitness, carpentry/construction. Home: 6984 S Pontiac Ct Englewood CO 80112 Office: Pryor Johnson Montoya et al Ste 1313 6400 S Fiddlers Green Cir Englewood CO 80111-4959

NIXON, SCOTT WEST, oceanography science educator; b. Phila., Aug. 24, 1943; s. Robert Scott West and Elizabeth (Wright) West Nixon; m. Pendleton Hall, (div.); children: Carter Hall, Elizabeth Pendleton; m. Virginia Lee. BA, U. Del., 1965; PhD, U. N.C., 1970. Prof. oceanography U. R.I., Kingston, 1970—, dir. sea grant coll. program, 1983—; owner Coastal Ecology, Wakefield, R.I., 1980—. Author: (with others) A Coastal Marine Ecosystem, 1978, The New England High Salt Marshes, 1982; editor-in-chief Estuaries, 1988—; also articles. Grantee NSF, NOAA, EPA, Office Water Resources Research, State of R.I. Mem. Am. Soc. Limnology and Oceanography (governing bd. 1984-87), Estuarine Research Fedn., Nat. Assn. State Univs. Land-Grant Colls. Office: Univ of RI Dept Of Oceanography Kingston RI 02881

NIZZE, JUDITH ANNE, physician assistant; b. L.A., Nov. 1, 1942; d. Robert George and Charlotte Ann (Wise) Swan; m. Norbert Adolph Otto Paul Nizze, Dec. 31, 1966. BA, UCLA, 1966, postgrad., 1966-76; grad. physician asst. tng. program, Charles R. Drew Sch. Postgrad., L.A., 1979; BS, Calif. State U., Dominguez, 1980. Cert. physician asst., Calif. Staff rsch. assoc. I-II Wadsworth Vet. Hosp., L.A., 1965-71; staff rsch. assoc. III-IV John Wayne Clinic Jonsson Comprehensive Cancer Ctr., UCLA, 1971-78; clin. asst. Robert S. Ozeran, Gardena, Calif., 1978; physician asst. family practice Fred Chasan, Torrance, Calif., 1980-82; sr. physician asst. Donald L. Morton prof., chief surg. oncology Jonsson Comprehensive Cancer Ctr., UCLA, 1983-91; administrv. dir. immunotherapy John Wayne Cancer Inst., Santa Monica, Calif., 1991—. Contbr. articles to profl. jours. Fellow Am. Acad. Physician Assts., Am. Assn. Surgeons Assts., Calif. Acad. Physician Assts.; mem. AAUW, Assn. Physician Assts. in Oncology. Republican. Presbyterian. Avocations: sailing, tennis, skiing, photography, computers. Home: Ste J 13243 Fiji Way Marina Dl Rey CA 90292-7079 Office: John Wayne Cancer Inst St John's Hosp & Health Ctr 1328 22d St 2 West Santa Monica CA 90404-2032

NOAKES, BETTY L., retired elementary school educator; b. Oklahoma City, Okla., Aug. 28, 1938; d. Webster L. and Willie Ruth (Johnson) Hawkins; m. Richard E. Noakes, Apr. 22, 1962 (dec.); 1 child, Michele Monique. Student, Oklahoma City U., MEd, 1971; BS, Cen. State U., 1962; postgrad., Cen. State U., Okla. State U. Elem. tchr. Merced (Calif.) Pub. Schs., 1966-67, Oklahoma City Schs., 1971-73, Mid-Del Schs., Midwest City, Okla., 1973-95; founder, owner Noakes-I Care Day Care, 1995—. 2d v.p. PTA, Pleasant Hill, 1991, cert. recognition, 1992-93; active Nat. PTA, 1991-92; charter mem. Nat. Mus. of Am. Indian-Smithsonian Instn. Recipient Cert. Appreciation YMCA, 1992-92, Disting. Svc. award Mid-Del PTA, 1992. Mem. NEA, AAUW, NAACP, Nat. Therapeutic Recreation Assn., Okla. Edn. Assn., Smithsonian Instn., Oklahoma City U. Alumni Assn., United Meth. Women Assn., Cen. State U. Alumni Assn., Okla. Ea. Star (Lilly of the Valley chpt. 7), Phi Delta Kappa sorority (sgt.-at-arms), Zeta Phi Beta sorority. Avocations: aerobics, singing, piano, clarinet, folk dancing. Home: 5956 N Coltrane Rd Oklahoma City OK 73121-3409

NOBACK, CHARLES ROBERT, anatomist, educator; b. N.Y.C., Feb. 15, 1916; s. Charles Victor and Beatrice (Cerny) N.; m. Eleanor Louise Loomis, Nov. 23, 1938 (dec. Mar. 24, 1981); children: Charles Victor, Margaret Beatrice, Ralph Theodore, Elizabeth Louise. BS, Cornell U., 1936; MS, NYU, 1938; postgrad., Columbia U., 1936-38; PhD, U. Minn., 1942. Asst. prof. anatomy U. Ga., 1941-44; faculty L.I. Coll. Medicine, 1944-49, asso. prof., 1948-49; mem. faculty Columbia Coll. Phys. and Surg., 1949—, assoc. prof. anatomy, 1953-68, prof., 1968-86, prof. emeritus, 1986—, spl. lectr., 1986-92, acting chmn. dept., 1974-75, lectr., 1996—. Author: The Human Nervous System, 1967, 75, 81, Spinal Cord, 1971, The Nervous System Introduction and Review, 1982, 77, 86, 91, (with R. Demarest) Human Anatomy and Physiology, 1990, 2d edit., 1992, 3d edit., 1995, (with D. Van Wyseberghe and R. Carola) Human Anatomy, 1992, (with N. Strominger and R. Demarest) The Human Nervous System, Structure and Function, 5th edit., 1996; editor: with R. Carola and H. Harley) The Primate Brain, 1970, Sensory Systems of Primates, 1978; sr. editor: Advances in Primatology: series editor: Contbns. to Primatology; contbr. articles to profl. jours., sects. to Ency. Britannica, McGraw Hill Ency. Sci. and Tech., Collier's Ency. Fellow N.Y. Acad. Scis. (past rec. sec.), AAAS; mem. Am. Assn. Anatomists, Histochem. Soc., Internat. Primatological Soc., Am. Soc. Naturalists, Cajal Club Am. (past pres.), Assn. Phys. Anthropologists, Harvey Soc., Am. Acad. Neurology, Soc. Neurosci., Sigma Xi. Home: 116 7th St Cresskill NJ 07626-2005 Office: Columbia U Anatomy And Cell Dept New York NY 10032

NOBACK, RICHARDSON KILBOURNE, medical educator; b. Richmond, Va., Nov. 7, 1923; s. Gustav Joseph and Hazel (Kilborn) N.; m. Nan Jean Gates, Apr. 5, 1947; children: Carl R., Robert K., Catherine E. MD, Cornell U., 1947; BA, Columbia U., 1993. Diplomate Am. Bd. Internal Medicine. Intern N.Y. Hosp., 1947-48; asst. resident Cornell Med. div. Bellevue Hosp., N.Y.C., 1958-50, chief resident, 1950-52; instr. medicine Cornell U., N.Y.C., 1950-53; asst. prof. medicine SUNY Upstate Med. Ctr., Syracuse, 1955-56; assoc. prof. medicine U. Ky. Med. Ctr., Lexington, 1956-64; exec. dir. Kansas City (Mo.) Gen. Hosp. and Med. Ctr., 1964-69; assoc. dean, prof. medicine U. Mo. Sch. Medicine, Columbia, 1964-69; founding dean U. Mo. Sch. Medicine, Kansas City, 1969-78, prof. medicine, 1969-90, prof. and dean emeritus, 1990—; cons. U. Tenn., U. Mich., U. Del., Northeastern Ohio Group, U. Mo., Eastern Va. Med. Sch., Tex. Tech. U. Contbr. numerous articles to profl. jours. Bd. dirs. Kansas City Gen. Hosp., Truman Med. Ctr., Wayne Miner Health Ctr., Jackson County Med. Soc., The Shepherd's Ctr., Am. Fedn. Aging Rsch., Mo. Gerontol. Inst., The Shepherd's Ctrs. of Am.; dir. Mo. Geriatric Edn. Ctr., 1985-88. Capt. USAF Med. Svcs. 1953-55. Recipient medal of honor Avila Coll., Kansas City, 1968, merit award Met. Med. Soc., 1991, recognition award Mo. Soc. Internal Medicine, 1993. Mem. AMA, Mo. Med. Assn. (former mem. ho. of dels., v.p. 1992), Am. Geriatric Soc., Alpha Omega Alpha, Phi Kappa Phi. Avocations: photography, writing, travel. Home: 2912 Abercorn Dr Las Vegas NV 89134-7440 Office: U Mo-Kansas City Sch Medicine Sch Medicine 2411 Holmes St Kansas City MO 64108-2741

NOBE, KEN, chemical engineering educator; b. Berkeley, Calif., Aug. 26, 1925; s. Sidney and Kiyo (Uyeyama) N.; m. Mary Tagami, Aug. 31, 1957; children: Steven Andrew, Keven Gibbs, Brian Kelvin. B.S., U. Calif., Berkeley, 1951; Ph.D., UCLA, 1956. Jr. chem. engr. Air Reduction Co., Murray Hill, N.J., 1951-52; asst. prof. chem. engring. UCLA, 1957-62, assoc. prof., 1962-68, prof., 1968—, chmn. dept. chem., nuclear and thermal engring., 1978-83, founding chmn. chem. engring., 1983-84. Div. editor: Jour. Electrochem. Soc, 1967-91, Electrochimica Acta, 1977-85. Served with U.S. Army, 1944-46. Mem. Electrochem. Soc. (Henry B. Linford award 1992), Am. Chem. Soc., Nat. Assn. Corrosion Engrs., Internat. Soc. Electrochemistry, Sigma Xi. Office: UCLA Dept Of Chemical Engin Los Angeles CA 90095

NOBEL, JOEL J., biomedical researcher; b. Phila., Dec. 8, 1934; s. Bernard D. and Golda R. (Nobel) Judovich; m. Bonnie Sue Goldberg, June 19, 1960 (div.); children—Erika, Joshua; m. Loretta Schwartz, Oct. 28, 1979; 1 child, Adam. AB, Haverford Coll., 1956; MA, U. Pa., 1958; MD, Thomas Jefferson Med. Coll., Phila., 1963. Intern Presbyn. Hosp., Phila., 1963-64; resident in surgery Pa. Hosp., Phila., 1964-65; resident in neurosurgery U. Pa. Hosp., 1965-66; practice medicine specializing in biomed. engring. rsch. and healthcare tech. assessment, Phila., 1968—; dir. research Emergency Care Research Inst., Plymouth Meeting, Pa., 1968-71; dir., pres. Emergency Care Research Inst., 1971—; pres. Plymouth Inst., 1979—; cons. in field; bd. dirs. Consumers Union, 1976-79, 80—, chmn. tech. policy com., exec. bd. Publisher Health Devices, 1971—, Health Devices Alerts, 1977—. Contbr. articles to profl. jours. Served with USNR, 1966-68. Smith, Kline & French fgn. fellow, 1962; grantee HEW, 1968-72; grantee Am. Heart Assn., 1965-66. Mem. AMA, APHA, Assn. Advancement Med. Instrumentation, Critical Care Med. Soc., Pa. Med. Assn., Navy League, U.S. Naval Inst., Sunday Breakfast Club. Home: 1434 Monk Rd Gladwyne PA 19035-1315 Office: ECRI 5200 Butler Pike Plymouth Meeting PA 19462-1241

NOBLE, DOUGLAS ROSS, museum administrator; b. Sturgis, Ky., Jan. 19, 1945; s. Roscoe and Robbie Rae (Martin) N.; m. Catherine Ann Richardson, Nov. 3, 1973; children: Kate Faxon, Jennifer Martin. BS, Okla. State U., 1967; MSA, Ga. Coll., 1978; D of Pub. Adminstrn., U. Ga., 1987. Asst. to dir. Savannah Sci. Mus., Ga., 1971-73; exec. dir. Mus. of Arts and Scis., Macon, Ga., 1973-80; dir. of museums Memphis Mus. System, 1980—; mem. mus. assessment program Inst. of Mus. Services, Washington, 1982—, grant reviewer, 1983—; cons. Mus. Mgmt. Program, Sarasota, Fla., 1985. Contbr. articles to profl. jours. Grad. Leadership Memphis, 1984; bd. dirs. Memphis in May Internat. Festival. 1st lt. U.S. Army, 1968-70; Vietnam. Decorated Bronze Star. Mem. Natural Sci. for Youth Found. (trustee 1980-87), Naumburg award 1978), Am. Assn. Museums (S.E. rep. 1984-87, chmn. mus. assessment program adv. com. 1987-89, treas., v.p. fin. 1990-92, bd. dirs. 1997—, chmn. nature ctr. accreditation com. 1985), Southeastern Museums Conf. (pres. 1982-84), Memphis Museums Roundtable (co-founder). Episcopalian. Home: 330 Belhaven St Memphis TN 38117-1602 Office: Memphis Pink Palace Mus & Planetarium 3050 Central Ave Memphis TN 38111-3316

NOBLE, ERNEST PASCAL, physician, biochemist, educator; b. Baghdad, Iraq, Apr. 2, 1929; came to U.S., 1946; s. Noble Babik and Barkev Grace (Kasparian) Babikian; m. Inga Birgitta Kilstromer, May 19, 1956; children—Lorna, Katharine, Erik. B.S. in Chemistry, U. Calif.-Berkeley, 1951; Ph.D. in Biochemistry, Oreg. State U., 1955; M.D., Case Western Res. U., 1962. Diplomate Nat. Bd. Med. Examiners. Sr. instr. biochemistry Western Res. U., Cleve., 1957-62; intern Stanford Med. Ctr., Calif., 1962-63, resident in psychiatry, 1963-66, research assoc., asst. prof., 1965-69; assoc. prof. psychiatry, psychobiology and pharmacology U. Calif.-Irvine, 1969-71, prof., chief neurochemistry, 1971-76, 79-81; dir. Nat. Inst. Alcohol Abuse and Alcoholism HEW, 1976-78, assoc. adminstr. sci., alcohol, drug abuse and mental health, 1978-79; Pike prof. alcohol studies, dir. Alcohol Research Ctr. UCLA Sch. of Medicine, 1981—. Mem. various med./sci. jour. editorial bds.; contbr. numerous articles to profl. jours., chpts. to books. v.p. Nat. Coun. on Alcoholism 1981-84; pres. Internat. Commn. for the Prevention of Alcoholism and Drug Dependency, 1988. Fulbright scholar, 1955-56; Guggenheim fellow, 1974-75; Sr. Fulbright scholar, 1984-85; recipient Career Devel. award NIMH, HEW, 1966-69. Fellow Am. Coll. Neuropsychopharmacology; mem. Internat. Soc. Neurochemistry, Am. Soc. Pharmacology and Exptl. Therapeutics, Research Soc. on Alcoholism. Office: UCLA 760 Westwood Plz Los Angeles CA 90024-8300

NOBLE, JAMES KENDRICK, JR., media industry consultant; b. N.Y.C., Oct. 6, 1928; s. James Kendrick and Orrel Tennant (Baldwin) N.; m. Norma Jean Rowell, June 16, 1951; children: Anne Rowell, James Kendrick III. Student, Princeton U., 1945-46; BS, U.S. Naval Acad., 1950; postgrad., USN Gen. Line Sch., 1955-56; MBA, NYU, 1961; postgrad., Sch. Edn., 1962-68. CFA. Commd. ensign USN, 1950; transferred to USNR, 1957; advanced through grades to capt. USNR, 1973; asst. gunnery officer in U.S.S. Thomas E. Fraser, 1950-51; student naval aviator USNR, 1951-52, pilot asst. ops. officer, 1952-55; instr. U.S. Naval Acad., 1956-57, Officer Candidate Sch., Newport, R.I., 1958; asst. to pres. Noble & Noble, Pub., Inc., N.Y.C., 1957-60, dir. spl. projects, 1960-62, v.p., 1962-65, exec. v.p., 1965-66, dir., 1957-65; dir., v.p. Transl. Pub. Co., N.Y.C., 1958-65, cons., 1965-66; v.p., dir. Elbon Realty Corp., Bronxville, N.Y., 1960-65; cons. Elbon Realty Corp., Bronxville, 1965-66; comdg. officer NAIRU R2, 1968-70; staff NARS W2, 1970-71, NRID 3-1, 1971-74; comdg. officer NRCSG 302, 1974-76; sr. analyst F. Eberstadt & Co., 1966-69; sr. analyst Auerbach, Pollak & Richardson, 1969-75, v.p., 1972-75, mgr. spl. rsch. projects, 1973-75, dir., 1975; v.p. rsch. Paine, Webber, Jackson & Curtis, Inc., 1975-77, assoc. dir. rsch., 1976-77; v.p. Paine Webber, N.Y.C., 1977-79; 1st v.p. Paine Webber, 1979-91; pres. Noble Cons., Bronxville, 1991-95; bd. dirs. Curriculum Info. Center, Inc., Denver, 1972-78; instl. investor All Am. Rsch. Team, 1972-90. Author: Ploob, 1949, rev., 1956; editor pub.: The Years Between, 1966; also articles in various publs. Mem. Bronxville Bd. Edn., 1968-74, pres., 1970-72; Rep. co-leader 21st Dist., Eastchester, N.Y., 1961-65; dir. Merit; cons., dir. Space and Sci. Train, 1962-63; trustee St. John's Hosp., Yonkers, N.Y., 1972-92, com. chmn., 1980-92. Freedom Forum Ctr. for Media Studies fellow, 1993-94. Fellow emeritus AAAS; mem. Info. Industry Assn. (disting. profl. mem.), Nat. Inst. Social Scis., N.Y. Soc. Security Analysts (mem. com. 1971-91, dir. 1975-84, v.p. 1977-81, exec. v.p.. 1981-82, pres. 1982-83), Am. Textbook Pub. Inst. (com. chmn. 1964-66), AIAA (mem. com. 1957-61), Media and Entertainment Analysts Assn. (pres. 1969-71), Fin. Analysts Fedn. (dir. 1984-87), Naval Res. Assn. (v.p. N.Y. Navy chpt. 1968-76), Wings Club, Siwanoy Country Club. Mem. Reformed Ch. Home: 409 Blue Heron Dr Port Aransas TX 78373 Office: Noble Cons PO Box 2709 Port Aransas TX 78373

NOBLE, JAMES WILKES, actor; b. Dallas, Mar. 5, 1922; s. Ralph Byrne and Lois Frances (Wilkes) N.; m. Carolyn Owen Coates, May 19, 1956; 1 child: Jessica Katherine. Student, North Tex. Coll., Arlington, 1939-41, So. Methodist U., Dallas, 1941-43, 1946-47. lectr. acting and mime Am. Acad. Dramatic Art, 1956-59. Mem. Lydia Tarnower Modern Dance Co., 1937-39; title role in 1st TV drama, The Egoist on Dumont TV, 1943; 1st N.Y. Stage appearance Helena's Room, 1947; 1st Broadway appearance: The Big Knife, 1949; others include: The Velvet Glove, 1949; Medea, 1951; Come of Age, 1952; A Far Country, 1961; Strange Interlude, 1963; 1776, 1971; The Runner Stumbles, 1976; mem. Am. Mime Theatre, 1952-59; appeared in numerous TV dramas and soap operas; appeared in more than 200 plays in theatres throughout the world most recent: Stratford Characters in Stratford-Upon-Avon, England, T.S. Eliot in The Poet's Theatre, Cambridge, Mass., 1996, Out of Order, Calgary, Alta., Can., 1997; TV appearances include the role of the Governor on Benson, ABC-TV, 1979-86, series First Impressions, CBS-TV, 1987—, series Archies, NBC-TV, 1990—, Law and Order, 1991; movies include: Dragonfly, 1965; The Sporting Club, 1967; 1776, 1972; Promises in the Dark, 1978; Ten, 1979; Being There, 1979; Airplane II, 1983; You Talkin' To Me?, 1986; Tiger's Tale, 1987, Chances Are, 1988, Absent Minded Professor, 1989, Law and Order, 1991, All My Children, 1992; numerous other appearances. Author jour. article on Am. mime. Served as lt. USNR, 1943-46, P.T.O. Named Hon. Gov., N.J., N.Y., 1982; appreciation award Am. Heart Assn., 1983. Mem. Actors Studio (life), Actors Equity, SAG, AFTRA. Democrat. Roman Catholic. Avocation: Photography. Office: Paradigm Agy 10100 Santa Monica Blvd Los Angeles CA 90067-4003

NOBLE, JOSEPH VEACH, fine arts administrator; b. Phila., Apr. 3, 1920; s. Joseph Haderman and Helen Elizabeth (Veach) N.; m. Olive Ashley Mooney, June 21, 1941 (dec. Sept. 1978); children: Josette, Ashley, Laurence; m. Lois Cook Cartwright, Oct. 27, 1979. Student, U. Pa., 1942. Cameraman, dir. DeFrenes and Co. Studios, Phila., 1939-41; studio mgr. WPTZ, Philco TV Sta., Phila., 1941-42, DeFrenes and Co. Studios, 1946-49; gen. mgr. Murphy-Lillis Prodns., N.Y.C., 1949-50; exec. v.p. Film Counselors, Inc., N.Y.C., 1950-56, dir., 1950-82; operating adminstr. Met. Mus. Art, 1956-67, vice dir. adminstrn., 1967-70; dir. Mus. City N.Y., 1970-85; exec. dir. Soc. Medalists, 1985-95; photog. salon exhibitor, from 1936; lectr. CCNY, 1949-51. Author: The Techniques of Painted Attic Pottery, 1965, The Historical Murals of Maplewood, 1961, Forgery of the Etruscan Terracotta Warriors, 1961; Contbr.: Ency. Brit, 1970. Trustee Corning Mus. of Glass, 1970—; mem. Morrow Meth. Ch., pres. trustees, 1972-77; chmn. N.Y. State Bd. Hist. Preservation 1972-76; co-chmn. Save Venice, Inc., 1972; trustee Brookgreen Gardens, 1971—, pres., 1976-90, chmn., 1990-95, chmn. emeritus, 1995—. With AUS, 1942-46. Recipient Venice Film Festival medal for photography in sci., 1948, Sigma Xi award 1963, Maple Leaf award Maplewood, N.J., 1966, 87, Gold medal for The Big Apple N.Y. Film Festival, 1979, Disting. Svc. award Maplewood C. of C., 1987. Fellow Soc. Antiquaries London; mem. N.Y. State Assn. Museums (pres. 1970-72), NAD (medal 1976), Nat. Sculpture Soc. (medal 1978, 91), Artists' Fellowship (medal 1978), Archeol. Inst. Am. (treas. 1963-70), Museums Council N.Y.C. (chmn. 1965-67), Am. Assn. Museums (pres. 1975-78, Disting. Svc. Awd., 1991), Cultural Instns. Group N.Y.C. (chmn. 1984-85), Soc. Promotion Hellenic Studies; Am. Watercolor Soc. (medal 1982). Clubs: Maplewood Country; Explorers (N.Y.C.), Century Assn. (N.Y.C.). Home: 107 Durand Rd Maplewood NJ 07040-2103 Office: Brookgreen Gardens Murrells Inlet SC 29576 *As a classical archaeologist I always have been guided by the ancient saying, "Let the light of the past illumine a pathway to the future.*

NOBLE, MARION ELLEN, retired home economist; b. Blanchardville, Wis., Feb. 18, 1914; d. Dwight Eldridge and Doris Edna (Parkinson) Baker; m. B. Frank Smyth (dec. 1979); children: William, Ann Smyth Marris, Robert, Larry, Margaret Smyth Decker; m. George C. Noble, 1981. BS, U. Wis., Madison, 1936. V.p. Smyth Bus Systems, Canton, Ohio, 1950; womens editor Radio Station WFAH, Alliance, Ohio, 1952-58; home economist extension svc. Stark County, Ohio State U., Canton, 1961-70. Contbr. articles to profl. jours. Named Woman of the Year Urban League, Canton, 1964. Mem. AAUW, Nat. Assn. Extension Home Economists, Pacific Pioneer Broadcasters, Home Econs. Club, Thimble Collectors Internat., Ladies Oriental Shrine of North Am., Phi Upsilon Omicron, Epsilon Sigma Phi. Republican. Methodist. Avocations: needlework, collecting thimbles and antique sewing items. Home: 3240 San Amadeo # A Laguna Hills CA 92653-3037

NOBLE, MERRILL EMMETT, retired psychology educator, psychologist; b. Las Vegas, N.Mex., July 25, 1923; s. Merrill Emmett and Martha (Van Petten) N.; m. Joy Lind, July 18, 1953; children: Margaret Lind, Eric Severin. B.A., N.Mex. Highlands U., 1947; M.A., Ohio State U., 1949, Ph.D., 1951. Research asso. Ohio State U., 1951-54, summers 1956, 58; mem. faculty Kans. State U., 1954-67, prof. psychology, 1961-67, chmn. dept., 1962-67; prof. psychology Pa. State U., 1967-89, chmn. dept., 1967-77, ret., 1989; Vis. scientist Inst. for Perception TNO, Soesterberg, Netherlands, 1973-74, 77-78, 80, also NATO vis. lectr. several univs. Mem. editorial bd. Psychol. Bull., 1963-64, Jour. Exptl. Psychology, 1967-78, Acta Psychologica, 1978-82, Human Performance, 1987-92. Bd. dirs. Environ. Research Found., Topeka, 1965-68. Fellow APA (com. on adv. svcs. for edn. and tng. 1967-70, accreditation com. 1979-82), AAAS, Psychonomic Soc., Midwestern Psychol. Assn. (mem. coun. 1967-70), Sigma Xi. Home: 2562 Calle Delfino Santa Fe NM 87505-6488

NOBLE, PHILLIP D., lawyer; b. Oakland, Calif., Aug. 1, 1946. BA, AD in Bus., U. Wash., 1968, JD, 1971. Bar: Wash. 1971. Law clk. to Hon. Morell Sharp Wash. State Supreme Ct., 1971, U.S. Dist. Ct. (we. dist.) Wash., 1972; with Helsell, Fetterman LLP, Seattle. Editor: Justice on Trial, 1971. Mem. ABA, Wash. State Bar Assn., Seattle-King County Bar Assn. Office: Helsell Fetterman LLP 1500 Puget Sound Plz 1325 4th Ave Seattle WA 98101-2509

NOBLE, RICHARD LLOYD, lawyer; b. Oklahoma City, Oct. 11, 1939; s. Samuel Lloyd and Eloise Joyce (Millard) N. AB with distinction, Stanford, 1961, LLB, 1964. Bar: Calif. 1964. Assoc. firm Cooper, White & Cooper, San Francisco, 1965-67; assoc., ptnr. firm Voegelin, Barton, Harris & Callister, Los Angeles, 1967-70; ptnr. Noble & Campbell, Los Angeles, San Francisco, 1970—; dir. Langdale Corp., L.A., Gt. Pacific Fin. Co., Sacramento; lectr. Tax Inst. U. So. Calif., 1970; mem. bd. law and bus. program Stanford Law Sch. Contbr. articles to legal jours. Bd. govs. St. Thomas Aquinas Coll. Recipient Hilmer Dehlman Jr. award Stanford Law Sch., 1962; Benjamin Harrison fellow Stanford U., 1967. Mem. ABA, State Bar Calif., L.A. Bar Assn., San Francisco Bar Assn., Commercial Club (San Francisco), Petroleum Club (L.A.), Capitol Hill Club (Washington), Pi Sigma Alpha. Republican. Home: 2222 Ave Of Stars Los Angeles CA 90067-5655 Office: Noble & Campbell 333 N Grand Ave Los Angeles CA 90012-2622

NOBLE, RONALD KENNETH, government official, lawyer; b. Ft. Dix, N.J., Sept. 24, 1956. BA cum laude, U. N.H., 1979; JD, Stanford U., 1982. Bar: Pa. 1983, N.J., 1983. Sr. law clk. to Hon. A. Leon Higginbotham Jr. U.S. Ct. Appeals for 3d Cir., Phila., 1982-84; asst. U.S. atty. for ea. dist. Pa. Office Atty. Gen., Phila., 1984-88; with U.S. Dept. Justice, Phila., 1988-89, dep. asst. atty. gen., chief staff, spl. counsel criminal divsn., 1988-89; assoc. prof. law NYU Sch. Law, 1989—; asst. sec. for enforcement U.S. Dept. Treasury, Washington, 1993-94, under sec. for enforcement, 1994-96; pres. Fin. Action Task Force, 1994—; mem. exec. com. INTERPOL, 1994—; mem. Root-Tilden Scholar Selection Bd., 1990—; chmn. Customs Ops. Adv. Com., 1993—; chmn. Bank Secrecy Act Adv. Com., 1993—. Articles editor Stanford Law Rev., 1981-82. Mem. Am. Law Inst. Office: NY U Sch of Law 40 Washington Sq S Rm 314 New York NY 10012-1005*

NOBLE, RONALD MARK, sports medicine facility administrator; b. Atlanta, Dec. 28, 1950; s. Dexter Ron and Judy (Puckett) N.; m. Teresa Lowder, Sept. 20, 1975; children: Kimberly, Heather, James, Ashlee. AS, Ricks Coll., 1974; BS cum laude, Troy State U., 1976; MS, U. Tenn., 1977. Grad. asst. U. Tenn., Knoxville, 1976-77; lectr. Tex. A&M U., College Station, 1977-79; asst. prof. U.S. Mil. Acad., West Point, N.Y., 1979-80; dir. clin. phys. NASA Med. Ctr., MSFC, 1980-85; exec. dir. Total Wellness Ctr., Huntsville, Ala., 1986-90, Preventive and Rehab. Sports Medicine Assocs., Huntsville, 1990—; clin. advisor Huntsville Med. Sch., U. Ala., 1990—, exec. dir. preventive and clin. advisor, preceptor, 1992—; adj. prof. U. Ala., Huntsville, 1982-85; sports medicine cons. Mex. Olympic Com., San Luis Potosi, 1980, Duke U. Basketball, Durham, N.C., 1987-95, U.S. Olympic Team, 1994-96; coord. U.S. Olympic Com. Nat. Rehab. Network; cons. USAF Dept. Manned Space Flight Ops., L.A., 1983-84, athletic dept. Ala. A&M U., 1994—; asst. coach U.S. Olympic Com., Colorado Springs, 1979-83; spl. advisor Pres. Coun. on Phys. Fitness and Sports, Huntsville, 1991; clin. advisor, preceptor U. Ala. Huntsville Med. Sch. Developer computer software in field; contbr. articles to profl. jours., also to USAF manual. Campaign mgr. Brooks for State Legislature, Huntsville, 1992; bd. dirs. Huntsville Boys Club, 1988-89, Big Bros./Sisters of No. Ala., Huntsville, 1988-89, Ala. affiliate Am. Heart Assn., Huntsville, 1980-88; commr. Ala. Gov.'s Com. on Phys. Fitness, 1991-94; mem. U.S. Olympic Com. Spkrs. Bur., 1978-80; U.S. Olympic Com., Nat. Rehab. Network for Elite Athletes. With U.S. Army, 1970-73, Vietnam. Named Outstanding Leader Jaycees of Ala., 1983; Paul Harris fellow Huntsville Rotary Club, 1987—. Mem. Huntsville Rotary (Paul Harris fellow), Kappa Delta Pi. Mem. LDS Ch. Avocations: family activities, sports, woodworking, gardening, service to others. Office: PRSM Sports Therapy 4715 Whitesburg Dr S Ste 200 Huntsville AL 35802-1632

NOBLE, (TERRY) THOM, film editor. Editor: (films) Fahrenheit 451, 1966, The Man Who Had Power over Women, 1970, Senza Ragione, 1972, And Now for Something Completely Different, 1972, The Strange Vengeance of Rosalie, 1972, The Apprenticeship of Duddy Kravitz, 1974, (with Peter Thornton) Rosebud, 1975, Inside Out, 1976, Joseph Andrews, 1977, Black Joy, 1977, Who Is Killing the Great Chefs of Europe?, 1978, All Things Bright and Beautiful, 1979, Boardwalk, 1979, Improper Channels, 1981, Tattoo, 1981, Red Dawn, 1984, Witness, 1985 (Academy award best film editing 1985), Poltergeist II: The Other Side, 1986, The Mosquito Coast, 1986, Switching Channels, 1988, Winter People, 1989, Mountains of the Moon, 1990, Thelma and Louise, 1991 (Academy award nomination best film editing 1991), Body of Evidence, 1993, The Hudsucker Proxy, 1994; editor, visual cons.: (films) First Blood, 1982; editorial cons.: (films) North Dallas Forty, 1979, Uncommon Valor, 1983; editor, prodn. designer: (films) Final Analysis, 1992. Office: The Gersh Agency 232 N Canon Dr Beverly Hills CA 90210-5302*

NOBLES, LAURENCE HEWIT, retired geology educator; b. Spokane, Sept. 28, 1927; s. Harry and Florence (Giffin) N.; m. Barbara Joanne Smith, Aug. 28, 1948; children: Heather C., Laurence F. BS, Calif. Inst. Tech., 1949, MS, 1949; PhD, Harvard, 1952. Instr. geology Northwestern U., 1952-55, asst. prof., 1955-61, assoc. prof., 1961-67, prof., 1967-90, prof. emeritus, 1990—; also asst. dean Northwestern U. (Coll. Arts and Scis.), 1961-67, asso. dean, 1968-70, acting dean, 1970-72, dean adminstrn., 1972-81, v.p. adminstrn. and fin. planning, 1981-86. Trustee Adler Planetarium, 1980-86; faculty rep. Big Ten Conf., 1976-81; trustee Chgo. Acad. Scis., 1967-87, pres., 1973-78, hon. trustee, 1987—. Mem. Am. Geophys. Union, Geol. Soc. Am.

NOBLETT, RUSSELL DON, medical and computer consultant; b. Lubbock, Tex., Oct. 25, 1957; s. Clois and Margaret (Scott) N. BA in Philosophy, North Tex. U., 1982; MD, U. Tex., Dallas, 1989. Resident internal medicine U. Va., Roanoke, 1992; cons.-liaison attending in internal medicine residency U. Va. Sch. Medicine, Roanoke, 1993-94, clin. instr. in internal medicine residency, 1994-95; chief emergency medicine VA Med. Ctr., Salem, Va., 1994-95; pres., owner, chief med. cons. in clin. software design Deming Internat. Cons.: Computer Cons. to Physicians, Roanoke, 1995—. Vol. physician Bradley Free Clinic, Roanoke, 1992—. Recipient Extra-Mile award for vol. work as a resident Bradley Free Clinic, Roanoke, 1992. Mem. ACP, Roanoke Acad. Medicine. Avocations: clinical computer software design, volunteer work. Home: PO Box 21561 Roanoke VA 24018 Office: Deming Internat Cons PO Box 20371 Roanoke VA 24018

NOBLIN, CHARLES DONALD, clinical psychologist, educator; b. Jackson, Miss., Dec. 16, 1933; s. Charles Thomas and Margaret (Byrne) N.; m. Patsy Ann Beard, Aug. 12, 1989. BA, Miss. Coll., 1955; MS, Va. Commonwealth U., 1957; PhD, La. State U., 1962. Lic. psychologist, Miss., N.J., N.C. Instr. to asst. prof. La. State U., Baton Rouge, 1961-63; asst. to assoc. prof. U. N.C., Greensboro, 1963-66; assoc. prof. Rutgers Med. Sch., New Brunswick, N.J., 1966-69; dir. clin. training Va. Commonwealth U., Richmond, 1969-72; chmn. dept. psychology Va. Tech., Blacksburg, 1972-82; dir. clin. training U. So. Miss., Hattiesburg, 1982-85, chmn. dept. psychology, 1985-91, prof., 1991-93, dir. clin. tng., 1993—. Contbr. over 60 articles and presentations. Recipient Clin. Tng. grant NIMH, 1983-86, Victim Behavior & Personal Space rsch. grant U.S. Dept. Justice, 1970-71, Trubeck Found. Rsch. award, 1968-69. Baptist. Avocation: antique art glass. Home: 7 Cane Cove Hattiesburg MS 39402-8716 also: PO Box 10036 Hattiesburg MS 39406-1000 Office: U So Miss Dept Psychology Hattiesburg MS 39406

NOBLITT, HARDING COOLIDGE, political scientist, educator; b. Marion, N.C., Oct. 31, 1920; s. Walter Tate and Nellie Mae (Horton) N.; m. Louise Hope Lester, July 3, 1943; 1 son, Walter Thomas. B.A., Berea Coll., 1942; M.A., U. Chgo., 1947, Ph.D., 1955. Mem. faculty Concordia Coll., Moorhead, Minn., 1950-90, prof. polit. sci., 1956-90, Wije Disting. prof., 1979-82; chmn. dept. Concordia Coll., 1964-72, prof. emeritus, 1990. Mem. editorial bd.: Discourse: A Review of the Liberal Arts, 1957-67, acting editor, 1959-60. Democratic candidate Congress, 1962; del. Dem. Nat. Conv., 1964; chmn. Profs. for Johnson-Humphrey, Minn., 1964; chmn. platform com. Dem. State Conv., 1968; mem. Gov's Citizens Council on Aging, 1963-68; mem. City Charter Commn., Moorhead, 1985—; mem. Minn. Higher Edn. Coordinating Bd., 1971-81, sec., 1974-75, pres., 1979-80. Served with AUS, 1943-46, ETO. Recipient 1st ann. Great Tchr. award Concordia Coll., 1960; recipient Flaat Disting. Service award Concordia Coll., 1982. Mem. Am. Polit. Sci. Assn., Am. Legion, Phi Kappa Phi, Pi Gamma Mu, Tau Kappa Alpha, Pi Kappa Delta. Presbyterian (elder). Home: 2014 4th St S Moorhead MN 56560-4131 Office: Concordia Coll Dept Polit Sci Moorhead MN 56560

NOBLITT, NANCY ANNE, aerospace engineer; b. Roanoke, Va., Aug. 14, 1959; d. Jerry Spencer and Mary Louise (Jerrell) N. BA, Mills Coll., Oakland, Calif., 1982; M.S. in Indsl. Engring., Northeastern U., 1990. Data red specialist, Universal Energy Systems, Beaver Creek, Ohio, 1981; aerospace engr. turbine engine div. components br. turbine group aero-propulsion lab. Wright-Patterson AFB, Ohio, 1982-84, engine assessment br. spl. engines group, 1984-87; lead analyst cycle methods computer aided engr. Gen. Electric Co., Lynn Mass., 1987-90, Lynn PACES project coord., 1990-91; software systems analyst Sci. Applications Internat. Corp., with artificial intelligence Sci. Applications Internat. Corp., Mc Lean, Va., 1991-92, software engring. mgr., intelligence applications integration, Sci. Applications Internat. Corp., Hampton, Va., 1992-93, mgr. test engring. and systems support, 1993-94, mgr. configuration mgmt., 1994, mgmt. asst. to TBMCS program mgr., 1994-95; sr. simulation engr. Chem Demil, 1995—. Math and sci. tutor Centerville Sch. Bd., Ohio, 1982-86, math. and physics tutor Marblehead Sch. Bd., Mass., 1988-90; tutor math, chemistry & physics Poquoson Sch. Bd., Va., 1994—; rep. alumnae admissions Mills Coll., Boston area, 1987-91; mem. bd. trustees/bd. govs. Mills Coll., 1995—; mem. Citizens for Hilton Area Revitalization, 1994—. Recipient Notable Achievement award U.S. Air Force, 1984; recipient Special award Fed. Lab. Consortium, 1987. Mem. Soc. Mfg. Engrs. (sec., exec. bd. 1997—). Avocation: book collecting. Home: 58 Hopkins St Newport News VA 23601-4034 Office: Sci Applications Internat Corp Hampton VA 23666

NOCAS, ANDREW JAMES, lawyer; b. Los Angeles, Feb. 2, 1941; s. John Richard and Muriel Phyliss (Harvey) N.; 1 child, Scott Andrew. B.S., Stanford U., 1962, J.D., 1964. Bar: Calif. 1965. Assoc. Thelen, Marrin, Johnson & Bridges, Los Angeles, 1964-71, ptnr., 1972-91; pvt. practice L.A., 1992—; del. Calif. Bar Conv., 1972-92. Served to capt. JAGC, USAR. Fellow Am. Bar Found.; mem. Los Angeles County Bar Assn. (chmn. sect. law office mgmt. 1980-82, chair errors & ommissions com. 1987-88, chair litigation sect. 1988-89), ABA (chmn. arbitration com. 1981), Am. Bd. Trial Advocates, Los Angeles County Bar Found. (trustee 1992—). Office: 201 N Figueroa St Ste 1300 Los Angeles CA 90012-2636

NOCE, WALTER WILLIAM, JR., hospital administrator; b. Neptune, N.J., Sept. 27, 1945; s. Walter William and Louise Marie (Jenkins) N.; m. Cinda Ann Miller, Apr. 15, 1967; children: Krista Suzanne, David Michael. B.A., LaSalle Coll., Phila., 1967; M.P.H., UCLA, 1969. Regional coordinator USPHS, Rockville, Md., 1969-71; v.p. Hollywood Presbyn. Hosp., Los Angeles, 1971-75; sr. v.p. Hollywood Presbyn. Med. ctr., 1975-77; v.p. adminstrn. Huntington Meml. Hosp, Pasadena, Calif., 1977-83; pres., chief exec. officer St. Joseph Hosp., Orange, Calif., 1983-90; pres. so. Calif. region St. Joseph Health System, 1987-90, exec. v.p., 1990-94; pres., CEO Children's Hosp., L.A., 1995—; preceptor UCLA Health Services Mgmt. Program, 1977—; chmn. bd. Health Plan of Am., 1985-91; chmn. Hosp. Coun. So. Calif., 1989. Exec. v.p. Mental Health Assn. in Los Angeles County, 1979-82; regional v.p. Calif. Mental Health Assn., 1982-83. W. Glenn Ebersole finalist Assn. Western Hosp., 1969; recipient USPHS letter commendation, 1971, leadership in health affairs award Healthcare Assn. So. Calif., 1997. Mem. Am. Coll. Hosp. Adminstrs., Am. Hosp. Assn. (ho. of dels. 1994—), Nat. Assn. Children's Hosps. (bd. dirs. 1995—), Calif. Assn. Cath. Hosps. (chmn. 1990-91), Calif. Assn. Hosps. and Health Sys. (chmn. 1992), UCLA Hosp. Adminstrn. Alumni Assn. (pres. 1979-80), Pasadena C. of C. (v.p. 1980-82). Home: 20388 Via Marwah Yorba Linda CA 92886-4522 Office: Children's Hosp Los Angeles 4650 W Sunset Blvd Los Angeles CA 90027-6062 *Ambition is necessary for success, but success achieved at the expense of others is failure.*

NOCHIMSON, DAVID, lawyer; b. Paterson, N.J., June 19, 1943; s. Samuel S. and Mildred (Singer) N.; m. Roberta Maizel, June 5, 1966 (div. 1972); m. Gail Burgess, May 26, 1978. BA, Yale U., 1965; LLB, Columbia U., 1968; LLM, Australian Nat. U., Canberra, 1969. Bar: N.Y. 1970, Calif. 1977. Assoc. Paul, Weiss, Rifkind, Wharton and Garrison, N.Y.C., 1970-72; sr. v.p. Comprop Equities Corp., N.Y.C., 1972-76; assoc. Mitchell, Silberberg and Knupp, L.A., 1977-80, ptnr., 1980-83; ptnr. Ziffren, Brittenham, Branca & Fischer, L.A., 1983—; adv. com. UCLA Entertainment Symposium, 1979—, co-chmn., 1981-82. Contbr. articles to Encyclopedia of Investments, 1982, profl. jours. Pres. Friends of the L.A. Free Clinic, 1994-96; trustee Santa Monica (Calif.) Mus. of Art, 1995—. Fulbright scholar, Australia, 1968-69. Mem. ABA (forum com. on entertainment and sports industries 1982—, editor The Entertainment and Sports Lawyer 1982-89, chmn. 1989-92), Internat. Bar Assn. (Vice chmn. entertainment com. 1986-90), Am. Bar Found., Beverly Hills Bar Assn. Democrat. Jewish. Avocations: tennis, racquetball, playing piano, hiking. Office: Ziffren Brittenham Branca & Fischer 1801 Century Park W Los Angeles CA 90067-6406

NOCHMAN, LOIS WOOD KIVI (MRS. MARVIN NOCHMAN), educator; b. Detroit, Nov. 5, 1924; d. Peter K. and Annetta Lois (Wood) Kivi; AB, U. Mich., 1946, AM, 1949; m. Harold I. Pitchford, Sept. 6, 1944 (div. May 1949); children: Jean Wood Pitchford Horiszny, Joyce Lynn Pitchford Undiano; m. Marvin A. Nochman, Aug. 15, 1953; 1 child, Joseph Asa. Tchr. adult edn., Honolulu, 1947, Ypsilanti (Mich.) H.S., 1951-52; spl. instr. English, Wayne State U., Detroit, 1953, 54; tchr. Highland Park (Mich.) Coll., 1950-51, instr. English, 1954-83. Mem. exec. bd. Highland Park Fedn. Tchrs., 1963-66, 71-72, mem. 1st bargaining team, 1965-66, 73, del. to Nat. Conv., 1964, 71-74, rep. higher edn. to Mich. Fedn. Tchrs. Exec. Com., 1972-76; mem. faculty adv. com. Gov.'s Commn. on Higher Edn., 1973—. Tchr. Baha'i schs., Davison, Mich., 1954-55, 58-59, 63-66, Beaulac, Que., Can., 1960, Greenacre, Maine, 1965; sec. local spiritual assembly Baha'is, Ann Arbor, 1953, sec., Detroit, 1954, chmn., 1955; mem. nat. com. Baha'is U.S., 1955-68; sec. Davison Bahai Sch. Com. and Council, 1956, 58, 63-68; Baha'i lectr. Subject of local TV show Senior Focus, 1992. Mem. NOW, Modern Lang. Assn., Nat. Coun. Tchrs. English, Mich. Coll. English Assn., Am. Fedn. Tchrs., Nat. Soc. Lit. and Arts, Women's Equity and Action League (sec. Mich. chpt. 1975-79), Alpha Lambda Delta, Alpha Gamma Delta. Contbr. poems to mags. Recipient Women's Movement plaque Women Lawyers Assn. Mich., 1975, Lawrence award Mich. Masters Swimming, 1991, 10 World Master Records In Age Group short course meters, 1994 Long Course Meters, 1995, 96, 23 Nat. Masters Records, 1994-96, 6 Nat. YMCA records, 1995, 2 U.S. Nat. Sr. Sports Classic Records, 1995, 2 World Sr. Games Records, 1993, All-Am. award, 1990-96, U.S. MS Long Distance All Star, 1995, U.S. MS Finals All Star, 1995, 6 World Sr. Games Records, 1996, MS Long Distance All Star, 1996; named one of 10 Best of 1995 Swim Mag. Avocation: U.S. Swimming Master Champion.

NOCKS, JAMES JAY, psychiatrist; b. Bklyn., Apr. 17, 1943; s. Henry and Pearl (Klein) N.; m. Ellen Jane Leblang, June 21, 1964; children: Randy, Jason. BA in English Lit., U. Pa., 1964, MD, 1968. Diplomate Nat. Bd. Med. Examiners, Am. Bd. Psychiatry and Neurology (psychiatry and addiction psychiatry), Am. Bd. Med. Mgmt. Rotating intern Chgo. Wesley Meml. Hosp., Northwestern U., 1968-69; resident psychiatry U. Pa., Phila., 1969-73; chief alcoholism program VA Med. Ctr., West Haven, Conn., 1975-87; asst. chief psychiatry svc. VA Med. Ctr., 1978-87; chief staff VA Med. Ctr., Coatesville, Pa., 1987-95; network dir. Balt. VISN, 1995—; sr. resident psychiatry U. Pa., 1971-72, chief resident psychiatry, 1972-73, asst. instr. psychiatry, 1971-73; clin. asst. prof. psychiatry Health Sci. Ctr. U. Tex., San Antonio, 1973-75; asst. clin. prof. psychiatry Yale U. Sch. Medicine, New Haven, 1975-80, assoc. clin. prof. psychiatry, 1980-87; clin. prof. psychiatry and human behavior Jefferson Med. Coll., Phila., 1987-91; prof. psychiatry Temple U. Sch. Medicine, Phila., 1991—. Contbr. chpts. in Psychiatry: Pre-Test, Self-Assessment and Review, 2d edit., 1982, 3d edit., 1984, Alcoholic Liver Disease, 1985; contbr. articles to profl. jours. Mem. exec. com. Med. Alumni Soc., U. Pa., 1989—. Major Med. Corps, USAF, 1973-75. Fellow Am. Psychiat. Assn. (cert. adminstrv. psychiatry Md.), Am. Soc. of Addiction Medicine (cert.), Am. Coll. Physician Execs.; mem. Assn. for Med. Edn. & Rsch. in Substance Abuse, Am. Assn. for Social Psychiatry, Am. Acad. Psychiatrists in Alcoholism & Addictions. Jewish. Avocations: bicycling, tennis, music. Office: VISN 5 849 International Dr Ste 275 Linthicum Heights MD 21090-2231

NODA, MITSUHIKO, diabetologist, medical educator; b. Seki, Gifu, Japan, Mar. 10, 1954; s. Goichi and Shigeko (Nishida) N.; m. Yasuko Hasemura, Nov. 3, 1986; 1 child, Shoko. B in Engring., U. Tokyo, 1976, M in Engring., 1978, MD, 1984. Authorized physician internal medicine, Japan. Resident U. Tokyo, 1984-85, Toshiba Ctrl. Hosp., Tokyo, 1985-86; internist U. Tokyo, 1986-91; asst. prof. Jichi Med. Sch., Omiya, Japan, 1991-95; vis. prof. Cornell U., Ithaca, N.Y., 1995—. Columnist Diabetes Frontier, 1990—; contbr. articles to profl. jours. Mem. AAAS, Am. Diabetes Assn., European Assn. for the Study of Diabetes, Japan Diabetes Soc. Avocations: golfing, singing.

NODDINGS, NEL, education educator, writer; b. Irvington, N.J., Jan. 19, 1929; d. Edward A. Rieth and Nellie A. (Connors) Walter; m. James A. Noddings, Aug. 20, 1949; children: Chris, Howard, Laurie, James, Nancy, William, Sharon, Edward, Vicky, Timothy. BA in Math., Montclair State Coll., 1949; MA in Math., Rutgers U., 1964; PhD in Edn., Stanford U., 1973; PhD (hon.), Columbia Coll., S.C., 1995. Cert. tchr., Calif., N.J. Tchr. Woodbury (N.J.) Publ Schs., 1949-52; tchr. math. dept. Matawan (N.J.) High Sch., 1958-62, chair, asst. prin., 1964-69; curriculum supr. Montgomery Twp. Pub. Schs., Skillman, N.J., 1970-72; dir. precollegiate edn. U. Chgo., 1975-76; asst. prof. Pa. State U., State College, 1973; from asst. prof. to assoc. prof. Stanford (Calif.) U., 1977-86, prof., 1986—, assoc. dean, 1990-92, acting dean, 1992-94, Lee L. Jacks prof. child edn., 1992—; bd. dirs. Ctr. for Human Caring Sch. Nursing, Denver, 1986-92; cons. NIE, NSF and various other sch. dists. Author: Caring: A Feminine Approach to Ethics and Moral Education, 1984, Women and Evil, 1989, (with W. Paul Shore) Awakening the Inner Eye: Intuition in Education, 1984, (with Carol Witherell) Stories Lives Tell, 1991, The Challenge to Care in Schools, 1992, Educating for Intelligent Belief or Unbelief, 1993, Philosophy of Education, 1995, (with Suzanne Gordon and Patricia Benner) Caregiving, 1996. Mem. disting. women's adv. bd. Coll. St. Catherine. NSF fellow Rutgers U., 1962-64; recipient Anne Roe award for Contbns. to Profl. devel. of Women, Harvard Grad. Sch. Edn., 1993, medal for disting. svc. Tchrs. Coll. Columbia, 1994, Spencer Mentor grant, 1995-97, grant Nat. Acad. Edn., 1996—. Fellow Philosophy of Edn. Soc. (pres. 1991-92); mem. Am. Ednl. Rsch. Assn., Am. Philos. Assn., John Dewey Soc. (pres. 1994-96), Phi Beta Kappa (vis. scholar), Kappa Delta Pi. Avocation: gardening. Office: Stanford U Sch of Edn Stanford CA 94305

NODDINGS, SARAH ELLEN, lawyer; b. Matawan, N.J.; d. William Clayton and Sarah Stephenson (Cox) Noddings; children: Christopher, Aaron. BA in Math., Rutgers U., New Brunswick, N.J., 1965, MSW, 1968; JD cum laude, Seton Hall U., Newark, 1975; postgrad., UCLA, 1979. Bar: Calif. 1976, Nev. 1976, N.J. 1975, U.S. Dist. Ct. (ctrl. dist.) Calif. 1976, U.S. Dist. Ct. N.J. 1975. Social worker Carteret (N.J.) Bd. Edn., 1970-75; law clk. Hon. Howard W. Babcock, 8th Jud. Dist. Ct., Las Vegas, Nev., 1975-76; assoc. O'Melveny & Myers, L.A., 1976-78; atty. Internat. Creative Mgmt., Beverly Hills, Calif., 1978-81, Russell & Glickman, Century City, Calif., 1981-83; atty. Lorimar Prodns., Culver City and Burbank, Calif., 1983-87, v.p., 1987-93; atty. Warner Bros. TV, Burbank, Calif., 1993—, v.p., 1993—. Dir. county youth program, rsch. analyst Sonoma County People for Econ. Opportunity, Santa Rosa, Calif., 1968-69; VISTA vol. Kings County Cmty. Action Orgn., Hanford, Calif., 1965-66; officer, PTA bd. Casimir Mid. Sch. and Arlington Elem. Sch. Mem. Acad. TV Arts and Scis. (nat. awards com. 1994—), L.A. Copyright Soc. (trustee 1990-91), Women in Film, L.A. County Bar Assn. (intellectual property sect.), Women Entertainment Lawyers, Media Dist. Intellectual Propr. Bar Assn. Avocations: travel, tennis, skiing, bicycling, swimming. Office: Warner Bros TV 300 Television Plz Burbank CA 91505-1372

NODEEN, JANEY PRICE, government official; b. Scotland Neck, N.C., Nov. 7, 1959; d. Wade Hampton and Joyce Ann (Councill) P.; m. Thomas Nodeen. BS in Computer Sci., Christopher Newport Coll., 1987; grad., Def. Sys. Mgmt. Coll., 1994; grad. advanced mgmt. program, Nat. Def. U., 1995. Engring. analyst Newport News (Va.) Shipbldg., 1978-86; mgr. submarine info. resources and computer ops. Dept. of the Navy, Washington, 1986-93, mem. exec. devel. program, 1993-96, sr. staff Navy Acquisition Reform Exec., 1995, dep. program exec. officer Submarines for Acquisition, 1996—; mil. legis. fellow for Congressman Sam Gejdenson, 1994; sr. exec. fellow John F. Kennedy Sch. Govt. Harvard U., class officer, 1994. Home: 6915 Ashbury Dr Springfield VA 22152-3221 Office: PEO SUB Ste 6e08 2531 Jefferson Davis Hwy Arlington VA 22242-0001

NODINE, LOREN L., critical care nurse, consultant; b. East St. Louis, Ill., Aug. 13, 1934; s. Hester Ruth Robinson (dec.); m. Billie R. Nodine, June 4, 1981 (dec.); children: Nancy, Kathy, Larry, Cynthia.; m. Debra J. Nodine, Sept., 1996. BSN, So. Ill. U., 1973; M in Vocat. Edn., U. N.Mex., 1983. Cert. trauma nurse specialist, cardiovascular nurse. Charge nurse St. Elizabeth's Med. Ctr., Granite City, Ill.; staff and charge nurse Lovelace Med. Ctr., Albuquerque; paramedic clin. instr. Albuquerque Fire Dept.; staff nurse St. Joseph Med. Ctr., Albuquerque. Mem. AACCN, Am. Heart Assn. Home: 1618 Hwy 63 Walnut Ridge AR 72476

NOE, ELNORA (ELLIE NOE), retired chemical company executive; b. Evansville, Ind., Aug. 23, 1928; d. Thomas Noe and Evelyn (West) Dieter. Student Ind. U.-Purdue U., Indpls. Sec., Pitman Moore Co., Indpls., 1946; with Dow Chem. Co., Indpls., 1960-90, pub. rels. asst. then mgr. employee comm., 1970-87, mgr. cmty. rels., 1987-90, DowBrands Inc., 1986-90; vice chmn. corp. affairs discussion group, 1988-89, chmn., 1989-90; mem. steering com. Learn About Bus. Recipient 2d pl. award as Businesswoman of Yr., Indpls. Bus. and Profl. Women's Assn., 1980, Indpls. Profl. Woman of Yr. award Zonta, Altrusa, Soroptomist & Pilot Svc. Clubs, 1985, DowBrands Great Things Cmty. Svc. award, 1991. Mem. Am. Bus. Women Assn. (Woman of Yr. award 1965, past pres.), Ind. Assn. Bus. Communicators (hon., Communicator of Yr. 1977), Women in Comm. (Louise Eleanor Kleinhenz award 1984), Zonta (dist. pub. rels. chmn. 1978-80, area dir. 1980-82, pres. Indpls. 1977-79, bd. dirs. 1993-95), Dow Indpls. Retiree Club (pres. 1995—).

NOE, FRED J., sports association administrator; b. Germany, May 19, 1936; m. Elizabeth Noe.; B Arts and Scis. in Fin., Northwestern U. Divsn. mgr. Eaton Corp.; CEO Stihl Inc., 1978-93; exec. v.p. U.S. Trotting Assn., Columbus, Ohio, 1993—. Office: US Trotting Assn 750 Michigan Ave Columbus OH 43215-1107

NOE, GUY, social services administrator; b. Brussels, Jan. 28, 1934; came to U.S., 1955, naturalized, 1961; s. Marinus Cornelis and Johana Dorothea (Beijne) N.; 1 dau., Jeanette Sue. B.S., Regional Agrl. Sch., Loiret, France, 1954. Social worker State of Wyo., Casper, 1962-66; dir. Natrona County (Wyo.) Dept. Public Assistance, Casper, 1966-79; dir. Wyo. Div. Mental Health, Cheyenne, 1979-82, asst. adminstr. Divsn. of Youth Svcs., 1992—; former mgr. Platte County Office Pub. Assistance and Social Services, Wheatland, Wyo., dir. low income energy assistance programs, 1994-95; lectr. in field. V.p. Wyo. chpt. Big Bros., 1976-77; chmn. adv. coun. social svcs. State of Wyo., 1969-79; bd. dirs. Casper United Way, 1970—, Casper Salvation Army, 1970—, Casper chpt. ARC, 1977—; mem. Gov.'s Drug Abuse Adv. Bd., 1992—; pres. State Employees Assn. Named Outstanding Adminstr. State of Wyo., 1976 ; recipient Youth Svcs. award Wyo. Human Resources Confederation, 1988. Mem. Am. Public Welfare Assn. (Wyo. membership chmn.), Am. Soc. Public Adminstrn., Wyo. State Employees Assn. (pres. 1996-97). Democrat. Club: Toastmasters. Home: 2731 Deming Blvd Cheyenne WY 82001-5709

NOE, JAMES ALVA, retired judge; b. Billings, Mont., May 25, 1932; s. James Alva Sr. and Laura Madlen (Parmenter) N.; m. Patricia Arlene Caudill, Aug. 4, 1956; children: Kendra Sue, Jeffrey James, Bradley John, Kirkwood Merle. BA in Polit. Sci., U. Wash., 1954, LLB, 1957; LittD hon., Christian Theol. Sem., 1986. Bar: Wash. 1958, U.S. Dist. Ct. (we. dist.) Wash. 1958, U.S. Ct. Appeals (9th cir.) 1959. Dep. prosecuting atty. King County, Seattle, 1958-61; trial lawyer Williams, Kastner & Gibbs, Seattle, 1961-67; judge Seattle Mcpl. Ct., 1967-71, King County Superior Ct., 1971-96; ret., 1996. Moderator Christian Ch. (Disciples of Christ) in the U.S. and Can., 1977-79. Fellow Am. Bar Found.; mem. ABA (ho. of dels. 1976-78, 82-87, 91-96, bd. govs. 1991-94, chmn. jud. divsn. 1988-89, nat. conf. state trial judges 1981-82), Wash. State Superior Ct. Judges Assn. (pres. 1984-85), Nat. Jud. Coll. (trustee 1988-91, 95—). Home: 8250 SE 61st St Mercer Island WA 98040-4902

NOE, JERRE DONALD, computer science educator; b. McCloud, Calif., Feb. 1, 1923; s. Charles J. and Mae H. Noe; m. Mary A. Ward, Oct. 20, 1943 (dec.); children: M. Sherill (Mrs. Michael F. Roberts), Jeffrey W., Russell H.; m. Margarete Wöhlert, Sept. 10, 1983. B.S., U. Calif., 1943; Ph.D., Stanford U., 1948. Rsch. assoc. Radio Research Lab. Harvard and Am. Brit. Lab., Malvern, Eng., 1943-45; devel. engr. Hewlett-Packard Co., Palo Alto, Calif., 1946-48; rsch. engr. Stanford Research Inst., Menlo Park, Calif., 1948-53; asst. dir. engring. rsch., 1954-60, exec. dir. info. sci. and engring., 1961-68; prof. computer sci. U. Wash., Seattle, 1968-89, prof. emeritus, 1990—; chmn. dept. U. Wash., 1968-76; lectr. Stanford U., 1955-68; vis. prof. Vrije Universiteit, Amsterdam, 1976-77; guest rsch. scientist Gesellschaft fur Mathematik und Datenverarbeitung (GMD), Bonn, Fed. Republic Germany, 1986-87; mem. Army Sci. Bd., 1984-90; trustee Internat. Computer Sci. Inst., 1991-93; panelist NRC, 1991-92. Mem. Assn. Computing Machinery, IEEE. (nat. chmn. profl. group electronic computers 1956-57), Sigma Xi, Eta Kappa Nu, Tau Beta Pi. Tech. dir., devel. 1st computer for banking industry Bank Am. ERMA system, 1950-56. Home: 7524 34th Ave NW Seattle WA 98117-4723 Office: U Wash Dept Computer Sci & Engring Sieg Hall Box 352350 Seattle WA 98195-2350

NOEHREN, ROBERT, organist, organ builder; b. Buffalo, Dec. 16, 1910; s. Alfred H. and Juliet (Egelhoff) N.; m. Eloise Southern, Aug. 27, 1938; children: Judith, Arthur. Student Inst. Mus. Art, N.Y.C., 1929-30, Curtis Inst. Music, Phila., 1930-31; BMus, U. Mich., 1948; DMus (hon.), Davidson Coll., 1957. Instr., Davidson Coll., 1946-49; prof., univ. organist U. Mich., 1949-77, prof. emeritus, 1977—; vis. prof. Eastman Sch. Music, 1967, U. Kans., 1975; organ builder; important instruments include organ in St. John's Roman Cath. Cathedral, Milw., 1st Unitarian Ch., San Francisco, 1st Presbyn. Ch., Buffalo, St. Andrew's Episc. Ch., Newport News, Va., Calvary Episc. Ch., Rochester, Minn.; designer, cons., 1954—; concert tours of Europe, 1948—; soloist Phila. Orch., Philharmonia Hungarica, New Sinfonia; rec. artist Lyrichord, Urania, Orion, Delos records; spl. research old organs Europe, 17th and 18th century organs in France. Recipient Grande Prix du Disque. Contbr. articles profl. jours. Composer pieces for organ, piano, voice, chorus. Patentee combination action for organs. Home: 17605 Drayton Hall Way San Diego CA 92128-2057

NOEL, DON OBERT, JR., newspaper columnist; b. Elizabeth, N.J., Nov. 27, 1931; s. Don O. and Catherine (Pyle) N.; m. Elizabeth Bradford Foulds, Aug. 29, 1953; 1 child, Emily Rebecca. BA in Am. Studies, Cornell U., 1954. Reporter Hartford (Conn.) Times, 1958-68, asst. mng. editor, 1968-69, editorial page editor, 1969-74, editor in chief, 1974-75; sr. corr. WFSB-TV, host Face the State Post-Newsweek Stas., 1975-84; polit. columnist op-ed page Hartford Courant, 1984—. Bd. sec. Blue Hills Civic Assn., Hartford, 1988—. Served alt. mil. duty Am. Friends Svc. Com., Tokyo, 1954-56. Recipient Sevellon Brown Meml. award New England AP, 1964, Nat. Journalism award AMA, 1972, Nat. Journalism award Am. Soc. Planning Officials, 1972, 74; fellow Alicia Patterson Found., 1966-67; finalist Pulitzer Prize for non-deadline reporting, 1964. Mem. Soc. of Friends. Avocations: gardening, birdwatching, language study. Home: 141 Ridgefield St Hartford CT 06112-1837 Office: Hartford Courant Co Op-Ed Page 285 Broad St Hartford CT 06115-2500

NOEL, EDWIN LAWRENCE, lawyer; b. St. Louis, July 11, 1946; s. Thomas Currie and Christine (Jones) N.; m. Nancy Carter Simpson, Feb. 7, 1970; children: Caroline, Edwin C. BA, Brown U., 1968; JD cum laude, St. Louis U., 1974. Bar: Mo. 1974, U.S. Dist. Ct. (ea. dist.) Mo. 1974, U.S. Ct. Appeals (8th cir.) 1974, U.S. Ct. Appeals (6th cir.) 1978, U.S. Ct. Appeals (7th cir.) 1994, U.S. Supreme Ct. 1986. Ptnr. Armstrong, Teasdale, Schlafly & Davis, St. Louis, 1974—, mng. ptnr., 1993—; bd. dirs. Corley Printing Co., Elcom Industries, St. Louis, Home Fed. Savs. Bank of Mo., 1988-93. Bd. dirs. Edgewood Children's Ctr., St. Louis, 1982-92, St. Louis Assn. for Retarded Citizens, 1984-87, Churchill Sch., 1988-94, Whitfield Sch., 1991—; chmn. Mo. Clean Water Com., Jefferson City, 1982-86; chmn. environ. com. St. Louis Regional Commerce and Growth Assn., 1982-88. Mem. Mo. Bar Assn., Bar Assn. Met. St. Louis, Attys. Liability Assurance Soc. (bd. dirs. 1995—). Republican. Episcopalian. Home: 301 S Mcknight Rd Saint Louis MO 63124-1884 Office: Armstrong Teasdale Schlafly & Davis 1 Metropolitan Sq Saint Louis MO 63102-2733

NOEL, FRANKLIN LINWOOD, federal chief magistrate judge; b. N.Y.C., Dec. 7, 1951; s. Charles Alexander and Mayme (Loth) N.; m. Ellen Barbara Perl, Sept. 15, 1979; children: Kate Alexandra, Charles David. BA, SUNY, Binghamton, 1974; JD, Georgetown U., 1977. Bar: D.C. 1977, U. S. Dist. Ct. D.C. 1978, U.S. Ct. Appeals (D.C. cir.) 1978, Pa. 1979, Minn. 1983, U.S. Ct. Appeals (8th cir.) 1983, U.S. Dist. Ct. Minn. 1984. Assoc. Arnold & Porter, Washington, 1977-79; asst. dist. atty. Phila. Dist. Attys. Office, 1979-83; asst. U.S. atty. U.S. Attys. Office, Mpls., 1983-89; U.S. magistrate judge U.S. Dist. Ct., St. Paul, 1989—; legal writing instr. U. Minn., Mpls., 1989-92, adj. prof. Law Sch., 1996—. Mem. League of Am. Wheelman, Phi Beta Kappa. Episcopalian. Avocation: bicycling. Office: US Dist Ct 300 S 4th St Minneapolis MN 55401-2233

NOEL, LARRY KENNETH, family physician; b. Kirksville, Mo., Oct. 9, 1939; s. Kenneth Carl and Marietta (Waddill) N.; m. Mary Lee Green, Oct. 26, 1963; children: Kent, Lance. BS, No. Mo. State U., 1965; DO, Kirksville Coll. Osteo. Med., 1969. Diplomate Am. Bd. Family Practice. Intern Normandy (Mo.) Osteo. Hosp., 1969-70; active staff Moberly (Mo.) Regional Med. Ctr., 1970—; pvt. practice Moberly, Mo., 1970—. Mayor City of Moberly, 1988—, mem. city coun., 1978—. With USN, 1957-60. Roman Catholic. Avocations: golf, horseback riding. Home: 419 Greenbrier Rd Moberly MO 65270-3214 Office: 1145 S Morley St Moberly MO 65270-1948

NOËL, LAURENT, bishop, educator; b. St. Just de Bretenieres, Que., Can., Mar. 19, 1920; s. Remi and Albertine (Nadeau) N. B.A., Coll. de Levis, 1940; L.Th., Laval U., 1944, L.Ph., 1948; D.Th., Inst. Angelicum, Rome, 1951. Ordained priest Roman Catholic Ch., 1944; prof. theology Laval U., 1946-48, 52-63, prof. ethics Med. Sch., 1952-63; vice rector Grand Sem., Sch. Theology, 1961-63; aux. bishop Que., 1963-74; apostolic administr. Diocese of Hauterive, 1974-75; bishop Diocese of Trois-Rivieres, Que., 1975—; Provincial chaplain Assn. des Infirmieres Catholiques, 1958—; chaplain Syndicat Profl. des Infirmieres Catholiques, 1958-63. Author: Precis de morale medicale, 1962. Address: 2 Rue Port Daubhim St, Succhz CP 459, PQ Canada G1R 4R6*

NOEL, NICHOLAS, III, lawyer; b. Pottstown, Pa., June 5, 1952; s. Nicholas Jr. and Elaine (Buckwalter) N.; m. Karen Bean Schomp, Oct. 28, 1978; children: Carol Elaine, Nicholas IV. BA magna cum laude, Lehigh U., 1974; JD, U. Detroit, 1977. Bar: Pa. 1977, U.S. Dist. Ct. (ea. dist.) Pa. 1979, U.S. Ct. Appeals (3rd cir.) 1980, U.S. Supreme Ct. 1986, U.S. Dist. Ct. (mid. dist.) Pa. 1989. Assoc. Hahalis Law Office, Bethlehem, Pa., 1977-84; assoc. Teel, Stettz, Shimer & DiGiacomo, Easton, Pa., 1984-87; ptnr. Teel, Stettz, Shimer & DiGiacomo, Easton, 1987—, sr. litigation ptnr., 1989—; adj. prof. Northampton County C.C., Bethlehem, 1990; solicitor Chiefs of Police Assn. of Mid. Ea. Pa., 1977—, Palmer Twp. Zoning Hearing Bd., Easton, 1989—; arbitrator Am. Arbitration Assn., 1986—. Contbr. to several books. Trustee Palmer Twp. Moravian Ch., 1985—; mem. Moravian Ch. No. Province Ch. and Soc. Com., 1990—, Palmer Moravian Day Sch. bd., 1991-94. Named Outstanding Young Man Am., 1974. Fellow Pa. Bar Found.; mem. ABA, Pa. Bar Assn. (civil rights chair 1989-92, vice chair legal edn. com. 1992, profl. stds. com. 1983), Northampton County Bar Assn. (legal ethics and responsibility com. 1987-94, bd. govs. 1991—, treas. 1995, v.p. 1996, pres.-elect 1997, pres. 1998). Avocations: most athletic events, sports. Home: 2840 Green Pond Rd Easton PA 18045-2504 Office: 400 S Greenwood Ave Ste 300 Easton PA 18045-3776

NOEL, RANDALL DEANE, lawyer; b. Memphis, Oct. 19, 1953; s. D.A. and Patricia G. Noel; m. Lissa Johns, May 28, 1977; children: Lauren Elizabeth, Randall Walker. BBA with honors, U. Miss., 1975, JD, 1978. Bar: Miss. 1978, U.S. Dist. Ct. (no. and so. dists.) Miss. 1978, Tenn. 1979, U.S. Dist. Ct. (we., mid. and ea. dists.) Tenn. 1979, U.S. Ct. Appeals (5th and 6th cirs.) 1984, U.S. Supreme Ct. 1986. Assoc. Armstrong, Allen, Braden, Goodman, McBride & Prewitt, Memphis, 1978-85; ptnr. Armstrong, Allen, Prewitt, Gentry, Johnston & Holmes, Memphis, 1985—, mgr. litig. practice group, 1990-94, mgmt. com., 1994-96, 97—. Mem. fin. com. Memphis in May Internat. Festival, 1980-81; pres. Carnival Memphis, 1996; bd. dirs. Christ United Meth. Ch., Memphis, 1984-87, 89-91, chmn. bd. trustees 1993; mem. Leadership Memphis, 1994-95. Fellow Am. Bar Found., Tenn. Bar Found.; mem. ABA (young lawyers divsn., fellow dir. 1988-90, editor The Affiliate newsletter 1987-88, dir. Affiliate Outreach project 1988—, vice chmn. Award of Achievement com. 1986, ALI-ABA bd. 1992-97, litig. sect. com. chair), Am. Counsel Assn. (pres.-elect 1995), Tenn. Bar Assn. (pres. young lawyers divsn. 1990, pres. litig. sect. 1988, bd. govs. 1989—, v.p. 1997, Pres.'s Disting. Svc. award 1988, 89), Memphis and Shelby Bar Assn. (mem. jud. recommendations, law week nominations and membership coms.), Miss. Bar Assn., Def. Rsch. Inst., Tenn. Def. Lawyers Assn., Am. Judicature Soc. (bd. dirs. 1992—). Home: 2938 Tishomingo Ln Memphis TN 38111-2627 Office: Armstrong Allen Prewitt Gentry Johnston & Holmes Brinkley Plaza 80 Monroe Ave Ste 700 Memphis TN 38103-2467

NOËL HUME, IVOR, retired archaeologist, consultant; b. London, Eng., 1927; s. Cecil and Gladys Mary (Bagshaw Mann) Noël H. Student, Framlingham Coll., Suffolk, 1936-39, St. Lawrence Coll., Kent, 1942-44; LHD (hon.), U. Pa., 1976, Coll. William and Mary, 1983. Archaeologist Guildhall Mus. Corp., London, 1949-57; chief archaeologist Colonial Williamsburg, Va., 1957-64; dir. dept. archaeology Colonial Williamsburg, 1964-72, resident archaeologist, 1972-87, ret., 1987; consulting curator Winthrop Rockefeller Archaeology Mus., 1987—; guest curator Steuben Glass Co., 1990, dir. Roanoke Project, 1991-93; rsch. assoc. Smithsonian Instn., 1959—; archaeol. cons. to Govt. of Jamaica, 1967-69; vice chmn. gov.'s adv. com. Va. Rsch. Ctr. for Hist. Archaeology, 1967-70, mem., 1971-76; mem. Va. Historic Landmarks Bd., 1985-87; mem. rev. Panel NEH, 1973-77; mem. Coun. Inst. Early Am. History and Culture, 1974-77; chair Jamestown Rediscovery Adv. Bd., 1994-95. Author: Archaeology in Britain, 1953, (with Audrey Noël Hume) Tortoises, Terrapins and Turtles, 1954, Treasure in the Thames, 1956, Great Moments in Archaeology, 1957, Here Lies Virginia, 1963, 1994, 1775: Another Part of the Field, 1966, Historical Archaeology, 1969, Artifacts of Early America, 1970, All the Best Rubbish, 1974, Early English Delftware, 1977, Martin's Hundred, 1982, The Virginia Adventure, 1994, Shipwreck: History from the Bermuda Reefs, 1995, In Search of This and That, 1996; contbr. articles to profl. jours.; Writer-dir.: (film) Doorway to the Past, 1968; writer, narrator: (TV movie) The Williamsburg File, 1976, Search for a Century, 1981; author pseudonymous novels, 1971, 72. Bd. dirs. Jamestown-Yorktown Found., 1987-91, Flowerdew Hundred Found., 1988—, Bermuda Underwater Exploration Inst., 1992—. With Indian Army, 1944-45. Recipient spl. award for hist. archaeology U. S.C., 1975, Achievement award Nat. Soc. Daus. Founders and Patriots Am., 1989, Nat. Soc. Daus. of the Am. Colonists, 1990; named Officer of the Brit. Empire (OBE), 1992. Fellow Soc. Antiquaries London, Am. Antiquarian Soc., Zool. Soc. London; mem. Soc. Hist. Archaeology (Harrington medal 1991), Soc. for Post-Medieval Archaeology (v.p. 1967-76), Kent Archaeol. Soc. (Gt. Britain), Va. Archeol. Soc. (hon., Profl. Archaeologist of Yr. award 1980), English Ceramic Circle, Glass Circle. Home: 2 West Cir Williamsburg VA 23185-1426

NOELKE, PAUL, lawyer; b. La Crosse, Wis., Feb. 10, 1915; s. Carl Bernard and Mary Amelia (O'Meara) N.; m. Mary Jo Kamps, May 4, 1943; children: Paul William, Mary Nesius, Ann Witt, Kate Helms. A.B. magna cum laude, Marquette U., 1936, J.D. cum laude, 1938; LL.M., U. Chgo., 1947; D.H.L. (hon.), Mt. Senario Coll., 1976. Bar: Wis. 1938, D.C. 1975, U.S. Dist. Ct. (ea. dist.) Wis. 1938, U.S. Supreme Ct. 1960. Assoc. firm Miller, Mack & Fairchild, 1938-40; asst. prof. law Marquette U., 1940-42; spl. agt. FBI, 1942-45; assoc. Quarles & Brady and predecessor firms, Milw., 1943-52, ptnr., 1952-85, of counsel, 1985—. Trustee emeritus Viterbo Coll., LaCrosse, Wis.; mem. adv. bd. Cardinal Stritch Coll., Milw.; past chmn. Pres.'s Coun. Marquette U.; past pres. Serra Internat., Chgo.; past chmn. Bd. Tax Rev., Village of Shorewood, Wis. Recipient Alumnus of Yr. award Marquette U., 1980; recipient Conf. award NCCJ, 1967. Mem. ABA, Wis. State Bar Assn., Milw. Bar Assn., Am. Judicature Soc., Order Holy Sepulchre, Alpha Sigma Nu. Roman Catholic. Home: 2462 N Prospect Ave Milwaukee WI 53211-4462 Office: 411 E Wisconsin Ave Milwaukee WI 53202-4409

NOELKEN, MILTON EDWARD, biochemistry educator, researcher; b. St. Louis, Dec. 5, 1935; s. William Henry Noelken and Agnes (Westbrook) Burkemper; m. Carol Ann Agne, June 9, 1962. BA in Chemistry, Washington U., St. Louis, 1957, PhD in Chemistry, 1962. Rsch. chemist Ea. Regional Rsch., Dept. Agr., Phila., 1964-67; asst. prof. dept. biochemistry U. Kans. Med. Ctr., Kansas City, 1967-71, assoc. prof., 1971-81, acting chmn., 1973-74, prof., 1981—, interim chmn., 1993-94; vis. prof. Fed. U. Minas Gerais, Brazil, 1978. Contbr. articles to profl. jours. Recipient Scholastic Achievement award Am. Inst. Chemists, Washington U., 1957; NSF fellow, Washington U., 1959. Mem. Am. Chem. Soc., Am. Soc. for Biochemistry and Molecular Biology, Protein Soc., Sigma Xi. Achievements include research in properties of antibody molecules related to antigen binding, stucture of collagen of basement membranes, and stability of proteins. Office: U Kans Med Ctr Dept Biochemistry 39th and Rainbow Blvd Kansas City KS 66160-7421

NOER, RICHARD J., physics educator, researcher; b. Madison, Wis., July 3, 1937; s. Rudolf J. and Anita M. (Showerman) N.; m. Raymonde Tasset, Aug. 17, 1967; children—Geoffrey, Catherine. B.A., Amherst Coll., 1958; Ph.D., U. Calif., Berkeley, 1963. Physicist Atomic Energy Research, Harwell, Eng., 1963-64; asst. prof. physics Amherst Coll., Mass., 1964-66; asst. prof. physics Carleton Coll., Northfield, Minn., 1966-68, assoc. prof. physics, 1968-72, prof. physics, 1972—, dept. chair, 1974-77, 89-92; vis. physicist U. Paris, Orsay, France, 1972-73; physicist Ames Lab., Iowa, summers 1977-80, 82-84; rsch. physicist U. Geneva, 1980-81, 84-85; vis. scientist Cornell U., summers 1986, 88-91; vis. physicist Centre d'Etudes Nucléaires, Saclay, France, 1992-93. Co-author: Revolutions in Physics, 1972; contbr. articles to profl. jours. Mem. Am. Phys. Soc., Am. Assn. Physics Tchrs., AAAS, Phi Beta Kappa, Sigma Xi. Home: 101 Winona St Northfield MN 55057-2232 Office: Carleton Coll Dept Physics Northfield MN 55057

NOETHER, EMILIANA PASCA, historian, educator; b. Naples, Italy; came to U.S., 1919; d. Guglielmo and Bianca (Dramis) Pasca; m. Gottfried E. Noether, Aug. 1, 1942; 1 dau., Monica Gail. AB, Hunter Coll., N.Y.C., 1943; MA, Columbia U., 1944, PhD, 1948. Instr., then asst. prof. history Douglass Coll., Rutgers U., 1947-52; research asso. Center Internat. Studies, Mass. Inst. Tech., 1952-54; from lectr. to prof. history Regis Coll., Weston., Mass., 1959-66; prof. history Simmons Coll., Boston, 1966-68, U. Conn., Storrs, 1968-87. Editor: Italian sect. Am. Hist. Rev, 1958-75, Recently Published Articles, 1976-90, Garland Modern History Dissertation Series (Italy), 1989— ; author: Seeds of Italian Nationalism, 2d edit, 1969, also articles.; co-editor, contbr.: Modern Italy: A Topical History Since 1861, 1974; contbg. editor: The American Constitution as a Symbol and Reality for Italy, 1989. AAUW fellow, 1946-47, 62-63; Bunting Inst. fellow, 1961-62; sr. Fulbright scholar Florence, Italy, 1965-66; Rome, 1982; research grantee Am. Philos. Soc., summer 1970; U. Conn. Research Found. grantee, 1969-71, 73-77, 81-86. Mem. Am. Hist. Assn. (council 1975-78, chmn. com. women historians 1976), Soc. Italian Studies (chmn. prize award and citation com. 1968-69, adv. council 1979-82, adv. council v.p. 1981-83, pres. 1983-85), Berkshire Conf. Women Historians (sec. 1962-64, pres. 1967-71), Coordinating Com. on Women in Hist. Profession, AAUW, Phi Beta Kappa, Pi Gamma Mu, Phi Kappa Phi. Home: 632 Fearrington Post Pittsboro NC 27312

NOFER, GEORGE HANCOCK, lawyer; b. Phila., June 14, 1926. B.A., Haverford Coll., 1949; J.D., Yale U., 1952. Bar: Pa. 1953. Pvt. practice Phila., 1953—; ret. ptnr. Schnader, Harrison, Segal & Lewis, Phila., 1961-91, sr. counsel, 1992—; lectr. probate law, 1955—. Pres. bd. sch. dirs. Upper Moreland Twp., Pa., 1965-73; trustee Beaver Coll., Glenside, Pa., 1969-76; bd. dirs. Fox Chase Cancer Ctr., Phila., 1989-94; elder, trustee, deacon Abington (Pa.) Presbyn. Ch.; bd. dirs. Phila. Presbyn. Homes, Inc.; bd. dirs. A.G. Bell Assn. for Deaf, Washington. Fellow Am. Coll. Trust and Estate Counsel (regent 1975—, pres. 1983-84, chmn. Pa. 1973-78), Am. Law Inst., Am. Bar Found.; mem. ABA (standing com. on specialization 1980-86, chmn. 1983-86), Pa. Bar Assn., Phila. Bar Assn., Internat. Acad. Estate and Trust Law, Phi Beta Kappa, Phi Delta Phi. Home: 241 Pine St Philadelphia PA 19106-4313 Office: Schnader Harrison Segal & Lewis 1600 Market St Ste 3600 Philadelphia PA 19103-7286

NOFFSINGER, ANNE-RUSSELL L., former nursing administrator, educator; b. Frankfort, Ky., Feb. 4, 1932; d. Charles Russell and Hettie Lee (Ward) Lillis; m. J. Philip Noffsinger, July 1, 1964; children: Ward, Gretchen, Hans. Diploma, Good Samaritan Hosp., Lexington, Ky., 1952; BA in English, U. Ky., 1966, MA in Counseling, 1968, EdD in Psychology, 1979; MSN, U. Tenn., 1986. Instr. fundamentals of nursing Good Samaritan Hosp., Lexington, 1955-56; assoc. dir. nursing St. Joseph Hosp., Lexington, 1958-61; instr. pediatric nursing Good Samaritan Hosp. Sch. Nursing, Lexington, 1961-68; prof., chmn. nursing Lexington C.C., 1977-94; asst. to pres. for instnl. advancement and rsch., 1994—. Co-author: Counseling: An Introduction for Health and Human Services, 1983. Recipient U. Ky. Alumni Great Teaching award; Helene Fuld grantee. Mem. ANA (del.), KNA (former pres.), Nat. League for Nursing, KLN (former pres.), ODK, KCADN, Sigma Theta Tau, Omicron Delta Kappa, Phi Delta Kappa.

NOFSINGER, WILLIAM MORRIS, engineering executive; b. Orange, N.J., Sept. 11, 1932; s. Charles William and Grace Elizabeth (Morris) N.; m. Bonnie Jean Haisler, Nov. 6, 1965; children: Barry Jean, Betsy Jayne. BS in Chem. Engring., U. Kans., 1955. Registered profl. engr. With The C.W. Nofsinger Co., Kansas City, Mo., various positions to v.p., 1959-78, pres., 1978—; mem. adv. bd. U. Kans. Dept. Chem. and Petroleum Engring.; v.p., mem. exec. com. Fractionation Rsch., Inc., Bartlesville, Okla. Lt. USAF, 1955-58, capt. Res. Fellow Am. Inst. Chem. Engrs.; mem. NSPE, Am. Chem. Soc., Mo. Soc. Profl. Engrs., Kans. Engring. Soc. Republican. Lodge: Rotary (v.p. 1983-84, pres. elect 1984-85, pres. 1985-86). Home: 6645 Brookside Rd Kansas City MO 64113-1837 Office: Nofsinger Inc 9400 Ward Pkwy Kansas City MO 64114-3319

NOGALES, LUIS GUERRERO, communications company executive; b. Madera, Calif., Oct. 17, 1943; s. Alejandro Cano and Florence (Guerrero) N.; children: Alicia Fipp, Maria Cristina. BA in Polit. Sci., San Diego State U., 1966; JD, Stanford U., 1969. Asst. to pres. Stanford U., Calif., 1969-72; White House fellow, asst. to sec. U.S. Dept. Interior, Washington, 1972-73; exec. v.p., dir. Golden West Broadcasters, L.A., 1973-80; pres. Nogales, Bermudex, Chase and Tamayo, L.A., 1981-82; chmn., chief exec. officer UPI, Washington, 1983-86; pres. ECO Internat. News Svc., 1987, Univision, 1987-88; gen . ptnr. Nogales Castro Ptnrs., 1989-90; pres. Nogales Ptnrs., L.A., 1990—; bd. dir. The Bank of Calif., San Francisco, Stanford U. Ctr. for Pub. Svc., The Ford Found. Bd. dirs. State of Calif. Bd. Higher Edn., Sacramento, 1973-79, Los Angeles Redevel. Agy., 1973-76, United Way Am., Alexandria, Va., 1984-88; trustee Claremont U. Ctr. and Grad. Sch., 1987, Stanford U.; chmn. MALDEF, 1980-82. Office: 1925 Century Park E Ste 830 Los Angeles CA 90067-2709*

NOGELO, ANTHONY MILES, retired health care company executive; b. Framingham, Mass., Apr. 2, 1943; s. Anthony Joseph and Lillian Carol (Nowick) N.; m. Gerry C. Stugis, Mar. 20, 1965; children: Laura Elizabeth, Michael Joseph. B.A. in Econs., Tufts U., 1964; M.B.A., Harvard Bus. Sch., 1968. Mgr. fin. planning and analysis Gen. Foods Corp., White Plains, N.Y., 1968-73; ptnr. Paul E. Dean, Greenwich, Conn., 1973-74; asst. treas. Ludlow Corp., Needham Heights, Mass., 1974-80; v.p., treas. Nat. Med. Care Inc., Boston, 1980-85; v.p., chief fin. officer, treas. Nat. Med. Care Inc., 1985-95; v.p., treas. Nat. Med. Care, Inc., 1995-96. Served to lt. j.g. USNR, 1964-66. Mem. Fin. Execs. Inst., Treas. Club Boston. Home: 19 Washington Dr Sudbury MA 01776-2935 Office: Nat Med Care Inc 1601 Trapelo Rd Waltham MA 02154-7333

NOGUCHI, THOMAS TSUNETOMI, author, forensic pathologist; b. Fukuoka, Japan, Jan. 4, 1927; came to U.S., 1952; s. Wataru and Tomika Narahashi N. D of Medicine, Nippon Med. Sch., Tokyo, 1951; LLD (hon.), U. Braz Cubas Fedn. Faculties Mogi Das Cruzes, Sao Paolo, Brazil, 1980; DSc (hon.), Worcester State Coll., 1985. Dep. med. examiner Los Angeles County Dept. Chief Med. Examiner, L.A., 1961-67, coroner, 1967-82; prof. forensic pathology U. So. Calif., L.A., 1982—. Author: Coroner, 1983 (N.Y. Times Bestseller 1984), Coroner At Large, 1985; (fiction) Unnatural Causes, 1988, Physical Evidence, 1990. Fellow Am. Acad. Forensic Sci. (chmn. sect. 1966); mem. Nat. Assn. Med. Examiners (pres. 1983), Calif. State Coroners Assn. (pres. 1974), World Assn. Med. Law (v.p.). Republican. Avocations: fine arts, gourmet Oriental cooking, painting stills and abstracts. Office: U So Calif Med Ctr 1200 N State St Rm 2520 Los Angeles CA 90033-4525

NOHE, RICHARD EDGAR, telecommunications executive; b. Greenville, S.C., June 9, 1963; s. Richard E. and Catherine D. (Cashin) N. BA, Augusta (Ga.) Coll., 1986; M in Profl. Studies, NYU, 1989; JD, N.Y. Law Sch., 1996. News dir. WRDW-TV CBS, Augusta, 1983-87; rschr. Columbia U., Ctr. Telecomm. and Info. Studies (name changed to Columbia Inst. Tele-Info.), N.Y.C., 1989-90; mgr. NTT Am., N.Y.C., 1990-93, sr. mgr., 1993-95, dir., 1995-97; v.p. corp. strategy, gen. mgr. NTT Am., Washington, 1997—; congl. fellow subcom. on oversight, ways and means com. U.S. Ho. of Reps., 1996. Contbr. articles to profl. publs. Mem. ABA, Brookings Instn. (congressional fellow 1996), Washington Export Coun. Avocations: golf, tennis, reading, films, writing. Office: NTT Am 700 13th St NW Ste 950 Washington DC 20005-3960 also: NTT Am 101 Park Ave 41st Fl New York NY 10178

NOHRDEN, PATRICK THOMAS, lawyer; b. Santa Cruz, Calif., Mar. 7, 1956; s. Thomas Allen and Roberta Eugenia (Brydon) N.; m. Debora Ann Heintz, Sept. 19, 1981; children: Steven, Laura, Maranda, Patricia. AS, SUNY, Albany, 1980; BA in English, San Jose State U., 1984; JD, U. Akron, 1992. Bar: Nev. 1993, U.S. Dist. Ct. Nev. 1993. Regional dir. CareerPro, Inc., Roseville, Calif., 1984-91; cons. Patrick T. Nohrden & Assocs., Youngstown, Ohio, 1991-93; pvt. practice, Las Vegas, Nev., 1993—; bd. dirs. Profl. Resume Svc., Inc., Las Vegas, Las Vegas Diamondbacks, Inc., Old Nev. Fin., Inc., Las Vegas. Sgt. U.S. Army, 1975-81. Recipient Spirit of Pro Bono award. Mem. ATLA, ABA (family law sect.), Fed. Bar Assn., Nev. Trial Lawyers Assn., State Bar Nev. (family law and bankruptcy sects.), Clark County Bar Assn., Phi Kappa Phi. Republican. Roman Catholic. Office: 608 S 8th St Las Vegas NV 89101-7005

NOHRNBERG, JAMES CARSON, English language educator; b. Berkeley, Calif., Mar. 19, 1941; s. Carson and Geneva Gertrude (Gibbs) N.; m. Stephanie Payson Lamport, June 14, 1964; children: Gabrielle L., Peter Carson L. Student, Kenyon Coll., 1958-60; BA, Harvard Coll., 1962, postgrad., 1965-68; PhD, U. Toronto, Ont., Can., 1970. Teaching fellow dept. English U. Coll., U. Toronto, 1963-64; jr. fellow Soc. of Fellows Harvard U., 1965-68; acting instr. dept. English Yale U., New Haven, 1968-69, lectr. dept. English, 1969-70, asst. prof. dept. English, 1970-75, assoc. prof., 1975; prof. English U. Va., Charlottesville, 1975—; adj. instr. English Harvard U., Cambridge, 1967; lectr. various univs., 1974-96; Gauss seminar in criticism lectr. Princeton U., 1987. Author: The Analogy of the Faerie Queene, 1976, 80, Like Unto Moses: The Constituting of an Interruption, 1995; mem. editl. bd. Spenser Ency., 1977-90; contbr. articles to profl. jours. and ed. vols. on Bible, Homer, Dante, Boiardo, Spenser, Milton, Thomas Pynchon, among others. Woodrow Wilson fellow, 1962, jr. fellow Harvard U., 1965-68, Morse fellow Yale U., 1974-75, U. Va. Ctr. for Advanced Studies fellow, 1975-78, Guggenheim fellow, 1981-82, Ind. U. Inst. for Advanced Studies fellow, 1991. Mem. MLA, Spenser Soc. Presbyterian. Avocations: writing poetry, collecting books and records. Home: 1874 Wayside Pl Charlottesville VA 22903-1631 Office: U Va Dept English Bryan Hall Charlottesville VA 22903

NOKES, JOHN RICHARD, retired newspaper editor, author; b. Portland, Oreg., Feb. 23, 1915; s. James Abraham and Bernice Alfaretta (Bailey) N.; m. Evelyn Junkin, Sept. 13, 1936; children: Richard Gregory, William G., Gail (Mrs. William M. Hulden), Douglas J., Kathy E. B.S., Linfield Coll., 1936, LHD (hon.), 1988. With The Oregonian, Portland, 1936-82, city editor, 1950-65, asst. mng. editor, 1965-71, mng. editor, 1971-75, editor, 1975-82; disting. vis. prof. journalism Linfield Coll., 1982-85; cons. editor The Hong Kong Standard, 1994. Author: American Form of Government, 1939, Columbia's River: The Voyages of Robert Gray 1787-1793, 1991; editor Oreg. Edn. Jour., 1944. Bd. dirs. Portland U.S.O., 1968-72, U.S. Coast Guard Acad. Found., 1972-74, Portland Opera Assn., 1976-78; trustee Linfield Coll., 1977-93; v.p. Oreg. UN Assn., 1983-85, chmn. Oreg. UN Day, 1983. Lt. (j.g.) USNR, 1944-46; comdr. Res. (ret.). Mem. Navy League U.S. (pres. Portland coun. 1969-71), Linfield Coll. Alumni Assn. (pres. 1940), World Affairs Coun. Oreg. (pres. 1973-74), AP Mng. Editors Assn. (dir. 1973-80), Am. Soc. Newspaper Editors, N.W. China Coun., Sigma Delta Chi (pres. Willamette Valley chpt. 1975-76). Republican. Methodist. Club: Multnomah Athletic (Portland). Home: 14650 SW 103rd Ave Tigard OR 97224-4740

NOKES, MARY TRIPLETT, former university president, counselor, artist; b. Weatherford, Okla., Sept. 6, 1920; d. Ernest Carlton and Eva Hannah (Claridge) Triplett; m. George Willis Malcom Nokes, July 11, 1937; 1 child, William Careton. BA, Cen. State U., 1943; Masters Degree, U. Okla., 1949, Doctors Degree, 1969. Tchr., sec. Okla. Edn. Assn., Oklahoma City, 1943-83; advisor Nat. Honor Soc., Oklahoma City, 1955-83; 1st v.p. Internat. Porcelain Artist, 1966-68, pres., 1968-70, sec. bd., 1979-92; pres. Okla. State U., 1975-91; ret., 1991; legis. rep. for Okla. Edn. Assn., 1979-92; presenter seminars on china painting, 1991-97. Sponsor Student Coun., 1955-83; pres. Okla. State China Painting Tchr., 1986-87; dir. Vacation Bible Sch., 1984-95, 96—; pres. Sooner Club, 1995-96, Sooner Art Club, 1996—. Named Vol. Woman of Yr. Salvation Army, Okla., 1992-93, Woman of Yr. Salvation Army, 1995-96, Personality of South, 1994-95, Cmty. Leader for Noteworthy Ams., 1994-95, Cmty. Leader Oklahoma City, 1994-95; recipient proclamation Mayor Oklahoma City, 1994-95, 95-96, named Amb. of Good Will by Governor of Okla. Mem. Internat. Porcelain Art Tchrs. (past v.p., past pres., regional chmn., sec. to internat. bd. dirs.), Intercontinental Biographical Assn., C. of C. (sec.), Les Lefeyetts Home Club (pres. 1941-43), Garden Club (pres.), Sooner Art Club (pres. 1991-97), Kermac Art Club, Alpha Phi Sigma, Kappa Delta Phi, Kappa Kappa Iota. Baptist. Home: 4125 NW 57th St Oklahoma City OK 73112-1505

NOLAN, ALAN TUCKER, retired lawyer; b. Evansville, Ind., Jan. 19, 1923; s. Val and Jeannette (Covert) N.; m. Elizabeth Clare Titsworth, Aug. 26, 1947 (dec. Nov. 1967); children: Patrick A., Thomas C., Mary F., Elizabeth T., John V.; m. Jane Ransel DeVoe, Feb. 7, 1970; adopted children: John C. DeVoe, Ellen R. DeVoe, Thomas R. DeVoe. AB in Govt., Ind. U., 1944, DHL (hon.), 1993; LLB, Harvard U., 1947. Bar: Ind. 1947. Law clk. U.S. Ct. Appeals (7th Cir.), Chgo., 1947-48; assoc. Ice, Miller, Donadio & Ryan, Indpls., 1948-58, ptnr., 1958-93, ret., 1993—; chmn. Disciplinary Commn. Supreme Ct. Ind., Indpls., 1966-73; vice-chmn. bd. dirs. Union City Body Co., Inc., 1982-92. Author: The Iron Brigade, 1961, As Sounding Brass, 1964, Lee Considered, 1991; contbg. editor The Civil War, 1985-89; contbr. numerous articles to profl. jours. Life mem. NAACP Indpls., v.p., 1950-54; bd. dirs., founder Ind. Civil Liberties Union, Indpls., 1953-60; bd. dirs. Indpls. Art League, 1981-87; chmn., bd. trustees Ind. Hist. Soc., Indpls., 1986—; trustee Eiteljorg Mus., Indpls., 1987-93. Fellow Co. Mil. Historians, Am. Bar Found.; mem. ABA, Ind. Bar Assn., Indpls. Bar Assn. (bd. mgrs. 1958-60, chmn. Grievance Com. 1960-64), Indpls. Civil War Round Table. Democrat. Roman Catholic. Avocations: travel, gardening, reading. Home: 4118 N Pennsylvania St Indianapolis IN 46205-2611 Office: PO Box 82001 1 American Sq Indianapolis IN 46282-0001

NOLAN, BARRY HANCE, publishing company executive; b. Easton, Pa., Sept. 15, 1942; s. Arthur James Nolan and Marion (Hance) Slater; m. Janet Lynch, Mar. 20, 1971 (dec. Mar. 1981); 1 child, Tracy; m. Catherine McDermott, Feb. 19, 1983; children: Craig, Kelsey. AB in Econs., Princeton U., 1964; MBA, Columbia U., 1966. Account exec. Papert, Koenig, Lois Advt., N.Y.C., 1966-68; group mgr. new bus.'s Butterick div. Am. Can, N.Y.C., 1969-72; dir. mktg. planning Current Inc. subs. Deluxe Check Printers, Colorado Springs, Colo., 1973-77, v.p. mktg., 1977-79, pres., chief exec. officer, 1980-89; pres., chief exec. officer ECM, Inc., Colorado Springs, Colo., 1991-96; asst. to pres. Pacific Water Works Supply Co., Seattle, 1979-80. Pres. bd. dirs. Pikes Peak br. Cystic Fibrosis Found., Colorado Springs, 1984-89, nat. trustee-at-large, Washington, 1985-92. Mem. Parcel Shippers Assn. (bd. dirs. 1987-89). Republican. Presbyterian. Clubs: Cheyenne Mountain Country (Colorado Springs); Sahalee Country (Redmond, Wash.), Broadmoor Golf, Garden of the Gods. Avocations: golf, landscape architecture, photography. Home: 35 Elm Ave Colorado Springs CO 80906-3169

NOLAN, EDMUND FRANCIS, management consultant; b. Buffalo, June 9, 1931; s. James Paul and Isabel Jane (Curry) N.; m. Chloe Dandison Nolan, Dec. 19, 1959 (div. Aug. 1979); children: Andrew Dandison, Jeffrey Stewart; m. Ann Hopkins Chadbourne, Aug. 18, 1979; stepchildren: Gay Chadbourne Canepa, Scott Holt Chadbourne. BA, Cornell U., 1953; MBA, Columbia U., 1957. Sales and mktg. staff Armstrong World Industries, Lancaster, Pa., 1957-63; mgmt. cons. Hay Group, Phila., 1963-72; dir. compensation and benefits Nashua (N.H.) Corp., 1972-76; sr. mgmt. cons. Coopers & Lybrand, N.Y.C., 1976-83; dir. compensation and benefits Svc. Systems Corp., Buffalo, 1983-87; mgmt. cons. Nolan Consulting, Falmouth, Mass., 1987—; bd. dirs. J R Hess & Co., Inc., Cranston, R.I.; mem. adv. bd. L F Giampietro, PC, Falmouth. Del. Rep. state conv., Boston, 1990, Econ. Devel. Com. Town of Falmouth, 1993—; mem. Bikeways Com., Town of Falmouth, 1990—; trustee Falmouth Pub. Libr., 1994—. 1st lt. U.S. Army, 1953-55, Korea. Mem. Cape Cod Cornellians (pres. 1987-89), Falmouth Sports Ctr., Woods Hole Theatre Co. (pres. 1990-95), Delta Phi (v.p. 1950—). Congregationalist. Avocations: teaching, acting, tennis, skiing, biking. Office: Nolan Consulting 101 Town Hall Sq Falmouth MA 02540-2754

NOLAN, JAMES PAUL, medical educator, scientist; b. Buffalo, June 21, 1929; s. James Paul and Isabel (Curry) N.; m. Christa Paul, July 23, 1956; children—Lisa, James, Christopher, Thomas. BA, Yale U., 1951, MD cum laude, 1955. Diplomate Am. Bd. Internal Medicine. Instr. in medicine Yale U., New Haven, 1961-63; intern Grace-New Haven Hosp., 1955-56, resident, 1958-60, chief med. resident, 1961-62, asso. physician, 1962-63; asst. prof. medicine SUNY, Buffalo, 1963-67; asso. prof. SUNY, 1967-69, prof., 1969—, vice-chmn. dept. medicine, 1973-77, acting chmn. dept., 1978-79, chmn. dept., 1979-95, disting. svc. prof., 1996—; chief of medicine Buffalo Gen. Hosp., 1969-80, attending, 1969—; asso. attending Edward J. Meyer Meml. Hosp., Buffalo, 1963-68; attending Edward J. Meyer Meml. Hosp., 1968-71, cons., 1971—; cons. physician Millard Fillmore Hosp., 1981—, Deaconess Hosp., 1973—; attending Buffalo VA Hosp., Children's Hosp. Buffalo; cons. Roswell Park Meml. Inst., 1970—; acting dir. dept. medicine Erie County Med. Center, 1978-80, dir. dept., 1980—; Trustee Buffalo Gen. Hosp., 1974—. Editorial adv. bd. Jour. Medicine Exptl. and Clin, 1971—; reviewer: Gastroenterology, 1973—; contbr. numerous articles to med. and sci. jours. Served to lt. comdr., M.C. USN, 1956-58. NIH grantee, 1979-86; Hartford Found. grantee, 1981. Mem. ACP (master, chair bd. regents 1994-95), Am. Fedn. Clin. Rsch., AAAS, Am. Gastroent. Assn. (procedures com.), Am. Assn. Study of Liver Disease, Reticuloendothelial Soc., N.Y. Acad. Sci., Am. Clin. and Climatol. Assn., Interurban Club, Ctrl. Soc. Clin. Rsch., Internat. Assn. Study of Liver, Assn. Am. Physicians, Assn. Profs. Medicine (pres. 1993-94), Phi Beta Kappa, Alpha Omega Alpha. Home: 213 Burbank Dr Buffalo NY 14226-3938 Office: 462 Grider St Buffalo NY 14215-3021

NOLAN, JOHN BLANCHARD, lawyer; b. Providence, Aug. 30, 1943; s. John O'Leary and Elizabeth Rita (Blanchard) N.; m. Marguerite Ruth Hartley, Mar. 1, 1969 (dec. Aug. 1988); children: Suzanne, Caroline, Danielle; m. Lillian B. Prestley, 1989. AB, Brown U., 1965; JD, Georgetown U., 1968. Bar: Conn. 1968, N.Y. 1974, U.S. Ct. Appeals (2d cir.) 1969, U.S. Dist. Ct. Conn.1969, U.S. Dist. Ct. (so. dist.) N.Y. 1973, U.S. Ct. Appeals (1st cir.) 1991, U.S. Dist. Ct. Ariz. 1994, U.S. Supreme Ct. 1995. Assoc. Day, Berry & Howard, Hartford, Conn., 1969-76, ptnr., 1976—; bd. dirs. Spiritus Wines, Inc., Hartford; chmn. Local Rules of Practice Adv. Com. to U.S. Bankruptcy Ct., 1981—. Corporator St. Francis Hosp. Med. Ctr., Hartford, 1982—; trustee St. Mary Home Found., 1983—, U. Hartford Art Sch., 1988-94; bd. dirs. Greater Hartford Arts Coun., Inc., 1993—, also v.p., mem. exec. com.; mem. parish coun. Ch. of St. Timothy. Mem. ABA, Am. Bankruptcy Inst., Conn. Bar Assn., Hartford County Bar Assn., Insolvency Internat., Loomis Chaffee Sch. Alumni Assn. (bd. dirs. 1996—), Hartford Golf Club. Democrat. Roman Catholic. Avocations: golf, skiing, travel, wines. Home: 150 Scarborough St Hartford CT 06105-1107 Office: Day Berry & Howard Cityplace Hartford CT 06103

NOLAN, JOHN EDWARD, retired electrical corporation executive; b. Bklyn., Apr. 15, 1925; s. John C. and Elizabeth (Reighton) N.; m. Dorothea Scheuermann, Aug. 23, 1952; children: Kathleen, Elizabeth, John Edward, James, Michael, Patricia, Maureen. BEE, Cooper Union, 1950; MSEE, U. Pitts., 1955. With Westinghouse Electric Corp., 1950-90, mem. staff Bettis Atomic Power Lab., 1951-69, with Advanced Reactors div., 1969-79, dir. Hanford Engring. Devel. Lab., 1980-87, pres. Westinghouse Hanford Co., 1988-90; ret., 1990. With U.S. Army, 1943-46, ETO. Mem. IEEE, ASME, Am. Nuclear Soc. Home: 411 Snyder Rd Richland WA 99352-1945

NOLAN, JOHN EDWARD, lawyer; b. Mpls., July 11, 1927; s. John E. and Teresa (Franey) N.; m. Joan Dobbins, June 3, 1950; children: Carol N. Klatt, John Edward III (dec.), Kelly N. Spencer, Richard Clark, Patricia N. McNeill. BS, U.S. Naval Acad., 1950; JD, Georgetown U., 1955. Bar: D.C. 1955, U.S. Supreme Ct. 1959, Md. 1961. Law clk. to Justice Clark U.S. Supreme Ct., 1955-56; adminstrv. asst. to Atty. Gen. Robert F. Kennedy, 1963-64; assoc. Steptoe & Johnson, Washington, 1956-62; ptnr. Steptoe & Johnson, 1962-63, 65—; assoc. counsel Cuban families com. Cuban Prisoners Exch., Havana, 1962-63; spl. counsel refugee subcom. Senate Jud. Com., Vietnam, 1967-68; mem. CPR Panel of Disting. Neutrals, Washington, U.S. Ct. Appeals mediator D.C. cir.; mem. exec. com. Lawyers Com. for Civil Rights Under the Law; bd. dirs. Hooper Holmes, Inc., Iomega Corp.; vis. fellow Wolfson Coll., Cambridge (Eng.) U., 1987, 92. Trustee Robert F. Kennedy Meml., 1969—; bd. dirs. Fund Dem. Majority; moderator Aspen Inst., 1980—. 2d. Lt. to Capt. USMC, 1950-54, Korea. Decorated Silver Star, Bronze Star with Combat V, Purple Heart. Mem. ABA, D.C. Bar Assn. (gov.), Am. Law Inst. Democrat. Roman Catholic. Clubs: Met. (Washington); Congl. Home: 7830 Persimmon Tree Ln Bethesda MD 20817-4520 Office: 1330 Connecticut Ave NW Washington DC 20036-1704

NOLAN, JOHN MICHAEL, lawyer; b. Conway, Ark., June 21, 1948; s. Paul Thomas and Peggy (Hime) N. BA, U. Tex., 1970, postgrad., 1971, JD, 1973; LLM in Taxation, George Washington U., 1976. Bar: Tex. 1973, U.S. Ct. Mil. Appeals 1973, U.S. Ct. Appeals (D.C. cir.) 1975, U.S. Tax Ct. 1975, U.S. Supreme Ct. 1975. Chief counsel to chief judge U.S. Ct. Mil. Appeals, Washington, 1976-77; assoc. Winstead, McGuire, Sechrest & Minick P.C., Dallas, 1977-81; shareholder Winstead Sechrest & Minick P.C., Dallas, 1981—. Editor in chief The Advocate, 1973-76. Served as capt. JAGC, U.S. Army, 1973-76. Named one of Outstanding Young Men in Am., U.S. Jaycess, 1976. Mem. ABA (real property, probate and trust sect., real property com., partnerships, joint ventures, and other investment vehicles), ALA (bd. dirs.), Tex. Bar Assn. (real property, probate and trust sect.), D.C. Bar Assn., Dallas Bar Assn. (real estate group), Tex. Coll. Real Estate Lawyers, Coll. State Bar Tex., Real Estate Coun., Salesmanship Club Dallas, Royal Oaks Country Club. Presbyterian. Home: 6681 Crest Way Ct Dallas TX 75230 Office: Winstead Sechrest & Minick 5400 Renaissance Tower 1201 Elm St Dallas TX 75270-2102

NOLAN, JOHN THOMAS, JR., retired oil industry administrator; b. Boston, Apr. 15, 1930; s. John T. Sr. and Margaret M. (Craig) N.; m. Mary Sharkey, May 7, 1955; children: Anne, Margaret, John T. III, Stephen, Michael. AB, Cath. U. Am., 1951; PhD, MIT, 1955. Chemist Texaco, Inc., Beacon, N.Y., 1955-59; group leader Texaco, Inc., Beacon, 1959-69, supr., 1969-79, asst. mgr., 1979-82, assoc. dir., 1982-87, dir. strategic rsch., 1987-92; mem. adv. bd. Dutchess County Sci. Fair, Poughkeepsie, N.Y., 1990—. Contbr. over 5 articles to profl. jours. Mem. blue ribbon panel Beacon Sch. Dist., 1987-92; chmn. bd. Dutchess C.C. Found., Poughkeepsie, 1989-92, chmn. planning com., 1992—. Mem. AAAS, Am. Chem. Soc., Greater So. Dutchess C. of C. (bd. dirs. 1989-92), Sigma Xi, Phi Beta Kappa. Achievements include patents in field. Home: 18 Relyea Ter Wappingers Falls NY 12590-5824

NOLAN, JOSEPH THOMAS, journalism educator, communications consultant; b. Waterbury, Conn., Apr. 11, 1920; s. Thomas Francis and Mary Margaret (Gaffney) N.; m. Virginia Theodate Tappin, May 6, 1943; children—Carol Nolan Rigolot, David J. A.B., Holy Cross Coll., 1942; MA in English Lit., Boston U., 1945; Ph.D. in Econs, NYU, 1973. Washington corr. UPI, 1943-49; writer, copy editor N.Y. Times, N.Y.C., 1949-55; mgr. editorial and press services RCA Corp., N.Y.C., 1955-62; sr. v.p. corporate communications Chase Manhattan Bank, N.Y.C., 1962-74; prof. journalism and pub. affairs U. S.C., Columbia, 1974-76; v.p. pub. affairs Monsanto Co., St. Louis, 1976-85; Gannett vis. prof. communications U. Fla., 1985-86; prof. communications U. North Fla., Jacksonville, 1986-92; adj. prof. bus. and comm. Flagler Coll., St. Augustine, Fla., 1992—. Contbr. articles to various mags. Fellow Pub. Rels. Soc. Am. Roman Catholic. Home: 30 Park Terrace Dr Saint Augustine FL 32084-5334

NOLAN, LONE KIRSTEN, financial advisor; b. Copenhagen, Oct. 9, 1938; d. Johannes and Elizabeth (Zachariassen) Jansen; came to U.S., 1957, naturalized, 1964; m. Gene Nolan, Mar. 19, 1973; children—Glenn Muller, Erik Muller. Lic. securities broker; adminstrv. asst. Am. Nat. Bank and Trust, Morristown, N.J., 1967-72; asst. cashier First Nat. Iron Bank, 1972; comptroller and ops. officer Panama City Nat. Bank, 1973-74; asst. v.p. Lee County Bank, Ft. Myers, Fla., 1974-76; Priscilla Murphy Realty, Sanibel, Fla., 1976-77; pres. Century 21 Nolan Realty, Ft. Myers, 1977-80; pres. AAIM Realty Group, Ft. Myers, 1980-81; real estate investment counselor Merrill Lynch, Boca Raton, Fla., 1982-85; mgr. Merrill Lynch Realty, Palm Beach, Fla., 1984-85; mgr. J.W. Charles Realty, Inc., Boca Raton, 1985-89; investment advisor Dean Witter Reynolds, Ft. Lauderdale, Fla., 1990-96; fin. planner FFP Securities, 1996—. Mem. NAFE, Nat. Assn. Security Dealers, Inst. Cert. Fin. Planners. Address: 7129 Promenade Dr A202 Boca Raton FL 33433 Office: FFP Securities Ste 355 One Park Pl 621 NW 53d St Boca Raton FL 33487

NOLAN, MARK GREGORY, advertising executive; b. San Francisco, July 3, 1958; m. Robyn Lynn Nolan, June 7, 1980. Founder, chief exec. officer Mark Nolan & Assocs., Inc., Citrus Heights, Calif., 1981-87; v.p., ptnr. Nolan Mktg. Group Inc., Citrus Heights, 1987—; mktg. dir., ptnr. Fin. Mktg. Corp., Citrus Heights, 1989—; keynote speaker Marin Self-Pubs. Assn., Ross, Calif., 1986; featured speaker Community Entrepreneurs Assn., Sacramento, 1986, home-based bus. conf., 1991; treas. COSMEP, San Francisco, 1986-88; lectr. UCLA, 1987. Author: The Instant Marketing Plan, 1995; editor: Info. Mktg., 1985-87. Mem. Better Bus. Bur., Eagle Scouts. Mem. S.C. Publicists Assn., Community Entrepreneurs Assn., Internat. Assn. Self-Pubs. (treas. 1986-88), Com. of Small Mag. Editors and Pubs., C. of C., Turtles, Oregon Advt. Club, Entrepreneurs Am., Active 20-30 Club. Avocations: wine appreciation, classic automobiles. Office: Nolan Mktg Group Inc PO Box 2570 Fair Oaks CA 95628-9570

NOLAN, OWEN, professional hockey player; b. Belfast, Northern Ireland, Feb. 12, 1972. Selected 1st round NHL entry draft Que. Nordiques, 190, right wing, 1990-96; right wing San Jose Sharks, 1996—; named to OHL All-Star 1st team, 1989-90; played in NHL All-Star Game 1992, 96. Recipient Emms Family award, 1988-89, Jim Mahon Meml. Trophy, 1989-90. Office: care San Jose Sharks 525 W Santa Clara St San Jose CA 95113

NOLAN, PATRICK JOSEPH, screenwriter, playwright, educator; b. Bronx, N.Y., Jan. 2, 1933; s. Patrick John and Catherine Katrina (O'Malley) N.; children: Patrick, Christian, Mark. BA, Villanova U., 1955; MA, U. Detroit, 1961; PhD, Bryn Mawr Coll., 1973. Teaching fellow and mem. faculty dept. English U. Detroit, 1959-62; instr. English Villanova (Pa.) U., 1962-80, prof., 1980—. Playwright: Chameleons, 1980, Midnight Rainbows, 1991; TV screenwriter: The Jericho Mile, 1979 (Emmy award). Served to lt. (j.g.) USNR, 1955-59, PTO. Recipient teaching excellence award Philadelphia mag., 1980, Alumni Medallion award Villanova U., 1986. Mem. Writers Guild Am. (West chpt.), Dramatists Guild. Roman Catholic. Avocations: swimming, biking. Office: Dept English Villanova U Villanova PA 19085

NOLAN, RICHARD THOMAS, clergyman, educator; b. Waltham, Mass., May 30, 1937; s. Thomas Michael and Elizabeth Louise (Leishman) N.; life ptnr. Robert C. Pingpank, Sept. 14, 1955. BA, Trinity Coll., 1960; cert. in clin. pastoral edn., Conn. Valley Hosp., 1962; diploma, Berkeley Divinity Sch., 1962; MDiv., Hartford Sem. Found., 1963; postgrad., Union Theol. Sem., N.Y.C., 1963; MA in Religion, Yale U., 1967; PhD, NYU, 1973; post doctoral, Harvard U., 1991. Ordained deacon Episcopal Ch., 1963, priest, 1965. Instr. Latin and English Watkinson (Conn.) Sch., 1961-62; instr. math. Choir Sch. of Cathedral of St. John the Divine, N.Y.C., 1962-64; instr. math. and religion, assoc. chaplain Cheshire (Conn.) Acad., 1965-67; instr. Hartford (Conn.) Sem. Found., 1967-68, asst. acad. dean, lectr. philosophy and edn., 1968-70; instr. Mattatuck C.C., Waterbury, Conn., 1969-70, asst. prof. philosophy and history, 1970-74, assoc. prof., 1974-78, prof. philosophy and social sci., 1978-92, prof. emeritus, 1992—; rsch. fellow in med. ethics Yale U., 1978, rsch. fellow in profl. and bus. ethics, 1987; vicar St. Paul's Parish, Bantam, Conn., 1974-88; pastor emeritus St. Paul's Parish, Bantam, 1988—; pres. Litchfield Inst., Conn. and Fla., 1984-96; mem. ethics com. Waterbury Hosp. Health Ctr., 1984-88; vis. and adj. prof. philosophy, theology and religious studies Trinity Coll., Conn., L.I. U., U. Miami, St. Joseph Coll., Conn., Pace U., Teikyo Post U., U. Conn., Hartford Grad. Ctr., Ctrl. Conn. State U., Broward C.C., Fla., 1964-95; lectr. philosophy and theology Barry U., Fla., 1973, 89-92, 97—; adj. assoc. in continuing edn. Berkeley Div. Sch. Yale U., 1987-89; Rabbi Harry Halpern Meml. lectr., Southbury, Conn., 1987; guest spkr. various chs. and orgns. including Cathedral of St. John the Divine, N.Y. and Trinity Cathedral, Miami; mem. faculty of consulting examiners Charter Oak State Coll., Conn., 1990-93; fellow Associated Fellows for Counseling and Psychotherapy, Inc., 1990-93; assoc. for edn. Christ Ch. Cathedral, Hartford, Conn., 1988-94, hon. canon, 1991—; cons. Dept. Def. Activity Non-Traditional Ednl. Support, Ednl. Testing Svcs., Princeton, 1990; vis. scholar Coll. Preachers Washington Nat. Cathedral, 1994; retired assisting priest Episcopal Ch. of Bethesda-by-the-Sea, Palm Beach, Fla., 1994—; spkr. seminars Barnes and Noble Palm Beach County, 1997—; cons. spl. projects Wadsworth Publ. Co., Belmont, Calif., 1997—. Author: (with H. Titus and M. Smith) Living Issues in Philosophy, 7th edit., 1979, Indonesian edit., 1984, 8th edit., 1986, 9th edit., 1995, (with F. Kirkpatrick) Living Issues in Ethics, 1982; editor, contbr. Diaconate Now, 1968; host Conversations with ..., 1987-89. Founding mem. The Heritage Soc. of The Episcopal Ch. of Bethesda-by-the Sea, Palm Beach. Mem. Am. Acad. Religion, Am. Philos. Assn., Authors Guild, Hemlock Soc., Boston Latin Sch. Alumni Assn., Tabor Acad. Alumni Assn., Cavalier King Charles Spaniel Club, Phi Delta Kappa. Avocation: Cavalier King Charles Spaniels. Home: 6342 Forest Hill Blvd # 350 West Palm Beach FL 33415-6158 *Who am I? By baptism I am a resurrected child of God born to love and be loved; my pilgrimage among others is lived within this baptismal identity, more enduring than any achievement.*

NOLAN, ROBERT, management consulting company executive; b. Hartford, Conn., Oct. 13, 1933; s. Robert Emmett and Marian (Sobanski) N.; m. Eileen Luke, July 7, 1955; children: Daniel, Kathleen, Michael, Pamela, Mary. BA, U. Conn., 1958. Sr. analyst Aetna Life & Casualty Co., Hartford, 1958-62; v.p. Serge A. Birn Co. Inc., Louisville, 1962-73; chmn., chief exec. officer Robert E. Nolan Co. Inc., Simsbury, Conn., 1973—; sr. examiner Malcolm Baldridge Nat. Quality Award, Gaithersburg, Md., 1988-89. Co-author: Work Measurement in Accounting, 1963, Office Work Measurement, 1970, Improving Productivity through Advanced Office Controls, 1980, White Collar Productivity, 1982. With USAF, 1950-54, Korea. Mem. Am. Soc. for Quality Control, Inst. Indsl. Engrs., Assn. for Systems Mgmt., Adminstrn. Mgmt. Soc. Office: Robert E Nolan Co Inc 90 Hopmeadow St Simsbury CT 06070-2413

NOLAN, STANTON PEELLE, surgeon, educator; b. Washington, May 29, 1933; s. James Parker and Ellen Dubose (Peelle) N.; m. Marion Faro, June 16, 1955; children—Stanton Peelle Jr., Tiphanie Ravenel. B.A., Princeton U., 1955; M.D., U. Va., 1959, M.S., 1962. Cert. Am. Bd. Surgery, Am. Bd. Thoracic Surgery. Intern U. Va. Med. Ctr., Charlottesville, 1959-60, asst. resident gen. surgery, 1960-61, research fellow surgery, 1961-62, sr. asst.

resident gen. surgery, 1962-64, chief resident gen surgery, 1964-65, chief resident thoracic cardiovascular surgery, 1965-66; sr. rsch. assoc. Clinic of Surgery Nat. Heart Inst., NIH, Bethesda, Md., 1966-68; asst. prof. surgery U. Va. Med. Ctr., Charlottesville, 1968-70, assoc. prof. surgery, 1970-74, surgeon in charge div. thoracic cardiovascular surgery, 1970-93, prof. surgery, 1974—, Claude A. Jessup prof. surgery, 1981—, med. dir. Thoracic Cardiovascular post-operative unit, 1989-93; established investigator Am. Heart Assn., 1969-74; mem. surgery A study sect. NIH, Washington, 1972-76, surgery and bioengring. study sect. 1984-87, chmn. 1985-87; cons. thoracic cardiovascular surgery VA Hosp., Salem, Va., 1968—, Am. Bd. Surgery to qualifying examination com., 1988-91; surg. cons. Bur. Crippled Children, Charlottesville, 1968-93; vis. cons. cardiothoracic surgery Aga Khan U., Karachi, Pakistan, 1995. Mem. editl. bd. Jour. Surg. Rsch., 1973-79, Annals of Thoracic Surgery, 1979-88; mem. sci. adv. bd. Jour. for Heart Valve Disease, 1993-94; mem. editl. adv. bd. ECRI Operating Rm. Risk Mgmt., 1992—; co-editor: Comprehensive Thoracic Surgery Curriculum, TSDA, 1995; contbr. numerous articles to profl. jours., chpts. to books. Recipient John Horsley Meml. prize U. Va. Med. Sch., 1962; Merit award Research Forum of Am. Coll. Chest Physicians, 1968; research fellow Va. Heart Assn., 1961-62, Am. Cancer Soc., 1963-64; grantee NIH, 1968-84, Am. Heart Assn., 1970-73, Medtronic Corp., 1975-81. Fellow ACS, Am. Coll. Cardiology, Am. Surg. Assn.; mem. Am. Assn. Thoracic Surgery (rep. to Assn. Am. Med. Colls., Am. Bd. Cardiovascular Perfusion, Am. Soc. Extracorporeal Tech., others), Am. Heart Assn. (coun. on cardiovascular surgery 1969—, anesthesiology, radiology and surgery study com. 1991-94), Andrew G. Morrow Soc., Assn. Acad. Surgery, Assn. Advancement of Med. Instrumentation (chair-elect 1996, co-chmn. cardiac valve prostheses stds. com. 1974—, mem. internat. stds. com. 1989—, bd. dirs. 1990—, stds. bd. 1991—, edn. com. 1992-93, nominating com. 1996—, exec. com. 1996—), Internat. Stds. Orgn. (chmn. subcom. on cardiovascular surg. implants 1982—), Assn. Clin. Cardiac Surgeons, Halsted Soc. (exec. com. 1985-89), Coord. Com. on Perfusion Affairs (chmn. 1990—), Internat. Assn. Cardiac Biol. Implants (sci. com. 1994), Internat. Cardiovascular Soc., Muller Surg. Soc. (pres. 1979), Soc. Internat. de Cirurgie, Soc. Vascular Surgery, Soc. Thoracic Surgeons (ad hoc com. on industry rels. 1992—, stds. and ethics com. 1993-95, edn. and resources com. 1996—), Soc. Univ. Surgeons, Southeastern Surg. Congress, So. Surg. Assn. (2d v.p. 1982), Va. Surg. Soc. (v.p. 1980-83, pres. 1984), Va. Vascular Soc. (exec. coun. 1985-86), Soc. Critical Care Medicine, Raven Soc., Assn. Am. Med. Colls. (rep. coun. acad. socs. 1992—), Alpha Omega Alpha, Omicron Delta Kappa. Clubs: Chevy Chase (Md.); Farmington Country (Va.); Princeton (N.Y.C.). Office: U Va Dept Surgery Box 181-6 Charlottesville VA 22908

NOLAN, THEODORE JOHN, professional hockey coach; b. Sault Ste. Marie, Ont., Can., Apr. 7, 1958. Center Detroit Red Wings, 1978-85, Buffalo (N.Y.) Sabres, 1985, Pitts. Penguins, 1985-86, Buffalo Sabres, 1986; asst. coach Hartford (Conn.) Whalers, 1994-95; head coach Buffalo Sabres, 1995—. Recipient Adams award Coach of the Yr., 1997. Office: Marine Midland Arena One Main St Buffalo NY 14203*

NOLAN, VAL, JR., biologist, lawyer; b. Evansville, Ind., Apr. 28, 1920; s. Val and Jeannette (Covert) N.; m. Susanne Howe, Dec. 23, 1946 (div. Aug. 29, 1980); children: Val, Ann Clare, William Alan; m. Ellen D. Ketterson, Oct. 17, 1980. A.B., Ind. U., 1941, J.D., 1949. Bar: Ind. 1949. Dep. U.S. marshal, 1941; agt. White House Detail, U.S. Secret Service, 1942; asst. prof. law Ind. U., 1949-52, assoc. prof., 1952-56, prof., 1956-85, prof. emeritus, 1985—, research scholar in zoology, 1957-68, prof. zoology, 1968-77, prof. biology, 1977-85; prof. emeritus, 1985—, acting dean Sch. Law, 1976, 80. Author: (with F.E. Horack, Jr.) Land Use Controls, 1955, Ecology and Behavior of the Prairie Warbler, 1978; editor Ind. Law Jour., 1945-46; co-editor Current Ornithology, 1994—. Served with USNR, 1942-46. Guggenheim fellow, 1957; recipient Ind. U. Disting. Alumni Svc. award, 1987; named to Acad. Law Alumni Fellows, Ind. U., 1988. Fellow AAAS, Am. Ornithologists Union (v.p. 1989-90, Brewster Meml. award 1986); mem. Brit. Ornithologists Union, Cooper Ornithol. Soc., Wilson Ornithol. Soc., Assn. Field Ornithologists, Ecol. Soc. Am., Am. Soc. Naturalists, Animal Behavior Soc., Deutsche Ornithologen-Gesellschaft, Nederlandse Ornithologische Unie, Soc. for Study of Reprodn., Phi Beta Kappa, Sigma Xi. Democrat. Home: 4675 E Heritage Woods Rd Bloomington IN 47401-9312

NOLAN, VICTORIA, theater director; b. Portland, Maine, June 15, 1952; d. Herbert Wallace and Diane Katharine (Kremm) N.; m. Clarkson Newell Crolius, Aug. 30, 1980; children: Covey Emmeline, Wilhelmina Adams. BA magna cum laude, U. Maine, 1976. Publicity asst. Loeb Drama Ctr. Harvard U., Cambridge, Mass., 1975; pub. rels. asst. to dir. Sch. for Arts Boston U., 1975-76; mgmt. asst. TAG Found., N.Y.C., 1976-77; mng. dir. Ram Island Dance Co., Portland, 1977-78; dir. devel. Ctr. Stage, Balt., 1979-81, assoc. mng. dir., 1981-87; mng. dir. Ind. Repertory Theatre, Indpls., 1988-93; mng. dir., assoc. prof. Yale Sch. Drama, Yale Repertory Theatre, New Haven, 1993—; cons. Fedn. for Ext. and Devel. Am. Profl. Theatre, N.Y.C., 1979-87; program evaluator Nat. Endowment for Arts, Washington, 1988—, panelist, 1991-95; mem. Indpls. Cultural Consortium, v.p., 1991-93; bd. dirs. Greater Indpls. Progress Com., Indpls. Urban League, Arts Coun. Indpls.; mem. nat. bd. Theatre Comm. Group, N.Y.C., treas., 1995—. Mem. exec. com. League Resident Profl. Theatres. Nat. Performing Arts Mgmt. fellow Exxon, Doner Fedn. and NEA, 1978. Home: 120 Rimmon Rd Woodbridge CT 06525-1915 Office: Yale Repertory Theater PO Box 208244 Yale Station 222 York St New Haven CT 06520-8244

NOLAND, CHARLES DONALD, lawyer, educator; b. Tulsa, July 31, 1946; s. Clyde Earl and Birdeen Elizabeth (White) N.; m. Elisabeth Hooper, June 27, 1987; 1 stepchild, Richard G. Reynolds. BA in Journalism, U. N.Mex., 1972, JD, 1978. Bar: N.Mex. 1978, U.S. Dist. Ct. N.Mex. 1979, U.S. Ct. Appeals (10th cir.) 1991, U.S. Supreme Ct. 1991. Reporter, copy editor New Mexican, Santa Fe, 1969; newsman AP, Des Moines, 1969-71, Albuquerque, 1973-74; editor programmed instrn. materials Systema Corp., Albuquerque, 1974-75; pvt. practice Albuquerque, 1978-79; asst. gen. counsel, then gen. counsel N.Mex. Dept. Edn., Santa Fe, 1979-83; asst. atty. gen. State of N.Mex., Santa Fe, 1984-85; pvt. practice Santa Fe, 1985-95; dep. gen. counsel N.Mex. Dept. Corrections, Santa Fe, 1995—; adj. prof. U. N.Mex. Grad. Sch. Edn., 1981, 92, N.Mex. Highlands U. Grad. Sch. Edn., 1985, Coll. Santa Fe, 1984-89; sole practitioner, pvt. practice Simons, Cuddy & Friedman, Santa Fe, 1985-95; cons. in field; hearing officer tchr. termination appeals N.Mex. Bd. Edn., 1980, 81; presenter N.Mex. Sch. Bds.; Assn. Law Conf., 1980-95; panelist pub. sch. reduction in force Nat. Sch. Bds. Assn. Conv., Dallas, 1981. Contbr. articles to profl. publs. Founding bd. dirs. Santa Fe Symphony Orch., 1984-85, corp. sec., 1985-88; community musician Santa Fe Concert Band, Santa Fe Brass Ensemble, 1983-89; mem. audit com. Christ the King Episc. Ch., 1996, chair 1997. With U.S. Army, 1971-72. Mem. State Bar N.Mex. (mem. trial practice sect.). Avocation: trombone. Home: 3 Pino Pl Santa Fe NM 87505-8750 Office: NMex Dept Corrections PO Box 27116 Santa Fe NM 87502-0116

NOLAND, CHRISTINE A., magistrate judge. BA, La. State Univ., JD. Law clk. to Hon. John V. Parker U.S. Dist. Ct. (La. mid. dist.), 5th circuit; magistrate judge U.S. Dist. Ct. (La. mid. dist.), 5th circuit, Baton Rouge, 1987—. Mem. ABA, La. State Bar, La. trial Lawyers Assn., Baton Rouge Bar Assn., Dean Henry George McMahon Inn of Ct. (counselor). Office: Russell B Long Fed Bldg & Courthouse 777 Florida St Rm 265 Baton Rouge LA 70801-1717

NOLAND, GARY LLOYD, vocation educational administrator; b. Lindsborg, Kans., July 29, 1942; s. Willard L. and Florence L. (Waggoner) N.; m. Deborah L. Homan, Mar. 20, 1981; children: Krista L., Timothy L. BSBA, Cen. Mo. State U., 1971, MEd, 1974. Cert. vocat. dir., Mo. V.p. sales First Nat. Land Co., Scottsdale, Ariz., 1961-66; student grad. asst. Cen. Mo. State U., Warrensburg, 1968-72; instr. State Fair CC., Sedalia, Mo., 1972-74, dir. job placement, 1974-79; dir. Statewide Job Placement Svc., Sedalia, 1979-84, State Fair Area Vocat. Sch., Sedalia, 1984—; dir. State Fair C.C. Found., Sedalia, 1986—; mgr. State Fair Coll. Farm, Sedalia, 1987-92. Author: Help Yourself to Successful Employment, 1980; author instructional modules. mem., chmn. ctrl. Mo. chpt. March of Dimes, Sedalia, 1979; v.p. Pettis County Farm Bur., Sedalia, 1987-91, pres., 1991-95; bd. dirs. Mo. Farm Bur., 1995—, Am. Cancer Soc., Sedalia, 1989-92. Named Outstanding Young Man Am., 1979, Outstanding Placement Specialist, Mo. Guidance and Placement, 1980, Outstanding Vocat. Program Area VII, U.S. Dept. Edn., 1982. Mem. VFW (life), Am. Simmental Assn., Am. Legion, Mo. Coun. Local Adminstrs., Mo. Assn. Secondary Prins., Mo. Cattleman's Assn., Pettis County Cattleman's Assn., Lions (pres. Sedalia 1979-80), Masons, Sedalia Area C. of C. (amb. 1975-92). Baptist. Avocations: farming, golfing, fishing. Home: 19776 Ridge Crest Pl Sedalia MO 65301-1514 Office: State Fair Area Vocat Sch 3201 W 16th St Sedalia MO 65301-2188

NOLAND, KENNETH CLIFTON, artist; b. Asheville, N.C., Apr. 10, 1924; s. Harry C. and Bessie (Elkins) N.; m. Cornelia Langer (div.); children: Cady, William L., Lyndon; m. Stephanie Gordon, 1967 (div.); m. Peggy Schiffer; children: Samuel Jesse (div.); m. Paige Rense, 1994. Student, Ozzip Zadkine, Paris, 1948-49; studied, Black Mountain Coll., N.C., summers, 1950, 51. Tchr. Inst. Contemporary Arts, 1950-52, Cath. U., 1951-60. One man shows include Galerie Creuze, Paris, 1949, Tibor de Nagy Gallery, N.Y.C., 1957, 58, Jefferson Pl. Gallery, 1958, French & Co., N.Y.C., 1959, Bennington Coll., 1961, Andre Emmerich Gallery, N.Y.C., 15 shows from 1960-83, Andre Emmerich Gallery, Zurich, Switzerland, 1973, 76, 79, 82, David Mirvish Gallery, Toronto, Can., 1965, 67, 74, 76, Jewish Mus., 1965, Salander O'Reilly Galleries, N.Y.C., 1989, Leo Castelli Gallery, N.Y., 1995, Gana Art Gallery, Seoul, 1995-96, also other galleries in Milan, Italy, Paris, Zurich, Dusseldorf, Hamburg and Cologne, Fed. Republic Germany, London, Montreal and Toronto, Can.; retrospective show Guggenheim Mus., N.Y.C., 1977; group shows include Kootz Gallery, N.Y.C., 1954, Norman Mackenzie Art Gallery, Regina, Sask., Can., 1963, Corcoran Gallery, Washington, 1956, 59, 63, 64, 67, 70, 75, Corcoran Gallery Biennial in Italy, 1964, Fogg Art Mus., Cambridge, Mass., 1965, 72, Mus. Modern Art, N.Y.C., 1965, 68, Nat. Gallery, Washington, 1968, U.S. Pavilion Expo 67, Montreal, Art Inst. Chgo., 1962, 70, 72, 76, Balt. Mus., 1957, 70, 77, Jewish Mus., 1963, Tate Gallery, London, 1964, 74, Guggenheim Mus., 1961, 66, 70, 73-74, 76-77, L.A. County Mus., 1964, Inst. Contemporary Art, Boston, 1964, 65, 67, Whitney Mus., N.Y.C., 1961-67, 69-73, 76, Met. Mus. N.Y.C., 1968, 70, Mus. Fine Arts, Boston, 1972, Albright-Knox Gallery, Buffalo, 1978, 80; represented in permanent collections Salander O'Reily Galleries, N.Y.C., Mus. of Fine Arts, Houston, 1994, Ft. Lauderdale, 1994; Arte Metro Roma, Rome Colosseum Ctrl. Subway Mosaic Installed, 1995. Trustee Bennington (Vt.) Coll. Recipient 1st prize Premio Nacional Internat., Inst. Torcuato de Tella, Buenos Aires, 1964, Creative Arts award Brandeis U., 1965, 4th prize Corcoran Biennale, 1967; recipient The N.C. Award/medal of arts, 1995. Home: Hall Farm RR 1 Box 45 North Bennington VT 05257-9703

NOLAND, MARCUS, economist, educator; b. Greensboro, N.C., Mar. 29, 1959. BA, Swarthmore Coll., 1981; PhD, Johns Hopkins U., 1985. Sr. fellow Inst. for Internat. Econs., Washington, 1985—; asst. prof. U. So. Calif., L.A., 1990-91; sr. economist Coun. Econ. Advisers, Washington, 1993-94; vis. prof. Saltama U., Urawa, Japan, 1988-89; vis. scholar Korea Devel. Inst., Swoul, 1991; vis. assoc. prof. Johns Hopkins U., Balt., 1991—; vis. prof. Tokyo U., 1996, U. Ghana, 1997; cons. N.Y. Stock Exch., 1990, Adv. Com. on Trade Policy, Washington, 1989-92, World Bank, Washington, 1990—. Author: Pacific Basin Developing Countries, 1991; co-author: Japan in the World Economy, 1988, Reconcilable Differences?, 1993; co-editor: Pacific Economic Dynamism, 1993. Japan Soc. for Promotion of Sci. fellow, 1988; Internat. Affairs fellow Coun. on Fgn. Rels., 1993. Mem. Coun. on Fgn. Rels. Office: Inst for Internat Econs 11 Dupont Cir NW Washington DC 20036

NOLAND, MARIAM CHARL, foundation executive; b. Parkersburg, W.Va., Mar. 29, 1947; d. Lloyd Henry and Ethel May (Beare) N.; m. James Arthur Kelly, June 13, 1981. BS, Case Western Res. U., 1969; M in Edn., Harvard U., 1975. Asst. dir admissions, fin. aid Baldwin-Wallace Coll., Berea, Ohio, 1969-72; asst. dir. admissions Davidson (N.C.) Coll., 1972-74; case writer Inst. Edn. Mgmt., Cambridge, Mass., 1975; sec., treas., program officer The Cleve. Found., 1975-81; v.p. The St. Paul Found., 1981-85; pres. Community Found. for S.E. Mich., 1985—; chair bd. trustees Coun. of Mich. Founds., Grand Haven, Mich., 1988—. Trustee Coun. on Founds., 1994—, Henry Ford Health System, 1994—, Alma Coll., 1994—. Mem. Detroit Com. Fgn. Rels. Office: Community Found Southeastern Mich 333 W Fort St Bsmt 2010 Detroit MI 48226-3134

NOLAND, ROBERT LEROY, retired manufacturing company executive; b. Lawrence, Kans., Sept. 7, 1918; s. Harry L. and Angela (Scola) N.; m. Delpha Mae Mierndorf, June 16, 1962; children: Gary, Fabra Jeanine, Derice Elizabeth. B.S. in Mech. Engring, Calif. Inst. Tech., 1941. Design and devel. rocket propelled devices Calif. Inst. Tech., 1941-45; supr. propulsions Naval Ordnance Test Sta., China Lake, Calif., 1945-46; asst. chief engr. Aerojet Gen. Corp., 1946-52; cons. engr. plastic components, rockets and missiles, 1952-54; exec. v.p. Rienhold Engring. and Plastics Co., 1954-57, pres., 1957-59; exec. v.p. Haveg Industries, Wilmington, Del., 1959-66; exec. v.p. Ametek, Inc., Paoli, Pa., 1966-68, pres., bd. dirs., 1968-88; pres., chief exec. officer, dir. Ketema Inc., Bensalem, Pa., 1988-92; ret., ret., 1992; chmn. bd. Myricom, 1994—. Home: 5555 East Lake Blvd Carson City NV 89704-9266

NOLAND, ROYCE PAUL, association executive, physical therapist; b. Walla Walla, Wash., Dec. 6, 1928; s. Homer Vernon and Mildred Bessie (Royce) N.; m. April Lynn Hawkes, Feb. 10, 1979; children—Royce Paul, Richard Mitchell. B.A., Whitman Coll., Walla Walla, Wash., 1951; Cert. in phys. therapy, Stanford U., 1952. Pvt. practice in phys. therapy Santa Cruz, Calif., 1961-68; exec. dir. Calif. chpt. Am. Phys. Therapy Assn., Santa Cruz, Calif., 1965-69; exec. dir. Am. Phys. Therapy Assn., Washington, D.C., 1969-87; pres., chief exec. officer Inst. Profl. Health Service Adminstrs., Alexandria, 1988-91; exec. dir., CEO Fedn. of State Bds. of Phys. Therapy, Alexandria, Va., 1992-97; CEO Nat. Phys. Rehab. Networks, Inc., Alexandria, 1997—. Co-inventor phys. therapy device; contbr. articles to profl. publs. Mem. Am. Soc. Assn. Execs. (cert.), Presdl. Commn. Employment of Handicapped, Am. Pub. Health Assn. Republican. Club: Belle Haven Country (Alexandria). Avocation: golf. Home: 2302 Popkins Ln Alexandria VA 22306-2443 Office: Nat Phys Rehab Networks Inc 601 Madison St Alexandria VA 22314

NOLD, CARL RICHARD, state historic parks and museums administrator; b. Mineola, N.Y., Nov. 26, 1955; s. Carl Frederick and Joan Catherine (Heine) N.; m. Mary Beth Krivoruchka (div.). BA in History magna cum laude, St. John's U., Jamaica, N.Y., 1977; MA in History Mus. Studies, SUNY, Oneonta, 1982. Pres. Gregory Mus., Hicksville, N.Y., 1977; registrar N.Y. State Hist. Assn., Cooperstown, 1978-80; dir., curator Gadsby's Tavern Mus., Alexandria, Va., 1980-84; dir. State Mus. Pa., Harrisburg, 1984-91; exec. dir. Mackinac State Hist. Parks, Lansing, Mackinac Island, Mich., 1992—; grant reviewer Inst. Mus. Svcs., Washington, 1982-90, 95—, mus. assessment prog. reviewer, 1985—, panelist, 1992-94; panelist mus. grant prog. Nat. Endowment for Humanities, 1990-93. Co-author: Gadsby's Tavern Mus. Interpretive Master Plan, 1984; contbr. articles to profl. jours. Mem. adv. bd. for Grad. History George Mason U., Fairfax, Va., 1982-84, adv. com. Susquehanna Mus. Art, Harrisburg, 189-91; bd. dirs. Harrisburg-Hershey-Carlisle Tourism and Visitor Bur., 1987-91, bd. sec., 1990-91; mem. mayor's adv. bd. city of Mackinac Island, 1993—. Mem. Midwest Mus. Assn., Mich. Mus. Assn. (bd. dirs. 1995—), Am. Assn. Mus. (vis. com. mus. accreditation 1989—), Am. Assn. for State and Local History (elections chmn. 1990), Cooperstown Grad. Assn. (bd. dirs. 1985-87).

NOLDE, SHARI ANN, pediatrics, critical care nurse; b. Bad Axe, Mich., Nov. 24, 1960; d. Kurt E. and Leona P. (Ruthkowski) Zinger; m. Bart David Nolde, May 22, 1982; children: Byron David, Bart William. BSN, Saginaw Valley State U., 1982. Cert. ACLS, PALS. Pediatric staff nurse Bay Medical Ctr., Bay City, Mich., 1982-83; medical/surgical nurse Sierra Vista Cmty., Sierra Vista, Ariz., 1983; pediatric nurse St. John's Hosp., Leavenworth, Kans., 1983-85; chief nurse ambulatory clinic U.S. Army Hosp., Fulda, Fed. Republic Germany, 1986-88; pediatric charge nurse Potomac Hosp., Woodbridge, Va.; staff nurse neonatal ICU Fairfax (Va.) Hosp., 1988-90; charge nurse NICU No. Mich. Hosp., Petroskey, Mich., 1990-94; staff nurse emergency rm. Tex. Children's Hosp., Houston, 1994; staff nurse Neonatal ICU Saginaw (Mich.) Gen. Hosp., 1994-95; emergency rm. nurse Bay Med. Ctr., 1995—; neonatal resusitation instr., 1992.

NOLEN, JERRY AFTEN, JR., physicist; b. Washington, Nov. 17, 1940; s. Jerry Aften and Roxie Ann (Stout) N.; m. Geraldine Janet Meads, Oct. 4, 1980; children by previous marriage: Greer Roxanne, Joyce Lynne, Paige Hamilton; stepchildren: Jeffrey Brian, Tara Leigh, Christopher Allen. BS, Lehigh U., 1961; PhD, Princeton U., 1965. Instr. Princeton (N.J.) U., 1965-66; postdoctoral appointee Argonne (Ill.) Nat. Lab., 1966-68; asst. prof. U. Md., College Park, 1968-70; assoc. prof. Mich. State U., East Lansing, 1970-76; prof. physics Mich. State U., 1976-92, assoc. dir. Nat. Superconducting Cyclotron Lab., 1984-92; Max Planck fellow Heidelberg, Ger., 1977; dir. Atlas Argonne Nat. Lab., Argonne, Ill., 1992—. Contbr. articles to profl. jours.; editor: (with W. Benenson) Atomic Masses and Fundamental Constants, 1980. Woodrow Wilson grad. fellow, 1961-62. Fellow Am. Phys. Soc. (mem. exec. com. div. nuclear physics 1989-91, mem. nuclear sci. adv. com. 1996-97); mem. Sigma Xi, Phi Beta Kappa, Tau Beta Pi. Home: # 4104 1816 N Orleans Chicago IL 60614 Office: Argonne Nat Lab Physics Div Bldg 203 Argonne IL 60439

NOLEN, ROY LEMUEL, lawyer; b. Montgomery, Ala., Nov. 29, 1937; s. Roy Lemuel Jr. and Elizabeth (Larkin) N.; m. Evelyn McNeill Thomas, Aug. 28, 1965; 1 child, Rives Rutledge. BArch, Rice U., 1961; LLB, Harvard U., 1967. Bar: Tex. 1968, U.S. Ct. Appeals (5th cir.) 1969. Law clk. to sr. judge U.S. Ct. Appeals (5th cir.), 1967-68; assoc. Baker & Botts, Houston, 1968-75, ptnr., 1976—; co-head Corp. Dept., 1985-90, mem. exec. com., 1988-91. Bd. dirs. Houston Ballet Found., 1980-92, Rice Design Alliance, 1995-96; exec. com. Contemporary Arts Mus., 1990-96; exec. com., gen. counsel Houston Symphony Soc., 1994—; sr. warden Christ Ch. Cathedral, 1991-92; chmn. Houston area devel. initiative Episcopal Diocese of Tex., 1997. 1st lt. USMC, 1961-64. Mem. ABA, State Bar of Tex., Houston Bar Assn., Coronado Club, Allegro, Paul Jones Dancing Club. Episcopalian. Office: Baker & Botts 3000 One Shell Plz 910 Louisiana St Houston TX 77002-4916

NOLEN, WILFRED E., church administrator. Pres. Brethren Benefit Trust. Office: 1505 Dundee Ave Elgin IL 60120-1605*

NOLEN, WILLIAM GILES, lawyer, accountant; b. Fayetteville, Ark., Aug. 4, 1931; s. William Jefferson and Marie (Giles) N.; m. Carole Turner, Aug. 25, 1957; children: Kathy, Thomas. B.S.B.A., U. Ark., 1960; J.D., U. Houston, 1980. Bar: Tex. 1980; CPA, Tex. Auditor Arthur Anderson & Co., Houston, 1960-66; sec., treas. Brown & Root (U.K.) Ltd., London, 1966-69; v.p. Highlands Ins. Co., Houston, 1969-73, sr. v.p., 1973-80, dir., 1973-88; v.p. Halliburton Co., Dallas, 1980-82; sr. v.p. Brown & Root, Inc., Houston, 1982-86; exec. v.p. Highlands Ins. Co., Houston, 1986-88; of counsel Whitmore, Sheppard & Pollicoff, Houston, 1988-92, Policoff, Smith & Myres LLP, Houston, 1992-95, Policoff, Smith, Myres & Remels LLP, Houston, 1995—. Maj. USAF, 1951-56. Mem. ABA, Am. Assn. Atty. CPAs (v.p., bd. dirs.), Tex. Soc. CPAs (Tex. CPA of Yr. 1961), Mensa. Presbyterian.

NOLF, DAVID MANSTAN, financial executive; b. Hartford, Conn., Nov. 25, 1942; s. Richard A. and Erreld I. (Manstan) N.; m. Linda J. Anderson, June 20, 1964; 1 child, Cristina E. BSChemE, Lafayette Coll., 1964; MBA, U. Conn., 1968. Prodn. engr. Am. Cyanamid, Wallingford, Conn., 1664-66; adminstrn. supr. Electric Boat Div. Gen. Dynamics, Groton, Conn., 1966-71; chief fin. and adminstrv. officer, corp. sec. Analysis and Tech. Inc., North Stonington, Conn., 1971—; bd. dirs. Analysis and Tech., Inc., North Stonington, Conn., Applied Sci. Assocs., Butler, Pa., Integrated Performance Decisions, Inc., North Stonington. Bd. dirs., sec. Sch. Bldg. Com., Stonington, 1989-92; chmn. Ch. Fin. Com., Westerly, R.I., 1996—; trustee Westerly Hosp., 1993—, New London Day Newspaper, 1997—. Mem. Nat. Contract Mgmt. Assn., Am. Mgmt. Assn., Def. Preparedness Assn., Tau Bet Pi, Beta Gamma Sigma. Avocations: fishing, golf. Home: 11 Meadow Rd Pawcatuck CT 06379-2013 Office: Analysis & Tech Inc Technology Park PO Box 220 North Stonington CT 06359-9801

NOLL, ANNA CECILIA, curator; b. Alexandria, Va., July 22, 1950; d. Louis Richard and Barbara Lucille (Curtice) N. BS in Psychology, Va. Poly. Inst. and State Univ., 1974; MA in Art History, George Washington U., 1983. Asst. curator Queens Mus., Flushing, N.Y., 1984-86; curator Fort Wayne (Ind.) Mus. Art, 1986-89, Heckscher Mus., Huntington, N.Y., 1989-95; curator of collections Tacoma Art Mus., 1996—; guest essayist June Kelly Gallery, N.Y.C., 1994, Bernice Steinbaum Gallery, N.Y.C., 1989; mem. benefit com. Ctr. for Book Arts Auction, N.Y.C., 1991. Vol. Gay Men's Health Crisis AIDS Dance-a-thon, N.Y.C., 1990, Cold Spring Harbor (N.Y.) Lab. Centennial Celebration, 1990. Hilla von Rebay fellow Solomon R. Guggenheim Mus., 1981, Univ. fellow George Washington U., 1981-83. Mem. Am. Assn. Mus. (mem. curators com., co-chair exhibit competition 1994-95), Coll. Art Assn. (presenter ann. meeting 1994, 97), Pacific Northwest Garden History Soc. (charter). Avocations: garden history, cooking, travel. Office: Tacoma Art Mus 1123 Pacific Ave Tacoma WA 98402-4303

NOLL, CHARLES HENRY, former professional football coach; b. Cleve., Jan. 5, 1932; m. Marianne Noll; 1 son, Chris. BE, U. Dayton, 1953. Football player Cleve. Browns, 1953-59; asst. coach San Diego Chargers, 1960-65, Balt. Colts, 1966-68; head coach Pitts. Steelers, 1969-91; winner Super Bowl games, 1975-76, 79-80; now admn. advisor Pittsburgh Steelers. Named Am. Football Conf. Coach of Yr., UPI, 1972; inductee Pro Football Hall of Fame, 1993. Office: 300 Stadium Cir Pittsburgh PA 15212-5729 Office: The Football Hall of Fame 2121 George Halas Dr NW Canton OH 44708-2630*

NOLL, JOHN F., sales and marketing executive, investment banker; b. Ft. Wayne, Ind., Feb. 2, 1945; s. Martin F. and Viola N.: m. Ann E. Files, Sept. 23, 1972; children: Eric, Scott. BA in Philosophy, Athanaeum of Ohio Coll., 1966; MA in English, Purdue U., 1968; MBA in Mktg., U. of Colo., 1970. From sales rep. to dist. mgr. Procter & Gamble, Cin., 1968-83; v.p. sales Software Distrbn. Svcs., Buffalo, 1983-85; adminstrv. v.p. trusts M&T Bank, Buffalo, 1985-88; dir. sales and mktg. Select Interior Door, Ltd., N. Java, N.Y., 1988-93; dir. corp. fin. Capital Formation Group, 1994—; co-founder, bd. dirs. NORAM Group, Ltd., Buffalo, 1988—; owner Sales Resources, Orchard Park, N.Y., 1989-90. Bd. dirs. Orchard Park Little League, 1973-85, Boys and Girls Club of Orchard Park, 1986-93; bd. dirs., pres. Eagle Ridge Recreation Assn., Orchard Park, 1986-88. Mem. Am. Mktg. Assn., Sales and Mktg. Execs. (bd. dirs. 1989-91), Resource Group (founder, bd. dirs. 1981—), Orchard Park Country Club. Republican. Presbyterian. Avocations: golf, skiing, tennis. Home and Office: 46 Knob Hill Rd Orchard Park NY 14127-3931

NOLL, ROGER GORDON, economist, educator; b. Monterey Park, Calif., Mar. 13, 1940; s. Cecil Ray and Hjordis Alberta (Westover) N.; m. Robyn Schreiber, Aug. 25, 1962; 1 child, Kimberlee Elizabeth. B.S., Calif. Inst. Tech., 1962; A.M., Harvard U., 1965, Ph.D. in Econs, 1967. Mem. social sci. faculty Calif. Inst. Tech., 1965-84, prof., 1973-82, Inst. prof., 1982-84, chmn. div. humanities and social scis., 1978-82; prof. econs. Stanford U., 1984—, dir. pub. policy program, 1986—, Morris M. Doyle centennial prof. of pub. policy, 1990—; Jean Monnet prof. European U. Inst., 1991; vis. fellow Brookings Instn., 1995-96; sr. staff economist Coun. of Econ. Advisors, Washignton, 1967-69; sr. fellow Brookings Instn., Washington, 1970-73; mem. tech. adv. bd. Com. for Econ. Devel., 1978-82; mem. adv. coun. NSF, 1978-89, SERI, 1982-90, NASA, 1978-81; mem. Pres.'s Commn. for Nat. Agenda for the Eighties, 1980; chmn. L.A.Sch. Monitoring Com., 1978-79; mem. Commn. on Behavioral Social Scis. and Edn., NAS, 1984-90; mem. energy rsch. adv. bd. Dept. Energy, 1986-89; mem. Sec. of Energy Adv. Bd., 1990-94. Author: Reforming Regulation, 1971, The Economics and Politics of Deregulation, 1991; co-author: Economic Aspects of Television Regulation, 1973, The Political Economy of Deregulation, 1983, The Technology Pork Barrel, 1991; editor: Government and the Sports Business, 1974, Regulatory Policy and the Social Sciences, 1985; co-editor: Constitutional Reform in California, 1995; supervisory editor Info. Econs. and Policy Jour., 1984-92. NSF grantee, 1973-82; Recipient 1st ann. book award Nat. Assn. Ednl. Broadcasters, 1974; Guggenheim fellow, 1983-84. Mem. Am. Econ. Assn., Calif. Coun. on Sci. and Tech. Democrat. Home: 4153 Hubbart Dr Palo Alto CA 94306-3834 Office: Stanford U Dept Econs Stanford CA 94305

NOLLAU, LEE GORDON, lawyer; b. Balt., Feb. 6, 1950; s. E. Wilson and Carolyn G. (Blass) N.; m. Carol A. Haughney, Aug. 12, 1978; children: Ann G., Catherine E., Margaret C. BA, Juniata Coll., 1972; MAS, Johns

Hopkins U., 1975; JD, Dickinson Sch. Law, 1976. Bar: Pa. 1976, U.S. Dist. Ct. (mid. dist.) 1982, U.S. Dist. Ct. (we. dist.) 1988, U.S. Ct. Appeals (3d cir.) 1980, U.S. Supreme Ct. 1982. Instr. Juniata Coll., Huntingdon, Pa., 1976-78; asst. dist. atty. Centre County, Bellefonte, Pa., 1978-80, dist. atty., 1981; assoc. Litke, Lee, Martin, Grine & Green, Bellefonte, 1981-83, Jubelirer & Assocs., State College, Pa., 1983-87; ptnr. Jubelirer, Nollau, Young & Blanarik, Inc., State College, 1988-89, Jubelirer, Rayback, Nollau, Walsh, Young & Blanarik, Inc., State College, 1989-94, Nollau & Young, State Coll., Pa., 1994—; mental health rev. officer Centre County, Bellefonte, 1982—; instr. Pa. State U. Smeal Coll. Bus. Adminstrn., 1995—; lectr. Pa. Bar Inst., 1995—. Mem. ABA, Pa. Bar Assn., Centre Co. Bar, Pa. Assn. Criminal Def. Lawyers. Presbyterian. Office: Nollau & Young 2153 E College Ave State College PA 16801-7204

NOLLER, HARRY FRANCIS, JR., biochemist, educator; b. Oakland, Calif., June 10, 1939; s. Harry Francis and Charlotte Frances (Silva) N.; m. Betty Lucille Parnow, Nov. 25, 1964 (div. 1969); 1 child, Maria Irene; m. Sharon Ann Sussman; 1 child, Eric Francis; stepchildren: Django Sussman, Seb Sussman. AB, U. Calif., Berkeley, 1960; PhD, U. Oreg., 1965. Postdoctoral fellow MRC Lab. of Molecular Biology, Cambridge, Eng., 1965-66, Inst. Molecular Biology, Geneva, Switzerland, 1966-68; asst. prof. biology U. Calif., Santa Cruz, 1968-73, assoc. prof., 1973-79, prof. biology, 1979—, Robert Louis Sinsheimer prof. molecular biology, 1987—; Harvey lectr. Rockefeller U., 1989; Sherman Fairchild Disting. scholar, Calif. Inst. Tech., 1990; dir. Ctr. Molecular Biology of RNA, 1992—. Mem. NAS, The RNA Soc. (pres.-elect 1997). Office: Sinsheimer Labs U Calif Santa Cruz High St Santa Cruz CA 95064-1099

NOLLETTI, JAMES JOSEPH, lawyer; b. Portchester, N.Y., Sept. 20, 1953; s. James Louis and Anne Marie (Mandracchia) N.; children: Jay, Justin, Jamie-Lynn, Jeff. BA, Villanova U., 1975; JD, Fordham U., 1978. Bar: N.Y. 1979, U.S. Dist. Ct. (so. dist.) N.Y., U.S. Supreme Ct. Asst. dist. atty. Westchester County Dist. Atty.'s Office, White Plains, N.Y., 1978-81; assoc. Sirlin & Sirlin, Mamaroneck, N.Y., 1981-84; ptnr. Sirlin, Sirlin & Nolletti, Mamaroneck, 1984—; village atty. Village of Mamaroneck, 1985—; mem. adv. bd. Westchester Abstract Co., White Plains, 1985-88; bd. dirs., legal advisor Orienta Beach CLUB, iNC., mAMARONECK, 1986-90. Commr. ABC bd. Westchester County, White Plains, 1984-88, Westchester County Pub. Employees Rels. Bd., 1986-88. Mem. N.Y. State Bar Assn., Westchester County Bar Assn., Westchester County Col. Lawyers Bar Assn. (bd. dirs., v.p. 1989-93). Office: Sirlin Sirlin Nolletti 211 Mamaroneck Ave Mamaroneck NY 10543-2602

NOLLY, ROBERT J., hospital administrator, pharmaceutical science educator; b. Amsterdam, N.Y., Jan. 8, 1947; m. Diera R. Lehtonen, June 21, 1969; children: Shelby Alexandra, Kirby Alycia, Kendall Alexis. BS in Pharmacy with honor, Albany Coll. Pharmacy, 1970; MSc in Hosp. Pharmacy, Ohio State U., 1979. Pharmacy extern Matt Pharmacy, Canajoharie, N.Y., 1967-70; pharmacy intern Park Row Drugs, Canajoharie, 1970-71, asst. mgr., 1971-72; staff pharmacist Mary Imogene Bassett Hosp., Cooperstown, N.Y., 1972-74, 75-77; med. svc. rep. Dista Products Co., Eli Lilly and Co., Indpls., 1974-75; resident hosp. pharmacy Grant Hosp., Columbus, Ohio, 1977-79; asst. dir. pharmacy svcs. City of Memphis Hosp., 1979-81; asst. dir. pharmacy svcs. U. Tenn. Bowld Hosp., Memphis, 1980-82, dir. pharmacy svcs. and materials mgmt., 1982-85, asst. adminstr. pharmacy svcs. and materials mgmt., 1985-91, adminstr., 1991—; asst. prof. dept. pharmacy practice Coll. Pharmacy U. Tenn., Memphis, 1979-83, asst. prof. dept. health sci. adminstrn. dept. pharmaceutics, 1983-92, assoc. prof. dept. clin. pharmacy divsn. pharmacy adminstrn., dept. pharm. scis., 1992—; attended confs., mgmt. tng. programs in field; lectr. Columbus Tech. Inst., 1978-79, City of Memphis Hosp., 1980-81; trustee Diversified Svcs., Inc., Tenn. Hosp. Assn., 1990-96, mem. pharmacy adv. com., 1990; bd. dirs. Ava Marie Nursing Home, chmn. nom. com., 1988, 89, mem. long-range planning com., 1989, 90, mem. constn. and by-laws com., 1990, mem. govtl. rels. com., 1991-93; presenter in field. Editor U. Tenn. Bowld Hosp. Pharmacy Newsletter, 1987-91; mem. editl. bd. Drug and Therapeutics Newsletter, U. Tenn. Coll. Pharmacy, 1989, 90. usher Ch. of Holy Spirit, 1988-96; mem. Am. Cancer Soc. Recipient Order of Sword award Am. Cancer Soc., 1992. Mem. Am. Soc. hosp. Pharmacists, Tenn. Soc. Hosp. Pharmacists (mem. com. 1980, constn. and by-laws com. 1985, 88, 89, 90, chmn. nominating com. 1989, orgn. and goals com. 1991, strategic planning com. 1992), Tenn. Pharmacists Assn. (pharmacy tech. task force 1988, 89, 90, ho. dels. 1988, 89, 90, 91, 92, 94, chmn. tech. curriculum com. 1991, tech. edn. accreditation com. 1991, 92, 94), Memphis Area Soc. Hosp. Pharmacists (pres.-elect 1984, pres. 1985, past pres. 1986, chmn. nominating com. 1991), Tenn. Hosp. Assn. (liaison Tenn. Med. Assn. com. 1991), Mid-South Healthcare Materials Mgmt. Assn. (co-chmn. founding orgnl. com. 1991), Kappa Psi, Rho Chi. Home: 2927 Mikeyair Dr Germantown TN 38138-7148 Office: UT Bowld Hosp 951 Court Ave Memphis TN 38103-2813

NOLTE, HENRY R., JR., lawyer, former automobile company executive; b. N.Y.C., Mar. 3, 1924; s. Henry R. and Emily A. (Eisele) N.; m. Frances Messner, May 19, 1951; children: Gwynne Conn, Henry Reed III, Jennifer Stevens, Suzanne. BA, Duke U., 1947; LLB, U. Pa., 1949. Bar: N.Y. 1950, Mich. 1967. Assoc. Cravath, Swaine & Moore, N.Y.C., 1951-61; assoc. counsel Ford Motor Co., Dearborn, Mich., 1961, asst. gen. counsel, 1964-71, assoc. gen. counsel, 1971-74, v.p., gen. counsel, 1974-89; v.p., gen. counsel Philco-Ford Corp., Phila., 1961-64; v.p., gen. counsel, sec. Ford of Europe Inc., Warley, Essex, Eng., 1967-69; gen. counsel fin. and ins. subs. Ford Motor Co., 1974-89; sr. ptnr. Miller, Canfield, Paddock & Stone, Detroit, 1989-93, of counsel, 1993—; bd. dirs. Charter One Fin., Inc. Formerly vice chmn. and trustee Cranbrook Ednl. Community; mem. Internat. and Comparative Law Ctr. of Southwestern Legal Found.; bd. dirs. Detroit Symphony Orch.; trustee Beaumont Hosp. Lt. USNR, 1943-46, PTO. Mem. ABA (past chmn. corp. law depts.), Mich. Bar Assn., Assn. Bar City N.Y., Assn. Gen. Counsel, Orchard Lake Country Club, Bloomfield Hills Country Club, Everglades Club (Fla.), Gulfstream Golf Club (Fla.), Ocean Club (Fla.). Episcopalian. Office: Miller Canfield Paddock & Stone 1400 N Woodward Ave Ste 100 Bloomfield Hills MI 48304-2855

NOLTE, NICK, actor; b. Omaha, 1941; m. Rebecca Linger, Feb. 19, 1984 (div. 1995); 1 child, Brawley King. Student, Pasadena City Coll., Phoenix City Coll.; studies with, John Paul, Allen Dutton. Actor: (play) The Last Pad, 1973, (TV movies) Winter Kill, 1974, The California Kid, 1974, Death Sentence, 1974, Adams of Eagle Lake, 1975, The Treasure Chest Murder, 1975, The Runaways, 1975, (mini-series) Rich Man, Poor Man, 1976, (films) The Deep, 1977, Return to Macon County, 1975, Who'll Stop the Rain, 1978, North Dallas Forty, 1979, Heart Beat, 1980, Cannery Row, 1982, 48 Hours, 1982, Under Fire, 1983, The Ultimate Solution of Grace Quigley, 1984, Teachers, 1984, Down and Out in Beverly Hills, 1986, Weeds, 1987, Extreme Prejudice, 1987, Farewell to the King, 1988, Three Fugitives, 1988, New York Stories, 1989, Everybody Wins, 1989, Q & A, 1990, Another 48 Hours, 1990, Prince of Tides, 1991, Cape Fear, 1991, Lorenzo's Oil, 1992, The Player, 1992, Blue Chips, 1994, I'll Do Anything, 1994, I Love Trouble, 1994, Jefferson in Paris, 1995, Mulholland Falls, 1996, Mother Night, 1996, Nightwatch, 1997, Afterglow, 1997, Stray Dogs, 1997. Address: 6153 Bonsall Dr Malibu CA 90265-3824

NOLTE, RICHARD HENRY, political science researcher, consultant; b. Duluth, Minn., Dec. 27, 1920; s. Julius Mosher and Mildred (Miller) N.; m. Jeanne McQuarrie, Mar. 27, 1945; children: Charles McQuarrie, Roger Reed, Douglas Mitchell, Jameson Jay. A.B., Yale, 1943, M.A., 1947; B.A. (Rhodes scholar), Oxford (Eng.) U., 1950, MA, 1954, Inst. Current World Affairs fellow, 1948-54; D.Sc. (hon.), U. Wis., Milw., 1979. Assoc. on Middle East Am. Univs. Field Staff, 1953-58; asst. dir. humanities Rockefeller Found., Inc., N.Y.C., 1958-59; exec. dir. Inst. Current World Affairs, N.Y.C., 1959-78, Alicia Patterson Found., N.Y.C., 1965-78; exec. v.p. Hamilton, Johnston & Co., Inc., N.Y.C., 1978-81; cons. Middle East Dillon, Read & Co., Inc., N.Y.C., 1981-82; assoc. for Middle East HME Internat. Adv. Assocs., Inc., N.Y.C., 1982-90; gen. ptnr. Washburn Island Res. Ltd. Partnership, East Falmouth, Mass., 1981-89; pres. Near East Found., N.Y.C., 1984-87, now bd. dirs.; ambassador to Egypt Cairo, 1967. Editor: The Modern Middle East, 1963. Vice chmn. Stamford Forum for World Affairs; bd. dirs. Pro Bono, Inc., 1994—; hon. trustee Inst. Current World Affairs, 1995—. Pilot USNR, 1943-45. Mem. Am. Geog. Soc. (pres. 1973-80, now chmn. emeritus bd.), Nat. Aphasia Assn. (bd. dirs. 1990—, bd. dirs. Fund for Peace 1993-96), Coun. on Fgn. Rels., Phi Beta Kappa. Clubs: Yale, Mid-Atlantic. Home and Office: 516 Harvest Commons Westport CT 06880-3950

NOLTE, WILLIAM HENRY, English language educator; b. Tulia, Tex., May 2, 1928; s. Eugene Arch Nolte and Myrtle (Burns) Goldman; m. Alice Froehling, June 12, 1954; 1 child, Katherine Ann. Student, Tex. Tech U., 1947-49; BA, U. Mo., 1951; MA, U. Tex., 1952; PhD, U. Ill., 1959. Teaching asst. U. Ill., Urbana, 1954-59; asst. prof. English U. Oreg., Eugene, 1959-65; assoc. prof. U. Mo., St. Louis, 1965-67; prof. U. S.C., Columbia, 1967-89, disting. prof. emeritus English, 1989—. Author: H.L. Mencken, Literary Critic, 1966, H.L. Mencken's Smart Set Criticism, 1968, Rock and Hawk: Robinson Jeffers and the Romantic Agony, 1978. Served to cpl. USAAF, 1946-47. Holder endowed chair U. S.C. Ednl. Found., Columbia, 1978. Democrat. Home: 4502 Storkland Ave Columbia SC 29206-1245 Office: Univ of SC Dept of English Lang & Lit Columbia SC 29208

NOLTING, EARL, academic administrator; b. Columbus, Ind., July 24, 1937; s. Earl Seeger and Gladys Marie (Veale) N.; m. Judith Lynn Tegeler, June 18, 1961; children: Susan, Matthew, David. BSBA, Ind. U., 1959, MS in Edn., 1961; PhD in Psychology, U. Minn., 1967. Lic. psychologist, Wis., Minn. Counselor, asst. prof. U. Minn., Mpls., 1966-68; assoc. dir. U. Wis., Madison, 1968-72, assoc. dean, assoc. vice-chancellor, 1970-74; assoc. prof. edn. Kans. State U., Manhattan, 1974-86, dean of students, 1974-86; dir. dept. counseling, Univ. Coll. U. Minn., Mpls., 1986-97, dir. student support svcs., Univ. Coll., 1997—; cons. psychologist Alberg and Assocs., Shoreview, Minn., 1989—. Contbr. articles to profl. publs. Exec. bd. Adult Learner Svcs. Network, St. Paul, 1989-90. 1st lt. U.S. Army, 1961-62. Mem. AACD, APA, Minn. Psychol. Assn., Am. Coll. Pers. Assn. (news editor 1977-82, sen. 1982-85, Presdl. award 1982), Am. Counseling Assn., Am. Coll. Counseling Assn., Acad. of Family Mediators. Avocations: canoeing, gardening, reading. Home: 3336 Lake Johanna Blvd Saint Paul MN 55112-7942 Office: 315 Pillsbury Dr SE Minneapolis MN 55455-0139

NOME, WILLIAM ANDREAS, lawyer; b. Springfield, Ohio, May 21, 1951; s. Reidar Andreas and Nancy Louisa (Smith) N.; m. Carolyn Ruth Johnson, Feb. 7, 1981. BA, Akron U., 1973; JD, Cleve. State U., 1976. Bar: Ohio 1976, U.S. Dist. Ct. (no. dist.) Ohio 1977, U.S. Ct. Appeals (6th cir.) 1985, U.S. Supreme Ct. 1987. Asst. prosecutor Portage County Prosecutor's Office, Ravenna, Ohio, 1977; pvt. practice Ravenna, 1977-82; assoc. Arthur & Clegg, Kent, Ohio, 1982-85; ptnr. Arthur, Nome & Assocs., Kent, 1985-96, Arthur, Nome, Can, Szymanski & Clinard, Kent, Cuyahoga Falls, Ohio, 1996—; legal advisor Portage Area Regional Transit Authority, Kent, 1986—. Chmn. Highland Home Health Care, Ravenna, 1980, Kent Bd. Bldg. Appeals, 1987, Portage County Mental Health Bd., 1988; trustee Kevin Coleman Mental Health Ctr., 1989-93, pres., 1991-93. Col. Ohio Mil. Res., 1986—. Recipient Cert. of Achievement, Emergency Mgmt. Inst., Fed. Emergency Mgmt. Agy., 1987, 93, 95. Mem. Ohio Bar Assn., Akron Bar Assn., Portage County Bar Assn. (sec.-treas. 1982-85), Portage County Estate Planning Coun., Delta Theta Phi. Republican. Lutheran. Avocations: gardening, cooking, target shooting, reading. Office: Arthur Nome et al 1325 S Water St Kent OH 44240-3845

NOMO, HIDEO, professional baseball player. Pitcher Kintetsu, Japan, 1990-94, L.A. Dodgers, 1995—; mem. Japanese Olympic Baseball team, 1988. Named Nat. League Rookie Pitcher of Yr. The Sporting News, 1995, Nat. League Rookie of Yr. Baseball Writers Assn., 1995; strikeout leader Japanese Pacific League, 1990-93, Nat. League, 1995. Office: care Los Angeles Dodgers 1000 Elysian Park Ave Los Angeles CA 90012-1112*

NOMURA, MASAYASU, biological chemistry educator; b. Hyogo-Ken, Japan, Apr. 27, 1927; s. Hiromichi and Yaeko N.; m. Junko Hamashima, Feb. 10, 1957; children—Keiko, Toshiyasu. Ph.D., U. Tokyo, 1957. Asst. prof. Inst. Protein Research, Osaka (Japan) U., 1960-63; assoc. prof. genetics U. Wis., Madison, 1963-66, prof., 1966-70, Elvehjem prof. in Life Sci. genetics and biochemistry, 1970-84, co-dir. Inst. for Enzyme Research, 1970-84; prof. biol. chemistry, Grace Bell chair U. Calif., Irvine, 1984—. Recipient U.S. Steel award in molecular biology Nat. Acad. Scis., 1971; recipient Acad. award Japanese Acad. Arts and Sci., 1972. Mem. Am. Acad. Arts and Scis., Nat. Acad. Scis., Royal Danish Acad. Scis. and Letters, Royal Netherlands Acad. Arts and Scis., Japanese Biochem. Soc. Home: 74 Whitman Ct Irvine CA 92612-4066 Office: U Calif Dept Biol Chemistry 240 D Med Sci I Irvine CA 92697-1700

NONET, PHILIPPE, law educator; b. Liège, Belgium, Feb. 25, 1939; s. Leon and Helene (Reginster) N.; m. Pamela Jean Utz, Mar. 21, 1978; children—Michael, Genevieve, Beatrice. Docteur en Droit, U. Liège, 1961; Ph.D., U. Calif., Berkeley, 1966. Prof. law U. Calif.-Berkeley, 1966—. Author: Administrative Justice, 1969; (with others) Law and Society in Transition, 1978. Mem. Am. Soc. for Polit. and Legal Philosophy, Amintaphil, Law and Soc. Assn. Home: 885 Creed Rd Oakland CA 94610-1853 Office: U Calif-Berkeley Sch Law Berkeley CA 94720

NONG, artist, sculptor; b. Seoul, Korea, Oct. 10, 1930; came to U.S., 1952, naturalized, 1958; Commr. Asian Art Commn. Asian Art Mus. San Francisco, The Avery Brundage Collection, City and County of San Francisco, 1981-84. One-man exhbns. paintings and/or sculpture include Ft. Lauderdale (Fla.) Mus. Arts, Santa Barbara (Calif.) Mus. Art, Crocker Art Mus., Sacramento, Calif., 1965, Ga. Mus. Art, Athens, 1967, El Paso (Tex.) Mus. Art, 1967, Nat. Mus. History, Taiwan, 1971, Nihonbashi Gallery, Tokyo, Japan, 1971, Shinsegye Gallery, Seoul, Korea, 1975, Nat. Mus. Modern Art, Seoul, 1975, San Francisco Zool. Garden, 1975, Tongin Art Gallery, Seoul, 1978, Consulate Gen. Republic of Korea, L.A., 1982, Choon Chu Gallery, Seoul, 1982, Mee Gallery, Seoul, 1984, 86, Leema Art Mus., Seoul, 1985, Tong-A Dept. Store, Taegu, Korea, 1986, Tongso Gallery, Masan, Korea, 1986, Han Kwang Art Mus., Pusan, Korea, 1986, Union de Arte, Barcelona, Spain, 1987, Acad. de Belles Arts, Sabadell, Spain, 1987, Nong Hyup Art Mus., Ft. Lee, N.J., 1995, The Info. Ctr. Korean Embassy, Washington, 1997; numerous group exhibits Mus. and Art Ctr., Douglaston, N.Y., 1961, Nat. Collection Fine Arts, Smithsonian Instn., Washington, 1961, Mus. Fine Arts, Springfield, Mass., 1961, Conn. Acad. Fine Arts, Hartford, Conn., 1962, Charles and Emma Frye Art Mus., Seattle, 1962, The Denver Art Mus., 1965, Jersey City Mus., 1967, U. Santa Clara (Calif.) Mus., 1967, U. Calif., Berkeley, 1968, Maison de la Culture du Havre, Le Havre, France, 1970, Oakland (Calif.) Art Mus., 1971, Gallerie des Champs Elysees, Paris, 1971, Nat. Sculpture Soc., Lever House, N.Y.C., 1971, Taipei Provincial Mus., Republic of China, 1971, San Francisco Mus. Modern Art, 1972, Galerie Hexagramme, Paris, 1975, Galeria de Arte Misrachi, Mexico City, 1979, The Mun Ye Art Ctr., Seoul, 1986, Salon de Artistes Francais, Paris, France, 1971, Salon d'Automne, Paris, 1969-71, Salon Grands et Jeunes d'Aujourd'hui, Paris, 1971-77, The Jane Voorhees Zimmerli Art Mus. Rutgers, New Brunswick, N.J., 1997, Chgo. Cultural Ctr., 1997; represented in numerous permanent collections including, Santa Barbara Mus. Art, Anchorage (Alaska) Hist. and Fine Art Mus., Museo de Arte, Lima, Peru, Govt. Peru, Nat. Mus. History, Govt. of Republic of China, Oakland (Calif.) Art Mus., Ga. Mus. Art, Athens, Korean Embassy, Lima, Peru, Nat. Mus. of Modern Art, Nat. Mus. Korea, Govt. of Republic of Korea, Seoul, Nat. Gallery of Modern Art, New Delhi, India, Asian Art Mus. San Francisco, Govt. of People's Republic China, Beijing and Shanghai, Palacio de la Zarzuela, Madrid, Palacio de la Moncloa, Madrid, The Korean Embassy, Madrid, Mus. Art de Sabadell, Spain, Mus. Nat. des Beaux-Arts, Monte Carlo, Monaco, The Philatelic Mus. Palais des Nations, Geneva, others; author: Nong Questions, 1982. Chmn. San Francisco-Seoul Sister City Com., City and County San Francisco, 1981-84. Served with U.S. Army, 1956-59; Served with USAF, 1959-60. Recipient numerous awards including citations from Republic of Korea, Cert. Disting. Achievement State of Calif., 1982, Proclamation City and County of San Francisco, 1982; Nong Stamp issued in his honor UNISEF, 1996. Home: 13694 Bent Tree Cir #202 Centreville VA 20121-4722 *Beauty and ugliness, good and bad, right and wrong. Which test should I choose to measure these? Then, how long can I rely on the test I choose?.*

NONNA, JOHN MICHAEL, lawyer; b. N.Y.C., July 8, 1948; s. Angelo and Josephine (Visconti) N.; m. Jean Wanda Cleary, June 9, 1973; children: Elizabeth, Caroline, Marianne, Timothy. AB, Princeton U., 1970; JD, NYU, 1975. Bar: N.Y. 1976, U.S. Dist. Ct. (so. dist.) N.Y. 1978, U.S. Ct. Appeals (2d cir.) 1978, U.S. Ct. Appeals (9th cir.) 1980, U.S. Dist. Ct. Conn. 1988. Law asst. to Hon. D.L. Gabrielli N.Y. Ct. Appeals, Albany, 1975-77; assoc. Reid & Priest, N.Y.C., 1977-84; ptnr. Werner & Kennedy, N.Y.C., 1984—. Contbr. articles to profl. jours. Dep. mayor, trustee Village of Pleasantville, N.Y., 1990-95, mayor, 1995—, acting justice, 1983-89. With USNR, 1970-75. U.S. Olympic Team, Munich, 1972, Moscow, 1980. Fellow Am. Bar Found.; mem. ABA (torts and ins. practice sect. com. chair 1986-87, 92-93), N.Y. State Bar Assn. (chair-elect comml. and fed. litigation sect. 1996—), Assn. Bar City N.Y., N.Y. Fencers Club (pres. 1990-93). Avocations: fencing, running, piano. Office: Werner and Kennedy 1633 Broadway Fl 46 New York NY 10019-6708

NOOLAN, JULIE ANNE CARROLL VIRGO, management consultant; b. Adelaide, South Australia, Australia, June 14, 1944; came to U.S., 1966; d. Archibald Henry and Norma Mae (Gillett) Noolan; m. Daniel Thuering Carroll, Aug. 20, 1977. M.A., U. Chgo., 1968, Ph.D., 1974, Exec. M.B.A., 1983. With State Library of South Australia, 1962-63, Repatriation Dept. South Australia, 1962-66; asst. librarian U. Chgo. Libraries, 1966-68; dir. edn. Med. Library Assn., Chgo., 1972-77; exec. dir. Assn. Coll. and Research Libraries, Chgo., 1977-84; exec. v.p., COO COO Carroll Group, Inc., Chgo., 1984-95, pres., 1995—; mem. faculty U. Chgo., 1968-89. Author: Libraries and Accreditation in Higher Education; contbr. articles to jours. U. Chgo. fellow, 1967-68, Higher Edn. Act fellow, 1969-72; Nat. Library of Medicine grantee, 1967-69; named Outstanding Young U.S. Leader 1985 Coun. on the U.S.,. Mem. ALA, Am. Soc. Assn. Execs., Am. Mgmt. Assn., Spol. Librs. Assn., Am. Soc. for Info. Scis. (past pres., doctoral award, Watson Davis award), ASTD, Nat. Tng. Labs. (bd. dirs. 1990-94), Orgn. Devel. Network, Internat. Assn. Neuro-Linguistic Programming (bd.dirs. 1990-93), Internat. Plant Genetic Resources Inst. (Rome, bd. dirs. 1991—), Internat. Ctr. Agrl. Rsch. in Dry Areas (Syris, bd. dirs. 1992—), Planning Forum, Beta Phi Mu.

NOONAN, FRANK R., business executive; b. Boston, July 21, 1942; s. Russell F. and Barbara (Yutronich) N.; m. Patricia Bernadette Saulnier, Aug. 22, 1964; children: Kathleen, Kelly, Kristin. BA, U. N.H., 1964. Fin. mgmt. trainee GE, Lynn, Mass., 1966-69; corp. auditor GE, Schenectady, N.Y., 1969-74, audit adminstr., 1974-76; fin. mgr. mechanical drive turbine dept. GE, Fitchburg, Mass., 1976-78; fin. mgr. air conditioning divsn. GE, Louisville, 1978-81; sr. v.p., chief fin. officer Union Mutual Ins. Co., Portland, Maine, 1981-86, UNUM Corp., Portland, 1986-89; sr. v.p., group fin. The Dun & Bradstreet Corp., N.Y.C., 1989-90; chmn., CEO Reuben H. Donnelly Corp., Purchase, N.Y., 1991—. Bd. dirs. United Hosp. Med. Ctr., 1995—, Maine Coll. Art; v.p. Found. Blood Rsch., Scarborough, Maine, 1982-89; mem. bd. govs. Buick Classic, 1996—. Mem. Yellow Pages Pubs. Assn. (bd. dirs. 1996—). Republican. Avocations: tennis, skiing, music, golf, model trains. Home: 8 Lincoln Ln Purchase NY 10577-2304 Office: Reuben H Donnelly Corp 1 Manhattanville Rd Purchase NY 10577-2100

NOONAN, GREGORY ROBERT, lawyer; b. Bridgeport, Conn., Dec. 15, 1960; s. John L. and Margaret B. (Petek) N. BA in Acctg. cum laude, N.C. State U., 1982; JD, Wake Forest U., 1985; LLM in Taxation, Villanova U., 1990. Bar: N.C. 1985, Pa. 1986, U.S. Dist. Ct. (ea. dist.) Pa. 1988, U.S. Ct. Claims 1991, U.S. Tax Ct. 1994, U.S. Ct. Appeals (3d cir.) 1994, N.J. 1995, U.S. Dist. Ct. N.J. 1995; CFE, 1995; CPA, N.C.; cert. fraud examiner. Acctg. cons. Ernst & Whinney, Raleigh, N.C., 1985-86; tax atty. Fox, Differ, Norristown, Pa., 1987-90, Solomon Berschler & Warren, Norristown, 1990; tax/bankruptcy atty. Koresko & Noonan, Norristown, 1990-92, Pizonka, Reilley & Bello, King of Prussia, Pa., 1992-94, Deyoung, Walfish & Noonan, King of Prussia, 1994—; instr. acctg., tax and bus. law Pierce Jr. Coll., Phila., 1990-92, Paralegal Inst. Mainline, Phila., 1990; instr. 2d pl. team Mock Trials of Pa. Young Lawyers Divsn. ABA, Norristown, 1989. Mem. ABA, AICPA, Pa. Bar Assn., N.C. Bar Assn., N.J. Bar Assn., Montgomery County Bar Assn., Norristown Jaycees (dir. 1990-94). Republican. Roman Catholic. Avocations: tennis, boating, chess, golf, watching college basketball. Home: 109 Stony Way Norristown PA 19403-4210 Office: Deyoung Walfish & Noonan PC 144 E Dekalb Pike Ste 200 Kng Of Prussa PA 19406-2150

NOONAN, JACQUELINE ANNE, pediatrics educator; b. Burlington, Vt., Oct. 28, 1928. BA, Albertus Magnus Coll., 1950; MD, U. Vt., 1954, DSc (hon.), 1980. Diplomate Am. Bd. Pediatrics, Am. Bd. Pediatric Cardiology. Intern N.C. Meml. Hosp., Chapel Hill, 1954-55; resident in pediatrics Children's Hosp., Cin., 1955-57; rsch. fellow Children's Med. Ctr., Boston, 1957-59; asst. prof. pediatrics State U. Iowa Sch. Medicine, 1959-61; asst. prof. pediatrics cardiology U. Ky. Coll. Medicine, Lexington, 1961-64, assoc. prof., 1964-69, prof., 1969—, chmn. dept. pediatrics, 1974-92; mem. embryology and human devel. study sect. NIH, 1973-78; mem. U.S.-USSR Symposium on Congenital Heart Disease, 1975; mem. sub. bd. pediatric cardiology Am. Bd. Pediatrics, 1977-82; examiner, mem. test. com. Nat. Bd. Med. Examiners, 1984-90, exec. com., 1991-95; participant various confs. in field; vis. prof. Vanderbilt U., Nashville, 1987; spkr. in field. Contbr. articles, revs. to med. publs.; mem. editl. bd. Am. Jour. Diseases Children, 1970-80, Am. Jour. Med. Edn., 1975-78, Pediatric Cardiology, 1978-90, Am. Heart Jour., 1994—, Clin. Pediatrics, 1990—. Mem. AMA, Am. Acad. Pediatrics (cardiology sect. chmn. 1972-74), Am. Coll. Cardiology (gov. Ky. chpt. 1989-92), Am. Fedn. Clin. Rsch., Assn. Med. Sch. Pediatric (dept. chmn. exec. com. 1978-81), Fayette County Med. Soc., Irish-Am. Pediatric Soc., Am. Pediatric Soc., Ky. State Med. Assn., NIH Alumni Assn., Soc. Pediatric Rsch., So. Soc. Pediatric Rsch. (pres. 1972). Office: U Ky Med Ctr Pediatrics Ky Clinic Lexington KY 40536-0284

NOONAN, JOHN G(ERARD), state financial management specialist; b. N.Y.C., June 5, 1958. BS in Econs., SUNY, Albany, 1980, MPA in Pub. Fin., 1981. Jr. profl. N.Y. State Dept. Commerce, Albany, 1979; rsch. analyst N.Y. State Legis. Commn. on Economy and Efficiency in Govt., Albany, 1980-82; mgmt. analyst State of Conn. Dept. Mental Retardation, East Hartford, 1983-87; prin. budget specialist State of Conn. Office of Policy and Mgmt., Hartford, 1987—; bd. dirs., treas. West Hartford Srs. Job Bank, Inc., 1987-90; grant solicitor Conn. Vol. Svcs. for Blind and Disabled, East Hartford, 1989. Coach Avon Canton, Farmington Youth Hockey, Avon, Conn., 1989-90; vol. Am. Heart Assn., Hartford, 1991—. Named one of Outstanding Young Men of Am., Jaycees, 1984. Mem. Am. Soc. Pub. Adminstrs., Govt. Fin. Officers Assn. (mem. budget presentation awards rev. panel), Nat. Assn. State Budget Officers (Conn. state rep.). Office: Office of Policy and Mgmt 450 Capitol Ave Hartford CT 06106-1308

NOONAN, JOHN T., JR., federal judge, legal educator; b. Boston, Oct. 24, 1926; s. John T. and Marie (Shea) N.; m. Mary Lee Bennett, Dec. 27, 1967; children: John Kenneth, Rebecca Lee, Susanna Bain. B.A., Harvard U., 1946, LL.B., 1954; student, Cambridge U., 1946-47; M.A., Cath. U. Am., 1949, Ph.D., 1951, LHD, 1980; LL.D., U. Santa Clara, 1974, U. Notre Dame, 1976, Loyola U. South, 1978; LHD, Holy Cross Coll., 1980; LL.D., St. Louis U., 1981, U. San Francisco, 1985; student, Holy Cross Coll., 1980, Cath. U. Am., 1980, Gonzaga U., 1986, U. San Francisco, 1986. Bar: Mass. 1954, U.S. Supreme Ct. 1971. Mem. spl. staff Nat. Security Council, 1954-55; pvt. practice Herrick & Smith, Boston, 1955-60; prof. law U. Notre Dame, 1961-66; prof. law U. Calif., Berkeley, 1967-86, chmn. religious studies, 1970-73, chmn. medieval studies, 1978-79; judge U.S. Ct. Appeals (9th cir.), San Francisco, 1985—; Oliver Wendell Holmes, Jr. lectr. Harvard U. Law Sch., 1972, Pope John XXIII lectr. Cath. U. Law Sch., 1973, Cardinal Bellarmine lectr. St. Louis U. Div. Sch., 1973, Baum lectr. U. Ill., 1988, Strassberger lectr. U. Tex., 1989; chmn. bd. Games Rsch., Inc., 1961-76; overseer Harvard U., 1991—. Author: The Scholastic Analyst of Usury, 1957; Contraception: A History of Its Treatment by the Catholic Theologians and Canonists, 1965; Power to Dissolve, 1972; Persons and Masks of the Law, 1976; The Antelope, 1977; A Private Choice, 1979; Bribes, 1984; editor: Natural Law Forum, 1961-70, Am. Jour. Jurisprudence, 1970. The Morality of Abortion, 1970. Chmn. Brookline Redevel. Authority, Mass., 1958-62; cons. Papal Commn. on Family, 1965-66, Ford Found., Indonesian Legal Program, 1968, NIH, 1973, NIH, 1974; expert Presdl. Commn. on Population and Am. Future, 1971; cons. U.S. Cath. Conf., 1979-86; sec., treas. Inst. for Research in Medieval Canon Law, 1970-88; pres. Thomas More-Jacques Maritain Inst., 1977—; trustee Population Council, 1969-76, Phi Kappa Found., 1970-76, Grad. Theol. Union, 1970-73, U. San Francisco, 1971-75; mem. com. theol. edn. Yale U., 1972-77; exec. com. Cath. Commn. Intellectual and Cultural Affairs, 1972-75; bd. dirs. Ctr. for Human Values in the Health Scis., 1969-71, S.W. Intergroup Relations Council, 1970-72, Inst.

for Study Ethical Issues, 1971-73. Recipient St. Thomas More award U. San Francisco, 1974, Christian Culture medal, 1975, Laetare medal U. Notre Dame, 1984, Campion medal Cath. Book Club, 1987; Guggenheim fellow, 1965-66, 79-80, Laetare medal U. Notre Dame, 1984, Campion medal, 1987, Alemany medal Western Dominican Province, 1988; Ctr. for advanced Studies in Behavioral Scis. fellow, 1973-74; Wilson Ctr. fellow, 1979-80. Fellow Am. Acad. Arts and Scis., Am. Soc. Legal Historians (hon.); mem. Am. Soc. Polit. and Legal Philosophy (v.p. 1964), Canon Law Soc. Am. (gov. 1970-72), Am. Law Inst., Phi Beta Kappa (senator United chpts. 1970-72, pres. Alpha of Calif. chpt. 1972-73). Office: US Ct Appeals 9th Cir 121 Spear St San Francisco CA 94105-1558*

NOONAN, NORINE ELIZABETH, academic administrator, researcher; b. Phila., Oct. 5, 1948; d. Alaric Edwin and Norine (Radford) Freeman. BA, summa cum laude, U. Vt., 1970; MA, Princeton U., 1972, PhD, 1976. Asst. prof. Coll. Vet. Medicine, U. Fla., Gainesville, 1976-81, assoc. prof., 1981; research assoc. prof. Georgetown U., Washington, 1981-82; Am. Chem. Soc. sci. fellow U.S. Senate Commerce Com., Washington, 1982-83; program and budget analyst Office Mgmt. and Budget, Washington, 1983-87, acting br. chief sci. and space programs, 1987-88, br. chief, 1988-92; v.p. rsch. Fla. Inst. Tech., Melbourne, 1992—, dean grad. sch., 1993—; bd. advisors U.S. Found. for the Internat. Space U., 1989-90; disting. lectr. MITRE Corp. Inst., 1991; vis. faculty Exec. Seminar Ctrs., Office Personnel Mgmt.; cons. Am. Chem. Soc. com. chem. and pub. affairs; mem. NASA space sci. adv. com.; mem. com. Antarctic policy & sci. NRC; mem. future of space sci. DOE environ. mgmt. sci. program NRC; councilor Oak Ridge Assn. Univs.; trustee Southeast Univs. Rsch. Assn., also chair finance com. Contbr. articles to sci. jours. Vol. Balt. City Fair, 1982-91; mem. editorial bd. Fla. Today, 1997. Bd. dirs. Brevard Symphony Orchestra, 1993-96, Wolf Trap Farm Pk. Assocs., Wolf Trap Farm Pk. for the Performing Arts, 1988-92, exec. com. 1990-92, exec. vice chmn., 1991-92, treas., 1992; mem. adv. coun. Brookings Instn. Ctr. for Pub. Policy Edn., 1989-93; treas. White House Athletic Ctr., 1990-92, Potomac Basset Hound Club, Space Coast Tiger Bay Club, bd. dirs 1996—. Recipient Spl. Performance award Office Mgmt. and Budget, 1987, 88; grantee Fla. div. Am. Cancer Soc., 1977, NIH, 1979, NSF, 1979. Fellow AAAS (mem. at large sect. gen. interest in sci. and tech. 1994-97, chair-elect 1997—, mem. sci., engring. and pub. policy com.); mem. Am. Soc. Cell Biology, Sigma Xi, Phi Beta Kappa (pres. Fla. chpt. 1980-81). Mem. United Ch. of Christ. Avocations: running, purebred dogs, fishing, cooking, aerobics. Home: 2480 Grassmere Dr Melbourne FL 32904-9715 Office: Fla Inst Tech 150 W University Blvd Melbourne FL 32901-6982

NOONAN, PATRICK FRANCIS, conservation executive; b. St. Petersburg, Fla., Dec. 2, 1942; s. Francis Patrick and Henrietta (Donovan) N.; m. Nancy Elizabeth Peck, Aug. 15, 1964; children: Karen Elizabeth, Dawn Wiley. A.B., Gettysburg Coll., 1961-65; M.City and Regional Planning, Catholic U. Am., 1967; M.B.A., Am. U., 1971. Dir. ops. The Nature Conservancy, Arlington, Va., 1969-73; pres. The Nature Conservancy, 1973-80; chmn. The Conservation Fund, 1985—. Trustee Nat. Geographi Soc., 1990—, Gettysburg Coll., 1978-91, Duke U. Sch. Environment, 1979—, Ind. Sector, 1984-91, dir. Ashland, 1991—, Internat. Paper, 1993—, Saul Ctrs., 1993—, Rushmore Funds, 1987—; mem. Pres.' Commn. on Am. Outdoors, 1985-87, Pres.' Commn. on Environ. Quality, 1991-93; trustee Am. Conservation Assn., 1986—, Natural Resources Coun. Am., 1996—. MacArthur Found. fellow, 1985-90. Home: 11901 Glen Mill Rd Potomac MD 20854-1920

NOONAN, STEPHEN JOSEPH, accounting firm executive; b. Millbury, Mass., June 13, 1945; s. Joseph Andrew and Evelyn Mary (Devoe) N.; m. Helen Stephanie Wolochowicz, May 20, 1967; children: John Patrick, Karen Marie. Diploma, N.E. Sch. Acctg., Worcester, 1965. Enrolled agt. Acct. George Cagan, CPA, Worcester, 1965-66; mgr. Greenberg, Rosenblat & Assocs., Worcester, 1966-85; proprietor Stephen J. Noonan Assocs., Millbury, Mass., 1985—; cons. Sisters of the Assumption, Worcester, 1991—. Mem. sch. com. Assumption Sch., Millbury, Mass., 1979—; youth soccer coach Sutton (Mass.) Soccer Club, 1979-87; organizer Good Shepherd Endowment Fund, Worcester, 1984. Mem. Mass. Soc. CPAs, Estate and Bus. Planning Coun. of Worcester County. Democrat. Roman Catholic. Avocations: wood carving, photography, writing, soccer, music. Home: 18 Juniper Dr Millbury MA 01527-1817 Office: Stephen J Noonan and Assocs PO Box 431 Millbury MA 01527-0431

NOONAN, SUSAN ABERT, public relations counselor; b. Lancaster, Pa., May 10, 1960; d. James Goodear and Carole (Althouse) Abert; m. David Lindsay Noonan, July 28, 1986; children: Caroline du Pont, Elizabeth Augusta. BA, Mt. Holyoke Col., 1982. Account exec. Merill Lynch, N.Y.C., 1982-83; sr. v.p. Cameron Assocs., N.Y.C., 1983-88; pres., founder Noonan/Russo Comm., N.Y.C., 1988—. Mem. Nat. Investor Rels. Inst. Office: Noonan Russo Comm Inc 220 Fifth Ave New York NY 10001-7708

NOONAN, THOMAS SCHAUB, history educator, Russian studies educator; b. N.Y.C., Jan. 20, 1938; s. Thomas M. and Martha M. (Schaub) N.; m. Norma L. Corigliano, May 19, 1937; 1 child, Thomas R. AB, Dartmouth Coll., 1959; MA, Ind. U., 1962, PhD, 1965. Cert. Russian Inst., Ind. U. Asst. prof. Otterbein Coll., Westerville, Ohio, 1965-66; asst. prof. dept. history U. Minn.-Mpls., 1966-74, assoc. prof., 1974-79, prof., 1979—; chmn. dept. Russian and East European studies, 1981-91; assoc. chmn. dept. history U. Minn.-Mpls., 1992-93, 94—; acting chmn. dept. history, 1994-95. Co-editor Archivum Eurasiae Medii Aevi, 1980—, Russian and East European Studies, 1986-95; adv. bd. Russian History, 1980-88, Soviet Studies in History, 1986-89; contbr. articles to profl. jours. Recipient Royal medal Swedish Numismatic Soc., 1984; Kraay vis. fellow Oxford U., 1983; Social Sci. Rsch. Coun. fellow, 1980-81; Reference Tools grantee NEH, 1990-91. Fellow Am. Numismatic Soc., Royal Numismatic Soc.; mem. Am. Hist. Assn., Am. Assn. Advancement Slavic Studies, Assn. Advancement Baltic Studies. Home: 10224 Rich Rd Minneapolis MN 55437-2503 Office: Univ Minn Dept History 614 Social Sciences Bldg Minneapolis MN 55455

NOONAN, WILLIAM DONALD, lawyer; b. Kansas City, Mo., Oct. 18, 1955; s. Robert Owen and Patricia Ruth Noonan. AB, Princeton (N.J.) U., 1977; JD, U. Mo., Kansas City, 1980; postgrad., Tulane U., 1981-83; MD magna cum laude, Oreg. Health Scis. U., 1991. Bar: Mo. 1980, U.S. Ct. Appeals (5th cir.) 1982, U.S. Patent & Trademark Office 1982, U.S. Ct. Appeals (D.C. cir.) 1984, Oreg. 1985, U.S. Ct. Appeals (9th Cir.) 1985. Assoc. Shurgue, Mion, Zinn, Washington, 1983-84, Keaty & Keaty, New Orleans, 1984-85; ptnr. Klarquist, Sparkman, Portland, Oreg., 1985—; adj. prof. patent law Tulane U., New Orleans, 1984-85, U. Oreg., 1992-93. Casenotes editor U. Mo. Law Rev., 1979. Mem. ABA, AMA (Leadership award 1994), Alpha Omega Alpha (pres. Oreg. chpt. 1990-91). Republican. Avocation: raising and showing horses. Office: Klarquist Sparkman 121 SW Salmon 1600 World Trade Ctr Portland OR 97201

NOONE, ROBERT BARRETT, plastic surgeon; b. Scranton, Pa., Oct. 30, 1939; s. Robert Patrick and Margaret Ann (Barrett) N.; m. Barbara Ellen Atkins, May 29, 1965; children: Robert B. Jr., Megan J., Genevieve C., Rebecca B., Theresa Ann. BS, U. Scranton, 1961; MD, U. Pa., 1965. Diplomate Am. Bd. Surgery, Am. Bd. Plastic Surgery. Rotating intern Hosp. of U. Pa., Phila., 1965-66, resident in surgery, 1966-71, resident in plastic surgery, 1971-73; asst. prof. surgery Sch. Medicine, U. Pa., Phila., 1974-83, clin. assoc. prof. surgery, 1983-89; clin. prof. surgery Sch. Medicine, U. Pa., 1989—; head sect. on plastic surgery Pa. Hosp., Phila., 1974-80; chief svc. plastic surgery Bryn Mawr Hosp., Bryn Mawr, Pa., 1977—, Lankenau Hosp., Phila., 1980-91; chmn. dept. surgery Bryn Mawr (Pa.) Hosp., 1991—; bd. dirs. Am. Bd. Plastic Surgery, Phila., 1987-94, vice chmn. 1993-94; bd. dirs. Plastic Surgery Ednl. Found., Chgo., 1981-91, pres. 1989-90. Contbr. articles to profl. jours. Bd. dirs., trustee Rosemont (Pa.) Sch. of the Holy Child, 1983-87. Capt. USAF, 1967-69. Recipient Frank J. O'Hara Disting. Alumnus award U. Scranton, 1986. Fellow Am. Coll. Surgeons (bd. govs. 1994—); mem. AMA (del. plastic surgery 1986-88), Am. Soc. Plastic and Reconstructive Surgery (bd. dirs. 1989-90, 92-95, chmn. bd. trustees 1994-95), Am. Assn. Plastic Surgeons (sec. 1995—), Northeastern Soc. Plastic Surgeons (pres. 1985-86), Robert H. Ivy Soc. (pres. 1982-83), Merion Cricket Club, Phila. Country Club. Republican. Roman Catholic. Avocations: golf, tennis, photography, swimming, travel, reading. Home: 234 Cheswold Hill Rd Haverford PA 19041-1814 Office: Plastic & Reconstructive Surg Assocs 888 Glenbrook Ave Bryn Mawr PA 19010-2506

NOONKESTER, JAMES RALPH, retired college president; b. Flatridge, Va., June 10, 1924; s. Reggie L. and Arcie (Parks) N.; m. Naomi Hopkins, June 10, 1947; children: Myron Craig, Lila. BA, U. Richmond, 1944, LLD, 1968; ThM, So. Bapt. Theol. Sem., 1947, PhD, 1949; LHD (hon.), Blue Mountain Coll., 1982; postgrad., Harvard U., 1980. Minister edn. 1st Bapt. Ch., Charlottesville, Va., 1950-52; prof., head div. religion and philosophy William Carey Coll., Hattiesburg, Miss., 1952-53; acad. dean William Carey Coll., 1953-56, pres., 1956-89, pres. emeritus, 1989—; pres. Miss. Found. Ind. Colls.; mem. Edn. commn. So. Bapt. Conv., chmn., 1983; bd. dirs. Miss. Sch. Bds. Assn. Workers Compensation Trust, 1993-95, chmn., 1994. Chmn. bd. dirs. Am. Cancer Soc., Miss. divsn., 1966; campaign chmn. United Givers Fund, 1975-76, pres. 1976-77; coun. chmn. Boy Scouts Am., dir. Planned Giving Pine Burr Area Boy Scouts Am., 1990-93; trustee Hattiesburg Pub. Schs., 1990-95, pres. bd. trustees, 1992-95. Recipient award Outstanding Grad. English U. Richmond, 1944; named Hattiesburg's Outstanding Young Man of 1956.; recipient Silver Beaver award Boy Scouts Am., 1981, HUB award, 1983; named Sales and Mktg. Execs. Man of Yr., 1983. Mem. NEA, Miss. Edn. Assn., Hattiesburg Concert Assn. (bd. dir.), So. Assn. Bapt. Colls. and Schs. (pres.), Miss. Assn. Colls. (pres.), Hattiesburg C. of C. (pres. 1966), Phi Beta Kappa, Phi Delta Kappa, Chi Beta Phi, Omicron Delta Kappa. Club: Kiwanian. Home: 100 Lesley Ln Hattiesburg MS 39402-2922

NOORDA, RAYMOND J., computer software company executive; b. Ogden, Utah.. BSEE, Utah, 1949. CEO Novell Inc., 1982—; chmn. MTI Inc, Anaheim, Calif. Office: MTI Technology Corp 4905 E La Palma Ave Anaheim CA 92807-1915*

NOORDERGRAAF, ABRAHAM, biophysics educator; b. Utrecht, Netherlands, Aug. 7, 1929; s. Leendert and Johanna (Kool) N.; m. Geertruida Alida Van Nee, Sept. 6, 1956; children: Annemiek (Mrs. James A. Young), Gerrit Jan, Jeske Inette, Alexander Abraham. B.Sc., U. Utrecht, 1953, M.S., 1955, Ph.D., 1956; M.A. (hon.), U. Pa., 1971. Teaching asst. U. Utrecht, 1949-50, asst. dept. physics, 1951-53, research asst. dept. med. physics, 1953-55, research fellow dept. med. physics, 1956-58, sr. research fellow dept. med. physics, 1959-65; tchr. math. and physics Vereniging Nijverheidsonderwijs, Utrecht, 1951; research asst. U. Amsterdam, Netherlands, 1952; vis. fellow dept. therapeutic research U. Pa., Phila., 1957-58; assoc. prof. biomed. engring. Moore Sch. Elec. Engring., 1964-70, acting head electromed. div., 1968-69, prof. biomed. engring., 1970—; prof. physiology Sch. Vet. Medicine, 1976—, prof. Dutch culture Sch. Arts and Scis., 1983—; prof. medicine Med. Sch. U. Pa., 1990—; assoc. dir. biomed. engring. tng. program Moore Sch. Elec. Engring., 1971-76, asso. dir. sch., 1972-74, chmn. grad. group in biomed. electronic engring., 1973-75, chmn. dept. bioengring., 1973-76, chmn. grad. group bioengring., 1975-76, dir. systems and integrative biology tng. program, 1979-84; vis. prof. biomed. engring. U. Miami, 1970-79, Erasmus U. Med. Sch., Rotterdam, The Netherlands, 1970-71, Tech. U., Delft, 1970-71, Polish Acad. Scis., Warsaw, 1975; hon. vis. prof. of physiology U. Ljubljana, 1994—; mem. cardiovascular study sect., 1985-89; cons. sci. affairs divsn. NATO, 1973—; participant numerous internat. confs. in field. Author: (with I. Starr) Ballistocardiography in Cardiovascular Research, 1967, Circulatory System Dynamics, 1978; contbg. author: Biological Engineering, 1969; Editor: (with G.N. Jager and N. Westerhof) Circulatory Analog Computers, 1963, (with G.H. Pollack) Ballistocardiography and Cardiac Performance, 1967, (with E. Kresch) The Venous System: Characteristics and Function, 1969, (with J. Baan and J. Raines) Cardiovascular System Dynamics, 1978, (with Reichenbach-Consten) Two Hundred Years of Netherlands-American Interaction; sci. editor Biophysics and Bioengring. Series, 1976-94; contbr. numerous articles to profl. jours.; Referee: Biophys. Jour., 1968—, Physics in Medicine and Biology, 1969—, Bull. Math. Biophysics, 1972-84, Circulation Research, 1973—; mem. editorial adv. bd.: Jour. Biomechanics, 1969-84; assoc. editor: Bull. Math. Biology, 1973-84. Vice pres. Haverford Friends Sch. PTA, 1968-70. Recipient S. Reid Warren Jr. award U. Pa. Sch. Engring. and Applied Sci., 1986, Christian and Mary Lindback award U. Pa., 1988. Fellow IEEE (mem. adminstrv. com. engring. in medicine and biology group 1967-70, mem. edn. com. group biomed. engring. 1968-70, sec. Phila. chpt. 1974-75, mem. regional council profl. group engring. in medicine and biology 1974-77), N.Y. Acad. Scis., AAAS, Explorers Club, Coll. Physicians Phila., Am. Coll. Cardiology, Royal Soc. Medicine London; mem. Nederlandse Natuurkundige Vereniging, Ballistocardiograph Research Soc. U.S.A. (sec.-treas. 1965-67, pres. 1968-70), Biophys. Soc. (charter), European Soc. for Noninvasive Cardiovascular Research (co-founder 1960, sec.-treas. 1960-61, mem. com. on nomenclature 1960-61, officer 1961-62, Herman C. Burger award 1978, Disting. Rsch. Award, 1993), Cardiovascular System Dynamics Soc. (co-founder 1976, pres. 1976-80, hon. life 1986), Franklin Inst., John Morgan Soc., Biomed. Engring. Soc. (founding mem., chmn. membership com. 1978-79, dir. 1972-75), Am. Heart Assn., Instrument Soc. Am. (sr. mem.), Soc. Math. Biology (charter mem.), Am. Physiol. Soc., Microcirculatory Soc., Am. Assn. Med. Systems and Informatics, Pa. Acad. Sci., Sigma Xi, Phi Zeta. Presbyterian. Home: 620 Haydock Ln Haverford PA 19041-1208 Office: U Pa 101 Hayden Hall Philadelphia PA 19104-6392

NORA, AUDREY HART, physician; b. Picayune, Miss., Dec. 5, 1936; d. Allen Joshua and Vera Lee (Ballard) H.; m. James Jackson Nora, Apr. 9, 1966; children: James Jackson Jr., Elizabeth Hart. BS, U. Miss., 1958, MD, 1961; MPH, U. Calif., 1978. Diplomate Am. Bd. Pediatrics, Am. Bd. Hematology and Oncology. Resident in pediatrics U. Wis. Hosp., Madison, 1961-64; fellow in hematology/oncology Baylor U., Tex. Childrens Hosp., Houston, 1964-66, asst. prof. pediatrics, 1966-70; assoc. clin. prof. pediatrics U. Colo. Sch. Medicine, Denver, 1970—; dir. genetics Denver Childrens Hosp., 1970-78; cons. maternal and child health USPHS, Denver, 1978-83, asst. surgeon gen. regional health adminstr., 1983-92; dir. maternal & child health bur., health resources and svc. adminstrn. USPHS, commd. med. officer, 1978, advanced through grades to asst. surgeon gen., 1983; adv. com. NIH, Bethesda, 1975-77; adv. bd. Metronet Health, Inc., Denver, 1986—, Colo. Assn. Commerce and Industry, Denver, 1985—. Author: (with J.J. Nora) Genetics and Counseling in Cardiovascular Diseases, 1978, (with others) Blakiston's Medical Dictionary, 1980, Birth Defects Encyclopedia, 1990, (with J.J. Nora and K. Berg) Cardiovascular Diseases: Genetics, Epidemiology and Prevention, 1991; contbr. articles to profl. jours. Recipient Virginia Apgar award Nat. Found., 1976. Fellow Am. Acad. Pediatrics; mem. Am. Pub. Health Assn. (governing coun. 1990-92, coun. mem. maternal and child health 1990—), Commd. Officers Assn., Am. Soc. Human Genetics, Teratology Soc., Western Soc. Pediatric Rsch. Presbyterian. Avocations: quilting, cooking, hiking. Office: USPHS Room 18-05 Parklawn Bldg 5600 Fishers Ln Rockville MD 20857-0001

NORA, JAMES JACKSON, physician, author, educator; b. Chgo., June 26, 1928; s. Joseph James and May Henrietta (Jackson) N.; m. Barbara June Fluhrer, Sept. 7, 1949 (div. 1963); children: Wendy Alison, Penelope Welbon, Marianne Leslie; m. Audrey Faye Hart, Apr. 9, 1966; children: James Jackson Jr., Elizabeth Hart Nora. AB, Harvard U., 1950; MD, Yale U., 1954; MPH, U. Calif., Berkeley, 1978. Intern Detroit Receiving Hosp., 1954-55; resident in pediatrics U. Wis. Hosps., Madison, 1959-61, fellow in cardiology, 1962-64; fellow in genetics McGill U. Children's Hosp., Montreal, Can., 1964-65; assoc. prof. pediatrics Baylor Coll. Medicine, Houston, 1965-71; prof. genetics, preventive medicine and pediatrics U. Colo. Med. Sch., Denver, 1971—; dir. genetics Rose Med. Ctr., Denver, 1980—; dir. pediatric cardiology and cardiovascular tng. U. Colo. Sch. Medicine, 1971-78; mem. task force Nat. Heart and Lung Program, Bethesda, Md., 1973; cons. WHO, Geneva, 1983—; mem. U.S.-U.S.S.R. Exchange Program on Heart Disease, Moscow and Leningrad, 1975. Author: The Whole Heart Book, 1980, 2d rev. edit., 1989; (with F.C. Fraser) Medical Genetics, 4th rev. edit., 1994, Genetics of Man, 2d rev. edit., 1986, Cardiovascular Diseases: Genetics, Epidemiology and Prevention, 1991; (novels) The Upstart Spring, 1989, The Psi Delegation, 1989, The Hemingway Sabbatical, 1996. Com. mem. March of Dimes, Am. Heart Assn., Boy Scouts Am. Served to lt. USAAC, 1945-47. Grantee Nat. Heart, Lung and Blood Inst., Nat. Inst. Child Health and Human Devel., Am. Heart Assn., NIH; recipient Virginia Apgar meml. award. Fellow Am. Coll. Cardiology, Am. Acad. Pediatrics, Am. Coll. Med. Genetics; mem. Am. Pediatric Soc., Soc. Pediatric Rsch., Am. Heart Assn., Teratology Soc., Transplantation Soc., Am. Soc. Human Genetics, Authors Guild, Authors League, Acad. Am. Poets, Mystery Writers Am., Rocky Mountain Harvard Club. Democrat. Presbyterian. Avocations: writing fiction, poetry.

NORBACK, CRAIG THOMAS, writer; b. Pitts., Nov. 14, 1943; s. Howard George and Maybelle Veronica Montaigne (Cosse) N.; m. Judith Carol Shaul, Oct. 12, 1976. BS, Washington U., St. Louis, 1967; postgrad., Drew U., 1986—. Author, co-author, compiler, producer over 150 books, including: The Misspeller's Dictionary, 1972, Everything You Can Get from the Government for Free or Almost for Free, 1975, The Dream Machine: The Golden Age of American Automobiles 1946-65, 1976, Great Songs of Madison Avenue, 1976, Great North American Indians, 1977, The Health Care Directory, 1977, The Older American's Handbook, 1977, The Educational Marketplace, 1978, Famous American Admirals, 1978, Newsweek Travel Guide to the U.S., 1978, The Dow Jones-Irwin Guide to Franchising, 1979, The Horseman's Catalog, 1979, The Must Words, 1979, The Practical Inventor's Handbook, 1979, ABC Complete Book of Sports Facts, 1980, ABC Monday Night Football, 1980-81, 1980, The Bible Almanac, 1980, Check Yourself Out, 1980, The Signet Book of World Winners, 1980, The TV Guide Almanac, 1980, The World's Great News Photos (1840-1980), 1980, The Allergy Encyclopedia, 1981, American Expressions, 1981, The Computer Invasion, 1981, The Consumer's Energy Handbook, 1981, 500 Questions New Parents Ask, 1982, Business Week Almanac, 1982, The International Yellow Pages, 1982, The Puzzle King's Bafflers, 1982, The Associated Press Sunday Crossword Puzzle Book, 1983, Chilton's Job Textbook Series: Advertising Management, 1983, Office Management, 1983, It's a Fact, 1983, National Education Association Parent and Child Success Library: Helping Your Child Read, 1983, How Letters Make Words, 1983, How to Prepare Your Child for School, 1983, Learning the Alphabet, 1983, Learning to Add, 1983, The Ultimate Toy Catalog, 1983, U.S. Publicity Directory, various years, Advertising and Promotion Management, 1983, America Wants to Know, 1983, Certified Professional Secretary modules I through VI, 1984, East Coast Publicity Directory, 1984, Human Resources Yearbook, 1987, 88, 89, 90, Princeton Area Job Finder, 1986-87, Career Encyclopedia, 1987, Travel Publicity Directory, 1987, 88, 89, 90, Arthur Young Guide to Venture Capital, 1987, Hazardous Chemicals on File, 1988, Joint Ventures, 1992. Home: 88 Parker Rd S Plainsboro NJ 08536

NORBECK, JANE S., nursing educator; b. Redfield, S.D., Feb. 20, 1942; d. Sterling M. and Helen L. (Williamson) N.; m. Paul J. Gorman, June 28, 1970; 1 child Sara J. Gorman. BA in Psychology, U. Minn., 1965, BSN, 1965; MS, U. Calif., San Francisco, 1971, DNSc, 1975. Psychiat. nurse Colo. Psychiat. Hosp., Denver, 1965-66, Langley Porter Hosp., San Francisco, 1966-67; pub. health nurse San Francisco Health Dept., 1968-69; prof. U. Calif. (San Francisco) Sch. of Nursing, 1975—, dept. chair, 1984-89, dean, 1989—; chair study sect. Nat. Inst. of Nursing Rsch., 1990-93, mem. editl. bd. Archives of Psychiat. Nursing, 1985-95, Rsch. in Nursing and Health, 1987—. Co-editor: Annual Review of Nursing Research, 1996-97; contbr. articles to profl. jours. Mem. ANA, Am. Acad. Nursing, Am. Orgn. Nursing Exec., Am. Assn. Coll. Nursing, Inst. of Medicine, Sigma Theta Tau. Office: U Calif Sch Nursing 501 Parnassus Ave San Francisco CA 94122-2722

NORBERG, ARTHUR LAWRENCE, JR., historian, physicist educator; b. Providence, Apr. 13, 1938; s. Arthur Lawrence Sr. and Margaret Helen (Riley) N.; m. Kerry J. Freedman. BS in Physics, Providence Coll., 1959; MS in Physics, U. Vt., 1962; PhD in History of Sci., U. Wis., 1974. Asst. prof. physics St. Michael's Coll., Winooski, Vt., 1961-63, 64-68; assoc. scientist Westinghouse Electric Co., Pitts., 1963-64; instr. in physics U. Wis., Whitewater, 1968-71; rsch. historian U. Calif., Berkeley, 1973-79; program mgr. NSF, Washington, 1979-81; dir. Charles Babbage Inst. for History of Info. Processing U. Minn., Mpls., 1981-93, prof. history of sci. and tech., 1995—, assoc. prof. computer sci., 1981-95, prof. computer sci., 1995—; del. Am. Coun. Learned Socs., N.Y.C., 1981-87; mem. adv. coun. NASA, Washington, 1988-93; endowed ERA Land Grant chair U. Minn., 1989-93. Editor: Annals of the History of Computing, 1982-93; adv. editor Tech. and Culture, 1985-92, (book) Transforming Computer Technology: Information Processing for the Pentagon; contbr. articles to profl. jours. Founding pres. City Works-A Tech. Ctr., Mpls., 1987-90; exec. dir. Charles Babbage Found., 1984-94; trustee Charles Babbage Found., 1993-96. Fellow AAAS; mem. History of Sci. Soc. (treas. 1975-80), Brit. Soc. for History of Sci., Soc. for History of Tech., Sigma Xi. Office: U Minn Dept Computer Sci 4-192 EE/CS Bldg Minneapolis MN 55455-0290

NORBERG, CHARLES ROBERT, lawyer; b. Cleve., July 25, 1912; s. Rudolf Carl and Ida Edith (Roberts) N. B.S. in Adminstrv. Engring, Cornell U., 1934; M.A. in Internat. Econs, U. Pa., 1937; LL.B., Harvard U., 1939. Bar: Pa. bar 1940, U.S. Supreme Ct. bar 1946, D.C. bar 1947. Lab. research asst. Willard Storage Battery Co., Cleve., 1934-35; asso. firm Hepburn and Norris, Phila., 1939-42; with Office of Assn. Sec. State for Public Affairs, Dept. State, 1948-51; asst. dir. psychol. strategy bd. Exec. Office of the Pres., 1952-54; mem. staff U.S. Delegation to UN Gen. Assembly, Paris, 1951; adviser U.S. Delegation to UNESCO Gen. Conf., Montevideo, 1954; assoc. firm Morgan, Lewis and Bockius, Washington, 1955-56; individual practice law Washington, 1956—; treas., gen. counsel Inter-Am. Comml. Arbitration Commn., 1968-83, dir. gen., 1983-95, hon. dir. gen., 1995—; chief Spl. AID Mission to Ecuador, 1961; spl. Aid Mission to Uruguay, 1961; mem. U.S. delegation to Specialized Inter-Am. Conf. on pvt. internat. law, Panama, 1975. Chmn. Internat. Visitors Info. Service, Washington, 1965-69; chmn. Mayor's Com. on Internat. Visitors, 1971-78; chmn., pres. Bicentennial Commn. of D.C., Inc., 1975-81. Served with USAF, 1942-46. Mem. Phila. Bar Assn., Pa. Bar Assn., Inter-Am. Bar Assn., Washington Fgn. Law Soc. (pres. 1959-63), Am. Soc. Internat. Law, Am. Law Inst., Am. Bar Assn. (chmn. internat. legal exchange program 1974-79), Bar Assn. of D.C. (chmn. internat. law com. 1977-79), Inter-Am. Bar Found. (founder, dir. 1957, pres. 1969-84, chmn. bd. 1984—), Diplomatic and Consular Officers Retired (Washington), Washington Inst. Fgn. Affairs, Academia Colombiana de Jurisprudencia, Inter-Am. Acad. Internat. and Comparative Law, Colegio de Abogados de Quito. Clubs: Met. (Washington); Dacor (Washington); Racquet (Phila.); Harvard (N.Y.C.). Home: 3104 N St NW Washington DC 20007-3413 Office: 1819 H St NW Washington DC 20006-3603

NORBERG, RICHARD EDWIN, physicist, educator; b. Newark, Dec. 28, 1922; s. Arthur Edwin and Melita (Roefer) N.; m. Patricia Ann Leach, Dec. 27, 1947 (dec. July 1977); children—Karen Elizabeth, Craig Alan, Peter Douglas; m. Jeanne C. O'Brien, Apr. 1, 1978. B.A., DePauw U., 1943; M.A., U. Ill., 1947, Ph.D., 1951. Research assoc., control sytems lab. U. Ill., 1951-53, asst. prof., 1953; vis. lectr. physics Washington U., St. Louis, 1954—; mem. faculty Washington U., 1955—, prof. physics, 1958—, chmn. dept., 1962-91. Mem. editl. bd. Magnetic Rsch. Rev. Served with USAAF, 1943-46. Fellow Am. Phys. Soc.; mem. Internat. Soc. Magnetic Research. Home: 7134 Princeton Ave Saint Louis MO 63130-2308 Office: Washington U Dept Physics PO Box 1105 Saint Louis MO 63188-1105

NORBY, MARK ALAN, lawyer; b. Cadillac, Mich., July 5, 1955; s. Walter Carl and Nadine Kaye (Hunt) N.; m. Connie Lynn Perrine, Feb. 26, 1983. BS in Polit. Sci., Agr., Oreg. State U., 1977; JD, U. Mich., 1980. Bar: Oreg. 1980, U.S. Dist. Ct. Oreg. 1980. Assoc. Stoel, Rives, Boley, Fraser & Wyse, Portland, 1980-86; ptnr. Stoel, RivesLLP, Portland, 1986—. Office: Stoel Rives Boley Jones & Grey 900 SW 5th Ave Portland OR 97204-1235

NORBY, WILLIAM CHARLES, financial consultant; b. Chgo., Aug. 10, 1915; s. Oscar Maurice and Louise (Godejohann) N.; m. Camilla Edbrooke, June 12, 1943; children: Martha Norby Fraundorf, Richard James. AB, U. Chgo., 1935. With Harris Trust & Savs. Bank, Chgo., 1935-70, v.p., 1953-64, sr. v.p., 1964-70; exec. dir. Fin. Analysts Fedn., N.Y.C., 1970-72; sr. v.p., bd. dirs. Duff & Phelps, Inc., Chgo., 1973-81; mem. Fin. Acctg. Standards Adv. Coun., 1975-79. mem. Fin. Acctg. Stds. Adv. Coun., 1975-79. Mem. AICPA (com. on auditors responsibilities 1975-78), Fin. Analysts Fedn. (bd. dirs. 1962-68, pres. 1963-64, Disting. Svc. award 1973, Nicholas Molodovsky award 1979), Investment Analysts Soc. Chgo. (pres. 1955-56), U. Chgo. Alumni Assn. (citation 1961), Phi Beta Kappa. Congregationalist (trustee 1950-56, chmn. 1955-56). Home: 337 Blackstone Ave La Grange IL 60525-2107

NORCEL, JACQUELINE JOYCE CASALE, educational administrator; b. Bklyn., Nov. 19, 1940; d. Frederick and Josephine Jeanette (Bestafka) Casale; m. Edward John Norcel, Feb. 24, 1962. BS, Fordham U., 1961; MS, Bklyn. Coll., 1966; 6th yr. cert. So. Conn. State U., 1980; postgrad. Bridgeport U.

Elem. tchr., pub. schs., N.Y.C., 1961-80; prin. Coventry Schs., Conn., 1980-84, Trumbull Schs., Conn., 1984—; guest lectr. So. Conn. State U., 1980—; cons. Monson Schs., Mass., 1984; mem. Conn. State Prin. Acad. Adv. Bd., 1986-88; mem. adj. faculty Sacred Heart U., Fairfield, Conn., 1985—, So. Conn. State U., summer 1991. Editor: Best of the Decade, 1980; mem. editorial adv. bd. Principal Matters; contbr. articles to profl. jours. Chmn. bldg. com. Trumbull Bd. Edn., 1978-80; chmn. Sch. Benefit Com., Trumbull, 1985-86; catechist Bridgeport Diocese, Roman Cath. Ch., Conn., 1975-85, youth minister, 1979-84, coord., evaluator leadership tng. workshops for teens and adults, 1979-84; mem. St. Stephen's Parish Coun., 1993-97, trustee, 1997—. Recipient Town of Trumbull Service award, 1982, Nat. Disting. Prin. award, 1988, Joseph Formica Disting. Svc. award EMSPAC, 1994. Mem. ASCD, N.E. Regional Elem. Prins. Assn. (rep. 1984-86, sec. 1986-87), Elem. Mid. Sch. Prins. Assn. (pres. 1985-86, Citizen of Year award, 1991, Pres.'s award 1981-85, state elected rep. 1989-90, fed. rels. coord. 1990-94, dist. dir. 1995-96),Adminstrn. and Supervision Assn. (sec. 1980-81, pres. 1981-82, exec. bd. 1982-93), Hartford Area Prins. and Suprs. Assn. (local pres. 1981-82), Nat. Assn. Elem. Sch. Prins. (zone I dir. 1987-90, del. to gen. assemblies 1984-90, bd. dirs. 1987-90), Conn. Assn. Supervision and Curriculum Devel., Trumbull Adminstrs. Assn. (pres.-elect 1989-91, pres. 1991-93), Eastern Conn. Council of Internat. Reading Assn., New Eng. Coalition Ednl. Leaders, Associated Tchrs. of Math. in Conn., Phi Delta Kappa (Disting. Fellow award 1992, v.p. rsch. and projects 1993-95), Pi Lambda Theta (Beta Sigma chpt.), Delta Kappa Gamma. Republican. Home: 5240 Madison Ave Trumbull CT 06611-1016 Office: Tashua Sch 401 Stonehouse Rd Trumbull CT 06611-1651

NORCIA, STEPHEN WILLIAM, advertising executive; b. N.Y.C., Jan. 21, 1941; s. William Matthew and Amelia (Marrone) N.; m. Martha Elizabeth Whelan, Apr. 22, 1978; children: Matthew F., Daniel P., Anne E. BA, U. Conn., 1962. Media planner and buyer SSC&B, N.Y.C., 1965-66; account exec. McCann-Erickson Co., Chgo., 1966-68; v.p., dep. mgr. McCann-Erickson Co., Milw., 1971-72; v.p., mgmt. supr. McCann-Erickson Co., N.Y.C., 1972-74; sr. v.p., gen. mgr. McCann-Erickson Co., Atlanta, 1974-78; exec. v.p., gen. mgr. McCann-Erickson Co., N.Y.C., 1978-81; exec. v.p., mem. exec. policy com., mem. mgmt. com. Lintas, N.Y.C., 1981-94, exec. v.p., 1989-91, world wide client dir., dir. bus. devel., 1991-94, also bd. dirs.; mng. ptnr. Earle Palmer Brown, N.Y.C., 1994-96; dir. global account DDB Needham, N.Y.C., 1996—; account exec. Needham, Harper & Steers, Chgo., 1968-70; dir. mktg. product devel. workshop Interpub., N.Y.C., 1970-71; bd. dirs. Communication Counselors Network. Bd. dirs. U. Ga. Master of Br. Mgmt. Program, 1985, 86, 87. 1st lt. U.S. Army, 1962-65. Recipient Robert E. Healy award Interpub. Group Cos., 1975, Effie award Am. Mktg. Assn., 1985, Grand Effie award Am. Mktg. Assn., 1984. Mem. Am. Assn. Advt. Agys., Advt. Club N.Y., Am. Yacht Club. Republican. Roman Catholic. Avocations: tennis, boating, skiing. Home: 1 Topsail Ln Rye NY 10580-3116 Office: DDB Needham 437 Madison Ave New York NY 10022-7001

NORCROSS, DAVID FRANK ARMSTRONG, lawyer; b. Camden, N.J., Mar. 30, 1937; s. David Kincaid and Elizabeth S. (Norcross) Armstrong; m. Laurie Lee Michel, Nov. 11, 1988; children: Spencer Kincaid Cook, Victoria Lynn Armstrong. BA, U. Del., 1958; LLB, U. Pa., 1961. Bar: N.J. 1961, U.S. Ct. Appeals (3d cir.) 1971, U.S. Supreme Ct. 1987, D.C. 1993. Ptnr. Archer & Greiner, Haddonfield, N.J., 1965-71; exec. asst. to gov. State of N.J., Trenton, 1971-73; exec. dir. N.J. Election Law Enforcement Commn., Trenton, 1973-76; of counsel Brandt, Haughey, Penberthy & Lewis, Haddonfield, 1976; ptnr. Myers, Matteo, Rabil & Norcross, Cherry Hill, N.J., 1977-89, Montgomery, McCracken, Walker & Rhoads, Washington, Cherry Hill, 1989-94, Blank, Rome, Comisky & McCauley, Washington, Cherry Hill, 1994—; cons. Fed. Election Com., Washington, 1976, White House Conf. Drug Free Am., 1987-88; dir. Rep. Inst. Internat., Washington, 1984—, gen. counsel, 1984-93; bd. dirs. Ctr. for Democracy, Washington, 1985-95; gen. counsel Rep. Nat. Com., 1993-97. rep. candidate U.S. Senate, N.J., 1976; chmn. N.J. Rep. Party, 1977-81; counsel to chmn. Rep. Nat. Com., Washington, 1983-89, mem. 1977-81, 92—; vice chmn. Commn. on Presdl. Debates, 1988-93. Mem. N.J. Bar Assn., Burlington County Bar Assn., D.C. Bar Assn., Camden County Bar Assn., St. Andrews Soc. Washington, Capitol Hill Club (Washington), Moorestown Field Club, Univ. Club, Army-Navy Country Club. Episcopalian. Office: Blank Rome Comisky McCauley 1156 15th St NW Ste 550 Washington DC 20005-1704

NORCROSS, DAVID WARREN, physicist, researcher; b. Cin., July 18, 1941; s. Gerald Warren and Alice Elizabeth (Downey) N.; children: Joshua David, Sarah Elizabeth. AB, Harvard Coll., 1963; MSc, U. Ill., 1965; PhD, Univ. Coll., London, 1970. Research assoc. U. Colo., Boulder, 1970-74; physicist Nat. Bur. Standards, Boulder, 1974—; chief quantum physics divsn. Nat. Inst. Stds. and Tech., 1989-93, dir. Boulder Labs., 1994—; fellow Joint Inst. Lab. Astrophysics, Boulder, 1976—. Contbr. articles to profl. jours. Recipient Bronze medal Nat. Bur. Standards, 1982, Silver medal U.S. Dept. Commerce, 1994. Fellow Am. Phys. Soc. Office: Nat Inst Standards & Tech 325 Broadway St Boulder CO 80303-3337

NORCROSS, MARVIN AUGUSTUS, veterinarian, retired government agency official; b. Tansboro, N.J., Feb. 8, 1931; s. Marvin A. and Katherine V. (McGuigan) N.; m. Diane L. Tuttle, Nov. 22, 1956 (div. 1991); children: James, Janet. Student, Rutgers U., 1954-55; VMD, U. Pa., 1959, PhD, 1966. Pathologist Merck Sharp & Dohme Rsch. Labs., Rahway, N.J., 1966-69; dir. clin. research Merck Sharp & Dohme Rsch. Labs., 1969-72, sr. dir. domestic vet. research, 1972-75; dir. div. vet. med. rsch. Ctr. Vet. Medicine, FDA, Rockville, Md., 1975-78; assoc. dir. for rsch. Ctr. Vet. Medicine, FDA, 1978-82, assoc. dir. for human food safety, 1982-84, assoc. dir. for new animal drug evaluation, 1984-87; asst. dep. adminstr., then dep. adminstr. Sci. and Tech., Food Safety and Inspection Svc. USDA, Washington, 1987-93, exec. asst. to the adminstr., 1993-94; U.S. coord. for Codex Alimentarius USDA, Washington, 1994-96, sr. sci. advisor to adminstr., 1996; cons. vet. medicine and food safety, 1996—; adj. prof. faculty Va.-Md. Regional Coll. Vet. Medicine, Blacksburg, Va., 1980-85. Contbr. articles to profl. jours. Trustee Scotch Plains (N.J.) Community Fund, 1969-72. Served to lt. AUS, 1952-54; col. Res., 1954-83 (ret.). Recipient FDA Merit award, 1978, Meritorious Presdl. Rank award, 1989. Mem. AVMA, AAAS, Am. Assn. Avian Pathologists, Assn. Mil. Surgeons U.S., Civil Affairs Assn., Inst. Food Technologists, Nat. Assn. Fed. Veterinarians, N.J. Acad. Sci., N.Y. Acad. Scis., Res. Officers Assn., Soc. Toxicologic Pathologists, Sigma Xi. Home and Office: 14304 Brickhowe Ct Germantown MD 20874-3431

NORD, ERIC THOMAS, manufacturing executive; b. Amherst, Ohio, Nov. 8, 1917; s. Walter G. and Virginia C. (Greive) N.; m. Jane H. Baker; children: Virginia, Emily, Carlotte, Richard. BS in Mech. Engring., Case Inst. Tech., 1939. Pres., chief exec. officer Nordson Corp., Amherst, Ohio, 1954-73; chmn. Nordson Corp., Amherst, 1973—. Pres. Oberlin (Ohio) Bd. Edn., 1965; chmn. Oberlin City Council, 1959; bd. trustees Oberlin Coll., 1977—.

NORD, HENRY J., transportation executive; b. Berlin, May 1, 1917; came to U.S., 1937, naturalized, 1943; s. Walter and Herta (Riess) N.; children: Stephen, Philip. Student, U. Oxford, Eng., 1934, Northwestern U., 1938-40, Ill. Inst. Tech., 1942; JD, De Paul U., 1949. CPA, Ill. Apprentice in export Hamburg, Germany, 1935- 37; with GATX Corp., Chgo., 1938-85; comptroller GATX Corp., 1961—, v.p., 1967-71, exec. v.p., 1971-78, sr. v.p., 1978-80, v.p., 1980-82, cons., 1982-84, fin. cons., 1982—, dir., 1964-78; dir. Planned Lighting, Inc. to 1988. Trustee DePaul U. Served to 1st lt. AUS, 1944-46. Mem. Internat. Law Assn. Club: Tavern (Chgo.). Home: 1000 N Lake Shore Dr Chicago IL 60611-1308 Office: 55 W Monroe St Ste 500 Chicago IL 60603-5003

NORD, PAUL ELLIOTT, accountant; b. Carona, N.Y., Mar. 22, 1936; s. Abe and Rose (Guss) N.; m. Marcia B. Gross, June 13, 1965; children: Howard, Aimee, Samuel. Student U. Utah, 1952-56; degree in acctg., LaSalle Extension Inst., 1966. CPA, Calif.; accredited estate planner. Staff acct. Robinson, Nowell & Co. (merged with Muncy McPherson & Co., Muncy McPherson McCune Dieckman 1967), 1966-73, ptnr., 1973-81, mng. ptnr., 1981-87, ptnr. BDO Seidman, 1988-95, sr. ptnr., 1995—. Bd. dirs. Congregation Beth Sholom, San Francisco, 1969—, pres., 1979-81; mem. budget and allocations com. Jewish Fedn., East Bay, 1981-84. With U.S. Army, 1957-58, 61-62. Ford Found. scholar. Mem. Am. Inst. C.P.A.s (acctg. standards exec. com. 1979-81), Nat. Assn. Accredited Estate Planners, Calif. Soc. C.P.A.s (chmn. sub-com. acctg. principles 1981-83), C.P.A. Assocs. (bd. dirs. 1986-87) San Francisco Estate Planning Coun., Mensa, Club One Valley Vista Club. Jewish. Home: 931 Walnut Ave Walnut Creek CA 94598-3738 Office: 1 Sansome St Fl 11 San Francisco CA 94104-4430

NORD, ROBERT EAMOR, lawyer; b. Ogden, Utah, Apr. 11, 1945; s. Eamor Carroll and Ella Carol (Winkler) N.; m. Sherryl Anne Smith, May 15, 1969; children: Kimberly, P. Ryan, Debra, Heather, Andrew, Elizabeth. BS, Brigham Young U., 1969; JD, U. Chgo., 1972. Bar: Ill. 1972, U.S. Dist. Ct. (no. dist.) Ill. 1972, U.S. Ct. Appeals (D.C. cir.) 1974, U.S. Dist. Ct. (mid. dist.) Fla. 1976, U.S. Ct. Appeals (7th cir.) 1977, U.S. Dist. Ct. (no. dist.) Ind. 1978, U.S. Dist. Ct. (no. dist.) Fla. 1979, U.S. Supreme Ct. 1981, U.S. Dist. Ct. (ea. dist.) Mich. 1984, U.S. Ct. Appeals (11th cir.) 1985, U.S. Ct. Appeals (3d cir.) 1996. Assoc. Chadwell & Kayser, Chgo., 1972-75; from assoc. to ptnr. Hinshaw & Culbertson, Chgo., 1975—. Republican. Mormon. Club: University (Chgo.). Home: 481 Woodlawn Ave Glencoe IL 60022-2175 Office: Hinshaw & Culbertson 222 N La Salle St Ste 300 Chicago IL 60601-1013

NORD, THOMAS ALLISON, hospital administrator; b. Boise, Idaho, Dec. 29, 1934; s. Everett Oliver and Alice Susan (Sherry) N.; m. Kay Hahn, Apr. 19, 1958; children: Mark Allison, Matthew Brendan, Julia Christian Nord Jenkins, Christopher Thomas. BSBA, Denver U., 1957, MBA, 1971; post-grad., Cornell U., 1974. Office mgr. Mountain States Sprinkler Supply, Denver, 1957-61; owner, mgr. Desert Rain, Roswell, N.Mex., 1961-68; sheriff Chaves County, Roswell, 1966-71; adminstr. St. Vincent Gen. Hosp., Leadville, Colo., 1972-78, Grand River Hosp. Dist., Rifle, Colo., 1980-83; planner, coord. outreach St. Mary's Hosp. and Med. Ctr., Grand Junction, Colo., 1978-80, assoc. adminstr., 1980; pres., CEO, Ivinson Meml. Hosp., Laramie, Wyo., 1983—; Mem. Garfield County Human Svc. Commn., 1980-83, chmn., 1982-83; mem. governing bd. Western Colo. Health Sys. Agy., 1980; chmn. steering com. Southeastern Colo. Health Sys. Agy., 1975, chmn. governing bd., 1976-79; mem. liaison com. for U. Wyo. Sch. Nursing, 1984-85; mem. strategic planning com. U. Wyo., 1995—; mem. clin. faculty programs in health svcs. adminstrn. U. Minn. Sch. Pub. Health, 1984; bd. dirs. Blue Cross/Blue Shield Wyo., 1988—, mem. exec. com., 1993—, chmn. bd. dirs. 1996—; mem. Wyo. Healthcare Reform Commn., 1994; chmn. bd. VHA Mountain States. Active Boy Scouts Am., United Way. Fellow Am. Coll. Healthcare Execs. (Wyo. regent 1994—); mem. Am. Hosp. Assn. (Colo. Hosp. Assn. del. 1980-83, mem. task force for input price adjustments 1988, del. regional policy bd. 1994-96), Wyo. Hosp. Assn. (bd. dirs. 1984—, chmn. 1986), Healthcare Forum (membership com. 1985, bd. dirs. 1986-89), Laramie C. of C., Rotary, Lions, Elks. Republican. Avocations: skiing, hunting, hiking, fishing, woodworking. Home: PO Box 155 Centennial WY 82055-0155 Office: Ivinson Memorial Hospital 255 N 30th St Laramie WY 82072-5140

NORD, WALTER ROBERT, business administration educator, researcher, consultant; b. Mt. Kisco, N.Y., July 2, 1939; s. Arthur William and Elizabeth (Reimstedt) N.; m. Ann Feagan, June 10, 1967. BA in Econs., Williams Coll., 1961; MS in Organizational Behavior, Cornell U., 1963; PhD in Social Psychology, Washington U., St. Louis, 1967. Asst. prof. organizational psychology Washington U., 1967-70, assoc. prof., 1970-73, prof., 1973-89; prof. mgmt. U. South Fla., 1989—; vis. prof. faculty commerce U. B.C. (Can.), Vancouver, 1975-76, Northwestern U., 1981. Author: (with S. Tucker) Implementing Routine and Radical Innovations, 1987; editor: Concepts and Controversy in Organizational Behavior, 1972, rev. edit, 1976; (with P. Frost and V. Mitchell) Organizational Reality, 1978, rev. edit., 1982, 86, 92; (with H. Meltzer) Making Organizations Humane and Productive, 1982; (with P. Frost and V. Mitchell) Managerial Reality, 1989, HRM Reality, 1992; (with A. Brief) Meanings of Occupational Work, 1990, (with S. Clegg and C. Hardy) Handbook of Organization Studies, 1996. Fellow Am. Psychol. Assn.; mem. Acad. Mgmt., Union for Radical Polit. Econs. Home: 6004 Pratt St Tampa FL 33647-1043 Office: U South Fla Sch Bus Tampa FL 33620-5500

NORDBERG, JOHN ALBERT, senior federal judge; b. Evanston, Ill., June 18, 1926; s. Carl Albert and Judith Ranghild (Carlson) N.; m. Jane Spaulding, June 18, 1947; children: Carol, Mary, Janet, John. Student, Carleton Coll., 1943-44, 46-47; J.D., U. Mich., 1950. Bar: Ill. 1950, U.S. Dist. Ct. (no. dist.) Ill. 1957, U.S. Ct. Appeals (7th cir.) 1961. Assoc. Pope & Ballard, Chgo., 1950-57; ptnr. Pope, Ballard, Shepard & Fowle, Chgo., 1957-76; judge Cir. Ct. of Cook County, Ill., 1976-82; judge U.S. Dist. Ct. (no. dist.) Ill., Chgo., 1982-95, sr. judge, 1995—. Editor-in-chief, bd. editors Chgo. Bar Record, 1966-74. Magistrate of Cir. Ct. and justice of peace Ill., 1957-65. Served with USN, 1944-46; PTO. Mem. ABA, Chgo. Bar Assn., Am. Judicature Soc., Law Club Chgo., Union League Club of Chgo., Legal Club Chgo., Order of Coif. Office: US Dist Ct 219 S Dearborn St Chicago IL 60604

NORDBY, EUGENE JORGEN, orthopedic surgeon; b. Abbotsford, Wis., Apr. 30, 1918; s. Herman Preus and Lucille Violet (Korsrud) N.; m. Olive Marie Jensen, June 21, 1941; 1 child, Jon Jorgen. B.A., Luther Coll., Decorah, Iowa, 1939; M.D., U. Wis., 1943. Diplomate Am. Bd. Orthopaedic Surgery. Intern Madison Gen. Hosp., Wis., 1943-44, asst. in orthopedic surgery, 1944-48; practice medicine specializing in orthopedic surgery Madison, Wis., 1948—; pres. Bone and Joint Surgery Assocs., S.C. 1969-91; chief staff Madison Gen. Hosp., 1957-63; assoc. clin. prof. U. Wis. Med. Sch., 1961—; chmn. Wis. Physicians Svcs., 1979—; dir. Wis. Regional Med. Program, Chgo. Madison and No. RR; bd. govs. Wis. Health Care Liability Ins. Plan; chmn. trustees S.M.S. Realty Corp.; mem. bd. attys. Profl. Responsibility of Wis. Supreme Ct., 1992—. Assoc. editor Clin. Orthopaedics and Related Research, 1964—; mem. adv. edtl. bd. Spine, 1994—. Pres. Vesterheim Norwegian Am. Mus., Decorah, Iowa, 1968—. Served to capt. M.C., AUS, 1944-46. Decorated Knight 1st class Royal Norwegian Order St. Olav; named Notable Norwegian Dane County Norwegian-Am. Fest, 1995; recipient Disting. Svc. award Internat. Rotary,1 987, Den Hoyeste Aere award Vesterheim, 1993. Mem. Acad. Orthopaedic Surgeons (bd. dirs. 1972-73), Clin. Orthopaedic Soc., Assn. Bone and Joint Surgeons (pres. 1973), Internat. Soc. Study Lumbar Spine, State Med. Soc. Wis. (chmn. 1968-76, treas. 1976—, Coun. award 1976), Am. Orthopaedic Assn., N.Am. Spine Soc., Internat. Intradiscal Therapy Soc. (sec. 1987—, exec. dir. 1996—), Wis. Orthopaedic Soc., Dane County Med. Soc. (pres. 1957), Nat. Exch. Club, Madison Torske Klubben (founder, pres. 1978—), Norwegian-Am. Orthopaedic Soc., Am. Acad. Orthopaedic Surgeons, Am. Orthopedic Assn., Phi Chi. Lutheran. Home: 6234 S Highlands Ave Madison WI 53705-1115 Office: 2704 Marshall Ct Madison WI 53705-2256
We must remember no matter how dedicated we are to the accumulation of knowledge, it isn't always what you know that matters but what you can think of in time.

NORDBY, GENE MILO, engineering educator; b. Anoka, Minn., May 7, 1926; s. Bert J. and Nina Grace N.; m. Arlene Delores Anderson, Aug. 27, 1949 (dec. Nov. 1974); children: Susan Pamela, Brett Gene, Lisa Lea; m. Dusilla Anne Rycroft, July 8, 1975 (div. July 1988); m. Catherine Lynn Short, Dec. 23, 1992. BSCE, Oreg. State U., 1948; MSCE, U. Minn., 1949, Ph.D. in Civil Engring., 1955. Registered profl. engr., Colo. Ariz. Grad. asst. U. Minn., 1948-50; structural designer Pfeiffer and Shultz, Mpls., summer 1950; instr., then asst. prof. civil engring. U. Colo., Boulder, 1950-56; assoc. prof., rsch. engr. Joint Hwy. Rsch. Project Purdue U., East Lafayette, Ind., 1956; engr. program dir. engring. scis. NSF, Washington, 1956-58; lectr. civil engring. George Washington U., Washington, 1956-58; dir., then chmn. adv. com. Ariz. Transp. and Traffic Inst. at univ., 1959-62; prof. engring. U. Okla., Norman, 1962-77, dean Coll. Engring, 1962-70, v.p. for adminstrn. and fin. Coll. Engring, 1969-77; v.p. for bus. and fin., prof. civil engring. Ga. Inst. Tech., Atlanta, 1977-80; chancellor U. Colo., Denver, 1980-85; chancellor emeritus, 1985—; prof. civil engring. U. Colo., Denver and Boulder, 1985-86; prof. civil engring, head dept. civil engring. U. Ariz., 1958-62; prof. agrl. engring. U. Ariz., Tucson, 1986-94, prof. emeritus, 1994—, head dept. agrl. engring., 1986-91; mem. Reinforced Concrete Research Council Engring. Found., 1954-60; trustee Frontiers of Science Found., Okla., 1963-70; pres. Tetracon Assos., Inc., 1968-86; cons. structural engring., research financing and programming, ednl. facilities planning and constrn., reinforced concrete, also higher edn. adminstrn., engring. program accreditation, NSF, 1984-87, panel engring. ctrs. of excellence, 1983-87; bd. dirs. Higher Edn. and the Handicapped, Am. Council on Edn., 1980-83; pres. Accreditation Bd. for Engring. and Tech., 1985-86, fellow, mem. Related Accreditation Commn., 1986-95, chair, 1993-94; gen. chmn. Nat. Congress on Engring. Edn., Washington, 1986; commr. at large N. Cen. Assn. Schs. and Colls., 1988-92. Co-author: Introduction to Structural Mechanics, 1960; Cons. editor, MacMillan Co., 1962-70. Mem. bd. vis. Air Force Inst. Tech., 1985-87. With AUS, 1943-46. Recipient Citation for Svc., State of Okla. Ho. Reps., 1977, Linton E. Grinter Disting. Svc. award Accreditation Bd. for Engring. and Tech., 1982. Fellow ASCE (com. on engring edn., 1964-68, com. on research needs, 1965-70, com. on ednl. research, 1976-79, Edmund Friedman Profl. Devel. award 1982); mem. Am. Soc. Engring. Edn. (projects bd. 1969-70, chmn. Curtis W. McGraw award com. 1968, Dean's Inst. com. 1966-69, accreditation process com. 1979-81), Nat. Soc. Profl. Engrs., Am. Arbitration Assn., Am. Soc. Agrl. Engrs. (com. in egring. and tech. accreditation 1987-93), Engrs. Council for Profl. Devel. (chmn. engring. edn. and accreditation com. 1970, dir. 1976-79, 83-87), Ariz. Soc. Profl. Engrs., Okla. Soc. Profl. Engrs. (dir. 1966-69), Nat. Assn. State Univs. and Land Grant Colls. (commn. edn. engring. profession 1966, 70-73), Engring. Colls. Adminstrv. Council (mem. exec. bd. 1966), Ga. Soc. Profl. Engrs. (bd. dirs. Atlanta chpt. 1978-79), Nat. Assn. Coll. and Univ. Bus. Officers (chmn. personnel com. 1977-79), Sigma Tau, Omicron Delta Kappa, Tau Beta Pi, Chi Epsilon, Alpha Epsilon. Club: Mason. Office: U Ariz PO Box 210038 403 Shantz Bldg 38 Tucson AZ 85721-0038

NORDEL, PATRICIA A. OLMSTEAD, medical/surgical, critical care, and obstetrical nurse; b. New Britain, Conn., Jan. 19, 1965; d. Lester B. and Patricia (Tufts) Olmstead; m. David R. Nordel; children: David M., Dominic X. BSN, U. Conn., 1987. Cert. med.-surg. nurse. Commd. 2d lt. USAF, 1987, advanced through grades to capt., 1991; staff nurse med.-surg. USAF, Scott AFB, Ill., Travis AFB, Calif.; charge nurse outpatient USAF, RAF Greenham Common, Eng.; staff nurse obstetrics USAF, RAF Upper Heyford, Eng., 1987-94; staff nurse Travel Nurse Broker Svc., Napa, Calif., 1994-95; RN Profl. Nursing Svcs., Suisun City, Calif., 1995-96; staff nurse Lake Meade Med. Ctr., Las Vegas, 1996—.

NORDELL, HANS RODERICK, journalist, retired editor; b. Alexandria, Minn., June 26, 1925; s. Wilbur Eric and Amelia (Jasperson) N.; m. Joan Projansky, Apr. 30, 1955; children: Eric Peter, John Roderick, Elizabeth Sabin. AB magna cum laude, Harvard U., 1948; B Litt, U. Dublin, 1951. Exec. editor World Monitor: The Christian Science Monitor Monthly; with Christian Sci. Monitor, Boston, 1948-93, arts editor, 1968-73, asst. chief editorial writer, 1973-83, home forum editor, 1983-85, feature editor, 1985-87; exec. editor World Monitor: The Chrstian Science Monitor Monthly, Boston, 1988-93. Bd. dirs. Cmty. Music Ctr., Boston, 1970-94, corp. chair, 1994—; bd. dirs. Young Audiences, 1970-88; mem. Com. for Harvard Theatre Collection, 1977-91; trustee Berklee Coll. Music, 1970-97, trustee emeritus, 1997—. With USMCR, 1943-46. Fellowship Rotary Found., 1950-51. Mem. St. Botolph Club, Phi Beta Kappa. Christian Scientist. Home: 25 Meadow Way Cambridge MA 02138-4635

NORDENBERG, MARK ALAN, law educator, university official; b. Duluth, Minn., July 12, 1948; s. John Clemens and Shirley Mae (Tappen) N.; m. Nikki Patricia Pirillo, Dec. 26, 1970; children: Erin, Carl, Michael. BA, Thiel Coll., 1970; JD, U. Wis., 1973. Bar: Wis. 1973, Minn. 1974, U.S. Supreme Ct. 1976, Pa. 1985. Atty. Gray, Plant, Mooty & Anderson, Mpls., 1973-75; prof. law Capital U. Law Ctr., Columbus, Ohio, 1975-77; prof. law U. Pitts., 1977—, acting dean Sch. Law, 1985-87, dean Sch. Law, 1987-93, interim univ. sr. vice chancellor and provost, 1993-94, Univ. Disting. Svc. prof., 1994—, interim univ. chancellor, 1995-96, univ. chancellor, 1996—; mem. U.S. Supreme Ct. Adv. Com. on Civil Rules, Washington, 1988-93, Pa. Supreme Ct. Civil Procedure Rules Com., Phila., 1986-92; mem. large and complex case panel Am. Arbitration Assn.; reporter civil justice adv. group U.S. Dist. Ct., Pitts., 1991-96. Author: Modern Pennsylvania Civil Practice, 1985, 2d edit., 1995. Trustee Thiel Coll., Greenville, Pa., 1987—; bd. dirs. Lawyers Concerned for Lawyers of Pa., Harrisburg, Inst. for Shipboard Edn., Pitts. High Tech. Coun., Urban League of Pitts., United Way of Allegheny County, World Affairs Coun. of Pitts., The Carnegie, Pitts.; vice chair Pitts.-Wuhan Friendship Com. Fellow Am. Bar Found.; mem. ABA, Pa. Bar Assn., Pa. Assn. Colls. and Univs. (bd. dirs.), Allegheny County Bar Assn., Acad. Trial Lawyers Allegheny County, Law Club Pitts., Univ. Club, Duquesne Club. Office: U Pitts 107 Cathedral of Learning Pittsburgh PA 15260-0001

NORDGREN, RONALD PAUL, engineering educator, researcher; b. Munising, Mich., Apr. 3, 1936; s. Paul A. and Martha M. N.; m. Joan E. McAfee, Sept 12, 1959; children: Sonia, Paul. BS in Engring., U. Mich., 1957, MS in Engring., 1958; PhD, U. Calif., Berkeley, 1962. Rsch. asst. U. Calif., Berkeley, 1959-62; mathematician Shell Devel. Co., Houston, 1963-68, staff rsch. engr., 1968-74, sr. staff rsch. engr., 1974-80, rsch. assoc., 1980-90; Brown prof. civil and mech. engring. Rice U., Houston, 1989—; mem. U.S. nat. com. on theoretical and applied mechanics NRC, 1984-86, U.S. nat. com. for rock mechanics, 1991-95. Contbr. tech. papers to profl. jours.; assoc. editor Jour. Applied Mechanics, 1972-76, 81-85; patentee in field. Fellow ASME; mem. NAE, ASCE, Soc. Industrial and Applied Math., Soc. Engring. Sci., Sigma Xi. Office: Rice U 6100 Main St Houston TX 77005-1827

NORDHAUS, ROBERT RIGGS, lawyer; b. Albuquerque, Mar. 27, 1937; s. Robert J. and Virginia (Riggs) N.; m. Jean Friedberg, June 27, 1964; children: Ronald E., Hannah E. BA, Stanford U., 1960; LLB, Yale U., 1963. Bar: N.Mex. 1963, D.C. 1981, U.S. Supreme Ct. 1982. Asst. counsel U.S. House Reps., Washington, 1963-74, counsel interstate and fgn. commerce com., 1975-76; asst. adminstr. FEA, Washington, 1977; gen. counsel Fed. Energy Regulatory Commn., Washington, 1977-80; ptnr. Van Ness, Feldman & Curtis, Washington, 1981-93; gen. counsel Dept. of Energy, Washington, 1993-97; ptnr. Van Ness Feldman, Washington, 1997—; adj. prof. Georgetown U. Law Ctr., Washington, 1980-85. 2d. lt. U.S. Army, 1960. Mem. Fed. Energy Bar Assn. (bd. dirs. 1989-92). Office: Van Ness Feldman 1050 Thomas Jefferson St NW Washington DC 20007-3837

NORDLAND, GERALD, art museum administrator, historian, consultant; b. Los Angeles. AB, U. So. Calif., JD. Dean of faculty Chouinard Art Sch., L.A., 1960-64; dir. Washington Gallery of Modern Art, 1964-66, San Francisco Mus. Art, 1966-72, Frederick S. Wight Art Galleries, UCLA, 1973-77, Milw. Art Mus., 1977-85; ind. curator, author, editor Chgo., 1985—. Author: Paul Jenkins, 1972, Gaston Lachaise/The Man and His Work, 1974, Richard Diebenkorn, 1987, Zhou Brothers, Chicago, 1994, Ynez Johnston, 1996. Gaston Lachaise Found. grantee, 1973-74; John Simon Guggenheim Found. fellow, 1985-86. Home and Office: 645 W Sheridan Rd Chicago IL 60613-3316

NORDLEY, GERALD DAVID, writer, investor; b. Mpls., May 22, 1947; s. V. Gerald and Evelyn May (Whitesel) N.; (div. 1973); 1 child, Sharon; m. Gayle Ann Wiesner, May 9, 1976; children: Jeffrey Goldberg, Andrew Nordley. BA in Physics, Macalester Coll., 1969; MS in System Mgmt., U. So. Calif., L.A., 1980. Enlisted USAF, 1969, commd. 2nd lt., 1970, advanced through grades to maj., 1982; inter-range ops. officer Network Ops. Div., Sunnyvale AFB, Calif., 1973-76; chief orbital ops. br. Def. Satellite Communications Directorate, L.A. AFB, 1976-81; chief spacecraft engr. br. DSCS III Program Office, L.A. AFB, 1981-82; battle dir. Mangilsan Liason Annex, Mang Il San, South Korea, 1983; chief advanced propulsion br. A.F. Rocket Propulsion Lab., Edwards AFB, Calif., 1984-86; rsch. staff mgr. ARIES office Astronautics Lab., Edwards AFB, 1986-89; ret. USAF, 1989; writer, pvt. investor Sunnyvale, 1990—. Mem. dir. Macalester Coll. Rep. Club, St. Paul, 1967-68; pres. Park Knowles Estates Property Owners Assn., Boron, Calif., 1988; co-chair Silicon Valley Writers Workshop, Cupertino, Calif., 1992, 93. Decorated Air Force Commendation medal with 4 oak leaf clusters, Meritorious Svc. medal with 1 oak leaf cluster; recipient Anlab award Analog Mag., 1992, 93. Fellow Brit. Interplanetary Soc.; mem. AIAA (elec. propulsion com. 1984-86), Air Force Assn., Sci. Fiction Writers Am., Whensday People Writers Group, Ft. Mason's Officers Club, Am. Legion. Unitarian. Avocation: amateur astronomy.

NORDLIE, ROBERT CONRAD, biochemistry educator; b. Willmar, Minn., June 11, 1930; s. Peder Conrad and Myrtle (Spindler) N.; m. Sally Ann Christianson, Aug. 23, 1959; children: Margaret, Melissa, John. B.S. St. Cloud State Coll., Minn., 1952; M.S., U. N.D., 1957, Ph.D., 1960.

Teaching and research asst. biochemistry U. N.D. Med. Sch., Grand Forks, 1955-60, Hill research prof. biochemistry, 1962-74, Chester Fritz disting. prof. biochemistry, 1974—, Cornatzer prof., chmn. dept. biochemistry and molecular biology, 1983—; hon. prof. San Marcos U., Lima, Peru, 1981, 82—; NIH fellow Inst. Enzyme Rsch., U. Wis., 1960-61; mem. biochemistry study sect. NIH; merit rev. com. VA, 1994—; cons. enzymology Oak Ridge, 1961—; vis. prof. Tokyo Biomed. Inst., 1984; mem. predoctoral fellowship rev. group Howard Hughes Inst., 1990-93. Mem. editorial bd.: Jour. Biol. Chemistry, Biochimca et Biophysica Acta. Research publs. on enzymology relating to metabolism of various carbohydrates in mammalian livers, regulation blood sugar levels. Served with AUS, 1953-55. Recipient Disting. Alumnus award St. Cloud State U., 1983; recipient Sigma Xi Rsch. award, 1969, Golden Apple award U. N.D., 1968, Edgar Dale award U. N.D., 1983, Burlington No. Faculty Scholar award, 1987, Thomas J. Clifford Faculty Achievement award for excellence in rsch. U. N.D. Found., 1993. Mem. AAAS, Am. Soc. Biol. Chemistry and Molecular Biology, Am. Chem. Soc., Internat. Union Biochemists, Soc. Exptl. Biology and Medicine, Am. Inst. Nutrition, Sigma Xi, Alpha Omega Alpha. Home: 162 Columbia Ct Grand Forks ND 58203-2947

NORDLING, BERNARD ERICK, lawyer; b. Nekoma, Kans., June 14, 1921; s. Carl Ruben Ebben and Edith Elveda (Freeburg) N.; m. Barbara Ann Burkholder, Mar. 26, 1949. Student, George Washington U., 1941-43; AB, McPherson Coll., 1947; JD, U. Kans., 1949. Bar: Kans. 1949, U.S. Dist. Ct. Kans. 1949, U.S. Ct. Appeals (10th cir.) 1970. Pvt. practice Hugoton, Kans., 1949—; ptnr. Kramer & Nordling, Hugoton, Kans., 1950-65, Kramer, Nordling & Nordling, Hugoton, Kans., 1966-94; of counsel Kramer, Nordling, Nordling & Tate, 1994—; city atty. City of Hugoton, 1951-87; county atty. Stevens County, Kans., 1957-63; Kans. mem. legal com. Interstate Oil Compact Commn., 1969-93; mem. supply tech. adv. com. nat. gas survey FPC, 1975-77. Editor U. Kans. Law Rev., 1949. Mem. Hugoton Sch. Bds., 1954-68, pres. grade sch. bd., 1957-63; trustee McPherson Coll., 1971-81, mem. exec. com., 1975-81; mem. Kans. Energy Adv. Coun., 1975-78, mem. exec. com., 1976-78. With AUS, 1944-46. Recipient Citation of Merit, McPherson Coll., 1987, Disting. Alumnus award Kans. U. Law Sch., 1993, Lifetime Achievement award Hugoton Kans. Area C. of C., 1994. Fellow Am. Bar Found. (Kans.); mem. ABA, Kans. Bar Assn., S.W. Kans. Bar Assn., Am. Judicature Soc., City Attys. Assn. Kans. (exec. com. 1975-83, pres. 1982-83), Nat. Assn. Royalty Owners (bd. govs. 1980—), S.W. Kans. Royalty Owners Assn. (exec. sec. 1968-94, asst. exec. sec. 1994—), U. Kans. Law Soc. (bd. govs. 1984-87), Kans. U. Endowment Assn. (trustee 1989—), Kans. U. Alumni Assn. (bd. dirs. 1992—), Order of Coif, Phi Alpha Delta. Home: 218 N Jackson St Hugoton KS 67951-2040 Office: 209 E 6th St Hugoton KS 67951-2613

NORDLUND, DONALD CRAIG, corporate lawyer; b. Chgo., May 23, 1949; s. Donald E. and Jane (Houston) N.; m. Sally Baum, Sept. 7, 1975; children: Courtney Elizabeth, Michael Andrew, Laurie Katherine. AB, Stanford U., 1971; JD, Vanderbilt U., 1974. Assoc. Ware & Freidenrich, Palo Alto, Calif., 1974-77; atty. Hewlett-Packard Co., Palo Alto, 1977-80, sr. atty., asst. sec., 1980-81, asst. sec., corp. counsel, 1981-85, sec., corp. counsel, 1985-86, sec., asst. gen. counsel, 1986-87, assoc. gen. counsel, sec., 1987—; bd. dirs. Hewlett-Packard Hellas, Palo Alto, Hewlett-Packard European Distbn., Ops., Inc., The Netherlands, Hewlett-Packard Labs. Japan, Inc., Hewlett-Packard Del. Holding Inc., Hewlett-Packard Employees Fed. Credit Union, other Hewlett-Packard subs.; sec. Hewlett-Packard Co. Found., Palo Alto, 1979—, Hewlett-Packard Fin. Co., Palo Alto, 1983—; pres. Hewlett-Packard Inter-Ams.; panelist ann. disclosure documents seminar Practicing Law Inst., 1982-97, also contbg. author to course handbook; cons. pub. guide series, CEB, 1991. Chmn., bd. dirs. Santa Clara County chpt. Jr. Achievement, 1995—. Mem. Am. Soc. Corp. Secs. Inc. (pres. San Francisco region 1986-88, bd. dirs. 1987-90, mem. exec. com. 1988-89, chmn. securities law com. 1995—), Am. Corp. Counsel Assn. (bd. dirs. San Francisco chpt. 1984—, nat. bd. dirs. 1995—, pres. 1989-90), Foothills Tennis and Swimming Club (Palo Alto). Avocations: tennis, skiing, sailing, golf. Office: Hewlett-Packard Co 3000 Hanover St Palo Alto CA 94304-1112

NORDLUND, DONALD ELMER, manufacturing company executive; b. Stromsburg, Nebr., Mar. 1, 1922; s. E.C. and Edith O. (Peterson) N.; m. Mary Jane Houston, June 5, 1948; children: Donald Craig, William Chalmers, Sarah, James. A.B., Midland Coll., 1943; J.D., U. Mich., 1948. Bar: Ill. 1949. With Stevenson, Conaghan, Hackbert, Rooks and Pitts, Chgo., 1948-55, A.E. Staley Mfg. Co., Decatur, Ill., 1956-85; v.p., dir., mem. exec. com. A.E. Staley Mfg. Co., 1958-65, pres., chief operating officer, 1965-80, dir., mem. exec. com., 1965-85, also chmn., 1975-85; chief exec. officer Staley Continental, Inc., Rolling Meadows, Ill., 1985-88, chmn. and chief exec. officer, 1985-88; bd. dirs. Sentry Ins., Sundstrand Corp. Past chmn. bd. trustees Millikin U., now hon. trustee; trustee Vanderbilt U., Mus. Sci. and Industry, Chgo., Rush-Presbyn. St. Lukes Med. Ctr., Chgo.; bd. dirs. Lyric Opera Chgo.; mem. grad. dirs. coun. Decatur Meml. Hosp. Mem. ABA, Chgo. Bar Assn., Corn Refiners Assn. (bd. dirs., past chmn., now hon. dir.), Legal Club, Comml. Club, Chgo. Club, Tavern Club, Barrington Hills Club, Phi Alpha Delta.

NORDLUND, WILLIAM CHALMERS, lawyer; b. Chgo., Aug. 29, 1954; s. Donald E. and Jane H. (Houston) N.; m. Elizabeth Apell, Oct. 1, 1983; children: William Chalmers Jr., Scott Donald. BA, Vanderbilt U., 1976; JD, Duke U., 1979; MM, Northwestern U., 1990. Bar: Ill. 1979, Md. 1991, Mich. 1992. Assoc. Winston & Strawn, Chgo., 1979-87, ptnr., 1987-90; atty. Constellation Holdings, Inc., 1990-91; v.p., sec., gen. counsel The Oxford Energy Co., Dearborn, Mich., 1991-92, sr. v.p., sec., gen. counsel, 1992-93; gen. counsel Panda Energy Corp., Dallas, 1993-94, v.p. and gen. counsel, 1994-95; v.p., gen. counsel Panda Energy Internat., Inc., Dallas, 1995-96, sr. v.p., gen. counsel, 1996-97, exec. v.p., CFO, 1997—. Bd. dirs. Orch. of Ill., Chgo., 1983-85; bd. dirs., sec. Literacy Vols. of Am.-Ill., Chgo., 1985-88, treas., 1988-90. Avocations: golf, tennis, skiing. Office: Panda Energy Internat Inc 4100 Spring Valley Rd Ste 1001 Dallas TX 75244-3646

NORDMAN, CHRISTER ERIC, chemistry educator; b. Helsinki, Finland, Jan. 23, 1925; came to U.S., 1948, naturalized, 1960; s. Eric Johan and Gertrud (Nordgren) N.; m. Barbara Lorraine Neal, Nov. 28, 1952 (div. 1993); children: Christina, Aleta, Eric, Carl; m. Outi Marttila, Dec. 28, 1994. Dipl. Ing., Finnish Inst. Tech., Helsinki, 1949; Ph.D., U. Minn., 1953. Research asso. Inst. Cancer Research, Phila., 1953-55; mem. faculty U. Mich., Ann Arbor, 1955—; prof. chemistry U. Mich., 1964-95; prof. emeritus, 1995—. Mem. U.S. Nat. Com. Crystallography, 1970-72. Served with Finnish Army, 1943-44. NIH spl. fellow, 1971-72. Fellow AAAS; mem. Am. Chem. Soc., Am. Phys. Soc., Am. Crystallographic Assn., Finnish Soc. Scis. and Letters. Home: 27 Haverhill Ct Ann Arbor MI 48105-1406 Office: Univ Mich Dept Chemistry Ann Arbor MI 48109

NORDMAN, RICHARD DENNIS, chemical company executive; b. Iowa, Sept. 30, 1946; s. Victor and Dorothy Nordman; m. Patricia Lynn Boehnke, Aug. 27, 1966; children: Sarah, Matthew, Angela. BSBA, Iowa State U., 1968. CPA, Ill. Mgr. Arthur Andersen & Co., Chgo., 1968-74; treas. Lawter Internat., Inc., Northbrook, Ill., 1974-80, v.p. fin., 1980-83, exec. v.p., 1983-86, pres., COO, 1986-96, bd. dirs., 1982. Trustee Cornerstone Found. Luth. Social Svcs. of Ill. Mem. AICPA, Ill. Soc. CPAs, Chgo. Sunday Evening Club (trustee), Econ. Club, Exec. Club. Avocations: golf, tennis, flying. Office: Lawter Internat Inc 990 Skokie Blvd Northbrook IL 60062-4005

NORDQVIST, ERIK ASKBO, shipping company executive; b. Copenhagen, Aug. 8, 1943; s. Joergen and Lissie (Moeller) A.; m. Kirsten Vibeke Kenholt, Sept. 17, 1970; children: Ken-Martin, Alexander. Student, Danish Comml. Coll. Commerce, London, 1963-64, U. S.C., London, 1964-65. Vice pres. Import Center W.S., L.A., 1964-65; mgr. Denning Freight Forwarders Ltd., Toronto, Ont., Can., 1965-66; sales dir. overseas Samson Transp. Co., Copenhagen, 1967-68; mng. dir., pres. Seair AS, Copenhagen, 1969-71, Nordbird Group, Vedbaek, Denmark, 1971—, Nordbird AS, 1971—; chmn. European Steamship Line, Vedbaek, 1995—, European Airline Sys., Vedbaek, 1995—; also Nordbird Oil, Nordbird Fin., Copenhagen, Nordbird Internat. Financing Ltd., Toronto, Ont.; v.p. N. Sea Products Inc., High Point, N.C., 1980—; bd. dirs. Fino Travel, Odense, Denmark, Annex Furniture Galleries, European Broadcast Comm., Vedbaek, On Holding Ltd., Gibraltar, Olsen & Nordqvist Holding, Holbaek, Denmark, pres., 1986—, NQ-Byg Aps, Holbaek, Auto Dan-Am., Holbaek, Autotel Internat., Roskilde, On Holding APS, Vedbaek Dansk-Fransk Osters Aps, 3 Danish Open, U.S., Gt. Britain, Japan,, Tins and Cans, Denmark; chmn. European Broadcast Comm., Charlottenlund, Denmark, London, European Aid Found., Vedbeak, Denmark, Lac, Albanien; cons. Frederikshavns. Skibsvaerf AS, Copenhagen Cmty. Chmn. European Broadcast Comm., Copenhagen and London, 1992—, European Aid Found., Copenhagen and N.Y.C.; del. Internat. Red Cross, Copenhagen, 1994—. Recipient Devel. honor for shipping City of Le Havre, France, 1971. Mem. Det Udenrigspolitiske Selskab, Funen Soc. (founder, past pres.). Conservative. Lutheran. Office: EAS/ESL/RSD, 35 Flintemarken, 2950 Vedbaek Denmark

NORDSIECK, KAREN ANN, custom design company owner; b. Ft. Campbell, Ky., Nov. 2, 1955; d. Reuben James and Shirley Jean (Walters) Simpson; m. Kenneth M. Farber, Mar. 5, 1977 (div. July 1982); children: Carissa Ann, Laurie Jean; m. Derrell E. Hiett, May 10, 1985 (div. May 1989); m. Michael Louis Nordsieck, June 2, 1989. Student, El Paso Community Coll., 1976, 84. Sales clk. Busy B Gift Shop, El Paso, Tex., 1973; svc. rep. Bell System, El Paso and Seattle, 1974-85; substitute tchr. Cleburne County Elem. Sch., Heflin, Ala., 1986; credit clk. Wakefields, Anniston, Ala., 1986-87; svc. rep. Ala. Power, Anniston, 1986-88; beauty cons. May Kay Cosmetics, El Paso and Heflin, Ala., 1983-88; mgr. Rock's T-Shirts & Screen Printing, El Paso, 1988-92; owner Custom Designs and Promotions, Richmond, Mo., 1992-96; svc. rep. Southwestern Bell Telephone Co., Kansas City, Mo., 1993—; owner Kreations by Karen, Richmond, 1996—; liaison for ptnrs. in edn. El Paso Ind. Sch. Dist., Rock's T-Shirts and Screen Print, El Paso, 1990—; co-chairperson Quality of Work Life Com. Southwestern Bell, El Paso, 1984; union steward Communication Workers Am., El Paso, 1974-75. Troop leaders Brownies, Girl Scouts U.S.A., troop # 126, Heflin, 1985-88, mag. chairperson, 1986; v.p. Clendenin Elem. PTA, El Paso, 1989-90, pres., 1990-92; family support leader Ft. Bliss Family Support, El Paso, 1990-91; mem. El Paso Ind. Sch. Dist. Strategic Planning Com., 1990-91; mem. campus improvement com. Clendenin Elem., 1991-92, vol. pub. schs., 1989-92; mem. parent adv. com. ctrl. area El Paso Ind. Sch. Dist., 1989-92; mem. Richmond PTA, 1992—; mem. com. Richmond A-Plus Sch. Planning, 1994-95; co-chairperson Jr. Class Parents After Prom/Project Graduation, 1995-96; mem. Battlefield Piece Makers Quilt Guild, 1995-97; chmn., editor CWA Local 6327 newsletter, The Localizer, 1997—, union steward, 1996—. Recipient Outstanding Troop Leader award Girl Scouts U.S.A., Anniston, 1987, cert. outstanding svc. Clendenin PTA, El Paso, 1990, 91, 92; cert. of honor Clendenin Elem. Sch., 1990, 91, 92, Cert. of Appreciation, 1991, 92; Cert. of Appreciation, Ft. Bliss Army Family Support, 1991, plaque Vols. in Pub. Sch., El Paso, 1991, 92, Ptnrs. in Edn., El Paso Ind. Sch. Dist., 1991, 92, Desert Storm vol. pin Ptnrs. in Edn., 1991, Pres. Appreciation award S.W. Bell, 1997. Mem. Order Ea. Star. Mem. Assembly of God. Avocations: sewing, painting, quilting, reading, sailing. Office: Kreations by Karen PO Box 187 Richmond MO 64085

NORDSTROM, BRUCE A., department store executive; b. 1933; married. BA, U. Wash., 1956. With Nordstrom, Inc., Seattle, 1956—; v.p., 1964-70, pres., 1970-75, chmn., 1975-77, co-chmn., 1977—, dir. Office: Nordstrom Inc 1501 5th Ave Seattle WA 98101-1603*

NORDSTROM, JOHN N., department store executive; b. 1937; married. BA, U. Wash., 1958. With Nordstrom, Inc., Seattle, 1958—, v.p., 1965-70, exec. v.p., 1970-75, pres., 1975-77, co-chmn., 1977—, dir.; bd. dirs. Fed. Res. Bank San Francisco. Office: Nordstrom Inc 1501 5th Ave Seattle WA 98101-1603*

NOREIKA, JOSEPH CASIMIR, ophthalmologist; b. Scranton, Pa., Aug. 21, 1950; s. Joseph C. and Joan (Stirna) N.; m. Joanne Elizabeth Keane, May 14, 1977; children: Sarah, Michael, Katya, Mathew. BS, U. Scranton, 1972; MD, Jefferson Med. Coll., 1976; MBA, Case Western Res. U., 1988. Diplomate Am. Bd. of Opthalmology. Intern Dartmouth Hosps., Hanover, N.H., 1976-77; resident in ophthalmology U. Pitts., 1977-80, assoc. clin. prof., 1981-83; fellow U. Calif., San Francisco, 1980-81; pvt. practice Medina, Ohio, 1983—; founding mem. Physician Resources Group, 1995, bd. dirs., mem. nominating com., chmn. compensation com., 1995, chmn. practice mgmt. physician adv. bd.; adj. cl in. staff Cleve. Clinic Found., 1980-92. Editl. advisor The Argus; sect. contbr.: Ocular Surgery News, editl. bd., Adminstrv. Ophthalmology; editl. bd. Eye World News Svc.; contbr. articles to profl. jours. Bd. dirs. Physician Resource Group. Recipient Shoemaker award Pa. Acad. Ophthalmology, 1979; Heed Found. fellow, 1980. Mem. AMA (Physician Recognition award 1984-96), Am. Acad. Ophthalmology (chmn. computerized patient record task force 1994-95, chair practice mgmt. com. 1997, managed care adv. com. 1994-95, Honor award 1996), Am. Soc. Cataract and Refractive Surgeons (sci. adv. bd. rep., rep. to AMA CPT adv. com., govt. rels. com.), Am. Soc. Ophthalmology Adminstrs. (editl. bd. Adminstrv. Ophthalmology, Ohio State Med. Assn., Ohio Ophthalmology Soc. (editor Managed Care-n Focus, chmn. managed care com.), Medina County Med. Soc. (past pres., program chmn.), Cleve. Ophthalmology Soc. (past pres.), Alpha Sigma Nu, Beta Gamma Sigma. Avocations: computers, collecting toy trains. Office: Eye Care Medina Inc 3637 Medina Rd Ste 70 Medina OH 44256-8155

NOREK, JOAN I., lawyer; b. Chgo., Jan. 26, 1945; d. Michael Stephen and Viola Catherine (Harbecke) N. BA in Chemistry, U. Ill., 1968; JD, DePaul U., 1975. Bar: Ill. 1975, U.S. Dist. Ct. (no. dist.) Ill. 1976, U.S. Ct. Appeals (7th cir.) 1976; registered patent atty. Assoc. William Brinks et al, Chgo., 1975-80; pvt. practice Chgo., 1980—. Mem. Am. Chem. Soc., Chgo. Intellectual Property Law Assn. (mem. bd. mgrs. 1989-91), Chgo. Bar Assn. Office: 180 N La Salle St Chicago IL 60601

NORELL, MARK ALLEN, paleontology educator; b. St. Paul, July 26, 1957; s. Albert Donald Norell and Helen Louise Soltau; m. Vivian Pan, Nov. 1, 1991; 1 child, Inga Pam. BS, Long Beach State U., 1980; MS, San Diego State U., 1983; PhD, Yale U., 1988. Assoc. curator Am. Mus., N.Y.C., 1989-96, chmn. dept., 1996—; adj. assoc. prof. dept. biology Yale U., New Haven, 1991—. Author: All You Need to Know About Dinosaurs, 1991, Discovering Dinosaurs, 1995, Searching for Velociraptor, 1996. Fellow Willi Hennig Soc., Explorers Club; mem. Soc. Vertebrate Paleontology (Romer prize 1987). Office: Am Mus Natural History 79th At Ctrl Park West New York NY 10024-5192

NOREM, RICHARD FREDERICK, SR., musician, music educator; b. Joliet, Ill., June 28, 1931; s. Oscar Lewis and Mabel Vera (Meyer) N.; m. Sally Lou Jarvis, July 24, 1954; 1 son, Richard Frederick II. Mus.B., U. Rochester, 1953, Mus.M., 1958; postgrad., Guildhall Sch., London, 1974. Instr. Joliet Musical Coll., Ill., 1951-53; tchr. Rochester Pub. Schs., N.Y., 1956-57; mem. faculty La. State U., Baton Rouge, 1957-95; prof., asst. dean music La. State U., 1969-84; prof. emeritus La. State U., Baton Rouge, 1995; dir., sec.-treas. Bank Commerce, 1983—; bd. dirs., sec.-treas. NBC Fin. Corp., 1988—. Mem. Baton Rouge Symphony Orch., 1957—, Timm Woodwind Quintet, 1957-95. With USMC Band, 1953-56. Mem. Am. Legion (past post comdr.), Rolls-Royce Owners Club (sec.-treas. So. Delta region), Norwegian Club Baton Rouge, La. State U. Faculty Club, Baton Rouge Model R.R. Club, Rotary. Republican. Episcopalian. Home: 4821 Sweetbriar St Baton Rouge LA 70808-8660 Office: La State U Sch Music Baton Rouge LA 70803 *I have been blessed by the divine creator with an artistic talent in music to which I have dedicated my life. Early during my performing career I knew I must share with others the knowledge I had obtained in music; consequently my goals have been to train and educate the hundreds of music students I have taught during my teaching career. I have also tried to continue to bring beauty to our world in my own way as an active performing musician.*

NOREN-IACOVINO, MARY-JO PATRICIA, insurance company executive; b. N.Y.C., Feb. 20, 1951; d. James Pierce and Grace Virginia (Keating) Keelty; m. Louis T. Iacovino, Sept. 23, 1989. Student, CUNY, 1971-72. Asst. v.p. Huntoon, Paige & Co., Inc., N.Y.C., 1972-79; v.p. Merrill Lynch Capital Mkts., N.Y.C., 1979-85, Security Pacific Merchant Bank, N.Y.C., 1985-89, Oxford Resources Corp., Woodbury, N.Y., 1989-90; securities products coord. Equitable Life, N.Y.C., 1990-94. Mem. Oratorio Soc. N.Y. (bd. dirs., mktg. dir. 1993), Women's Life Underwriters Coun., Nat. Assn. Life Underwriters. Avocations: choral singing, photography, travel. Home: 15 Park Ave # 15B New York NY 10016 Office: The Equitable Fl 32 1221 Ave of the Americas New York NY 10020-1088

NORFOLK, WILLIAM RAY, lawyer; b. Huron, S.D., Mar. 15, 1941; s. James W. and Helen F. (Thompson) N.; m. Marilyn E. Meadors; children: Stephanie G., Allison T., Meredith H. BA, Miami U., Oxford, Ohio, 1963; student, U. London, 1963-64; LLB, Duke U., 1967. Bar: N.Y. 1968, U.S. Dist. Ct. (so. and ea. dists.) N.Y. 1969, U.S. Ct. Appeals (2d cir.) 1969, U.S. Ct. Appeals (9th cir.) 1977, U.S. Ct. Appeals (5th cir.) 1979, U.S. Ct. Appeals (3d and 11th cirs.) 1981, U.S. Dist. Ct. (ea. dist.) Mich. 1986, U.S. Ct. Appeals (6th and 8th cirs.) 1986, U.S. Ct. Appeals (Fed. cir.) 1990, U.S. Ct. Internat. Trade 1990, U.S. Dist. Ct. (we. dist.) Mich. 1992. Assoc. Sullivan & Cromwell, N.Y.C., 1967-74, ptnr., 1974—. Trustee N.Y. Meth. Hosp. Mem. ABA, N.Y. State Bar Assn., Am. Soc. Internat. Law. Office: Sullivan & Cromwell 125 Broad St New York NY 10004-2400

NORGLE, CHARLES RONALD, SR., federal judge; b. Mar. 3, 1937. BBA, Northwestern U., Evanston, Ill., 1964; JD, John Marshall Law Sch., Chgo., 1969. Asst. state's atty. DuPage County, Ill., 1969-71, dep. pub. defender, 1971-73, assoc. judge, 1973-77, 78-81, cir. judge, 1977-78, 81-84; judge U.S. Dist. Ct. (no. dist.) Ill., Chgo., 1984—; mem. exec. com. No. Dist. Ill.; mem. 7th Cir. Jud. Coun., 7th Cir. Jud. Conf. planning com., subcom. grant requests Fed. Defender Orgn., Fed. Defender Svcs. Com. Mem. ABA, Fed. Bar Assn., Ill. Bar Assn., DuPage Bar Assn., Nat. Attys. Assn., DuPage Assn. Women Attys., Chgo. Legal Club, Northwestern Club. Office: US Dist Ct 219 S Dearborn St Ste 1703 Chicago IL 60604-1706

NORGREN, C. NEIL, retired manufacturing company executive; b. Silt, Colo., Aug. 23, 1923; s. Carl August and Juliet (Lien) N.; m. Carolyn Sutherland, Apr. 12, 1980; children by previous marriage: Jeraldine Leigh, Carol Ann, John Carl, David Laurence. Student, U. Colo., 1941-43. With C.A. Norgren Co. (mfrs. pneumatic products), Englewood, Colo., 1938-84; asst. gen. mgr. C.A. Norgren Co. (mfrs. pneumatic products), 1947-53, v.p., 1953-55, exec. v.p., 1955-62, pres., 1962-84, also dir.; chmn., chief exec. officer Butler Fixture Co., Denver, 1984-91; dir. United Bank of Denver (mem. exec. com. 1957-90). Bd. dirs. Bus. and Industry Polit. Action Com., 1967-89, Carl A. Norgren Found., 1955-90, Unitog Co., 1971-84; pres. Met. Denver chpt. Jr. Acheivement, 1954-56, nat. exec. com. 1956-62; bd. dirs. Denver Mus. Natural History, 1st v.p., 1983-88, pres., 1988-91; pres. C. Neil and Carolyn S. Norgren Found., 1990—; bd. dirs. U. Colo. Found., 1961-68, 81—, vice chmn., 1985-87, chmn., 1987-90, chmn. exec. com., 1990-92; Colo. divsn. exec. com. Am. Cancer Soc., 1961-67. Staff sgt. USAAF, 1942-46. Mem. NAM (bd. dirs. 1964-87, regional v.p. 1966-71, divsn. v.p. 1972-78, exec. com. 1966-78), Nat. Fluid Power Assn., Nat. Coun. Profit Sharing Industries (past chmn. exec. com.), Nat. Western Stock Show Assn. (former bd. dirs.), Inst. Dirs. London, Met. Denver Execs. Club (co-founder, past pres.), Athletic Club, Pinehurst Country Club, Air Force Acad. Golf Club (Colorado Springs), Met. Club, Glenmore Country Club, Flatirons Club, Beta Theta Pi. Home: 3319 Marsden Point Keswick VA 22947-9133

NORGREN, WILLIAM ANDREW, religious denomination administrator; b. Frostburg, Md., May 5, 1927; s. William Andrew and Martha Elizabeth Leona (Richardson) N. BA, Coll. William and Mary, 1948; STB, now STM, Gen. Theol. Sem., N.Y.C., 1953; LittB, Oxford (Eng.) U., 1959; DD (hon.), Gen. Theol. Sem., N.Y.C., 1984, Berkeley Div. Sch. at Yale, 1995. Ordained to ministry Episcopal Ch., 1953. Chaplain Christ Ch. Cathedral, Oxford, 1955-59; exec. dir. Commn. on Faith and Order Nat. Coun. Chs. of Christ in U.S.A., N.Y.C., 1959-71; mem. gen. bd. Nat. Coun. Chs. in Christ in U.S.A., N.Y.C., 1979-95; pastoral asst. Trinity Ch., N.Y.C., 1972-74; assoc. ecumenical officer Episcopal Ch., N.Y.C., 1975-79, ecumenical officer, 1979-94, theol. cons., 1995—; observer 2d Vatican Coun., Roman Cath. Ch., Vatican City, 1963-65; mem. assemblies World Co. Chs., various cities, 1961, 68, 83, 91. Editor: Living Room Dialogues, 1965, Implications of the Gospel, 1988, Toward Full Communion and Concordat of Agreement, 1991; compiler: What Can We Share, 1985. Fellow Gen. Theol. Sem., 1953-55. Democrat. Avocations: art, music, theatre, walking. Office: Episcopal Church Ctr 815 2nd Ave New York NY 10017-4503

NORICK, RONALD J., mayor; b. Oklahoma City, Aug. 5, 1941; m. Carolyn Marshall, July 28, 1961; children: Allyson, Lance. BS in Mgmt., Oklahoma City U., 1964, LHD (hon.), 1990. Pres. Norick Bros., Inc., 1981-92; mayor City of Oklahoma City, Oklahoma City, 1987—; gen. ptng. Norick Investment Inc.; former chmn. bd. Norick Software, Inc. Trustee Community Ch. of Redeener; mem. Ctrl. Okla. Transp. and Parking Authority, Oklahoma City Water Utilities Trust, Myriad Gardens Authority; bd. dirs. Okla. State Fair' mem. McGee Creek Authority; bd. dirs. Oklahoma City Philharm.; mem. exec. com. Oklahoma City U., Allied Arts Found. Mem. Nat. League Cities, U.S. Conf. Mayors, Okla. Mcpl. League, Oklahoma City C. of C. (bd. dirs.), South Oklahoma City C. of C. (bd. dirs.). Avocations: golf, fishing, boating. Office: Office of Mayor City Hall 200 N Walker Ave Oklahoma City OK 73102-2232*

NORIEGA, RUDY JORGE, hospital administrator; b. Havana, Cuba, Apr. 23, 1937; s. Rodolfo and Iris (Santini) N.; came to U.S., 1961; naturalized, 1966; BS, Masonic U., 1960; m. Rosa E. Del Castillo, Jan. 2, 1960; children: Rudy A., George. Acct., Continental Can Co., Havana, 1961, Am. Fgn. Ins. Assn., N.Y.C., 1961-62, North Miami Gen. Hosp., Miami, Fla., 1962-64; asst. controller Jackson Meml. Hosp., Miami, 1964-65; asst. adminstr. Plantation (Fla.) Gen. Hosp., 1965-72, adminstr., trustee, 1972-80; v.p., trustee Internat. Hosp., Miami, 1980-83; exec. v.p., COO Gen. Health L.P., Miami, 1983-93, 94-96; sr. v.p. Ornda So. Fla., 1993—; chmn. Golden Glades Gen. Hosp., 1991-95; bd. dirs. Pkwy. Gen. Hosp., 1995—; mem. sch. bldg. com. U. Miami Law Sch., 1989—; bd. dirs. Kendall Hosp., 1989—; coord. health needs for Pope John Paul II's U.S. Visit, 1987-91. Mem. jud. nominating commn. 3rd dist. Ct. Appeals, Fla., 1987-91. Fellow Am. Coll. Health Care Execs., Am. Coll. Hosp. Adminstrs.; mem. So. Fla. Hosp. Assn. (pres. 1979-80), Broward County Hosp. Assn. (pres. 1978-79), Fla. League Hosps. (pres. 1974-75), Fedn. Am. Hosps. (dir. 1973-74), Hosp. Fin. Mgmt. Assn. (dir. 1971-72), Plantation C. of C. (pres. 1978-79), Kiwanis (v.p. 1978-79). Office: Gen Health LP 11880 Bird Rd Miami FL 33152

NORINS, ARTHUR LEONARD, physician, educator; b. Chgo., Dec. 2, 1928; s. Russell Joseph and Elsie (Lindemann) N.; m. Mona Lisa Wetzer, Sept. 12, 1954; children: Catherine, Nan, Jane, Arthur. B.S. in Chem. Engring, Northwestern U., 1951, M.S. in Physiology, 1953, M.D., 1955. Diplomate: Am. Bd. Dermatology; subcert. in dermatopathology. Intern U. Mich., Ann Arbor, 1955-56; resident in dermatology Northwestern U., Chgo., 1956-59; asst. prof. Stanford U., 1961-64; prof., chmn. dept. dermatology, prof. pathology Ind. U. Sch. Medicine, Indpls., 1964-93, prof. emeritus, 1993—, mem. staff Riley Children's Hosp., Univ. Hosp., Wishard Hosp.; cons. VA Hosp. Contbr. articles to profl. jours. Capt. M.C. U.S. Army, 1959-61. Recipient Pres.' award Ind. U., 1979. Fellow ACP; mem. Am. Acad. Dermatology (bd. dirs.), Am. Dermatol. Assn., Soc. Pediatric Dermatology (founder, past pres.), Am. Soc. Dermatopathology, Am. Soc. Photobiology (founder), Soc. Investigative Dermatology. Home: 1234 Kirkham Ln Indianapolis IN 46260-1637 Office: 550 University Blvd Ste 3240 Indianapolis IN 46202-5149

NORINS, LESLIE CARL, publisher; b. Balt., Mar. 23, 1937; s. Abe and Patricia N.; m. Ann Rainey Hammatt, Nov. 19, 1994. AB, Johns Hopkins U., Balt., 1958; MD, Duke U., 1962; PhD, U. Melbourne, Australia, 1966. M.D., N.C. Lab. dir. Ctrs. for Disease Control, Atlanta, 1966-72; pres. Am. Health Cons., Atlanta, 1972-87, Global Success Corp., Naples, Fla., 1990—; cons. World Health Orgn., Geneva, 1970, NIH, Bethesda, Md., 1972, Pharmaceutical Mfrs., N.J. and N.Y., 1972-76; bd. dirs. Newsletter Publishers Assoc. Contbr. articles to sci. jours. Recipient Best Med. Student Rsch. award Borden Found., 1962; student of Sir MacFarlane Burnet, Nobel Laureate. Fellow Infectious Disease Soc. of Am.; Nat. Press Club (Washington). Home: 4301 Gulf Shore Blvd N Apt 1404 Naples FL 34103-3481

NORKIN, CYNTHIA CLAIR, physical therapist; b. Boston, May 6, 1932; d. Miles Nelson and Carolyn (Green) Clair; m. Stanislav A. Norkin, Feb. 19, 1955 (dec. 1970); 1 child, Alexandra. BS in Edn., Tufts U., 1954; cert. phys. therapy Bouve Boston Coll., 1954; MS, Boston U., 1973, EdD, 1984. Instr. Bouve-Boston Coll., 1954-55; staff phys. therapist New Eng. Med. Center, Boston, 1954-55; staff phys. therapist Abington Meml. Hosp., Abington, Pa.,

1965-70, Eastern Montgomery County Vis. Nurse Assn., 1970-72; asst. prof. phys. therapy Sargent Coll., Boston U., 1973-84; assoc. prof. phys. therapy, dir., founder Sch. Phys. Therapy, Ohio U., Athens, 1984-95; cons. Boston Center Ind. Living, Cambridge Vis. Nurse Assn., Mass. Medicaid Cost Effectiveness Project, 1978; sec. Health Planning Council Greater Boston, 1976-78; book, manuscript reviewer F.A. Davis Co., 1986—; mem. arthritis adv. com. Ohio Dept. Health. Trustee Brimmer and May Sch., 1980. Mem. AAAS, Am. Phys. Therapy Assn. (on site evaluator commn. on accreditation 1986—), Mass. Phys. Therapy Assn. (chmn. Mass. quality assurance com. 1980-83), Am. Public Health Assn., Mass. Assn. Mental Health, Athens County Vi. Nurse Assn. (sec. adv. coun. 1984-95). Episcopalian. Author: (with P. Levangie) Joint Structure and Function: A Comprehensive Analysis, 1983, 2d edit., 1992; (with D.J. White) Joint Measurement: A Guide to Goniometry, 1985, 2d edit., 1995.

NORLAND, DONALD RICHARD, retired foreign service officer; b. Laurens, Iowa, June 14, 1924; s. Norman and Aletta (Brunsvold) N.; m. Patricia Bamman, Dec. 13, 1952; children: Richard Boyce, David, Patricia D. Student, Iowa State Tchrs. Coll., 1941-43, N.W. Mo. State Tchrs. Coll., 1943-44; BA, U. Minn., 1948, MS, 1950; postgrad., U. Mich., 1951-52, Grenoble (France) U., 1948-49. Instr. history and polit. sci. U. No. Iowa, 1949-51; teaching fellow U. Mich., 1951-52; with Fgn. Svc., U.S. Dept. State, 1952-81; posts include Rabat, Morocco, 1952-56, Washington, 1956-58, Abidjan, Ivory Coast, 1958-60; mem. NATO del., Paris, 1961-63, NATO delegation, The Hague, The Netherlands, 1964-69; dep. chief mission Conakry, Guinea, 1970-72; U.S. Dept. State fellow Stanford (Calif.) U., 1969-70; dep. dir. Office Mil. Assistance and Sales, Bur. Politico-Mil. Affairs, Dept. State, Washington, 1972-73, chief polit. officers counseling br. Office Pers., 1973-75; dep. dir. Office Mgmt. Ops., 1975-76; amb. to Botswana, Lesotho and Swaziland Gaborone, Botswana, 1976-79; amb. to Chad, 1979-81; ret. Fgn. Svc., U.S. Dept. State, 1981; lectr. African affairs; internat. cons., specialist econ. devel.; chmn. African studies Fgn. Svc. Inst. of U.S. Dept. of State, Washington, 1987-89; program dir. Ctr. for Internat. Pvt. Enterprise affiliate U.S. C. of C., Washington, 1990-91; sr. cons. World Space, Inc., 1995, sr. policy advisor, 1996—. Bd. dirs. Calvert New Africa Fund, 1995. Lt. (j.g.) USNR, 1943-46. Mem. Am. Fgn. Svc. Assn. (v.p. for retirees 1993-95, sec. 1995—, mem. editl. bd. Fgn. Svc. Jour. 1992-95). Home: 4000 Cathedral Ave NW Apt 138B Washington DC 20016-5249

NORMAN, ALBERT GEORGE, JR., lawyer; b. Birmingham, Ala., May 29, 1929; s. Albert G. and Ila Mae (Carroll) N.; m. Catherine Marshall DeShazo, Sept. 3, 1955; children: Catherine Marshall, Albert George III. BA, Auburn U., 1953; LLB, Emory U., 1958; MA, U. N.C., 1960. Bar: Ga. 1957. Assoc. Moise, Post & Gardner, Atlanta, 1958-60, ptnr., 1960-62; ptnr. Hansell & Post, Atlanta, 1962-86, Long, Aldridge & Norman, Atlanta, 1986—; dir. Atlanta Gas Light Co. Served with USAF, 1946-49. Mem. ABA, Ga. Bar Assn., Atlanta Bar Assn., Lawyers Club Atlanta (pres. 1973-74), Am. Law Inst., Am. Judicature Soc. (dir. 1975-78), Old War Horse Lawyers Club, (pres. 1991-92), Cherokee Town and Country Club. Episcopalian.

NORMAN, ALLINE L., health facility administrator; b. Homerville, Ga., Dec. 20, 1938; d. John F. and Alline D. N. BS, Ga. Coll., 1960; cert. Sch. for Med. Records, U.S. Pub. Health Svc., 1961. U.S. pub. svc. offcr. U. Cin., 1961-65; asst. chief and chief med. records U.S. Pub. Health Svc. Hosps., New Orleans, Chgo., Norfolk, 1965-70; chief med. info. section, Med. Adminstrn. Svc. VA Med. Ctr., N.Y., 1970-72, Miami, 1972-75; asst. chief Med. Adminstrn. Svc. VA Med. Ctr., East Orange, N.J., 1975-80, Miami, 1980-83; chief Med. Adminstrn. Svc. VA Med. Ctr., Augusta, Ga., 1983-85; chief field ops. divsn., Med. Adminstrn. Svc. VA Med. Ctr., Atlanta, 1988-89; from dep. dir. to dir. Med. Adminstrn. Svc. VHA, 1990-93, dir. Adminstrn. Svc. Office, 1993-94; dir. VA Med. Ctr., Lake City, Fla., 1994—; chmn. combined fed. campaign Vets. Health Adminstrn., 1991, co-chmn. chief med. dir.'s adv. com. on diversity, 1992-96, mem. task force subcom. on recommendations of commn. on future structure of vets. health car, 1992; mem. White House Nat. Health Care Task Force on Integration Govt. Sys., 1993, Sec.'s Adv. Group on Sexual Harassment, 1993-96, Interagy. Inst., 1993-94. Bd. dirs. Suwanee United Way, 1994-95, Lake City C.C. Found., 1995-96, Am. Cancer Soc., Lake City, 1995-96. Recipient Fed. Leadership award, 1992, cert. achievement Fed. Women's Interagency Bd., 1993, Sec. Meritorious Svc. award, 1994, Under Sec. Health Honor award, 1994. Mem. VA Sr. Execs. Assn. (bd. dirs. 1994). Methodist. Office: VA Med Ctr Lake City FL 32025

NORMAN, ANTHONY WESTCOTT, biochemistry educator; b. Ames, Iowa, Jan. 19, 1938; s. A. Geoffrey and Marian Ester (Foote) N.; children—Thea C., Jacqueline E., Derek P.G. M.S., U. Wis., 1960, Ph.D., 1963. From asst. prof. to prof. dept. biochemistry U. Calif., Riverside, 1963—, chmn. dept., 1975-80, prof. biomedical scis., 1986—, divisional dean biomed. scis., 1986-91; asst. dean UCLA Sch. Medicine, 1986-91. Recipient Ernst Oppenheimer award Endocrine Soc., 1977; Prix Andre Lichwitz award French Govt., 1981; Fulbright fellow, 1970. Mem. AAAS, Am. Inst. Nutrition (Mead Johnson award 1977, Osborne-Mendel award 1989), Am. Chem. Soc., Am. Soc. Biol. Chemists, Am. Soc. Bone & Mineral Rsch. (William Neuman award 1995). Home: 7225 Lenox Ave Riverside CA 92504-4922 Office: U of Calif-Riverside Dept of Biochemistry Riverside CA 92521

NORMAN, ARLENE PHYLLIS, principal; b. Seattle; d. Samuel Edward and Connie Solveig (Jorgensen) Hendricksen; m. Charles Edward Norman; children: Tamara, Mark, Todd, Lisa. BA, Wash. State U.; MAT, Lewis and Clark Coll., 1980; postgrad., Portland State U. Tchr. Salem (Oreg.) Sch. Dist., 1956; tchr. Beaverton (Oreg.) Sch. Dist., 1973-83, prin. Terra Linda Sch., 1984-94; prin. Aloha Park Sch., 1994; presenter children's seminar Nat. Coun. Tchrs. Eng. Confs. Contbr. articles to mags. Mem. selection com. Associated Oreg. Industries, 1994, 95. Named Prin. of Excellence, Assoc. Oreg. Industries, 1991, sch. named Sch. of Excellence, 1991. Mem. NASEP, N.W. Women in Ednl. Adminstrn., Profl. Assistance Com. for State of Oreg., Toastmasters (pres.), Phi Delta Kappa, Pi Lambda Theta (pres.).

NORMAN, ARNOLD MCCALLUM, JR., engineer; b. Little Rock, May 1, 1940; s. Arnold McCallum and Ann Carolyn (Gibson) N.; m. Sylvia Burton, July 1, 1962 (div. 1967); m. Marisha Irene Malin, June 7, 1969; children: Frank Lee, Paul James. BS in Physics, Ga. Inst. Tech., 1962. Test engr. Rocketdyne div. Rockwell Internat., Canoga Park, Calif., 1962-64, engr. in charge of various programs, 1964-75, engr. in charge, project engr. large chem. lasers, 1975-85, project engr. space sta. propulsion system, 1985-87, project engr. nat. launch system health mgmt. systems, 1987-92, project engr. kinetic energy weapons, 1993-94; project engr. advanced propulsion systems Rockwell Internat., Canoga Park, Calif., 1994-95, sr. engring. specialist, 1995-96; health mgmt. sys. team head, x-33 Aerospike rocket engine Boeing-N.Am. Rocketdyne Divsn., Canoga Park, Calif., 1996-97; cons. rocket propulsion sys., ops. and health mgmt., 1997—; mem. ops. com. health mgmt. ctr. U. Cin., 1988-94; mem. program com. Ann. Internat. Conf. on Engring. Applications of Artificial Intelligence, 1988-90; presenter in field. Mem. editorial bd. Jour. Applied Intelligence, 1990-94; author numerous papers in field. Fellow AIAA (assoc., sect. chair sr. adv. com. 1991-93, San Fernando Valley sect., chmn. 1989-90, sys. effectiveness & safety com. 1995—), Inst. Advancement Engring; mem. Tau Beta Pi. Home: 4053 Bones Rd Sebastopol CA 95472

NORMAN, CHARLES HENRY, broadcasting executive; b. St. Louis, June 13, 1920; s. Charles Henry and Grace Vincent (Francis) N. BS, U. So. Calif., L.A., 1942. Announcer WIL, KSTL Radio Stas., St. Louis, 1948-55; owner Norman Broadcasting Co., St. Louis, 1961—. Lt. USN, 1943-45. Mem. St. Louis Ambassadros, Phi Kappa Phi. Episcopalian. Office: Portland Towers 275 Union Blvd Ste 1315 Saint Louis MO 63108-1236

NORMAN, CHRISTINA REIMARSDOTTER, secondary education language educator; b. Stockholm, Jan. 7, 1947; came to U.S., 1968; d. Leif Reimar and Hilma Birgitta (Berg) Norman; m. Geoffrey Robert Norman, May 27, 1968; children: Catarina Louise, Camilla Elizabeth. Fil. Mag., Stockholm U., 1968; MA, SUNY, Albany, 1973. Cert. tchr., N.Y., Conn. Tchr. French Our Lady of Grace Sch., Stratford, Conn., 1970-71; tchr. French, German Burnt Hills (N.Y.)-Ballston Lake Jr. High Sch., 1971-74; tchr. English Colegio Ayalde, Lujua, Vizcaya, Spain, 1975-78; tchr. French, English, Spanish Hillcrest Jr. High Sch., Trumbull, Conn., 1979-83; tchr. Spanish, French Saxe Mid. Sch., New Canaan, Conn., 1983-94; tchr. Spanish New Canaan H.S., 1994—. Mem. Conn. Orgn. Lang. Tchrs. Avocations: travel, skiing, reading. Office: New Canaan High Sch Farm Rd New Canaan CT 06840

NORMAN, COLIN ARTHUR, astrophysics educator; b. Melbourne, Australia, May 3, 1948; came to U.S., 1984; s. Howard Arthur Norman and Jean Olice (Macgregor) Downing; m. Wen Shen, June 2, 1988; children: Alexandra Jean, Arthur Shen, Victoria Amelia. BE with honours, U. Melbourne, 1969; DPhil, Oxford U., 1973. Rsch. fellow Magdalen Coll., Oxford (Eng.) U., 1973-77, U. Calif., Berkeley, 1975-77; asst. prof. U. Leiden (Netherlands), 1977-84; prof. physics and astronomy Johns Hopkins U., Balt., 1984—, head acad. affairs div. Space Telescope Sci. Inst., 1987-91, head Hubble Fellow program Space Telescope Sci. Inst., 1991-94; sr. rsch. fellow Inst. Astronomy, Cambridge, Eng., 1981-84, European So. Obs., Munich, 1983-84; vis. prof. U. Paris, 1983; bd. dirs. Norman Bros. Pty. Ltd., Melbourne; trustee Norman Family Trusts, Melbourne. Editor: Stellar Populations, 1987, Quasar Absorption Lines, 1988, Massive Stars and Star Formations, 1991; contbr. articles to astrophysics jours. Rhodes scholar, 1970-73. Fellow Royal Astron. Soc.; mem. Am. Phys. Soc., Am. Astron. Soc., Amnesty Internat., Greenpeace, Johns Hopkins Club, Hamilton St. Club. Office: Johns Hopkins U Dept Physics and Astronomy Baltimore MD 21218

NORMAN, DENNIS KEITH, psychologist, educator; b. Oklahoma City, Aug. 31, 1949; s. B.J. and Gertrud (Thuringer) N.; m. Wendy McNeal (div. Mar. 1973; children: Tamsen, Jakob; m. Carol Goodwin Taylor, Apr. 21, 1978; children: Ross, Jessie. BS in Psychology, U. Oregon, 1971; MEd in Allied Health Edn., U. Houston, 1975; MA in Child Psychology, Tufts U., 1978; EdD Human Devel. & Counseling Psychology, Harvard U., 1981. Lic. psychologist, Mass.; cert. health care provider in psychology, Mass. Chief psychologist child psychiatry svc. Mass. Gen. Hosp., Boston, 1985—, dir. psychology tng., 1989—, chief of psychology, 1990—; asst. prof. psychology Harvard Med. Sch., Boston, 1986-95, assoc. prof. psychology, 1995—; vice chmn. Bd. of Registration of Psychology, Boston, 1995—. Contbr. over 50 articles to profl. jours. Jessie Noyes scholar Baylor Coll. of Medicine, 1975. Fellow APA, Mass. Psychol. Assn., Soc. Personality Rsch. Home: 4 Fieldstone Way Boxford MA 01921-1639 Office: Mass Gen Hosp Psychology Office Bullfinch 5 Boston MA 02114

NORMAN, DONALD ARTHUR, cognitive scientist; b. N.Y.C., Dec. 25, 1935; s. Noah N. and Miriam F. N.; m. Martha Karpati (div.); children—Cynthia, Michael; m. Julie Jacobsen; 1 child, Eric. BSEE, MIT, 1957; MSEE, U. Pa., 1959, PhD in Psychology, 1962; degree in psychology (hon.), U. Padua, Italy, 1995. Lectr. Harvard U., 1962-66; Prof. dept. psychology U. Calif.-San Diego, La Jolla, 1966-92, prof. emeritus, 1992—, prof., chair dept. cognitive sci., 1988-92, chair dept.psychology, 1974-78, dir. cognitive sci. program, 1977-88, dir. Inst. for Cognitive Sci., 1981-89; Apple fellow Apple Computer Inc., Cupertino, Calif., 1993-95, v.p. advanced tech., 1993—; mem. sci. adv. bd. Naval Pers. Rsch. Ctr., San Diego, 1982-86; cons. to industry on human computer interaction and user-centered design. Author: Learning and Memory, 1982, Human Information Processing, 2d edit., 1977, User Centered System Design, 1986, The Psychology of Everyday Things, 1988, The Design of Everyday Things, 1989, Turn Signals Are the Facial Expressions of Automobiles, 1992, Things That Make Us Smart, 1993; editor: Perspectives on Cognitive Science, 1981, Exploration in Cognition, 1975, Cognitive Sci. Jour., 1981-85; series editor Cognitive Sci. Series Lawrence Earlbaum Assoc., 1979—. Recipient Excellence in Rsch. award U. Calif., 1984. Fellow Am. Psychol. Soc., Am. Acad. Arts and Scis.; mem. Am. Assn. Arts and Scis., Am. Assn. for Artificial Intelligence, Assn. for Computational Machinery, Cognitive Sci. Soc. (chmn. founding mem.). Office: Apple Computer Inc MS 301-4D 1 Infinite Loop Cupertino CA 95014-2083

NORMAN, DUDLEY KENT, hospital administrator, nurse; b. Cleve., July 27, 1949; s. George R. and Coral L. (Henrickson) N.; m. Martha Alice; children: David, Nicholas. BS in Edn., MEd, Kent State U., 1976; BS in Nursing, Case Western Res. U., 1976; MS, MSN, Tex. Women's U., 1981; EdD, U. Houston, 1990. RN; cert. nursing home adminstr. Tchr. Beachwood City Schs., Cleve., 1972-74; clin. nurse Univ. Hosp., Cleve., 1976-78; asst. adminstr. Parkland Hosp., Dallas, 1979-83, St. Lukes Hosp./Tex. Heart Inst., Tex. Children's Hosp., Houston, 1983-84; asst. dean U. Tex. Med. Sch., Houston, 1984-85; adminstr. U. Tex. Mental Scis. Inst., Houston, 1985-87; asst. adminstr. U. Tex.-Harris County Psychiat. Ctr., Houston, 1987-90; adminstr. U. Tex. Med. Br., Galveston, 1990-96; pres., CEO Tex. Univs. Health Plan, Inc., 1996—; cons. St. Lukes Hosp., N.Y.C., 1980; dir. nurse tng. Bd. Nurse Examiners Approved Program, Dallas, 1979-81. Recipient Chemistry Scholar prize Lubrizol Found., Cleve., 1971, Cushing Robb prize Case Western Res. U., Cleve., 1976; named One of Outstanding Young Men of Am., U.S. Jaycees, 1978. Fellow Am. Coll. Health Care Execs.; mem. ANA, Assn. for Study of Higher Edn., Healthcare Fin. Mgmt. Assn., Sigma Theta Tau. Methodist.

NORMAN, E. GLADYS, business computer educator, consultant; b. Oklahoma City, June 13, 1933; d. Joseph Eldon and Mildred Lou (Truitt) Biggs; m. Joseph R.R. Radeck, Mar. 1, 1953 (div. Aug. 1962); children: Jody Matti, Ray Norman, Warren Norman (dec. May 1993), Dana Norman; m. Leslie P. Norman, Aug. 26, 1963 (dec. Feb. 1994); 1 child, Elayne Pearce. Student, Fresno (Calif.) State Coll., 1951-52, UCLA, 1956-59, Linfield Coll., 1986-95. Math. aid U.S. Naval Weapons Ctr., China Lake, Calif., 1952-56, computing systems specialist, 1957-68; systems programmer Oreg. Motor Vehicles Dept., Salem, 1968-69; instr. in data processing, dir. Computer Programming Ctr., Salem, 1969-72; instr. in data processing Merritt-Davis Bus. Coll., Salem, 1972-73; sr. programmer, analyst Teledyne Wah Chang, Albany, Oreg., 1973-79; sr. systems analyst Oreg. Dept. Vets. Affairs, Albany, 1979-80; instr. in bus. computers Linn-Benton Community Coll., Albany, 1980-95; ret., 1995; computer cons. for LBCC Ret. Sr. Vol. Program, 1995—; presenter computer software seminars State of Oreg., 1991-93, Oreg. Credit Assoc. Conf., 1991, Oreg. Regional Users Group Conf., 1992; computer tchr. Linn-Benton C.C., 1996-97; computer cons. Oremet Titanium, 1996-97; computer cons. in field. Mem. Data Processing Mgmt. Assn. (bd. dirs. 1977-84, 89-95, region sect. 1995-96, assoc. v.p. 1988, Diamond Individual Performance award 1985). Democrat. Avocations: drawing, painting, sewing.

NORMAN, EDWARD COBB, psychiatrist, educator; b. Prince George, B.C., Can., Oct. 5, 1913; s. Arthur J. and Lilla E. (Cobb) N.; m. June Marie Morris, Sept. 24, 1949; children: Donald, Cornelia, Sharon. BS, U. Wash., 1935; MD, U. Pa., 1940; MPH, Tulane U., 1965. Intern, Phila. Gen. Hosp., 1940-42; resident, Pa. Hosp., 1942-43; resident Michael Reese Hosp., 1946-49; asst. surgeon, USPHS, 1943-46; pvt. practice psychiatry, Chgo., 1949-53, New Orleans, 1953—; clin. instr. psychiatry U. Ill., Chgo., 1949-53; asst. prof. clin. psychiatry Tulane U., New Orleans, 1953-60, assoc. prof., 1960-64, prof., 1964-79; emeritus, 1979-96; dir. community mental health sect. Tulane U. Sch. Pub. Health Tropical medicine, 1967-79; assoc. dir. Pain Rehab. Unit Hotel Dieu Hosp., 1978—; adminstr. Learning Procedures, Inc., New Orleans, 977-78, v.p., 1978-96; cons. to govt. agys. Fellow APHA, Am. Psychiat. Assn. (life), Am. Acad. Psychoanalysis; mem. N.Y. Acad. Scis., Forum for Improvement of Quality of Life (sec.), Delta Omega (pres. Eta chpt.). Contbr. numerous articles to profl. jours. Home: 1209 Washington Ave New Orleans LA 70130-5747

NORMAN, GEOFFREY ROBERT, financial executive; b. Orpington, Kent, Eng., Jan. 31, 1944; came to U.S., 1968, naturalized, 1974; s. Leonard Robert and Minnie Rose (Carter) N.; m. Christina Norman, June 8, 1968; children—Catarina, Camilla. B.A., St. Catharine's Coll., Cambridge, Eng., 1966, M.A., 1968. Corp. auditor Gen. Electric Co., Schenectady, 1971-74, comptroller GE Española, Bilbao, Spain, 1974-78, cons. corp. fin., Fairfield, Conn., 1978-81, mgr. fin., Bridgeport, Conn., 1981-83; v.p., treas. Gen. Electric Fin. Services, Inc. and Gen. Electric Capital Corp., N.Y.C., 1983-85, Stamford, Conn., 1985-88; exec. v.p. GE Investments, 1988—. State scholar U.K. Govt., 1962, Open Exhbn. scholar St. Catharine's Coll., 1962. Office: GE Investments 3003 Summer St Stamford CT 06905-4316

NORMAN, GREGORY JOHN, professional golfer; b. Mt. Isa, Australia, Feb. 10, 1955; m. Laura Norman; children: Morgan-Leigh, Gregory. Profl. golfer, 1976—. Winner Martini Internat., 1977, 79, 81, French Open, 1980, Australian Open, 1980, 85, 87, Dunlop Masters, 1981, 82, Hong Kong Open, 1981, Australian Masters 1981, 83, 84, 87, 89, 90 State Express Classic, 1982, Benson and Hedges, 1982, Canadian Open, 1984, 92, Kemper Open, 1984, Las Vegas Invitational, 1986, Kemper Open, 1986, British Open, 1986, 93, European Open, 1986, Suntory World Match, 1986, Queensland Open, 1986, New South Wales Open, 1985, 86, 88, Australian Tournament Players Championship, 1988, 89, Heritage Classic, 1988, Italian Open, 1988, Doral Ryder Open, 1990, 93, Memorial Tournament, 1990, Tournament Players Championship, 1994, Johnnie Walker Asian Classic, 1994, winner Vardon trophy, 1989, 90, 94; recipient Arnold Palmer award for leading money winner, 1995, Byron Nelson trophy for the lowest scoring average, 1995; ranked #1 by Sony; named PGA Player of Yr., 1995, PGA Tour Player of Yr., 1995. Leading Money Winner PGA Tour 1986, 90. Address: Great White Shark Enterprises Inc PO Box 1189 Hobe Sound FL 33475-1189*

NORMAN, JACK LEE, church administrator, consultant; b. Lancaster, Ohio, Aug. 5, 1938; s. Clearence Herbert and Jeanette Belle (Bennett) N.; m. Boneda Mae Coppock, June 30, 1957; children: Anthony Lee, Becky Lynn Norman Hux. Student, Circleville Bible Coll., Olivet U. Ordained min. Ch. of Christ, 1961. Pastor Chs. of Christ in Christian Union, Chillicothe, Ohio, 1959-62, 65-90, Winchester, Ohio, 1962-65; dist. supt. Chs. of Christ in Christian Union, Circleville, Ohio, 1990—; trustee Chs. of Christ in Christian Union, mem. dist. bd., mem. ch. ext. bd., mem. bd. exam. and ordination, mem. Evang. Christian Youth Bd. Trustee Circleville Bible Coll. Sgt. USNG, 1956-59. Avocations: fishing, boating, classic cars. Office: Ch of Christ in Christian Union PO Box 30 Circleville OH 43113-0030

NORMAN, JEAN REID, journalist; b. Phoenix, Feb. 13, 1957; d. James August and V. Janice (Radford) R.; m. James E. Norman, Jr., Dec. 30, 1982; children: James R., Janiece C. BS in Journalism, Northwestern U., 1979. Reporter Fallon (Nev.) Eagle-Standard, 1979-80; reporter, spl. sections editor North Las Vegas Valley Times, 1980-81; mng. editor Good Times, Santa Cruz, Calif., 1981-83; copy editor Daily Review, Hayward, Calif., 1983-85, Journal-Bulletin, Providence, R.I., 1986-89, Contra Costa Times, Walnut Creek, Calif., 1989, The Washington Post, 1990, USA Today Money Sect., Rosslyn, Va., 1990-93; mng. editor Navy Times, Springfield, Va., 1993—. Vestry mem. St. Mark's Episcopal Ch., 1996—. Democrat. Office: Navy Times 6883 Commercial Dr Springfield VA 22151-4202

NORMAN, JESSYE, soprano; b. Augusta, Ga., Sept. 15, 1945; d. Silas Sr. and Janie (King) N. B.M. cum laude, Howard U., 1967; postgrad., Peabody Conservatory, 1967; M.Mus., U. Mich., 1968; MusD (hon.), U. South, 1984, Boston Conservatory, 1984, U. Mich., 1987, U. Edinburgh, 1989, Cambridge U., 1989. Debut, Deutsche Oper, Berlin, 1969, Italy, 1970; appeared: in operas Die Walküre, Idomeneo, L'Africaine, Marriage of Figaro, Aida, Don Giovanni, Tannhauser, Gotterdammerung, Ariadne auf Naxos, Les Troyens, Dido and Aeneas, Oedipus Rex, Hérodiade, Les Contes d'Hoffmann; debut in operas, La Scala, Milan, Italy, 1972, Salzburg Festival, 1977, U.S. debut, Hollywood Bowl, 1972, appeared with, Tanglewood Festival, Mass., also Edinburgh (Scotland) Festival, debut, Covent Garden, 1972; appeared in 1st Great Performers recital, Lincoln Center, N.Y.C., 1973—; other guest performances include, L.A. Philharm. Orch., Boston Symphony Orch., Am. Symphony Orch., Chgo. Symphony Orch., San Francisco Symphony Orch., Cleve. Orch., Detroit Symphony, N.Y. Philharm. Orch., London Symphony Orch., London Philharm. Orch., BBC Orch., Israel Philharm. Orch., Orchestre de Paris, Nat. Symphony Orch., English Chamber Orch., Royal Philharm., London Phila. Orch., Milw. Symphony Orch., Stockholm Philharm. Orch., Vienna Philharm. Orch., Berlin Philharm. Orch.; tours, Europe, S. Am., Australia, numerous recs., Columbia, EMI, Philips Records; PBS TV spcls. include Kathleen Battle and Jessye Norman Sing Spirituals, 1991, Concert at Avery Fisher Hall, 1994; recordings include Amazing Grace, Brava, Jessye!, Jessye Norman at Notre Dame, Lucky to Be Me, Sacred Songs, With a Song in My Heart. Recipient 1st prize Bavarian Radio Corp. Internat. Music Competition, 1968, Grand Prix du Disque, Acad. du Disque Francais, 1973, 76, 77, 82, 84, Deutsche Schallplatten, Preis, 1975, 81, Alumni award U. Mich., 1982, Outstanding Musician of Yr. award Musical Am., 1982, Grand Prix du Disque Academie Charles Cros, 1983, Commandeur de l'Ordre des Arts et des Lettres, France, 1984, Grammy awards, 1980, 82, 85, numerous other awards; named hon. life mem. Girl Scouts U.S., 1987. Mem. Royal Acad. Music (hon.), Alpha Kappa Alpha, Gamma Sigma Sigma, Sigma Alpha Iota, Pi Kappa Lambda. Club: Friday Morning Music (Washington). Office: PO Box 5 Crugers NY 10521 also: Philips Records Polygram 825 8th Ave New York NY 10019*

NORMAN, JOHN BARSTOW, JR., designer, educator; b. Paloa, Kans., Feb. 5, 1940; s. John B. and Ruby Maxine (Johnson) N.; m. Roberta Jeanne Martin, June 6, 1967; children: John Barstow III, Elizabeth Jeanne. BFA, U. Kans., 1962, MFA, 1966. Designer and illustrator Advt. Design, Kansas City, Mo., 1962-64; asst. instr. U. Kans., Lawrence, 1964-66; art dir. Hallmark Cards, Inc., Kansas City, Mo., 1966-69; instr. dept. art U. Denver, 1969-73, asst. prof., 1973-78, assoc. prof., 1978-93, Disting. prof., 1980 , prof. emeritus, 1993—; sr. designer Mo. Coun. Arts and Humanities, 1966-67; cons. designer Rocky Mountain Bank Note Corp., Denver, 1971—, Signage Identity System, U. Dever; bd. dirs. communications U. Denver; tech. cons. Denver Art Mus., 1974—, designed exhbns., 1974-75; adv., cons. Jefferson County (Colo.) Sch., System, 1976—; chmn. Design and Sculpture Exhbn., Colo. Celebration of the Arts, 1975-76. One man shows include: Gallery Cortina, Aspen, Colo., 1983; commd. works include: Jedda, Saudi Arabia, Synegistics Corp., Denver; represented in permanent collections Pasadena Ctr. for the Arts, N.Y. Art Dirs. Club, Calif. State U./Fiber Collection, Pasadena (Calif.) Ctr. for the Arts, 1984, N.Y. Art Dirs. Club, 1985 Midland Art Coun./Fiber Collection, 1985, Geologic Soc. Am.; represented in traveling exhbns. L.A. Art Dirs. Show and N.Y. Art Dirs. Show, U.S., Europe, Japan, 1985; fearured in Denver Post, 1984, Post Electric City Mag., 1984, Rocky Mt. News, 1984, Douglas County Press, 1984, Mile High Cable Vision, 1985, Sta. KWGN-TV, 1985, Les Krantz's Am. Artists, 1988, Illustrated Survey of Leading Contemporaries, 1988, U.S. Surface Design Jour., 1988; co-work represented in film collection Mus. Modern Art, N.Y.C.; selected fashion show designs displayed to Sister City dels., Denver, 1987. Co-recipient Silver Medal award N.Y. Internat. Film and Video Competition, 1976, Design awards Coun. Advancement and Support of Edn., 1969, 71, 73, 76, Honor Mention award L.A. Art Dirs. Club, 1984, Honor Mention award N.Y. Art Dirs. Club, 1984, Native Am. Wearable Art Competition, 1985, 5th pl. Nat. Wind Sail Am. Banners Competition, Midland, Mich., 1985, also awards for surface designs in Colo. Ctr. for the Arts Wearable Art Competition, 1984-85, Foothills Art Gallery Nat. Wearable Art Competition, 1984-85, Fashion Group of Denver Competition, 1984-85. Mem. Art Dirs. Club Denver (Gold medals 1974-82, Best of Show Gold medal 1983, Honor Mention award, 1984, 3 Gold medals 1989), Univ. Art Dirs. Assn. Home: PO Box 302 751 Willow Lake Dr Franktown CO 80116 Office: U Denver Sch Art 2121 E Asbury Ave Denver CO 80210-4303

NORMAN, JOHN EDWARD, petroleum landman; b. Denver, May 22, 1922; s. John Edward and Ella (Warren) N.; m. Hope Sabin, Sept. 5, 1946; children—J. Thomas, Gerould W., Nancy E., Susan G., Douglas E. BSBA, U. Denver, 1949, MBA, 1972. Clk., bookkeeper Capitol Life Ins. Co., Denver, 1940-42, 45-46; salesman Security Life and Accident Co., Denver, 1947; bookkeeper Central Bank and Trust Co., Denver, 1947-50; automobile salesman H.A. Hennies, Denver, 1950; petroleum landman Continental Oil Co. (name changed to Conoco Inc. 1979), Denver, 1950-85; ind. petroleum landman, 1985; ind. investor 1985—. Lectr. pub. lands Colo. Sch. Mines, 1968-85; lectr. mineral titles and landmen's role in oil industry Casper Coll., 1969-71. Mem. Casper Mcpl. Band Commn., 1965-71, mem. band, 1961-71, mgr., 1968-71; former musician, bd. dirs. Casper Civic Symphony; former bd. dirs. Jefferson Symphony, performing mem., 1972-75. Served with AUS, World War II. Mem. Am. Assn. Petroleum Landmen (dir. at large, chmn. publs. for regional dir.), Wyo. Assn. Petroleum Landmen (pres.), Denver Assn. Petroleum Landmen, Rocky Mountain Oil and Gas Assn. (pub. lands com. 1981-85), Rocky Mountain Petroleum Pioneers. Episcopalian (mem. choir, vestryman, past dir. acolytes). Club: Elks. Home and Office: 2710 S Jay St Denver CO 80227-3856

NORMAN, LALANDER STADIG, insurance company executive; b. Binford, N.D., Apr. 10, 1912; s. John and Corinne (Stadig) N.; m. Garnet Johnston, Nov. 8, 1941; children: Eric John, Martha Mary Norman Neely,

Carol Jean Norman Wellborn, Shirley Ann Norman Cook. A.B., U. Mich., 1935, M.B.A., 1937. Actuarial asst. Central Life Ins. Co. of Ill., Chgo., 1937-40; mgr. Eastern dept. Central Life Ins. Co. of Ill., 1940-41; actuary Mich. Life Ins. Co., Detroit, 1941-43; asst. actuary Guarantee Mut. Life Co., Omaha, 1946-49; asso. actuary Am. United Life Ins. Co., Indpls., 1949; actuary Am. United Life Ins. Co., 1950-77, dir., 1959-77, v.p., 1962-69, sr. v.p., 1969-77; ret., 1977; bd. mgrs. AUL Fund B, 1969-84, chmn., 1973-84; actuary Ind. Dept. Ins., 1977-79. Bd. dirs. Cypress Village Assn., 1981, 83-85. Served with USNR, 1943-46. Recipient Navy Commendation award, 1946, Theta Xi Distinguished Service award, 1958. Fellow Soc. Actuaries; mem. Am. Acad. Actuaries, Indpls. Actuarial Club (past pres.), Woodland Country Club (Carmel), Sugarmill Woods Golf and Racquet Club, So. Woods Golf Club, Phi Beta Kappa, Theta Xi (regional dir. 1953-59), Phi Kappa Phi, Beta Gamma Sigma. Republican. Home: Sugarmill Woods 21 Graytwig Ct W Homosassa FL 34446-4727 Office: 1 American Sq Indianapolis IN 46282-0001

NORMAN, MARSHA, playwright; b. Louisville, Sept. 21, 1947; d. Billie Lee and Bertha Mae (Conley) Williams; m. Michael Norman (div. 1974); m. Dann C. Byck Jr., 1978 (div.); m. Timothy Dykman; 2 children: Angus, Katherine. B.A., Agnes Scott Coll., 1969; M.A.T., U. Louisville, 1971. Author: (plays) Getting Out, 1977 (John Gassner New Playwrights medallion, Outer Critics Circle award 1979, George Oppenheimer-Newsday award 1979), Third and Oak, 1978, Circus Valentine, 1979, The Holdup, 1980, 'Night, Mother, 1982 (Susan Smith Blackburn prize 1982, Tony award nomination for best play 1983, Pulitzer prize for Drama 1983, Elizabeth Hull-Kate Warriner award Dramatists Guild 1983), Traveler in the Dark, 1984, Sarah and Abraham, 1987, D. Boone, 1992; (book of musical, lyrics) The Secret Garden, 1991 (Tony award for best book of musical 1991, Tony award nominee for best original score 1991, Drama Desk award for best book of musical 1991; Loving Daniel Boone (play) 1992, Trudy Blue (play), 1995, The Red Shoes (book and lyrics), 1992; (screenplay) 'Night, Mother, 1986; (teleplays) It's the Willingness, 1978, In Trouble at Fifteen, 1980, The Laundromat, 1985, Third and Oak: The Pool Hall, 1989, Face of a Stranger, 1991; (novel) The Fortune Teller, 1987; (collection) Four Plays by Marsha Norman, 1988. NEA grantee, 1978-79, Rockefeller playwright-in-residence grantee, 1979-80, Am. Acad. and Inst. for Arts and Letters grantee; recipient Lit. Lion award N.Y. Pub. Libr., 1986. Office: Jack Tantleff 375 Greenwich St Ste 700 New York NY 10013-2376*

NORMAN, MARY MARSHALL, counselor, therapist, educator; b. Auburn, N.Y., Jan. 10, 1937; d. Anthony John and Zita Norman. BS cum laude, LeMoyne Coll., 1958; MA, Marquette, U., 1960; EdD, Pa. State U., 1971. Cert. alcoholism counselor. Tchr., St. Cecilia's Elem. Sch., Theinsville, Wis., 1959-60; vocat. counselor Marquette U., Milw., 1959-60; dir. testing and counseling U. Rochester (N.Y.), 1960-62; dir. testing and counseling, dean women, asso. dean coll., asst. dean students, dir. student activities, asst. prof. psychology Corning (N.Y.) C.C., 1962-68; rsch. asst. Center for Study Higher Edn., Pa. State U., University Park, 1969-71; dean faculty South Campus, C.C. Allegheny County, West Mifflin, Pa., 1971-72, campus pres., coll. v.p., 1972-82; pres. Orange County C.C., 1982-86; alcohol counselor Sullivan County Alcohol Drug Abuse Svc., 1985-90; sr. counselor Horton Family Program, 1990-96; ednl. cons., writer, 1996—; cons. Boricua Coll., N.Y.C., 1976-77; reader NSF, 1977-78; mem. govtl. commn. com. Am. Assn. Cmty. and Jr. Colls., 1976-79, bd. dirs., 1982—; mem. and chmn. various middle state accreditation teams. Bd. dirs. Orange County United Way; bd. dirs. Orange County Alcoholism and Drug Abuse Coun., 1993—. Mem. Am. Assn. Higher Edn., Nat. Assn. Women Deans Counselors, Am. Assn. Women in Community and Jr. Colls. (charter, Woman of Yr. 1981), Pa. Assn. Two-Yr. Colls., Pa. Assn. Acad. Deans, Pitts. Council Women Execs. (charter), Am. Council on Edn. (Pa. rep. identification women for adminstrn. 1978—), Pa. Council on Higher Edn., Orange County C. of C. (bd. dirs.), Kiwanis, Gamma Pi Epsilon. Contbr. articles to profl. jours. Home: 9 S Park St Seneca Falls NY 13148

NORMAN, PETER MINERT, fundraising consulting company executive; b. Rochester, N.Y., Mar. 23, 1932; s. Jesse George and Doris (Colony) N.; m. Janet G. Wasson, Sept. 6, 1952; children: Susan Jane, Paula Lea, Christa MacLeod, Peter Minert II. BA, Trinity Coll., Hartford, Conn., 1954; MDiv, Yale U., 1957. Ordained priest Episcopal Ch., 1957; lic. nursing home adminstr. Curate St. Stephen's Episc. Ch., Rochester, 1957-60; rector Zion Episc. Ch., Avon, N.Y., 1960-68; cons. Health and housing programs, Rochester and Washington, 1968-73; dir. Ward, Dreshman, Reinhardt, Worthington, Ohio, 1973-77; v.p. Seabury Western Sem., Evanston, Ill., 1977-80; exec. dir. Cathedral Found., Jacksonville, Fla., 1980-82; chmn. CEO Ward, Dreshman & Reinhardt, Worthington, 1982-92, WDR Community Svcs., Worthington, 1990-92; exec. v.p. Goettler Assocs., Columbus, Ohio, 1992-93; corp. v.p. of devel. svcs. St. Francis Acad., Salina, Kans., 1993-94; exec. officer devel. Episcopal Retirement House, Cin., 1994—; pres. Clan MacLeod Soc. U.S.A., 1988-89; chmn. Dunvegan Fund, N.Y./Edinburgh, 1988; chmn. World Fundraising Counsel, Amsterdam, 1990-92. Author: How to Assure Successful Every Member Canvass, 1979, Hospital Prayer Book, 1958. Mem. Worthington Hills Country Club, Am. Assn. Fundraising Counsel (treas. 1989-90, vice-chmn. 1990-91), Phi Beta Kappa, Pi Gamma Mu. Republican. Home: 1308 Clubview Blvd S Columbus OH 43235-1643 Office: Episcopal Retirement Homes 3870 Virginia Ave Cincinnati OH 45227-3431

NORMAN, PHILIP SIDNEY, physician; b. Pittsburg, Kans., Aug. 4, 1924; s. P. Sidney and Mildred A. (Lawyer) N.; m. Marion Birmingham, Apr. 15, 1955; children: Margaret Reynolds, Meredith Andrew, Helen Elizabeth. A.B., Kans. State Coll., 1947; M.D. cum laude, Washington U., St. Louis, 1951. Intern Barnes Hosp., St. Louis, 1951-52; resident Vanderbilt U. Hosp., Nashville, 1952-54; fellow Rockefeller Inst., 1954-56; instr. medicine Johns Hopkins U. Sch. Medicine, Balt., 1956-59; asst. prof. Johns Hopkins U. Sch. Medicine, 1959-64, assoc. prof., 1964-75, prof., 1975—, chief allergy and immunology div., 1971-91. Editor Jour. of Allergy and Clin. Immunology, 1993—; contbr. chpt. to books, articles to profl. jours. Served with USAAF, 1943-46; served with USPHS, 1954-56. Fellow Am. Acad. Allergy (pres. 1975); mem. Am. Fedn. Clin. Research, Am. Assn. Immunologists, Am. Soc. Clin. Investigation, Am. Assn. Physicians, N.Y. Acad. Scis., Soc. Exptl. Biology and Medicine, Am. Thoracic Soc., Am. Clin. and Climatol. Assn., Johns Hopkins Med. Soc., Alpha Omega Alpha. Episcopalian. Home: 13500 Manor Rd Baldwin MD 21013-9775 Office: Johns Hopkins U Asthma and Allergy Ctr 5501 Hopkins Bayview Cir Baltimore MD 21224-6821

NORMAN, RALPH LOUIS, physicist, consultant; b. Kingston, Tenn., Mar. 25, 1933; s. Walter Hugh and Helen Irene (Smith) N.; m. Agnes Irene Pickel, Sept. 5, 1964; children: Mark Alan, Max Alvin. B.S., U. Tenn., 1959; LL.B., Blackstone Sch. Law, 1967, J.D., 1971; certificate, Indsl. Coll. Armed Forces, 1969; M.A. in Pub. Adminstrn, U. Okla., 1971; D.Sci. (hon.), Apollo Research Inst., 1976. Engr. Chrysler Corp. Missile Div., Huntsville, Ala., 1959-60; physicist Army Rocket & Guided Missile Agy., Redstone Arsenal, Ala., 1960-61; asst. project mgr. Army Missile Command, Redstone Arsenal, 1961-62; project mgr. Army Missile Command, 1962-89, ret., 1989; cons. to several def. constractors, 1989—; faculty Athens (Ala.) Coll., 1970-71, Calhoun Jr. Coll., Decatur, Ala., 1971-74, 85-90, U. Montevallo, Ala., 1973-74, U. Ala. at Huntsville, 1976-77, Columbia (Mo.) Coll., 1977-79; cons. firm Bishop and Sexton, 1973—, Athens (Ala.) State Coll.; reviewer NSF, 1974-76; FAA examiner. Contbr. articles profl. jours. Served with USN, 1951-55. Recipient Dept. Def. commendations, 1961, 65, Dept. Army commendation, 1972. Mem. N.Y. Acad. Scis., Assn. U.S. Army. Home: 13889 Dupree Worthey Rd Harvest AL 35749-7321 *I strive to make the knowledge gained through my research benefit all mankind.*

NORMAN, RICHARD ARTHUR, humanities educator; b. Columbus, Ohio, July 11, 1915; s. Norman Oscar and Marie (Falter) Kuhnheim. BA, George Washington U., 1951; MA, Columbia U., 1952, PhD, 1957. Instr. Columbia U., N.Y.C., 1952-57; asst. prof. English Barnard Coll., 1957-64, asso. prof., 1964-72, prof., 1972-81, spl. lectr., 1981-85, prof. emeritus, 1985—; instr. grad. div. Hunter Coll., 1960-62; Speech cons. CBS News, 1971-85; reader Talking Books Am. Found. for Blind, 1973-80. Radio announcer, producer, actor, 1934-50; commentator for chamber music concert; broadcast, from Library of Congress, Washington, 1948-50; Author: (with George W. Hibbitt) A Guide to Speech Training, 1964; radio series The Wonder of Words, 1962. Vice pres. Axe-Houghton Found., now emeritus. Served to capt. USAAF, 1942-45. Home: 9 Branchville Rd Ridgefield CT 06877-5012

NORMAN, SHERI HANNA, artist, educator, cartographer; b. Chgo., Dec. 15, 1940; d. L.J. and Margaret Maxine (Kuyper Fleischer) Hanna; m. Donald Lloyd Norman, Febr. 28, 1963 (div. 1996); 1 child, Ronald Wayne Norman. BA, U. Wyo., Laramie, 1963; attended, Dayton (Ohio) Art Inst., 1975; MFA, San Francisco Art Inst., 1993. Substitute tchr. Arlington, Va. and Yellow Springs, Ohio Pub. Sch. Dists., 1965-71; tech. illustrator, draftsperson U. Tex. Austin, Geotek, Inc., Denver, 1976-85; cartographer British Petroleum, San Francisco, 1985-87; draftsperson Earth Scis. Assocs., Palo Alto, Calif., 1988-92; intern, printmaking asst. Crown Point Press, San Francisco, 1991-92; freelance cartographer San Francisco, 1993—; educator pub. printmaking & papermaking workshops, San Francisco, 1995-96, Napa, Calif., 1997—; pub. printmaking demonstrations San Francisco Women Artists Gallery, 1995, 96; leader pub. nature/women's ceremony-ritual, San Francisco, 1991-93; artist in residence Villa Montalvo Ctr. for the Arts, Saratoga, Calif., 1996, Dorland Mountain Arts Colony, Temecula, Calif., 1996. Author, illustrator: (book) Envisioning An Unbroken Arc, 1992, Vol. 11, 1992; participating artist San Francisco Bay Area Presses, Visual Arts Ctr., Bluffton (Ohio) Coll., 1996; contbg. artist Visual Aid's BIG DEAL, San Francisco, 1996, Florence Crittenton Svcs., San Francisco, 1995, San Francisco Women Artists Gallery, 1995—. Contbg. artist Florence Crittenton Svcs., San Francisco, 1995, San Francisco Women Artists Gallery, 1995—. Mem. Calif. Soc. Printmakers (mem. exhbn. com. 1995), No. Calif. Women's Caucus For Art, Graphic Arts Workshop. Avocations: ongoing nature studies, early mythologies and desert travel, advocacy. Home and Studio: 2834 Monticello Rd Napa CA 94558

NORMAN, STEPHEN PECKHAM, financial services company executive; b. Norwich, Conn., May 20, 1942; s. Richard Leonard and Mary Ellen (Carr) N.; m. Jacqueline Mary Batten, June 29, 1968; children—Adrian Gates, Hilary Batten, Philip Douglas, Matthew Jeremy Mitchell. B.A., Yale U., 1964; J.D., U. Pa., 1967. Bar: Conn. 1967, N.Y. 1972. Atty. Am. Express Co., N.Y.C., 1970-78, v.p. corp. office, 1978-82, sec., 1982—; Mem. bd. editors Corp. Governance. Served to sgt. U.S. Army, 1968-70; Vietnam. Mem. Am. Soc. Corp. Secs. (past chmn.), Conn. Bar Assn., N.Y. Bar Assn., U.S. Working Com. Group 30. Republican. Episcopalian. Club: Am. Yacht (Rye). Home: 6 Highland Park Pl Rye NY 10580-1736 Office: Am Express Co World Fin Ctr 200 Vesey St New York NY 10281-1009

NORMAN, WILLIAM STANLEY, travel and tourism executive; b. Roper, N.C., Apr. 27, 1938; s. James Colbitt and Josephine Cleo (Woods) N.; m. Elizabeth Patricia Patterson, May 31, 1969; children: Lisa Renée, William Stanley II. BS, West Va. Wesleyan U., 1960; MA, Am. U., 1967; exec. program, Stanford U., 1976. Math. tchr. Washington High Sch., Norfolk, 1961; commd. USN, 1962; advanced through grades to comdr., 1973; naval flight officer Airborne Early Warning Squadron Eleven, 1962-65; asst. combat info. ctr. officer U.S.S. Constellation, 1965; staff officer air weapons systems analysis Office Chief Naval Ops., Pentagon, Washington, 1965-66; history and fgn. affairs instr. U.S. Naval Acad., 1967-69; social aide The White House, 1967-69; carrier div. staff officer SE Asia, 1969-70, spl. asst. to Chief Naval Ops. for Minority Affairs, 1970-72, asst. to Chief Naval Ops. for Spl. Projects, 1972-73; dir. corp. action Cummins Engine Co. Inc., Columbus, Ind., 1973-74, exec. dir. corp. responsibility, 1974-76; exec. mktg. mgr., 1976-77; exec. dir. distbn. mktg. Cummins Engine Co. Inc., Columbus, Ind., 1977-78; v.p. eastern divsn., 1978-79; v.p. sales and mktg. Amtrak, Washington, 1979-81, group v.p., 1981-84, exec. v.p., 1984-94; pres., CEO Travel Industry Assn. of Am., Washington, 1994—; bd. dirs. CPC Internat., Englewood Cliffs, N.J., Logistics Mgmt. Inst., McLean, Va. Bd. dirs. USN Meml. Found., Washington, 1980—, Internat. Consortium on Health Effects of Radiation, 1993—, An-Bryce Found., 1993—; bd. visitors Am. U. Kogod Sch. of Bus.; bd. overseers Hospitality Industry Hall of Honor and Archives, 1995—. Capt. USNR. Mem. Travel Industry Assn. Am. (bd. dirs. 1980—, chmn. bd. 1987-89, chmn. bd. dirs. of found. 1990-92), UN Assn. U.S. (bd. dirs. 1983—, bd. govs. 1985—), Coun. on Fgn. Rels., Inst. Cert. Travel. Agts., Bretton Woods Com., Travel and Tourism Govt. Affairs Coun. (bd. dirs. 1988—). Democrat. Episcopalian. Avocations: golf, tennis, jogging, walking, cycling. Home: 1308 Timberly Ln Mc Lean VA 22102-2504 Office: Travel Industry Assn of Am 1100 New York Ave Ste 450 Washington DC 20005-3934

NORMAND, ROBERT, utility industry executive; b. Montreal, Que., Can., Jan. 9, 1940; s. Albert and Germaine (Levesque) N.; m. Pauline Ross, July 14, 1962; children—Patrice, Isabelle. Bus. cert., U. Montreal, 1966. Chartered acct., Can. External auditor Richter Usher Vineberg, Montreal, 1962-65, Coopers & Lybrand, Montreal, 1966-67; chief acct. Tioxide of Can., Tracy, 1967-68; comptroller Scott Lasalle Ltd., Montreal, 1969-71; v.p. Gaz Metropolitain Inc., Montreal, 1972—; bd. dirs. Daubois Inc., Montreal, Fonds Investments REA, TQM Pipeline, Vt. Gas. Roman Catholic. Avocation: tennis. Home: 177 Grande Cote, Rosemere, PQ Canada J7A 1H5

NORMAND, ROBERT, lawyer; b. Montreal, Que., Can., Sept. 24, 1936; s. Lucien and Eva (Rochon) N.; m. Madeleine Scott, Sept. 16, 1961; children: Eric, Yves, Genevieve. BA, U. Montreal, 1956; LLL, U. Sherbrooke, Que., 1960; diploma, Inst. d'etudes politiques, Paris, 1962. Bar: Que. 1960. Legal adviser Nat. Assembly, Quebec City, 1962-67, law clk., 1967-71; asst. dep. min. justice Que. Govt., Quebec City, 1970-71, dep. min. justice, 1971-77, dep. min. intergovtl. affairs, 1977-82, dep. min. fin., 1982-87; pres., pub. Le Soleil (Hollinger), Quebec City, 1987-93; v.p. corp. affairs UniMedia Inc., 1993-94, dep. min. internat. affairs, 1994-96; pres., dir. gen. Télé-Québec, 1996—; sec. Study Com. on Expropriation 1965-67; guest prof. legis. law faculty Laval U., Ottawa U., 1971; pres. Que. Police Inst., 1974; chmn. Com. Supervising Olympic Security, 1974-76; chmn. Uniform Law Conf. Can.; dir. Caisse de Dèpot et Placement du Quèbec, 1982-87; v.p. Can. del. Diplomatic Conf. on travel contracts, Brussels, 1970; pres. Can. del. at convs. Internat. Inst. French Lang. law, 1974, 76. V.p. Hosp. du Saint-Sacrement, Quebec City, 1988-94; vice chmn. Inst. Rsch. on Pub. Policy, Montreal, 1988-94; pres. Que. Symphony Orch., Quebec City, 1989-92; consul gen. Sweden, Quebec City, 1989-94; co-pres. United Way Campaign Greater Quebec Region, 1989, hon. chmn. Telethon for Cerebral Palsy, 1990; mem. Citizens Forum, Spicer Commn., 1990-91. Capt. Can. Army, 1954-60. Named Queen's Counsel, 1971; recipient Pub. Adminstrn. award of excellence Nat. Sch. Pub. Adminstrn. Alumni, Quebec City, 1986. Mem. Investment Dealers Assn. Can. (dir. 1989-94), Que. Garrison Club (dir. 1991—), Profl. Liability Ins. of Que. Bar (dir. 1991-94), Que. Bar (supervisory com. 1988-93), Can. Bar Assn., la Commanderie de Bordeaux. Roman Catholic. Avocations: fishing, hunting. Home: 2750 de L'Anse, Sainte-Foy, PQ Canada G1W 2G5 Office: Télé-Québec, 1000 Fullum, Montreal, PQ Canada H2K 3L7

NORMANDEAU, ANDRE GABRIEL, criminologist, educator; b. Montreal, Que., Can., May 4, 1942; s. Gabriel E. and Laurette D. (Sauve) N.; m. Pierrette La Pointe, Aug. 14, 1965; children: Alain, Louis, Jean. M.A. in Criminology, U. Pa., 1965, Ph.D. in Sociology, 1968. Asst. prof. criminology U. Montreal, 1968-71, assoc. prof., 1971-76, prof., 1976—, chmn. dept. criminology, 1970-80, dir. Internat. Ctr. Comparative Criminology, 1983-89, dir. Rsch. Inst. on Police, 1990—. Author: Public Attitudes and Crime, 1970, The Measurement of Crime, 1975, Patterns of Robbery, 1980, Crimes of Violence, 1985, A Vision of the Police, 1990, Crime Prevention, 1993, Justice and Minorities, 1995, Community Policing, 1997. Woodrow Wilson fellow, 1964-68. Mem. Internat. Soc. Criminology, Am. Soc. Criminology, Am. Sociol. Assn., Can. Criminal Justice Assn. Roman Catholic. Home: 3150 Ave Kent, Montreal, PQ Canada H3S 1N1 Office: Dept Criminology U Montreal, Montreal, PQ Canada H3C 3J7 *Happiness is achieved by working for it, not by waiting for it to come to you.*

NORMENT, ERIC STUART, newspaper editor; b. Butler, Pa., July 26, 1956; s. Hillyer Gavin and Reva Lucille (Shepherd) N.; m. Ann Hobin, Aug. 22, 1987; children: Timothy Hobin, Peter John, Laura Mary. BA, U. Chgo., 1979; MS, Northwestern U., Evanston, Ill., 1980. Reporter Paddock Publs., Arlington Heights, Ill., 1980-83; asst. night editor Cape Cod Times, Hyannis, Mass., 1983; copy editor The Boston Herald, 1983-84, copy desk chief news, 1984-88, features prodn. editor, 1987-88, asst. Sunday editor, 1988-94, Sunday editor, 1994—; instr. journalism Northeastern U., Boston, 1984. Recipient Peter Lisagor Pub. Svc. award Chgo. Headline Club, 1981, Edn. Reporting award Ill. Press Assn., 1981. Office: Boston Herald 1 Herald St Boston MA 02118-2200

NORQUIST, JOHN OLOF, mayor; b. Princeton, N.J., Oct. 22, 1949; s. Ernest O. and Jeannette (Nelson) N.; m. Susan R. Mudd, Dec. 1986; 1 child, Benjamin Edward. Student, Augustana Coll., Rock Island, Ill., 1967-69; BS, U. Wis., 1971, MPA, 1988. Assemblyman Wis. State Assembly, Madison, 1974-82, co-chmn. state joint com. fin., 1980-81; mem. Wis. State Senate, 82-88, asst. majority leader, 1984-85, 87; mayor City of Milw., 1988—. Sgt. USAR, 1971-77. Mem. Nat. League of Cities, Wis. Alliance of Cities. Democrat. Presbyterian. Avocation: map collecting. Office: Office of Mayor City Hall Rm 201 200 E Wells St Milwaukee WI 53202-3515*

NORRBY, KLAS CARL VILHELM, pathology educator; b. Shanghai, China, Jan. 8, 1937; s. Åke Vilhelm and Ingrid Maria (Wedblad) N.; m. Ulla Margareta Hjort, June 17, 1961; children: Katarina, Cecilia, Jacob. MB, Göteborg (Sweden) U., 1959, MD, 1964, PhD, 1970. Asst. prof. pathology Göteborg U., 1967-71, prof. pathology, regal chair, 1985—; sr. lectr. in pathology Linköping U., 1972-84, chmn. Inst. Med. Microbiology and Pathology, 1980-84; vis. prof. in cell biology Harvard Med. Sch., Boston, 1989-90. Author over 200 articles to profl. jours. Sub.-lt. Royal Swedish Navy Med. Corps, 1972-86. Fellow European Study Group for Cell Proliferation, European Histamine Rsch. Soc., N.Y. Acad. Sci. Avocations: hiking, sailing, skiing, classical music. Office: Sahlgrenska U Hosp, Dept Pathology, S-413 45 Goteborg Sweden

NORRELL, MARY PATRICIA, nursing educator; b. Seymour, Ind., Jan. 3; d. William C. and Mary Elizabeth (Elkins) Ulrey; m. Robert Gerald Norrell, Aug. 17, 1974; children: Shannan, Richard, Trisha. BSN, Ball State U., 1971; MS, Ind. U. Cert. inpatient obstetrics. Team leader Mt. Sinai Med. Ctr., Miami Beach, Fla., 1971-73; charge nurse Jackson County Schneck Meml. Hosp., Seymour, 1971, 73-74; nurse Camp Matoaka, Oakland, Maine, 1973; master instr. Ivy Tech. State Coll., Columbus, Ind., 1974—; item writer Nat. Coun. Licensure Exam. for Practical Nurses, 1992. Mem. Assn. of Women's Health, Obstetric and Neonatal Nurses, Ind. Soc. for Healthcare Edn. and Tng. Home: 572 Shawnee Ct Seymour IN 47274-1956

NORRID, HENRY GAIL, osteopath, surgeon, researcher; b. Amarillo, Tex., June 4, 1940; s. Henry Horatio and Johnnie Belle (Combs, Cummins) N.; m. Andreia Maybeth Hudson, Jan. 29, 1966 (dec. 1988); children: Joshua Andrew, Noah Adam; m. Cheryll Diane Payne, Mar. 19, 1989; stepchildren: Kim Sheri Payne, Matthew Dominic Payne. AA, Amarillo Coll., 1963; BA, U. Tex., 1966; MS, West Tex. State U., 1967; DO, Kirksville Coll. Osteo. Medicine, 1973. Diplomate Bd. Osteo. Physicians and Surgeons, Nat. Bd. Examiners Osteo. Physicians and Surgeons; cert. basic sci. tchr. Iowa, Tex., Colo. Intern Interboro Gen. Hosp., Bklyn., 1973-74; attending physician dept. gen. practice Osteo. Hosp. and Clinic N.Y., N.Y.C., 1974-77; gen. practice medicine specializing in osteo., Amarillo, Tex., 1978—; emergency care physician Amarillo Emergency Receiving Ctr. Amarillo Hosp. Dist., Tex., 1978-79, Ready Care Emergency Center, Arlington and Bedford, Tex., 1990-92; emergency room physician St. Anthony Hosp., Amarillo, Tex., 1992; emeritus mem. consulting staff physician dept. family practice Northwest Tex. Hosp., Amarillo, 1995; emergency/trauma physician Tex. EM Care, 1995—; mem. mass casualty nat. disaster response team ARC, 1995; contract staff physician Tex. Tech Univ. Sch. Medicine and Health Scis. Ctr., med. dept. and infirmary Tex. Dept. Corrections, Tex. Dept. Criminal Justice; med. cons. rehab. medicine vocat. rehab. divsn Tex. Rehab. Commn., Plano; cattleman, ranch owner, Van Zandt County, Tex.; lectr. osteo. prins. and practice, The Osteo. Hosp. and Clinic N.Y., 1974-77, mem. credentials com., 1975-76; mem. exec. com. Southwest Osteo. Hosp., Amarillo, 1983-84, chief of staff, 1984-85; sec. dept. family practice Northwest Tex. Hosp., Amarillo, 1981-82, mem. credentials com., 1984-85, joint practice com. dept. family practice, 1986-87; mem. orgnl. com. for devel. of dept. osteo. prins. and practices, chmn. N.Y.C. group N.Y. Coll. Osteo. Med., 1977; mem. North Tex. Amputee Support Group, Dallas. Contbr. articles to Tex. Jour. Sci., other publs. Scout physician Llano Estecato council Boy Scouts Am., Texas, 1978-85. Served to E-4 U.S. Army, 1956-63. Recipient William M. Giltner Meml. Fund award 1972, Humanitarian award Am. Cath. Conf., 1979, Century award Boy Scouts Am., 1982; Maxwell D. Warmer Meml. scholar 1973; scholar Kirksville Coll. Osteo. Medicine, 1970, Tex. Legislature, 1969-73, Pfizer, 1973; named to Eminent Soc. Border Legionaires, 11th Armored Cavalry Regiment, Germany, 1958. Mem. Am. Coll. Gen. Practitioners, Tex. Osteo. Med. Assn. (pres. dist. I, mem. ho. of dels. 1981-82, 95), Sons of Am. Revolution, The Sons of Republic of Tex., Am. Congress Rehab. Medicine, Am. Osteo. Assn., World Future Soc. (profl.), Gen. Soc. War of 1812, Tex. & Southwest Cattle Raisers Assn., N.Y. Acad. Scis., Ex-Student's Assn. of The Univ. Tex. (life), 11th Armored Cavalry Regiment Assn., 36th (Tex.) Inf. Divsn. Assn. (life), Baron of the Magna Charta (Sommerset chpt. 1994—), Masons, Am. Legion, Trinity Fellowship, Beta Beta Beta, Sigma Sigma Phi (pres. 1972), Alpha Phi Omega, Psi Sigma Alpha, Theta Psi, Theta Psi Clowns (1969-73). Avocations: astronomy, short wave listening, camping, fishing, anthropology. Office: 1422 S Tyler St Ste 102 Amarillo TX 79101-4238

NORRIE, ELEANOR E., government official; married; 3 children. Grad., Provincial Normal Coll. Sch. tchr., owner family restaurant bus.; mem. for constituency Truro-Bible Hill MLA, 1993—; Min. Human Resources N.S. Govt., 1993-95, mem. Priorities and Planning Secretariat, 1993—, Min. Housing and Consumer Affairs, 1995-96, Min. Natural Resources, 1996—; min. responsible for Sport and Recreation Commn., Adv. Coun. on Status of Women. Vice chair Colchester Regional Hosp. Found.; past pres. Truro Attic Painters; exec. Truro Head Start, Truro Sch. Band Aux., Home and Sch. Assn.; chair Nova Scotia Sport Heritage Centre, Truro Sport Heritage Soc. Mem. Truro Centurion Swim Club (past pres.). Avocations: swimming, tennis, cross-country skiing, politics. Office: Dept Housing & Consumer Min, PO Box 815 Stn Main 40 Alderney Dr Fl 5, Dartmouth, NS Canada B2Y 3Z3

NORRIE, K. PETER, manufacturing executive; b. Madison, Wis., Mar. 7, 1939; s. Kenneth Peter and Clara Frances (Storey) N.; m. Susan Kelliher, Sept. 6, 1960 (dec. 1975); children: Peter Clark, David Doherty, Charles Kelliher; m. Betty Buzard, Oct. 14, 1978 (div. Apr. 1989); m. Vicki Wheeler, May 30, 1996. BCE, Gonzaga U., 1961; MBA, Harvard U., 1964. Estimator H. Halvorsen Contractors, Spokane, Wash., 1961-62; gen. mgr. Boise (Idaho) Cascade Corp., 1964-70, mgr. gen. sales, 1970-72, v.p., 1972-76, sr. v.p., gen. mgr. paper group, 1976-89; chmn. bd. dirs. Specialty Paperboard, Inc., Brattleboro, Vt., 1989—; pres. Parma (Idaho) Labs., Inc., 1993—. Trustee UCLA Found. With USMCR, 1956-62. Recipient Disting. Alumni Merit award Gonzaga U., 1987. Republican. Roman Catholic. Avocation: golf.

NORRIS, ALAN EUGENE, federal judge; b. Columbus, Ohio, Aug. 15, 1935; s. J. Russell and Dorothy A. (Shrader) N.; m. Nancy Jean Myers, Apr. 15, 1962 (dec. Jan. 1986); children: Tom Edward Jackson, Tracy Elaine; m. Carol Lynn Spohn, Nov. 10, 1990. BA, Otterbein Coll., 1957, HLD (hon.), 1991; cert., U. Paris, 1956; LLB, NYU, 1960; LLM, U. Va., 1986. Bar: Ohio 1960, U.S. Dist. Ct. (so. dist) Ohio 1962, U.S. Dist. Ct. (no. dist) Ohio 1964. Law clk. to judge Ohio Supreme Ct., Columbus, 1960-61; assoc. Vorys, Sater, Seymour & Pease, Columbus, 1961-62; ptnr. Metz, Bailey, Norris & Spicer, Westerville, Ohio, 1962-80; judge Ohio Ct. Appeals (10th dist.), Columbus, 1981-86, U.S. Ct. Appeals (6th cir.), Columbus, 1986—. Contbr. articles to profl. jours. Mem. Ohio Ho. of Reps., Columbus, 1967-80. Named Outstanding Young Man, Westerville Jaycees, 1971; recipient Legislator of Yr. award Ohio Acad. Trial Lawyers, Columbus, 1972. Mem. Ohio Bar Assn., Columbus Bar Assn. Republican. Methodist. Lodge: Masons (master 1966-67). Office: US Ct Appeals 328 US Courthouse 85 Marconi Blvd Columbus OH 43215-2823

NORRIS, ALBERT STANLEY, psychiatrist, educator; b. Sudbury, Ont., Can., July 14, 1926; s. William and Mary (Zell) N.; m. Dorothy James, Sept. 2, 1950; children: Barbara Ellen, Robert Edward, Kimberly Ann. M.D., U. Western Ont., 1951. Intern Ottawa (Ont.) Civic Hosp., 1951-52; resident in psychiatry U. Iowa, Psychopathic Hosp., Iowa City, 1953-55, Boston City Hosp., 1955-56; practice medicine Kingston, Ont., Can., 1956-57; instr. Queen's U., Kingston, 1956-57; asst. prof. psychiatry U. Iowa, 1957-62, asso. prof., 1962-64, 1965-66, prof., 1966-72; asso. prof. U. Oreg., 1964-65; prof.

So. Ill. U. Sch. Medicine, Springfield, 1972-84, chmn. dept. psychiatry, 1972-82; prof. emeritus, 1984—; practice medicine specializing in psychiatry Cedar Rapids, Iowa, 1984—; vis. prof. U. Auckland, N.Z., U. Otago, New Zealand, U. Liverpool. Contbr. chpts. to books, articles to med. jours. Fellow Am. Psychiat. Soc. (life); mem. AMA, Am. Psychopath. Assn., Soc. Biol. Psychiatry, Can. Psychiat. Soc., Am. Soc. Psychosomatic Ob-Gyn, Royal Soc. Medicine. Republican. Presbyterian. Home: 5 Penfro Dr Iowa City IA 52246-4927 Office: 1730 1st Ave NE Ste 133 Cedar Rapids IA 52402-5433 *A life is only fulfilled by a quest, a vision of the future and a commitment to a greater value than one's self. A flickering candle is poor light, unless there is no other.*

NORRIS, ALFRED LLOYD, theological seminary president, clergyman; b. Bogalusa, La., Feb. 6, 1938; s. Leslie Henry Peter and Adele Theresa (Washington) N.; m. Mackie Lyvonne Harper, Sept. 9, 1961; children: Alfred Lloyd II, Angela Renee. BA, Dillard U., 1960; MDiv, Gammon Theol. Sem., Atlanta, 1964, DD (hon.), 1976; DD (hon.), Centenary Coll., 1989; LLD, Dillard U., 1989. Ordained ministry United Meth. Ch., 1963. Pastor Haven United Meth. Ch., New Orleans, 1963-66, Peck United Meth. Ch., New Orleans, 1966-68, First Street United Meth. Ch., New Orleans, 1972-74, Mt. Zion United Meth. Ch., New Orleans, 1980-85; dist. supt. New Orleans dist. United Meth. Ch., New Orleans, 1974-80; dir. recruitment Gammon Theol. Sem., 1968-72, pres., 1985—; now bishop of New Mexico United Methodist Church, Albuquerque, N.Mex.; mem. Am. Preaching Mission, 1967; mem. bd. publs. United Meth. Pub. House, Nashville, 1980—; bd. dirs. Gulfside Assembly, Waveland, Miss., 1975—; mem. La. Conf. Bd. Higher Edn. and Campus Ministry; chmn. bd. ordained ministry La. Ann. Conf., 1980-88; guest preacher Liberia, West Africa, 1988. Trustee Centenary Coll., Shreveport, La., 1979—; mem. exec. com. NAACP, New Orleans, 1980-85; bd. dirs. New Orleans Urban League, 1981-84, Wesley Homes, Inc., Atlanta, 1986—; mem. exec. com. Met. Area Com., New Orleans, 1983-85; chmn. bd. dirs. Lafon Home for Elderly, New Orleans, 1983-85. Crusade scholar, 1961-63. Mem. Assn. United Meth. Theol. Schs. (sec. 1986-88), Adminstrv. Deans' Coun. (v.p. 1986—), Masons, Sigma Pi Phi, Theta Phi. Democrat. Avocations: reading, spectator sports. *

NORRIS, ANDREA SPAULDING, art museum director; b. Apr. 2, 1945; d. Edwin Baker and Mary Gretchen (Brendle) Spaulding. BA, Wellesley Coll., 1967; MA, NYU, 1969, PhD, 1977. Intern dept. western European arts Met. Mus. Art, N.Y.C., 1970, 72; rsch. and editorial asst. Inst. Fine Arts NYU, 1971, lectr. Washington Sq. Coll., 1976-77; lectr. Queens Coll. CUNY, 1973-74; asst. to dir. Art Gallery Yale U., New Haven, 1977-80, lectr. art history, 1979-80; chief curator Archer M. Huntington Art Gallery, Austin, Tex., 1980-88; lectr. art history Dept. Art U. Tex., Austin, 1984-88; dir. Spencer Mus. Art U. Kans., Lawrence, 1988—. Co-author: (catalogue) Medals and Plaquettes from the Molinari Collection at Bowdoin College, 1976; author: (exhbn. catalogues) Jackson Pollock: New-Found Works, 1978; exhbn. The Sforza Court: Milan in the Renaissance 1450-1535, 1988-89. Mem. Renaissance Soc. Am., Coll. Art Assn., Assn. Art Mus. Dirs., Phi Beta Kappa. Office: Spencer Mus Art U Kans Lawrence KS 66045

NORRIS, CHUCK (CARLOS RAY), actor; b. Ryan, Okla., Mar. 10, 1940; m. Dianne Norris (div.); children: Mike, Eric. Appeared in films The Wrecking Crew, 1969, Return of the Dragon, 1972, Breaker, Breaker, 1976, Good Guys Wear Black, 1977, Force of One, 1978, The Octagon, 1979, An Eye for an Eye, 1980, Silent Rage, 1981, Forced Vengeance, 1981, Lone Wolf McQuade, 1982, Missing in Action, 1984, Missing in Action II-The Beginning, 1985, Code of Silence, 1985, (co-screenwriter) Invasion, U.S.A., 1985, Delta Force, 1986, Firewalker, 1986, (co-screenwriter) Braddock: Missing in Action III, 1987, Hero and the Terror, 1988, Delta Force 2: Operation Stranglehold, 1990, The Hitman, 1991, (co-exec. prodr.) Sidekicks, 1993, Top Dog, 1994, Forrest Warrior, 1995; TV series Walker: Texas Ranger, 1993—; author: The Secret Power Within Zen Solutions to Real Problems, 1996; (with Joe Hyams) The Secret of Inner Strength: My Story, 1988; host: The Ultimate Stuntman: A Tribute to Dar Robinson. Profl. world middleweight karate champion, 1968-74. Office: 144 S Beverly Dr Ph Beverly Hills CA 90212

NORRIS, CURTIS BIRD, writer, journalist; b. Quincy, Mass., July 14, 1927; s. Lowell Ames and Helen (Curtis) N.; m. Eileen Patricia Schindler, Mar. 23, 1959; children: Katharine Eileen, Helen Carolyn, Suzanne Elizabeth. AB, Middlebury Coll., 1951; postgrad., Bridgewater (Mass.) State Coll., 1986-95. Free-lance writer, 1945—; writer Sikorsky Aircraft Co., Stratford, Conn., 1957-59, N.Am. Aviation, Downey, Calif., 1959-61; editor Hughes Aircraft Co., Fullerton, Calif., 1961-62, Whitman (Mass.) News, 1962-65; sci. writer U. Vt., 1965-66; editor Wareham (Mass.) Courier, 1966-69; med. sci. editor Brown U., Providence, 1969-77; dir. pub. affairs Stonehill Coll., North Easton, Mass., 1977-83; staff columnist Quincy (Mass.) Patriot Ledger, 1982—; news dir. Bridgewater State Coll., 1985-87; indsl. rels. dir. Morgan Meml. Goodwill Industries, Boston, 1987-89; instr. Stonehill Coll., North Easton, 1991—; lectr., feature writer Boston Sunday Herald-Traveler, 1963-76, Yankee mag., 1963—; staff investigative reporter Globe Communications, Montreal, Can., 1973—; bd. dirs. pub. rels. programs Composite Tech. Alloys Co., Attleboro, Mass., 1975—; coord. Ea. Writers Conf., Salem, Mass., 1982; cons. pub. rels., 1983—; instr. Stonehill Coll., 1991. Author: Seldom Heard Tales of New England, 1964, American Holocaust, 1975, Phantom P. 40, 1981, Little Known Mysteries of New England, 1992, Ghosts I Have Known, 1993, The Boston Bogeyman, 1995, The Man Who Talked to Trees, 1995, Clue of the Talking Potato - And More of Connecticut's Forgotten Crimes, 1996, Horror on the Midnight Bus, and Other Massachusetts True Crime Mysteries, 1997; assoc. editor: Stonehill Alumni News, 1977-81; editor: Stonehill Rev., 1977-83; originator (TV programs) Health Call, Science Call, Providence; prodr.: (cable TV program) Seldom Heard Tales of New Eng., 1986-88; represented in anthologies including Yankees Under Steam, 1970, Mysterious New England, 1971, Danger, Disaster and Horrid Deeds, 1974, Best Detective Cases, 1975-77, True Police Yearbook, 1975, 77, Startling Detective Yearbook, 1975-77, The World Wars Remembered, 1979, Best of Old Farmers Almanac, 1991; author manuscripts in Norris Collection, Brown U.; contbr. numerous stories to mags., TV Unsolved Mysteries, 1989. Chmn. publicity Wareham chpt. Am. Cancer Soc., 1966, cmty. chmn., 19678-69; assoc. mem. Federated Ea. Indian League; bd. dirs. Opera New Eng. of Greater Brookton. With USAAF, 1945-57; maj. Mass. N.G. Recipient Grand award Coun. Advancement and Support of Edn., 1976-77, Philippine Liberation medal Philippine Govt., 1994. Mem. New Eng. Press Assn., Am. Defenders of Bataan and Corregidor, Am. Med. Writers Assn., Assn. Am. Med. Colls., Mystery Writers Am., State Def. Force Assn. of U.S., Ret. Officers Assn., U.S. Coast Guard Aux. Flotilla 1108, Kappa Delta Rho. Unitarian. Home: 166 E Main St Norton MA 02766-2310 *Life can be like a jaunt thru a candy store, full of tasty morsels for the creative and adventurous to grasp. Always observe nobless oblige and the ten commandments - you will be rewarded severalfold. My most useful knowledge? High school Latin. Regrets? Unable to return to Bataan or to visit English roots.*

NORRIS, DARELL FOREST, insurance company executive; b. Pontiac, Mich., Oct. 19, 1928; s. Forest Ellis and Mabel Marie (Smith) N.; m. Thordis Marie Johansen, Aug. 21, 1955; children: Dara Lee, Jennifer, Lisa, Nancy. BS, U. Kans., 1950. CLU, chartered fin. cons. Reporter, sports staff Kansas City Star, Mo., 1950-51; pilot TWA, 1955-56; div. agy. mgr. Merced region Farmers Group, Inc., Calif., 1959, sales rep., Colorado Springs region, 1962, regional agy. mgr., Aurora, Ill., 1964, regional sales mgr., Santa Ana, Calif., 1966, mgmt. tng. program staff, dir. agys., L.A., 1969, regional mgr., Austin, Tex., 1971, v.p. sales, L.A., 1973, v.p. field ops. midwestern zone, 1976, v.p. field ops., western zone, 1979—; pres. Farmers New World Mgmt. Co., 1977-81, v.p. staff ops., 1981-85, sr. v.p. life co. ops. and staff support svcs., 1985-90, farmers cons., 1990-93; gen. ins. cons., 1993—; bd. dirs. Northridge Hosp. Med. Found. Chmn. bd. deacons First Baptist Ch., Granada Hills, Calif., 1977-89; sustaining mem. Rep. Nat. Com. Capt. USAF, 1951-55. Mem. Am. Soc. CLUs, Chartered Fin. Cons. (San Fernando Valley chpt.), Ins. Edn. Assn. (trustee 1982-84).

NORRIS, DAVID RANDOLPH, recording artist, philanthropist; b. Oakland, Calif., Sept. 19, 1952; s. Joseph Lloyd and Corene (Keenom) N. AA, Gulf Coast Community Coll., Panama City, Fla., 1974. Touring/recording artist worldwide; cons. accoustic and electric 12-string guitar. Artist: (records recorded in 1990) Cindy, Loosing You, Why Is She Cruel, Alone, Just An Old Sargent, Carolina, VA Two Step, Establishment Ties, No More, Hoot Owl Trail, Blond Child. Carpenter/contractor Pres. Carter's Habitat for Humanity, project team leader, 1990. With USAF, 1972-73, Vietnam. Decorated Silver Star, Bronze Star with cluster, Purple Heart with clusters; pub. svc. honoree Rep. Party/NRA, Washington, 1970-90, honored by Pres. Reagan at White House, 1988. Mem. NRA (life mem.), Calif. Rifle and Pistol Assn. (Pub. Svc. award 1988). Republican. Avocations: carpenter, trap shooter, fisherman, philanthropist. Home: PO Box 5488 Santa Monica CA 90409-5488

NORRIS, DENNIS E., religious organization executive. Dir. Am. Baptist Chs. Cleve. Region.

NORRIS, DOLORES JUNE, elementary school educator; b. Belmore, N.Y., Feb. 10, 1938; d. Abe and Doris Cyril (Stahl) Wanser; m. William Dean Norris, June 11, 1960; children: William Dean II, Ronald Wayne, Darla Cyrille. BS in Elem. Edn., So. Nazarene U., 1959; MS in Computer Edn., Nova U., 1988, EdS in Computer Applications, 1990. Cert. elem. edn. and computer sci. tchr., Fla. Tchr. 4th and 5th grades Ruskin (Fla.) Elem. Sch., 1959-61; tchr. 5th grade Emerson Elem. Sch., Kansas City, Kans., 1961-63; tchr. 1st grade Hickman Mills, Mo., 1964-65; tchr. 3d and 4th grades Lake Mary Elem. Sch., Sanford, Fla., 1968-72; tchr. 1st grade St. Charles Cath. Sch., Port Charlotte, Fla., 1976-77; primary tchr. Meadow Park Elem. Sch., Port Charlotte, 1977-89; computer specialist Vineland Elem. Sch., Rotanda West, Fla., 1989-90; computer specialist Myakka River Elem. Sch., Port Charlotte, 1990—, tech. trainer, 1995—; reading coun. Charlotte County Schs., Port Charlotte, 1987—, rep., 1989-90, in-svc. com. 1990-93; program planner Meadow Park Elem. Sch., 1988-89; program planner Myakka River Elem. Sch. 1991-93. Mem. Rotary, Punta Gorda, Fla., 1982-86; co-dir. teens Touring Puppet Group, Punta Gorda, 1982-86; puppet co-dir. NOW Teens, Punta Gorda, 1976-80. Mem. Fla. Assn. Computers in Edn. Avocations: piano, swimming, travel. Home: 1171 Richter St Pt Charlotte FL 33952-2870

NORRIS, FLOYD HAMILTON, financial journalist; b. L.A., Sept. 6, 1947; s. Floyd H. and Martha Leota (Buntin) N.; m. Mary Christine Bockelmann, Oct. 5, 1984; 1 child, John Buntin. Student, U. Calif., Irvine, 1965-68; MBA, Columbia U., 1982. Reporter Coll. Press Svc., Washington, 1969-70, Manchester (N.H.) Am., 1970-72, Concord (N.H.) Monitor, 1972-74, UPI, Vt. and Ala., 1974-77; press sec. Sen. John Durkin, Washington, 1977-78; fin. writer AP, N.Y.C., 1978-81; columnist Barron's, N.Y.C., 1982-88; fin. columnist N.Y. Times, N.Y.C., 1988—. Office: N Y Times 229 W 43rd St New York NY 10036-3913

NORRIS, FRANKLIN GRAY, surgeon; b. Washington, June 30, 1923; s. Franklin Gray and Ellie Narcissus (Story) N.; m. Sara Kathryn Green, Aug. 12, 1945; children: Gloria Norris Sales, F. Gray III. BS, Duke U., 1947; MD, Harvard U., 1951. Resident, Peter Bent Brigham Hosp., Boston, 1951-54, Bowman Gray Sch. Medicine, 1954-57; practice medicine specializing in thoracic and cardiovascular surgery, 1957—; prof. anatomy and physiology, Valencia C.C., Orlando, Fla., 1995—; pres. Norris Assocs., Orlando, 1985—; mem. staff Brevard Meml. Hosp., Melbourne, Fla., Waterman Meml. Hosp., Eustis, Fla., West Orange Meml. Hosp., Winter Garden, Fla., Orlando Regional Med. Ctr., Fla. Hosp., Lucerne Hosp., Arnold Palmer Children Hosp., Princeton, Fla. Hosp. N.E. and South (all Orlando). Bd. dirs. Orange County Cancer Soc., 1958-64, Ctrl. Fla. Respiratory Disease Assn., 1958-65. Served to capt. USAAF, 1943-45. Decorated Air medal with 3 oak leaf clusters. Diplomate Am. Bd. Surgery, Am. Bd. Thoracic and Cardiovasc. Surgery, Am. Bd. Gen. Vascular Surgery. Mem. Fla. Heart Assn. (dir. 1958—), Orange County Med. Soc. (exec. com. 1964-75, pres. 1971-75), Cen. Fla. Hosp. Assn. (bd. dirs., 1980-85), ACS, Soc. Thoracic Surgeons, So. Thoracic Surg. Assn., Am. Coll. Chest Physicians, Fla. Soc. Thoracic Surgeons (pres. 1981-82), Am. Coll. Cardiology, So. Assn. Vascular Surgeons, Fla. Vascular Soc., Phi Kappa Psi. Presbyterian (elder). Clubs: Citrus, Orlando Country. Home: 1801 Bimini Dr Orlando FL 32806-1515 Office: Norris Assocs 1801 Bimini Dr Orlando FL 32806-1515

NORRIS, GENIE M., senior government official; b. N.Y.C., July 15, 1951; d. Eugene and Peggy (Carter) Martell; m. Larry Specht, Apr. 22, 1982; children: Amanda Michele, Joshua Albert, Rachel Elizabeth. Adminstr. Senator Patrick Moynihan, N.Y.C., 1976; exec. asst. U.S. Senate, Washington, 1982-86; dep. field dir. Carter/Mondale Presdl. Campaign, Washington, 1979; dep. dir. Dem. Nat. Com., Washington, 1980-81; dir., sr. assoc. Francis Assocs., Ltd., Washington, Germany, 1981-82; exec. asst. Senator Patrick Moynihan, Washington, 1982-86; guest lectr. USIA, Washington, 1987-90; mgr. Amb. Residence, Bonn, Germany, 1987-90; sr. assoc. FMR Group, Washington, 1990; dep. exec. dir. Dem. Congl. Campaign Com., Washington, 1990-91, exec. dir., 1991-94; dep. asst. sec. for ops. Dept. of State, Washington, 1995—; com. rep. Dem. Nat. Com. South Africa, 1980, Dem. Congl. Campaign Com., Republic of China, 1992; Peace Corp. transistion team leader Pres. Transition Team, Washington, 1992-93; South Africa elections obs. UN, 1994. With U.S. Army, 1975-78. Democrat. Roman Catholic. Avocations: art history, 1st edition books, horseback riding, music, antiques. Home: 3014 Dent Pl NW Apt 14E Washington DC 20007

NORRIS, GEOFFREY, geology educator, consultant; b. Romford, Essex, Eng., Aug. 6, 1937; came to Can., 1964; s. Alfred Frederick Henry and Winifred Lucy (Camps) N.; m. Anne Frances Facer, Sept. 20, 1958; children—Grant, Theresa, Brett, Sonia. BA, Cambridge U., Eng., 1959, MA, 1962, PhD, 1964. Sci. officer N.Z. Geol. Survey, Lower Hutt, 1961-64; postdoctoral fellow McMaster U. Hamilton, Ont., Can., 1965; rsch. scientist Pan Am. Petroleum, Tulsa, Okla., 1965-67; prof. U. Toronto, Ont., Can., 1967—, chmn. dept. geology, 1980-90; rsch. assoc. Royal Ont. Mus., Toronto, 1967—; A.V. Humboldt fellow Cologne U., W.Ger., 1976; Ptnr. Austin and Cumming Exploration, Calgary, Alta., Can., 1980-87; vis. scientist Fla. Marine Research Lab., St. Petersburg, 1986, Fla. Mus. Natural History, U. Fla., Gainesville, 1994. Contbr. articles to profl. jours. Pres. White Light Hospice Found., Toronto, 1987-96; dir. Metro Toronto Residents Action Com. for Rail Safety, 1980-95; bd. dirs. Can. Geol. Found., 1997—. Recipient numerous operating, equipment and travel grants, Nat. Scis. and Engring. Research Council of Can., 1967—. Fellow Am. Assn. Stratigraphic Palynologists (pres. 1972), Royal Soc. Can. (sec. divsn. earth, ocean and atmospheric scis. 1990-92, dir. 1993-96), Geol. Assn. Can. (councilor 1987-90), Geol. Soc. Am.; mem. Can. Assn. Palynologists (pres. 1982), Internat. Commn. Palynology (sec.-treas. 1975-80), Internat. Union Geol. Scis. (Can. nat. com. 1990—). Home: 12 Astley Ave, Toronto, ON Canada M4W 3B4 Office: U Toronto, Dept Geology, Toronto, ON Canada M5S 3B1

NORRIS, H. THOMAS, pathologist, academic administrator; b. Johnson City, Tenn., Nov. 24, 1934; s. Herbert Thomas and Ruth M. (Church) N.; m. Patricia Henry, June 19, 1956; children: Ruth Eileen, Margaret Ann, Edward Robert. BS with honors, Wash. State U., 1956; MD, U. So. Calif., 1959. Diplomate Am. Bd. Anatomic and Clin. Pathology. Resident pathology Mallory Inst. Pathology, Boston, 1960-62, 64-65; instr. Tufts U. Sch. Medicine, Boston, 1964-66; fellow Harvard Med. Sch., Cambridge, Mass., 1966-67; from asst. prof. to prof. U. Wash. Sch. Med., 1967-83; prof., chmn. East Carolina U. Sch. Medicine, Greenville, N.C., 1983—; asst. pathologist Mallory Inst. Pathology, Boston, 1965-66; asst. chief lab svc. VA Hosp., Seattle, 1967-74; dir. hosp. pathology U. Hosp., Seattle, 1974-83; chief pathology Pitt County Meml. Hosp., Greenville, 1983—. Editor: Contemporary Issues in Surgical Pathology, 1983, Pathology of the Colon, Small Intestine and Anus, 1991; contbr. articles to profl. jours. Bd. dirs. Am. Cancer Soc., Greenville, 1984—. Capt. USAR, 1962-64. Recipient Cert. Outstanding Achievement with Honorarium U.S. Army Sci. Conf., West Point, N.Y., 1964. Fellow ACP, Am. Soc. Clin. Pathologists, Coll. Am. Pathologists, Am. Pathology Found.; mem: AAAS, AMA, Am. Gastroent. Assn., Internat. Acad. Pathology, U.S. and Can. Acad. Pathology, Am. Assn. Pathologists, Arthur Purdy Stout Soc. Surg. Pathologists, Acad. Clin. Lab. Physicians and Scientists, Assn. Pathology Chmn., Am. Men and Women Sci., N.Y. Acad. Scis., Mass. Med. Soc., N.C. Med. Assn., N.C. Soc. Pathologists, Pitt County Med. Soc., Gastrointestinal Pathology Club (charter), Alpha Omega Alpha, Sigma Xi. Office: East Carolina U Sch Medicine Dept Pathology Lab Medicine Greenville NC 27858-4354

NORRIS, JAMES ARNOLD, engineering company executive; b. Fargo, N.D., May 26, 1937; s. Cedric Leon and Gladys Louise (Arnold) N.; m. Catherine Anne Wright, Mar. 2, 1963; children: Suzanne, Erica, James. SB, MIT, 1959, SM, 1965; PhD, U. Calif., 1963. Economist US AID, Tunis, Tunisia, 1966-71, Jakarta, Indonesia, 1971-76, Cairo, 1976-80; dir. Bangladesh-India office US AID, Washington, 1980-82; mission dir. US AID, Dhaka, Bangladesh, 1982-84, Islamabad, Pakistan, 1988-92, Moscow, 1992-96; counselor to agy. US AID, Washington, 1984-85, dep. adminstr. Asia and Near East, 1985-88; project dir. Ralph M. Parsons Co., St. Petersburg, Russia, 1996—. Recipient Presdl. Meritorious Svc. award President U.S., 1984, 87, Presdl. Disting. Svc. award President U.S., 1989.

NORRIS, JAMES HAROLD, lawyer; b. New Kensington, Pa., Sept. 18, 1953; s. J. Harold and Eleanore Rose (Arch) N.; m. Ann Marie Annase, Nov. 25, 1988; children: Ryan, Scott, Nicholas. BA, Washington Jefferson Coll., 1975; JD, Duquesne U., 1978. Bar: Pa. 1978, U.S. Dist. Ct. (we. dist.) Pa. 1978, U.S. Ct. Appeals (3d cir.) 1994, U.S. Dist. Ct. (no. dist.) Va. 1996. Assoc. Ruffin Hazlett Snyder Brown & Stabile, Pitts., 1979-83; ptnr. Eckert Seamans Cherin & Mellott, Pitts., 1983—, vice chmn. litigation dept., 1995. Bd. dirs. Summit Acad., 1996. Mem. Allegheny County Bar Assn., Pa. Bar Assn. (chmn. adminstrv. law sect. 1992-94, sect. del., sports, entertainment and art law com., spl. achievement award 1993). Home: 2545 Country Side Ln Wexford PA 15090-7941 Office: Eckert Seamans Cherin & Mellott 600 Grant St Pittsburgh PA 15219-2702

NORRIS, JOHN ANTHONY, health sciences executive, lawyer, educator; b. Buffalo, Dec. 27, 1946; s. Joseph D. and Maria L. (Suite) N.; m. Kathleen E. Mullen, July 13, 1969; children: Patricia Marie, John Anthony II, Joseph Mullen, Mary Kathleen, Elizabeth Mary. BA, U. Rochester, 1968; JD, MBA with honors, Cornell U., 1973; cert., Harvard U. Sch. Govt., 1986. Bar: Mass. 1973. Assoc. Peabody, Brown, Boston, 1973-75; assoc. Powers Hall, Boston, 1975-76, ptnr., mem. exec. com., 1976-80, v.p., dir., 1979-80, chmn. adminstrv. com., 1976-79, chmn. hiring com., 1979-80; chmn. bd., pres., chief exec. officer, founder Norris & Norris, Boston, 1980-85; dep. commr. and chief operating officer FDA, Washington, 1985-88, chmn. action planning and cap coms., 1985-88, chmn. reye syndrome com., 1985-87, chmn. trade legis. com., 1987-88; corporate exec. v.p. Hill & Knowlton, Inc., N.Y.C., 1988-93; worldwide dir. Health Scis. Cons. Group., 1988-93, chmn. health scis. policy coun., 1989-93; chmn. bd., pres., CEO, founder John A. Norris, Esq., P.C., Boston, 1993—; pres., CEO Nat. Pharm. Coun., Reston, Va., 1995-96; mem. faculty Tufts Dental Sch., 1974-79, Boston Coll. Law Sch., 1976-80; Boston U. Law Sch., 1979-83, Harvard U. Pub. Health Sch., 1988—; mem. bd. editors FDA Drug Bull. and FDA Consumer Report, 1985-88; bd. dirs. Summit Tech., Inc., Cytologics, Inc., Horus Therapeutics Inc., Nat. Applied Scis. Founder, faculty editor-in-chief Am. Jour. Law and Medicine, 1973-81, emeritus 1981—; editor-in-chief Cornell Internat. Law Jour., 1971-73; reviewer New Eng. Jour. Medicine Law-Medicine Notes, 1980-81; assoc. editor Medicolegal News, 1973-75. Mem. U.S. Del. to Japan (chmn.), Austria, Saudi Arabia, 1987, mem., chmn. Finland, Denmark, Italy, 1986; chmn. Mass. Statuatory Adv. Com. on Regulation of Clin. Labs., 1977-83; chmn. Boston Alumni and Scholarship Com., U. Rochester, 1979-85; mem. trustees coun. U. Rochester, 1979-85; mem. exec. com. Cornell Law Sch. Assn., 1982-85; mem. Mass. Gov.'s Blue Ribbon Task Force on DON, 1979-80, bd. trustees Jordan Hosp., 1978-80, mem. exec. com., 1979-80, chmn., chief exec. officer search com., 1980; chmn. Joseph D. Norris, Esq. Health Law and Pub. Policy Fund., 1979—; chmn. bd. Boston Holiday Project, 1981-83; mem. U.S. Pres. Chernobyl Task Force, 1986, vice-chmn. health affects sub.-com.; mem. U.S. Intra-Govtl. AIDS Task Force, 1987; mem. IOM Drug Devel. Forum, 1986-88, co-chmn. end points sub-com., 1987-88, Fed. Pain Commn., 1984-85. With U.S. Army, 1972-73. Fed. Comprehensive Health Planning fellow, 1970-73; recipient Kansas City Hon. Key award, 1988, Nat. Health Fraud Conf. award, 1988, TOYL award, 1982, FDA Award of Merit, 1987, 88, PHS award, 1987, HHS Sec. award, 1988. Mem. ABA (vice chmn. medicine and law com. 1977-80), Mass. Bar Assn., Am. Soc. Hosp. Attys., Nat. Health Lawyers, Am. Soc. Law and Medicine (1st v.p. 1975-80, chmn. bd. 1981-84, life mem. award 1981), Soc. Computer Applications to Med. Care (bd. dirs. 1984-85), Internat. Coun. for Global Health Progress (bd. dirs. 1989-95), Phi Kappa Phi. Home: 531 W Washington St Hanson MA 02341-1067 also: 2209 Burgee Ct Reston VA 22091

NORRIS, JOHN HART, lawyer; b. New Bedford, Mass., Aug. 4, 1942; s. Edwin Arter and Harriet Joan (Winter) N.; m. Anne Kiley Monaghan, June 10, 1967; children: Kiley Anne, Amy O'Shea. BA, Ind. U., 1964; JD, U. Mich., 1967. Bar: Mich. 1968, U.S. Ct. Mil. Appeals 1969, U.S. Supreme Ct. 1974, U.S. Ct. Claims 1975, U.S. Tax Ct. 1979. Assoc., then ptnr. Monaghan, Campbell, LoPrete, McDonald and Norris, 1970-83; of counsel Dickinson, Wright, Moon, Van Dusen & Freeman, 1983-84, ptnr.1985—; natural gas law counsel to claims mediator Columbia Gas Transmission Corp.; chpt. 11 bankruptcy proceedings in Wilmington, Del. Bankruptcy Ct., 1992—; bd. dirs. Prime Securities Corp., Ray M. Whyte Co., Ward-Williston Drilling Co. Mem. Rep. State Fin. Com.; founder, co-chmn. Rep. majority club; bd. trustees Boys and Girls Clubs of Southeastern Mich., 1979—, Mich. Wildlife Habitat Found., Mercy Coll., Detroit, Detroit Hist. Soc., 1984—; bd. trustees, bd. dirs. African Wildlife Found.; trustee and 1st vice chmn. Salk Inst. With M.I., U.S. Army, 1968-70. Recipient numerous civic and non-profit assn. awards. Fellow Mich. State Bar Found.; mem. ABA (litigation and natural resources sects.), Mich. Oil and Gas Assn. (legal and legis. com.), State Bar Mich. (chmn. environ. law sect. 1982-83, probate and trust law sect., energy conservation task force, oil and gas com.), Oakland County Bar Assn., Detroit Bar Assn. (pub. adv. com.), Am. Arbitration Assn., Fin. and Estate Planning Council of Detroit, Def. Orientation Conf. Assn., Detroit Zool. Soc., Blue Key Nat. Hon. Fraternity, Phi Delta Phi. Roman Catholic. Clubs: Bloomfield Hills Country; Thomas M. Cooley, Detroit Athletic, Economic (Detroit); Hundred, Prismatic, Turtle Lake, Yondotega. Contbr. articles to profl jours. Home: 1325 Buckingham Ave Birmingham MI 48009-5881 Office: Dickinson Wright 525 N Woodward Ave Bloomfield Hills MI 48304-2971

NORRIS, JOHN WINDSOR, JR., manufacturing company executive; b. Marshalltown, Iowa, Feb. 10, 1936; s. John Windsor Norris and Mary Merrill Margerin; m. Terry Reibsamen, Dec. 26, 1956; children: John Windsor III, Julie, Jeffrey. B.S. in Bus. Adminstrn, M.I.T., 1960. With Lennox Industries Inc., Dallas, 1960—, sr. v.p., 1975-77; pres. Lennox Industries Inc., 1977-80, past pres., chief exec. officer, 1980—, dir.; past pres., chief exec. officer Lennox Internat., Dallas, now chmn. bd., CEO; dir. Central Life Assurance Co., Des Moines. Chmn. parents div., mem. ann. gifts council Tex. Christian U. Mem. ARI (dir. at large, vice chmn. cert. programs and policy com., vice chmn. communications com.), GAMA (chmn. furnace div. 1978-79, chmn. bd. 1980). Club: Bent Tree Country (Dallas). Office: Lennox Industries Inc PO Box 799900 Dallas TX 75379*

NORRIS, KARL HOWARD, optics scientist, agricultural engineer; b. Glen Richey, Pa., May 23, 1921; married, 1948; 2 children. BS, Pa. State U., 1942. Radio engr. Airplane & Marine Instruments Co., 1945-46; electronic engr. U. Chgo., 1946-49; lab. dir. Instrumentation Rsch. Lab., Agrl. Rsch. Svc., USDA, 1950-77; chief instrument rsch. lab. Sci. & Edn. Adminstr., 1977-88; retired. Recipient McCormick Gold medal Am. Soc. Agrl. Engrs., 1974; Recipient Alexander von Humboldt award, 1978, Maurice F. Hasler award Soc. Applied Spectroscopy, 1991. Mem. Nat. Acad. Engrs., Am. Soc. Agrl. Engrs., Soc. Applied Spectros. Achievements include research in instrumentation for the measurement of quality factors of agricultural products. Office: 11204 Montgomery Rd Beltsville MD 20705-2820

NORRIS, KATHARINE EILEEN, communications professional, educator; b. Norwalk, Calif., Feb. 2, 1960; d. Curtis Bird and Eileen Patricia N. BA, Salem State Coll., 1982; MA, Brown U., 1987. Feature writer The Enterprise newspaper, Brockton, Mass., 1984, 87-88; editor Assoc. Newspapers, Stoughton, Mass., 1987-88, The Mansfield (Mass.) News, 1988-89; coll. instr. Bristol C.C., Fall River, Mass., 1989—, Mt. Ida Coll., Newton Centre, Mass., 1990-95, Bridgewater (Mass.) State Coll., 1991—; radio talk host WPEP, Taunton, Mass., 1991—; dir. pub. rels. Zeiterion Theatre, New Bedford, Mass., 1995—. Asst. editor: The Guide for Students and Parents to 101 of the Best Values in America's Colleges and Universities, 1993. Active Big Bros./Big Sisters. Mem. Nathaniel Hawthorne Soc. Avocations: study of czarist Russia, collector of old New Eng. post cards.

NORRIS, LOIS ANN, elementary school educator; b. Detroit, May 13, 1937; d. Joseph Peter and Marguerite Iola (Gourley) Giroux; m. Max Norris, Feb. 9, 1962 (div. 1981); children: John Henry, Jeanne Marie, Joseph Peter. BS in Social Sci., Ea. Mich. U., 1960, MA, 1960; cert. adminstr., Calif. State U., Bakersfield, 1983. Kindergarten tchr. Norwalk-LaMirada Unified Sch. Dist., 1960-62; tchr. various grades Rialto Unified Sch. Dist., 1962-66; kindergarten tchr. Inyokern (Calif.) Sch., 1969-82; 1st grade tchr. Vieweg Basic Sch, 1982-92, kindergarten tchr., 1992-96; retired, 1996; head tchr. Sierra Sands Elem. Summer Sch.; adminstrv. intern Sierra Sands Adult Sch., master tchr., head tchr., counselor. Ofcl. scorekeeper, team mother, snack bar coord. China Lake Little League; team mother, statistician Indian Wells Valley Youth Football; bd. mem. PTA; pres. Sch. Site Coun.; treas. Inyokern Parents Club; run coord. City of Hope; timekeeper, coord. Jr. Olympics; mem. planning com. Sunshine Festival; active Burros Booster Club. Recipient Hon. Svc. award PTA, 1994. Mem. NEA, Calif. Tchrs. Assn., Desert Area Tchrs. Assn., Assn. Calif. Sch. Adminstrs., Inyokern C. of C. (sec.), Am. Motorcycle Assn., NRA, Bakersfield Coll. Diamond Club. Republican. LDS Ch. Avocations: swimming, physical fitness, music, American history. Home: PO Box 163 201 N Brown Rd Inyokern CA 93527

NORRIS, MARTIN JOSEPH, lawyer; b. N.Y.C., Mar. 23, 1907; s. Louis and Esther (Wohlgemuth) Knaris; m. Helen Stella Hecht, June 5, 1930; 1 child, Barbara. LL.B., Bklyn. Law Sch., 1930. Bar: N.Y. 1932. Pvt. practice law N.Y.C., 1932-35; atty. U.S. Shipping Bd. Bur., Dept. Commerce, Washington, 1935-36, U.S. Maritime Commn., Washington and N.Y.C., 1936-42, War Shipping Adminstrn., N.Y.C., 1945-50; admiralty trial atty. admiralty and shipping sect. Dept. Justice, N.Y.C., 1950-56; adminstrv. law judge U.S. Coast Guard, N.Y.C., 1956-70; lectr. Sch. for World Trade, N.Y.C., Practicing Law Inst., N.Y.C., Lawyers Sq. Club, N.Y.C., U.S. Merchant Marine Acad., N.Y. State Maritime Coll.; cons. maritime law, shipping. Author: Your Boat and the Law, 1965, The Law of Seamen, 3 vols., 4th edit., 1985, The Law of Maritime Personal Injuries, 2 vols., 4th edit., 1990, The Law of Salvage, 1990; contbr. articles in field to legal jours. Served to capt. U.S. Army, 1942-45. Mem. Am. Soc. Writers on Legal Subjects. Jewish.

NORRIS, MELVIN, lawyer; b. Cambridge, Mass., Aug. 17, 1931. BA, Northeastern U., Boston, 1954; JD, Boston Coll., 1959. Bar: Mass. 1959, U.S. Supreme Ct. 1965. Atty. FTC, Boston, 1960-62; pvt. practice Boston, Boston, 1962-76; ptnr. Norris, Kozody, Krasnoo & Fong, Boston, 1976-90, Norris, Kozody & Fong, Boston, 1991-96; pvt. practice Newton, Mass., 1997—. Bd. editors Mass. Lawyers Weekly, 1984-93. Vice-chmn. Newton Crime Commn., 1966-67; mem. Newton Bldg. Code Revision Com., 1972-73; chmn. bd. dirs., pres. Waterville Estates Assn., Campton, N.H., 1992-94. With USCG, 1954-56. Mem. Fed. Bar Assn. (pres. Boston chpt. 1977-78, v.p. 1st circuit 1978—, exec. com. 1982-83, Cert. Appreciation 1996), Mass. Bar Assn. Address: 220 Boylston St Chestnut Hill MA 02167-2005

NORRIS, RICHARD ANTHONY, accountant; b. Birmingham, Eng., July 6, 1943; s. Albert Edward and Audrey (Rowley) N.; m. Geri M., Jan. 20, 1947; 1 child, Karen Louise. BA, U. Leeds, York, Eng., 1966. Chartered acct., Can. Auditor Price Waterhouse & Co., Bristol, Eng., 1966-70; mgr. Price Waterhouse & Co., Montreal, Que., Can., 1970-78; from mgr. corp. acctg. to controller Can. Pacific Enterprises, Montreal and Calgary, Alta., Can., 1978-85; v.p. fin. U.S. Ops. Laidlaw Waste Systems Inc., North Richland Hills, Tex., 1986-96; exec. v.p., CFO Thermo-Serv Inc., Dallas, 1997—. Home: 2401 Hillside Ct Southlake TX 76092-8793

NORRIS, RICHARD PATRICK, museum director, history educator; b. Galveston, Tex., May 21, 1944; s. William Gerard and Iris Elsa (Allington) N.; m. Therese Louise Aalid, July 26, 1974; children: William Gerard, John Patrick. BA, Ohio State U., 1966; MA, SUNY, Binghamton, 1968; PhD, U. Minn., 1976. Instr. U. Minn., Mpls., 1970-76; lectr. U. Md., Europe/Asia, 1976-78; dir. Chippewa Valley Mus., Eau Claire, Wis., 1978-80, Kalamazoo Valley Mus., 1985—; curator of history Mus. Sci. & Hist., Fort Worth, 1980-85; lectr. Tex. Christian U., Fort Worth, 1981-85; cons. Am. Assn. Mus., Washington, 1979—, NEH, 1989; grant reviewer Inst. Mus. Svcs., Washington, 1984—, Mich. Coun. Humanities, Lansing, 1985—; adj. prof. Western Mich. U., Kalamazoo, 1986—. Author: History by Design, 1984; book reviewer Mus. News, History News; contbr. articles to profl. jours. Dir. Downtown Kalamazoo Inc., 1995—, dir. at large Arts Coun. Greater Kalamazoo, 1987-93; chmn. internat. com. Ft. Worth 150 Com., 1984. 1st lt. U.S. Army, 1968-70. Mem. Am. Assn. Mus., Am. Assn. State and Local Hist., Internat. Coun. Mus., Midwest Mus. Conf., Tex. Assn. Mus., Rotary (dir. Kalamazoo club 1991-93). Democrat. Roman Catholic. Office: Kalamazoo Valley Museum PO Box 4070 230 N Rose St Kalamazoo MI 49003-4070

NORRIS, ROBERT MATHESON, geologist; b. Los Angeles, Apr. 24, 1921; s. Robert DeWitt and Jessie (Matheson) N.; m. Virginia Grace Oakley, Jan. 5, 1952; children—Donald Oakley, James Matheson, Elizabeth Anne. A.B., UCLA, 1943, M.A., 1949; Ph.D. Scripps Inst. Oceanography, U. Calif., San Diego, 1951. Teaching asst. UCLA, 1946-49; asso. marine geology Scripps Inst. Oceanography, 1951-52; mem. faculty U. Calif., Santa Barbara, 1952—; prof. geology U. Calif., 1968-86, prof. emeritus, 1986—; also dir. Channel Islands Field Sta., 1970-75. Contbr. articles profl. jours. Served with USNR, 1944-46. Fulbright scholar, 1961-62. Mem. Geol. Soc. Am., Geol. Soc. N.Z., Nat. Assn. Geology Tchrs. (pres. 1988-89), Am. Assn. Petroleum Geologists, Soc. Econ. Paleontologists and Mineralogists, Sigma Xi, Phi Kappa Sigma, Phi Delta Kappa. Congregationalist. Address: 4424 Nueces Dr Santa Barbara CA 93110-2006

NORRIS, ROBERT WHEELER, lawyer, military officer; b. Birmingham, Ala., May 22, 1932; s. Hubert Lee and Georgia Irene (Parker) N.; m. Martha Katherine Cummins, Feb. 19, 1955; children—Lisha Katherine Norris Utt, Nathan Robert. B.A. in Bus. Adminstrn., U. Ala., 1954, LL.B., 1955; LL.M., George Washington U., 1979; postgrad., Air Command & Staff Coll., 1968, Nat. War Coll., 1975. Commd. 2d lt. USAF, advanced through grades to maj. gen.; dep. judge advocate gen. USAF, Washington, 1983-85, judge advocate gen., 1985-88; gen. counsel Ala. Bar Assn., Montgomery, 1988-95; ptnr. London & Yancey, Birmingham, Ala., 1995—. Decorated D.S.M., Legion of Merit, Meritorious Svc. medal. Mem. ABA. Methodist. Office: London & Yancey 2001 Park Pl Ste 1000 Birmingham AL 35203-2770

NORRIS, TERRY, professional boxer; b. Campo, Calif., June 17, 1967. WBC super welterweight champion, 1990; lost to Simon Brown to give up WBC Super Welterweight champion, 1993; regained WBC Super Welterweight champion, 1994; lost to Luis Santana giving up WBC Super Welterweight champion, 1994; regained WBC Super Welterweight championship, 1995, IBF Jr. Middleweight champion, 1995. Office: Internat Boxing Fedn 134 Evergreen Pl Ste 9 East Orange NJ 07018-2012

NORRIS, WILLIAM ALBERT, federal judge; b. Turtle Creek, Pa., Aug. 30, 1927; s. George and Florence (Clive) N.; m. Merry Wright, Nov. 23, 1974; children: Barbara, Donald, Kim, Alison; m. Jane Jelenko. Student, U. Wis., 1945; B.A., Princeton U., 1951; J.D., Stanford U., 1954. Bar: Calif. and D.C. 1955. Assoc. firm Northcutt Ely, Washington, 1954-55; law clk. to Justice William O. Douglas U.S. Supreme Ct., Washington, 1955-56; sr. mem. firm Tuttle & Taylor, Inc., L.A., 1956-80; judge U.S. Ct. Appeals (9th cir.), L.A., 1980-94, sr. judge, 1994—; spl. counsel Pres.' Kennedy's Com. on Airlines Controversy, 1961; mem., v.p. Calif. State Bd. Edn., 1961-67. Trustee Calif. State Colls., 1967-72; pres. L.A. Bd. Police Commrs., 1973-74; Democratic nominee for atty. gen. State of Calif., 1974; founding pres. bd. trustees Mus. Contemporary Art, L.A., 1979—; trustee Craft and Folk Art Mus., 1979—. With USN, 1945-47. Home: 1473 Oriole Dr West Hollywood CA 90069-1155 Office: US Ct Appeals 9th Cir 312 N Spring St Los Angeles CA 90012-4701*

NORSTRAND, IRIS FLETCHER, psychiatrist, neurologist, educator; b. Bklyn., Nov. 21, 1915; d. Matthew Emerson and Violet Marie (Anderson) Fletcher; m. Severin Anton Norstrand, May 20, 1941; children: Virginia Helene Norstrand Villano, Thomas Fletcher, Lucille Joyce. BA, Bklyn. Coll., 1937, MA, 1965, PhD, 1972; MD, L.I. Coll. Medicine, 1941. Diplomate Am. Bd. Psychiatry and Neurology with supplementary cert. in geriatric psychiatry. Med. intern Montefiore Hosp., Bronx, N.Y., 1941-42; asst. resident in neurology N.Y. Neurol. Inst.-Columbia-Presbyn. Med. Ctr., N.Y.C., 1944-45; pvt. practice Bklyn., 1947-52; resident in psychiatry Bklyn. VA Med. Ctr., 1952-54, resident in neurology, 1954-55, staff neurologist, 1955-81, asst. chief neurol. svc., 1981-91, staff psychiatrist, 1991-95; neurol. cons. Indsl. Home for Blind, Bklyn., 1948-51; clin. prof. neurology SUNY Health Sci. Ctr., Bklyn., 1981—; attending neurologist Kings County Hosp., Bklyn., State U. Hosp., Bklyn. Contbr. articles to med. jours. Recipient spl. plaque Mil. Order Purple Heart, 1986, Spl. Achievement award PhD Alumni Assn. of CUNY, 1993, Lifetime Achievement award Bklyn. Coll., 1995, and others. Fellow Am. Psychiat. Assn., Am. Acad. Neurology, Internat. Soc. Neurochemistry, Am. Assn. U. Profs. Neurology, Am. Med. EEG Soc. (pres. 1987-88), Nat. Assn. VA Physicians (pres. 1989-91, James O'Connor award 1987), N.Y. Acad. Scis., Sigma Xi. Democrat. Presbyterian. Avocations: writing, piano, travel, reading. Home: 7624 10th Ave Brooklyn NY 11228

NORTH, ANITA, secondary education educator; b. Chgo., Apr. 21, 1963; d. William Denson and Carol (Linden) N. BA, Ind. U., 1985; MS in Edn., Northwestern U., 1987. Cert. tchr., Ill. High sch. social studies and English tchr. Lake Park High Sch., Roselle, Ill., 1987-89; high sch. social studies tchr. West Leyden High Sch., Northlake, Ill., 1989—; exch. program coord. West Leyden High Sch., 1989—, head coach boys' tennis team, 1989—, asst. coach girls' tennis team, 1994—, asst. speech coach, 1992-93. Humanities fellow Nat. Coun. Humanities, 1995; recipient Fern Fine Tchg. award West Leyden H.S., 1992. Mem. AAUW, Nat. Coun. for Social Studies, Ill. Coun. for Social Studies, Orgn. Am. Historians, Ill. Tennis Coaches Assn., Phi Delta Kappa. Christian. Avocations: wilderness backpacking, tennis, orienteering, gardening, antique books and maps.

NORTH, DANIEL WARNER, consulting analyst; b. N.Y.C., Mar. 12, 1941; s. James Dennis and Margaret P. North; m. Diane M. Tarantino, Nov. 26, 1978 (div. May 27, 1993); 1 child, Evan Armstrong; m. Cheryl Jeanne Bonham, May 27, 1993. BS, Yale U., 1962; MS, Stanford U., 1964, PhD, 1970. Analyst SRI Internat., Menlo Park, Calif., 1967-74, asst. dir. decision analysis dept., 1974-77; sr., v.p. Decision Focus Inc., Mountain View, Calif., 1977—; consulting prof. Dept. of Eng.-Econ. Sys., Stanford U., 1977—; mem. sci. adv. bd. EPA, Washington, 1978—, gov.'s sci. adv. panel Calif. Propostion 65, 1987-89, Nuc. Waste Tech. Review Bd., 1989-94. Mem. Soc. Risk Analysis, (pres. 1991-92), Inst. Ops. Rsch. Mgmt. Sci., Sigma Xi. Office: Decision Focus Inc 650 Castro St Ste 300 Mountain View CA 94041-2057

NORTH, DAVID MORGAN, editor; b. Oswego, N.Y., Dec. 31, 1934; s. Joseph Irving and Mable Marie (Hants) N.; m. Victoria K. King, Oct. 7, 1967; children: Erik Morgan, Tristan Morgan, Kendra Victoria. BS, U.S. Naval Acad., 1957; MS in Comm., Rensselaer Poly. Inst., 1965. Commd. ens. USN, 1957, advanced through grades to lt. comdr., resigned, 1967; transport editor Aviation Week, Washington, 1976-79, bus. flight editor, 1979-86, Washington bur. chief, 1987-88, mng. editor, 1988-95, editor-in-chief, 1995—. Avocations: flying, sailing, skiing. Office: Aviation Week 1200 G St NW Ste 922 Washington DC 20005-3814

NORTH, DORIS GRIFFIN, retired physician, educator; b. Washington, Nov. 30, 1916; d. Edward Lawrence and Ruth Gladys (Spray) Griffin; m. Victor North, Nov. 2, 1940 (dec. 1984); children: James, Daniel, Frederick. BA, U. Kans., 1938, MT, 1939; MD, Kans. U., 1947. Med. tech. Ralph G. Ball, M.D., Manhattan, Kans., 1939-40, St. Francis Hosp., Pitts., 1940-41, John Minor, M.D., Washington, 1941-43; intern Wesly Hosp., Wichita, Kans., 1947-48; resident in pediat. and internal medicine Sedgwick Hosp., Wichita, 1948-49; pvt. practice family physician Wichita, Kans., 1951-96; ret., 1996; clin. asst. prof. medicine Kans. State U. Sch. Medicine, Wichita, 1974-96. Mem. AMA, Am. Acad. Family Practice, Kans. Med. Soc., Med. Soc. Sedgwick County, Phi Beta Kappa, Alpha Omega Alpha. Home: 1000 S Woodlawn St Apt 408 Wichita KS 67218-3641

NORTH, DOUGLASS CECIL, economist, educator; b. Cambridge, Mass., Nov. 5, 1920; s. Henry Emerson and Edith (Saitta) N.; m. Elisabeth Willard Case, Sept. 28, 1972; children by previous marriage: Douglass Alan, Christopher, Malcolm Peter. B.A., U. Calif., Berkeley, 1942, Ph.D., 1952; D Rer. Pol. (hon.), U. of Cologne, Federal Republic of Germany, 1988, U. Zurich, Switzerland, 1993, Stockholm Sch. of Econs., Sweden, 1994, Prague Sch. Econs., 1995. Asst. prof. econs. U. Wash., 1950-56, assoc. prof., 1957-60, prof., 1960-83, prof. emeritus, 1983—, chmn. dept., 1967-79; dir. Inst. Econ. Research, 1960-66, Nat. Bur. Econ. Research, 1967-87; Luce prof. law and liberty, prof. econs. Washington U., St. Louis, 1983—; Pitt prof. Am. history and instns. Cambridge U., 1981-82; fellow Ctr. for Advanced Study on Behavioral Scis., 1987-88. Author: The Economic Growth of the U.S. 1790-1860, 1961, Growth and Welfare in the American Past, 1966, (with L. Davis) Institutional Change and American Economic Growth, 1971, (with R. Miller) The Economics of Public Issues, 1971, 74, 76, 78, 80, (with R. Thomas) The Rise of the Western World, 1973, Structure and Change in Economic History, 1981, Institutions, Institutional Change and Economic Performance, 1990. Guggenheim fellow, 1972-73; grantee Social Sci. Rsch. Coun., 1962, Rockefeller Found., 1960-63, Ford Found., 1961, 66, NSF, 1967-73, Bradley Found., 1986—. Recipient Nobel Prize in Economic Science, Nobel Foundation, 1993. Fellow Am. Acad. Arts and Scis.; mem. Am. Econ. Assn., Econ. History Assn., The British Acad. (corr. mem.). Office: Washington U Dept Econs Campus Box 1208 Saint Louis MO 63130-1208

NORTH, GERALD DAVID WILLIAM, lawyer; b. N.Y.C., Feb. 15, 1951; s. David North and Isabella (Leonard) Cadgene; m. Jeanne Curtis, Nov. 1970 (div. 1977); m. Carmela Benvenuto, Feb. 21, 1980; 1 child, David II. BA honors and distinction, U. Iowa, 1972, JD high distinction, 1975; postgrad., Oxford (Eng.) U., 1975-76. Bar: Iowa 1975, Ill. 1977, U.S. Dist. Ct. (no. dist.) Ill. 1977, U.S. Supreme Ct. 1982, U.S. Dist. Ct. (no. dist. trial bar) Ill. 1983, U.S. Ct. Appeals (fed. cir.) 1984, Ariz. 1985, U.S. Dist. Ct. Ariz. 1985, U.S. Ct. Appeals (9th cir.) 1985. Assoc. Sidley & Austin, Chgo., 1976-81; ptnr. Brace & North, Chgo., 1981-82; v.p., gen. counsel Trans-Global Group, Chgo., 1983-84; of counsel McCabe, Polese, Pietzsch, Phoenix, 1984-87; founder, shareholder North & Barron, Phoenix, 1987-92; sr. shareholder North & Vaira, Phila., Phoenix, 1992-93; chmn. bd. Fibrin Techs., Inc., Wilmington, Del., 1993—; prin. counsel MinTec, Inc., Freeport, Bahamas, 1994-96; dir. Fenders Auto Leasing Inc., Vancouver, Can., 1996—. Contbg. author: European Investment in U.S. and Canadian Real Estate, 1990, Directory of Asian High Tech Companies in the U.S., 1991. Fellow Ariz. Bar Found.; mem. ABA (antitrust, litigation, patent trademark and copyright sects.), Am. Intellectual Property Law Assn., Assn. Trial Lawyers Am., Fed. Cir. Bar Assn., Order of Coif, Monte Carlo Country Club, Fisher Island Club, Phi Beta Kappa, Omicron Delta Kappa. Avocations: skiing, sailing, tennis. Address: PO Box 80127 Phoenix AZ 85060-0127

NORTH, HELEN FLORENCE, classicist, educator; b. Utica, N.Y.; d. James H. and Catherine (Debbold) N. A.B., Cornell U., 1942, M.A., 1943, Ph.D., 1945; LL.D. (hon.), Rosary Coll., 1982; D.Litt. (hon.), Trinity Coll., Dublin, 1984; L.H.D. (hon.), La Salle U., 1985, Yale U., 1986. Instr. classical lang. Rosary Coll., River Forest, Ill., 1946-48; mem. faculty Swarthmore Coll., 1948-91, prof. classics, 1961-91, chmn. dept., 1959-91, emerita, 1991—, Centennial prof. classics, 1966-73, 78-91, Kenan prof., 1973-78; vis. asst. prof. Cornell U., summer 1952—; vis. assoc. prof. Barnard Coll., 1954-55; vis. prof. LaSalle Coll., Phila., 1965, Am. Sch. Classical Studies, Athens, 1975, 87; Blegen disting. vis. rsch. prof. Vassar Coll., 1979. Author: Sophrosyne: Self-Knowledge and Self-Restraint in Greek Literature, 1966, From Myth to Icon: Reflections of Greek Ethical Doctrine in Literature and Art, 1979; translator: John Milton's Second Defense of the English People, 1966; editor: Interpretations of Plato: A Swarthmore Symposium, 1977; co-editor: Of Eloquence, 1970; editor: Jour. History of Ideas; mem. editorial bd.: Catalogus Translationum et Commentariorum, 1979—. Bd. dirs. Am. Coun. Learned Socs., 1977-85; chmn. bd. trustees LaSalle U., 1991-93; trustee King's Coll., Am. Acad. in Rome; chmn. com. on Classical Sch. Recipient Harbison prize Danforth Found., 1969; named Distinguished Daughter of Pa., 1989, del. of Am. Philological Assn. to Am. Coun. Learned Studies, 1991-95 ; grantee Am. Council Learned Socs., 1943-45, 73, fellow, 1971-72, 87-88; Mary Isabel Sibley fellow Phi Beta Kappa Found., 1945-46, Ford Fund Advancement Edn. fellow, also Fulbright fellow Rome, 1953-54; grantee Danforth Found., 1962, Lindbach Found., 1966; fellow AAUW, 1963-64; NEH sr. fellow, 1967-68; NEH Coll. Tchrs. fellow, 1983-84; Martin classical lectr. Oberlin Coll., 1972; Guggenheim fellow, 1958-59, 75-76; Centennial medal Am. Acad. Rome, 1995. Mem. Am. Philol. Assn. (dir. 1968—, pres. 1976—, Charles J. Goodwin award of merit 1969, Disting. Svc. medal 1996), Classical Assn. Atlantic States, Catholic Commn. Intellectual and Cultural Affairs (chmn. 1968-69), Am. Acad. Arts and Scis., Am. Philos. Soc., Soc. Religion Higher Edn., Phi Beta Kappa (mem. bd. vis. scholars 1975-76, senate 1991—), Phi Kappa Phi. Home: 604 Ogden Ave Swarthmore PA 19081-1131

NORTH, JOHN ADNA, JR., accountant, real estate appraiser; b. Atlanta, Oct. 20, 1944; s. John Adna and Julia Osborn (Napier) N.; m. Alexa Ruth Bryans, Mar. 20, 1976; 1 child, William Bryans. BA in Econs., U. Ga., 1966; M of Profl. Accountancy, Ga. State U., 1977, M of Taxation, 1980; JD, Woodrow Wilson Coll. Law, Atlanta, 1980. CPA, Ga.; cert. real estate appraiser. Trust adminstr. Trust Co. Bank, Atlanta, 1968-71; fin. produce sales exec. Dean Witter Reynolds Inc., Atlanta, 1971-73; with acctg. firm and in pvt. practice Atlanta, 1973-80; multi-state tax, staff, gen. tax counsel Texaco Inc., White Plains, N.Y., 1980-87; mgr. multi-state tax Price Waterhouse, Atlanta, 1987-88; dir. various corps. MacMillan Bloedel (USA) Inc., Wilmington, Del., 1988-91; pres. Cobb Svc. Assocs. Inc., Marietta, Ga., 1991—; chmn. supervisory com. Texaco Fed. Credit Union, Atlanta, 1980-88; bd. dirs., treas. Atlanta Credit Union League, 1986-87; v.p. The Planning Forum, Atlanta, 1984-85. Alumni trustee The Lovett Sch., Atlanta, 1985-89. Capt. U.S. Army, 1966-68. Mem. Ga. Soc. CPAs, Nat. Soc. Scabbard and Blade, Mil. Order of Stars and Bars, Beta Alpha Psi. Anglican. Avocations: personal computers, building custom fly fishing rods, genealogy. Home: 3242 Old Mill Trce Marietta GA 30067-5119

NORTH, JOHN E., JR., lawyer; b. Omaha, Feb. 26, 1952; s. John E. and Joyce (Zimmerman) N.; m. Pamela K. Black, Nov. 22, 1978; children: Stuart, Jeremy, Katherine, Jacqueline, Rebecca. BSBA, Univ. Nebr., 1974; JD, Creighton Univ., Nebr., 1977. Bar: Nebr. 1977, U.S. Dist Ct. Nebr. 1977, U.S. Ct. Appeals (8th cir.) Nebr. 1979, U.S. Tax Ct. Nebr. 1980, U.S. Dist Ct. (no. dist.) Texas, 1993. Assoc. McGrath, North, Dwyer, O'Leary & Martin, Omaha, 1977-78, Lathrop, Albright & Swenson, Omaha, 1978-80; ptnr. Fromkin, Herzog, Jabenis & North, Omaha, 1980-84; prin. North & Black, P.C., Omaha, 1984-89, McGrath, North, Mullin & Kratz, P.C., Omaha, 1989—. Mem. ABA, Nebraska State Bar Assn., Omaha Bar Assn., Nebraska Assn. Trial Attys. Office: McGrath North Mullin & Kratz 222 S 15th St Ste 1400 Omaha NE 68102-1632

NORTH, MARJORIE MARY, columnist; b. Mt. Clemens, Mich., Oct. 21, 1945; d. Robert Haller and Hilla Beryl (Willard) Wright; m. William B. Hirons; children: Laura, Christina, Angela. Student, Wayne State U., 1963-65. Features editor Elizabeth City (N.C.) Daily Advance, 1966-69; news/mng. editor Brandon (Fla.) News, 1977-78; city editor Leesburg (Fla.) Daily Comml., 1978-79; metro editor Sarasota (Fla.) Herald Tribune, 1979-80, Fla. West editor, 1980-85, daily columnist, 1985—. Author: Sarasota: A City For All Seasons, 1994, (play) With the Best Intentions, 1994. Recipient Layout, Creativity and Overall Publ. awards Fla. Press Assn., numerous comty. awards and citations; winner Fla. shorts competition Fla. Studio Theater New Play Festival, 1994; Paul Harris fellow, 1994. Avocations: sailing, tennis, entertaining, theater. Office: Sarasota Herald-Tribune PO Box 1719 Sarasota FL 34230-1719

NORTH, PHIL RECORD, retired banker; b. Fort Worth, July 6, 1918; s. James M. and Lottie R. North; m. Janis Harris, July 28, 1944; children: Phillip Kevin (dec.), Kerry Lawrence, Mairin Kathleen, Deirdre Aine. A.B., U. Notre Dame, 1939. With Fort Worth Star Telegram, 1937-62, exec. editor, 1956-62, asst. gen. mgr., 1959-62; v.p. Carter Publs., Inc., 1949-62; with Tandy Corp., Fort Worth, 1966-82; chief exec. officer Tandy Corp., 1978-81, pres., 1978-81, chmn. bd., 1978-82; chmn. bd. 1st City Nat. Bank, Ft. Worth, 1982-86; chmn. bd. dirs. JMJ Fin. Corp., Ft. Worth, CXE, inc., Plano, Tex., Haeco II, Inc., Hillsboro, Ohio; bd. dirs. Del Norte Tech., Euless, Tex. Served to maj. AUS, 1940-46. Decorated Bronze Star. Mem. Ft. Worth Club, River Crest Club, Shady Oaks Club, Rockport Country Club, Rockport Yacht Club, Corpus Christi Yacht Club. Roman Catholic.

NORTH, RICHARD BOYDSTON, neurological surgery educator; b. Summit, N.J., Nov. 28, 1948; s. William Borsum and Geraldine H. (Flitcraft) N.; m. Catherine Basgal Anderson, Nov. 15, 1983; children: Richard B. Jr., Jacqueline R. Student, Harvard U., 1966-68; BA, Johns Hopkins U., 1970, MD, 1973. Diplomate Am. Bd. Neurol. Surgery. Fellow in biomed. engring. Johns Hopkins U., Balt., 1973-78; intern in surgery Duke U. Med. Ctr., Durham, N.C., 1978-79; resident, fellow in neurosurgery Johns Hopkins U., Balt., 1979-83, from instr. to asst. prof. Neurosurgery, 1983-91, assoc. prof. Neurosurgery, 1991-97, prof. neurosurgery, anesthesiology & critical care medicine, 1997—, dir. div. Functional Neurosurgery, co-dir. spine svc., 1991—; cons. Applied Physics Lab. Johns Hopkins U., Balt., 1974-78. Contbr. articles to profl. jours. Mem. AMA, Assn. for Advancement of Med. Instrumentation (co-chair Implanted Neurosimulator subcom.), Am. Assn. Neurol. Surgeons (chmn. sect. on pain), Congress of Neurol. Surgeons, Am. Pain Soc., Internat. Assn. for Study of Pain, Am. Soc. Functional and Stereotactic Neurosurgery, World Soc. Functional and Stereotactic Neurosurgery. Office: Johns Hopkins Hosp Dept Neurosurg Meyer 7-113 600 N Wolfe St Baltimore MD 21205-2110

NORTH, ROBERT CARVER, political science educator; b. Walton, N.Y., Nov. 17, 1914; s. Arthur W. and Irene (Davenport) N.; m. Dorothy Anderson, Mar. 12, 1977; children by previous marriage: Woesha Kristina, Mary Davenport, Elizabeth Katrynka, Robert Cloud, Renya Catarina. A.B., Union Coll., 1936; M.A., Stanford U., 1948, Ph.D., 1957. Tchr. English, History Milford (Conn.) Sch., 1939-42; research asst. Hoover Instn., Stanford, Calif., 1948-50, research assoc., 1950-57; assoc. prof. polit. sci. Stanford (Calif.) U., 1957-62, prof., 1962-85, prof. emeritus, 1985—. Author: Revolt in San Marcos, 1941 (Commonwealth Gold medal), Moscow and Chinese Communists, 1952, The World That Could Be, 1976, (with Nazli Choucri) Nations in Conflict, 1975, War, Peace, Survival, 1990, (with Nazli Choucri and Susumu Yamakage) The Challenge of Japan: Before World War II and After, 1992. Served to capt. USAAF, 1942-46. Mem. Am. Polit. Sci. Assn. (Conflicts Processes Sect. Lifetime Achievement award 1993), Internat. Studies Assn. (pres. 1970-71), Internat. Peace-Sci. Assn., Explorers Club. Democrat. Unitarian. Office: Stanford U Dept Polit Sci Stanford CA 94305

NORTH, ROBERT JOHN, biologist; b. Bathurst, Australia, Aug. 22, 1935; s. Herbert John North and Loraine (Grace) Lamrock. BS, Sydney U., Australia, 1958; PhD, Nat. U., Canberra, Australia, 1967; DSc (hon.), SUNY, 1992. Vis. investigator Trudeau Inst., Saranac Lake, N.Y., 1967-70; assoc. mem. Trudeau Inst., 1970-74, mem., 1974-76, dir., 1976—. Mem. editorial bd. Jour. Exptl. Medicine, Infection and Immunity, Cancer Immunology and Immunotherapy; contbr. articles on immunity to infections and cancer to profl. jours. Recipient Friedrich Sasse sci. prize, 1984, rsch. award Soc. of Leukocyte Biology, 1990; grantee NIH, Am. Cancer Soc. Mem. Am. Assn. Immunologists, Reticuloendothelial Soc. (pres. 1983), Transplantation Soc., AAAS, Am. Soc. Microbiologists. Avocation: classical music. Office: Trudeau Inst Inc PO Box 59 Saranac Lake NY 12983-0059

NORTH, STEVEN EDWARD, lawyer; b. Bklyn., Oct. 16, 1941; s. Irving J. and Barbara (Grubman) N.; m. Sue J. Buznitsky, Dec. 24, 1966; children: Jennifer, Samantha. B.A., CCNY, 1963; J.D., Bklyn. Law Sch., 1966; LLM, NYU, 1967. Bar: N.Y. 1967, U.S. Dist. Ct. (so. and ea. dists.) N.Y. 1970, U.S. Supreme Ct., 1971. Asst. dist. atty. homicide bur. N.Y. County Dist. Attys. Office, N.Y.C., 1967-71; spl. asst. atty. gen., bur. chief N.Y. State Atty. Gen.'s Office, N.Y.C., 1972-75; sole practice, N.Y.C., 1975—; mem. adv. com. Ann. Civil Litigation Inst., Practising Law Inst., 1996; chmn. Assn. Bar Subcom. on Investigation into Imposition of Legis. Limits on Awards for Non-Econ. Damages, 1995; mediator U.S. Dist. Ct. (so. dist.) N.Y., 1994—; mem. adv. coms. solo law practice Practising Law Inst., 1991, adv. bd. tort litigation, 1989—; commentator Court TV, Eyewitness News, Talk News TV; vis. faculty Sch. Law NYU, faculty workshop Cardoza Sch. Law. Author: Prevention and Detection of Fraud in Industry, 1973, Deposition Strategy, Law and Forms, vol. 1 (Introduction and Law), vol. 5 (Medical Malpractice), vol. 8 (Personal Injury), 1981, (course handbooks) Trial Mechanics and Discovery, 1985, 86, Medical Malpractice Litigation, 1988, Managing the Multi-Million Dollar Case, 1990, Fundamentals of

Medical Malpractice Litigation, 1991, Damage Update, 1992, 93, 94, 95—, Proving & Defending Damages, 1993, Conducting & Defending Depositions, 1993; author chpts to books; editor Cancer Litigation Bull., 1994—; contbg. editor Law and Order mag.; med.-legal editor Perinatology, 1983; contbr. articles to legal jours.; commentator Eyewitness News, 1994, Court TV, 1994-95, Talk News TV, 1996. Leadership coun. So. Poverty Law Ctr. Mem. ATLA, NOW (benefits com.), U.S. Holocaust Mus. (charter mem.), Am. Bd. Trial Lawyers, Soc. Med. Jurisprudence, Nat. Conf. Christians and Jews (lawyers divsn., annual dinner com.), N.Y. State Bar Assn. (faculty), N.Y. State Trial Lawyers Assn. (bd. dirs. 1990—), Lotos Club, Nat. Eagle Scout Assn., State Trial Lawyers Assn. (bd. dirs. 1990—, seminar faculty chmn. 1993, faculty decisions program 1991—, Law Day dinner com.), N.Y. County Lawyers Assn. (exec. com. med. malpractice sect., exec. com. gen. tort law sect.), Assn. of Bar of City of N.Y. (civil ct. com. 1980-83, legal and continuing edn. com. 1983—, legal referral svc. com., med. malpractice mediator, 1994—, chmn. subcom. on imposition of legislative limits to awards for non-econ. damages), Vol. Lawyers for the Arts, Mensa. Home: 6 Saddle Rock Ter Great Neck NY 11023-1921 Office: 148 E 74th St New York NY 10021-3542

NORTH, WARREN JAMES, government official; b. Winchester, Ill., Apr. 28, 1922; s. Clyde James and Lucille Adele (Bishop) N.; m. Mary Strother; children—James Warren, Mary Kay, Susan Lee, Diane. B.S. in Engring, Purdue U., 1947; M.S., Case Inst. Tech., 1954, Princeton, 1956. Engr. and test pilot NACA, Cleve., 1947-55; asst. chief aerodynamics br. NACA, 1955-59; chief manned satellites NASA, Washington, 1959-62; chief flight crew support div. NASA (Manned Spacecraft Center), Houston, 1962-71; asst. dir. space shuttle NASA (Flight Ops. Directorate), 1972-85; pres. Spalding Edn. Found., Glendale, Ariz., 1986—. Contbr. articles to profl. jours. Served with USAAF, 1943-45. Recipient DeFlorez tng. award, 1966; NASA award for exceptional service, 1968, 69. Mem. Am. Inst. Aero. and Astronautics (asso. fellow 1955), Tau Beta Pi, Pi Tau Sigma. Club: Mason. Home: 6933 W Kimberly Way Glendale AZ 85308-5757 Office: Spalding Edn Found 2814 W Bell Rd Ste 1405 Phoenix AZ 85023-7531

NORTH, WHEELER JAMES, marine ecologist, educator; b. San Francisco, Jan. 2, 1922; s. Wheeler Orrin and Florence Julia (Ross) N.; m. Barbara Alice Best, Apr. 25, 1964; children: Hannah Catherine, Wheeler Orrin. BS in Engring, Calif. Inst. Tech., 1944, BS in Biology, 1949; MS in Oceanography, U. Calif. at San Diego, 1953; Ph.D., 1953. NSF postdoctoral fellow Cambridge (Eng.) U.; Electronics engr. U.S. Navy Electronics Lab., Point Loma, Calif., 1947-48; asst. research biologist Scripps Inst. Oceanography, U. Calif. at San Diego, 1953, Rockefeller postdoctoral fellow, 1955-56; asst. research biologist Inst. Marine Resources Scripps Inst. Oceanography, 1956-63; assoc. prof. Calif. Inst. Tech., Pasadena, 1963-70; prof. Calif. Inst. Tech., 1970-92, prof. emeritus, 1992—; Cons. marine biology U.S. Govt., State of Calif., San Francisco, Los Angeles, San Diego, numerous industries, 1957—; Phi Beta Kappa vis. scholar, 1973-74; mem. Calif. Adv. Commn., 1972-73, Nav. and Ocean Devel. Commn., 1973-76; dir. Marine Biol. Cons. Contbr. articles to profl. jours. Recipient NOGI award Underwater Soc. Am., 1975. Mem. Am. Littoral Soc. (James Duggan award), AAAS, Am. Soc. Limnology and Oceanography, Am. Soc. Zoology, Soc. Gen. Physiology, Calif. Acad. Sci., Fish Protective Assn. (dir.), N.Y. Acad. Sci., Am. Geophys. Union, Smithsonian Instn., Am. San Diego museums, Marine Tech. Soc., Western Soc. Naturalists, Calif. Soc. Profl. Engrs., Am. Zoomalac Soc., Internat. Oceanographic Found., Sigma Xi. Home: 205 Carnation Ave Apt 5 Corona Del Mar CA 92625-2807 Office: Calif Inst Tech Div Engring and Applied Sci Pasadena CA 91125

NORTH, WILLIAM HAVEN, foreign service officer; b. Summit, N.J., Aug. 17, 1926; s. Eric M. and Gladys (Haven) N.; m. Jeanne Foote, Sept. 2, 1950; children: Jeannette Haven, William Ashby, Charles Eric. B.A. with high distinction and honors in History, Wesleyan U., Middletown, Conn., 1949; M.A. In History, Columbia, 1951. Program officer ICA, Ethiopia, 1953-57; then dep. chief program div. ICA (African-European Regional Office), Washington; asst. dir. for program Lagos, Nigeria, AID, until 1965; dir. Ctrl. and Western African affairs AID, Washington, 1966-70, U.S. AID mission to Ghana, 1970-76; dep. asst. adminstr. Africa Bur. AID, 1976-82, spl. asst. Office of the Adminstr., 1982-83, assoc. asst. adminstr. Ctr. Devel. Info. and Evaluation, 1983-89, ret.; pvt. cons. Internat. Devel. for World Bank, 1989—, UN Devel. Program USAID, 1989—; coord. Evaluation of Global Environ. Facility, 1993; fellow Ctr. for Internat. Affairs, Harvard U., 1965-66; chmn. experts group on evaluation Devel. Assistance Commn., OECD, 1985-88; vice-chmn. editl. bd. Fgn. Svc. Jour., 1983-86; mem. adv. panel on evaluation Inter-Am. Devel. Bank, 1993-94; prin. evaluator Internat. Fin. Corp., 1994-95, U.S. AID Africa Program; program dir. U.S. Fgn. Assistance Oral History Program, 1995—. Served with AUS, 1944-46. Recipient Meritorious Svc. award for exemplary achievement in pub. adminstrn., W.A. Jump Honor cert., Superior Honor award for Nigerian Relief Adminstrn., Equal Employment Opportunity award, Disting. Honor award AID, Presdl. Meritorious Svc. medal, Adminstrs. Career Svc. award. Mem. Soc. for Internat. Devel., African Studies Assn., Assn. Diplomatic Studies and Tng., Am. Evaluation Assn., Applachian Mountain Club. Methodist. Home and Office: Internat Development 6748 Brigadoon Dr Bethesda MD 20817-5436

NORTHCUTT, CLARENCE DEWEY, lawyer; b. Guin, Ala., July 7, 1916; s. Walter G. and Nancy E. (Homer) N.; m. Ruth Eleanor Storms, May 25, 1941; children: Gayle Marie (Mrs. John J. Young), John E. A.B., U. Okla., 1939, LL.B., 1938. Bar: Okla. 1938. Pvt. practice Ponca City, 1938—; Mem. bd. visitors U. Okla. Served with AUS, 1941-46. Decorated Bronze Star, Air medal with oak leaf cluster., Order St. John of Jerusalem; named Outstanding Citizen of Ponca City, 1982. Fellow Am. Coll. Trial Lawyers, Am. Coll. Trust and Estate Attys., Am. Bar Found.; mem. Acad. Univ. Fellows, Internat. Soc. Barristers, Am. Bd. Advocacy, Internat. Acad. Trial Lawyers, Okla. Bar Assn. (pres. 1975, bd. govs.), Ponca City C. of C. (past pres.). Democrat. Baptist. Clubs: Mason, Kiwanian. Home: 132 Whitworth Ave Ponca City OK 74601-3438 Office: PO Box 1669 Ponca City OK 74602-1669

NORTHEN, CHARLES SWIFT, III, banker; b. Birmingham, Ala., Jan. 25, 1937; s. Charles Swift and Jennie Hood (Hunt) S.; m. Margaret Carson Robinson, Dec. 27, 1959 (div. 1972); children—Margaret Allen, Charles Swift IV, Bryce Robinson,; m. Betty Jean Taylor, Oct. 3, 1981. B.A. cum laude, Vanderbilt U., 1959, M.A., 1961. Chartered fin. analyst. Mem. staff trust dept. Birmingham Trust Nat. Bank, 1960-64; with First Ala. Bank Birmingham, 1964-80, sr. v.p., trust officer, 1975-80; sr. v.p., trust officer Central Bank of South, Birmingham, 1981-85; exec. v.p. 1st Ala. Bancshares, 1985-95, Corp. Investment Officer, 1993-95; mng. dir. Sterne, Agee & Leach, Inc., Birmingham, 1995—; lectr. So. Trust Sch., Birmingham So. Coll.; pres. First Ala. Investments Inc.; dir. Hubbard Press, Findlay, Ohio. Bd. dirs. United Presbyn. Found., N.Y.C., 1977—; mem. Birmingham Com. Fgn. Relations, 1970—. Mem. Ala. Security Dealers Assn. (pres.), Ala. Soc. Fin. Analysts (pres.), Inst. Chartered Fin. Analysts, Newcomen Soc., SAR. Presbyterian. Clubs: Mountain Brook, The Club. Lodge: Kiwanis. Home: 3024 N Woodridge Rd Birmingham AL 35223-2748 Office: 1901 6th Ave N Ste 2100 Birmingham AL 35203-2618

NORTHINGTON, DAVID KNIGHT, III, research center director, botanist, educator. BA in Biology, U. Tex., 1967, PhD in Systematic Botany, 1971. Prof. Texas Tech U., 1971-84; exec. dir. Nat. Wildflower Rsch. Ctr., Austin, Tex., 1984—; vis. assoc. prof. Southwest Tex. State U., 1985-95; adj prof. dept. botany U. Tex., 1984—; curator E.L. Reed Herbarium Tex. Tech. U.; dir. Tex. Tech. Ctr., Junction. Co-author 3 books; contbr. numerous articles to profl. jours., mags., newspapers, newsletters. Mem. Am. Assn. Bot. Gardens and Arboreta, Am. Soc. Plant Taxonomists, Nature Conservancy. Office: Nat Wildflower Rsch Ctr 4801 La Crosse Ave Austin TX 78739-1702

NORTHRIP, ROBERT EARL, lawyer; b. Sleeper, Mo., May 8, 1939; s. Novel and Jessie (Burch) N.; m. Linda Kay Francis, June 15, 1968; children: Robert E. Jr., William F., Darryl F., David F. BA, Southwest Mo. State, 1960; MA, U. N.C., 1965; JD, U. Mo., 1968. Bar: Mo. 1968, U.S. Dist. Ct. (we. dist.) Mo. 1968, U.S. Ct. Appeals (10th cir.) 1976, U.S. Ct. Appeals (8th cir.) 1980, U.S. Ct. Appeals (9th cir.) 1983, U.S. Ct. Appeals (3d cir.) 1987, U.S. Supreme Ct. 1978. Ptnr. Shook, Hardy & Bacon, Kansas City, Mo., 1968—. Active Nelson Art Gallery, Soc. of Fellows, Kans. City, Mo. 1st lt. US Army, 1963-65. Mem. ABA, Mo. Bar Assn., Lawyers Assn. Kansas City, Mo. Orgn. Def. Lawyers, Kansas City Met. Bar Assn., U. Mo. Alumni Assn. (past pres. Kansas City chpt.), Nat. Soc. Arts and Letters. Republican. Avocations: baseball, football. Office: Shook Hardy & Bacon 1200 Main St Kansas City MO 64105

NORTHROP, EDWARD SKOTTOWE, federal judge; b. Chevy Chase, Md., June 12, 1911; s. Claudian Bellinger and Eleanor Smythe (Grimke) N.; m. Barbara Middleton Burdette, Apr. 22, 1939; children: Edward M., St. Julien (Mrs. Kevin Butler), Peter. LL.B., George Washington U., 1937. Bar: Md. 1937. Village mgr. Chevy Chase, Md., 1934-41; pvt. practice Rockville, Md., Washington, D.C., 1937-61; mem. Md. Senate, 1954-61, chmn. fin. com., joint com. taxation fiscal affairs, majority leader, 1959-61; judge U.S. Dist. Ct. Md., Balt., 1961—; chief judge U.S. Dist. Ct. of Md., Balt., 1970-81; mem. Met. Chief Judges Conf., 1970-81; mem. Jud. Conf. Com. on Adminstrn. of Probation System, 1973-79, Adv. Corrections Council U.S., 1976—, Jud. Panel on Multidist. Litigation, 1979—; judge U.S. Fgn. Intelligence Surveillance Ct. of Rev., 1985—. Trustee Woodberry Forest Sch.; founder Washington Met. Area Coun. Govts. & Mass Transp. Agy. Served to comdr. USNR, 1941-45. Decorated Army commendation medal, Navy commendation medal; recipient Profl. Achievement award George Washington U., 1975, Disting. Citizen award State of Md., 1981, Spl. Merit citation Am. Judicature Soc., 1982. Mem. ABA, Md. Bar Assn. (Disting. Svc. award 1982), D.C. Bar Assn., Montgomery County Bar Assn., Barristers, Washington Ctr. Met. Studies. Democrat. Episcopalian. Club: Chevy Chase (Md.). Lodge: Rotary. Office: US Dist Ct 101 W Lombard St Baltimore MD 21201-2626

NORTHROP, MARY RUTH, mental retardation nurse; b. Washington, June 5, 1919; d. William Arthur and Emma Aurelia (Kaech) N. Diploma in nursing, Georgetown U., 1951, BS in Nursing cum laude, 1952; MS, U. Md., 1958; MA in Anthropology, U. Va., 1970. RN, Va. Asst. dir. nursing U. Md. Hosp., Balt., 1958-60; dir. nursing Georgetown U. Hosp., Washington, 1961; nursing rep. ARC, Pa., 1962; regional dir. nursing ARC, New Eng. and N.Y., 1963-68; pediatric nursing cons. Va. Dept. Health, Richmond, 1971-84; clin. nursing specialist Va. Dept. Mental Health and Mental Retardation, Petersburg, Va., 1988—; adj. asst./assoc. prof. U. Md. Sch. Nursing, Balt., 1958-60. Nursing fellow rsch. HEW, Bethesda, U. Md., Bethesda, 1957-68, nursing fellow anthropology U. Va., 1968-70; recipient Recognition Georgetown U. Alumni Assn., Richmond, 1987. Mem. ANA, Va. Nursing Assn., DAR (chpt. regent 1983-86, dist. treas. 1992-95), Nat. Soc. Women Descendants Ancient and Hon. Arty. Co. (treas. Va. chpt. 1995—), Daus. of Founders and Patriots of Am. (registrar Va. 1997—), Order of First Families of R.I. and Providence Plantation (charter), Sons and Daus. of Colonial and Antebellum Bench and Bar (charter), Mensa, Sigma Theta Tau. Republican. Roman Catholic. Avocations: genealogy, reading, travel. Home: 300 W Franklin St # 401E Richmond VA 23220-4904 Office: Southside Va Tng Ctr PO Box 4110 Petersburg VA 23803-0110

NORTHROP, STUART JOHNSTON, manufacturing company executive; b. New Haven, Oct. 22, 1925; s. Filmer Stuart Cuchow and Christine (Johnston) N.; divorced; children: Christine Daniell, Richard Rockwell Stafford; m. Judith S. Northrop. BA in Physics, Yale U., 1948. Indsl. engr. U.S. Rubber Co., Naugatuck, Conn., 1948-51; head indsl. engring. dept. Am. Cyanamid Co., Wallingford, Conn., 1951-54; mfg. mgr. Linear, Inc., Phila., 1954-57; mgr. quality control and mfg. Westinghouse Electric Co., Pitts., 1957-58; mfg. supt. SKF Industries, Phila., 1958-61; v.p. mfg. Am. Meter Co., Phila., 1961-69; founder, v.p., gen. mgr. water resources div. Singer Co., Phila.; pres., dir. Buffalo Meter Co., Four Layne Cos.; dir. Gen. Filter Co., 1969-72; chmn., CEO Huffy Corp., Dayton, Ohio, 1972-85, chmn. exec. com., 1985-94; bd. dirs. Union Corp., N.Y.C., DSLT, Inc., St. Clair, Mich., Elbit Sys. Am., Ft. Worth. County fin. chmn. George Bush Presdl. campaign, 1980; presdl. appointee Pres.'s Commn. on Ams. Outdoors, 1985-86; chmn. nat. hwy. safety adv. com. Dept. Transp., 1986—; founder, dir. emeritus Recreation Roundtable, Washington. Served with USAAF, 1944-45. Named Chief Exec. Officer of Yr. for leisure industry Wall Street Transcript, 1980. Mem. Del. Valley Investors (past pres.), Interlocutors, Elihu, Am. Bus. Conf. (founding), Fin. Commn. of Funds Am. Future, Boulders Club (Scottsdale), KOA Soc., Delta Kappa Epsilon. Home: 615 Via Mezner #1702 Naples FL 34108 Office: Huffy Corp 7701 Byers Rd Miamisburg OH 45342-3657

NORTHRUP, HERBERT ROOF, economist, business executive; b. Irvington, N.J., Mar. 6, 1918; m. Eleanor Pearson, June 3, 1944; children: James Pearson, Nancy Warren, Jonathan Peter, David Oliver, Philip Wilson. A.B., Duke U., 1939; A.M., Harvard U., 1941, Ph.D., 1942. Instr. econs. Cornell U., 1942-43; sr. hearing officer Nat. War Labor Bd., 1943-45; asst. prof. econs. Columbia U., 1945-49; labor economist Nat. Indsl. Conf. Bd., 1949-52; indsl. relations cons. Ebasco Services, 1952-55; v.p. indsl. relations Penn-Texas Corp., N.Y.C., 1955-58; employee relations mgr. Gen. Electric Co., 1958-61; prof. industry Wharton Sch., U. Pa., Phila., 1961-88; prof. emeritus Wharton Sch. U. Pa., Phila., 1988—; chmn. dept. industry Wharton Sch., U. Pa., 1964-69, dir. indsl. research unit, 1964-88, chmn. Labor Relations Council, 1968-85; cons. and expert witness on manpower, pers. and labor rels. problems for many cos.; arbitrator in labor rels. disputes. Author: Organized Labor and the Negro, 1944, Unionization of Professional Engineers and Chemists, 1946, Economics of Labor Relations, 1950, 9th edit., 1981, Government and Labor, 1963, Readings in Labor Economics, 1963, Boulwarism: Labor Policies of General Electric Company, 1964, Negro and Employment Opportunity, 1965, Hours of Labor, 1965, Compulsory Arbitration and Government Intervention in Labor Disputes, 1966, Restrictive Labor Practices in Supermarket Industry, 1967, Negro in the Automobile Industry, 1968, Negro in the Aerospace Industry, 1968, Negro in the Rubber Tire Industry, 1969, Negro in Paper Industry, 1969, Negro in the Tobacco Industry, 1970, Negro Employment in Basic Industry, 1970, Negro Employment in Southern Industry, 1970, Negro Employment in Land and Air Transport, 1971, Impact of Government Manpower Programs, 1975, Open Shop Construction, 1975, The Impact of OSHA, 1978, Objective Selection of Supervisors, 1978, Black and Other Minority Participation in the All-Volunteer Navy and Marine Corps, 1979, Manpower in the Retail Pharmacy Industry, 1979, The Impact of the ATT-EEO Consent Decree, 1979, Multinational Collective Bargaining Attempts, 1979, Multinational Union Organizations in the Manufacturing Industries, 1980, Employee Relations and Regulations in the 80s, 1982, Internat. Transport Workers' Federation and Flag of Convenience Shipping, 1983, Open Shop Construction Revisited, 1984, Personnel Policies for Engineers and Scientists, 1985, Doublebreasted Operations and Pre-Hire Agreements in Construction: The Facts and the Law, 1987, The Federal Government as Employer: The Federal Labor Relations Authority and the PATCO Challenge, 1988, The Changing Role of Women in Research and Development, 1988, Government Protection of Employees in Mergers and Acquisitions, 1989, The Railway Labor Act, 1990, Union Corporate Campaigns and Inside Games as a Strike Form, 1994, also over 300 articles in field. Mem. Am. Econ. Assn., Indsl. Relations Research Assn., Am. Arbitration Assn., Phi Beta Kappa. Clubs: Harvard (N.Y.C.); Harvard-Radcliffe (Phila.); University (Washington), Faculty (U. Pa.). Home and Office: 205 Avon Rd Haverford PA 19041-1612

NORTHUP, ANNE MEAGHER, state legislator; b. Louisville, Jan. 22, 1948; d. James L. and Floy Gates (Terstegge) Meagher; m. Robert Wood Northup, Apr. 12, 1969; children: David, Katherine, Joshua, Kevin, Erin, Mark. BA in Econs. and Bus., St. Mary's Coll. Notre Dame, South Bend, Ind., 1970. Mem. Ky. Ho. of Reps., Frankfort, 1987-96, 105th Congress from 3d Ky. dist., 1997—; mem. fin. adv. bd. EPA, 1989-93; mem. home econs. adv. bd. U. Ky. Coll. Agr., 1992—. Mem. exec. com. Partnership Ky. Sch. Reform, 1990—; bd. dirs. Greater Louisville Pub. Radio, 1993—, Hospice Louisville, 1994—, Ky. Cancer Consortium, 1992—; mem. cmty. adv. bd. Jr. League Louisville, 1993—. Named Outstanding Woman of Achievement St. Matthews BPW, 1990; recipient Cath. Schs. Disting. Alumni award, 1991, U. Notre Dame award of the yr. Ky. Alumni Assn., 1991, Clearing the Air award Am. Lung Assn. of Ky., 1991, Svc. Above Self award St. Matthews Rotary Club, 1992, Pub. Svc. award Am. Heart Assn., 1992, Sacred Heart Acad. Alumna award, 1994, NFIB Guardian of Small Bus. award, 1996. Mem. Nat. Order Women Legislators, Nat. Conf. State Legislators, Nat. Rep. Legis. Conf., Inst. Rep. Women, So. Legis. Conf. (alternat from Ky. to fiscal affairs and governmental com.). Roman Catholic. Home: 3340 Lexington Rd Louisville KY 40206-3050 Office: US Ho Reps 1004 Longworth House Office Bldg Washington DC 20515

NORTHUP, BEVERLY A. BAKER, principal chief; b. Columbia, Mo., Feb. 14, 1938; d. Charles Clayton Rupard and Annie Cecil Barnes Rupard Collins; m. Erbie M. Baker, Sept. 10, 1955 (div. Sept. 1970); children: Sherry, Peggy, Erbie Jr., Phillip, Jason; m. Robert Lionel Northup, June 29, 1991. Oper. room sec. Ellis Fischel Cancer Hosp., Columbia, Mo., 1976-77; sec. Mo. Cancer Registry, Columbia, 1977-78, U. Mo. Dept. of Fisheries & Wildlife, Columbia, 1980-84; sec. sterile processing U. Mo. Hosp., Columbia, 1984-85; sec. Ctrl. Mo. Regional Ctr., Columbia, 1985-86; rsch. dir. No. Cherokee Nation, Columbia, 1986-88; propr. Physicians Eyewear & Hearing Aid Ctr., Columbia, 1989—; prin. chief No. Cherokee Nation, Columbia, 1984—; pres. bd. No. Cherokee Tribe, Inc., Columbia, 1984—; Indian task force to the gov. Mo. Dept. of Econ. Dev., Jefferson City, Mo., 1994; tribal historian, spokesperson, consulting geneologist, No. Cherokee Nation, Columbia, 1984—. Author: History of the Northern Cherokee Nation Part I, 1993, History of the Northern Cherokee Nation Part II, 1996. Del. Boone County Rep. Conv., Columbia, 1992, Ninth Dist. Mo. Rep. Conv., Columbia, 1992, Mo. Rep. Conv., 1992; bd. dirs. Boone County Elections Verification Bd., Columbia, 1992. Grantee Adminstrn. for Native Ams., 1986, 87, 88, United Meth. Ch., 1986, 87, 88. Mem. Nat. Am. Indian Coun. (tribal del. 1994—), Nat. Orgn. for the Unification of Native Ams. (tribal del. 1994—), White House Com. for the Recognition of all Indian People (tribal del. 1995—), No. Cherokee Cmty. Assn. (bd. dirs. 1983—). Republican. Baptist. Avocations: pianist, Sunday School teacher, horticulture, travel. Office: No Cherokee Nation Old LA Territory 1012 Old Hwy 63N Columbia MO 65201

NORTHUP, JOHN DAVID, management consultant, inventor; b. Toledo, Sept. 8, 1910; s. Charles S. and Alice Delia (Bachelder) N.; m. Ruth Bender, Jan. 15, 1937; children: John David, Mary Elizabeth, Nancy Ross (Mrs. H.T. Lehrkind). B.S., MIT, 1932. With Owens-Ill. Glass Co., 1933-74; mgr. Owens-Ill. Glass Co., Clarion, Pa., 1943-46, Charleston, W.Va., 1946-47; gen. purchasing agt. glass container div. Owens-Ill. Glass Co., 1947-49, gen. mgr. corrugated package ops., 1949-53, dir. engring., 1953-55, v.p. adminstrv. div., 1956-61, v.p., gen. mgr. Closure div., 1961-72, v.p. charge glass container mfg., 1972-74; ind. inventor, mgmt. cons., 1974—; chmn. closure com. Glass Container Mfrs. Inst., 1966-69; tech. adviser on poison prevention packaging FDA, 1971-72. Mem. Inverness Club, Beta Theta Pi. Republican. Home: 2460 Underhill Rd Toledo OH 43615-2332

NORTON, ANDRE ALICE, author; b. Cleve., Sept. 17, 1912; d. Adalbert and Bertha Stemm N. Librarian Cleve. Public Library, until 1951. Author: 125 books including The Sword is Drawn (Dutch Gov. award 1946) 1944, Sword in Sheath (Ohioana Juevenile award Honor Book 1950) 1949, Starhunter (Hugo award nomination World Sci. Fiction Convention 1962) 1961, Witch World (Hugo award nomination World Sci Fiction Convention 1964) 1963, Night of Masks (Boy's Club of Am. Certificate of Merit 1965) 1964; series include Swords Trilogy, Star Ka'at Sci. Fiction Series, Witch World Fantasy Series. Recipient Invisible Little Man award Westercon XVI, 1963, Phoenix award 1976, Gandalf Master Fantasy award World Sci. Fiction Convention, 1977, Andre Norton award Women Writers of Sci. Fiction, 1978, Balrog Fantasy award 1979, Ohioana award, 1980, Fritz Leiber award, 1983, E.E. Smith award, 1983, Nebula Grand Master award Sci. Fiction Writers of Am., 1984, Jules Verne award, 1984, Second Stage Lensman award, 1987; named to Ohio Hall of Fame, 1981. Mem. Sci. Fiction Writers Am.

NORTON, AUGUSTUS RICHARD, political science educator; b. Bklyn., Sept. 2, 1946; m. Deanna Lampros, Dec. 27, 1969; 1 child, A. Timothy. BA in Polit. Sci. magna cum laude, U. Miami, Fla., 1974, MA in Polit. Sci., 1974; PhD in Polit. Sci., U. Chgo., 1984. Commd. 2d lt. U.S. Army, 1967, advanced through grades to col., 1990, ret., 1993; prof. polit. sci., dept. social scis. U.S. Mil. Acad., West Point, N.Y., 1981-93; prof. internat. rels. Boston U., 1993—, prof. anthropology, 1996—; dir. Civil Soc. in Mid. East program NYU, 1992-94. Author: Amal and the Shi'a: Struggle for the Soul of Lebanon, 1987; co-author: International Terrorism: An Annotated Bibliography and Research Guide, 1980, UN Peacekeepers: Soldiers with a Difference, 1990, Political Tides in the Arab World, 1992; contbr., sr. editor: Studies in Nuclear Terrorism, 1979, The International Relations of the PLO, 1989, Touring Nam: The Vietnam War Reader, 1989; editor: Civil Society in the Middle East, vol. I, 1995, vol II, 1996; mem. editl. bd. Ethics and Internat. Affairs, 1990, Current History, 1992—, Global Governance, 1995-97. Sr. rsch. fellow Internat. Peace Acad., 1990-92, Woodrow Wilson Nat. fellow, 1990-97; Fulbright rsch. prof., Norway, 1989; grantee NEH summer 1986, MacArthur Found., 1989-90, Ford Found., 1991—, Rockefeller Found., 1993-94, 96-97. Fellow Inter-Univ. Seminar on Armed Forces and Soc.; mem. Am. Polit. Sci. Assn., Coun. Fgn. Rels., Internat. Inst. Strategic Studies, Mid. East Studies Assn., Am. Rsch. Ctr. Egypt, Am. Mid. East Women's Studies Assn., Columbia Univ. Seminar on Middle East, Mid. East Inst. Columbia U., Conf. Group on Mid. East (co-founder), Phi Kappa Phi, Pi Sigma Alpha. Office: Dept Internat Rels Boston U 152 Bay State Rd Boston MA 02215-1501

NORTON, DAVID C., federal judge; b. Washington, July 25, 1946; s. Charles Edward and Louise Helen (Le Feber) N.; m. Dee Holmes, June 16, 1973; children: Phoebe Elizabeth, Christine Baron. BA in History, U. of the South, 1968; JD, U. S.C., 1975. Assoc. Holmes & Thomson, Charleston, S.C., 1975-77, 80-82, ptnr., 1982-90; dep. solicitor 9th Jud. Ct., Charleston, 1977-80; U.S. Dist. judge Charleston, 1990—. With USN, 1969-72. Mem. Fed. Judges Assn., Charleston County Bar Assn. (sec.-treas. 1983-90), S.C. Def. Trial Attys. Assn. (exec. com. 1988-90), S.C. Bar Assn. (Ho. Dels. 1986-90). Episcopalian. Avocations: boating, racquet ball. Office: Hollings Judicial Ctr PO Box 835 Broad & Meeting Sts 3rd Fl Charleston SC 29402-0835

NORTON, DAVID JERRY, mechanical research engineer; b. Manhattan, Kans., Oct. 23, 1940; married; 1 child, Kristin. BS, MS, Tex. A&M U., 1963; PhD, Purdue U., 1968. Sr. rsch. engr. Jet Propulsion Lab., 1968-70; from asst. prof. to prof. aerospace engring. Tex. A&M U., 1970-86; asst. dir. Tex. Engring. Exptl. Station Tex. A&M U., 1981-86, v.p. rsch. Houston Advanced Rsch. Ctr., 1986—; bd. dirs. Space Found. Fellow AIAA (assoc.); mem. ASME, Am. Soc. Engring. Edn., Sigma Xi. Office: Houston Advanced Rsch Ctr 4800 Research Forest Dr Bldg I The Woodlands TX 77381-4142

NORTON, DELMAR LYNN, candy company executive, video executive; b. Vernal, Utah, Sept. 6, 1944; s. La Mar and Velma (Hullinger) N.; m. Connie Jean Bryan, Mar. 10, 1967; children: Bryan Lynn, Christopher Max, Wendy, Nicholas Delmar. Student, U. Utah, 1962-63, Famous Artists Sch., 1966-69. Nat. sales mgr. Maxfield Candy Co., Salt Lake City, 1965-72; sec.-treas. Ice Cream & Candy Shops, Salt Lake City, 1972-73; pres., gen. mgr. Ostlers' Candy Co., Salt Lake City, 1973—; chmn. bd. Nat. Mktg. Co., Salt Lake City, 1974—; pres., gen. mgr. Rent-A-Flick, Inc., Salt Lake City.; v.p. Redi-Therm Insulation, Inc., Salt Lake City., 1991-94; nat. sales mgr. Uphill Down U.S.A., 1994—. Mem. Ch. Jesus Christ of Latter-Day Saints (missionary). Home: 4240 S 1650 E Salt Lake City UT 84124-2556 Office: PO Box 71470 Salt Lake City UT 84171-0470

NORTON, DOUGLAS RAY, auditor general; b. Portales, N.Mex., Mar. 23, 1933; s. Clayton G. and Lillian W. (Powers) N.; m. Wanda Jones, May 23, 1951 (div. July 1979); children: Debbie Norton Goodman, Vicki Norton Hulet, Denise Norton Jolley. BS, U. Ariz., 1963. CPA, Ariz. Staff acct., audit supr. Ernst & Ernst, Tucson, Ariz., 1963-67; ptnr. Baker, Price & Norton, Prescott, Ariz., 1968-75, Lester Witte & Co., Prescott, Ariz., 1975-76; auditor gen. State of Ariz., Phoenix, 1976—; mem. Profl. Adv. Bd. Sch. Acctg. Ariz. State U., Tempe; mem. acctg. bd. advisors U. Ariz. Pres. Prescott Bd. Edn., 1976. Served with U.S. Army, 1953-55. Mem. AICPA, Ariz. Soc. CPAs, Nat. Assn. State Auditors, Comptrollers and Treasurers (pres. 1993-94), Nat. State Auditors Assn. (pres. 1982-83), Lions (pres. Prescott chpt. 1973-74). Home: PO Box 1251 Phoenix AZ 85001-1251 Office: Office Ariz Auditor Gen 2910 N 44th St Ste 410 Phoenix AZ 85018-7256

NORTON, DUNBAR SUTTON, economic developer; b. Hoquiam, Wash., Jan. 30, 1926; s. Percy Dunbar and Anna Fedelia (Sutton) N.; m. Kathleen Margaret Mullarky, Dec. 21, 1948 (dec. Apr. 1994); children: Priscilla K., Rebecca C., Jennifer A., Douglas S.; m. Mary Ethel Wolff, May 25, 1996. Student, U. Oreg., 1946-48; diploma, U.S. Army Command & Gen. Staff, 1964. Enlisted U.S. Army, 1944, commd. 2d lt., 1948, advanced through grades to lt. col., ret., 1974; dir. econ. devel. dept. Yuma (Ariz.) County C. of C., 1974-83; exec. v.p. Lakin Enterprises, Yuma, 1983-87; owner Norton Cons., Yuma, 1987—; corp. mem. Greater Yuma Econ. Devel. Corp., 1984-96, vice chmn., 1993-95. Mem. Yuma County Indsl. Devel. Authority, 1984-90, 92—, pres., 1992—; chmn. fundraising com. Yuma Cross Park Coun., 1984-88, sec., 1988-90, v.p., 1990-92, bd. dirs., 1982-96; bd. dirs. Yuma Leadership, 1990-93; chmn. devel. com. Yuma County Airport Authority, 1985-92, v.p., 1992—; vice chmn. Yuma Main St. Bd., 1988-90, Yuma County Geog. Info. Sys. Task Force, 1991-95, Yuma Kids Voting, 1990-91, bd. dirs. Ariz. Partnership Air Transp., 1990-96, v.p. 1993-95; bd. dirs. Yuma County Civic Trusteeship, 1993-95; chmn. The Southwest Inst., 1995-96, What's Best for Our Kids, 1995-96, Yuma Sch. Dist. No. 1 New Elem. Sch. Planning Com., 1996-97; mem. bd. trustees Yuma County Libr., 1996—. Decorated Legion of merit with oak leaf cluster, Bronze Star. Mem. Ariz. Assn. for Econ. Devel. (bd. dirs. 1975-82, pres. 1982-83, legis. affairs com. 1987—, Developer of Yr. 1977), Yuma Execs. Assn. (sec.-treas., exec. dir. 1987—). Republican. Episcopalian. Avocations: golf, swimming, singing. Home: 12267 E Del Norte Yuma AZ 85367-7356 Office: 11411 S Fortuna Rd Ste 205 Yuma AZ 85367-7827

NORTON, ELEANOR HOLMES, congresswoman, lawyer, educator; b. Washington, June 13, 1937; d. Coleman and Vela (Lynch) Holmes; m. Edward W. Norton (div.); children: Katherine Felicia, John Holmes. BA, Antioch Coll., 1960; MA in Am. Studies, Yale U., 1963, LLB, 1964. Bar: Pa., 1965, U.S. Supreme Ct., 1968. Law clk. to Judge A. Leon Higgonbotham Fed. Dist. Ct., 1964-65; asst. legal dir. ACLU, 1965-70; exec. asst. to mayor City of N.Y., 1971-74; chmn. N.Y.C. Commn. on Human Rights, 1970-77, EEOC, Washington, 1977-81; sr. fellow Urban Inst., Washington, 1981-82; prof. law Georgetown U., Washington, 1982—; mem. 100th-105th Congresses from D.C. dist., 1990—; lead Dem. mem. D.C. subcom., water resources and environ. subcom., pub. bldgs. and econ. devel. subcom. Office: 1424 Longworth HOB Washington DC 20515 also: Georgetown U Law Ctr 600 New Jersey Ave NW Washington DC 20001-2075*

NORTON, ELIZABETH WYCHGEL, lawyer; b. Cleve., Mar. 25, 1933; d. James Nicolas and Ruth Elizabeth (Cannell) Wychgel; m. Henry Wacks Norton Jr., July 16, 1954 (div. 1971); children: James, Henry, Peter, Fred; m. James Cory Ferguson, Dec. 14, 1985 (div. Apr. 1988). BA in Math., Wellesley Coll., 1954; JD cum laude, U. Minn., 1974. Bar: Minn. 1974. Summer intern Minn. Atty. Gen.'s Office, St. Paul, 1972; with U.S. Dept. Treasury, St. Paul, 1973; assoc. Gray, Plant, Mooty, Mooty & Bennett, P.A., Mpls., 1974-79, prin., 1980-94, of counsel, 1995-96; mem. Minn. Lawyers Bd. Profl. Responsibility, 1984-89; mem. U. Minn. Law Sch. Bd. Visitors, 1987-92. trustee YWCA, Mpls., 1979-84, 89-91, co-chmn. deferred giving com., 1980-81, chmn. by-laws com., bd. dirs., 1976-77, lectr.; treas. Minn. Women's Campaign Fund, 1985, guarantor, 1982-83, budget and fin. com. bd. dirs., 1984-87; trustee Ripley Meml. Found., 1980-84; treas. Jones-Harrison Home, 1967, bd. dirs., 1962-69, 2d v.p., chmn. fin., 1968-69; mem. Sen. David Durenberger's Women's Network, 1983-88. Durant scholar. Fellow Am. Bar Found.; mem. ABA (mediation task force family law sect. 1983-84), Minn. Bar Assn. (human rights com. family law sect., task force uniform marital property act 1984-85), Minn. Bar Found. (dir. 1991-94), Hennepin County Bar Assn. (pres. 1987-88, chmn. task force on pub. edn. 1984, chmn., mem. exec. com. family law sect. 1979-94), Minn. Inst. Legal Edn., Minn. Women's Lawyers (exec. com.), U. Minn. Law Sch. Alumni Assn. (dir. 1975-81, exec. com. 1981-83), Wellesley Club, Phi Beta Kappa. Home: 4980 Dockside Dr # 204 Fort Myers FL 33919-4657

NORTON, EUNICE, pianist; b. Mpls., June 30, 1908; d. Willis I. and Charlotte (O'Brien) N.; m. Bernard Lewis, May 4, 1934; 1 child, Norton Lewis. Student, U. Minn., 1922-24, Tobias Matthay Pianoforte Sch., London, 1924-31, Artur Schabel Master Piano Classes, Ger., 1931-33, Arthur Schabel Master Piano Classes, Italy, 1933; MusD (hon.), Wooster Coll., 1977. vis. prof. piano Carnegie Mellon U.; lectr. U. Pitts., Cath. U. Am.; lectr., condr. master piano classes univs.; condr. pvt. master classes, Pitts., N.Y.C., Vt.; dir. Peacham (Vt.) Piano Festivals; founder, musical dir. Pitts. New Friends of Music, Pitts. Concert Artists. Concert pianist in U.S. and Europe, 1927—; soloist with numerous symphony orchs., including N.Y. Philharm., Boston, Phila., Pitts., Mpls., London, Berlin symphony orchs., also orchs. in Leipzig, Germany, Vienna, Austria, Birmingham, Eng., Manchester, Eng.; chamber musician with Budapest, Juilliard and Griller string quartets, Am. Chember Orch.; recorded Well Tempered Clarier (J.S. Bach); performed Beethoven's entire piano sonatas, Carlow Coll., Pitts., 1983, U. Pitts., 1988, recorded ltd. edit., 1988; recorded 4 one-hour illustrated lectrs. on video Teaching of Arthur Schnabel, U. Pitts., 1987, video The Teaching of Tobias Matthay, 1995; her complete piano repertoire produced on CD's (over 150 works from Bach through Stravinsky including 48 preludes and fugues of Well Tempered Clavier and Beethoven's 32 sonatas), 1995. Pres. Norvard Co. Classic CDs. Recipient Bach prize, 1927; recipient Chappell Gold medal Chappell Piano Co., London, 1928. Mem. Am. Matthay Piano Assn. (founder mem.), Sigma Alpha Iota (hon.). Club: Tuesday Musical (hon.) (Pitts.). Home: 5863 Marlborough Ave Pittsburgh PA 15217-1415 *I am convinced that music is not an ornament but an essential part of life. It is a serious activity. I live with the principle of uncompromising adherence to musical values without regard for popular approval and economic gain.*

NORTON, FLOYD LIGON, IV, lawyer; b. Shreveport, La., Oct. 23, 1950; s. Floyd Ligon III and Grace Louise (Julian) N.; m. Kathleen Fair Patterson, Nov. 24, 1979; children: Caroline, Elizabeth. BA with honors, U. Va., 1972, JD, 1975. Bar: Va. 1975, D.C. 1975. Assoc. Reid & Priest, Washington, 1975-83, ptnr., 1983-95; ptnr. Morgan Lewis & Bockius, 1995—. Mem. ABA, Fed. Energy Bar Assn. Episcopalian. Home: 4107 Bradley Ln Bethesda MD 20815-5236 Office: Morgan Lewis & Bockius 1800 M St NW Washington DC 20036-5802

NORTON, GALE A., state attorney general; b. Wichita, Mar. 11, 1954; d. Dale Bentsen and Anna Jacqueline (Lansdowne) N.; m. John Goethe Hughes, Mar. 26, 1990. BA, U. Denver, 1975, JD, 1978. Bar: Colo. 1978, U.S. Supreme Ct. 1981. Jud. clk. Colo. Ct. of Appeals, Denver, 1978-79; sr. atty. Mountain States Legal Found., Denver, 1979-83; nat. fellow Hoover Instn. Stanford (Calif.) U., 1983-84; asst. to dep. sec. U.S. Dept. of Agr., Washington, 1984-85; assoc. solicitor U.S. Dept. of Interior, Washington, 1985-87; pvt. practice law Denver, 1987-90; atty. gen. State of Colo., Denver, 1991—; Murdock fellow Polit. Economy Rsch. Ctr., Bozeman, Mont., 1984; sr. fellow Ind. Inst., Golden, Colo., 1988-90; policy analyst Pres. Coun. on Environ. Quality, Washington, 1985-88; lectr. U. Denver Law Sch., 1989; transp. law program dir. U. Denver, 1978-79. Contbr. chpts. to books, articles to profl. jours. Participant Rep. Leadership Program, Colo., 1988, Colo. Leadership Forum, 1989; past chair Nat. Assn. Attys. Gen. Environ. Com.; co-chair Nat. Policy Forum Environ. Coun.; candidate for 1996 election to U.S. Senate, 1995—. Named Young Career Woman Bus. and Profl. Wome, 1981, Young Lawyer of Yr., 1991. Mem. Federalist Soc., Colo. Women's Forum, Order of St. Ives. Republican. Methodist. Avocation: skiing. Office: Colo Dept of Law 1525 Sherman St Fl 5 Denver CO 80203-1700

NORTON, GERALD PATRICK, lawyer; b. West Roxbury, Mass., Jan. 25, 1940; s. Thomas W. and Genevieve (Sweeny) N.; m. Judith C. Ralphs, Apr. 24, 1965 (dec. Oct. 1969); children: Jeremy, Elizabeth; m. Amanda B. Norton, Sept. 25, 1971; 1 child, Adam. AB magna cum laude, Princeton U., 1961; LLB magna cum laude, Columbia U., 1964. Bar: N.Y. 1964, D.C. 1966. Law clk. to judge U.S. Ct. Appeals (2d cir.), N.Y.C., 1964-65; assoc. Covington & Burling, Washington, 1965-73; asst. to solicitor gen. Dept. Justice, Washington, 1973-75; dep. gen. counsel FTC, Washington, 1975-79; ptnr. Pepper Hamilton & Scheetz, Washington, 1979-92, Harkins Cunningham, Washington, 1992—; mem. com. on admissions and grievances D.C. Cir., 1988-94; mediator U.S. Dist. Ct. for D.C.; lectr. various seminars. Mng. and research editor Columbia U. Law Rev., 1963-64; contbr. articles to profl. jours. Bd. dirs. Washington Lawyer Com. for Civil Rights & Urban Affairs, 1984—; 1st v.p., bd. dirs. Washington Met. Planning and Housing Assn., 1969-70; vol. atty. ACLU, Washington. Recipient Arthur E. Flemming award Jaycees of Nat. Capital Area, 1979; named Grad. of Yr., Province I Phi Delta Phi, 1964. Mem. D.C. Bar (spl. com. on profl. responsibility for govt. employees, legal ethics com. 1989-95, com. on rev. of rules of profl. conduct 1995—), Nat. Assn. Attys. Gen., Supreme Ct. Moot Ct. (panel). Democrat. Office: Harkins Cunningham 1300 19th St NW Washington DC 20036-1609

NORTON, GLYN PETER, French literature educator; b. Exeter, Devonshire, Eng., May 22, 1941; s. Trevor Thomas and Betty (Marshall) N.; m. Victoria Josefina Perez, Oct. 28, 1966; children—Alexandra, Leslie. A.B., U. Mich., 1963, A.M., 1965, Ph.D., 1968. Asst. prof. Dartmouth Coll., Hanover, N.H., 1968-71; prof. French lit. Pa. State U., University Park, 1971-88; prof. French lit., chmn. dept. romance langs, dir. Ctr. for Fgn. Langs., Lits. and Cultures Williams Coll., Williamstown, Mass., 1988-93, Willcox B. and Harriet M. Adsit prof. Internat. Studies, 1993—. Author: Montaigne and the Introspective Mind, 1975; The Ideology and Language of Translation in Renaissance France, 1984; editor: The Cambridge History of Literary Criticism, vol. III; contbr. articles to ednl. jours. NEH fellow, 1973-74, Guggenheim fellow, 1986-87; Am. Council of Learned Socs. grantee, 1980-81, 85; recipient medal City of Melun, France, 1985. Fellow Camargo Found., mem. MLA, Renaissance Soc. Am., Soc. Franç aise des Seiziemistes. Avocations: music; gardening; traveling. Office: Williams Coll Dept Romance Langs Weston Hall Williamstown MA 01267

NORTON, HUGH STANTON, economist, educator; b. Delta, Colo., Sept. 18, 1921; s. Cecil A. and Olive S. (Stanton) N.; m. Miriam Jarmon, Dec. 19, 1949 (dec. 1983); children: Pamela, John; m. Mary Jo Roberts. A.B., George Washington U., 1947, Ph.D., 1956. Johnson prof. econs. U. S.C., Columbia, 1968—; disting. prof. emeritus U. S.C., 1988—; cons. anti-trust and transp. econs. to indsl. firms. Author: The Role of the Economist in Government Policy Making, 1969, The World of the Economist, 1973, 2d edit., 1977, The Employment Act and the Council of Economic Advisers 1946-76, 1977, The Quest for Economic Stability: Roosevelt to Reagan, rev. edit., 1990. Served with Signal Corps AUS, 1942-45. Club: Cosmos (Washington). Home: 3335 Overcreek Rd Columbia SC 29206-5145

NORTON, JAMES J., union official; b. Boston, June 9, 1930; s. Patrick P. and Annie (Flaherty) N.; m. Patricia A. Tuley, Sept. 19, 1953; children: James, Ann Marie, Robert, Thomas, Donald, David, Brian. Treas. Boston Photo Engravers Union, 1957-60, pres., 1960-62; internat. rep. Graphic Arts Union, Boston, 1962-78; sec. treas. Graphic Arts Union, Washington, 1979-83; rec. and fin. sec. Graphic Communications Internat. Union, 1983-85, pres., 1983—; exec. coun. AFL-CIO, Union Labor Life Ins. Co.; bd. govs. ARC. Coach Peewee-Bantum level Dorchester Youth Hockey Program, Boston, 1958-79; coach Midget level Fairfax (Va.) Hockey Program, 1980-81; exec. bd. mem. ARC. Mem. AFL-CIO (exec. coun.), Montclair C. of C. Roman Catholic. Lodge: K.C. Office: Graphic Comms Internat Union 1900 L St NW Washington DC 20036-5002

NORTON, JOAN JENNINGS, English language educator; b. Starke, Fla., Oct. 21, 1931; d. Thomas Joseph and Marie Louise (Wade) Jennings; m. James T. Norton (div. 1972); 1 child, Jeanne Marie. BS in edn., U. Ala., 1953; MEd, U. Fla., 1963. Cert. Tchr., Fla. Tchr. soc. studies Reinhold Jr. High, Green Cove Springs, Fla., 1958-61, tchr. soc. studies, English, 1961-67; tchr. English tchr., dept head Clay Jr., Sr. High, Greencove Springs, 1967-71, Clay H.S., Green Cove Springs, 1971-83; ret., 1993; sec. Clay County Tchrs. Assoc.,1954, mem. nom. com. FEA, Clay County, 1968, nom. com. Fla. P-R-I-D-E Writing Awards, 1979-80. Mem. Clay County Dem. Com., 1958-59, Sunday Sch. & Bible Sch. Tchr. 1st Presbyterian Green Cove Springs, 1940, 60. Recipient Clay's County Outstanding Young Tchr. award C. of C., Green Cove Springs, 1958. Mem. Clay COunty Retired Tchrs. Assoc., Clay County Historical Soc. Democratic. Presbyterian. Avocations: reading, travel, writing, piano, politics. Home: PO Box 372 Green Cove Springs FL 32043

NORTON, JODY (JOHN DOUGLAS NORTON), English language educator; b. Princeton, N.J., Nov. 13, 1943; s. Paul Foote and Alison Edmunds (Stuart) N.; m. Alexandra Holt Morey, Aug. 20, 1977; children: Joselle, Jackson, Tayo. BA, U. Mass., Amherst, 1966; MA, U. Calif., Berkeley, 1981, PhD, 1988. Vis. asst. prof. Rice U., Houston, 1988-89, Albion (Mich.) Coll., 1989-94; lectr. Ea. Mich. U., Ypsilanti, 1994—. Contbr. articles to profl. jours. Fellow U. Calif., 1979-80, 80-81, 84-85, 87-88, Yale U., 1966-67; faculty rsch. grantee Albion Coll., 1992, 93, 94. Mem. MLA, Midwest MLA, Soc. for Critical Exch., Popular Culture Assn., Phi Beta Kappa, Phi Kappa Phi. Avocations: tennis, mountain climbing, camping, playing electric bass, blues and country western music. Home: 2820 Kimberley Rd Ann Arbor MI 48104 Office: Eastern Mich U Dept English Lang & Lit Ypsilanti MI 48197

NORTON, JUDY, actress; b. Santa Monica, Calif., Jan. 29; d. Harry Vincent and Constance (Glazebrook) Norton; m. Randy Apostle, Apr. 8, 1991, 1 child: Devin Aric. Participated in 2 world skydiving records. Appeared in film Hotel, 1966; actress repertory co. The Stable Players, 1969-71, Cinderella, 1981, Annie Get Your Gun, 1983, I Ought to Be in Pictures, 1983, Perfect Pitch, 1984, Spring at Marino, 1984, Times of Your Life, 1985, Social Security (Stage West, Calgary, Can.), 1987, Sound of Music, 1989, Alive & Kicking, 1989, Move Over, Mrs. Markham (Stage West, Can.), 1991, Weekend Comedy (Stage West, Can.), 1991, Volstead Blues (Souris Valley Theatre, Can.), 1993, Ranchers & Rustlers (Can.), 1994, Ranchers & Rustlers, Mayfield Theatre 1996, 97; TV movies include The Homecoming, 1971, Valentine, 1978, Valentine's Day-A Love Story, 1982, A Day of Thanks, 1982; appeared in TV series The Waltons, 1972-81, also Circus of the Stars, 1983, 84; TV movie A Walton Thanksgiving, 1993, A Walton Wedding, 1995, A Walton Easter, 1996; TV guest appearances in The Love Boat, 1981, Trial by Jury, 1989, (mini series) Lost Daughter, 1996; co-writer Knaughty Knights, 1992, Ranchers And Rustlers, 1992; co-dir., co-writer Laura & Johnny Were Lovers, 1992, Hot Summer Nights, 1992, Gillian's Island, 1992, Murder on the Prairie Express, 1993, Mugs and Molls, 1993, I Dream of Jimmy, 1993, Rock N Roll Candidate, 1993, Star Trax, 1993, There's No Life Like It, 1993, He Shoots, She Scores, 1994, Of Course, Elvis Will Be Here, 1994, Monster High Reunion, 1994, Don't Touch That Dial, 1994, Ranchers and Rustlers II, 1994, Captain Vancouver & The Land Pirates, 1995, Philip Harlow, 1995, Phantom of the Theatre, 1995, Fantasy Island, 1995, Crystal's Palace, 1995, Super Heroes in Retirement Land, 1996, Big Bonanza Barn Burner, 1996, Impossible Mission, 1996. Mem. AFTRA, SAG, Actors Equity, Can. Actors Equity, ACTRA.

NORTON, KENNETH HOWARD, professional football player; b. Jacksonville, Ill., Sept. 29, 1966; s. Ken Norton. Student, UCLA. Linebacker Dallas Cowboys, 1988-93, San Francisco 49ers, 1994—. Selected to Pro Bowl, 1991-95; played in Super Bowls XXVII-XXIX, 1992-94. Office: San Francisco 49ers 4949 Centennial Blvd Santa Clara CA 95054-1229*

NORTON, MARY BETH, history educator, author; b. Ann Arbor, Mich., Mar. 25, 1943; d. Clark Frederic and Mary Elizabeth (Lunny) N. BA, U. Mich., 1964; MA, Harvard U., 1965, PhD, 1969; DHL (hon.), Siena Coll., 1983, Marymount Manhattan Coll., 1984, De Pauw U., 1989; DLitt (hon.), Ill. Wesleyan U., 1992. Asst. prof. history U. Conn., Storrs, 1969-71; from asst. prof. to prof. Cornell U., Ithaca, N.Y., 1971-87, Mary Donlon Alger prof. Am. history, 1987—. Author: The British-Americans: The Loyalist Exiles in England, 1774-1789, 1972, Liberty's Daughters: The Revolutionary Experience of American Women, 1750-1800, 1980 (Berkshire prize for Best Book Woman Historian 1980), Founding Mothers and Fathers: Gendered Power and the Forming of American Society, 1996; co-author: A People and A Nation, 1982, 4th rev. edit., 1994 (finalist Pulitzer prize in history 1997); editor: AHA Guide to Historical Literature, 3d rev. edit., 1995; co-editor: Women of America: A History, 1979, To Toil the Livelong Day: America's Women at Work, 1790-1980, 1987, Major Problems in American Women's History, 1989, 2nd rev. edit., 1995; contbr. articles to profl. jours. Trustee Cornell U., 1973-75, 83-88; mem. Nat. Coun. Humanities, Washington, 1979-84. Woodrow Wilson Found. fellow, 1964-65, NEH fellow, 1974-75, Shelby Cullom Davis Ctr. fellow Princeton U., 1977-78, Rockefeller Found. fellow, 1986-87, Soc. for Humanities fellow Cornell U., 1989-90, John Simon Guggenheim Meml. Found. fellow, 1993-94. Fellow Soc. Am. Historians (exec. bd. 1974-87, Allan Nevins prize 1970); mem. Am. Hist. Assn. (v.p. for rsch. 1985-87) Orgn. Am. Historians (exec. bd. 1983-86), Berkshire Conf. Women Historians (pres. 1983-85). Democrat. Methodist. Office: Cornell U Dept History 440 Mcgraw Hall Ithaca NY 14853-4601

NORTON, NATHANIEL GOODWIN, marketing executive; b. Chgo., Jan. 7, 1948; s. Wilbur H. and Eva (Geneen) N.; m. Ariel Taylor, Nov. 15, 1980 (div. July 1987). BA, U. N.C., 1969. Mktg. mgr. Canteen Corp., Chgo., 1971-74; sr. v.p. Mathieu, Gerfen & Bresner, N.Y.C., 1974-83; pres., ptnr. Rand Pub. Rels., N.Y.C., 1983-89; ind. marketing cons. North Hampton, N.H., 1989—.

NORTON, NORMAN JAMES, exploration geologist; b. Du Quoin, Ill., Apr. 26, 1933; s. James Harlan Norton and Helen Jane (Riley) Norton Rosen; m. Bettie Jean Greer, July 7, 1955; children—Matthew James, Jane Alison. B.S., So. Ill. U., 1958; M.S., U. Minn., 1960, Ph.D., 1963. Successively, asst., assoc., then full prof. biology Hope Coll., Holland, Mich., 1964-74; prof., chmn. dept. biology Ball State U., Munice, Ind., 1974-78, acting v.p. acad. affairs, 1978-79; acting dean Coll. Arts and Scis. Ball State U., 1979-81; provost, v.p. acad. affairs Ind. U. Pa., 1981-83; cons. geologist Gulf Oil Corp., Houston, 1970-83; sr. staff geologist Gulf Oil Exploration and Prodn. Co., Houston, 1983-85; biostratigrapher, stratigraphic services, exploration Chevron Overseas Petroleum Inc., San Ramon, Calif., 1985-91; supr. biostratigraphy sect. Chevron U.S.A., Inc., Houston, 1991-93; acting divsn. geologist Chevron U.S.A., Inc., Houston, 1993-95, divsn. geologist, 1995—, geol. cons., 1997—. Contbr. articles to profl. jours. Served with USAF, 1952-56. Recipient Outstanding Tchr. Educator award Sr. Class of Hope Coll., 1969, acad. citation for disting. achievement Mich. Acad. Scis., Art and Letters, 1969, Outstanding Achievement award Chevron Overseas Petroleum Inc., 1990. Mem. Am. Assn. Stratigraphic Palynologists (Disting. Svc. award 1978, chmn. bd. trustees found., archives com. 1970—, constrn. revision com.). Home: 4419 St Michaels Ct Sugar Land TX 77479-2989 Office: CPDN PO Box 1635 Houston TX 77251-1635

NORTON, ROBERT HOWARD, entertainer, musical arranger, author; b. N.Y.C., July 19, 1946; s. Howard R. and Lena (Triano) N.; m. Eileen Williams, Sept. 29, 1966 (div. 1976); children: Brian, Lelania. Student, Broward C.C., Ft. Lauderdale, Fla., 1970-75; community antenna TV engr. cert., Nat. Cable TV Inst., 1976. Rec. session artist Motown and various other recording labels, 1964—; entertainer various concerts, 1964—; systems technician Selkirk Communications, Ft. Lauderdale, Fla., 1979-81; cable TV engr. Gen. Instrument Corp., Hatboro, Pa., 1981-84; entertainer (with Leilani Chandler) The Sophisticats, Ft. Pierce, Fla., 1984—; owner, author, software writer Norton Music, Ft. Pierce, Fla., 1990—. Author: The Artist's and Entertainer's Tax Bible, 1990, Entertainer's Guide to Cruising, 1991—; writer mus. software 175 User Styles, 1991, Band-in-a-Box Supercharger, 1993, 5 Band-in-a-Box Fake Disks, 1994—, 6 Band-in-a-Box User Style Disks, 1993—; writer software 475+ Gen. MIDI Sequences, 1993—; composer numerous songs; arranger of more than 400 songs. Home and Office: Norton Music PO Box 13149 Fort Pierce FL 34979-3149

NORTON, ROBERT LEO, SR., mechanical engineering educator, researcher; b. Boston, May 5, 1939; s. Harry Joseph and Kathryn (Warren) N.; m. Nancy Auclair, Feb. 27, 1960; children: Robert L., Jr., MaryKay, Thomas J. AS in Mechanical Engring. cum laude, Northeastern U., 1962, BS in Indsl. Tech. summa cum laude, 1967; MS in Engring. Design, Tufts U., 1970. Registered profl. engr., Mass. Engr. Polaroid Corp., Cambridge, Mass., 1959-66, sr. engr., Waltham, 1979-81; project engr. Jet Spray Cooler, Inc., Waltham, Mass., 1966-69; bio-med. engr. Tufts surg. rsch. dept. N.E. Med. Ctr. Hosps., Boston, 1969-71; rsch. assoc. Tufts surg. svc. Boston City Hosp., 1971-74; lectr. bio-med. engring. Franklin Inst., Boston, 1973-76; instr. dept. surgery, Tufts U., Boston, 1970-82, asst. prof. engring. design, Medford, 1974-79; prof. mech. engring. Worcester Poly. Inst., Mass., 1981—; pres. Norton Assocs., Norfolk, Worcester, 1970—. Patentee (13) in field; contbr. articles to profl. jours; author engring. textbooks including Design of Machinery: An Introduction to the Synthesis and Analysis of Mechanisms and Machines, 1992, internat. edit., 1992, Korean translation, 1995, Spanish translation, 1996, Machine Design: An Integrated Approach, 1996, internat. edit., 1996, Chinese Translation, 1997, others; reviewer IFTOMM Jour. Mechanism and Machine Theory; presenter in field. Fellow ASME (reviewer Jour. Mechanisms, Transmission, and Automation in Design); mem. Am. Soc. Engring. Edn. (program chmn. computers in edn. divsn. 1985-86, sec. computers in edn. divsn. 1986-87, pres. computers in edn. divsn. 1988-90, reviewer Jour. Prism, J.F. Curtis award 1984, Merle Miller award 1987, 92), Pi Tau Sigma, Sigma Xi. Democrat. Avocations: sailing, computers. Office: Worcester Poly Inst Dept Mechanical Engring 100 Institute Rd Worcester MA 01609-2247

NORTON, ROBERT R., JR., food products executive; b. 1946. BS, Mo. Western State Coll., 1966; MBA, N.W. Mo. State U., 1968. Sec., treas. Dugdale Packing Co., St. Joseph, Mo., 1966-86; with BeefAmerica Operating Co., Inc., Omaha, 1986—, pres., 1988—. Office: Beef Am 14748 W Center Rd Ste 201 Omaha NE 68144-2029*

NORTON, RUTH ANN, education educator; b. Sioux City, Iowa, Mar. 7, 1947; d. Burton Ellwood and Mildred Ruth (Schneider) N.; m. Jack William Moskal, May 30, 1985. BA, U. No. Iowa, 1969; MS, Syracuse U., 1984, EdD, 1985. Cert. tchr., Iowa, Vt. Tchr. Cedar Falls (Iowa) Unified Sch. Dist., 1969-79; asst. didr. Area 7 Tchr. Ctr., Waterloo, Iowa, 1979-80; tchr. Moretown (Vt.) Elem. Sch., 1980-81; doctoral candidate Syracuse (N.Y.) U., 1981-85; prof. Calif. State U., San Bernardino, 1985—, dir. student teaching, 1989-95; cons. tech. tng. inst. Calif. State U., San Bernardino, Constl. Heritage Inst.; trainer supervision workshops Calif. State U., San Bernardino; cons. Lime St. Elem. Sch., Hesperia, Calif.; bd. dirs. Redlands Ednl. Partnership Found.; chairperson Reflections Com. for Redlands PTA Coun. Contbr. articles to profl. jours. Recipient Affirmative Action Faculty Devel. grant Calif. State U., 1986, Profl. Devel. Monetary grant Calif. State U., 1987, Meritorious Performance & Profl. Promise award Calif. State U., 1988. Mem. ASCD, Am. Ednl. Rsch. Assn., Assn. Tchr. Educators, Calif. Assn. for Supervision and Curriculum Devel., Calif. Coun. for Social Studies, Nat. Coun. for Social Studies, So. Calif. Assn. Tchr. Educators, Phi Delta Kappa. Avocations: gardening, camping, swimming, needlework, reading. Office: Calif State U 5500 University Pky San Bernardino CA 92407-2318

NORTON, STEPHEN ALLEN, geological sciences educator; b. Newton, Mass., May 21, 1940; m. Anne Peer, Apr. 25, 1970; children: David S., Lisa A., Stephen A. B.A., Princeton U., 1962; M.A., Harvard U., 1963, Ph.D., 1967. Prof. geol. scis. U. Maine, Orono, 1978—; chmn. dept. U. Maine-Orono, 1978-82, 93-97, dean arts and scis., 1984-86. Fellow Geol. Soc. Am.; mem. Am. Soc. Limnology and Oceanography. Office: U Maine Dept Geol Scis Bryand Ctr Orono ME 04469-5790

NORTON, WILLIAM ALAN, lawyer; b. Garretsville, Ohio, Apr. 26, 1951; s. Hugh Delbert and Tommie (Leet) N.; m. Denise Ann, May 2, 1991; children: Rachel, Sarah Megan, William Tucker. AA, U. Fla., 1972, BS, 1973, JD, 1976. Bar: Fla. 1977, U.S. Dist. Ct. (so. and mid. dist.) Fla. 1995. Assoc. Law Office of David Paul Horan, Key West, Fla., 1978-79; asst. pub. defender 16th Jud. Cir., Monroe County, Fla., 1979-81, 1st Jud. Cir., Ft. Walton Beach, Fla., 1981-85; assoc. Jones & Foster, P.A., West Palm Beach, Fla., 1985-88, Montgomery Searcy & Denney, West Palm Beach, 1988-89, Searcy Denney Scarola Barnhart & Shipley, P.A., 1989-93; atty./shareholder Searcy Denney Scarola Barnhart & Shipley, P.A., West Palm Beach, 1989—, shareholder; lectr. in civil trial and securities litigation. Bd. dirs. Ctr. for Children in Crisis, West Palm Beach, 1994—. Mem. Fla. Bar Assn. (cert. civil trial litigation), Pub. Investors Arbitration Bar Assn., Palm Beach County Bar Assn., Acad. Fla. Trial Lawyers. Home: 8152 Needles Dr Palm Beach Gardens FL 33418 Office: Searcy Denney Scarola et al 2139 Palm Beach Lakes Blvd West Palm Beach FL 33409-6601

NORVELL, PATSY, artist; b. Greenville, S.C., July 13, 1942; d. Wendell Norvell and Margaret Marie (Schaefer) Nichols; m. Robert Rahway Zakanitch, May 2, 1982; 1 child, Amelia Zakanitch Norvell. BA, Bennington Coll., 1964; studied with David Smith, Bolton Landing, N.Y., 1964; MA, CUNY-Hunter Coll., 1970. Asst. instr. Colo. Springs (Colo.) Fine Arts Ctr., 1967; instr. dept. art Rutgers U., Newark, 1969-70, Montclair (N.J.) State Coll., 1970-74; assoc. in sculpture Columbia U., N.Y.C., 1977; instr.

pvt. studio seminar, N.Y.C, 1973-74; adj. lectr. in sculpture SUNY, Queens, 1978-79; adj. asst. prof. dept. art Hunter Coll., N.Y.C., 1979-81, vis. asst. prof., 1982-83; vis. artist N.Y. Exptl. Glass Workshop, 1980, 84; cons. sculpture panel N.Y. State Creative Artist Pub. Svc., 1980, 81; panelist sculpture fellowship N.J. State Coun. Arts, 1983, gen. svc. adminstrn. NEA, 1984, Hunter's Point Selection Com., 1987; presenter numerous seminars. One woman shows include A.I.R. Gallery, N.Y.C., 1973, 75, 78, 80, 82, 87, LaGrangeville, N.Y., 1977, Vassar College & Barrett Ho., Poughkeepsie, N.Y., 1979, Avery Fisher Hall, Lincoln Ctr., N.Y.C., 1980, Sidney James Gallery, N.Y.C., 1982, Norton Gallery of Art, West Palm Beach, Fla., 1983, Matthew Hamilton Gallery, Phila., 1984, Art Awareness, Lexington, N.Y., 1995; exhibited in group shows at 117 Prince St, N.Y.C., 1972, Kent (Ohio) State Galleries, 1972, Alonzo Gallery, N.Y.C., 1972, Newark Mus., 1973, Nancy Hoffmann Gallery, N.Y.C., 73, Erotic Art Gallery, N.Y.C., 1973, Indpls. Mus. Art, Cin., 1974, Taft Mus., Cin., 1974, Central Hall Gallery, Port Washington, N.Y., 1975, 77, Skidmore Coll., Saratoga Springs, N.Y., 1975, Fine Arts Bldg., N.Y.C., 1976, Webb and Parsons, Bedford Village, N.Y., 1976, Hurlbutt Gallery, Greenwich, Conn., 1977, County Mus. Fine Arts, Roslyn, N.Y., 1977, Whitney Downtown Mus., N.Y.C., 1978, 79, Robert Freidus Gallery, N.Y.C., 1978, Ginza Kaigaken, Tokyo, 1978, Battery Park Landfill, N.Y.C., 1978, Thorpe Intermedia Gallery, Sparkill, N.Y., 1979, Perkins Ctr. Arts, Moorestown, N.J., 1979, McKintosch/Drysdale Gallerym Washington, 1980, Danforth (Mass.) Mus., 1981, Berkshire (Mass.) Mus., 1981-82, Women's Hall of Fame, Seneca Falls, N.Y., 1981, U. Houston, 1981, Sidney Janis Gallery, N.Y.C., 1982, Norton Gallery Art, West Palm Beach, Fla., 1983, High Mus. Art, Atlanta, 1983, Nat. Gallery Art, Washington, 1984, Palladium, N.Y.C., 1985, Vanderwoude/Tanabaum Gallery, N.Y.C., 1985, Contemporary Arts Ctr., Cin., 1986, Lowe Art Mus., Coral Gables, Fla., 1987, Max Protetch Gallery, N.Y.C., 1987, Toledo Mus. Art, 1988, Fort Wayne (Ind.) Mus. Art, 1988, The Home Saving Tower, L.A., 1989, Md. Coll. Art and Design, 1989, Bernice Steinbaum Gallery, 1989-93, Noyes Mus., Oceanville, N.J., 1990, Art Mus., Southampton, N.Y., 1991, Midtown-Payson Gallery, 1992, Willow Gallery, N.Y.C., 1993, Steinbaum-Krauss Gallery, N.Y.C., 1993, Parish Art Mus., Southampton, N.Y., 1994, Paine Webber Art Gallery, N.Y.C., 1994, Cribbs Mus. Art, Charleston, C.C., 1996, Gallery 128, N.Y.C., 1996, others; commd. works include glass, mirror, railing, and stone sculptures for Nicholas Recital Hall, Douglass Coll., New Brunswick, N.H., 1981-82, Bridgeport (Conn.) Fed. Bldg. and Courthouse, 1983-85, Battery Park City Authority, N.Y.C., 1983-86, 4600 East-West Hwy, Bethesda, Md., 1984-88, Bellevue Hosp., 1986, Home Savings Am. Tower, L.A., 1987-88, 14th St. Union Sq. Local Devel. Corp., 1988—, Beverly and Cortelyou Subway Stas., M.T.A., N.Y., 1992-96; represented in permanent collections including Jim Henson Apt., N.Y.C., Brown's Residence, Bethesda, Md., Steinbaum Residence, L.I., N.Y., Bill and Norma Roth Collection, Winterhaven, Fla. Recpient Spl. Recognition award Art Commn. N.Y.C., 1993; Nat. Endowment for Arts artist fellow, 1976-77; Patlock/Krasner Artist fellow, 1995; artist residency grantee Art Awareness, Lexington, N.Y., 1995, 96; Elxir Napenthe grantee, 1996-97. Home: 78 Greene St New York NY 10012-5100

NORVILLE, DEBORAH, news correspondent; b. Aug. 8, 1958; m. Karl Wellner; 2 children: Karl Nikolai, Kyle Maximilian. BJ, U. Ga., 1979. Reporter Sta. WAGA-TV, Atlanta, 1978-79, anchor, reporter, 1979-81; anchor, reporter Sta. WMAQ-TV, Chgo., 1982-86; anchor NBC News, N.Y.C., 1987-89; news anchor Today Show, NBC, N.Y.C., 1989, co-anchor, 1990-92; corr. Street Stories, CBS, N.Y.C., 1992-94; co-anchor America Tonight, CBS, N.Y.C., 1994; anchor Inside Edition, King World Prodns., 1994—; contbg. editor McCall's, N.Y.C. Bd. dirs. Greater N.Y. coun. Girl Scouts U.S. Recipient Outstanding Young Alumni award Sch. Journalism, U. Ga., Emmy award, 1985-86, 89; named Person of Yr., Chgo. Broadcast Advt. Club, 1989, Anchor of Yr. 2000, Washington Journalism Rev., 1989. Mem. Soc. Profl. Journalists. Office: Inside Edition King Worl Prod 402 E 76th St New York NY 10021-3104*

NORWOOD, BERNARD, economist; b. Boston, Nov. 21, 1922; s. Hyman and Rose (Fink) N.; m. Janet Lippe, June 25, 1943; children: Stephen Harlan, Peter Carlton. BA, Boston U., 1947; MA, Fletcher Sch. Law and Diplomacy, 1948, PhD, 1957. Internat. economist State Dept., 1949-58; joined U.S. Fgn. Svc., 1955; 1st. sec. U.S. mission to European Communities, Brussels, Belgium, 1958-62; asst. chief comml. policy and treaties divsn. Dept. State, 1962; chmn. trade staff com. Office Spl. Rep. for Trade Negotiations, Exec. Office Pres., 1963-67; assigned The Nat. War Coll., 1967-68; advisor divsn. internat. fin. bd. govs. Fed. Res. Sys., 1968-75; prin. assoc., sr. cons. Nathan Assocs., Inc., 1975-94; mem. U.S. del. to negotiations and confs. GATT, Geneva, 1953-67. Served with AUS, 1943-46. Home and Office: 5610 Wisconsin Ave 21D Chevy Chase MD 20815-4415

NORWOOD, CAROLE GENE, middle school educator; b. Odessa, Tex., Feb. 27, 1943; d. Perry Eugene and Jeffie Lynn (Stephens) Knowles; m. James Ralph Norwood, Aug. 4, 1973. BA, U. Tex., 1966; MA, U. North Tex., 1975; cert. ESL, Our Lady of the Lake U., San Antonio, 1988. Cert. Sec. Edn. English, Spanish, ESL. Student intern Dept. of the Interior, Washington, 1962; receptionist Senate Chambers, Austin, Tex., 1965; English instr. Universidade Mackenzie, Sao Paulo, Brazil, 1966-67, Uniao Cultural Brasil-Estados Unidos, Sao Paulo, 1966-67; tchr. Terrell (Tex.) Jr. Sr. High Sch., 1967-68, Agnew Jr. High Sch., Mesquite, Tex., 1968-70; teaching asst. U. North Tex. Denton, Tex., 1970-71; sec. to pres. The Village Bank, Dallas, 1971-72; tchr. Plano (Tex.) High Sch., 1972-74; ESL adult edn. tchr. Dallas, 1972-73; tchr., yearbook sponsor Brentwood Middle Sch., San Antonio, 1975-90; instructional specialist Gus Garcia Jr. High Sch., San Antonio, 1990—, interdisciplinary team leader, 1992-93, 96—; yearbook and newspaper sponsor, Agnew Jr. High Sch., 1969-70. Contbr. articles to profl. jours. Mem. World Wildlife Fund, Audubon Soc., Nat. Wildlife Fedn., Nature Conservancy, San Antonio Museum Assn., San Antonio Zoological Soc., Los Padrinos (Mission Rd. Devel. Ctr.); U.I.L. coach 1976-87, 92-93. Named Outstanding Young Woman of Am., 1972. Mem. AAUE, NEA, ADCD, Nat. Coun. Tchrs. English, San Antonio Area Coun. Tchrs. English, Tex. State Tchrs. Assn., Edgewood Classroom Tchrs. Assn. (faculty rep. 1991-94), Longhorn Singers Alumni Assn., Delta Kappa Gamma (chpt. pres. 1990-92, San Antonio coord. coun. chair 1995-96, state program com. mem. 1995—). Presbyterian. Office: Edgewood Ind Sch Dist Gus Garcia Jr School 3306 Ruiz St San Antonio TX 78228-6226

NORWOOD, CAROLYN VIRGINIA, business educator; b. Florence, S.C., Dec. 11; d. James Henry and Mildred (Jones) N. BS, N.C. A&T State U., 1956; MA, Columbia U., 1959; postgrad., Seton Hall U., Temple U.; cert. scholarly distinction, Nat. Acad. Paralegal Studies, 1991. Instr. Gibbs. Jr. Coll., St. Petersburg, Fla., Fayetteville State Coll., N.C.; asst. prof. Community Coll. Phila.; prof. Essex County Coll., Newark, 1968—; cons. Mercer County Coll., Trenton, N.J.; mem. assessment team Mid.-States Commn., Phila., 1980—. Co-author: Alphabetic Indexing, 1989. Recipient Eddy award Gregg/McGraw-Hill Co., N.Y.C., 1986, Who's Who in N.J. Bus. Edn. award N.J. Dept. Edn. Divsn. Vocat. Edn., 1990, Cert. of Recognition of Outstanding and Dedicated Svc., Mid. States Assn. Colls. and Schs., Commn. on Higher Edn., 1994; profiled in NBEA Yearbook chpt. on Leadership in Bus. Edn., 1993; doctoral fellow Temple U., Phila., 1977-78. Mem. AAUW, NAFE, NAACP, Nat. Bus. Edn. Assn. (bd. dirs. 1982-85), Ea. Bus. Edn. Assn. (pres. 1986-87, membership dir. 1976-85, Educator of the Yr. 1994), Nat. Coun. Negro Women, N.J. Bus. Edn. Assn., Alpha Kappa Alpha, Phi Delta Kappa, Delta Pi Epsilon. Avocations: bowling, photography. Office: Essex County Coll 303 University Ave Newark NJ 07102-1719

NORWOOD, CHARLES W., JR., congressman; b. Valdosta, Ga., July 27, 1942; m. Gloria Norwood; 2 children. BS, Ga. So. U., 1964; DDS, Georgetown U., 1967. Pvt. practice Augusta, Ga., 1969—; owner Norwood Tree Nursery, 1984—; mem. 104th Congress from 10th Ga. dist., 1995—, 105th Congress from 10th Ga. dist., 1996—. Capt. U.S. Army, 1967-69, Vietnam. Decorated Combat Medic badge, Bronze Star for Meritorious Svc., Bronze Star for Meritorious Achievement. Mem. Ga. Dental Assn. Republican. Methodist. Office: US Ho of Reps 1707 Longworth Bldg Washington DC 20515-1010

NORWOOD, COLVIN GAMBLE, JR., lawyer; b. New Orleans, Dec. 10, 1947; s. Colvin Gamble and Dorothy P. (Pecot) N.; m. Susan Clark, Dec. 29, 1971; children: Benjamin, Colvin Gamble III. BS in Physics, Tulane U., 1969, JD, 1972. Bar: La. 1972. Assoc. Deutsch, Kerrigan & Stiles, New Orleans, 1972-73, Schumacher, McGlinchey, Stafford & Mintz, New Orleans, 1974-75; ptnr., dir., mng. dir. McGlinchey Stafford, New Orleans, 1986—. Chmn. law firm solicitation United Fund of Greater New Orleans, 1983; trustee Xavier U. of La.; bd. dirs., treas., New Orleans Pro Bono Project. Served to 1st lt. U.S. Army, 1971-73. Fellow Am. Coll. of Trial Lawyers, La. Bar Found.; mem. ABA, Internat. Assn. Def. Counsel, Product Liability Adv. Coun., World Trade Ctr., La. Supreme Ct. Hist. Soc., Sigma Pi Sigma, Omicron Delta Kappa, Sigma Alpha Epsilon. Avocations: photography, computer programming, office automation. Home: 6031 Perrier St New Orleans LA 70118-5940 Office: McGlinchey Stafford 643 Magazine St New Orleans LA 70130-3405

NORWOOD, DEBORAH ANNE, law librarian; b. Honolulu, Nov. 12, 1950; d. Alfred Freeman and Helen G. (Papsch) N.; 1 child, Nicholas. BA, U. Wash., 1972; JD, Willamette U., 1974; M in Law Librarianship, U. Wash., 1979. Bar: Wash., U.S. Dist. Ct. (we. dist.) 1975, U.S. Ct. Appeals (9th cir.) 1980. Ptnr. Evans and Norwood, Seattle, 1975-79; law librarian U.S. Courts Library, Seattle, 1980-89; state law librarian Wash. State Law Libr., Olympia, 1989—, reporter of decisions, 1994—. Mem. ALA, Am. Assn. Law Librs. (chmn. state, ct. and county spl. interest section 1995-96). Office: Wash State Law Libr PO Box 40751 Temple of Justice Olympia WA 98504-0751

NORWOOD, JANET LIPPE, economist; b. Newark, Dec. 11, 1923; d. M. Turner and Thelma (Levinson) Lippe; m. Bernard Norwood, June 25, 1943; children—Stephen Harlan, Peter Carlton. BA, Douglass Coll., 1945; MA, Tufts U., 1946; PhD, Fletcher Sch. Law and Diplomacy, 1949; LLD (hon.), Fla. Internat. U., 1979; LL.D. (hon.), Carnegie Mellon U., 1984. Instr. Wellesley Coll., 1948-49; economist William L. Clayton Ctr., Tufts U., 1953-58; with Bur. Labor Stats., U.S. Dept. Labor, Washington, 1963-91; dep. commr., then acting commr. Bur. Labor Stats. Dept. Labor, Washington, 1975-79, commr. labor stats., 1979-92; sr. fellow The Urban Inst., Washington, 1992—; dir. Republic Nat. Bank, Nat. Opinion Rsch. Ctr., Consortium for Internat. Earth Scis. Info. Network, chair adv. coun. unemployment compensation, 1993-96; mem. com. on nat. stats. NAS. Author papers, reports in field. Recipient Disting. Achievement award Dept. Labor, 1972, Spl. Commendation award, 1977, Philip Arnow award, 1979, Elmer Staats award, 1982, Pub. Svc. award, 1984; named to Hall Disting. Alumni, Rutgers U., 1987; recipient Presdl. Disting. Exec. rank, 1988. Fellow AAAS, Am. Statis. Assn. (pres. 1989), Royal Statis. Soc., Nat. Assn. Bus. Economists; mem. Am. Econ. Assn., Indsl. Rels. Rsch. Assn., Internat. Statis. Inst., Internat. Assn. Ofcls. Stats., Nat. Acad. Pub. Adminstrn., Nat. Inst. Statis. Sci. (bd. trustees); mem. Cosmos Club (pres. 1995-96), Douglas Coll. Soc. Disting. Achievement. Home: Apt PH 21-D 5610 Wisconsin Ave Chevy Chase MD 20815-4415 Office: The Urban Inst 2100 M St NW Washington DC 20037-1207

NOSANOW, BARBARA SHISSLER, art association administrator; b. Roanoke, Va.; d. Willis Morton and Kathryn Sabin (Bradford) Johnson; m. John Lewis Shissler Jr., July 28, 1957 (dec. May 1972); children: John Lewis Shissler III, Ada Holland Shissler; m. Lewis Harold Nosanow, Oct. 15, 1973. AB, Smith Coll., 1957; MA, Case Western Res. U., 1958. Asst. mng. editor Jour. Aesthetics and Art Criticism, Cleve. Mus. Art, 1958-63; dir. publs. and rsch. Mpls. Inst. Arts, 1963-72; dir. U. Minn. Gallery, Mpls., 1972-76; dir. exhbns. and edn. Nat. Archives, Washington, 1976-79; curator of edn. Smithsonian Instn., Washington, 1979-82; asst. dir. Nat. Mus. Am. Art, Smithsonian Instn., 1982-88; dir. Portland (Maine) Mus. Art, 1988-93, Art Spaces, 1993—. past mem. various rev. panels NEH, Washington. Bd. dirs. Md. Com. for Humanities, Balt., 1980-83. Mem. Internat. Women's Forum (Maine Women's Forum divsn.). Avocation: travel. Office: Art Spaces 23 Wildwood Cir Portland ME 04103-2778

NOSEK, LAURA J., health facility administrator; b. Cleve.; d. LeRoy VanPelt and Florence Isabel (Acker) John; m. Frank Joseph Nosek, Sept. 9, 1961; children: Karin Beth, Kevin Bruce. Diploma in nursing, Grace New Haven Sch. Nursing, 1958; BSN, Case We. Res. U., 1961, MSN, 1981, PhD, 1986. RN, Vt. Adminstrv. nurse clin. U. Hosps. Cleve., dir. nursing mgmt. svcs.; asst. clin. prof. nursing Case Western Res. U., Cleve.; assoc. v.p. nursing and patient svcs. Med. Ctr. Hosp. Vt., Burlington, 1990-93, v.p. nursing and patient svcs., 1993-94; assoc. hosp. dir., nurse exec. Edward Hines Jr. V.A. Hosp., Hines, Ill., 1995-97, assoc. hosp. dir. clin. support, 1997—; adj. assoc. prof. nursing U. Vt., 1990—, Loyola U., Chgo., 1996—; cons. Mt. Sinai Med. Ctr., N.Y.C. Contbr. articles to profl. jours. Mem. ANA, AONE, Nat. Commn. on Edn., NLN, Am. Nurses Found., Vt. Nurses Assn. (past pres.), Vt. Orgn. Nurse Execs. (past pres.), Sigma Theta Tau (Info. Resources Tech. award). Office: Edward Hines Jr VA Hosp PO Box 5000/002 Hines IL 60141

NOSKO, MICHAEL GERRIK, neurosurgeon; b. Montreal, Que., Can., Feb. 24, 1957; came to U.S., 1991; s. Joseph John and June Elizabeth (Salter) N.; m. Deborah Anne Branciere, May 23, 1981; children: Douglas Joseph, Denise Elizabeth, Keith Michael. BS, McMaster U., 1978; MD, U. Toronto, 1982; PhD, U. Alberta, 1986. Intern U. Toronto (Ont., Can.) Gen. Hosp., 1982-83; resident U. Alberta Hosps., Edmonton, Can., 1986-91; asst. prof. neurosurgery Robert Wood Johnson Med. Sch., New Brunswick, N.J., 1991—, chief, divsn. neurosurgery, 1991—; cons. and presenter in field. Contbr. articles to profl. jours., chpts. to books. Rsch. fellow Alberta Heritage Found., 1983-86; Chancellor' scholar McMaster U., 1975, Univ. scholar, 1976, Edwin Marwin Dalley Meml. scholar, 1977; recipient Acad. award Am. Acad. Neurological Surgery, 1986. Fellow Am. Coll. Surgeons (Resident Rsch. award 1986), Royal Coll. Surgeons Can., Acad. Medicine N.J.; mem. AMA, Am. Assn. Neurol. Surgeons, Can. Neurosurg. Soc., N.J. Neurosurg. Soc., N.Y. Acad. Scis., Middlesex County Med. Soc., Soc. Critical Care Medicine, Congress Neurol. Surgeons, Alpha Omega Alpha. Anglican. Avocations: aircraft/helicopter pilot, fishing. Office: Divsn Neurosurgery 125 Paterson St Ste 2100 New Brunswick NJ 08901-1962

NOSLER, ROBERT AMOS, sports company executive; b. Ashland, Oreg., Apr. 21, 1946; s. John Amos and Louise (Booz) N.; m. Joan Kathleen Hilliard, July 15, 1967; children: Christie Lynn, Jill Ann, John Robert. Student, U. Oreg., 1965. V.p., gen. mgr. Nosler Bullets, Inc., Bend, Oreg., 1974-88; pres., chief exec. officer Nosler Bullets, Inc., 1988-90; pres., CEO Nosler, Inc., Bend, 1990—. Editor: Nosler Reloading Manual #1, 1976. Bd. dirs. Bend C. of C., 1984-88, treas., 1988; chmn. Central Oreg. Welcome Ctr. Steering Com., 1988. With USN, 1966-70; trustee Ctrl. Oreg. Community Coll. Found., 1992—; trustee Nat. Rifle Assn. Found., 1997—. Recipient Pres.' award Bend C. of C., 1984, 87, 88. Mem. Nat. Reloading Mfrs. Assn. (bd. dirs. 1982-86, 90-93, pres. 1984-86), Oreg. Grad. Inst. Sci. & Tech. Chief Exec. Roundtable, Greater Bend Rotary (dir. 1989-91). Republican. Lutheran. Avocations: hunting, outdoors, sports. Office: Nosler Inc 107 SW Columbia St Bend OR 97702-1014

NOSTRAND, HOWARD LEE, language and literature educator; b. N.Y.C., Nov. 16, 1910; s. Elijah H. and Ida Josephine (Maeder) N.; m. Frances Anne Levering, June 23, 1933 (div. Aug. 1967); children: David L., Richard L., Robert M.; m. Frances Helen Brewer, Aug. 9, 1967. BA, Amherst Coll., 1932; MA, Harvard U., 1933; D, l'Université de Paris, 1934. Tchr. U. Buffalo, 1934-36, U.S. Naval Acad., 1936-38, Brown U., 1938-39; prof. romance langs. U. Wash., Seattle, 1939-81, chmn. dept., 1939-64, prof. emeritus, 1981—; vis. prof. Coll. de France, 1975, Simon Fraser U., 1982.; Fulbright lectr., France, 1970-71; cons. Am. Coun. on Teaching Fgn. Langs., 1982, chair Nat. Commn. on Ethnography, 1974-80; Am. Assn. of Tchr. of French (pres.1960-62); Nat. Commn. Profl. Stds., 1986—; mem. Nat. Commn. on Profiency, 1986-93, mem., chair Nat. Commn. on Telematics, 1990-92; co-chair Nat. Commn. on Cultural Competence, 1992-96; mem. Nat. Commn. Student Stds., 1993—; cons. Ednl. Testing Svc., 1988—. Author: Le Theatre Antique, 1934, Mission of the University, 1944, The Cultural Attaché, 1947, Research on Language Teaching...International Bibliography, 1962, 2d edit., 1965, The University and Human Understanding, 1963, Film-Recital of French Poems and Cultural Commentary, 1964, Background Data for the Teaching of French, 1967; (with others) La France en mutation, 1979, Savoir vivre en français, 1988, Databases: Our Third Technical Revolution, 1991, Acquiring Cross-Cultural Competence, 1996; contbr. articles to profl. jours. Bd. mem. Seattle Nantes Sister City Assn., 1980-90, pres., 1987-89; bd. mem. U.S. Com. for a Cmty. Democracies, 1983-92, hon. chair, Seattle, 1986-92. Guggenheim fellow, 1953-54; named Order of Sun Peru, 1947, French Govt. Palmes Académiques, 1950, Chevalier, Legion d'Honneur, 1962, Officer, 1994; recipient Pro Lingua award Wash. Assn. Fgn. Lang. Tchrs., 1977, award for leadership N.E. Conf. on Teaching Fgn. Langs., 1978, Nelson Brooks award Am. Coun. Teaching Fgn. Langs., 1980, Outstanding Pub. Svc. award U. Wash. Alumni, 1980, award for vision and leadership Vols. of Bonjour Seattle Festival, 1979-80. Mem. Assn. pour la recherche interculturelle (hon.). Democrat. Unitarian. Home: U Washington 18550 29th Ave NE Seattle WA 98155-4137

NOTARBARTOLO, ALBERT, artist; b. N.Y.C., Jan. 12, 1934; s. Leopold and Elvira (Caputo) N.; m. Valerie Cervelli, June 1, 1962. Student (scholar), Nat. Acad. Fine Arts, 1950; apprentice to mural painter, Ignacio LaRussa, 1951-53. Tchr., 1967—. Represented in permanent collections, Smithsonian Instn., Washington, Mus. Modern Art, N.Y.C.; one-man shows include Hemisphere Gallery of Time-Life Inc., 1973, U. P.R., 1966, David Gavin Gallery, Millerton, N.Y., 1993; exhibited group shows, Tate Gallery, London, 1965, Corcoran Gallery Art, Washington, 1968, Del. Art Mus., Wilmington, 1970, Mus. Modern Art, N.Y.C., 1971, 74, 76, Nat. Gallery Art, Washington, 1976, Smithsonian Instn., Washington, 1976, Santa Barbara (Calif.) Mus. Art, 1976, Taft Mus., Cin., Bell Gallery, Greenwich, Conn., 1977, Huntsville (Ala.) Mus. Art, 1978, Hokin Gallery, Palm Beach, Fla., 1982. Served with AUS, 1957-59. Recipient Nat. Community Art Competition award HUD, 1973; U.S. Bicentennial Flag Competition award, A Flag for the Moon, 1976. Mem. Nat. Soc. Lit. and the Arts. Home: 99 Battery Pl Apt 27H New York NY 10280-1329 *When I turned thirteen my Aunt Rosa Pucci gave me a gift—a small packet of reproductions of Raphael's paintings. On the overleaf she inscribed, "Art does affect the lives of men; it moves to ecstasy, thus giving colour and movement to what be otherwise a rather grey and trivial affair." The intonation of this phrase today makes me believe that an act of art echoes on, invoking a continuing music, a vitality for the future while all else turns into the dust of history.*

NOTARI, PAUL CELESTIN, communications executive; b. Chgo., Sept. 8, 1926; s. Peter and Mae Rose (Luvisi) N.; m. Marlene Fineman, Feb. 21, 1969; children: Cathy Notari Davidson, Kenneth, Sharon Notari Christian, Mindy Nielsen, Debbie McGrath. B.S. in Physics, DePaul U., 1952; M.S. in Comml. Sci., Rollins Coll., 1968. Mgr. publs. and tng. Motorola Inc., Chgo., 1952-65; supr., publs. engr. Martin Co., Orlando, Fla., 1966-67; dir. communications Bus. Equipment Mfrs. Assn., N.Y.C., 1967-70; dir. publs., pub. jour. Am. Water Works Assn., Denver, 1971-79; mgr. tech. info. Solar Energy Research Inst., Denver, 1979-91; pres. SciTech Communications, Inc., Denver, 1992—; lectr. bus. communications Northwestern U. Served with USNR, 1944-46. Mem. Assn. Computer Programmers and Analysts (founding pres. 1970-73), Soc. Tech. Writers and Pubs. (chmn. chpt. 1965-66), Am. Solar Energy Soc. (nat. chmn. 1990-91). Office: SciTech Comm Inc 1000 S Monaco Pky Ste 77 Denver CO 80224-1603 *In this complex world we live in, a nation lives or dies by its technological achievements, made possible by a steady flow of information between scientists, engineers, technicians and producers. I believe I have made a significant contribution on this behalf.*

NOTARO, MICHAEL R., data processing and computer service executive; b. Chgo., Nov. 1, 1914; s. Anthony and Felicia (Franzese) N.; m. Irene Hapsude, May 5, 1936 (dec.); children: Michael R., Phyllis Ann; m. Ruth Bostrom, Mar. 10, 1984. Student, Northwestern U. Sch. Commerce, 1930-36, Chgo. Law Sch., 1930-32; LL.D., DePaul U. dir. St. Paul Fed. Savs. Bank. Bd. dirs. Cath. Charities of Archdiocese of Chgo., Boys Clubs Chgo., Loyola U.; trustee De Paul U. Decorated knight Malta, knight St. Gregory, Knight comdr. Order Merit Italy). Roman Catholic (lay trustee). Clubs: Union League, Mid-Am., Tavern, Chgo. Athletic Assn. (Chgo.); Butterfield Country (Hinsdale, Ill.). Home & Office: 1400 Bonnie Brae River Forest IL 60305-1202

NOTEBAERT, RICHARD C., telecommunications industry executive; b. 1947; married. With Wisconsin Bell, 1969-83; v.p. marketing and operations Ameritech, Chicago, 1983-86; pres. Ameritech Mobile Comm., 1986-89, Indiana Bell Telephone Co., 1989-92; pres. Ameritech Services, 1992-93, pres., COO, 1993-94; chmn., pres., CEO Ameritech Corp., Chicago, 1994—. Office: Ameritech Corp 30 S Wacker Dr Chicago IL 60606-7413

NOTHERN, MARJORIE CAROL, nursing administrator; b. Bonners Ferry, Idaho, June 23, 1936; d. Carl John and Ione Faye (Hobson) Frank; m. Abbott Burton Squire, Dec. 15, 1956 (div. Aug. 5, 1972); m. William Thomas Nothern, Aug. 5, 1972. Diploma, Deaconess Hosp. Sch. Nursing, Spokane, Wash., 1956; BA, Stephens Coll., Columbia, Mo., 1981; MBA, Golden Gate U., San Francisco, 1987. Cert. nursing adminstrn. advanced ANCC. Relief head nurse Deaconess Hosp., Spokane, Wash., 1956-57; staff nurse Kadlec Meth. Hosp., Richland, Wash., 1957-58, Southern Pacific Hosp., San Francisco, 1958-59; relief evening supr. The Gen. Hosp., Eureka, Calif., 1959-60; med. office nurse Ely & Davis, Eureka, Calif., 1960-66; head nurse Redbud Cmty. Hosp., Clear Lake, Calif., 1968-72, dir. nurses, 1972-77; supr. Hosp. Nursing Kaiser Found. Hosp., Martinez, Calif., 1977-78; dir. med. ctr. nursing Kaiser Permanente Med. Ctr., Richmond, Calif., 1978-80; asst. hosp. adminstr. Kaiser Found. Hosp., Hayward, Calif., 1980-94; assoc. M2, Inc., San Francisco, 1996—; nurse evaluator II Calif. Dept. Health Svcs., San Francisco, 1996—. Mem. health sci. adv. commn. Ohlone Coll., Fremont, Calif., 1980-94; mem. med. aux. and nursing adv. com. Chabot Coll., Hayward, Calif., 1980-94; mem. Grad. Coll. Nursing adv. bd. San Francisco State U., 1986—; mem. Stephens Coll. Alumnae Coun., 1996-98. Recipient Leadership award Sigma Theta Tau, Alpha Gamma, San Jose State U., 1990. Mem. ANA-Calif., Orgn. Nurse Execs.-Calif., East Bay Orgn. Nurse Execs., Assistance League Diablo Valley, Blackhawk Country Club, Blackhawk Bus. Women, Sigma Theta Tau., Alpha Gamma, Nu Xi. Republican. Avocations: philately, gardening. Home: 363 Jacaranda Dr Danville CA 94506-2124

NOTHMANN, RUDOLF S., legal researcher; b. Hamburg, Fed. Republic of Germany, Feb. 4, 1907; came to U.S., 1941, naturalized, 1943; s. Nathan and Henrietta G. (Heymann) N. Referendar, U. Hamburg, 1929, PhD in Law, 1932; postgrad. U. Liverpool Law Sch. (Eng.), 1931-32. Law clk. Hamburg Cts., 1929-31, 32-33; export, legal adviser, adviser ocean marine ins. various firms, Ger., Eng., Sweden, Calif., 1933-43, 46-47; instr. fgn. exchange, fgn. trade Extension div. UCLA, 1947-48, vis. assoc. prof. UCLA, 1951; asst. prof. econs. Whittier Coll., 1948-50, assoc. prof., 1950-51; contract work U.S. Air Force, U.S. Navy, 1953-59; contract negotiator space projects, space and missile systems orgn. USAF, L.A., 1959-77; pvt. researcher in internat. comml. law, Pacific Palisades, Calif., 1977—. With U.S. Army, 1943-45; ETO. Recipient Gold Tape award Air Force Systems Command, 1970. Mem. Internat. Bar Assn. (vice chmn. internat. sales and related comml. trans. com. 1977-82), Am. Econ. Assn., Calif. Bar Assn. (internat. law sect.), Am. Soc. Internat. Law, Uebersee Club (Hamburg, Germany). Author: The Insurance Certificate in International Ocean Marine Insurance Law and Foreign Trade, 1932; The Oldest Corporation in the World: Six Hundred Years of Economic Evolution, 1949. Home: PO Box 32 Pacific Palisades CA 90272-0032

NOTKIN, LEONARD SHELDON, architect; b. N.Y.C., Apr. 1, 1931; s. Murry and Evelyn (Mofshatz) N.; m. Ann Mathilda Stefanko, Nov. 24, 1956; children: Jennifer, Mead. BArch, U. Pa., 1954. Registered architect, N.Y., Mass., Ohio, Pa., Nat. Coun. Archtl. Registration Bds. Architect, Percival Goodman (Architect), N.Y.C., 1956-58; Architect Bloch and Hesse (Architects), N.Y.C., 1958-59, Resnick and Green (Architects), N.Y.C., 1959-60; architect, prin., v.p. The Architects Collaborative, Inc., Cambridge, Mass., 1960-95; chief design critic Boston Archtl. Center, 1964-69; mem. Lexington (Mass.) Design Adv. Com., 1970-73, chmn., 1972; profl. studio critic Harvard Grad. Sch. Design, 1974-76; pres. Boston Design Assocs., Inc., Waltham, Mass., 1995—. Major recent works include Intermediate Sch. 137, Bronx, N.Y., 1976, Visual Arts Instructional Facility SUNY, Purchase, 1976, Lahey Clinic Med. Ctr., Burlington, Mass., 1976—, W. Penn Hosp., Pitts., 1977, St. Francis/St. George Hosp., Cin., 1978, Blue Cross/Blue Shield of Conn. Hdqrs., North Haven, Temple U. Hosp., Phila., composite hosp. Loring AFB, Limestone, Maine, Med. Facilities, Fort Drum, N.Y., Health Care Internat. Ltd., Glasgow, Scotland, Intensive Care Hosp. and Hotel, Univ. Ky. Cancer Rsch. Ctr., Children's Hosp. Med. Ctr. Rsch. Lab., Cin., new main entrance, lobby and admissions facilities Hosp. of U. Pa., Phila., Childrens Hosp., Kuwait, 1996, Health Facilities, Algiers,

Algeria, 1996. Served with U.S. Army, 1954-56. Recipient Design award for IBM Hdqrs., Gaithersburg, Md. Progressive Architecture mag., 1964; 1st pl. award for Worcester (Mass.) Community Center AIA, 1966; Design award for Worcester Found. Exptl. Biology bldg. Mass. chpt. AIA, 1968; Design award NIH Research Lab., Bethesda, Md. GSA, 1972; Best Bldg. of Yr. award for Norwalk (Conn.) High Sch. Assn. for Better Community Design, 1972; Honor award Conn. Soc. Architects AIA, 1974. Mem. AIA, Mass. State Assn. Architects, Boston Soc. Architects (dir. 1976-79, spl. design citation 1993). Office: Boston Design Assocs Inc 393 Totten Pond Rd Waltham MA 02154-2013

NOTO, LUCIO R., gas and oil industry executive; b. Apr. 24, 1939. BS in Physics, U. Notre Dame; MBA, Cornell U.; Woodrow Wilson Fell., U. Notre Dame; Bache Fell., Cornell U. With Mobil Corp., 1962—; pres. Mobil Saudi Arabia, 1981-85, chmn., 1985-86; v.p. planning and econs. Mobil Corp./Mobil Oil Corp., 1986-88, CFO, 1989-93, pres., 1993—, chmn. bd., CEO, COO, 1994—. Internat. Business Machines Corp. (dir.), Amer. petroleum Inst. Public Policy Committee, The Business Council, The Council on Foreign Relations & Business Roundtable. Office: Mobil Corp 3225 Gallows Rd Fairfax VA 22031-4872

NOTOPOULOS, ALEXANDER ANASTASIOS, JR., lawyer; b. Altoona, Pa., Jan. 29, 1953; s. Alexander Anastasios Sr. and Christine (Economou) N.; m. Alexis J. Anderson, Aug. 4, 1984. BA, Amherst Coll., 1974; JD, Harvard U., 1977. Bar: Mass. 1978, U.S. Dist. Ct. Mass. 1979. Law clk. to judge U.S. Ct. Appeals (3d cir.), Phila., 1977-78; assoc. Sullivan & Worcester, Boston, 1978-85, ptnr., 1985—. Home: 96 Shornecliffe Rd Newton MA 02158-2421 Office: Sullivan & Worcester One Post Office Sq Boston MA 02109

NOTTAY, BALDEV KAUR, microbiologist; b. Nairobi, Kenya, East Africa, Jan. 15, 1936; d. Santa Singh and Swaran (Kaur) N. B.S. with honors, U. Bombay, 1960; M.Sc., U. Bombay, 1964. Research student Polio Research Unit, Haffkine Inst., Bombay, India, 1962-63; assoc. head poliovirus research Virology Dept., Med. Research Lab., Nairobi, 1964-71; vis. assoc. viral reagents Ctrs. Disease Control, Atlanta, 1972-74, vis. assoc. enteric virology br., 1974-78, research microbiologist molecular biology section, respiratory and enterovirus br., div. viral and rickettsial diseases, 1978-96, retired, 1996. Contbr. articles to profl. jours. Home: 5574 Wylstream St Norcross GA 30093-4153

NOTTINGHAM, EDWARD WILLIS, JR., federal judge; b. Denver, Jan. 9, 1948; s. Edward Willis and Willie Newton (Gullett) N.; m. Cheryl Ann Card, June 6, 1970 (div. Feb. 1981); children: Amelia Charlene, Edward Willis III; m. Janis Ellen Chapman, Aug. 18, 1984; 1 child, Spencer Chapman. AB, Cornell U., 1969; JD, U. Colo., 1972. Bar: Colo. 1972, U.S. Dist. Ct. Colo. 1972, U.S. Ct. Appeals (10th cir.) 1973. Law clk. to presiding judge U.S. Dist. Ct. Colo., Denver, 1972-73; assoc. Sherman & Howard, Denver, 1973-76, 78-80, ptnr., 1980-87; ptnr. Beckner & Nottingham, Grand Junction, Colo., 1987-89; asst. U.S. atty. U.S. Dept. Justice, Denver, 1976-78; U.S. dist. judge Dist. of Colo., Denver, 1989—. Bd. dirs. Beaver Creek Met. Dist., Avon, Colo., 1980-88, Justice Info. Ctr., Denver, 1985-87, 21st Jud. Dist. Victim Compensation Fund, Grand Junction, Colo., 1987-89. Mem. ABA, Colo. Bar Assn. (chmn. criminal law sect. 1983-85, chmn. ethics com. 1988-89), Order of Coif, Denver Athletic Club, Delta Sigma Rho, Tau Kappa Alpha. Episcopalian. Office: US Dist Ct 1929 Stout St Denver CO 80294-0001

NOTTINGHAM, ROBINSON KENDALL, life insurance company executive; b. Balt., Apr. 4, 1938; s. Robinson Jr. and Juliet (Moore) N.; m. Elizabeth LeViness, Aug. 26, 1960; children: Robinson Kendall Jr., Charles Denmead. BA in Polit. Sci., Johns Hopkins U., 1959; postgrad., Johns Hopkins U., Washington, 1965. With Am. Internat. Group, Inc., Hong Kong and Bangkok, 1968-71; chief exec. officer for Japan and Korea Am. Internat. Group, Inc., Tokyo, 1986-89; mng. dir. Hanover Ins. Co., Universal Ins. Co., Bangkok, 1971-73, Am. Internat. Ins. Co., Lagos, Nigeria, 1973-75; regional pres. African div. Am. Internat. Underwriters, N.Y.C., 1975-78, Middle Ea. div., 1978-83, European div., 1983-86; chmn., bd. dirs., CEO Am. Life Ins. Co., Wilmington, Del., 1989—; bd. dirs. AIG Overseas Fin. (Japan) Inc., Tokyo, Am. Home Assurance Co., N.Y.C., AIU Ins. Co., N.Y.C. Pres. USO Coun., Tokyo, 1987-89; mem. world bd. govs. USO, Washington, 1987—; mem. adv. coun. Johns Hopkins U. Sch. Advanced Internat. Studies, Washington, 1984—. Served to lt. comdr. USNR, 1960-68. Mem. Princeton Club (N.Y.C.), Short Hills Club (N.J.), Bay Head Yacht Club (N.J.), Baltusrol Club (Springfield, N.J.), Chevy Chase (Md.) Club, Delta Phi. Republican. Episcopalian. Avocation: sailing. Home: 393 Charlton Ave South Orange NJ 07079-2405 Office: Am Life Ins Co 1 Alico Plz Wilmington DE 19899

NOTTINGHAM, WILLIAM JESSE, retired church mission executive, minister; b. Sharon, Pa., Nov. 22, 1927; s. Jess William and Alice May (Green) N.; m. Patricia Clutts, Feb. 1, 1949; children: Theodore Jess, Deborah Joan Selke, Nancy Alice, Gregory Philip. BA, Bethany Coll., W.Va., 1949, DD (hon.), 1987; BD, Union Theol. Sem., N.Y.C., 1953; PhD, Columbia U., 1962; DD (hon.), Christian Theol. Sem., Indpls., 1984. Ordained to ministry Christian Ch. (Disciples of Christ), Oct. 21, 1945. Pastor Ch. of Christ, Canoe Camp and Covington, Pa., 1949-50; field worker Ch. of the Master, N.Y.C., 1950-53; assoc. min. Nat. City Christian Ch., Washington, 1954-58; fraternal worker Coun. on Christian Unity, France, 1958-65; with CIMADE and Centre de Glay; with youth dept. World Coun. of Chs., Geneva, 1965-68; exec. sec. for Latin Am. and Caribbean Divsn. Overseas Ministries, Christian Ch. (Disciples of Christ and United Ch. Christ), Indpls., 1968-76, exec. sec. East Asia and Pacific, 1976-83, exec. sec. Europe, pres., 1984-94; affiliate prof. mission Christian Theol. Sem., 1995—; ret., 1994. Author: Christian Faith and Secular Action: An Introduction to the Life and Thought of Jacques Maritain, 1968, The Practice and Preaching of Liberation, 1986, The Social Ethics of Martin Bucer 1491-1551, 1962; translator: God's Underground, 1970, Prayer at the Heart of Life, 1975, Materialist Approaches to the Bible, 1985, Madeleine Barot, 1991; contbr. articles to profl. jours. Mem. Ind. Interfaith Com. for Worker Justice. Fulbright scholar, Strasbourg, France, 1953-54. Mem. Nat. Coun. Chs. of Christ in USA (gen. bd.), Assn. Disciples for Theol. Discussion, Christians Associated for Relations with Eastern Europe, Am. Maritain Assn. Democrat.

NOTZ, JOHN KRANZ, JR., arbitrator and mediator, retired lawyer; b. Chgo., Jan. 5, 1932; s. John Kranz and Elinor (Trostel) N.; m. Janis Wellin, Apr. 23, 1966; children: Jane Elinor, John Wellin. BA, Williams Coll., 1953; JD, Northwestern U., 1956. Bar: Ill. 1956, Fla. 1957, Wis. 1989, U.S. Supreme Ct. 1960. Assoc. 1st Nat. Bank Chgo., 1954, 1956; from assoc. to ptnr. Gardner, Carton & Douglas, Chgo., 1960-95, of counsel, 1990-95; ret., 1996; arbitrator, mediator CPR Inst. for Dispute Resolution, Am. Arbitration Assn., Nat. Assn. Securities Dealers Regulatory Body, Nat. Futures Assn., N.Y. Stock Exch., Am. Stock Exch. Contbr. numerous articles to profl. jours. Sec. State Corp. Acts Adv. Com., 1982-95, chmn., 1987-89; bd. dirs., pres. Chgo. Lit. Club; bd. dirs. Ill. Inst. Continuing Legal Edn., 1980-91, chmn., 1990-91; bd. dirs., treas. Inspired Ptnrs.; bd. trustees Graceland Cemetery, Beloit Coll., pub. mem. Bus. Conduct Commn., Chgo. Bd. Options Exchange. 1st lt. USAF, 1957-60. Recipient Svc. award Northwestern U., 1978. Fellow Am. Bar Found. (life), Ill. Bar Found. (life), Chgo. Bar Found. (life); mem. Am. Law Inst., Ill. State Bar Assn., Chgo. Bar Assn., Wis. State Bar, Law and Legal Club City Chgo., Racquet Club Chgo., Lake Geneva (Wis.) Country Club, Mid-Day Club (Chgo., bd. trustees, v.p.), Literary Club (Chgo., pres.), Caxton Club (Chgo.). Office: care Gardner Carton & Douglas 3300 Quaker Tower 321 N Clark St Chicago IL 60610-4715

NOVA, CRAIG, writer; b. Los Angeles, July 5, 1945; s. Karl and Elizabeth (Sinclair) N.; m. Christina Barnes, July 2, 1977; children: Abigail, Tate. B.A., U. Calif.-Berkeley, 1967; M.F.A., Columbia U., 1969. Author: Turkey Hash, 1972, The Geek, 1975, Incandescence, 1978, The Good Son, 1982, The Congressman's Daughter, 1986, Tornado Alley, 1989, Trombone, 1992, The Book of Dreams, 1994, The Universal Donor, 1997. Recipient Harper-Saxton prize Harper and Row, Pubs., 1972; recipient award in lit. Am. Acad. and Inst. Arts and Letters; Guggenheim Found. fellow, 1977; fellow Nat. Endowment for Arts, 1973, Nat. Endowment for Arts, 1975, Creative Artists Pub. Service, 1976; NEA fellow, 1985; story included in Best Am. Short Stories, 1987.

NOVACEK, JAY MCKINLEY, professional football player; b. Martin, S.D., Oct. 24, 1962. BS in Indsl. Edn., U. Wyoming, 1986. With St. Louis Cardinals, 1985-87, Phoenix Cardinals (formerly St. Louis Cardinals), 1988-89; tight end Dallas Cowboys, 1990—; player Pro Bowl, 1991-93, Super Bowl XXVII, 1992, XXVIII, 1993. Office: Dallas Cowboys 1 Cowboys Pky Irving TX 75063-4945*

NOVACK, ALVIN JOHN, physician; b. Red Lodge, Mont., Mar. 11, 1925; s. John and Anna Geraldine (Maddio) N.; m. Betty P. Novack, Jan. 10, 1952; children—Vance, Deborah, Michelle, Mitchel, Craig, Brad, Mary Ellen, Garth. M.D., U. Wash., 1952. Intern Harper Hosp., Detroit, 1952; resident in surgery Harper Hosp., 1953; resident in otolaryngology Johns Hopkins U., 1954-57; resident in surgery Columbia-Presbyn. Med. Center, N.Y.C., 1957-60; fellow head and neck surgery Columbia-Presbyn. Med. Center, 1957-60; dir. head and neck surgery Swedish Hosp., Seattle, 1960-91; dir. otolaryngology Children's Orthopedic Hosp., Seattle, 1965-78; ret., 1991. Contbr. articles to med. jours. Served to lt. AUS, 1940-43. Nat. Cancer Inst. fellow, 1957-60. Fellow A.C.S.; mem. AMA, Am. Acad. Otolaryngology and Head and Neck Surgery, Soc. Head and Neck Surgeons, North Pacific Surg. Assn., Pacific Coast Surg. Assn., Seattle Surg. Soc.

NOVACKY, ANTON JAN, plant pathologist, educator; b. Bratislava, Czechoslovakia, June 3, 1933; came to U.S., 1968; s. Jan Martin and Katarina (Fischer) N.; m. Dorothy Edit Hyross, June 28, 1958; children: Andrea Novacky Congdon, Thomas Martin. Student, Charles U., Prague, Czechoslovakia; BS, Comenius U., Bratislava, 1955, MS, 1956; PhD, Czechoslovak Acad. Sci., Prague, 1965. Postgrad. fellow U. Moscow, Russia, 1964; postdoctoral fellow U. Ky., Lexington, 1966-69; postdoctoral rsch. assoc. U. Mo., Columbia, 1969-70, asst. prof., 1970-74, assoc. prof., 1974-82, prof., 1982—; rsch. phytopathologist Inst. Exptl. Phytopathology and Entomology, Bratislava, Czechoslovakia, 1962-68. Author: (with R.N. Goodman) The Hypersensitive Reaction in Plants to Pathogens, 1994; speaker various seminars and meeting presentations; contbr. articles to profl. jours. Grantee NSF, 1986-89, 1978-82, USDA, 1978-83, 93-95, MSMC, 1986-89; fellow Japanese Soc. for Promotion of Sci. Rsch., 1984; recipient German Academic Exch. award, 1976, Alexander von Humboldt Sr. U.S. Scientist, 1983. Mem. AAAS, Am. Phytopathol. Soc. (fellow 1986, chair 1984-85), Am. Soc. Plant Physiologists, Sigma Xi. Roman Catholic. Home: 311 Crown Pt Columbia MO 65203-2202 Office: U Mo 108 Waters Hall Columbia MO 65211

NOVAK, ALFRED, retired biology educator; b. Chgo., Jan. 28, 1915; s. Phillip and Celia (Kaplan) N.; m. Helen Ascher, Feb. 19, 1944 (dec. Oct. 20, 1985); children—Paul, Gregory, David. A.A., U. Chgo., 1934, B.S., 1936; M.S., 1941; M.Ed., Chgo. Tchrs. Coll., 1940; Ph.D., Mich. State U., 1950. Mem. faculty Mich. State U., 1945-61, asso. prof. biology, 1951-55, prof., 1955-61; sci. coordinator, prof. emeritus biology Stephens Coll., Columbia, Mo., 1961-80; prof. biology div. U. Mo., Columbia, 1980-81; cons., writer Biol. Sci. Curriculum Study, Boulder, Colo., 1960-61; cons. sci. curriculum, facilities planning for colls. and univs., 1955—; heart damage research U. Bologna (Italy) Med. Sch., 1972; bd. dirs. Allied Health Programs. Adv. biology editor, writer: Ency. Americana, 1959-69. Served with USAAF, 1941-44. Recipient Favilli medal Istituto di Patologia Generale, Bologna, 1972; Guggenheim fellow Cambridge (Eng.) U., 1957-58; NIH fellow Cal. Inst. Tech., 1950. Mem. Am. Assn. Gen. Liberal Edn. (past pres.), Nat. Assn. Biology Tchrs., AAAS. Discovered cold pack treatment for mumps orchitis, 1945. Home: 4954 W 60th Ter Mission KS 66205-3079 *I have lived through two major wars, the 1929 depression, the turbulent 60's, distressing inflation of the 70's and rejuvenation in the early 80's. I am dismayed with bureaucratic waste, the decay in character, honesty & morality. I am also appalled by the ineptitude of the U.S. judicial system. There are too many laws and too many corrupt lawyers. Our freedoms are being eroded, yet democracy is still the greatest hope of the world.*

NOVAK, BARBARA, art history educator; b. N.Y.C.; d. Joseph and Sadie (Kaufman) N.; m. Brian O'Doherty, July 5, 1960. B.A., Barnard Coll., 1951; M.A., Radcliffe Coll., 1953, Ph.D., 1957. TV instr. Mus. Fine Arts, Boston, 1957-58; mem. faculty Barnard Coll., Columbia U., N.Y.C., 1958—; prof. art history Barnard Coll., Columbia U., 1970—, Helen G. Altschul prof., 1984—; adv. council Archives of Am. Art, NAD. Author: American Painting of the 19th Century, 1969, Nature and Culture, 1980, The Thyssen-Bornemisza Collection 19th Century American Painting, 1986, Alice's Neck, 1987, The Ape and the Whale, 1995, (play) The Ape and the Whale: Darwin and Melville in Their Own Words, 1987 (performed at Symphony Space 1987), Dreams and Shadows: Thomas H. Hotchkiss in 19th Century Italy, 1993; co-editor: Next to Nature, 1980; mem. editorial bd. Am. Art Jour. Commr. Nat. Portrait Gallery; trustee N.Y. Hist. Soc. Fulbright fellow Belgium, 1953-54; Guggenheim fellow, 1974; Nat. Book Critics nominee, 1980; Los Angeles Times Book Award nominee, 1980; Am. Book Award paperback nominee, 1981. Fellow Soc. Am. Historians, Phila. Atheneum; mem. Soc. Am. Historians, Am. Antiquarian Soc., Coll. Art Assn. (dir. 1974-77), N.Y. Hist. Soc. (trustee), PEN. Office: Barnard Coll Art History Dept 606 W 120th St New York NY 10027-5706

NOVAK, CHRISTINE ALLISON, advertising agency executive; b. Glen Ridge, N.J., May 14, 1953; d. Richard F. and Joyce S. (Borgesen) N. BA, Yale U., 1975; MBA, Harvard U., 1979. Account exec., v.p., then mgmt. dir. Foote Cone & Belding, N.Y.C., 1979-86; sr. v.p., mgmt. supr. Doyle, Graf, Mabley Advt., N.Y.C., 1987; sr. v.p., dir. client svcs. Euramerica Internat. Advt. (an Ogilvy Group Co.), N.Y.C., 1988—. Account exec. TV campaign, Clairol products, 1982 (Clio award 1982); mgmt. dir., Frito-Lay products, 1984 (Effie award 1986), Nabisco products, 1986 (Addy award 1986). Mem. Founders' Soc., N.Y. Community Ctr., 1988. Mem. Harvard Bus. Sch. Club N.Y. Office: Ogilvy and Mather Advt 390 W 49th St New York NY 10019-7303

NOVAK, DARWIN ALBERT, JR., engineering company executive, chemical engineer; b. Quincy, Ill., Nov. 25, 1935; s. Darwin Albert and Mildred Luisa (Schuermann) N.; m. Carol Joan Stephany, Apr. 22, 1961; children: Robert Brian, Linda Susan. B Chem. Engring., Cornell U., 1958; MS, Washington U., St. Louis, 1966, DSc, 1973. Registered profl. engr., Mo. Pilot plant engr. Mallinckrodt, St. Louis, 1958-60; rsch. engr. Monsanto Co., St. Louis, 1960-64; with tech. svc. dept. Monsanto Co., Brussels, 1964-66; engring. specialist Monsanto Co., St. Louis, 1966-81, mgr. engring., 1981-87; dir. engring. Henkel, Ambler, Pa., 1987-92; consulting engr. BE&K DE, Newark, Del., 1992-95; mgr. engring. Cabot Performance Materials, Boyertown, Pa., 1995-96, sr. technologist, 1997—; affiliate prof. Washington U., 1984-87; mem. assessment bd. NAE, Gaithersburg, Md., 1981-86. Patentee for detergent process, oil recovery. Fellow AIChE (dir., chmn. mgmt. div. 1986-89); mem. NSPE, Am. Chem. Soc. Republican. Avocations: photography, personal computing. Home: 27 Timber Rd Horsham PA 19044-3810 Office: Cabot Performance Materials County Line Rd Boyertown PA 19512

NOVAK, DAVID, Judaic studies educator, rabbi; b. Chgo., Aug. 19, 1941; s. Syd and Sylvia (Wien) N.; m. Melva Ziman, July 3, 1963; children: Marianne, Jacob George. AB in Classics and Ancient History, U. Chgo., 1961; M in Hebrew Lit., Jewish Theol. Sem. Am., 1964; PhD, Georgetown U., 1971. Ordained rabbi, 1966. Rabbi Shaare Tikvah Congregation, 1966-69; dir. Jewish chaplaincy St. Elizabeth's Hosp., 1966-69; rabbi Emanuel Synagogue, Oklahoma City, 1969-72, Beth Tfiloh Congregation, Balt., 1972-77, Congregation Beth El, Norfolk, Va., 1977-81, Congregation Darchay Noam, Far Rockaway, N.Y., 1981-89; Edgar M. Bronfman prof. modern Judaic studies U. Va., Charlottesville, 1989-97; chair of Jewish studies U. Toronto, 1997—; lectr. philosophy Oklahoma City U., 1969-72, New Sch. for Social Rsch., 1982-84; lectr. Jewish studies Balt. Hebrew Coll., 1972-77; adj. asst. prof. philosophy Old Dominion U., 1977-81; vis. assoc. prof. Talmud Jewish Theol. Sem. Am., 1986-88; adj. assoc. prof. Baruch Coll., CUNY, 1984-88, adj. prof., 1989; founder, v.p., coord. panel Halakhic Inquiry Union Traditional Judaism/Inst. Traditional Judaism; disting. vis. prof. religion and corp. ethics Drew U., 1995. Contbg. editor First Things. Sec.-treas. Inst. on Religion and Pub. Life. Essay winner Hyman G. Enelow prize Jewish Theol. Sem. Am., 1975; recipient Rabbi Jacob B. Augus award Jewish Theol. Sem. Am., 1984; Woodrow Wilson Internat. Ctr. for Scholars fellow, 1992-93. Fellow Acad. for Jewish Philosophy; mem. Am. Theol. Soc., Assn. for Jewish Studies, Am. Acad. Religion, Jewish Law Assn., Leo Baeck Inst. Office: Univ Coll Dept Religious Studies, 15 King's College Cir, Toronto, ON Canada M5S 3H7

NOVAK, DENNIS E., family practice physician; b. East Liverpool, Ohio, Jan. 5, 1946. BA, Bklyn. Coll., 1966; Lic. in Med. Scis., U. Brussels, 1972; MD, Rutgers U., 1974. Diplomate Am. Bd. Family Practice, Nat. Bd. Med. Examiners. Resident in family practice Monmouth Med. Ctr., Long Branch, N.J., 1974-77; clin. instr. to clin. asst. prof. Robert Wood Johnson Med. Sch., 1977—, chmn. dept. family practice; pvt. practice specializing in family medicine, 1977—; attending physician utilization rev. com. Comty. Meml. Hosp., 1987-88, quality assurance com., 1988, dept. family practice quality assurance com.; physician reviewer, quality assurance Garden State Rehab. Hosp.; physican exec. com. Cmty. Med. Assocs. Mem. exec. adv. bd. Ocean County coun. Boy Scouts Am.; bd. trustees United Way Ocean County., Area VII Physician Rev. Org., 1983-86. Fellow Am. Acad. Family Practice; mem. Ocean County Acad. Family Practice (v.p. 1983), Ocean County Med. Soc. (bd. trustees 1983-87). Avocations: photography, scuba. Address: PO Box 780 1001 Lacey Rd Forked River NJ 08731

NOVAK, HARRY R., manufacturing company executive; b. Chgo., Sept. 30, 1951; s. Edward M. and Rose (Loncar) N.; m. Shawn Sternquist, Sept. 7, 1975; children: Andrea, Jacob, Bethany. BS in Econs., MacMurray Coll., Jacksonville, Ill., 1973; MBA in Fin., DePaul U., 1977. Ops. mgr. to v.p., regional mgr. Heller Fin. Inc., Chgo., 1974-87; v.p. Golenberg & Assocs., Cleve., 1987-88; sr. v.p., CFO Gibson-Homans Co., Twinsburg, Ohio, 1988—. Congregation pres. First Luth. Ch., Strongsville, Ohio, 1987-92; founder Strongsville Area Youth Group, 1992; mem. Strongsville Choral Boosters, 1991-94. Mem. Cleve. Growth Assn. Avocations: chess, golf, pocket billards, computers. Office: Gibson-Homans Co 1755 Enterprise Pky Twinsburg OH 44087-2203

NOVAK, JOSEPH DONALD, science educator, knowlege studies specialist; b. Mpls., Dec. 2, 1930; s. Joseph Daniel and Anna (Podany) N.; m. Joan Owen, July 18, 1953; children: Joseph Mark, Barbara Joan, William John. BS, U. Minn., 1952, MA, 1954, PhD, 1958. Teaching asst. U. Minn., Mpls., 1952-56, instr., 1956-57; asst. prof. Kans. State Tchrs. Coll., 1957-59; asst. prof. Purdue U., West Lafayette, Ind., 1959-62, assoc. prof., 1962-67; prof. Cornell U., Ithaca, N.Y., 1967-95, prof. emeritus, 1995—; knowledge constrn. and orgn. cons. to Procter & Gamble and other cos.; cons. to over 300 schs. and colls., 1975—; vis. fellow Harvard U., 1965-66; disting. vis. prof. U. N.C., Wilmington, 1980, U. Western Fla., 1987-88; vis. prof. U. South Fla., 1995. Author: Learning How to Learn, 1984, in 10 langs. 1984-96, Educational Psychology: A Cognitive View, 1978, A Theory of Education, 1977, Aprendizaje Significativo: Techieas y Aplicaciones, 1997; 15 others; contbr. over 100 articles to profl. jours. Fellow Tozer Found., Lydia Anderson, 1955-56; research assoc. Harvard U., 1965-66; Fulbright-Hayes Sr. Scholar, Australia, 1980. Fellow AAAS (sec. sect. Q); mem. APA, NSTA, Am. Inst. Biol. Scis., Nat. Assn. Rsch. in Sci. Tchr. (Outstanding Contbns. Sci. Tchg. Through Rsch. award 1990), Nat. Assn. Biology Tchrs. (hon.), Assn. for Edn. of Tchrs. of Sci., Am. Ednl. Rsch. Assn., Sigma Xi. Avocations: hiking; swimming; dancing; music. Home: 1403 Slaterville Rd Ithaca NY 14850-6207 Office: Cornell U Dept Edn Kennedy Hall Ithaca NY 14853

NOVAK, JULIE COWAN, nursing educator, researcher, clinician; b. Peoria, Ill., Oct. 2, 1950; m. Robert E. Novak, 1972; children: Andrew, Christopher, Nicholas. BS in Nursing, U. Iowa, 1972, MA in Nursing of Children, 1976; D.N.Sc., U. San Diego, 1989. RN, Va., Calif. Charge nurse surg. and med. ICU U. Iowa Hosp. and Clinics, 1972-73; instr. med. sur. nursing St. Luke's Sch. Nursing, Cedar Rapids, Iowa, 1973-74; instr. family and cmty. health U. Iowa Coll. of Nursing, 1974-75; perinatal nurse clinician U. Iowa Hosps., 1976-77; pediatric nurse practitioner Chicano Cmty. Health Ctr., 1978-80; lectr., asst. prof. child health nursing and physical assesstment San Diego State U., 1977-79; child health nurse practitioner program coord. U. Calif., San Diego, 1978-82; pediatric nurse practitioner San Diego City Schs., 1980-82; coord. infant spl. care ctr. follow-up program U. Calif., San Diego, 1982-83, assoc. clin. prof. intercampus grad. studies, 1983-90, dir. health promotion divsn. cmty. and family medicine, 1985-90; assoc. clin. prof. dept. cmty. family medicine U. Calif. Divsn. Health Care Sci., San Diego, 1990-94; assoc. prof. San Diego State U. Sch. Nursing, 1990-94, Calif. Nursing Students Assn. faculty advisor, 1992-94; pediatric nurse practitioner Naval Hosp., 1990-92, Comp. Health Clinic, 1990-94; prof., dir. Master's in Primary Care/Family Nurse Practitioner, Pediatric Nurse Practitioner, Women's Health Practitioner programs U. Va. Schs., Charlottesville, 1994—; cons. child health San Diego State U. Child Study Ctr.; mem. accident prevention com. Am. Acad. Pediats.; mem. adv. bd. Albemarle County Sch Health, 1995—, Camp Holiday Trails, 1995—; mem. reg. adv. bd. Am. Lung Assn., 1997—. Contbr. numerous articles to profl. jours. and book chpts. to 7 texts; co-author: Ingall's & Salerno's Maternal Child Nursing, 1995, Mosby Year Book; mem. editl. bd. Jour. Perinatal and Neonatal Nursing, 1986-93, Children's Nurse, 1982-88, ; mem. editl. bd., reviewer Jour. Pediatric Health Care, 1987-93; speaker in field. Chair Ann. Refugee Clothing Drive, East San Diego, ESL Program, Car Seat Roundup U. Calif., San Diego, 1983-85; mem. telethon March of Dimes; mem. steering com. Healthy Mothers/Healthy Babies Coalition; chair ways and means com. Benchley-Weinberger Elem. Sch. PTA, 1985-87, pres., 1988-90; v.p., pres. Friends Jamul Schs. Found.; co-chair teen outreach program Jr. League San Diego, 1987-88, chair, 1989-90, bd. dirs., 1990-92; educator presch. health San Carlos Meth. Ch.; mem. Head Start Policy Coun., 1992-94, San Diego County Dropout Prevention Roundtable, 1991-93, Western Albemarle H.S. Planning Team, 1994—. Recipient Svc. award Benchley-Weinberger Elem. Sch. PTA, 1988, Hon. Youth Svc. award Calif. Congress Parents and Tchrs., Loretta C. Ford Award for excellence as an nurse practitioner in edn. U. Colo., 1990, March of Dimes Svc. commendation, 1983, Project Hope Svc. commendation, 1983, Hon. Svc. award Calif. Congress of Parents, Tchrs. & Students, 1988, Doctoral Student fellowship U. San Diego, 1986, and numerous others. Mem. ANA (mem. ANCC rsch. coalition on credentialing 1997—), Nat. Certification Bd. Pediatric Nurse Practitioners and Nurses (pres.), Nat. Assn. Pediat. Nurse Practioners Assoc. (chpt. pres., program com., coord. legis. field, nat. cert. chair 1992—), Calif. Nurse Assn., Pi Lamda Theta, Sigma Theta Tau (mem. nominations com. 1990-91, pres. elect Gamma Gamma chpt. 1993-94, Beta Kappa 1995—, Media award, 1992). Home: 2415 Harmony Dr Charlottesville VA 22901-8990

NOVAK, KIM (MARILYN NOVAK), actress; b. Chgo., Feb. 13, 1933; d. Joseph A. and Blanche (Kral) N.; m. Richard Johnson, April 1965 (div.); m. Robert Malloy, Jan. 1977. Student, Wright Jr. College, Chgo.; A.A., Los Angeles City College, 1958. appeared in: (films) The French Line, 1953, Pushover, 1954, Phffft, 1954, Five Against the House, 1955, Son of Sinbad, 1955, Picnic, 1955, The Man with the Golden Arm, 1956, The Eddie Duchin Story, 1956, Jeanne Eagles, 1957, Pal Joey, 1958, Vertigo, 1958, Bell, Book and Candle, 1958, Middle of the Night, 1959, Strangers When We Meet, 1960, Pépé, 1960, Boys' Night Out, 1962, The Notorious Landlady, 1962, Of Human Bondage, 1964, Kiss Me Stupid, 1964, The Amorous Adventures of Moll Flanders, 1965, The Legend of Lylah Clare, 1968, The Great Bank Robbery, 1969, Tales That Witness Madness, 1973, The White Buffalo, 1977, Just a Gigolo, 1979, The Mirror Crack'd, 1980, The Children, 1990, Liebestraum, 1991; (TV movies) Third Girl from the Left, 1974, Satan's Triangle, 1975, Malibu, 1983; (TV series) Falcon Crest, 1986-87, Alfred Hitchcock Presents, 1985. Named one of 10 most popular movie stars by Box-Office mag. 1956, All-Am. Favorite 1961, Brussels World Fair poll as favorite all-time actress in world 1958. Office: William Morris Agency 151 S El Camino Dr Beverly Hills CA 90212-2704

NOVAK, MARLENA, artist, educator, writer, curator; b. Brownsville, Pa., Mar. 6, 1957; d. Anthony Edward and Mary Margaret (Shader) N.; m. Jay Alan Yim, June 28, 1990. BFA in Painting, Carnegie-Mellon U., 1982; MFA in Art Theory and Practice (Painting), Northwestern U., 1986. tchr. art, Northwestern U., Evanston, Ill., 1985, 89, 96, De Paul U., Chgo., 1986-92, 94, 96, Amsterdams Inst. voor Schilderkunst, The Netherlands, 1996; asst. prof. U. N.Mex., Albuquerque, 1992-93. One person shows include Handled With Care Gallery, Provincetown, Mass., 1983, Dittmar Gallery, Evanston, 1986, Carson Street Gallery, Pitts., 1989, C.G. Jung Inst. Chgo.,

Evanston, 1990, Wabash Coll., Crawfordsville, Ind., 1990, Esther Saks Gallery, Chgo., 1991, MC Gallery, Mpls., 1992, Ruschman Gallery, Indpls., 1993, Kay Garvey Gallery, Chgo., 1994, 95, Three Ill. Ctr., Chgo., 1994, Galerie Vromans, Amsterdam, 1995; exhibited in group shows at Harrisburg (Pa.) Mus., 1984, Govt. Ctr., Boston, 1984, Univ. Kobe (Japan), 1985, Union Art Gallery, Milw., 1986, Rockford (Ill.) Mus., 1986, Gracie Mansion Gallery Mus. Store, N.Y.C., 1987, George Walter Vincent Smith Art Mus., Springfield, Mass., 1988, East West Contemporary Art Gallery, Chgo., 1989, Provincetown Art Assn. and Mus., 1989, 94, Eve Mannes Gallery, Atlanta, 1990, Mary and Leigh Block Gallery, Northwestern U., Ill., 1990, Deson-Saunders Gallery, Chgo., 1990, Chgo. Cultural Ctr., 1990, Art Inst. Chgo., 1990, Esther Saks Fine Art, Chgo., 1991, 92, DePaul U. Art Gallery, Chgo., 1992, Ruschman Gallery, 1992, 94, MC Gallery, 1992, Lowe Gallery, Atlanta, 1992, Kay Garvey Gallery, 1992, 93, 95, Charlotte Jackson Fine Art, Santa Fe, 1993, John Sommers Gallery, 1993, CWCA, Chgo., 1993, Klein Art Works, 1993, Greenpeace Fund Benefit, Chgo., 1994, Bethany Coll. Fine Art Ctr., Mankato, Minn., 1994, Galerie Vromans, 1994, 95, Wabash Coll., 1994, Global Focus, Beijing, 1995, Stichting Amazone, Amsterdam, 1995, Galerie Beeld & Ambeeld, Enschede, The Netherlands, 1996, Galerie Waszkowiak, Berlin, 1996; contbr. articles to various publs. Avocations: travelling, sailing. Home: 835 N Wood St Apt 102 Chicago IL 60622-5044

NOVAK, MARTHA LOIS, elementary education educator; b. Cape Girardeau, Mo., Sept. 14, 1938; d. Roy Edward and Mable Mae (Clinton) Partain; m. Raymond Victor Novak, Nov. 29, 1968; children: Carolyn, Edward. BA, U. Calif., Fresno, 1964. Cert. tchr., Calif. Tchr. kindergarten Clovis (Calif.) Unified Sch. Dist., 1964; tchr. Magnolia Sch. Dist., Anaheim, Calif., 1964-69, Burr Oak Sch. Dist., Chgo., 1969-70, Buttonwillow (Calif.) Sch. Dist., 1970-72, Richland Sch. Dist., Shafter, Calif., 1972-80, St. Francis Sch., Bakersfield, Calif., 1980-84, Standard Sch. Dist., Bakersfield, 1984-93, St Joseph Sch., Pekin, Ill., 1994—; chmn. honor chorus Kern County Schs., Bakersfield, 1974-75; 2d v.p. cen. sect. Calif. Music Educators Assn., 1976-78; pres. Standard Sch. Dist. Tchrs. Assn., Bakersfield, 1988-92; mentor tchr. Standard Sch. Dist., 1990-93; presenter Kern County Music Educators, 1986, Kern County Reading Assn., 1986-90, Calif. State Reading Assn., 1988; presenter music workshops Kern County Spl. Edn. Tchrs., 1989-93. Author manuals. Female lead in musical prodns. Shafter (Calif.) High Patrons Orgn., 1978-83; grand marshall Potato Festival parade City of Shafter, 1979; commr. of heritage Kern County Govt., Bakersfield, 1990-93. Recipient Tchr. of Yr. award Tchrs. Assn. Standard Sch. Dist., 1992; named Citizen of Yr. City of Shafter, 1979. Fellow ASCD, PTA (past officer), Nat. Tchrs. Assn., Calif. Tchrs. Assn. (local pres. 1988-92), Delta Kappa Gamma (local music chmn. 1988-92). Avocations: singing, golf, camping, reading. Home: 809 S Capitol St Pekin IL 61554-4411

NOVAK, MICHAEL (JOHN), religion educator, author, editor; b. Johnstown, Pa., Sept. 9, 1933; s. Michael John and Irene (Sakmar) N.; m. Karen Ruth Laub, June 29, 1963; children: Richard, Tanya, Jana. AB summa cum laude, Stonehill Coll., North Easton, Mass., 1956; BT cum laude, Gregorian U., Rome, 1958; MA, Harvard U., 1966; LLD, Keuka (N.Y.) Coll., 1970, Stonehill Coll., Mass., 1977, Thomas More Coll., 1992; LHD, Davis and Elkins (W.Va.) Coll., 1971, LeMoyne (N.Y.) Coll., 1976, Sacred Heart U., 1977, Muhlenberg Coll., 1979, D'Youville Coll., 1981, Boston U., 1981, New Eng. Coll., 1983, Rivier Coll., 1984, Marquette U., 1987; D en Ciencias Sociales, U. Francisco Marroquin, Guatemala, 1993; Jacksonville U., 1994; HHD, Saint Xavier U., 1995. Teaching fellow Harvard U., 1961-63; asst. prof. Stanford U., 1965-68; assoc. prof. philosophy and religious studies State U. N.Y., Old Westbury, 1968-71; assoc. dir. humanities Rockefeller Found., N.Y.C., 1973-75; provost Disciplines Coll., SUNY, Old Westbury, 1969-71; vis. prof. Jan. session Carleton Coll., Northfield, Minn., 1970, Immaculate Heart Coll., Hollywood, Calif., 1971; vis. prof. U. Calif., Santa Barbara, 1972, Riverside, 1975; Ledden-Watson disting. prof. religion Syracuse U., 1977-79; journalist nat. elections Newsday, 1972; writer in residence The Washington Star, 1976, syndicated columnist, 1976-80, 84-89; columnist Forbes Mag., 1989—; resident scholar in religion and public policy Am. Enterprise Inst., Washington, 1978—, George Frederick Jewett chair pub. policy research, 1983—, dir. social and polit. studies, 1987—; chmn. working seminar on family and Am. welfare policy Ind., 1986; faculty U. Notre Dame, Ind., 1986-87, vis. W. Harold and Martha Welch Prof. Am. Studies, 1987, 88; judge Nat. Book awards, 1971, DuPont Broadcast Journalism awards, 1971-80; speechwriter nat. polit. campaigns, 1970, 72; mem. Bd. Internat. Broadcasting, 1983—; mem. Presdl. Task Force Project Econ. Justice, 1985-87, Council Scholars Library of Congress, 1986—; mem. monitoring panel UNESCO, 1984; vice chmn. Lay Commn. Cath. Social Teaching and U.S. Economy, 1984-86; U.S. Ambassador to Experts Meeting on Human Contacts of the Conf. On Security and Cooperation in Europe, Bern, Switzerland, 1986; U.S. rep. to human rights commn. UN, 1981-83; hon. prof. U. Cuyo, Argentina, 1992. Author: novel The Tiber was Silver, 1961, A New Generation, 1964, The Experience of Marriage, 1964, The Open Church, 1964, Belief and Unbelief, 1965, 3d edit., 1994, A Time to Build, 1967, A Theology for Radical Politics, 1969, American Philosophy and the Future, 1968, Story in Politics, 1970, (with Brown and Herschel) Vietnam: Crisis of Conscience, 1967; Politics: Realism & Imagination, 1971, Ascent of the Mountain, Flight of the Dove, 1971, A Book of Elements, 1972, All the Catholic People, 1971, novel Naked I Leave, 1970, The Experience of Nothingness, 1970, The Rise of the Unmeltable Ethnics, 1972, Choosing Our King, 1974, The Joy of Sports, 1976, The Guns of Lattimer, 1978, The American Vision, 1978, Rethinking Human Rights I and II, 1981, 82, The Spirit of Democratic Capitalism, 1982, Confession of a Catholic, 1983, Moral Clarity in the Nuclear Age, 1983, Freedom with Justice, 1984, Human Rights and the New Realism, 1986, Will It Liberate? Questions About Liberation Theology, 1986, Character and Crime, 1986, The New Consensus on Family and Welfare, 1987, Taking Glasnost Seriously: Toward an Open Soviet Union, 1988, Free Persons and the Common Good, 1989, This Hemisphere of Liberty, 1990, The Spirit of Democratic Capitalism, 1991 (Anthony Fisher award 1992), Choosing Presidents, 1992, The Catholic Ethic and the Spirit of Capitalism, 1993, Awakening from Nihilism, Joy of Sports, rev. 1995; Belief and Unbelief, rev. 1995; Business as a Calling, 1996; To Empower People, anniv. ed, 1995; numerous other articles and books transl. into all maj. langs.; assoc. editor Commonweal mag., 1966-69; contbg. editor Christian Century, 1967-80, Christianity and Crisis, 1968-76, Jour. Ecumenical Studies, 1967—, This World, 1982-89, First Things, 1990—; religion editor Nat. Rev., 1979-86; founder, pub. Crisis, 1982—, editor-in-chief, 1993—. Decorated K.M.G., Soverign Mil. Order of Malta, 1987; Kent fellow, 1961—; fellow Hastings Inst., 1970-76; named Most Influential Prof. Sr. Class Stanford U., 1967, 68; Man of Yr. Johnstown, Pa., 1978; recipient Faith and Freedom award Religious Heritage Am., 1978, HIAS Liberty award, 1981, Friend of Freedom award, 1981; Newman Alumni award CCNY, 1984; George Washington Honor medal, 1984; award of Excellence, Religion in Media, 8th annual Angel Awards, 1985, Ellis Island Honor medal, 1986, Anthony Fisher award, 1992, Wilhelm Weber Prize, 1993, Templeton Progress in Religion prize, 1994; Internat. prize Inst. World Capitalism, 1994; diploma as vis. prof. U. Francisco Marroquin, 1985; named acad. corr. mem. from U.S., Argentina Nat. Acad. Scis., Morals & Politics, 1985, others. Mem. Soc. Religion in Higher Edn. (ctrl. com. 1970-73), Am. Acad. Religion (prog. dir. 1968-72), Coun. Fgn. Rels., Cath. Theol. Soc., Soc. Christian Ethics, Inst. Religion and Democracy (dir. 1981—), Nat. Ctr. Urban and Ethnic Affairs (dir. 1982-86). Office: Am Enterprise Inst 1150 17th St NW Washington DC 20036-4603 *Many persons have found a certain emptiness at the heart of human life —an experience of nothingness. Hidden in it, implicit in it, are prior commitments to honesty, courage, freedom, community. To increase the frequency of such acts in our lives is to grow, and to feel them diminish is to wither.*

NOVAK, RAYMOND FRANCIS, research institute director, pharmacology educator; b. St. Louis, July 26, 1946; s. Joseph Raymond and Margaret A. (Cerutti) N.; m. Frances C. Holy, Apr. 12, 1969; children: Jennifer, Jessica, Janelle, Joanna. BS in Chemistry, U. Mo., St. Louis, 1968; PhD in Phys. Chemistry, Case Western Res. U., 1973. Assoc. in pharmacology Northwestern U. Med. Sch., Chgo., 1976-77, asst. prof. pharmacology, 1977-81, assoc. prof., 1981-86, prof., 1986-88; prof. pharmacology Wayne State U. Sch. Medicine, Detroit, 1988—; dir. Inst. Chem. Toxicology Wayne State U., Detroit, 1988—, dir. NIEHS Ctr. in Molecular and Cellular Toxicology with Human Application, 1994—; mem. toxicology study sect. NIH, Bethesda, Md., 1984-88; adj. sci. Inhalation Toxicology Rsch. Inst., Lovelace Biomed. and Environ. Rsch. Inst., 1991—; program leader Epidemiology and Environ. Carcinogenesis, Karmanos Cancer Inst. and Comprehensive Cancer Ctr., 1996—. Assoc. editor Toxicol. Applied Pharmacology, 1992-96; editor Drug Metabolism and Disposition, 1994—; mem. editorial bd. Jour. Toxicology and Environ. Health, 1987-92, In Vivo, 1986—, Toxic Substances Jour., 1993—; mem. bd. pub. trustees Am. Soc. Pharmacology and Experimental Therapeutics, 1994—; contbr. articles to profl. jours. Recipient Disting. Alumni award U. Mo., St. Louis, 1988; grantee Nat. Inst. Environ. Health Sci., 1979—, Gen. Medicine sect. NIH, 1979—. Mem. Am. Soc. for Biochem. and Molecular Biology, Soc. Toxicology (councilor 1996—, chmn. cont. edn. com. 1995-96), Am. Assn. for Cancer Rsch., Am. Soc. for Pharmacology and Exptl. Therapeutics (bd. publ. trustees 1994—), Am. Soc. Hematology, Am. Chem. Soc., Biophys. Soc., Internat. Soc. for Study Xenobiotics. Office: Wayne State U Inst Chem Toxicology 2727 2nd Ave Rm 4000 Detroit MI 48201-2671

NOVAK, ROBERT DAVID SANDERS, newspaper columnist, television commentator; b. Joliet, Ill., Feb. 26, 1931; s. Maurice Pall and Jane Anne (Sanders) N.; m. Geraldine Williams, Nov. 10, 1962; children: Zelda, Alexander. AB, U. Ill., 1952; LLD (hon.), Kenyon Coll., 1987. Reporter Joliet (Ill.) Herald-News, 1947-51, Champaign-Urbana (Ill.) Courier, 1951-52, AP, Omaha, Lincoln, Nebr., Indpls. and Washington, 1954-58, Wall St. Jour., Washington, 1958-63; syndicated columnist N.Y. Herald-Tribune, Washington, 1963-66; commentator Corinthian Broadcasting, Washington, 1963-65, Metromedia, Washington, 1966-76, RKO-Features, Washington, 1976-78; syndicated columnist Chgo. Sun-Times, Washington, 1966—; commentator Cable News Network, Washington, 1980—, Nat. Empowerment TV, 1993—; pub. Evans-Novak Polit. Report, Washington, 1967—, Evans-Novak Tax Report, Washington, 1985-92, Evans-Novak Japan Report, Washington, 1989-92; roving editor Readers Digest, 1979—. Author: The Agony of the GOP, 1965, (with Rowland Evans) Lyndon B. Johnson: The Exercise of Power, 1967, Nixon In The White House, 1971, The Reagan Revolution, 1981. Trustee Bullis Sch., Potomac, Md., 1987—, Phillips Found., 1991—. 1st lt. U.S. Army, 1952-54. Recipient ACE award Cable Broadcasting Industry, 1990. Mem. Soc. Profl. Journalists, Washington Gridiron Club, Nat. Press Club, Army and Navy Club. Home: 801 Pennsylvania Ave NW Washington DC 20004-2615 Office: Ste 1312 1750 Pennsylvania Ave NW Washington DC 20006-4501

NOVAK, ROBERT LOUIS, civil engineer, pavement management consultant; b. Chgo., Feb. 29, 1928; s. Louis and Frances (Kucera) N.; m. Virginia Staas, Jan. 22, 1955 (div. 1962); children: Susan Grace, Nina Louise; m. Joyce Eloise Keen, May 7, 1966; stepchildren: Robert John Moore, William Keen Moore, Marilyn Joyce Moore, James Clifford Moore. BCE, Ga. Inst. Tech., 1948. With Am. Bridge Co., 1948-49; soils engr. Soil Testing Svc., Chgo., 1952-54; chief materials engr. Skidmore Owings and Merrill USAF Acad., Colorado Springs, 1954, dir. field invest; asst. dir. engring. O'Hare field constrn. Naess & Murphy, Chgo., 1958-60; pres. Novak, Dempsey & Assocs., Palatine, Ill., 1960-85; ptnr. Infrastructure Mgmt. Svcs., Arlington Heights, Ill., 1985-89, cons., 1989—. Contbr. articles to profl. jours. With U.S. Army, 1950-52. Mem. ASTM, Am. Pub. Works Assn. (life; Meritorious Svc. award 1990), Transp. Rsch. Bd. Achievements include development of one of the first pavement management programs. Home: 1066 Truman St Nokomis FL 34275-4401

NOVAK, TERRY LEE, public adminstration educator; b. Chamberlain, S.D., Sept. 1, 1940; s. Warren F. and Elaine M. N.; m. Barbara Hosea, Aug. 29, 1981; 1 child, David. B.Sc., S.D. State U., 1962; postgrad. (Rotary fellow), U. Paris, 1962-63; M.P.A., Colo. U., 1965, Ph.D., 1970. Asst. city mgr. City of Anchorage, 1966-68; city mgr. City of Hopkins, Minn., 1968-74, City of Columbia, Mo., 1974-78, City of Spokane, Wash., 1978-91; v.p. bus. and fin. Ea. Wash. U., Cheney, 1991-92, prof. public adminstrn., 1992—, dir. grad. program pub. adminstrn., 1994-95; dir. Spokane Joint Ctr. for Higher Edn., 1995—; asst. adj. prof. U. Mo., Columbia, 1975, 77; adj. instr. Gonzaga U., Spokane, 1986-88; mem. nat. adv. coun. on environ. policy and tech. EPA. Author: Special Assessment Financing in American Cities, 1970; contbr. articles to profl. jours. Mem. Internat. City Mgrs. Assn. (Acad. Profl. Devel.), Am. Soc. Public Adminstrn. Episcopalian. Office: 665 N Riverpoint Blvd Spokane WA 99202-1648

NOVAK, VICTOR ANTHONY, semi-retired manufacturing company executive; b. Antigo, Wis., Mar. 23, 1930; s. Joseph F. and Mary C. (Jirovec) N.; m. Marcella A. Tessmer, Nov. 3, 1951; children: Deborah, Mark, Jeffrey, Lori. Cert. in Mgmt., Marquette U., 1980. Mgr. repairshop Novak's Machineshop, Antigo, 1947-52; model maker AC Spark Plug co., Oakcreek, Wis., 1952-66; supr. experimental div. Oster Corp., Glendale, Wis., 1966-72; gen. foreman toolroom Square D Co., Milw., 1972-82, mgr. tool engring., 1982-89; sr. mfg. engr. Square D Co., Milw., Wis., 1993—; tchr. Milw. Area Tech. Coll., 1973—. Avocations: golf, bowling, fishing, skiing. Home: 7724 W Heather Ave Milwaukee WI 53223-2504 Office: Square D Co 4080 N 1st St Milwaukee WI 53212-1239

NOVAKOV, GEORGE JOHN, JR., gifted and talented educator; b. New Orleans, Apr. 1, 1945; s. George John Novakov Sr. and Gloria (Edwards) Frost; m. Ann Marie Mariano, Dec. 27, 1969; children: Jay, Jaime. BA, U. New Orleans, 1967, MEd, 1970, postgrad., 1985; postgrad., Tulane U., Loyola U., 1985. Tchr. New Orleans Pub. Schs., 1967—, adminstrv. asst. Edna Karr Magnet Sch., 1994—; grant writer asst. New Orleans Pub. Libr., 1987-89. Author: (play) The Christmas Caper, 1980. Ind. Study Humanities fellow, 1991. Mem. La. Assn. of Computer Using Educators (assoc. editor newsletter, 1992), Greater New Orleans Coun. of Tchrs. of English. Democrat. Roman Catholic. Avocations: opera, science fiction, computers. Home: 7340 Edward St New Orleans LA 70126-2012 Office: Edna Karr Magnet Sch 3332 Huntlee Dr New Orleans LA 70131-7046

NOVALES, RONALD RICHARDS, zoologist, educator; b. San Francisco, Apr. 24, 1928; s. William Henry and Dorothy (Richards) N.; m. Barbara Jean Martin, Dec. 19, 1953; children: Nancy Ann, Mary Elizabeth. B.A., U. Calif., Berkeley, 1950, M.A., 1953, Ph.D., 1958; postgrad., U. Calif., Los Angeles, 1951-52. Asst. prof. biol. scis. Northwestern U., Evanston, Ill., 1958-64; assoc. prof. Northwestern U., 1964-70, prof., 1970-80, prof. neurobiology and physiology, 1981-93, emeritus prof. neurobiology and physiology, 1993—; cons. A.J. Nystrom Co., 1969. Mem. editorial bd.: The American Zoologist, 1969-73; Contbr.: articles to profl. jours. Ency. Brit. Book of Year. Served with U.S. Army, 1953-55. NSF research grantee, 1959-73, 75-78. Fellow AAAS. Unitarian. Home: 2008 Mcdaniel Ave Evanston IL 60201-2125 *Remember not to "die on the barbed wire" of all the conflicting demands of your work. It is possible for you to cut through the individual strands and to make a successful rush for the enemy's trench.*

NOVALES-LI, PHILIPP, neuropharmacologist; b. Manila, Philippines, May 27, 1962; s. Angelita Tobillo de Novales-Li. DMSc, PhD, Gifu U. Sch. Medicine, Japan, 1989; DPhil, U. Oxford, U.K., 1993. Rsch. fellow U. Oxford, U.K., 1990-94; fellow U. So. Calif. Sch. Medicine, L.A., 1994, project mgr., 1995; pres. St. Hugh's Coll. MCR, U. Oxford, 1991, exec. officer, 1992, pharmacology tutor, 1993; cons. Novales-Li Rsch., Ltd., 1994. Columnist Manila Bull., 1994-95; contbr. articles to sci. jours. Monbusho Rsch. scholar Ministry Edn. & Culture, Tokyo, 1986-89; recipient Outstanding Youth award City of Manila, 1979, ORS award CVCP, London, 1989-92. Mem. Internat. Brain Rsch. Orgn., World Fedn. Mental Health, European Neuroscis. Assn., Oxford Union Soc., Gridiron Club, Oxford Soc. (hon. sec. So. Calif. 1995), Phi Kappa Phi, Phi Epsilon, Phi Sigma (Acad. Excellence in Biol. award 1984). Home: 1201 Maria Orosa St, Ermita Manila 1000, The Philippines Office: 3225 Promontory Cir San Ramon CA 94583 also: U So Calif Sch Medicine 1540 Alcazar St # 205 Los Angeles CA 90033-4500

NOVAS, JOSEPH, JR., advertising agency executive; b. Bueu, Pontevedra, Spain, Sept. 21, 1921; came to U.S., 1928; s. Joseph and Josephine (Regueira) N.; m. Carmen Ramos, Feb. 9, 1989; children by previous marriage: Stephen, Robert, Paul, Patricia. A.B., Brown U., 1946; postgrad., Columbia U., 1948-49. Asst. advt. mgr. Colegate-Palmolive, Jersey City, 1946-49; internat. advt. mgr. The Gillette Co., Boston, 1949-53; founder, pres. Laradiotel, C.A., Havana, Caracas, Mexico, San Juan, N.Y.C., 1953-58; founder Telefilms, C.A., Venezuela, 1955; founder, pres. Novas-Criswell Advt., Caracas, Mexico City, Madrid, Bogota, Sao Paulo, San Juan, Buenos Aires, 1958-74; chmn. and mem. exec. com. Leo Burnett Co., Inc., Spain, Portugal, 1974-77; sr. v.p. Leo Burnett Co., Inc., Chgo., 1977-83, also bd. dirs.; chmn. Leo Burnett Europe/ME Ltd., London, 1983-86; cons. CMQ-TV, Havana, Cuba, 1953-54, Channel 2, Caracas, Venezuela, 1951-58, Heinz Co., Europe, 1985-87, Leo Burnett, 1986-93; lectr. Caracas Central U., Caracas Andres Bello U., Mich. State U., Ohio U., Eastern Ill. U., McGill U., Montreal, Can. Served to lt. (j.g.) USN, 1942-46. Named Advt. Man of Yr., Venezuela. Mem. Internat. Advt. Assn. (world pres. 1974-76), Sales and Mktg. Execs. (pres. Venezuela chpt. 1962-64), Broken Sound Club (Boca Raton). *Frankness, forthrightness—always with the cards on the table. You lose some but you win most, and you always look in the mirror with pride and self respect.*

NOVECOSKY, PETER WILFRED, abbot; b. Humboldt, Sask., Can., Apr. 27, 1945; s. Martin Benedict and Elizabeth (Suchan) N. BA, St. John's U., 1966, MST, 1970. Abbot St. Peter's Abbey, Muenster, Sask., 1970—. Roman Catholic. Address: PO Box 10, Muenster, SK Canada S0K 2Y0

NOVELLO, DON, writer, comedian, actor; b. Ashtabula, Ohio, Jan. 1, 1943; s. A.J. and Eleanor (Finnerty) N. BA, U. Dayton, 1964. Writer, performer TV show Smothers Brothers Show, 1975; author novel The Lazlo Letters, 1977; writer, performer TV show Saturday Night Live, 1978-80; performer feature film Gilda Live, 1979; writer, performer rec. Live At St. Douglas Convent, 1980; producer TV series SCTV, 1982; author novel The Blade, 1985; performer TV spl. Father Guido Sarducci Goes To College, 1985; writer, performer rec. Breakfast in Heaven, 1986; performer feature film Head Office, 1986; performer TV spl. The Vatican Inquirer, 1987; performer feature film Tucker, 1988, N.Y. Stories, 1989, Godfather III, 1990, La Pastorela, 1991. Author: (children's mus.) Full Moon Over Tutti, 1992, (novel) Citizen Lazlo, 1992; contbr. articles to Rolling Stone, Playboy, Washington Post, Mother Jones, Spy mag.; performer feature film Casper, 1995, One Night Stand, 1995, Jack, 1996, Touch, 1997. Founder The People's Cath. Ch. Mem. AFTRA, Writers Guild Am., Screen Actors Guild. Club: Cavalier's. Office: PO Box 245 Fairfax CA 94978-0245

NOVETZKE, SALLY JOHNSON, former ambassador; b. Stillwater, Minn., Jan. 12, 1932; married; 4 children. Student, Carlton Coll., 1950-52; HHD (hon.), Mt. Mercy Coll., 1991. Amb. to Malta, Am. Embassy, Valletta, 1989-93. Past mem., legis. rep. Nat. Coun. on Vocat. Edn.; past mem. adv. coun. for career edn., past mem. planning coun. Kirkwood C.C.; bd. dirs., life trustee Cedar Rapids (Iowa) Cmty. Theater; bd. dirs. James Baker III Pub. Policy Inst., Rice U.; trustee Shattuck-St. Mary's Sch., Faribault, Minn., Mt. Mercy Coll., Cedar Rapids; vice chmn., life trustee, mem. exec. com. Hoover Presdl. Libr., 1982—; state chmn. Iowa Rep. Ctrl. Com., 1985-87; chmn. Linn County Rep. Com., 1980-83; mem. adv. bd. Iowa Fedn. Rep. Women, 1987-89; vice chmn. campaign adv. bd. Nat. Fedn. Rep. Women, 1987-89; co-chmn. V.P. Bush Inauguration, 1980; Iowa co-chmn. George Bush for Pres., 1988; bd. dirs. Greater Cedar Rapids Found., also chmn. grants com.; mem. Coun. Am. Ambs.; bd. dirs. Ambs. Forum; mem. nat. bd. New Designs for Two Yr. Insts. Higher Edn.; co-chair Rep. Party Iowa, 1982-84. Decorated dame Order of Knights of Malta; recipient Disting. Alumnus award Stillwater High Sch., 1991; Disting. Alumni award for outstanding achievement Carleton Coll., 1994. Home: 4747 Mount Vernon Rd SE Cedar Rapids IA 52403-3941

NOVICK, ANDREW CARL, urologist; b. Montreal, Apr. 5, 1948; came to U.S., 1974; s. David and Rose (Ortenberg) N.; m. Thelma Silver, June 29, 1969 (div. Dec. 1983); 1 child, Lorne J.; m. Linda Friedman, May 24, 1992; children: Rachel H., Eric D. BSc, McGill U., Montreal, 1968, MD, CM, 1972. Diplomate Am. Bd. Urology. Resident in surgery Royal Victoria Hosp., Montreal, 1972-74; resident in urology Cleve. Clinic Found., 1974-77, staff dept. urology, 1977—, head sect. renal transplant, 1977—, chmn. dept. urology, 1985—, chmn. Organ Transplant Ctr., 1985—; trustee Am. Bd. Urology, 1995—. Editor: Vascular Problems in Urology, 1982, Stewart's Operative Urology, 1989, Renal Vascular Disease, 1995; contbr. over 400 articles to profl. jours. Fellow ACS, Med. Coun. Can.; mem. Am. Urol. Assn., Am. Assn. Genito-Urinary Surgeons, Clin. Soc. Genito-Urinary Surgeons. Home: 22325 Canterbury Ln Cleveland OH 44122-3901 Office: Cleve Clinic Found 9500 Euclid Ave Cleveland OH 44195-0001

NOVICK, JULIUS LERNER, theater critic, educator; b. N.Y.C., Jan. 31, 1939; s. Solomon Joseph and Ethel (Lerner) N.; m. Phyllis Belle Spaeth, May 27, 1983; 1 child, Ilana. B.A., Harvard U., 1960; D.F.A., Yale U., 1966. Theatre critic WNDT-TV, Channel 13, N.Y.C., 1968-70; asst. prof. English NYU, N.Y.C., 1969-72; assoc. prof. lit. SUNY-Purchase, 1972-80, prof., 1980—; theatre critic The Village Voice, N.Y.C., 1958-89, The N.Y. Observer, N.Y.C., 1987-91, Newsday, N.Y.C., 1992-94; vis. lectr. drama div. Juilliard Sch., N.Y.C., 1968-71; dramaturg The Acting Co., N.Y.C., 1971-73; vis. critic Dartmouth Summer Repertory Co., Hanover, N.H., 1976, 79, 80, 82, 83, 84; master critic Nat. Critics Inst., Waterford, Conn., 1971—. Author: Beyond Broadway, 1968. Fulbright scholar, 1960-61; Woodrow Wilson fellow, 1961-62; Guggenheim fellow, 1977; recipient George Jean Nathan award for dramatic criticism, 1981-82. Mem. Am.Soc. for Theatre Rsch., Am. Theatre Critics Assn. Jewish.

NOVICK, MARVIN, investment company executive, former automotive supplier executive, accountant; b. N.Y.C., July 16, 1931; s. Joseph and Anna Novick; m. Margaret A. Blau, Apr. 9, 1960; children: Jeffrey, Stuart, Barry. BBA, CCNY, 1952; MBA, NYU, 1955, postgrad., 1955-58. CPA, N.Y., Mich., La., N.C. Sr. v.p. Mich. Blue Cross/Blue Shield, Detroit, 1961-70; v.p., dir. fin. Meadowbrook Ins., Southfield, Mich., 1970-72; ptnr. Touche Ross and Co., Detroit, 1972-84; vice chmn. Dura Corp., Southfield, 1984-87, Wesnovtek Corp., Birmingham, Mich., 1987-91; pres. R&M Resources Inc., Birmingham, 1991—; advisor Meadowbrook Ins. Group, Southfield, Mich., 1995—. Chmn. Oak Park-Huntington Woods-Pleasant Ridge (Mich.) Dem. Orgn., 1970-72, 18th Dem. Congl. Dist., 1972-74; trustee Mich. Assn. for Emotional Children, 1965—, also past pres.; trustee Providence Hosp., Southfield, 1975-83, also past chmn., trustee bldg. bd., 1982-89; trustee Oak Park (Mich.) Bd. Edn., 1964-71, also past pres.; trustee Temple Beth El, Birmingham, Mich., 1968—, also past pres.; trustee, vice chmn. Union of Am. Hebrew Congregation, 1981—; chmn. fin. com., fin. sec. World for Prog. Judaism-Internat., 1985—; chmn. pers. com. Jewish Welfare Found., 1987-91, assoc. chmn. cultural and edn. fedn. com., 1984—, chmn. subcom. Israel and Overseas Com., 1988—; mem. com. Jewish Agy. in Israel, 1987—; vice chmn. fin. com., trustee Sinai Hosp., 1988-92, mem. audit com., 1995—; trustee fin. com. Mich. Cancer Found., 1992—; trustee Mariners Inn, 1996—; bd. dirs. B'nai B'rith Centennial Lodge, 1970-79, past v.p.; trustee, mem. exec. com. Rose Hill Ctr., Inc., 1992—; mem. com. Hillel Ctr., U. Mich.; mem. various coms. Jewish Welfare Fedn. Recipient Honor and Service cert. Oak Park Bd. Edn., 1972, Past Pres. award Mich. Assn. Emotionally Disturbed Children, 1986; named one of Outstanding Young Men of Am., Outstanding Am. Found., 1968. Mem. Am. Inst. CPA's, Mich. Assn. CPA's, N.Y. State Assn. CPA's. Home: 12820 Burton St Oak Park MI 48237-1679

NOVICK, NELSON LEE, dermatologist, internist, writer; b. Bklyn., June 27, 1949; s. Benjamin and Vivian (Meltzer) N.; m. Meryl Sohnis, June 20, 1971; children: Yonatan, Yoel, Ariel, Daniel, Avraham. BA in Biology magna cum laude, Bklyn. Coll., 1971; MD, Mt. Sinai Sch. Medicine, 1975. Diplomate Am. Bd. Internal Medicine, Am. Bd. Dermatology, Am. Bd. Med. Examiners. Resident in internal medicine Mt. Sinai Med. Ctr., N.Y.C., 1975-78, assoc. attending, 1980—, postgrad. preceptee, 1980-83, outpatient dept. clinic chief, dermatology svc., 1983; resident Skin and Cancer Unit NYU Med. Ctr., N.Y.C., 1978-80; assoc. clin. prof. Mt. Sinai Sch. Medicine, N.Y.C., 1980—; cons. Westwood-Squibb Skin Care Info. Ctr., Vaseline Intensive Care Rsch., Bausch & Lomb, Schering-Plough, Sandoz Internat., Procter & Gamble, Lever-2000, Novartis, Bradley Pharms., Inst. for Med. Info. Author: Saving Face, Skin Care for Teens, Super Skin, Baby Skin, You Can Do Something About Your Allergies, You Can Look Younger at Any Age, Diseases of the Mucus Membranes, (novel) In the Path of the Wolf; co-author: The External Ear; reviewer Annals Internal Medicine, Jour. Am. Acad. Dermatology, Jour. Dermatol. Surgery and Oncology, Internat. Jour. Dermatology; edtl. advisor Exec. Health's Good Health Report, Snyder Comm., Your Baby Wallboard Program; former med. editor Current Podiatric Medicine, Jour. Am. Angalgesia Soc.; contbr. articles to profl. publs. Regent's Coll. scholar, 1971, Max and Leah Strauss Fund scholar, 1971, Grand St. Found. scholar, 1971. Fellow ACP (direct election), Am. Acad. Dermatology, Am. Soc. Dermatol. Surgery, Am. Acad. Cosmetic Surgery,

Skin Cancer Found. (hon.); mem. AMA, AAAS, Soc. Investigative Dermatology, Skin Phototrauma Found., Internat. Soc. for Androgenic Disorders, Skin Cancer Found. (charter), N.Y. Acad. Scis., N.Y. County Med. Soc., Am. Soc. Dermatologic Surgery, Am. Analgesia Soc. (past bd. dirs.), Nature Conservancy, Audubon Soc., Nat. Geog. Found., N.Y. Zool. Soc., Am. Mus. Natural History, Smithsonian Instn., Nat. Wildlife Fedn., The Wilderness Soc., Author's Guild, Author's League Am., Phi Beta Kappa. Jewish. Office: 328 E 75th St New York NY 10021-3317 *The true measure of a person's success in life is not how much he accomplished, but how much of his God-given potential he has used.*

NOVICK, ROBERT, physicist, educator; b. N.Y.C., May 3, 1923; s. Abraham and Carolyn (Weisberg) N.; m. Bernice Lehrman, July 2, 1947; children: Beth, Amy, Peter. M.E., Stevens Inst. Tech., 1944, M.S., 1949; Ph.D., Columbia, 1955. Microwave engr. Wheeler Lab., Inc., Great Neck, L.I., N.Y., 1946-47; instr. physics Columbia U., 1952-54, research assoc., 1954-57, assoc. prof. physics, dir. radiation lab., 1960-62, prof., co-dir. Astrophysics Lab., 1968-77, 86-92, dir. Astrophysics Lab., 1977-86, prof., 1977-93, prof. of physics emeritus, 1993—, chmn. dept. physics, 1983-88; asst. prof. physics U. Ill., Urbana, 1957-59, assoc. prof., 1959-60; Cons to labs., research insts.; chmn. subpanel on atomic and molecular physics Nat. Acad. Sci., 1964-65; mem. NASA Commn. on Sci. Uses of Space Sta., 1984-86. Recipient Exceptional Sci. Achievement medal NASA, 1980, Honor award Stevens Inst. Tech., 1989; A.P. Sloan fellow, 1958-70. Fellow Am. Phys. Soc., IEEE, AAAS; mem. Am. Astron. Soc. (sec.-treas. high energy astrophysics sect. 1975-78), Internat. Astron. Union. Research, publs. on atomic physics, atomic collisions, quantum electronics, atomic frequency standards, nuclear spins and moments, X-ray astronomy. Home: 366 W 245th St Bronx NY 10471-3902 Office: Dep Physics Columbia Univ 538 W 120th St New York NY 10027-6601

NOVICK, SHELDON M., author, lawyer; b. N.Y.C., June 19, 1941; s. Irving and Ruth (Rosenblatt) N.; m. Carolyn M. Clinton; 1 child, Michael Clinton; 1 child by previous marriage: Melia Bensussen. BA, Antioch Coll., 1963; JD, Washington U., 1977. Adminstr. Center for Biology of Natural Systems, Washington U., St. Louis, 1966-69; assoc. editor Environment mag., St. Louis, 1964-69; editor Environment mag., 1969-77, pub., 1972-74; assoc. firm Milgrim Thomajan Jacobs & Lee, N.Y.C., 1977-78; regional counsel U.S. EPA, Phila., 1978-86; staff atty. Environ. Law Inst., 1986-87; scholar in residence Vt. Law Sch., 1987—. Author: The Careless Atom, 1969, The Electric War, 1976, Law of Environmental Protection, 1987, Honorable Justice: The Life of Oliver Wendell Holmes, 1989, Henry James: The Young Master, 1996; editor: (with Dorothy Cottrell) Our World in Peril, 1971, The Collected Works of Justice Holmes, Vols. I-III, 1995. Town agt., grand juror Strafford Twp., 1988-96; pres. South Strafford Cafe, Inc., 1994—; mem. Vt. Water Resources Bd., 1988-92; bd. trustees Vt. Coun. for Humanities, bd. dirs., 1996—. Home: PO Box 259 South Strafford VT 05070-0259

NOVIKOFF, HAROLD STEPHEN, lawyer; b. N.Y.C., Apr. 5, 1951; s. Eugene Benjamin and Vivian (Hirsch) N.; m. Amy Pearl, Aug. 20, 1972; children: Sara Heather, Elyse Fana. AB, Cornell U., 1972; JD, Columbia U., 1975. Bar: N.Y. 1976, U.S. Dist. Ct. (so. dist.) N.Y. 1976. Ptnr. Wachtell, Lipton, Rosen & Katz, N.Y.C., 1975--. Mem. ABA, N.Y. State Bar Assn. (bankruptcy com. 1981--), Assn. Bar City N.Y. Office: Wachtell Lipton Rosen Katz 51 W 52nd St New York NY 10019-6119

NOVITCH, MARK, physician, educator, retired pharmaceutical executive; b. New London, Conn., Apr. 23, 1932; s. Charles Weinger and Mary (Margolick) N.; m. Katherine Louise Henderson, Oct. 9, 1971; 1 dau., Julia Drummond. A.B., Yale U., 1954; M.D., N.Y. Med. Coll., 1958. Intern, asst. resident in medicine Boston City Hosp., 1958-60; rsch. fellow Harvard Med. Sch., 1960-62, asst. in medicine, 1962-64, instr. medicine, 1964-67; mem. med. staff Peter Bent Brigham Hosp., Boston, 1962-67; asst. physician Univ. Health Svcs., Harvard U., 1961-67; asst. to dep. asst. sec. for health and sci. affairs HEW, Washington, 1967-71; dep. assoc. commr. for med. affairs FDA, Washington, 1971-78; assoc. commr. for health affairs FDA, 1978-81; dep. commr. food and drugs HHS, 1981-85; corp. v.p. The Upjohn Co., Kalamazoo, 1985-86, sr. v.p. sci. adminstrn., 1986-88, exec. v.p., 1989-90, vice-chmn. bd. dirs., 1991-93; prof. health scis. George Washington U., Washington, 1994—; bd. dirs. Biomed. Svcs. Bd. ARC, Guidant Corp. Calypte Biomed., Inc., Neurogen Corp., Osiris Therapeutics, Inc., Alteon, Inc., Food and Drug Law Inst.; trustee and past pres. U.S. Pharmacopeial Conv. Inc. Bd. dirs. Nat. Fund Med. Edn. USPHS fellow, 1960-62; Brookings Instn. fed. exec. fellow, 1970-71. Mem. AMA, Mass. Med. Soc., Am. Pub. Health Assn., Am. Soc. Clin. Pharmacology and Therapeutics, Nat. Acad. Social Ins. Home: 3558 Albemarle St NW Washington DC 20008-4214

NOVITSKI, CHARLES EDWARD, biology educator; b. Rochester, N.Y., Oct. 3, 1946; s. Edward and Esther Ellen (Rudkin) N.; m. Margaret Thornton Sime, June 15, 1968; children: Nancy Ellen, Linda Nicole, Elise Michelle. BA in Biology, Columbia Coll., 1969; PhD in Biophysics, Calif. Inst. Tech., 1979. Rsch. fellow and assoc. City of Hope Nat. Med. Ctr., Duarte, Calif., 1977-80; sr. tutor in biochemistry Monash U., Victoria, Australia, 1980-82, lectr. in biochemistry, 1982-84; program leader and rsch. scientist in nematode control Agrigenetics Advanced Sci. Co., Madison, Wis., 1985-88; assoc. prof. molecular biology Cen. Mich. U., Mt. Pleasant, 1989—. Assoc. editor Jour. Nematology, 1994—; contbr. articles to various profl. jours. Mem. Soc. of Nematologists, Internat. Soc. of Plant Molecular Biology. Achievements include patent for Nematode Control; research in the molecular genetics of mitochondria and of nematodes. Home: 1208 E Preston Rd Mount Pleasant MI 48858-3927 Office: Cen Mich U Dept Biology Mount Pleasant MI 48859

NOVITZ, CHARLES RICHARD, television executive; b. Chgo., Oct. 25, 1934; m. Eve Krzyzanowski, Feb. 11, 1988; 1 child, Alexandra Maris. BS in Journalism, U. Ill., Champaign-Urbana, 1956; MS, Columbia U., 1960; MPA, NYU, 1971. Reporter, writer, editor City News Bur., Chgo., 1956-57, UPI, Chgo., 1957-59; editor, writer, field producer NBC News, N.Y.C. and Chgo., 1959-60; with ABC News, 1960-79; mgr. ABC News (TV network syndication), 1973-79; mng. dir. Ind. TV News Assn., N.Y.C., 1979-81; producer, exec. NBC News, N.Y.C., 1982-85, 87; assoc. Rowan & Blewitt, Inc./Exec. TV Workshop, N.Y.C., 1985-95; pres. NovaNews Comm. Cons., N.Y.C., 1994—; on-air talent Money Call News, 1988; freelance TV producer, cable and pub. TV series, 1985—; adj. instr. LIU, 1967-69, NYU, 1969-70; asst. adj. prof. Lehman Coll., 1970-71; adj. prof., producer interactive televised course CUNY, 1972-75. Mem. Broadcast Pioneers, Radio TV News Dirs. Assn., Alumni Assn. Columbia Grad. Sch. Journalism (pres. 1979, Deadline Club (N.Y.C.; pres. 1969), Soc. Profl. Journalists-Sigma Delta Chi (pres. 1981-82). Office: 160 W End Ave Apt 29D New York NY 10023-5616

NOVOGROD, NANCY ELLEN, editor; b. N.Y.C., Jan. 30, 1949; d. Max and Hilda (Kirschbaum) Gerstein; m. John Campner Novogrod, Nov. 7, 1976; children: James Campner, Caroline Anne. AB, Mt. Holyoke Coll., 1971. Sec. fiction dept. The New Yorker, N.Y.C., 1971-73, reader, 1973-76; asst. editor Clarkson N. Potter, Inc., N.Y.C., 1977-78, assoc. editor, 1978-80, editor, 1980-83, sr. editor, 1984-86, exec. editor, 1987; sr. editor HG (formerly House and Garden mag.), N.Y.C., 1987-88, editor-in-chief, 1988-93; editor-in-chief Travel & Leisure, N.Y.C., 1993—. Bd. dirs. N.Y. Bot. Garden, 1991, Mount Holyoke Coll., 1992—. Office: Travel & Leisure 1120 Avenue Of The Americas New York NY 10036-6700

NOVOTNEY, DONALD FRANCIS, superintendent of schools; b. Streator, Ill., July 10, 1947; s. Andrew Stephen and Irene Marie (Lux) Novotney; m. Jane Francis Loeffelholz, June 3, 1973; children: Nicole, Tara, Thomas, Michael, Theresa. BA, Loras Coll., 1969; MS in Tchg., U. Wis., Platteville, 1973; MS, U. Dayton, 1985. Cert. tchr., Wis.; cert. tchr. and adminstr., Ohio. Prin. Holy Ghost Sch., Dickeyville, Wis., 1969-75, St. John Sch., Green Bay, Wis., 1975-76, Beaver Dam (Wis.) Cath. Schs., 1976-83; coord. Jordan Cath. Schs., Rock Island, Wis., 1983-85; supt. schs. Diocese of Fargo, N.D., 1985-86, Diocese of La Crosse, Wis., 1987—. Mem. Nat. Cath. Edn. Assn. (del. to nat. congress for cath. schs.). Republican. Roman Catholic. Avocations: athletics, travel. Home: 3314 33rd St S La Crosse WI 54601-7706 Office: Diocese of La Crosse 3710 East Ave S La Crosse WI 54601-7215

NOVOTNY, DONALD WAYNE, electrical engineering educator; b. Chgo., Dec. 15, 1934; s. Adolph and Margaret Novotny; m. Louise J. Eenigenburg, June 26, 1954; children: Donna Jo Kopp, Cynthia Mason. BEE, Ill. Inst. Tech., 1956, MS, 1957; PhD, U. Wis., 1961. Registered profl. engr., Wis. Instr. Ill. Inst. Tech., 1957-58; mem. faculty U. Wis., Madison, 1958—, prof. elec. engring., 1969—, chmn. dept. elec. and computer engring., 1976-80, Grainger prof. power electronics, 1990—; vis. prof. Mont. State U., 1966, Eindhoven (The Netherlands) Tech. U., 1974, Tech. U. Louvain, Belgium, 1986; Fulbright lectr. Tech. U. Ghent, Belgium, 1981; dir. Wis. Elec. Machines and Power Electronics Consortium, 1981—; assoc. dir. Univ.-Industry Rsch. Program, 1982-93; chmn. elec. engring. program Nat. Technol. U., 1989—; cons. to industry. Author: Introductory Electromechanics, 1965, Vector Control and Dynamics of AC Drives, 1996; also rsch. papers; assoc. editor: Electric Machines and Power Systems, 1976—. Recipient Kiekhofer tchg. award U. Wis., 1964, Benjamin Smith Reynolds tchg. award, 1984, Holdridge tchg. award, 1995; Outstanding paper award Engring. Inst. Can., 1966; fellow GE, 1956, Ford Found., 1960; grantee numerous industries and govt. agys. Fellow IEEE (prize paper awards 1983, 84, 86, 87, 90, 91, 93, 94); mem. Am. Soc. Engring. Edn., Sigma Xi, Tau Beta Pi, Eta Kappa Nu. Congregationalist. Lodge: Rotary. Home: 1421 E Skyline Dr Madison WI 53705-1132 Office: U Wis Dept Elec and Computer Engring 1415 Johnson Dr Madison WI 53706-1607

NOWACKI, JAMES NELSON, lawyer; b. Columbus, Ohio, Sept. 12, 1947; s. Louis James and Betty Jane (Nelson) N.; m. Catherine Ann Holden, Aug. 1, 1970; children: Carrie, Anastasia, Emma. AB, Princeton U., 1969; JD, Yale U., 1973. Bar: Ill. 1973, N.Y. 1982, U.S. dist. Ct. (no. dist.) Ill. 1973, U.S. Ct. Appeals (7th cir.) 1978, U.S. Ct. Appeals (6th cir.) 1987, U.S. Supremem Ct. 1992. Assoc. Isham, Lincoln & Beale, Chgo., 1976-80; ptnr. Kirkland & Ellis, Chgo., 1980—. Mem. Winnetka Sch. Bd. Dist. 36, Ill. 1983-91, bd. pres., 1989-91. Harlan Fiske Stone prize Yale U., 1972. Mem. ABA (forum com. on constrn. industry, litigation sect.), Mid-Am. Club, Skokie Country Club. Home: 708 Prospect Ave Winnetka IL 60093-2320 Office: Kirkland & Ellis 200 E Randolph St Chicago IL 60601-6436

NOWAK, JACQUELYN LOUISE, administrative officer, realtor, consultant; b. Harrisburg, Pa., Sept. 2, 1937; d. John Henry and Irene Louise (Clark) Snyder; children: Andrew Alfred, IV, Deirdre Anne. Student, Pa. State U., 1973-74; BA, Lycoming Coll., 1975. Editorial writer Patriot News Co., Harrisburg, Pa., 1957-58; dir. West Shore Sr. Citizens Ctr., New Cumberland, Pa., 1969-72; exec. dir. Cumberland County Office Aging, Carlisle, Pa., 1972-80; bur. dir. Bur. Advocacy, Pa. Dept. Aging, Harrisburg, 1980-88; exec. asst. to Pa. Senator John D. Hopper, Senate Com. on Aging and Youth, 1989; owner D&J Prodns., Art and Handcrafted Teddy Bears 1986, Ted E. Bear's Emporium, Harrisburg, 1988-92; assoc. Century 21 Piscioneri Realty, Inc., Camp Hill, Pa.; spl. projects coord. Pa. div. Am. Trauma Soc., 1991-93; adminstr. Country Meadows of West Shore II. Mechanicsburg, Pa., 1993-94; admininstrv. officer Am. Trama Soc., 1994—; recorder Pa. Gov's. Coun. Aging Cen. Region, 1972-74; chmn. pub. rels., 1973-74; mem. state planning com. Pa. State Conf. Aging, 1974, panelist, 1975-78; mem. state bd. Pa. Coun. Homemakers-Home Health Aide Svcs., 1972-80, v.p., 1975, chmn. ann. meeting, 1973-75; sr. citizens subcom. chmn. Pa. Atty. Gens. Commn. to Prevent Shoplifting, 1983; mem. adv. com. Tri-County Ret. Sr. Vol. Program, 1972-74; bd. dirs. Coun. Human Svcs. Cumberland, Dauphin, and Perry Counties, 1973-74; mem. svc. com. Family and Children's Svc. Harrisburg, 1970-74, mem. policy com., 1973-74, bd. dirs. Cumberland County unit Am. Cancer Soc., 1964-76, state del., 1964-66, chmn. county pub. rels., 1965-66, cancer crusade chmn., 1964. Recipient Herman Melitzer award, Pa. Conf. Aging, 1978; named Woman of the Yr. Sta. WIOO Radio, Carlisle, Pa., 1979. Mem. Nat. Assn. Area Ags. on Aging (bd. dir. 1975-80, pres. 1976-77; sec. 1978-79), Nat. Soc. Decorative Painters (bd. dirs. Penns Woods painters chpt. 1995—), Pa. Watercolor Soc., Harrisburg Art Assn., Mechanicsburg Art Ctr. (pres. 1987-90, bd. dirs. 1984-95), Am. Trauma Soc. (Pa. div. state bd. 1985-88), Older Women's League (founder chpt.), Lycoming Coll. Alumni Assn. (exec. bd. 1987-89), Pa. Fedn. of Women's Club (div. chmn. 1972-76), Torch Club (pres. 1987-88, 2d v.p. 1985-86), Zonta Internat. (sec. 1986-89). Home: 15 Paddock Ln Camp Hill PA 17011-1268

NOWAK, JAN ZDZISLAW, writer, consultant; b. Warsaw, Poland, May 15, 1913; came to U.S., 1977; s. Waclaw Adam and Elisabeth (Piotrowski) Jezioranski; m. Jadwiga Zaleski, Sept. 7, 1944. M.S., U. Poznan, Poland, 1936; Doctorate honoris causa, U. Poznan. Sr. researcher U. Poznan, 1937-39; emissary Polish resistance movement, 1941-45; editor BBC, London, 1947-51; dir. Polish Service Radio Free Europe, Munich, Fed. Republic of Germany, 1951-76; nat. dir. Polish Am. Congress, Washington, 1979-96; cons. Nat. Security Coun., 1979-92. Author: Courier from Warsaw, 1982, War on Airways, 1985, Poland From Afar, 1988; contbr. articles to mags. Served to maj. Polish Army, 1939-45. Decorated Virtuti Militari; decorated Cross of Valour, King's medal for Courage, Order of White Eagle, Poland, gt. ribbon Polonia Restituta, Comdrs. Cross of Merit with star (Poland), Presdl. Medal of Freedom, 1996. Roman Catholic. Home: 3815 Forest Grove Dr Annandale VA 22003-1959

NOWAK, JOHN E., law educator; b. Chgo., Jan. 2, 1947; s. George Edward and Evelyn (Bucci) N.; m. Judith Johnson, June 1, 1968; children: John Edwin, Jeffrey Edward. AB, Marquette U., 1968; JD, U. Ill., 1971. Law clk. Supreme Ct. of Ill., Chgo., 1971-72; asst. prof. U. Ill., Urbana, 1972-75, assoc. prof., 1975-87, law prof., 1978—, grad. coll. faculty, 1982—, Baum Prof. Law, 1993—; chmn. Constl. Law Sch. Sect.; faculty rep. Big Ten Intercollegiate Conf., Schaumburg, Ill., 1981-91; vis. prof. law U. Mich., Ann Arbor, 1985; Lee Disting. vis. prof. Coll. William and Mary, 1993. Coauthor: Constitutional Law, 5th edit. 1995, Treatise on Constitutional Law, 1986, 2nd edit., 1992, Story's Commentaries on the Constitution, 1987. Scholar-in-Residence, U. of Ariz., Tucson, 1985, 87. Mem. Assn. of Am. Law Schs. (chm. constl. law sect., accreditation com. 1980-88), Nat. Collegiate Athletic Assn. (mem. infractions com. 1987—), Am. Law Inst., Am. Bar Assn., Ill. Bar Assn., Order of the Coif (Triennial Book award com.). Roman Catholic. Home: 1701 Mayfair Rd Champaign IL 61821-5522 Office: U Ill Coll Law 504 E Pennsylvania Ave Champaign IL 61820-6909

NOWAK, JOHN MICHAEL, retired air force officer, company executive; b. Grand Rapids, Mich., Dec. 17, 1941; s. John F. and Dorothy F. (Smigiel) N.; m. Maureen K. Henry, Apr. 20, 1963; children: Kimberly, Susan, John, Michael, Lynn. BA in Sociology and Polit. Sci., Aquinas Coll., Mich., 1963; M in Mgmt., U. So.Calif., 1973. Commd. 2d lt. U.S. Air Force, 1963, advanced through grades to lt. gen., 1993; dir. maintenance Ogden Air Logistics Ctr., Hill AFB, Utah, 1984-86; dep. chief staff for maintenance Air Force Logistics Command, Wright-Patterson AFB, Ohio, 1986-89; dep. chief staff for logistics and engring. Hdqrs. Mil. Airlift Command, Scott AFB, Ill., 1989-92; dep. chief staff for logistics Hdqrs. Air Mobility Command, Scott AFB, 1992; dir. of supply Hdqrs. U.S. Air Force, Washington, 1992-93, dep. chief for logistics, 1993-1995; pres., CEO Logtec, Fairborn, OH, 1995—. Decorated DSM, Legion of Merit, Bronze Star medal, Meritorious Svc. medal with 3 oak leaf clusters, Air Force Commendation medal. Avocations: golf, boating, fishing. Office: Logtec 2900 Presidential Dr Fairborn OH 45324-6210

NOWAK, JUDITH ANN, psychiatrist; b. Albany, N.Y., Feb. 18, 1948; d. Jacob Frank and Anne Patricia (Romanowski) N. BA, Cornell U., Ithaca, N.Y., 1970, MD, 1974. Bd. cert. Psychiatry. Resident Univ. Va. Hosp., Charlottesville, 1974-77; fellow in psychiatry Cornell U. Med. Coll. Westchester Div., White Plains, N.Y., 1977-78, clin. affiliate, 1k978-79; staff psychiatrist Chestnut Lodge Hosp., Rockville, Md., 1979-81; med. officer psychiatry St. Elizabeth's Hosp., Washington, 1981; pvt. practice Washington, 1981—; clin. asst. prof. of psychiatry, George Washington U., Washington, 1981-89; clin. assoc. prof. psychiatry, George Washington U. 1989-94, clin. prof. psychiatry, 1994—. Mem. Am. Psychiat. Soc. (pub. affairs rep. 1995), Am. Psychoanalytic Soc., Washington Psychiat. Soc. (sec. 1989-90, pres. 1991-92),. Office: 908 New Hampshire Ave NW Washington DC 20037-2346

NOWAK, NANCY STEIN, judge; b. Des Moines, Sept. 17, 1952; d. Russell D. and Christine (Evanoka) Stein; m. Raymond A. Nowak, May 26, 1973. BA, Drake Univ., Iowa, 1974, MA, 1976; JD, George Washington Univ., D.C., 1980. Bar: D.C. 1980, Iowa 1982, Tex. 1986. Briefing atty. Judge Jamie Boyd, 1983-84, Judge Edward Prado, 1984-87; asst. U.S. atty., 1987-88, asst. U.S. trustee, 1988-89; magistrate judge U.S. Dist. Ct. (Tex. we. dist.), 5th circuit, San Antonio, 1989—. Office: US Courthouse 655 E Durango Blvd San Antonio TX 78206-1102

NOWAK, ROBERT MICHAEL, chemist; b. South Milwaukee, Wis., Oct. 28, 1930; s. Casimer M. and Anita Marie (Anderson) N.; m. Susan Lora Boyd, Oct. 12, 1957; children: Karen Sue Nowak Sapsford, Janet Lynn Nowak McMorris. Student, U. Wis., Racine, 1949-51; BS, U. Wis., Madison, 1953; PhD, U. Ill., 1956. Rsch. chemist Phys. Rsch. Lab. , Dow Chem. Co., Midland, Mich., 1956-64, from group leader to asst. lab dir., 1964-72; dir. rsch. and devel. plastics dept. Dow Chem. Co., Midland, 1972-73, dir. rsch. and devel. Olefin and Styrene plastics depts., 1973-78, dir. rsch. and devel. plastics dept., 1978-83, dir. cen. rsch., 1983-90, chief scientist, dir. cen. rsch. and devel., 1990-94; pres., CEO Mich. Molecular Inst., Midland, 1994—. Contbr. articles to profl. jours.; patentee organic reaction mechanisms and reinforced plastics. Mem. NAE, AIChE, Am. Chem. Soc., Soc. Chem. Industry. Office: MI Molecular Inst 1910 W Saint Andrews Rd Midland MI 48640-2657

NOWEL, DAVID JOHN, marketing professional; b. New Britain, Conn., Mar. 29, 1935; s. John Joseph and Sophie C. (Nowel) Bonkowski; m. July 20, 1961 (div. 1979); children: Lynn Marie, Bruce Edward. BA in Chemistry and Psychology, Hobart Coll., 1959; MA in Bus., Bklyn. Coll. of Pharmacy, 1964. Neurophysiology rsch. technician Inst. of Living Rsch. Lab., Hartford, 1955-57; sales rep. Sandoz Pharms., Bklyn., 1961-65, Becton Dickenson, Huntington Beach, Calif., 1965-71; sales mgr. Scott Labs., N. Hollywood, Calif., 1971-79; area mgr. Beckman Instruments, Fullerton, Calif., 1979-86; sales rep. Indsl. Tng. Corp.; sales mgr. Pacific Toxicology Lab., L.A., 1987-89, The Mark Group, Santa Ana, Calif., 1989-91; dir. of mktg. Remedial Mgmt. Corp., Newport Beach, Calif., 1991-92; bus. devel. mgr. Tech. Waste Inc., Placentia, Calif., 1993-94; sales engr. Nat. Tech. Sys., Calabasas, Calif., 1994-95; dir. sales and mktg. Western Environ. Engring. Co., Santa Ana, Calif., 1995—. Author: Space Station "ARK," 1987, 2d edit., 1995. Chairperson energy Orange County C. of C., 1989, mem. air subcom., 1991; co-chairperson environment Irvine C. of C., 1989. With USN, 1959-61. Mem. Assn. of Hazardous Materials Profls. Republican. Unitarian. Avocations: weight training, painting, public speaking, writing, psychology. Home: 19585 Seagull Ln Huntington Beach CA 92648-3034 Office: Western Environ Engring Co 1780 E Mcfadden Ave Ste 117 Santa Ana CA 92705-4648

NOWELL, GLENNA GREELY, librarian, consultant, city manager; b. Gardiner, Maine, Apr. 15, 1937; d. Bion Mellon and Faith Louise (Hutchings) Greely; m. Dana Richard Nowell, Sept. 1, 1956 (div. 1971); children: Dana A., Mark R., Dean E. BA in English, U. Maine, 1986. Dir. Gardiner Pub. Libr., 1974-97; city mgr. Gardiner, 1997—; bd. dirs. Gardiner Bd. Trade; mem. Maine Libr. Commn., 1980-88, Gov.'s Commn. Employment of Handicapped, 1978-81; mem. adv. bd. Gardiner Savs. Bank, 1986—; trustee J. Walter Robinson Welfare Trust, 1986—. Creator, editor Who Reads What publ., 1988—. Mem. Gardiner Econ. Devel. Com., 1989—; interim city mgr. City of Gardiner, 1991; bd. dirs. Kennebec Valley Mental Health, 1995-97; mem. State Ct. Libr. Com., 1996—. Recipient Hugh Hefner 1st Amendment award Playboy Found., 1987, Outstanding Libr. award Maine Libr. Assn., 1993, Cmty. Svc. award Kennebec Valley C. of C., 1993. Mem. Rotary (pres. Gardiner chpt. 1993-94). Office: City of Gardiner 6 Church St Gardiner ME 04345

NOWELL, PETER CAREY, pathologist, educator; b. Phila., Feb. 8, 1928; s. Foster and Margaret (Matlack) N.; m. Helen Worst, Sept. 9, 1950; children: Sharon, Timothy, Karen, Kristin, Michael. B.A., Wesleyan U., Middletown, Conn., 1948; M.D., U. Pa., 1952. Intern Phila. Gen. Hosp., 1952-53; resident pathology Presbyn. Hosp., Phila., 1953-54; med.-teaching, research specializing in cancer Phila., 1956—; from instr. to prof. pathology Sch. Medicine U. Pa., 1956—, chmn. dept. pathology, 1967-73; dir. (Cancer Center), 1973-75. Served to lt., M.C. USNR, 1954-56. Recipient Research Career award USPHS, 1964-67, Parke-Davis award, 1965, Lindback Disting. Teaching award, 1967, Passano award, 1984, Rous-Whipple award Am. Assn. Pathology, 1986, de Villers award Leukemia Soc. Am., 1987, Mott prize GM Cancer Rsch. Found., 1989, 3M award, FASEB, 1993. Home: 345 Mt Alverno Rd Media PA 19063-5313 Office: U Pa Sch Medicine Dept Pathology & Lab Medicine Philadelphia PA 19104-6082

NOWICK, ARTHUR STANLEY, metallurgy and materials science educator; b. N.Y.C., Aug. 29, 1923; s. Hyman and Clara (Sperling) N.; m. Joan Franzblau, Oct. 30, 1949; children: Jonathan, Steven, Alan, James. A.B., Bklyn. Coll., 1943; A.M., Columbia U., 1948, Ph.D., 1950. Physicist NACA, Cleve., 1944-46; instr. U. Chgo., 1949-51; asst. prof., then assoc. prof. metallurgy Yale U., 1951-57; mgr. metallurgy research IBM Corp Research Center, Yorktown Heights, N.Y., 1957-66; prof. metallurgy Columbia U., 1966-90, Henry Marion Howe prof. metallurgy and materials sci., 1990—; A. Frank Golick lectr. U. Mo., 1970; vis. prof. Technion, Haifa, Israel, 1973; co-chmn. Internat. Conf. Internal Friction, 1961, 69 (medal 1989); cons. in field. Author: Crystal Properties Via Group Theory, 1995; co-author: Anelastic Relaxation in Crystalline Solids, 1972; co-editor: Diffusion in Solids, 1975, Diffusion in Crystalline Solids, 1984; contbr. articles to profl. jours. Named David Turnbull lecturer Materials Rsch. Soc., 1994. Fellow AIME, Am. Phys. Soc.; mem. Materials Rsch. Soc. (Turnbull lectr. 1994), Sigma Xi (pres. Kappa chpt. 1983-85). Office: 1144 Mudd Bldg Columbia U New York NY 10027

NOWICKI, GEORGE LUCIAN, retired chemical company executive; b. Rutherford, N.J., Dec. 4, 1926; s. Justin Nowicki; m. Mary Elisabeth Baker, Aug. 30, 1947; children: Barbara, Peter, Paul, James. BSChemE, CCNY, 1949; MSChemE, NYU, 1956. Registered profl. engr., N.Y., Pa. Chemist Ideal Toy Co., N.Y.C., 1949; chem. engr. Bklyn. Union Gas Co., 1949-50, Sonotone Corp., Elmsford, N.Y., 1950-52; dept. head Burroughs Wellcome Co., Tuckahoe, N.Y., 1952-70; v.p. mfg. Quaker Chem. Corp., Conshohocken, Pa., 1970-79, v.p. domestic ops., 1984-89; ret. Quaker Chem. Corp., Conshohocken, 1989; pres. Selby Batersby Co., Phila., 1979-81; mng. dir. Quaker Chem. Holland BV, Uithoorn, The Netherlands, 1981-84; chmn. bd. Overdale Corp., Alsip, Ill., 1987-89, Quaker Chem. Can. Ltd., Toronto, 1985-89. Pres. Ctrl. Sch. Dist. 7, Hartsdale, N.Y., 1960-69, Westchester County Sch. Bds. Assn., White Plains, N.Y., 1965; bd. dirs. Suburban Gen. Hosp., Norristown, Pa., 1986; mem. governing bd. Vt. Common Cause, 1993—; bd. dirs. Martha Canfield Libr., Arlington, Vt., 1994—; counselor Svc. Corps Ret. Execs., 1993-95. Mem. Am. Inst. Chem. Engrs., Mfrs. Assn. Del. Valley (bd. dirs. 1987-89). Avocations: swimming, skiing, video photography, stamps. Home: RR 1 Box 1809 Arlington VT 05250-9716

NOWLAN, DANIEL RALPH, engineering executive; b. Hammond, Ind., Feb. 23, 1947; s. Kenneth Edwin and Patricia Jane (Prendergast) N.; m. Sharon Louise Greichunos, Sept. 7, 1968; children: Daniel Ralph Jr., Kevin Anthony, Cynthia Ann. BSEE, Purdue U., 1969, MSEE, 1969. Engr./scientist McDonnell Douglas Astronautics Co, Santa Monica, Calif., 1969-75; engring. mgr. McDonnell Douglas Aerospace-West, Huntington Beach, Calif., 1975-96; tax preparer Tax Corp. of Am., Montrose, Calif., 1975-76; cons. in field; MDC fellow McDonnell Douglas Aerospace-West, 1996—. Eucharistic minister to convalescent homes St. Vincent De Paul Soc., Huntington Beach, 1993—; youth soccer coach Am. Youth Soccer Orgn., Westminster and Huntington Beach, 1975-82; bldg. fund dr. capt. St. Vincent De Paul Cath. Ch., Huntington Beach, 1979, 82, 97. Recipient Popular Sci. Achievement award, 1993, Space Frontier award, 1994, Engring. Project Achievement award, L.A. & Orange County Engring. Coun., 1994. Mem. AIAA (sr.), IEEE, Phi Kappa Theta, Tau Beta Pi, Eta Kappa Nu, Phi Eta Sigma. Roman Catholic. Avocations: arranging music for piano and keyboard, study of modern physics, study of philosophy. Home: 15931 Diamond St Westminster CA 92683-7203 Office: McDonnell Douglas Aerospace M/C:HO13-C306 5301 Bolsa Ave Huntington Beach CA 92647-2048

NOWLAN, GEORGE JOSEPH See DAVIS, DANNY

NOWLIN, JAMES ROBERTSON, federal judge; b. San Antonio, Nov. 21, 1937; s. William Forney and Jeannette (Robertson) N. B.A., Trinity U.,

1959, M.A., 1962; J.D., U. Tex., Austin, 1963. Bar: Tex. 1963, Colo. 1993, U.S. Dist. Ct. D.C. 1966, U.S. Ct. Claims 1969, U.S. Supreme Ct. 1969, U.S. Dist. Ct. (we. dist.) Tex. 1971. Assoc. Kelso, Locke, & King, San Antonio, 1963-65; assoc. Kelso, Locke & Lepick, San Antonio, 1966-69; legal counsel U.S. Senate, Washington, 1965-66; propr. Law Offices James R. Nowlin, San Antonio, 1969-81; mem. Tex. Ho. of Reps., Austin, 1967-71, 73-81; judge U.S. Dist. Ct. (we. dist.) Tex., Austin, 1981—; instr. Am. govt. and history San Antonio Coll., 1964-65, 71-73. Served to capt. U.S. Army, 1959-60, USAR, 1960-68. Life fellow State Bar Found; mem. Travis County Bar Assn., San Antonio Bar Assn., Colo. Bar Assn. Republican. Presbyterian. Avocations: pilot; skiing; hiking; jogging. Office: US Courthouse 200 W 8th St Austin TX 78701-2333

NOWOSATKO, JEROME RAYMOND, software engineer; b. Detroit, Apr. 30, 1965; s. Raymond Peter and Sophie Helen (Pendzik) N. AA in Computer Sci., U. Md., Naples, Italy, 1989, BS in Info. Systems, 1989; MS in Software Engring., Colo. Tech., 1996. Cert. data processor, sys. profl., computing profl. Commd. E-4 U.S. Army, 1984; software engr. Compuware Corp., Detroit, 1990-91, Columbus, Ohio, 1991-92, Colorado Springs, 1992—. Mem. Data Processing Mgmt. Assn., Inst. for Certification of Computing Profls., Project Mgmt. Inst., Buckley Sch. Forensic Soc., Project Mgmt. Inst. Republican. Roman Catholic. Avocations: hiking, skydiving, reading, writing, skiing. Home: 7215 Big Valley Ct Colorado Springs CO 80919-1035 Office: Compuware Corp 5575 Tech Center Dr Ste 212 Colorado Springs CO 80919-2392

NOYCE, PHILLIP, film director; b. Griffith, New South Wales, Austalia, Apr. 27, 1950; films include: (dir., writer): Backroads, 1977 (also prodr.), Newsfront, 1979, Heatwave, 1983; (dir.): Shadows of the Peacock, 1987 (in U.S. as Echoes of Paradise, 1989), Dead Calm, 1989, Blind Fury, 1990, Patriot Games, 1992, Sliver, 1993, Clear and Present Danger, 1994, The Saint, 1997; television work includes (as dir.): The Dismissal, 1983, The Cowra Breakout, 1985, The Hitchhiker (The Curse), 1986, Nightmare Cafe (pilot), 1992. Office: ICM 8942 Wilshire Blvd Beverly Hills CA 90211-1934*

NOYES, H(ENRY) PIERRE, physicist; b. Paris, Dec. 10, 1923; s. William Albert and Katharine Haworth (Macy) N.; m. Mary Wilson, Dec. 20, 1947; children—David Brian, Alan Guinn, Katharine Hope. AB magna cum laude, Harvard U., 1943; Ph.D., U. Calif., Berkeley, 1950. Physicist MIT, 1943-44, U. Calif., Berkeley, 1949-50; Fulbright fellow U. Birmingham, Eng., 1950-51; asst. prof. U. Rochester, N.Y., 1951-55; group leader Lawrence Livermore Lab., 1955-62; Leverhulme lectr. U. Liverpool, Eng., 1957-58; adminstrv. head theory sect. Stanford Linear Accelerator Center, 1962-69; asso. prof. Stanford U., 1962-67, prof., 1967—; vis. scholar Center Advanced Study Behavioral Scis., Stanford, 1968-69; cons. in field. Author papers in field. Chmn. Com. for Direct Attack on Legality of Vietnam War, 1969-72; mem. steering com. Faculty Political Action Group, Stanford U., 1970-72; mem. policy com. U.S. People's Com. on Iran, 1977-79. Served with USNR, 1944-46. Fellow NSF, 1962; Fellow Nat. Humanities Faculty, 1970; recipient Alexander von Humboldt U.S. Sr. Scientist award, 1979. Mem. Alternative Natural Philosophy Assn. (pres. 1979-87, 1st alternative natural philosopher award 1989), Am. Phys. Soc., AAAS, Sigma Xi. *What success I may have had has come because I have tried to bring together my physics and politics and family to serve the people. I aim to achieve a unified materialist philosophy that might help others to greater success than my own. I sum up this philosophy as "fixed past - uncertain future".*

NOYES, JUDITH GIBSON, library director; b. N.Y.C., Apr. 19, 1941; d. Charles II and Alice (Klauss) Gibson; m. Paul V. Noyes, June 1, 1991; children from previous marriage: Andrea Elizabeth Green, Michael Charles Green. BA, Carleton Coll., 1962; MLS, U. Western Ont., London, Can., 1972. Librarian edn. U. New Brunswick, 1972-86; libr. Can. Inst. Sci. and Tech. Info., Ottawa, Ont., Can., 1975-86; univ. librarian Colgate U., Hamilton, N.Y., 1986—; mem. OCLC Adv. Com. on Coll. and Univ. Librs., 1991-94; pres. bd. trustees Ctrl. N.Y. Libr. Resources Coun., 1992-96. Mem. ALA, Am. Coll. and Rsch. Librs. (nominating com. 1988-89, 92-93, legis. com. coll. libr. sect. liaison 1989-91, chair task force on intellectual freedom, 1992-94), Internat. Stds. Orgn. (tech. com. 46, 1981-89), N.Y. Libr. Assn. (ASLS bd. 1996—). Office: Colgate U Everett Needham Case Libr 13 Oak Dr Hamilton NY 13346-1338

NOYES, RICHARD HALL, bookseller; b. Evanston, Ill., Feb. 12, 1930; s. George Frederick and Dorothy (Hall) N.; m. Judith Claire Mitchell, Oct. 10, 1953; children—Catherine, Stephanie, Matthew. B.A., Wesleyan U., 1952. Tng. program, elementary-high sch. salesman Rand McNally & Co., Colo., Utah, Idaho, Wyo., 1955-59; founder, owner, mgr. The Chinook Bookshop, Colorado Springs, Colo., 1959—. Contbr. to A Manual on Bookselling, 1974, The Business of Book Publishing, 1984; contbr. articles to newspapers and trade jours. Co-chmn. Colo. Media Coalition, 1974—; bd. dirs. Colorado Springs Fine Arts Ctr., 1977-81, Citizens Goals for Colorado Springs, 1976-88; trustee Fountain Valley Sch., 1979-81; vice chmn. Colorado Springs Charter Rev. Commn., 1991-92. Served with AUS, 1952-54. Recipient Intellectual Freedom award Mountain Plains Librs. Assn., 1977, Disting. Svc. award U. Colo., 1980, Recognition award Pikes Peak Arts Coun., 1989, Charles S. Haslam award, 1990), Entrepreneur of Yr. award U. Colo., 1992, Gordon Saull award for outstanding bookseller Mountains and Plains Booksellers Assn., 1996. Mem. Am. Booksellers Assn. (pres., dir.). Home: 1601 Constellation Dr Colorado Springs CO 80906-1609 Office: The Chinook Bookshop Inc 210 N Tejon St Colorado Springs CO 80903-1314

NOYES, ROBERT EDWIN, publisher, writer; b. N.Y.C., June 22, 1925; s. Clarence A. and Edith (LaDouns) N.; m. Janet Brown, Mar. 24, 1952 (div. June 1963); children—Keith, Steven, Mark, Geoffrey; m. Mariel Jones, July 24, 1964; children—Rebecca, Robert. B.S. in Chem. Engring, Northwestern U., 1945. Chem. engr. Am. Cyanamid Co., Pearl River, N.Y., 1947; sales exec. Titanium Pigment Corp., N.Y.C., 1948-55; market research mgr. U.S. Indsl. Chem. Co., N.Y.C., 1956-58; sales mgr. atomic energy Curtiss Wright Export, N.Y.C., 1958-60; founder, pres., chmn. bd. Noyes Data Corp., Westwood, N.J., 1960—; pub. Noyes Press, Noyes Publs., Westwood, 1961—. Author numerous books in fields of internat. fin., devel., tech. Served to lt. (j.g.) USNR, 1945-47. Mem. AIAA, Am. Chem. Soc., Am. Inst. Chem. Engrs., Indian Harbor Yacht Club (Conn.), N.Y. Yacht Club. Episcopalian. Office: 369 Fairview Ave Westwood NJ 07675-1704

NOYES, RONALD TACIE, agricultural engineering educator; b. Leedey, Okla., Jan. 4, 1937; s. Johnnie Lyle and Anna Madeline (Allen) N.; m. Zona Gail McMillen, Apr. 16, 1960; children: Cynthia Gail, Ronald Scott, David Eric. BS in Agrl. Engring., Okla. State U., 1961, MS in Agrl. Engring., 1964; postgrad., Purdue U., 1966-68, U. Okla., 1988-97. Profl. engr., Ind., Okla. Asst. prof. Purdue U., West Lafayette, Ind., 1964-68; chief engr. Beard Industries, Inc., Frankfort, Ind., 1968-81, v.p. engring., 1981-85; assoc. prof. Okla. State U., Stillwater, 1985-88, prof., 1988—; cons. Ronald T. Noyes, Profl. Agrl. Engr., Stillwater, 1988—. Co-author: Designing Pesticide and Fertilizer Containment Facilities, 1991, revised edit., 1995; contbr. chpts. to books. 1st lt. U.S. Army, 1961-63. Recipient Disting. Svc. award U.S. Dept. Agr., 1992, Outstanding Ext. Faculty award Okla. State U., 1991. Fellow Am. Soc. Agrl. Engrs.; mem. Aircraft Owners and Pilots Assn., Nat. Agrl. Aviation Assn. (assoc.), Exptl. Aircraft Assn. Achievements include 6 patents in field; developed new aeration management procedure for controlling insects in stored grain that reduces chemical use, manifolded phosphine fumigation process for grain tanks and silos that reduces chemical use. Home: 1116 Westwood Dr Stillwater OK 74074-1116 Office: Oklahoma St Univ Biosyss & Agrl Engring Dept 224 Ag Hall Stillwater OK 74078-6020

NOYES, RUSSELL, JR., psychiatrist; b. Indpls., Dec. 25, 1934; s. Russell and Margaret (Greenleaf) N.; m. Martha H. Carl, Nov. 13, 1960; children: Marjorie Noyes-Aamot, Nancy Heifner, James R. BS, DePauw U., 1956; MD, Ind. U., 1959. Diplomate Am. Bd. Psychiatry and Neurology. Intern Phila. Gen. Hosp., 1959-60; residency U. Iowa, Iowa City, 1961-63; asst. prof. psychiatry U. Iowa, 1966-71, assoc. prof., 1971-78, prof., 1978—. Editor: Handbook of Anxiety, 1988-91; contbr. articles to profl. jours. With USN, 1963-65. Fellow Am. Psychiat. Assn., Acad. Psychosomatic Medicine (pres. 1990-91); mem. Iowa Psychiat. Soc. (pres. 1986-87). Republican. Lutheran. Avocation: gardening. Home: 326 Macbride Dr Iowa City IA 52246-1716 Office: Psychiatry Rsch Med Edn Bldg Iowa City IA 52242-1009

NOZERO, ELIZABETH CATHERINE, lawyer; b. Detroit, June 13, 1953; d. Peter J. and Pauline R. (Reeves) N.; m. Stephen A. Catalano, May 23, 1981 (div. May 1993); 1 child: Alexandra L. BA in history, U. Calif., 1975; JD, U. San Diego, 1978. Bar: Calif. 1979, Nev. 1980. Counsel State Industrial Ins. System, Las Vegas, 1980-81; sr. legal counsel Reynolds Elec. & Engring. CO., Las Vegas, 1981-85; asst. gen. counsel U. Nev., Las Vegas, 1985-89; v.p., gen. counsel Harrah's Casino Hotels, Las Vegas, 1989-95; sr. legal counsel Sierra Health Svcs., Inc., 1996—; mem. exec. bd. Nev. Bar Assn. Fee Dispute com. 1982-88, Nev. Law Found., 1980-88. Chairperson S. Nev. Area Health Edn. Ctr., Las Vegas, 1990-94; former chair Nev. Adv. Com. U.S. Commn. on Civil Rights, Nev., 1989-94; gov.'s com. Infrastructive Financing, 1994-95. Recipient Woman of Achievement award Las Vegas C. of C., 1992, Silver State Citizen award Nev. Atty. Gen., 1992. Mem. Nev. Gaming Attys. (v.p. 1994-95), Nev. Resort Assn. (chairperson, regulations com. 1993-95). Office: Sierra Health Svcs Inc PO Box 15645 2724 N Tenaya Way Las Vegas NV 89114-5645

NOZICK, ROBERT, philosophy educator, author; b. Bklyn., Nov. 16, 1938; s. Max and Sophie (Cohen) N.; m. Barbara Fierer, Aug. 15, 1959 (div. 1981); children: Emily, David; m. Gjertrud Schnackenberg, Oct. 5, 1987. A.B., Columbia U., 1959; A.M., Princeton U., 1961, Ph.D., 1963; A.M. (hon.), Harvard U., 1969; DHL (hon.), Knox Coll., 1983. Asst. dir. Social Sci. Research Council Summer Inst., 1962; instr. philosophy Princeton U., 1962-63, asst. prof., 1964-65; Fulbright scholar Oxford (Eng.) U., 1963-64; asst. prof. philosophy Harvard U., Cambridge, Mass., 1965-67; prof. Harvard U., 1969—, chmn. dept., 1981-84, Arthur Kingsley Porter prof., 1985—, sr. fellow Soc. Fellows; assoc. prof. Rockefeller U., 1967-69. Author: Anarchy, State, and Utopia, 1974 (Nat. Book award 1975), Philosophical Explanations, 1981 (Ralph Waldo Emerson award 1982), The Examined Life, 1989, The Nature of Rationality, 1993, Socratic Puzzles, 1997; mem. bd. editors Philosophy and Pub. Affairs; contbr. articles to profl. jours. Fellow Ctr. Advanced Study Behavioral Scis., 1971-72, Rockefeller Found. humanities fellow, 1979-80, NEH fellow, 1987-88, Guggenheim fellow, 1996-97. Mem. Am. Philos. Assn. (pres.-elect ea. divsn.), Am. Acad. Arts and Scis., Council of Scholars, Library of Congress, Phi Beta Kappa. Office: Harvard U Emerson Hall Cambridge MA 02138

NRIAGU, JEROME OKON, environmental geochemist; b. Ora-eri Town, Anambra, Nigeria, Oct. 24, 1942; came to U.S., 1993; s. Martin and Helena (Anaekwe) N.; children: Chinedu Delbert, Uzoma Vivian, Osita Jide. BSc with honors, U. Ibadan, Nigeria, 1965, DSc, 1987; MS, U. Wis., 1967; PhD, U. Toronto, Ont., 1970. Rsch. scientist Environment Can., Burlington, Ont., 1970-93; prof. environ. chem. sch. of pub. health U. Mich., Ann Arbor, 1993—; dir. environ. health scis. program, 1996-99; assoc. rsch. scientist Ctr. for Human Growth and Devel., U. Mich., 1997—; adj. prof. U. Waterloo, Ont., 1985—; vis. scientist NOAA, Ann Arbor, 1992. Author: Lead and Lead Poisoning in Antiquity, 1983; editor book series: Advances in Environmental Science and Technology, 1982—; editor 24 books on various environ. topics, 1979—; editor Sci. of the Total Environment, 1983—; contbr. articles to profl. jours.; editl. bd. 9 jours. Recipient Rigler medal Can. Soc. Limnologists, 1988. Fellow Royal Soc. Can.; mem. Geochem. Soc. Roman Catholic. Avocations: photography, reading (African authors), travel. Office: Univ of Michigan Environ/Indsl Health 109 Observatory St Ann Arbor MI 48109-2029

NTLOLA, PETER MAKHWENKWE, retired translator; b. Phillipstown, Cape, South Africa, July 7, 1908; s. Fanteni and Sarah Notsitsa (Bonani) N.; m. Constance Nomalanga Siningwa, July 7, 1949 (dec. Mar. 1976). Pub. serials on Man's Footprints on the Moon in state-sponsored monthly, 1963-76; columnist to 3 African monthly periodicals. Journalist, editor, reporter, proofreader, photographer, layout artist 5 books translated from English, 1966-86. Served as sgt. in World War II. Home: PO Box 77396, Mamelodi West 0101, South Africa

NUCCI, LEO, baritone; b. nr. Bologna, Italy, 1942. Studied with, Guiseppe Marchesi, Ottaviano Bizzarri. Mem. chorus La Scala, Milan, Italy, 1969-75. Debut as Figaro in The Barber of Seville at Spoleto, 1967, Covent Garden, London, 1987, San Francisco, 1987; appeared in La Boheme, La Fenice, Venice, Italy, 1975, as Rodrigo in Don Carlo, La Scala, Milan, as Belcore in L'Elisir d'amore, as Francesco Foscari in I due Foscari, as Miller in Luisa Miller, Covent Garden, 1978, as Renato in Un Ballo in Maschera, Met. Opera, N.Y., 1980, Paris Opera, 1981, La Scala, 1987, Barber of Seville Met. Opera, 1984, Falstaff, London, Adriana Levouvreur, San Francisco Opera, 1985, La Traviata, Met. Opera, 1985, Don Carlo, 1986, Madame Butterfly, 1986, Aida, 1986, Rigoletto, Hamburg, Barcelona, Spain, 1987, Il Trovatore, Lyric Opera Chgo., 1987, Met. Opera, 1987; The Force of Destiny, Lyric Opera Chgo., 1988, Macbeth, Marseille, 1988, Il Trovatore and Barber of Seville, Met. Opera, 1988, Rigoletto, Met. Opera, 1989, Un Ballo in Maschera, Salzburg Festival, 1989, Rigoletto, Houston Grand Opera, 1990, Elisir d'Amore, Vienna State Opera, 1990, Rigoletto and Simone Boccanegra, Vienna, Rigoletto Lyric Opera Chgo., 1990, Rigoletto in Bologna, Italy and Munich, 1990, Luisa Miller, Ballo in Maschera Met. Opera, 1991; Otello Chgo. Symphony; Rigoletto Rome Opera, Verona Festival, Covent Garden, 1991, Simon Boccanegra in Santiago, Chile, Trovatore in Torino, Rigoletto in Venice, 1992; opera recs. include La Rondine, Le Villi, Andrea Chenier, The Barber of Seville, Don Pasquale, Tosca, Turco in Italia, Ernani, Aida, Falstaff, Don Carlo, Macbeth, 1987, Un Ballo in Maschera, Simone Boccanegra, Otello, Rigoletto, bel canto arias Il Viaggio a Reims, Idomeneo, Elisir d'Amore, Simon Boccanegra Popular Italian Songs, Gianni Schicchi, Italian Songs, Bel Canto Arias from Puritani, Pirata, Beatrice di Tenda, Guglielmo Tell, Poliuto, Duca d'Alba, Don Sebastiano, Favorita; films include: Macbeth, 1987. Office: care Allied Artists Agency, 42 Montpellier Square, London SW7 152, England

NUCCIARONE, A. PATRICK, lawyer; b. Denville, N.J., Aug. 29, 1947; s. H. Joseph and Alice Marie (McGuirk) N. BA, U. So. Calif., 1969; JD, George Washington U., 1973. Bar: N.J. 1973, N.Y. 1981, Vt. 1984, U.S. Dist. Ct. N.J. 1973, U.S. Dist. Ct. (no. dist.) Ohio 1986, U.S. Ct. Appeals (3d cir.) 1976, U.S. Supreme Ct. 1995. Com. staff asst. U.S. House of Reps., Washington, 1971-72; staff asst. Exec. Office of Pres. of U.S., Washington, 1972-73; asst. U.S. Atty. Office of U.S. Atty., Newark, 1974-83, chief environ. sect., 1978-83; spl. asst. Atty. Gen. Office of Atty. Gen., Montpelier, Vt., 1984; ptnr. Hannoch Weisman, Roseland, N.J., 1984-91, Dechert, Price & Rhoads, Princeton, N.J., 1991-95; co-chmn. N.J. Hazardous Task Force, Trenton, 1978-83; supr. Rutgers U. Environ. Law Clinic, Newark, 1978-83; mem. Environ. Expn. Adv. Bd., Trenton, 1985-90; chmn. ann. seminar on impacts of environ. law bus. trans. Practicing Law Inst., 1986-92; mem. faculty NYU Summer Inst. on Environ. Law, 1991-94. Contbr. articles to profl. jours. Recipient Outstanding Service award U.S. Dept. Justice, Washington, 1980, Spl. Achievement awards U.S. Dept. Justice, 1978, 79, Presdl. Citation for Excellent Performance Exec. Office of Pres., Washington, 1973. Mem. ABA (vice chmn. sect. on natural resources, energy and environ. law 1987-93), N.J. State Bar Assn. (bd. dirs. environ. law sect. 1985-89), Monmouth County Bar Assn. Avocations: flying, sailing, skiing, hiking. Office: 321 Broad St Red Bank NJ 07701-2101

NUCE, MADONNA MARIE, military officer; b. Denver, Jan. 15, 1952; d. Donald William and Marie Dorothy (Ruscio) N.; m. Edward Ray Geron, Oct. 9, 1982; 1 child, Maria Louise. BA, U. No. Colo., 1974; grad., Command and Gen. Staff Coll., Ft. Leavenworth, 1993. Enlisted U.S. ANG, 1973; commd. 2d lt. U.S. Army, 1981, advanced through grades to lt. col., 1993; admistrv. supply tech. Colo. Army Nat. Guard, Denver, 1974-79; supply technician Colo. Army Nat. Guard, Golden, Colo., 1979-81; tng. officer Colo. Army Nat. Guard, Aurora, Colo., 1981-84, adminstrv. officer, 1984-85; maintenance officer Colo. Army Nat. Guard, Golden, Colo., 1985-86, asst. supply officer, 1986-91, data processing chief, 1991-92, supply mgmt. officer, 1992-93, comptr., 1993-94, dir. maintenance, 1994-96; logistics officer Colo. Army Nat. Guard, Golden, 1996—; Mem. Colo. Nat. Guard Assn. (sec. 1981-83, bd. dirs. 1983-85), Assn. of the U.S. Army (treas. 1986-88), Colo. Artists Assn. Group leader 5th grade Archdiocese of Denver Jr. Great Books Program, St. Anne Sch., 1987-89, group leader 7th grade Holy Family, 1991-92; bd. dirs. 9 Health Fair, Denver, 1985-90. Decorated Meritorious Svc. medal, Army Commendation medal, Army Achievement medal, Air Force Achievement medal. Mem. Colo. Nat. Guard Assn. (sec. 1981-83, bd. dirs. 1983-85), Assn. of U.S. Army (treas. 1986-88). Roman Catholic. Avocations: reading, skiing, watercolor painting. Office: Colo Army Nat Guard 6848 S Revere Pky Englewood CO 80112-3904

NUCKOLLS, JOHN HOPKINS, physicist, researcher; b. Chgo., Nov. 17, 1930; s. Asa Hopkins and Helen (Gates) N.; m. Ruth Munsterman, Apr. 21, 1952 (div. 1983); children—Helen Marie, Robert David; m. Amelia Aphrodite Liaskas, July 29, 1983. B.S., Wheaton Coll., 1953; M.A., Columbia U., 1955; D.Sc. (hon), Fla. Inst. Tech., 1977. Physicist U. Calif., Lawrence Livermore Nat. Lab., 1955—, assoc. leader thermonuclear design div., 1965-80, assoc. leader laser fusion program, 1975-83, div. leader, 1980-83, assoc. dir. physics, 1983-88, dir., 1988-94, assoc. dir. at large, 1994—; mem. adv. com. Princeton Plasma Physics Lab.; dir. Cen. Intelligence Nonproliferation adv. panel, U.S. Strategic Command Strategic adv. group; cons. def. sci. bd. Dept. Def. Recipient E.O. Lawrence award Pres. and AEC, 1969, Fusion Leadership award, 1983, Edward Teller medal Internat. Workshop Laser Interaction and Related Plasma Phenomena, 1991, Resolution of Appreciation, U. Calif. Regents, 1994, Sec. of Def. Outstanding Pub. Svc. medal, 1996, Disting. Assoc. award U.S. Dept. Energy, 1996, Career Achievement award Fusion Power Assocs., 1996. Fellow AAAS, Am. Phys. Soc. (J.C. Maxwell prize 1981); mem. NAE. Office: Lawrence Livermore Nat Lab PO Box 808 Livermore CA 94551-0808

NUCKOLLS, LEONARD ARNOLD, retired hospital administrator; b. Park City, Utah, Feb. 22, 1917; s. Harry Leonard and Mabel Hill (Ganson) N.; m. Rachel A. Beckner, Apr. 18, 1942; children: Rachel Nuckolls Conine, Peter Leonard. AB, Pueblo Jr. Coll., 1938; BA, U. Colo., 1940. Commd. U.S. Army, 1942, advanced through grades to lt. col., 1962; adj. gen. 2d Army Div., Ft. Hood, Tex., 1960-62; ret., 1962; acct. Colo. State Hosp., Pueblo, 1963-64; caseworker N.Mex. Dept. Pub. Welfare, Clovis, 1964-66; unit coord. N.Mex. Dept. Hosps. and Instns., Las Vegas State Hosp., 1966-69; hosp. adminstr. Las Vegas Med. Ctr., 1969-76; adminstr. Vista Sandia Hosp., Albuquerque, 1980-83. Vol. Internat. Exec. Svc. Corp. Mem. Ret. Officers Assn., Mensa. Home: 810 Faldas De La Sierra Santa Fe NM 87501-1252

NUCKOLS, FRANK JOSEPH, psychiatrist; b. Akron, Ohio, Apr. 7, 1926; s. William Alexander Jr. and Jean (Harrison) N.; m. Jane Fleetwood McIntosh, June 16, 1948; children: Claud Alexander, John Andrew. BA, U. Louisville, 1946; MD, U. Ala., 1951. Diplomate Am. Bd. Psychiatry and Neurology. Intern Holy Name Jesus Hosp., Gadsden, Ala., 1951; ward physician Ala. State Hosp., Tuscaloosa, 1951-52; resident U. Louisville, USPHS Hosp., Lexington, Ky., 1953-56; mem. faculty dept. psychiatry U. Ala. Med. Ctr., Birmingham, 1958-68, dir. tng. psychiat. residents, 1964-68, head div. community psychiatry, 1964-68, head continuing psychiat. edn. for physicians, 1964-68; chief psychiat. staff in-patient svc. U. Hosp., Birmingham, 1966-68; dir. tng. Hill Crest Hosp., Birmingham, 1975-79; pvt. practice Birmingham, 1968-93; cons. Ala. Div. Disability Determinations, Birmingham, 1993—; staff Med. Ctr. East Hosp., Birmingham, Bapt. Med. Ctr. Montclair, Birmingham; cons. staff St. Vincent's Hosp., Birmingham, Lloyd Noland Hosp., Birmingham, South Highland Hosp., Birmingham; vis. faculty, mem. interuniv. forum in cmty. psychiatry Harvard U., Boston, 1963-66; vis. faculty Baylor U. Med. Sch., Houston, 1967-71. Ensign USNR, 1941-43; sr. surgeon USPHS, 1956—. Fellow Am. Psychiat. Assn. (life), So. Psychiat. Assn.; mem. Med. Assn. Ala., So. Med. Assn., Jefferson County Mental Health Assn. (v.p. 1960), Jefferson County Med. Soc., Mental Health Assn. State Ala. (chmn. profl. adv. com. 1961), Nat. Assn. Disability Examiners, Phi Beta Pi, Tau Kappa Epsilon. Home and Office: 3741 River Oaks Cir Birmingham AL 35223-2117

NUCKOLS, WILLIAM MARSHALL, electrical goods manufacturing executive; b. Washington, Nov. 1, 1939; s. Edgar Marshall Jr. and Helen Abigail (Potter) N.; m. Margaret Louise Beebe, July 9, 1963 (div. 1980); children: Teryl K., Kerena A.; m. Maureen Joy Ryan, July 18, 1981 (div. 1990); children: Lauren E., Lindsay A.; m. Tuula Elina Renko, June 8, 1991; children: Wilson M., Julia A. BEE, Cornell U., 1962; MS in Indsl. Mgmt., MIT, 1965. Ops. and fin. analyst Ebasco Industries, N.Y.C., 1965-69; mktg. mgr. Gen. Cable Corp., N.Y.C., 1970-73; dir. corp. planning Gen. Cable Corp., Greenwich, Conn., 1974, group v.p., 1975-81; v.p. ops. devel. Penn Ctrl. Corp., Greenwich, 1982-83; group v.p. electronics Burndy Corp., Norwalk, Conn., 1984-89; dir. bus. devel. Uponor Group, Helsinki, Finland, 1990-91; chmn., pres., CEO Pass & Seymour/Legrand, Syracuse, N.Y., 1991—; bd. dirs. Ctrl. N.Y. Tech. Devel. Orgn., Pass & Seymour Can., Inc., The Watt Stopper, Inc.; v.p. Legrand Holding, Inc., 1991—. Dir. Hiawatha coun. Boy Scouts Am., Syracuse, 1992—. Mem. IEEE, Elec. Mfrs. Club, Am. Electronics Assn. (dir. 1985-88), Mfrs. Assn. Ctrl. N.Y. (dir. 1993—). Avocations: sailing, skiing, genealogy, shop, computers. Home: 5209 Harvest Hill Dr Jamesville NY 13078-9309

NUERNBERG, WILLIAM R(ICHARD), lawyer; b. Pitts., July 7, 1946; s. William W. and Frances (Hubler) N. BA cum laude, Denison U., 1968; JD cum laude, U. Mich., 1971. Bar: Pa. 1971, U.S. Dist.Ct. (we. dist.) Pa. 1971, Fla. 1995. Mem. Eckert Seamans Cherin & Mellott LC, Miami, 1981—. Bd. govs. Big Bros. Big Sisters Greater Miami. Pitt fellow U. Pitts. Sch. Bus., 1987-88. Mem. ABA, Pa. Bar Assn., Fla. Bar Assn., Rivers Club. Office: Eckert Seamans Cherin & Mellott LC 701 Brickell Ave Ste 1850 Miami FL 33131-2834

NUESSE, CELESTINE JOSEPH, retired university official; b. Sevastopol, Wis., Nov. 25, 1913; s. George and Salome Helen (Martens) N.; m. Margaret O'Donoghue, 1969. B.E., Central State Tchrs. Coll., Stevens Point, Wis., 1934; M.A., Northwestern U., 1937; Ph.D., Cath. U. Am., 1944, L.H.D., 1982; LL.D., Merrimack Coll., 1960. Tchr. social studies Pub. High Sch., Antigo, Wis., 1934-40; instr. sociology Coll. St. Catherine, St. Paul, 1943, Marquette U., 1943-45; instr. Cath. U. Am., Washington, 1945-48, asst. prof., 1948-52, assoc. prof., 1952-64, prof., 1964-81, prof. emeritus, 1981—, dean Sch. Social Sci., 1952-61, exec. v.p., 1967-81, provost, 1968-79, provost emeritus, 1981—; Spl. rep. in Germany, Nat. Cath. Welfare Conf., 1950-51; mem. U.S. Nat. Commn. for UNESCO, 1950-56, 63-69, exec. com., 1954-56; mem. gov. bd. UNESCO Youth Inst., Munich, Germany, 1955-59; mem. U.S. Bd. Fgn. Scholarships, 1954-58, chmn., 1956-58; mem. D.C. Commr.'s Council Human Relations, 1958-64, D.C. Commn. on Postsecondary Edn., 1975-80. Author: The Social Thought of American Catholics, 1634-1829, 1945, The Catholic University of America: A Centennial History, 1990; co-author, co-editor: The Sociology of the Parish, 1951; staff editor New Cath. Ency., 1963-66, chmn. editl. bd. supplements, 1973-79; contbr. articles to profl. jours. Mem. Am. Cath. Hist. Assn., Am. Cath. Sociol. Soc. (pres. 1954), Am. Sociol. Assn., Cath. Assn. Internat. Peace (pres. 1954-56), Cath. Commn. Intellectual and Cultural Affairs, Inst. Internat. Sociologie, Internat. Conf. on Sociology of Religion (past v.p.), Nat. Cath. Ednl. Assn., Cath. Interracial Council Washington (pres. 1962-66), Phi Beta Kappa (hon.), Alpha Kappa Delta, Pi Gamma Mu, Sigma Tau Delta, Phi Sigma Epsilon. Club: Cosmos (Washington). Lodge: KC. Home: 8108 River Crescent Dr Annapolis MD 21401-8414

NUESSLE, WILLIAM RAYMOND, surgeon; b. Bismarck, N.D., Sept. 17, 1951; s. Robert Frederick and Margaret Elizabeth (Bergeson) N.; m. Anna Maria Marlow, June 26, 1982; children: Aaron, Alexa, Matthew. BS, U. N.D., 1973, BS Medicine, 1975; MD, U. Ala., 1977. Diplomate Am. Bd. Surgery and Colon and Rectal Surgery. Resident gen. surgery Ochsner Found., New Orleans, 1977-1982; resident colon and rectal surgery U. La., Shreveport, 1982-83; colon and rectal surgeon Quain and Ramstat Clinic, Bismarck, N.D., 1983-90, Clinic for Colon & Rectal Surgery, Huntsville, Ala., 1990—, Huntsville (Ala.) Hosp., 1990—, Crestwood Hosp., Huntsville, 1990—. Fellow Am. Coll. Surgeons, Am. Soc. Colon and Rectal Surgeons; mem. SAGES. Avocations: tennis, fishing, music. Office: Clinic for CRS 303 Williams Ave SW Ste 1011 Huntsville AL 35801-6001

NUGENT, CHARLES ARTER, physician; b. Denver, Nov. 18, 1924; s. Charles Arter and Florence (Cohn) N.; m. Margaret Flint, Aug. 30, 1950; children—Stephen, Sara, Daniel. Student, U. Chgo., 1941-43, Ill. Inst. Tech., 1943, U. Minn., 1944, U. S.D., 1945-46; M.D., Yale U., 1951. Intern, asst. resident New Haven Hosp., 1951-53; resident Salt Lake County Gen. Hosp., Salt Lake City, 1954-56; mem. faculty U. Utah Coll. Medicine, 1956-67, assoc. prof. medicine, 1965-67; prof. dept. internal medicine U. Hawaii

Med. Sch., 1967-70; prof. sect. endocrinology dept. internal medicine U. Ariz. Coll. Medicine, Tucson, 1970—. Contbr. articles to profl. jours. Served with U.S. Army, 1943-46, 53. James Hudson Brown Meml. fellow, 1949-50. Mem. AAUP, Endocrine Soc., Western Assn. Physicians, Physicians Forum, Am. Soc. Clinical Investigators. Home: 3242 E 5th St Tucson AZ 85716-4902 Office: Dept Medicine Rm 6411 PO Box 245021 1501 N Campbell Ave Tucson AZ 85724-5021

NUGENT, CONSTANCE MARIE JULIE, health facility administrator; b. Lewiston, Maine, July 3, 1933; d. Joseph E.W. Sr. and Beatrice M.J. (Levasseur) Lessard; m. John Thomas Nugent Sr., Jan. 2, 1954 (dec. Feb. 27, 1982); children: John Thomas Jr., Michael Joseph. Diploma in nursing, Maine Gen. Hosp., 1953; BA, St. Joseph's Coll., Windham, Maine, 1974; family nurse practitioner cert., U. Maine Sch. of Nursing, 1976; M in Health Svc. Adminstrn., St. Joseph's Coll., Windham, Maine, 1995. RNNP, Maine, Calif., Ariz. Staff nurse med. surg., peds., gyn. Maine Med. Ctr., Portland, 1953-57; staff nurse ob-gyn. Mercy Hosp., Portland, Maine, 1957-59; emergency rm. nurse Huntington Meml. Hosp., Pasadena, Calif., 1959-63; supr. critical care unit Osteopathic Hosp. of Maine, Portland, 1963-69; clin. instr. sch. nursing Mercy Hosp., Portland, 1969; supr. ICU Dallas (Tex.) Osteopathic Hosp., 1970; adminstr. Nat. Med. Care of Portland, 1970-80; dir. nursing svcs. Lassen Cmty. Hosp., Susanville, Calif., 1980-87, Hospice of Monterey Peninsula, Carmel Valley, Calif., 1987; adminstr. Ukiah (Calif.) Convalescent Hosp., 1988—; cons. Office of Alcohol Drug Abuse Prevention, Augusta, Maine, 1975-77; mem. adv. com. Home Health Care, Portland, 1974-76, adv. coun. Bur. of Elderly, Portland, 1975-80, Provider Health Forum, Susanville, 1983-87. Sec. Lassen County Mental Health Bd., Susanville, 1980-81; co-facilitator Diabetic Clinic, Susanville, 1983-87; vice-chair Lassen County Health Human Svcs. Bd., Susanville, 1985-87. Mem. Bus. and Profl. Women (treas., v.p. 1990-94), Calif. Assn. Health Facilities, Coun. of Long Term Care Nurses of Calif. (pres. Redwood Empire chpt. 1989-92). Republican. Roman Catholic. Avocations: photography, travel, golf, reading. Office: Ukiah Convalescent Hosp 1349 S Dora St Ukiah CA 95482-6512

NUGENT, DANIEL EUGENE, business executive; b. Chgo., Dec. 18, 1927; s. Daniel Edward and Pearl A. (Trieger) N.; m. Bonnie Lynn Weidman, July 1, 1950; children: Cynthia Lynn, Mark Alan, Dale Alan. BSME, Northwestern U., 1951. With U.S. Gypsum Co., Chgo., 1951-71, dir. corp. devel., to 1971; pres. Am. Louver Co., Chgo., 1971-72; v.p. ops. ITT Corp., Cleve., 1972-74; exec. v.p. ITT Corp., St. Paul, 1974-75; v.p., ops. Pentair, Inc., St. Paul, 1974-75, pres., COO, 1975-81, pres., CEO, 1981-86, chmn., CEO, 1986-92, chmn. exec. com., 1992—; chmn. nominating com., dir. Pentair, Inc.; bd. dirs., audit, exec., compensation and corp. governance coms. Apogee Enterprises, Inc. Vice-chmn. local planning commn., 1968-72; co-chmn. Wellspring, 1989-92; trustee Harper Coll., Palatine, 1970-73; mem. adv. commn. McCormick Engring. and Kelloggg Schs. at Northwestern U., MBA Sch. of St. Thomas U., St. Paul; mem. exec. com. Indian Head coun. Boy Scouts Am. With AUS, 1946-47. Mem. North Oaks Golf Club, Mpls. Club. Republican. Presbyterian.

NUGENT, DENISE SMITH, holistic nurse; b. Winston Salem, N.C., July 27, 1959; d. Richard Delane and Betty Jean (Williams) Smith; m. Francis William Nugent Jr., Sept. 19, 1980. RN, Cabarrus Hosp. Sch. Nursing, Concord, N.C., 1980; cert., Internat. Inst. Reflexology, St. Petersburg, Fla., 1990, cert. in reflexology, 1996. RN, N.C., Va., Pa., Mass., Ariz., Calif. Staff nurse oncology dept. Bapt. Hosp., Winston Salem, 1980-82; staff nurse diabetes dept. Lehigh Valley Hosp., Allentown, Pa., 1982-83; staff nurse home health Berks Vis. Nurse Assn., Reading, Pa., 1983-85; staff nurse diabetic educator Moses Taylor Hosp., Scranton, Pa., 1990-93; staff nurse, supr. In Home Health, San Mateo, Calif., 1993-94; holistic nurse, cons. in pvt. practice Foster City, Calif., 1995—; dir. profl. svcs. Olsten Health Care, Scranton, 1992-93; cons., 1995—; tchg. Reiki, 1995—; Qi Gong Practitioner, 1997—. Mem. Am. Holistic Nurses Assn. (cert. program holistic nursing, bd. cert. holistic nurse), Inst. Noetic Sci., Calif. Concention-Holistic Nurses, Foster City C. of C. Avocations: mind-body practices, prosperity consciousness, energy healing, sex education, Qi Gong. Home: 44 Rock Harbor Ln Foster City CA 94404-3565 Office: 969G Edgewater Blvd # 764 Foster City CA 94404-3760

NUGENT, JANE KAY, utility executive; b. Detroit, Aug. 31, 1925; d. Albert A. and Celia (Betzing) Kay; m. Robert L. Nugent, Apr.3, 1991. BS, U. Detroit, 1948; MA, Wayne State U., 1952; MBA, U. Mich., 1963. Sr. personnel interviewer employment Detroit Edison Co., 1948-60, personnel coord. for women, 1960-65, office employment adminstr., 1965-70, gen. employment adminstr., 1970-71, dir. personnel svcs., 1971-72, mgr. employee rels., 1972-77, asst. v.p. employee rels., 1977-78, v.p. employee rels., 1978-82, v.p. adminstrn., 1982-90, ret., 1990; bd. dirs. First Am. Bank-SE Mich., 1986-90, Bon Secours of Mich. Healthcare System, Inc., 1984-93, Detroit Exec. Svc. Corp., 1990—; tchr. U. Detroit Evening Coll. Bus. and Adminstrn., 1963-75; seminar leader div. mgmt. edn. U. Mich., 1968-74, Waterloo Mgmt. Edn. Centre, 1972-77. Mem. Mich. Employment Security Adv. Coun., 1967-81; chmn. bd. dirs. Detroit Inst. Commerce, 1976-79; exec. bd. NCCJ, 1980-91, nat. trustee, 1984-88; bd. dirs. Childrens Home Detroit, 1991-94, 1st v.p. 1994-96, pres. 1996—. Recipient Alumni Tower award U. Detroit, 1967, Headliner award Women Wayne State U., 1970, Wayne State U. Alumni Achievement award, 1974, Career Achievement award Profl. Panhellenic Assn., 1973, Bus. Achievement award Assn. Bus. Deans, 1989, Svcs. Older Citizens All Star award, 1996; named one of Top Ten Working Women of Detroit, 1970, Alumnus of Yr., U. Detroit, 1981, Woman of Yr. Am. Lung Assn., 1991, Sr. Profl. in Human Resources Soc. Human Resource Mgmt.; cert. Adminstrv. Mgr. Am. Mgmt. Soc.; inducted in Mich. Women's Hall of Fame, 1988. Mem. Internat. Assn. Personnel Women (pres. 1969-70), Women's Econ. Club (v.p. 1971-72, pres. 1972-73), Am. Soc. Employees (bd. dirs. 1979-90), Personnel Women Detroit (pres. 1960-61), U. Detroit Alumni Assn. (pres. 1964-66), Phi Gamma Nu (nat. v.p. 1955-57), Boys and Girls Club S.E. Mich. (pres. 1987-89), Econ. Club Detroit (v.p. 1981-90), Internat. Womens Forum.

NUGENT, JOHN HILLIARD, communications executive; b. Paterson, N.J., Aug. 20, 1944; s. James Joseph and Jacqueline Ann (Storms) N.; m. Mary Elizabeth Maher, June 3, 1967; 1 child, Jill Frances. BA, Columbia U., 1970; MS, Southeastern U., 1978; DBA, Bus. Sch. of Lausanne, Switzerland, 1989. Adminstr. Chase Manhattan Bank, N.Y.C., 1970-71; analyst U.S. Dept. of Army, Washington, 1971-72; chmn. Strategic Planning & Rsch. Corp., Dallas, 1977-95; pres. AT&T Aviation Tech. and Sys., Ltd., Arlington, Va., Hong Kong, Beijing, 1993; exec. CDX, Inc., Dallas, 1995; v.p., bd. dirs. SA Telecomm., Inc., Richardson, Tex., 1996—, also bd. dirs., v.p., 1996; v.p., fin. acct. AdCon Inc./Internat. Bank, Reston, Va., 1971-79; CFO HDS, Inc., Reston, 1979-82; pres. Group L Corp., Herndon, Va., 1983-85; pres., bd. dirs. AT&T/Datotek, Dallas, 1985-92. Author: Corporate Decline: Causes, Symptoms, and Prescriptions for a Turnaround, 1989. Cpl. USMC, 1962-66. Mem. AICPAs, D.C. Inst. CPAs, Tex. Soc. CPAs, Nat. Assn. Accts., Dallas Com. on Fgn. Rels., Columbia Club of N.Y. Republican. Avocation: reading. Home: RR 1 Box 285c1 Mc Kinney TX 75070-9758 Office: SA Telecommunications Inc 1600 Promenade Ctr Fl 15 Richardson TX 75080-5400

NUGENT, LORI S., lawyer; b. Peoria, Ill., Apr. 24, 1962; d. Walter Leonard and Margery (Frost) Meyer; m. Shane Vincent Nugent, June 14, 1986; 1 child, Justine Nicole. BA in Polit. Sci. cum laude, Knox Coll., 1984; JD, Northwestern U., Chgo., 1987. Bar: Ill. 1987, U.S. Dist. Ct. (no. dist.) Ill. 1988, U.S. Ct. Appeals (7th cir.) 1995. Assoc. Peterson & Ross, Chgo., 1987-94; assoc. Blatt, Hammesfahr & Eaton, Chgo., 1994, ptnr., 1994—. Co-author: Punitive Damages: A Guide to the Insurability of Punitive Damages in the United States and Its Territories, 1988, Punitive Damages: A State-by-State Guide to Law and Practice, 1991, Japanese edit., 1995; contbr. articles to law jours. Mem. Def. Rsch. Inst. Office: Blatt Hammesfahr & Eaton 333 W Wacker Dr Ste 1900 Chicago IL 60606-1226

NUGENT, NELLE, theater, film and television producer; b. Jersey City, May 24, 1939; d. John Patrick and Evelyn Adelaide (Stern) N.; m. Donald G. Baker, June 6, 1960 (div. 1962); m. Benjamin Janney, June 22, 1969 (div. Apr., 1980); m. Jolyon Fox Stern, Apr. 7, 1982; 1 child, Alexandra Fox Stern. BS, Skidmore Coll., 1960, DHL (hon.), 1981. Chmn. bd. McCann & Nugent, Prodns. Inc., N.Y.C., 1976-86; pres. Foxboro Prodns., Inc., N.Y.C., 1985-94; pres., CEO Foxboro Entertainment, 1990-94; pres. The Foxboro Co., Inc.; co-prin. Golden Fox Films, Inc. Stage mgr. various off-Broadway shows, 1960-64; prodn. asst.: Broadways plays Any Wednesday, 1963-64, Dylan, 1964, Ben Franklin in Paris, 1964-65; stage mgr. Broadway shows, 1964-68; prodn. supr., then gen. mgr., 1969-76, assoc. mng. dir. Nederlander Corp., operating theaters and producing plays in, N.Y.C. and on tour, 1970-76; prodr.: Dracula, 1977 (Tony award), The Elephant Man, 1978 (Tony award, Drama Critics award), Morning's at Seven, 1980 (Tony award), Home, 1980 (Tony nomination), Amadeus, 1981 (Tony award); also produced: Rose and Piaf, 1980, The Life and Adventures of Nicholas Nickleby, 1981 (Tony award, Drama Critics award), The Dresser (Tony award nominee), 1981, Mass Appeal, 1981; The Lady & The Clarinet, 1982; The Glass Menagerie (revival), 1983; Painting Churches (Obie award), 1983; Total Abandon, 1983; All's Well That End's Well, 1983 (Tony nominee); Pilobolus Dance Company, 1983; Pacific Overtures (revival), 1984; Much Ado about Nothing/Cyrano de Bergerac (repertory) (Tony award nominees), 1984; Leader of the Pack (Tony award nominee), 1985, The Life and Adventures of Nicholas Nickleby (revival) (Tony award nominee), 1986; prodr.: TV spls.: Morning's At Seven, Piaf; Pilobolus; prodr. A Fighting Choice, Walt Disney Prodns., 1986, Phoenix Entertainment Group, 1986-88, A Conspiracy of Love, CBS, 1987, The Final Verdict, TNT, 1990 (Cable Ace award nominee Best Picture); exec. prodr. (TV pilot) Morning Maggie, 1987, Dick Clark Prodns., 1988-90, (feature films) Student Body, 1993, Pictures of Baby Jane Doe, 1996; (Showtime) In the Presence of Mine Enemies, 1995-96, Dinner at The Homesick Restaurant, 1997, (USA) A Town Has Turned to Dust, 1997. Mem. Am. Women's Econ. Devel. Corp. (bd. dirs.). Office: Foxboro Co Inc 133 E 58th St Ste 301 New York NY 10022-1236

NUGENT, ROBERT J., JR., fast food company executive; b. 1942. BBA, U. Cin., 1964. loan officer Citizens Savs., 1964-67; asst. v.p. Gem City Savs., 1967-69; v.p. Ponderosa System Inc., 1969-78, Ky. Fried Chicken, 1978-79; v.p. Foodmaker Inc., San Diego, from 1979, exec. v.p. ops., mktg., 1985-95; CEO, pres. Foodmaker Inc., 1995—. Office: Foodmaker Inc 9330 Balboa Ave San Diego CA 92123-1516*

NUGENT, THEODORE ANTHONY, musician; b. Detroit, Dec. 13, 1948; s. Warren Henry and Marion Dorothy (Johnson) N.; divorced; children: Sasha Emma, Theodore Tobias. Ed., Oakland Community Coll., Detroit. Also profl. off-road racer, 1981—. Guitarist, 1958—, mem. group, Amboy Dukes, 1965, solo artist, 1965—; recs. include: (with Amboy Dukes) Ted Nugent and the Amboy Dukes, 1968, Journey to the Center of the Mind, 1968, Marriage on the Rocks, 1970, Survival of the Fittest, 1974, Call of the Wild, 1974, Tooth, Fang, and Claw, 1975; (solo albums) Ted Nugent, 1975, Free for All, 1976, Cat Scratch Fever, 1977, Double Live Gonzo, 1977, Weekend Warriors, 1978, State of Shock, 1979, Scream Dream, 1980, Great Gonzos/The Best of, 1981, Intensities in Ten Cities, 1981, Penetrator, 1984, Little Miss Dangerous, 1986, If You Can't Lick 'Em...Lick 'Em, 1988, Spirit of the Wild, 1995; (with Damn Yankees) Damn Yankees, 1990, Don't Tread, 1992. Mem. ASCAP, Nat. Rifle Assn. (life), Ducks Unlimited (life sponsor), Nat. Trappers Assn., Mich. Bowhunters, Safari Club Internat. Address: PO Box 15108 Ann Arbor MI 48106-5108 also: Sony Music Entertainment Inc. 550 Madison Ave New York NY 10022-3211*

NUGENT, WALTER TERRY KING, historian; b. Watertown, N.Y., Jan. 11, 1935; s. Clarence A. and Florence (King) N.; children from previous marriage: Katherine, Rachel, David, Douglas, Terry, Mary; m. Suellen Hoy, 1986. A.B., St. Benedict's Coll., 1954, D.Litt., 1968; M.A., Georgetown U., 1956; Ph.D., U. Chgo., 1961. Instr. history Washburn U., 1957-58; asst. prof. Kans. State U., 1961-63; asst. prof. history Ind. U., 1963-64, assoc. prof., 1964-68, prof., 1968-84, assoc. dean Coll. Arts and Scis., 1967-71, dir. overseas study, 1967-76, chmn. history dept., 1974-77; Andrew V. Tackes prof. history U. Notre Dame, 1984—; Paley lectr., Fulbright vis. prof. Hebrew U., Jerusalem, 1978-79; vis. prof. U. Hamburg, 1980, U. Warsaw, 1982; Mary Ball Washington Fulbright prof. U. Coll., Dublin, 1991-92; summer seminar dir. NEH, 1979, 84, 86; bd. mem. U.S.- Israel Ednl. Found., 1985-89. Author: The Tolerant Populists, 1963, Creative History, 1967, The Money Question During Reconstruction, 1967, Money and American Society 1865-1880, 1968, Modern America, 1973, From Centennial to World War: American Society 1876-1917, 1977, Structures of American Social History, 1981, Crossings: The Great Transatlantic Migrations 1870-1914, 1992. Newberry Libr. fellow, 1962; Guggenheim fellow, 1964-65; Huntington Libr. fellow, 1979, 85; Beinecke fellow Yale U., 1990. Mem. Western Hist. Assn., Soc. Am. Historians, Coun. on Fgn. Rels. Democrat. Office: U Notre Dame Notre Dame IN 46556

NUGTEREN, CORNELIUS, air force officer; b. Colton, S.D., Feb. 7, 1928; s. Adrian Joe and Marie Johanna N.; m. Liane Albrecht, Sept. 22, 1956; children: Cecile, Aneli. B.A., Central Coll., Pella, Iowa, 1951. Commd. 2d lt. USAF, 1953, advanced through grades to maj. gen., 1980; advisor Vietnam Air Force, 1970-71, served in Germany, 1971-77; vice comdr. (Air Logistics Center), Utah, 1977-79; comdr. (Aerospace Rescue and Recovery Service), Scott AFB, Ill., 1979-81; chief (Joint U.S. Mil. Aid Group), Greece, 1981-82; comdr. Air Logistics Ctr., Robins AFB, Ga, 1983-88, ret.; cons. for def. industries Warner Robins, Ga., 1988—; v.p. Chem. Tech. Internat., Warner Robins, Mercer U. Engring. Rsch. Ctr., Warner Robins, 1988—. Decorated D.S.M., Legion of Merit, Bronze Star, Superior Service medal; recipient USAF EEO award, 1979. Mem. Air Force Assn., Order Daedalians, Internat. Order Hansen, Order of the Sword. Office: 114 Holly Dr Warner Robins GA 31088-6615 *Service to one's country is not just a job...it's a calling. Integrity to and within the institution to which you belong is an absolute necessity. Loyalty to peers and subordinates is equally important as loyalty to your superiors. Attitude toward life, humankind and profession is key determinant to success. Goals should be set high enough so as to be unattainable. Standard of conduct must always include duty, honor, country.*

NULAND, ANTHONY C. J., lawyer; b. N.Y.C., 1943. AB cum laude, Princeton U., 1965; JD, NYU, 1968. Bar: N.Y. 1969, D.C. 1977, Ga. 1978. Asst. dir. divsn. market regulation SEC, 1975-76, assoc. dir. divsn. market regulation, 1976-77; now ptnr. Seward & Kissel, N.Y.C. Office: Seward & Kissel 1200 G St NW Ste 350 Washington DC 20005-3814

NULAND, SHERWIN, surgeon, author; b. N.Y.C., Dec. 8, 1930; s. Meyer and Violet (Lutsky) N.; m. Sarah Peterson, May 29, 1977; children: Victoria Jane, Andrew Meyer, William Peterson, Amelia Rose. BA, NYU, 1951; MD, Yale U., 1955. Surgeon Yale-New Haven Hosp. (Conn.), 1962-91; clin. prof. surgery Yale Sch. Medicine, New Haven, 1962—. Author: The Origins of Anesthesia, 1983, Doctors: the Biography of Medicine, 1988, Medicine: The Art of Healing, 1991, The Face of Mercy, 1993, How We Die: Reflections on Life's Final Chapter, 1994 (Nat. Book award for non-fiction 1994, Pulitzer prize finalist 1995), The Wisdom of the Body, 1997. Pres. med. com. Jewish Home Aged, New Haven, 1985-87; v.p. Conn. Hospice, New Haven, 1978-80. Fellow ACS; mem. New Eng. Surg. Soc., Assocs. of Yale Med. Sch. Libr. (chmn. 1982-94), Yale-China Assn. (chmn. med. 1988-93). Democrat. Jewish. Avocation: tennis. Home: 29 Old Hartford Tpke Hamden CT 06517-3523 Office: PO Box 6356 Hamden CT 06517-0356

NULL, JACK ELTON, schools superintendent; b. New Haven, Ind., May 22, 1938; s. Clifford Lewis and Violet Alice (Shuler) N.; 1 child, Richard Lance; m. Bonnie Bermes Ottenweller, Dec. 2, 1995. BS in Bus. Mgmt., Ind. U., 1960; MA in Elem. Edn., Ball State U., 1963; EdD in Ednl. Adminstrn., Ariz. State U., 1974. Cert. elem. edn. tchr., prin., bus. mgr., supt., Ariz. Adminstrv. asst. to dir. of purchasing Cummins Engine Co., Columbus, Ind., 1960-61; tchr. Randolph Cen. Schs., Winchester, Ind., 1963; tchr., coach East Allen County Schs., New Haven, 1963-66; from prin. to adminstrv. asst. to supt. Wilson Sch. Dist. 6, Phoenix, 1966-73; acting supt., exec. asst. Washington Sch. Dist. 7, Phoenix, 1973-79; supt. Fowler Sch. Dist. 45, Phoenix, 1979—; supt.'s chmn. Westside IMPACT, Phoenix, Tolleson, Avondale, Goodyear and Litchfield, Ariz., 1988-92; All Ariz. Supt., 1992-93; bd. dirs. Ariz. Sch. Bd. Assn. Ins. Trust, 1997—. Football ofcl. PAC-10, Big Sky, Ariz. C.C. Athletic Conf., Ariz. Interscholastic Assn., 1966-95, basketball ofcl., 1963-85; clock operator NFL, Phoenix, 1987—; vice chmn. West Phoenix Cactus League Baseball Coalition, 1991-93, Ariz. Edn. Revorm Com., 1993—. Sgt. USAFR, 1961-66. Named Football Ofcl. Yr. ACCAC, 1990, 94. Mem. Am. Assn. Sch. Adminstrs., Ariz. Sch. Adminstrs. Inc. (charter; chmn. lgeis. com. 1992—, bd. dirs. supts. divsn. 1993—, pres. 1995-96, exec. bd. 1994—), Maricopa County Supt. Assn. (treas. 1970-71, pres. 1971-72, Westmarc adv. bd. 1997—), Greater Phoenix Supts. Assn., Century Club. Democrat. Mem. United Ch. of Christ. Avocations: investments, sports.

NULL, MICHAEL ELLIOT, lawyer; b. Chgo., Feb. 14, 1947; s. Samuel Joseph and Rose (Baren) N.; m. Eugenia Irene Frack, Dec. 21, 1969; children: Jennifer Susan, Emily Lauren. B.S. in Psychology, U. Ill., 1969; J.D., Ill. Inst. Tech. Chgo. Kent Law Sch., 1974. Bar: Ill. 1974, U.S. Dist. Ct. (no. dist.) Ill. 1974, U.S. Dist. Ct. (ea. dist.) Mich., 1985, U.S. Dist. Ct. (ea. dist.) Wis., 1986, U.S. Ct. Appeals (7th cir.) 1981, U.S. Ct. Appeals (6th cir.) 1985, U.S. Supreme Ct., 1985. Prin. Michael Null And Assocs., Chgo., 1977—. Author: Truths: A Guide to Practical Metaphysics; composer musical selections. Mem. ABA, 1st Amendment Lawyers Assn. Office: 155 N Michigan Ave Chicago IL 60601

NULL, PAUL BRYAN, minister; b. Oakland, Calif., May 7, 1944; s. Carleton Elliot and Dorothy Irene (Bryan) N.; m. Renee Yvonne Howell, Aug. 23, 1969; children: Bryan Joseph, Kara Renee. BS, Western Bapt. Coll., 1973; MDiv, Western Conservative Bapt. Sem., 1979; DMin, Trinity Theol. Sem., 1994. Ordained to ministry Bapt. Ch., 1982. Asst. pastor Bethel Bapt. Ch., Aumsville, Oreg., 1972-74, sr. pastor, 1974-87; sr. pastor The Calvary Congregation, Stockton, Calif., 1987-94; pastor Sierra Comty. Ch., South Lake Tahoe, Calif., 1994—; trustee Conservative Bapt. Assn. of Oreg., 1982-85, mem. Ch. extension com., 1975-85. Radio show commentator Food for Thought, 1987. Panel mem. Presdl. Anti-Drug Campaign, 1984. Served with U.S. Army, 1965-67. Named Outstanding Young Man Am., 1979. Mem. Conservative Bapt. Assn. of Am., No. Calif. Conservative Bapt. Assn. (pres. 1992-93), Delta Epsilon Chi. Avocations: weight training, aerobics, writing, hiking, cross-country skiing. Home: 1399 Iroquois Cir South Lake Tahoe CA 96150-4728 Office: Sierra Comty Ch 1165 Sierra Blvd South Lake Tahoe CA 96150-3005

NULTON, WILLIAM CLEMENTS, lawyer; b. Pittsburg, Kans., Feb. 22, 1931; s. Perley Edgar and Mary Celia (Anderson) N.; m. Vicki Smith, Aug. 20, 1956; children: Carnie, Erica. BA, Kans. U., 1953, LLB with honors, 1958; postgrad., NYU, 1953-54. Bar: Kans. 1958, Mo. 1959. Sr. atty. Great Lakes Pipe Line Co., Kansas City, Mo., 1958-66, asst. sec., 1961-66; assoc. Blackwell, Sanders, Matheny, Weary & Lombardi, Kansas City, 1966-68, ptnr., 1968-81; assoc. Shughart Thomson & Kilroy, Kansas City, 1981-83, ptnr., 1983-94. Contbr. articles to profl. jours. Bd. dirs. Corinth Hills Home Assn., Shawnee Mission, 1974-76; pres. Beta Theta Pi Kansas City Alumni Assn., 1977; mem., elder Village United Presbyn. Ch., Prairie Village, Kans., 1976—, trustee, 1992-94, mem. found. bd., 1997—; bd. dirs. Kansas City Civil Rights Consortium, 1993—, Marillac Acad., 1994—; mem. Kans. adv. com. U.S. Civil Rights Commn., 1994—; mem. Shawnee Mission Unified Bd. Edn., 1969-73, v.p., 1973; pres. Corinth Elem. Bd. Edn., Johnson County, Kans., 1969; chmn. Full Employment Task Group on Employment Disabled, Kansas City, 1987. Summerfield scholar Kans. U., 1949-53, Root-Tilden scholar NYU, 1953-54. Mem. ABA (mgmt. chmn. labor and employment law sect., com. on arbitration and collective bargaining 1989-92), Am. Acad. Hosp. Attys. (co-chmn. task group on bylaws for small rural hosps. 1992-93), Mo. Bar Assn. (chmn. labor law com. 1982), Nat. Health Lawyers Assn. (co-chmn. task group on alternative dispute resolution in health care field 1990-91), Phi Beta Kappa. Republican. Home: 7908 El Monte St Shawnee Mission KS 66208-5047

NUMBERE, DAOPU THOMPSON, petroleum engineer, educator; b. Buguma, Nigeria, Mar. 30, 1951; came to the U.S., 1975; s. Thompson and Norah (West) N.; m. Tonye Eugenia Higgwe, Dec. 29, 1987. BS in Mech. Engring., U. Coll. Swansea, 1975; MS in Petroleum Engring., Stanford U., 1977; PhD, U. Okla., 1982. Asst. prof. U. Mo., Rolla, 1982-88, assoc. prof., 1988-96, prof., 1996—, head dept. petroleum engring., 1996—; cons. Sigma Cons., Mattoon, Ill., 1987-93. Author: Petroleum Reservoir Class Manual, 1991, Notes on Water Flooding, 1994. Recipient Shell-BP award, 1971-75, Selwyn Caswell prize U. Coll. Seansea, 1975, Okla. Rsch. award Okla Rsch. Coun., 1981. Mem. ASME, Internat. Soc. for Computer Methods and Adv. in Geomechanics, Soc. Petroleum Engrs., Sigma Xi. Achievements include development of an innovative method for streamline generation for oil recovery prediction, simultaneous prediction of oil recovery and water influx for oil and gas reservoirs. Office: U Mo Rolla 119 Mcnutt Hall Rolla MO 65401

NUNES, GEOFFREY, lawyer, corporate executive; b. N.Y.C., July 7, 1930; s. Kenneth Neville and Helen (Landsberg) N.; m. Clare Harwood, Sept. 13, 1958; children: Geoffrey Jr., John Kenneth, Margaret Hamilton Nunes Rogers. AB, Princeton U., 1952; LLB, Harvard U., 1957. Bar: N.Y. 1957, N.J. 1968, Mass. 1978. Assoc. atty. Breed Abbott & Morgan, N.Y.C., 1957-61, Shea & Gould, N.Y.C., 1961-66; v.p., gen. counsel Lenox, Inc., Princeton, N.J., 1966-76; sr. v.p., gen. consel Millipore Corp., Bedford, Mass., 1976—; bd. dirs. Reebok Internat., Stoughton, Mass., Scottish Widows Internat. Mut. Found. Trustee, bd. dirs. DeCordova Mus., Lincoln, Mass., Boston Biomed. Rsch. Inst., 1992; bd. overseers New Eng. Conservatory, 1996. Office: Millipore Corp 80 Ashby Rd Bedford MA 01730-2237

NUÑEZ DE, MARIA IRENE, small business owner, consultant; b. Caibarien, Cuba, Jan. 19, 1940; came to U.S., 1956; d. Candido Gregorio and Sofia Irene Diaz; m. Antonio Luis Nuñez de Villavicencio, July 15, 1960; children; Ana Maria, Jacqueline, Mark Allan, Paul Anthony, Jennifer Susan. Student, Marsh Bus. Sch., Atlanta, 1960, Bentley Coll., 1989. With accounts receivable dept. GE Credit Corp., Atlanta, 1960-62; cashier Digital Equipment Corp., Marlboro, Mass., 1981-83, auditor, 1983-87; with profit and loss statements dept. Digital Equipment Corp., Maynard, Mass., 1987-92; owner, v.p. ops., cons. AMN Assocs., Westboro, Mass., 1991-94; with AMN Enterprises, 1994—, Hobe Sound, Fla., 1996—. Roman Catholic. Avocations: investing, reading, travel, swimming, trap shooting. Home and Office: 8305 SE Paurotis Ln Hobe Sound FL 33455 Address: PO Box 1476 Hobe Sound FL 33475-1476

NUNEZ-PORTUONDO, RICARDO, investment company executive; b. N.Y.C., June 9, 1933; s. Emilio and Maria (Garcia) N-P.; m. Dolores Maldonado, Sept. 7, 1963; children—Ricardo Jose, Emilio Manuel, Eduardo Javier. LL.D., U. Havana, Cuba; postdoctoral in law, U. Fla., 1975. Bar: Cuba, Fla. Editor Latin Am. div. USIA, Miami, Fla., 1961-71; editor Latin Am. div. USIA, Washington, 1961-71; nat. dir. Cuban Refugee Program, Washington, 1975-77; pres. Cultural Pub., Inc., Miami, 1994—, Central Investment Trust, Coral Gables, Fla., 1977—; chmn. bd. Interstate Bank of Commerce, Miami, 1986-88; v.p. Century 21, Coral Gables, 1989—. Author: A Critique on the Linowitz Report, 1975, Cuba: La Otra Imagen, 1994, Un Procer Cubano, 1994, Cuban Refugee Program, The Early Years, 1995. dir. Nat. Hispanic Scholarship Fund, San Francisco, 1978—; dir. COSSMHO, Washington, 1980—; trustee emeritus Fla. Internat. U., 1984—; pres. Mercy Hosp. Found., Miami, 1985—; bd. dirs. ARC, Greater Miami. Recipient numerous awards for civic contbns. including day named in honor Ricardo Nunez Day, Miami, 1975. Mem. Cuban Lawyers Assn., Cuban Acad. History, Metro. Club, Lyford Cay Club, Ocean Reef Club, Key Biscayne Yacht Club, Big Five Club, 200 Club. Republican. Roman Catholic. Home: 675 Solano Prado Miami FL 33156-2373 Office: PO Box 141720 Coral Gables FL 33114-1720

NUNIS, DOYCE BLACKMAN, JR., historian, educator; b. Cedartown, Ga., May 30, 1924; s. Doyce Blackman and Winnie Ethel (Morris) N. B.A., U. Calif., Los Angeles, 1947; M.S., U. So. Calif., 1950, M.Ed., 1952, Ph.D., 1958. Lectr. U. So. Calif., 1951-56; instr. El Camino Coll., 1956-59; asst. prof. edn. and history UCLA, 1959-65; assoc. prof. history U. So. Calif., 1965-68, prof., 1968-89, emeritus, 1989—; asst. research historian U. Calif., Los Angeles, 1959-63; asso. U. Calif., 1963-65, lectr., 1960-61, asst. prof. edn. and history, 1961-64, asso. prof., 1964-65. Author: Andrew Sublette, Rocky Mountain Prince, 1960, Josiah Belden, 1841 California Overland Pioneer, 1962, The Golden Frontier: The Recollections of Herman Francis Rinehart, 1851-69, 1962, The California Diary of Faxon Dean Atherton, 1836-39, 1964, Letters of a Young Miner, 1964, The Journal of James H. Bull, 1965, The Trials of Isaac Graham, 1967, The Medical Journey of Pierre Garnier in California, 1851, 1967, Past is Prologue, 1968, Hudson's Bay Company's First Fur Brigade to the Sacramento Valley, 1968, Sketches of a

Journey on Two Oceans by H.J.A. Alric, 1850-1867, 1971, San Francisco 1856 Vigilance Committee: Three Views, 1971, The Drawings of Ignatio Tirsh, Los Angeles and Its Environs in the 20th Century, A Bibliography, 1973, A History of American Political Thought, 2 vols, 1975, The Mexican War in Baja California, 1977, Henry Hoyt's A Frontier Doctor, 1979, Los Angeles from the Days of the Old Pueblo, 1981, The 1769 Transit of Venus, 1982, The Missionary Letters of Jacob Baegert, 1982, Men, Medicine and Water, 1982, Southern California Historical Anthology, 1984, George Coe's Frontier Fighter, 1984, Life of Tom Horn, 1987, A Guide to the History of California, 1989, Great Doctors of Medicine, 1990, The Bidwell-Bartleson Party, 1991, The Life of Tom Horn Revisited, 1992, Southern California's Spanish Heritage, 1992, Southern California Local History, A Gathering of W.W. Robinson's Writings, 1993, From Mexican Days to the Gold Rush, 1993, Tales of Mexican California, 1994, Women in the Life of Southern California, 1996, Hispanic California Revisited, 1996, The Presidio of San Francisco under Spain and Mexico, 1775-1848, 1996; editor So. Calif. Quar., 1962—; contbr. articles to profl. jours. Trustee Mission Santa Barbara Archives-Libr., 1970—, pres., 1972—. Decorated Benemerenti, Papal medal, 1984; recipient Distinction award Calif. Com. for Promotion of History, 1985, Merit award Calif. Conf. Hist. Socs., 1986, Franciscan Hist. award, 1990, Disting. Emeritus award U. So. Calif., 1993, Knight Comdr. of St. Gregory, 1993, Order of Isabel the Cath. (Spanish Govt.), 1995, Oscar Lewis award Book Club of Calif., 1996; Henry E. Huntington Libr. grantee-in-aid, 1960, Am. Philos. Soc. grantee, 1969; Guggenheim fellow, 1963-64. Fellow Calif. Hist. Soc. (trustee 1987-93, v.p. 1989-93, Henry R. Wagner award 1988), Hist. Soc. So. Calif.; mem. Am. Antiquarian Soc., Am. Hist. Assn., Orgn. Am. Historians, Western Hist. Assn., Zamorano Club, L.A. Corral Westerners, Phi Alpha Theta, Pi Sigma Alpha. Home: 4426 Cromwell Ave Los Angeles CA 90027-1250

NUNIS, RICHARD A., amusement parks executive; b. Cedartown, Ga., May 30, 1932; s. Doyce Blackman and Winnie E. (Morris) N.; m. Mary Nunis; children: Richard D., Lisa Parks, Corey Vanelli. B.S. in Edn, U. So. Calif., 1954; D honoris causa, U. Ctrl. Fla., 1996. With The Walt Disney Co., 1955—; dir. ops. Disneyland, Calif., 1961-68; chmn. park ops. com. Disneyland, 1968-74; corp. v.p. Disneyland Ops. (Disneyland, Walt Disney World, Tokyo Disneyland), 1968-91, Walt Disney World, Orlando, Fla., 1971—; exec. v.p., then pres. Walt Disney Attractions and Disneyland Internat., 1972-91; chmn. Walt Disney Attractions, 1991—; mem. Recreation Roundtable; bd. dirs. Suntrust, Orlando, Fla. Exec. adv. bd. dirs. Give the Kids the World; bd. dirs. Fla. Progress Bd., U. Ctrl. Fla. Found., Inc.; chmn. bd. dirs. Fla. Coun. of 100, 1995-96; bd. dirs. United Arts of Ctrl. Fla.; vice chair bd. dirs. Enterprise Fla. Inc., 1996-97; mem. adv. bd. In Roads/Ctrl. Fla. Inc.; chmn. Heart of Fla. United Way, 1993. Named First Acad. All-Am. U. So. Calif., 1952, Richard L. McLaughlin Fla. Econ. Devel. Vol. of Yr., 1995. Mem. Fla. Isleworth Golf and Country Club. Republican. Avocations: sports, fishing, golf. Office: Walt Disney Attractions Inc PO Box 10000 Lake Buena Vista FL 32830-1000 *Do the best job you can with the job you are given to do. Those who look over the hill never climb the mountain.*

NUNN, CHARLES BURGESS, religious organization executive; b. Richmond, Va., May 1, 1931; s. Charles Burgess Sr. and Virginia Atkinson (Goode) N.; m. Helen Agnes Parker, Sept. 1, 1957; children: Patsy Virginia, Catherine Louise, Stephen Charles, Stewart Gavin. BA in Econs., Randolph Macon Coll., 1953; BD, Southwestern Bapt. Theol. Sem., 1959, MDiv, 1969; DMin, Pitts. Theol. Sem., 1979. Ordained to Gospel ministry, 1954. Pastor Warwick Rd. Bapt. Chapel, Richmond, Va., 1952-53, Garrett's Bluff Bapt. Ch., Arthur City, Tex., 1954-56, Plymouth Haven Bapt. Ch., Alexandria, Va., 1959-68, First Bapt. Ch., Bluefield, W.Va., 1968-77; exec. dir. missions Richmond (Va.) Bapt. Assn., 1977-97; trustee Bluefield (W.Va.) Coll., 1972-82, U. Richmond, Va., 1989-93; first v.p. Va. Bapt. Gen. Bd., Richmond, 1974-75; dir. Home Mission Bd., So. Bapt. Conv., Atlanta, 1976-84. Author: (children's book) Following Jesus, 1968. Commr. Bluefield (W.Va.) Urban Renewal Authority, 1971-74; chmn. Bluefield (W.Va.) Beautification Commn., 1972-73; pres. North Chamberlayne Civic Assn., Richmond, 1989-91. Recipient Disting. Svc. award City of Bluefield, 1970, Disting. Alumnus award Alumni Soc. Randolph Macon, Ashland, Va., 1992, Vol. Missions award Richmond Regional Devel. Coun. of the Fgn. Mission Bd., So. Bapt. Conv., 1995. Mem. Richmond Rotary Club (bd. dirs. 1990-92), Omicron Delta Kappa. Avocations: traveling, fishing, photography, baseball. Office: Richmond Bapt Assn 3111 Moss Side Ave Richmond VA 23222-2523

NUNN, G. RAYMOND, history educator; b. Pirbright, Surrey, Eng., May 18, 1918; came to U.S., 1951; s. Alfred Gerald Cole and Sybil Amy (Bolton) N.; m. E. Margaret Brown; children: Pamela Elizabeth, Michael David, Lesley Margaret. BA honours, U. London, 1951, Dip. Librarianship, 1952; MA, U. Mich., 1954, PhD Far Eastern studies, 1957. Head Asia Library Univ. Mich. Library, Ann Arbor, 1951-61; instr. history Univ. Mich., Ann Arbor, 1959-61; prof. history U. Hawaii, Honolulu, 1961-64, prof. history and Asian studies, 1964-92, dir. rsch. collections East-West Ctr., 1961-64; prof. history, chair Asian studies program U. Hawaii, 1990-92, prof. emeritus, 1993—. Author: Canada and Asia, a Guide to Archive and Manuscript Sources in Canada, 1997, Asia and Oceania, A Guide to Archival and Manuscript Sources in the U.S., 1985, Publishing in Mainland China, 1966, Southeast Asian Periodicals an International Union List, 1977, Japanese Periodicals and Newspapers in Western Languages and Newspapers in Western Languages an International Union List, 1979, Asia Reference Works, 1980, Asia, a Selected and Annotated Guide to Reference Works, 1971. Maj. inf., Indian Army, 1940-47. Ford Found. fellow, 1956. Mem. Assn. for Asian Studies, Internat. Assn. Orientalist Librs. (pres. 1976-80). Episcopalian. Home: 2631 Ferdinand Ave Honolulu HI 96822-1740 Office: U Hawaii SHAPS 1890 E West Rd Honolulu HI 96822-2318

NUNN, GRADY HARRISON, political science educator emeritus; b. Arlington, Tex., Apr. 12, 1918; s. William Roy and Floy Brooke (Dugan) N.; m. Ann Torrey Welsh, June 15, 1951 (dec. 1980); 1 child, Therese von Hohoff.; m. Virginia Cotton Chivington, Dec. 18, 1982. B.A., U. Okla., 1939, M.A., 1941; Ph.D. (Penfield fellow), N.Y.U., 1961. Instr. N.Y.U., 1946-49; from instr. to asso. prof. U. Ala., Tuscaloosa, 1949-65; prof., chmn. dept. polit. sci. U. Ala., Birmingham, 1969-83, prof. emeritus, 1983—; vis. asst. prof. Ind. U., 1960-61; asst. prof., asso. prof. U. Pitts. at Ahmadu Bello U., Nigeria, 1964-68; assoc. prof. U. Pitts., 1968, Auburn U., 1968-69; Bd. dirs. Unitarian Universalist Service Com., 1978-84, v.p., 1981-82. Assoc. editor: Background on World Politics, 1957-62; Contbr. to: Readings in Government in American Society, 1949, Federalism in the Commonwealth, 1963, The Politics and Administration of Nigerian Government, 1965; editorial bd.: Jour. of Politics, 1971-74. Served to capt., F.A. AUS, 1942-46. Ford Found. Fgn. Area fellow, 1956-57. Mem. Am. Polit. Sci. Assn., So. Polit. Sci. Assn. (exec. council 1974-77), Royal African Soc., AAUP (pres. Ala. conf.), Phi Beta Kappa, Pi Sigma Alpha, Phi Eta Sigma, Alpha Tau Omega, Omicron Delta Kappa. Unitarian. Home: 1152 52nd St S Birmingham AL 35222-3925

NUNN, ROBERT WARNE, lawyer; b. Salem, Oreg., Sept. 20, 1950; s. Warne Harry and Delores (Netz) N.; m. Kandis Brewer; 1 child, Hayley Elisabeth. Student, U. Vienna, Austria, 1971; BS, Willamette U., 1972; MS in Acctg., Northeastern U., Boston, 1973; JD, U. Oreg., 1976. Bar: Oreg 1976, U.S. Dist. Ct. Oreg. 1977, U.S. Ct. Appeals (9th cir.) 1977, U.S. Supreme Ct. 1982, Wash. 1986. Ptnr. Schwabe, Williamson &, Wyatt, Portland, Oreg., 1976-92; ptnr., chmn. corp. dept. Preston, Gates & Ellis, Portland, 1992-96; founder, mng. ptnr. Nunn & Motschenbacher LLP, Portland, 1996—. Mem. exec. com. Am. Leadership Forum, 1988-94, sr. fellow, 1988—; bd. mgrs. Multnomah Metro Br. YMCA, Portland, 1983-86, chmn., 1984-85; pres. Oreg. divsn. Am. Cancer Soc., Portland, 1986-87, bd. dirs., 1982-88; trustee Marylhurst Coll., Oreg., 1985-91, Willamette U., 1991—; trustee World Affairs Coun. Oreg., 1991-97, pres., 1995-96; bd. dirs. United Way of Columbia-Willamette, Portland, 1984-87. Am. Leadership fellow, 1987; named Order of Red Sword Am. Cancer Soc., 1985. Mem. ABA, Oreg. Bar Assn. (chmn. CPA joint com., past chmn. legal assts. and legal investigators com., cert. subcom., fee arbitration panel), Internat. Bar Assn., Nat. Assn. Bond Lawyers (vice-chmn. mcpl. utility obligations com.), Pacific N.W. Internat. Trade Assn., Portland C. of C. (chmn. internat. trade com.), Univ. Club, Multhnomah Athletic Club (Portland). Republican. Lutheran. Avocations: computers, skiing, sailing. Office: Nunn & Motschenbacher LLP 733 SW 2nd Ave Ste 212 Portland OR 97204-3116

NUNN, SAMUEL (SAM NUNN), former senator; b. Perry, Ga., Sept. 8, 1938; s. Samuel Augustus and Elizabeth (Cannon) N.; m. Colleen O'Brien, Sept. 25, 1965; children: Michelle, Brian. Student, Ga. Tech. Coll., 1956-59; A.B., LL.B., Emory U., 1962. Bar: Ga. 1962. Legal counsel armed services com. U.S. Ho. Reps., 1963; mem. firm Nunn, Geiger & Rampey, Perry, Ga., 1964-73; mem. Ga. Ho. Reps., 1968-72; U.S. senator from Ga., 1972-96; ranking Dem. mem. armed svcs. com.; mem. govtl. affairs com., small bus. com., senate Dem. steering and coord. com.; ptnr. King & Spalding, Atlanta, 1997—; ranking Dem. Permanent Subcom. on Investigations of Govt. Affairs; farmer, Perry, 1964—. Office: King & Spalding 191 Peachtree St Atlanta GA 30303*

NUNN, THOMAS CALVIN, school supervisor, retired army officer; b. Weleetka, Okla., Mar. 28, 1928; s. Ernest Howard and Beatrice (Thomas) N.; m. Agnes Ruth Zaletel, Sept. 2, 1950; children: Thomas C. Jr., Pamela, Becky, Marilyn, Linda. BA, Okla. State U., 1952; MA, U.S. Army Command & Gen. Staff Coll., 1967. Cert. sch. supr. Platoon leader 1st armored div. U.S. Army, Ft. Hood, Tex., 1950-52; provost marshal U.S. Army, Fairbanks, Alaska, 1953-55; co. comdr. 1st cav. div. U.S. Army, Korea, 1960-61; ops. officer U.S. Army, Berlin, 1963-65; battalion comdr. 25th infantry div. U.S. Army, Vietnam, 1967-68; chief plans and ops. fifth hdqrs. U.S. Army, Ft. Sheridan, Ill., 1968-72; dep. comdr. criminal investigation command U.S. Army, Heidleberg, Germany, 1972-74; supr. Lafourche Parish Sch. Bd., Thibodaux, La., 1974-95; dir. army inst. LaFourche Parish Sch. Bd., Thibodaux, 1974-95. Co-chmn. Civic Com., Thibodaux, 1979. Lt. Col. U.S. Army, 1950-74. Decorated Legion of Merit (3 awards), D.F.C., Purple Heart (3 awards), others; named Outstanding La. Educator, State Dept. Edn., Baton Rouge, 1981; recipient Svc. award Citizen of Yr. City Svc. League, Thibodaux, 1990, Outstanding Civilian Svc. medal Dept. of the Army, 1995, Outstanding Vol. Activist award S.E. L.A. Area, 1994. Mem. DAV (life), VFW (life), Purple Heart Assn. (life), Am. Legion (v.p. 1975-79), Gulf South Suprs. Assn., La. Sch. Suprs. Assn., Lions Club (prs. 1978-79, Lion of Yr. 1979-80). Avocations: fishing, golfing, gardening. Home: 305 Edgewood Dr Thibodaux LA 70301-3809

NUNN, TREVOR ROBERT, director; b. Ipswich, Eng., Jan. 14, 1940; s. Robert Alexander and Dorothy May (Piper) N.; m. Janet Suzman, 1969 (div. 1985); 1 child; m. Sharon Lee Hill, 1986 (div. 1991); 2 children; m. Imogen Stubbs, 1994; 2 children. Student, Ipswich Coll., Downing Coll., Cambridge, Eng.; LLD, U. Warwick, 1982; MA (hon.), U. Newcastle-upon-Tyne, 1982. Trainee dir. Belgrade Theatre, Coventry; assoc. dir. Royal Shakespeare Co., Warwickshire, Eng., 1964-68, artistic dir., 1968-78, joint artistic dir., 1978-86, chief exec., 1968-86, dir. emeritus, 1986—; artistic dir. Royal Nat. Theatre, London, 1997—. Dir. plays including Tango, 1965, The Revenger's Tragedy, 1965, 69, The Taming of the Shrew, The Relapse, The Winter's Tale, 1969, Hamlet, 1970, Henry VIII, 1970, Roman Season: Antony and Cleopatra, Coriolanus, Julius Caesar, Titus Andronicus, 1970, Macbeth, 1974, 76, Hedda Gabler (own version) 1975, Romeo and Juliet, 1976, Comedy of Errors, 1976, The Alchemist, 1977, As You Like It, 1977, Every Good Boy Deserves Favour, 1977, Three Sisters, 1978, The Merry Wives of Windsor, 1979, Once in a Lifetime, 1979 (Evening Standard Best Dir. award), Juno and the Paycock, 1980, The Life and Adventures of Nicholas Nickleby (with John Caird), 1980 (Tony Best Dir. award 1981, Evening Standard Best Dir. award), touring revival, 1985, Cats, 1981 (Best Dir. Tony award 1982), All's Well That Ends Well, 1981, Henry IV (parts I and II), 1981, 82, Peter Pan (with John Caird), 1982, Starlight Express, 1984, Les Miserables (with John Caird), 1985 (Tony award for best dir. 1987), Fair Maid of the West, 1986, Chess, 1986, Aspects of Love, 1989, Othello, 1989, The Baker's Wife, 1989, Timon of Athens, 1991 (Evening Standard Best Dir. award, Best Dir. Critics' Cir. award), The Blue Angel, 1991, Measure for Measure, 1991, Heartbreak House, 1992, Arcadia, 1993, Sunset Boulevard, 1993 (Tony nominee - Direction of a Musical, 1995); (opera) Idomeneo, 1982, Porgy and Bess, 1986, revived 1987,92, Cosi Fan Tutte, 1991, Peter Grimes, 1992, Katya Kabanova, 1994; TV shows Include: Anthony and Cleopatra, 1975, Comedy of Errors, 1976, Every Good Boy Deserves Favour, 1978, Three Sisters, 1978, Macbeth, 1978, Great Hamlets, 1983, Othello, 1990, Porgy and Bess, 1993; writer, dir. Shakespeare Workshops Word of Mouth, 1979, films Hedda, Lady Jane, 1985, Twelfth Night, 1996; author: British Theatre Design, 1989. Recipient London Theatre Critics Best Dir. award, 1969; Soc. Film and TV Arts award, 1975, Ivor Novello award for best Brit. Musical, 1976; numerous others. Office: Royal Nat Theatre, Upper Ground South Bank, Cambridge Circus London SE1 9PX, England

NUNNALLY, DOLORES BURNS, retired physical education educator; b. Strong, Ark., Jan. 2, 1932; d. Marion Saunders Burns and Emma Jo (Burns) Baca; m. Curtis Jerome Nunnally, Apr. 16, 1954; 1 child, Jo Lynn Nunnally Blair. BSE, Ark. State Tchrs. Coll., 1953; MSE, State Coll. Ark., 1964; EdD, U. Sarasota, 1981. Phys. edn. tchr. El Dorado (Ark.) Pub. Schs., 1953-72; real estate salesman Continental Real Estate, Downers Grove, Ill., 1972-74; phys. edn. instr. Triton Coll., River Grove, Ill., 1973-74; substitute tchr. DuPage and Kane County Schs., Ill., 1972-74; phys. edn. tchr. Wheeling (Ill.) Sch. Dist. 21, 1974-91; tennis coach El Dorado Pub. Schs., 1953-73; tennis pro El Dorado Racquet Club, City of El Dorado, summers 1965-72. Contbr. articles to profl. jours. Pres. Ark. Sq. Dance Fedn., Little Rock, 1971-72, Progressive Sunday Sch., El Dorado, 1994—. Recipient All Star Coaches Clinic award Ark. H.S. Coaches Assn., 1971. Mem. NEA, AAHPERD (pres. 1969-70, State Honor award 1972), Ark. Assn. Health, Phys. Edn., Recreation and Dance (life), Ill. Assn. Health, Phys. Edn., Recreation and Dance (Quarter Century award 1981, Svc. award 1991), U.S. Tennis Assn., Order Eastern Star, Delta Phi Kappa. Methodist. Avocations: league tennis, swimming. Home: PO Box 641 1415 Huttig Hwy Strong AR 71765

NUNNELLEY, CAROL FISHBURNE, editor newspaper; b. Montgomery, Ala., Dec. 25, 1942; m. William A. Nunnelley; 1 child, Meg. BA, Samford U., 1965; postgrad., U. Ky., 1965-66. Reporter The Birmingham (Ala.) News, 1966, city editor, 1978, mng. editor, 1992. Recipient reporting and writing awards Ala. Soc. Porfl. Journalists, Ala. Press Assn., Ala. Associated Press, Journalist of the Yr. award Troy State U., Achievement award Birmingham Emancipation Assn. Mem. Soc. Profl. Journalists, Leadership Birmingham, The Women's Network. Office: The Birmingham News 2200 4th Ave N Birmingham AL 35203-3802

NUNZ, GREGORY JOSEPH, program manager, aerospace engineer, educator, entrepreneur; b. Batavia, N.Y., May 28, 1934; s. Sylvester Joseph and Elizabeth Marie (Loesell) N.; m. Georgia Monyea Costas, Mar. 30, 1958; children: Karen, John, Rebecca, Deirdre, Jaimie, Marta. BSChemE, Cooper Union, 1955; postgrad., U. So. Calif., Calif. State U.; MS in Applied Math., Columbia Pacific U., 1991, PhD in Mgmt. Sci., 1993. Adv. design staff, propulsion mgr. U.K. project Rocketdyne div. Rockwell, Canoga Park, Calif., 1955-65; mem. tech. staff Aerospace Corp., El Segundo, Calif., 1965-70; mem. tech. staff propulsion div. Jet Propulsion Lab., Pasadena, Calif., 1970-72; chief. monoprop. engring. Bell Aerospace Corp., Buffalo, N.Y., 1972-74; group supr. comb. devices Jet Propulsion Lab., Pasadena, 1974-76; asst. div. leader, program mgr. internat. HDR geothermal energy program, project mgr. space-related projects Los Alamos (N.Mex.) Nat. Lab., 1977—; assoc. prof. electronics L.A. Pierce Coll., Woodland Hills, Calif., 1961-72; instr. No. N.Mex. C. C., Los Alamos, 1978-80, div. head scis., 1980-92; adj. prof. math. U. N.Mex., Los Alamos, 1980—; sr. mgmt. rep. Excel Telecommunications, Inc., 1995—. Author: Electronics Lab Manual I, 1964, Electronics in Our World, 1972; co-author: Electronics Mathematics, vol. I, II, 1967; contbg. author Prentice-Hall Textbook of Cosmetology, 1975, Alternative Energy Sources VII, 1987; contbr. articles to profl. jours.; inventor smallest catalytic liquid N2H4 rocket thrustor, co-inventor first monoprop/biprop bimodal rocket engine, tech. advisor internat. multi-prize winning documentary film One With the Earth. Mem. Aerial Phenomena Research Orgn., L.A., 1975. Fellow AIAA (assoc.); mem. Tech. Mktg. Soc. Am., Math. Assn. Am., ARISTA, Shrine Club, Masons, Ballut Abyad Temple. Avocations: travel, archaeology, fgn. langs., golf. Office: Los Alamos Nat Lab PO Box 1663 MS D460 Los Alamos NM 87545

NURENBERG, DAVID, oil company executive; b. N.Y.C., Mar. 25, 1939; s. Abraham S. and Katherine G. N.; m. Brenda G. Schwait, Sept. 1963; children—Jill Suzanne, Brian Michael. B.S. in Marine Engring, U.S. Mcht. Marine Acad., 1960; M.S. in Indsl. Mgmt, Columbia U., 1963, Ph.D. in Mgmt. Sci, 1965. With Exxon Corp., 1963-67; employee relations mgr. Esso Pappas, Athens, Greece, 1968-72; labor relations and compensation mgr. Esso Europe, London, 1972-77; corp. sec. Esso Eastern Inc., Houston, 1977-82; mgr. exec. compensation Exxon Corp., N.Y.C., 1982-90; mgr. compensation and exec. programs Exxon Corp., Irving, Tex., 1990—; mem. coun. exec. compensation Conf. Bd., past chmn.; adj. prof. Union Inst. Mem. exec. edn. adv. bd. Wharton Sch., U. Pa.; mem. adv. bd. Ctr. for Effective Orgns., U. So. Calif. Mem. Am. Compensation Assn. (bd. dirs., chmn., exec. comp. coun., bd. steering com.). Office: Exxon Corp 5959 Las Colinas Blvd Irving TX 75039-4202

NURNBERGER, JOHN I., JR., psychiatrist, educator; b. N.Y.C., July 18, 1946; married; 3 children. BS in Psychology magna cum laude, Fordham U., 1968; MD, Ind. U., 1975, PhD, 1983. Diplomate Am. Bd. Psychiatry and Neurology. Resident in psychiatry Columbia Presbyn. Med. Ctr., N.Y.C., 1975-78, med. officer sect. psychogenetics, 1977-78; sr. staff fellow, outpatient clinic adminstr. sect. psychogenetics NIH, Bethesda, Md., 1978-83, staff psychiatrist, chief NIMH Outpatients Clinic, 1983-86, acting chief sect. clin. genetics, 1986; prof. psychiatry, dir. Inst. Psychiatric Rsch., rsch. coord. dept. psychiatry Ind. U. Med. Ctr., Indpls., 1986—; prof. med. neurobiology Ind. U. Grad. Sch., Indpls., 1987—; clin. cons. Cold Spring VA Hosp., 1986—; cons., lectr. in field. Editor-in-chief: Psychiatric Genetics; field editor: Neuropsychiatric Genetics; contbr. articles to profl. jours. NSF fellow, 1968; recipient NAMI Exemplary Psychiatrist award Nat. Alliance Mentally Ill, 1992, 94. Fellow Am. Psychiatric Assn., Am. Psychpathological Assn.; mem. AAAS, Am. Soc. Human Genetics, Internat. Soc. Psychiatric Genetics (bd. dirs.), Am. Coll. Neuropsychopharmacology, Soc. Light Treatment and Biol. Rhythms, Soc. Neursci., Assn. Rsch. in Nervous and Mental Disease, Soc. Biol. Psychiatry, Sigma Xi. Office: Ind U Sch Medicine Psychiatric Rsch Inst 791 Union Dr Indianapolis IN 46202-2873

NUROCK, ROBERT JAY, investment analysis company executive; b. Phila., May 25, 1937; s. Abe and Sid (Smokler) N.; m. Doris L. Whitliff, Oct. 19, 1974 (div.); m. 2d, Bridget A. McManus, June 16, 1984; children: Megan, Andrew. BA, Pa. State U., 1958. Owner, pres. Md. Brake Alignment Service, Balt., 1959-67; v.p. investor support Merrill Lynch & Co., Inc., N.Y.C., 1967-79; 1st v.p. market strategy Butcher & Singer, Inc., Phila., 1979-82; pres., market strategist Investor's Analysis, Inc., 1982—; lectr. various ednl. and fin. orgns., 1973—. Panelist program Wall St. Week, Pub. Broadcasting System TV, 1970-89; author, pub. Bob Nurock's Advisory/Pvt. Elves Report, Santa Fe, 1979—; contbg. editor The Hume Moneyletter, Atlanta, 1982—; creator E$P-Elves $hortterm Predictor, EMI-Elves Market Index, TMI-Tech. Market Index. Bd. dirs. Tredyffrin/Easttown Edn. Found., Wharton Esherick Mus., Paoli, 1989—, Friends of Indian Art, Mus. of N.Mex. Found. Mem. Market Technicians Assn. (chartered market technician, v.p. 1977-78), N.Y. Soc. Security Analysis, Assn. for Investment Mgmt. and Rsch., Analysts Club (pres. 1979), Rolls Royce Owners Club (dir. Keystone region). Office: PO Box 460 Santa Fe NM 87504-0460

NUSBACHER, GLORIA WEINBERG, lawyer; b. N.Y.C., July 22, 1951; d. Murray and Doris (Togman) Weinberg; m. Burton Nusbacher, Aug. 4, 1974; 1 child, Shoshana. BA, Barnard Coll., 1972; JD, Columbia U., 1975. Bar: N.Y. 1976. Assoc. Hughes Hubbard & Reed, N.Y.C., 1975-83, counsel, 1983-91, ptnr., 1991—; atty. specializing in exec. compensation and employee benefits; lectr. in field. Contbr. articles to profl. jours. Troop leader, leader trainer Girl Scouts USA. Mem. ABA (employee benefits and exec. compensation com. 1987—, fed. regulation securities com., subcom. employee benefits and exec. compensation 1983—, task force Sect. 16, 1991—, chmn. subcom. fed. and state securities laws of com. employee benefits and exec. compensation 1994—, task force exec. compensation 1992-94), Phi Beta Kappa. Office: Hughes Hubbard & Reed LLP 1 Battery Park Plz New York NY 10004-1405

NUSBAUM, GEOFFREY DEAN, psychotherapist; b. Berkeley, Calif., Apr. 1, 1946; s. Wayne Dale and Jeanne (Hankins) N.; m. Barbara Ann Pierfy, June 1, 1986; 1 child, Michael Wayne. BA, Washington U., St. Louis, 1967; MA, Hartford Sem. Fdn. Consortium, 1971, PhD, 1978. Diplomate Am. Bd. Med. Psychotherapy; cert. therapist Am. Assn. for Marriage and Family Therapy; lic. therapist, N.J. Pvt. practice Marlton, N.J. and Phila., 1972—; cons. N.Y. Fertility Rsch. Found., N.Y.C., 1978-83, Bancroft Sch., Haddonfield, N.J., 1983-87; fellow Internat. Coun. Sex. Edn. and Parenthood Am. U. Author: Community, Self Identity, 1978; peer manuscript reviewer to sci. jours. Bd. dirs. Calcutta House AIDS Hospice. Mem. Am. Soc. for Reproductive Medicine, Am. Soc. for Psychosomatic Ob-Gyn., N.Y. Acad. Scis. Office: PO Box 256 Mount Ephraim NJ 08059-0256

NUSIM, STANLEY HERBERT, chemical engineer, consultant; b. N.Y.C., Oct. 2, 1935; s. Seymour and Ranna T. (Weiner) N.; m. Marcia Anne Borsig, Feb. 21, 1960; children: David Mark, Jill Wendi. BSChemE, CCNY, 1957; MSChemE, N.Y. U., 1960, PhD, 1967. Rsch. engr. Battelle Meml. Inst., Columbus, Ohio, 1956; researcher, chem. engring. rsch. and devel. Merck Rsch. Labs. Div., Rahway, N.J., 1957-68; sect. mgr. Merck Rsch. Labs. Div., Rahway, 1968-70; tech. svcs. mgr. Merck Chem. Mfg. Div., Rahway, 1970-73, mfg. mgr., 1973-80; dir. subsidiary projects Merck Internat. Div., Rahway, 1981-82, exec. dir. Latin Am., Far East, Near East ops., 1982-88; exec. dir. licensee, Latin Am., Far East, Asia ops. Merck Pharm. Mfg. Div., Rahway, 1989-92; exec. dir. licensee ops. worldwide Merck mfg. divsn. Merck & Co. Inc., Whitehouse Station, N.J., 1992-94; pres. S.H. Nusim Assocs., Inc., Hollywood, Fla., 1994—; v.p. mfg. and ops. Therics, Inc., Princeton, N.J., 1994—; adv. bd. CCNY Sch. Engring., 1982—. Author: Kinetic Studies on C4 Hydrocarbon Systems, 1967. V.p. men's club Temple Beth Shalom, Livingston, N.J., 1975-78; rep. to bd. edn. Livingston Home and Sch. Assn., 1982-83; bd. govs. Turnberry Isle Yacht and Racquet Club, Aventura, Fla., 1992-94. Mem. Am. Inst. Chem. Engrs. (bd. dir. N. Jersey sect. 1968-71, scholarship award 1955), Am. Chem. Soc., Tau Beta Pi, Garden State Yacht Club (bd. govs. 1987-88). Achievements include U.S. and foreign patents on the continuous manufacture of halogenated acetone, development of "clean room" concepts for pharmachemical manufacturing, development of sophisticated training techniques for sterile pharmaceutical manufacturing. Home: Apt 4L 19355 Turnberry Way Aventura FL 33180 Office: SH Nusim Assocs 686 N Dixie Hwy Hollywood FL 33020-3906 : 115 Campus Dr Princeton NJ 08540

NUSINOVICH, GREGORY SEMEON, physicist, researcher; b. Berdichev, Russia, July 18, 1946; came to U.S., 1991; s. Semeon and Esther (Burdo) N.; m. Yelena Naydich, July 2, 1968; children: Maria, Liza, Paulina. MSc, Gorky (Russia) State U., 1968, PhD, 1975. Rsch. scientist Radiophys. Rsch. Inst., Gorky, 1968-77; sr. rsch. scientist, group leader Inst. Applied Physics, Acad. Scis. of Russia, Gorky, 1977-90; sr. rsch. scientist Inst. for Plasma Rsch., U. Md., College Park, 1991—; mem. sci. coun. on phys. electronics Acad. Scis. Russia, 1981-90; cons. Phys. Scis., Inc., Alexandria, Va., 1991-93, Sci. Applications Internat. Corp., McLean, Va., 1991-93, Omega-P, New Haven, Conn., 1995—. Co-editor: Gyrotron, 1981, Gyrotrons, 1989; contbr. chpts. to books. Mem. IEEE (sr.), Am. Phys. Soc. Achievements include development of the theory of multimode gyrotrons, the nonlinear theory of relativistic gyrodevices and the gyrotron producing 100 KW power at the frequency of 500 GHZ. Office: University of Maryland Inst for Plasma Rsch College Park MD 20742

NUSS, ELDON PAUL, casket manufacturer; b. Sumner, Iowa, Apr. 24, 1933; s. Paul John and Helen (Nolting) N.; m. Carolyn Ann Krug, June 6, 1959 (dec. Dec. 1996); children—Susan Elizabeth, Laurie Ann. Student, Grinnell Coll., 1950; BS with honors, U. Iowa, 1954; postgrad., Harvard, 1971. With Arthur Young & Co. CPAs, 1957-68; prin. Arthur Young & Co. CPAs, Houston, 1967-68; v.p. Marathon Mfg. Co., Houston, 1969-71; exec. v.p., dir. Marathon Mfg. Co., 1972-75; pres., CEO PMI Industries, Houston, 1975-91; chmn. The York Group, Houston, 1991—. Served with USNR, 1955-57. Mem. Assn. for Corporate Growth, AICPA. Lutheran (council 1966-67). Club: Lakeside Country. Home: 327 Knipp Forest St Houston TX 77024-5030 Office: 9430 Old Katy Rd Houston TX 77055-6340

NUSS, SHIRLEY ANN, computer coordinator, educator; b. Madison, Min., Oct. 22, 1946; d. Woodland Henry and Aileen Thelma (Mattox) Cover; m. Sheldon Edward Nuss, May 29, 1970; 1 child, Melissa Ann. BEd, Trinity U., Washburn U., 1969; MA, Mich. State U., 1982, PhD, 1990. 3d grade tchr. Topeka Pub. Schs. System, 1969-70; 6th grade tchr. McCune (Kans.)

Middle Sch., 1970-72; 7th grade English tchr. Muskego (Wis.) Norway Sch. Dist., 1972-78; intermediate level. tchr. Gibson Sch. for Gifted Children, Redford, Mich., 1979-82; 3d grade tchr. Cranbrook Edn. Community, Bloomfield Hills, Mich., 1982-89, computer coord., instr., 1989—; ednl. adv. bd. Henry Ford Mus. and Greenfield Village, Dearborn, 1988-91; Renaissance Outreach for Detroit Area Schs; task force Mich. Coun. for the Humanities, Lansing, 1991-92; speaker, presenter on tech. Mich. Sci. Tchr. Assn., Lansing, 1992-96, Mich. Assn. Computer Users in Learning, Ind. Sch. Assn. Ctrl. States; tchr. adv. bd. Teaching and Computer Magazine, 1988-90; developer grades 1-5 multimedia/computer curriculum Brookside Sch., Cranbrook, 1995-96. Author: (museum activities) Henry Ford Museum, Greenfield Village, 1991. Space camp fellowship Mary Bramson award Huntsville, Ala., 1992; Detroit Edison Conservation grantee Detroit Edison, 1992, ROADS Mimi grant Mich. Coun. for Humanities, Lansing, 1993. Mem. Assoc. Supervision Curriculum Development, Cranbrook Schs. Faculty Coun. (pres., v.p. 1993-95). Republican. Presbyterian. Avocations: antique collecting, reading, gardening, computers and technology. Home: 32671 W 11 Mile Rd Farmingtn Hls MI 48336-1005 Office: Cranbrook Schs Brookside 550 Cranbrook Rd # 801 Bloomfield Hills MI 48304-2715

NUSSBAUM, A(DOLF) EDWARD, mathematician, educator; b. Rheydt, Fed. Republic Germany, Germany, Jan. 10, 1925; came to U.S., 1947; s. Karl and Franziska (Scheye) N.; m. Anne Ebbin, Sept. 1, 1957; children: Karl, Franziska. MA, Columbia U., 1950, PhD, 1957. Mem. staff electronic computer project Inst. Advanced Study, Princeton, N.J., 1952-53; mem. Inst. Advanced Study, 1962-63; instr. math U. Conn., Storrs, 1953-55; asst. prof. Rensselaer Poly. Inst., Troy, N.Y., 1956-58; vis. scholar Stanford U., Calif., 1967-68; asst. prof., then assoc. prof. Washington U., St. Louis, 1958-66, prof., 1966-95, prof. emeritus, 1995—. Contbr. articles to profl. jours. Grantee NSF, 1960-79. Mem. Am. Math. Soc. Home: 8050 Watkins Dr Saint Louis MO 63105-2517 Office: Washington U Dept Math Saint Louis MO 63130

NUSSBAUM, BERNARD J., lawyer; b. Berlin, Mar. 11, 1931; came to U.S., 1936; s. William and Lotte (Frankfurther) N.; m. Jean Beverly Enzer, Sept. 4, 1956; children—Charles, Peter, Andrew. A.B., Knox Coll., 1948-52; J.D., U. Chgo., 1955. Assoc. Proskauer Rose Goetz & Mendelsohn, N.Y.C., 1955-56; assoc. Sonnenschein Nath & Rosenthal, Chgo., 1959-65, sr. ptnr., 1965—; master bencher Am. Inns of Ct., 1986—; appointed to com. on civility 7th cir. U.S. Ct. Appeals, 1989-92. Editor U. Chgo. Law Rev., 1954-55; mem. nat. adv. bd. BNA Civil Trial Man., 1985—; contbr. articles to profl. jours. Mem. vis. com. U. Chgo. Law Sch., 1977-83. Served to capt. U.S. Army, 1956-59. Fellow Am. Bar Found., Ill. Bar Found. (charter); mem. ABA, Chgo. Bar Assn. (chmn. com. on fed. civil procedure 1968-69, mem. com. on judiciary 1970-76), Ill. Bar Assn. (council Antitrust sect. 1971-73, assembly del. 1972-80), U. Chgo. Law Sch. Nat. Alumni Assn. (pres. 1981-83), Law Club Chgo., Legal Club Chgo. Avocations: skiing; cycling. Office: Sonnenschein Nath & Rosenthal 8000 Sears Tower 233 S Wacker Dr Chicago IL 60606-6306

NUSSBAUM, HOWARD JAY, lawyer; b. N.Y.C., Dec. 17, 1951; s. Norman and Ruth (Rand) N.; children: Martin Garrett, Daniel Todd. BA, SUNY, Binghamton, 1972; JD, Boston Coll., 1976. Bar: Fla. 1977, U.S. Dist. Ct. (so. dist. trial and bankruptcy bar) Fla. 1977, U.S. Ct. Appeals (5th and 11th cirs.) 1981. Mng. atty. Legal Aid. Svc., Ft. Lauderdale, Fla., 1976-88; ptnr. Weinstein, Zimmerman & Nussbaum, P.A., Tamarac, Fla., 1988-92; pres. Howard J. Nussbaum, P.A., 1993—; chmn. Legal Aid com. North Broward Bar Assn., Pompano Beach, Fla., 1986-87; cons. Police Acad. of Broward County, Ft. Lauderdale, 1985-87. Author: Florida Landlord/Tenant Law and the Fair Housing Act, 1989. Gen. coun. Registered Apt. Mgrs. Assn. South Fla., 1993—, Wynmoor Cmty. Coun., 1993—, Skyline Properties, Inc., Ft. Lauderdale, 1994—, Accutrack Tracking Sys., Inc., 1996. Regents scholar N.Y. State, 1968-72, Presdl. scholar Boston Coll. Law Sch., 1973-76. Mem. ABA (litigation sect.), ATLA, Acad. Fla. Trial Lawyers, Broward Bar Assn., Justice Lodge J.C.C. Avocations: softball, tennis, swimming. Office: Howard J Nussbaum PA 2400 E Commercial Blvd Ste 205 Fort Lauderdale FL 33308-4022

NUSSBAUM, JEFFREY JOSEPH, musician; b. N.Y.C., July 7, 1952; s. Eli and Dorothy (Wolkowitz) N.; m. Alison Knopf (div. 1984); m. Joan Feigenbaum, April 5, 1990; 1 child, Samuel Leon Baum. BA in Music, Hunter Coll., N.Y., 1977; MA in Edn., Bklyn. Coll., 1987; MFA in Early Music, Sarah Lawrence Coll., Bronxville, Tex., 1989. Cert. N.Y.S., N.Y.C. Freelance musician (trumpet, cornetto, natural trumpet), 1979—; tchr. music park West H.S., N.Y., 1984—; pres., founder Historic Brass Soc., N.Y., 1989—; dir. Manhattan Early Wind Ensemble, N.Y., 1992—, Pan Brass Quintet, N.Y., 1978-84; organized Internat. Hist. Brass Symposium, Amherst, Mass., 1995; organizer Early Brass Colloquium, Royal Acad. Music, London, 1997. Contbr. articles to jours. in field. Mem. Am. Fedn. Musicians, Am. Musicological Soc., Internat. Trumpet Guild, Galpin Soc. Jewish. Home: 148 W 23rd St Apt 2A New York NY 10011-2447

NUSSBAUM, LEO LESTER, retired college president, consultant; b. Berne, Ind., June 27, 1918; s. Samuel D. and Margaret (Mazelin) N.; m. Janet Nell Gladfelter, Nov. 25, 1942; children: Felicity Ann, Luther James, Margaret Sue. BS, Ball State U., 1942, MA, 1949; PhD, Northwestern U., 1952; Postgrad., U. Mich., 1963. Tchr. Monmouth High Sch., Decatur, Ind., 1946-48; dean men, asst. prof. bus. Huntington Coll., (Ind.), 1948-51; dean coll. liberal arts, assoc. prof. edn. and psychology U. Dubuque, (Iowa), 1952-60; dean coll., prof. edn. and psychology Austin Coll., 1960-67; dean coll., prof. psychology Coe Coll., 1967-70, pres., 1970-82, pres. emeritus, 1982—; dir. Acad. Sr. Profls. Eckerd Coll., 1983-87; dir. PEL-ASPEC Project, 1988-95; coord. faculty ASPEC Colleagues, St. Petersburg, 1992—; cons. pvt. practice St. Petersburg, Fla., 1982—; Fulbright lectr. U. Mysore (India), 1958-59; cons., evaluator So. Assn. Colls. and Schs., Atlanta, 1963-67, North Cen. Assn. Colls. and Schs., 1959-60, 67-82, dir. I.E. Industries and Iowa Electric Light and Power Co., Cedar Rapids, 1982-91, dir. emeritus, 1991-92. Contbr. articles to scholastic and profl. jours. and periodicals. Bd. dirs. Cedar Rapids Symphony, 1968-70; mem. cabinet Cedar Rapids United Way, 1980-82; elder Presbyn. Ch., moderator Presbytery of S.W. Fla., 1989. Sgt. U.S. Army, 1942-46. Recipient Disting. Alumnus award Ball State U., 1976, Alumni Merit award Northwestern U., 1977. Mem. Assn. Colls. Midwest (chmn. 1975-77), Iowa Assn. Ind. Colls. and Univs. (chmn. 1976-77), Danforth Assocs., Rotary (Cedar Rapids, pres. 1975-76), Phi Delta Kappa, Blue Key, Pi Gamma Mu. Home: Apt 336 6909 9th St S Saint Petersburg FL 33705-6207

NUSSBAUM, MARTHA CRAVEN, philosophy and classics educator; b. N.Y.C., May 6, 1947; d. George and Betty (Warren) Craven; m. Alan Jeffrey Nussbaum, Aug., 1969 (div. 1987); 1 child, Rachel Emily. BA, NYU, 1969; MA, Harvard U., 1971, PhD, 1975; LHD (hon.), Kalamazoo Coll., 1988, Grinnell Coll., 1993. Asst. prof. philosophy and classics Harvard U., Cambridge, 1975-80, assoc. prof., 1980-83; vis. prof. philosophy, Greek and Latin Wellesley (Mass.) Coll., 1983-84; assoc. prof. philosophy and classics Brown U., Providence, R.I., 1984-85, prof. philosophy, classics and comparative lit., 1985-87, David Benedict prof. philosophy, classics and comparative lit., 1987-89, prof., 1989-95; prof. law and ethics U. Chgo., 1995-96, Ernst Freund prof. law and ethics, 1996—; rsch. advisor World Inst. Devel. Econs. Rsch., Helsinki, Finland, 1986-93; vis. prof. law U. Chgo., 1994. Author: Aristotle's De Motu Animalium, 1978, The Fragility of Goodness, 1986, Loe's Knowledge, 1990, The Therapy of Desire, 1994, Poetic Justice: The Literary Imagination and Public Life, 1996, For Love of Country, 1996; editor: Language and Logos, 1983; (with A. Rorty) Essays on Aristotle's De Anima, 1992, (with A. Sen) The Quality of Life, 1993, (with J. Brunschwig) Passions & Perceptions, 1993, (with J. Glover) Women, Culture and Development, 1995. Soc. Fellows Harvard U. jr. fellow, 1972-75, Humanities fellow Princeton U., 1977-78, Guggenheim Found. fellow, 1983, NIH fellow, vis. fellow All Souls Coll., Oxford, Eng., 1986-87; recipient Brandeis Creative Arts award, 1990, Spielvogel-Diamondstein award, 1991; Gifford lectr. U. Edinburgh, 1993. Fellow Am. Acad. Arts and Scis. (membership com. 1991-93, coun. 1992-96), Am. Philos. Soc.; mem. Am. Philos. Assn. (exec. com. Ea. divsn. 1985-87, chair com. internat. coop., ex-officio mem. nat. bd. 1989-92, chair com. on status of women 1994-97), Am. Philol. Assn., PEN. Office: U Chicago The Law Sch 1111 E 60th St Chicago IL 60637-2702

NUSSBAUM, MICHEL ERNEST, physician; b. L.A., Nov. 7, 1947; s. Schymen and Jeannette Eleanor (Pequignot) N.; m. Joyce Wendy Laudon, Nov. 1, 1981; children: Eleanor, Anna. BA, Cornell U., 1969; MD, Free U. Brussels, 1977. Intern internal medicine N.Y. Hosp. Med. Ctr. of Queens, 1977-78, resident, 1978-80, fellow gastroenterology, 1980-82; attending physician N.Y. Hosp. Med. Ctr. of Queens, Flushing, N.Y., 1982—; physician pvt. practice, Flushing, N.Y., 1982—; attending physician Flushing Hosp. Med. Ctr., 1987—; clin. instr. medicine Cornell U. Med. Coll., N.Y.C., 1994—; med. dir. Franklin Nursing Home, Flushing, 1995—; physician in charge endoscopic svcs. N.Y. Hosp. Med. Ctr. of Queens, 1990—, pres. med. staff soc., 1992-96, vice chmn. med. bd., 1994-96, chmn., 1997. Fellow Am. Coll. Physicians, Am. Coll. Gastroenterology. Office: 14243 Booth Memorial Ave Flushing NY 11355-5343

NUSSBAUM, PAUL EUGENE, journalist; b. Upland, Ind., Aug. 30, 1952; s. Elmer N. and Ruth Ellen (Shugart) N.; m. Debra Stone, Oct. 31, 1987; children: Molly Elizabeth, Matthew Connor. Student, Taylor U., 1970-71; BS, Ball State U., 1974. Reporter Muncie (Ind.) Star, 1973-74, Indpls. Star, 1974, Anchorage Times, 1975-76; staff writer Anchorage Daily News, 1976-78, metro editor, 1978-80; staff writer L.A. Times, 1980-82; staff writer Phila. Inquirer, 1982-91, dep. fgn. editor, 1991-94; mng. editor Phila. Inquirer Mag., 1994—. Recipient Best Editorial award Alaska Press Club, 1978, Best News Story award Sigma Delta Chi, 1984, Best Mag. Story, Sigma Delta Chi Soc. of Profl. Journalists, 1991, 1st Pl. news reporting award Pa. AP Mng. Editors, 1985. Methodist. Office: Phila Inquirer 400 N Broad St Philadelphia PA 19130-4015

NUSSBAUM, V. M., JR., former mayor; b. Ft. Wayne, Ind., June 25, 1919; m. Terry O'Hayer, 1943 (dec.); 9 children. Student, Holy Cross Coll., Univ. Pa., Harvard Univ. City councilman Greensboro, N.C., 1973-81; mayor City of Greensboro, Greensboro, 1987-93; founder, pres. So. Food Svc. Inc., 1954, So. Foods, 1960. Gen. chmn. united fund drive United Way, 1971, pres., 1972; former pres. United Arts Coun., Boy Scouts Am., Gen. Greene Coun. Lt. comdr. USN. Recipient Nat. Greene award Greensboro C. of C., 1983, Citizen of Yr. award, 1993; named N.C. Entrepreneur of Yr., 1995. Home: 9 Saint Augustine Sq Greensboro NC 27408-3834

NUSSBAUMER, GERHARD KARL, metals company executive; b. Linz, Austria, Mar. 25, 1959; came to U.S., 1987; s. Franz and Stefanie (Hinternberger) N. MBA, U. Vienna, 1982. Jr. auditor Price Waterhouse, Vienna, 1983-85; corp. staff contr. Oesterreichische Industrieholding AG, Vienna, 1985-87; v.p. fin. Voest-Alpine Internat. Corp., N.Y.C., 1987-92, pres., 1993—; bd. dirs. Voest-Alpine Internat. Corp., N.Y.C., Voest-Alpine Svcs. and Technologies, Pitts., Voest-Alpine Tubular Corp., Houston, Voest-Alpine M.C.E. Corp., Berlin, Voest-Alpine Steel Products Corp., N.Y.C. Mem. U.S. Austrian C. of C., Am. Mgmt. Assn. Avocations: theatre, constitutional law, history, tennis, skiing. Office: Voest-Alpine Internat Corp 60 E 42nd St New York NY 10165

NUSSDORF, BERNARD, wholesale distribution executive. CEO Quality King Distributors. Office: Quality King Distribution 2060 9th Ave Ronkonkoma NY 11779-6253*

NUSSENBAUM, SIEGFRIED FRED, chemistry educator; b. Vienna, Austria, Nov. 21, 1919; came to U.S., 1939; s. Marcus and Susan Sara (Rothenberg) N.; m. Celia Womark, Feb. 20, 1951; children; Deborah M., Evelyn R. BS in Chemistry, U. Calif., Berkeley, 1941, MS in Food Tech., 1948, PhD in Comparative Biochemistry, 1951. Analytical chemist Panam. Engrng. Co., Berkeley, 1942-43; asst. chief chemist Manganese Ore Co., Las Vegas, 1943-45; rsch. assoc. U. Calif., Berkeley, 1951-52; dir. master clin. lab. sci. program U. Calif., San Francisco, 1969-87; from instr. to prof. Calif. State U., Sacramento, 1952-90, chair dept. chemistry, 1958-65; cons. biochemist Sacramento County Hosp., 1958-70; lectr. U. Calif. Davis Med. Ctr., 1970-93, guest lectr., 1993—. Author: Organic Chem-Principles and Applications, 1963; contbr. articles to profl. jours. Sgt. U.S. Army, 1945-47. Fellow AAAS; mem. Am. Chem. Soc., Am. Assn. Clin. Chemistry (Outstanding Contbn. in Edn. award no. sect. 1991), Nat. Acad. Clin. Biochemistry. Achievements include research in pectic enzymes, mechanism of amylopectin formation and differentiation from amylose, phenotyping of lipemias. Home: 2900 Latham Dr Sacramento CA 95864-5644

NUSSLE, JAMES ALLEN, congressman; b. Des Moines, June 27, 1960; s. Mark S. and Lorna Kay (Fisher) N.; m. Leslie J. Harbison, Aug. 23, 1986. BA, Luther Coll., Decorah, Iowa, 1983; JD, Drake U., 1985. Bar: Iowa 1985. Pvt. practice law Manchester, Iowa, 1986; states atty. Delaware County Atty., Manchester, 1986-90; mem. 102nd-105th Congresses from 2d Iowa dist., Washington, 1991—; mem. house ways and means com., budget com. 102nd-105th Congresses from 2d Iowa dist. Lutheran. Avocation: guitar. *

NUTE, DONALD E., JR., philosophy educator; b. Maysville, Ky., Aug. 12, 1947; s. Donald E. Sr. and Virginia (Boyd) N.; m. Jane Greifenkamp, Aug. 17, 1968; 1 child, Achsa Lynn. BA, U. Ky., 1969; PhD, Ind. U., 1974. Assoc. instr. Ind. U., Bloomington, 1970-71; asst. prof. U. Ga., Athens, 1973-78, assoc. prof., 1978-83, prof. philosophy, 1983—, dir. MS in artificial intelligence program, 1987—, head dept. philosophy, 1989—, dir. artificial intelligence ctr., 1994—; vis. prof. U. Tubingen, Germany, 1985; pres. AI Assocs., Athens, 1987—; rsch. assoc. U. Antwerp, Belgium, 1989. Author: Topics in Conditional Logic, 1980, Essential Formal Semantics, 1981; coauthor: Prolog Programming in Depth, 1988, 2d edit., 1997. Mem. Am. Philos. Assn., Am. Assn. Artificial Intelligence, So. Soc. for Philosophy and Psychology, Assn. for Symbolic Logic, Soc. for Exact Philosophy, Phi Beta Kappa. Office: U Ga Dept Philosophy Athens GA 30602

NUTT, ROBERT L., lawyer; b. New Castle, Pa., Mar. 30, 1945; s. James Earl and Dorothy Nutt; m. Virginia Anne Maurer, Aug. 16, 1969; children: David, Jonathan. BA, Grove City Coll., 1967; JD, U. Pa., 1970. Bar: N.Y., Mass. Law clerk U.S. Ct. Appeals (2d cir.), N.Y.C., 1970-71; assoc. Ropes & Gray, Boston, 1971-79, ptnr., 1979—; lectr. in law Boston U., 1989—. Contbr. articles to profl. jours. Trustee Shore County Day Sch., Beverly, Mass., 1986-94; moderator First Ch. of Christ, Marblehead, Mass., 1993—. Mem. ABA, Boston Bar Assn. (bus. law sect. chair 1990-93). Congregationalist. Avocations: skiing, golf, upland bird hunting. Office: Ropes & Gray One International Pl Boston MA 02110-2624

NUTTALL, MICHAEL LEE, engineer, educator; b. Salem, Mass.; s. Leonard John IV and Ethel (Pecukonis) N.; m. Susan Patricia Wade, July 12, 1988; children: Leonard John VI, Andrew Norman, Michelle Leigh, Patricia Katherine. BSChemE, Brigham Young U., 1987; MEE, U. Utah, 1994. Japanese linguist Utah Army N.G., Provo, 1984-87; math tutor Utah Valley C.C., Provo, 1987; engr. Micron Tech., Boise, Idaho, 1988-89, lead engr., 1989-91, process devel. engr., 1994—; instr. Salt Lake C.C., Salt Lake City, 1991-92. Patentee in field. Home: 1469 N Deep Creek Way Meridian ID 83642-4215 Office: Micro Tech 8000 Federal Way Boise ID 83716-9632

NUTTALL, RICHARD NORRIS, state agency administrator; b. Hamilton, Ont., Can., Feb. 7, 1940; s. James William and Margaret Gay (Walsh) N.; m. Ethel Jane Pickering, July 9, 1977; children: Andrew Richard, John Patrick. BSA, U. Toronto, 1961; MPA, Harvard U., 1964; MB, BS, U. London, Eng., 1974. Cert. Coll. Family Physicians Can., Mgmt. Cons. Zone dir. Health and Welfare Can., Prince Rupert, B.C., 1977-79; regional dir. Health and Welfare Can., Edmonton, Alta., 1980-82; pres. Rutland Consulting Group, Ltd., Vancouver, B.C., 1982-87, Richmond Assocs. Internat., Vancouver, 1988-90; med. health officer Govt. N.W. Ters., Yellowknife, B.C., 1990-93, Regina Health Dist., 1993—. Fellow Am. Coll. Preventive Medicine, Am. Coll. Healthcare Execs.; mem. Can. Pub. Health Assn. (bd. dirs. 1991-93), Rotary Club North Regina. Office: Regina Health Dist, 1910 McIntyre St, Regina, SK Canada S4P 2R3

NUTTER, DAVID GEORGE, urban planner; b. Manchester, Conn., Nov. 25, 1939; s. George Huitt and Catherine Lavina (Casey) N.; m. Ellen Marie Manfredonia, Sept. 7, 1968; children: Susan Katharine, Anne Amelia. BA in English, Tufts U., 1961; MS in Urban Planning, Columbia U., 1967. City planner Balt. City Planning Commn., 1967-69; dir. planning Charles Ctr.-Inner Harbor Mgmt., Inc., Balt., 1969-72, v.p., 1972-76; pvt. cons. Balt., 1976-83; dir. downtown mall mgmt. dist. Denver Partnership, Inc., 1983-85; exec. dir. Rochester (N.Y.) Downtown Devel. Corp., 1985-87; prin. Nutter Assocs., Rochester, 1987—. Author: Selecting a Developer, 1983. Bd. dirs. Soc. Preservation of Fed. Hill, Balt., 1969-73, Arts for Greater Rochester, 1986-90; chmn. Town of Brighton (N.Y.) Conservation Bd., 1992-95; active Downtown Coalition, Rochester, 1995—. Sgt. U.S. Army, 1962-65. William F. Kinne Travelling fellow Columbia U., 1967. Mem. Am. Inst. Cert. Planners, Am. Planning Assn., Urban Land Inst. (assoc.), N.Y. Canal Soc., N.Y. Planning Fedn. Avocations: historical map and atlas collecting, American and English history, computer mapping, hiking. Home: 240 Allens Creek Rd Rochester NY 14618

NUTTER, FRANKLIN WINSTON, lawyer; b. Charleston, W.Va., Apr. 17, 1946; s. Frank Hamilton and Marie Agnes (Pyles) N.; m. Linda Jean Davis, Sept. 2, 1972; children: Alycia Marie, Aaron Davis. BBA in Econs., U. Cin., 1968; JD, Georgetown U., 1974. Bar: D.C., Va., U.S. Dist. Ct. (no. dist.) Va., U.S. Ct. Appeals (9th and D.C. cirs.), U.S. Supreme Ct. 1993. Gen. counsel Nat. Flood Ins. Assn., Washington, 1975-78; gen. counsel Reins. Assn. Am., Washington, 1978-81, pres., 1981-84, 91—; pres. Alliance Am. Insurers, Schaumburg, Ill., 1984-91, Property Loss Research Bur., Schaumburg, 1984-91; bd. overseers Inst. Civil Justice subs. Rand Corp.; chair Natural Disaster Coalition. Bd. dirs. Advs. for Hwy. and Auto Safety; trustee Nat. Commn. Against Drunk Driving. Lt. (j.g.) USN, 1968-72. Mem. ABA (torts and injury practice sect., past chmn. internat. ins. law, excess and surplus lines and reins. com., coun. tort and ins. practice sect.), Va. Bar Assn., Ins. Inst. Hwy. Safety (bd. dirs.), Workers' Compensation Rsch. Inst., Industry Sector Adv. Coun. on Svcs. Home: 8458 Portland Pl Mc Lean VA 22102-1708 Office: 1301 Pennsylvania Ave NW Washington DC 20004-1701

NUTTER, ZOE DELL LANTIS, retired public relations executive; b. Yamhill, Oreg., June 14, 1915; d. Arthur Lee Lantis and Olive Adelaide (Reed) Lantis-Hilton; m. Richard S. West, Apr. 30, 1941 (div. Nov. 1964); m. Ervin John Nutter, Dec. 30, 1965. Assoc. in Bus., Santa Ana Jr. Coll., 1944. Cert. gen. secondary sch. tchr., Calif.; FAA cert. lic. commercial, instrument, single/multi engine land airplanes pilot. Promoter World's Fair & Comml. Airlines Golden Gate Internat. Expn., San Francisco, 1937-39; pirate theme girl, official hostess Treasure Island's World Fair, San Francisco, 1939-40; prin. dancer San Francisco Ballet, 1937-41; artist, 1941-45; program dir. Glenn County High Sch., Willows, Calif., 1952-58; pub. rels. Monarch Piper Aviation Co., Monterey, Calif., 1963-65; pilot, pub. rels. Elano Corp., Xenia, Ohio, 1968-85; bd. dirs. Nat. Aviation Hall of Fame, Dayton, Ohio, pres., chmn., 1989-92, bd. trustees, 1976—, chmn. bd. nominations, 1992—; bd. trustees Ford's Theatre, Washington, Treasure Island Mus., San Francisco; charter mem. Friends of First Ladies, Smithsonian, Washington, 1990-93. Assoc. editor KYH mag. of Shikar Safari Internat., 1985-87; contbg. columnist Scripps Howard San Francisco News, 1938. Bd. dirs. Cin. May Festival, 1976-80; cen. com. Glenn County Rep. Party, Willows, 1960-64; state cen. com. Rep. Party, 1962-64; adv. bd. Women's Air & Space Mus., Dayton, 1987-94. Warrant officer, Civil Air Patrol, 1967-69. Recipient Civic Contbn. Honor award Big Brothers/Big Sisters, 1991, John Collier Nat. award Camp Fire Girls & Boys, 1988, Tambourine award Salvation Army, 1982, State of Ohio Gov.'s award for Volunteerism, 1992; named Most Photographed Girl in World, News Burs. & Clipping Svcs., 1938-39. Mem., founder Dancers Over 40, NYC; Fellow Pres.'s Club U. Ky., Ohio State U., Wright State U.; mem. 99's Internat. Women Pilots Orgn. (life, hospitality chmn. 1968), Monterey Bay Chapter 99's (mem. chmn. 1964-65), Walnut Grove Country Club, Lost Tree Country Club, Windstar County Club (Naples, Fla.), Rotary (Paul Harris fellow 1987), Old Port Yacht Club, Shikar Safari Internat. (host com. 1976), Country Club of the North. Avocations: flying, horseback riding, hunting, shooting, fashion. Home: 986 Trebein Rd Xenia OH 45385-9534

NUTTING, GEORGE OGDEN, newspaper publisher; b. Washington, Oct. 21, 1935; s. George Kegley and Margaret Lawson (Ogden) N.; m. Betty S. Woods; children—William Ogden, Robert McLain. B.A., Williams Coll., 1956. With Martinsburg (W.Va.) Jour., 1956, Wheeling (W.Va.) News Register, 1957; with Ogden Newspapers, Inc., Wheeling, 1958—; pres., gen. mgr. Ogden Newspapers, Inc., 1970—; chmn. bd. United Nat. Bank North, Wheeling; bd. dirs. Stone & Thomas, United Bankshares. Bd. dirs. Bethany Coll.; mem. Wheeling Park Commn., Linsly Sch., Ohio Valley Indsl. and Bus. Devel. Corp., W.Va. U. Found. Mem. So. Newspaper Pubs. Assn. Republican. Episcopalian. Office: Wheeling News-Register 1500 Main St Wheeling WV 26003-2826

NUTTING, PAUL A., medical educator, medical science administrator; b. Aug. 24, 1944; m. Kaia M. Gallagher; children: Paul James, Kaia Elise. AB in Psychology, Cornell U., 1966; MD, U. Kans., 1970; MSPH, U. Colo., 1988. Diplomate Am. Bd. Family Practice, Am. Bd. Preventive Medicine. Intern in pediat. U. Pitts., 1970-71; resident in preventive medicine U. Ariz., 1973-75; clin. dir. Santa Rosa (Ariz.) Clinic Indian Health Svc., 1971-72, maternal and child health officer Sells (Ariz.) Svc. Unit, 1972-73; med. rsch. office Office of R&D Indian Health Svc., Tucson, 1973-77, assoc. dir. rsch. Office of R&D, 1977-83; sr. scholar-in-residence Inst. Medicine-NAS, Washington, 1983-84; dir. Office of Primary Care Studies Health Resources and Svcs. Adminstrn., DHHS, Rockville, Md., 1984-86; resident in family medicine Mercy Med. Ctr., Denver, 1986-88; dir. rsch. Indian Health Svc., Tucson, 1989-90; dir. divsn. primary care and dep. dir. Ctr. for Gen. Health Svcs. Rsch., DHHS, Rockville, 1990-93; dir. Ambulatory Sentinel Practice Network, Denver, 1993—; prof. family medicine dept. family medicine U. Colo. Health Scis. Ctr., 1993—; rsch. assoc. prof. dept. family and cmty. medicine U. Ariz., 1981-87, 88-90; clin. assoc. prof. dept. family and family medicine Georgetown U. Sch. Medicine, 1983-86; mem. subcom. on cardiovascular disease Sec.'s Task Force on Black and Minority Health, 1984-85; mem. interagy. com. on infant mortality USHPS, 1990-93, chair rsch. subcom., clin. preventive svcs. steering com., 1991-93, nat. steering com. primary care-substance abuse linkage initiative, 1991-93; chairperson Workshop on Early Detection of Prostate Cancer, Nat. Cancer Inst., Bethesda, Md., 1993; cons. in field. Author: (with L.A. Green) From Research to Policy to Practice: Closing the Loop in Clinical Policy Development in Primary Care, 1994; editor: Community-Oriented Primary Care: From Principle to Practice, 1987, co-editor: Primary Care Research: Theory and Methods, 1991; mem. editl. bd. Jour. Cmty. Health, 1981-84, Jour. Family Practice, 1990—, Am. Family Physician, 1990—, Jour. Rural Health, 1994—; contbr. chpts. to books and articles to profl. jours. Capt. USPHS, 1982. Recipient Cert. appreciation Nat. Indian Health Bd., 1982, Modern Medicine award for disting. achievement, 1993. Mem. APHA (sect. in med. care, epidemiology, internat. health), Inst. Medicine-NAS, Am. Acad. Family Physicians (liaison mem. com. on rsch. 1993—), Am. Acad. Pediat. (mem. steering com. pediat. rsch. in office settings 1993—), N.Am. Primary Care Rsch. Group (bd. dirs. 1994—, chair com. on bldg. capacity for rsch. in family practice 1994—), Soc. for Epidemiologic Rsch., Soc. Tchrs. Family Medicine. Office: Ambulatory Sentinel Practice Network 1650 Pierce St Denver CO 80214-1433*

NUTTING, PAUL JOHN, city official; b. Oswego, N.Y., July 6, 1952; s. Robert Truman and Joan Violet (Joyce) N. BA, SUNY, Oswego, 1974; MPA, SUNY, Albany, 1977. Adminstrv. asst. City of League City, Tex., 1978-79, acting city adminstr., 1979-80, 81, asst. city adminstr., 1980-81, exec. asst. to mayor, 1981-82, city adminstr., 1982-95; city mgr. City of Springfield, Tenn., 1995—; bd. dirs. Tenn. Natural Gas Acquisition Corp. Bd. dirs. League City Family Welfare Coun., 1978-89, United Way, Robertson County; mem. exec. bd. Mainland Communities United Way, Texas City, Tex., 1991-94; adv. dir. League City Mchts. and Bus. Assn., 1989-95, North Galveston County C. of C., Dickinson, Tex., 1989-95. Mem. Internat. City/County Mgmt. Assn., Tenn. City Mgmt. Assn., Texas City Mgmt. Assn., Am. Soc. for Pub. Adminstrn. (pres. Houston area chpt. 1991-93, dir. 1990-91, 93-95), Springfield-Robertson County C. of C., League City Rotary Club (pres. 1985-86, 93-94), Rotary Club of Springfield. Avocations: golf, tennis. Home: 130 Pepper Grove Cv Springfield TN 37172-2125 Office: City of Springfield 405 N Main St Springfield TN 37172-2408

NUTTING, WALLACE HALL, army officer; b. Newton, Mass., June 3, 1928; s. Gerry B. and Ethel M. (Hall) N.; m. Jane Anne Walker, June 17, 1950; children: Elizabeth J., John T., Katherine A., Sally W. BS, U.S. Mil. Acad., 1950; MA in Internat. Affairs, George Washington U., 1963; postgrad., Naval War Coll., 1963, Nat. War Coll., 1968. Commd. cavalry officer

U.S. Army, 1950, advanced through grades to gen.; asst. dir. plans Dept. Army, Washington, 1968-70; dep. dir. plans Dept. Army, 1973-74; comdr. 11th Armored Cavalry Regiment, Vietnam, 1970-71; dep. comdr. ops. 1st brigade 5th Inf. Div., Vietnam, 1971; Army mem. chmn.'s staff group Orgn. Joint Chiefs of Staff, Washington, 1971-73; comdg. gen. 1st Inf. div. forward, Fed. Republic Germany, 1974-75; dir. strategy plans and policy Dept. Army, 1975-77; comdg. gen. 3d Armored div., Fed. Republic Germany, 1977-79; comdr. in chief U.S. So. Command, Quarry Heights, Panama, 1979-83; comdr.-in chief U.S. Readiness Command, dir. Joint Deployment Agy., MacDill AFB, Fla., 1983-85; assoc. fellow Ctr. for Internat. Affairs, Harvard U., 1986; sr. fellow Inst. Higher Def. Studies, Nat. Def. U., Washington, 1986-96. Mem. exec. bd., Panama Canal Council, Boy Scouts Am., 1979-83; mem. Gulf Ridge council, Boy Scouts Am., 1983-85. Decorated Defense D.S.M. with oak leaf cluster, Silver Star, Legion of Merit with 2 oak leaf clusters, Soldier's medal, Bronze Star with oak leaf cluster, Air medal (7), Purple Heart with oak leaf cluster, Army Commendation medal with oak leaf cluster, Presdl. Unit citation, Korean Svc. medal with 5 stars, Vietnam Svc. medal with 4 stars, U.N. Svc. medal, JCS Identification badge, Gen. staff Identification badge, Vietnamese Cross of Gallantry with palm and silver star, Brazilian Order Mil. Merit, Order Mil. Merit Dominican Republic, Cross of Venezuelan Armed Forces, Mil. Star Armed Forces Chile, Cross Armed Force Republic of Honduras, Order Mil. Merit in grade grand officer (Argentina), Order Mil. Merit (Panama), Korea Campaign medal, Vietnamese Campaign medal; recipient Silver Beaver award. Mem. U.S. Armor Assn., Assn. U.S. Army. Congregationalist. Home: PO Box 96 Biddeford Pool ME 04006-0096 Office: Dept of Army Gen Officer Mgmt Office Washington DC 20310

NUTZLE, FUTZIE (BRUCE JOHN KLEINSMITH), artist, author, cartoonist; b. Lakewood, Ohio, Feb. 21, 1942; s. Adrian Ralph and Naomi Irene (Rupert) Kleinsmith; children: Adrian David, Arielle Justine and Tess Alexandra (twins). Represented by The Pope Gallery, Santa Cruz, Calif. Author: Modern Loafer, Thames and Hudson, 1981, (authobiography) Futzie Nutzle, 1983, Earthquake, 1989, Run the World: 50 Cents Chronicle Books, 1991; illustrator: The Armies Encamped Beyond Unfinished Avenues (Morton Marcus), 1977, Box of Nothing, 1982, The Duke of Chemical Birds (Howard McCord), 1989, Book of Solutions, 1990, Fact and Friction, 1990, Managing for the 90s, 1992, Soundbites for Success, 1994; feature cartoonist Rolling Stone, N.Y.C., 1975-80, The Japan Times, Tokyo and L.A., 1986—, The Prague Post, Czechoslovakia, 1991—; contbr. exhbns. include Inaugural, 1966, Cupola, 1967, Rolling Renaissance, San Francisco, 1968, 100 Acres, O.K. Harris 1971, N.Y.C., San Francisco Mus. Art, 1972, Indpls. and Cin. Mus. Art, 1975, Leica, L.A., 1978, Santa Barbara Mus. Annex, Calif., 1978, Swope, Santa Monica, West Beach Cafe, Venice, Calif., 1985, Les Oranges, Santa Monica, Correspondence Sch., 1970-78, 1st Ann. Art-A-Thon, N.Y.C., 1985, Am. Epiphany with Phillip Hefferton, 1986, Polit. Cartoon Show, Braunstein, San Francisco, Komsomolskaya Pravda, 1988, retrospective Eloise Packard Smith, 1990, exemplary contemporary, Cowell, U. Calif. Santa Cruz, 1991, Silicon Graphics Inc., Computer Graphics for NAB, Las Vegas, 1993, Prague Eco-Fair, 1991; represented in pvt. and pub. collections (complete archives) Spl. Collections, McHenry Libr., U. Calif., Santa Cruz, Mus. Modern Art, N.Y.C., San Francisco Mus. Modern Art, Oakland Mus., San Francisco Mus. Cartoon Art, Whitney Mus. Am. Art, N.Y.C. regular contbr. The Japan Times. Ltd., Tokyo. Address: PO Box 325 Aromas CA 95004-0325

NUWER, HENRY JOSEPH (HANK NUWER), journalist, educator; b. Buffalo, N.Y., Aug. 19, 1946; s. Henry Robert and Teresa (Lysiak) N.; m. Alice May Cerniglia, Dec. 28, 1968 (div. Mar. 1980); 1 child, Henry Christian; m. Jenine Howard, Apr. 9, 1982; 1 child, Adam. BS in English, SUNY, Buffalo, 1968; MA in English, N.Mex. Highlands U., 1971; PhD, Ball State U., 1987. Freelance author, journalist, 1969—; asst. prof. Clemson (S.C.) U., 1982-83; assoc. prof. Ball State U., Muncie, Ind., 1985-89; sr. editor Rodale Press, Emmaus, Pa., 1990-91; editor in chief Arts Ind. Mag., Indpls., 1993-95; assoc. prof. journalism U. Richmond, Va., 1995-97; Hazing expert-lectr., Richmond, 1990—; Hazing cons. NBC Movie-of-the-Week Moment of Truth: Broken Pledges, Indpls., 1994. Author: Steroids, 1990, Broken Pledges: The Deadly Rite of Hazing, 1990, How to Write Like an Expert, 1995; mem. editl. bd. Chic Mag., 1976-77; contbr. articles to profl. jours. Grantee Nat. Endowment for the Arts, 1976, Idaho Humanities Coun., 1985, Gannett Found., 1988; named Mag. Adviser of Yr., Coll. Media Advisers, 1988. Mem. Soc. Profl. Journalists, Investigative Reporters and Editors. Democrat. Roman Catholic. Office: 1108 Meridian Plaza 1106 Meridian Plz Ste 668 PO Box 33 Anderson IN 46016

NUZMAN, CARL EDWARD, retired hydrologist; b. Topeka, Aug. 5, 1930; s. Loren Manuel and Loraine Lillian (Bowler) N.; B.S. in Agrl. Engring., Kans. State U., 1953; M.S. in Water Resources Engring., U. Kans., 1966; m. Janet Ruth Steck, Aug. 23, 1952. Engr. div. water resources Kans. Bd. Agr., Topeka, 1957-65; hydrologist Kans. Water Resources Bd., Topeka, 1965-66; hydrology supr., sales engr. Layne-Western Co., Inc., Shawnee Mission, Kans., 1967-72, mgr. hydrology div., 1972-86; v.p., chief hydrologist, Groundwater Mgmt. Inc., 1986-88; chief hydrologist Layne Western Co. Inc., 1988-92; v.p., chief hydrologist Layne GeoSci., Inc., 1992-97; ret., 1997; hydrology cons., 1997—. Treas. local sch. bd., 1958-59. Served to 1st lt. USAF, 1953-56. Registered profl. engr., Kans., Mo.; cert. hydrologist Am. Inst. Hydrology. Mem. Am. Soc. Agrl. Engrs., ASCE, Am. Geophys. Union, Kans. Engring. Soc. (sec.-treas. 1965-68, Outstanding Young Engr. award Topeka chpt. 1965), Nat. Soc. Profl. Engrs., Alpha Kappa Lambda, Sigma Tau, Steel Ring. Elk. Contbr. articles to profl. jours.; author, inventor. Home: 3314 NW Huxman Rd Silver Lake KS 66539-9243

NUZUM, JOHN M., JR., banker; b. Milw., Dec. 22, 1939; s. John M. and Helen (Ollis) N.; m. Margaret Bolway, Feb. 25, 1967; children: Kimberly, Courtney, Leah, Jonathan. AB, Princeton U., 1962; MBA, U. Pa., 1964. Sr. v.p. Chase Manhattan Bank, N.Y.C., 1965—; mem. governing bd. Credit Rsch. Ctr., Georgetown U., Washington, 1995—. Project Reach Youth, Bklyn., 1977—, Park Slope Family Ctr., Bklyn., 1984-95. Mem. Montauk Club (bd. dirs. 1985-94), Heights Casino Club, Princeton Club. Office: 270 Park Ave New York NY 10017-2014

NUZUM, ROBERT WESTON, lawyer; b. Evanston, Ill., Dec. 11, 1952; s. John Weston and Janet Marie (Talbot) N.; m. Julia Ann Abadie, Sept. 16, 1983. BS in Fin., La. State U., 1974, JD, 1977; LLM in Taxation, N.Y.U., 1978. Bar: La. 1977, D.C. 1979. Assoc. Office Chief Counsel, Washington, 1978-81, Jones, Walker, Waechter, Poitevent, Carrere & Denegre, New Orleans, 1981-85; ptnr. Jones, Walker, Waechter, Potevent, Carrere & Denegre, New Orleans, 1985-88, Deutsch, Kerrigan & Stiles, New Orleans, 1988-89, Phelps & Dunbar and predecessor firm, New Orleans, 1989—; adj. instr. Tulane U., New Orleans, 1984—. Editor La. Law Rev., 1977; contbr. articles to profl. jours. Wallace scholar N.Y.U., 1978. Mem. La. Bar Assn. (program chmn. tax sect. 1992-93, sec.-treas. 1993-94, vice-chmn. 1994-95, chmn. 1995-96), Tulane Tax Inst. (planning com. 1993—, tax specialization adv. commn. 1997—), Order of Coif. Republican. Roman Catholic. Avocations: golf, reading, fishing. Office: Phelps Dunbar LLP 400 Poydras St New Orleans LA 70130-3245

NUZZO, SALVATORE JOSEPH, defense, electronics company executive; b. Norwalk, Conn., Aug. 6, 1931; s. Rocco and Angelina (Renzull) N.; m. Lucille Cocco, Oct. 3, 1953; children: James, David, Thomas, Dana. B.S. in Elec. Engring, Yale U., 1953; M.S. in Bus, Columbia U., 1974. With Hazeltine Corp., Greenlawn, N.Y., 1953-88, v.p. govt. products and mktg., 1969-73, v.p. govt. products div., 1973-74, sr. v.p. ops., 1974-76, exec. v.p., chief oper. officer, 1976, pres., chief oper. officer, 1977-88, chief exec. officer, 1980-87, chmn., 1986-88, ret., 1988; chmn., Technautics Corp., Cleve., 1991-94; chmn. Marine Mech. Corp., Cleve., 1994—; bd. mem. Avnet Inc.; chmn. SL Industries; chmn., CEO, bd. dirs. Datron, Inc., 1996—. Fellow Poly. Inst. N.Y. Mem. Yale Sci. and Engring. Assn. (former pres.). Home: 118 St Mellions Dr Pinehurst NC 28374 also: 1101 Waterfront on Ocean 800 Ocean Dr Juno Beach FL 33408

N'VIETSON, TUNG THANH, civil engineer; b. Bien Hoa, Vietnam, Nov. 12, 1949; came to U.S., 1979; s. Cu Van and Dao Thi Nguyen; m. Phan Thi, Oct. 12, 1973; children: Trucle C., Leyna C., Tung Thanh Jr. BS in Civil Engring., Nat. Inst. Tech., Saigon, Vietnam, 1973. Registered profl. engr., La., Va., D.C., Md., Fla., Tex. Asst. province engr. Darlac Province Pub. Works, Banmethuot, Vietnam, 1973-75; design engr. Daklak Province, Dept.. of Transp., Banmethuot, 1975-79, Burk & Assocs. Inc., New Orleans, 1980-85; project engr. David Volkert & Assocs. Inc., Metairie, La., 1985-87, Cervantes & Assocs. P.C., Fairfax, Va., 1987-88, Progressive Engring. Cons. Inc., Fairfax, 1988-89; sr. project mgr. Sheladia Assocs. Inc., Rockville, Md., 1989-93; v.p. Guillot-Vogt Assocs., Inc., Metairie, La., 1993-94; sr. project mgr. Evans-Graves, Metairie, 1994—. Mem. ASCE. Roman Catholic. Home: 3945 Tall Pines Dr New Orleans LA 70131-8419 Office: 1 Galleria Blvd Ste 1216 Metairie LA 70001-7508

NWAGBARA, CHIBU ISAAC, industrial designer, consultant; b. Umuahia, Abia, Nigeria, Apr. 24, 1957; s. Marcus and Catherine (Onyemairo) N.; m. Chioma Adamma Ariwodo, Apr. 26, 1997; children: Obinna Alex, Amara Joy. BS, No. Ill. U., 1984, MS, 1986; MS, Purdue U., 1990, PhD, 1993. Cert. indsl. technologist. Tech. mgr. 3M Internat., Lagos, Nigeria, 1977-80; founder, pres. ChiMarc Assocs., DeKalb, Ill., 1981-84; rsch. asst. No. Ill. U., DeKalb, Ill., 1985-86; assoc. editor Purdue U., West Lafayette, Ind., 1987-89, rsch. assoc., 1990-91, grad. lectr., 1990-93; cons. Arthur Andersen & Co., St. Charles, Ill., 1993-95; program mgr. Allen-Bradley Co., Milw., 1995-96; project mgr. BellSouth Telecom. Inc., Atlanta, 1997—; cons. Arnett Clinic, Lafayette, 1992-93, Chimarc Assocs., DeKalb, 1986—, GoldMark Ltd., Lagos, 1985-90. Coord. community outreach program Purdue U. Afro-Am. Studies and Rsch. Ctr., West Lafayette, 1990-91; coach Am. Youth Soccer Orgn., West Lafayette, 1987-90. Named one of Outstanding Young Men of Am., 1989, Men of Achievement, 1995. Mem. Inst. Indsl. Engrs., Am. Soc. for Quality Control, Am. Edn. Rsch. Assn., Nat. Assn. Indsl. Tech., Internat. Soc. for Performance and Instrn., World Future Soc. Methodist. Avocations: enjoys travel, reading, meeting people, music, sports. Home: 1025 B Oak Chase Dr Tucker GA 30084 Office: BellSouth Telecom Inc 675 W Peachtree St NW Atlanta GA 30375-0001

NWANGWU, JOHN TOCHUKWU, epidemiologist, public health educator; b. Ogidi, Anambra, Nigeria, Apr. 16, 1952; came to U.S., 1973; s. Sidney N. and Phoebe Nwangwu; m. Chioma Ugonwa Nwokolo, Sept. 3, 1988; children: Nmadinobi, Tobenna. MB, U. Nebr., Omaha, 1979; MPH, Loma Linda U., 1981; PhD, Columbia U., 1988; postgrad., Erasmus U., Rotterdam, The Netherlands, 1991. Cons. WHO, 1982-87; instr. Columbia U., N.Y.C., 1983-85, St. Joseph's Coll. Hosp., Bklyn., 1986-88; asst. prof. SUNY, Westbury, 1988-89; chief epidemiologist Kern County Health Dept., Bakersfield, Calif., 1989-90, dir. epidemiology and data mgmt., 1990; assoc. prof. pub. health Conn. State U., New Haven, 1991-95, prof. pub. health, 1995—; vis. prof. Calif. State U., Bakersfield, 1990, Yale U., New Haven, 1992; epidemiologist/rsch. affiliate faculty Yale U. Sch. Medicine, 1993—; cons. Hosp. of St. Raphael, New Haven, 1995—; cons. to fgn. countries, 1982—; presenter in field. Contbr. articles to profl. publs. Fellow Royal Soc. Medicine, Am. Coll. Epidemiology; mem. APHA, Internat. Epidemiol. Assn., N.Y. Acad. Scis., Assn. Tchrs. Preventive Medicine. Avocations: badminton, squash, reading. Home: 898 Greenway Rd Woodbridge CT 06525-2413 Office: Conn State U Dept Pub Health 144 Farnham Ave New Haven CT 06515-1202 also: Yale U Sch Medicine Dept Epidemiology and Pub Health 60 College St New Haven CT 06510-3210

NWOFOR, AMBROSE ONYEGBULE, vocational assessment evaluator; b. Amandugba, Nigeria, Dec. 7, 1947; came to the U.S., 1975; s. Wewe Ogbuihe and Nwanyi-Ihuoma (Olujie) N.; m. Clara Chinyere, June 14, 1975; children: Chiugo, Chiedoziem, Uzonna, Nnanaka, Ozioma. Diploma in elec. engring., Inst. Mgmt. & Tech. Engring., Enugu, Nigeria, 1973; BS in Electronics, Norfolk State U., 1977; MS in Ind. Tech., Ea. Mich. U., 1978; MEd in Ednl. Adminstrn., Ariz. State U., 1980. Electronic engr. Geoservices (Nigeria) Ltd., Nigeria, 1973-74, Taylor Electronics, Ariz., 1979-80; internat. svcs. engr. Dowell Schlumberger Overseas, Brazil, 1981-82; engring. lab. dir. U. Port Harcourt, Nigeria, 1982-83; sr. rsch. fellow, computer cons. Fed. U. Tech., Nigeria, 1983-89; pvt. specialist N.Y., 1989-91; elec. vocat. tchr. N.Y. Bd. Edn., 1991-93, vocat. assessment evaluator, 1993—; H.S. bd. mem. Amandugba Tech. Sch., Nigeria, 1984-88; pvt. vocat. assessment cons., 1989—. Inventor in field. Active Amandugba (Nigeria) Alms, 1973—, Amandugba (Nigeria) Dynamic Front, 1987—; chmn. Amandugba (Nigeria) Water Project, 1982-89; pres. Amandugba Fed. Union, Inc., 1992—. Mem. IEEE, Am. Vocat. Assn., Soc. Mfg. Engrs., Nat. Tech. Assn., Sci. Assn. Nigeria, N.Y. State Occupl. Assn. Roman Catholic. Avocation: video recording. Home: 702 Sturgis Pl Baltimore MD 21208

NWOSU, KINGSLEY CHUKWUDUM, research and development scientist, educator; b. Onitsha, Nigeria, Jan. 13, 1961; came to U.S., 1981, naturalized, 1996; s. Emmanuel Nwachukwu and Josephine (Nwokedike) N.; m. Nneka Veronica Anuligo, Jan. 11, 1996. BS, U. Southwestern La., Lafayette, 1984; MS, U. Okla., 1987; PhD, Syracuse U., 1993. Grad. rsch. asst. U. Okla., Norman, 1986-88, La. State Law Inst., Baton Rouge, 1988; assoc. sys. engr. IBM, Kingston, N.Y., 1989-91, sr. assoc. sys. engr., 1991-93, R&D staff, 1993-94; mem. tech. staff Lucent Technologies, Whippany, N.J., 1994—; adj. prof. dept. math. and computer sci. Rutgers U., Newark, 1995—; vis. prof. dept. math. and computer sci. Montclair State U., Upper Montclair, N.J., 1995—; program chair, com. mem. several IEEE/Assn. Computing confs. Author: (with P.B. Berra and B. Thuraisingham) Multimedia Database Systems: Design and Implementation Strategies, 1996; contbr. articles to profl. jours. Mem. IEEE, Assn. Computing Machinery, Nat. Soc. on Sys. Engring., Nat. Soc. Black Engrs., Assn. African Computing Engrs. and Scientists (pres. 1994—), Math. Assn. Am., N.Y. Acad. Scis. Avocations: soccer, tennis, jazz. Office: Lucent Technologies 67 Whippany Rd Rm 2e-223A Whippany NJ 07981-1406

NYBERG, DONALD ARVID, oil company executive; b. Ridgewood, N.J., Aug. 23, 1951; s. Arvid H. and Rita T. (Tenwick) N.; m. Susan Radis, Feb. 16, 1985; children: Matthew D., Ryan T. BA, St. Lawrence U., 1973; MBA, Harvard U., 1975. Mgr. marine ops. Standard Oil, L.A., 1982-83; mgr. ops. planning Standard Oil, Cleve., 1984-85, dir. strategic studies, 1986; divsn. mgr. Brit. Petroleum, Ltd., London, 1987-88; v.p., gen. mgr. U.S. gas bus. BP Exploration, Houston, 1989, v.p., gen. mgr. tech., 1990; v.p. BP Exploration, Anchorage, 1991-94; pres., CEO BP Pipelines, Anchorage, 1991-94; pres. Marya Resources, 1994—; v.p. MAPCO, 1996; pres. Tesoro Marine Svcs., 1996—. mem. devel. coun. Tex. Children's Hosp. Mem. C Club of Houston, Houston Racquet Club. Avocations: running, weight lifting, reading. Office: 9426 Telephone Rd Houston TX 77075-2020

NYBERG, STANLEY ERIC, cognitive scientist; b. Boston, Jan. 30, 1948; s. Leroy Milton and Anna Maria (Olson) N. PhD, SUNY, Stony Brook, 1975; M of Pub. and Pvt. Mgmt., Yale U., 1984. Postdoctoral fellowship U. Calif., Berkeley, 1975-76; asst. prof. North Pk. Coll., Chgo., 1976-79, Barnard Coll., Columbia U., N.Y.C., 1979-82; sys. mgmt. Interactive Data Corp., Lexington, Mass., 1984-88, Dept. of Revenue, Commonwealth of Mass., Boston, 1988—; bd. dirs. Children's Home of Cromwell, Conn. Co-author: Human Memory: An Introduction to Research and Theory, 1982. Bd. dirs. Childrens Home of Cromwell, Conn., 1988-94, Decade Fund, Yale U. Sch. Mgmt., 1984-85; ch. coun. Luth. Ch. of Redeemer, Woburn, Mass., 1991-97, West Roxbury Rugby Football Club, 1984-87, v.p., sec. L Street Running Club, South Boston, 1987—; mem. divsn. ecumenism New Eng. Synod, Evang. Luth. Ch. in Am., 1997—. Fellow Am. Psychol. Soc.; mem. Soc. for Applied Rsch. in Memory and Cognition, Eastern Psychol. Assn., Midwestern Psychol. Assn., Am. Psychol. Assn. Home: PO Box 1849 GMF Boston MA 02205

NYCE, DAVID SCOTT, electronics company executive; b. Norristown, Pa., Jan. 25, 1952; s. Jonathan J. and Emma R. (Dusza) N.; m. Gwen Ann Gordon, Apr. 26, 1975; children: Timothy S., Christopher D., Megan S. BSEE, Temple U., 1973. Cert. pvt. pilot; cert. firearms instr. N.C. Project engr. Robinson-Halpern Co., Plymouth Meeting, Pa., 1973-77; sr. devel. engr. Honeywell, Ft. Washington, Pa., 1977-78; chief engr. Chatlos Systems, Inc., Whippany, N.J., 1978-79; mgr. engring. Environ. Tectonics Corp., Southampton, Pa., 1979-80; v.p., dir. engring. Neutronics, Inc., Exton, Pa., 1980-90; dir. engring. measurement and automation group MTS Systems Corp., Research Triangle Park, N.C., 1990—; cons. in field; proprietor Nyce Sporting Equipment, Apex, N.C., 1985—, Nyce Sounds, Trappe, Pa., 1987-90. Tchr. aerodynamics and rocketry Apex Sch. System, 1990—; merit badge counselor Boy Scouts Am. Recipient Vaaler award Chem. Engring. Mag., 1988. Mem. AAAS, Aircraft Owners and Pilots Assn., Instrument Soc. Am. (sr.), NRA (life, cert. instr., sharpshooter), Lower Providence Rod and Gun Club (capt. pistol team 1987-89, high on team 1988-89), U.S. Hang Gliding Assn., U.S. Parachute Assn., U.S. Judo Assn. (brown belt), Nat. Assn. Rocketry, Nat. Trappers Assn., Acad. Model Aero., The Planetary Soc., Tripoli Rocketry Assn. Achievements include patents for low power magnetostriction, threshold compensating detector, bandwidth limiting, densimeter. Office: MTS Systems Corp Sensors Divsn 3001 Sheldon Dr Cary NC 27513-2006

NYCE, ROBERT EUGENE, state legislator, tax accountant; b. Allentown, Pa., Oct. 14, 1946; s. Preston Nyce and Flora Louise (Beck) Jones; m. Maria Irene Datta, Oct. 3, 1970; 1 child, Jennifer. BA in Acctg., Moravian Coll. Tax acct. Lehigh Portland Cement Co., 1970-72; mgr. credit, taxes & ins. Frick Co., 1973-75; sr. tax acct. Bethlehem Steel Corp., 1975-85; asst. v.p., tax dir. Chrysler First, Inc., 1985-90; mem. Ho. of Reps. Commonwealth of Pa., Harrisburg, 1990-96; mem. edn. com., mem. spl. sub-com. Ho. Resdl. 37, higher edn. and basic edn. subcoms., fin. com., chmn. spl. task force on local tax reform, 1995-96, game & fish, policy com., Gov.'s motor carrier adv. bd., 1991-92, 93-94, 95-96; mem. tuition account adv. bd., 1993-94, 95-96. Mem. Northampton (Pa.) Sch. Bd., 1984-90, pres., 1987-89, v.p., 1986-87; mem. Bethlehem Area Vo-Tech Joint Com., 1984-90, chmn., 1986-87, vice chmn., 1985-86, 88-89; mem. East Allen Twp. Mcpl. Authority, 1979-84, former chmn.; Rep. candidate auditor gen. of Pa., 1996. Mem. Masons, Lehigh Consistory, Rajah Temple, Star Grange, Am. Legion, East Bath Rod & Gun Club, Pa. Soc. Republican. Lutheran. Avocations: fishing, tennis, skiing, cars. Home: 7416 Carol Ln Northampton PA 18067-9074 Office: 333 Market St Fl 14 Harrisburg PA 17101-2210

NYCKLEMOE, GLENN WINSTON, bishop; b. Fergus Falls, Minn., Dec. 8, 1936; s. Melvin and Bertha (Sumstad) N.; m. Ann Elizabeth Olson, May 28, 1960; children: Peter Glenn, John Winston, Daniel Thomas. BA, St. Olaf Coll., 1958; MDiv, Luther Theol. Sem., St. Paul, 1962; D of Ministry, Luth. Sch. Theology, Chgo., 1977. Ordained to ministry Am. Luth. Ch., 1962. Assoc. pastor Our Savior's Luth. Ch., Valley City, N.D., 1962-64; assoc. pastor Our Savior's Luth. Ch., Milw., 1964-67, co-pastor, 1967-73; sr. pastor Our Savior's Luth. Ch., Beloit, Wis., 1973-82, St. Olaf Luth. Ch., Austin, Minn., 1982-88; bishop Southeastern Minn. Synod, Evang. Luth. Ch. in Am., Rochester, 1988—; bd. dirs. Luth. Social Svcs. of Minn., Mpls., Bd. of Social Ministries, St. Paul, Minn. Coun. Chs., Mpls. Mem. bd. regents St. Olaf Coll., Northfield, Minn., 1988—. Avocations: skiing, trap shooting, golf. Office: SE Minn Synod Evang Luth Ch Am Assist Heights Box 4900 Rochester MN 55903

NYCUM, SUSAN HUBBELL, lawyer. B.A., Ohio Wesleyan U., 1956; J.D., Duquesne U., 1960; postgrad., Stanford U. Bar: Pa. 1962, U.S. Supreme Ct. 1967, Calif. 1974. Sole practice law Pitts., 1962-65; designer, adminstr. legal rsch. sys. U. Pitts., Aspen Sys. Corp., Pitts., 1965-68; mgr. ops. Computer Ctr., Carnegie Mellon U., Pitts., 1968-69; dir. computer facility Computer Ctr., Stanford U., Calif., 1969-72, Stanford Law and Computer fellow, 1972-73; cons. in computers and law, 1973-74; sr. assoc. MacLeod, Fuller, Muir & Godwin, Los Altos, Los Angeles and London, 1974-75; ptnr. Chickering & Gregory, San Francisco, 1975-80; ptnr.-in-charge high tech. group Gaston Snow & Ely Bartlett, Boston, NYC, Phoenix, San Francisco, Calif., 1980-86; mng. ptnr. Palo Alto office Kadison, Pfaelzer, Woodard, Quinn & Rossi, Los Angeles, Washington, Newport Beach, Palo Alto, Calif., 1986-87; sr. ptnr., chmn. U.S. IP/IT practice group Baker & McKenzie, Palo Alto, 1987—, mem. U.S. leadership team, 1987-96, mem. Asia Pacific regional coun., 1995—; trustee EDUCOM, 1978-81; mem. adv. com. for high tech. Ariz. State U. Law Sch., Santa Clara U. Law Sch., Stanford Law Sch., U. So. Calif. Law Ctr., law sch. Harvard U., U. Calif.; U.S. State Dept. del. OECD Conf. on Nat. Vulnerabilities, Spain, 1981; invited speaker Telecom, Geneva, 1983; lectr. N.Y. Law Jour., 1975—, Law & Bus., 1975—, Practicing Law Inst., 1975—; chmn. Office of Tech. Assessment Task Force on Nat. Info. Sys., 1979-80. Author:(with Bigelow) Your Computer and the Law, 1975, (with Bosworth) Legal Protection for Software, 1985, (with Collins and Gilbert) Women Leading, 1987; contbr. monographs, articles to profl. publs. Mem. Town of Portola Valley Open Space Acquisition Com., Calif., 1977; mem. Jr. League of Palo Alto, chmn. evening div., 1975-76. NSF and Dept. Justice grantee for studies on computer abuse, 1972—. Mem. ABA (chmn. sect. on sci. and tech. 1979-80), Internat. Bar Assn. (U.S. mem. computer com. of corps. sect.), Assn. Computing Machinery (mem. at large of coun. 1976-80, nat. lectr. 1977—, chmn. standing com. on legal issues 1975—, mem. blue ribbon com. on rationalization of internat. proprietary rights protection on info. processing devel. in the '90s, 1990—), Computer Law Assn. (v.p. 1983-85, pres. 1986—, bd. dirs. 1975—), Calif. State Bar Assn. (founder first chmn. econs. of law sect., vice chmn. law and computers com.), Nat. Conf. Lawyers and Scientists (rep. ABA), Strategic Forum on Intellectual Property Issues in Software of NAS. Home: 35 Granada Ct Portola Vally CA 94028-7736 Office: Baker & McKenzie PO Box 60309 Palo Alto CA 94306

NYDICK, DAVID, school superintendent; b. N.Y.C., Feb. 10, 1929; s. Irving and Minnie (Bilibom) N.; m. Gilda Pivnick, June 14, 1953; children: Leslie Ruth, Jay Scott. BA, NYU, 1950, MA, 1952, profl. Diploma, 1960, postgrad., 1960—. Tchr. pub. schs., Great Neck, N.Y., 1954-60; prin. asst. supt. Princeton Pub. Schs., N.J., 1961-65; asst. supt. Jericho Pub. Schs., N.Y., 1965-68, supt., 1968-84; exec. dir. Guide Dog Found., Smithtown, N.Y., 1984-89; supt. Syosset (N.Y.) Pub. Schs., 1989-90, Bethpage (N.Y.) Pub. Schs., 1991—; assoc. prof. L.I. U., 1975—, Hofstra U., 1976—, Pace U., 1978—; asst. prof. Bklyn. Coll., 1979—; arbitrator Am. Arbitration Assn., Better Bus. Bur., Nat. Assn. Securities Dealers, N.Y. Stock Exchange, various N.Y. state agys. Syndicated columnist UPI, Copley News, DANY News, 1962—. Pres., East Plains Mental Health Ctr., 1964—. Served with U.S. Army, 1952-54. Recipient Edn. Achievement award NCCJ, 1975. Mem. N.Y.U. Alumni Assn. (pres. 1971-72), Am. Assn. Sch. Adminstrs., Ednl. Writers Assn., Overseas Press Club, Nat. Press Club, Masons. Home and Office: 22 Lesley Dr Syosset NY 11791-5222

NYDLE, NANCY EVE, clinical nursing educator, critical care nurse; b. Ottumwa, Iowa, Sept. 23, 1946; d. Francis Vernon and Luana Elizabeth (Walker) N. RN diploma, St. Joseph Hosp. Sch. Nursing, Ottumwa, 1968; BSN, Graceland Coll. CCRN, RN, Iowa; cert. BLS, ACLS. Staff nurse St. Francis Hosp., Waterloo, Iowa, 1968-69, head nurse CCU, 1969-71; staff nurse ICU Mt. Zion Hosp., San Francisco, 1971-76, supr. ICU, 1976-79, staff devel. ICU, 1979-80, day shift charge RN ICU, 1980-82; supr. ICU Lake Havasu Regional Hosp., Lake Havasu City, Ariz., 1982-85; staff nurse MICU U. Iowa Hosps. and Clinics, Iowa City, 1985-86; staff nurse ICU Ottumwa Regional Health Ctr., 1986—; clin. nursing instr. Indian Hills C.C., Ottumwa, 1989-95; adj. faculty Mohave C.C., Lake Havasu City, 1983-84; mem. Indian Hills C.C. faculty senate, Ottumwa, 1992-95, sec.-treas., 1993-94. Mem. AACN. Democrat. Home and Office: 227 E Main St Agency IA 52530-0193

NYE, DANIEL WILLIAM, elementary school educator; b. Harrisburg, Pa., Apr. 14, 1942; s. Daniel J. and Clarice L. (Stonesifer) N.; m. Carol A. Stewart, Aug. 10, 1968; 1 child, Michael S. BS in Health Edn., West Chester (Pa.) U., 1964; MEd in Elem. Edn., Towson (Md.) U., 1970. Cert. tchr., Md. Tchr. phys. edn. elem. sch. Harford County Pub. Schs., Bel Air, Md., 1964-72, 74—, tchr. phys. edn. mid. sch., 1972-73; rep. United Rep. Life Ins. Co., Harrisburg, Pa., 1981-85. Mem. AAHPERD, NEA, Md. State Tchrs. Assn., Harford County Edn. Assn., Md. chpt. AAHPERD. Republican. Avocations: avid golfer, antique car collector and restorer, stamp collector. Home: 1119 Carrs Mill Rd Bel Air MD 21014-2414 Office: Harford County Pub Schs 45 E Gordon St Bel Air MD 21014-2915

NYE, EDWIN PACKARD, mechanical engineering educator; b. Atkinson, N.H., Jan. 29, 1920; s. Eben W. and Gertrude Florence (Dunn) N.; m. Persephone Fern Drumheller, Aug. 12, 1944; children: David Edwin, Sarah Leone, Benjamin Alfred. BS with high honor, U. N.H., 1941; ScM, Harvard U., 1947. Registered profl. engr., Pa., Conn. Service engr. Bailey Meter Co., Cleve., 1941-42; instr. mech. engring. U. N.H., 1942-44; project engr. NACA, 1944-46; from instr. to assoc. prof. mech. engring. Pa. State U., 1947-59; Hallden prof. Trinity Coll., Hartford, Conn., 1959-83; chmn. dept. engring. Trinity Coll., 1960-70, dean of faculty, 1970-79; pres. Charter Oak Coll., 1989; sec. Univ. Research Inst. Conn., 1964-68, pres., 1968-71, chmn., 1971-74; bd. dir. Hallden Machine Co.; chmn. coll. work Episcopal Diocese Conn., 1960-64. Co-author: Steam Power Plants, 1952, Power Plants, 1956,

Thermal Engineering, 1959. Mem. bd. edn., Bloomfield, Conn., 1961-65; mem. State Bd. Acad. Awards, 1974-94, dean faculty, 1979-83; corporator Hartford Pub. Libr., 1978-82. Mem. ASME, Am. Soc. Engring. Edn., Conn. Acad. Sci. and Engring., Phi Kappa Phi, Pi Tau Sigma. Home: Bug Hill Rd Ashfield MA 01330

NYE, ERIC WILLIAM, English language and literature educator; b. Omaha, July 31, 1952; s. William Frank and Mary Roberta (Lueder) N.; m. Carol Denison Frost, Dec. 21, 1980; children: Charles William, Ellen Mary. BA, St. Olaf Coll., 1974; MA, U. Chgo., 1976, PhD, 1983; postgrad., Queens' Coll., Cambridge, England, 1979-82. Tutor in coll. writing com. U. Chgo., 1976-79, tchg. intern, 1978; tutor Am. lit. Cambridge (Eng.) U., 1979-82; asst. prof. English U. Wyo., Laramie, 1983-89, assoc. prof., 1989—; v.p., bd. dirs. Plainview Tel. Co., Nebr.; hon. vis. fellow U. Edinburgh (Scotland) Inst. for Advanced Studies in the Humanities, 1987; guest lectr. NEH summer Inst., Laramie, Wyo., 1985, Carlyle Soc. of Edinburgh, 1987, Wordsworth summer Conf., Grasmere, Eng., 1988, cons. NEH. Contbr. articles and reviews to profl. jours. Mem. Am. Friends of Cambridge U., Gen. Soc. Mayflower Descendants; elected mem. Wyo. Coun. for Humanities, 1992-96, mem. exec. com., 1993-94; mem. adv. bd. Wyo. Ctr. for the Book, 1995—. Named Nat. Merit Scholar St. Olaf Coll., 1970-74; recipient Grad. Fellowship, Rotary Found., 1979-80, grant Am. Coun. of Learned Socs., 1988, Disting. Alumnus award, Lincoln (Neb.) E. High Sch., 1986. Mem. MLA (del. assembly 1991-93), Assn. for Documentary Editing, Biblog. Soc. London, Assn. for Computers and the Humanities, Assn. for Lit. and Linguistic Computing, Coleridge Soc. (life), Friends of Dove Cottage (life), Charles Lamb Soc., Carlyle Soc., Rsch. Soc. for Victorian Periodicals, Soc. for History of Authorship, Reading and Pub., The Victorians Inst., Gen. Soc. Mayflower Descs., The Tennyson Soc., Penn Club (London), Queens Coll. Club (Cambridge) Phi Beta Kappa (pres., v.p., sec. Wyo. chpt. 1988—). Home: 1495 Apache Dr Laramie WY 82070-6966 Office: U Wyo Dept English PO Box 3353 Laramie WY 82071-3353

NYE, ERLE ALLEN, utilities executive, lawyer; b. Ft. Worth, June 23, 1937; s. Ira Benjamen N.; m. Alice Ann Grove, June 5, 1959; children: Elizabeth Nye Janzen, Pamela Nye Schneider, Erle Allen Jr., Edward Kyle, Johnson Scott. BEE, Tex. A&M U., 1959; JD, So. Meth. U., 1965. With Dallas Power & Light Co., 1960-75, v.p., 1975-80; exec. v.p. Tex. Utilities Co., Dallas, 1980-87, pres., 1987—, CEO and pres., 1995—; pres. Chaco Energy Co., Dallas, 1994-96, CEO, 1996—; pres. Tex. Utilities Mining Co., Dallas, 1982-96, CEO, 1996—; CEO Tex. Utilities Svcs., Inc., Dallas, 1982—; chmn. bd., CEO Tex. Utilities Electric Co., Dallas, 1987—; CEO Basic Resources Inc., Dallas, 1994—, Chaco Energy Co., Dallas, 1994—, TU Svcs., 1982—, Tex. Utilities Commn., Dallas, 1995—; pres. Tex. Utilities Fuel Co., 1982—; chmn. Tex. Utilities Australia Pty., Ltd., 1996—. Bd. dirs. Dallas Bar Found., 1980-83, Dallas Cen. Bus. Plan Com., 1980-83, Inroads/Dallas-Ft. Worth Inc., 1984-88, trustee Baylor Dental Coll., Dallas, 1985-94; mem. Dallas Together Forum, 1989—, Dallas Com. Fgn. Rels., 1991—, Bd. of Boys & Girls Clubs of Am., 1991—; The Dallas Found., 1994—; The Science Pl., Dallas, 1995—; The Salvation Army's Dallas County Adv. Bd., 1995—. Mem. ABA, Dallas Bar Assn., Tex. State Bar Assn., Dallas C. of C. (bd. dirs. 1991-95, vice chmn. 1992-95). Methodist. Clubs: Engineers (pres. 1982-83), Northwood (Dallas). Home: 6924 Desco Dallas TX 75225-1716 Office: Texas Utilities Company 41st Floor 1601 Bryan St Fl 41 Dallas TX 75201-3402

NYE, GENE WARREN, art educator; b. Sacramento, July 3, 1939; s. Charles Frederick and Dorthy Dell Nye; m. Alena Mae Nye, Sept. 20, 1974; children: Dirk, Ronni, Anthony, Timothy. AA, American River Coll., Sacramento, 1962; AB, Sacramento State U., 1964; cert. Secondary Art Tchr., U. Calif., Berkeley, 1966. Printer Roseville (Calif.) Press Tribune, 1957-60; typographer Oakland (Calif.) Tribune, 1960-65; tchr. art Long Beach (Calif.) Unified Sch. Dist., 1965-67; tchr., chair art dept. Woodland (Calif.) Unified Sch. Dist., 1967—; freelance artist Wildcat Art, Sacramento, 1985—; cons. N.Mex. Ctrl. Coun. Student Activities, 1991; workshop presenter. Author: (workbook set and video) Posters Made EZ, 1990. Mem. task force Constn. Revision of CADA, L.A., 1988-89. Named to Calif. Assn. Dirs. of Activities Hall of Fame, 1992. Mem. NEA (life), Calif. Tchrs. Assn., Woodland Edn. Assn. (v.p. 1971-72), Calif. Art Edn. Assn., Nat. Art Edn. Assn., Calif. League Mid. Schs., U. Calif.-Berkeley Alumni Assn. (life). Home: 2200 Eastern Ave Sacramento CA 95864-0805 Office: Lee Jr HS 520 West St Woodland CA 95695-3705

NYE, JOHN CALVIN, agricultural engineer, educator; b. Anthony, Kans., Mar. 24, 1945; s. Paul Everet and Alice Anna (Schmidt) N.; m. Gloria Tara Giese, Dec. 8, 1974; children: Donn, Paul, Jaffe. BS in Agrl. Engring., Kans. State U., 1968; MS in Agrl. Engring., Purdue U., 1970, PhD, 1971. Registered profl. engr., La., Ind., Del. Asst. prof. Purdue U., West Lafayette, Ind., 1971-73, assoc. prof., then prof., 1975-84; chief agrl. permit team region V U.S. EPA, Chgo., 1974-75; prof., head agrl. engring. dept. La. State U., Baton Rouge, 1984-91; dean Coll. of Agrl. Scis. U. Del., Newark, 1991—; chair joint coun. food and agrl. sci. USDA, 1994-95; bd. dirs. Accreditation Bd. Engring. and Tech., Delmarva Poultry Industries, Inc. Bd. dirs. La. Sci. and Engring. Fair, Baton Rouge, 1986-91. 1st lt. U.S. Army, 1971. Recipient Disting. Svc. award La. Acad. Sci., 1990, Professionalism award La. Engring. Found., 1990. Fellow Am. Soc. Agrl. Engrs. Home: 204 Wilson Rd Newark DE 19711-3629 Office: U Del Coll Agrl Scis 133 Townsend Rd Newark DE 19717-7905

NYE, JOSEPH S(AMUEL), JR., government studies educator, administrator; b. N.J., Jan. 19, 1937; s. Joseph S. and Else (Ashwell) N.; m. Molly Harding, June 10, 1961; children—John Bundy, Joseph Benjamin, Daniel Tupper. A.B. in Pub. Affairs, Princeton U., 1958; B.A. in Philosophy, Politics and Econs., Oxford U., Eng., 1960; Ph.D. in Polit. Sci., Harvard U., 1964. Prof. govt. Harvard U., Cambridge, Mass., 1969—, dir. Ctr. for Internat. Affairs, assoc. dean internat. rels.; dep. undersec. Dept. State, Washington, 1977-79, cons., 1979; cons. Dept. Energy, Washington, 1979; U.S. rep. UN Adv. Bd. on Disarmament; chmn. Nat. Intelligence Coun., 1992—. Co-author: Power and Interdependence, 1977; author: Nuclear Ethics, 1986, Understanding International Conflict, 1993; editor, co-author: The Making of America's Soviet Policy, 1984, Hawks, Doves and Owls, 1985; co-editor: Fateful Visions, 1988, Bound to Lead: The Changing Nature of American Power, 1990. Recipient Disting. Honor award Dept. State, 1979; Rhodes scholar Oxford U., 1958-60. Fellow Am. Acad. Arts and Scis., Aspen Inst. (sr.); mem. Internat. Inst. Strategic Studies (council), Coun. Fgn. Rels., Trilateral Commn., Am. Acad. Diplomacy. Office: Harvard U CSIA Ctr for Internat Affairs 737 Cambridge St Cambridge MA 02141-1428

NYE, THOMAS RUSSELL, retired drafting, reproduction and surveying company executive; b. Arlington, Mass., July 16, 1928; s. Russell Van Buren and Sibyl (Partridge) N.; m. Patricia Bentley, Dec. 14, 1951; children: Bradford V. B., Debra Nye Moran. AB, Brown U., 1950; MBA, Harvard U., 1952. Salesman Russell Nye Co., Inc., Boston, 1951-52; assignment dir., sr. assoc. Bruce Payne & Assocs., N.Y.C., 1953-59; with Keuffel & Esser Co., Morristown, N.J., 1959-84, exec. v.p., 1970, pres., 1970-82, chief exec. officer, 1971-82; bd. dirs. J.K. Adams Co., Inc.; arbitrator N.Y. Stock Exch., Nat. Assn. Securities Dealers. Author articles. Bd. dirs. United Way, Madison, N.J., 1968-73, Madison YMCA, 1970-72; mem. corp. United Way Morris County, 1973-91; mem. adv. bd. R & D Coun. N.J., 1980-88, Morristown Meml. Hosp. Corp., 1985-91. Lt. USAF, 1952-53. Mem. Assn. Reproduction Materials Mfrs. (pres. 1978, bd. dirs.), Am. Mgmt. Assn., NAM, Internat. Assn. Blueprinters and Allied Industries, Am. Congress Mapping and Surveying, Soc. Advancement Mgmt., Lake Sunapee Country Club, Boca Grande Club, Morris County Golf Club. Baptist. Home: PO Box 936 The Seasons New London NH 03257

NYE, W. MARCUS W., lawyer; b. N.Y.C., Aug. 3, 1945; s. Walter R. and Nora (McLaren) N.; m. Eva Johnson; children: Robbie, Stephanie, Philip, Jennifer. BA, Harvard U., 1967; JD, U. Idaho, 1974. Bar: Idaho 1974, U.S. Dist. Ct. Idaho 1974, U.S. Ct. Appeals (9th cir.) 1980; lic. pilot. Ptnr. Racine, Olson, Nye, Cooper & Budge, Pocatello, Idaho, 1974—; vis. prof. law U. Idaho, Moscow, 1984; adj. prof. Coll. Engring. Idaho State U., 1993—; bd. dirs. Idaho State U. Found. Recipient Alumni Svc. award U. Idaho, 1988. Fellow ABA (mem. ho. dels. 1988—, state chmn. ho. of dels. 1991—, bd. of govs. 1997—), Am. Bar Found. (stat. chmn. 1992-95); mem. Am. Bd. Trial Advs., Am. Coll. Trial Lawyers, Idaho Bar Assn. (commr. 1985—, pres. bd. commrs. 1987-88), Idaho Def. Counsel Assn. (pres. 1982), Idaho State Centennial Found. (commr. 1985-90), 6th Dist. Bar Assn. (pres. 1982). Avocation: flying. Home: 173 S 15th Ave Pocatello ID 83201-4056 Office: Racine Olson Nye Cooper & Budge PO Box 1391 Pocatello ID 83204-1391

NYENHUIS, JACOB EUGENE, college official; b. Mille Lacs County, Minn., Mar. 25, 1935; s. Egbert Peter and Rosa (Walburg) N.; m. Leona Mae Van Duyn, June 6, 1956; children: Karen Joy, Kathy Jean, Lorna Jane, Sarah Van Duyn. AB in Greek, Calvin Coll., 1956; AM in Classics, Stanford U., 1961, PhD in Classics, 1963. Asst. in classical langs. Calvin Coll., Grand Rapids, Mich., 1957-59; acting instr. Stanford (Calif.) U., 1962; from asst. prof. to prof. Wayne State U., Detroit, 1962-75, dir. honors program, 1964-75, chmn. Greek and Latin dept., 1965-75; prof. classics, dean for humanities Hope Coll., Holland, Mich., 1975-78, dean for arts and humanities, 1978-84, provost, 1984—; cons. Mich. Dept. Edn., Lansing, 1971-72, Gustavus Adolphus Coll., St. Peter, Minn., 1974, Northwestern Coll., Orange City, Iowa, 1983, Whitworth Coll., Spokane, Wash., 1987, The Daedalus Project, 1988; reviewer NEH, Washington, 1986-87, panelist, 1991; reviewer Lilly Endowment, Indpls., 1987-89, U.S. Dept. Edn., 1993; vis. assoc. prof. U. Calif., Santa Barbara, 1967-68, Ohio State U., Columbus, 1972; vis. rsch. prof. Am. Sch. Classical Studies, Athens, Greece, 1973-74, also mem. mng. com.; vis. scholar Green Coll. Oxford U., 1989. Co-author: Latin Via Ovid, 1977, rev. edit., 1982; editor: Petronius: Cena Trimalchionis, 1970, Plautus: Amphitruo, 1970; articles in field. Elder Christian Reformed Ch., Palo Alto, Calif., 1960-62; elder, clk. Christian Reformed Ch., Grosse Pointe, Mich., 1964-67; elder, clk. Christian Reformed Ch., Holland, Mich., 1976-85, v.p., 1988-91, mem. exec. com., 1994-95; chmn. human rels. coun. Open Housing Com., Grosse Pointe, 1971-73. Mem. Am. Philol. Assn., Danforth Assocs. (chmn. regional com. 1975-77), Mich. Coun. for Humanities (bd. dirs., 1976-84, 88-92, chmn. 1980-82, 96-99, Disting. Svc. award 1984), Nat. Fedn. State Humanities Couns. (bd. dirs. 1979-84, pres. 1981-83), Gt. Lakes Colls. Assn. (bd. dirs. 1991-93), Coun. on Undergrad. Rsch. (councilor-at-large 1993—). Democrat. Avocations: photography, carpentry, cross-country skiing. Home: 51 E 8th St Ste 200 Holland MI 49423-3501 Office: Hope Coll Office of the Provost 141 E 12th St PO Box 9000 Holland MI 49422-9000

NYERE, ROBERT ALAN, banker; b. Aberdeen, Wash., July 19, 1917; s. George Louis and Augusta (Draheim) N.; m. Jeanne Fortier, Nov. 8, 1941; children: Sharon L. Nyere Olson, Barbara J. Nyere Slevin. B.A., U. Wash., 1939; M.B.A., Harvard U., 1941; grad., Stonier Sch. Banking, Rutgers U., 1951. With First Nat. Bank of Boston, 1941-79, asst. mgr., mgr., asst. v.p., 1948-58, v.p., 1958-69, sr. v.p., 1969-79; global dir. Mastercard Internat. Corp., FNBC Acceptance Corp., 1st La. Acceptance Corp., Boston Trust & Savs., Ltd.; cons., dir. Credit Card Services Corp., Springfield, Va., 1981-83; mem. Sr. Corps Ret. Execs., SBA, 1980-85. Served from ensign to lt. USNR, 1942-46. Fellow U. Ky., 1995. Mem. Algonquin Club, U. Ky. Faculty Club, The Lexington Club, The Lafayette Club, Spindletop Hall U. Ky., Masons (32 deg.), Shriners, Alpha Kappa Psi. Episcopalian. Home: 4922 Hartland Pky Lexington KY 40515-1109

NYERGES, ALEXANDER LEE, museum director; b. Rochester, N.Y., Feb. 27, 1957; s. Sandor Elek and Lena (Angeline) N.; 1 child, Robert Angeline. BA, George Washington U., 1979, MA, 1981. Intern The Octagon, Washington, 1976-79; archeol. asst. Smithsonian Instn., Washington, 1977, curatorial intern Nat. Mus. Am. History, 1978-79; adminstrv. asst. George Washington U., Washington, 1979-81; exec. dir. DeLand Mus. Art, Fla., 1981-85, Miss. Mus. Art, Jackson, 1985-92; dir. Dayton (Ohio) Art Inst., 1992—; grants panel Nat. Endowment for the Arts, 1988—; field surveyor Inst. Mus. Svcs., Washington, 1985-88, nat. review panel, 1990-92; treas., bd. dirs. Volusia County Arts Coun., Daytona Beach, Fla., 1983-85. Contbr. articles to profl. jours. Bd. dirs. West Volusia Hist. Soc., 1984-85; pres. Miss. Inst. Arts and Letters, 1987-88; trustee Cultural Arts Ctr., DeLand, 1984-85, Miami Valley Cultural Alliance, 1993—, Intermus. Conservation Lab., 1993—, Montgomery county arts and culture district, 1994—. U.S. Dept. Edn. scholar, 1973. Mem. DeLand Area C. of C. (bd. dirs., tourist adv. com. 1984-85), Assn. Art Mus. Dirs., Am. Assn. Mus. (SE regional rep. to nonprint media com. 1983-85, nat. legis. com. 1986-93), Miss. Mus. Assn., Assn. Art Mus. Dirs., Southeastern Mus. Conf. (bd. dirs. 1991-92), Fla. Mus. Assn., Fla. Art Mus. Dirs. Assn., Cultural Roundtable (pres. 1993—), Ohio Mus. Assn. (trustee 1993—), Phi Beta Kappa. Avocations: restoring old houses, gardening, music, writing, sports, scuba diving. Home: 1719 Auburn Ave Dayton OH 45406-4513 Office: Dayton Art Inst 456 Belmonte Park N Dayton OH 45405-4700

NYERGES, GEORGE LADISLAUS, lawyer; b. Cleve., Aug. 27, 1925; s. Constantine L. and Irene (Schneider) N.; m. Joanne Mayo, Aug. 2, 1958; children: James George, Susan Joanne. BS, Case Western Reserve U., 1946; LLB, Cleveland-Marshall Law Sch., 1951, LLM, 1956; JD, Cleve. State U., 1969. Bar: Ohio 1951, U.S. Dist. Ct. (no. dist.) Ohio 1954, U.S. Ct. Appeals (6th cir.) 1985, U.S. Supreme Ct. 1991; lic. USCG. Lawyer, sole practice Cleve., 1951—; lectr. legal and med. ethics Cuyahoga C.C., Cleve., 1989; pvt. and ct. interpreter Hungarian lang., 1955—; ind. real estate broker, Ohio, 1960—; cons. to various religious groups, 1985—. Mem. Magyar Club of Cleve., 1952—, sec., 1954-57, pres. 1958; mem. "Night in Budapest Com." in Cleve., 1958-65, Vermilion (Ohio) Yacht Club, 1973—, sec., 1974-76; coach girls baseball Summer Recreational Jr. Girls Baseball, Westlake, Ohio, 1980, coach boys football Fall Recreational Jr. Boys Football, Westlake, 1980-82; former precinct committeeman Dem. Party, Westlake, 1990. Recipient Cert., Am. Judicature Soc., 1961, Plaque Am. Arbitration Assn., 1970, Cert. of Appreciation, Cleve. Bar Assn., 1987-88. Mem. ATLA, ABA, FBA, Ohio State Bar Assn. (Cert. of Appreciation 1991). Democrat. Presbyterian. Avocations: former comdr., including lesser chairs and charter mem. of Rocky River Power Squadron. Home: 1999 Dover Center Rd Westlake OH 44145-3151 Office: United Office Bldg 2012 W 25th St Ste 803 Cleveland OH 44113-4131

NYGAARD, RICHARD LOWELL, federal judge; b. 1940. BS cum laude, U. So. Calif., 1969; JD, U. Mich. Mem. Orton, Nygaard & Dunlevy, 1972-81; judge Ct. Common Pleas, 6th Dist. Pa., Erie, 1981-88, U.S. Ct. Appeals (3d cir.) Pa., Erie, 1988—. Councilman Erie County, 1977-81. With USNR, 1958-64. Mem. ABA, Pa. Bar Assn., Erie County Bar Assn. Office: US Ct Appeals 3d Cir 500 First Nat Bank Bldg 717 State St Erie PA 16501-1341*

NYGAARD, THOMAS WILLIAM, cardiologist; b. Stavanger, Norway, Jan. 23, 1952; s. Isak and Bernice (Thomas) N.; m. Ellen Gebhardt, Aug. 9, 1980; children: Anna K., Gretchen E., Erik T. BS in Chemistry, Vanderbilt U., 1974, MD, 1978. Diplomate Nat. Bd. Med. Examiners, Am. Bd. Internal Medicine, Cardiovascular Disease. Intern in internal medicine Johns Hopkins Hosp., Balt., 1978-79, resdient in internal medicine, 1979-81; fellow in cardiovascular diseases U. Va. Hosp., Charlottesville, 1981-83, asst. prof., internal medicine, 1983-86; dir. cardiac cath. lab. Lynchburg (Va.) Gen. Hosp., 1986—; chief of staff Cen. Health/Lynchburg Gen. and VA Hosp., 1992, also bd. dirs. Contbr. articles to profl. jours. and publs. Recipient Weinstein prize in medicine, Vanderbilt U., 1978, Amos Christie prize in pediatrics, 1978, others. Fellow Am. Coll. Cardiology, Am. Coll. Physicians, Am. Heart Assn.; mem. John Hopkins Med. and Surg. Assn., Phi Beta Kappa, Alpha Omega Alpha. Office: Cardiology Assocs Ctrl Va 2215 Landover Pl Lynchburg VA 24501

NYGARD, HOLGER OLOF, English and folklore educator; b. Vasa, Finland, Feb. 24, 1921; came to U.S., 1953, naturalized, 1958; s. Victor N. and Maria (Bergman) Nygard; m. Margaret C. Rodger, Oct. 11, 1944; Jennifer K., Stephen V., Kerstin M., Karl Erik. B.A., U. B.C., Vancouver, 1944; M.A., U. Calif.-Berkeley, 1949, Ph.D., 1955. Instr. U. B.C., 1945-47; asst. prof. U. Kans., Lawrence, 1953-57; assoc. prof. U. Tenn., Knoxville, 1957-60; prof. English Duke U., Durham, N.C., 1960-90, prof. emeritus, 1990—. Author: (Chgo. Folklore prize 1959) The Ballad of Heer Halewijn, 1958. Fellow Am. Council Learned Socs., 1952; Guggenheim fellow, 1966; fellow Inst. Advanced Studies Humanities, U. Edinburgh, Scotland, 1979; NEH fellow, 1980. Mem. Am. folklore Soc., MLA. Home: 4015 Cole Mill Rd Durham NC 27712-2907

NYHAN, WILLIAM LEO, pediatrician, educator; b. Boston, Mar. 13, 1926; s. W. Leo and Mary N.; m. Christine Murphy, Nov. 20, 1948; children: Christopher, Abigail. Student, Harvard U., 1943-45; M.D., Columbia U., 1949; M.S., U. Ill., 1956, Ph.D., 1958; hon. doctorate, Tokushima U., Japan, 1981. Intern Yale U.-Grace-New Haven Hosp., 1949-50, resident, 1950-51, 53-55; asst. prof. pediatrics Johns Hopkins U., 1958-61, assoc. prof., 1961-63; prof. pediatrics, biochemistry U. Miami, 1963-69, chmn. dept. pediatrics, 1963-69; prof. U. Calif., San Diego, 1969—; chmn. dept. pediatrics U. Calif., 1969-86; mem. FDA adv. com. on Teratogenic Effects of Certain Drugs, 1964-70; mem. pediatric panel AMA Council on Drugs, 1964-70; mem. Nat. Adv. Child Health and Human Devel. Council, 1967-71; mem. research adv. com. Calif. Dept. Mental Hygiene, 1969-72; mem. med. and sci. adv. com. Leukemia Soc. Am., Inc., 1968-72; mem. basic adv. com. Nat. Found. March of Dimes, 1973-81; mem. Basil O'Connor Starter grants com., 1973-93; mem. clin. cancer program project rev. com. Nat. Cancer Inst., 1977-81; vis. prof. extraordinario U. del Salvador (Argentina), 1982. Author: (with E. Edelson) The Heredity Factor, Genes, Chromosomes and You, 1976,Genetic & Malformation Syndromes in Clinical Medicine, 1976, Abnormalities in Amino Acid Metabolism in Clinical Medicine, 1984, Diagnostic Recognition of Genetic Disease, 1987, (with P. Ozan) Atlas of Metabolic Disease, 1997; editor: Amino Acid Metabolism and Genetic Variation, 1967, Heritable Disorders of Amino Acid Metabolism, 1974; mem. editorial bd. Jour. Pediatrics, 1964-78, King Faisal Hosp. Med. Jour., 1981-85, Western Jour. Medicine, 1974-86, Annals of Saudi Medicine, 1985-87, mem. editorial com. Ann. Rev. Nutrition, 1982-86; mem. editorial staff Med. and Pediatric Oncology, 1975-83. Served with U.S. Navy, 1944-46; U.S. Army, 1951-53. Nat. Found. Infantile Paralysis fellow, 1955-58; recipient Commemorative medallion Columbia U. Coll. Physicians and Surgeons, 1967. Mem. AAAS, Am. Fedn. Clin. Rsch., Am. Chem. Soc., Soc. Pediatric Rsch. (pres. 1970-71), Am. Assn. Cancer Rsch., Am. Soc. Pharmacology and Exptl. Therapeutics, Western Soc. Pediatric Rsch. (pres. 1976-77), N.Y. Acad. Sci., Am. Acad. Pediatrics (Borden award 1980), Am. Pediatric Soc., Am. Inst. Biol. Scis., Soc. Exptl. Biology and Medicine, Am. Soc. Clin. Investigation, Am. Soc. Human Genetics (dir. 1978-81), Am. Assn. Clin. Chemistry, Am. Coll. Human Genetics, Inst. Investigaciones Citologicas (Spain, corr.), Biochem. Soc., Société Française de Pediatrie (corr.), South African Human Genetics (hon.), Sigma Xi, Alpha Omega Alpha. Office: U Calif San Diego Dept Pediatrics #0830 9500 Gilman Dr La Jolla CA 92093-5003

NYHART, ELDON HOWARD, JR., biopharmaceuticist, biomedical engineer; b. Indpls., Nov. 19, 1955; s. Eldon H. Nyhart and Jane (Eaglesfield) Darlington; m. Deborah Elaine Fortune, Sept. 7, 1991. BS in Biomed. Engring., Vanderbilt U., 1978; PhD in Biopharmaceutics, Purdue U., 1984. Rsch. asst. Indpls. Ctr. for Advanced Rsch., Fortune-Fry Lab., 1978; rsch. asst./tchg. asst. dept. industrial and physical pharmacy Purdue U., West Lafayette, Ind., 1979-84; sr. scientist Eli Lilly and Co., Indpls., 1984—. Contbr. articles to profl. jours. Mem. Ind. Mus. Art, Indpls., 1992; amb. People to People Program, Washington, 1972. Recipient David Ross fellowship Purdue U., 1981-83. Mem. Am. Assn. Pharm. Scientists, Rho Chi, Sigma Xi, Alpha Tau Omega (pres. 1974), Univ. Club Indpls. Avocations: market timing, soccer. Home: 40 E Ash St Zionsville IN 46077-1402 Office: Eli Lilly and Co Lilly Clinic 1001 W 10th St Indianapolis IN 46202-2859

NYHUS, LLOYD MILTON, surgeon, educator; b. Mt. Vernon, Wash., June 24, 1923; s. Lewis Guttorm and Mary (Shervem) N.; m. Margaret Goldie Sheldon, Nov. 25, 1949; children: Sheila Margaret, Leif Torger. B.S., Pacific Luth. Coll., 1945; M.D., Med. Coll. Ala., 1947; Honoris Doctoris Causa, Aristotelian U., Thessalonika, Greece, 1968, Uppsala U., Sweden, 1974, U. Chihuahua, Mex., 1975, Jagallonian U., Cracow, Poland, 1980, U. Gama Filho, Rio de Janeiro, 1983, U. Louis Pasteur, Strasbourg, France, 1984, U. Athens, 1989. Diplomate Am. Bd. Surgery (chmn. 1974-76). Intern King County Hosp., Seattle, 1947-48; resident in surgery King County Hosp., 1948-55; practice medicine specializing in surgery Seattle, 1956-67, Chgo., 1967—; instr. surgery U. Wash., Seattle, 1954-56; asst. prof. U. Wash., 1956-59, assoc. prof., 1959-64, prof., 1964-67; Warren H. Cole prof., head dept. surgery U. Ill. Coll. Medicine, 1967-89, emeritus head, 1989—, prof. emeritus, 1993; emeritus surgeon-in-chief U. Ill. Hosp.; sr. cons. surgeon Cook County, West Side VA, Hines (Ill.) VA hosps.; cons. to Surgeon Gen. NIH, 1965-69. Author: Surgery of the Stomach and Duodenum, 1962, 4th edit., 1986, named changed to Surgery of the Esophagus, Stomach and Small Intestine, 5th edit., 1995, Hernia, 1964, 4th edit., 1995, Abdominal Pain: A Guide to Rapid Diagnosis, 1969, 95, Spanish edit., 1996, Manual of Surgical Therapeutics, 1969, latest rev. edit., 1996, Mastery of Surgery, 1984, 2d edit., 1992, 3rd edit., 1997, Surgery Ann., 1970-95, Treatment of Shock, 1970, 2d rev. edit., 1986, Surgery of the Small Intestine, 1987; editor-in-chief Rev. of Surgery, 1967-77, Current Surgery, 1978-90, emeritus editor, 1991—; assoc. editor Quar. Rev. Surgery, 1958-61; editl. bd. Am. Jour. Digestive Diseases, 1961-67, Scandinavian Jour. Gastroenterology, 1966—, Am. Surgeon, 1967-89, Jour. Surg. Oncology, 1969—, Archives of Surgery, 1977-86, World Jour. Surgery, 1977-95; contbr. articles to profl. jours. Served to lt. M.C. USNR, 1943-46, 50-52. Decorated Order of Merit (Poland); postdoctoral fellow USPHS, 1952-53; recipient M. Shipley award So. Surg. Assn., 1967, Rovsing medal Danish Surg. Soc., 1973; Disting. Faculty award U. Ill Coll. Medicine, 1983, Disting. Alumnus award Med. Coll. Ala., 1984, Disting. Alumnus award U. Wash., 1993; Guggenheim fellow, 1955-56. Fellow ACS (1st v.p. 1987-88), Assn. Surgeons Gt. Brit. and Ireland (hon.), Royal Coll. Surgeons Eng. (hon.), Royal Coll. Surgeons Ireland (hon.), Royal Coll. Surgeons Edinburgh (hon.), Royal Coll. Physicians and Surgeons Glasgow (hon.); mem. Am. Gastroent. Assn., Am. Physiol. Soc., Pacific Coast Surg. Assn., Am. Surg. Assn. (recorder 1976-81, 1st v.p. 1989-90), Western Surg. Assn., Ctrl. Soc. Clin. Rsch., Chgo. Surg. Soc. (pres. 1974), Ctrl. Surg. Assn. (pres. 1984), Seattle Surg. Soc., St. Paul Surg. Soc. (hon.), Kansas City Surg. Soc. (hon.), Inst. Medicine Chgo., Internat. Soc. Surgery (pres. U.S. sect. 1986-88, pres. 34th World Congress 1991, internat. pres. 1991-93), Internat. Soc. Surgery Found. (sec. treas. 1992—), Collegium Internat. Chirurgiae Digestivae (pres III world congress Chgo. 1974, internat. pres. 1978-84), Soc. for Surgery Alimentary Tract (sec. 1969-73, pres. 1974), Soc. Clin. Surgery, Soc. Surg. Chmn., Soc. U. Surgeons (pres. 1967), Duetschen Gesellschaft für Chirurgie (corr.), Polish Assn. Surgeons (hon.), L'Academie de Chirurgie (France) (corr.), Nat. Acad. of Medicine (France and Brazil), Swiss Surg. Soc. (hon.), Brazilian Coll. Surgeons (hon.), Surg. Biology Club, Warren H. Cole Soc. (pres. 1981), Japan Surg. Soc. (hon.), Assn. Gen. Surgeons of Mex. (hon.), Columbian Surg. Soc. (hon.), Internat. Fedn. Surg. Colls. (hon. treas. 1992—), Sigma Xi, Alpha Omega Alpha, Phi Beta Phi. Home: 310 Maple Row Winnetka IL 60093-1036 Office: M/C 958 840 S Wood St Chicago IL 60612-7317

NYIRJESY, ISTVAN, obstetrician, gynecologist; b. Budapest, Hungary, Nov. 14, 1929; came to U.S., 1954, naturalized, 1960; s. Sandor D. and Margit (Bertalan) N.; m. Michelle Shoepp, June 16, 1956; children—Francis, Paul, Christine. M.D., Catholic U. Louvain, Belgium, 1955. Diplomate: Am. Bd. Ob-Gyn. Intern Cath. U. Louvain and Little Co. Mary Hosp., Evergeen Park, Ill., 1954-55; resident in gynecology obstetrics, 1960-63; chief obstetrical research Nat. Naval Med. Center, Bethesda, Md., 1966-68; ret., 1968; practice medicine specializing in Ob-Gyn Bethesda, 1968—; clin. prof. Ob-Gyn Georgetown U., 1968—; cons. NIH, 1974—, FDA, 1977-88. Lit. editor Breast Disease: contbr. articles to med. jours.; author: Prevention and Detection of Gynecologic and Breast Cancer, 1994. Pres., Internat. Found. for Gynecol. Cancer Detection and Prevention, 1993—. Officer M.C. USN, 1956-68; advanced through grades to comdr. Recipient Sword of Hope pin Am. Cancer Soc., 1973, Vicennial medal Georgetown U., 1988. Fellow ACOG (Host award 1964), Internat. Coll. Surgeons; mem. Montgomery County (Md.) Med. Soc. (chmn. profl. edn. com. 1971-72), Gynecol. Soc. Study of Breast Disease (past pres.), Assn. Profs. Ob-Gyn., Am. Fertility Soc., Washington Gynecol. Soc. (v.p. 1993-94, 1st v.p. 1994-95, pres. 1996-97). Office: 5301 Westbard Cir Ste 5 Bethesda MD 20816-1425

NYKIEL, KAREN ANN, retirement facility administrator, religious studies instructor; b. Chgo., July 27, 1945; d. John Marion and Dorothy Ann (Lasko) N. BA, Coll. St. Benedict, St. Joseph, Minn., 1969; MSNS, Seattle U., 1975; MA, Mundelein Coll., Chgo., 1989. Tchr. science Benet Acad., Lisle, Ill., 1969-73; adult edn. coord. St. Joan of Arc Ch., Lisle, 1973-77; adj. faculty chemistry Coll. DuPage, Glen Ellyn, Ill., 1975-92; campus min. Diocese of Joliet, Ill., 1982-92; adminstr. Queen of Peace Ctr., Lisle, 1992-97; cons. Nat. Fusion Co., Plainfield, Ill., 1980-82; mem. Benedictine Sisters Sacred Heart, Lisle, 1965—, bd. dirs., 1980-92; state coord. Pax Christi Ill.,

1994—; pres. Queen of Peace Ctr., Inc., Lisle, 1992-97; adj. faculty religious studies Coll. DuPage, Benedictine U., Coll. St. Francis; mem. med. team Republic of the Congo, 1996. Mem. C. of C., Lisle, 1992—. Grantee NSF, 1971, 72, 73, 74. Mem. Am. Chemical Soc., Assn. Sr. Svc. Providers, Rotary Internat. (Lisle chpt. chair internat. com., pres. 1997—). Democrat. Roman Catholic. Avocations: playing guitar, reading, lecturing. Home: 1910 Maple Ave Lisle IL 60532-2164 Office: Sacred Heart Monastery 1910 Maple Ave Lisle IL 60532-2164

NYKROG, PER, French literature educator; b. Copenhagen, Nov. 1, 1925; came to U.S., 1979; s. Kai S. Nathanson and Karen E. (Olsen) Nykrog; m. Vibeke H. Rasmussen, 1951 (dec. 1977); children: Thomas, Jakob; m. Usha Saksena Nilsson, Jan. 2, 1981. Grad., U. Copenhagen, 1952; PhD, U. Aarhus, Denmark, 1957. Asst. prof. U. Aarhus, 1953-57, prof., 1957-79; prof. French lang. and lit. Harvard U., Cambridge, Mass., 1979—. Author: Les Fabliaux, 1957, La Pensée de Balzac, 1965, L'Amour et la Rose, 1986, La Recherche du Don perdu, 1987, Chrétien de Troyes romancier discutable, 1995. Mem. Royal Soc. Scis. Denmark. Home: 243 Concord Ave Cambridge MA 02138-1360 Office: Harvard U Dept Romance Langs Boylston Hall Cambridge MA 02138

NYKVIST, SVEN VILHEM, cinematographer; b. Moheda, Sweden, Dec. 3, 1922; s. Gustaf Nathanael and Gerda Emilia (Nilson) N.; 1 son, Carl-Gustaf. Student, Stockholm Photog. Sch.; hon. doctorate, Am. Film Inst., 1991. Asst. cameraman Stockholm, 1941-44; co-owner film prodn. co. Josephson-Nykvist, Stockholm. Dir. photography over 100 feature films, including 22 films directed by Ingmar Bergman, 1945—; cinematographer: (films) Sawdust and Tinsel, 1953, The Virgin Spring, 1960, Winter Light, 1962, Karin Mansdotter, The Silence, 1963, Loving Couples, 1964, Persona, 1966, Hour of the Wolf, 1968, One Day in the Life of Ivan Denisovich, 1971, The Dove, 1973, Cries and Whispers, 1973, Scenes from a Marriage, 1973, Black Moon, 1975, The Magic Flute, 1975, Face to Face, 1976, The Tenant, 1976, The Serpent's Egg, 1977, Autumn Sonata, 1978, King of the Gypsies, 1978, Pretty Baby, 1978, Hurricane, 1979, Starting Over, 1979, Willie and Phil, 1980, The Postman Always Rings Twice, 1981, Cannery Row, 1982, Fanny and Alexander, 1983, Star 80, 1983, Swann in Love, 1984, Agnes of God, 1985, Dream Lover, 1986, The Sacrifice, 1986, The Unbearable Lightness of Being, 1988 (nominated Oscar award), Brothers, 1988, segment of film New York Stories, 1988-89, Crimes and Misdemeanors, 1989, Sleepless in Seattle, 1992, Him, 1993, Gilbert Grape, 1993, Him, 1993, Night Before Christmas, 1993, Kirsten Laviansdatter, 1994; (TV) Bergman, 1995 (Golden Eagle 1996); dir. film The Vine Bridge, 1965; dir., cinematographer The Ox, 1991, Charlie, 1992; dir. With Honors, 1993; author: Resan Till Lambarene. Recipient Acad. award Am. Acad. Motion Picture Arts and Scis. for Cries and Whispers, 1974, for Fanny and Alexander, 1984, Caesar French Acad. award, Swedish Acad. award, nominee for best fgn. film for the Ox, 1991, Doctorate Am. Film Inst., 1991. Mem. Swedish Film Acad., Am. Soc. Cinematographers (Life Achievement award 1996), Svenska Teaterforbundet. Office: care Milton Forman 433 N Palm Dr Beverly Hills CA 90210

NYLANDER, JANE LOUISE, museum director; b. Cleve., Jan. 27, 1938; d. James Merritt and Jeannette (Crosby) Cayford; m. Daniel Harris Giffen, Nov. 30, 1963 (div. 1970); children: Sarah Louise, Thomas Harris; m. Richard Conrad Nylander, July 8, 1972: 1 child, Timothy Frost. AB, Brown U., 1959; MA, U. Del., 1961; postgrad., Attingham (Eng.) Summer Sch., 1970; PhD (hon.), New England Coll., 1994. Curator Hist. Soc. York (Pa.) County, 1961-62, N.H. Hist. Soc., Concord, 1962-69; instr. New England Coll., Henniker, N.H., 1964-65, Monadnock Community Coll., Peterborough, N.H., 1966-69; curator of textiles and ceramics Old Sturbridge (Mass.) Village, 1969-85; adj. assoc. prof. Boston U., 1978-85; sr. curator Old Sturbridge Vill., 1985-86; dir. Strawbery Banke Mus., Portsmouth, N.H., 1986-92, Soc. Preservation New England Antiquities, Boston, 1992-93; pres. Soc. for Preservation of New Eng. Antiquities, 1993—; adj. asst. prof. art history and Am. studies Boston U., 1993—; trustee Worcester (Mass.) Hist. Mus., 1978-84, Hist. Deerfield (Mass.), Inc., 1981-94, hon. trustee, 1994—, Hist. Mass. Inc., 1991-93, Decorative Arts Trust, 1991—, Portsmouth Athenaeum, 1988-90, Japan Soc. N.H., 1988-92; mem. adv. bd. Concord (Mass.) Mus., 1986-94, Wentworth-Coolidge Commn., 1991-96, John Nicholas Brown Ctr. for Am. Studies, Providence, 1995—; mem. adv. bd. dept. Am. decorative arts Mus. Fine Arts, Boston, 1971—; mem. coun. Colonial Soc. Mass., 1993-96; cons. in field. Author: Fabrics for Historic Buildings, 4th edit., 1990, Our Own Snug Fireside: Images of the New England Home 1760-1860, 1993, paperback edit., 1994; mem. editorial bd. Hist. New Hampshire; 1993—, The Dublin Seminar, 1984—; contbr. numerous articles to profl. jours. Mem. adv. bd. New Eng. Heritage Ctr., 1993—; active State House Adv. Com., Boston, 1984-85, Gov.'s Coun. for Wentworth Coolidge Mansion, Concord, 1964-66; mem. Com. for Preservation of N.H. State Flags, 1989-92; mem. H.F. duPont award com. Winterthur Mus., 1993—, Mt. Vernon adv. com. for 1999, 1996—, collections com. N.J. Hist. Soc., 1996—. Recipient Charles F. Montgomery Prize Decorative Arts Soc., 1985, (with Richard C. Nylander) The Anne and Roger Webb award Historic Massachusetts, Inc., 1996. Mem. Am. Antiquarian Soc., Am. Assn. for State and Local History, Nat. Trust Hist. Preservation, Royal Oak Assn., Portsmouth Athenaeum, New Eng. Mus. Assn., Trustees of Reservations, Soc. Winterthur Fellows, Hist. Mass., Soc. Preservation of N.H. Forests, N.H. Audubon Soc., N.H. Humanities Coun., New Eng. Hist. Genealogical Soc., Hist. Houses Trust NSW, Costume Soc. Am. (bd. dirs. 1977-83), Dublin Seminar, Nat. Soc. Colonial Dames in N.H. (bd. dirs. 1967-73), Colonial Soc. of Mass., The Garden Conservancy, N.H. Hist. Soc., Friends of Hist. Deerfield, Nat. Soc. Colonial Dames in Mass. (courtesy), Brown Club N.H. (trustee 1988-93). Episcopalian. Home: 17 Franklin St Portsmouth NH 03801-4501 Office: Soc Preservation New England Antiquities 141 Cambridge St Boston MA 02114-2702

NYMAN, CARL JOHN, JR., university dean and official; b. New Orleans, Oct. 21, 1924; s. Carl John Sr. and Dorothy (Kraft) N.; m. Betty Spiegelberg, July 15, 1950; children: Gail Katherine, John Victor, Nancy Kraft. B.S., Tulane U., 1944, M.S., 1945; Ph.D., U. Ill., 1948. Jr. technologist Shell Oil Co., Wilmington, Cal., 1944; instr. chemistry U. Ill., 1948, Wash. State U., Pullman, 1948-50; asst. prof. Wash. State U., 1950-55, assoc. prof., 1955-61, prof., 1961-88, prof. emeritus, 1988—, vice provost for rsch., 1981-86, acting dean grad. sch., 1968-69; dean, 1969-87; dean and vice provost emeritus for rsch. grad. sch. Wash. State U., 1988—; vis. asst. prof. Tulane U., summer, 1950, adj. prof., 1986-87; vis. fellow Cornell U., 1959-60, Imperial Coll. Sci. and Tech., 1966-67; vis. fellow Swiss Fed. Inst. Tech., Zurich, 1973; chmn. Acad. Coun. Ctr. Grad. Study, Richland, Wash., 1968-70, N.W. Assn. Colls. and Univs. for Sci., 1969; mem. Gov.'s Adv. Coun. on Nuclear Energy, 1968-70, Washington State High Tech. Coord. Bd., 1984-86. Author: (with G. B. King and J. A. Weyh) Problems for General Chemistry and Qualitative Analysis, 4th edit., 1980, (with R. E. Hamm) Chemical Equilibrium, 1967, (with W. E. Newton) Procs. of the 1st Internat. Conf. Nitrogen Fixation; contbr. articles to profl. jours. Mem. Am. Chem. Soc. (chmn. Wash.-Idaho border sect. 1961-62), AAAS, Sigma Xi, Phi Lambda Upsilon, Alpha Chi Sigma, Omicron Delta Kappa. Home: East 1419 Cambridge Ln Spokane WA 99203

NYMAN, GEORGIANNA BEATRICE, painter; b. Arlington, Mass., June 11, 1930; d. Daniel Eugene Nyman and Irene Krans (Müller) Lombardi; m. David Aronson, June 10, 1956; children: Judith, Benjamin, Abigail. Diploma, Boston Mus. Sch. Art., 1952, student, 1952-54; postgrad., Longy Sch. Music, Cambridge, Mass., 1965-73. Portraits displayed in Brookline (Mass.) Hosp., Inst. Critical Care Medicine, U. Pitts., McClosky Inst. Voice Therapy, Boston, U.S. Supreme Ct., Washington, New Eng. Sch. of Law, Boston, 1991, Milton (Mass.) Acad., Boston Acad. Music; group exhbns. include Shore Studio Gallery, Boston, 1960,61, Lee Nordness Gallery, N.Y.C., 1963, Copley Soc., Boston, 1980, Nat. Acad. Design, N.Y.C., 1990; solo exhbns. include Nancy Lincoln Gallery, Brookline, 1990; represented in permanent collections Rose Art Mus., Brandeis U., U. Pitts. Sch. Medicine; commd. portraits include Justice Sandra Day O'Connor, Mr. and Mrs. Pieh--headmaster Milton Acad., 1992, Justice Harry A. Blackmun, 1993, Julie Harris Am. actress, 1994, Hon. James R. Lawton, 1994, Richard Conlow, opera singer, dir. Boston Acad. Music, 1994, Justice Clarence Thomas, 1995, David Leisner, 1995. Jurist Art and Mental Illness--An Itinerary Boston U., 1989; active in LeMoyne Found., Fla., 1989. Recipient Bidi prize, 1951, cert. of merit NAD, 1992; Kate Morse fellow Boston Mus. Fine Arts, 1953. Mem. Women's Indsl. Inst. (life), Mass. Soc. Mayflower Descendants. Avocations: music, vocal recitals. Home and Studio: 137 Brimstone Ln Sudbury MA 01776-3200 also: RR 2, Cornwall, PE Canada C0A 1HO

NYMAN, MICHAEL LAWRENCE, composer; b. London, Eng., Mar. 23, 1944; s. Mark and Jeanette N.; m. Aet Toome, May 16, 1970; 2 children. Attended, King's Coll., London, 1964-67; B.Mus., Royal Acad. of Music, 1965; attended, Conservatoire and Folklore Inst., Bucharest, 1965-66. Music critic Spectator, New Statesman, The Listener, 1968-78; founder Michael Nyman Band, 1977. Music dir., composer, performer: (film scores) 1-100, 1977, A Walk Through H, 1977, Tom Philips, 1977, Vertical Features Remake, 1978, The Falls, 1980, Brimstone and Treacle, 1982, Frozen Music, 1983, Nelly's Version, 1983, The Draughtsman's Contract, 1983, The Cold Room, 1984, L'ange frenetique, 1985, A Zed and Two Noughts, 1985, Ballet Mechanique, 1986, The Disputation, 1986, Photographic Exhibits, 1987, Drowning By Numbers, 1988, La Traversee de Paris, 1989, The Cook, the Thief, His Wife, Her Lover, 1989, Monsieur, 1989, Prospero's Books, 1991, Les enfants volants, 1991, Le Mari de la Coiffeuse, 1991, The Piano, 1993; musical performer, composer: (theatre) The Masterwork/Award-Winning Fishknife, 1979, , (ballets) Portraits in Reflection, 1985, And Do They Do, 1986, (dance works) The Fall of Icarus, 1989, Garden Party, 1990; composer: (ballets) A Broken Set of Rules, 1984, Touch the Earth, 1987, (dance works) Miniatures, 1989, (operas) The Man Who Mistook His Wife for a Hat, 1986, La Princesse de Milan, 1991, Letters, Riddles and Writs, 1992, (TV spls.) Act of God, 1980, The Man Who Mistook His Wife for a Hat, 1987, Fairly Secret Army Series 2, 1987, Dancing in Numbers, 1988, Touch the Earth, 1988, Out of the Ruins, 1989, Death in the Seine, 1989, Men of Steel, 1990, Letters, Riddles and Writs, 1991, The Final Score, 1992, The Fall of Icarus, 1992; author: (music criticism) Experimental Music: Cage and Beyond, 1975; recs. include The Convertibility of Lute Strings, 1993, For John Cage, 1993, Goodbye Frankie, Goodbye Benny, 1993. Office: care Screen Composer of Am 2451 Nichols Canyon Rd Los Angeles CA 90046-1734*

NYQUIST, JOHN DAVIS, retired radio manufacturing company executive; b. Peoria, Ill., May 28, 1918; s. Eliud and Linnea (Widen) N.; m. Alice Schmidt, June 5, 1942; 1 child, Sarah Lynn. B.S. in Mech. Engring. U. Ill., 1941. With Collins Radio Co., Cedar Rapids, Iowa, 1941—; v.p., gen. mgr. Iowa region Collins Radio Co., Cedar Rapids, 1965-69; v.p. operations Collins Radio Co., 1969-70, sr. v.p., 1970-73, also dir.; ret., 1973; cons. Rockwell-Collins; dir. Norwest Bank Iowa N.A. (formerly Peoples Bank & Trust Co.), Cedar Rapids. Bd. dirs. Am. Cancer Soc., YMCA, St. Lukes Hosp. Recipient award for outstanding achievement Am. Inst. Indsl. Engrs., 1966, Indsl. Engring. award, 1969, Coll. Engring. Alumni Honor award, 1977; both U. Ill.). Mem. Iowa Mfrs. Assn., Am. Mgmt. Assn., Am. Inst. Indsl. Engrs., IEEE, Cedar Rapids C. of C. (dir.). Club: Cedar Rapids Country. Home: 3279 Jordans Grove Rd Springville IA 52336-9786

NYQUIST, KATHLEEN A., publishing executive; b. Biloxi, Miss., May 14, 1955; d. Clarence and Marianne M. (Mahoney) Boehm; m. John D. Nyquist, Nov. 5, 1983; children: Lindsay, Eric. BS in Edn., Miami U., Oxford, Ohio, 1977. High sch. biology tchr. Ill., 1978-79; home tutor Fed. Homebound Program, Ill., 1980; from sci. editor to editorial v.p. Scott Foresman & Co., Glenview, Ill., 1981-89, creative dir., 1990, pub., 1992, pres., 1993-95; author, ednl. cons., 1996—. Parent rev. com. mem. Sch. Dist. 96, Buffalo Grove, Ill., 1991-92. Mem. ASCD, Nat. Coun. Tchrs. Math., Nat. Sci. Tchrs. Assn., Chgo. Book Clinic.

NYQUIST, THOMAS EUGENE, consulting business executive, mayor; b. Froid, Mont., June 20, 1931; s. Richard Theodore and Lydia (Baker) N.; m. Corinne Elaine Johnson, Dec. 22, 1956; children: Jonathan Eugene, Lynn Marie Nyquist Bergstrausser. BA, Macalester Coll., 1956; MA, U. Mont., 1958; PhD, Northwestern U., 1966. Prof. SUNY, New Paltz, 1968-76; adminstr. cen. div. SUNY, Albany, 1976-90; pres. Nyquist Assocs., New Paltz, N.Y., 1991—; mem. adv. bd. George Washington's Hdqrs., Newburgh, N.Y., 1980-92; acad. dir. N.Y. Edn. Dept., Kenya, 1982; head del. House of Peace and Friendship/Village of New Paltz delegation, St. Petersburg, Russia, 1992. Author: (monograph) Urban Africans in South Africa, 1977, (book) African Middle Class Elite, 1983. Mem. Ulster County Legislature, 1976-79; dep. mayor Village of New Paltz, 1983-87, mayor, 1987—; chmn. New Paltz Centennial Com., 1986-87; bd. dirs. Ulster Region Credit Union, Kingston, N.Y., 1976-87, Partnership in Svc. Learning, 1985—, Ulster Performing Arts Ctr., 1978-82, Friends of Cuttington Coll., Liberia, 1994—; treas. Lower Hudson Conf., 1988, 89-90, 91-92. With U.S. Army, 1952-54. Fellow SUNY, South Africa, 1975; Ford Found. grantee, 1986. Mem. African Studies Assn., N.Y. African Studies Assn. (exec. bd. dirs. 1973—, co-editor newsletter 1974—), Am. Polit. Sci. Assn. (chmn. Japan com. 1997—). Democrat. Avocations: hiking, cross county skiing. Home: 62 S Chestnut St New Paltz NY 12561-1936 Office: Office of Mayor Village Hall 25 Plattekill Ave New Paltz NY 12561-1918 also: Nyquist Assocs 62 S Chestnut St New Paltz NY 12561

NYREN, NEIL SEBASTIAN, publisher, editor; b. Boston, June 13, 1948; s. Karl Edwin and Dorothy Elizabeth (Smith) N.; m. Lois Miriam Sharfman, Oct. 11, 1970; 1 child, Alexander. B.A., Brandeis U. v.p. G.P. Putnam's Sons Pub., N.Y.C., 1997—; editor Random House Pubs., N.Y.C., 1974-77; Editor Arbor House Pubs., N.Y.C., 1977-78; exec. editor Atheneum Pubs., N.Y.C., 1978-84; sr. editor G.P. Putnam's Sons Pub., N.Y.C., 1984-86, editor-in-chief, 1986—, pub., 1989—. Democrat. Jewish. Office: GP Putnam's Sons 200 Madison Ave New York NY 10016-3903

NYROP, DONALD WILLIAM, airline executive; b. Elgin, Nebr., Apr. 1, 1912; s. William A. and Nellie (Wylie) N.; m. Grace Cary, Apr. 19, 1941; children: Nancy, William, Karen, Kathryn. A.B., Doane Coll., 1934; LL.B., George Washington U., 1939. Bar: D.C. 1938. Atty. Gen. Counsel's Office, CAA, Washington, 1939-41; exec. officer to chmn. CAB, 1942, chmn., 1952; rep. U.S. airlines; mem. ofcl. U.S. delegations Internat. Civil Aviation Orgn. Assemblies, 1946, 47; dep. adminstr. for ops. CAA, 1948-50, adminstr., 1950-51; chmn. CAB, 1951-52; pres. Northwest Airlines, Inc., 1954-78. Served with Air Transport Command USAAF, 1942-46. Decorated Legion of Merit. Clubs: Minneapolis, Minnesota. Home: 4505 Golf Ter Minneapolis MN 55424-1510

NYSTRAND, RAPHAEL OWENS, university dean, educator; b. Maryville, Mo., Nov. 6, 1937; s. Phillip Owens and Emily (Martin) M.; m. Suzanne Rose Duval, Apr. 1, 1961; children: Kathryn Lee, Kristin Sue. B.A., Cornell Coll., 1959; M.A.T., Johns Hopkins U., 1960; Ph.D., Northwestern U., 1966. Tchr. Lyons Twp. High Sch., La Grange, Ill., 1960-64; research assoc. Research Council of Great Cities Program for Sch. Improvement, Chgo., 1965-66; asst. prof. Coll. Edn., Ohio State U., Columbus, 1967-69, assoc. prof., 1969-71, prof., chmn. dept., 1972-78; dean Sch. Edn., U. Louisville, 1978—, prof., 1978—; sec. edn. and humanities cabinet Commonwealth of Ky., 1984 (on leave); postdoctoral fellow U. Chgo., 1966-67, vis. lectr., 1967; vis. prof. U. Victoria, B.C., Can., 1977; cons. various sch. dists., state agys.; v.p. Holmes Group, 1990—; mem. Nat. Policy Bd. for Ednl. Adminstrn., 1991-93, Nat. Coun. Accreditation tchr. Edn. State Partnership Bd., 1994—. Co-author: The Organization and Control of American Schools, 6th edit., 1990, Introduction to Educational Administration, 6th edit., 1983; co-editor: Educational Administration: The Developing Decades, 1977, Strategies for Educational Change, 1981. Trustee Columbus Met. Sch., 1974-78, Fairmount Fund, 1980—, Louisville Youth Choir, 1983-85, Louisville Art Gallery, 1985-87, Wesley Comty. House, 1986-90, Stage One, 1989-91, Ky. Derby Festival, 1990-92; adv. bd. Inst. Creative Learning, Inc., Louisville, 1980-90, Jr. League Louisville, 1984-87, Gov.'s Sch. for Arts, 1986-87; mem. Ky. Edn. Profl. Stds. Bd., 1993—. Mem. Am. Ednl. Rsch. Assn., Nat. Soc. Study Edn., Phi Delta Kappa. Methodist. Home: 3015 Springcrest Dr Louisville KY 40241-2755 Office: U Louisville Belknap Campus Louisville KY 40292

NYTKO, EDWARD C., printing company executive; b. Chgo., Feb. 20, 1943; s. Edward Frank and Helen Nytko; m. Deborah Harriet Nytko, Nov. 21, 1980; children: Jeffrey Daniel, Christopher Edward. BBA in Mktg., U. Tex., 1965; MBA in Fin., Loyola U., Chgo., 1969. Mgmt. trainee W.F. Hall Printing Co., Chgo., 1965-67, group v.p. Gravure, 1980-81, pres., chief operating officer, 1981, pres., chief exec. officer, 1982-85; pres., chief exec. officer Ringier Am. (fomerly Krueger Ringier Inc., W.F. Hall Printing Co.), Itasca, Ill., 1985-96. Mem. Gravure Assn. Am. (bd. dirs. 1987—).

NZEYIMANA, NOAH, bishop. Bishop Free Meth. Ch. N.Am., Winona Lake, Ind., 1987—. Office: Free Meth Ch N Am PO Box 535002 Indianapolis IN 46253-5002*

OAK, CLAIRE MORISSET, artist, educator; b. St. Georges, Quebec, Can., May 31, 1921; came to U.S., 1945; d. Louis and Bernadette (Coulombe) Morisset; m. Alan Ben Oak, July 2, 1947. Student, Ecole des Beaux Arts, 1938-42, Parsons Sch. Design, N.Y.C., 1945, Art Students League, N.Y.C., 1945-46. Staff artist Henry Morgan & R. Simpson, Montreal, 1942-45; artist illustrator W.B. Golovin Advt. Agy., N.Y.C., 1947-49; freelance illustrator Arnold Constable & Advt. Agy., N.Y.C., 1948-50, Le Jardin des Modes, Paris, 1950-51, May & Co., L.A., 1956, Katten & Marengo Advt., Stockton, Calif., 1962-84; pvt. practice illustrator, designer San Joaquin Valley, Calif., 1984-92; art instr. San Joaquin Delta Coll., Stockton, 1973—; owner Fashion Illustrator's Workshop, N.Y.C., 1953-54; instr. Bauder Coll., Sacramento, 1975-76; painting workshop leader Lodi Art Ctr., 1991—; watercolor workshop leader D'Pharr Painting Adventures, Virginia City, Nev., 1992; ongoing watercolor workshop Galerie Iona, Stockton, Calif., 1993—. Named S.B. Anthony Woman of Achievement in the Arts, U. Pacific, 1982. Mem. Stockton Art League, Lodi Art Ctr., Ctrl. Calif. Art League, The League of Carmichael Artists, Delta Watercolor Soc. (bd. mem. 1988—). Avocations: outdoor painting, drawing from a model. Home: 2140 Waudman Ave Stockton CA 95209-1755 *You are a success in the visual arts if you teach others how to see.*

OAK, H. LORRAINE, academic administrator, geography educator; b. Toronto, July 19, 1951; d. James Wilfred George and Helen Mary (Towers) O.; m. Athol Denis Abrahams, Jan. 3, 1976; 1 child, Geoffrey James Oak Abrahams. BA Honours, U. Alta., 1973; PhD in Geomorphology, Macquarie U., Sydney, 1982. Acad. editor Assn. Am. Geographers, Washington, 1981-85; rsch. adminstr. SUNY, Buffalo, 1987-92, asst. vice provost rsch., 1992-93, dep. provost, 1993-96, assoc. dean for interdisc. affairs Sch. Med. & Biomed. Scis., 1996—; Mem. Environ. Inst. Task Force, SUNY, Buffalo, 1994—. Freelance tech. editor, 1985-86; contbr. articles to profl. jours. and reviews. Me. Assn. Am. Geographers (nat. acad. leadership round table 1995—), N.Y. Sea Grant Inst. (bd. govs. 1993—), Sigma Xi (pres. SUNY Buffalo chpt. 1993-94). Avocations: travel, reading. Office: SUNY 155 Biomed Edn Bldg Sch Med and Biomed Scis Buffalo NY 14214

OAK, RONALD STUART, health and safety administrator; b. Fargo, N.D., Dec. 20, 1956; s. Duane Lyle and Beverly Alice (Anderson) O. BS in Environ. Health, Colo. State U., 1979. Cert. indsl. hygienist Am. Bd. Indsl. Hygiene, cert. hazardous materials mgr. Inst. Hazardous Materials Mgmt. Compliance officer Wyo. Occupational Health and Safety Dept., Cheyenne, 1980-82, OSHA consultation program cons., 1982-84; indsl. hygienist Hager Labs., Inc., Denver, 1984-86; from assoc. to sr. indsl. hygienist Ecology and Environment, Inc., Denver, 1987-91; sr. indsl. hygienist Harding Lawson Assocs., Inc., Santa Ana, Calif., 1991-92; health and safety mgr. IT Corp., San Jose, Calif., 1993—. Mem. adv. com. Wyo. Gov.'s Com. on Hazardous Materials Response, Cheyenne, 1983-84; nat. mem. Smithsonian Assocs., Washington, 1990—, contbg. mem., 1995—. Mem. AAAS, N.Y. Acad. Scis., Am. Indsl. Hygiene Assn. Achievements include diverse work on the investigation and remediation of hazardous waste sites, environmental emergency response, occupational health and safety management, industrial hygiene evaluations and indoor air quality assessments. Office: IT Corp 2055 Junction Ave San Jose CA 95131-2105

OAKAR, MARY ROSE, lawyer, former congresswoman; b. Cleve., Mar. 5, 1940; d. Joseph M. and Margaret Mary (Ellison) O. BA in English, Speech and Drama, Ursuline Coll., Cleve., 1962, LHD (hon.); MA in Fine Arts, John Carroll U., Cleve., 1966; LLD (hon.), Ashland U., 1978, Ursuine Coll., 1984, St. Mary's Notre Dame, 1989, Baldwin Wallace Coll., 1988; LHD (hon.), Trinity Coll., 1987. Instr. English and drama Lourdes Acad., Cleve., 1963-70; asst. prof. English, speech and drama Cuyahoga Community Coll., Cleve., 1968-75; mem. Cleve. City Council from 8th Ward, 1973-76, 95th-102nd Congresses from 20th Dist. Ohio, 1977-92; mem. Pepper Commn. on Long Term Health Care, chair subcom. internat. devel., fin., trade and monetary policy, chair task force on social security, elderly, women; chair subcom. on personnel and police, mem. banking, fin. and urban affairs com., select com. on aging, post office and civil service com., com. on house adminstrn., also numerous subcoms.; ptnr. Mary Rose Oakar and Assocs.; apptd. to Sec. Conf. to Establish Nat. Action Plan on Breast Cancer, 1994, by Pres. Clinton to bd. dirs. Bldrs., For Peace, 1994, to policy to White House Conf. on Aging. Founder, vol.-dir. Near West Side Civic Arts Center, Cleve., 1970; ward leader Cuyahoga County Democratic Party, 1972-76; mem. Ohio Dem. Central Com. from 20th Dist., 1974; trustee Fedn. Community Planning, Cleve., Health and Planning Commn. Cleve., Community Info. Service Cleve., Cleve. Soc. Crippled Children, Public Services Occupational Group Adv. Com., Cuyahoga Community Coll., Cleve. Ballet, Cleve. YWCA. Recipient Outstanding Service awards OEO, 1973-78, Community Service award Am. Indian Center, Cleve., 1973, Community Service award Nationalities Service Center, 1974, Community Service award Club San Lorenzo, Cleve., 1976, Cuyahoga County Dem. Woman of Yr., 1977, Ursuline Coll. Alumna of Yr. award, 1977, awards Irish Nat. Caucus, awards West Side Community Mental Health Center, awards Am. Lebanese League, awards Cleve. Fedn. Am.-Syrian Lebanese Clubs, Breast Cancer Awareness award Nat. Women's Health Resource Ctr., 1989, 1st lay recipient Barbara Bohen-Pfeiffer award Italian-Am. Found. Cancer Rsch., 1989, Disting. Svc. award Am. Cancer Soc., 1989, Myrl H. Shoemaker award Ohio Dem. Party, 1992, Philip Hart award Consumer Fedn. Am., 1987; cert. appreciation City of Cleve.; Woman of Yr. award Cuyahoga County Women's Polit. Caucus, 1983; decorated Knight of Order of St. Ladislaus of Hungary, Women in Aerospace Outstanding Ach. award, Black Focus Woman of the Decade award. Office: 2621 Lorain Ave Cleveland OH 44113-3414*

OAKES, JAMES L., federal judge; b. Springfield, Ill., Feb. 21, 1924; m. Evelena S. Kenworthy, Dec. 29, 1973; one son, two daus. by previous marriage. AB, Harvard U., 1945, LLB, 1947; LLD, New Eng. Coll., 1976, Suffolk U., 1980, Vt. Law Sch., 1995. Bar: Calif. 1949, Vt. 1950. Pvt. practice Brattleboro, Vt.; spl. counsel Vt. Pub. Service Commn., 1959-60; counsel Vt. Statutory Revision Commn., 1957-60; mem. Vt. Senate, 1961-65; atty. gen. Vt., 1967-69, U.S. dist. judge, 1970-71; U.S. cir. judge 2d Cir. Ct. Appeals, Brattleboro, 1971—; chief judge 2d Circuit Ct. Appeals, 1989-92; adj. faculty Duke U. Law Sch., 1985-96, Iowa U. Coll. Law, 1993—. Office: US Ct Appeals PO Box 696 Brattleboro VT 05302-0696

OAKES, JOHN BERTRAM, writer, editor; b. Elkins Park, Pa., Apr. 23, 1913; s. George Washington Ochs Oakes and Bertie (Gans) Ochs; m. Margery C. Hartman, Oct. 24, 1945; children: Andra N., Alison H., Cynthia J., John G. H. A.B. magna cum laude, Princeton U., 1934; A.B., A.M. (Rhodes scholar), Queen's Coll., Oxford, 1936; LL.D. (hon.), U. Hartford, 1960; L.H.D. (hon.), Chatham Coll., 1969; Litt.D. (hon.), CUNY, 1976. Reporter Trenton (N.J.) State Gazette, Trenton Times, 1936-37; polit. reporter Washington Post, 1938-41; editor Rev. of the Week, Sunday N.Y. Times, 1946-49; mem. editorial bd. N.Y. Times, 1949-76; columnist on conservation environ., 1951-61, editor of edit. page, 1961-76; originator Op.-Ed. page N.Y. Times, 1970, contbg. columnist, 1977-90. Author: The Edge of Freedom, 1961; contbr.: Essays Today, 1955, Foundations of Freedom, 1958, Tomorrow's American, 1977, On the Vineyard, 1980, The March to War, 1991, Cast a Cold Eye, 1991. Mem. adv. bd. Nat. Parks Dept. Interior, 1955-62; Pres.'s Commn. White House Fellows, 1964-69; founding trustee Natural Resources Def. Coun., 1970—; adv. coun. U.S. Bur. Land Mgmt., 1980-81; mem. N.Y. State Commn. on Future of Adirondacks, 1989-90; past trustee Nat. Parks Conservation Assn., Fisk U., Chatham Coll., N.Y. Found., Sierra Club, Wilderness Soc., Nature Conservancy, Washington Journalism Ctr., Temple Emanu-El. Decorated Bronze Star, Order Brit. Empire, Croix de Guerre, Medaille de Reconnaissance (France); recipient Columbia-Catherwood award for disting. journalism, 1961, Dept. Interior Conservation award 1963, George Polk Meml. award, 1965, Silurian Soc. award, 1969, Woodrow Wilson award Princeton U., 1970, Audubon medal Nat. Audubon Soc., 1976, UN Environ. award, 1982, Lawrenceville Sch. medal, 1994, other. Mem. Am. Philos. Soc., Coun. Fgn. Rels., Phi Beta Kappa, Century Assn. (N.Y.C.), Cosmos Club (Washington, D.C.). Jewish. Home: 1120 Fifth Ave New York NY 10128-0144

OAKES, LESTER CORNELIUS, retired electrical engineer, consultant; b. Knoxville, Oct. 11, 1923; s. Charles Vaughn and Maude Cornelia (Harrison) O.; m. Kathleen Clark, Dec. 27, 1947; children: Michael, Richard, Cynthia, Melissa. B.S. in E.E., U. Tenn., 1949, M.S., 1962. Registered profl. engr., Tenn. Engr. Fairchild Engring. and Aircraft, Oak Ridge, 1949-51; engr. I&C div. Oak Ridge Nat. Lab., 1951-68, dep. head I&C div., 1968—, asst. dir. I&C div., 1971-90; cons. Oak Ridge Nat. Lab., electric Power Rsch. Inst., Nuclear Regulatory Commn., 1990—. Contbr. articles to profl. jours.; patentee in field. Served with USAF, 1943-46. Martin Marietta Corp. fellow. Fellow IEEE. Presbyterian. Home: 710 Pleasant Hill Rd Maryville TN 37803-7337

OAKES, ROBERT JAMES, physics educator; b. Mpls., Jan. 21, 1936; s. Sherman E. and Josephine J. (Olson) O.; children: Cindy L., Lisa A. B.S., U. Minn., 1957, M.S., 1959, Ph.D., 1962. NSF fellow Stanford U., 1962-64; asst. prof. physics, 1964-68; assoc. prof. physics Northwestern U., 1968-70, prof. physics, 1970-76, prof. physics and astronomy, 1976—; vis. staff mem. Los Alamos Sci. Lab., 1971—; vis. scientist Fermi Nat. Accelerator Lab., 1975—; faculty assoc. Argonne Nab. Lab., 1982—; U.S. scientist NSF-Yugoslav joint program, 1982—; panelist Nat. Rsch. Coun., 1990—. A.P. Sloan fellow 1965-68; Air Force Office Sci. Rsch. grantee, 1969-71, NSF grantee 1971-87, Dept. Energy grantee, 1987—; named Fulbright-Hays Disting. prof. U. Sarajevo, Yugoslavia, 1979-80; recipient Natural Sci. prize China, 1993. Fellow Am. Phys. Soc., AAAS; mem. N.Y. Acad. Sci., Ill. Acad. Sci., Physics Club (Chgo.), Sigma Xi, Tau Beta Pi. Club: Physics (Chgo.). Office: Northwestern U Dept Physics 633 Clark St Evanston IL 60208-0001

OAKES, THOMAS WYATT, environmental engineer; b. Danville, Va., June 14, 1950; s. Wyatt Johnson and Relia (Sceacre) O.; m. Terry Lynn Jenkins, June 15, 1974; 1 child, Travis Wyatt. BS in Nuclear Engring., Va. Polytechnic U., 1973, MS in Nuclear Engring., 1975; MS in Environ. Engring., U. Tenn., 1981. Ordained deacon Bapt. Ch., 1989. Health physics asst. Va. Polytechnic U., Blacksburg, 1972-74; radiation engr. Babcock and Wilcox Co., Lynchburg, Va., 1974-75; dept. mgr. Oak Ridge (Tenn.) Nat. Lab., 1975-78, environ. mgr., 1978-85; corp. environ. coord. Martin Marietta, Oak Ridge, 1985-87; asst. v.p. Sci. Applications Internat. Corp., Oak Ridge, 1987-90; environ. mmgr. Westinghouse Environ. and Geotech. Svcs., Knoxville, Tenn., 1990-91; mgr. S.E. region environ. svcs. ATEC & Assocs., Inc., Marietta, Ga., 1991-93; asst. v.p. environ. svcs. Scitek, Ft. Campbell, Ky., 1993—. Contbr. over 107 articles to scholarly and profl. jours. Recipient Spl. Recognition award Union Carbide Corp., 1980, Best Paper award Nat. Safety Coun., 1982, Tech. Publs. award Soc. Tech. Communications, 1987. Mem. AAAS, Am. Indsl. Hygiene Assn., N.Y. Acad. Scis., Health Physics Soc. (sec.-treas. environ. sect. 1984-85), Am. Naval Soc., Am. Soc. for Quality Control. Office: Scitek PO Box 527 Fort Campbell KY 42223

OAKES, WALTER JERRY, pediatric neurosurgeon; b. De Soto, Mo., July 10, 1946; s. Marvin Melton and Mildred Florene (Link) O.; m. Linda Helen Maas (div. Jan. 1985); 1 child, Kathleen Suzanne; m. Jean Evans, Dec. 1988; children: Matthew Marvin, Peter Clifford. BA in Chemistry, U. Mo., 1968; MD, Duke U., 1972. Diplomate Am. Bd. Neurol. Surgeons. Neurosurgery resident Duke U., Durham, N.C., 1972-78, asst. prof. neurosurgery, 1979-90, assoc. prof. neurosurgery, 1991—, asst. prof. pediatrics, 1981-92; assoc. prof. pediatrics Duke U., 1992; pediatric neurosurgery resident U. Toronto Hosp. for Sick Children, Ont., Can., July-Dec., 1975; registrar pediatric neurosurgery U. London Hosp. for Sick Children, Eng., Sept., 1978-Feb., 1979; prof. neurosurgery and pediatrics U. Ala. Birmingham, 1992—. Fellow ACS. Office: Children's Hosp of Ala 1600 7th Ave S Ste 400 Birmingham AL 35233-1711

OAKEY, JOHN MARTIN, JR., lawyer; b. Roanoke, Va., Jan. 29, 1935; s. John Martin and Mildred Hunter (Urquhart) O.; m. Jean Lindsey, May 7, 1966; children: John M. III, Daniel L., Christopher K. BA, U. Va., 1957, LLB, 1963. Law clk. U.S. Dist. Ct. (ea. dist.) Va., Richmond, 1963-64; assoc. McGuire, Woods & Battle, Richmond, 1964-69, ptnr., 1969-87; ptnr. McGuire, Woods, Battle & Boothe, Richmond, 1987—; mem. 4th Cir. Jud. Conf., Richmond, 1976—; chmn. Bar Com. on Unprofl. Conduct, 1977, Com. on Rules of Evidence, 1984-85. Chmn. Richmond Bd. Housing Appeals, 1975; pres. Richmond Tennis Patrons Assn., 1979. Served to lt. USN, 1958-61. Fellow Am. Coll. Trial Lawyers; mem. Va. Bar Assn., Richmond Bar Assn., Va. Assn. Def. Attys. (pres. 1994-95), Def. Rsch. Inst., Boyd Graves Conf. (chair 1991-94), Bull and Bear Club, Westwood Club, Phi Beta Kappa, Omicron Delta Kappa. Episcopalian. Avocations: tennis, travel. Home: 11 Roslyn Rd Richmond VA 23226-1609 Office: McGuire Woods Battle & Boothe 1 James Ctr Richmond VA 23219

OAKLEY, ANDREW ARTHUR, journalist, educator; b. Chgo., Oct. 22, 1958; s. Arthur George and Dolores Margarite (Hernandez) O.; m. Suzanna Pinter, Sept. 7, 1985; 1 child, Glen Matthias. BS in Journalism, Northwestern U., 1980, MS, 1981. Reporter Woodstock (Ill.) Daily Sentinel, 1980-81; police reporter Herald-Palladium, St. Joseph, Mich., 1981-82; city hall reporter Daily Herald, Arlington Heights, Ill., 1982-84; instr. journalism Oakton C.C., Des Plaines, Ill., 1984-85; features editor North Shore Mag., Winnetka, Ill., 1985-86; news editor City and State, Chgo., 1986-93; journalism editor P.O. Publ. Co., Port Murray, N.J., 1993-96; newsletter editor All Aboard for Hackettstown, N.J., 1996—; lectr. Northwestern U., Evanston, Ill., 1990-96; columnist Daily Herald, Arlington Heights, Ill., 1995-96. Author: Eighty-Eight, 1988, Issues Confronting City and State Governments, 1992, Beginning Journalism Packet, 1994; cons. editor P.O. Pub. Co., Skokie, Ill., 1988-92. Lifetime mem. N Club, 1980—; commr. Skokie Human rels. Commn., 1987-94; co-chmn. Skokie Centennial Events Com., 1987-88; advisor Mcpl. Alliance Lit. Club, 1997—. Mem. No. Ill. Newspaper Assn. (Pub. Affairs Reporting award 1983), Ill. Press Assn. (Edn. Reporting award 1983), Suburban Press Club Chgo. (Investigative Series award 1984), Soc. Profl. Journalists (Peter Lisagor award 1984), Investigative Reporters and Editors, Chgo. Headline Club, Assn. for Edn. in Journalism and Mass Comm., Medill Alumni Assn., Evanston Running Club. Methodist. Avocations: distance running, weight lifting, writing, Spanish language.

OAKLEY, BILL, television producer; m. Rachel Pulido, Jan. 27, 1991. AB in History, Harvard U., 1988. Co-writer Lampoon parodies USA Today, Time, also others.; co-writer Spy, Nat. Lampoon, America's Most Wanted. Writer The Simpsons, from 1992, also story editor, supervising prodr., now exec. prodr. (Emmy award 1995). Office: care Fox Publicity PO Box 900 Beverly Hills CA 90213

OAKLEY, DEBORAH JANE, researcher, educator; b. Detroit, Jan. 31, 1937; d. George F. and Kathryn (Willson) Hacker; m. Bruce Oakley, June 16, 1958; children: Ingrid Andrea, Brian Benjamin. BA, Swarthmore Coll., 1958; MA, Brown U., 1960; MPH, U. Mich., 1969, PhD, 1977. Dir. teenage and adult programs YWCA, Providence, 1959-63; editorial asst. Stockholm U., 1963-64; rsch. investigator, lectr. dept. population planning U. Mich., 1971-77; asst. prof. community health programs U. Mich., Ann Arbor, 1977-79, asst. prof. nursing rsch., 1979-81, assoc. prof., 1981-89, prof., 1989—, interim dir. Ctr. Nursing Rsch., 1988-90; prin. investigator NIH-funded Rsch. grants on family planning and women's health, mem. nat. adv. com. nursing rsch., 1993-97; mem. adv. workshop on Nat. Survey on Family Growth, 1994—; co-chair Mich. Initiative for Women's Health, 1993-95. Author: (with Leslie Corsa) Population Planning, 1979; contbr. articles to profl. jours. Bd. dirs. Planned Parenthood Fedn. Am., 1975-80. Recipient Margaret Sanger award Washtenaw County Planned Parenthood, 1975; Outstanding Young Woman of Ann Arbor award by Jaycees, 1970, Dist. Faculty award, Mich. Assn. Gov. Bds., 1992, Blue Cross Blue Shield Found. of Mich. award for Excellence in Health Policy, 1996. Mem. Am. Pub. Health Assn. (chmn. population sect. council), Internat. Union Sci. Study Population, Midwest Nursing Rsch. Soc., Population Assn. Am., Nat. Family Planning and Reproductive Health Assn. (nat. comms.), Delta Omega, Sigma Theta Tau (hon.). Democrat. Home: 5200 S Lake Dr Chelsea MI 48118-9481 Office: U Mich Sch Nursing Ann Arbor MI 48109-0482

OAKLEY, DIANE, insurance executive, benefit consultant; b. Teaneck, N.J., Dec. 27, 1953; d. Geard Joseph and Joan B. (Peterson) O. BS, Fairfield U., 1975; MBA, Fordham U., 1984. Actuarial asst. TIAA-CREF, N.Y.C., 1975-79, benefit plan counselor, 1979-82, adv. officer, 1982-85; branch mgr., 2nd v.p. TIAA-CREF, Bethesda, Md., 1985-89, v.p., assns. & govt. rels., 1989-95, v.p., 1995—. Bd. dirs. Nat. Assn. Coll. and Univ. Bus. Officers; bd. trustees Fairfield U. Mem. Am. Assn. Higher Edn., Am. Assn. Women in C.C.'s, Nat. Assn. Women in Edn., Women in Govt. Rels., Working in Employee Benefits. Roman Catholic. Home: 4400 East-West Hwy #432 Bethesda MD 20814 Office: TIAA-CREF 601 13th St NW Ste 1100N Washington DC 20005-3807

OAKLEY, FRANCIS CHRISTOPHER, history educator, former college president; b. Liverpool, Eng., Oct. 6, 1931; came to U.S., 1957, naturalized, 1968; s. Joseph Vincent and Siobean (NiCurean) O.; m. Claire-Ann Lamenzo, Aug. 9, 1958; children: Deirdre, Christopher, Timothy, Brian. BA, Corpus Christi Coll., Oxford U., 1953, MA, 1957; postgrad., Pontifical Inst. Medieval Studies, Toronto, 1953-55; MA, Yale U., 1958, PhD, 1960; LLD, Amherst Coll., 1986; Wesleyan U., 1989; LHD, Northwestern U., 1990, North Adams State Coll., 1993, Bowdoin Coll., 1993; LittD, Williams Coll., 1994. Mem. faculty Yale U., 1959-61; Mem. faculty Williams Coll., Williamstown, Mass., 1961—, prof. history, 1970—, dean faculty, 1977-84, Edward Dorr Griffin prof. history of ideas, 1984-85, 94—, pres., 1985-94, pres. emeritus, 1994—; hon. fellow Corpus Christi Coll., Univ. Oxford, 1991—; vis. lectr. Bennington (Vt.) Coll., 1967; mem. Inst. Advanced Study Princeton, 1981-82; assoc. Nat. Humanities Ctr., 1991; guest scholar Woodrow Wilson Internat. Ctr. for Scholars, 1994; chair bd. dirs. Am. Coun. Learned Socs., 1993—; trustee Sterling and Francine Clark Art Inst., 1985—, MassMoCA Found., 1995—, Wililamstown Art Conservation Ctr., 1995—, Nat. Humanities Ctr., 1996—; mem. MassMoCA Cultural Devel. Commn., 1988—. Author: The Political Thought of Pierre d'Ailly: The Voluntarist Tradition, 1964, Kingship and the Gods: The Western Apostasy, 1968, Council over Pope?, Towards a Provisional Ecclesiology, 1969, Medieval Experience: Foundations of Western Cultural Singularity, 1974, rev. England edit., The Crucial Centuries, 1979, Spanish edit., 1980, 95, Medieval Acad. edit., 1988, 93, The Western Church in the Later Middle Ages, 1979, rev. edit., 1985, 88, 91, Natural Law, Conciliarism and Consent in the Late Middle Ages, 1984, Omnipotence, Covenant and Order: An Excursion in the History of Ideas, 1984, Community of Learning: The American College and the Liberal Arts Tradition, 1992, Scholarship and Teaching: A Matter of Mutual Support, 1996; editor: (with Daniel O'Connor) Creation: The Impact of an Idea, 1969; contbr. articles to profl. jours. Lt. Brit. Army, 1955-57. Goldsmith's Co. London fellow, 1953-55, Social Sci. Rsch. Coun. fellow, 1963, Am. Coun. Learned Socs. fellow, 1965, 69-70, Weil Inst. fellow, 1965, Folger Shakespeare Libr. fellow, 1974, NEH fellow, 1976, 81-82. Fellow Medieval Acad. Am.; mem. Am. Hist. Assn., Am. Cath. Hist. Assn., Am. Ch. History Soc., New Eng. Medieval Conf., Am. Coun. Learned Socs. (chair bd. dirs. 1993—), The Century Assn. Democrat. Roman Catholic. Office: Williams Coll Oakley Ctr for Humanities and Social Scis Williamstown MA 01267

OAKLEY, GARY WILLIAM, travel incentive executive; b. Norfolk, Va., Dec. 29, 1942; s. Francis and Mabel (Waters) O.; m. Suzy Bridge Oakley, Apr. 3, 1982; div. 1980; children Gary W. Jr., Sara W. BA in Econs., Amherst Coll., 1960-64; MBA in Mktg., U. Pa., 1968. Assoc. N.W. Ayer & Sons, Inc., Phila., 1968-70; group. prodn. mgr. Lever Bros., Inc., N.Y.C., 1970-73; mktg. dir. Am. Can Co., Greenwich, Conn., 1973-78; cons., chmn., CEO The Saugatuck Group, Westport, Conn., 1980-93; chmn., CEO The Saugatuck Travel Co., Westport, Conn., 1987-93, Media Mktg. Svcs., Atlanta, 1994—. Mem. Country Club New Canaan, Edgartown (Mass.) Yacht Club, The Mornings Club (Vero Beach, Fla.). Home: 243 White Oak Shade Rd New Canaan CT 06840-6833

OAKLEY, GODFREY PORTER, JR., health facility administrator, medical educator; b. Greenville, N.C., June 1, 1940; s. Godfrey Porter and Carrie O.; m. Mary Ann Bryant, Sept. 2, 1961; children: Martha Gray, Susan Herndon, Robert Bryant. Student, Duke U., 1958-61; MD, Bowman Gray Sch. of Medicine, 1965; MS in Preventive Medicine, U. Washington, 1972. Diplomate Am. Bd. Pediatrics, Nat. Bd. Med. Examiners, Am. Bd. Preventive Medicine, Am. Bd. Med. Genetics. Intern in straight pediatrics Cleve. Met. Gen. Hosp., 1965-66, resident in pediatrics, 1966-68; sr. fellow in teratology and human embryology U. Washington Sch. of Medicine, Ctrl. Lab. Human Embryology, Dept. of Pediatrics, Seattle, 1970-72; sr. fellow U. Washington Sch. Pub. Health and Community Medicine, Seattle, 1971-72; EIS officer leukemia sect. Ctrs. Disease Control and Prevention (CDC), Atlanta, 1968-70, chief etiology studies sect., bur. epidemiology, cancer and birth defects, 1972-81; chief birth defects br., chronic diseases divisn. Nat. Ctr. Environ. Health, Ctrs. Disease Control and Prevention, Atlanta, 1981-85, dir. divsn. birth defects and devel. disabilities, 1985—; clin. asst. prof. pediatrics divsn. med. genetics Emory U., Atlanta, 1968-70, 72—, clin. asst. prof. gynecology-obstetrics divsn. med. genetics, 1981—; mem. visiting med. staff Grady Meml. Hosp., Atlanta, 1974—; med. adv. bd. Ctrs. Disease Control & Prevention (CDC); mem. task force on predictors of hereditary disease or congenital defects NIH Consensus Conf., 1979; mem. genetics coordinating com. NIH/CDC; mem. adv. com. biometric and epidemiological methodology FDA/CDC; cons. bur. med. svcs. FDA; mem. Chronic Diseases Surveillance Working Group; mem. patient registry com. Cystic Fibrosis Found., med. adv. coun., 1978—; mem. drug experience coordinating com. Dept. Health, Edn. and Welfare; mem. genetics com. Ga. Dept. Human Resources, 1980—; ex-officio mem. genetic diseases rev. and adv. com. Health Svcs. Adminstrn., 1981; mem. master community health program, interdisciplinary faculty com., curriculum com. Emory U.; mem. working group on heart disease epidemiology Nat. Heart, Lung and Blood Insts., 1978; mem. ad hoc com. on Alpha-fetoprotein Pub. Health Svc.; mem. profl. adv. coun. Spina Bifida Assn. Am., 1981—; mem. WHO EURO-China Consultation, Beijing, China, 1983; lectr. in field. Mem. editorial bd. Pediatric & Perinatal Epidemiology, 1987-89; contbr. articles to profl. jours., chpts. to books. Nancy Lybrook Lasater scholar 1961-67; recipient Physician's Recognition award AMA, 1973-76, Outstanding Svc. medal Pub. Health Svc., 1981, Meritorious Svc. award, 1988, Spl. Recognition award, 1993, President's Excellence award Spina Bifida Assn. Am., 1988-89, Disting. Alumnus award U. Washington Sch. Pub. Health, 1990, Hebert L. Needleman award Am. Pub. Health Assn., 1996; named Person of Week, World News Tonight, 1996. Mem. Am. Acad. Pediatrics (past com. drugs/CDC liaison, com. genetics 1990, exec. com. 1990—, CDC rep. Ga. chpt. 1993), Am. Soc. Human Genetics, Am. Coll. Epidemiology, Am. Coll. Med. Genetics, Atlanta Genetics Soc., Greater Atlanta Pediatric Soc., Atlanta Obstetrical and Gynecological Soc. (assoc.), Soc. Epidemiologic Rsch., Soc. Pediatric Rsch., Teratology Soc. (pres. elect 1983-84, pres. 1984-85, editorial bd. Teratology 1978-83, edn. com. 1988), Internat. Clearinghouse Birth Defects Monitoring Systems (chmn. 1981-82, vice chmn. 1982-83, chmn. 1983-84), Pub. Health Leadership Inst., Alpha Omega Alpha. Home: 2224 Kodiak Dr NE Atlanta GA 30345-4152 Office: CDC NCEH BDDD 4770 Buford Hwy NE # F34 Atlanta GA 30341-3717

OAKLEY, JOHN BILYEU, law educator, lawyer, judicial consultant; b. San Francisco, June 18, 1947; s. Samuel Heywood and Elsie-Maye (Bilyeu) O.; m. Fredericka Barvitz, May 25, 1969; children: Adélie, Antonia. BA, U. Calif., Berkeley, 1969; JD, Yale U., 1972. Bar: Calif. 1972, U.S. Dist. Ct. (no. dist.) Calif. 1974, U.S. Dist. Ct. (ctrl. and ea. dists.) Calif. 1975, U.S. Supreme Ct. 1977, U.S. Ct. Appeals (5th cir.) 1979, U.S. Ct. Appeals (9th cir.) 1992. Rsch. atty. chief justice Donald R. Wright Supreme Ct. of Calif., 1972-73, sr. rsch. atty. chief justice Donald R. Wright, 1974-75; sr. law clk. chief judge M. Joseph Blumenfeld U.S. Dist. Ct. Conn., Hartford, 1973-74; acting prof. law U. Calif., Davis, 1975-79, prof. law, 1979—; reporter Speedy Trial Planning Group, U.S. Dist. Ct., Sacramento, 1977-82, Civil Justice Reform Act Adv. Group, 1991-94, U.S. Jud. Conf. Com. on Fed.-State Jurisdiction, 1991-96, Western Regional Conf. on State-Fed. Jud. Relationships, 1992-93; scholar-in-residence, sr. trial atty. Civil Rights Divsn., U.S. Dept. Justice, Washington, 1979-80; vis. scholar U. Coll., Oxford (Eng.) U., 1982-83; apptd. counsel death penalty appeal Supreme Ct. Calif., 1984-96; cons. Calif. Jud. Coun. Commn. on the Future of the Cts., 1992-93. Co-author: Law Clerks and the Judicial Process, 1980, An Introduction to the Anglo-American Legal System, 1980, 2d edit., 1988, Civil Procedure, 1991, 2d edit., 1996; contbr.: Restructuring Justice, 1990. Pub. mem. New Motor Vehicle Bd. Calif., Sacramento, 1976-82; bd. dirs. Fallen Leaf Lake (Calif.) Mutual Water Co., 1980-82, 94—; western regional assoc., field assoc. Duke U. Primate Ctr., 1986-91. With U.S. Merchant Marine, 1969, Vietnam. Nat. Merit scholar, 1964. Mem. Am. Law Inst. (reporter project on revision of fed. jud. code 1995—), Assn. Am. Law Schs. (chair sect. on civil procedure 1979-80, 96-97), Phi Beta Kappa. Avocations: aviation, photography, railroads, rugby, running. Office: Univ Calif Sch Law Davis CA 95616

OAKLEY, MARY ANN BRYANT, lawyer; b. Buckhannon, W.Va., June 22, 1940; d. Hubert Herndon and Mary F. (Deeds) Bryant; m. Godfrey P. Oakley, Jr., Sept. 2, 1961; children: Martha, Susan, Robert. AB, Duke U., 1962; MA, Emory U., 1970, JD, 1974. Tchr., Winston-Salem/Forsyth County Schs., N.C., 1961-65; assoc. Margie Pitts Hames, Atlanta, 1974-80; ptnr. Stagg Hoy & Oakley, Atlanta, 1980-83, Oakley & Bonner, Atlanta, 1984-90; pvt. practice, 1990-96; ptnr. Holland & Knight, Atlanta, 1996—; adj. prof. trial practice Ga. State U., 1986-95; adj. prof. pretrial practice Emory U. Law Sch., 1991, 95—; bd. dirs. Nat. Employment Lawyers Assn., 1989-94; founding coodr. NELA, Ga.; mem. Ga. Supreme Ct. Commn. on Racial and Ethnic Bias, 1994-95. Contbr. articles to law jours. Notes and Comments editor Emory Law Jour., 1973-74. Author: Elizabeth Cady Stanton, 1972; bd. dirs. Atlanta Met. YWCA, 1975-79, 1st v.p., 1978-79; mem. Leadership Atlanta, 1979; bd. dirs. Ga. chpt. ACLU, 1981-83; trustee Unitarian Universalist Congregation Atlanta, 1977-80, pres., 1979-80, mem. Unitarian Universalist Commn. Appraisal, 1980-85; bd. dirs. Unitarian Universalist Service Com., 1984-90, v.p., 1986-88, pres. 1988-90. Nat. Merit scholar, 1958. Mem. ABA, Am. Judicature Soc., State Bar Ga. (chmn. individual rights sect. 1979-81), Atlanta Bar Assn., Lawyers Club Atlanta, No. Dist. Bar Council, 1982-86, Ga. Assn. Women Lawyers, Ga. State Bar Disciplinary Bd. (investigative panel 1985-88, chmn., 1987-88), Bleckley Inn of Ct. (pres. 1996—), Gate City Bar Assn., Ga. Legal Svcs. Program Bd., LWV, Phi Beta Kappa, Order of Coif. Home: 2224 Kodiak Dr NE Atlanta GA 30345-4152 Office: 1201 W Peachtree St 1 Atlantic Ctr Ste 2000 Atlanta GA 30309-3400

OAKLEY, PHYLLIS ELLIOTT, diplomat; b. Omaha, Nov. 23, 1934; d. Thomas Myron Elliott and Elsa (Kerkow) Elliott Garabedian; m. Robert Bigger Oakley, June 8, 1958; children: Mary Oakley Kress, Thomas Elliott. B.A., Northwestern U., 1956; M.A., Fletcher Sch. Law and Diplomacy, 1957. Commd. fgn. svc. officer Dept. State, 1957-58, 74—, asst. cultural affairs officer, Kinshasa, Zaire, 1979-82, desk officer, Afghanistan, 1982-85, Pearson Exchange officer Senator Mathias, 1985-86; dep. spokesman, 1986-86, AID Afghan Humanitarian Assistance program, Islamabad, 1989-91, dep. asst. sec. INR Bur., 1991-93, sr. dep. PRM, 1993-94, asst. sec. PRM, 1994—. Mem. Coun. Fgn. Rels., Cosmos Club, Phi Beta Kappa. Office: Dept of State Bur Population Refugees & Migration 2201 C St NW Washington DC 20520-0001*

OAKLEY, ROBERT LOUIS, law librarian, educator; b. N.Y.C., Nov. 6, 1945; s. Bert Tuttle Oakley and Allese (Duffin) Vestigo; m. Madeleine Cohen, Aug. 13, 1971; children: Esther Shulamit, Daniel Isaac-Meir. BA, Cornell U., 1968; MLS, Syracuse U., 1972; JD, Cornell U., 1976. Bar: N.Y. 1977, U.S. Dist. Ct. (no. dist.) N.Y. 1977. Assoc. dir. law libr. Cornell U., Ithaca, N.Y., 1976-79; dir. law libr., assoc. prof. Boston U. Law, 1979-82; dir. law libr., assoc. prof. Georgetown U., Washington, 1982-87, dir. law libr., prof., 1987—. Contbr. articles to profl. jours. Mem. Libr. of Congress, mem. Network Adv. Com., 1986-92, 95—; adv. nat. commn. on Preservation and Access, 1988-94; bd. dirs. Montgomery County (Md.) Pub. Librs., 1988-92. Mem. ABA, ALA, Am. Assn. Law Librs. (Washington Affairs rep. 1989—, mem. exec. bd. 1991-94), Assn. Am. Law Schs., Libr. of Congress Fgn. Law Classification Adv. Com. Avocations: photography, music, personal computers, amateur radio. Office: Georgetown U Law Ctr 111 G St NW Washington DC 20001-1417

OAKS, B. ANN, plant physiologist, educator; b. Winnipeg, Man., Can., June 4, 1929; d. H.A. and Bernice (Farlinger) O. BA with honors, U. Toronto, Ont., Can., 1951; MA, U. Sask., Can., 1954, PhD, 1959. Alexander von Humbolt assoc. Rsch. Inst. for Dairying, Freising, Fed. Republic Germany, 1958-60; rsch. assoc. Purdue U., West Lafayette, Ind., 1960-64, Oak Ridge (Tenn.) Nat. Lab., 1964-65; asst. prof. biology McMaster U., Hamilton, Ont., 1965-68, assoc. prof., 1968-74, prof., 1974-89; prof. emeritus McMaster U., Hamilton, 1989—; prof. U. Guelph, Ont., 1989—; vis. prof. Wash. State U., 1979-80, U. Nancy, France, 1980, Chiba U., Japan, 1984; adj. prof. U. Guelph, 1987-89; affiliated scientist NRC Lab., Saskatoon, Sask., 1988-92. Assoc. editor Biochemistry and Cell Biology, 1988-90; mem. editl. bd. Plant Physiology, 1970-89, Jour. Plant Physiology, 1984-95, Physiologia Plantarium, 1995-96, Plant and Cell Physiology, 1989-93; contbg. author various books; contbr. articles to profl. jours. Rsch. grantee in field. Fellow Royal Soc. Can.; mem. Can. Soc. Plant Physiologists (treas. 1974-76, Gold medal 1989), Am. Soc. Plant Physiologists. Avocations: skiing, hiking, naturalist, writing letters to members of parliament. Office: U Guelph, Dept Botany, Guelph, ON Canada N1G 2W1

OAKS, DALLIN HARRIS, lawyer, church official; b. Provo, Utah, Aug. 12, 1932; s. Lloyd E. and Stella (Harris) O.; m. June Dixon, June 24, 1952; children: Sharmon, Cheri Lyn, Lloyd D., Dallin D., TruAnn, Jenny June. BA with high honors, Brigham Young U., 1954, LLD (hon.), 1980; JD cum laude, U. Chgo., 1957; LLD (hon.), Pepperdine U., 1982, So. Utah U., 1991. Bar: Ill. 1957, Utah 1971. Law clk. to Chief Justice Earl Warren U.S. Supreme Ct., 1957-58; with firm Kirkland, Ellis, Hodson, Chaffetz & Masters, Chgo., 1958-61; mem. faculty U. Chgo. Law Sch., 1961-71, assoc. dean and acting dean, 1962, prof., 1964-71, mem. vis. com., 1971-74; pres. Brigham Young U., Provo, Utah, 1971-80; also prof. law J. Reuben Clark Law Sch., 1974-80; justice Utah Supreme Ct., 1981-84; mem. Coun. of Twelve Apostles Ch. Jesus Christ of Latter Day Sts., 1984—; legal counsel Bill of Rights com. Ill. Constl. Conv., 1970. Author: (with G.G. Bogert) Cases on Trusts, 1967, 78, (with W. Lehman) A Criminal Justice System and The Indigent, 1968, The Criminal Justice Act in the Federal District Courts, 1969, (with M. Hill) Carthage Conspiracy, 1975, Trust Doctrines in Church Controversies, 1984, Pure in Heart, 1988, The Lord's Way, 1991; editor: The Wall Between Church and State, 1963. Mem. Wilson coun. Woodrow Wilson Internat. Ctr. for Scholars, 1973-80; trustee Intermountain Health Care Inc., 1975-80; mem. adv. com. Nat. Inst. Law Enforcement and Criminal Justice, 1974-76; bd. dirs. Notre Dame Ctr. for Constl. Studies, 1977-80, Rockford Inst., 1980—; bd. dirs. Pub. Broadcasting Svc., 1977-85, chmn., 1980-85; bd. dirs. Polynesian Cultural Ctr., 1987-96, chmn., 1988-96. Fellow Am. Bar Found. (exec. dir. 1970-71); mem. Am. Assn. Pres. Ind. Colls. and Univs. (pres. 1975-78, dir. 1971-78), Order of Coif. Mem. Ch. of Jesus Christ of Latter-day Saints (regional rep. 1974-80; past 1st counselor Chgo. South Stake). Address: 47 E South Temple Salt Lake City UT 84150

OAKS, LUCY MOBERLEY, retired social worker; b. Lexington, Ky., May 10, 1935; d. Shelton Neville Moberley and Jane Emison (Roberts) Meadors; m. William Bryant Oaks, Nov. 10, 1956; children: Bryant, Michael, Kevin, Richard, Deborah. BA in Social Work, U. Ky., 1957; MA in Counseling Psychology, Bowie (Md.) State Coll., 1979. Cert. mental health counselor, Wash. Youth dir. Calvary Bapt. Ch., Renton, Wash., 1960-64, ch. tng. dir., 1980-87; youth dir. Temple Bapt. Ch., Redlands, Calif., 1965-68, Calvary Bapt. Ch., Morgantown, W.Va., 1971-73; cmty. coll. parent educator Bellevue (Wash.) Cmty. Coll., 1980-89; pvt. counselor Renton, 1980-90; Christians social svcs. dir. Puget Sound Bapt. Assn., Federal Way, Wash., 1984-87; program dir. ACAP Child and Family Svcs., Auburn, Wash., 1989-93; assoc. dir. ACAP Child and Family Svcs., Auburn, 1994-96; parent instr. APPLE Parenting, Auburn, 1990-92; seminar presenter, Puget Sound, Wash., 1980-95; therapeutic program cons. ACAP Child and Family Svcs., 1997—. Bd. trustee Valley Cmty. Players, Renton, 1995; bd. dirs. Calvary Bapt. Ch., Renton, 1981-87. Mem. Puget Sound Adlerian Soc. (bd. dirs. 1981-83), Nat. Assn. Adlerian Psychologists (assoc. mem.), Wash. Counseling Assn., Kiwanis (chmn. interclub com., membership chmn. 1994-95). Democrat. Avocations: drama, reading, walking, traveling, bowling. Home: 2218 177th Pl NE Redmond WA 98052

OAKS, MAURICE DAVID, retired pharmaceutical company executive; b. Everett, Pa., Jan. 22, 1934; s. Jacob Garvin and Hannah Alma (Young) O.; m. Judith Ann Rayne; 1 child, Kimberly. BS in Biology, Franklin and Marshall Coll., 1956. Sales rep. Squibb Pharm, Salisbury and Balt., Md., 1959-69; div. sales mgr. Squibb Pharm., Columbus, Ohio, 1969-71; product mgr. Squibb Pharm., Princeton, N.J., 1971-76, group product dir. antibiotics, cardiovasculars, and insulin, 1976-78, dir. product planning, U.S., 1979-80, v.p. world wide mktg. devel., 1980-82, v.p. mktg. svcs., 1983-85, pres. Princeton Pharm. Products, 1985-89; exec. v.p. Squibb Pharm. Group U.S., Princeton, N.J., 1989-90; v.p. worldwide ops. planning Bristol-Myers Squibb

Pharms. Ops., Princeton, 1990-92; bd. dirs. Nat. Pharm. Coun., McLean, Va., 1985-90, mem. exec. com., 1988-90; bd. dirs., mem. audit com. Penn Engring. Mfg., Danboro, Pa. Mem. coun. Franklin and Marshall Coll. Commn. on Found. and Corp. Support, Lancaster, Pa., 1987-90, ann. fund class capt., 1991—; mem., pres. Mid-Atlantic regional adv. coun. Franklin and Marshall Coll., also mem. phys. scis. labs. renovation com., 1996—; bd. dirs. Surf's Edge Condo Assn., Ocean City, Md., 1995—; active YMCA, Doylestown, Pa. With U.S. Army, 1956-58. Mem. Doylestown (Pa.) Country Club. Republican. Methodist. Avocations: tennis, golf, bicycling.

OATES, ADAM R., professional hockey player; b. Weston, Ont., Can., Aug. 27, 1962. Attended, Rensselaer Polytech. Inst., 1985. With Detroit Red Wings, 1985-89, St. Louis Blues, 1989-92, Boston Bruins, 1992—; player NHL All-Star Game, 1991-94. Named NCAA All-American, 1984-85; named to Sporting News All-Star Team, 1990-91. Office: Boston Bruins 1 Fleet Ctr Ste 250 Boston MA 02114-1303*

OATES, CARL EVERETTE, lawyer; b. Harlingen, Tex., Apr. 8, 1931; s. Joseph William and Grace (Watson) O.; m. Eileen N. Hudnall; children: Carl William, Gregory Carl Hudnall, Patricia O. Chase, Matthew Noble Hudnall. BS, U.S. Naval Acad., 1955; LLB, So. Meth. U., 1962. Bar: Tex. 1962, D.C. 1977, Nebr. 1985. Assoc. Akin, Gump, Strauss, Hauer & Feld, Dallas, 1962-64, ptnr., 1965-91. Asst. atty. gen. State of Texas, 1992-94, spl. coun., Tex. Dept. Banking, 1994-95, prin. Carl E. Oates, P.C. Chmn. bd. trustees S.W. Mus. Sci. and Tech., Dallas; v.p. S.W. Sci. Mus. Found., Dallas; bd. dirs. Kiwanis Wesley Dental Ctr., Inc., Dallas; pres. Wesley Dental Found., Dallas. Served to lt. USN, 1955-59. Mem. ABA, D.C. Bar Assn., Tex. Bar Assn., Dallas Bar Assn., Nebr. Bar Assn., Barristers, Northwood Club, Delta Theta Phi.

OATES, JAMES G., advertising executive; b. Kenton, Ohio, Apr. 2, 1943; m. Sue Ann Minter; 2 children. BS, Ohio State U. Trainee Leo Burnett USA, Chgo., 1966-68, asst. acct. exec., 1968-69, acct. exec., 1969-73, acct. supv., 1973-74, v.p., 1974-77, acct. supv. GM Olds acct., 1977-80, mgmt. dir. Philip Morris account, 1980-84, sr. v.p., 1984-86, exec. v.p., 1986-90, vice chmn., dir. client svcs., 1990-92, chmn., bd. dirs., mem. exec. com., 1992—, group pres. Asia/Pacific, 1993-97; pres. Leo Burnett Co., 1997—; bd. dirs. The Advt. Coun. mem. MBA adv. bd. Ohio State U.; Kellogg Adv. Bd.; active Chgo. Crime Commn. Mem. Am. Assn. Advt. Agys. (bd. govs. Chgo. chpt.). Office: Leo Burnett Co Inc 35 W Wacker Dr Chicago IL 60601-1614*

OATES, JOHN ALEXANDER, III, medical educator; b. Fayetteville, N.C., Apr. 23, 1932; s. John Alexander and Isabelle (Crowder) O.; m. Meredith Stringfield, June 12, 1956; children: David Alexander, Christine Larkin, James Caldwell. BS magna cum laude, Wake Forest Coll., 1953; MD, Bowman Gray Sch. Medicine, 1956. Intern, then asst. resident medicine N.Y. Hosp.-Cornell U. Med. Center, N.Y.C., 1956-58, 61-62; clin. assoc., then sr. investigator Nat. Heart Inst., 1958-63; mem. faculty Vanderbilt U. Sch. Medicine, 1963—, prof. medicine and pharmacology, 1969—, Werthan prof. investigative medicine, 1974-84, chmn. dept. medicine, 1983—; mem. drug research bd. Nat. Acad. Scis.-NRC, 1967-71; chmn. pharmacology and toxicology tng. com. Nat. Inst. Gen. Med. Scis., 1969-70; mem . adv. coun. Nat. Heart, Lung and Blood Inst., 1985-89. Fellow ACP, Am. Acad. Arts & Scis.; mem. Am. Fedn. Clin. Rsch. (pres. 1970-71), Am. Soc. Clin. Investigation (v.p. 1976-77), Assn. Am. Physicians (pres. 1981-82), Am. Soc. Pharmacology and Exptl. Therapeutics (chmn. exec. com. divsn. clin. pharmacology 1967-69), Inst. of Medicine. Participated in discovery antihypertensive effect of methyldopa, elucidation of a number of interactions between drugs in man; research on the biochemistry and pathophysiology of eicosanoids. Home: 6440 Brownlee Dr Nashville TN 37205-3162 Office: Vanderbilt U Med Ctr Dept Internal Medicine D3100 MCN Nashville TN 37232-2358

OATES, JOHN FRANCIS, classics educator; b. Holyoke, Mass., Aug. 7, 1934; s. William Adrian and Lilian (Woods) O.; m. Rosemary Walsh, June 27, 1957; children: Elizabeth, Emily, John Francis, Sarah. B.A., Yale U., 1956, M.A., 1958, Ph.D., 1960; postgrad. (Fulbright fellow), Am. Sch. Classical Studies in Athens, Greece, 1956-57. Instr. classics Yale U., 1960-63, asst. prof., 1963-67; asso. prof. ancient history Duke U., 1967-71, prof., 1971—, chmn. dept. classical studies, 1971-80, chmn. Humanities Council, 1975-80, dir. database of documentary papyri, 1982—, dir. papyrus catalog project, 1992-95; Hon. research asst., Morse fellow Univ. Coll. London (Eng.), 1965-66; vis. prof. Smith Coll., Northampton, Mass., 1967, 68; mem. mng. com. Intercollegiate Center Classical Studies in Rome, Italy, 1972-77, Am. Sch. Classical Studies in Athens, 1973—, mem. com. on coms., 1975-77; mem. Council for Internat. Exchange of Scholars, 1974-77; v.p., trustee Triangle Univs. Center for Advanced Study, Inc., 1975-90; trustee Nat. Humanities Center, 1977-90, trustee emeritus, 1990—; adv. council Sch. Classical Studies, Am. Acad. in Rome, 1976—; dir. summer seminar Nat. Endowment Humanities, 1978; dir. Nat. Fedn. State Humanities Councils, 1980-83; mem. N.C. Humanities Com., 1977-83, chmn. 1980-82. Author: The Status Designatin, 1963 (with A.E. Samuel and C.B. Welles) Yale Papri in the Beinecke Library, 1967, (with W.H. Willis and R.S. Bagnall) A Checklist of Papyrological Editions, 4th edit., 1992, (with Willis) Duke Data Bank of Documentary, Papyri (CD-ROM), 1996, The Basilikos Grammateus, 1995; mem. adv. bd. Greek, Roman and Byzantine Studies, 1977—, Humanities Report, 1981-83. Am. Council Learned Socs. fellow, 1973-74. Mem. Am. Philol. Assn. (chmn. com. computer activities 1974-75, dir. 1975-78, mem. nominating com. 1980-83), Archaeol. Inst. Am., Am. Hist. Assn., Am. Soc. Papyrologists (v.p. 1971-73, pres. 1976-80, dir.), Assn. Internationale de Papyrologues, Classical Assn. Middle West and South (v.p. 1972-74, pres. So. sect. 1974-76). Home: 2416 Alpine Rd Durham NC 27707-3818 Office: Dept of Classical Studies Duke U Durham NC 27708-0103

OATES, JOHNNY LANE, professional baseball team manager; b. Sylva, N.C., Jan. 21, 1946. BS in Health and Phys. Edn., Va. Tech. U. Player minor league team Chgo. White Sox, 1967; player minor league team Balt. Orioles, 1967-71, player, 1970, 72, mgr. minor league team, 1988, coach, 1989-91, mgr., 1991-94; player Atlanta Braves, 1973-75, Phila. Phillies, 1975-76, L.A. Dodgers, 1977-79; player N.Y. Yankees, 1980, minor league coach, 1981-83; coach Chgo. Cubs, 1984-87; mgr. Texas Rangers, 1995—. Named Internat. League Mgr. of Yr., 1988, coach Am. League All-Star Team, 1993, 95, Am. League Mgr. of the Year by The Sporting News, 1993, 96, co Am. League Mgr. of the Year by Baseball Writers' Assn. of Am., 1996. Office: The Ballpark in Arlington 1000 Ballpark Way Arlington TX 76011-5168*

OATES, JOYCE CAROL, author; b. Lockport, N.Y., June 16, 1938; d. Frederic James and Caroline (Bush) O.; m. Raymond Joseph Smith, Jan. 23, 1961. BA, Syracuse U., 1960; MA, U. Wis., 1961. Instr. English U. Detroit, 1961-65, asst. prof., 1965-67; prof. English U. Windsor, Ont., Can., 1967-87; writer-in-residence Princeton (N.J.) U., 1978-81, prof., 1987—. Author: (short story collections) By the North Gate, 1963, Upon the Sweeping Flood, 1966, The Wheel of Love, 1970, Marriages and Infidelities, 1972, The Hungry Ghosts, 1974, The Goddess and Other Women, 1974, Where Are You Going, Where Have You Been?: Stories of Young America, 1974, The Poisoned Kiss and Other Stories From the Portuguese, 1975, The Seduction and Other Stories, 1975, Crossing the Border, 1976, Night-Side, 1977, All the Good People I've Left Behind, 1978, The Lamb of Abyssalia, 1980, A Sentimental Education: Stories, 1981, Last Days: Stories, 1984, Wild Nights, 1985, Raven's Wing: Stories, 1986, The Assignation, 1988, Heat: And Other Stories, 1991, Where is Here?, 1992, Haunted: Tales of the Grotesque, 1994, Will You Always Love Me? and Other Stories, 1995; (novels) With Shuddering Fall, 1964, A Garden of Earthly Delights, 1967 (Nat. Book award nomination 1968), Expensive People, 1967 (Nat. Book award nomination 1969), them, 1969 (Nat. Book award for fiction 1970), Wonderland, 1971, Do With Me What You Will, 1973, The Assassins, 1975, Childwold, 1976, The Triumph of the Spider Monkey, 1976, Son of the Morning, 1978, Unholy Loves, 1979, Cybele, 1979, Bellefleur, 1980 (L.A. Times Book award nomination 1980), A Sentimental Education, 1981, Angel of Light, 1981, A Bloodsmoor Romance, 1982, Mysteries of Winterthorn, 1984, Solstice, 1985, Marya, 1986, You Must Remember This, 1987, (as Rosamond Smith) The Lives of the Twins, 1987, American Appetites, 1989, (as Rosamond Smith) Soul-Mate, 1989, Because It Is Bitter, and Because It Is My Heart, 1990, (as Rosamond Smith) Nemesis, 1990, I Lock My Door Upon Myself, 1990, The Rise of Life on Earth, 1991, Black Water, 1992, (as Rosamond Smith) Snake Eyes, 1992, Foxfire: Confessions of a Girl Gang, 1993, What I Lived For, 1994 (PEN/Faulkner award nomination 1995); (poetry collections) Women in Love, 1968, Expensive People, 1968, Anonymous Sins, 1969, Love and Its Derangements, 1970, Angel Fire, 1973, Dreaming America, 1973, The Fabulous Beasts, 1975, Season of Peril, 1977, Women Whose Lives are Food, Men Whose Lives are Money: Poems, 1978, The Stepfather, 1978, Celestial Timepiece, 1981, Invisible Women: New and Selected Poems, 1970-1972, 1982, Luxury of Sin, 1983, The Time Traveller, 1987; (plays) The Sweet Enemy, 1965, Sunday Dinner, 1970, Ontological Proof of My Existence, 1970, Miracle Play, 1974, Three Plays, 1980, Daisy, 1980, Presque Isle, 1984, Triumph of the Spider Monkey, 1985, In Darkest America, 1990, I Stand Before You Naked, 1990, The Perfectionist and Other Plays, 1995; (essays) The Edge of Impossibility, 1972, The Hostile Sun: The Poetry of D.H. Lawrence, 1973, New Heaven, New Earth, 1974, Contraries: Essays, 1981, The Profane Art, 1984, On Boxing, 1987, (Woman) Writer: Occasions and Opportunities, 1988; editor, compiler: Scenes from American Life: Contemporary Short Fiction, 1973, (with Shannon Ravenel) Best American Short Stories of 1979, 1979, Night Walks, 1982, First Person Singular: Writer's on Their Craft, 1983, (with Boyd Litzinger) Story: Fictions Past and Present, 1985, (with Daniel Halpern) Reading and Fights, 1988, The Oxford Book of American Short Stories, 1992, The Sophisticated Cat: An Anthology, 1992; editor (with Raymond Smith) Ontario Rev.; contbr. to nat. mags. including N.Y. Times Book Rev., Mich. Quarterly Rev., Mademoiselle, Vogue, North Am. Rev., Hudson Rev., Paris Rev., Grand Street, Atlantic, Poetry, Esquire. Recipient O. Henry award, 1967, 73, Rosenthal award Nat. Inst. Arts and Letters, 1968, O. Henry Spl. award continuing achievement, 1970, 86, Award of Merit Lotos Club, 1975, St. Louis Lit. award, 1988, Rea award for the Short Story, 1990, Alan Swallow award for fiction, 1990, Nobel Prize in Lit. nomination, 1993; Guggenheim fellow, 1967-68, Nat. Endowment for the Arts grantee, 1966, 68. Mem. Am. Acad. and Inst. Arts and Letters. Office: care John Hawkins 71 W 23rd St Ste 1600 New York NY 10010-4102

OATES, JOYCE MARIE, psychiatrist; b. Salt Lake City, Mar. 31, 1948; d. Douglas Francis and Lois Joy (Allgaier) O. BS magna cum laude, U. Utah, 1970, MD, 1974. Diplomate Am. Bd. Psychiatry and Neurology. Intern Pa. Hosp., Phila., 1974-75; resident in psychiatry Inst. of Pa. Hosp., Phila., 1975-78; physician Intensive Treatment unit Copper Mountain Community Mental Health Ctr., Salt Lake City, 1978-79; pvt. practice psychiatry Salt Lake City, 1980-88; med. dir. psychiatry Yuma (Ariz.) Reg. Med. Ctr., 1988-90; psychiatrist locum tenens CompHealth, Salt Lake City, 1990; pvt. practice psychiatrist Las Vegas, 1990—; med. dir. Cinnamon Hills residential treatment, 1993—; med. dir., part owner Vista Treatment Ctr., St. George, Utah, 1995-96. Mem. Latter Day Saints. Avocations: writing, weaving, spinning.

OATES, SHERRY CHARLENE, portraitist; b. Houston, Sept. 11, 1946; d. Charles Emil and Berniece Faye (Lohse) O. Student, North Tex. State U., 1965-66; student under Martin Kellogg; BA in English, Health and Phys. Edn., Houston Bapt. U., 1968. Cert. art tchr., Tex. Tchr. Jackson Jr. High Sch., Houston, 1968-69, Percy Priest Sch., Nashville, 1969-70, Franklin (Tenn.) High Sch., 1970-84; freelance illustrator Bapt. Sunday Sch. Bd., Nashville, 1978-85, United Meth. Pub. House, Nashville, 1980-85; portraitist in oils, owner Portraits, Ltd., Nashville, 1984—. Portraits include corp. leaders, educators, politicians, hist. and equestrian subjects, society figures and children; participated in various exhbns. at Bapt. Sunday Sch. Bd. and All State and Ctr. South Exhibits at the Parthenon. Recipient 3d place in graphics Ctrl. South Exhbn. at The Parthenon-Tenn. Art League, 1986. Mem. Tenn. Art League. Republican. Baptist. Avocations: antiques, photography. Studio: 816 Kirkwood Ave Nashville TN 37204-2602

OATES, STEPHEN BAERY, history educator; b. Pampa, Tex., Jan. 5, 1936; s. Steve Theodore and Florence (Baer) O.; divorced; children: Gregory Allen, Stephanie; m. Marie Phillips. B.A. magna cum laude, U. Tex., 1958, M.A., 1960, Ph.D., 1968; Litt.D. (hon.), Lincoln Coll., 1981. Prof. history U. Mass., Amherst, 1971—; now also Paul Murray Kendall prof. biography U. Mass., adj. prof. English, 1980—. Author: Confederate Cavalry West of the River, 1961, Rip Ford's Texas, 1963, Republic of Texas, 1968, Visions of Glory, 1970, To Purge This Land With Blood: A Biography of John Brown, 1970, Portrait of America, 2 vols., 1973, rev. edits., 1976, 83, 86, 90, 94, The Fires of Jubilee: Nat Turner's Fierce Rebellion, 1975, With Malice Toward None: The Life of Abraham Lincoln (Christopher award for outstanding lit., Barondess/Lincoln award N.Y. Civil War Round Table 1977), Our Fiery Trial: Abraham Lincoln, John Brown, and the Civil War Era, 1979, Let the Trumpet Sound: The Life of Martin Luther King, Jr., 1982 (Christopher award, Robert F. Kennedy Meml. Book award), Abraham Lincoln, The Man Behind the Myths, 1984, Biography as High Adventure: Life Writers Speak on Their Art, 1986, William Faulkner: The Man and the Artist, 1987, A Woman of Valor: Clara Barton and the Civil War, 1994, The Approaching Fury: Voices of the Storm, 1820-1861, 1997; contbr. articles and essays to periodicals; lectr. Recipient Chancellor's medal for outstanding scholarship U. Mass., 1976, Disting. Teaching award, 1981, Faculty fellowship award, 1981; Presdl. Writers award, 1985; Master Tchr. award U. Hartford, 1985; Silver Medal award Case Council for Advance and Support of Edn., Prof. of Yr., 1986, 87, Kidger award New Eng. History Tchrs. Assn., Nevins-Freeman award Chgo. Civil War Round Table, 1993; Guggenheim fellow, 1972; sr. summer fellow NEH, 1978. Fellow Tex. State Hist. Assn.; mem. Tex. Inst. Letters, Soc. Am. Historians, Am. Antiquarian Soc., Phi Beta Kappa. Office: U Mass Dept History Amherst MA 01003

OATES, THOMAS R., university executive; married; 4 children. BA in English and Philosophy, St. Louis U., 1964, MA in English, 1970; postgrad., Am. Film Inst. Ctr., Beverly Hills, Calif., 1971; PhD in Am. Lit., St. Louis U., 1979. Coord., dir. program assts. and counselors upward bound pgm. Webster Coll., 1970-71, dir. media/journalism degree program, 1974-81, coord. MA program in media comms., 1975-81; chair, assoc. prof. dept. journalism St. Michael's Coll., 1981-85; campus dean U. Wis. Ctr., Richland Center, 1985-89; dir. U.S. ops. and acad. programs Coop. Assn. of States for Scholarships, Georgetown U., Washington, 1989-94; pres. Spalding U., Louisville, 1994—; mem. media adv. com. Mo. State Coun. of Arts, 1973-77; mem. planning commn. State Dept. of Higher Edn., Baton Rouge, 1979-80; mem., rep. Mo.'s ind. colls. and univs. Cen. Ednl. Network Mo., 1979-81; mem. adv. bd. Tri-State Bilingual Tng. Program, St. Michael's Coll., 1981-83; mem. Vt. Cath. Press Assn. Bd., 1984-85; mem., appointed chair Internat. Edn. Coun., U. Wis. Sys., 1987-88, designer, author Ctr. of Excellence project, 1988; mem. acad. staff adv. bd., U. Wis. Ctr. Sys., 1987-89, chair acad. staff grievance com., 1988; mem. 9-person state commn. to develop criteria for legal evaluations of devel. projects reviewed under Act 250 environ. law, Vt., 1984-85; presenter on internat. ednl. regional and nat. meetings of various orgns. Author, designer: (slide-tape program on history of early French and English explorers in mid-west) Old Land, New Land, 1985; author, designer: (book) Images, Values, and Development in Chittenden County, 1984; prodr.: (documentary photographic study on 5 rural Alaskan comtys.) Images of Continuity, Images of Change, 1977; prodr., dir.: (16mm documentary film) The Faces of British Honduras, 1974. Grantee Mo. Coun. on Arts, 1972, 76, NEH, 1975, U. Alaska, 1978, Mo. Coun. on Humanities, 1979, Vt. Coun. on Humanities, 1981, IBM, 1982, U. Wis. Ext., 1988, Wis. Coun. for Humanities, 1989, Orgn. for Petroleum Exporting Countries, 1992, C.C.'s for Internat. Devel., 1992. Office: Spalding U Office pres 851 S 4th St Louisville KY 40203-2115*

OATES, WILLIAM ARMSTRONG, JR., investment company executive; b. Pitts., July 27, 1942; s. William Armstrong and Margaret (Nichols) O.; m. Elizabeth Dick Macy, Sept. 7, 1968; children: Elizabeth N., Katherine M., Emily E.A. BA, Colby Coll., 1965; MBA, Harvard U., 1972. Asst. treas. Morgan Guaranty Trust, N.Y.C., 1966-70; trustee, dir. Northeast Investors Trust, Boston, 1972—; pres. Northeast Investors Growth Fund, Boston, 1980—; ptnr. Guild, Monrad & Oates, Inc., 1984—; dir. Horn Corp., Ayer, Mass., Furman Lumber Co., Boston, Clifford Inc., Bethel, Vt. Pres. bd. trustees Groton (Mass.) Sch., 1979; trustee, treas. Roxbury Latin Sch., West Roxbury, Mass., 1975—. Served to 2d lt. Army N.G., 1966-70. Republican. Episcopalian. Clubs: Harvard (Boston); Brookline Country (Brookline, Mass.); Somerset (Boston). Home: 201 Village Ave Dedham MA 02026-4230 Office: Guild, Monrad & Oates Inc 50 Congress St Boston MA 02109-4002

OATWAY, FRANCIS CARLYLE, corporate executive; b. Bermuda, Nov. 29, 1936; s. Charles Y. and Josephine (McLellan) O.; m. Ann Thomason; children—Stephen F., Karen E., Andrew C., Christopher M. BSBA, Boston Coll., 1960. C.P.A., Mass., N.Y., others. With Deloitte Haskins & Sells, N.Y.C., 1960-80, ptnr., 1970-80; v.p. taxation Continental Group, Inc., Stamford, Conn., 1980-81, v.p. treasury and taxation, 1981-82, v.p. fin., 1982-83, v.p., chief fin. officer, 1983; exec. v.p., pres., dir. Continental Forest Industries, Inc., Stamford, Conn., 1984-85; pres. Hargro Assocs., Stamford, Conn., 1985—; pres., CEO, dir. Hargro Enterprises, Inc., Stamford, 1985—; chmn., CEO, bd. dirs. NER Data Products, Glassboro, N.J., 1985—; pres., bd. dirs. Covent Ins. Co. Ltd., Hamilton, Bermuda, 1980-85; chmn. bd., mng. dir. CCC Finanz A.G., Zug, Switzerland, 1980-85; mng. dir. Continental Group Overseas Fin. N.V., Curacao, Netherlands Antilles, 9181-85; bd. dirs. Hansa Reins Co. Am., Tarrytown, N.Y., chmn. bd. Apple Syndicate Corp., Westport, Conn., 1983-85. Contbg. editor: Federal Income Taxation of Banks and Financial Institutions, 1968, Professional Responsibility in Federal Tax Practice, 1970; contbr. articles to fin. jours. Trustee Convent of Sacred Heart, Greenwich, Conn., 1979-83; mem. acctg. adv. bd. Columbia U. Grad. Sch. Bus., N.Y.C., 1982-86; mem. exec. com. Boston Coll. Wall St. Coun., 1989—; trustee Conn. Pub. Expenditure Coun., Inc., Hartford, 1984-85; mem. pres.'s adv. bd. Weston Sch. Theology, Cambridge, 1993—. Roman Catholic. Clubs: Union League (N.Y.C.); Landmark (Stamford); Country of New Canaan (Conn.). Office: Hargro Assocs One Landmark Sq Stamford CT 06901

OBAIDAT, MOHAMMAD SALAMEH, electrical and computer engineering educator; b. Kofrsoum, Irbid, Jordan, Dec. 22, 1952; came to U.S., 1981; s. Salameh Mohammad and Wardeh Ahmed Obaidat; m. Balqies I. Sadoun, June 1, 1988. BSEE, Aleppo U., Syria, 1975; MSEE, MS in Computer Engring., Ohio State U., 1982, PhD in Elec. and Computer Engring., 1986. Chief engr. video dept. Jordan TV, Amman, 1975-81; grad. rsch. asst. elec. engring. Ohio State U., 1981-86; asst. prof. elec. engring. U. Sci. and Tech., Irbid, 1986-89; asst. prof., dir. computer engring. rsch. lab. U. Mo., Columbia, 1989-92; assoc. prof. elec. engring. CUNY, 1992-96; prof., chmn. dept. computer sci. Monmouth U., West Long Branch, N.J., 1996—; vis. rschr. Ohio State U., 1987; organizer, prin. instr. workshop Jordan U. Sci. and Tech., 1989; instr. engr.-in-tng. course U. Mo., Truman, 1990; reviewer many jours. and confs. including IEEE Trans. Sys. Man and Cybernetics, Computers and Elec. Engring. Jour., Info. Scis. Jour., Simulation Jour., Internat. Jour. in Computer Simulation, IEEE Transactions Instrumentation & Measurement Conf. on Distributed Computing Systems; presenter numerous seminars. Mem. editl. bd. IEEE Transactions on Instrumentation and Measurement, ACM Applied Computing Rev.; assoc. editor Modeling and Simulation, 1991, 92, IEEE Trans. Sys. Man, Cybernetics, SCS Simulation Jour., Jour. Computers & Elec. Engring.; guest editor Simulation Jour., 1992, 95, 97, IEEE Trans. on SMC on neural networks applications, 1996, IEEE Trans. System Man. Cybernetics, 1996-97; contbr. numerous articles to profl. jours. Grantee Gerhard Cibis Inc., 1992, Mo. Rsch. Asst. Act and TransSoft 32 Ltd., 1991-93, Intel Corp., 1991, Tex. Instruments, 1991, U. Mo. at Columbia, 1991, Motorola, 1990, 95, U. Mo. at Columbia/U. Mo. at Kans. City Engring., 1990, ODA, 1989, U. Mo., 1991, CUNY, 1993-96, Nat. Security Agy., 1995, 96, NSA. Mem. IEEE (sr. admission and advancement com. 1991-92, ACM dist. vis. lectr. 1995-96, tutorial chair IPCCC conf. 1993-95, program chair internat. conf. electronics, circuits & sys. 1995, program chair internat. Phoenix conf. on computers and comms. 1996, vice gen. chair internat. performance, computing, and comm. conf., 1997, program co-chair, 1997, summer computer simulation conf., vice gen. chair 1997 IEEE Internat. performance, computing, and comm. conf., Disting. Spkr. award 1994—, others), IEEE Computer Soc. (chmn. Kansas City chpt. 1991-92, co-founder, CSAB evaluator, vice chmn. Kansas City chpt. 1990-91, recognition certs., reviewer jours., transactions, participant, organizer numerous confs.), Soc. for Computer Simulation (chair numerous conf. sessions and tracks, presenter numerous seminars), Assn. for Computing Machinery (chair numerous confs., sessions and tracks).

O'BANNON, ED, professional basketball player; b. Aug. 14, 1972; 1 child, Aaron. Grad., UCLA. Forward N.J. Nets, 1995—. Recipient John Wooden award as Nat. Player of Yr., Chevrolet/CBS, Most Outstanding Player in Final Four, Player of Yr. USBWA; named to 1st Team All-Am., AP. Office: NJ Nets 405 Murray Hill Pkwy East Rutherford NJ 07073-2136

O'BANNON, FRANK LEWIS, governor, lawyer; b. Louisville, Jan. 30, 1930; s. Robert Pressley and Rosella Faith (Dropsey) O'B.; m. Judith Mae Asmus, Aug. 18, 1957; children: Polly, Jennifer, Jonathan. AB, Ind. U., 1952, JD, 1957. Ind. 1957. Pvt. practice Corydon; ptnr. Hays, O'Bannon & Funk, Corydon, 1966-80, O'Bannon, Funk & Simpson, Corydon, 1980-94, Funk, Simpson, Thompson & Byrd, Corydon, 1995—; mem. Ind. Senate, Corydon, 1970-89, minority floor leader, 1979-89, asst. minority floor leader, 1972-76; lt. gov. State of Ind., Corydon, 1989-96, gov., 1997—; chmn., dir. O'Bannon Pub. Co., Inc. Served with USAF, 1952-54. Mem. Ind. Dem. Editorial Assn. (pres. 1961), Am. Judicature Soc., Am. Bar Assn., Ind. Bar Assn. Democrat. Methodist. Office: Office of the Gov State Capitol Rm 206 Indianapolis IN 46204*

O'BARA, KENNETH J., physician; b. Detroit, Feb. 27, 1947; s. John Joseph and Catherine (Levens) O'Bara; m. Marianne Schwartz, July 29, 1972; children: Thomas, Mickel. BSE, U. Mich., Ann Arbor, 1969, MD, 1976. Diplomate Am. Bd. Emergency Medicine. Resident Truman Med. Ctr., Kansas City, Mo., 1976-79; mem. staff St. Joseph Mercy Hosp., Ann Arbor, 1979-80, Centralia (Wash.) Gen. Hosp., 1980-81, St. Helen's Hosp., Chehalis, Wash., 1980-81, Valley Med. Ctr., Renton, Wash., 1981—; ACLS affiliate faculty Am. Heart Assn., Seattle, 1982-86; co-dir. Assn. Emergency Physicians, Seattle, 1983-85. Fellow Am. Coll. Emergency Physicians, Wash. State Med. Soc., King County Med. Soc. Office: 8009 S 180th St Ste 103 Kent WA 98032-1042

OBEAR, FREDERICK WOODS, academic administrator; b. Malden, Mass., June 9, 1935; s. William Fred and Dorothea Louise (Woods) O.; m. Patricia A. Draper, Aug. 30, 1959 (dec. Dec. 1993); children: Jeffrey Allan, Deborah Anne, James Frederick. BS with high honors, U. Mass., Lowell, 1956, LHD, 1985; PhD, U. N.H., 1961. Mem. faculty dept. chemistry Oakland U., Rochester, Mich., 1960-81, prof., 1979-81, v.p. for acad. affairs, provost, 1970-81; chancellor U. Tenn., Chattanooga, 1981—; mem. nat. addv. panel Nat. Commn. on Higher Edn. Issues, 1981; mem. pres. commn. NCAA, 1991-94. Trustee Marygrove Coll., 1973-79. Am. Council Edn. fellow, 1967-68. Mem. AAAS, Am. Assn. State Colls. and Univs. (bd. dirs. 1992—, chair 1995), Am. Chem. Soc., Am. Assn. Higher Edn., Sigma Xi. Roman Catholic. Office: U Tenn Office of Chancellor 615 Mccallie Ave Chattanooga TN 37403-2504

OBENBERGER, THOMAS E., lawyer; b. Milwaukee, Wis., Nov. 29, 1942. AB, Marquette U., 1965, JD, 1967. Bar: Wis. 1967. Law clk. to Hon. E. Harold Hallows Wis. Supreme Ct., 1967-68; mem. Michael, Best & Friedrich, Milw. Mem. editorial bd. Marquette Law Rev., 1966-67. Mem. ABA. Office: Michael Best & Friedrich 100 E Wisconsin Ave Milwaukee WI 53202-4107

OBENDORF, SHARON KAY, fiber science educator; b. Lewis, Kans., Nov. 25, 1939; d. Emery H. and Pauline (Mahan) Randel; m. Ralph L. Obendorf, Mar. 11, 1967; children: Michael, Kevin. BS, Kans. State U., 1962; MS, U. Ill., 1963, Cornell U., 1974; PhD, Cornell U., 1976. Instr. textiles and clothing Washington State U., Pullman, 1963-65; lab. technician U. Calif., Davis, 1965-66; asst. prof. textiles and clothing Cornell U., Ithaca, N.Y., 1966-71, lectr. design and environ. analysis, 1971, grad. rsch. asst. in chemistry, 1973-75, postdoctorate assoc. in biochemistry, 1975-78, assoc. prof. design and environ. analysis, 1978-85, prof. textiles and apparel, 1985—, chair dept., 1985-95; vis. asst. Inst. Cancer Rsch., Phial., 1972-73. Contbr. articles to profl. jours. Mem. ASTM, Internat. Textiles and Apparel Assn., Am. Chem. Soc., Am. Assn. Textile Chemists and Colorists, Am. Family and Consumer Sci. Assn. (Manufactured Fiber award 1986), Fiber Soc. (lectr. 1985-86). Home: 24 Dart Dr Ithaca NY 14850-1111 Office: Cornell Univ 288 Van Rensselaer Hall Ithaca NY 14853-4401

OBER, ROBERT FAIRCHILD, JR., retired government official, school administrator; b. Hartford, Conn., June 8, 1935; s. Robert Fairchild and

Celia (Mahoney) F.; m. Elizabeth Ann Stone, Aug. 22, 1959; children: Elise, Abigail, Robert III. AB, Princeton U., 1958; JD, Harvard U., 1961; MA in History, Ind. U., 1969. Fgn. svc. officer U.S. Dept. of State, Washington, 1961-87; econ. counselor Am. Embassy, Moscow, 1985-87; dir. devel., alumni sec. Kent (Conn.) Sch., 1987—; fgn. svc. included assignments in Hamburg, Warsaw, New Delhi, Athens, Washington, Moscow (3 times). Contbr. articles to mags. and newspapers including Washington Post, Christian Sci. Monitor, Cleve. Plain Dealer, Orbis. Trustee Internat. Coll., Beirut, Lebanon, 1987—. Recipient Superior Honor awards, Dept. State, Washington, 1974, 80; named State Dept. fellow Coun. on Fgn. Rels., 1981-82. Episcopalian. Home: 187 West Woods Rd Sharon CT 06069 Office: Kent Sch Devel Dept Kent CT 06757

OBER, RUSSELL JOHN, JR., lawyer; b. Pitts., June 26, 1948; s. Russell J. and Marion C. (Hampson) O.; m. Kathleen A. Stein, Apr. 8, 1972; children: Lauren Elizabeth, Russell John III. BA, U. Pitts., 1970, JD, 1973. Bar: Pa. 1973, U.S. Dist. Ct. (we. dist.) Pa. 1973, U.S. Tax Ct. 1982, U.S. Ct. Appeals (4th cir.) 1976, U.S. Ct. Appeals (3d cir.) 1979, U.S. Ct. Appeals (D.C. cir.) 1985, U.S. Ct. Appeals (2d cir.), 1990, U.S. Ct. Appeals (7th cir.) 1993, U.S. Supreme Ct. 1976. Asst. dist. atty. Allegheny County, Pitts., 1973-75; ptnr. Wallace Chapas & Ober, Pitts., 1975-80, Rose, Schmidt, Hasley & DiSalle, Pitts., 1980-92, Meyer, Unkovic & Scott, Pitts., 1992—. Bd. dirs. Parent and Child Guidance Ctr., Pitts., 1983-90, treas., 1985-86, pres., 1986-88; bd. mgmt. South Hills Area YMCA, 1989-91; mem. Mt. Lebanon Traffic Commn., 1976-81; bd. dirs. Whale's Tale Youth Family Counseling Ctr., 1990-95. Mem. ABA (discovery com. litigation sect. 1982-88, ho. of dels. young lawyers div. 1982-83), Pa. Bar Assn. (ho. of dels. 1983—), Allegheny County Bar Assn. (chmn. young lawyers sect. 1983, bd. govs. 1984, fin. com. 1984-88, mem. coun. civil litigation sect. 1991-93), Nat. Bd. Trial Advocacy (diplomate), Acad. Lawyers Allegheny County (fellow 1983—, bd. govs. 1988-90) U. Pitts. Law Alumni Assn. (bd. govs. 1984-89, v.p. 1985-87, pres. 1987-88), Rivers Club. Office: Meyer Unkovic & Scott 1300 Oliver Bldg Pittsburgh PA 15222

OBER, STUART ALAN, investment consultant, book publisher; b. N.Y.C., Oct. 2, 1946; s. Paul and Gertrude E. (Stollerman) O.; m. Joanne Michaels, Sept. 20, 1981 (div. July 27, 1995); 1 child Erik Kenneth. BA, Wesleyan U., Middletown, Conn., 1968; postgrad., U. Sorbonne, Paris, 1970, CUNY, 1976-77. Pres., editor-in-chief, chmn. bd. Beekman Pubs. Inc., N.Y.C., 1972—; investment cons., 1972—; investment cons., expert witness Loeb, Rhoades & Co., 1976-77; div. dir. tax investment dept. Josephthal & Co., Inc., 1977; mgr. tax investment dept. Bruns, Nordeman, Rea & Co., 1978-80; pres. Ober Tax Investment Cons., 1980—, Securities Investigations, Inc., 1981—; sr. v.p. Cash Franchise Mgmt., Inc., 1988-89. Author: Everybody's Guide to Tax Shelters; editor-in-chief: Ober Income Letter, 1983-88; pub.: Tax Shelter Blue Book, 1983—. Bd. dirs., pres. Woodstock Playhouse Assn., 1985-87; trustee Maverick Concerts, 1986—; chmn. Woodstock Arts and Cultural Com., 1988. Mem. Inst. Cert. Fin. Planners (fin. standards product bd. 1986—, treas. 1988—, bd. dirs.). Office: PO Box 888 Woodstock NY 12498-0888

OBERDANK, LAWRENCE MARK, lawyer, arbitrator; b. Cleve., Nov. 1, 1935; s. Leonard John and Mary (Pavelich) O.; m. Arlene C. Baldini, Aug. 25, 1962; 1 child, Karen A. BA, Western Res. U., 1958, JD, 1965. Bar: Ohio 1965, U.S. Dist. Ct. (no. dist.) Ohio 1966, U.S. Ct. Appeals (6th cir.) 1968, U.S. Supreme Ct. 1970. Assoc. Law Offices Mortimer Riemer, Cleve., 1965-69; ptnr. Riemer and Oberdank, Cleve., 1969-76; prin. Lawrence M. Oberdank Co., L.P.A., Cleve., 1976—; arbitrator Ohio Employment Rels. Bd., 1985-89, Cleve. Civil Svc. Commn., 1983—, FMHA, 1989—; chmn. mandatory arbitration panel Ct. Common Pleas; mem. Nat. Mediation Bd., 1986—; instr. indsl. rels. law Cleve. State U., 1982-85; instr. labor rels. Cuyahoga C.C., 1983; arbitrator/mediator U.S. Dist. Ct. (no. dist.) Ohio, ea. divsn. fee dispute panel Cleve. Bar Assn.; mem. securities arbitration panel Am. Stock Exch., N.Y. Stock Exch., 1995—. Lt. USNR, 1958-62. Mem. ABA (labor and employment sect., labor arbitration, law collective bargaining agreements, alternate dispute resolution sect., fed. ct. annexed/connected programs com., sr. lawyers sect.), Am. Arbitration Assn. (securities arbitrator, nat. labor panel 1973—, comml. arbitration panel, nat. panel of employment arbitrators), Nat. Assn. Securities Dealers, Inc. (bd. mediators), Bar Assn. Greater Cleve. (labor law com.), Cuyahoga County Bar Assn., Fed. Bar Assn., Am. Judicature Soc., Internat. Soc. Labor Law and Social Legislation, Ohio State Bar Assn. (chmn. labor law sect. 1970-73), Indsl. Rels. Rsch. Assn., Pub. Sector Labor Rels. Assn., Soc. Profls. in Dispute Resolution (bd. dirs. Southwest Ohio chpt.), Nat. Inst. Dispute Resolution (assoc.), Masons, Phi Gamma Delta. Roman Catholic. Avocations: golf, Civil War history. Home: 8051 Lakeview Ct N Royalton OH 44133-1214 Office: 6450 Rockside Woods Blvd S Cleveland OH 44131-2230

OBERDORF, JOHN J., lawyer; b. N.Y.C., Aug. 19, 1946. AB, Georgetown U., 1968; JD, Fordham U., 1973; LLM in Taxation, NYU, 1975. Bar: N.J. 1973, U.S. Dist. Ct. N.J. 1973, U.S. Tax Ct. 1975. Ptnr. St. John & Wayne, Newark; adj. prof. taxation Fairleigh Dickinson U., 1977-79. Mem. ABA (taxation, corporation and banking and bus. law sects.), N.J. State Bar Assn. (taxation sect.). Address: St John & Wayne 2 Penn Plz E Newark NJ 07105-2246

OBERDORFER, LOUIS F., federal judge; b. Birmingham, Ala., Feb. 21, 1919; s. A. Leo and Stella Maud (Falk) O.; m. Elizabeth Weil, July 31, 1941; children: John Louis, Kathryn Lee, Thomas Lee, William L. A.B., Dartmouth, 1939; LL.B., Yale, 1946. Bar: Ala. bar 1946, D.C. bar 1949. Law clk. to Justice Hugo L. Black, 1946-47; pvt. practice, 1947-51; mem. firm Wilmer, Cutler, & Pickering (and predecessors), 1951-61, 65-77; asst. atty. gen. tax div. Dept. of Justice, 1961-65; judge, now sr. judge U.S. Dist. Ct. (D.C. dist.), 1977—; vis. lectr. Yale Law Sch., 1966-71; adv. com. Fed. Rules Civil Procedure, 1962-84; co-chmn. lawyers com. Civil Rights Under Law, 1967-69; adj. prof. law Georgetown U., Washington, 1993—. Editor-in-chief Yale Law Jour., 1941. Served to capt. AUS, 1941-46. Mem. ABA, D.C. Bar Assn. (bd. govs. 1972-77, pres. 1977), Ala. Bar Assns., Am. Law Inst., Yale Law Sch. Assn. (pres. 1971-73). Office: US Dist Ct US Courthouse Rm 2309 333 and Constitution Ave NW Washington DC 20001*

OBERDORSTER, GUNTER, toxicology educator and researcher; b. Cologne, Germany, Feb. 27, 1939; came to U.S., 1979; s. Ewald and Liesel (Selbach) O.; m. Ingeborg Gerda Karden, Mar. 22, 1968; children—Jan, Eva, Uta. D.V.M., U. Giessen, 1964, Ph.D. (Dr. Med. Vet.), 1966. Diplomate in pharmacology and toxicology. Scientist Pharm. Industry, Cologne, Fed. Republic Germany, 1965-67; asst. prof. U. Cologne, 1968-71; mem. sci. staff Fraunhofer Inst., Grafschaft, Fed. Republic Germany, 1971-79; assoc. prof. toxicology U. Rochester, N.Y., 1979-89, full prof., 1989—, head divsn. respiratory biology and toxicology; mem. contact group heavy metals European Commn., Brussels, 1977-79; cons. WHO, Geneva, 1983—, sci. adv. bd. EPA, Washington, 1984—, UNEP, Geneva, 1985, N.Y. State Health Dept., 1987. Contbr. articles to profl. jours.; editorial bd. Jour. Aerosols in Medicine, Inhalation Toxicology. Recipient Joseph von Fraunhofer prize, 1982; grantee EPA-Dept. Energy, 1979-81, NIH, 1982—. Mem. Am. Thoracic Soc., Soc. Toxicology (career achievement award inhalation specialty sect. 1996), Am. Conf. of Govtl. and Indsl. Hygienists, Internat. Soc. Aerosols in Medicine. Avocations: literature, skiing, rowing. Home: 121 Southern Pky Rochester NY 14618-1052 Office: U Rochester Dept Environ Medicine Rochester NY 14642

OBERG, LARRY REYNOLD, librarian; b. Midvale, Idaho; s. Gustav Wilhelm and Esther Marie (Watkins) O.; m. Marilyn Ann Gow, Jan. 1, 1964 (div. 1985); 1 child, Marc Aurelien. AB in Anthropology, U. Calif., Berkeley, 1977, MLS, 1978. Reference librarian Stanford (Calif.) U., 1979-80, U. Calif., Berkeley, 1981-82; dir. libr. Lewis-Clark State Coll., Lewiston, Idaho, 1984-86; dir. library Albion (Mich.) Coll., 1986-92; univ. libr. Willamette U., Salem, Oreg., 1992—. Author: Human Services in Postrevolutionary Cuba, 1985 (named a Choice Outstanding Acad. Book, Choice Editors 1984-85); mem. editl. bd. College and Research Libraries; mem. adv. bd. Jour. Info. Ethics; contbr. articles to profl. jours. Mem. Am. Library Assn., Oreg. Library Assn., Phi Beta Kappa. Democrat. Office: Willamette U Mark O Hatfield Libr 900 State St Salem OR 97301-3930

OBERG, MURIEL CURNIN, community health nurse, health facility manager; b. Bridgeport, Conn., July 12, 1925; d. James P. and Lillian (Bannister) Curnin; m. Leonard E. Oberg, Nov. 9, 1946; 1 child, Douglas P. Diploma in Nursing, St. Vincent's Med. Ctr., Bridgeport, 1946; BSN, U. Bridgeport, 1963, MS, 1972; postgrad., Fairfield U., 1991. RN, Conn.; cert. in nursing adminstrn.; cert. profl. educator. Inservice edn. supr. Bridgeport Hosp., 1963-65, health careers counselor Sch. of Nursing, 1966-69; health careers counselor Quinnipiac Coll., 1970-71; asst. dir. maternal and child health Vis. Nurse Assn., New Haven, 1972-81; dir. pub. health nursing Dept. Health City of New Haven, New Haven, 1981—. Recipient USPH traineeship, 1962. Mem. ANA, Conn. Nurses Assn. Home: 240 Hillside Rd Fairfield CT 06430-2145

OBERG, ROGER WINSTON, management educator; b. Mpls., Oct. 5, 1919; s. Ezra Nathaniel and Adele Erika Wilhelmina (Boquist) O.; m. Pansy Jane Sherrill, June 29, 1957; children: Sherrill Katherine, Roger Winston, Keith Eric, Elizabeth Jane. Student, North Park Coll., 1937-38; B.B.A. with distinction, U. Minn., 1941; M.B.A., Ohio State U., 1947; Ph.D., M.I.T., 1955. Mgmt. trainee Sears Roebuck & Co., 1941-43; grad. asst. Ohio State U., 1946-47, M.I.T., 1947-50; human relations research analyst Prudential Ins. Co., Newark, 1950-51; personnel specialist Esso Research & Engring. Co., Linden, N.J., 1952-57; assoc. prof. mgmt. Mich. State U., 1957-65, prof. mgmt., 1965-86, prof. emeritus, 1986—; vis. prof. Leeds U., Eng., 1959, U. Rio Grande do Sul, Brazil, 1959-61, Stanford U., 1964, North European Mgmt. Inst., Norway, 1974-76; World Bank cons. to Bangladesh univs., 1985. Served to 2d lt. USAAF, 1943-46, PTO. Recipient Forensic medal U. Minn., 1941, Lit. Rev. prize, 1941. Mem. Beta Gamma Sigma, Delta Sigma Rho. Mem. Evangelical Covenant Ch. Clubs: University (Mich. State U.), Scandinavian Am. Home: 1585 Hillside Dr Okemos MI 48864-2319

OBERHELMAN, HARRY ALVIN, JR., surgeon, educator; b. Chgo., Nov. 15, 1923; s. Harry Alvin and Beatrice (Babel) O.; m. Betty Jane Porter, June 12, 1946; children: Harry Alvin III, James I., Robert P., Thomas L., Nancy L. Student, Yale U., 1942-43; B.S., U. Chgo., 1946, M.D., 1947. Diplomate: Am. Bd. Surgery. Intern U. Chgo. Clinics, 1947-48, resident in surgery, 1948-51, 52-57; asst. prof., then assoc. prof. surgery U. Chgo. Sch. Medicine, 1957-60; mem. faculty Stanford (Calif.) Sch. Medicine, 1960—, prof. surgery, 1964-95, prof. emeritus, 1995—; mem. div. licensing Calif. Bd. Med. Quality Assurance, 1970-82. Author papers in field. Served with USAF, 1951-53. Mem. AMA, Calif. Med. Assn., Soc. Univ. Surgeons, Am., Western, Pacific Coast surg. assns., Soc. Alimentary Tract, Halsted Soc., Fedn. State Med. Bds. U.S. (bd. dirs. 1979-82). Home: 668 Cabrillo St Stanford CA 94305-8404

OBERHUBER, KONRAD JOHANNES, art museum curator, educator; b. Linz/Donau, Austria, Mar. 31, 1935. Ph.D., U. Vienna, Austria, 1959, Dozent, 1971. Asst. U. Vienna; delegated as research fellow to Austrian Inst. in Rome, 1959-61; asst., then curator Albertina, Vienna, 1961-71; research curator Nat. Gallery Art, Washington, 1971-74; guest lectr. Fogg Art Mus., Harvard U., Cambridge, Mass., spring 1974; curator of drawings, prof. fine arts Fogg Art Mus., Harvard U., 1974-85, Ian Woodner curator of drawings, prof. fine arts, 1985-87; dir. Graphische Sammlung Albertina, Vienna, 1987—; T.A.O. prof. U. Vienna, 1991; Italian Ministry of Culture scholar, Rome, winter 1958; asst. prof. Smith Coll., 1964-65; Kress fellow Harvard Center for Renaissance Studies, Florence, Italy, 1965-66; guest prof. Cambridge (Eng.) U., 1968. Author: Raphael, Die Zeichnungen, 1983, Poussin, The Early Years in Rome, 1988; contbr. articles to profl. jours. fellow Inst. Advanced Study Princeton, N.J., 1974-75; Nat. Endowment Humanities grantee, 1979-80; Gerda Henkel Stiftung grantee, 1983-84. Office: Graphische Sammlung Albertina, Augustinerstrasse 1, A-1010 Vienna Austria

OBERLANDER, CORNELIA HAHN, landscape architect; b. Muelheim-Ruhr, Germany, June 20, 1924; arrived in U.S., 1939; d. Franz and Lotte Beate (Jastrow) H.; m. H. Peter Oberlander, Jan. 2, 1953; children: Judith A., Timothy A., Wendy E. BA, Smith Coll., 1944; B of Landscape Architecture, Harvard U., 1947; LLD (hon.), U. British Columbia, 1991. guest prof. U. B.C. Dept. Landscape Architecture, 1992; lectr. for guided tour Renaissance Gardens of No. Italy, Smith Coll. Alumni Assn., 1988; mem. adv. com. on design Nat. Capital Commn., 1975-82; mem. adv. panel, co-founder Children's Play Resource Centre, Vancouver, 1978—; lectr. in field. Prin. works include C.K. Choi Bldg., U. B.C., 1992-96, New Pub. Library, 1992—, Asian Inst., U. B.C., 1993—, Thunderbird Housing, U. B.C., 1992—, Kwantlen Coll., 1991—, Cariboo Coll., 1991—, N.W. Territories Legis. Bldg., 1991—, UN Peacekeeping Meml., 1990—, Ritsumeikan U. B.C. Ho., 1990—, Ottawa City Hall, 1989—, Environ. Sci. Bd., Ward Environ. Garden, Trent U., 1989—, Nat. Gallery Can., 1983-88, Canadian Chancery, Washington D.C., 1983-89. Recipient medal Smith Coll., 1982, Regional Honor award and Nat. Merit award Christopher Phillips Landcape Architects, Inc., 1992, Allied Arts medal Royal Archtl. Inst. Can., 1995, Cathedral Place, 1983-88, Nat. Gallery of Can., Ottawa, Ontario, Can. Chancery Am. Assn. of Nurserymen, 1990, Grand award for L'Ambassade du Can., Landscape Contractors Assn., 1989, Can. Architect award of Excellence, Matsuzaki Wright Architects, Inc., 1989, Amenity award City of Vancouver for Robson Square, 1986, Citation award Can. Soc. of Architects for Chancery & Nat. Gallery, 1990. Fellow Am. Soc. Landscape Architects, Can. Soc. Landscape Architects; mem. Order of Can., Royal Can. Acad. Arts, Archtl. Inst. B.C. (hon.). Home: 1372 Acadia Rd, Vancouver, BC Canada V6T 1P6

OBERLANDER, HERBERT, insect physiologist, educator; b. Manchester, N.H., Oct. 2, 1939 s. Solomon and Minnie (Shapiro) O.; m. Barbara Judith Marks, June 12, 1962; children: Jonathan, Beth. BA cum laude in Zoology, U. Conn., 1961; PhD in Biology, Western Res. U., 1965. Postdoctoral fellow U. Zurich (Switzerland), 1965-66; asst. prof. Brandeis U., Waltham, Mass., 1966-71; rsch. physiologist USDA, Agrl. Rsch. Svc., Gainesville, Fla., 1971-76, rsch. leader, physiology unit, insect attractants lab., 1976-84, lab. dir. insect attractants, behavior and basic biology rsch. lab., Gainesville, 1984-96; dir. Ctr. for Med. Agrl. and Vet. Entomology, Gainesville, 1996—; prof. entomology U. Fla., Gainesville, 1979—. NSF fellow, 1961-65; NIH fellow, 1965-66; NSF Research grantee, 1966-71, 83; grantee U.S.-Israel BARD, 1989-93. Fellow Entomol. Soc. Am. (Founders' Meml. award 1995); mem. Tissue Culture Assn., Entomol. Soc. Am. (Founders Award, 1995), Phi Beta Kappa, Sigma Xi, Phi Kappa Phi. Contbr. chpts. to books, articles to profl. jours. Office: USDA Insect Attractant Behav Lab PO Box 14565 1700 SW 23rd Dr Gainesville FL 32604-2565

OBERLIES, JOHN WILLIAM, physician organization executive; b. Rochester, N.Y., June 9, 1939; s. Hubert H. and Martha (Voght) O.; m. Mary Teresa Sundholm, Sept. 29, 1962; children: Katie, Daniel. BCE, Villanova U., 1961; MBA, U. Rochester, 1978. From surveyor to purchasing agt. Rochester Gas & Electric Co., 1959-79, gen. mgr., 1979-82, v.p., 1982-87, sr. v.p., 1988-90; chief ops. officer Le Chase Constrn., Inc., Rochester, 1990-95; COO Rochester Individual Practice Assn. Inc., 1995—; bd. dirs. Transmation, Inc. Trustee Aquinas Inst., Rochester, 1986-93; bd. dirs. Cath. Charities, Rochester, 1984-85; chmn. bd. Preferred Care, Inc., Rochester, 1986-90; mem. Diocesan Pastoral Coun., Health Futures of Rochester Commn.; bd. dirs. Rochester Area Found., 1984-85, Highland Hosp.; chmn. nominations com. United Way, Rochester; mem. Rochester Housing Partnership Commn. With U.S. Army, 1961-62. Mem. Rochester C. of C. (chmn. polit. action com. 1987). Republican. Avocation: fishing. Home: 242 Shoreham Dr Rochester NY 14618-4112 Office: Rochester Individual Practice Assn Inc 2000 Winton Rd S Rochester NY 14618-3922

OBERLY, KATHRYN ANNE, lawyer; b. Chgo., May 22, 1950; d. James Richard and Lucille Mary (Kraus) O.; m. Daniel Lee Goelzer, July 13, 1974 (div. Aug. 1987); 1 child, Michael W. Student, Vassar Coll., 1967-69; BA, U. Wis., 1971, JD, 1973. Bar: Wis. 1973, D.C. 1981, N.Y. 1995. Law clk. U.S. Ct. Appeals, Omaha, 1973-74; trial atty. U.S. Dept. Justice, Washington, 1974-77, spl. asst., 1977-81, spl. litigation counsel, 1981-82, asst. to Solicitor Gen., 1982-86; ptnr. Mayer, Brown & Platt, Washington, 1986-91; assoc. gen. counsel Ernst & Young LLP, Washington, 1991-94; vice chair, gen. counsel Ernst & Young LLP, N.Y.C., 1994—. Mem. ABA, Am. Law Inst., Wis. State Bar Assn., D.C. Bar Assn. Democrat. Office: Ernst & Young LLP 787 7th Ave New York NY 10019-6018

OBERMAN, MICHAEL STEWART, lawyer; b. Bklyn., May 21, 1947; s. Hyman Martin and Gertrude O.; m. Sharon Land, Oct. 8, 1975; 1 child, Abigail Land. AB, Columbia U., 1969; JD, Harvard U., 1972. Bar: N.Y. 1973, U.S. Dist. Ct. (so. and ea. dists.) N.Y. 1973, U.S. Ct. Appeals (2d cir.) 1973, U.S. Supreme Ct. 1976, Calif. 1981, U.S. Dist. Ct. (no. dist.) Calif. 1981, U.S. Ct. Appeals (9th cir.) 1981, U.S. Dist. Ct. (so. and cen. dists.) Calif. 1982, U.S. Ct. Appeals (5th cir.) 1989, D.C. 1992, U.S. Ct. Appeals (7th cir.) 1993. Law clk. to Hon. Milton Pollack, U.S. Dist. Ct. (so. dist.) N.Y., 1972-73; assoc. Kramer, Levin, Naftalis & Frankel, N.Y.C., 1973-79, ptnr., 1980—. Contbr. articles to profl. jours. Recipient Nathan Burkan prize ASCAP, 1973. Mem. N.Y. State Bar Assn. (mem. ho. of dels. 1989-91, exec. com. comml. and fed. litigation sect.). Office: Kramer Levin Naftalis & Frankel 919 3rd Ave New York NY 10022

OBERMAN, SHELDON ARNOLD, writer, educator; b. Winnipeg, Man., Can., May 20, 1949; s. Allan and Dorothy Oberman; m. Lee Anne Block, Sept. 8, 1973 (div. Mar. 9, 1990); children: Adam, Mira; m. Lisa Ann Dveris, Sept. 2, 1990; 1 child: Jesse. BA in English, U. Winnipeg, 1972; BA in English with honors, U. Jerusalem, Israel, 1973; teaching cert., U. Man., 1974. tchr. W. C. Millar Collegiate, Altona, Man., Can., 1975-76, Joseph Wolinsky Collegiate, Winnipeg, Man., Can., 1976-95. Author: The Folk Festival Book, 1983, Lion in the Lake: A French English Alphabet Book, 1988, Julie Gerond and the Polka Dot Pony, 1988, TV Sal and the Game Show From Outer Space, 1993, This Business With Elijah, 1993, The Always Prayer Shawl, 1994, The White Stone in the Castle Wall, 1995, By the Hannukah Light, 1997; co-editor: A Mirror of a People: The Canadian Jewish Experience in Poetry and Prose, 1985. Nat. Jewish Book award Jewish Book Coun., 1995, Sydney Taylor award, 1995, Best Book of the Yr. A Child's Mag., 1994, Pick of the List award Am. Bookseller, 1994, Can. Author Short Story award Canadian Author's Assn., 1987; Bliss Carmen Poetry prize Banff Sch. of Fine Arts, 1980; various writer and film maker grants. Avocations: public address, acting, collage sculptor, canoeing. Home: 822 Dorchester Ave, Winnipeg, MB Canada R3M 0R7

OBERMAN, STEVEN, lawyer; b. St. Louis, Sept. 21, 1955; s. Albert and Marian (Kleg) O.; m. Evelyn Ann Simpson, Aug. 27, 1977; children: Rachael Diane, Benjamin Scott. BA in Psychology, Auburn U., 1977; JD, U. Tenn., 1980. Bar: Tenn. 1980, Tenn. Supreme Ct. 1980, Tenn. Criminal Ct. Appeals 1980, U.S. Dist. Ct. (ea. dist.) Tenn. 1980, U.S. Ct. Appeals (4th cir.) 1981, U.S. Ct. Appeals (6th cir.) 1983, U.S. Supreme Ct. 1985. Law clk. Daniel, Duncan & Claiborne, Knoxville, Tenn., 1978-80; assoc. Daniel, Claiborne & Lewallen, Knoxville, Tenn., 1980-82; ptnr. Daniel, Claiborne, Oberman & Buuck, Knoxville, 1983-85, Daniel & Oberman, Knoxville, 1986—; pres., Project First Offender, Knoxville, 1983-86;bd. dirs. Fed. Defender Svcs. Eastern Tenn., Inc., v.p. 1994-96; guest instr. U. Tenn. 1988-96; guest lectr. U. Tenn. Law Sch., 1982-88; guest instr. U. Tenn. Grad. Sch. Criminal Justice Program, 1983, 84; guest speaker Ct. Clk's Meeting, Cambridge, Eng., 1984; guest instr. legal clinic , trial advocacy program U. Tenn., 1987-88; adj. prof. U. Tenn. Law Sch., 1993— (Forrest W. Lacey award for outstanding faculty contbn. to U. Tenn. Coll. Law Moot Ct. Program, 1993-94; coach U. Tenn. Law Sch. Nat. Trial Team, 1991—; spl. judge Criminal Divsn. Knox County Gen. Sessions Court; founding mem. Nat. Coll. for DUI Def.; speaker in field. Author: D.U.I.: The Crime and Consequences in Tennessee, 1991, supplemented annually; co-author: D.W.I. Means Defend With Ingenuity, 1987; contbr. legal articles on drunk driving to profl. jours. Bd. dirs. Knoxville Legal Aid Soc., Inc., 1986-88 (pres. 1990), Arnstein Jewish Community Ctr., 1987-91, pres. 1990; bd. dirs. Knoxville Racquet Club, 1991-93, pres. 1992-93. Col. Aide de Camp Tenn. Gov.'s Staff, 1983, Moot Ct. Bd. Spl. Svc. award, 1995-96. Mem. ATLA, Nat. Assn. Criminal Def. Lawyers (co-chair DUI advocacy com. 1995-97), Tenn. Assn. Criminal Def. Lawyers (bd. dirs. 1983-89), Knoxville Bar Assn. Jewish. Office: Daniel & Oberman 550 W Main St Ste 950 Knoxville TN 37902-2567

OBERMANN, RICHARD MICHAEL, governmental technology and policy analyst; b. May 21, 1949; s. Baird J. and Phyllis L. (Weber) O. BS of Engring. in Aerospace and Mech. Scis. cum laude, Princeton U., 1971, PhD in Engring., Aerospace and Mech. Scis., 1977; MS of Engring. in Astronautics and Aeros., Stanford U., 1972; postgrad., Va. Poly. Inst. and State U., Am. U. With MITRE Corp., McLean, Va., 1977-88, engr. transp. systems analysis, transp. energy analysis, telecommunications, project leader, mem. tech. staff in communications and system design; sr. staff officer aeros. and space engring. bd. NRC, Washington, 1988-90, study dir. and analyst technol. and policy issues; mem. profl. staff for space subcom. U.S. Ho. of Reps. Com. on Sci., Space and Tech., Washington, 1990-95; minority staff dir., space subcom. U.S. House of Reps. Com. on Sci., Washington, 1995—. Author tech. papers and presentations. Fellow AIAA (assoc.), Brit. Interplanetary Soc.; mem. N.Y. Acad. Scis., IEEE, Internat. Inst. Communications, Japan-Am. Soc., Asia Soc., Am. Astronaut. Soc. (v.p.), Nat. Space Club, Pacific Telecommunications Coun., Women in Aerospace (bd. dirs.). Avocations: Japanese, Chinese and Spanish langs., sports, trumpet.

OBERMAYER, HERMAN JOSEPH, newspaper publisher; b. Phila., Sept. 19, 1924; s. Leon J. and Julia (Sinsheimer) O.; student U. Geneva (Switzerland), 1946; AB cum laude, Dartmouth, 1948; m. Betty Nan Levy, June 28, 1955; children: Helen O. Levy-Myers, Veronica O. Atnipp, Adele O. Malpass, Elizabeth Rose. Reporter, L.I. Daily Press, Jamaica, N.Y., 1950-53; classified advt. mgr. New Orleans Item, 1953-55; asst. to pub. Standard-Times, New Bedford, Mass., 1955-57; editor, pub. Long Branch (N.J.) Daily Record, 1957-71, No. Va. Sun, Arlington, 1963-89; adj. prof. journalism U. Md., 1989-93; vis. lectr. U. West Indies, Jamaica, 1994-95; Pulitzer Prize juror, 1983, 84; publ. com. Commentary Mag., 1989—; chmn. fin. com. Washington Journalism Rev., 1990-91; lectr publs. mgmt. seminars, Warsaw, Budapest, Barbados, Jamaica, Vilnius, Lithuania, Riga, Latvia, Tallinn and Tartu, Estonia, Ljubljana, Slovenia, 1990-96, Ctr. Fgn. Journalists, 1992—. Bd. dirs. Monmouth Med. Center, 1958-71; mem. exec. coun. Monmouth Boy Scouts Am., 1958-71, mem. exec. com. Nat. Capital coun., 1971-79, v.p., 1974-77; mem. Va. Legis. Alcohol Beverage Control Study Commn., 1972-74; trustee Arlington (Va.) Bicentennial Commn., Am. Jewish Com. (Cmty. Svc. award 1986, nat. bd. govs., 1989-96, nat. coun. 1995—, v.p. Washington chpt.; trustee Inst. for Learning in Retirement, Marymount U., 1994-95. Served with AUS, 1943-46; ETO. Rhineland Campaign; Recipient Silver Beaver award Boy Scouts of Am., 1977, Knight Internat. Press fellow, 1994-95. Mem. Am. Soc. Newspaper Editors, So. Newspapers Pubs. Assn. (dir. 1981-84), Soc. Profl. Journalists, Sigma Chi. Jewish. Rotarian. Clubs: Nat. Press (Washington), Cosmos (Washington), Washington Golf and Country (Arlington, Va.), Dartmouth (N.Y.C.), Econ. (Washington). Contbr. articles to numerous mags. and newspapers. Home: 4114 N Ridgeview Rd Arlington VA 22207-4711

OBERNAUER, MARNE, corporate executive; b. Pitts., Mar. 6, 1919; s. Arthur H. and Anna (Somerman) O.; m. Joan Strassburger, Aug. 1, 1941; children: Marne Jr., Wendy Damon. Grad., Cornell U., 1941. Chmn. exec. com. Devon Group, Inc., Stamford, Conn.; chmn. Beverage Distbrs. Corp. and BDH Inc., Aurora, Colo.; pres. Doric Securities Co.; bus. cons., pvt. investor. Pres., bd. dirs. The Obernauer Found., Inc. Served to lt. USNR, 1942-45. Mem. Hillcrest Country Club (L.A.), Concordia Club (Pitts.), Century Country Club (Purchase, N.Y.), Banyan Golf Club (Palm Beach, Fla.). Office: Devon Group Inc 281 Tresser Blvd # 501 Stamford CT 06901-3238

OBERNAUER, MARNE, JR., business executive; b. Lakehurst, N.J., July 1, 1943; s. Marne and Joan Carolyn (Strassburger) O.; m. Marion Fleck Gislason, Aug. 22, 1976 (dec. Jan. 1996); children: Matthew Gene, Michael Sidney. BA, Yale U., 1965; MBA, Harvard U., 1972. With First Nat. City Bank (Citibank, N.A.), N.Y.C., 1965-70, Donaldson, Lufkin & Jenrette, N.Y.C., 1972-74; with Devon Group, Inc., N.Y.C. and Stamford, Conn., 1974—, pres., 1978, chief exec. officer, 1980—, chmn. bd., 1986—; bd. dirs. Devon Group Inc., Beverage Distbrs. Corp. Trustee Trinity Sch., The Obernauer Found., Inc.; bd. dirs. Com. for Responsible Fed. Budget, Assocs. of Harvard Bus. Sch. Mem. Am. Bus. Conf. (bd. dirs., vice chmn.), Yale Club of N.Y.C. Office: Devon Group Inc 450 Park Ave New York NY 10022-2605

OBERNDORF, MEYERA E., mayor; m. Roger L. Oberndorf; children: Marcie, Heide. BS in Elem. Edn., Old Dominion U., 1964. Broadcaster Sta. WNIS, Norfolk, Va.; mem. city coun. City of Virginia Beach, Va., 1976—, vice-mayor, 1986, mayor, 1988—. Mem. exec. bd. Tidewater coun. Boys Scouts Am.; bd. dirs. Virginia Beach Pub. Libr., 1966-76, chmn. bd., 1967-76. Mem. AAUW, U.S. Conf. Mayors, Va. Mcpl. League (exec. bd.), Nat. League Cities (vice-chmn.), Princess Anne Women's Club. Jewish. Home: 5404 Challedon Dr Virginia Beach VA 23462-4112 Office: Office of the Mayor Municipal Ctr City Hall Bldg Virginia Beach VA 23465*

OBERNE, SHARON BROWN, elementary education educator; b. Lakeland, Fla., Sept. 2, 1955; d. Morris C. and Amy (Beecroft) Brown; m. Ronald Allan Oberne, Mar. 29, 1980; children: Laura, Aaron, Kelley. AA in Pre-tchg., Hillsborough C.C., Tampa, Fla., 1975; BA in Elem. Edn., U. South Fla., 1976, cert., 1980, AA in Acctg., 1980. Cert. tchr. K-8. 3rd grade tchr. Zolfo Springs Elem., Wauchula, Fla., 1976-77, 2nd grade tchr., 1977-79; 1st grade tchr. Westgate Christian Sch., Tampa, Fla., 1979-80; 5th grade tchr. Pasoc Elem., Dade City, Fla., 1980-81; 3rd grade tchr. San Antonio Elem., Dade City, 1981-86; temporary reading tchr. Chesterfield Heights Elem., Norfolk, Va., 1986-87; 2nd grade tchr. Ocean View Elem., Norfolk, 1987—; dir. Ocean View Writing Club, Norfolk, 1992—. Author: Pink Monkey, 1994, Space Traveler, 1995, Daisy Dolphin (Spelling in Context). Pres. USS Guam's Wife's Club, Norfolk Naval Base, 1990-91; amb. of goodwill USS Guam, 1990-91; founder AmeriKids of Ocean View, Norfolk, 1991-93; liaison Adopt-A-Sch. Program, Norfolk, 1991—. Recipient Good Neighbor award NEA, 1994. Mem. Norfolk Reading Coun., Nat. Autism Soc., CHADD. Avocations: writing, reading, swimming, walking. Home: 8243 Briarwood Cir Norfolk VA 23518-2862

OBERREIT, WALTER WILLIAM, lawyer; b. Paterson, N.J., Oct. 7, 1928; s. William and Gertrud (Limpert) O.; m. Anne-Marie Gohier, July 6, 1955; children: Stephan, Alexis, Jerome. BA, U. Mich., 1951; diploma, U. Paris Inst. Polit. Studies, 1955; JD, Yale U., 1958. Bar: N.Y. Assoc. Cleary, Gottlieb, Steen & Hamilton, N.Y.C., 1958-62, Paris, 1962-66; assoc. Cleary, Gottlieb, Steen & Hamilton, Brussels, 1966-67, ptnr., 1967—. Contbr. articles to profl. jours., chpts. to books. Lt. (j.g.) USN, 1953-55. Mem. ABA, Assn. of Bar of City of N.Y. (co-chmn. com. on rels. with European Bars 1981—), Am. Arbitration Assn., Ctr. European Policy Studies, Inst. Royal Rels. Internat., Union Internat. Des Avocats. Clubs: Cercle Royal Gaulois, Cercle Nations, Am. Common Market (Brussels). Avocations: sailing, tennis, skiing. Home: Ave Geo Bernier 7, 1050 Brussels Belgium Office: Cleary Gottlieb Steen & Hamilton, rue de la Loi 23, 1040 Brussels Belgium

O'BERRY, CARL GERALD, air force officer, electrical engineer; b. Lansing, Mich., Apr. 11, 1936; s. Gerald Ray and Edith Lenore (Watson) O'B.; m. Charlene Marice Bussche, June 21, 1958; children: Brian, Eileen, Kevin, Bradley, Kathleen. BSEE, N.Mex. State U., 1972; MS in Systems Mgmt., Air Force Inst. Tech., 1977. Commd. 2d lt. USAF, 1961, advanced through grades to lt. gen., 1993; comdr. 2019 Communications Squadron, Griffiss AFB, N.Y., 1974-76; project engr. Rome Air Devel. Ctr., Griffiss AFB, 1979-81; asst. dep. chief of staff requirements Air Force Systems Command, Andrews AFB, Md., 1982-84; comdr. Rome Air Devel. Ctr., Griffiss AFB, 1984-86; joint program mgr. WWMCCS info. system Hdqrs. USAF, Washington, 1986-88; dir. command, control and communications U.S. European Command, Stuttgart, Fed. Republic Germany, 1988-90; dir. command control systems and logistics U.S. Space Command, Peterson AFB, Colo., 1990-92; command control comm. and computers DCS, HQ USAF, Washington, 1992-95; v.p., dir. strategic planning Motorola Govt. & Space Tech. Group, Scottsdale, Ariz., 1995—; v.p. Motorola, Inc. Mem. Air Force Assn., Armed Forces Communications-Electronics Assn., Soc. Logistics Engrs. Roman Catholic. Office: 8201 E Mcdowell Rd Scottsdale AZ 85257-3812

O'BERRY, PHILLIP AARON, veterinarian; b. Tampa, Fla., Feb. 1, 1933; s. Luther Lee and Marjorie Mae (Mahlum) O'B.; m. Terri Martin, July 31, 1960; children: Kelly, Eric, Holly, Danny, Andy, Toby, Michael Asefa. BS in Agr., U. Fla., 1955; DVM, Auburn U., 1960; PhD, Iowa State U., 1967. With Agrl. Rsch. Svc. USDA, 1956—; asst. to dir. vet. scis. rsch. div. USDA, Beltsville, Md., 1967-72; asst. dir. Nat. Animal Disease Ctr., Ames, Iowa, 1972-73, dir., 1973-88, nat. tech. transfer coord., 1988—; prin. scientist Office Agr. Biotech., USDA, 1988-90; adj. prof. Coll. Vet. Medicine, Iowa State U., 1973—; mem. expert panel livestock infertility FAO; sci. adv. com. Pan Am. Zoonosis Ctr., Buenos Aires; mem. Fed. Coun. Sci. and Tech.; mem. com. animal health, world food and nutrition study NRC; cons. Govt. of Italy, USDA; mem. nat needs grad. fellowship rev. panel USDA, 1989-91, cons. agr. biotech. rsch. adv. com.; mem. sci. adv. bd. Biotech. R&D Corp., 1992—, sci. review bd. Am. Jour. Vet. Rsch., 1990-92; mem. USDA Patent Review Com., 1988—. Author 27 research publs. Recipient Cert. of Merit, Agrl. Rsch. Svc., 1972, 84, Alumni Merit award Iowa State Club of Chgo., 1982, Cert. Appreciation, 1988, Tech. Transfer award 1989, USDA Disting. Alumnus award Auburn U., 1991; named Hon. Diplomate Am. Coll. of Vet. Microbiologists, 1995. Mem. APHA, AVMA, AAAS, Nat. Assn. Fed. Vets., Iowa Vet. Med. Assn., N.Y. Acad. Scis., Conf. Rsch. Workers Animal Diseases, Am. Soc. Microbiology, Am. Assn. Lab. Animal Sci., U.s. Animal Health Assn., Am. Assn. Bovine Practitioners, Livestock Cons. Inst., Sigma Xi, Phi Zeta, Phi Kappa Phi, Gamma Sigma Delta (Alumni award Merit 1976), Alpha Zeta, Spades, Blue Key. Democrat. Home: 3319 Woodland St Ames IA 50014-3550 Office: Nat Soil Tilth Lab Rm 114 Ames IA 50011

OBERSTAR, JAMES L., congressman; b. Chisholm, Minn., Sept. 10, 1934; s. Louis and Mary (Grillo) O.; m. Jo Garlick, Oct. 12, 1963 (dec. July 1991); children: Thomas Edward, Katherine Noelle, Anne-Therese, Monica Rose; m. Jean Kurth, Nov. 1993; stepchildren: Corinne Quinlan Kurth, Charles Burke Kurth, Jr. B.A. summa cum laude, St. Thomas Coll., 1956; postgrad. in French, Laval U., Que., Can.; M.S. in Govt. (scholar), Coll. Europe, Bruges, Belgium, 1957; postgrad. in govt, Georgetown U. Adminstrv. asst. Congressman John A. Blatnik, 1963-74; adminstr. Pub. Works Com. U.S. Ho. of Reps., 1971-74; mem. 94th-105th Congresses from 8th Minn. Dist., 1975—; ranking minority mem. transp. and infrastructure com. 94th-104th Congresses from 8th Minn. Dist. Mem. Am. Polit. Sci. Assn. Office: US Ho of Reps 2366 Rayburn HOB Washington DC 20515-2308

OBERSTEIN, MARYDALE, geriatric specialist; b. Red Wing, Minn., Dec. 30; d. Dale Robert and Jean Ebba-Marie (Holmquist) Johnson; children: Kirk Robert, Mark Paul, MaryJean. Student, U. Oreg., 1961-62, Portland State U., 1962-64, Long Beach State U., 1974-76. Cert. geriatric specialist, Calif. Florist, owner Sunshine Flowers, Santa Ana, Calif., 1982—; pvt. duty nurse Aides in Action, Costa Mesa, Calif., 1985-87; owner, activity dir., adminstr. Lovelight Christian Home for the Elderly, Santa Ana, 1987—; activity dir. Bristol Care Nursing Home, Santa Ana, 1985-88; evangelist, speaker radio show Sta. KPRZ-FM, Anaheim, Calif., 1985-88; adminstr. Leisure Lodge Resort Care for Elderly in Lake Forest, Lake Forest, Calif., 1996—; nursing home activist in reforming laws to eliminate bad homes, 1984-90; founder, tchr. hugging classes/laughter therapy terminally ill patients, 1987—; founder healing and touch therapy laughter Therapy, 1991-93; bd. dirs. Performing Arts Ctr.; speaker for enlightenment and healing. Author (rewrite) Title 22 Nursing Home Reform Law, Little Hoover Commn.; model, actress and voiceovers. Bd. dirs. Orange County Coun. on Aging, 1984—; chairperson Helping Hands, 1985—, Pat Robertson Com., 1988, George Bush Presdl. Campaign, Orange County, 1988; bd. dirs., v.p. Women Aglow Orange County, 1985—; evanglist, pub. spkr., v.p. Women Aglow Huntington Beach; active with laughter therapy and hugging classes for terminally ill. Recipient Carnation Silver Bowl, Carnation Svc. Co., 1984-85, Gold medal Pres. Clinton, 1994; named Woman of Yr., Kiwanis, 1985, ABI, 1990, Woman of Decade, Am. Biog. Soc., 1995, Little Hoover Commn., 1995; honored AM L.A. TV Show, Lt. Gov. McCarthy, 1984. Mem. Calif. Assn. Residential Care Homes, Orange County Epilepsy Soc. (bd. dirs. 1986—), Calif. Assn. Long Term Facilities. Home: 2722 S Diamond St Santa Ana CA 92704-6013

OBERT, CHARLES FRANK, banker; b. Cleve., Apr. 28, 1937; s. Carl William and Irene Frances (Urban) O.; m. Linda Marie Thoss, June 3, 1961; children—Lisa Marie, Charles David. Student, Ohio State U., 1955-57. With Ameritrust Corp., Cleve., 1958—, sr. v.p. affiliate bank div., 1975-80, sr. v.p. corp. service div., 1980-87, sr. v.p. br. adminstrn., 1987-92, mgmt. cons., 1993—; pres. Acoustical Cleaning Systems Inc. Mem. Solon (Ohio) Recreation Commn., 1978-94, Solon Bd. Edn., 1986-94. Mem. Am. Inst. Banking, Am. Bankers Assn., Ohio Bankers Assn., Bank Adminstrn. Inst., Internat. Assn. Laryngectomees, Cleve. Hearing and Speech Ctr., Greater Cleve. Growth Assn., Solon C. of C. Home and Office: 8270 Pebble Creek Ct Chagrin Falls OH 44023-4866

OBERT, JESSIE CRAIG, nutritionist, consultant; b. Port Byron, Ill., Mar. 26, 1911; d. Walter Thomas and Clara D.C. Craig; m. Carl B. Obert, Dec. 7, 1935 (dec. 1943). BA, Park Coll., Parkville, Mo., 1931; SM, U. Chgo., 1943; PhD, Ohio State U., 1951. Nutritionist Chgo. Welfare Dept., 1937-42; dir. nutrition ARC, Phoenix, 1943-47; instr. Ohio State U., Columbus, 1947-51, UCLA, 1952-53; chief div. nutrition L.A. County Health Dept., L.A., 1953-76; ind. nutrition cons. L.A., 1976—. Author college textbook: Community Nutrition, 1986. Named Disting. Alumna, Ohio State U., 1976, Park Coll., 1978; recipient recognition for svc. Am. Home Econs. Assn., 1970. Mem. APHA, Am. Dietetic Assn. (del. 1965-71), Calif. Dietetic Assn. (outstanding mem. award 1977, Dolores Nyhus award 1989). Avocations: travel, genealogy, exercise, vegetable gardening. Home: 2400 S Fremont Ave Alhambra CA 91803-4319

OBERT, PAUL RICHARD, lawyer, manufacturing company executive; b. Pitts., Aug. 24, 1928; s. Edgar F. and Elizabeth T. (Buchele) O. B.S., Georgetown U., 1950; J.D., U. Pitts., 1953. Bar: Pa. 1954, D.C. 1956, Ohio 1972, Ill. 1974, U.S. Supreme Ct. 1970. Sole practice Pitts., 1954-60; asst. counsel H.K. Porter Co., Inc., Pitts., 1960-62, sec., gen. counsel, 1962-71; sec., gen. counsel Addressograph-Multigraph Corp., Cleve., 1972-74; v.p. law Marshall Field & Co., Chgo., 1974-82, sec., 1976-82; v.p., gen. counsel, sec. CF Industries, Inc., Long Grove, Ill., 1982—, also officer, dir. various subs. Served to lt. col. USAF. Mem. ABA (corp. gen. counsel com.), Pa. Bar Assn., Allegheny County Bar Assn., Ill. Bar Assn., Chgo. Bar Assn., Am. Soc. Corp. Secs., Am. Retail Fedn. (bd. dirs. 1977-80), Georgetown U. Alumni Assn. (bd. govs.), Pitts. Athletic Assn., Univ. Club (Chgo.), Delta Theta Phi. Office: CF Industries Inc 1 Salem Lake Dr Long Grove IL 60047-8401

OBEY, DAVID ROSS, congressman; b. Okmulgee, Okla., Oct. 3, 1938; s. Orville John and Mary Jane (Chellis) O.; m. Joan Therese Lepinski, June 9, 1962; children: Craig David, Douglas David. BS in Polit. Sci, U. Wis., 1960, MA, 1962. Mem. Wis. Gen. Assembly, 1963-69, asst. minority leader, 1967-69; mem. 91st-105th Congresses from 7th Wis. dist., 1969—; ranking minority mem. appropriations com., ranking minority mem. labor, HHS and edn. subcom., mem. joint econ. com.; mem. adminstrv. com. Wis. Dem. Com., 1960-62. Named Edn. Legislator of Yr., Rural div. NEA, 1968; recipient Legislative Leadership award Eagelton Inst. Politics, 1964, award of merit Nat. Council Sr. Citizens, 1976, citation for legis. statesmanship Council Exceptional Children, 1976. Office: US Ho of Reps 2462 Rayburn HOB Washington DC 20515*

OBIORA, CHRIS SUNNY, architect; b. Lagos, Nigeria, Sept. 2, 1954; came to U.S., 1978; s. Patrick M. and Virginia E. Obiora. Diploma in Physics, Chemistry, and Biology, Christ the King Coll., Onitsha, Anambra, 1974; A in Econs. and Current Affairs, Christ the King Coll., 1976; postgrad., Tex. A&M U., 1986, Coll. Profl. Mgmt., Lintas, Lagos, 1992. CFP; cert. tng. adminstr. Accounts clk. Lintas, Ltd., Lagos, 1976-78, media accounts clk., 1977-78; with San Jacinto Jr. Coll., Houston, Tex., 1980-81; The Wacherhit Corp., Coral Gables, Fla., 1980-84; gen. merchant Joncod Overseas Ltd., Lagos, 1974—; world trade strategist Joncod Overseas Ltd., Houston, 1987—; retail trader Star Liquor Store, Hempstead, Tex., 1987—; owner, prin. Chris & Chris Assocs., 1989; coord. Jancod/Bexpharm, Houston, 1987-88; cost acct. Jancod Overseas Ltd., Houston, 1980—; founder, pres. Joncod Internat., Inc., 1987—; founder, com. group head Star Liquor Store, Hempstead, 1987—. Active ARC, 1967-70, PTO, also numerous charitable activities, Lagos, 1970-74. Recipient Professionalism Cert. AMA, 1994, Meritorious Svc. award AIA Students, 1985, Recognition award Nat. Fire Protection Assn., 1986. Fellow The Highlanders Club (svcs. prof. 1993—), Nat. Shrine, Oxford Club, Oblates Mission Mary Immaculate; mem. NAFE, N.Y. Acad. Sci., Am. Chem. Soc., Am. Fin. Assn., Nat. Audubon Soc., Internat. Assn. Fin. Planners, Soc. Applied Learning Tech., Assn. Corp. Tech. Computer Profls., Instr. of Profl. Mgmt. and Adminstrn., Internat. Assn. of Account Practitioners, Constrn. Specs. Inst., Nat. Hist. Soc. Avocations: table and lawn tennis, photography, swimming. Office: Joncod Overseas Ltd PO Box 87483 Houston TX 77287-7483

OBLIGACION, FREDDIE RABELAS, sociology educator, researcher; b. Legazpi City, Albay, The Philippines, July 20, 1959; came to U.S., 1988; s. Wilfredo and Lourdes Rances (Rabelas) O. BS magna cum laude, U. Philippines, Quezon City, 1980, MBA, 1981; MA, Ohio State U., 1990, PhD, 1995. Exec. asst. Concrete Aggregates, Quezon City, 1980-82; asst. prof. Bicol U., Legazpi City, 1982-88; rsch. asst. Ohio State U., Columbus, 1988-89, teaching asst., 1989-92; asst. prof. sociology SUNY Suffolk C.C., Selden, 1992-93; reviewer Academic Text Rev., Columbus, 1994—; asst. prof. sociology Moorhead (Minn.) State U., 1994-95; with faculty Wyo. Coll. Advanced Studies, 1996—; asst. prof. sociology, distance learning sch. faculty Western New Eng. Coll., Springfield, Mass., 1996—; prof. lectr. Devine Word Grad. Sch. Bus., 1982-88; mem. faculty Grad. Sch. Aquinas U., 1982-88. Contbr. essays and articles to profl. jours. Rsch. grantee Soc. for Psychol. Studies and Social Issues, U. Mich., 1992, Ohio State U. Grad. Sch., 1992, summer rsch. award Western New Eng. Coll. Mem. Am. Sociol. Assn., Internat. Inst. Sociology, Soc. for Applied Sociology (cons. 1992—), Soc. for Psychol. Study Social Issues, Assn. for the Sociology of Religion, Assn. Humanist Sociol., Phi Kappa Phi, Phi Beta Delta. Avocations: travel, playing piano and violin.

O'BLOCK, ROBERT PAUL, management consultant; b. Pitts., Mar. 9, 1943; s. Paul Joseph and Mary Elizabeth (Galicic) O'B.; m. Megan Marie. BSME, Purdue U., 1965; MBA, Harvard U., 1967. Rsch. and teaching fellow in fin., econs. and urban mgmt., Harvard U., 1967-70; assoc. in real estate mgmt. and fin. McKinsey & Co., Inc., Boston, 1969-78, prin., 1979-84, dir., 1984—; gen. and mng. ptnr. Freeport Center, Clearfield, Utah, 1971—; vis. lectr. urban econs. Yale Law Sch., Princeton U.; cons. Mass., N.J. housing fin. agys., Rockefeller Assn., HUD, 1968-76; chmn. mgmt. com. Snowbird Lodge (Utah), 1974-86. Mem. nat. adv. bd. Snowbird Arts Inst., 1977-83; mem. budget com. N.Y. Pub. Libr., 1977-79; mem. adv. bd. Internat. Tennis Hall of Fame, 1986-89, bd. dirs., 1989-95; mem. bd. overseers Boston Symphony Orch., 1988—, vice-chmn. bd. overseers, 1992-95, chmn., 1995—; mem. bd. trustees U.S. Ski Ednl. Found., 1989—. Rsch. fellow Harvard U., 1967. Roman Catholic. Clubs: Devon Yacht, Maidstone (East Hampton, N.Y.), Natl. Golf Links Am. (Southampton, N.Y.), Alta (Salt Lake City), The Country Club (Brookline, Mass.). Contbr. articles to profl. jours. Office: McKinsey & Co Inc 75 Park Pl 3d Fl Boston MA 02116

OBLOY, LEONARD GERARD, priest; b. Cleve., Sept. 1, 1951; s. Henry Joseph and Ruth Elsie (Walter) O. AB, Borromeo Coll. of Ohio, 1973; MDiv, St. Mary's Seminary, 1977; SSL, Pontifical Biblical Inst., Rome, 1983, postgrad., 1984. Ordained priest Roman Cath. Ch., 1977. Assoc. pastor St. Helen Parish, Newbury, Ohio, 1977-80, St. Rose of Lima Parish, Cleve., 1984-88; vice-rector St. Mary's Sem., Emmitsburg, Md., 1988-97; vice rector, asst. prof. sacred scripture and computer sci. Mt. St. Mary's Sem., Emmitsburg, Md., 1988—; adj. prof. St. Mary's Sem., Cleve., 1984-88, dir. auxiliary svcs., 1997—; curriculum com. Cath. Distance U., Paeonian Springs, Va., 1986—, dean grad. divsn., 1995—; guest lectr. Our Lady of Holy Cross Coll., New Orleans, 1988—; lectr. in field. Author, narrator pub. TV series And God Said, Witness; author various pamphlets/audio casettes for Cath. Distance U. Mem. IEEE Computer Soc., Assn. for Computing Machinery, N.Y. Acad. Scis., Cath. Bibl. Fedn., Cath. Distance U., Corp. for Pub. Broadcasting, Nat. Cath. Edn. Assn., Sacred Congregation for Doctrine of Faith, Vatican Radio, Eternal Word TV Network. Avocations: computers, audio engineering, audio recording, auto mechanics. Home and Office: Mt St Mary's Sem Emmitsburg MD 21727

OBNINSKY, VICTOR PETER, lawyer; b. San Rafael, Calif., Oct. 12, 1944; s. Peter Victor and Anne Bartholdi (Donston) O.; m. Clara Alice Bechtel, June 8, 1969; children: Mari, Warren. BA, Columbia U., 1966; JD, U. Calif., Hastings, 1969. Bar: Calif. 1970. Sole practice, Novato, Calif., 1970—; arbitrator Marin County Superior Ct., San Rafael, 1979—; superior ct. judge pro tem, 1979—; lectr. real estate and partnership law. Author: The Russians in Early California, 1966. Bd. dirs. Calif. Young Reps., 1968-69, Richardson Bay San. Dist., 1974-75, Marin County Legal Aid Soc., 1976-78; baseball coach Little League, Babe Ruth League, 1970-84; mem. nat. panel consumer arbitrators Better Bus. Bur., 1974-88; leader Boy Scouts Am., 1970-84; permanent sec. Phillips Acad. Class of 1962, 1987—; mem. Phillips Acad. Alumni Council, 1991-95; bd. community advisors Buck Ctr. for Rsch. on Aging. Mem. ABA, State Bar Calif., Marin County Bar Assn. (bd. dirs. 1985-91, treas. 1987-88, pres.-elect 1989, pres. 1990), Phi Delta Phi, Phi Gamma Delta. Republican. Russian Orthodox. Office: 2 Commercial Blvd Ste 103 Novato CA 94949-6121 *An all-out intellectual attempt to understand baseball thoroughly may give sufficient insight to understand oneself; the so-called "designated hitter" rule should be abolished immediately.*

OBOLENSKY, IVAN, investment banker, foundation consultant, writer, publisher; b. London, May 15, 1925; s. Serge and Alice (Astor) O. (parents Am. citizens); m. Claire McGinnis, 1949 (div. 1956); children—Marina Ava, Ivan Serge, David; m. Mary Elizabeth Morris, 1959; 1 child, Serge. AB, Yale U., 1947. Pres. Hotel Investments, Inc., N.Y.C., 1950-58; v.p., treas. Serge Obolensky Assocs., 1952-75; Ivan Obolensky Inc. and Astor books, pubs. Ivan Obolensky Inc., pubs., 1956-65; dir. Silver Bear Inc., Atlanta; ptnr. A.T. Brod & Co., investment bankers, Dominick & Dominick Inc., investment bankers, 1965-70, Middendorf Colgate, investment bankers, 1970-73; v.p. C.B. Richard, Ellis/Moseley Hallgarten, investment bankers, 1974-81, Sterling Grace & Co., investment bankers, N.Y.C., 1982-87; sr. v.p. Jesup, Josephthal & Co., investment bankers, N.Y.C., 1987-90; gen. ptnr. Astor Capital Mgmt. Assocs., 1980—; v.p. Capital Mgmt. Assocs., N.Y.C., 1990—; v.p. Shields & Co., N.Y.C., 1990—; bd. dirs. Gold Canyon Resources, 1996—; cons. and lectr. in field. Author: Rogues' March, 1956; contbr. to Nihon Keizai Shimbun, Tokyo, on precious metals, 1985—, program com. N.Y. Soc. of Security Analysts for pub., oil and gas; contbr. articles to profl. publs. Bd. dirs. Police Athletic League, N.Y.C., 1975-85, exec. com., 1980-85, 96—, U.S.O., 1987—, Audubon Canyon Ranch, Calif., 1989—, Tolstoy Found., 1994—, Soldiers', Sailors' and Airmen's Club, 1976—, pres., 1987—, Russian Nobility Assn. in Am., 1990—, treas., 1991—, v.p., 1995—, Musicians Emergency Fund, 1985-93, pres., 1987-92, Children's Blood Found., N.Y. Hosp., 1952—, pres., 1981-95, pres. emeritus, 1995—; pres., dir. Josephine Lawrence Hopkins Found., 1971—; pres. Whitemarsh Found., 1980-90. Lt. (j.g.) USNR, 1943-45, ret., 1980. Published works by James Agee: A Death in the Family and Tad Mosel; All the Way Home, which received Pulitzer prizes, 2 Caldecott awards. Mem. Am. Legion, Mil. Order Loyal Legion U.S. (sr. vice-comdr. 1955, comdr. 1967-70), St. Elmo Soc., Met. Mus. Art (life), Knickerbocker Club, N.Y. Yacht Club, New Eng. Soc. N.Y., St. Georges Soc. N.Y., The Navy League, Army and Navy Club, Explorer's Club, Masons (Holland #8 master 1981, dist. dep. grand master 1st Manhattan 1983-84, grand treas. 1994-96). Office: Shields & Co 140 Broadway New York NY 10005-1101

OBOLENSKY, MARILYN WALL (MRS. SERGE OBOLENSKY), metals company executive; b. Detroit, Aug. 13, 1929; d. Albert Fraser and Christine (Frischkorn) Wall; m. Serge Obolensky, June 3, 1971. Student, Duschesne Jr. Coll., 1947. Chmn. bd. Wall-Colmondy Corp., Detroit, 1959-61, exec. sec., 1961—; chmn. bd. Wall-Gases Inc., Morrisville, Pa., 1959-61; pres. Serge Obolensky Assocs. Bd. dirs. Heart and Lung Assn. N.Y.C., 1963—. Republican. Roman Catholic. Clubs: Bathing Corp. (Southampton, N.Y.), Southampton. Home: New York NY 10021 Address: 45 Preston Pl Grosse Pointe MI 48236-3035

OBOMSAWIN, ALANIS, director, producer; b. Lebanon, N.H., Aug. 31, 1932; arrived in Can., 1933; d. Herman and Maria (Benedict) O.; 1 child Kisos. Dir., prodr. numerous filmstrips, 2 multimedia packages, 2 vignettes, 6 half hour 16mm films for ednl. TV; dir. 17 documentaries, short fiction film for children about racism; author, composer album Bush Lady, 1988. Former chair bd. dirs. Native Women's Shelter Montreal; former mem. Can. Coun.'s Native Adv. Com. Recipient several prizes for her films. Mem. Order of Can. Office: care Nat Film Bd CAN, CP 6100 Succ A, Montreal, PQ Canada H3C 3H5

O'BOYLE, ROBERT L., landscape architect; b. Alma, Mich., Oct. 26, 1935; s. Frederick and Ella (Keefer) O'B.; m. Kay Louise Wells, Dec. 18, 1954; children—Robert M., Brian P., Cathleen S., Andrew F. B.A., Alma Coll., 1958; B.S. in Landscape Architecture, Mich. State U., 1960. Registered landscape architect, Mich. Landscape designer Jane Smith Assocs., Lansing, Mich., 1959-61; park planner State of Mich., Lansing, 1961-62; landscape architect Light's Landscape, Richland, Mich., 1962-64; pres. O'Boyle, Cowell, Blalock & Assocs., Inc., Kalamazoo, 1964—; mem. Bd. Licensing and Registration, State of Mich., 1970-76. Contbr. articles to profl. jours. Bd. dirs. Kalamazoo Nature Ctr., 1971-76, Kalamazoo County Parks Commn., 1974-78; bd. dirs. Kalamazoo Flower Fest, Inc., 1983-89, pres., 1987-88; Parchment Downtown Devel. Authority, 1991—. Fellow Am. Soc. Landscape Architects (trustee Mich. chpt., v.p. 1991-92, award 1980, 89); Kalamazoo County C. of C. (chair transp. com. 1993-95), Rotary (editorian 1985—). Methodist. Avocations: sailing; photography; wood working. Home: 311 E Thomas Ave Kalamazoo MI 49004-1446 Office: O'Boyle Cowell Blalock & Assocs 521 S Riverview Dr Kalamazoo MI 49004-1230

OBRAMS, GUNTA IRIS, research administrator; b. Düsseldorf, Germany, Sept. 2, 1953; came to U.S., 1961; d. Robert and Olga (Baltins) O.; m. Malcolm DeWitt Patterson, Dec. 22, 1975; 1 child, Andrew McDougal Patterson. BS in Biology cum laude, Rensselaer Poly. Inst., 1977; MD, Union U., Albany, N.Y., 1977; MPH, Johns Hopkins U., 1982, PhD, 1988. Resident in obstetrics and gynecology Ea. Va. Grad. Sch. Medicine, Norfolk, 1977-78; community physician Southampton Meml. Hosp., Franklin, Va., 1978-81; resident in gen. preventive medicine sch. hygiene and pub. health Johns Hopkins U., Balt., 1981-84, project dir., 1983-85, med. dir., 1985-86; med. officer divsn. cancer etiology Nat. Cancer Inst., Bethesda, Md., 1986-89, dep. chief, 1989-90, chief, 1990-96, dir. extramural epidemiology & genetics program, 1996—. Editor: (with M. Potter): The Epidemiology and Biology of Multiple Myeloma, 1991; contbr. articles to profl. jours. With USPHS, 1987—. Recipient Nat. Cancer Inst. Nat. Rsch. Svc. award, 1981, Rsch. Career award Nat. Inst. Occupational Safety & Health; scholar Am. Med. Women's Assn., 1977. Mem. Phi Beta Kappa, Delta Omega, Alpha Omega Alpha. Office: National Cancer Institute 6130 Executive Blvd Ste 535 Bethesda MD 20892

O'BREADY, JACQUES, city administrator; b. Sherbrooke, Que., Can., June 15, 1936; s. Hertel O'Bready and Lucienne Lacroix; m. Pierrette Marquis, Sept. 9, 1961; children: Michel, Marc, Maryse. BA, U. Montreal, Que., 1956; LLL, U. Sherbrooke, 1959, JD (hon.), 1994. Bar: Que. 1960. Mayor City of Sherbrooke, 1974-82; dep. min. Mcpl. Affairs, Quebec, Que., 1984-88; pres. Commn. d'Accès à l'Information, Quebec, 1988-90, Commn. Mcpl. Quebec, 1990—. Roman Catholic. Home: 581 Bouchette, Sherbrooke, PQ Canada J1J 2T4 Office: Commn Mcpl Que, 20 Rue Chauveau, Quebec, PQ Canada G1R 4J3

O'BRIAN, BONNIE JEAN, library services supervisor; b. Great Bend, Kans., Oct. 19, 1940; d. Claude Marion and Mildred Geraldine (Schmaider) Baker; m. Patrick Gilbert Gibson (div.); 1 child, Debra Kathleen; m. John Robinson O'Brian, Nov. 2, 1968. BS, UCLA, 1961; MS, Calif. State U., Northridge, 1977; Credential in Libr. Media Svcs., Calif. State U., Long Beach, 1978. Libr. L.A. Unified Sch. Dist., Northridge, 1978-84; supr. chpt. 2 L.A. Unified Sch. Dist., L.A., 1984, coord. field libr., 1984-87, supr. libr. svcs., 1987—; asst. prof. libr. sci. Calif. State U., L.A.; condr. workshops in field. Recipient N.W. Valley Parent Tchr. Student award 1978, San Fernando Valley Reading Assn. Myrtle Shirley Reading Motivation award 1986. Mem. ALA, Am. Assn. Sch. Librs., Calif. Sch. Libr. Assn. (pres.), So. Calif. Coun. on Lit. for Children and Young People, White House Conf. on Libr. and Info. Svcs. Republican. Office: Los Angeles Unifed Sch Dist 1320 W 3rd St Los Angeles CA 90017-1410

O'BRIAN, JAMES, broadcast executive. Pres. James Intercable, Inc., Englewood, Colo. Office: Jones Intercable Inc 9697 E Mineral Ave Englewood CO 80112*

O'BRIEN, ANNMARIE, education educator; b. N.Y.C., Nov. 10, 1949; d. Hugh and Margaret (Doherty) O'B.; m. William James McGinty, Dec. 30, 1976; children: Michael Hugh, Liam Patrick. BS in Elem. Edn., Boston U., 1971; MS in Early Childhood Edn., Queens Coll., 1976; EdD in Ednl.

Leadership, Portland State U., 1994. Tchr. St. Gerard Majella Elem. Sch., Hollis, N.Y., 1972-76, Lower Kuskokwim Sch. Dist., Bethel, Alaska, 1977-85; child sexual abuse prevention coord. Resource Ctr. for Parents and Children, Fairbanks, Alaska, 1986; grad. asst., project evaluator Portland (Oreg.) State U., 1989-92, student tchr. supr., 1992; prof. edn., rsch. assoc. Inst. Social and Econ. Rsch. U. Alaska, Anchorage, 1993-96; prin. Old Harbor Sch., Kodiak Island Borough Sch. Dist., Kodiak, Alaska, 1996—. Author: A Child Abuse Prevention Training Manual for Educators, 1976; co-author: The Academy for Future Educators Guidebook, 1992. Recipient scholarship Portland State U., 1991. Mem. AAUW, Kappa Delta Pi. Office: Old Harbor Sch PO Box 49 Old Harbor AK 99643

OBRIEN, BARBARA ANN, speech and language pathologist; b. Albany, N.Y., Nov. 13, 1946; d. William Henry and Katherine (Garrow) O. BA, SUNY, Albany, 1969; MEd, U. Va., 1971. Lic. speech pathologist; cert. tchr., Va. Speech pathologist Fairfax County Pub. Schs., Falls Church and McLean, Va., 1971—; autism resource tchr. Fairfax County Pub. Schs., 1994—; merit tchr., peer observer Fairfax County Pub. Schs., Vienna, Va., 1989—, colleague lead clinician, 1990—; writer, presenter Future Directions, Arlington, Va., 1984; pvt. practice, Falls Church, 1987-89; assoc. Nelson Ctr., Annandale, Va., 1990—; mem. speech and lang. adv. coun. Fairfax County Pub. Schs., 1993. Mem. NEA, Am. Speech Hearing Lang. Assn., Va. Speech Hearing Assn. Home: 8360 Greensboro Dr Mc Lean VA 22102-3511 Office: Cooper Intermediate Sch 977 Balls Hill Rd Mc Lean VA 22101-2020

O'BRIEN, CHARLES H., lawyer, retired state supreme court chief justice; b. Orange, N.J., July 30, 1920; s. Herbert Rodgers and Agnes Sidman (Montanya) O'B.; m. Anna Belle Clement, Nov. 9, 1966; children: Merry Diane, Steven Shawn (dec.), Heather Lynn. LLB, Cumberland U., 1947. Rep. Tenn. Legislature, Memphis, 1963-65, senator, 1965-67; assoc. judge Tenn. Ct. Criminal Appeals, Crossville, 1970-87; assoc. justice Tenn. Supreme Ct., 1987-94, chief justice, 1994-95; ret., 1995; pvt. practice, Crossville, 1995—. Bd. dirs. Lake Tansi Village Property Owners Assn., 1984-89, chmn., 1989. With U.S. Army, 1938-45, ETO, 1950, UN Command, Tokyo. Decorated Bronze Star, Purple Heart with oak leaf cluster. Fellow Tenn. Bar Found.; mem. ABA, Tenn. Bar Assn., Cumberland County Bar Assn., Am. Legion, Lake Tansi Village Chowder and Marching Soc. (pres.). Democrat. Avocation: outdoor activities.

O'BRIEN, CHARLES P., psychiatrist, educator. BA, Tulane U., 1960, MS, 1964, MD, 1966, PhD in Neurophysiology, 1964. Resident in internal medicine Mass. Gen. Hosp., 1964-65; neurologist, psychiatrist Tulane U., 1965-67, Nat. Hosp. Nervous Disorders, 1967-68; psychiatrist U. Pa., Phila., 1968-69, from instr. to asst. prof. to assoc. prof., 1969-78, prof. psychiatry, 1978—, vice chmn., 1986—; tchg. asst. neurophysiology Tulane Med. Sch., 1965-66, instr., 1966-67; vis. prof. Sch. Medicine Hahnemann U., 1980-95; Pfizer vis. prof. Albert Einstein Coll. Medicine, 1990. Fellow APA, Am. Coll. Neuropsychopharmacology; mem. Psychiat. Rsch. Soc., Am. Acad. Neurol., Soc. Psychotherapy Rsch., Am. Psychosomatic Soc., Inst. Medicine NAS, Coll. on Problems of Drug Dependence, Soc. Neurosci., Assn. Rsch. Nervous and Mental Dis. (pres. 1989-90). Office: U Pa VA Med Ctr 3900 Chestnut St Philadelphia PA 19104-3120

O'BRIEN, CONAN, writer, performer, talk show host; b. Brookline, Mass., Apr. 18, 1963. BA Am. Hist., Lit., Harvard U., 1981-85. staff mem. The Harvard Lampoon, 1981-85 (pres. 1983, 84). Stage appearances with: The Groundlings (L.A.) 1985-87; writer, performer The Happy Happy Good Show (L.A., Chgo.) 1988; writer (TV) Not Necessarily the News (HBO) 1985-87, Saturday Night Live, 1988-91 (NBC, Emmy Outstanding Writing in Comedy series 1989), Lookwell (NBC) 1991; writer, prodr. The Simpsons (Fox) 1991-93, The Wilton North Report (syndicated) 1987, Late Night with Conan O'Brien (NBC) 1993—. Office: Late Night with Conan O'Brien NBC 30 Rockefeller Plz New York NY 10112*

O'BRIEN, DANIEL DION, track and field athlete, Olympic athlete; b. Portland, Oreg., July 18, 1966. Student, U. Idaho, 1989. Track and field athlete Reebock Racing Club; pub. personality Reebok. Winner Decathlon World Championship, 1991, 93; ranked No.1 in Decathlon Track & Field News, 1991; recipient Gold medal Atlanta Olympics, 1996. Office: USA Track and Field Press Info Dept PO Box 120 Indianapolis IN 46204*

O'BRIEN, DANIEL WILLIAM, lawyer, corporation executive; b. St. Paul, Jan. 6, 1926; s. Daniel W. and Kathryn (Zenk) O'B.; m. Sarah Ward Stoltze, June 20, 1952; children: Bridget Ann, Daniel William, Kevin Charles, Timothy John. Student, U. Dubuque, 1943, Ill. State U., 1944; B.S.L., U. Minn., 1948, LL.B., 1949. Bar: Minn. 1949. Practice in St. Paul, 1950—; partner Randall, Smith & Blomquist, 1955-65; of counsel Doherty, Rumble & Butler, 1965—; pres. F.H. Stoltze Land & Lumber Co., 1964—, Maple Island, Inc., 1968—; dir. Villaume Industries, Inc., Evercolor Corp. Served to ensign USNR, 1943-46. Mem. Minn., Ramsey County bar assns., World Pres's. Orgn., Chief Execs. Orgn. Home: 4734 Bouleau Rd White Bear Lk MN 55110-3355 Office: 2497 7th Ave E Ste 105 North Saint Paul MN 55109-2902

O'BRIEN, DARCY, English educator, writer; b. Los Angeles, July 16, 1939; s. George and Marguerite (Churchill) O'B.; m. Ruth Ellen Berke, Aug. 26, 1961 (div. 1968); 1 child, Molly; m. Suzanne Beesley, Feb. 27, 1987. A.B., Princeton U., 1961; postgrad., Cambridge (Eng.) U., 1963-64; M.A., U. Calif., Berkeley, 1963, Ph.D., 1965. Asst. prof. English Pomona Coll., Claremont, Calif., 1965-70, assoc. prof., 1970-75, prof., 1975-78; prof. English U. Tulsa, 1978-96. Author: The Conscience of James Joyce, 1968, W.R. Rodgers, 1971, Patrick Kavanagh, 1975, A Way of Life, Like Any Other (Ernest Hemingway Found. award 1978), Moment By Moment, 1978, The Silver Spooner, 1981, Two of a Kind, 1985, Murder in Little Egypt, 1989, Margaret in Hollywood, 1991, A Dark and Bloody Ground, 1993, Power to Hurt, 1996. Woodrow Wilson fellow, 1961-62; U. Ill. Ctr. for Advanced Study fellow, 1969-70; Mellon Found. fellow, 1973-74; Guggenheim fellow, 1978-79. Mem. PEN, James Joyce Soc., Internat. Assn. Crime Writers, Authors Guild, Am. Irish Hist. Soc., Screen Writers Guild. Address: 2936 S Delaware Ave Tulsa OK 74104

O'BRIEN, DAVID A., lawyer; b. Sioux City, Iowa, Aug. 30, 1958; s. John T. and Doris K. (Reisch) O'B. BA, George Washington U., 1981; JD, U. Iowa, 1984. Bar: Iowa 1985, U.S. Dist. Ct. (no. dist.) Iowa 1985, Nebr. 1990, U.S. Dist. Ct. Nebr. 1990. Legis. asst. Nat. Transp. Safety Bd., Washington, 1978-81; assoc. O'Brien, Galvin & Kuehl, Sioux City, 1985-88; ptnr. O'Brien, Galvin Moeller & Neary, Sioux City, 1989-94; chair Wage Appeals Bd. & Bd. of Svc. Contract Appeals U.S. Dept. Labor, Washington, 1994-96, acting dir. Office Adminstrv. Appeals, 1995-96, chair adminstrv. review bd., 1996—. Dem. candidate for Congress, 6th dist. of Iowa, Sioux City, 1988; chmn. Woodbury County Dem. Party, Sioux City, 1992-94, chair Iowa campaign Clinton for Pres., Des Moines, 1992; bd. dirs. Mid-Step Svcs. Inc., Sioux City, 1986-91, Mo. River Hist. Devel., Sioux City, 1989-94. Mem. Nat. Assn. Trial Lawyers, Iowa Trial Lawyers Assn. (bd. govs. 1991-94). Roman Catholic. Avocations: sports, politics. Office: O'Brien Galvin Moeller & Neary PO Box 3223 922 Douglas St Sioux City IA 51101-1026

O'BRIEN, DAVID MICHAEL, law educator; b. Rock Springs, Wyo., Aug. 30, 1951; s. Ralph Rockwell and Lucile O'Brien; m. Claudine M. Mendelovitz, Dec. 17, 1982; children: Benjamin, Sara, Talia. BA, U. Calif., Santa Barbara, 1973, MA, 1974, PhD, 1977. Fulbright lectr. Oxford (Eng.) U., 1987-88; lectr. U. Calif., Santa Barbara, 1976-77; asst. prof. U. Puget Sound, Tacoma, Wash., 1977-79; Spicer prof. U. Va., Charlottesville, 1979—; Fulbright rschr., Tokyo, Kyoto, Japan, 1993-94; jud. fellow U.S. Supreme Ct., Washington, 1982-83; vis. postdoctoral fellow Russell Sage Found., N.Y.C., 1981-82; lectr. USIA, Burma, Japan, France, 1994-95. Author: Supreme Court Watch, 1991—, Constitutional Law and Politics, 2 vols., 3d edit., 1997, Storm Center: The Supreme Court in American Politics, 4th edit., 1996, To Dream of Dreams: Constitutional Politics in Postwar Japan, 1996, To Dream of Dreams: Religious Freedom in Postwar Japan, 1996; editor: Views from the Bench, 1985. Rappatour, jud. selection 20th Century Fund Task Force, N.Y., 1986-87. Tom C. Clark Jud. Fellow, Jud. Fellows Commn., Washington, 1983. Mem. ABA (Silver Gavel award 1987), Am. Judicature Soc., Am. Polit. Sci. Assn., Supreme Ct. Hist. Soc. (editl. bd. 1982—), Internat. Polit. Sci. Assn. Democrat. Avocations: painting, travel. Home: Rt 12 Box 64A Charlottesville VA 22901 Office: U Va 232 Cabell Hall Charlottesville VA 22901

O'BRIEN, DAVID PETER, oil company executive; b. Montreal, Que., Can., Sept. 9, 1941; s. John Lewis and Ethel (Cox) O'B.; m. Gail Baxter Corneil, June 1, 1968; children: Tara, Matthew, Shaun. B.A. with honors in Econs., Loyola Coll., Montreal, 1962; B.C.L., McGill U., 1965. Assoc. and ptnr. Ogilvy, Renault, Montreal, 1967-77; v.p., gen. counsel Petro-Can., Calgary, Alta., 1977-81; sr. v.p. Petro-Can., Calgary, 1982-85, sr. v.p. fin. and planning, 1982-85, exec. v.p., 1985-89; pres., chief exec. officer Noverco Inc., Montreal, 1989; chmn. bd., pres., chief exec. officer PanCan. Petroleum Ltd., Calgary, Alta., Can., 1990-94; pres., COO Can. Pacific Ltd., Montreal, 1995-96; chmn., pres., CEO Can. Pacific Ltd., Calgary, 1996—; bd. dirs. Westburne Inc., Fording Coal Ltd., Laidlaw Inc., Inco Ltd., Royal Bank Can., Conf. Bd. Can., Bus. Coun. Nat. Issues, Inco Ltd.; chmn. bd. dirs. PanCan. Petroleum Ltd. Mem. Quebec Bar Assn., Glencoe Club, Calgary Petroleum Club, Calgary Golf and Country Club. Home: 906 Riverdale Ave SW, Calgary, AB Canada T2S 0Y6 Office: 1800 Bankers Hall East, 855 2nd St SW, Calgary, AB Canada T2P-4Z5

O'BRIEN, DELLANNA WEST, religious organization administrator; b. Wichita Falls, Tex.; d. Paul H. and B. West; m. William R. O'Brien; children: Denise O'Brien Basden, Erin O'Brien Puryear, William Ross. BS, Hardin Simmons U., 1953; MEd, Tex. Christian U., 1972; EdD, Va. Tech. and State U., 1983; LHD (hon.), Judson Coll., 1992; D in Social Svc. (hon.), U. Richmond, 1993. Tchr. elem. schs., Tex., 1953-63; missionary So. Baptist Conv., Indonesia, 1963-71; tchr. elem. schs., Va., 1972-88; pres. Internat. Family and Children's Ednl. Svcs., Richmond, Va., 1988-89; exec. dir., treas. Woman's Missionary Union, Birmingham, Ala., 1989—; exec. com Bapt. World Alliance, budget and fin. com., Bapt. world aid com., global resource panel for women in evangelism; mem. N. Am. Bapt. Fellowship. Co-author: In Christ's Name; contbr. articles to religious mags.: The Commission, The Student, Baptist Heritage Update, Pioneer, Open Windows. Past mem. Henrico County (Va.) Sch. Bd. Recipient Disting. Alumni award Hardin Simmons U., Abilene, Tex., 1990. Avocations: reading, music, gardening. Office: Woman's Missionary Union PO Box 830010 Birmingham AL 35283-0010

O'BRIEN, DONAL CLARE, JR., lawyer; b. N.Y.C., May 16, 1934; s. Donal Clare and Constance (Boody) O'B.; m. Katharine Louise Slight, June 20, 1956; children: Donal Clare III, Constance Nancy O'Brien Ashforth, Katharine Louise O'Brien Rohn, Caroline Clare Thomas. BA, Williams Coll., 1956; LLB, U. Va., 1959. Bar: N.Y. 1961. Assoc. Milbank, Tweed, Hadley & McCloy, N.Y.C., 1959-67, ptnr, 1967-83, 91—; chief legal counsel Rockefeller Family & Assoc., N.Y.C., 1968-91; pres., CEO Rockefeller Trust Co., N.Y.C., 1986-91; bd. dirs. Greenacre Found., N.Y.C., Quebec Labrador Found., Ipswich, Mass., Nat. Audubon Soc., N.Y.C. Chmn. bd. dirs. Atlantic Salmon Fedn., N.Y.C.; trustee N.Am. Wildlife Found., Wendell Gilley Mus., Southwest Harbor, Maine, Waterfowl Rsch. Found., N.Y.C., Am. Bird Conservancy, Washington, The JDR 3d Fund, N.Y.C., Trust for Mut. Understanding, Winthrop Rockefeller Charitable Trust, Little Rock; mem. coun. Rockefeller U.; commr. State of Conn. Bd. Fisheries and Game, 1971-72; mem. Coun. on Environ. Quality, Conn., 1971-76, 91—. Mem. Century Assn. Anglers Club of N.Y. Home: 436 Trinity Pass Rd New Canaan CT 06840-2530 Office: Milbank Tweed Hadley & McCloy 1 Chase Manhattan Plz New York NY 10005-1401

O'BRIEN, DONALD EUGENE, federal judge; b. Marcus, Iowa, Sept. 30, 1923; s. Michael John and Myrtle A. (Toomey) O'B.; m. Ruth Mahon, Apr. 15, 1950; children: Teresa, Brien, John, Shuivaun. LL.B., Creighton U., 1948. Bar: Iowa bar 1948, U.S. Supreme Ct. bar 1963. Asst. city atty. Sioux City, Iowa, 1949-53; county atty. Woodbury County, Iowa, 1955-58; mcpl. judge Sioux City, Iowa, 1959-60; U.S. atty. No. Iowa, 1961-67; pvt. practice law Sioux City, 1967-78, U.S. Dist. judge, 1978—; chief judge U.S. Dist. Ct. (no. dist.) Iowa, Sioux City, 1985-92, sr. judge, 1992—; rep. 8th cir. dist. ct. judges to Jud. Conf. U.S., 1990—. Served with USAAF, 1943-45. Decorated D.F.C., air medals. Mem. Woodbury County Bar Assn., Iowa State Bar Assn. Roman Catholic. Office: US Dist Ct PO Box 267 Sioux City IA 51102-0267

O'BRIEN, EDWARD IGNATIUS, lawyer, private investor; b. N.Y.C., Sept. 15, 1928; s. Edward I. and Marguerite (Malone) O'B.; m. Margaret M. Feeney, June 29, 1957; children: Edward Ignatius III, Margaret Mary, Thomas Gerard, John Joseph. AB, Fordham U., 1950; LLB, St. John's U., 1954; grad., Advanced Mgmt. Program, Cornell U., 1965. Bar: N.Y. 1954. With firm Hale, Kay & Brennan, N.Y.C., 1954-55; with Bache & Co., Inc., N.Y.C., 1955-74, gen. counsel, 1960, gen. ptnr., 1964, sec., 1968, v.p., 1965-68, sr. v.p., mem. exec. com., 1969, exec. v.p., 1969, chmn. exec. com., 1971-74; pres. Securities Industry Assn., 1974-93; retired, 1993; bd. dirs. 8 corps.; lectr. Am. Law Inst., Practising Law Inst., Am. Mgmt. Assn.; exch. ofcl. Am. Stock Exch., 1972; mem. adv. bd., mem. exec. com. Securities Regulation Inst., U. Calif., 1975—. Mem. Cardinal's com. Laity Cath. Archdiocese N.Y., mem. Cardinal's com. for edn.; chmn. Fordham U. Coun., 1971-73; bd. dirs. 3 non-profit orgns.; chmn. corp. devel. com. Fordham U.; trustee, chmn. bd. trustees Fordham Prep. Sch., 1975-77, Capt. USAR. Mem. N.Y. State Bar Assn., Am. Arbitration Assn., Am. Soc. Internat. Law, Guild Cath. Lawyers, Securites Industry Assn. (chmn. publicly owned firms com. 1972), Nat. Assn. Securities Dealers (dist. com. 1973-74), City Midday Club, Shenorock Shore Club (Rye, N.Y.), Town Club (Scarsdale, N.Y.), Met. Club (Washington). Home and Office: 12 Woods Ln Scarsdale NY 10583-6408

O'BRIEN, ELMER JOHN, librarian, educator; b. Kemmerer, Wyo., Apr. 8, 1932; s. Ernest and Emily Catherine (Reinhart) O'B.; m. Betty Alice Peterson, July 2, 1966. A.B., Birmingham So. Coll., 1954; Th.M., Iliff Sch. Theology, 1957; M.A., U. Denver, 1961. Ordained to ministry Methodist Ch., 1957; pastor Meth. Ch., Pagosa Springs, Colo., 1957-60; circulation-reference librarian Boston U. Sch. Theology, Boston, 1961-65; asst. librarian Garrett-Evang. Theol. Sem., Evanston, Ill., 1965-69; librarian, prof. United Theol. Sem., Dayton, Ohio, 1969-96, prof. emeritus, 1996—; abstractor Am. Bibliog. Center, 1969-73; dir. Ctr. for Evang. United Brethren Heritage, 1979-96; chmn. div. exec. com. Dayton-Miami Valley Libr. Consortium, 1983-84; rsch. assoc. Am. Antiquarian Soc., 1990. Author: Bibliography of Festschriften in Religion Published Since 1960, 1972, Religion Index Two: Festschriften, 1960-69; contbg. author: Communication and Change in American Religious History, 1993, Essays in Celebration of the First Fifty Years, 1996; pub. Meth. Revs. Index, 1818-1985, 1989-91; contbr. essay to profl. jour. Recipient theol. and scholarship award Assn. Theol. Schs. in U.S. and Can., 1990-91; Assn. Theol. Schs. in U.S. and Can. library staff devel. grantee, 1976-77, United Meth. Ch. Bd. Higher Edn. and Ministry research grantee, 1984-85. Mem. ALA, Acad. Libr. Assn. Ohio, Am. Theol. Libr. Assn. (head bur. personnel and placement 1969-73, dir. 1973-76, v.p. 1977-78, pres. 1978-79), Am. Antiquarian Soc. (rsch. assoc. 1990), Delta Sigma Phi, Omicron Delta Kappa, Eta Sigma Phi, Kappa Phi Kappa. Club: Torch Internat. (v.p. Dayton club 1981-82, pres. 1982-83). Home: Apt 281 4840 Thunderbird Dr Boulder CO 80303

O'BRIEN, FRANCIS ANTHONY, retired lawyer; b. Albany, N.Y., Sept. 23, 1936; s. Francis Joseph and Helen Marie (Smith) O'B.; m. Maryanne Delia Mahoney, May 2, 1964; children—John, Dennis, Kathleen, Eileen. AB, Hamilton Coll., 1958; LLB, Cornell U., 1961. Bar: N.Y. 1962, D.C. 1968. Trial atty. FTC, Washington, 1962-68; assoc. Howrey & Simon, Washington, 1968-70, ptnr., 1971-86; prin., ret. Francis A. O'Brien & Assocs., Washington. Alumni trustee Hamilton Coll., Clinton, N.Y., 1980-84; mem. Chesterbrook Woods Citizen Assn., McLean, Va., 1976—. Mem. ABA, Fed. Bar Assn., N.Y. Bar Assn., D.C. Bar Assn. Roman Catholic. Avocations: basketball; soccer; Civil War history. Home: 1600 Forest Ln Mc Lean VA 22101-3314

O'BRIEN, FRANK B., manufacturing executive; b. Evanston, Ill., Dec. 5, 1946; s. Frank B. and Barbara (Greene) O'B.; m. Karen Eby, Oct. 12, 1974; children: Frank B. IV, Caroline Ann, Mary Karen, Margaret Greene, John Patrick, William Thomas. BSBA, Ohio State U., 1972. CPA, Ohio. Acct. Ernst & Whinney, Cleve., 1973-80; asst. to v.p. fin. The N.Am. Coal Corp., Cleve., 1980-82, mgr. corp. planning, 1982-87; v.p. corp. devel. NACCO Industries, Inc., Cleve., 1987-93, sr. v.p. corp. devel., chief fin. officer, 1994—; chmn. corp. planning coun. Mfrs.' Alliance for Productivity and Innovation, Washington, 1987—. Bd. dirs. The Guidance Ctr., Boy Scouts of Am., Boys Hope, 1993; founder Children's Little Theater Endowment Fund, Cleve., 1987—. Sgt. U.S. Army, 1968-71. Mem. Assn. for Corp. Growth, Mayfield Country Club, Cleve. Playhouse Club, Pine Lake Trout Club. Republican. Roman Catholic. Office: NACCO Industries Inc 5875 Landerbrook Dr Mayfield Heights OH 44124

O'BRIEN, GEOFFREY PAUL, editor; b. N.Y.C., May 4, 1948; s. Joseph Aloysius and Margaret Dorothy (Owens) O'B.; m. Carly Francis O'Brien, Mar. 18, 1977; 1 child, Heather. Student, Yale U., 1966-67, SUNY, Stony Brook, 1968-70. Editor Reader's Catalog, N.Y.C., 1987-91; exec. editor Libr. of Am., N.Y.C., 1992—. Author: Hardboiled America, 1981, Dream Time, 1988, A Book of Maps, 1989, The Phantom Empire, 1993, The Hudson Mystery, 1994, Floating City: Selected Poems 1978-95, 1996; contbr. poetry, essays and revs. to profl. jours.; contbg. writer The Village Voice, 1982-90; editor: Frogpond, 1980-81; co-editor: Montemora, 1974-76. Recipient Writing award Whiting Found., 1988. Office: Libr of Am 14 E 60th St New York NY 10022-1006

O'BRIEN, GEORGE DENNIS, retired university president; b. Chicago, Ill., Feb. 21, 1931; s. George Francis and Helen (Fehlandt) O'B.; m. Judith Alyce Johnson, June 21, 1958; children: Elizabeth Belle, Juliana Helen, Victoria Alyce. AB in English, Yale, 1952; PhD in Philosophy, U. Chgo., 1961. Tchr. humanities, Carnegie rsch. fellow U. Chgo., 1956-57; successively instr., asst. prof., asst. dean coll. Princeton (N.J.) U., 1958-65; on leave in Athens, Greece, 1963-64; spl. honors seminars LaSalle Coll., spring 1963, fall 1964, spring 1965; assoc. prof. philosophy Middlebury (Vt.) Coll., 1965-71, prof., 1971-76, dean of men, 1965-67, dean of coll., 1967-74, dean faculty, 1975-76; pres. Bucknell U., 1976-84, U. Rochester, N.Y., 1984-94; ret., 1994; dir. Salzburg Seminar in Am. Studies. Author: Hegel on Reason in History, 1975, God and the New Haven Railway, 1986, What to Expect from College, 1991, All the Essential Half-Truths About Higher Education, 1997; contbr. articles to profl. jours. Trustee LaSalle Coll., Phila., 1965—; bd. dirs. Union Theol. Sem., 1985-90, Rsch. Librs. Group, 1994—; v.p. Commonweal Found., 1994—. Fellow Am. Coun. Learned Socs., London, 1971-72; Nat. Phi Beta Kappa scholar, 1996-97. Mem. Am. Philos. Assn., Phi Beta Kappa. Home: RR 3 Box 510 Middlebury VT 05753-8728

O'BRIEN, GERALD JAMES, utilities executive; b. St. Paul, May 1, 1923; s. Dewey Joseph and Henrietta Elizabeth O'B.; m. Patricia Margaret McCorison, Feb. 23, 1946; children: Kathleen, Thomas, John, Andrew. Student, St. Thomas Coll., 1940-41, 45-46; B.C.S., Drake U., 1948. Staff acct. Haskins & Sells, Mpls., 1948-50; with Donovan Cos., Inc., St. Paul, 1950-81; sec., asst. treas. Donovan Cos., Inc., 1977-81; utility rate cons., 1981-84; dir. Alumbaugh Coal Co., Donovan Constrn. Co., So. Tier Gas Corp., Gas Distbrs. Info. Service. Served with U.S. Army, 1942-45. Decorated Purple Heart. Address: 13313 W Meeker Blvd Sun City West AZ 85375-3808

O'BRIEN, GREGORY MICHAEL ST. LAWRENCE, university official; b. N.Y.C., Oct. 7, 1944; s. Henry Joseph and Mary Agnes (McGoldrick) O'B.; m. Mary K. McLaughlin, Dec. 28, 1968; children: Jennifer Jane, Meredith Kathleen. A.B. with honors, Lehigh U., 1966; A.M., Boston U., 1968, Ph.D., 1969. Assoc. in psychology Lab. Community Psychology, Harvard Med. Sch., Boston; dir. Human Svcs. Design Lab., Sch. Applied Social Scis., Case Western Res. U., Cleve., 1970-74; dean, prof. Sch. Social Welfare, U. Wis., Milw., 1974-78; provost, prof. psychology U. Mich.-Flint, 1978-80; prof. social work and psychology, v.p. acad. affairs U. South Fla., Tampa, 1980-83, provost, 1983-87, prof. mgmt., 1986-87; chancellor U. New Orleans, 1987—; evaluation research cons. Cambridge Dept. Health and Hosps. and USPHS, 1968; bd. dirs. WLAE-TV (PBS), Bank One New Orleans Region, Entergy New Orleans, NACFAM, NASULGC. Contbr. chpts. to books, articles to profl. jours. State of La. Econ. Devel. Coun., 1997—; vice chmn. State of La. Film and Video Commn., 1993-94, mem., 1993—; chmn. Metro. Coun. Govts. MetroVision, 1992—; adv. mem. Bus. Coun. New Orleans and the River Region; bd. dirs. The Chamber/New Orleans and the River Region, 1988—; mem. Kellogg Commn. on Future of Land Grant Colls. and State Univs., 1996—. NIMH fellow, 1968-69. Fellow Am. Coll. Mental Health Adminstrs. (founding fellow, pres. 1984-86); mem. NCAA (chair pres. commn. 1992-93), Nat. Assn. Social Workers, Nat. Conf. Social Welfare, Soc. Gen. Systems Research, Am. Psychol. Assn., Am. Public Health Assn., Metrovision Partnership Found. (1992-93), Council Social Work Edn. (presdl. task force on structure of assn.), Indsl. Relations Research Assn. Roman Catholic. Home: 2468 Lark St New Orleans LA 70122-4322 Office: U New Orleans Office of Chancellor New Orleans LA 70148

O'BRIEN, J. WILLARD, lawyer, educator; b. N.Y.C., Oct. 19, 1930; s. J. Willard and Anna C. (Carroll) O.'B.; m. Peggy J. O'Brien. B.S., Fordham U., 1952, J.D., 1957. Bar: N.Y. 1957. Assoc. Cahill, Gordon, Reindel & Ohl, N.Y.C., 1957-62; asst. prof. law Syracuse U. Coll. Law, 1962-65; prof. law Villanova (Pa.) U. Sch. Law, 1965—, dean, 1972-83, dir. Connelly Inst. Law and Morality, 1983-95; mem. Pa. Fed. Jud. Nominating Commn., 1977-80, vice chmn., 1978-80; mem. Pa. Law and Justice Inst., 1972-73, chmn. exec. com., 1973-75, pres., 1975-77. Editor-in-chief Fordham Law Rev, 1956-57. Bd. dirs. Nat. Inst. on Holocaust, 1984-85; bd. dirs. Phila. Coordinating Council on the Holocaust, 1983—. Served with USAF, 1952-54; Served with N.Y. Air N.G., 1954-58. Mem. ABA, N.Y. State Bar Assn., Pa. Bar Assn., Canon Law Soc. Am. Roman Catholic.

O'BRIEN, JACK GEORGE, artistic director; b. Saginaw, Mich., June 18, 1939; s. J. George and Evelyn (MacArthur Martens) O'B. A.B., U. Mich., 1961, M.A., 1962. Asst. dir. APA Repertory Theatre, N.Y.C., 1963-67; asso. dir. APA Repertory Theatre, 1967-69; worked with San Diego Nat. Shakespeare Festival, 1969-82, A.C.T., 1970-80, Loretto Hilton, 1975, Ahmanson, Los Angeles, 1978-80, San Francisco Opera, Houston Grand Opera, Washington Opera Soc., N.Y.C. Opera. Lyricist: Broadway prodn. The Selling of the President, 1972; dir.: on Broadway Porgy and Bess (Tony award nominee 1977), Most Happy Fella, Street Scene, Two Shakespearean Actors, 1993, Damn Yankees, 1994, Hapgood, 1994, others; artistic dir.: Old Globe Theatre, San Diego, 1981. Mem. Actors' Equity, Am. Soc. Composers and Performers, Soc. Stage Dirs. and Choreographers, Dirs. Guild Am. *

O'BRIEN, JAMES ALOYSIUS, foreign language educator; b. Cin., Apr. 7, 1936; s. James Aloysius and Frieda (Schirmer) O'B.; m. Rumi Matsumoto, Aug. 26,1961. B.A., St. Joseph's Coll., 1958; M.A., U. Cin., 1960; Ph.D., Ind. U., 1969. Instr. English St. Joseph's Coll., Rensselaer, Ind., 1960-62; asst. prof. Japanese U. Wis.-Madison, 1968-74, assoc. prof., 1974-81, chmn. East Asis langs. and lit., 1979-80, 82-85, prof. Japanese, 1981—. Author: Dazai Osamu, 1975, Akutagawa and Dazai: Instances of Literary Adaptation, 1988; translator: Selected Stories and Sketches (Dazai Osamu), 1983, Three Works (Muro Saisei), 1985, Crackling Mountain and Other Stories (Dazai Osamu), 1989. Mem. Middleton City Common Coun., 1996—. Ford Found fellow, 1965-66; Fulbright-Hays and NDEA fellow, 1966-68; Social Sci. Research Council fellow, 1973-74; Japan Found. fellow, 1977-78. Mem. Assn. Asian Studies, Assn. Tchrs. of Japanese (exec. com. 1981-84, dir. devel. 1981-83, pres. 1984-90). Home: 2533 Branch St Middleton WI 53562-2812 Office: U Wis Dept East Asian Langs & Lit 1220 Linden Dr Madison WI 53706-1525

O'BRIEN, JAMES JEROME, construction management consultant; b. Phila., Oct. 20, 1929; s. Sylvester Jerome and Emma Belle Filer (Fulforth) O'B.; m. Carmen Hiester, June 10, 1952 (div. Aug. 1, 1984); children: Jessica Susan, Michael, David; m. Rita F. Gibson, Nov. 1, 1984. BCE, Cornell U., 1952; postgrad., U. Houston, 1957-58. Registered profl. engr., N.Y., N.J., Pa., Ga., Conn., Maine. Project engr. Rohm & Haas, Phila. and Tex., 1955-59, RCA Corp., Moorestown, N.J., Greenland and Alaska, 1959-62; cons. Mauchly Assocs., Fort Washington, Pa., 1962-65; founding ptnr., exec. v.p. Meridian Engring. Co., Phila., 1965-68; pres. MDC Systems, Cherry Hill, 1968-72; ptnr. James J. O'Brien P.E., Cherry Hill, 1972-77; pres. O'Brien-Kreitzberg & Assocs., N.Y.C., Pennsauken, San Francisco, 1977-80, chief exec. officer, 1980-89, chmn. bd. dirs., 1989-93, vice chmn., 1993—. Author: CPM in Construction Management-Scheduling by the Critical Path Method, 1965, CPM in Construction Management-Project Management with CPM, 4th edit., 1993, Management Information Systems-Concepts, Techniques and

Applications, 1970, Management with Computers, 1972, Construction Inspection Handbook, 1974, 4th edit., 1997, Value Analysis in Design and Construction, 1976, Construction Delay-Risks, Rsponsibilities and Litigation, 1976, Preconstruction Estimating: Budget to Bid, 1994, Construction Documentation, 3d edit., 1995; co-author: Construction Management: A Professional Approach, 1974; editor: Recollections (L.D. Miles), 1987; author, editor: Scheduling Handbook, 1969, Contractor's Management Handbook, 1971, 2d edit., 1990, Standard Handbook of Heavy Construction, 3d edit., 1996; contbr. articles to profl. jours. Lt. 1952-55, USN. Recipient Profl. Mgr. award N.Y. chpt. Soc. Advancement Mgmt., 1969. Fellow ASCE (Constrn. Mgmt. award 1976, v.p. 1985, pres. South Jersey br. 1985, Disting. Engr. South Jersey br. 1986, pres. N.J. sect. 1987-89, mem. com. on quality in civil engring. profession 1990—), Project mgmt. Inst. (sec. 1971, v.p. 1972, pres. 1973, chmn. bd. 1974-75, award for contbn. to project mgmt. 1983, Fellow award 1989), Constrn. Mgmt. Assn. Am. (bd. dirs. 1990-92, Fellow award 1993, Constrn. Mgr. of Yr. award N.Y.-N.J. chpt. 1994), Cornell Soc. Engrs. (dean's adv. com. sch. civil and environ. engring. 1986-87); mem. Am. Inst. Indsl. Engrs. (sr.), Am. Assn. Cost Engring., Soc. Am. Value Engrs. (cert. value specialist, v.p. N.E. region 1986-87, Fallon Value-in-Life award 1993), Miles Value Found. (bd. dirs. 1987-90, trustee 1990—), Soc. Advancement Mgmt. (v.p. CPM divsn. 1970), Tau Beta Pi, Chi Epsilon. Home: 2 Linden Ave Riverton NJ 08077-1124 Office: Cross Roads Corp Ctr 3150 Brunswick Pike Lawrenceville NJ 08648

O'BRIEN, JAMES PHILLIP, lawyer; b. Monmouth, Ill., Jan. 6, 1949; s. John Matthew and Roberta Helen (Cavanaugh) O'B.; m. Laurene Reason, Aug. 30, 1969 (div. 1980); m. Lynn Florsheim, Sept. 5, 1987. BA, Western Ill. U., 1971; JD, U. Ill., 1974. Bar: Ill. 1974. Asst. atty. gen. State Ill., Springfield, 1974-75; jud. clerk Ill. Appellate Ct., Springfield, 1975-76; assoc. Graham & Graham, Springfield, 1976-81; corp. counsel Am. Hosp. Assn., Chgo., 1981-84; ptnr., co-chmn. health care dept. Katten, Muchin & Zavis, Chgo., 1984—; task force med. malpractice reform legislation Am. Hosp. Assn., 1983-84, tax adv. com., 1987-91, tax reporting and compliance com., 1990-91; spkr. in field. Contbr. numerous articles to profl. jours. Recipient cert. recognition Ill. Dept. Children and Family Svcs., 1981; Edward Arthur Mellinger Found. scholar, Western Ill. U. 1971. Mem. Nat. Health Lawyers Assn., Am. Soc. Hosp. Attys., Am. Acad. Hosp. Attys., Am. Arbitration Assn. (Task Force Health Care Dispute Resolution 1982-84). Office: Katten Muchin & Zavis 525 W Monroe St Ste 1600 Chicago IL 60661-3629

O'BRIEN, JOHN CONWAY, economist, educator, writer; b. Hamilton, Lanarkshire, Scotland; s. Patrick and Mary (Hunt) O'B.; m. Jane Estelle Judd, Sept. 16, 1966; children: Kellie Marie, Kerry Patrick, Tracy Anne, Kristen Noël. B.Com., U. London, 1952, cert. in German lang., 1954; tchr.'s cert., Scottish Edn. Dept., 1954; AM, U. Notre Dame, 1959, PhD, 1961. Tchr. Scottish High Schs., Lanarkshire, 1952-56; instr. U. B.C., Can., 1961-62; asst. prof. U. Sask., Can., 1962-63, U. Dayton, Ohio, 1963-64; assoc. prof. Wilfrid Laurier U., Ont., Can., 1964-65; from asst. to full prof. Econs. and Ethics Calif. State U., Fresno, 1965—; vis. prof. U. Pitts., 1969-70, U. Hawaii, Manoa, 1984; keynote speaker Wageningen Agrl. U., The Netherlands, 1987; presenter papers 5th, 6th, 10th World Congress of Economists, Tokyo, 1977, Mexico City, 1980, Moscow, 1992; presenter Schmoller Symposium, Heilbronn am Neckar, Fed. Republic Germany, 1988, paper The China Confucius Found. and "2540" Conf., Beijing, 1989, 6th Internat. Conf. on Cultural Econs., Univ. Umeå, Sweden, 1990, Internat. Soc. Intercommunication New Ideas, Sorbonne, Paris, 1990, European Assn. for Evolutionary Polit. Economy, Vienna, Austria, 1991; active rsch. U. Göttingen, Fed. Republic Germany, 1987; acad. cons. Cath. Inst. Social Ethics, Oxford; presenter in field. Author: Karl Marx: The Social Theorist, 1981, The Economist in Search of Values, 1982, Beyond Marxism, 1985, The Social Economist Hankers After Values, 1992; editor: Internat. Rev. Econs. and Ethics, Internat. Jour. Social Econs., Ethical Values and Social Econs., 1981, Selected Topics in Social Econs., 1982, Festschrift in honor of George Rohrlich, 3 vols., 1984, Social Economics: A Pot=Pourri, 1985, The Social Economist on Nuclear Arms: Crime and Prisons, Health Care, 1986, Festschrift in honor of Anghel N. Rugina, Parts I and II, 1987, Gustav von Schmoller: Social Economist, 1989, The Eternal Path to Communism, 1990, (with Z. Wenxian) Essays from the People's Republic of China, 1991, Festschrift in honor of John E. Elliott, Parts I and II, 1992, Communism Now and Then, 1993, The Evils of Soviet Communism, 1994, Ruminations on the USSR, 1994, The Future Without Marx, 1995, Essays in Honour of Clement Allan Tisdell, 1996, Essays in House of Clement Allan Tisdell, part I, 1996, part II, 1997; translator econ. articles from French and German into English; contbr. numerous articles to profl. jours. With British Royal Army Service Corps, 1939-46, ETO, NATOUSA, prisoner of war, Germany. Recipient GE Corp. award Stanford U., 1966, Ludwig Mai Svc. award Assn. for Social Econs., Washington, 1994; named Disting. Fellow of Internat. Soc. for Intercomm. of New Ideas, Paris, 1990. Fellow Internat. Inst. Social Econs. (mem. coun., program dir. 3d World Cong. Social Econs. Fresno Calif. 1983, keynote spkr. 4th conf. Toronto 1986), Internat. Soc. for Intercomm. New Ideas (disting.); mem. Assn. Social Econs. (dir. west region 1977—, pres.-elect 1988-89, program dir. conf. 1989, pres. 1990, presdl. address Washington 1990, Thomas Divine award 1997), Western Econ. Assn. (organizer, presenter 1977-95), History Econs. Soc., Soc. Reduction Human Labor (exec. com.), European Assn. Evolutionary Polit. Econs. Roman Catholic. Avocations: jogging, collecting miniature paintings, soccer, tennis, photography. Home: 2733 W Fir Ave Fresno CA 93711-0315 Office: Calif State U Econs And Ethics Dept Fresno CA 93740

O'BRIEN, JOHN F., insurance company executive. Pres., CEO First Allmerica Fin. Life Ins. Co., Worcester, Mass., 1989—; also bd. dirs. State Mut. Life Assurance Co. Am., Worcester, Mass.; pres. Allmerica Fin. Life Ins. and Annuity Co., Worcester, 1989—; pres., CEO Allmerica Property & Casualty Co., Inc., Worcester, 1992—; also bd. dirs. Citizens Corp.; pres., CEO Citizens Corp., Worcester, 1992—, Allmerica Fin. Corp., Worcester, Mass., 1995—; chmn. The Hanover Ins. Co., Worcester; pres., dir., CEO Allmerica Property & Casualty Cos., Inc., First Allmerica Life Ins. Co.; pres., CEO, chmn. bd. Citizens Corp; pres., chmn. bd. Allmerica Fin. Life Ins. and Annuity Co.; chmn. bd. Hanover Ins. Co., Citizens Ins. Co. Am.; bd. dirs. Am. Coun. Life Ins., Cabot Corp.; trustee Worcester Poly. Inst.; vis. com. bd. overseers Harvard Coll., 1990—, com. on univ. resources, 1990—, com. on mng. acad. resources, 1990—. Mem. Am. Coun. Life Ins. (bd. dirs. 1992—), Life Ins. Assn. Mass. (bd. dirs. 1989—), Harvard Alumni Assn. (exec. com. 1991—, past pres.). Office: Allmerica Fin 440 Lincoln St Worcester MA 01653-0002*

O'BRIEN, JOHN FEIGHAN, investment banker; b. Cleve., Aug. 8, 1936; s. Francis John and Ann (Feighan) O'B.; m. Regina Quaid Harahan, June 27, 1959 (div. 1976); children: Regina, Victoria, Julie, John Jr.; m. Marilyn E. Schreiner. BS, Georgetown U., 1958. Salesman Appliance Mart, Cleve., 1958-59, ptnr., 1960-66; investment broker McDonald & Co. Investments, Cleve., 1966-71, ptnr., 1971-83, exec. v.p., 1983-88, mng. dir., 1988-91, sr. mng. dir., 1993—. Bd. dirs. Hitchcock House, Cleve., 1978-89; chmn. Alcoholism Svcs. of Cleve., 1989-92, Alcohol and Drug-Addiction Svcs. Bd. of Cuyahoga County, 1992—; trustee St. Edward H.S., Lakewood, Ohio, chmn. capital campaign, 1993-95. Named Good Fellow of Yr. Irish Good Fellows Club Cleve., 1995. Mem. Leadership Cleve., Greater Cleve. Growth Assn., Georgetown U. Alumni Assn. (alumni bd. senator), Westwood Country Club, Cleve. Yacht Club, Catawba Island Club. Home: 1031 Brook Ln Cleveland OH 44116-2184 Office: McDonald & Co Investments 800 Superior Ave E Ste 2100 Cleveland OH 44114-2601

O'BRIEN, JOHN STEININGER, clinical psychologist; b. Lewisburg, Pa., June 3, 1936; s. Peck Zanders and Esther (Steininger) O'B.; m. Joan Irene Romanos, Nov. 1, 1976; children: Peck David, Timothy. AB, Pa. State U., 1967; MA, So. Ill. U., 1969; PhD, Boston U., 1980. Diplomate Internat. Acad. Profl. Psychotherapists, Internat. Acad. Behavioral Medicine/Psychotherapy. Asst. tchr. educable retarded children Selin's Grove (Pa.) State Sch., 1964-66; clin. rsch. asst. Pa. State U., State Coll., 1966-67; rsch. technician Anna (Ill.) State Hosp., 1968; intern Boston City Hosp., 1968-69, from coord. alcohol study unit to psychologist, 1969-73; clin. instr. psychiatry Sch. Medicine Tufts U., St. Elizabeth's Hosp., Brighton, Mass., 1973-81; dir. psychol. svcs. Baldpate Hosp., Georgetown, Mass., 1981—, dir. outpatient substance abuse rehab. program, 1991—; bio-behavioral cons. Behavioral Medicine Inst., Quincy, Mass., 1985-88; clin. dir. Social Learning Ctr., Quincy, 1971—; behavioral therapist, clin. coord. TAP Boston Childrens Svc., 1973-76. Author: Moments with Peck, 1982; contbr. 45 articles to profl. jours. Mem. Am. Psychol. Assn., Nat. Register Health Svcs. in Psychology, Soc. Study of Addiction, Assn. Advancement Behavioral Therapy, Am. Assn. Clin. Counselors, Biofeedback Soc. Am., Internat. Acad. Profl. Counselors and Psychotherapists. Avocations: ocean cruising, deep sea fishing, photography, gardening. Home and Office: 250 Copeland St Quincy MA 02169-4073

O'BRIEN, JOHN THOMAS, illustrator, cartoonist; b. Phila., Nov. 18, 1953; s. John Thomas and Esther Anne (Carideo) O'B; 1 child, Terase. BFA, Phila. Coll. Art, 1975. lifeguard North Wildwood (N.J.) Beach Patrol, 1970—, lt., 1986—. Author and illustrator: Sam and Spot, 1995, The Idle Wizards, 1995; illustrator: Six Creepy sheep, 1992, Daffy Down Dillies, 1992, Funny You Should Ask, 1992, What His Father Did, 1992, Brother Billy Bronto's Bygone Blues Band, 1992, Fast Freddie Frog, 1993, The Twelve Days of Christmas, 1993, This Is Baseball, 1993, Six Snowy Sheep, 1994, Tyranosaurus Tex, 1994, Mother Hubbards Christmas 1996, Dear Old Donegol, 1996, others; illustrator: The Saracen Maid; (mag. covers) Highlights for Children, The New Yorker, Global Fin.; cartoonist (mags.) Omini, Worth, Electronic Engring. Times; (newspaper) The Washington Post, The N.Y. Times, The Village Voice. Banjo profl. various dixieland bands. Recipient Pewter Plate awards Highlights for Children. Mem. U.S. Lifeguard Assn., Soc. Children's Book Writers and Illustrators, Cartoonist Assn. Avocations: running, crossword puzzles, bagpipes, piano.

O'BRIEN, JOHN WILFRID, economist, emeritus university president, educator; b. Toronto, Ont., Can., Aug. 4, 1931; s. Wilfred Edmond and Audrey (Swain) O'B.; m. Joyce Helen Bennett, Aug. 4, 1956; children—Margaret Anne, Catherine Audrey. B.A., McGill U., 1953, M.A., 1955, Ph.D., 1962, LL.D., 1976; postgrad., Inst. Polit. Studies, Paris, France, 1954; D.C.L., Bishop's U., 1976. Lectr. econs. Sir George Williams U., Montreal, 1954-57; asst. prof. Sir George Williams U., 1957-61, assoc. prof., 1961-63, asst. dean U., 1961-63, dean arts, 1963-68, vice prin. acad., 1968-69, prof., 1965-96, prin., vice chancellor, pres., 1969-74; rector, vice chancellor, pres. Concordia U., Montreal, 1974-84; rector emeritus Concordia U., 1984—; mem. Provincial Ednl. TV Com., Dept. Edn. Que., 1962-66, dep. chmn., 1965-66, mem. tchr. tng. planning com., 1964-66; mem. Gauthier Ad Hoc Com., Univ. Operating Budgets, 1965-68, Council Univs., 1969-76; pres. Conf. Rectors and Prins. Que. Univs., 1974-77; mem. council Assn. Commonwealth Univs., 1975-78; bd. dirs. Assn. Univs. and Colls., Can., 1977-79; mem. Conseil Consultatif sur l'Immigration, Que. Gov., 1977-79, Corp. Higher Edn. Forum, 1983-84; bd. govs. YMCA, 1969-89, Vanier Coll., 1975-79, Fraser-Hickson Inst., 1975—, pres. 1989-92, Que. div. Can. Mental Health Assn., 1977-79, Montreal World Film Festival, 1985—; sec., treas., mem. bd. dirs., Cinematheque Can., 1988-96, bd. dirs.; sec., treas. World Film Fest. Found., 1989-96; mem., bd. dirs., 1989—, exec. mem. Alliance Que., 1989-96; chmn. Alliance Que., 1990-91, 92-96; hon. mem. Corp. Higher Edn. Forum, 1984—; hon. v.p. Que. Provincial council Boy Scouts Can., 1974-90; hon. councillor Montreal Mus. Fine Arts, 1969—. Author: Canadian Money and Banking, 1964, (with G. Lermer) 2d edit., 1969.

O'BRIEN, JOHN WILLIAM, JR., investment management company executive; b. Bronx, N.Y., Jan. 1, 1937; s. John William and Ruth Catherine (Timon) O'B.; B.S., MIT, 1958; M.S., UCLA, 1964; m. Jane Bower Nippert, Feb. 2, 1963; children: Christine, Andrea, Michael, John William III, Kevin Robert. Sr. assoc. Planning Research Corp., Los Angeles, 1962-67; dir. fin. systems group Synergetic Scis., Inc., Tarzana, Calif., 1967-70; dir. analytical services div. James H. Oliphant & Co., Los Angeles, 1970-72; chmn. bd., chief exec. officer, pres. Wilshire Assocs. formerly O'Brien Assocs., Inc., Santa Monica, Calif., 1972-75; v.p. A.G. Becker Inc., 1975-81; chmn., chief exec. officer Leland O'Brien Rubinstein Assocs., 1981—. Served to 1st lt. USAF, 1958-62. Recipient Graham and Dodd award Fin. Analysts Fedn., 1970; named Businessman of Yr. Fortune Mag., 1987. Mem. Delta Upsilon. Home: 332 Piazza Lido Newport Beach CA 92663-4646 Office: Leland O'Brien Rubinstein Assocs 523 W 6th St Ste 220 Los Angeles CA 90014-1228

O'BRIEN, KENNETH ROBERT, life insurance company executive; b. Bklyn., June 18, 1937; s. Emmett Robert and Anna (Kelly) O'B.; m. Eileen M. Halligan, July 1, 1961; children: Joan Marie, Margaret Mary, Kathy Ann. B.S. in Bus. Adminstrn., Coll. Holy Cross, Worcester, Mass., 1959. With N.Y. Life Ins. Co., N.Y.C., 1962—; 2d v.p. N.Y. Life Ins. Co., 1973-77, v.p. investments, 1977-82, sr. v.p. pensions, 1982-87, sr. v.p. individual products, 1987-89, exec. v.p., 1989-91; chief exec. officer Aurora Nat. Life Assurance Co., L.A., 1991-96; founder, pres., CEO O'Brien Asset Mgmt., Inc., 1993—. Served to 1st lt. USAF, 1959-62. Mem. Nat. Consumer Fin. Assn., Fin. Forum, N.Y. Soc. Security Analysts. Home: 165 Loines Ave E Merrick NY 11566-3211

O'BRIEN, KEVIN J., lawyer; b. N.Y.C., Mar. 12, 1934; s. George and Kathleen (Fox) O'B.; m. Winifred Gallagher, Aug. 23, 1958; children: Karen A., Kevin J., Susan M. BS, Fordham U., 1959; LLB, Columbia U., 1962. Bar: N.Y. 1962, U.S. Ct. Appeals (2d cir.) 1971, U.S. Dist. Ct. (so. dist.) N.Y. 1972, U.S. Tax Ct. 1972. Law clk. to presiding justice U.S. Ct. Appeals (2d. cir.), N.Y.C., 1962-63; assoc. Paul, Weiss, Rifkind, Wharton & Garrison, N.Y.C., 1963-70, ptnr., 1970—. Contbr. articles to profl. jours. Trustee Convent of Sacred Heart, Greenwich, Conn., 1979-82; mem. Cardinal's Com. of Laity, N.Y.C., 1986—. Served with USN, 1952-55. Mem. ABA, N.Y. State Bar Assn. (exec. com. tax sect. 1979-83), Assn. of Bar of City of N.Y. Office: Paul Weiss Rifkind Wharton & Garrison 1285 Avenue Of The Americas New York NY 10019-6028

O'BRIEN, MARGARET HOFFMAN, educational administrator; b. Melrose, Mass., Aug. 22, 1947; d. John Francis and Margaret Mary (Colbert) Hoffman; m. Edward Lee O'Brien, June 13, 1970 (div. Sept. 1988); children: John Hoffman, Elizabeth Lee; m. Michael Ellis-Tolaydo, Mar. 9, 1991. AB, Trinity Coll., Washington, 1969; LHD (hon.), Trinity Coll., 1994; MA, Cath. U., 1971; LHD (hon.), Georgetown U., 1991; PhD, Am. U., 1993. English tchr. D.C. Pub. Schs., Washington, 1969-73; edn. coord. Street Law, Georgetown Law Ctr., Washington, 1973-75; owner, mgr. Man in the Green Hat Restaurant, Washington, 1976-81; head of edn. Folger Shakespeare Libr., Washington, 1981-94; dir. Teaching Shakespeare Inst., Washington, 1983-94; v.p. edn. Corp. for Pub. Broadcasting, Washington, 1994—; mem. faculty Prince of Wales Shakespeare Sch., Stratford on Avon, Eng., 1993; edn. dir. Fairfax (Va.) Family Theatre, 1988-93, Md. Shakespeare Festival, St. Mary's City, 1988-91; head of faculty Atlantic Shakespeare Inst., Wroxton, U.K., 1985-90. Gen. editor: Shakespeare Set Free, 1993-95; pub.: Shakespeare Mag. Bd. dirs. Edmund Burke Sch., Washington, 1993—, Capitol Hill Day Sch., 1994—, Fillmore Arts Ctr., Washington, 1991-93, Capitol Hill Arts Workshop, Washington, 1989-91, Horizons Theatre, 1991, Janice F. Delaney Found., 1991—; site visitor U.S. Dept. Edn., Washington, 1990; mem. nat. adv. bd. Orlando Shakespeare Festival, 1990-93. Mem. Shakespeare Assn. Am., Nat. Coun. Tchrs. English., Nat. Coun. Tchrs. English Commn. on Media. Office: Corp for Pub Broadcasting 901 E St NW Washington DC 20004-2037

O'BRIEN, MARGARET JOSEPHINE, retired community health nurse; b. N.Y.C., Dec. 5, 1918; d. John J. and Nellie (Coyle) O'B. BS, St.John's U., 1954, MS, 1962; MPH, Columbia U., 1964. With Health Dept., City of New York, 1943-81, assoc. dir. Bur. Pub. Health Nursing, dir. Pub. Health Nursing Svc., asst. commr. pub. health nursing; retired. Contbr. articles to profl. jours. Recipient Outstanding Alumnus of Columbia U. Sch. of Pub. Health award, 1994. Mem. ANA, APHA, NLN, N.Y. State Nurses Assn., N.Y.C. Pub. Health Assn. Home: 11055 72nd Rd Forest Hills NY 11375-5472

O'BRIEN, MARK STEPHEN, pediatric neurosurgeon; b. West New York, N.J., Jan. 2, 1933; s. Mark Peter and Hannah (Dempsey) O'B.; m. Mary Morris Johnson, June 3, 1961 (div.); children: David, Derek, Marcia; m. Karen-Marie Sampson, June 1, 1984; children: Blythe, Blake, Lauren-Blair, Connor. A.B. cum laude, Seton Hall U., 1955; M.D., St. Louis U., 1959. Diplomate Am. Bd. Neurol. Surgery, Am. Bd. Pediat. Neurol. Surgery. Intern St. John's Hosp., St. Louis, 1959-60; resident in surgery St. John's Hosp., 1960; resident in neurology Charity Hosp., New Orleans, 1962-63; resident in neurosurgery St. Vincent's Hosp., N.Y.C., 1963-64; resident in surgery St. Vincent's Hosp., 1965; sr. resident, chief resident Cin. Children's Hosp., U. Cin., 1965-68, research fellow in neurosurgery, 1966-67, 67-68; NIH spl. fellow in neuroradiology Albert Einstein Coll. Medicine, N.Y.C., 1968-69; mem. faculty dept. surgery Emory U. Sch. Medicine, Atlanta, 1969—; prof. surgery, assoc. prof. pediatrics Emory U. Sch. Medicine, 1979—; chief neurosurgery Henrietta Egleston Hosp. for Children, Atlanta, 1971—; trustee Elaine Clark Center for Exceptional Children; mem. med. adv. bd. Nat. Found., March of Dimes; trustee Henrietta Egleston Hosp. for Children; mem. profl. adv. panel Spina Bifida Assn. Am. Editorial bd. Pediatric Neurosurgery; contbr. chpts. to books, articles to med. jours. Served with USNR, 1960-62. Mem. Am. Assn. Neurol. Surgeons, Soc. Neurol. Surgeons, Congress Neurol. Surgeons, Internat. Soc. Pediatric Neurosurgery, Greater Atlanta Pediatric Soc., Med. Soc. Atlanta, AMA, ACS, Ga. Neurosurg. Soc., Am. Acad. Pediatrics, Am. Soc. Pediatric Neurosurgery, Pediatric Oncology Group, Am. Bd. Pediatric Neurol. Surgery (sec.), Acad. Pediatric Neurosurgeons. Home: 82 Huntington Rd Atlanta GA 30309 Office: 1900 Century Blvd NE Ste 4 Atlanta GA 30345-3307

O'BRIEN, MARY DEVON, communications executive, consultant; b. Buenos Aires, Argentina, Feb. 13, 1944; came to U.S., 1949, naturalized, 1962; d. George Earle and Margaret Frances (Richards) Owen; m. Gordon Covert O'Brien, Feb. 16, 1962 (div. Aug. 1982); children: Christopher Covert, Devon Elizabeth; m. Christopher Gerard Smith, May 28, 1983. BA, Rutgers U., 1975, MBA, 1976. Project mgmt. cert., 1989. Contr. manpower Def. Comm. divsn. ITT, Nutley, N.J., 1977-80, adminstr. program, 1977-78, mgr. cost, schedule control, 1978-79, voice processing project, 1979-80; mgr. project Avionics divsn. ITT, Nutley, 1980-81, sr. mgr. projects, 1981-93, cons. strategic planning, 1983-95; pres. Anamex, Inc., 1995—; bd. trustees South Mountain Counseling Ctr., 1987—, chmn. bd. trustees, 1994—; bd. dirs. N.J. Eye Inst.; session leader Internet Conf., Florence, Italy, 1992; session moderator, panel mem. MES Conf., Cairo, Egypt, 1993, spkr., session leader Vancouver, 1994, keynote spkr. New Zealand, 1995; lectr. in field;. Author: Pace: System Manual, 1979, Voices, 1982; contbr. articles to profl. jours. and Maplewood Community calendar. Chmn. Citizens Budget Adv. Com., Maplewood, N.J., 1984-87, chmn. recreation, libr., pub. svcs., 1982-83, 94-96, chmn. pub. safety, emergency svcs., 1983-84, chmn. schs. and edn., 1984-85; first v.p. Maplewood Civic Assn., 1987-89, pres., 1989-91, sec. 1993-94, bd. dirs., officer, 1984—; chmn. Maple Leaf Svc. award Com., 1987-89, 94—, Community Svc. Coun. of Oranges and Maplewood Homelessness, Affordable Housing, Shelter Com., 1988—; chmn. speaker's bur. United Way, 1989-93; bd. trustees United Way Essex and West Hudson Cmty. Svc. Coun., 1988—; v.p. mktg. United Way Community Svc. Coun. of Oranges and Maplewood, 1990-93, v.p. 1994; mem. Maplewood Zoning Bd. of Adjustment, 1983-95; officer, mem. exec. bd. N.J. Project Mgmt. Inst., 1985—, pres., 1987-88, 95—, v.p. adminstrn., 1994—; bd. dirs. Performance Mgmt. Assn.; chmn. Charter Com.; chmn. Internat. Project Mgmt. Inst. Jour. and Membership survey, 1986-87, mktg. com., 1986-89, long range planning and steering com., 1987—; bd. dirs., vice chmn. Coun. Chpt. Pres. Interaction Com., 1986-90, chmn., 1991—, pres. Internat. Project Mgmt. Inst., 1991, chmn., 1992, v.p. Region II, 1989-90; adv. bd. Project Mgmt. Jour., 1987-90, N.J. PMI Ednl., 1987—; liaison officer, PMI internat. liaison to Australian Inst. of Project Mgmt. and Western Australia Project Mgmt. Assn.; apptd. fellow Leadership N.J., 1993—, Internat. Project Mgmt. Inst. and Performance Mgmt. Assocs.; mem. MCA/N.J. Blood Bank Drive; chmn. Maplewood Community Calendar, 1990—; trustee community svc. coun. and edn. program United Way Essex and West Hudson, 1988—, also, chmn. leadership div., chmn. speakers bur., 1991— and mem. communications com.; pres. N.J. Project Mgmt. Inst., 1995—; chmn. Maplewood Republican County Com., 1996. Recipient Spl. commendation for Community Svc. Twp. Maplewood, 1987; First Place award Anti-Shoplifting Program for Distributive Edn. Club Am., 1981, N.J. Fedn. of Women's Clubs, 1981, 82, Retail Mchts. Assn., 1981, 82; Commendation and Merit awards Air Force Inst. Tech., 1981; Pres.'s Safety award ITT, 1983; State award 1st Pl. N.J. Fedn. of Women's Clubs Garden Show, 1982, Outstanding Pres. award Internat. Project Mgmt. Inst., 1988, Outstanding Svc. and Contbrn. award 1986-87; Cert. Spl. Merit award N.J. Fedn. of Women's Clubs, 1982, Disting. Contbn. award United Way, 1990, Pursuit of Exellence Cost Savings Achievement award ITT Avionics, 1990, Meritorious Svc. Recognition award Internat. Project Mgmt. Inst., 1989-90, Maple Leaf award for outstanding community svc., 1992, Phoebe and Benjamin Shackelford award United Way, 1992, U.S. Ho. Reps. citation, 1992, N.H. Gen. Assembly Senate resolution for Community Leadership and Svc., 1992, resolution of Appreciation Township of Maplewood; N.J. Leadership fellow, 1993, awarded fellow of Internat. Project Mgmt. Inst., 1995. Mem. Internat. Platform Speakers Assn., Grand Jury Assn., Telecommunications Group and Aerospace Industries Assn., Women's Career Network Assn., Nat. Security Indsl. Assn., Assn. for Info. and Image Mgmt., Internat. Project Mgmt. Inst. (liaison officer pres. 1991—), Performance Mgmt. Assn, Indsl. Rels. Rsch. Assn., ITT Mgmt. Assn., NAFE, Rutger's Grad. Sch. Bus. Mgmt. Alumni Assn., Maplewood LWV (chair women and family issues com., voter registration bd. dirs.), Maplewood Women's Evening Membership Div. (pres. 1980-82), Lions (Maplewood dir. 1992-95, program chmn. 1991-92, treas. 1994-95, N.J. dist. 16E zone chmn. 1992-93, 95-96, cabinet sec. internat. dist., region chmn. 1993-94, 96—, trustee Eye Bank N.J., internat. dist. 16-E cabinet sec. 1994-95, dist. 16-E chmn. peace poster contest 1995—, pres. Newark 1995—, N.J. State chmn. youth outreach and quest 1995—). Home: 594 Valley St Maplewood NJ 07040-2616 Office: 21 Madison Plz Ste 152 Madison NJ 07940-2354

O'BRIEN, SISTER MAUREEN, school system administrator; b. Manchester, England, Dec. 3, 1939. BEd (equivalent), U. Durham, Eng., 1960; BA, U. Pacific, 1969; diploma in secondary sch. adminstrn., Manchester Poly., Eng., 1978. Joined Daus. of Cross of Liège, 1962. Tchr. St. Ambrose Secondary Sch., Rawtenstall, Calif., Eng., 1960-62, St. Philomena's Collegiate Sch., Carshalton, Eng., 1962-67; tchr. St. Bernard Sch., Tracy, Calif., 1969-76, vice prin., 1972-76; vice prin. Holy Cross Coll., Bury, Eng., 1976-84; prin. St. Bernard Sch., 1985-93; supt. schs. Roman Cath. Diocese of Stockton, Calif., 1993—. Office: Office Supt Schs PO Box 4237 Stockton CA 95204-0237

O'BRIEN, MORGAN EDWARD, communications executive. BA, Georgetown U., 1966; JD, Northwestern U., 1969. Bar: Ill. 1969, Washington 1971. Lawyer Mobile Svcs. divsn. Common Carrier Bur. FCC, 1970-72; asst. bur. chief Spectrum Mgmt. Pvt. Radio Bur. FCC, 1976-87; co-founder, chmn. bd. Nextel Comm., Inc., McLean, Va., 1987-96; vice chmn. Nextel Comm., Inc., McLean, 1996—; ptnr. Jones, Day, Reavis & Pogue, 1986-90; pvt. practice, 1979—. Bd. dirs. Am. Mobile Telecomm. Assn., Cellular Telecomm. Industry Assn. Office: Nextel Comm Inc 1505 Farm Credit Dr Ste 100 Mc Lean VA 22102

O'BRIEN, NANCY PATRICIA, librarian, educator; b. Galesburg, Ill., Mar. 17, 1955; d. Leo Frederick O'Brien and Yvonne Blanche (Uhlmann) O'Brien Tabb; 1 child, Nicole Pamela. AB in English, U. Ill., 1976, MS in LS, 1977. Vis. instr. U. Ill., Urbana, 1977-78, asst. prof. libr. adminstrn., 1978-84, assoc. prof., 1984-91, prof., 1991—, serials bibliographer, 1977-78, social sci. bibliographer collection devel. div., 1979-81, project dir. Title II-C grant, 1987-88, acting libr. and info. sci. libr., 1989-90, head Edn. and Social Sci. Libr., 1994—, coord. social scis. divsn., 1996—, edn. subject specialist, 1981—; discussion leader Ill. White House Conf. on Libr. and Info. svcs., 1990; mem. nat. adv. bd. Office Ednl. Rsch. and Improvement, U.S. Dept. Edn., 1989-91; grant proposal reviewer NEH, 1991; mem. adv. bd. Ctr. for Children's Books, 1992—; cons. Ark. Coll., 1989; chmn. rev. team Instrnl. Materials Ctr., U. Wis., Madison, 1989; presenter in field. Author: Test Construction: A Bibliography of Resources, 1988, (with Emily Fabiano) Core List of Books and Journals in Education, 1991; co-editor Media/Microforms column Series Rev., 1979-82; mem. editl. bd. Bull. Bibliography, 1982-90; asst. editor Libr. Hi Tech., 1983-85; editor EBSS Newsletter, 1990-91; contbr. articles to profl. jours., chpts. to books. Mem. ALA (Whitney-Carnegie grantee 1990-91), Am. Ednl. Rsch. Assn. (spl. interest group on libr. resources and info. tech.), Assn. Coll. and Rsch. Librs. (access policy guidelines task force 1990-95, vice chmn., chmn.-elect edn. and behavioral scis. sect. 1993—, chmn. 1994-95, acad. status com. 1996—), Libr. Adminstrn. and Mgmt. Assn. (edn. and tng. com. pub. rels. sect. 1990-95), Resources and Tech. Svcs. Divsn.(micropub. com. 1982-85, chmn. 1983-85, cons. 1985-87). Office: U Ill Edn & Social Sci Libr 100 Main Libr 1408 W Gregory Dr Urbana IL 61801-3607

O'BRIEN, ORIN YNEZ, musician, educator; b. Hollywood, Calif., June 7, 1935; s. George Joseph and Marguerite Graham (Churchill)

O'Brien. Studied with Frederick Zimmermann and, Milton Kestenbaum; diploma, The Juilliard Sch., 1957. Double bassist N.Y.C. Ballet Orch., Saidenberg Little Symphony, Am. Symphony, 1956-66, N.Y. Philharm., N.Y.C., 1966—; faculty YMHA Sch. Music, 1967-71, Manhattan Sch. Music, N.Y.C., 1969—, Mannes Coll. Music, N.Y.C., 1988—, The Julliard Sch., N.Y.C., 1990—; co-chair double bass dept., 1992—; participant numerous chamber music festivals, including Marlboro; featured in 1st performances of Gunther Schuller Quartet for 4 double basses; artist for GM, CBS and RCA Recording cos. Mem. Am. Fedn. Musicians, Internat. Soc. Bassists. Avocations: reading, writing, cooking.

O'BRIEN, PATRICK MICHAEL, library administrator; b. Newport, R.I., Mar. 17, 1943; s. Joseph Xavier and Loretta (DeCotis) O'B.; m. Roberta Luther, Nov. 27, 1977; children—Megan MacRae, Brendan Watters. B.A. in Eng. Lit., Merrimack Coll., North Andover, Mass., 1964; M.L.S., U. R.I., Kingston, 1965; M.B.A., Case Western Res. U., Cleve., 1983. Reference libr. Newsweek mag., N.Y.C., 1965-72; asst. dir. rsch. FIND/SVP, N.Y.C., 1972-74; head cen. libr., cultural ctr. Chgo. Pub. Libr., 1974-79; dir. Cuyahoga County Pub. Libr., Cleve., 1979-84; dir. librs. Dallas Pub. Libr., 1984-92; dir. Alexandria (Va.) Libr., 1992—. Mem. editorial bd. Handel's Nat. Directory for Performing Arts; contbr. articles to profl. jours. Participant, alumnus Leadership Dallas Program, 1984-85, Leadership Cleve. Program, 1981; mem. nat. adv. com. to Libr. of Congress; mem. adv. coun. Tex. State Libr., Libr. Svcs. and Constrn. Act, 1986-89; co-chair, del. selection com. Tex. Conf. on Librs. and Info. Svcs.; mem. com. Goals for Dallas, 1985; mem. exec. bd. univ. librs. So. Meth. U., 1985—; bd. dirs. Urban Community Sch., Cleve., 1982-84, Mus. African-Am. Life and Culture, 1985-86; mem. client data base com. Dallas Assn. Svcs. to Homeless, 1988-90; mem. Latchkey Children's Task Force, 1985-90. Recipient Servant as Leader award City of Dallas, 1989, Disting. Alumnus award U. R.I. Grad. Sch. Libr. and Info. Studies, 1990. Mem. ALA (coun. mem. 1987-95), Am. Libr. Trustee Assn. (bd. dirs.), Pub. Libr. Assn. (pres. 1985-86), Pub. Libr. Systems Sect (pres. 1983), Tex. Libr. Assn. (legis com. 1986-92), Tex. Women's Univ. Sch. Libr. and Info. Studies Vis. Com., Tex. Ctr. for Book Dallas Pub. Libr., Cleve. Area Met. Libr. Systems (pres. bd. 1980), Chgo. Libr. Club (pres. 1978), D.C. Libr. Assn., Va. Pub. Libr. Dirs. Assn. (bd. dirs. 1994—), Va. Libr. Assn., Online Computer Libr. Ctr. (bd. trustees 1992—), The White House Conf. on Librs. and Info. Svcs. (del. 1991), Pub. Lib. Adminstrs. N.Tex. (pres. 1990-91), Dallas 40, Rotary of Alexandria (bd. dirs. 1996—), Beta Gamma Sigma. Office: Alexandria Libr 717 Queen St Alexandria VA 22314-2420

O'BRIEN, PATRICK WILLIAM, lawyer; b. Chgo., Dec. 5, 1927; s. Maurice Edward and Ellen (Fitzgerald) O'B.; m. Deborah Bissell, July 2, 1955; children: Kathleen, Mariellen, Patrick, James, Patricia. BS in Mech. Engring., Northwestern U., 1947, JD, 1950. Bar: Ill. 1951, U.S. Dist. Ct. (no. dist.) Ill. 1954, U.S. Dist. Ct. (so. dist.)Ill. 1956, U.S. Ct. Appeals (7th cir.) 1955, U.S. Ct. Appeals (8th cir.) 1972, U.S. Supreme Ct. 1970. Assoc. Bell, Boyd, Marshall & Lloyd, Chgo., 1950-51; assoc. Mayer, Brown & Platt, Chgo., 1953-62, ptnr., 1962-94, sr. counsel, 1995—. Served to capt. USAF, 1951-53. Fellow Am. Coll. Trial Lawyers; mem. ABA, Ill. Bar Assn., Chgo. Bar Assn. Republican. Roman Catholic. Clubs: Chgo., Mid-Day, University, Westmoreland Country, Cliff Dwellers, Dairymen's Country. Home: 1119 Judson Ave Evanston IL 60202-1314 Office: Mayer Brown & Platt 190 S La Salle St Chicago IL 60603-3410

O'BRIEN, PAUL HERBERT, surgeon; b. Evanston, Ill., Sept. 12, 1930; s. Maurice Edward and Nellie (Fitzgerald) O'B.; m. Ann Hope Miller, Aug. 28, 1965; children—Jennifer, Paul Edward. B.S., Northwestern U., 1950, M.D., 1954. Diplomate: Am. Bd. Surgery. Intern Northwestern U. Hosp., Chgo., 1954-55; asst. prof. surgery Northwestern U. Hosp., 1967-69; resident in surgery Cook County Hosp., Chgo., 1957-62; sr. resident Meml. Sloan Kettering Inst. Cancer and Allied Diseases, N.Y.C., 1962-65; also USPHS sr. fellow; assoc. prof. Med. U. S.C., Charleston, 1970-72, prof., 1972—, Am. Cancer Soc. clin. prof. oncology, 1974-79; chief Gold Surgery. Contbr. articles to profl. jours. Served to capt. AUS, 1955-57. Recipient career devel. award Schweppe Found. Mem. A.C.S., Soc. Surg. Oncology, Am. Cancer Soc. (past pres. profl. edn. com.), AMA, Halsted Soc., AAUP, Chgo. Surg. Soc. Anglo Catholic. Home: 1467 Burningtree Rd Charleston SC 29412-2602 Office: 171 Ashley Ave Charleston SC 29425-0001

O'BRIEN, RAYMOND FRANCIS, transportation executive; b. Atchison, Kans., May 31, 1922; s. James C. and Anna M. (Wagner) O'B.; m. Mary Ann Baugher, Sept. 3, 1947; children: James B., William T., Kathleen A., Christopher R. B.S. in Bus. Adminstrn., U. Mo., 1948; grad., Advanced Mgmt. Program, Harvard, 1966. Accountant-auditor Peat, Marwick, Mitchell & Co., Kansas City, Mo., 1948-52; contr., treas. Riss & Co., Kansas City, Mo., 1952-58; regional contr. Consol. Freightways Corp. of Del., Indpls., also, Akron, Ohio, 1958-61; contr. Consol. Freightways, Inc., San Francisco, 1961—; v.p., treas. Consol. Freightways, Inc., 1962-63, bd. dirs., 1966, v.p. fin., 1967-69, exec. v.p., 1969-75, pres., 1975—, chief exec. officer, 1977-88, 90-91, chmn., 1988—, now chmn. emeritus; pres. CF Motor Freight subs. Consol. Freightways, Inc., 1973; dir. Transam. Corp., Watkins-Johnson, Inc.; past chmn. WesternHwy. Inst., Champion Road Machinery, Ltd. Former mem. bus. adv. bd. Northwestern U., U. Calif., Berkeley; bd. dirs., regent, former chmn. bd. trustees St. Mary's Coll.; bd. dirs., regent Charles Armstrong Sch., 1991—; mem. Pres.'s Adv. Herbert Hoover Boys and Girls Club; dir. Boy Scouts Am. Bay Area Coun.; adv. coun. Nat. Commn. Against Drunk Driving. Served to 1st lt. USAAF, 1942-45. Recipient Disting. Svc. Citation Automotive Hall Fame, 1991; named Outstanding Chief Exec. five times Financial World Mag. Mem. Am. Trucking Assn. (bd. dirs. Found., exec. com.), Pacific Union Club, World Trade Club, Commonwealth Club (San Francisco), Burning Tree Country Club, Menlo Country Club. Home: 26347 Esperanza Dr Los Altos CA 94022-2601 Office: Consol Freightways Inc 3000 Sand Hill Rd Ste 130 Menlo Park CA 94025-7116

O'BRIEN, RAYMOND VINCENT, JR., banker; b. Bronx, N.Y., Sept. 23, 1927; s. Raymond Vincent and Blanche (Harper) O'B.; m. Theresa Sweeney, Mar. 29, 1952 (dec. June 1981); children: Susan, Raymond, Christopher, Sean, Carol, Nancy Meisenzahl; m. Ellen Boyle, July 24, 1982. A.B., Fordham U., 1951, J.D., 1958; postgrad., Advanced Mgmt. Program, Harvard U., 1969. With Chase Manhattan Bank (N.A.), N.Y.C., 1953-74; chief exec. officer, chmn. bd. Emigrant Savs. Bank, N.Y.C., 1978-92; dir. Emigrant Savs. Bank, 1974—; bd. dirs. Emigrant Savs. Bank, Internat. Shipholding Corp. Trustee Fordham U., 1979-92; chmn. bd. trustees Regis High Sch., 1988-92; past chmn. Community Bankers Assn., N.Y., Nat. Assn. Community Bankers. Served with AUS, 1946-47, 51-53. Mem. N.Y. State Bar Assn., Guild Cath. Lawyers, Sky Club, Econ. Club, Navesink Country Club (Middletown, N.J.), Sawgrass Country Club (Ponte Vedra, Fla.), Plantation Country Club (Ponte Vedra), Knights of Malta, Friendly Sons St. Patrick. Republican. Roman Catholic. Home: 102 Lands End Ponte Vedra Beach FL 32082-3906

O'BRIEN, RICHARD FRANCIS, advertising agency executive; b. Everett, Mass., Aug. 3, 1942; s. James Raymond and Gertrude Lucille O'B.; m. Clare Lynch, Apr. 7, 1973; children: Catherine Lynch, Miles Edward. A.B. magna cum laude, Boston Coll., 1964; M.A., Ind. U., 1965; M.B.A., Columbia U., 1967. With Grey Advt. Inc., N.Y.C., 1967-83; v.p., mgmt. supr. Grey Advt. Inc., 1973-77, sr. v.p., mgmt. rep., 1977-80, exec. v.p., mgmt. rep., 1980-83; exec. v.p., mgmt. dir. Dancer Fitzgerald Sample, Inc. (name changed to Saatchi & Saatchi Advt.), N.Y.C., 1983-88; vice chmn. Dancer Fitzgerald Sample, Inc. (became Saatchi & Saatchi Advt.), N.Y.C., 1988—; bd. dirs. Saatchi & Saatchi Advt. Worldwide, 1989—. Bd. dirs. Spl. Olympics Internat., 1983—. Office: Saatchi & Saatchi Advt 375 Hudson St New York NY 10014-3658

O'BRIEN, RICHARD L(EE), academic administrator, physician, cell biologist; b. Shenandoah, Iowa, Aug. 30, 1934; s. Thomas Lee O'B. and Grace Ellen (Sims) Parish; m. Joan Frances Gurney, June 29, 1957; children: Sheila Marie, Kathleen Therese, Michael James, Patrick Kevin. M.S. in Physiology, Creighton U., 1958, M.D., 1960. Diplomate: Nat. Bd. Med. Examiners. Intern and resident Columbia med. div. Bellevue Hosp., N.Y.C., 1960-62; postdoctoral fellow in biochemistry Inst. for Enzyme Research, U. Wis., 1962-64; asst. prof. to prof. pathology Sch. Medicine, U. So. Calif., Los Angeles, 1966-82, dep. dir. Cancer Ctr., 1975-80, dir. research and edn. Cancer Ctr., 1980-81; dir. Cancer Ctr. Sch. Medicine, U. So. Calif., 1981-82; dean Sch. Medicine Creighton U., Omaha, 1982-92; acting v.p. health scis. Creighton U., 1984-85, v.p. health scis., 1985—; vis. prof. molecular biology U. Geneva, 1973-74; cons. in field; mem. cancer control research grants rev. com. NIH, Nat. Cancer Inst.; mem. Cancer Ctr. Support grant rev. com. Nat. Cancer Inst., 1984-88, chmn. 1987-88; co-chmn. United Way/CHAD Pacesetter campaign, 1988, 94. Contbr. articles; editor various profl. jours. Served to capt. U.S. Army, 1964-66. Spl. fellow Nat. Cancer Inst., 1967-69; Combined Health Agys. Drive—Health Citizen of Yr., 1986. Mem. ACP, Am. Assn. Pathologists, Am. Assn. Cancer Rsch., Am. Assn. Cancer Edn., AAAS, Am. Assn. Cancer Insts. (dir. 1982-83), Assn. Am. Med. Colls. (chmn. MCAT evaluation panel 1987-88, liaison com. on med. edn., 1988-93, co-chmn, 1989-93, adv. panel Strategic Planning Health Care Reform 1992-96), Assn. Acad. Health Ctrs. (long-range planning com. 1986, nominating com. 1987, 96, Task Force Health Care Delivery 1992, mem. task force on leadership and instl. values 1993—), Am. Cancer Soc. (adv. com. Inst. rsch. Grants 1977-80, Outstanding Leadership award, dir. Calif. div. 1980-82, dir. Nebr. divsn. 1992-96), Am. Hosp. Assn. (com. on med. edn. 1986-89), Alpha Omega Alpha. Home: 142 N Elmwood Rd Omaha NE 68132-2714 Office: Creighton Univ VP Health Sci California at 24th Omaha NE 68178

O'BRIEN, ROBERT BROWNELL, JR., investment banker, consultant, yacht broker, opera company executive; b. N.Y.C., Sept. 6, 1934; s. Robert Brownell and Eloise (Boles) O'B.; m. Sarah Lager, Nov. 28, 1958; children: Robert Brownell III, William Stuart, Jennifer. BA, Lehigh U., 1957; postgrad., NYU, Am. Inst. Banking. Asst. treas., credit officer, br. locations officer Bankers Trust Co., N.Y.C., 1957-63; v.p., dir. bus. devel. George A. Murray Co., gen. contractors, N.Y.C., 1964; also v.p. Bowery Savs. Bank, 1964-69; dir., chief exec. officer Fed. Savs. & Loan Ins. Corp., Washington, 1969-71; chmn. exec. com. Fed. Home Loan Bank Bd., 1969-71; v.p. Bowery Savs. Bank, N.Y.C., 1972; exec. v.p. First Fed. Savs. & Loan Assn., N.Y.C., 1973-75; chmn., chief exec. officer Carteret Savs. Bank, Morristown, 1975-91, also bd. dirs.; mng. dir. Printon Kane Group Inc., Short Hills, N.J., 1991-94; dir., former chief exec. officer Govs. Bank Corp., West Palm Beach, 1992—; bd. dirs. Fed. Home Loan Bank N.Y., Govs. Bank Corp.; vice chmn. 1st Mortgage Capital Corp., Vero Beach, Fla.; chmn. Neighborhood Housing Svcs. Am., 1972-91; vice chmn., bd dirs. U.S. League Savs. Instns., Washington, O'Brien Yacht Sales. Contbr. articles to trade mags. Trustee Trinity Pawling Sch., Palm Beach County Housing Partnership, Lehigh U.; chmn. Housing Opportunities Found.; trustee, past chmn. Cmty. Found. of N.J., 1987—; vice chmn., bd. dirs. Dalt Found.; chmn. adv. bd. Palm Beach Maritime Mus., Peanut Island, Fla.; active Nat. Commn. on Neighborhoods; past chmn., exec. dir. N.J. State Opera. Mem. Nat. Coun. Savs. Instns. (past chmn.), Essex County Savs. and Loan League (past chmn.), N.J. Savs. League (past chmn.), N.J. Hist. Soc. (past chmn.), Greater Newark C. of C. (bd. dirs.), N.J. C. of C. (bd. dirs.), Union League Club, Delray Beach Yacht Club (past commodore), New York Yacht Club, Morris County Golf Club, Somerset Hills Golf Club, Palm Beach Yacht Club, Bay Head Yacht Club (past commodore). Republican. Episcopalian. Home: 12 Banyan Rd Gulf Stream FL 33483-7425 Office: 1400 Centrepark Blvd Ste 909 West Palm Beach FL 33401-7412

O'BRIEN, ROBERT JAMES, financial consultant, business owner; b. Waterbury, Conn., Nov. 22, 1940; s. Stephen Joseph and Ada Florence (Schiardli) O'B.; m. Janyce Leah Bruni, Sept. 24, 1966; children: Gayle Elizabeth O'Brien Blachura, Julie Maureen O'Brien Orlando. BA, U. Conn., 1964. Registered investment advisor SEC; CFP; registered fin. cons.; CLU. Commd. ensign USN, 1964, advanced through grades to comdr., ret., 1984; fin. cons. Davenport-Dukes Assocs., Virginia Beach, Va., 1984-97, prin., ptnr., 1992-97; prin., mng. ptnr. Fin. Guardian Group, Inc., 1997—; pres. Fin. Guardian Adv., Inc., 1997—; adj. instr. Commonwealth Coll., Virginia Beach, 1988-91. Elder Kempsville Presbyn. Ch., Va. Beach, 1987—; bd. dirs. Edmarc Children's Hospice, Portsmouth, Va., 1988-92, pres. bd. dirs., 1992; bd. dirs. Bethany Christian Svcs., Va. Beach, Dec. 1995-96. Mem. Nat. Assn. Life Underwriters (Million Dollar Round Table 1994, 95, 96), Internat. Assn. Registered Fin. Cons. Republican. Avocations: golf, reading, chess. Home: 4841 Kempsville Greens Pky Virginia Beach VA 23462 Office: Fin Guardian Group Inc 448 Viking Dr Virginia Beach VA 23452

O'BRIEN, ROBERT JOHN, JR., public relations executive, former government official, air force officer; b. Wheeling, W. Va., Apr. 16, 1935; s. Robert John and Martha Virginia (Hunter) O'B.; m. Margaret Eugenia Schultz. B.S. in Journalism, Northwestern U., 1957; M.A. in Journalism, U. Wis., 1970; grad., Indsl. Coll. Armed Forces, 1977. Commd. officer U.S. Air Force, 1957, advanced through grades to col.; dir. pub. affairs N. Am. Air Def. Command, Colorado Springs, Colo., 1977-80, Air Force Systems Command, Camp Springs, Md., 1980-82; dir. def. info. Office Sec. Def., Washington, 1982-83, dep. asst. sec. def., 1983-86; dir. pub. rels., Washington McDonnell Douglas Corp., Arlington, Va., 1986—. Decorated D.S.M., Legion of Merit, Bronze Star, Air medal, Medal of Honor (Republic Vietnam). Mem. Air Force Assn., Pub. Rels. Soc. Am., Aviation/Space Writers Assn., U.S. Space Found., Ret. Officers Assn., U.S. C. of C. (pub. affairs com.), Hidden Creek Country Club (Reston, Va.), Nat. Aviation Club, Nat. Press Club. Republican. Methodist. Avocations: golf; stamp collecting; model railroading. Home: 13804 Leighfield St Chantilly VA 22021-2503

O'BRIEN, ROBERT KENNETH, insurance company executive; b. Worcester, Mass., Dec. 8, 1934; s. Robert Ivor O'Brien and Arline Mary (Lanois) Knight; m. Barbara Ann Hickey, Dec. 28, 1957; children: Kevin Robert, Brendan Robert. BS in Edn., Worcester State Coll., 1958. CLU. Group underwriter State Mut. of Am., Worcester, 1958-74, v.p. group underwriting, 1974-86, v.p. bus. unit, 1987, v.p. reins., 1988-90; pres. Health Reins. Mgmt., Inc., Salem, Mass., 1990—; v.p., bd. dirs. Bibliomania, Inc., West Yarmouth, Mass, 1982-87. Pres. Westboro PTA, 1965; chmn. Young Reps. Conv., Mass., 1960. Mem. Health Ins. Assn. Am., Life Office Mgmt. Assn., Am. Soc. CLUs, Self-Ins. Inst. Am., Am. Arbitration Assn. Avocations: boating, fishing, scuba diving, flying, golf. Office: Health Reinsurance Mgmt Inc 27 Congress St Salem MA 01970-5575

O'BRIEN, ROBERT S., state official; b. Seattle, Sept. 14, 1918; s. Edward R. and Maude (Ransom) O'B.; m. Kathryn E. Arvan, Oct. 18, 1941 (dec. June 1984). Student pub. schs. With Kaiser Co., 1938-46; restaurant owner, 1946-50; treas. Grant County, Wash., 1950-65, State of Wash., 1965-89; chmn. Wash. State Fin. Com., 1965-89, Wash. Public Deposit Protection Commn., 1969-89, Wash. Public Employees Retirement Bd., 1969-77, Law Enforcement Officers and Firefighters Retirement System, 1971-77, Wash. State Investment Bd., 1981-89; retired, 1989; mem. Wash. Data Processing Adv. Bd., 1967-73; Gov.'s Exec. Mgmt. and Fiscal Affairs Com., 1978-80, Gov.'s Cabinet Com. on Tax Alternatives, 1978-80; trustee Wash. Tchr.'s Retirement System, 1965-89; bd. dirs. Centennial Bank, Olympia, Wash. Recipient Leadership award Joint Council County and City Employees-Fedn. State Employees, 1970, Eagles Leadership award, 1967. Mem. Nat. Assn. State Auditors, Comptrollers and Treasurers (pres. 1977), Nat. Assn. Mcpl. Fin. Officers, Nat. Assn. State Treasurers, Western State Treasurers Assn. (pres. 1970), Wash. County Treas. Assn. (pres. 1955-56), Wash. Assn. Elected County Ofcls. (pres. 1955-58), Olympia Area C. of C., Soap Lake C. of C. (pres. 1948). Democrat. Clubs: Elks (hon. life); Moose, Eagles, Lions, Olympia Yacht, Olympia Country and Golf; Empire (Spokane); Wash. Athletic (Seattle). Address: 3613 Plummer St SE Olympia WA 98501-2126

O'BRIEN, STEPHEN JAMES, geneticist; b. Rochester, N.Y., Sept. 30, 1944; s. Bernard Carroll and Kathryn Marie O'Brien; m. Diane Louise Rockhill, Nov. 28, 1968; children: Mary, Meghan. BS, St. Francis Coll., Loretto, Pa., 1966; PhD, Cornell U., 1971. Postdoctoral fellow genetics-biochemistry Gerontology Rsch. Ctr., Balt., 1971-72; NIH postdoctoral fellow Nat. Cancer Inst., NIH, Bethesda, Md., 1972-73; staff fellow Lab. Viral Carcinogenesis, Nat. Cancer Inst., NIH, Bethesda, 1973-78; rsch. geneticist Lab. Viral Carcinogenesis, Nat. Cancer Inst., NIH, Frederick, Md., 1978-80; chief sect. of genetics Lab. Viral Carcinogenesis, Nat. Cancer Inst., NIH, Frederick, 1980—, acting chief, 1983-85, chief, 1986—; zoology and botany tchg. asst. St. Francis Coll., 1965-66; gen. genetics lab. instr. and lectr. Cornell U., 1966-71, biology and soc. tchg. asst., 1969-71, human genetics discussion leader, 1970-71; adj. prof. genetics George Washington U., 1974—; adj. grad. advisor dept. biology Am. U., 1979—, Hood Coll., 1982—; adj. prof. dept. zoology U. Md., 1982—, dept. biology Johns Hopkins U., 1982—; faculty affiliate dept. pathology Colo. State U., 1994—; affiliate prof. dept. biology George Mason U., 1994—; apptd. rsch. fellow Smithsonian Instn., Washington, 1982—; bd. trustees Am. Type Culture Assn., Rockville, Md., 1983—; apptd. exec. bd. Am. Type Culture Collection, Rockville, 1984—, sec.-treas. bd. trustees, 1987— ; founder, co-dir. New Opportunities in Animal Health Scis., Ctr. for Wildlife Scis., Smithsonian Instn., 1985—; mem. cat specialist group Internat. Union for Conservation of Nature, Geneva, 1985—, mem. captive breeding specialist group species survival commn., 1986—; lectr. in field. Editor Isozyme Bulletin, 1975-78, Genetic Maps, 1980—; exec. editor Jour. Heredity, Am. Genetics Assn., 1987—; assoc. editor Genomics, 1987-91, Mammalian Genome, 1990—, Molecular Phylogenetics and Evolution, 1990—; guest editor Current Biology, 1993; jour. adv. bd. Cosmos, 1994; contbr. numerous articles to profl. jours. Mem. AAAS, Genetics Soc. Am., Am. Soc. Naturalists, Tissue Culture Assn., Am. Genetics Assn. (bd. dirs. 1984—, chmn. long range planning com. 1985—), Am. Assn. Zool. Pks. and Aquariums (advisor spl. survival plan-cheetah 1986—), N.Y. Acad. Sci., Cosmos Club. Achievements include research in molecular genetics, developmental and cell biology, genetics of oncology, viral oncology, immunology and reproductive physiology, molecular evolution, paleontology, cytology, populations genetics. :

O'BRIEN, THOMAS GEORGE, III, lawyer; b. N.Y.C., Aug. 26, 1942; s. Thomas George Jr.and Margaret Patricia (Arctander) O'B.; m. Alison Marie Rich, Aug. 26, 1967; children: Christian Arctander, Kylin Stafford. AB magna cum laude, U. Notre Dame, 1964; LLB, Yale U., 1967. Bar: N.Y. 1967, Fla. 1988. Assoc. Carter, Ledyard & Milburn, N.Y.C., 1971-78; assoc. gen. counsel Frank B. Hall & Co Inc., Briarcliff Manor, N.Y., 1978-79, v.p., sec., gen. counsel, 1979-86; exec. v.p., sec., gen. counsel CenTrust Savs. Bank, Miami, 1986-87; of counsel Steel Hector & Davis, Miami, 1987-88, ptnr., West Palm Beach, Fla., 1988—; Author: Florida Law of Corporations and Business Organizations, 1990, 92-97. Trustee Bus. Vols. for Arts, Miami, 1986-88, Fla. Repertory Theatre, West Palm Beach, 1989-91, chmn., 1990-91; mem. vestry Episcopal Ch. Bethesda-by-the-Sea, 1991-94, sr. warden, 1992-94; bd. dirs. Bus. Devel. Bd. Palm Beach County, 1991—, sec., 1992-93, chmn., 1993-94; bd. dirs. Palm Beach Fellowship Christians and Jews, 1993—, sec., 1996—; bd. dirs. Directions 21st Century, 1995—, chmn., 1996—. Lt. USNR, 1967-71, Vietnam. Mem. ABA (com. on legal opinions 1992—), N.Y. State Bar Assn., Fla. Bar (mem. corps./securities law com. 1988—, vice-chmn. 1989-90, chmn. 1990-91, chmn. com. on opinion standards 1988-95, exec. coun. bus. law sect. 1989-93), Am. Soc. Corp. Secs. (sec. N.Y. regional group 1984-86), Palm Beach Yacht Club, PGA Nat. Club (Palm Beach Gardens). Home: 81 Sandbourne Ln Palm Beach Gardens FL 33418-8085 Office: 1900 Phillips Point W 777 S Flagler Dr West Palm Beach FL 33401-6161

O'BRIEN, THOMAS HENRY, bank holding company executive; b. Pitts., Jan. 16, 1937; s. J. Vick and Georgia (Bower) O'B.; m. Maureen Sheedy; children—Thomas Henry, Lauren C., Timothy B. BS in Commerce, U. Notre Dame, 1958; MBA, Harvard U., 1962. Joined Pitts. Nat. Bank, 1962, v.p., 1967-73, sr. v.p., 1973-80, exec. v.p., 1980-83, vice chmn., 1983-84; pres., bd. dirs., chief exec. officer PNC Fin. Corp., 1984—; also chmn. PNC Fin. Corp., Pitts., 1988—; now chmn., CEO PNC Bank Corp.; bd. dirs. Hilb, Rogal & Hamilton Co., Bell Atlantic Corp., Internat. Monetary Conf. Bd. dirs. United Way Southwest Pa., Allegheny Health, Edn. and Rsch. Found., Extra Mile Found., Carnegie Museums of Pitts., Pitts. Opera, Allegheny Conf. Cmty. Devel., U. Pitts., Res. City Bankers; mem. bd. visitors U. Pitts. Grad. Sch. Bus. Named Industrialist of Yr. Soc. Indsl. and Office Realtors, 1996. Mem. Assn. Res. City Bankers, Pa. Bankers Assn., Fox Chapel Golf Club. Roman Catholic. Clubs: Duquesne, Allegheny (bd. dirs.), Pitts. Field, Rolling Rock, Laurel Valley Golf. Avocation: golf. Office: PNC Bank Corp 249 5th Ave Pittsburgh PA 15222-2707 also: Pitts Pirates 600 Stadium Cir Pittsburgh PA 15212-5731

O'BRIEN, THOMAS IGNATIUS, lawyer; b. Troy, N.Y., Dec. 24, 1925; s. Timothy F. and Catherine M. (McCarthy) O'B.; m. Barbara Lasher; children: Kathleen, Stephanie, Alicia. BAE, Rensselaer Poly. Inst., 1946; LLB, JD, Georgetown U., 1951. Bar: N.Y. 1951, U.S. Ct. Appeals (3d cir.) 1968, U.S. Dist. Ct. N.Y. (so. dist.) 1973, U.S. Ct. Appeals (9th cir.) 1973, U.S. Ct. Appeals (2d cir.) 1975, U.S. Ct. Appeals (fed. cir.) 1982, Conn. 1988. Patent examiner U.S. Patent Office, Washington, 1946-51; patent atty. North Am. Phillips, Irvington, N.Y., 1951, Pollard, Johnston, Smythe & Robertson, N.Y.C., 1952-54; patent atty. Union Carbide Corp., Danbury, Conn., 1954-90, chief patents counsel, 1969-90; counsel Morgan & Finnegan, N.Y.C., 1991—. Mem. ABA (chmn. coms.), Am. Intellectual Property Law Assn. (bd. dirs. 1986-89), Pacific Indsl. Property Assn. (pres.), Assn. Corp. Patent Counsel (pres.), Chem. Mfrs. Assn., Internat. Patent and Trademark Assn., Intellectual Property Orgn. (bd. dirs.), Assn. Bar City N.Y. Home: 58 Stonehenge Dr New Canaan CT 06840-3524 Office: Morgan & Finnegan 345 Park Ave New York NY 10154-0004

O'BRIEN, THOMAS JOSEPH, bishop; b. Indpls., Nov. 29, 1935. Grad., St. Meinrad Coll. Sem. Ordained priest Roman Catholic Ch., 1961. Bishop of Phoenix, 1982—. Office: Catholic Diocese 400 E Monroe St Phoenix AZ 85004-2336*

O'BRIEN, TIMOTHY ANDREW, writer, journalist, lawyer; b. N.Y.C., July 11, 1943; s. Timothy Andrew and Hildegarde J. (Schenkel) O'B.; m. Maria de Guadalupe Margarita Moreno, Jan. 15, 1971; children: Theresa Marie, Tim A. BA in Comm., Mich. State U., 1967; MA in Polit. Sci., U. Md., 1972; postgrad., Tulane U., 1974-75; JD, Loyola U., New Orleans, 1976. Bar: La. 1976, D.C. 1977, U.S. Supreme Ct 1981. News writer, reporter, anchorman WKBD-TV, Detroit, 1968-69, WTOP-TV, Washington, 1969-72, WDSU-TV, New Orleans, 1972-74, WVUE-TV, New Orleans, 1974-77; Leo Goodwin prof. law Nova Southeastern Law Sch., 1997—; Leo Goodwin Prof. Law Southeastern U., 1997. Contbr. articles to profl. jours. Bd. govs. Woodward Acad., College Park, Ga. Recipient AP award for outstanding reporting of extraordinary event, 1976, New Orleans Press Club award for non-spot news reporting, 1976, Emmy award for documentary on D.C., 1969, ABA awards of merit, 1979 (2), 80, 85, Gavel award for documentary, 1980, Nat. award for human rights reporting Women in Comm., 1981, Disting. Alumnus award Mich. State U., 1996. Mem. Am. Law Inst., Radio-TV Corrs. Assn. Washington, Am. Judicature Soc. (bd. dirs. 1991—), Sigma Delta Chi, Pi Sigma Alpha, Phi Kappa Phi. Office: ABC News Washington Bur 1717 Desales St NW Washington DC 20036-4401

O'BRIEN, TIMOTHY JAMES, lawyer; b. Detroit, Nov. 4, 1945; m. Hyon Baek, Jan. 31, 1970; children: Jean, Jane. AB, Yale U., 1967; JD, Harvard U., 1976. Bar: N.Y. 1977, U.S. Dist. Ct. (so., ea. and we. dists.) N.Y. 1978. Assoc. Cleary, Gottlieb, Steen & Hamilton, N.Y.C., 1976-80; ptnr. Coudert Bros., N.Y.C., 1980—; lectr. symposium on internat. investment Southwestern Law Found., 1995. Mem. Harvard Law Rev., 1975-76. Assoc. dir., vol. Peace Corps, Republic of Korea, 1967-73. Mem. ABA (co-chmn. conf. on Korea-U.S. trade and investment 1990-92), Assn. of Bar of City of N.Y. (internat. law com., Asian affairs com. 1989-94), The Korea Soc. (N.Y.)(sec., bd. dirs. 1996—). Office: Coudert Bros 1114 Avenue Of The Americas New York NY 10036-7703

O'BRIEN, WILLIAM JEROME, II, lawyer; b. Darby, Pa., Oct. 22, 1954; s. Richard James O'Brien and Margaret (McGill) Hahn. BA in Econ. and Polit. Sci., Merrimack Coll., 1976; JD, Del. Law Sch., 1981. Bar: Pa. 1982, U.S. Dist. Ct. (ea. dist.) Pa. 1983, U.S. Supreme Ct. 1986. Law clk. Commonwealth Ct. of Pa., Harrisburg, 1982-83; assoc. Philips, Curtin and DiGiacomo, Phila., 1983-86, O'Brien & Assocs. PC, Phila., 1986—; bd. dirs. New Manayunk Corp., Phila, counselor, 1987—. Bd. dirs. North Light Inc., 1986-94, sec., 1988-90, pres., 1990-92; bd. dirs. Manayunk Cmty. Ctr. for Arts, 1988-90, chmn. Chaminouix Mansion, 1989—, chmn., 1991—; spl. asst. to U.S. Senator H. John Heinz, 1976-78; Rep. candidate for Phila. City Coun., 1991, for Phila. City Contr., 1997. Mem. Phila. Bar Assn., Pa. Bar Assn., Del. Law Sch. Alumni Assn. (sec. 1985-87), Bus. Assn. Manayunk (bd. dirs. 1987-89), Union League, Racuet Club (mem. com. 1985-87). Roman Catholic. Avocations: squash, court tennis, scuba, golf. Office: O'Brien & Assocs PC 4322 Main St Philadelphia PA 19127-1421

O'BRIEN, WILLIAM JOHN, ecology researcher; b. Summit, N.J., Nov. 30, 1942; m. Mavion Meier, 1964; children: Connor, Shay, Lia. BA, Gettysburg Coll., 1965; postgrad., Cornell U., 1965-69; PhD, Mich. State U., 1970. sch. rsch. assoc. Ctr. Northern Studies, 1977; disting. lectr. Kans. Acad. Sci., 1990. From asst. prof. to prof. aquatic ecology U. Kans., Lawrence, 1971—; chair dept. sys. & ecology U. Kans., 1991—, rsch. scientist ecosystem ctr. Marine Biol. Lab., 1986—. Grantee NSF, 1975—. Mem. Am. Soc. Limnology & Oceanography, Ecol. Soc. Am., Internat. Assn. Theoretical and Applied Limnology, Am. Fisheries Soc., Animal Behavioral Soc. Office: Univ Kansas Kansas Ecological Reserves Lawrence KS 66045-2106 Office: U Kans Dept Biology 6010 Haworth Lawrence KS 66045*

O'BRIEN, WILLIAM JOSEPH, materials engineer, educator, consultant; b. N.Y.C., July 25, 1940; s. William P. O'Brien; divorced; children: Anne Marie, Matthew. BS, CCNY, 1960; MS, NYU, 1962; PhD, U. Mich., 1967. Assoc. dir. rsch. J.F. Jelenko Inc., N.Y.C., 1956-61; from asst. to assoc. prof. Marquette U., Milw., 1961-67; mech. engr., dir. Biomaterials Rsch. Ctr., Milw., 1967-70; prof. biologic and materials scis. U. Mich., Ann Arbor, 1970—, dir. Biomaterials Rsch. Ctr., 1994—; cons. WHO, N.Y.C., 1967-70, Johnson & Johnson, Inc., New Brunswick, N.J., 1970-83; chmn. rsch. com. Sch. Dentistry U. Mich., 1987-91. Editor: (book) Dental Materials, 1989; inventor Magnesia Ceramic, 1985. Recipient UN Cert., 1967, Disting. Contbn. award Mexican Prosthodontics Soc., 1991. Mem. Materials Rsch. Soc., Acad. Dental Materials, Adhesion Soc., Dental Materials Group (pres. 1985). Office: U Mich Biomaterials Rsch Ctr 1011 N University Ave Ann Arbor MI 48109-1078

OBRIG, ALICE MARIE, nursing educator; b. Bklyn., Apr. 1, 1939; d. Gordon A. and Virginia (Morgan) O.; BSN, Cornell U., 1961; MS, Boston U., 1964; CNM, John Hopkins U., 1968; EdD, Tchrs. Coll., Columbia U., 1987. Asst. head nurse N.Y. Hosp., N.Y.C., 1961-62; pub. health nurse N.Y.C. Vis. Nurses, 1962-63; instr. Russell Sage Coll., Troy, N.Y., 1964-67, Yale U., New Haven, 1969-72; asst. prof. Fairfield U., Conn., 1973—; cons. and lectr. in field.; contbr. chpt. to book. Mem. APHA, Am. Coll. Nurse Midwives, Nat. League for Nursing, Conn. Pub. Health Assn., Cornell U.-N.Y. Hosp. SON Alumnae Assn. (sec.), Sigma Theta Tau, Delta Kappa Gamma (mem. nominating com., alpha kappa state). Episcopalian. Home: 50 Lafayette Pl Greenwich CT 06830-5405 Office: Fairfield U N Benson Rd Fairfield CT 06430

O'BRYAN, WILLIAM HALL, insurance executive; b. Tulia, Tex., June 15, 1919; s. Barnett and Goldie (Hall) O'B.; m. Marjorie Mae Lewis, Apr. 14, 1962; children: Richard L., Clelie S. Student, Internat. Bus. Coll., El Paso, Tex., 1936-37, Hills Bus. U., Oklahoma City, 1937, Tulsa Law Sch., 1939. With Okla. Compensation Rating Bur., Oklahoma City, 1937; underwriter, v.p. Tri State Ins. Co., Tulsa, 1937-61; pres. Occidental Fire & Casualty Co., Denver, 1961-72; founder, owner Am. Underwriters, Denver, 1972-74; pres., chmn. bd. Prime Ins. Corp., 1973-74, exec. v.p., 1976-77; v.p. Asso. Internat. Mgmt., 1974-75; conservator Equity Educators Assurance Co., Denver, 1974-75; spl. dep. Colo. ins. commr. acting as receiver Equity Educators Assurance Co., 1975-77; receiver Mfrs. & Wholesalers Indemnity Exchange, 1975-77; pres. Mo. Profl. Liability Ins. Assn., Jefferson City, Mo., 1977-86; pres. subs. Providers Ins., 1981-86; dep. receiver Profl. Mut. Ins. Co., Kansas City, Mo., 1987-96, Protective Casualty Ins. Co., Kansas City, Mo., 1991-96; pres. Liquidation and Asset Recovery, LLC, 1996—. Capt. AUS, 1942-46. Episcopalian. Home: 5404 S Fulton Ct Englewood CO 80111-3660

O'BRYAN, WILLIAM MONTEITH, lawyer; b. Manning, S.C., Apr. 27, 1912; s. Samuel Oliver and Frances (Davis) O'B.; m. Jeane Barrett, Nov. 22, 1942; 1 dau., Donna. Student, U. Miami, Fla., 1931-32; LL.B., U. Fla., 1937. Bar: Fla. bar 1937. Practice in Miami, 1937-50, in Ft.Lauderdale, 1950—; partner firm Fleming, O'Bryan & Fleming (and predecessor), 1950—; Regional v.p. Def. Research Inst., 1963-65. Served to lt. USNR, 1942-45. Fellow Am. Coll. Trial Lawyers, Internat. Acad. Trial Lawyers; mem. Internat. Assn. Ins. Counsel (exec. com. 1964-67), Sigma Chi. Presbyn. Clubs: Mason (Shriner), Rotarian (pres. Ft. Lauderdale 1954-55). Home: 707 NE 26th Ave Fort Lauderdale FL 33304-3613 Office: 1415 E Sunrise Blvd Fort Lauderdale FL 33304-2339

O'BRYANT, CECYLE ARNOLD, secondary English educator; b. Middlesex, N.C.; d. Hubert Leon and Oma Cecyle (Sugg) Arnold; children: Charles III, Hubert A., Patrick C.. BA in English and Polit. Sch., Wake Forest U.; MEd in English Edn., U. N.C., Greensboro; postgrad., various schs. and subjects.; degree in academically gifted students. English tchr. Broadway High Sch., N.C., Hepzibah High Sch., Ga., High Point Cen. High Sch, N.C.; 10th grade advanced placement English tchr. Atkins High Sch., N.C.; tchr. academically gifted students; sponsor Nat. Honor Soc., Hepzibah High Sch., High Point Cen., Great Books Club High Point Cen.; adv. coun. sch. improvement team, Atkins Sch. Mem. Winston-Salem, Forsyth Tchrs. Adv. Coun. on Exceptional Children; tchr. Sunday Sch.; pres. Bapt. Women; ind. vol. work for charitable and civic causes; chmn. So. Assn. of Credentials Comml. Dept. Grantee PTA Coun.; recipient N.C. Sch. of Arts Drama scholarship two consevutive summers; tchr. winner N.C. Ctr. for Advancement of Teachers, 1989, 93; named Atkins Tchr. of Yr.; semifinalist W.S. Forsyth County Schs. Tchr. of Yr. Mem. ASCD, Forsyth Assn. Classroom Tchrs., World Coun. of Exceptional Children, N.C. Assn. Educators, N.C. Tchrs. of English, Arts Coun. (sch. rep), Internat. Honorary Ednl. Orgn., Delta Kappa Gamma. Home: PO Box 291 Oak Ridge NC 27310-0291

O'BRYON, JAMES FREDRICK, defense executive; b. Schenectady, N.Y., Oct. 1, 1941; s. Frederick Stanley and Elizabeth Mary O'B.; m. Margaret Adina Bell, Oct 23, 1965; children: Daniel, Douglas, Cris, Kera. BS in Math., King's Coll., Briarcliff, N.Y., 1964; MSA in Ops. Rsch., George Washington U., 1973; SM Through Elec. Engring. Dept., MIT, 1975. Mathematician Ballistics Rsch. Lab. Aberdeen (Md.) Proving Ground, 1966-74, asst. to dir. Ballistics Rsch. Lab., 1975-76, ops. rsch. analyst smart munitions group Ballistics Rsch. Lab., 1976-79, chmn. red-on-blue working group Joint Tech. Coord. Group, 1979-85, chief combat survivability and tech. U.S. Army Materiel Systems Analysis Activity, 1985-86; asst. dep. undersec. def. Office Sec. Def., Washington, 1986-88, dir. live-fire testing, 1988-95, dep. dir. operational test and evaluation, 1995—; dir. Joint Live Fire Program, Washington, 1986—; mem. Conventional Systems Com., Washington, 1987—. Co-author: (manual) Red-on-Blue Weapons, Effects, 1983; contbr. over 50 articles to profl. jours. Active edn. coun. MIT, Cambridge, 1980—; trustee King's Coll., Briarcliff Manor, N.Y., 1988—. With U.S. Army, 1964-66. Named Outstanding Young Man in Am., Jaycees, 1970, Disting. Lectr., Def. Systems Mgmt. Coll., 1988. Fellow Ctr. Advanced Engring. Study MIT; mem. Am. Def. Preparedness Assn. (chmn. test and evaluation divsn.), Internat. Test and Evaluation Assn., Assn. Governing Bds. of Univs. and Colls., Sigma Xi. Home: 1608 S Tollgate Rd Bel Air MD 21015-5825 Office: The Pentagon Rm 1C730 DOT&E OSD Washington DC 20301-0001

O'BRYON, LINDA ELIZABETH, television station executive; b. Washington, Sept. 1, 1949; d. Walter Mason Ormes and Iva Genevieve (Batrus) Ranney; m. Dennis Michael O'Bryon, Sept. 8, 1973; 1 child, Jennifer Elizabeth. BA in Journalism cum laude, U. Miami, Coral Gables, Fla. News reporter Sta. KCPX, Salt Lake City, 1971-73; documentary and pub. affairs producer Sta. WPLG-TV, Miami, Fla., 1974-76; producer, reporter, anchor, news dir. then v.p. for news and pub. affairs, exec. editor, sr. v.p. The Nightly Business Report Sta. WPBT-TV (PBS), Miami, 1976—. Recipient award Fla. Bar, Tallahasse, 1977, 2 awards Ohio State U., 1976, 79, local Emmy award So. Fla. chpt. Nat. Acad. TV Arts and Scis., 1978, award Corp. for Pub. Broadcasting, 1978, Econ. Understanding award Amos Tuck Sch. Bus. Dartmouth Coll., Hanover, N.H., 1980, award Fla. AP, 1981, 1st prize Nat. Assn. Rea Hors, 1986, Bus. News Luminary award Bus. journalism Rev., 1990, Am. Women in Radio and TV award, 1995. Mem. Nat. Acad. TV Arts and Scis. (former So. Fla. bd. dirs.), Radio-TV News Dirs. Assn., Sigma Delta Chi. Republican. Roman Catholic. Avocations: aerobics, tennis, golf. Office: Sta WPBT 14901 NE 20th Ave Miami FL 33181-1121

OBST, LYNDA ROSEN, film company executive, producer, screenwriter; b. N.Y.C., Apr. 14, 1950; d. Robert A. and Claire (Shenker) Rosen; m. David Obst (div.); 1 child, Oliver. BA, Pomona Coll., 1972; degree in philosophy, Columbia U., 1974. Editor Rolling Stone History of 60's, N.Y.C., 1974-76, New York Times mag., N.Y.C., 1976-79; exec. Polygram Pictures, Los Angeles, 1979-81, Geffen Films, Los Angeles, 1981-83; co-producer Paramount Pictures, Los Angeles, 1983-85, Disney Pictures, Los Angeles, 1986—. Author: Hello He Lied and Other Truths From the Hollywood Trenches, 1996; assoc. prodr. Flashdance, 1983; prodr. Adventures in Babysitting, 1987, Heartbreak Hotel, 1988, The Fisher King, 1991, This is My Life, 1992, One Fine Day, 1996, Contact, 1996, Hope Floats, 1997; exec. prodr. Sleepless in Seattle, 1993, Bad Girls, 1994; contbr. articles to mags. Mem. Writers Guild Am. Office: Lynda Obst Prodns Bldg 43 care 20th Century Fox 10201 W Pico Blvd Los Angeles CA 90064-2606

O'BYRNE, ELIZABETH MILIKIN, pharmacologist, researcher, endocrinologist; b. Miami, Fla., May 19, 1944; d. Richard Mershon and Anne (Smith) Milikin; m. Brian Kenneth O'Byrne, July 1, 1972; children: Lucy Milikin, Kenneth Daniel. AB in Chemistry, Emory U., 1965, MS in Biochemistry, 1968; PhD in Biochemistry, N.Y. Med. Coll., 1985. Assoc. scientist Eli Lilly Rsch. Labs., Indpls., 1968-70; sr. rsch. scientist CIBA-GEIGY Pharms., Summit, N.J., 1970-96; staff scientist Novartis Pharms., Summit, N.J., 1997—. Contbr. articles to profl. jours. Mem. AAAS, N.Y. Acad. Sci., Inflammation Rsch. Assn., Osteoarthritis Rsch. Soc. Achievements include isolation, characterization and development of radioimmunoassay for hormone relaxin to monitor production and secretion, of assays of cytokine and enzyme degradation of cartilage in vitro and in vivo, of proton and sodium magnetic resonance properties of cartilage; demonstration of therapeutic efficacy of matrix metalloprotease inhibitors to retard tissue damage in animal models of diseases; co-founder of CIBA-GEIGY Partnership in Sci. in which scientists work with teachers to bring hands-on experiences in laboratory investigation to high school students. Home: 234 Sagamore Rd Millburn NJ 07041-2136 Office: Novartis Morris Ave Summit NJ 07901

O'BYRNE, PAUL J., bishop; b. Calgary, Alta., Can., Dec. 21, 1922. Ordained priest Roman Catholic Ch., 1948; bishop of Calgary, 1968—. Office: Cath Pastoral Care Ctr, 120 17th Ave SW, Calgary, AB Canada T2S 2T2*

O'CALLAGHAN, JERRY ALEXANDER, government official; b. Klamath Falls, Oreg., Feb. 23, 1922; s. Jeremiah Patrick and Marie Jane (Alexander) O'C.; m. Florence Marie Sheehan, Aug. 6, 1949; children—Jane Mary, Susan Margaret. B.S. with honors, U. Oreg., 1943, M.A. with honors, 1947; Ph.D., Stanford, 1951. Acting instr. history Stanford, 1951-52, U. Wyo., 1952-53; oil editor Tribune-Herald, Casper, Wyo., 1953-55; acting asst. prof. U. Wyo., 1955-56; legis. asst. to Senator Joseph O'Mahoney (Wyo.), 1956-60; exec. asst. to Senator Joseph Hickey(Wyo.), 1961; asst. dir. lands and minerals mgmt. Bur. Land Mgmt., Dept. Interior, 1961-62, asst. dir. plans and legislation, 1962-64, chief legislation and office coop. relations, 1964-69, chief div. coop. relations, 1969-80, chief hist. studies, 1980-82, historian emeritus, 1982—. Author: Disposition of the Public Domain in Oregon, 1960, America 200—The Legacy of Our Lands, 1976. Bd. govs. St. Columba's Episc. Nursery Sch., 1959-71; vestryman Episc. Ch., 1964-68, outreach leader, 1985-90; lay ministry St. Columba's, 1990—. With AUS, 1943-46. Mem. Soc. of Forest History, Fed. Profl. Assn. (pres. 1972), Fossils, Phi Kappa Psi. Home: 5607 Chesterbrook Rd Bethesda MD 20816-1301

O'CALLAGHAN, PATTI LOUISE, court program administrator; b. Bklyn., Mar. 26, 1953; d. Cornelius Leo and Louise Patricia (Casey) O'C.; m. Mark A. Diekman, Dec. 17, 1977; children: Casey, Brian. BA in Biology, NYU, 1975; MS in Physiology, Colo. State U., 1983. Cert. in program adminstrn. Grad. asst. Colo. State U., Ft. Collins, 1975-78; rsch. technician Iowa State U., Ames, 1978-80; counselor trainer Tecumseh Planned Parenthood, Lafayette, Ind., 1985; program coord. Date-rape Awareness and Edn., Lafayette, 1986-89; dir. Tippecanoe Ct. Apptd. Spl. Advocates, Lafayette, 1989—; mem. adv. commn. Ind. State Supreme Ct., Indpls., 1992—, chair, 1995—; mem. Tippecanoe Child Abuse Prevention, 1992—, pres. 1996-97; mem. Tippecanoe County Child Protection Team, 1995—. Editor tng. manuals; contbr. articles to profl. jours. Mem. adv. com. Jour. and Courier, Lafayette, 1992-93; vol. adv. Urban Ministries Homeless Shelter, Lafayette, 1992-93; coach Tippecanoe Soccer Assn., West Lafayette, Ind., 1989—; coach girls soccer West Lafayette H.S., 1994—; sec., v.p., pres. West Lafayette Sch. Bd., 1988—; mem. Tippecanoe County Child Protection Team, 1994—; mentor Mothers Adv. Bd., 1994—. Named Ind. Child Adv. of Yr., 1992, Nat. CASA Dir. of Yr., 1995; D.A.T.E. grantee Ind. Bd. Health, 1988. Mem. Ind. Chpt. for Prevention of Child Abuse, Ind. Advs. for Children (program com. 1991-92), Ind. Sch. Bd. Assn. (legis. com. 1991-92), Ctrl. Ind. Assn. Vol. Adminstrs., Assn. of Women in Sci., Nat. Ct.Apptd. Spl. Adv. Assn., West Lafayette Swim Club (v.p. 1989-92). Democrat. Christian. Avocations: soccer, swimming, reading, camping, travel. Office: Tippecanoe CASA Tippecanoe Superior Ct 3 County Courthouse Lafayette IN 47901

O'CALLAGHAN, ROBERT PATRICK, lawyer; b. Mpls., Aug. 8, 1924; s. Robert Desmond and Claire Marie (Moe) O'C.; married Albina Julie Sepich, June 4, 1949; children: Michael, Edward, Catherine, Diana, Robert, Daniel. BA, Drake U., 1949; JD, U. Denver, 1951. Bar: Colo. 1951, U.S. Dist. Ct. Colo. 1956, U.S. Tax Ct. 1971, U.S. Ct. Appeals (10th cir.) 1978. Pvt. practice law Denver, 1952-53, Rangely, Colo., 1953-63; real estate broker Grand Junction, Colo., 1963-65; ptnr. Bellinger, Faricy, Tursi & O'Callaghan, Pueblo, Colo., 1965-73; pvt. practice law Pueblo, 1973-76; ptnr. Lattimer, O'Callaghan & Ware P.C., Pueblo, 1978-81; of counsel Quiet & Dice, Denver, 1981-83; pvt. practice law Pueblo, 1983—; atty. Town of Rangely, 1953-63; bd. atty. Pueblo Bd. Realtors, 1971-82; instr. real estate U. Colo., 1968-79; sr. cert. valuer Internat. Real Estate Inst. Pres. Homes for Sr. Citizens Inc., Pueblo, 1978-80; pres. Mt. Carmel Credit Union, 1972-74; adv. bd. dirs. Pueblo Salvation Army, 1987-91. With USNR, 1943-46. Mem. ABA, Colo. Bar Assn., Pueblo County Bar Assn., Nat. Network Estate Planning Attys., B.P.O., Elks (exalter ruler Rangley Lodge No. 1907). Republican. Roman Catholic. Avocation: photography. Address: Union Depot 132 W B St Ste 230 Pueblo CO 81003-3402

OCASIO BELÉN, FÉLIX E., real estate development company executive; b. San Germán, P.R., Feb. 21, 1939; s. Epifanio and Leonor (Belén) O.; m. Nereida Montalvo, July 11, 1957 (div. Aug. 1981); children: F=248lix E., José E., Luis E., Jorge E.; m. Beda Torres, June 5, 1982; 1 child, Gustavo E. B.Econs. cum laude, Inter-Am. U. P.R., 1970, M.Fin. magna cum laude, 1975. Asst. libr. Inter-Am. U. P.R., San Germán, 1960-64, jr. acct., 1964-66, pers. officer, 1966-68, budget dir., 1969-78, v.p. adminstrn., 1978-94; exec. dir. Empresas Interex, Inc., San Juan, P.R., 1994—; treas. P.R. N.G. Mil. Stores, San Juan, 1993—; pres. Credit Union, San Germán, 1963-70. Pres. Boy Scouts Am., San Juan, 1994-96, instnl. rep. cub scouts, 1990-94, com. pres., 1994-97. With U.S. Army, 1959-60, brig. gen. Army N.G., 1960—. Decorated Meritorious Svc. medal with 10 oak leaf clusters, Army Commendation medal; named Disting. Alumnus Inter-Am. U. of P.R., 1986; inducted into Inf. Hall of Fame, U.S. Army, 1992. Mem. Nat. Assn. Coll. and Univ. Bus. Officers, N.G. Assn. of U.S., N.G. Assn. P.R., Nat. Assn. Coll. Aux. Svcs., P.R. Assn. Univ. Pers. Roman Catholic. Avocations: jogging, swimming, rifle and pistol matches. Home: Urb Boringuen Gardens Samaniego 1938 San Juan PR 00926 Office: PO Box 3786 92d in Bde Prar San Juan PR 00904

OCASIO-MELENDEZ, MARCIAL ENRIQUE, history educator; b. San Juan, P.R., Aug. 22, 1942; s. Manuel C. and Amparo (Melendez) Ocasio; m. Mimi Rivera, Apr. 15, 1973 (div. 1976). BA, U. P.R., 1964, MA, 1977; PhD, Mich. State U., 1988. Tchr. sci. P.R. Dept. Edn., San Juan, 1966-67; tchr. sci., history Nyack (N.Y.) Schs., 1967-71; tchr. sci. Robinson Prep. Sch., Condado, P.R., 1971-72; instr., asst. prof. P.R. Jr. Coll., Rio Piedras, 1972-80; teaching asst. Mich. State U., E. Lansing, 1979-83; instr. history Caribbean U., Bayamon, P.R., 1983-85; instr. Inter Am. U., Bayamon, 1985-87, U. P.R., Rio Piedras, 1983-87; vis. asst. prof. Mich. State U., E. Lansing, 1987-88; asst. prof. history U. Mich., Flint, 1988-91; assoc. prof. history U. P.R., Rio Piedras, 1991—, dir. grad. program history, 1991-93, assoc. dean acad. affairs Coll. Humanities, 1993-95, dir. internat. studies, 1995—; bd. dirs. Spanish Speaking Info. Ctr., Flint, Internat. Studies U. Puerto Rico, 1995-97; lectr. Universidad del Valle, Cali, Universidad de Los Andes, Bogota, Universidad Pedagogica Nacional, Tunja, U. del Norte Barranquilla, Colombia; dir. Rockefeller Found. Caribbean 2000 Project, U. P.R., 1994-95, Urban Preservation Project of Rio Piedras, P.R., 1994-95; mem. editorial bd. Caribbean Studies, 1994—. Author: Rio Piedras Notas, 1985. Geografia e Historia Am. Latina, 1997; Fulbright scholar (Colombia) 1989, 90; NEH fellow, 1973, 78-79, 91. Mem. U.S. Nexus, Social Sci. Studies Assn., Coun. L.Am. History, Am. Hist. Assn., L.Am. Studies Assn., Assn. P.R. Historians (pres. 1995-97), Joint Border Rsch. Inst., Assn. Caribean Historians, Hispanic Coun. on Internat. Rels., Phi Alpha Theta. Office: Univ PR History Dept PO Box 23350 San Juan PR 00931-3350

OCCHIATO, MICHAEL ANTHONY, city official; b. Pueblo, Colo.; s. Joseph Michael and Joan Occhiato; m. Peggy Ann Stefonowicz, June 27, 1964 (div. Sept. 1983); children: Michael, James, Jennifer; m. Patsy Gay Payne, June 2, 1984; children: Kim Carr, Jerry Don Webb. BBA, U. Denver, 1961; MBA, U. Colo., 1984; postgrad., U. So. Colo. Sales mgr. Tivoli Brewing co., Denver, 1965-67, acting brewmaster, prodn. control mgr., 1967-68, plant mgr., 1968-69; adminstrv. mgr. King Resources Co., Denver, 1969-70; ops. mgr. Canners Inc., Pepsi-Cola Bottling Co., Pueblo, 1970-76; pres. Pepsi-Cola Bottling Co., Pueblo, 1978-82; gen. mgr. Pepsi-Cola Bottling Group div. PepsiCo., Pueblo, 1982, area v.p., 1982-83; ind. cons. Pueblo, 1983—; broker assoc. Sound Venture Realty, Pueblo, 1996—; v.p. Colo. Soft Drink Assn., 1978, pres., 1979; regional dir. Pepsi Cola Mgmt. Inst. divsn. Pepsi Co., 1979-82; pres. Ethnic Foods Internat. dba Taco Rancho, Pueblo; chmn. Weifang (China) Sister City Del., 1991—; bd. dirs. HMO So. Colo. Health Plan, 1988-93; rancher, 1976—; land devel. real estate broker assoc., 1996—. V.p. Colo. Soft Drink Assn., 1979-80, pres., 1980-81; mem. coun. City of Pueblo, 1978-93, pres., 1986, 87, 90, 91; mem. bd. health, 1978-80, regional planning commn., 1980-81, Pueblo Action Inc., 1978-80, Pueblo Planning and Zoning Commn., 1985; chmn. Pueblo Area Coun. Govts., 1980-82; mem. Pueblo Econ. Devel. Corp., 1983-91; chmn. fundraising Pueblo chpt. Am. Heart Assn., 1983—; bd. dirs. El Pueblo Boys Ranch, 1971-73; del. 1st World Conf. Local Elected Orcls. to 1st UN Internat. Coun. for Local Environ. Initiative; active Earth Wise Pueblo, 1991. Lt. USN, 1961-65. Mem. So. Colo. Emergency Med. Technicians Assn. (pres. 1975), Am. Saler Assn., Am. Quarter Horse Assn., Colo. Cattle Assn., Pueblo C. of C., Rotary, Pi Kappa Alpha (v.p. 1960). Home and Office: 11 Harrogate Ter Pueblo CO 81001-1723

OCH, MOHAMAD RACHID, psychiatrist, consultant; b. Damascus, Syria, Apr. 1, 1956; came to U.S., 1981; s. Seifeddine and Souad (Oubari) O.; m. Marianne Noonan, July 24, 1960; children: Seifeddine, Adam. MD, Aleppo (Syria) U., 1980. Psychiat. cons. Human Resource Inst., Brookline, Mass., 1985; med. dir. Spectrum House, Westboro, Mass., 1986-87; assoc. med. dir. Boston Rd. Clinic, Shrewsbury, Mass., 1985—, v.p., 1989—; med. dir. mental health unit Holden (Mass.) Hosp., 1988-90; med. dir. Basic Health Mgmt., Worcester, Mass., 1988-90; asst. med. dir. Boston Rd. Clinic, Shrewsbury, 1986—, Holden Hosp., 1988—, Basic Health Mgmt., Worcester, 1988—; attending psychiatrist, asst. prof. U. Mass. Med. Ctr., Worcester; dir. mental health unit Milford Whitinsville Hosp., 1990—, chmn. dept. psychiatry, 1991-92; med. dir. Seven Hills Intensive Residential Treatment Program, 1990—; asst. chief psychiatry St. Vincent's Hosp., 1996—; mem. adv. bd. Pfeizer, 1996—; med. dir. HMA behaviral health, 1995—. Mem. Am. Psychiat. Assn., AMA. Moslem. Office: Boston Road Clinic 108 Belmont St Worcester MA 01605-2937

OCHBERG, FRANK MARTIN, psychiatrist, foundation administrator; b. N.Y.C., Feb. 7, 1940; s. Gerald Frank and Belle (Solomon) O.; m. Lynn Jeffie Wescott, July 1, 1962; children: Billie Jennifer, Jesse Frank, Abigail Kathryn. A.B., Harvard U., 1961; M.D., Johns Hopkins U., 1965; postgrad. in psychiatry, Stanford U., 1966-69. Diplomate: Am. Bd. Psychiatry and Neurology. Intern USPHS Hosp., San Francisco, 1965-66; resident in psychiatry Stanford (Calif.) U. Med. Ctr., 1966-69; with NIMH, 1969-79, dir. div. mental health service programs, 1973-76; dir. Mich. Dept. Mental Health, 1979-81; pres. Victimization Research and Tng. Inst., 1981—; Med. dir. St. Lawrence Mental Health Center, Lansing, 1981-84; med. dir. Dimondale Stress Reduction Ctr., 1983-85; clin. prof. psychiatry and behavioral medicine, adj. prof. criminal justice, adj. prof. journalism, Mich. State U., East Lansing, 1979—; psychiat. adviser FBI, 1977—, U.S. Secret Service, 1978—; rep. Dart Found., 1991—. Co-editor: Violence and the Struggle for Existence, 1970, The Victim of Terrorism, 1982; editor: Post Traumatic Therapy and Victims of Violence, 1988. Fellow Am. Psychiat. Assn. (past chmn. coun. on nat. affairs 1979-87); mem. Internat. Soc. for Traumatic Stress Studies (founding bd. dirs.). Address: 4211 Okemos Rd Ste 6 Okemos MI 48864-3287

OCHELTREE, RICHARD LAWRENCE, lawyer, retired forest products company executive; b. Springfield, Ill., Oct. 9, 1931; s. Chalmer Myerly and Helen Margaret (Camm) O.; m. Ann Maureen Washburn, Apr. 11, 1958; children: Kirstin Ann, Lorraine Page, Tracy Lynn. A.B., Harvard U., 1953, LL.B., 1958. Bar: Calif. 1959. Sec., gen. counsel Am. Forest Products Corp./Bendix Forest Products Corp., San Francisco, 1961-81; v.p. adminstrn., sec., gen. counsel Am. Forest Products Co., 1981-87. Served with USAF, 1953-55. Mem. Am., San Francisco bar assns. Home: 1446 Floribunda Ave Apt 102 Burlingame CA 94010-3810

OCHMAN, B. L., public relations executive, writer; b. N.Y.C., Mar. 13, 1949; d. Reuben and Dorothy (Bussel) Friedman. BA in Journalism, U. Bridgeport (Conn.), 1968. Account exec. Leo Miller Assocs., Westport, Conn., 1968-74; pub. rels. dir. M Hohner Inc., L.I., N.Y., 1974-76; editorial dir. Ruder & Finn Pub. Rels., N.Y.C., 1976-78; account supr. Ben Kubasik Pub. Relations, N.Y.C., 1978-79; pres. Rent-A-Kvetch, Inc., N.Y.C., 1979—; pres. B.L. Ochman Pub. Relations, N.Y.C., 1979—. Mem. N.Y. C. of C., N.Y. New Media Assn. Office: 594 Broadway Rm 809 New York NY 10012-3257

OCHMANEK, DAVID ALAN, defense analyst; b. Oak Park, Ill., Apr. 10, 1951; s. Edwin Joseph and Phyllis Jean (Straass) O.; m. Barbara Jane Larson, June 16, 1973; children: James Edwin, Anne Skaaden. BS in Internat. Affairs, Polit. Sci., USAF Acad., 1973; MPA in Pub. Affairs and Internat. Rels., Princeton U., 1980. Fgn. svc. officer U.S. Dept. State, 1980-85; profl. staff The Rand Corp., 1985-93, 95—; dep. asst. sec. of def. for strategy Washington, 1993-95; def. analyst The RAND Corp., Washington, 1995—. Co-author: (with Edward L. Warner III) Next Moves: An Arms Control Agenda for the 1990's, 1989, (with Christopher Bowie et al) The New Calculus, 1993, (with Zalmay Khalilzad) Strategic Appraisal, 1997; contbr. articles to profl. jours., chpts. to books. Capt. USAF, 1973-78. Lutheran. Office: The RAND Corp 1333 H St NW Washington DC 20005-4707

OCHOA, MANUEL, JR., oncologist; b. N.Y.C., Apr. 22, 1930; s. Manuel and Maria (Diaz) O.; m. Suzanne Ellen Recca, Sept. 1, 1956; children: Elizabeth, Suzanne Elise. AB, Columbia Coll., 1951; MD, Columbia U., 1955. Diplomate Am. Bd. Internal Medicine; lic. physician, N.Y., Mass. Asst. in medicine U. Rochester (N.Y.) Med. Sch., 1958-61; instr. medicine, assoc., asst. prof. Columbia U., N.Y.C., 1964-68; attending physician Meml. Sloan-Kettering Cancer Ctr., N.Y.C., 1973—; investigator Marine Biol. Lab., Woods Hole, Mass., 1965; assoc. prof. clin. medicine Cornell U., N.Y.C., 1982-96, prof., 1996—; cons. Harlem Hosp. Ctr., N.Y.C., 1966-68, Kingston (N.Y.) Hosp., 1970-85; vis. prof. U. Hawaii, Honolulu, 1971, U. Mex., Mexico City, 1979. Contbr. articles to profl. jours. Capt. USAF, 1956-58, ETO. Fellow Lalor Found., 1965. Fellow ACP, ACS. Republican. Roman Catholic. Achievements include discovering genetic code and protein synthesis in cancer cells, cancer chemotherapy. Home: 82 E Middle Patent Rd Bedford NY 10506 Office: Meml Sloan-Kettering Cancer Ctr 1271 York Ave New York NY 10021-6007

OCHS, CAROL REBECCA, theologian, philosophy and religion educator; b. N.Y.C., May 7, 1939; d. Herman and Clara Florence (Michaels) Blumenthal; m. Michael Ochs, Sept. 27, 1959; children: Elisabeth Amy, Miriam Adina. BA, CUNY, 1960, MA, 1964; PhD, Brandeis U., 1968. Philosophy lectr. CUNY, 1964-65; from asst. prof. to prof. philosophy Simmons Coll., Boston, 1967-92, prof. emerita, 1992—; adj. faculty Grad. Sch., Union Inst., Cin., 1992—, Hebrew Union Coll.-Jewish Inst. Religion, N.Y.C., 1994—; cons. Inst. for Svc. to Higher Edn., Chestnut Hill, Mass., 1972, St. Mary's Coll., South Bend, Ind., 1980; scholar-in-residence Hollins Coll., Roanoke, Va., 1987, Temple Beth El, Rochester, N.Y., 1990; mem. selection com. Kent Postdoctoral Fellowships, Bunting Inst., Radcliffe Coll.; lectr. in field. Author: Behind the Sex of God: Toward a New Consciousness Transcending Matriarchy and Patriarchy, 1977, Women and Spirituality,

1983, 2d edit., 1997, An Ascent to Joy: Transforming Deadness of Spirit, 1989, The Noah Paradox: Time as Burden, Time as Blessing, 1991, Song of the Self: Biblical Spirituality and Human Holiness, 1994; contbr. articles to profl. jours. Mem. Jewish-Cath. Dialogue, Boston, 1989-93; mem. Cath.-Jewish com. Archdiocese of Boston, 1989-93. Fellow NEH, 1976, 88, Nat. Humanities Inst., U. Chgo., 1978-79, Danforth Found., 1981-86, Coolidge Rsch., Colloquium, 1985, Resource Theologian, 1995-97. Fellow Soc. for Values in Higher Edn. (bd. dirs. 1982-88, chair ctrl. com. 1985-87), Assn. for Religion and Intellectual Life (mem. editl. bd. 1986—).

OCHS, MICHAEL, editor, librarian, music educator; b. Cologne, Germany, Feb. 1, 1937; came to U.S., 1939, naturalized, 1945; s. Isaac Julius and Claire (Baum) O.; m. Carol Rebecca Blumenthal, Sept. 27, 1959; children—Elisabeth Amy, Miriam Adina. B.A., CCNY, 1958; M.S., Columbia U., 1963; A.M., NYU, 1964; D.A., Simmons Coll., 1975. Cataloguer CCNY, 1963-65, lectr. in music, 1964; music libr. Brandeis U., Waltham, Mass., 1965-68; creative arts libr. Brandeis U., Waltham, 1968-74; asst. prof. libr. sci. Simmons Coll., Boston, 1974-78; libr. Eda Kuhn Loeb Music Libr., Harvard U., Cambridge, Mass., 1978-88; Richard F. French libr. Eda Kuhn Loeb Music Libr., Harvard U., Cambridge, 1988-92; lectr. music Harvard U., Cambridge, Mass., 1978-81, sr. lectr. music, 1981-92, also libr. cons., 1977-78; music editor W. W. Norton and Co., N.Y.C., 1992—; libr. cons. Biblioteca Berenson, Florence, Italy, 1983, Columbia U., 1987; project dir. U.S. Répertoire International des Sources Musicales Manuscript Inventory Ctr. at Harvard U., NEH, Cambridge, Mass., 1985-88. Editor Notes, Jour. Music Libr. Assn., 1987-92, Music Librarianship in America, 1991; contbr. articles to profl. jours., 1976—. Mem. Internat. Assn. Music Librs. (pres. rsch. librs. br. 1987-90), Music Libr. Assn. (chmn. New Eng. chpt. 1968-69, chmn. com. on bibliog. description 1971-73, chmn. music libr. adminstrn. com. 1975-76, chmn. fin. com. 1976-78, bd. dirs. 1976-78, chmn. publs. com. 1983-87, pres. 1993-95). Office: W W Norton and Co 500 5th Ave New York NY 10110

OCHS, ROBERT DAVID, history educator; b. Bloomington, Ill., Mar. 27, 1915; s. Herman Solomon and Fannie Leah (Livingston) O. A.B., Ill. Wesleyan U., 1936; M.A., U. Ill., 1937, Ph.D., 1939; M.A., Oxford U., Eng., 1964. Research dir. Anti-Defamation League, 1939-41; mem. faculty U. S.C., 1946—, prof. history, 1957-76, disting. prof. emeritus, 1976—, chmn. dept., 1960-74; acting dean U. S.C. (Coll. Arts and Sci.), 1970-71; asso. editor U. S.C. Press, 1950-53; vis. prof. Merton Coll., Oxford U., 1964; Mem. S.C. Archives Commn., 1960-74. U.S. cons.: History of The 20th Century, 1967. Bd. dirs. Columbia Music Festival Assn., 1957-64, 77-85, v.p., 1961-62, pres., 1962-63; dir. Columbia Lyric Opera, Columbia Mus. Art, 1966-69, 74-77, McKissick Mus., 1991-96. Maj. AUS, 1941-46; lt. col. Mem. Am. Hist. Assn., So. Hist. Assn. (exec. council 1973-76), S.C. Hist. Assn. (editor 1947-55, pres. 1956-57), Am. Studies Assn., Orgn. Am. Historians, Southeastern Am. Studies Assn. (pres. 1960-61), Omicron Delta Kappa. Home: 100 Sunset Blvd Apt 401 West Columbia SC 29169-7565

OCHS, SIDNEY, neurophysiology educator; b. Fall River, Mass., June 30, 1924; s. Nathan and Rose (Kniaz) O.; m. Bess Ratner; children—Rachel F., Raymond S. Susan B. Ph.D., U. Chgo., 1952. Research assoc. Ill. Neuropsychiat. Inst., Chgo., 1952-54; research fellow Calif. Inst. Tech., Pasadena, 1954-56; asst. prof. dept. physiology U. Tex. Med. Br., Galveston, 1956-58; assoc. prof. dept. physiology Ind. U., Indpls., 1958-61; prof. Ind. U., 1961-94, prof. emeritus, 1994—. Author: Elements of Neurophysiology, 1965; Axoplasmic Transport and Its Relation to Other Nerve Functions, 1982; founding editor, editor-in-chief Jour. Neurobiology, 1969-76; assoc. editor Jour. Neurobiology, 1977-86. Served with U.S. Army, 1943-45. Mem. Internat. Brain Rsch. Orgn., Am. Physiol. Soc., Soc. Neurosci., Am. Soc. Neurochemistry, Peripheral Nerve Soc. Democrat. Jewish. Office: Ind U Med Ctr Dept Physiology/Biophys 635 Barnhill Dr Indianapolis IN 46202-5126

OCHSNER, JOHN LOCKWOOD, thoracic-cardiovascular surgeon; b. Madison, Wis., Feb. 10, 1927; s. Edward William Alton and Isabel (Lockwood) O.; m. Mary Lou Hannon, Mar. 20, 1954; children: John L., Joby Hannon, Katherine Lockwood, Frank Hannon. MD, Tulane U., 1952. Diplomate Am. Bd. Thoracic Surgery (chmn.), Am. Bd. Surgery, Am. Bd. Vascular Surgery. Intern Univ. Mich. Hosp., Ann Arbor, 1952-53, resident, 1953-54; resident Baylor U. Affilliated Hosp., Houston, 1956-58, 1958-59; chief surg. resident Tex. Children's Hosp., 1959-60; instr. Baylor U., Houston, 1960-61; mem. staff Ochsner Clinic, New Orleans, 1961-66, chmn. dept. surgery, 1966-87, chmn. emeritus dept surgery, 1987—; clin. asst. prof. Tulane U., New Orleans, 1961-65, clin. assoc. prof., 1965-70, clin. prof. surgery, 1970—. Author: (with others) Coronary Artery Surgery, 1978. Pres. Tennis Patrons Assn. New Orleans, 1972; image amb. City of New Orleans, 1982; bd. dirs. Internat. Trade Mart, New Orleans, 1983. Capt. USAF, 1954-56. Recipient award Life Mag., 1961, Golden Plate Acad. Achievement award, 1962, medal of honor, Ecuador, 1981. Mem. Internat. Soc. Cardiovascular Surgery (pres. N.Am. chpt. 1983-84, internat. pres. 1989-91), Am. Assn. Thoracic Surgery (sec. 1979-83, pres. 1992-93), New Orleans Surg. Soc. (pres. 1977-78), So. Surg. Assn. (pres. 1991), So. Assn. for Vascular Surgery (pres. 1983), Boston Club, La. Club, New Orleans Country Club, City Club, Alpha Omega Alpha. Republican. Home: 84 Audubon Blvd New Orleans LA 70118-5540 Office: Ochsner Clinic & Hosp 1514 Jefferson Hwy New Orleans LA 70121-2429*

OCHSNER, SEYMOUR FISKE, radiologist, editor; b. Chgo., Nov. 29, 1915; s. Albert Henry Ochsner and Fleda Fiske; m. Helen Keith, Sept. 8, 1945 (dec. Jan. 1976; children: Anne, Diana, Lida; m. Bobbie Sue Mercer, Dec. 31, 1981. AB, Dartmouth Coll., 1937; MD, U. Pa., Phila., 1947. Diplomate Am. Bd. Radiology, 1953. Intern Johnston-Willis Hosp., Richmond, Va., 1949-50; staff radiologist Ochsner Clinic, New Orleans, 1953-89, also chmn. dept., 1969-77; clin. prof. radiology Tulane Med. Sch., New Orleans, 1955-75; editor Orleans Parish Med. Bulletin, New Orleans, 1985-91. Contbr. articles to profl. jours. Pres. PTA, Metairie, La., 1964. Recipient Disting. Svc. medal So. Med. Assn., 1972, Disting. Svc. award AMA, 1993; fellow Acton Ochsner Med. Found., New Orleans, 1950-53. Mem. Radiol. Soc. La. (pres. 1965), So. Radiol. Conf. (pres. 1968), Am. Coll. Radiology (pres. 1972, Gold medal 1982), Am. Roentgen Ray Soc. (pres. 1975, Gold medal 1986), Rex Orgn., So. Yacht Club, Candlewood Club. Republican. Episcopalian. Avocations: reading, gardening, travel, sailing. Home: 107 Holly Dr Metairie LA 70005-3915

OCKERBLOOM, RICHARD C., newspaper executive; b. Medford, Mass., Dec. 19, 1929; s. Carl F. and Helen C. (Haraden) O.; m. Anne Joan Torpey, Sept. 17, 1955; children: Catherine, Carl, Gail, Mark, John, Peter. BSBA, Northeastern U., 1952; D Pub. Svc. (hon.), Westfield State Coll., 1989; LLD (hon.), Northeastern U., 1995. With Boston Globe, 1948—, salesman, 1955-63, asst. nat. advt. mgr., 1963-70, nat. advt. mgr., 1970-72, asst. advt. dir., 1972-73, advt. dir., 1973-77, v.p. mktg. and sales, 1977-81, exec. v.p., 1981—, gen. mgr., chief operating officer, 1984-86, pres., chief operating officer, 1986-93, vice chmn., 1993-94; ret.; retired; chmn. bd. Met. Sunday Newspapers. Bd. dirs. Greater Boston Conv. and Visitors Bur., Winchester Hosp., United Way Mass. Bay; trustee Northeastern U.; adv. bd. U. Mass., Boston. With U.S. Army, 1952-54. Mem. Algonquin Club (pres.), WInchester Country Club, Phi Kappa Phi. Nat. Honor Soc. Home: 80 Arlington St Winchester MA 01890-3735

OCKERMAN, HERBERT W., agricultural studies educator; b. Chaplin, Ky., Jan. 16, 1932; m. Frances Ockerman (dec.). BS with Distingtion, U. Ky., 1954, MS, 1958; PhD, N.C. State U., 1962; postgrad., Air Univ., 1964-70, Ohio State U., 1974, 83, 87. Asst. prof. Ohio State U., Columbus, 1961-66, assoc. prof., 1966-71, prof., 1971—; former mem. Inst. Nutrition and Food Tech.; judge regional and state h.s. sci. fairs, 1965—, Ham Contest, Ky. State Fair, Sausage and Ham Contest, Ohio Meat Processing Groups; cons. various food companies, 1975—, Am. Meat Inst., 1977-88, USDA, 1977-88, CRC Press., Inc., 1988—; bd. examiners U. Calcutta, 1987-88; examiner U. Mysore, India, 1990-97; expert witness, various firms, 1992—, UN expert 95; presenter in field. Contbr. over 1300 chpts. to books, abstracts and over 65 articles to profl. jours, conf. proceedings. Comdr, USAF, 1955-58. Fisher Packing scholar; named Highest Individual in Beef Grading, Kansas City Meat Judging Contest, 1952; recipient Cert. of Appreciation, Ohio Assn. Meat Processors, 1987-91, Profl. Devel. award Cahill faculty, commendation for internat. work in agr. Ohio Ho. of Reps., badge of merit for svc. to agr. Polish Govt., plaque Argentina Nat. Meat Bd., animal sci. award Roussel UCALF, France, U. Assiuit, Egypt, silver platter Nat. Meat Bd., Sec. Agr., Livestock and Fishery, Argentina, Svc. award Coun. Grad. Students, Pomerance Tchg. award, Outstanding Alumni award U. Ky., also named to Hall of Disting. Alumni, 1995, award for outstanding ednl. achievements Argentine Soc. Agr., Coop. award vet. faculty U. Cordoba, Svc. award Panoma Legis. Br., Brazil; veterinary faculty U. Cordoba, Spain, 1982, 94, Nat. Chung-Hsing U., 1982, 95, Vet. Mus. Ciechanowcu, Poland. Mem. NAS, NCR, ASTM, Am. Meat Sci. Assn., Am. Soc. Animal Sci. (rsch. award 1987), Reciprocal Meat Conf., European Meeting of Meat Rsch. Workers, Polish Vet. Soc. (hon.), Inst. Food Technologists (nat. and OVS chpts.), Can. Meat Sci. Assn., Internat. Congress Meat Sci. and Tech., Rsch. in Basic Sci., Phi Beta Delta (treas. 1987, pres. 1991, internat. scholar award 1991, internat. faculty award 1991, Presdl. medallion award), Gamma Sigma Delta (rsch. award 1977, internat. award of merit 1988), Sigma Xi (outstanding advisor in coll. award 1995), Phi Beta Kappa (Pomerene Tchg. Enhancement award 1997, Outstanding Internat. Faculty award 1997). Office: Ohio State U Meat Lab Animal Sci 2029 Fyffe Rd Columbus OH 43210-1007

OCKERSE, THOMAS, graphic design educator; b. Dutch Bandung, Java, Apr. 12, 1940; came to U.S., 1957, naturalized, 1964; s. Willem Fedor Pieter and Louise Johanna (Tideman) O.; m. Susan Carol Florence, Aug. 31, 1963; children: Kirsten Ingred, Eerin Irene, Tara Manisses. B.F.A., Ohio State U., 1963; M.F.A., Yale U., 1965. Sr. designer Fogleman Assos., Morristown, N.J., 1965-67; asst. prof. Ind. U., Bloomington, 1967-71; prof. graphic design R.I. Sch. Design, Providence, 1971—; head graphic design dept. R.I. Sch. Design, 1973-93, program head grad. studies in graphic design, 1976—; ptnr., prin. Ockerse Ltd. (design cons.); ptnr. Humanity Found. Inc.; mem. adv. bd. Visible Lang.; adj. faculty Jan van Eyck Acad., Maastricht, Netherlands, 1992—. Artist, poet, freelance graphic designer, Providence, 1972—; author: SP-VII, 1968, Stamps-To, 1968, The A-Z Book, 1969, T.O.P., 1970, TV Documentracing, 1974, Son of Fury, 1974, Time, 1974, 26 Poems 1, 1975, Word and Image Equations, 1975, Fact of Fiction, 1976, Stamps-USA, 1975, Graphic Design Education: An Exposition, 1977, Space Window, 1977, Semiotics and Graphic Design Education, Chance/Choice, 1988, Spirals, 1993. Recipient Edn. award Am. Ctr. for Design, 1991; faculty rsch. grantee Ind. U., 1969, RISD, 1992, Scottish Internat. Trust grantee for edn. and art, 1972. Mem. Am. Inst. Graphic Arts (v.p. 1980-85, chmn. edn. com.), Indsl. Design Soc. Am., Semiotic Soc. Am., Am. Ctr. for Design, Theosophical Soc. (pres. Blavatsky br. 1957-67, 89—), Sigma Chi. Home: 37 Woodbury St Providence RI 02906-3509 Office: RI Sch Design Graphic Design Dept 2 College St Providence RI 02903-2717

O'CONNELL, ANTHONY J., bishop; b. Lisheen, County Clare, Ireland, May 10, 1938. Ed., Mt. St. Joseph Coll., Cork, Ireland; Mungret Coll., Mangret Coll., Limerick, Ireland; ed., Kenrick Sem., St. Louis. Ordained priest Roman Cath. Ch., 1963. Bishop Diocese of Knoxville, 1988—. Office: Bishop of Knoxville 805 Northshore Dr Knoxville TN 37919

O'CONNELL, BRIAN, community organizer, public administrator, writer, educator; b. Worcester, Mass., Jan. 23, 1930; s. Thomas J. and Mary (Carroll) O'C.; m. Ann C. Brown, July 11, 1953; children: Todd, Tracey, Matthew. B.A., Tufts Coll., 1953; postgrad., Maxwell Sch. Citizenship and Pub. Adminstrn., 1953-54; also numerous hon. degrees. Field rep. Am. Heart Assn., Pa., 1954-56; exec. dir. Am. Heart Assn., Md., 1956-61, Calif., 1961-66; exec. dir. Nat. Assn. Mental Health, 1966-78, dir. emeritus, 1978—; pres. Nat. Council on Philanthropy, 1978-80; exec. dir. Coalition of Nat. Vol. Orgns., 1978-80; pres. Ind. Sector, 1980-95, founding pres., 1980—; prof. pub. svc. Tufts U., Medford, Mass., 1995—; mem. U.S. Pres.'s Com. Employment of Handicapped, 1966-68; chmn. Liaison Group Mental Health, 1969-72. Author: Effective Leadership in Voluntary Organizations, 1976, Finding Values That Work: The Search for Fulfillment, 1977, America's Voluntary Spirit, A Book of Readings, 1983, The Board Members Book, 1985, Philanthropy in Action, 1987, Our Organization, 1987, Volunteers in Action, 1989, People Power: Service Advocacy, Empowerment, 1994, Board Overboard, 1995, Powered By Coalition: The Story of Independent Sector, 1997. Mem. Alumni Coun. Tufts U., 1970-80, trustee, 1988—, chmn. pres. search com., 1992; trustee Points of Light Found., 1989-95; bd. dirs. Hogg Found., 1990-95; chmn. organizing com., co-chmn., chmn. exec. com. Civicus: World Alliance for Citizen Participation, 1992-95; bd. dirs. E.M. Kaufman Found., 1994—. Recipient outstanding agy. prof. award United Way Am., 1979, Lincoln Filene Citizenship award, 1985, John W. Gardner Leadership award, 1994, Gold Key award, 1994, Chmns. award, NSFBE, 1994. Fellow Am. Pub. Health Assn., Nat. Acad. Pub. Adminstrn. (trustee 1993—), Nat. Com. Patients' Rights (chmn. 1975-77). Home: 50 Chase St Chatham MA 02633-2404 Office: Lincoln Filene Ctr Tufts U Medford MA 02155

O'CONNELL, BRIAN JAMES, priest, former university president; b. Hartford, Conn., Aug. 21, 1940; s. Jerry and Mary (Moloney) O'C. AB, Mary Immaculate Sem., 1964, MDiv, 1968; MA, St. John's U., Jamaica, N.Y., 1970; PhD, Ohio State U., 1974. Ordained priest Roman Cath. Ch., 1968. Social studies tchr. St. John's Prep. Sch., Bklyn., 1968-70; lectr. sociology St. John's U., Jamaica, 1970-71, asst. prof. sociology, 1974-79, assoc. prof., 1979-87, assoc. dean arts and scis., 1987-88, also bd. dirs., 1989—; exec. v.p. Niagara U., N.Y., 1988-89, pres., 1989-95; chaplain Providence Hosp., Washington, 1996—. Author: Blacks in White Collar Jobs, 1979; also articles. Cons. Bklyn. Ecumenical Coops., 1981-88. Mem. Niagara Falls C. of C. (bd. dirs. 1989-95).

O'CONNELL, DANIEL CRAIG, psychology educator; b. Sand Springs, Okla., May 20, 1928; s. John Albert and Letitia Rutherford (McGinnis) O'C. B.A., St. Louis U., 1951, Ph.L., 1952, M.A., 1953, S.T.L., 1960; Ph.D., U. Ill., 1963. Joined Soc. of Jesus, 1945; asst. prof. psychology St. Louis U., 1964-66, asso. prof., 1966-72, prof., 1972-80, trustee, 1973-78, pres., 1974-78; prof. psychology Loyola U., Chgo., 1980-89; prof. psychology Georgetown U., Washington, 1990—, chmn., 1991-96; vis. prof. U. Melbourne, Australia, 1972, U. Kans., 1978-79, Georgetown U., 1986; Humboldt fellow Psychol. Inst. Free U. Berlin, 1968; sr. Fulbright lectr. Kassel U., W. Ger., 1979-80. Author: Critical Essays on Language Use and Psychology, 1988; contbr. articles to profl. jours. Recipient Nancy McNeir Ring award for outstanding teaching St. Louis U., 1969; NSF fellow, 1961, 63, 65, 68; Humboldt Found. grantee, 1973; Humboldt fellow Tech. U. of Berlin, 1987. Fellow Am., Mo. psychol. assns., Am. Psychol. Soc.; mem. Midwestern, Southwestern, Eastern psychol. assns., Psychologists Interested in Religious Issues, Psychonomic Soc., Soc. for Scientific Study of Religion, N.Y., Mo. acads. sci., AAUP, AAAS, Phi Beta Kappa. Home and Office: Georgetown U Dept Psychology 37th & O Sts NW Washington DC 20057 *Were it over, it would have been more than my expected share already. The challenge of learning to serve others has moved it along at a quick pace, and I am grateful that I have always received more than I've been able to give in return—from the Lord and from many good people.*

O'CONNELL, DANIEL F., lawyer; b. Orange, N.J., May 5, 1943. BS with honors, Villanova U., 1965; JD, Rutgers U., 1968. Bar: N.J. 1968, N.Y. 1980, U.S. Supreme Ct. 1980. Ptnr. Shanley & Fisher, P.C., Morristown, N.J.; mem. Supreme Ct. N.J. Dist. VII Ethics Com., 1978-83, sec., 1980-83; chmn. N.J. Commn. Legal and Ethical Problems in the Delivery of Health Care, 1986-90. Mem. ABA (labor and employment law sect., antitrust law sect., health law sect. 1977—), N.J. State Bar Assn. (labor law sect., health and hosp. law sect.), Somerset County Bar Assn. (exec. com. 1977-81, pres. 1980). Office: Shanley & Fisher PC 131 Madison Ave Morristown NJ 07960-6086

O'CONNELL, EDWARD JAMES, JR., psychology educator, computer applications and data analysis consultant; b. Sterling, Ill., Aug. 15, 1932; s. Edward James and Elizabeth E. (Clapham) O'C.; m. Pamelia Canon Floyd, Aug. 21, 1959; children—Edward James III, John Matthew. B.S. in Psychology, Ill. Inst. Tech., 1958; M.A. in Psychology, Northwestern U., 1961, Ph.D. in Psychology, 1962. NSF postdoctoral fellow Carnegie Inst. Tech., Pitts., 1962-63; asst. prof. psychology Carnegie Inst. Tech., 1963-65; psychology faculty Syracuse (N.Y.) U., N.Y., 1965-93; prof. Syracuse (N.Y.) U., 1975-93, prof. emeritus, 1993—; cons. Rand Corp., Santa Monica, Calif., 1962-64, Abt Assocs., Boston, 1970-73, Marcy Psychiat. Hosp., N.Y., 1979-82. Served to cpl. U.S. Army, 1952-54. NSF predoctoral fellow, 1959-62; NSF postdoctoral fellow, 1962-63; Northwestern U. predoctoral fellow, 1958-59. Mem. Am. Psychol. Assn., Assn. Computing Machinery, Sigma Xi. Democrat. Avocations: billiards; computer programming. Home: 508 Halsted Rd Cashiers NC 28717 Address: PO Box 570 Cashiers NC 28717-0570

O'CONNELL, EDWARD JOSEPH, III, financial executive, accountant; b. Evergreen Park, Ill., Aug. 9, 1952; s. Edward Joseph Jr. and Mary Jane O'C.; m. Mary M. Witt, May 30, 1976; children: Kelly, Edward IV, Molly, Kevin. BBA, U. Notre Dame, 1974. CPA, Ill. Mem. audit staff Coopers and Lybrand, Chgo., 1974-78, audit mgr., 1978-81; controller Union Spl. Corp., Chgo., 1981-83, v.p., treas., 1983-85, v.p., chief fin. officer, 1985-89, exec. v.p. fin. and adminstrn., chief. fin. officer, 1989-91; sr. v.p. fin., chief fin. officer GenDerm Corp., Lincolnshire, Ill., 1991-95; COO Keck, Mahin & Cate, Chgo., 1995—. Mem. Am. Inst. CPA's, Ill. Soc. CPA's, Fin. Execs. Inst., Machinery and Allied Products Inst. (fin. council II). Roman Catholic. Club: Notre Dame of Chgo. (bd. govs. 1984-86). Avocations: rugby, running, reading, golf. Home: 10420 Lamon Ave Oak Lawn IL 60453-4743 Office: Keck Mahin & Cate 77 W Wacker Dr Chicago IL 60601

O'CONNELL, FRANCIS JOSEPH, lawyer, arbitrator; b. Ft. Edward, N.Y., Mar. 19, 1913; s. Daniel Patrick and Mary (Bowe) O'C.; m. Adelaide M. Nagro, Sept. 27, 1937; children: Chris, Mary Gaynor Lavonas. AB, Columbia U., 1934; JD, Fordham U., 1938; SJD summa cum laude, Bklyn. Law Sch., 1945. Bar: N.Y. 1938, U.S. Dist. Ct. (so. dist.) N.Y. 1942, U.S. Tax Ct. 1941. Counsel and asst. to chmn. exec. com. for labor law and litigation Allied Chem. Corp., N.Y.C., 1942-70; ptnr. Bill & O'Connell and predecessor, Garden City, N.Y., 1970-76; pvt. practice Garden City, N.Y., 1976-85, Cutchogue, N.Y., 1985—; arbitrator, fact-finder, mediator Fed. Mediation and Conciliation Svc., 1970—, N.Y. State Mediation Bd., Am. Arbitration Assn., N.Y. State, Nassau and Suffolk County pub. employment rels. bds., 1970—; adminstrv. law judge N.Y. State Dept. Health, 1979—; instr. labor law and labor rels. Cornell U.; U.S. del. ILO, Geneva, 1948, 59, 69, 72. Author: Labor Law and the First Line Supervisor, 1945, Restrictive Work Practices, 1967, National Emergency Strikes, 1968. Trustee Village of Garden City, 1948-50; mem. bd. edn. Diocese of Rockville Centre (N.Y.), 1972-80; pres. various civic orgns., 1942—. Mem. ABA (labor and internat. law sects.), N.Y. State Bar Assn. (labor com.), Bar Assn. Nassau County (labor and arbitration coms., former chmn. arbitration andlabor law coms.), Mfg. Chemists Assn. (chmn. indsl. rels. com.), U.S. C. of C. (indsl. rels. com.), Southold Indian Mus. (bd. dirs.). Republican. Roman Catholic. Office: PO Box 819 Cutchogue NY 11935-0819

O'CONNELL, FRANCIS V(INCENT), textile printing company executive; b. Norwich, Conn., July 8, 1903; s. Thomas Francis and Isabelle (Gelino) O.'C.; LL.B., Blackstone Coll. Law, 1932, J.D., 1940, LL.M., 1942; m. Marie Louise Lemoine, Nov. 7, 1940. Textile screen printer U.S. Finishing Co. Norwich, 1921-30; foreman Ahern Textile Print Co., Norwich, 1930-36; pres., owner Hand Craft Textile Print Co., Plainfield, Conn., 1936—. Roman Catholic. Home: 25 14th St Norwich CT 06360-2823 Office: Bishop's Crossing Plainfield CT 06374

O'CONNELL, HAROLD PATRICK, JR., banker; b. Chgo., Sept. 11, 1933; s. Harold P. and Charlotte Anne (Woodward) O'C.; m. Geraldine Taylor McLaughlin, 1979; children: Alexandra T. Close, Geraldine S. Kuchman, Peter B. McLaughlin Jr. AB, Dartmouth Coll., 1955; JD, U. Mich., 1958. V.p. Continental Ill. Nat. Bank and Trust Co., Chgo., 1958-83, No. Trust Co., Chgo., 1983-86; dir. Terra Mus. of Am. Art, Chgo., 1987-92; chmn. exec. com. Mid-Am. Nat. Bank, 1989-92, pres., CEO, dir., 1992-93, chmn. bd., 1993—. Trustee Better Govt. Assn. Chgo., 1974—, pres., 1979-83; governing mem. Chgo. Symphony Orchestra, 1979—; sustaining fellow Art Inst. Chgo., 1982—; bd. dirs. Rehab. Inst. Chgo., 1980—. Mem. Chgo. Club, Racquet Club, Econ. Club, Casino Club (pres. 1988-91), Onwentsia Club (Lake Forest, Ill.), Shoreacres (Lake Bluff, Ill.), Old Elm Club (Highland Park, Ill.), Cypress Point Club (Pebble Beach, Calif.). Home: 435 Thorne Ln Lake Forest IL 60045-2343 Office: PO Box 81044 Chicago IL 60681-0044

O'CONNELL, HENRY FRANCIS, lawyer; b. Boston, Jan. 4, 1922; s. Henry F. and Anna (Cunning) O'C. BA, Boston Coll., 1943, JD, 1948. Bar: Mass. 1948, U.S. Supreme Ct. 1956. House counsel electronics div. Am. Machine & Foundry Co., Boston, 1951-54; sole practice Boston, 1954-60; assoc. Glynn & Dempsey, Boston, 1960-70, Avery, Dooley, Post & Avery, Boston, 1970-88; asst. atty. gen. mcpl. affairs State of Mass., Boston, 1969-88; mcpl. cons. State of Mass., Winthrop, 1989—. Mem. Winthrop Bd. of Selectmen, 1958-64, 68-72, chmn., 1960-61, 68-69, 71-72. Lt. USCGR, WWII, ret. capt. Mem. VFW (life), Internat. Platform Assn., Mass. Bar Assn., Mass. Chiefs of Police Assn., Nat. Boating Fedn. (life, past pres.), Mass. Selectmen's Assn. (life), Mass. Boating and Yachts Club Assn. (life, past commodore), Mass. Boating and Club Assn. (past commodore), Port Norfolk Yacht Club (hon. life mem.), Cottage Pk. Yacht Club (life), Pleasant Pk. Yacht Club, Port Norfolk Yacht Club (hon. life, Dorchester, Mass.), Res. Officers Assn. (life), Ret. Officers Assn. (life), Winthrop Yacht Club (life, past commodore), Commodore Club Am. (life), U.S. Sailing Assn. (Portsmouth, R.I.), Yachting Club Am. (Marco Island, Fla.), KC (hon., life), Elks (life), Am. Legion (life). Home and Office: 20 Belcher St Winthrop MA 02152-3014

O'CONNELL, HUGH MELLEN, JR., retired architect; b. Oak Park, Ill., Nov. 29, 1929; s. Hugh M. and Helen Mae (Evans) O'C.; m. Frances Ann Small, Apr. 13, 1957; children—Patricia Lynn, Susan Marie, Jeanette Maureen. Designer, John Mackel. Student mech. engring., Purdue U., 1948-50; B.S. in Archtl. Engring, U. Ill., 1953. Registered architect, Ariz., Calif., La., Nev., Nat. Council Archtl. Registration Bds. Structural engr. Los Angeles, 1955-57; architect Harnish & Morgan & Causey, Ontario, Calif., 1957-63; self-employed architect Ventura, Calif., 1963-69; architect Andrews/O'Connell, Ventura, 1970-78; dir. engring. div. Naval Constrn. Bn. Center, Port Hueneme, Calif., 1978-91; supervisory architect Naval Constrn. Bn. Center, Port Hueneme, 1991-93; ret., 1993; mem. tech. adv. com. Ventura Coll., 1965-78; sec. Oxnard Citizens' Adv. Com., 1969-79, v.p., 1970-72, pres., 1972—; chmn. Oxnard Beautification Com., 1969, 74, Oxnard Cmty. Block Grant adv. com., 1975-76; mem. Oxnard Planning Commn., 1976-86, vice chmn., 1978-79, chmn., 1980-81. Mem. Oxnard Art-in-Pub. Places Commn., 1988—. Served with AUS, 1953-55. Mem. AIA (emeritus, pres. Ventura chpt. 1973), Am. Concrete Inst., Soc. Am. Registered Architects (Design award 1968, dir. 1970), Am. Legion, Soc. for Preservation and Encouragement of Barbershop Quartet Singing in Am. (chpt. pres. 1979, chpt. sec. 1980-83), Acad. Model Aeros. (#9190 1948—), Channel Islands Condors Club (treas. 1986—), Sports Flyers Assn., Alpha Rho Chi. Presbyterian (elder 1963, deacon 1967). Lodges: Kiwanis (pres. 1969, div. sec. 1974-75), Elks. Home and Office: 520 Ivywood Dr Oxnard CA 93030-3527

O'CONNELL, JAMES JOSEPH, port official; b. Lockport, Ill., Feb. 7, 1933; m. Phyllis Ann Berard, Aug. 1, 1953; children: Lynn, Kathryn, Julie. BSBA, Lewis U., 1958. lic. pvt. pilot FAA. Recorder Will County, Joliet, Ill., 1976-88; dir., treas., corp. sec., v.p. Joliet Regional Port Dist., 1972-96; dir. Des Plaines Valley Enterprise Zone, Joliet; reg. lobbyist Ill. Assn. Pt. Dists. Nat. dir., nat. U.S. pres. Internat. O'Connell Clan, Kerry County, Ireland, 1996—; precinct committeeman Will County, Joliet, 1962-72, exec. cen. committeeman, 1965-70, dir. Will County Young Reps., Joliet, 1984, sec. Will County Econ. Affairs Commn., Joliet; candidate for U.S. Congress, 1994. With U.S. Army, 1953-54, Korea. Mem. Ill. Assn. Port Dists. (sec., treas. 1982—), Ill. Jaycees (senate pres. 1972-73, named to Hall of Fame 1993, Disting. Svc. award 1977), Joliet Flying Club (sec.), Joliet Navy League (pres. 1996—), KC (past Grand Knight 1972, 91), Joliet Exch. Club, Three Rivers Mfg. Assn. (pub. affairs com.), Joliet Columbian Club (pres.), Am. Legion (life, former post officer), VFW (life), others. Roman Catholic. Office: 1009 Western Ave Joliet IL 60435-6801

O'CONNELL, JEFFREY, law educator; b. Worcester, Mass., Sept. 28, 1928; s. Thomas Joseph and Mary (Carroll) O'C.; m. Virginia Kearns, Nov. 26, 1960; children: Mara, Devin. Grad. cum laude, Phillips Exeter Acad., 1947; AB cum laude, Dartmouth Coll., 1951; JD, Harvard U., 1954. Bar: Mass. 1954, Conn. 1954, Va. 1983, hon. admittance to Ark. and Minn. bar. Instr. speech Tufts U., 1953-54; assoc. Sherburne, Powers & Needham, 1954-57, Hale & Dorr, Boston, 1958-59; asst. prof., then assoc. prof. law U. Iowa

Coll. Law, 1959-62; assoc. dir. automobile claims study Harvard Law Sch., 1963-64; assoc. prof. law U. Ill. Coll. Law., 1964-65, prof., 1965-79; prof. law U. Va. Law Sch., 1980-83, John Allan Love prof., 1983-90, Samuel H. McCoy II prof., 1990—, Class of 1948 rsch. prof., 1994-97; summer vis. prof. Northwestern U., 1963, U. Mich., 1966, 75, So. Meth. U., 1972, U. Tex., 1977, U. Wash., 1979; John Marshall Harlan vis. prof. N.Y. Law Sch., 1991; vis. fellow Centre for Socio-Legal Studies, Wolfson Coll., Oxford (Eng.) U., 1973, 79; Thomas Jefferson vis. fellow Downing Coll. Cambridge U., Eng., 1989; mem. U. Va. Ctr. for Advanced Study, 1980-83. Author: (with R.E. Keeton) Basic Protection for the Traffic Victim, 1965, After Cars Crash: The Need for Legal and Insurance Reform, 1967, (with Arthur Myers) Safety Last: An Indictment of the Auto Industry, 1966, (with R.E. Keeton, John McCord) Crisis in Car Insurance, 1968, (with Wallace Wilson) Car Insurance and Consumer Desires, 1969, The Injury Industry, 1971, (with Rita James Simon) Payment for Pain and Suffering, 1972, Ending Insult to Injury: No-Fault Insurance for Products and Services, 1975, (with Roger Henderson) Tort Law, No-Fault and Beyond, 1975, The Lawsuit Lottery: Only the Lawyers Win, 1979, (with C. Brian Kelly) The Blame Game: Injuries, Insurance and Injustice, 1986, (with Lester Brickman and Michael Horowitz) Rethinking Contingency Fees: A Proposal to Align the Contingency Fee System with its Policy Roots and Ethical Mandates, 1994, (with Peter Bell) Accidental Justice: The Dilemmas of Tort Law, 1997;. Mem. Nat. Hwy. Safety Adv. Com., 1967-70; edn1. adv. bd. John Simon Guggenheim Found., 1973-87; bd. dirs. Consumers Union, 1970-76; mem. com. on competitive safeguards and med. aspects of sports NCAA, 1985-87. Served as 1st lt. USAF, 1954-57. Recipient Robert B. McKay award for ins. scholarship Tort and Ins. Practice sect. ABA, 1992; Guggenheim fellow, 1972-73, 79-80. Mem. ABA, Va. Bar Assn., Casque and Gauntlet, Phi Beta Kappa, Phi Upsilon, Farmington Country Club. Democrat. Roman Catholic. Home: 4 Oak Cir Charlottesville VA 22901-3220 Office: U Va Sch Law 580 Massie Rd Charlottesville VA 22903-1738

O'CONNELL, KENNETH JOHN, state justice; b. Bayfield, Wis., Dec. 8, 1909; s. Daniel W. and Kathryn B. (Smith) O'C.; m. Evelyn L. Wachsmuth, June 2, 1938; children: Daniel, Thomas; m. Esther Erickson, July 3, 1964. LL.B., U. Wis., 1933, S.J.D., 1934; LL.D. (hon.), Willamette U., 1983. Bar: Wis. 1933, Oreg. 1944. Assisted preparation Restatement of Law of Property, Am. Law Inst.; asst. atty. Wis. Tax Commn., 1934; pvt. practice law Eugene, Oreg., 1944-47; mem. Oreg. Supreme Ct., 1958-77, chief justice, 1970-76; asst. prof. law U. Oreg. Law Sch., 1935-40, asso. prof., 1940-44, prof., 1947-58; Mem. faculty N.Y. U. Law Sch. Appellate Judges Seminar, 1966, 67; Disting. vis. prof. law U. Oreg., 1977; vis. prof. law Willamette U. Sch. Law, 1977-79, adj. prof., 1981-85; Chmn. Oreg. Statute Revision Council, 1950-54; mem. 2d Triennial Coif Award Com., 1965, Oreg. Jud. Reform Commn., 1971—; vice chmn. Constl. Revision Com., Oreg., 1961-63; mem. exec. com. Conf. Chief Justices.; Chmn. Oreg. Rhodes Scholarship Selection Com., 1969—; elector N.Y.U. Hall of Fame for Great Ams. Author article, monographs legal topics. Recipient Oreg. State Bar award of merit, 1953, Disting. Service award U. Oreg., 1967, Herbert Harley award Am. Judicature Soc., 1976, Cert. Distinction award U. Wis., 1983, E.B. McNaughton award ACLU, 1984, Legal Citizen of Yr., Oreg. Law Related Edn. Project, 1984, Disting. Service award U. Oreg. Law Sch., 1985. Center Advanced Study Behavioral Scis., 1965-66. Mem. Oreg. Jud. Council, Oreg. State Bar, Order of Coif, Omicron Delta Tau, Phi Delta Phi. Home: 3393 Country Club Rd S Salem OR 97302-9710

O'CONNELL, KEVIN, lawyer; b. Boston, Sept. 4, 1933; s. Michael Frederick and Kathryn Agnes (Kelley) O'C.; m. Mary Adams, July 14, 1990; children: Tiffany W., Elizabeth H., Dana A., Liesel E. A.B., Harvard, 1955, J.D., 1960. Bar: Calif. 1961. Assoc. firm O'Melveny & Myers, L.A., 1960-63; asst. U.S. atty. criminal div. Cen. Dist. Calif., L.A., 1963-65; staff counsel Gov. Calif. Commn. to Investigate Watts Riot, L.A., 1965-66; ptnr. Tuttle & Taylor, L.A., 1966-70, Coleman & O'Connell, L.A., 1971-75; pvt. practice law L.A., 1975-78; of counsel firm Simon & Sheridan, L.A., 1978-89; ptnr. Manatt, Phelps & Phillips, L.A., 1989—. Bd. editors: Harvard Law Rev, 1958-60. Mem. Los Angeles County (Calif.) Democratic Central Com., 1973-74; bd. dirs. Calif. Supreme Ct. Hist. Soc. Lt. USMCR, 1955-57. Mem. Am. Law Inst. Home: 426 N Mccadden Pl Los Angeles CA 90004-1026 Office: Manatt Phelps & Phillips Trident Ctr E Tower 11355 W Olympic Blvd Los Angeles CA 90064-1614

O'CONNELL, KEVIN GEORGE, priest, foreign missionary, former college president; b. Boston, May 22, 1938; s. George Lawrence and Mary Margaret (Cohan) O'C. BA, Boston Coll., 1962, MA, 1963; PhD, Harvard U., 1968; MDiv, Weston Sch. Theology, Cambridge, Mass., 1969. Joined S.J., 1956; ordained priest Roman Cath. Ch., 1969. Asst. prof. Old Testament Weston Sch. Theology, Cambridge, 1971-77, dir. field edn., 1972-75, assoc. prof. Old Testament, 1977-80; assoc. prof., chmn. dept. religious studies John Carroll U., Cleve., 1981-87; pres., prof. Le Moyne Coll., Syracuse, N.Y., 1988-93; provincial asst. for capital devel. Soc. of Jesus of New Eng., Boston, 1994-96; fgn. missionary and pastor for English-speaking Caths. Amman, Jordan, 1996—; vis. prof. O.T., Woodstock Coll., Balt., 1969-70; vis. prof. theology U. San Francisco, 1970; William K. Warren Disting. vis. prof. Roman Cath. studies U. Tulsa, 1987; sabbatical John Carroll U., University Heights, Ohio, 1993-94; chmn. bd. Joint Archeol. Expdn. to Tell el-Hesi, Israel, 1982—. Author: The Theodotionic Revision of the Book of Exodus, 1972; editor: The Tell el-Hesi Field Manual, 1980, Tell el-Hesi: Modern Military Trenching and Muslim Cemetery, 1985, Tell el-Hesi: The Persian Period (Stratum V), 1989, Tell el-Hesi: The Site and the Expedition, 1989, Tell el-Hesi: The Muslim Cemetery in Fields V and VI/IX (Stratum II), 1993; mem. editorial adv. bd. Bible Rev., 1987—. Bd. dirs. Hiawatha coun. Boy Scouts Am., 1988-93, Syracuse Opera, 1991-94; trustee Albright Inst. Archeol. Rsch., Jerusalem, Israel, 1982—; trustee Am. Schs. Oriental Rsch., Balt., 1983-96, vice chmn., 1993-96; trustee Boston Coll., 1988-96, Loyola U. Chgo., 1990-96, U. Scranton, 1992-96. Kent fellow Danforth Found., 1965-67; Am. Coun. Learned Socs. study fellow, 1970-71, grantee, 1980-81; Grauel Faculty fellow John Carroll U., 1986-87. Mem. Cath. Bibl. Assn., Soc. Bibl. Lit., Internat. Fedn. Cath. Univs. (trustee, v.p., mem. coun. 1988-94). Office: The Jesuit Ctr, PO Box 212074, Amman 11121, Jordan

O'CONNELL, LAWRENCE B., lawyer; b. Corpus Christi, Tex., July 18, 1947; s. Lawrence M. and Isabelle Susan (Strawbridge) O.; m. Carolyn Janet Rush, Sept.24, 1967; children: Suzanne Michelle, Elizabeth Danielle, Jason Lawrence. BA, Purdue U., 1970; JD, Ind. U., Indpls., 1975. Bar: Ind. 1975, U.S. Dist. Ct. (no. and so. dists.) Ind. 1975. Chief investigator Consumer Protection Div. Office of the Ind. Atty. Gen., Indpls., 1974-75; dep. atty. gen. Office of the Ind. Atty. Gen., Indpls., 1975; assoc. Schultz, Ewan & Burns Law Firm, Lafayette, Ind., 1975-79; ptnr. Schultz, Ewan, Burns & O'Connell, Lafayette, 1979-82, Gothard, Poelstra & O'Connell, Lafayette, 1982-86, Profl. Assn. Gothard & O'Connell, Lafayette, 1987-93; pvt. practice, 1994—; atty. Tippecanoe County, Lafayette, 1983-95. Edn. cons. Ind. U., 1973-75; treas. Ind. Young Rep. Fedn. 1976-77, chmn. 1977-79; Hoosier Assoc. Ind. Reps., 1980—. Recipient Sagamore of the Wabash citation, Gov. Otis R. Bowen, M.D., Ind. 1978, Gov. Robert D. Orr, Ind. 1980. Mem. ABA, Ind. Bar Assn., Tippecanoe County Bar Assn. (treas. 1976-77), Columbia Club (Indpls.), Ind. Soc. of Chgo., Ind. Mcpl. Lawyers Assn. (bd. dirs. 1989-95, pres. 1994-95). Office: Lawrence B O'Connell Esq # 558 223 Main St Lafayette IN 47901-1261

O'CONNELL, MARGARET ELLEN, editor, writer; b. N.Y.C., May 2, 1947; d. Daniel Gregory O'Connell and Anastasia Marie Crowley. BA, Hunter Coll., 1969; std. cert., Am. Inst. Banking, 1974; postgrad., Pace U., 1995. Circulation dir., book reviewer, office mgr. Emmanuel Mag., N.Y.C., 1984-85; assoc. editor The Christophers, Inc., N.Y.C., 1985-96, sr. rsch. editor, 1996—. Editor: Christopher Book, Calendar, Pocket Planner, 1986—; book reviewer Cath. News Svc.; contbr. book revs. and articles to periodicals. Bd. dirs. Brewster-Carver Coop. Apts., Bronxville, N.Y., 1987-88, pres. bd. dirs., 1988-89; lay min. of the Eucharist, lector St. Francis of Assisi Ch., 1987—. Mem. AAUW, Internat. Union of Cath. Press, Cath. Press Assn., St. Benedict the Moor Fraternity (gov. coun., rec. sec. 1982-88, 91-95), Secular Franciscan Order N.Y.C. Avocations: concerts, theater, opera and operettas, urban walking, museums. Office: The Christophers Inc 12 E 48th St New York NY 10017-1008

O'CONNELL, MARY ANN, state senator, business owner; b. Albuquerque, Aug. 3, 1934; d. James Aubrey and Dorothy Nell (Batsel) Gray; m. Robert Emmett O'Connell, Feb. 21, 1977; children: Jeffery Crampton, Gray Crampton. Student, U. N.Mex., Internat. Coun. Shopping Ctrs. Exec. dir. Blvd. Shopping Ctr., Las Vegas, Nev., 1968-76, Citizen Pvt. Enterprise, Las Vegas, 1976; media supr. Southwest Advt., Las Vegas, 1977—; owner, operator Meadows Inn, Las Vegas, 1985—, 3 Christian bookstores, Las Vegas, 1985—; state senator Nev. Senate, 1985—; chmn. govtl. affairs; vice chmn. commerce and labor; mem. taxation com.; vice chmn. Legis. Commn., 1985-86, 95-96; mem., 1987-88, 91-93; commr. Edn. Commn. States; rep. Nat. Conf. State Legislators; past vice chair State Mental Hygiene & Mental Retardation Adv. Bd. Pres. explorer div. Boulder Dam Area coun. Boy Scouts Am., Las Vegas, 1979-80, former mem. exec. bd.; mem. adv. bd. Boy Scouts Am.; pres., bd. dirs. Citizens Pvt. Enterprise, Las Vegas, 1982-84, Secret Witness, Las Vegas, 1081-82; vice chmn. Gov.'s Mental Health-Mental Retardation, Nev., 1983—; past mem. community adv. bd. Care Unit Hosp., Las Vegas; past mem. adv. bd. Kidney Found., Milligan Coll., Charter Hosp.; tchr. Young Adult Sunday Sch. Recipient Commendation award Mayor O. Grayson, Las Vegas, 1975, Outstanding Citizenship award Bd. Realtors, 1975, Silver Beaver award Boy Scouts Am., 1980, Free Enterprise award Greater Las Vegas C. of C., Federated Employers Assn., Downtown Breakfast Exch., 1988, Award of Excellence for Women in Politics, 1989, Legislator of Yr. award Bldg. and Trades, 1991, Legislator of Yr. award Nat. ASA Trade Assn., 1991, 94, Guardian of Liberty award Nev. Coalition of Conservative Citizens, 1991, Internat. Maxi Awards Promotional Excellence, Guardian of Small Bus. award Nat. Fedn. Ind. Bus., 1995-96; named Legislator of Yr., Nev. Retail Assn., 1992. Mem. Retail Mchts. Assn. (former pres., bd. dirs.), Taxpayers Assn. (bd. dirs.), Greater Las Vegas C. of C. (past pres., bd. dirs., Woman of Achievement Politics women's coun. 1988). Republican. Mem. Christian Ch. Avocations: china painting, reading. Home: 7225 Montecito Cir Las Vegas NV 89120-3118 Office: Nev Legislature Senate 401 S Carson St Carson City NV 89701-4747

O'CONNELL, MAURICE DANIEL, lawyer; b. Ticonderoga, N.Y., Nov. 9, 1929; s. Maurice Daniel and Leila (Geraghty) O'C.; m. Joan MacLure Landers, Aug. 2, 1952; children: Mark M., David L., Ann M., Leila K., Ellen A. Grad., Phillips Exeter Acad., 1946; A.B., Williams Coll., 1950; LL.B., Cornell U., 1956. Bar: Ohio 1956. Since practiced in Toledo; assoc. Williams, Eversman & Black, 1956-60; ptnr. Robison, Curphey & O'Connell, 1961-95, of counsel, 1996—; spl. hearing officer in conscientious objector cases U.S. Dept. Justice, 1966-68; mem. complaint rev. bd. Bd. Commrs. on Grievance and Discipline of Supreme Ct. Ohio, 1987. Mem. Ottawa Hills Bd. Edn., 1963-66, pres., 1967-69; former trustee Toledo Soc. for Handicapped; past trustee Woodlawn Cemetery; past trustee Toledo Hearing and Speech Center, Easter Seal Soc.; mem. alumni council Phillips Exeter Acad. Served to 1st lt. USMCR, 1950-53. Fellow Ohio State Bar Found.; mem. NW Ohio Alumni Assn. of Williams Coll. (past pres.), ABA, Ohio Bar Assn., Toledo Bar Assn. (chmn. grievance com. 1971-74), Kappa Alpha, Phi Delta Phi. Club: Toledo. Home: 3922 W Bancroft St Toledo OH 43606-2533 Office: Four SeaGate 9th Fl Toledo OH 43604

O'CONNELL, PATRICK MICHAEL, naval officer; b. Washington, Nov. 11, 1948; s. William Patrick O'Connell and Audrey Lucille (Inscoe) Robertson; married; children: Patrick Michael, Mary Kelly, Caitlin Elizabeth, Thomas Earl. BA, U. Va., Monterey, Calif., 1970; MS, Naval Postgrad. Sch., Va., 1977; PhD, George Washington U., 1990. Cert. USN Aerospace Engr., project mgmt. profl., naval aviator. Commd. USN, advanced through grades to capt.; project mgr. Space and Naval Warfare Systems Command, Washington, 1982-83; program mgr. Tactical Jet Airdraft KA-6D USN, Norfolk, Va., 1986-89; project mgr. cruise missiles program USN, Washington, 1989-91, joint project mgr. unmanned aerial vehicles, 1990-91, major program mgr. Nat. Reconnaissance Office, 1991-95; dir. Space R&D Office Naval Rsch., Washington, 1995—; Chmn. U.S. Space Tech. Consrotium, Washington; adj. prof. George Washington U., Washington. Head soccer coach Springfield (Va.) Youth Club, 1980-96. Recipient Meritorious Svc. award USN, 1987, 90, Def. Meritorious Svc. award Dept. Def., 1992, Joint Svc. Commendation award USN, 1994. Mem. IEEE (sr.), Project Mgmt. Inst. Avocations: power lifting, jogging. Home: 8007 Pyracantha Ct Springfield VA 22153 Office: Office Naval Rsch 800 N Quincy St Arlington VA 22203-1906

O'CONNELL, PAUL EDMUND, publisher; b. Cambridge, Mass., Dec. 15, 1924; s. William Henry and Catherine O'C.; m. Phyllis B. Borgeson, July 18, 1970; children—Eileen Lucy, Brian Paul, Philip Bartlett, Douglas John, Donald Paul, Lori Ann, Stephanie Elizabeth, Kirsten Lynn. A.B., Harvard U., 1949. Salesman Am. Tobacco Co., 1949-50; sales rep. dept. coll. texts Prentice-Hall Co., 1950-58, editor, 1958-62, exec. editor, asst. v.p., 1963-68; chmn. Winthrop Pubs. Inc. subs. Prentice Hall Co., Cambridge, Mass., 1969-81; cons., 1981-82; sr. acquisition editor Bobbs-Merrill Ednl. Pubs., 1983-84; sr. editor Dorsey Press, 1985-88, Lexington Books, 1988-91; pub. cons., 1991—. Served with AC U.S. Army, 1943-47. Decorated Purple Heart. Home: 60 Pleasant St Apt 221 Arlington MA 02174-6519

O'CONNELL, PHILIP RAYMOND, retired lawyer, paper company executive; b. N.Y.C., June 2, 1928; s. Michael Joseph and Ann (Blaney) O'C.; m. Joyce McCabe, July 6, 1957; children: Michael, Kathleen, Jennifer, David. AB, Manhattan Coll., 1949; LLB, Columbia U., 1956; grad., Advanced Mgmt. Program, Harvard U., 1967. Bar: N.Y. 1956, U.S. Supreme Ct. 1961, Conn. 1988. Assoc. Dewey, Ballantine, Bushby, Palmer & Wood, N.Y.C., 1956-61, 62-64; gen. counsel, sec. Laurentide Finance Corp., San Francisco, 1961-62; gen. counsel Wallace-Murray Corp., 1964-66, div. mgr., 1966-70; pres., chief exec. officer, dir. Universal Papertech Corp., Hatfield, Pa., 1970-71; sec. Champion Internat. Corp., Stamford, Conn., 1972-90, v.p., 1979-81, sr. v.p., 1981-90; mem. legal adv. com. N.Y. Stock Exch., 1985-88, corp. governance subcom., legal adv. com., 1985-94; chmn. lawyers steering com. corp. governance task force The Bus. Roundtable, 1981-87, mem., 1981-94. Mem. Champion Internat. Found., 1979-90; mem. bd. visitors Fairfield Univ. Sch. Bus., 1981-93, chmn., 1983-93; bd. dirs. Kearney-Nat. Corp., 1975-78. With USNR, 1951-54. Mem. Am. Soc. Corp. Secs. (hon.; chmn. 1988-89).

O'CONNELL, ROBERT FRANCIS, physics educator; b. Athlone, Ireland, Apr. 22, 1933; came to U.S., 1958; s. William and Catherine (O'Reilly) O'C.; m. Josephine Molly Buckley, Aug. 3, 1963; children: Adrienne Molly, Fiona Catherine, Eimear Kathleen. BSc, Nat. U. Ireland, Galway, 1953, DSc, 1975; PhD, U. Notre Dame, 1962. Telecommunications engr. Dept. Posts and Telegraphs, Dublin, Ireland, 1954-58; scholar Inst. Advanced Studies, Dublin, 1962-63; systems analyst IBM, Dublin, 1963-64; sr. rsch. assoc. Inst. Space Studies, N.Y.C., 1966-68; asst. prof. physics La. State U., Baton Rouge, 1964-66, assoc. prof., 1966-69, prof., 1969-86, Boyd prof., 1986—. Editor for theoretical physics Hadronic Jour.; bd. mem. Phys. Rev. A; contbr. articles to profl. jours. Named Disting. Rsch. Master, La. State U., 1975; NAS-NRC fellow, 1966-68, Sci. Rsch. Coun. (Eng.) sr. vis. fellow, 1976. Fellow Am. Phys. Soc.; mem. Am. Astron. Soc., Internat. Astronomy Union, Internat. Soc. Gen. Relativity and Gravitation. Republican. Roman Catholic. Avocation: tennis. Home: 522 Bancroft Way Baton Rouge LA 70808-4807 Office: La State Univ Dept Physics and Astronomy Baton Rouge LA 70803-4001

O'CONNELL, ROBERT JOHN, insurance company executive; b. N.Y.C., May 16, 1943; m. Claire M. Costantini; children: Kristin, Jared. BA, Fordham U., 1965; MA, U. Pa., 1966. With N.Y. Life Ins. Co., N.Y.C., 1970-89, v.p., 1983-86, sr. v.p., 1986-89; sr. v.p. group mgmt. divsn. AIG, 1989-91; pres., CEO AIG Life Ins. Cos., 1991—; also bd. dirs. A.I. Life; bd. dirs. AIG Life Ins. Co., AIG Equity Sales Corp., Delam Life Ins. Co.; mem. adv. com. to Cato Inst. project on Social Security Privatization. Mem. State Dept. Fin. Svcs. Corps Mission to Czechoslovakia. Mem. Am. Coun. Life Ins., Am. Internat. Life Assn. N.Y. (bd. dirs.). Home: 3040 North St Fairfield CT 06430-1624

O'CONNELL, WILLIAM EDWARD, JR., finance educator; b. N.Y.C., Sept. 16, 1937; s. William Edward and Helen Margaret (Brazel) O'C.; m. Janet Elinor Shields, Aug. 15, 1965; children: William Edward III, Cathleen Anne. AB, Manhattan Coll., 1959; MBA, Columbia U., 1961; D in Bus. Adminstrn. with honors, Ind. U., 1967; JD, Coll. William & Mary, 1974. Fin. analyst Pfizer, Inc., N.Y.C., 1962-64; asst. prof. U. Conn., Storrs, 1967-69; Morris prof. banking U. Va., Charlottesville, 1988; Chessie prof. bus. Coll. William and Mary, Williamsburg, Va., 1969—; mem. faculty Va. Bankers Sch., Chrlottesville, 1975—, Stonier Grad. Sch. Banking, Newark, 1977—, Bank Adminstrn. Inst., Madison, Wis., 1978—; dir. Citizens & Farmers Bank. Author: Asset & Liability Management, 1979, Advanced Financial Planning, 1984, Financial Planning for Credit Unions, 1989, Strategic Financial Management for Commercial Banks, 1993. Mem. Am. Fin. Assn., Fin. Mgmt. Assn., Beta Gamma Sigma, Omicron Delta Epsilon. Roman Catholic. Home: 102 Overlook Dr Williamsburg VA 23185-4434 Office: Coll William & Mary Sch Bus Williamsburg VA 23187-8795

O'CONNELL, WILLIAM RAYMOND, JR., educational consultant; b. Richmond, Va., Jan. 4, 1933; s. William Raymond and Mary Helen (Wenenger) O'C.; m. Peggy Annette Tucker, June 29, 1957; 1 child, William Raymond III. BMusEd, Richmond Profl. Inst., 1955; MA, Columbia U., 1962, EdD, 1969; HLD (hon.), New Eng. Coll., 1995. Asst. to provost Richmond (Va.) Profl. Inst., 1955-57, dean of men, 1957-59, dean of students, dean of men, 1959-61; asst. to provost, dir. student info. ctr. Tchrs. Coll. Columbia U., N.Y.C., 1962-65, rsch. asst. inst. of higher edn. Tchrs. Coll., 1965-66; rsch. assoc. So. Regional Edn. Bd., Atlanta, 1966-69, dir. spl. programs, 1969-73, project dir., undergrad. edn. reform, 1973-79; dir. curriculum and faculty devel. Assn. Am. Colls., Washington, 1979-80, v.p. for programs, 1980-82, v.p., 1982-85; pres. New Eng. Coll., Henniker, N.H., 1985-95; dir. health edn. and leadership program Nat. Assn. Student Personnel Adminstrs., 1996—; cons. Coun. for Advancement Small Colls., 1975; mem. adv. com. project on instnl. renewal through improvement of teaching Soc. for Values in Higher Edn., 1975-78; mem., evaluator N.H. Postsecondary Edn. Commn., 1987-95, vice chmn., 1990-92, chmn., 1992-94; evaluator Nat. Ctr. for Rsch. to Improve Postsecondary Teaching and Learning, 1987-90, New Eng. Assn. Schs. and Colls., 1988, 91; mem. higher edn. rev. panel awards for pioneering achievements in higher edn. Charles A Dana Found., 1988, 89. Author, editor articles in field. Pres. Richmond Cmty. Amb. Project, 1958-60, bd. dirs., 1960-61; bd. dirs. Alumni Assn. Acad. divsn. Va. Commonwealth U., 1970-73; trustee Atlanta Boys Choir, Inc., 1978-79, chmn. fundraising com., 1976-77; trustee Atlanta Coun. for Internat. Visitors, 1973-76, 78-79; pres. UN Assn., Atlanta, 1976, 77; mem. steering com. Nat. Coun. chpt. and divsn. pres. UN Assn. U.S., 1977-79, nat. coun., 1980-90; mem. steering com. Leadership Concord, 1992-95, chmn., 1994-95. Named Community Amb. to Sweden Community Amb. Project of the Experiment in Internat. Living, 1956. Fellow Royal Soc. of the Arts (U.K.); mem. Am. Assn. Higher Edn., Newcomen Soc. U.S., N.H. Coun. on World Affairs (bd. dirs. 1993-95), Greater Concord C. of C. (bd. dirs. 1989-93), Phi Delta Kappa. Methodist. Avocations: antiques, travel.

O'CONNER, LORETTA RAE, lawyer; b. Denver, Dec. 23, 1958; d. Ronald Lee and Norma Jareene (Warner) Barkdoll; m. George Ellis Bentley, Dec. 31, 1976 (div. 1979); m. Donald Hugh O'Conner, Feb. 3, 1987; children: Justin Lee, Brandon Craig. AS, Denver Acad. Ct. Reporting, 1983; BA summa cum laude, Regis U., 1992; JD, U. Colo., 1996. Bar: Colo., 1996. Ct. reporter Denver, 1983-87; dist. ct. reporter Judicial Dept., State of Colo., Pueblo, 1987-91; ct. reporter Pueblo, 1991-93; student atty. Pueblo County Legal Svcs.; pvt. practice Pueblo, 1996—. Chief justice Student Govt. Ct., U. So. Colo., Pueblo, 1992; trained facilitator Kettering Found., Pub. Policy Inst., Dayton, Ohio, 1992; sec. So. Colo. Registered Interpretors for Deaf, Pueblo, 1991. President's scholar U. So. Colo., 1991-92, Alumni Assn. scholar, 1991-92; grantee Kettering Found., 1992; Colo. Legislature grantee and scholar Regis U., 1992; Colo. Legislature grantee U. Colo. Sch. Law, 1993-95, Dean's scholar, Dazzo Scholar, King scholar U. Colo. Sch. Law, 1993-96. Mem. ATLA, ABA, Nat. Ct. Reporters Assn., Colo. Trial Lawyers Assn., Colo. Bar Assn., Colo. Womens Bar Assn., Colo. Ct. Reporters Assn., Boulder Bar Assn., Golden Key Soc., Phi Delta Phi (clk. 1994-95). Avocations: women's studies, political activism. Home and Office: 1911 N Santa Fe Ave Pueblo CO 81003

O'CONNOR, BETTY LOU, service executive; b. Phoenix, Oct. 29, 1927; d. Georg Eliot and Tillie Edith (Miller) Miller; m. William Spoeri O'Connor, Oct. 10, 1948 (dec. Feb. 1994); children: Thomas W., William K., Kelli Anne. Student, U. So. Calif., 1946-48, Calif. State U., Los Angeles, 1949-50. V.p. O'Connor Food Svcs., Inc., Jack in the Box Restaurants, Granada Hills, Calif., 1983-93; pres. O'Connor Food Svcs., Inc., Granada Hills, Calif., 1994—, Western Restaurant Mgmt. Co., Granada Hills, 1986—; mem. adv. bd. Bank of Granada Hills; bd. dirs. Nat. Franchise Purchasing Coop., nc. Recipient Frannie award Foodmaker, Inc., Northridge, Calif., 1984, First Rate award, 1992. Mem. Jack in the Box Franchisee Assn., Spurs Hon. (sec. U. So. Calif. 1947-48), Associated Women Students (sec. U. So. Calif. 1946-47), Gamma Alpha Chi (v.p. 1947-48), Chi Omega. Republican. Roman Catholic. Avocation: sewing. Office: Western Restaurant Mgmt Co 17545 Chatsworth St Granada Hills CA 91344-5720

O'CONNOR, CARROLL, actor, writer, producer; b. N.Y.C., Aug. 2, 1924; s. Edward Joseph and Elise Patricia (O'Connor) O'C.; m. Nancy Fields, July 28, 1951; 1 son, Hugh (dec.). B.A., Nat. U. Ireland, 1952; M.A., U. Mont., 1956, L.H.D. (hon.), 1985. Actor, Dublin, Cork, Limerick, Galway, London, Paris, Edinburgh, 1950-54; appeared in: Ulysses in Nightown, 1958, The Big Knife, 1959, Brothers, 1983, Home Front, 1984; TV appearance in The Sacco and Vanzetti Story, 1960; TV guest appearances on Armstrong Circle Theater; films include: Fever in the Blood, 1961, By Love Possessed, 1961, Lad a Dog, 1961, Lonely Are the Brave, 1962, Cleopatra, 1963, Not With My Wife, You Don't, 1966, Warning Shot, 1967, What Did You Do In The War Daddy?, 1968, Marlowe, 1969, Death of a Gunfighter, 1969, Kelly's Heroes, 1970, Doctors' Wives, 1971, Law and Disorder; TV film Brass, 1985; star TV series: All in the Family, 1971-79, Archie Bunker's Place, 1979-83, (also co-exec. producer) In The Heat of the Night, 1987-94; star TV spls. including: The Funny Papers, 1972, Of Thee I Sing, 1972, The Carroll O'Connor Special, 1973, The Last Hurrah, 1973. Recipient Emmy award for best actor, 1973, 77, 78, 79, 89; recipient George Foster Peabody award for broadcasting excellence, 1980; named to Hall of Fame Acad. TV Arts and Scis., 1990. Mem. The Players, Sigma Phi Epsilon. Address: 201 Tilden Ave Los Angeles CA 90019 *Everyone should rid himself of the illusion that his fulfillments are of much interest to anyone else.*

O'CONNOR, CHARLES P., lawyer; b. Boston, Sept. 29, 1940; m. Mary Linda Hogan; children: Jennifer, Amy, Austin, Catherine. Bachelors degree, Holy Cross Coll., Worcester, Mass., 1963; LLB, Boston Coll., 1966. Bar: Mass. 1966, D.C. 1968, U.S. Supreme Ct. 1974. Atty., gen. counsel's office NLRB, Washington, 1966-67; assoc. Morgan, Lewis & Bockius, LLP, Washington, 1968-71; ptnr. Morgan, Lewis & Bockius, Washington, 1971—, chmn. labor and employment law sect., 1996—, mng. ptnr. Washington office, 1995-97; gen. counsel Major League Baseball Player Rels. Com., N.Y.C., 1989-94. Contbr. numerous articles on labor and employment law to law jours. spl. counsel elections com. U.S. Ho. of Reps., Washington, 1968-69. Mem. ABA, D.C. Bar Assn., Belle Haven Country Club, N.Y. Athletic Club. Home: 6121 Vernon Ter Alexandria VA 22307-1152 Office: Morgan Lewis & Bockius 1800 M St NW Ste 800 Washington DC 20036-5802

O'CONNOR, DANIEL WILLIAM, retired religious studies and classical languages educator; b. Jersey City, Mar. 17, 1925; s. Daniel William and Emma Pauline (Ritz) O'C.; m. Carolyn Lockwood, June 26, 1954; children—Kathlyn Forssell Beal, Daniel William III. B.A., Dartmouth Coll., 1945; M.A., Columbia U., 1956, Ph.D., 1960; M.Div., Union Theol. Sem., 1950. Ordained to ministry United Ch. of Christ, 1950. Mem. exec. com., bd. home missions Congl. Chs., 1946-51; pastor Paramus Congl. Ch., N.J., 1950-55; assoc. sec. Student Christian Movement YMCA, N.Y., 1947-48; exec. sec. Earl Hall Columbia U., N.Y.C., 1948-50; tutor asst., dept. N.T. Union Theol. Sem., N.Y.C., 1958-59; successively asst. prof., assoc. prof., prof. religious studies and classical langs. St. Lawrence U., Canton, N.Y., 1959-67, dir. summer session, 1966, assoc. dean coll., 1967-68, Charles A. Dana prof. religious studies and classical langs., 1967-89, chmn. dept. religious studies and classical langs., 1974-89, Charles A. Dana emeritus prof., 1989—. Author: Peter in Rome, 1969; contbr. articles to Ency. Britannica and profl. jours., also revs. Trustee Silver Bay Assn. YMCA, N.Y., 1978-86, 86-92, Lit. Vols. Am., St. Lawrence County, N.Y., 1991-94; bd. dirs. U.S. Power Squadron, St. Lawrence Squadron, N.Y., 1972-75. With USNR, 1943-45. Grantee Lilly Found., Columbia U., 1969-70, Mellon Found., Am. Schs. Oriental Research, Jerusalem, 1979. Mem. AAUP, Am. Assn. Ret. Persons, Adirondack Mountain Club, Rotary (pres. Canton Club 1972-73, Rotary Found. scholarship selection com. dist. 7040 1983-87, 96—, dist. gov.

7040 1987-88, dist. 7040 ext. com. 1988-89, youth exch. com. dist. 7040 1990-93, lit. com. 1991-93). Home: 3 Hillside Cir Canton NY 13617-1409

O'CONNOR, DONALD THOMAS, lawyer; b. Lackawana, N.Y., Apr. 14, 1935; s. Thomas Joseph and Edna Mabel (Thomas) O'C.; children: Kevin M., David T., Donna M., Cheryl L. Grad., U. Buffalo, 1957; LLB, Boston Coll., 1966. Bar: Mass., Pa. Asst. pers. supr. Continental Can Co., Tonawanda, N.Y., 1957-62; pers. supr. Continental Can Co., Natick, Mass., 1962-65; asst. div. mgr. labor rels. Weyerhaeuser Co., Fitchburg, Mass., 1956-66; field atty. NLRB, Pitts., 1966-67; assoc. Berkman, Ruslander, Pohl, Lieber & Engel, Pitts., 1967-71; ptnr. Randolph & O'Connor, P.C., Pitts., 1971-74; ptnr. Buchanan Ingersoll, P.C., Pitts., 1974—, chmn. labor sect., 1984-88, co-chmn. labor sect., 1988-90; speaker in field. Contbr. articles to profl. jours. Solicitor Twp. of Penn Hills, Pa., 1971. Mem. ABA, Pa. Bar Assn., Allegheny County Bar Assn. (chmn. labor sect. 1971-73), St. Thomas More Soc. (treas. 1970-72), Rivers Club, Alcoma Golf Club (Penn Hills). Republican. Avocations: golf, sailing, water skiing, reading, dancing. Home: 1414 Towne Square Dr Allison Park PA 15101-1951 Office: Buchanan Ingersoll One Oxford Ctr 301 Grant St Ste 20 Pittsburgh PA 15219-1408

O'CONNOR, DORIS JULIA, non-profit fundraiser, consultant; b. N.Y.C. Apr. 30, 1930; d. Joseph D. and Mary (Longinotti) Bisagni; m. Gerard T. O'Connor, Oct. 8, 1950 (div. Dec. 1972); 1 dau., Kim C. BA cum laude in Econs., U. Houston, 1975. Adminstrv. asst. Shell Cos. Found., Inc., N.Y.C., 1966-71, asst. sec., Houston, 1971-73, sec., 1973-76, sr. v.p., dir., mem. exec. com., 1976-93; prin. Doris O'Connor & Co., 1993—; Corp. assoc. United Way of Am., Washington, 1976-93; corp. advisor Bus. Com. of Arts, N.Y.C., 1976-91; del. Bus. Com. of Arts, Houston, 1982-87; dir. Ind. Sector, Washington, 1981-89, vice chmn., 1983-87; mem. contbns. coun. Conf. Bd., N.Y.C., 1976-93; advisor Coun. of Better Bus. Burs., Washington, 1975-94, vice chmn., 1983-87; commr. adv. commn. on work based learning Dept. Labor, 1991-93; mem. Houston/Harris County Arts Task Force, 1991-93, Houston Ind. Sch. Dist. Task Force, 1991-93; bd. trustees Houston Grand Opera, 1993—, Houston Symphony Orch., 1993—, Houston Symphony Soc., 1993—, Soc. Performing Arts, 1993—, Cultural Arts Coun., 1993-96, Greater Houston Coalition Edn. Excellence, 1993-96; mem. adv. bd. Ctr. for Edn. Rice U., The Houston Zool. Soc., 1993—. Mem. Nat. Soc. Fundraising Execs. (Houston com. on fgn. rels. 1993—), Omicron Delta Epsilon. Club: Pla. (bd. govs. 1987-89).

O'CONNOR, EARL EUGENE, federal judge; b. Paola, Kans., Oct. 6, 1922; s. Nelson and Mayme (Scheetz) O'C.; m. Florence M. Landis, Nov. 3, 1951 (dec. May 1962); children: Nelson, Clayton; m. Jean A. Timmons, May 24, 1963; 1 dau., Gayle. B.S., U. Kans., 1947, LL.B., 1950. Bar: Kans. 1950. Practiced in Mission, Kans., 1950-51; asst. county atty. Johnson County, Kans., 1951-53; probate and juvenile judge, 1953-55; dist. judge 10th Jud. Dist., Olathe, Kans., 1955-65; justice Kans. Supreme Ct., 1965-71; judge U.S. Dist. Ct., Dist. of Kans., Kansas City, 1971—, chief judge, 1981-92; mem. Jud. Conf. U.S., 1988-91. Served with AUS, World War II, ETO. Mem. ABA, Nat. Conf. Fed. Trial Judges, Kans. Bar Assn., Phi Alpha Delta. Office: 628 US Courthouse 500 State Ave Kansas City KS 66101-2403

O'CONNOR, EDWARD CORNELIUS, army officer; b. Middlesex County, Mass., June 22, 1931; s. Edward Denis and Gladys Marie (Devine) O'C.; m. Charlotte Hubble, June 1, 1958. A.B., Boston Coll., 1952; M.S., U. N.C., 1966; M.S. George Washington U., 1979. Commd. 2d lt. U.S. Army, 1952, advanced through grades to maj. gen., 1981; asst. for NATO Affairs, Office of Sec. Def., 1970-72; sec. Joint Staff, Vietnam, 1972; chief staff Joint Mil. Commn., Vietnam, 1973; arty. comdr. 1st Armored Div., Europe, 1973-74; Fed. Exec. fellow Brookings Inst., Washington, 1975-76; chief Army Initiatives Group, Army Staff, Pentagon, 1976-77; dep. dir. ops. Nat. Mil. Command Center, Joint Chiefs of Staff, Washington, 1977-78; asst. div. comdr. (maneuver) 1st Armored Div., Europe, 1978-79; chief nuclear activities SHAPE, Belgium, 1979-82; dir. ops., readiness and mobilization ODCSOPS, Dept. Army, 1982-83; comdg. gen. Security Affairs Command Army Material Command, 1983-86; chief exec. officer, pres. Global Mktg. Corp. (doing bus. as GMA Internat., Inc.), 1986—; chmn. Contraves, Inc., Pitts., 1992—; mem. policy working group U.S. State Dept. Def. Trade Adv. Group, Washington, 1994—; internat. lectr. in field. Author: Performance Appraisal, 1966. Chmn. Harvard U. Grad. Sch. rels. com. Decorated D.S.M., Legion of Merit with 3 oak leaf clusters, Bronze Star, Air medal with 6 oak leaf clusters, Army Commendation medal with V device and 7 oak leaf clusters, Def. Meritorious Service medal, Def. Superior Service medal, Joint Service Commendation with oak leaf cluster, Identification Badges of Sec. Def. Office, Joint Chiefs of Staff and Army Gen. Staff. Mem. Harvard U. Alumni Assn. (bd. dirs. 1989-93). Address: 10202 Eagle Landing Ct Burke VA 22015-2524

O'CONNOR, EDWARD GEARING, lawyer; b. Pitts., May 5, 1940; s. Timothy R. and Irene B. (Gearing) O'C.; m. Janet M. Showalter, June 17, 1972; children: Mark G., Susan M. BA, Duquesne U., 1962, JD, 1965. Bar: Pa. 1965, U.S. Dist. Ct. (we. dist.) Pa. 1965, U.S. Ct. Appeals (3d cir.) 1968, U.S. Supreme Ct. 1976. Assoc. Eckert, Seamans, Cherin & Mellott, Pitts., 1965-72, ptnr., 1973—; mem. adv. com. on appellate ct. rules Supreme Ct. Pa., 1986-92. Editor Duquesne U. Law Rev., 1964-65. Chmn. Hampton (Pa.) Twp. Planning Commn., 1986-87; mem. Hampton (Pa.) Twp. Zoning Hearing Bd., 1997—; bd. dirs. Pa. Health Choice Plan, St. Francis Health Sys., Duquesne U.; trustee Noble J. Dick Edn. Fund, 1989—. Recipient Disting. Alumni award Duquesne U. Law Rev., 1985, Disting. Law Alumni award Duquesne U. Sch. Law, 1991, Disting. Svc. award Hampton Twp., 1991, McAnulty Svc. award Duquesne U., 1992; named Century Club Disting. Alumni, Duquesne U., 1985. Fellow Am. Bar Found., Pa. Bar Found.; mem. Pa. Bar Assn. (ho. of dels. 1985-90), Acad. Trial Lawyers Allegheny County (bd. govs. 1986-89), Duquesne U. Alumni Assn. (pres. 1980-82, 88-90, bd. govs. 1982-90, bd. dirs. 1988-89), Duquesne Club, Pitts. Athletic Assn. Republican. Roman Catholic. Home: 4288 Green Glade Ct Allison Park PA 15101-1202 Office: Eckert Seamans Cherin & Mellott 600 Grant St Ste 42D Pittsburgh PA 15219-2703

O'CONNOR, FRANCIS PATRICK, state supreme court justice; b. Boston, Dec. 12, 1927; s. Thomas Lane and Florence Mary (Hagerty) O'C.; m. Ann Elizabeth O'Brien; children: Kathleen, Francis P., Brien T., Maureen T., Ellen M., Ann E., Jane C., Joyce E., Thomas J., Matthew P. AB, Holy Cross Coll., 1950; LLB, Boston Coll., 1953; JD (hon.), Suffolk U., 1983, New Eng. Sch. Law, 1984. Bar: Mass. 1953. Assoc. Friedman, Atherton, Sisson & Kozol, Boston, 1954-57, Mason, Crotty, Dunn & O'Connor, Worcester, Mass., 1957-73, Wolfson, Moynihan, Dodson & O'Connor, Worcester, 1974-75; judge Mass. Superior Ct., 1976-81; assoc. judge Mass. Supreme Ct., 1981—. Office: Mass Supreme Jud Ct Pemberton Sq 1300 New Courthouse Boston MA 02108

O'CONNOR, FRANCIS X., financial executive; b. Bklyn., May 7, 1929; s. Richard B. and Mary (McCafferty) O'C.; m. Leona A. Windorf, June 30, 1951; children: Francis X., Edward K., Brendan T., Richard B. III, A. Bruce, Marianne, Margaret, Leona. BS, St. Peter's Coll., 1951. CPA, N.Y., N.J. Audit mgr. Coopers & Lybrand, N.Y.C., 1951-65; controller Ward Foods, Inc., N.Y.C., 1965-66, v.p. fin., CFO, 1966-72, also bd. dirs., 1968-73; v.p. fin., CFO UMC Industries, Inc., N.Y.C., 1973-76; v.p. fin. and corp. devel., CFO SKF Industries, Inc., King of Prussia, Pa., 1976-87; v.p. corp. fin. Moore & Schley Securities Corp., Morristown, N.J., 1987-89; mng. dir. Sterling Manhattan Corp. Investment Bankers, N.Y.C., 1989-93; adv. bd. Boyden Cons. Corp. Mem. AICPA, AIM, N.Y. State Soc. CPAs. Fin. Excs. Inst., Nat. Conf. on Power Transmission (trustee), Machinery and Allied Products Inst. Fin. Coun., St. Peter's Coll. Alumni Assn. (trustee, past pres. Monmouth chpt.), Navy League U.S., Spring Lake Golf Club, (past pres., trustee), Seaview Country Club (N.J.), Green Gables Croquet Club (past pres.), Legacy Golf Club (Ft. Pierce, Fla.). Home: 2355 NE Ocean Blvd Stuart FL 34996-2945

O'CONNOR, GAYLE MCCORMICK, law librarian; b. Rome, N.Y., July 8, 1956; d. John Joseph and Barbara Jane (Molyneaux) McC. Head libr. Bolling, Walter & Gawthrop, Sacramento, 1987-88, Weintraub, Genshlea & Sproul, Sacramento, 1988-93, Brobeck, Phleger & Harrison, San Diego, 1993-96; legal cons., author, 1996—; instr. law Lincoln U., Sacramento. Contbr. articles to profl. jours. Mem. ABA (tech. show bd.), No. Calif. Assn. Law Librs., So. Calif. Assn. Law Librs., Am. Assn. Law Librs., Spl. Librs. Assn. (chair legal divsn. 1997—). Avocations: bodybuilding, skiing.

O'CONNOR, SISTER GEORGE AQUIN (MARGARET M. O'CONNOR), college president, sociology educator; b. Astoria, N.Y., Mar. 5, 1921; d. George M. and Joana T. (Loughlin) O'C. B.A., Hunter Coll., 1943; M.A., Catholic U. Am., 1947; Ph.D. (NIMH fellow), NYU, 1964; LL.D. Manhattan Coll., 1983; DPed (hon.), Dowling Coll., 1997; DHL, St. Francis Coll., 1997, St. Joseph's Coll., 1997. Mem. faculty St. Joseph's Coll., Bklyn., 1946—; prof. sociology and anthropology St. Joseph's Coll., 1966—, chmn. social sci. dept., 1966-69, pres., 1969—; Fellow African Studies Assn., Am. Anthrop. Assn.; Bklyn. C. of C. (dir. 1973—), Alpha Kappa Delta, Delta Epsilon Sigma. Author: The Status and Role of West African Women: A Study in Cultural Change, 1964. Office: Saint Joseph's Coll Office of Pres 245 Clinton Ave Brooklyn NY 11205-3602

O'CONNOR, G(EORGE) RICHARD, ophthalmologist; b. Cin., Oct. 8, 1928; s. George Leo and Sylvia Johanna (Voss) O'C. AB, Harvard U., 1950; MD, Columbia U., 1954. Resident in ophthalmology Columbia-Presbyn. Med. Center, N.Y.C., 1957-60; research fellow Inst. Biochemistry, U. Uppsala, Sweden, 1960-61, State Serum Inst., Copenhagen, 1961-62; asst. prof. ophthalmology U. Calif., San Francisco, 1962-68; prof. U. Calif., 1972-84; dir. Francis I. Proctor Found. for Research in Ophthalmology, 1970-84; mem. Nat. Adv. Eye Council NIH, 1974-78. Author: (with G. Smolin) Ocular Immunology, 1981; asso. editor: Am. Jour. Ophthalmology, 1976-81. Served with USPHS, 1955-57. Recipient Janeway prize Coll. of Physicians and Surgeons, Columbia U., 1954; Doyne medal Oxford U., 1984; NIH grantee, 1962-84. Mem. Am. Bd. Ophthalmology (examiner), Assn. for Rsch. in Vision and Ophthalmology (trustee 1979-83, pres. 1982-83, Weisenfeld award 1990), AMA, Am. Ophthal. Soc., Calif. Med. Assn., Frederic C. Cordes Eye Soc., Pan Am. Ophthal. Assn. Republican. Presbyterian. Club: Faculty. Home: 22 Wray Ave Sausalito CA 94965-1831 Office: U Calif Med Ctr 315-S San Francisco CA 94143

O'CONNOR, JAMES ARTHUR, theatre educator; b. Buffalo, Nov. 24, 1937; s.Bernard and Elsie (Thoman) O'C.; children: Anita, Lisa. BS, SUNY, 1960; MA, U. N.Mex., 1963; MFA, Pa. State U., 1969. Assoc. prof. art N.Mex. Inst. Tech., 1963-70; prof. theatre Purdue U., West Lafayette, Ind., 1978-97, chair theatre divsn., 1986-97, dir. theatre, 1987-97; chair, artistic dir. U. S.C., 1997—; stage dir. Repertory Theatre St. Louis, 1980-95, Stage West, Springfield, Mass., 1983, Alley Theatre, Houston, 1984, Walnut St. Theatre, Phila., 1995, others. Recipient Cleve. Critics Cir. award for Direction; nominated Joseph Jefferson award for Direction. Mem. Univ./Resident Theatre Assn. (v.p. 1986-92, pres. 1992-96). Office: U SC Dept Theatre Speech Dance Columbia SC 29208

O'CONNOR, JAMES JOHN, utility company executive; b. Chgo., Mar. 15, 1937; s. Fred James and Helen Elizabeth O'Connor; m. Ellen Louise Lawlor, Nov. 24, 1960; children: Fred, John (dec.), James, Helen Elizabeth. BS, Holy Cross Coll., 1958; MBA, Harvard U., 1960; JD, Georgetown U., 1963. Bar: Ill. 1963. With Commonwealth Edison Co., Chgo., 1963—, asst. to chmn. exec. com., 1964-65, comml. mgr., 1966, asst. v.p., 1967-70, v.p., 1970-73, exec. v.p., 1973-77, pres., 1977-87, chmn., 1980—; CEO, also bd. dirs.; chmn., CEO Unicom Corp., 1994—; bd. dirs. Corning, Inc., Chgo. Bd. of Trade, Tribune Co., United Air Lines, Scotsman Industries, Am. Nat. Can., 1st Chgo. NBD Corp., 1st Nat. Bank Chgo.; past chmn. Nuc. Power Oversight Com., Edison Electric Inst., bd. dirs.; chmn. Advanced Reactor Corp. Mem. The Bus. Coun.; bd. dirs. Assocs. Harvard U. Grad. Sch. Bus. Adminstrn., Lyric Opera, Helen Brach Found.; bd. dirs., trustee Mus. Sci. and Industry; past chmn. Met. Savs. Bond Campaign; trustee Northwestern U.; bd. dirs., past chmn. Chgo. Urban League, Chicagoland C. of C.; past chmn. bd. trustees Field Mus. Natural History; life trustee Adler Planetarium; mem. exec. bd. Chgo. area Coun. Boy Scouts Am.; chmn. Cardinal Bernardin's Big Shoulders Fund; exec. v.p. The Hundred Club Cook County; dir., past pres. Cath. Charities; past chmn., hon. dir. Am. Cancer Soc., Chgo. Conv. and Tourism Bur. With USAF, 1960-63. Mem. ABA, Ill. Bar Assn., Chgo. Bar Assn., Chgo. Assn. Commerce and Industry (bd. dirs., chmn.), Ill. Bus. Roundtable, Chicagoland C. of C. (dir., past chmn.). Home: 1500 N Lake Shore Dr # 5C Chicago IL 60610-1607 Office: Commonwealth Edison Co PO Box 767 1 1st Nat Plz Chicago IL 60690-0767

O'CONNOR, JENNIFER, lawyer; b. Somerville, Mass., Feb. 12, 1966; m. Paul J. Meyer, Nov. 13, 1993. BA in Govt. magna cum laude, Harvard U., 1987; MPA, Columbia U., 1992; JD magna cum laude, Georgetown U., 1997. Dep. press sec., econ. devel. assoc. Office of Manhattan Borough Pres Ruth Messinger, N.Y.C., 1990-92; budget specialist, N.E. regional polit. dir. Presdl. Transition Office, Little Rock, 1992-93; dep. dir. Office of Mgmt. and Adminstrn. The White House, Washington, 1993, spl. asst. to Pres. for Cabinet affairs, 1993-95, spl. asst. to Pres. Office Dep. Chief of Staff, 1995-96; dep. asst. sec. policy U.S. Dept. Labor, Washington, 1997—; field. dir. N.Y. primary campaign, polit. dir. N.J. primary campaign, dep. mgr. at Dem. Nat. Conv., state dir. Vt. gen. election campaign Clinton for Pres./Clinton-Gore '92, 1992. Democrat. Roman Catholic. Office: Office Asst Sec Policy US Dept Labor Washington DC 20210

O'CONNOR, JOHN DENNIS, academic administrator; b. Chgo., Mar. 20, 1942; married, 1964; 3 children. B.S., Loyola U, Chgo., 1963; M.S., DePaul U., 1966; Ph.D., Northwestern U., 1968. NIH fellow Mich. State U., East Lansing, 1968-70; asst. prof. biology UCLA, 1969-74, assoc. prof., 1974-77, prof. biology, 1977-81, chmn. biology, 1979-81, dean, life scis., 1981-87; vice chancellor for research, dean of grad. sch., prof. biology U. N.C.; prof. biology U. N.C., Chapel Hill, 1988-91; chancellor, prof. biology U. Pitts., 1991-95; provost Smithsonian Instn., Washington, 1996—; vis. prof. U. Nijmegen, Netherlands, 1975-76, Monash U., 1977. Fellow AAAS; mem. Am. Soc. Zoology, Soc. Devel. Biology, Am. Soc. Molecular Biology and Biochemistry, Bus. Higher Edn. (vice chair 1994-96, chair 1996—). Office: Smithsonian Instn Office of Provost 1000 Jefferson Dr SW Washington DC 20560-0008

O'CONNOR, JOHN JAY, III, lawyer; b. San Francisco, Jan. 10, 1930; s. John Jay and Sally (Flynn) O'C.; m. Sandra Day, Dec. 20, 1952; children: Scott, Brian, Jay. AB, Stanford U., 1951, LLB, 1953. Bar: Calif. 1953, Ariz. 1957, D.C. 1981. Mem. Fennemore, Craig, von Ammon & Udall, Phoenix, 1957-81, Miller & Chevalier, Washington, 1982-88; ptnr. Bryan Cave, Washington and Phoenix, 1988—; judge pro-tem Superior Ct. State of Ariz., 1979-81. Chmn. Ariz. Crippled Children's Services, 1968; Chmn. planning and zoning commn. Town of Paradise Valley, 1967; Chmn. Maricopa County Young Republicans, 1960, Ariz. Young Rep. League, 1962; bd. dirs. Ariz. Tax Research Assn., 1966-81; chmn. bd. dirs. Maricopa County Gen. Hosp., 1967-70; exec. com. bd. visitors Stanford Law Sch., 1976-80; pres. Stanford Law Fund, 1980-82; mem. nat. council Salk Inst. Biol. Studies, San Diego, 1977-90; pres. Phoenix-Scottsdale United Way, 1977-79; bd. dirs. World Affairs Council of Phoenix, 1970-81, Legal Aid Soc. Phoenix, Maricopa County Mental Health Assn.; trustee Meridian House Internat., Washington, 1982-88; mem. policy devel. com. Phoenix Community Service Fund, 1978; mem. exec. com. Valley Leadership, 1979-81; bd. dirs. Trusteeship for St. Luke's Hosp., 1979-81; mem. adv. com. Nat. Postal Mus., Washington, 1992—. Served to 1st lt. AUS, 1954-57. Mem. ABA, Stanford Assocs., Paradise Rotary (pres. 1977-78), Paradise Valley Country Club, Ariz. Club (pres. 1979-81), Valley Field Riding and Polo Club, Stanford Club of Phoenix (pres.), Iron Springs Club (pres. 1974-76), Bohemian Club, Met. Club, Alfalfa Club, Alibi Club, Ariz. Acad. Delta Upsilon, Phi Delta Phi. Office: Bryan Cave 700 13th St NW Washington DC 20005-3960

O'CONNOR, JOHN JOSEPH, insurance company executive; b. Worcester, Mass., Apr. 26, 1950; s. John J. and Alice M. (Grogan) O'C.; m. Mary Ellen Nyberg, July 10, 1976; children: Ryan J., Caitlin Mary, Kevin T. Assoc. Mech. Engring., Quinsigamond Community Coll., Worcester, 1971; BSBA cum laude, Worcester State Coll., 1988. Account rep. Wausau Ins. Cos., Worcester, 1975-81, field sales mgr., 1981-85; regional sales mgr. Wausau Ins. Cos., Boston, 1985-91; asst. v.p., corp. sales mgr. Wausau (Wis.) Ins. Cos., 1991-93, v.p. mktg. Mid Atlantic divsn., 1993—, dir. standard accounts, 1995—. Designer A to Z Strategic Planning Guide, Sales and Sales Management Fin. Planning Disk, 1991; creator Risk Mgmt. Audiocassette Tng. Tape. Exec. bd. Boy Scouts Am., Wausau, 1992—, den leader, 1987-91; pres. Holden (Mass.) Baseball, 1991, Everest Soccer Assn., Schofield, Wis., 1992—. Recipient Citizenship award Town of Holden/Holden Soccer, 1991, Outstanding Leadership award Boston Region, 1986. Mem. Exchange Club (bd. dirs. 1980-82, Merit award 1982). Avocations: biking, downhill skiing, youth sports coaching. Home: 1066 Victory Dr Yardley PA 19067-4517 Office: Wausau Ins Co 1700 Market St Philadelphia PA 19103-3913

O'CONNOR, JOHN JOSEPH, operations executive; b. Smyrna, Tenn., June 1, 1959; s. John O'Connor and Dolores Jane (Bell) Brem; m. Lea Ann Bradford, Sept. 6, 1986; 1 child, Colleen Michelle. BS, Tex. A&M U., 1981. Cert. marine engr. 3rd asst. engr. Marine Engrs. Beneficial Assn., Houston, 1981-84; asst. engr. Biehl Ship Mgmt., Houston, 1984; balance technician Hickham Industries, Inc., LaPorte, Tex., 1984-86, prodn. scheduler/Sulzer, 1986-87, project engr./Sulzer, 1987-88, engring. mgr./Sulzer, 1988-89; ops. mgr./Sulzer Hickham Industries, Inc., Huntington Beach, Calif., 1989-93; sr. engr., corp. mergers and acquisitions Hickham Industries, Inc., La Porte, Tex., 1993-94; tech. and field svc. mgr. Sulzer Turbosys. Internat., Houston, 1994—; guest speaker Tex. A&M U., Galveston, Tex., College Station, Tex., 1981-89, U. Houston, 1986-89; moderator Power Machinery and Compressor Conf., Houston, 1989. Prin. engr. inventions in field (Achievement awards 1989); author: Steam Turbine Overhaul and Repair Specifications, 1994. Bd. dirs. Cedar Lawn Assn., East End Presch. Recipient Outstanding Records in Engring., Gulf Oil Corp., Galveston, 1981. Mem. ASME (guest speaker convs.), Pacific Energy Assn. (guest speaker convs. 1990-92), Assn. of Former Students/Tex. A&M. Avocations: hiking, camping, travel, automotive restoration, litigation.

O'CONNOR, JOHN JOSEPH CARDINAL, archbishop, former naval officer; b. Phila., Jan. 15, 1920; s. Thomas Joseph and Dorothy Magdalene (Gomple) O'C. M.A., St. Charles Coll., 1949, Catholic U. Am., 1954; Ph.D., Georgetown U., 1970; D.R.E., Villanova (Pa.) U., 1976. Ordained priest Roman Cath. Ch., 1945, elevated to monsignor, 1966, consecrated bishop, 1979, created cardinal, 1985; served in Chaplain Corps U.S. Navy, 1952, advanced through grades to rear adm.; assigned to Atlantic and Pacific fleets U.S. Navy, Okinawa and Vietnam; sr. chaplain U.S. Naval Acad.; chief of chaplains U.S. Navy, Washington; aux. bishop, vicar gen. Mil. Vicariate, 1979-83; apptd. bishop of Scranton Pa., 1983-84; archbishop Archdiocese of N.Y., 1984—; Exec. bd. Nat. USO, Georgetown Center Strategic and Internat. Studies, Marine Corps Found. Author: Principles and Problems of Naval Leadership, 1958, A Chaplain Looks at Vietnam, 1969, In Defense of Life, 1981, (with Edward I. Koch) His Eminence and Hizzoner: A Candid Exchange, 1989, (with Elie Wiesel) A Journey of Faith, 1990. Decorated DMS, Legion of Merit (3), Meritorious Service medal. Mem. Am. Polit. Sci. Assn. Office: Archdiocese NY 452 Madison Ave New York NY 10022-6810*

O'CONNOR, JOHN MORRIS, III, philosophy educator; b. Evanston, Ill., Sept. 21, 1937; s. John Morris and Clare Evelyn (Merrick) O'C.; m. Mary Bittner, Dec. 31, 1960 (div.); 1 dau., Emily; m. Miranda E. P. Ind, Aug. 14, 1971 (div.); 1 dau., Amanda. Student, Georgetown U., 1955-56; B.A., Cornell U., 1959; M.A., Harvard U., 1962, Ph.D., 1965. Instr. Vassar Coll., 1964-66, asst. prof. philosophy, 1966-68; asst. prof. Case Western Res. U., Cleve., 1968-70, assoc. prof., 1970-77; exec. sec. Am. Philos. Assn. U. Del., Newark, 1977-84, assoc. prof., 1977-83; asst. dir. for programs Nat. Humanities Ctr., Research Triangle Park, N.C., 1983-87; dean Sch. Humanities William Paterson Coll., Wayne, N.J., 1987-91, dean Sch. Humanities, Mgmt. and Social Scis., 1991-92, coord. spl. projects Office of Provost, 1992-93, prof. philosophy, 1992—. Contbr. articles to profl. jours.; editor: (with others) Introductory Philosophy, 1967, Modern Materialism, 1969, Moral Problems in Medicine, 1976. Woodrow Wilson nat. fellow, 1959-60. Office: William Paterson Coll Dept Philosophy Wayne NJ 07470

O'CONNOR, JOHN T., civil engineering educator; b. N.Y.C., Feb. 11, 1933; married, 1966; 2 children. BCE, Cooper Union, 1955; MSCE, N.J. Inst. Tech., 1958; EngD, Johns Hopkins U., 1961. Sanitary engr. Elson T. Killam Sanit & Hydraulic Consulting Engrs., 1955-56; civil engr. George A. Fuller Constrn. Co., N.Y., 1956-57; sanitary engr. Parsons, Brinckerhoff, Quade & Douglas, 1957; asst. assoc. prof. sanitary engr. U. Ill., Urbana-Champaign, 1961-69, prof. civil engring., 1969-75; prof. civil engring. U. Mo., Columbia, 1975-92, chmn. dept., 1975-89; chief Ill. State Water Survey, 1992-95; pres. H20'C Ltd., 1995—. Mem. ASCE, Am. Chem. Soc., Am. Water Works Assn., Am. Soc. Limnology and Oceanography, Water Environment Fedn. Achievements include research on drinking water treatment processes; removal of microorganisms, organic substances, iron and manganese, radionuclides; wastewater treatment and disinfection; solid and hazardous waste site remediation. Address: 2118 Robert Dr Champaign IL 61821-6535

O'CONNOR, JOSEPH A., JR., lawyer; b. N.Y.C., Aug. 12, 1937; s. Joseph A. and Louise G. (Lucht) O'C.; children: Joseph A. III, Edward W. BA, Yale U., 1959; LLB, Columbia U., 1962. Bar: N.Y. 1963, U.S. Supreme Ct. 1968, Pa. 1973, Fla. 1978. Assoc. Davis, Polk & Wardwell, N.Y.C., 1963-72; ptnr. Morgan, Lewis & Bockius, Phila., 1972—. Mem. ABA, N.Y. State Bar Assn., Pa. Bar Assn., Fla. Bar Assn., Phila. Bar Assn., Assn. of Bar of City of N.Y. Roman Catholic. Club: Racquet (Phila.). Office: Morgan Lewis & Bockius LLP 2000 One Logan Sq Philadelphia PA 19103

O'CONNOR, JUDE, special education educator, consultant; b. Mt. Holly, N.J., Feb. 18, 1950; d. John Edward and Mary (Walsh) Rogerson; m. Kevin Francis O'Connor, July 7, 1973; children: Heather Jude, Kevin Francis Jr. BS in Elem. Edn. cum laude, Coll. of St. Joseph, Rutland, Vt., 1972; MA in Moderate Spl. Needs, Assumption Coll., Worcester, Mass., 1986. Cert. elem. and spl. edn. tchr., Mass. Tchr. spl. edn. Hoosick Falls (N.Y.) Elem. Sch., 1972-73; spl. edn. cons. Williams Syndrome Soc., 1976-80; spl. edn. tchr. Naquag Elem. Sch., Rutland, Mass., 1986-96, Holliston (Mass.) Middle Sch., 1996—; spl. edn. cons. Williams Syndrome Soc., Rutland, 1976—; leader insvc. tng. Wachusett Sch. Union, Holden, 1992. Author, pub.: I'm Not Lazy or Dumb, I Just Learn Differently, 1996; author of poetry. Coach Holden (Mass.) Softball League, 1985, 86, Naquag Basketball Team, Rutland, 1987-92. Mem. Am. Soc. for Learning Disabilities. Avocations: writing poetry and children's literature, reading. Home: 190 Lovell Rd Holden MA 01520-1602 Office: Holliston Middle Sch Linden St Holliston MA 01743

O'CONNOR, KARL WILLIAM, lawyer; b. Washington, Aug. 1, 1931; s. Hector and Lucile (Johnson) O'C.; m. Sylvia Gasbarri, Mar. 23, 1951 (dec.); m. Judith Ann Byers, July 22, 1972 (div. 1983); m. Eleanor Celler, Aug. 3, 1984 (div. 1986); m. Alma Hepner, Jan. 1, 1987 (div. 1996); children: Blair, Frances, Brian, Brendan. BA, U. Va., 1952, JD, 1958. Bar: Va. 1958, D.C. 1959, Am. Samoa 1976, Calif. 1977, Oreg. 1993. Law clk. U.S. Dist. Ct. Va., Abingdon, 1958-59; practice law Washington, 1959-61; trial atty. U.S. Dept. Justice, Washington, 1961-65; dep. dir. Men's Job Corps OEO, Washington, 1965-67; mem. civil rights div. Dept. of Justice, chief criminal sect., prin. dep. asst. atty. gen., 1967-75, spl. counsel for intelligence coordination, 1975; v.p., counsel Assn. of Motion Picture and Television Producers, Hollywood, Calif., 1975-76; assoc. justice Am. Samoa, 1976, chief justice, 1977-78; sr. trial atty. GSA Task Force, Dept. Justice, 1978-81; insp. gen. CSA, 1981-82; spl. counsel Merit Systems Protection Bd., Washington, 1983-86; U.S. atty. for Guam and the No. Marianas, 1986-89, ret.; pvt. practice Medford, Oreg., 1989—; Am. counsel O'Reilly Vernier Ltd., Hong Kong, 1992-93; ptnr. O'Connor & Vernier, Medford, Oreg., 1993-94; pvt. practice Medford, 1994—. Served with USMC, 1952-55. Mem. Oreg. Bar Assn., D.C. Bar Assn., Va. Bar Assn., Calif. Bar Assn., Am. Samoa Bar Assn., Phi Alpha Delta, Sigma Nu. Home: Box 112 4804 Dark Hollow Rd Medford OR 97501-0008 Office: 916 W 10th St Medford OR 97501-3018

O'CONNOR, KAY, state legislator; b. Everett, Wash., Nov. 28, 1941; d. Ernest S. and Dena (Lampers) Wells; m. Arthur J. O'Connor, Sept. 1, 1959; 6 children. Diploma, Lathrop H.S., Fairbanks, Alaska, 1959. Office mgr. Blaylock Chemicals, Bucyrus, Kans., 1981-84; store mgr. Copies Plus, Olathe, Kans., 1984-86; acct. Advance Concrete Inc., Spring Hill, Kans., 1986-92; mem. Kansas Ho. of Reps., 1993—; appropriations com., legis. edn. planning joint com. Kansas Ho. of Reps.; bd. dirs. Hometel Ltd.; author sch. voucher legis. for State of Kans., 1994, 95, 96. Republican. Roman Catholic. Avocations: choir dir., statue renovations, spkr. on sch. vouchers.

Home: 1101 N Curtis St Olathe KS 66061-2709 Office: PO Box 2232 Olathe KS 66051-2232

O'CONNOR, KEVIN JOHN, psychologist; b. Jersey City, N.J., July 18, 1954; s. John Lanning and Marilyn (Reynolds) O'C.; m. Ryan Michael, Matthew Benham. BA, U. Mich., 1975; PhD, U. Toledo, 1981. Clin. psychologist Blythedale Children's Hosp., Valhalla, N.Y., 1980-83; dir. Psychol. Svcs. Walworth Barbour Am. Internat. Sch., Kfar Shmaryahu, Israel, 1983-84; adjunct asst. prof. Dept. Psychology Iona Coll., New Rochelle, N.Y., 1984; clin. psychologist Northern Westchester Guidance Clinic, Mt. Kisco, N.Y., 1985; exec. dir., newsletter editor Assn. for Play Therapy, Fresno, Calif., 1982—; consulting psychologist Fresno (Calif.) Treatment Ctr., 1986-87, Diagnostic Sch. for Neurologically Handicapped Children, Fresno, Calif., 1986-90; adjunct faculty Pacific Grad. Sch. of Psychology, Palo Alto, Calif., 1987—, Calif. Sch. Profl. Psychology, Berkeley, Calif., 1988-89; prof. Calif. Sch. Profl. Psychology, Fresno, 1985—. Contbr. numerous presentations in field. Named Psychologist of Yr. San Joaquin Psychol. Assn., 1994. Fellow APA; mem. Assn. for Play Therapy, Mental Health Assn. Greater Fresno, San Joaquin Psychol. Assn., Western Psychol. Assn., Coun. for Nat. Register of Health Svc. Providers in Psychology. Democrat. Avocations: travel, art, ceramics. Office: Calif Sch Profl Psych 5130 E Clinton Way Fresno CA 93727-2014

O'CONNOR, MARY SCRANTON, public relations executive; b. New Haven, May 9, 1942; d. James T. and Mary E. (Scranton) O'C. BA, Manhattanville Coll., 1964. Women's editor Hartford Times, Conn., 1964-68; pub. rels. account exec. Wilson, Haight & Welch, Hartford, 1968-72, v.p., dir. pub. rels., 1972-75; pub. rels. cons. O'Connor/PR, Farmington, Conn., 1975-76; v.p. pub. rels. Lowengard & Brotherhood, Hartford, 1976-78, pres., 1978-83; pres. Harland, O'Connor, Tine & White, Hartford, 1983-84; v.p. communications Conn. Mut. Life Ins. Co., Hartford, 1984-88; pres. Bradford Advt., Inc., Old Saybrook, Conn., 1988-90; prin. Strategic Communications, Old Lyme, Conn., 1990-95; dir. com. and pub. rels. N.E. region Kaiser Permanente, Farmington, 1995-96; dir. pub. rels. and responsibility ConnectiCare, Inc., Farmington, 1996—; instr. pub. rels. mgmt. Manchester Community Coll., 1975. Bd. dirs. Child and Family Svcs., Inc., Hartford, 1980-89, Better Bus. Bur., 1980-83, Criminal Justice Edn. Ctr., 1981; trustee The Mark Twain House, Hartford, 1994-96. Recipient Woman of Yr. award YWCA, 1980. Mem. Pub. Rels. Soc. Am. (Merit award 1992), Greater Hartford C. of C. (bd. dirs. 1983-86). Office: ConnectiCare Inc 30 Batterson Park Rd Farmington CT 06032-2502

O'CONNOR, NEAL WILLIAM, former advertising agency executive; b. Milw., Aug. 25, 1925; s. Arthur J. and Helen (Radell) O'C.; m. Nancy K. Turner, July 8, 1950; children: Robert W., Thomas N., David J. B.S. cum laude, Syracuse U., 1949. With N.W. Ayer Inc., N.Y.C., 1949-80; v.p., mgr. N.Y. service N.W. Ayer Inc., 1962-65, pres., 1965-73, chmn. bd., 1973-76, chief exec. officer, 1966-76, chmn. exec. com., 1976-80; Past dir. Advt. Council; past. chmn. Am. Assn. Advt. Agys.; past pres. Consumer Research Inst. Pres. Found. for Aviation WWI, 1980—; past chmn. and pres. League of WWI Aviation Historians. With inf. AUS, 1943-45, ETO. Decorated Bronze Star, Combat Inf. badge. Mem. Beta Theta Pi, Alpha Delta Sigma. Clubs: Pretty Brook Tennis, Wings (N.Y.C.). Home: 10 Constitution Hl E Princeton NJ 08540-6749 Office: PO Box 212 Princeton NJ 08542-0212

O'CONNOR, PATRICIA RANVILLE, secondary and special education educator; b. Flint, Mich., Feb. 24, 1951; d. Marcel L. and Ruth Ellen (Smith) Ranville. BS, Ea. Mich. U., 1973, MA, 1978; MS in Adminstrn., Pepperdine U., 1995. Cert. tchr. (life) Calif., severely handicapped and learning handicapped, multiple subject, resource specialist. Spl. edn. tchr. Genessee Intermediate Sch. Dist., Flint, 1974-78, Barstow (Calif.) Unified Sch. Dist., 1978-81, Westport Sch., L.A., 1981-83; resource specialist Culver City (Calif.) Unified Sch. Dist., 1983-96, mentor tchr., chmn. dept. spl. edn., coord. sch. improvement program; asst. prin. mid. sch. El Segundo (Calif.) Unified Sch. Dist., 1996—; chair sch. site coun., self review com. Coordinated Compliance Review; chair lang. arts curriculum com. dist. El Segundo; team leader dept. edn. program quality rev. State of Calif.; mem. C.A.R.E. Team; reader, scorer Calif. Assessment Program; coord. sch. wide goal setting esteem program Striving for My Personal Best. Recipient Hon. Svc. award PTA. Mem. NEA, Calif. Tchrs. Assn. Home: 5460 White Oak Ave Apt 210C Encino CA 91316-2408

O'CONNOR, PAUL DANIEL, lawyer; b. Paterson, N.J., Nov. 24, 1936; s. Paul Daniel and Anne Marie Christopher O'C.; children: Steven Paul, Sheryl Lynn, Laura Ann. B.S. in Engring, U.S. Naval Acad., 1959; LL.B., U. Va., 1965. Bar: N.Y. 1965, Calif. 1995. Assoc. firm Winthrop, Stimson, Putnam & Roberts, N.Y.C., 1965-72; partner Winthrop, Stimson, Putnam & Roberts, 1972-80; sr. v.p., gen. counsel Singer Co., Stamford, Conn., 1980-86; chief exec. officer Citation Builders, 1986-95; trustee Valley Trusts, San Ramon, Calif., 1986—. 1st lt. USAF, 1959-62. Mem. Assn. of Bar of City of N.Y., Bar Assn. of San Francisco, Alameda County Bar Assn., Am. Horse Shows Assn., Fairfield County Hunt Club. Home: Unit 2 1150 Lombard St San Francisco CA 94109 Office: Valley Trusts 1999 Harrison St Ste 2040 Oakland CA 94612-3517

O'CONNOR, R. D., health care executive. BS Psychology, Sociology, U. So. Miss., 1960, MS Adminstrv. Personnel, 1961, PhD Mgmt., Orgnl. Communication, 1983. Asst. dean student affairs Holmes Jr. Coll., Goodman, Mo., 1961-64; spl. counselor vocat. rehab. divsn. Dept. Edn., Jackson, Mo., 1964-65; asst. adminstr. Hinds Gen. Hosp., Jackson, Mo., 1965-68; adminstr. Rankin Gen. Hosp., Brandon, Mo., 1968-76; v.p. Human Resources/ Mktg. Delta Mgmt. Systems, Metairie, La., 1976-79; asst. to exec. dir. Baptist Med. Ctr., Jacksonville, Fla., 1979-82; pres. RiverGroup Riverside Hosp., Rivercorp Inc., Riverside Found., Jacksonville, Fla., 1982-87; owner O'Connor & Assocs., Jacksonville, Fla., 1987-91; pres. Fla. 1st: Managed Health Care, Winter Haven, Orlando & Tampa, Fla., 1991-94; dir. orgn. devel. Mid Florida Med. Svcs. Inc., Winter Haven, Fla., 1994—; instr. U. So. Miss., Hattiesburg, Ms.; tchr., lectr. various univs., C.C.s, military acads.; grad. faculty coord. Webster U. Contbr. articles to profl. jours. and books. Commr. Cleary Heights Sewer Dist., 1978-79; pres'. selective task force Induction Procedures, 1969; chmn. personnel com. San Jose Baptist Ch., 1981-86, strategic planning com., 1986-87; gov's. com. Statewide Planning Vocat. Rehab., 1968; bd. dirs. Rankin County C. of C., 1970-73, exec. com., chmn. health affairs com., 1970-72, chmn. highway com. 1970-74, fin. com. 1971-73), Family Blood Assurance Program, 1972-77, v.p. 1977, Vol. Action Coun., 1973-76, United Givers Fund, 1973-76. With Air Nat. Guard, Med. Svc. Corps., ret. Fellow Am. Coll. Healthcare Execs.; mem. Fla. Hosp. Assn. (com. chmn. 1984), Greater Jacksonville Area Hosp. Coun. (chmn. 1985), Jackson-Vicksburg Hosp. Coun. (chmn. 1974), Nat. Assn. Mental Health (bd. dirs. 1973-74), Miss. Assn. Mental Health (pres. 1972-74), Miss. Hosp. Assn. (bd. dirs .1973-76, exec. devel. com. 1972-75, mgmt. engring. adminstrv. bd. 1973, fin. com. 1972-74, chmn. nominating com. 1971, coord. divsn. profl. practice 1970). Home: 2 Casarena Ct Winter Haven FL 33881-1290

O'CONNOR, RALPH STURGES, investment company executive; b. Pasadena, Calif., Aug. 27, 1926; s. Thomas Ireland and Edith Masury (Sturges) O'C.; m. Alice Maconda Brown, Apr. 28, 1950; children—George Rufus, Thomas Ireland III, Nancy Isabel, John Herman. B.A., Johns Hopkins, 1951. With Highland Resources, Inc., Houston, 1951-87, exec. v.p., 1961-64; pres. Highland Resources, Inc., 1964-87; pres., chief exec. officer Ralph S. O'Connor and Assocs., 1987—; chmn. bd. Arnaud's Restaurant, New Orleans, PanEnergy. Trustee emeritus Rice U., Houston Oldfields Sch., Glencoe, Md., Nat. Found. Advancement in the Arts. With USAAF, 1943-46. Mem. NAS (Pres.'s Circle), Am. Assn. Petroleum Landmen, All Am. Wildcatters. Clubs: Bayou (Houston), Ramada (Houston), River Oaks Country (Houston). Home: 5627 Indian Cir Houston TX 77056-1006 Office: Ralph S O'Connor & Assocs 1001 Fannin St Ste 622 Houston TX 77002-6707

O'CONNOR, RICHARD DENNIS, lawyer; b. Worcester, Mass., Oct. 22, 1937. BS, Coll. of Holy Cross, 1959; LLB, Georgetown U., 1964. Bar: Conn. 1964, U.S. Dist. Ct. Conn. 1964, U.S. Ct. Appeals (2d cir.) 1969, U.S. Dist. Ct. D.C. 1971, U.S. Supreme Ct. 1973, U.S. Ct. Appeals (D.C. cir.) 1974, Mass. 1985, U.S. Dist. Ct. Mass. 1985. Law clk. to hon. judge Clarie U.S. Dist. Ct. Conn., Hartford, 1964-65; prin., founding ptnr. Siegel, O'Connor, Schiff & Zangari, P.C., Hartford, 1965—; spkr. on labor issues, Conn., 1985-90; arbitrator Am. Arbitration Assn., Conn.; mem. Magistrate Reappointment Rev. Com., Conn.; arbitrator panel Gov.'s State Bd. of Edn., Conn., 1987—. Lt. USN, 1959-61. Mem. ABA (labor and employment law internat. labor law com. mgmt. co-chmn. 1992-95), ATLA, Conn. Bar Assn., Mass. Bar Assn., Fed. Bar Coun., Am. Assn. Hosp. Attys., Conn. Sch. Attys.' Coun. Office: Siegel OConnor Schiff & Zangari PC 150 Trumbull St Hartford CT 06103-2403

O'CONNOR, ROBERT JAMES, gynecologist, consultant; b. S.I., N.Y., Dec. 11, 1919; s. Robert and Anna (Lindsey) O'C.; B.S., Wagner Coll., 1941; M.A., Columbia U., 1947; M.D., SUNY, 1951; m. Olive Errington, Feb. 21, 1943; children: Robert, Carol, Richard. Intern S.I. Hosp., 1951-53; resident in ob-gyn, Woman's Hosp. N.Y., 1955-58; practice medicine specializing in ob-gyn, N.Y.C. and S.I., 1958—; attending physician in gynecology Sea View Hosp. and Home, S.I., 1958—; attending physician in gynecology S.I. Hosp., 1951—, chief of staff, 1976-78; dir. quality assurance S.I. Univ. Hosp., 1989—; cons. in gynecology USPHS Hosp., 1958—; mem. med. appeals unit N.Y. State Worker's Compensation Bd; mem. N.Y. State Bd. Profl. Med. Conduct, 1991—. Bd. dirs. S.I. chpt. ARC, 1974—, Health Systems Agy., N.Y.C. 1982—, Meals on Wheels, S.I., 1980—, N.Y.C., 1982—; trustee S.I. Hosp., 1979-93, sr. trustee, 1993—; elder Calvary Presbyn. Ch., 1958—; trustee and sec. of bd. Wagner Coll., S.I., 1985-92; chmn. bd. trustees S.I. Inst. Arts & Scis., 1989-94. Served to lt. USN, 1942-46. Diplomate Am. Bd. Ob-Gyn. Fellow Am. Coll. Ob-Gyn, Internat. Coll. Surgeons, Am. Soc. Abdominal Surgeons, N.Y. Micros. Soc.; mem. Med. Soc. N.Y. State (chmn. coordinating coun. 1st dist. br. 1977—, dir. div. med. svcs. 1979-84, dep. exec. v.p. 1984-87), Richmond County Med. Soc. (pres. 1972), AMA, S.I. Inst. Arts and Scis. (chmn. bd., 1989-94), S.I. C. of C. (dir. 1964-66). Republican. Club: Kiwanis (pres. 1968). Home: 33 Valencia Ave Staten Island NY 10301-2023 Office: SI Univ Hosp Sea View Ave Staten Island NY 10305

O'CONNOR, ROD, chemist, inventor; b. Cape Girardeau, Mo., July 4, 1934; s. Jay H. and Flora (Winters) O'C.; m. Shirley Ann Sander, Aug. 7, 1955; children: Mark Alan, Kara Ann, Shanna Suzanne, Timothy Patrick. BS, S.E. Mo. State Coll., 1955; PhD, U. Calif., Berkeley, 1958. Asst. prof. chemistry U. Omaha, 1958-60, Mont. State Coll., 1960-63; assoc. prof. chemistry Mont. State U., Bozeman, 1963-66; assoc. prof., coordinator gen. chemistry Kent (Ohio) State U., 1966-67; prof., dir. 1st year chemistry U. Ariz., Tucson, 1968-72; staff assoc. Adv. Council on Coll. Chemistry Stanford (Calif.) U., 1967-68; vis. prof. Wash. State U., Pullman, 1972-73; prof. chemistry Tex. A&M, College Station, 1973-86; pres. Texas ROMEC Inc., College Station, 1983—; prof. environ. studies Baylor U., Waco, Tex., 1996—; cons. insect venoms Hollister-Stier Labs., Spokane, Wash., 1963-67; lab. separates editor W.H. Freeman Co., 1968-78; ednl. cons. TUCARA-4 Media Resources, Inc., 1971-74; mem. Coll. Chemistry Cons. Service; vis. scientist, tour lectr. Am. Chem. Soc., 1970—. Author: (with T. Moeller) Ions in Aqueous Systems, 1972, Fundamentals of Chemistry, 1981, (with C. Mickey and A. Hassell) Solving Problems in Chemistry, 1981, (with L. Peck and K. Irgolic) Fundamentals of Chemistry in The Laboratory, 1981, (with T.E. Taylor and P. Glenn) Toward Success in College, 1981; films Laboratory Safety, 1971; Contbr. articles to profl. jours.; patentee in field. Recipient nat. teaching award Mfg. Chemists Assn., 1978; 4 regional teaching awards. Fellow AAAS, Am. Inst. Chemists; mem. Internat. Soc. Toxinology, Am. Chem. Soc., Sigma Xi. Office: Texas ROMEC Inc 1300 Angelina Cir College Station TX 77840-4855 *Only those who truly care can ever be hurt ... or know real joy.*

O'CONNOR, SANDRA DAY, United States supreme court justice; b. El Paso, Tex., Mar. 26, 1930; d. Harry A. and Ada Mae (Wilkey) Day; m. John Jay O'Connor, III, Dec. 1952; children: Scott, Brian, Jay. AB in Econs. with great distinction, Stanford U., 1950, LLB, 1952. Bar: Calif. Dep. county atty. San Mateo, Calif., 1952-53; civil atty. Q.M. Market Ctr., Frankfurt am Main, Fed. Republic of Germany, 1954-57; pvt. practice Phoenix, 1958-65; asst. atty. gen. State of Ariz., 1965-69; Ariz. state senator, 1969-75, chmn. com. on state, county and mcpl. affairs, 1972-73, majority leader, 1973-74; judge Maricopa County Superior Ct., 1975-79, Ariz. Ct. Appeals, 1979-81; assoc. justice U.S. Supreme Ct., 1981—; referee juvenile ct., 1962-64; chmn. vis. bd. Maricopa County Juvenile Detention Home, 1963-64; mem. Maricopa County Bd. Adjustments and Appeals, 1963-64, Anglo-Am. Legal Exchange, 1980, Maricopa County Superior Ct. Judges Tng. and Edn. Com., Maricopa Ct. Study Com.; chmn. com. to reorganize lower cts. Ariz. Supreme Ct., 1974-75; faculty Robert A. Taft Inst. Govt.; vice chmn. Select Law Enforcement Rev. Commn., 1979-80. Mem. bd. editors Stanford (Calif.) U. Law Rev. Mem. Ariz. Pers. Commn., 1968-69, Nat. Def. Adv. Com. on Women in Svcs., 1974-76; trustee Heard Mus., Phoenix, 1968-74, 76-81, pres., 1980-81; mem. adv. bd. Phoenix Salvation Army, 1975-81; trustee Stanford U., 1976-81, Phoenix County Day Sch.; mem. citizens adv. bd. Blood Svcs., 1975-77; nat. bd. dirs. Smithsonian Assocs., 1981—; past Rep. dist. chmn.; bd. dirs. Phoenix Cmty. Coun., Ariz. Acad., 1969-75, Jr. Achievement Ariz., 1975-79, Blue Cross/Blue Shield Ariz., 1975-79, Channel 8, 1975-79, Phoenix Hist. Soc., 1974-78, Maricopa County YMCA, 1978-81, Golden Gate Settlement. Recipient Ann. award NCCJ, 1975, Disting. Achievement award Ariz. State U., 1980; named Woman of Yr., Phoenix Advt. Club, 1972; inducted, National Women's Hall of Fame, 1995. Lodge: Soroptimists. Office: US Supreme Ct Supreme Ct Bldg 1 First St NE Washington DC 20543*

O'CONNOR, SHEILA ANNE, freelance writer; b. Paisley, Scotland, Jan. 20, 1960; came to the U.S., 1988; d. Brian Aubrey Witham and Margaret Kirk (Reid) Davies; m. Frank Donal O'Connor, Aug. 9, 1986; children: David Michael, Andrew James, Christine Charlotte. BA in French and German, Strathclyde U., 1980, postgrad. diploma in office studies, 1981, MBA, 1992. Office asst. BBC, London, 1982-83; asst. to mng. dir. Unimatic Engrs. Ltd., London, 1983-84; freelance word processing operator London, 1984-88; staff asst. Internat. Monetary Fund, Washington, 1988-94; prin. Internat. Media Assn., Washington, 1988—. Contbr. numerous articles to various publs. Mem. Am. Mktg. Assn., Bay Area Travel Writers Assn., Calif. Writers Club. Avocations: animals, travel. Home and Office: 2531 39th Ave San Francisco CA 94116-2752

O'CONNOR, SINEAD, singer, songwriter; b. Dublin, Dec. 8, 1966; 1 child, Jake. Albums include The Lion and The Cobra, 1987, I Do Not Want What I Haven't Got (Grammy award for Best Alternative Performance), 1990, My Special Child, 1991, Am I Not Your Girl?, 1992, Universal Mother, 1994. Office: Chysalis Records 810 7th Ave Frnt 4 New York NY 10019-5818*

O'CONNOR, THOMAS EDWARD, petroleum geologist, world bank officer; b. Boston, Dec. 16, 1936; s. John Stephen and Lucille (Arnold) O'C.; m. Jeannette Canuel, June 30, 1962 (dec. Mar. 1976); children: Kevin Patrick, David Andrew, Shelley Elizabeth; m. Moufida Banawi, Apr. 28, 1977; children: Tammer Thomas, Amr Adel Hammouda. BSc, Stanford U., 1958; MSc., U. Colo., 1961. Geologist Amoco Prodn. West, Denver, 1963-67, Amoco Netherlands, Utrecht, 1968-69, Amoco Europe, London, 1969-74; chief geologist Gulf of Suez Petroleum Co., Cairo, 1974-79; geol. mgr. Amoco Africa, Mid East, Houston, 1979-80; v.p. Aminoil, Houston, 1980-84; prin. petroleum engr. The World Bank, Washington, 1985—. Presenter numerous sci. confs., seminars, workshops in U.S. and abroad, 1976—. Lt. USNR, 1960-63. Mem. AAAS, Am. Assn. Petroleum Geologists (cert. petroleum geologist), Geol. Soc. Am., Houston Geol. Soc. Moslem. Home: 3637 Winfield Ln NW Washington DC 20007-2350 Office: The World Bank 1818 H St NW Washington DC 20433-0001

O'CONNOR, TOM, corporate executive, management consultant; b. Boston, June 11, 1942; s. Thomas Henry and Blanche (Cosgrove) O'C.; m. Mary Alice Kelly; 1 child, Michael Kelly O'Connor. BA in econs., U. Mass., 1971; postgrad., U. Wis., Milw., 1971-73, U. Del., 1978, Am. U., 1980. Economist Interstate Commerce Commn., Washington, 1973-74; mgr. planning U.S. Railway Assn., Washington, 1974-75; cons. transp. R.L. Banks & Assocs., Washington, 1975-77; asst. dir. Conrail, Phila., 1977-79; asst. v.p. econs. Assn. Am. R.R.'s, Washington, 1979-82; v.p. DNS Assocs., Inc., Washington, Lexington (Mass.), 1982-88; v.p., ptnr. Snavely, King, Majoros, O'Connor & Lee, Inc., Washington, 1988—; chmn. surface freight transport regulation com. Transp. Rsch. Bd., 1994—. Pres. Green Briar Civic Assn., Fairfax, Va., 1985, Greenbriar Dem. Club, Fairfax, 1984-89, Greenbriar Community Ctr., Fairfax, 1984; v.p. Greenbriar West PTA, Fairfax, 1986-88. Sgt. U.S. Army, 1963-66. Mem. Am. Econ. Assn., Am. Statis. Assn., Coun. Logistics Mgmt., Transp. Rsch. Forum (pres. Washington chpt. 1987-89), Nat. Def. Assn. (bd. dirs. 1991-94), Air Force Assn., Phi Beta Kappa, Phi Kappa Phi. Democrat. Roman Catholic. Avocations: camping, reading, counseling. Home: 13222 Point Pleasant Dr Fairfax VA 22033-3515 Office: Snavely King Majoros O'Connor & Lee Inc 1220 L St NW Washington DC 20005-4018

O'CONNOR, WILLIAM MICHAEL, executive search company executive; b. Chgo., Sept. 28, 1947; s. Maurice Francis and Margaret (Brand) O'C.; m. Karen Jean Gipson, Jan. 30, 1972; children: Sean, Mary, William, David. BA in History, Loyola U., Chgo., 1970. Interviewer Ill. State Employment Svc., Chgo., 1970-73; ins. agt. Equitable Life Assurance Soc., Chgo., 1973-76; recruiting officer U.S. Army, Chgo., 1977-78; profl. employment rep. GTE Network Systems, Northlake, Ill., 1978-81; employment mgr. Molex, Inc., Lisle, Ill., 1981-85, Rand McNally & Co., Skokie, Ill., 1986; v.p. Richards Cons., Ltd., Chgo., 1987-88; v.p., ptnr. Chestnut Hill Ptnrs., Deerfield, Ill., 1988-95; v.p. Kennedy & Co., Chgo., 1995—. Mem. Art Inst. Chgo., Smithsonian Inst., Field Mus. Natural History, Rep. Nat. Com., 1984—. Lt. col. USAR, 1971—. Mem. Res. Officers Assn., U.S. Armor Assn. (Order of St. George), Mil. Police Assn., 337th Cavalry Regiment (Order of the Spur), Bus. Mobilized for Loyola U. Roman Catholic. Home: 521 E Circle Hill Dr Arlington Heights IL 60004-3116 Office: Kennedy & Co 20 N Wacker Dr Chicago IL 60606-2806

O'CONNOR, WILLIAM NOEL, pathologist; b. Cork, Ireland, Dec. 28, 1949; came to U.S., 1972, naturalized, 1981; s. William Francis and Marguerite (Constant) O'C. M.B.,B.Ch., Nat. U. Ireland, Cork, 1972. Lic. physician, Ireland, D.C., Ky. Rotating intern St. Mary's Hosp., Waterbury, Conn., 1972-73; resident in pathology Georgetown U. Hosp., Washington, 1973-75; instr. pathology Georgetown U., Washington, 1975-76; instr. pathology U. Ky., Lexington, 1976-77, asst. prof. dept. pathology, 1977-81, assoc. prof., 1982-94, prof., 1994—, assoc. prof. Grad. Ctr. for Toxicology, 1991—, dir. residency tng. program dept. pathology/lab. medicine, 1989—; mem. attending staff Georgetown U. Hosp., 1975-76; cons. dept. pathology VA Med. Ctr., Lexington, 1977—; mem. med. staff Univ. Hosp., Lexington, 1978—, St. Claire Med. Ctr., Morehead, Ky., 1978—; grant reviewer peer rev. com. Am. Heart Assn., Ky. affiliate, Louisville, 1980-92, rsch. com., 1993—; vis. prof. U. London, England, 1994—; lectr. in field; condr. workshops in field. Manuscript reviewer Histotechnology, 1978—, Stain Tech., 1978, Am. Jour. Cardiology, 1978—, Jour. Am. Coll. Cardiology, 1982—, Am. Jour. Pathology, 1993—; contbr. numerous articles and abstracts to profl. jours., chpts. to books. Grantee Am. Heart Assn., Ky. affiliate, 1978-79, 82-88, 90-91, BRSG, 1979-81, U. Ky. Dept. Pathology Acad. Enrichment Funds, 1980-82, Tobacco and Health Rsch. Inst. and NIH, 1985-88, NIH, 1988-91, 91—, Children Miracle Network Telethon Fund, 1991-92, 92-93. Fellow Am. Bd. Pathology, Coll. Am. Pathologists, Am. Coll. Cardiology; mem. AMA, Soc. for Cardiovascular Pathology, Ky. Med. Assn., Fayette County Med. Soc., Southeastern Pediatric Cardiology Soc., Ky. Soc. Pathologists, Irish and N.Am. Pathologists Soc., Irish and Am. Pediatric Soc., U.S.-Can. Acad. Pathology, Am. Soc. Clin. Pathologists, Am. Assn. Pathologists, Am. Heart Assn. (Ky. affiliate), Assn. Clin. Scientists, Children's Cancer Study Group, Brit. Heart Found., Alpha Omega Alpha. Democrat. Roman Catholic. Avocations: collecting provincial Irish georgian silversmith work, Kurdish textiles. Office: Univ of Kentucky Med Ctr Lab Medicine Dept Pathology 800 Rose St MS 141 Lexington KY 40536-0001

OCVIRK, OTTO GEORGE, artist; b. Detroit, Nov. 13, 1922; s. Joseph and Louise (Ekle) O.; m. Betty Josephine Lebie, June 11, 1949; children: Robert Joseph, Thomas Frederick, Carol Louise. B.F.A., State U. Iowa, 1949, M.F.A., 1950. Advt. artist apprentice Bass-Luckoff Advt. Agy., Detroit, 1941; engring. draftsman Curtiss-Wright Aircraft Corp., Buffalo, 1942; faculty Bowling Green (Ohio) State U., 1950—, assoc. prof., 1960-65, prof. art, 1965-85, prof. emeritus, 1985—. Exhibited in group shows at, Denver Mus. Art, 1949, 50, 53, Detroit Inst. Art, 71948, 49, 50, 53, 56, Dayton (Ohio) Art Inst., 1950, 51, 56, Ohio State U., 1953, Walker Art Center, Mpls., 1948, 49, Library of Congress, Washington, 1949, Bklyn. Mus., 1949, Joslyn Mus., Omaha, 1949, Colorado Springs Fine Arts Center, 1949; represented in permanent collections, Detroit Inst. Arts, Dayton Art Inst., Friends of Am. Art, Grand Rapids, Mich., State U. Iowa, Iowa City, Bowling Green State U.; (Recipient 24 nat., regional juried art exhbn. awards 1947-57, others.); Author: (with R. Stinson, P. Wigg, R. Bone and David Cayton) Art Fundamentals—Theory and Practice, 1960-97, 7th edit., 1994, 8th edit., 1997. Scoutmaster Toledo Area council Boy Scouts Am., 1960-63, asst. scoutmaster, 1963-74, dist. commr., 1978-80. Served with AUS, 1943-46. Recipient Silver Beaver award Boy Scouts Am., 1976, Magnifico award Medici Circle, Bowling Green State U., 1987. Mem. Delta Phi Delta (hon.). Methodist. Home and Office: 231 Haskins Rd Bowling Green OH 43402-2206 *"Freedom for expression" keys creative thought into a productive whole.*

ODA, TAKUZO, biochemist, educator; b. Shinichicho, Japan, Oct. 20, 1923; s. Ryoichi and Misu Oda; M.D., Okayama U., 1947, Ph.D., 1953; m. Kazue Matsui, Dec. 8, 1946; children: Mariko, Yumiko. Intern, Okayama U. Hosp., 1947-48, mem. faculty, 1949—, prof. biochemistry, 1965—, dir. Cancer Inst., from 1969; dean Okayama U. Med. Sch., 1985-87; prof. Okayama U. Sci., 1989—; pres. and prof. Niimi Women's Coll., 1993—; postdoctoral trainee Inst. Enzyme Research, U. Wis., Madison, 1960-62. Fellow Rockefeller Found., 1959-60, grantee, 1964; USPHS grantee, 1963-68. Mem. Japanese Soc. Electron Microscopy (Seto prize 1966), Japanese Soc. Biochemistry, Japanese Soc. Cancer, Japan Soc. Human Genetics, Japanese Soc. Histochemistry, Japanese Soc. Virology, Am. Soc. Microbiology. Author: Biochemistry of Biological Membranes, 1969, Mitochondria, Handbook of Cytology; editor, writer: Cell Biology series, 1979—; chief editor Acta Medica Okayama, 1975-85 . Home: 216-38 Maruyama, Okayama 703, Japan Office: Niimi Women's Coll, 1263-2 Nishikata, Niimi City Okayama 718, Japan

O'DAIR, BARBARA, editor. Editor US mag., N.Y.C. Office: US mag 1290 Avenue Of The Americas New York NY 10104-0199*

O'DAY, ANITA BELLE COLTON, entertainer, singer; b. Chgo., Oct. 18, 1919; d. James and Gladys (Gill) C. Student, Chgo. public schs. Singer and entertainer various Chgo. Music Clubs, 1939-41; singer with Gene Krupa's Orch., 1941-45, Stan Kenton Orch., 1944, Woody Herman Orch., 1945, Benny Goodman Orch., 1959; singing tours in U.S. and abroad, 1947—; rec. artist Polygram, Capitol, Emily Records, Verve, GNP Crescendo, Columbia, London, Signature, DRG, Pablo; million-seller songs include Let Me Off Uptown, 1941, And Her Tears Flowed Like Wine, 1944, Boogie Blues, 1945; appeared in films Gene Krupa Story, 1959, Jazz on a Summer's Day, 1960, Zigzag, 1970, Outfit, 1974; TV shows 60 Minutes, 1980; Tonight Show, Dick Cavett Show, Today Show, Big Band Bash, CBS Sunday Morning, CNN Showbiz Today, others. Author: High Times, Hard Times, 1981, rev. edit., 1989; performed 50 yr. anniversary concert Carnegie Hall, 1985, Avery Fisher Hall, 1989, Tanglewood, 1990, Town Hall, 1993, Rainbow and Stars, 1995, JVC Festival Carnegie Hall, 1996, currently touring worldwide; albums include Drummer Man, Kenton Era, Anita, Anita Sings The Most, Pick Yourself Up, Lady is a Tramp, An Evening with Anita O'Day, At Mr. Kelly's, Swings Cole Porter, Travelin' Light, All the Sad Young Men, Waiter Make Mine Blues, With the Three Sounds, I Told Ya I Love Ya Now Get Out, Uptown, My Ship, Live in Tokyo, Anita Sings the Winners, Incomparable, Anita 1975, Live at Mingos, Anita O'Day/The Big Band Sessions, Swings Rodgers and Hart, Time for Two, Tea for Two, In a Mellowtone (Grammy nomination 1990), At Vine St. Live, Mello'Day, Live at the City, Angel Eyes, The Night Has a Thousand Eyes, The Rules of the Road, Jazz Masters, Skylark, Swingtime in Hawaii, others. Jazz Masters fellow Nat. Endowment for the Arts, 1997. Mem. AFTRA, Screen Actors Guild, BMI. Office: 1862 Vista Del Mar St Los Angeles CA 90028-5208 *From the time I was twelve or thirteen, my life was music. I never thought about being on top. I only wanted to be a part of the scene.*

O'DAY, DENIS MICHAEL, ophthalmologist, educator; b. Melbourne, Victoria, Australia, Dec. 10, 1935; came to U.S., 1967; s. Kevin John and Bernadette John (Hay) O'D.; m. Ann Georgina Despard, May 28, 1966;

children: Luke Gerard, Simon Patrick, Edward Daniel. Diploma, Xavier Coll., 1953; MBBS, Melbourne U., 1960. Diplomate Am. Bd. Ophthalmology. Intern St. Vincent's Hosp./U. Melbourne, 1961; resident in internal medicine St. Vincent's Hosp., 1962-64, chief resident dept. medicine, 1964, clin. asst. medicine, 1965-66; 3d asst., mem. asst. Royal Victoria Eye & Ear Hosp., Melbourne, 1967-70; resident in ophthalmology U. Calif., San Francisco, 1970; Wellcome rsch. fellow in corneal disease Inst. Opthalmology, London, 1970-72; asst. prof. ophthalmology Vanderbilt U. Sch. Medicine, Nashville, 1972-74, assoc. prof. ophthalmology, 1974-77; prof. ophthalmology, now chmn. Vanderbilt U. Sch. Medicine, 1977; cons. ophthalmologist Royal Commonwealth Soc. of Blind, Nigeria, 1972; cons. VA Hosp., 1973-74, active staff, 74; mem. active staff Nashville Gen. Hosp., 1974, Park View Hosp., 1980, Vanderbilt Hosp., 1972; mem. cons. staff St. Thomas Hosp.; bd. dirs. Am. Bd. Ophthalmology, Phila., 1988—; proctor lectr. U. Calif., San Francisco, 1993; co-med. dir. Lions Eye Bank and Sight Svc., 1973-86, med. dir. 1986—; bd. dirs. Lions Eye Bank Mid. Tenn., 1987—; ad-hoc mem. NIH Visual Sci. Study Sect., 1977. Author: Management of Functional Impairment due to Cataract, 1993; contbr. numerous articles, abstracts to profl. publs., chpts. to books. Chair ethics com. Cath. Pub. Policy Commn., Nashville, 1991—. Joyn Hayden rsch. fellow, 1965; recipent Felton Bequest and Potter Found. awards, 1967, recognition award Alcon Rsch. Inst., 1983, Sr. Sci. Investigator award Rsch. to Prevent Blindness, 1987, Health Profl. of Yr. award Tenn. chpt. Assn. for Edn. and Rehab. of Blind and Visually Impaired, 1990. Fellow ACS, Royal Australia Coll. Physicians, Royal Soc. Medicine, Am. Acad. Ophthalmology (sec. quality of care com. 1993—, Honor award for Ednl. Contbns. 1981-85, dir. clin. alert program, pub. health com. 1985-88); mem. AMA, AAUP, Am. Ophthalmol. Soc., Assn. for Rsch. in Vision and Ophthalmology, Nashville Acad. Medicine, Nashville Acad. Ophthalmology (v.p. 1980-81), Oxford Ophthalmol. Soc., Royal Australasian Coll. Physicians, Tenn. Acad. Medicine, Tenn. Acad. Ophthalmology. Roman Catholic. Avocation: sailing. Office: Vanderbilt U Med Ctr East Dept Ophthal and Vis Scis Fl 8 Nashville TN 37232-8808

O'DAY, KATHLEEN LOUISE, food products executive; b. Chgo., July 10, 1951; d. Alfred Anton and Maria (Weidinger) Schuld; m. Gary Michael O'Day, Oct. 25, 1975; children: Colleen Marie, Daniel Michael. BS in Biology, Mundelein Coll., 1973; Assoc. Mid-Mgmt. & Mktg., McHenry County Coll., Crystal Lake, Ill., 1986; MBA, Keller Grad. Sch. Mgmt., 1995. Food techologist Park Corp., Barrington, Ill., 1973-84; sr. product devel. scientist J.W. Allen & Co., Wheeling, Ill., 1984—. Mem. v.p. Transfiguration Sch. Bd., Wauconda, Ill., 1983-85; team mem. Transfiguration RCIA Orgn., Wauconda, 1992. Mem. Am. Assn. Cereal Chemists, Inst. Food Technologists, Bakers Club Chgo. Republican. Roman Catholic. Home: 3287 Kings Point Ct Island Lake IL 60042-9752

O'DAY, PAUL THOMAS, trade association executive; b. May 2, 1935; s. James Thomas and Jeannette Irene (Deschenes) O'D.; m. Nancy Frances Eitler, June 16, 1962; children: Kathleen, Maureen, Michael, Ellen. B.A., Am. Internat. Coll., Springfield, Mass., 1958; J.D., Georgetown U., 1963; MPA, Am. U., 1967. Bar: D.C. 1964, U.S. Supreme Ct. 1974. Patent examiner U.S. Patent Office, Washington, 1959-62; exec. sec. panel high-speed ground transp., auto. air poll. Dept. Commerce, Washington, 1965-66, staff asst. to sec., 1967-69, exec. asst. to sec., 1969-71, dep. dir. bur. domestic commerce, 1972-74; dep. dir. Nat. Bus. Coun. for Consumer Affairs, Washington, 1971-72; cons. to Gen. Counsel GE, Fairfield, Conn., 1974-75; asst. trade rep. Exec. Office of the Pres., Washington, 1975-77; dep. asst. sec. U.S. Dept. Commerce, Washington, 1978-84; pres. Am. Fiber Mfrs. Assn., Washington, 1984—; chmn. Fiber Econs. Bur., 1984—; pres. Eisenhower World Affairs Inst., 1993—. Corporator Am. Internat. Coll., 1974—; mem. governing coun. Shakespeare Theater Guild, 1989—. Recipient Constl. Law award Georgetown U. Law Ctr., 1962; Alumni award Am. Internat. Coll., 1970; Pres.'s Meritorious Exec. award., 1984; Nat. Inst. Pub. Affairs fellow Princeton U., 1964. Mem. World Econ. Forum, AAAS, Am. Chem. Soc., Cosmos Club, Jefferson Islands Club (bd. dirs. 1993—), Federal City Club. Home: 8261 Private Ln Annandale VA 22003-4471 Office: Am Fiber Mfrs Assn 1150 17th St NW Washington DC 20036-4603

O'DAY, ROYAL LEWIS, former banker; b. Avon, N.Y., Apr. 28, 1913; s. Roy Lyday and Winifred (Heath) O'D.; m. Elizabeth M. Fearon, Oct. 12, 1952; children: Margaret (Mrs. Thomas W. Wright), Patti (Mrs. Warner Blow), Timothy N. BS, Syracuse U., 1936. With Gen. Motors Acceptance Corp., 1936-42; sr. v.p. Mchts. Nat. Bank & Trust Co., Syracuse, N.Y., 1942-61; exec. v.p. Marine Midland Bank—Central, Syracuse, 1961-68; pres. Marine Midland Bank—Central, 1968-71, chmn. bd., 1971-76, chief exec. officer, 1973-76, cons., 1976—; bd. dirs. Syracuse Chiefs Baseball Club. Bd. dirs. Syracuse Rsch. Corp.; past pres. Met. Devel. Assn., Syracuse, Syracuse Rep. Citizens Com.; past chmn. bd. trustees, now trustee Syracuse U.; past chmn. bd. N.Y. divsn. Am. Cancer Soc.; trustee Crouse Irving Meml. Hosp., Syracuse. Lt. USNR, WWII. Named Outstanding Man in Syracuse Area in Bus. and Fin. Syracuse Herald Jour., 1963; recipient Torch of Liberty award Anti-Defamation League of B'nai B'rith, 1974. Mem. Nat. Alumni Assn. Syracuse U. (pres. 1965-69), Automobile Club Syracuse (dir., vice chmn.) Hosp. Svcs. Assn. Cen. N.Y. (dir.), Greater Syracuse C. of C. (past pres.), Masons (33 deg., Shriner, Jester), Onondaga Golf and Country Club (Fayetteville, N.Y.), Royal Poinciana Golf Club (Naples, Fla.), Phi Gamma Delta. Mem. Dewitt Community Ch. (finance com.). Clubs: Mason (Fayetteville, N.Y.) (33 deg., Shriner, Jester), Onondaga Golf and Country (Fayetteville, N.Y.), Royal Poinciana Golf (Naples, Fla.). Home: 714 Scott Ave Syracuse NY 13224-2160 Office: 360 S Warren St Syracuse NY 13202-2017

O'DAY, STEPHEN EDWARD, lawyer; b. Indpls., Nov. 8, 1953; s. George R. and M. Kate (Harrington) O'D.; m. Fran Bold, Dec. 16, 1973; children: Jeremy, Kelly, Rory, Curry. Student, Ga. Inst. Tech., 1971-72; BA summa cum laude, Furman U., 1976; JD cum laude, Harvard U., 1979. Bar: Ga. 1979, U.S. Dist. Ct. (no. dist.) Ga. 1979, U.S. Ct. Appeals (5th cir.) 1979, U.S. Ct. Appeals (11th cir.) 1981, U.S. Claims Ct. 1981, U.S. Supreme Ct. 1986. Assoc. Hurt, Richardson, Garner, Todd & Cadenhead, Atlanta, 1979-85, former ptnr.; now mem. Smith, Gambrell & Russell, Atlanta; trustee Ga. Conservancy, Atlanta, 1981-91, sec. 1984-85, vice chmn. 1986; bd. dirs. Southern Environ. Law Ctr., Charlottesville, Va., 1985—. Youth dir. Episcopal Ch. of St. Peter and St. Paul, Marietta, Ga., 1982-84, vestry, 1984-85; bd. trustees Upper Chattahoochee River Keeper, 1996—. Mem. ABA (mem. natural resources, energy and environ. sect., mem. litigation sect.), Ga. Bar Assn. (chmn. com. on the handicapped, 1980-81, mem. young lawyers sect., vice chmn. environ. sect. 1995), Phi Beta Kappa, Phi Eta Sigma, Pi Gamma Mu. Democrat. Home: 950 Poplar Springs Rd Dallas GA 30132-6512 Office: Smith Gambrell & Russell 1230 Peachtree St NE Atlanta GA 30309-3575

ODDEN, ALLAN ROBERT, education educator; b. Duluth, Minn., Sept. 16, 1943; s. Robert Norman and Mabel Eleanor (Bjornnes) O.; m. Eleanor Ann Rubottom, May 28, 1966; children: Sarina, Robert. BS, Brown U., 1965; MDiv, Union Theol. Sem., 1969; MA, Columbia U., 1971, PhD, 1975. Tchr. N.Y.C. Pub. Schs., 1967-72; rsch. assoc. Teachers' Coll. Columbia U., N.Y.C., 1972-75; dir. policy Edn. Commn. of the States, Denver, 1975-84; prof. U. So. Calif., L.A., 1984-93, U. Wis., Madison, 1993—; rsch. dir. Sch. Fin. Commns. Conn., 1974-75, S.D., 1975-76, Mo. 1975-76, 93, 94, N.Y., 1978-81, N.J., 1991-92; co-dir. Consortium for Policy Rsch. in Edn.; cons. Nat. Govs. Assn., Nat. Conf. State Legislatures, U.S. Sec. Edn., U.S. Senate, U.S. Dept. Edn. and many state legislatures and govs.; nat. rsch. coun. task force on sch. fin. equity adequacy and productivity, 1996—. Author: Education Leadership for America's Schools, 1995; co-author: Paying Teachers for What They Know and Do, 1997, School Finance: A Policy Perspective, 1992; editor: Education Policy Implementation, 1991, Rethinking School Finance, 1992; contbr. articles to profl. jours., chpts. to books. Mem. L.A. Chamber Edn. and Human Resources Commn., 1986, Gov.'s Sch. Fin. Commn., Calif., 1987, Calif. Assessment Policy Com., Gov.'s Edn. Task Force, Wis., 1996, Carnegie Corp. Task Force on Edn. in the Early Years, 1994-96. Grantee Dept. Edn., Carnegie Corp., Spencer Found., Ford Found., Mellon Found., Carnegie Corp., Pew Charitable Trusts. Mem. Am. Ednl. Rsch. Assn., Am. Ednl. Fin. Assn. (pres. 1979-80), Nat. Tax Assn., Politics of Edn. Assn., Nat. Soc. for Study of Edn. Democrat. Avocations: Lionel train collector, youth soccer and baseball coach. Home: 3128 Oxford Rd Madison WI 53705-2224 Office: U Wis Sch Edn Wis Ctr Edn Rsch 1025 W Johnson St # 653E Madison WI 53706-1706

ODDIS, JOSEPH ANTHONY, social services administrator; b. Greensburg, Pa., Nov. 5, 1928; s. Giacinto and Felicetta (D'Amico) O.; m. Jeanne Trevena, July 10, 1954; children—Joseph Michael, Marie Thersa. B.S., Duquesne U., 1950; D.Sc. (hon.), Mass. Coll. Pharmacy, 1975, Phila. Coll. Pharmacy and Sci., 1975, Albany Coll. Pharmacy, Union U., 1976, Duquesne U., 1989, Mercer U., 1995; LHD (hon.), L.I. U., 1991. Staff pharmacist Mercy Hosp., Pitts., 1950-51; asst. chief pharmacist Mercy Hosp., 1953-54; chief pharmacist Western Pa. Hosp., Pitts., 1954-56; staff rep. hosp. pharmacy Am. Hosp. Assn., Chgo., 1956-60; dir. div. hosp. pharmacy Am. Pharm., Washington, 1960-62; exec. v.p. Am. Soc. Health-System Pharmacists, Washington, 1960—; pres. Am. Soc. Hosp. Pharmacists Research and Edn. Found., 1986—. Active Boy Scouts Am., Camp Fire Girls; Sec. Am. Soc. Health-System Pharmacists Research and Edn. Found., 1970-86. Served with AUS, 1951-53. Recipient 1st cert. Honor award Duquesne U. Sch. Pharmacy, 1969, named Outstanding Alumnus, 1978; recipient Harvey A.K. Whitney award Am. Soc. Hosp. Pharmacists, 1970, Julius Sturmer Meml. Lecture award Rho Chi soc. Phila., 1971, Howard C. Newton Lecture award 1977, Samuel Melendy Lecture award, 1978, Hugo H. Schaefer award, 1983, Reed and Alice Henninger Lecture award, 1984, Donald E. Francke medal, 1986, Remington medal award, 1990. Fellow AAAS; mem. Am. Pharm. Assn., Am. Soc. Hosp. Pharmacists, Am. Inst. History Pharmacy, Internat. Pharm. Fedn. (pres. hosp. pharmacy sect. 1977-81, v.p. 1984-86, pres. 1986-90), Drug Info. Assn., Am. Soc. Assn. Execs., Can. Soc. Hosp. Pharmacists (hon.), Soc. Hosp. Pharmacists Australia (hon.), Pharm. Soc. Gt. Britain (hon.), Pharm. Soc. Nigeria (hon.), Nat. Coun. Patient Info. and Edn. (sec. 1982-85), Israel Pharm. Soc. (hon.), Rho Chi, Kappa Psi (hon.), Duquesne U. Century Club (charter). Home: 6509 Rockhurst Rd Bethesda MD 20817-1661 Office: Am Soc Health-System Pharmacists 7272 Wisconsin Ave Bethesda MD 20814-4836*

O'DEA, DENNIS MICHAEL, lawyer; b. Lowell, Mass., Nov. 1, 1946; s. James Lawrence and Carol Frances (Gibbons) O'D.; children: Emily C., Dennis C., Daniel P.; m. Mary Gail Frawley. BA in Govt., U. Notre Dame, 1968; JD magna cum laude, U. Mich., 1972. Bar: Mass. 1972, D.C. 1980, Ill. 1981, N.Y. 1994. Assoc. Goodwin, Procter & Hoar, Boston, 1972-74, Fine & Ambrogne, Boston, 1974-77; assoc. prof. Syracuse U. Coll. Law, 1977-78; vis. assoc. prof. Nat. Law Ctr., George Washington U., 1978-80; ptnr. Keck, Mahin & Cate, N.Y.C., 1980—. Co-dir. The Gilmore Inst., 1995—. Mem. Order of the Coif (Mich.), Chgo. Literary Club (pres. 1993). Presbyterian. Home: 75 N Broadway Nyack NY 10960-2624 Office: Keck Mahin & Cate 100 Maiden Ln Ste 1600 New York NY 10038-4818

O'DELL, CHARLENE ANNE AUDREY, lawyer; b. Warwick, N.Y., Feb. 27, 1963; d. Charles Edward and Stella Ruth (Brazil) O'D. Student, Fordham U., 1981-83; BA summa cum laude with distinction, Boston U., 1985; JD, NYU, 1988. Bar: N.Y. 1989, U.S. Dist. Ct. (so. and ea. dists.) N.Y. 1989, D.C. 1990, Ct. Internat. Trade 1991. Assoc. Winston & Strawn (previously Cole & Deitz), N.Y.C., 1988-90; assoc. Graham & James, N.Y.C., 1990-95, spl. counsel, 1996—. Editor Moot Ct., NYU, 1987-88. Recipient Moot Ct. Advocacy award NYU, 1987. Mem. ABA, N.Y. State Bar Assn. Avocations: reading, tennis, photography. Office: Graham & James 885 3rd Ave New York NY 10022-4834

O'DELL, EDWARD THOMAS, JR., lawyer; b. Lowell, Mass., Nov. 26, 1935; s. Edward Thomas and Helen Louise (Shaw) O'D.; m. Kerstin Lilly Sjoholm, Mar. 18, 1962; children: Edward Thomas III, Brian Patrick, Christine Marie. BA, Brown U., 1957; JD, U. Chgo., 1960. Bar: N.Y. 1961, Mass. 1968, U.S. Dist. Ct. Mass. 1968, U.S. Ct. Appeals (1st cir.) 1968. Ptnr. Goodwin, Procter and Hoar, Boston, 1966—. Trustee Gov. Dummer Acad., Byfield, Mass, 1982-87. Mem. ABA, Mass. Bar Assn., Internat. Bar Assn. (sec. 1986-88, chmn. investment cos. com. 1994—). Home: 96 Wildwood Rd Andover MA 01810-5126 Office: Goodwin Procter & Hoar Exchange Pl Boston MA 02109

ODELL, FRANK HAROLD, banker; b. Hobart, N.Y., May 17, 1922; s. Harold E. and Naomi (Cole) O.; m. Elizabeth J. Hetherington, Dec. 29, 1946; children: Thomas A., Nancy E., Susan. AB, U. Ala., 1943; MBA, Harvard U., 1949; postgrad., Stonier Grad. Sch. Banking, Rutgers U., 1958. With State Bank of Albany, N.Y., 1949-71; v.p. State Bank of Albany, 1963-69, sr. v.p. in charge bank's loan portfolio, 1969-71; exec. v.p. Norstar Bancorp Inc., Albany, 1971-72; also vice chmn. Norstar Bancorp Inc.; chmn., chief exec. officer Norstar Bank of Upstate N.Y., 1972-87, also bd. dirs. Bd. dirss. YMCA, Saratoga Performing Arts Ctr.; bd. dirs. Albany Inst. History and Art, Robert Morris Assn., Capital Region Tech. Devel. Council, Mayor's Downtown Adv. Com., N.Y. State Banking Bd., Albany Med. Ctr., Albany chpt. ARC, United Way, Russell Sage Coll., Sta. WMHT-TV. Capt. C.E., AUS, 1943. Mem. Harvard Club (N.Y.C.), Harvard Club of Naples (pres.), Fort Orange Club (past pres.), Club Pelican Bay, Forum Club of Collier County, Moorings Country Club, Masons. Republican. Presbyterian.

ODELL, HERBERT, lawyer; b. Phila., Oct. 20, 1937; s. Samuel and Selma (Kramer) O.; m. Valerie Odell; children: Wesley, Jonathan, James, Sarah, Samuel. BS in Econs., U. Pa., 1959; LLB magna cum laude, U. Miami, 1962; LLM, Harvard U., 1963. Bar: Fla. 1963, Pa. 1968. Trial atty. tax div. U.S. Dept. Justice, Washington, 1963-65; assoc. Walton, Lantaff, Schroeder, Carson & Wahl, Miami, Fla., 1965-67; from assoc. to ptnr. Morgan, Lewis & Bockius, Phila., 1967-89; ptnr. Zapruder & Odell, Washington, 1989—; adj. prof. U. Miami, Villanova U.; lectr. various tax insts. Contbr. articles to profl. jours. Ford fellow, 1962-63. Mem. ABA, Fla. Bar Assn., Pa. Bar Assn., Phila. Bar Assn., Phi Kappa Phi, Omicron Delta Kappa, Beta Alpha Psi. Clubs: Harvard, U. Pa. Avocations: sailing, running, tennis, scuba diving. Office: Zapruder & Odell 401 E City Ave Ste 415 Bala Cynwyd PA 19004-1122

O'DELL, JAMES E., newspaper publishing executive. V.p. ops. and techs. Chgo. Tribune. Office: Chgo Tribune 777 W Chicago Ave Chicago IL 60610-2423*

ODELL, JOHN H., construction company executive; b. Toledo, Oct. 31, 1955; s. John H. and Doris Irene Odell; m. Kathryn Lau, Oct. 1, 1988; children: Ceara, Heather, Victoria. B of Environ. Design, U. Miami, Oxford, Ohio, 1977. Staff architect Richard Halford and Assocs., Santa Fe, 1978-79; ptnr. B.O.A. Constrn., Santa Fe, 1980-84; assoc. Stanley Design Works, Santa Fe, 1984-85; owner John H. Odell Constrn., Santa Fe, 1985—; v.p. Los Pintores Inc., Santa Fe, 1990-92; pres. Uncle Joey's Food Svcs. Inc., 1991—, John H. Odell Assocs. Inc., Santa Fe, 1995—. Musician Santa Fe Community Orch., 1982, Huntington Community Orch., Huntington, W.Va., 1972-73. Recipient Historic Preservation award City of Santa Fe, 1997. Mem. AIA (assoc. mem., treas., bd. dirs. Santa Fe chpt. yearly 1988-95, mem. liaison com. on design 1987—, Cmty. Svc. award 1993), Vine and Wine Soc. (N.Mex. No. Rio Grande chpt. pres., bd. dirs., v.p.). Avocations: skiing, scuba, handball, racquetball. Home: PO Box 2967 Santa Fe NM 87504-2967 Office: John H Odell Assn 729 Dunlap St Santa Fe NM 87501-2541

O'DELL, LYNN MARIE LUEGGE (MRS. NORMAN D. O'DELL), librarian; b. Berwyn, Ill., Feb. 24, 1938; d. George Emil and Helen Marie (Pesek) Luegge; student Lyons Twp. Jr. Coll., La Grange, Ill., 1957; student No. Ill. U., Elgin Community Coll., U. Ill., Coll. of DuPage; m. Norman D. O'Dell, Dec. 14, 1957; children—Jeffrey, Jerry. Sec., Martin Co., Chgo., 1957-59; dir. Carol Stream (Ill.) Pub. Library, 1964—; chmn. automation governing com. DuPage Library System, v.p., 1982-85, pres. exec. com. adminstrv. librarians, 1985-86, chair automation search com., 1991-92. Named Woman of Yr., Wheaton Bus. and Profl. Woman's Club, 1968. Mem. ALA, Ill. Library Assn., Library Adminstrs. Conf. No. Ill. Lutheran. Home: 182 Yuma Ln Carol Stream IL 60188-1917 Office: 616 Hiawatha Dr Carol Stream IL 60188-1616

ODELL, MARY JANE, former state official; b. Algona, Iowa, July 28, 1923; d. Eugene and Madge (Lewis) Neville; m. Garry Chinn, 1945 (dec.); m. Jonn Odell, Mar. 3, 1967 (dec.); m. Ralph Sigler, Nov. 22, 1987; children: Brad, Chris. B.A., U. Iowa, 1945; hon. doctorate, Simpson Coll., 1982. Host public affairs TV programs Des Moines and Chgo., 1953-79; with Iowa Public Broadcasting Network, 1975-79, host Assignment Iowa, 1975-78, host Mary Jane Odell Program, 1975-79; sec. of state State of Iowa, 1980-87; ret., 1987—; tchr. grad. classes in communications Roosevelt U., Chgo., Drake U., Des Moines. Chmn. Iowa Easter Seals campaign, 1979-83; mem. Midwest Com. Future Options; bd. dirs. Iowa Shares; mem. exec. bd. Iowa Peace Inst., 1985-92. Recipient Emmy award, 1972, 75; George Washington Carver award, 1978; named to Iowa Women's Hall of Fame, 1979. Republican. Address: 6129 Meadow Crest Dr Apt 206 Johnston IA 50131-2106

ODELL, PATRICK LOWRY, mathematics educator; b. Watonga, Okla., Nov. 29, 1930; s. Max Vernon and Pamela (Massey) O.; m. Norma Lou Maddox, Aug. 16, 1958 (dec. May, 1980); children: James M., David L., Michael R.L., Julie K., Patricia L., Deborah L.; m. Dovalee Dorsett, Aug. 3, 1985. BS, U. Tex., 1952; postgrad., UCLA, 1953-54; MS, Okla. State U., 1958, PhD, 1962. Mathematician White Sands (N.Mex.) Proving Grounds, 1952-53, Kaman Nuclear, Albuquerque, 1958-59, U.S. Naval Nuclear Ordnance Evaluation Unit, 1959-62, Ling-Temco Vought Aeros., 1962; asst. prof. math. U. Tex., Austin, 1962-66; prof., chmn. dept. math. Tex. Technol. U., Lubbock, 1966-71, coordinator insts., dir. rsch., Coll. Arts and Sci., 1971-72; prof math. scis. and environ. scis. U. Tex., Dallas, 1972-88, prof. emeritus, 1988—, exec. dean grad. studies and rsch., 1972-75; prof. math. sci. Baylor U., Waco, Tex., 1988—; assoc. dir. Tex. Ctr. for Rsch., Austin, 1964-66; rsch. scientist Def. Rsch. Lab., 1963-65; cons. math statistician, 1962—. Capt. USAF, 1953-57. Fellow Tex. Acad. Sci. (Disting. Tex. Scientist award 1994), Am. Statis. Assn.; mem. Soc. Indsl. and Applied Math. Home: 3200 Windsor Ave Waco TX 76708-3113

ODELL, WILLIAM DOUGLAS, physician, scientist, educator; b. Oakland, Calif., June 11, 1929; s. Ernest A. and Emma L. (Mayer) O.; m. Margaret F. Reilly, Aug. 19, 1950; children: Michael, Timothy, John D., Debbie, Charles. AB, U. Calif., Berkeley, 1952; MD, MS in Physiology, U. Chgo., 1956; PhD in Biochemistry and Physiology, George Washington U., 1965. Intern, resident, chief resident in medicine U. Wash., 1956-60, postdoctoral fellow in endocrinology and metabolism, 1957-58; sr. investigator Nat. Cancer Inst., Bethesda, Md., 1960-65; chief endocrine service NICHD, 1965-66; chief endocrinology Harbor-UCLA Med. Center, Torrance, Calif., 1966-72; chmn. dept. medicine Harbor-UCLA Med. Center, 1972-79; vis. prof. medicine Auckland Sch. Medicine, New Zealand, 1979-80; prof. medicine and physiology U. Utah Sch. Medicine, Salt Lake City, 1980-96, chmn. dept. medicine, 1980-96, prof. medicine and physiology, 1996—. Mem. editorial bds. med. jours.; author 6 books in field; contbr. over 300 artilces to med. jours. Served with USPHS, 1960-66. Recipient Disting. Svc. award U. Chgo., 1973, Pharmacia award for outstanding contbns. to clin. chemistry, 1977, Gov.'s award State of Utah Sci. and Tech., 1988, also rsch. awards, Mastership award ACP, 1987. Mem. Am. Soc. Clin. Investigation, Am. Physiol. Soc., Assn. Am. Physicians, Am. Soc. Andrology (pres.), Endocrine Soc. (v.p., Robert Williams award 1991), Soc. Study of Reprodn. (bd. dirs.), Pacific Coast Fertility Soc. (pres.), Western Assn. Physicians (pres.), Western Soc. Clin. Rsch. (Mayo Soley award), Soc. Pediatric Rsch., Alpha Omega Alpha. Office: U of Utah Med Ctr 50 N Medical Dr Salt Lake City UT 84132-0001

O'DELL, WILLIAM FRANCIS, retired business executive, author; b. Detroit, Jan. 24, 1909; s. Frank Trevor and Garnett (Aikman) O'C.; m. Bess Baer, June 10, 1933 (dec. July 1986); m. Helen M. Porter, May 16, 1987 (dec. 1997); children: Peggy, David. B.S., U. Ill., 1930. With Penton Pub. Co., 1933-37; v.p. Ross Fed. Research Corp., 1937-44; mng. dir. Statis Research Co., 1944-45; pres. Market Facts, Inc., 1946-64, chmn., 1964-74; pres. ROC Internat., 1961-64; mem. census adv. bd. Dept. Commerce, 1963-73; prof. mktg. McIntire Sch. Commerce U. Va., 1965-78; vis. prof. Chinese U. of Hong Kong, 1969. Author: Marketing Decision, 1968, Marketing Decision Making, 1976, 4th edit., 1988, How to Make Lifetime Friends—With Peers and Parents, 1978, Twelve Families—An American Experience, 1981, Effective Business Decision Making and the Educated Guess, 1991; mem. editorial rev. bd. Jour. Mktg, 1964-73. Recipient Leader in Mktg. award, 1970, Jour. Mktg. Research editorial award, 1979; William F. O'Dell professorship in commerce named in his honor U. Va., 1983. Mem. Am. Mktg. Assn. (pres. 1960-61), Colonnade Club (Charlottesville), Univ. Club of Ft. Myers, Rotary, Delta Upsilon, Beta Gamma Sigma. Home: 5707 Junonia Ct Fort Myers FL 33908-1667

ODEM, JOYCE MARIE, human resources specialist; b. Des Moines, Mar. 21, 1936; d. Robert Gibson and Minnie Anna (Godown) Hague; m. Phillip Wayne Odem, May 23, 1954; children: Vickie, Phillip, Beth, Amy, Keith. Student, Merced C.C., 1976-78. Legal sec. C. Ray Robinson, Merced, Calif., 1959-60; office mgr., legal aid Kane & Canelo, Merced, Calif., 1960-65; recorder disciplinary control bd. U.S. Army Civil Svc., Okinawa, Japan, 1965-69; legal aid, office mgr. Courtney & Sharrow, Merced, 1969-72; adminstr. USAF Civil Svc., Okinawa, 1972-75; asst. indsl. rels. mgr. Maracay Mills Divsn. Mohasco, Merced, 1975-78; safety dir., personnel mgr. Keller Industries, Merced, 1978-83; mgr. employee rels. McLane Pacific, Merced, 1983-85; corp. dir. human resources McLane Co., Inc., Temple, Tex., 1983—; mem. adv. bd. Pvt. Industry Coun., Merced, 1980-85. Mem. Temple Human Resource Mgrs. Assn., Soc. Human Resource Mgrs. Avocations: sporting clays, golf, hunting. Office: McLane Co Inc 4747 McLane Pky Temple TX 76503

ODEN, ROBERT RUDOLPH, surgeon; b. Chgo., Dec. 2, 1922; s. Rudolph J.E. and Olga H. (Wahlquist) O.; m. Nancy Clow; children: Louise, Boyd, Beach, Lisbeth. BS, U. Ill., 1943; MD, Northwestern U., 1947, MS in Anatomy, 1947. Intern Augustana Hosp., Chgo., 1947-48, resident in surgery, 1948-49; resident in orthopaedics Hines Vets. Hosp., Chgo., 1949-51; resident in children's orthopaedics Shriner's Hosp., 1953-54; pvt. practice Chgo., 1954-57, Aspen, Colo., 1957—; clin. assoc. prof. in orthopaedics U. Colo.; orthopaedic surgeon U.S. Olympic Com., 1960, 72, 76, 80. Assoc. editor: Clin. Orthopaedics and Related Rsch. Trustee U.S. Ski Ednl. Found., 1967-82, Aspen Valley Hosp., 1978-86; founder Aspen Orthopaedic and Sports Medicine Pub. Found., 1985, Aspen Inst. for Theol. Futures, 1978, Great Tchrs. and Preachers Series Christ Episc. Ch., 1989; mem. organizing com. Aspen World Cup, 1976-92; founder, trustee Pitkin County Bank, 1983—; founder Aspen Pitkin Employee Housing, 1975. Recipient Blegan award for most outstanding svc. to U.S. skiing, 1985, Halsted award U.S. Ski Assn., 1987, inducted into Aspen Hall of Fame, 1996. Mem. Am. Acad. Orthopaedic Surgeons, ACS, Internat. Coll. Surgeons, Western Orthopaedic Assn., SICOT, Am. Assn. Bone & Joint Surgeons, Rocky Mountain Traumatologic Soc., Canadian Orthopaedic Assn., Am. Orthopaedic Soc. for Sports Medicine, Internat. Ski Safety Soc., ACL Study Group, Internat. Soc. Knee, Internat. Knee Inst., Phi Beta Kappa. Home: PO Box 660 Aspen CO 81612-0660 Office: 100 E Main St Aspen CO 81611-1778

ODEN, WILLIAM BRYANT, bishop, educator; b. McAllen, Tex., Aug. 3, 1935; s. Charles Alva and Evea (Bryant) O.; m. Marilyn Brown, July 12, 1957; children: Danna Lee Oden Bowen, William Dirk, Valerie Lyn, Charles Bryant. BA, Okla. State U., 1958; MDiv, Harvard U., 1961, postgrad., 1974; ThD, Boston U., 1964; DD (hon.), Oklahoma City U., 1980; LHD (hon.), Centenary Coll., 1990. Ordained to ministry Meth. Ch., 1961. Pastor Aldersgate United Meth. Ch., Oklahoma City, 1963-69, St. Stephen's United Meth. Ch., Norman, Okla., 1969-76, Crown Heights United Meth. Ch., Oklahoma City, 1976-83; prof. Phillips Grad. Sem., Enid, 1976-88; pastor 1st United Meth. Ch., Enid, 1983-88; bishop United Meth. Ch., Baton Rouge, 1988-96; bishop for the Dallas area United Meth. Ch., 1996—; pres. SCJ Coll. of Bishops, 1989-90; del. Gen. Conf., 1976, 80, 84, 88; chmn. Okla. Del. to Gen. and Jurisdictional Confs., 1984, 88; Jackson lectr. Perkins Sch. Theology, So. Meth. U., 1975, Wilson lectr. SCJ Bishop's Week, 1989; co-chair World Meth.-Anglican Dialogue, 1991—; bd. dirs. Wesley Works Project; pres. Gen. Bd. Higher Edn. & Ministry, 1996—. Author: Oklahoma Methodism in the Twentieth Century, 1968, Liturgy as Life Journey, 1976, Wordeed: Evangelism in Biblical and Wesleyan Perspective, 1978; contbr.: Send Me: The Itenerancy in Crisis, 1991. Trustee Oklahoma City U., 1980-88, Southwestern U., Winfield, Kans., 1983-88, Centenary Coll., 1988—, Dillard U., 1988—, So. Meth. U., 1996—. Mem. Am. Acad. Homiletics. Avocations: writing, reading biographies, mountain climbing, backpacking. Home: PO Box 8127 Dallas TX 75205-0127

ODENWELLER, ROBERT PAUL, philatelist, association executive, airline pilot; b. Colon, C.Z., Sept. 19, 1938; s. Charles Joseph and Robina Katharine (Watson, O.; m. Jane Blackistone Rawlings, June 24, 1965; 1

stepchild, Joy McCorriston; 1 child, Liesl Hasbrouck. BS U.S. Air Force Acad., 1960. Commd. USAF, 1956, advanced through grades to capt., 1963, resigned, 1956-66; mem. Collectors Club, Inc., N.Y.C., 1964—, gov. 1969—, program chmn., 1970-80, mem. editl. bd., 1975—, sec. 1979-82, v.p., 1983-86, pres. 1987-90, trustee, 1992—; trustee, vice chmn. then chmn. expert com. Philatelic Found., N.Y.C., 1970—. Author: The FIP Guide to Exhibiting and Judging Traditional and Postal History Exhibits, 1993; author, Editor: Philatelic Vocabulary in Five Languages, 1978 (Vermeil medal 1979); editor: Opinions VI, 1992 (Gold medal); contbr. articles to profl. pubs. Recipient Grand Prix d' Honneur, Zeapex Orgn., 1980; selected to sign Roll of Disting. Philatelists, Brit. Philatelic Fedn., 1991, Alfred Lichtenstein Meml. award Collectors Club, N.Y., 1993, TWA Flight Ops. Meritorious Achievement award, 1995, award of Excellence, 1995. Fellow Royal Philatelic Soc. London, Royal Philatelic Soc. N.Z.; mem. Fedn. Internationale de Philatelie (pres. commn. traditional philately 1978-96; Grand Prix d' Honneur 1980, Svc. medal 1996), Am. Philatelic Soc. (bd. dirs. 1981-84, 89-90, named Champion of Champions 1973, Luff award), Assn. Internationale Des Experts Philateliques (expert 1980—, bd. dirs. 1987—), Fedn. New Zealand Philatelic Socs., Grand Prix Club Internat. (sec., treas. 1980-89, bd. dirs. 1989-92, 94—, v.p. 1994-96, pres. 1996—), Soc. Australasian Specialists (pres. 1969-72), U.S. Chess Fedn. Republican. Episcopalian. Avocations: stamp collecting; photography; languages; chess; bridge. Home: Chalon Round Top Rd Bernardsville NJ 07924 Office: Collector's Club Inc 22 E 35th St New York NY 10016-3806

ODER, BROECK NEWTON, school emergency management consultant; b. Highland Park, Ill., Apr. 20, 1953; s. Bruce Newton and Mary Louise (Roe) O.; m. Jolene Marie Peragine, June 28, 1975 (dec. June 1979). BA in History, U. San Diego, 1974, MA in History, 1975; postgrad., U. N.Mex., 1976-77. Life C.C. teaching credential, Calif. Rsch. asst. to pres. U. San Diego, 1975; grad. asst. U. N.Mex., Albuquerque, 1976-79; tchr. history, chmn. dept. Santa Catalina Sch., Monterey, Calif., 1979—, asst. dean students, 1981-83, dir. ind. study, 1981-95, dean students, 1983-91, dir. emergency planning, 1986—, dean campus affairs, 1991-94, dir. security, 1994—; mem. disaster preparedness coun. Monterey County Office Edn., 1988—; chair Diocesan Sch. Emergency Preparedness Coun., 1991—. Mem. bd. of tchrs. The Concord Rev.; contbr. articles to profl. publs. Participant Jail and Bail, Am. Cancer Soc., Monterey, 1988, 89; reviewer sch. emergency plans, Monterey, 1989—. Recipient award of merit San Diego Hist. Soc., 1975, Outstanding Tchr. award U. Chgo., 1985, Outstanding Young Educator award Monterey Peninsula Jaycees, 1988, resolution of commendation Calif. Senate Rules Com., 1988, cert. of commendation Calif. Gov.'s Office Emergency Svcs., 1991, nat. cert. of achievement Fed. Emergency Mgmt. Agy., 1991. Mem. ACLU, NRA (life), Congress Racial Equality, Am. Hist. Assn., Orgn. Am. Historians, Nat. Coun. on History Edn., Soc. for History Edn., Second Amendment Found., Individual Rights Found., Phi Alpha Theta. Avocations: reading, sports, target shooting. Office: Santa Catalina Sch 1500 Mark Thomas Dr Monterey CA 93940-5238

ODER, FREDERIC CARL EMIL, retired aerospace company executive, consultant; b. Los Angeles, Oct. 23, 1919; s. Emil and Katherine Ellis (Pierce) O.; m. Dorothy Gene Brumfield, July 2, 1941; children—Frederic E., Barbara Oder Debes, Richard W. B.S., Calif. Inst. Tech., 1940, M.S., 1941; Ph.D., UCLA, 1952. Commd. 2d lt. U.S. Army Air Force, 1941; advanced through grades to col. U.S. Air Force, 1960; ret., 1960; asst. dir. and program mgr. for research and engring. Apparatus and Optical div. Eastman Kodak Co., Rochester, N.Y., 1960-66; with Lockheed Missiles & Space Co., Sunnyvale, Calif., 1966-91; v.p., asst. gen. mgr. div. space systems Lockheed Missiles & Space Co., 1972-73, v.p., gen. mgr. div. space systems, 1973-84, exec. v.p., 1984-85; cons., 1985-91; mem. Def. Intelligence Agy. Sci. Adv. Com., 1972-76, assoc. mem., 1976-78; mem. Air Force Studies Bd., Assembly Engring., NRC, 1975-79, Def. Sci. Bd. Summer Study, 1975, Rev. Panel, 1979, Space Applications Bd., 1985-88. Contbr. articles to profl. publs. Decorated Legion of Merit. Fellow AIAA; mem. NAE, Masons, Sigma Xi. Episcopalian. Home: 224 La Puerta Way Palm Beach FL 33480

ODERMATT, ROBERT ALLEN, architect; b. Oakland, Calif., Jan. 3, 1938; s. Clifford Allen and Margaret Louise (Budge) O.; m. Diana Birtwistle, June 9, 1960; children: Kristin Ann, Kyle David. BArch, U. Calif., Berkeley, 1960. Registered architect, Calif., Oreg., Nev., Colo., Hawaii; cert. Nat. Coun. Archtl. Registration Bds. Draftsman Anderson Simonds Dusel Campini, Oakland, 1960-61; architect James R. Lucas, Orinda, Calif., 1961-62, ROMA Architects, San Francisco, 1962-76; architect, pres. ROMA Architects, 1976-84; prin. ROMA Design Group, San Francisco, 1962-92; pres. The Odermatt Group, Orinda, Calif., 1992—; prin. speaker Internat. Conf. on Rebuilding Cities, Pitts., 1988; mem. U.S. Design in Am. Program, Sofia, Bulgaria, Armenian Disaster Assn. Team, 1989; prin. State of Calif. Bay Area Facilities Plan, 1992; princ. Greece Resort Privatization Program, 1993. Prin. designer U.S. Embassy, Bahrain, Grand Canyon Nat. Park, 1977, Yosemite Nat. Park, 1987; prin. planner hotel complex Westin Hotel, Vail, Colo., 1982, Kaanapali Resort, 1987, Las Montanas Resort, San Diego; master plan U. Calif., Berkeley, 1988, Kohanaiki and Mauna Lani resorts, 1989, Calif. State Strategic Real Estate Plan, 1992, Greek Resort/Marina Privatization Program, 1993, Tektronix Strategic Plan, 1994, United Labs, Manila Master Plan, 1995, State of Calif. Reorganization Plan, 1996, Ford Island Pearl Harbor Master Plan, 1996. Mem. Oakland Mayor's Com. on High Density Housing, 1982, Oakland Gen. Plan Congress, 1994, waterfront plan adv. com. City of Oakland, 1996. Fellow AIA (dir. East Bay chpt. 1969-71, pres. 1980-81, dir. Calif. coun. 1979-81, Disting. Svc. award 1991, nat. dir. 1983-86, nat. v.p. 1986-87, chair AIA internat. steering com. 1993-94, graphic stds. adv. com. 1991-92, U. Calif. archtl. review commn. 1992-96, exec. com. Coll. Fellows 1996—).

ODIER, PIERRE ANDRE, educator, writer, photographer, artist; b. Lausanne, Switzerland, May 24, 1940; came to U.S., 1959; s. Leon Odier and Gretha (Vesper) Hough; m. Mary Ellen Patton, Apr. 2, 1967 (div. Apr. 1984); children: Yvette, Debbi. BA, U. Puget Sound, 1967; MFA, Calif. State U., L.A., 1974; postgrad., UCLA, 1976-83. Cert. tchr., Calif. Owner restaurant The End, Tacoma, Wash., 1961-64; owner gallery Place des Arts, Tacoma, 1964-65; interpeter Weyerhauser Corp., Tacoma, 1964; chairperson dept. fine arts Hoover H.S., Glendale, Calif., 1967—. Author: The Rock, A History of Alcatraz, 1983, Lummis Inside his Habitat, 1977 (State Hist. Soc. award 1981), A Discovery of Age, Students Look at Aging Process, 1992, A Discovery of Destitution, Students Look at Extreme Poverty; editor: Nat. Photographers Assn. quar., 1980-84. Served with U.S. Army, 1959-62. Recipient Tchr. of Yr. award Parent Tchrs. Student Assn., Glendale, Calif., 1979, Tchr. of Yr. award Glendale C. of C., 1983, Hon. Tchr. award Puiching Sch. China, 1994. Mem. Glendale Tchrs. Assn. (contract negotiator 1977), Nat. Photography Instrs. Assn. (chmn. election com., pres. 1980-85, chairperson conv. 1982), China Exploration and Rsch. Soc. (v.p., editor newsletter, expedition leader China, Mongolia, Siberia, Russia, U.S.A. 1994), NEA, Adventurers Club (1st v.p.), Explorers Club. Democrat. Lutheran. Home: 1255 Hill Dr Los Angeles CA 90041-1610 Office: Hoover High Sch 651 Glenwood Rd Glendale CA 91202

ODLE, ROBERT CHARLES, JR., lawyer; b. Port Huron, Mich., Feb. 15, 1944; s. Robert Charles and Elizabeth Dagmar (Lassen) O.; m. Lydia Ann Karpinol, Aug. 2, 1969. B.A., Wayne State U., Detroit, 1966; J.D., Detroit Coll. Law, 1969, LLD (hon.), 1992. Staff asst. to pres. of U.S., 1969-71; dir. adminstrn. Com. Re-election of President, 1971-73; dep. asst. sec. HUD, 1973-76; Washington corp. affairs rep. Internat. Paper Co., 1976-81; asst. sect. Dept. Energy, 1981-85; ptnr. Weil, Gotshal & Manges, 1985—. Mem. Mich. Bar Assn., D.C. Bar Assn., Delta Theta Phi. Republican. Roman Catholic. Club: University (Washington). Home: 476 S Union St Alexandria VA 22314 Office: Weil Gotshal & Manges 1615 L St NW Washington DC 20036-5610

ODLIN, RICHARD BINGHAM, retired banker; b. Olympia, Wash., Nov. 22, 1934; s. Reno and Edith Mary (Murphy) O.; m. 1963 (div. 1969); children: Julia Eleanor Odlin Lord, Tracy Edith Odlin Pacek; m. Barbara Ellen Button, Aug. 8, 1985. AB, Whitman Coll., 1957. With Wells Fargo Bank, San Francisco, 1957-63; various positions to sr. v.p., sec. Puget Sound Nat. Bank, Tacoma, Wash., 1963-92; pres. New Tacoma Parking Corp., 1969-91. Bd. dirs. Tacoma-Pierce County chpt. ARC, 1964-69, vice chmn., 1969; active Wash. State Hist. Soc., treas., 1971-92. Mem. Am. Contract Bridge League (life master), Tacoma Country and Golf Club, Columbia Tower Club (Seattle), Tacoma Club, Balboa Club (Mazatlan, Mex.), Kappa Sigma. Republican. Avocations: duplicate bridge, opera, old time radio. Home: 507 N 3d St Apt 301-A Tacoma WA 98403-2753

O'DOHERTY, BRIAN, writer, filmmaker; b. Ballaghadereen, County Roscommon, Ireland; came to U.S., 1957; m. Barbara Novak, 1960. M.D., Univ. Coll. Dublin, Nat. U. Ireland, 1952, D.P.H. with honors, 1955; MS in Hygiene, Harvard U., 1958; TV host programs Mus. Fine Arts, Boston, 1958-61; art critic N.Y. Times, 1961-64; host Dialogue, WNBC, 1961-64; vis. prof. Berkeley U., 1967; dir. visual arts Nat. Endowment for Arts, 1969-76, dir. media arts, 1976-94; dir. Millennium Projects, 1994-96; prof. visual & media arts Long Island U., Southampton, 1997—; art and architecture critic Today Program, 1971-76; adj. prof. Barnard Coll., 1969-96; univ. prof. L.I. U.-Southhampton Campus, 1997—. Author: Object and Idea: A New York Art Journal 1961-67, 1967; editor: Museums in Crisis, 1972, American Masters, The Voice and the Myth, 1973 2d. revised edit., 1988, Inside the White Cube, 1986, The Strange Case of Mlle. P, 1992. Contbr. articles to profl. jours. Smith-Mundt fellow; recipient Mpls. Citizens award, 1961; Emmy nominations; Eire Soc. Gold medal for contbns. to Culture, 1963; Grand Prix Montreal Internat. Festival of Arts Film award, 1982; Sagittarius award London, 1993. Mem. Am. Irish Historical Soc. (bd. dirs.), N.Y., Irish Mus. of Modern Art (bd. dirs.), Dublin, Whitney Mus. Am. Art (bd. dirs.), Coll. Art Assn. (life mem., Mather award 1964). Office: 15 W 67th St New York NY 10023-6226

ODOM, FLOYD CLARK, surgeon; b. Cisco, Tex., 1946. MD, U. Tex., San Antonio, 1972. Diplomate Am. Bd. Colon & Rectal Surgery, Am. Bd. Surgery. Intern Bexar County Hosp., San Antonio, 1972-73, resident in gen. surgery, 1973-77; fellow in colon & rectal surgery Baylor Med. Ctr., Dallas, 1977-78; with Presbyn. Hosp., Dallas. Fellow ACS, Am. Soc. Colon and Rectal Surgeons. Office: 8220 Walnut Hill Ln Dallas TX 75231-4406

ODOM, GUY LEARY, retired physician; b. New Orleans, May 20, 1911; s. Guy Leroy and Marion (Brown) O.; m. Suzanne Price, Aug. 19, 1933 (dec. Nov. 1965); children—Guy Leary, Linda P. (Mrs. Wesley Cook), Carolyn (Mrs. Terry H. Little); m. Mataline Nye, Dec. 29, 1968. M.D., Tulane U., 1933. Diplomate: Am. Bd. Neurol. Surgery (sec.-treas. 1964-70, chmn. 1970-72). Intern, resident E. La. State Hosp., Jackson, 1933-37; practice medicine, specializing in neurol. surgery Montreal, Que., Can., 1937-42, New Orleans, 1942-43, Durham, N.C., 1943-81; instr. Montreal Neurol. Inst., 1937-42; assoc. surgery La. State U., 1942-43; faculty Duke Med. Sch., 1943-81, prof. neurosurgery, 1950-81, chmn. dept., 1960-75, James B. Duke prof. neurol. surgery, 1974; cons. VA Hosp., Durham; cons. neurosurgery Watts Hosp. Durham, Womack Army Hosp., Ft. Bragg, N.C.; Mem. Adv. Bd. Med. Specialists. Mem. A.M.A., Pan Am. Med. Assn., N.C., Durham-Orange County med. socs., World Fedn. Neurol. Surgery, Internat. Soc. Neurol. Surgery, Am. Acad. Neurol. Surgeons (pres. 1967), Soc. Neurol. Surgeons (pres. 1970-71), Am. Surg. Assn., So. Neurol. Soc. (pres. 1968), Am. Assn. Neurol. Surgeons (pres. 1972). Home: 2812 Chelsea Cir Durham NC 27707-5133

ODOM, WILLIAM ELDRIDGE, army officer, educator; b. Cookeville, Tenn., June 23, 1932; s. John Albert and Callie Frances (Everhart) O.; m. Anne Weld Curtis, June 9, 1962; 1 child, Mark Weld. BS, U.S. Mil. Acad., 1954; MA, Columbia U., 1962, PhD, 1970; DSc (hon.), Middlebury Coll., 1987. Commd. 2nd lt. U.S. Army, 1954, advanced through grades to lt. gen., 1984; mem. U.S. Mil. Liaison Mission to Soviet Forces, Germany, 1964-66; from asst. prof. to assoc. prof. govt. U.S. Mil. Acad., West Point, 1966-69, 74-76; asst. Army attache U.S. embassy, Moscow, 1972-74; nat. security staff mem. White House, 1977-81; asst. chief of staff for intelligence Dept. Army, Washington, 1981-85; dir. Nat. Security Agy., Fort Meade, Md., 1985-88; dir. nat. security studies Hudson Inst., 1988—; adj. prof. pol. sci. Yale U., 1989—; bd. dirs. Nichols Rsch., Am. Sci. and Engring., V-ONE (Virtual Open Network Environs.). Author: The Soviet Volunteers, 1973, On Internal War, 1992, Trial After Triumph, 1992, America's Military Revolution, 1993, (with Robert Dujarric) Commonwealth or Empire? Russia, Central Asia and The Transcaucasus, 1995; contbr. articles to profl. jours. Trustee Middlebury Coll. Bd., 1987—. Decorated Def. Disting. medal with oak leaf cluster, DSM with oak leaf cluster, Legion of Merit, Nat. Security medal, Nat. Intelligence Disting. Svc. medal; grand cross Order of Merit with Star (Fed. Republic Germany); Order Nat. Security Merit (Republic of Korea), officer Nat. Order of Merit (France). Mem. Coun. on Fgn. Rels., Am. Assn. for Advancement of Slavic Studies, Internat. Inst. for Strategic Studies, Am. Polit. Sci. Assn., Acad. Polit. Sci. Conglist. Office: Hudson Inst 1015 18th St NW Ste 300 Washington DC 20036-5215

ODOMS, DAVE, collegiate athletic coach. Head coach-basketball Wake Forest U., Winston-Salem, N.C. Office: Wake Forest U PO Box 7265 Winston Salem NC 27109*

O'DONNELL, EDWARD FRANCIS, JR., lawyer; b. Waterbury, Conn., May 13, 1950; s. Edward Francis and Dorothy Patricia (Breheny) O'D.; m. Jayne Ann DeSantis, Dec. 29, 1972; children: Ryan Anderson, Brooke Stires. BA, St. Anselm Coll., Manchester, N.H., 1972; JD, U. Conn., 1977. Bar: S.C. 1978, Conn. 1977, U.S. Dist. Ct. S.C. 1978, U.S. Dist. Ct. Conn. 1980, U.S. Ct. Appeals (1st and 2d cirs.) 1980. Assoc. Ogeltree, Deakins, Nash, Smoak & Stewart, Greenville, S.C., 1977-79; ptnr. Siegel, O'Connor, Schiff & Zangari, Hartford, Conn., 1979—. Contbr. articles to profl. jours. Mem. ABA, Conn. Bar Assn., S.C. Bar Assn., Hartford Bar Assn., Wampanoag Country Club, Phi Alpha Theta. Roman Catholic. Office: Siegel O'Connor Schiff & Zangari 370 Asylum St Hartford CT 06103-2025

O'DONNELL, EDWARD JOSEPH, bishop, former editor; b. St. Louis, July 4, 1931; s. Edward Joseph and Ruth Mary (Carr) O'D. Student, Cardinal Glennon Coll., 1949-53; postgrad., Kenrick Sem., 1953-57. Ordained priest Roman Cath. Ch., 1957, consecrated bishop, 1984; assoc. pastor in 5 St. Louis parishes, 1957-77; pastor St. Peter's Ch., Kirkwood, Mo., 1977-81; assoc. dir. Archdiocesan Commn. on Human Rights, 1962-70; dir. Archdiocesan Radio-TV Office, 1966-68, Archdiocesan Vocation Council, 1965; editor St. Louis Rev., 1968-81; vicar-gen. Archdiocese of St. Louis, 1981-84, aux. bishop, 1984-94; bishop Diocese of Lafayette, Lafayette, LA, 1994—; bd. dirs. Nat. Cath. Conf. for Interracial Justice, 1980-85, NAACP, 1964-66, Urban League St. Louis, 1962-68; chmn. Interfaith Clergy Coun. Greater St. Louis, 1963-67. Named to Golden Dozen Internat. Soc. Weekly Newspaper Editors, 1970, 77. Mem. Cath. Press Assn., Nat. Assn. TV Arts and Scis. Office: PO Box 3387 Lafayette LA 70502-3387

O'DONNELL, F. SCOTT, banker; b. Brownsville, Pa., Sept. 20, 1940; s. Francis Horner and Rebecca (Warren) O'D.; m. Ann Bukmir, Dec. 30, 1976. BA, Grove City (Pa.) Coll., 1962; postgrad., U. Wis. Grad. Sch. Banking, 1970, Internat. Sch. Banking, U. Colo., 1972. Nat. bank examiner Comptroller of Currency, Cleve., 1965-71; supt. of banks State of Ohio, Columbus, 1975-77; sr. v.p. First Nat. Bank, Steubenville, Ohio, 1971-75; exec. v.p. Heritage Bancorp, Steubenville, 1977-80; from v.p. to sr. v.p. Soc. Corp., Cleve., 1980-95; dep. tax commr. State of Ohio, Columbus, 1996—; mem. state banking bd. Div. of Banks, Columbus, 1979-85, govt. affairs com. Ohio Bankers Assn., 1982-84. Served with USCG, 1963-69. Mem. Columbus Athletic Club, Pitts. Univ. Club, Belmont Hills Country Club. Avocations: golfing, antiques. Home: 31830 Lake Rd Avon Lake OH 44012-2022 Office: Dept Taxation 22nd floor 30 E Broad St Fl 22 Columbus OH 43215-3414

O'DONNELL, BROTHER FRANK JOSEPH, principal; b. Phila., Aug. 6, 1942; s. Francis J. and Eleanor E. (Doney) O'D. BA, U. Dayton, 1963; MLS, Cath. U. Am., 1964; MEd, Loyola Coll., 1971; JD, U. Md., 1991. Faculty mem. Cardinal Gibbons High Sch., Balt., ednl. media coord., libr., 1964—, prin., 1969—; dir. tenant advocacy program Justice Ctr. Balt., 1991; N.Y. prov. dir. of edn., 1993. Mem. ABA, Nat. Assn. Secondary Sch. Prins., Nat. Cath. Edn. Assn.

O'DONNELL, G. DANIEL, lawyer; b. Scranton, Pa., 1951. BA summa cum laude, U. Notre Dame, 1973; JD, U. Pa., 1976. Bar: Pa. 1976. Ptnr., chmn. bus. dept. Dechert Price & Rhoads, Phila. Mem. Order of Coif. Home: 102 West Chestnut Hill Ave Philadelphia PA 19118 Office: Dechert Price & Rhoads 4000 Bell Atlantic Tower 1717 Arch St Philadelphia PA 19103-2713

O'DONNELL, JAMES FRANCIS, health science administrator; b. Cleve., July 22, 1928; s. John Michael and Mary Louise (Hayes) O'D.; m. Winifred Locke, Sept. 10, 1955; children—Anne Catherine, Patrick John, Mary Elizabeth. B.S. in Biology, St. Louis U., 1949; Ph.D. in Biochemistry, U. Chgo., 1957. Asst., then. assoc. prof. biol. chemistry and exptl. medicine Coll. Medicine, U. Cin., 1957-68; grants assoc., div. research grants NIH, Bethesda, Md., 1968-69; program dir. population and reprodn. grants br. Ctr. for Population Research, Nat. Inst. Child Health and Human Devel., NIH, 1969-71; asst. dir. div. research resources NIH, Bethesda, 1971-76, dep. dir. div. research resources, 1976-90, acting dir. div. research resources, 1981-82, dir. Office of Extramural Programs, Office of the Dir., 1990—. Served with U.S. Army, 1950-52. Home: 11601 Bunnell Ct S Rockville MD 20854-3603 Office: NIH 6701 Rockledge Dr Rm 6182 Bethesda MD 20817-1813

O'DONNELL, JOHN JOSEPH, JR., optometrist; b. Phila., Oct. 26, 1956; s. John Joseph and Mary Agnes (Hungrige) O'D.; m. Jane Susan Betz, June 28, 1980; children: Kathryn Marie, John Joseph III, Michael Charles. BS in Biology, St. Joseph U., 1978; BS in Ocular Sci., Pa. Coll. Optometry, 1981, OD with honors, 1983. Cardio-pulmonary perfusionist Hosp. U. Pa., Phila., 1978-80; staff optometrist Pa. Eye Assocs., Harrisburg, 1983-85; staff chief optometric svcs. Meml. Eye Inst., Harrisburg, 1986-93; optometrist, ptnr. Premier Eye Care Group, Harrisburg, 1994—; trustee Optometric Svc. Corp. Pa., Harrisburg, 1989. Contbr. articles to profl. jours. Fellow Am. Acad. Optometry; mem. Am. Optometric Assn., Pa. Optometric Assn. (trustee 1987-94, pres. 1994), Ctrl. Pa. Optometric Soc. (pres. 1985-86). Republican. Roman Catholic. Avocations: golf, computers, writing, photography. Office: Premier Eye Care Group Inc 92 Tuscarora St Harrisburg PA 17104-1667

O'DONNELL, JOHN LOGAN, lawyer; b. Chgo., Mar. 6, 1914; s. William Joseph and Elizabeth (McLogan) O'D.; m. Mary Ellen Sipe, Sept. 2, 1939 (dec. Dec. 29, 1979); 1 son, John Logan; m. Michele G. Fischer, May 9, 1981. B.A., Williams Coll., 1934; J.D., Northwestern U., 1937. Bar: Ill. 1937, N.Y. 1943, D.C. 1977. Asso. firm Defrees, Buckingham, Jones and Hoffman, Chgo., 1937-38; staff atty. Office Gen. Counsel, SEC, 1938-41; instr. Cath. U. Law Sch., 1938-41; assoc. Cravath, Swaine & Moore, N.Y.C., 1941-52; ptnr. Olwine, Connelly, Chase, O'Donnell & Weyher, N.Y.C., 1952-91, of counsel, 1991; of counsel Aron, Twomey, Hoppe & Gallanty, N.Y.C., 1991—. Bd. dirs. Near East Found., 1968-84. Fellow Am. Coll. Trial Lawyers; mem. Assn. Bar City N.Y., Am., Fed., bar assns., Beta Theta Pi, Phi Delta Phi. Roman Catholic. Clubs: Union, Univ., Williams, (N.Y.C.). Avocations: piano, sports. Home: 181 E 73rd St New York NY 10021-3549 Office: Aron Twomey Hoppe & Gallanty 757 3rd Ave New York NY 10017-2013

O'DONNELL, KEVIN, retired metal working company executive; b. Cleve., June 9, 1925; s. Charles Richard and Ella (Kilbane) O'D.; m. Ellen Blydenburgh, Aug. 16, 1965; children: Kevin, Susan, Michael, John, Maura, Neil, Megan, Hugh. AB, Kenyon Coll., Gambier, Ohio, 1947, PhD in Law (hon.), 1980; MBA, Harvard U., 1947; PhD in Econs. (hon.), Pusan (Korea) Nat. U., 1970; Ph.D. in Humanities (hon.), Ohio Wesleyan U., 1972. Gen. sales mgr. Steel Improvement & Forge Co., Cleve., 1947-60; mgmt. cons. Booz, Allen and Hamilton, Cleve., 1960-62; gen. mgr., dir. Atlas Alloys-Rio Algom Corp., Cleve., 1963-66; dir. Peace Corps, Seoul, 1966-70; dir. adminstrn. and fin., then dep. acting dir. Peace Corps, 1970-71; assoc. dir. internat. ops. ACTION, 1971-72; exec. v.p. SIFCO Industries, Inc., Cleve., 1972-75; pres., chief oper. officer SIFCO Industries, Inc., 1976-83, pres., chief exec. officer, 1983-89, chief exec. officer, 1989-90, chmn., exec. comm., 1990-94; bd. dirs. Nat. Machinery, Tiffin, Ohio, Central Park Media Corp., N.Y.C., R.P.M. Inc., Medina, Ohio. Trustee Alcohol Svcs. Cleve., 1993—, Cleve. Coun. World Affairs, Nat. Peace Corps Assn.; mem. Coun. Fgn. Rels., N.Y.C., Washington Inst. Fgn. Affairs, Cleve. Com. Fgn. Rels., chmn., 1979-82; chmn. CCWA, 1982-89; pres. Guest House, Inc., 1990-92. Decorated Order Civil Merit (Republic of Korea). mem. Harvard Bus. Sch. Club Cleve., Harvard Bus. Sch. Alumni Assn. (dir. Boston 1991-94), First Friday Club, 50 Club, Union Club, Pepper Pike Country Club, Westwood Country Club, Army-Navy Club (Washington), Knights of Malta (master knight). Republican. Roman Catholic. Avocations: golf, reading.

O'DONNELL, LAURENCE GERARD, editorial consultant; b. Bklyn., June 30, 1935; s. Thomas Edward and Dorothy (Clark) O'D.; m. Joan M. Coniglio, Jan. 9, 1960; children: Christopher, Carolyn, Jeffrey, Anthony. AB, Holy Cross Coll., 1957. Reporter Wall Street Jour., N.Y.C., 1958-66, chief Detroit Bur., 1966-74, asst. mng. editor, N.Y.C., 1974-77, mng. editor, 1977-83; assoc. editor Dow Jones & Co., Inc., N.Y.C., 1983-90; cons. Dow Jones & Co., Inc., 1991—; pres. Dow Jones Newspaper Fund, 1988-93; bd. dirs. Dow Jones Newspaper Fund, Inter Am. Press Assn.; vis. lectr. Queens Coll./CUNY, 1992—. Trustee Holy Cross Coll., 1982-90; mem. journalism adv. bd. Queens Coll./CUNY, 1989—; juror Pulitzer Prize, 1982, 83. Mem. Am. Soc. Newspaper Editors. Office: Dow Jones Newspaper Fund PO Box 300 Princeton NJ 08543-0300

O'DONNELL, LAWRENCE, III, lawyer; b. Houston, Dec. 14, 1957; s. Lawrence Jr. and Annell (Haggart) O'D.; m. Dare Boswell, May 22, 1981; children: Linley, Lawrence IV. BS in Archtl. Engring., U. Tex., 1980; JD cum laude, U. Houston, 1983. Bar: Tex. 1983. Assoc. Wood, Campbell, Moody & Gibbs, Houston, 1983-84; ptnr. Campbell & Riggs, Houston, 1984-91; dep. gen. counsel Baker Hughes Inc., Houston, 1991-94; v.p., gen. counsel Baker Hughes Oilfield Ops., Houston, 1993-95; corp. sec. Baker Hughes Inc., Houston, 1991-96, v.p., gen. counsel, 1995—; bd. dirs. Spring Br. Edn. Found., Am. Arbitration Assn. Trustee Houston Police Activities League. Mem. ABA, Tex. State Bar (corp. law com. of bus. law sect.), Houston Bar Assn., Am. Corp. Counsel Assn., Am. Soc. Corp. Sec., Tex. Bus. Law Found., Houston Bar Assn., Am. Soc. Civil Engrs., Order of Barons, Phi Delta Phi. Avocations: golf, tennis, sailing, skiing. Office: Baker Hughes Inc 3900 Essex Ln Ste 1200 Houston TX 77027-5112

O'DONNELL, LAWRENCE FRANCIS, JR., author; b. Boston, Nov. 7, 1951; s. Lawrence Frances and Frances Marie (Buckley) O'D.; m. Kathryn Hunter Harrold; 1 child, Elizabeth Buckley Harrold. AB, Harvard U., 1976. Writer self-employed, Boston and N.Y.C., 1976-84, 84-87; sr. advisor Senator Daniel Patrick Moynihan, Washington, 1988-92; chief of staff U.S. Senate Com. on Environment and Pub. Works, Washington, 1992-93, U.S. Senate Com. on Fin., Washington, 1993-95. Author: Deadly Force, 1983; assoc. producer: A Case of Deadly Force, 1986. Mem. Writers Guild of Am. Home: 324 Palisades Ave Santa Monica CA 90402 Office: 1505 4th St Ste 215 Santa Monica CA 90401-2381

O'DONNELL, PIERCE HENRY, lawyer; b. Troy, N.Y., Mar. 5, 1947; s. Harry J. and Mary (Kane) O'D.; m. Dawn Donley, Mar. 17, 1995; children: Meghan Maureen, Brendan Casey, Courtney Dawn. BA, Georgetown U., 1969, JD, 1972; LLM, Yale U., 1975. Bar: D.C. 1973, U.S. Supreme Ct. 1975, Calif. 1978. Law clk. to Justice Byron R. White U.S. Supreme Ct.; law clk. to Judge Shirley M. Jufstedler U.S. Dist. Ct. (9th cir.); assoc. Williams & Connolly, Washington, 1975-78; ptnr. Beardsley, Hufstedler & Kemble, L.A., 1978-81, Hufstedler, Miller, Carlson & Beardsley, L.A., 1981-82, O'Donnell & Gordon, L.A., 1982-88, Kaye, Scholer, Fierman, Hays & Handler, L.A., 1988-95, O'Donnell, Reeves & Shaeffer, LLP, L.A., 1996—; exec. asst. U.S. Sec. Edn., 1979; spl. counsel Commn. Jud. Performance, San Francisco, 1979; chmn. Nat. Media, Inc., 1984-92. Co-author: Fatal Subtraction: The Inside Story of Buchwald v Paramount, 1992; contbr. articles to profl. jours. Chmn. Friends Calif. Tech. YMCA, 1983-84, Verduga-San Rafael Urban Mountain Park Fund, 1980-84; bd. dirs. Friends of Altadena Libr., 1979-81, Pasadena-Foothill Urban League; bd. dirs. Foothill Family Svc., 1979-85, chmn., 1984-85; bd. dirs. Interfaith Ctr. To Reverse Arms Race, 1984-90, pres., 1987-88. Mem. PEN, NAACP, Am. Law Inst., Econ. Round Table L.A., Sierra Club, Bel Air Country Club, Gridiron Club (Georgetown U.). Roman Catholic. Home: 405 Linda Vista Ave Pasadena CA 91105-1237 Office: O'Donnell Reeves & Shaeffer LLP 633 W 5th St Ste 1700 Los Angeles CA 90071-2005

O'DONNELL, ROBERT MICHAEL, electrical engineering executive; b. Lynn, Mass., Aug. 31, 1941; s. Michael Cornelius and Katherine (Niland)

O'D.; m. Margaret Ann Connell, Aug. 20, 1968 (div. 1978); children: Michael, Meghan; m. Janice Elaine Nickerson, Aug. 1, 1983; children: Brian, Andrew. BS in Physics, MIT, 1963; MS in Physics, U. Pa., 1964, PhD in Physics, 1970. Mem. tech. staff MITRE Corp., Beford, Mass., 1969-73, MIT Lincoln Lab., Lexington, Mass., 1973-83; mgr. systems engring. RCA, Moorestown, N.J., 1983-86; v.p., chief scientist ISC Def. and Space Group, Lancaster, Pa., 1986-88; sr. staff MIT Lincoln Lab., Lexington, Mass., 1988—. Contbr. numerous articles to profl. jours. Mem. IEEE Aerospace Elec. Sys. Soc. (bd. govs. 1997—), IEEE (sr., vice-chmn. radar panel 1983-84, chmn. 1985-86). Mem. United Ch. Christ. Avocations: amateur radio, classical music. Office: MIT Lincoln Lab 244 Wood St Lexington MA 02173-6426

O'DONNELL, ROSIE, comedienne, actress; b. Commack, N.Y., 1962; 1 son: Parker Jaren. Attended, Dickinson Coll., Boston Univ. Appearances include (TV series) Gimme A Break, 1986-87, Stand By Your Man, 1992, Women Aloud, 1992, Stand-up Spotlight, VH-1 (American Comedy award nomination best female performer in a TV special 1994, Cable ACE award nomination best entertainment host 1994), (TV) Host, The Rosie O'Donnell Show, 1995—; (film) A League of Their Own, 1992, Sleepless in Seattle, 1993 (American Comedy award nomination best supporting female in a motion picture 1994), Another Stakeout, 1993 (American Comedy award nomination best actress in a motion picture 1994), Car 54, Where Are You?, 1994, The Flintstones, 1994, Exit to Eden, 1994, Now and Then, 1995, Beautiful Girls, 1996, Harriet the Spy, 1996, A Very Brady Sequel, 1996 (uncredited), Wide Awake, 1996; (theatre) Grease (Broadway prodn.), 1994. Office: Internat Creative Mgmt 8942 Wilshire Blvd Beverly Hills CA 90211-1934*

O'DONNELL, SCOTT RICHARD, aviation administrator; b. Pitts., Sept. 27, 1950; s. Robert Thomas and Corinne Ann (Phelps) O'D.; m. Patricia Lea Donnelly, Sept. 1, 1978; children: Ronald, Michael, Daniel. BA, Geneva Coll., 1972. Cert. secondary edn. teaching. Tchr. Montour High Sch., McKees Rocks, Pa., 1973-74; project adminstr. Allegheny County Law Dept., Pitts., 1974-76; adminstrv. asst. Allegheny County Police Dept., Pitts., 1976-77; exec. asst. Allegheny County Commr., Pitts., 1977-80; dir. adminstrn. Allegheny County, Pitts., 1980-88, dir. aviation, 1988-94, dir. property assessment appeals, 1994; v.p. airports Lockheed Air Terminals (now Airport Group Internat.), 1994—. Chmn. Higher Edn. Bldg. Authority, Pitts., 1983-90; dir. Allegheny West Authority, Pitts., 1988-94; mem. Mediate, Moon Twp., Pa., 1991-94. Recipient Disting. Alumni award Geneva Coll., Beaver Falls, Pa., 1988, Disting. Svc. award FAA, Jamaica, N.Y., 1992; named Man of Yr. in Law and Govt., Vectors, Pitts., 1992. Mem. Am. Soc. Pub. Adminstrn. (past pres., exec. bd.), Airport Area C. of C. (exec. bd. 1988-94), Airport Coun. Internat., Am. Assn. Airport Execs. Democrat. Presbyterian. Avocation: golf. Home: 20241 Ruston Rd Woodland Hills CA 91364-5642 Office: 330 N Brand Blvd Ste 300 Glendale CA 91203-2308

O'DONNELL, TERESA HOHOL, software development engineer, antennas engineer; b. Springfield, Mass., Nov. 25, 1963; d. Marion Henry and Lena Ann (Zajchowski) Hohol; m. Patrick Alan O'Donnell; children: Kelly Marle, Tracy Alana. BS in Computer Engring., MIT, 1985, BSEE, 1985, MSEE, MS in Computer Sci., 1986. Rsch. asst. MIT Rsch. Lab for Electronics, Cambridge, 1985-86; lead VHSIC insertion engr. USAF Electronic Systems Div., Hanscom AFB, Mass., 1986-88; intelligent antennas engr. USAF Rome Lab., Hanscom AFB, Mass., 1988-91; software devel. engr. Arcon Corp., Waltham, Mass., 1991—. Composer: (choral mass setting) Mass of Rejoicing, 1989; inventor: U.S. patents on Cab to Cap Gap Filler Apparatu, 1996, Weather Seal Strip, 1996. Performer Zbeide's Harem, Tewksbury, Mass., 1986-93; organist/composer St. Theresa's Choir, Billerica, Mass., 1987-95. Maj. USAF and USAFR, 1986—. Decorated Commendation medal (2), Joint Svc. Achievement medal. Mem. IEEE, Nat. Assn. Pastoral Musicians, Am. Guild Organists, Assn. for Computing Machinery, Res. Officers Assn., Sigma Xi, Eta Kappa Nu (v.p. 1985-86). Roman Catholic. Avocations: music, dancing, theater, composing, roller skating. Office: Arcon Corp 260 Bear Hill Rd Waltham MA 02154-1018

O'DONNELL, TERRENCE, lawyer; b. N.Y.C., Mar. 3, 1944; s. Emmett and Lorraine (Muller) O'Donnell; m. Margaret Lynne Kidder; children: Stephanie T., Erin K., Victoria L. BS, U.S. Air Force Acad., 1966; JD, Georgetown Law Sch., 1971. Bar: D.C. 1971, U.S. Ct. Appeals (D.C. cir.) 1978, U.S. Ct. Appeals (4th cir.) 1987, U.S. Dist. Ct. Md. 1986, U.S. Ct. Mil. Appeals 1990, U.S. Ct. Fed. Claims, U.S. Supreme Ct., others. Commd. 2d lt. USAF, 1966, advanced through grades to capt.; various positions USAF, Washington and Republic of Vietnam, 1966-72; resigned USAF, 1972; spl. asst. Pres. of U.S., The White House, Washington, 1972-77; appointments sec. Pres. Ford, Washington, 1974-77; assoc. Williams & Connolly, Washington, 1977-82, ptnr., 1982-89; gen. counsel Dept. Def., Washington, 1989-92; ptnr. Williams and Connolly, Washington, 1992—; Presdl. appointee to bd. visitors U.S. Air Force Acad., Colorado Springs, 1982-87, chmn., 1985-86; U.S. corr. and rep. UN Program to Prevent Crime, Washington and N.Y.C., 1977-81; bd. dirs. IGI Inc., MLC Holdings. Trustee Gerald R. Ford Found., Grand Rapids, Mich., 1987—; mem. Adminstrv. Conf. U.S., 1991-92; mem. claims ct. adv. com., mem. code com. U.S. Ct. Mil. Appeals, 1993—; bd. dirs. Falcon Found., 1988—. Decorated Bronze star; recipient Disting. Pub. Svc. medal Dept. of Def., 1992, Disting. Svc. award U.S. Atty. Gen., 1992. Mem. ABA, D.C. Bar Assn., Fed. Bar Assn., Bar of U.S. Supreme Ct., Bar of U.S. Ct. Appeals, Bar of U.S. Dist. Ct. of Md., Bar of Mil. Ct. Appeals, Bar Fed. Ct. Claims. Home: 5133 Yuma St NW Washington DC 20016-4336 Office: Williams and Connolly 725 12th St NW Washington DC 20005-3901

O'DONNELL, THOMAS FRANCIS, vascular surgeon, health facility administrator; b. Providence, R.I., Sept. 7, 1941; s. Thomas Francis and Mary Jo O'Donnell; m. Carolyn Eva Rogean, Aug. 28, 1965; children: Thomas F. III, Hugh Jackson. AB, Harvard Coll., 1963; MD, Tufts U., 1967. Vascular fellow St. Thomas Hosp., London, 1974-75, Mass. Gen. Hosp., Boston, 1975; vascular surgeon, chief vascular surgery New Eng. Med. Ctr., Boston, pres., CEO, chmn. dept. surgery; Andrews profl surgery Tufts U. Sch. Medicine; Kinmouth meml. lectr. Vascular Soc. of Great Britain and Ireland, 1989. Author numerous book chpts. on vascular surgery; reviewer jour. publs. Coach Wellesley Youth Work, Wellesley Youth Hockey, 1977-80. Lt. comdr. USN, 1969-71. Fellow Royal Soc. Medicine; mem. Soc. Vascular Surgery (head membership com.), Internat. Vascular Soc. (N.Am. chpt.), N.E. Soc. for Vascular Surgery (pres. 1994). Roman Catholic. Avocations: tennis, golf. Home: 49 Cliff Rd Wellesley MA 02181-3025 Office: New Eng Med Ctr 750 Washington St Boston MA 02111-1526*

O'DONNELL, THOMAS LAWRENCE PATRICK, lawyer; b. Taunton, Mass., Aug. 12, 1926; s. Patrick Francis and Ellen Balfe (Brady) O'D.; m. Carol Hodgdon, Feb. 16, 1952; children—Ellen, Thomas, Janet Gael, Christopher Hodgdon. A.B. magna cum laude, Harvard U., 1947, LL.B., 1949. Bar: Mass. 1950. Assoc. Ropes & Gray, Boston, 1949-52, 54-61, ptnr., 1962—, chmn., 1984-90; dir. Rath & Strong, Inc., 1985-96. Trustee, Trustees of Reservations, 1970—, chmn. bd., 1975-76; bd. dirs. Mass. Land Conservation Trust, 1975—, chmn. bd., 1986—; bd. dirs. Mass. Taxpayers Found., 1972—, chmn. bd., 1977-79, 93-95, mem. exec. com., 1976—; bd. dirs. Boston Mcpl. Rsch. Bur., 1965—, chmn. bd., 1967-72; mem. pub. pension task force Mass. Bus. Roundtable, 1983-86; bd. dirs., sec. Jobs for Mass., Inc., 1981-83; moderator Town of Hingham, 1967—; del. Rep. Nat. Conv., 1972, all Rep. State convs., 1960-94; dir. Rep. Club of Mass., 1974—; overseer Harvard U., 1986-92; bd. dirs. United Way Mass. Bay, 1987—, mem. exec. com. 1993—, chmn. bd. 1997—. Lt. USNR, 1994-45, 52-54. Recipient Cushing award Labor Guild of Archdiocese Boston, 1973; Pub. Servant award Sons of Italy, Hingham, 1978; mem. Knights of Malta, 1983—. Fellow Am. Bar Found.; mem. ABA, Mass. Bar Assn., Boston Bar Assn., Am. Arbitration Assn., New England Legal Found. (Mass. adv. coun. 1980—), Indsl. Rels. Rsch. Assn. (pres. Boston chpt. 1980), Harvard Alumni Assn. (bd. dirs. 1978-81; 1st marshal class of 1947). Roman Catholic. Clubs: Harvard of Boston (bd. govs. 1985-91), Union of Boston; Hingham Yacht, Comml. Home: 7 South Ln Hingham MA 02043-2446 Office: Ropes & Gray 1 International Pl Boston MA 02110-2602

O'DONNELL, THOMAS MICHAEL, brokerage firm executive; b. Cleve., Apr. 9, 1936; s. John Michael and Mary L. (Hayes) O'D.; m. Nancy A. Dugan, Feb. 4, 1961; children—Christopher, Colleen, Julie. BBA, U. Notre Dame, 1959; MBA, U. Pa., 1960. Cert. Chartered Fin. Analyst. Fin. analyst Saunders Stiver & Co., Cleve., 1960-65; rsch. dir. McDonald & Co., Cleve., 1965-66, exec. v.p. corp. fin., 1967-83, gen. ptnr., 1968-83; pres. McDonald & Co. Investments, Inc./McDonald & Co. Securities, Cleve., 1984-88; chmn., chief exec. officer McDonald & Co. Securities, Cleve., 1988—; bd. dirs. Seaway Food Town; mem. regional firms adv. com. N.Y. Stock Exch., 1986-92, chmn., 1991-92; dir. C.I.D. Venture Funds. Author: The Why and How of Mergers, 1968. Bd. dirs. Greater Cleve. Growth Assn., Inroads Northeast Ohio, PlayHouse Square Found.; bd. regents St. Ignatius High Sch., Cleve.; steering com. Leadership Cleve. Mem. Cleve. Soc. Security Analysts (cert.), Securities Industry Assn. (dir. 1988-94, chmn. 1993), Union Club, Westwood Country Club, 50 Club Cleve., Pepper Pike Club, Double Eagle Club. Roman Catholic. Avocation: golf. Home: 1325 Timber Lea Ct Cleveland OH 44145-2648 Office: McDonald & Co Securities Inc 800 Superior Ave E Ste 2100 Cleveland OH 44114-2601

O'DONNELL, VICTORIA J., communications educator; b. Greensburg, Pa., Feb. 12, 1938; d. Victor C. and Helen A. (Detar) O'D.; children from previous marriage: Christopher O'Donnell Stupp, Browning William Stupp; m. Paul M. Monaco, Apr. 9, 1993. BA, Pa. State U., 1959, MA, 1961, PhD, 1968. Asst. prof. comm. Midwestern State U., Wichita Falls, Tex., 1965-67; prof. dept. chair comm. U. No. Tex., Denton, 1967-89; prof., dept. chair comms. Ore. State U., Corvallis, 1989-91; prof. comm., basic course dir. Mont. State U., Bozeman, 1991-93, prof. comm., dir. honors program, 1993—; prof. Am. Inst. Fgn. Studies, London, 1988; cons. Arco Oil & Gas, Dallas, 1983-86, Federal Emergency Mgrs. Agy., Salt Lake City, 1986; speechwriter Sen. Mae Yih, Salem, Ore., 1989-91; steering com. Ore. Alliance Film & TV Educators, 1990-91. Author: Introduction to Public Communication, 1992, 2d edit., 1993; co-author: Persuasion, 1982, Propaganda and Persuasion, 1986, 2d edit., 1992; producer: (video) Women, War and Work, 1994; mem. editl. bd. Am. Comm. Jour. Bd. dirs. Friends of the Family, Denton, 1987-89, Bozeman Film Festival, 1991—; del. Tex. Dem. Convention, Denton, 1976. Grantee Mont. Com. for the Humanities, 1993, Oreg. Coun. for the Humanities, 1991, NEH, 1977. Mem. Nat. Collegiate Honors Coun., Speech Comm. Assn., Internat. Comm. Assn., Western States Comm. Assn. Home: 290 Low Bench Rd Gallatin Gateway MT 59730-9741 Office: Univ Honors Program Mont State U Bozeman MT 59717

O'DONNELL, WILLIAM DAVID, construction firm executive; b. Brockton, Mass., Aug. 21, 1926; s. John Frank and Agnes Teresa (Flanagan) O'D.; m. Dixie Lou Anderson, Jan. 31, 1951; children—Craig Patrick, Ginger Lynn. BS, U. N.Mex., 1953. Registered profl. engr., Ill., 1958. Engr. State of Ill., 1953-59; with Gregory-Anderson Co., Rockford, Ill., 1959—, gen. mgr., 1960-61, sec., 1961-81, pres., 1981—; bd. dirs. Growth Enterprise, Davis Meml. Park, BankOne, Rockford. Dir. St. Anthony Med. Ctr., Youth Svcs. Network; bd. dirs. Rockford YMCA, pres., 1984. Served with USN, 1943-47. Recipient Friend of the Boy award Optimist Club, 1966, Excalibur award for community service Rockford Register Star, 1971; named Titan of Yr., Boylan High Sch., 1974. Fellow ASCE, NSPE, Soc. Am. Mil. Engrs.; mem. No. Ill. Bldg. Contractors, Aircraft Owners and Pilots Assn., Balloon Fedn. Am., World Future Soc., Am. Polar Soc., Sigma Tau, Chi Epsilon, Tau Beta Pi. Clubs: Forest Hills Country (Rockford), Metropolitan Club (Chgo.); Adventurers (Chgo.). Lodges: Rotary (Service Above Self award 1972; v.p. Rockford chpt. 1983, pres. 1984). Home: 2004 Bradley Rd Rockford IL 61107-1258 Office: Gregory Anderson Co PO Box 900 Rockford IL 61105-0900

O'DONNELL, WILLIAM HUGH, English educator; b. San Diego, June 17, 1940; s. William Henry and Ella (McMullen) O'D.; m. Gloria Roach, June 5, 1967; children: Kerry Susan, Clare Louise. BA, U. Wash., 1962; MA, Princeton U., 1969, PhD, 1971. Asst., then assoc. prof. English Pa. State U., University Park, 1971-86; prof. English, chmn. dept. U. Memphis, 1986-93, prof., 1986—. Author: Guide to Prose Fiction of Yeats, 1984, Poetry of W.B. Yeats, 1986; editor: Speckled Bird, 1977, Prefaces and Introductions by W.B. Yeats, 1989, Later Essays of W.B. Yeats, 1994. Served with USN, 1962-67. NEH grantee, 1973-74; fellow Am. Council of Learned Societies, 1977-78. Mem. MLA, Am. Com. Irish Studies, Internat. Assn. Study Anglo-Irish Lit., South Atlantic MLA, Assn. for Asian Studies. Office: U Memphis English Dept Campus Box 526176 Memphis TN 38152-6176

O'DONNELL, WILLIAM JAMES, engineering executive; b. Pitts., June 19, 1935; s. William James and Elizabeth (Rau) O'D.; m. Joanne Mary Kusen, Jan. 31, 1959; children—Suzanne, Janice, William, Thomas, Kerry, Amy. B.S.M.E., Carnegie Inst. Tech., 1957; M.S.M.E., U. Pitts., 1959, Ph.D., 1962. Jr. engr. Westinghouse Research Lab., 1957-58, asso. engr., 1958; with Westinghouse Bettis Atomic Power Lab., West Mifflin, Pa., 1961-70, adv. engr., 1966-70; pres., chmn. bd. O'Donnell & Assos., Inc., Pitts., 1970—. Contbr. numerous articles on engring. and mechanics to profl. jours.; holder patents on processes and devices. Served with C.E. AUS, 1963-64. Recipient Machinery's Achievement award as outstanding mech. designer, 1957, Pi Tau Sigma Gold medal for achievements in engring., 1967, Pressure Vessel and Piping award Am . Soc. of Mechanical Engineers, 1994. Fellow ASME (nat. award for outstanding contbn. to engring. profession 1973, internat. award for best publ. in pressure vessels and poping 1988, Engr. of Yr. award 1988, Pressure Vessel and Piping medal 1994); mem. NSPE, AAAS, ASTM, Soc. Exptl. Mechanics, Am. Nuclear Soc., Am. Soc. Metals Internat., The Minerals, Metals and Materials Soc., Sigma Xi. Home: 3611 Maplevue Dr Bethel Park PA 15102-1423 Office: O'Donnell Consulting Engrs 3611 Maplevue Dr Bethel Park PA 15102-1423

O'DONOHUE, WALTER JOHN, JR., medical educator; b. Washington, Sept. 23, 1934; s. Walter John and Mavis Leota (Terry) O'D.; m. Cynthia Ann Halmintoller, Aug. 10, 1957 (div. 1978); 1 child, Diane Louise; m. Maria Theresa Sauer, Nov. 27, 1978; children: Walter John III, Mary Theresa. BA, Va. Mil. Inst., 1957; MD, Med. Coll. Va., 1961. Diplomate Am. Bd. Internal Medicine, Am. Bd. Pulmonary Medicine. Resident internal medicine Med. Coll. Va., Richmond, 1961-63, 65-66, chief med. resident, 1966-67, cardio-pulmonary fellow, 1967-69, asst. prof. medicine, 1968-73, assoc. prof., 1973-77; prof. Creighton U., Omaha, Nebr., 1977—, chief pulmonary medicine div., 1977—, chmn. dept. medicine, 1985-96; assoc. chair for edn., 1996—, dir. internal medicine program, 1995—. Editor: Current Advances in Respiratory Care, 1984, Long-term Oxygen Therapy: Scientific Basis and Clinical Application, 1995; contbr. over 100 articles to med. jours., chpts. to books. Served to capt. M.C., U.S. Army, 1963-65. Fellow ACP, Am. Coll. Chest PHysicians (regent 1986-88, gov. for Nebr. 1982-88); mem. AMA (CPT adv. com. 1992—), Am. Lung Assn. (bd. dirs. 1981-87), Nebr. Lung Assn. (bd. dirs., pres. 1979-81), Am. Assn. Respiratory Care (chmn. bd. med. advisors 1986-87), Assn. Profs. Medicine, Nat. Assn. Med. Dirs. on Respiratory Care (pres. 1995-97). Republican. Roman Catholic. Avocations: hunting, fishing. Home: 12773 Izard St Omaha NE 68154-1243 Office: Creighton U Sch Medicine 601 N 30th St Omaha NE 68131-2137

O'DONOVAN, LEO JEREMIAH, university president, theologian, priest; b. N.Y.C., Apr. 24, 1934; s. Leo J. Jr. O'D. AB, Georgetown U., 1956; Licentiate in Philosophy, Fordham U., 1961; STB, Woodstock Coll., 1966, Licentiate in Sacred Theology, 1967; ThD, U. Münster, Fed. Republic Germany, 1971. Joined S.J., 1957, ordained priest Roman Cath. Ch., 1966. Instr. philosophy Loyola Coll., Balt., 1961-63; asst. prof. Woodstock (Md.) Coll., 1971-74; assoc. prof. Weston Sch. Theology, Cambridge, Mass., 1974-81, prof., 1981-89; pres. Georgetown U., Washington, 1989—; provincial asst. formation Md. Province S.J., Balt., 1985-88; cons. Nat. Conf. Cath. Bishops, Washington, 1986-89; vis. fellow Woodstock Theol. Ctr.; bd. dirs. The Riggs Nat. Bank, Walt Disney Co. Co-editor: The Society of Jesus and Higher Education in America, 1965; (author preface) Faithful Witness: Foundations of Theology for Today's Church, 1989; assoc. editor Jour. Am. Acad. Religion, 1985-89; mem. adv. bd. America mag., 1985-89; contbr. numerous articles to America, Washington Post, Theol. Studies, Communio, Cross Currents. Bd. dirs. U. Detroit Mercy, 1986-95; vice chair Consortium of Univs. of Washington Met. Area, 1993-94, chair, 1994-96, trustee, 1989—; mem. campaign for communities com. Local Initiatives Support Corp., 1993—; mem. exec. com. Fed. City Coun., 1993-95; bd. dirs. Nat. Assn. Ind. Colls. and Univs., 1991-94, Consortium on Financing Higher Edn., 1990—; active Bus.-Higher Edn. Forum, 1989—, Nat. Coun. on Arts, 1994—; exec. com. Campus Compact, 1990—. Fulbright scholar Fulbright Found., U. Lyon, France, 1956-57; Danforth fellow Danforth Found., 1956-71; Assn. Theol. Schs. grantee on teaching, 1978-79. Fellow Soc. for Values in Higher Edn.; mem. Assn. of Jesuit Colls. and Univs. (fed. rels. com. 1994—), Assn. Cath. Colls. and Univs. (bd. dirs. 1994—), Boston Theol. Soc., University Club. Office: Georgetown U Office of President 37th O St NW Washington DC 20057

O'DOR, RON, physiologist, marine biology educator; b. Kansas City, Mo., Sept. 20, 1944; s. Claude Marvin O'Dor and Opal LaMoyne (Sears) Mathes; m. Janet Ruth Spiller, Dec. 30, 1967; children: Matthew Arnold, Stephen Roderick. AA, El Camino Coll., 1965; AB, U. Calif., Berkeley, 1967; PhD, U. B.C., Can., 1971. From asst. prof. to prof. Dalhousie U., Halifax, N.S., Can., 1973—, chairperson dept. biology, 1997—; dir. Aquatron Lab., Halifax, 1986-93; summer scientist Laboratoire Arago, Banyuls-sur-Mer, France, 1979-85; vis. scientist Pacific Biol. Sta., Nanaimo, B.C., 1980, U. Papua New Guinea, Motupore Island, 1989-91, Port Elizabeth Mus., South Africa, 1994; vis. prof. U. B.C., Vancouver, 1986-87; sessional prof. Bamfield (B.C.) Marine Sta., 1987; cons. UN, Rome, 1987—; adv. space sta. Can. Space Agy., Ottawa, 1992—; mem. mgmt. com. Ocean Prodn. Enhancement Network, Halifax, 1993-95. Author, editor: Cephalopod Fishery Biology, 1993, Physiology of Cephalopod Molluscs, 1994; contbg. author Cephalopod Life Cycles, Vol. I, 1983, Vol. II, 1987; contbr. articles and revs. to profl. jours. Scholar Med. Rsch. Coun. Can., 1968; fellow MRC, Cambridge U., Eng., 1971-73, Stazione Zoologica, Naples, Italy, 1971-73; recipient Hon. Mention Rolex Awards Enterprise, 1987. Mem. Can. Soc. Zoologists (councillor 1989-92), Can. Fedn. Biological Socs., Soc. Integrative and Comparative Biology, Am. Soc. Gravitational and Space Biology, Cephalopod Internat. Adv. coun. (councillor, pres. 1988-91), Phi Beta Kappa. Achievements include co-development of acoustic pressure transducer/transmitters and radio-linked tracking systems for monitoring cephalopod bioenergetics in nature; co-organization of projects in the Azores, South Africa and Papua New Guinea to monitor squid and nautilus, first international cephalopod research conference in Japan, experiment with Aquatic Research Facility Space Shuttle STS-77, 1996. Home: 1181 South Park St, Halifax, NS Canada B3H 2W9 Office: Dalhousie University, Biology Dept, Halifax, NS Canada B3H 4J1

O'DOWD, DONALD DAVY, retired university president; b. Manchester, N.H., Jan. 23, 1927; s. Hugh Davy and Laura (Morin) O'D.; m. Janet Louise Fithian, Aug. 23, 1953; children: Daniel D., Diane K., James E., John M. BA summa cum laude, Dartmouth Coll., 1951; postgrad. (Fulbright fellow), U. Edinburgh, Scotland, 1951-52; MA, Harvard U., 1955, PhD, 1957. Instr., asst. prof. psychology, dean freshmen Wesleyan U., Middletown, Conn., 1955-60; assoc. prof., prof. of psychology, dean Univ. Oakland Univ., Rochester, Mich., 1960-65, provost, 1965-70; pres. Oakland U., Rochester, Mich., 1970-80; exec. vice chancellor SUNY, Albany, 1980-84; pres. U. of Alaska Statewide System, 1984-90. Sr. cons. Assn. Governing Bds. Univs. and Colls. Carnegie Corp. fellow, 1965-66. Mem. APA, AAAS, Phi Beta Kappa, Sigma Xi. Home and Office: 1550 La Vista Del Oceano Santa Barbara CA 93109-1739

O'DRISCOLL, MARILYN LUTZ, elementary school educator; b. L.A.; d. Robert Thomas and Helen Mary (Cardamone) Lutz; m. John P. O'Driscoll Jr., Jan. 15, 1966 (dec. 1978); children: Kelley, John, Patrick. BS in Edn., U. So. Calif., 1961, cert. lang. devel. specialist, 1990. Cert. tchr., Calif. Tchr. kindergarten Montebello (Calif.) Sch. Dist., 1961-64, Garvey Sch. Dist., Rosemead, Calif., 1964—; program quality reviewer San Gabriel Consortium, 1988-94; mem. parent bd. Incarnation Sch., Glendale, Calif., 1990-92, chmn. sch. site coun., 1990-93; participant ednl. TV program, 1989—. Pres. Incarnation Parish Coun., 1993-95. Mem. ASCD, NEA, Garvey Edn. Assn., Calif. Tchrs. Assn., Women of Troy (life), Spirit of Troy (life), Trojan Guild, Kappa Delta.

ODZA, RANDALL M., lawyer; b. Schnectady, May 6, 1942; s. Mitchell and Grace (Mannes) O.; m. Rita Ginness, June 19, 1966; children—Kenneth, Keith. B.S. in Indsl. and Labor Relations, Cornell U., 1964, LL.B., 1967. Bar: N.Y. 1967, U.S. Ct. Appeals (2d cir.) 1970, U.S. Dist. Ct. (no., so. and ea. dists.) N.Y. 1969, U.S. Dist. Ct. (we. dist.) N.Y. 1970, Fed. Dist. Ct. (we. dist.) N.Y. Assoc. Proskauer, Rose, Goetz & Mendelsohn, N.Y.C., 1967-69; assoc. Jaeckle, Fleischmann & Mugel, Buffalo, 1969-72, ptnr., 1972—. Trustee, legal counsel, past treas. Temple Beth Am. Recipient Honor award Western N.Y. Retail Mchts. Assn., 1980. Mem. Indsl. Relations Rsch. Assn. Western N.Y., ABA, Erie County Bar Assn., N.Y. State Bar Assn. Office: Jaeckle Fleischmann & Mugel 12 Fountain Plz Buffalo NY 14202-2222

OECHLER, HENRY JOHN, JR., lawyer; b. Charlotte, N.C., Apr. 9, 1946; s. Henry J. and Convere Jones (McAden) O. AB, Princeton U., 1968; JD, Duke U., 1971. Bar: N.Y. 1972, U.S. Ct. Appeals (2d cir.) 1974, U.S. Ct. Appeals (D.C. cir.) 1975, U.S. Ct. Appeals (8th cir.) 1986, U.S. Ct. Appeals (9th cir.) 1995. Assoc. Chadbourne & Parke, N.Y.C., 1971-80, ptnr., 1980—. Avocations: studying airline schedules. Office: Chadbourne & Parke 30 Rockefeller Plz New York NY 10112

OEHLER, RICHARD WILLIAM, lawyer; b. N.Y.C., Nov. 24, 1950; s. John Montgomery and Florence Mae (Jahn) O.; m. Linda Tyson. BA, Dartmouth Coll., 1972; JD, Harvard U., 1976. Bar: Calif. 1976, Wash. 1987, D.C. 1988, U.S. Dist. Ct. (no. dist.) Calif. 1976, U.S. Dist. Ct. Wash. 1987, U.S. Claims Ct. 1979, U.S. Ct. Appeals (fed. cir.) 1982, U.S. Ct. Appeals (9th cir.) 1976. Assoc. Pillsbury, Madison & Sutro, San Francisco, 1976-78; trial atty. U.S. Dept. Justice, Washington, 1978-87; of counsel Perkins Coie, Seattle, 1987-90, ptnr., 1990—. Mem. ABA, Nat. Contract Mgmt. Assn. (Spl. Achievement award 1990-92), Wash. State Bar Assn. Office: Perkins Coie 1201 3rd Ave Fl 40 Seattle WA 98101-3099

OEHLERT, WILLIAM HERBERT, JR., cardiologist, administrator, educator; b. Murphysboro, Ill., Sept. 11, 1942; s. William Herbert Sr. and Geneva Mae (Roberts) O.; m. L. Keith Brown, Mar. 14, 1976; children: Emily Jane, Amanda Elizabeth. BA, So. Ill. U., 1967; MD, Washington U., St. Louis, 1967. Diplomate Nat. Bd. Med. Examiners, Am. Bd. Internal Medicine, Am. Bd. Cardiovascular Disease, North Am. Soc. Pacing and Electrophysiology. Intern Union Meml. Hosp., Balt., 1967-68, resident, 1968-69; resident U. Iowa, Iowa City, 1969-70, cardiology fellow, 1970-72; asst. prof. medicine, dir. coronary care units U. Okla. Health Sci. Ctr., Oklahoma City, 1972-74, asst. clin. prof. medicine, 1974-82, assoc. clin. prof. medicine, 1982-88, clin. prof. medicine, 1988—; chmn. dept. cardiology Bapt. Med. Ctr., 1992-95; pvt. practice Oklahoma City, 1974—; med. dir. cardiovasc. svcs. Integris Bapt. Med. Ctr., 1993—; pres. Cardiovasc. Clinic, Oklahoma City, 1987-91, chmn. exec. com., 1987-91; pres., med. dir. Cardiovasc. Imaging Svcs. Corp., Oklahoma City, 1987-92; v.p. Plaza Med. Group, 1992-93; CEO W.H. Oehlert, MD, P.C., 1993—. Author: Arrhythmias, 1973, Cardiovascular Drugs, 1976; contbr. articles to profl. jours. Fellow Am. Heart Assn. (nat. program com. 1979-82, pres. Okla. affiliate 1985-86, bd. dirs. 1974-88, ACLS nat. affiliate faculty 1987-90), Am. Coll. Cardiology; mem. AMA, ACP, Nat. Assn. Residents and Interns, Am. Soc. Internal Medicine, Am. Coll. Physician Execs., Okla. County Med. Assn. (chmn. quality of care com. 1990-91), Okla. State Med. Assn., Okla. City Clin. Soc., Okla. Cardiac Soc. (pres. 1978-79), Osler Soc., Soc. Nuclear Medicine, Okla. Found. for Med. Quality (bd. dirs. 1995—), Wilderness Med. Soc., Stewart Wolf Soc., Phi Eta Sigma, Phi Kappa Phi. Home and Office: 3017 Rock Ridge Pl Oklahoma City OK 73120-5713

OEHME, FREDERICK WOLFGANG, medical researcher and educator; b. Leipzig, Germany, Oct. 14, 1933; came to U.S., 1934; s. Friedrich Oswald and Frieda Betha (Wohlgamuth) O.; m. Nancy Beth MacAdam, Aug. 6, 1960 (div. June 1981); children: Stephen Frederick, Susan Lynn, Deborah Ann, Heidi Beth; m. Pamela Sheryl Ford, Oct. 2, 1981; 1 child, April Virginia. BS in Biol. Sci., Cornell U., 1957, DVM, 1958; MS in Toxicology and Medicine, Kans. State U., 1962; DMV in Pathology, Justus Liebig U., Giessen, Germany, 1964; PhD in Toxicology, U. Mo., 1969. Diplomate Am. Bd. Toxicology, Am. Bd. Vet. Toxicology, Acad. Toxicological Scis. Resident intern, Large Animal and Ambulatory Clinic Cornell U., 1957-58; gen. practice vet. medicine, 1958-59; from asst. to assoc. prof. medicine Coll. Vet. Medicine Kans. State U., 1959-66, 69-73, dir. comparative toxicology labs., 1969—, prof. toxicology, medicine and physiology Coll. Vet. Medicine, 1974-96, prof. toxicology, pathology, medicine and physiology, 1996—;

postdoctoral research fellow in toxicology, NIH U. Mo., 1966-69; cons. FDA, Washington, Ctr. for Vet. Medicine, Rockville, Md., Animal Care com. U. Kans., Lawrence, 1969-76, Syntex Corp., Palo Alto, Calif., 1976-77; mem. sci. adv. panel on PBB Gov.'s Office, State of Mich., 1976-77, Coun. for Agrl. Sci. and Tech. Task Force on Toxicity, Toxicology and Environ. Hazard, 1976-83; cons., mem. adv. group on pesticides EPA, Cin., 1977—; expert state and fed. witness; advisor WHO, Geneva; presenter more than 580 papers to profl. meetings; numerous other activities. Author over 680 books and articles on toxicology and vet. medicine; editor, pub. Vet. Toxicology, 1970-76, Vet. and Human Toxicology, 1977—; assoc. editor Toxicology Letters; mem. editl. bd. Am. Jour. Vet. Rsch., 1975-83, Toxicology, 1979-85, Clin. Toxicology, Jour. Toxicologie Medicale, Toxicology and Indsl. Health, Poisindex, Jour. Analytical Toxicology, Companion Animal Practice; reviewer Toxicology and Applied Pharmacology, Jour. Agrl. and Food Chemistry, Spectroscopy, numerous others. Mem. council Luth. Ch. Am., sr. choir, numerous coms., adv. council Cub Scouts Am., Eagle Scouts, mgr., coach Little League Baseball; council rep., treas. area council, various coms. PTA; mem. Manhattan Civic Theatre; bd. trustees Manhattan Marlin Swim Team; dir. meet Little Apple Invitational Swim Meet, 1984. Recipient Disting. Grad. Faculty award Kans. State U., 1977-79, Dir.'s Letter of Commendation, FDA, 1983, Kenneth P. DuBois award Midwest Soc. Toxicology, 1991, Kenneth F. Lampe award Am. Acad. Clin. Toxicology, 1993, John Doull award Ctrl. States Soc. Toxicology, 1994, medal Azabu U., 1994, Silver award Aristotelian U., 1995, others; project fellow Morris Animal Found., 1967-69. Fellow Am. Acad. Clin. Toxicology (charter, past pres., numerous coms.), Am. Acad. Vet. and Comparative Toxicology (past sec.-treas., numerous coms.); mem. Soc. Toxicology (past pres., numerous coms.), World Fedn. Clin. Toxicology Ctrs. and Poison Control Ctrs. (past pres.), Soc. Toxicologic Pathologists, N.Y. Acad. Scis., Am. Vet. Med. Assn. (com. on environmentology 1971-73, adv. com. council on biol. and therapeutic agts. 1971-74, various others), Nat. Ctr. Toxicological Rsch. (vet. toxicology rep. sci. adv. bd.), Nat. Rsch. Coun. (subcom. on organic contaminants in drinking water, safe drinking water com., adv. ctr. on toxicology assembly life scis. 1976-77, panel on toxicology marine bd., assembly of engring. 1976-79, com. on vet. med. scis. assembly life scis. 1976-78), Nat. Ctr. for Toxicological Rsch. (grad. edn. subcom., sci. adv. bd. 1974-77), Cornell U. Athletic Assn, Omega Tau Sigma, Phi Zeta, Sigma Xi, numerous others. Republican. Clubs: Cornell U. Crew; Manhattan Square Dance. Avocations: hist. readings, sci. writings, nature tours and walks, travel. Home: 148 S Dartmouth Dr Manhattan KS 66503-3079 Office: Kans U Comparative Toxicology Labs Manhattan KS 66506

OEHME, REINHARD, physicist, educator; b. Wiesbaden, Germany, Jan. 26, 1928; came to U.S., 1956; s. Reinhold and Katharina (Kraus) O.; m. Mafalda Pisani, Nov. 5, 1952. Dr. rer. nat., U. Goettingen, Germany, 1951; Diplom Physiker, U. Frankfurt am Main, Germany, 1948. Asst. Max Planck Inst. Physics, Goettingen, 1949-53; research asso. Fermi Inst. Nuclear Studies, U. Chgo., 1954-56; mem. faculty dept. physics and Fermi Inst., 1958—, prof. physics, 1964—; mem. Inst. Advanced Studies, Princeton, 1956-58; vis. prof. Inst. de Fisica Teórica, São Paulo, Brazil, 1952-53, U. Md., 1957, U. Vienna, Austria, 1961, Imperial Coll., London, Eng., 1963-64, U. Karlsruhe, Fed. Republic Germany, 1974, 75, 77, U. Tokyo, 1976, 88; vis. scientist Internat. Centre Theoretical Physics, Miramare-Trieste, Italy, Brookhaven Nat. Lab., Lawrence Radiation Lab., U. Calif., Berkeley, CERN, Geneva, Switzerland, Max Planck Inst., Munich, Fed. Republic Germany, Rsch. Inst. for Fundamental Physics, Kyoto (Japan) U. Author articles in field, chpts. in books. Guggenheim fellow, 1963-64; recipient Humboldt award, 1974, Japan Soc. for Promotion of Sci. Fellowship awards, 1976, 88. Fellow Am. Phys. Soc. Office: Univ of Chicago Enrico Fermi Inst 5640 S Ellis Ave Chicago IL 60637-1433

OEHME, WOLFGANG WALTER, landscape architect; b. Chemnitz, Germany, May 18, 1930; came to the U.S., 1957; s. Walter Gustav and Elisabeth Elsa (Neumann) O.; 1 child, Roland. Degree in horticulture, Bitterfeld Trade Sch., 1950; degree in landscape architecture, U. Berlin, 1954. Exch. student Waterer & Sons Nurseries, Bagshot, United Kingdom, 1954-56; landscape architect Baltimore County Planning, Towson, Md., 1958-65, The Rouse Co., Columbia, Md., 1965-66; asst. prof. U. Pa., Phila., 1962-64, U. Ga., Athens, 1965; pvt. practice Balt., 1965-74; CEO Oehme, Van Sweden and Assocs., Inc., Washington, 1974—. Co-author: Bold Romantic Gardens, 1990, Gardening with Water, 1995, Process Architecture, 1996, Gardening with Nature, 1997. Named to Hall of Fame, Towson Devel. Corp., 1995; named Man of Yr., German Soc. Md., 1996. Fellow Am. Soc. Landscape Architects; mem. Perennial Plant Assn. (Disting. Svc. 1988), Garden Writers Assn. (Quill and Trowel award 1991). Home: 511 A W Joppa Rd Baltimore MD 21204 Office: 800 G St SE Washington DC 20003-2816

OELBAUM, HAROLD, lawyer, corporate executive; b. Bklyn., Jan. 9, 1931; s. Max and Betty (Molomet) O.; m. Nancy Rothkopf, June 28, 1968; children—Louise, Andrew, Jennifer. A.B., Franklin and Marshall Coll., 1952; J.D., Harvard, 1955; LL.M., N.Y. U., 1959. Bar: N.Y. 1955, Mass. 1960. Atty. Hellerstein & Rosier, Esqs., N.Y.C., 1955-59; gen. atty. Raytheon Co., Lexington, Mass., 1959-68; sr. atty. Revlon, Inc., N.Y.C., 1968-72; pres., dir., mem. exec. com. Kane-Miller Corp., Tarrytown, N.Y., 1972—. Home: 77 Chestnut Rd Bedford Corners NY 10549 Office: Kane-Miller Corp 555 White Plains Rd Tarrytown NY 10591-5109

OELBERG, DAVID GEORGE, neonatologist, educator, researcher; b. Waukon, Iowa, May 26, 1952; s. George Robert and Elizabeth Abigail (Kepler) O.; m. Debra Penuel, Aug. 4, 1979; 1 child, Benjamin George. BS with highest honors, Coll. William and Mary, 1974; MD, U. Md., 1978. Diplomate Am. Bd. Pediatrics, Am. Bd. Neonatal-Perinatal Medicine. Intern U. Tex. Med. Br., Galveston, 1978-79, resident, 1979-81, pediatric house staff, 1978-81; postdoctoral fellow in neonatal medicine U. Tex. Med. Sch., Houston, 1981-84, asst. prof. dept. pediatrics, 1984-90, assoc. prof., 1990-93; assoc. prof. dept. pediatrics, head perinatal rsch. Ctr. Pediatric Rsch., Ea. Va. Med. Sch., 1993—; mem. hosp. staff Hermann Hosp., Houston, 1983-93; physician Crippled Children's Services Program, Houston, 1985-93; mem. hosp. staff Lyndon B. Johnson County Hosp., 1990-93; visiting prof. Wyeth-Ayerst Labs., 1992; med. dir. Office Rsch. Children's Hosp. King's Daughter, Sentara Norfolk Gen. Hosp., 1993—. Mem. editorial adv. bd. jour. Neonatal Intensive Care; contbr. articles to profl. jours; ad hoc reviewer profl. jours.; patentee in field. Physician cons. Parents of Victims of Sudden Infant Death Syndrome, Houston, 1984. Recipient award in analytical chemistry Am. Chem. Soc., 1974, NIH Clin. Investigator award Nat. Heart, Lung and Blood Inst., 1989-94; rsch. grantee Am. Lung Assn., 1989-90, NIH, 1989-94. Fellow Am. Acad. Pediatrics, N.Y. Acad. Scis.; mem. AMA, NAS, Soc. Exptl. Biology and Medicine, So. Soc. Pediatric Rsch. (councilor), Soc. Pediatric Rsch. Achievements include a method for optical measurement of bilirubin in tissue. Avocations: sailing, gardening. Home: 1624 W Little Neck Rd Virginia Beach VA 23452-4720 Office: Ea Va Med Sch Ctr Pediatric Rsch 855 W Brambleton Ave Norfolk VA 23510-1005

OELGESCHLAGER, GUENTHER KARL, publisher; b. Jersey City, Apr. 19, 1934; s. Herman Wilhelm and Frieda Johanna (Onken) O.; m. Jacqueline L. Braley, July 16, 1962; children: Stacey, Lauren, Amy. BA cum laude, Princeton U., 1958; postgrad., Columbia U., 1959. Nat. sales mgr. Harper & Row Pubs., N.Y.C., 1959-67; dir. coll. div. F.A. Praeger Co., N.Y.C., 1968; v.p., gen. mgr. D.C. Heath & Co., Lexington, Mass., 1969-72; pres., dir. Ballinger Pub. Co., Cambridge, Mass., 1973-78; v.p., dir. J.B. Lippincott Co., Phila., 1973-78; pres. Oelgeschlager, Gunn & Hain, Pubs., Inc., Cambridge, 1979—; pres. bd. dirs. Falcon Software Inc., Wellesley, Mass. With U.S. Army, 1954-56. Mem. Software Pubs. Assn. Democrat. Episcopalian. Home: 245 Merriam St Weston MA 02193-1350

OELMAN, ROBERT SCHANTZ, retired manufacturing executive; b. Dayton, Ohio, June 9, 1909; s. William Walter and Edith (Schantz) O.; m. Mary Coolidge, Oct. 17, 1936; children: Bradford Coolidge, Robert Schantz, Jr., Kathryn Peirce, Martha Forrer. A.B. summa cum laude, Dartmouth Coll., 1931, M.A., 1963, LL.D. (hon.), 1981; postgrad., U. Vienna, 1931-32; H.H.D. (hon.), U. Dayton, 1959; LL.D. (hon.), Miami U., Oxford, Ohio, 1960, Wright State U., 1976; L.H.D. (hon.), Wilmington Coll. (Ohio), 1965. With NCR Corp., Dayton, 1933-80; asst. to pres. NCR Corp., 1942-45, v.p., 1946-50, exec. v.p., 1950-57, pres., 1957-62, chmn., pres., 1962-64, chmn., 1962-74, chmn. exec. com., 1974-80, dir., 1948-80; ret., 1980; former dir. Koppers Co., Inc., Pitts., Winters Nat. Bank & Trust Co., Dayton, Citibank and Citicorp, N.Y.C., Ford Motor Co., Detroit., Ohio Bell Telephone, Cleve., Procter & Gamble, Cin. Trustee Dartmouth Coll., 1961-76; Mem. Bus. Council, 1965—; chmn. bd. trustees Wright State U., 1961-76; bd. dirs. Miami Conservancy, 1967-79, pres., 1975-79; chmn. Air Force Mus. Found., Dayton, 1970-80; trustee C.F. Kettering Med. Center, 1971-80; ind. dir. tournament policy bd. PGA Tour, Ponte Vedra, Fla., 1974-83, chmn., 1978-83. Mem. Country Club of Fla., Ocean Club of Fla., Augusta Nat. Club (Ga.), Delray Beach Yacht Club. Clubs: Country of Fla., Ocean of Fla., Augusta (Ga.), Delray Beach Yacht.

OEMLER, AUGUSTUS, JR., astronomy educator; b. Savannah; Ga., Aug. 15, 1945; s. Augustus and Isabelle Redding (Clarke) O.; children: W. Clarke, Bryan S. AB, Princeton U., 1969; MS, Calif. Inst. Tech., 1970, PhD, 1974. Postdoctoral assoc. Kitt Peak Nat. Obs., Tucson, 1974-75; instr. astronomy Yale U., New Haven, 1975-77, asst. prof., 1977-79, assoc. prof., 1979-83, prof., 1983-96, chmn. dept., 1988-96; dir. Obs. Carnegie Instn. Washington, Pasadena, Calif., 1996—. Contbr. articles to profl. jours. Alfred P. Sloan fellow, 1978-80. Mem. Am. Astronom. Soc., Internat. Astronom. Union. Republican. Roman Catholic. Home: 88 Mulberry Farms Rd Guilford CT 06437-3215 Office: Carnegie Obs 813 Santa Barbara St Pasadena CA 91101-1232

OERTEL, GOETZ K. H., physicist, professional association administrator; b. Stuhm, Germany, Aug. 24, 1934; came to U.S., 1957; s. Egon F.K. and Margarete W. (Wittek) O.; m. Brigitte Beckmann, June 17, 1960; children: Ines M.H. Oertel Downing, Carsten K.R. Abitur, Robert Mayer, Heilbronn, Fed. Republic Germany, 1953; vordiplom, U. Kiel, Fed. Republic Germany, 1956; PhD, U. Md., 1963. Aerospace engr. Langley Ctr. NASA, Hampton, Va., 1963-68; chief solar physics NASA, Washington, 1968-75; analyst Office of Mgmt. and Budget, Washington, 1974-75; head astronomy div. NSF, Washington, 1975; dir. def. and civilian nuclear waste programs U.S. Dept. Energy, Washington, 1975-83; acting mgr. sav. river ops. office Aiken, S.C., 1983-84; dep. mgr. ops. office Albuquerque, 1984-85; dep. asst. sec. EH Washington, 1985-86; pres. Assn. Univs. for Rsch. in Astronomy, Inc. (AURA, Inc.), Washington, 1986—, also bd. dirs.; cons. Los Alamos Lab., N.Mex., 1987-92, Westinghouse Electric, 1988—; bd. dirs. AURA, Inc., Inst. for Sci. and Soc., Ellensburg, Wash., IUE Corp., Inst. for Computational Scis. and Informatics, George Mason U., Nat. Rsch. Coun., U.S. Com. for CODATA, 1993—. Patentee in field. Fulbright grantee, 1957. Fellow AAAS; mem. Am. Phys. Soc., Am. Astron. Soc., Internat. Astron. Union, N.Y. Acad. Scis., Internat. U. Exch., Inc. (bd. dirs.), Cosmos Club, Sigma Xi. Lutheran. Avocations: fitness, chess, computing. Home: 9609 Windcroft Way Potomac MD 20854-2864 Office: Assn Univs for Rsch in Astronomy 1200 New York Ave NW Ste 350 Washington DC 20005-3929

OERTEL, YOLANDA CASTILLO, pathologist, educator, diagnostician; b. Lima, Peru, Dec. 14, 1938; came to U.S., 1966; d. Leonardo A. and Dalila (Ramirez) C.; m. James E. Oertel, Sept. 24, 1969. MD, Cayetano Heredia, Lima, 1964. Diplomate Am. Bd. Pathology (mem. test com. for cytopathology 1988-94). Internat. postdoctoral fellowship NIH, Bethesda, Md., 1966-68; asst. prof. pathology Sch. Medicine George Washington U., Washington, 1975-78, assoc. prof., 1978-84, prof., 1984—; cons. Registry Cytology Armed Forces Inst. Pathology, Washington, 1981—. Author: Fine Needle Aspiration of the Breast, 1987; contbr. chpts. to books and articles to profl. jours. Recipient Francisco A. Camino prize Peruvian Med. Assn., 1965, cert. Meritorious Svc. Armed Forces Inst. Pathology, 1974; named Disting. Alumna Cayetano Heredia Med. Sch., 1989. Mem Internat. Acad. Cytology, Assn. Mil. Surgeons (hon), Colombian Soc. Pathology (hon.), Argentinian Soc. Pathology (hon.), Peruvian Soc. Pathologists (hon.), Argentinian Soc. Cytopathology, (hon.), Am. Soc. Cytology, Internat. Acad. Pathology, Soc. Latinoamericana Patologia, Am. Soc. Clin. Pathologists (coun. on cytopathology 1982-88). Avocations: reading, gardening. Office: George Washington U Med Ctr 901 23rd St NW Washington DC 20037-2327

OESTERLE, DALE ARTHUR, law educator; b. West Lafayette, Ind., Oct. 25, 1950; s. Eric Clark and Germaine Dora (Seelye) O.; m. Patricia Marie Pessemier, May 6,1972; children: Helen, Ann, William. BA, U. Mich., 1972, M in Pub. Policy, 1974, JD, 1975. Bar: N.Y., Va. Law clk. to Robert R. Merhige, Jr. U.S. Dist. Ct., Richmond, Va., 1975-76; assoc. Hunton & Williams, Richmond, 1976-79; prof. law Cornell U., Ithaca, N.Y., 1979-92; Monfort prof. comml. law U. Colo., Boulder, 1992—. Author: Mergers, Acquisitions and Reorganizations, 1991; contbr. articles to profl. jours. Sir William Henry Cooper fellow U. Auckland, New Zealand, 1992. Office: Univ Colo Law Sch Campus Box 401 Boulder CO 80309

OESTERLE, ERIC ADAM, lawyer; b. Lafayette, Ind., Dec. 2, 1948; s. Eric Clark and Germaine Dora (Seelye) O.; m. Carolyn Anne Scherer, Sept. 16, 1973; children: Adam Clark, Allison Margaret. BS, U. Mich., 1970, JD, 1973. Bar: Ill. 1973, U.S. Dist. Ct. (no. dist.) Ill. 1973, U.S. Ct. Appeals (7th cir.) 1987, U.S. Supreme Ct. 1986. Assoc. Sonnenschein, Carlin, Nath & Rosenthal, Chgo., 1973-80; ptnr. Sonnenschein Nath & Rosenthal, Chgo., 1980—. Mem. ABA, Ill. Bar Assn., Chgo. Bar Assn. Home: 645 Lake Rd Glen Ellyn IL 60137-4249 Office: Sonnenschein Nath & Rosenthal 8000 Sears Tower 233 S Wacker Dr Chicago IL 60606-6306

OESTERLING, JOSEPH EDWIN, urologic surgeon; b. Greensburg, Ind., May 28, 1956; s. Walter Bernard and Leona Martha (Muckerheide) O.; m. Carmen Teresa Noguera, June 9, 1984; children: Christopher Charles, Jennifer Marie. BA, Columbia Coll., 1978; MD, Columbia U., 1982. Diplomate Nat. Bd. Med. Examiners, Am. Bd. Urology; lic. in Md., Fla., Ariz., Minn., Mich. Intern, dept. gen. surgery Johns Hopkins U. Sch. of Med., Balt., 1982-83, resident, dept. gen. surgery, 1983-84, resident, dept. urology, 1984-87, chief resident, dept. urology, 1988, instr., dept. urology, 1988-89; cons. dept. urology Mayo Clinic, Rochester, Minn., 1989-94; asst. prof. urology Mayo Med. Sch., Rochester, 1989-93; assoc. prof. urology Mayo Clinic, Rochester, 1993-94; prof., urologist-in-chief, dir. Mich. Prostate Inst., U. Mich., Ann Arbor, 1994—; dir. Mich. Prostate Inst., U. Mich. Med. Ctr., Ann Arbor, 1994—; cons./researcher in field; mem. Comprehensive Cancer Ctr. U. Mich.; physician cons. Ann Arbor Vet. Adminstrn. Hosp.; mem. prostate cancer adv. com. Mich. Cancer Consortium, 1988. Author: The ABCs of Prostate Cancer: The Book That Could Save Your Life, 1997; cons. The Jour. of Urology, The Prostate, 1990, Cancer, 1990, Cancer Rsch., 1990, New Eng. Jour. Medicine, Jour. Am. Med. Assn., 1991, Jour. Andrology, 1992, So. Med. Jour., 1992, The Clin. Jour. of Pain, 1992; editor-in-chief Urology; book editor: Urologic Oncology, Prostate-specific antigen: The Best Tumor Marker for Prostate cancer; mem. editl. bd. Annals of Surg. Oncology, 1993, Urology Times, 1994, Men's Confidential, 1994, Jour. Urologic Pathology, 1995, Jour. Clin. Outcomes Mgmt., 1996, Infections in Urology, 1996, Prostate Diseases, 1996, Urology Bulletin, 1996. Recipient Emil T. Hofman Chemistry award Univ. Notre Dame, 1975, Albert B. Schweitzer award for Acad. Excellence, Columbia Coll., 1978, Salutatorian, Columbia Coll., 1978, Samuel W. Rover and Lewis C. Rover Biochemistry award Coll. of Physicians and Surgeons of Columbia U., 1982, Valedictorian, 1982, Am. Soc. Clin. Oncology Rsch. award 1987, Devel. award Am. Cancer Soc., 1988, others in field. Fellow ACS; mem. AMA, Am. Urol. Assn. (voting mem., Grand Champion prize 1991 Western sect., Prostate Educator of Yr. 1995, mem. BPH guidelines com., prostate cancer guidelines com.), N.Y. Acad. Sci., Sci. Rsch. Soc., Nat. Assn. Residents and Interns, Minn. State Med. Assn., Minn. Urol. Soc., Zumbro Valley Med. Soc., So. Minn. Med. Assn., Mich. Urol. Soc., Am. Soc. Andrology, Am. Assn. Clin. Urologists, Am. Geriatrics Soc., Am. Soc. Clin. Oncology, Can. Urol. Assn., European Assn. Urology, Endourol. Soc., Pan-Pacific Surg. Assn., Soc. for Basic Urologic Rsch., Soc. Internat. Urology, Johns Hopkins Med. and Surg. Assn., Soc. Univ. Urologists, North Cen. Sect. Am. Urologic Assn. (1st prize Clin. Rsch. 1986, 87, 1st prize Lab. Rsch. 1987), Mayo Alumni Assn., Sigma Xi. Avocations: landscape photography, cross country skiing, downhill skiing, sailing, gardening. Home: 5410 Meadowcrest Dr Ann Arbor MI 48105 Office: Mayo Clinic Dept Urology 200 1st St SW Rochester MN 55902-3008

OESTERLING, THOMAS OVID, pharmaceutical company executive; b. Butler, Pa., Mar. 6, 1938; s. Victor Kenneth and Marjorie Gertrude (Oswald) O.; m. Janet Westrick, Dec. 30, 1960 (div. 1983); children: Thomas, Jennifer, Daniel; m. Cynthia Adler, 1984 (div. 1987). B.S., Ohio State U., 1962, M.S., 1964, Ph.D., 1966. Research asso., research head Upjohn Co., Kalamazoo, 1966-76; dir. research and devel., dermatol. div. Johnson & Johnson Corp., New Brunswick, N.J., 1976-78; dir. pharm. research and devel. Johnson & Johnson Corp., 1978-79; v.p. med. products research and devel. Mallinckrodt, Inc., St. Louis, 1979-83; sr. v.p. research and devel. Collaborative Research Inc., Bedford, Mass., 1984-86; pres. Collaborative Research Inc., 1986-89; pres., chief exec. officer Gliatech, Inc., Cleve., 1989—; faculty mem. Arden House Conf. on Stability Evaluation Pharm. Dosage Forms, 1979. Contbr. numerous sci. articles to profl. jours. Recipient Disting. Alumni award Ohio State U. Coll. Pharmacy, 1982; Parke Davis research grantee, 1962-64; Am. Found. for Pharm. Edn. fellow, 1964-66. Mem. Am. Chem. Soc., Soc. Nuclear Medicine, Acad. Pharm. Scis., Soc. for Neurosci. Patentee in field. Office: Gliatech Inc 23420 Commerce Park Cleveland OH 44122-5813

OESTERREICHER, JAMES E., department stores executive; b. 1941. B.S., Mich. State U., 1964. With J. C. Penney Co. Inc., 1964—; pres. Western Region J. C. Penney Co. Inc., 1987-88, exec. v.p., 1988-94; vice chm., CEO J.C. Penny Co. Inc., 1994—. Office: J C Penney Co Inc 6501 Legacy Dr Plano TX 75024-3612*

OESTMANN, MARY JANE, retired senior radiation specialist; b. Chgo., May 22, 1924; d. Charles Edward and Harriet Evelyn (Stoltenberg) O. BA in Math, Chemistry with honors, Denison U., 1946; MS, U. Wis., 1948, PhD, 1954; DSc., Denison U., 1975. Research chemist Inst. for Atom Energy, Oslo, 1954-55; vis. scientist AB Atom Energy, Stockholm, 1955-56; vis. prof. chem. dept. U. Iowa, Iowa City, 1957; sr. scientist Battelle Meml. Inst., Columbus, Ohio, 1957-61; assoc. chemist Argonne (Ill.) Nat. Lab, 1961-71; environ. project mgr. U.S. AEC, Washington, 1971-75; sr. radiation specialist U.S. Nuclear Regulatory Commn., Glen Ellyn, Ill., 1975-87; bd. dirs. U. Wis.-Madison Alumni Assn. of the So. Lakes, 1992—. Contbr. numerous articles to scientific jours. Mem. planning and zoning commn. Town of Burlington; bd. trustees Plymouth Congl. UCC Ch. Burlington, 1993-96. Recipient Internat. Women's Yr. award Nuclear Regulatory Commn., 1975. Fellow Am. Inst. Chemists, Am. Nuclear Soc. (bd. dirs. 1983-86); mem. Am. Chem. Soc., Inst. Environ. Scis. (sr. mem.), Health Physics Soc. (sec.-treas. Midwest chpt. 1978, exec. com. 1983-86), N.Y. Acad. Scis., Wis. Acad. Scis., Arts and Letters, Sigma Xi, Phi Beta Kappa, Sigma Delta Epsilon, Iota Sigma Pi. Clubs: Burlington (Wis.) Women's Club, Browns Lake Yacht (Burlington), Rep. Women Racing County-West (v.p. 1992-93, sec. 1994, pres. 1995-97). Home: 2520 Cedar Dr Burlington WI 53105-9174

OESTREICH, CHARLES HENRY, president emeritus; b. Columbus, Ohio, June 8, 1932; s. Henry F. and Martha (Schwartz) O.; m. Rhoda J. Haseley, Aug. 26, 1957; children: Martha, Mary, David. BS, Capital U., 1954; MS, Ohio U., 1956, PhD, 1961; LLD, Capital U., 1986. Instr. chemistry Va. Military Inst., 1956-57; instr. Capital U., Columbus, 1960-62; asst. prof. chemistry Capital U., 1962-64, assoc. prof. chemistry, 1965-69; acad. dean Tex. Luth. U., Seguin, 1969-76; interim pres. Tex. Luth. U., 1976-77, pres., 1977-94; area rep. Evang. Luth. Ch. Found., New Braunfels, Tex., 1994—; pres. emeritus Tex. Luth. U., Seguin, 1995—; postdoctoral research fellow Vanderbilt U., 1965-66. Bd. dirs. Mid-Tex. Symphony. Mem. Seguin Rotary Club (past prs.). Home: 2269 S Abbey Loop New Braunfels TX 78130-8965

OETTGEN, HERBERT FRIEDRICH, physician; b. Cologne, Germany, Nov. 22, 1923; came to U.S., 1958; s. Peter and Minna (Kaul) O.; m. Trudi Hesberg, Feb. 16, 1957; children: Hans Christoph, Joerg Peter, Anne Barbara. MD, U. Cologne, 1951. Diplomate Bd. Internal Medicine, Fed. Republic of Germany. Resident in pathology City Hosp., Cologne, 1952-54, resident in medicine, 1955-58; fellow Meml. Sloan-Kettering Cancer Ctr., N.Y.C., 1958-62, assoc. to assoc. mem., 1963-69, mem., 1972—, attending physician, 1971—; prof. medicine Cornell U. Med. Coll., N.Y.C., 1972—; assoc. dir. Cancer Rsch. Inst., N.Y.C., 1985—. Author over 350 publs. in hematology, cancer rsch., immunology and clin. oncology. Recipient award for cancer rsch. Wilhelm Warner Found., Hamburg, Fed. Republic Germany, 1970, Lisec-Artz award for cancer rsch. Friedrich Wilhelm U., Bonn, Fed. Republic of Germany, 1982. Presbyterian. Avocations: violin, woodworking. Home: 48 Overlook Dr New Canaan CT 06840-6825 Office: Meml Sloan-Kettering Cancer Ctr 1275 York Ave New York NY 10021-6007

OETTINGER, ANTHONY GERVIN, mathematician, educator; b. Nuremberg, Germany, Mar. 29, 1929; came to U.S., 1941, naturalized, 1947; s. Albert and Marguerite (Bing) O.; m. Marilyn Tanner, June 20, 1954; children: Douglas, Marjorie. A.B., Harvard U., 1951, Ph.D., 1954; Henry fellow, U. Cambridge, Eng., 1951-52; Litt.D. (hon.), U. Pitts., 1984. Mem. faculty Harvard, 1955—, asso. prof. applied math., 1960-63, prof. linguistics, 1963-75, Gordon McKay prof. applied math., 1963—, chmn. program on info. resources policy, 1972—, mem. faculty of govt., 1973—, prof. info. resources policy, 1975—; mem. command control comm. and intelligence bd. Dept. Navy, 1978-83; mem. sci. adv. group Def. Comm. Agy., 1979-90; chmn. bd. visitors Joint Mil. Intelligence Coll., 1986—; chmn., dir. Ctrl. Intelligence Advanced Tech. Panel, 1995—; cons. Arthur D. Little, Inc., 1956-80, Office Sci. and Tech., Exec. Office of Pres., 1960-73, Bellcomm, Inc., 1963-68, Sys. Devel. Corp., 1965-68, Nat. Security Coun., Exec. Office of Pres., 1975-81, Pres.'s Fgn. Intelligence Adv. Bd., 1981-90; chmn. Computer Sci. and Engring. Bd., Nat. Acad. Scis., 1968-73; mem. Mass. Cmty. Antenna TV Commn., 1972-79, chmn., 1975-79; mem. rsch. adv. bd. Com. for Econ. Devel., 1975-79; trustee Babbage Inst., 1991—; panel mem. Naval Studies Bd. NAS/NRC, 1993-95. Author: A Study for the Design of an Automatic Dictionary, 1954, Automatic Language Translation: Lexical and Technical Aspects, 1960, Run Computer Run: The Mythology of Educational Innovation, 1969, High and Low Politics: Information Resources for the 80s, 1977, Behind the Telephone Debates, 1988, Mastering the Changing Information World, 1993; editor: Proc. of a Symposium on Digital Computers and Their Applications, 1962. Fellow Am. Acad. Arts and Scis., AAAS, IEEE, Assn. Computing Machinery (mem. coun. 1961-68, chmn. com. U.S. Govt. Rels. 1964-66, editor computational linguistics sect. Commn. 1964-66, pres. 1966-68); mem. Soc. Indsl. and Applied Math. (mem. coun. 1963-67), Coun. on Fgn. Rels., Phi Beta Kappa, Sigma Xi. Clubs: Cosmos (Washington); Harvard (N.Y.C.). Home: 65 Elizabeth Rd Belmont MA 02178-3819 Office: Harvard U Program Info Resources Policy 200 Aiken Cambridge MA 02138-2901

OETTINGER, JULIAN ALAN, lawyer, pharmacy company executive. BS, U. Ill., 1961; JD, Northwestern U., 1964. Bar: Ill. 1964. Atty. SEC, 1964-67; atty. Walgreen Co., Deerfield, Ill., 1967-72, sr. atty., 1972-78, dir. law, 1978-89, v.p., gen. counsel, corp. sec., 1989—. Office: Walgreen Co 200 Wilmot Rd Deerfield IL 60015-4620

O'FARRELL, MARK THEODORE, religious organization administrator; b. Milw., Apr. 13, 1948; s. Theodore Wolfred and Ernestine (Shelhammer) O.; m. Phillis Gilley, Sept. 18, 1948; children: Gwen, Kevin. BA, Columbia Bible Coll., 1970; DD, Toccan Falls Coll., 1996. Asst. pastor 1st Alliance Ch., Macon, Ga., 1970-71; sr. pastor 1st Alliance Ch., Port Charlotte, Fla., 1981-86, Belle Glade (Fla.) Alliance Ch., 1971-81; asst. to dist. supt., ext. dir. Southeastern Dist. of Christian and Missionary Alliance, Orlando, Fla., 1986-93, dist. supt., 1993—. Recipient Spiritual Aims award Kiwanis. Home: Christian & Missionary Alliance Southeastern District 2450 Donaldson Dr Orlando FL 32812 Office: PO Box 720430 Orlando FL 32872-0430

OFFENBERGER, ALLAN ANTHONY, electrical engineering educator; b. Wadena, Sask., Can., Aug. 11, 1938; s. Ivy Viola (Hagglund) O.; m. Margaret Elizabeth Patterson, Apr. 12, 1963; children: Brian, Gary. BS, U. B.C., 1962, MS, 1963; PhD, MIT, 1968. Asst. prof. U. Alta., Edmonton, Can., 1968-70, assoc. prof., 1970-75, prof., 1975-95, prof. emeritus, 1996—; cons. Lawrence Livermore (Calif.) Nat. Lab., 1996—; vis. prof. U.K. Atomic Energy Agy., Abingdon, Oxon, Eng., 1975-76; project dir. Laser Fusion Project, Edmonton, 1984-91; mem. strategic adv. com. Nat. Fusion Program, Atomic Energy of Can. Ltd., Chalk River, Ont., 1987-96; vis. prof. U. Oxford, U.K., 1992. Mem. editorial bd. Laser and Particle Beams, 1987—; contbr. over 100 sci. articles on lasers and plasma physics. Killam Rsch. fellow Can. Coun., 1980-82. SERC rsch. fellow, Eng., 1992. Mem. Can.

Assn. Physicists (exec. officer, v.p. elect 1987-88, pres. 1989-90), Am. Phys. Soc., Sigma Xi. Home: 412 Lessard Dr. Edmonton, AB Canada T6M 1A7 Office: Dept Elec Engring, U Alta, Edmonton, AB Canada T6G 2G7

OFFENHARTZ, EDWARD, aerospace executive; b. Bklyn., Mar. 1, 1928; s. Hyman and Anna (Konecky) O.; m. Edith Enevoldsen, Nov. 4, 1951; children: Debra, Marc, Beth, Kay, David. BSME, Poly. Inst. Bklyn., 1948; postgrad., U. Va., 1949-50; student Program for Mgmt. Devel., Harvard U., 1970. Registered profl. engr., Mass. Aero. research scientist NACA, Langley, Va., 1948-56; with Avco Corp., Wilmington and Lowell, Mass., 1956-67, successively research engr., group leader, project engr., sr. project engr., project mgr., project dir., 1956-67; project dir., asst. gen. mgr. ops. Perkin-Elmer Corp., 1967-70; program dir. spl. projects Grumman Aerospace Corp., Bethpage, N.Y., 1970-73, program dir. Earth Limb Measurements Satellite program, 1973-75, mem. def. sci. bd. shuttle task force, 1974-75, program dir. internat. offset mgmt., 1975-82, program dir. mktg. planning, 1982-84; dir. strategic planning Grumman Data Systems Div., Woodbury, N.Y., 1984-90; pres. E.O. Assocs., 1991—; lectr. UCLA, 1965—. Contbr. articles to profl. jours. Mem. AIAA, Sci. Research Soc. Am., Am. Mgmt. Assn. Home: 4 Glen Ln Weston CT 06883-2308 Office: EO Assocs 4 Glen Ln Weston CT 06883-2308

OFFER, DANIEL, psychiatrist; b. Berlin, Germany, Dec. 24, 1930; married; 3 children. Grad., U. Chgo., 1957. Intern Ill. Research and Ednl. Hosps., Chgo., 1957-58; resident Inst. Psychosomatics and Psychiat. Research and Tng. Michael Reese Hosp., Chgo., 1958-61; psychiatrist Chgo. Inst. Psychoanalysis, 1963-68; career investigator Nat. Inst. Mental Health, Psychosomatic and Psychiat. Inst., Michael Reese Hosp., 1961-64; asst. dir. Inst. Psychosomatics and Psychiat. Research and Tng., Chgo., 1961-64; assoc. dir. Inst. Psychosomatics and Psychiat. Research and Tng., 1965-74, co-dir., 1974-76, acting chmn., 1976-77, chmn., 1977-87; dir. Ctr. for Study of Adolescence, 1987-90; assoc. prof. psychiatry U. Chgo., 1969-73, prof., 1973-90, prof. psychiatry Northwestern U., 1991—; fellow Center for Advanced Studies in Behavioral Scis., Stanford, 1973-74. Author: Normality: Theoretical and Clinical Concepts of Mental Health, 1966, rev. edit., 1973, new edit., 1984, The Psychological World of the Teen-ager, 1969, From Teenage to Young Manhood: A Psychological Study, 1975, Psychological World of the Juvenile Delinquent, 1979, The Adolescent: A Psychological Self Portrait 1981, Patterns of Adolescent Self-Image, 1984, The Leader, 1985, The Teenage World, 1988, The Diversity of Normal Behavior, 1991, Adolescent Suicide and Homicide, 1994; also numerous articles.; editor in chief Jour. Youth and Adolescence. Served with Israeli Army. Fellow Chgo. Inst. Medicine, Am. Soc. Adolescent Psychiatry (pres. 1972-73, Schonfeld Meml. award for rsch. 1985, John P. Hill Meml. award 1990). Office: Northwestern U Med Sch Dept Psychiatry & Behavioral Scis 303 E Ohio St Chicago IL 60611

OFFER, STUART JAY, lawyer; b. Seattle, June 2, 1943; m. Judith Spitzer, Aug. 29, 1970; children: Rebecca, Kathryn. BA, U. Wash., 1964; LLB, Columbia U., 1967. Bar: D.C. 1968, U.S. Tax Ct. 1968, Calif. 1972. Atty.-advisor U.S. Tax Ct., Washington, 1967-68; assoc. Morrison & Foerster, LLP, San Francisco, 1972-76; ptnr. Morrison & Foerster, San Francisco, 1976—. Mem. San Francisco Dir.'s Adv. Com. 1985. Served as capt. U.S. Army, 1968-72. Mem. ABA (chmn. taxation sect., corp. tax com. 1991-92, coun. dir. 1995—), Internat. Fiscal Assn., Am. Coll. Tax Counsel. Office: Morrison & Foerster LLP 425 Market St San Francisco CA 94105

OFFERMAN, JOSE ANTONIO DONO, professional baseball player; b. San Pedor de Macoris, Dominican Republic, Nov. 8, 1968. Student, Colegio Biblico Cristiano, Dominican Republic. Shortstop L.A. Dodgers, 1990—, Kansas City Royals, 1996—. Selected to N.L All-Star Team, 1995. Office: Kansas City Royals PO Box 419969 Kansas City MO 64141-6969*

OFFIT, MORRIS WOLF, investment management executive; b. Balt., Jan. 22, 1937; s. Michael and Rhea (Wolf) O.; m. Nancy Silverman, Nov. 26, 1959; children: Ned S., Daniel W. BA in History, Johns Hopkins U., 1957; MBA in Fin., U. Pa., 1959. V.p. investment dept. Mercantile Safe Deposit and Trust, Balt., 1960-68; gen. ptnr. Salomon Bros. Inc., N.Y.C., 1970-80; pres. Julius Baer Securities, N.Y.C., 1980-82, Offit Assocs. Inc., N.Y.C., 1983—; now CEO OffitBank, N.Y.C.; bd. dirs. Merc. Bancshares Corp., Balt. Trustee, former chmn. bd. trustees Johns Hopkins U.; mem. adv. coun. Sch. Advanced Internat. Studies, Washington; trustee Jewish Mus., former chmn.; trustee Union Theol. Sem., Jewish Theol. Sem. Mem. Coun. Fgn. Rels. Office: Offitbank 520 Madison Ave New York NY 10022-4213

OFFIT, SIDNEY, writer, educator; b. Balt., Oct. 13, 1928; s. Barney and Lillian (Cohen) O.; m. Avodah Crindell Komito, Aug. 8, 1952; children: Kenneth, Michael Robert. B.A., Johns Hopkins U., 1950. Editorial staff Mercury Publs., N.Y.C., 1952-53, Macfadden Publs., N.Y.C., 1953-54; contbg. editor Baseball mag., Washington, 1955-58; mem. faculty N.Y. U., 1964—, adj. prof. creative writing, 1977—; asso. editor Intellectual Digest, 1970-72, sr. editor, 1972-74; lectr. creative writing New Sch. Social Research, 1965—; curator George Polk Awards for Journalism, 1977—; mem. nat. bd. Nat. Book Com., 1973-75; commentator Channel 5 TV, N.Y.C., 1975-85, Channel 11 TV, 1992. Author: He Had it Made, 1959, The Other Side of the Street, 1962, Soupbone, 1963, Topsy Turvey, 1965, the Adventure of Homer Fink, 1966, The Boy Who Made a Million, 1968; short stories Not All the Girls Have Million Dollar Smiles, 1971; Only a Girl Like You, 1972, What Kind of Guy Do You Think I Am?, 1977, Memoir of the Bookie's Son, 1995; series sports books for boys, 1961-65, also essays, revs., short stories; book editor: Politics Today, 1978-80. Mem. selection com. Dist. Sch. Bd., N.Y.C., 1968; Mem. exec. bd. Lexington Democratic Club, 1957-60, N.Y. Dem. County Com., 1966—; chmn. 19th Precinct Community Council of N.Y.C., 1964-80. Recipient Disting. Alumni award Valley Forge Mil. Acad., 1961, Otty Community Svc. award, 1975, Teaching Excellence award NYU, 1981, commendation for achievment as teacher, scholar, communicator N.Y. State Legislature, 1983, proclamation for contbns. to city, N.Y.C. Coun., 1983, Police Athletic League citation for svc. to children of N.Y.C., 1991, 96, Honors Convocation award Marymount Manhattan Coll., 1994, Detlev W. Bronk award Johns Hopkins Alumni Assn., 1994. Mem. Tudor and Stuart Club, Authors Guild Found. (pres. 1993—), Authors Guild (coun. 1970-77, 79—, v.p. 1993-95), Authors League (nat. coun. 1976-79), Am. Ctr. PEN (exec. com. 1969-88, 89-96, v.p. 1970-74, internat. del. 1971, 72, 74). Clubs: Century Assn. (N.Y.C.), Coffee House (N.Y.C.). Home: 23 E 69th St New York NY 10021-4919 *I have been guided by a strong devotion to my family and friends and moderate ambition. In both these priorities I have been influenced by my parents. With my writing I have tried to fulfill my own needs, and for the most I have been satisfied by the reception. I do not aspire to fame or great fortune, and this leaves me free to enjoy the sharing of experiences with my friends and family. I consider myself a lucky man and this keeps me grateful to whatever forces there are that contrive man's fortune.*

OFFNER, ERIC DELMONTE, lawyer; b. Vienna, Austria, June 23, 1928; came to U.S., 1941, naturalized, 1949; s. Sigmund J. and Kathe (Delmonte) O.; m. Julie Cousins, 1955 (dec. 1959); m. Barbara Ann Shotton, July 2, 1961; 1 son, Gary Douglas; m. Carol Sue Marcus, Jan. 12, 1980 (dec. 1983). B.B.A., CCNY, 1949; LL.B. in Internat. Affairs, Cornell U., 1952. Bar: N.Y. 1952. Assoc. Langner, Parry, Card & Langner, N.Y.C., 1952-57; ptnr. Haseltine, Lake, Waters & Offner, N.Y.C., 1957-77; sr. ptnr. Offner & Kuhn, 1978-83; pvt. practice N.Y.C., 1983—; instr. George Washington U. Law Sch., Cornell U. Law Sch.; spl. prof. law Hofstra Law Sch., 1974-92, Cornell Law Sch., 1979. Author: International Trademark Protection, 1964, Japanese edit., 1977, International Trademark Service, Vols. I-III 1970, Vol. IV, 1972, Vol. V., 1973, Vol. VI, 1976, Vol. VII, 1981, Vols. I-VII, 2d edit., 1981, Legal Training Course on Trademarks, 1982; editor in chief: Cornell Law Forum, 1950-51; mem. editorial bd.: Trademark Reporter, 1961-64, 69-72; book reviewer Jour. Humanism and Ethical Religion; contbr. articles to profl. jours. V.p. Riverdale Mental Health Clinic, N.Y.C., 1966-67; pres. Riverdale Mental Health Assn., 1967-69, Ethical Culture Soc., Riverdale-Yonkers, 1964-67, Ethical Cultural Retirement Ctr., 1975-94; trustee Am. Ethical Union, 1967-73, Internat. Alliance of Holistic Lawyers; bd. dirs. Fit Kids. Mem. N.Y. Patent Law Assn. (assoc. editor Bull. 1961-66, gov. 1973-76), ABA, City N.Y. Bar Assn. (sec. 1962-64), U.S. Trademark Assn., World Peace Through Law (charter), Trademark Soc. Washington (charter), Inst. Trade Mark Agts. (London), Australian Patent Inst., Internat. Assn. Protection Indsl. Property, Nat. Coun. Patent Law Assn., Internat. Patent, Trademark Assn., Phi Alpha Delta. Home: 20 Joy Dr New Hyde Park NY 11040-1109 *Do unto others so as to elicit the best in them and thereby the best in yourself.*

OFFUTT, SUSAN ELIZABETH, economist; b. Newport, R.I., Apr. 17, 1954; d. William Franklin and Carol Dorothy (Chieves) O. BS, Allegheny Coll., 1976; MS, Cornell U., 1980, PhD, 1982. Asst. prof. agrl. econs. U. Ill., Urbana, 1982-87; sect. leader Econ. Rsch. Svc. USDA, Washington, 1987-88; chief agr. br. U.S. Office Mgmt. and Budget, Washington, 1988-92; exec. dir., bd. agr. Nat. Rsch. Coun., Washington, 1992-96; adminstr. U.S. Dept. Agrl./Econ. Rsch. Svc., Washington, 1996—. Office: Econ Rsch Svc 1301 New York Ave NW Washington DC 20005-4708

O'FLAHERTY, PAUL BENEDICT, lawyer; b. Chgo., Feb. 11, 1925; s. Benedict Joseph and Margaret Celestine (Harrington) O'F.; m. Catherine Margaret Bigley, Feb. 13, 1954; children: Paul, Michael, Kathleen, Ann, Neil. JD cum laude, Loyola U., Chgo., 1949. Bar: Ill. 1949, U.S. Dist. Ct. (no. dist.) Ill. 1949, U.S. Ct. Appeals (7th cir.) 1956, U.S. Supreme Ct. 1959. Ptnr. Madden, Meccia, O'Flaherty & Freeman, Chgo., 1949-56; ptnr. Groble, O'Flaherty & Hayes, Chgo., 1956-63, Schiff Hardin & Waite, Chgo., 1963—; mem. adj. faculty Loyola U., 1959-65. Author: (with others) Illinois Estate Administration, 1983; contbr. articles to profl. jours. Bd. advisors Cath. Charities, Chgo., 1979-92; trustee Clarke Coll., Dubuque, Iowa, 1982—. Served to 2d lt. U.S. Army, 1943-46. Fellow Am. Coll. Trust and Estate Counsel; mem. ABA, Ill. Bar Assn. (past chmn. fed. taxation sect. council), Chgo. Bar Assn. (past chmn. trust law com.), Chgo. Estate Planning Council. Clubs: Union League, Metropolitan (Chgo.). Office: Schiff Hardin & Waite 7200 Sears Tower Chicago IL 60606-6327

O'FLAHERTY, TERRENCE, journalist; b. What Cheer, Iowa, July 15, 1917; s. Leo J. and Lelia (Thomas) O'F. B.A., U. Calif. at Berkeley, 1939. Hist. researcher Metro-Goldwyn-Mayer Studios, 1940-42; columnist San Francisco Chronicle, 1949-86; writer nationally syndicated TV column, 1960-86; mem. bd. Peabody Awards for Radio and TV, 1952-84. Host: TV program PM West, San Francisco, 1961-62; created The Terrence O'Flaherty TV Collection for UCLA TV Archives and Theater Arts Library, 1987; author: Masterpiece Theatre: A Celebration, 1995; contbr. articles to McCalls, Reader's Digest, TV Guide. Served as lt. USNR, 1942-46. Recipient Gov.'s award (Emmy) NATAS, 1988. Mem. Beta Theta Pi. Subject of UCLA oral history program. Home and Office: 4 Whiting St San Francisco CA 94133-2419

O'FLARITY, JAMES P., lawyer; b. Yazoo City, Miss., Oct. 15, 1923; s. James P. and Jessie E. (Marshall) O'F.; m. Betty Reichman, Apr. 9, 1955; children: Michael J., Deborah J. O'Flarity James, Steven M., Pamela G. BS, Millsaps Coll., 1950; postgrad., Miss. Coll. Sch. Law, 1948, 53-54; J.D., U. Fla., 1965. Bar: Miss. 1954, Fla. 1966, U.S. Dist. Ct. (so. dist.) Miss. 1954, U.S. Ct. Mil. Appeals 1957, U.S. Dist. Ct. (so. and mid. dists.) Fla. 1966, U.S. Dist. Ct. (no. dist.) Fla. 1967, U.S. Ct. Appeals (5th cir.) 1957, U.S. Ct. Appeals (11th cir.) 1981, U.S. Supreme Ct. 1957; state ct. cert. arbitrator. Assoc. law firm Cone, Owen, Wagner, Nugent & Johnson, West Palm Beach, Fla., 1966-69; sole practice law West Palm Beach, 1969—; mem. Supreme Ct. Matrimonial Law Commn. Fla., 1982-85; ABA observer family ct. proc. Nat. Jud. Coll., 1983; mem. U. Fla. Law Ctr. Coun., 1972—, mem. legal edn. com., 1973, chmn. membership and fin. com., 1977-78; lectr. on marital and family law; leader del. for legal exchange on family law to Ministry of Justice, Peoples Republic of China, 1984. Contbr. articles to profl. publs. Mem. U. Fla. Pres.'s Council; mem. U.S Rep. Senatorial Inner Circle, 1988—; col. La. Gov.'s Staff, 1982—. With USAAF, 1942-45. Decorated Air medal with five oak leaf clusters. Fellow Royal Geog. Soc. (life), Am. Bar Found. (life), Roscoe Pound-Am. Trial Lawyers Found. (life), Am. Acad. Matrimonial Lawyers (nat. pres. 1985-86, nat. bd. of govs. 1977-88, founding pres. Fla. chpt. 1976-80, bd. mgrs. Fla chpt. 1976—, hon. permanent pres. emeritus 1982—), Internat. Acad. Matrimonial Lawyers (convenor, founder), Trusler Soc., Fla. Bar Found. (life, exec. dir. screening com. 1976, chmn. projects com. 1976-77, asst. sec. 1973-79, dir. 1977-81); mem. Internat. Soc. Family Law, Internat. Bar Assn. (assoc.), Am. Law Inst. (consultative group law of family dissolution 1990—, Nat. Conf. Bar Pres'. 1991), ABA (chmn. coms. 1973-75, 78-81, 82-83, editor Family Law Newsletter 1975-77, mem. council family law sect. 1976-85, vice-chmn. sect. 1981-82, chmn. sect. 1983-84, mem. conf. sect. chairmen 1982-85, mem. adv. bd. jour. 1978-80), Assn. Trial Lawyers Am. (Fla. State committeeman 1973-75, 1st chmn. family law sect. 1971-72, 72-73), Fla. Supreme Ct. Hist. Soc., Fla. Council Bar Assn. Presidents (life mem.), U. Fla. Law Ctr. Assn. (life), Acad Fla. Trial Lawyers (dir. 1974-77, coll. diplomates 1977), Fla. Bar (exec. council 1973-84, sec.-treas. family law sect. 1973-74, chmn. family law sect. 1974-75, 75-76, guest editor spl. issue jour. 1978, chmn. jour. and news editorial bd. 1978-79, mem. bd. legal specialization and edn. 1982-91, 92-95, jud. nominating procedures com. 1992-93, Family Law Rules com. 1992-95), Palm Beach County Bar Assn. (cir. ct. civil adv. com. 1981, mem. cir. ct. juvenile domestic rels. adv. com. 1971-80, 81-83, adv. com. chmn. 1974-78), Solicitor's Family Law Assn. (Eng.), Gov.'s Club of Palm Beach (founder, life, gov's. coun.), Explorers Club (life, vice chmn. South Fla. chpt. 1990-95), Circumnavigators Club, Travelers Century Club (life), Phi Alpha Delta (life), Sigma Delta Kappa. Home: 908 Country Club Dr North Palm Beach FL 33408-3714 Office: Ste 960 Esperante 222 Lakeview Ave West Palm Beach FL 33401

OFNER, J(AMES) ALAN, management consultant; b. East Orange, N.J., Mar. 23, 1922. Student, Newark U., 1941; B.A., Antioch Coll., 1949. Trainee, L. Bamberger & Co., Newark, 1941; asst. dept. mgr. Carson Pierie Scott Co., Chgo., 1949; sr. personnel rep. Argonne (Ill.) Nat. Lab., 1950-55; mgmt. cons. McKinsey & Co., Chgo. and San Francisco, 1955-60; mgr. orgn. planning J.C. Penney Co., Inc., N.Y.C., 1960-65; dir. orgn. devel. J.C. Penney Co., Inc., 1965-74, div. v.p., 1974-82, dir. corp. personnel planning, 1976-82; pres. Mng. Change, Inc., 1981—. Served with USAAF, 1941-44. Mem. Exec. Forum Group, Strategic Leadership Forum, Human Resources Planning Soc., World Future Soc., Nat. Retail Fedn., Inst. Mgmt. Cons., N.C. Citizens for Bus. and Industry, Soc. for Human Resource Mgmt., Princeton Club. Office: Mng Change Inc PO Box 98387 Raleigh NC 27624-8387

OFNER, WILLIAM BERNARD, lawyer; b. L.A., Aug. 24, 1929; s. Harry D. and Gertrude (Skoss) Offner; m. Florence Ila Maxwell, Apr. 13, 1953 (div. 1956). AA, L.A. City Coll., 1949; BA, Calif. State U., L.A., 1953; LLB, Loyola U., L.A., 1965; postgrad. Sorbonne, 1951, cert. de Langue Francaise, 1987; postgrad. U. So. Calif., 1966, Glendale Community Coll., 1986-92. Bar: Calif. 1966, U.S. Dist. Ct. Calif. 1966, U.S. Supreme Ct. 1972. Assoc. Thomas Moore and Assocs., L.A., 1967-69; pvt. practice, L.A., 1969-70, 74—; assoc. Peter Lam, L.A., 1981-94, mgn. atty. 1993—; assoc. C.M. Coronel, 1986-87, Jack D. Janofsky, 1987-89, Mario P. Gonzalez, 1990-92, Genaro Legorreta, Jr., 1997—; lectr. Van Norman U., 1975. With USNR, 1947-54. Mem. Inst. Gen. Semantics, Inst. for Antiquity and Christianity, Soc. des Amis De l'Universite de Paris, Safari Athletic Club. Democrat. Avocations: painting, photography, linguistics, French tutoring, travel. Office: 4091 Riverside Dr # 101 Chino CA 91710-6501

OFTE, DONALD, retired engineering executive, consultant; b. N.Y.C., Aug. 23, 1929; s. Sverre and Ingeborg Ofte; m. Margaret Mae McHenney, July 23, 1955; children: Marc Christian, Nancy Carolyn Ofte Appleby, Kirk Donald Jr. BA in Chemistry, Dana Coll., 1952; postgrad. study metall. engring., Ohio State U., 1958-60. Jr. chemist Inst. Atomic Research, Ames, Iowa, 1952-53; sr. research chemist Monsanto Research Corp., Miamisburg, Ohio, 1958-66; ops. engr. AEC, Miamisburg, 1966-69; br. chief, div. dir. ops. office AEC, Albuquerque, 1969-73; mgr. Pinellas area office AEC, Largo, Fla., 1973-79; mgr. Rocky Flats area office Dept. Energy, Golden, Colo., 1979-82; asst. mgr. devel. and prodn. Dept. Energy, Albuquerque, 1982-83, dep. mgr. ops. office, 1983-84; prin. dep. asst. sec. Dept. Energy Defense Programs, Washington, 1984-87; mgr. ops. office Dept. Energy, Idaho Falls, Idaho, 1987-89; mgmt. cons. Idaho Falls, 1989-92; v.p. govt. ops. United Engrs. and Constructors, Denver, 1992-93; v.p. Adv. Scis., Inc., Albuquerque, 1993-94; pres. FERMCO, Cin., 1994-96; ret., 1996; v.p. Fluor-Daniel, Inc., 1994-96; affiliate prof. Idaho State U., 1990-92; bd. dirs. Denver Fed. Exec. Bd., 1979-82. Author: (with others) Plutonium 1960, 1965, Physicochemical Methods in Metallurgical Research; contbr. articles to profl. jours. on metallurgy and ceramics. Campaign chmn. United Way Pinellas, St. Petersburg, Fla., 1978; bd. dirs. Bonneville County United Way, Idaho Rsch. Found.; mem. adv. bd. Teton Peaks Council Boy Scouts of Am., 1987-92, Eastern Idaho Tech. Coll.; chmn. Excellence in Edn. Fund Com., 1990-92; vice chmn., bd. dirs. Rio Grande Ch. ARC, Albuquerque, 1982-84. Served to lt. (j.g.) USN, 1953-57. Recipient citation AEC for Apollo 12 SNAP 27 Radioisotope Generator, 1969, High Quality Performance award AEC, 1968, Group Achievement award NASA, 1972; Meritorious Svc. award Dept. Energy, 1985, Disting. Career Svc. award, 1989. Mem. Am. Chem. Soc., Am. Nuclear Soc., Am. Soc. Metals, Nat. Contract Mgmt. Assn., Am. Soc. Pub. Adminstrs., Suncoast Archeol. Soc., Idaho Falls C. of C. (bd. dirs., cmty. svc. award 1990), Rotary Internat. (Paul Harris fellow). Avocations: reading, bridge, gardening, golf. Home: 1129 Salamanca NW Albuquerque NM 87107

OGAN, RUSSELL GRIFFITH, business executive, retired air force officer; b. Reading, Pa., Nov. 20, 1923; s. Russell John and Edna Gwendlyn (Griffith) O.; m. Gloria Mae Withers, Oct. 30, 1943; children: Susan Ann (Mrs. Greg Gunn), Russell Lee. Student, Wyomissing Polytech. Inst., 1942, Air Command Staff Coll., 1948, Nat. War Coll., 1963. Enlisted as pvt. U.S. Army, 1942; advanced through grades to brig. gen. USAF, 1970; fighter squadron comdr. Dover AFB, Del., 1951; dir. combat operations (11th Air Div.), Ladd AFB, Alaska, 1951-53; dir. (Combat Operations Center), Hamilton AFB, Calif., 1953-56; with (Hdqrs. Air Def. Command), Ent AFB, Colo., 1956-60; dir. (Aerospace Def. Systems Office, Air Force Ballistic Missile Div.), 1960-62; from dep. dir. plans to comdr. Sector Operation Ctr. NATO, Germany, 1963-66; dep. dir. personnel data and records (USAF Mil. Personnel Center), Randolph AFB, Tex., 1966-68; comdr. 71st Missile Warning Wing, then vice comdr. (14th Aerospace Force), Ent AFB, Colo., 1968-71; dep. dir. personnel programs Hdqrs. USAF, Washington, 1971-72; dir. Prisoner of War and Missing in Action Affairs, Office Sec. Def., Washington, 1972-74; former pres. Vacation Interval Mktg.; real estate broker Fishermen's Village, Punta Gorda, Fla. Decorated D.S.M., Legion of Merit with bronze oak leaf cluster, Air medal with 1 silver and 1 bronze oak leaf cluster. Mem. Daedalians, T.R.O.A., Venice Golf and Country Club. Home: 528 Cheval Dr Venice FL 34292-4605

OGATA, KATSUHIKO, engineering educator; b. Tokyo, Jan. 6, 1925; came to U.S., 1952; s. Fukuhei and Teruko (Yasaki) O.; m. Asako Nakamura, Sept. 6, 1961; 1 son, Takahiko. B.S., U. Tokyo, 1947; M.S., U. Ill., 1953; Ph.D., U. Calif., Berkeley, 1956. Research asst. Sci. Research Inst., Tokyo, 1948-51; fuel engr. Nippon Steel Tube Co., Tokyo, 1951-52; mem. faculty U. Minn., 1956—, prof. mech. engring., 1961—; prof. elec. engring. Yokohama Nat. U., 1960-61, 64-65, 68-69. Author: State Space Analysis of Control Systems, 1967, Modern Control Engineering, 1970, 2d edit., 1990, 3d edit., 1996, Dynamic Programming, 1973, Ingenieria de Control Moderna, 1974, 2d edit., 1990, Metody Przestrzeni Stanow w Teorii Sterowania, 1974, System Dynamics, 1978, 2d edit., 1992, Engenharia de Controle Moderno, 1982, 2d edit., 1993, Teknik Kontrol Automatik, 1985, Discrete-Time Control Systems, 1986, 2d edit., 1995, Gendai Seigyo Riron, 1986, Dinamica de Sistemas, 1987, Solving Control Engineering Problems with MATLAB, 1994, Gendai Seigyo Kogaku, 1994, Designing Linear Control Systems with MATLAB, 1994, Sistemas de Control en Tiempo Discreto, 1996, Projeto de Sistemas Lineares de Controle com MATLAB, 1996, Solucao de Problemas de Engenharia de Controle com MATLAB, 1997. Recipient Outstanding Adv. award Inst. of Tech., U. Minn., 1981. Fellow ASME; mem. Sigma Xi, Pi Tau Sigma. Office: U Minn Dept Mech Engring Minneapolis MN 55455

OGAWA, DENNIS MASAAKI, American studies educator; b. Manzanar, Calif., Sept. 7, 1943; s. Frank M. and Alice T. (Tanaka) O.; m. Amy Ranko, Jan. 1, 1973; children: Quin, Owen, Autumn. BA, UCLA, 1966, MA, 1967, PhD, 1969. Prof. Am. studies U. Hawaii at Manoa, Honolulu, 1969—; dir. Nippon Golden Network, Honolulu, 1982—. Author: Jan Ken Po, 1973, Kodomo No Tame Ni, 1978; co-author: Ellison Onizuka: Remembrance, 1986. Dir. Japanese Cultural Ctr., Hawaii, 1992—, Olelo: Corp. Cmty. Television, 1994—, Hawaii Internat. Film Festival, 1994-97. Danforth Found. assoc., 1975; named Disting. Historian Hawaiian Hist. Soc., 1992; fellow Japan Soc. Promotion of Sci., 1978, East West Ctr., Honolulu, 1979. Mem. Assn. Asian-Am. Scholars. Democrat. Office: Univ Hawaii Am Studies Dept 1890 E West Rd Honolulu HI 96822-2318

OGAWA, HIDEMICHI, anesthesiologist, researcher; b. Asahikawa, Hokkaido, Japan, Nov. 14, 1932; s. Taizui and Toyoko (Hata) O.; m. Hisako Mizushina, Mar. 15, 1935; children: Hideaki, Toshiaki, Masaaki. MD, Sapporo Med. U., 1957, PhD, 1962. Diplomate Japan Soc. Anesthesiology; cert. anesthesiologist, Min. Health and Welfare, Japan. Asst. Sapporo (Japan) Med. U., 1962, asst. prof., 1962-65, assoc. prof., 1965-73; dir. dept. anesthesiology Kushiro (Japan) City Hosp., 1973-76; prof., chmn. dept. anesthesiology Asahikawa (Japan) Med. Coll., 1976-82, prof., chmn. dept. anesthesiology and critical care medicine, 1992—; vis. prof. Nanjing (China) U. of TCM, 1991—, Sun Yat-Sen U. of Med. Scis., Guang Zhou, China, 1993—, The Fourth Mil. U., Xian, China, 1993—, Tian Jin U. Medicine, China, 1994—, Su Zhou Med. Coll., China, 1996—, Guang Zhou U. of TCM, 1996—; hon. prof. China-Japan Friendship Hosp., Beijing, 1992—; hon. cons. U. Wash., Seattle, 1992—. Editor Clin. Pharmacology and Therapy, 1992—, The Clin. Report, 1992—, Japanese Jour. Oriental Medicine, 1993—. Hon. pres. Aging Soc. Devel. Found., Sapporo, 1990—; mem. spl. com. Coun. of Propulsion for Devel. of Acute Care, Asahikawa, Japan, 1992—; spl. lectr. Hokkaido Coll. of High Tech., Eniwa, Japan, 1992—, Hokuto Coll. Health and Welfare, Asahikawa, Japan, 1995—. Recipient Hokkaido Gov.'s prize for Med. Scis., 1985, prize for med. advancement Hokkaido Med. Assn./Hokkaido Gov., 1985; Cleve. Clin. Found. fellow, 1969-71. Fellow Internat. Coll. Surgeons; mem. Am. Assn. Advancement of Med. Instrumentation, Am. Soc. Artificial Internal Organs (assoc.), N.Y. Acad. Scis. Avocations: art appreciation, gardening, horticulture, photography, golf. Home: Chuoku Minami-15, Nishi-13 1-30 Sapporo, Hokkaido 064, Japan Office: Asahikawa Med Coll Dept Anes and Critical Care Medicine, Nishikagura 4-5 3-11, Hokkaido 078, Japan

OGAWA, MAKIO, physician; b. Otsu, Shiga, Japan, Jan. 22, 1940; s. Takeo and Yasuko (Sugata) O.; m. Mary-Jane Trevithick, June 21, 1969; children: Terry, Lesley. MD, Osaka U. Med. Sch., Japan, 1964; PhD, Toronto U., Can., 1973. Diplomate Am. Bd. Internal Medicine, Am. Bd. Hematology. Rotating intern U.S. Naval Hosp., Yokosuka, Japan, 1964-65; resident in Medicine Osaka U. Hosp., 1965-66; resident in Medicine Dartmouth Med. Sch. Affiliated Hosp., Hanover, N.H., 1966-68, fellow in Hematology, 1968-70; asst. prof. medicine Med. U. S.C., Charleston, 1973-77, assoc. prof., 1977-80, prof., 1980—, dir. div. exptl. hematology, 1984—; ACOS for R and D Va. Med. Ctr., Charleston, 1993—. Recipient W.S. Middleton award Dept. Vets. Affairs, 1989, William Dameshek prize Am. Soc. Hematology, 1991, Behring-Kitasato award in immunology, 1994; Leukemia Soc. Am. scholar, 1975-80; med. investigator Dept. Vets Affairs, 1980-85, 87-92. Mem. So. Soc. Clin. Investigation, Am. Soc. Clin. Investigation, Internat. Soc. Exptl. Hematology (pres. 1989-90), Assn. Am. Physicians. Office: VA Med Ctr 109 Bee St Charleston SC 29401-5703

OGBURN, CHARLTON, writer; b. Atlanta, Mar. 15, 1911; s. Charlton and Dorothy (Stevens) O.; m. Mary C. Aldis, June 6, 1945 (div. 1951); 1 child, William O. Aldis; m. Vera Weidman, Feb. 24, 1951; children: Nyssa, Holly. S.B. cum laude, Harvard, 1932; grad., Nat. War Coll., 1952. Writer Alfred P. Sloan Found., 1937-39; book reviewer Book-of-the-Month Club, 1940-41; with Div. Southeast Asian Affairs, Dept. of State, 1946-50, polit. adviser, acting U.S. rep. com. good offices on Indonesia UN Security Council, 1947-48, policy planning adviser Bur. Far Eastern Affairs, 1952-54, chief div. research for Near East, South Asia and Africa,, 1954-57. Author: The White Falcon, 1955, The Bridge, 1957, Big Caesar, 1958, The Marauders, 1959, U.S. Army, 1960, The Gold of the River Sea, 1965, The Winter Beach, 1966, The Forging of Our Continent, 1968, The Continent in Our Hands, 1971, Winespring Mountain, 1973, The Southern Appalachians: A Wilderness Quest, 1975, The Adventure of Birds, 1976, Railroads: The Great American Adventure (Nat. Geog. Soc.), 1977, The Mysterious William Shakespeare: the Myth and the Reality, 1984, 2d edit., 1992, The Man Who Was Shakespeare, 1995; contbr. to mags. Served to capt. AUS, 1941-46, India-Burma. Recipient John Burroughs medal, 1967, Indonesian Order of Svc. medal, 1995. Home: 403 Hancock St Beaufort SC 29902-4717

OGBURN, HUGH BELL, chemical engineer, consultant; b. Lexington, Va., July 13, 1923; s. Sihon Cicero Jr. and Bettie Mae (Bell) O.; m. Anne Wotherspoon, Mar. 2, 1946 (div.); children: Margaret Mathews Berenson, Scott A.; m. Nancy Wrenn Petersen, Sept. 5, 1974. B.S, Princeton U., 1944, M.S., 1947, Ph.D., 1954. Sect. dir. research and devel. dept. Atlantic Refining Co., Phila., 1950-61; mgr. process engring. M.W. Kellogg Co., N.Y.C., London, 1961-67; dir. research and engring. Union Carbide Corp., N.Y.C., 1967-69; dir. new bus. devel. Weyerhaeuser Co., Tacoma, 1969-72; pres. H.B. Ogburn Assoc., Greenwich, Conn. and Honolulu, 1971—; v.p., dir. Incontrade Inc., Stamford, Conn., 1973-78; v.p. Pacific Resources Inc., Honolulu, 1978-83; chmn. Pacific Oasis, Los Angeles, 1983-85; dir. Danmore Corp., Planning Research Corp.; cons. AEC; prof. chem. engring. Drexel U., Phila., 1951-61. Contbr. articles to profl. jours.; patentee in field. Pres. bd. trustees Woman's Hosp., Phila., 1954-62, Kapiolani Women's and Children's Med. Ctr., 1980-90; mem. adv. bd. Princeton U., 1960-70. Served to lt. j.g. USNR, 1942-46, PTO. Mem. AIChE, Am. Chem. Soc., Research Engrs. Soc., Pacific (Honolulu) Club, Greenwich Field (Conn.) Club, Princeton (N.Y.C.) Club, Phi Beta Kappa, Sigma Xi, Tau Beta Pi. Republican. Presbyterian. Home and Office: 4340 Pahoa Ave Apt 16 A Honolulu HI 96816-5032

OGBURN, WAYNE LEE, health science facility administrator; b. Tulsa, July 23, 1947; s. Luther Calveston and LaDessa Malvina (Bohrer) O.; m. Kay McAdoo, Dec. 27, 1969 (div. July 1984); children: Vicki Elizabeth, Donna Marie; m. Cherry Lynn Manuel Roberts, Feb. 1, 1986; 1 child, Jared Brandon Roberts. BA, Tex. A&M U., 1970; MS, Trinity U., 1972. Adminstrv. resident St. Paul Hosp., Dallas, 1973; asst. adminstr. Tarrant County Hosp. Dist., Ft. Worth, 1973-75, assoc. adminstr., 1975, acting dep. adminstr., 1976; adminstr. Caney Valley Meml. Hosp., Wharton, Tex., 1976-79; v.p. Hendrick Med. Ctr., Abilene, 1979-88, Hendrick Med. Devel. Corp., Abilene, 1979-88, Western Hosp. Affiliates, Inc., Abilene, 1985-88; sr. v.p. Dallas County Hosp. Dist.. Parkland Meml Hosp, Dallas, 1988-91; CEO Titus County Meml. Hosp., Mt. Pleasant, Tex., 1991-95, Brazos Valley Med. and Surg. Ctrs., College Station, Tex., 1995-96, Healthcare Mgmt. Cons., 1996—, Specialty Hosp. of San Fernando Valley, 1997—; commr. Houston/Galveston Area Hosp. System Agy., Houston, 1976-79; bd. mem. Group One, Inc., 1989-91; mem. Tex. State Bd. Vocat. Nurse Examiners, 1987-91, sec.-treas. 1988-89). Loaned exec. Abilene United Way, 1980-81, com. mem., 1986-87. Served with U.S. Army, 1970-71. Fellow Am. Coll. Healthcare Exec. (regents adv. coun. 1993-95); mem. Am. Hosp. Assn. (alt. del. regional policy bd. dirs. 1996—), Tex. Hosp. Assn. (bd. dirs. 1995-97, divsn. sec. 1980-81), N.W. Tex. Hosp. Assn. (bd. dirs. 1985-88, pres. 1987-88), Wharton C. of C. (chmn. com. 1977), Mt. Pleasant C. of C. (bd. dirs. 1992-95). Methodist. Avocations: antique autos, photography. Home: 1800 Via Petirrojo Apt J Thousand Oaks CA 91320 Office: Brazos Valley Med Ctr 1604 Rock Prairie Rd College Station TX 77845-8345

OGDEN, ALFRED, lawyer; b. Bklyn., Oct. 14, 1909; s. Alfred Trecartin and Sophronia (Wisner) O.; m. Mary Fell Jordan, June 25, 1938; 1 child, Alfred Trecartin II. Grad., Phillips Acad., 1928; B.A., Yale, 1932; LL.B., Harvard, 1935. Bar: N.Y. 1936. Since practiced N.Y.C.; partner Alexander & Green, 1955-75; of counsel firm Morgan, Lewis & Bockius, 1979-80, c/o Reboul, MacMurray, Hewitt, Maynard & Kristol, 1980—; Pres., dir. C. Tennant, Sons & Co., N.Y.C., 1952-54. Trustee Fay Sch., Southborough, Mass., 1950-70, Population Reference Bur., 1963-68, Daniel and Florence Guggenheim Found., 1972—, Lavenberg Found., 1986—; trustee Mystic Seaport Mus., Mystic, Conn., 1959—, chmn., 1982-83, chmn. emeritus, 1983—; bd. mgrs., bd. overseers Meml. Sloan Kettering Cancer Ctr., 1959—; trustee, exec. com. Robert Coll., Istanbul, Turkey, 1952-73, chmn., 1955-63; bd. dirs., v.p. English Speaking Union U.S., 1950-92, acting pres., 1983-84; bd. dirs., mem. exec. com. Winston Churchill Meml. Fund., 1966—; trustee Planned Parenthood N.Y.C., 1977-83; bd. dirs. Children's Mus. Manhattan, 1985-87. Served to lt. col. Gen. Staff Corps AUS, 1942-46. Decorated Legion of Merit. Mem. ABA, Internat. Law Assn., Soc. Colonial Wars, Pilgrims of U.S., Coun. on Fgn. Rels., Century Assn., Yale Club (N.Y.C.), Wadawanuck Club (Stonington, Conn.), Cosmopolitan Club, Thursday Evening Club. Home: 150 E 73rd St New York NY 10021-4362 Also: PO Box 214 Stonington CT 06378-0214 Office: 10th Fl 45 Rockefeller Plz Fl 10 New York NY 10111-1099 *There is nothing permanent except change.*

OGDEN, ANITA BUSHEY, nursing educator; b. Malone, N.Y., May 23, 1938; d. John Richard and Eleanor Miriam (Wright) Bushey; m. William Alan Ogden, Dec. 27, 1972. Nursing diploma, N.Y. Med. Coll., 1959; BSN, Columbia U., 1962; MS in Adult Health, SUNY, Buffalo, 1968; PhD, Cornell U., 1984. Faculty Flower-Fifth Ave. Sch. Nursing, N.Y.C., 1959-62, Meth. Hosp., Bklyn. Sch. Nursing, N.Y.C., 1962-66, Hartwick Coll., Oneonta, N.Y., 1968-73; faculty, chair divsn. nursing edn. Corning (N.Y.) C.C., 1973-89; faculty Alfed U., Alfed Station, N.Y., 1984-88; prof., dir. nurse edn. Elmira (N.Y.) Coll., 1989—; clin. staff nurse various orgns., 1959—; cons. curriculum devel., 1978—. Mem. adv. coun. Alfed U., Alfed Station, 1984-87; mem. bd. dirs. Cmty. Health Svcs. for Elderly, Elmira, 1992—; nursing cons. St. Kitts/Nevis U.S. Aid Ptnrs. Ams., 1986-87. Mem. ANA (various offices), N.Y. State Nurses Assn. (various offices), Internat. Resources Instructional Svcs. (faculty 1990—), Nat. League for Nursing (regional bd. dirs. 1973—, ednl. cons. 1982—), LWV (regional coord.), Order Ea. Star (various offices), Delta Kappa Gamma (scholarship award 1981, 83), Delta Kappa Gamma (pres., bd. dirs. 1970), Sigma Theta Tau. Republican. Avocations: bicycling, hand crafts, cats. Home: 104 Fairview Ave Painted Post NY 14870-1215

OGDEN, DANIEL MILLER, JR., government official, educator; b. Clarksburg, W.Va., Apr. 28, 1922; s. Daniel Miller and Mary (Maphis) O.; m. Valeria Juan Munson, Dec. 28, 1946; children: Janeth Lee Martin, Patricia Jo Hunter, Daniel Munson. BA in Polit. Sci., Wash. State U., 1944; MA, U. Chgo., 1947, PhD, 1949. From instr. to assoc. prof. Wash. State U., Pullman, 1949-61; staff asst. resources program U.S. Dept. Interior, 1961-64; asst. dir. U.S. Bur. Outdoor Recreation, 1964-67; dir. budget U.S. Dept. Interior, Washington, 1967-68; dean Coll. Humanities and Social Scis. Colo. State U., Ft. Collins, 1968-76; disting. vis. prof. Lewis and Clark Coll. and Portland (Oreg.) State U., 1977-78; dir. Office of Power Mktg. Coordination U.S. Dept. Energy, 1978-84; mgr. Pub. Power Coun., Portland, Oreg., 1984-88, ret., 1988; mem. profl. staff com. interstate and fgn. commerce U.S. Senate, 1956-57; spll. asst. to chmn. Dem. Nat. Com., 1960-61; lectr. Mgmt. Devel. Ctrs., U.S. Office Pers. Mgmt., 1966—. Co-author: Electing the President, rev. edit., 1968, American National Government, 7th edit., 1970, American State and Local Government, 5th edit., 1972, Washington Politics, 1960, How National Policy is Made, 3d edit., 1997. Committeeman Wash. Dem. Ctrl. Com., 1952-56; chmn. Whitman County Dem. Ctrl. Com., 1958-60; chmn. 49th Legis. Dist. Dem. Com., 1990-94; chmn. Clark County Dem. Ctrl. com., 1994—. With inf. U.S. Army, 1943-46. Mem. Phi Beta Kappa, Phi Kappa Phi, Pi Sigma Alpha, Sigma Delta Chi. Mem. Unitarian Ch. Home: 3118 NE Royal Oak Dr Vancouver WA 98662-7435

OGDEN, DAVID WILLIAM, lawyer; b. Washington, Nov. 12, 1953; s. Horace Greeley and Elaine Celia (Condrell) O.; m. Wannett Smith, 1988; children: Jonathan Smith, Elaine Smith. BA summa cum laude, U. Pa., 1976; JD magna cum laude, Harvard U., 1981. Bar: D.C. 1983, Va. 1986, U.S. Dist. Ct. D.C. 1984, U.S. Dist. Ct. (ea. dist.) Va. 1988, U.S. Ct. Appeals (D.C. cir.) 1984, U.S. Ct. Appeals (4th cir.) 1986, U.S. Ct. Appeals (1st cir. 1989), U.S. Ct. Appeals (10th cir.) 1991, U.S. Supreme Ct. 1987. Law clk. to presiding judge U.S. Dist. Ct. (so. dist.) N.Y., N.Y.C., 1981-82; law clk. to assoc. justice Harry A. Blackmun U.S. Supreme Ct., Washington, 1982-83; assoc. atty. Ennis, Friedman, Bersoff & Ewing, Washington, 1983-85; atty., ptnr. Ennis, Friedman & Bersoff, Washington, 1986-88, Jenner & Block, Washington, 1988-94; legal counsel, dep. gen. counsel U.S. DOD, Washington, 1994-95; assoc. dep. atty. gen. U.S. Dept. Justice, Washington, 1995-97, counselor to the atty. gen., 1997—; adj. prof. law Georgetown U. Law Ctr., 1992-95. Author: (with Jerald A. Jacobs) Legal Risk Management for Associations, 1995. Recipient Disting. Pub. Svc. medal Dept. Def., 1995. Mem. ABA, D.C. Bar Assn., Phi Beta Kappa. Democrat.

OGDEN, DAYTON, executive search consultant. Pres. Spencer Stuart & Assocs., Stamford, Conn. Office: Spencer Stuart & Assocs Fin Centre 695 Main St Stamford CT 06901-2141 Office: 277 Park Ave New York NY 10172

OGDEN, JAMES RUSSELL, marketing educator, consultant, lecturer, trainer; b. Paris, Ill., Nov. 4, 1954; s. Russell Lee and Marianne (Johnson) O.; children: David James, Anne Marie, Kari Kristine; m. Denise T. Alarid, 1989. B of Bus. Edn., Ea. Mich. U., 1978; MS, Colo. State U., 1981; PhD, U. No. Colo., 1986. Grad. fellow Colo. State U., Ft. Collins, 1979-81, asst. mgr. family housing, 1979-81; placement counselor U. No. Colo., Greeley, 1981-83, mktg. instr., 1982-83; CEO, pres. Ogden Latshaw & Assocs., Allentown, Pa., 1982—; chair advt. and mktg. dept., assoc. prof. Adams State Coll., Alamosa, Colo., 1983-89; dept. chair, prof. mktg. Coll. Bus., Kutztown (Pa.) U., 1989—, bd. bus. advisors Students in Free Enterprise, 1996—; interim dir. Small Bus. Devel. Ctr., Adams State Coll., 1988-89; adj. prof. Ctrl. Mich. U., Mt. Pleasant, 1987—, Cedar Crest Coll., Allentown, 1989—, Pa. State U., 1994-95, Nova Southeastern U., Ft. Lauderdale, Fla., 1995—; spkr. in field; mktg. and advt. cons.; corp. trainer; textbook reviewer, editl. cons. Merrill Pub. Co., Allyn & Bacon, Inc., Richard Irwin, Inc., Macmillan Pub., John Wiley & Sons, Inc., Prentice-Hall, Houghton & Mifflin Co., Austen Press, Simon & Schuster; textbook reviewer Fairchild Books and Visuals, Inc.; tech. editor Rsch. and Edn. Assn. Co-author: The Best Test Preparation for the CLEP College-Level Examination Program Principles of Marketing, 1996; contbg. author, editor: Principles of Business, 1991, Essentials of Advertising, 1992, rev. edit., 1994; editor: Essentials of Marketing, 1994; contbr. over 40 articles to profl. jours. Treas. Com. to Elect Jorge Amaya County Commr., Colo., 1985, Bob Pastore for Senate Com.; senator Assoc. Student and Faculty Senate, Adams State Coll., 1984-85; bd. dirs. Am. Advt. Fedn. Acad. Com., 1991—, Alamosa Personnel Bd., 1986-88, Alamosa County Devel. Corp., 1987-89, Alamosa Tourism Com., 1988-89, trustee bd. dirs. Creede Repertory Theatre, 1987-89; expert witness in tourism and mktg. State of Colo.; advisor student team entries into Nat. Student Advt. Competition, Coll. World Series of Advt., 1989, 90, 93—; trustee Dr. R.L. Ogden Meml. Scholarship, Colo. State U. Found., 1992—; faculty advisor Students in Free Enterprise (SIFE) nat. competition, 1997—; faculty advisor, mem. bus. adv. bd. Kutztown U. chpt. of Students in Free Enterprise (SIFE). Recipient award for Excellence in Econ. Edn., Freedoms Found. Valley Forge, 1986, Capital award for contbn. to edn., Nat. Leadership Coun., 1991-92, Disting. Leadership award for Excellence in Mktg. Edn., Am. Biog. Inst., 1988; named Outstanding Educator of Sch. of Bus., Adams State Coll., 1987-88; Sam Walton fellow Students in Free Enterprise, 1997. Fellow Direct Mktg. Assn.; mem. Am. Advt. Fedn. (faculty advisor 1987-89, 90—, bd. dirs. acad. com. 1991—), Western Mktg. Educators Assn. (paper reviewer), Nat. Guild Hypnotists (cert. hypnotherapist), Acad. Mktg. Sci., Advt. Club N.Y., Point of Purchase Advt. Inst., Am. Collegiate Retailing Assn., Assn. Nat. Advertisers, Nat. Assn. Hispanic Profs. of Bus. Adminstrn. and Econs., New Eng. Bus. Adminstrn. Assn., Ctrl. Pa. Advt. Club, Phi Kappa Phi, Alpha Sigma Alpha (fin. advisor 1992—), Alpha Kappa Psi (dist. dir.). Democrat. Avocations: scuba, music, traveling. Office: Kutztown U Coll Bus Dept Mktg Kutztown PA 19530

OGDEN, LOUANN MARIE, dietitian, consultant; b. Enid, Okla., Dec. 16, 1952; d. Raymond Michael Schiltz and Donna Mae Stuever; m. Wendell Edwin Ogden, Jan. 5, 1979; 1 child, Gregory Jacob Jeremiah. BS in Home Econs., Okla. State U., 1974, MS, 1977. Registered dietitian; lic. dietitian, Tex. Dietetic intern Ind. U. Med. Ctr., Indpls., 1974; therapeutic dietitian-clin. svcs. and trayline ops. Bapt. Med. Ctr. Okla., Oklahoma City, 1975-76; grad. teaching asst. lower and upper level food preparation Okla. State U., Stillwater, 1976-77, teaching assoc. lower and upper level food preparation, 1977; chief clin. dietitian adminstrv. and clin. coordination Borgess Hosp., Kalamazoo, 1978; dietary cons. nutrition program Iowa Commn. on Aging, Des Moines, 1979-80; asst. food svc. dir., adminstrv. dietitian Timberlawn Psych. Hosp., Dallas, 1980-92; rep. group one purchasing program, mem. student tng. program Zale Lipshy U. Hosp., Dallas, 1992-93, food svc. cons., 1993—. Mem. Am. Dietetic Assn., Am. Soc. Hosp. Food Svc. Adminstrn. (nat. nominating com. 1990-91, Disting. Health Care Food Svc. Adminstr. 1992, North ctrl. Tex. chpt.: corr. sec. 1985-86, comms. chair 1986-87, rec. sec. 1987-89, pres.-elect 1989-90, pres. 1990-91, nominating com. chair, health care food svc. week com. chair 1991-92, Outstanding Mem. award 1992), Tex. Dietetic Assn., Dallas Dietetic Assn. Democrat. Roman Catholic. Avocations: photography, traveling. Home and Office: 3302 Oxford Dr Rowlett TX 75088-5936

OGDEN, MAUREEN BLACK, retired state legislator; b. Vancouver, B.C., Nov. 1, 1928; came to U.S., 1930; d. William Moore and Margaret Hunter (Leitch) Black; m. Robert Moore Ogden, June 23, 1956; children: Thomas, Henry, Peter. BA, Smith Coll., 1950; MA, Columbia U., 1963; M in City and Regional Planning, Rutgers U., 1977. Researcher, staff asst. Ford Found., N.Y.C., 1951-56; staff assoc. Fgn. Policy Assn., N.Y.C., 1956-58; mem. Millburn (N.J.) Twp. Com., 1976-81; mayor Twp. of Millburn, N.J., 1979-81; mem. N.J. Gen. Assembly, Trenton, 1982-96; chmn. Assembly Environment Com., N.J. Gen. Assembly; chmn. Energy and Pub. Utilities Com., Coun. State Govts., 1991-92; mem. adv. bd. Sch. Policy and Planning, Rutgers Univ., New Brunswick, N.J., 1992-96. Author: Natural Resources Inventory, Township of Millburn, 1974. Bd. govs. N.J. Hist. Soc., Newark, 1990—; trustee N.J. chpt. The Nature Conservancy; hon. trustee Paper Mill Playhouse, Millburn, 1990—; former trustee St. Barnabas Med. Ctr., Livingston, N.J.; former pres. N.J. Drug Abuse Adv. Coun.; chair Gov.'s Coun. on N.J. Outdoors, 1996—; mem. Palisades Interstate Park Commn., 1996—. Recipient citation Nat. Assn. State Outdoors Recreation Liaison Officers, 1987, cert. appreciation John F. Kennedy Ctr. for the Performing Arts, The Alliance for Art Edn., 1987, disting. svc. award Art Educators N.J., 1987, ann. environ. quality award EPA Region II, 1988, citation Humane Soc. U.S., 1989, award N.J. Hist. Sites Coun., 1989, N.J. Sch. Conservation, 1990, pres.'s award The Nature Conservancy, 1995, pub. policy award Nat. Trust for Hist. Preservation, 1995. Republican. Episcopalian. Home: 59 Lakeview Ave Short Hills NJ 07078-2240

OGDEN, PEGGY A., personnel director; b. N.Y.C., Mar. 21, 1932; d. Stephen Arnold and Margaret (Stern) O. BA with honors, Brown U., 1953; MA, Trinity Coll., Hartford, Conn., 1955. Asst. dir. YMCA Counseling Svc., Hartford, 1953-55; employment interviewer R.H. Macy & Co., N.Y.C., 1955; asst. pers. dir. Inst. Internat. Edn., N.Y.C., 1956-59; pers. advisor Girl Scouts U.S.A., N.Y.C., 1959-61; store and pers. mgr. Ohrbachs, Inc., N.Y.C., 1961-74; dir. pers. N.Y.C. Tech. Coll. CUNY, Bkyn., 1974—; arbitrator Better Bus. Bur., N.Y.C., 1988—; cons. Girl Scout Coun. N.Y., N.Y.C., 1988-89. Mem APA, Am. Assn. U. Adminstrs., Women in Human Resources, N.Y. Pers. Mgmt. Assn. Home: 1100 Park Ave New York NY 10128-1202 Office: NYC Tech Coll 300 Jay St Brooklyn NY 11201-1909

OGDEN, VALERIA JUAN, management consultant, state representative; b. Okanogan, Wash., Feb. 11, 1924; d. Ivan Bodwell and Pearle (Wilson) Munson; m. Daniel Miller Ogden Jr., Dec. 28, 1946; children: Janeth Lee Ogden Martin, Patricia Jo Ogden Hunter, Daniel Munson Ogden. BA magna cum laude, Wash. State U., 1946. Exec. dir. Potomac Coun. Camp Fire, Washington, 1964-68, Ft. Collins (Colo.) United Way, 1969-73, Designing Tomorrow Today, Ft. Collins, 1973-74, Poudre Valley Community Edn. Assn., Ft. Collins, 1977-78; pres. Valeria M. Ogden, Inc., Kensington, Md., 1978-81; nat. field cons. Camp Fire, Inc., Kansas City, Mo., 1980-81; exec. dir. Nat. Capital Area YWCA, Washington, 1981-84, Clark County YWCA, Vancouver, Wash., 1985-89; pvt. practice mgmt. cons. Vancouver, 1989—; mem. Wash. Ho. of Reps., 1991—; mem. adj. faculty pub. adminstrn. program Lewis and Clark Coll., Portland (Oreg.) State U., 1979-94; mem. Pvt. Industry Coun., Vancouver, 1986-95; mem. regional Svcs. Network Bd. Mental Health, 1993—. Author: Camp Fire Membership, 1980. County vice chmn. Larimer County Dems., Ft. Collins, 1974-75; mem. precinct com. Clark County Dems., Vancouver, 1986-88; mem. Wash. State Coun. Vol. Action, Olympia, 1986-90; treas. Mortar Bd. Nat. Found., Vancouver, 1987-96; bd. dirs. Clark County Coun. for Homeless, Vancouver, 1989—, chmn., 1994; bd. dirs. Wash. Wil life and Recreation Coalition, 1995—, Human Svcs. Coun., 1996—; chair arts and tourism com. Nat. Coun. State Legis., 1996-97; bd. Wash. State Hist. Soc., 1996—. Named Citizen of Yr. Ft. Collins Bd. of Realtors, 1975; recipient Gulick award Camp Fire Inc., 1956, Alumna Achievement award Wash. State U. Alumni Assn., 1988. Mem. Internat. Assn. Vol. Adminstrs. (pres. Boulder 1989-90), Nat. Assn. YWCA Exec. Dirs. (nat. bd. nominating com. 1988-90), Sci. and Society Assn. (bd. dirs. 1993—), Women in Action, Philanthropic and Ednl. Orgn., Phi Beta Kappa. Democrat. Avocation: hiking, travel. Home: 3118 NE Royal Oak Dr Vancouver WA 98662-7435 Office: John L O'Brien Bldg Rm 342 State Ave NE Olympia WA 98504-1134

OGDON, WILBUR, composer, music educator; b. Redlands, Calif., Apr. 19, 1921; s. Alfred Benjamin and Ethel (Brooks) O.; m. Beverly Jean Porter, Aug. 22, 1958; children—Bethany, Benjamin, Erica. MusB, U. Wis., 1942; MA, Hamline U., 1947; postgrad., U. Calif., Berkeley, 1949-50; pvt. composition studies with René Leibowitz, Paris, 1952-53; composition studies with Ernst Krenek, composition studies with Roger Sessions; Ph.D., Ind. U., 1955. Asst. prof. U. Tex., 1947-50; prof. Coll. St. Catherine, St. Paul, 1955-56; assoc. prof. Ill. Wesleyan U., 1956-65; dir. music Pacifica Found., KPFA, Berkeley, Calif., 1962-64; coordinator music programming U. Ill., 1965-66; prof. music U. Calif., San Diego, 1966-91, chmn. dept. music, 1966-71, research fellow Project for Music Expt., 1973-74. Author: (with Krenek and Stewart) Horizons Circled, 1974; mem. editorial bd. Perspective of New Music; composer: Three Sea Choruses, 1960-62, String Quartet, 1960, By the Isar, 1969, Un Tombeau de Cocteau, I, 1964, II, 1972, III, 1975, Sappho, The Awakening (chamber opera), 1976-80, Capriccio and Five Comments for Orch, 1980, Images, A Winter's Calendar (Soprano, piano and 3 winds), 1980, Six Small Trios for trumpet, marimba and piano, 1982, Five Preludes for violin and piano, 1982, Summer Images and Reflections, 1984-85, Five Preludes for Violin and Chamber Orchestra, 1985, Two Serenades for Wind Quintet, 1987, 90-94, Two Sea Chanteys for soprano, baritone and percussion, 1987-88, Seven Piano Pieces, 1987, 7 pieces and a Capriccio for violin and piano, 1988-89, Four D.H. Lawrence Songs for Soprano and Chamber Ensemble, 1989, 13 Expressions for solo violin and chamber ensemble, 1993, others. Bd. dirs. San Diego Opera Inc., 1967-70, La Jolla Civic Orch. and Chorus Assn., 1967-72, 80-82; hon. dir. N.C. Gov.'s Bd. Music, 1964—. Served with AUS, 1942-46. Nat. Endowment of Arts fellow, 1975. Mem. Anton Webern Soc. (charter), Music Execs. Calif., Calif. Profl. Music Tchrs. Assn. (hon.). Home: 452 15th St Del Mar CA 92014-2521 Office: U Calif at San Diego Dept Music La Jolla CA 92037 *As years pass, one becomes increasingly aware of an indebtedness to others: to those who taught, encouraged, tolerated and even sacrificed. That increasing sense of indebtedness serves to sustain one's own efforts to teach and encourage.*

OGE, MARGO TSIRIGOTIS, environmentalist; b. Athens, Greece, Feb. 20, 1949; came to U.S., 1968; d. John Tsirigotis and Joana Lambrinakos; m. Cuneyt Oge, Aug. 24, 1975; children: Nicole, Marisa. Degree in Plastic Tech., Lowell U., 1972, degree in Plastic Engring., 1975. Chem. engr. EPA, Washington, 1980-83, sect. chief, 1983-85, dep. dir. toxic substances office, 1986-88, dir. radon divsn., 1988—; legis. asst. to Sen. Chafee U.S. Senate, Washington, 1985. Avocations: reading, tennis, skiing, travel. Office: EPA Mobile Sources Office 401 M St SW Washington DC 20460-0001

OGEDEGBE, HENRY, medical technologist, clinical laboratory scientist, chemist, consultant; b. Benin City, Nigeria, Mar. 25, 1946; came to U.S., 1971; s. Edmund Iduorobo and Esther Amadin (Uwaifo) O.; m. Patricia O'Brien, Aug. 12, 1973 (div. Oct. 1975); m. Esther Osagie, June 5, 1982; children: Henry, Stanley. BA in Biology and Chemistry, Linfield Coll., 1978; MS in Biology and Health Sci., Ctrl. Conn. State U., 1993; PhD in Biomed. Scis., The Union Inst., 1996. Cert. clin. lab. scientist Nat. Cert. Agy.; cert. technologist in chemistry, cert. specialist in chemistry, cert. technologist blood banking Am. Soc. Clin. Pathologists; registered clin. chemist Nat. Registry in Clin. Chemistry. Lab. technician Hartord (Conn.) Coll., 1971-75, ARC, Farmington, Conn., 1974-76, Mount Sinai Hosp., Hartford, Conn., 1976-77; lectr. Sch. Health Tech., Benin City, Nigeria, 1980-83; lab. dir. Imasi Biomedica Labs., Benin City, Nigeria, 1983-89; med. technologist Manchester (Conn.) Meml. Hosp., 1989—; instr. Fox Inst. Bus., Hartford, Conn., 1992-95; clin. cons. in field. Mem. AAAS, Am. Assn. Clin. Chemists, Am. Soc. Clin., Am. Mus. Natural History, Conn. Sci. Educators Assn., N.Y. Acad Sci. Avocations: reading, walking, music. Home: 54 Queen Ct Apt A Manchester CT 06040-8119 Office: Manchester Meml Hosp 71 Haynes St Manchester CT 06040-4112

OGG, GEORGE WESLEY, retired foreign service officer; b. Washington, June 13, 1932; s. William Raymond and Carrie (Blair) O.; m. Frances Zabilsky, Sept. 17, 1954; children: David Stuart, Carolyn Ogg Tripp. A.B., Colgate U., N.Y., 1954; M.A., George Washington U., Washington, 1970; postgrad., U. Md., College Park, 1968-69, Nat. Def. Coll., Can., 1977-78. Chief econ. sect. U.S. Embassy, San Jose, Costa Rica, 1974-77; chief commodities and developing countries div. Dept. of State, 1978-80; dep. dir. Office Canadian Affairs, Dept. of State, 1980-82; consul gen. U.S. Consulate Gen., Vancouver, B.C., Can., 1982-86; prof. internat. rels. Nat. Defense U., Washington, 1986-91. Served to 1st lt. USAF, 1954-57. Recipient Superior Honor award U.S. Dept. State, 1974, Meritorious Honor award, 1980. Avocations: tennis, photography.

OGG, JAMES ELVIS, microbiologist, educator; b. Centralia, Ill., Dec. 24, 1924; s. James and Amelia (Glammeyer) O.; m. Betty Jane Ackerson, Dec. 27, 1948; children—James George, Susan Kay. B.S., U. Ill., 1949; Ph.D., Cornell U., 1956. Bacteriologist Biol. Labs., Ft. Detrick, Md., 1950-53; cons. Biol. Labs., 1953-56, med. bacteriologist, 1956-58; prof. microbiology Colo. State U., Ft. Collins, 1958-85, prof. emeritus, 1985—; asst. dean Grad. Sch., 1965-66, head dept. microbiology, 1967-77; dir. Advanced Sci. Edn. Program div. grad. edn. in sci. NSF, Washington, 1966-67; Fulbright-Hays sr. lectr. in microbiology, Nepal, 1976-77, 81; acad. adminstrn. advisor Inst. Agr. and Animal Sci., Tribhuvan U., Nepal, 1988-91; cons. NASA, 1968-69, NSF, 1968-73, Martin Marietta Corp., 1970-76; cons.-evaluator North Central Assn. Colls. and Secondary Schs., 1974-89; cons. Consortium for Internat. Devel., 1990—, Winrock Internat. Inst. for Agrl. Devel., 1992—. Contbr. articles to profl. jours. Served with AUS, 1943-46, 50-51. Fellow AAAS, Am. Acad. Microbiology; mem. Am. Soc. Microbiology (chmn. pub. service and adult edn. com. 1975-80). Home: 1442 Ivy St Fort Collins CO 80525-2348

OGG, ROBERT DANFORTH, corporate executive; b. Gardiner, Maine, June 10, 1918; s. James and Eleanor B. (Danforth) O.; m. Nancy Foote, Oct. 21, 1978; children by previous marriage: Richard Aasgaard, Robert Danforth, James Erling. Student U. Calif., Berkeley, Stanford U. Utilities engr. State of Calif., 1946-48; gen. mgr. Danforth Anchors, Berkeley, 1948-51, pres., chief exec. officer, 1951-59; mng. dir. Danforth div. The Eastern Co., 1959-79, dir., 1972-80; dir. Hodgdon Bros., East Boothbay, Maine, 1961-65; pres. Brewers Boatyard, West Southport, Maine, 1963-65; v.p. Henry R. Hinckley Co., Manset, Maine, 1974-79; pres. Ogg Oceans Systems, 1980—; chmn. Alpha Ocean Systems, 1983—. Author: Anchors & Anchorin (8 editions); contbr. chpts. to books, articles to profl. jours.; patentee in field; inventor The Danforth Anchor, Inertial Altimeter, Digital Depth Sounder, others. Mem. adv. com. U. Calif. Rsch. Expeditions Program, 1979, co-chmn., 1983—; trustee U. Calif.-Berkeley Found., 1981, exec. com., 1983—, chmn. audit com., 1984-89, fellow, 1990, lifetime emeritus trustee; advisor Lawrence Hall Sci.; founder, sr. warden St. Ann's Episcopal Ch., Windham, Maine, 1976-79; life fellow U. Calif., Berkeley; contbr. to ABC and BBC documentaries on Pearl Harbor. With USN Intelligence, 1941-46. Recipient Wheeler Oak meritorious award U. Calif., 1987. Fellow Explorers Club (life), Calif. Acad. Scis. (life); mem. Navy League (founder Marin coun.), Soc. Naval Architects & Marine Engrs., Am. Soc. Naval Engrs., Am. Boat & Yacht Coun., Boating Writers Internat., Am. Geophys. Union, IEEE, Chancellors Cir. U. Calif., Sports Adv. Coun. U. Calif., Bodega Marine Lab., U.S. Naval Inst., R.G. Sproul Assocs., Tail Hook Assocs., Woodshole Assocs., Bunčke Microsurgical Found. (bd. dirs. 1994—), Sierra Club, U. Calif.-Berkeley Alumni Assn., Engring. Alumni Assn., N.Y. Yacht Club, Pacific Union Club, Elks Club, Bear Backers Club, U. Calif. Berkeley Chancellor's Circle Club, U. Calif. San Francisco Heritage Club. Address: 11490 Franz Valley Rd Calistoga CA 94515-9549

OGG, WILSON REID, lawyer, poet, retired judge, lyricist, curator, publisher, educator, philosopher, social scientist, parapsychologist; b. Alhambra, Calif., Feb. 26, 1928; s. James Brooks and Mary (Wilson) O. Student Pasadena Jr. Coll., 1946; A.B., U. Calif. at Berkeley, 1949, J.D., 1952; Cultural D in Philosophy of Law, World Univ. Roundtable, 1983. Bar: Calif. Assoc. trust Dept. Wells Fargo Bank, San Francisco, 1954-55; pvt. practice law, Berkeley, 1955—; adminstrv. law judge, 1974-93; real estate broker, cons., 1974—; curator-in-residence Pinebrook, 1964—; owner Pinebrook Press, Berkeley, Calif., 1988—; rsch. atty., legal editor dept. of continuing edn. of bar U. Calif. Extension, 1958-63; psychology instr. 25th Sta. Hosp., Taegu, Korea, 1954; English instr. Taegu English Lang. Inst., Taegu, 1954. Trustee World U., 1976-80; dir. admissions Internat. Soc. for Phil. Enquiry, 1981-84; dep. dir. gen. Internat. Biographical Centre, Eng.,

1986—; dep. gov. Am. Biographical Inst. Research Assn., 1986—; ind. rep. Excel Comm., Inc. Served with AUS, 1952-54. Cert. community coll. instr. Mem. VFW, AAAS, ABA, ASCAP, State Bar Calif., San Francisco Bar Assn., Am. Soc. Composers, Am. Arbitration Assn. (nat. panel arbitrators), Calif. Soc. Psychical Study (pres., chmn. bd. 1963-65), Internat. Soc. Unified Sci., Internat. Soc. Poets, (life), Internat. Platform Assn., Amnesty Internat., Am. Civil Liberties Union, Intertel, Internat. Soc. Individual Liberty, Triple Nine Soc., Wisdom Soc., Inst. Noetic Scis., Men's Inner Circle of Achievement, Truman Libr. Inst. (hon.), Am. Legion, City Commons Club (Berkeley), Commonwealth Club of Calif., Town Hall Club of Calif., Marines Meml. Club, Masons, Shriners, Elks. Unitarian. Contbr. numerous articles profl. jours; contbr. poetry to various mags. including American Poetry Anthology Vol. VI Number 5, Hearts on Fire: A Treasury of Poems on Love, Vol. IV, 1987, New Voices in American Poetry, 1987, The Best Poems of the 90's, Distinguished Poets of America, The Poetry of Life A Treasury of Moments Am. Poetry Anthology, Vol. VII, 1988, Nat. Libr. Poets, 1992, Disting. Poets Of Am., 1993, The Best Modern Writer of 1994, Parnassus of World Poets, 1994, 95, 96, Best Poems of 1995, 96, 97; elected Internat. Poetry Hall Fame Nat. Libr. Poetry, 1997. Home: Pinebrook 8 Bret Harte Way Berkeley CA 94708-1609 Office: 1104 Keith Ave Berkeley CA 94708-1607 also: 39193 Liberty St Fremont CA 94538-1501 *Judge Ogg's career combines outstanding achievement in the legal profession with a major analysis of the problems of distinguishing co-existence from causality in medicine and science. He has also formulated the two-way flow theory of matter and consciousness under which principles of quantum mechanics, black notes, light, suppression and contraction of manifestation, and physical and biological evolutions are derivative from the basic postulates of the theory.*

OGIDA, MIKIO, history of religion educator; b. Akita, Japan, Jan. 20, 1938; s. Shigeji and Kiyono (Sato) O.; m. Noriko Yamamoto, May 3, 1966; 1 child, Satoshi. BD, Doshisha U., Kyoto, Japan, 1961; S.T.M., Doshisha U., 1963; ThM, Harvard U., 1969. Assoc. minister Heian Ch., United Ch. of Christ in Japan, Kyoto, 1963-66; lectr. Kobe Jogakuin U., Nishinomiya, Hyogo, Japan, 1969-72; assoc. prof. Kobe Jogakuin U., 1972-81, prof., 1981—, dean students, 1989-93. Author: Religions of the World, 1981. Mem. Japan Soc. Christian Studies, Soc. Hist. Studies Christianity Japan, Classical Soc. Japan. Avocation: igo, skiing. Home: 4 11 1 108 Makami cho, Takatuki shi Osaka, Japan Office: Kobe Jogakuin U, 4 1 Okadayama, Nishinomiya Hyogo, Japan

OGIER, WALTER THOMAS, retired physics educator; b. Pasadena, Calif., June 18, 1925; s. Walter Williams and Aileen Vera (Polhamus) O.; m. Mayrene Miriam Gorton, June 27, 1954; children: Walter Charles, Margaret Miriam, Thomas Earl, Kathryn Aileen. B.S., Calif. Inst. Tech., 1947, Ph.D. in Physics, 1953. Research fellow Calif. Inst. Tech., 1953; instr. U. Calif. at Riverside, 1954-55, asst. prof. physics, 1955-60; asst. prof. physics Pomona Coll., Claremont, Calif., 1960-62, assoc. prof., 1962-67, prof. physics, 1967-89, prof. emeritus, 1989—, chmn. dept., 1972-89. Contbr. articles on metals, liquid helium, X-rays and proton produced X-rays to profl. jours. Served with USNR, 1944-46. NSF Sci. Faculty fellow, 1966-67. Mem. Am. Phys. Soc., Am. Assn. Physics Tchrs. (pres. So. Calif. sect. 1967-69), Tau Beta Pi. Home: 8555 San Gabriel Rd Atascadero CA 93422-4928

OGILVIE, DONALD GORDON, bankers association executive; b. N.Y.C., Apr. 7, 1943; s. John B. and Ann (Stephens) O.; m. Fan Staunton, Apr. 18, 1966; children: Jennifer B., Adam C. B.A., Yale U., 1965; M.B.A., Stanford U., 1967. Systems analyst Dept. of Def., Washington, 1967-68; pres., dir. ICF Inc., Washington, 1969-73; dep. assoc. dir. Office of Mgmt. and Budget, Washington, 1973-74, assoc. dir., 1974-76; assoc. dean Yale U., New Haven, 1977-80; v.p. Celanese Corp., N.Y.C., 1980-85; exec. v.p. Am. Bankers Assn., Washington, 1985—; dir. Colonial Bancorp, 1979-85, MacDermid Corp., 1986—, Marine Spill Response Corp., 1991—. Bd. dirs. N.Y.C. Ballet, 1981-88, Hospiec Edn. and Rsch., New Haven, 1978-81; mem. adv. bd. Yale Sch. Orgn. and Mgmt., 1992-94. Home: 1425 34th St NW Washington DC 20007-2804 Office: Am Bankers Assn 1120 Connecticut Ave NW Washington DC 20036-3902*

OGILVIE, KELVIN KENNETH, university president, chemistry educator; b. Windsor, N.S., Can., Nov. 6, 1942; s. Carl Melbourn and Mabel Adelia (Wile) O.; m. Emma Roleen, May 7, 1964; children: Kristine, Kevin. B.Sc. with honors, Acadia U., 1964, D.Sc. honoris causa, 1983; Ph.D., Northwestern U., 1968; D.Sc. honoris causa, U. N.B., Can., 1991. Assoc. prof. U. Man., Winnipeg, 1968-74; prof. chemistry McGill U., Montreal, 1974-88, Can. Pacific prof. biotech., 1984-87; bd. dirs. Sci. Adv. Bd., Biologicals, Toronto, Ont., 1979-84; dir. Office of Biotech. McGill U., 1984-87; v.p. acad. affairs, prof. chemistry Acadia U., Wolfville, N.S., 1987-93, pres., vice-chancellor, 1993—; invited lectr. on biotech. Tianjin, People's Republic of China, 1985; Snider lectr. U. Toronto, 1991; Gwen Leslie Meml. lectr., 1991; mem. Nat. Adv. Bd. Sci. and Tech., 1994-95; chair selection com. Indsl. Postgrad. Scholarship program NSERCC, 1994; mem. Coun. N.S. U. Pres. 1993—; mem. Coun. of Applied Sci. and Tech. for N.S., 1988-93; mem. Nat. Biotech. Adv. Com., 1988—; mem. Fisher (Can.) Biotech. Adv. Ctr., 1989-92; mem. sci. adv. bd. Allelix Biopharms., 1991-93; bd. dirs. Hyal Pharm. Corp.; chair adv. bd. NRC Inst. for Marine Bioscis., 1990-93; mem. steering com. on biotech. labor Can., 1990-92; chair Atlantic regional com. Prime Min.'s Awards for Tchg. Excellence in Sci., Tech. and Math., 1993-95; chair regional planning forum for a pharm. industry, Atlantic, Can., 1993; mem. Atomic Energy Control Bd., Can., 1997—. Mem. editorial bd. Nucleosides and Nucleotides, 1981-92; contbr. over 150 articles to profl. jours.; holder 14 patents. Bd. dirs. Plant Biotech. Inst., 1987-90. Decorated Knight of Malta, 1985, Order of Can., 1991, Hon. Col. 14th Air Maintenance Squadron, Can. Air Force, 1995—; recipient Commemorative medal for 125th Anniversary of Confedn. Can., 1992, Buck-Whitney medal, 1983, Manning Prin. award, 1992; named to McLean's Honor Roll of Canadians Who Made a Difference, 1988; E.W.R. Steacie Meml. fellow, 1982-84; named Hon. Col. Can. Air Force, 1995. Fellow Chem. Inst. Can.; mem. Am. Chem. Soc., Ordre des Chemists of Que., Assn. Canadienne Française pour l'Advancement des Scis., Assn. Univs. and Colls. Can. (standing com. on rsch. 1993—), Atlantic Univ. Athletic Assn. (pres. 1995-97). Achievements include inventing of BIOLF-62 (ganciclovir), antiviral drug used worldwide; developed general synthesis of RNA; developed original 'gene machine'; developed complete chemical synthesis of large RNA molecules. Home: PO Box 307, Canning, NS Canada B0P 1H0 Office: Acadia U, Office of Pres, Wolfville, NS Canada B0P 1X0

OGILVIE, RICHARD IAN, clinical pharmacologist; b. Sudbury, Ont., Can., Oct. 9, 1936; s. Patrick Ian and Gena Hilda (Olson) O.; m. Ernestine Tahedl, Oct. 9, 1965; children—Degen Elisabeth, Lars Ian. M.D., U. Toronto, 1960. Intern Toronto (Ont.) Gen. Hosp., 1960-61; resident Montreal Gen. and Univ. Alta. hosps., 1962-66; fellow in clin. pharmacology McGill U., Montreal, 1966-68; asst. prof. medicine, pharmacology and therapeutics McGill U., 1968-73, assoc. prof., 1973-78, prof., 1978-83, chmn. dept. pharmacology and therapeutics, 1978-83; clin. pharmacologist Montreal Gen. Hosp., 1968-83, dir. div. clin. pharmacology, 1976-83; prof. medicine and pharmacology U. Toronto, 1983—; dir. div. cardiology Toronto Western Hosp., 1983-88, div. clin. pharmacology, 1983-91; mem. pharm. grants com. Med. Research Coun. Can., 1977-82, chmn. 1980-82; mem. med. adv. com. Que. Heart Found., 1976-82, chmn. 1977-81. Editor Hypertension Canada, 1989—. Bd. dirs. PMAC Health Care Found., 1986-92; hon. sec.-treas. Banting Research Found., 1984-87, chmn. grant rev. com., 1985-86. Decorated knight comdr. Sovereign Mil. Order St. John of Jerusalem, Knights of Malta, 1987, nat. chmn., recipient prize in med. ethics, 1988—, sci. advisor to the prior, 1987—, Knight Grand Cross, 1990; jury mem. Can. Prix Galien, 1994—; grantee Can. Kidney Found., J.C. Edwards Found., Med. Rsch. Coun., Que. Heart Found., Can. Found. Advancement Therapeutics, Conseil de la recherche en sante du Que. Fellow ACP, Royal Coll. Physicians of Can.; mem. Can. Soc. Clin. Investigation (coun. 1977-80), Can. Hypertension Soc. (bd. dirs. 1979-81, 89—, v.p. 1991-92, pres. 1992-93), Can. Found. Advancement Clin. Pharmacology (dir. 1978-86), Canadian Soc. for Clin. Pharmacology (pres. 1979-82, Sr. Investigator award 1993), Internat. Union Pharmacology (coun. mem. clin. pharmacology sect. 1981-84, chmn. 1984-87), Pharm. Soc. Can., Can. Cardiovascular Soc., Am. Soc. Pharmacology and Exptl. Therapeutics, Am. Soc. Clin. Pharm., Am. Fedn. Clin. Rsch., Toronto Hypertension Soc. (pres. 1988—). Home: 79 Collard Dr, King City, ON Canada L7B 1E4 Office: Toronto Hosp Western Div, 399 Bathurst St, Toronto, ON Canada M5T 2S8

OGILVIE, T(HOMAS) FRANCIS, engineer, educator; b. Atlantic City, Sept. 26, 1929; s. Thomas Fleisher and Frances Augusta (Wilson) O.; m. Joan Husselton, Sept. 11, 1950; children: Nancy Louise, Mary Beth, Kenneth Stuart. B.A. in Physics, Cornell U., 1950; M.Sc. in Aero. Engring., U. Md., 1957; Ph.D. in Engring. Sci., U. Calif., Berkeley, 1960; D in Naval Arch./Marine Engring. (hon.), Nat. Tech. U. Athens, 1996. Physicist, David Taylor Model Basin, Dept. Navy, Bethesda, Md., 1951-62, 64-67; liaison scientist Office of Naval Research, London, 1962-63; asso. prof. naval architecture and marine engring. U. Mich., Ann Arbor, 1967-70; prof. fluid mechanics U. Mich., 1970-81, chmn. dept. naval architecture and marine engring., 1973-81; prof. ocean engring. MIT, Cambridge, 1982-96, prof. emeritus, 1996—, head dept., 1982-94; vis. prof. naval architecture Osaka (Japan) U., 1976; vis. prof. math. U. Manchester, Eng., 1976. Contbr. articles to profl. jours. Recipient Meritorious Pub. Svc. award U.S. Dept. of Transp., 1982. Fellow Soc. of Naval Architects and Marine Engrs.; mem. Soc. Naval Architects and Marine Engrs. (coun. 1977-82, exec. com. 1978-80, 83-84, William H. Webb medal 1989), Sigma Xi, Phi Beta Kappa. Home: 110 Gray St Arlington MA 02174-6337 Office: MIT Dept Ocean Engring Cambridge MA 02139

OGLE, EDWARD PROCTOR, JR., investment counseling executive; b. Inglewood, Calif., Dec. 20, 1935; s. Edward Proctor and Allene Emma (Blumenthal) O.; m. Elizabeth Lovejoy Myers, Mar. 28, 1958; children: Kathryn Ogle Nava, Terry Ogle Nelson, Wendy Ogle Reeves. BA, U. So. Calif., 1964; MA, Claremont Grad. Sch., 1980. Cert. fin. planning practitioner. Zone mgr. Investors Diversified Svcs., Pasadena, Calif., 1964-66; asst. mgr. Merrill Lynch Pierce Fenner Smith, Pasadena, 1966-72; mgr. Clark Dodge & Co-Capital Place Dept., L.A., 1972-74; sr. v.p. Security Pacific Bank - Pacific Century Group, L.A., 1974-86; mgr., registered prin. Brown Bros. Harriman & Co., L.A., 1986—. Author: (booklet) Role of Bank Trust Department, 1981; editor (booklet) Parade Operations Manual, 1992, 93. Com. sec. Tournament of Roses Assn., Pasadena, 1976—; mem. Town Hall of Calif., L.A., 1977—; mem. Rep. Presdl. Task Force, Orange County, Calif., 1984—; mem. L.A. World Affairs Coun., 1985—; elder Presbyn. Ch. Recipient Corp. Fund Raising Cert. United Way, L.A., 1978-80, Exec. Mgmt. Cert. Claremont Grad. Sch., 1979, Mgmt. and Exec. Cert. Security Pacific Bank, L.A., 1981. Mem. Internat. Assn. Fin. Planners, Drucker Ctr. Mgmt. Assn., Claremont Grad. Sch. Alumni Assn. (pres. 1984-86), Pasadena Bond Club, Bond Club L.A., Jonathan Club. Republican. Avocations: photography, golf, basketball, music, travel. Office: Brown Bros Harriman & Co 355 S Grand Ave Ste 3250 Los Angeles CA 90071-1592

OGLE, ROBBIN SUE, criminal justice educator; b. North Kansas City, Mo., Aug. 28, 1960; d. Robert Lee and Carol Sue (Gray) O. BS, Ctrl. Mo. State U., 1982; MS, U. Mo., 1990; PhD, Pa. State U., 1995. State probation and parole officer Mo. Dept. Corrections, Kansas City, 1982-92; collector J.C. Penney Co., Mission, Kans., 1990-92; instr. U. Mo., Kansas City, 1990-92; grad. lectr. Pa. State U., University Park, 1992-95; prof. criminal justice dept. U. Nebr., Omaha, 1995—. Contbr. articles to profl. jours. Athletic scholar Ctrl. Mo. State U., Warrensburg, 1978-82. Mem. AAUW, ACLU, NOW, Am. Soc. Criminology, Acad. Criminal Justice Scis., Am. Correctional Assn., Phi Kappa Phi. Avocations: reading, watching basketball, walking dog. Home: 9535 Western Cir Apt 4 Omaha NE 68114-6714 Office: Univ Nebr 1100 Neihardt Criminal Justice Dept Lincoln NE 68588-0630

OGLESBY, BEVERLY CLAYTON, kindergarten educator; b. Jacksonville, Fla., Mar. 11, 1950; d. Willie Edward Clayton and Venetta (Preston) Singleton; m. Eugene Oglesby, June 23, 1974; children: Venetta, Erin. BS, Fla. Meml. Coll., 1971; MEd, U. North Fla., 1982. Cert. tchr., Fla. 3d grade tchr. S. Bryan Jennings Elem. Sch., Orange Park, Fla., 1971-75, kindergarten tchr., 1975-77, 83-90, 1993-94, 2d grade tchr., 1977-82, 1st grade tchr., 1982-83, devel. 1st grade tchr., 1990-92, devel. 2d grade tchr., 1992-93, devel. kindergarten tchr., 1994—; kindergarten team leader S. Bryan Jennings Elem. Sch. 1975-90; mem. instrnl. material coun. Clay County Schs., Green Cove Springs, Fla., 1989, devel. dist. com. 1990-92; presenter Clay County Whole Lang. Clay County Reading Coun., Orange Park, 1988-89, So. Early Childhood Assn. and Early Childhood Assn. of Fla. Confs. SACS com. mem. Forest Hill Elem. Sch., Jacksonville, 1973; SECA rep. State of Fla.; mem. PTA bd. Oceanway Jr. High Sch., Jacksonville, 1980. Named S. Bryan Jenning Elem. Sch. Tchr. of Yr., 1989-90. Mem. Early Childhood Assn. Fla. (pres. 1992-93, SECA rep. 1995—), So. Early Childhood Assn. (chair membership com. 1993-95, rep. to Early Childhood Assn. Fla., 1995—), Nat. Assn. for Edn. Young Children, Assn. Childhood Edn. Internat., North Fla. Assn. Young Children (pres. 1986-87), Early Childhood Assn. Fla. (pres. 1993-94), Phi Delta Kappa. Avocations: reading and collecting children's books, walking. Home: 215 Corona Dr Orange Park FL 32073

OGLESBY, SABERT, JR., retired research institute administrator; b. Birmingham, Ala., May 14, 1921; s. Sabert Sr. and Myrtle (Dunn) O.; m. Carolyn Vance, Mar. 4, 1944; 1 child, Donald Thomas. B.S.E.E., Auburn U., 1943; M.S.E.E., Purdue U., 1951. Registered profl. engr., Ala. Research engr. So. Research Inst., Birmingham, 1946-48; various positions So. Research Inst., 1951-80, pres., 1980-87, pres. emeritus, 1987—; instr. Purdue U., West Lafayette, Ind., 1948-51. Author: Heat Pump Application; Electrostatic Precipitation. Mem. exec. bd. Birmingham Music Club, 1982—. 1st lt. Signal Corps, U.S. Army, 1943-46. Named to Ala. Engring. Hall of Fame, 1989. Mem. Internat. com. on Electrostatic Precipitation (steering com. 1978-85), Kiwanis (bd. dirs. 1982-83, 85-86), Vestavia Country Club, Sigma Xi, Tau Beta Pi, Eta Kappa Nu. Republican. Presbyterian. Avocations: golf; gem cutting; music. Home: 1348 Panorama Dr Birmingham AL 35216-3013

OGLIARUSO, MICHAEL ANTHONY, chemist, educator; b. Bklyn., Aug. 10, 1938; s. Andrea and Anna (Bianco) O.; m. Basila Gallo, Apr. 2, 1961; 1 child, Michael Dana. B.S., Poly. Inst. Bklyn., 1960, Ph.D., 1965. Postdoctoral research asso. UCLA, 1965-67; asst. prof. chemistry Va. Poly. Inst. and State U., Blacksburg, 1967-72; assoc. prof. Va. Poly. Inst. and State U., 1972-78, prof., 1978-95, assoc. dean Coll. Arts and Scis., 1984-95; ret. Coll. Arts and Scis. Contbr. articles to profl. jours. Served with C.E. U.S. Army, 1960-61. Mem. Am. Chem. Soc., Va. Acad. Sci., Sigma Xi, Phi Lambda Upsilon. Office: Va Poly Inst and State U Dept Chemistry Davidson Hall Blacksburg VA 24061 *I have been fortunate to be associated with the most personally rewarding profession available today, the professional education of young men and women. This career is best suited to persons who wish to remain young in spirit, since regardless of your age you are always surrounded with students who are between 18 and 22 years old. This is the best way I know to remain spiritually young.*

OGNIBENE, ANDRE J(OHN), physician, army officer, educator; b. N.Y.C., Nov. 18, 1931; s. Morris S. and Josephine C. (Macaluso) O.; m. Margaret A. Haug, Apr. 21, 1957; children: Judy, Andrea, Adrienne, Marc, Eric. B.A. cum laude, Columbia U., 1952; M.D., NYU, 1956. Diplomate Am. Bd. Internal Medicine, Am. Bd. Geriatrics, Am. Bd. Med. Mgmt. Intern in medicine Bellevue Hosp., N.Y.C., 1956-57; resident in medicine Bellevue Hosp., 1957-59; commd. capt. U.S. Army M.C., 1957, advanced through grades to brig. gen., 1978; resident in medicine Manhattan VA Hosp., N.Y.C. and chief resident in medicine, 1959-60; chief med. service U.S. Army Hosp., Nurnburg, Germany, 1961-62; chief dept. medicine U.S. Army Hosp., 1962-64; fellow in cardiology Walter Reed Gen. Hosp., Washington, 1964-65; asst. in cardiology Walter Reed Gen. Hosp., 1965-66, asst. chief dept. medicine, 1969-72; chief dept. medicine, chief profl. services U.S. Army Hosp., Ft. Meade, Md., 1966-68; cons. in medicine Hdqrs. U.S. Army, Vietnam, 1969; asst. chief Dept. of Medicine Walter Reed Army Med. Ctr., 1970-72; chief dept. medicine Brooke Army Med. Center, Ft. Sam Houston, Tex., 1972-76; dir. med. edn. Brooke Army Med. Center, 1976-78, dep. comdr. and chief profl. services, 1976-78, comdr., 1978-81; hosp. dir. San Antonio State Chest Hosp., 1981-85; program dir. internal medicine Canton, Ohio, 1985-95; assoc. dean for med. edn., med. dir. Columbia Mercy Med. Ctr., Canton, 1995—; prof. medicine N.E. Ohio U., Rootstown, 1985—; chmn. dept. medicine N.E. Ohio U., 1989—; instr. medicine NYU, 1960; assoc. clin. prof. Georgetown U., 1970-72; clin. prof. U. Tex. Health Sci. Center, San Antonio, 1973-85, mem. postgrad. adv. com., 1977-78; mem. Instl. Rev. Bd., 1981-85; pres. Bexar Met. unit Am. Cancer Soc., 1984; dir. Eisenhower Nat. Bank; bd. dirs. Cancer Therapy and Research Ctr.; chmn. South Tex. Epilepsy Found., 1985. Contbr. articles to med. publs. and chpts. to books; editor, prin. author Internal Medicine in Vietnam, Vol. II, 1982; editor-in-chief: Internal Medicine in Vietnam, vol. I, 1977. Bd. trustees Regina Health Ctr., 1992—. Decorated Disting. Service medal, Legion of Merit, Meritorious Service medal, Army Commendation medal. Fellow ACP (laureate, master tchr.), Am. Coll. Physician Execs.; mem. N.Y. Acad. Scis., Am. Fedn. Clin. Rsch., Bexar County Med. Soc., Stark County Med. Soc., Assn. Profs. Medicine, Alpha Omega Alpha. Home: 1409 Harbor Dr NW Canton OH 44708-3098 Office: 1320 Mercy Dr NW Canton OH 44708-2614 *Compassion must remain the universal prescription in medical practice. Technology can provide no solutions in the absence of humanity.*

OGNIBENE, EDWARD JOHN, research and development mechanical engineer; b. Aug. 27, 1965; s. Peter Edward and Dorothy May (Gasdaska) O.; m. Donna Lee Paul, Dec. 14, 1991; children: Ariana JoAnn, Corinne Elizabeth. B. Engring. in Mech. Engring., SUNY, Stony Brook, 1989; MS in Mech. Engring., MIT, 1991, PhD, 1995. Engring. asst., intern Baker Engring., Inc., Elmsford, N.Y., summer 1988; rsch. intern Schlumberger-Doll Rsch., Ridgefield, Conn., summer 1989; rsch. asst. MIT, Cambridge, 1989-91, 92-95, postdoctoral assoc., 1995; mech. engr. United Technologies, Norden Sys., Norwalk, Conn., 1991-92; rsch. engr./cons. Praxair Inc., Tarrytown, N.Y., 1992; R&D engr. SatCon Tech. Corp., Cambridge, Mass., 1995—. Recipient Grumman Corp. Award for Scholastic Excellence, 1988. Mem. ASME, Sigma Xi, Tau Beta Pi. Achievements include patent pending on steam generating dynamometer. Avocations: chess, cycling, hiking, photography, sailing. Home: 19 Marion Rd Belmont MA 02178-3655

O'GORMAN, JAMES FRANCIS, art educator, writer; b. St. Louis, Sept. 19, 1933; s. Paul Joseph and Dorothy Frances (Hogan) O'G.; m. Jean Baer, Feb. 9, 1957 (div. 1987); children—Christopher, Harold, Michael (dec.), Samuel. B.Arch., Washington U., St. Louis, 1956; M. Arch., U. Ill., 1960; Ph.D., Harvard U., 1966. Grace Slack McNeil prof. Am. art Wellesley Coll., Mass., 1975—. Author: H.H. Richardson and His Office: Selected Drawings, 1973; This Other Gloucester, 1976; H.H. Richardson. Architectural Forms for an American Society, 1987; ThreeAmerican Architects: Richardson, Sullivan, and Wright, 1865-1915, 1991, Living Architecture: A Biography of H.H. Ricghardson, 1997, ABC of Architecture, 1997; (with others) The Architecture of Frank Furness, 1974; editor, translator: Paul Frankl, Principles of Architectural History, 1968. Phila. Athenaeum fellow, 1985. Office: Wellesley Coll Dept Art 106 Central St Wellesley MA 02181-8203

O'GORMAN, PETER JOSEPH, retail company executive; b. Surbiton, Surrey, Eng., May 25, 1938; came to U.S., 1981; s. Peter and Noreen (O'Gorman) McCormack; m. Rosemary Anne Underhill, July 20, 1974; 1 child, Ruth. B in Nautical Sci., Nellists Nautical Coll., Gt. Britain, 1959; M in Nautical Sci., Auckland U., New Zealand, 1963. Cert. master mariner. Supermarket mgr., later sr. v.p. devel. Tesco Stores Ltd., London, 1964-81; pres. Doody Co., Columbus, Ohio, 1981-83; sr. v.p. devel. and mktg. Great Atlantic and Pacific Tea Co., Montvale, N.J., 1983-90, exec. v.p. real estate, store devel. and mktg., 1990-95, exec. v.p. internat. devel., 1996—. Bd. dirs. Bergen County (N.J.) United Way; mem. food industry steering com. Efficient Consumer Response; mem. svcs. com., trustee food industry Food Industry Campaign Against Hunger. Office: Gt Atlantic & Pacific Tea Co Inc 2 Paragon Dr Montvale NJ 07645-1718

OGRA, PEARAY L., physician, educator; b. Srinagar, Kashmir, India, Mar. 19, 1939; came to U.S., 1961, naturalized, 1969; s. Govinda Kaul and Gunvati (Daftari) O.; m. Kathleen Marie Ogra; children: Sanjay, Monica. MB, Christian Med. Coll., Ludhiana, India, 1961. Intern Binghamton (N.Y.) Gen. Hosp., 1962-63; resident U. Chgo., 1963-64; resident N.Y. U.-Bellevue Med Center, 1964-66, fellow infectious diseases, 1966-68; asst. prof. pediatrics SUNY, Buffalo, 1968-71; assoc. prof. pediatrics and microbiology SUNY, 1972-74, prof., 1974-91; John Sealy disting. chair and prof., chmn. dept. pediatrics U. Tex. Med. Br., Galveston, 1991—; dir. div. virology Children's Hosp. Buffalo, 1969-81, chief dept. infectious diseases, 1970-91; dir. Clin. Labs. Children's Hosp., 1985-90; mem. study sect. NIH, 1979-85, maternal child health com., 1987-91; mem., chmn. bd. Internat. Pediat. Rsch. Found., Inc., 1984-89, respiratory diseases steering com. WHO. Recipient E. Mead Johnson award for Pediatric Research Am. Acad. Pediatrics, 1978; Kalhana award Kashmir Sci. Culture and Soc., 1984; Stockton Kimball award SUNY, 1985; Buswell fellow, 1968-71. Fellow Royal Soc. Medicine, Assn. Am. Physicians, Am. Acad. Pediatrics, Am. Acad. Microbiology; mem. Am. Soc. Clin. Investigation, Soc. Pediatric Rsch., Infectious Disease Soc. Am., Soc. Exptl. Biology and Medicine, Am. Assn. Immunologists, Am. Soc. Microbiology, AAAS, Am. Fedn. Clin. Rsch., Reticuloendothelial Soc., Am. Soc. Virology. Home: 9 Colony Park Cir Galveston TX 77551

O'GRADY, BEVERLY TROXLER, investment executive, counselor; d. Robert Andrew and Beverly Beam (Barrier) Troxler; m. Robert Edward O'Grady, Aug. 6, 1966. BA, St. Mary's Coll., 1963; MA, Columbia U., 1965. Exec. v.p. Wilkinson & Hottinger Inc., N.Y.C., 1973-94, Helvetia Capital Corp., N.Y.C., 1987-94; pres. Wilkinson O'Grady & Co., Inc., N.Y.C., 1994—; mem. adv. bd. Charles Schwab Fin., San Francisco, 1991-93. Active Women's Nat. Rep. Club, N.Y.C., 1991-94. Mem. Assn. Investment Mgrs., N.Y. Soc. Security Analysts, Women's Bond Club (pres. 1992-94), Univ. Club. Roman Catholic. Office: Wilkinson O'Grady & Co Inc 520 Madison Ave New York NY 10022-4213

O'GRADY, DENNIS JOSEPH, lawyer; b. Hoboken, N.J., Nov. 16, 1943; s. Joseph A. and Eileen (Broderick) O'Grady; m. Mary Anne Amoruso, Sept. 9, 1966 (div. Apr. 1984); 1 child, Kara Anne. AB, Seton Hall Coll., 1965; MA, U. So. Calif., 1969; JD, Rutgers U., 1973. Bar: N.J. 1973, U.S. Ct. Appeals (3d cir.) 1975, U.S. Dist. Ct. N.J. Ptnr. Riker, Danzig, Scherer, Hyland & Perretti, Newark, Trenton and Morristown, N.J., 1974—; adj. asst. prof. of bus. law St. Peter's Coll., Jersey City, 1973—; adj. prof. law Rutgers U. Law Sch., 1997—. Mem. ABA (bus./bankruptcy sect.), N.Y. State Bar Assn. (debtor/creditor sect.), Fed. Bar Assn., Am. Bankruptcy Inst. (health care subcom., bd. profl. cert.). Democrat. Roman Catholic. Office: Riker Danzig Scherer Hyland & Perretti 1 Speedwell Ave Morristown NJ 07960-6838

O'GRADY, JOHN JOSEPH, III, lawyer; b. N.Y.C., Mar. 21, 1933; s. John Joseph and Terese (O'Rourke) O'G.; m. Mary E. McHugh, June 28, 1958; children—Glennon, Ellen, Carol, Paul. A.B., Holy Cross Coll., 1954; J.D., Harvard U., 1957. Bar: N.Y. 1958. Assoc. Cadwalader, Wickersham & Taft, N.Y.C., 1958-66, ptnr., 1966-96, counsel, 1997—. Mem. ABA. Office: Cadwalader Wickersham & Taft 100 Maiden Ln New York NY 10038-4818

O'GRADY, MARY J., editor, foundation consultant; b. Chgo., Sept. 25, 1951; d. Valentine Michael and Lillian Mary (Quinlan) O'G. Student, St. Mary's Coll., Rome, Italy, 1970-71; BFA, Manhattanville Coll., 1973; MA, Georgetown U., 1996. Assoc. editor Magnum Photos, N.Y.C., 1973-76; asst. picture editor Modern Photography Mag., N.Y.C., 1976-78; freelance photographer N.Y.C., 1978-80; sr. producer Trans-Atlantic Enterprises, N.Y.C., L.A., 1981-82; dir. pub. info. World Wildlife Fund, Washington, 1983-84; sr. analyst Mead Data Cen., Washington, 1985-87; editor photos U.S. News and World Report, Washington, 1987-90; program dir. Sacharuna Found., 1990-92; adminstr. Roland Films, 1991-92; assoc. dir. AIDS Control and Prevention Project Family Health Internat., 1994—; cons. Time, Inc., N.Y.C., 1981, Exxon Corp., N.Y.C., 1981-82, U.S. News and World Report, Washington, 1987, The German Marshall Fund of U.S., Conservation Internat., Washington, 1992, W. Alton Jones Found., 1993-94. Asst. editor: The Family of Woman, 1978; producer (TV shows) A Conversation With..., 1982, The Helen Gurley Brown Show, 1982, Outrageous Opinions, 1982; photo editor America's Best Colleges, 1989, 90, Great Vacation Drives, 1989. Recipient Editorial Excellence award Natural Resources Coun. Am., 1984. Mem. Soc. Environ. Journalists, Worldwide Women in Environment and Devel., Monitoring the AIDS Pandemic Network.

O'GRADY, THOMAS B., Canadian provincial official; m. Betty O'Grady. Commr. Can. Police Cmty. Recipient Police Exemplary Svc. medal, The Can. 125 medal. Mem. Can. Chiefs of Police Assn. (v.p., immediate past pres.), Ont. Pub. Svc. Quarter Century Club (immediate past pres.), Order of St. John of Jerusalem (officer). Office: 777 Memorial Ave, Orillia, ON Canada L3V 7V3

OGREAN, DAVID WILLIAM, sports executive; b. New Haven, Feb. 7, 1953; s. Richard Berton and Dorothy (Nystrom) O.; m. Maryellen Harvey, Aug. 10 1974; children: Matthew David, Tracy Erin, Dana Marie. BA in English cum laude, U Conn., 1974; MS in Film, Boston U., 1978. Asa S. Bushnell intern Ea. Coll. Athletic Conf., Centervill, Mass., 1977-78; pub. rels. dir. Amateur Hockey Assn. U.S., Colorado Springs, Colo., 1978-80; mng. editor Am. Hockey and Arena mag., 1979-80; communications rep. ESPN, Inc., Bristol, Conn., 1980-83, program mgr., 1983-88; asst. exec. dir. for TV Coll. Football Assn., Boulder, Colo., 1988-90; dir. of broadcasting U.S. Olympic Com., Colorado Springs, 1990-93, chmn. legis. com., 1997—; exec. dir. USA Hockey, Colorado Springs, 1993—; pres. Colorado Springs Sports Corp., 1996-97; chair legis. com. U.S. Olympic Com., 1997—. Mem. Country Club Colo. Office: USA Hockey 4965 N 30th St Colorado Springs CO 80919-4102

OGREN, CARROLL WOODROW, retired hospital administrator; b. Mpls., Mar. 22, 1927; s. Peter L. and Mabel (Wohleen) O.; m. Patricia Ann Sweeney. B.A., U. Minn., 1952; M.Hosp. Adminstrn., Washington U., St. Louis, 1958. Asst. adminstr. Washoe Med. Center, Reno, 1958-59; adminstr. Washoe Med. Center, 1959-80, Jean Hannah Clark Rehab. Center, Las Vegas, Nev., 1980-92. Served with USNR, 1944-46, 50-54, PTO. Mem. Am. Coll. Hosp. Adminstrs., Am. Hosp. Assn. (nat. com. state hosp. assn. 1967—), Nev. Hosp. Assn. (pres. 1961-62, sec. 1961-66). Club: Gourmet Toastmasters (Reno) (pres. 1960). Home: 5860 Via Manigua Las Vegas NV 89120-2348

OGREN, ROBERT EDWARD, biologist, educator; b. Jamestown, N.Y., Feb. 9, 1922; s. David Paul and Mary Gladys (Ahlstrom) O.; m. Jean Blose Jackson, Aug. 28, 1948; children: Paul Robert, Philip Edward. B.A., Wheaton Coll., 1947; M.S., Northwestern U., 1948; Ph.D., U. Ill., 1953. Asst. prof. biology Ursinus Coll., Collegeville, Pa., 1953-57, Dickinson Coll., Carlisle, Pa., 1957-63; mem. faculty Wilkes Coll., Wilkes-Barre, Pa., 1963—, prof. biology, 1981-86, prof. emeritus, 1986—. Contbr. articles to profl. lit. Bd. dirs. Northeastern Pa. chpt. Am. Heart Assn., 1971-88; chmn. bd. Northeastern Pa. chpt. Am. HeartAssn., 1973-76; bd. dirs. Wyo. Valley West Sch. Dis., 1973-79, pres., 1979. Served with AUS, 1943-46. Recipient Frank B. Shepela Meml. Vol. award Northeastern Pa. Heart Assn., 1977; NSF grantee, 1960, 63, 65. Fellow AAAS; mem. Am. Soc. Zoologists, Am. Soc. Parasitologists, Am. Micros. Soc., Soc. Protzoologists, Electron Micros. Soc. Am., Wyo. Commemorative Assn., Pa. Acad. Sci. (editor procs. 1961-62 Darbaker award 1989), Soc. Systematic Zoology, N.Y. Acad. Sci., Helminthological Soc. Washington, AAUP, Ecol. Soc. Am., Nat. Audubon Soc., Western N.Y. Geneol. Soc., Wyo. Hist. and Geol. Soc., Sigma Xi (chpt. pres. 1981-82). Republican. Presbyterian. Home: 88 Lathrop St Wilkes Barre PA 18704-4811 Office: Wilkes Univ Dept Biology S Franklin St Wilkes Barre PA 18701-1201 *To be involved as a citizen in some aspect of community life. To use academe as an opportunity to prepare scholarly works for publication advancing knowledge in your discipline. To work beyond your limitations. To recognize opportunities and use them for making progress. To be positive, honest, creative and persevering. To enjoy the fruits of your labor and the freedom of expression and movement in our great land.*

OGUL, MORRIS SAMUEL, political science educator, consultant; b. Detroit, Apr. 15, 1931; s. Jack and Sarah (Zimmerman) O.; m. Eleanor Simon, Aug. 26, 1954. B.A., Wayne State U., 1952; M.A., U. Mich., 1953, Ph.D., 1958. Instr. polit. sci. U. Pitts., 1957-59, asst. prof., 1959-64, assoc. prof., 1964-67, prof., 1967—; cons. U.S. Ho. of Reps., 1973, 83, U.S. Office Personnel Mgmt., Washington, 1975—, U.S. Senate, 1977. Author: (with William J. Keefe) American Legislative Process, 1964, 7th edit., 1989, 8th edit., 1993, 9th edit., 1997, Congress Oversees the Bureaucracy, 1976. Carnegie Corp. research grantee, 1965-68. Mem. Am. Polit. Sci. Assn., Midwest Polit. Sci. Assn. (council 1982-84), Pa. Polit. Sci. Assn. Democrat. Home: 1500 Cochran Rd Apt 814 Pittsburgh PA 15243-1068 Office: U Pitts Dept Polit Sci 4n25 Forbes Quadrangle Pittsburgh PA 15260-7454

OH, JOHN KIE-CHIANG, political science educator, university official; b. Seoul, Korea, Nov. 1, 1930; came to U.S., 1954, naturalized, 1971; s. Sung-Jun and Duk-Cho (Kim) O.; m. Bonnie Cho, Sept. 5, 1959; children: Jane J., Marie J., James J. B.S., Marquette U., 1957; postgrad., Columbia U., 1957-58; Ph.D., Georgetown U., 1962. Asst. prof. St. Thomas Coll., St. Paul, 1962-66; assoc. prof. polit. sci. Marquette U., Milw., 1967-71, prof., chmn., 1971-77, dean grad. sch., 1977-85; acad. v.p. Cath. U. Am., Washington, 1985-89, prof. politics dept., 1990—. Author: Korea: Democracy on Trial, 1968, (with Peter Cheng et. al.) Emerging Roles of Asian Nations in the 1980's, 1979, Democratization and Economic Development in Korea, 1990; contbr. articles to profl. jours. Chmn. scholarship com. World Affairs Council, 1976-78; mem. Wis. Gov.'s Commn. for UN, Madison, 1971-74; chmn. Korean Studies com., Assn. Asian Studies, 1975-76. Grantee Hill Found., 1963, Relm Found., 1968, Social Sci. Rsch Coun., 1973, Am. Coun. Learned Socs., 1973. Mem. Am. Polit. Sci. Assn., Assn. Asian Studies, Internat. Polit. Sci. Assn., Midwest Conf. Assn. Affairs (pres. 1970-71, nat. chmn. China-Japan-Korea-The Philippines-Thailand sect.) Fulbright Hays Program, Assn. Cath. Colls. and Univs. (bd. dirs. 1983-87). Roman Catholic. Home: 8807 Maxwell Dr Potomac MD 20854-3123 Office: Cath U Am Politics Dept Washington DC 20064

OH, KEYTACK HENRY, industrial engineering educator; b. Hamduk, Korea, Mar. 16, 1938; s. DalPyong and Kee-Sook (Yang) O.; m. Youngsim Lee, Sept. 15, 1967; children: Jeanne, Susan. BS, Hanyang U., Seoul, Korea, 1962; MS, Okla. State U., 1966; PhD, The Ohio State U., 1974. Supr. East Gate Telephone Exch., Seoul, Korea, 1958-61; ops. rschr. Western Elec. Co., Oklahoma City, 1966-68; MIS staff mem. Western Elec. Co., Columbus, Ohio, 1968-72; logistics engr. Ross Labs., Columbus, Ohio, 1972-75; asst. prof. U. Mo./St. Louis Grad. Engring. Ctr., Rolla, 1975-82; assoc. prof. U. Toledo, 1982—; pres. Oh Enterprises Corp., Toledo, 1995—. Author: The Perfect Wedding—Starting with Proper Invitations and Announcements, 1980, Computers and Industrial Engineering, 1994, Productivity and Quality Research Frontiers, 1995. Chmn. bd. trustees Korean Acad., Toledo, 1995. Recipient presdl. fellowship Okla. State U., 1965. Mem. Inst. Indsl. Engrs. (pres. Toledo chpt. 1984), Am. Soc. for Engring. Edn., Anthony Wayne Toastmasters (pres. 1994), Toastmasters Internat. (area gov. 1995, divsn. gov. 1996), Korean Assn. of Greater Toledo (pres. 1996—). Republican. Presbyterian. Avocations: tennis, golf. Home: 2817 Westchester Rd Toledo OH 43615-2245 Office: U Toledo Dept Industrial Engring Toledo OH 43606

OH, SE-KYUNG, immunochemist; b. Seoul, South Korea, Jan. 11, 1943; came to U.s., 1966; s. Bang-Whan and Pong-Ho (Park) O. BS, Seoul Nat. U., 1965; M in Nutritional Sci., Cornell U., 1968; PhD, U. Ga., 1972. Fellow Scripps Clinic and Rsch. Found., La Jolla, Calif., 1972-74; vis. scientist Cornell U., Ithaca, N.Y., 1974-76, NIA, NIH, Balt., 1974-76; lectr. Harvard Med. Sch., Boston, 1976-79; from asst. prof. to assoc. prof. Boston U. Sch. Medicine, 1979-92; staff scientist Chiron Diagnostics, Walpole, Mass., 1992-97, sr. staff scientist, 1997—; adj. prof. biochemistry, Boston U. Sch. Medicine, 1992—. Editor Jour. Nutritional Biochemistry, 1990—. NIH grantee, 1979-86. Mem. Am. Assn. Immunologists, Am. Assn. Cancer Rsch., Korean Scientists and Engring. Assn. (mem. coun. 1990-93), Boston Cancer Rsch. Assn. (pres. 1992-93). Presbyterian. Achievements include patent and patent pending in field. Office: Ciba-Corning Diagnostics 333 Coney St East Walpole MA 02032-1597

OH, TAI KEUN, business educator; b. Seoul, Korea, Mar. 25, 1934; s. Chin Young and Eui Kyung (Yun) O.; came to U.S., 1958, naturalized, 1969; B.A., Seijo U., 1957; M.A., No. Ill. U., 1961; M.L.S., U. Wis., 1965, Ph.D., 1970; m. Gretchen Brenneke, Dec. 26, 1964; children: Erica, Elizabeth, Emily. Asst. prof. mgmt. Roosevelt U., Chgo., 1969-73; assoc. prof. Calif. State U., Fullerton, 1973-76, prof. mgmt., 1976—; vis. prof. U. Hawaii, 1983-84, 86; advisor Pacific Asian Mgmt. Inst., U. Hawaii; internat. referee Asia-Pacific Jour. of Mgmt., 1990—; cons. Calty Design Research, Inc. subs. Toyota Motor Corp. The Employers Group; seminar leader and speaker. Named Outstanding Prof., Sch. Bus. Adminstrn. and Econs., Calif. State U., Fullerton, 1976, 78. NSF grantee, 1968-69, recipient Exceptional Merit Service award Calif. State U., 1984, Meritorious Performance and Profl. Promise award Calif. State U., 1987. Mem. Acad. Mgmt., Indsl. Relations Research Assn., Acad. Internat. Bus. Editorial bd. Acad. Mgmt. Rev., 1978-81; contbg. author: Ency. Profl. Mgmt., 1978, Handbook of Management 1985; contbr. articles to profl. jours. Home: 2044 E Eucalyptus Ln Brea CA 92821-5911 Office: Management Dept Calif State U Fullerton CA 92634

OH, WILLIAM, physician; b. The Philippines, May 22, 1931; came to U.S., 1958, naturalized, 1970; s. Bun Kun and Chay Suat (Lim) O.; m. Mary Oh, June 4, 1960; children—Kenneth Albert, Kerstin Amy. M.D., U. Santo Tomas, Phillipines, 1958; M.A. (hon.), Brown U., 1974. Diplomate Am. Bd. Pediatrics, Am. Bd. Neonatal Perinatal Medicine. Intern Deaconess Hosp., Milw., 1958-59; resident in pediatrics Michael Reese Hosp., Chgo., 1959-63; fellow in neonatology Kavolinska Inst., Stockholm, 1963-65; dir. neonatology Michael Reese Hosp., Chgo., 1965-69; dir. neonatology, assoc. prof. pediatrics UCLA, 1969-73, prof., 1973-74; prof. pediatrics and obstetrics Brown U., Providence, 1974-88, Sylvia Hassenfeld prof. pediatrics, chmn. dept., 1989—; pediatrician-in-chief Women and Infants Hosp. of R.I., Providence, 1974—, R.I. Hosp.; prof., chmn. dept. pediatrics Brown U., 1989—; mem. NIH study sect. on human embryology and devel., chmn., 1985—; mem. pediatric test com. Bd. Med. Exam., 1985-89; mem. sub-bd. of neonatal-perinatal medicine Am. Bd. Pediatrics, 1982-88; chair com. on Fetus and Newborn, Am. Acad. Pediatrics; mem. Nat. Adv. Coun. for Child Health, 1995—. Author book in field; contbr. chpts. to books, numerous articles to profl. jours.; editor profl. jour. Adv. com. Nat. Found. of March of Dimes. NIH grantee. Mem. Am. Pediatric Soc., Am. Acad. Pediatrics (fetus and newborn com. 1986—), Soc. Pediatric Research, Perinatal Research Soc. (pres. 1981), Am. Inst. Nutrition, Fedn. Am. Socs. Exptl. Biology. Roman Catholic. Club: University. Home: 24 Robbins Dr Barrington RI 02806-2612 Office: 101 Dudley St Providence RI 02905-2401

O'HAGAN, JAMES JOSEPH, lawyer; b. Chgo., Dec. 29, 1936; s. Francis James and Florence Agnes (Dowgialo) O'H.; m. Suzanne Elizabeth Wiegand, June 28, 1958; children: Timothy, Karen, Peggy, Kevin. B in Commerce, De Paul U., 1958, JD, 1962. Law clk. Querrey & Harrow, Chgo., 1958-62, assoc., 1963-67, ptnr., 1968—, chmn. mgmt., 1985—; lawyer Chgo. Claim Mgrs. Assn., Chgo., 1992-93. Bd. dirs. Park Ridge (Ill.) Fine Arts Soc., 1984—, pres., 1992-94. Mem. ABA, Ill. Bar Assn. Chgo. Bar Assn. (mediator mediation program), Internat. Assn. Def. Coun., Trial Lawyers Club. Roman Catholic. Avocations: golf, tennis, physical conditioning, painting, reading. Office: Querrey & Harrow 180 N Stetson Ave Chicago IL 60601-6710

O'HALLORAN, THOMAS ALPHONSUS, JR., physicist, educator; b. Bklyn., Apr. 13, 1931; s. Thomas Alphonsus Sr. and Nora (Sheehan) O'H.; m. Barbara Joyce Hug, June 4, 1954; children: Theresa Joyce, Maureen Ann, Kevin Thomas, Patrick Joseph. Student, San Jose State U., 1948-50; BS in Physics & Math., Oreg. State U., 1953, MS in Physics, 1954; PhD, U. Calif., Berkeley, 1963. Rsch. asst. Lawrence Berkeley Lab., U. Calif., 1963-64; rsch. fellow Harvard U., Cambridge, Mass., 1964-66; asst. prof. physics U. Ill., Urbana, 1966-68, assoc. prof., 1968-70, prof., 1970-93, prof. emeritus, 1993—; vis. scholar U. Utah, Salt Lake City, 1990-93, rsch. prof. physics, 1993—; mem. program adv. com. Argonne Nat. Lab., Lemont, Ill., Fermi Lab., Batavia, Ill., Brookhaven Nat. Lab., Upton, L.I.; vis. scientist Lawrence Berkeley Lab., U. Calif., 1979-80. Contbr. numerous articles on elem. particle physics to profl. jours. Lt. USN, 1954-58. Guggenheim fellow, 1979-80. Fellow Am. Phys. Soc.; mem. Molly Green Club. Home: 4614 Ledgemont Dr Salt Lake City UT 84124-4735 Office: U Utah Physics Dept 201 Jfb Salt Lake City UT 84112

OHANIAN, MIHRAN JACOB, nuclear engineering educator, research dean; b. Istanbul, Turkey, Aug. 7, 1933; came to U.S., 1956, naturalized, 1967; s. Mark and Mary Catherine (Sayabalian) O.; m. Sandra Jean Blair, Apr. 22, 1962; children: Heather Jean Allen, Holly Lynn. B.S.E.E. with high honors, Robert Coll. Engring. Sch., Istanbul, 1956; M.E.E., Rensselaer Poly. Inst., 1960, Ph.D. in Nuclear Engring. and Sci., 1963. Lectr. nuclear engring. Rensselaer Poly. Inst., 1963, instr., 1958-62; asst. prof. nuclear engring. U. Fla., Gainesville, 1964-67, assoc. prof., 1967-70, prof., 1970—, chmn. dept., 1969-79, assoc. dir. Engring. and Indsl. Expt. Sta., 1977—, assoc. dean for research, 1979-90, assoc. dean for adminstrn. and planning, 1990-91, assoc. dean for rsch. and adminstrn., 1991—; sabbatical leave Inst. Energy Analysis, Oak Ridge, 1976-77; on assignment Inst. Energy Analysis, 1977-78; cons. Fla. Power Corp., Batelle Meml. Inst., Fla. Nuclear Assos., Oak Ridge Nat. Lab., Inst. Energy Analysis, Argonne Nat. Lab., Savannah River Lab., U. Va., Tex. Higher Edn. Bd., NSF; U. Fla. rep. U.S. Nuc. Energy Inst., 1972—, mem. adv. council, 1972-80; U. Fla. rep. to Oak Ridge Assoc. Univs., 1972-76; mem. engring. accreditation commn. Accreditation Bd. Engring. and Tech., 1984-88; mem. rev. com. Reactor Analysis and Safety div. Argonne Nat. Lab, 1982-88, chmn. 1986-87, mem. rev. com. Reactor Engring. div., 1992—; mem. adv. com. Consol. Fuel Reprocessing Program Oak Ridge Nat. Lab., 1982-88; mem. com. on univ. research reactors Energy Engring. Bd., NRC, 1986-88; mem. U.S. Dept. Energy's Adv. Com. on Nuclear Facility Safety (ACNFS), 1988-90; bd. dirs., chmn. Fla. Inst. Phosphate Rsch., 1990—. Contbr. articles to profl. jours. Trustee Fla. Defenders of the Environment, 1969-71, treas., 1969-70, mem., 1969—. Recipient valor medal Am. Legion, 1966, Disting. Faculty award Fla. Blue Key, 1984; Alumnus fellow Rensselaer Poly. Inst., 1994. Fellow AAAS, Am. Nuclear Soc. (v.p., pres.-elect 1989-90, pres. 1990-91, bd. dirs. 1974-77, 84-93, vice chmn., chmn. edn. divsn. 1975-76, exec. com. nuclear fuel cycle divsn. 1978-81, mem. profl. devel. and accreditation com., chmn. tech. program of internat. conf. Washington, 1980, mem. nominating com., 1980-81, 87-88, chmn., 1991-92, exec. com., 1986-92, Exceptional Svc. award 1980, adv. editor Nuclear Sci. and Engring. Jour. 1989—, hon. chmn. ann. conf. 1997), Engrs.'s Coun. Profl. Devel. (dir. 1976-78), Am. Assn. Engring. Socs. (awards com. 1985-86, bd. dirs. 1990-91, exec. com. 1990-95, sec.-treas., 1992, chair-elect 1993, chair 1994, chair nominating com. 1995, chair awards com. 1996), Am. Soc. Engring. Edn. (adv. com. Ford Found. Resident Fellow Program 1971-79, sec.-treas. nuclear engring. divsn. 1981-82, vice-chmn. 1982-83, chmn. 1983-84, projects bd. 1981-87, chmn. awards com. 1985-87; mem. Nat. Audubon Soc. (pres. 1965-66), Sigma Xi, Tau Beta Pi (eminent engr.), Alpha Nu Sigma (pres. 1981-83), Eta Kappa Nu, Phi Kappa Phi, Rotary (Paul Harris fellow. Presbyterian. Home: 315 NW 28th St Gainesville FL 32607-2565

OHANNESSIAN, GRISELDA JACKSON, publishing executive; b. N.Y.C., Feb. 5, 1927; d. Schuyler Brinckerhoff and Katharine Savage (Townsend) Jackson; m. Garo Ohannessian, May 5, 1955 (dec.); children: Ani Maria, Lucia Victoria, Mary Margaret. BA, Barnard Coll., 1949; MA, Columbia U., 1951. Asst. to prodn. mgr. Scribners Pub. Co., N.Y.C., 1951-53; music and movie reviewer Al Nida, Beirut, Lebanon, 1955-56; promotion and prodn. mgr. New Directions Pub., N.Y.C., 1956-60, publicity dir., gen. asst., 1972-83, v.p., trustee, 1983-93, mng. dir., trustee, 1994—. Democrat. Episcopalian. Avocations: piano playing, reading, attending concerts. Office: New Directions Pub Co 80 8th Ave New York NY 10011-5126

O'HARA, ALFRED PECK, lawyer; b. Patterson, N.Y., Apr. 27, 1919; s. Peter and Anna L. (Peck) O'H.; m. Muriel A. Sandberg, Aug. 30, 1940 (dec.); children: Jane Ann O'Hara Toth, Margaret Kathleen O'Hara Duff, Peter James, John Edward; m. 2d Thelma deVries (div.); m. 3d Martha Stein, June 22, 1984. B.A., Syracuse U., 1940; LL.B., Fordham U., 1942. Bar: N.Y. bar 1942, U.S. Supreme Ct 1956. Sec. to U.S. Dist. Ct., 1942-43; partner firm McLaughlin & Stickles, 1946-52; asst. U.S. atty., chief civil div. So. Dist. N.Y., 1953-56; cons. to atty. gen. N.Y. State, 1956; sr. ptnr. firm Rogers Hoge & Hills, N.Y.C., 1958-86; of counsel Kelley, Drye & Warren, N.Y.C., 1986—; counsel U.S. Trademark Assn., 1967-70; pres., chmn. bd. Bacardi Corp., 1976-87; bd. dirs. Guiding Eyes for the Blind, chmn., 1994—. Mem. ABA, NAM (bd. dirs. 1978-90), N.Y. State Bar Assn., Assn. Bar City N.Y., Fed Bar Coun., Am. Law Inst. (life), Internat. Patent adn Trademark Assn., Quaker Hill Club, Key Biscayne Yacht Club, Son Am. Rev. Home: RR 4 Box 55 Birch Hill Rd Patterson NY 12563 Office: Kelley Drye & Warren 101 Park Ave New York NY 10178

O'HARA, JAMES THOMAS, lawyer; b. Hazleton, Pa., Oct. 11, 1936; s. Thomas James and Bridget Helen (Campbell) O'H.; m. Kathleen M. Shane, Aug. 3, 1963; children: Colleen, Michael, Brian. BS in Acctg., Kings Coll., 1958; LLB, Cath. U., 1962; LLM, Georgetown U., 1967. Bar: D.C. 1962. Ptnr. Casey, Tyre et al, N.Y.C., 1969-73, Jones, Day, Reavis & Pogue, Washington, 1973—; adj. prof. tax Georgetown U., Washington, 1976—; bd. advisers Corp. Taxation. Contbr. articles to profl. jours. Trustee St. Bonaventure U., 1996—. Served with USAR, 1959. Fellow Am. Bar Found.; mem. ABA (chmn. subcom. tax sect. 1982-86), Am. Coll. Tax Counsel. Democrat. Roman Catholic. Clubs: Metropolitan (Washington); Union (Cleve.). Home: 1610 44th St NW Washington DC 20007-2025 Office: Jones Day Reavis & Pogue 1450 G St NW Ste 600 Washington DC 20005-2001

O'HARA, JOHN PATRICK, lawyer, accountant; b. N.Y.C., Jan. 11, 1930; s. Thomas James and Anne (Henry) O'H.; m. Mary Ann Leavey, Oct. 15, 1955; children: Ann O'Hara Carroll, Kathleen O'Hara Geary, Maureen Elizabeth. BBA, St. John's U., N.Y.C., 1952; JD, U. Balt., 1960. Bar: Md. 1960. Spl. agt. FBI, 1955-62; chief counsel, staff dir. subcom. on investigations and oversight Com. on Pub. Works and Transp., Ho. of Reps., Washington, 1962-86; dir. corp. security Flying Tiger Ln., L.A., 1986-89; ptnr. Burgess & O'Hara, Upper Marlboro, Md., 1990-91; cons. Legal Svcs. Corp., Washington, 1990-91, pres., 1991-94. 1st lt. USMC, 1952-54. Decorated Nat. Def. Svc. medal, UN medal, Korean Svc. medal. Mem. Md. Bar Assn., Bolling AFB Officers Club, Marines Meml. Assn., Am. Legion. Home: 5904 Mount Eagle Dr Apt 518 Alexandria VA 22303-2537

O'HARA, JOHN PAUL, III, orthopaedic surgeon; b. Detroit, June 10, 1946; m. Randy Baird, Mar. 11, 1987; children: Riley Anne, Nolan Baird, Evan John. BA, U. Mich., 1968, MD, 1972. Resident U. Va. Med. Ctr., Charlottesville, 1973-77; fellow Nuffield Orthopaedic Ctr., Oxford, Eng., 1977; practice medicine specializing in orthopaedic surgery Southfield, 1978—; staff Providence Hosp., Southfield, Mich., 1978—, pres. elect med. staff, 1990, pres. med. staff, 1991; sect. chief orthopedics; pres. Providence Hosp. Med. Staff Research Found., 1984-85, bd. dirs., 1982—; bd. dirs. Mich. Master Health Plan, Southfield, 1982. Contbr. articles to profl. jours. Recipient Disting. Alumni award Brother Rice High Sch., 1986. Fellow Am. Acad. Orthopaedic Surgery, Mid Am. Orthopaedic Soc.; mem. Detroit Orthopaedic Soc., Mich. Orthopaedic Soc., Detroit Acad. Orthopaedic Surgeons (past pres.), Oakland Hills Country Club (Birmingham, Mich.), Beverly Hills (Mich.) Club. Avocations: earthwatch vol., travel, sports. Home: 627 Waddington St Bloomfield Hills MI 48301-2346 Office: Porretta & O'Hara Orthopaedic Surgeons PC 22250 Providence Dr Ste 401 Southfield MI 48075-6212

O'HARA, TAMARA LYNN, public health nurse, consultant; b. Cleve., Apr. 30, 1963; d. Ronald Charles and Sally Ann (Wilson) Marsho; m. Michael Tracy O'Hara, July 14, 1984; children: Ryan Michael, Megan Marie, Matthew Charles. BSN, Ursuline Coll., 1986. Staff nurse Fairview Gen. Hosp., Cleve., 1986-92; pub. health nurse Lakewood (Ohio) Divsn. Health, 1992—; nurse coord. Bur. Children with Med. Handicaps, Lakewood, 1992—, head poisoning prevention educator; family chair Cuyahoga County Early Intervention Local Collaborative Group, 1994-95, family, clin. faculty Case Western Res. U., Cleve., 1994-97; clin. site facilitator Ursuline Coll., 1994-97. Contbr. articles to newsletter. Recipient Collaboration award Cuyahoga County Early Intervention Local Collaborative Group, 1994-95, Nursing Recognition award 1990. Avocations: downhill skiing, boating, physical fitness, nutrition. Office: Lakewood Divsn Health 12805 Detroit Ave Lakewood OH 44107-2835

O'HARA, THOMAS EDWIN, professional administrator executive; b. Springfield, Mo., July 28, 1915; s. Robert John and Olga Florence (Lindberg) O'H.; m. Eleanor McLennan Urquhart, May 6, 1950; children: Thomas Edwin, Robert Andrew, Shelley Janette. AB, Wayne State U., 1938. Accountant Nash-Kelvinator Corp., 1938-39, Gen. Electric Co., 1938-41, Ernst & Ernst, 1941-42; dir. payrolls Detroit Bd. Edn., 1942-58; chmn. bd. trustees Nat. Assn. Investment Clubs, Madison Heights, Mich., 1951—; treas. Sunshine Fifty, Inc., 1969-77; vice chmn. H.W. Rickel & Co., 1971-76; dir. N.Y. Stock Exch., 1973-75; mem. adv. com. individual investors, 1988—; dir. Investment Edn. Inst., 1962—; chmn. NAIC Growth Fund, Inc., 1990—. Bd. dirs. William Tyndale Coll.; chmn. N.Y. Stock Exch. Individual Investors Adv. Com., 1987-89; mem. U.S. Securities and Exch. Commn. Consumers Affairs Adv. Com. and Compensation Practices Com. With USAAF, 1942-45. Recipient Disting. Service award in investment edn., 1969, Disting. Alumni award Wayne State U. Sch. Bus. Adminstrn., 1987, Roalman award Nat. Investor Rels. Inst., 1987. Mem. World Fedn. Investment Clubs (dir., chmn. 1985-90), Arab Frat., Gamma Beta Phi. Presbyn. Home: 367 Sycamore Ct Bloomfield Hills MI 48302-1173 Office: National Assoc of Investors Corp 711 W 13 Madison Heights MI 48071

O'HARA, THOMAS PATRICK, managing editor; b. Phila., July 15, 1947; s. Hugh James and Agatha Mary (Gilroy) O'H.; m. Juliet Munro, 1970 (div. 1974); m. Pamela Smith, Oct. 8, 1977; children: Rachel Kathleen, Patrick Graham. BA in English, Rutgers South Jersey, 1972; MA in Communications, U. Fla., 1974. Sports reporter Gainesville SUN, 1972-74; reporter Orlando (Fla.) Sentinel, 1974-76, Daytona Beach (Fla.) News Jour., 1976-78; various editing and reporting positions Miami (Fla.) Herald, 1978-86, city editor Palm Beach ed., 1985-86; asst. met. editor Palm Beach Post, West Palm Beach, Fla., 1986-87; met. editor Palm Beach Post, West Palm Beach, 1987-88, asst. mng. editor, 1988-89, mng. editor, 1989—. Sgt. USAF, 1969-71. Home: 107 Seabreeze Ave Delray Beach FL 33483-7017 Office: Palm Beach Post PO Box 24700 2751 S Dixie Hwy West Palm Beach FL 33405

O'HARE, DEAN RAYMOND, insurance company executive; b. Jersey City, June 21, 1942; s. Francis and Ann O'H.; m. Kathleen T. Walliser, Dec. 2, 1967; Dean, Jason. BS, NYU, 1963; MBA, Pace U., 1968. Trainee Chubb Corp., N.Y.C., 1963-64, tax advisor, 1964-67, asst. v.p., mgr. corp. fin. devel., 1968-72, sr. v.p., mgr. corp. fin. devel. dept., from 1979, chief fin. officer, 1979-94, pres., 1986-88, chmn., chief exec. officer, 1988—; chmn. Chubb Life Ins. Co. N.H., 1981—; chmn., pres. Fed. Ins. Co., 1988—, Vigilant Ins. Co., 1988—; chmn., dir. Bellemead Devel. Corp., 1973—; chmn. Colonial Life Ins. Co. Am., 1980—, Chubb Life Ins. Co. Am., 1980—; bd. dirs. Chubb Ins. Co. Can., Fed. Ins. Co., Vigilant Ins. Co. Dir. Coalition Svc. Industries, The N.J. Partnership; trustee com. for econ. devel., WDC. Mem. Am. Ins. Assn. (current chmn.), The Links Club (N.Y.C.), India House. Home: 370 Lake Rd Far Hills NJ 07931-2314 Office: Chubb Corp PO Box 1615 15 Mountain View Rd Warren NJ 07061

O'HARE, JAMES RAYMOND, energy company executive; b. Evergreen Park, Ill., July 20, 1938; s. Raymond Clarence and Helen (Nickel) O'H.; m. Nan Jane Raleigh, Sept. 18, 1965; children: Joan, Daniel, Colleen, Patrick. B.S., Marquette U., 1960; M.B.A., U. Calif. at Los Angeles, 1961. C.P.A., Ind., Ill., Ky., Calif., Tex. Mgr. Peat, Marwick, Mitchell & Co., Chgo., 1961-68, South Bend, Ind., 1968-69; controller Essex Internat., Inc., Fort Wayne, Ind., 1969-76, Am. Air Filter Co., Inc., Louisville, 1976-80; fin. v.p. and treas. Petrolane Inc., Long Beach, Calif., 1980-85; treas. Tex. Eastern Corp., Houston, 1985-87, v.p., treas., 1987-88; sr. v.p. fin. and adminstrn. Texas Eastern Gas Pipeline Co., Houston, 1988-89; v.p., CFO Enclean Inc., Houston, 1991-93; fin. cons., 1993-97; v.p., CFO Ascendant Healthcare Group, Inc., Houston, 1997—. Served with USNR, 1962-68. Mem. AICPA, Evans Scholars, Fin. Execs. Inst., The Woodlands Country Club, Beta Gamma Sigma.

O'HARE, JOHN DIGNAN, library director; b. Glen Cove, N.Y., Mar. 23, 1949; s. James and Eileen Mary (Dignan) O'H.; m. Mary Earlene Wright, Oct. 19, 1974; children: Elizabeth Catherine, Emily Suzanne. BA in English, St. Vincent Coll., Latrobe, Pa., 1971; MS in LS, Long Island U., Greenvale, N.Y., 1974; MA in Comm. Arts, N.Y. Inst. Tech., Old Westbury, 1984. Cert. tchr. secondary English, pub. libr., N.Y. English tchr. Mattituck-Cutchogue Union Free Sch. Dist., Mattituck, N.Y., 1973-87; reference libr. Bayport-Blue Point Pub. Libr., Blue Point, N.Y., 1987-93, libr. dir., 1993—; part-time reference libr. Shoreham-Wading River Pub. Libr., Shoreham, N.Y., 1980—; chair home econs. adv. coun. Cornell Coop. Extension, Riverhead, N.Y., 1993—; sec. system technology adv. Suffolk Coop. Libr., Bellport, N.Y., 1995—; mem. Librs. Exploring Automation Procurement Com., Bellport, 1995—; judge Ednl. Film Libr. Assn. Film Festival, N.Y.C., 1988-89. Mem. ednl. adv. com. Comsewogue Union Free Sch. Dist., Port Jefferson Station, N.Y., 1977-78; mem. com. sch. consolidation task force Shoreham-Wading River Ctrl. Sch. Dist., 1993-94. Mem. Pub. Libr. Dirs. Assn. Suffolk County (v.p.), Suffolk County Libr. Assn. Democrat. Roman Catholic. Avocations: long-distance running, biking, golf. Home: 48 Cross Rd PO Box 93 Wading River NY 11792 Office: Bayport-Blue Point Pub Libr 203 Blue Point Ave Blue Point NY 11715

O'HARE, JOSEPH ALOYSIUS, academic administrator, priest; b. N.Y.C., Feb. 12, 1931; s. Joseph Aloysius and Marie Angela (Enright) O'H. AB, Berchmans Coll, Cebu City, Philippines, 1954, MA, 1955; STL, Woodstock Coll., Md., 1962; PhD, Fordham U., 1968; DHL (hon.), Fairfield U., 1980, Rockhurst Coll., Kansas City, Mo., 1984, Ateneo de Manila U., 1990, CUNY, 1991, Coll. of St. Rose, Albany, N.Y., 1995, St. Francis Coll., Bklyn., 1996; DLitt (hon.), Coll. of New Rochelle, 1984. Joined S.J., 1948, ordained priest Roman Cath. Ch., 1961. Instr. Ateneo de Manila U., 1955-58, prof. philosophy, 1968-72; assoc. editor Am. Mag., N.Y.C., 1972-75, editor-in-chief, 1975-84; pres. Fordham U., Bronx, N.Y., 1984—. Author weekly column Of Many Things (Best Original Column award Cath. Press Assn. 1976, 78, 81, 84). Chmn. N.Y.C. Campaign Fin. Bd. Office: Fordham U Office of Pres New York NY 10458

O'HARE, LINDA PARSONS, management consultant; b. Robinson, Ill., Nov. 30, 1947; d. William Wayne and Silvetta (Simmons) Parsons; m. John M. O'Hare, Oct. 5, 1968 (div. May 1983). BS, U. Ill., 1965-68, 72; M in Mgmt., Northwestern U., 1984. Various positions Harvard U., Cambridge, Mass., 1968-71; mgr. employment dept. Leo Burnett Co., Inc., Chgo., 1972-75; various positions Booz, Allen & Hamilton, Inc., Chgo., 1975-81; pres. The Bridge Orgn., Inc., Chgo., 1981—, also bd. dirs.; bd. dirs. All Am. Bank Chgo.; former mem. adv. bd. human resources devel. Northeastern Ill. U., Chgo., 1980-93; mem. Kellogg Alumni Adv. Bd., 1989—. Steering com. Kellogg Alumni Club Cmty. Svcs. Project, Chgo., 1986-95; gov. bd. Ill. Coun. on Econ. Edn., 1992—. Mem. Inst. Mgmt. Cons. (bd. dirs., v.p. 1986-91), Chgo. Fin. Exch. (bd. dirs., sec. 1988-89, v.p. 1990-91, pres. 1991-92), Nat. Assn. Women Bus. Owners (bd. dirs. 1981-84), Chgo. Health Execs. Forum, Univ. Club Chgo. (bd. dirs. 1993—), Execs. Club Chgo. (bd. dirs. 1993—), Econ. Club Chgo., Chgo. Network, Wis. Arabian Horse Assn. Avocation: Arabian horses. Home: N1212 Academy Rd Lake Geneva WI 53147-4212 Office: Bridge Orgn Inc N1212 Academy Rd Lake Geneva WI 53147-4212

O'HARE, MARILYNN RYAN, artist; b. Berkeley, Calif., Aug. 6, 1926; d. Lawrence and Linnie Marie (Ryan) Atkins; m. Lawrence Bernard O'Hare, Sept. 20, 1947; children: Timothy Lawrence, Kevin Roy, Shannon John, Kacey Sophia, Kelly Katherine. Student, Jean Turner Art Sch., San Francisco, 1944, 45, 46. Artist Cherubs children's dept. store, San Francisco, 1946, 47, Emporium Art Dept., San Francisco, 1947-54; freelance artist Capwells-Emporium, Liberty House, San Francisco, Oakland, 1955-64; artist-in-residence, coord. art program Childrens Fairyland USA, Oakland, 1962—; commissioned painting for Moffit Hosp., San Francisco, 1970, Havens Sch. Libr., Piedmont, Calif., 1975. Painter children's portraits; designer greeting cards; executed murals Children's Fairyland, Oakland, 1965, 66, 73, Kaiser Hosp., Martinez, Calif., 1974. Vol. art tchr. Oakland Pub. Schs., 1958-62; vol. Oak Mus., 1965—, Convelescant Hosp., Berkeley, Calif., 1975—. Named Mother of Yr., City of Oakland, 1993. Mem. Oakland Art Assn. Democrat. Avocations: reading, craft design, garage sales. Home: 3361 Burdeck Dr Oakland CA 94602-2624

O'HARE, SANDRA FERNANDEZ, elementary education educator, adult education educator; b. N.Y.C., Mar. 19, 1941; d. Ricardo Enrique and Rosario de Los Angeles (Arenas) Fernandez; m. S. James O'Hare, Oct. 12, 1963; children: James, Richard, Michael, Christopher. BA, Marymount Coll., 1962; MA, U. San Francisco, 1980. Cert. elem. and coll. tchr.; bilingual and lang. devel. specialist. Instr. adult edn. Guam, 1964-66, Spanish Speaking Ctr., Harrisburg, Pa., 1977-79; tchr. Colegio Salesiano, Rota, Spain, 1973, 84, Alisal Sch. Dist., Salinas, Calif., 1979-81, Liberty Sch., Petaluma, Calif., 1981-85, Cinnabar Sch., Petaluma, 1985—; instr. Chapman U., 1994—; also summer migrant edn. programs Cinnabar Sch., Petaluma, 1990, 91; instr. Santa Rosa (Calif.) Jr. Coll., 1982-83; mem. math. curriculum com. Sonoma County Office Edn., Santa Rosa, 1988; mem. Summer Sci. Connections Inst., Sonoma State U., 1994, Redwood Empire Math. Acad., summer 1995; mem. Sonoma County Math Project, 1995-96; summer '96 NEH stipend to Harvard U. Translator: Isabel la Catolica, 1962. Mem. Asian relief com. ARC, Harrisburg, 1975, Boy Scouts Am., Petaluma, 1983, Mechanicsburg, Pa., 1974, Monterey, Calif., 1971, Sonoma County Adult Literacy League, 1996—. Sarah D. Barder fellow Johns Hopkins U., 1990. Mem. NEA, AAUW (chair edn. founds. com. 1985-86), Calif. Assn. Bilingual Educators, Club Hispano-Americano Petaluma (pres. 1987-89), M3 Investment Club. Roman Catholic. Avocation: travel. Home: 1289 Glenwood Dr Petaluma CA 94954-4326

O'HARE, VIRGINIA LEWIS, legal administrator; b. Pitts., May 2, 1951; d. Robert Edward and Ellen Marie (Saylor) Lewis; m. John Francis O'Hare, Sept. 17, 1994; 1 child, Merit Elisabeth. BS in Edn., U. Pitts., 1973; MS in Human Resources Mgmt., Laroche Coll., 1984. Legal asst. Meyer, Darragh, Buckler, Bebenek & Eck, Pitts., 1973-85; legal office mgr. Rockwell Internat., Pitts., 1985-86; pers. mgr. Rose, Schmidt, Hasley & DiSalle, Pitts., 1986-88; legal adminstr. Duquesne Light Co., Pitts., 1988—. Mem. Assn. Legal Adminstrs., Pitts. Legal Adminstrn. Assn. (sec. 1989-93, membership chair 1993—), Pa. Bar Assn., Allegheny Bar Assn., Pitts. Pers. Assn. Republican. Avocations: horseback riding, target shooting, walking, biking. Office: Duquesne Light Co 411 7th Ave # 16 006 Pittsburgh PA 15219-1905

O'HAREN, THOMAS JOSEPH, financial services executive; b. Shenandoah, Pa., Apr. 1, 1934; s. James Francis and Elizabeth Margaret (Sauer) O'H.; m. Virginia Ann Kobylinski, Mar. 4, 1957; children: Michelle, Timothy, Terrence, Anne, David, Mary. BS, Pa. State U., 1956. CLU, CHFC. Sales rep. Conn. Gen., Houston, 1957-62, asst. mgr., 1962-66; mgr. Conn. Gen., Atlanta, 1966-85, regional v.p., 1985—; regional v.p. Faculty Leadership Inst. Am. Coll., Atlanta, 1990—; adj. prof. mgmt. Am. Coll., Bryn Mawr, Pa., 1995, chmn. curriculum com., palnned Giving Com. Am. Coll., 1995; mem. pres.'s adv. coun., mentor program. Editor, contbr. Mgrs. Mag., 1987, Gen. Agts. & Mgrs. News, 1987. Fin. chmn. Mattingly Senate Camapign, 1980, Bell Gubernatorial Campaign, 1987; pres. Cobb County C. of C., 1980; co-chmn. Ga. Rep. Found.; chmn. bd. trustees Gama Found., 1990-97, bd. trustees Ga. State U. Ednl. Found., 1996—; Newt Gingrich Fin. Com., 1992-95, Millner Gubernatorial Campaign, 1994. Lt. (j.g.) USNR, 1956-58. Named to the Gama Hall of Fame, 1992, Cigna Fin. Advisors Hall of Fame, 1995; recipient Gordon Setchel award for Contbn. to Agy. Mgmt., 1994. Mem. Gen. Agts. and Mgrs. (Master Agy. award 1983-94, John W. Yates Meml. award 1990, chmn. GAMC Found. 1990-97), CLUs, Chartered Fin. Counsellors, Gen. Agts. Assn. (pres. Atlanta, 1976-77, nat. bd. dirs., 1979-84, nat. pres. 1987-88), Advanced Assn. Life Underwriters (polit. involvement com.), Nat. Assn. Life Underwriters, Million Dollar Roundtable (Top of Table 1988), Atlanta Country Club (bd. dirs. 1986-92, pres. 1988-90), Georgian Club (bd. dirs. 1985 pres.), Equestrian Order of the Holy Sepulchre (knight). Republican. Roman Catholic. Avocations: golf, tennis, reading. Home: 280 Pine Valley Rd Marietta GA 30067-4822 Office: Conn Gen 1800 Parkway Pl SE Marietta GA 30067

OHASHI, SHOICHI, business administration educator; b. Seto, Aichi, Japan, Mar. 7, 1932; s. Mitsuo and Yoshie Ohashi; m. Kimiko Ohashi, Nov. 20, 1957; 1 child, Reisaku; *Wife Kimiko Ohashi studied drawing, having received some prizes at prefectural exhibitions during college. These days she engages herself as leader of a regional voluntary worker group for the aged. Son Reisaku Ohashi works as section chief of a security corporation*. MBA, Kobe (Japan) U., 1957, DBA, 1967. Acad. asst. Kansai U., Suita, Japan, 1957-60, lectr., 1960-63, assoc. prof., 1963-70, prof. bus. adminstrn., 1970—, vice dean students div., 1972-74, vice dean faculty commerce, 1977-78, dean faculty commerce, 1979-80, dean vocat. div., 1982-86, acad. v.p., 1986-92, dean of entrance divsn., 1993—; lectr. Osaka U. Fgn. Studies, 1968-74, Kobe U., 1971, Ritsumeikan U., Kyoto, Japan, 1971-73, Kwanseigakuin U., Nishinomiya, Japan, 1979-80, 94—. Author: Theories on Works Community, 1966, Theory of Business Administration, 1992; co-uthor: Workers' Participation, 1979; co-editor: Information Society Business, 1988, Business Administration, 1991, Lexicon of Business Administration, 1994, An Inquiry into the Japanese Management, 1996. Researcher com. Rsch. Fund Commn. Japan Ministry Edn., 1987-89. Mem. Japan Soc. Bus. Adminstrn. (internat. com. 19880-83, exec. com. 1983-89, 92-95, vice pres. 1995—), Assn. for Comparative Study of Mgmt. (exec.com. 1980-84, pres. 1994-96), Soc. for the History of Mgmt. Theories (exec. com. 1993-96, v.p. 1996). Home: 5-40-602 Mukogawacho, Takarazuka Hyogo 665, Japan Office: Kansai U, 3-3-35 Yamate-cho, Suita Osaka564, Japan *Books published as author, editor or co-editor since a first book in 1966, a dissertation book, until 1997 are 24. Being engaged these days in research into Japanese management system sponsored by Japan Ministry of Education and Japan Society for the promotion of Science. Recent accomplishments as Dean of Entrance Division include a successful increase of about 10% in applicants for Kansai University in 1997 entrance examination amid overall decrease of the applicable in Japan.*

OHE, SHUZO, chemical engineer, educator; b. Tokyo, Mar. 31, 1938; s. Kunio and Chizu (Tabata) O.; m. Nobuko Motegi, Oct. 31, 1975; 1 child, Kenzo. BS, Sci. U. Tokyo, 1962; D of Engring., Tokyo Met. U., 1971. Chem. engr. Ishikawajima-Harima Heavy Indsl. Co. Ltd., Tokyo, 1962-65, reseracher, then rsch. mgr., 1966-80; assoc. prof. Tokai U., Tokyo, 1980-82; prof. chem. engring. Tokai U., 1982-91, Sci. U. of Tokyo, 1991—; vis. researcher Fractionation Rsch., Inc., South Pasadena, Calif., 1973; cons. Chiyoda Engring. Co. Ltd., 1986-89, NKK, Tokyo, 1988—, Sibata Scientific Tech. Ltd., Siber Instrument Co. Ltd. Inventor angle tray distillation tower; author, editor: Computer-Aided Data Book of Vapor Pressure, 1976, Vapor-Liquid Equilibrium Data, 1988, Vapor-Liquid Equilibrium Data at High Pressure, 1990, Vapor-Liquid Equilibrium Data-Salt Effect, 1991; author: Chemical Engineering Design By P.C., 1985. Mem. AAAS, AIChE, Kanagawa Micon Club (pres. 1988—), Japan Info. Ctr. Sci. and Tech., Japan Soc. Chem. Engring., N.Y. Acad. Scis. Avocation: golf. Office: Sci Univ Tokyo, 1-3 Kagurazaka Shinjuku-ku, Tokyo 162, Japan

O'HEARN, JAMES FRANCIS, chemical company executive; b. Fall River, Mass., Nov. 5, 1935; s. Francis Henry and Eileen Eleanor (James) O'H.; m. Sabrina Sieley Hu, Dec. 31, 1966; children: Kevin, Claudine. BS in Edn., Bridgewater Coll., 1960; student, Sofia U., 1962-63. Tchr. Freetown (Mass.) Elem. Sch., 1960-62, Dept. Def., Tokyo, 1962-63; regional mgr. Reynolds Metals Co., Hong Kong, L.A., 1963-69; regional mgr. Uniroyal Chems., Hong Kong, Singapore, 1969-76, Akron, Ohio, 1976-77; dir. mktg. Uniroyal Chems., Brussels, 1977-80; pres. Premier Chem. Co., Taipei, Taiwan, 1980—; dir. USA-ROC Econ. Coun., Taipei, 1991—, chmn. chem. group, 1986—. Mem. Petrochem. Ind. Assn. Taipei (dir. 1981-86), Am. Club in China (pres. 1993-94), Am. C. of C. (pres. 1991, 92), Am. Univ. Club (dir. 1992—). Republican. Roman Catholic. Avocations: golf, tennis, aerobics, mountain climbing. Home: 229 Chung Shan N Rd Sec 7, Taipei Taiwan Office: Premier Chem Co Ltd, 205 Tun Hwa N Rd Ste 704, Taipei Taiwan

O'HEARN, MICHAEL JOHN, lawyer; b. Akron, Ohio, Jan. 29, 1952; s. Leo Ambrose and Margaret Elizabeth (Clark) O'H. BA in Econs., UCLA, 1975; postgrad., U. San Diego, 1977; JD, San Fernando Valley Coll. Law, 1979. Bar: Calif. 1979, U.S. Dist. Ct. (cen. dist.) Calif. 1979. Document analyst Mellonics Info. Ctr., Litton Industries, Canoga Park, Calif., 1977-79; pvt. practice Encino, Calif., 1979-80; atty. VISTA/Grey Law Inc., L.A., 1980-81; assoc. Donald E. Chadwick & Assocs., Woodland Hills, Calif., 1981-84, Law Offices of Laurence Ring, Beverly Hills, Calif., 1984-85; atty., in-house counsel Coastal Ins. Co., Van Nuys, Calif., 1985-89; atty. Citrus Glen Apts., Ventura, Calif., 1989-92; pvt. practice Ventura County, Calif., 1992—. Recipient Cert. of Appreciation, Agy. for Vol. Svc., 1981, San Fernando Valley Walk for Life, 1988, Cert. of Appreciation, Arbitrator for the Superior and Mcpl. Cts., Ventura County Jud. Dist., 1996. Mem. KC, Ventura County Bar Assn., Ventura County Trial Lawyers Assn., Secular Franciscan Order. Republican. Roman Catholic. Avocation: golf. Home: 1741 Fisher Dr Apt 201 Oxnard CA 93035 Office: 3650 Ketch Ave Oxnard CA 93035-3029

O'HEARN, ROBERT RAYMOND, stage designer; b. Elkhart, Ind., July 19, 1921; s. Robert Raymond, Sr. and Ella May (Stoldt) O'H. B.A., Ind. U., 1939-43; student, Art Students League, 1943-45. Designer Brattle Theatre, Cambridge, Mass., 1948-52; prof. stage design, chmn. design dept. Sch. Music Ind. U., 1989—; instr. Studio and Forum Scenic Design, 1968-88. Stage designer: Broadway shows The Relapse, 1950, Loves Labor's Lost, 1953, Othello, Festival, 1955, The Apple Cart, Child of Fortune, 1956; asst. designer: Broadway shows Kismet, 1953, Pajama Game, 1955, My Fair Lady, 1956, West Side Story, 1958; designer: for film A Clerical Error, 1955; designer prodns. Central City Opera House, 1959-63, Opera Soc. Washington, 1958-61, L'Elisir D'Amore at Met. Opera House, 1960, Die Meistersinger, 1962, Aida, 1963; stage designer: As You Like It, Stratford, Conn., 1961, Troilus and Cressida, Stratford, 1961, Kiss Me Kate, Los Angeles Civic Light Opera, 1964, N.Y.C. Center, 1965, Samson and Delila, Met. Opera, 1964, La Sylphide, Am. Ballet Theatre, 1964, Italian Symphony, 1971, Adam Cochrane, Broadway, 1964, Pique Dame, Met. Opera, 1965, La Ventana, 1966, Die Frau Ohne Schatten, 1966, Porgy and Bess, Vienna Volksoper, 1965, Bregenzer Festspiele, 1971, Otello, Boston Opera, also Hamburg State Opera, 1967, Hansel and Gretel, Met. Opera, 1967, Nutcracker Ballet, San Francisco Ballet, 1967, L.A. Ballet, 1979, La Traviata, Santa Fe Opera, 1968, Rosalinda, L.A. Civic Light Opera, 1968, Der Rosenkavalier, Met. Opera, 1969, Tallis Fantasia, N.Y.C. Ballet, 1969, Boris Godunov (unproduced), Met. Opera, 1970, Parsifal, Met. Opera, 1970, Porgy and Bess, Bregenz Festspiel, Austria, 1971, Falstaff, Marriage of Figaro, Gianni Schicci, Central City Opera House, 1972, Barber of Seville, 1973, The Enchanted, Kennedy Center, 1973, The Mind with the Dirty Man, Los Angeles, 1973, Midsummer Night's Dream, Central City Opera, 1974, Coppelia, Ballet West, 1974, Carmen, Strasbourg, 1974, The Pearl Fishers, Miami Opera, 1974, N.Y.C. Opera, 1980, Don Pasquale, Miami Opera, 1976, Scipio Africanus, Central City Opera, 1975, Swan Lake, Strasbourg, 1975, Marriage of Figaro, Met. Opera, 1975, Die Meistersinger, Karlsruhe, Germany, 1975, Girl of the Golden West, Houston Opera, 1976, N.Y.C. Opera, 1977, Vienna Staatsoper, 1976, Boris Godunov, Strasbourg, 1976, Der Rosenkavelier, Karlsruhe, 1976, Don Quixote, Ballet West, 1977, Die Meistersinger, Chgo. Lyric Opera, 1977, Adriana Lecouvreur, Miami Opera, 1978, La Boheme, 1978, Coppelia, Pacific N.W. Dance, Seattle, 1978, Andrea Chenier, N.Y.C. Opera, 1978, Der Rosenkavelier, Can. Opera Co., Toronto, 1978, Taming of the Shrew, Pa. State U., 1980, Die Fledermaus, Miami Opera, 1980, Tosca, Miami Opera, 1981, West Side Story, Bregenz Festspiel, Austria, 1981, Mich. Opera Theatre, 1985; Pique Dame, San Francisco Opera, 1982, La Traviata, Miami Opera, 1982, Of Mice and Men, Miami Opera, 1982, Carousel, Annie Get Your Gun, Miami Opera, 1984, Lucia di Lammermoor, 1984, L'Italiana in Algeri, 1985, Porgy and Bess, Met. Opera, 1985, West Side Story, Mich. Opera Theatre, 1985, Aida, Don Giovanni, Opera Colo., 1986, My Fair Lady, Mich. Opera Theatre, 1986, Samson and Delilah, Manon Lescaut Opera Colo., 1987, Annie Get Your Gun, Paper Mill Playhouse, 1987, Peter Grimes, Ind. U., 1987, Madama Butterfly, N.J. State Opera, 1990. Mem. vis. com. Costume Inst., Met. Museum. Mem. United Scenic Artists. Home: 2604 E 2nd St Bloomington IN 47401-5351

O'HERN, DANIEL JOSEPH, state supreme court justice; b. Red Bank, N.J., May 23, 1930; s. J. Henry and Eugenia A. (Sansone) O'H.; m. Barbara Ronan, Aug. 8, 1959; children: Daniel J., Eileen, James, John, Molly. AB, Fordham Coll., 1951; LLB, Harvard U., 1957. Bar: N.J. 1958. Clk. U.S. Supreme Ct., Washington, 1957-58; assoc. Abramoff, Apy & O'Hern, Red Bank, N.J., 1966-78; commr. N.J. Dept. Environ. Protection, 1978-79; counsel to Gov. N.J. Trenton; justice N.J. Supreme Ct., Trenton, 1981—; former mem. adv. com. profl. ethics N.J. Supreme Ct. Past trustee Legal Aid Soc. Monmouth County, (N.J.); mayor Borough of Red Bank, 1969-78, councilman, 1962-69. Served as lt. (j.g.) USNR, 1951-54. Fellow Am. Bar Found.; mem. ABA, N.J. Bar Assn., Monmouth County Bar Assn., Harvard Law Sch. Assn. N.J. (past pres.). Office: NJ Supreme Ct 151 Bodman Pl Red Bank NJ 07701-1070 also: NJ Supreme Ct CN 970 Trenton NJ 08625*

O'HERN, ELIZABETH MOOT, microbiologist, writer; b. Richmondville, N.Y., Sept. 1, 1913; s. Carl Melvin and Margaret Esther (Dibble) Moot; B.A., U. Calif., Berkeley, 1945, M.A., 1947; Ph.D. (grad. fellow), U. Wash., 1956; m. William J. O'Hern, Jan. 4, 1952. Instr. SUNY, Bklyn., 1957-62; asst. prof. George Washington U., Washington, 1962-65; prin. investigator rsch. Bionetics Rsch. Lab., Kensington, Md., 1965-67; adminstr. rsch. grants in microbiology, genetics and anesthesiology NIH, Nat. Inst. Gen. Med. Scis., Bethesda, Md., 1968-75, spl. asst. to dir., 1975-77, adminstr. spl. programs, 1977-86, also programs adminstr. Mem. bd. examiners in basic scis. Commn. on Licensure to Practice Healing Arts in D.C., 1974-75; panel mem. Washington Area Office, U.S. Civil Svc. Commn., 1977-86; program cons. U. Calif., 1990. Fellow Am. Acad. Microbiology; mem. AAUW (pres. Washington br. 1967-69, trustee edn. found. 1976-81), AAAS, Am. Inst. Biol. Sci., Am. Public Health Assn., Am. Soc Cell Biology, Am. Soc. Microbiology (chmn. status of women in the profession 1975-78), Am. Soc. Tropical Medicine and Hygiene, Med. Mycology Soc. Am., Mycol. Soc. Am., N.Y. Acad. Sci., Wash. Acad. Sci., Assn. Women in Sci., Astron. Soc. Pacific, Planetary Soc., Grad. Women in Sci. (nat. sec. 1974-77, chpt. pres. 1979-80, historian 1994-97), Sigma Xi. Author: Profiles of Pioneer Women Scientists. Contbr. articles to profl. publs. Home: 522 Russell Ave Gaithersburg MD 20877

O'HERN, JANE SUSAN, psychologist, educator; b. Winthrop, Mass., Mar. 21, 1933; d. Joseph Francis and Mona (Garvey) O'H. BS, Boston U., 1954, EdD, 1962; MA, Mich. State U., 1956. Instr. Mercyhurst Coll., 1954-55, Hofstra Coll., 1956-57, State Coll., Salem and Boston, 1957-60; asst. prof. Boston U., 1962-67, assoc. prof., 1967-75, prof. edn. and psychiat. (psychology), 1975-95, prof. emeritus, 1995—, chmn. dept. counseling psychology, 1972-75, 88-89, dir. mental health edn. program, 1975-81, dir. internat. edn., 1978-81, asst. v.p. internat. edn., 1981; pres. ASSIST Internat., Inc., 1989—; adv. bd. Internat. Study Cons., 1994—. Contbr. articles to profl. jours. Trustee Boston Ctr. Modern Psychoanalytic Studies, 1980-92. Recipient grants U.S. Office Edn., NIMH, Dept. of Def. Mem. Assn. Counselor Edn. and Suprs., Am. Counseling Assn., North Atlantic Assn. Counselor Edn. and Supervision (past pres.), Mass. Psychol. Assn., Am. Psychol. Assn., Mortar Bd., Pi Lamda Theta, Sigma Kappa, Phi Delta Kappa, Phi Beta Delta. Home: 111 Perkins St Apt 287 Boston MA 02130-4324

OHGA, NORIO, electronics executive; b. Numazu, Japan, Jan. 29, 1930; m. Midori Ohga. Grad., Tokyo Nat. U. Fine Arts and Music, 1953, Kunst U., Berlin, 1957. Cons., advisor Tokyo Tsushin Kogyo (later Sony Corp.), 1953-59; gen. mgr. tape recorder divsn., product planning divsn., indsl. design divsn. Sony Corp., Tokyo, 1959, bd. dirs., 1964-72, mng. dir., 1972-74, sr. mng. dir., 1974-76, dep. pres., 1976-82, pres., chief oper. officer, 1982-89, pres. and CEO, 1989-95, chmn. and CEO, 1995—; sr. mng. dir. CBS/Sony Group, Inc., 1968-70, pres., 1970-80, chmn., 1980-91; chmn. Sony Corp. Am., 1988—, Sony Software Corp., 1991—. Decorated Medal of Honor with Blue Ribbon by J.M. the Emperor of Japan, 1988, Cmdrs. Cross First Class of the Order of Merit of the Rep. of Austria, 1987, Officier de l'Ordre Nat. de la Legion d'Honneur France, 1996. Mem. Japan Fedn. Econ. Orgn. (chmn. com. on new bus.), Tokyo C. of C. and Industry (vice chmn.). Office: Sony Corp, 7-35 Kitashinagawa 6-chome, Shinagawa-ku Tokyo 141, Japan Office: Sony Corp Am 550 Madison Ave New York NY 10022-3211

OHINOUYE, TSUNEO, automobile manufacturing executive; b. Tokyo, Mar. 13, 1932; came to U.S., 1977; s. Tatsuo and Haru (Ito) O.; m. Tomie Murate, Oct. 23, 1958; children: Mariko Itoh, Yuko Ohinouye. B Mech. Engring., Kyoto (Japan) U., 1954; M Automobile Engring., Cranfield Inst. Tech., Bedford, Eng., 1964. Mgr. engine design Mitsubishi Heavy Industries, Kyoto, 1955-77; pres. Mitsubishi Motors Corp. Svcs., Southfield, Mich., 1977-80; chief coord. vehicle devel. passenger car ctr. Mitsubishi Motors Corp., Okazaki, Japan, 1980-85; corp. chief engr. export product planning Mitsubishi Motors Corp., Tokyo, 1985-87; pres. Mitsubishi Motors Am., Southfield, 1987-91; pres., CEO Diamond-Star Motors (subs. Mitsubishi Motors Corp.), Normal, Ill., 1991-95; chmn., CEO Mitsubishi Motor Mfg. of Am., Inc., Normal, 1995—. UN fellow Cranfield Inst. Tech. Mem. Bloomington C. of C. (bd. dirs. 1993—). Office: Mitsubishi Motor Mfg America Inc 100 N Mitsubishi Motorway Normal IL 61761-8099

OHIRA, KAZUTO, theatre company executive, writer; b. Hiroshima, Japan, Jan. 5, 1933; s. Kitaro and Ryo (Sugimoto) O.; m. Evelyn Lanham, Sept. 3, 1964. BA, Waseda U., Tokyo, 1956. Theatre mgr. Toho's La Brea Theatre, L.A., 1961-63; gen. mgr. Toho Cinema, N.Y.C., 1963-64; publicity mgr. Towa Co., Ltd., Tokyo, 1965-69; rep., dir., mgr. Toho Internat. Inc., N.Y.C., 1969, chief exec. officer, 1988-97; pres. Internat. Cultural Prodn. Inc., N.Y.C. Producer (dance performance and drama) Yasuko Nagamine's Musume Dojoji, 1982, Mandara, 1985, (drama) Yukio Ninagawa's Media, 1987, Takarazuka Show at Radio City Music Hall, N.Y., 1989, KanashibetsU: Furano Group at La Mama, Takarazuka Dance Concert at Joyce Theater, 1992, Sotoba Komachi, Yasuko Nagamine and Co., Beauty of Tokyo, Met. Tokyo, City Ctr., N.Y., 1993; author: Broadway parts I and II, 1982, 2d edit., 1987, Broadway, Broadway, 1987, Performing Arts of New York, 1989, Haiku Collection: Though The Travel is Short, The Charms of Broadway, 1994, Broadway Criticism, 1995, Japanese translation of Show Business Is No Business by Al Hirshfeld, 1997. Bd. dirs. Japan Musical Award Com. in U.S., 1994—, N.Y. Symphony Ensemble, Saeko Ichinohe Dance Co. Recipient 2d Fumiko Yamaji Cultural award, 1985. Mem. UNESCO, Internat. Theatre Critics Assn., Internat. Theatre Inst. Japan, N.Y. Waseda Univ. Alumni Assn. (hon. dir.), Players Club. Avocation: golf. Home: Island House 555 Main St Apt 1204S New York NY 10044-0123 Office: ICP Inc 235 W 48th St Apt 33B New York NY 10036-1431

OHKAWA, TIHIRO, physicist; b. Kanazawa, Ishikawa, Japan, Jan. 3, 1928; came to U.S., 1955; s. Ryoichi and Ryuko (Kitagawa) O.; m. Yoko Hitomi, June 2, 1959; children: Risa, Taro, Hana. B.S. in Physics, U. Tokyo, 1950, Ph.D., 1955, D.Sc., 1958. Research asso. Midwestern U. Research Assn., Madison, Wis., 1955-57; prof. physics U. Tokyo, 1958; with European Orgn. Nuclear Research, Geneva, 1959-60; vice chmn. Gen. Atomics, San Diego, 1960-95; pres. Toyo Techs., Inc., San Diego, 1996—; mem. joint high level adv. panel U.S.-Japan Agreement on Cooperation in R & D in Sci. and Tech., 1988-89; bd. councilors Nat. Inst. for Fusion Sci., Japan, 1989—; adj. prof. physics U. Calif., San Diego. Inventor doublet device, 2-beam FFAG accelerator, helical field stabilization of plasma devices; co-inventor multipole machine; contbr. articles to profl. publs. Fellow Am. Phys. Soc. (award 1979), Am. Nuclear Soc. (award 1984), Fusion Power Assn. (award 1984). Address: 9515 La Jolla Farms Rd La Jolla CA 92037-1130

OHL, RONALD EDWARD, academic administrator; b. Warren, Ohio, May 30, 1936; s. Howard Edward and Ella May (Van Auker) O.; m. Joan Ann Elizabeth Eschenbach, June 29, 1974. BA, Amherst Coll., 1958; MA, Columbia U., 1961; M in Divinity, Union Theol. Sem., N.Y.C., 1964; PhD, U. Pa., 1980. Ordained minister Congregationalist Ch., 1964. Counselor to grad. students Columbia U., N.Y.C., 1960-62; asst. dean students, asst. prof. history Elmhurst (Ill.) Coll., 1964-67; spl. asst. to dean of men Temple U., Phila., 1967-68; assoc. dean coll., dean student affairs, instr. in edn. Colo. Coll., Colorado Springs, 1968-74; with Fairleigh Dickinson U., Rutherford, N.J., 1975-83, successively acting v.p. for external relations, asst. to pres., acting chmn. and cons. relations div. univ. resources and pub. affairs; pres. Salem (W.Va.)-Teikyo U., 1983—, trustee, 1989—, also bd. dirs.; bd. dirs. One Valley Bank, Clarksburg. Contbr. articles to profl. jours. Bd. dirs. Sta. WNPB-TV, 1992—. Recipient Edward Poole Lay Traveling fellowship award Amherst Coll., 1958-59, Young Am. Artists' Dirs. award U.S. Embassy, Rome, 1959-60; Rockefeller Bros. Fund fellow, 1961-62; named Research Asst., U. Pa., 1967-68. Mem. W.Va. Assn. Ind. Colls. (pres. 1985-89), North Ctrl. Assn. Colls. and Schs. (cons.-evaluator 1987—), W.Va. Found. for Ind. Colls. (acad. vice chmn. 1992-94), Clarksburg C. of C. (bd. dirs. 1985-91, 93-96), Univ. Club, W.Va. Christopher Quincentenary Commn., Rotary. Avocations: reading, writing, aviation, skiing, backpacking. Home: 63 Terrace Ave Salem WV 26426-1124

OHLGREN, JOEL R., lawyer; b. Mpls., July 21, 1942. BA, UCLA, 1965, JD, 1968. Bar: Calif. 1969. Ptnr. Sheppard, Mullin, Richter & Hampton, L.A. Fellow Am. Coll. Bankruptcy; mem. ABA, State Bar Calif., Los Angeles County Bar Assn. (past chmn. comml. law and bankruptcy sect.), Order of Coif. Office: Sheppard Mullin Richter & Hampton 333 S Hope St Fl 48 Los Angeles CA 90071-1406

OHLKE, CLARENCE CARL, public affairs consultant; b. Kansas City, Mo., Feb. 16, 1916; s. William Erdman and Amanda (Rubin) O.; m. Frances Woodley Nicholson, Oct. 9, 1954; children: Daniel N., Carl E., Amanda A. A.A., Kansas City Jr. Coll., 1935; B.S., U. Mo., 1940. Personnel examiner, rsch. asst. to city mgr. Mcpl. Govt., city of Kansas City, 1940-41; personnel specialist WPB, Washington, 1942; dir. civilian personnel Chief Naval Operations, Washington, 1946-47; successively personnel specialist, asst. dir. community ops., dir. contracts br., prodn. div. AEC, Washington, 1947-58, spl. asst. to chmn. and commr., 1959-61; asst. dir. operations div. contracts AEC, 1961, asst. to asst. gen. mgr. ops., 1962-63, dir. Office Econ. Impact and Conversion, 1964-66; spl. asst. to dir., head congl. and pub. affairs, govt. and pub. programs dir. NSF, Washington, 1966-73; cons., dir. Center Urban Research and Environ. Studies Drexel U., 1973-75; cons. pub.

affairs, 1976—. Served to lt. USNR, 1942-46. Recipient Disting. Service award NSF, 1973; resolution of commendation Pres.' Nat. Sci. Bd., 1973. Mem. AAAS (public understanding of sci. com. 1977-80). Home: Bear Branch Farms 7380 Ira Sears Rd Adamstown MD 21710-8501

OHLMAN, DOUGLAS RONALD, commodities and securities trader, investment consultant, lawyer; b. Rockville Centre, N.Y., Mar. 25, 1949; s. Maxwell and Miriam (Frucht) O.; m. Elat Menashe, Dec. 4, 1983 (div. Nov. 1996). B.A., Columbia Coll., 1971; J.D., Hofstra U., 1974. Bar: N.Y. 1975, U.S. Dist. Ct. (so. and ea. dists.) N.Y. 1976, (no. and we. dists.) N.Y. 1978, U.S. Tax Ct. 1978, U.S. Supreme Ct. 1978, U.S. Ct. Claims 1978, U.S. Customs Ct. 1978. V.p. Info. & Research Services, Inc., Roslyn, N.Y., 1975-81; assoc. Baer & Marks, N.Y.C., 1974-75, Rains, Pogrebin & Scher, Mineola, N.Y., 1975-76, Weisman, Celler, Spett, Modlin & Wertheimer, N.Y.C., 1976-79, Hoffberg, Gordon, Rabin & Engler, N.Y.C., 1979-80, Bergner & Bergner, Blum & Ruditz, N.Y.C., 1980-81; gen. counsel Greenfield Ptnrs., N.Y.C., 1981-86, gen. ptnr., 1982-86, dep. mng. ptnr., 1984-86, chief operating officer, sr. v.p., sec., dir. V.W. Investors, Inc., J.L. Investors, Inc., N.Y.C., 1985-88; commodities and securities trader for proprietary accts. Highland Beach, Fla., 1988—; dir. Track Data Corp., N.Y.C., 1983-87; allied mem. N.Y. Stock Exchange, Inc., 1982-88, options prin., 1985, 87. Mem. radio news team WKCR-FM, N.Y.C. (Writers Guild award, Peabody nomination 1968); notes and comments editor Hofstra Law Rev., 1973-74. Communications dir., dep. radiol. officer Nassau County Civil Def., Town of Roslyn, N.Y., 1964-74; mem. com. Nassau County Liberal Party, 1982. Mem. ABA, N.Y. State Bar Assn., N.Y. County Lawyers Assn., Assn. of Bar of City of N.Y. Home: 401 N E Mizner Blvd Apt T502 Boca Raton FL 33432

OHLMEYER, DONALD WINFRED, JR., film and television producer; b. New Orleans, Feb. 3, 1945; s. Donald W. and Eva Claire (Bivens) O.; m. Adrian Perry, Feb. 11, 1978; 1 son, Kemper Perry; children by previous marriage: Justin Drew, Christopher Brett, Todd Bivens. BA in Communications, U. Notre Dame, 1967. Pres. Roadblock Prodns., 1977—; chmn. bd., chief exec. officer Ohlmeyer Communications, Los Angeles, 1982—; pres. west coast NBC, Burbank, Calif. Assoc. dir. ABC Sports, N.Y.C., 1967-70, dir., 1971-72, producer, 1972-77; dir. Olympic Games, 1972, Walt Disney World's 4th of July Spectacular; producer, dir. Summer and Winter Olympics, 1976; producer Monday Night Football, 1972-76; exec. producer NBC Sports, N.Y.C., 1977-82; exec. producer: 1980 Olympic Games, Crime of Innocence, Under Siege, Bluffing It, Right to Die; exec. producer: (movies) Special Bulletin, The Golden Moment: An Olympic Love Story; producer Battle of the Network Stars. Recipient 11 Emmy awards 1975-83, Cine Golden Eagle award, 1979, Miami Film Festival award 1979. Mem. Dirs. Guild Am., Acad. TV Arts and Scis. Clubs: Bel-Air (Calif.); Deepdale (N.Y.); Outrigger Canoe, Waialae Country (Honolulu). Office: NBC 3000 W Alameda Blvd Burbank CA 91523-0001*

OHLSON, DOUGLAS DEAN, artist; b. Cherokee, Iowa, Nov. 18, 1936; s. Lloyd E. and Effie O. (Johnson) O. B.A., U. Minn., 1961. Prof. art Hunter Coll., N.Y.C., 1964—. One man shows include Fischbach Gallery, N.Y.C., 1964, 66-70, 72, Susan Caldwell Gallery, N.Y.C., 1974, 76, 77, 79, 81, 82, 83, Portland (Oreg.) Ctr. for Visual Arts, 1977, Ruth Siegel Gallery, N.Y.C., 1985, 87, Andre Zarre Gallery, N.Y.C., 1985, 90, 92, 93, 95, Gallery 99, Miami, Fla., 1986, Nina Freudenheim Gallery, Buffalo, 1986, Jaffe Gallery, Miami, 1989; group shows include Mus. Modern Art, N.Y.C., 1968, Tate Gallery, London, 1969, Whitney Mus., N.Y.C., 1969, 71, Corcoran Gallery, Washington, 1972, 73, UCLA, 1975; represented in permanent collections Met. Mus. Art, N.Y.C., Nat. Gallery Art, Washington, Am. Fedn. Art, Mus. Modern Art, Frankfurt, Fed. Republic Germany, Mus. Contemporary Art, Helsinki, Mpls. Inst. Art, Dallas Mus., Bklyn. Mus., Born in Iowa: The Homecoming, 1986-87; invitational Am. Acad. Arts and Letters, 1992, 94, 97. Served with USMC, 1955-58. Guggenheim fellow, 1968; Creative Artists Public Service grantee, 1974; Nat. Endowment for Arts grantee, 1976. Home and Studio: 35 Bond St New York NY 10012-2426

OHM, HERBERT WILLIS, agronomy educator; b. Albert Lea, Minn., Jan. 28, 1945; s. Wilhelm Carl and Lena Ann (Finkbeiner) O.; m. Judy Ann Chrisinger, Aug. 8, 1964; children: Cari Lynn, David William. BS in Agrl. Edn., U. Minn., St. Paul, 1967; MS in Plant Breeding, N.D. State U., 1969; PhD in Plant Genetics and Breeding, Purdue U., 1972. Cert. agronomist. Asst. prof. Purdue U., West Lafayette, Ind., 1972-77, assoc. prof. agronomy, 1977-83, prof., 1983—; team leader Interdisciplinary Wheat and Oat Genetics and Breeding Program, West Lafayette, 1980—, Interdisciplinary Purdue/AID Devel. Program, Burkina Faso, West Africa, 1983-85; mgr. hard red winter wheat rsch. Pioneer Hi-Bred Internat., Inc., Hutchinson, Kans., 1980. Contbr. book chpts. Recipient Soils and Crops Merit award Ind. Crop Improvement Assn., 1988, Merit award Orgn. of African Unity, 1989, Meritorious Svc. award Sci., Tech. and Rsch. Commn., 1989, Agronomic Acheivement award American Soc. of Agronomy, 1994. Fellow Am. Soc. Agronomy (Agronomic Achievement award), Crop Sci. Soc. Am. (chmn. divsn. 1991); mem. Am. Oat Workers Conf. (chmn.), Nat. Oat Improvement Coun. (chmn.), Coun. Agrl. Sci. and Tech., Am. Registry Cert. Profls. in Agrl. Crops and Soils (cert.). Avocations: woodworking, music. Office: Purdue U Dept Agronomy Lilly Hall Life Scis West Lafayette IN 47907-7899

OHMAN, DIANA J., state official, former school system administrator; b. Sheridan, Wyo., Oct. 3, 1950; d. Arden and Doris Marie (Carstens) Mahin. AA, Casper Coll., 1970; BA, U. Wyo., 1972, MEd, 1977, postgrad., 1979—. Tchr. kindergarten Natrona County Sch. Dist., Casper, Wyo., 1971-72; tchr. rural sch. K-8 Campbell County Sch. Dist., Gillette, Wyo., 1972-80, rural prin. K-8, 1980-82, prin. K-6, 1982-84, assoc. dir. instrn., 1984-87; dir. K-12 Goshen County Migrant Program, Torrington, Wyo., 1988-89; prin. K-2 Goshen County Sch. Dist., Torrington, Wyo., 1987-90; state supt. pub. instrn. State of Wyo., Cheyenne, 1991-94, secretary of state, 1995—; chmn. Campbell County Mental Health Task Force, 1986-87; mem. Legis. Task Force on Edn. of Handicapped 3-5 Yr. Olds, 1988-89. State Committeewoman Wyo. Rep. Party, 1985-88. Recipient Wyo. Elem. Prin. of Yr. award, 1990; named Campbell County Tchr. of Yr. 1980, Campbell County Profl. Bus. Woman of Yr. 1984, Outstanding Young Woman in Am., 1983. Mem. Coun. of Chief of State Sch. Officers (Washington chpt.), Internat. Reading Assn., Wyo. Assn. of Sch. Adminstrs., Kappa Delta Pi, Phi Kappa Phi, Phi Delta Kappa. Republican. Lutheran. Office: Sec State Office State Capitol Cheyenne WY 82002-0020

OHMERT, RICHARD ALLAN, architect; b. Davenport, Iowa, Apr. 13, 1925; s. Richard George and Jeanette Marie (Ackerman) O.; m. Bonnie Lou Bruyere, June 26, 1948 (div. June 1964); children: Richard, Jennifer, Jan, Kenneth; m. Violet Maria Alto Holmes, Dec. 31, 1971; stepchildren: Candyce, Cynthia. Student, Gallery Fine Arts Sch. Design, 1940-41, UCLA, 1954-56. Registered architect Calif., Nev., accredited Nat. Coun. Archtl. Registration Bds. Assoc. Kistner Wright & Wright, L.A., 1950-71; asst. mgr. architecture Voorhis, Trindle, Nelson Corp., Irvine, Calif., 1971-74; assoc. Davis-Duhaime Assocs., Anaheim, Calif., 1974-89; firm assoc. Neptune-Thomas-Davis, Corona, Calif., 1989—; cons. architect E&O Corp., Irvine, 1985—. Pres. Groves Homeowners Assn., Irvine, 1981-82; bd. mgrs. YMCA, Irvine, 1988-89; pres. bd. dirs. Orange County Child Abuse Prevention Ctr., 1991. Mem. Soc. Am. Registered Architects (sec.-treas. 1990-92, pres. Orange County chpt. 1993—), Irvine Chpt. of Nat. Exch. Club (pres. 1983-84, dist. dir. 1986-87, Calif.-Nev. dist. pres. 1988-89, pres. Sunrise chpt. 1993-94, 94—, Exchangite of Yr. award 1990). Democrat. Episcopalian. Avocations: oil painting, astronomy, miniature car collecting, cooking. Home: 5200 Irvine Blvd Spc 18 Irvine CA 92620-2016 Office: Neptune-Thomas-Davis Architects 357 N Sheridan St Ste 101 Corona CA 91720-2028

OHNAMI, MASATERU, mechanical engineering educator; b. Kyoto, Japan, Apr. 6, 1931; s. Eijiro and Hisae O.; m. Hiroko Ohnami, Oct. 10, 1959; 1 child, Masahiro. B in Engring., Ritsumeikan U., Kyoto, Japan, 1954; D in Engring., Kyoto U., 1960; D Internat. Rels. (honoris causa), Am. U., Washington, 1995; LLD (honoris causa), B.C. U., Can., 1997, U. B.C., Can., 1997. Asst. prof. Kyoto U., 1955-61; assoc. prof. Ritsumeikan U., Kyoto, 1961-67, prof., 1967—, dean acad. affairs, 1978-80, dean faculty sci. & engring., 1988-90, pres., 1991—; vis. rsch. prof. Columbia U., N.Y.C., 1963-64; mng. dir. Japan Assn. Pvt. Colls. and Univs., Tokyo, 1991—; v.p. Japanese Univ. Accreditation Assn., Tokyo, 1997—; mem. Sci. Coun., Ministry Edn., 1984-86, 88-91, Univ. Formation Coun., 1993—, Coun. Colls. and Univs., Ministry Edn., Tokyo, 1995—, steering com. ctr. entrance exam., 1996—. Author: Plasticity and High Temperature Strength of Materials, 1988, Fracture and Society, 1992. Mem. Deutscher Verband für Materialforschung und prüfung undaunted prüfung e.V. (hon. 1992—), Soc. of Materials Sci. Japan (bd. dirs. 1971-74, 81-84, 85-88, Prize 1971), Japanese Soc. of Strength and Fracture of Materials (bd. dirs. 1984—), Sci. Coun. Japan (material rsch. liaison com. 1988-94), Engring. Acad. Japan. Avocations: oil painting, reading. Home: 8-10 Hyugacho, Takatsuki Osaka 569, Japan Office: Ritsumeikan Univ, 56-1 Tojiin Kitamachi, Kita-ku Kyoto 603-77, Japan

OHNISHI, STANLEY TSUYOSHI, biomedical director, biophysicist; b. Ohtsu City, Japan, Dec. 17, 1931; came to U.S., 1966; s. Teruhiko and Miyoko (Tomoda) O.; m. Tomoko Kirita, Mar. 25, 1958; children: Hiroshi, Noriko. MS in Chemistry, Kyoto (Japan) U., 1956; PhD in Biophysics, Nagoya (Japan) U., 1959. Rsch. prof. dept. hemtology Hahnemann U., Phila., 1984, rsch. prof. dept. biochemistry, 1984; dir. Membrane Rsch. Inst., Phila., 1989—; dir. developing chomotherapeutic drugs Phila. Biomed Rsch. Inst., King of Prussia, Pa., 1989—. Editor: Experimental Techniques in Biomembranes, 1967, Mechanisms Gated Calcium Transport, 1981, Cellular Membranes, 1993, Membrane Abnormalities in Sickle Cell Disease, 1994, Malignant Hyperthermia, 1994, Central Nervous System Trauma, 1995, 2 others; contbr. 150 articles to Biochem. Biophys. Pharmacology. Buddhist. Achievements include 5 patents in field. Office: Phila Biomed Rsch Inst 100 Ross and Royal Rd King of Prussia PA 19406-2110

OHNO, SUSUMU, research scientist; b. Seoul, Korea, Feb. 1, 1928; came to U.S., 1953; s. Kenichi and Toshiko (Saito) O.; m. Midori Aoyama, Jan. 7, 1951; children: Azusa, Yukali, Takeshi. DVM, Tokyo U. Agr. and Tech., 1949; PhD, Hokkaido U., 1956, DSc, 1961; DSc, U. Pa., 1984; HHD (hon.), Kwansei Gakuin U., 1983. Rsch. staff pathology Tokyo U., 1950-53; rsch. assoc. City of Hope, Duarte, Calif., 1953-66, chmn. biology, 1966-81, disting. scientist, 1981-95, emeritus, 1996—; vis. prof. Albert Einstein Med. Sch., Bronx, N.Y., 1969, Basel Inst. for Immunology, Switzerland, 1976, Nat. Inst. Genetics of Japan, 1997; prof. at large Tohoku U., Japan, 1987—; bd. dirs. Beckman Rsch. Inst., Duarte, Calif. Author monographs. Recipient Kihara prize Genetic Soc. Japan, Tokyo, 1983. Fellow AAAS (Amory prize 1981); mem. NAS, Royal Danish Acad. Scis. and Letters (fgn.). Avocations: horsemanship, dressage, fishing, musical transformation of gene DNA sequences. Office: Beckman Rsch Inst City of Hope 1450 Duarte Rd Duarte CA 91010-3011

O'HOLLAREN, PAUL JOSEPH, former international fraternity administrator; b. Portland, Oreg., Dec. 24, 1927; s. Charles Edward and Helen Henrietta (McHugh) O'H.; m. Patricia Marie Foley, June 27, 1953; children: Mark T., Kevin J., Brian T., Patrick S., Kelly P. JD, Northwestern Coll. of Law, 1954. Bar: Oreg., 1954. Atty. Oreg. State Bar, 1954—; mem. supreme coun. Moose Internat., Inc., Mooseheart, Ill., 1968-79; supreme gov. Loyal Order of Moose, Mooseheart, Ill., 1978-79, dir. gen., 1984-94, retired, 1994; chmn. exec. bd. Moose Internat., Inc., 1994—. With U.S. Army, 1945-46. Named Jr. First Citizen, U.S. Jr. C. of C., Portland, 1959; recipient Oreg. State Bar award of Merit, 1979. Mem. Multnomah Athletic Club, Loyal Order of Moose. Republican. Roman Catholic. Avocation: golf. Office: 1850 Benjamin Franklin Plz 1 SW Columbia St Portland OR 97258-2002

O'HORGAN, THOMAS FOSTER, composer, director; b. Chgo., May 3, 1924. BA, MA, DePaul U. Chgo. Debut performance in Fallout; off-Broadway revue, 1959; directing debut with prodn. The Maids, 1964; dir.: Hair (Tony award nominee 1968), Lenny (Drama Desk award 1971), Jesus Christ Super Star, Inner City, Six from La Mama, The Hessian Corporal, Futz (Obie award 1967, Drama Desk award 1968), Tom Paine (Drama Desk award 1968), Massachusetts Trust, Dude, The Leaf People, Sergeant Pepper's Lonely Hearts Club Band on the Road, Capitol Cakewalk, 1990, The Architect and The Emperor of Abyssinia; composer: music for numerous prodns. including Open Season at Second City Senator Joe (also dir.), 1989, The Body Builder's Book of Love, 1990; music for films including Futz, 1969, Alex in Wonderland, 1970, Rhinocerous, 1974; performer in: film All Men Are Apes, 1965. Recipient Creative Arts award Brandeis U., 1968. Office: care Dirs Guild Am 110 W 57th St New York NY 10019-3319*

OHRENSTEIN, ROMAN ABRAHAM, economics educator, economist, rabbi; b. Slomniki, Poland, June 12, 1920; came to U.S., 1951, naturalized, 1957; s. Joseph Barukh and Gena (Fiefkopf) O.; m. Ruth Silberstein, Aug. 30, 1953; children: Gena Ann, Ilana Rose. M.A. in Econs., U. Munich, 1948, Ph.D. cum laude in Econs., 1949, postgrad. in medicine, 1949-51; M.H.L., Jewish Theol. Sem. Am., 1955; postgrad., Columbia U., 1963-64. Ordained rabbi, 1955. Rabbi Auburn, N.Y., 1955-57, Pittsfield, Mass., 1957-60, Atlanta, 1960-62, N.Y.C., 1962-66; prof. econs. Nassau Coll., SUNY-Garden City, 1964—, chmn. econs. dept., 1976-78, 82-84, campus chaplain, 1970—; chaplain Nassau County Civic Preparedness, N.Y., 1965—; prof. econs. Am. Coll. Jerusalem, 1968-73, mem. Coll. Council, 1967-73; vis. prof. U. Newcastle, Australia, 1985, vis. rsch. prof., 1989; past chaplain Kiwanis, Police Dept. Cayuga County, N.Y., 1955-57, Mt. Sinai Hosp., N.Y.C., 1963-64; nat. dir. Jewish Rights Council; mem. Council of Orgns., U.S.A., 1978-85; mem. spl. com. on Jewish law Rabbinical Assembly, 1971; condr. seminars U. Queensland, Sydney U., Nat. Univ., all Australia, 1989, Sorbonne, Paris, 1990; lectr., guest speaker on radio, TV, Jewish civic and profl. orgns. Author: (series) Economic Thought in Talmudic Literature, 1968, 70, 83, 86, 87, 89, 91-93, 96, Inventories During Business Fluctuations, 1973, Inventory Control as an Economic Shock Absorber, 1975, Economic Analysis in Talmudic Literature, 1992; mem. editl. adv. bd. Internat. Rev. Econs. and Ethics; contbr. articles to profl. jours. Mem. nat. exec. comm. Am. Profs. for Peace in the Mid. East, 1971-73; mem. adv. bd. Am. Acad. Alliance for Israel, 1995—. Recipient 1st Faculty Disting. Achievement award Nassau Coll., SUNY, 1992, 95; SUNY fellow, 1968, 70. Mem. Nat. Assn. Jewish Chaplains, Rabbinical Assembly N.Y. Bd. Rabbis, Am. Econ. Assn., History of Econs. Soc., Assn. Social Econs., Learned Soc., N.Y. Acad. Scis., Internat. Soc. for Intercommunication New Ideas, Literati Club (Eng.). Home: 28-74 208th St Bayside NY 11360-2421 Office: Nassau Coll Dept Econ Stewart Ave Garden City NY 11530 *I kept my faith in God coupled with loyalty to tradition, sharpened my mind while maintaining discipline of the heart; tenacity in the face of adversity, turning stumbling blocks into stepping stones while never losing sight of life's supreme purpose: to leave the world a little better than I found it.*

OHRN, NILS YNGVE, chemistry and physics educator; b. Avesta, Sweden, June 11, 1934; came to U.S., 1966; s. Nils E. and Gerda M. (Akerlund) O.; m. Ann M.M. Thorsell, Aug. 24, 1957; children: Elisabeth, Maria. M.S., Uppsala U., 1958, Ph.D., 1963, F.D., 1966. Research assoc. Uppsala (Sweden) U., 1963-66; assoc. prof. U. Fla., Gainesville, 1966-70, prof. chemistry and physics, 1971—, assoc. dir. Quantum Theory Project, 1976-77, dir. Quantum Theory Project, 1983—, chmn. dept. chemistry, 1977-83. Editor: Internat. Jour. Quantum Chemistry, 1970—. Fulbright grantee Com. for Internat. Exchange of Scholars, Washington, 1961-63; recipient Bicentennial Gold medal King of Sweden, 1980; Fla. Acad. Scis. medal, 1984. Fellow Am. Phys. Soc., Chaire Francqui Interuniversitaires Belgium; mem. Am. Chem. Soc. (Fla. award 1997), Royal Acad. Scis. Sweden (fgn.), Finnish Acad. Scis. (fgn.), Royal Danish Acad. Scis. (fgn.), Sigma Xi, Phi Beta Kappa. Home: 1823 NW 11th Rd Gainesville FL 32605-5323 Office: U Fla Quantum Theory Project 362 Williamson Hall Gainesville FL 32611-2085

OHSOL, ERNEST OSBORNE, consulting chemical engineer; b. Washington, May 28, 1916; s. Johann Gottfried and Klara Elizabeth (Karpowitz) O.; m. Mary Rosamond Montgomery, June 15, 1940 (div. Jan. 4, 1977); children: Frederick M., Richard B., Barbara Alison Allen, Elizabeth Anne Gustafson; m. Barbara I. Handy, Mar. 24, 1977. Student, Fed. Polytech. Inst., Zurich, Switzerland, 1934-35; B.S., Coll. City N.Y., 1936; Sc.D., Mass. Inst. Tech., 1939. Registered profl. engr., N.J. Devel. engr. Standard Oil Devel. Co., Linden, N.J., 1939-50; mgr. process devel. chem. div. Gen. Elec. Co., Pittsfield, Mass., 1950-52; dir. research and devel. Pitts. Coke and Chem. Co., 1953-60; v.p. Haveg Industries, Inc. (plastics), Wilmington, Del., 1960-65, Chem. Constrn. Corp., N.Y.C., 1965-67, Escambia Chem. Co., N.Y.C., 1967; dir. chem. engring. dept. Am. Cyanamid Co. (central research div.), Stamford, Conn., 1967-72; cons. chem. engr. Plainfield, N.J., 1973; chief process engr. Eastern group Jacobs Engring. Co., Mountainside, N.J., 1973-75; corp. mgr. European fluid processing Selas Corp. Am., Munich, W. Ger., 1975-78; coordinator C.H. Dexter div. Dexter Corp., Windsor Locks, Conn., 1978-80; cons. Scallop Corp., Houston, Shell Nigerian Oil Co., Aramco, Tek-Rap, Petromin Shell, EnviroKinetics; chmn. emeritus Unipure Corp., 1993—; adj. prof. Grad. Sch., Stevens Inst. Tech., 1946-50. Patentee in field. Naumburg fellow CCNY, 1934-35; Arthur D. Little fellow Mass. Inst. Tech., 1937-38. Fellow Am. Inst. Chem. Engrs. (dir. 1973); mem. Am. Chem. Soc., Chemists Club N.Y.C., Sigma Xi. Episcopalian (vestryman 1963-65). Home and Office: 711 Hyannis Port North Crosby TX 77532-5515

OIKAWA, HIROSHI, materials science educator; b. Sakhalin, Japan, Oct. 15, 1933; s. Torao and Tomi (Kumagai) O.; m. Ayako Otomo, May 4, 1963; children: Makoto, Junko. BE, Tohoku U., Sendai, Japan, 1956, ME, 1958, D in Engring., 1961. Instr. Tohoku U., Sendai, 1961-63, lectr., 1963-64, assoc. prof., 1964-82; rsch. fellow U. Fla., Gainesville, 1966-68; prof. Tohoku U., Sendai, 1982-97, councilor, 1993-95, dean faculty engring., 1995-97; prof. emeritus Tohuku U., Sendai, 1997—; prof. Nat. Instn. for Acad. Degrees, Yokohama, 1997—, Nat. Instn. Acad. Degrees, Yokohama, Japan, 1997—. Co-editor: Metals Handbooks, 1990, Metals Databook, 1993. Mem. Engring. Acad. of Japan, Japan Inst. Metals (bd. dirs. 1992-94, 96—, bd. dirs. Tohoku chpt. 1991-93, pres. 1996-97), Iron and Steel Inst. of Japan (bd. dirs. 1990-92), Japan Inst. Light Metals (bd. dirs. 1989-95), Minerals, Metals and Materials Soc., ASM Internat., Inst. Materials. Office: Nat Instn Acad Degrees, 4529 Nagatsuda Midori-ku, Yokohama 226, Japan

OJALVO, MORRIS, civil engineer, educator; b. N.Y.C., Mar. 4, 1924; s. Nissim and (Fanny) O.; m. Anita Bedein, Dec. 26, 1948; children—Lynne, Joseph, Howard, Isobel. B.C.E., Rensselaer Poly. Inst., Troy, N.Y., 1944, M.C.E., 1952; Ph.D., Lehigh U., Bethlehem, Pa., 1960; J.D., Ohio State U., Columbus, 1978. Bar: Ohio bar 1979. Draftsman Am. Bridge Co., Elmira, N.Y., 1946-47; tutor civil engring. CCNY, 1947-49; instr. Rensselaer Poly. Inst., 1949-51; asst. prof. Princeton U., 1951-58; research instr. Lehigh U., 1958-60; mem. faculty Ohio State U., 1960—, prof. civil engring., 1964-82, prof. emeritus, 1982—; vis. prof. U. Tex.-Austin, 1982-83. Author: Thin-Walled Bars With Open Profiles, 1990; contbr. papers in field. Served with USNR, 1944-46. Mem. ASCE, Structural Stability Research Council. Patentee warp restraining device. Home and Office: 1024 Fairway Ln Estes Park CO 80517

OJIMA, IWAO, chemistry educator; b. Yokohama, Japan, June 5, 1945; came to U.S., 1983; s. Masaharu and Sumiko (Takatsuki) O.; m. Yoko Ogino, Apr. 24, 1971. BS, U. Tokyo, 1968, MS, 1970, PhD in Organic Chemistry, 1973. Rsch. fellow Sagami Inst. for Chem. Rsch., Japan, 1970-76, sr. rsch. fellow, group leader, 1976-83; assoc. prof. chemistry SUNY, Stony Brook, 1983-84, prof., 1984-91, leading prof., 1991-95, disting. prof., 1995—; lectr. Tokyo Inst. Tech., 1978-79, 83, Tokyo U. Agr. and Tech., 1983; prin. investigator NSF, 1983—, N.Y. Sci. Tech. Found., 1985—, NIH, 1986—, ACS prof. 1987—; vis. prof. U. Claude Bernard I, Lyon, France, 1989, U. Tokyo, 1996, Scripps Rsch. Inst., 1997; mem. adv. com., NIH, 1988—, NSF, 1992, Dept. Energy, 1992; mem. editl. adv. bd. Elsevier Pubs., Lausanne, Switzerland, 1986-95; cons. Nippon Steel Corp., Yokohama, 1989—, Rhone-Poulenc Rorer, Vitry, France, 1991—, Ajinomoto Co., Inc., Kawasaki, 1995—. Editor: Catalytic Asymmetric Synthesis, 1993, Taxane Anticancer Agents, 1994; contbr. numerous articles to profl. jours.; numerous patents in field. Named fellow J.S. Guggenheim Meml. Found., 1995-97. Mem. AAAS, Am. Chem. Soc. (editl. adv. bd. 1995—, A.C. Cope Scholar award 1994), Chem. Soc. Japan (Nat. Young Investigator award 1976), N.Y. Acad. Scis., Sigma Xi. Achievements include research in homogenous catalysis of transition metal complexes; asymmetric synthesis; organic synthesis by means of organometallic reagents; peptides and peptide mimetics; beta-lactam chemistry; organo flourine chemistry, medicinal chemistry especially in regard to enzyme inhibitors and taxane anticancer agents. Home: 6 Ivy League Ln Stony Brook NY 11790 Office: State U New York Dept Chemistry Stony Brook NY 11794-3400

OKA, TAKESHI, physicist, chemist, astronomer, educator; b. Tokyo, June 10, 1932; arrived in Can., 1963, naturalized, 1973; s. Shumpei and Chiyoko O.; m. Keiko Nukui, Oct. 24, 1960; children: Ritsuko, Noriko, Kentaro, Yujiro. B.Sc., U. Tokyo, 1955, Ph.D., 1960. Research asso. U. Tokyo, 1960-63; fellow NRC Can., Ottawa, Ont., 1963-65; asst. NRC Can., 1965-68, asso., 1968-71, sr. research physicist, 1971-80; prof. U. Chgo., 1981—; Robert A. Millikan disting. prof., 1989—; prof. Enrico Fermi inst., 1993—. Mem. editorial bd. Chem. Physics, 1972—, Jour. Molecular Spectroscopy, 1973—, Jour. Chem. Physics, 1975-77. Recipient Steacie prize, 1972; Earle K. Plyler prize, 1982, William F. Meggers award, 1997. Fellow Royal Soc. Can., Royal Soc. London, Am. Phys. Soc., Optical Soc. Am., Am. Acad. Scis. and Arts; mem. Am. Astron. Soc. Office: U Chgo Dept Chemistry Astronomy & Astrophysics Chicago IL 60637

OKADA, RONALD MASAKI, insurance agent; b. Tokyo, Oct. 23, 1941; s. Robert M. Okada and Betty (Nakai) Chung; m. Barbara Moo Ching Lau, May 1, 1971; 1 child, Evie Michi. BBA, U. Hawaii, 1964. CLU; ChFC; CFP, Coll. for Fin. Planning. Ops. supr. Cen. Pacific Bank, Honolulu, 1964-68; mgmt. trainee Bank of Hawaii, Honolulu, 1968-70; life ins. agt. Conn. Mut. Life, Honolulu, 1970-96, Mass. Mutual, Honolulu, 1996—. Chmn. bd. dirs. Hawaii Bapt. Found., Honolulu, 1993—; exec. bd. dirs. Hawaii Bapt. Conv., Honolulu, 1977-80; deacon, tchrs., various coms., Sunday Sch. dir. Mililani Bapt. Ch., Mililani Town, Hawaii, 1975—. Mem. Hawaii State Assn. Life Underwriters (pres. 1994-95, Life Ins. Profl. of Yr. runner-up 1984), Nat. Assn. Life Underwriters (nat. sales achievement award, nat. quality award, Million Dollar Round Table), Am. Soc. CLU's and ChFC's (com. chmn. 1984-87, 91-92), West Honolulu Assn. Life Underwriters (bd. dirs. 1982-87), Hawaii Estate Planning Coun., Assn. Health Ins. Agts. Office: MassMutual City Financial Tower 201 Merchant St Ste 2200 Honolulu HI 96813-2929

OKADA, RYOZO, medical educator, clinician and researcher; b. Kiryu, Gummaken, Japan, July 20, 1931; s. Kenji and Sachi (Ishihara) O.; m. Shigeko Shindo, May 25, 1958; children: Kyoko, Taro. MD, Tokyo U., 1956, PhD, 1961. Intern then resident; asst. Sch. Med. Tokyo U., 1962-63; research fellow Hektoen Inst. Cook County Hosp., Chgo., 1963-66; attending physician Yoikuin Hosp., Tokyo, 1966-68; assoc. prof. Sch. Med. Juntendo U., Tokyo, 1968-83, prof., 1983-97, dir. cardiovascular lab., 1985-97, prof. emeritus, 1997—; rector Gumma PAS Coll. of Nursing Sci., Japan; cons. Migita Hosp., Tokyo, 1968—; councilor Cardiovascular Inst. Roppongi, Tokyo, 1990—, Indsl. Medicine Found., 1995—. Contbr. articles to med. jours. and books. Active group study specific intractable diseases Met. Office of Tokyo, 1972—, congenital heart disease Ministry of Health and Welfare, Japan, 1974—, occupational diseases Ministry of Labor, Japan, 1987—; bd. dirs. Shirane Kaizen Sch., Gumma, Japan. Fellow Am. Geriatrics Soc., Cardiac Pathology, Internat. Electrocardiology, Internat. Union Angiology, Coun. Prevention Heart Disease, Japanese Coll. Cardiology, Japanese Angiology Soc., Japanese Geriatrics Soc.; mem. Japanese Soc. Medicine. Avocation: travel. Home: 53 Asahigaoka, Kanagawa-ku, Yokohama 221, Japan

OKADA, TAKUYA, retail executive; b. Sept. 19, 1925; m. Yasuko Okada; children: Motoya, Katsuya, Masaya. BA, Waseda U., Japan, 1948. Pres. Jusco (USA), Inc., Tokyo; founder, chmn., CEO JUSCO Co. Ltd., Tokyo; chmn. Talbots, pres. JUSCO (U.S.); bd. dirs. Laura Ashley Holdings, Plc, U.K.; chmn. Japan Shopping Ctrs. Assn., 1995—, Japan Retailers Assn., 1995—. Vice chmn. Tokyo C. of C., 1987—, spl. advisor Japanese C. of C., 1987—; exec. dir. Fedn. Ecol. Orgns. (Keidanren), 1979; chmn. AEON Group Environs. Found., Okada Found. for Promotion of Hometown, Culture Found. Okada; bd. dirs. N.Y.C. Ballet. Recipient Blue ribbon decoration 1985, Japanese Prime Minister commendation 1986, Internat. medal Nat. Retail Fedn., 1985; named Hon. Comdr. Order Brit. Empire, 1989. Mem. Japan Shopping Ctrs. Assn. (chmn. 1995—), Japan Retailers Assn. (chmn. 1995—), Tokyo C. of C. and Industry (vice chmn. 1987—), Japanese C. of C. (spl. adv. 1986—), Fedn. of Ecol. Orgn. (Keidanren) (exec. dir. 1979).

OKAMURA, ARTHUR, artist, educator, writer; b. Long Beach, Calif., Feb. 24, 1932; s. Frank Akira and Yuki O.; m. Elizabeth Tuomi, Aug. 7, 1953

(div.); children: Beth, Jonathan, Jane, Ethan; m. Kitty Wong, 1991. Student, Art Inst. of Chgo., 1950-54, U. Chgo., 1951, 52, 57, art seminar Yale, 1954. Faculty Central YMCA Coll., Chgo., 1956, 57, Evanston Art Center, 1956-57, Art Inst. Chgo., North Shore Art League, Winnetka, Ill., Acad. Art, San Francisco, 1957, Calif. Sch. Fine Arts, 1958, Ox Bow Summer Art Sch., Saugatuck, Mich.; faculty Calif. Coll. Arts and Crafts, 1958-59, prof. arts, 1966—; instr. watercolor painting, 1987; dir. San Francisco Studio Art, 1958; tchr. watercolor workshops, Bali, Indonesia, 1989, 92; lectr. in field. Author: (with Robert Creeley) 1, 2, 3, 4, 5, 6, 7, 8, 9, 0, 1971, (with Joel Weishaus) Ox-Herding, 1971, (with Robert Bly) Basho, 1972, Ten Poems by Issa, 1992, (with Steve Kowit) Passionate Journey, 1984, Magic Rabbit, 1995; one-man shows include Charles Feingarten Galleries, Chgo., 1956, 58, 59, San Francisco, 1957, Santa Barbara Mus. Art, 1958, Oakland Mus. Art, 1959, Legion Honor, San Francisco, 1961, Dallas, 1962, La Jolla (Calif.) Mus., 1963, U. Utah, 1964, San Francisco Mus. Art, 1968, Hanssen Gallery, 1968, 71, Ruth Braunstein, San Francisco, 1981, 82, 84, 86-88, 90, 94; exhibited in group shows including Pa. Acad. Fine Art, U. Chgo., U. Wash., U. Ill., Art Inst. Chgo., L.A. County Mus., Am. Fedn. Art, Denver Mus., NAD, De Young Mus., San Francisco, Knoedler Gallery, N.Y.C., Feingarten Galleries, Whitney Mus. Art, others; retrospective at Bolinas Mus. and Claudia Chapline Galleries, Stinson Beach, Calif., 1995; represented in permanent collections including Art Inst. Chgo., Borg-Warner Collections, Chgo., Whitney Mus. Art, N.Y.C., Santa Barbara Mus. Art, San Francisco Mus. Art, Ill. State Normal, Corcoran Mus., Nat. Collection Fine Arts, Smithsonian Instn., 1968, many others. Served as pvt. AUS, 1955-56. Recipient 1st prize religious art U. Chgo., 1953; Ryerson travelling fellow, 1954; Martin Cahn award contemporary Am. paintings Art Inst. Chgo., 1957; purchase award U. Ill., 1959; purchase award Nat. Soc. Arts and Letters, N.Y.C., 1960; Neysa McMein purchase award Whitney Mus. Art, 1960; Schwabacher-Frey award 79th Ann. of San Francisco Mus. Art, 1960. Mem. Commonweal (bd. dirs. 1993-94). Home: 210 Kale Rd Bolinas CA 94924 Office: Calif Coll Arts and Crafts 5212 Broadway Oakland CA 94618-1426

OKAY, JOHN LOUIS, telecommunications executive; b. Emmett, Mich., Mar. 27, 1942; s. Stanley John and Mildred Isabell (Little) O.; m. Judith Ann Gerlach, Aug. 22, 1964; children: Stephen, Christopher, Douglas. BS in Agr., Mich. State U., 1964, MS in Agrl. Econs., 1967, PhD in Resource Econs., 1974. Agrl. economist U.S. Soil Conservation Svc., East Lansing, Mich., 1967-73; program analyst U.S. Soil Conservation Svc., Washington, Mich., 1974-83; dir. info. systems U.S. Soil Conservation Svc., Washington, 1983-85; assoc. dir. info. systems USDA, Washington, 1985-91, dir. info. systems, 1991-95; dep. commr. Fed. Telecom. Svc., GSA, Falls Church, Va., 1995—. Recipient Meritorious Exec. award Pres. of U.S., 1989. Mem. Armed Forces Comms. and Electronics Assn. (bd. dirs. 1994—), Sr. Execs. Assn. (bd. dirs. 1989—, vice chair 1994—). Office: Fed Telecom Svc GSA 7799 Leesburg Pike Ste 210 Falls Church VA 22043-2413

OKE, JOHN BEVERLEY, astronomy educator; b. Sault Ste. Marie, Ont., Can., Mar. 23, 1928; s. Charles Clare and Lyla Jane (Partushek) O.; m. Nancy Sparling, Aug. 20, 1955; children—Christopher, Kevin, Jennifer, Valerie. B.A., U. Toronto, 1949, M.A., 1950; Ph.D., Princeton U., 1953. Lectr. U. Toronto, 1953-55, asst. prof., 1955-58; asst. prof. Calif. Inst. Tech., Pasadena, 1958-61, assoc. prof., 1961-64, prof., 1964-92; assoc. dir. Hale Observatories, 1970-78; vis. Dominion Astrophysical Observatory, 1992—. Mem. Astron. Soc. of the Pacific, Am. Astronomical Soc. (councillor 1969-72), Internat. Astronomical Union. Office: Dominion Astrophysical Obs, 5071 W Saanich Rd, Victoria, BC Canada V8X 4M6

O'KEEFE, EDWARD FRANKLIN, lawyer; b. S.I., N.Y., June 9, 1937; s. Francis Franklin and Bertha (Hall) O'K.; m. Toni Lynne McGohan; children: Kira Kathleen, Douglas Franklin, Andrew Franklin, Alison Elizabeth, Theadore William, Nigel Francis. A.B., U. N.C., 1959; J.D., U. Denver, 1961. Bar: Colo. 1962. Law clk. Colo. Supreme Ct., Denver, 1962-63; assoc. gen. counsel Hamilton Mgmt. Corp., Denver, 1966-69; sec. Hamilton Mgmt. Corp., 1968-76, v.p. legal, gen. counsel, 1969-76; now mng. ptnr. Moye, Giles O'Keefe, Vermeire & Gorrell, Denver; assoc. gen. counsel, sec. ITT Variable Annuity Ins. Co., Denver, 1969, v.p. legal, gen. counsel, 1969-70; sec. Hamilton Funds Inc., Denver, 1968-76. Served with USNR, 1963-66. Mem. Nat. Assn. Security Dealers (dist. conduct com., chmn. 1976), Colo. Assn. Corporate Counsel (pres. 1974-75). Home: 6300 Montview Blvd Denver CO 80207-3947 Office: Moye Giles O'Keefe Vermeire 1225 17th St Fl 29 Denver CO 80202-5534

O'KEEFE, GERALD FRANCIS, bishop, retired; b. St. Paul, Mar. 30, 1918; s. Francis Patrick and Lucille Mary (McDonald) O'K. Student, St. Paul Sem., 1938-44; B.A., Coll. St. Thomas, 1945; LLD (hon.), St. Ambrose Coll., 1967, Loras Coll., 1967; LHD, Marycrest Coll., 1967. Ordained priest Roman Cath. Ch., 1944. Asst. St. Paul Cathedral, 1944, rector, 1961-67; chancellor Archdiocese of St. Paul, 1945-61, aux. bishop, 1961-67, vicar gen., 1962-67; bishop Diocese of Davenport, Iowa, 1967-93; ret., 1993; instr. St. Thomas Acad., St. Paul, 1944-45. Home: 2706 Gaines St Davenport IA 52804-1914

O'KEEFE, JOHN DAVID, investment specialist; b. N.Y.C., Nov. 16, 1941; s. Timothy J. and Agnes V. (Timlin) O.; m. Stefanie Carreau Keegan, Jan. 28, 1978; children: Douglas G., Hillary C., John M., Meredith B. BBA, Iona Coll., 1963; MBA, L.I. U., 1968. Analyst L.I. Lighting Co., Mineola, N.Y., 1965-69, Pershing and Co., N.Y.C., 1969-72; mng. dir. Kidder, Peabody and Co., Inc., N.Y.C., 1972-89; v.p. Smith Barney, N.Y.C., 1989-92. Bd. dirs. Heisman Found. Sgt. USMC, 1963-65. Mem. Securities Industry Assn. Republican. Club: Down Town Athletic (gov. 1986, 88, chmn. Heisman Trophy com. 1987, 88). Home: 31 Linden Tree Rd Wilton CT 06897-1613 Office: Smith Barney 1 Village Sq Westport CT 06880-3211

O'KEEFE, KATHLEEN MARY, state government official; b. Butte, Mont., Mar. 25, 1933; d. Hugh I. and Kathleen Mary (Harris) O'Keefe; B.A. in Communications, St. Mary Coll., Xavier, Kans., 1954; m. Nick B. Baker, Sept. 18, 1954 (div. 1970); children—Patrick, Susan, Michael, Cynthia, Hugh, Mardeen. Profl. singer, mem. Kathie Baker Quartet, 1962-72; research cons. Wash. Ho. of Reps., Olympia, 1972-73; info. officer Wash. Employment Security Commn., Seattle, 1973-81, dir. public affairs, 1981-90, video dir., 1990-95, ret., 1995; freelance writer, composer, producer, 1973—. Founder, pres. bd. Eden, Inc., visual and performing arts, 1975—; public relations chmn. Nat. Women's Democratic Conv., Seattle, 1979, Wash. Dem. Women, 1976-85; bd. dirs., composer, prodr., dir. N.Y. Film Festival, 1979; Dem. candidate Wash. State Senate, 1968. Recipient Silver medal Seattle Creative Awards Show for composing, directing and producing Rent A Kid, TV pub. svc. spot, 1979. Mem. Wash. Press Women. Democrat. Roman Catholic. Author: Job Finding In the Nineties, The Third Alternative, handbook on TV prodn., (children) So You Want to be President, 1995; composer numerous songs, also writer, dir., producer Job Service spots, Immigration & Naturalization Svc. spots, U.S. Dept. Labor spots, Dept. VA spots. Home: 4426 147th Pl NE # 12 Bellevue WA 98007-3162

O'KEEFE, MICHAEL DANIEL, lawyer; b. St. Louis, Jan. 3, 1938; s. Daniel Michael and Hanoria (Moriarty) O'K.; m. Bonnie Bowdern, July 11, 1964; children: Collen Coyne, Daniel Michael. AB, St. Louis U., 1961, LLB, 1961; postgrad., George Washington U., 1963. Bar: Mo. 1961, U.S. Ct. Appeals (8th cir.) 1961, U.S. Dist. Ct. (ea. dist.) Mo. 1961, Ill. 1975, U.S. Dist. Ct. (so. dist.) Ill. 1975, U.S. Ct. Appeals (5th and 7th cirs.) 1983, (10th cir.) 1995. Asst. atty. U.S. Ct. Appeals, St. Louis, 1962-63, 64-65; pvt. practice St. Louis, 1964-67; ptnr. Lucas, Murphy & O'Keefe, St. Louis, 1967-74, Thompson & Mitchell, St. Louis, 1974-96; adj. prof. trial practice Sch. of Law, St. Louis U., 1992—. Editor: American Maritime Cases, 1985—. Active Port Commn., St. Louis; trustee St. Louis U. Capt. USAF, 1962-64. Fellow Am. Coll. Trial Lawyers; mem. Internat. Assn. Def. Counsel, Fedn. Ins. and Corp. Counsel, Maritime Law Assn., USAZ, Nat. Assn. Railroad Trial Counsel, Am. Law Inst. Democrat. Roman Catholic. Avocations: reading, tennis, fencing, archaeology, microbiology. Home: 372 Walton Row Saint Louis MO 63108-1909 Office: Thompson Coburn Ste 3300 1 Mercantile Ctr Saint Louis MO 63101-1643

O'KEEFE, ROBERT JAMES, retired banker; b. Boston, Dec. 30, 1926; s. James J. and Irene (Egan) O'K.; m. Mary U. Hughes, Oct. 12, 1951 (dec.); children—Mary F., Robert James; m. Simone A. Charbonneau, Apr. 3, 1976. A.B., Boston Coll., 1951; grad., Advanced Mgmt. Program, Harvard, 1968. Mem. staff Mass. Inst. Tech., Cambridge, 1951-55; cons. Arthur D. Little, Inc., Cambridge, 1955-58; with Chase Manhattan Bank, N.Y.C., 1958-79, v.p., 1964-69, sr. v.p., 1969-79; sr. v.p. Am. Security Bank, Washington, 1979-89; exec. v.p. MNC Info. Svcs., Balt., 1989-90, ret. Trustee Boston Coll., 1974-82, trustee assoc., 1982-86; mem. computer sci. and engrng. bd. Nat. Acad. Sci., 1971-73. Served with AUS, 1945-46. Recipient Alumni medal Boston Coll., 1970. Mem. Boston Coll. Alumni Assn. (pres. 1973-74), Country Club at Jacaranda West, Am. Legion, KC. Home: 944 S Doral Ln Venice FL 34293-3808

O'KEEFE, THOMAS JOSEPH, metallurgical engineer; b. St. Louis, Oct. 2, 1935; s. Thomas and Hazel (Howard) O'K.; m. Jane Gilmartin, Aug. 31, 1957; children—Thomas, Kathleen, Matthew, Daniel, Margaret, Robert. B.S., Mo. Sch. Mines, 1958; Ph.D., U. Mo., Rolla, 1965. Process control engr. Dow Metal Products Co., Madison, Ill., 1959-61; mem. faculty U. Mo., Rolla, 1965—, prof. metall. engring., 1972—, Curators prof. metall. engring., 1985-86, Curators Disting. prof., 1986—; rsch. technologist NASA, Houston, summer 1965; rsch. metall. engr. Ames (Iowa) Lab., 1966-67; rsch. metall. engr., cons. Cominco Ltd., Trail, B.C., Can., 1970-71. Recipient Alumni Merit award U. Mo., Rolla, 1971, Outstanding Tchg. award, 1979, Silver medal paper award AESF, 1994; Jefferson-Smurfit fellow, 1984-85; named Disting. Hydrometallurgy lectr. U. B.C., 1992. Mem. AIME (dir. 1976-77, 79-81, EMD lectr. 1991), Testing Materials Soc., The Metall. Soc., Sigma Xi, Alpha Sigma Mu, Tau Beta Pi, Phi Kappa Theta (dir. 1965-77, cert. commendation 1970, pres. citation 1986). Home: 905 Southview Dr Rolla MO 65401-4720 Office: Material Research Center Univ Mo Rolla MO 65401

O'KEEFE, THOMAS MICHAEL, foundation executive; b. St. Cloud, Minn., Mar. 25, 1940; s. Thomas William and Genevieve B. (McCormick) O'K.; m. Kathleen Marie Gnifkowski, Aug. 20, 1966; children: Steven Michael, Ann Catherine. Student, Marquette U., 1961-65, BS, 1965; MS in Nuclear Physics, U. Pitts., 1968; DHL, Hamline U., 1989. Dir. edn. planning HEW, Washington, 1969-70, dep. asst. sec., 1977-80; v.p. Carnegie Found. for Advancement of Teaching, Washington, 1980-83; pres. Consortium for Advancement Pvt. Higher Edn., Washington, 1983-89; exec. v.p. McKnight Found., Mpls., 1989—; dir. Washington internships in edn. George Washington U., 1970-73; dir. policy analysis and evaluation U. Ill., Chgo., 1973-74, assoc. v.p. acad. affairs, 1974-77; head U.S. del. to Orgn. Econ. Coop. and Devel., 1979, 80; mem. Carnegie Forum on Edn. and the Economy, 1985-88; mem. N.J. Commn. on Ind. Higher Edn., 1986-88; mem. task force on ind. higher edn. Edn. Commn. States, 1987-89; co-chair Program on Edn. in a Changing Soc., The Aspen Inst., 1987—. Contbg. editor and contbr. articles on fed. edn. programs, acad. policies and internships Change mag., 1985—; bd. dirs. Editl. Projects in Edn., 1984-93. Bd. dirs. The Edn. Resources Inst., Boston, 1987-94, Minn. Coun. on Founds., 1994—; trustee Buena Vista Coll., Storm Lake, Iowa, 1984-90; mem. Coun. on Fgn. Rels., 1995—; bd. regents U. Minn., 1996—. Mem. Minn. Club St. Paul, Mpls. Club. Democrat. Office: McKnight Found 121 S 8th St Ste 600 Minneapolis MN 55402-2825

O'KEEFE, VINCENT THOMAS, clergyman, educational administrator; b. Jersey City, Jan. 10, 1920; s. James and Sarah (Allen) O'K. A.B., Georgetown U., 1943; M.A., Woodstock Coll., 1945, Ph.L., 1944; Th.L., St. Albert de Louvain, Belgium, 1951; student, Muenster (Germany) U., 1951-52; S.T.D., Gregorian U., Rome, 1954. Ordained priest Roman Cath. Ch., 1950. Instr. Latin and math. Regis High Sch., N.Y.C., 1944-47; assoc. prof. fundamental theology Woodstock Coll., 1954-60; acad. v.p. Fordham U., Bronx, N.Y., 1960-62; exec. v.p. Fordham U., 1962-63, pres., 1963-65, rector Jesuit community, 1984-88; gen. asst. to superior gen. Soc. of Jesus, Rome, 1965-83; v.p. spl. projects Jesuit Conf. Soc. of Jesus, 1988-90; superior, writer provincial residence Soc. of Jesus, Bronx, 1990-94; superior Am. House, N.Y.C., 1994—; Mem. regents exams. and scholarship center N.Y. State Dept. Edn.; pres., dir., mem. exec. com. Council Higher Ednl. Instns. of N.Y.C. Author: The History and Meaning of Ex Attrito Fit Contritus, 1957; Contbr. articles to religious publs., also book reviews. Dir. N.Y. World's Fair, 1964-65; Corp. Bd. mgrs. New York Bot. Garden; dir., mem. bd. Center Intercultural Formation, Cuernavaca, Mexico; trustee Fordham U. Fellow Royal Soc. Encouragement Arts Mfrs. and Commerce (London); mem. Council Higher Edn. City N.Y., Religion Council Cath. Secondary Schs. Archdiocese of N.Y., Cath. Bibl. Assn., Cath. Theol. Assn. Am., Religion Ednl. Assn., NEA, Jesuit Ednl. Assn., Nat. Cath. Edn. Assn., Internat. Assn. Univs., Soc. Cath. Coll. Tchrs. Sacred Doctrine, Phi Beta Kappa. Office: 106 W 56th St New York NY 10019-3803

OKEH, SAMSON EWRUJE, psychiatric nurse; b. Abraka, Nigeria, Nov. 5, 1943; s. Ovaguono Okeh; m. Pauline Okeh, Dec., 1969; children: Helen, Sunday, Debra, Abraka, John, Amber. Diploma, Bapt. Sch. Nursing, Eku Sapele, Nigeria, 1967; BA, U. Ill., Chgo., 1979; MA in Pub. Admistrn., Northeastern Ill. U., 1981. RN, Ill., Md., Calif. Asst. head nurse Loretto Hosp., Chgo.; nursing supr. Greater Laurel (Md.) and Beltsville Hosp.; charge nurse, part time supr. South Wood Hosp., Chula Vista, Calif.; asst. nurse mgr. Cedars Sinai Med. Ctr., L.A., 1991—. Mem. L.A. World Affairs Coun., 1994—. Mem. United Nurses Assn. Calif., Nigerian Assn. San Diego (pres. 1990-91), URHOBO Assn. So. Calif. (pres. 1992-93), Acad. Polit. Sci., L.A. World Affairs Coun. Home: PO Box 48151 Los Angeles CA 90048-0151 Office: Cedars Sinai Med Ctr 8700 Beverly Blvd Los Angeles CA 90048-1804

O'KEHIE, COLLINS EMEKA, lawyer, consultant; b. Aba, Nigeria, Apr. 4, 1952; came to U.S., 1976; s. Simon A. and Elizabeth Jane (Oledibe) O.; m. Justina Amuche Nnadi, Aug. 6, 1983; children: Pamela, Collins Emeka Jr., Stanley, Charles. Assoc. in Bus., Ellsworth Coll., 1977; BS, U. Tex., Richardson, 1979; MBA, N. Tex. State U., 1981; JD, Tex. So. U., 1984. Bar: Tex. 1985, U.S. Ct. Appeals (5th cir.) 1986, U.S. Dist. Ct. (so. dist.) Tex. 1987, Internat. Ct. of Trade 1990, U.S. Ct. Appeals (fed. cir.) 1990, U.S. Supreme Ct. 1992. Ptnr. Gregg, O'Kehie & Cashin, Houston, 1985-90; prin. O'Kehie & Assocs., Houston, 1990—; legal cons. various cos. and law firms in Eng., France, Belgium, Holland, Nigeria, 1985—. Mem. ABA, Tex. Bar Assn., Tex. Trial Lawyers Assn, Coll. of State Bar Tex., Assn. Trial Lawyers Am., Internat. Bar Assn., MBA Execs. Assn., Chartered Ins. Inst. London, Internat. Bar Assn., Internat. Platform Assn., Phi Delta Phi. Roman Catholic. Avocations: tennis, jogging. Office: O'Kehie and Assocs 1300 Main St Ste 1930 Houston TX 77002-6814 *In my life I have found that one should use an opportunity to help less fortunate people and that the reward comes from sources other than the recipients.*

O'KELLEY, WILLIAM CLARK, federal judge; b. Atlanta, Jan. 2, 1930; s. Ezra Clark and Theo (Johnson) O'K.; m. Ernestine Allen, Mar. 28, 1953; children: Virginia Leigh O'Kelley Wood, William Clark Jr. AB, Emory U., 1951, LLB, 1953. Bar: Ga. 1952. Pvt. practice Atlanta, 1957-59; asst. U.S. atty. No. Dist. Ga., 1959-61; partner O'Kelley, Hopkins & Van Gerpen, Atlanta, 1961-70; U.S. dist. judge No. Dist. Ga., Atlanta, 1970—, chief judge, 1988-94; mem. com. on adminstrn. of criminal law Jud. Conf. U.S., 1979-82, exec. com., 1983-84, subcom. on jury trials in complex criminal cases, 1981-82, dist. judge rep. 11th cir., 1981-84, mem. adv. com. of fed. rules of criminal procedure, 1984-87; bd. dirs. Fed. Jud. Ctr., 1987-91, adv. com. history program, 1989-91, com. on orientation of newly appointed dist. judges, 1985-88; mem. Com. Jud. Resources, 1989-94; mem. Jud. Coun. 11th Cir., 1990-96, exec. com., 1990-96; mem. Fgn. Intelligence Surveillance Ct., 1980-87; mem. Alien Terrorist Removal Ct., 1996—; corp. sec., dir. Gwinnett Bank & Trust Co., Norcross, Ga., 1967-70. Mem. exec. com., gen. counsel Ga. Republican Com., 1968-70; mem. fin. com. Northwest Ga. Girl Scout Coun., 1958-70; trustee Emory U., 1991—. Served as 1st lt. USAF, 1953-57; capt. USAFR. Mem. Fed. Bar Assn., Ga. State Bar, Atlanta Bar Assn., Dist. Judges Assn. 5th Cir. (sec.-treas. 1976-77, v.p. 1977-78, pres. 1978-80), Lawyers Club Atlanta, Kiwanis (past pres.), Atlanta Athletic Club, Sigma Chi, Phi Delta Phi, Omicron Delta Kappa. Baptist. Home: 550 Ridgecrest Dr Norcross GA 30071-2158 Office: US Dist Ct 1942 US Courthouse 75 Spring St SW Atlanta GA 30303-3309

OKERLUND, ARLENE NAYLOR, university official; b. Emmitsburg, Md., Oct. 13, 1938; d. George Wilbur and Ruth Opal (Sensenbaugh) Naylor; m. Michael Dennis Okerlund, June 6, 1959 (div. Apr. 1983); 1 dau., Linda Susan. B.A., U. Md., 1960; Ph.D., U. Calif.-San Diego, 1969. Instr. sci. Mercy Hosp. Nursing Sch., Balt., 1959-63; prof. English San Jose State U., Calif., 1969-80, 94—, dean humanities and arts, 1980-86, acad. v.p., 1986-93; cons. Ednl. Testing Service, Berkeley, Calif., 1976-80. Editor: San Jose Studies, 1975-80; contbr. articles on the humanities to profl. jours. Bd. dirs. World Forum Silicon Valley, Am. Beethoven Soc. Grantee NEH, 1979; grantee San Jose State U., 1971-72. Mem. Philol. Assn. Pacific Coast (sec.-treas. 1975-78), MLA (del. to assembly, west coast rep. 1976-77), Internat. Coun. Fine Arts Deans, Calif. Coun. Fine Arts Deans (pres. 1984-86), Am. Beethoven Soc. (bd. dirs.). Democrat. Office: San Jose State U Dept English Washington Sq San Jose CA 95192

OKEZIE, B. ONUMA, food scientist, nutritionist, educator; b. Obizi, Imo, Nigeria, Mar. 31, 1936; came to U.S., 1962; s. Chief Anyanwu and Lolo Ihuoma (Ogbediya) O.; m. Monique Chika Offurum, Sept. 4, 1971; children: Uchechi, Okezie II, Ihuoma, Oluchi. BS, U. Calif., Davis, 1966, MS, 1966; PhD, Cornell U., 1975. Cert. nutrition specialist. Sci. officer Ministry of Animal Health, Enugu, Biafra, 1967-68; advisor on nutrition Rehab. Commn., Okigwe, Biafra, 1968-70; rsch. fellow U. Ife, Ile-Ife, Nigeria, 1970; exec. advisor on nutrition Internat. Union for Child Welfare, Geneva, 1970-71; teaching and rsch. asst. Cornell U., Ithaca, N.Y., 1971-74; rsch. assoc., 1974; asst. prof. Howard U., Washington, 1975; assoc. prof. food sci. & nutrition Ala. A&M U., Huntsville, 1975-82, prof., 1982—, dir. internat. programs, 1979—; spl. asst. to pres. Ala. A&M U., 1988-90; trustee S.E. Cons. for Internat. Devel., Washington, 1980—, vice chair bd. trustees, 1992-93, chair-elect, 1993-94, chair, 1995-96; bd. dirs. USAID-Peanut-Collaborative Rsch. Support Program, Washington, 1982—, chair-elect, 1994, chair, 1995-97; bd. dirs. Peanut Collaborative Rsch. Support Program; chair Assn. Dirs. Internat. Agr. Progs. 1992-96; pres. Aries Enterprises, Inc., Huntsville, 1983—; disting. lectr. Berger Found. Cornell U., Ithaca, N.Y., 1993. Author: International Dimensions in Human Ecology, 1975, Effective Participation in Technical Assistance Programs, 1982; contbr. articles to profl. jours. NSF fellow, 1959-60, U.S. AID sci. fellow, 1962-66. Fellow Am. Coll. Nutrition; mem. Am. Dietetic Assn., Am. Coll. Nutrition, Inst. Food Technologists (chair-elect internat. divsn., 1991-92, chair 1992-93, div. com. chair of two coms., 1990-93, mem. IFT awards com., 1993-95), Assn. Nigerians in North Ala. (pres. 1994-96), Am. Assn. Cereal Chemists, Am. Chem. Soc., So. Assn. Agr. Scientists, Ala. Acad. Sci., Ala. Coun. for Internat. Programs (exec. com.), Assn. Internat. Edn. Adminstrn., North Ala. Internat. Trade Assn., Huntsville C. of C. (small bus. com. 1985-87), Alpha Zeta, Phi Tau Sigma, Phi Beta Delta. Avocations: tennis, jogging, photography. Home: 561 Hurricane Rd New Market AL 35761-8204 Office: Ala A&M U Office of Internat Programs Normal AL 35762

OKHAMAFE, IMAFEDIA, English literature and philosophy educator; b. Otuo, Nigeria; s. Obokhe and Olayemi (Bello) O. Double PhD, Purdue U., 1984. Prof. philosophy and English U. Nebr., Omaha, 1993—. Office: U Nebr Annex 39 Omaha NE 68182-0208 also: U Nebr Philosophy Dept. Omaha NE 68182-0265

OKI, BRIAN MASAO, software engineer; b. Inglewood, Calif., Oct. 17, 1958; s. Masao and Chiyoe (Yata) O. BS summa cum laude, U. Calif., Irvine, 1980; MS, MIT, 1983, PhD, 1988. Mem. rsch. staff Xerox Palo Alto (Calif.) Rsch. Ctr., 1988-92; sr. mem. tech. staff Teknekron Software Systems, Inc., Palo Alto, 1992-94; sr. tech. staff Oracle Corp., Redwood Shores, Calif., 1994-96; staff engineer, software Sun Microsystems, Inc., Menlo Park, Calif., 1996—. Mem. IEEE, Assn. Computing Machinery, Phi Beta Kappa, Sigma Xi. Avocations: competitive ballroom dancing, golf. Home: 493 Mill River Ln San Jose CA 95134-2420 Office: Sun Soft Inc 2550 Garcia Ave Mountain View CA 94043-1109

OKIISHI, THEODORE HISAO, mechanical engineering educator; b. Honolulu, Jan. 15, 1939; s. Clifford Muneo and Dorothy Asako (Tokushima) O.; m. Rae Wiemers, May 28, 1963; children: Christopher Gene, John Clifford, Mark William, Kenneth Edward. Student, U. Hawaii, 1956-57; BS, Iowa State U., 1960, MS, 1963, PhD, 1965. Registered profl. engr., Iowa, Ohio. From asst. prof. to assoc. dean coll. engring. Iowa State U., Ames, 1967—; cons. on fluid dynamics. Contbr. articles to profl. jours. Served to capt. C.E., U.S. Army, 1965-67. Decorated Joint Services Commendation award; named Outstanding Prof., Iowa State U. student sect. ASME, 1983, Mech. Engring. Dept. Prof. of Yr., Iowa State U., 1977, 86, 90; recipient award for research NASA, 1975; Ralph R. Teetor award Soc. Automotive Engrs., 1976, Engring. Coll. Superior Teaching award Iowa State U., 1987, Cardinal Key Iowa State U., 1991. Fellow ASME (Melville medal 1989); mem. AIAA, Sigma Xi. Republican. Mem. Ch. of Jesus Christ of Latter-day Saints. Club: Osborn Research. Home: 2940 Monroe Dr Ames IA 50010-4362 Office: Iowa State U 104 Marston Hall Ames IA 50011

OKINAGA, LAWRENCE SHOJI, lawyer; b. Honolulu, July 7, 1941; s. Shohei and Hatsu (Kakimoto) O.; m. Carolyn Hisako Uesugi, Nov. 26, 1966; children: Carrie, Caryn, Laurie. BA, U. Hawaii, 1963; JD, Georgetown U., 1972. Bar: Hawaii 1972, U.S. Dist. Ct. Hawaii 1972, U.S. Ct. Appeals (9th cir.) 1976. Administrv. asst. to Congressman Spark Matsunaga, Honolulu, 1964, 1965-69; law clk. to chief judge U.S. Dist. Ct. Hawaii, Honolulu, 1972-73; assoc. Carlsmith, Ball, Wichman Murray and Ichiki, Honolulu, 1973-76, ptnr., 1976—; mem. Gov.'s Citizens Adv. Com. Coastal Zone Mgmt., 1974-79; sec. Hawaii Bicentennial Corp., 1975-77, chmn., 1985-87; vice chmn., mem. Jud. Selection Commn., State of Hawaii, 1979-87, vice chmn., 1986; mem. consumer adv. coun. Fed. Res. Bd., 1984-86; chmn. State of Hawaii Judicial Conduct Commn., 1991-94; apptd. mem. Fed. Savings and Loan Adv. Council, Washington, 1988-89; mem. nat. adv. coun. U.S. Small Bus. Adminstrn., 1994—; mem. adv. coun. on small bus. and agr. Fed. Reserve Bank of San Francisco, 1995—. Bd. dirs. Moiliili Community Ctr., Honolulu, 1965-68, 1973-86; bd. visitors Georgetown U. Law Ctr., 1993—; trustee Kuakini Med. Ctr., 1984-88, 89-96. Served to capt. USAFR, 1964-72, 1974-76. Mem. ABA (house of delegates 1991-94, mem. standing com. on judicial selection tenure and compensation, 1993-96), Hawaii Bar Assn. (sec., bd. dirs. 1981), Am. Judicature Soc. (v.p. 1990-92, bd. dirs. 1986—, sec. 1993-95, treas. 1995—), Georgetown U. Law Alumni Assn. (bd. dirs. 1986-91), Omicron Delta Kappa. Office: Carlsmith Ball Wichman Case & Ichiki PO Box 656 Honolulu HI 96809-0656

OKITA, GEORGE TORAO, pharmacologist educator; b. Seattle, Jan. 18, 1922; s. Kazuo and Fusao (Muguruma) O.; m. Fujiko Shimizu, Nov. 29, 1958; children: Ronald Hajime, Sharon Mariko, Glenn Torao. Student, U. Cin., 1943-44; BA, Ohio State U., 1948; PhD, U. Chgo., 1951. Rsch. asst., rsch. assoc., instr., then asst. prof. U. Chgo., 1949-63; assoc. prof. Northwestern U., 1963-66, prof. pharmacology, 1966-90, prof. emeritus, 1990—, acting chmn. dept., 1968-70, 76-77. Contbr. articles to profl. jours.; Asst. editor: Jour. Pharmacology and Exptl. Therapeutics, 1965-68. Served with AUS, 1944-46. NIH Postdoctoral fellow, 1952. Mem. AAAS, AAUP, Am. Soc. Pharmacology and Exptl. Therapeutics, Internat. Soc. Biochem. Pharmacology, Am. Heart Assn., Cardiac Muscle Soc., Sigma Xi. Achievements include research in med. field. Home: 8619 Vineyard Ridge Pl San Jose CA 95135-2153

OKO, ANDREW JAN, art gallery director, curator; b. London, Sept. 7, 1946; arrived in Can., 1948; s. Jan Kazimierz and Julia Helena (Suska) O.; m. Helen Marie Blanc, Dec. 21, 1972; children: Sonya Celeste, Michelle Kathleen. BA, U. Calgary, 1968; MA, U. Toronto, 1972. Preparator Glenbow Mus., Calgary, Alta., 1972-73, curatorial asst., 1973-74, asst. curator, 1974-77; curator Art Gallery of Hamilton, Ont., 1977-86; dir. MacKenzie Art Gallery, Regina, Sask., 1986-96. Author: Country Pleasures: The Angling Art of Jack Cowin, 1984, (with others) Art Gallery Handbook 1982; author/curator: (exhbn. catalogue) The Frontier Art of R.B. Nevitt, 1974, T.R. MacDonald 1908-1978, 1980, The Society of Canadian Painter-Etchers and Engravers in Retrospect, 1981, The Prints of Carl Schaefer, 1983, Canada in the Nineteenth Century: The Bert and Barbara Stitt Family Collection, 1984, Jan Gerrit Wyers 1888-1973, 1989, (with James D. Campbell) Masks and Shadows: The Art of Ivan Eyre, 1996. Mem. Can. Mus. Assn., Can. Art Mus. Dirs.' Orgn., Sask. Arts Alliance (pres. 1991-93), Rotary. Avocations: flyfishing, swimming, music.

OKOLSKI, CYNTHIA ANTONIA, psychotherapist, social worker; b. N.Y.C., July 26, 1954; d. Augusto and Valerie (Toffolo) Zaccari; m. Andrzej L. Okolski, Jan. 8, 1983; children: Gabriel, Christian. BA, Hofstra U., 1976; MA, Columbia U., 1978, MSW, 1983; cert. psychoanalytic psychotherapy, Advanced Ctr. Analytic Therapy, 1986. Counselor, instr. Hofstra U.,

Hempstead, N.Y., 1975-76; recreational dir. Residence for Young Adults Hostel, Hempstead, 1976-78; rsch. asst. Ctr. Policy Rsch., N.Y.C., 1978-79, Ctr. Psychosocial Studies, N.Y.C., 1979-81; group leader Fidel Sch., Glen Cove, N.Y., 1981; rsch. asst. Assn. of Jr. League, N.Y.C., 1982; social worker Children's Aid Soc., N.Y.C., 1983-84, Manhattan Psychiat. Ctr., N.Y.C., 1984-85; psychotherapist Advanced Inst. Analytic Psychotherapy, Jamaica, N.Y., 1986—; supervising psychotherapist in therapeutic foster care program St. Christopher-Ottillie, 1994—. Mem. NASW, Acad. Cert. Social Workers, Alpha Kappa Delta.

OKRENT, DANIEL, magazine editor, writer; b. Detroit, Apr. 2, 1948; s. Harry and Gizella (Adler) O.; m. Cynthia Jayne Boyer, June 23, 1969 (div. Aug. 1977); m. Rebecca Kathryn Lazear, Aug. 28, 1977. BA, U. Mich., 1969; DHL, North Adams (Mass.) State Coll, 1988. Editor Alfred A. Knopf, Inc., N.Y.C., 1969-73; editorial dir. Grossman Pubs., Inc., N.Y.C., 1973-76; editor-in-chief Harcourt Brace Jovanovich, N.Y.C., 1976-77; pres. Hilltown Press, Inc., Worthington, Mass., 1978-91, Tex. Monthly Press, Inc., Austin, 1978-83; editor New Eng. Monthly, Northampton, Mass., 1984-89; asst. mng. editor Life mag., N.Y.C., 1991-92, mng. editor, 1992-96; editor new media Time Inc., N.Y.C., 1996—; columnist Esquire mag., N.Y.C., 1985-89. Author: Nine Innings, 1985, The Way We Were: New England Then and Now, 1989; co-author: Baseball Anecdotes, 1989; co-editor: The Ultimate Baseball Book, 1979. Mem. Am. Soc. Mag. Editors (bd. dirs. 1987-89), Cuttyhunk Yacht Club, Century Assn. Jewish. Office: Time Inc 1271 6th Ave New York NY 10020

OKRENT, DAVID, engineering educator; b. Passaic, N.J., Apr. 19, 1922; s. Abram and Gussie (Pearlman) O.; m. Rita Gilda Holtzman, Feb. 1, 1948; children—Neil, Nina, Jocelyne. M.E., Stevens Inst. Tech., 1943; M.A., Harvard, 1948, Ph.D. in Physics, 1951. Mech. engr. NACA, Cleve., 1943-46; sr. physicist Argonne (Ill.) Nat. Lab., 1951-71; regents lectr. UCLA, 1968, prof. engring., 1971-91, prof. emeritus, rsch. prof., 1991—; vis. prof. U. Wash., Seattle, 1963, U. Ariz., Tucson, 1970-71; Isaac Taylor chair Technion, 1977-78. Author: Fast Reactor Cross Sections, 1960, Computing Methods in Reactor Physics, 1968, Reactivity Coefficients in Large Fast Power Reactors, 1970, Nuclear Reactor Safety, 1981; contbr. articles to profl. jours. Mem. adv. com. on reactor safeguards AEC, 1963-87, also chmn., 1966; sci. sec. to sec. gen. of Geneva Conf., 1958; mem. U.S. del. to all Geneva Atoms for Peace Confs. Guggenheim fellow, 1961-62, 77-78; recipient Disting. Appointment award Argonne Univs. Assn., 1970, Disting. Service award U.S. Nuclear Regulatory Commn., 1985. Fellow Am. Phys. Soc., Am. Nuclear Soc. (Tommy Thompson award 1980, Glenn Seaborg medal 1987), Nat. Acad. Engring. Home: 439 Veteran Ave Los Angeles CA 90024-1956

OKSAS, JOAN KAY, economist, educator; b. Chgo., Feb. 21, 1927; d. John Joseph and Antoinette (Pestinick) Kazanauskas; m. Casimir G. Oksas, Nov. 3, 1956; children: Stephen, Mary. BS, Northwestern U., 1944; MS in Edn., Chgo. State U., 1975, Northern Ill. U., 1981; EdD, Loyola U., Chgo., 1986. From instr. to assoc. prof. Chgo. State U., 1976-89, prof., 1989-93; ret., 1993; chair dept. libr. sci. and communication Chgo. State U., 1986-88; judge Am. Film and Video Festival, N.Y., Chgo., 1980-93, Chicagoland History Fairs, 1986—; mem. vis. com. North Ctrl. Assn. Accreditation, Chgo., 1980-93; cons. Adopt-a-Sch. program, 1984; bd. dirs. Mut. Fedn. Savs. and Loan, Chgo. Contbr. articles, revs. to profl. jours. Recipient Faculty Excellence award Chgo. State U., 1991. Mem. Ill. Libr. Assn., Phi Delta Kappa, Delta Kappa Gamma (Ill. Gamma Alpha chpt.) (bd. dirs. 1982—, pres. 1986-88). Republican. Roman Catholic.

OKUI, KAZUMITSU, biology educator; b. Ohta, Japan, July 8, 1933; s. Sadajiroh and Ume (Tanaka) O.; m. Mizue Aoki Okui, May 6, 1961; children: Teiichiroh, Ari. B Agr., Tokyo U. Agr., 1962, M Agr., 1964, D Agr., 1967. Lectr. biology Denki-Tsushin U., Tokyo, 1968-70; lectr. biology Kitasato U., Sagamihara, Japan, 1970-73, asst. prof. biology, 1973-82, prof. ethology, 1982—, dean Ednl. Ctr. of Liberal Arts and Sci., 1995—, councilor, 1995—; v.p. Internat. Centre of Wild Silkworm, 1990—; vis. rsch. prof. Waikato U., New Zealand, 1991; mem. book rev. com. Yomiuri Shimbun, Tokyo, 1981-85, Sankei Shimbun, Tokyo, 1990—. Author: Entomology, 1976, Ethology, 1976, General Zoology, 1984, General Zoology, 1985, General Entomology, 1992, Human Ethology, 1992, Essay of Insects, 1993, Textbook For Ethology, 1994. Mem. Internat. Soc. Wild Silkworm (sec. 1988—, v.p. 1990—), Japan Cosmo-Biol. Soc. (councilor 1987-89), Japan Wild Silkworm Soc. (v.p. 1994—), Sci. Coun. of Japan (mem. rsch. com. 1994—). Home: 972-7 Yumoto-machi, Kanagawa-ken 250-03, Japan Office: Ednl Ctr Liberal Arts/Sci, 1-15-1 Kitasato, Sagamihara, Kanagawa 228, Japan

OKULSKI, JOHN ALLEN, principal; b. Mineola, N.Y., July 28, 1944; s. John Joseph and Rose (Zebrowski) O.; m. Martina Carol Schoneboom, July 16, 1966; children: Richard, Peter, John. BS, Rutgers U., 1966; MS, C.W. Post Coll., 1972; postgrad., Hofstra U., 1975-76, Queens Coll., 1973. Social studies tchr. Long Beach (N.Y.) Jr. H.S., 1966-67, Lynbrook (N.Y.) H.S., 1967-69, Herricks H.S., New Hyde Park, N.Y., 1969-72; guidance counselor Herricks Jr. H.S., 1972-75; dept. chmn. sec. sch. guidance Herricks pub. schs., 1975-78; asst. prin. Herricks H.S., 1978-87; prin. Bay Shore (N.Y.) H.S., 1987-92, Garden City (N.Y.) H.S., 1992—. Cubmaster Boy Scouts Am., New Hyde Park, 1975-83; v.p. New Hyde Park Little League, 1978-83. Recipient Outstanding Achievement award Garden City C. of C., 1995. Mem. L.I. Pers. and Guidance Assn. (officer), Mid. States Accreditation Assn. (adv. com. N.Y. chpt.), Garden City C. of C. (Outstanding Achievement award 1995). Presbyterian. Home: 1505 Washington Ave New Hyde Park NY 11040-4332 Office: Garden City High Sch 170 Rockaway Ave Garden City NY 11530-1430

OKUMA, ALBERT AKIRA, JR., architect; b. Cleve., Feb. 10, 1946; s. Albert Akira Sr. and Reiko (Suwa) O.; m. Janice Shirley Bono, July 17, 1971; children: Reiko Dawn, Benjamin Scott. BS in Archtl. Engring, Calif. Poly. State U., San Luis Obispo, 1970, BArch, 1975; ednl. facility planning cert., U. Calif., Riverside, 1990. Lic. architect, Calif., Mont., Ariz., Ill., Nev., N.Mex., Oreg., Maine; cert. Nat. Coun. Archtl. Bds. Architect USN, Point Mugu, Calif., 1975-76; designer Wilson Stroh Wilson Architects, Santa Paula, Calif., 1976-79; architect, project mgr. W.J. Kulwiec AIA & Assocs., Camarillo, Calif., 1979-83, Wilson & Conrad Architects, Ojai, Calif., 1983-84, Dziak, Immel & Lauterbach Services Inc., Oxnard, Calif., 1984-85; ptnr. Conrad & Okuma Architects, Oxnard, 1985-96; architect So. Calif. Edison/Edison Internat., Ventura, 1996—; commr. Calif. Bd. Archtl. Examiners, 1985—, City of San Buenaventura Hist. Preservation Commn., 1990-94, chmn., 1991-93, City of San Buenaventura Planning Commn., 1994—, City of San Buenaventura Design Rev. Com., 1994—, vice chair 1994—; peer reviewer Am. Cons. Engrs. Coun., 1987—; lectr. U. Calif. Ext., Riverside, 1991—. Prin. works include Hobson Bros. Bldg. (reconstrn. and preservation), Ventura, Calif., (Design for Excellence award 1991, Historic Bldg. of Yr. award 1992, Archtl. Rev. Design award 1993), Oxnard (Calif.) Main Post Office Renovation (Design for Excellence award 1994). Mem. Spiritual Assembly Baha'is of Ventura, Calif., 1978—, treas., 1978-79, 84, 86-88, chmn., 1992-93; treas.'s rep. Nat. Spiritual Assembly Baha'is U.S., Wilmette, Ill., 1981-91, dist. tchg. com., 1992-93; treas. Parents and Advs. for Gifted Edn., 1988-89; chmn. Ventura Unified Sch. Dist. Citizens Budget Adv. Com., 1990-92, adult edn. adv. com., 1992; mem. City of San Buenaventura specific plan citizens com., 1990-93, multicultural/cmty. heritage task force of the cultural arts plan com., 1991-92, strategic planning citizens adv. com., 1992-93; emergency svcs. vol. State of Calif., 1994—. 1st lt. U.S. Army, 1971-73. Mem. AIA (chpt. bd. dirs. 1976-79, 81—, chpt. sec. 1981, v.p. 1982, pres. 1983, Intern Devel. Program Outstanding Firm award 1993), Am. Planning Assn., Internat. Conf. Bldg. Ofcls., Nat. Trust for Hist. Preservation, Calif. Preservation Found., Constrn. Specifications Inst., Design Methods Group, Coalition for Adequate Sch. Housing, Coun. Ednl. Facility Planners Internat., Structural Engrs. Assn. So. Calif. (affiliate), Ventura County Econ. Devel. Assn. (impact II adv. com. 1993-94, edn. com. 1992-94), Calif. Polytech. State U. Alumni Assn. (life), Toastmasters Internat. Office: So Calif Edison/Edison Internat New Constrn Svcs/EE 10180 Telegraph Rd Ventura CA 93004-1703 *Personal philosophy: Live a life of service to others while keeping a global perspective on life and maintaining a clear vision of one's future goals. This service must be balanced among our own faith, family, and career.*

OKUN, DANIEL ALEXANDER, environmental engineering educator; b. N.Y.C., June 19, 1917; s. William Howard and Leah (Seligman) O.; m. Elizabeth Griffin, Jan. 14, 1946; children: Michael Griffin, Tema Jon. BS, Cooper Union, 1937; MS, Calif. Inst. Tech., 1938; ScD, Harvard U., 1948. Registered profl. engr., N.C., N.Y. With USPHS, 1940-42; tchg. fellow Harvard U., 1946-48; with Malcolm Pirnie, N.Y.C., 1948-52; from assoc. prof. dept. environ. scis. and engring. to prof. U. N.C., Chapel Hill, 1952-73, Kenan prof., 1973-82, Kenan prof. emeritus, 1982—, head dept. environ. scis. and engring., 1955-73; chmn. faculty Water Resources Rsch. Inst., 1970-73; vis. prof. Tech. U. Delft, 1960-61, Univ. Coll., London, 1966-67, 73-75, Tianjin U., 1981; editor environ. scis. series Acad. Press, 1968-75; cons. to industry, cons. engrs., govtl. agys. World Bank, WHO, UNDP, with spl. svc. in Switzerland, Israel, Jordan, Peru, Egypt, Colombia, Brazil, Venezuela, Thailand, Indonesia, Kenya, Zambia, Tunisia, Australia, Taiwan, Bangladesh, Argentina, Chile, Jamaica, Turkey, Finland, Eng., Morocco, China; mem. environ. coun. Rohm & Haas Co., Inc., 1985-92; chmn. expert panel on N.Y.C. water supply EPA, 1992-93. Author: (with Gordon M. Fair and John C. Geyer) Water and Wastewater Engineering, 2 vols., 1966-68, Elements of Water Supply and Wastewater Disposal, 1971; (with George Ponghis) Community Wastewater Collection and Disposal, 1975; Regionalization of Water Management—A Revolution in England and Wales, 1977; editor: (with M.B. Pescod) Water Supply and Wastewater Disposal in Developing Countries, 1971; (with C.R. Schulz) Surface Water Treatment for Communities in Developing Countries, 1984; contbr. to publs. in field. Chmn. Chapel Hill Fellowship for Sch. Integration, 1961-63; mem. adv. bd. Ackland Meml. Art Mus., 1973-78; bd. dirs. Warrren Regional Planning Corp., 1971-77, Inter-Faith Coun. Housing Corp., 1975-83, N.C. Water Quality Coun., 1975-77; mem. adv. com. for med. rsch. Pan Am. Health Orgn., 1976-79; chmn. Washington Met. Area Water Supply Study Com., 1976-80, NAS-NRC; mem. bd. sci. and tech. for internat. devel. NRC, 1978-81, vice chmn. environ. studies bd., 1980-83, chmn. water sci. and tech. bd., 1991-94; mem. com. on human rights NAS, 1988-94; pres. Chapel Hill chpt. N.C. Civil Liberties Union, 1991-93. Maj. AUS, 1942-46. Recipient Harrison Prescott Eddy medal for research Water Pollution Control Fedn., 1950, Gordon Maskew Fair award Am. Acad. Environ. Engrs., 1973, Thomas Jefferson award U. N.C. at Chapel Hill, 1973, Gordon Y. Billard award N.Y. Acad. Scis., 1975, 1st Thomas R. Camp Meml. lectr. Boston Soc. Environ. Engrs., Gordon Maskew Fair medal Water Pollution Control Fedn., 1978, First Allen Hazen lectr. New England Water Works Assn., 1990, Donald R. Boyd award Assn. Met. Water Agys., 1993; Friendship medal Inst. Water Engrs. and Scientists (Gt. Britain), 1984; NSF fellow, 1960-61; Fed. Water Pollution Control Adminstrn. fellow, 1966-67; Fulbright-Hayes lectr., 1973-74. Mem. NAE, AAUP (pres. U. N.C. chpt. 1963-64), ASCE (hon., chmn. environ. engring. divsn. 1967-68, 1st Simon W. Freese award 1977), Am. Water Works Assn. (hon., N.C. Fuller award 1983, Best Paper award ednl. divsn. 1985, Abel Wolman award of Excellence 1991), Inst. Medicine, Water Environ. Fedn. (hon., chmn. rsch. com. 1961-66, dir.-at-large 1969-72), Am. Acad. Environ. Engring. (pres. 1969-70, hon. diplomate, Kappe lectr. 1995), Assn. Environ. Engring. Profs. (Founders' award 1994), N.C. Pub. Health Assn. (Jarrett award 1994), U. N.C. Order of Golden Fleece), Sigma Xi (pres. U. N.C. chpt. 1968-69). Home: 204 Carol Woods 750 Weaver Dairy Rd # 204 Chapel Hill NC 27514 Office: U NC CB 8060 Chapel Hill NC 27599

OKUN, HERBERT STUART, ambassador, international executive; b. N.Y.C., Nov. 27, 1930; s. Irving and Ida Muriel (Levine) O.; m. Lorraine Joan Price, Dec. 5, 1954 (div. 1985); children: Jennifer, Elizabeth, Alexandra; m. Enid Curtis Bok Schoettle, Dec. 27, 1990. AB with gt. distinction, Stanford U., 1951; postgrad., Syracuse U., 1951-52, Princeton U., 1952; Hochschule fuer Politische, Wissenschaft, Munich, Fed. Republic of Germany, 1956-57; MPA, Harvard U., 1959. Mem. U.S. Fgn. Service, 1955-91; vice consul U.S. Fgn. Service, Munich, Fed. Republic Germany, 1955-57; with bur. intelligence & research Office of Soviet Union Affairs, Dept. State, 1959-61, alt. dir., 1971-73; 2d sec. Am. embassy U.S. Fgn. Service, Moscow, 1961-63; consul, prin. officer U.S. Fgn. Service, Belo Horizonte, Brazil, 1964-65; 1st sec., prin. officer embassy U.S. Fgn. Service, Brasilia, Brazil, 1965-66, counsellor embassy, prin. officer, 1967-68; assigned Naval War Coll. U.S. Fgn. Svc., 1968-69; spl. asst. to Sec. of State U.S. Fgn. Service, 1969-71, dep. chmn. U.S. Del., U.S.-USSR Talks on Prevention Incidents at Sea, 1971-72; spl. asst. for internat. affairs to comdr.-in-chief NATO So. Command, Naples, Italy, 1973-74; minister-counsellor, dep. chief mission Am. Embassy, Lisbon, Portugal, 1975-78; dep. chmn. U.S. del. SALT, Geneva, 1978-79, U.S. del. to trilateral U.S.-U.K.-USSR Talks on comprehensive test ban treaty, Geneva, 1979-80; ambassador to German Democratic Republic East Berlin, 1980-83; ambassador-in-residence Aspen Inst., Washington, 1983-85; ambassador, dep. permanent rep. of U.S. to the UN N.Y.C., 1985-89; rep. of U.S. to 40th, 41st, 42d and 43d sessions of Gen. Assembly of UN, to UN Security Coun., 1985-89, to 29th and 30th sessions of Com. on Peaceful Uses of Outer Space, 1986, 87, to Disarmament Commn. of UN, 1985-89, to Commn. Human Rights, to 27th and 29th session of com. on program and coordination of Econ. and Social Coun., 1987, 89; amb. in residence Carnegie Corp. of N.Y., 1989-90; mem. UN sec. Gen.'s Expert Group on Enhancing UN Structure for Drug Abuse Control, 1990; exec. dir. Fin. Svcs. Vol. Corps, N.Y.C., 1990-97; vis. lectr. Yale Law Sch., New Haven, 1991—; spl. adviser to the personal envoy of the sec. gen. UN, Yugoslavia and Nagorno-Karabakh, 1991-92; spl. adv., dep. co-chmn. Internat. Conf. on former Yugoslavia, 1992-93; U.S. mem., v.p. UN Internat. Narcotics Control Bd., Vienna, Austria, 1992—; adv. bd. Chazen Inst. Internat. Bus. Grad. Sch. Bus., Columbia U.; mem. bd. dirs. World Rehab. Fund; mem. adv. bd. Minority Rights Group U.S.A.; spl. advisor Carnegie Commn. on Preventing Deadly Conflict. Commr. U.S.-Poland Action Commn; mem. Internat. Coun., Found. Inter-Ethnic Rels., The Hague, The Netherlands, 1995—, mem. Adv. Com., Human Rights Watch, N.Y., 1995—, mem. Internat. Adv. Coun., Internat. Com. Red Cross, Geneva, 1996—; bd. overseers Curtis Inst. Music., Phila.; adv. bd. internat. security studies Yale U., New Haven; mem. adv. bd. Portuguese-Am. Leadership Coun. U.S. Served with AUS, 1952-54. Recipient Meritorious Honor award Dept. of State, 1972, Superior Honor award Dept. of State, 1980, Presdl. Meritorious Svc. award, 1983. Mem. Am. Fgn. Svc. Assn., Coun. Fgn. Rels., Am. Fgn. Policy (nat. com.), Am. Acad. Diplomacy, Washington Inst. Fgn. Affairs, Phi Beta Kappa. Home: 1133 Park Ave New York NY 10128-1246

OKUN, NEIL JEFFREY, vitreoretinal surgeon; b. St. Louis, Nov. 21, 1957; s. Edward and Barbara J. (Braham) O.; m. Joan A. Sosnoff, May 19, 1984; children: David E., Sarah E. AB, Dartmouth Coll., 1980; MD, Washington U., 1984. Diplomate Am. Bd. Ophthalmology. Intern internal medicine Jewish Hosp. at Washington U., St. Louis, 1984-85; resident ophthalmology Washington U. Med. Ctr., St. Louis, 1985-88; fellow vitreoretinal Retina Cons., Ltd., Washington U., St. Louis, 1988-89; vitreoretinal surgeon Fla. Retina Inst., Jacksonville, Fla., 1990-91, Retina Assocs. Ctrl. Fla., Orlando, 1991—; instr. dept. ophthalmology Washington U. Sch. Medicine, St. Louis, 1988-89; clin. asst. prof. dept. ophthalmology U. South Fla., Tampa, 1992—; chmn. dept. ophthalmology Fla. Hosp. Orlando, 1996—. Recipient Upjohn Achievement award for endocrinology and metabolism Washington U. Sch. Medicine, St. Louis, 1984. Fellow ACS, Am. Acad. Ophthalmology; mem. AMA (Physicians's Recognition award for continuing med. edn. 1992—), Assn. for Rsch. in Vision and Ophthalmology, Fla. Med. Assn., Fla. Soc. Ophthalmology, Ctrl. Fla. Soc. Ophthalmology, Orange County Med. Soc., Vitreous Soc., Paul Cibis Club. Avocations: music, art. Office: Retina Assocs Ctrl Fla 2501 N Orange Ave Ste 401 Orlando FL 32804-4643

OKUNIEFF, PAUL, radiation oncologist, physician; b. Chgo., Mar. 8, 1957; s. Michael and Beverly Okunieff; m. Debra Trione, Sept. 7, 1989. SB in Elec. Engring. & Biology, MIT, 1978; MD, Harvard U., 1982. Diplomate Nat. Bd. Med. Examiners; cert. in therapeutic radiology Am. Bd. Radiology. Intern in medicine Beth Israel Hosp., Boston, 1982-83; resident in radiation oncology Mass. Gen. Hosp., Boston, 1983-86, fellow in radiation oncology, 1986-87, asst. prof. radiation oncology, 1987-93; chief dept. radiation oncology NIH, Bethesda, Md., 1993—; instr. in radiation medicine Harvard Med. Sch., Boston, 1987, asst. prof. radiation oncology, 1988-93; asst. radiation therapist Waltham (Mass.) Hosp. Med. Ctr., 1989-93, Mt. Auburn Hosp., Cambridge, Mass., 1989-93; assoc. radiation oncologist Univ. Hosp., Boston, 1990-93, co-dir. radiation therapy, 1990-93; chief radiation neuro-oncology Mass. Gen. Hosp., Boston, 1991-93; chief radiation oncology br. Nat. Cancer Inst., Bethesda, 1993—; invited lectr. various med. schs., congresses & confs. Contbr. over 80 articles to profl. jours., also chpts. to books. Recipient Essay award IEEE, 1978, Young Oncologist Essay award Am. Radium Soc., 1987, travel award Am. Coll. Radiology, 1987, Young Investigator travel award VIth Internat. Meeting on Chem. Modifiers of Cancer Treatment, 1988, Basic Sci. travel grant ASTRO Ann. Meeting, 1989, USNC/UICC travel grant UICC Meeting, Hamburg, Germany, 1990, Melvin H. Knisely award Internat. Soc. Oxygen, 1991; grantee/fellow Am. Cancer Soc., 1985-86, 86-87, 89-92, Mass. Gen. Hosp., 1986, NIH, 1988-93. Office: NCI-Radiation Oncology Branch Bldg 10 B3 9000 Rockville Pike B Bethesda MD 20814-1436

OKUSANYA, OLUBUKANLA TEJUMOLA, ecologist; b. Ikenne-Remo, Ogun, Nigeria, Aug. 22, 1941; s. Samuel Tayo and Esther Oyeyinka (Bolorunde) O.; m. Iretiola Hope Titilola Omoleye, Sept. 25, 1971; children: Tolulope, Omotayo, Ibukunolu, Olugbenga. BS, U. Ibadan, 1966; MS, U. North Wales, 1970; PhD, U. Lancaster, 1976; MI Biol., Inst. Biology, London, 1971; FLS, Linnean Soc., London, 1977. Tchr. Ijebu-Ode Grammar Sch., Nigeria, 1966-68; asst. prof. U. Lagos, Nigeria, 1971-83, assoc. prof., 1983-85, prof., 1985-92, head of botany dept., 1984-85, dean, Sch. Postgrad. Studies, 1986-90; vis. rsch. prof. Ohio U., Athens, 1985, U. Agr., Abeokuta, Nigeria, 1990-91; adj. lectr. Ocean County Coll., Toms River, N.J., 1992-94; cons. Ministry of Sci. and Tech., Lagos, 1989-92. Editorial bd. Nigerian Jour. of Botany, 1993; contbr. articles to profl. jours. Pres. Lagos chpt. Lancaster U. Grad. Assn., 1990-92; commr. Civil Svc., Ogun State, Abeokuta, Nigeria, 1978-80. Recipient commonwealth scholarship Assn. Commonwealth U., London, 1968, 74, commonwealth travel fellowship, 1991. Mem. Botanical Soc. Nigeria (coun. mem. 1986-92), Ecol. Soc. Nigeria (coun. mem. 1989-94), Nigerian Inst. Biology (v.p. 1990-94). Anglican. Achievements include identification of some tropical legumes for growing in saline areas to increase land productivity; salt stress alleviation by mineral nutrients in halophytes is species specific; contrary to exptl. nom, in germination studies, it is necessary to state not only the date of seed collection, but also very important to state prevailing environ. factors - especially temperature and soil characteristics at time of seed prodn. and collection. Home: 869 Astoria Dr Toms River NJ 08753-4462

OKUYAMA, SHINICHI, physician; b. Yamagata, Japan, Dec. 4, 1935; s. Kinzo Okuyama and Asayo Hasegawa; m. Masako Fujii, Dec. 4, 1966 (dec.); children: Yuriko, Izumi, Takashi, Jun; m. Junko Hsun Chen, Mar. 21, 1983; children: Midori, Shaw. MD, Tohoku (Japan) U., 1961, PhD, 1966. Intern Saiseikan Hosp., Yamagata, 1961-62; resident in radiology Tohoku U. Research Inst., Sendai, Japan, 1962-66; research assoc. Tohoku U. Inst. Tb, Leprosy and Cancer, 1966-73, assoc. prof. radiology, 1974-80; dir. radiology Tohoku Rosai Hosp., Sendai, 1980—. Author: Diagnostic Bone Scintigraphy, 1974, Compton Radiography, 1979, Induction of Cancer Rediffer-entiation, 1983, Evolution of Cancer, 1990, Origin of Reed-Sternberg cell in Hodgkin's Disease, 1991, Evolution of Human Diseases, 1991, Morphogenesis of Reed-Sternberg Cells, 1994, Pirarubicin Pasting for Radiotherapy of Colorectal Cancer, 1996, The First Radioisotopic Evaluation of the Integrity of the Nose-Brain Barrier, 1997. Recipient Compton Tomography-Radiotherapy Planning award Japanese Ministry of Edn., 1980. Mem. AAAS, Japanese Soc. Radiology, Japanese Soc. Nuclear Medicine, Japanese Soc. Reticuloendothelial Systems, Japanese Soc. Internal Medicine, N.Y. Acad. Scis. Achievements include reinforcing aerosol cisplatin for radiotherapy of laryngeal cancer, pasting chemotherapy for radiotherapy of uterine, rectal, penile and esophageal cancer, antibiotic pasting for putrefactive cancers, reduced perfusion of the cerebral basal ganglia for micro-aspiration pneumonia. Home: Kamo 4-4-5, Izumi-ku, Sendai 981-31, Japan Office: Tohoku Rosai Hosp, Dainohara 4-3-21, Aoba-ku Sendai 981, Japan

OLAFSON, FREDERICK ARLAN, philosophy educator; b. Winnipeg, Man., Can., Sept. 1, 1924; s. Kristinn K. and Fredericka (Björnson) O.; m. Allie Lewis, June 20, 1952 (dec.); children—Peter Niel, Christopher Arlan, Thomas Andrew. A.B., Harvard U., 1947, M.A., 1948, Ph.D., 1951. Instr. philosophy and gen. edn. Harvard U., 1952-54; asst. prof. philosophy, then assoc. prof. Vassar Coll., 1954-60; assoc. prof. Johns Hopkins U., 1960-64; prof. edn. and philosophy Harvard Grad. Sch. Edn., 1964-71; prof. philosophy U. Calif., San Diego, 1971-91, chmn. dept., 1973-76, assoc. dean grad. studies and research, 1980-85. Author: Principles and Persons, 1967, Ethics and Twentieth Century Thought, 1973, The Dialectic of Action, 1979, Heidegger and the Philosophy of the Mind, 1987, What Is A Human Being?, 1995. Served to lt. (j.g.) USNR, 1943-46. Mem. Nat. Acad. Edn. Home: 6081 Avenida Chamnez La Jolla CA 92037-7404

OLAGUNJU, AMOS OMOTAYO, computer science educator, consultant; b. Igosun, Kwara, Nigeria, Nov. 27, 1954; came to U.S., 1980; s. Solomon Atoyebi and Ruth Ebun (Adegoke) O.; 1 child, Amanda. EdD, U. N.C., Greensboro, 1987; PhD, Kensington U., 1990; cert. in cryptography and info. systems, MIT, 1996. Mgmt. info. system dir. Barber-Scotia Coll., Concord, N.C., 1981-82; lectr. N.C. A&T State U., Greensboro, 1982-87, asst. prof., 1987-90; mem. tech. staff Bell Communications Rsch., Piscataway, N.J., 1986-90; vis. prof. Mich. State U., East Lansing, 1990-91; coord. acad. computing, assoc. prof. Del. State U., 1991-92, prof., chair dept. math. and computer sci., 1992—; cons. NSF, Washington, 1991-93, Edn. Testing Agy., Princeton, N.J., 1995—. Author: Lecture Notes Series in Language C, Systems Programming, Database Systems, Theoretical Aspects of Computing, File Structures, Introduction to Computer Science and Scientific and Engineering Applications of Fortran, 1991-96; contbr. articles to Software Metrics, Automatic Indexing, Perfect Hashing, Number Theory, Efficient Statis. Algorithms, Del. State News. Pres. Ahmadu Bello Assn. Computer Univ. Students, Zaria, Nigeria, 1976, Orgn. United Africans, Concord, N.C., 1982. Recipient Queen's Grad. award Queen's Univ., Kingston, Ont., 1979, Creative Rsch. Achievement award Del. State U., 1997; named Outstanding Young Man of Am., 1989; Navy fellow Am. Soc. for Engring. Edn., 1997. Mem. Assn. for Modelling and Simulation in Enterprises (program chair 1989-90, editor), Assn. for Computing Machinery (reviewer), N.C. Acad. Scis. (program chair 1991—), N.Y. Acad. Scis. Achievements include invention of the Bell Communication Rsch. Software Daily Software Report and Analysis Measurement System and General Adminstrative Quantitative Decision Support System. Home: 121 Red Oak Dr Dover DE 19904

OLAH, GEORGE ANDREW, chemist, educator; b. Budapest, Hungary, May 22, 1927; came to U.S., 1964, naturalized, 1970; s. Julius and Magda (Krasznai) O.; m. Judith Agnes Lengyel, July 9, 1949; children: George John, Ronald Peter. PhD, Tech. U. Budapest, 1949, D (hon.), 1989; DSc (hon.), U. Durham, 1988, U. Munich, 1990, U. Crete, Greece, 1994, U. Szeged, Hungary, 1995, U. Veszprem, Hungary, 1995, Case Western Res. U., 1995, U. So. Calif., 1995, U. Montpellier, 1996. Mem. faculty Tech. U. Budapest, 1949-54; assoc. dir. Ctrl. Chem. Rsch. Inst., Hungarian Acad. Scis., 1954-56; rsch. scientist Dow Chem. Can. Ltd., 1957-64, Dow Chem. Co., Framingham, Mass., 1964-65; prof. chemistry Case Western Res. U., Cleve., 1965-69, C.F. Mabery prof. rsch., 1969-77; Donald P. and Katherine B. Loker disting. prof. chemistry, dir. Hydrocarbon Rsch. Inst., U. So. Calif., L.A., 1977—; vis. prof. chemistry Ohio State U., 1963, U. Heidelberg, Germany, 1965, U. Colo., 1969, Swiss Fed. Inst. Tech., 1972, U. Munich, 1973, U. London, 1973-79, L. Pasteur U., Strasbourg, 1974, U. Paris, 1981; hon. vis. lectr. U. London, 1981; cons. to industry. Author: Friedel-Crafts Reactions, Vols. I-IV, 1963-64; (with P. Schleyer) Carbonium Ions, Vols. I-V, 1969-76, Friedel-Crafts Chemistry, 1973, Carbocations and Electrophilic Reactions, 1973, Halonium Ions, 1975; (with G.K.S. Prakash and J. Somer) Superacids, 1984; (with Prakash, R.E. Williams, L.D. Field and K. Wade) Hypercarbon Chemistry, 1987; (with R. Malthotra and S.C. Narang) Nitration, 1989, Cage Hydrocarbons, 1990; (with Wade and Williams) Electron Deficient Boron and Carbon Clusters, 1991; (with Chambers and Prakash) Synthetic Fluorine Chemistry, 1992; (with Molnar) Hydrocarbon Chemistry, 1995; also chpts. in books, numerous papers in field; patentee in field. Recipient Alexander von Humboldt Sr. U.S. Scientist award, 1979, Calif. Scientist of Yr. award, 1989, Pioneer of Chemistry award Am. Inst. Chemists, 1993; Mendeleev medal Russian Acad. Scis., 1992, Kapitsa medal Russian Acad. Natural Scis., 1995; Nobel prize in Chemistry, 1994; Guggenheim fellow 1972, 88. Fellow AAAS, Chem. Inst. Can.; mem. NAS, Italian NAS, Royal Soc. London (fgn.), European Acad. Arts, Scis. and Humanities, Italy Chem. Soc. (hon.), Hungarian Acad. Sci. (hon.), Am. Chem. Soc. (award petroleum chemistry 1964, Leo Hendrik Baekeland award N.J. sect. 1966, Morley medal Cleve. sect. 1970, award Synthetic organic chemistry 1979, Roger Adams award in organic chemistry 1989), German Chem. Soc., Brit. Chem. Soc. (Centenary lectr. 1978). Home: 2252 Gloaming Way Beverly Hills CA 90210-1717 Office: U So Calif Labor Hydrocarbon Rsch Inst Los Angeles CA 90007 *America still is offering a* *new home and nearly unlimited possibilities to the newcomer who is willing to work hard for it. It is also where the "main action" in science and technology remains.*

OLAJUWON, HAKEEM ABDUL, professional basketball player; b. Lagos, Nigeria, Jan. 21, 1963; s. Salaam and Abike O. Student, U. Houston, 1980-84. With Houston Rockets, 1984—. Named to Sporting News All-Am. First Team, 1984, NBA All-Rookie Team, 1985, All-Star team, 1985-90, 92-94, All-NBA First Team, 1987-89, 93-94, NBA All-Defensive First Team, 1987-88, 90, 93-94; named MVP 1993-94, NBA Defensive Player of Yr., 1993-94, mem. NBA championship team, 1994-95; named MVP NBA finals, 1994-95; recipient award IBM, 1993. Office: Houston Rockets The Summit Two Greenway Pl E Houston TX 77046-3865*

OLAN, WILLIAM JOSEPH, III, banker; b. N.Y.C., Apr. 6, 1947; s. William J. Jr. and Alice Nettleton (Edwards) N.; m. Wendy Collison French, Mar. 21, 1981; children: William J. IV, Anina Chrysler. Student, Hackley Sch., Tarrytown, N.Y., 1958-65; E.S.U. scholar, Eastbourne Coll., U.K., 1966; BA, Colgate U., 1970; MBA, Stanford U., 1973. V.p. Bankers Trust Co., N.Y.C., 1973-83; mng. dir. Becker-Paribas, N.Y.C., 1983-84; exec. v.p., treas. PaineWebber, N.Y.C., 1984—. Bd. dirs. Adirondack Mus. (Blue Mountain), 1996—. Mem. Pub. Securities Assn. (money market exec. com. 1985-89, chmn. 1987, bd. dirs. 1988-91, treas. 1990), Adirondack League, Piping Rock Club, Union Club of N.Y.C. Home: 1088 Park Ave New York NY 10128-1132 Office: PaineWebber Inc 1285 6th Ave New York NY 10019-6028

OLANDER, RAY GUNNAR, retired lawyer; b. Buhl, Minn., May 15, 1926; s. Olof Gunnar and Margaret Esther (Meisner) O.; m. Audrey Joan Greenlaw, Aug. 1, 1959; children: Paul Robert, Mary Beth. BEE, U. Minn., 1949, BBA, 1949; JD cum laude, Harvard U., 1959. Bar: Minn. 1959, Wis. 1962, U.S. Patent Office 1968. Elec. engr. M. A. Hanna Co., Hibbing, Minn., 1950-56; assoc. Leonard, Street & Deinard, Mpls., 1959-61; comml. atty. Bucyrus Internat. Inc., South Milwaukee, Wis., 1961-70, dir. contracts, 1970-76, v.p. comml., 1976-88, gen. atty., 1978-80, corp. sec., 1978-88, gen. counsel, 1980-88, vice chmn., dir., 1988-92; ret. Bd. dirs. Ballet Found. Milw., Inc., 1978-92, Pub. Expenditure Rsch. Found., Inc., Madison, Wis., 1978-94, Pub. Expenditure Survey Wis., Madison, 1978-82. With USN, 1944-46. Mem. ABA, Wis. Bar Assn., Wis. Intellectual Property Law Assn., Am. Soc. Corp. Secs., Inc., Am. Corp. Counsel Assn., VFW, Harvard Club (N.Y.C.), Harvard of Wis. Club, Bonita Bay Club. Republican. Roman Catholic. Home: 3708 Woodlake Dr Bonita Springs FL 34134-8605 *Strive for success in whatever you endeavor in every honorable way. Respect the dignity and rights of all persons with whom you come in contact, irrespective of their station in life. Recognize your own shortcomings and allow for those of others.*

O'LAUGHLIN, DONNA, editor periodical. Mng. editor The Appraisal Jour., Chgo. Office: The Appraisal Jour 875 N Michigan Ave Ste 2400 Chicago IL 60611-1877

O'LAUGHLIN, SISTER JEANNE, university administrator; b. Detroit, May 4, 1929. Pres. Barry U., Miami. Office: Barry U Office of the President 11300 NE 2nd Ave Miami FL 33161-6628*

OLAYAN, SULIMAN SALEH, finance company executive; b. Onaiza, Saudi Arabia, Nov. 5, 1918; s. Saleh and Heya (Al Ghanem) O.; student public schs., Bahrain Islands; m. Mary Perdikis, Feb. 22, 1974; children: Khaled, Hayat, Hutham, Lubna. Rsch. specialist Arabian Am. Oil Co., 1937-47; founder and chmn. The Olayan Group, Saudi Arabia, 1947—, which includes Olayan Investments Co. Establishment, Olayan Europe Ltd., Olayan Devel. Corp., Ltd., Olayan Am. Corp., Crescent Holding GmbH, Competrol Real Estate Ltd., Competrol Establishment, Olayan Financing Co., Olayan Saudi Holding Co. Saudi Arabian Oil Co., Supreme Coun. (mem., 1989—); chmn. bd. The Saudi Brit. Bank, Riyadh, Saudi Arabia, 1977-89; adv. bd. Am. Internat. Group, 1982—; mem. internat. coun. J.P. Morgan & Co. Inc. N.Y., 1979-90; internat. councillor, mem. adv. bd. Ctr. for Strategic and Internat. Studies, Washington, 1977-95; bd. dirs. CS First Boston, Inc., 1988-95. Decorated Knight Comdr. of Brit. Empire, 1987, comdr. 1st class Royal Order of the Polar Star (Sweden), 1988; recipient Great Cross of the Order of Merit, Spain, 1984, Medal of Honor, Madrid C. of C., 1985. Mem. internat. adv. coun. SRI Internat., Menlo Park, Calif., 1965—. Alumnus Mem. The Rockefeller U. Coun., N.Y.C., 1978—; trustee Am. U. of Beirut, 1979-84; co-chmn. U.S.-Saudi Arabian Businessmen's Dialogue under the U.S.-Saudi Arabian Joint Commn. on Econ. Cooperation, 1980-92; Mem. Internat. Coun. Inst. Europeen de Adminstrn. des Affaires (INSEAD), Internat. Indsl. Conf., San Francisco (participant, internat. chmn. 1985), Inst. for Internat. Econs., Washington (bd. dirs.), The Conf. Bd. of N.Y. (sr. mem., internat. counselor), Royal Inst. Internat. Affairs, 1979-91, London, Riyadh Handicapped Children Assn. (vice chmn., 1983-88). Islam. Clubs: Equestrian (Riyadh), Knickerbocker, N.Y. Athletic (N.Y.C.), Pacific-Union and Bohemian (San Francisco), Royal Automobile (London). Office: The Olayan Group, PO Box 8772, Riyadh 11492, Saudi Arabia

OLAZABAL, JOSE MARIA, professional golfer; b. Fuenterrabla, Spain, Feb. 5, 1966. Profl. golfer, 1985—; mem. European Ryder Cup Team, 1987, 89, 91, 93, Kirin Cup Team, 1987, Four Tours World Championship Team, 1989, 90, World Cup Team, 1989, Dunhill Cup Team, 1986, 87, 88, 89, 92. Winner Italian Amateur award, 1983, Spanish Amateur award, 1983, European Masters-Swiss Open, 1986, Belgian Open, 1988, German Masters, 1988, Tenerife Open, 1989, Dutch Open, 1989, Benson & Hedges Internat., 1990, Irish Open, 1990, Lancome Trophy, 1990, Visa Talhoyo Club Masters, 1990, Catalonia Open, 1991, Turespana Open de Tenerife, 1992, Open Mediterrania, 1992, Masters, 1994; tour victories include NEC World Series of Golf, 1990, The Internat., 1991. Avocations: music, cinema. Office: care PGA 100 Avenue Of Champions Palm Beach Gardens FL 33418*

OLBERMANN, KEITH, sportcaster; b. Jan. 27, 1959. BS in Comm. Arts, Cornell U., 1979. Sports reporter UPI Radio, N.Y.C., 1979-80, RKO Radio, N.Y.C., 1980-82, WNEW-AM, N.Y.C., 1980-83; nat. sports reporter, anchor CNN, N.Y.C., 1981-84, WCVB-TV, Boston, 1984; weeknight sports anchor, reporter KTLA-TV, L.A., 1985-88; sports commentator KNX-AM, L.A., 1996-91; sports anchor, host The Keith Olbermann Show KCBS-TV, L.A., 1988-91; weekend co-host ESPN Sports Radio, 1992-93; co-anchor, co-host SportsCenter ESPN, Bristol, Conn., 1992—; co-anchor SportsNight ESPN2, 1993-94. Recipient 11 Golden Mike awards Best Sportscaster, 1985, 86, 87, 88, 89, 90, Best Sportscast Calif. Radio and TV News Assn., 1985-91, Cable Ace award Best Sportscaster Nat. Acad. Cable Programming, 1995; voted Calif. A.P. Sportscaster of Yr., 1985, 87, 89. Office: ESPN Inc Comms Dept 935 Middle St Bristol CT 06010-1000*

OLCOTT, JOHN WHITING, aviation executive; b. Orange, N.J., Oct. 20, 1936; s. Egbert Whiting and Marion Richmond (Braillard) O.; m. Hope Bennett Phillips, May 14, 1966 (div. Feb. 1987); children: David Whiting, Bradley Phillips, Carter Howell; m. Isobel Waxman Ritter, Nov. 25, 1989. BS in Aero. Engring., Princeton U., 1960, MS in Aero. Engring., 1964; MBA in Gen. Mgmt., Rutgers U., 1970. V.p. Linden (N.J.) Flight Svc., 1960-66; flight rsch. specialist Princeton (N.J.) U., 1966-68; v.p. corp. devel., sr. cons. Aero. Rsch. Assocs. Princeton, Inc., 1968-74; v.p., group pub., editorial dir. McGraw-Hill Aviation Week Group, Rye Brook, N.Y., 1973-92; pres. Nat. Bus. Aircraft Assn., Inc., 1992—; rsch. engring. and devel. adv. com. FAA, 1990—; mem. bd. govs. Flight Safety Found., 1992—; bd. dirs. ARINC, Inc., Annapolis, Md. Crew chief, mem. New Vernon (N.J.) Vol. First Aid Squad, 1974-92; bd. dirs. Aviation Rsch. and Edn. Found., Washington, 1988-92; mem. bd. visitors Aircraft Owner and Pilots Assn. Air Safety Found., Frederick, Md., 1988-93; trustee Embry-Riddle Aero. U., Daytona Beach, Fla., 1988-93, 95—; chmn. panel on gen. aviation and commuter tech. NASA, Washington, 1974-86; chmn. panel gen. aviation safety FAA, Washington, 1983-88. Recipient Meritorious Svc. award Flight Safety Found., 1983, Dir.'s award FAA Ctral Region, 1984, Commendation cert. FAA, 1984, Gill Robb Wilson award Embry-Riddle Aero. U., 1986, Journalism award Helicopter Assn. Internat., 1990. Republican. Presbyterian. Office: NBAA 1200 18th St NW Washington DC 20036 also: 3808 N Richmond St Arlington VA 22207

OLCOTT, WILLIAM ALFRED, magazine editor; b. Bklyn., June 29, 1931; s. W. Alfred and Margaret Mary (Carr) O.; m. Anne Maria Gorman, Sept. 7, 1963; children: Christopher, James, Katharine, William, Terence. B.A. in Philosophy, Mary Immaculate Sem. and Coll., Northampton, Pa., 1956; postgrad., Columbia U. Reporter, writer AP, 1960-66; with McGraw-Hill Publs. Co., 1966-80, 81-84, chmn. editorial bd., 1976-77, editor in chief 26 Plus mag., 1973-77, editor in chief Nat. Petroleum News mag., 1977-81, editor in chief Office Adminstrn. and Automation mag., 1984; editor in chief Fund Raising Mgmt. mag., Garden City, N.Y., 1985-96; publs. exec. editor Hoke Communications, Garden City, 1989-96. Mem. adv. com. Garden City Bd. Edn., N.Y., 1976—; prin. religious edn. home program St. Joseph's Roman Cath. Ch., Garden City, 1976—, mem. pastoral coun., 1990-94. Recipient Jesse H. Neal Editorial Achievement award Am. Bus. Press, 1974, 80, Golden Mike award Nat. Religious Broadcasters, 1989. Home and Office: 70 Greensboro Rd Hanover NH 03755-3101

OLD, BRUCE SCOTT, chemical and metallurgical engineer; b. Norfolk, Va., Oct. 21, 1913; s. Edward H.H. and Eugenia (Smith) O.; m. Katharine G. Day, Oct. 7, 1939; children: Edward H., Randolph B., Lansing G., Ashlee Virginia, Barbara Stuart. B.S., U. N.C., 1935; Sc.D., M.I.T., 1938. Research engr. devel. and research dept. Bethlehem Steel Corp., 1938-41; with Arthur D. Little, Inc., Cambridge, Mass., 1946-78; v.p. Arthur D. Little, Inc., 1950-60, sr. v.p., 1960-78; pres. Bruce S. Old Assos., Inc., 1979—; pres., chmn. Cambridge Corp., 1952-53; pres. Nuclear Metals, Inc., 1954-57; dir. Mass. Investors Trust and 13 other mut. funds in MFS group, 1973-85; chief metallurgy and materials br., div. research AEC, 1947-49; mem. Sci. Adv. Com. to Pres., 1952-56. Co-author: The Game of Singles in Tennis, 1962, Stroke Production in the Game of Tennis, 1971, The Game of Doubles in Tennis, 1956, Tennis Tactics, 1983; Contbr. articles to profl. publs.; patentee in field. Comdr. USNR, 1941-46. Fellow AAAS, Am Soc. Metals, Am. Inst. Chemists; mem. N.Y. Acad. Scis., Nat. Acad. Engring., Wianno (Mass.) Club, Sigma Xi, Tau Beta Pi. Address: 10 Longwood Dr Unit 106 Westwood MA 02090

OLD, HUGHES OLIPHANT, research theologian, clergyman; b. Redondo Beach, Calif., Apr. 13, 1933; s. Shadburne Edward and Emma Coulter (Oliphant) O.; m. Mary Chase McCaw, June 12, 1982; children: Hannah Chase, Isaac Houghton Chambers. BA, Centre Coll., 1955; BD, Princeton Theol. Sem., 1958; postgrad., U. Tubingen, 1964-66; ThD, U. Neuchatel, 1971. Ordained to ministry Presbyn. Ch., 1959. Minister Presbyn. Ch., Atglen, Pa., 1959-64, Faith Presbyn. Ch., West Lafayette, Ind., 1972-85; mem. Ctr. for Theol. Inquiry, Princeton, N.J., 1985—. Author: Patristic Roots of Reformed Worship, 1975, Worship, 1984, Shaping of the Reformed Baptismal Rite, 1992, Leading in Prayer, 1995, Themes and Variations for A Christian Doxology, 1992; contbr. numerous articles to scholarly jours. Fellow N.Am. Acad. Liturgy; mem. Union League Phila. Republican. Avocations: painting, music. Home: 818 Lower Ferry Rd Trenton NJ 08628-3501

OLD, LLOYD JOHN, cancer biologist; b. San Francisco, Sept. 23, 1933; s. John H. and Edna A. (Marks) O.;. BA, U. Calif., Berkeley, 1955; MD, U. Calif., San Francisco, 1958; MD (hon.), Karolinska Inst., 1994, U. Lausanne, Switzerland, 1995. Rsch. fellow Sloan-Kettering Inst. Cancer Rsch., N.Y.C., 1958-59, rsch. assoc., 1959-60, assoc., 1960-64, assoc. mem., 1964-67, mem., 1967—; rsch. assoc. biology Sloan-Kettering div. grad. sch. Med. Scis., Cornell U., N.Y.C., 1960-62, asst. prof. biology, 1962-66, assoc. prof. biology, 1966-69, prof. biology, 1969-81, prof. immunology, 1981—; acting assoc. dir. research planning Sloan-Kettering Inst. Cancer Rsch., N.Y.C., 1972, v.p., assoc. dir., 1973-76, v.p., assoc. dir. for sci. devel., 1976-83; assoc. dir. for research Meml. Sloan-Kettering Cancer Ctr. and Meml. Hosp., N.Y.C., 1973-83, William E. Snee Chair cancer immunology, 1983—; Harvey Soc. lectr., 1972, G.H.A. Clowes Meml. lectr., 1980; assoc. med. dir. N.Y. Cancer Rsch. Inst. Inc., 1970; med. dir. Cancer Rsch. Inst., Inc., 1971-74, dir. sci. adv. coun., 1974—; vis. prof. clin. investigation GM Cancer Rsch. Found., Dana-Farber Cancer Inst.; vis. prof. pathology Harvard U., 1986; fgn. adj. prof. med. faculty Karolinska Inst., 1994—; cons. in field. Adv. editor: Jour. Exptl. Medicine, 1971-76, 90-95; Progress in Surface and Membrane Sci., 1972-74; assoc. editor: Virology, 1972-74; editl. adv. bd.: Cancer Rsch., 1967-70, Cancer, 1968-71, Recent Results in Cancer Rsch., 1972, editl. bd. Immunobiology, 1987—. Sci. dir., mem. Emeritus Sci. Com., Ludwig Inst. Cancer Rsch., 1971-86, chmn. sci. com. 1988—, bd. dirs. 1989—, CEO, 1995, dir. N.Y. unit, 1990; mem. rsch. coun. Pub. Health Rsch. Inst. City N.Y., 1977-80, bd. dirs., 1979-89, vice chmn. exec. com. 1984-89; adv. bd. biology div. N.Y. Hall of Sci., 1985—; mem. med. and sci. adv. bd., trustee Leukemia Soc. Am. Inc., 1970-73; mem. sci. adv. bd. Jane Coffin Childs Meml. Fund for Med. Rsch., 1970-75. Recipient Roche award, 1957; Alfred P. Sloan award cancer research, 1962, Lucy Wortham James award James Ewing Soc., 1970, Louis Gross award, 1972, Founders Tumor Immunology award Cancer Research Inst., 1975, Rabbi Shai Shacknai Meml. award, 1976; Research Recognition award Noble Found., 1978; Robert Roesler de Villiers award, 1981; N.Y. Acad. Medicine medal, 1985, Robert Koch prize, 1990. Mem. NAS, AAAS, N.Y. Acad. Scis., Harvey Soc., Am. Acad. Arts and Scis., Am. Assn. Cancer Research (bd. dirs. 1980-83), Am. Assn. Immunologists, Inst. Medicine of Nat. Acad. Scis., Phi Beta Kappa, Sigma Xi, Alpha Omega Alpha. Office: Ludwig Inst Cancer Rsch 1345 Avenue Of The Americas New York NY 10105-0302

OLDAKER, BRUCE GORDON, physicist, military officer; b. Albuquerque, June 3, 1950; s. Marion Joseph and Minerva Rae (Rogers) O.; m. Patricia Rose Cooney, Feb. 17, 1973; children: Ian Joseph, Kathleen Marie. B Math., U. Minn., 1972; MS, U. Colo., 1981; PhD, MIT, 1990. Commd. 2d lt. U.S. Army, 1972, advanced through grades to col., 1996; asst. prof., now assoc. prof. physics U.S. Mil. Acad. U.S. Army, West Point, N.Y., 1981—; dir. Photonics Rsch. Ctr. U.S. Mil. Acad., West Point, N.Y., 1990-94, program dir., advanced physics courses, 1994—. Contbr. articles to sci. jours. Hertz Found. fellow, 1985-89. Mem. Am. Phys. Soc., Assn. U.S. Army, Sigma Xi, Phi Kappa Phi. Achievements include proving that momentum distribution of atoms after interaction with a photon field can be used to study properties of the photon field. Office: US Mil Acad Dept Physics West Point NY 10996

OLDEN, ANNA BEATRICE, former educator; b. Pinehurst, N.C., Mar. 15, 1931; d. Allen and Anna (Wallace) Bethea; B.A., Bennett Coll., 1952; postgrad. Bank Street Coll., N.Y.C., Am. U., Marywood Coll., Loyola Coll. m. Simon J. Olden Jr., July 12, 1953 (div.); children: Darryl Craig, Pamela Lynette, Brian Kevin. Tchr. Kannapolis (N.C.) Public Schs., 1952-53, Rochdale Sch., Jamaica, N.Y., 1955-69, Carousel Sch., Jamaica, N.Y. and Headstart tchr., curriculum coordinator, supr., St. Albans, N.Y., 1955-69; tchr. Cecil County (Md.) Public Schs., 1969-90, ret., 1990. Active Arthritis Found.; chef Black History luncheon MBNA, 1994. Mem. NEA, NEAR, NAACP (exec. bd.), Md. Tchrs. Assn., Del. Ret. Tchrs. Assn., Cecil County Tchrs. Assn., Internat. Reading Assn., Heal and Cease (nat. chpt., Pa. chpt.), Cecil County Reading Assn., Cecil County Retired Tchr.'s Assn., Bennett Coll. Alumnae Assn. (Delaware Valley & nat. chpts.). Methodist. Club: Grandma's. Home: 1 Bristol Way New Castle DE 19720-3906

OLDEN, KENNETH, science administrator, researcher; b. Parrottsville, Tenn., July 22, 1938; s. Mack L. and Augusta (Christmas) O.; m. Sandra L. White; children: Rosalind, Kenneth, Stephen, Heather. BS, Knoxville Coll., 1960; MS, U. Mich., 1964; PhD, Temple U., 1970. Rsch. fellow, physiology instr. Harvard U., Cambridge, Mass., 1970-74; sr. staff fellow NIH, Nat. Cancer Inst., Bethesda, Md., 1974-77, biochemistry expert, 1977-78, rsch. biologist, 1978-79; assoc. dir. rsch. Howard U. Med. Sch. Cancer Ctr., Washington, 1979-82, dep. dir., 1982-85, dir., 1985-91; dir. Nat. Inst. Environ. Health Scis. and Nat. Toxicology Program NIH, Rsch. Triangle Park, N.C., 1991—. Author numerous books; assoc. editor Cancer Rsch., 1990—, Jour. Nat. Cancer Inst., 1990—, Molecular Biology of the Cell, 1991-93, Environ. Health Perspectives, 1992—; contbr. articles to profl. jours. Mem. awards bd. Gen. Motors Cancer Rsch. Found., Detroit, 1992-96. Recipient Presidential Meritorious Exec. Rank award, City of Medicine award, Durham, N.C., 1996; Porter Devel. Postdoctoral fellow Am. Physiol. Soc., 1970, Postdoctoral fellow NIH, 1970-73, Macy Faculty fellow Macy Found., 1973-74. Mem. Am. Soc. Cell Biology, Am. Soc. Biol. Chemistry, So. Biol. Response Modifiers, Metastasis Rsch. Soc., Inst. Medicine, Internat. Soc. Study Comparative Oncology. Baptist. Avocations: tennis, hiking, cycling, cooking. Home: 19 Quail Ridge Rd Durham NC 27705-1870 Office: Nat Inst Environ Health Scis & Nat Toxicology Prog PO Box 12233 Research Triangle Park NC 27709-2233

OLDENBURG, CLAES THURE, artist; b. Stockholm, Sweden, Jan. 28, 1929; s. Gosta and Sigrid Elisabeth (Lindforss) O.; m. Patricia Joan Muschinski, Apr. 13, 1960 (div. Apr. 1970); m. Coosje van Bruggen, July 22, 1977. B.A., Yale, 1951; student, Art Inst., Chgo., 1952-54. One-man shows include Reuben Gallery, N.Y.C., 1960, Green Gallery, N.Y.C., 1962, Sidney Janis Gallery, N.Y.C., 1964-70, Galerie Ileana Sonnabend, Paris, 1964, Robert Fraser Gallery, London, 1966, Moderna Museet, Stockholm, 1966, 77, Mus. Contemporary Art, Chgo., 1967, 77, Irving Blum Gallery, Los Angeles, 1968, Mus. Modern Art, N.Y.C., 1969, U. Calif. at Los Angeles Art Gallery, 1970, Stedelijk Mus., Amsterdam, 1970, 77, Tate Gallery, London, 1970, Nelson-Atkins Mus., Kansas City, 1972, Art Inst. Chgo., 1973, Leo Castelli Gallery, N.Y.C., 1974, 76, 80, 90, Kunstmus., Basel, 1992, Margo Leavin Gallery, Los Angeles, 1975, 76, 78, 88, Art Gallery of Toronto, Ont., 1976, Centre Georges Pompidou Musée National d'Art Moderne, Paris, 1977, Kröller-Muller Mus., 1979, Mus. Ludwig, Cologne, 1979, Wave Hill, Bronx, N.Y., 1984, Pace Gallery, 1992, 94, Nat. Gallery of Art, Washington, 1995, Mus. Contemporary Art, L.A., 1995, Solomon R. Guggenheim Mus., N.Y.C., 1995, Kunst und Ausstellungshalle der Bundersrepublik Deutschland, Bonn, 1996, Hayward Gallery, London, 1996; group shows include Martha Jackson Gallery, N.Y.C., 1960, 61, Dallas Mus. Contemporary Art, 1961, 62, Sidney Janis Gallery, 1962, 64, Inst. Contemporary Arts, London, 1963, Art Inst. Chgo., 1962, 63, Allen Art Mus. Oberlin (Ohio) Coll., 1963, Mus. Modern Art, N.Y.C., 1963, 88, 90, 91, Washington Gallery Modern Art, 1963, Am. Pavilion, Venice, 1964, Moderna Museet, Stockholm, 1964, Gulbenkian Found. Tate Gallery, London, 1964, Rochester (N.Y.) Meml. Mus., 1964-65, Worcester (Mass.) Mus., 1965, Met. Mus. Art, N.Y.C., 1969, Walker Art Center, 1975, others, numerous commd. works, rep. permanent collections at, Guggenheim Mus., N.Y.C., Mus. Modern Art, Albright-Knox Art Gallery, Buffalo, Centre Georges Pompidou, Stedelijk Mus., Tate Gallery, Mus. Ludwig, Moderna Museet, Rose Art Mus. Brandeis U., Waltham, Mass., Oberlin Coll., Nat. Gallery Art, Canberra, Art Gallery Ont., Toronto, Art Inst. Chgo., Hirshorn Gallery and Sculpture Garden, Whitney Mus. Modern Art, N.Y.C., Mus. Contemporary Art, L.A., many others; Numerous outdoor works in corporate and private collections. (Recipient Creative Arts citation Brandeis U. 1971, Sculpture award Am. Ann., Chgo. Art Inst. 1976, medal AIA 1977, Wilhelm Lehmbruck Sculpture award 1981); author: Store Days, 1967, Proposals for Monuments and Buildings, 1969, Notes in Hand, 1971, Raw Notes, 1973, Multiples in Retrospect, 1991, Claes Oldenburg Coosje van Bruggen: Large Scale Projects. Recipient Sculpture award Brandeis U., 1971, Skowhegan Sculpture medal, 1972, Wilhelm Lehmbruck Sculpture award, 1981, Wolf Prize in Arts, 1989, Jack I. and Lillian Poses medal Brandeis U., 1993, Lifetime Achievement award Contemporary Sculpture Internat. Sculpture Ctr., 1994. Mem. Am. Acad. & Inst. Arts & Letters. Office: care Pace Gallery 32 E 57th St New York NY 10022-2513*

OLDENBURG, RICHARD ERIK, auction house executive; b. Stockholm, Sept. 21, 1933; came to U.S., 1936, naturalized, 1959; s. Gösta and Sigrid Elisabeth (Lindforss) O.; m. Harriet Lisa Turnure, Dec. 17, 1960. A.B., Harvard U., 1954. Mgr. design dept. Doubleday & Co., Inc., N.Y.C., 1958-61; mng. editor trade div. Macmillan Co., Inc., N.Y.C., 1961-69; dir. publs. Mus. Modern Art, N.Y.C., 1969-72, dir., 1972-94, dir. emeritus, hon. trustee, 1995—; chmn. Sotheby's North and South America, N.Y.C., 1995—. Served with AUS, 1956-58. Home: 447 E 57th St New York NY 10022-3064 Office: Sotheby's Inc 1134 York Ave New York NY 10021-8300

OLDER, RICHARD SAMUEL, elementary school music educator; b. Cuba, N.Y., Aug. 10, 1947; s. Laurence Charles and Ann Nell (Reese) O.; m. Harriet Karangelan, June 24, 1972 (div. Mar. 28, 1978); m. Helen Mary DiOrio, Nov. 8, 1986; 1 child, Michelle Ann. B in Music Edn., Westminster Choir Coll., 1971. Cert. tchr. of music, N.J. Tchr. 8th grade vocal and gen. music Columbia Jr. H.S., Berkeley Heights, N.J., 1971-81; tchr. vocal and gen. music Woodruff and Mountain Park elem. schs., Berkeley Heights, 1981-88, Woodruff and T.P. Hughes schs., Berkeley Heights, 1988—. Recipient 20 Yrs. of Svc. award PTA Woodruff Sch., 1990. Mem. N.J. Edn. Assn. (local rep. 1986-87), Foxhollow Golf Club. Republican. Presbyterian. Avocations: golf, bowling, swimming, piano, guitar. Home: 43 River Bend Rd Berkeley Heights NJ 07922-1812 Office: Woodruff Elem Sch Briarwod W Berkeley Heights NJ 07922

OLDERMAN, GERALD, retired medical device company executive; b. N.Y.C., July 16, 1933; s. Cass and Hilda (Klein) O.; m. Myrna Ruth Schwartz, Aug. 3, 1958; children: Sharon, Neil, Lisa. BS in Chemistry, Rensselaer Poly Inst., 1958; MS Phys. Chemistry, Seton Hall U., 1971, PhD, 1972. Rsch. chemist Nat. Cash Register, Dayton, Ohio, 1958-61; tech. mgmt. positions Johnson & Johnson, New Brunswick, N.J., 1961-75, dir. R & D, bd. dirs. surg. products hosp. divsn., 1972-75; v.p. R & D, Surgikos divsn. Johnson & Johnson, New Brunswick, 1975-78, bd. dirs. Surgikos divsn., 1975-78; v.p. R & D, bd. dirs. Am. Convertors divsn. Am. Hosp. Supply corp., Evanston, Ill., 1978-85; v.p. internat. rsch. and devel. Pharmaseal divsn. Baxter Healthcare Corp., Valencia, Calif., 1985-91; v.p. R & D, bd. dirs. cardiopulmonary divsn. C.R. Bard, 1991-96, ret., 1996; cons. R.F. Caffrey & Assoc., Inc., Brownsville, Vt., 1996—. Served with USMC, 1954-56. Recipient Robert Wood Johnson medal, Johnson & Johnson, 1969. Fellow Am. Inst. Chemists; mem. Assn. Advancement Med. Instrumentation, INDA, Assn. Nonwovens Industry (bd. dirs., corp. rep. 1986, 87), Nat. Fire Protection Assn. (industry rep.), Am. Soc. Artificial Internat. Organs. Home: 17 Pickman Dr Bedford MA 01730-1009 Office: RF Caffrey & Assoc Inc PO Box 319 Brownsville VT 05037

OLDERSHAW, LOUIS FREDERICK, lawyer; b. New Britain, Conn., Aug. 30, 1917; s. Louis A. and Annie Louise (Bold) O.; m. Virginia Wakelin, Nov. 30, 1940; children: Peter W., Robert J., David L. A.B., Dartmouth Coll., 1939; LL.B., Yale U., 1942. Bar: Mass. 1946, Fed. 1947. Mem. legal staff Army Ordnance Dist., Springfield, Mass., 1942-43; with firm Lyon, Green, Whitmore, Doran & Brooks, Holyoke, Mass., 1947-49; partner firm Davenport, Millane & Oldershaw, Holyoke, 1949-64; treas. Nat. Blank Book Co., Inc., Holyoke, 1964-65; pres. Nat. Blank Book Co., Inc., 1965-78, chmn. bd., 1978-83; group v.p., dir. Dennison Mfg. Co., Framingham, Mass., 1967-82; counsel Bulkley, Richardson & Gelinas, Springfield, Mass., 1983—. Mem. editorial bd.: Yale Law Jour, 1941-42. Trustee Mt. Holyoke Coll., 1966-76, Greater Holyoke YMCA; bd. dirs. Holyoke Community Coll. Found., The Ctr. Redevel. Corp subs. Mt. Holyoke Coll., South Hadley, Mass., Sta. WGBY-TV. Lt. USNR, 1943-47. Republican. Mem. United Congl. Ch. Clubs: Longmeadow (Mass.) Country; Mill Reef (Antigua). Lodge: Rotary. Home: 1 Brookwood Rd Holyoke MA 01040-9510 Office: Baybank Tower 1500 Main St Ste 2700 Springfield MA 01115-0001

OLDFATHER, CHARLES EUGENE, lawyer; b. Brady, Nebr., Oct. 7, 1927; s. Harold and Marcia (Hazlett) O.; m. Diane C. Harris, June 15, 1957; children: David H., Jane Oldfather Light. Student, U. Colo., 1945, Kearney (Nebr.) State Tchrs. Coll., 1946-48, U. Cal. at Berkeley, 1949; A.B., U. Nebr., 1950; J.D. with distinction, U. Mich., 1953. Bar: Nebr. bar 1953. Since practiced in Lincoln; asso. Cline, Williams, Wright & Johnson, 1953-58; partner Cline, Williams, Wright, Johnson & Oldfather, 1958-80, of counsel, 1980—. Bd. editors: U Mich Law Rev, 1952-53. Past pres. Family Svc. Assn., Lincoln, Nebr. State Hist. Soc. Found.; trustee U. Nebr. Found. Served with Adj. Gen. Divsn. AUS, 1946-48. Mem. Am., Nebr., Lincoln bar assns., Lincoln C. of C. (past dir.), Phi Kappa Psi, Phi Delta Phi. Republican. Presbyn. Club: Lincoln Country. Home: 6719 Old Cheney Rd Lincoln NE 68516-3561 Office: 1900 First Bank Bldg Lincoln NE 68508

OLDFIELD, A(RTHUR) BARNEY, writer, radio commentator; b. Tecumseh, Nebr., Dec. 18, 1909; s. Adam William and Anna Ota (Fink) O.; m. Vada Margaret Kinman, May 6, 1935. AB, U. Nebr., 1933, LittD (hon.), 1992. Commd. 2d lt. U.S. Army, 1932, advanced through grades to lt. col., 1945; advanced through grades to col. USAF, 1947, ret., 1962; columnist, feature writer Jour., Lincoln, Nebr., 1932-40; publicist Warner Bros. Studio, Burbank, Calif., 1946-47; corp. dir. internat. rels. Litton Industries, Beverly Hills, Calif., 1963-89; founder, treas. Radio & TV News Dirs. Found. Author: Never a Shot in Anger, Operation Narcissus, 1991, Those Wonderful Men in the Cactus Starfighter Squadron; contbr. to collections: Yanks Meet Reds, Sale I Made Which Did Most for Me, Road to

Berlin. Founder, sec.-treas. Found. of Ams. for Handicapped, Washington; bd. mem., trustee Triple L Youth Ranch Ctr., Colo., 1978-88; trustee USAF Mus.; mem. bd. nominations Aviation Hall of Fame, Dayton, Ohio. Recipient Humanitarian award Am. Rsch. and Med. Svcs. Anaheim, 1978; named Disting. Nebraskalander of Yr., 1983, VFW Disting. Citizen, 1992; inducted Hall of Champions Invent Am., 1989; his uniform displayed in Celebrities in Uniform sect. USAF mus., 1997; 5 miles of U.S. highway designated Col. Barney Oldfield Meml. Hwy., Tecumseh, Nebr., 1997. Mem. Aviation/Space Writers Assn. (founder Aviation/Space Writers Found., Disting. Svc. award 1977), Radio and TV News Dirs. Assn. (founder, treas. Radio and TV News Dirs. Found. 1968, John F. Hogan Disting. Svc. award for establishment of Radio and TV News Dirs. Found. 1978, Col. Barney Oldfield Disting. Svc. award 1994), Overseas Press Club Am., Greater L.A. Press Club, Radio and TV News Assn. So. Calif., Writers Guild Am. West, Armed Forces Broadcasters Assn., Air Force Assn. (life), Navy League (life), Soc. for Preservation of English Lang. and Lit. (hon.). Republican. Avocation: philanthropy. Office: PO Box 1855 Beverly Hills CA 90213-1855

OLDFIELD, BARNEY, entertainment executive; b. Boston, June 28, 1956; s. Wilbur Joseph and Thelma Florence (Coombs) O. AB, Harvard U., 1979, Cert. Advanced Studies, 1981; Cert. Bus. Entertainment, NYU, 1996. Editor Musicians, 1979-83; copy editor Social Register Assocs., N.Y.C., 1983-87; advt. dir. Local Listings, N.Y.C., 1987-89; mkt. dir. Societa Italiana Lavor Oro, N.Y.C., 1989-90; bus. mgr. Al-Bab Internat., N.Y.C., 1990-92, McKenzie Internat., N.Y.C., 1992-96; bd. dirs. Anthology Film Archives, N.Y.C., 1995—. Columnist So. Voice newspaper, 1976-79. Mem. Soc. Calif. Pioneers, San Francisco, 1981—. Mem. NATAS, Friars Club of Calif., Harvard Club of N.Y., Harvard Club of Boston, Harvard Club of So. Calif., Harvard Faculty Club, Union League Club N.Y. Republican. Anglican Ch. Avocations: squash, tennis. Home: 143 E 97th St New York NY 10029 Office: Harvard Club Box 92 27 W 44th St New York NY 10036-6613

OLDFIELD, EDWARD CHARLES, JR., retired naval officer, communications company executive; b. Hampton, Va., July 21, 1919; s. Edward Charles and Alice Toomer (Parrish) O.; m. Lucy Garnett Jordan, Apr. 19, 1941; children: Edward Charles III, William Marshall, Henry Jordan. BS in Commerce, U. Va., 1940; MBA with distinction, Harvard U., 1950; grad., Naval War Coll., 1956. Commd. ensign USN, 1942, advanced through grades to capt., 1962, served in ships of Atlantic and Pacific fleets and major naval installations, 1942-70; dep. comdr. Def. Indsl. Supply Ctr., Phila., 1966-68; comdg. officer Naval Supply Ctr., Newport, R.I., 1968-70; dir. U.S. Naval Audit Svc., S.E. U.S., 1970-71; ret. USN, 1971; asst. to pres. TeleCable Corp., Norfolk, Va., 1971-73; treas. TeleCable Corp., Norfolk, 1973-74, v.p. corp. devel., 1974-83; v.p., asst. to chmn. Landmark Communications Inc., Norfolk, 1983-88; ret., 1988. Mem. dean's adv. com., bd. dirs. ctr. for econ. edn., lectr. Old Dominion U. Sch. Bus. and Pub. Adminstrn., Norfolk, 1985-88. Baker scholar Harvard U., 1950. Mem. Tower Club-So. Cable TV Assn., Alpha Kappa Psi, Beta Gamma Sigma, Kappa Alpha, Harbor Club (Norfolk, bd. dirs. 1980-86, pres. 1986-88), Norfolk Yacht and County Club. Republican. Roman Catholic. Home: 3100 Shore Dr Apt 1121 Virginia Beach VA 23451

OLDFIELD, JAMES EDMUND, nutrition educator; b. Victoria, B.C., Can., Aug. 30, 1921; came to U.S., 1949; s. Henry Clarence and Doris O. Oldfield; m. Mildred E. Atkinson, Sept. 4, 1942; children: Nancy E. Oldfield McLaren, Kathleen E. Oldfield Sansone, David J., Jane E. Oldfield Imper, Richard A. BSA, U. B.C., 1941, MSA, 1949; PhD, Oreg. State U., 1951. Faculty Oreg. State U., Corvallis, 1951-90, head dept. animal sci., 1967-83, dir. Nutrition Research Inst., 1986-90; mem. nat. tech. adv. com. on water supply U.S. Dept. Interior, Washington, 1967-68; bd. dirs. Coun. for Agrl. Sci. and Tech., Ames, Iowa, 1978-84; mem. nutrition study sect. NIH, Bethesda, Md., 1975-80, 85-87; cons. Selenium Tellurium Devel. Assn., Grimbergen, Belgium, 1990—. Editor: Selenium in Biomedicine, 1967, Sulphur in Nutrition, 1970, Selenium in Biology and Medicine, 1987; author: Selenium in Nutrition, 1971. Served to maj. Can. Army, 1942-46, ETO. Fulbright research scholar U.S. Dept. State, 1974, Massey U., New Zealand. Fellow Am. Soc. Animal Sci. (pres. 1966-67, Morrison award 1972), Am. Inst. Nutrition; mem. Am. Chem. Soc., Am. Registry Profl. Animal Scientists (pres. 1990, editor: Profl. Animal Scientist 1993-96), Fedn. Am. Socs. Exptl. Biol. Republican. Episcopalian. Lodge: Kiwanis (pres. 1964, lt. gov. 1986). Home: 1325 NW 15th St Corvallis OR 97330-2604 Office: Oreg State Univ Dept Animal Sci Corvallis OR 97331

OLDFIELD, RUSSELL MILLER, lawyer; b. Salem, Ohio, Aug. 18, 1946; s. Donald W. and Virginia Alice (Harold) O.; m. Mary Lou Kubrin, May 28, 1966; children: Lindsey Marie, Grant Russell. AB, Youngstown State U., 1971; JD, Ohio No. U., 1974. Bar: Ohio 1974, Tenn. 1984. Assoc. counsel Gulf. and Western Industries, Nashville, 1979-83; v.p., gen. counsel, sec. Rogers Group Inc., Nashville, 1983—. Served with U.S. Army, 1966-68. Mem. ABA, Nashville Bar Assn., Am. Corp. Counsel Assn. (pres. Tenn. chpt. 1994-95), Samaritan, Inc. (chmn. 1991-92), Univ. Club. Episcopalian. Home: 101 Sioux Ct Hendersonville TN 37075-4634 Office: Rogers Group Inc PO Box 25250 Nashville TN 37202-5250

OLDHAM, BILL W., mathematics educator; b. Paris, Tex., Oct. 30, 1934; s. H.H. and Margaret Irene (McDowna) O.; m. Monda Underwood, Jan. 30, 1954; children: Clifford, Brent, Bill. BA in Math., Abilene Christian U., 1956; MS in Math., Okla. State U., 1963; EdD in Math. Edn., U. No. Colo., 1972. Tchr. math. Mcpl. Sch., Ft. Summer, N.Mex., 1956-61; prof. math. Harding U., Searcy, Ark., 1961—. Mem. Math. Assn. Am., Nat. Coun. Tchrs. Math., Am. Coun. Tchrs. Math., Phi Delta Kappa. Ch. of Christ. Home: 1403 W Arch Ave Searcy AR 72143-5105 Office: Harding Univ PO Box 764 Searcy AR 72149-1001

OLDHAM, CHARLES HERBERT GEOFFREY, physicist, science consultant; b. Harden, Yorkshire, Eng., Feb. 17, 1929; s. Herbert Cecil and Evelyn Selina (Brooke) O.; m. Brenda Mildred Raven, Sept. 1, 1951; children: David Charles (dec.), Jon Geoffrey, Janice Kathryn, Keith Andrew. BSc, U. Reading, Eng., 1950, BSc with spl. honours, 1951; MA in Physics, U. Toronto, Ont., Can., 1952, PhD in Physics, 1954. Geophysicist Standard Oil Co. Calif., La Habra, 1954-57; sr. geophysicist Standard Oil Co. Calif., San Francisco, 1957-60; fellow Inst. Current World Affairs, Hong Kong, 1960-66; dep. dir. Sci. Policy Rsch. Unit, Sussex, Eng., 1966-80, dir., 1980-92; hon. prof. Sci. Policy Rsch. Unit U. Sussex, 1996—; sci. advisor Internat. Devel. Rsch. Ctr., Ottawa, Ont., Can., 1992-96; chmn. adv. com. on sci. and tech. for devel. UN, N.Y.C., 1990-92; U.K. del. UN Commn. Sci. and Tech. for Devel., 1992—; chmn. Gender Working Group, Ottawa, 1993-95. Sci. editor World Devel., 1975-90; contbr. articles on sci. policy and Chinese Sci. to profl. jours. Decorated comdr. Order Brit. Empire, 1990. Fellow Royal Soc. Arts, Manufactures and Commerce; mem. Lewes Golf Club. Avocations: golf, long distance train travel, swimming, hiking, theatre. Home: The Block House Barcombe Pl, The Clock House Bascombe Pl, Barcombe Bascombe BN8 5DL, England K1N 9M5 Office: U Sussex, Sci Policy Rsch Unit, Brighton BN1 9RF, England

OLDHAM, DALE RALPH, life insurance company executive, actuary; b. Topeka, May 31, 1943; s. Ralph W. and Anna Marie (Minch) O.; m. Marilyn D. Morris, June 5, 1965; children: Kent D., Kevin L. BS magna cum laude, Washburn U., 1965; AM, U. Mich., 1967. Asst. actuary Nat. Res. Life, Topeka, Kans., 1967-72, assoc. actuary, 1972-74, v.p., assoc. actuary, 1974-76, v.p., chief actuary, 1976-84; also bd. dirs.; sr. v.p. adminstrn. Security Benefit Group, Topeka, 1984-88, sr. v.p. affiliated products, services, 1988-89; pres., COO, Savers Life Ins. Co. Am., 1989-90, pres., CEO, chmn. bd., 1990-94, pres., CEO 1994-95; v.p., actuary Centennial Life Ins. Co., Lenexa, Kans., 1995-96, sr. v.p., actuary, bd. dirs., 1996—. Bd. dirs., treas. United Way Greater Topeka, 1988-89; mem. adv. council Unified Sch. Dist., Topeka, 1981-84; trustee Meml. Hosp. Corp. Topeka, 1984-89, chmn., 1989; mem. adv. bd. Ctr. Ins. Edn., 1987-89. Fellow Soc. Actuaries; mem. Am. Acad. Actuaries, Kansas City Actuaries Club (pres. 1980-81), Adminstrv. Mgmt. Soc. (bd. dirs. 1975-82, 84—, pres. 1981-82, Merit award 1980, Diamond Merit award 1987), Topeka Geneal. Soc. (pres. 1988-89). Republican. Lodge: Kiwanis (Topeka pres. 1980). Home: 12414 Wedd St Overland Park KS 66213-1841 Office: Centennial Life Ins Co 8735 Rosehill Rd Lenexa KS 66215-4610

OLDHAM, DARIUS DUDLEY, lawyer; b. Beaumont, Tex., July 6, 1941; s. Darius Saran and Mary Francis (Carraway) O.; m. Judy J. White, Jan. 23, 1965; children: Steven, Michael. BA, U. Tex., Austin, 1964; JD, U. Tex., 1966. Bar: Tex. 1966, U.S. Dist. Ct. (so., no., ea. and we. dists.) Tex. 1966, U.S. Supreme Ct. 1974, U.S. Ct. Appeals (5th and 11th cirs.) 1968. Assoc. Fulbright & Jaworski, Houston, 1966-74, ptnr., 1974—, mem. policy com., 1980—; mem. faculty grad. litigation program U. Houston; lectr. on corp. def. ins. and product liability. Mem. bd. editors Aviation Litigation Reporter, Personal Injury Def. Reporter; country corr. Internat. Ins. Law Rev.; contbr. articles to profl. jours. Mem. Nat. Jud. Coll. Coun. for the Future; bd. dirs., former sec.-treas. FIC Found., 1979-87; past bd. dirs. Houston Pops Orch.; mem. liberal arts adv. coun. U. Tex. Fellow Am. Coll. Trial Lawyers (complex litigation com.), Tex. Bar Found. (life), Am. Bar Found. (life), Houston Bar Found. (life), Am. Bd. Trial Advs.; mem. ABA (vice chmn. aviation com. tips sect. 1980-82, chmn. aviation com. litigation sect. 1982-84, vice chmn. econs. law practice com. 1985-86, mem. coun. tort and ins. practice sect. 1988-91, vice chair 1991-92, chair-elect 1992-93, chmn. ann. meeting program com. 1987, chmn. professionalism com. 1990-91, fin. com. 1986-93, chmn. long range planning com. 1991-92, chair tort and ins. practice sect. 1994-95, presdl. emissary 1993-95), Tex. Bar Assn. (liaison law schs. and law students com. 1983-86, PEER com. 1979-82, chmn. liaison fed. jud. com. 1989-90, pattern jury charges Vol. IV com. 1988-92), Tex. Young Lawyers Assn. (bd. dirs., chmn.), Fed. Ins. and Corp. Counsel (exec. v.p., pres.-elect 1988-89, pres. 1989-90, chmn. bd. 1990-91, exec. com. 1988-91, coord. com. 1984-87, sec.-treas. 1987-88), Tex. Assn. Def. Counsel, Maritime Law Assn. U.S., Am. Counsel Assn. (bd. dirs. 1982-83, 89-94), Def. Rsch. Inst. (chmn. aerospace com. 1984-87, vice chmn. 1983-84, Presdl. Achievement award 1987, bd. dirs. 1989-92, exec. com. 1991-92), Lawyers for Civil Justice (bd. dirs. 1988-92, 95—, exec. com. 1990-92, 95—, pres. elect 1996, pres. 1996-97), River Oaks Country Club, Houston Ctr. Club, Sigma Chi, Phi Delta Phi. Office: Fulbright & Jaworski 1301 Mckinney St Fl 51 Houston TX 77010-3031

OLDHAM, ELAINE DOROTHEA, retired elementary and middle school educator; b. Coalinga, Calif., June 29, 1931; d. Claude Smith Oldham and Dorothy Elaine (Hill) Wilkins. AB in History, U. Calif., Berkeley, 1953; MS in Sch. Adminstrn., Calif. State U., Hayward, 1976; postgrad. U. Calif., Berkeley, Harvard U., Mills Coll. Tchr. Piedmont Unified Sch. Dist., Calif., 1956-94, ret., 1994. Pres., bd. dirs. Camron-Stanford House Preservation Assn., 1979-86, adminstrv. v.p., bd. dirs., 1976-79, 86—; mem. various civic and community support groups; bd. dirs. Anne Martin Children's Ctr., Lincoln Child Ctr., pres. Acacia br. Children's Hosp. Med. Ctr., No. Light Sch. Aux., East Bay League II of San Francisco Symphony, Piedmont Hist. Soc., pres. Children's Hosp. Med. Ctr. Mem. Am. Assn. Museums, Am. Assn. Mus. Trustees, Internat. Council Museums, Inst. Internat. Edn., Am. Assn. State and Local History, Am. Decorative Arts Forum, Oakland Mus. Assn. (women's bd.), DAR (regent, Outstanding Tchr. Am. History award), Colonial Dames Am., Magna Charta Dames, Daus. of Confederacy (bd. dirs.), Huguenot Soc. (bd. dirs.), Plantagenent Soc., Order of Washington, Colonial Order of Crown, Americans of Royal Descent, Order St. George and Descs. of Knights of Garter, San Francisco Antiques Show (com. mem.), U. Calif. Alumni Assn. (co-chmn. and chmn. of 10th and 25th yr. class reunion coms.), Internat. Diplomacy Coun. (San Francisco chpt.), Internat. Churchill Soc., English Speaking Union, Pacific Mus. Soc., Prytanean Alumnae Assn. (bd. dirs.), Phi Delta Kappa, Delta Kappa Gamma. Republican. Episcopalian. Clubs: Harvard (San Francisco), Bellevue.

OLDHAM, JOE, editor; b. Bklyn., Aug. 1, 1943. B.S., NYU, 1965. Editor Car Model OLR Pub., North Arlington, N.J., 1966-68; assoc. editor Automobile Internat. Johnston Internat. Publs., N.Y.C., 1968-70; spl. projects editor Magnum-Royal Publs., N.Y.C., 1970-72; book devel editor Hearst Corp., N.Y.C., 1972-77; editor Motor Mag. Hearst Corp., 1977-81, exec. editor Popular Mechanics, 1981-85, editor-in-chief Popular Mechanics, 1985—; contbr. numerous articles to various mags. Recipient cert. of appreciation Nat. Inst. for Automotive Service Excellence, 1976; recipient cert. of appreciation Automotive Service Councils, 1979, cert. of appreciation Northwood Inst., 1981, cert. of appreciation Automotive Hall of Fame, 1981. Mem. Internat. Motor Press Assn. (pres. 1973-74, 81-82), Am. Soc. Mag. Editors, Soc. Profl. Journalists, Am. Auto Racing Writers and Broadcasting Assn. Club: Detroit Press. Office: Popular Mechanics The Hearst Corp 224 W 57th St New York NY 10019-3212*

OLDHAM, JOHN MICHAEL, physician, psychiatrist, educator; b. Muskogee, Okla., Sept. 6, 1940; s. Henry Newland and Alice Gray (Ewton) O.; m. Karen Joan Pacella, Apr. 24, 1971; children: Madeleine Marie, Michael Clark. BS in Engring., Duke U., 1962; MS in Neuroendocrinology, Baylor U., 1966, MD, 1967. Licensed physician N.Y., N.J., Tex.; diplomate in psychiat. Am. Bd. Psychiatry and Neurology. Intern pediatrics St. Luke's Hosp., N.Y.C., 1967-68; resident psychiat. Columbia U. Dept. Psychiat., N.Y.S. Psychiatric Inst., N.Y.C., 1968-70, chief resident in psychiat., 1970-71; candidate Columbia Psychoanalytic Ctr., N.Y.C., 1977; dir. psychiatric emergency svcs. Roosevelt Hosp., N.Y.C., 1973-74, dir. residency tng. dept. psychiat., 1974-77; dir. short term diagnostic and treatment unit N.Y. Hosp. Westchester Divsn., White Plains, N.Y., 1977-80; dir. divsn. acute treatment svcs. N.Y. Hosp. Westchester Divsn., White Plains, 1980-84; deputy dir. N.Y. State Psychiatric Inst., N.Y.C., 1984-89, acting dir., 1989-90, dir., 1990—; assoc. chmn. dept. psychiatry Columbia U. Coll. Physicians & Surgeons, N.Y.C., 1986-96, vice chmn., 1996—; chief med. officer N.Y. State Office Mental Health, Albany, 1989—; instr. clin. psychiat. Columbia U. Coll. Physicians & Surgeons, 1974-76, assoc. clin. psychiat., 1976-77, lectr. psychiat., 1977-84, assoc. prof. clin. psychiat., 1984-88, prof. clin. psychiat., 1988-96, Elizabeth K. Dollard profl. clin. psychiatry medicine & law, 1996—; asst. prof. psychiat. Cornell U. Med. Coll., N.Y.C., 1977-83, assoc. prof. clin. psychiat., 1983-84; attending staff dept. psychiat. Roosevelt Hosp., N.Y.C., 1973-77; assoc. attending psychiat., N.Y. Hosp., 1977-84, Presbyn Hosp., N.Y.C., 1984-88, attending psychiat., 1988—; tng., supervising psychoanalyst Columbia Psychoanalytic Ctr., N.Y.C., 1983—; coord. med. student edn., Cornell U. Med. Coll. Dept. Psychiat., Westchester Divsn., White Plains, N.Y., 1977-84; coord. clin. clerkships in psychiat. Roosevelt Hosp., Columbia U. Coll. Physicians & Surgeons, N.Y.C., 1974-77; mem. acad. adv. com. Pfizer vis. professorship program in psychiat., 1990-92; mem. Sandoz Clozaril nat. adv. bd; spl. adv. bd. Freedom From Fear, Inc.; examiner Am. Bd. Psychiatry and Neurology; chmn. acute divisin rsch. group, Westchester Divsn., N.Y. Hosp., 1981-84, co-project dir. borderline rsch. group, 1982-84, co-prin. investigator familial transmission DSM III personality disorders, 1982-84; prin. investigator personality disorders in bulimia, N.Y.S. Psychiatric Inst., 1985-90, structured DSM III assessment psychoanalytic patients, Columbia Psychoanalytic Ctr., 1986-91; co-prin. investigator validity DSM III R personality disorders, N.Y. State Psychiatric Inst., 1987-94; co=investigator NIMH, 1996—. Author: (with L.B. Morris) The Personality Self-Portrait, 1990; editor Jour. Practical Psychiatry and Behavioral Health; contbg. editor Jour. Personality Disorders; sect. editor Psychiatry; mem. editl. adv. bd. Am. Psychiat. Press, Inc.; mem. exec. editl. bd. Psychiat. Quar.; reviewer Psychiat. Svcs., Jour. of Neuropsychiatry; contbr. numerous articles to profl. jours.; more than 100 presentations in field. Recipient John J. Weber prize Excellence in Psychoanalytic Rsch. Columbia Psychoanalytic Ctr., 1990. Fellow Am. Coll. Psychiatrists, Am. Psychiat. Assn. (chmn. com. psychoanalytic liaison N.Y. County dist. br. 1986-87, pres. 1989-90, com. rsch. psychiat. treatment 1987-93, coun. rsch., steering com. practice guidelines, chmn. sci. program com. 1992-95, cons. 1991-92, 95-96), Am. Psychopath. Assn., N.Y. Acad. Medicine;mem. Am. Psychoanalytic Assn. (cert.), Assn. Psychoanalytic Medicine (pres. 1989-91), Internat. Psychoanalytical Assn., N.Y. Acad. Sci., N.Y. State Med. Soc., Assn. Rsch. Personality Disorders (bd. dirs.). Office: NY State Psychiatric Inst 722 W 168th St New York NY 10032-2603

OLDHAM, MAXINE JERNIGAN, real estate broker; b. Whittier, Calif., Oct. 13, 1923; d. John K. and Lela Hessie (Mears) Jernigan; m. Laurance Montgomery Oldham, Oct. 28, 1941; 1 child, John Laurence. AA, San Diego City Coll., 1973; student Western State U. Law, San Diego, 1976-77, LaSalle U., 1977-78; grad. Realtors Inst., Sacramento, 1978. Mgr. Edin Harig Realty, LaMesa, Calif., 1966-70; tchr. Bd. Edn., San Diego, 1959-66; mgr. Julia Cave Real Estate, San Diego, 1970-73; salesman Computer Realty, San Diego, 1973-74; owner Shelter Island Realty, San Diego, 1974—. Author: Jernigan History, 1982, Mears Geneology, 1985, Fustons of Colonial America, 1988, Sissoms. Mem. Civil Svc. Commn., San Diego, 1957-58. Recipient Outstanding Speaker award Dale Carnegie. Mem. Nat. Assn. Realtors, Calif. Assn. Realtors, San Diego Bd. Realtors, San Diego Apt. Assn., Internationale des Professions Immobilieres (internat. platform speaker), DAR (vice regent Linares chpt.), Colonial Dames 17th Century, Internat. Fedn. Univ. Women. Republican. Roman Catholic. Avocations: music, theater, painting, geneology, continuing edn. Home: 3348 Lowell St San Diego CA 92106-1713 Office: Shelter Island Realty 2810 Lytton St San Diego CA 92110-4810

OLDHAM, TODD, fashion designer; b. Corpus Christi, Tex., 1960; s. Jack and Linda Oldham. Founder Times 7, Dallas; founder, designer Todd Oldham, N.Y.C., 1989—; design dir. Escada, Munich, Germany, 1994—. Host, dir. Todd Time MTV House of Style, 1993-96; guest Tracy Takes On with Tracy Ullman, 1994, The Nanny, 1996, Roseanne, 1996; designer spl. collection for Batman Forever, 1995, MTV's Choose or Lose bus, 1996, GM Bravada to raise money for cancer rsch., 1997; music video co-dir. (with Hype Williams) Maxi Priest's That Kind of Girl, 1996; music video dir. Us3's Come on Everybody, 1997. Active Design Industries Found. for AIDS, People for the Ethical Treatment of Animals, POWARS, Pet Pals. Recipient Rising Star award Internat. Apparel Mart, Dallas, 1991, Fashion Excellence award Internat. Apparel Mart, Dallas, 1993; named Designer of Yr. Calif. Fashion Industry Friends of AIDS Project, 1996. Mem. Coun. Fashion Designers Am. (Perry Ellis award for new fashion talent 1991). Office: Todd Oldham Store NY 123 Wooster St New York NY 10012-3106 Office: Todd Oldham Miami Beach 160 8th St Miami Beach FL 33139-6286

OLDS, ELIZABETH, dancer; b. Mpls.. Attended, SouthWest Ballet Ctr., Nat. Acad. of Arts, Ill., Royal Winnipeg (Man., Can.) Ballet Sch. Dancer Royal Winnipeg Ballet, 1982-85, soloist, 1985-89, prin. dancer, 1989—; various guest performances in U.S. and Can. Dance performances include Nuages, Symphony in D, Four Last Songs, Romeo & Juliet, Adagio Hammerklavier, Three Pieces, Giselle, Fall River Legend, Rodeo, Dark Elegies, Deuce Coupe, The Nutcracker, Tarantella, Apollo, Scotch Symphony, Roses, There is a Time, Lilac Garden, The Sleeping Beauty, Gâité Parisienne, many others. Master of ceremonies Western Can. Summer Games, 1990, Access Awareness Week, 1991; chairperson Easter Seals Campaign, 1994. Avocations: pottery, gardening. Office: Royal Winnipeg Ballet, 380 Graham Ave, Winnipeg, MB Canada R3C 4K2*

OLDS, JACQUELINE, psychiatrist, educator; b. Springfield, Mass., Jan. 4, 1947; d. James and Marianne (Ejier) O.; m. Richard Stanton Schwartz, Aug. 26, 1978; children: Nathaniel Leland, Sarah Elizabeth. BA, Radcliffe Coll., 1967; MD, Tufts U., 1971. Diplomate Am. Bd. Psychiatry and Neurology. Resident in adult psychiatry Mass. Mental Health Ctr., Boston, 1974; resident in child psychiatry McLean Hosp., Belmont, Mass., 1976, assoc. attending child psychiatrist, 1979—; psychiatrist-in-charge inpatient unit McLean Hall-Mercer Children's Ctr., Belmont, 1976-79; assoc. child psychiatry Beth Israel Hosp., Boston, 1979—; cons. in child psychiatry Mass. Gen. Hosp., Boston, 1994—; instr. psychiatry Harvard U. Med. Sch, Boston, 1976-86; asst. prof. clin. psychiatry, 1986—; cons. North Shore Mental Health Ctr., Salem, 1981-82. Author: Overcoming Loneliness in Every Day Life, 1996; contbr. articles to profl. jours. Sec. Cambridge (Mass.) Nursery Sch. Bd., 1982-84. Fellow Am. Psychiat. Assn.; mem. Mass. Psychiat. Soc. (ethics com. 1988-93, mem. pub. affairs com. 1992—), Am. Acad. Child Psychiatry, Am. Psychoanalytic Assn., New England Coun. Child and Adolescent Psychiatry (bd. dirs.). Democrat. Avocations: piano, writing, skating, watercolors.

OLDS, JOHN THEODORE, banker; b. N.Y.C., Dec. 24, 1943; s. Richard J. and Barbara (Moses) O.; m. Candace Rose; children: Richard W., Samantha. Grad., Hill Sch., 1961; BA, U. Pa., 1965. With Morgan Guaranty Trust Co. N.Y., N.Y.C.; now mng. dir. J.P. Morgan & Co., N.Y.C. Trustee The Browning sch., N.Y. Hist. Soc. Mem. Univ. Club, Bedford Golf and Tennis Club, Mid-Ocean Club, Knickerbocker Club. Episcopalian. Home: 7 Plateau Ln Bedford NY 10506-1339 Office: Morgan Guaranty Trust Co 9 W 57th St New York NY 10019

OLDSHUE, JAMES Y., chemical engineering consultant; b. Chgo., Apr. 18, 1925; s. James and Louise (Young) O.; m. Betty Ann Wiersema, June 14, 1947; children: Paul, Richard, Robert. B.S. in Chem. Engring., Ill. Inst. Tech., 1947, M.S., 1949, Ph.D. in Chem. Engring., 1951. Registered engr., N.Y. With Mixing Equipment Co., Rochester, N.Y., 1950-92, dir. research, 1960-63, tech. dir., 1963-70, v.p. mixing tech., 1970-92; pres. Oldshue Techs. Internat., Inc., Fairport, N.Y., 1992—; adj. prof. chem. engring. Beijing Inst. Chem. Tech., 1992—. Author: Fluid Mixing Technology, 1983; contbr. chpts. and articles to books and jours. Chmn. budget com. Internat. div. YMCA; bd. dirs. Rochester YMCA. Served with AUS, 1945-47. Recipient 1st Disting. Svc. award N.E. YMCA Internat. Com., 1979, J.E. Purkynse medal Czech Republic Acad. Sci.; named Rochester Engr. of Yr., 1980. Fellow AIChE (pres. 1979, treas. 1983-89, chmn. internat. activities com. 1989-92, Founders award 1981, Eminent Chem. Engr. award 1983, Svc. to Soc. award 1989); mem. NAE, Am. Assn. Engring. Socs. (chmn. 1985, K.A. Roe award 1987), Am. Chem. Soc., Internat. Platform Assn., World Congress Chem. Engrs. (v.p. 1986, pres. 1994—), N.Am. Mixing Forum (chmn. 1990-93, Mixing Achievement rsch. award 1992), Interam. Confedn. Chem. Engrs. (sec. gen. 1991-93, v.p. 1993-95, pres. 1995-96), Victor Marquez award 1983), Rochester Engring. Soc. (pres. 1992-93). Mem. Reformed Ch. in Am. (gen. program coun.). Achievements include design and scale-up procedures in field of fluid mixing. Home: 141 Tyringham Rd Rochester NY 14617-2522 Office: 811 Ayrault Rd Fairport NY 14450-8964

OLDSON, WILLIAM ORVILLE, history educator; b. Hampton, Va., Jan. 23, 1940; s. James Orville and Kathryn Francis (Zephir) O.; m. Judith Ann Kinsinger, June 11, 1967; children: Scott Ryan, Darren Randall. BA magna cum laude, Spring Hill Coll., Mobile, Ala., 1965; MA, Ind. U., 1966, PhD, 1970. Mem. Soc. of Jesus, 1959-65. Asst. prof. dept. history Fla. State U., Tallahassee, 1969-74; assoc. prof. history Fla. State U., 1974-79, assoc. chmn. undergrad. affairs, 1973-75, 83-84, dir. hist. adminstrn. and pub. history prog., 1987—, prof. history, 1979—, dir. history computer programs and rsch., 1993—, assoc. chmn. grad. affairs, 1994; dir. grievances and arbitration United Faculty of Fla., 1978-80, chief negotiator, 1980-81; dir. Social Sci. Interdisciplinary Program, Fla. State U., Panama City campus, 1986-90; charter mem. Pres.'s Coun. for Excellence in Coll. Tchg., 1990; assoc. dir. Holocaust Study Summer Inst. for Secondary Sch. Tchrs., 1996—. Author: The Historical and Nationalistic Thought of Nicolae Iorga, 1973, A Providential Anti-Semitism: Nationalism and Polity in Nineteenth Century Romania, 1991; author numerous hist. manuals. Recipient Outstanding Tchr. award Phi Eta Sigma, 1990, John Frederick Lewis award Am. Philos. Soc., 1991, Univ. Tchg. award, 1988, 95, travel grant Internat. Rsch. & Exch. Bd., 1996; NDEA fellow, 1966-67; Russian and East European Inst. fellow Ind. U., 1965-66; Fulbright fellow, 1967-68, Internat. Rsch. and Exch. Bd. fellow, 1973; Loyola U. of New Orleans honors fellow, Romanian State fellow, 1967-68; Holocaust Ednl. Found. fellow, 1994, 96; Inst. on the Holocaust and Jewish Civilization fellow Northwestern U., 1996; Coun. Rsch. and Creativity Planning grantee, 1994-95; Wolfson Found. grantee, 1995; Louis E. and Patrice J. Wolfson Found. grantee, 1995; Wolfson Family Found. grantee, 1996. Mem. Sigma Pi Sigma, Delta Tau Kappa, Phi Alpha Theta (Prof. of Yr. 1988). Democrat. Roman Catholic. Home: 1116 Sandhurst Dr Tallahassee FL 32312-2530 Office: Fla State U History Dept Tallahassee FL 32306-2029

OLEARCHYK, ANDREW, cardiothoracic surgeon, educator; b. Peremyshl, Ukraine, Dec. 3, 1935; s. Simon and Anna (Kravets) O.; m. Renata M. Sharan, June 26, 1971; children: Christina N., Roman A., Adrian S. Grad., Med. Acad., Warsaw, Poland, 1961; med. edn. grad., U. Pa., 1970. Diplomate Am. Bd. Surgery, Am. Bd. Thoracic Surgery. Chief divsn. anesthesiology, asst. dept. surgery Provincial Hosp., Kielce, Poland, 1963-66; resident in gen. surgery Geisinger Med. Ctr., Danville, Pa., 1968-73; resident in thoracic, cardiac surgery Allegheny Gen. Hosp., Pitts., 1980-82; pvt. practice medicine specializing in cardiac, thoracic and vascular surgery Phila. and Camden, N.J., 1982—. Contbr. articles to med. jours., also 7 monographs. Achievements include internal repair of the coronary sinus (Valsalva) aneurysm 1996; grating of the internal thoracic to coronary arteries without touching the atherosclerotic ascending aorta, on cardiopulmonary bypass with a beating, warm and vented heart and bradycardia induced by beta-blocker; design of double occlusion clamps for the ascending aorta, Olearchyk R Triple Ringed Cannula Spring Clip to secure vein grafts over blunted cannulas in coronary artery bypass surgery; demonstration of safety of simultaneous use of fluothane and curare as gen. anesthesia; intro. of endarterectomy and external prosthetic grafting of ascending and transverse aorta under hypothermic circulatory arrest; pioneering promotion of grafting of the left anterior descending coronary artery sys. during resection of cardiac aneurysms, and of diffusely diseased coronary arteries with the internal thoracic artery; first to combine insertion of the inferior vena cava filter with iliofemoral venous thrombectomy; combined right femoral and iliac retroperitoneal surgical approach to remove retained intraaortal balloon device; applied a technique for early antegrade flow from an axillary to main graft during replacement of the ascending aorta in proximal aortic dissection. Address: 129 Walt Whitman Blvd Cherry Hill NJ 08003-3746

O'LEARY, DANIEL FRANCIS, university dean; b. Boston, Apr. 17, 1923; s. Dennis Joseph and Catherine Mary (O'Connell) O'L. BA, Oblate Coll., 1950; EdM, U. Buffalo, 1953, EdD, 1956. Tchr. gen. sci., biology Bishop Fallon High Sch., Buffalo, 1951-62, asst. prin., 1962-65; dir. edn. Oblate Fathers, Washington, 1963-68; prin. Bishop Fallon High Sch., Buffalo, 1968-74; dir. spl. programs Niagara U. (N.Y.), 1974-77, dean spl. programs, 1977-81, prof. edn., 1982—, dean edn. and continuing studies, 1982-88, prof., dean Coll. Edn., 1988—; adj. prof. Mt. St. Joseph's Tchrs. Coll., Buffalo, 1956-64, edn. evaluator reading clinic, 1956-64. Asst. dir. family life dept. Diocese of Buffalo, 1953-64. Mem. AAIP, ASCD, ATE, Am. Assn. Sch. Adminstrs., Nat. Coun. for Adminstrn. Tech. Edn., N.Y. State Assn. Tchr. Educators, Am. Assn. Colls. for Tchr. Edn., Phi Delta Kappa. Roman Catholic. Office: Niagara U Dept Edn Niagara University NY 14109

O'LEARY, DANIEL VINCENT, JR., lawyer; b. Bklyn., May 26, 1942; s. Daniel Vincent and Mary (Maxwell) O'L.; m. Marilyn Irene Gavigan, June 1, 1968; children: Daniel, Katherine, Molly, James. AB cum laude, Georgetown U., 1963; LLB, Yale U., 1966. Bar: Ill. 1967. Assoc. Wilson & Mc Ilvaine, Chgo., 1967-75, ptnr., 1975-1987; ptnr. Peterson & Ross, Chgo., 1987-94, Schwartz & Freeman, Chgo., 1994-95; of counsel Davidson, Goldstein, Mandell & Menkes, Chgo., 1995—; pres., bd. dirs. Jim's Cayman Co., Ltd., 1992—; bd. dirs. TV and Radio Purchasing Group Inc.; asst. sec. L.M.C. Ins. Co. Bermuda, 1990—; pres. Wagering Ins. N.Am. P.G. Ltd., 1997—. Lt. comdr. USNR, ret. Mem. Kenilworth Sailing Club (commodore 1985-87). Roman Catholic. Avocations: fishing, scuba diving. Office: Davidson Goldstein Mandell & Menkes 303 W Madison St Ste 1900 Chicago IL 60606-3308

O'LEARY, DAVID MICHAEL, priest, educator; b. Lynn, Mass., Mar. 11, 1958; s. Edward William and Kathryn O'L. BA, St. John's Sem., Boston, 1981, MDiv, 1984; MEd, Boston Coll., 1986; STL, Weston Sch. of Theology, 1990. Ordained priest Roman Catholic Ch., 1986; cert. alcohol counselor. Deacon intern Immaculate Conception Parish, Malden, Mass., 1984-86; parochial vicar Immaculate Conception Parish, Everett, Mass., 1986-91, St. Augustine's Parish, South Boston, 1991-93; priest St. Theresa's Ch., North Reading, Mass., 1993-95; prof. St. Mary's Sem. and U., Balt., 1995—; spl. edn. tchr., 1977-81, coll. dir. St. John's spl. edn. program, 1980-81, rschr., writer, film editor Office Religious Edn., Boston diocese, Brighton, Mass., 1981-82; group therpy leader, case worker Brigham and Women's Hosp., Kenmore Sq. De-Tox, 1982-83; substance abuse counselor St. John/ St. Hugh Parish, Roxbury, Mass., 1983-84; lectr. Pro-Life Archdiocese of Boston, 1986—, Basic Tchr. and Intermediate Tchr Trainer and Cert., 1987; vis. lectr. coll. level, 1991, 92; cons. in counseling. Contbr. articles to religious and other pubs. Counselor Camp Fatima Exceptional Citizens Week, 1978-90, asst. resident dir., 1991, resident dir., 1992; founding mem. Everett Ltd. Equity Coop. Project, 1988; mem. steering com., synthesizer and co-editor report to Nat. Conf. Cath. Bishops on Women's Pastoral, 1989; active mem. South Boston Pastoral Com., 1991; mem. Instn. Rev. Bd. Human Subjects Com., U. Mass., 1992; founder spiritual support group for AIDS victims and families, 1992. Mem. KC (life). Democrat. Avocation: long distance running. Home and Office: St Mary's Sem and U 5400 Roland Ave Baltimore MD 21210

O'LEARY, DENIS JOSEPH, retired physician, insurance company executive; b. Ireland, Feb. 5, 1924; came to U.S., 1949, naturalized, 1954; s. Joseph and Mary Christine (Dennis) O'L.; m. Audrey Mary Ryan, Nov. 26, 1952; children: Michael, Brian, Denis, Kevin. MD, Nat. U. Ireland, Cork, 1947. Intern St. Michael's Hosp., Toronto, Ont., Can., 1947-48; resident St. Michael's Hosp., 1948-49, St. Vincent's Hosp., N.Y.C., 1949-50, Triboro Hosp., Jamaica, N.Y., 1950-51; with N.Y. Life Ins. Co., N.Y.C., 1952-88; med. dir. employees' health N.Y. Life Ins. Co., 1961-70, v.p., 1970-82, sr. v.p., 1982-88; asst. attending physician Bellevue Hosp., N.Y.C., 1955-69; assoc. attending physician Bellevue Hosp., 1969-77, attending physician, 1977-84, sr. attending physician, 1984-87; instr. medicine, Columbia U., 1958-63, assoc. in medicine, 1963-68; asst. prof. clin. medicine NYU, 1968-86; sec. N.Y. Lung Assn., 1962-67, 69-71, v.p., 1967-69, dir., 1961-86, pres.-elect, 1983, pres., 1985-86. Bd. dirs. Nat. Council on Alcoholism, N.Y.C., 1979-86, pres., 1984-86. Served as capt. M.C. AUS, 1953-55. Fellow Am. Coll. Chest Physicians, Am. Occupational Med. Assn., Am. Pub. Health Assn.; mem. AMA, N.Y. State, New York County med. socs., Am. Thoracic Assn., Soc. Alumni Bellevue Hosp., N.Y. Occupational Med. Assn. (exec. com. 1967—, pres. 1973-74). Club: Scarsdale (N.Y.) Golf (gov. 1981-84), Rancho Bernardo Golf.

O'LEARY, DENNIS JOSEPH, lawyer; b. Phila., Jan. 11, 1941; s. Joseph P. and Catherine (Brannigan) O'L.; married; children: Dennis J., Terrance P., Patricia M., Maryann M. BS, Villanova U., 1963; JD, Temple U., 1972. Bar: Pa. 1972. Ptnr. White and Williams, Phila., 1972—. Mem. Pa. Bar Assn., Phila. Bar Assn., Defense Rsch. Inst., Pa. Defense Inst. Roman Catholic. Avocations: photography, travel, fishing, gardening. Office: White & Williams 1650 Market St Philadelphia PA 19103-7301

O'LEARY, DENNIS PATRICK, biophysicist; b. Dec. 24, 1939; married, 1964; 2 children. BS, U. Chgo., 1962; PhD, U. Iowa, 1969. Asst. prof. surg. and anatomy UCLA, 1971-74; rsch. assoc. prof. otolaryngology and pharmacology U. Pitts., 1974-78, assoc. prof. otolaryngology and physiology, 1978-84; prof. depts. otolaryngology, physiology, biomed. engring. U. So. Calif., 1984—; USPHS rsch. fellow UCLA, 1969-70. Mem. AAAS, Inst. Medicine-Nat. acad. Sci., Am. Physiol. Soc., Soc. Neurosci., Internat. Brain Rsch. Orgn. Office: U So Calif Parkview Med Bldg C103 1420 San Pablo St Los Angeles CA 90033-1042*

O'LEARY, DENNIS SOPHIAN, medical organization executive; b. Kansas City, Mo., Jan. 28, 1938; s. Theodore Morgan and Emily (Sophian) O'L.; m. Margaret Rose Wiedman, Mar. 29, 1980; children: Margaret Rose, Theodore Morgan. BA, Harvard U., 1960; MD, Cornell U., 1964. Diplomate Am. Bd. Internal Medicine, Am. Bd. Hematology. Intern U. Minn. Hosp., Mpls., 1964-65, resident, 1965-66; resident Strong Meml. Hosp., Rochester, N.Y., 1966-68; asst. prof. medicine and pathology George Washington U. Med. Ctr., Washington, 1971-73, assoc. prof., 1973-80, prof. medicine, 1980-86, assoc. dean grad. med. edn., 1973-77, dean clin. affairs, 1977-86; pres. Joint Commn. on Accreditation Healthcare Orgns., Chgo., 1986—; med. dir. George Washington U. Hosp., 1974-85, v.p. Univ. Health Plan, 1977-85; pres. D.C. Med. Soc., 1983. Chmn. editorial bd. Med. Staff News, 1985-86; contbr. articles to profl. jours. Founding mem. Nat. Capital Area Health Care Coalition, Washington, 1982; trustee James S. Brady Found., Washington, 1982-87; bd. dirs. D.C. Polit. Action Com., 1982-84. Maj. U.S. Army, 1968-71. Recipient Community Service award D.C. Med. Soc., 1981, Key to the City, Mayor of Kansas City, Mo., 1982. Fellow Am. Coll. Physician Execs.; mem. ACP, AMA (resolution commendation 1981), Am. Soc. Internal Medicine, Soc. Med. Adminstrs., Am. Hosp. Assn. (del. 1984-86, resolution commendation 1981), Internat. Club (Chgo.). Avocation: tennis.

O'LEARY, EDWARD CORNELIUS, former bishop; b. Bangor, Maine, Aug. 21, 1920; s. Cornelius J. and Annabel (McManus) O'L. B.A., Holy Cross Coll., Worcester, Mass., 1942; S.T.L., St. Paul's U. Sem., Ottawa, Can., 1946. Ordained priest Roman Cath. Ch., 1946, named monsignor, 1954, consecrated bishop, 1971; vice-chancellor, then chancellor of Diocese of Portland, Maine; diocesan consultor, pro-synodal judge of diocese, pres. priests senate, mem. finance com. of diocese, also dir. Commodity Service Corp., 1969-75; titular bishop of Moglaena, aux. bishop Portland, 1971-74; bishop Roman Cath. Diocese Portland, 1974-89, bishop emeritus, 1989—; mem. Maine Office Religious Coop., from 1973. Mem. Nat. Conf. Cath. Bishops. Address: 307 Congress St Portland ME 04101-3638*

O'LEARY, JAMES JOHN, economist; b. Manchester, Conn., May 7, 1914; s. James Henry and Helen Agnes (Hogan) O'L.; m. Rita Marie Phelps, May 31, 1941; children: James Phelps, Martha Ellen, Paul Howard, Mark Evans. B.A., Wesleyan U., 1936, M.A., 1937; Ph.D., Duke, 1941. Instr. econs. Wesleyan U., 1939-42, asst. prof., 1943-46, instr. air navigation U.S. Naval Flight Preparatory Sch., 1943-44; cons. Conn. Gen. Life Ins. Co., 1945-46; assoc. prof. econs. Duke, 1946-47; dir. investment research, economist Life Ins. Assn. Am., 1947-59, v.p., dir. econ. research, economist, 1959-67; chmn., chief economist Lionel D. Edie & Co., 1967-69; exec. v.p., economist U.S. Trust Co. of N.Y., 1969-70, vice chmn., 1970-80, econ. cons., 1980-91; bd. dirs. Bowery Savs. Bank, Guardian Life Ins. Co. Am., Atlantic Mut. Ins. Co.; dir. rsch. Com. on Pub. Debt Policy, 1946-47; mem. com. on rsch. in fin. Nat. Bur. Econ. Rsch.; alt. mem. nat. com. vol. credit restraint program Fed. Res. Bd., 1951-52. Author: Stagnation or Healthy Growth? The Challenge to the United States Economy in the Nineties, 1992; contbr. articles to profl. publs. Bd. dirs. Student Loan Mktg. Assn., Fed. Nat. Mortgage Assn., Kennecott/Copper Co., GAF/Corp., Excelsior Income Shares; mem. adv. com. Grad. Sch. Bus. NYU; trustee Wesleyan U.; bd. dirs. Nat. Bur. Econ. Rsch., chmn., 1976-80; trustee St. Joseph Coll. Recipient Silver Anniversary Sports Illustrated All Am. award, 1961, Disting. Alumnus award Wesleyan U., 1965, William Butler award for excellence in econs., 1985. Mem. Am. So. econ. assns., Am. Finance Assn., Am. Statis. Assn., Phi Beta Kappa, Pi Gamna Mu, Alpha Chi Rho. Club: University (N.Y.C.). Home: 8 Crooked Mile Rd Westport CT 06880-1123

O'LEARY, KATHLEEN A., legal secretary, writer; b. Washington, Dec. 17, 1946; d. Patrick Christopher and Hilda Elizabeth (Gobrecht) O'Leary; children—Kara Ann, Scott Patrick, Ryan Arthur Thompson, Kelly Marie. Student Montgomery Jr. Coll., 1964-66; Colo. State U., 1974; BS in Bus. Adminstrn., U. Md., 1975. Acct. exec. Sta. WSBT-AM-FM-TV, South Bend, Ind., 1972-74; mgr. advt. and promotion Sta. WGHP-TV, High Point, N.C., 1978-83; account exec. Wheat, First Securities, Greensboro, N.C., 1983-85; investment broker Legg Mason Wood Walker, Greensboro, 1985-88; investment exec. Ferris, Baker Watts, Inc., Bethesda, Md., 1988-90; legal sec., paralegal complex civil and criminal investigation and def. practice Washington, 1988-94; lectr. in investment field. Exec. producer TV show Classic Memories, 1985. Founder, 1st pres., bd. dirs. Big Bros./Big Sisters of High Point, 1981-85; founder, sec.-treas. Furniture City Classic, Inc., High Point, 1981-88; founder, bd. dirs. Henredon Classic LPGA Golf Tournament, High Point, 1981-88; mem. Leadership High Point, 1987-89; Challenge: High Point grad. and steering com. mem. High Point C. of C., 1984-85; bd. dirs. met. bd. YMCA of High Point, 1981, 82, Adams Meml. YWCA, High Point, 1985-87, Salvation Army Boys Club, 1980-81, Vols. to Ct., Guilford County, 1980-81; Sunday sch. tchr. Immaculate Heart of Mary Ch., High Point, 1980-87; exec. bd. mem. Greater Washington Open LPGA Golf Tournament, 1989-90. Democrat. Roman Catholic. Avocations: creative writing; classical piano. Office: Morgan Lewis Bockins LLP 1800 M St NW Washington DC 20036

O'LEARY, MARION HUGH, university dean, chemist; b. Quincy, Ill., Mar. 24, 1941; s. J. Gilbert and Ruth Elizabeth (Kerr) O'L.; m. Sandra E. Eisemann, Sept. 5, 1964 (div. 1979); children—Catherine, Randall, Jessica; m. Elizabeth M. Kean, Jan. 24, 1981. B.S., U. Ill., 1963; Ph.D., MIT, 1966. Asst. prof. chemistry and biochemistry U. Wis., Madison, 1967-73, assoc. prof., 1973-78, prof. chemistry and biochemistry, 1978-89; prof. and head dept. biochemistry U. Nebr., Lincoln, 1989-96; dean Sch. Natural Scis. and Math., Calif. State U., Sacramento, 1996—; cons. Institut Pertanian Bogor, Indonesia, 1983-84; vis. prof. Universitas Andalas, Padang, Indonesia, 1984-85, Australian Nat. U., 1982-83. Author: Contemporary Organic Chemistry, 1976. Editor: Isotope Effects on Enzyme-Catalyzed Reactions, 1977. Contbr. articles to sci. pubs. Grantee, NSF, U.S. Dept. Agr., Dept. Energy, NIH; Guggenheim Found. fellow, 1982-83; Sloan Found. fellow, 1972-74. Fellow AAAS; mem. Am. Chem. Soc., Am. Soc. Biochemists and Molecular Biologists. Home: 920 Entrada Rd Sacramento CA 95864-5314 Office: Calif State U Sch Natural Scis and Math 6000 J St Sacramento CA 95819-2605

O'LEARY, PAUL GERARD, investment executive; b. Boston, June 22, 1935; s. Gerard Paul and Marie Agnes (Hennessey) O'L.; m. Elizabeth Jane Pollins, Oct. 14, 1961; children: Paul Hennessey, William Gerard, Mary Elizabeth, James Daniel. AB cum laude, Harvard U., 1956; MBA, U. Pa., 1958. Alumni dir. Wharton Grad. Sch., U. Pa., Phila., 1958-60; asst. sec. Empire Trust Co., N.Y.C., 1960-65; sr. investment analyst Blyth & Co., Inc., N.Y.C., 1965-70; v.p. William D. Witter, Inc., N.Y.C., 1970-76, also bd. dirs.; v.p. portfolio mgmt. Prudential Ins. Corp. Am., Newark, 1977—; instr. fin. U. Pa., 1957-60. V.p. Prudential Found., Newark, 1986-96. Mem. Inst. Chartered Fin. Analysts, Am. Nuclear Insurers (chmn. investment com. West Hartford, Conn. 1989-96), Assn. Ins. and Fin. Analysts (pres. 1973-74), Ins. Inst. for Hwy. Safety (investment com. 1983—), N.Y. Property Ins. Underwriting Assn. (investment com. 1994—), N.Y. Soc. Security Analysts, Harvard Club of N.J. (pres. 1983-84), Boston Latin Sch. Alumni Assn., Indian Trail Club (Franklin Lakes, N.J.), Upper Ridgewood Tennis Club. Roman Catholic. Avocations: tennis, squash, philately, cartography, history. Home: 719 Belmont Rd Ridgewood NJ 07450-1300 Office: Prudential Investment Corp Gateway Ctr Two Newark NJ 07102

O'LEARY, THOMAS HOWARD, resources executive; b. N.Y.C., Mar. 19, 1934; s. Arthur J. and Eleanor (Howard) O'L.; m. Cheryl L. Westrum; children: Mark, Timothy, Thomas, Denis, Daniel, Mary Frances. A.B., Holy Cross Coll., 1954; postgrad., U. Pa., 1959-61. Asst. cashier First Nat. City Bank, N.Y.C., 1961-65; asst. to chmn. finance com. Mo. Pacific R.R. Co., 1966-70, v.p. finance, 1971-76, dir., 1972-82, chmn. finance com., 1976-82; treas. Mo. Pacific Corp., St. Louis, 1968-71; v.p. finance Mo. Pacific Corp., 1971-72, exec. v.p., 1972-74, dir., 1972-82, pres., 1974-82; chmn. bd., CEO Mississippi River Transmission Corp., 1974-82; vice chmn. Burlington No., Inc., Seattle, 1982-89; chmn., CEO Burlington Resources, 1989—; bd. dirs. BF Goodrich, Kroger Co. Served to capt. USMC, 1954-58. Mem. Blind Brook Club (N.Y.C.), Chgo. Club. Office: Burlington Resources Inc 999 3rd Ave Ste 2810 Seattle WA 98104-4097

O'LEARY, THOMAS MICHAEL, lawyer; b. N.Y.C., Aug. 16, 1948; s. James and Julia Ann (Conolly) O'L.; m. Luise Ann Williams, Jan. 13, 1978; 1 child, Richard Meridith. BA, CUNY, 1974; JD, Seattle U Sch. of Law (formerly U. Puget Sound Law Sch.), 1977. Bar: Wash. 1977, U.S. Ct. Mil. Appeals 1978, U.S. Supreme Ct. 1983, U.S. Ct. Appeals (9th cir.). Dep. pros. atty. Pierce County, Tacoma, 1978; commd. 1st lt. U.S. Army, 1978, advanced through grades to capt., 1978; chief trial counsel Office of Staff Judge Adv., Fort Polk, La., 1978-79, trial def. counsel trial def. svc., 1979-81; chief legal advisor Office Insp. Gen., Heidelberg, Fed. Republic of Germany, 1981-82; sr. def. counsel Trial Def. Svc., Giessen, Germany, 1982-84; asst. chief adminstrv. law U.S. Army Armor Ctr., Fort Knox, Ky., 1984-85, chief adminstrv law, 1985, chief legal asst., 1985-86; sr. trial atty. Immigration and Naturalization Svc., Phoenix, 1987; sector counsel, spl. asst. U.S. atty., U.S. Border Patrol, Tucson, 1987-90; enforcement counsel U.S. Immigration and Naturalization Svc., Tucson, 1990-95, asst. dist. counsel Phoenix litigation, 1995-97; apptd. U.S. Immigration Judge, U.S. Immigration Ct., Imperial, Calif., 1997—. Decorated Purple Heart, Cross of Gallantry (Vietnam). Mem. Judge Advs. Assn., Wash. State Bar Assn. Home: 9080 E 25th St Tucson AZ 85710-8675 Office: US Immigration Ct 2409 La Brucherie Rd Imperial CA 92251-9501

OLEJAR, PAUL DUNCAN, former information science administrator; b. Hazelton, Pa., Sept. 13, 1906; s. George and Anna (Danco) O.; m. Ann Ruth Dillard, Jan. 6, 1933 (dec. Oct. 1978); 1 child, Peter; m. Martha S. Ross, Sept. 8, 1979. AB, Dickinson Coll., 1928. Dir. edn. W.Va. Conservation Commn., 1936-41; coordinator U.S. Fish and Wildlife Service, 1941-42; chief press and radio Bur. Reclamation, Dept. Interior, 1946-47; editor Plant Industry Sta. AGRI, 1948-51; chmn. spl. reports Agrl. Research Adminstrn., 1951-56; dir. tech. info. Edgewood Arsenal, Md., 1956-63; chief, tech. info. plans and programs Army Research Office, Washington, 1963-64; chmn. chem. info. unit NSF, Washington, 1965-70; dir. drug info. program Sch. Pharmacy, U. N.C., Chapel Hill, 1970-73, ret., 1973. Author: West Virginia Units in Conservation, 1939, Rockets in Early American Wars, 1946, A Taste of Red Onion, 1981, Sentinel at the Crossroads, 1991, Thoughts Along the Way, 1996: editor: Computer-Based Information Systems in the Practice of Pharmacy, 1971; newspaper columnist, editor AP, Pa. and W.Va.; editor Hanover Record-Herald, Pa. Served with AUS, 1942-46. Decorated Army Commendation medal. Mem. Ravens Claw, Mil. Order of The World Wars (lt. col.), Masons (32 degree), Theta Chi, Omicron Delta Kappa. Methodist. Home: 407 Russell Ave # 111 Gaithersburg MD 20877

OLEJKO, MITCHELL J., lawyer; b. Jersey City, June 15, 1951; s. Frank Edward and Eugenia Joan Olejko; m. Jill Wolcott, Aug. 5, 1988. AB, Boston Coll., 1973; JD, Washington U., St. Louis, 1977. Bar: Wash. 1977, U.S. Dist. Ct. (we. dist.) Wash. 1977, (ea. dist.) Wash. 1978, Oreg. 1992, U.S. Dist. Ct. Oreg. 1992, U.S. Ct. Appeals (9th cir.) 1980. Assoc. Davis, Wright, Todd, Riese & Jones, Seattle, 1977-82; ptnr. Davis, Wright & Jones, Seattle, 1982-92; chief legal officer, sr. v.p. Legacy Health System, Portland, Oreg., 1992—. Contbr. Ambulatory Care Management, 2d edit., 1991. Mem. Am. Acad. Hosp. Attys., Wash. State Soc. Hosp. Attys. (pres. 1991-92). Office: Legacy Health System 1919 NW Lovejoy St Portland OR 97209-1566

OLEKSIW, DANIEL PHILIP, consultant, former foreign service officer; b. Wilkes Barre, Pa., Feb. 5, 1921; s. Rev. Michael Nicholas and Maria Helena (von Kotzko) O.; m. Elizabeth Louise Hyatt, Aug. 21, 1948 (dec. 1990); children: Barbara Anne, Daniel Hyatt. Student, Duke U., 1938-39; BA, Pa. State U., 1940; student, Duke U.; postgrad., U. Mo., Princeton U., 1941-42; grad., Nat. War Coll., 1962. Reporter, editor small newspapers Mo. and Mich.; advt. copywriter Cleve.; info. specialist Civilian Prodn. Adminstrn., Washington, 1946; dep. chief press br. pub. rels. USAF Hdqrs., Washington, 1947, 48; pub. advt. newspapers Arlington and Alexandria, Va., 1948, 49; pub. rels. officer U.S. Mission for Aid to Turkey, 1949-50; attache Am. embassy, USIS, Ankara, 1951; press attache Am. embassy, Cairo, 1952-55; 1st sec. Am. embassy, dep. pub. affairs officer USIS, Tehran, 1956-58; consul, pub. affairs officer consulate gen. Bombay, 1958-61; program coord. Africa USIA, 1962-63, dep. area dir. Africa, 1963-64, dir. media content, 1964-65; spl. asst. to permanent rep. U.S. mission to UN, 1966; area dir. for East Asia and Pacific USIA, 1966-70; minister-counselor pub. affairs Am. Embassy, New Delhi, 1970-73; dir. USIS, India; sr. faculty adviser Nat. War Coll., 1973; insp. gen. USIA, Washington, 1973-78; dir. ednl. programming Middle East Svcs., Inc., Washington, 1979-80; dir. Washington Export Info., Inc., 1980-89; program evaluation cons. Bur. Cultural and Ednl. Affairs, USIA, 1984-85; dir. Dan Oleksiw & Assocs., Washington; cons. program evaluator Brit.-Am. Project Johns Hopkins U. Sch. Advanced Internat. Studies, 1986-95, Royal Inst. Internat. Affairs, Coun. for Internat. Devel. on Mercy Fund programs in Burkina Faso, Eselen Inst. San Francisco, 1988, U.S. Bus Leadership Exchange Program, USSR, 1988, Washington, 1987, Fgn. Svc. Inst., Dept. State, 1989-90. 2d lt. inf. AUS, 1942-45. Recipient Disting. Service award USIA, 1966. Roman Catholic. Home: 3003 Van Ness St NW Washington DC 20008-4824

OLEN, MILTON WILLIAM, JR., marketing executive; b. Providence, Sept. 15, 1950; s. Milton William and Elizabeth Amanda (Goodrich) O.; m. Marsha Elizabeth Broughton, Mar. 15, 1971. Student, Fla. So. Coll., 1969-72; BS in Behavioral Scis. magna cum laude, Nova U., 1978. Lic. comml. pilot, USCG capt.; lic. residential contractor, Fla. Mfr.'s rep. for Fla., The Siemens Corp., Ft. Lauderdale, Fla., 1972-77; product mgr., exec. salesman, sales mgr. The Ritter Dental Co., Romulus, Mich., 1977-85; gen. mgr., exec. salesman Olen Homes Internat. Inc., West Palm Beach, Fla., 1981—. Mem. Nat. Assn. Home Builders, C. of C. Miami Beach, Better Bus. Bur. Roman Catholic. Avocation: boating, travel. Office: PO Box 70156 Fort Lauderdale FL 33307-0156

OLENDER, JACK HARVEY, lawyer; b. McKeesport, Pa., Sept. 8, 1935; m. Lovell Olender. BA, U. Pitts., 1957, JD, 1960; LLM, George Washington U., 1961. Bar: D.C. 1961, U.S. Supreme Ct. 1965, Md. 1966, Pa. 1985; diplomate Am. Bd. Trial Advocates,Inner Cir. Advocates. Pvt. practice Washington, 1961-79; prin. Jack H. Olender & Assocs., P.C., Washington, 1979—. Contbr. articles to profl. jours. Active World Peace through Law, Washington. Named to Hall of Fame Nat. Assn. Black Women Attys., 1987; recipient Presdl. award Nat. Bar Assn., 1996. Fellow Am. Coll. Trial Lawyers, Internat. Acad. Trial Lawyers; mem. Am. Bd. Profl. Liability Attys. (bd. dirs.), Assn. Trial Lawyers Am., Trial Lawyers Pub. Justice (bd. dirs.). Office: Jack H Olender & Assocs PC 888 17th St NW Fl 4 Washington DC 20006

OLENGINSKI, JAN ANTHONY, surgeon; b. West Point, N.Y., May 29, 1964; s. Jan Anthony and Patricia Ann (Grabowski) O. BS, U. Scranton, 1986; DO, U. Health Scis., 1990. Intern Suburban Gen. Hosp., Norristown, Pa., 1990-91; resident Phila. Coll. Osteo. Medicine, 1991-95, chief resident, 1994-95; surgeon Grad. Hosp., Phila., 1995—; chmn. gen. surgery Pa. Osteopathic Med. Assn. (POMA); adj. faculty Phila. Coll. of Osteopathic Medicine; staff surgeon vascular surgery Allegheny Parkview City Ave., Elkins Park Divsns., Del. Valley Med. Ctr., Northeastern Hosp. Vascular surgery fellow Phila. Coll. Osteo. Medicine, 1995-96. Mem. Am. Osteo. Assn., Am. Coll. Osteo. Surgeons, Am. Assn. Osteo. Postgrad. Physicians, Pa. Osteo. Med. Assn., Pa. Med. Soc. Republican. Roman Catholic. Avocations: golf, sports, running, art. Home: 349 Peachtree Dr Jenkintown PA 19046 Office: Ste 2110 1331 E Wyoming Ave Philadelphia PA 19124

OLER, WESLEY MARION, III, physician, educator; b. N.Y.C., Mar. 8, 1918; s. Wesley Marion Jr. and Imogene (Rubel) O.; m. Virginia Carolyn Craemer, Dec. 8, 1951; children: Helen Louise (dec.), Wesley Marion IV, Stephen Scott. Grad., Phillips Andover Acad., 1936; AB, Yale U., 1940; MD, Columbia U., 1943. Intern Bellevue Hosp., N.Y.C., 1944; resident Bellevue Hosp., 1948-50; fellow Hosp. U. Pa., 1951; practice medicine specializing in internal medicine Washington, 1952-93; mem. emeritus staff, vice chmn. dept. medicine Washington Hosp. Ctr., 1962-64; v.p. med. bd. Washington Hosp. Center, 1971-72, trustee, 1973-81, emeritus, 1994; clin. prof. medicine emeritus Med. Sch. Georgetown U. Contbr. articles on old musical instruments to jours. Founder, past pres. Washington Recorder Soc.; bd. dirs. Am. Recorder Soc. Maj. M.C. U.S. Army (paratroops), 1944-47. Fellow ACP (gov. 1980-84); mem. SAR, Mensa, Osler Soc. Washington (past pres.), Met. Club, Cosmos Club, Chevy Chase Club. Republican. Episcopalian. Home: Apt 612N 8101 Connecticut Ave Chevy Chase MD 20815-2805

OLERUD, JOHN GARRETT, professional baseball player; b. Seattle, Aug. 5, 1968; s. John E. Olerud. Student, Washington State U. With Toronto Blue Jays, 1989-96, NY Mets, 1997—; mem. Am. League All-Star Team, 1993. winner A.L batting title, 1993. Office: NY Mets 123-10 Roosevelt Ave Flushing NY 11368*

OLES, PAUL STEVENSON (STEVE OLES), architect, perspectivist, educator; b. San Antonio, Sept. 26, 1936; s. Paul Stevenson Sr. and Suda (Willis) O.; m. Carole Simmons, Oct. 11, 1963 (div. 1991); children: Brian Thomas, Julia Oles Carr; m. Susan Thompson, Sept. 26, 1992. BArch, Tex. Tech U., 1960; MArch, Yale U., 1963. Registered architect, Mass. Draftsman The Architects Collaborative, Cambridge, Mass., 1963-65, Cambridge Seven Assocs., Cambridge, 1965-67; architect MIT, Cambridge, 1968-70; prin. architect Interface Architects, Newton, Mass., 1971—; vis. faculty RISD, Providence, 1974-79; lectr. architecture Harvard Grad. Sch. Design, Cambridge, 1984-88, vis. scholar, 1989-91. Author: Architectural Illustration, 1979, Drawing the Future, 1988. Mem. vestry Episcopalian Ch., 1995—. Named Loeb fellow Harvard Grad. Sch. Design, 1982. Fellow AIA (inst. honor 1983, fellow 1989), Boston Soc. Architects, Am. Soc. Archtl. Perspectivists (founder, pres. 1986-90, bd. dirs. 1993—, Hugh Ferriss Meml. prize 1996). Democrat. Avocations: music, painting, photography. Office: Interface Architects 1 Gateway Ctr Ste 501A Newton MA 02158-2802

OLES, STUART GREGORY, lawyer; b. Seattle, Dec. 15, 1924; s. Floyd and Helen Louise (La Violette) O.; B.S. magna cum laude, U. Wash., 1947, J.D., 1948; m. Ilse Hanewald, Feb. 12, 1954; children: Douglas, Karl, Stephen. Admitted to Wash. bar, 1949, U.S. Supreme Ct. bar, 1960; dep. pros. atty. King County (Wash.), 1949, chief civil dept., 1949-50; gen. practice law, Seattle, 1950-95; sr. partner firm Oles, Morrison & Rinker and predecessor, 1955-90, of counsel, 1991-95. Author: A View From the Rock, 1994. Chmn. Seattle Community Concert Assn., 1955; pres. Friends Seattle Pub. Library, 1956; mem. Wash. Pub. Disclosure Commn., 1973-75; trustee Ch. Div. Sch. of Pacific, Berkeley, Calif., 1974-75; mem. bd. curators Wash.

State Hist. Soc., 1983; former mem. Seattle Symphony Bd.; pres. King County Ct. House Rep. Club, 1950, U. Wash. Young Rep. Club, 1947; Wash. conv. floor leader Taft, 1952, Goldwater, 1964; Wash. chmn. Citizens for Goldwater, 1964; chmn. King County Rep. convs., 1966, 68, 76, 84, 86, 88, 90, 92, 96, Wash. State Rep. Conv., 1980. Served with USMCR, 1943-45. Mem. ABA (past regional vice chmn. pub. contract law sect.), Wash. Bar Assn., Order of Coif, Scabbard and Blade, Am. Legion, Kapoho Beach Club (pres.), Am. Highland Cattle Assn. (v.p. and dir.), Phi Beta Kappa, Phi Alpha Delta. Episcopalian (vestryman, lay-reader). Home: 22715 SE 43rd Ct Issaquah WA 98029-5200 Office: Oles Morrison & Rinker 701 5th Ave Ste 3300 Seattle WA 98104-7082

OLESEN, DOUGLAS EUGENE, research institute executive; b. Tonasket, Wash., Jan. 12, 1939; s. Magnus and Esther Rae (Myers) O.; m. Michaele Ann Engdahl, Nov. 18, 1964; children: Douglas Eugene, Stephen Christian. B.S., U. Wash., 1962, M.S., 1963, postgrad., 1965-67, Ph.D., 1972. Research engr. space research div. Boeing Aircraft Co., Seattle, 1963-64; with Battelle Meml. Inst., Pacific NW Labs., Richland, Wash., 1967-84, mgr. water resources systems sect., water and land resources dept., 1970-71, mgr. dept., 1971-75, dep. dir. research labs., 1975, dir. research, 1975-79, v.p. inst., dir. NW div., 1979-84; exec. v.p., chief operating officer Battelle Meml. Inst., Columbus, Ohio, 1984-87, pres., chief exec. officer, 1987—. Patentee process and system for treating wast water. Trustees Capital Univ., Columbus Mus. of Art, Riverside Hosp., INROADS/Columbus Inc., Franklin County United Way; bd. dirs. Ohio State U. Found. Mem. Ohio C. of C. (trustee). Office: Battelle Meml Inst 505 King Ave Columbus OH 43201-2696*

OLESKIEWICZ, FRANCIS STANLEY, retired insurance executive; b. Chicopee, Mass., Jan. 2, 1928; s. Francis and Agata (Gniady) O.; m. Ruth M. Ventrice, June 16, 1951; children—Francis H., Laurie. B.S., Am. Internat. Coll., Springfield, Mass., 1953; LL.B, Western New Eng. Coll., 1961. Bar: Mass. 1962. With Ins. Co. N.Am., Boston, 1953-67; property mgr. Employers-Comml. Union, Boston, 1967-69; pres., chmn. Lexington Ins. Co., Boston, 1969-86; v.p. Am. Internat. Group, N.Y.C., 1979-86; retired, 1986; limited sole practice law Framingham, Mass., 1986—; ins. arbitrator; chmn. bd. Risk Specialists Cos., Inc., Boston; vice chmn. Starr Assocs., N.Y.C., C.V. Starr & Co., Inc., Calif.; bd. dirs. Audubon Ins. Co., Baton Rouge, Union Atlantique d'Assurances S.A., Brussels; bd. trustees, mem. devel. com. We. New England Coll., Springfield, Mass., 1987—. Served as pfc. USMC, 1946-47, PTO. Mem. Mass. Bar Assn. (vol. law speaker, 1988—), Marine Corps League, Amvets, Am. Legion, Alpha Chi. Home: 19 Hickory Hill Ln Framingham MA 01702-6113 also: 3328 Providence Plantation Ln Charlotte NC 28270-3719

OLESON, RAY JEROME, computer service company executive; b. Windom, Minn., June 20, 1944; s. Ray Jerome and Evah Oleson; m. Kathleen Ruth Johnson, July 2, 1966; children: Michelle Dawn, Carrie Elisabeth. BS in Math., Mankato State U., 1966; MS in Applied Stats., Villanova U., 1970. Mgr., dir. Sperry Univac, Egan, Minn., 1966-77; v.p. Computer Scis. Corp., Moorestown, N.J., 1977-84; from v.p. mktg. to pres. Systems and Applied Scis. Corp., Vienna, Va., 1984-87; pres. systems devel. and implementation div. CACI, Inc., Arlington, Va., 1987-90; pres., COO CACI, Inc., Arlington, 1990—. Mem. Armed Forces Electronic and Comm. Assn. (pres. Phila. chpt. 1980-82), River Bend Country Club. Democrat. Lutheran. Avocations: golf, bridge, home computing. Home: 1312 Tulip Poplar Ln Vienna VA 22182-1340 Office: CACI 1100 N Glebe Rd Arlington VA 22201-4798

OLEXY, JEAN SHOFRANKO, English language educator; b. Plymouth, Pa., Oct. 23, 1938; d. John Andrew and Elizabeth (Lawrence) Shofranko; m. Joseph P. Olexy Jr., Oct. 29, 1960; children: Lysbeth Olexy Kilcullen, Joseph P. Olexy III, Douglas L. Olexy. BA in English, Wilkes U., Wilkes-Barre, Pa., 1960; MEd in Teaching and Curriculum, Pa. State U., Harrisburg, 1992. Secondary English tchr. Wilkes-Barre (Pa.) City Schs., 1960-61, Brick Township Sch. Dist., Brick Town, N.J., 1964-66, Upper Merion Area Sch. Dist., King of Prussia, Pa., 1968—; lectr., cons. dept. fgn. langs. Safarik U., Slovak Republic, 1992; mem. strategic plan steering com. Ctrl. Montgomery County Area Vocat. Tech. Ctr., Norristown, Pa., 1995-96, bd. dirs., 1996—; curriculum cons. Evang. Lyceum, Bratislava, Slovakia, 1992; vol. reading specialist, mem. Norristown Literacy Coun. Mem. Balch Inst. for Ethnic Studies, Phila., 1982-93; mem. N.E. Pa. Slovak Heritage Soc., Wilkes-Barre, Pa., 1982—; sec. Valley Forge-Exch. Club, King of Prussia, Pa., 1985-89; bd. dirs. Francisvale Home for Smaller Animals, Wayne, Pa., 1987-88; mem. bd. strategic planning Montgomery County Area Vocat.-Tech. Ctr., Norristown, Pa., 1996—. Named Outstanding Educator of Yr. Beta Pi Chpt. Delta Kappa Gamma, King of Prussia, Pa., 1988; Nat. Faculty Acad. fellow Pa. State U., 1993. Mem. NEA, ASCD, Nat. Coun. Tchrs. English, Pa. Edn. Assn., N.E. Pa. Slovak Heritage Soc., Upper Merion Edn. Assn., Delta Kappa Gamma (pres. Beta Pi chpt. 1994-96). Lutheran. Avocations: music, reading, gardening, genealogy research, handcrafts. Home: 382 Maiden Ln King Of Prussia PA 19406-1803 Office: Upper Merion Area Sch Dist Crossfield Rd King Of Prussia PA 19406

OLI, MADAN KUMAR, wildlife ecologist; b. Pokhari, Terathum, Nepal, May 27, 1961; s. Bishnu P. and Laxmi K. (Thapaliya) O.; m. Monika Förstl, June 8, 1993; 1 child, Muna Oli. Diploma in sci., Tribhuvan U., Kathmandu, Nepal, 1983, MS, 1986; MPhil, U. Edinburgh, Scotland, 1992. Field biologist Red Panda Project, WWF-U.S., Nepal, 1987; co-investigator Nar-Phu Valley Project, WWF, Nepal, 1987; rsch. officer Annapurna CA Project, Nepal, 1988-92; prin. investigator Snow Leopard project WWF-U.S., Nepal, 1990-92; rsch. asst. Miss. State U., 1993-95; grad. asst. Auburn (Ala.) U., 1995—; rsch. dir. Wildland Rsch. Nepal program San Francisco State U., 1987. Contbr. articles to sci. jours. Recipient Young Scientist award UNESCO, South and Ctrl. Asia, 1988, 90, Tech. Coop. Tng. award Brit. Coun., Eng., 1989. Mem. Internat. Union for Conservation of Nature and Natural Resources (World Conservation Union, species survival commn., cat specialist group), Am. Soc. Mammalogists, Internat. Assn. Bear Rsch. & Mgmt., Internat. Snow Leopard Trust, Wildlife Soc., Smithsonian Assocs., Wildlife Conservation Soc., Sigma Xi. Home: 513 E University Dr Auburn AL 36830 Office: Dept Zoology and Wildlife Auburn U Auburn AL 36849-5414

OLIAN, JOANNE CONSTANCE, curator, art historian; b. N.Y.C., d. Richard Edward and Dorothy (Singer) Wahrman; m. Howard Olian; children: Jane Wendy, Patricia Ann. Student, Syracuse U.; BA, Hofstra U., 1969; MA, NYU/Inst. Fine Arts, 1972. Grad. internship Met. Mus., N.Y.C., 1973; asst. curator Mus. of City of N.Y., 1974, curator costume collection, 1975-91; cons. curator Costume Collection, 1992-95, curator emeritus, 1995—; lectr. Parsons Sch. Design; vis. lectr. Musée des Arts Decoratifs, Paris, summer 1983, 84, 85. Author: The House of Worth: The Gilded Age, 1860-1918, 1982; editor: Authentic French Fashions of the Twenties, 1990, Everyday Fashions of the Forties, 1992, Children's Fashions from Mode Illustre 1860-1912, 1994, Wedding Fashions, 1862-1912, 1994, Everyday Fashions, 1909-1920, 1995; contbr. articles to profl. jours., chpts. to books. Mem. Internat. Council Mus. (costume com.), Costume Soc. Am. (dir. 1976-79, 83-86), Fashion Group (bd. dirs. 1985-86), Centre Internat. d'Etude des Textiles Anciens. Club: Cosmopolitan (N.Y.C.). Home: Shepherds Ln Port Washington NY 11050 Office: Shepherds Ln Sands Point NY 11050

OLIAN, ROBERT MARTIN, lawyer; b. Cleve., June 14, 1953; s. Robert Meade and Doris Isa (Hessing) O.; m. Terri Ellen Ruther, Aug. 10, 1980; children: Andrew Zachary, Alix Michelle, Joshua Brett. AB, Harvard U., 1973, JD, M in Pub. Policy, 1977. Bar: Ill. 1977, U.S. Dist. Ct. (no. dist.) Ill. 1977, U.S. Ct. Appeals (7th cir.) 1983, U.S. Dist. Ct. (no dist. trial bar) Ill. 1992, U.S. Dist. Ct. (we. dist.) Mich. 1994. Assoc. Sidley & Austin, Chgo., 1977-84, ptnr., 1985—. Editor: Illinois Environmental Law Handbook, 1988. Panel atty. Chgo. Vol. Legal Svcs., Chgo., 1983—; mem. regional strategic planning/mktg. com. Alexian Bros. Ill., Inc., Elk Grove, 1985-88; trustee North Shore Congregation Israel, 1990—, sec., 1995-96, v.p., 1996—. Mem. ABA, Chgo. Bar Assn., Std. Club, Harvard Club (Chgo.). Jewish. Home: 85 Oakmont Rd Highland Park IL 60035-4111 Office: Sidley & Austin 1 First Natl Plz Chicago IL 60603-2003

OLIANSKY, JOEL, author, director; b. N.Y.C., Oct. 11, 1935; s. Albert and Florence (Shaw) O.; children: Ingrid, Adam. M.F.A., Yale, 1962; B.A., Hofstra U., Hempstead, N.Y., 1959. Playwright-in-residence Yale, 1962-64; co-founder Hartford Stage Co., 1963; writer Universal Studios, 1974—. Author: Shame, Shame on the Johnson Boys!, 1966; writer, dir.: The Competition, 1980, The Silence at Bethany, 1987, Bird, 1988. Recipient Emmy award, 1971, Humanitas prize, 1975, Writers Guild award 1975. *I have, I think, used less than 1 percent of my talent. If I have achieved anything, it is because others have used even less of theirs.*

OLICK, ARTHUR SEYMOUR, lawyer; b. N.Y.C., June 15, 1931; s. Jack and Anita (Babsky) O.; m. Selma Ada Kaufman, June 27, 1954; children: Robert Scott, Karen Leslie. B.A., Yale U., 1952, LL.B., J.D., 1955. Bar: N.Y. 1956. Asst. instr. polit sci. Yale U., New Haven, Conn., 1953-55; instr. polit. sci.-bus. law U. Ga., 1955-57; assoc. atty. Casey, Lane & Mittendorf, N.Y.C., 1957-62; asst. U.S. atty. So. Dist. N.Y., 1962-68; chief civil div., 1965-68; partner Otterbourg, Steindler, Houston & Rosen, N.Y.C., 1968-71, Kreindler, Relkin, Olick & Goldberg, N.Y.C., 1971-74; officer, dir. Anderson, Kill & Olick, P.C. and predecessor firms, N.Y.C., 1974—; ptnr. Anderson, Kill & Olick, P.C. and predecessor firms, Washington, 1979—, Phila., 1990—, Newark, 1991—, San Francisco, 1992—, Phila., 1994—, Phoenix, 1994—; lectr. Practicing Law Inst., N.Y.C., 1965—, Bklyn. Bar Assn., Comml. Law League, Nat. Jud. Coll.; lectr., CLE instr. Fordham Law Sch.; candidate N.Y. State Supreme Ct., 1971; counsel Tarrytown (N.Y.) Urban Renewal Agy., 1968-73, 75-77; town atty., Greenburgh, N.Y., 1974; spl. counsel, Town of New Castle, N.Y., 1979-94; village atty., Tarrytown, N.Y., 1968-73, 75-77, Dobbs Ferry, N.Y., 1975-77, North Tarrytown, N.Y., 1978-81; dir. Westechester County (N.Y.) Legal Aid Soc., 1976-79. Pres. Hartsdale (N.Y.) Bd. Edn., 1968-72; bd. dirs. Westchester County Mcpl. Planning Fedn., 1976-78, Circle in the Sq. Theater, 1978-96; trustee Calhoun Sch., N.Y.C., 1973-80. Served with U.S. Army, 1955-57. Fellow Am. Bankruptcy Coll.; mem. ABA (bus. bankruptcy com., chmn. sect. subcom., ad hoc com. on partnerships in bankruptcy), Am. Bar Found., N.Y. State Bar Assn., Assn. of Bar of City of N.Y. (com. on profl. reposnibility), Fed. Bar Coun., Am. Arbitration Assn. (nat. panel arbitrators), Am. Law Inst., Bklyn. Soc. for Prevention Cruelty to Children (bd. dirs. 1994—), Yale Club, Merchants Club (N.Y.C.), Nat. Lawyers Club (Washington), Rockefeller Ctr. Club, Phi Beta Kappa. Home: 300 E 54th St New York NY 10022-5018 also: 611 Masters Way Palm Beach Gardens FL 33410 Office: 1251 Avenue Of The Americas New York NY 10020-1104 also: 2000 Pennsylvania Ave NW Washington DC 20006-1812

OLICK, PHILIP STEWART, lawyer; b. N.Y.C., Oct. 2, 1936; s. Jack and Anita (Babsky) O.; m. Alice D. Chait, Mar. 25, 1961; children: Jonathan A., Jeffrey K., Diana M. B.A., Columbia U., 1957; LL.B., NYU, 1960. Bar: N.Y. 1961, Mo. 1966. Ptnr. Benjamin, Galton, Robbins & Flato, N.Y.C., 1961-65; gen. counsel, v.p., sec. Nat. Bellas Hess, Inc., Kansas City, Mo., 1965-69; dir. Nat. Bellas Hess, Inc., 1970-76; ptnr. Burke & Burke, N.Y.C., 1970-73, Townley & Updike, 1973-89, Moses & Singer, 1989—; bd. arbitrators N.Y. Stock Exch. Bd. dirs. Univ. Glee Club N.Y.C.; bd. dirs. The Young Peoples Chorus of N.Y.C. With AUS, 1960-61. Mem. N.Y. Bar Assn., Assn. of Bar of City of N.Y., Univ. Club (N.Y.C.), Columbia Club. Home: 860 5th Ave 19J New York NY 10021-5856 Office: 1301 Avenue Of The Americas New York NY 10019-6022 also: 4 Rosebud Ln East Quogue NY 11942-3627

OLIENSIS, SHELDON, lawyer; b. Phila., Mar. 19, 1922. AB with honors, U. Pa., 1943; LLB magna cum laude, Harvard U., 1948. Bar: N.Y. State 1949. With Kaye Scholer Fierman Hays & Handler, N.Y.C., 1960—; chair N.Y.C. Conflicts of Interest Bd., 1990—. Pres.: Harvard Law Rev., 1948. Trustee Harvard Law Sch. Assn., 1973-77, 1st v.p., 1980-82, pres., 1982-84, trustee, N.Y.C., 1962-65, v.p., 1972-73, pres., 1978-79; nat. chmn. Harvard Law Sch. Fund, 1973-75; mem. Harvard U. overseers com. to visit law sch., 1981-87; spl. master appellate divsn. 1st dept. N.Y. State Supreme Ct., 1983-89, 91—; bd. dirs. Legal Aid Soc., 1969-88, pres., 1973-75; vice chmn. N.Y.C. Cultural Coun., 1968-75; bd. dirs. Cultural Coun. Found., 1968-88, pres., 1968-72, v.p., 1972-82; bd. dirs. Park Assn. N.Y.C., Inc., 1963-73, exec. com., 1967-73, pres., 1965-67; bd. dirs. Gateway Sch., N.Y.C., 1968-83, chmn. bd. trustees, 1968-70; dir. officer Wiltwyck Sch. for Boys, Inc., 1951-71; bd. dirs. East Harlem Tutorial Program, 1972-80, Fund for Modern Cts., 1979-91, N.Y. Lawyers for Pub. Interest, 1980-85, 91-94; bd. dirs. Vols. of Legal Svc. Inc., 1984—, pres., 1984-87, trustee Lawyers' Com. for Civil Rights Under Law, 1978-91. Fellow Am. Coll. Trial Lawyers; mem. N.Y. State Bar Assn., N.Y. County Lawyers Assn., Assn. of Bar of City of N.Y. (exec. com. 1961-65, v.p. 1974-75, 86-87, pres. 1988-90, chmn. com. state legis. 1959-61, com. revision of constn. and by-laws 1965-66, com. electric power and environ. 1971-74, com. on grievances 1975-78, com. on access to legal svcs. 1982-87, com. on fee disputes and conciliation 1987-89, nominating com. 1991, mem. task force on N.Y. state constn. conv. 1994-96). Office: Kaye Scholer Fierman et al 425 Park Ave New York NY 10022-3506

OLIKER, DAVID WILLIAM, healthcare management administrator; b. Elkins, W.Va., Mar. 29, 1948; married; 3 children. BA in Sociology and Anthropology, East Carolina U., 1970; MA in Social Anthropology, Am. U., 1973; Cert. in Healthcare Adminstrn., George Washington U., 1977. Health svcs. specialist United Mine Workers Am. Health and Retirement Funds, 1976-78; health planner Health Sys. Agy. Western Md., Cumberland, 1978-79; ops. mgr. Md.-Individual Practice Assn., Inc., Rockville, 1979-81; project dir. N.Y. Health Maintenance Plan, Inc., N.Y.C., 1981-82; pres., CEO MVP Health Plan, Schenectady, N.Y., 1982—. Mem. APHA, Am. Assn. Health Plans, N.Y. State HMO Conf. (bd. dirs.), Nat. Managed Care Inc. (chmn.). Office: MVP Health Plan 111 Liberty St Schenectady NY 12305-1827

OLIKER, VLADIMIR, mathematician, educator; b. Ulianovsk, Russia, Oct. 7, 1945; came to U.S. 1975, naturalized 1980; s. Yosef and Sonia (Bakelman) O.; m. Elena Matis, Mar. 20, 1969; children—Olga, Aviva, Josef Matis. M.S., Leningrad U., Russia, 1967; Ph.D., Leningrad U., 1971. Sr. researcher Hydrometeorological Inst., Leningrad, Russia, 1970-72; group leader Dept. Transportation, 1972-74; vis. prof. Temple U., Phila., 1975-77; assoc. prof. to prof. U. Iowa, Iowa City, 1977-80, 80-84; prof. math. Emory U., Atlanta, 1984—; vis. mem. Math Scis. Research Inst., Berkeley, Calif., 1983; vis. prof. U. Florence, Italy, 1983, Technische U., Berlin, 1982, U. Heidelberg, Fed. Republic Germany, 1981. Contbr. articles to profl. jours. Jewish. Home: 1565 Adelia Pl NE Atlanta GA 30329-3805 Office: Emory U Dept Math and Computer Sci Atlanta GA 30322

OLIN, KENT OLIVER, banker; b. Chgo., July 27, 1930; s. Oliver Arthur and Beatrice Louise (Thompson) O.; m. Marilyn Louise Wood, May 27, 1956. BS in Econs., Ripon Coll., 1955. Dist. sales rep. Speed Queen Corp., Ripon, Wis., 1955-57; v.p. United Bank, Denver, 1957-71; exec. v.p., pres. Bank One Boulder (formerly Affiliated First Nat. Bank), Boulder, Colo., 1971-74; pres., CEO Bank One Colorado Springs, Colorado Springs, 1974-86; pres., CEO Bank One Colo. (formerly Affiliated Bankshares of Colo.), Denver, 1986-91, vice chmn. bd., 1992-94, also bd. dirs. Trustee Colo. Coll., Colorado Springs, 1983-89, Falcon Found., Colorado Springs, 1983—, El Pomar Found., Colorado Springs, 1992—, Colorado Springs Fine Arts Ctr., 1992-95; sec.-treas. Air Force Acad. Found., Colorado Springs, 1988; bd. dirs. Rocky Mountain Arthritis Found., Denver, 1989-94, Goodwill Industries, Colorado Springs, 1994. Staff sgt. USAF, 1950-54. Mem. Broadmoor Golf Club (dir. 1975-88, 93-97). Office: El Pomar Found 10 Lake Cir Colorado Springs CO 80906-4201

OLIN, ROBERT FLOYD, mathematics educator and reseacher; b. Evanston, Ill., Oct. 8, 1948; s. Floyd Thomas and Anne Elanor (Knutson) O.; m. Linda Renee King, Aug. 23, 1969; children: Kristopher Robert, Susan Michelle. BSc, Ottawa U., 1970; PhD, Ind. U., 1975. Asst. prof. math. Va Poly. Inst. and State U., Blacksburg, 1975-80, assoc. prof., 1980-87, prof., 1987—, dept. head, 1994—; vis. assoc. prof. Ind. U., Bloomington, 1985; rschr. NSF, 1975-94, grad. chmn., 1993-94; chmn. rsch. commn., 1993-94. Co-author: A Functional Calculus for Subnormal Operators II, 1977, Subnormal Operators, and Representations of Bounded Analytic Functions and Other Uniform Algebras, 1985. Pres. Southwestern Va. Soccer Assn., Blacksburg, 1989-90; tchr. Sunday Sch. Blacksburg Bapt. Ch., 1983—; treas. Margaret Beeks PTA, 1993-95; chmn. steering com. Southeastern Analysis Meeting, 1984—. Named Hon. Faculty Mem., Sichuan U., Chengdu, China, 1988; recipient cert. Math. Edn. Devel. Ctr., Ind. U., Bloomington, 1976. Mem. N.Y. Acad. Scis., Va. Acad. Scis., Am. Math. Soc., Math. Assn. Am., Nat. Coun. Tchrs. Math., Coun. Undergrad Rsch., Am. Assn. Higher Edn., Sigma Xi, Pi Mu Epsilon. Avocations: racquetball, cooking, computers, soccer. Home: 707 Draper Rd SW Blacksburg VA 24060-4654 Office: Va Poly Inst and State U Math Dept Blacksburg VA 24061

OLIN, WILLIAM HAROLD, orthodontist, educator; b. Menominee, Mich., Mar. 7, 1924; s. Harold H. and Lillian (Hallgren) O.; m. Bertha Spitters, May 6, 1950; children—William Harold, Paul Scott, Jon Edward. D.D.S., Marquette U., 1947; M.S., U. Iowa, 1948. Asst. prof. orthodontics Univ. Hosps., U. Iowa, Iowa City, 1948, assoc. prof., 1963-70, prof., 1970-93; prof. emeritus, 1995; chmn. bd. Hills Bank, Iowa. Author: Cleft Lip and Palate Rehabilitation, 1960; contbr. articles on treatment of craniofacial deformities to profl. jours. Served to capt. U.S. Army, 1952-54. Mem. Angle Orthodontic Soc. Midwest (pres. 1982), Midwest Orthodontic Soc. (pres. 1968-69), Iowa Orthodontic Soc. (pres. 1959), Am. Cleft Palate Assn. (pres. 1970), Am. Acad. for Sports Dentistry (bd. dirs., sec./treas. 1989—). Republican. Methodist. Club: Univ. Athletic (bd. dirs.) (Iowa City). Lodge: Rotary (pres. Iowa City). Avocations: coins, antique music boxes, sports, travel, political memorabilia. Home: 426 Mahaska Dr Iowa City IA 52246-1610 Office: University Hospitals Iowa City IA 52242

OLINGER, CARLA D(RAGAN), medical advertising executive; b. Cin., Oct. 8, 1947; d. Carl Edward and Selene Ethel (Neal) Dragan; m. Chauncey Greene Olinger, Jr., May 30, 1981. B.A., Douglass Coll., 1975. Mgr. info. retrieval services Frank J. Corbett, Inc., N.Y.C., 1976-77; editor, proofreader, prodn. asst. Rolf W. Rosenthal, Inc., N.Y.C., 1977-78, copywriter, 1978-80, copy supr., 1980-82, v.p. copy dept., 1982-83; v.p., group copy supr., adminstrv. copy supr. Rolf W. Rosenthal, Inc., div. Ogilvy & Mather, 1984-89, v.p., assoc. creative dir. RWR Advt., 1989; v.p., copy supr. Barnum & Souza, N.Y.C., 1990-92; v.p., copy supr. Botto, Roessner, Horne & Messinger, Ketchum Comm., N.Y.C., 1992-95, Lyons Lavey Nickel Swift, N.Y.C., 1995—. Editor: Antimicrobial Prescribing (Harold Neu), 1979. Mem. Am. Med. Writers Assn., Ch. Club N.Y., St. George's Soc. N.Y. Office: Lyons Lavey Nickel Swift 488 Madison Ave New York NY 10022-5702

OLINGER, SHEFF DANIEL, neurologist, educator; b. Olinger, Va., Oct. 23, 1930; s. Sheff Daniel and Ada Sue O.; m. Norma Lanier, June 25, 1953; children: Nancy, Sheff D. III, Amy. BS, Va. Mil. Inst., 1949; MD, U. Va., 1953. Diplomate Am. Bd. Psychiatry and Neurology. Intern Tripler Army Hosp., Honolulu, 1953-54; resident in neurology U. Mich., Ann Arbor, 1956-59, clin. instr., 1958-59; instr. Southwestern Med. Sch., Dallas, 1960-82, assoc. prof. neurology, 1982—; pvt. practice in neurology Dallas, 1959-72; dir. dept. neurology Baylor U. Med. Ctr., Dallas, 1972-90, dir. stroke unit and EEG dept., 1972-90; cons. Presbyn. Hosp., Dallas, 1960—, Parkland Hosp., Dallas, 1960—, Timberlawn Psychiatric Hosp., 1960-90, also U.S. Dept. Labor, Dallas Mil. Entrance Processing Sta. Contbr. articles to profl. jours. Fellow Am. Acad. Neurology; mem. AMA, Tex. Med. Assn., Tex. Neurol. Soc. (founding pres. 1975), Dallas County Med. Soc., Dallas So. Clin. Soc. Home: 3564 Colgate Ave Dallas TX 75225-5009 also: 119 Cattle Trail Way Georgetown TX 78628

OLINS, ROBERT ABBOT, communications research executive; b. Cambridge, Mass., Sept. 25, 1942; s. Harry and Janice Olins; m. Irma Westrich, June 16, 1967; 1 son, Matthew Abbot. Student, Hobart Coll., 1961-62, San Francisco Art Inst., 1962; BA, U. Mass., 1967; postgrad., U. Tampa, 1968; MA, U. Mo., 1969, PhD, 1972. With Marsteller, 1972, N.W. Ayer, 1972, Post, Keys & Gardner, Chgo., 1973; with Young & Rubicam, Chgo., 1973-76, mng. dir. comm. rsch. divsn., 1976-77; pres., CEO, subs. Comm. Rsch. Inc., Chgo., 1978—; owner, chmn. Comm. Rsch. Inc., 1979—; pres., chief exec. officer Insights, Chgo., 1976—. Contbr. articles to profl. jours. Recipient Chgo./4 award for creative excellence, 1974; overall winner Chgo. Mackinac race, 1981; Am. Assn. Advt. Agys. grantee, 1968-71. Mem. Am. Mktg. Assn., Lake Michigan Yachting Assn., U.S. Yacht Racing Union, Chgo. Yacht Club (chmn. membership, bd. dirs.), Skyline Club. Avocations: skiing, sailing, power boating. Office: Communications Rsch Inc 233 E Wacker Dr Apt 2105 Chicago IL 60601-5110

OLIPHANT, BETTY, ballet school director; b. London, Eng., Aug. 5, 1918. Studied classical ballet under Tamara Karsavina and Laurent Novikoff; student, Queen's and St. Mary's Colls.; LLD (hon.), Queen's U., 1978, Brock U., 1978, U. Toronto., 1980; DLitt, York U., 1992. Prin. dancer and arranger Prince & Emile Littler Prodns., London, 1936-46; dance arranger Howard & Wyndham, London, 1936-46; tchr. ballet London, 1936-40; dancer, dance arranger and ballet mistress Blue Pencils Concert Party, Eng., 1944-46; tchr. ballet Oliphant Sch., Toronto, Can., 1948-59; ballet mistress Nat. Ballet of Can., Toronto, 1951-62; prin. and dir. Nat. Ballet Sch., 1959; assoc. artistic dir. Nat. Ballet of Can., 1969-75, artistic dir., 1975-89; founder Nat. Ballet Sch., 1991—; founder reorganized Ballet Sch. of Royal Swedish Opera, 1967, Royal Danish Theatre, 1978; mem. jury Internat. Ballet Competition, Moscow, 1977-81, III Internat. Ballet Competition, Jackson, MIss., 1986. Author: Miss O: My Life in Dance, 1996; contbr. articles on dance and teaching to profl. publs. Decorated officer Order of Can., 1972, Companion Order of Can., 1985; recipient Centennial medal, 1967, Molson prize, 1978, Diplome d'Honneur Can. Conf. Arts, 1982, Lifetime Achievement award, Toronto Arts Awards Found., 1989, Order of Napoleon, France, 1990, Commemorative medal 125th Anniversary Can., 1992; fellow Ont. Inst. for Studies in Edn., 1985. Fellow Imperial Soc. Tchrs. of Dancing (examiner), Ont. Inst. Studies in Edn., 1985; mem. Can. Dance Tchrs. Assn. (founder, past pres.), Internat. Soc. of Tchrs. of Dancing, Can. Assn. Profl. Dance Orgns. (founding mem.). Office: Nat Ballet Sch, 105 Maitland St, Toronto, ON Canada M4Y 1E4

OLIPHANT, CHARLES FREDERICK, III, lawyer; b. Chattanooga, Sept. 25, 1949; s. Charles Frederick and Jayne (Shutting) O.; m. Nancy Ann Stewart, May 15, 1976; children: James Andrew, Alexander Stewart. AB in Econs., U. N.C., 1971; JD, U. Mich., 1975. Bar: D.C. 1975. Assoc. Miller & Chevalier, Chartered, Washington, 1975-81, mem. firm, 1982—. Bd. adv. Jour. of Taxation of Employee Benefits. Mem. ABA, Bar Assn. D.C. Episcopalian. Avocations: music, reading. Office: Miller & Chevalier Chartered 655 15th St NW Ste 900 Washington DC 20005-5701

OLIPHANT, CHARLES ROMIG, physician; b. Waukegan, Ill., Sept. 10, 1917; s. Charles L. and Mary (Goss) R.; student St. Louis U., 1936-40; m. Claire E. Canavan, Nov. 7, 1942; children: James R., Cathy Rose, Mary G., William D. Student, St. Louis U., 1936-40, MD, 1943; postgrad. Naval Med. Sch., 1946. Intern, Nat. Naval Med. Ctr., Bethesda, Md., 1943; pvt. practice medicine and surgery, San Diego, 1947—; pres., CEO Midway Med. Enterprises; former chief staff Balboa Hosp., Doctors Hosp., Cabrillo Med. Ctr.; chief staff emeritus Sharp Cabrillo Hosp.; mem. staff Mercy Hosp., Children's Hosp., Paradise Valley Hosp., Sharp Meml. Hosp.; sec. Sharp Sr. Health Care, S.D.; mem. exec. bd., program chmn. San Diego Power Squadron, 1985-93, 95. Charter mem. Am. Bd. Family Practice. Served with M.C., USN, 1943-47. Recipient Golden Staff award Sharp Cabrillo Hosp. Med. Staff, 1990. Fellow Am. Geriatrics Soc. (emeritus), Am. Acad. Family Practice, Am. Assn. Abdominal Surgeons; mem. AMA, Calif. Med. Assn., Am. Acad. Family Physicians (past pres. San Diego chpt., del. Calif. chpt.), San Diego Med. Soc., Public Health League, Navy League, San Diego Power Squadron (past comdr.), SAR. Clubs: San Diego Yacht, Cameron Highlanders. Home: 4310 Trias St San Diego CA 92103-1127

OLIPHANT, JAMES S., lawyer; b. Evanston, Ill., Apr. 17, 1945; s. Laurence E. and Adele (Stern) O.; m. Audrey Mae Oliphant, Aug. 15, 1982; children: James S., Mark P. BA, Northwestern U., Evanston, Ill., 1967; JD, Ohio State U., 1971. Bar: Ohio, U.S. Dist. Ct. (so. dist.) Ohio, U.S. Ct. Appeals (6th cir.). Assoc. Wright, Harbor, Morris & Arnold, Columbus, 1971-77; ptnr. Porter, Wright, Morris & Arthur, Columbus, 1977—. Fellow Am. Coll. Trial Lawyers; mem. Am. Bd. Trial Advocates (advocate), Def. Rsch. Inst. (bd. dirs. 1988-91, v.p. 1991-93, pres.-elect 1993-94, pres. 1994—), Internat. Assn. Def. Counsel, Ohio Assn. Civil Trial Attys. (pres. 1985). Democrat. Roman Catholic. Office: Porter Wright Morris & Arthur 41 S High St Columbus OH 43215-6101

OLIPHANT, PATRICK, cartoonist; b. Adelaide, Australia, July 24, 1935; came to U.S., 1964; s. Donald K. and Grace L. (Price) O.; children: Laura, Grant, Susan. L.H.D. (hon.), Dartmouth Coll., 1981. Copyboy, press artist Adelaide Advertiser, 1953-55, editorial cartoonist, 1955-64; world tour to study cartooning techniques, 1959; editorial cartoonist Denver Post, 1964-75, Washington Star, 1975-81, L.A. Times Syndicate, 1965-80, Universal Press Syndicate, 1980—; represented by Susan Conway Gallery, Washington. Author: The Oliphant Book, 1969, Four More Years, 1973, An Informal Gathering, 1978, Oliphant! A Cartoon Collection, 1980, The Jellybean Society, 1981, Ban this Book, 1982, But Seriously Folks, 1983, The Year of Living Perilously, 1984, Make My Day, 1985, Between a Rock and a Hard Place, 1986, Up to There in Alligators, 1987, Nothing Basically Wrong, 1988, What Those People Need Is a Puppy, 1989, Fashions for the New World Order, 1991, Just Say No, 1992, Why do I Feel Uneasy?, 1993, Waiting for the Other Shoe to Drop, 1994, Off to the Revolution, 1995, Maintain The Status Quo, 1996. Recipient 2d Place award as funniest cartoonist Internat. Fedn. Free Journalists in Fleet St., London, 1958, Profl. Journalism award Sigma Delta Chi, 1966, Pulitzer prize for editl. cartooning, 1967, Cartoonist of Yr. award Nat. Cartoonist Soc., 1968, 72, Best in Bus. award Washington Journalism Rev., 1985, 87, Premio Satira Politica award Forte de Marmi, 1992, Thomas Nast award, 1992. Office: Universal Press Syndicate 4900 Main St Fl 9 Kansas City MO 64112-2630 also: care Susan Conway Gallery 1214 30th St NW Washington DC 20007-3401

OLITSKI, JULES, artist; b. Snovsk, USSR, Mar. 27, 1922; came to U.S., 1923, naturalized, 1943; s. Jevel and Anna (Zarnitsky) Demikovsky; m. Gladys Katz, 1944 (div. 1951); 1 dau., Eve; m. Andrea Hill Pearce, Jan. 21, 1956 (div. 1974); 1 dau., Lauren; m. Kristina Gorby, Feb. 29, 1980. Student, Academie de la Grande Chaumiere, Paris, 1949-50; BA, NYU, 1952, MA, 1954; postgrad., Beaux Arts Inst., N.Y.C., 1940-42, Nat. Acad. Design, N.Y.C., 1940-42, Ednl. Alliance, N.Y.C., 1947, Zadkine Sch. Sculpture, Paris, 1949. Assoc. prof. art SUNY, New Paltz, N.Y., 1954-55; curator Art Edn. Gallery, NYU, 1955-56; chmn. fine arts div. C.W. Post Coll. L.I. U., Greenvale, N.Y., 1956-63; tchr. Bennington Coll., 1963-67. Exhibited in many one-man shows including Galerie Huit, Paris, 1951, Iolas Gallery, N.Y.C., 1958, French & Co., N.Y.C., 1959-61, Poindexter Gallery, N.Y.C., 1961-68, Bennington (Vt.) Coll., 1962, Kasmin, Ltd., London, 1964-75, 89, Galerie Lawrence, Paris, 1964, David Mirvish Gallery, Toronto, Ont., Can., 1964-78, Nicholas Wilder, L.A., 1966, Corcoran Gallery, Washington, 1967, 74, Am. Pavillion, Venice Biennale Art Exhbn., 1966, 88, Andre Emmerich Gallery, N.Y.C., 1966-96, Zurich, Switzerland, 1973-78, Met. Mus. Art, N.Y.C., 1969, Inst. Contemporary Art, U. Pa., 1968, 86, Lawrence Rubin Gallery, N.Y.C., 1969, 71, 72, 73, Knoedler Contemporary Art, 1973-77, 79, 81, 83, 85, 87, Dart Gallery, Chgo., 1975, FIAL, Paris, 1976, Berlinische Galerie, 1977, Downstairs Gallery, Edmonton, Can., 1980, 82, Janus Gallery, L.A., 1981, Gallery One, Toronto, 1980-90, Yares Gallery, Scottsdale, Ariz., 1986-89, Galerie Wentzel, Hamburg and Cologne, Fed. Republic Germany, 1975, 77, 81, 89, Mus. Fine Arts, Boston, 1973, 77, Whitney Mus. Am. Art, 1973, Galleria Dell'Ariete, Italy, 1974, Corcoran Gallery Art, 1974-76, Waddington Gallery, London, 1975, Galerie Templon, Paris, 1984-85, Hirshhorn Mus., Washington, 1977, Edmonton (Alta., Can.) Art Gallery, 1979, Martha White Gallery, Louisville, 1982, Harcus/Krakow Gallery, Boston, 1978, 81, 82, Harcus Gallery, Boston, 1984, 86, Meredith Long, Houston, 1981, 82, 87, 90, (retrospective) Fondation du Chateau de Jau, Perpignon, France, 1984, La Musee de Valence, France, 1985, Hokin Gallery, Palm Beach, Fla., 1988, Associated Am. Artists, N.Y.C., 1989, (retrospective) Buschlen/Mowatt Gallery, Vancouver, B.C., Can., 1990, Salander-O'Reilly Galleries, N.Y.C., 1990, 92, 94, Gallery Camino Real, Boca Raton, Fla., 1987, 88, 90, 92, 94, 95, 96, Thorne-Sagendorph Art Gallery, Keene, N.H., 1993, 96, Long Fine Arts, N.Y.C., 1994, 95, 97, U. Miami, Coral Gables, Fla., 1994, C.S. Schulte Gallery, Milburn, N.J., 1995, 97, Drabinsky Friedland Gallery, Naples, Fla., and Toronto, 1996, 97, Dorthy Blau Gallery, Bay Harbor Island, Fla., 1996, 97, Virginia Lynch Gallery, Tiverton, R.I., 1997; exhibited in many group shows including Carnegie Internat., Pitts., 1961, 1965, Washington Gallery Modern Art, 1963, Los Angeles County Mus., 1964, Fogg Art Mus. Harvard, 1965, Pasadena Art Mus., 1965, Mus. Basel, Switzerland, 1965, 74, Whitney Mus. Am. Art, 1972, 73, Musée d'Art Contemporain, Montreal, 1973, Hirshhorn Mus., 1974, Corcoran Gallery Art, 1975, Everson Mus. Art, Syracuse, N.Y., 1976, Bass Mus., Miami, Am. Embassy, Madrid, 1984, Ft. Worth Art Mus., Mus. Art, Ft. Lauderdale, 1986, Joseloff Gallery, Hartford, Conn., 1994, Galerie Piltzer, Paris, 1994, N.Y. Studio Sch., N.Y., 1996; represented in permanent collections including Mus. Modern Art, N.Y.C., Art Inst. Chgo., Whitney Mus., Corcoran Art Gallery, Nat. Gallery Can., Met. Mus. Art, N.Y.C., Bklyn. Mus., Hirshhorn Mus., Washington, Everson Mus. Art, Syracuse, N.Y., Mus. Fine Arts, Boston, Norman MacKensie Art Gallery, Regina, Can., also pvt. collections; subject book Jules Olitski by Kenworth Moffett, 1981, Nat. Acad. Design, N.Y., 1993. Recipient 2d prize Carnegie Internat. 1961, 1st prize Corcoran Biennial, Washington, 1967, Award for Distinction in the Arts Univ Union, U. S.C., 1975, The Milton and Sally Avery Disting. Professorship, Bard Coll., 1987; named Assoc. Nat. Academician Nat. Acad. of Design, 1993. Fellow AAAS, Nat. Acad. Arts and Scis. also: c/o Salanders O'Reilly Galleries Inc 20 E 79th St New York NY 10021

OLIVA, LAWRENCE JAY, academic administrator, history educator; b. Walden, N.Y., Sept. 23, 1933; s. Lawrence Joseph and Catherine (Mooney) O.; m. Mary Ellen Nolan, June 3, 1961; children: Lawrence Jay, Edward Nolan. BA, Manhattan Coll., 1955; MA, Syracuse U., 1957, PhD, 1960; postgrad., U. Paris, 1959; DHL (hon.), Manhattan Coll., 1987; LLD (hon.), St. Thomas Aquinas Coll., 1988; DHL (hon.), Hebrew Union Coll., 1992; DLitt, Univ. Coll., Dublin, 1993; PhD, Tel Aviv U., 1994. Prof. history NYU, 1969—, assoc. dean, 1969-70; vice dean N000, 1970-71; dean faculty NYU, 1971-72, dep. vice chancellor, 1970-75, v.p. acad. planning and services, 1975-77, v.p. acad. affairs, 1977-80, provost, exec. v.p. acad. affairs, 1980-83, chancellor, exec. v.p., 1983-91, pres., 1991—. Author: Misalliance: A Study of French Policy in Russia during the Seven Years' War, 1964, Russia in the Era of Peter the Great, 1969; editor: Russia and the West from Peter to Kruschev, 1965, Peter the Great, 1970, Catherine the Great, 1971; contbr. article and revs. to profl. lit. Trustee Inst. Internat. Edn.; active Onassis Found., UN Assn. of N.Y. Adv. Coun., N.Y.C. Partnership, Assn. for Better N.Y., Am. Mus. Immigration; bd. dirs. Chatham House, Royal Inst. Internat. Affairs, Am. Bd. Dirs. Coun. for U.S. and Italy Nat. Collegiate Athletic Assn., Pres.'s Commn., N.Y. State Commn. on Nat. and Cmty. Svc.; adv. bd. U. Athletic Assn., Pres.'s Coun. Fribourg fellow, 1959; recipient Medal of Sorbonne, U. Paris, 1992, Man. in Edn. award Italian Welfare League, Ellis Island medal of honor. Mem. Am. Coun. Edn., Assn. Colls. and Univs. of State of N.Y., Irish-Am. Cultural Inst., Soc. Fellows NYU, Phi Beta Kappa, Phi Gamma Delta. Home: 33 Washington Sq W New York NY 10011-9154 Office: NYU 70 Washington Sq S New York NY 10012-1019*

OLIVA, TERENCE ANTHONY, marketing educator; b. Rochester, N.Y., Feb. 21, 1943; s. Anthony J. and Teresa (Savasta) O.; children: Mark, Andrea. BA in Math. and Art, St. Mary's Coll., Calif., 1964; MBA with distinction, Fresno State U., 1971; PhD, U. Ala., 1974. Assoc. prof. mgmt. La. State U., Baton Rouge, 1974-82; vis. assoc. mktg. Columbia U., N.Y.C., 1982-83; assoc. prof., mktg. Rutgers U., Newark, 1983-88; vis. assoc. prof. Wharton Sch., U. Pa., Phila., 1985-87, assoc. prof., 1989-90; prof. Temple U., 1990—; mem. editl. bd. Org. Sci., 1993—. Author: Production Mgmt., 1981, editor, 1983; reviewer Behavioral. Sci., 1978—, Jour. Mktg., 1987—, Jour. Consumer Rsch., 1988—; assoc. editor Mgmt. Sci. Dept. Tech., 1989-91; editl. bd. mem. Org. Sci.; contbr. articles to profl. jours. Capt. USAF, 1965-69, Vietnam. Decorated Bronze Star; recipient Andrisani/Frank Undergrad Teaching award. Mem. Am. Mktg. Assn., Inst. for Mgmt. Sci. Avocation: restoring old Victorian homes. Office: 1810 Nth St Philadelphia PA 19122-6038 *Swimming upstream is often very productive. Just be prepared to jump obstacles and have a hard head.*

OLIVARES, RENE EUGENIO, translator; b. Santiago, Chile, Feb. 20, 1941; came to U.S., 1979; s. Luis Armando and Amelia del Carmen (Leiva) O. MS, U. Chile, 1971. Engr. Soquimich (Chile), Antofagasta, 1969-71, Codelco (Chile), Santiago, 1971-75; terminologist Entel (Chile), Santiago, 1975-79; translator UN, N.Y.C., 1979—. Editor: Tesauro de la Industria Extractiva del Cobre, 1974, Tesauro de Telecomunicaciones, 1978. Mem. AAAS, Am. Math. Soc., Math. Assn. Am., Blue Army of Fatima. Roman Catholic. Avocations: math, programming. Home: 32 W 40th St Apt 3L New York NY 10018-3991 Office: UN 1 United Nations Plz New York NY 10017-3515

OLIVE, DAVID MICHAEL, magazine writer, magazine editor; b. Toronto, Ont., Canada, Nov. 9, 1957; s. Harold Leslie and Alison Linton (Black) O.; m. Margaret Anne O'Reilly, Feb. 13, 1982 (div. June 1992). B of Applied Arts in Journalism, Ryerson Polytech. U., 1979. Copy editor Toronto Life Mag., 1979-81; assoc. editor Can. Bus. Mag., Toronto, 1981-84; sr. writer Report on Bus. Mag., Toronto, 1984-87, Toronto Life Mag., 1988-90; editorial writer The Globe and Mail, Toronto, 1990-91, current affairs columnist, 1991-92, bus. ethics columnist, 1996—; editor Report on Bus. Mag., 1991-97, sr. writer, 1997—; dir. Can. Ctr. for Ethics and Corp. Policy, 1988-91, Jessie's Ctr. for Teenagers, 1994—; pres. Jessie's Ctr. Non-Profit Homes Corp., 1994—; pres. Nat. Mag. Awards Found., 1988-90. Author: Just Rewards: The Case for Ethical Reform in Business, 1987, White Knights and Poison Pills: A Cynic's Dictionary of Business Jargon, 1990, Political Babble: The 1,000 Dumbest Things Ever Said by Politicians, 1992, Gender Babble: The Dumbest Things Men Ever Said About Women, 1993, Canadian Political Babble: A Cynic's Dictionary of Political Jargon, 1993, More Political Babble: The Dumbest Things Ever Said by Politicians, 1996, Canada Inside Out: How We See Ourselves, How Others See Us, 1996. Recipient Nat. Mag. awards Silver, 1987, Gold, 1988, hon. mention, 1983, 85, 87, 89, 96, Nat. Bus. Writing awards, 1983, 85, hon. mention, 1986, Nat. Journalism award, 1983. Mem. Can. Soc. Mag. Editors, Ethics Practitioners Assn. Can. Office: The Globe and Mail, 444 Front St W, Toronto, ON Canada M5V 2S9

OLIVEIRA, ELMAR, violinist; b. Waterbury, Conn., June 28, 1950. Student, Hartt Coll. Music, Hartford, Conn., Manhattan Sch. Music; studied with Raphael Bronstein, Ariana Bronne, John Oliveira; MusD (hon.), Manhattan Sch. Music, 1985. Prof. violin Manhattan Sch. Music, N.Y.C., 1990-91; vis. prof. Harper Coll., Binghamton, N.Y.; guest artist Chamber Music Soc. Lincoln Ctr., N.Y.C., 1994-95. Debut with Hartford Symphony Orch.; appeared on nat. TV as soloist with Young People's Concert series of N.Y. Philharmonic; N.Y.C. debut in Town Hall, 1973; appeared in recitals at Alice Tully Hall, 1976, 77; appeared with orchs. of Atlanta, Balt., Chgo., Cin., Cleve., Dallas, Minn., Phila., Pitts., St. Louis, Denver, Portland (Oreg.), also appeared with Nat. Symphony, L.A. Chamber Orch., L.A. Philharmonic Orch., Boston Symphony Orch., Milw. Orch., Ton Halle Orch., Zurich, London Philharmonic Orch., Gewand Haus Orch., Leipzig, Casals Festival Orch., and in Europe, Far East, S. Am.; appeared TV CBS Sunday Morning, Good Morning Am.; appeared with Madeira Bach Festival, 1980; Carnegie Hall debut, 1979; honored by Pres. Carter, 1978; recs. include Elmar Oliveira; cs. for CBS, Angel, EMI, MMG, RCA, Delos, IMP, VOX Unique, Elan. Winner 1st prize G.B. Dealey-Dallas News award, 1975, 1st Naumberg Internat. Violin Competition, 1975, Gold medal in violin Tchaikovsky Internat. Competition, 1978, Avery Fisher prize, 1983. Office: Seldy Cramer Artists 3436 Springhill Rd Lafayette CA 94549-2535

OLIVEIRA, MARY JOYCE, middle school education educator; b. Oakland, Calif., Feb. 16, 1954; d. Joseph and Vivian (Perry) O. BA, U. Calif., Berkeley, 1978; student, Holy Names Coll., Oakland, 1992; grad. in math., Calif. State U., Hayward, 1994. Cert. tchr., Calif.; cert. single subject math. credential, Hawaii. Recreation specialist Oakland Parks and Recreation, 1977-89; substitute tchr. Diocese of Oakland, 1989-90; tutor Oakland Pub. Schs., 1991; substitute tchr. Alameda (Calif.) Unified Sch. Dist., 1991—, Piedmont (Calif.) Unified Sch. Dist., 1993-96; tchr. summer program Wood Mid. Sch., Alameda, 1993, 96, Chipman Mid. Sch., Alameda, 1994, Encinal H.S., Alameda, 1995; math. tutor Calif. State U., Hayward, 1996, Intersession, Bay Farm Sch., Alameda, 1996; math tutor, 1996—. Creator children's sock toys Oliveira Originals, 1985. Vol. in art therapy oncology ward Children's Hosp., Oakland, 1985; vol. Berkeley Unified Sch. Dist., 1990-91. Mem. Nat. Coun. Tchrs. Math., Calif. Math. Coun., Math. Assn. Am., Alameda Swimming Pool Assn. Avocations: swimming, weight lifting, reading, arts and crafts.

OLIVELLA, BARRY JAMES, financial executive; b. Can., 1947. BA, York U., Toronto, Ont., Can., 1968. Chartered acct., Ont. Ptnr. Arthur Young Clarkson Gordon and Woods Gordon (name now Ernst & Young), Toronto, 1968-87; v.p. fin. Bombardier Inc., Montreal, Que., Can., 1987-89, v.p. planning and acquisitions, 1989-93, v.p. acquisitions and strategic alliances, 1993—; bd. dirs. NovaBus Corp. Pres. Uxbridge (Ont.) C. of C., 1986-87. Mem. Inst. Chartered Accts. Ont. and Can., Nat. Club (Toronto). Office: Bombardier Inc Ste 2900, 800 Rene-Levesque Blvd W, Montreal, PQ Canada H3B 1Y8

OLIVER, ANN BREEDING, fine arts education curator; b. Hollywood, Fla., Sept. 21, 1945; d. Harvey James and Ruth (Lige) Breeding; m. John Russell Kelso, July 22, 1972 (div. Feb. 1984); 1 child, Anna Liege; m. Ted J. Oliver, June 29, 1996. BA in Fgn. Lang., U. Ky., 1967; MA in History of Art, Ohio State U., 1971. Curatorial intern Lowe Art Mus., Coral Gables, Fla., 1972; adj. faculty Fla. Atlantic U., Boca Raton, Fla., 1972-73, 78; lectr. Miami (Fla.) Dade Community Coll., 1974, with art-music workshop, 1980-81; lectr.-cons., 1972—; adj. faculty music dept. Miami Dade (Fla.) Community Coll., 1991; curator of edn. Ctr. for the Fine Arts, Miami, 1987-92, High Mus. of Art, Atlanta, Ga., 1992-96; mem. Artists in Edn. Panel, Ga. Coun. for Arts, 1994; field reviewer Inst. Mus. Svcs., 1994; adj. faculty in art history Kennesaw State U., Marietta, Ga., 1996—. Contbg. editor African Art: An Essay for Teachers, 1993; project mgr. and contbg. author: Rings: Five Passions in World Art: Multicultural Curriculum Handbook, 1996. Recipient Nat. award for graphics Mead Paper Co., 1989, Gold Medal of Honor publication design S.E. Mus. Educators Publ. Design, 1994. Mem. Am. Assn. of Mus., Inst. Mus. Svcs., Nat. Art Edn. Assn., Fla. Art Edn. Assn. (dir. mus. divsn.), Ga. Art Edn. Assn. (dir. mus. divsn., Mus. Educator of Yr. 1993). Home: 2420 Mitchell Rd Marietta GA 30062-5321

OLIVER, DANIEL, foundation fellow, lawyer; b. N.Y.C., Apr. 10, 1939; s. Andrew and Ruth (Blake) O.; m. Anna Louise Vietor, Sept. 16, 1967; children: Anna Louise, Andrew II, Daniel Jr., Susan F., Peter A. AB, Harvard U., 1964; LLB, Fordham U., 1967. Bar: N.Y. 1967. Assoc. Hawkins, Delafield & Wood, N.Y.C., 1967-70; editorial asst. Nat. Rev. mag., N.Y.C., 1970-71, exec. editor, 1973-76; assoc. Alexander & Green, N.Y.C., 1971-73, 76-79; pvt. cons., 1980-81; gen. counsel U.S. Dept. Edn., Washington, 1981-83, USDA, Washington, 1983-86; chmn. FTC, Washington, 1986-89; disting. fellow The Heritage Found., Washington, 1989-91, Citizens for a Sound Economy Found., Washington, 1991-93; sr. fellow The Heritage Found., Washington, 1993-96; vice chmn. bd. Preferred Health Systems LLC, Bethesda, Md., 1996—; coun. Adminstrv. Conf. U.S., 1983-89. Vestryman Christ Ch., Greenwich, Conn. 1972-75, St. Andrews Ch., Edgartown, Mass., 1985-87, Ch. of Ascension and St. Agnes, 1991-94. Mem. Federalist Soc. Law Pub. Policy Studies (v.p. 1984, 86), Phila. Soc. (pres. 1991-92), Mont Pelerin Soc. Republican. Office: Preferred Health Systems 7500 Old Georgetown RdSte 900 Bethesda MD 20814

OLIVER, DEBBIE EDGE, elementary education educator; b. Houston, Jan. 8, 1953; d. John Orval and Charlotte (Laird) Edge; m. Lawrence Allen Oliver, July 21, 1973; 1 child, Kelly Dawn. BA in Teaching, Sam Houston State U., 1975, kindergarten cert., 1975. Cert. elem. tchr., Tex. Tchr. 3rd grade Big Sandy Ind. Sch. Dist., Livingston, Tex., 1975—; mem. site-based decision group, mem. textbook com., tech. com., gifted and talented com., Big Sandy Ind. Sch. Dist., 1989—; H.E.B. Edn. 2000 rep., 1993—; mem. grant writing com. Telecomms. Infrastructure Fund, 1997. Hon. mem. Future Farmers Am., Livingston, 1987; rodeo sec. Polk County Youth Rodeo Assn., Livingston, 1984—; adult leader 4-H, Livingston, 1984—. Recipient Disting. Svc. award Future Farmers Am., 1989; Title II math./sci. minigrantee Edn. Svc. Ctr., Huntsville, Tex., 1992. Mem. Ch. of Christ. Home: RR 3 Box 60 Livingston TX 77351-9501 Office: Big Sandy Ind Sch Dist RR 3 Box 422 Livingston TX 77351-9507

OLIVER, DIANE FRANCES, publisher, writer; b. N.Y.C., Feb. 7, 1935; m. Ben Martin Oliver, Sept. 3, 1960 (div. 1973). BA, Syracuse U., 1955. Reporter Millinery Rsch. mag., N.Y.C., 1956-58; with N.Y.C. Bur., London Daily Mail and London Daily Sketch, 1964-69; editor The Celebrity Bull., Celebrity Svc. Inc., N.Y.C., 1971-78; pub. The Celebrity Bull., pres., owner Celebrity Svc. Ltd., London, 1978—; former publicist Lake Lucerne (N.Y.) Playhouse, Bklyn. Acad. Music, Statler Hilton Hotel, N.Y.C. Author: Older Woman/Younger Man, 1975; columnist Palm Beach Social Pictorial mag., 1981-85. Avocations: music, ballet, films, theater, travel. Home: 44 Lennox Gardens, London SW1X 0DJ, England Office: Celebrity Svc Ltd, 93/97 Regent St, London W1R 7TA, England

OLIVER, EDWARD CARL, state senator, retired investment executive; b. St. Paul, May 31, 1930; s. Charles Edmund and Esther Marie (Bjugstad) O.; m. Charlotte Severson, Sept. 15, 1956; children—Charles E., Andrew T., Peter A. B.A., U. Minn., 1955. Sales rep. Armstrong Cork Co., N.Y.C., 1955; registered rep. Piper, Jaffray & Hopwood, Mpls., 1958; mgr. Mut. Funds, Inc. subs. Dayton's, Mpls., 1964; mgr. NWNL Mgmt. Corp. subs. Northwestern Nat. Life Ins. Co., Mpls., 1968-72, v.p., 1972-81, pres., dir., 1981-90; mem. Minn. Senate, 1992—; arbitrator/mediator, Nat. Assn. Securities Dealers, 1988—; bd. dirs. Minn. World Trade Ctr. Corp. Commr. Great Lakes Commn., 1993—. Served to sgt. USAF, 1951-52. Mem. Internat. Assn. Fin. Planners (past pres. Twin City chpt., nat. governing com.), Psi Upsilon. Presbyterian (elder). Club: Mpls. Athletic. Home: 20230 Cottagewood Rd Deephaven MN 55331-9300 Office: Washington Sq Securities Inc 100 Washington Ave S Ste 1639 Minneapolis MN 55401-2154

OLIVER, ELIZABETH KIMBALL, writer, historian; b. Saginaw, Mich., May 21, 1918; d. Chester Benjamin and Margaret Eva (Allison) Kimball; m. James Arthur Oliver, May 3, 1941 (div. July 1967); children: Patricia Allison (dec.), Dexter Kimball. BA, U. Mich., 1940. Tchr. Dexter (Mich.) High Sch., 1940-41; libr. Sherman (Conn.) Libr. Assn., 1966-75; pres. Sherman (Conn.) Libr. Assn., 1983-84; writer, historian, 1976—; reporter Sherman Sentinel, 1965-70; editor newsletter Sherman Hist. Soc., 1977-78; columnist Citizen News, Fairfield County, Conn., 1981-83. Author: History of Staff Wives-AMNH, 1961, Background and History of the Palisades Nature Association, 1964, History and Architecture of Grace United Methodist Church, 1990, Legacy to St. Augustine, 1993; guest columnist Mandarin News, 1995—. Vol. N.Y. Hist. Soc., N.Y.C., 1961-65; treas. Coburn Cemetery Assn., Sherman, 1976-82; historian Greenbrook-Palisades Nature Assn., Tenafly, N.J., 1962-64, Wesley Manor/Wesley Village Retirement Cmty., 1995-97; mem. St. Augustine Hist. Soc., Naromi Land Trust (life), Cedar Key Hist. Soc.; adv. bd. ABI, 1996—. Mem. AAUW, Friends of Libr. (life), Inst. Am. Indian Studies, Marjorie Kinnan Rawlings Soc. (charter), St. Augustine Woman's Club (archivist, cert. of appreciation 1990), Sherman Hist. Soc., Mandarin Hist. Soc. Republican. Congregationalist. Avocations: sacred choral music, research, reading, piano and dulcimer playing, botany. Home: 2292 Commodores Club Blvd Saint Augustine FL 32084 *There are four words which I endeavor to live up to in my work, my personal contacts and every day life. They are the guideposts which I use in all I do: love, courage, integrity and steadfastness.*

OLIVER, EUGENE ALEX, speech and language pathologist; b. East Palatka, Fla., Apr. 18, 1938; s. John T. and Ida (McBride) O.; m. Barbara Ann Gainer, Apr. 20, 1963; 1 child, Zulika Bonita. BA, Fla. A&M Univ., 1962; MA (equiv.), Southern Conn. State Univ., 1983; cert. advanced studies (equiv.), Fairfield Univ., 1989. Cert. speech and language pathology, Conn., lic. speech pathologist, Conn. Speech and lang. pathologist Florence (S.C.) Pub. Schs., 1962-63, Baltimore Pub. Schs., 1963-66, Imperial County Supt.'s Office, El Centro, Calif., 1967-69, Danbury (Conn.) Pub. Schs., 1969-80, Albuquerque Pub. Schs., 1980-81, Monzano H.S., Albuquerque, 1980-81; speech and lang. pathologist & coord. Cuba (N.Mex.) Pub. Schs., 1981-84; speech and lang. pathologist Waterbury (Conn.) Pub. Schs., 1985—; specialist comm. disorders on H.S. level Crosby H.S., Waterbury, 1986—, specialist Wilson Learning Ctr., Waterbury, 1985—. Founding mem. Black Congress, New Milford Conn., 1969; cons. Kwanzaa Celebrations, Conn., 1993; mem. Greater Bridgeport, Conn. chpt. NAACP, 1994—. Recipient Spl. Recognition, speech dept. Waterbury Pub. Sch., 1993, Wilson Learning Ctr., 1991. Mem. NEA, Conn. Speech Lang. Hearing Assn., Conn. Edn. Assn., Waterbury Tchrs. Assn. Avocations: tennis, horseback riding, archery, swimming, writing. Home: 289 Fan Hill Rd Monroe CT 06468-1316 Office: Waterbury Pub Schs 236 Grand St Waterbury CT 06702-1930

OLIVER, G(EORGE) BENJAMIN, educational administrator, philosophy educator; b. Mpls., Sept. 17, 1938; s. Clarence P. and Cecile (Worley) O.; m. Paula Rae Foust, Sept. 15, 1963; children: Paul Benjamin, Rebecca Lee. B.A. with honors, U. Tex., 1960; M.Div., Union Theol. Sem., N.Y.C., 1963; M.A., Northwestern U., 1966, Ph.D., 1967. Lectr. Northwestern U., Evanston, Ill., 1966-67; asst. prof. Hobart & William Smith Coll., Geneva, N.Y., 1967-71, chmn. dept. philosphy, 1969-77, assoc. prof., 1971-77; prof., 1977; dean Southwestern U., Georgetown, Tex., 1977-89, provost, 1986-89; pres. Hiram (Ohio) Coll., 1989—; chmn. Coun. of Acad. Deans and V.P.s of Tex., 1987-88. Contbr. articles to profl. jours. Trustee John Cabot Univ., Rome, 1989—, Grand River Acad., Austinburg, Ohio, 1991—, Northeast Ohio Coun. Higher Edn., 1991—, Ohio Found. Ind. Colls., 1989—, vice-chair elect, 1997-98; trustee Assn. Ind. Colls. and Univ. of Ohio, 1993—, Am. Coun. Edn. Commn. Govtl. Rels., 1994-97; chmn., bd. trustees, East Central Coll. Consortium, 1993-95. Rockefeller Found. fellow, 1960-61, Internat. fellow Columbia U., 1962-63; research grantee NEH, 1973-74. Mem. AAUP, Am. Coun. Edn. (mem. commn. on govtl. rels.), Soc. for Values in Higher Edn., Assn. Indep. Coll. and Univ. of Ohio (treas. 1993-94), East Ctrl. Colls. Consortium (chair, bd. trustees, 1993-95), Ohio Found. Ind. Colls. (exec. com. 1994—, vice chair elect 1997—), Am. Assn. Higher Edn. Episcopalian. Office: Hiram Coll Office of Pres Hiram OH 44234

OLIVER, HARRY MAYNARD, JR., retired brokerage house executive; b. Kansas City, Mo., Jan. 21, 1921; s. Harry Maynard and Marie (Curtin) O. BA, Williams Coll., 1943. Pres. M.A. Gesner & Co., Marsh & McLennan Co., Chgo., 1947-88. Chmn. Chgo. Commn. for Sr. Citizens, 1960-69; mem. Chgo. Bd. Edn., 1966-69; pres. Vol. Agys. Chgo., 1956-86; mem. vis. com. Sch. Edn. and div. of social scis., U. Chgo.; pres., bd. dirs. Benton House Settlement, 1953-58; bd. dirs. Adult Edn. Council Greater Chgo., Nat. Fedn. Settlements and Community Centers, 1961-67; trustee Old Peoples Home Chgo., Pub. Sch. Tchrs. Pension and Retirement Fund Chgo., 1966-69, George M. Pullman Ednl. Found., Field Mus. Natural History, 1971-75. Served to lt. (j.g.) USNR, World War II. Mem. Chgo. Club, Racquet Club, Commonwealth Club, Tavern Club, Onwentsia Club (Lake Forest, Ill.), Chi Psi. Home: 1948 N Lincoln Ave Chicago IL 60614-5404 also: PO Box 1319 Big Pine Key FL 33043 also: New Richmond PO Box 100 Fennville MI 49408

OLIVER, JACK ERTLE, geophysicist; b. Massillon, Ohio, Sept. 26, 1923; s. Chester L. and Marie (Ertle) O.; m. Gertrude van der Hoeven, Apr. 16, 1964; children: Cornelia Oliver, Amy Oliver. AB, Columbia U., 1947, MA, 1950, PhD, 1953; DSci (hon.), Hamilton Coll., 1988. Rsch. asst., then rsch. assoc. Columbia, 1947-55, mem. faculty, 1955-73, prof. geology, 1961-71, chmn. dept., 1969-71, adj. prof., 1971-73; Irving Porter Church prof. engring. dept. geol. scis. Cornell U., 1971-93, prof. emeritus, 1993—, chmn. dept., 1971-81; chmn. exec. com. COCORP; terrestrial physicist USAF Cambridge (Mass.) Rsch. Labs., 1951; dir. Inst. for Study of the Continents, 1981-88; cons. AEC, 1969-72, ACDA, 1962-74, USAF Tech. Applications Ctr., 1959-65; mem. Polar Rsch. Com., 1959-71, also nat. commn. uppermantle program, 1963-71; mem. panel solid earth problems NAS, 1962; mem. adv. com. U.S. Coast and Geodetic Survey, 1962-66, on seismology, 1960-72, chmn., 1966-70; mem. Geophysics Rsch. Bd., 1969-70; U.S. coord. 2d U.S.-Japan Earthquake Prediction Conf., Palisades, 1966; earth sci. panel NSF, 1962-65; mem. USAF Sci. Adv. Bd., 1960-63, 64-69; mem. geophysics adv. panel Office Sci. Rsch., USAF, 1961-74, chmn., 1966-68; U.S. del. Test Ban Conf., Geneva, Switzerland, 1958-59; intergovtl. meeting seismology and earthquake engring., mem. exec. com. IASPEI, 1968-71; mem. governing com. Internat. Seismol. Summary Commn., 1963-67, 75-76; mem. exec. com. UNESCO, Paris, France, 1964, U.S.-Japan Earthquake Prediction Conf., Tokyo, 1964; mem. UNESCO Joint Com. on Seismology and Earthquake Engring., 1965-71; chmn. exec. com. Office Earth Scis., NRC, 1976-79, Internat. Seismol. Centre, 1976-78; mem. U.S. Geodynamics Com., 1979-87, chmn., 1984-87; mem. Geol. Scis. Bd., Assembly of Math. and Phys. Scis., NRC, 1981-84; Cabot Disting. vis. scholar U. Houston, 1985-86; commn. on phys. scis., math. and resources NRC, 1987-90, commn. on geoscis., environ. and resources, 1990—. Served with USNR, 1943-46. Recipient Hedberg award Inst. for Study of Earth and Man, So. Meth. U., 1990. Fellow Am. Geophys. Union (pres. seismology sect. 1964-68, Walter H. Bucher medal 1981), Geol. Soc. Am. (coun. 1970-73, v.p. 1986, pres. 1987, Woollard medal 1990), Geol. Soc. London (hon.); mem. AAAS (chmn. geol. geog. sect. 1993), NAS, Seismol. Soc. Am. (pres. 1964-65, bd. dirs. 1961-70, 72-76, Eighth medal 1984), Soc. Exploration Geophysicists (Virgil Kauffman Gold medal 1983), European Union Geoscis. (hon. fgn. fellow), Sigma Xi. Home: 125 Cayuga Park Rd Ithaca NY 14850-1405

OLIVER, JAMES JOHN, lawyer; b. Norristown, Pa., Feb. 18, 1944; s. James Adam and Geraldine M. (Bartlett) O.; m. Judy M. Oliver; children: Justin J., Christine P. BA, St. Mary's U., Halifax, N.S., Can., 1967; LLB, Dalhousie U., Halifax, 1970; student, Harvard U. Law Sch., 1982. Bar: Pa. 1972, U.S. Dist. Ct. Pa. 1973, U.S. Ct. Appeals (3rd cir. 1973). Atty. Nationwide Ins. Co., Phila., 1970-73, Wright, Manning, Kinkead & Oliver, Norristown, Pa., 1974-90; ptnr. Murphy & Oliver, P.C., Norristown, Pa., 1990—. Author/listed in Contemporary Poets of America, 1980, New Voices in American Poetry, 1983. Vice-chmn. East Norristown Bd. Suprs., 1974-79; pres. Am. Cancer Soc., Norristown, 1974-82; chmn. ARC, Norristown, 1975-76; v.p. Child Devel. Found., 1974—; bd. advisor Gwynedd Mercy Coll., 1984-86; dir. Montgomery County Higher Edn. Authority, 1993—. Recipient Spl. Recognition award Montgomery County Assn. for Retarded Citizens, 1993, Individual award of Excellence, 1994, Award for Excellence, Am. Cancer Soc., 1994. Mem. ABA, ATLA, Am. Arbitration Assn. (panel of arbitrators), Montgomery County Bar Assn. (mem. ins. com., med. legal com., trial com.), Pa. Bar Assn. (mem. torts com., med. legal com., trial com.), Pa. Trial Lawyers Assn., Assn. Trial Lawyers of Am., Nat. Coll. Trial Advocacy, Million Dollar Advocates Forum, Tail Twisters/Lions Club. Avocations: sailing, hiking. Office: Murphy & Oliver 43 E Marshall St Norristown PA 19401-4818

OLIVER, JOHN PRESTON, chemistry educator, academic administrator; b. Klamath Falls, Oreg., Aug. 7, 1934; s. Robert Preston and Agnes May (McCornack) O.; m. Elizabeth Ann Shaw, Aug. 12, 1956; children: Karen Sue Oliver Vernon, Roy John, Gordon Preston. BA, U. Oreg., 1956; PhD, U. Wash., 1959. Asst. prof. chemistry Wayne State U., Detroit, 1959-64, assoc. prof., 1964-67, prof., 1967—, assoc. dean R&D, Coll. Liberal Arts, 1987-91, acting dean, 1991-92, interim dean Coll. Sci., 1992-93, dep. v.p. for acad. affairs, 1996—; chmn. organizing com. XIV Internat. Conf. on Organometallic Chemistry. Mem. Ferndale (Mich.) Bd. Edn., 1984-88. Mem. Am. Chem. Soc., Detroit sect. Am. Chem. Soc., Sigma Xi. Office: Wayne State Univ Rm 4101 FAB Detroit MI 48202-3489

OLIVER, JOHN WILLIAM POSEGATE, minister; b. Vincennes, Ind., Apr. 9, 1935; s. Dwight L. and Elizabeth (Posegate) O.; m. Cristina Shepard Hope, Oct. 19, 1968; children: John William Posegate Jr., Sloan Christian Shepard. BA, Wheaton Coll., 1956; BD, Fuller Theol. Sem., 1959; ThM, So. Bapt. Theol. Sem., 1963; DD, Western Sem., 1996. Ordained to ministry Presbyn. Ch. in Am., 1962. Asst. pastor Covenant Presbyn. Ch., Hammond, Ind., 1964-66, Trinity Presbyn. Ch., Montgomery, Ala., 1966-69; pastor 1st Presbyn. Ch., Augusta, Ga., 1969-97, Trinity Presbyn. Ch., Montgomery, Ala., 1997—; moderator Ctrl. Ga. Presbytery, Presbyn. Ch. in Am., 1976. Founder, trustee Westminster Schs., Augusta, 1972-97; trustee Trinity Sch., Montgomery, 1997—; chmn. clergy Augusta United Way Campaign, 1974; mem. exec. bd. clergy staff Univ. Hosp., Augusta, 1975-76; mem. bd. commrs. Augusta Housing Authority, vice-chmn., 1976-93; trustee, chmn. bd. Columbia Internat. U., 1978—; mem. ministerial adv. bd. Reformed Theol. Sem., 1978-85, 89-93, 96—; bd. dirs. Mission to the World, Presbyn. Ch. in Am., 1984-89, 92-96; dir. Bailey Manor Retirement Ctr., Clinton, S.C., 1992-97. Mem. Evang. Theol. Soc., Nassau Club of Princeton, Augusta Country Club, Montgomery Country Club, Kappa Sigma. Address: 1728 S Hull St Montgomery AL 36104-5597

OLIVER, MARY, poet; b. Maple Heights, Ohio, Sept. 10, 1935; d. Edward William and Helen Mary (Vlasak) O. Student, Ohio State U., 1955-56, Vassar Coll., 1956-57. Chmn. writing dept. Fine Arts Work Ctr., Provincetown, 1972-73, mem. writing com., 1984; Banister poet in residence Sweet Briar Coll., 1991-95; William Blackburn vis. prof. creative writing Duke U., 1995; Catharine Osgood Foster prof. Bennington Coll., 1996—. Author: No Voyage and Other Poems, 1963, enlarged edit., 1965, The River Styx, Ohio, 1972, The Night Traveler, 1978, Twelve Moons, 1979, American Primitive, 1983, Dream Work, 1986, House of Light, 1990, new and Selected Poems, 1992, A Poetry Handbook, 1994, White Pine, 1994, Blue Pastures, 1995, West Wind, 1997; contbr. to Yale U. Rev., Kenyon Rev., Poetry, Atlantic, Harvard mag., others. Recipient Shelley Meml. award, 1970, Alice Fay di Castagnola award, 1973; Cleve. Arts prize for lits., 1979; Achievement award Am. Acad. and Inst. Arts and Letters, 1983; Pulitzer prize for poetry, 1984; Christopher award, 1991, L.L. Winship award, 1991, Nat. Book award, 1992; Nat. Endowment fellow, 1972-73; Guggenheim fellow, 1980-81. Mem. PEN, Authors Guild. Home: care Molly Malone Cook Lit Agy PO Box 338 Provincetown MA 02657

OLIVER, ROBERT BRUCE, retired investment company executive; b. Brockton, Mass., Aug. 1, 1931; s. Stanley Thomas and Helen (Sabine) O.; m. Sylvia E. Bell, Feb. 17, 1954; children: Susan Pamela, Robert Bruce. A.B., Harvard U., 1953; postgrad., Bus. Sch., 1971, Boston U. Law Sch., 1955-57; M.A., Mich. State U., 1958. Ret. chmn., pres., chief exec. officer John Hancock Income Securities Trust, Boston, 1989; ret. chmn., pres. chief exec. officer John Hancock Investors Trust, John Hancock Bond Trust, John Hancock Growth Trust, John Hancock Tax Exempt Cash Mgmt. Trust, John Hancock Govt. Securities Trust, John Hancock Tax Exempt Income Trust, John Hancock Cash Mgmt. Trust, John Hancock Spl. Equities Trust, John Hancock Global Trust, John Hancock World Trust, John Hancock High Income Trust, John Hancock Tax Exempt Series Trust; chmn., dir. John Hancock Distbrs.; vice chmn., chief exec. officer John Hancock Advisers, Inc.; chmn., mng. dir. John Hancock Advisers Internat. Ltd. 1st lt. USMCR, 1953-55. Mem. Marine Corps League, Harvard Club of Naples. Home: 6619 Trident Way Naples FL 34108-8243

OLIVER, ROBERT WARNER, economics educator; b. L.A., Oct. 26, 1922; s. Ernest Warner and Elnore May (McConnell) O.; m. Darlene Hubbard, July 1, 1946 (dec. Mar. 1987); children: Lesley Joanne Oliver McClelland, Stewart Warner; m. Jean Tupman Smock, July 15, 1989. AB, U. So. Calif., 1943, AM, 1948; AM, Princeton U., 1950, PhD, 1958. Tchg. asst. U. So. Calif., 1946-47; instr. Princeton U., 1947-50, Pomona Coll., L.A., Calif., 1950-52; asst. prof. U. So. Calif., L.A., 1952-56; economist Stanford Rsch. Inst., South Pasadena, Calif., 1956-59; mem. faculty dept. econs. Calif. Inst. Tech., 1959-88, prof. econs., 1973-88, prof. emeritus, 1988—; urban economist World Bank, Washington, 1970-71; cons. Brookings Instn., 1961, OECD, Paris, 1979; vis. prof. U. So. Calif., 1985; vis. scholar Pembrook Coll., Cambridge (Eng.) U., 1989-90. Author: An Economic Survey of Pasadena, 1959, International Economic Cooperation and the World Bank, 1975, reissued with new intro., 1996, Bretton Woods: A Retrospective Essay, 1985, Oral History Project: The World Bank, 1986; contbg. author: Ency. of Econs., 1981, 93, George Woods and the World Bank, 1995. Mem. Human Rels. Com. City of Pasadena, 1964-65, Planning Commn., 1972-75, 91-95; bd. dirs. Pasadena City Coun., 1965-69; mem. Utilities Adv. Commn., 1984-88, 96—, Strategic Planning Com., 1985; pres. Pasadena Beautiful Found., 1972-74; bd. dirs. Pasadena Minority History Found., 1984—, Jackie Robinson Meml. Found., 1994—, UN Assn., Pasadena chpt., 1996—; trustee Pasadena Hist. Soc., 1992-94. Lt. (j.g.) USN, 1942-46. Social Sci. rsch. fellow London Sch. Econs., 1954-55; Rockefeller Found. fellow, 1974, 91; Danforth assoc., 1981; recipient Outstanding Tchg. award, 1982, Master of the Student Houses, 1987; Hon. Alumnus, 1987—. Mem. Am. Econs. Assn., Royal Econs. Assn., Athenaeum Club, Phi Beta Kappa, Phi Kappa Phi, Delta Tau Delta. Democrat. Methodist. Home: 3197 San Pasqual St Pasadena CA 91107-5330 Office: 1201 E California Blvd Pasadena CA 91125-0001 *The world is so full of beauty, natural and man-made, that human intelligence should seek to comprehend and enjoy it. Observation and reflection which lead to understanding are more important than performance, and the most important performance is service to others. The greatest human virtue is love, which is why family is important. If there be a God, I believe He works His will amongst civilized men through love, and He manifests His works through beauty.*

OLIVER, RONALD, retired medical technologist; b. New Orleans, July 16, 1949; s. Wilbert and Everlina (Theard) O.; m. Ora Grant, July 12, 1995; children: Nannette Marie, Joseph Byron. Diploma in bus. adminstrn., Meadows-Draughon Coll., New Orleans, 1972; AS in Environ. Health Tech., Delgado C.C., New Orleans, 1976; BS in Biology Edn., So. U., 1980, BS in Chemistry Edn., 1983; MA in Hosp. Adminstrn., Southwest U., La., 1986; PhD in Hosp. Adminstrn., Southwest U., 1987; cert., Charity Hosp. Sch. Nuclear Med, 1986; PhD in Pub. Health, Columbia State U., La., 1992; PhD in Health Adminstrn., Kennedy-Western U., 1993; PhD in Environ. Engring., Kensington U., Glendale, Calif., 1994; PhD in Electrophysiology, Summit U., New Orleans, 1995. Med. technologist, med. technologist supr. Charity Hosp., New Orleans, 1969-95, retired, 1995; mem. faculty Pacific Western U., 1993—, Kensington U.; mem. faculty Kensington Univ., Glendale, Calif., 1996—. Author 7 books, including A Primer in Electrocardiography with Technical and Some Evaluative Values, 1991, 2d edit., 1995, Electrocardiography, Theories, Applications and Practice, 1997; also articles. Recipient Outstanding Svc. award Charity Hosp., 1972, acknowledgement letter Nobel Found., 1992, cert. of acknowledgement Coll. Am. Pathologists, 1981, Am. Ex-mem. Assn. Profl. Cons.; candidate Pulitzer Prize, 1995. Mem. Am. Med. Technologists, Am. Coll. Healthcare Execs. (cert. of acknowledgment), La. Environ. Health Assn. Methodist. Achievements include over 30 copyrights in the field of electrophysiology in Library of Congress; discovered the sigma wave in electracardiography, the electrical alternan theory, the intracerebral-intracranial theories; patentee in field, 1 reg. U.S. Dept. Commerce. Home: 8851 N Bunkerhill Rd Apt B New Orleans LA 70127-5319

OLIVER, ROSEANN, lawyer; b. Chgo., Oct. 9, 1947. BA, Northwestern U., 1969; JD, Loyola U., 1972. Bar: Ill. 1972, U.S. Dist. Ct. (no. dist.) Ill. 1974, U.S. Ct. Appeals (7th cir.) 1974. legal writing instr. I.I.T. Chicago-Kent Coll. Law, 1973-74, Loyola U., 1974-75; mem. Cook County Bd. Ethics. Articles editor Loyola Law Jour., 1971-72; contbr. articles to profl. jour. Mem. Ill. State Bar Assn., Chgo. Bar Assn. (spl. counsel 1981-82, chmn. standing com. on litigation 1985-88, amicus curiae com. 1989-95), 7th Cir. Bar Assn., Inns of Ct. Office: Cahill Christian & Kunkle 224 S Michigan Ave Ste 1300 Chicago IL 60604-2500

OLIVER, SAMUEL WILLIAM, JR., lawyer; b. Birmingham, Ala., Apr. 18, 1935; s. Samuel William and Sarah Pugh (Coker) O.; m. Anne Holman Marshall, Aug. 26, 1961; children: Sarah Bradley Oliver Crow, Samuel William III, Margaret Nelson Oliver Little. BS, U. Ala., 1959, JD, 1962. Bar: Ala. 1962, U.S. Dist. Ct. (no. dist.) Ala. 1963. Law clk. Supreme Ct. Ala., Montgomery, 1962-63, U.S. Dist. Ct. (no. dist.) Ala., Birmingham, 1963; assoc. Burr & Forman (formerly Thomas, Taliaferro, Forman, Burr), Birmingham, 1964-65, ptnr., 1966—, also chmn. bus./corp. law sect., 1990-93; dir. Metalplate Galvanizing Inc., Birmingham; mem. panel arbitrators commercial Am. Arbitration Assn., Atlanta and Nashville, 1981—. Chmn. bd. govs. The Relay House, Birmingham, 1985-89; mem. Leadership Birmingham, 1990; mem. adv. bd. Jr. League Birmingham, 1975-77; bd. dirs. Jr. Achievement Greater Birmingham, Inc., 1975—; sr. warden St. Stephen's Episcopal Ch., Birmingham, 1979; mem. diocese coun. Episcopal Diocese Ala., Birmingham, 1981-85; chmn. bd. trustees Highlands Day Sch. Found., Inc., Birmingham, 1980-81; bd. dirs. Ala. Kidney Found., Birmingham, 1990-94. With U.S. Army, 1956-58. Mem. ABA (bus. law sect. 1965—, negotiated acquisitions com. 1990—, task force on joint venture and asset purchase agreements 1994—, sect. internat. law and practice), Internat. Bar Assn. (corp. law sect.), Southeastern Corp. Law Inst. (planning com. 1996—), Birmingham Bar Assn., Country Club Birmingham, Summit Club (bd. govs.), Monday Morning Quarterback Club, Rotary Club, Venture Club. Episcopalian.

OLIVER, SANDRA KAY, nursing researcher; b. Orangeburg, S.C., Oct. 20, 1945; d. John Walthall and Miriam (Garrick) O.; m. R. Wayne Matthews, Dec. 28, 1977; children: Joseph Lenear Oliver Matthews, Miriam Elizabeth Oliver Matthews. BSN, U. Tex. Med. Br., 1967; MA, U. Iowa, 1971, PhD, 1981. Cert. CCRN, CNS. Staff nurse U. Iowa Hosp. and Clinic, Iowa City, 1971-81; asst. prof. U. Iowa, Iowa City, 1971-81, U. S.C., Columbia, 1981-82; assoc. prof. S.C. State Coll., Orangeburg, 1983-84, Tex. Woman's U., Dallas, 1984-86; asst. prof. Tex. A&M Health Sci. Ctr., Temple, 1990—; Temple site MSN coord. Tex. A&M at Corpus Christi, 1992—; rsch. assoc. Scott and White Meml. Hosp., Temple, 1986—. Contbr. articles to profl. jours. Pres. Agens Waddson chpt. DAR, Belton, Tex., 1992—; lay leader 1st United Meth. Ch., Temple, 1993—; adult leader Tigertown 4H, Belton, 1987—; dist. commr. Heart of Tex. Coun. Boy Scouts Am., Waco, 1992-94. Mem. Tex. League for Nursing (pres. 1993-95), Tex. Nurses Assn. (govt. affairs com. 1993-95, pres. dist. VII 1991-93), Sigma Theta Tau (Excellence in Rsch. award Epsilon Theta chpt. 1995), Pi Lambda Theta, Phi Delta Kappa. Democrat. United Methodist. Office: Scott and White Meml Hosp 2401 S 31st St Temple TX 76508-0001

OLIVER, STEPHANIE STOKES, magazine editor; b. Seattle; m. Reginald Oliver; 1 child, Anique. BA in Journalism cum laude, Howard U., 1974. Former fashion & beauty merchandising editor Glamour Mag.; editor contemporary living sect. Essence Mag., N.Y.C., 1978-80, sr. editor, 1980-84; West Coast editor Essence Mag., Seattle, 1984-85; editor of mag. Essence Mag., N.Y.C., 1986-94; editor-in-chief Heart & Soul Mag., N.Y.C., 1994—; keynote and panel spkr.; First William Randolph Hearst vis. prof. Howard U. Sch. Comms., 1996. Bd. trustees Women's Sports Found., 1997—. Recipient Outstanding Alumnae award Howard U., 1986. Mem. Am. Soc. Mag. Editors (former sec. bd. dirs.), Nat. Assn. Black Journalists, Black Women in Pub., Women in Comm., Inc. Office: Heart & Soul 733 3rd Ave Fl 15 New York NY 10017-3204

OLIVER, STEVEN WILES, banker; b. Los Angeles, May 27, 1947; s. Frank Wiles and Hazel Gloria (Patton) O.; m. Susan Elizabeth Peace, Nov. 27, 1971; children: Andrew Wells, Elizabeth Patton, Laura Rice. AB cum laude, Claremont Men's Coll., 1969; JD, Vanderbilt U., 1972. Officer Citibank, N.A., S.E. Asia, 1972-79; mng. dir. Lazard Asia Ltd., Hong Kong, 1980-88, Lazard Freres & Co. Ltd., London, 1988-90; gen. ptnr. Lazard Frères & Co., N.Y.C., 1988-94; mng. dir. Lazard Frères K.K., Tokyo, 1990-95; founding ptnr. Lazard Asia Ltd., Singapore, 1995; non-exec. dir. Lazard Bros. & Co. Ltd., London, 1989. Mem. Tokyo Lawn Tennis Club, Tokyo Am. Club, Hong Kong Country Club, Penang Club, Leland Country Club. Presbyterian. Office: Lazard Freres & Co 30 Rockefeller Plz New York NY 10112 also: Lazard Asia Ltd, #22-20 UOB Plz II 80 Raffles, Singapore 048624, Singapore

OLIVER, THORNAL GOODLOE, health care executive; b. Memphis, Aug. 26, 1934; s. John Oliver and Evelyn Doris (Goodloe) Mitchell; m. Pauline Reid, Oct. 1, 1959. B.S., Tenn. State U., Nashville, 1956; M.H.A., Washington U., St. Louis, 1973. Cert. nursing home adminstr., Mo. Asst. dir., King Meml. Hosp., Kansas City, Mo., 1973-75; evening mgr. Truman Med. Ctr., Kansas City, Mo., 1975-77; asst. adminstr. Mid-Am. Radiation Ctr. U. Kans. Coll. Health Sci., Kansas City, Kans., 1977-81; dir. CHS, Inc., Leawood, Kans., 1981-82; adminstr. Poplar Bluff Hosp., Mo., 1982-83; adminstr. The Benjamin F. Lee Health Ctr., Wilberforce, Ohio, 1983-86; asst. clin. prof. Dept. Community Medicine, Wright State U., Dayton, 1986-89; asst. patent adminstr. Munson Army Hosp., Ft. Leavenworth, Kans., 1987—; cons. Urban Health Assocs., Nashville, 1986-87, others. Contbr. articles to profl. jours. Served with U.S. Army, 1957-59, USAR, 1959-63. Fellow Am. Coll. Hosp. Adminstrs.; mem. Am. Hosp. Assn., Nat. Assn. Health Services Execs., Am. Med. Record Assn., Mo. League of Nursing Home Adminstrs. Home: 10641 N Grand Ave Kansas City MO 64155-1655 Office: Munson Army Hosp Fort Leavenworth KS 66027

OLIVER, WILBERT HENRY, religious organization administrator; b. Corozal Town, Belize, Oct. 3, 1958; came to the U.S., 1967; s. Wilbert and Ofelia (Rojas) O.; m. Elaine P. Powell, Aug. 26, 1984; children: Jessica D., Julian T. BA in Theology, West Indies Coll., 1979; MA in Religion, Andrews U., 1981; MA in Sociology, Columbia U., 1988, postgrad. in sociology, 1990. Youth pastor Grand Concourse Temple of Seventh-Day Adventists, N.Y.C., 1982-83; sr. pastor Tabernacle of Joy Seventh-Day Adventist Ch., N.Y.C., 1983-87, Maranatha Seventh-Day Adventist Ch., N.Y.C., 1987-88; assoc. youth ministries dir. Greater N.Y. Conf. Seventh-day Adventists, 1988-89, dir. youth ministries and family ministries, 1989-93; dir. youth ministries and family ministries Atlantic Union Conf. Seventh-day Adventists, South Lancaster, Mass., 1994-95; dir. family ministries and Pathfinder Camp Ministries N.Am. Divsn. Seventh-Day Adventists, Silver Spring, Md., 1996—. Contbr. articles to profl. jours. Named one of Outstanding Young Men Am., 1983. Mem. Assn. Adventist Family Life Profls., Am. Assn. Christian Counselors, Nat. Coun. on Family Rels., Ministerial Assn. Seventh-Day Adventists, Am. Sociol. Assn., N.Y. Acad. Scis. Avocations: golf, reading, skiing, travel. Home: 14808 Athey Rd Burtonsville MD 20866 Office: Seventh Day Adventists North American Divsn 12501 Old Columbia Pike Silver Spring MD 20904-6601

OLIVER, WILLIAM ALBERT, JR., paleontologist; b. Columbus, Ohio, June 26, 1926; s. William Albert and Mary-Maud (Thompson) O.; m. Johanna L. Kramer, Sept. 1, 1948 (dec.); children: Robert A., James A. B.S., U. Ill., 1948; M.A., Cornell U., 1950, Ph.D., 1952. Instr., then asst. prof. geology Brown U., Providence, 1952-57; research geologist-paleontology U.S. Geol. Survey, Washington, 1957-93, emeritus scientist, 1993—; mem. U.S. Nat. Com. on Geology, 1975-79, chmn., 1978-79; U.S. rep. Internat. Subcommn. on Devonian Stratigraphy, 1973-92; chmn., 1984-89; rsch. assoc. dept. paleobiology U.S. Nat. Mus. Natural History-Smithsonian Instn., Washington, 1993—. Contbr. articles to profl. jours. Fellow AAAS (coun. 1971-73), Geol. Soc. Am.; mem. Paleontol. Soc. (councilor 1964-69, 73-76, editor Jour. 1964-69, pres. 1974-75), Paleontol. Assn. (London), Palaeontol. Rsch. Inst. (trustee 1976-89, pres. 1984-86, Harris award, 1994), Am. Geol. Inst. (dir. 1974-77, v.p. 1975-76, pres. 1976-77), Internat. Assn. for Study of Fossil Cnidaria (coun. 1971-88, pres. 1983-88), Internat. Palaeontological Assn. (sec. gen. 1984-89). Home: 4203 McCain Ct. Kensington MD 20895-1321 Office: Natural Hist Bldg MRC137 Smithsonian Inst E-305 Washington DC 20560

OLIVER, WILLIAM DONALD, orthodontist; b. Montreal, Que., Can., Dec. 14, 1944; s. Austen William and Margaret Kay (Donald) O.; B.S. in Physics, Mt. Allison U., 1964; D.D.S., McGill U., 1968; M.S.D. in Orthodontics, U. Pa., 1970. Pres., Othodontic Enterprises Internat., Geneva, Switzerland, 1973-78; practice dentistry specializing in orthodontics, Pawtucket, R.I., 1979; instr. Frankfurt Carolinium, 1972-74; witness Senate Armed Services Com., 1975. Inventor Pezio Electric Bone Healing. Served with USAF, 1970-73. Recipient Carter Meml. Award, 1964; M. T. Dohan Prize, 1966. Mem. Am. Dental Assn., Canadian Assn. Orthodontists, Am. Assn. Orthodontists, European Orthodontic Soc., Canadian Dental Assn., Fedn. Internat. d'Automobile (qualified and registered mem.). Republican. Clubs: Royal Ocean Racing. Mem. Olympic Ski Team, Squaw Valley, 1960; contbr. articles on orthodontics to profl. jours. Office: 10812 Bothell Hwy SE Everett WA 98208-3828

OLIVER, WILLIAM JOHN, pediatrician, educator; b. Blackshear, Ga., Mar. 30, 1925; s. John Wesley and Katherine (Schalwig) O.; m. Marguerite Bertoni, May 28, 1949; children: Ralph Scott, Catherine, Susan. Student, Ga. Southwestern Coll., 1942-43, Mercer U., 1943-44; MD cum laude, U. Mich., 1948. Diplomate Am. Bd. Pediatrics (examiner), Subsplty. Bd. Pediatric Nephrology. Intern, resident U. Mich. Med. Center, 1948-53, dir. pediatric labs., 1959-67; pvt. practice medicine specializing in pediatrics Ann Arbor, Mich., 1953—; instr. dept. pediatrics U. Mich., 1953-56, asst. prof., 1956-61, assoc. prof., 1961-65, prof., 1965, chmn. dept. pediatrics, 1967-79; chief pediatric service Wayne County Hosp., 1958-61; co-chmn. task force on recent advances of coordinating com. on continuing edn. and recertification Am. Bd. Pediats. and Am. Acad. Pediats., 1977-80; mem. task force for pediatric rev. edn. program, 1980-88; mem. com. program for renewal certification in pediat. Am. Bd. Pediat., 1989-91, mem. exam writing com. for cert. pediatric nephrology, 1989-93, PRCP pilot test com., 1993-96; mem. rev. and question writing com. for Pediat. in Rev. Am. Acad. Pediat., 1991—; cons. U. Riyadh, Saudi Arabia, 1980, Rsch. Rev. Com. on Pediat., 1989; ednl. cons. dept. pediat. Stanford U. Hosps., 1991—; mem. self-assessment program for Pediat. in Rev., 1990—; investigator adaptation primative So. Ams. Indians, 1976—, African Pygmies, 1987—. Mem. editl. bd. IRCS Jour. Med. Sci., 1975-90. Pres. Mich. Kidney Disease Found., 1969, Washtenaw County br. Mich. Childrens Aid Soc., 1964; trustee Ann Arbor Hands-On Mus., 1983-88; pres. bd. trustees Perry Nursery Sch., Ann Arbor, 1989-90. With USNR, 1950-52. Fellow Am. Acad. Pediatrics (chmn. com. med. edn. 1974-80, chmn. council on pediatric edn. 1975-80, chmn. task force oversight of pediatric rev. and edn. program 1984-88, Clifford G. Grulee award 1979); mem. Soc. Pediatric Research, Midwest Soc. Pediatric Research (pres. 1968), Am. Soc. Nephrology, Assn. Med. Sch. Pediatric Dept. Chairmen (mem. council 1977-79), Soc. for Exptl. Biology and Medicine, Am. Pediatric Soc., Alpha Omega Alpha, Gamma Sigma Epsilon. Home: 2892 Bay Ridge Dr Ann Arbor MI 48103-1704

OLIVERO, GARY, insurance company executive, financial planner; b. Newark, Oct. 1, 1949; s. Anthony and Anna Maria (Borra) O.; m. Nancilee E. Yannetta, May 25, 1952; children: Jason Matthew, Eric John, Stephanie Anne. Student, U. Mo., 1967-69. ChFC, CLU. Sales rep. METLIFE, Somerville, N.J., 1972-75, sales mgr., 1975-77; tng. mgr. METLIFE, N.Y.C., 1977-79; dist. sales mgr. METLIFE, Rutherford, N.J., 1979-83; territorial dir. annuity mktg. METLIFE, Tampa, Fla., 1991-92; nat. dir. variable products METLIFE, N.Y.C., 1992-94; regional sales mgr. ea. Pa. METLIFE, Allentown, Pa., 1994—; regional v.p. METLIFE-L.I. and Hudson Valley, Melville, N.Y., 1995—; gen. agt. Life of Va., Tampa, 1983-87; regional dir. recruiting Century 21 Ins. Svcs., Tampa, 1987-91. Author: (tng. guide) Annuity Resource Guide, 1991, (tng. video) Seminar Marketing to Seniors, 1992; co-author: (tng. video) Variable Life Markets, 1991. Councilman Borough of Bound Brook, N.J., 1974-75; county coord. U.S. Senator Frank Lautenberg, Somerset, N.J., 1983; bd. mem. Urban League, Jersey City, 1979-83; advisor campaign funding Tampa Bay Performing Arts, 1984-86; corp. fund raising solicitor United Way, Tampa, 1986-88; com. chmn. troop 11 Boy Scouts Am., Valrico, Fla., 1986-88. With U.S. Army, 1969-72. Named Keyman of Yr. Somerville Jaycees, 1975. Mem. Am. Soc. CLUs, Gen. Agts. Mgrs. Assn. (v.p. 1984-88). Avocations: photography, camping, cooking, racquetball, trap shooting. Home: 41 Twixt Hill Road Saint James NY 11780-1621 Office: Metlife 135 Pinelawn Rd Ste 220 Melville NY 11747-3133

OLIVER-SIMON, GLORIA CRAIG, human resources advisor, consultant, lawyer; b. Chester, Pa., Sept. 19, 1947; d. Jesse Harper and Lavinia Craig Cuff; m. James Russell Norwood, Sept. 1970 (div.); 1 child, James Russell Jr.; m. Joseph M. Simon, Jan. 1993. BS, U. Md., 1987; JD, Am. U., 1990, MS, 1992. Bar: Pa. 1991, U.S. Ct. Appeals (fed. cir.) 1994, D.C. 1997. Pers. specialist VA Med. Ctr., Phila., 1974-80; pers./human resources specialist VA Ctrl. Office, Washington, 1980-90, human resources mgr., 1990-97; mem. VA Work Group on Minority Initiatives, 1990, 93—; VA coord., rep. Coun. for Excellence in Govts. Spkrs. Bur. Project, 1991-92, Pub. Employees Roundtable for Pub. Svc. Recognition Week, 1991-92; subcom. chair Student Employee Programs, Office of Pers. Mgmt. Work Group, 1993; coord. VA Caring and Courtesy Campaign Focus Group, 1993; mem. VA Veterans Health Adminstrn. Nursing Shortage Task Group, 1987, 93, VA Work Group on the Nat. and Cmty. Svc. Program, 1993-94, 95-96, Veterans Health Adminstrn. Healthcare Reform Work Group on Customer Svc., 1993-94; VA's Nat. Com. on Employment of Disabled Vets. and People with Disabilities, 1992-93; VA Office Human Resources Mgmt. coord. Pres.'s Com. on Employment of Persons with Disabilities/Dept. of Def. Student Employment Initiative, 1994-95; VA Office of Human Resources Mgmt. steering com. 1994-96; mem. Dept. of Energy Student Employment Task Group, 1994-96; coord. Welfare to Work Program, 1997—. Mem. ABA, Fed. Bar Assn., Nat. Bar Assn., Fed. Cir. Bar Assn., D.C. Bar Assn., Bar Assn. of D.C., Phi Delta Phi, U. Md. Alumni Assn. (mentor program), Am. U. Alumni Assn. (admissions com.), AKA Sorority Inc., DAV Aux. (fed. unit 1). Avocations: reading, traveling. Home: 809 Braeburn Dr Tantallon Fort Washington MD 20744-6022 Office: Dept Vets Affairs 810 Vermont Ave NW Washington DC 20420-0001

OLIVER-WARREN, MARY ELIZABETH, retired library science educator; b. Hamlet, N.C., Feb. 23, 1924; d. Washington and Carolyn Belle (Middlebrooks) Terry; m. David Oliver, 1947 (div. 1971); children: Donald D., Carolyn L.; m. Arthur Warren, Sept. 14, 1990 (dec. Feb. 1995). BS, Bluefield State U., 1948; MS, South Conn. State U., 1958; student, U. Conn., 1977. Cert. tchr., adminstr. and supr., Conn. Media specialist Hartford (Conn.) Pub. Schs., 1952-86; with So. Conn. State U., New Haven, 1972—, asst. prof. Sch. Libr. Sci. and Instructional Tech., 1987-95, ret., 1995; mem. dept. curriculum com. So. Conn. State U., 1987-95, adj. prof., 1995—; cert. substitute tchr. Somerset County Pub. Schs., 1997—. Author: My Golden Moments, 1988, The Elementary School Media Center, 1990, Text Book Elementary School Media Center, 1991, I Must Fight Alone, 1991, (textbook) I Must Fight Alone, 1994. Mem. ALA, Conn. Ednl. Media Assn., Black Librs. Network N.J. Inc., Assn. Ret. Tchrs. Conn., Black and Hispanic Consortium, So. Conn. State U. Women's Assn., Cicuso Club (v.p.), Friends Club (v.p.), Delta Kappa Gamma, Alpha Kappa Alpha. Avocations: reading, music, piano, walking. Home: 6 Freeman Rd Somerset NJ 08873-2925 Office: So Conn State U 501 Crescent St New Haven CT 06515-1330

OLIVETI, SUSAN GAIL, sales promotion and public relations executive; b. Bklyn., Nov. 1, 1938; d. Peter and Nancy Jane (Wolk) Randolph; m. Fosco Anthony Oliveti, Sept. 18, 1970 (div. 1990); children by previous marriage: Lois, Peter, Elizabeth, Ruben. BBA, CCNY, 1967; student, NYU, 1968-69; diploma in nursing, Jewish Hosp. Sch. Nursing, 1960. Estimator, media rsch. Ogilvy & Mather, N.Y.C., 1966-68; TV rep. Adam Young, Inc., N.Y.C., 1968-69; exec. asst. Paramount Pictures, N.Y.C., 1969-80; mgr. conv. and media events Warner Amex Satellite Enterprise Co. (now MTV Networks), N.Y.C., 1980-83; exhibits and pub. rels. specialist Siemens Med. Systems, Iselin, N.J., 1983-85; meetings and pub. rels. mgr. U.S. Trademark Assn., N.Y.C., 1985; v.p. corp. communications J.R. Heimbaugh, Inc., 1986; mgr. sales promotions, pub. relations meetings, convs. Lightolier, Inc., Secaucus, N.J., 1986-90; exec. v.p. Globefern USA, Inc., 1990-95; sales & mktg. exec. marriott Sr. Living Svcs., 1995—. Recipient spl. honors United Airlines, 1978. Mem. Meeting Profls. Internat. (reception com., edn. com.), Pub. Rels. Soc. Am. Democrat. Jewish. Avocations: knitting, gardening, designing jewelry. Office: 1425 S Congress Ave Boynton Beach FL 33426

OLIVETO, FRANK LOUIS, recreation consultant; b. Bellaire, Ohio, Oct. 9, 1956; s. Donald Albert and Patricia Edna (Pezdriz) O.; m. Ann Marie Mongelli, Mar. 13, 1982; children: Leah Marie, Hannah Emily. BS, Pa. State U., 1980. Intern, then asst. dir. recreation Kiawah Island Resort, Charleston, S.C., 1980; dir. recreation Seabrook Island Resort, Charleston, 1981-85, Innisbrook Resort, Tampa, Fla., 1985-88; pres., owner Recreation Mgmt. Assn., Tampa, 1988—. Contbr. articles to mags. Elder, home group leader In the Name of Jesus World Outreach Ctr., Odessa, Fla., 1989. Mem. Resort and Comml. Recreation Assn. (founding mem., pres. 1983, exec. dir. 1988—), Fla. Recreation and Park Assn., Nat. Recreation and Park Assn. Republican. Avocations: travel, public speaking, racquetball, photography. Home: 6850 Larchmont Ave New Port Richey FL 34653-5921 Office: Recreation Mgmt Assn PO Box 215 New Port Richey FL 34656-0215

OLKINETZKY, SAM, artist, retired museum director and educator; b. N.Y.C., Nov. 22, 1919; s. Isidor and Jennie O.; m. Sammie Lee Sturdevant, Dec. 20, 1959; children: Jov Shan, Tova Shana. B.A., Bklyn. Coll., 1942; postgrad., Inst. Fine Arts, N.Y. U., 1946-47. Asst. prof. art and humanities Okla. A&M U., Stillwater, 1947-57; vis. asst. prof. art U. Okla., Norman, 1957-58; assoc. prof. art Mus. of Art, 1959—; dir. Mus. Art U. Okla., Norman, 1959-83; vis. prof. art and humanities U. Ark., Fayetteville, 1962-63, 67-68, Langston (Okla.) U., 1969-70; art cons. Kerr-McGee Industries, Inc.; advisor State of Okla. Visual Arts; mem. State Art Collection Com.; Mem. Norman Arts and Humanities Council. One-man exhbns. include Arts Place II, Okla. Art Ctr., Firehouse Art Ctr., Norman, 1989; other exhbns. include Mus. Non-Objective Art, N.Y.C., Mus. Modern Art, N.Y.C.; 50-yr. Retrospective Exhbn., 1942-92, Norick Art Ctr., Oklahoma City, 1992; represented in permanent collections Philbrook Art Ctr., Tulsa, Okla. Art Ctr., Mus. Art U. Okla. Served with USAAF, 1942-45. Recipient Gov.'s Art award, 1981. Mem. Okla. Museums Assn. (pres. 1978-79), Internat. Council Museums, Mountain-Plains Museums Assn., Am. Assn. Museums, Art Mus. Assn.

OLLEMAN, ROGER DEAN, industry consultant, former metallurgical engineering educator; b. Cornelia, Ga., Nov. 25, 1923; s. Faye Erlando and Esther (Perkins) O.; m. Elizabeth Ann Deutsch, May 24, 1947; children—Esther Jean, Ruth Ellen, Mark Charles. B.S. in Mech. Engring, U. Wash., 1948; M.S. in Metall. Engring, Carnegie Inst. Tech., 1950; Ph.D., U. Pitts., 1955. Group leader Westinghouse Research Labs., Pitts., 1950-55; asst. br. head, dept. metall. research Kaiser Aluminum & Chem. Corp., Spokane, Wash., 1955-59; mem. faculty dept. mech. and metall. engring. Oreg. State U., Corvallis, 1959-76, now courtesy prof.; pres. Accident and Failure Investigations, Inc., 1974—; cons. to industry, also Lawrence Radiation Lab., 1965-66, U.S. Bur. Mines Metallurgy Research Ctr., Albany, 1962-72. Bd. dirs. Benton Assn. Retarded Children. Served with AUS, 1944-46. Recipient Lloyd Carter award outstanding teaching Sch. Engring., Oreg. State U., 1962. Mem. ASTM (Templin award 1953), ASME (past sec., nonferrous subcom. boiler and pressure vessle code), Am. Soc. Engring. Edn., Am. Soc. Metals Internat., Am. Inst. Mining, Metall. and Petroleum Engrs., Sigma Xi, Tau Beta Pi, Pi Tau Sigma. Home: 1005 NW 30th St Corvallis OR 97330-4441

OLLER, WILLIAM MAXWELL, retired energy company executive, retired naval officer; b. Lancaster, Pa., Apr. 7, 1924; s. John Secrist and Mabel Margaret (Coffman) O.; m. Doris Seitz Greenleaf, June 15, 1946; children: Arthur G., J. Richard. BS, U.S. Naval Acad., 1946; MBA, George Washington U., 1960. Commd. ensign USN, 1946, advanced through grades to rear adm., 1972; svc. in Samoa, Philippines and Italy; exec. officer Naval Supply Ctr., Newport, R.I., 1966-67, Ships Parts Control Ctr., Mechanicsberg, Pa., 1970-72; comdr. Def. Fuel Supply Ctr., Alexandria, Va., 1972-76; comdg. officer Naval Supply Ctr., Norfolk, Va., 1976-77; gen. mgr. corp. supply and distbn. Champlin Petroleum Co., Houston, 1977-79, Ft. Worth, 1979-81; sr. v.p. Petroleum Ops. and Support Svcs., Inc., New Orleans, 1981-82, pres., 1982-84; spl. asst. to pres., CEO Kaneb Svcs., Inc., Houston, 1984-85; exec. v.p. Tex. Ea. Products Pipeline Co., Houston, 1986-90. Pres. Am. Leadership Forum, Houston, 1986. Decorated Legion of Merit with gold star, Meritorious Svc. medal with gold star, Joint Svc. Commendation medal. Mem. Lansdowne (Va.) Golf Club, Army Navy Country Club (Arlington, Va.). Home: 46847 Grissom St Sterling VA 20165

OLLEY, ROBERT EDWARD, economist, educator; b. Vendun, Que., Can., Apr. 16, 1933; s. Edwin Henry and Elizabeth (Reed) O.; m. Shirley Ann Dahl, Jan. 19, 1957; children—Elizabeth Anne, George Steven, Susan Catherine, Maureen Carolyn. B.A., Carleton U., Can., 1960; M.A., Queen's U., Can., 1961, Ph.D. in Econs., 1969. Vis. asst. prof. Queen's U., Kingston, Ont., Can., 1967-68; asst. prof. econs. U. Sask., Saskatoon, Can., 1963-67, 68-69, assoc. prof., 1969-71, 73-75, prof., 1975-93, prof. emeritus, 1993—; pres. Gen. Econs. Ltd., 1993—; dir. rsch. Royal Commn. on Consumer Problems and Inflation, 1967-68; econ. advisor Bell Can., Montreal, Que., 1971-73, 78-79, Can. Telecom. Carriers Assn., 1978-85, Sask. Power Corp., 1980-83; econ. advisor AT&T, 1980-90, Waste Mgmt., Inc., 1990-92, SaskTel, 1989-93; chmn. adv. com. on consumer stds. Stds. Coun. Can., 1992-93; Can. rep. to ISO/COPOLCO, Geneva, 1992-93. Author, editor: Consumer Product Testing, 1979; Consumer Product Testing II, 1981; Consumer Credit in Canada, 1966; Economics of the Public Firm: Regulation, Rates, Costs, Productivity Analysis, 1983, Total Factor Productivity of Canadian Telecommunications, 1984; Consumer Reps. Conf. Procs., 1st-4th, 1982-91. Bd. dirs. Can. Found. for Econ. Edn., 1974-82, Can. Gen. Standards Bd., 1977-81. Recipient Her Magesty The Queen silver Jubilee medal, 1977, Can.'s Jean P Carriere Exptl. Contbr. Vol. Standardization award, 1995. Mem. Royal Econ. History Soc., Royal Econs. Assn., Econ. History Assn., Am. Econ. Assn., Can. Econ. Assn., Consumers Assn. Can. (v.p. 1967-75, chmn. 1975-77), Can. Stds. Assn. (dir., mem. exec. com. 1971-93, vice chmn. 1985-87, chmn. 1987-89, Award of Merit 1995), Consumer's Assn. Found. Can. (v.p. 1989-95), Can. Comms. Rsch. Ctr. (dir. 1992—), Internat. Telecom. Soc. (bd. dirs. 1986—), Shaw Guild. Home and office: PO Box 1040, 374 Queen St, Niagara on the Lake, ON Canada L0S 1J0

ÖLLING, EDWARD HENRY, aerospace engineer, consulting firm executive; b. Zion, Ill., Feb. 18, 1922; s. Edward and Lydia Ester (Amstudz) O.; children—Linda S., Charles R., Carole L. B.S.M.E., Purdue U., 1949; postgrad., UCLA, 1952-54, U. Houston, 1963-66. Registered profl. engr., Tex. Sr. thermodynamics engr. Lockheed Aircraft Corp., Burbank, Calif., 1954-56; project mgr. NASA Project Mercury, Garret Airesearch Corp., Los Angeles, 1956-60; dep. asst. Apollo project mgr., chief Future Projects Office chief advanced earth orbital missions office and space sta. office NASA, Houston, 1960-70; dir. Galaxy Engring. Inc., Captiva Island, Fla., 1971-90; cons. in oceanography, energy, environment, conservation. Pres. Captiva Island Wildlife Sci. Research Found.; pres. Satellite-TV Communications Enterprises; surrogate astronaut, 1962-69; cons.-dir. Orbita Space Sta., 1985-94, revised space sta., 1990-94; pres. Seaboard Stamp Svc., 1980-94; leader Hong Kong-China Progress Studios; cons. People to People Ambassadors, China Space Progress Tour and Survey; delaer rare books and antiques, big band era records; pres. Nouveaux Terra Electic Motion Corp., Generator Electrics. Contbg. author: Enciclopedia Mondadori, Italy; Contbr. articles to profl. jours.; Inventor, developer auto rsch. engring. devel. patent applications; inventor, patentee and devel. APU Electric Car. Bd. dirs. Captiva Seaside Flora and Fauna Research Found. Center; bd. dirs. Concerned Captiva Citizens.; mem. exec. com. Lee County (Fla.) Democratic Party; Nat. campaign worker John Glenn for Pres., 1984 Dem. State Conv.; campaign worker Frank Mann for Fla. Gov., 1986; founder, dir. Restoration of Mars Found., 1975-94; CEO Les Nouveaux Mars Found.; dir. Found. for Restoration Pyramids, Stonehenge. Served with USAAC, 1942-46. Recipient Sustained Superior Performance awards NASA, Inventions and Contbns. awards. Mem. Nat. Space Inst., Nat. Energy Inst., Nat. Audubon Soc. (pres. Theodore Roosevelt chpt.), Am. Assn. Concerned Scientists, Sanibel Captiva Conservation Assn., Captiva Civic Assn., Am., Fla. Stamp Dealers Assns., Am. Topical Assn., Rocket Mail Soc., Tex. Profl. Engring. Soc., Am. Legion, LBJ Space Center Stamp Club, Jack Knight Aerospace Philatelic Assn., Am. Soc. Polar Philatelists, Strengthen Am. Def. Assn., Support Nuclear Energy Soc. (pres.), Purdue Club S. W. Fla., Danish Am. Genealogy Rsch. Assn., High Flight Soc. (search for Noah's Ark divsn.), Scientists So. Fla., Imaginarium Ft. Meyers, Conquest Space Philatelic Soc., Orbital Space Covers, Lea. Co. Edison Philatelic Soc., Alligator Deltrology Soc., Sunshine Postcard Club, Tropical Postcard Club, Edison Inventor Assn. (dir.). Address: 2581 Palm Ave Fort Myers FL 33916-5347

OLLINGER, W. JAMES, lawyer; b. Kittanning, Pa., Apr. 5, 1943; s. William James and Margaret Elizabeth (Reid) O.; m. Susan Louise Gerspacher, Oct. 20, 1979; children: Mary Rebecca, David James. BA, Capital U., Columbus, Ohio, 1966; JD, Case Western Res. U., 1968. Bar: Ohio 1968, U.S. Dist. Ct. (no. dist.) Ohio 1971. Ptnr. Baker & Hostetler, Cleve., 1968—; bd. dirs. Parts Assocs., Inc., Cleve., 1975—. Mem. Bentleyville (Ohio) Village Coun., 1990-93. Mem. Wembley Club, Order of Coif, Phi Delta Phi. Office: Baker & Hostetler 3200 Nat City Ctr 1900 E 9th St Cleveland OH 44114-3401

OLLWERTHER, WILLIAM RAYMOND, newspaper editor; b. Neptune, N.J., Jan. 1, 1950; S. William Frederick and Daphne Marie (Hawkins) O.; m. Arlene Judith Newman; children: Geoffrey Vaughan, Alyssa Irene. BA, Princeton U., 1971; MS, Northwestern U., 1972. Reporter Asbury Park (N.J.) Press, 1972-76, bur. chief, 1977-78, night suburban editor, 1979-82, asst. to editor, 1982-84; asst. mng. editor Asbury Park (N. J.) Press, Neptune, 1985-87, exec. editor, 1988—, v.p. news, 1994—; adj. prof. Rutgers U., New Brunswick, N.J., 1988; bd. trustees Daily Princeton Pub. Co., 1996—. Editor: The Shore Catch, 1987. Commr. Ocean County Cultural & Heritage Commn., Toms River, N.J., 1977-78. Mem. Am. Soc. Newspaper Editors. Unitarian. Office: Asbury Park Press PO Box 1550 3601 Hwy 66 Neptune NJ 07754-1550

OLMSTEAD, CECIL JAY, lawyer; b. Jacksonville, Fla., Oct. 15, 1920; s. Cecil Jay Sr. and Bessie (Irby) O.; m. Frances Hughes; children: Cecil Jay III, Frank Hughes, Jane Olmstead Murphy, Amy Olmstead Vanecek. B.A., U. Ga., 1950, LL.B., 1951; Sterling Grad. fellow, Yale Law Sch., 1951-52; LL.D. (hon.), U. Hull, Eng., 1978. Bar: Ga. 1950, U.S. Supreme Ct 1964, D.C. 1978. Asst. to legal adviser Dept. State, counsel Mut. Security Agy., counsel Hoover Commn. on Orgn. Exec. Br. of Govt., 1952-55; prof. N.Y. U. Sch. Law, 1953-61; dir. Inter-Am. Law Inst., 1958-61, adj. prof. law, 1961-69; atty. Texaco, Inc., N.Y.C., 1961-62; asst. to chmn. bd. Texaco, Inc., 1962-70, v.p., asst. to chmn. bd., 1970, v.p., asst. to pres., 1970-71, v.p., asst. to chief exec. officer, 1971-73, exec. dept., v.p., 1973-80; mem. firm Steptoe & Johnson, Washington, 1980—; Wang Disting. vis. prof. St. Johns U., 1987-90; mem. adv. panel on internat. law to sec. state; adv. com. law of sea State Dept.; also adv. com. transnat. enterprise; U.S. del. UN Com. on Law of Sea, 1972-73; U.S. del. UN Conf. on Law of Sea, 1974-76; Eisenhower lectr. Nat. War Coll., 1973; mem. U.S. del. UN Conf. on Code of Conduct for Transnat. Corps., ann. 1984-90; mem. World Bank's panel of conciliatiors of the Internat. Ctr. for Settlement of Investment Disputes, 1988-95; vis. fellow All Souls Coll., Oxford U., 1988; vis. scholar Yale Law Sch., 1990-91. With USAF, 1943-46, 8th and 20th Air Force. Recipient Gold medal City of Brussels (Belgium, 1973, Gold medal City of Paris (France), 1984; named Commdr. Brit. Empire (hon.), 1990. Mem. Internat. Law Assn. (pres. Am. br. 1966-73, pres. 1972-75, vice chmn. exec. coun. 1975-86, chmn. exec. coun. 1986-88, patron 1989), Am. Law Inst. (assoc. reporter Restatement of the Fgn. Rels. Law of the U.S., 1d eidt. 1964, advisor 3d edit.), Coun. on Fgn. Rels., Washington Inst. Fgn. Affairs, Nat. Fgn. Trade Coun. (dir.), Am. Coun. on Germany (hon. dir.), Coun. on Ocean Law (dir.), Knickerbocker Club, Yale Club (N.Y.C.), Fairfield County Hunt Club (Westport), Order of Coif, Phi Beta Kappa. Clubs: Knickerbocker, Yale (N.Y.C.); Fairfield County Hunt (Westport); 1925 F Street, Cosmos (Washington). Home: 4 Sprucewood Ln Westport CT 06880-4021 Office: 1330 Connecticut Ave NW Washington DC 20036-1704

OLMSTEAD, FRANCIS HENRY, JR., plastics industry executive; b. Corning, N.Y., June 21, 1938; s. Francis Henry and Josephine (Andolino) O.; B.S., Detroit U., 1960; M.S., Purdue U., 1962; postgrad. program for mgmt. devel. Harvard, 1976; m. Mary Helen Nelson, Sept. 2, 1961; children: Kathleen, Ann, John. Foreman, Corning Glass Works, 1962, sect. foreman, 1963-64, dept. foreman, 1965-66, prodn. supt., 1967-69, plant mgr., 1970-71, mgr. mktg., 1972-73, gen. sales and mktg. mgr., 1973-75, bus. mgr. lighting products, 1976-79, bus. mgr. TV products, 1979-80, v.p., gen. mgr. TV products, 1981—, gen. mgr. elec. products div., 1982-83 ; exec. v.p. N.Am. Philips Lighting Corp., Bloomfield, N.J., 1984-86, exec. v.p., gen. mgr., Somerset, N.J., 1986-88; pres., chief operating officer Anchor Advanced Products, Inc., Knoxville, Tenn., 1988-90, chmn., pres., chief exec. officer, 1990—; instr. bus. adminstrn. Elmira Coll., 1972-73; vis. lectr. Purdue U., 1973. Mem. exec. bd. Steuben area council Boy Scouts Am., 1975—, v.p. fin., 1977-79, coun. pres., 1979-84, bd. dirs. N.E. region, 1984-88, pres. N.J. Area, 1985-88, pres., bd. dirs. South region Boy Scouts Am., 1988-91, v.p. S.E. region, 1991-93, pres. Southeast region, 1993-95, nat. bd. dirs., 1993—, nat. commr., 1995—; mem. dean's adv. coun. Krannert Sch. Purdue U., Coll. Engring. U. Detroit.; bd. dirs. Knoxville Symphony, 1994—, v.p. devel., 1996. Served to capt. U.S. Army, 1961-62. Recipient Silver Beaver award, Silver Antelope award, Silver Buffalo award, St. George Catholic award, Boy Scouts Am., Disting. Alumni award Purdue U. Mem. ASME, Am. Soc. Plastics Engrs., Am. Brush Mfg. Assn., Cosmetics, Toiletry and Fragrance Assn., Corning C. of C., Krannert Sch. Alumni Assn. Purdue U. (pres.), Corning Country Club, Cherokee Country Club, Tau Beta Pi, Pi Tau Sigma. Republican. Roman Catholic. Home: 7328 Misty Meadow Pl Knoxville TN 37919-7219 Office: Anchor Advanced Products 1111 Northshore Dr NW Ste N-600 Knoxville TN 37919-4005

OLMSTEAD, MARJORIE ANN, physics educator; b. Glen Ridge, N.J., Aug. 18, 1958; d. Blair E. and Elizabeth (Dempwolf) O. BA in Physics, Swarthmore Coll., 1979; MA in Physics, U. Calif., Berkeley, 1982, PhD, 1985. Rsch. staff Palo Alto (Calif.) Rsch. Ctr. Xerox Corp., 1985-86; asst. prof. physics U. Calif., Berkeley, 1986-90; asst. prof. physics U. Wash., Seattle, 1991-93, assoc. prof., 1993—; prin. investigator materials sci. divsn. Lawrence Berkeley Lab., 1988-93. Contbr. articles to profl. jours. Named Presdl. Young Investigator, Nat. Sci. Found., 1987; recipient Devel. awards IBM, 1986, 87. Fellow Am. Vacuum Soc. (Peter Mark Meml. award 1994); mem. Am. Assn. Physics Tchrs., Am. Phys. Soc. (Maria Goeppart-Mayer award 1996), Materials Rsch. Soc., Assn. Women in Sci., Phi Beta Kappa, Sigma Xi. Office: Univ Washington Dept Physics PO Box 351560 Seattle WA 98195-1560

OLMSTEAD, WILLIAM EDWARD, mathematics educator; b. San Antonio, June 2, 1936; s. William Harold and Gwendolyn (Littlefield) O.; m. Adele Cross, Aug. 14, 1957 (div. 1967); children: William Harold, Randell Edward. BS, Rice U., 1959; MS, Northwestern U., 1962, PhD, 1963. Mem. research staff S.W. Research Inst., San Antonio, 1959-60; Sloan Found. postdoctoral fellow Johns Hopkins, 1963-64; prof. applied math. Northwestern U., Evanston, Ill., 1964—, chmn. dept. engring. scis. and applied math., 1991-93; vis. mem. Courant Inst. Math. Scis., NYU, 1967-68; faculty visitor Univ. Coll. London, Eng., 1973, Calif. Inst. Tech., 1987, 90. Contbr. articles to profl. jours. Named Technol. Inst. Tchr. of Yr., 1980; recipient Award for Tchg. Excellence, Northwestern Alumni Assn., 1993; appointed Charles Deering McCormick prof., 1994. Mem. Am. Acad. Mechanics, Am. Math. Soc., Am. Phys. Soc., Soc. Indsl. and Applied Math., Am. Contract Bridge League (silver life master), John Evans Club, Sigma Xi, Tau Beta Pi, Sigma Tau. Episcopalian. Home: 141 Lockerbie Ln Wilmette IL 60091-2947 Office: Northwestern U Dept Engring Scis and Applied Math Evanston IL 60208

OLMSTED, AUDREY JUNE, communications educator; b. Sioux Falls, S.D., June 5, 1940; d. Leslie Thomas and Dorothy Lucille (Else) Perryman; m. Richard Raymond Olmsted; 1 child, Quenby Anne. BA, U. No. Iowa, 1961, MA, 1963; PhD, Ind. U., 1971. Comm. instr. Boston U., 1964-71, acting chair comm., 1972-73, asst. prof. comm., 1971-74; debate coach R.I. Coll., Providence, 1978-92, asst. prof. comm., 1987—, internat. student advisor, 1980—; text editor Prentice-Hall Pub., 1986-88. Recipient Faculty award R.I. Coll. Alumni Assn., 1987. Mem. Nat. Assn. Fgn. Student Advisors, Eastern Comm. Assn., Nat. Comm. Assn. Democrat. Office: RI Coll Dept Comm 600 Mount Pleasant Ave Providence RI 02908-1924

OLMSTED, JERAULD LOCKWOOD, telephone company executive; b. Des Moines, Aug. 26, 1938; s. George Hamden and Virginia (Camp) O.; m. Mary Karen Autenrieth, June 20, 1962 (div. Dec. 1986); children: Scott H., Victoria L., Jerauld; m. Gisele A. Child, June 17, 1988. B.S., Iowa State U., 1961; M.B.A., George Washington U., 1979; Cert. mgmt. accountant. Vice-pres. First Nat. Bank of Washington, 1969; v.p., dir. Intermediate Credit Corp., 1969-73; v.p., dir. Internat. Gen. Industries, Inc., 1974-79, pres., dir., 1980-82; pres., dir. IB Credit Corp., 1982-85, N.Am. Communications, Inc., Bethesda, Md., 1985—; sr. v.p., dir. Internat. Bank, 1978-85. Bd. govs. Iowa State U. Found., 1980—; chmn. corporate adv. bd. div. arts and humanities U. Md., 1982—; sec.-treas. George Olmsted Found., 1970—. Served with U.S. Army, 1961-63. Decorated Knight of Malta, Order of St. John. Mem. Fin. Execs. Inst., Mensa, Soc. Cincinnati, Beta Alpha Psi., Beta Gamma Sigma. Republican. Episcopalian. Clubs: Metropolitan, City, Georgetown (Washington). Home & Office: 7735 Arrowood Ct Bethesda MD 20817-2821

OLMSTED, PATRICIA PALMER, educational researcher; b. Chgo., Sept. 19, 1940; d. Richard O. and Marion E. (Huffman) Palmer. BA in Psychology, Mich. State U., 1962; postgrad. Stanford U., 1962-63; MA, Columbia U., 1965; PhD, U. Fla., 1977. Grad. research asst. Columbia U., N.Y.C., 1964, pub. health trainee psychopathology, 1964-65; assoc. rsch. scientist dept. med. genetics Psychiat. Inst., N.Y.C., 1965-66; asst. rsch. coord. Merrill-Palmer Inst., Detroit, 1966-68, instr., 1966-69, rsch.coord., 1966-69; instr. Coll. Edn. U. Fla., Gainesville, 1969-71, asst. in edn., 1971-73, assoc. in edn., 1973-77; clin. asst. prof. Sch. Edn., U. N.C., Chapel Hill, 1977-82, clin. assoc. prof., 1982-86, dir. parent edn. follow-through program, 1977-86; rsch. assoc. High/Scope Ednl. Rsch. Found., 1986-91, sr. rsch. assoc., 1991—, dep. coord. internat. child care study, 1986—; grantee, 1977-86, cons. various pub. schs., 1969—. Contbr. articles on rsch. in edn. to profl. jours., chpts. to books. Dept. Edn. grantee, 1977-84. Mem. APA, Soc. Rsch. Child Devel., Am. Ednl. Rsch. Assn., Nat. Assn. Edn. Young Children, Phi Delta Kappa. Office: High/Scope Ednl Rsch Found 600 N River St Ypsilanti MI 48198-2821

OLMSTED, RONALD DAVID, foundation executive, consultant; b. Portland, Oreg., June 27, 1937; s. Clifford Wolford and Ruth Emily (Driesner) O.; m. Susan Mary Spare, Dec. 27, 1961 (div. June 1972); 1 child, Craig William. Student, Lewis and Clark Coll., 1955-57, U. So. Calif., L.A., 1959-62. V.p., exec. dir. L.A. Ctr. for Internat. Visitors, 1961-67; assoc. dir. devel. U. Chgo., 1967-71; v.p. devel. and pub. affairs Northwestern Meml. Hosp., Chgo., 1971-79; dir. devel. Marimed Found., Honolulu, 1989-93; exec. dir. Alzheimer's Assn., Honolulu, 1995-96; cons. on health, edn. and human svc. orgns., Ill., Mich., Oreg., Hawaii, 1979—; mem. Honolulu Mayor's Com. on People with Disabilities, 1995-96. Contbr. articles on African travels and African affairs to profl. publs. Co-founder, treas. Civic Found. of Chelsea, Mich., 1982-83; treas. Chelsea Area C. of C., 1981-83; trustee Harris Sch., Chgo., 1972-73, Ogden Dunes (Ind.) Town Bd., 1971-72; bd. dirs. United Way Porter County, Ind., 1969-71; mem. L.A. Com. on Fgn. Rels., 1965-69; bd. dirs. Am. Friends of Africa, 1965-68, Nat. Coun. for Cmty. Svcs. to Internat. Visitors, 1965-67; mem. exec. com. L.A. Mayor's Coun. for Internat. Visitors and Sister Cities, 1964-68; vice chmn. Greater L.A. Com. Internat. Student Svcs., 1966. Recipient Koa Anvil award Pub. Rels. Soc. Am.-Honolulu, 1992, multiple awards Assn. Am. Colls., 1975-79, multiple MacEachern awards Am. Acad. Hosp. Pub. Rels., 1974-79, multiple awards Nat. Assn. for Hosp. Devel., 1975-79. Mem. Nat. Soc. Fund Raising Execs. Presbyterian. Avocations: cooking, gardening, sailing, wines. Home and Office: 469 Ena Rd Apt 1506 Honolulu HI 96815-1710

OLNESS, KAREN NORMA, pediatrics and international health educator; b. Rushford, Minn., Aug. 28, 1936; d. Norman Theodore and Karen Agnes (Gunderson) O.; m. Hakon Daniel Torjesen, 1962. BA, U. Minn., 1958, BS, MD, 1961. Diplomate Am. Bd. Pediatrics, Am. Bd. Med. Hypnosis. Intern Harbor Gen. Hosp., Torrance, Calif.; resident Nat. Children's Hosp. Med. Ctr., Washington; asst. prof. George Washington U., Washington, 1970-74; assoc. prof. U. Minn., Mpls., 1974-87; prof. pediatrics, family medicine and internat. health Case Western Res. U., Cleve., 1987—. Named Outstanding Woman Physician, Minn. Assn. Women Physicians, 1987. Fellow Am. Acad. Pediatrics, Am. Acad. Family Physicians, Am. Soc. Clin. Hypnosis (pres. 1984-86), Soc. Clin. and Exptl. Hypnosis (pres. 1991-93); mem. Soc. for Behavioral Pediatrics (pres. 1991-92), Northwestern Pediatric Soc. (pres. 1977). Office: Case Western Res U 11100 Euclid Ave Cleveland OH 44106-1736

OLNEY, JAMES, English language educator; b. Marathon, Iowa, July 12, 1933; s. Norris G. and Doris B. (Hawk) L.; 1 child, Nathan. B.A., U. Iowa, 1955; M.A., Columbia U., 1958, Ph.D., 1963. Asst. prof. Drake U., Des Moines, 1963-67; Fulbright lectr. Cuttington Coll., Liberia, 1967-69; prof. English N.C. Central U., Durham, 1970-83; Voorhies prof. English La. State U., Baton Rouge, 1983—; vis. prof. Northwestern U., 1974, Amherst Coll., 1978-79. Author: Metaphors of Self, 1972, Tell Me Africa, 1973, the Rhizome & the Flower, 1980, The Language(s) of Poetry, 1993; editor: Autobiography, 1988; editor So. Rev., 1983—. Fellow NEH, 1975-76, Guggenheim Found., 1980-81, Nat. Humanities Ctr., Research Triangle Park, N.C., 1980-81. Mem. MLA (exec. council 1983-87). Home: 1744 Pollard Pky Baton Rouge LA 70808-8854 Office: La State U Southern Review 43 Allen Hall Baton Rouge LA 70803

OLNEY, ROBERT C., diversified products manufacturing executive; b. Bklyn., Aug. 19, 1926; s. Herbert Mason and Martha L. (Otten) O.; m. Wanda G. Olney, July 17, 1948 (dec. 1988); children: Robert C. Jr., Thomas J., Douglas P.; m. Ann Waters Bell, Mar. 14, 1992. BA in Econs., Cornell U., 1946. With Chem. Bank, N.Y.C., 1946-48; various mgmt. positions 3M Co., from 1948; v.p., gen. mgr. 3M-Nat. Adv. Co., Bedford Pk., Ill., 1976-80; chmn., mng. dir. 3M UK plc, Bracknell, Eng., 1980-86; dir. Yale-Valor plc, Chiswick, London, Eng., 1986-91; chmn. Nutone Inc., Cin., 1987-91; cons. Outdoor Consulting Inc., N.Y.C.; bd. dirs. Revere Holdings Inc., Balt., Merton Assocs. Ltd., Honeytree Inc., Mich. Mem. Hinsdale (Ill.) Golf Club, Worshipful Co. of Upholders (London), Royal Automobile Club (London). Avocation: skiing. Home: PO Box 223 Montchanin DE 19710 also: Oatlands Park, 32 Lakeside Grange, Weybridge Surrey KT139ZE, England KT139ZE also: PO Box 1764 Avon CO 81620-1764

OLOFSON, ROY LEONARD, retail executive; b. Kenmore, N.Y., Jan. 13, 1939; s. Eric Leonard and Karin (Smith) O.; m. Lillian Dimich, Apr. 28, 1962; children—Eric Leonard, Erin Diane, Roy Andrew. B.S., UCLA, 1965; A.M.P., Harvard U., 1980. C.P.A., Calif. Mgr. Price Waterhouse, Los Angeles, 1965-70; v.p., Carter, Hawley, Hale Stores, Inc., Los Angeles, 1970-82; CEO Fedco, Inc., Santa Fe Springs, Calif., 1982-96; pres., dir. Fedco Credit Corp., Santa Fe Springs, 1983-96; exec. v.p., CFO Pia Merchandising Co., Inc., Irvine, 1996—. Served with USMC, 1956-59. Mem. Am. Inst. C.P.A.s, Calif. Soc. C.P.A.s. Clubs: Jonathan (Los Angeles), Los Angeles Athletic. Office: Pia Merchandising Co Inc 19900 Macarthur Blvd Irvine CA 92612-2445

OLOFSON, TOM WILLIAM, electronics executive; b. Oak Park, Ill., Oct. 10, 1941; s. Ragnar V. and Ingrid E. Olofson; BBA, U. Pitts., 1963; m. Jeanne Hamilton, Aug. 20, 1960; children: Christopher, Scott. Various mgmt. positions Bell Telephone Co. of Pa., Pitts., 1963-67; sales mgr. Xerox Corp., Detroit, 1967-68, nat. account mgr., Rochester, N.Y., 1968, mgr. govt. planning, Rochester, 1969, mgr. Kansas City (Mo.) br., 1969-74; corp. v.p. health products group Marion Labs., Inc., Kansas City, Mo., 1974-78, sr. v.p., mem. Office Pres., 1978-80; exec. v.p., dir. Electronic Realty Assocs., Inc., 1980-83; chmn. bd., CEO Emblem Graphic Systems, Inc., 1983-88, Electronic Processing, Inc., 1988—; dir. DemoGraFX, Wordenglass & Electricity, Inc., Elinco Internat., Access Industries, Inc., Saztec Internat., Capital Ptnrs. Bd. visitors U. Pitts. Joseph M. Katz Grad. Sch. Bus.; past trustee Barstow Sch.; past chmn. bd. trustees Village United Presbyn. Ch. Mem. Carlton Club (Chgo.), Omicron Delta Kappa, Sigma Chi. Republican. Presbyterian. Club: Kansas City. Home: 400 W 49th Ter Kansas City MO 64112-2303 Office: Electronic Processing Inc 501 Kansas Ave Kansas City KS 66105-1309

O'LOUGHLIN, JOHN KIRBY, retired insurance executive; b. Bklyn., Mar. 31, 1929; s. John Francis and Anne (Kirby) O'L.; m. Janet R. Tag, July 5, 1952; children: Robert K., Steven M., Patricia A., John A. BA in Econs., St. Lawrence U., Canton, N.Y., 1951. State agt. Royal Globe Ins. Group, 1953-58; with Allstate Ins. Co., 1958—, mktg. v.p., group v.p., then exec. v.p., 1972—; pres. Allstate Life Ins. Co., 1977—; chmn. bd. Allstate Ins. Co. and Life Co. Can., 1976—, sr. exec. v.p., chief planning officer, 1980-90; ret.; bd. dirs. all cos. in Allstate Ins. Group and Allstate Enterprises, Inc.; former pres. Allstate Enterprises, Inc.; pres., CEO JKO Cons. Ltd., Lake Forest, Ill., Royal Links Ventures Ltd. Trustee St. Lawrence U.; bd. trustees U.S. Marine Corps U. Found., Inc.; bd. dirs. Marine Corps Assn., Am. Ireland Fund, USMC Scholarship Found. Inc., Coun. on Ind. Colls.; past chmn. No. Suburban Chgo. United Way; elder 1st United Presbyn. Ch., Lake Forest, Ill. Capt. USMCR, 1951-53. Mem. Sales and Mktg. Execs. Internat. (bd. dirs., past chmn., pres.), Met. Club (Chgo.), Knollwood Club, Whispering Woods Golf Club, Pinehurst Country Club, Lahinch Club, Country Club of N.C. Office: JKO Cons Ltd 133 E Laurel Ave Lake Forest IL 60045-1205

O'LOUGHLIN, SANDRA S., lawyer; b. Buffalo, Jan. 15, 1942. BA summa cum laude, Rosary Hill Coll., 1973; JD cum laude, U. Buffalo, 1978. Bar: N.Y. 1979. Atty. Hiscock & Barclay, Buffalo; mem. character & fitness com. appellate divsn. 4th dept. 8th jud. cir. N.Y. Supreme Ct., 1986—; adj. prof. SUNY Law Sch., Buffalo. Note editor Buffalo Law Rev., 1977-78. Mem. Erie County Legis. Task Force Mental Health, 1979-81; mem. adv. bd. Congregation of Sisters of St. Joseph, 1987—. Mem. ABA, Am. Arbitration Assn., N.Y. State Bar Assn. (ethics com. 1984-94, vice chair 1987-92), Erie County Bar Assn. (ethics com. 1984-87, chair 1987-89, corp. law com. 1984, grievance com. 1993—, judiciary com. 1996—), Women Lawyers of Western N.Y. Office: Hiscock & Barclay Ste 301 Key Bank Towers 50 Fountain Plz Buffalo NY 14202-2212

OLPIN, ROBERT SPENCER, art history educator; b. Palo Alto, Calif., Aug. 30, 1940; s. Ralph Smith and Ethel Lucille (Harman) O.; m. Mary Florence Catharine Reynolds, Aug. 24, 1963; children: Mary Courtney, Cristin Lee, Catharine Elizabeth, Carrie Jean. BS, U. Utah, 1963; AM, Boston U., 1965, PhD, 1971. Lectr. art history Boston U., 1965-67; asst. prof. U. Utah, Salt Lake City, 1967-72, assoc. prof., 1972-76, prof., 1976—, chmn. dept., 1975-82, dir. art history program, 1968-76, 83-84, dean Coll. Fine Arts, 1987—; cons. curator Am. and English art Utah Mus. Fine Arts, 1973—. Grantee U. Utah, 1972, 85, Utah Mus. Fine Arts, 1975, Utah Bicentennial Commn., 1975, Ford Found., 1975, Utah Endowment for Humanities, 1984, 85, Quinney Found., 1986, U. Utah, 1987, State Utah, 1989, Christensen Found., 1993, Eccles Found, 1994, 95; trustee Pioneer State Theatre Found., 1988—; vice chair Utah Arts Coun., 1993-95, chair, 1995—, Utah Sci. Ctr. Authority, 1995-97; vice chair adv. bd. U. Utah Fine Arts, 1996-97, chair, 1997—. Mem. NASULGC (commn. on the arts, 1989-93), Utah Arts Coun., Utah Sci. Authority, Archives Am. Art Smithsonian Instn., Coll. Art Assn. Am., Utah Acad. Scis. Arts Letters, Assn. Historians Am. Art, Internat. Coun. Fine Arts Deans, Phi Kappa Phi, Sigma Nu. Republican. Mormon. Author: Alexander Helwig Wyant, 1836-92, 1968, Mainstreams/Reflections-American/Utah Architecture, 1973, American Painting Around 1850, 1976, Art-Life of Utah, 1977, Dictionary of Utah Art, 1980, A Retrospective of Utah Art, 1981, Waldo Midgley: Birds, Animals, People, Things, 1984, A Basket of Chips, 1985, The Works of Alexander Helwig Wyant, 1986, Salt Lake County Fine Arts Collection, 1987, Signs and Symbols...Utah Art, 1988, J.A.F. Everett, 1989, George Dibble, 1989, Utah Art, 1991; contbd. articles to profl. jours. including Utah, State of the Arts, 1993, Utah History Ency., 1994, Macmillan's Dictionary of Art, 1996, Garland's Dutch Art Ency., 1997. Home: 887 Woodshire Ave Salt Lake City UT 84107-7639 Office: U Utah Coll Fine Arts 250 Art & Architecture Ctr Salt Lake City UT 84112 *Personal philosophy: Not to reduce what I think about life to a motto.*

OLSAK, IVAN KAREL, civil engineer; b. Nitra, Czechoslovakia, Apr. 30, 1933; came to the U.S., 1970; s. Innocenc and Jolana (Rutkovska) O.; m. Renata Gabriela Franclova, Sept. 26, 1959; children: Ruth E., Patricia L. Degree in civil and sanitary engring., Slovak Tech. U., 1958. Registered profl. engr., Pa., Fla. Chief engr. Keramoproject, Bratislava, Czechoslovakia, 1961-63; chief of commune hygien Slovak Dept. Health, Bratislava, 1963-68; draftsman Crippen Acres Ltd., Winnipeg, Canada, 1969-71; design engr. Bouguard & Assocs., Harrisburg, Pa., 1971-72; chief dept. engring. Adair & Brady, Inc., West Palm Beach, Fla., 1972-74; profl., engr., ptnr. Weimer & Co., Inc., West Palm Beach, 1974-75; pvt. practice Olsak & Assocs., West Palm Beach, 1975-96. Rep. Presdl. Task Force, Washington, 1986—, Nat. Com., Washington, 1989-97, Citizens Against Govt. Waste, Washington, 1988—; hon. mem. Fla. Sherrif's Assn., 1992—. Recipient Cert. of Appreciation Palm Beach County Bar Assn., 1990, Fla. Assn. State Troopers, 1987. Mem. NSPE, Fla. Engring. Soc., Profl. Engrs. in Pvt. Practice. Roman Catholic. Achievements include research in oil refinery construction, influence of oil exfiltration on ground water system. Home: 308 Greymon Dr West Palm Beach FL 33405-1922 Office: PO Box 6727 West Palm Beach FL 33405-6727

OLSCHWANG, ALAN PAUL, lawyer; b. Chgo., Jan. 30, 1942; s. Morton James and Ida (Ginsberg) O.; m. Barbara Claire Miller, Aug. 22, 1965; children: Elliot, Deborah, Jeffrey. B.S., U. Ill., 1963, J.D., 1966. Bar: Ill. 1966, N.Y. 1984, Calif. 1992. Law clk. Ill. Supreme Ct., Bloomington, 1966-67; assoc. Sidley & Austin, and predecessor, Chgo., 1967-73; with Montgomery Ward & Co., Inc., Chgo., 1973-81, assoc. gen. counsel, asst. sec., 1979-81; ptnr. Seki, Jarvis & Lynch, Chgo., 1981-84, dir., mem. exec. com.; exec. v.p., gen. counsel, sec. Mitsubishi Electric Am., Inc., N.Y.C., 1983-91, Cypress, Calif., 1991—. Mem. ABA, Am. Corp. Counsel Assn., Calif. Bar Assn., Ill. Bar Assn., Chgo. Bar Assn., N.Y. State Bar Assn., Bar Assn. of City of N.Y., Am. Arbitration Assn. (panel arbitrators). Office: Mitsubishi Electric Am 5665 Plaza Dr Cypress CA 90630-5023

OLSEN, ALFRED JON, lawyer; b. Phoenix, Oct. 5, 1940; s. William Hans and Vera (Bearden) O.; m. Susan K. Smith, Apr. 15, 1979. B.A. in History, U. Ariz., 1962; MS in Acctg., Ariz. State U., 1964; J.D., Northwestern U., 1966. Bar: Ariz. 1966, Ill. 1966; C.P.A., Ariz., Ill. cert. tax specialist. Acct. Arthur Young & Co., C.P.A.s, Chgo., 1966-68; dir. firm Ehmann, Olsen & Lane (P.C.), Phoenix, 1969-76; dir. Streich, Lang, Weeks & Cardon (P.C.), Phoenix, 1977-78; v.p. Olsen-Smith, Ltd., Phoenix, 1978—. Bd. editors: Jour. Agrl. Law and Taxation, 1978-82, Practical Real Estate Lawyer, 1983-95. Mem. Phoenix adv. bd. Salvation Army., 1973-81. Fellow Am. Coll. Trust and Estate Counsel, Am. Coll. Tax Counsel; mem. State Bar Ariz. (chmn. tax sect. 1977-78), ABA (chmn. com. on agr., sect. taxation 1976-78, chmn. CLE com. sect. taxation 1982-84), Am. Law Inst. (chmn. tax planning for agr. 1973-84), Cen. Ariz. Estate Planning Coun. (pres. 1972-73), Nat. Cattlemen's Assn. (tax com. 1979-88), Internat. Acad. Estate and Trust Law (exec. coun. 1994—), Sigma Nu Internat. (pres. 1986-88). Office: 3300 Virginia Financial Pla 301 E Virginia Ave Phoenix AZ 85004-1215

OLSEN, ARTHUR MARTIN, physician, educator; b. Chgo., Aug. 29, 1909; s. Martin I. and Aagot (Rovelstad) O.; m. Yelena Pavlinova, Sept. 16, 1936; children: Margaret Ann (Mrs. Frank A. Jost), David Martin, Karen Yelena (Mrs. Dori Kanellos), Mary Elizabeth. AB, Dartmouth Coll., 1930; MD, U. Chgo., 1935; MS, U. Minn., 1938. Diplomate Am. Bd. Internal Medicine. Intern Cook County Hosp., Chgo., 1935-36; fellow in medicine, resident Mayo Found., U. Minn., 1936-40, from instr. to prof. medicine, 1950-57, prof., 1957—; cons. medicine Mayo Clinic, Rochester, Minn., 1940-76, chmn. divsn. thoracic diseases, 1968-71. Author numerous publs. on diseases of the lungs and esophagus. Mem. nat. heart and lung adv. coun. NIH, 1970-71; trustee Mayo Found., 1961-68, mem. subsplty. bd. pulmonary diseases, 1958—, chmn., 1961-63. Recipient Alexander B. Vishnevski medal Inst. Surgery, Moscow, 1966, Andres Bello medal Govt. of Venezuela, 1987, Disting. Alumnus award Rush Med. Coll., U. Chgo., 1989. Fellow ACP, Am. Coll. Chest Physicians (master, regent 1955—, chmn. 1959-66, pres. 1970, Disting. Fellow award 1978, dir. internat. activities 1976-83, cons. internat. activities 1983-85); mem. AMA (Billings gold meadl for exhibit on esophagitis 1955), Am. Soc. Gastrointestinal Endoscopy (pres. 1962-63), Minn. Respiratory Health Assn. (pres. 1964-68), Minn. Med. Assn., Am. Assn. Thoracic Surgery, Am. Thoracic Soc., Minn. Thoracic Soc. (pres. 1952), Am. Bronchoesophagol. Assn. (pres. 1969-70, Chevalier Jackson award 1973), Internat. Bronchoesophagol. Soc. (pres. 1979-81), Minn. Soc. Internal Medicine, Brit. Thoracic Soc. (hon.), Nat. Acad. Medicine of Buenos Aires (hon.), Portuguese Soc. Respiratory Pathology (corr.), Sigma Xi, Alpha Omega Alpha. Episcopalian. Home: 211 2nd St NW Apt 2002 Rochester MN 55901-3101 Office: Mayo Clinic Rochester MN 55901

OLSEN, CLIFFORD WAYNE, retired physical chemist, consultant; b. Placerville, Calif., Jan. 15, 1936; s. Christian William and Elsie May (Bishop) O.; m. Margaret Clara Gobel, June 16, 1962 (div. 1986); children: Anne Katherine Olsen Cordes, Charlotte Marie; m. Nancy Mayhew Kruger, July 21, 1990 (div. 1994). AA, Grant Tech. Coll., Sacramento, 1955; BA, U. Calif.-Davis, 1957, PhD, 1962. Physicist, project leader, program leader, task leader Lawrence Livermore Nat. Lab., Calif., 1962-93; ret., 1993, lab. assoc., 1993-95, 96—; cons. Keystone Internat., 1996-97, Am. Techs. Inc., 1997—; mem. Containment Evaluation Panel, U.S. Dept. Energy, 1984—, mem. Cadre for Joint Nuclear Verification Tests, 1988; organizer, editor procs. for 2nd through 7th Symposiums on Containment of Underground Nuclear Detonations, 1983-93. Contbr. articles to profl. jours. Mem. bd. convocators Calif. Luth. U., 1976-78. Recipient Chevalier Degree, Order of DeMolay, 1953, Eagle Scout, 1952. Mem. AAAS, Am. Radio Relay League, Seismol. Soc. Am., Livermore Amateur Radio Klub (pres. 1994-96), Sigma Xi, Alpha Gamma Sigma (life), Gamma Alpha (U. Calif.-Davis chpt. pres. 1960-61). Democrat. Lutheran. Avocations: photography, amateur radio, music, cooking.

OLSEN, DAVID ALEXANDER, insurance executive; b. Bklyn., Nov. 29, 1937; s. Alexander and Meile (Anderson) O.; m. Roberta Ruth Garverick, May 11, 1963; children: Bradford, Amy. BA, Bowdoin Coll., 1959. With marine dept. Gt. Am. Ins. Co., N.Y.C. and Chgo., 1959-62; acct. exec. Johnson & Higgins, San Francisco, 1966-71; v.p., mgr. marine dept. Johnson & Higgins, Chgo., 1971-78, exec. v.p. Ill. br., 1978-79; br. mgr., exec. v.p. Johnson & Higgins, Houston, 1979-80, chmn., bd. dirs. Tex. br., 1980-85; exec. v.p. Johnson & Higgins, N.Y.C., 1985-87, pres., COO, 1987-93, CEO, 1990—, chmn., 1991—; trustee, exec. com. Am. Inst. Chartered Property Casualty Underwriters, Ins. Inst. Am., Coll. of Ins., N.Y.C., 1994—, U.S. Coun. Internat. Bus., N.Y.C., 1995; bd. dirs. U.S. Trust Corp., U.S. Trust Co. N.Y. Vice-chmn. South St. Seaport Mus., N.Y.C.; v.p. bd. overseers Bowdoin Coll., Brunswick, Maine; bd. dirs. United Way, N.Y.C., N.Y.C. Partnership; bd. dirs. corp. congress N.Y. Pub. Libr.; co-chmn. Corp. Coun. The N.Y. Botanical Garden. 1st lt. U.S. Army, 1960-62. Mem. India House (bd. dirs.), River Club, Econ. Club N.Y., Psi Upsilan. Republican. Avocations: art, photography, antiques, scuba diving, tennis, skiing. Home: 1120 Park Ave New York NY 10128-1242 Office: Johnson & Higgins 125 Broad St New York NY 10004-2400

OLSEN, DOUGLAS H., superintendent. Supt. Southfield Christian Schs., Mich. Recipient Blue Ribbon award, 1990-91. Office: Southfield Christian Sch 28650 Lahser Rd Southfield MI 48034-2020*

OLSEN, EDWARD JOHN, geologist, educator; b. Chgo., Nov. 23, 1927; s. Edward John and Elizabeth (Bornemann) O.; children—Andrea, Ericka. A.B., U. Chgo., 1951, M.S., 1955, Ph.D., 1959. Geologist Geol. Survey Can., 1953, U.S. Geol. Survey, 1954—, Canadian Johns-Manville Co., Ltd., 1956, 57, 59; asst. prof. Case Inst. Tech., also Western Res. U., 1959-60; curator mineralogy Field Mus. Natural History, 1960-91, chmn. dept. geology, 1974-78; research assoc. prof. dept. geophys. scis. U. Chgo., 1977—; adj. prof. U. Ill., Chgo. Circle, 1970-91. Assoc. editor Geochim. et Cosmochim. Acta., 1985-91. Fellow Mineral. Soc. Am.; mem. Mineral. Assn. Can., Geochem. Soc., Meteoritical Soc. Spl. research stability relations of minerals in earth's mantle and meteorites. Office: U Chgo Dept Geophys Sci Chicago IL 60637

OLSEN, FRANCES ELISABETH, law educator, theorist; b. Chgo., Feb. 4, 1945; d. Holger and Ruth Mathilda (Pfeifer) O.; m. Harold Irving Porter, June 8, 1984. Cert., Roskilde (Denmark) Højskole, 1967; BA, Goddard Coll., 1968; JD, U. Colo., 1971; SJD, Harvard U., 1984. Bar: Colo. 1972, U.S. Dist. Ct. Colo. 1972. Law clk. hon. Arraj U.S. Dist. Ct. Colo., Denver, 1972; lawyer Am. Indian Movement, Wounded Knee, S.D., 1973; pvt. practice Denver, 1973-74; law prof. U. Puget Sound, Tacoma, Wash., 1975-79, St. John's U., Jamaica, N.Y., 1982-83, UCLA, 1984—; vis. fellow New Coll., Oxford, Eng., 1987; vis. prof. U. Mich., Ann Arbor, 1988, Harvard U., Cambridge, Mass., 1990-91; Fulbright prof. U. Frankfurt, Germany, 1991-92, Ochanomizu U., Tokyo, 1997, U. Tokyo, 1997, Cornell U., 1997; overseas fellow Churchill Coll. Faculty of Law, Cambridge (Eng.) U., 1997—; del. UN 4th World Conf. on Women, Beijing, China, 1995, NGO Forum, Huairou, China, 1995. Co-author: Cases and Materials on Family Law: Legal Concepts and Changing Human Relationships, 1994; editor: Feminist Legal Theory I: Foundations and Outlooks, 1995, Feminist Legal Theory II: Positioning Feminist Theory Within the Law, 1995; contbr. articles to law revs. Named Outstanding Alumnus U. Colo., 1989. Mem. Am. Assn. Law Schs. (chair jurisprudence sect. 1987-88, chair women in law tchg. sect. 1995-96), European Conf. Critical Legal Studies. Avocations: wind-surfing, bicycling, mountain climbing. Office: UCLA Sch Law 405 Hilgard Ave Los Angeles CA 90095-9000

OLSEN, GORDON, retired lawyer; b. Pitts., July 5, 1927; s. ALvin Gordon and Alma (Wollbrandt) O.; m. Nancy Smith, Dec. 26, 1955; children: Lars Andrew, Lisa Olsen Lerch (dec.). Student, Duquesne U., 1947-48; B.A., Pa. State U., 1951; LL.B., Fordham U., 1957; student, Ariz. State U., 1986. Bar: Ariz. 1958. Sr. asst. furniture buyer Macy's, N.Y.C., 1953-54; practice law Phoenix, until 1986, ret.; law clk. to justice Ariz. Supreme Ct., 1957-58; assoc. Lewis & Roca, 1958-63, ptnr., 1963-86. Bd. dirs. Family Svc. Phoenix, 1962-68, pres., 1966-67; bd. dirs. Ariz. Assn. for Health and Welfare, 1967-70, 1st v.p., 1967-68; bd. dirs. Community Coun., 1969-75; commr. LEAP Commn., Phoenix Community Action Agy., 1971-75, chmn., 1972-73; mem. plan steering com. Comprehensive Health Planning Coun., 1973-75; mem. CETA Manpower Adv. Coun., 1974-76, chmn., 1974-75, vice chmn., 1975-76; bd. dirs. Planned Parenthood Cent. and No. Ariz., 1975-81, pres., 1977-78; pres. Trinity Luth. Ch. of Maricopa County, 1989-91. Seaman 1st cl. USNR, 1945-46; 1st lt. USAF, 1951-53. Home: 232 W Frier Dr Phoenix AZ 85021-7233

OLSEN, GREG SCOTT, chiropractor; b. Anaheim, Calif., June 28, 1968; s. John Carlos and Gloria (Brownmiller) Frazier. D Chiropractic, L.A. Coll. Chiropractic, Whittier, Calif., 1994. Pvt. practice, Huntington Beach, Calif., 1994; postgrad. tchg. asst. Internat. Coll. Applied Kinesiology, L.A., 1995—. Mem. Am. Chiropractic Assn., Internat. Chiropractic Assn., Internat. Coll. Applied Kinesiology, Calif. Chiropractic Assn. Avocations: running, bicycling, snow skiing, dancing. Office: GO Chiropractic 16168 Beach Blvd Ste 135 Huntington Beach CA 92647-3814

OLSEN, HANS PETER, lawyer; b. Detroit, May 21, 1940; s. Hans Peter and Paula M. (Olsen) O.; m. Elizabeth Ann Gayton, Sept. 14, 1968; children: Hans Peter, Heidi Susanne, Stephanie Elizabeth. BA, Mich. State U., 1962; JD, Georgetown U., 1965; LLM, NYU, 1966. Bar: Mich. 1967, Pa. 1969, R.I. 1974. Law clk. firm Monaghan, McCrone, Campbell & Crawmer, Detroit, 1964; law clk. U.S. Ct. of Claims, Fed. Appellate Ct., Washington, 1966-68; assoc. firm Pepper, Hamilton & Scheetz, Phila., 1968-72; ptnr. firm Hinckley, Allen, & Snyder, Providence and Boston, 1972—; adv. planning com. U. R.I. Fed. Taxation Inst.; continuing legal edn. adv. bd., tax symposium adv. bd. Bryant Coll.; mem. Gov.'s State Task Force, R.I. Pub. Expenditure Coun.; cons. Bur. Nat. Affairs; liaison Bar Assn. and North Atlantic region IRS; tax adminstrs. adv. com. R.I.; lectr. tax insts. and other profl. groups N.Y., L.A., Phila., Boston, R.I.; advisor R.I. Econ. Policy com. Contbr. numerous articles on taxation to legal jours. Fellow Am. Bar Found.; mem. ABA (sect. taxation, exempt orgns. com., subcom. healthcare, corp.-shareholders rels. com., partnerships com.), R.I. Bar Assn. (sect. taxation, sec.-treas. 1977-80, liaison with CPAs, specialization com., mem. various coms.), Providence C. of C., R.I. C. of C. (chmn. com. on bus. taxes and public spending, mem., past chmn. legis. action council), Mich. State Bar, Pa. State Bar. Home: 274 Olney St Providence RI 02906-2305 Office: 1500 Fleet Ctr Providence RI 02903

OLSEN, HAROLD FREMONT, lawyer; b. Davenport, Wash., Oct. 17, 1920; s. Oscar E. and Dorothy (Sprowls) O.; m. Jeanne L. Rounds, Aug. 30, 1942; children: Eric O., Ronald R., Margaret Ruth. B.A., Wash. State U., 1942; LL.B., Harvard U., 1948. Bar: Wash. 1948, U.S. Ct. Claims 1970, U.S. Supreme Ct. 1982; C.P.A., Wash. Instr. Oxford Bus. Sch., Cambridge, Mass., 1946-47; examiner Wash. State Dept. Pub. Utilities, 1948; with firm Perkins Coie (and predecessors), Seattle, 1949—, ptnr., 1954-88, of counsel, 1989—; bd. dirs. Exotic Metals Forming Co.; dir. Barker Ranch, Inc., pres., 1997—; trustee Exec. Svcs. Corp. Wash., 1990-96. Bd. dirs. Northwest Hosp. Found., Northwest Hosp., 1980-90; trustee Wash. State U. Found., chmn. 1986-88; mem. adv. coun. Wash. State U. Sch. Bus. and Econs., 1978-90; trustee, mem. exec. com., pres. Mus. of Flight, 1991-92, chmn., 1993; trustee Horizon House, 1994-97. Maj. USAAF, 1942-45, NATOUSA, Mid. East, ETO. Decorated Silver Star. Mem. ABA, Wash. Bar Assn., Seattle Bar Assn., Aircraft Industry Assn. (chmn. legal com. 1957), Nat. Contract Mgmt. Assn., Alumni Assn. Wash. State U. (pres. 1956), Mcpl. League Seattle and King County, Seattle C. of C., Internat. Law Soc., Am. Judicature Assn., Phi Beta Kappa, Phi Kappa Phi, Tau Kappa Epsilon, Rainier Club, Seattle Golf Club (pres. 1986-87), Sr. N.W. Golf Assn. Congregationalist. Home: 8875 Overlake Dr W Medina WA 98039-5347 Office: 1201 3rd Ave Ste 4500 Seattle WA 98101-3000

OLSEN, HARRIS LELAND, real estate and international business executive, educator, diplomat; b. Rochester, N.H., Dec. 8, 1947; s. Harries Edwin and Eva Alma (Turmelle) O.; m. Mimi Kwi Sun Yi, Mar. 15, 1953; children: Garin Lee, Gavin Yi, Sook Ja. AS, SUNY, Albany, 1983, BS, 1988; MA in Polit. Sci., U. Hawaii, 1990; PhD in Internat. Bus. Adminstrn., Kennedy Western U., Idaho, 1993. Enlisted USN, 1967, advanced through grades to; served in various nuclear power capacities USN, Conn., 1971-76, Hawaii, 1976-87; ret. USN, 1987; v.p. Waiono Land Corp., Honolulu, 1981-92, dir., 1993-95; v.p. Asian Pacific Electricity, Honolulu, 1988-89, Kapano Land Assocs., Honolulu, 1988-92, 94-95, MLY Networks, Inc., Honolulu, 1989—, THO Consultants Cor., 1991—, Clarix Internat. Corp., 1994; staff cons. Mariner-Icemakers, Honolulu, 1982-84, Transpacific Energy Corp., Honolulu, 1982-84; dir. Asian Pacific Devel. Bank, 1983; sr. cons. Western Rsch. Assocs., Honolulu, 1984-87, 94-95; quality assurance cons. Asian Pacific, Inc., Hoholulu, 1987-88; instr., lectr. Asian history and culture U. Chaminade in Honolulu, 1991; nuclear reactor plant specialist Pearl Harbor Emergency Recall Team, 1991-95; instr. nuclear reactor theory Pearl Harbor, Hawaii, 1992-95; v.p. Schwartz, inc., 1992—, dir. Schwartz Jewelry Sch., 1996—; cons. Waiono/Kapano Devel. Co., 1993; bd. dirs., sec. Pacific Internat. Engring. Corp., 1994-95; Keiretsu sec. Global Ocean Cons., Inc. and Assocs., 1994-95; joint venture Premier Fisheries Pty. Ltd., Papua New Guinea, 1995—; cons. BFD Devel. Group, 1995-96; co-drafter Nat. Tuna Industry Devel. Plan for Papua New Guinea, 1995; quality analyst, Pearl Harbor, 1995; rep. for Min. for Fisheries, Papua New Guinea, Bi-lateral Fisheries Access Rights Japan and Papua New Guinea, 1996—, drafter Bi-Lateral Fishing Treaty Japan and Papua New Guinea, 1996; U.S. del. to 4th World Tuna Conf., Manila, 1995, U.S. del. to 5th Aquatic Continent Conf., Maui, Hawaii, 1995, 6th, 1996; apptd. rep. Abau Electorate, Papua New Guinea Timber Sales, 1995—; apptd. hon. counsel gen. and trade rep. for Govt. of Papua New Guinea in Honolulu, 1996—; bd. dirs. Papua New Guinea Devel. Corp., 1997—. Inventor, alternate power supply system; contbr. articles to profl. publs. Head coach USN Men's Softball, Honolulu, 1978-79; pres. Pearl Harbor (Hawaii) Welfare and Recreation Com., 1983-84; mem. Bishop Mus, Rep. Senatorial Inner Cir.; commd. hon. consul gen. Ind. State Papua, New Guinea, 1996. Named Alumnus of Yr., Kennedy Western U., 1993; recipient Citation of Leadership, Rep. Nat. Com., 1996. Mem. ASCD, AAAS, Internat. Fedn. Profl. and Tech. Engrs., Am. Polit. Sci. Assn., Semiotic Soc. Am., N.Y. Acad. Scis., Toronto Semiotics Cir., USCG Aux., Am. Legion, Fleet Res. Assn., Internat. Platform Assn., Navy League, U.S. Naval Inst., UN Assn., U.S. Submarine Vets., Honolulu Acad. Arts, U. Hawaii Founders Assn., U. Hawaii Coll. Arts and Sci. Found., Plaza Club, Delta Epsilon Sigma. Republican. Buddhist. Avocations: chess, philosophy, Japanese haiku poetry. Home: 94-1025 Anania Cir Apt 56 Mililani HI 96789-2045 Office: Ban of Am Bldg 1357 Kapiolani Blvd Ste 1440 Honolulu HI 96814-4509

OLSEN, JACK, writer; b. Indpls., June 7, 1925; s. Rudolph O. and Florence (Drecksage) O.; m. Su Peterson, 1966; children: John Robert, Susan Joyce, Jonathan Rhoades, Julia Crispin, Evan Pierce, Barrie Elizabeth, Emily Sara Peterson, Harper Alexander Peterson. Student, U. Pa., 1946-47. Newspaper reporter San Diego Union Tribune, 1947-48, San Diego Jour., 1949-50, Washington Daily News, 1950- 51; TV news editor and broadcaster sta. WMAL-TV, Washington, 1950-51; newspaper reporter New Orleans Item, 1952-53, Chgo. Sun-Times, 1954-55; corr. Time mag., 1956-58, Midwest chief, 1959-59. Author: The Mad World of Bridge, 1960, (pseudonym Jonathan Rhoades) Over the Fence is Out, 1961, The Climb up to Hell, 1962, (with Charles Goren) Bridge Is My Game, 1965, Black is Best: The Riddle of Cassius Clay, 1967, The Black Athlete: A Shameful Story, 1968, Silence on Monte Sole, 1968, Night of the Grizzlies, 1969, The Bridge at Chappaquiddick, 1970, Aphrodite: Desperate Mission, 1970, Slaughter the Animals, Poison the Earth, 1971, The Girls in the Office, 1971, The Girls on the Campus, 1972, Sweet Street, 1973, The Man with the Candy, 1974, Alphabet Jackson, 1974, Massy's Game, 1976, The Secret of Fire Five, 1977, Night Watch, 1979, Missing Persons, 1981, Have You Seen My Son?, 1982, Son: A Psychopath and His Victims, 1983, Give a Boy a Gun, 1985, Cold Kill, 1987, Doc: The Rape of the Town of Lovell, 1990, Predator, 1991, The Misbegotten Son, 1993, Charmer: A Ladies Man and His Victims, 1994, Salt of the Earth, 1996; work included in numerous anthologies. Served with OSS AUS, 1943-44. Recipient Edgar award Mystery Writers Am., Page One award Chgo. Newspaper Guild; Nat. Headliners award; Wash. Gov.'s award; citations U. Ind., Columbia U.

OLSEN, JOHN RICHARD, education consultant; b. St. Paul, Aug. 6, 1930; s. Richard Lewis and Anita Marie (Cavanaugh) O.; m. Marlene Dorothy Delaria, June 5, 1954; children: Mary Elizabeth Olsen Lavalley, Teresa Louise Olsen Preston. BS in Edn., U. St. Thomas, St. Paul, 1953; MEd, U. St. Thomas, 1959; PhD in Ednl. Tech., Cath. U. Am., 1969. Cert. tchr., Minn. Tchr. Minn. Pub. Schs., Holdingford, Minn., 1953-54; commd. 2d lt. USAF, 1954, advanced through grades to col., 1980; with res. USAFR; br. chief Ctr. for Disease Control, Atlanta, 1964-70; div. dir. FDA, Washington, 1970-72; tng. dir. SAODAP, White House, Washington, 1972-74; prevention dir. Nat. Inst. on Drug Abuse, Washington, 1974-77; prin. advisor USN, Pensacola, Fla., 1977-79; pres. Tranex, Pensacola, 1979—; cons. Office Substance Abuse, Washington, 1985-95, USN, Washington, 1986-89, CRS, Inc., 1989-92, Mantec Math., Washington, 1988-91. Author: Model Community Handbook, 1989; co-author: Transition Assistance Program, 1990; editor: Drug Abuse Evaluation, 1977; contbg. editor NSPI Jour., 1962-87; contbr. articles to profl. jours. Pres. Found. for Internat. Cooperation, 1979-83, Nat. Inst. for the Family, 1980-81; chmn. Human Rights Adv. Com., Pensacola, 1987, Escambia Dem. Exec. Com., Pensacola, 1986—; bd. dirs. Avant Garde, Pensacola, 1991; mem. Leadership Pensacola, 1981. Decorated Meritorious Svc. medal; named Citizen of Yr. PTA, Escambia, Fla., 1983, Profl. of Yr., Pensacola C. of C., 1984; recipient Disting. Svc. award Tng. Officers Conf., 1973, 1990. Mem. Internat. Soc. for Performance and Instrn. (life, treas. 1964, chpt. pres. 1965, 89), Fla. Alcohol and Drug Abuse Assn. (prevention chmn. 1984-89), Krewe of Neptune, Krewe of Lafitte, K.C. (grand knight coun. 8450, 1994-97, dist. dep. 1997—). Roman Catholic. Avocations: photography, sailing.

OLSEN, KENNETH HAROLD, geophysicist, astrophysicist; b. Ogden, Utah, Feb. 20, 1930; s. Harold Reuben and Rose (Hill) O.; m. Barbara Ann Parson, June 15, 1955; children: Susan L., Steven K., Christopher P., Richard Scott. BS, Idaho State Coll., 1952; MS, Calif. Inst. Tech., 1954, PhD, 1957. Grad. rsch. asst. Calif. Inst. Tech., Mt. Wilson and Palomar Obs., Pasadena, 1952-57; staff member, group leader Los Alamos (N.Mex.) Nat. Lab., 1957-89; lab. assoc. Los Alamos Nat. Lab., 1989—; geophys. cons. GCS Internat., Lynnwood, Wash., 1989—; vis. rsch. fellow Applied Seismol. Group, Swedish Nat. Def. Inst., Stockholm, Sweden, 1983; sr. vis. scientist fellow Norwegian Seismic Array, Oslo, Norway, 1983; vis. scholar Geophysics Program, Univ. Wash., Seattle, 1989-91. Author, editor: Continental Rifts: Evolution, Structure, Tectonics, 1995; contbr. articles to profl. jours. Mem. Am. Geophys. Union, Geol. Soc. Am., Seismol. Soc. Am., Am.

Astron. Soc., Royal Astron. Soc. Home: 1029 187th Pl SW Lynnwood WA 98036-4986

OLSEN, KURT, investment company executive, adviser; b. Astoria, Oreg., Nov. 2, 1924; s. Matt J. and Irene (Lindholm) O.; m. Lois Helen Giberson, Mar. 23, 1947; children: Kurt F., Eric J., Mark C. BS, U. Oreg., 1949. RR mgr. and ptnr. Foster & Marshall, Eugene, Oreg., 1948-61; mgr., v.p., dir. Harris, Upham Inc., Portland, Oreg., 1961-70; v.p., dir. Foster & Marshall Inc., Portland, 1971-76; pres. Alpen Securities, Inc., Portland, 1977—. Mem. adv. bd. Columbia Pacific coun. Boy Scouts Am., mem. nat. coun., 1966-73; bd. dirs. United Way Columbia and Willamette, 1973-77, Oreg. Law Found., 1986-89. With USNR, 1944-46. Mem. Nat. Assn. Securities Dealers (chmn. dist. 1 1967), Investment Bankers Assn. Am. (bd. govs. 1968-70), Sigma Alpha Epsilon, Rotary. Home: 1127 SW Myrtle Dr Portland OR 97201-2270 Office: Alpen Securities Inc 1425 Yeon Bldg Portland OR 97204

OLSEN, MARK NORMAN, small business owner; b. Seattle, Mar. 3, 1947; s. Norman Henry and Agnes Carolyn (Hansen) O.; m. Antoinette Marie Korman, June 20, 1991. Student, U. Wash., Western Wash. U., 1965-67, BHM Tech. Coll., 1968. Cert. autobody journeyman, estimator, inter-industry conf. auto collision repair. Mgr. body shop Fraser Chevrolet, Bellingham, Wash., 1967-83; owner Olsen Auto Body, Bellingham, 1983—. Bd. dirs. Bellingham Tech. Coll. Mem. Auto Body Craftsman (treas.). Home: 1117 N Shore Dr Bellingham WA 98226-9420 Office: Olsen Auto Body 1919 Humboldt St Bellingham WA 98225-4204

OLSEN, REX NORMAN, trade association executive; b. Hazeltown, Idaho, Apr. 9, 1925; s. Adolph Lars and Pearl (Robbins) O. B.J., B.A. in English, U. Mo., 1950. Editor Clissold Pub. Co., Chgo., 1950-54; copy editor Am. Peoples Ency., Chgo., 1955; asst. editor Am. Hosp. Assn., Chgo., 1956-59; mng. editor Am. Hosp. Assn., 1959-64, dir. jours. div., 1964-69, dir. publs. bur., 1969-75, exec. editor, asso. pub., 1975-79; v.p., treas. Am. Hosp. Pub., Inc., 1980-85; pres. Words Ltd., 1985—. Served with USNR, 1943-46. Mem. Am. Pub. Health Assn., Am. Med. Writers Assn., Soc. Nat. Assn. Pubs. (sec. 1975-76, 2d v.p. 1976-77, 1st v.p. 1977-78, pres. 1978-79), Chgo. Bus. Publs. Assn. (dir. 1974-78, 4th v.p. 1978-79), Sigma Delta Chi. Home and Office: 3845 N Alta Vista Ter Chicago IL 60613-2907

OLSEN, RICHARD GALEN, biomedical engineer, researcher; b. Colorado Springs, Colo., Aug. 10, 1945; s. Floyd Edwin and Ruth Elizabeth (Robinson) O.; m. Karen Fidler Brubaker, June 17, 1973; children: Kathryn Elizabeth, Nickolas Robert. BSEE, U. Mo., Rolla, 1968; MS, U. Utah, 1970, PhD, 1975. Registered profl. engr., Fla. Engr. Bendix Corp., Kansas City, Mo., 1968-69; elec. engr. Naval Aerospace Med. Rsch. Lab., Pensacola, Fla., 1975-79, chief engring. systems div., 1979-82, head bioengring. divsn., 1982-94; head bioengring. dept. Naval Med. Rsch. Inst. Detachment, Brooks AFB, Tex., 1994—; tech. cons. Armstrong Lab., USAF, 1991—, German Ministry of Def., Munster, 1994, Naval Surface Warfare Ctr., Dahlgren, Va., 1989-95, Naval Sea Sys. Command, Arlington, Va., 1989-91. Contbr. articles to profl. jours. and books. With U.S. Army, 1970-72. Recipient NDEA fellowship U. Utah, 1969, Fred A. Hitchcock award Aerospace Physiologist Soc. of Aerospace Med., 1987; named Engr. of the Yr., N.W. Fla. Engrs. Coun., 1991. Mem. IEEE (sr., chmn. Pensacola sect. 1982-83, radio frequency and microwave measuring methods com. 1982—, nonionizing radiation hazards com. 1983—, SCC-28 com., Cert. of Appreciation 1983), Bioelectromagnetics Soc. (charter, editl. bd. 1990-96), Aerospace Med. Assn. (editl. cons. 1986—), Rotary (bd. dirs. Suburban West 1980-81), Sigma Xi, Eta Kappa Nu, Tau Beta Pi, Phi Kappa Phi. Republican. Adventist. Achievements include conducting the first shipboard measurements of specific absorption rate (SAR) and of electromagnetic pulse (EMP) induced body current, obtaining the first evidence of reduced RF heating in wrists and ankles from wearing conductive gloves and socks; patents in RF coil for hypothermia resuscitation, RF dosimetry system, personal microwave and RF detector, and RF warming of submerged extremities. Home: 1503 N Baylen St Pensacola FL 32501-2101 Office: Naval Med Rsch Inst Detach 8308 Hawks Rd Brooks AFB TX 78235-5324 *Live an ordinary life except in attainment.*

OLSEN, RICHARD W., advertising executive; b. Flushing, N.Y., Jan. 27, 1952; s. Harold William and Hilda (Flanner) O.; m. Patricia Lynn Richards, Apr. 22, 1978; children: Lindsay Hunt, Caroline Wallace. BA History, Bethany Coll., 1974. Acct. exec. SSC&B Lintas, N.Y.C., 1975-77, Marschalk Co., N.Y.C., 1977-79; sr. v.p. mgmt. supr. Saatchi & Saatchi, N.Y.C., 1979-90; sr. v.p. mgmt. rep. Bozell Inc., N.Y.C., 1990-92; exec. v.p. gen. mgr. Cliff Freeman and Ptnrs., N.Y.C., 1992-96; pres., CEO Saatchi & Saatchi Can., Toronto, 1997—. Republican. Avocations: sailing, golf. Home: 35 Christie Hill Rd Darien CT 06820-3726 Office: Saatchi and Saatchi Can, 145 King St E, Toronto, ON Canada M5C 2Y8

OLSEN, ROBERT ARTHUR, finance educator; b. Pittsfield, Mass., June 30, 1943; s. Arthur Anton and Virginia O.; BBA, U. Mass., 1966, MBA, 1967; PhD, U. Oreg., 1974; m. Maureen . Joan Carmell, Aug. 21, 1965. Security analyst Am. Inst. Counselors, 1967-68; rsch. assoc. Center for Capital Market Rsch., U. Oreg., 1972-74; asst. prof. fin. U. Mass., 1974-75; prof. fin., chmn. dept. fin & mktg. Calif. State U., Chico, 1975—; cons. bus. feasibility studies for Fin. Svc. Industry, Calif. State U., Chico, Endowment Fund, U.S. Forest Svc. Stonier Banking fellow, 1971-72, Nat. Assn. Mut. Savs. Banks fellow, 1975-76; scholar Stanford U., 1986, rsch. fellow Decision Research, Inc., 1986, 95, 96. Recipient Research award Calif. State U.-Chico, 1983, 86, 96, Profl. Achievement award, 1985. Mem. Am. Fin. Assn., Fin. Execs. Inst., Western Fin. Assn. (Trefftzs award 1974), Southwestern Fin. Assn., Fin. Mgmt. Assn., Eastern Fin. Assn., Sierra Club. Contbr. articles to profl. jours. Office: Calif State U Sch Bus Chico CA 95929

OLSEN, STANLEY SEVERN, minister; b. Denver, Mar. 10, 1944; s. Olaf S. and Margaret Ruth (Hook) O.; m. Patricia Joy Wahlen, Sept. 17, 1966; children: Nathaniel S., Nisse J. BA, Bethel Coll., 1966; postgrad., U. Minn., 1968; MA in Christian Edn., Bethel Theol. Sem., 1969; postgrad., U. Mid. Am., 1975; Theol. Orientation, North Park Theol. Sem., 1984; D of Ministry, Trinity Divinity Sch., 1997. adj. prof. Bethel Theol. Sem., St. Paul, 1980-85; chmn. N.W. Covenant Conf. Bd. of Christian Edn., Mpls., 1980-84, Nat. Bd. of Christian Edn. and Discipleship, 1987-93; pres. Nat. Assn. Dirs. Christian Edn., 1981-85; vis. prof. AIM Pastors Conf., Nairobi, Kenya, 1995; ednl. cons. Greater Europe Mission, 1994—. Minister Christian edn. Aldrich Ave. Presbyn. Ch., Mpls., 1969-71; minister children, dir. children's ctr. Grace Cmty. Ch., Tempe, Ariz., 1972; minister Christian edn. Bethel Reformed Ch., Bellflower, Calif., 1973-77; assoc. pastor First Covenant Ch., Mpls., 1977-85; exec. pastor Hillcrest Covenant Ch., Prairie Village, Kans., 1985—; adj. prof. Bethel Theol. Sem., St. Paul, 1980-85, St. Paul Bible Coll., St. Bonifacious, 1969-71; chmn. N.W. Covenant Conf. Bd. of Christian Edn., Mpls., 1980-84, Nat. Bd. of Christian Edn. and Discipleship, 1987-93; vis. instr. Con Mex. Christian Edn. Project, Mexico City, 1992-94; pres. Nat. Assn. Dirs. Christian Edn., 1981-85; vis. prof. AIM Pastors Conf., Nairobi, Kenya, 1995, Ecuadorian Pastor's Seminar, Quito, 1996; coord. Spanish Writing Conf., Kansas City, 1997; co-dir. Covenant Spanish Writing Project for Curriculum, 1993-97. Pub., editor (mag.) Infocus, 1981-85; author: (with others) Introduction to Christian Education, 1991, Adult Education in the Church, 1992; keynote speaker Christian Edn. Meeting of Seminarians, Dallas, 1992. Mem. Young Reps., Mpls., 1966-69; pres. Bellflower (Calif.) Ministerial Assn., 1974-77; sec. Downtown Pastors Ministerial Assn., Mpla., 1981-84; citizenship chmn. Mission Valley PTA, 1995—. Mem. Profl. Assn. Christian Educators (bd. dirs., v.p. 1986-93). Republican. Avocations: hist. fiction, antique fishing gear. Office: Hillcrest Covenant Ch 8801 Nall Ave Shawnee Mission KS 66207-2106

OLSEN, THOMAS RICHARD, SR., air force officer; b. Houston, June 28, 1934; s. Oscar Leonard and Catherine (Byers) O.; m. Dorothy Kendrick Taylor, July 7, 1956; children: Thomas Richard Jr., Lisa Kendrick Olsen Wesolick. BSME, Tex. A&M U., 1956; MS in Internat. Affairs, George Washington U., 1968. Mech. engr. Tex. Gas Corp., Houston, 1956; commd. 2d lt. USAF, 1957, advanced through grades to maj. gen., 1986; pilot trainee Greenville AFB, Miss., 1957-58; fighter pilot 326 FIS/526 FIS, U.S. and Fed. Republic Germany, 1958-65, 614 TFS/615 TFS, England AFB, La., 615 TFS, Phan Rang AB, Vietnam, 1966-67; instr. U.S. Naval Amphibious Sch., Coronado, Calif., 1968-71; fighter pilot 391 TFS, Mt. Home AFB, Idaho, 1971-72; squadron ops. officer, squadron comdr. 391 TFS, Mt. Home AFB, 1972-74; chief rated officer Mgmt. Hdqrs. AFMPC, Randolph AFB, Tex., 1975-78; chief of staff Hdqrs. 9th Air Force, Shaw AFB, S.C., 1978-79; dep. comdr. Hdqrs. 314th Air Div., Seoul, Republic of Korea, 1979-81; dir. ops. Hdqrs. 5th Air Force, Yokota AFB, Japan, 1981-82; wing comdr. 51 TFW, Osan AB, Republic of Korea, 1982-83; dep. dir. ops. Hdqrs. Pacific Command, Camp Smith, Hawaii, 1983-85; asst. chief of staff ops. Hdqrs. AFCENT, NATO, Brunsuum, The Netherlands, 1985-87; dep. comdr., chief of staff Hdqrs. 4 ATAF, NATO, Heidelberg, Fed. Republic Germany, 1987-89; vice comdr. Hdqrs. 9th Air Force, Shaw AFB, S.C., 1989-91; dep. comdr. U.S. Cen. Command Air Forces (Desert Shield/Desert Storm), Riyadh, Saudi Arabia, 1990-91; ret., 1991. Mem. Optimist Club, Coronado, 1969-71. Mem. Air Force Assn., Ret. Officers Assn., Daedalians, Kiwanis, Rotary. Presbyterian. Home: 1006 Golfcrest Rd Sumter SC 29154-6179

OLSEN, TILLIE, author; b. Omaha, Nebr., Jan. 14, 1912; d. Samuel and Ida (Beber) Lerner; m. Jack Olsen; children: Karla, Julie, Kathie, Laurie. LittD (hon.), U. Nebr., 1979, Knox Coll., 1982, Hobart and William Smith Coll., 1984, Clark U., 1985, Albright Coll., 1986, Wooster Coll., 1991, Mills Coll., 1995. Writer-in-residence Amherst Coll., 1969-70; vis. faculty Stanford U., 1972; Writer-in-residence, vis. faculty English M.I.T., 1973-74, U. Mass., Boston, 1974; internat. vis. scholar Norway, 1980; Hill prof. U. Minn., spring 1986; writer-in-residence Kenyon Coll., 1987—; Regents lectr. U. Calif. at San Diego, 1977—, UCLA, 1987; commencement spkr. English dept. U. Calif., Berkeley, 1983, Hobart and William Smith Coll., 1984 Bennington Coll., 1986. Author: Tell Me A Riddle, 1961 (title story received First prize O'Henry award 1961), Rebecca Harding Davis: Life in the Iron Mills, 1972, Yonnondio: From the Thirties, 1974, Silences, 1978, The Word Made Flesh, 1984; editor: Mother to Daughter, Daughter to Mother, 1984; Preface Mothers and Daughters, That Special Quality: A Exploration in Photographs, 1989; short fiction published in over 200 anthologies; books translated in 11 langs. Recipient Am. Acad. and Nat. Inst. of Arts and Letters award, 1975, Ministry to Women award Unitarian Universalist Fedn., 1980, Brit. Post Office and B.P.W. award, 1980, Mari Sandoz award Nebr. Libr. Assn., 1991, REA award Dungannon Found., 1994, Disting. Achievement award Western Lit. Assn., 1996; Grantee Ford Found., 1959, NEA, 1968; Stanford Univ. Creative Writing fellow, 1962-64, Guggenheim fellow, 1975-76, Bunting Inst. Radcliffe Coll. fellow, 1985; Tillie Olsen Day designated in San Francisco, 1981. Mem. Authors Guild, PEN, Writers Union. Home: 1435 Laguna St Apt 6 San Francisco CA 94115-3742

OLSHAN, KENNETH S., business executive, advisor; b. Evansville, Ind., July 15, 1932; s. Harry and Ethel (Hamburg) O.; m. Patricia E. Shane, Aug. 25, 1954; children: Margot E., Mathew S., John K. BA, Ind. U., 1954; postgrad., Grad. Sch. Bus. Washington U., 1955. Trainee, TV-radio buyer Batten Barton Durstine & Osborn (Advt.), N.Y.C., 1958-60; v.p., account exec. Doherty, Clifford, Steers & Shenfield, N.Y.C., 1960-64; sr. v.p., account mgmt. supr. McCaffrey & McCall, N.Y.C., 1964-67; pres. Olshan, Smith & Gould, N.Y.C., 1967-69, Doherty, Mann & Olshan, N.Y.C., 1969-76; exec. v.p. creative Wells, Rich, Greene, N.Y.C., 1976-80; pres. Wells, Rich, Greene/East, 1980-81; chmn. Wells, Rich, Greene/USA, 1981-82, also dir.; chmn. Wells, Rich, Greene/World Wide, 1982-90, chmn. bd. dirs.; chief exec. officer Wells Rich Greene BDDP Inc., 1990-95; vice-chmn. BDDP Advt. Agy. Group, 1990-95; lectr. journalism Miriam Meloy Sturgeon Ind. U., 1981; mem. Advt. Coun. Campaigns Rev. Com., 1992-96; bd. dirs. Am. Assn. Advt. Agys., 1992-95, mem. ops. com., 1993-95; bd. dirs. Footstar, chmn. nominating com., 1996—. Trustee Westport Pub. Libr., 1976-83; bd. dirs. Nat. Multiple Sclerosis Found., 1984-96; trustee Poly. U. Promise Bd., 1988-96, trustee Central Park Conservancy, 1992—, chmn. mktg. com., 1992—. With U.S. Army, 1954-56. Mem. Blue Key, Sigma Alpha Mu. Office: 866 3rd Ave Fl 26 New York NY 10022-6221

OLSHEN, RICHARD A., statistician, educator; b. Portland, Oreg., May 17, 1942; s. A.C. and Dorothy (Olds) O.; m. Susan Abroff, 1979. AB, U. Calif., Berkeley, 1963; PhD, Yale U., 1966. Rsch. staff statistician, lectr. Yale U., New Haven, 1966-67; asst. prof. of statistics Stanford (Calif.) U., 1967-72; assoc. prof. of statistics and math. U. Mich., Ann Arbor, 1972-75; assoc. prof. of math. U. Calif., San Diego, 1975-77, prof. of math., 1977-89, dir. lab. for math. and statistics, 1982-89; prof. of biostatistics Sch. Medicine Stanford U., 1989—, prof. by courtesy dept. statis., 1990—, prof. by courtesy dept. elec. engring., 1995—. Office: Stanford U Sch Medicine Hrp Bldg Stanford CA 94305

OLSHIN, SAMUEL E., architect. BA in Design of the Environment, U. Pa., 1982, MArch, 1986. Registered architect, Pa. Arch. Atkin, Olshin, Lawson-Bell & Assocs., Phila., 1986—; juror Temple U., U. Pa., Drexel U., Bryn Mawr Coll., Villanova U., Phila. Coll. Textiles and Sci.; asst. prof. U. Pa., fall 1988; lectr. Bryn Mawr Coll., 1990—. Prin. works include Jaffe History of Art Bldg. at U. Pa., Hitchings Residence (Merit award Cedar Shake and Shingle Bur. 1989, 1st prize Sympathetic Additions category Nat. Trust Hist. Preservation 1990), Mitchell Residence (Merit award Builder Mag. 1991), Historic Kesher Israel Synagogue renovation, Pensacola St. Beach Pavilion, Seaside, Fla.; one man shows include AIA, Phila., 1995. Phila. Chpt. scholar Victorian Soc., summer 1991. Office: Atkin Olshin Lawson-Bell & Assocs Archs 125 S 9th St Ste 900 Philadelphia PA 19107-5125

OLSHWANGER, RON, photojournalist. Freelance photographer St. Louis Post-Dispatch. Recipient Pulitzer prize for spot news photography, 1989. Home: 1447 Meadowside Dr Saint Louis MO 63146

OLSON, BARBARA FORD, physician; b. Iowa City, June 15, 1935; d. Leonard A. and Anne (Swanson) Ford; m. Robert Eric Olson, 1959 (div. 1973); children: Katherine Gee, Eric Ford, Julie Marie. BA, Gustavus Adolphus Coll., 1956; MD, U. Minn., 1960. Diplomate Am. Bd. Family Practice (cert. added qualifications geriatric medicine). Intern St. Paul-Ramsy Med. Ctr., 1960-61; resident in anesthesiology U. Hosp. Cleve., 1961-62, U. Minn. Hosp., Mpls., 1962-63; pvt. practice anesthesiology St. Johns Hosp. and Devine Redeemer Hosp., St. Paul, 1963-67, Mercy Hosp., Coon Rapids, Minn., 1967-74; staff physician Oak Terrace Nursing Home, Minnetonka, Minn., 1974-88; med. dir. nursing home care unit VA Med. Ctr., St. Cloud, Minn., 1988—. Pres., bd. dirs. Alpha Epsilon Iota Med. Found., Mpls., 1980-86. Mem. Minn. Med. Assn., Minn. Women Physicians (pres. 1981-82), Minn. Nursing Home Med. Dirs. Home: PO Box 7306 Saint Cloud MN 56302-7306 Office: VA Med Ctr 4801 8th St N Saint Cloud MN 56303-2015

OLSON, BETTY-JEAN, elementary education educator; b. Camas, Wash., Apr. 26, 1934; d. Earl Raymond and Mabel Anna (Burden) Clemons; m. Arthur H. Geda, Dec. 31, 1957; children: Ann C. Geda, Scott A. Geda; m. Conrad A. Olson, June 14, 1980. AA, Clark Coll., 1954; BA in Edn., Cen. Wash. Coll. Edn., 1956; MEd, No. Monn. Coll., 1975. Cert. elem. tchr. class I, Mont., supr. K-9 class III. Supervising tchr., demo. teaching No. Mont. Coll.; kindergarten, 1st grade instr. Glasgow, Mont.; supervisor, head tchr. Reading Lab, Glasgow AFB, Mont.; 1st grade instr., kindergarten tchr., elem. adminstr. K-7 Medicine Lake (Mont.) Dist. 7; certification stds. and practices Adv. Coun. to the State Bd. Pub. Edn.; mem. bd. examiners Nat. Coun. for Accred. of Tchr. Edn., adv. com. Western Mont. Coll., U. Mont.; workshop leader and presenter in field. Mem. Sheridan County Community Protective Svcs. Com., Med-Lake Scholarship Com. Mem. NEA, ASCD, Internat. Reading Assn., Nat. Coun. Social Studies, Nat. Elem. Prin. Assn., Medicine Lake Edn. Assn. (past pres.), Mont. Edn. Assn. (rev. bd., officerships), Mont. Elem. Prin., N.E. Mont. Reading Coun. (v.p.), Delta Kappa Gamma (state pres., chpt. pres., exec. bd., committeeships, mem. internat. exec. bd.). Home: 108 E Antelope Antelope MT 59211-9607

OLSON, BOB MOODY, marketing executive; b. Memphis, June 18, 1934; s. Nels Antone and June Esther (Hogan) O.; m. Sandra Holmes, Oct. 2, 1956; children: Jeffrey, Sandra Leigh, Karen Louise. AB in Econs., Princeton (N.J.) U., 1955; postgrad., U. Va., 1974; MBA in Bus., Fordham U., 1977. With IBM Corp., 1955-80, industry dir. ins., 1969-74; account exec. IBM Corp., N.Y.C., 1974-80; sr. v.p. sales and mktg. div. ITT World Communications, Inc., N.Y.C., 1980-83; v.p. sales and mktg. div. Siemens/Databit, Hauppauge, N.Y., 1983-85, Amdahl Communications, Richardson, Tex., 1985-86; v.p. U.S. div. Gandalf Techs., Inc., Nepean, Ont., Can., 1986-88; sr. dir. Motorola Info. Systems Group, King of Prussia, Pa., 1988—. Capt. USAF, 1956-59. Mem. Charter Club (bd. govs. 1968-85), Princeton Club of N.Y. Republican. Avocations: tennis, golf. Home: 222 Nevin Ln Lower Gwynedd PA 19002-2033 Office: Motorola ISG 660 Am Ave Ste 105 King Of Prussia PA 19406

OLSON, CAL OLIVER, golf architect; b. Grindstone, S.D., Oct. 18, 1939; s. Harold John and Maxine Lorraine (Knutson) O.; m. Paula Lavon Hancock, Dec. 27, 1971. BSCE, Calif. Poly., Pomona, 1974. Prin. Peridian Group, Irvine, Calif., 1966-78; v.p. L.D. King Engring., Ontario, Calif., 1978-79; prin. Cal Olson Golf Architect, Costa Mesa, Calif., 1979—. Author: Turfgrass Science, 1983. Mem. ASCE, Am. Soc. Landscape Architects. Republican. Lutheran. Avocation: golf. Office: Cal Olson Golf Architect 3070 Bristol St Ste 460 Costa Mesa CA 92626-3070

OLSON, CAROL LEA, lithographer, educator, photographer; b. Anderson, Ind., June 10, 1929; d. Daniel Ackerman and Marguerite Louise Olson. AB, Anderson Coll., 1952; MA, Ball State U., 1976. Pasteup artist Warner Press, Inc., Anderson, 1952-53, apprentice lithographer stripper, 1953-57, journeyman, 1957-63, lithographic dot etcher, color corrector, 1959-73, prepres coord. art dept., 1973-81, prepres tech. specialist, 1981-83, color film assembler, 1983-96; part-time photography instr. Anderson Univ.; tchr. photography Anderson Fine Arts Ctr., 1976-79; instr. photography, photographics Anderson U., 1979—; mag. photographer Bd. Christian Edn. of Ch. of God, Anderson, 1973-86; freelance photographer. One person show Anderson U., 1979; exhibited in group shows Anderson U., 1980-93, Purdue U., 1982. Instr. 1st aide ARC, Anderson, 1969-79; sec. volleyball Anderson Sunday Sch. Athletic Assn., 1973—. Recipient Hon. mention, Ann Arbor, Mich., 1977, Anderson Fine Arts Ctr., 1977, 78, 83, 1st Pl., 1983, Hon. Mention, 1983, 2d Pl., 1988, Hon. Mention, 1988, 93, Best of Show, 1983, 91, 92, Best Nature Catagory Anderson Fine Arts Ctr., 1994. Mem. AAUW, Associated Photographer Internat., Nat. Inst. Exploration, Profl. Photographers Am. Mem. Ch. of God. Avocations: camping, travel, canoeing. Home: 2604 E 6th St Anderson TN 46012-3725

OLSON, CLARENCE ELMER, JR., newspaper editor; b. Edgerton, Wis., July 1, 1927; s. C. Elmer and Helen (Turnbull) O.; m. Arielle North, Sept. 4, 1954; children: Randall Jack, Christina North, Jens Sterling Elmer. B.S., U. Wis., 1950. News editor Edgerton Reporter, 1953; photographer, writer Madison (Wis.) Capital Times, 1953-59; writer St. Louis Post-Dispatch Pictures mag., 1959-65, asst. editor, 1965-68; asst. mng. editor Careers Today mag., Delmar, Calif., 1968-69; book editor St. Louis Post-Dispatch, 1969-91, ret., 1991. Served with USNR, 1945-46. Home: 236 N Elm Ave Saint Louis MO 63119-2420

OLSON, CLIFFORD LARRY, management consultant, entrepreneur; b. Karlstad, Minn., Oct. 11, 1946; s. Wallace B. and Lucille I (Pederson) O.; m. B.A. Blue Blodgett, March 18, 1967; children: Derek, Erin. B in Chemical Engring., U. Minn., 1969, B in Physics, 1969; MBA, U. Chgo., 1972; Licence en Sciences Economiques, U. de Louvain, Brussels, 1972. CPA, Cert. mgmt. cons. Project engr. Procter & Gamble, Chgo., 1969-71; engagement mgr. McKinsey & Co., Chgo., 1972-75; ptnr., midwest regional dir. mgmt. consulting Peat, Marwick, Mitchell, St. Louis, 1976-87; chmn. Casson Industries Inc., Mpls., 1987—; bd. dirs. Castlerock Group, Inc., Chevron, Inc. Mem. AICPA, Union League Club Chgo., Tavern Club, Interlache Country Club. Episcopalian. Avocations: skiing, carpentry. Office: 5804 Schaefer Rd Minneapolis MN 55436-1116

OLSON, CLINTON LOUIS, foreign service officer, former ambassador; b. S.D., Mar. 31, 1916; s. William H. and Allie (Sparling) O.; m. Ethel Hoover, June 14, 1943; children: Merilee, Peter, David, Steven. B.S., Stanford U., 1939, M.B.A., 1941. Petroleum engr. with Robert S. Lytle, 1939-40; partner Chino Homes, Inc. (realtors), 1946- 47; pres. EXIM of Calif., 1946-48; with U.S. Fgn. Service, 1948-75; 2d sec. U.S. legation, Vienna, Austria, 1948-52; consul. French West Indies, 1953-55; budget examiner State Dept., 1956; exec. dir. bur. Inter-Am. Affairs, 1957-59; assigned Nat. War Coll., 1959-60; counselor of embassy London, Eng., 1960-62; counselor econ. affairs Am. embassy, Vienna, 1962-66; charge d'affaires, minister-counselor Am. embassy, Lagos, Nigeria, 1966-70; sr. fgn. service insp., 1970-72; U.S. ambassador to Sierra Leone, 1972-75; internat. cons., 1975—. Served to lt. col., ordnance AUS, 1941-46, Russia, Iran. Fellow Explorers Club; mem. Fgn. Service Assn., Theta Xi. Clubs: Rolling Rock (Ligonier, Pa.); Ross Mountain (Pa.); Mill Reef (Antigua, W.I.). Home: Ross Mountain Club New Florence PA 15944

OLSON, CURTIS D., advertising executive. Sr. ptnr., exec. creative dir. Tatham Euro RSCG, Chgo. Office: Tatham Euro RSCG 980 N Michigan Ave Chicago IL 60611-4501

OLSON, DALE C., public relations executive; b. Fargo, N.D., Feb. 20, 1934; s. Arthur Edwin and Edith (Weight) Olson Neubauer. Sr. v.p., prin., pres. motion picture divsn. Rogers and Cowan, Inc., Beverly Hills, Calif., 1967-85; prin. Dale C. Olson & Assocs., Beverly Hills, 1985—; cons. Filmex, L.A., 1972-83; U.S. del. Manila Film Festival, 1982-83. Editor L.A. edit. Theatre ann. Best Plays, 1963-67. V.p. Diamond Cir. City of Hope, Duarte, Calif., 1980-83; mem. adv. bd. Calif. Mus. Sci. and Industry, L.A., 1975-81; mem. bd. govs. Film Industry Workshops, Inc., 1965-80; pres. Hollywood Press Club, 1963-66; assoc. Los Angeles County Art Mus., 1981-83; bd. trustees Hollywood Arts Coun. Recipient Golden Key, Pub. Rels. News, 1982, Les Mason and pub. svc. awards Publicists Guild. Mem. NATAS, Acad. Motion Picture Arts and Scis. (chmn. pub. rels. coordinating com. 1982—), Actors Fund Am. (chmn. Western coun. 1991, trustee 1992), Hollywood Arts Coun. (bd. dirs.), Pres.'s Club, Thalians. Lutheran. Office: 6310 San Vicente Blvd Ste 340 Los Angeles CA 90048-5426

OLSON, DAVID JOHN, political science educator; b. Brantford, N.D., May 18, 1941; s. Lloyd and Alice Ingrid (Black) O.; m. Sandra Jean Crabb, June 11, 1966; 1 dau., Maia Kari. B.A., Concordia Coll., Moorhead, Minn., 1963; Rockefeller fellow Union Theol. Sem, N.Y.C., 1963-64; M.A. (Brookings Instn. predoctoral research fellow 1968-69), U. Wis., Madison, 1966, Ph.D. (univ. fellow 1967), 1971. Community planner Madison Redvel. Authority, 1965-66; lectr. U. Wis., 1966-67; from lectr. to asso. prof. polit. sci. Ind. U., Bloomington, 1969-76; prof. polit. sci. U. Wash., Seattle, 1976—; chmn. dept. U. Wash., 1983-88, Harry Bridges endowed chairlabor studies, 1992-94; bd. dirs. Harry Bridges Inst.; dir.Ctr. Labor Studies U. Wash., 1992-94; Disting. lectr. in labor studies San Francisco State U., 1994; vis. prof. U. Bergen, 1987, Harvard U., 1988-89, U. Hawaii, 1989, U. Calif., Berkeley, 1996. Co-author: Governing the United States, 1978, Commission Politics, 1977, To Keep the Republic, 1975, Black Politics, 1971; co-editor: Theft of the City, 1974. Recipient Disting. Teaching award Ind. U., 1973, faculty fellow, 1973. Mem. Am. Polit. Sci. Assn., Western Polit. Sci. Assn. (v.p. 1984, pres. 1985), Midwest Polit. Sci. Assn., So. Polit. Sci. Assn. Democrat. Lutheran. Home: 6512 E Green Lake Way N Seattle WA 98103-5418 Office: Univ Wash Dept Polit Sci Seattle WA 98195

OLSON, DENNIS OLIVER, lawyer; b. Seminole, Tex., Oct. 19, 1947; s. Edwin and Beulah Matilda (Strang) O.; m. Leonee Lynn Claud, Jan. 30, 1971; children: James Edwin, Stacy Rae. BA in English, U. Tex., 1969; JD, Tex. Tech U., 1974. Cert. consumer bankruptcy law, bus. bankruptcy law, bankruptcy law examiner, Tex. Bar: Tex. 1974, U.S. Ct. Mil. Appeals 1974, U.S. Dist. Ct. (no. dist.) Tex. 1978, U.S. Dist. Ct. (we. dist.) Tex. 1978, U.S. Ct. Appeals (5th cir.) 1984, U.S. Supreme Ct. 1985. Commd. USMC, 1969, advanced through grades to capt., 1973, infantry officer various locations including Vietnam, 1969-74, judge advocate, various locations, 1974-78, resigned, 1978; assoc. Carr, Evans, Fouts & Hunt, and predecessor, Lubbock, Tex., 1978-81, ptnr., 1981-85; sole practice, Dallas, 1985-88; shareholder, co-chmn. bankruptcy sect. Godwin & Carlton, P. C., Dallas, 1989-94; ptnr. Olson Gibbons Nicoud Birne Sussman & Gueck, LLP, and predecessor, Dallas, 1994—. Bd. dirs. Presbyn. Ctr. Doctor's Clinic, Lubbock, 1983-85, United Campus Ministry, Tex. Tech U., Lubbock, 1984-85; elder Canyon Creek Presbyn. Ch., Richardson, Tex.; treas. bd. dirs. Lubbock chpt. ARC, 1981-82, v.p., bd. dirs. Quantico (Va.) chpt. ARC, 1975-77; vol. Lubbock United Way, 1978-80. Decorated Bronze Star; named Outstanding Young Man of Am., 1983. Fellow Tex. Bar Found.; mem. Dallas County Bar Assn., Lubbock County Bar Assn. (bd. dirs. 1983-85), Tex. Young Lawyers Assn. (bd. dirs. 1981-83), Judge Advocates Assn. (bd. dirs. 1976-78), Lubbock C. of C. (grad. Leadership Lubbock program 1981), Phi Delta Phi. Home: 407 Fall Creek Dr Richardson TX 75080-2508

OLSON, DIANE LOUISE, secondary education educator; b. Ft. Dodge, Iowa, Dec. 15, 1951; d. Ralph Leroy and Donna Marie (Solbeck) O.; m. Michael John Schroeder, June 1, 1991. BA in English Edn., U. No. Iowa, 1974; MA in English Edn., N.E. Mo. State U., 1986. Cert. tchr., Iowa. Tchr. English, drama, composition and speech Lamoni (Iowa) Community Schs., 1974-76; tchr. English Rockwell (Iowa)-Swaledale Community Schs., 1977-80; tchr. English and skills for adolescence Wayne Community Schs., Corydon, Iowa, 1980—; workshop presenter and speaker in field. Author pamphlets for workshops; editor, writer: The Story of Cambria, 1990; columnist Humeston New Era, 1995—; contbr. articles to profl. jours. Mem. adminstrv. bd. Christian-United Meth. Ch., Humeston, 1982—, lay leader, 1994, 95, youth group leader, 1996—; actress, reader Wayne County Arts Coun., Corydon, 1987-93; actress, dir. Humeston Theater Group, 1992; writer, actress Wayne County Sesquicentennial Pageant, 1994-96. Recipinet Ednl. Achievement award Corydon Optimist Club, 1996; named Outstanding Young Woman of Am., 1986, Outstanding Writing Tchr., Writing Conf., 1991; State of Iowa grantee, 1980. Mem. NEA, AAUW (pres. 1993-95), Nat. Coun. Tchrs. English, Iowa Edn. Assn., Iowa Coun. Tchrs. English, Wayne Cmty. Edn. Assn., Mormon Trail Chamber and Devel. Corp., Beta Sigma Phi (treas., v.p.). Democrat. Avocations: reading, writing, hiking, biking, travel. Home: 511 Guy Porter St Humeston IA 50123-1004 Office: Wayne Community Schs PO Box 308 Corydon IA 50060-0308

OLSON, DONALD RICHARD, mechanical engineering educator; b. Sargent, Nebr., Dec. 26, 1917; s. Harry T. and Gyneth E. (Wittemyer) O.; m. Nancy Walker Benton, June 17, 1944; children: Walter H., Sally, Timothy W. B.S., Oreg. State U., 1942; M.Engring., Yale U., 1944, D.Engring., 1951. Profl. engr., Conn. Asst. prof., asso. prof. mech. engring. Yale U., New Haven, 1951-62; prof. mech. engring. Pa. State U., University Park, 1962-83; prof. emeritus Pa. State U., 1983—; head underwater power plants Applied Research Lab., 1962-72, head dept. mech. engring., 1972-83; mem. engring. accreditation commn., 1979-82. Contbr. tech. papers in field to publs. Mem. ASME, Soc. Automotive Engrs. (dir. 1968-71), Sigma Xi. Home: 621 Glenn Rd State College PA 16803-3475

OLSON, EDWARD CHARLES, entrepreneur, conservationist, film industry executive, writer, environmental consultant, business consultant; b. Jacksonville, Fla., July 6, 1956; s. Edward Charles and Marcine Era (Hall) O.; m. Krista Lynn Neuberger, Aug. 5, 1978; children: Laura Ellen, Edward Charles, Natalie Rose. BS, Miami U., Oxford, Ohio, 1978; MS, Wash. State U., 1980; PhD, Ohio State U., 1983. State dir. Nature Conservancy, Columbus, Ohio, 1983-86; pres., CEO Florida Keys Land & Sea Trust, 1986-93, Catalina Island Conservancy, Avalon, Calif., 1993-96, E.C. Olson & Assocs., 1996—; ptnr. Oceanwatch Prodn. Group, 1996—; cons. non-profit orgns., 1987—; pres. Man-O-War Clothing, Co., 1996—. Editor: Guide to the Florida Keys, 1989. Bd. dirs. Catalina Cmty. Pub. Radio, 1993-96, Fla. Nat. Parks and Monuments Assn., Homestead, 1988-93, Fla. Keys Meml. Hosp., Key West, 1989-91, Fla. Keys Guidance Clinic, Marathon, 1990-92. Recipient Leadership Fla. Grad. award Fla. C. of C., 1990, Outstanding Young Floridian, Fla. Jaycees, 1991; named Man of Yr., Marathon Jaycees, 1990. Avocations: fishing, travel, reading, writing, Civil War study. Office: 205 Olive Ave Port Saint Lucie FL 34952-1347

OLSON, FERRON ALLRED, metallurgist, educator; b. Tooele, Utah, July 2, 1921; s. John Ernest and Harriet Cynthia (Allred) O.; m. Donna Lee Jefferies, Feb. 1, 1944; children: Kandace, Randall, Paul, Jeffery, Richard. BS, U. Utah, 1953, PhD, 1956. Ordained bishop LDS Ch., 1962. Research chemist Shell Devel. Co., Emeryville, Calif., 1956-61; assoc. research prof. U. Utah, Salt Lake City, 1961-63, assoc. prof., 1963-68, chmn. dept mining, metall. and fuels engring., 1966-74, prof. dept. metallurgy and metall. engring., 1968-96, prof. emeritus, 1996—; cons. U.S. Bur. Mines, Salt Lake City, 1973-77, Ctr. for Investigation Mining and Metallurgy, Santiago, Chile, 1978; dir. U. Utah Minerals Inst., 1980-91. Author: Collection of Short Stories, 1985, (novel) Harriet Cynthia Allred Olson, 1995; contbr. articles to profl. jours. Del. State Rep. Conv., Salt Lake City, 1964; bishop, 1962-68, 76-82, missionary, 1988. With U.S. Army, 1943-46, PTO. Named Fulbright-Hayes lectr., Yugoslavia, 1974-75, Disting. prof. Fulbright-Hayes, Yugoslavia, 1980, Outstanding Metallurgy Instr., U. Utah, 1979-80, 88-89, Disting. Speaker U. Belgrade-Bor, Yugoslavia, 1974. Mem. Am. Inst. Mining, Metall. and Petroleum Engrs. (chmn. Utah chpt. 1978-79), Am. Soc. Engring. Edn. (chmn. Minerals div. 1972-73), Fulbright Alumni Assn., Am. Bd. Engring. and Tech. (bd. dirs. 1975-82). Republican. Achievements include research on explosives ignition and decomposition; surface properties of thoria, silica gels, silicon monoxide in ultra high vacuum; kinetics of leaching of Chrysocolla, Malachite and Bornite; electrowinning of gold; nodulation of copper during electrodeposition. Home: 1862 Herbert Ave Salt Lake City UT 84108-1832 Office: U Utah Dept Metallurgy 412 Browning Building Bldg Salt Lake City UT 84112-1118

OLSON, FRANK ALBERT, car rental company executive; b. San Francisco, July 19, 1932; s. Alfred and Edith Mary (Hazeldine) O.; m. Sarah Jean Blakely, Oct. 19, 1957; children: Kimberly, Blake, Christopher. AA, City Coll. San Francisco, 1961. V.p. and gen. mgr. Barrett Transp. Inc., San Francisco, 1950-64; v.p., gen. mgr. Valcar Co. subs. Hertz Corp., San Francisco, 1964-68; mgr. N.Y. zone Hertz Corp., N.Y.C., 1968-69, v.p., mgr. Ea. region, v.p., gen. mgr. rent-a-car divsn., exec. v.p. rent-a-car divsn. gen. mgr., also bd. dirs., 1973-77, pres., CEO, 1977-80, chmn. bd. dirs., 1980, also dir., CEO, from 1982; chmn., CEO Allegis Corp., 1987; pres., CEO United Airlines, 1987; chmn., CEO Hertz Corp., Park Ridge, N.J., 1987—; bd. dirs. Becton Dickinson & Co., Cooper Industries, Fund Am. Holdings, Inc. Bd. dirs., mem. exec. com. World Travel & Tourism Coun. Mem. Am. Assn. Sovereign Mil. Order of Malta, Olympic Club (Calif.), Pine Valley Golf Club (N.J.), Royal and Ancient St. Andrews (Scotland), Turnberry Golf Club (Scotland), Arcola Country Club (Paramus, N.J.), Met. Club (N.Y.C.), Seminole Golf Club (Fla.). Republican. Roman Catholic. Office: Hertz Corp 225 Brae Blvd Park Ridge NJ 07656-1870

OLSON, FREDERICK IRVING, retired history educator; b. Milw., May 30, 1916; s. Frank and Clara (Hansen) O.; m. Jane Marian Correll, June 8, 1946; children: David Frederick, Donald Frank, Roger Alan. B.A. magna cum laude, Harvard U., 1938, M.A. (George W. Dillaway fellow 1938-39), 1939, Ph.D. in History, 1952. Mem. faculty U. Wis., Milw., 1946-85, prof. history, 1956-85, chmn. com. on univ. future, 1959-60, chmn. dept. history, 1960-62, 67-70, assoc. dean Coll. Letters and Sci., 1971-76, acting dean Sch. Library Sci., 1977-79; exec. dir. Milw. Humanities Program, 1979-84; vis. prof. history U. Wis.-Madison, summer 1957; assoc. dean U. Wis. extension, Mil., 1960-68; dir. Ridge Stone Fin. Svcs., Brookfield, 1995—. Author: (with Harry H. Anderson) Milwaukee: At the Gathering of the Waters, 1981, 2d edit., 1984, (with Frank Cassell and J. Martin Klotsche) The University of Wisconsin-Milwaukee: A Historical Profile, 1885-92, 1992, (with Jane Correll Olson) Dear Jane: A Soldier's Letters from Africa and the Middle East, 1942-45, 1994; contbr. articles and book revs. to profl. jours. Trustee Milw. Pub. Mus., 1951-52; bd. dirs. Milw. County Hist. Soc., 1947-85, 95—, pres., 1953-57, 72-75; bd. curators State Hist. Soc. Wis., 1961-91; mem. Milw. Landmarks Commn., 1964-71, Milw. County Landmarks Commn., 1976—, chmn., 1976-82; mem. rev. bd. Wis. Hist. Preservation, 1978-89; bd. dirs. Wis. Heritages, Inc., 1983-93, pres., 1989-90; bd. dirs. Wauwatosa Hist. Soc., 1984-96. With AUS, 1942-45. Mem. Orgn. Am. Historians, Wis. Acad. Scis., Arts and Letters, Lincoln Group (Boston), North Hills Country Club (Waukesha, Wis.), Phi Beta Kappa, Phi Alpha Theta, Phi Kappa Phi. Lutheran. Home: 2437 N 90th St Milwaukee WI 53226-1809

OLSON, GARY ROBERT, banker; b. Milw., May 9, 1946; s. Ward Louis and Mary Jane (Brown) O.; m. Mia Kristina Sohn, Feb. 26, 1972; children: Kristin Anne, Brian Ward. Student, Loyola U., Rome, 1966-67; AB, Marquette U., 1968; M Internat. Mgmt., Am. Grad. Sch. Internat. Mgmt., Glendale, Ariz., 1973. Instr. Sogang Jesuit U., Seoul, 1968-70, Hankuk U. Fgn. Studies, Seoul, 1971-72; grad. asst. Am. Grad. Sch. Internat. Mgmt., 1972; credit analyst Chase Manhattan Bank, N.A., N.Y.C. and Tokyo, 1973-75; asst. treas. Chase Manhattan Bank, N.A., N.Y.C., 1975-77; 2d v.p. Chase Manhattan Bank, N.A., Madrid, 1977, Paris, 1977-80; v.p., mgr. Regional Banking Office Chase Manhattan Bank, N.A., Chgo., 1980-83; v.p., regional mgr. Case Nat. Corp. Svcs., San Francisco, 1983-87; sr. v.p. Chase Bank Ariz., Phoenix, 1987-90; v.p. Bklyn. and S.I. commercial mgr. Chase Manhattan Bank, N.A., Bklyn., 1990-93; v.p., team leader Nassau mid. mkt. mgr. Chase Manhattan Bank, N.A., Melville, L.I., 1993—. Advisor English program USIS, Seoul, 1969; alumni domestic counselor Am. Grad. Sch. Internat. Mgmt. Marquette U., 1990—; vol. Spl. Olympics, Phoenix, 1988-89; fund drive capt. Phoenix Econ. Growth Corp., 1988; trustee, bd. dirs. Variety Pre-schooler's workshop, 1994—; bd. bd.dirs. L.I. chpt. Robert Morris Assocs., 1994—, chmn., 1995—; mem. devel. com. Hecksher Mus., Huntington, N.Y., 1995—. Mem. Robert Morris Assocs. (assoc.), Econ. Club Phoenix, World Trade Club. Republican. Roman Catholic. Avocations: reading, skiing, swimming, golf. Office: Chase Manhattan Bank NA 395 N Svc Rd Melville NY 11747-3133

OLSON, GREGORY BRUCE, materials science and engineering educator, academic director; b. Bklyn., Apr. 10, 1947; s. Oscar Gustav Fritz and Elizabeth Rose (Dorner) O.; m. Jane Ellen Black, May 10, 1980; 1 child, Elise Marie. BS, MS in Materials Sci. and Engring., MIT, 1970, ScD in Materials Sci. and Engring., 1974. Rsch. assoc. dept. materials sci. and engring. MIT, Cambridge, 1974-79, prin. rsch. assoc., 1979-85, sr. rsch. assoc., 1985-88; prof. materials sci. and engring. Northwestern U., Evanston, Ill., 1988—; cons. Army Materials Tech. Lab., Watertown, Mass., 1975-88, Lawrence Livermore (Calif.) Nat. Lab., 1983-89; Jacob Kurtz Exchange Scientist Technion-Israel Inst. Tech., 1979; SERC vis. prof. U. Cambridge, 1992; now assoc. chmn. dept. materials sci. and engring. Northwestern U., dir. materials rsch. ctr.-steel rsch. group, 1985—. Editor: Innovative UHS Steel Technology, 1990, Martensite, 1992; contbr. numerous papers and articles to jours., encys., and symposia; inventor hydrogen-res. UHS steel, stainless bearing steel. Fellow AMAX Found., 1972-74; named N.Mex. Disting. lectr. in Materials, 1983; recipient Creativity Extension award NSF, 1983-85; Wallenberg grantee Jacob Wallenberg Found., Sweden, 1993, Technology Recognition award NASA, 1994. Fellow ASM (chmn. phase transformation com. 1987-90, Boston chpt. Saveurmeml. lectr. 1986, Alpha Sigma Mu lectr. 1996), ASM Internat.; mem. AAAS, Materials Rsch. Soc., Internat. Soc. Martensitic Transformation, Internat. Conf. Martensitic Transformation (co-chmn. 1992), TMS-AIME (student affairs com.), ISS-AIME (M.R. Tenebaum award 1993). Lutheran. Avocations: sports cars, jazz trumpet. Office: Northwestern U Dept Materials Sci and Engring 2225 N Campus Dr Evanston IL 60208-3108

OLSON, HARRY ANDREW, JR., communications consultant; b. Nashwauk, Minn., Jan. 8, 1923; s. Harry Arnold and Elizabeth C. (Wigen) O.; m. Dorothy M. Kuntz July 25, 1946 (div. 1978); children: Dana, Sarah, Cara, Christopher, Eric, Todd. B.S., U. Minn., 1948; LL.B., St. Paul Coll. Law, 1950. Bar: Minn. 1950. Investment analyst Investors Diversified, Mpls., 1954-57; dir. investment div. Investors Diversified, 1958-61; pres., dir. Am. Plan, Mpls., 1961-66; v.p. investments Fireman's Fund, San Francisco, 1966-67, Fund Am., 1967-69; v.p. corp. devel. Am. Express Co., N.Y.C., 1969-72; sr. v.p. corp. personnel Am. Express Co., 1974-78, sr. v.p. investment planning and adminstrn., 1978-80, sr. v.p. fin. analysis and investor relations, 1980-81; pres. dir. Am. Express Investment Mgmt. Co., 1972-74; pres. Partnership for Neighborhood Safety, 1982-83; v.p. Nat. Exec. Svc. Corps, N.Y.C., 1983-87, nat. coord. affiliates network, 1990-91; adminstr. Diocese of the Armenian Ch. of Am., N.Y.C., 1992-94; comm. cons. ELF Techs., Mercer Island, Wash., 1994-95. Founder, pres. Found. Disadvantaged Youth. Unitarian. Office: 505 Court St Apt 5R Brooklyn NY 11231-3951

OLSON, HERBERT THEODORE, trade association executive; b. Bridgeport, Conn., Feb. 9, 1929; s. Herbert Theodore and Inez Evelyn (Lindahl) O.; children: Christina, Victoria; m. Kathleen A. Harrison, Dec. 27, 1988. Student Heidelberg Coll., 1947-49; A.B., Ohio U., 1951, postgrad., 1951-52. Asst. to dean of men Ohio U., Athens, 1951-52; with Union Carbide Corp., 1952-71, mgr. employee relations, coordinator pub. affairs, N.Y.C., 1969-71; exec. v.p. Am. Assn. for Aging, Washington, 1971-75; dir. spl. projects Am. Health Care Assn., Washington, 1975-79; pres. Promotional Products Assn. Internat., Irving, Tex., 1979-96, pres. emeritus 1996—; adv. bd. Allied Bank. Mem. long-term care for elderly research rev. and adv. com. Dept. Health, 1972-77; mem. Longterm Care grant rev. com. HEW, 1972-77; mem. planning commn. City of Torrance, Calif., 1962-64, city councilman, 1964-67; mem. nat. exploring com., vice chmn. nat. events com., ann. meetings com., mem.-at-large nat. council Boy Scouts Am.; chmn. Gov's Operation Leegit; treas. U.S. Found. for Internat. Scouting, 1988—, chmn. audit com. 1984-87; adv. bd. Irving Hosp.; bd. dirs. Irving Cancer Soc. Served with USAR. Lord Baden Powell fellow, 1986; recipient Disting. Eagle award Boy Scouts Am., 1974, Silver Beaver award, 1968; named Person of Yr. in Promotional Products UN Counselor MAg, 1995, Hall of Fame Promotional Products Assn. Can., Hall of Fame Promotional Products Assn. Internat., 1997. Mem. Meeting Planners Internat. (charter), Am. Soc. Assn. Execs., U.S. C. of C., Washington Soc. Assn. Execs., Nat. Assn. Exhibit Mgrs., Small Bus. Legal Council (chmn. bd. 1993-95), Dallas Ft. Worth Soc. Assn. Execs. (v.p. 1985-87), Irving C. of C. (past bd. dirs.), Am. Advt. Fedn., Tex. Soc. Assn. Execs. Lutheran. Club: Las Colinas Country. Lodges: Rotary (past bd. dirs.), Masons, Shriners. Home: 2910 Pacific Ct Irving TX 75062-4624 Office: 3125 Skyway Cir N Irving TX 75038-3541

OLSON, HILDING HAROLD, surgeon, educator; b. Burlington, Wash., Apr. 30, 1916; s. Adolph and Gerda (Gerdin) O.; m. Donna D. Anderson, Aug. 14, 1943; children: Sheila K. Richardson, Susan L. LeClerq, Daniel L. BS, U. Wash., 1939; MD, U. Oreg., 1943. Diplomate Am. Bd. Surgery. Intern King County Hosp., Seattle, 1944-45, resident, 1945-51, attending surgeon, 1951—; clin. prof. surgery U. Wash., Seattle, 1964-87, emeritus, 1987—; mem. staff Providence Med. Ctr., Harborview Med. Ctr., Swedish Hosp. Med. Ctr., Univ. Hosp.; teaching fellow Dept. Anatomy, U. Oreg., 1940-43; dir. surgical clerkship program U. Wash. Dept. Surgery, 1954-73; dir. residency program Providence Med. Ctr., U. Wash. Dept. Surgery, 1976-87. Author: A Retrospective View of Northwest Medicine: The Early History of the Department of Surgery and the Health Sciences of the University of Washington, 1989; co-author: Saddlebags to Scanners: The First 100 Years of Medicine in Washington State, 1989; contbr. numerous articles to profl. jours. Served with U.S. Army, 1941-43, 46. Recipient Outstanding Tchr. award U. Wash. Sch. Medicine, 1958, 68, 85. Fellow Am. Coll. Surgeons; mem. AMA, Western Surg. Assn., Pacific Coast Surg. Assn. (pres. 1982-83), North Pacific Surg. Assn., Seattle Surg. Soc. (pres. 1975), Internat. Soc. Surgeons, King County Med. Assn., Pan Pacific Surg. Assn. Avocations: piano, pipe organ. Home and Office: 401 100th Ave NE Apt 317 Bellevue WA 98004-5456

OLSON, JAMES CLIFTON, historian, university president; b. Bradgate, Iowa, Jan. 23, 1917; s. Arthur Edwin and Abbie (Anderson) O.; m. Vera Blanche Farrington, June 6, 1941; children: Elizabeth, Sarah Margaret. AB, Morningside Coll., 1938, LLD, 1968; MA, U. Nebr., 1939, PhD, 1942, LittD, 1980; LittD, Chonnam Nat. U., Korea, 1978. Instr. Northwest Mo. State Tchrs. Coll., summers 1940-42; dir. Nebr. State Hist. Soc., 1946-56; lectr. U. Omaha, 1947-50; lectr. U. Nebr., 1946-54, part-time assoc. prof., 1954-56, prof., chmn. dept. history, 1956-65, Bennett S. and Dorothy Martin prof. history, 1962-65; dean Grad. Coll., univ. research adminstr., 1966-68, vice chancellor, 1968; chancellor U. Mo.-Kansas City, 1968-76; interim pres. U. Mo. System, 1976-77, pres., 1977-84, pres. emeritus, 1984—; OAS prof. Am. history El Colegio de Mexico, Mexico City, 1962; vis. prof. U. Colo., summer 1965; commr. N. Cen. Assn. Colls. and Schs.; bd. dirs. Uhlmann Co. Author: J. Sterling Morton, 1942, The Nebraska Story, 1951, History of Nebraska, 1955, 3d edit. (with Ronald C. Naugle), (with Vera Farrington Olson) Nebraska is My Home, 1956, This is Nebraska, 1960, Red Cloud and the Sioux Problem, 1965, paper edit., 1975, 79, (with Vera Farrington Olson) The University of Missouri: An Illustrated History, 1988, Serving the University of Missouri: A Memoir of Campus and System Administration, 1993; contbg. author: The Army Air Forces in World War II, 1951, 53; editor: Nebraska History, 1946-56; contbr. articles to profl. jours., encys. Bd. dirs. Mid-Am. Arts Alliance; trustee Midwest Rsch. Inst., Kansas City. Mem. Am. Assn. State and Local History, Coun. Basic Edn., Am. Hist. Assn., Orgn. Am. Historians, State Hist. Soc. Mo. (exec. com.), Nebr. State Hist. Soc., We. Hist. Assn., Cosmos Club, Phi Beta Kappa, Omicron Delta Kappa, Phi Kappa Phi, Pi Gamma Mu.

OLSON, JAMES RICHARD, transportation company executive; b. Alexandria, Minn., Mar. 11, 1941; s. Orie D. and Theresa Marie (Erickson) O.; m. Ronna Lee, Feb. 1, 1969 (dec.); 1 child, Trevor James. BS, N.D. State U., 1963; LLD, U. Minn., 1966; MBA, Harvard U., 1968. Asst. to v.p. finance Cargill Inc., Mpls., 1968-69; with Graco Inc., Mpls., 1969-75; v.p. finance Graco Inc., 1972-75; exec. v.p. finance Ponderosa System, Inc., Dayton, Ohio, 1975-77; v.p. planning Pillsbury Co., Mpls., 1977-79; v.p. restaurant group Pillsbury Co., 1979-80; group v.p.-restaurants The Carlson Cos., Inc., Mpls., 1981-83; exec. v.p., chief fin. and adminstrv. officer Schneider Nat., Inc., 1983-87, pres. van group, 1987-92, pres. transp. sector, 1992—; mem. corp. bd. dirs. Curative Rehab. Ctr.; mem. bd. dirs The Ground Round, Inc. Mem. Financial Execs. Inst., Citizens League Mpls.-St. Paul, Harvard Bus. Sch. Club Minn. (past pres.). Lutheran. Home: 2512 Riverside Dr Green Bay WI 54301-1950 Office: PO Box 2545 Green Bay WI 54306-2545

OLSON, JAMES ROBERT, consulting engineer; b. Columbus, Nebr., Nov. 23, 1940; s. Robert August and Jean Elizabeth O.; 1 child, Eric Robert. Student, U.S. Naval Acad., 1962; BA, U. Nebr., 1965; MA, Cen. Mich. U., 1977; diploma Nat. Def. U., 1981. Commd. ensign USN, 1965, advanced through grades to comdr., 1980; svc. in S.W. Pacific, Philippines and Vietnam; designated Space Systems Ops. Subspecialist, 1982; ret., 1983; sr. systems engr. G.E. Space Systems Div., Valley Forge, Pa., 1983-92; mem. faculty Def. Intelligence Sch., 1970-71; mem. Naval Insp. Gen. Staff, 1982. Decorated Bronze Star with combat V, Air medal (5), Republic of Vietnam Cross of Gallantry, numerous others. Mem. NRA (life), VFW (life), Inst. Navigation, Fla. Gulf Coast R.R. Mus., Rlwy. and Locomotive Hist. Soc. (life), Colo. R.R. Hist. Found. (life), Am. Swedish Hist. Found., VASA Order of Am., Am. Legion, Phi Alpha Theta, Isles Yacht Club (Punta Gorda). Methodist. Home: 1424 Surfbird Ct Punta Gorda FL 33950-7616

OLSON, JAMES WILLIAM PARK, architect; b. St. Louis, Oct. 6, 1940; s. James William Park; s. Louis Garfield and Gladys Helen (Schuh) O.; m. Katherine Fovargue, June 11, 1971; children: Park, Reed. BArch, U. Wash., 1963. Registered architect, Wash., Oreg., Calif., Ill., Colo. Ptnr. Olson/Sundberg Architects, Seattle, 1985—; assoc. architect New Seattle Art Mus., 1991. Prin. works include Pike and Virginia Bldg. (AIA Honor award 1980), Seattle's Best Coffee Retail Locations (AIA Honor award 1984), Hauberg Residence Complex (AIA Citation award 1996), Olympic Block Bldg. (Outstanding Merit award Wash. Trust Hist. Preservation 1986), numerous residences nationwide. Bd. dirs. On The Bds., Ctr. Contemporary Art, Seattle, 1982-86, Artist Trust, Seattle, 1986-90, U. Wash. Henry Art Gallery, Seattle, 1986-92, Seattle Art Mus. Recipient Best Architect award Seattle Mag., 1985. Fellow AIA; mem. IFRAA, NEA (juror). Avocation: art. Work published in numerous mags, jours., including The AD 100 Architects, N.Y. Times, Archtl. Digest, Archtl. Record, Global Architecture and others. Office: Olson/Sundberg Architects 108 1st Ave S Fl 4 Seattle WA 98104-2502

OLSON, JEANNE INNIS, technology/technical management; b. South Bend, Ind., May 10, 1960; d. Francis Bedford and Mary Ann (Szachnia) Innis; m. Thomas Hilton Olson, Apr. 12, 1992. Student, Purdue U., 1978-80; BS in Tech. & Mgmt. summa cum laude, U. Md., 1986; MS in Sys. Mgmt. with honors, U. So. Calif., 1991. Analyst Potomac Rsch., Inc., Alexandria, Va., 1980-82; staff specialist SWL, Inc., McLean, Va., 1982-87; sr. staff Advanced Tech., Inc., El Segundo, Calif., 1987-89; prin. staff/section mgr. PRC, Inc., El Segundo, Calif., 1989-95, deputy dir. space sys. acquisition support, 1995-96, dir. space sys. acquisition support and LA operations, 1997—. Mem. South Bay Friends Planned Parenthood, Calif., 1992—, v.p. fund raising, 1994. Recipient Vol. Recognition award Planned Parenthood L.A., 1994, 96. Mem. Innes Clan Soc. (v.p. 1984-91, pres. 1991-92), Innes Clan Ctr. Assn. (bd. dirs. 1993—), Phi Kappa Phi. Avocations: skiing, music, travel, Scottish heritage, family planning edn. Office: PRC Inc 222 N Sepulveda Blvd Ste 1310 El Segundo CA 90245-4353

OLSON, JOHN KARL, lawyer; b. Springfield, Mass., Aug. 14, 1949; s. Harold Gunnar and Louise Theodora (Shukis) O.; m. Anne Catherine Sullivan, June 16, 1973; children: Elizabeth Ann, Katherine Louise. AB, Harvard Coll., 1971; JD, Boston Coll., 1975. Bar: Fla. 1975, U.S. Dist. Ct. (mid. and so. dists.) Fla. 1976, U.S. Ct. Appeals (5th cir.) 1979, U.S. Supreme Ct. 1979; U.S. Ct. Appeals (11th cir.) 1981. From assoc. to ptnr. Carlton, Fields, Ward et al., Tampa, Fla., 1975-86; exec. v.p., gen. counsel, dir. Jet Fla., Inc., Miami, 1986-88; ptnr. Stearns Weaver Miller Weissler Alhadeff & Sitterson P.A., Tampa, 1988—. Author: Creditors and Debtors Rights in Florida, 1979, 89, Collier Bankruptcy Practice Guide, 1986. Trustee Tampa Mus. Art, 1992—. Fellow U. Tampa, 1986—. Mem. ABA (vice-chmn. backruptcy com. 1984-86), Fla. Bar (chmn. bus. law sect. 1988-89), Harvard Club (pres. 1982-84), Turnaround Mgmt. Assn. (Ctrl. Fla. chpt. pres. 1995-96). Home: 2632 W Prospect Rd Tampa FL 33629-5358 Office: Sun Trust Fin Ctr 401 E Jackson St Tampa FL 33602

OLSON, JOHN MICHAEL, lawyer; b. Grafton, N.D., Feb. 9, 1947; s. Clifford Inguold and Alice M. (Schwandt) O.; children: Dana Michel, Kirsten Lee. BA, Concordia Coll., Moorhead, Minn., 1969; JD, U. N.D., 1972. Bar: N.D. 1972. Asst. atty. gen. N.D. Atty. Gen.'s Office, Bismarck, 1972-74; state's atty. Burleigh County, Bismarck, 1974-82; pvt. practice Bismarck, 1983-91; mem. 49th dist. N.D. Senate, Bismarck, 1983-91, minority leader, 1987-91; ptnr. Olson Cichy Bismarck, Bismarck, 1994—, Olson Cichy Attys., Bismarck, 1994—. Recipient Disting. Svc. award N.D. Peace Officers Assn., 1981, Outstanding Bismarcker award Bismarck Jaycees, 1981. Mem. N.D. Bar Assn. Republican. Lutheran. Office: 115 N 4th St Bismarck ND 58501-4002

OLSON, JUDY MAE, geography, cartography educator, consultant; b. Waupaca, Wis., May 15, 1944; d. Leonard A. and Hilma R. (Johnson) O. B.S., Wis. State U., Stevens Point, 1966, M.S., U. Wis., Madison, 1968, Ph.D., 1970. Asst. prof. U. Ga., Athens, 1970-74; asso. prof. Boston U., 1974-83; prof. geography Mich. State U., East Lansing, 1983—, chair dept. 1989-94; vis. asst. prof. U. Minn., Mpls., 1973, vis. assoc. prof., 1981; cons. U.S. Bur. Census, Washington, 1975, U.S. Army Engr. Topog. Labs., Washington, 1983, 84, U.S. Dept. Transp., Boston, 1980. Editor: The Am. Cartographer, 1977-82; U.S. Nat. Report to ICA, 1984; co-editor Geography's Inner Worlds, 1992; contbr. articles to profl. jours. Recipient Presdl. citation Am. Congress Surveying and Mapping, 1979, 80, 84, 85; AAG hon., 1990. Fellow Am. Congress Surveying and Mapping (dir. 1976-79, 81-82); mem. Am. Cartographic Assn. (pres. 1981-82), Assn. Am. Geographers councillor 1990-93, sec. 1991-93, pres. 1995-96), U.S. Nat. Com. for ICA (chmn. 1985-88), Internat. Cartographic Assn. (v.p. 1992—). Office: Mich State U Dept Geography 315 Natural Sci Bldg East Lansing MI 48824

OLSON, KEITH WALDEMAR, history educator; b. Poughkeepsie, N.Y., Aug. 4, 1931; s. Ernest Waldemar and Elin Ingeborg (Rehnstrom) O.; m. Marilyn Joyce Wittschen, Sept. 10, 1955; children—Paula, Judy. B.A., SUNY-Albany, 1957, M.A., 1959; Ph.D., U. Wis., 1964. Mem. history faculty Syracuse U., N.Y., 1963-66; mem. history faculty U. Md., College Park, 1966—; prof. history U. Md.; Fulbright prof. U. Tampere, Finland, 1986-87, U. Oulu, 1993, U. Jyväskylä, 1994. Author: The G.I. Bill, the Veterans and the Colleges, 1974; Biography of a Progressive: Franklin K. Lane, 1979. Pres. Am. Scandinavian Found., Washington, 1977-79. Served with U.S. Army, 1952-54. U.S. Office Edn. grantee, 1965-66; U. Md. grantee, 1971, 76, 78. Mem. Am. Hist. Assn., Orgn. Am. Historians, Wis. Hist. Soc., Swedish Am. Hist. Soc., Finnish Hist. Soc., Soc. Historians of Am. Fgn. Rels., Cen. Study of Presidency. Unitarian. Home: 10746 Kinloch Rd Silver Spring MD 20903-1226 Office: Dept History U Md College Park MD 20742

OLSON, KENNETH HARVEY, computer company executive; b. Souris, N.D., May 7, 1927; s. Oscar L. and Clara (Haugen) O.; m. Darlene R. Gronseth, Aug. 19, 1950 (div. 1987); children: Kenneth David, Martha C., Marie K. BA, Concordia Coll., Moorhead, Minn., 1950; MS, U. N.D., 1953; postgrad., U. Minn., 1955. Instr. math. U. N.D., Grand Forks, 1952-54; programming supr. Convair, San Diego, 1955-59; mgr. software Control Data Corp., Mpls., 1959-61, product mgr., 1961-62; sales mgr. Control Data Corp., San Diego, 1962-70; v.p. Automated Med. Analysts, San Diego, 1970-90; pres., dir. Focus 100 Group, San Diego, 1975—; pres., dir. Health Care Svcs. Corp., San Diego, 1971-74, H.C.S. Corp., San Diego, 1972-75; v.p., trustee Calif. Prepaid Health Plan Coun., 1971-74; trustee HMO Assn. Am., 1974-75; bd. dirs. Touch Techs., Inc., San Diego. Editor: Approximations for the 1604 Computer, 1960; contbr. papers to Computer Applications, 1957-61. Pres. Lemon Grove (Calif.) Luth. Ch., 1957-59; treas. St. Luke's Luth. Ch., La Mesa, Calif., 1992-93; founder San Diego Nat. Bank, 1980, mem. bus. adv. com., 1981-85. Named Subcontractor of Yr., Small Bus.

Assn. and SAI Corp., 1985; day proclaimed in his honor Mayor of San Diego, 1986; recipient Pres.'s award for disting. svc. Concordia Coll., 1991. Mem. Assn. for Computing Machinery, Sons of Norway. Republican. Avocations: photography, travel, classical concerts.

OLSON, LEROY CALVIN, retired educational administration educator; b. Kane, Pa., Mar. 7, 1926; s. Vernon Reinhold and Gertrude Viola (Hutchins) O.; m. Miriam Marie Vogler, June 19, 1954; children—David Lee, Thomas Edward, Steven Andrew. B.S., Clarion State Coll., 1949; M.Ed., Pa. State Coll., 1950; Ed.D., Pa. State U., 1962; postgrad., U. Del., 1964-65. Tchr.-counselor Boiling Springs (Pa.) High Sch., 1950-52, Gordon Jr. High Sch., Coatesville, Pa., 1952-54; guidance dir. Cen. Dauphin Sch. Dist., Harrisburg, Pa., 1954-57; coordinator pupil personnel services, asst. supt. for instrn. and personnel, acting supt. Alfred I. duPont Sch. Dist., Wilmington, Del., 1957-65; prof. ednl. adminstrn. Temple U., Phila., 1965-92, prof. emeritus, 1992—; cons. to schs. bds. and dists., also Nat., Wis., Pa. sch. bds. assns. Contbr. articles to profl. jours. Trustee Luth. Ch., 1963-66, chmn. bd., 1976-78, chmn. various coms., discussion groups. Served with USNR, 1944-46, PTO. Recipient Disting. Alumni award Clarion State Coll., 1972. Mem. Am. Personnel and Guidance Assn., AAUP, Am. Assn. Sch. Personnel Adminstrs., Assn. Supervision and Curriculum Devel., Council Profs. Instrn. Supervision, Nat. Staff Devel. Council, Am. Legion, Phi Delta Kappa, Phi Kappa Phi. Republican. Home: 231 Prospect Dr Wilmington DE 19803-5331 *God's gift of life is a marvelous thing. My attempt to make the best use of that gift is to try to live an integrated and balanced life. This means that active attention must be paid to the physical, social, spiritual, and recreational aspects as well as to the work or career dimension. It also means we must share that gift through loving and caring about others.*

OLSON, LUTE, university athletic coach; b. Mayville, N.D., Sept. 22, 1934; s. Albert E. and Alinda E. (Halvorson) O.; m. Roberta R. Russell, Nov. 27, 1953; children: Vicki, Jodi, Gregory, Christi, Steven. B.A., Augsburg Coll., Mpls., 1956; M.A., Chapman Coll., Orange, Calif., 1964. Cert. counselor. Head basketball coach Mahonomen High Sch., Minn., 1956-57, Two Harbors High Sch., Minn., 1957-61; dean of boys Baseline Jr. High Sch., Boulder, Colo., 1961-62; head basketball coach Loara High Sch., Anaheim, Calif., 1962-64, Marine High Sch., Huntington Beach, Calif., 1964-69, Long Beach City Coll., Calif., 1969-73, Long Beach State U., 1973-74, U. Iowa, Iowa City, 1974-83; head basketball coach U. Ariz. Wildcats, 1983—, head coach NCAA Divsn. 1A basketball, ranked #10, 1992, head coach NCAA Tournament winner West Region, semifinalist (overall), 1994, head coach NCAA Tournament champions, 1997. Author: Passing Game Offense, 1980, Multiple Zone Attack, 1981, Pressure Defense, 1981, Match-up Zone, 1983. Crusade chmn. Am. Cancer Soc., Iowa, 1982. Named Coach of Yr. Orange League, 1964; named Coach of Yr. Sunset League, 1968, Coach of Yr. Met. Conf. Calif., 1970-71, Coach of Yr. PCAA, 1974, Coach of Yr. Big Ten Conf., 1979, 80. Mem. Nat. Assn. Basketball Coaches (Coach of Yr. 1980). Lutheran. Office: U Ariz Mckale Ctr Tucson AZ 85721*

OLSON, LYNN, sculptor, painter, writer; b. Chgo., Mar. 23, 1952; s. Ellen (Nelson) Olson. instr. direct cement sculpture workshops Montoya Art Studios, West Palm Beach, Fla., 1988-89, Alta. Sculptors Assn., Edmonton, Can., 1990, Mendocino (Calif.) Art Ctr., 1992-93, Sierra Nev. Coll. at Lake Tahoe, Incline Village, 1993, Lighthouse Art Ctr., Crescent City, Calif., 1990-96, Elisabet Ney Sculpture Conservatory, Austin, Tex., 1995, Tarrant County Jr. Coll., Ft. Worth, 1995. Prin. works include Good Shepherd, Ch. Good Shepherd, Albion, Ind., Kneeling Figure, Manta Ray. World of Concrete, Addison, Ill., Rose, Carter Meml., Chesterton, Ind., Redwood Tree, Lighthouse Art Ctr., Crescent City, Calif., George Bartholomew Meml., Bellefontaine, Ohio, Color Concerto, Purdue U., Hammond, Ind., Continuity III, Tower East, Shaker Heights, Ohio, Aluma Beam, Aluma Corp., Toronto; author, pub.: Sculpting with Cement, 1981-97; contbr. over 50 articles to mags. Mem. Am. Concrete Inst. (com. 124 concrete aesthetics). Home and Office: Steelstone 4607 Claussen Ln Valparaiso IN 46383-1526

OLSON, MARIAN EDNA, nursing consultant, social psychologist; b. Newman Grove, Nebr., July 20, 1923; d. Edward and Ethel Thelma (Hougland) Olson; diploma U. Nebr., 1944, BS in Nursing, 1953; MA, State U. Iowa, 1961, MA in Psychology, 1962; PhD in Psychology, UCLA, 1966. Staff nurse, supr. U. Tex. Med. Br., Galveston, 1944-49; with U. Iowa, Iowa City, 1949-59, supr. 1953-55, asst. dir. 1955-59; asst. prof. nursing UCLA, 1966-67; prof. nursing U. Hawaii, 1967-70, 78-82; dir. nursing Wilcox Hosp. and Health Center, Lihue, 1970-77; chmn. Hawaii Bd. Nursing, 1974-80; prof. nursing No. Mich. U., 1984-88; cons., ind. nursing svcs. adminstr. practice & curriculum, 1988—. Bd. trustees Bay de Noc C.C., 1988—. Home and Office: 6223 County 513 T Rd Rapid River MI 49878-9595

OLSON, MARIAN KATHERINE, emergency management executive, consultant, publisher, information broker; b. Tulsa, Oct. 15, 1933; d. Sherwood Joseph and Katherine M. (Miller) Lahman; m. Ronald Keith Olson, Oct 27, 1956, (dec. May 1991). BA in Polit. Sci., U. Colo., 1954, MA in Elem. Edn., 1962; EdD in Ednl. Adminstrn., U. Tulsa, 1969. Tchr. public schs., Wyo., Colo., Mont., 1958-67; teaching fellow, adj. instr. edn. U. Tulsa, 1968-69; asst. prof. edn. Eastern Mont. State Coll., 1970; program assoc. research adminstrn. Mont. State U., 1970-75; on leave with Energy Policy Office of White House, then with Fed. Energy Adminstrn., 1973-74; with Dept. Energy, and predecessor, 1975—, program analyst, 1975-79, chief planning and environ. compliance br., 1979-83; regional dir. Region VIII Fed. Emergency Mgmt. Agy., 1987-93; exec. dir., Search and Rescue Dogs of the U.S., 1993—; pres. Western Healthclaims, Inc., Golden, Co.; pres. Marian Olson Assocs., Bannack Pub. Co.; mem. Colo. Nat. Hazards Mitigation Coun. Contbr. articles in field. Grantee Okla. Consortium Higher Edn., 1969, NIMH, 1974. Mem. Am. Soc. for Info. Sci., Am. Assn. Budget and Program Analysis, Assn. of Contingency Planners, Internat. Assn. Ind. Pubs., Assn. of Contingency Planners, Nat. Inst. Urban Search and Rescue (bd. dirs.), Nat. Assn. for Search and Rescue, Colo. Search and Rescue, Search and Rescue Dogs of U.S., Colo. Emergency Mgmt. Assn., Front Range Rescue Dogs, Colo. State Fire Chiefs Assn., Kappa Delta Pi, Phi Alpha Theta, Kappa Alpha Theta. Republican. Home: 203 Iowa Dr Golden CO 80403-1337 Office: Western Healthclaims Inc 203 Iowa Dr Ste B Golden CO 80403-1337

OLSON, MAXINE LOUISE, artist, lecturer; b. Kingsburg, Calif., June 29, 1931; d. Alfred and Lena A. Marshall; divorced; children: Todd Olson, Terry Olson. BA, Calif. State U., Fresno, 1973, MA, 1975. Asst. prof. U. Ga., Athens, 1986-89; lectr. Coll. of Sequoias, Visalia, Calif., 1973-96; lectr. Fresno City Coll., 1990, Calif. State U., Fresno, intermittently 1973-96; tchr. U. Ga., Contona, Italy, 1987, 93. Exhibited works at Oakland Mus., Palazzo Casali, Venice, Italy, Forum Gallery, N.Y.C., Soho 20, N.Y., The World's Women on-line/UN 4th World Conf. on Women, Beijing, China, William Sawyer Gallery, Palm Springs Mus., Calif. Recipient Gold award Art of Calif. Mag., 1992. Mem. Coll. Art Assn. Roman Catholic. Avocations: painting, drawing, digital art. Home: 1555 Lincoln St Kingsburg CA 93631-1804

OLSON, NORMAN FREDRICK, food science educator; b. Edmund, Wis., Feb. 8, 1931; s. Irving M. and Elva B. (Rhinerson) O.; m. Darlene Mary Thorson, Dec. 28, 1957; children: Kristin A., Eric R. BS, U. Wis., 1953, MS, 1957, PhD, 1959. Asst. prof. U. Wis.-Madison, 1959-63, assoc. prof., 1963-69, prof., 1969-93, dir. Walter V. Price Cheese Research Inst., 1976-93; dir. Ctr. Dairy Research, 1986-93; disting. prof. U. Wis., 1993—. Author: Semi-soft Cheeses; inventor enzyme microencapsulation; sr. editor Jour. Dairy Sci., 1996—. Lt. U.S. Army, 1953-55. Fellow Inst. Food Technologists (Macy award 1986); mem. Am. Dairy Sci. Assn. (v.p. 1984-85, pres. 1985-86, Pfizer award 1971, Dairy Rsch. Inc. award 1978, Borden Found. award 1988), Inst. Food Technologists. Democrat. Lutheran. Avocation: cross-country skiing. Home: 114 Green Lake Pass Madison WI 53705-4755 Office: U Wis Dept Food Sci Babcock Hall Madison WI 53706

OLSON, PATRICIA JOANNE, artist, educator; b. Chgo., Aug. 22, 1927; d. Fred William and Fern Leslie (Shaffer) Kohler; m. Paul J. Olson, Jan. 21, 1950 (dec. July 1968); adopted children: Paulette, Dominic; stepchildren: Cindy, Katie, Larry, Daniel. BA, Northeastern Ill. U., 1976; MA, Loyola U., 1981. Advt. art dir. Chas. A. Stevens Dept. Store, Chgo., 1950-55; art dir. McCann, Erickson Advt. Agy., Chgo., 1955-57; pres. Olson Studio, Chgo., 1957-75; dept. chair, mem. faculty Chgo. Acad. Fine Art, 1974-78; exhibiting artist Chicago and Santa Barbara, Calif., 1981—; instr. Old Town Triangle Art Ctr., Chgo., 1978—, Bernard Horwich Ctr., Chgo., 1982-86, Art Inst. Chgo., 1987; prof. Columbia Coll., Chgo., 1978—; panelist Chgo. Cultural Ctr.; spkr., demonstrator Skokie Cultural Ctr., 1992, Joliet Art Ctr., 1992; guest spkr. AAUW, Evanston, Ill., 1991, Columbia Coll. Humanities, Chgo., 1992. Author: Women of Different Sizes, 1981; contbr. poetry to mags.; one woman shows include Artemesia Gallery, 1985, Highland Park H.S., 1987, One Ill. Ctr., 1987, Gallery 6000, 1988, Countryside Gallery of New Work, 1991, Old Town Triangle Gallery, 1991, Loyola U. Gallery, 1991; exhibited in group shows New Horizons, Art Inst. Gallery, 1975, 90, Beverly Art Ctr., 1978, 79, 82, 87, 89, 90, Beacon St. Gallery, 1984, 89, Art Inst. Chgo., 1984, Galex 19 Internat., Galesburg, Ill., 1985, Suburban Art League, 1986, Natalini Gallery, 1987, Societe des Pastellistes de France, 1987, Campanile Gallery, 1987, Artemsia Gallery, 1987, Delora Cultural Ctr., 1988, Alexandrian Mus., 1988, Gallery Genesis, 1988, 89, Adler Cultural Ctr., 1989, Post Rd. Gallery, 1989, Evanston Co-op Gallery, 1990, Pilsen Gallery, 1991, Old Town Triangle Gallery, 1991, Loyola U. Gallery, 1991, Chgo. Soc. Artists, 1992, R.H. Love Gallery, 1992, Chgo. Cultural Ctr., 1992, Wood St. Gallery, 1994, North Lakeside Cultural Ctr., 1994, State of Ill. Bldg. Chgo. Sr. Citizen Art Network (award), others. Hostess Rogers Park (Ill.) Hist. Soc., 1993. Named to Sr. Hall of Fame, Mayor Daley, Chgo., 1991, Womens Mus., Washington. Mem. Chgo. Soc. Artists, Chgo. Womens Caucus for Art (curator 1989-90), North Lakeside Cultural Ctr. (mem. art adv. bd. 1990—), Am. Jewish Art Club (juror, curator, speaker 1991), Wizo (juror 1989), Sr. Citizens Art Network. Democrat. Avocations: writing poetry, theatre, photography, hiking, reading. Home: 1955 W Morse Ave Chicago IL 60626-3111

OLSON, PAUL RICHARD, Spanish literature educator, editor; b. Rockford, Ill., Nov. 2, 1925; s. Oscar Wilhelm and Jenny Ingeborg (Taube) O.; m. Phyllis Elizabeth Edwards, Jan. 10, 1953; children: Thomas Jeremy, John Stephen, Carl Philip, Paul Andrew. A.B., U. Ill., 1948, A.M., 1950; Ph.D., Harvard U., 1959. Instr. Dartmouth Coll., Hanover, N.H., 1956-59, asst. prof., 1959-61; asst. prof. modern Spanish lit. Johns Hopkins U., Balt., 1961-63, assoc. prof., 1963-67, prof., 1967-91, prof. emeritus, 1991—. Author: Circle of Paradox, 1967, Unamuno: Niebla, 1984, Unamuno and the Primacy of Language, 1989; editor: Unamuno: Como se hace una novela, 1977; gen. editor: Modern Lang. Notes, 1983-86. Guggenheim Found. fellow, 1964; Fulbright grantee, 1964-65; Am. Council Learned Socs. grantee, 1969. Mem. MLA, Acad. Lit. Studies, Asociacion Internacional Hispanistas.

OLSON, PAUL S., nuclear engineer; b. Cambridge, Mass., May 2, 1933; s. Charles Louis and Mary Agnis (Navin) O.; m. Elaine Marylyn Selvitella, Nov. 25, 1956; children: Cheryl McCarthy, Christine Baginski, Karen Barbarick. BSChemE, Northeastern U., 1957; MS Nuclear Engring., U. Cin., 1962. Registered prof. engr. Calif. Commd. 2d lt. Rockwell, 1952; advanced through ranks to col. U.S. Army, 1978, retired, 1985; engr. GE, Cin., 1958-62, Rockwell, Canoga Park, Calif., 1962—. Bd. dirs. Univ. Mo. NE, Rolla, 1994-97, St. Anthony Home for Troubled Youngsters, Canoga Park, 1983-89. Fellow ASTM (chmn. 1958—, Merit award 1983); mem. K.C. (Grand Knight 1980—, Merit award 1985), Tau Beta Pi, Sigma Xi. Democrat. Roman Catholic. Avocation: outdoor activities. Home: 1365 Van Antwerp Rd # M-128 Niskayuna NY 12309-4441 Office: Rockwell 6633 Canoga Ave Canoga Park CA 91303-2703

OLSON, PHILLIP DAVID LEROY, agriculturist, chemist; b. Anchorage, Feb. 3, 1940; s. Marvin Willard and Bernadette (McName) O.; m. Deborah Andreé Butler, Apr. 10, 1982; children from a previous marriage: Jamie Kay, Samuel Phillip, Jill Andre. BS, U. Idaho, 1963; MS, Oreg. State U., 1972. Technician U. Calif., Riverside, 1963-65; rsch. staff Oreg. State U., Corvallis, 1965-75; mgr. R & D, Hoechst-Roussel Agri-Vet Co., Somerville, N.J., 1975-91; owner, pres. Profl. Agrl. Cons., Indio, Calif., 1991—; R & D cons. and quality assurance rsch. contractor Elf Atochem N.A., Bryan, Tex., 1991—, Dupont, Wilmington, Del., 1991—, Ciba-Geigy, Greensboro, N.C., 1991—, BASF, Research Triangle Park, N.C., 1991, ISK-Bioscis., Fresno, Calif., 1992—, Rhone-Plulenc, Durham, N.C., 1992—, Sandoz Agro, Inc., Des Plaines, Ill., 1992—, Zeneca, Inc., Richmond, Calif., 1992—, Stewart AG, Macon, Mo., 1995—; cons. in field. Mem. Soc. Quality Assurance, Pacific Regional Quality Assurance Soc., Oreg. State U. Found. (hon.), Smithsonian Instn., Archaeol. Soc. Am., Acad. Model Aeronautics, Elks. Avocations: reading, fishing, RC model building, rose gardening.

OLSON, PHILLIP ROGER, naval officer; b. Elmhurst, Ill., June 23, 1939; s. Willard Clarence and Carol (Schulz) O.; m. Marsha Andrea Lippert, July 10, 1966; children: Christine Carole, Phillip Roger Jr. B in Naval Sci., U.S. Naval Acad.; M in Physics, Naval Postgrad. Sch. Commd. ens. USN, 1962, advanced through grades to rear adm., 1987; instr. ship material readiness group USN, Idaho Falls, 1978-81; commdg. officer USS Pharris (FF 1094) USN, Norfolk, Va., 1981-82; commdg. officer USS Mississippi (CGN 40) USN, Norfolk, 1983-86; sr. instr. ship material readiness group USN, Newport, R.I., 1986-87; dep. dir. ops. Joint Staff USN, Washington, 1987-88, dep. dir. strategy & policy Joint Staff, 1988-89; comdr. logistics group two USN, Norfolk, 1989-90; comdr. cruiser-destroyer group one USN, San Diego, 1990-92; pres. bd. inspection & survey USN, Norfolk, 1992-96; retired, 1996. Decorated Disting. Svc. medal. Mem. Surface Navy Assn. Lutheran. Avocations: golf, tennis.

OLSON, RENÉE ALICIA, magazine editor; b. Evanston, Ill., Jan. 15, 1962; d. Samuel Paul and Barbara Mae (Mulligan) Mizerack. BA in Journalism, Ind. U., 1984; AB in Spanish, U. Ill., 1987, MS in Libr. Sci., 1987. Head reference svcs. Reading (Mass.) Pub. Libr., 1987-94; news and features editor Sch. Libr. Jour., N.Y.C., 1994—. Editor: New Eng. Librs. newsletter of New Eng. Libr. Assn., 1990-94, Bay State Libr. newsletter of Mass. Libr. Assn., 1989-90; contbr. articles to profl. jours. Visitor guide Bklyn. Bot. Garden, 1995—. Mem. ALA, Ednl. Press Assn. Avocation: travel. Office: Sch Libr Jour 245 W 17th St New York NY 10011-5300

OLSON, RICHARD DAVID, psychology educator; b. Reading, Pa., Oct. 10, 1944; s. Milton Stuart and Sarah Ellen (Moyer) O.; m. M. Gayle Augustine, Aug. 26, 1967. B.A., U. Redlands, 1966; M.S., St. Louis U., 1968, Ph.D., 1970. Lic. psychologist, La. Asst. prof. psychology U. New Orleans, 1970-74, assoc. prof., chmn. dept. psychology, 1974-79, prof., chmn. dept., 1979-81, assoc. dean Grad. Sch., 1981-82, dean, 1982-88, vice chancellor, 1984-88, rsch. prof., 1988—; chmn. dept. psychology, 1995—; cons. psychologist, New Orleans, 1973—; pres. Statis. Cons. of New Orleans, 1977-82. Editor: Learning in the Classroom, 1971, The Comma After Love, The Selected Poems of Raeburn Miller, 1994; contbr. articles to profl. jours. Grantee HEW, 1976-81. Fellow APA, Am. Psychol. Soc.; mem. Soc. for Neuroscis., Am. Statis. Assn. Home: 103 Doubloon Dr Slidell LA 70461-2715 Office: U New Orleans Dept Psychology Lake Front New Orleans LA 70148

OLSON, RICHARD EARL, lawyer, state legislator; b. Elmhurst, Ill., Apr. 24, 1953; s. Earl Leroy and Helen Ellen (Wanamaker) O.; m. Patricia Michelle McKinney, May 16, 1976; children: Shelley, Rachel, Eric. BA, U. Miss., Oxford, 1975; JD, So. Meth. U., 1978. Bar: N.Mex. 1978. Ptnr. Hinkle, Cox, Eaton, Coffield & Hensley, Roswell, N.Mex., 1978—; mem. N.Mex. Ho. of Reps., 1989-95, mem. various coms.; bd. trustees Eastern N.Mex. Med. Ctr., 1995—. Mem. Roswell City Coun., 1986-88, chmn. sts. and alleys com., mem. various other coms.; past chmn. pastor-parish rels. com. 1st United Meth. Ch., Roswell; bd. dirs. Roswell Econ. Forum, Roswell Mus. and Art Ctr. Found., city coun. liaison; bd. dirs. Assurance Home, 1980—, former v.p.; mem. N.Mex. 1st, former bd. dirs. Mem. ABA, Am. Legis. Exec. Coun. (civil justice task force), Def. Rsch. Inst., Noon Optimist Club, Order of Coif, Phi Kappa Phi. Republican. Home: 5003 Thunderbird Ln Roswell NM 88201-9386 Office: Hinkle Cox Eaton Coffield & Hensley PO Box 10 Roswell NM 88202-0010

OLSON, ROBERT EDWARD, coal mining executive; b. Phila., Aug. 5, 1927; s. Oscar E. and Marie B. (Kilgallon) O.; m. Jean Emilie Wadsworth, Dec. 31, 1955; children: Grace Olson Carmichael, Nancy Olson Ashcraft, Karen Olson Culbertson. Student U. Richmond, 1945, Duke, 1945-46, U. Pa., 1946; BS in Mining Engring., Pa. State U., 1952. Registered profl. engr., Pa., W.Va. Indsl. engr. Island Creek Coal Co., Holden, W.Va., 1952-55; dir., treas., sr. assoc. Coal Standards, Inc., mgmt. cons., Charleston, W.Va., 1955-61; v.p. adminstrn. Rochester & Pitts. Coal Co., Indiana, Pa., 1961-81; pres., chief operating officer, Valley Camp Coal Co., Oil City, Pa., 1981-86, vice chmn., dir., mem. exec. com., 1986-88, ret., 1988; past pres., dir. Kanawha and Hocking Coal & Coke Co., Kelley's Creek and Northwestern R.R. Co., Valley Camp Coal Sales Co.; pres., chief exec. officer Gt. Lakes Coal & Dock Co.; chmn., dir. Donaldson Mine Co., Elm Grove Coal Co., Shrewsbury Coal Co., Helen Mining Co., Valley Camp of Utah Inc.; chmn., CEO Pa. and W.Va. Supply Co.; bd. dirs. Strickland Constrn. Co. Bd. dirs. United Way of Venango County, 1983-88; pres. bd. trustees Venango County Community Area Found., 1988-94, former dir.; mem. Ind. County C. of C. 1973-81, pres. 1976-77; mem. vestry Christ Episc. Ch., Oil City, 1989-92. With USN, 1945-47. Mem. Wanango Country Club, Univ. Club, Franklin Club, Rotary Internat., Theta Delta Chi, Sigma Phi Sigma. Home: 8 Glenwood Dr Oil City PA 16301-2104

OLSON, ROBERT EUGENE, physician, biochemist, educator; b. Minn., Jan. 23, 1919; s. Ralph William and Minnie (Holtin) O.; m. Catherine Silvoso, Oct. 21, 1944; children: Barbara Lynn, Robert E., Mark Alan, Mary Ellen, Carol Louise. A.B., Gustavus Adolphus Coll., 1938; Ph.D., St. Louis U., 1944; M.D., Harvard, 1951; M.D. (hon.), Chiang Mai U., Thailand, 1983. Diplomate: Nat. Bd. Med. Examiners, Am. Bd. Nutrition (pres. 1962-63). Postgrad. research asst. biochemistry St. Louis U. Sch. Medicine, 1938-43, asst. biochemistry, 1943-44, Alice A. Doisy prof. biochemistry, chmn. dept. biochemistry, 1965-82, assoc. prof. medicine, 1966-72, prof. medicine, 1972-82; vis. prof. (sabbatical) dept. biochemistry U. Freiburg, Breisgau, West Germany, 1970-71; also Hoffman-La Roche Co., Basel, Switzerland, 1970-71; instr. biochemistry and nutrition Harvard Sch. Pub. Health, 1946-47; research fellow Nutrition Found., 1947-49; research fellow Am. Heart Assn., 1949-51, established investigator, 1951-52; house officer Peter Bent Brigham Hosp., Boston, 1951-52; prof., head dept. biochemistry and nutrition Grad. Sch. Pub. Health U. Pitts.; lectr. medicine Sch. Medicine, 1952-65; mem. panel malnutrition Japan-U.S. Med. Scis. Program, 1965-69; dir. Nutrition Clinic, Falk Clinic, 1953-65; mem. sr. staff Presbyn. Hosp., dir. metabolic unit, 1960-65; mem. staff St. Louis U. Hosp., 1965-81; prof. biochemistry, prof. medicine, assoc. dean acad. affairs U. Pitts. Sch. Medicine, 1982-84; prof. medicine, prof. pharm. scis. SUNY-Stony Brook, 1984-90, prof. emeritus, 1990-94; prof. pediatrics U. South Fla., Tampa, 1994—; cons. Mercy Hosp., U. Pitts. Med. Center; assoc. in medicine St. Margaret's Meml. Hosp., Pitts., dir. metabolic unit, 1954-60; cons. div. research grants USPHS, 1954-69, 72-76; dir. Anemia and Malnutrition Center, Chiang Mai, Thailand, 1967-77; vis. scholar dept. biochemistry Oxford (Eng.) U., 1961-62; vis. prof. dept. biochemistry U. Freiburg, West Germany, 1970-71; mem. food and nutrition bd. NRC, 1977-83; mem. adv. council Nat. Inst. Arthritis, Diabetes, Digestive and Kidney Diseases, 1981-85; William A. Noyes lectr. U. Ill., Urbana, 1980. Assoc. editor Nutrition Revs., 1954-56, editor, 1978-88; assoc. editor Am. Jour. Medicine, 1956-65, Circulation Rsch., 1956-76, Am. Heart Jour., 1958-65, Am. Jour. Clin. Nutrition, 1960-66, Methods in Med. Rsch., 1963-70, Biochem. Medicine, 1967-90, Molecular and Cellular Cardiology, 1967-78; assoc. editor Ann. Rev. Nutrition, 1979-84, editor, 1984-94; co-editor: Vitamins and Hormones, 1975-81. Bd. dirs. Nat. Nutrition Consortium, 1977-81, Am. Council on Sci. and Health, 1984-91. Served as lt. (j.g.) USNR, 1944-46. Recipient Fulbright award, 1961-62; Guggenheim Found. award, 1961-62, 70-71; McCollum award, 1965; Joseph Goldberger award, 1974; Atwater Meml. lectr., 1978; Geiger Meml. lectr., 1979, William A. Noyes lectr. U. Ill., 1980, H. Brooks James lectr. N.C. State U., 1981, Virginia Beal lectr. U. Mass., 1990. Fellow ACP, Am. Pub. Health Assn. (chmn. food and nutrition sect. 1960-61), Am. Inst. Nutrition (Pres. 1981-82), Assn. Am. Physicians; mem. AAAS (sec. med. scis. N. sect. 1965-67), Am. Assn. Cancer Research, Am. Heart Assn., AMA (mem. council food and nutrition 1959-67, vice chmn. 1962-67), Royal Soc. Health (London), N.Y. Acad. Scis., Am. Fedn. Clin. Research, Am. Soc. Clin. Investigation, Boyleston Med. Soc., Am. Chem. Soc. (pres. biochemistry group Pitts. sect. 1960-61), Am. Soc. Biol. Chemists, Soc. Exptl. Biology and Medicine, Am. Soc. Clin. Nutrition (pres. 1961-62, McCollum award 1965), Assn. Med. Sch. Depts. Biochemistry (pres. 1979-80), Pa., St. Louis, Allegheny County med. socs., Am. Soc. Study Liver Diseases, Phi Beta Kappa, Sigma Xi, Phi Lambda Upsilon, Alpha Omega Alpha, Alpha Sigma Nu. Clubs: Cosmos (Washington), Countryside Country Club (Tampa). Home: 2673 Camille Dr Palm Harbor FL 34684-2217 Office: U South Fla Dept Pediatrics 1 Davis Blvd Ste 307 Tampa FL 33606-3422

OLSON, ROBERT GOODWIN, philosophy educator; b. Mpls., May 8, 1924; s. Goodwin Carl and Mary Helen (Hutchins) O. B.A., U. Minn., 1943; Docteur (French Govt. scholar 1951), U. Paris, 1953; Ph.D., U. Mich., 1957. Staff editor Grolier Soc., N.Y.C., 1946-48; historian Office Mil. Govt., Berlin, Germany, 1948-49; asst. prof. philosophy Ripon (Wis.) Coll., 1953-56; instr. philosophy U. Mich., 1956-58; asst. prof. Columbia U., 1958-61; asso. prof., chmn. dept. philosophy Rutgers U., 1961-65, prof., chmn. dept. philosophy, 1965-69; prof., chmn. dept. philosophy L.I. U., Bklyn., 1969-97, prof. emeritus, 1997—. Author: An Introduction to Existentialism, 1962, The Morality of Self-Interest, 1965, A Short Introduction to Philosophy, 1967, Meaning and Argument, 1969, Ethics: A Short Introduction, 1977; Contbr. articles to profl. jours. Served with USAAF, 1943-46. Mem. Am., L.I. philos. assns., AAUP, United Fedn. Coll. Tchrs. Home: 2 Cornelia St New York NY 10014-5668 Office: Long Island U Dept Philosophy Bklyn Ctr Brooklyn NY 11201

OLSON, ROBERT GRANT, lawyer; b. Ft. Dodge, Iowa, Mar. 29, 1952; s. Grant L. and R. June (Pohlmann) O.; m. Cynthia Lynn Murray, Sept. 7, 1978; children: Brendon, Elisabeth, Jeffrey, Daniel. BS, Iowa State U., 1973; JD, U. Iowa, 1976. Bar: Mo., 1976, Ill. 1977. Ptnr. Thompson & Mitchell, St. Louis, 1976-92, Riezman & Blitz, P.C., St. Louis, 1992—. Editor Jour. Corp. Law, 1975-76. Vol. Gephardt for Pres. Campaign, 1988, Carnahan for Lt. Gov. Campaign, 1988, Carnahan for Gov. Campaign, 1992. Mem. ABA, Mo. Bar Assn., Ill. Bar Assn., Met. St. Louis Bar Assn., Downtown St. Louis Lions Club (pres. 1990-91). Home: 424 E Jackson Rd Saint Louis MO 63119-4128 Office: Riezman & Blitz PC 120 S Central Ave Saint Louis MO 63105-1705

OLSON, ROBERT HOWARD, lawyer; b. Indpls., July 6, 1944; s. Robert Howard and Jacquline (Wells) O.; m. Diane Carol Thorsen, Aug. 13, 1966; children: Jeffrey, Christopher. BA in Govt. summa cum laude, Ind. U., 1966; JD cum laude, Harvard U., 1969. Bar: U.S. Dist. Ct. (no. dist.) Ohio 1970, U.S. Dist. Ct. (no. Dist.) Ind. 1970, U.S. Dist. Ct. (so. Dist.) Ohio 1971, U.S. Supreme Ct. 1973, Ariz. 1985. Assoc. Squire, Sanders & Dempsey, Cleve., 1969, 70-71, 76-81, ptnr., 1981—, ptnr., Phoenix, 1985—; sr. law clk. U.S. Dist. Ct., No. Dist. Ind. 1969-70; chief civil rights div. Ohio Atty. Gen.'s Office, Columbus, 1971-73, chief consumer protection, 1973-75, chief counsel, 1975, 1st asst. (chief of staff), 1975-76; instr. Law Sch., Ohio State U., Columbus, 1974; mem. Cen. Phoenix com. to advise city council and mayor, 1987-89; bd. dirs. Orpheum Theater Found., 1989—, sec., 1989-90, pres., 1990-97, mem. exec. com., 1997—; bd. dirs. The Ariz. Ctr. for Law in the Pub. Interest, 1988—, mem. exec. com., 1990-94, treas. 1992-93, v.p., 1993-94; mem. Ariz. Ctr. for Disability Law, 1994-96, treas. 1994-95; mem. Valley Leadership Class XIV, Ariz. Town Hall, 1977. Author monograph on financing infrastructure, 1983; also law rev. articles on civil rights, consumer protection. Bd. dirs. 1st Unitarian Ch. Phoenix, v.p., 1987-89; bd. dirs. 1st Unitarian Ch. Found., 1987-93, pres., 1990-93. Mem. Ariz. State Bar Assn., Phi Beta Kappa. Democrat. Home: 5201 E Paradise Dr Scottsdale AZ 85254-4746 Office: Squire Sanders & Dempsey 40 N Central Ave Ste 2700 Phoenix AZ 85004-4424

OLSON, ROBERT LEONARD, retired insurance company executive; b. Auburn, Mass., Aug. 11, 1930; s. Henry Leroy and Marie Albertina (Holquist) O.; m. Muriel E. Storms, Mar. 22, 1958; children: Cynthia L., Mark W., Keith E. AAS, Becker Jr. Coll., 1956; BBA, Clark U., 1958; grad. exec. program, Dartmouth Coll., 1986. Supr. payroll and expense acctg. State Mut. Life Assurance Co. Am., Worcester, 1958-66, asst. mgr. budget fiscal planning, 1966-68; mgr. cost acctg. State Mut. Life Assurance Co. Am., Worcester, Mass., 1968-72, asst. contr., 1972-75, asst. v.p., 1975-82, 2d v.p. fin. planning and reporting, 1982-85, v.p. fin. planning and reporting, 1985-87, v.p., contr., 1987-90, also bd. dirs. Asst. treas. Mass. affiliate Am. Heart Assn., 1982-90, mem. budget, fin. and audit com., 1983-90; treas. Auburn Dist. Nursing Assn., 1972—. Mem. Inst. Mgmt. Accts., Fin. Execs. Inst., Bus. Planning Bd., Am. Mgmt. Assn. (cert. mgmt. course 1982). Avocations: antique and classic cars. Home: 7 Ridgewood Dr Auburn MA 01501-2316 Office: Allmerica Fin Corp 440 Lincoln St Worcester MA 01653-0002

OLSON, ROBERT WYRICK, lawyer; b. Madison, Wis., Dec. 19, 1945; s. John Arthur and Mary Katherine (Wyrick) O.; m. Carol Jean Duane, June 12, 1971; children: John Hagan, Mary Catherine Duane. BA, Williams Coll., 1967; JD, U. Va., 1970. Assoc. Cravath, Swaine & Moore, N.Y.C., 1970-79; asst. gen. counsel Penn Cen. Corp., Cin., 1979-80, assoc. gen. counsel, 1980-82, v.p., dep. gen. counsel, 1982-87; sr. v.p., gen. counsel, sec. Am. Premier Underwriters, Inc. (formerly Penn Cen. Corp.), Cin., 1987-95, Chiquita Brands Internat., Inc., Cin., 1995—. Mem. ABA. Office: Chiquita Brands Internat 25th Fl 250 E 5th St Ste 25 Cincinnati OH 45202-4154

OLSON, ROBERTA JEANNE MARIE, art historian, author, educator; b. Shawano, Wis., June 1, 1947; d. Robert Bernard Olson and Emma Pauline (Dallmann) Hoops; m. Alexander Buchanan Vance Johnson, June 15, 1980; 1 child, Allegra Alexandra Olson Johnson. BA, St. Olaf Coll., 1969; MA, U. Iowa, 1971; MFA, Princeton U., 1973, PhD, 1976. Preceptor Princeton (N.J.) U., 1972-74; contbg. editor Arts Mag., N.Y.C., 1973-75; art news editor The Soho Weekly News, N.Y.C., 1976-78; asst. prof., assoc. prof. Wheaton Coll., Norton, Mass., 1975-88, prof., 1988—, chmn. art dept., 1987-89, 92-93; A. Howard Meneely chair Wheaton Coll., 1990-92; faculty chair in the arts Wheaton Coll., 1997—; cons. Smithsonian Instn., Washington, 1984-86; bd. dirs. The Drawing Soc., N.Y.C., 1989-94, The Friends of Art; bd. advisers Halley's Comet Soc., 1986—; mem. vis. com. drawing and print dept. Met. Mus. Art, 1993—. Author: Italian Nineteenth Century Drawings and Watercolors: An Album, 1976, Italian Drawings 1780-1890, 1980 (N.Y. Times Best Art Book award 1981, Whole Earth Book award), Fire and Ice: A History of Comets in Art, 1985, Italian Renaissance Sculpture, 1992, French edit., 1993, Ottocento: Romanticism and Revolution in 19th Century Italian Painting, 1993: contbr. articles to profl. jours., including Burlington Mag., Art Bull., Master Drawings, Jour. History of Astronomy, Artibus et Historiae, Sci. Am., Mitteilungen des Kunsthistorischen Insts. in Florenz, Arte Cristiana, Gazette des Beaux-Arts, Antologia di Belle Arti, Astronomy and Astrophysics, Print Quarterly, Art Jour., Studies in History of Art; contbr. articles to art exhbn. catalogs, including Six Centuries of Sculptors Drawings, The Drawing Ctr., N.Y.C., 1981, Desegni di Tommaso Minardi, 2 vols., 1982, Old Master Drawings from the Mus. Art RISD, 1983; guest curator Art Mus. Princeton U., 1974, Nat. Gallery Art, 1980, N.Y. Hist. Soc., 1990. Fellow Samuel H. Kress Found., 1973-74, Whiting Found. for Humanities, 1974-75, NEH, 1982-83; grantee NEH, 1987-88, Am. Philos. Soc., 1989, Am. Coun. Learned Socs., 1990-91, Getty sr. rsch. grantee, 1994-95, Samuel H. Kress Found., 1996. Mem. Coll. Art Assn. Am., Assn. Univ. Profs. Italian, Drawing Soc., Phi Beta Kappa (pres. 1980-82, Kappa chpt.). Avocations: running, squash, collecting. Home: 35 Howard St Norton MA 02766-2734 Office: Wheaton Coll Watson Hall Norton MA 02766

OLSON, ROGER NORMAN, health service administrator; b. Spokane, July 3, 1936; s. Harry Leonard and Evelyn Helen (Pearson) O.; m. Joyce Marlene Markert, June 28, 1959; children: Leonard Mark, Brent Norman. BA, Pacific Luth. U., 1958; MDiv, Augustana Theol. Sem., 1962; MSW, U. Wash., 1970. Pastor Christ Luth. Ch., Des Moines, 1962-64; asst. pastor First Immanuel Luth. Ch., Portland, Oreg., 1964-68; planner Tri-County Community Coun., Portland, 1970-71; project coord. City-County Commn. on Aging, Portland, 1971-73; evaluation coord. Portland Bur. of Human Resources, 1973-74; asst. dir. Multnomah County Project Health Div., 1974-83; interim pastor Augustana Luth. Ch., 1984-85; dir. family support svcs. Met. Family Svc., 1985-91; dir. planning and rsch. Met. Family Svcs., 1992-94; dir. info. exch. Luth. Family Svc., 1994—. Rockefeller Bros. fellowship Rockefeller Fund for Theol. Edn., 1958-59, fellowship NIMH, 1968-69, Adminstn. on Aging, 1969-70. Democrat. Lutheran. Avocations: music, reading, theatre. Home: 3939 NE 21st Ave Portland OR 97212-1432 Office: Luth Family Svc 605 SE 39th Ave Portland OR 97214-3216

OLSON, RUE EILEEN, librarian; b. Chgo., Nov. 1, 1928; d. Paul H. and Martha M. (Fick) Meyers; m. Richard L. Olson, July 18, 1964; children: Catherine, Karen. Student Herzl Coll., 1946-48, Northwestern U., 1948-50, Ill. State U., 1960-64, Middle Mgmt. Inst. Spl. Librs. Assn., 1985-87. Acct. Ill. Farm Supply Co., Chgo., 1948-59; asst. libr. Ill. Agrl. Assn., Bloomington, 1960-66, libr., 1966-86, dir. libr. svcs., 1986-96, ret., 1996; bd. dirs. Corn Belt Libr. System, 1989-94, sec., 1991-94. Mem. area Com. Nat. Libr. Week, 1971, area steering com., 1972; mem. steering com. Illinet/OCLC, 1985-87; mem. adv. council of librs. Grad. Sch. Libr. Sci. U. Ill., 1976-79; mem. Ill. State Libr. Adv. Com. for Interlibr. Cooperation, 1979-80; del. Ill. White House Conf. on Libr. and Info. Svcs., 1978; coordinator Vita Income Tax Assistance, Bloomington, Ill., 1986-89, 95—, preparer 1978—; sec. Hawthorne Village Homeowner's Assn., 1995—. Mem. Am., Ill., McLean County (pres. 1970-71) Libr. Assns., Spl. Librs. Assn. (pres. Ill. chpt. 1977-78, first to be named Disting. Mem. food, agr. and nutrition div. 1989), Ill. OCLC Users Group (treas. 1988-90, bd. dirs. 1991-92), Internat. Assn. Agrl. Librs. and Documentalists, Am. Soc. Info. Sci., Am. Mgmt. Assn., USAIN, Mended Hearts, Inc. (sec. Ill. chpt. 250 1994-95, v.p. 1995-96, pres., 1996—, newsletter editor, 1994-96), Zonta (pres. 1987-89), Bloomington Club. Home: 8 Aspen Ct Bloomington IL 61704

OLSON, RUSSELL L., pension fund administrator; b. Elizabeth, N.J., Jan. 3, 1933; s. Harold B. and Edythe M. (Roberts) O.; m. Jeanette A. Sanderson, Aug. 9, 1958; children: Tracy, Stephen, Heather. BA, Rutgers U., 1954; MBA, Harvard U., 1971. Trainee Eastman Kodak Co., Rochester, N.Y., 1954-56, with pub. rels. dept., 1957-69, coordinator internt. info. svcs., 1964-69, treas. staff, 1971-74; adminstrv. asst. pension investments Eastman Kodak Co., Rochester, 1974-82, dir. pension investments worldwide, 1982—. With USAF, 1954-56. Presbyterian. Office: Eastman Kodak Co 343 State St Rochester NY 14650-0001

OLSON, STANLEY WILLIAM, physician, educator, medical school dean; b. Chgo., Feb. 10, 1914; s. David William and Agnes (Nelson) O.; m. Lorraine Caroline Lofdahl, June 26, 1936; children: Patricia Ann, Richard David, Robert Dean. BS, Wheaton Coll., 1934, LLD (hon.), 1956; MD, U. Ill., 1938; MS in Medicine (fellow), U. Minn., 1943; ScD, U. Akron, 1979, N.E Ohio U., 1985, Morehouse Sch. Medicine. Diplomate: Am. Bd. Internal Medicine. Intern Cook County Hosp., Chgo., 1938-40; asst. dir. Mayo Found., from 1947; cons. medicine Mayo Clinic, 1947—; instr. medicine grad. sch. U. Minn., 1947-50; dean and prof. coll. medicine, med. dir. Rsch. and Ednl. Hosp. U. Ill., 1950-53; dean and prof. Coll. Medicine Baylor U., Tex. Med. Ctr., Houston, 1953-66; prof. medicine Vanderbilt U.; clin. prof. medicine Meharry Med. Coll., 1966-68; dir. Tenn. Mid-South Regional Med. Program, 1967-68; dir. Div. Regional Med. Programs Svc. USPHS, 1968-70; pres. S.W. Found. for Rsch. and Edn., San Antonio, 1970-73; provost Coll. Medicine N.E. Ohio U., 1973-79, cons. med. edn. Morehouse Coll. Medicine, 1980-81; dean Morehouse Sch. Medicine, Atlanta, 1985-87; past chmn. med. bd., chief staff Ben Taub Hosp., Jefferson Davis Hosp., Houston; nat. adv. council for health research facilities NIH, 1963-68; rev. panel constrn. med. schs. USPHS, 1964-65; spl. cons. div. Regional Med. Programs NIH, 1966-68; med. cons. bd. trustees. SUNY, 1949; cons. to Hoover Commn., 1954; mem. bd. trustees. Wheaton Coll., Ill., 1953-68. Contbr. articles to profl. jours. Capt., M.C. AUS, 1943-46. Mem. AMA, Houston Philos. Soc. (pres. 1962-63), Tex. Philos. Soc., Assn. Am. Med. Colls., Alumni Assn. Mayo Found., Sigma Xi, Alpha Kappa Kappa, Alpha Omega Alpha. Baptist. Home: 5901 Churchview Dr Unit 25 Rockford IL 61107

OLSON, STEPHEN M(ICHAEL), lawyer; b. Jamestown, N.Y., May 4, 1948; s. Charles R. and Marilyn (Dietzel) O.; m. Linda C. Hanson, Aug. 24, 1968; children: Kevin, Darren. AB cum laude, Princeton U., 1970; JD, U. Chgo., 1973. Bar: Pa. 1973, U.S. Dist. Ct. (we. dist.) Pa. 1973, U.S. Ct. Appeals (3d cir.) 1975, U.S. Ct. Appeals (1st and D.C. cirs.) 1986, U.S. Ct. Appeals (7th cir. and 8th cir. 1988), U.S. Supreme Ct. 1986. Assoc. Kirkpatrick & Lockhart, Pitts., 1973-81, ptnr., 1981—. Mem. bd. editors HealthSpan. Vice chair bd. trustees Chatham Coll.; bd. dirs. Competitive Employment Opportunities. Mem. ABA (rwy./airline labor law com.), Pa. Bar Assn., Allegheny County Bar Assn., Princeton Alumni Assn. West Pa., Duquesne Club, Edgeworth Club. Avocations: photography, music, tennis. Office: Kirkpatrick & Lockhart 1500 Oliver Building Bldg Pittsburgh PA 15222-2312

OLSON, THEODORE ALEXANDER, former environmental biology educator; b. Oakes, N.D., Sept. 12, 1904; s. Henry Martin and Anna R. (Anderson) O.; m. Grace Myrtle Lundberg, Jan. 5, 1929; children—Theodore A., R. Thomas, Robert C. B.S., U. Minn., 1926; M.A., Harvard, 1938, Ph.D., 1958. Econ. entomologist U. Wis., 1926; instr. entomology U. Minn., 1926-28; prof. environmental biology Sch. Pub. Health, 1938-73, prof. emeritus, 1973—; biologist Minn. Dept. Health, 1928-38; Cons. health depts., Minn., N.Y., Wash.; Cons. health depts. Ohio River Valley Sanitation Commn., WHO, Norwegian Inst. Water Research, NIH; participant internat. study rodent control, Europe, Mid East, Pacific WHO, 1965, Internat. Conf., Munich, 1966. Author 1 book and over 100 profl. publs. Served from 1st lt to lt. col. San. Corps AUS, 1942-46. Rockefeller fellow, 1947; WHO fellow Caribbean, 1955; USPHS fellow N. Europe, 1962. Mem. AAAS, Am. Pub. Health Assn. (sect. vice chmn., chmn. lab. sect., governing council 1960-70), Am. Soc. Limnology and Oceanography, Am. Micros. Soc., Entomol. Soc. Am., State and Territorial Lab. Dirs. Assn., Sigma Xi, Internat. Assn. Great Lakes Research (dir., pres. 1968—). Clubs: University Minnesota, Harvard. Research on basic limnology of Lake Superior. Home: 3663 Park Ctr Blvd Apt 604 Minneapolis MN 55416-2519

OLSON, THEODORE BEVRY, lawyer; b. Chgo., Sept. 11, 1940; 2 children. B.A., U. Pacific, 1962; LL.B., U. Calif.-Berkeley, 1965. Bar: Calif. 1965, D.C. 1982. Assoc. Gibson, Dunn & Crutcher, Los Angeles, 1972-81, 84—, ptnr., 1972-81; asst. atty. gen. Dept. Justice, Washington, 1981—. Mem. Calif. Commn. on Uniform State Laws, 1972-74; del. Republican Nat. Conv., 1976, 80. Fellow Am. Acad. of Appellate Lawyers, Am. Coll. Trial Lawyers; mem. ABA, L.A. County Bar Assn. Office: Gibson Dunn & Crutcher 1050 Connecticut Ave NW Ste 90 Washington DC 20036

OLSON, THOMAS FRANCIS, II, communications company executive; b. Chgo., July 31, 1948; s. Thomas Francis and Nora Theresa (Shaw) O.; m. Maureen Eunice Walsh, July 28, 1972; children: Amy Michelle, Danielle Renee. B in Bus. Mktg., Western Ill. U., 1970. Sales exec. Sta. WQAD-TV, Moline, Ill., 1970-73; computer salesman Honeywell, Inc., Springfield, Ill., 1973; project mgr. Olson Bros. and Sons Constrn. Co., Chgo., 1973-75; sales exec. Katz Communications, Chgo., 1975-77, sales team mgr., 1977-81; v.p., nat. sales mgr. Katz Communications, N.Y.C., 1981-83, v.p., gen. sales mgr., 1983-84, div. pres., 1984-90, exec. v.p. TV group, 1991-92; pres. Katz TV Group, N.Y.C., 1992—; pres. chief exec. officer Katz Media Group, Inc., 1994—. Mem. Nat. Assn. Broadcasters, I.R.T.S., Sta. Reps. Assn. (past pres.). Roman Catholic. Avocations: running, skiing, hiking, sailing, scuba diving. Office: Katz Media Grp Inc 125 W 55th St New York NY 10019-5369

OLSON, WALTER GILBERT, lawyer; b. Stanton, Nebr., Feb. 2, 1924; s. O.E. Olson and Mabel A. Asplin; m. Gloria Helen Bennett, June 26, 1949; children: Clifford Warner, Karen Rae Olson. BS, U. Calif., Berkeley, 1947, JD, 1949. Bar: Calif. 1950, U.S. Dist. Ct. (no. dist.) Calif. 1950, U.S. Tax Ct. 1950, U.S. Ct. Appeals (9th cir.) 1950. Assoc. Orrick, Herrington and Sutcliffe (formerly Orrick, Dahlquist, Herrington and Sutcliffe), San Francisco, 1949-54, ptnr., 1954-88, of counsel, 1989—; bd. dirs. Alltel Corp., Little Rock, 1988-94; mem. Commn. to Revise Calif. Corp. Securities Law, 1967-69, Securities Regulatory Reform Panel, 1978-80; mem. corp. security adv. com. Calif. Commr. of Corps, 1975—. Editor-in-chief Calif. Law Review, 1948-49. Bd. dirs. Internat. Ho., Berkeley, 1981-86. With U.S. Army, 1943-46, ETO. Fellow Am. Bar Found.; mem. ABA (trust divsn. nat. conf. of lawyers and reps. of Am. Bankers Assn.), Calif. Bar Assn. (chmn. corps com. 1975-76, exec. com. bus. law sect. 1977-78), San Francisco Bar Assn., U. Calif. Alumni Assn., Boalt Hall Alumni Assn. (bd. dirs. 1982-90, sec. 1985, v.p. 1987, pres. 1988), Order of Coif, Menlo Country Club (Woodside, Calif.), Pacific-Union Club. Office: Orrick Herrington & Sutcliffe 400 Sansome St San Francisco CA 94111-3304

OLSON, WALTER JUSTUS, JR., management consultant; b. Paterson, N.J., July 27, 1941; s. Walter Justus and Viola Patricia (Trautvetter) O. BS, BA, Brown U., 1964; MBA, Columbia U., 1967. CPA, Va. Design engr. Rockwell Internat., Inc., Downey, Calif., 1964-65; mgmt. officer CIA, Washington, 1969-73; sr. cons. Booz, Allen and Hamilton, Inc., Washington, 1973-78; corp. planning coordinator Washington Gas Light Co., Washington, 1978-82; prin. Walter J. Olson and Assoc., McLean, Va., 1982-83; dep. asst. sec. for export adminstrn. U.S. Dept. Commerce, Washington, 1983-86; prin. Walter J. Olson & Assoc., Washington, 1986—. Vice-chmn. fin. com. Fairfax County (Va.) Reps., 1982-83. Served to 1st lt., USAF, 1967-69. Mem. AICPA, Greater Wash. Soc. CPAs, Strategic Leadership Forum (pres. Washington chpt. 1990-91). Republican. Episcopalian. Home: 7348 Dartford Dr Mc Lean VA 22102-7348 Office: 1815 H St NW Ste 600 Washington DC 20006-3604

OLSON, WARREN KINLEY, operations research analyst, engineer, physicist; b. Minot, N.D., Aug. 11, 1943; s. Arthur Conrad and Dorothy Elenor (Kinley) O.; m. Colleen Kay Ude, Dec. 18, 1965; children: Christine Kay, Cynthia Dorine. BA in Physics and Math., St. Olaf Coll., 1965; MS in Stats., U. Del., 1974; postgrad., George Mason U., 1995—. Mathematician Ballistics Rsch. Lab., Aberdeen Proving Ground, Md., 1962-69; ops. rsch. analyst Army Materiel Systems Analysis Agy., Aberdeen Proving Ground, 1969-76; br. chief USA TRADOC Systems Analysis Activity, White Sands Missile Range, N. Mex., 1976-85; dir. rsch. USA TRADOC Ops. Rsch. Activity, White Sands Missile Range, 1985-86; div. chief USA TRADOC Analysis Command, White Sands Missile Range, 1986, dir. rsch., 1986-87; sr. staff engr. Honeywell Defense Systems Group, Edina, Minn., 1987-90, Alliant Techsystems, Inc., Hopkins, Minn., 1990-93; rsch. mem. Inst. for Def. Analysis, Alexandria, Va., 1993—; mem. sci. staff NATO Joint Field Trials, Munich, Germany, 1973-74; chmn. U.S. Army ABCA QWG/AOR Spl. Work Group, White Sands, 1979-87; mem. def. sci. bd. MOBA Study, 1994; tech. expert on computer simulation, virtual reality. Co-author: (with others) (text) Military Strategy and Tactics, 1975, (handbook) Military Operations Research, 1994; contbr. tech. reports to profl., military publs., 1965-97. Elder Peace Luth. Ch., El Paso, Tex., 1985-87; mem. St. Olaf choir, 1963-65. Recipient Citizenship award, DAR, 1956, Civilian Svc. Commander's award, U.S. Army, Washington, 1979. Mem. Soc. for Preservation and Encouragement of Barber Shop Quartet Singing (bd. dirs. El Paso 1977-79, Internat. medalist 1991, 92, 93, Gt. No. Union Chorus), Mil. Ops. Rsch. Soc., Am. Def. Preparedness Assn., Sigma Pi Sigma. Avocations: music, skiing, scuba diving, photography, model railroading, chess. Home: 4657 Longstreet Ln Unit 302 Alexandria VA 22311-4940 Office: Inst Defense Analyses Simulation Ctr 1801 N Beauregard St Alexandria VA 22311-1733

OLSON, WILLIAM CLINTON, international affairs educator, author, lecturer; b. Denver, Aug. 19, 1920; s. Albert Merrill and Frances (Murray) O.; m. Mary Elizabeth Matthews, Aug. 16, 1943; children: Jon Eric, Peter Murray, Elizabeth Ann. AB, U. Denver, 1942; PhD, Yale U., 1953; DHL (hon.), U. Denver, 1992. Staff officer Social Sci. Found., Denver, 1947-49; chmn. com. on internat. rels. Pomona Coll., 1953-61; sr. mem. St. Antonys Coll. Oxford (Eng.) U., 1959-60; assoc. dean sch. internat. affairs Columbia U., N.Y.C., 1965-67; assoc. dir. for social scis. Rockefeller Found., N.Y.C., 1967-79; prof. internat. affairs. Am. U. Sch. Internat. Svc., Washington, 1979-90; prof. emeritus Am. U., Washington, 1990—; dean Am. U. Sch. Internat. Svc., Washington, 1979-86; vis. rsch. fellow Royal Inst. Internat. Affairs, London, 1986-87; dir. Bellagio Study and Conf. Ctr. of Rockefeller Found., Villa Serbelloni, Italy, 1970-79; vis. prof. Grad. Inst. Internat. Studies, Geneva, 1976-78; life fellow Clare Hall, Cambridge; cons. to vice chancellor U. Colombo, Sri Lanka, 1983; lectr. Johns Hopkins U., Washington, 1961-65, Bologna, 1973-75. Author, editor: The Theory and Practice of International Relations, 1960, 9th edit., 1994; contbr.: International Relations: British and American Perspectives, 1985, The Aberystwth Papers, 1972, Jahrbuch des offentlichen Rechts der gegenwart, 1972, 74, 78, 80, Internat. Affairs, 1976, 91; co-author: Internat. Relations Then and Now: Origins and Trends in Interpretation, 1991. Trustee Experiment in Internat. Living, 1959-65, Social Sci. Found. U. Denver, 1967-76, 80-92, 94—; co-founder Am. Friends Wilton Park, Inc., 1986. Recipient Disting. Alumnus award Grad. Sch. Internat. Studies, Denver, 1986; received medal and named Hon. Ancien, NATO Def. Coll., 1989. Mem. Coun. Fgn. Rels., Washington Inst. Fgn. Affairs, Internat. Studies Assn. (nat. pres. 1968-69), British International. Studies Assn., Cosmos Club (Washington), Phi Beta Kappa (pres. Gamma of Calif. 1957-58), Sigma Iota Rho (founder).

OLSON, WILLIAM HENRY, neurology educator, administrator; b. Haxtun, Colo., Sept. 2, 1936; s. William Henry and Burdene (Anderson) O.; m. Shirley Gorden, July 24, 1967; children: Erik, Marnie. B.A., Wesleyan U., 1959; M.D., Harvard U., 1963. Diplomate: Am. Bd. Psychiatry and Neurology. Intern Beth Israel Hosp., Boston, 1963-65; resident Children's Hosp. Med. Ctr., Boston, 1965-67; staff assoc. NIH, Bethesda, Md., 1969-70; asst. prof. neurology and anatomy Vanderbilt U., Nashville, 1970-73, assoc. prof. neurology and anatomy, 1973-75; prof., chmn. dept. adult neurology U. N.D., Fargo, 1975-80; chmn., prof. dept. neurology U. Louisville, 1980—. Co-author: Practical Neurology and the Primary Care Physician, 1981, Symptom Oriented Neurology, 1994. Fulbright scholar Tubingen, Germany, 1958-59. Fellow Am. Acad. Neurology; mem. Phi Beta Kappa. Home: 331 Zorn Ave # 1 Louisville KY 40206-1542 Office: Univ Louisville Dept Neurology Louisville KY 40292

OLSON, WILLIAM JEFFREY, lawyer; b. Paterson, N.J., Oct. 23, 1949; s. Walter Justus and Viola Patricia (Trautvetter) O.; m. Janet Elaine Bollen, May 22, 1976; children: Robert J., Joanne C. AB, Brown U., 1971; JD, U. Richmond, 1976. Bar: Va. 1976, D.C. 1976, U.S. Ct. Claims 1976, U.S. Ct. Appeals (4th and D.C. cirs.) 1976, U.S. Supreme Ct. 1982. Assoc. Jackson & Campbell, Washington, 1976-79; ptnr. Gilman, Olson & Pangia, Washington, 1980-92; prin. William J. Olson PC, McLean, Va. and Washington, 1992—; sec., treas. bd. dirs. Victims Assistance Legal Orgn., Virginia Beach, Va., 1979—; presdl. transition team leader Legal Svcs. Corp., Washington, 1980; chmn. and bd. dirs. nat. Legal Svcs. Corp., 1981-82; mem. Pres.'s Export Coun. Subcom. on Export Adminstrn., Washington, 1982-84; spl. counsel bd. govs. U.S. Postal Svc., Washington, 1984-86. Author: Tuition Tax Credits and Alternatives, 1978; co-author: Debating National Health Policy, 1977. Trustee Davis Meml. Goodwill Industries, Washington, 1980-86, 88-93; chmn. Fairfax County Rep. Com., Fairfax, Va., 1980-82; mem. Rep. State Ctrl. Com., Richmond, Va., 1982-86. Mem. Va. Bar Assn., Assn. Trial Lawyers Am., Va. Trial Lawyers Assn., Christian Legal Soc. Republican. Baptist. Avocation: gardening. Office: 8180 Greensboro Dr Ste 1070 Mc Lean VA 22102-3823

OLSON-HELLERUD, LINDA KATHRYN, elementary school educator; b. Wisconsin Rapids, Wis., Aug. 26, 1947; d. Samuel Ellsworth and Lillian (Dvorak) Olson; m. H. A. Hellerud, 1979; 1 child, Sarah Kathryn. BS, U. Wis.-Stevens Point, 1969, teaching cert., 1970, MST, 1972; postgrad. U. Wis. at Madison, 1969-70; MS, U. Wis. Whitewater, 1975; EdS, U. Wis.-Stout, 1978; cert. k-12 reading tchr. and specialist. Clk., Univ. Counseling Ctr., U. Wis., Stevens Point, 1965-69; elementary sch. tchr., Wisconsin Rapids, 1970-76, sch. counselor, 1976-79, dist. elem. guidance dir., 1979-82, elem. and reading tchr., 1982—, also cons.; advocate Moravian Ch. Sunday sch. Mem. NEA, Wisconsin Rapids Edn. Assn., Internat. Reading Assn., Wis. Reading Assn., Ctrl. Wis. Reading Assn., Wis. State Hist. Soc., Wood County Hist. Soc., Wood County Literacy Coun. (cons.). Mem. United Ch. of Christ.Avocations: gardening, piano. Home: 1011 16th St S Wisconsin Rapids WI 54494-5371 Office: Howe Elem Sch Wisconsin Rapids WI 54494

OLSSON, ANN-MARGRET See ANN-MARGRET

OLSSON, BJÖRN ESKIL, railroad supply company executive; b. Kristianstad, Sweden, Oct. 7, 1945; came to U.S., 1990; m. Cecilia Lindblad, July 6, 1968; children: Fredrik, Karin, Eva. M Bus. and Adminstrn., U. Lund, Sweden, 1968. Internal auditor Kockums Mek. Verkstad, Malmö, Sweden, 1969-71, mgr. acctg., 1971-74; v.p. fin. and adminstrn. Kockums Industri, Söderhamn, Sweden, 1974-76, Linden Alimak, Skellefteå, Sweden, 1976-81, Sonessons, Malmö, 1981-82; pres. Sab-Nife, Malmö, 1982-87; v.p. corp. devel. Investment AB Cardo, Malmö, 1987-90; pres., CEO Harmon Industries Inc., Blue Springs, Mo., 1990—; bd. dirs. Deve Schindler, Stockholm, Green & Co., Malmö; mem. adv. bd. Ctrl. Mo. State U. Bus. Sch., Warrensburg, 1991—. Staff sgt. Swedish Army, 1964-65. Avocations: golf, skiing. Office: Harmon Industries Inc 1300 NW Jefferson Ct Blue Springs MO 64015-7265

OLSSON, CARL ALFRED, urologist; b. Boston, Nov. 29, 1938; s. Charles Rudolph and Ruth Marion (Bostrom) O.; m. Mary DeVore, Nov. 4, 1962; children: Ingrid, Leif Eric. Grad., Bowdoin Coll., 1959; MD, Boston U., 1963. Diplomate Am. Bd. Urology (trustee 1988-94, pres. 1993-94). Asst. prof. urology Boston U. Sch. Medicine, 1971-72, assoc. prof., 1972-74, prof., chmn. dept., 1974-80; dir. urology dept. Boston City Hosp., 1974-77; chief urology dept. Boston VA Med. Ctr., 1971-75; urologist-in-chief Univ. Hosp., Boston, 1971-80; John K. Lattimer prof., chmn. dept. urology Coll. Phys. and Surgs., Columbia U., N.Y.C., 1980—; dir. Squier Urol. Clinic, urology service Presbyn. Hosp., N.Y.C.; lectr. surgery Tufts U. Sch. Medicine. Boston Interhosp. Organ Bank, 1976-79; mem. working cadre Nat. Prostate Cancer Project, Nat. Cancer Inst., 1979-84; mem. adv. coun. Nat. Inst. Diabetes, Digestive Disease and Kidney. Editl. bd. Jour. Prostate, World Jour. Urology, Jour. Urodynamics and Neurourology, Jour. Urology; asst. editor Jour. Urology, 1978-89; contbr. chpts. to books, articles to med. jours. Recipient Disting. Alumnus award Boston U., 1985. Fellow ACS; mem. Am. Urol. Assn. (coord. continuing med. edn. New Eng. sect. 1977-80, del. rsch. com., Gold Cystoscope award 1979, Grayson-Carroll award 1971, 73), Boston Surg. Soc. (exec. com. 1976-80), Am. Assn. Clin. Urologists, Am. Surg. Assn., Am. Assn. Genitourinary Surgeons, Clin. Soc. Genitourinary Surgeons, Transplantation Soc., Soc. Urologic Oncology (pres. 1993), Soc. Univ. Urologists (pres. 1990), N.Y. Sect. Am. Urol. Assn., Am. Fertility Soc., AMA, Assn. Acad. Surgery, Am. Soc. Artificial Internal Organs, Am. Soc. Transplant Surgeons, Assn. Med. Colls., Can. Urol. Assn., Societe Internationale d'Urologie, Internat. Urodynamics Soc., Mass. Med. Soc., Soc. Govt. Urologists, Australasian Urol. Soc. (hon.), New Eng. Handicapped Sportsmen's Assn. (exec. com. 1977-81), U.S. Yacht Racing Union, Yacht Racing Union L.I. Sound Club, N.Y. Yacht Club, Cottage Park Yacht Club, Larchmont Yacht Club, Storm Trysail Club, Alpha Omega Alpha. Episcopalian. Home: 18 Elm Ave Larchmont NY 10538-3649 Office: Columbia-Presbyn Hosp P&S Box 44 630 W 168th St New York NY 10032-3702

OLSSON, NILS WILLIAM, former association executive; b. Seattle, June 11, 1909; s. Nils A. and Mathilda (Lejkell) O.; m. Dagmar T. Gavert, June 15, 1940; children: Karna B., Nils G. and Pehr C. (twins). Student, North Park Coll., Chgo., Northwestern U., U. Minn., 1929-34; A.M., U. Chgo., 1938, Ph.D., 1949; Ph.D., U. Uppsala, Sweden, 1968; LHD, North Park Coll., Chgo., 1990. Admissions counselor, instr. Swedish North Park Coll., 1937-39; asst. Scandinavian U. Chgo., 1939-42, instr., 1945-50, asst. prof., 1950; mem. U.S. diplomatic service, 1950-67; 2d sec., pub. affairs officer Am. legation, Reykjavik, Iceland, 1950-52; attache, pub. affairs officer Am. embassy, Stockholm, Sweden, 1952-55; 1st sec., consul Am. embassy, 1955-57; pub. affairs adviser Dept. State, 1957-59; chief Am. sponsored schs. abroad, 1959-62; 1st sec. Am. embassy, Oslo, Norway, 1962-64; counselor for polit. affairs Am. embassy, 1964-66; diplomat in residence Ind. U., 1966-67; dir. Am. Swedish Inst., Mpls., 1967-73; exec. dir. Swedish Council of Am., 1973-84. Author: Swedish Passenger Arrivals in New York 1820-1850, 1967, Swedish Passenger Arrivals in U.S. Ports (except New York) 1820-1850, 1979, Tracing Your Swedish Ancestry, 1974, (with Erik Wiken) Swedish Passenger Arrivals in the U.S. 1820-1850, 1995; editor: A Pioneer in Northwest America, 1841-1858, vol. I, 1950, vol. II, 1959, Veckobladet, 1934-35; editor, pub.: Swedish American Genealogist, 1981—; editor: A Swedish City Directory of Boston 1881, 1986; contbr. to hist. and ednl. jours. Mem. bd. Evang. Covenant Hist. Commn., Chgo., 1958; asst. naval attache Am. legation, Stockholm, 1943-45. Served from lt. (j.g.) to lt. comdr. USNR, 1942-45. Decorated knight Order Vasa 1st class, knight comdr. Order North Star, Sweden; recipient Swedish Pioneer Centennial medal, 1948; King Carl XVI Gustaf Bicentennial Gold medal, Carl Sandburg medal Swedish Pioneer Hist. Soc., 1982, Charlotta medal Emigrant Inst. Växjö, Sweden; named Swedish Am. of Yr. Stockholm, 1969; recipient Hans Mattsson Plaque, Önnestad, Sweden, 1992; Victor Örnberg prize, Sweden, 1994. Fellow Geneal. Soc. (Finland), Geneal. Soc. (Sweden), Am. Soc. Genealogists; mem. Wermländska Sällskapet Stockholm (hon.), Nat. Geneal Soc., Carl Johan Soc. Sweden, Swedish-Am. Hist. Soc. (exec. sec. 1949-50, 57-68, pres. 1986-88), Royal Acad. Belles Lettres, History and Antiquities (Sweden, fgn. corr.), Pro Fide et Christianismo (Sweden, hon.), Royal Soc. Pub. Manuscripts Dealing with Scandinavian History (Sweden, fgn.). Clubs: Skylight (Mpls.); Grolier (N.Y.C.); Cosmos (Washington); Explorers (Central Fla.); Univ. (Winter Park, Fla.). Lodge: Rotary. Home: Winter Park Gardens Apt # G-21 700 Melrose Ave Winter Park FL 32789

OLSTAD, ROGER GALE, science educator; b. Mpls., Jan. 16, 1934; s. Arnold William and Myra (Stroschein) O.; m. Constance Elizabeth Jackson, Aug. 20, 1955; children: Karen Louise, Kenneth Bradley. B.S., U. Minn., 1955, M.A., 1959, Ph.D., 1963. Instr. U. Minn., Mpls., 1956-63; asst. prof. U. Ill., Urbana, 1963-64; mem. faculty U. Wash., Seattle, 1964—; asso. prof. sci. edn. U. Wash., 1967-71, prof., 1971-95, asso. dean grad. studies Coll. Edn., 1971-85; prof. emeritus, 1995—. Fellow AAAS; mem. NSTA (bd. dirs.) Wash. Sci. Tchrs. Assn. (pres. 1973-74), Nat. Assn. Rsch. Sci. Teaching (pres. 1977-78, bd. dirs.), N.W. Sci. Assn. (chmn. 1966-68), Assn. Edn. Tchrs. in Sci. (regional pres. 1966-68, pres. 1991-92), Nat. Assn. Biology Tchrs., Biol. Scis. Curriculum Study (chmn., bd. dirs. 1989-94), U. Wash. Faculty Club, Phi Delta Kappa. Home: 20143 53rd Ave NE Seattle WA 98155-1801 Office: U Wash Coll Edn Seattle WA 98195

OLSTOWSKI, FRANCISZEK, chemical engineer, consultant; b. N.Y.C., Apr. 23, 1927; s. Franciszek and Marguerite (Stewart) O.; A.A., Monmouth Coll., 1950; BSCE, Tex. A&M U., 1954; m. Rosemary Sole, May 19, 1952; children: Marguerita Antonina, Anna Rosa, Franciszek, Anton, Henryk Alexander. Research and devel. engr. Dow Chem. Co., Freeport, Tex., 1954-56, project leader, 1956-65, sr. research engr., 1965-72, research specialist, 1972-79, research leader, 1979-87; dir. Tech. Cons. Services, Freeport, 1987—. Lectr. phys. scis. elementary and intermediate schs., Freeport, 1961-85. Vice chmn. Freeport Traffic Commn., 1974-76, chmn., 1976-79, vice-chmn. 1987-89, chmn., 1989-92. With USNR, 1944-46. Fellow Am. Inst. Chemist; mem. AAAS, Am. Chem. Soc., Electrochem. Soc. (sec. treas. South Tex. sect. 1963-64, vice chmn. 1964-65, chmn. 1965-67, councillor 1967-70), N.Y. Acad. Sci, Velasco Cemetery Assn. (sec.-treas. 1992-95). Patentee in synthesis of fluorocarbons, natural graphite products, electrolytic prodn. magnesium metal and polyurethane tech.

OLSZEWSKI, EDWARD JOHN, art history educator; b. Detroit, Jan. 7, 1937; s. John Peter and Mary Catherine (Kaminski) O.; m. I. Monica Foltarz (dec.). BS, U. Detroit, 1958, MS, 1962; PhD, U. Ill., 1964, U. Minn., 1974. Rsch. assoc. prof. U. South Fla., Tampa, 1964-65; rsch. chemist Archer Daniels Midland, Mpls., 1965-68; asst. prof. art history Case Western Res. U., Cleve., 1971-77, assoc. prof., 1977-89, prof., 1989—. Author: Art of Painting, 1977, Draftsman's eye, 1981, Drawings in Midwestern collections, 1996. Fellow NEH, 1979, Fulbright-Hays fellow, 1980, fellow Gladys Krieble Delmas Found., 1986. Mem. Coll. Art Assn., Midwest Art History Soc. (pres. 1981-84), Renaissance Soc. Am. Avocation: travel. Office: Case Western Reserve U University Cir Cleveland OH 44106

OLTMAN, C. DWIGHT, conductor, educator; b. Imperial, Nebr., May 27, 1936; s. George L. and Lois Beryl (Wine) O.; m. Shirley Jean Studebaker, May 30, 1966; children—Michelle Leigh, Nicole Alicia. B.S., McPherson Coll., 1958; M.Mus., Wichita State U., 1963; postgrad., U. Cin., 1967-70; student, Nadia Boulanger, Paris, 1960, Pierre Monteux, 1963. Asst. prof. music Manchester Coll., North Manchester, Ind., 1963-67; prof. of conducting, music dir. symphony orch. and Bach Festival Baldwin-Wallace Coll., Berea, Ohio, 1970—; music dir. Ohio Chamber Orch., Cleve., 1972-92, laureate conductor, 1992—; music dir., prin. condr. Cleve. Ballet, 1976—; music dir. Cullowhee Music Festival, N.C., 1977-79; guest conductor Europe, Can., U.S.A. Mem. Am. Symphony Orch. League, Conductor's Guild. Democrat. Avocations: reading; walking; theater; spectator sports. Home and Office: 21631 Cedar Branch Trl Strongsville OH 44136-1287

OLTZ, RICHARD JOHN, minister, publishing executive; b. Duluth, Minn., Sept. 20, 1945; s. Donald F. and Helen J. (Richardson) O.; m. Mary Jane Willman, June 1969; children: Shawn Richard, Jennifer Marie. Student, Olivet Coll., 1963-64; pastorial ministries, Berean Coll., 1980-83, counseling, 1984. Sr. pastor First Missionary Ch., Bad Axe, Mich., 1985-87; exec. dir. Bethel Pub., Elkhart, Ind., 1987—; sr. pastor Grace Chapel, N. Liberty, Ind., 1990—; pastor Oslo Missionary Ch., Elkhart, 1995. Mem. Christian Booksellers Assn., Anabaptist Pubs., Christian Mgmt. Assn., Evang. Christian Pubs. Assn., Am. Assn. Christian Counselors. Office: Bethel Pub Co 1819 S Main St Elkhart IN 46516-4212 *No matter how successful life may appear to be, no matter what you may have accomplished, God must get all the glory or you will have labored in vain.**

OLVER, JOHN WALTER, congressman; b. Honesdale, Pa., Sept. 3, 1936; s. Helen Fulleborn Olver; m. Rose Alice Richardson, Sept. 12, 1959; children: Martha. BS, Rensselaer Poly. Inst., 1955; MS, Tufts U., 1956; PhD, MIT, 1961. Asst. prof. chemistry, U. Mass., Amherst, 1962-68; mem. Mass. Ho. of Reps., Boston, 1969-72, Mass. Senate, 1973-91; mem. 101st-105th Congresses from 1st Mass. dist., 1991—, mem. com. on appropriations, mem. subcoms. on transp. and mil. constrn. Contbr. articles to profl. jours. Democrat. Avocations: hiking; gardening; tennis. Office: US Ho of Reps 1027 Longworth HOB Washington DC 20515-2101

OLVER, MICHAEL LYNN, lawyer; b. Seattle, June 22, 1950; s. Manley Deforest and Geraldine (Robinson) O.; m. Wendy Kay, July 6, 1974; children: Erin, Christina. BA, U. Wash., 1972; JD, Calif. Western Sch. of Law, 1976. Assoc. Robbins, Merrick & Kraft, Seattle, 1976-77; lawyer, sole practitioner Michael L. Olver, Seattle, 1977-80; ptnr., pres. Merrick & Olver, P.S., Seattle, 1980—; bd. dirs. Found. for Handicapped, Seattle, 1988-93; commr. pro tem Ex part Dept. King County Superior Ct., Seattle, 1992—. Author: Wills and Trusts for the Disabled, 1989, Living Trusts--Pros and Cons, 1992, Special Needs Trusts After OBRA '93, 1994, Bascomb's Rogue, 1994, Medicaid Lien Recovery, 1994, Medicaid Trusts and Lien Recovery, 1995, Sole Support Trusts, 1995, Nursing Home Litigation, 1996, Community Spousal Sole Benefit Trusts, 1996, Complex Trial Issues, GAL Training, 1996, others; editor Calif. Western Internat. Law Jour., 1975-76. Chmn. Ann. Cath. Appeal, Assumption Parish, Seattle, 1989-90. Mem. Nat. Acad. Elder Law Attys. (dir. Wash. chpt. 1994—), Wash. State Trial Lawyers Assn. Office: Merrick & Olver PS 9222 Lake City Way NE Seattle WA 98115-3268

OLWIN, JOHN HURST, surgeon; b. Robinson, Ill., May 28, 1907; s. Charles Hurst and Etta (Campbell) O.; m. Betty Smothers, Apr. 17, 1943; children: Holly Corinne, Barbara Hurst. BA, U. Ill., 1929; MD, U. Chgo., 1934. Diplomate: Am. Bd. Surgery. Intern Presbyn. Hosp., Chgo., 1935-36, surg. resident, 1937-39; practice in Chgo., 1938—; clin. prof. surgery Rush Med. Coll., 1942—; attending surgeon Presbyn.-St. Luke's Hosp., Chgo., Rush North Shore Med. Ctr.; clin. prof. surgery U. Ill. Coll. Medicine, 1959-71; chmn., dir. TEI Analytical Inc., 1970—. Contbr. more than 175 articles to profl. jours. Bd. dirs. Vascular Disease Rsch. Found., 1963—. Lt. col. M.C., AUS, 1940-46. Decorated Bronze Star. Mem. AMA, Chgo., Western, Central surg. assns., Soc. Vascular Surgery (recorder 1960-66), Internat. Cardiovascular Soc., Internat. Surg. Soc. Episcopalian (warden). Home: 1508 Hinman Ave Evanston IL 60201-4664 Office: 9631 Gross Point Rd Skokie IL 60076-1264

OLYPHANT, DAVID, cultural, educational association executive; b. N.Y.C., Feb. 3, 1936; s. John Kensett Olyphant and Adele (Hammond) Emery; m. Pamela Moore, Apr. 27, 1962 (div. Aug. 1988); children: Hillary, Fanny, David K., Elgin, Flora; m. Tatyana Doughty, Oct. 22, 1988. BA, Harvard U., 1958. V.p. Citibank, N.Y.C., 1959-75; ptnr. Harold Denton Assocs., Princeton, N.J., 1975-76; owner/operator Cluaran Farm, Pittstown, N.J., 1976-87; exec. dir., sec. The English Speaking Union US, N.Y.C., 1987-93; dir. Plays For Living, Inc., N.Y.C.; treas./sec. Am. Trust for The British Libr., 1992—. Fellow Met. Mus. Art (life), NAD (life); mem. St. Andrew's Soc. (life), Harvard Club of N.Y., Porcellian Club (Cambridge, Mass.), The Pilgrims of the U.S. Republican. Presbyterian. Office: The English-Speaking Union US 16 E 69th St New York NY 10021-4906

O'MAHONEY, ROBERT M., retired lawyer; b. Indpls., Jan. 4, 1925; s. Joseph Francis and Evelyn (O'Connor) O'M.; m. Mary C. Mitchell, Sept. 12, 1953; children: Terrance M., Patrick J., Mary E., Susan M., Sharon A. B.S., Purdue U., 1948; J.D., Georgetown U., 1954. Bar: D.C. 1954, Ind. 1954, U.S. Supreme Ct. 1959. Assoc. Ross McCord, Ice and Miller, Indpls., 1954-55; dep. atty. gen. Ind., 1954-59; gen. counsel Def. Air Transp. Adminstrn., 1959; dep. asst. gen. counsel for transp. Dept. Commerce, 1959-66; adviser to dep. asst. sec. state for transp. and communications, 1966-67; asst. gen. counsel Fed. Hwy. Adminstrn., 1968-69; commr. transp. and telecommunications service GSA, 1969-73; transp. cons. EPA, 1973; atty. Fed. Power Commn., Washington, 1973-77, Fed. Energy Regulatory Commn., Washington, 1977-80; sales assoc. Shannon & Luchs, Potomac, Md., 1980-83, Merrill Lynch Realty, Potomac, Md., 1983-85, Long & Foster Realtors, Rockville, Md., 1985-86. Co-author: Great Lakes Pilotage Act, 1960. Served with USAAF, 1943-45; Served with USAF, 1950-52. Decorated Air medal with oak leaf cluster. Mem. Phi Alpha Delta. Republican. Roman Catholic.

O'MALLEY, BERT WILLIAM, cell biologist, educator, physician; b. Pitts., Dec. 19, 1936; s. Bert Alloysius O'M.; m. Sally Ann Johnson; children: Sally Ann, Bert A., Rebecca, Erin K. BS, U. Pitts., 1959, MD summa cum laude, 1963; DSc (hon.), N.Y. Med. Coll., 1979, Nat. U. Ireland, 1985; MD (hon.), Karolinska Inst., Stockholm, 1984. Intern, resident Duke U., Durham, N.C., 1963-65; clin. assoc. Nat. Cancer Inst., NIH, Bethesda, Md., 1965-67, head molecular biology sect., endocrine br., 1967-69; Lucius Birch prof., dir. Reproductive Biology Ctr. Vanderbilt U. Sch. Medicine, Nashville, 1969-73; Tom Thompson prof., chmn. dept. cell biology Baylor Coll. Medicine, Houston, 1973—, Disting. Svc. prof., 1985, dir. Baylor Ctr. for Reproductive Biology, 1973—; mem. endocrine study sect., NIH, 1970-73, chmn., 1973-74; chmn. CETUS-UCLA Symposium on Gene Expression, 1982; con., mem. coun. rsch. and clin. investigation awards Am. Cancer Soc., 1985-87. Author: (with A.R. Means) Receptors for Reproductive Hormones, 1973, (with L. Birnbaumer) Hormone Action, vols. I and II, 1977, vol. III, 1978, (with A.M. Gotto) The Role of Receptors in Biology and Medicine, 1986; co-author: Methods in Enzymology: Hormone Action: Calmodulin and Calcium-Binding Proteins, 1983, Mechanism of Steriod Hormone Regulation of Gene Transcription, 1994; editor: Gene Regulation: UCLA Symposium on Molecular Cellular Biology, 1982; contbg. author to over 400 publs. Lt. comdr. USPHS, 1965-69. Recipient Ernst Oppenheimer award Am. Endocrine Soc., 1975, Gregory Pincus medal, 1975, Lila Gruber Cancer award, 1977, Disting. Achievement in Modern Medicine award, 1978, Borden award Assn. Am. Med. Colls., 1978, Dickson prize for Basic Med. Rsch., 1979, Philip S. Hench award U. Pitts., 1981, Axel Munthe Reproductive Biology award, Capri, Italy, 1982, Bicentennial Medallion of Distincton U. Pitts., 1987. Mem. AAAS, NAS, Inst. Med. NAS, Am. Soc. Biol. Chemists, Am. Acad. Arts and Scis., Endocrine Soc. (pres. 1985, Fred Conrad Koch medal 1988), Am. Soc. Clin. Investigation, Am. Inst. Chemists, Fedn. Clin. Rsch., Harvey Soc., Alpha Epsilon Delta, Phi Beta Kappa, Alpha Omega Alpha. Democrat. Roman Catholic. Office: Baylor Coll Medicine Dept Neuroscience One Baylor Pla Houston TX 77030-3411

O'MALLEY, CARLON MARTIN, judge; b. Phila., Sept. 7, 1929; s. Carlon Martin and Lucy (Bol) O'M.; m. Mary Catherine Lyons, Aug. 17, 1957; children: Carlon Martin III, Kathleen B. O'Malley Aikman, Harry Tighe, John Todd, Cara M. B.A., Pa. State U., 1951; LL.B., Temple U., 1954. Bar: Pa. 1955, Fla. 1973, U.S. Supreme Ct. 1973. Practiced law, 1957-61; asst. U.S. atty. for Middle Dist. Pa., Dept. Justice, 1961-69, U.S. atty., 1979-82; ptnr. O'Malley & Teets, 1970-72, O'Malley, Jordan & Mullaney (and predecessor firms), 1976-79; pvt. practice Pa. and Fla., 1972-79, 82-87; judge Ct. Common Pleas of Lackawanna County (45th Judicial Dist.), 1987—; dir. pub. safety City of Scranton, 1983-86; lectr. Lackawanna Jr. Coll., 1982-86. Editorial bd.: Temple Law Rev, 1952-53. Pres. Lackawanna County (Pa.) unit Am. Cancer Soc., 1966-67; bd. dirs. Pa. Cancer Soc., 1967-68, Lackawanna county chpt. ARC, 1967-69; mem. solicitation team, govtl. divsn. Lackawanna United Fund, 1963-68, B.P.O.E. Judiciary Com., 1985-89, 94-95, justice grand forum B.P.O.E., 1995—; chmn. profl. divsn. Greater Scranton (Pa.) YMCA Membership Drives; trustee Everhart Mus., Scranton, 1987—; justice Grand Forum Elks, 1991, chief justice, 1992-93. Pilot USAF, 1955-57, Pa. N.G., 1957-59. Mem. Am. Judges Assn., Nat. Assn. Former U.S. Attys., Pa. Bar Assn., Lackawanna County Bar Assn., Fla. Bar Assn., Country Club of Scranton, Elks (pres. Pa. chpt. 1978-79), K.C., Phi Kappa (pres.), Delta Theta Phi (pres.). Democrat. Office: Judges Chambers Lackawanna County Courthouse Scranton PA 18503

O'MALLEY, EDWARD, physician, consultant; b. Hudson, N.Y., May 30, 1926; s. Thomas Patrick and Helen Mary (Cornell) O. BS, St. John's U., Bklyn., N.Y., 1949; MS, Loyola U., Chgo., 1952, PhD, 1954; MD, SUNY, Bklyn., 1958. Diplomate Am. Bd. Forensic Examiners. Psychiat. cons. dept. of corrections N.Y.C., 1962-68; psychiatrist Cath. Charities, N.Y.C., 1963-68; dir. of mental health Suffolk County Govt., Hauppauge, N.Y., 1968-70; commr. of mental health Orange County, Goshen, N.Y., 1970-72; dir. drug abuse services State of N.Y., Bronx, 1972-78; lic. sch. psychiatrist N.Y.C. Bd. of Edn., 1962-82; chief psychiatry services VA, Huntington, W.Va., 1982-86; med. cons. State of Calif., San Diego, 1986—, psychiat. cons. dept. of corrections, 1987—; asst. prof. psychiatry N.J. Med. Sch., Newark, 1975—; examiner Am. Bd. of Psychiatry and Neurology, Los Angeles, 1980; assoc. prof. psychiatry U. Calif., San Diego, 1980—; prof. psychiatry Marshall U. Sch. of Medicine, Huntington, 1982-86; dir. com. on sea cadets Navy League, San Diego, 1987—; cons. HHS, Social Security Adminstrn., Office of Hearings and Appeals, 1989—. Contbr. articles to profl. jours. Bd. dirs. Suffolk Community Council, Hauppauge, 1968-70, United Fund of Long Island, Huntington, 1968-70. Served to capt. USN, 1978-81. Scholar N. Y. State Coll., 1946-49, SUNY Joseph Collins Med. Sch., 1955-58; Teaching and Research fellow Loyola U., 1952-54. Fellow Am. Psychiat. Assn.; mem. San Diego Psychiat. Soc., Soc. of Med. Cons. to the Armed Forces, Soc. of Mil. Surgeons of U.S.A., N.Y. Celtic Med. Soc., Union Am. Physicians and Dentists (steward 1990—), State Employed Physicians Assn. (bd. dirs. 1993—). Roman Catholic. Home: 3711 Alcott St San Diego CA 92106-1212

O'MALLEY, JAMES TERENCE, lawyer; b. Omaha, Nov. 24, 1950; s. John Austin and Mayme Bernice (Zentner) O'M.; m. Colleen L. Kizer, May 22, 1972; children: Erin C., Michael B., James P. BA magna cum laude, U. Notre Dame, 1972; JD, Stanford U., 1975. Bar: Calif. 1975. Ptnr. Gray, Cary, Ames & Frye, San Diego, 1975-87, of counsel, 1987-91, ptnr., 1991—; vice chmn., exec. v.p., gen. counsel Noble Broadcast Group, Inc., San Diego, 1987-91; chmn. CEO Gray Care Ware & Freidenrich PC, San Diego, 1996—. Bd. dirs. Children's Mus., San Diego, 1986-87, Am. Ireland Fund. Mem. Am. Judicature Soc., San Diego Taxpayers Assn. (pres. 1986-87), Order of Coif. Avocation: jogging, music. Office: Gray Cary Ware & Freidenrich PC 401 B St San Diego CA 92101-4223

O'MALLEY, JOHN DANIEL, law educator, banker; b. Chgo., Dec. 18, 1926; s. William D. and Paula A. (Skaugh) O'M.; m. Caroline Tyler Taylor, July 12, 1958; children: John Daniel, Taylor John. Grad., St. Thomas Mil. Acad., 1945; B.S., Loyola U., Chgo., 1950, M.A., 1952, J.D., 1953; grad., U.S. Army Intelligence Sch., 1962, Command & Gen. Staff Coll., 1965. Bar: Ill. 1953, Mich. 1954, U.S. Supreme Ct. 1962. Asst. prof. law Loyola U., 1953-59, asso. prof., 1959-65; formerly spl. counsel and bond claims mgr. Fed. Ins. Co.; prof. law Loyola U. Grad. Sch. Bus., 1965—, chmn. dept. law, 1968-86; trust officer, v.p. First Nat. Bank Highland Park (Ill.), Marina City Bank, Chgo., Hyde Park Bank & Trust Co., 1970-75; exec. v.p. Harris Bank Winnetka, Ill., 1975-95. Author: Subrogation Against Banks on Forged Checks, 1967, Common Check Frauds and the Uniform Commercial Code, 1969; Contbr. articles to profl. jours. and law revs. Served to maj. AUS, 1945-47, 61-62. Decorated Army Commendation medal; knight grand officer Papal Order of Holy Sepulchre, Knight Comdr. with star Constantinian Order of St. George (Italy), knight Order of St. Maurice and St. Lazarus (Italy). Mem. ABA, Chgo., Ill., Mich. bar assns., Chgo. Crime Commn., French Nat. Hon. Soc., Am., Chgo. bus. law assns., Mil. Govt. Assn. Home: 1040 Chestnut Ave Wilmette IL 60091-1732 Office: Loyola U 820 N Michigan Ave Chicago IL 60611-2103

O'MALLEY, JOHN PATRICK, dean; b. Hoosick Falls, N.Y., Nov. 27, 1928; s. Thomas Joseph and Mary Alice (Mulvihill) O.'M.; m. Margaret Parlin, June 24, 1989. BA, Villanova U., 1950; MA, PhD, Cath. U., 1969. Tchr. Archbishop Carroll High Sch., Washington, 1954-68, prin., 1987-89; asst. prof. Cath. U., Washington, 1968-69; asst. prof. Merrimack Coll., North Andover, Mass., 1969-74, dean humanities, 1976-78; chair edn. dept. Emmanuel Coll., Boston, 1974-76; dean coll. arts and scis. Villanova (Pa.) U., 1978-84; provost St. Thomas U., Miami, Fla., 1985-86; assoc. prof. Widener U., Chester, Pa., 1990—. Editor: Non-Fiction, Books I and II, 1968. Mem. Assn. Tchr. Edn., Middle Atlantic States Philosophy of Edn. Soc., ASCD, Assn. Ind. Liberal Arts Colls. for Tchr. Edn. Home: 64 Crestline Rd Wayne PA 19087-2669 Office: Widener U 1 University Pl Chester PA 19013

O'MALLEY, JOSEPH JAMES, lawyer; b. Wilkes-Barre, Pa., Oct. 24, 1923; s. Edward Leo and Mary Catherine (Moran) O'M.; m. Helen Alberta Hyde, Mar. 21, 1952 (div. Jan. 1979); children: Patricia, Katherine, Sharon, Edward, Joseph James; m. Theresa Hernandez, Jan. 20, 1979 (div. Dec. 1995); 1 child, James Christopher; m. Constance R. McKenney, Feb. 15, 1997. B.A., U. Scranton, 1946; J.D., Georgetown U., 1956. Bar: D.C. 1956, Calif., 1977, U.S. Supreme Ct. 1967. Sr. trial atty. antitrust div. Dept. Justice, Washington, 1957-65; assoc. chief counsel Comptroller of Currency, Washington, 1965-68; asst. dir. FTC, Washington, 1968-76; ptnr. Paul, Hastings, Janofsky & Walker, Los Angeles, 1976-94; pvt. practice Glendale, Calif., 1994—; guest lectr. Georgetown U., 1966-68. Mem. ABA, L.A. County Bar Assn. (exec. com. antitrust sect. 1990—), KC (grand knight 1963-64, state dep. 1971). Office: Law Offices Joseph O'Malley 801 N Brand Blvd Ste 950 Glendale CA 91203-1243

O'MALLEY, KATHLEEN M., federal judge; b. 1956. AB magna cum laude, Kenyon Coll., 1979; JD, Case Western Reserve, 1982. Law clk. to Hon. Nathaniel R. Jones U.S. Ct. of Appeals, 6th circuit, 1982-83; with Jones, Day, Reavis & Pogue, Cleve., 1983-84, Porter, Wright, Morris & Arthur, Cleve., 1985-91; chief counsel, first asst. atty. gen., chief of staff Office of Atty. Gen., Columbus, 1991-94; district judge U.S. Dist. Ct. (Ohio no. dist.), 6th circuit, Cleve., 1994—. Mem. Am. Bar Assn., Fed. Bar Assn., Ohio State Bar Assn., Cleve. Bar Assn. Office: US Courthouse 201 Superior Ave E Ste 135 Cleveland OH 44114-1201*

O'MALLEY, KEVIN FRANCIS, lawyer, writer, educator; b. St. Louis, May 12, 1947; s. Peter Francis and Dorothy Margaret (Cradick) O'M.; m. Dena Hengen, Apr.2, 1971; children: Kevin Brendan, Ryan Michael. AB, St. Louis U., 1970, JD, 1973. Bar: Mo. 1973, U.S. Ct. Appeals D.C. 1974, U.S. Ct. Appeals (8th cir.) 1979, Ill. 1993. Trial lawyer U.S. Dept. Justice, Washington, 1973-74, Los Angeles, 1974-77, Phoenix, 1977-78; asst. U.S. atty. U.S. Dept. Justice, St. Louis, 1978-83; adj. prof. law St. Louis U., 1979—; lectr. Ctrl. and Ea. European Law Initiative, Russian Fedn., 1996. Author: (with Devitt, Blackmar, O'Malley) Federal Jury Practice and Instruction, 1990, 92; contbr. articles to law books and jours. Community amb. Expt. in Internat. Living, Prague, Czechoslovakia, 1968; bd. dirs. St. Louis-Galway (Ireland) Sister Cities. Capt. U.S. Army, 1973. Recipient Atty. Gen.'s Disting. Service award U.S. Dept. Justice, 1977, John J. Dwyer Meml. Scholarship award, 1967-70. Mem. ABA (chmn. govt. litigation counsel com. 1982-86, chmn. jud. com. 1986-87, chmn. com. on ind. and small firms, chmn. trial practice com. 1991-94, health care litigation 1994—), Am. Law Inst., Met. Bar Assn. St. Louis (chmn. criminal law sect.), Nat. Inst. Trial Advocacy, Mo. Athletic Club. Roman Catholic. Office: 10 S Brentwood Blvd Ste 102 Saint Louis MO 63105-1694

O'MALLEY, MARJORIE GLAUBACH, health care executive; b. Orange, N.J., Apr. 28, 1950; d. Robert M. and Joanne (Weil) Glaubach; m. Charles A. O'Malley III, Dec. 27, 1969; children: Gregory, Ashley. BA in Econs., U. Pa., 1969. With Old Stone Bank, Providence, 1970-75, v.p., 1975-76; sr. v.p., treas. Old Stone Bank and Old Stone Corp., Providence, 1976-80; dir. corp. fin. Conn. Gen. Corp., Hartford, 1980-81; 2d v.p., dept. head mktg. pensions Cigna Corp., Hartford, 1981-85, v.p. fin. employee benefit group, 1985-89; v.p. corp. acctg. and planning Cigna Corp., 1989-90; v.p., contr. employee benefits div. Cigna Corp., Hartford, 1990-92, pres. Rx Prime, 1993-95; pres. Strategic Healthcare Cons., Avon, Conn., 1995—. Mem. health Planning Coun. R.I., 1976-79, Statewide Planning Coun. R.I., 1978; mem. bd. Health Sys. Agy.-North Cen. Conn., Hartford, 1980. Mem. Life Ins. Mktg. and Rsch. Assn. (chmn. group and pension com. 1989), New Eng. Econ. Project (bd. mem. 1976-79, treas. 1978-79). Home: 23 Henley Way Avon CT 06001-4067 Office: Strategic Healthcare Cons 23 Henley Way Avon CT 06001-4067

O'MALLEY, PATRICIA, critical care nurse; b. Boston, May 13, 1955; d. Peter and Catherine (Dwyer) O'M. BSN, Coll. Mt. St. Joseph, Cin., 1977; MS, Ohio State U., 1984, postgrad., 1990—. Cert. critical care nurse. Primary nurse critical care unit Miami Valley Hosp., Dayton, Ohio, nurse educator, clin. nurse specialist, cons.; adj. faculty Wright State U., Dayton. Contbr. articles to profl. jours., textbooks. Recipient honors Dayton Area Heart Assn., Ohio Ho. of Reps., 1994, Ohio Dept. Health, 1996. Mem. AACN (bd. dirs. Dayton-Miami Valley), Soc. Critical Care Medicine, Midwest Nursing Rsch. Soc., Sigma Theta Tau. Office: Miami Valley Hosp 1 Wyoming St Dayton OH 45409-2722

O'MALLEY, PETER, professional baseball club executive; b. N.Y.C., Dec. 12, 1937; s. Walter F. and Kay (Hanson) O'M.; m. Annette Zacho, July 10, 1971; children: Katherine, Kevin, Brian. B.S. in Econs, U. Pa., 1960. Dir. Dodgertown, Vero Beach, Fla., 1962-64; pres., gen. mgr. Spokane Baseball Club, 1965-66; v.p. Los Angeles Dodgers Baseball Club, 1967-68, exec. v.p., from 1968; pres. Los Angeles Dodgers, Inc., 1970—, also bd. dirs.; bd. dirs. Tidings newspaper. Bd. dirs. L.A. Police Meml. Found., L.A. World Affairs Coun., Jackie Robinson Found., L.A.-Gungzhou (Republic of China) Sister City Assn., Amateur Athletic Found.; pres. Little League Found.; active L.A. County Bd. Govs., Music Ctr., So. Calif. Com. for the Olympic Games. Mem. Korean-Am. C. of C. of L.A. Office: LA Dodgers 1000 Elysian Park Ave Los Angeles CA 90012-1112*

O'MALLEY, ROBERT EDMUND, JR., mathematics educator; b. Rochester, N.H., May 23, 1939; s. Robert E. and Jeanette A. (Dubois) O'M.; m. Candace G. Hinz, Aug. 31, 1968; children: Patrick, Timothy, Daniel. B.S. in Elec. Engring., U. N.H., 1960, M.S., 1961; Ph.D., Stanford U., 1966. Mathematician Bell Labs., Gen. Electric Research Co., RCA, summers 1961-63; asst. prof. U. N.C., Chapel Hill, 1965-66; vis. mem. Courant Inst., NYU, 1966-67; research mem. Math. Research Ctr., Madison, Wis., 1967-68; asst. prof., assoc. prof. NYU, N.Y.C., 1968-73; prof. math. U. Ariz., Tucson, 1973-81, chmn. applied math. program, 1976-81; prof. math. Rensselaer Poly. Inst., Troy, N.Y., 1981-90, chmn. dept. math. scis., 1981-84, Ford Found. prof., 1989-90; prof., chair applied math. U. Wash., Seattle, 1990-93, prof., 1993—; sr. vis. fellow U. Edinburgh, (Scotland), 1971-72; guest prof. Tech. U. Vienna, 1987-88; vis. Univ. Lyon 1 and Univ. of Cambridge, 1994-95. Author: Introduction to Singular Perturbations, 1974; editor: Asymptotic Methods and Singular Perturbations, 1976, Singular Perturbation Methods for Ordinary Differential Equations, 1991, ICIAM 91 procs., Thinking About Ordinary Differential Equations, 1997; contbr. numerous articles to profl. jours. Mem. Soc. for Indsl. and Applied Math. (pres. 1991-92), Am. Math. Soc. Roman Catholic. Home: 3415 W Laurelhurst Dr NE Seattle WA 98105-5345 Office: U Wash Dept Applied Math FS # 20 Seattle WA 98195

O'MALLEY, SEAN, bishop; b. Lakewood, Ohio, June 29, 1944. Ed., St. Fidelis Sem., Herman, Pa., Capuchin Coll. and Cath. U., Washington. Ordained priest Roman Cath. Ch., 1970. Episcopal vicar of priests serving Spanish speakin Washington archdiocese, 1978-84; exec. dir. Spanish Cath. Ctr., Washington, from 1973; bishop Roman Cath. Ch., St. Thomas, V.I., 1985-92, Fall River, NH, 1992—. Office: Bishop of Fall River PO Box 2577 47 Underwood St Fall River MA 02722*

O'MALLEY, SUSAN, professional basketball team executive. Degree in Bus. and Finance, Mt. St. Mary's, 1983. Dir. advt. Washington Bullets, 1986-87, dir. mktg., 1987-88, exec. v.p., 1988-91, pres., 1991—; pres. Washington Capitals, 1995-96. Avocations: tennis, vacations. Office: Washington Bullets USAir Arena Landover MD 20785*

O'MALLEY, THOMAS ANTHONY, gastroenterologist, internist; b. St. Helens, Lancashire, Eng., Jan. 21, 1932; s. Michael and Margaret (Melia) O'M.; m. Margaret May O'Kane, Apr. 7, 1958 (dec. Apr. 1985); m. Marianne Rapier, Jan. 23, 1988; children: Anne, Patricia, Katherine, Jane, Margaret. MBChB, U. Liverpool, Eng., 1956; Lic. Medicine, U. State N.Y., 1964. Diplomate Am. Bd. Internal Medicine, State Bd. Med. Examiners Fla. House physician Royal Infirmary, Liverpool, 1956-57; house surgeon Royal Liverpool Children's Hosp., 1957; resident in medicine C.S. Wilson Meml. Hosp., Johnson City, N.Y., 1957-58; fellow internal medicine Lahey Clinic, Boston, 1958-59; USPHS trainee in gastroenterology U. Rochester (N.Y.), Strong Meml. Hosp., 1959-60; chief resident medicine/Segal Watson fellow gastroenterology Genesee Hosp., Rochester, 1960-61; gastroenterologist Cancer Clinic, Regina, Sask., Can., 1963; asst. dir. med. edn. Genesee Hosp., U. Rochester, 1967-72; clin. assoc. prof. medicine U. South Fla., Tampa,

1973—; chief medicine Sarasota (Fla.) Meml. Hosp., 1973, Doctors Hosp., Sarasota, 1985. With RAF, 1961-62. Recipient Physician of Yr. award Doctors Hosp. Sarasota, 1985. Fellow ACP, Am. Coll. Gastroenterology, Chevalier du Tastevin (comdr. 1985—), Cavalieri del Vini Nobili (amb. 1989—, pres. 1997). Office: O'Malley & Hall MD PA 2650 Bahia Vista St Sarasota FL 34239-2635

O'MALLEY, THOMAS D., diversified company executive; b. N.Y.C., 1941. Grad., Manhattan Coll., 1963. Vice chmn., dir. Salomon, Inc. (formerly Phibro-Salomon, Inc.), N.Y.C.; former chmn., chief exec. officer, pres. Phibro Energy Inc., Greenwich, Conn.; chmn. Argus Investments (formerly Argus Resources), Stamford, Conn., from 1987; now chmn., chief exec. officer Tosco Corp., Conn. Office: Tosco Corp Hdqrs 72 Cummings Point Rd Stamford CT 06902-7919*

O'MALLEY, THOMAS PATRICK, academic administrator; b. Milton, Mass., Mar. 1, 1930; s. Austin and Ann Marie (Feeney) O'M. BA, Boston Coll., 1951; MA, Fordham U., 1953; STL, Coll. St.-Albert de Louvain, 1962; LittD, U. Nijmegen, 1967; LLD (hon.), John Carroll U., 1988. Entered Soc. of Jesus, 1952. Instr. classics Coll. of Holy Cross, Worcester, Mass., 1956-58; asst. prof., chmn. dept. classics Boston Coll., 1967-69, assoc. prof., chmn. dept. theology, 1969-73; dean Boston Coll. (Coll. Arts and Scis.), 1973-80; pres. John Carroll U., Cleve., 1980-88; vis. prof. Cath. Inst. W. Africa, 1988-89; assoc. editor AMERICA, N.Y.C., 1989-90; rector Jesuit Com. Fairfield U., 1990-91; pres. Loyola Marymount U., L.A., 1991—. Author: Tertullian and the Bible, 1967. Trustee Boston Theol. Inst., 1969-73, Fairfield U., 1971-82, 89-91, John Carroll U., 1976-88, Xavier U., 1980-86, U. Detroit, 1982-88, Boston Coll. H.S., 1986-88, Boys Hope, 1986-88, Loyola Marymount U., 1991—, St. Joseph's U., 1996—. Mem. AAUP, Soc. Bibl. Lit., N.Am. Patristic Soc.

OMAN, HENRY, retired electrical engineer, engineering executive; b. Portland, Oreg., Aug. 29, 1918; s. Paul L. and Mary (Levonen) O.; m. Winifred Eleanor Potter, June 17, 1944 (dec. Nov. 1950); m. Earlene Mary Boot, Sept. 11, 1954; children: Mary Janet, Eleanor Eva, Eric Paul. BSEE, Oreg. State U., 1940, MSEE, 1951. Registered profl. engr., Wash. Application engr. Allis Chalmers Mfg. Co., Milw., 1940-48; rsch. engr. Boeing Co., Seattle, 1948-63, engring. mgr., 1963-91. Author: Energy Systems Engineering Handbook, 1986; contbr. numerous articles to profl. jours. Mem. team that restarted amateur radio communication to the outside world from the People's Republic of China, 1981. Recipient prize paper award Am. Inst. Elec. Engrs., 1964. Fellow IEEE (founder power electronics systems confs., 1970—, v.p. Aerospace and Electronics Systems Soc. 1984-88, Harry Mimno award 1989, editor-in-chief IEEE Aerospace and Electronic Sys. mag. 1995—/rated in top two by Inst. for Scientific Info.), AIAA (assoc.); mem. AAAS (bd. dir. Pacific divsn. 1992—). Republican. Methodist. Achievements include development of concepts for solar power satellite which generates power in geo-synchronous orbit 24 hours per day and beams it to the Earth surface with a microwave beam; research in simple battery-powered electric bicycles for low-cost, pollution-free transportation in developing nations. Home: 19221 Normandy Park Dr SW Seattle WA 98166-4129

OMAN, RALPH, lawyer; b. Huntington, N.Y., July 1, 1940; s. Henry Ferdinand and Annamarie (Retelsdorf) O.; m. Anne K. Henehan, Oct. 21, 1967; children: Tabitha Russell, Caroline Adams, Charlotte Ericsson. Diploma, Sorbonne U., Paris, 1961; BA, Hamilton Coll., 1962; LLD, Georgetown U., 1973. Bar: D.C. 1973, U.S. Dist. Ct. Md. 1973, U.S. Ct. Appeals (4th cir.) 1974, U.S. Supreme Ct. 1977. Law clk. to U.S. Dist. Ct. judge U.S. Dist. Ct. Md., Balt., 1973-74; trial atty U.S. Dept. Justice, Washington, 1974-75; chief minority counsel patents, trademarks and copyrights subcom. U.S. Senate, Washington, 1975-77; legis. dir. Senator Charles Mathias, Washington, 1977-78; minority counsel judiciary com. U.S. Senate, Washington, 1978-81, chief counsel, staff dir. criminal law subcom., 1981-82, chief counsel patents, copyrights and trademarks subcom., 1982-85; register of copyrights U.S. Copyright Office, Washington, 1985-94; adj. prof. copyright law George Washington U.; speaker in field. Contbr. numerous articles to profl. jours. Served to lt. USN, 1965-70, Vietnam. Mem. ABA, Fed. Bar Assn. (pres. Capitol Hill chpt.). Episcopalian. Home: 1110 E Capitol St NE Washington DC 20002-6225 Office: Dechert Price and Rhoads 1500 K St NW Ste 500 Washington DC 20005-1209

OMAN, RICHARD GEORGE, museum curator; b. Salt Lake City, Oct. 15, 1945; s. Dorse Miles and Margaret (Call) O.; m. Susan Staker, May 31, 1970 (div. 1983); children: Sarah Elizabeth, Nathan Bryan, Bevin Marie; m. Pamela Fillmore, Oct. 4, 1984; children: Emily Anne, Lisa Meleana. AA, Big Bend Community Coll., 1965; BA in History, Brigham Young U., 1970; BA in Art History, U. Wash., 1971, postgrad., 1971-75. Dir. audio-visual sect. Seattle Art Mus., 1973-75; mgr. mus. sect., hist. dept. Ch. of Jesus Christ of Latter-day Saints, Salt Lake City, 1975-86; curator acquisitions Mus. Ch. History and Art, Salt Lake City, 1986—; high priest missionary to Quebec and Ontario, 1965-67; v.p., Import Broker, Salt Lake City, 1984—; instr. Brigham Young U., Provo, 1979; cons., Utah State Hist. Soc., Salt Lake City, 1980—, Utah Endowment for Humanities, Salt Lake City, 1981; bd. dirs., Utah Children's Mus., Salt Lake City, 1981-83. Contbg. author: Arts and Inspiration, 1980, Utah Folk Art, 1980, Encyclopedia of Mormonism, 1992, Mormon Americana, 1995, Encyclopedia of Utah, 1995; co-author: Images of Faith: Art of the Latter-day Saints, 1995; contbr. articles to numerous publs. Asst. commr., Salt Lake City area Boy Scouts Am., 1979-82; chmn. Cen. City Parks Com., Salt Lake City, 1980-83; cons. L.D.S. Hosp. Found., Salt Lake City, 1984; cons., judge, Dixie Coll. Ann. Art Exhbn., St. George, Utah, 1987—, Springville (Utah) Mus. Art; cons. art mus., Brigham Young U., 1984-87; mem. sesquicenten nial com., Mormon Ch., Salt Lake City, 1980. Mem. Utah Mus. Assn. (pres. 1979-81), Am. Assn. State and Local History, Am. Assn. Mus., Mormon History Assn. Republican. Mormon. Avocations: skiing, camping, gardening, sailing, gourmet cooking. Home: 3266 Bonview Dr Salt Lake City UT 84109-3704 Office: Mus Ch History and Art 45 N West Temple Salt Lake City UT 84150-1003

OMAN, RICHARD HEER, lawyer; b. Columbus, Ohio, Jan. 4, 1926; s. B. R. Oman and Marguerite H. (Oman) Andrews; m. Jane Ellen Wert, Oct. 5, 1963; children: Sarah H., David W. B.A., Ohio State U., 1948, J.D., 1951. Bar: Ohio 1951. Atty. Ohio Nat. Bank, Columbus, 1951-55; partner firm Isaac, Postlewaite, O'Brien & Oman, Columbus, 1955-71; dir. Columbus Found., 1955-77, counsel, 1955—; partner firm Porter, Wright, Morris and Arthur (and predecessor firm), Columbus, 1972-89; of counsel Vorys, Sater, Seymour and Pease, Columbus, 1990; ptnr. Vorys, Sater, Seymour and Pease, 1991-96, of counsel, 1997—. Mem. Columbus Airport Commn., 1960-64; trustee Reinberger Found., Cleve., 1980—, Columbus Acad., 1981-87, Grant Hosp., 1978-86, Harding Hosp., 1978-86; sr. warden Trinity Epsic. Ch., 1985-88. Fellow Ohio State Bar Found.; mem. ABA, Am. Coll. Trust and Estate Counsel, Ohio State Bar Assn. (past mem. bd. govs. probate and trust law sect.), Columbus Bar Assn., Columbus Club, Rocky Fork Hunt and Country Club, Nantucket (Mass.) Yacht Club, Kit Kat Club. Republican. Episcopalian. Office: Vorys Sater Seymour & Pease PO Box 1008 52 E Gay St Columbus OH 43216

O'MARA, JOHN ALOYSIUS, bishop; b. Buffalo, Nov. 17, 1924; s. John Aloysius and Anna Theresa (Schenck) O'M. Student, St. Augustine's Sem., Toronto, Ont., Can., 1944-51; J.C.L., St. Thomas U., Rome, 1953. Ordained priest Roman Catholic Ch., 1951; mem. chancery Archdiocese of Toronto, 1953-69; pres., rector St. Augustine's Sem., Toronto, 1969-75; pastor St. Lawrence Parish, Scarboro, Ont., 1975-76; bishop Diocese of Thunder Bay, Ont., 1976-94, Diocese of St. Catharines, Ont., 1994—; pres. Ont. Conf. Cath. Bishops, 1986-92. Bd. dirs. Ont. Hosp. Assn., 1961-65; mem. Ont. Hosp. Services Commn., 1964-69. Named hon. prelate of Papal Household with title monsignor, 1954. Mem. Cath. Ch. Ext. Soc. (bd. dirs. 1992-96). Address: 122 Riverdale Rd, Saint Catharines, ON Canada L2R 4C2

O'MARA, ROBERT EDMUND GEORGE, radiologist, educator; b. Flushing, N.Y., Dec. 8, 1933; s. George Harold and Leonora (Potter) O'M.; m. Brenda Mae Millard, Feb. 15, 1964; children—Robert, Susan, Bridget. B.S., U. Rochester, 1955; M.D., Albany Coll. Medicine, 1959. Diplomate: Am. Bd. Radiology, Am. Bd. Nuclear Medicine (sec. 1982—, chmn. 1983-84). Resident in radiology St. Vincent's Hosp., N.Y.C., 1963-66; fellow in nuclear medicine Upstate Med. Center SUNY, Syracuse, 1966-67; instr. radiology Upstate Med. Center SUNY, 1967-68, asst. prof. radiology, 1968-71; assoc. prof. radiology, dir. nuclear medicine U. Ariz., Tucson, 1971-74; prof., dir. nuclear medicine U. Ariz., 1974-75; prof. radiology, chief div. nuclear medicine U. Rochester Sch. Medicine and Dentistry, 1975—; acting chmn. dept. radiology U. of Rochester, 1987-88, chmn. dept. radiology, 1988-93; med. dir. nuclear medicine tech. program Rochester Inst. Tech., 1976-92. Contbr. articles to med. jours. Pres. Clover Hills Assn., Rochester, N.Y., 1978-79; pres. Fruchtendler Parent Tchr. Assn., Tucson, 1974-75. Served with M.C. USAF, 1960-62. Fellow Am. Coll. Radiology (councillor 1983-89), Am. Coll. Nuclear Physicians (pres. 1980, trustee 1972-80), N.Y. State Radiol. Soc. (pres. 1989-90); mem. Soc. Nuclear Medicine (trustee 1978-82, v.p. 1985-86, Gold medal for sci. exhibit 1977), Radiol. Soc. N.Am., Assn. Univ. Radiologists. Office: 601 Elmwood Ave Rochester NY 14642-0001

O'MARA, THOMAS PATRICK, manufacturing company executive; b. St. Catharine's, Ont., Can., Jan. 17, 1937; s. Joseph Thomas and Rosanna Patricia (Riordan) O'M.; m. Nancy Irene Rosevear, Aug. 10, 1968; children: Patricia Catharine, Tracy Irene, Sara Megan. B.S., Allegheny Coll., 1958; M.S., Carnegie Inst. Tech., 1960. Mktg. analyst U.S. Steel Corp., Pitts., 1960-65; dir. info. systems AMPCO Pitts. (formerly Screw & Bolt Corp.), Pitts., 1965-68; v.p., gen. mgr. Toy div. Samsonite Corp., Denver, 1968-73; regional mgr. Mountain Zone, Hertz Corp., Denver, 1973-75; asst. to chmn. Allen Group, Melville, N.Y., 1975-76; group exec. v.p. fin. and adminstrn. Bell & Howell Co., Chgo., 1976-77; corp. controller Bell & Howell Co., 1977-78, corp. v.p., 1978-85, pres. visual communications, 1978-85; pres., chief operating officer, dir. Bridge Product Inc., Northbrook, Ill., 1985-87; chmn., chief exec. officer Micro Metl Corp., Indpls., 1987-91; chmn. Omara Ptnrs., 1992—; bd. dirs. Loyola U. Press; trustee Barat Coll., 1994—. Mem. Lake Forest H.S. Bd., 1989-96, pres. 1993-96. With USAR, 1961-66. Mem. Econs. Club Chgo., Newcomen Soc. U.S., Sigma Alpha Epsilon, Knollwood Club. Home: 1350 Inverleith Rd Lake Forest IL 60045-1540

O'MEALLIE, KITTY, artist; b. Bennettsville, S.C., Oct. 24, 1916; d. Earle and Rosa Estelle (Bethea) Chamness; m. John Ryan O'Meallie, June 27, 1939 (dec. Apr. 26, 1974); children—Sue Ryan, Kathryn Bethea; m. Lee Harnie Johnson, Aug. 21, 1976. BFA Tulane U., 1937; postgrad., 1954-59. One-woman shows include Masur Mus., Monroe, La., 1979, Marlboro County Mus. of S.C., 1975, Meridian Mus. Art, Miss., 1981, 85; exhibited in group shows at New Orleans Mus. Art, Contemporary Art Ctr., Meadows Mus., Cushing Gallery, SE Ctr. of Contemporary Art, Art 80, Art Expo West, Art Expo 81. Represented in permanent collections New Orleans Mus. Art, Tulane U. Pan-Am. Life Ctr., Masur Mus. Art, Meridian Mus. Art. Nat. officer Newcomb Coll. Alumnae Assn., 1964-66; lectr. exhibitor for many charitable orgns. Recipient award WYES-TV, 1979, Hon. Invitational New Orleans Women's Caucus, 1986, numerous awards and prizes in competitive exhibitions; grant St. Charles Ave. Presbyn. Ch., New Orleans, 1995-96. Mem. Womens Caucus for Art, New Orleans Womens Caucus for Art, Chi Omega Alumnae Assn. (pres. mothers' club 1964), Town and Country Garden Guild (pres. 1970, 1986). Avocations: bird-watching; bridge. Home and Office: 211 Fairway Dr New Orleans LA 70124-1018

O'MEARA, JOHN CORBETT, federal judge; b. Hillsdale, Mich., Nov. 4, 1933; s. John Richard and Karolyn Louise (Corbett) O'M.; m. Penelope Reingier Appel, June 9, 1962 (div. Feb. 1975); children: Meghan Appel, John Richard, Corbett Edge, Patrick Fitzpatrick, Tighe Roberts; m. Julia Donovan Darlow, Sept. 20, 1975; 1 child, Gillian Darlow. AB, U. Notre Dame, 1955; LLB, Harvard U., 1962. Bar: Mich. 1962. Assoc. Dickinson, Wright, Moon, Van Dusen & Freeman, Detroit, 1962-70; mem. faculty U. Detroit, 1965-70; ptnr. Dickinson, Wright, Moon, Van Dusen & Freeman, Detroit, 1970-94, head of labor group, 1985-94; judge U.S. Dist. Ct., Detroit, 1994—; bd. dirs. Mich. Opera Theatre, Detroit. Contr. articles to profl. jours. Fin. chmn. Dem. Party Mich., 1968-70; chmn. U.S. Cts. Com. State Bar Mich., 1984-94. Lt. USN, 1955-59. Fellow Am. Coll. Trial Lawyers, Am. Bar Found.; mem. ABA, U.S. Supreme Court Bar, Am. Judicature Soc., Mich. State Bar Assn., 6th Cir. Court Appeals Bar (life mem., 6th Cir. Jud. Conf. 1986). Office: US Dist Ct 231 W Lafayette Blvd Detroit MI 48226-2720

O'MEARA, MARK, professional golfer; b. Goldsboro, N.C., Jan. 13, 1957. Grad., Long Beach State U. Profl. golfer, 1980—. Named All-Am., Long Beach State U., Rookie of Yr., 1981; mem. Ryder Cup team, 1985, 89, 91; won U.S. Amateur, 1979, Greater Milw. Open, 1984, Bing Crosby Pro-Am., 1985, Hawaiian Open, 1985, Fuji Sankei Classic, 1985, Australian Masters, 1986, Lawrence Batley Internat., 1987, AT&T Pebble Beach Nat. Pro-Am., 1989, 90, 92, H-E-B Tex. Open, 1990, Walt Disney World/Oldsmobile Classic, 1991, Tokia Classic, 1992, Argentine Open, 1994, Honda Classic, 1995, Bell Can. Open, 1995, Mercedes Championships, 1996, Greater Greensboro Open, 1996; tied (with Corey Pavin) Bob Hope Chrysler Classic, 1990. Office: c/o PGA Box 109601 Ave of Champions Palm Beach Gardens FL 33410

O'MEARA, ONORATO TIMOTHY, academic administrator, mathematician; b. Cape Town, Republic of South Africa, Jan. 29, 1928; came to U.S., 1957; s. Daniel and Fiorina (Allorto) O'M.; m. Jean T. Fadden, Sept. 12, 1953; children—Maria, Timothy, Jean, Kathleen, Eileen. B.Sc., U. Cape Town, 1947, M.Sc., 1948; Ph.D., Princeton U., 1953; LLD (hon.), U. Notre Dame, 1987. Asst. lectr. U. Natal, Republic South Africa, 1949; lectr. U. Otago, New Zealand, 1954-56; mem. Inst. for Advanced Study, Princeton, N.J., 1957-58, 62; asst. prof. Princeton, 1958-62; prof. math. U. Notre Dame, Ind., 1962-76; chmn. dept. U. Notre Dame, 1965-66, 68-72, Kenna prof. math., 1976—, provost, 1978-96, provost emeritus, 1996—; vis. prof. Calif. Inst. Tech., 1968; Gauss prof. Göttingen Acad. Sci., 1978; mem. adv. panel math. scis. NSF, 1974-77, cons., 1960—. Author: Introduction to Quadratic Forms, 1963, 71, 73, Lectures on Linear Groups, 1974, 2d edit., 1977, 3d edit., 1988, Russian translation, 1976, Symplectic Groups, 1978, 82, Russian translation, 1979, The Classical Groups and K-Theory (with A.J. Hahn), 1989; contbr. articles on arithmetic theory of quadratic forms and isomorphism theory of linear groups to Am. and European profl. jours. Mem. Cath. Commn. Intellectual and Cultural Affairs, 1962—; bd. govs., trustee U. Notre Dame Australia, 1990—, life trustee, 1996—. Recipient Marianist award U. Dayton, 1988; Alfred P. Sloan fellow, 1960-63. Mem. Am. Math. Soc., Am. Acad. Arts and Scis., Collegium (bd. dirs. 1992-96). Roman Catholic. Home: 1227 E Irvington Ave South Bend IN 46614-1417 Office: U Notre Dame Office of Provost Emeritus Notre Dame IN 46556

O'MEARA, PATRICK O., political science educator; b. Cape Town, South Africa, Jan. 7, 1938; came to U.S., 1964.; s. Daniel and Fiorina (Allorto) O'M. B.A., U. Capetown, 1960; M.A., Ind. U., 1966, Ph.D., 1970. Dep. dir. African studies program, asst. prof. polit. sci. Ind. U., Bloomington, 1970-72, dir. African studies program, 1972—, assoc. prof. polit. sci. and pub. and environ. affairs, 1972-81, prof. polit. sci. and pub. and environ. affairs, 1981—, dean office of internat. programs, 1993—; cons. in field. Author: Rhodesia: Racial Conflict or Coexistance?, 1975; editor: (with Gwendolen M. Carter) Southern Africa in Crisis, 1977, African Independence: The First Twenty-Five Years, 1985, Southern Africa: The Continuing Crisis, 1979, International Politics in Southern Africa, 1982 (with Phyllis M. Martin) Africa, 1977, 2d edit. 1986, 3d edit. 1995, (with C.R. Halisi and Brian Winchester) Revolutions of the Late Twentieth Century, 1991; contbr. articles to profl. jours., book chpts. Mem. African Studies Assn., Pi Alpha Alpha. Roman Catholic. Office: Ind U Woodburn Hall # 211 Bloomington IN 47405

O'MEARA, THOMAS FRANKLIN, priest, educator; b. Des Moines, May 15, 1935; s. Joseph Matthew and Frances Claire (Rock) O'M. MA, Aquinas Inst, Dubuque, Iowa, 1963; PhD, U. Munich, Germany, 1967. Ordained priest Roman Cath. Ch., 1962. Assoc. prof. Aquinas Inst. of Theology, Dubuque, Iowa, 1967-69; prof. U. Notre Dame, South Bend, Ind., 1981-84, William K. Warren prof. of theology, 1985—. Author 14 books, including: Romantic Idealism and Roman Catholicism, 1983, Theology of Ministry, 1985, Church and Culture, 1991, Thomas Aquinas: Theologian, 1997. Mem. Catholic Theol. Soc. Am. (pres. 1980). Office: U Notre Dame Dept Of Theology Notre Dame IN 46556

OMELENCHUK, JEANNE, mayor pro tem, owner; b. Detroit, Mar. 25, 1931; d. Harry Douglas and Blanche (George) Robinson; m. George Omelenchuk (dec.); 1 child, Kristin. BA in Fine Arts, Wayne State U., 1954, M in Art Edn., 1962, postgrad. Art tchr., English tchr. grades 1-9 Detroit Pub. Schs., 1955-74; mem. U.S. Olympic Team Speed Skating, Squaw Valley, Calif., 1960, Grenoble, France, 1968, Sapporo, Japan, 1972; mem. World Championship Teams, Oostersund, Sweden, 1960, Edmonton, Can., 1963, West Allis, Wis., 1965, Flint, Mich., 1967, Helsinki, 1968, Grenoble, France, 1969, St. Paul, 1970; mem. U.S. Team vs. Can., Saskatoon, Sask., Can., 1965, Edmonton, 1967, Winnipeg, Man., Can., 1969; owner Grandfather Clock Headquarters, 1976-91; mem. Warren City Coun., 1985-91, pres., mayor pro tem, 1991-95; owner Metro Bus, Inc., 1980-95; ret., 1995. Coach, sponsorship Macomb Bicycle Racing Club, 1965-86; sponsorship, meet dir. Detroit Speed Skating Clubs Ann. Gold & Silver Skates Meet, 1974-83; vol. instr., coach Mich. Spl. Olympics, Traverse City, 1986-93; founder Warren's Thanksgiving Day Parade, 1986. Recipient Nat. Bicycle Racing Championship Titles, 1951, 55, 57-59, Nat. Championship Masters, 1978, 79, 80, 81, Nat. Speed Skating Championship Titles, St. Paul, 1954, 57-72, Nat. Champ Masters, 1987, 88, 89, 90, 91, Five N.Am. Championships 1957, 58, 59, 62, 63, Nat. Bicycle Racing Championship, Antwerp, Belgium, 1957; inducted into Athletic Hall of Fame, Wayne State U., 1979, Amateur Skating U.S. Hall of Fame, 1979, Mich. Amateur Athletic Hall of Fame, 1981, U.S. Amateur Skating Union Hall of Fame, Chgo., 1984, Mich. Sports Hall of Fame, Cobo Hall, Detroit, 1984, Mich. Women's Hall of Fame, Lansing, Mich., 1994; recognized by YWCA for outstanding contbns. to world of sports on Nat. Women's Sports Day, 1996; recipient Internat. World Speedskating Championship, Master's Class, 1997, Pettit U.S. Olympic Tng. facility, 1997. Mem. Southern Mich. Athletic Assn. (founding mem., sponsor). Achievements include one mile national record. Home: 27544 Sutherland Ave Warren MI 48093-4830

O'MELIA, CHARLES RICHARD, environmental engineering educator; b. N.Y.C., Nov. 1, 1934; s. Charles James and Anne Frances (Dobbin) O'M.; m. Mary Elizabeth Curley, Oct. 27, 1956; children: Kathleen Marie, Mary Margaret, Charles James, Anne Marie, John Thomas, Michael Joseph. BCE, Manhattan Coll., 1955; M San. Engring., U. Mich., 1956, PhD in San. Engring., 1963. Registered profl. engr., Ga. Asst. engr. Hazen & Sawyer Engrs., N.Y.C., 1956-67; teaching fellow, rsch. asst. U. Mich., 1957-61; asst. prof. san. engring. Ga. Inst. Tech., Atlanta, 1961-64; postdoctoral fellow Harvard U., Cambridge, Mass., 1964-65, lectr., 1965-66; assoc. prof. environ. scis. and engring. U. N.C., Chapel Hill, 1966-70, prof., 1970-80, dep. chmn. dept., 1977-80; prof. Johns Hopkins U., Balt., 1980—, chmn. dept. geography and environ. engring., 1990-95; vis. scientist Swiss Fed. Inst. Tech., summer 1971; vis. scholar Woods Hole Oceanographic Inst., summer 1975; vis. prof. Calif. Inst. Tech., Pasadena, 1973-74; guest prof. Eidgenössische Anstalt für Wasserversorgung Abwasserreinigung und Gewässerschutz, Zurich, Switzerland, 1988-89, 96; mem. engring and urban health scis. study sec. EPA, 1970-72, com. on rsch. needs in water supply, pollution control processes peer rev. panel, 1980—, sci. adv. bd., 1981-89; mem. program com. Water Pollution Control Fedn., 1980-86, chmn. rsch. symposium subcom., 1980-85; chmn. waste disposal com. Marine Scis. Coun. N.C., 1970-72; dep. chmn. Gordon Rsch. Confs., Environ. Scis.: Water, 1976, chmn. 1984; mem. com. on non-phosphorus detergent builders Internat. Joint Commn., 1976-83; cons. Monsanto Chem. Co., Union Carbide Corp., Office Gov. Puerto Rico, EPA, others. Contbr. numerous articles to profl. jours, chpts. to books. Recipient Best Lectr. award Environ. Engring Students U. N.C., 1969-70, 71-71, Pergammon Press Publs. award Internat. Assn. on Water Pollution Rsch. and Control, 1988. Mem. NAE (co-chmn. safe drinking water com., subcom. on particulate contaminants 1976, com. on water treatment chemicals 1983-85, wastewater mgmt. in coastal zones com. 1989—), ASCE (Simon W. Freese lectr. 1985, rsch. award 1969), Am. Acad. Environ. Engrs. (cert.), Am. Chem. Soc. (assoc. editor Environ. Sci. and Tech. 1975-83, chmn. water program environ. chemistry div. 1970-72), Am. Soc. Limnology and Oceanography, Am. Water Works Assn. (Publs. award 1965, 85, Best Paper award rsch. div. 1989, A.P. Black award 1990), Water Environment Fedn. (Gordon Maskew Fair medal 1993), AAAS, Assn. Environ. Engring. Profs. (Disting Faculty award 1972, Engring Sci. award 1975, CH2M-Hill award 1988, 96, Outstanding Publ. award 1984, 91, bd. dirs. 1977-80, 88—, v.p. 1978-79, pres. 1979-80), Sigma Xi, Chi Epsilon. Roman Cathlic. Office: Johns Hopkins U 34th And Charles St Baltimore MD 21218

OMENN, GILBERT STANLEY, university dean, physician; b. Chester, Pa., Aug. 30, 1941; s. Leonard and Leah (Miller) O.; m. Martha Darling; children: Rachel Andrea, Jason Montgomery, David Matthew. AB, Princeton U., 1961; MD, Harvard U., 1965; PhD in Genetics, U. Wash., 1972. Intern Mass. Gen. Hosp., Boston, 1965-66; asst. resident in medicine Mass. Gen. Hosp., 1966-67; research assoc. NIH, Bethesda, Md., 1967-69; fellow U. Wash., 1969-71, asst. prof. medicine, 1971-74, assoc. prof., 1974-79, investigator Howard Hughes Med. Inst., 1976-77, prof., 1979—, prof. environ. health, 1981—, chmn. dept., 1981-83, dean Sch. Pub. Health and Community Medicine, 1982—; bd. dirs. Rohm & Haas Co., Amgen, BioTechniques Labs. Inc., Immune Response Corp., Clean Sites, Inc., Population Svcs. Internat., Pacific N.W. Pollution Prevention Rsch. Ctr.; White House fellow/spl. asst. to chmn. AEC, 1973-74; assoc. dir. Office Sci. and Tech. Policy, The White House, 1977-80; assoc. dir. human resources Office Mgmt. and Budget, 1980-81; vis. sr. fellow Wilson Sch. Pub. and Internat. Affairs, Princeton U., 1981; sci. and pub. policy fellow Brookings Instn., Washington, 1981-82; cons. govt. agys., Lifetime Cable Network; mem. Nat. Com. on the Environment, environ. adv. com. Rohm & Haas, Rene Dubos Ctr. for Human Environments, AFL-CIO Workplace Health Fund., Electric Power Rsch. Inst., Carnegie Commn. Task Force on Sci. and Tech. in Jud. and Regulatory Decision Making, adv. com. to dir., Ctrs. Disease Control, 1992—, adv. com. Critical Technologies Inst., RAND; mem. Pres.'s Coun., U. Calif., 1992—. Co-author: Clearing the Air, Reforming the Clean Air Act, 1981. Editor: (with others) Genetics, Environment and Behavior: Implications for Educational Policy, 1972; Genetic Control of Environmental Pollutants, 1984; Genetic Variability in Responses to Chemical Exposure, 1984, Environmental Biotechnology: Reducing Risks from Environmental Chemicals through Biotechnology, 1988, Biotechnology in Biodegradation, 1990, Biotechnology and Human Genetic Predisposition to Disease, 1990, Annual Review of Public Health, 1991, 92, 93, 94, Clinics in Geriatric Medicine, 1992; assoc. editor Cancer Rsch., Cancer Epidemiology, Biomarkers and Prevention, Environ. Rsch., Am. Jour. Med. Genetics, Am. Jour. Preventive Medicine; contbr. articles on cancer prevention, human biochem. genetics, prenatal diagnosis of inherited disorders, susceptibility to environ. agts., clin. medicine and health policy to profl. publs. Mem. President's Council on Spinal Cord Injury; mem. Nat. Cancer Adv. Bd., Nat. Heart, Lung and Blood Adv. Council, Wash. State Gov.'s Commn. on Social and Health Services, Ctr. for Excellence in Govt.; chmn. awards panel Gen. Motors Cancer Research Found., 1985-86; chmn. bd. Environ. Studies and Toxicology, Nat. Rsch. Coun., 1988-91; mem. Bd. Health Promotion and Disease Prevention, Inst. Medicine; mem. adv. com. Woodrow Wilson Sch., Princeton U., 1978-84; bd. dirs. Inst. for Sci. in Society; trustee Pacific Sci. Ctr., Fred Hutchinson Cancer Research Ctr., Seattle Symphony Orch., Seattle Youth Symphony Orch., Seattle Chamber Music Festival, Santa Fe Chamber Music Festival; mem. Citizens for a Hunger-Free Washington; chmn. rules com. Democratic Conv., King County, Wash., 1972. Served with USPHS, 1967-69. Recipient Research Career Devel. award USPHS, 1972; White House fellow, 1973-74. Fellow ACP, AAAS, Nat. Acad. Social Ins., Western Assn. Physicians, Hastings Ctr., Collegium Ramazzini; mem. Inst. Medicine of NAS, White House Fellows Assn., Am. Soc. Human Genetics, Western Soc. Clin. Rsch. Jewish. Home: 5100 NE 55th St Seattle WA 98105-2821 Office: U Wash Dean Sch Pub Health Box 357230 Seattle WA 98195-7230

OMENS, SHERWOOD, cinematographer. Prodr.: (documentary) Somebody Waiting, 1971 (Academy award nomination best documentary short subject 1971); cinematographer: (TV movies) Ishi, the Last of His Tribe, 1978, The Man in the Santa Claus Suit, 1979, Stone, 1979, Madame X, 1981, The Facts of Life Goes to Paris, 1982, Fire on the Mountain, 1982, Policewoman Centerfold, 1983, Grace Kelly, 1983, The Red Light Sting, 1984, Why Me?, 1984, An Early Frost, 1985 (Emmy award outstanding cinematography 1986), Blade in Hong Kong, 1985, Evergreen, 1984 (Emmy award nomination outstanding cinematography 1985), I Saw What You Did, 1987 (Emmy award outstanding cinematography 1988), (TV series) Magnum P.I., 1981 (Emmy award nomination outstanding cinematography 1982),

Alfred Hitchcock Presents ("Road Hog"), 1985 (Emmy award nomination outstanding cinematography 1986), (TV pilots) Lime Street, 1985, Heart of the City, 1986 (Emmy award outstanding cinematography 1987), (films) History of the World, Part I, 1981, Coming to America, 1988, Harlem Nights, 1989, Boomerang, 1992. Office: 6647 Morella Ave North Hollywood CA 91606-1629*

OMER, GEORGE ELBERT, JR., orthopaedic surgeon, hand surgeon, educator; b. Kansas City, Kans., Dec. 23, 1922; s. George Elbert and Edith May (Hines) O.; m. Wendie Vilven, Nov. 6, 1949; children: George Eric, Michael Lee. B.A., Ft. Hays State U., 1944; M.D., Kans. U., 1950; M.Sc. in Orthopaedic Surgery, Baylor U., 1955. Diplomate Am. Bd. Orthopaedic Surgery, 1959, re-cert. orthopaedics and hand surgery, 1983 (bd. dirs. 1983-92, pres. 1987-88), cert. surgery of the hand, 1989. Commd. 1st lt. U.S. Army, 1949; advanced through grades to col., 1967; ret. U.S. Army, 1970; rotating intern Bethany Hosp., Kansas City, 1950-51; resident in orthopaedic surgery Brooke Gen. Hosp., San Antonio, 1952-55, William Beaumont Gen. Hosp., El Paso, Tex., 1955-56; chief surgery Irwin Army Hosp., Ft. Riley, Kans., 1957-59; cons. in orthopaedic surgery 8th Army Korea, 1959-60; asst. chief orthopaedic surgery, chief hand surgeon Fitzsimons Army Med. Center, Denver, 1960-63; dir. orthopaedic residency tng. Armed Forces Inst. Pathology, Washington, 1963-65; chief orthopaedic surgery and chief Army Hand Surg. Center, Brooke Army Med. Center, 1965-70; cons. in orthopaedic and hand surgery Surgeon Gen. Army, 1967-70; prof. orthopaedics, surgery, and anatomy, chmn. dept. orthopaedic surgery, chief div. hand surgery U. N.Mex., 1970-90, med. dir. phys. therapy, 1972-90, acting asst. dean grad. edn. Sch. Medicine, 1980-81; mem. active staff U. N.Mex. Hosp., Albuquerque, chief of med. staff, 1984-86; cons. staff other Albuquerque hosps.; cons. orthopedic surgery USPHS, 1966-85, U.S. Army, 1970-92, USAF, 1970-78, VA, 1970—; cons. Carrier Tingley Hosp. for Crippled Children, 1970—, interim med. dir., 1970-72, 86-87, mem. bd. advisors, 1972-76, chair, 1994-96. Mem. bd. editors Clin. Orthopaedics, 1973-90, Jour. AMA, 1973-74, Jour. Hand Surgery, 1976-81; trustee Jour. Bone and Joint Surgery, 1993—, sec., 1993-96, chmn., 1997—; contbr. more than 200 articles to profl. jours., numerous chpts. to books. Decorated Legion of Merit, Army Commendation medal with 2 oak leaf clusters; recipient Alumni Achievement award Ft. Hays State U., 1973, Recognition plaque Am. Soc. Surgery Hand, 1989, Recognition plaque N.Mex. Orthopaedic Assn., 1991; recognized with Endowed Professorship U. N.Mex. Sch. Medicine, 1995. Fellow ACS, Am. Orthopaedic Assn. (pres. 1988-89, exec. dir. 1989-93), Am. Acad. Orthopaedic Surgeons, Assn. Orthopaedic Chmn., N.Mex. Orthopaedic Assn. (pres. 1979-81), La. Orthopaedic Assn. (hon.), Korean Orthopaedic Assn. (hon.), Peru Orthopaedic Soc. (hon.), Caribbean Hand Soc., Am. Soc. Surgery Hand (pres. 1978-79), Am. Assn. Surgery of Trauma, Assn. Bone and Joint Surgeons, Assn. Mil. Surgeons U.S., Riordan Hand Soc. (pres. 1967-68), Sunderland Soc. (pres. 1981-83), Soc. Mil. Orthopaedic Surgeons, Brazilian Hand Soc. (hon.), S.Am. Hand Soc. (hon.), Groupe D'Etude de la Main, Brit. Hand Soc., Venezuela Hand Soc. (hon.), South African Hand Soc. (hon.), Western Orthopaedic Assn. (pres. 1981-82), AAAS, Russell A. Hibbs Soc. (pres. 1977-78), 38th Parallel Med. Soc. (Korea) (sec. 1959-60); mem. AMA, Phi Kappa Phi, Phi Sigma, Alpha Omega Alpha, Phi Beta Pi. Achievements include pioneer work in hand surgery. Home: 316 Big Horn Ridge Rd NE Sandia Heights Albuquerque NM 87122 Office: U N Mex Dept Orthopaedic Surgery 2211 Lomas Blvd NE Albuquerque NM 87106-2745

OMER, ROBERT WENDELL, hospital administrator; b. Salt Lake City, Feb. 10, 1948; s. Wayne Albert and Melva Bernice (Thunell) O.; m. Deborah Jackson, May 4, 1972;children: Melinda, Carmen, Creighton, Preston, Allison. BS in Biology, U. Utah, 1972; MHA, Washington U., St. Louis, 1975. V.p. St. Luke's Hosp., Cedar Rapids, Iowa, 1974-80; asst. adminstr. Franciscan Med. Ctr., Rock Island, Ill., 1980-82, Latter Day Saints Hosp., Salt Lake City, 1982-85; asst. adminstr. Clarkson Hosp., Omaha, 1985-93, v.p., COO, 1993—; bd. dirs. ARC, Heartland chpt. Omaha; bd. dirs. Nebr. Scanning Svcs. Lt. col. USAR, 1972. Fellow Am. Coll. Healthcare Execs. (regent); mem. Nebr. Hosp. Assn., Omaha C. of C. (Leadership Omaha award 1978), Omaha Healthcare Execs. Group (pres. 1989-90), Rotary (bd. dirs. 1990). Republican. Mem. LDS Ch. Avocations: jogging, history, cycling, backpacking, racquetball. Home: 14111 Cedar Cir Omaha NE 68144-2120

OMINSKY, ALAN JAY, lawyer, medical educator; b. Phila., Apr. 7, 1938; s. Benjamin B. and Ida S. (Snydman) O.; m. Marlene Lachman, Nov. 1, 1992; 1 child, Sara. BA, U. Pa., Phila., 1958, MD, 1962, JD, 1988. Bar: Pa. 1989, U.S. Supreme Ct. 1994; cert. Am. Bd. Anesthesiology, Am. Bd. Psychiatry. Assoc. prof. anesthesiology U. Pa., Phila., 1972-88, assoc. prof. psychiatry, 1975-88; assoc. Bernstein Silver & Agins, Phila., 1089-96. Mem. ABA, Pa. Bar Assn., Phila. Bar Assn. (chiar medicolegal com. 1993-95, mem. sr. lawyers, state civil, and computer users coms.), Assn. Trial Lawyers Am., Pa. Trial Lawyers Assn., Phil. Trial Lawyers Assn., Am. Soc. Anesthesiologists, Am. Psychiat. Soc., Lawyers Club Phila., Phi Beta Kappa. Home: 233 S 6th St Apt 701 Philadelphia PA 19106-3751

OMINSKY, HARRIS, lawyer; b. Phila., Sept. 14, 1932; s. Joseph and Lillian (Herman) O.; m. Rosalyn Rita Rutenberg, June 4, 1961; children—Michelle, David. B.S. in Econs., U. Pa., 1953, LL.B., 1956. Bar: Pa. 1956. Ptnr. Ominsky & Ominsky, Phila., 1958-64; ptnr. Blank, Rome, Comisky & McCauley, Phila., 1964—, mem. mgmt. com., 1981-84, 88-92, co-chmn. real estate dept., 1988-93; lectr. Law Sch., Temple U., Phila., 1969-71, lectr. Real Estate Inst., 1996—. Author: Real Estate Practice: New Perspectives, 1996; contbr. numerous articles to profl. jours. Pres. bd. Phila. Singing City Choir, 1984-88; chmn. zoning com. Merion Civic Assn., Pa., 1984-91. Fellow Am. Bar Found.; mem. ABA (Harrison Tweed spl. merit award 1988), Pa. Bar Assn. (ho. of dels. 1984—), Pa. Bar Inst. (bd. dirs. 1981—, exec. com. 1986-93, v.p. 1988-89, pres. 1989-90, lectr., planner 1969—), Phila. Bar Assn. (chmn. real estate taxes subcom. 1984-85, real property sect. 1991-92, Leon J. Obermayer Edn. award 1989), Am. Coll. Real Estate Lawyers (chmn. publs. com. 1987-91, bd. govs. 1993-95), Order of Coif. Home: 526 Baird Rd Merion Station PA 19066-1302 Office: Blank Rome Comisky & McCauley 4 Penn Center Plz Philadelphia PA 19103-2521

OMIROS, GEORGE JAMES, medical foundation executive; b. Uniontown, Pa., Oct. 26, 1956; s. Chris George and Alice (Zervoudi) O.; m. Sophia Florent, June 28, 1980; children: Christopher George, Alicia Helene. BS in Polit. and Philosophy, U. Pitts., 1978; M, Cen. Mich. U., 1982. Campaign coordinator, program assoc. SW Pa. chpt. Am. Heart Assn., Greensburg, 1979, fundraising dir., 1979-80, dir. devel., 1980-84; v.p. devel., ops. Western Pa. chpt. Am. Heart Assn., Pitts., 1984-85, dep. exec. v.p., 1985-87, exec. v.p., 1987-88; exec. dir. Leukemia Soc. Am., Pitts., 1988—, nat. mktg. rep., 1988—, asst. v.p. nat. office, 1991-93; sr. exec. dir., nat. dir. Don Devel., Pitts., 1993-95, sr. exec. dir., group dir., nat. dir. comm. camp., 1995—. Cons. devel. Greek Orthodox Archdiocese, Pitts., 1982—, v.p. 1987—; chair Pitts. Metro. Com. Internat. Orthodox Christian Charities, Balt., 1993—; mem. coun., rev. com. Health Sys. Agy. Southwest Pa., Pitts., 1983-87; mem. parish coun. St. Spyridon Greek Orthodox Ch., Monessen, Pa., 1982—; met. chmn. Internat. Orthdox Christian Charities; devel. com. Persad Ctr. Mem. Nat. Soc. Fundraising Execs. (cert., founder 1980, pres. 1985-87, Outstanding Fundraising Exec. 1990), Pitts. Planned Giving Coun. (founding com. 1983—), Friends of George C. Marshall (steering com. 1990-92), Uniontown Country Club, Uniontown Rotary (local treas. 1985, sec. 1986, v.p. 1987, pres. 1988), Pitts. Rotary, Masons. Republican. Greek Orthodox. Avocations: stained glass work, art collections, gardening, antiques. Office: Leukemia Soc Am 13 North 2 Gateway Ctr Pittsburgh PA 15222-1402

OMMAYA, AYUB KHAN, neurosurgeon; b. Pakistan, Apr. 14, 1930; came to U.S., 1961, naturalized, 1968; s. Sultan Nadir and Ida (Counil) Khan; children: David, Alexander, Shana, Aisha, Iman, Sinan. M.D., U. Punjab, Pakistan, 1953; M.A., Oxford U., Eng., 1956. Diplomate Am. Bd. Neurological Surgery. Intern Mayo Hosp., Lahore, Pakistan, 1953-54; resident in neurosurgery Radcliffe Infirmary, Oxford, Eng., 1954-61; vis. scientist NIH, Bethesda, Md., 1963-63, assoc. neurosurgeon, 1963-68, head sect. applied rsch., 1968-74, chief neurosurgery, 1974-79; clin. prof. George Washington U. Med. Sch., 1970—; cons. VA Armed Forces Radiobiology Rsch. Inst.; chmn. Inter-Agy. Com. for Protection Human Rsch. Subjects of Fed. Coordinating Coun. for Sci., Engring. and Tech., NAS; chmn. biomechanics adv. com. com. Nat. Hwy. Traffic Safety Adminstrn.; mem. adv. com. Nat. Ctr. Injury Control & Prevention, Atlanta; inaugural Lewin Meml. lectr. U. Cambridge, Eng., 1983; mem. adv. coun. CDC; Shively lectr. Am. Assn. Auto. Medicine, 1988; Ibn-Sina lectr. Islamic Med. Assn. N.Am. Contbr. articles to profl. jours.; inventor, patentee spinal fluid flow driven artificial organs for diabetes and degenerative diseases of the nervous system. Pres. Found. for Fundamental and Applied Neurosci., Bethesda; v.p., dir. rsch. Cyborgan, Inc., Bethesda. Recipient J. W. Kirkdaldy prize Oxford U., 1956, Lifetime Achievement award Internat. Coll. Surgeons, 1996; recipient Sitara-i-Imtiaz for Achievements in Neurosurgery Govt. Pakistan, 1981; Hunterian prof. Royal Coll. Surgeons, 1968; Rhodes scholar, 1954-60. Fellow ACS, Third World Acad. Scis. (assoc., med. scis. com.), Royal Coll. Surgeons Eng.; mem. ASME (exec. affiliate), Soc. for Neurosci., Am. Assn. Neurol. Surgeons, Rsch. Soc. Neurosurgeons, Brit. Soc. Neurol. Surgeons, Am. Assn. Pakistani Physicians (pres.), Internat. Brain Rsch. Orgn. (life), Pan-Am. Med. Assn. Home: 8901 Burning Tree Rd Bethesda MD 20817-3007 Office: 8006 Glenbrook Rd Bethesda MD 20814-2608 *My research on how consciousness is disrupted and restored after brain injuries is serving as a paradigm for my current investigations into the mind-body problem. In this work my scientific training as well as experiential work in both Eastern and Western modes are useful.*

OMMODT, DONALD HENRY, dairy company executive; b. Flom, Minn., July 7, 1931; s. Henry and Mabel B. (Kvidt) O.; m. Evelyn Mavis Blilie, June 15, 1957; children—Linette, Kevin, Lee, Jodi. Student, Interstate Bus. Coll., Fargo, N.D. Acct. Farmers State Bank, Waubun, Minn., 1950-53; chief acct. Cass-Clay Creamery, Inc., Fargo, 1953-61, office mgr., 1961-65, gen. mgr., 1965-83, pres., 1983—. Pres. Messiah Luth. Ch., Fargo, 1976-78; mem. Minn. Dairy Task Force Com., 1988-90; bd. dirs. Communicating for Agr., Fergus Falls, Minn., 1977-80, Blue Cross of N.D., Fargo, 1971-88. Recipient Builder of the Valley award Minn. Red River Valley Devel. Assn., 1991, N.D. Milky Way award, 1993. Mem. N.D. Dairy Industries Assn. (bd. dirs., past pres.), Am. Dairy Assn. (bd. dirs. N.D. 1970-80), N.D. Dairy Product Promotion Commn. (bd. dirs. 1970-80), Messiah Found. Christian Communications (pres. 1987—), Moorhead C. of C. Office: Cass-Clay Creamery Inc 1220 Main Ave # 2947 Fargo ND 58103-8201

OMOIKE, ISAAC IRABOR, chemist, publisher, author; b. Iruekpen, Nigeria, Apr. 29, 1957; came to U.S., 1976; s. Matthew Ighodalo and Rosaline Alice (Amiolemen) O.; m. Brenda Gail Roberts, Sept. 20, 1980 (div. Dec. 1993); children: Ann, Angel, Jeremey. BS in Biology and Chemistry, U. Southwestern La., 1980; MS in Food Sci. and Biochemistry, La. State U., 1986, Cert. Law Enforcement/Pvt. Investigation, 1995. Teaching asst. chemistry dept. La. State U., Baton Rouge, 1984, rsch. asst. food sci. dept., 1985-86; lab. analyst Fina Oil and Chem. Co., Caraville, La., 1987-88; chemist, supr. Bio-Now Lab. Inc., Amelia, La., 1989; lab. analyst Cibageigy corp., St. Gabriel, La., 1989-90; chemist West Paine Lab., Baton Rouge, 1991; dir. Isaac Omoike Books, Baton Rouge, 1990—; owner Family Pizza Lover Restaurant, Baton Rouge; pres. rsch. and investigations Baton Rouge, 1990—. Author: Genocide The Ultimate Threat of the Next milleniums, 1991, Insider America, 1993, Euthanasia Right or Wrong (Tell-Tale Signs of Murder), 1995. Mem. ALA, Am. Chem. Soc., U.S. Soccer Referees, Am. Civil Liberties Union, PUb. Mktg. Assn. Avocations: soccer, volleyball, ping-pong, bowling, athletics. Home: 1910 America St Baton Rouge LA 70806 Office: 8867 Highland Rd Ste 252 Baton Rouge LA 70808-6856

O'MORCHOE, CHARLES CHRISTOPHER CREAGH, administrator, anatomical sciences educator; b. Quetta, India, May 7, 1931; came to U.S., 1968; s. Nial Francis C. and Jessie Elizabeth (Joly) O'M.; m. Patricia Jean Richardson, Sept. 15, 1955; children: Charles Eric Creagh, David James Creagh. B.A., Trinity Coll., Dublin (Ireland) U., 1953, M.B., B.Ch., B.A.O., 1955, M.A., 1959, M.D., 1961, Ph.D., 1969, DSc, 1981. Resident Halifax Gen. Hosp., U.K., 1955-57; lectr. in anatomy Sch. Medicine Trinity Coll., Dublin (Ireland) U., 1957-61, 63-65, lectr. in physiology, 1966-67, assoc. prof. in physiology, 1967-68; instr. in anatomy Harvard Med. Sch., Boston, 1962-63; vis. prof. physiology U. Md. Sch. Medicine, Balt., 1961-62, assoc. prof. anatomy, 1968-71, prof. anatomy, 1971-74; chmn. anatomy bd. State of Md., 1971-73; prof., chmn. dept. anatomy Stritch Sch. Medicine Loyola U., Maywood, Ill., 1974-84; dean Coll. Medicine, U. Ill., Urbana-Champaign, 1984—, prof. anat. scis. and surgery, 1984—; WHO cons., vis. prof. physiology Jaipur, India, 1967, S.M.S. Med. Coll., U. Rajasthan, vis. prof. anatomy, 1971. Assoc. editor: Anatomical Record, 1978—, Am. Jour. Anatomy, 1987-91; contbr. articles to profl. jours. Elected fellow Trinity Coll., Dublin U., 1966; named faculty mem. of yr. Loyola U., Chgo., 1982. Mem. AMA, Am. Soc. Nephrology, N.Am. Soc. Lymphology (v.p. 1982-84, pres. 1984-86, sec. 1993—, Cecil K. Drinker award 1992), Am. Assn. Anatomy Chairmen (emeritus), Am. Assn. Anatomists (dir. placement svc. 1981-91), Internat. Soc. Lymphology (exec. com. 1987—, pres. 1993-95), Ill. State Med. Soc., Champaign County Med. Soc., Alpha Omega Alpha. Mem. Church of Ireland. Home: 2709 Holcomb Dr Urbana IL 61802-7724 Office: U Ill Coll Medicine 190 Med Sci Bldg 506 S Mathews Ave Urbana IL 61801-3618

O'MORCHOE, PATRICIA JEAN, pathologist, educator; b. Halifax, Eng., Sept. 15, 1930; came to U.S., 1968; d. Alfred Eric and Florence Patricia (Pearson) Richardson; m. Charles Christopher Creagh O'Morchoe, Sept. 15, 1955; children: Charles E.C., David J.C. BA, Dublin U., Ireland, 1953, MB, Bch., BAO, 1955, MA, 1966, MD. Intern Halifax (Yorkshire) Gen. Hosp., Eng., 1955-57; instr., lectr. physiology Dublin U., 1957-61, 63-68; instr. pathology Johns Hopkins U., Balt., 1961-62, 68-72, asst. prof. pathology, 1972-74; rsch. assoc. surgery, pathology Harvard U., Boston, 1962-63; asst. prof. anatomy U. Md., 1970-74; assoc.prof., prof. pathology, anatomy Loyola U. Chgo., 1974-84; prof. pathology, cell and structural biology U. Ill., Urbana, 1984—; head dept. pathology coll. medicine U. Ill., Urbana-Champaign, 1994—; staff pathologist VA Hosp., Danville, Ill., 1989—; assoc. head dept. pathology U. Ill., 1991-94; courtesy staff pathologist Covenant Hosp., Urbana, 1984—, Carle Clinic, Urbana, 1990—. Contbr. numerous articles to profl. jours. Recipient Excellence in Teaching award U. Ill., 1996. Mem. Internat. Acad. Cytology, Internat. Soc. Lymphology (auditor 1989-91, exec. com. 1991-93), N.Am. Soc. Lymphology (sec. 1988-90, treas. 1990-92, v.p. 1992-94, pres. 1994—), Am. Soc. Cytology, Am. Assn. Anatomists, Ill. Soc. Cytology. Avocations: boating, needlework. Home: 2709 Holcomb Dr Urbana IL 61802-7724 Office: U Ill Coll Med 506 S Mathews Ave Urbana IL 61801-3618

OMURA, GEORGE ADOLF, medical oncologist; b. N.Y.C., Apr. 30, 1938; s. Bunji K. and Martha (Pilger) O.; m. Emily Fowler, Dec. 27, 1962; children: June Ellen, Susan, Ann, George Fowler. B.A. magna cum laude, Columbia U., 1958; M.D., Cornell U., 1962. Intern Bellevue Hosp., N.Y.C., resident, 1965-67; fellow Meml. Sloan Kettering Cancer Ctr., N.Y.C., 1967-70; asst. prof. medicine U. Ala., Birmingham, 1970-73, assoc. prof. medicine, 1973-78, prof. medicine, 1978-95, prof. emeritus, medicine, 1995—, prof. ob-gyn., 1991-95; v.p. clin. devel. BioCryst Pharms., Inc., Birmingham, 1995—, med. dir., 1996—; prof. emeritus, ob-gyn U. Ala., Birmingham, 1996—; cons. Nat. Cancer Inst., 1975—; chmn. Southeastern Cancer Study Group, 1983-87; cons. to FDA, 1994-95. Contbr. articles to profl. jours. Served with USNR, 1963-65. Am. Cancer Soc. jr. faculty clin. fellow, 1971-74. Fellow A.C.P.; mem. Gynecol. Oncology Group (co-prin. investigator for Ala. 1988, prin. investigator cancer and leukemia Group B for Ala. 1986), Am. Soc. Clin. Oncology, Am. Soc. Hematology, Am. Assn. Cancer Research, Phi Beta Kappa, Alpha Omega Alpha. Home: 3621 Crestside Rd Birmingham AL 35223-1514 Office: 2190 Parkway Lake Dr Ste B Birmingham AL 35244-2812

OMURA, YOSHIAKI, physician, educator; b. Tomari, Toyama-ken, Japan, Mar. 28, 1934; came to U.S., 1959, naturalized, 1979; s. Tsunejiro and Minako (Uozu) O.; m. Rose Ninon Alexander, Sept. 8, 1962 (separated); children: Alexander Kenji, Vivienne Midori, Richard Itsuma; assoc. degree in elec. engring. and pre-med., Nihon U., 1952-54; BSc in Applied Physics, Waseda U., 1957; MD, Yokohama City U., 1958, postgrad. exptl. physics, Columbia U., 1960-63; ScD (Med.), Coll. Physicians and Surgeons, Columbia U., 1965. Diplomate Am. Acad. Pain Mgmt., 1992—, Am. Bd. Forensic Medicine. Rotating intern Tokyo U. Hosp., 1958, Norwalk (Conn.) Hosp., 1959; rsch. fellow cardiovascular surgery Columbia U., N.Y.C., 1960, resident physician in surgery, Francis Delafield Hosp., Cancer Inst., Columbia U., 1961-65; asst. prof. pharmacology and instr. surgery N.Y. Med. Coll., 1966-72; vis. prof. U. Paris, summers 1973-77; Maitre de recherche, Disting. Fgn. Scientist program of INSERM, Govt. of France, 1977; rsch. cons. orthopedic surgery Columbia U., 1965-66; part-time emergency rm. physician Englewood Hosp., 1965-66; rsch. cons. pharmacology dept. N.Y. Down State Med. Center, SUNY, 1966; co-founder, cons. Lincoln Hosp. Acupuncture Drug Detoxification Program, 1974-75; chmn. Columbia U. Affiliation and Cmty. Medicine com., Community Bd., Francis Delafield Hosp., 1974-75; vis. rsch. prof. dept. elec. engring., Manhattan Coll., 1962—; chmn. Sci. Div., Children's Art & Sci. Workshops, N.Y.C., 1971-92; dir. Med. Rsch., Heart Disease Rsch. Found., Bklyn., 1972—; adj. prof. dept. pharmacology Chgo. Med. Sch., 1982-93; adj. prof. physiology Sch. Med., Showa U., Tokyo, 1988-96; attending physician Dept. Neurosci., L.I. Coll. Hosp., 1980-88; cons. New York Pain Center, 1988-92; prof. dept. non-orthodox medicine Ukrainian Nat. Med. U., Kiev, 1993—; adj. prof. preventive medicine N.Y. Med. Coll., 1997—; v.p. Internat. Kirlian Rsch. Assn., 1981—; mem. N.Y. State Bd. Medicine, 1984-94; mem. alumni council Coll. Phys. and Surg. Columbia U., 1986—; founder, editor-in-chief Acupuncture & Electro-Therapeutics Rsch. Internat. Jour., 1974—. Mem. editorial bd. Alternative Medicine, 1985—, Scandinavian Jour. Acupuncture and Electrotherapy, 1987—, Functional Neurology, 1988—; editorial cons. Jour. Electrocardiology, 1980-86; cons. NIH Rsch. Grant Evaluation, 1994—. Columbia U. rsch. fellow, 1960; Am. Cancer Soc. Inst. grantee, 1961-63; John Polacek Found. grantee, 1966-72; NIH grantee, 1967-72; Heart Disease Rsch. Found. grantee, 1972—; recipient: Acupuncture Scientist of the Year award, Internat. Congress of Chinese Medicine, 1989, Qi Gong Scientist of Yr. award Int. Congress of Chinese Medicine & Qi Gong, 1990, granted 4 U.S. patents and 3 Japanese patents. Fellow Internat. Coll. Acupuncture and Electro-Therapeutics (pres. 1980—), Am. Coll. Angiology, Am. Coll. Acupunture, N.Y. Cardiol. Soc.; mem. Internat. Assn. for Study of Pain (founding mem. 1975—), N.Y. Acad. Sci., Japan Bi-Digital O-Ring Test Assn. (pres. 1986—), Japan Bi-Digital O-Ring Test Med. Soc. (pres. 1990—), Am. Soc. Artificial Internal Organs, N.Y. Japanese Med. Soc. (pres. 1963-73), others. Author 6 books, also chpts. in books; contbr. over 160 articles to profl. jours. Home: 800 Riverside Dr Apt 8-I New York NY 10032-7400

ONAK, THOMAS PHILIP, chemistry educator; b. Omaha, July 30, 1932; s. Louis Albert and Louise Marie (Penner) O.; m. Sharon Colleen Neal, June 18, 1954. BA, Calif. State U., San Diego, 1954; PhD, U. Calif., Berkeley, 1957. Research chemist Olin Mathieson Chem. Corp., Pasadena, Calif., 1957-59; asst. prof. Calif. State U., Los Angeles, 1959-63, assoc. prof., 1963-66, prof. chemistry, 1966—. Author: Organoborane Chemistry, 1975; Contbr. articles to profl. jours., chpts. to books. Recipient Rsch. Career award NIH, 1973-78, Nat. award Am. Chem. Soc., 1990, Outstanding Prof. award Calif. State U., System, 1993-94; named Calif. Prof. of Yr. Carnegie Found. and Coun. for the Advancement and Support of Edn., 1995; Fulbright Rsch. fellow U. Cambridge, Eng., 1965-66. Home: PO Box 1477 South Pasadena CA 91031-1477 Office: Calif State U Dept Chemistry 5151 State U Dr Los Angeles CA 90032

ONA-SARINO, MILAGROS FELIX, physician, pathologist; b. Manila, May 8, 1940; came to U.S., 1965, naturalized, 1983; d. Venancio Vale Ona and Fidela Torres Felix; m. Edgardo Formantes Sarino, June 11, 1966; children: Edith Melanie, Edgar Michael, Edenn Michele. AA, U. Santo Tomas, Manila, 1959, MD meritissimus cum laude 1964; postgrad. W. Va. U., 1997—. Diplomate Am. Bd. Pathology; med. licensure N.Y., N.J., W.Va. Rotating intern N.Y. Infirmary, pediatrics, Roosevelt Hosp., N.Y.C., 1965-66; resident in anatomic and clin. pathology Lenox Hill Hosp., N.Y.C., 1966-71, asst. adj. pathologist, 1972-74; assoc. pathologist St. Francis Med. Ctr., Trenton, N.J., 1974-84, Hamilton Hosp., N.J., 1974-84; pathologist, chief pathology and lab. medicine svc., med. dir. blood bank Louis A. Johnson VA Med. Ctr., Clarksburg, W.Va., 1984—; clin. instr. pathology Columbia U. Coll. Physicians and Surgeons, N.Y.C., 1973-85; clin. assoc. prof. pathology, W.Va. U. Sch. Medicine. Fellow Am. Soc. Clin. Pathologists, Coll. of Am. Pathologists (cert. inspector); mem. Internat. Acad. Pathology, N.Y. Acad. Scis. (life). Office: Louis A Johnson VA Med Ctr Dept Pathology Clarksburg WV 26301

ONDETTI, MIGUEL ANGEL, chemist, consultant; b. Buenos Aires, Argentina, May 14, 1930; came to U.S., 1960, naturalized, 1971; s. Emilio Pablo and Sara Cecilia (Cerutti) O.; m. Josephine Elizabeth Garcia, June 6, 1958; children: Giselle Christine, Gabriel Alexander. Licensiate in Chemistry, U. Buenos Aires, 1955, D.Sc., 1957. Prof. chemistry Inst. Tchrs., Buenos Aires, 1957-60; instr. organic chemistry U. Buenos Aires, 1957-60; rsch. scientist Squibb Inst. Med. Rsch., Buenos Aires, 1957-60; rsch. investigator Squibb Inst. Med. Rsch., Princeton, N.J., 1960-66; rsch. supr. Squibb Inst. Med. Rsch., 1966-73, sect. head, 1973-76, dir. biol. chemistry, 1976-79; assoc. dir. Squibb Inst., 1980-82, v.p. rsch. cardiopulmonary disease, 1982-86, sr. v.p. cardiovascular rsch., 1987-91; pharm. cons., 1991—; ad-hoc cons., sculptor NIH; mem. adv. com. dept. chemistry Princeton U., 1982-86. Patentee in field (115); contbr. articles to sci. jours. Served with Argentine Army, 1950-51. Recipient Thomas Alva Edison Patent award R&D Coun. N.J., 1983, Ciba award for hypertension rsch. Am. Heart Assn., 1983, Perkins medal Soc. Chemistry Industry, 1991, Warren Alpert Found. award, 1991; scholar Brit. Coun., 1960, Squibb, 1956. Mem. AAAS, Am. Chem. Soc. (Alfred Burger award 1981, Creative Invention award 1992, Perkin medal 1992), Am. Soc. Biol. Chemists. Home: 79 Hemlock Cir Princeton NJ 08540-5405

ONDRICEK, MIROSLAV, cinematographer. Cinematographer: (films) If..., 1969, Slaughterhouse Five, 1971, Taking Off, 1971, O Lucky Man!, 1973, Hair, 1979, Ragtime, 1981 (Academy award nomination best cinematography 1981), The World According to Garp, 1982, Silkwood, 1983, The Divine Emma, 1983, Amadeus, 1984 (Academy award nomination best cinematography 1984), Heaven Help Us, 1985, F/X, 1986, Big Shots, 1987, Funny Farm, 1988, Valmont, 1989, Awakenings, 1990, A League of Their Own, 1992, The Preacher's Wife, 1996. Office: The Gersh Agency 232 N Canon Dr Beverly Hills CA 90210-5302*

ONDRUSEK, DAVID FRANCIS, discount store chain executive; b. Johnson City, N.Y., Aug. 8, 1955; s. Frank Joseph and Juanita Elizabeth (Seeley) O.; m. Tina G. Papapavlos, July 11, 1981; children: Stephanie Ann Albina, Michael David. BA, St. Michael's Coll., Winooski, Vt., 1977; BS, Idaho State U., Pocatello, 1980. Asst. mgr. Osco Drugs, Wenatachee, Wash., 1980, Richland, Wash., 1981-83; asst. mgr. Thrift Drug, Williamsport, Pa., 1983; mgr. Revco Drug, Williamsport, 1983-88; dist. mgr. Revco Drug, Morgantown, W.Va., 1988-92, pharmacy supr., 1992; pharmacy mgr. Wal-Mart, Salisbury, Md., 1992-94; dist. mgr. Wal-Mart, Lewisburg, Pa., 1994—. Head coach Lycoming Coll. Lacrosse Team, Williamsport, 1983-88. Mem. Am. Pharm. Assn., Nat. Assn. Retail Druggists, Wash. State Pharm. Assn., Pa. Assn. Chain Drug Stores (bd. dirs. 1996—). Avocation: golf. Home: 157 Ridgeway Dr Lewisburg PA 17837-9235 Office: 125 Rt 15 N Lewisburg PA 17837

O'NEAL, EDGAR CARL, psychology educator; b. St. Louis, Apr. 30, 1939; s. Clarence Edgar O'Neal and Alyce (Mullins) Redwine; m. Ellen Rose Luther, Aug. 31, 1963; children—Colleen Ruth, Patrick Blaine. B.A., Duke U., 1961; M.Div., Drew U., 1964; M.A., U. Mo., 1968, Ph.D., 1969. Ordained to ministry United Meth. Ch., 1964. Minister Community Meth. Ch., Cold Spring Harbor, N.Y., 1962-65; NIMH fellow U. Mo., Columbia, 1966-69; asst. prof., assoc. prof. psychology Tulane U., New Orleans, 1969-76, chmn. dept. psychology, 1978-84, prof. psychology, 1977—. Editor: Perspectives on Aggression, 1976; mem. editl. bd. Jour. Personality and Social Psychology, 1991-97, Jour. Non-verbal Behaviour, 1991-94, Aggressive Behavior, 1995—; contbr. articles to profl. jours. Fellow APA (coun. 1982-85); mem. Sigma Xi, Sigma Chi. Democrat. Home: 7219 O'Neil Dr Harahan LA 70123-4844 Office: Tulane U Dept Psychology 2007 Stern Hall New Orleans LA 70118

O'NEAL, EDWIN A., geologist, geophysicist, petroleum engineer; b. Gulfport, Miss., Jan. 5, 1929; s. Aurelius Pericles and Eula Lee (Walker) O'N.; m. Nelle Gray Fulton, Feb. 10, 1952 (dec. Dec. 25, 1994); children: David Edwin, Kerry Christian. BS in Petroleum Geology, Miss. State U., 1952; MS in Geology, Tulane U., 1973. Geophysicist Western Geophysical Co., Shreveport, La., 1954-56; asst. dist. geologist Ark. Fuel Oil Corp., Shreveport, 1956-59; mgr. exploration and prodn. Whitaker Oil Co., Carthage, Tex., 1959-64; geologist Internat. Helium Inc., Longview, Tex.,

1964-66, Robbins Drilling Co., Longview, 1966-67; prof., dean engring. and indsl. tech. Delgado C.C., New Orleans, 1967-88; geologist, resource evaluation Minerals Mgmt. Svc., New Orleans, 1988-96. 1st lt. Army Artillery, 1952-54, Korea. Mem. Am. Assn. Petroleum Geologists, Soc. Petroleum Engrs. Avocations: lapidary, camping. Home: 806 Franklin Ct Slidell LA 70458

ONEAL, GLEN, JR., retired physicist; b. Gt. Falls, Mont., Feb. 2, 1917; s. Glen and Marion (Sherrard) O.; B.S., Mont. State Coll., 1940; M.S., U. Pa., 1947; m. Lois Fay, May 23, 1941 (div. Aug. 1968); 1 child, Fay O. Redwine; m. Evelyn Spies Hessenbruch, May 5, 1975. Jr. engr. physicist Public Rds. Adminstrn. Washington, 1941; asso. physicist Naval Ordnance Lab., Washington, 1941-45; physicist Sun Oil Co., Newtown Square, Pa., 1947-55; research physicist Am. Viscose Corp., Marcus Hook, Pa., 1955-63; research physicist Am. Viscose div. FMC Corp., 1963-70, chem. group research, 1970-81, sr. physicist corp. engring. and constrn., 1981-82. Research asso. Nat. Bur. Standards, 1968-70. Prodn. chmn. Rose Valley Chorus, Media, Pa., 1950-67; bd. dirs. Media (Pa.) Fellowship House, 1971-77. Mem. Am. Phys. Soc., ASTM, IEEE, Sigma Xi. Mem. Soc. of Friends. Home: 128 Yale Ave Swarthmore PA 19081-2021

O'NEAL, HANK, entertainment producer, business owner; b. Kilgore, Tex., June 5, 1940; s. Harold Lee and Sarah (Christian) O'N.; m. Shelley M. Shier, May 14, 1985. BA, Syracuse U., 1962. With CIA, Washington and N.Y.C., 1963-76; exec. v.p. Hammond Music Enterprises, N.Y.C., 1980-83; pres., owner Chiaroscuro Records Co./Downtown Sound recording studio, N.Y.C., 1970-80, 85—; exec. v.p. HOSS, Inc., N.Y.C., 1983—; instr., dept. head New Sch. for Social Rsch., N.Y.C., 1970-92; bd. dirs. Composer's and Choreographer's Theater, N.Y.C.; pres. SOS Prodns., Wilkes Barre, Pa., 1987—. Author: Eddie Condon Scrapbook of Jazz, 1973, A Vision Shared, 1976, Berenice Abbott-American Photographer, 1982, Djuna Barnes 1978-81, 1990, Charlie Parker/The Funky Blues Date, 1995; author/photographer: The Floating Jazz Festival, 1985, The Ghosts of Harlem, 1997; photographer: (books) Allegra Kent's Water Beauty Book, 1976, All the King's Men, 1990; producer, cover photographer/designer numerous record albums, 1967—. Capt. U.S. Army, 1963-67. Recipient various awards and prizes for books. Mem. Phi Gamma Delta. Home: Glenside Box 101 River Rd Thornhurst PA 18424 Office: Chiaroscuro Records 830 Broadway New York NY 10003-4827

O'NEAL, HARRIET ROBERTS, psychologist, psycholegal consultant; b. Covington, Ky., Dec. 28, 1952; d. Nelson E. and Georgia H. (Roberts) O'N. Student, U. Paris Sorbonne, 1972; BA in Psychology, Hollins Coll., 1974; JD, U. Nebr., 1978, MA in Psychology, 1980, PhD in Psychology, 1982. Therapist Richmond Maxi Ctr., San Francisco, 1979-81; clin. coord., therapist Pacifica (Calif.) Youth Svc. Bur., 1981-83; staff psychologist Kaiser Permanente Med. Ctr., Walnut Creek, Calif., 1983-91; pvt. practice psychotherapy Pleasant Hill, Calif., 1985—, San Francisco, 1995—; psycholegal cons., Nebr., 1975-79, Calif. Bd. Behavioral Sci. Examiners, Sacramento, 1982—; psycholegal cons., presenter San Francisco State U., 1980, U. Calif., San Francisco, 1980, VA Med. Ctr., San Francisco, 1983; cons. Employee Assistance Program, Pacific Bell, San Francisco, 1996—. Cons. Nebr. Gov.'s Commn. on Status of Women, 1975, 78; vol. Make-A-Wish Found., 1992—. NIMH fellow, 1974-79. Mem. APA, Employee Assistance Profls. Assn., Phi Beta Kappa, Psi Chi. Avocations: dancing, swimming, hiking, travel, cycling.

O'NEAL, LESLIE CORNELIUS, professional football player; b. Pulaski County, Alaska, May 7, 1964. Student, Okla. State U. Defensive end San Diego Chargers, 1986—. Named to Sporting News Coll. All-Am. 1st Team, 1984-85; selected to Pro Bowl, 1989, 90, 92-94. Holder of NFL rookie-season record for most sacks, 1986. Office: San Diego Jack Murphy Stadium PO Box 609609 San Diego CA 92160-9609*

O'NEAL, MICHAEL RALPH, state legislator, lawyer; b. Kansas City, Mo., Jan. 16, 1951; s. Ralph D. and Margaret E. (McEuen) O'N.; m. Tammy E. Miller, Dec. 30, 1978 (div.); children: Haley Anne, Austin Michael. BA in English, U. Kans., 1973, JD, 1976. Bar: Kans. 1976, U.S. Dist. Ct. Kans. 1976, U.S. Ct. Appeals (10th cir.) 1979. Intern Legis. Counsel State of Kans., Topeka, 1975-76; assoc. Hodge, Reynolds, Smith, Peirce & Forker, Hutchinson, Kans., 1976-77; ptnr. Reynolds, Peirce, Forker, Suter, O'Neal & Myers, Hutchinson, 1980-88, Gilliland & Hayes, P.A., Hutchinson, 1988—; mem. Kans. Ho. of Reps., chmn. jud. com., 1989-90, 92-96, minority whip, 1991-92, majority whip, 1995-96, chmn. edn. com., 1997—, mem. fiscal oversight com., 1997—; instr. Hutchinson C.C., 1977-88. Vice chmn. Rep. Ctrl. Com., Reno County, Kans., 1982-86; bd. dirs. Reno County Mental Health Assn., Hutchinson, 1984-89, YMCA, 1984-86, Crime Stoppers (ex-officio), Hutchinson; chmn. adv. bd. dirs. Wesley Towers Retirement Cmty., 1984-96; mem. Kans. Travel and Tourism Commn., 1990-94; bd. govs. U. Kans. Law Sch., 1991—. Recipient Leadership award Kans. C. of C. and Industry, 1985; named one of Outstanding Young Men Am., 1986. Mem. ABA, ATLA, Nat. Conf. State Legislatures (criminal justice com.), Kans. Assn. Def. Counsel, Def. Rsch. Inst., Kans. Bar Assn. (prospective legis. com., Outstanding Svc. award), Hutchinson C. of C. (ex-officio bd. dirs., Leadership award 1984), Am. Coun. Young Polit. Leaders (del. to Atlantic conf. biennial assembly), Kans. Jud. Coun., Commn. on Uniform State Laws. Avocations: basketball, tennis, golf. Home: 8 Windemere Ct Hutchinson KS 67502-2020 Office: Gilliland & Hayes PA 335 N Washington St Ste 2977 Hutchinson KS 67501-4863

O'NEAL, MICHAEL SCOTT, SR., lawyer; b. Jacksonville, Fla., Dec. 22, 1948; s. Jack Edwin and Lucille (Colvin) O'N.; m. Barbara Louise Hardie, Jan. 30, 1971 (div. Sept. 1974); 1 child, Jennifer Erin; m. Helen Margaret Joost, Mar. 18, 1985; children: Mary Helen, Angela Marie, Michael Scott O'Neal Jr. AA, Fla. Jr. Coll., 1975; BA in Econs. summa cum laude, U. No. Fla., 1977; JD cum laude, U. Fla., 1979. Bar: Fla. 1980, U.S. Dist. Ct. (mid. dist.) Fla. 1980, U.S. Dist. Ct. (no. dist.) Fla. 1981, U.S. Ct. Appeals (5th and 11th cirs.) 1981, U.S. Supreme Ct. 1986. Assoc. Howell, Liles, Braddock & Milton, Jacksonville, Fla., 1980-83; ptnr. Commander, Legler, Werber, Dawes, Sadler & Howell, Jacksonville, 1983-91, Foley & Lardner, Jacksonville, 1991-93, Howell O'Neal & Johnson, Jacksonville, 1993-96, Howell & O'Neal, Jacksonville, 1996—; pro bono atty. Legal Aid Soc., Jacksonville, 1980—; practicing atty. Lawyers Reference, Jacksonville, 1980—; pres. N.E. Fla. Med. Malpractice Claims Coun., 1996. Pres. Julington Landing Homeowners Assn., Jacksonville, 1980-83. Served to staff sgt. USAF, 1968-74. Mem. ABA, Jacksonville Bar Assn., Fed. Bar Assn., Assn. Trial Lawyers Am., Fla. Def. Lawyers Assn., Jacksonville Assn. Def. Counsel (treas. 1996, sec. 1997), Internat. Assn. Def. Counsel. Republican. Methodist. Clubs: University, San Jose Country (Jacksonville). Avocations: golf, music. Home: 1299 Norwich Rd Jacksonville FL 32207-7525 Office: Howell O'Neal 200 N Laura St Ste 1100 Jacksonville FL 32202-3500

O'NEAL, SHAQUILLE RASHAUN, professional basketball player; b. Newark, Mar. 6, 1972; s. Philip A. Harrison and Lucille O'Neal. Student, La. State U. Center Orlando Magic, 1992-96, L.A. Lakers, 1996—. Appeared in movie Blue Chips, 1994, Kazaam, 1996. Named to Sporting News All-American first team, 1990-91; recipient Rookie of the Yr. award NBA, 1993; mem. NBA All-Star team, 1993, 94, Dream Team II, 1994; first pick overall, 1992 draft. Office: LA Lakers PO Box 10 Inglewood CA 90306

O'NEAL, TATUM, actress; b. Nov. 5, 1963; d. Ryan and Joanna (Moore) O'N.; m. John McEnroe, Aug. 1, 1986; 3 children: Kevin, Sean, Emily. Ed., pvt. schs. and tutors. Appearences include (films) Paper Moon, 1973 (Acad. award for best supporting actress), The Bad News Bears, 1976, Nickelodeon, 1976, International Velvet, 1978, Little Darlings, 1979, Circle of Two, 1981, Certain Fury, 1985, Little Noises, 1992, Basquiat, 1996; (TV movies) Woman on the Run: The Lawrencia Bambenek Story, 1993. Office: care Innovative Artists 1999 Ave of the Stars Ste 2850 Century City CA 90067-6082*

O'NEIL, CHARLOTTE COOPER, environmental education administrator; b. Chgo., Sept. 21, 1949; d. Adolph H. and Charlotte Waters (Edman) Cooper; m. William Randolph O'Neil, Nov. 18, 1972; children: Sean, Megan. BA in Polit. Sci., Okla. State U., 1969; BS in Edn., U. Tenn., 1988. Cert. tchr., Tenn. Intern Senator Charles H. Percy, Washington, 1969; state treas., state hdqrs. office mgr. Jed Johnson for U.S. Senate, Okla., 1972; mem. acct. staff Pacific Architects & Engrs., Barrow, Alaska, 1973; tchr. social studies Jefferson Jr. High Sch., Oak Ridge, Tenn., 1988; edn. specialist Sci. Applications Internat. Corp., Oak Ridge, Tenn., 1988-94, mgr. environ. edn. and info. tech. sect., 1994-95, mgr. comm. edn. and pub. info. sect., 1995-96, mgr. pub. rels., edn. and multimedia/engring. design, 1996—; mem. edn. strategies com. Dept. of Transp./Fed. Hwy. Adminstrn./Intelligent Transp. Sys. Edn. 1995—; mem. steering com. Am. Mus. of Sci. and Energy, 1st Annual ASME Tribute to Tech. Competition, 1996—. Author: Science, Society and America's Nuclear Waste, 1992, 2d edit., 1995, Technical Career Opportunities in High-Level Waste Management, 1993, The Environmental History of the Tonawanda Site, 1994, FAA Community Involvement Training: Better Decisions through Consensus, 1996; contbr. articles to profl. jours. Publicity chair, mem. steering com. Am. Mus. Sci. & Energy Tribute to Tech. Mem. ASCD, AAUW, Triangle Coalition, Tenn. Geography Alliance, Nat. Coun. for Social Studies (culture, sci. and tech. com., sci. and society com., sec.-treas. 1991—), Earthwatch, Internat. Alliance for High-Level Radioactive Waste Mgmt., Golden Key, Atomic City Aquatic Club (chair constl. rev. com. 1991—). Office: Sci Applications Internat PO Box 2502 Oak Ridge TN 37831-2502

O'NEIL, CHLOE ANN, state legislator; m. John G.A. O'Neil (dec.); children: Beth Ann Rice, John A.S. BS in Psychology, SUNY, Potsdam, 1967, MS in Edn. Tchr. Hermon-DeKalb Ctr. Sch.; tchr. SUNY, Canton, N.Y., Potsdam; elem. tchr. Parishville (N.Y.)-Hopkinton Ctrl. Sch.; mem. N.Y. State Assembly, 1993—. Past mem. St. Mary's Sch. Bd. Edn.; active St. Michael's Ch. in Parishville, N.Y. Mem. N.Y. State United Tchrs. Home: Cassidy Rd Hopkinton NY 12940 Office: NY State Assembly State Capitol Albany NY 12224*

O'NEIL, CLEORA TANNER, personnel specialist; b. Roosevelt, Utah, Sept. 1, 1946; d. Frank and Pearl (Mecham) Tanner; divorced; 1 child, Sylvia Boroughs. AA, Drury Coll., 1983; BA, Westminster U., 1985. Sec. USAF, Hill AFB, Utah, 1966-74, U.S. Army, Ft. Leonard Wood, Mo., 1981-83, VA Hosp., Salt Lake City, 1983-86; employee rels. specialist USAF, McClellan AFB, Calif., 1986-90; pers. specialist USAF, Washington, 1990-94; employee rels. specialist, fed. women's program mgr. USAF, McClellan AFB, 1994—; resident in upper managerial tng. Civilian Air Staff Tng., USAF, Washington, 1990-92. Recipient Outstanding USAF Civilian Pers. Program Specialist award, 1989. Mem. Toastmasters (v.p. Aerospace chpt. 1989-90, Toastmaster of Yr. 1989, pres. Am. River chpt. 1989-90, Pres.' award 1990, internat. gov. 1989-90). Avocations: writing, studying, travel, square dancing.

O'NEIL, DANIEL JOSEPH, science research executive, university consultant; b. Boston, June 5, 1942; s. Daniel Joseph and Grace Veronica (Francis) O'N.; m. Elizabeth Noone, Nov. 14, 1964; children: Elizabeth Grace, Daniel Joseph, Dara Veronica. BA, Northeastern U., 1964; MS, So. Conn. State U., 1967; PhD, U. Dublin, 1972. Sr. rsch. chemist Raybestos-Manhattan Advanced Rsch. Lab., Stratford, Conn., 1964-67; unit leader Hitco Materials Sci. Ctr., Gardena, Calif., 1967-68; tech. dir. Euroglas Ltd., Middlesex, Eng., 1970-72, Kildare, Ireland, 1970-72; founding faculty mem., dir. external liaison and coop. edn., lectr. polymer sci. U. Limerick, Ireland, 1972-75; chief exec. European Rsch. Inst. Ireland, Limerick, 1981-83; sr. rsch. scientist Ga. Tech. Rsch. Inst., Atlanta, 1975-78, prin. rsch. scientist, 1978-91, dir. energy and materials sci. lab., 1988-90, group dir. office of dir., 1990-91; v.p. and dean grad. coll. U. Okla., Norman, 1991-93, prof. chemistry, 1991-93; pres., dir. Sarkeys Energy Ctr. Univ. Okla. Rsch. Corp., Norman, 1992-93; founder, mng. dir. Okla. Energy Rsch. Ctr., Atlanta, 1992-93; chmn., pres. CRADA Corp., Atlanta, 1993, pres., 1993—; bd. dirs. U. Okla. Rsch. Corp., Okla. Ctr. for Advancement of Sci. and Tech., Okla. Exptl. Program Stim. Comp. Res.; mem. adv. bd. Gov.'s Energy Coun.; mem. Okla. Higher Edn. State Regents Coun. on Rsch. and Grad. Edn., 1991-93; panelist bd. on sci. and tech. for internat. devel. NAS/NRC, Washington, 1978-79, 86-87; cons. EEC, Brussels, 1982, 87, 89, U.S. rep., 1989; mem. nat. policy rev. panel U.S. Dept. Energy, Washington, 1986; witness, cons. energy R & D com. U.S. Senate, Washington, 1986-88; reviewer small bus. innovation rsch. program U.S. Dept. Energy, Washington, 1988-90; active Israel Tech. Project Com., Atlanta Jewish Fedn., Jewish Agy for Israel, 1990-91; rep., lectr. Fedn. Arab. Sci. Rsch. Coun., Arab Bur. Edn. for Gulf States, 1987. Author, co-author of 100 reports and publs. including USDOE Solar Thermal Tech., 1989, Energy from Biomass and Wastes XIII, 1989, Internat. Conf. Pyrolysis/Gasification, 1989, High Flux Materials Treatment, 1990, Energy Initiative and Competitive Strategies, 1991, Research Innovation and the University, 1992, University Research and Economic Development, 1992, University Strategic Planning, 1993, Institutional Strategy for Increasing Sponsored Research, 1996. Pres. U. Okla. Res. Corp, 1982-83, bd. dirs., 1992-93; mng. dir. Okla. Energy Res. Ctr., 1992-93; expert evaluator NBS Office Energy-Related Inventions, Gaithersburg, Md., 1978-86; adv. bd. dirs. tech. utilization USDOC Office Minority Bus. Enterprises, Washington, 1977-86; U.S. del. U.S.-Brazil energy workshop U.S. Dept. State, Washington and Brazil, 1980; active Okla. Higher Edn. State Regents Coun. on Rsch. and Grad. Edn., 1991-93; Okla. Ctr. Advancement of Sci. and Tech., 1991-94; mem. Team Ireland com. Atlanta Olympics, 1995-96; mem. White House Conf. Trade and Investment, Ireland, 1995—; mem. No. Ireland and Border Countries Trade and Investment Coun., Inc., 1995—. Fellow Am. Inst. Chemists, Soc. Rsch. Adminstrs.; mem. AAAS, Com. Grad. Rsch., Oak Ridge Associated Univs., Univ. Rsch. Assn., Midwest Assn. Grad. Schs., Nat. Assn. State Univs. and Land Grant Colls., Nat. Coun. Univ. Rsch. Adminstrs., Am. Chem. Soc., Assn. Big Eight Univs., Biomass Energy Rsch. Assn. (bd. dirs. 1990—), Coun. on Rsch., Edn. and Tech., Ga. Acad. Sci. (councillor 1990-91), Ga. Inst. Chemistry (pres. 1988-90), Assn. Western U. (bd. dirs. 1991-93), Univ. Okla. Assn., Trinity Coll. Dublin Alumni Assn., Japan-Okla. Soc., Internat. Club of Atlanta (founder), Petroleum Club of Okla., Husky Club Northeastern U., Sigma Xi. Office: CRADA Corp Atlanta HQ 2660 Goodfellows Rd Tucker GA 30084-2702

O'NEIL, JAMES PETER, financial printing company executive; b. Bloomfield, N.J., Dec. 8, 1944; s. John F. and Mary (Kane) O'N.; m. Jo Anne Elizabeth Schweitzer, Oct. 10, 1970; children: Pamela, James, Kathleen. BBA, Seton Hall U., 1966. CPA, N.J. Ptnr. J.H. Cohn and Co., N.Y.C., 1968-84; from v.p. fin. to exec. v.p., COO Bowne and Co., Inc., N.Y.C., 1984-95, pres., 1996—. Sgt. U.S. Army, 1966-68. Decorated twice Bronze Star with Valor. Office: Bowne & Co Inc 345 Hudson St New York NY 10014-4502

O'NEIL, J(AMES) PETER, elementary education educator, computer software designer; b. Rockville Center, N.Y., Apr. 2, 1946; s. Clement Lee and Frances Rita (Theis) O'N.; m. Carol Ann Sypniewski, June 8, 1968; children: Kelly Ann, Thomas Joseph. BA in Psychology, Loyola U., Chgo., 1968; M in Sci. Edn., Webster Coll., St. Louis, 1972. Cert. elem. tchr. K-8, Mo., elem. tchr. K-8, Wis., dir. instruction, Wis. Tchr., student tchr. Sacred Heart Sch., Florissant, Mo., 1968-73; tchr. sci. Waunakee (Wis.) Mid. Sch., 1973-96, chmn. K-8 sci. dept., chmn. K-12 dept., 1984-92; dir. Waukakee Summer Sci. Program, 1975-91; dir. instrn./tech. Brodhead Wis., 1996—; designer sci. curriculum computer CD-ROM programs Sci. Curriculum Assistance Program and Elem. Sci. Curriculum Assistance Program, 1990—. Editor: Science Scope, 1989-96; contbr. over 30 activities and articles to profl. jours. Group worker settlement houses Chgo., St. Louis; mem. Parish Coun.; dir. Waunakee Area Edn. Found. Named Master Tchr. NSF, Waunakee, 1986-96; recipient Tchr. of Yr. award Waunakee, 1984, 90, 92, Kohl Found. award, 1992, Mid. Sch. Tchr. of Yr. award Wis., 1992-93. Mem. Nat. Sci. Tchrs. Assn., Wis. Soc. Sci. Tchrs., Wis. Elementary Sci. Tchrs., NEA, Wis. Edn. Assn. Roman Catholic. Avocations: computers, sports, writing, jogging. Home: 119 Simon Crestway Waunakee WI 53597-1721 Office: Brodhead Sch Dist 2501 W Fifth Ave Brodhead WI 53520

O'NEIL, JOHN, artist; b. Kansas City, Mo., June 16, 1915; s. Michael and Emma (Harms) O'N. BFA, U. Okla., 1936, MFA, 1939; student, Taos Sch. Art, 1942, U. Florence, Italy, 1951. Dir. U. Okla. Sch. Art, 1951-65; chmn. dept. fine arts Rice U., Houston, 1965-70; dir. Sewall Art Gallery, 1972-77, Joseph and Joanna Nazro prof. art and art history, 1979-81; vis. lectr. NYU, U. Mich., U. Mass., l'Accademia di Belle Arti, Rome, Moana Olu Coll., Hawaii. One-man show, Mus. Art, U. Okla., Sask. (Can.) Art Centers, Seattle Art Mus., M-59 Galleries, Copenhagen, Denmark, Los Robles Galleries, Calif., La. Gallery, Houston, Philbrook Art Ctr., Tulsa, Firehouse Art Ctr., Norman, Okla.; works exhibited, Carnegie Inst., Artists West of Mississippi at Colorado Springs, Denver Art Mus., San Francisco Mus., Art Inst. of Chgo., U. Ill., Dallas Mus., Cin. Mus., Sadeer Gallery, Kuwait, Kauffman Galleries, Houston, Graham Gallery, Houston, Wierzbowski Gallery, Houston, N.Y. World's Fair, Pickard Gallery, Oklahoma City, U.S. Art Expo, San Francisco; rep. collections, Philbrook Art Center, U. Mich., Denver Art Mus., Dallas Mus., Am. Arts., Kansas City, Chgo., others. Recipient 30 painting and graphics awards. Painting fellow Huntington Hartford Found., MacDowell Colony, Montalvo Assn. Mem. Coll. Art Assn., Southwestern, Mid-Am. art confs., Delta Phi Delta. Home: 1701 Hermann Dr Apt 901 Houston TX 77004-7326

O'NEIL, JOHN JOSEPH, lawyer; b. Detroit, July 20, 1943; s. John J. and Dora J. (Collins) O'N.; children: Meghan, Kathryn. BA, Trinity Coll., 1965; LLB, U. Va., 1968. Bar: N.Y. 1969, U.S. Ct. Appeals (2d cir.) 1969, Fla. 1979, D.C. 1982. Assoc. Jackson & Nash, N.Y.C., 1968-71; assoc. Paul, Weiss, Rifkind, Wharton & Garrison, N.Y.C., 1971-77, ptnr., 1977—. Fellow Am. Coll. Trusts and Estates Counsel; mem. ABA (com. on spl. problems of aged), N.Y. State Bar Assn. (com. on taxation, trusts and estates sect.), Assn. Bar City N.Y. (com. on trusts and estates), Pi Gamma Mu. Office: Paul Weiss Rifkind Wharton & Garrison 1285 Avenue Of The Americas New York NY 10019-6028

O'NEIL, JOHN P(ATRICK), athletic footwear company executive; b. Malden, Mass., 1921; s. Jeremiah James and Elizabeth Agnes (McMahon) O'N.; m. nancy Hodgkins, Dec. 21, 1944; children: John W., Michael P., Martha E., Timothy P. B.S., Tufts U., 1943. Vice pres. prodn. Granite State div. Converse Inc., Berlin, N.H., 1946-66; v.p. mfg. Converse Rubber Co., Malden, Mass., 1966-70; v.p. ops. Converse Rubber Co., Wilmington, Mass., 1970-73, exec. v.p., 1974; pres. Converse Inc., Wilmington, 1974-87, vice chmn., 1987—; dir. Footwear Industries Am., Washington; chmn. Athletic Footwear Council, North Palm Beach, Fla., 1981-90; trustee Mass. Bank for Savs., Reading, 1982-87. Bd. overseers for athletics, Tufts Univ. 1st lt. U.S. Army, 1943-46. Named Businessman of Yr. Dr. I. Fund Found., N.Y.C., 1982. Mem. Internat. Athletic Footwear and Apparel Mfg. Assn. (pres.), Rubber and Plastics Footwear Mfg. Assn. (pres.), Internat. Athletic Footwear Assn. (pres. worldwide). Roman Catholic. Clubs: Lanam (Andover, Mass.); Meadow Brook Golf (Reading, Mass.) (bd. dirs. 1980-86), Country Club of New Seabury (Mass.), Mariner Sands Country (Stuart, Fla.); Tufts of Boston. Office: Converse Inc 1 Fordham Rd North Reading MA 01864-2619

O'NEIL, JOSEPH FRANCIS, association executive; b. Chicopee, Mass., Oct. 3, 1934; s. Joseph Francis and Mary Agnes (Sheehan) O'N.; m. Carol Marie Quindlen, June 12, 1975; 1 child, Anna Lyons. B.A., Holy Cross Coll., 1956; M.S. in Theology, St. Mary's U., Balt., 1960; M.S. in Journalism, Columbia U., 1965. Mem. editorial staff Cath. Observer, Springfield, Mass., 1961-64; asst. editor Cath. Observer, 1965-69, editor, 1969-74; editor Child Devel. Asso. Consortium, Washington, 1975-77; asst. exec. sec. Am. Council Independent Labs., Washington, 1977-80; exec. dir. Am. Council Independent Labs., 1981—. Chmn. Bus. Coalition for Fair Competition, 1983-90; sec., treas. Bus. Coalition for Fair Competition, 1990-92; chmn., cons. coun. Nat. Inst. Bldg. Scis., 1992-93; bd. dirs. Small Bus. Legis. Coun. Mem. Am. Nat. Standards Inst. (bd. dirs.), Assn. Chief Execs. Coun. Home: 1712 N Jefferson St Arlington VA 22205-2817 Office: Am Coun Ind Labs 1629 K St NW Washington DC 20006-1602

O'NEIL, LEO E., bishop; b. Holyoke, Mass., Jan. 31, 1928. Ed. Mary-knoll Sem., St. Anselm's Coll., Manchester, N.H., Grand Sem., Montreal, Que., Can. Ordained Roman Cath. priest, 1955; ordained titular bishop of Bencenna and aux. bishop of Springfield (Mass.), 1980-89, co-adjutor bishop Manchester, N.H., 1989-90, bishop, diocese of Manchester, 1990—. Office: Bishop of Manchester 657 N River Rd Manchester NH 03104-1955*

O'NEIL, MARY AGNES, health science facility administrator; b. Bridgeport, Conn., Sept. 26, 1926. Diploma in nursing, St. Vincent's Hosp., Bridgeport, 1947; BS, St. Joseph's Coll., Emmitsburg, Md., 1952; MS in Nursing Services Adminstrn., Boston Coll., 1960; LLD (hon.), Sacred Heart U., Bridgeport, 1974. Nurse St. Vincent's Hosp., 1947-48, dir. nursing, 1961-63, assoc. adminstr., 1969, adminstr., 1969-74, chmn. bd. dirs., 1969-76, coordinator constrn., in-residence chmn. bd. dirs., 1973—; 3d directress Sisters of Charity Sem., Emmitsburg, 1949-54; supr. nursing services Carney Hosp., Boston, 1954-57, dir. nursing svcs., 1957-60, adminstrv. asst. patient care svcs., 1960-61, asst. to pres., 1981-83; assoc. adminstr. St. Mary's Hosp., Troy, N.Y., 1963, adminstr., 1963-69, pres., chief exec. officer, chmn. bd. dirs., ex-officio lay adv. bd., 1976—; sr. v.p., chmn. bd. dirs. Good Samaritan Hosp., Pottsville, Pa., 1983-86, chmn. bd. dirs., v.p. corp. affairs, 1986, chmn. corp. reorgn., chmn. bd. dirs., bd. liaison, 1986—; acting bd. chair Sisters of Charity Hosp., Buffalo, N.Y., 1991-92; mem. Upper Hudson sub-area council, mem. project rev. com. Health Systems Agy. of Northeastern N.Y.; mem. regional bd. Nat. Comml. Bank and Trust Co., N.Y., 1979; bishop's rep., mem. legis. com. N.Y. State Council Cath. Hosps., 1980; rep. governing bd. Iroquois Hosp. Consortium, Inc., N.Y., 1980; mem. Green Island Bridge Task Force Com., Troy, 1981; mem. Northeast Province Health Commn., 1987, Devel. Corp. Good Samaritan Hosp., Pottsville, Pa., 1989-90, chmn. bd. dirs., 1983-90; provincial health councillor Dau. of Charity Northeast Province De Paul Provincial House, Albany, N.Y., 1990-93, provincial asst., 1991-93; acting bd. chairperson Sisters of Charity Hosp., Buffalo, N.Y., 1991-92; bd. dirs. Carney Hosp., Boston, St. Vincent's Med. Ctr., Bridgeport, Conn., Sisters of Charity Hosp., Buffalo, N.Y., Dau. of Charity of St. Vincent de Paul, Northeast Province, Inc.; sec. regional corp. DCNHS-NE, bd. dirs., treas., Daus. of Charity Nat. Health System; bd. dirs. St. Mary's Hosp., Troy, N.Y., chair, 1993-94; chair Our Lady Lourdes Meml. Hosp., Binghamton, N.Y, 1993-94; chair Seton Health Sys., Inc., Troy, N.Y., 1994—, Mount St. Mary's Hosp. of Niagara Falls, Lewiston, N.Y., 1997. V.p. Greater Bridgeport C. of C., 1975; mem. mayor's human rights commn. City of Troy, 1976; bd. dirs. Northeastern/Southeastern Shared Services of Daus. of Charity, 1977, treas. Eastern Coop. Services, 1980, chmn. investment com., 1981, mem. health adv. commn. N.E. Province, 1986; v.p. govtl. relations City of Troy, 1978; hon. chmn. Upper Hudson area chpt. Am. Diabetes Assn., Inc., 1978-79; bd. dirs. Blue Cross of Northeastern N.Y., 1977; bd. dirs. Lourdes Hosp., Binghamton, N.Y., 1985, chmn. evaluation com., 1987; mem. adv. bd. Jr. League, Troy, 1979; mem. St. Mary's Hosp. Found. Bd., 1981; provincial asst. Daus. of Charity, Buffalo, 1991. Recipient Cmty. Svcs. award City of Troy, 1968, Leadership and Svc. cert. Conn. Hosp. Assn., 1973, Cmty. Svc. and Accomplishment award Sta. WICC-FM, 1975, Cmty. Svc. award Sta. WNAB-FM, 1975, Key to City of Bridgeport, 1975, Caritas award Seton Health Sys. Found., 1995; named one of Outstanding Women of State of Conn., Gov. Ella Grasso, 1976; Sister Mary Agnes Day proclaimed by City of Bridgeport, 1976, by City of Troy, 1981. Fellow Am. Coll. Hosp. Adminstrs.; mem. Hosp. Assn. Northeastern N.Y. (mem. program com. 1978, chmn. bylaws com. 1979). Democrat. Avocations: music, walking, swimming. Home: Sacred Heart Sisters' Residence 76 Adams Ave Cohoes NY 12047-3502 Office: Mount St Marys Hosp Niagara Falls 5300 Military Rd Lewiston NY 14092-1903

O'NEIL, MICHAEL JOSEPH, opinion survey executive, marketing consultant; b. Springfield, Mass., June 22, 1951; s. James Francis and Mary Helen (Apolis) O'N.; m. Catherine Mary Zirkel, Sept. 10, 1983; children: Heather Rose, Sean Michael, Ryan Joseph, Matthew James. BA, Brown U., 1974, MA, 1975; PhD, Northwestern U., 1977. Mem. faculty Northwestern U., 1976-77, U. Ill., Chgo., 1977; mem. faculty U. Mich., Ann Arbor, 1977-79, postdoctoral fellow Survey Rsch. Ctr., Inst. Social Rsch., 1977-79; dir. Pub. Opinion Rsch. Ctr. Ariz. State U., Tempe, 1979-81; pres. O'Neil Associates, Tempe, 1981—; reviewer grant proposals NSF, Washington, 1977—; mem. mktg. com. Phoenix Art Mus., 1992-96; mem. bd. dirs. Phoenix Children's Hosp. Found., 1993—. Manuscript reviewer Social Problems, 1977—, Pub. Opinion Quar., 1977—, Urban Affairs Quar., 1977—, Jour. Ofcl. Statistics, 1990—, Sociological Methods and Rsch., 1993; contbr. articles to profl. jours. Chmn. Tempe Union High Sch. Dist. Bus. Edn. adv. com., 1986-88; mem. mktg. com. Mesa Assn. Retarded Citizens, 1985-87; bd. dirs. East Valley Camelback Hosp., Mesa, 1985-90, v.p., 1988-90; active Valley Leadership, Ariz. Acad./Ariz. Town Halls, Maricopa County Citizens' Jud. Adv. Coun., Ariz. Coalition for Tomorrow; mem. Phoenix Pride Commn., 1991-94; bd. dirs. Class X, 1997—. Mem. Am. Mktg. Assn., Am. Assn. Pub. Opinion Rsch., Alumni Assn. Brown U. (bd. dirs. 1985-90), Brown U. Club of Phoenix (pres. 1984—), Phoenix City Club (bd. dirs. 1987-93, pres.

1990-91), East Valley Partnership (mem. bd. dirs. 1993—), Phi Beta Kappa. Democrat. Avocation: tennis. Home: 418 E Erie Dr Tempe AZ 85282-3711 Office: O'Neil Assocs 412 E Southern Ave Tempe AZ 85282-5212

O'NEIL, PATRICK MICHAEL, political scientist, educator; b. Norwich, N.Y., Dec. 3, 1947; s. Thomas Doyle and Edith (Byrne) O.'N. MA in English Lit., SUNY, Binghamton, 1973, MA in Philosophy, 1979, MA in History, 1981, PhD in History, 1993. Adj. instr. SUNY-Morrisville, Norwich, N.Y., 1985-90; assoc. prof. in humanities and social scis. Broome C.C., Binghamton, 1985—; adj. instr., tutor Empire State Coll., Binghamton, 1985-91; tour leader, guide Travelearn, Lakeville, Pa., 1993. Contbr. articles to profl. jours.; reporter, critic, reviewer: Sun Bulletin, 1971-72; editorial asst. ethics and religion sect. Evening Press, 1981-84. Congrl. candidate, Binghamton, 1972; chmn. Broome County Conservative Ctrl. Com., 1976-80, Chenango County Conservative Ctrl. Com., Norwich, 1980-90. Mem. Am. Hist. Assn. (life), Am. Philos. Assn. (life), Am. Acad. Polit. Sci. (life). Republican. Roman Catholic. Avocations: hunting, fishing, chess. Home: 75 Colfax Ave Binghamton NY 13905-2106 Office: Broome CC Upper Front St Binghamton NY 13902

O'NEIL, ROBERT MARCHANT, university administrator, law educator; b. Boston, Oct. 16, 1934; s. Walter George and Isabel Sophia (Marchant) O'N.; m. Karen Elizabeth Elson, June 18, 1967; children—Elizabeth, Peter, David, Benjamin. A.B., Harvard U., 1956, A.M., 1957, LL.B., 1961; LL.D., Beloit Coll.,, 1985, Ind. U., 1987. Bar: Mass. 1962. Law clk. to justice U.S. Supreme Ct., 1962-63; acting assoc. prof. law U. Calif.-Berkeley, 1963-66, prof., 1966-67, 1969-72; exec. asst. to pres., prof. law SUNY-Buffalo, 1967-69; provost, prof. law U. Cin., 1972-73, exec. v.p., prof. law, 1973-75; v.p., prof. law Ind. U., Bloomington, 1975-80; pres. U. Wis. System, 1980-85; prof. law U. Wis.-Madison, 1980-85; prof. law U. Va., Charlottesville, 1985—, pres., 1985-90; gen. counsel. AAUP, 1970-72, 91-92. Author: Civil Liberties: Case Studies and the Law, 1965, Free Speech: Responsible Communication Under Law, 2d edit., 1972, The Price of Dependency: Civil Liberties in the Welfare State, 1970, No Heroes, No Villians, 1972, The Courts, Government and Higher Education, 1972, Discriminating Against Discrimination, 1976, Handbook of the Law of Public Employment, 1978, 2d rev. edit., 1993, Classrooms in the Crossfire, 1981, Free Speech in the College Community, 1997; co-author: A Guide to Debate, 1964, The Judiciary and vietnam, 1972, Civil Liberties Today, 1974. Trustee Tchrs. Ins. and Annuity Assn.; bd. dirs. Commonwealth Fund, James River Corp., Sta. WVPT Pub. TV. Home: 1839 Westview Rd Charlottesville VA 22903-1632 Office: Thomas Jefferson Ctr 400 Peter Jefferson Pl Charlottesville VA 22911-8691

O'NEIL, SHARON LUND, educator; b. Spokane, Wash., June 23, 1942; d. Thorvald J. and Lulu B. (Wentland) Lund; m. Roger G. O'Neil, June 6, 1971. BA, Walla Walla (Wash.) Coll., 1964, MA, 1967; PhD, U. Ill., 1976. Instr. U. Ill./Ill. Comml. Coll., Champaign-Urbana, 1971-76; bus. edn. tchr. various pub. schs., 1964-72; dir. pupil pers. New Milford (Conn.) pub. schs., 1976-79; chair, ITEC dept., prof. bus. edn., assoc. vice provost U. Houston, 1979—; cons. on bus. practices; lectr. and presenter in field. Author: Office Information Systems, 1990; co-author: Supervision Today!, 1995; editor, contbg. author 6 books; contbr. articles to profl. jours. Active various charitable orgns. Recipient numerous grants, Faculty Excellence and Teaching Excellence awards U. Houston and U. Ill., others. Mem. Nat. Assn. Tchr. Educators in Bus. Edn. (pres. 1990-92, dist. svc. award), Mountain-Plains Bus. Edn. Assn. (pres. 1990-91, Tchr. of Yr. 1991, Leadership award 1993), Nat. Bus. Edn. Assn. (yearbook editor 1990, exec. bd. dirs. 1991-94, Coll. Educator of Yr. 1993, Gregg Lifetime Achievement award 1995), Policies Commn. for Bus. and Econ. Edn. (chair 1989-90), Am. Voc. Assn. (exec. bd. bus. edn. div., Award of Merit 1991), Nat. Assn. for Bus. Tchr. Educators (rsch. coord. 1991-93), Phi Kappa Phi (U. Houston chpt. pres. 1987-88, Delta Pi Epsilon (nat. v.p. 1992-93, exec. bd. 1992-97, nat. pres. 1994-95), Pi Omega Pi (sponsor 1981—). Avocations: golf, skiing, reading, travel. Home: 2349 Bellefontaine St Houston TX 77030-3203 Office: U Houston Coll Tech Sr VP's Office 4800 Calhoun Rd Houston TX 77004-2610

O'NEIL, THOMAS MICHAEL, physicist, educator; b. Hibbing, Minn., Sept. 2, 1940; married; 1 child. BS, Calif. State U., Long Beach, 1962; MS, U. Calif., San Diego, 1964, PhD in Physics, 1965. Rsch. physicist Gen. Atomic, 1965-67; prof. physics U. Calif., San Diego, 1967—; mem. adv. bd. Inst. Fusion Studies, 1980-83, Inst. Theoretical Physics, 1983-86. Assoc. editor Physics Review Letters, 1979-83; correspondent Comments Plasma Physics & Controlled Fusion, 1980-84. Alfred P. Sloan fellow, 1971; recipient Alumni Disting. Tchg. award UCSD, 1996. Fellow Am. Phys. Soc. (award for excellence in plasma physics 1991, James Clerk Maxwell prize 1996). Achievements include research in theoretical plasma physics with emphasis on nonlinear effects in plasmas and on non-neutral plasmas. Office: Univ of California Dept of Physics 9500 Gilman Dr La Jolla CA 92093-5003

O'NEIL, WAYNE, linguist, educator; b. Kenosha, Wis., Dec. 22, 1931; s. L.J. and Kathryn (Obermeyer) O'N.; married; children: Scott Leslie, Patrick Sean, Elizabeth Erla. AB, U. Wis., 1955, AM, 1956, PhD, 1960; AM (hon.), Harvard U., 1965. Asst. prof. linguistics and lit. U. Oreg., 1961-65; prof. linguistics and edn. Harvard U., 1965-68, lectr. edn., 1968-72, vis. prof. edn., 1978-86; prof. linguistics and humanities MIT, 1968—, chmn. lit. faculty, 1969-75, chmn. linguistics program, 1986—, head dept. linguistics and philosophy, 1989—; lectr. bilingualism Wheelock Coll., Boston, 1991—; lectr. Beijing Normal U., 1980, Beijing and Shanghai Fgn. Lang. Insts., 1981; lectr. linguistics Shandong (China) U., 1982-83, prof., 1984—; prof. Summer Inst. on Lang. Change, NEH, 1978; vis. prof. Tsuda Coll., Tokyo, 1983; co-dir. MIT-Tokyo U. mind articulation project, 1996—. Mem. editorial group Radical Teacher, 1975—; author: (in Chinese) English Transformational Grammar, 1981, Linguistics and Applied Linguistics, 1983, (with S.J. Keyser) Rule Generalization and Optionality in Language Change, 1985, (with S. Flynn) Linguistic Theory in Second Language Acquisition, 1988, (with S. Flynn and G. Martohardjono) Generative Grammar in Second Language Acquisition, 1997. Mem. steering com. Resist, 1967—, Peoples Coalition for Peace and Justice, 1970-72; co-founder, mem. Linguistics for Nicaragua, 1985—. With U.S. Army, 1952-54. Fulbright fellow in Iceland, 1961; Am. Council Learned Socs. study fellow M.I.T., 1964-65. Mem. AAAS, Linguistic Soc. Am., Nat. Coun. Tchrs. English, Native Am. Langs. Inst., Soc. Pidgin and Creole Linguistics. Office: MIT Dept Linguistics and Philosophy Cambridge MA 02139-4307

O'NEIL, WILLIAM FRANCIS, academic administrator; b. Worcester, Mass., Mar. 26, 1936; s. John J. and Mary A. (Trahant) O'N.; m. Mary Elizabeth Dillon, Aug. 22, 1959; children: Kathleen, Mary Elizabeth. BS, Boston U., 1960; MEd, Worcester State Coll., 1963; diploma, U. Conn., 1970; EdD, Wayne State U., 1972. Tchr. Worcester Pub. Schs., 1960-68, community sch. dir., 1968-73; assoc. prof., dir. community edn. devel. ctr. Worcester State Coll., 1973-75, dir. community svc., 1975-77, dean grad. and continuing edn., 1977-83, exec. v.p., 1983-85; exec. v.p. Mass. Coll. Art, Boston, 1985-86, acting pres., 1986-87, pres., 1987-96; exec. officer Mass. State Coll. Coun. Pres., 1996—. Contbr. articles to profl. jours. Mem. Worcester Dem. City Com., Ward I Dem. Com., 1980—; pres., trustee Worcester Pub. Libr., 1977-82; mem. Mass. Bd. Libr. Commrs., 1984-89. Recipient Outstanding Alumni award field of edn. Worcester State Coll., 1996, citation Mass. Ho. of Reps., 1977, key City of Worcester, 1982; Mott fellow Charles Stewart Mott Found., 1971. Mem. Mass. Pub. Colls. and Univs. Pres. and Chancellors Assn. (chair 1991-92), Assn. Ind. Colls. Art and Design (bd. dirs.), Mass. Cmty. Edn. Assn. (life; bd. dirs. 1972-77), Mass. State Colls. Pres. Assn. (chair 1992-93), Profl. Arts Consortium (v.p. Boston, pres. 1993-94), Emerald Club. Roman Catholic. Office: Mass Coll Art Office Pres 621 Huntington Ave Boston MA 02115-5801

O'NEIL BIDWELL, KATHARINE THOMAS, fine arts association executive, performing arts executive; b. Dayton, Ohio, Mar. 23, 1937; d. Charles Allen and Margaret Stoddard (Talbott) Thomas; children: Margaret, Stephen, Thomas; m. J. Truman Bidwell. B.A., Sarah Lawrence Coll., Bronxville, N.Y., 1959. Mng. dir. Met. Opera Assn., 1977-86, v.p., 1979-86; first v.p. Met. Opera Guild, N.Y.C., 1978-79, pres., chief exec. officer, 1979-86; dir. spl. projects Lincoln Ctr., N.Y.C., 1986-96; bd. dirs. Norlin Corp. Bd. dirs. Lincoln Ctr. for Performing Arts, N.Y.C., Assn. of Mentally Ill Children, 1975-76, Valerie Bettis Sch. of Theater/Dance, 1976-79, Salisbury Sch., Conn., 1982-84; trustee Sarah Lawrence Coll., 1977-86; Westminster Choir Coll., 1986-91, Greenwall Found., 1986, Vol. Cons. Group, 1986. Mem. Assn. Sarah Lawrence Coll. (pres. 1975-77). Republican. Episcopalian. Home: 455 E 57th St New York NY 10022-3065

O'NEILL, ALBERT CLARENCE, JR., lawyer; b. Gainesville, Fla., Nov. 25, 1939; s. Albert Clarence and Sue Virginia (Henry) O'N.; m. Vanda Marie Nigels, Apr. 26, 1969; 1 child, Heather Marie. B.A. with high honors, U. Fla., 1962; LL.B. magna cum laude, Harvard U., 1965. Bar: Fla. bar 1965. Law clk. to judge U.S. Dist. Ct. (mid. dist.) Fla., Jacksonville, 1965-66; assoc. Fowler, White, Collins, Gillen, Humkey & Trenam, Tampa, Fla., 1966-69; ptnr. Trenam, Simmons, Kemker, Scharf & Barkin, Tampa, 1970-77; mem. firm Trenam, Kemker, Scharf, Barkin, Frye, O'Neill & Mullis (P.A.), Tampa, 1977—, also bd. dirs.; vis. lectr. law Stetson Law Sch., 1970-73; bd. dirs. Am. Bar Retirement Assn. Exec. editor: Harvard Law Rev, 1964-65; contbr. articles to profl. jours. Bd. dirs. Fla. Gulf Coast Symphony, Inc., 1975-86, U. Fla. Found., Inc., 1976-84, Fla. Orch., 1988-95. Mem. ABA (chmn. tax sect. 1992-93), Am. Law Inst., Am. Coll. Tax Counsel, Fla. Bar (chmn. tax sect. 1975-76), Phi Beta Kappa. Office: Trenam Kemker Scharf Barkin Frye O'Neill & Mullis 2800 Barnett Plz Tampa FL 33602

O'NEILL, BEVERLY LEWIS, mayor, former college president; b. Long Beach, Calif., Sept. 8, 1930; d. Clarence John and Flossie Rachel (Nicholson) Lewis; m. William F. O'Neill, Dec. 21, 1952. AA, Long Beach City Coll., 1950; BA, Calif. State U., Long Beach, 1952, MA, 1956; EdD, U. So. Calif., 1977. Elem. tchr. Long Beach Unified Sch. Dist., 1952-57; instr., counsellor Compton (Calif.) Coll., 1957-60; curriculum supr. Little Lake Sch. Dist., Santa Fe Springs, Calif., 1960-62; women's advisor, campus dean Long Beach City Coll., 1962-71, dir. Continuing Edn. Ctr. for Women, 1969-75, dean student affairs, 1971-77, v.p. student svcs., 1977-88, supt.-pres., 1988—, exec. dir. Found., 1983—; mayor City of Long Beach, Calif. Advisor Jr. League, Long Beach, 1976—, Nat. Coun. on Alcoholism, Long Beach, 1979—, Assistance League, Long Beach, 1982—; bd. dirs. NCCJ, Long Beach, 1976—, Meml. Hosp. Found., Long Beach, 1984-92, Met. YMCA, Long Beach, 1986-92, United Way, Long Beach, 1986-92. Named Woman of Yr., Long Beach Human Rels. Commn., 1976, to Hall of Fame, Long Beach City Coll., 1977, Disting. Alumni of Yr., Calif. State U., Long Beach, 1985, Long Beach Woman of Yr. Rick Rackers, 1987, Assistance League Aux., 1987; recipient Hannah Solomon award Nat. Coun. Jewish Women, 1984, Outstanding Colleague award Long Beach City Coll., 1985, NCCJ Humanitarian award, 1991, Woman of Excellence award YWCA, 1990, Community Svc. award Community Svcs. Devel. Corp., 1991, Citizen of Yr. award Exch. Club, 1992, Pacific Regional CEO award Assn. Community Coll. Trustees, 1992. Mem. Assn. Calif. Community Coll. Adminstrs. (pres. 1988-90, Harry Buttimer award 1991), Calif. Community Colls. Chief Exec. Officers Assn., Rotary, Soroptomists (Women Helping Women award 1981, Hall of Fame award 1984). Democrat. Office: Office of the Mayor 333 W Ocean Blvd Long Beach CA 90802-4604*

O'NEILL, BRIAN, research organization administrator; b. Bristol, Eng., Sept. 20, 1940; s. Raymond and Phyllis Mary (Marshall) O'N.; m. Alayne O'Neill, Aug. 31, 1969 (div. Sept. 1987); children: Allison Sarah, Stuart Douglas, Lesley Alexandra; m. Karen O'Neill, Feb. 20, 1988. BSc in Math. and Stats., Bath. U. Tech., 1965. Cons. in stats. and ops. research Unilever Ltd., London, 1965-66; research assoc. Tech. Ops. Inc., Ft. Belvoir, Va., 1966-67; mgr. applied math. dept. Wolf Research & Devel. Corp., Riverdale, Md., 1967-69; v.p., sr. v.p., exec. v.p. Ins. Inst. for Hwy. Safety, Washington, 1969-85, pres., 1985—; v.p., sr. v.p., exec. v.p. Hwy. Loss Data Inst., Washington, 1969-85, pres., 1985—; witness at numerous fed. and state hearings on hwy. safety and transp. Contbr. numerous articles to profl. jours.; also presentations at profl. confs. Mem. Am. Pub. Health Internat. Com. on Alcohol Drugs and Traffic Safety, Royal Statis. Soc., Soc. Automotive Engrs. Office: Ins Inst for Hwy Safety 1005 N Glebe Rd Ste 800 Arlington VA 22201-4751

O'NEILL, BRIAN BORU, lawyer; b. Hancock, Mich., June 7, 1947; s. Brian Boru and Jean Anette (Rimpela) O'N.; m. Ruth Bohan Sept. 18, 1991; children: Brian Boru, Maggie Byrne, Phelan Boru, Ariel Margaret. B.S., U.S. Mil. Acad., 1969; J.D. magna cum laude U. Mich., 1974. Bar: Mich. 1974, U.S. Ct. Mil. Appeals 1975, U.S. Ct. Appeals (6th cir.) 1975, Minn. 1977, U.S. Dist. Ct. Minn. 1977, U.S. Ct. Appeals (8th cir.) 1977. U.S. Ct. Claims, 1981, U.S. Supreme Ct. 1981, U.S. Ct. Appeals (fed. cir.) 1983, U.S. Ct. Appeals (7th cir.) 1985, U.S. Ct. Appeals (10th cir.) 1986, U.S. Ct. Appeals (9th cir.) 1990. Asst. to gen. counsel Dept. Army, Washington, 1974-77; assoc., ptnr. Faegre & Benson, Mpls., 1977—; mem. com. vis. Mich. Law Sch., 1994—; counsel Defenders of Wildlife, Washington, 1977—, also bd. dirs; counsel Sierra Club, Audubon Soc. Mng. editor Mich. Law Rev., 1973-74; contbr. articles to law jours. Served to capt. U.S. Army, 1969-77. Named Environmentalist of Yr., Sierra Club North Star, 1982, 96; recipient William Douglas award Sierra Club, 1985, Trial Lawyer of the Yr. award Trial Lawyers for Public Justice, 1995. Fellow Am. Coll. Trial Lawyers; mem. Order Coif. Clubs: Mpls. Golf, Mpls. Athletic. Office: Faegre & Benson 2200 Norwest Tower 90 S 7th St Minneapolis MN 55402-3903

O'NEILL, BRIAN DENNIS, lawyer; b. Phila., Feb. 21, 1946; s. Harry William and Margaret Elizabeth (Miller) O'N.; m. Bonnie Anne Ryan, Aug. 17, 1968; children: Aimee Kathleen, Catherine Margaret. BA, Fla. State U., 1968, JD, 1971. Bar: Fla. 1971, D.C. 1975, U.S. Ct. Appeals (D.C. cir.) 1978, U.S. Ct. Appeals (5th and 11th cirs.) 1981, U.S. Ct. Appeals (10th cir.) 1985. Trial atty. Fed. Power Commn., Washington, 1972-75; assoc. Farmer, Shibley, McGuinn & Flood, Washington, 1975-80; ptnr. LeBoeuf, Lamb, Greene & MacRae, Washington, 1980—; lectr. in field. Editorial bd. Energy Law Jour., Washington, 1983-84; contbr. articles to profl. jours. Bd. dirs. Immaculata Coll., Rockville, Md., 1989-91; bd. advisors Acad. of the Holy Cross, Kensington, Md., 1994—; bd. visitors Fla. State U. Coll. of Law, 1994—. 2d lt. USAF, 1971-72. Mem. Fla. Bar Assn. (pub. utilities com. 1985-90), Fed. Energy Bar Assn. (chmn. coms. 1983-84), Montgomery Village Golf Club (Gaithersburg, Md.) (bd. dirs. 1984-88), Congl. Country Club (Bethesda, Md.), Phi Alpha Delta. Democrat. Roman Catholic. Office: LeBoeuf Lamb Green & MacRae 1875 Connecticut Ave NW Washington DC 20009-5728

O'NEILL, CATHERINE R., emergency nurse, nurse manager; b. Lexington, Va., Oct. 11, 1946; d. Donald Franklin Sr. and Virginia Hazel (Birch) Ruth; m. John Joseph O'Neill Jr., Aug. 16, 1969; children: John Joseph III, Catherine Ann. Diploma, Church Home and Hosp., Balt., 1968; BS in Bus. Adminstrn., U. Balt., 1993; postgrad., U. Ctrl. Mich., 1996—. Cert. emergency nurse, trauma nurse core course, pediatric advanced life support, emergency nurse pediatric course, ACLS, EMT, haz-mat. Staff nurse Church Home and Hosp., 1968-70; intravenous therapy staff nurse Franklin Sq. Hosp., 1970-71; charge nurse in emergency rm. Mercy Med. Ctr., 1972-90; nurse mgr. emergency dept. Homewood Hosp. Ctr., 1990-91, North Arundel Hosp., 1991—. Co-author: White Paper on Over Crowding in ERs, ENA Legislative Manual. Mem. Orgn. Nurse Execs., Emergency Nurses Assn. Home: 2402 Charlton Ct Monkton MD 21111-1914

O'NEILL, CHARLES KELLY, marketing executive, former advertising agency executive; b. Springfield, Mo., Apr. 2, 1933; s. Charles Chester and Frances (Kelly) O'N.; m. Kyoko Hirano, June 2, 1981. B.J., U. Mo., 1955. With Galvin-Farris-Alvine, Kansas City, Mo., 1957-58; copy chief Galvin-Farris-Alvine, 1958; with Potts-Woodbury, Inc., Kansas City, 1958-61; chief time buyer Potts-Woodbury, Inc., 1960-61; with Gardner Advt. Co., St. Louis, 1962-88; assoc. media dir. Gardner Advt. Co., 1964-65, media dir., 1965-69, v.p., 1966-76, corp. media dir., dir. co., 1969-88, sr. v.p., 1976-78, pres., 1978-88; gen. mgr. Advansweers div., 1971-72; pres. Advansweers Media/Programming, Inc., 1973-78, chmn., 1978-88; v.p. Wells, Rich, Greene, N.Y.C., 1974-88; exec. v.p. Wells, Rich, Greene, 1979-88, dir., 1978-88; vice chmn. WRG-USA, 1981-88; chmn. O'Neill Mktg., Honolulu, 1988—; exec. v.p. Kyoko O'Neill, Inc., 1993—; dir. Colony Surf Ltd., Honolulu, 1990-94, chmn., bd. dirs., 1994. Bd. dirs. Waialae Iki Ridge Cmty. Assn., Honolulu, 1991—, 1st v.p., 1993-94. Lt. (j.g.) USN, 1955-57. Mem. St. Louis Advt. Club (gov. 1981-83), Outrigger Canoe Club (Honolulu), N.Y. Athletic Club, St. Louis Club, St. Louis Racquet Club, The Bridge (Navy League of the U.S.-Honolulu), Labrador Retriever Club of Hawaii, Sigma Chi, Alpha Delta Sigma. Episcopalian. Home: 1594 Hoaaina St Honolulu HI 96821-1345

O'NEILL, DONALD EDMUND, health science executive; b. Port Angeles, Wash., Feb. 10, 1926; s. Edward I. and Christine (Williamson) O'N.; m. Violet Elizabeth Oman, June 12, 1948; children: Shelly O'Neill Lane, Erin O'Neill Kennedy, Shawn O'Neill Hoffman. B.S., U. Wash., 1949. With G.D. Searle & Co., 1950-71, regional sales dir., 1962-64, dir. med. service, 1964-68, dir. mktg., 1968-71; with Warner-Lambert Co., 1971—, v.p., 1974-77, exec. v.p. pharm. group, 1977, exec. v.p.; chmn. Internat. profl. group, 1974-76; pres. Parke-Davis & Co., 1976-78; pres., exec. dir. Warner-Lambert/Parke Davis Research Div., 1978, pres. Health Care Group, 1978-81; pres. Parke-Davis Group, 1981, Health Techs. Group, 1982-86, Internat. Ops., 1986-89; exec. v.p., chmn. internat. ops. Warner-Lambert Co, 1989-91; ret., 1991; bd. dirs. Fujisawa U.S.A., Alliance Pharm. Immunogen Co., Fuisz Techs., Cytogen, Targeted Genetics. With USAAF, 1944-46. Mem. John's Island and Bent Pine Golf Clubs, Morris County Golf Club, Elk River Country Club.

O'NEILL, ELIZABETH STERLING, trade association administrator; b. N.Y.C., May 30, 1938; d. Theodore and Pauline (Green) Sterling: m. W.B. Smith, June 18, 1968 (div. Aug., 1978); 1 child, Elizabeth S. Kroese; m. Francis James O'Neill, May 19, 1984. BA, Cornell U., 1958; postgrad. studies, Northwestern U., 1959-60. Social sec. Perle Mesta Ambassador Luxembourg, N.Y.C.; spl. asst. Vivian Beaumont Allen, philanthropist, N.Y.C.; rep. Prentice-Hall Pub. Co., Eastern Europe; exec. dir. New Caanan (Conn.) C. of C., 1985-97; speaker various orgns. including Lions Club, Exchange Club, Kiwanis, Rotary, Poinsettia Club; apptd. Commn. Small Bus. State of Conn., 1996. Pres. Newcomers, New Caanan, Conn.; pub. rels. rep. Girl Scouts of U.S., Fairfield County; bd. dirs. Young Women's Rep. Club; mem. Gov. Weicker's Com. for Curriculum Reform; mem. community bd. Waveny Care Ctr., New Caanan; apptd. mem. Gov. John Roland's Commn. on Small Bus., Conn., 1996—. Recipient Service awards New Caanan YMCA, N.Y. ASPCA, certs. of appreciation New Caanan Lions Club, President Bush. Mem. AAUW (bd. dirs. New Canaan chpt.), Kiwanis. Christian Scientist. Avocations: tennis, horses, travel. Home: 17 Lance Rd Lebanon NJ 08833

O'NEILL, EUGENE FRANCIS, communications engineer; b. N.Y.C., July 2, 1918; s. John J. and Agnes (Willmeyer) O'N.; m. Kathryn M. Walls, Oct. 24, 1942; children—Kathryn Anne, Kevin, Jane A., Andrew Thomas. B.S. in Elec. Engring, Columbia U., 1940, M.S., 1941; D.Sc. (hon.), Bates Coll.; D.Engring. (hon.), Politecnico di Milano; D.Sc. (hon.), St. John's U., N.Y.C. With Bell Telephone Labs., Holmdel, N.J., until 1983, engaged in radar devel., 1941-45, coaxial and submarine cable and microwave radio relay, 1945-56, headed devel. of speech interpolation terminals which doubled capacity submarine telephone cables, 1956-60, dir. Telstar satellite projects, 1960-66, exec. dir. network projects, 1966-83. Pulitzer prize; scholar Columbia, 1936-40. Fellow IEEE; mem. Nat. Acad. Engring., Sigma Xi, Tau Beta Pi. Home: 17 Dellwood Ct Middletown NJ 07748-3010

O'NEILL, EUGENE MILTON, mergers and acquisitions consultant; b. Richmond, Calif., Nov. 4, 1925; s. John Milton and Vivian Elda (Vogel) O'N.; m. Jane Prigmore; children: Karen, Kay, Mary. B.S. in Bus. and Pub. Adminstrn., Washington U., St. Louis, 1949. CPA, Mo. Acct., Jeff K. Stone & Co., St. Louis, 1948-52; controller Campbell Holton & Co. (div. Gen. Grocer Co.), Bloomington, Ill., 1953-54; pres. Campbell Holton & Co. (div. Gen. Grocer Co.), 1955-57; v.p. Gen. Grocer Co., St. Louis, 1957-60, pres., 1960-74, chmn. bd., pres., 1974-83. Sec., trustee Food Industry Crusade Against Hunger. With Army Air Corp., 1943-45. Mem. Nat. Wholesale Am. Grocers Assn. (past chmn.). Home: 8 Deacon Dr Saint Louis MO 63131-4803

O'NEILL, FRANCIS XAVIER, III, marketing executive; b. Hampton, Va., June 25, 1953; s. Francis Xavier Jr. and Elizabeth Theresa (Javorsky) O'N. BA in History cum laude, So. Conn. State U., 1980. Clk. FBI, Washington, N.Y.C., 1975-78; rsch. analyst McGavren Guild Radio, N.Y.C., 1981; rsch. mgr. McGavren Guild Radio, 1982, rsch. dir., 1982-84; v.p. mktg. rsch. div. Interep, 1984-90; mgr. mktg. devel. The Arbitron Co., N.Y.C., 1990-93, cons. mktg. comm. and joint ventures, 1994-95; dir. sports rsch. CBS TV Network, N.Y.C., 1995-96, dir. media and sports rsch., 1996-97, dir. sports and cable rsch., 1997—. Author (booklets) Radio's Got Rhythm, 1984, Flying to Succeed: Frequent Business Air Travelers, 1988, The Vital Link: Adults 35-54 in American Society, 1988, On The Air: American Team Sports and the Media, 1989, Seasonal Listening Trends, 1991, Frequent Moviegoers, 1994, Reaching The Non-Prescription Drug Consumer, 1994. Campaigner Francis O'Neill Jr. for State Rep., Conn., 1980-92. Avocations: writing, music, biking, tennis. Home: 213 Crosswood Rd Branford CT 06405 Office: 51 West 52nd St New York NY 10019

O'NEILL, GEORGE DORR, business executive; b. N.Y.C., Dec. 27, 1926; s. Grover and Catharine (Porter) O'N.; m. Abby Milton, June 22, 1949; children: George D. Jr., Abby Caulkins, David M., Catharine Broderick, Wendy Wang, Peter M. BA, Harvard Coll., 1950. Registered rep. Harris Upham & Co., N.Y.C., 1949-53; with Chase Manhattan Bank, N.Y.C., 1953-58; chmn. exec. com. Equity Corp., N.Y.C., 1959-63, Train Cabot & Assocs., N.Y.C., 1963-76; chmn. Meriwether Capital Corp., N.Y.C., 1977—; chmn., bd. dirs. Chemstone Corp., Strasburg, Va., 1984-94, Victoreen Inc., Cleve., 1990—, C&W Fabricators, Inc., Gardner, Mass., 1996—. Trustee Colonial Williamsburg (Va.) Found., 1966-94, Inc. Village of Oyster Bay (N.Y.) Cove, 1989—, Ednl. Broadcasting Corp., N.Y.C., 1991—; commr. The Port Authority of N.Y. and N.J., N.Y.C., 1991—. With U.S. Merchant Marine Cadet Corps, 1945-46. Office: Meriwether Capital Corp 30 Rockefeller Plz Ste 5432 New York NY 10112-5499

O'NEILL, HARRY WILLIAM, survey research company executive; b. Atlantic City, Jan. 30, 1929; s. Harry William and Marian Elizabeth (Kuhl) O'N.; m. Carmel Gullo, Sept. 21, 1952; children: Sharon Ruth, Randal Bruce. B.A., Colgate U., 1950; M.S., Pa. State U., 1951. Lic. practicing psychologist, N.J. Research analyst Prudential Ins. Co., Newark, 1957-62; with Opinion Research Corp., Princeton, N.J., 1962-87; sr. v.p. Opinion Research Corp., 1970-73, exec. v.p., 1973-80, pres., 1980-85, vice chmn., 1985-87; vice chmn. Roper Starch Worldwide, N.Y.C., 1988—; mem. coadj. faculty Rutgers U., 1959-64; vis. lectr. Woodrow Wilson Sch., Princeton U., 1980-82;. Editor Marketing Research: A Magazine of Management & Applications, 1988-93. Pres. Nat. Coun. Pub. Polls, 1984-94, trustee, 1994—; bd. dirs. Roper Ctr. for Pub. Opinion Rsch., 1984-94, chmn., 1994—; bd. dirs. Coun. Am. Survey Rsch. Orgns., 1981-83, chmn., 1982-83; vice chmn. Rsch. Industry Coalition, 1993-94, chmn., 1994-95; mem. Highland Park (N.J.) Human Rights Commn., 1973-77; bd. dirs. Del-Raritan Lung Assn., 1974-88, v.p., 1977-82, chmn., 1982-84; fin. chmn. Highland Park Rep. Orgn., 1977-89. Served with USAF, 1951-54. Recipient Maroon citation Colgate U., 1975. Mem. Am. Psychol. Assn., Ea. Psychol. Assn., Am. Assn. Pub. Opinion Rsch., Assn. Consumer Rsch., Am. Mktg. Assn., Market Rsch. Coun., Highland Park Rep. Club, Masons, Elks. Presbyterian. Office: Roper Starch Worldwide 205 E 42nd St New York NY 10017-5706

O'NEILL, JAMES ANTHONY, JR., pediatric surgeon, educator; b. N.Y.C., Dec. 7, 1933; m. Susan Pokorny; children: James Anthony III, Elizabeth, Kathryn S. BS, Georgetown U., 1955; MD, Yale U., 1959. Diplomate Am. Bd. Surgery (bd. dirs. 1981-87, sr. 1988—), Am. Bd. Thoracic Surgery; lic. surgeon, Ohio, La., Tenn., Pa.; cert. instr. advanced trauma life support. Intern Vanderbilt U. Hosp., 1959-60, asst. resident, 1960-64, resident, instr. surgery, 1964-65; chief burn study divsn. U.S.A. Surgl Rsch. Unit Brooke Army Med. Ctr., 1965-67; resident, USPHS fellow in pediatric oncology Columbus Children's Hosp., 1967-69; instr. pediatric surgery Coll. Medicine Ohio State U., 1967-69; asst. prof. surgery and pediatrics, chief pediatric surg. svc. Sch. Medicine La. State U., 1969-70, assoc. prof. surgery, chief sect. pediatric surgery, 1970-71; prof. surgery, chmn. dept. pediatric surgery Sch. Medicine Vanderbilt U., 1971-81, chief med. staff Med. Ctr., 1976-77; prof. pediatric surgery Sch. Medicine U. Pa., Phila., 1981-95, C.E. Koop prof. pediatric surgery, 1988-95; surgeon-in-chief Children's Hosp. Phila., 1981-95; chmn. of surgery, J.C. Foshee Disting. prof. surgery Vanderbilt U. Med. Ctr., Nashville, 1995—; site visitor residency rev. com. for surgery AMA; mem. trauma care subcom. med. adv. com. Phila. Emergency Med. Svcs. Coun.; surg. cons. U.S. Army Inst. Surg.

Rsch., Ft. Sam Houston, Tex. Mem. editorial bd. Jour. Burn Care and Rehab., Jour. Enteral and Parenteral Nutrition, Jour. Surg. Rsch., Peduatrics, 1984—, Pediatric Emergency Care, 1984—, Pediatric Surgery, Pediatric Surgery Internat., 1988; mem. assoc. editorial bd. Jour. Pediatric Surgery; sect. editor Jour. Trauma, 1983—, Jour Vascular Surgery, 1992; contbr. 350 articles to med. jours. Mem. med. adv. bd. Hope Found.; mem. adv. bd. James Whitcomb Riley Rsch. Found., 1986-89; mem. standards com. State Pa. Found. for Trauma Care. Fellow Am. Acad. Pediatrics (surg., pediatric trauma care coord. Pa. chpt., sect. on oncology-hematology chmn. surg. sect. program com. 1975-77, adv. com. postgrad. edn. 1979-81, exec. com. surg. sect. 1977-80, chmn. 1980-81); mem. ACS (founding, cancer liason physician, Met. Phila. chpt., exec. com. trauma com. 1975-77, adv. coun. pediatric surgery 1977-83, 86-88, 90—, postgrad. edn. com. 1979-82, continuing edn. com. 1981-88, nominating com. 1986, regental ad hoc com. on legis issues in trauma in emergency med. svcs. 1987—, bd. govs. 1990—, com. to study fiscal affairs coll. 1992-93, subcom. on burns, spl. soc. gov. from. AM. Pediatric Surg. Assn. 1992—, coun. on acad. surgery 1993—, v.p. Phila chpt. 1993-94), Am. Assn. for Surgery Trauma, Am. Trauma Soc. (bd. dirs. 1974-78), Am. Burn Assn., Am. Pediatric Surg. Assn. (sec. 1976-79, chmn. edn. com. 1984-87, pres.-elect 1987-88, pres. 1988-89, manpower, trauma and issues and ethics coms.), Am. Surg. Assn., Assn. for Acad. Surgery (membership com. 1973-74), Soc. for Surgery Alimentary Tract, Soc. Univ. Surgeons (edn. com. 1974-75), Assn. Program Dirs. in Surgery (steering com. 1990-94), Internat. Soc. for Burn Injuries, Internat. Soc. Parenatal Nutrition, Brit. Assn. Pediatric Surgeons, S.E. Surg. Congress (program com. 1979-82), So. Gut Club, So. Soc. for Pediatric Rsch., So. Surg. Assn., Tenn. Med. Assn. (del. 1976, 77), Tenn. Pediatric Soc., New Orleans Surg. Soc., Phila. Acad. Surgery, Phila Peduatric Soc., Coll. Physicians Phila. (coun. 1988-91), Portland Surg. Soc. (hon.), Nashville Surg. Soc., Davidson County Med. Assn., James D. Rives Surg. Soc., Halsted Soc. (bd. govs. 1986-89), Alpha Omega Alpha. Office: Vanderbilt Univ Med Ctr Dept of Surgery D-4316 MCN Nashville TN 37232-2730

O'NEILL, JOHN H., JR., lawyer; b. Bainbridge, Md., Oct. 20, 1946; s. John Hardin and Lois May (Schnepfe) O'N.; m. Vivian Lidwina Gemelli, Nov. 29, 1969; children: Eric Michael, David Christopher, Sean Timothy, Daniel Ryan. BS with distinction in Naval Engring., U.S. Naval Acad., 1968; JD, Yale U., 1976. Bar: Md. 1976, D.C. 1977, U.S. Supreme Ct., U.S. Dist. Ct. D.C.; lic. to supervise operation, maintenance naval nuclear propulsion power plants AEC. Commd. ensign USN, 1968, officer on nuclear submarines, 1968-73; resigned, 1973; ptnr., chmn. energy practice group Shaw, Pittman, Potts & Trowbridge, Washington, 1976—; gen. counsel various nuclear industry cos.; cons. in field to fgn. govs. Mem. ABA, Internat. Bar Assn., Internat. Nuclear Law Assn., SERL (chmn. com. on nuclear energy). Republican. Roman Catholic. Avocations: squash, tennis, skiing. Office: Shaw Pittman Potts & Trowbridge 2300 N St NW Washington DC 20037-1122

O'NEILL, JOHN JOSEPH, speech educator; b. De Pere, Wis., Dec. 6, 1920; s. John Joseph and Elizabeth (Murray) O'N.; m. Dorothy Jane Arnold, Dec. 28, 1943; children—Katherine, Thomas, John, Philip. B.S., Ohio State U., 1947, Ph.D., 1951. From instr. to assoc. prof. speech Ohio State U., 1949-59; prof. speech U. Ill. at Champaign, 1959-91, prof. emeritus, 1991—; prof. audiology U. Ill. Coll. Medicine, Chgo., 1965-79, head speech and hearing sci. dept., 1973-79; research assoc. U.S. Naval Sch. Aviation Medicine, summers 1953, 54; cons. in field. Co-author: Visual Communication, 1961, 81;, Hard of Hearing, 1964, Applied Audiometry, 1966. Pres. Columbus Hearing Soc., 1956-58; Bd. dirs. Champaign County Assn. Crippled-United Cerebral Palsy, 1961-63. Served with inf. AUS, 1942-46. Decorated Purple Heart, Bronze Star with oak leaf cluster; recipient Disting. Alumnus award dept. speech Ohio State U., 1969, recipient honors, 1979. Fellow Am. Speech and Hearing Assn. (pres. 1969), Ohio Psychol. Assn.; mem. Am. Bd. Examiners Speech Pathology and Audiology (pres. 1967-68), Acad. Rehabilitative Audiology (pres. 1969). Home: 1203 W University Ave Champaign IL 61821-3224

O'NEILL, JOHN JOSEPH, JR., business consultant, former chemical company executive; b. N.Y.C., Sept. 13, 1919; s. John Joseph and Margaret (Patterson) O'N.; m. Irene Ray, Apr. 18, 1940; children—Anne, Mary (Mrs. George Schuler). B.S. in Chem. Engring, Mo. Sch. Mines, 1940, Chem. Engr., 1951. Research engr. Western Cartridge Co., 1940-49; with Olin Industries, Inc., 1949-60, dir. prodn. explosives operations, energy div., 1959-60; with Olin Mathieson Chem. Corp., 1960-71, asst. to pres., 1963-64, staff v.p. planning, 1964-65, v.p. comml. devel., chems. group, 1965-67, corporate v.p. plastics, 1967-70, corporate v.p. product diverification, 1970-71; cons., 1971-72; exec. v.p., chief operating officer Kleer-Vu Inc., N.Y.C., 1972-76; v.p. planning and devel. Vertac Consol., 1976-77; pres., chief exec. officer Vertac, Inc., 1977-78, cons., 1979-80, vice chmn. bd., chief oper. officer, 1980-81; cons., 1981—; pres. Jonco, Inc., 1986-89. Contbr. articles to profl. jours.; patentee explosives, chemicals, ordnance items. Emeritus trustee St. Mary-of-Woods Coll., Terre Haute, Ind. Fellow Am. Inst. Chemists; mem. Am. Inst. Chem. Engring. Club: Chemists (N.Y.C.). Home and Office: 7 Castlewood Ln PO Box 429 Pinehurst NC 28370-0429

O'NEILL, JOHN ROBERT, airline executive; b. Bronxville, N.Y., Feb. 13, 1937; s. John R. and Hazel (Edwards) O'N.; m. Laura M. Bellmer, May 25, 1962; children: Amy, Wendy. B.A., Hamilton Coll., 1958. Various positions in scheduling Eastern Airlines, Miami, Fla., 1961-71, dir. schedule planning, 1971-74, systems dir. schedule planning, 1974-75, dir. current schedules, 1975-80, dir. schedules, 1980-81, v.p. schedules, 1981-87; v.p. scheduling TWA Airlines, 1987—. Mem. Phi Beta Kappa. Presbyterian. Office: TWA Airlines 515 N 6th St Saint Louis MO 63101-1842

O'NEILL, JOHN T., toy company executive; b. N.Y.C., Oct. 25, 1944; s. John and Rhoda (Dillon) O'N; m. Lois E. McGarry, Oct. 8, 1966; children: John, Margaret, Gregory, Brian. BS in Acctg., Providence Coll., 1962-66. Acct. Arthur Andersen & Co., Providence, 1966-67; ptnr. Peat Marwick, KPMG, Providence, 1970-84; mng. ptnr. Peat Marwick KPMG, 1984-87; sr. v.p. fin. Hasbro, Inc., Pawtucket, R.I., 1987-88; sr. v.p., chief fin. officer Hasbro, Inc., 1988-89, exec. v.p., chief fin. officer, 1990—; mem. pres. coun. Providence Coll.; bd. dirs., past pres. Jr. Achievement R.I.; pres., bd. dirs. Galaxy Funds. Trustee Women and Infants Hosp. R.I., Providence; treas., bd. dirs. R.I. Philharmonic Orch., Providence, C. of C.; chmn. Catholic Charity Fund, Providence. Capt. Med. Svc. Corps, U.S. Army, 1967-70. Decorated Bronze Star. Mem. AICPA, R.I. CPA Soc., Inst. Mgmt. Accts., Fin. Execs. Inst., Warwick Country Club, Hope Club, Dunes Club, Bonita Bay Club, Univ. Club. Avocations: golf, outdoors, art. Office: Hasbro Inc 200 Narragansett Park Dr Pawtucket RI 02861-4338

O'NEILL, JUNE ELLENOFF, economist; b. N.Y.C., June 14, 1934; d. Louis and Matilda (Liebstein) Ellenoff; m. Sam Cohn, 1955 (div. 1961); 1 child, Peter; m. David Michael O'Neill, Dec. 24, 1964; 1 child, Amy. BA, Sarah Lawrence Coll., Bronxville, N.Y., 1955; PhD, Columbia U., 1970. Econs. instr. Temple U., Phila., 1965-68; rsch. assoc. Brookings Instn., Washington, 1968-71; sr. economist Pres.'s Coun. Econ. Advisors, Washington, 1971-76; chief human resources budget Congl. Budget Office, Washington, 1976-79; sr. rsch. assoc. The Urban Inst., Washington, 1979-86; dir. Office Policy and Rsch. U.S. Commn. Civil Rights, Washington, 1986-87; prof. econs. and fin., dir. Ctr. for Study Bus. and Govt. Baruch Coll., CUNY, 1987-95; dir. Congl. Budget Office U.S. Congress, Washington, 1995—; adj. scholar Am. Enterprise Inst., 1994-95; mem. Nat. Adv. Com., The Poverty Inst., U. Wis., 1988-95. Contbr. articles to profl. jours. Rsch. grantee, U.S. Dept. Labor, NICHD, Dept. Health & Human Svcs., others. Mem. Am. Econs. Assn. (past bd. dirs. com. on status of women), Nat. Acad. Social Ins. Republican. Jewish. Home: 420 Riverside Dr New York NY 10025-7773 Office: Congressional Budget Ofc Ford HOB US Congress Washington DC 20515

O'NEILL, MARY JANE, health agency executive; b. Detroit, Feb. 24, 1923; d. Frank Roger and Kathryn (Rice) Kilcoyne; Ph.B. summa cum laude, U. Detroit, 1944; postgrad. U. Wis., 1949-50; m. Michael James O'Neill, May 31, 1948; children: Michael, Maureen, Kevin, John (dec.), Kathryn. Editor, East Side Shopper, Detroit, 1939-45; club editor Detroit Free Press, 1945-48; reporter UP, Milw. and Madison, Wis., 1949; dir. pub. rels. Fairfax-Falls Church (Va.) Cmty. Chest, 1955-60; copy editor Falls Ch. Sun-Echo, 1958-60; free-lance writer, Washington, 1960-63; assoc. editor Med. World News, Washington, 1963-66; dir. public relations Westchester Lighthouse, N.Y. Assn. for Blind, 1967-71; dir. public edn. The Lighthouse, N.Y.C., 1971-73, dir. pub. rels., 1973-80; exec. dir. Eye-Bank for Sight Restoration, Inc., 1980—. Mem. N.Y. State Transplant Coun., 1991—; bd. dirs. N.Y. Organ Donor Network, 1987-91, 94—, Pro Mujer, 1997—. Mem. Women in Communications (pres. N.Y. chpt. 1980-81), Eye Bank Assn. Am. (lay adv. bd. 1981-83, dir. 1983-86, pres. N.E. Region, 1993-96, exec. com. 1994-96), Pub. Rels. Soc. Am., Women Execs. in Pub. Rels. (dir. 1982-88, pres. 1986-87), N.Y. Acad. Scis., Cosmopolitan Club. Office: Eye-Bank for Sight Restoration 120 Wall St New York NY 10005-3902

O'NEILL, MICHAEL FOY, business educator; b. Milw., Apr. 16, 1943; s. Edward James and Marcellian (Wesley) O'N.; m. Karen Lynn Shoots, June 13, 1968; children: Kristine, Brenna. BBA, Ohio State U., 1966; PhD in Bus. Adminstrn., U. Oreg., 1978. Cons. Robert E. Miller and Assocs., San Francisco, 1969-73; mem. faculty Calif. State U., Chico, 1971-73, 1980—, U. Oreg., Eugene, 1974-77, U. Ariz., Tucson, 1977-79; pres. Decision Sci. Inst., Atlanta, 1986-87, v.p., 1985-86. Contbr. articles to profl. jours. Served with U.S. Army, 1962-68. Recipient Dean's Research award Calif. State U., Chico, 1981. Avocations: golf, fly fishing. Home: 2819 North Ave Chico CA 95973-0916 Office: Calif State U Dept Fin and Mktg Chico CA 95926

O'NEILL, MICHAEL JAMES, editor, author; b. Detroit, Nov. 19, 1922; s. Michael J. and Ellen Mary (Dacey) O'N.; B.A., U. Detroit, 1946, L.H.D. (hon.), 1977; postgrad. Fordham U., 1946-47; m. Mary Jane Kilcoyne, May 31, 1948; children: Michael, Maureen, Kevin, Kathryn. Writer Standard News Assn., N.Y.C., 1946-47; with UPI, 1947-56; Washington corr. N.Y. Daily News, 1956-66, asst. mng. editor, 1966-68, mng. editor, 1968-74, exec. editor, 1974-75, editor, 1975-82, v.p., 1971-79, exec. v.p., 1979-82, also dir.; freelance writer, lectr., 1983—. Mem. Nat. Adv. Coun. Health Professions Edn., 1967-71. Served with U.S. Army, 1943-45; ETO. Decorated Bronze Star. Recipient Nat. Affairs Reporting award Nat. Headliner's, 1956. Mem. Overseas Writers (pres. 1965), Am. Soc. Newspaper Editors (pres. 1981-82), Council Fgn. Relations. Club: Century (N.Y.C.). Author: (with L. Tanzer) The Kennedy Circle, 1961; China Today, 1976, Terrorist Spectaculars: Should TV Coverage Be Curbed, 1986, The Roar of the Crowd, How TV and People Power are Changing the World, 1993, (with K.M. Cahill) Preventive Diplomacy, 1996. Address: 23 Cayuga Rd Scarsdale NY 10583-6941

O'NEILL, PATRICK HENRY, consulting mining engineer; b. Cordova, Alaska, Aug. 11, 1915; s. Harry I. and Florence (Leahy) O'N.; m. Sandra Dorris, Dec. 5, 1967; children: Kevin Reddy, Erin Dorris, Patrick Henry, Timothy Hazleton, Frederick Leahy. B.S., B.Min.E., U. Alaska, 1941, E.M., 1953, D.Sc. (hon.), 1976. Engr. and supt. U.S. Smelting Refining & Mining Co., Fairbanks, Alaska, 1939-41, 46-53; chief engr. Compañia Minera Choco Pacifico, Colombia, 1953-54; v.p. South Am. Gold & Platinum Co., N.Y.C., 1954-57; exec. v.p. Internat. Mining Corp. (formerly SAG&P Co.), 1957-70; chmn. Frontino Gold Mines Ltd., London, 1958-76; pres. S.Am. Placers, Bolivia, 1960-76; chmn. Pato Consol. Gold Dredging Ltd., Can., 1961-76, Consol. Purchasing and Designing, San Francisco, 1961-77; pres. Internat. Mining Corp., 1970-76; sr. v.p. Rosario Resources Corp., N.Y.C., 1977-80; exec. v.p. Rosario Resources Corp., 1981-82; mining cons., 1982—; bd. dirs. Zemex Corp., Toronto, Ont. Chmn. bd. trustees Joslin Diabetes Ctr., Boston, 1981-94. Served to maj. USAAF, 1941-46. Mem. Mining and Metall. Soc. Am., Am. Inst. Mining, Metall. and Petroleum Engrs., Can. Inst. Mining and Metallurgy, Arctic Inst., NAM (gov., chmn. 1972-73), Pioneers of Alaska, Instn. Mining and Metallurgy London, Am. Geog. Soc. (councilor), Ireland-U.S. Coun. for Commerce and Industry (dir.), Explorers Club, Chemists Club, Wings Club, Met. Club (N.Y.C.), Darien Country Club, Woodway Country Club. Home and Office: 42 Dunning Rd New Canaan CT 06840-4008

O'NEILL, PAUL ANDREW, professional baseball player; b. Columbus, Ohio, Feb. 25, 1963. BS, Otterbein Coll. With Cin. Reds, 1985-92; outfielder N.Y. Yankees, 1993—. Recipient Am. League Batting Champion, 1994; named to Am. League All-Star Team, 1994-95, Nat. League All-Star Team, 1991. Mem. World Series Champions. Office: New York Yankees Yankee Stadium E 161 St and River Ave Bronx NY 10451*

O'NEILL, PAUL HENRY, aluminum company executive; b. St. Louis, Dec. 4, 1935; s. John Paul and Gaynald Elsie (Irvin) O'N.; m. Nancy Jo Wolfe, Sept. 4, 1955; children: Patricia, Margaret, Julie, Paul Henry. BA, Fresno State Coll., 1960; Haynes Found. fellow, Claremont Grad. Sch., 1960-61; postgrad., George Washington U., 1962-65; MPA, Ind. U., 1966; hon. degree, Clarkson U., 1993. Site engr. Morrison-Knudsen, Inc., Anchorage, 1955-57; systems analyst VA, Washington, 1961-66; budget examiner Bur. of Budget, Washington, 1967-69; chief human resources program div. U.S. Govt. Office of Mgmt. and Budget, Washington, 1969-70; asst. dir. U.S. Govt. Office of Mgmt. and Budget, 1971-72, assoc. dir., 1973-74, dep. dir., 1974-77; v.p. Internat. Paper Co., N.Y.C., 1977-81, sr. v.p., 1981-85, pres., dir., 1985-87; chmn., CEO Aluminum Co. Am., Pitts., 1987—, also bd. dirs.; bd. dirs. Rand Corp, chmn.; bd. dirs. Lucent Techs., Coun. for Excellence; chmn. Pres.'s Edn. Policy Adv. Com., 1989-92. Bd. dirs. Gerald R. Ford Found., 1981—; dir. Manpower Demonstration Rsch. Corp., 1981—, Coun. for Excellence; trustee Am. Enterprise Inst., H. John Heinz III Ctr. for Sci., Econs. and the Environment; mem., coun. mem. Miller Ctr. at U. Va. Recipient Nat. Inst. Pub. Affairs Career Edn. award, 1965, William A. Jump Meritorious award, 1971; Fellow Nat. Inst. Pub. Affairs, 1966. Mem. Bus. Coun., Bus. Roundtable (policy com.), Nat. Acad. Social Ins. (founding mem.), Inst. Internat. Econs. (bd. dirs.), Inst. Rsch. on Econs. of Taxation, Internat. Primary Aluminum Inst. (former chmn.), Mgmt. Exec. Soc. Methodist. Office: Alumninum Co Am 425 6th Ave Ste 31 Pittsburgh PA 15219-1819

O'NEILL, PAUL JOHN, retired psychology educator; b. Taunton, Mass., Apr. 12, 1936; s. Clarence Bernard and Edna Mary (Burke) O'N.; 1 child, Maureen Kelly O'Neill. BA, St. Bonaventure (N.Y.) U., 1960; MA, Boston U., 1961; EdD, U. Ga., 1973. Lic. psychologist. Prof. psychology Jackson (Miss.) State U., 1972—, 1972-93; dir. critical thinking and outcome measures program Jackson (Miss.) State U., 1987-93. Contbr. articles to profl. jours. With U.S. Army, 1954-56, Germany. Home: 7005 Copper Cv Ridgeland MS 39157-1044

O'NEILL, PHILIP DANIEL, JR., lawyer, educator; b. Boston, Sept. 19, 1951; s. Philip Daniel Sr. and Alice Maureen (Driscoll) O'N.; m. Lisa G. Arrowood, June 25, 1983; children: Alexander Edwin, Sean Matthew, Madeleine Clarice. BA, Hamilton Coll., 1973; JD cum laude, Boston Coll., 1977. Bar: Mass. 1977, N.Y. 1985, R.I. 1988. Assoc. Hale and Dorr, Boston, 1977-83, ptnr., 1983-87; ptnr. Edwards & Angell, Boston, 1987—; adj. rsch. fellow John F. Kennedy Sch. Govt., Ctr. for Sci. and Internat. Affairs Harvard U., 1983-86; adj. prof. law Boston U., 1992, Boston Coll., 1988—; cons. Arms Control and Disarmament Agy. U.S. Dept. Def., 1983-84; guest lectr., commentator Boston Coll. Law Sch., Harvard U. Bus. Sch., Kennedy Sch. Govt., 1985, Boston U. Law Sch., 1990-91, Harvard Law Sch., 1994-95; internat. and domestic comml. arbitrator Am. Arbiration Assn., Hong Kong Ctr. for Internat. Arbitration, N.Am. Free Trade Agreement, Internat. C. of C. Ct. Arbitration Paris, Inter-Am. Comml. Arbitration Commn., Japanese Comml. Arbitration Assn., Cairo Regional Ctr., Euro-Arab C. of C., World Intellectual Property Orgn.; panelist in internat. and domestic legal programs. Contbr. chpts. to books and articles to profl. jours. Fellow Chartered Inst. Arbitrators (Eng.); mem. ABA, Internat. Law Assn. (chmn. am. br. arbitration com. 1985-89, rep. internat. arbitration com. 1989—), Boston Bar Assn. (chmn. internat. law sect. 1994-96, past chmn. internat. litigation and arbitration com.), Am. Soc. Internat. Law. Home: 11 Blackburnian Rd Lincoln MA 01773-4317 Office: Edwards & Angell 101 Federal St Boston MA 02110-1817

O'NEILL, RICHARD PAUL, federal agency administrator; b. Balt., Nov. 19, 1943; m. Nichole Rose Phillips; children: Shannon, Colin. BS in Chem. Engring., U. Md., MBA in Ops. Rsch., Math., PhD in Ops. Rsch., Math. Asst. prof. U. Md., Coll. Park, 1969-73, La. State U., Baton Rouge, 1973-78; dir. oil and gas analysis Energy Info. Adminstrn., Washington, 1978-86; dir. pipeline and producer regulation Fed. Energy Regulatory Commn., Washington, 1986-88, chief economist, dir. office of econ. policy, 1988—. Office: Dept Energy FERC Econ Policy 888 1st St NE Washington DC 20426-0001

O'NEILL, ROBERT CHARLES, inventor, consultant; b. Buffalo, Dec. 3, 1923; s. Albert T. and Helen (Lynch) O'N.; m. Agnes Balischak; 1 dau., Eileen Anne. BS in Chemistry, Rensselaer Poly. Inst., 1945; PhD in Organic Chemistry, Mass. Inst. Tech., 1950. Sr. chemist Merck & Co., Inc., Rahway, N.J., 1950-56, marketing devel. specialist, 1956-58; v.p. Stauffer Pharms. div. Stauffer Chem. Co., N.Y.C., 1958-61; v.p., dir. R & D Cooper Labs., Inc., 1961-70, exec. v.p., 1970-76, gen. mgr., 1975-76, pres., 1976-77, also dir.; cons., inventor, 1977—. Contbr. articles to profl. jours. Served with USNR, 1943-46. Mem. Am. Chem. Soc., Chemists Club N.Y. Patentee in field. Home: 10 Whitlaw Close Chappaqua NY 10514-1008

O'NEILL, ROBERT EDWARD, business journal editor; b. N.Y.C., Aug. 30, 1925; s. Joseph Michael and Ethel Agnes (Seymour) O'N.; m. Phyllis Ann Schreck, Apr. 19, 1952; children: Keith, Kathy, Kim, Karen. B.A. in Journalism, Syracuse (N.Y.) U., 1950. Reporter Southeasterner, Long Island, N.Y., 1950-51; rep. Bklyn. Daily, 1952; asso. editor Progressive Grocer, N.Y.C., 1952-62; sr. editor Progressive Grocer, 1962-69, exec. editor, 1970-86; editor in chief Monitor mag., Stamford, Conn., 1986-92; editorial dir. Progressive Grocer; dir. Sopro Foods, Inc. Contbg. author/editor: Foodtown Study, 1954, Super Valu Study, 1957, Dillon Study, 1959, Colonial Study, 1961, Outstanding New Super Markets, 1961, Consumer Dynamics, 1963, A & P Study, 1970, Merchandising in Action, 1972, Consumer Behavior Study, 1976, Brand Power Study, 1977. Served with USN, 1944-47. Mem. Am. Bus. Press (editorial com. 1974-75, co-winner, Jesse H. Neal award 1961, 66, 74, 89, 90, Points of Light award 1991), Glacier Hills Assn. (pres. 1964-66), Sigma Delta Chi. Club: Overseas Press. Home: 67 Moraine Rd Morris Plains NJ 07950-2752 Office: O'Neill Assocs 67 Moraine Rd Morris Plains NJ 07950-2752

O'NEILL, SALLIE BOYD, education educator, business owner, sculptor; b. Ft. Lauderdale, Fla., Feb. 17, 1926; d. Howard Prindle and Sarah Frances (Clark) Boyd; AA, Stephens Coll., 1945; m. Roger H. Noden, July 8, 1945; children: Stephanie Ann Ballard, Ross Hopkins Noden; m. Russell R. O'Neill, June 30, 1967. Course coord. UCLA Extension, 1960-72, specialist continuing edn. dept. human devel., acad. appointment, 1972-83; pres. Learning Adventures, Inc., 1985-86; v.p., CFO The Learning Network, Inc., 1985-86; ednl. cons., 1986—; sculptor, 1987—. Bd. dirs. Everywoman's Village, Sherman Oaks, Calif., 1988—, v.p. 1993-95. Mem. Women in Bus. (v.p., bd. dirs. 1976-77, 86-87), Golden State Sculpture Assn., UCLA Assn. Acad. Women. Democrat. Home and Studio: 15430 Longbow Dr Sherman Oaks CA 91403-4910

O'NEILL, SHEILA, principal. Prin. Cor Jesu Acad., St. Louis. Recipient Blue Ribbon award U.S. Dept. Edn., 1990-91. Office: Cor Jesu Acad 10230 Gravois Rd Saint Louis MO 63123-4030

O'NEILL, THOMAS NEWMAN, JR., federal judge; b. Hanover, Pa., July 6, 1928; s. Thomas Newman and Emma (Cornpropst) O'N.; m. Jeanne M. Corr., Feb. 4, 1961; children: Caroline Jeanne, Thomas Newman, III, Ellen Gitt. A.B. magna cum laude, Catholic U. Am., 1950; LL.B. magna cum laude, U. Pa., 1953; postgrad. (Fulbright grantee), London Sch. Econs., 1955-56. Bar: Pa. 1954, U.S. Supreme Ct. 1959. Law clk. to Judge Herbert F. Goodrich U.S. Ct. Appeals (3d cir.), 1953-54; to Justice Harold H. Burton U.S. Supreme Ct., 1954-55; assoc. firm Montgomery, McCracken, Walker & Rhoads, Phila., 1956-63; ptnr. Montgomery, McCracken, Walker & Rhoads, 1963-83; judge U.S. Dist. Ct. (ea. dist.) Pa., 1983—; counsel 1st and 2d Pa. Legis. Reapportionment Commns., 1971, 81; lectr. U. Pa. Law Sch., 1973. Articles editor: U. Pa. Law Rev, 1952-53. Former trustee Lawyers Com. for Civil Rights Under Law; former mem. Gov.'s Trial Ct. Nominating Commn. for Phila. County; former mem. bd. overseers U. Pa. Mus. Fellow Am. Coll. Trial Lawyers; mem. Am. Law Inst. (life), Phila. Bar Assn. (chancellor 1976), Pa. Bar Assn. (gov. 1978-81), U. Pa. Law Alumni Soc. (pres. 1976-77), Pa. Conf. County Bar Officers (pres. 1981-82), Am. Inn of Ct. (founding chmn. U. Pa.), Order of Coif (pres. U. Pa. chpt. 1971-73), Merion Cricket Club, Edgemere Club, Broadacres Trouting Assn., Phi Beta Kappa, Phi Eta Sigma. Office: US Dist Ct 14613 US Courthouse 601 Market St Philadelphia PA 19106-1713

O'NEILL, TIMOTHY, federal agency administrator; m. Virginia O'Neill; children: Elizabeth Porter, John Timothy Jr., David Elliott. Degree in fgn. svc. magna cum laude, Georgetown U., 1976; JD, Harvard U., 1980. Legis. dir. U.S. Senator John Heinz of Pa., Washington; dep. dir. congl. affairs U.S. AID, Washington; sr. legis. mgr. for internat. affairs U.S. Dept. Treasury, Washington; dir. congl. affairs Fed. Housing Fin. Bd., Washington, dir., 1995—; ptnr. O'Connor & Hannan, Washington. Office: Fed Housing Fin Bd 1777 F St NW Washington DC 20006-5210*

O'NEILL, TIMOTHY P., lawyer; b. Shotts, Scotland, Sept. 23, 1940; came to U.S., 1953; s. Thomas P. and Catherine (O'Connor) O'N.; m. Maria E. Karagianis, May 19, 1982; children: Katherine, Elizabeth. STB, Gregorian U., Rome, 1965; MA, Brandeis U., 1970; JD, Boston U., 1971. Bar: Mass. 1972, U.S. Dist. Ct. Mass. 1982, U.S. Ct. Appeals (1st cir.) 1982. Asst. dist. atty. Suffolk County, Mass., 1972-81; assoc. Driscoll and Gillespie, Lynn, Mass., 1981-83; ptnr. Murphy, DeMarco & O'Neill, Boston, 1983-93, Hanify & King, P.C., Boston, 1993—; clin. supr. Sch. Law Harvard U., Cambridge, Mass., 1976-81; lectr. Mass. Continuing Legal Edn., 1988—. Chmn. fin. com. City of Boston, 1984-86. Recipient Disting. Prosecutor award Citizens for Decency Through Law, Phoenix, 1981. Mem. ABA, Internat. Assn. Defense Coun., Mass. Bar Assn., Inns Ct. Avocations: skiing, reading, classical music. Home: 145 Dudley Ln Milton MA 02186-4019 Office: Hanify & King PC One Federal St Boston MA 02110

O'NEILL, WILLIAM LAWRENCE, history educator; b. Big Rapids, Mich., Apr. 18, 1935; s. John Patrick and Helen Elizabeth (Marsh) O'N.; m. Elizabeth Carol Knollmueller, Aug. 20, 1960; children: Cassandra Leigh, Catherine Lorraine. A.B., U. Mich., 1957; M.A., U. Calif., Berkeley, 1958, Ph.D., 1963. Asst. prof. history U. Colo., 1964-66; asst. prof. U. Wis., 1966-69, asso. prof., 1969-71; prof. Rutgers U., New Brunswick, N.J., 1971—; vis. asst. prof. U. Pitts., 1963-64; vis. asso. prof. U. Pa., 1969-70. Author: Divorce in the Progressive Era, 1967, Everyone Was Brave: The Rise and Fall of Feminism in America, 1969, rev. and repub. as: Feminism in America: A History, 1989, Coming Apart: An Informal History of America in the 1960's, 1971, The Last Romantic: A Life of Max Eastman, 1978, 2d edit., 1991, A Better World: The Great Schism: Stalinism and the American Intellectuals, 1982, repub. as: A Better World: Stalinism and the American Intellectuals, 1989, American High: The Years of Confidence, 1945-60, 1986, A Democracy at War: America's Fight at Home and Abroad in World War II, 1993. Nat. Endowment Humanities fellow, 1979-80. Mem. Am. Hist. Assn. Office: Rutgers U Dept History New Brunswick NJ 08903

O'NEILL, WILLIAM PATRICK, lawyer; b. Joplin, Mo., Sept. 14, 1951; s. Fred Charles and Dorothy Isabel (Snyder) O'N.; m. Mary Louise Richardson, June 17, 1989. BA, U. Kans., 1973; JD, U. Mich., 1976. Bar: Ill. 1976, U.S. Dist. Ct. (no. dist.) Ill. 1976, U.S. Dist. Ct. D.C. 1982. Assoc. Kirkland & Ellis, Chgo., 1976-81, Sidley & Austin, Chgo., 1982-85, Skadden, Arps, Slate, Meagher & Flom, N.Y.C., 1986-87; assoc. Crowell & Moring, Washington, 1987-88, ptnr., 1988—; gen. counsel Ill. Common Cause, Chgo., 1979-81. Editor, author: (with others) Successfully Acquiring A U.S. Business, 1990; editorial chmn. Antitrust Law Jour., 1984-89. Mem. University Club of Chgo. Office: Crowell & Moring 1001 Pennsylvania Ave NW Washington DC 20004-2505

O'NEILL, WILLIAM WALTER, physician, educator; b. Nov. 24, 1951; m. Carol; children: Brian, Katie, Julie, Molly. BS, U. Mich., 1972; MD, Wayne State U., 1977. Diplomate Am. Bd. Internal Medicine, Am. Bd. Cardiology. Intern in internal medicine U. Wis., Madison, 1977-78; resident in internal medicine Wayne State U., Detroit, 1978-80; fellow U. Mich., Ann Arbor, 1980-82, instr. internal medicine, 1982-83, asst. prof., 1983-86, assoc. prof., 1986-87; dir. cardiac catheterization lab. U. Mich. Hosp., Ann Arbor, 1984-87; dir. divsn. cardiology William Beaumont Hosp., Royal Oak, Mich., 1987—; attending cardiologist VA Hosp., Ann Arbor, 1982-90; chmn. govt. rels. subcom. Nat. Cardiovasc. Network; rsch. peer rev. com. Am. Heart Assn. Mich., 1988-89; chmn. publs. com. Mansfield Scientific Balloon Valvuloplasty Registry; bd. govs. William Beaumont Hosp. Rsch. Inst.; presenter in field. Author: Myocardial Revascularization by Coronary Angioplasty or Bypass Surgery During MI in Acute Myocardial Infarction:

New Approaches to Evaluation and Therapy, 1986, (chpt.) Acute Coronary Intervention, 1987, Current Perspective in Coronary Care, 1987, Interventional Cardiovascular Medicine, 1994, Acute Coronary Care, 2d edit., 1995; co-author: (chpts.) Cardiovascular Review, 6th edit., 1985, 8th edit., 1987, Tissue Plasminogen Activator in Thrombolytic Therapy, 1987, Techniques and Applications in Interventional Cardiology, 1991, Atherectomy, 1992, Emergency Medicine: A Comprehensive Study Guide, 3d edit., 1992, Adjunctive Therapy for Acute Myocardial Infarction, 1992, Manual of Interventional CArdiology, 1992, Cura Intensiva Cardiologica, Primary Coronary Angioplasty in Acute Myocardial Infarction; author, co-author: (chpt.) Interventional Cardiovascular Medicine, 1994; editl. cons. Jour. Intervention Cardiology; mem. editl. bd. Catheterization Cardiovasc. Diagnosis; contbr. over 400 articles to profl. publs. Grantee Smith/Kline Beecham, 1989-90, 90—, Advanced Cardiovasc. Sys., Inc., 1988-90, 90—, Midwest Heart Rsch. Found., Abbott Labs., 1990—, Duke U., 1990—, William Beaumont Hosp. Rsch. Inst., 1990—. Fellow Am. Coll. Cardiology (chpt. sec.-treas. 1993-94, reimbursement com.), Am. Coll. Chest Physicians, Coun. Clin. Cardiology; mem. AMA, ACP, Internat. Andreas Gruentzig Soc. Office: William Beaumont Hosp. 3601 W 13 Mile Rd Royal Oak MI 48073-6712

ONEK, JOSEPH NATHAN, lawyer; b. N.Y.C., Jan. 9, 1942; s. Jacob J. and Doris (Aaronson) O.; m. Margot Debrah Piore, June 29, 1963; children: David, Matthew. A.B. magna cum laude, Harvard Coll., 1962; M.A., London Sch. Econs., 1964; LL.B. magna cum laude, Yale Law Sch., 1967. Bar: D.C. 1968. Law clk. to chief judge David L. Bazelon, U.S. Ct. Appeals (D.C. cir.), 1967-68; law clk. Justice William J. Brennan, U.S. Supreme Ct., 1968-69; staff Senate Adminstrv. Practice and Procedure Subcom., Senate Labor and Pub. Welfare Commn., 1969-71; dir., atty. Ctr. for Law and Social Policy, 1971-76; adj. prof. U. Md. Law Sch., Health Care Law, 1976-77; dir. health policy analysis Carter-Mondale Transition Planning Group, 1976-77; assoc. dir. for health and human resources Domestic Policy Staff, White House, 1977-79; dep. counsel to Pres., White House, 1979-81; ptnr. Onek, Klein & Farr, Washington, 1981-91; ptnr. Crowell & Moring, 1991—; presdl. appointee to D.C. Jud. Nominating Com., 1994—. Marshall scholar, 1962. Mem. ABA, Phi Beta Kappa. Home: 3723 Ingomar St NW Washington DC 20015-1819 Office: Crowell & Moring 1001 Pennsylvania Ave NW Washington DC 20004-2595

ONESTI, SILVIO JOSEPH, psychiatrist; b. San Francisco, Jan. 3, 1926; s. Silvio Joseph and Johanna (Kristoffy) O.; m. Jean Thomas, May 12, 1956; children: Sally Joanna, Stephen Thomas. BS, Stanford U., 1947; MD, McGill U., 1951. Diplomate Am. Bd. Psychiatry and Neurology. Instr. pediatrics Yale Med. Sch., New Haven, 1956-58; career tchr. psychiatry NIMH, Harvard Med. Sch., Beth Israel Hosp., Boston, 1963-65; head child psychiatry unit Beth Israel Hosp., Boston, 1965-73; dir. child and adolescent psychiatry McLean Hosp., Belmont, Mass., 1973-91; dir. Hall-Mercer Ctr. for children and adolescents McLean Hosp., Belmont, 1973-91; dir. child and adolescent psychiat. tng., 1973-92; dir. clin. svcs. McLean Hosp., Belmont, 1981-83; asst. prof. psychiatry Harvard Med. Sch., Boston, 1969—; faculty Boston Psychoanalytic Soc. and Inst. Inc., Boston, 1971-81. Contbr. articles to profl. jours. With USN, 1944-46. Fellow Am. Psychiat. Assn., Am. Acad. Child and Adolescent Psychiatry, Am. Coll. Psychiatrists; mem. Group for Advancement of Psychiatry (fellow 1959-61, bd. dirs. 1987-89), Boston Psychoanalytic Soc. and Inst. Inc., Mass. Med. Soc., Alpha Omega Alpha. Home: 4 Gray Gdns W Cambridge MA 02138-2312 Office: McLean Hosp 115 Mill St Belmont MA 02178-1041

ONG, CHEE-MUN, engineering educator; b. Ipoh, Perak, Malaysia, Nov. 23, 1944; came to U.S., 1978; s. Chin-Kok Ong and Say-Choo Yeoh; m. Penelope Li-Lok, July 17, 1971; children: Yi-Ping, Yi-Ching, Chiew-Jen. BE with honors, U. Malaysia, 1967; MS, Purdue U., 1968, PhD, 1974. Registered profl. engr. Ind., Eng. Plant engr. Guinness Brewery, Malaysia, 1967; asst. lectr. U. Malaysia, 1968-73, lectr., 1976-78; rsch. asst. Purdue U., West Lafayette, Ind., 1973-74, vis. asst. prof., 1975-76, asst. prof., 1978-81, assoc. prof., 1981-85, prof., 1985—; cons. SIMTECH, West Lafayette, 1978-85, L.A. Water and Power Co., 1986-88, Caterpillar, 1993-94. Contbr. articles to jours. in field. Fulbright-Hayes scholar, 1967-68; UNESCO fellow, 1969-70. Fellow Inst. Elec. Engrs. (U.K.); mem. IEEE (sr.). Avocations: gardening, fishing, reading. Office: Purdue U Dept Elec Engring 1285 Elec Engring Bldg West Lafayette IN 47907

ONG, JOHN DOYLE, lawyer; b. Uhrichsville, Ohio, Sept. 29, 1933; s. Louis Brosee and Mary Ellen (Liggett) O.; m. Mary Lee Schupp, July 20, 1957; children: John Francis Harlan, Richard Penn Blackburn, Mary Katherine Caine. BA, Ohio State U., 1954, MA, 1954; LLB, Harvard, 1957; LHD, Kent State U., 1982. Bar: Ohio 1958. Asst. counsel B.F. Goodrich Co., Akron, 1961-66, group v.p., 1972-73, exec. v.p., 1973-74, vice chmn., 1974-75, pres., dir., 1975-77, pres., chief operating officer, dir., 1978-79, chmn. bd., pres., chief exec. officer, 1979-84, chmn. bd., chief exec. officer, 1984-96, chmn. bd., 1996—; asst. to pres. Internat. B.F. Goodrich Co., Akron, 1966-69, v.p., 1969-70, pres., 1970-72; bd. dirs. Cooper Industries, Ameritech Corp., The Kroger Co., Asarco, Inc., Geon Co., TRW, Inc. V.p. exploring Great Trail coun. Boy Scouts Am., 1974-77; bd.d irs. Nat. Alliance of Bus., 1981-84; trustee Mus. Arts Assn., Cleve., Bexley Hall Sem., 1974-81, Case Western Res. U., 1980-92, Kenyon Coll., 1983-85, Hudson (Ohio) Libr. and Hist. Soc., pres., 1971-72, Western Res. Acad., Hudson, 1975-95, pres. bd. trustees, 1977-95; nat. trustee Nat. Symphony Orch., 1975-83, John S. and James L. Knight Found., 1995—; mem. bus. adv. com. Transp. Ctr. Northwestern U., 1975-78, Carnegie-Mellon U. Grad. Sch. Indsl. Adminstrn., 1978-83; trustee U. Chgo., 1991—; chmn. Ohio Bus. Roundtable, 1994—. Mem. Ohio Bar Assn. (bd. govs. corp. counsel sect. 1962-74, chmn. 1970), Rubber Mfrs. Assn. (bd. dirs. 1974-84), Chem. Mfrs. Assn. (bd. dirs. 1988-91, 94-97), Conf. Bd., Bus. Roundtable (chmn. 1992-94), Bus. Coun., Portage Country Club, Union Club, Links, Union League, Ottawa Shooting Club, Met. Club, Rolling Rock Club, Castalia Trout Club, Phi Beta Kappa, Phi Alpha Theta. Episcopalian. Home: 230 Aurora St Hudson OH 44236-2941

ONG, MICHAEL KING, mathematician, educator, banker; b. Manila, Philippines, Dec. 16, 1955; s. Sanchez and Remedios (King) O. BS in Physics cum laude, U. Philippines, 1978; MA in Physics, SUNY, Stony Brook, 1979, MS in Applied Math., 1981, PhD in Applied Math., 1984. Asst. prof. Bowdoin Coll., Brunswick, Maine, 1984-91; sr. mathematician, fin. analyst Chgo. Rsch. & Trading Group Ltd., 1990-92; v.p., sr. rsch. analyst First Chgo. Corp., 1993-94, head market risk analysis unit, 1994—, 1st v.p., head corp. rsch. unit, 1996-97; sr. v.p., head treasury bus. rsch. ABN-AMRO Bank, Chgo., 1997—; adj. prof. fin. markets and trading program Stuart Sch. Bus. Ill. Inst. Tech., 1990—. Mem. editl. bd. Jour. Fin. Regulation & Compliance; contbr. articles to profl. jours. Mem. Am. Fin. Assn., Am. Math. Soc., Math. Assn. Am., Soc. Indsl. and Applied Math., Consortium for Math. and Its Applications, Am. Phys. Soc., Phi Kappa Phi. Avocations: writing, singing, traveling, painting. Home: 2650 N Lakeview Ave Apt 4106 Chicago IL 60614-1833 Office: ABN-AMRO Bank 181 W Madison St Fl 31 Chicago IL 60602-4510

ONG, WALTER JACKSON, priest, English educator, author; b. Kansas City, Mo., Nov. 30, 1912; s. Walter Jackson and Blanche Eugenia (Mense) O. AB, Rockhurst Coll., 1933; PhL, St. Louis U., 1940, AM, 1941, STL, 1948; PhD, Harvard U., 1955; various hon. degrees. Joined S.J., Roman Cath. Ch., 1935, ordained priest, 1946. Newspaper, comml. positions until, 1935; instr. English and French Regis Coll., Denver, 1941-43; asst. English St. Louis U., 1944-47, instr., 1953-54, asst. prof., 1954-57, assoc. prof., 1957-59; prof., 1959—, prof. humanities in psychiatry Sch. Medicine, 1970—, Univ. prof. humanities, 1981—, prof. emeritus, 1984—; mem. Fulbright nat. selection com., France, 1957-58, chmn., 1958; regional asso. Am. Coun. Learned Socs., 1957-66; mem. White House Task Force on Edn., 1966-67, Nat. Coun. on Humanities, 1968-74, vice chmn., 1971-74; co-chmn. adv. com. on sci., tech. and human values NEH, 1974-78; mem. Rockefeller Found. Commn. on Humanities, 1978-80; vis. prof. U. Calif., 1960; Terry lectr., Yale, 1963-64; vis. lectr. U. Poitiers, 1962; Berg prof. English N.Y. U., 1966-67; McDonald lectr. McGill U., 1967-68; Willett vis. prof. humanities U. Chgo., 1968-69; nat. Phi Beta Kappa vis. scholar, 1969-70; Lincoln lectr. Central and West Africa, 1973-74; Messenger lectr. Cornell U., 1979-80; Alexander lectr. U. Toronto, 1981; vis. prof. comparative lit. Washington U., 1983-84; Wolfson Coll. lectr. Oxford U., 1985. Author: Frontiers in American Catholicism, 1957, Ramus, Method, and the Decay of Dialogue, 1958, Ramus and Talon Inventory, 1958, Am. Cath. Crossroads, 1959, The Barbarian Within, 1962, In the Human Grain, 1967, The Presence of the Word, 1967, Rhetoric, Romance and Technology, 1971, Why Talk?, 1973, Interfaces of the Word, 1977, Fighting for Life: Contest, Sexuality, and Consciousness, 1981, Orality and Literacy, 1982, Hopkins, the Self and God, 1986, Faith and Contexts, 3 vols., 1992-95; co-author, editor: Darwin's Vision and Christian Perspectives, 1960, Knowledge and the Future of Man, 1968; editor: Petrus Ramus and Audomarus Talaeus, Collectaneae praefationes epistolae, orationes, 1969, Petrus Ramus, Scholae in liberales artes, 1970; co-editor, translator: Logic (John Milton), 1982; mem. editl. bd. Studies in English Literature, 1962—; editl. adv. bd. Philosophy and Rhetoric, 1967—, The English Literary Renaissance, 1969—, Manuscripta, 1957—, others; contbr. articles, chpts. to learned and popular publs. Mem. adv. bd. John Simon Guggenheim Meml. Found., 1962-84; trustee Nat. Humanities Faculty, 1968-76, chmn., 1974-76. Decorated chevalier l'Ordre des Palmes Académiques (France); Guggenheim fellow, 1949-50, 51-52; fellow Ctr. Advanced Studies, Wesleyan U., Middletown, Conn., 1961-62; fellow Sch. Letters, Ind. U., 1965—; fellow Ctr. for Advanced Study in Behavioral Scis., Stanford, 1973-74. Fellow Am. Acad. Arts and Scis.; mem. AAUP, MLA (pres. 1978), Renaissance Soc. Am. (adv. coun. 1957-59), Modern Humanities Rsch. Assn., Nat. Coun. Tchrs. English, Cambridge Bibliog. Soc. (Eng.), Catholic Commn. Intellectual and Cultural Affairs (exec. com. 1962-63), Milton Soc. of Am. (pres. 1967), Phi Beta Kappa, Alpha Sigma Nu. Office: Saint Louis University Saint Louis MO 63103

ONGMAN, JOHN WILL, lawyer; b. Chgo., July 19, 1951; s. John Warner and Helen Will (Dunbar) O.; m. Joanne Patricia Sawicki, Oct. 17, 1981. BS, Purdue U., 1972; MS, U. Ill., 1973; JD, Northwestern U., 1976. Bar: Ill. 1976, D.C. 1984, N.Y. 1990. Law clk. to Hon. Walter J. Cummings U.S. Ct. Appeals 7th cir., Chgo., 1976-77; assoc. Sidley & Austin, Chgo. and Washington, 1977-83; ptnr. Pepper, Hamilton & Scheetz, Washington, 1983—. Contbr. numerous articles to law jours. Mem. University Club of Chgo., Metropolitan Club of Washington. Office: Pepper Hamilton & Scheetz 1300 19th St NW Washington DC 20036-1609

ONKEN, GEORGE MARCELLUS, lawyer; b. Bklyn., Aug. 15, 1914; s. William Henry and Lillian Charlotte (Dawe) O.; m. Mildred Ann Tausch, Dec. 13, 1958; children: Jane Elizabeth, Nancy Catherine. AB, Princeton U., 1936; LLB, Columbia U., 1948; LLM, NYU, 1952. Bar: N.Y. 1949. Asst. to pres. Welsbach Engring. and Mgmt. Corp., Phila., 1939-43; mem. legal staff L.I. R.R., 1949-78, gen. counsel, 1963-78, v.p., 1966-78, sec., 1968-78. Bd. dirs. Orphan Asylum Soc., Bklyn., 1958—, YMCA Greater N.Y., 1963-80, Pop Warner Little League, 1976-78; bd. mgrs. Pa. R.R. br. YMCA, N.Y.C., 1957-80, chmn., 1967-80; trustee Bklyn. YWCA, 1976-92. Lt. (j.g.) USNR, 1943-46. Recipient Man of Year award YMCA, 1977; Outstanding Svc. award Bklyn. Chpt. ARC Greater N.Y., 1994. Mem. Newcomen Soc. N.Am. Republican. Episcopalian (vestry 1958-64, 76-85). Clubs: Union League (N.Y.C.), Univ. (N.Y.C.), Church (N.Y.C.); Rembrandt (Bklyn.), Heights Casino (Bklyn.), Ihpetonga (Bklyn.). Home: 215 Adams St Brooklyn NY 11201-2856

ONO, CHERYL EIKO, senior controls engineer; b. Chgo., Feb. 26, 1965; d. Mitsuo and Sachiye (Ikeda) O. BS, Eastern Ill. U., 1987, MS, 1988. Grad. asst. Eastern Ill. U., Charleston, 1987-88; intern GE Co., Mattoon, Ill., 1988, mfg./quality engr., 1988-92; controls engr. GE Co., Ravenna, Ohio, 1992-94; advanced process engr. GE Co., Nela Park, Cleve., 1994-95, sr. controls engr., 1995-97; Black Belt, Six Sigma Quality Engr. Black Belt, Six Sigma Quality Engr., Nela Park, Cleve., 1997—. Mem. Am. Soc. Quality Engrs., Epsilon Pi Tau. Avocations: camping, aerobics, biking. Office: GE Lighting 1975 Noble Rd Cleveland OH 44112-1719

ONORATO, NICHOLAS LOUIS, program director, economist; b. South Barre, Mass., Feb. 24, 1925; s. Charles and Amalia (Tartaglia) O.; m. Elizabeth Louise Settergren, July 19, 1947; children: Gary, Deborah, Nicholas, Jeffrey, Glenn, Charles, Lisa. B.S. in Pub. Relations, Boston U., 1951; M.A. in Econs, Clark U., 1952, Ph.D., 1959. Mem. faculty Becker Jr. Coll., Worcester, Mass., 1952-54; prof. econs. Worcester Poly. Inst., 1955-68, chmn. dept. econs., govt., bus., 1968-74, dir. Sch. Indsl. Mgmt., 1972—; prof. emeritus Worcester (Mass.) Poly Inst., 1994; vis. prof. Clark U., Worcester, 1964-66; fin. cons. Coz Chem. Co., Northbridge, Mass., 1959-95. Contbr. to newspapers and mags. Trustee Bay State Savs. Bank, Worcester. Served with USNR, 1943-46. Mem. Am. Finance Assn., Am. Econ. Assn., Am. Accounting Assn., Phi Kappa Theta. Club: Torch (pres. Worcester 1967, 87, 95). Home: 39 Knollwood Dr Shrewsbury MA 01545-3329 Office: Institute Rd Worcester MA 01609

ONSAGER, JEROME ANDREW, research entomologist; b. Northwood, N.D., Apr. 8, 1936; s. Alfred and Anne Marie (Kielbauch) O.; m. Bette Lynn Stanton, Aug. 16, 1958. B.S., N.D. State U., 1958, M.S., 1960, Ph.D., 1963. Research entomologist USDA Agrl. Research Service, Sidney, Mont., 1963—. Contbr. articles on biology, ecology, population dynamics of rangeland grasshoppers to profl. jours. Fellow NSF, 1960. Mem. Entomol. Soc. Am., Entomol. Soc. Can., Orthopterist Soc., Sigma Xi, Alpha Zeta. Lutheran. Avocations: fishing; big game hunting; equestrian activities. Home: 309 4th St SE Sidney MT 59270-5011 Office: USDA ARS No Plains Agrl Rsch Lab 1500 N Central Ave Sidney MT 59270-4202

ONSANIT, TAWACHAI, physician; b. Trang, Thailand, Jan. 14, 1940; arrived in U.S., 1965; s. Toon and Tanomchit (Kongsong) O.; m. Bubpha Janturagit, May 8, 1966; children: Krittika, Addie. MD, Chulalongkorn Med., Bangkok, 1964. Rotating intern Queens Gen. Hosp., N.Y.C., 1965-66; resident in gen. surgery Med. Coll. of Ohio, Toledo, 1966-70; resident in colon and rectal surgery Allentown (Pa.) Gen. Hosp., 1970-72; mem. staff Coaldale (Pa.) Hosp., 1973-77, Sentara Hosp., Virginia Beach, Va., 1977—; pvt. practice, 1973—; asst. prof. clin. surgery Ea. Va. Med. Sch., Norfolk, Va., 1993. Fellow ACS, Am. Soc. Colon and Rectal Surgery; mem. Soc. Am. Gastrointestinal Endoscopic Surgeons. Avocations: photography, ballroom dancing, reading. Office: 1020 Independence Blvd Ste 204 Virginia Beach VA 23455-5542

ONSLOW FORD, GORDON MAX, painter; b. Wendover, Buckinghamshire, Eng., Dec. 26, 1912; came to U.S., 1947, naturalized, 1952; s. Max and Maud Elizabeth (Woollerton) Onslow Ford; m. Jacqueline Marie Johnson, May 5, 1941. Grad., Royal Naval Coll., Dartmouth, Eng., 1929; grad., Royal Naval Coll., Greenwich, Eng., 1930. Mem. Surrealist Group, Paris, London, N.Y.C., 1938-43. One-man shows include New Sch. for Social Rsch., N.Y.C., 1940, Nierendorf Gallery, N.Y.C., 1946, San Francisco Mus. Art, 1948, M.H. DeYoung Mus., San Francisco, 1962, San Francisco Mus., 1951, 59, 70, Oakland (Calif.) Mus., 1977, Art Gallery Greater Victoria, B.C., 1971, Samy Kinge Gallery, Paris, 1985; group shows: Paris, 1983, London, 1940, N.Y.C., 1943, L.A. County Mus., 1950, 61, 70, 87, Newport Harbor Mus., 1986, Mus. Rath, Geneva, 1987, Centro Atlantico De Arte Moderno, Gran Canaica, Spain, 1989, Laguna Art Mus., 1990, U. Calif.-Berkeley Art Mus., 1990, Pepperdine U. Art Mus., 1992, Harcourt Gallery, San Francisco, 1993, Pavillion Gallery, Munich, 1993, Brochier Gallery, Munich, 1993, Mus. Bochum, Germany, 1994, Museo de Arte Contemporáneo, Santiago, Chile, 1995, Kunsthaus foram, Bonn, Germany, 1996, Arts & Consciousness Gallery, Berkeley, Calif., 1996; permanent collections: San Francisco Mus. Modern Art, Tate Gallery, London, M.H. deYoung Mus., Oakland Mus., Guggenheim Mus., N.Y.C., Whitney Mus. Modern Art, N.Y.C., Denver Mus., Fogg Mus., U. Mass., U. Calif.-Davis, L.A. County Mus. Art, Chgo. Art Inst.; author: Toward A New Subject in Painting, 1947, Painting in the Instant, 1964, Creation, 1978, Yves Tanguy and Automatism, 1983, Insights, 1991, Ecomorphology, 1993.

ONSTEAD, RANDALL, consumer goods company executive. Pres. Randall's Food & Drug Inc., Houston, 1976—. Office: Randall's Food & Drug Inc 3663 Briarpark Dr Houston TX 77042-5205*

ONSTEAD, ROBERT R., consumer goods company executive; b. 1931. Student, North Tex. State Tchrs. Coll., 1952-54. With IBM Co., Dallas, 1954-55, Randall's Super Valu, Houston, 1955-57; v.p. Randall's #1, Inc., Houston, 1957-64, pres., 1964-66; pres. & COO Randall's Food Markets, Inc., Houston, 1966-1996, now chmn. bd., 1996—. With USAF, 1951-52. Office: Randalls Food Markets Inc 3663 Briarpark Dr Houston TX 77042-5205

ONTJES, DAVID AINSWORTH, medicine and pharmacology educator; b. Lyons, Kans., July 19, 1937; s. Max S. and Elizabeth (Ainsworth) O.; m. Sherri James, Aug. 27, 1960; children: Linden F., Sarah E., Ethan A., Jason A. B.A., U. Kans., 1959; M.A., Oxford U., 1961; M.D., Harvard U., 1964. Am. Bd. Internal Medicine, sub-board endocrinology. Intern, resident Boston City Hosp., 1964-66; research assoc. NIH, Besthesda, Md., 1966-69; asst. prof. dept. medicine and pharmacology U. N.C., Chapel Hill, 1969-72, assoc. prof., 1972-76, prof., 1976—, Eunice Bernhardt Disting. prof., 1982—. Contbr. articles in field to profl. jours. Served with USPHS, 1966-69. Rhodes scholar Oxford U., 1959-61; USPHS grantee Nat. Ints. Arthritis and Metabolic Diseases, NIH, 1969-82; recipient Basic Sci. Teaching award U. N.C., 1978. Fellow ACP; mem. Endocrine Soc., Am. Soc. Clin. Investigation, Am. Soc. Pharmacology and Exptl. Therapeutics, Assn. Profs. Medicine. Republican. Presbyterian. Office: U NC Sch Medicine Dept Medicine Chapel Hill NC 27599-7527

ONUCHIC, JÓSE NELSON, biophysics educator, electrical engineer; came to U.S., 1990; BS in Elec. Engring., U. Sao Paulo, Brazil, 1980, BS in Physics, 1981, MS in Applied Physics, 1982; PhD in Chemistry, Calif. Inst. Tech., 1987. Asst. prof. physics Inst. Physics and Chemistry Sao Carlos U. Sao Paulo, Brazil, 1987-90; asst. prof. physics U. Calif. San Diego, 1990-92, assoc. prof. physics, 1992-95, prof. of physics, 1995—. Contbr. articles to profl. jours. Sr. fellow San Diego Wupercomputer Ctr., 1997—; recipient Engring. Inst. prize, Sao Paulo, 1980, Internat. Ctr. for Theoretical Physics Prof. Werner Heisenberg prize, Trieste, Italy, 1988; elected assoc. mem. Acad. Scis. Estado de Sao Paulo, 1991; named Beckman Young Investigator, 1992. Fellow Am. Phys. Soc. Office: Univ Calif at San Diego Dept Physics La Jolla CA 92093 Office: U Calif San Diego Dept Physics 9500 Gilman Dr La Jolla CA 92093-5003

ONUFROCK, RICHARD SHADE, pharmacist, researcher; b. Colorado Springs, Colo., July 5, 1934; s. Frank and Mildred Joy (Overstreet) O.; m. Karen Faye Larson, June 15, 1958 (div. 1980); children: Richard Alan (dec.), Amy Mildred. BS in Pharmacy, U. Colo., 1961; diploma, Famous Artists Schs., 1963. Registered pharmacist, Colo., Ariz., South Africa. Pharmacist Aley Drug Co., Colorado Springs, 1961-75, St. Joseph Hosp., Denver, 1976-77, Navajo Nation Health Found., Ganado, Ariz., 1977-81, Kearny (Ariz.) Kennecott-Samaritan Hosp., 1984-85, NIH, Warren G. Magnuson Clin. Ctr., Bethesda, Md., 1988—; dir. pharmacy, chief pharmacist Tintswalo Hosp., South Africa, 1981-84; pharmacist, chief pharmacist Miami (Ariz.)-Inspiration Hosp., 1985-88; instr. Coll. of Ganado, 1979-80; asst. in textbook revision and illustration U. Colo., 1961; cons. Heritage Health Care Ctr., Globe, Ariz., 1988. Illustrator Pharmacy for Nurses, 1961, Colo. Jour. of Pharmacy, 1962-64; illustrations exhibited Colo. Springs Fine Art Ctr., 1964-66, Gilpin County Art Assn., Central City, Colo., 1968-74, 1st Nat. Space Art Show, Denver, 1969. dem. precinct committeeman, 1974-76; den leader Boy Scouts Am., com. mem., 1975-76; fireman, lt. Ganado Vol. Fire Dept., 1977-81; compassionate med. missionary Nazarene Ch., Tintswalo Hosp. Gazankulu, South Africa, 1981-84;bd. dirs. Friends of Libr., Kearny, 1985-87; active Grace Episcopal Ch. Mem. Am. Pharm. Assn., Am. Soc. Hosp. Pharmacists, Washington Met. Soc. Hosp. Pharmacists, Phi Delta Chi, Delta Sigma Phi. Avocations: traveling, bicycling, hiking, skiing, computers. Home: 4831 36th St NW Apt 202 Washington DC 20008-4917 Office: NIH Clin Ctr 9000 Rockville Pike Bethesda MD 20814-1436

OOLIE, SAM, manufacturing and investment company executive; b. N.Y.C., Aug. 11, 1936; s. Bernadt S. and Rose (Moyel) O.; m. Marjorie R. Oolie, Dec. 3, 1961; children: Janis, Caroline, Tara. BS in Metallurgy, MIT, 1958; MBA, Harvard U., 1961. Chmn. Food Concepts, Inc., Rutherford, N.J., 1962-85; pres. CFC Venture Capital Corp., Fairfield, N.J., 1984-90; chmn. Oolie Enterprises, Upper Saddle River, N.J., 1985—; vice chmn. Am. Mobile, Inc., Secaucus, N.J., 1986-89; chmn. The Nostalgia Network, N.Y.C., 1987-90, New Thermal Corp., Keasbey, N.J., 1991-95; chmn., CEO NoFire Tech., Inc., Upper Saddle River, N.J., 1995—; bd. dirs. Avesis, Inc., Phoenix, Comverse Tech., N.Y.C., Noise Cancellation Tech., Stamford, Conn. Mem. exec. com. State of N.J.-Israel Commn., 1989—; commr. Essex County Improvement Authority, 1987-88; trustee Coun. Jewish Fedns., 1986—; bd. govs. Haifa U., 1986-90, 93—; trustee Garden State Cancer Ctr., 1989—, Beth Israel Med. Ctr., 1990-96, Assn. Reform Zionists Am., 1990-97, Am. Joint Distbn. Com., 1990—; pres. United Jewish Fedn. Met. West N.J., 1988-90; vice chmn. United Jewish Appeal, 1986-96; chmn. Beth Israel Health Care Found., 1993-96. Recipient Gates of Jerusalem award Boys Town of Jerusalem, 1990, Israel 40th Ann. medal State of Israel Bonds, 1988. Mem. World Bus. Coun., Harvard Club of N.Y., Greenbrook Country Club. Avocations: golf, numismatics. Office: 21 Industrial Ave U Saddle Riv NJ 07458-2301

OOMS, VAN DOORN, economist; b. Chgo., Oct. 29, 1934; s. Casper William and Ruth P. (Miller) O.; m. Theodora J. Parfit, June 17, 1961; children: Katrina, Alex, Tamara. BA summa cum laude, Amherst Coll., 1956, LHD (hon.), 1981; BA with 1st class honors, Oxford (Eng.) U., 1958, MA, 1962; M.A., Yale U., 1960, Ph.D., 1965. Lectr. Yale U., 1962, asst. prof. econs., to 1968; assoc. prof. Swarthmore Coll., 1968, prof., to, 1978; chief economist U.S. Senate Budget Com., Washington, 1977-78; asst. dir. for econ. policy U.S. Office Mgmt. and Budget, Washington, 1978-81; chief economist U.S. House Budget Com., Washington, 1981-91, exec. dir. for policy, 1989-91; sr. v.p., dir. rsch. Com. for Econ. Devel., Washington, 1991—. Rhodes scholar, Oxford U., 1958; Ford Found. Dissertation fellow Yale U., 1965. Office: 2000 L St NW Ste 700 Washington DC 20036-4915

OORT, ABRAHAM HANS, meteorologist, researcher, educator; b. Leiden, The Netherlands, Sept. 2, 1934; came to U.S., 1961; s. Jan Hendrik and Johanna Maria (Graadt Van Roggen) O.; m. Bineke Pel, May 20, 1961; children: Pieter Jan, Michiel, Sonya. MS, MIT, 1963; PhD in Meteorology, U. Utrecht, The Netherlands, 1964. Rsch. meteorologist Koninklyk Nederlands Meteorologisch Instituut, De Bilt, The Netherlands, 1964-66; rsch. meteorologist Geophys. Fluid Dynamics Lab/NOAA, Washington, 1966-68; rsch. meteorologist Geophys. Fluid Dynamics Lab/NOAA, Princeton, N.J., 1968-77, sr. rsch. meteorologist, 1977-96, ret., 1996; prof. dept. geological and geophys. scis. Princeton U., 1971—. Author: Physics of Climate, 1992; contbr. monographs in field. 2nd lt. Netherlands Air Force, 1959-61. NATO sci. fellow MIT, Cambridge, 1961-63; 10th Victor P. Starr Meml. lectr. MIT, 1988; recipient Gold medal U.S. Dept. Commerce, Washington, 1979. Fellow N.Y. Acad. Scis., Am. Meteorol. Soc. (Jule G. Charney award 1993), Royal Meteorol. Soc.; mem. Am. Geophys. Union. Democrat. Avocations: sculpture, shiatsu, meditation. Office: Princeton U NOAA Box 308 Princeton NJ 08542

OPALA, MARIAN P(ETER), state supreme court justice; b. Lódz, Poland, Jan. 20, 1921. BSB in Econs., Oklahoma City U., 1957, JD, 1953, LLD, 1981; LLM, NYU, 1968; HHD, Okla. Christian U. Sci. & Arts, 1981. Bar: Okla. 1953, U.S. Supreme Ct. 1970. Asst. county atty. Oklahoma County, 1953-56; practiced law Oklahoma City, 1956-60, 65-67; referee Okla. Supreme Ct., Oklahoma City, 1960-65; prof. law Oklahoma City U. Sch. Law, 1965-69; asst. to presiding justice Supreme Ct. Okla., 1967-68; administrv. dir. Cts. Okla., 1968-77; presiding judge Okla. State Indsl. Ct., 1977-78; judge Workers Compensation Ct., 1978; justice Okla. Supreme Ct., 1978—, chief justice, 1991-93; adj. prof. law Okla. City U., 1962—, U. Okla. Coll. Law, 1969—; prof. law U. Tulsa Law Sch., 1982—; mem. permanent faculty Am. Acad. Jud. Edn., 1970—; mem. NYU Inst. Jud. Adminstrn.; mem. faculty Nat. Jud. Coll., U. Nev., 1975—; chmn. Nat. Conf. State Ct. Adminstrs., 1976-77; mem. Nat. Conf. Commrs. on Uniform State Laws, 1982—. Co-author: Oklahoma Court Rules for Perfecting a Civil Appeal, 1969. Mem. Adminstrn. Conf. U.S., 1993-95. Recipient Herbert Harley award Am. Judicature Soc., 1977, Disting. Alumni award Oklahoma City U., 1979, Americanism medal Nat. Soc. DAR, 1984, ABA/Am. Law Inst. Harrison Tweed Spl. Merit award, 1987, Humanitarian award NCCJ, 1991, Jour. Record award, 1995, Constn. award Rogers U., 1996. Mem. ABA (edn. com. appellate judges conf. 1984-93), Okla. Bar Assn. (Earl Sneed Continuing Legal Edn. award 1988), Okla. County Bar Assn., Am. Soc. Legal History, Oklahoma City Title Lawyers Assn., Am. Judicature Soc. (bd. dirs. 1988-92), Am. Law Inst. (elected), Order of Coif, Phi Delta Phi (Oklahoma

City Alumni award). Office: Okla Supreme Ct State Capitol Rm 238 Oklahoma City OK 73105

OPARA, EMMANUEL CHUKWUEMEKA, biochemistry educator; b. Lagos, Nigeria, July 4, 1951; came to U.S., 1984; s. Eugene Uba and Caroline (Adanma) O.; m. Clarice Adaku Njemanze, Mar. 28, 1980; children: Ogechi, Chiedu, Chukwuka, Ikenna. BS with honors, U. Nigeria, 1976; MS, U. Surrey, Eng., 1980; PhD, U. London, 1983. Assoc. Royal Coll. of Pathologists. Inspecting officer Food and Drug Adminstrn., Lagos, 1977-78; clin. biochemist Epsom (Eng.) Hosp. Labs., 1978-81; teaching asst. Chelsea Coll., London, 1981-83; rsch. fellow Mayo Clinic, Rochester, Minn., 1984-86; vis. fellow NIH, Bethesda, Md., 1986-88; rsch. assoc. Duke U. Med. Ctr., Durham, N.C., 1988-89; asst. prof. Duke U. Med. Ctr., 1989—. Contbr. articles to numerous scientific and med. jours. Com. chairperson Holy Cross Ch., Durham, 1992. WHO fellow, Geneva, 1984; Fogarty Internat. fellow, Bethesda, 1986; recipient Cystic Fibrosis Found. grant, 1990, Am. Diabetes Assn. grant, 1993. Mem. Am. Fedn. for Clin. Rsch., Am. Diabetes Assn., Am. Pancreatic Assn., Assn. Clin. Biochemists (U.K.), Biochemistry Soc., Am. Gastroenterological Assn. Democrat. Roman Catholic. Avocations: tennis, walking, current affairs, reading, television. Home: 2 Scarsdale Pl Durham NC 27707-5526 Office: Duke U Med Ctr Dept of Surgery PO Box 3065 Durham NC 27710

OPARIL, SUZANNE, cardiologist, educator, researcher; b. Elmira, N.Y., Apr. 10, 1941; d. Stanley and Anna (Penkova) O. AB, Cornell U., 1961; MD, Columbia U., 1965. Diplomate Am. Bd. Internal Medicine. Intern in medicine Presbyn. Hosp., N.Y.C., 1965-66; sr. asst. resident in medicine Mass. Gen. Hosp., Boston, 1967-68, clin. and rsch. fellow in medicine, cardiac unit, 1968-71; asst. prof. medicine Med. Sch., U. Chgo., 1971-75, assoc. prof., 1975-77; assoc. prof. dept. medicine U. Ala., Birmingham, 1977-81, asst. prof. physiology and biophysics, 1980-81, assoc. prof., 1981—, prof. medicine, 1981—, dir. vascular biology and hypertension program, 1985—; mem. vis. faculty Nat. High Blood Pressure Edn. Program, 1974—, Joint Nat. Com. on Detection, Evaluation and Treatment High Blood Pressure, 1991; mem. bd. sci. advisors Sterling Drug, Inc., 1988-91; lectr. in field; Selkurt lectr. Ind. U. Sch. Medicine, 1994; hon. prof. Peking Union Med. Coll., 1994. Author books on hypertension; editor Am. Jour. Med. Scis., 1984-94; assoc. editor Hypertension, 1979-83, mem. editl. bd., 1984—; assoc. editor Am. Jour. Physiology-Renal, 1989-91; mem. editl. bd. Jour. Hypertensioin, 1989—; contbr. over 300 articles to profl. jours., chpts. to books. Recipient Young Investigator award Internat. Soc. Hypertension, 1979, ann. award Med. Coll. Pa., 1984; fellow Am. Coll. Cardiology, 1992. Fellow Am. Coll. Cardiology; mem. Inst. Medicine of NAS (corr. com. on human rights 1992, chmn. com. advise Dept. Def. 1993 Breast Cancer Rsch. Program), AAAS, Endocrine Soc., Inter-Am. Soc. Hypertension, Am. Soc. Hypertension (pub. policy com. 1990—, sci. program com. 1990-92), Assn. for Women in Sci., Am. Heart Assn. (coun. for high blood pressure rsch., 1973—, exec. com. 1985-90, vice chmn. 1986, coun. on basic scis. 1978—, mem.-at-large, exec. com. 1979-81, mem.-at-large bd. dirs. 1992, chmn. Louis B. Katz Prize com. 1984-86, chmn., 1988-90, chmn. budget com. 1990-91, v.p. Ala. affiliate 1986-87, pres.-elect Ala. affiliate 1987-88, 93-94, pres. Ala. affiliate 1988-89, nat. pres.-elect 1993-94, nat. pres. 1994—, Lewis K. Dahl Meml. Lectr. 1993), Am. Physiol. Soc. (clin. physiology adv. com. 1992—), Am. Soc. for Clin. Investigation (sec.-treas. 1983-86), Soc. Exptl. Biology and Medicine (councillor 1993—), So. Soc. for Clin. Investigation (Founder's award 1995), Assn. Am. Physicians, Am. Fedn. for Clin. Rsch. (midwest councillor 1974-75, nat. councillor 1975-78, sec.-treas. 1978-80, pres. 1981-82), Phi Beta Kappa, Sigma Xi, Alpha Omega Alpha (mem. nat. bd. dirs., dir.-at-large 1991, treas. 1993). Avocations: horseback riding, tennis, hiking, travel. Office: U Ala Sch Medicine 1034 Zeigler Research Bldg Birmingham AL 35294*

OPDYCKE, LEONARD EMERSON, retired secondary education educator, publisher; b. Boston, May 22, 1929; s. Leonard and Frances (Prescott) O.; m. Susan Wolcott, 1951 (div.); children: Susan, Deborah, Margot; m. Jeanne Bernhard, 1963 (div.); children: Sarah, Frances; m. Sandra S. Auchincloss, 1976. BA, Harvard U., 1951; MA, U. Rochester, 1965. Tchr. Southfield Sch., Shreveport, L.A., 1952-53, Dedham (Mass.) Country Day, Harley Sch., Rochester, N.Y., 1956-64; dir. Poughkeepsie (N.Y.) Day Sch., 1965-72; chair English dept. Rhinebeck (N.Y.) High Sch., 1974-77; adj. prof. Marist Coll., Poughkeepsie, N.Y., 1977-84, 93-95. Editor, pub. WWI Aero, 1961—; pub. Skyways, 1987—. Mem. Phi Beta Kappa. Avocations: building aircraft, linguistics, education. Home and Office: 15 Crescent Rd Poughkeepsie NY 12601

OPEL, JOHN R., business machines company executive; b. Kansas City, Mo., Jan. 5, 1925; s. Norman J. and Esther (Roberts) O.; m. Julia Carole Stout, Dec. 28, 1953; children: Robert, Nancy, Julia, Mary, John. AB, Westminster Coll., 1948; MBA, U. Chgo., 1949. With IBM Corp., Armonk, N.Y., 1949—, salesman, various mgmt. positions, 1949-66, v.p., 1966-68, mem. mgmt. com., 1967, v.p. corp. finance and planning, 1968-69, sr. v.p. finance and planning, 1969-72, group exec. data processing group, 1972-74, dir., 1972-94, pres., 1974-83, chief exec. officer, 1981-85, chmn., 1983-86, chmn. exec. com., 1986-93, ret. chmn., 1993. Trustee, Westminster Coll. Served with U.S. Army, 1943-45. Mem. Bus. Coun., Coun. on Fgn. Rels. Office: IBM Corp 590 Madison Ave New York NY 10022-2524

OPEL, WILLIAM, medical research administrator. MBA, U. So. Calif.; PhD, Claremont Grad. Sch. Exec. dir. Huntington Med. Rsch. Inst., Pasadena, Calif.; lectr. in technology, mgmt., Pepperdine U. Mem. Beta Gamma Sigma, Phi Kappa Phi. Office: Huntington Med Rsch Inst 734 Fairmount Ave Pasadena CA 91105-3104

OPENSHAW, HELENA MARIE, investment company executive, portfolio manager; b. Beirut, July 30, 1953; d. Hubert J. and Lucile Openshaw. BA, U. South Fla., 1975, MA, 1977; PhD, SUNY, Buffalo, 1986. Tchg. asst. instr. SUNY, 1977-83; analyst specialist ValueLine, Inc., N.Y.C., 1986-88, sr. analyst, mem. portfolio mgmt. team, 1988-93; equity portfolio mgr. Ganz Capital Mgmt., Miami, Fla., 1993-94; v.p., sr. portfolio mgr. Comerica FSB, Ft. Lauderdale, Fla., 1994-95, Comerica Inc., Detroit, 1995—. Mem. Assn. for Investment Mgmt. and Rsch., Fin. Analysts Soc. Detroit. Office: Comerica Inc One Detroit Ctr 500 Woodward Ave Detroit MI 48226-3423

OPFER, NEIL DAVID, construction educator, consultant; b. Spokane, Wash., June 3, 1954; s. Gus Chris and Alice Ann (Blom) O. BS in Bldg. Theory cum laude, Wash. State U., 1976, BA in Econs. cum laude, 1977, BA in Bus. cum laude, 1977; MS in Mgmt., Purdue U., 1982. Cert. cost engr., cert. project mgr. Estimator Standard Oil (Chevron), Richmond, Calif., 1975; gen. carpenter forman Opfer Constrn. Corp., Spokane, 1976; assoc. engr. Inland Steel Corp., East Chgo., Ind., 1977-78; millwright supr. Inland Steel Corp., 1978-79, field engr., 1979-82, project engr., 1982-84, sr. engr., 1984-87; asst. prof. construction and construction mgmt. Western Mich. U., Kalamazoo, 1987-89; asst. prof. construction and construction mgmt. U. Nev., Las Vegas, 1989-95, assoc. prof. construction and construction mgmt., 1995—. Contbr. articles to publs. Bd. dirs. Christmas in April, 1993—, Habitat for Humanity, 1991—. Mem. Am. Welding Soc. (bd. dirs. 1982-87), Am. Inst. Constructors, Am. Assn. Cost Engrs. (nat. bd. dirs. 1995-97, Order of Engr. award 1989), Project Mgmt. Inst., Constrn. Mgmt. Assn., Tau Beta Pi (life), Phi Kappa Phi (life). Methodist. Avocations: biking, running, marathons, triathlons. Home: 1920 Placid Ravine Las Vegas NV 89117 Office: Univ Nev 4505 S Maryland Pkwy Las Vegas NV 89154-9900

OPHULS, MARCEL, film director and producer; b. Frankfurt, Germany, Nov. 1, 1927; came to U.S., 1947, naturalized, 1950; s. Max and Hilda (Wall) Oppenheimer; m. Regine Ackermann, Aug. 21, 1956; children: Catherine Julie, Danielle, Jeanne Dorothee. Student, Occidental Coll., Los Angeles, 1946-49; Licencie es Letters, U. Paris, 1950; DArts (hon.), Columbia Coll., Chgo., 1983. Asst. dir. films France, 1951-56; tchr. film Princeton U., 1973-74, also sr. vis. fellow council humanities and mem. adv. council sociology dept. Program dir. TV and radio plays, Sudwestfunk, Fed. Republic of Germany, 1956-60; dir. feature films, Paris, 1961-65; producer, dir. documentary films, 1966—; dir.: (sketch) Love at Twenty, 1961, (films) including Banana Peel, 1963, Fire at Will, 1964, Munich, or Peace in Our Time, 1966, The Sorrow and The Pity, 1971, America Revisited, 1972, A Sense of Loss, 1972, The Memory of Justice, 1976, Kortner Geschichten, 1980, Yorktown, The Sense of A Battle, 1982, Hotel Terminus: The Life and Times of Klaus Barbie, 1988 (Acad. award best documentary feature 1989), November Days, 1990; The Troubles We've Seen, 1993, contbg. editor Am. Film. Served with AUS, 1946-47. Decorated knight of arts and letters French Ministry Culture; recipient film and TV awards including Best Documentary award, 1988, award Brit. Acad., 1972, 88, Best Documentary French Authors' Soc., 1994, Achievement award Acad. of Motion Pictures, 1995; MacArthur fellow, 1991. Mem. German Acad. Arts, French Authors Guild, French Dirs. Guild, Am. Acad. Arts and Scis. Address: 10 Rue Ernest Deloison, Neuilly sur Seine France also: French Film Office 745 Fifth Ave New York NY 10150 *I believe that individuals shape history, but are also shaped by it.*

OPIE, WILLIAM ROBERT, retired metallurgical engineer; b. Butte, Mont., Apr. 3, 1920; s. Ellison Stuart and Myrtle (Williams) O.; m. Constance E. Kickuth, Oct. 14, 1944; children: Lyle Margaret, Guy William. B.S., Mont. Sch. Mines, 1942, M.E. (hon.), 1965; Sc.D., MIT, 1949; student, Advanced Mgmt. Program, Harvard U., 1967; Sc.D. (hon.), Mont. Coll. Mineral Sci. and Tech., 1980. Foundry metallurgist Wright Aero Corp., Paterson, N.J., 1942-45; research asso. MIT, Cambridge, 1946-48; research metallurgist Am. Smelting and Refining, Perth Amboy, N.J., 1948-50; research supr. Nat. Lead Co., Sayreville, N.J., 1950-60; pres. Amax Base Metals Research & Devel., Inc., Carteret, N.J., 1960-85; cons., 1985—. Contbr. articles to profl. jours. Served with U.S. Navy, 1945-46. Fellow AIME, Am. Soc. Metals; mem. Nat. Acad. Engring. Patentee in field. Home: 119 Crawfords Corner Rd Holmdel NJ 07733-1947

OPITZ, JOHN MARIUS, clinical geneticist, pediatrician; b. Hamburg, Germany, Aug. 15, 1935; came to U.S., 1950, naturalized, 1957; s. Friedrich and Erica Maria (Quadt) O.; m. Susan O. Lewin; children: Leigh, Teresa, John, Chrisanthi, Emma. BA, State U. Iowa, 1956, MD, 1959; DSc (hon.), Mont. State U., 1983; MD (hon.), U. Kiel, Germany, 1986. Diplomate Am. Bd. Pediatrics, Am. Bd. Med. Genetics. Intern, State U. Iowa Hosp., 1959-60, resident in pediatrics, 1960-61; resident and chief resident in pediatrics U. Wis. Hosp., Madison, 1961-62; fellow in pediatrics and med. genetics U. Wis., 1962-64, asst. prof. med. genetics and pediatrics, 1964-69, assoc. prof., 1969-72, prof., 1972-79; dir. Wis. Clin. Genetics Ctr., 1974-79; clin. prof. med. genetics and pediatrics U. Wash., Seattle, 1979—; adj. prof. medicine, biology, history and philosophy, vet. rsch. and vet. sci. Mont. State U., Bozeman, 1979-94, McKay lectr., 1992, Univ. prof. med. humanities MSU, Bozeman, 1994—; adj. prof. pediatrics, med. genetics U. Wis., Madison, 1979—, Class of 1947 Disting. prof., U. of Wis., 1992; coordinator Shodair Mont. Regional Genetic Svcs. Program, Helena, 1979-82; chmn. dept. med. genetics Shodair Children's Hosp., Helena, 1983-94; dir. Found. Devel. and Med. Genetics, Helena, Mont.; pres. Heritage Genetics P.C., Helena, 1996; Farber lectr. Soc. Pediatric Pathology, 1987; Joseph Garfunkel lectr. So. Ill. U., Springfield, 1987, McKay lectr. Mont. State U., 1992; Warren Wheeler vis. prof. Columbus (Ohio) Children's Hospital, 1987; Bea Fowlow lectr. in med. genet. U. Calgary, 1996; 1st vis. prof. Hanseatic U. Found. of Lübeck, 1996. Editor, author 14 books; founder, editor in chief Am. Jour. Med. Genetics, 1977—; mng. editor European Jour. Pediatrics, 1977-85; contbr. numerous articles on clin. genetics. Chair Mont. Com. for Humanities, 1991. Recipient Pool of Bethesda award for excellence in mental retardation rsch. Bethesda Luth. Home, 1988, Med. Alumni Citation U. Wis., 1989, Col. Harlan Sanders Lifetime Achievement award for work in the field of genetic scis. March of Dimes, Purkinje medal Czech Soc. Medicine, Mendel medal Czech Soc. Med. Genetics, 1996, Internat. prize Phoenix-Anni Verdi for Genetic Rsch., 1996. Fellow AAAS, Am. Coll. Med. Genetics (founder); mem. German Acad. Scientists Leopoldina, Am. Soc. Human Genetics, Am. Pediatric Soc., Soc. Pediatric Rsch., Am. Bd. Med. Genetics, Birth Defects Clin. Genetic Soc., Am. Inst. Biol. Scis., Am. Soc. Zoologists, Teratology Soc., Genetic Soc. Am., European Soc. Human Genetics, Soc. Study Social Biology, Am. Acad. Pediatrics, German Soc. Pediatrics (hon.), Western Soc. Pediatrics Rsch. (emeritus), Italian Soc. Med. Genetics (hon.), Israel Soc. Med. Genetics (hon.), Russian Soc. Med. Genetics (hon.), So. Africa Soc. Med. Genetics (hon.), Japanese Soc. Human Genetics (hon.), Sigma Xi. Democrat. Roman Catholic. Home: 2930 E Craig Dr Salt Lake City UT 84109 Office: U Utah Sch Medicine Primary Childrens Med Ctr 100 N Medical Dr Salt Lake City UT 84113-1103

OPOTOWSKY, MAURICE LEON, newspaper editor; b. New Orleans, Dec. 13, 1931; s. Sol and Fannie (Latter) O.; m. Madeleine Duhamel, Feb. 28, 1959 (dec.); children: Didier Sol Duhamel, Joelle Duhamel, Arielle Duhamel (dec.); m. Bonnie Feibleman, May 4, 1991. Student, Tulane U., 1949-51; BA cum laude, Williams Coll., 1953. Reporter Berkshire Eagle, Pittsfield, Mass., 1951-53; pub. Sea Coast Echo, Bay St. Louis, Miss., 1953-54; reporter UPI, 1956-62; feature editor Newsday, Ronkonkoma, N.Y., 1962-64; Suffolk day editor Newsday, 1964-65, Nassau night editor, 1965-67, nat. editor, 1967-70, Suffolk editor, 1970-72; dir. L.I. Mag., 1972; day editor Press-Enterprise, Riverside, Calif., 1973-84, mng. editor features/adminstrn., 1984-87, sr. mng. editor, 1987-92, mng. editor, 1992—; chief N.Y. State Syndicate Service, 1961-74; mem. Calif. Freedom of Info. Exec. Com., sec., 1979-80, treas., 1980-81, v.p., 1981-82, pres., 1982-83. Trustee Harbor Country Day Sch., 1970-72; bd. dirs. Calif. Newspaper Editor Conf. Bd., 1978-83; mem. Smithtown (N.Y.) Hunt, 1970-73, West Hills Hunt, 1976-80, Santa Fe Hunt, Whip, 1985—; co-chmn. Calif. Bench-Bar Media Com.; mem. adv. coun. dept. comm. Calif. State U., Fullerton, 1995—. Served with AUS, 1954-56. Recipient Lifetime Achievement award Calif. 1st Amendment Assembly, 1997. Mem. AP News Execs. Calif. (chmn. 1986-87), Calif. 1st Amendment Coalition (pres., treas.), Calif. Soc. Newspaper Editors (bd. dirs., vice chmn. steering com. 1983), AP Mng. Editors Assn., Am. Soc. Newspaper Editors. Office: Press Enterprise Co 3512 14th St Riverside CA 92501-3814

OPPEDAHL, JOHN FREDRICK, publisher; b. Duluth, Minn., Nov. 9, 1944; s. Walter H. and Lucille (Hole) O.; m. Alison Owen, 1975 (div. 1983); m. Gillian Coyro, Feb. 14, 1987; 1 child, Max. B.A., U. Calif., Berkeley, 1967; M.S., Columbia U., 1968. Reporter San Francisco Examiner, 1967; reporter, asst. city editor Detroit Free Press, 1968-75, city editor, 1975-80, exec. city editor, 1981, exec. news editor, 1981-82, asst. mng. editor, 1983; nat. editor Dallas Times Herald, 1983-85, asst. mng. editor, 1985-87; mng. editor/news L.A. Herald Examiner, 1987-89; mng. editor Ariz. Republic, Phoenix, 1989-93; exec. editor Phoenix Newspapers, 1993-95; pub., CEO Phoenix Newspapers, Inc., 1996—. Trustee Walter Cronkite Sch. Journalism and Telecomm., Ariz. State U.; bd. dirs. Found. for Am. Comms., Downtown Phoenix Partnership, Valley of the Sun United Way, 1996-97 (campaign cabinet), Greater Phoenix Econ. Coun., Ariz. Communities in Schs., COMPAS; mem. Greater Phoenix Leadership. Mem. Am. Soc. Newspaper Editors, AP Mng. Editors, Newspaper Assn. of Am. Office: The Arizona Republic 200 E Van Buren St Phoenix AZ 85004-2238

OPPEDAHL, PHILLIP EDWARD, computer company executive; b. Renwick, Iowa, Sept. 17, 1935; s. Edward and Isadore Hannah (Gangstead) O.; B.S. in Naval Sci., Navy Postgrad. Sch., 1963, M.S. in Nuclear Physics, 1971; M.S. in Systems Mgmt., U. S.C., 1978; m. Sharon Elaine Ree, Aug. 3, 1957 (dec. Aug. 1989); children: Gary Lynn, Tamra Sue, Sue Ann, Lisa Kay. Commd. ensign U.S. Navy, 1956, advanced through grades to capt., 1977; with Airborne Early Warning Squadron, 1957-59, Anti-Submarine Squadron, 1959-65; asst. navigator USS Coral Sea, 1965-67; basic jet flight instr., 1967-69; student Armed Forces Staff Coll., 1971; test group dir. Def. Nuclear Agy., 1972-74; weapons officer USS Oriskany, 1974-76; program mgr. for armament Naval Air Systems Command, Washington, 1977-79; test dir. Def. Nuclear Agy., Kirtland AFB, N.Mex., 1979-82, dep. comdr. Def. Nuclear Agy., 1982-83; pres., chief exec. officer Am. Systems, Albuquerque, 1983—; dir., bd. dirs. BASIS Internat., 1991—. Pres., bd. dirs. Casa Esperanza, 1990-92. Decorated Disting. Service medal. Mem. Naval Inst., Am. Nuclear Soc., Aircraft Owners and Pilots Assn., Assn. Naval Aviation Navy League. Lutheran. Author: Energy Loss of High Energy Electrons in Beryllium, 1971; Understanding Contractor Motivation and Incentive Contracts, 1977. Home and Office: 5850 Eubank Blvd NE # B 49 Albuquerque NM 87111 *Personal philosophy: The remainder of my life is dedicated to giving back to the universe the life, love and energy that the universe has given me.*

OPPEL, ANDREW JOHN, computer systems consultant; b. Kerrville, Tex., Dec. 22, 1952; s. Wallace Churchill and Anne Kathryn (Smith) O.; m. Laura Lee Partridge, Aug. 26, 1972; children: Keith Andrew, Luke Andrew. BA in Computer Sci., Transylvania U., 1974. Computer programmer Johns Hopkins U., Balt., 1974-77; data base programmer Equitable Trust Co., Balt., 1977-78; sr. programmer, analyst Md. Casualty Co., Balt., 1978-79; sr. programmer, analyst Levi Strauss & Co., San Francisco, 1979-82, sr. requirements mgr., 1982-84, tech. cons., 1984-91, tech. advisor, 1991-93, mgr. database mgmt. sys., 1994-96, sr. sys. architect, 1996-97; sr. cons. Triadigm Internat., San Francisco, 1997—; instr. U. Calif. Extension, Berkeley, 1983—. Ops. officer Alameda County Radio Amateur Civil Emergency Svc., San Leandro, Calif., 1980-92; cub master Boy Scouts Am., Alameda, Calif., 1991-92; referee U.S. Soccer Fedn., Alameda, 1988—, referee instr., 1996—. Democrat. Episcopalian. Avocation: amateur radio. Home: 1308 Burbank St Alameda CA 94501-3946 Office: Triadigm Internat Ste 1220 345 California St San Francisco CA 94104-2621

OPPENHEIM, ALAN VICTOR, electrical engineering educator; b. N.Y.C., Nov. 11, 1937; s. Sydney and Dorothy (Arenz) O.; m. Phyllis Arnold, June 20, 1964; children: Justine Ruth, Jason Philip. S.B., MIT, 1961, S.M., 1961, Sc.D., 1964; D (hon.), Tel Aviv U., 1995. Asst. prof. dept. elec. engring. MIT, 1964-69, assoc. prof. dept. elec. engring. and computer scis., 1969-76, prof. dept. elec. engring. and computer sci., 1976-90, Disting. prof. elec. engring., 1990-96, Ford prof. engring., 1996—, MacVicar faculty fellow, 1997—; staff scientist Lincoln Lab., 1967-69, assoc. head data systems divsn., 1978-80; cons. Lincoln Lab., Atlantic Aerospace Inc., Sanders Assocs., Inc. Co-author: Digital Signal Processing, 1975, Signals and Systems, 1983, 2d edit. 1997, Discrete-Time Signal Processing, 1989, others; editor: Applications of Digital Signal Processing, 1978, (with others) Advanced Topics in Signal Processing, 1988; contbr. articles to profl. jours. Guggenheim fellow, 1972-73. Fellow IEEE (Edn. medal 1988, other awards); mem. Nat. Acad. Engring., Sigma Xi, Eta Kappa Nu, Tau Beta Pi. Office: MIT Dept Electric Engring & Computer Sci 50 Vassar St Cambridge MA 02139-4309

OPPENHEIM, ANTONI KAZIMIERZ, mechanical engineer; b. Warsaw, Poland, Aug. 11, 1915; came to U.S., 1948, naturalized, 1954; s. Tadeusz and Zuzanna (Zuckerwar) O.; m. Lavinia Stephens, July 18, 1945; 1 dau., Terry Ann. Diploma in Engring., Warsaw Inst. Tech., London, 1943; PhD in Engring., U. London, 1945; diploma of Imperial Coll., 1945; DSc, U. London, 1976; Dr. Honoris Causa, U. Poitiers, France, 1981, Tech. U., Warsaw, 1989, Imperial Coll., 1995. Registered profl. engr., Calif. Research asst. City and Guilds Coll., 1942-48, lectr., 1946-48; asst. prof. mech. engring. Stanford U., 1948-50; faculty U. Calif. at Berkeley, 1950—, prof. mech. engring., 1958-86, Miller prof., 1961-62, prof. emeritus, 1986—; fellow Imperial Coll., 1995; vis. prof. Sorbonne, Paris, 1960-61, U. Poitiers, France, 1973, 80; staff cons. Shell Devel. Co., 1952-60. Editor-in-chief: Acta Astronautica, 1974-79; contbr. articles to profl. jours., also monographs. Chmn. Heat Transfer and Fluid Mechanics Inst., 1958; IAA Com. on Gasdynamics of Explosions, 1968—; organizer Internat. Colloquia on Gas Dynamics of Explosions and Reactive Systems, 1967, 69, 71, 73, 75, 77, 79, 81, 83; mem. NASA, adv. com. fluid mechanics, 1963-69. Recipient Water Arbitration prize Inst. Mech. Engrs., 1948, Numa Manson medal Inst. for Dynamics of Explosions and Reactive Sys., 1981, Dionizy Smolenski medal Polish Acad. Scis., 1987, Alfred C. Egerton medal The Combustion Inst., 1988, citation U. Calif., Berkeley, 1988. Spl. research compressible fluid flow, gas turbines and internal combustion engines, heat transfer, combustion, detonation and blast waves. Home: 54 Norwood Ave Kensington CA 94707-1119

OPPENHEIM, DAVID JEROME, musician, educational administrator; b. Detroit, Apr. 13, 1922; s. Louis and Julia (Nurko) O.; m. Judy Holliday, 1948; 1 child, Jonathan; m. Ellen Adler, Apr. 14, 1957; children: Sara, Thomas; m. Pat Jaffe, June 13, 1987. Student, Julliard Sch. Music, 1939-40; MusB, U. Rochester, 1943. Dir. Masterworkd div. Columbia Records, N.Y.C., 1950-59; producer, dir., writer network news CBS-TV, N.Y.C., 1962-68; exec. producer Pub. Broadcasting Lab., N.Y.C., 1968-69; dean Tisch Sch. of the Arts NYU, N.Y.C., 1969-92, dean emeritus, 1992—; adv. com. Sta. WNCN; mem. Tony awards com., 1983-88. Clarinet soloist Casals Festival, Prades, France, 1955, San Juan, P.R., 1959, recs. include Budapest Quartet, Brahms Clarinet Quintet, Opus 115 and Mozart Clarinet Quintet in A Maj., (Stravinsky conducting) L'Histoire du Soldat, Octet, Septet, Bernstein Sonata, Leonard Bernstein, piano (dedicated to David Oppenheim), (with Julliard Quartet) Copland Sextet, (with New Music Quartet) Douglas Moore Quintet; co-producer (play) Saul Bellow's Last Analysis on Broadway, 1962; producer documentary films on Stravinsky and Casals, CBS News. Bd. dirs. emeritus Film Soc. Lincoln Center, Inc., Town Hall Found.; bd. dirs. Am. Stefan Wolpe Soc.; bd. advisors New Sch. Concerts. With AUS, World War II, ETO. Recipient Prix Italia Radiotelevisione Italiana, 1964. Mem. Nat. Soc. Lit. and Arts, Internat. Council Fine Arts Deans, N.Y. State Arts Deans, Town Hall Found., Soc. of Fellows (charter), Am. Fedn. Arts (film program). Avocations: camping, reading, gardening, hiking.

OPPENHEIM, IRWIN, chemical physicist, educator; b. Boston, June 30, 1929; s. James L. and Rose (Rosenberg) O.; m. Bernice Buresh, May 18, 1974; 1 child, Joshua Buresh. A.B. summa cum laude, Harvard U., 1949; postgrad., Calif. Inst. Tech., 1949-51; Ph.D., Yale, 1956. Physicist Nat. Bur. Standards, Washington, 1953-60; chief theoretical physics Gen. Dynamics/Convair, San Diego, 1960-61; assoc. prof. chemistry MIT, Cambridge, 1961-65; prof. MIT, 1965—; lectr. physics U. Md., 1953-60; vis. assoc. prof. physics U. Leiden, 1955-56, Lorentz prof., 1983; vis. prof. Weizmann Inst. Sci., 1958-59, U. Calif., San Diego, 1966-67; Van der Waals prof. U. Amsterdam, 1966-67. Author: (with J.G. Kirkwood) Chemical Thermodynamics, 1961; editor: Phys. Rev. E, 1992—. Fellow Am. Phys. Soc., Am. Acad. Arts and Scis., Washington Acad. Sci.; mem. Phi Beta Kappa, Sigma Xi. Research in quantum statis. mechanics, statis. mechanics of transport processes, thermodynamics. Home: 140 Upland Rd Cambridge MA 02140-3623 Office: MIT 77 Massachusetts Ave #6-221 Cambridge MA 02139-4301

OPPENHEIM, JUSTIN SABLE, business executive; b. N.Y.C., Aug. 17, 1923; s. Ferdinand S. and Esther D. (Hirsch) O.; m. Joyce Marrits, June 26, 1949; children: Janet Wexler, Judith, Jeffrey, Ann Harrisburg. BS, NYU, 1943; postgrad., Cambridge U., Eng., 1945, New Sch. for Social Research, 1963. V.p. Consol. Mercantile Industries, N.Y.C., 1946-52; adminstrn. and mgmt. Norden div. United Aircraft Co., 1952-60; pres., gen. mgr. Potentiometer div. Litton Industries, 1960-68; pres. Office Products Ctrs. div., 1968-70; v.p. Litton Industries, 1970-84; chmn., pres. Joyce Internat., 1984-85, dir., 1985-89; chmn. Joyce Furniture (Can.), 1984-86; also v.p. Litton Bus. Systems, Inc., Litton Bus. Equipment Ltd., Can., Standard Desk Ltd., Can. to 1985; pres., dir. Streater Industries Ltd. 1968-85; lectr. on advt. NYU, CCNY, 1954-57. Contbr. articles to profl. jours. including the N.Y. Times. Mem. adv. com. N. Hempstead Housing Authority, 1956-59; mem. Nassau County Republican Com., 1961-73; founding mem. Ctr. Econ. Rsch., L.I. U.; hon. dep. sheriff Westchester County, 1967; mem. Hon. Legion Police Dept. City of N.Y., 1978; bd. dirs. Sephardic House, N.Y.C.; trustee Am. Jewish Hist. Soc., L.I. Stage, 1985-87, Friends of Touro Synagogue, 1989—, life mem. Served with AUS, 1943-45; Hon. Adm. Tex. Navy, 1969. Recipient citation Borough Pres. Manhattan, N.Y.C., 1980, key to Albert Lea, Minn., key to Selma, Ala. Mem. SAR, Actor's Fund (life), Am. Arbitration Assn., Mosaic (charter mem), So. Jewish Hist. Soc., Alpha Epsilon Pi. Jewish. Club: Lambs (N.Y.) (life). Lodge: Masons. Home: 6691 S Pine Ct West Palm Beach FL 33418-6960

OPPENHEIMER, FRANZ MARTIN, lawyer; b. Mainz, Germany, Sept. 7, 1919; s. Arnold and Johanna (Mayer) O.; m. Margaret Spencer Foote, June 17, 1944; children: Martin Foote, Roxana Foote, Edward Arnold. B.S., U. Chgo., 1942; student, U. Grenoble, France, 1938-39; LL.B. cum laude (note editor Law Jour. 1945), Yale U., 1945. Bar: N.Y. 1946, D.C. 1955. Rsch. asst. com. human devel. U. Chgo., 1942-43; law clk. to Judge Swan, U.S. Circuit Ct. of Appeals, N.Y., 1945-46; assoc. atty. Chadbourne, Wallace, Parke & Whiteside, N.Y.C., 1946-47; atty. IBRD, Washington, 1947-57; individual practice law, 1958-59; ptnr. firm Leva, Hawes, Symington, Martin & Oppenheimer, 1959-83, Fort & Schlefer, Washington, 1984-94; pvt. practice Washington, 1995-96; sr. of counsel Swidler & Berlin, Washington, 1996—. Contbr. articles to profl. and other jours. Bd. dirs. Internat. Student House; founding mem. Company of Christian Jews. Decorated officer's cross Order of Merit (Fed. Republic Germany), chevalier Nat. Order of Merit (France). Mem. ABA, Am. Soc. Internat. Law (treas. 1964-76), Coun. Fgn. Rels., Yale Club, Century Assn. (N.Y.), City Tavern, Met. Club

(Washington). Anglican. Home: 3248 O St NW Washington DC 20007-2847 Office: 3000 K St NW Ste 300 Washington DC 20007-5109

OPPENHEIMER, JACK HANS, internist, scientist, educator; b. Egelsbach, Hesse, Germany, Sept. 14, 1927; came to U.S., 1937; s. Julius and Elsa (Reis) O.; m. Ann Ehrlich, Dec. 20, 1953; children: Mark, Lawrence, Adele Oppenheimer Brown. BA, Princeton U., 1949; MD, Columbia U., 1953. Diplomate Am. Bd. Internal Medicine. Intern Boston City Hosp., 1953-54; fellow Sloan Kettering Inst., N.Y.C., 1954-55, Columbia Presbyn. Hosp., N.Y.C., 1959-60; resident Duke U., 1957-59; asst. prof. to prof. medicine Albert Einstein Coll. Medicine, Bronx, N.Y., 1964-76; prof. medicine U. Minn., Mpls., 1976-97, Cecil J. Watson prof., dir. divsn. endocrinology, 1986-93, emeritus prof., 1997; staff physician Montefiore Hosp. Med. Ctr., Bronx, 1960-76. Contbr. over 270 articles to profl. jours.; editor 2 books. Capt. U.S. Army, 1955-57. Fellow ACP; mem. Endocrine Soc. (coun. 1974-78, Astwood award 1978), Am. Thyroid Assn. (pres. 1985-86, Van Meter award 1965, Parke-Davis award 1984), Am. Soc. Clin. Investigation, Assn. Am. Physicians. Home: 4100 Kerry Ct Minnetonka MN 55345-1825 Office: U Minn 520 Delaware St SE Minneapolis MN 55455-0356

OPPENHEIMER, MARTIN J., lawyer; b. Apr. 11, 1933; s. Julius and Sylvia (Haas) O.; m. Suzanne Rosenhirsch, July 3, 1958; children: Marcy, Evan, Joshua, Alexandra. BS with honors, U. Pa., 1953; LLB, Yale U., 1956. Assoc. Hays, Sklar & Hertzberg, Mendes & Mount; ptnr. Proskauer Rose Goetz & Mendelsohn, N.Y.C., 1958—. Contbr. articles to profl. jours. Chmn. City Ctr. of Music and Drama, Lincoln Ctr., N.Y., 1984—; vice chmn. N.Y.C. Opera, 1985—; bd. dir. 92nd St. YWCA, N.Y., 1985—, Lincoln Ctr. for Performing Arts, 1987—. Fulbright scholar Goethe U., Frankfurt, Fed. Republic Germany, 1956-57. Home: 400 Claflin Ave Mamaroneck NY 10543-3906 Office: Proskauer Rose et al 1585 Broadway New York NY 10036-8200

OPPENHEIMER, MAX, JR., foreign language educator, consultant; b. N.Y.C., July 27, 1917; s. Max and Louise (Pourfuerst) O.; m. Christine Backus, Oct. 14, 1942; children: Edmund Max, Carolyn Christine Oppenheimer Burns. Bachelier ès Lettres, U. Paris, 1935; BA cum laude, NYU, 1941; MA, UCLA, 1942; PhD, U. So. Calif., 1947. Instr. fgn. langs. San Diego State Coll., 1947-49; asst. prof. Romance langs. Washington U., St. Louis, 1949-51; assoc. prof. modern langs. Fla. State U., Tallahassee, 1958-61; prof., chmn. dept. Russian U. Iowa, Iowa City, 1961-67; prof. SUNY, Fredonia, 1967-76, prof. emeritus, 1976—, chmn. dept. fgn. langs., 1967-74; prof. English Yunnan Normal U., Kunming, Peoples Republic of China, 1985-86; intelligence officer CIA, 1956-58. Author: Outline of Russian Grammar, 1962; translator: Theory of Molecular Excitons (Davydov), 1962, Theory of Ship Waves and Wave Resistance (Kostyukov), 1968, The Fake Astrologer (Calderón de la Barca), 1976, 94, The Lady Simpleton (Lope de Vega), 1976, Don Juan (Tirso de Molina), 1976, Swim First and Last, 1981; contbr. articles to scholarly and profl. jours. Active YMCA, 1936—. Served to lt. col., MI, AUS, 1942-46, lt. col. Res., ret. Decorated Bronze Star; Fla. State U. grantee, 1961, Office Naval Rsch. grantee, 1965, SUNY grantee, 1973. Mem. MLA, Am. Soc. Geolinguistics (pres. 1975-76), Am. Soc. Dowsers, Ariz. Soc. for Profl. Hypnosis, Dobro Slovo, Am. Mensa Ltd., Elks, Phi Beta Kappa, Sigma Delta Pi, Pi Delta Phi (nat. pres. 1946-51), Alpha Mu Gamma. Avocation: swimming. Home: 10963 Coggins Sun City AZ 85351 *When you speak, always say what you think, not what you think you should say for the sake of expediency. Steadfastly, stubbornly, cling to your ideals, principles and beliefs, but be flexible enough to change whenever changing them reflects wisdom, not weakness or compromise. Avoid ego trips or being awed by your own alleged accomplishments.*

OPPENHEIMER, MICHAEL, physicist; b. Bklyn., Feb. 28, 1946; s. Harry and Shirley (Meyer) O.; m. Leonie Haimson, Dec. 31, 1986; 1 child, Chloe. S.B., MIT, 1966; Ph.D., U. Chgo., 1970. Research fellow Harvard Coll., 1971-73; lectr. astronomy Harvard U., 1973-81; physicist Harvard-Smithsonian Center for Astrophysics, Harvard U., 1973-81, Environ. Def. Fund, N.Y.C., 1981—; mem. panel on atmospheric effects of aviation NRC, 1995—; chmn. adv. panel on global warming Am. Mus. Natural History, 1990-93; mem. environ. adv. com. to N.Y. Gov. Cuomo, 1991-94. Author: Dead Heat: The Race Against the Greenhouse Effect, 1990; contbr. articles to profl. jours. Union Carbide fellow, 1969-70; A.F. Morrison fellow, 1979; Guggenheim fellow, 1978-79. Mem. AAAS, Am. Phys. Soc., Am. Geophys. Union, Am. Meteorol. Soc. Office: Environ Def Fund 257 Park Ave S New York NY 10010-7304

OPPENHEIMER, PAUL EUGENE, English comparative literature educator, poet, author; b. N.Y.C., May 1, 1939; s. Fred R. Oppenheimer and Gertrude Samuels; children: Julie Sarah, Ben. BA, Princeton U., 1961; MA, Columbia U., 1963, PhD, 1970. Lectr. Hunter Coll. CUNY, N.Y.C., 1964-67, lectr., poet-in-residence City Coll., 1967-70, from asst. prof. to assoc. prof. City Coll., 1970-84, prof. City Coll., 1984—; exch. prof., dir. CUNY student exch. program Sorbonne nouvelle, Paris, 1984-85; exch. prof. U. North London, Eng., 1989-90, Univ. Coll. London, 1993, German Dept., 1993, 95, 97; Fulbright prof. U. Osnabrück, Germany, 1993-94. Author: Before a Battle and Other Poems, 1967, Beyond the Furies, New Poems, 1985, The Birth of the Modern Mind: Self, Consciousness, and the Invention of the Sonnet, 1989, Evil and Demonic: A New Theory of Monstrous Behavior, 1996, An Intelligent Person's Guide to Modern Guilt, 1997; author, translator: Till Eulenspiegel: His Adventures, 1972, 91, 95. Woodrow Wilson fellow, 1961-62, Alfred Hodder fellow, 1969-70, Fulbright sr. fellow, Germany, 1993-94. Mem. Dante Soc. Am. Home: 50 W 67th St New York NY 10023-6227 Office: CCNY Dept English and Comparative Lit NAC 138 St and Convent Ave New York NY 10031

OPPENHEIMER, STEVEN BERNARD, biology educator; b. Bklyn., Mar. 23, 1944; s. Hugo and Irma (Schellenberg) O.; m. Carolyn Roberta Weisenberg, May 23, 1971; 1 child, Mark. BS magna cum laude, Bklyn. Coll., 1965; PhD, Johns Hopkins U., 1969. Am. Cancer Soc. postdoctoral fellow U. Calif., San Diego, 1969-71; asst. prof. biology Calif. State U., Northridge, 1971-74, assoc. prof., 1974-77, prof., 1977—, dir. Sch. Sci. and Math. Ctr. for Cancer and Devel. Biology; panel mem. NSF, Washington, 1985, NIH, 1987, 94, 96; cons. Northridge Hosp., 1984-92. Author: introduction to Embryonic Development, 1980, 2d rev. edit., 1984, 3d rev. edit., 1989, Cancer Biological and Clinical Introduction, 1982, 2d rev. edit., 1985, 3d rev. edit., 1995, Cancer Prevention Guidebook, 1984, 2d rev. edit., 1991, Atlas of Embryonic Development, 1984; editor Cancer, Longevity Letter, 1984-85; editor Jour. of Student Rsch. Abstracts, 1995—; writer (film) Cancer Prevention, A Way of Life, 1986; contbr. articles to profl. jours. Recipient Disting. Prof. award Calif. State U., 1977, Statewide Outstanding Prof. award Bd. Trustees of 19 Campuses, 1984, Excellence in Sci. Edn. award Calif. Sci. Tchrs. Assn., 1988; grantee Nat. Cancer Inst., 1972-84, NSF, 1981—, NICHHD, 1986-88, NIH, 1993—, Joseph Drown Found., 1988—, NASA, 1988-95, Urban Cmty. Svc. Program, 1992-95, Eisenhower Program, 1990-96, others; Exxon fellow, 1982, Thomas Eckstrom Trust fellow, 1982—. Fellow AAAS; mem. Am. Soc. Zoologists (nat. program chmn., devel. biology and nat. membership chmn. 198-85), Am. Soc. Cell Biology, Soc. Devel. Biology, Am. Cancer Soc. (bd. dirs. San Fernando Valley chpt. 1985-89, Pub. Edn. award 1985, grantee 1977-86), Sigma Xi (Disting. Rsch. award 1984), Phi Kappa Phi. Home: 8933 Darby Ave Northridge CA 91325-2706 Office: Calif State U Dept Biology 18111 Nordhoff St Northridge CA 91330-0001

OPPENHEIMER, SUZI, state senator; b. N.Y.C., Dec. 13, 1934; d. Alfred Elihu Rosenhirsch and Blanche (Schoen) O.; m. Martin J. Oppenheimer, July 3, 1960; children: Marcy, Evan, Josh, Alexandra. BA in Econs., Conn. Coll. for Women, 1956; MBA, Columbia U., 1958. Security analyst McDonnell & Co., N.Y.C., 1958-60, L.F. Rothschild Co., N.Y.C., 1960-63; mayor Village of Mamaroneck, N.Y., 1977-85; mem. N.Y. State Senate, Albany, 1985—; ranking mem. environ. conservation, mem. fin., edn., alcoholism, transp., water resources and drugs com., chmn. Senate Dem. Task Force on Women's Issues, treas. Legis. Women's Caucus, pres. Senate Club. Former pres. Mamaroneck LWV, Westchester County Mcpl. Ofcls. Assn., Westchester Mcpl. Planning Fedn. Recipient Humanitarian Svc. award Am. Jewish Com., 1988, Legis. Leadership award Young Adult Inst., 1988, Legis. award Westchester Irish Com., 1988, Hon. Svc. award Vis. Nurses Svcs., 1989, Humanitarian Svc. award Project Family, 1990, Meritorious Svc. award N.Y. State Assn. Counties, 1990, Friend of Edn. award N.Y. State United Tchrs., 1991, Assn. Health Care Providers award, 1993, Govtl. award Cmty. Opportunity Program, 1994, Spl. Recognition award Open Door Family Med. Group, 1995, Appreciation award, Careers for People with Disabilities, 1996, Dominican Sisters Family Health Svcs., 1996, Vets. Svc. award JWV, 1997; honoree Windward Sch. Ann. Dinner, 1992, others; named Legislator of Yr., N.Y. State Women's Press Club. Democrat. Jewish. Dist Office: 222 Grace St Port Chester NY 10573

OPPENHEIMER-NICOLAU, SIOBHAN, think tank executive; married; 5 children. MD, Goucher Coll. Supr. internat. svcs. Fuller, Smith and Ross Advt., N.Y.C., 1952-56; asst. to commr. N.Y.C. Cmty. Devel. Agy., 1966-68; program office divsn. nat. affairs Ford Found., N.Y.C., 1968-81; cons. to pres. Hallmark Corp., Kansas City, Mo., 1989-91; cons. to ct. apptd. spl. master The Buck Trust, Marin County, Calif., 1992; cons. to chmn. and pres. Enterprise Found., Columbia, Md., 1981—; with Univision TV Network, Miami, 1992; pres., founder Hispanic Policy Devel. Project, N.Y.C., Washington, 1982—; cons. Levi-Straus Found., Marin County, 1990, U.S. Dept. Labor, 1995, Acad. for Ednl. Devel., N.Y.C., 1993—, The Ewing Marion Kauffman Found., Kansas City; cmty. spokesperson for TV network GEMS Internat. TV, Miami, 1992—; dir. annual seminar Aspen Inst., 1987—; bd. dirs. Edn. Pub. Co., Ewing Marion Kauffman Found., other cos. Contbr. articles to profl. jours. Bd. dirs. Hispanic Women's Project; trustee First Nations' Fin. Inst., Mus. of the Am. Indian; pres., bd. dirs. Internat. Inst. for the Arts. Mem. Women's Prison Assn. (trustee). Home: 36 E 22nd St Fl 9 New York NY 10010-6124 Office: 125 E 10th St New York NY 10003-7504

OPPENLANDER, ROBERT, retired airline executive; b. N.Y.C., May 20, 1923; s. Robert and Lillian (Ahrens) O.; m. Jessie I. Major, Sept. 30, 1950; children: Kris Oppenlander Austin, Robert Kirk, Tenley. B.S., MIT, 1944; M.B.A., Harvard U., 1948. With Metals & Controls Corp., Attleboro, Mass., 1948-53; prin. Cresap, McCormick & Paget, N.Y.C., 1953-58; comptroller, treas. Delta Air Lines, Inc., Atlanta, 1958-88; v.p. fin. Delta Air Lines, Inc., 1964-67, sr. v.p. fin., treas., 1967-78, sr. v.p. fin., 1978-83, vice chmn. bd., chief fin. officer, 1983-88, ret., 1988, also adv. dir. Served to lt. USNR, 1944-46. Club: Capital City. Home: 3944 Powers Ferry Rd NW Atlanta GA 30342-4026

OPPERMAN, DANNY GENE, packaging professional, consultant; b. Fostoria, Ohio, June 29, 1938; s. Roy and Iva Ann (Dotson) O.; m. Dorothy Rae Bugner, Dec. 30, 1957; children: Carrie Rae Opperman Hammond, Melissa Ann Opperman Lee, Jon Aaron, Christopher Douglas. Assoc., ICS, 1960. Tool engr. Ford Motor Co., Fostoria, 1957-68; packaging engr. Allied-Signal Corp., Fostoria, 1968-86; machine designer ITS Tech., Toledo, 1987; prodn. engr. TRW, Elyria, Ohio, 1987-88; pres. packaging consulting firm Opperman/Assocs., Inc., Fostoria, 1988—. Pres. Fostoria Jaycees, 1970-71; advisor Fostoria Teen Ctr., Inc., 1960-66. Mem. ASTM (D-10 packaging com), Inst. Packaging Profls. (cert., chpt. bd. dirs. 1984-92), Packaging Cons. Coun., Elks (exalted ruler 1984-85), Masons.

OPPERMAN, DWIGHT DARWIN, publishing company executive; b. Perry, Iowa, June 26, 1923; s. John H. and Zoa L. Opperman; m. Jeanice Wifvat, Apr. 22, 1942 (dec.); children: Vance K., Fane W. JD, Drake U., 1951. Bar: Iowa 1951, U.S. Supreme Ct. 1976, U.S Ct. Internat. Trade, 1988. Editor, asst. editorial counsel West Pub. Co., St. Paul, Minn., 1951-64, mgr. reporters and digest depts., 1964-65; v.p. West Pub. Co., 1965-68, pres., 1968-93, CEO, 1978-96, chmn., 1993-96; chmn. emeritus West Info. Publ. Group, Eagan, 1996; chmn. Key Investment, Mpls., 1996—; dir. Inst. Judicial Adminstrn. V.p., trustee Supreme Ct. Hist. Soc.; dir. Inst. Jud. Adminstrn.; bd. govs., mem. nat. task force Drake U., Des Moines; dir. Minn. D.A.R.E. Inc.; dir. Brennan Ctr. for Justice, Nat. Legal Ctr. for Pub. Interest. Recipient Herbert Harley award Am. Judicature Soc., 1984, Justice award, 1992, 1st George Wickersham Founder's award Friends of Law Libr. of Congress, 1993. Fellow Am. Bar Found.; mem. ABA, Fed. Bar Assn., Am. Judicature Soc., Am. Law Inst., Drake U. Nat. Alumni Assn. (disting. svc. award 1974, Centennial award 1981, Outstanding Alumni award 1988), Minn. Club (pres. 1975-76). Office: Key Investment 601 2d Ave S Ste 520 Minneapolis MN 55402*

OPPERMANN, JOSEPH KAY, architect; b. Galveston, Tex., Apr. 15, 1949; s. Gustav John and Katherine (Shuberg) O.; m. Langdon Edmunds, Oct. 24, 1987; children: Joseph Sjöberg, Frances Edmunds. BA in Liberal Arts, U. Tex., 1971, BArch, 1975, MArch, 1975, cert. in mus. conservation, 1986. Registered architect, N.C., S.C., Ga., Ky., La., D.C. Grants mgr. Tex. Hist. Commn., Austin, 1976-79, dir. tech. svcs., 1979-81, dep. state hist. preservation officer, 1981-87; prin. C. Phillips & Co., Winston-Salem, N.C., 1987; pres. Phillips & Oppermann, P.A., Winston-Salem, 1988—; mem. hist. Am. bldgs. survey team Winedale Inst., 1975; architect mem. nat. register adv. com. N.C. Dept. Cultural Resources; lectr. in field. Contbr. articles to profl. publs. Architect mem. task group to prepare mandatory growth plan City of Austin, 1986; architect mem. rev. panel for hist. facade grants City of Winston-Salem, 1990-91; bd. advisors Hist. Preservation Found. N.C.; bd. advisors grad. archtl. program in hist. preservation Tex. A&M U., 1986-87; bd. dirs. Preservation Action, 1984-87; bd. dirs. Nat. Conf. State Hist. Preservations Officers, 1984-86, chmn. grants appropriations com.; pres. Tex. chpt. Soc. Archtl. Historians, 1980-82. Recipient Tower award for Outstanding Restoration, 1992, 93, 94, 96. Mem. AIA (mem. hist. resources com. N.C. chpt.), Assn. for Preservation Tech., Soc. Archtl. Historians (pres. Tex. chpt. 1980-82), Am. Inst. Conservation of Hist. and Artistic Works, Vernacular Archtl. Forum. Office: Phillips & Oppermann PA 539 N Trade St Winston Salem NC 27101-2914

OPPMANN, ANDREW JAMES, newspaper editor; b. Hopkinsville, Ky., Apr. 3, 1963; s. Patrick George Oppmann and Elizabeth Anne (Freeman) Peace; m. Emily Elise Wey, Oct. 8, 1988. BA in Journalism, U. Ky., 1985. Staff writer The Orange County Register, Santa Ana, Calif., 1985-86; copy editor, staff writer Lexington (Ky.) Herald-Leader, 1986-87, bur. chief, asst. metro editor, 1988-91; urban affairs writer The Knoxville (Tenn.) News-Sentinel, 1987-88; asst. city editor The Houston Post, 1991-92, dep. met. editor, 1992, asst. to mng. editor, 1992, met. editor, 1992-94; Ky. editor The Cin. (Ohio) Enquirer, 1994—; supervising editor The Ky. Enquirer, Ft. Mitchell, 1994—. Bd. vis. U. Ky. Sch. Journalism, 1994—; bd. dirs. Soc. Profl. Journalists Queen City chpt. Fellow U. Ky., 1984; recipient Gannett Newsroom Supr. Recognition award, 1995. Mem. U. Ky. Journalism Assn. (v.p. 1997—), Soc. Profl. Journalists (bd. dirs. Queen City chpt. 1995—). Office: The Ky Enquirer 226 Grandview Dr Fort Mitchell KY 41017-2702

OPRE, THOMAS EDWARD, magazine editor, film company executive, corporate travel company executive; b. Evansville, Ind., Nov. 6, 1943; s. William Jennings and Ruth (Strouss) O.; children: Thomas Andrew, William Hartley. A.B. in Journalism, Ind. U., 1965. Writer sports and outdoors Decatur (Ill.) Herald and Rev., 1965-66; outdoor editor Detroit Free Press, 1966-90; field editor Midwest div. Field and Stream mag., 1971-81; editorial dir. Gt. Lakes Sportsman mag., 1972-75; editor-at-large and sports vehicles editor Outdoor Life mag., 1981-93; pres. Tom Opre Prodns., 1967—; pres. TOP Safaris, Inc., 1986—. Author numerous articles in outdoor and travel fields. Recipient James Henshall award Am. Fish Tackle Mfrs. Assn., 1969, Teddy award Internat. Outdoor Travel Film Festival, 1973, Environ. award EPA, 1977, Nat. Writer's award Safari Club Internat., 1977, Deep Woods Writing award OWAA, 1977, Conservation Service award Ducks Unltd., 1977; World Wildlife Found. award, 1981; named to Internat. Fishing Hall of Fame, 1968, Conservation Communicator of Yr., 1985. Mem. Outdoor Writers Assn. Am. (past dir., pres., v.p., chmn. bd.), Assn. Gt. Lakes Outdoor Writers (past dir., chmn. bd., pres., v.p.), Mich. Outdoor Writers Assn. (v.p., pres., chmn. bd. dirs.), Alpha Tau Omega. Home and Office: PO Box 964 Royal Oak MI 48068-0964

O'QUINN, APRIL GALE, physician, educator; b. Columbia, Miss., Apr. 21, 1936; d. R.V. and Anna Pauline (Cook) O'Q.; diploma Scott and White Hosp. Sch. Nursing, 1965; A.A., Temple Jr. Coll., 1965; B.S. with honors, Baylor U., 1968; M.D., U. Tex. Med. Br., 1971. Intern, U. Tex. Med. Br., Galveston, 1971-72, resident ob-gyn., 1972-75; fellow in oncology M.D. Anderson Hosp., Houston, Tex., 1976-78; practice medicine specializing in ob-gyn., Galveston, 1978-81; asst. prof. dept. ob-gyn. U. Tex. Med. Br., Galveston, 1975-81; practice medicine specializing in ob-gyn, New Orleans, 1981—; mem. staff John Sealy Hosp., St. Mary's Hosp., Galveston, Tulane Med. Center, New Orleans Charity Hosp., So. Baptist Hosp. and Touro Infirmary, New Orleans; assoc. prof., dir. div. gynecol. oncology dept. ob-gyn Tulane U. Sch. Medicine, New Orleans, 1981-85, prof., 1985-89, prof., chair dept. ob.-gyn., 1989—. Diplomate Am. Bd. Ob-Gyn. Fellow Willard R. Cooke Obstet. and Gynecol. Soc., Am. Coll. Ob-Gyn.; mem. AMA, Soc. Gynecologic Oncologists, Western Assn. Gynecol. Oncologists, Coun. Univ. Chmn. in Ob-Gyn., Assn. Profs. in Ob-Gyn., New Orleans Gynecol. and Obstet. Soc., La. Med. Assn., Galveston County Med. Soc., Felix Rutledge Soc. Orleans Parish. Republican. Baptist. Home: 5100 Bancroft Dr New Orleans LA 70122-1218 Office: Tulane U Sch Medicine Ob Gyn Dept New Orleans LA 70112

ORAM, ROBERT W., library administrator; b. Warsaw, Ind., June 11, 1922; s. George Harry and Lottie Mae (Gresso) O.; m. Virginia White, June 16, 1949; 1 child, Richard W. B.A., U. Toledo, 1949; M.S. in Library Adminstrn., U. Ill., 1950. Asst. to librarian U. Mo.-Columbia, 1950-56; circulation librarian U. Ill.-Urbana, 1956-67, dir. pub. service, 1968-71, assoc. univ. librarian, 1971-79, acting univ. librarian, 1975-76; dir. Central Univ. Libraries So. Meth. U., Dallas, 1979-89, dir. emeritus, 1989; mem. adv. com. Ill. State Library, Springfield, 1975-79. Contbr. articles to profl. jours. Exec. sec. Friends of So. Meth. U. Librs., 1980-89; former mem. bd. dirs. Urbana Free Libr., Lincoln Trails Libr. Sys., Champaign, Ill.; trustee Friends Austin (Tex.) Pub. Libr., 1994—. Mem. ALA (life, pub. com. 1975-79), Friends of Libraries U.S.A. (exec. bd. 1980-86), Ill. Library Assn. (treas. 1972-73),. Democrat. Avocations: reading; music. Home: 8410 Lone Mesa Austin TX 78759-8025

ORAN, ELAINE SURICK, physicist, engineer; b. Rome, Ga.; d. Herman E. and Bessye R. (Kolker) Surick; m. Daniel Hirsh Oran, Feb. 1, 1969. AB, Bryn Mawr Coll., 1966; MPh, Yale U., 1968, PhD, 1972. Rsch. physicist Naval Rsch. Lab., Washington, 1972-76, supervisory rsch. physicist, 1976-88, sr. scientist reactive flow physics, 1988—; head Ctr. for Reactive Flow and Dynamical Systems, 1985-87; mem. adv. bd. NSF; cons. to U.S. govt., agys., NATO. Author: Numerical Simulation of Reactive Flow, 1987, Numerical Approaches to Combustion Modeling, 1991. Assoc. editor Jour. Computational Physics; mem. adv. bd. Computers in Physics; editl. bd. Prog. Ener. Comb. Sci., Combustion and Flame; contbr. numerous articles to profl. jours., chpts. to books. Recipient Arthur S. Flemming award, 1979, Women in Sci. and Engring. award, 1988; grantee USN, NASA, USAF, Def. Advanced Rsch. Projects Agy. Mem. Aero. Adv. Coun. NASA, 1995—. Fellow AIAA (pubs. com. 1986—, v.p. publs. 1993-97), Am. Phys. Soc. (exec. com. fluid dynamics divsn. 1986, 88, exec. com. computational physics 1989—, chair 1991-92); mem. Am. Inst. Aeronautics and Astronautics, Am. Phys. Soc., Am. Geophys. Union, Combustion Inst. (bd. dirs. 1990—), Internat. Colloquium Dynamic Energy Systems (bd. dirs. 1989—), Soc. of Indsl. and Applied Math., Sigma Xi. Office: Naval Rsch Lab Code 6404 # 6004 Washington DC 20011

ORAN, GERALDINE ANN, assistant principal; b. Burleson, Tex., June 27, 1938; d. Clyde Lloyd and Ruth (Baxley) Renfro; m. Francis Larry Oran, Dec. 18, 1960; children: Angelique Michelle, Jeremy Lloyd. AS summa cum laude, Roane State Community Coll., Harriman, Tenn., 1976; BS summa cum laude, U. Tenn., 1978, MS summa cum laude, 1990. IBM instr., office mgr. Kelsey-Jenney Bus. Coll., San Diego, 1958-61; exec. sec. Bendix Corp., San Diego, 1961-62; ednl. adminstr. South Harriman Bapt. Ch., 1964-74; sec. West Hills Presbyn. Ch., 1974-78; tchr. Midtown Elem., Harriman, 1979-89; adminstrv. intern, prin. preparation program Danforth Found. Leadership 21, 1989; asst. prin. Cherokee Mid. Sch., Kingston, Tenn., 1990—. Mem., sec., treas., pres. PTA and PTO, Harriman, 1967-81; active Cancer, Heart Fund and March of Dimes, Harriman, 1979—; dir. vacation Bible sch. South Harriman Bapt. Ch., 1983-86, tchr. women's Bible sch., 1965—; club sponsor Tenn. Just Say No to Drugs Team, Roane County, 1985-87; mem. Task Force on Mid. Schs., Tenn. Dept. Edn., 1990; selection com. Tenn. Mid. Sch. Tchr. of Yr., 1992. Named Tchr. of Yr., Roane County, 1987. Mem. ASCD, NEA (del. rep. 1985-86), Tenn. Assn. Supervision and Curriculum Devel., Tenn. Assn. Middle Schs., Nat. Assn. of Secondary Sch. Prins., Tenn Edn. Assn. (del. rep. 1984-86, Outstanding Svc. award 1985-86), Roane County Edn. Assn. (membership chair 1984-85, pres. 1985-86), Roane County Adminstrs. Assn. (pres. 1993), Gamma Phi Beta, Kappa Delta Pi, Phi Kappa Phi, Delta Kappa Gamma. Baptist. Avocations: reading, painting, crafts, sculpting, walking. Home: PO Box 917 Harriman TN 37748-0917 Office: Cherokee Mid Sch Paint Rock Ferry Rd Kingston TN 37763-2914

ORBACH, RAYMOND LEE, physicist, educator; b. Los Angeles, July 12, 1934; s. Morris Albert and Mary Ruth (Miller) O.; m. Eva Hannah Spiegler, Aug. 26, 1956; children: David Miller, Deborah Hedwig, Thomas Randolph. BS, Calif. Inst. Tech., 1956; PhD, U. Calif., Berkeley, 1960. NSF postdoctoral fellow Oxford U., 1960-61; asst. prof. applied physics Harvard U., 1961-63; prof. physics UCLA, 1963-92, asst. vice chancellor acad. change and curriculum devel., 1970-72, chmn. acad. senate L.A. divsn., 1976-77, provost Coll. Letters and Sci., 1982-92; chancellor U. Calif., Riverside, 1992—; mem. physics adv. panel NSF, 1970-73; mem. vis. com. Brookhaven Nat. Lab., 1970-74; mem. materials rsch. lab. adv. panel NSF, 1974-77; mem. Nat. Commn. on Rsch., 1978-80; chmn. 16th Internat. Conf. on Low Temperature Physics, 1981; Joliot Curie prof. Ecole Superieure de la Physique et Chimie Industrielle de la Ville de Paris, 1982, chmn. Gordon Rsch. Conf. on Fractals, 1986; Lorentz prof. U. Leiden, Netherlands, 1987; Raymond and Beverly Sackler lectr. Tel Aviv U., 1989; faculty rsch. lectr. UCLA, 1990; Andrew Lawson lectr. U. Calif., Riverside, 1992; mem. external rev. com. Nat. High Magnetic Fields Lab., 1994—. Author: (with A.A. Manenkov) SpinLattice Relaxation in Ionic Solids, 1966; Div. assoc. editor Phys. Rev. Letters, 1980-83, Jour. Low Temperature Physics, 1980-90, Phys. Rev., 1983—; contbr. articles to profl. jours. Alfred P. Sloan Found. fellow, 1963-67; NSF sr. postdoctoral fellow Imperial Coll., 1967-68; Guggenheim fellow Tel Aviv U., 1973-74. Fellow Am. Phys. Soc. (chmn. nominations com. 1981-82, counselor-at-large 1987-91, chmn. divsn. condensed matter 1990-91); mem. AAAS (chairperson steering group physics sect.), NSF (mem. rsch. adv. com. divsn. materials 1992-93), Phys. Soc. (London), Univ. Rsch. Assn. (chair coun. pres. 1993), Sigma Xi, Phi Beta Kappa, Tau Beta Pi. Home: 4171 Watkins Dr Riverside CA 92507-4738 Office: U Calif Riverside Chancellor's Office Riverside CA 92521-0101

ORBACZ, LINDA ANN, physical education educator; b. Schenectady, N.Y., June 29, 1948; d. Victor and Genevieve (Stempkowski) O. AAS, Ulster C.C., Stone Ridge, N.Y., 1969; BS, So. Ill. U., 1972; MA, George Washington U., 1982. Cert. permanent tchr., N.Y. Tchr., coach Ellenville (N.Y.) Ctrl. Sch., 1972-73, New Fairfield (Conn.) Sch., 1973-75, Middletown (N.Y.) City Sch., 1975-84, Liberty (N.Y.) Ctrl. Sch., 1984-86; dir. athletics, phys. edn. tchr., coach Newburgh (N.Y.) Enlarged City Sch., 1986—; alumni adv. Ulster County C.C., Stone Ridge, 1981—. Softball, soccer and basketball coach, Newburgh, 1987-92, softball, field hockey, basketball and cheerleading coach Ellenville, Middletown, New Fairfield, Liberty, 1972-86. Recipient Presdl. Sports award Sports Fitness, Washington, 1988, 94. Mem. Am. Alliance Health, Phys. Edn., Recreation and Dance, N.Y. State Alliance Health, Phys. Edn., Recreation and Dance. Avocations: nautilus weight tng., phys. conditioning, in-line skating, skiing, aerobic exercise. Office: Gardnertown Fundamental Magnet Sch 6 Plattekill Tpke Newburgh NY 12550-1708

ORBAN, EDMOND HENRY, political science educator; b. Heron, Liege, Belgium, Apr. 25, 1925; emigrated to Can., 1961; s. Edmond and Maria (Jamar) O.; m. Anne Marie Anciaux, May 10, 1955; children: Margaret, Christine, Yvon, Francois, Benoit. Ph.D. in Polit. Sci., U. Louvain, Belgium, 1967. Asst. adminstr. Province of Kasaï Govt. of Belgium, 1951-59, adminstr. Province of Kasaï, 1961; prof. polit. sci. U. Montreal, Que., Can., 1961—. Author: La Presidence moderne, 1974, Le Conseil legislatif, 1967, Le Conseil nordique, 1978; author-editor: Mecanismes constitutionnels, 1982, Dynamique de la Centralisation dans l'Etat Fédéral, 1984, Le Systeme politique des Etats-Unis, 1987, Federalism and Supreme Courts, 1991, Federalism, 1992, Systéme Politique Américain, 1994. Served as info.-commando Belgium Army, 1950-51. Decorated Medal of the Resistance, 1945, chevalier de l'Ordre de la Couronne (Belgium), 3 other decorations. Roman Catholic. Home: 337 Lac des chats, Saint-Sauveur, PQ Canada J0R 1R1 Office: U

Montreal Dept Sci Politique, 2900 Boul Edouard Montpetit, Montreal, PQ Canada H3C 3J7

ORBAN, KURT, foreign trade company executive; b. S.I., N.Y., Aug. 6, 1916; s. Kurt and Gertrude (Astfalck) Orbanowski; children: Robert Arnold, Robin Ann, Kurt-Matthew, Jonathan; m. 2d, Ann Norris, Oct. 1986. Grad. steel fgn. trade course, Stahlunion-Export GmbH, Duesseldorf, Germany, 1938. Fgn. trade corr. Stahlunion, Dusseldorf, 1938; rep. Stahlunion, Bulgaria, 1939-40; steel export trader Steel Union Sheet Piling Co., N.Y.C., 1941; v.p. North River Steel Co., N.Y.C., 1941; chmn., pres. Kurt Orban Co., Inc., Wayne, N.J., from 1946; now sr. ptnr. Kurt Orban Ptnrs. Mem. field hockey games com. U.S. Olympic Com., 1948-61; playing mgr. U.S. Field Hockey Team., London, Eng., 1948, playing coach, Melbourne, Australia, 1956; U.S. rep. Bur. Internat. Hockey Fedn., Brussels, 1954-62. Served to 1st lt. USAAF, 1943-45. Field Hockey Assn. Am. named its cup for each yrs. men's team competition for him. Mem. Am. Inst. Imported Steel (pres. 1966-68, 78-80, bd. dirs. N.Y.C.), Am. Exporters and Importers Assn. (pres. 1972-73, bd. dirs.), West Coast Metal Importers Assn. (bd. dirs.), Wire Assn. Internat. Climbed Mt. Shasta, Calif. (14, 203') and Mt. Kilimanjaro (20, 103'), 1987. Avocation: sr. tennis, skiing, photography, languages. Address: 450 Kings Rd Brisbane CA 94005-1650

ORBEN, JACK RICHARD, investment company executive; b. Bklyn., June 16, 1938; s. Stanley Souza and Helena Emily (Hall) O.; AA, Valley Forge, 1956; BA, Tufts U., 1960; m. Patricia Wells, Dec. 17, 1960; children: Stacey Souza, Stephanie Anne, Bradford Richard. Sales mgr. nat. accounts N.Y. Tel. Co., 1960-66; founder, exec. v.p. Facts, Inc., 1966-69; with Orben Assocs., Inc., N.Y.C., 1970—, pres., 1979—; chmn. CEO Associated Family Svcs., Inc., Starwood Corp., Fiduciary Counsel, Inc.; chmn. Estate Mgmt. Co., Seward, Groves, Richard & Wells; bd. dirs. Vintage Holdings, Vintage Funds, Vintage Advisors, vice chmn. Chmn. White Plains Charter Revision Commn.; mem. Fin. Com. City of White Plains; past pres. White Plains Child Day Care Assn., Thomas Slater Ctr.; past chmn., bd. dirs. YMCA Ctrl. and No. Westchester. With USNG, 1960-66. Clubs: Larchmont Yacht, N.Y. Yacht, City Midday, Union League, Windemere Island, University, Down Town Assn. Home: 177 Soundview Ave White Plains NY 10606-3825 Office: The AFS Group 40 Wall St New York NY 10005-2301

ORBEN, ROBERT, editor, writer; b. N.Y.C., Mar. 4, 1927; s. Walter August and Marie (Neweceral) O.; m. Jean Louise Connelly, July 25, 1945. Humor and speech writer for entertainment personalities, bus. execs., politicians, 1946—; writer Jack Paar Show, N.Y.C., 1962-63, Red Skelton Hour, Hollywood, Calif., 1964-70; editor Orben's Current Comedy, Wilmington, Del., 1971-89; cons. to Vice Pres. Gerald R. Ford, Washington, 1974; speechwriter Pres. Gerald R. Ford, Washington, 1974-75; spl. asst. to pres., dir. White House speechwriting dept., Washington, 1976-77; speaker on uses of humor in communication, 1977—. Author: 2500 Jokes to Start 'Em Laughing, 1979, 2100 Laughs for All Occasions, 1983, 2400 Jokes to Brighten Your Speeches, 1984, 2000 Sure-Fire Jokes for Speakers, 1986; numerous other books of humor for performers and public speakers. Recipient World Humor award Workshop Libr. on World Humor, 1992; Literary fellow Acad. Magical Arts, 1996. Mem. Writers Guild Am. Unitarian. Club: Nat. Press (Washington). Avocations: travel, theater. Home: # 205 E 3709 S George Mason Dr Falls Church VA 22041-3760 *I have spent most of my lifetime creating laughter and consider it a lifetime well spent. Laughter is one of the glories of the human experience. It warms, amuses, instructs, and opens emotional doors. For me, laughter has been a living and a loving as well.*

ORCHARD, HENRY JOHN, electrical engineer; b. Oldbury, Eng., May 7, 1922; came to U.S., 1961, naturalized, 1973; s. Richard John and Lucy Matilda O.; m. Irene Dorothy Wise, Sept. 13, 1947; 1 child, Richard John; m. Marietta Eugenie Gayet, Aug. 2, 1971. B.Sc., U. London, 1946, M.Sc., 1951. Prin. sci. officer Brit. Post Office, London, 1947-61; sr. staff GTE Lenkurt Inc., San Carlos, Calif., 1961-70; mem. faculty UCLA, 1970—, prof. elec. engring., 1970-91, prof. emeritus, 1991—, vice chmn. dept., 1982-91. Author. Fellow IEEE (Best Paper award group circuit theory 1968). Republican. Patentee in field. Home: 828 19th St Unit E Santa Monica CA 90403-1906 Office: UCLA Elec Engring Dept Los Angeles CA 90095-1594

ORCHARD, ROBERT JOHN, theater producer, educator; b. Maplewood, N.J., Dec. 3, 1946; s. Robert Orchard and Beatrice (Gould) Todd; m. Pamela Marcy Pritchard, Sept. 6, 1969; children: Christopher, Katherine. Student, The Lawrence Acad., 1965; BA, Middlebury Coll., 1969; MFA, Yale U., 1972. Gen. mgr. Peterborough (N.H.) Players, 1967-70; asst. mng. dir. Yale Repertory Theatre, 1971-72, artistic admistr., 1972-73; instr. Yale Sch. Drama, 1972-73; mng. dir. Yale Repertory Theatre and Sch. Drama, 1973-79, Am. Repertory Theatre, Cambridge, Mass., 1979—; assoc. prof., co-chmn. Theatre Adminstrn. Tng. Program Yale Sch. Drama, 1975-79; mng., dir. Loeb Drama Ctr., Inst. for Advanced Theatre Tng. Harvard U., 1979—. Bd. dirs. Theatre Comms. Group; pres. bd. Mass. Cultural Edn. Collaborative; former bd. dirs. Am. Arts Alliance, Peterborough Players, Cambridge Multi-Cultural Arts Ctrs.; former exec. com. League of Residents Theatres; chmn. NEA, Profl. Theatre Cos. Panel. Office: Am Repertory Theatre 64 Brattle St Cambridge MA 02138-3443

ORCUTT, JAMES CRAIG, ophthalmologist; b. Holyoke, Colo., July 22, 1946; s. John Potter and Irene M. (Falk) O.; m. Barbara McCallum, Feb. 9, 1974; children: John, Gale. BPh in Pharmacy, U. Colo., Boulder, 1969; PhD in Pharmacology, U. Colo., Denver, 1976, MD, 1977. Diplomate Am. Bd. Ophthalmology. Intern U. Wash., Seattle, 1977-78, resident, 1978-81; fellow in orbital disease Moorfields Eye Hosp., London, 1981-82; fellow in neuro-ophthalmology Hosp. for Nervous Diseases and Great Ormond St. Hosp., London, 1982; asst. prof. ophthalmology U. Wash., Seattle, 1983-88, adj. prof. otolaryngology, 1987-88, assoc. prof. ophthalmology/adj. assoc. prof. otolargyngology, 1988-95, prof. ophthalmology, 1995—; chief ophthalmology Seattle Vets. Affairs Ctr., 1983—; ophthalmology cons. Vets. Affairs Ctrl. Office, Washington, 1993—. Pres. bd. trustees Northwest Sch., Seattle, 1996—. Avocations: Northwest history, postal history, antique resotration. Office: U Wash Dept Ophthalmology Box 356485 Seattle WA 98195

ORD, LINDA BANKS, artist; b. Provo, Utah, May 24, 1947; d. Willis Merrill and Phyllis (Clark) Banks; m. Kenneth Stephen Ord, Sept. 3, 1971; children: Jason, Justin, Kristin. BS, Brigham Young U., 1970; BFA, U. Mich., 1987; MA, Wayne State U., 1990. Asst. prof. Sch. Art U. Mich., Ann Arbor, 1994—; juror Southeastern Mich. Scholastic Art Award Competition, Pontiac, 1992, Scarab Club Watercolor Exhbn., Detroit, 1991, Women in Art Nat. Exhbn., Farmington Hills, Mich., 1991, U. Mich. Alumni Exhbn., 1989-90. One-woman shows Atrium Gallery, Mich., 1990, 91; group shows include Am. Coll., Bryn Mawr, Pa., Riverside (Calif.) Art Mus., Kirkpatrick Mus., Oklahoma City, Montgomery (Ala.) Mus. Fine Arts, Columbus (Ga.) Mus., Brigham Young U., Provo, Utah, Kresge Art Mus., Lansing, Mich., U. Mich., Ann Arbor, Detroit Inst. Arts, Kirkpatrick Ctr. Mus. Complex, Oklahoma City, 1994, Riverside (Calif.) Art Mus., 1995, San Bernadino County Mus., Redlands, Calif., 1996, Neville Mus., Green Bya, Wis., 1996, Downey Mus. Art, Calif., 1996, Detroit Inst. Arts, 1996, Gallery Contemporary Art, U. Colo., Colorado Springs, 1996; works in many pvt. and pub. collections including Kelly Svcs., Troy, Mich., FHP Internat., Fountain Valley, Calif., Swords Into Plowshares Gallery, Detroit; work included in: (books) The Artistic Touch, 1995, Artistic Touch 2, 1996; (mag.) Watercolor, An Am. Artist, 1996. Chairperson nat. giving fund Sch. Art, U. Mich., 1993; Sch. Art rep. Coun. Alumni Socs., U. Mich., 1992—. Recipient 1st Pl. award Swords Into Plowshares Internat. Exhbn., Detroit, 1989, Silver award Ga. Watercolor Soc. Internat. Exhbn., 1991, Pres.'s award Watercolor Okla. Nat. Exhbn., Oklahoma City, 1992, Flint Jour. award Buckham Gallery Nat. Exhbn., 1993, Ochs Meml. award N.E. Watercolor Soc. Nat. Exhbn., Goshen, N.Y., 1993, Color Q award Ga. Watercolor Soc., 1994, St. Cuthberts award Tex. Watercolor Soc., 1996, many state and nat. painting awards. Mem. U. Mich. Alumni Assn. (bd. dirs. 1992—, Sch. Art rep.), U. Mich. Sch. Art Alumni Soc. (bd. dirs. 1989-91, pres.), Mich. Watercolor Soc. (chairperson 1992-93, bd. dirs. adv. 1993-94). Avocations: music, theatre, tennis, golf, reading.

ORDAL, CASPAR REUBEN, business executive; b. Martell, Wis., May 5, 1922; s. Zakarias John and Sina Carlovna (Wulfsberg) O.; m. Ann Elizabeth Brady, June 7, 1947; Christopher Rolf, Peter Stuart. B.S., Harvard Coll., 1946; M.P.A., Harvard U., 1947. Supr. central indsl. relations staff Ford Motor Co., Dearborn, Mich., 1947-53; dir. orgn. planning and mgmt. devel. Colgate-Palmolive Co., N.Y.C., 1953-65; v.p., gen. mgr. New Holland div. Sperry Rand Corp., (Pa.), 1965-76; corp. v.p. personnel Norton Simon Inc., N.Y.C., 1976-78; sr. v.p. adminstrn. Max Factor & Co., Hollywood, Calif., 1978-85. Served to 1st lt. USAAF, 1943-46. Mem. Personnel Round Table (chmn. 1983-84), Am. Mgmt. Assn. (Adv. council 1977-82), Phi Beta Kappa. Republican. Lutheran. Club: Lancaster (Pa.) Country.

ORDEN, TED, gasoline service stations executive; b. 1920. With Thrifty Oil Co., Inc., Downey, Calif., 1959—, now pres., also bd. dirs. Office: Thrifty Oil Co Inc 10000 Lakewood Blvd Downey CA 90240-4020*

ORDIN, ANDREA SHERIDAN, lawyer; m. Robert Ordin; 1 child, Maria; stepchildren: Allison, Richard. AB, UCLA, 1962, LLB, 1965. Bar: Calif. 1966. Dep. atty. gen. Calif., 1965-72; So. Calif. legal counsel Fair Employment Practices Commn., 1972-73; asst. dist. atty. Los Angeles County, 1975-77; U.S. atty. Central Dist. Calif. Los Angeles, 1977-81; adj. prof. UCLA Law Sch., 1982; chief asst. atty. gen. Calif. L.A., 1983-90; ptnr. Morgan, Lewis & Bockius, L.A., 1993—. Mem. Los Angeles County Bar Assn. (past pres., past exec. dir.). Office: Morgan Lewis & Bockius 801 S Grand Ave Fl 22 Los Angeles CA 90017-4613

ORDINACHEV, JOANN LEE, educator; b. Rogers, Ark., Mar. 17, 1936; d. Floyd Andrew and Irene Elnora Elizabeth (Slinkard) Walkenbach; m. J. Dean Harter, Dec. 24, 1953 (div. 1977); m. Miles Donald Ordinachev, Mar. 11, 1978. B.S. cum laude, U. Mo., 1971; M.A.T., Webster U., 1974; PhD, St. Louis U., 1989. Cert. spl. ed. adminstr., dir., counselor. Office mgr. Edwards Constrn. Co., Joplin, Mo., 1954-58; with Jasper Welfare Office, Joplin, 1958-61; tchr. St. Louis Archdiocese, 1963-68, 70-71; TV personality, tchr. Sta. KDMO Cablevision, Carthage, Mo., 1968-69; tech. reading and remedial math. specialist applied tech. divsn. Spl. Sch. Dist., St. Louis, 1974-89, crisis counselor and co-chair guidance office, 1989-90, chair guidance office, 1990—; owner Jody's Dyslexia Lab., Concord Village, Mo., 1982—. Bd. dirs. Heritage House Apts., Heritage Housing Found., Inc., Metro St. Louis Tchrs. Housing Corp., 1989-92; bd. trustees St. Louis C.C., 1995; active League of Women Voters. Mem. NEA, Am. Vocat. Assn., Mo. Vocat. Assn., Spl. Dist. Tchrs. Assn. (pres. 1980-81), Orton Dyslexia Soc., Sch. Psychologists Assn., Council Exceptional Children, Network for Women Psychologist. Democrat. Eastern Orthodox. Office: Spl Sch Dist 1700 Derhake Rd Florissant MO 63033-6419

ORDONEZ, NELSON GONZALO, pathologist; b. Bucaramanga, Santander, Colombia, July 20, 1944; came to U.S., 1972; s. Gonzalo and Itsmenia Ordonez; m. Miranda Lee Ferrell, Dec. 18, 1976 (div. June 1983); 1 child, Nelson Adrian; m. Catherine Marie Newton, Nov. 6, 1987; 1 child, Sara Catherine Itsmenia. BA and Sci., Instituto Daza Dangond, Bogota, Colombia, 1962; MD, Nat. U. Colombia, Bogota, 1970. Resident pathology U. N.C., Chapel Hill, 1972-73; resident pathology U. Chgo., 1974-76, asst. prof. pathology, 1977-78; asst. prof. pathology U. Tex. M.D. Anderson Cancer Ctr., Houston, 1978-82, assoc. prof., 1983-85, prof., 1985—, dir. immunocytochemistry sect., 1981—, dir. electron microscopy sect., 1996—. Author: (with others) Renal Biopsy Pathology and Diagnostic and Therapeutic Implications, 1980, Tumors of the Lung, 1991; contbr. chpts. to books, numerous articles to med. jours. Nat. Kidney Found. fellow, 1977-78. Mem. AMA, Am. Assn. Pathologists, Internat. Acad. Pathology, Am. Soc. Clin. Pathologists, Am. Soc. Sytology, Am. Soc. Investigative Pathology, Internat. Acad. Cytology, Arthur Purdy Stout Soc. Surg. Pathologists, Latin-Am. Soc. Pathology. Office: U Tex MD Anderson Cancer Ctr 1515 Holcombe Blvd Houston TX 77030-4009

ORDORICA, STEVEN ANTHONY, obstetrician, gynecologist, educator; b. N.Y.C., Jan. 4, 1957; s. Vincent and Rose (Goiricelaya) O. BA magna cum laude, NYU, 1979; MD, Stony Brook U., 1983. Diplomate Am. Coll. Obstetrics and Gynecology, speciality cert. maternal-fetal medicine; lic. Nat. Bd. Med. Examiners. Resident obstetrics and gynecology NYU-Bellevue Hosp. Ctr., 1983-87, fellow maternal-fetal medicine, 1987-89, instr. obstetrics-gynecology, 1989-91; clin. instr. obstetrics-gynecology NYU, 1986-89, asst. prof. ob/gyn., 1991-93; dir. perinatal clinics and prenatal diagnostic unit Gouverneur Hosp., N.Y.C., 1989-94; perinatal cons. Bellevue Hosp. Ctr., N.Y.C., 1989—; faculty mem. perinatal div. NYU Med. Ctr., 1989—; presenter in field. Contbr. articles to Surgery, Am. Jour. Obstetrics and Gynecology, Am. Jour. Perinatal, Surgery, Obstetrics and Gynecology, Jour. Reproductive Medicine, Acta Geneticae Medicae et Gemellologiae, Jour. Rheumatology. Mem. Am. Coll. Obstetrics and Gynecology, Soc. Perinatal Obstetricians, N.Y. Acad. Scis., N.Y. State Perinatal Soc., AMA, Phi Beta Kappa, Beta Lambda Sigma. Achievements include research in investigating aspects of maternal-fetal physiology. Office: NYU Med Ctr 530 1st Ave Ste 10Q New York NY 10016-6451

ORDOVER, ABRAHAM PHILIP, lawyer, mediator; b. Far Rockaway, N.Y., Jan. 18, 1937; s. Joseph and Bertha (Fromberg) O.; m. Carol M. Ordover, Mar. 23, 1961; children: Andrew Charles, Thomas Edward. BA magna cum laude, Syracuse U., 1958; JD, Yale U., 1961. Bar: N.Y. 1961, U.S. Dist. Ct. (so. and ea. dists.) N.Y., U.S. Ct. Appeals (2d cir.), U.S. Supreme Ct. Assoc. Cahill, Gordon & Reindel, N.Y.C., 1961-71; prof. law Hofstra U., Hempstead, N.Y., 1971-81; L.Q.C. Lamar prof. law Emory U., Atlanta, 1981-91; CEO Resolution Resources Corp., Atlanta, 1991—; mediator and arbitrator; vis. prof. Cornell U., Ithaca, N.Y., 1977; vis. lectr. Tel Aviv U., 1989, Am. Law Inst.; team leader nat. program Nat. Inst. Trial Advocacy, Boulder, Colo., 1980, 82, 84, 86, 89, tchr. program Cambridge, Mass., 1979-84, 88, adv. program Gainesville, Fla., 1978-79, northeast regional dir., 1977-81; team leader SE regional program, 1983; team leader Atlanta Bar Trial Tech. Program, 1981-91; lectr. in field. Author: Argument to the Jury, 1982, Problems and Cases in Trial Advocacy, 1983, Advanced Materials in Trial Advocacy, 1988, Alternatives to Litigation, 1993, Cases and Materials in Evidence, 1993, Art of Negotiation, 1994; producer ednl. films; contbr. articles to profl. jours. Bd. dirs. Atlanta Legal Aid Soc., 1984-91, 7 Stages Theatre, 1991-96. Recipient Gumpert award Am. Coll. Trial Lawyers, 1984, 85, Jacobsen award Roscoe Pound Am. Trial Lawyer Found., 1986. Mem. ABA, N.Y. State Bar Assn., Assn. Am. Law Schs. (chair litigation sect.), Atlanta Lawyers Club, Am. Law Inst. Avocation: photography.

ORDWAY, FREDERICK IRA, III, educator, consultant, researcher, author; b. N.Y.C., Apr. 4, 1927; s. Frederick Ira and Frances Antoinette (Wright) O.; m. Maria Victoria Arenas, Apr. 13, 1950; children: Frederick Ira IV, Albert James, Aliette Marisol. SB, Harvard, 1949; postgrad., U. Alger, 1950, U. Paris, France, 1950-51, 53-54, U. Barcelona, Spain, 1953, U. Innsbruck, Austria, 1954, Air U., 1952-63, Alexander Hamilton Bus. Inst., 1952-58, Indsl. Coll. Armed Forces, 1953, 63; DSc (hon.), U. Ala., 1992. Various geol., engring. positions Mene Grande Oil Co., San Tome, Venezuela, 1949-50, Orinoco Mining Co., Cerro Bolivar, Venezuela, 1950, Reaction Motors, Inc., Lake Denmark, N.J., 1951-53; with guided missiles divsn. Republic Aviation Corp., 1954-55; pres. Gen. Astronautics Research Corp., Huntsville, Ala., 1955-59, 65-66; v.p. Nat. R & D Corp., Atlanta, 1957-59; asst. to dir. Saturn Systems Office, Army Ballistic Missile Agy., Huntsville, 1959-60; chief space information systems br. George C. Marshall Space Flight Center NASA, 1960-64; prof. sci. and tech. applications Sch. Grad. Studies and Rsch., U. Ala. Rsch. Inst., 1967-73; cons. Sci. and Tech. Policy Office, NSF, 1974-75; cons. ops. analysis divsn. Gen. Rsch. Corp., 1974-75; asst. to adminstr. ERDA, 1975-77; Dept. Energy, 1977-94, policy and internat. affairs dir. spl. projects office, 1994—; aerospace cons., 1994—; also participant internat. energy devel. program Office of Asst. Sec. Internat. Affairs, Dept. Energy, 1978-79; cons. to industry, Ency. Britannica, Am. Coll. Dictionary of English Lang., M.G.M. film 2001: A Space Odyssey, 1965-66, Paramount Picture Corp., The Adventurers, 1968-69; internat. lectr. space flight and energy programs. Author: (with C.C. Adams) Space Flight, 1958, (with Ronald C. Wakeford) International Missile and Spacecraft Guide, 1960, Annotated Bibliography of Space Science and Technology, 1962, (with J.P. Gardner, M.R. Sharpe, Jr.) Basic Astronautics: An Introduction to Space Science, Engineering and Medicine, 1962, (with Adams, Wernher von Braun) Careers in Astronautics and Rocketry, 1962, (with Gardner, Sharpe, R.C. Wakeford) Applied Astronautics: An Introduction to Space Flight, 1963, (with Wakeford) Conquering the Sun's Empire, 1963, Life in Other Solar Systems, 1965, (with Roger A. MacGowan) Intelligence in the Universe, 1966, (with W. von Braun) History of Rocketry and Space Travel, 1966, 1969, 75, L'Histoire Mondiale de l'Astronautique, 1968, 70, Rockets Red Glare, 1976, (with C.C. Adams, M.R. Sharpe) Dividends from Space, 1972, Pictorial Guide to Planet Earth, 1975, (with W. von Braun) New Worlds, 1979, (with M.R. Sharpe) The Rocket Team, 1979, (with F.C. Durant and R.C. Seamans) Between Sputnik and the Shuttle, 1981, (with E.M. Emme) Science Fiction and Space Futures, 1982, (with von Braun, Dave Dooling) Space Travel: A History, 1985, (with Ernst Stuhlinger) Wernher von Braun: Aufbruch in den Weltraum, 1992, Wernher von Braun: Crusader for Space (2 vols.), 1994, revised 1996, also single vol. edition, 1996, (with Randy Liebermann) Blueprint for Space, 1992; editor: Advances in Space Science and Technology, vols. I-XII, 2 supplements, 1959-72, (with R.M.L. Baker, N.W. Makemson) Introduction to Astrodynamics, 1960, (with others) From Peenemünde to Outer Space, 1962, Astronautical Engineering and Science, 1963; mem. editorial bd.: (with others) IX Internat. Astronautical Congress procs., 2 vols, 1959, Xth Congress procs., 2 vols, 1960; guest editor: Acta Astronautica, 1985, 94, History of Rocketry and Astronautics, Vol. IX, 1989, Digital book Mars: Target for Tomorrow Microsoft Network & Internet, 1996; Co-creation of biographical Film "Conquered Space, Discovery channel, 1996, History of Astromatics Vedio, 1996, Inter-active CD Rom, 1997; contbr. (with others) numerous articles to profl. jours., U.S. and fgn. encys., chpts. to books, sects. to others; organizer Blueprint for Space exhbn., 1991-95, U.S. Space and Rocket Ctr., IBM Gallery of Sci. and Art, NASA Vis. Ctr., Houston, Spaceport USA, Cape Canaveral, Fla., Nat. Air and Space Mus., Washington, Va. Air and Space Ctr., Hampton and numerous others. Served with USNR, 1945. Recipient (with W. von Braun) diplôme d'honneur French Commn. d'Histoire, Arts et Letters, Paris, 1969; commended for contbns. to U.S. Space and Rocket Ctr., Ala. Space Sci. Exhibit. Fellow AAAS, AIAA (history com. 1975—, internat. activities com. 1980-89, Pendray award 1974, Hermann Oberth award 1977), Brit. Interplanetary Soc.; mem. Internat. Acad. Astronautics (history of astronautics com. 1983—, chmn. 1989-95, space activities and soc. com. 1986—, peer rev. com. 1985—, co-recipient Luigi Napolitano Lit. award 1992), Am. Astron. Soc. (Emme award 1994), Brit. Interplanetary Soc., Nat. Space Soc. (bd. dirs. 1986—, mem. publs. com. 1987-88, nominating com. 1990-92), Royal Soc. Arts, Mfrs. and Commerce, Eurasian Acad. Scis., Cosmos Club (bd. mgmt. 1986-91), v.p. 1988-90), Harvard Club N.Y. Home: 2401 N Taylor St Arlington VA 22207

ORDWAY, JOHN DANTON, retired pension administrator, lawyer, accountant; b. Mpls., Mar. 19, 1928; s. John Dunreath Ordway and Inez Adelaide (Stahl) Larson; m. Mary E. Bateman, June 16, 1951(div. 1978); 1 child, David. BBA, Am. U., 1963, JD, 1965. Bar: U.S. Dist. Ct. D.C. 1966; CPA, Minn. Dir. ins. Nat. Automobile Dealers Assn., Washington, 1957-69; v.p. Edward H. Friend and Co., Washington, 1969-74; exec. v.p. and CEO Pension Bds. United Ch. of Christ, N.Y.C., 1974-96. Alt. mem. Planning Bd., Stamford, Conn., 1982-86. With U.S. Army, 1946-47. Mem. AICPAs. Republican. Mem. United Ch. of Christ. Club: Westwood Country (Vienna, Va.); Quail Run Golf Club (Naples, Fla.). Lodge: Kena Temple. Home: 206 Woodshire Ln Naples FL 34105-7429

O'REAR, EDGAR ALLEN, III, chemical engineering educator; b. Jasper, Ala., Feb. 24, 1953; s. Edgar Allen O'Rear Jr. and Edith Idzorek. B-SChemE, Rice U., 1975; SM in Organic Chemistry, MIT, 1977; PhD, Rice U., 1981. Rsch. engr. Exxon Rsch. and Engring., Baytown, Tex., summer 1975; from asst. prof. to assoc. prof. U. Okla., Norman, 1981-91, Conoco disting. lectr., 1987-92, prof., 1991—, assoc. dean rsch. Coll. Engring., 1995—; vis. sr. rschr. Hitachi Cen. Rsch. Lab., Kokubumji, Japan, summer 1988; vis. scientist RIKEN-Inst. for Phys. and Chem. Rsch., Wako-Shi, Japan, summer 1992; cons. Boehringer-Mannheim, Indpls., Baxter-Travenol, Deerfield, Ill., Associated Metallurgists, Norman; co-founder Inst. for Applied Surfactant Rsch.; organizer symposia; reviewer for funding agys. and profl. jours. Co-author: Fluid Mechanics Exam File, 1985; contbr. tech. articles to profl. jours. Usher, mem. parish coun. St. Thomas More U. Parish, Norman, GlenMary Home Missioners; People to People Physiacal Scientist Del. to China; mentor Big Bros.,Big Sisters, Norman, 1984-86. Recipient Faculty Rsch. award Sigma Xi, 1986; rsch. grantee NSF, NIH, NASA, AHA, Dept. of Def. Mem. AIChE, AAAS, Internat. Soc. Biorheology (sec. gen. 1992-98), Am. Chem. Soc., Tau Beta Pi. Roman Catholic. Achievements include patent for production of polymeric films from a surfactant template; method and composition for treatment of thrombosis in a mammal. Avocations: reading, hiking, stamp collecting. Office: U Okla Dept Chem Engring SEC T335 100 E Boyd St Norman OK 73019-1000

OREAR, JAY, physics educator, researcher; b. Chgo., Nov. 6, 1925; s. Leslie and Edna (Tragnitz) O.; m. Jeanne Bliven, Mar. 10, 1951; children—Scott, Robin, Wendy; m. Virginia Watts, Sept. 6, 1974. Ph.B., U. Chgo., 1944, Ph.D., 1953. Research assoc. U. Chgo., 1953-54; instr. to asst. prof. Columbia U., N.Y.C., 1954-58; assoc. prof. Cornell U., Ithaca, N.Y., 1958-64, prof. physics, nuclear studies, 1964—; Chmn. Fedn. Am. Scientists, 1967-68; rschr., group leader in proton-antiproton elastic scattering Fermilab Tevatron. Author: Nuclear Physics, 1951, Fundamental Physics, 1961, Programmed Manual, 1963, Statistics for Physicists, 1958, 82, Physics, 1979. Served with USNR, 1944-46. Fellow AAAS, Am. Phys. Soc. (editor Forum Newsletter 1972-74); mem. Phi Beta Kappa, Sigma Xi. Office: Cornell U Newman Lab Ithaca NY 14853 *"Whatever you do, or dream you can, begin it. Boldness has genius, power and magic in it. Begin it now." J. W. Goethe. "To sin by silence when they should protest makes cowards of men." Abe Lincoln. "Neither those who know, nor those who know they do not know make mistakes. Those who do not know and think that they know are disgraceful and mischievous." Plato.*

O'REGAN, DEBORAH, association executive, lawyer; b. New Prague, Minn., Aug. 30, 1953; d. Timothy A. and Ermalinda (Brinkman) O'R.; m. Ron Kahlenbeck, Sept. 29, 1984; 1 child, Katherine. BA, Coll. of St. Catherine, 1975; JD, William Mitchell Coll. of Law, 1980. Bar: Ala. 1982, Minn. 1980. Asst. city atty. City of Bloomington, Minn., 1978-81, asst. city mgr., 1981-82; CLE dir. Alaska Bar Assn., Anchorage, 1982-84, exec. dir., 1985—; mem. task force on gender equality State Fed. Joint Commn., Anchorage, 1991—; mem. selection com. U.S. Magistrate Judge, U.S. Dist of Ala., 1992; mem. adv. bd. Anchorage Daily News, 1991-93. Mem. Nat. Assn. Bar Execs. (exec. com. 1993-97). Avocations: travel, outdoors, rollerblading. Office: Alaska Bar Assn 510 L St Ste 602 Anchorage AK 99501-1959

O'REGAN, RICHARD ARTHUR, editor, retired foreign correspondent; b. Boston, July 15, 1919; s. Arthur R. and Amelia H. (Egbers) O'R.; m. Elizabeth A. Hill, Mar. 23, 1946; children—John K., Michael L. Student, Temple U., 1940-41, Vienna U., Austria, 1953-54. With London Daily Mail and London Daily Sketch, 1938-39; reporter, night city editor Phila. Bull., 1939-43; writer Russian-German war specialist UPI, 1943-45; fgn. corr. AP, 1945-84; assigned AP, London, Paris, Germany, 1945-50; chief bur. AP, Vienna, 1950-55, Germany, 1956-66, London, 1966-77; dir. gen. for AP, Europe, Africa and Middle East, 1977-84; mng. dir., editor-in-chief Oriole Internat. Publs., Geneva, 1987—; bd. dirs. A.P. Ltd. Co-author: International Geneva (ann.). Mem. Assn. Am. Corrs. in London (pres. 1969). Clubs: Overseas Press (N.Y.C.); Press (Frankfurt, Germany) (past pres.); London Press, London Directors. Home: 33 Chemin de Grange Canal, 1208 Geneva Switzerland

O'REILLY, ANTHONY JOHN FRANCIS, food company executive; b. Dublin, Ireland, May 7, 1936; s. John Patrick and Aileen (O'Connor) O'R.; m. Susan Cameron, May 5, 1962 (div.); children: Susan, Cameron, Justine, Gavin, Caroline, Tony; m. Chryss Goulandris, Sept. 14, 1991. Student, Belvedere Coll., Dublin, Univ. Coll., Dublin, Wharton Bus. Sch. Overseas, 1965; B.C.L.; D.C.L. (hon.), Ind. State U.; Ph.D. in Agrl. Mktg, U. Bradford, Eng.; LL.D. (hon.), Wheeling Coll., 1974, Trinity Coll., Dublin, 1978, Allegheny Coll., 1983, De Paul U., Chgo., 1988; D in Bus. Studies (hon.), Rollins Coll., 1978; D in Civil Law honoris causa, Ind. State U., 1980; DBA (hon.), Boston Coll., 1985; D in Econ. Sci. (hon.), Nat. U. Ireland, 1989. Indsl. cons. Weston Evans, 1958-62; personal asst. to chmn. Suttons Ltd., Cork, Ireland, 1960-62; lectr. dept. applied psychology Univ. Coll., Cork, 1960-62; dir. Robert McCowen & Sons Ltd., Tralee, Ireland, 1961-62; mng. dir. An Bord Bainne/Irish Dairy Bd., 1962-66; dir. Agrl. Credit Corp. Ltd., 1965-66, Nitrigin Eireann Teoranta, 1965-66; mng. dir., chief exec. officer Comhlucht Siuicre Eireann Teo. (Irish Sugar Co.) and Erin

Foods Ltd., Dublin, 1966-69; joint mng. dir. Heinz-Erin Ltd., 1967-70; mng. dir. H.J. Heinz Co. Ltd., Eng., 1969-71; sr. v.p. N.Am. and Pacific H.J. Heinz Co., 1971-72; exec. v.p., chief operating officer H.J. Heinz Co., Pitts., 1972-73, pres., chief operating officer, 1973-79, pres., chief exec. officer, 1979-90, also chmn., 1978—, also bd. dirs., now chmn., CEO; chmn. Fitzwilton Plc.,Independent Newspapers Plc., Atlantic Resources, Dublin, Am. Ireland Fund.; ptnr. Cawley Sheerin Wynne and Co., solicitors, Dublin; bd. dirs. Bankers Trust N.Y. Corp., Bankers Trust N.Y. Corp., Washington Post Co., London Tablet Found. Inc., Starkist Foods Inc., Ore-Ida Foods Inc. Author: Prospect, 1962, Developing Creative Management, 1970, The Conservative Consumer, 1971, Food for Thought, 1972. Bd. govs. Hugh O'Brian Found., L.A.; mem. counc. Rockefeller U., N.Y.C.; bd. dirs. Assocs. Grad. Sch. Bus. Adminstrn. of Harvard U., Cambridge, Mass.; sr. bd. dirs. The Conf. Bd.; trustee U. Pitts., Com. for Econ. Devel.; mem. Nat. Com. Whitney Mus. Am. Art. Named Hon. Officer Order of Australia, 1988. Fellow Brit. Inst. Mgmt., Royal Soc. Arts; mem. Inst. Dirs., Inc., Law Soc. Ireland (treas.), Grocery Mfrs. Am. (sec., bd. dirs.), Am. Irish Found., Internat. Life Scis. Inst. Nutrition Found. (chmn., chief exec. officer council), Irish Mgmt. Inst. (council), Exec. Council Fgn. Diplomats (bd. dirs.). Clubs: St. Stephens Green, Kildare St., University (Dublin); Annabels, Les Ambassadeurs, Marks (London); Union League, The Links, The Bd. Room (N.Y.C.); Duquesne, Allegheny, Pitts. Golf, Fox Chapel Golf, Pitts. Press, Pitts. Golf (Pitts.); Rolling Rock (Ligonier) (bd. govs.); Lyford Cay (Bahamas). Office: H J Heinz Co PO Box 57 600 Grant St Pittsburgh PA 15219-2857 also: Mobil Corp 150 E 42nd St New York NY 10017-5612*

O'REILLY, CHARLES TERRANCE, university dean; b. Chgo., May 30, 1921; s. William Patrick and Ann Elizabeth (Madden) O'R.; m. Rosella Catherine Neilland, June 4, 1955; children—Terrance, Gregory, Kevin, Joan Bridget, Kathleen Ann. B.A., Loyola U., Chgo., 1942, M.S.W., 1948; postgrad., U. Cattolica, Milan, Italy, 1949-50; Ph.D., U. Notre Dame, 1954. Instr. DePaul U., Chgo., 1948-49; asst. in psychology U. Cattolica, 1949-50; caseworker Cath. Charities, N.Y.C., 1953-54; exec. dir. Family Service, Long Branch, N.J., 1954-55; asst. prof. Loyola U., 1955-59; vis. lectr. Ensiss Sch. Social Work, Milan, 1959-60; asso. prof. U. Wis.-Milw., 1961-64; prof., asso. dir. U. Wis. Sch. Social Work, Madison, 1965-68; dean social welfare, v.p. acad. affairs SUNY-Albany, 1969-76; dean social work Loyola U., Chgo., 1976-92, dean emeritus, sr. prof., 1994—; vis. prof. sch. social work SS Maria Asunta, Rome, 1992-93. Author: OAA Profile, 1961, People of Inner Core North, 1965, Men in Jail, 1968; contbr. articles to profl. jours. Pres. Community Action Commn. Dane County, Wis., 1967-68; bd. dirs. Council Community Services, Albany, Family and Children's Service, Albany; mem. adv. bd. Safer Found.; vice chmn. Ill. Pub. Aid Citizens Council. Served with AUS, 1942-46, 51-52. Fulbright scholar, 1949-50; fellow, 1959-60. Mem. AAUP, Nat. Assn. Social Workers. Roman Catholic. Home: 4073 Bunker Ln Wilmette IL 60091-1001 Office: Sch Social Work Loyola Univ Chicago IL 60611*

O'REILLY, DON, reporter, writer, photographer; b. Attleboro, Mass., May 1, 1913; s. Dennis Charles and Helen Louise (Barden) O'R.; m. Edith Lillian Macomber, July 9, 1938; 1 child, Howard (dec.). Owner, operator Eagle Press, 1930-37; reporter, photographer Attleboro (Mass.) Sun, 1937-39, N. Attleboro Chronicle, 1939-40, New London (Conn.) Day, 1940-42, Washington Post, 1945-47; editor, pub. Speed Age Mag., Washington, 1947-53; mgr. NASCAR News Bur., Daytona Beach, Fla., 1953-56; sports broadcaster NBC Radio Monitor, various locations, 1956-59, Stas. WESH-TV, WROD, Daytona Beach, 1956-59; dir. pub. rels. Atlanta Internat. Raceway, 1959-64; mgr. automotive divsn., writer, prodn. asst., unit mgr. sports documentaries Dynamic Films, Inc., 1964-68; pub. rels. Am. Motor Corp., 1971-75; broadcaster Mutual, ABC, NBC, 1968-80; writer Popular Mechanics, Sat. Evening Post, Stock Car Racing, Argosy, Small Cars, Illustrated Speedway News, others, 1968-80; bur. chief, reporter, photographer News-Jour., Daytona Beach, 1976-80; feature writer Circle Track Mag., Speed Age, Stock Car Racing, Racing Pictorial, others, 1980-90; columnist various newspapers, 1980-90; feature writer newspapers, mags., books, 1991—; stringer Boston Post, Globe, Herald-Traveler, 1937-39; dir. press rels. U.S. Grand Prix; self-syndicated columnist Inside Auto Racing, Motorcade USA, 1956-85. Author: Mr. Hockey: The World of Gordie Howe, The Complete Book of Motor Camping, Sports Review-Motorspeed, Auto Racing Guide, (with Curtis Crider) The Road to Daytona. Chief photographers mate U.S. Coast Guard, 1942-45. Elected to Nat. Auto Racing Hall of Fame by Nat. Old Timers Auto Racing Club, Flemington, N.J., 1988; named Living Legend of Auto Racing by Living Legends, Port Orange, Fla., 1993, Hon. Order of Ky. Cols., Louisville, 1990. Mem. Nat. Motorsports Press Assn., Ea. Motorsports Press Assn. (1st pl. award in feature writing 1990), Nat. Press Club, Am. Assn. Auto Racing Writers (v.p.), Nat. Press Photographers Assn. (charter, life), Am. Auto Racing Writers and Broadcasters Assn. (Best Column of Yr. 1989), Nat. Sportswriters and Sportscasters Assn., Soc. Profl. Journalists, Nikon Profl. Svcs., Fla. Freelance Writers Assn., Halifax Hist. Soc., Bay State Old Timers Racing Assn., Williams Grove Old Timers, Indpls. 500 Old Timers Club (charter, life). Home and Office: 198 Sea Pines Cir Daytona Beach FL 32114-1166

O'REILLY, HUGH JOSEPH, restaurant executive; b. Emporia, Kans., July 20, 1936; s. Henry Charles and Mary Esther (Rettiger) O'R.; m. Eileen Ellen Browne, Feb. 11, 1961; 1 child, Hugh Jr. Student, St. Benedicts Coll., Atchison, Kans., 1954-57, Kansas City Conservatory of Music, 1957-58. Banquet mgr. Stouffer Corp., N.Y.C., 1958-61; gen. mgr. Howard Johnsons, L.I., N.Y., 1961-65; regional mgr. Malt Village Corp., St. Louis, 1965-68; ops. cons. McDonald's Corp., Chgo., 1966-78; pres., chief exec. officer O'Reilly Mgmt. Corp., Emporia, Kans., 1978—; nat. advt. cons. McDonalds Operators Assn., Oak Brook, Ill., 1980-84. Republican. Roman Catholic. Lodge: Shriner. Avocations: golf, fishing. Office: 907 Commercial St Emporia KS 66801-2916

O'REILLY, JAMES THOMAS, lawyer, educator, author; b. N.Y.C., Nov. 15, 1947; s. Matthew Richard and Regina (Casey) O'R.; children: Jean, Ann. BA cum laude, Boston Coll., 1969; JD, U. Va., 1974. Bar: Va. 1974, Ohio, 1974, U.S. Supreme Ct. 1979, U.S. Ct. Appeals (6th cir.) 1980. Atty. Procter & Gamble Co., Cin., 1974-76, counsel, 1976-79, sr. counsel for food, drug and product safety, 1979-85, corp. counsel, 1985-93, assoc. gen. counsel, 1993—; adj. prof. in adminstrv. law U. Cin., 1980—; cons. Adminstrv. Conf. U.S., 1981-82, 89-90, Congl. Office of Compliance, 1995—; arbitrator State Employee Relations Bd.; mem. Ohio Bishops Adv. Council, Mayor's Infrastructure Commn, Cin. Environ. Adv. Coun. Author: Federal Information Disclosure, 1977, Food and Drug Administration Regulatory Manual, 1979, Unions' Rights to Company Information, 1980, Federal Regulation of the Chemical Industry, 1980, Administrative Rulemaking, 1983, Ohio Public Employee Collective Bargaining, 1984, Protecting Workplace Secrets, 1985, Emergency Response to Chemical Accidents, 1986, Product Defects and Hazards, 1987, Toxic Torts Strategy Deskbook, 1989; Protecting Trade Secrets Under SARA, 1988, Complying With Canada's New Labeling Law, 1989, Solid Waste Mgmt., 1991, Ohio Products Liability Handbook, 1991, Toxic Torts Guide, 1992, ABA Product Liability Resource Manual, 1993, RCRA and Superfund Practice Guide, 1993, Clean Air Permits manual, 1994, United States Environmental Liabilities, 1994, Elder Safety, 1995, Environmental and Workplace Safety for University and Hospital Managers, 1996, Sick of Safe Buildings, 1997; contbr. articles to profl. jours.; editorial bd. Food and Drug Cosmetic Law Jour. Mem. Hamilton County Dem. Central Com. Served with U.S. Army, 1970-72. Mem. Food and Drug Law Inst. (chair program com.), ABA (chmn. AD law sect.), Fed. Bar Assn., Leadership Cin. Democrat. Roman Catholic. Office: Procter & Gamble Co PO Box 599 Cincinnati OH 45201-0599

O'REILLY, KENNETH WILLIAM, military officer; b. N.Y.C., July 17, 1953; s. Thomas Michael and Dorothy Marie (Garvin) O'R.; m. Ginger Lee Jacobs, Apr. 22, 1978; children: Ryan, Erin. AAS, SUNY, Farmingdale, 1973; BS, Dowling Coll., 1975; MA, Webster U., 1982. Sales rep. N.W. Airlines, N.Y.C., 1976-78; commd. 2d lt. USAF, 1978—, advanced through grades to lt. col.; student navigator 452 Flight Tng. Squadron, Mather AFB, Calif., 1979-80; KC135 unit navigator 11th Air Refueling Squadron, Altus AFB, Okla., 1980-83; instr. navigator 11th Air Refueling Squadron, Altus AFB, 1984-85; wing exec. officer 340 Air Refueling Wing, Altus AFB, 1984-85; chief of navigation 34 Strategic Squadron, Zaragoza AB, Spain, 1985-88; strategic plans advisor 2 Airborne Command and Control Squadron, Offutt AFB, Nebr., 1988-91; action officer Hdqrs. SAC/Directorate of Strategic Plans, Offutt AFB, 1991-92; chief of tanker plans Hdqrs. Air Mobility Command/Dir. Ops. and Transp., 1992-93, chief personnel mgmt. br., 1993-96; chief opers. watch divsn., headqrs., dir. opers. and plans The Pentagon, 1996—. Committeeman Levittown South-North Wantagh, Rep. Club, N.Y.C., 1971-78. Decorated 2 Meritorious Svc. medal, 2 Commendation medals, others. Mem. Air Force Assn., Inst. of Navigation, Airlift Tanker Assn. Roman Catholic. Home: 7017 Petunia St Springfield VA 22152 Office: HQ USAF/X000 1480 Air Force Pentagon # Usaf Washington DC 20330-1480

O'REILLY, MICHAEL JOSEPH, lawyer, real estate investor; b. Columbus, Ohio, May 19, 1958; s. John Joseph and Virginia Joyce (Bradley) O'R.; m. Angelique I. Gaal, Feb. 25, 1995. AB, Miami U., Oxford, Ohio, 1980; JD, Ohio State U., 1984. Bar: Ohio 1984. Lawyer The Galbreath Corp., Columbus, 1984-89; gen. counsel R.J. Solove & Assocs. Mgmt./Devel., Inc., Columbus, 1989-95; pvt. practice Law Offices of Michael J. O'Reilly, Columbus, 1995—; pres. Franklin & Union Land Title Agy., Inc., 1996—; seminar spkr. Ohio CLE Inst., Nat. Bus. Inst. Mem. Ohio State Bar Assn., Columbus Bar Assn. Roman Catholic. Office: PO Box 340228 Columbus OH 43234-0228

O'REILLY, PATTY MOLLETT, psychometrist, consultant. BA in Psychology, U. Ala., 1978, MA in Devel. Learning and Psychometrics, 1979. Resource tchr. pub. schs., Madison, Ala., 1979-86, Huntsville, Ala., 1986-90; owner, mgr. Huntsville Ednl. Svc., cons., diagnostics, tutoring, 1988—; supr. grad. teaching students U. Ala., summers 1985-87, lectr. psychology, summer 1993. Mem. Coun. for Exceptional Children. Office: Huntsville Ednl Svc PO Box 1131 Huntsville AL 35807-0131

O'REILLY, RICHARD BROOKS, journalist; b. Kansas City, Mo., Feb. 19, 1941; s. Charles Alfred and Wilma Faye (Brooks) O'R.; m. Anne Pustmeuller, June 27, 1964 (div. 1978); children—Kathleen Marie, Randall Charles; m. Joan Marlene Sweeney, Jan. 1, 1981 (div. 1996). B.A., U. Denver, 1966. Reporter Washington Park Times, Denver, 1963-64; mng. editor Aurora Advocate, Colo., 1964; police reporter Rocky Mountain News, Denver, 1964-66, night rewrite reporter, 1966, city hall reporter, 1966-67, statehouse reporter, 1967-68, investigative reporter, 1971-74; minority affairs reporter Denver Post, 1968-70; freelance writer St. Georges, Grenada, 1970; investigative reporter Orange County edition Los Angeles Times, 1974-78, chief county bur., 1978, asst. met. editor, 1978-80, environ. reporter, 1980-84, computer columnist, syndicated columnist, 1983-96, coord. tech. resources, 1984-89, dir. editorial computer analysis, 1989—; adj. prof. journalism U. So. Calif., 1990-92; mem. electronic filing adv. com. Calif. Sec. of State, 1995. Named Colo. Journalist of Yr., Sigma Delta Chi, 1972; recipient Pub. Svc. award U.S. Justice Dept., 1973, McWilliams award Denver Press Club, 1974, Investigative Reporting award Orange Country Press Club, 1977, 95, Los Angeles Times, 1977, 97, Nat. Journalism award Soc. Profl. Engrs., 1983, Clean Air award Am. Lung Assn., 1985, award for non-deadline reporting Sigma Delta Chi, 1996, medal for investigative reporting Investigative Reporters and Editors, 1996. Democrat. Avocations: flying; sailing; camping. Office: Los Angeles Times Times Mirror Sq Los Angeles CA 90012

O'REILLY, THOMAS EUGENE, human resources consultant; b. Wichita, Kans., Sept. 7, 1932; s. Eugene William and Florence Irene (Gustner) O'R.; m. Lorraine Bryant, Feb. 9, 1957; children: Thomas Jr., Patricia, Susan, Gregory, Pamela. BA, Iona Coll., 1954; MBA, NYU, 1958. Mem. human resources staff Chase Manhattan Bank, N.Y.C., 1957-69; dir. employee rels. Chase Manhattan Bank, 1969-71, mgr. internat. personnel, 1971-75, dir. internal staffing, 1976-77, dir. mgmt. resources, 1978-80; dir. exec. resources Chase Manhattan Bank, N.Y.C., 1980-87; v.p., sr. cons. Lee Hecht Harrison, Inc., N.Y.C., 1988-93. Spl. agt. counter-intelligence corps, U.S. Army, 1954-57. Mem. Nat. Fgn. Trade Coun., Exec. Issues Forum. Republican. Roman Catholic. Home and Office: 6200 E Cielo Run Cave Creek AZ 85331-7645

O'REILLY, TIMOTHY PATRICK, lawyer; b. San Lorenzo, Calif., Sept. 12, 1945; s. Thomas Marvin and Florence Ann (Ohlman) O'R.; m. Susan Ann Marshall, July 18, 1969; children: T. Patrick Jr., Sean M., Colleen K. BS, Ohio State U., 1967; JD, NYU, 1971. Bar: Pa. 1971, U.S. Dist. Ct. (ea. dist.) Pa. 1971, U.S. Dist. Ct. (mid. dist.) Pa. 1972, U.S. Ct. Appeals (3d cir.) 1977, U.S. Supreme Ct. 1988. Ptnr. Morgan, Lewis & Bockius, Phila., 1978—. Editor: Developing Labor Law, 1989; contbr. articles to profl. jours. V.p. Chester Valley Bd. Govs., Malvern, Pa., 1980-85; bd. dirs. Notre Dame Acad. and Devon Preparatory Sch. Mem. ABA (chmn. com. on devel. of the law under the Nat. Labor Relations Act., editor-in-chief The Developing Labor Law jour.), Pa. Bar Assn., Phila. Bar Assn., Ohio State U. Alumni Assn. Avocation: golf. Home: 1127 Cymry Dr Berwyn PA 19312-2056 Office: Morgan Lewis & Bockius 2000 One Logan Sq Philadelphia PA 19103

OREL, HAROLD, literary critic, educator; b. Boston, Mar. 31, 1926; s. Saul and Sarah (Wicker) O.; m. Charlyn Hawkins, May 25, 1951; children: Sara Elinor, Timothy Ralston. BA cum laude, U. N.H., 1948; MA, U. Mich., 1949, PhD, 1952; postgrad., Harvard U., 1949. Teaching fellow U. Mich., 1948-52; instr. dept. English, U. Md., 1952-54, 55-56; overseas program U. Md., Germany, Austria, Eng., 1954-55; tech. editor Applied Physics Lab., Johns Hopkins U., Balt., 1953-56; flight propulsion lab. dept. Gen. Electric Co., Cin., 1957; asso. prof. U. Kans., Lawrence, 1957-63; prof. U. Kans., 1963-74, Disting. prof. English, 1975—, asst. dean faculties and research adminstrn., 1964-67; cons. to various univ. presses, scholarly jours., Can. Coun. Arts, Nat. Endowment of Humanities, Midwest Rsch. Inst., 1958—; lectr., Japan, 1974, 88, India, 1985. Author: Thomas Hardy's Epic-Drama: A Study of The Dynasts, 1963, The Development of William Butler Yeats, 1885-1900, 1968, English Romantic Poets and the Enlightenment: Nine Essays on a Literary Relationship in Studies in Voltaire and the Eighteenth Century, vol. CIII, 1973, The Final Years of Thomas Hardy, 1912-1928, 1976, Victorian Literary Critics, 1984, The Literary Achievement of Rebecca West, 1985, The Victorian Short Story: Development and Triumph of a Literary Genre, 1986, The Unknown Thomas Hardy: Lesser-Known Aspects of Hardy's Life and Career, 1987, A Kipling Chronology, 1990, Popular Fiction in England, 1914-1918, 1992, The Historical Novel from Scott to Sabatini, 1995; contbg. author: Thomas Hardy and the Modern World, 1974, The Genius of Thomas Hardy, 1976, Budmouth Essays on Thomas Hardy, 1976, Twilight of Dawn: Studies in English Literature in Transition, 1987; contbr. numerous articles on English lit. history and criticism to various mags.; editor: The World of Victorian Humor, 1961, Six Essays in Nineteenth-Century English Literature and Thought, 1962, Thomas Hardy's Personal Writings: Prefaces, Literary Opinions, Reminiscences, 1966, British Poetry 1880-1920: Edwardian Voices, 1969, The Nineteenth-Century Writer and his Audience, 1969, Irish History and Culture, 1976, The Dynasts (Thomas Hardy), 1978, The Scottish World, 1981, Rudyard Kipling: Interviews and Recollections, 2 vols., 1983, Victorian Short Stories: An Anthology, 1987, Critical Essays on Rudyard Kipling, 1989, Victorian Short Stories 2: The Trials of Love, 1990, Sir Arthur Conan Doyle: Interviews and Recollections, 1991, Critical Essays on Sir Arthur Conan Doyle, 1992, Gilbert and Sullivan: Interviews and Recollections, 1994, Critical Essays on Thomas Hardy's Poetry, 1995, The Brontës: Interviews and Recollections, 1997; delivered orations Thomas Hardy ceremonies, Westminster Abbey, 1978, 90. With USN, 1944-46. Recipient Higuchi Endowment Rsch. Achievement award, 1990; grantee Am. Coun. Learned Socs., 1966, NEH, 1975, Am. Philos. Soc., 1964, 80. Fellow Royal Soc. Literature; mem. Thomas Hardy Soc. (v.p. 1968—), Am. Com. on Irish Studies (v.p. 1967-70, pres. 1970-72). Unitarian. Home: 713 Schwarz Rd Lawrence KS 66049 Office: U Kans Dept English Lawrence KS 66045

OREM, CASSANDRA ELIZABETH, health systems administrator, educator, author, holistic health practitioner, entrepreneur; b. Balt., Sept. 26, 1940; d. Ira Julius and Mabel Ruth (Peeples) O. Diploma, Ch. Home and Hosp. Sch. Nursing, 1962; BS with honors, The Johns Hopkins U., 1968; MS, U. Md., 1972; cert., Balt. Sch. Massage, 1988; MA in Applied Psychology, U. Santa Monica, 1991, cert. in advanced applied psychology, 1992; cert., Waitley Masters Coaching Prog., 1996. Staff, charge nurse Ch. Home and Hosp., Balt., 1962-63; asst. instr. Ch. Home and Hosp. Sch. Nursing, Balt., 1963-64, instr., 1964-70, rsch., clin.-primary investigator, 1971-72; clin. nurse specialist Johns Hopkins Hosp., Balt., 1972-77, rsch., clin. co-investigator, 1975, asst. dir. nursing, 1977-79, asst. adminstr., dir. nursing, 1979-87; clin. assoc. faculty The Johns Hopkins U. Sch. of Nursing, 1984-87; program dir., instr. intermediate massage course Balt. Sch. Massage, 1988—, instr. advanced massage course, 1991—, program dir. advanced massage course, 1996—, curriculum devel. coord., 1996—, network mktg. cons., 1991—; ptnr., educator UBP Assocs., 1990-91; pres. Nursing Edn. and Cons. Svc., Inc., Balt., 1976-78, Oasis Health Systems, Inc., Balt., 1987—; spkr. workshop facilitator, cons. profl. topics, Health and Wellness, Personal Growth, Time Mgmt., 1973—. Author profl. booklet & audio publs., Patient Education Book and Related Materials, 1977, Time Management/Organizing System, 1995; contbr. chpts. and articles to profl. publs. Vol. Office on Aging, Balt., 1982-83, Boy Scouts Am., Balt., 1984-85. Mem. NOW, NAFE, Am. Holistic Nurses Assn., Nat. Assn. Nurse Massage Therapists, Am. Massage Therapy Assn., Md. Assn. Massage Practitioners (advisor to nurse's coalition 1992), Ch. Home and Hosp. Sch. Nursing Alumni Assn. (treas. 1970-72, pres.-elect 1975-76), Johns Hopkins U. Alumnae Assn., Sigma Theta Tau. Democrat. Episcopalian. Avocations: camping, photography, pets, birding, music.

OREM, HENRY PHILIP, retired chemist, chemical engineer, consultant; b. Campbellsburg, Ky., Feb. 28, 1910; s. Mal Lee and Alice (Green) O.; m. Lydia C. Orem (dec. Feb. 1988). BS Indsl. Chemistry, U. Ky., 1932, MS, 1934; postgrad., Pa. State U., 1934-36. Grad. asst. phys. chemistry U. Ky., 1933; grad. rsch. scholar Pa. State Coll., 1934-37; with rsch. dept. Calco Chem. Co. subs. Am. Cyanamid Co., Bound Brook, N.J., 1937-39; plant rschr./process developer Am. Cyanamid Co., Bound Brook, 1939-42; asst. chief chemist Azo Dye and Intermediate divsn. Am. Cyanamid Co., Bound Brook, N.J., 1942-46; departmental chemist Azo Dye and Intermediate divsn. Am. Cyanamid Co., Bound Brook, 1947, tech. supt., 1947-50; rsch. chemist Sloss Sheffield Steel and Iron Co. (now U.S Pipe and Foundry Co. subs. Jim Walter Co.), Birmingham, Ala., 1950-52, rsch. ehcm. engr., 1952-65, group leader, 1965-75, ret., 1975; cons. Jim Walter Resources, Inc., Arichem, Inc. (now subs. Jim Walter Resources, Inc.). Contbr. articles to on black powder and ballistics to publs. Fellow Am. Inst. Chemists (profl. accredited chemist); mem. AIChE (life, 1st sec. N.J. sect. 1949-50, chmn. 1963, treas. Ala. sect. 1971, 72), Am. Chem. Soc. (emeritus life, sec.-treas. Raritan Valley group N.J. sect. 1948, chmn. 1950, sec. Ala. sect. 1956-57), NRA (life), Nat. Muzzle Loading Rifle Assn. (life, contbr. and reviewer articles Muzzle Blasts, technical advisor muzzle blasts, powder and ballistics), U.S. Revolver Assn. (life), Ala. Gun Collectors Assn. (life), Magic City Gun Club (life), Va. Gun Collectors Assn. (life), Kate Carpenter Muzzleloaders Inc., Stonewall Rifle and Pistol Club (Churchville, Va.), Shenandale Gun Club (Buffalo Gap, Va.), Homestead Shooting Club (Hot Springs, Va.), Va. Muzzle Loading Rifle Assn., Va. State Rifle and Revolver Assn., Ft. Lewis Hunting Club (life), Am. Def. Preparedness Assn., Sigma Xi. Achievements include 22 patents in field (U.S. and Can.), numerous publs. in chemistry and ballistics. Home: HCR 02 Box 259 Warm Springs VA 24484-9508

OREN, BRUCE CLIFFORD, newspaper editor, artist; b. Mineola, N.Y., Aug. 31, 1952; s. Ralph and Bernice (Lands) O.; 1 child, Adam Nathaniel; m. Angela Malone Williams, Mar. 4, 1990. Student, U. Md., College Park, 1970-74. Archtl. sculptor Universal Restoration Inc., Washington, 1974-76; tech. illustrator Tex. Instruments, Stafford, Tex., 1976-77; graphic artist Houston Chronicle, 1977-79, photo editor, 1979-86, artist, 1986—; artist L.A. Times Syndicate, 1987-91. Recipient Bronze medal Soc. Newspaper Design, 1992. Jewish. Office: 801 Texas St Houston TX 77002-2906

OREN, JOHN BIRDSELL, retired coast guard officer; b. Madison, Wis., Dec. 27, 1909; s. Arthur Baker and Lucile Grace (Comfort) O.; m. Harriet Virginia Prentis, Feb. 9, 1934; children—Virginia Joan (Mrs. Luther Warren Strickler II), John Edward. B.S., USCG Acad., 1933; M.S. in Marine Enging, MIT, 1942. Commd. ensign USCG, 1933, advanced through grades to rear adm., 1964; chief engring. div. (11th Coast Guard Dist.), 1957-59, (12th Coast Guard Dist.), 1960-61; dep. chief (Office Engring.), Washington, 1962-63; chief Office of Engring. (Office Engring.), 1964-68; now ret.; Mem. Mcht. Marine Council, 1964—; chmn. ship structures com. Transp. Dept., 1964—; exec. dir. Maritime Transp. Research Bd., Nat. Acad. Scis., 1968—; mem. nat. adv. bd. Am. Security Council. Recipient Legion of Merit. Mem. Soc. Am. Mil. Engrs. (pres. 1966, Acad. of Fellows), Am. Soc. Naval Engrs. (pres. 1965), Internat. Inst. Welding (vice chmn. Am. coun. 1964), Ret. Officers Assn. (bd. dirs. 1978), Pan Am. Inst. Naval Engring., Masons. Republican. Episcopalian. Home: 6521 Old Dominion Dr #221 Mc Lean VA 22101

ORENSTEIN, (IAN) MICHAEL, philatelic dealer, columnist; b. Bklyn., Jan. 6, 1939; s. Harry and Myra (Klein) O.; m. Linda Turer, June 28, 1964; 1 child, Paul David. BS, Clemson U., 1960; postgrad., U. Calif., Berkeley, 1960-61. Career regional mgr. Minkus Stamp & Pub. Co., Calif., 1964-70; mgr. stamp div. Superior Stamp & Coin Co., Inc., Beverly Hills, Calif., 1970-90; dir. stamp divsn. Superior Galleries, Beverly Hills, Calif., 1991-94; dir. space memorabelia Superior Stamp and Coin. Co., Inc., Beverly Hills, Calif., 1992-94; dir. stamp and space divsn. Superior Stamp & Coin an A-Mark Co., Beverly Hills, 1994—; stamp columnist L.A. Times, 1965-93, Brookman Times, 1997—, Scott Stamp Monthly, 1997—, The Brookman Times, Scott Stamp Monthly; bd. Adelphi U. N.Y. Inst. Philatelic and Numismatic Studies, 1978-81. Author: Stamp Collecting Is Fun, 1990; philatelic advisor/creator The Video Guide To Stamp Collecting, 1988; writer The Brookman Times, Scott Stamp Mo. With AUS, 1962-64. Mem. Am. Stamp Dealers Assn., C.Z. Study Group, German Philatelic Soc., Confederate Stamp Alliance, Am. Philatelic Soc. (writers unit 1975-80, 89-93), Internat. Fedn. Stamp Dealers, Internat. Soc. Appraisers: Stamps, Space Memorabilia. Republican. Avocation: fishing. Office: Superior Stamp & Coin An A-Mark Co 9478 W Olympic Blvd Beverly Hills CA 90212-4246

ORENSTEIN, WALTER A., health facility administrator; b. N.Y.C., Mar. 5, 1948; m. Diane Rauzin; children: Eleza Tema, Evan William. BS, CCNY, 1968; MD, Albert Einstein Coll. Medicine, 1972. Intern U. Calif., San Francisco, 1972-73, resident in pediat., 1973-74; EIS officer divsn. immunization Ctr. for Disease Control, Atlanta, 1974-76, med. epidemiologist divsn. immunization, 1976-77, 80-82; resident pediat. Childrens Hosp. L.A., 1977-78; fellow infectious diseases U. So. Calif. Med. Sch., 1978-80; resident preventive medicine Ctrs. Disease Control, Atlanta, 1980-82, chief surveillance and investigations sect., 1982-88, dir. divsn. immunization, 1988-93; dir. nat. immunization program Ctrs. for Disease Control and Prevention, Atlanta, 1993—; cons. smallpox eradication program WHO, Uttar Pradesh, India, 1974-75; med. adv. bd. Ctrs. Disease Control, Atlanta, 1981-84, nat. vaccine adv. com., 1988—, adv. commn. on childhood vaccines, 1989—; clin. assoc. prof. dept. cmty. health Emory U. Sch. Medicine, 1985; adj. prof. The Rollins Sch. Pub. Health, 1992—; cons. and presenter in field. Editor Pediat. Infectious Disease Jour., 1987; contbr. articles to profl. jours. Asst. surgeon gen. USPHS, 1995. Fellow Am. Acad. Pediat. (liaison mem., com. on infectious diseases 1989—, nat. vaccine adv. com.), Infectious Diseases Soc. Am., Pediat. Infectious Diseases Soc. (chmn. publs. com., mem. coun.); mem. APHA, Am. Epidemiological Soc., Soc. for Epidemiologic Rsch., Coun. the Pediat. Infectious Diseases Soc. Home: 50 Battle Ridge Dr Atlanta GA 30342-2451 Office: Nat Immunization Program Mailstop EO5 Atlanta GA 30333*

ORESKES, IRWIN, biochemistry educator; b. Chgo., June 30, 1926; s. Herman and Clara (Rubenstein) O.; m. Susan E. Nagin, June 18, 1949; children: Michael, Daniel, Naomi, Rebecca. B.S. in Chemistry, CCNY, 1949; M.A. in Phys. Chemistry, Bklyn. Coll., 1956; Ph.D. in Biochemistry, CUNY, 1969. Cert. clin. lab. dir. N.Y.C., N.Y. State. Chemist Tech. Tape Co., Bronx, N.Y., 1949; technician NYU Sch. Medicine, 1950-51; phys. chemist Kingsbrook Jewish Med. Ctr., 1951-56; research fellow Poly. Inst., N.Y., 1957-58; research assoc. Mt. Sinai Hosp., N.Y., 1959-68, dir. arthritis lab., 1961-90; rsch. asst. prof. Mt. Sinai Sch. Medicine, 1969-74, rsch. assoc. prof., 1974-91; assoc. prof. Hunter Coll. Sch. Health Scis., CUNY, 1970-74, prof., 1974—, dean, 1977-80; mem. doctoral faculty in biochemistry Grad. Center, CUNY, 1970—; vis. prof. Johns Hopkins U. Sch. Health Services, 1976-77; cons to diagnostic reagent and instrument mfrs., 1953—; mem. Internat. Sci. Council, Albert Einstein Research Inst., Buenos Aires, Argentina, 1969-79; mem. bd. examiners for clin. labs. N.Y.C. Dept. Health, 1973-75; sr. cons. Biotech. Rev. Assocs., 1983-92. Co-editor: Rheumatology for the Health Care Professional, 1991; contbr. numerous articles to profl. jours. Served with U.S. Army, 1944-46. Nat. Inst. Arthritis and Metabolic Diseases grantee, 1961-69; Arthritis Found. grantee, 1961-65, 69, 72; Lupus Found. grantee, 1975-76; CUNY Found. grantee, 1982-83. Mem. Am. Chem. Soc., Am. Coll. Rheumatology, AAAS, N.Y. Acad. Scis., Am. Assn. Immunologists, Am. Assn. Clin. Chemistry, Harvey Soc., Nat. Acad. Clin. Biochemistry, Acad. Clin. Lab. Physicians and Scientists, Clin. Immunology Soc., Sigma Xi, Phi Lambda Upsilon. Home: 670 W End Ave New York NY 10025-7313 Office: Hunter Coll Sch Health Sci 425 E 25th St New York NY 10010-2547 *I have always tried to live and work by the idea that strength is not harshness, caring is not sentimentality, and honesty is not vulnerability.*

ORESKES, NAOMI, earth sciences educator, historian; b. N.Y.C., Nov. 25, 1958; d. Irwin Oreskes and Susan Eileen Nagin Oreskes; m. Kenneth Belitz, Sept. 28, 1986; children: Hannah Oreskes Belitz, Clara Oreskes Belitz. BSc with honors, Imperial Coll., London, 1981; PhD, Stanford U., 1990. Geologist Western Mining Corp., Adelaide, Australia, 1981-84; rsch. and tng. asst. Stanford (Calif.) U., 1984-89; vis. asst. prof. Dartmouth Coll., Hanover, N.H., 1990-91, asst. prof., 1991-96; asst. prof. NYU, 1996—; consulting geologist Western Mining Corp., 1984-90; consulting historian Am. Inst. Physics, N.Y.C., 1990—. Contbr. articles to profl. jours. Recipient Lindgren prize Soc. Econ. Geologists, 1993, Young Investigator award NSF, 1994—; fellow NEH, 1993. Mem. Geol. Soc. Am., History Sci. Soc. Jewish. Home: 110 Bleecker St New York NY 10012 Office: NYU Dept Earth Scis 715 Broadway 806 B New York NY 10003

ORESKES, SUSAN, private school educator; b. N.Y.C., May 24, 1930; d. Morris and Sarah (Rudner) Nagin; m. Irwin Oreskes, June 19, 1949; children: Michael, Daniel, Naomi, Rebecca. BA, Queens Coll., 1952; dance student, Eddie Torres Sch., Manhattan, N.Y., 1984-90. Organizer Strycker's Bay Neighborhood Coun., N.Y.C., 1961-75; dir. weekly column cmty. newspaper Enlightenment Press, N.Y.C., 1975-85; assoc. tchr. Riverside Ch. Weekday Sch., N.Y.C., 1985-95. Organizer, v.p. F.D.R.-Woodrow Wilson Polit. Club, Manhattan, 1961-71; organizer Hey Brother Coffee House, 1968. Democrat. Jewish. Avocations: music, dance, travel with husband. Home: 670 W End Ave New York NY 10025-7313

ORFIELD, MYRON WILLARD, JR., state legislator, educator; b. Mpls., July 27, 1961. BA summa cum laude, U. Minn., 1983; grad., Princeton U., 1983-84; JD, U. Chgo., 1987. Bar: Minn. 1988. Law clk. Judge Gerald W. Heaney, U.S. Ct. Appeals, 8th Cir., 1987-88; rsch. assoc. Ctr. for Studies in Criminal Justice, U. Chgo., 1988-89; assoc. Faegre & Benson, 1989; asst. atty. gen. Minn. Atty. Gen.'s Office, 1989—; Bradley fellow Ctr. for Studies in Criminal Justice, U. Chgo., 1990-91; rep. Minn. Ho. of Reps. Dist. 60B, Mpls., 1991—; adj. prof. law U. Minn., 1991—, Hamline U., 1991—; dir. Met. Area Protram, Mpls.' mem. com. on improving future of U.S. cities through improved met. governance Nat. Acad. Scis., 1996—. Author: Metropolitics, 1997; contbr. articles to profl. jours. Mem. Assn. Pub. Policy Analysis and Mgmt. (bd. dirs. 1997). Office: 521 State Office Bldg Saint Paul MN 55155

ORFORD, ROBERT RAYMOND, consulting physician; b. Winnipeg, Manitoba, Can., Apr. 18, 1948; came to U.S., 1988; s. Robert Raymond and Sarah Gloria L. (Gullden) O.; m. Dale Laura Stuart, June 2, 1972; children: Carolyn Tiffany, Andrew Craig, Loren Brent. BS, McGill U., 1969, MD, 1971; MS, U. Minn., 1975; MPH, U. Wash., 1976. Assoc. prof. cmty. medicine U. Alberta, Edmonton, Can., 1978-88; dir. med. svcs. Govt. of Alberta, Edmonton, Can., 1979-81, exec. dir. occupational health svcs., 1981-85, deputy min. cmty. occupational health, 1985-88; med. dir. employee health U. Alberta Hosp., Edmonton, Can., 1988; sr. assoc. cons. Mayo Clinic, Rochester, Minn., 1988-91, cons. preventive medicine, 1991-96; cons. preventive medicine Mayo Clinic, Scottsdale, Ariz., 1996—; asst. prof. Mayo Med. Sch., Rochester, 1988—; mem. Alberta Energy Resource Conservation Bd., 1988-89. Contbr. articles to profl. jours. Mem. Olmsted County Environ. Commn., Rochester, 1991-96, chair, 1994. Govt. of Can. Nat. Health fellow, 1975-76. Fellow Royal Coll. Physicians & Surgeons Can., Am. Coll. Occupational and Environ. Medicine, Am. Coll. Preventive Medicine, Aerospace Med. Assn.; mem. North Ctrl. Occupational and Environ. Medicine Assn. (pres. 1995), Internat. Commn. Occupational Health Medicine. Presbyterian. Avocations: volleyball, skiing, travel. Home: 15516 E Acacia Way Fountain Hills AZ 85268-3158 Office: Mayo Clinic Scottsdale Divsn Preventive Medicine 13400 E Shea Blvd Scottsdale AZ 85259

ORGANSKI, ABRAMO FIMO KENNETH, political scientist, educator; b. Rome, May 17, 1923; came to U.S., 1939, naturalized, 1944; s. Menasce and Anna (Feinstein) O.; m. Katherine Davis Fox, May 29, 1947 (dec. Feb. 1973); children: Eric Fox, Elizabeth Anna; m. Patricia Joan Bard, June 14, 1986. BA, NYU, 1947, MA, 1948, PhD, 1951; student, Ginnasio Liceo Torquato Tasso, Rome, 1933-38. From asst. prof. to prof. polit. sci. Bklyn. Coll., CUNY, 1952-64; prof. polit. sci. U. Mich., Ann Arbor, 1965—, James Orin Murfin prof. polit. sci., 1985-87, sr. scientist, program dir. Ctr. Polit. Sci., Inst. Social Research, 1969—; adj. prof. polit. sci. Grad. Sch. Pub. Adminstrn. NYU, 1960; vis. assoc. prof. pub. law and govt. Columbia U., N.Y.C., 1961-62; vis. prof. Fletcher Sch. Law and Diplomacy, 1963-66, Dartmouth Coll., 1963-64, U. Pa., 1983, U. Catania, 1975, 77, U. Florence, Italy, 1990, U. Turin, Italy, 1991; sr. cons., bd. dirs. Policon Corp., 1982—, Decision Insights, 1991—; lectr., cons. to various pvt. and govlt. instns., U.S. and abroad, 1960—, European Inst., Florence, 1993; vis. scholar The Hoover Instn., Stanford U., 1991, 92, 93; vis. scholar in residence Agnelli Found., 1991. Author: World Politics, 1958, 68, (with Katherine Organski) Population and World Power, 1961, Stages of Political Development, 1965, (with Jacek Kugler) The War Ledger, 1980, (with Kugler, Y. Cohen and T. Johnson) Births, Deaths and Taxes: The Political and Demographic Transition, 1984, The 36 Billion Dollar Bargain: Strategy and Politics in U.S. Assistance to Israel, 1990; bd. editors: Affari Sociali Internazionali, Comparative Politics, International Interactions. Served with U.S. Army, 1943-45. Decorated Cavaliere della Republic Italy; recipient Disting. Faculty Achievement award U. Mich., 1983; Social Sci. Rsch. Coun. fellow, 1976, Fulbright fellow, 1977. Mem. Am. Polit. Sci. Assn. (coun. 1969, Lifetime Achievement award conflict processes sect., 1992), Internat. Polit. Sci. Assn. Avocations: skiing, tennis. Home: 460 Hillspur Rd Ann Arbor MI 48105-1049 Office: U Mich Ctr Polit Studies Inst Social Rsch Ann Arbor MI 48106-1248

ORGEBIN-CRIST, MARIE-CLAIRE, biology educator; b. Vannes, France, Mar. 20, 1936. License Natural Scis., License Biology, Sorbonne, U. Paris, 1957; D. Scis., Lyons U., France, 1961. Stagiaire dept. biochemistry faculty medicine Paris, France, 1957-58; stagiaire Centre Nat. de la Recherche Scientifique, Paris, 1958-60, attachee de recherche, 1960-62; research assoc. Population Council (Med. Div.), N.Y.C., 1962-63; research assoc. dept. ob/gyn Vanderbilt Sch. Medicine, 1963-64, research instr., 1964-66, asst. prof., 1966-70, assoc. prof., 1970-73, Lucius E. Burch prof. reproductive biology, 1973—, prof. dept. anatomy, 1975—; dir. Vanderbilt Sch. Medicine (Center Reproductive Biology Research.), 1973—; Editor-in-Chief Jour. Andrology, 1983-89. Recipient Career Devel. award NIH, 1968-73, NIH Merit award, 1986,; Fogarty Internat. sr. fellow, 1977; Disting. Scientist award Am. Soc. Reproductive Medicine, 1996. Mem. Am. Assn. Anatomists, Am. Soc. Cell Biology, Am. Soc. Andrology (v.p. 1994-95, pres. 1995-96, Disting. Svc. award 1997), Internat. Com. on Andrology, Endoccrine Soc., Soc. for Study Fertility (Eng.), Soc. for Study Reprodn., N.Y. Acad . Scis. Office: Vanderbilt U Sch Med Ctr Reproductive Biology Rsch Rm D-2303 MCN Nashville TN 37232

ORIANI, RICHARD ANTHONY, metallurgical engineering educator; b. El Salvador, July 19, 1920; came to U.S., 1929, naturalized, 1943; s. Americo and Berta (Siguenza) O.; m. Constance Amelia Gordon, June 26, 1949; children—Margaret, Steven, Julia, Amelia. B. Chem.Engring, CCNY, 1943; M.S., Stevens Inst. Tech., 1946; M.A., Princeton U., 1948, Ph.D., 1949. Lab. asst. CCNY, 1943; chemist Bakelite Corp., Bloomfield, N.J., 1943-46; instr. physics Miss Fine's Finishing Sch., Princeton, N.J., 1946-47; research asso. Gen. Electric Corp. Research Lab., Schenectady, 1949-59; asst. dir. U.S. Steel Corp. Research Lab., Monroeville, Pa., 1959-80; prof. U. Minn., Mpls., 1980-89, dir. Corrosion Rsch. Ctr., 1980-87, prof. and dir. emeritus, 1989—; cons. in field. Contbr. chpts. to books, articles to profl. jours. Founder, mem. Foxwood Civic Assn., Monroeville, 1959-80; founder, v.p. Monroeville Public Library, 1960-80. Recipient Alexander von Humboldt Sr. Scientist award, 1984, W.R. Whitney award, 1987. Fellow Am. Soc. for Metals, Am. Inst. Chemists, N.Y. Acad. Scis., Nat. Assn. Corrosion Engrs., Electrochem. Soc.; mem. AAAS, Am. Phys. Soc., Am. Inst. Metall. Engrs. Republican. Home: 4623 Humboldt Ave S Minneapolis MN 55409-2264 Office: U Minn 112 Amundson Hall 221 Church St SE Minneapolis MN 55455-0152

ORIANS, GORDON HOWELL, biology educator; b. Eau Claire, Wis., July 10, 1932; s. Howard Lester and Marion Meta (Senty) O.; m. Elizabeth Ann Newton, June 25, 1955; children: Carlyn Elizabeth, Kristin Jean, Colin Mark. BS, U. Wis., 1954; PhD, U. Calif., Berkeley, 1960. Asst. prof. zoology U. Wash., Seattle, 1960-64, assoc. prof., 1964-68, prof., 1968-95, prof. emeritus, 1995—; active Wash. State Ecol. Commn., Olympia, 1970-75, ecology adv. com. EPA, Washington, 1974-79; assembly life scis. NAS/NRC, Washington, 1977-83, environ. studies and toxicology bd., 1991—. Author: Some Adaptations of Marsh Nesting Blackbirds, 1980, Blackbirds of the Americas, 1985, Life: The Science of Biology, 1995; editor: Convergent Evolution in Warm Deserts, 1968. 1st lt. U.S. Army, 1955-56. Mem. AAAS, NAS, Am. Inst. Biol. Scis. (Disting. Svc. award 1994), Am. Ornithologists Union (Brewster award 1976), Am. Soc. Naturalists, Animal Behavior Soc., Royal Netherlands Acad. Arts and Scis., Orgn. for Tropical Studies (pres. 1988-94), Ecol. Soc. Am. (v.p. 1975-76, pres. 1995-96). Avocations: hiking, opera. Office: U Wash Dept Zoology Box 351800 Seattle WA 98195

ORIHEL, THOMAS CHARLES, parasitology educator, research scientist; b. Akron, Ohio, Feb. 10, 1929; s. Joseph Andrew and Mary Susannah (Barno) O.; m. Dorothy Lila Williams, Dec. 27, 1952; children—Timothy Stewart, Charles Theodore, Susan Ethra, Adrianne Louise. B.S., U. Akron, 1950; M.S., U. Wash., 1952; Ph.D., Tulane U., 1959. Sr. scientist Tulane Delta Primate Ctr., Covington, La., 1963-85; prof. parasitology Tulane Med. Ctr., New Orleans, 1972—; William Vincent prof. tropical diseases Tulane Med. Ctr., 1982—; dir. Tulane U. Internat. Collaboration Infectious Diseases Rsch. Program, New Orleans, 1976-89; cons. NIH, Bethesda, Md., 1973-77; mem. expert panel WHO, Geneva, 1973-83; mem. U.S.-Japan Cooperative Med. Sci. Program, Bethesda, 1974-78; external examiner U. Queensland, Australia, U. Guelph, Ont., Can., U. Claude Bernard, Lyon, France, U. Malaya, Kuala Lumpur, Malaysia; external assessor U. Malaya, Kuala Lumpur, U. Pertanian Malaysia, Selangor. Author books on subject of medical parasitology, 1976, 81, 84, 90, 94, 95, 97; contbr. articles to Am. and internat. jours. Served to 1st lt. Med. Service Corps, U.S. Army, 1953-56, Korea. Mem. Am. Soc. Tropical Medicine and Hygiene (councilor 1975-78), Royal Soc. Tropical Medicine and Hygiene, Am. Soc. Microbiology, Southwestern Assn. Parasitologists (v.p. 1972-73), Am. Soc. Parasitologists, Sigma Xi. Avocations: gardening; woodworking. Home: 115 Bertel Dr Covington LA 70433-4815 Office: Tulane Med Ctr Dept Tropical Medicine 1430 Tulane Ave New Orleans LA 70112-2699

ORING, STUART AUGUST, visual information specialist, writer, photographer; b. Bronx, N.Y., Aug. 28, 1932; s. Irving and Helen Flora (Greenhut) O.; m. Mary Carolyn Barth, Aug. 22, 1957; children: Carlene Marie Oring, Sheri Alyce Oring. AAS, Rochester Inst. Tech., 1957; BFA, R.I. Tech., 1959; MA, Am. U., 1970. Photo lab asst. Nat. Geographic, Washington, summer 1957; photography asst. I.J. Becker, Studio Assocs. and Art Green Inc., N.Y.C., 1959-61; freelance photographer pvt. practice, Washington, 1961; indsl. photographer Vitro Corp., Rockville, Md., 1962-64; health photographer Nat. Ctr. Radiol. Health, Rockville, Md., 1964-67; visual info. specialist ARS Info. div. USDA, Washington, 1967-69; audio visual specialist Nat. AV Ctr., Washington, 1969-71; photojournalist Office of Econ. Opportunity, Washington, 1971-74; visual info. specialist ASCS, U.S. Dept. Agr., Washington, 1974-94; ret., 1994; mgr., owner ISIS Visual Comms.; photography tchr. Prince George's C.C., Largo, Md., 1975—; guest lectr. U. Md. Balt. County, Towson, Corcoran Gallery of Art, Washington; program spkr. Conf. Internat. Soc. Psychopathology of Expression, 13th ann. conf. in lit. and psychology. Author, editor and pub.: (textbook/gallery text) Understanding Pictures-A Teacher's Planning Guide, 1994, Understanding Pictures-Theories, Exercises and Procedures, 1990, rev. 1992, rev. 1995; contbr. numerous articles to profl. jours.; photos published in books, mags., brochures, pamphlets. Pub. rels. Calvert County Humane Soc., 1990. Photographer with U.S. Army, 1952-55. Recipient Cert. Recognition award Eastman Kodak Co., 1973, Nat. Ctr. Radiol. Health, Rockville, Md., 1965. Mem. Soc. Photographic Edn., Am. Soc. Psychopathology of Expression, Inst. for Psychol. Study of Arts (program spkr. internat. conf.), Am. Psychology Assn. Avocations: chess, swimming, classical music, oriental philosophy, art. Home and Office: 2570 Redbud Ln Owings MD 20736-4308

ORITSKY, MIMI, artist, educator; b. Reading, Pa., Aug. 14, 1950; d. Herbert and Marcia (Sarna) O. Student, Phila. Coll. Art, 1968-70; BFA, Md. Inst. Coll. Art, 1975; MFA, U. Pa., 1979. Artist, supr. subway mural projects Crisis Intervention Network, Phila., 1978-83; instr. painting U. Arts, Phila., 1984, 89-93, Abington Art Ctr., Jenkintown, Pa., 1989—, Main Line Art Ctr., Haverford, Pa., 1993—. One-woman shows include Gross McCleaf Gallery, 1980-82, Callowhill Art Gallery, Reading, Pa., Amos Eno Gallery, N.Y.C., 1986, 89, 91, 94, 96, Hahnemann U. Gallery, Phila.,1 988, Kaufmann Gallery, Shippensburg, Pa., 1989, Kimberton (Pa.) Gallery, 1990, Rittenhouse Galleries, Phila., 1992-94; group exhbns. include Current Representational Painting in Phila., 1980, Gross McCleaf Gallery, 1980-82. Recipient Purchase award Pa. Coun. Arts/Beaver Coll., 1983, Reading Pub. Mus., 1984; fellow Artists for Environment Found., 1980, Millay Colony for Arts, 1983. Mem. Coll. Art Assn.

ORKAND, DONALD SAUL, management consultant; b. N.Y.C., Mar. 2, 1936; s. Harold and Sylvia (Wagner) O.; children: Dara Sue, Katarina Day. BS summa cum laude, NYU, 1956, MBA, 1957, PhD, 1963. Statistician, Western Electric Co., N.Y.C., 1956-58; group v.p. Ops. Rsch., Inc., Silver Spring, Md., 1960-69; pres. Ops. Rsch. Industries, Ltd., Ottawa, Ont., Can., 1968-69; pres., CEO The Orkand Corp., Tysons Corner, Va., 1970—; bd. dirs. U. Md. Found., Inc., College Park, 1993—. Contbr. articles to profl. jours. Bd. visitors coll. of bus. and mgmt. U. Md., College Park, 1985—; trustee Suburban Hosp., 1994—. 1st lt. Ordnance Corps, USAR, 1958-60. Mem. Am. Econs. Assn., Am. Statis. Assn., Ops. Rsch. Soc. Am. Republican. Jewish. Avocations: reading, theater, travel, exercise. Office: The Orkand Corp 7799 Leesburg Pike Ste 700N Falls Church VA 22043-2413

ORKAND, RICHARD KENNETH, neurobiologist, researcher, educator; b. N.Y.C., Apr. 23, 1936. BS, Columbia U., 1956; PhD, U. Utah, 1961; MA, U. Pa., 1974. Fellow U. Coll. London, 1961-64, Harvard U., Boston, 1964-66; asst. prof. U. Utah, Salt Lake City, 1966-68; prof. UCLA, 1968-74; prof., chmn. U. Pa., Phila., 1974-86; dir. Inst. Neurobiology U. P.R., San Juan, 1986-96; Benjamin Meaker prof. U. Bristol, 1993; adj. prof. biology Calif. Poly. U., San Luis Obispo, 1993—; exec. dir. Caribbean Neurosci. Found., 1987—; mem. adv. coun. Conservation Trust of P.R., 1990-94; councilor AAAS, Caribbean, 1990-95. Co-author: Introduction to Nervous Systems, 1977; contbr. over 80 articles to profl. jours. Mem. com. Dem. Party, Phila., 1981. Fellow AAAS. Achievements include research in studies of physiology of neuroglia and neuron-glia interaction. Office: U PR Inst Neurobiology 201 Calle Blvd Del Vly San Juan PR 00901-1123

ORKIN, LOUIS RICHARD, physician, educator; b. N.Y.C., Dec. 23, 1915; s. Samuel David and Rebecca (Rish) O.; m. Florence Fine, Mar. 5, 1938; 1 dau., Rita. B.A., U. Wis., 1937; M.D., N.Y. U., 1941; AAS in Marine Tech., Kingsborough Coll., 1992. Intern Bellevue Hosp., N.Y.C., 1942; resident anesthesiology Bellevue Hosp., 1946-48; practice medicine specializing in anesthesiology Bronx, N.Y., 1946—; dir. anesthesiology Backus Hosp., Norwich, Conn., 1948-50; asst. prof. anesthesiology N.Y. U. Coll. Medicine, 1950-55; prof., chmn. dept. anesthesiology Albert Einstein Coll. Medicine, 1955-82, Disting. univ. prof., 1982-86, dist. univ. prof. emeritus, 1986—; vis. prof. depts. bioengring., anesthesiology U. Calif., San Diego, 1971; Cons. VA, USPHS, USN; mem. com. anesthesiology Nat. Acad. Scis., 1964-69; mem. com. anesthetic drugs FDA, Dept. Health, Edn. and Welfare, 1970—. Author: Patient in Shock, 1965, Physiology of Obstetrical Anesthesia, 1969; Contbr. articles to profl. jours. Vice pres., trustee Wood Library Mus. Served to capt. M.C. AUS, 1942-45. Decorated Bronze Star. Fellow Am. Coll. Chest Physicians, N.Y. Acad. Sci., N.Y. Acad. Medicine, Am. Coll. Anesthesiology (past chmn. bd. govs.); mem. N.Y. State Soc. Anesthesiologists (past pres.). Home: 11 Stuyvesant Oval New York NY 10009-2001 Office: Albert Einstein Coll Medicine Dept Anesthesiology Bronx NY 10461

ORLAND, FRANK, oral microbiologist, educator; b. Little Falls, N.Y., Jan. 23, 1917; s. Michael and Rose (Dorner) O.; m. Phyllis Therese Mrazek, May 8, 1943; children: Frank R., Carl P., June Rose, Ralph M. AA, U. Chgo., 1937, SM, 1945, PhD, 1949; BS, U. Ill., 1939, DDS, 1941. Diplomate Am. Bd. Med. Microbiology. With U. Chgo., 1941—; intern Zoller Meml. Dental Clinic, U. Chgo., 1941-42; Zoller fellow, asst. in dental surgery U. Chgo., 1942-49, instr., asst. prof., assoc. prof., prof. dental sci., 1949-88, prof. emeritus, 1988—, from instr. to assoc. prof. microbiology, 1950-58, rsch. assoc. prof., 1958-64; dir. Zoller Meml. Dental Clinic, 1954-66; prof. Fishbein Ctr. for Study History Sci. and Medicine, 1980-88, prof. emeritus, 1988—; attending dentist Country Home for Convalescent Children; past cons. Nat. Inst. Dental Rsch., NIH, Bethesda, Md.; mem. panel on dental drugs The Nat. Formulary; past chmn. dental adv. bd. Med. Heritage Soc. Author: The First Fifty-Year History of the International Association for Dental Research, 1973, Microbiology in Clinical Dentistry, 1982, William John Gies-His Contributions to the Advancement of Dentistry, 1992; editor: Jour. Dental Rsch., 1958-69, (Centennial brochure) Loyola U. Sch. Dentistry, 1983; editor, contbr. Microbiology in Clinical Dentistry, 1982; writer, prodr. 50th anniversary booklet Zoller Meml. Dental Clinic U. Chgo., 1987; contbr. articles to profl. jours. Past chmn. adv. coun. Forest Park (Ill.) Bd. Edn.; mem. Forest Park Citizens Com. for Better Schs.; past pres. Garfield Sch. PTA, 1953-55; chairperson heritage com. Bicentennial Commn. on Forest Park, 1983-85; editor Chronicles of Forest Park, 1976—. Recipient Rsch. Essay award Chgo. Dental Soc., 1955, Cook County Sheriff Medal of Honor award, 1993; named Citizen of Yr., Forest Park, 1989. Fellow AAAS, Inst. Medicine Chgo. (chmn. com. publ. comm.), Am. Acad. Microbiology (William J. Gies award 1994), Am. Coll. Dentists; mem. ADA (past chmn. coun. dental therapeutics), Internat. Assn. Dental Rsch. (pres. 1971-72, past councilor Chgo. sect., past chmn. program com., past chmn. com. on history), Am. Assn. Dental Schs. (past chmn. conf. oral microbiology past chmn. com. on advanced edn.), Am. Assn. Dental Editors (William Gies Editl. award 1968), Ill. State Dental Soc. (chmn. com on history), Fedn. dentaire Internat. (Commn. on History Rsch.), Am. Acad. History Dentistry (pres. 1976-77, Hayden-Harris award 1980), Hist. Soc. Forest Park (pres.), Soc. Med. History Chgo. (past pres.), Chgo. Lit. Club, Sigma Xi. Home: 519 Jackson Blvd Forest Park IL 60130-1807 Office: 521 Jackson Blvd Forest Park IL 60130-1807

ORLANDO, ALEXANDER MARIANO, international marketing and trade consultant; b. Naples, Italy, Oct. 10, 1962; came to U.S., 1987; s. Pasquale and Maria (Adaldo Anna Feo) Orlando. BS in Electronic Data Processing, Arts and Scis. Inst., Liceo Mercalli, Naples, 1982; AA in Gen. Studies, Essex C.C., Balt., 1989; BS in Fin. cum laude, U. Balt., 1991, MBA, 1992; PhD, U. So. Calif., 1996. Cert. mgmt. cons. Export devel. mgr. various indsl. coops, Italy, 1981-87; sr. mgmt. cons., CEO, v.p. mktg. Allyn Group, Inc., 1987-95, v.p., 1995—; sales analyst Black & Decker, 1992; mgmt. cons. Kellett Venture Mgmt. Group, Boston, 1992-94; v.p. mktg. Allyn Internet Svcs., Timonium, Md., 1994—; CEO Ciao Inc. Coop. Italian Artisans Overseas, Inc., 1996—; v.p. Tradex Com, Inc., 1995; mgmt. cons. Delizie Trading, Inc., 1995; mgmt. cons First Adv. Svcs. Internat., Inc. 1996; pres. Coop. Italian Artisans Overseas, Inc., 1995—. With Italian mil., 1981-83. Tae kwon do gold medalist, 1979, 80, 81. Avocations: visiting art museums and stock markets, new classical music, symphony, coins, antiques and precious metals. Office: Allyn Group Inc 1921 York Rd Timonium MD 21093

ORLANDO, CARL, medical research and development executive; b. Palermo, Italy, Sept. 26, 1915; came to U.S., 1928; s. Peter and Maria (Bongiorno) O.; m. Ann Bovè, May 29, 1943; children: Ann Marie, Francine, Patricia, Charleen, Joan. BS, Columbia U., 1941; postgrad., Rochester U., 1943. Chief photo optics U.S. Army Elec. Commd., Ft. Monmouth, N.J., 1945-75; cons. pvt. practice, New Shrewsbury, N.J., 1975-79; v.p. rsch. & devel. Analytical R&D Inc., Eatontown, N.J., 1979-88; cons. rsch. & devel. Engring. Devel. Co., Tinton Falls, N.J., 1986-88; pres., rsch. & devel. dir. Sens-O-Tech Indsutries Inc., Eatontown, N.J., 1988—; chmn. bd. dirs. Sens-O-Tech Industries, 1988-92. Contbr. articles to profl. jours. Bd. dirs. Monmouth Regional High Sch., Tinton Falls, 1974; com. mem. Tinton Falls Environ. Unit, 1984; chmn. Entertainment Activities St. Dorothaas Ch., Eatontown, 1983. With USN, 1945. Recipient Monetary Suggestion award Signal Corp. Engring. Lab., 1948. Mem. Soc. Photographic Scientist & Engrs. (sr. mem.), Soc. Imaging Sci. & Tech., N.Y. Acad. Scis., Elks, Battle Ground Country Club. Republican. Roman Catholic. Achievements include over 20 patents in various fields including non-invasive heart and breathing alarm monitors, moving target indicator, photographic reproduction in 0.2 second, one step photographic technic, image stabilization system, perk-type automatic drip coffee maker, military tactical image interpretation facility, production and reconstruction of holograms, device for intensifying photoelectrostatic images, bandwidth compression of photographic images, Natinol photographic high speed shutter. Home and Office: 47 Willow Rd Eatontown NJ 07724

ORLANDO, GEORGE (JOSEPH), union executive; b. N.Y.C., Nov. 27, 1944; s. Joseph and Anita O.; m. Joan Perrotta, Nov. 5, 1967; children: Gregory, Valerie, Dana, Christopher, Lauren. B.A. in Polit. Sci., St. John's U., Bklyn., 1966. Adminstrv. asst. Distillery, Wine and Allied Workers Internat., Englewood, N.J., 1966-67; internat. v.p. Distillery, Wine and Allied Workers Internat., 1968-74, gen. sec.-treas., 1974-85, gen. pres., 1985-95; trustee Distillery, Wine and Allied Workers Internat. Social Security fund, 1974, chmn. bd. trustees, 1985; trustee pension fund; mem. exec. bd. dept. food and allied svc. trades AFL-CIO, 1975; pres. Wine, Liquor & Distillery Workers Union Local 1D, 1985—; internat. v.p. United Food & Comml. Workers Internat. Union (dir. Distillery, Wine & Allied Workers Divsn. 1995—). Office: Distillery Wine & Allied Workers Divsn UFCW 66 Grand Ave PO Box 567 Englewood NJ 07631

ORLANDO, JOSEPH MICHAEL, sales executive; b. Paterson, N.J., Mar. 31, 1945; s. Costabile Enrico and Giovanna Mafalda (La Pastina) O.; m. Denise Lynn Veneziano, Oct. 29, 1978. Grad. high sch., Paterson, 1963. Lic. travel agt. Salesman Keystone Automotive, Kennilworth, N.J.; owner Jodeno Inc., Paterson. Gives polit. anlaysis and opinion on N.J. Radio, WCTC-AM; contbr. polit. columns to newspapers. Pres. Clark (N.J.) Rep. Club, 1988-91; active Am. Conservative Union, Washington, Heritage Found., Washington; former mem. planning bd., mem. bd. adjustment, Clark, N.J. Republican. Avocations: reading non-fiction, writing, gourmet cooking. Home: 1168 Lake Ave Clark NJ 07066-2745

ORLEN, JOEL, professional society administrator; b. Holyoke, Mass., Aug. 1, 1924; s. Barnet and Fannie (Fuchs) O.; m. Yana Sorra Edmundson, Nov. 24, 1963; 1 stepson, Charles. BA, U. Chgo., 1950, MA, 1952. Fgn. svc. officer U.S. Dept. State, Washington, 1952-56; fgn. affairs officer AEC, Washington, 1956-58; officer NAS, Washington, 1958-63; asst. dir. Desert Rsch. Inst., Reno, 1963-65; exec. officer, provost MIT, Cambridge, 1965-80; v.p. Sci. Mus. Minn., St. Paul, 1980-86; exec. officer Am. Acad. Arts and Scis., Cambridge, 1986-96; dir. Mounds Park Acad., St. Paul, 1983-86; cons. MIT, 1980-82; exec. sec. Mass. Tech. Devel. Corp., Boston, 1978-80; advisor U.S. del. to UN, N.Y.C. and Geneva, 1952-63. Contbr. chpts. to several books. Staff sgt. U.S. Army, 1943-46, ETO. Home: 931 Mass Ave Cambridge MA 02139-3173

ORLIK, PETER BLYTHE, media educator, author, musician; b. Hancock, Mich., Sept. 30, 1944; s. Harry Victor and Ruth Estelle (Blythe) O.; m. Christina Grace Bear, Aug. 18, 1967; children: Darcy Anne, Blaine Truen. BA with distinction, Wayne State U., 1965, MA, 1966, PhD, 1968. Copywriter Robin Prodns., Huntington Woods, Mich., 1962-63; announcer Sta. WQRS-FM, Detroit, 1963; copywriter Campbell-Ewald Advt., Detroit, 1965; asst. music dir. Sta. WDET-FM, Detroit, 1965-66; instr. Wayne State U., Detroit, 1966-69; from asst. prof. to assoc. prof. to prof. Cen. Mich. U., Mt. Pleasant, Mich., 1969—; univ. Merit prof. Cen. Mich. U., Mt. Pleasant, 1988, 92, 96, also founder, head dept. Broadcast and Cinematic Arts, 1969-79, chmn. dept., 1996—; freelance copywriter Mt. Pleasant, 1979—; prof. clarinetist various Mich. ensembles, Detroit, Saginaw, 1965—; asst. dir. creative svcs. Sta. WXYZ-TV, Detroit, 1982; coord. prior learning assessment external degree program Ctrl. Mich. U., 1978-85; cons. various univs.,

1980—; judge Thomas Jefferson Broadcast Awards, Dept. Def., 1994. Author: Broadcast/Cable Copywriting, 1978, 5th edit., 1994, Mass Media Description and Performance, 1979, Critiquing Radio and Television Content, 1988, The Electronic Media: An Introduction to the Profession, 1992, 2d edit., 1997, Electronic Media Criticism, 1994; mem. editl. bd. Media Mgmt. Rev.; contbr. articles to profl. jours. Lectr., liturgical clarinet soloist, eucharistic minister Sacred Heart Parish, Mt. Pleasant, 1969—, mem. religious edn. bd., 1978-84; adjudicator various H.S. speech and drama competitions, Mich., 1971-80; vice chmn. Zoning Bd. Appeals, Mt. Pleasant, 1974-78, 89-91, chmn., 1978-82, 91-97; mem. faculty adv. com. Mus. Broadcast Comms.; mem. Mt. Pleasant Planning Commn., 1997—. Named one of Outstanding Young Men Am. Nat. Jaycees, 1979; Nat. Assn. TV Program Execs. Faculty fellow, 1982. Mem. Broadcast Edn. Assn. (chmn. courses and curricula divsn. 1974-76, 80-82, bd. dirs. 1989-93, chmn. faculty internship com. 1990-91, chmn. nat. scholarship com. 1991—), Assn. for Edn. in Journalism and Mass Comms., Nat. Assn. TV Program Execs., Alpha Epsilon Rho (nat. v.p. profl. alumni rels. 1976-77, legis. coord. 1979-82), Phi Kappa Phi. Avocations: ice hockey, history, memorabilia. Home: 613 Kane St Mount Pleasant MI 48858-1949 Office: Cen Mich U 343 Moore Hall Mount Pleasant MI 48859

ORLIN, JAMES BERGER, mathematician, management scientist, educator; b. Buffalo, Apr. 19, 1953; s. Albert Norman and Roslyn Louise (Berger) O.; m. Donna Lynn Hogan, Jan. 3, 1982; children: Jennifer Robin, Benjamin Aaron, Caroline Anne. BA, U. Pa., 1974; MS, Caltech, 1976; MMath, U. Waterloo, Ont., Can., 1976; PhD, Stanford U., 1981. Asst. prof. MIT, Cambridge, Mass., 1979-83, assoc. prof., 1983-87, prof., 1987—; vis. prof. Erasmus U., Rotterdam, The Netherlands, 1984-85; vis. sci. Collaborative Rsch. Inc., Waltham, Mass., 1992-93, Whitehead Inst., 1993-96. Coauthor: Network Flows: Theory, Algorithms and Applications, 1993; assoc. editor Networks, 1992—; contbr. over 60 articles to profl. jours. Fulbright Rsch. grantee, 1984-85, UPS fellow, 1991-94, 95-96; recipient Presdl. Young Investigator award NSF, 1985-90. Mem. Informs (co-recipient Lanchester prize 1993), Assn. Computing Machinery, Math. Programming Soc., Soc. Indsl. and Applied Math. Home: 10 Taft Dr Winchester MA 01890-3748 Office: MIT E53-357 77 Massachusetts Ave # E53-357 Cambridge MA 02139-4301

ORLOFF, CHET, cultural organization administrator; b. Bellingham, Wash., Feb. 22, 1949; s. Monford A. and Janice (Diamond) O.; m. Wendy Lynn Lee, Sept. 20, 1970; children: Callman Labe, Hannah Katya, Michele Alison. BA, Boston U., 1971; MA, U. Oreg., 1978; postgrad., Portland State U. Tchr. Peace Corps, Afghanistan, 1972-75; asst. dir. Oreg. Hist. Soc., Portland, 1975-86, dir., 1991—; dir. Ninth Cir. Hist. Soc., Pasadena, Calif., 1987-91. Editor: Western Legal History, 1987-91, Law for the Elephant, 1992; sr. editor: Oreg. Hist. Quar.; contbr. articles to profl. jours. Commr. Met. Arts Commn., Portland, 1981-84, Portland Planning Commn., 1989-92; pres. Nat. Lewis and Clark Bicentennial Coun., 1996—. Mem. Phi Alpha Theta. Avocations: reading, tennis. Office: Oregon Historical Society 1200 SW Park Ave Portland OR 97205-2441

ORLOFF, NEIL, lawyer; b. Chgo., May 9, 1943; s. Benjamin R. and Annette (Grabow) O.; m. Jan Krigbaum, Oct. 9, 1971 (div. 1979); m. Gudrun Mirin, Oct. 2, 1992. BS, MIT, 1964; MBA, Harvard U., 1966; JD, Columbia U., 1969. Bar: D.C. 1969, N.Y. 1975, Calif. 1989, Utah 1993. Ops. officer World Bank, Washington, 1969-71; dir. regional liaison staff EPA, Washington, 1971-73; legal counsel Pres.'s Council on Environ. Quality, Washington, 1973-75; prof. dept. environ. engring. Cornell U., Ithaca, N.Y., 1975-88, sch. law UCLA, 1992; dir. Ctr. for Environ. Research, 1984-87, Am. Ecology Corp., 1986-88; of counsel Morgan, Lewis & Bockius, N.Y.C., 1986-87; ptnr. Irell & Manella, Los Angeles, 1986-92, Parsons, Behle & Latimer, Salt Lake City, 1992—; vice chmn. bd. dirs. S.W. Research and Info. Ctr., Albuquerque, 1975-84; vice chmn. air quality commn. ABA, Chgo., 1983-92, co-chmn. intensive course in environ. law ABA, 1994—, co-chmn. roundtable sr. environ. lawyers ABA, 1996—. Author: The Environmental Impact Statement Process, 1978, The National Environmental Policy Act, 1980, Air Pollution-Cases and Materials, 1980, Community Right-to-Know Handbook, 1988; mem. editorial bd. Natural Resources and Environment, 1984-87. Adviser Internat. Joint Com. Can., 1979-81; governing bd. N.Y. Sea Grant Inst., 1984-87; vice chmn. City of Ithaca Environ. Commn., 1976-77; adviser N.Y. Dept. Environ. Conservation, 1984-87.

ORLOVSKY, DONALD ALBERT, lawyer; b. East Orange, N.J., May 15, 1951; s. Manuel Martin and Eleanor Marie (Karr) O.; m. Nancy Ann Richmond, Nov. 21, 1987; children: Kyle Lee, Donald Albert Jr. AB, Cornell U., 1973; JD, Rutgers U., 1976. Bar: Fla. 1976, U.S. Ct. Appeals (5th cir.) 1976, N.J. 1977, U.S. Dist. Ct. (so. dist.) Fla. 1977, U.S. Dist. Ct. N.J. 1977, U.S. Supreme Ct. 1980, U.S. Ct. Appeals (11th cir.) 1981. Assoc. Smathers & Thompson, Miami, 1976-77; ptnr. McCune, Hiaasen, Crum, Ferris & Gardner, P.A., Ft. Lauderdale, Fla., 1978-86, Kamen & Orlovsky PA, West Palm Beach, 1988—; bd. dirs. Comprehensive Alcoholism Treatment Program, Inc., 1992—; supervising monitor and counselor, Fla. Lawyers Assistance, Inc., 1991—. Author: Nova U. Law Review, 1977, U. Miami Law Review, 1978. Alumni bd. St. Andrew's Sch., Boca Raton, Fla., 1996—. Recipient All-Am. recognition in springboard diving, 1966-69; inducted Hall of Fame Newark Acad., Livingston, N.J., 1997. Mem. ABA, Fla. Bar (civil procedure rules com. 1981), Acad. Fla. Trial Lawyers, Assn. Trial Lawyers Am. Episcopalian. Office: 1601 Belvedere Rd Ste 402 S West Palm Beach FL 33406-1542

ORLOWSKA-WARREN, LENORE ALEXANDRIA, art educator; b. Detroit, May 22, 1951; d. William Leonard and Aloisa Clara (Hrapkiewicz) Orlowski; m. Donald Edward Warren, May 11, 1990. AA, Henry Ford C.C., 1972; BS in Art Edn., Wayne State U., 1974, M Spl. Edn., 1978. Tchr. arts and crafts Detroit Pub. Schs., 1974—; cons. Arts Detroit Cmty. Plan, TRIACO Arts & Crafts, 1996—. Contbr. to Sch. Arts Mag. Mem. exec. bd. Springwells Pk. Assn., 1989—, pres., 1994-96; mem. Dearborn cmty. art coun. Art on the Ave., 1993—; chair Nat. Woman's History Month workshop, 1995; mem. LWV, Cranbrook Acad. Art, Art Inst. Chgo. Mem. Nat. Art Edn. Assn. (electronic gallery coord. 1992—), Mich. Art Edn. Assn. (presenter art advocacy workshop), Am. Craft Coun., Detroit Artist Market, Detroit Inst. Arts-Founders Soc., Dearborn Cmty. Arts Coun. Avocations: fiber art, travel, colonial gardening, reading colonial history and biographies. Home: 10 Berwick Ln Dearborn MI 48120-1102

ORLOWSKI, KAREL ANN, elementary education educator; b. Fremont, Ohio, Dec. 22, 1949; d. Karl and Angeline Marie (Oudersluys) Kooistra; m. Paul Joseph Orlowski, Apr. 28, 1973; 1 child, Jennifer Frann. BA in Music Edn., U. Mich., 1971; MS in Elem. Edn., Dowling Coll., Oakdale, N.Y., 1978. Cert. tchr., N.Y. Tchr. vocal music Patchogue (N.Y.)-Medford Schs., 1971—, lead tchr. music dept., 1986-88, 91-94; dir. of musicals Eagle Elem. Sch., 1990-94; dir. drama dept. River Elem. Sch., Patchogue, 1974-90, Chosen Few show choir South Ocean Mid. Sch., Patchogue, 1984-90, Notation! show choir Eagle Elem. Sch., 1990-94, 95—, A Chords show choir Barton Elem. Sch., 1994-95. Mem. N.Y. State Sch. Music Assn., Suffolk County Music Educators Assn. (co-chmn. so. divsn. I chorus 1993-95, divsn. II S.W. chorus 1996-97; asst. v.p. divsn. I festivals 1997—). Republican. Episcopalian. Avocations: gardening, Renaissance music, vocal jazz, NASCAR figure-eight racing. Home: 37 Detmer Rd East Setauket NY 11733-1912 Office: Patchogue-Medford Schs 241 S Ocean Ave Patchogue NY 11772-3732

ORLOWSKY, MARTIN L., executive manager; b. N.Y.C., Dec. 7, 1941; s. Solomon and Sylvia (Levine) O.; m. Carolyn Louise Brady, Mar. 25, 1973; children—Daniel, Keith, Matthew. B.A., Long Island U., N.Y.C., 1963. Media planner Compton Advertising, N.Y.C., 1968-69; media planner Young & Rubicam Inc., N.Y.C., 1969-71; v.p. media Grey Advertising, N.Y.C., 1971-76; sr. v.p., media and mktg. services Needham, Harper & Steers, N.Y.C., 1976-77; media dir. R.J. Reynolds Tobacco Co., Winston-Salem, N.C., 1977-80, dir. mktg. services, 1980-82, v.p. brand mktg., 1982-84, sr. v.p. mktg., 1984-85, exec. v.p., 1986; pres. Grocery div. Nabisco Brands, U.S.A., Parsippany, N.J., 1986—, Planters and Life Savers div. Nabisco Brands, U.S.A., Parsippany, N.J., 1987—, DKM Holdings, 1988-90; sr. v.p. mktg. Lorillard Tobacco Co., N.Y.C., 1990-92, exec. v.p. mktg. and sales, 1992-95, pres., 1995—. Vol., Peace Corps, Bolivia, 1963-65. Served to sgt. U.S. Army, 1966-68. Avocations: fishing; tennis. Home: 15 Manette Rd Morristown NJ 07960-6345

ORMAN, LEONARD ARNOLD, lawyer; b. Balt., June 15, 1930; s. Samuel and Bertie (Adler) O.; m. Barbara Gold, June 9, 1978; children: Richard Harold, Robert Barton. AB summa cum laude, U. Md., 1952, JD, 1955. Bar: Md. 1955, U.S. Ct. Appeals (4th cir.) 1956, U.S. Dist. Ct. Md. 1955, Ct. Appeals Md. 1955, U.S. Supreme Ct. 1977, U.S. Ct. Claims 1990, D.C. Ct. Appeals 1987; cert. civil trial advocate by Nat. Bd. Trial Advocacy. Law clk. Hon. Frederick W. Brune, Chief Judge Md. Ct. of Appeals, 1955-56; mem. dept. legis. reference Md. Legislature, 1957-58; mem. Gov.'s Commn. to Revise Criminal Code, 1958-59; pvt. practice law Balt., 1956—; lectr. trial tactics. Mem. editorial bd.: Md. Law Rev, 1953-55; Contbr. articles to profl. jours. Pres. Young Dems. 2d Dist., Balt., 1960-63. With AUS, 1948-49; lt. col. USAF Res. ret. Rosco Pound Found. fellow, trustee. Mem. Md. State Bar Assn. (various coms.), Balt. City Bar Assn. (various coms.), Nat. Coll. Trial Advocacy (trustee), Assn. Trial Lawyers Am. (numerous coms./offices, including nat. committeeman 1976-80, bd. govs. 1985—, exec. com. 1988-90, chmn. orgn. rev. com., home office and budget com., orgn. and home office com., election com., key man com., past mem. steering com., past mem. publ. com., past mem. ednl. adv. group 1989-90, co-chair Hall of Fame com., Stalwarts com., past vice-chair ABA-ATLA liaison com., M Club, co-chair conv. site planning com., co-chairpolit. insight com., long-range planning com., auth-hwy. adv. com., toy safety conf., med. malpractice adv. com., product liability adv. com., co-chair home office capital improvements adv. com., co-chmn. conv. planning com. Washington, Wysocki award), Md. Trial Lawyers Assn. (bd. govs., pres. 1984-85), Order of Coif, Masons. Home: 2 Celadon Rd Owings Mills MD 21117-3010 Office: 5 Light St Rear 1100 Baltimore MD 21202-1209

ORME, ANTONY RONALD, geography educator; b. Weston-Super-Mare, Somerset, Eng., May 28, 1936; came to U.S., 1968; s. Ronald Albert and Anne (Parry) O.; m. Amalie Jo Brown, Nov. 18, 1984; children: Mark Antony, Kevin Ronald, Devon Anne. B.A. with 1st class honors, U. Birmingham, 1957, Ph.D., 1961. Lectr. Univ. Coll., Dublin, Ireland, 1960-68; mem. faculty UCLA, 1968—, prof. geography, 1973—, dean social scis., 1977-83; cons. geomorphology various orgns., throughout U.S., 1968—. Editor-in-chief Phys. Geography; mem. editorial bd. Catena, Springer-Verlag, Berlin, U. Calif. Press. Recipient Award of Merit Am. Inst. Planners, 1975; recipient Outstanding Service award USAF, 1977-80. Mem. Geol. Soc. Am., Assn. Am. Geographers, Assn. Geography Tchrs. Ireland (pres. 1964-68), Inst. Brit. Geographers, Internat. Geog. Union. Home: 5128 Del Moreno Dr Woodland Hills CA 91364-2426 Office: UCLA Dept Geography Los Angeles CA 90095-1524

ORME, MELISSA EMILY, mechanical engineering educator; b. Glendale, Calif., Mar. 12, 1961; d. Myrl Eugene and Geraldine Irene (Schmuck) O.; m. Vasilis Zissis Marmarelis, Mar. 12, 1989; children: Zissis Eugene and Myrl Galinos (twins). BS, U. So. Calif., L.A., 1984, MS, 1985, PhD, 1989. Rsch. asst. prof. U. So. Calif., 1990-93; asst. prof. U. Calif., Irvine, 1993-96, assoc. prof., 1996—; panel reviewer NSF, Arlington, Va., 1993—; cons. MPM Corp., Boston, 1993—. Contbr. articles to profl. jours. Recipient Young Investigator award NSF, 1994, Arch T. Colwell Merit award SAE, 1994. Mem. AAUW, AIAA, ASME, Am. Phys. Soc., Minerals, Metals and Materials Soc. Achievements include 4 U.S. patents. Office: U Calif Dept Mech Engring Irvine CA 92697-3975

ORME-JOHNSON, WILLIAM HENRY, III, chemist, educator; b. Phoenix, Apr. 23, 1938; s. William Henry and Jean Mary (McGhee) O.; m. Nanette Roberts, May 27, 1957 (div. 1982); m. Carol Chamberlain, Aug. 23, 1983; children: Doris Helen, Ruth David, McGhee Charles, Heather. Student, Rice U., 1955-57; BS, U. Tex., 1959, PhD, 1964. Postdoctoral fellow U. Wis., Enzyme Inst., Madison, 1965-67, asst. prof., 1967-70; asst. prof. U. Wis., Dept. Biochemistry, Madison, 1970-71, assoc. prof., 1971-73, 1973-79, prof., 1973-79; prof. MIT, Dept. Chemistry, Cambridge, Mass., 1979—; sci. cons. various chem. and biotechs. Contbr. over 150 articles to sci. jours. V.p. The Lyric Stage, Boston, 1990-92. Grantee NIH, 1967—. Fellow AAAS; mem. Am. Chem. Soc., Am. Soc. Biol. Chemists. Unitarian. Avocations: guitar, cello, choral singing, acting, sailing. Home: 48 Massachusetts Ave Cambridge MA 02139-4312 Office: MIT 77 Massachusetts Ave Cambridge MA 02139-4301

ORMES, JONATHAN FAIRFIELD, astrophysicist, science administrator, researcher; b. Colorado Springs, Colo., July 18, 1939; s. Robert Manly and Suzanne (Viertel) O.; m. Karen Lee Minnick, Dec. 26, 1960 (div.); 1 child, Laurie Kylee; m. Janet Carolyn Dahl, Sept. 12, 1964; children: Marina, Nicholas. BS, Stanford U., 1961; PhD, U. Minn., 1967. NRC assoc. Goddard Space Flight Ctr., NASA, Greenbelt, Md., 1967-69, astrophysicist, 1969, head cosmic radiations br., 1981-82, head nuclear astrophysics br., 1983-87, assoc. chief lab. for high energy astrophysics, 1987-90, chief lab. for high energy astrophysics, 1990—; acting head high energy physics NASA hdqrs., Washington, 1982-83, mem. high energy astrophysics mgmt. ops. working group, 1975-83, mem. cosmic ray program working group, 1984-91; mem. com. on space and solar physics, com. on cosmic ray physics Nat. Acad. Sci., Washington, 1991-94. Editor: Essays in Space Science, 1987; assoc. editor astrophysics Phys. Rev. Letters, 1991-93; contbr. Astrophysics Jour., Phys. Rev. Letters, Astronomy and Astrophysics. Trustee Paint Br. Unitarian Universalist Ch., Adelphi, Md., 1987-88, chair bd. trustees, 1989, numerous positions, 1972-91. Fellow Am. Phys. Soc. (various div. offices); mem. Internat. Astron. Union, Am. Astron. Soc. (sec.-treas. High Energy Astrophysics div. 1985-87), Am. Geophys. Union. Achievements include discovery of unusual isotopic abundance of Ne in galactic cosmic rays; research on high energy spectra of cosmic rays, on anti-protons in galactic cosmic rays. Office: NASA Code 660 Goddard Space Flight Ctr Greenbelt MD 20771

ORMISTON, PATRICIA JANE, elementary education educator; b. Flint, Mich., Aug. 22, 1938; d. Elmer A. and Katheryn Lucille (Day) Knudson; m. Lester Murray Ormiston, June 13, 1964; 1 child, Brian Todd. BS, Minot State U., 1962; postgrad., U. Mont., 1963—, Mont. State U., 1963—, Western Mont. Coll., 1987. Elem. tchr. Lowell Sch., Gt. Falls, Mont., 1958, Webster Sch., Williston, N.D., 1958-59, Plaza (N.D.) Pub. Sch., 1959-61, Cen. Sch., Helena, Mont., 1962-63, Elrod Sch., Sch. Dist. 5, Kalispell, Mont., 1963—; core team Onward to Excellence, Sch. Dist. 5, Kalispell, 1989-92; participant Rocky Mountain Nat. Outcome-Based Edn. Conf., Greeley, Colo., 1990; presenter Kendall Hunt Lit. Reading Unit, Phi Delta Kappa, Kalispell, 1991, Mont. Assn. Gifted Talented Edn., 1991, Word Conf., Seattle, 1993; inst. presenter, symposium spkr. Utah Coun. Internat. Reading Assn. 28th Ann. State Reading Conf., Salt Lake City, 1994; univ. supr. student tchrs. Mont. State U., Bozeman, 1994—; mem. adv. bd. Kendall Hunt Pub. Co., Dubuque, Iowa, 1991—; symposium spkr., mem. reading coun., coun. tchrs. English S.D. State Conf., Mitchell, 1994; symposium spkr. Five Valleys Reading Conf. U. Mont., Missoula, 1994; insvc. presenter South Whidbey Intermediate Sch., Langley, Wash., 1994. Contbr. author lit. based reading units 2d grade level Kentall Hunt Pub. Co., Dubuque, Iowa, 1989—; author: PEGASUS Integrating Themes in Literature and Language Correlated to Gages Lake, Illinois State Goals for Learning Language Arts, Grades K-6, 1993, PEGASUS Integrating Themes in Literature and Language Correlated to State of Georgia Quality Core Curriculum for English and Language Arts, Grades K-6, 1994, PEGASUS Integrating Themes in Literature and Language Correlated to State of Indiana Essential Skills English/Language Arts, Grades K-6, 1994, PEGASUS Integrating Themes in Literature and Language Correlated to Dade County Public Schools Competency-Based Curriculum for Language Arts, Grades K-5, 1994. Vol. Conrad Mansion Restoration, Kalispell, 1976—; presenter 34th ann. conv. Lit. Base Reading Internat. Reading Assn., New Orleans, 1989. Named Tchr. of Yr., Kalispell Sch. Dist. 5, 1986; Chpt. 2 grantee, 1987-88; Gertrude Whipple Prof. Devel. grantee IRA, 1988. Mem. NEA, Internat. Reading Assn. (symposium speaker 38th ann. conv. San Antonio 1993), Nat. Coun. Tchrs. English, Kalispell Edn. Assn. (bldg. rep. 1987-88, chmn. profl. acknowledgement com. 1988-93), Nat. Hist. Preservation, Phi Delta Kappa, Delta Kappa Gamma. Avocations: reading, writing, hiking, skiing, golf. Home: PO Box 64 Kalispell MT 59903-0064 Office: Elrod Sch 3rd Ave W Kalispell MT 59901-4426

ORMSBY, ERIC LINN, educator, researcher, writer; b. Atlanta, Oct. 16, 1941; s. Robert and Virginia (Haire) O.; m. Dorothy Louise Hoffmann, July 22, 1967; children: Daniel Paul, Charles Martin. BA summa cum laude, U. Pa., 1971; MA, Princeton U., 1973, PhD, 1981; MLS, Rutgers U., 1978. Near East bibliographer libr. Princeton U., N.J., 1975-77; Near East curator libr. Princeton U., 1977-83; libr. dir. Cath. U. Am., Washington, 1983-86; libr. dir. McGill U., Montreal, Can., 1986-96, assoc. prof. Inst. Islamic Studies, 1986-96, prof., 1996—; cons. NYU, 1981-82; mem. libr. com. Mid. East Inst., Washington, 1985-87, Al Akhawayn U., Morocco, 1994-95, Saudi Arabian Monetary Agy., Riyadh, 1995-96; chmn. continuing edn. com. Washington Consortium, 1983-86; mem. bd. Ctr. Rsch. Librs., 1989-95. Author: Theodicy in Islamic Thought, 1984 (Choice Mag. award 1984), Bavarian Shrine and Other Poems, 1990 (QSPELL award for poetry 1991), (poems) Coastlines, 1992, For a Modest God: New and Selected Poems, 1997, (with others) Handlist of Arabic Manuscripts, 1986, For a Modest God: New and Selected Poems, 1997; editor: Moses Maimonides and His Time, 1989; contbr. articles and book revs. to profl. jours., poetry to various mags., including New Republic, New Yorker, Grand St., Shenandoah, So. Rev. and Chelsea. Instr. Princeton Adult Sch., 1978-80. DAAD fellow German Acad. Exch., 1973-74; recipient Ingram Merrill award, 1993. Mem. Middle East Librs. Assn. (v.p. 1981-82, pres. 1982-83), Hoelderlin Gesellschaft, Can. Assn. Rsch. Librs. (v.p. 1988-89), Can. Libr. Assn., Assn. pour l'Avancement des Scis. et des Techniques de la Documentation, Conseil des recteurs et des principaux des univs. du Québec, Sous-Comité des Bibliotheques (pres. 1989-91). Roman Catholic. Avocations: natural history, writing, cooking, photography. Office: McGill U Inst Islamic Studies, 3458 McTavish St, Montreal, PQ Canada H3A 1Y1

ORNAUER, RICHARD LEWIS, retired educational association administrator; b. Bklyn., Oct. 19, 1922; s. Edwin L. and Emma (Handler) O.; m. Jane Robb, May 15, 1955 (div. Jan. 7, 1976); children: David S., Michael J., SaraJo; m. J. Rexene Ashford, Nov. 24, 1985. BJ, U. Mo., 1947. Wire editor Coastal Georgian, Brunswick, Ga., 1947-48; reporter copyreader, night editor, city editor Nassau Daily Rev.-Star, Rockville Centre, N.Y., 1948-53; city editor L.I. Press, Jamaica, N.Y., 1953-71; asst. commr. Nassau County Dept. Social Services, Mineola, 1971-74; pub. health info. program officer Nassau County Dept. Health, Mineola, 1974-87; adminstr. Bur. Epidemiology, 1979-84; dir. communications N.Y. State Sch. Bds. Assn., Albany, 1987-89; instr. Queens Coll., Flushing, N.Y., 1955-59; instr., mentor 55/Alive mature driving program AARP, Dover, Del., 1994—; asst. state coord. Kent County, Del., 1996—; mem. exec. bd. Hofstra U. Sch. Bd. Forum, 1969-87; chmn. Merrick Planning Com., 1959-61; mem. publs. com. N.Y. State Sch. Bds. Assn., 1961-64, cons. to com., 1980-81, mem. BOCES com., 1971-74; vice chmn. State Sch. Bd. Leaders Com., 1975-79, cons. to com., 1980, bd. dirs., 1979-87, v.p., 1981, 84, 85, 86, 87, mem. exec. com., 1981-87, cons. to disting. service com., 1984, 85; cons. cities com., 1986, cons. grants com., 1987; del. L.I. Ednl. Conf. Bd., 1967-86; trustee Merrick Bd. Edn., 1962-87, pres., 1966-71; trustee Bd. Coop. Ednl. Services Nassau County, 1967-87, v.p., 1967-71, pres., 1971-87; mem. exec. com. Nassau-Suffolk Sch. Bds. Assn., 1962-87, v.p., 1974-77, pres., 1977-79; mem. exec. com. Merrick Citizens Com. for Pub. Schs., 1959-87; mem. fed. relations network 4th Congl. dist. Nat. Sch. Bds. Assn., 1973-87, study com. on career edn., 1976-78, sub-chmn. for N.E. region presdl. task force on edn. of handicapped children, 1977-78, presdl. task force on critical viewing of TV by children, 1979-80; del. Northeast Region, Nat. Sch. Bds. Assn., 1980-87, vice chmn., 1985-87, chmn., 1987; adv. com. N.Y. State Senate Standing Com. on Civil Service and Pensions, 1978-79; mem. Instructional Service Television Com. WLIW-TV/Channel 21, pres., 1973-82; mem. Com. for Better Schs. of Merrick, 1975-87, Hist. Soc. Merricks, 1976-88; bd. dirs. L.I. Coalition Fair Broadcasting, 1979-82; mem. commr.'s adv. council N.Y. State Edn. Dept., 1980-87; mem. City of Dover Pub. Safety Issues Implementation Studies Commn., 1993—; comms. officer Dover AFB Mus., 1995-96. Mem. citizens addv. com. Dover Met. Planning Orgn., 1993—, chmn. 1995—; del. Planned Parenthood, United Way; ptnr. Spl. Olympics, Medic Alert Internat.; active Sta. WHYY, Wilmington-Phila., Del. Hospice, Nat. Wildflower Rsch. Ctr., Am. Farmland Trust, Southern Poverty Law Ctr.; Kent County rep. to the prioritization sys. steering com. Del. Dept. Transp.; founding mem. FDR Meml. With AUS, 1942-45, PTO. Recipient citations N.Y. State Police Conf., 1949, citations Rockville Centre Police Benevolent Assn., 1953, citations Nassau Div. Am. Cancer Soc., 1961, citations Nassau Am. Legion, 1963, citations Nassau Library System, 1964, citations Firemen's Assn. of Nassau County, 1964, citations Nassau County Scholastic Press Assn., 1965, citations United Fund of L.I., 1970, citations Kiwanis Clubs Internat., 1971, citations Jewish War Vets., 1972, citations WLIW-TV, 1982; Educator of Yr. award Hofstra U. chpt. Phi Delta Kappa, 1973; Educator of Yr. award Assn. for the Help of Retarded Children, Nassau County chpt., 1977; Disting. Service award Nassau-Suffolk Sch. Bds. Assn., 1979, 87, Spl. Merit award Nassau-Suffolk Sch. Bds. Assn., 1987; named Educator of Yr. U.S. Congress, 1987, County of Nassau, 1987, Town of Hempstead (N.Y.), 1987, Merrick Bd. Edn., 1987, various depts. Nassau County Bd. Coop. Ednl. Services, 1987, Merrick Sch. Dist. Faculty Assn., 1987; named Man of Yr. L.I. Spl. Edn. Adminstrs. Assn., 1979, Man of Yr. Merrick C. of C., 1980, Man of Yr. N.Y. State Legislature, 1980, 87, Man of Yr. Nassau-L.I. dist. N.Y. State Congress Parents and Tchrs., 1980. Mem. Nat. Sch. Pub. Rels. Assn. (exec. com. N.Y. State chpt., Capital Dist. chpt.), Edn. Writers Assn., Am. Newspaper Guild, Nat. Congress Parents and Tchrs. (life), N.Y. State Congress Parents and Tchrs. (life), N.Y. State Pub. Health Assn., Assn. Emotionally Handicapped Children, Assn. to Help Retarded Children, Assn. Children With Learning Abilities, N.Am. Assn. Environ. Edn., N.Y. Citizens Com. Pub. Schs., Nat. Soc. Autistic Children, Am. Assn. Career Edn., Ad Hoc Planning Com. Mobilized Community Resources, L.I. Sch.-Community Relations Assn., N.Y. Civil Svc. Employees Assn., N.Y. State Outdoor Edn. Assn., Nat. Parks and Conservation Assn., Nat. Arbor Day Found., Conf. Sch. Bds. Assn. Communicators, Am. Assn. Retired Persons (Greater Dover area chpt., bd. dirs. 1995—), Ednl. Press Assn. Am., U. Mo. Alumni Assn., Boise State U. Alumni Assn., Albany Inst. History and Art (charter mem.), N.Y. State Mus. Assocs., Smithsonian Inst. Assocs., Libr. Congress Assocs. (charter), U.S. Holocaust Meml. Mus. Assocs. (charter), Ret. Pub. Employees Assn. N.Y. State, Nat. Geographic Soc., Nat. Wildlife Fedn., Newtonville Neighborhood Assn., Mifflin Rd. Neighborhood Assn. (gov. rels. chmn., exec. com.), Deerfield Civ. Assn., Consumer Union Assocs., Common Cause, Nat. Com. to Preserve Social Security and Medicare, Soc. Profl. Journalists, Sigma Delta Chi (life, Empire State chpt.), Alpha Epsilon Pi (life). Jewish. Home: 17 Mifflin Rd Dover DE 19904-3316

ORNDUFF, ROBERT, botany educator; b. Portland, Oreg., June 13, 1932; s. Robert and Kathryn (Davis) O. B.A., Reed Coll., 1953; M.Sc., U. Wash., 1956; Ph.D., U. Calif.-Berkeley, 1961. Asst. prof. Reed Coll., 1962, Duke U., 1963; asst. prof. botany U. Calif., Berkeley, 1963-66, assoc. prof., 1966-69, prof., 1969-93, prof. emeritus, 1993—, dir. Jepson Herbarium, 1968-83, dir. Univ. Herbarium, 1975-83, exec. dir. Miller Inst. for Basic Research in Sci., 1984-87, chmn. dept. botany, 1986-89. Dir. Stanley Smith Hort. Trust, 1992—. Fellow AAAS, Calif. Acad. Scis.; mem. Calif. Native Plant Soc. (pres. 1972-73), Am. Soc. Plant Taxonomists (pres. 1975). Home: 490 Arlington Ave Berkeley CA 94707-1609 Office: Dept Integrative Biology U Calif Berkeley CA 94720-3140

ORNE, EMILY CAROTA, psychologist; b. Boston, Sept. 7, 1938; d. Emil and Ruth (Farrell) Carota; m. Martin T. Orne, Feb. 3, 1962; children: Franklin Theodore, Tracy Meredith. BA, Bennington Coll., 1959. Rsch. assoc. Mass. Mental Health Ctr., Boston, 1963-64; rsch. psychologist Unit. for Exptl. Psychiatry, Phila., 1964-79, sr. rsch. psychologist, 1979-83, co-dir., 1982—; rsch. assoc. psychology U. Pa. Sch. Medicine, Phila., 1983—; trustee Inst. Exptl. Psychiatry Rsch. Found., Mass., 1964—, assoc. co-dir., 1987. Contbr. articles to profl. jours.; assoc. editor Internat. Jour. Clin. and Exptl. Hypnosis, 1977—. Recipient Benjamin Franklin Gold medal Internat. Soc. Hypnosis, 1982, Roy M. Dorcus award Soc. Clin. and Exptl. Hypnosis, 1985, Bernard B. Raginsky award, 1993, Morton Prince award Soc. Clin. and Exptl. Hypnosis and APA, 1994. Avocations: fishing, swimming, reading. Office: U Pa Sch Medicine 1013 Blockley Hall 423 Guardian Dr Philadelphia PA 19104-6021

ORNITZ, RICHARD MARTIN, lawyer, business executive; b. Annapolis, Md., July 4, 1945; s. Martin Nathaniel and Beatrice Cynthia (Swick) O.; m. Margareth Adams, June 15, 1971 (div. Apr. 1977); m. Janet Alma Steen, Dec. 5, 1981; children—Alexandra, Zachary, Darren, Erik, Nicholas. B.S. in Metall. Engring., Cornell U., 1967; J.D., NYU, 1970; grad. sr. exec.

program, MIT, 1985. Bar: N.Y. 1971, U.S. Dist. Ct. (ea. dist.) 1972, U.S. Supreme Ct. 1984. Assoc. Cravath, Swaine & Moore, N.Y.C., 1972-77; v.p., gen. counsel, sec. Degussa Corp., Teterboro, N.J. 1977-90, mem. mgmt. com., 1987-90; of counsel, Hughes, Hubbard & Reed, N.Y.C., 1985-92; dir. Degussa Corp. subs., 1980-92; ptnr. Stroock, Stroock & Lavan, 1991-95; ptnr., chmn., fin. Coudert Bros., 1996—; speaker Risk Ins. Mgmt. Soc., 1984, 85, 86, IBA, 1986, ACCA, 1986, European Co. Lawyers Assn., 1986; Swiss Co. Lawyers Assn., 1987; Norwegian Co. Lawyers Assn., 1988; mem. pvt. law adv. com. Office of Legal Adv. U.S. Dept. State, adv. bd. Nat. Inst. Preventive Maintenance, adv. bd. corp. counsel Am. Arbitration Assn. Assoc. editor Ann. Survey of Law, NYU, 1970. Fin. com. Conn. Spl. Olympics; bd. dirs. Old Greenwich Civic Assn. Served to 1st lt. U.S. Army, 1970-72. Mem. ABA (chmn. European law sect., human relations and labor law, 1987-90), N.Y. State Bar Assn., Internat. Bar Assn., Am. Corp. Counsel Assn. (chmn. of internat. sect. com., 1986-90) European Am. Gen. Counsels Group (chmn. 1986-87), N.J. Gen. Counsels Group, Cornell Soc. Engrs. Republican. Jewish. Clubs: Old Greenwich Republican (Conn.), Innis Arden, Rocky Point. Home: 18 Meadowbank Rd Old Greenwich CT 06870-2312 Office: Coudert Bros 1411 Avenue Of The Americas New York NY 10019-2512

ORNSTEIN, DONALD SAMUEL, mathematician, educator; b. N.Y.C., July 30, 1934; s. Harry and Rose (Wisner) O.; m. Shari Richman, Dec. 20, 1964; children—David, Kara, Ethan. Student, Swarthmore Coll., 1950-52; Ph.D., U. Chgo., 1957. Fellow Inst. for Advanced Study, Princeton, N.J., 1955-57; faculty U. Wis., Madison, 1958-60; faculty Stanford (Calif.) U., 1959—, prof. math., 1966—; faculty Hebrew U., Jerusalem, 1975-76. Author: Ergodic Theory Randomness and Dynamical Systems, 1974. Recipient Bocher prize Am. Math. Soc., 1974. Mem. NAS, Am. Acad. Arts and Sci. Jewish. Office: Dept Math Stanford U Stanford CA 94305

ORNSTEIN, LIBBIE ALLENE, primary school educator; b. Miami, Fla., Mar. 3, 1949; d. Raymond Gerald and Rose Elaine (Feinberg) Blasberg; m. Morton Jay Ornstein, June 16, 1978; children: Randy Brian, Mark Justin. BEd, U. Miami, Coral Gables, Fla., 1971; MS in Early Childhood Edn., Fla. Internat. U., 1980. Cert. elem., early childhood and spl. edn. tchr., Fla. Spl. edn. tchr. F. Douglas Elem. Sch., Phila., 1973-75; 4th grade tchr. Lorah Park Elem. Sch., Miami, Fla., 1975-76; kindergarten tchr. Charles Drew Elem. Sch., Miami, 1976-79; nursery sch. tchr. Temple Beth Ahm, Cooper City, Fla., 1982-83; 2d grade tchr. Myrtle Grove Elem. Sch., Miami, 1983-86; pk 4 tchr. Univ. Sch., Nova U., Davie, Fla., 1986-88; kindergarten tchr. Pines Lakes Elem. Sch., Pembroke Pines, Fla., 1988—. Cub scout den mother Boy Scouts Am., Plantation, Fla., 1987; mem. ORT, Plantation, 1990. Democrat. Jewish. Avocations: reading, needlework, crafts, sewing. Home: 145 NW 98th Ter Fort Lauderdale FL 33324-7215

ORNSTEIN, NORMAN JAY, political scientist; b. Grand Rapids, Minn., Oct. 14, 1948; s. Joseph and Dorothy (Latz) O.; m. Judith Linda Harris, May 29, 1977; children—Matthew, Daniel. BA, U. Minn., 1967; MA, U. Mich., 1968, PhD, 1972. Asst. prof. Johns Hopkins U., Bologna, Italy, 1971-72; prof. Cath. U. Am., Washington, 1972-84; staff mem., staff dir. Senate Com. on Com. System, Washington, 1976-77; fellow Ctr. for Advanced Study in Behavioral Scis., Palo Alto, Calif., 1979-80; resident scholar Am. Enterprise Inst., Washington, 1980—; co-dir. Renewing Congress Project, Washington, 1992—, Times Mirror-Gallup Study: The People, the Press and Politics, 1987-90, Times Mirror Ctr. for People and Press (now Pew Rsch. Ctr.), 1991—; columnist Roll Call newspaper, 1993—; columnist, bd. contbrs. USA Today, Washington, 1996—; polit. editor Lawmakers program Sta. WETA-TV, Washington, 1980-84; cons. CBS News Election Unit, N.Y.C., 1982—; commentator, cons. MacNeil/Lehrer News Hour, Washington and N.Y.C., 1983—; moderator Calif. Congl. Report, Sta. KCET-TV, L.A., 1983. Author: Interest Groups Lobbying and Policy, 1978: (with others) The New Congress, 1981, Vital Statistics on Congress, 1995-96, Debt and Taxes, 1994; writer, editor, co-host: (TV series) Congress: We the People, 1984 (cert. of merit 1985); columnist USa Today, 1996—. Fortieth Anniversary Fulbright Disting. fellow, 1986-87. Mem. Coun. on Fgn. Rels., Am. Polit. Sci. Assn. (coun. 1984-86, Congl. fellow 1969-70), Nat. Commn. Pub. Svc. (bd. dirs., Volcker commn. 1987-90), Phi Beta Kappa (vis. scholar 1986-87). Jewish. Home: 5818 Surrey St Bethesda MD 20815-5419 Office: Am Enterprise Inst 1150 17th St NW Washington DC 20036-4603

ORNSTON, DARIUS GRAY, JR., psychiatrist; b. Phila., Sept. 13, 1934; s. Darius Gray and Marie Elizabeth (Wallace) O. BA, U. Pa., 1955, MD, 1959. Intern U. Mich., 1959-60; resident Yale U., New Haven, 1960-62, chief resident, 1963, fellow dept. student mental hygiene, 1964, psychiatrist dept. student mental hygiene, 1964-72; assoc. clin. prof. Yale U., New Haven, S.C., 1972-86; pvt. practice psychiatry New Haven, 1964-85, Greenville, S.C., 1986—; mem. dept. psychiatry Greenville (S.C.) Hosp., 1986—, chmn. dept. psychiatry, 1990-94; clin. prof. U. S.C., Columbia, 1988—, Med. U. S.C., Charleston, 1988—. Editor: Translating Freud, 1993.

OROMANER, DANIEL STUART, marketing consultant; b. N.Y.C., Apr. 4, 1947; s. Mervin Louis and Sophie O.; m. Judith Ray Schaer, May 30, 1968 (div. June 1978); children—Michael Lawrence, Deborah Lynne; m. Claudia Alexandra Paulhiac, Sept. 25, 1996. B.A., Queens Coll., 1967; M.B.A., Bernard M. Baruch Coll., 1974. Dept. mgr. Mid-Island Dept. Stores, Seaford, N.Y., 1970-71; tng. dir. County of Suffolk, Hauppauge, N.Y., 1971-75; asst. prof. L.I. U., Greenvale, N.Y., 1975-81; sr. trainer Nat. Productivity Ctr., N.Y.C., 1981-82; v.p. Solutions, Inc., Locust Valley, N.Y., 1982-84, ptnr., 1984-87; founder, pres. The Qualitative Difference, Inc., 1987—. Contbr. articles to profl. jours.; speaker numerous confs.; Recipient Disting. Faculty award L.I. U., 1980. Mem. Am. Mktg. Assn. (exec. mem., chair bus. to bus., 1992—), ASTD (chair programs N.Y. chpt. 1983-84), Qualitative Rsch. Cons. Assn., Advt. Research Found. Avocations: sailing, photography, target shooting. Office: The Qualitative Difference 56 Beechwood Ave Port Washington NY 11050-3902

O'RORKE, JAMES FRANCIS, JR., lawyer; b. N.Y.C., Dec. 4, 1936; s. James Francis and Helen (Weber) O'R.; m. Carla Phelps, Aug. 6, 1964. A.B., Princeton U., 1958; J.D., Yale U., 1961. Bar: N.Y. 1962. Assoc. Davies, Hardy & Schenck, 1962-69; ptnr. Davies, Hardy, Ives & Lawther, 1969-72, Skadden, Arps, Slate, Meagher & Flom, N.Y.C., 1972—; dir. Clinipad Corp.; mem. adv. bd. Chgo. Title Ins. Co. N.Y. Trustee Mus. Am. Indian-Heye Found., 1977-80. Mem. ABA, N.Y. State Bar Assn., Assn. Bar City N.Y., Am. Coll. Real Estate Lawyers, Princeton Club N.Y.C. Office: Skadden Arps Slate Meagher & Flom 919 3rd Ave New York NY 10022

OROST, JOSEPH MARTIN, internet applications architect; b. Jersey City, Aug. 30, 1956; s. Joseph and Jean (Hawkins) O.; m. June Deli, Oct. 4, 1980; 1 stepchild, Jeffrey Liscik. BS in Computer Sci., Thomas A. Edison State Coll., 1991; MS in Computer Sci., Rutgers U., 1995. Programmer Interdata, Oceanport, N.J., 1974-78; sr. cons. tech. staff Concurrent Computer Corp., Tinton Falls, N.J., 1978-91, project leader, 1985-91; tech. staff AT&T Echo Logic, Holmdel, N.J., 1991-93; tech. mgr. AT&T Labs., Holmdel, 1994—. Author: UNIX compress, 1985, BENCH++, 1995. Past advancement chmn. Troop 82 Boy Scouts Am., Jackson, N.J. Mem. Assn. Computing Machinery, Internat. Platform Assn. Ukrainian Orthodox. Avocations: music, electronics. Home: 91 Pecan Ln Freehold NJ 07728-4124 Office: AT&T Labs 101 Crawfords Corner Rd Holmdel NJ 07733-3030

O'ROURKE, C. LARRY, lawyer; b. Colusa, Calif., Dec. 10, 1937; s. James Harold and Elizabeth Janice (Jenkins) O'R.; m. Joy Marie Phillips, May 22, 1965; children: Ryan, Paula. BSEE, Stanford U., 1959, MBA, 1961; JD, George Washington U., 1972. Bar: Va. 1971, D.C. 1974, U.S. Ct. Appeals (fed. cir.) 1973, U.S. Patent and Trademark Office 1971, U.S. Supreme Ct. Patent atty. Westinghouse Elec., Washington, 1969-70, Pitts., 1970-73; assoc. Finnegan, Henderson, Farabow, Garrett & Dunner, Washington, 1974-79, ptnr., 1979—; dir. Finnegan, Henderson, Farabow, Garrett & Dunner, Palo Alto, Calif.; dir. Zest Inc., Md., 1988, chmn. bd. dirs., 1990-95. Mem. ABA, Am. Intellectual Property Law Assn. Democrat. Presbyterian. Office: Finnegan Henderson Farabow Garrett & Dunner 1300 I St NW Ste 700 Washington DC 20005-3314

O'ROURKE, DENNIS, lawyer; b. Whiteclay, Nebr., Oct. 31, 1914; s. Frank L. and Jerene (Rebbeck) O'R.; m. Ruth Rouss, Jan. 21, 1940; children: Susan, Kathleen, Brian, Dennis, Ruth, Dolores. A.B. cum laude, Nebr. Tchrs. Coll., 1935; J.D. with distinction, George Washington U., 1939; LLD (hon.), Chadron State Coll., 1993. Bar: D.C. 1939, U.S. Supreme Ct 1945, Colo. 1946. Typist, auditor GAO, Washington, 1935-39; lawyer solicitor's office U.S. Dept. Agr., Washington, 1939-45; chief basic commodity div. U.S. Dept. Agr., 1945; gen. counsel Group Health Assn., Washington, 1943, Holly Sugar Corp., Colorado Springs, Colo., 1945; v.p. Holly Sugar Corp., Colorado Springs, 1953-63, pres., 1963-67, chmn. bd., 1967-69, dir., 1983-88; vice chmn. bd., mem. exec. com. Holly Sugar Corp. (merged with Imperial Sugar Co.), Colorado Springs, 1986-88; v.p., gen. counsel Holly Oil Co., 1955-63; sr. ptnr. Rouss & O'Rourke, Colorado Springs and Washington; U.S. counsel Union Nacional de Productores de Azucar, Mexico, 1970-82; pres. Man Exec., Inc., Colorado Springs and Washington; chmn. examining com. 1st Nat. Bank Colorado Springs, 1983-84. Contbr. articles financial and bus. jours. Bd. dirs. Colo. Pub. Expenditure Coun., vice chmn., exec. com., 1968-76; dir. Nat. C. of C. of the U.S., 1968-70; trustee, pres. Colorado Springs Fine Arts Center, 1961-62, 68-71, 73, chmn. adv. com., 1981-84, hon. trustee, 1988; founder, 1st chmn. Colo. Com. (now Coun.) on Arts and Humanities, 1963; Mem. Bus. and Industry Adv. Com. OECD, Paris, France, 1969-71; adviser U.S. dels. Internat. Sugar Confs., Geneva, 1965, Mexico City, 1959; chmn. Colorado Springs-El Paso County Citizens' Task Force on Local Govt. Reorgn., 1976-77. Mem. Am. Soc. Sugar Beet Technologists, Internat. Soc. Sugar Cane Technologists, Fed. Bar Assn., Colo. Bar Assn., El Paso County Bar Assn, Order of Coif, Cheyenne Mountain Country Club, El Paso Club, Garden of Gods Club, Sugar Club, Met. Club (Washington), Rotary, Phi Delta Phi. Home: 8 Heather Dr Broadmoor Colorado Springs CO 80906 Office: PO Box 572 Colorado Springs CO 80901-0572

O'ROURKE, JAMES LOUIS, lawyer; b. Bridgeport, Conn., July 5, 1958; s. James G. and Margaret Elizabeth (Fesco) O'R.; m. Margaret C. DiCicco, Sept. 18, 1994. BS, U. Bridgeport, 1984, JD, 1987. Bar: Conn. 1988, U.S. Dist. Ct. Conn. 1989, Mashantucket Pequot Tribal Bar 1995. Pvt. practice Stratford, Conn., 1987—. With USN, 1976-79. Mem. ABA, Assn. Am. Trial Lawyers Assn., Conn. Trial Lawyers Assn., Conn. Bar Assn., Greater Bridgeport Bar Assn. Roman Catholic. Avocations: boating, cycling, swimming, golf. Office: 2526 Main St Stratford CT 06497-5811

O'ROURKE, P. J. (PATRICK JAKE O'ROURKE), writer, humorist; b. Toledo, Ohio, Nov. 14, 1947; s. Clifford Bronson and Delphine (Loy) O'R. BA, Miami U. of Ohio, 1969; MA, Johns Hopkins U., 1970. Writer Nat. Lampoon mag., from 1973, former prin. editor; freelance writer, wrote screenplays, 1980s; writer Rolling Stone mag., 1981—, now fgn. affairs desk chief. Author: Modern Manners: An Etiquette Book for Rude People, 1983, The Bachelor Home Companion: A Practical Guide to Keeping House Like a Pig, 1987, Republican Party Reptile, 1987, Holidays in Hell, 1988, Parliament of Whores: A Lone Humorist Attempts to Explain the U.S. Government, 1991, Give War a Chance: Eyewitness Accounts of Mankind's Struggle Against Tyranny, Injustice and Alcohol-Free Beer, 1992, All the Trouble in the World: The Lighter Side of Overpopulation, Famine, Ecological Disaster, Ethnic Hatred, Plague and Poverty, 1994, Age and Guile Beat Youth, Innocence and a Bad Haircut, 1995. Office: care Rolling Stone 1290 Avenue Of The Americas New York NY 10104-0199

O'ROURKE, RICHARD LYNN, lawyer; b. Bklyn., Nov. 27, 1949; s. Joseph and Loretta (Casey) O'R.; m. Renee Marie Kupiec, July 17, 1971; children: Shannon, Kathleen. BA, SUNY, Geneseo, 1971; MA, Bowling Green State U., 1972; JD, Pace U. Sch. Law, 1981. Bar: N.Y. 1982, U.S. Ct. Appeals (10th cir.) 1983, U.S. Ct. Appeals (2d cir.) 1994, U.S. Dist. Ct. (all dists.) N.Y. 1982. Dir. career planning Pace U., Pleasantville, N.Y., 1977-81; assoc. Keane & Beane P.C., White Plains, N.Y., 1981-86, ptnr., v.p., 1986—. Judge Village of Brewster, N.Y., 1992—; pres. Brewster Edn. Found., 1992-94; town atty. Southeast Brewster, 1986-89, chmn. zoning bd. appeals, 1986-86; adv. bd. Jr. Achievement West, White Plains, 1977-82. Mem. Putnam County Magistrates Assn. (v.p. 1994-96, pres. 1997—). Avocations: golf, history. Office: Keane & Beane One N Broadway White Plains NY 10601

O'ROURKE, THOMAS DENIS, civil engineer, educator; b. Pitts., July 31, 1948; s. Lawrence Robert and Adel Mildred (Moloski) O'R.; m. Patricia Ann Lane, Aug. 12, 1978; 1 child, Adele Christina; BSCE, Cornell U., Ithaca, N.Y., 1970; MSCE, U. Ill., 1973, PhD., 1975. Soils engr. Dames & Moore, N.Y.C., 1970; research asst. U. Ill., Urbana, 1970-75, asst. prof., 1975-78; asst. prof. Cornell U., 1978-80, assoc. prof., 1981-87, prof, 1987—. Elected to Nat. Acad. Engring., 1993. Mem. ASCE (pres. Ithaca sect. 1981-82, Collingwood prize 1983, Huber prize 1988, C. Martin Duke award 1995), ASME, ASTM (C.A. Hogentogler award 1976), Earthquake Engring. Research Inst., Internat. Soc. Engring. Geology, Internat. Soc. Rock Mechanics, U.S. Nat. Com. on Tunnelling Tech. (chmn. 1987-88). Home: 10 Twin Glens Rd Ithaca NY 14850-1041 Office: Cornell U Sch Civil Environ Engring 265 Hollister Hall Ithaca NY 14853-3501

ORPHANIDES, NORA CHARLOTTE, ballet educator; b. N.Y.C., June 4, 1951; d. M.T. and Mary Elsie (Tilly) Feffer; m. James Mark Orphanides, July 1, 1972; children: Mark, Elaine, Jennine. BA, CUNY, 1973; student, Joffrey Ballet Sch., N.Y.C., 1970-75; postgrad., Princeton Ballet Sch., 1976-86. Cert. speech and hearing handicapped tchr. Sr. sales assoc. Met. Mus. Art, N.Y.C., 1970-86; membership asst. Patrons Lounge, M.M.A., N.Y.C., 1987—; mem. faculty Princeton (N.J.) Ballet Sch., 1983—, trustee emeritus, 1992—. Mem. cast Princeton Ballet ann. Nutcracker, 1985-90, now Am. Repertory Ballet Co., 1993—; appeared in Romeo & Juliet, 1995-96. Fundraising gala chmn. Princeton Ballet, 1985, 86, 91-92, chmn. spl. events, 1987—, trustee, 1986—, chmn. Nutcracker benefit, 1990—, Dracula benefit, 1991; dept. chmn. June Fete to benefit Princeton Hosp., 1988, 90-91, 92, 96; mem. worship and arts commn. Nassau Presbyn. Ch., 1989, 90, dinner chmn. Bach Music Festival, 1989, Cambridge Singers, 1990; vol. Nat. Hdqrs. Recording for the Blind, 1991-93; trustee Princeton Youth Fund, 1991-92; dinner chmn. Nassau Ch. Music Festival, 1992, Handel Festival, Nassau Ch., 1993, Princeton Chamber Symphony, 1993; vol. Cmty. Park Sch. Libr., 1992-93; hon. chmn. Princeton Ballet Gala, 1993; chmn. Christmas Boutique, Princeton Med. Ctr., 1993; trustee, Princeton Med. Ctr. Auxilary Bd., 1992—, pres. 1997—, trustee 1995—. Democrat. Avocations: piano, aerobics, skiing, swimming, tennis. Home: 35 Brearly Rd Princeton NJ 08540-6767 Office: 301 N Harrison St Princeton NJ 08540-3512

ORR, BETSY, business education educator; b. Dermott, Ark., Nov. 24, 1954; d. Doy and Peggy (Johnson) Ogles; m. Gary Orr, July 10, 1976; children: Brent, Shane. BA, U. Ark., 1975, bus. edn. cert., 1978, MEd, 1987, EdD, 1994. Cert. tchr., Ark. Tchr. Springdale (Ark.) High Sch., 1978-89; instr. bus. edn. U. Ark., Fayetteville, 1989-94, asst. prof., 1994—. Mem. Nat. Bus. Edn. Assn., Ark. Bus. Edn. Assn. (editor 1989-92), AAUW, Delta Pi Epsilon (pres. 1992—), Phi Delta Kappa. Avocations: walking, reading. Home: 1006 NW N St Bentonville AR 72712-4526 Office: U Ark Grad Edn 108 Fayetteville AR 72701

ORR, BOBBY (ROBERT GORDON ORR), former hockey player; b. Parry Sound, Ont., Can., Mar. 20, 1948; m. Peggy Orr; children: Darren, Brent. With Boston Bruins, 1966-76; with Chgo. Black Hawks, 1976-77, asst. coach, 1976-77; spokesman Nabisco Brands, Inc., N.Y.C., Bay Banks, Inc., Boston; asst. to the pres. Pandick New Eng.; host Hockey Legends program CBC; bd. dirs. numerous cos. Winner Calder Meml. trophy, 1967, Art Ross trophy, 1970, 75, James Norris Meml. trophy, 1968-75, Hart Meml. trophy, 1970-72, 2 Conn Smythe trophies, Lou Marsh trophy, 1970; named Male Athlete of Yr., Can. CP Poll, 1970, Athlete of Yr., Sport Mag. and Sports Illustrated, Most Valuable Player, Can. Cup, 1976. Address: 647 Summer St Boston MA 02210-2189*

ORR, BOBETTE KAY, diplomat; b. Oak Park, Ill., Oct. 28, 1941; d. Robert Jay and Neta (Hoobler) Pottle; m. William Rucker Orr, Oct. 11, 1974; step children: Bridgette, Brietta, Alyson, William Jr. BA in Econs., Conn. Coll. for Women, 1963; student auditor Internat. Econs., London Sch. of Econs., 1964; postgrad. studies in Econs., George Washington U., 1964-65. Rsch. asst. C. of C. USA, Washington, 1965-66; country desk officer for Scandanavia U.S. Dept. Commerce, Washington, 1966-69, country desk officer for France, 1970-72, 79-81, country desk officer for Belgium, Netherlands, Luxembourg, 1974-77, country desk officer for Japan, 1981-82; mkt. rsch. officer United States Trade Ctr., Stockholm, 1973; trade promotion officer United States Trade Ctr., London, 1977-78; asst. comml. attache Am. Embassy, Paris, 1982-87; comml. attache Am. Consulate Gen., Auckland, New Zealand, 1988-92; consul gen. Am. Consulate Gen., Edinburgh, Scotland, 1992-95; comml. counselor Am. Embassy, London, 1995—; mem. bd. dirs. U.S. Dept. Commerce Fed. Credit Union, Washington, D.C., 1972-77, pres., 1976-77, mem. supervisory com., 1979-81; equal employment opportunity counselor for Greater Washington Met. Area, 1972-75; mission dir. for USDOC's Concrete Constrn. Techniques Seminar Mission to Hong Kong, Singapore, Malaysia, 1980; detailed to Office of Dir. Fgn. Comml. Svc. as evaluator of candidates for Fgn. Comml. Svc., 1981. Author: (with others) 10 pamphlet series, on free enterprise, The Power of Choice, 1966; contbr. to Bus. Am., 1966-81, Overseas Bus. Reports 1966-76 (Dept. Commerce publs.). Mem. Am. Women's Club of Edinburgh, (hon. pres.), The English Speaking Union. Avocations: skiing, bicycle riding. Home: PO Box 63 Great Falls VA 22066 Office: Am Embassy, 24 Grosvenor Sq, London England W1A 1AE

ORR, CAROL WALLACE, book publishing executive; b. Newton, Mass., Dec. 17, 1933; d. Barton Stuart Wallace and Mary (Blanthorne) Stigler; children: Brett Amanda, Ross Wallace. Student, Boston U., 1951-53; BA, Douglass Coll., 1966. Successively permissions mgr., paperback editor, reprint editor, asst. to assoc. dir. Princeton (N.J.) U. Press, 1966-75, exec. asst. to dir. then asst. dir., 1975-78; dir. U. Tenn. Press., Knoxville, 1978-91; aerobics instr., freelance editor, 1992—. Mem. editorial bd. Book Rsch. Quar., 1988-92; contbr. articles to Scholarly Pub. jour., 1974-86. Recipient Book Woman award Women's Nat. Book Assn., 1987, Disting. Career award Needham (Mass.) H.S., 1995. Mem. Assn. Am. Univ. Presses (pres. 1987-88), Internat. Assn. Scholarly Pubs. (sec.-gen. 1980-83), Women in Scholarly Pub. (first pres. 1980-81), AAUP Lang. Task Force (chair 1989-91), AAUP Golden Fluke Award Com. (chair 1984-91), Phi Beta Kappa, Phi Kappa Phi. Avocations: jogging, aerobics, gardening, travel, music.

ORR, DANIEL, educator, economist; b. N.Y.C., May 13, 1933; s. Robert Connell and Lillian (Nagle) O.; m. Mary Lee Hayes, Oct. 12, 1957; children—Rebecca, Matthew, Sara. A.B., Oberlin Coll., 1954; Ph.D., Princeton, 1960. Ops. analyst Procter & Gamble Co., 1956-58; instr. econs. Princeton U., 1959-60; asst. prof. econs. Amherst Coll., 1960-61, Grad. Sch. Bus., U. Chgo., 1961-65; mem. faculty U. Calif. at San Diego, 1965-78, chmn. econs. dept., 1969-72; prof. econs., cons. in field; prof., head dept. econs. Va. Poly. Inst. and State U., 1978-89; prof. econs. U. Ill., Champaign-Urbana, 1989—, dept. head, 1989-94; vis. prof. U. Nottingham, Eng., 1972, U. Calif., 1988, U. Warsaw, 1992. Author: Cash Management and the Demand for Money, 1970, Property, Markets and Government Intervention, 1976. Trustee Oberlin (Ohio) Coll., 1993—. Served with AUS, 1958. Mem. Am. Econ. Assn., Crystal Downs Country Club. Home: 515 S Willis Ave Champaign IL 61821-3917 Office: U Ill 330 Commerce Bldg W 1206 S 6th St Champaign IL 61820-6915

ORR, FRANKLIN MATTES, JR., petroleum engineering educator; b. Baytown, Tex., Dec. 27, 1946; s. Franklin Mattes and Selwyn Sage (Huddleston) O.; m. Susan Packard, Aug. 30, 1970; children: David, Katherine. BSChemE, Stanford U., 1969; PhDChemE, U. Minn., 1976. Asst. to dir. Office Fed. Activities EPA, Washington, 1970-72; research engr. Shell Devel. Co., Houston, 1976-78; sr. engr. N.Mex. Petroleum Recovery Research Ctr., Socorro, 1978-84; assoc. prof. petroleum engring. Stanford (Calif.) U., 1985-87, prof., 1987—, interim dean Sch. Earth Scis., 1994-95, dean Sch. Earth Scis., 1995—. Contbr. articles to profl. jours. Bd. dirs. Wolf Trap Found. for the Performing Arts, 1988-94, Monterey Bay Aquarium Rsch. Inst., 1987—, Am. Geol. Inst. Found., 1997—; chair sci. adv. com. David and Lucile Packard Found. Fellowships for Sci. and Engring. With USPHS, 1970-72. Mem. Soc. Petroleum Engrs. (named Distin. Lectr. 1988-89, Disting. Achievement award for petroleum engring. faculty 1993), AIChE, AAAS, Soc. Indsl. and Applied Math. Office: Stanford U Sch Earth Scis Mitchell Bldg Rm 101 Stanford CA 94305

ORR, J. SCOTT, newspaper correspondent. Coor., wash. bur. The Star-Ledger, Newark, N.J. Office: New House New Service 1101 Connecticut Ave NW Ste 300 Washington DC 20036-4352*

ORR, JAMES F., III, insurance company executive; b. Mpls., 1943. BA, Villanova U., 1962; MA, Boston U., 1969. With New Eng. Mchts. Bank, Boston, 1965-67, Bache & Co., N.Y.C., 1967-69; ptnr. Cardinal Mgmt. Co., Boston, 1969-75; exec. v.p., treas. Conn. Bank and Trust Corp., 1975-86; with UNUM, 1986—, formerly pres., COO; chmn. bd., CEO UNUM Corp.; also pres., chmn., CEO UNUM Life Ins. Co. (subs.). Office: UNUM Corp 2211 Congress St Portland ME 04122-0002*

ORR, JIM (JAMES D. ORR), columnist, writer, publicist; b. Buffalo, Feb. 7, 1960; s. David James and Doris Kathleen (Wolos) O.; m. JoEllen Black, June 4, 1994. B in Journalism, Ind. U. of Pa., 1982, M in Comm., 1987. Station mgr. Sta. WIUP-TV, Ind., Pa., 1983-84; sports writer, news writer Ind. (Pa.) Gazette, 1984-88; edn. reporter Stuart (Fla.) News, 1988-89; staff writer, columnist Gannett Rochester (N.Y.) Newspapers, 1989-96. Columnist Orrdinary People, 1994-95; freelance writer, publicist, 1996—. Moderator polit. debate Edu-Cable Corp., Greece, N.Y., 1993. Recipient Agrl. Writing 1st Place award Penn-Ag Industries, 1985, 2d place Keystone State Press award Pa. Newspaper Pub. Assn., 1987. Home and Office: 4413 N Fruit Ave Fresno CA 93705

ORR, JOSEPH NEWTON, recreational guide, outdoor educator; b. San Francisco, Oct. 25, 1954; s. James Neewah and Verna Louise (Butler) O. BA in Spanish, Sul Ross State U., 1981. Cert. swiftwater rescue technician; cert. wilderness first responder; cert. open water SCUBA diver; cert. Utah river guide, Grand Canyon river guide. Instr. astronomy lab. Sul Ross State U., Alpine, Tex., 1972-75; svc. sta. attendent, store clerk Nat. Park Concessions, Big Bend Nat. Park, 1975-78; surveyor's aide Gila Nat. Forest U.S. Dept. Agriculture, N. Mex., 1979; instr. ESL Centro Universitario de Idiomas, Mexico City, 1981; English and Spanish tutor Ctr. Student Devel. Sul Ross State U., 1980-83; instr. ESL, Intensive Summer Lang. Tng. Inst. Sul Ross State U., Alpine, Tex., 1980-83; ednl. cons. Chihuahuan Desert Rsch. Inst., Alpine, Tex., 1983; editor The Skyline (student newspaper) Sul Ross State U., 1984; interpreter, translator, guide Dr. John M. Miller, Mexico, 1980-85; guide in U.S., Mex., Belize, Guatemala and Honduras for Far Flung Adventures, 1986-94, Remarkable Journeys, 1994—. Active Four Corners Sch. Outdoor Edn., Canyonlands Fld Inst., Crow Canyon Archeol. Ctr., Grand Canyon River Guides, Mus. No. Ariz., Friends of Lowell Obs., Grand Canyon Trust, others. Mem. Soc. for Am. Archaeology, Nat. Space Soc., Am. Rock Art Rsch. Assn., Astron. Soc. of Pacific, Planetary Soc., Internat. Dark Sky Assn., Grand Canyon Assn., Rock Art Found., Beta Beta Beta. Democrat. Avocations: astronomy, archaeology. Home: 223 N Guadalupe # 429 Santa Fe NM 87501-1850 Office: Remarkable Journeys PO Box 31855 Houston TX 77231-1855

ORR, KENNETH BRADLEY, academic administrator; b. Charlotte, N.C., Mar. 15, 1933; s. Frank Wylie and Kate Harriett O.; m. Janice Jarrett, July 15, 1960; children: Kevin, Jeffrey, Jonathan. BA, Duke U., 1954; MDiv, Union Theol. Sem., 1960, ThM, 1961; PhD, U. Mich., 1978; LittD, Carroll Coll., 1990. Ordained to ministry, Presbyn. Ch., 1961. Minister West End Presbyn. Ch., Roanoke, Va., 1961-64; asst. to pres. Union Theol. Sem., Richmond, Va., 1964-68; v.p. Union Theol. Sem., 1968-74; pres. Presbyn. Sch. Christian Edn., Richmond, 1974-79, Presbyn. Coll., Clinton, S.C., 1979-97; past mem. coun. presidents Nat. Assn. Intercollegiate Athletics, Kansas City, Mo.; chmn. South Atlantic Conf., 1989-91. Contbr. to religious and ednl. publs. Mem. Nat. Adv. Com. on Instnl. Quality and Integrity, 1994—. Capt. USAF, 1955-57. Mem. Assn. Presbyn. Colls. and Univs. (pres. 1994, exec. com.), Coun. Ind. Colls. (bd. dirs. 1993-96), Laurens County C. of C. (past pres.), Kiwanis. Democrat. Avocations: reading, camping, travel, tennis, classical music.

ORR, PARKER MURRAY, former lawyer; b. Cleve., Mar. 29, 1927; s. Stanley Lutz and Katherine (Murray) O.; m. Joan Luttrell, June 8, 1946; children: Kathleen Orr Guzowski, Parker Murray, Louise Orr Black, Kevin J. B.A., Western Res. U., 1948, LL.B., 1950. Bar: Ohio 1950. Atty. Leckie, McCreary, Schlitz, Hinslea & Petersilge, Cleve., 1950-51; owner Orr Constrn.

Co., Cleve., 1951-57; assoc. firm Baker & Hostetler, Cleve., 1957-67, ptnr., 1967-88; ret. Chmn. City of Willoughby Hills Planning Commn., Ohio, 1964-78. Mem. ABA, Ohio Bar Assn., Greater Cleve. Bar Assn. Republican. Club: Mayfield Country (Cleve.). Home: 2800 Hemlock Dr Willoughby OH 44094-9485 Office: Baker & Hostetler 3200 National City Ctr Cleveland OH 44114

ORR, RICHARD TUTTLE, journalist; b. Springfield, Ill., Feb. 19, 1915; s. Thomas Edward and Anna Maude (Tuttle) O.; m. Lois Marie Hollesen, June 3, 1939. B.S. in Journalism, U. Ill., 1937. Reporter City News Bur., Chgo., 1941-42; reporter Chgo. Tribune, 1941-49, farm editor, 1949-83, editorial writer, 1961-72, rural affairs writer, 1983—. Served with USAF, 1943-46. Recipient Edward Scott Beck award Chgo. Tribune, 1962, Oscar in Agr. award DeKalb Agrl. Research Inc., 1969, Pfizer Agr. Communications award Pfizer Genetics Inc., 1969, Champion Media award Dartmouth Coll., 1982, Hall of Fame award Saddle and Sirloin Club, 1972. Mem. Nat. Assn. Agrl. Journalists (pres. 1958, J.S. Russell Meml. award 1965, Nat. Farm Features award 1977, 79, Nat. Farm Column award 1981), Chgo. Press Club (pres. 1966), Chgo. Press Vets. Assn. (chmn. 1968). Republican. Methodist. Avocations: photography; watercolor painting; jazz records; western Americana. Home: 2933 N Sheridan Rd Apt 809 Chicago IL 60657-5938 Office: Chgo Tribune PO Box 25340 Chicago IL 60625-0340

ORR, ROBERT F., justice; b. Norfolk, Va., Oct. 11, 1946. AB, U. N.C., 1971, JD, 1975. Bar: N.C. 1975. News reporter, part-time photographer Sta. WSOC-TV, 1965-68, 71; pvt. practice Asheville, N.C., 1975-86; assoc. judge N.C. Ct. Appeals, 1986-94; assoc. justice N.C. Supreme Ct., Raleigh, 1994—; mem. N.C. Beverage Control Commn., 1985-86; adj. prof. appellate advocacy N.C. Ctrl. U. Sch. Law, 1989—. Mem. Asheville-Revitalization Commn., 1977-81, Asheville-Buncombe Hist. Resources Commn., 1980-81; bd. trustees Hist. Preservation Found. N.C., 1982-85; mem. Nat. Park Sys. Adv. Bd., 1990-95, chmn., 1992-93; bd. visitors U. N.C.-Chapel Hill, 1996—; mem. N.C. Commn. on the Delivery of Civil Legal Svcs. With U.S. Army, 1968-71. Mem. N.C. State Bar, 28th Jud. Dist., N.C. Bar Assn. Republican. Office: PO Box 1841 Raleigh NC 27602-1841 also: 304 Justice Bldg 2 E Morgan St Raleigh NC 27601

ORR, RONALD STEWART, lawyer; b. L.A., Nov. 19, 1946; s. Ashley S. and Nancy (McKenna) O.; divorced; children: Justin, Hailey. BSEE, Leland Sanford Jr. U., 1968; JD, U. So. Calif., 1972, MBA, 1987. Bar: Calif. 1973, U.S. Dist. Ct. (so. dist.) Calif. 1973, U.S. Ct. Appeals (9th cir.) 1974, U.S. Supreme Ct. 1983. Mem. tech. staff Hughes Aircraft Co., L.A., 1968-72; ptnr. Shutan and Trost, L.A., 1972-80, Gibson, Dunn and Crutcher, L.A., 1980—. Co-author: Secured Creditors Under the New Bankruptcy Code, 1979, Entertainment Contracts, 1986. Trustee U. So. Calif., L.A., 1986-91; exec. com. Nancy Regan Ctr., L.A., 1988-89. Mem. U. So. Calif. Alumni Assn. (bd. dirs. 1984-89), Order of Coif. Office: Gibson Dunn & Crutcher 333 S Grand Ave Los Angeles CA 90071-1504

ORR, SAN WATTERSON, JR., lawyer; b. Madison, Wis., Sept. 22, 1941; s. San Watterson and Eleanor Augusta (Schalk) O.; m. Joanne Marie Ruby, June 26, 1965; children: San Watterson III, Nancy Chapman. BBA, U. Wis., 1963, JD, 1966. Bar: Wis. 1966; CPA, Wis. Sec., tres., bd. dirs. Yawkey Lumber Co., Wausau, Wis., 1971—; chmn. exec. com. Wausau Paper Mills Co., 1977—, chmn. bd., 1989—; pres. Woodson Fudiciary Corp., Wilmington, Del., 1979—, also bd. dirs.; pres. Forewood, Inc., Wausau, 1979—, also bd. dirs.; chmn. Marathon Electric Mfg. Corp., Wausau, 1982-97; chmn. Mosinee (Wis.) Paper Corp., 1987—, also bd. dirs.; dir. M&I First Am. Bank, Wausau, 1988—; vice chmn. Marshall & Ilsley Corp., 1997—; bd. dirs. Wausau Ins. Cos., Marshall & Ilsley Corp., Wausau, M&I Marshall & Ilsley Bank, Milw., MDU Resources Group, Inc., Bismarck, N.D. Editor: U. Wis. Law Rev., 1962-63. Bd. dirs. The Aytchmonde Woodson Found., Inc., Wausau, 1966—, The Leigh Yawkey Woodson Art Mus., Inc., Wausau, 1981—, Wis. Taxpayers Alliance, Madison, 1983—, Competitive Wis., Inc., Milw., 1989—, U. Wis. Found., Madison, 1991—; dir. Wis. Policy Rsch. Inst., Milw., 1995—; mem. bd. regents U. Wis. Sys., Madison, 1993—; v.p., bd. dirs. Wausau YMCA Found., 1979—; bd. dirs. U. Wis. Hosp. and Clinics Authority, 1995—. Mem. Wis. Bar Assn., Am. Law Inst., Wausau Club. Office: Yawkey Lumber Co 500 3rd St Ste 602 Wausau WI 54403-4857

ORR, STANLEY CHI-HUNG, financial executive; b. Shanghai, China, May 19, 1946; s. Chiu-Lai and Chiu-Chun (Ma) O.; children: Simon K., Edmund K., Norman K. Grad., Hong Kong Bapt. U., 1966; M in Econs., Chu Hoi Coll., Hong Kong, 1973; post grad., East Anglia U., Eng., 1975; MBA, Bradford U., Eng., 1977, West Coast U., L.A., 1980. CPA, Calif.; CMA, Eng.; notary pub. Chief acct. Cordial Knitting Factory Ltd., Hong Kong, 1966-69, mgr., 1969-71; chief acct. for Asia Mark Holding Co. Ltd., Hong Kong, 1971-74; chief fin. officer Knits-Cord Ltd., Montebello, Calif., 1977—; broker Dept. of Real Estate, 1992—. Treas., sec. World Univs. Svc., Hong Kong, 1965-66. Mem. AICPA, Chinese-Am. CPA Soc. (chmn., pres. 1991), Calif. Soc. CPAs. Republican. Office: Knits-Cord Ltd 1600 Date St Montebello CA 90640-6371

ORR, STEVEN R., health facility administrator; b. 1947. Undergrad. degree, Macalester Coll.; M in Hosp. Adminstrn., U. Minn., 1973. Tchr., coord. master's degree program in hosp. adminstrn. U. Minn., 1974-76; v.p. corp. planning, v.p. managed and affiliated hosp. divsn. Fairfield Community Hosps., Mpls., 1976-81; COO Mid-Atlantic Health Group, 1981-83; adminstr. Monmouth Med. Ctr. Mid-Atlantic Health Group, Long Branch, N.J., 1981-83; ptnr., cons. Peat, Marwick, Main & Co., Mpls., 1984-88; chmn., pres., CEO Lutheran Health Systems, Fargo, N.D., 1988—. Office: Luth Health System PO Box 6200 Fargo ND 58106-6200

ORR, SUSAN PACKARD, foundation administrator. Pres. Packard Found., Los Altos, Calif. Office: The Packard Foundation 300 2nd St Ste 200 Los Altos CA 94022-3632

ORR, TERRENCE S., dancer; b. Berkeley, Calif., Mar. 12, 1943; m. Cynthia Gregory (div.); m. Marianna Tcherkassky. Student, San Francisco Ballet Sch. With San Francisco Ballet, 1959-65; with Am. Ballet Theatre, N.Y.C., 1965—, soloist, 1967-72, rehearsal asst., 1970-73, prin. dancer, 1972-78, assoc. ballet master, 1973-78, ballet master, 1978—; Mounted prodns. for the Royal Winnipeg Ballet, The National Ballet of Mexico, Teatro alla Scala in Millan, National ballet de Nancy in France, Teatro Colon in Buenos Aires, Pittsburgh Ballet Theatre, Boston Ballet, Ballet West, Dance theatre of Harlem, New York City Ballet, the Cleveland/San jose Ballet, the San Francisco Ballet and Ballet Arizona. Repertoire includes (with San Francisco Ballet) The Nutcracker, Fantasma, Divertissement d'Auber, Jeu des Cartes, Con Amore, (with Am. Ballet Theatre) Billy the Kid, Coppelia, La Fille Mal Gardee, Petrouchka, The River, Rodeo, Don Quixote, (leading roles) At Midnight, Dark Elegies, Fancy Free, Graduation Ball, Harbinger, Variations for Four, Pulcinella Variations, Brahms Quintet, Schubertiade, Mendelssohn Symphony, Polyandrion, (featured roles) Giselle, Swan Lake, La Sylphide, Gartenfest, Ontogeny; prodr., dir. Gala Performance, 1984, 86; stage prodns. La Sylphide, Rodeo, Fancy Free, Graduation Ball, Etudes, Billy the Kid, Fall River Legend, Giselle. Office: care Am Ballet Theatre 890 Broadway New York NY 10003-1211

ORR, T(HOMAS) J(EROME) (JERRY ORR), airport terminal executive; b. Charlotte, N.C., Feb. 25, 1941; m. Marcia Mincey; 3 children. BS in Civil Engring., N.C. State U., 1962. Registered profl. engr., N.C. Pvt. practice land surveyor Charlotte, 1962-75; with Charlotte/Douglas Internat. Airport, 1975—, asst. mgr. airport ops., until 1989, aviation dir., 1989—. Chmn. employes campaign United Way of Ctrl. Carolinas, 1990; active Neighborhood Task Force, Charlotte's Cities in Schs. Program. Recipient Outstanding Support award N.C. Air Nat. Guard, 1989, Spirit award Charlotte-MJecklenburg Spirit Sq. Ctr. for Arts, 1990. Mem. N.C. Airports Assn. (past pres.), Airport Operators Coun. Internat. Office: Charlotte/Douglas Internat Airport PO Box 19066 Charlotte NC 28219-9066

ORREGO-SALAS, JUAN ANTONIO, composer, retired music educator; b. Santiago, Chile, Jan. 18, 1919; came to U.S., 1961; s. Fernando M. and Filomena E. (Salas) Orrego-S.; m. Carmen Benavente, Apr. 17, 1943; children: Juan Cristian, Francisca, Juan Felipe, Juan Miguel, Juan Matias. Bachillerato, Liceo AlemÁn, Santiago, 1938; MusM, State U., 1942; MusD, Conservatorio Nacional de Música, Santiago, 1942; architect diploma, Cath. U. Chile, 1943; postgrad., Columbia U., 1944-45, Princeton U., 1945-46; MusD, U. Chile, Santiago, 1953; D Honoris Causa, Cath. U., Santiago, 1973. Condr. Cath. U. Choir, Santiago, 1938-57; prof. composition and musicology U. Chile, Santiago, 1942-61; editor Revista Musical Chilena, 1949-53; music critic El Mercurio, Santiago, 1950-61; dir. Instituto de Extension Musical, 1957-59; founder, chmn. dept. music Cath. U., Santiago, 1959-61; prof. music, dir. Latin Am. Music Center, Sch. Music, Ind. U., Bloomington, 1961-87, now prof. emeritus; chmn. composition dept. Latin Am. Music Center, Sch. Music, Ind. U., 1975-79; mem. Contemporary Music Panel, NEA, Washington, 1978-80; hon. prof. U. Autonoma, Madrid, Spain, 1997. Composer Canciones Castellanas, 1948, Concertos for piano and orch., 1950, 85, Sextet, 1954, 5 symphonies, 1949, 54, 61, 66, 95, 96, string quartets, 1957, 95, The Tumbler's Prayer Ballet, 1960, Sonata a Quattro, 1986, Missa, 1968, The Days of God, 1976, The Celestial City, 1992, Concertos for violin and orch., 1983, concertos for cello and orchestra, 1993, Riley's Merriment, 1986, Partita, 1988, (operas) The Dawn of the Poor King, 1952, Widows, 1990, (cantata) The Heavenly City, 1992, others, inluding chamber music, ballet, choral and solo instrumental music; contbr. articles to profl. jours. and encys. Mem. Frei Found. 5th Centennial of Discovery Commn., 1992. Served with Army of Chile, 1938. Recipient Olga Cohen prize Cohen Found., 1955, 58, Biennial Chilean Music Festival awards, 1948, 50, 54, 58, 60, InterAm. Mistral Cultural prize OAS, 1987, de National Prize Chilean Gov't., 1992; fellow Rockefeller Found., 1944, Guggenheim Found., 1945, 54; grantee Nat. Endowment for the Arts, 1975, 87. Mem. Am. Soc. Univ. Composers, Latin Am. Studies Assn., Interam. Music Council, Nat. Acad. Art (Chile), Broadcast Music Inc. Roman Catholic. Avocations: gardening, water coloring. Home: 490 Serena Ln Bloomington IN 47401-9226

ORRICK, WILLIAM HORSLEY, JR., federal judge; b. San Francisco, Oct. 10, 1915; s. William Horsley and Mary (Downey) O.; m. Marion Naffziger, Dec. 5, 1947; children: Mary-Louise, Marion, William Horsley III. Grad., Hotchkiss Sch., 1933; B.A., Yale, 1937; LL.B., U. Calif.-Berkeley, 1941. Bar: Calif. 1941. Partner Orrick, Dahlquist, Herrington & Sutcliffe, San Francisco, 1941-61; asst. atty. gen. civil div. Dept Justice, 1961-62, antitrust div., 1963-65; dep. under sec. state for adminstrn. Dept. State, 1962-63; practice law San Francisco, 1965-74; former partner firm Orrick, Herrington, Rowley & Sutcliffe; U.S. dist. judge No. Dist. Calif., 1974—. Past pres. San Francisco Opera Assn., Trustee, World Affairs Council; former trustee San Francisco Law Library, San Francisco Found., Children's Hosp. San Francisco, Grace Cathedral Corp. Served to capt. M.I. AUS, 1942-46. Recipient Alumnus of Yr. award Boalt Hall Alumni Assn., U. Calif., 1980. Fellow Am. Bar Found.; mem. Bar Assn. San Francisco (past trustee, treas.). Office: US Dist Ct PO Box 36060 450 Golden Gate Ave San Francisco CA 94102

ORRINGER, MARK BURTON, surgeon, educator; b. Pitts., Apr. 19, 1943; s. Harry B. and Alta (Moses) O.; m. Susan Michaels, June 20, 1964; children: Jeffrey Scott, Lisa Jill. BA, U. Pitts., 1963, MD, 1967. Diplomate Am. Bd. Surgery, Am. Bd. Thoracic Surgery. Resident Johns Hopkins Hosp., Balt., 1967-73; from asst. prof. to prof. surgery U. Mich. Med. Sch., Ann Arbor, 1973-80, prof. surgery, 1980—, John Alexander disting. prof. thoracic surgery, 1996; head sect. thoracic surgery U. Mich. Med. Sch., Ann Arbor, 1985—; dir. Am. Bd. Thoracic Surgery, 1988-95. Co-editor: (with Waldhausen) Complications in Cardiothoracic Surgery, Mosby Year Book, 1991, (with Zuidema) Shackelford's Surgery of the Alimentary Tract, vol. 1 - The Esophagus, 3d edit., 1991, 4th edit. 1995; contbr. over 150 articles to profl. jours., over 95 chpts. to books. Capt. USAR, 1974-76. Named among the best med. specialists in the U.S., Town and Country mag., 1984, 89, among the 400 best drs. in Am., Good Housekeeping mag., 1991; recipient Bicentennial Medal of Distinction, U. Pitts., 1987. Fellow ACP; mem. Thoracic Surgery Dirs. Assn. (sec., treas. 1991-95, pres. elect 1996), Soc. Thoracic Surgeons, Am. Coll. Chest Physicians, Am. Assn. Thoracic Surgery, Soc. Univ. Surgeons, Internat. Soc. Surgery, Am. Surg. Assn., Internat. Soc. Diseases Esophagus, Halsted Soc., Phi Beta Kappa, Alpha Omega Alpha. Avocations: swimming, scuba diving, hiking. Office: U Mich Med Ctr 1500 E Med Ctr Dr Ann Arbor MI 48109

ORRMONT, ARTHUR, writer, editor; b. Albany, N.Y., July 3, 1922; m. Lora Orenstein, Oct. 6, 1956 (div. 1965); m. Leonie Rosenstiel, Aug. 22, 1995. Student, U. Ala., 1941, U. Mich., 1942-45, Cornell U., 1945; BA, U. Mich., 1945. Editl. dept. head Farrar, Straus & Co., N.Y.C., 1945-51; sr. editor Popular Libr., N.Y.C., 1951-55; exec. editor Fawcett Books, N.Y.C., 1955-57; pres., editl. dir. Author Aid Assocs., N.Y.C., 1967—; v.p. Rsch. Assocs. Internat., N.Y.C., 1980—; lectr. creative writing CCNY, 1966, Columbia U., 1967. Author: Love Cults and Faith-Healers, 1961, (with Capt. Marion Aten) Last Train Over Rostov Bridge, 1962, Brit. edit., 1962, Indestructible Commodore Matthew Perry, 1962, Japanese edit., 1963, Amazing Alexander Hamilton, 1964, Portuguese edit., 1965, Chinese Gordon: Hero of Khartoum, 1966, Fighter Against Slavery: Jehudi Ashmun, 1966, Mr. Lincoln's Master Spy: Lafayette Baker, 1966, Diplomat in Warpaint: Chief Alexander Gillivray of the Creeks, 1967, Richard Burton, 1969, Brit. edit., 1969, James Buchanan Eads: The Man Who Mastered the Mississippi, 1970, (with Fr. Joseph Lauro) Action Priest, 1970, French edit., 1970, Requiem for War: The Life of Wilfred Owen, 1972; editor: (with Leonie Rosenstiel) Literary Agents of North America, 1984, 5th edit., 1995; editor Nat. Hall of Fame Biography series, 1970-72. With U.S. Army, 1942. Recipient Avery Hopwood award for short story U. Mich., 1943, 44, 45.

ORSATTI, ALFRED KENDALL, organization executive; b. Los Angeles, Jan. 31, 1932; s. Alfredo and Margaret (Hayes) O.; m. Patricia Decker, Sept. 11, 1960; children: Scott, Christopher, Sean. B.S., U. So. Calif., 1956. Assoc. prodr., v.p. Sabre Prodns., L.A., 1957-58; assoc. prodr. Ror Vic Prodns., L.A., 1958-59; bus. rep. AFTRA, L.A., 1960-61; Hollywood exec., sec. SAG, L.A., 1961-81, nat. exec. dir., 1981—; trustee Pension Welfare Plan SAG, 1971—; del. Los Angeles County Fedn. Labor, Los Angeles, Hollywood Film Council, Los Angeles; v.p., mem. exec. Calif. Fedn. Labor; v.p. Calif. Theatrical Fedn.; chmn. arts, entertainment and media com. dept. profl. employees AFL-CIO. Mem. Mayor's Film Devel. Com., Los Angeles. Mem. Hollywood C. of C. (bd. dirs.), Actors and Artists Am. Assn. (1st v.p.). Office: SAG 5757 Wilshire Blvd Los Angeles CA 90036-3635

ORSBON, RICHARD ANTHONY, lawyer; b. North Wilkesboro, N.C., Sept. 23, 1947; s. Richard Chapman and Ruby Estelle (Wyatt) O.; m. Susan Cowan Shivers, June 13, 1970; children: Sarah Hollingsworth, Wyatt Benjamin, David Allison. BA Disting. mil. grad. ROTC, Davidson Coll., 1969; JD, Vanderbilt U., 1972; honor grad. Officers Basic Course, U.S. Army, 1972. Bar: N.C. 1972, U.S. Dist. Ct. (we. dist.) N.C., 1972; cert. specialist in probate and fiduciary law. Assoc. Kennedy, Covington, Lobdell & Hickman, Charlotte, N.C., 1972-75; assoc. Parker, Poe et al, Charlotte, 1975-77, ptnr. 1978—; lectr. on estate planning, probate. Assoc. editor, contbr. Vanderbilt Law Rev., 1971-72. Pres. ECO, Inc., Charlotte, 1982—; bd. dirs. Charlotte United Way, 1983—; mem. planning bd. Queens Coll. Estate Planning Day, 1978—, chmn., 1991; active Myers Park United Meth. Ch., chmn. adminstrv. bd., 1994-96; trustee Davidson Coll., 1990-91, Camp Tekoa. Hendersonville, N.C.; mem. YMCA basketball com., Dem. precinct chmn., 1980-86; mem. Dem. state exec. com., 1980; bd. dirs. law explorer program Boy Scouts Am., Charlotte, 1976-78; bd. vis. Johnson C. Smith Univ., 1986-89. 1st lt. U.S. Army, 1972-73. Named Outstanding Vol., Charlotte Observer/United Way, 1984; Patrick Wilson Merit scholar Vanderbilt U. Law Sch., 1969-72. Mem. ABA (real property probate sect.), N.C. State Bar (cert. specialist estate planning and probate, 1987), N.C. Bar Assn. (probate and fiduciary law sect., author, speaker 1987-92), N.C. Bar Assn. Coll. of Advocacy, Mecklenburg County Bar Assn. (law day com., vol. lawyers program, bd. dirs., chmn. 1988-89, grievance com. 1987-88), Deans Assn. of Vanderbilt U. Law Sch. (bd. dirs.), Davidson Coll. Alumni Assn. (bd. dirs. 1983, class alumni sec. 1986—, pres.-elect 1989-90, pres. 1990-91, bd. dirs. Wildcat Club 1989—, pres. 1993—), Charlotte Estate Planning Coun. (exec. com., 1992—, sec. 1994—, pres. 1996-97), Foxcroft Swim and Racquet Club (pres. 1986-87, bd. dirs. 1985-88), Omicron Delta Kappa. Home: 2819 Rothwood Dr Charlotte NC 28211-2623 Office: Parker Poe Thompson 2600 Charlotte Plz Charlotte NC 28244

ORSEE, JOE BROWN, library director; b. Fulton, Ky., Oct. 25, 1949; divorced; children: Amy, Matthew. BS in Libr. Sci., Murray State U., 1971, MS in Libr. Sci., 1972. Assoc. regional libr. Barren River Regional Libr., Russellville, Ky., 1972-73; dir. interlibr. cooperation Ky. Dept. Libr. and Archives, Frankfort, 1973-76; libr. cons. Miss. Libr. Commn., Jackson, 1976, asst. dir. adminstrn., 1976-78, dir., 1978-80; dir. pub. libr. svcs. Ga. Dept. Edn., Atlanta, 1980-95; dir. N.W. Ga. Regional Libr., Daton, Ga., 1995—; co-chmn. Gov.'s Conf. on Libr. and Info. Svcs.; past vice-chmn. White House Conf. Libr. and Info. Svcs. Task Force.; del. 1st and 2d White House Confs. Libr. and Info. Scis. Contbr. articles to profl. jours., fed. and state docs.; guest spkr. in field. Mem. ALA, S.E. Libr. Assn. (pres.), Ga. Libr. Assn. Home: 214 Calhoun Ave Calhoun GA 30701 Office: NW Ga Regional Libr 310 Cappes St Dalton GA 30720-4123

ORSER, EARL HERBERT, insurance company executive; b. Toronto, Ont., Can., July 5, 1928; s. Frank Herbert and Ethel Marjorie (Cox) O.; m. Marion Queenie Ellis, Aug. 4, 1951; children: Darlene, Barbara, Beverley, Nancy. B in Comm., U. Toronto, 1950, Chartered Acct., 1953. bd. dirs. London, Ont.; chmn. bd. dirs. SPAR Aerospace Ltd., Inter-Provincial Pipe Line Ltd. With Clarkson Gordon, 1950-61, ptnr., 1958-61; treas. Anthes Imperial Ltd., 1961-63, v.p. fin., 1963-68, also bd. dirs.; sr. v.p. Molson Industries Ltd., 1968-70, also bd. dirs.; v.p. fin. Air Can., Montreal, Que., 1970-73; with T. Eaton Co. Ltd., Toronto, 1973-77, pres., CEO, 1975-77; exec. v.p., COO London Life Ins. Co. subs. Lonvest Corp., Ont., 1978-80; pres. London Life Ins. Co. subs. London Ins. Group, 1980-81, COO, 1980-81, CEO, 1981-89, chmn. bd. dirs.; Mem. univ. coll. com. U. Toronto, Ont., Can., Geneva Assn., Brit.-N.Am. Com. Mem. London Club (Ont.), Granite Club, St. James' of Montreal Club, Toronto Club, Nat. Toronto Rosedale Golf Club, London Hunt and Country Club. Mem. Can. Life and Health Ins. Assn. (chmn. 1987-88), London Club (Ont.), Granite Club, St. James' of Montreal Club, Toronto Club, Nat. Toronto Rosedale Golf Club, London Hunt and Country Club. Office: London Life Ins Co, 255 Dufferin Ave, London, ON Canada N6A 4K1

ORSILLO, JAMES EDWARD, computer systems engineer, company executive; b. Elmira, N.Y., Oct. 30, 1939; s. Giacomo and Irene (Heppy) O.; 1 child, June Lynne. BEE, RCA Insts., 1962; BS in Elec. Engring. and Math., Ind. Inst. Tech., 1964; MS, Rensselaer Poly., 1968; BS in Nuclear Engring., Capital Radio Electronic Inst., 1974. Communications engr. Bell Telephone Labs., Holmdel, N.J., 1962-63; video engr. Westinghouse, Elmira, N.Y., 1965-66; computer engr. GE, Pittsfield, Mass., 1966-67; systems specialist Control Data Corp., Mpls., 1968-70; software specialist Computer Sci. Corp., Morristown, N.Y., 1970-72; prin. cons. Computer Cons. Assocs., Elmira, 1972-78; CEO ORTHSTAR, Inc., Elmira, 1974—; acquired Hughes Tng., Inc. Rail Simulation Bus., 1996—; owner, pres. Shadowstand Properties, Inc. (FKA O-K Properties), Elmira, 1984—, Thundering Hooves Stables, Elmira, 1985—. Mem. IEEE, Am. Nuclear Soc., Soc. Indsl. and Applied Math., Am. Helicopter Soc., Army Aviation Assn. Am., Internat. Flying Engrs., USAF Assn., U.S. Naval League, U.S. Polo Assn. Republican. Achievements include invention of Integrated Data Acquisition System (IDAS), of Thread Algebra used in simulation development, of Extended Sentient Non-linear Ensemble (ESNE). Office: ORTHSTAR Inc Airport Corp Park PO Box 459 Big Flats NY 14814

ORSINI, ERIC ANDREW, army official; b. Lodi, N.J., Jan. 7, 1918; s. Serafino and Valentina Lena (Dinino) O.; m. Mildred Jean Andre, Feb. 8, 1947; children: Donna Jean, Debra Jane. BS, GED, Fort Knox, Ky., 1948; student, Def. Sys. Mgmt. Coll., Ft. Belvoir, Va., 1978, Harvard U., 1982, George Washington U., 1986. Registered mech. engr. Commd. 2d lt. armor U.S. Army, 1943, advanced through grades to col., 1965, transfer to Ordinance Corps., 1958, ret., 1971, appt. dep. asst. sec. for logistics, 1971—. Developer policy guidance mil. identification symbology technologies LOGMARS, 1982; policy developer mil. ordnance/maintenance policies and procedures. Decorated Purple Heart, Silver Star, Bronze Star, Legion of Merit; named to Ordnance Hall of Fame, 1991; recipient Presdl. Meritorious Exec. award, 1991, 94. Avocations: golf, fishing. Office: Office Asst Sec Army Installations Logistics 110 Army Pentagon Washington DC 20310-0110

ORSINI, MYRNA J., sculptor, educator; b. Spokane, Wash., Apr. 19, 1943; d. William Joseph Finch and Barbara Jean (Hilby) Hickenbottom; m. Donald Wayne Lundquist, Mar. 31, 1962 (div. Mar. 1987); children: Laurie Jeanine Winter, Stephanie Lynne Lundquist. BA, U. Puget Sound, 1969, MA, 1974; postgrad., U. Ga., 1987. Tchr. Tacoma (Wash.) Pub. Schs., 1969-78; owner, pres. Contemporary Print Collectors, Lakewood, Wash., 1978-81, Orsini Studio, Tacoma, 1985—. Sculptor: works include Vartai symbolic gate for Ctrl. Europas Park, Vilnius, Lithuania, 1994; Menat steel and neon corp. commn. completed in Tacoma, Wash. 1995. Chair Supt.'s Supervisory Com., Tacoma, 1978-79; lobbyist Citizens for Fair Sch. Funding, Seattle, 1979; art chair Women's Pres. Coun., Tacoma, 1987-88; founder, bd. dirs. Monarch Contemporary Art Ctr., Wash. Recipient 1st pl. sculpture award Pleinair Symposium Com., Ukraine, 1992, Peron Symposium Com., Kiev, Ukraine, 1993; recognized 1st Am. sculptor to exhibit work in Ukraine, 1993; prin. works include seven monumental sculptures worldwide. Mem. N.W. Stone Sculptors Assn. (coun. leader 1989—), Pacific Gallery Artists, Internat. Sculpture Ctr., Tacoma City Club. Avocations: reading, sailing, biking. Office: Orsini Studio PO Box 1125 Tenino WA 98589

ORSINI, PAUL VINCENT, music educator; b. Albany, N.Y., Oct. 4, 1955; s. Paul Vincent and Lucia (Rutolo) O.; m. Yvette Louise Kirk, Apr. 11, 1987. MusB in Music Edn., SUNY, Potsdam, 1977; MusM in Performance, Syracuse U., 1979. Cert. K-12 music tchr., N.Y. Musician Mirage, 1978-79; entertainer The Carmen Canavo Show, Tampa, Fla., 1979-83; freelance entertainer Albany, 1983-86; substitute tchr. Suburban Coun. Schs., Albany, 1983-86; tchr. Corinth (N.Y.) Sch. Dist., 1986-87, Shenendehowa Sch. Dist., Clifton Park, N.Y., 1987—; owner, leader High Society Big Band, Clifton Park, 1988-91. Premiered trumpet compositions of Dr. Brian Israel Syracuse Univ., 1977-79. Advisor Shenendehowa Crisis Intervention Team, Clifton Park, 1988-93; faculty rep., exec. bd. Friends of Music of Shenendehowa, Clifton Park, 1993; active Shenendehowa Partnership Team, 1995—. Mem. Albany Musicians Assn., Internat. Trumpet Guild, N.Y. State Congress of Parents and Tchrs. (hon. life mem.). Avocations: fishing, sports, travel, reading, jazz. Home: 54 Via Da Vinci Clifton Park NY 12065-2906

ORSKI, C. KENNETH, consulting company executive, lawyer; b. Warsaw, Poland, Mar. 7, 1932; came to U.S., 1946; naturalized, 1953; s. Thaddeus and Irene Orski; m. Jocelyne Schule, Aug. 27, 1968; children—Karine N., Monica J.; m. Barbara K. Klema, Apr. 28, 1978; 1 child, Christopher P. A.B., Harvard U., 1953, LL.B., J.D., 1956. Atty. U.S. Atomic Energy Commn., 1956-61; asst. to pres. Gen. Dynamics Corp., Washington, 1961-66; dir. OECD, Paris, fgn. svc. officer. U.S. Dept. State, 1966-73; assoc. adminstr. U.S. Dept. Transp., Washington, 1974-78; pres. Urban Mobility Corp., Washington, 1982—. Contbg. author books in field, 1982, 85; editor, pub. Innovation Briefs, 1991—; contbr. articles to profl. jours. Recipient Outstanding Pub. Service award U.S. Dept. Transp., 1985, Disting. Service award, 1977, Meritorious Service award, 1975. Republican. Home: 4504 Dalton Rd Chevy Chase MD 20815 Office: Urban Mobility Corp 1050 17th St NW Ste 600 Washington DC 20036-5517

ORSZAG, PETER RICHARD, economist; b. Boston, Dec. 16, 1968; s. Steven Alan and Reba (Karp) O.; m. Cameron Rachel Hamill. AB summa cum laude, Princeton U., 1991; MS, London Sch. Econs., 1992, PhD, 1997. Econ. advisor Ministry of Fin., Moscow, 1992-93; staff economist Coun. Econ. Advisers, Washington, 1993-94; prof. rsch. staff London Sch. Econs., 1994-95; sr. economist Coun. Econ. Advisers, Washington, 1995-96, sr. adviser, 1996; sr. econ. advisor Nat. Econ. Coun., 1997—. Marshall scholar, 1991-92. Mem. Am. Econ. Assn., Am. Stats. Assn., Coun. on Fgn. Rels., Phi Beta Kappa. Office: Nat Econ Coun The White House Washington DC 20502

ORTH-AIKMUS, GAIL MARIE, police chief; b. Kansas City, Dec. 31, 1956; d. Ben Roy and Janet Ferrell (Buckner) O.; m. Frank Henry Aikmus Jr., Oct. 5, 1980 (div. Oct. 1990); 1 child, Brian Russell. Cert. law enforcement officer, Mo.; cert. drug canine handler; cert. vanner. Patrol officer Parkville (Mo.) Police Dept., 1977-78; deputy Platte County Sheriff, Platte City, Mo., 1978-79; patrol officer, sgt., lt. Pleasant Valley (Mo.) Police Dept.,

1979-85, police chief, 1985-95; police chief Avondale (Mo) Police Dept., 1995-96; dep. sheriff Clay County Police Dept., Liberty, Mo., 1996—; bd. dirs. Clay County Investigative, pres. bd. dirs., 1991-93; guest spkr. Clay County Mcpl. Judges Conf.; testified before House Com. with Mo. Ho. of Reps., 1994. Appeared in fraud investigation on ABC 20/20 mag., 1980. Named Officer of Yr. Vets. Fgn. Wars Aux., Kansas City, 1991; recipient Key to Manor Pleasant Valley Manor, 1990, Puppy Trucker award Heart of Am. Van Club, 1994, Lifesaving award ribbon, 1996, Unit citation ribbon, 1996. Mem. Mo. Police Chief's Assn., Mo. Peace Officer's Assn., Kansas City Police Chief's Assn., Kansas City Major Case Squad, Kansas City Women in Law Enforcement, Nat. Assn. Chief's of Police, NRA, Weimaraner Club Am., Weimaraner Club Greater Kansas City (pres. 1991—), World Wide Race Fans. Avocations: hunting, dog training, dogs shows, camping, crafts. Home: 8405 Kaill Rd Pleasant Valley MO 64068 Office: Clay County Sheriffs Liberty MO 64068

ORTHWEIN, WILLIAM COE, mechanical engineer; b. Toledo, Jan. 27, 1924; s. William Edward and Millie Minerva (Coe) O.; m. Helen Virginia Poindexter, Feb. 1, 1948; children—Karla Frances, Adele Diana, Maria Theresa. B.S., M.I.T., 1946; M.S., U. Mich., 1951, Ph.D., 1959. Registered profl. engr., Ill., Ind., Ky. Aerophysicist Gen. Dynamics Co., Ft. Worth, 1951-52; research asso. U. Mich., 1952-59; adv. engr. IBM Corp., Owego, N.Y., 1959-61; dir. computer centers U. Okla., Norman, 1961-63; research scientist Ames Lab., NASA, Moffett Field, Calif., 1963-65; mem. faculty So. Ill. U., Carbondale, 1965—; prof. engring. So. Ill. U., 1967—; cons. in field. Author: Clutches and Brakes, 1986, Machine Component Design, 1990; papers, revs., books in field. Pres. Jackson County (Ill.) Taxpayers Assn., 1976. Served with AUS, 1943-46. Mem. ASME (Outstanding Svc. award 1972), Am. Gear Mfrs. Assn., Am. Acad. Mechanis, Soc. Automotive Engrs., Ill. Acad. Sci., Ill. Soc. Profl. Engrs. (chmn. salary and employment com. 1974, chmn. ad hoc com. continuing edn. 1975), NRA, Aircraft Owners and Pilots Assn., Sigma Xi. Mem. LDS Ch. Home: 879 Springer Ridge Rd Carbondale IL 62901-7906 Office: So Ill U Dept Engring Carbondale IL 62901 *Success in engineering is, I believe, contingent upon one's ability to see the world as it really is, to quickly gain insight enough to detect fundamental parameters that determine behavior of the system in question, to conduct a straightforward check of one's analysis, and to simply synthesize a means of modifying and/or controlling the parameters to obtain the desired results. These ingredients apply to both physical mechanisms and to human organizations—only the means of implementation differ.*

ORTIQUE, REVIUS OLIVER, JR., city official; b. New Orleans, June 14, 1924; s. Revius Oliver and Lillie Edith (Long) O.; m. Miriam Marie Victorianne, Dec. 29, 1947; children—Rhesa Marie (Mrs. Alden J. McDonald). AB, Dillard U., 1947; MA, Ind. U., 1949; JD, So. U., 1956; LLD (hon.), Campbell Coll., 1960; LHD (hon.), Ithaca Coll., 1971; LLD (hon.), Ind. U., 1983, Morris Brown Coll., 1992, Loyola U. South, 1993, Dillard U., 1996. Bar: La. 1956, U.S. Dist. Ct 1956, Eastern Dist. La 1956, U.S. Fifth Circuit Ct. of Appeals 1956, U.S. Supreme Ct 1956. Practiced in New Orleans, 1956-79; judge Civil Dist. Ct. for Orleans Parish, 1979-92; assoc. justice La. Supreme Ct., 1993-94; chmn. New Orleans Aviation Bd., 1994—; lectr. labor law Dillard U., 1950-52, U. West Indies, 1986-94; formerly assoc. gen. counsel Cmty. Improvement Agy.; gen. counsel 8th Dist. A.M.E. Ch.; mem. Fed. Hosp. Coun., 1966, Pres.'s Commn. on Campus Unrest, 1970, Bd. Legal Svcs. Corp., 1975-83; chief judge civil cts. Orleans Parish, 1986-87; spkr. in field. Contbr. articles to profl. jours. Former pres. Met. Area Com.; former mem. Bd. City Trusts, New Orleans, New Orleans Legal Assistance Corp. Bd., Ad Hoc Com. for Devel. of Ctrl. Bus. Dist. City of New Orleans; bd. dirs. Cmty. Rels. Coun., Am. Lung Assn.; trustee Antioch Coll. Law, New Orleans chpt. Operation PUSH, 1981—; pres. Louis A. Martinet Soc., 1959; active World's Fair, New Orleans, 1984, Civil Rights Movement, 1960-79; bd. dirs., mem. exec. com. Nat. Sr. Citizens Law Ctr., L.A., 1970-76, Criminal Justice Coordinating Com., UN Assn. New Orleans, 1980—; former mem. exec. bd. Nat. Bar Found.; mem. exec. com. econ. Devel. Coun. Greater New Orleans; past chmn. Health Edn. Authority of La.; trustee, mem. exec. com. Dillard U.; former mem. bd. mgmt. Flint Goodridge Hosp.; mem. adv. bd. League Women Voters Greater New Orleans; mem. men's adv. bd. YWCA; trustee AME Ch., aldo connectional trustee; chancellor N.O. Fedn. Chs.; bd. dirs. Nat. Legal Aid and Defender Assn.; bd. trustees Civil Justice Found.; served on over 50 bds., commns. 1st lt. AUS, 1943-47, PTO. Recipient Arthur von Briesen medal Disting. Svcs. Disadvantaged Ams. NLADA, 1971, Weiss award NCCJ, 1975, Brotherhood award NCCJ, 1976, Nat. Black Achievement award, 1979, Poor People's Banner award, 1979, William H. Hastie award, 1983, Outstanding Citizen award Kiwanis of Pontchartrain, 1986, Civil Justice award, 1989, Daniel E. Byrd award NAACP, 1991, A.P. Tureaud Meml. medal La. State NAACP, 1993; Revius O. Ortique Jr. Law Libr. named in his honor, Lafayette, La., 1988; named Outstanding Young Man Nat. Urban League, 1958, Outstanding Person in La. Inst. Human Understanding, 1976, Citizen of Yr. Shreveport, 1993. Mem. ABA (del., Legal Svcs. program, Nat. adv. coun., 1964-71, jud. divsn.), Nat. Bar Assn. (pres. 1965-66, exec. bd., Raymond Pace Alexander award, jud. coun. 1987, William Hastie award 1982, Gertrude E. Rush award 1991), La. State Bar Assn. (former mem. ho. of dels., Lifetime Achievement award 1986), Nat. Legal Aid and Defender Assn. (past pres., mem. exec. bd.), La. District Judges Assn., Am. Judicature Soc. (bd. dirs. 1975-79), Civil Justice Found. (trustee), Louis A. Martinet Legal Soc., World Peace Through Law (charter mem.), Blue Key Honor Soc., Phi Delta Kappa, Alpha Kappa Delta. Home: 10 Park Island Dr New Orleans LA 70122-1229 Office: New Orleans Aviation Bd PO Box 20007 New Orleans LA 70141-0007 *In 1989 the National Black Law Journal in cooperation with the UCLA Law Center published: Struggle: A Power Reserved to the People, which was distributed nationwide in commemoration of Black History month, the State of Louisiana thru the office of the Secretary of State has permanently installed a life size portrait of Justice Ortique in the gallery of the State Archives the Law Day Celebration on college campuses, 1992. "With little or no effort on our part, life unfolds with opportunities and rewards, except that we permit our frailties to enslave our ambitions. I am grateful that there are only horizons."*

ORTIZ, ANGEL VICENTE, church administrator; b. L.A., Nov. 9, 1956; s. Benjamin and Petra (Santiago) O.; m. Michele Annette Gaunt, May 5, 1979; children: Angela Nicole, Michael David. BS in Bibl. Studies, Ft. Wayne (Ind.) Bible Coll., 1982. Ordained to ministry Christian and Missionary Alliance, 1987. Pastor, ch. planter Christian and Missionary Alliance, Chula Vista, Calif., 1983-90; supt. Spanish western dist. Christian and Missionary Alliance, Escondido, Calif., 1991-96, also nat. conf. speaker, evangelist; asst. to the pres. for program devel. Nyack (N.Y.) Coll., 1996—. Republican. Avocations: camping, woodworking, refinishing, travel, teaching. Home: 21A College Ave Nyack NY 10960

ORTIZ, FERNANDO, JR., small business consultant; b. Havana, Cuba, Dec. 2, 1951; came to the U.S., 1961; m. Frances K. Ortiz; children: William, Fernando III. Attended, Miami-Dade C.C., 1972-74, U. Miami, Coral Gables, Fla., 1974-75, Fla. Internat. U., Miami, 1975-76; MD, U. Centro Estudios Technicos, Santo Domingo, Dominican Republic, 1981. Mgr. Ortiz Transp., Miami, 1981-84; ptnr. Astrum, Syracuse, N.Y., 1984-91; bus. developer Rebuild Syracuse, Inc., 1991-92; coord. Urban Bus. Opportunity Ctr. City of Syracuse, 1992-96, sr. econ. devel. officer, 1996—; mem. adv. bd. Greater Syracuse Small Bus. Loan Program, 1993—. Sec. bd. dirs. Onondaga Spanish Action League, Syracuse, 1994-95, pres., 1996; bd. dirs. Leadership Greater Syracuse, 1994—, Frank H. Hiscock Legal Aid Soc., Syracuse, 1996—; active Onondaga Citizens League, Syracuse, 1995; corp. mem. United Way Ctrl. N.Y.; mem. bus. and industry adv. bd. Onondaga C.C. Named Min. Small Bus. Adv. of Yr., U.S. SBA, Syracuse, 1995. Mem. U.S. Assn. Small Bus. and Entrepreneurship. Avocations: reading, gardening, music. Home: 1412 Lemoyne Ave Syracuse NY 13208 Office: City of Syracuse Office Econ Devel 221 City Hall Syracuse NY 13202

ORTIZ, FRANCIS VINCENT, JR., retired ambassador; b. Santa Fe, Mar. 14, 1926; s. Francis Vincent and Margaret Mary (Delgado) O.; m. Dolores Duke, May 2, 1953; children: Christina, Francis, Stephen, James. BS, Georgetown U., 1950, postgrad., 1951-53; postgrad., U. Madrid, Spain, 1950, Am. U. Beirut, Lebanon, 1952; MS, George Washington U., 1967; LLD (hon.), U. N.Mex., 1986. Joined U.S. Fgn. Service, 1951; asst. officer charge Egyptian affairs State Dept., 1951-53; 3d sec. embassy Addis Ababa, Ethiopia, 1953-55; 2d sec. Am. embassy, Mexico City, 1955-57; spl. asst. to ops. coordinator Office Undersec. State, 1957-60, staff asst. to asst. sec. interam. affairs, 1960-61; spl. asst. Am. ambassador to Mexico, 1961-63; officer charge Spanish affairs State Dept., 1963-66; assigned Nat. War Coll., 1966; chief polit. sect. Am. embassy, Lima, Peru, 1967-70; dep. chief of mission Am. embassy, Montevideo, Uruguay, 1970-72; charge' d'affairs Am. embassy, 1973; country dir. for Argentina, Uruguay and Paraguay, 1973-75; dep. exec. sec. Dept. State, 1975-77; ambassador to Barbados and Grenada, spl. rep. to Antigua, Dominica, St. Christopher-Nevis-Anguilla, St. Lucia & St. Vin, 1977-79; U.S. ambassador to Guatemala, 1979-80; spl. advisor for polit. affairs U.S. So. Command, Panama, 1980-81; U.S. ambassador to Peru, 1981-83, to Argentina, 1983-86; diplomat-in-residence U. N.Mex., Santa Fe, 1986-88; spl. asst. to under sec. of state for mgmt., 1988-90, ret., 1990. With USAAF, 1944-46. Decorated Air medal; Knight of Malta; recipient Honor award Dept. State, 1952, Superior Service award, 1964, Unit Superior Service award, 1973, Meritorious Civilian Svc. award U.S. Sec. of Def. 1981; Orden del Quetzal (Guatemala), 1980; Gran Cruz Merito Civil award (Spain), 1980; Gran Cruz Orden de Mayo (Argentina), 1991; U.S., Mexican Presdl. Chamizal Commemorative medals, 1964. Mem. Am. Fgn. Service Assn., Sigma Chi. Roman Catholic.

ORTIZ, GERMAINE LAURA DE FEO, secondary education educator, counselor; b. Astoria, N.Y., Aug. 6, 1947; d. Andrew and Germaine Laura (Fournier) De Feo; m. Dennis Manfredo, June 6, 1970 (annulled July 1975); m. Angel Manuel Ortiz, July 11, 1975; 1 child, Germaine Angela. AA, Suffolk County C.C., Selden, N.Y., 1969; BA magma cum laude, SUNY, Stony Brook, 1971, MALS, 1974; MS in Edn. with distinction, Hofstra U., 1989. Cert. N-6, 7-12 social studies tchr., sch. counselor, N.Y.; cert. rank II social studies, jr. coll. tchr., sch. counselor, Fla. Tchr. social studies Connetquot Cen. Sch. Dist. Islip, Bohemia, N.Y., 1971—. Mem. ASCD, NEA, N.Y. State Unified Tchrs., Connetquot Tchrs. Assn., Nat. Coun. for Social Studies, N.Y. Coun. for Social Studies, L.I. Coun. for Social Studies, Hofstra U. Alumni Assn., Suffolk County C.C. Alumni Assn., DAV Aux., Vietnam Vets. Am. Aux. Roman Catholic. Avocations: swimming, exercise, meteorology. Home: 5 Honey Ln W Miller Place NY 11764-1719 Office: Connetquot Cen Sch Dist Islip 780 Ocean Ave Bohemia NY 11716-3631

ORTIZ, JAMES GEORGE, data information services company executive; b. Boston, June 6, 1961. BA suma cum laude, Monterey Inst. Internat. Studies, 1989, MA, 1990. Instr. lang. Blue Mountain C.C., Pendleton, Oreg., 1990—; pres., CEO, Data Info. Svc., Inc., Toppenish, Wash., 1991-93; safety dir. Marlette Homes, Inc., Hermiston, Oreg., 1993—. Regional dir. CASA of Oreg., Hermiston, 1990. Scholar Chevron Co., 1988-89. Mem. Am. Soc. Safety Engrs. Republican. Adventist. Avocations: marathon running, scuba diving, piloting small engine aircraft.

ORTIZ, KATHLEEN LUCILLE, travel consultant; b. Las Vegas, N.Mex., Feb. 8, 1942; d. Arthur L. and Anna (Lopez) O. BA, Loretto Hghts. Coll., 1963; MA, Georgetown U., 1966; cert. tchg., Highlands U., 1980; cert. travel, ABQ Travel Sch., 1984. Mgr. Montezuma Sq., Las Vegas, 1966-70; office mgr. Arts Food Market, Las Vegas, 1971-75; tchr. Robertson H.S., Las Vegas, 1976-80; registered rep. IDS Fin. Svcs., N.Mex., 1980-84; travel cons. VIP Travel & Tours, Albuquerque, 1985-86, New Horizons Travel, Albuquerque, 1986-87, All World Travel, Albuquerque, 1987-90, Premium Travel Svcs., Albuquerque, 1990-91; travel cons., group tours Going Places Travel, Albuquerque, 1991—. Contbr. 100 articles to newspapers. Founding mem. Citizens Com. for Hist. Preservation, Las Vegas, 1977-79; fund raiser St. Anthony's Hosp., Las Vegas, 1969-75; mem. Hispanic Geneol. Rsch. Ctr., 1996—. Mem. LWV (numerous positions), Internat. Airlines Travel Agent Network, Airlines Reporting Corp. Agent, Georgetown Club of N.Mex. (bd. dirs. at large 1991-94), Hispanic Geneal. Rsch. Ctr. N.Mex. Avocations: tennis, langs., photography, writing. Home: 7600 Adele Pl NE Albuquerque NM 87109-5362 Office: Going Places Travel 6400 Uptown Blvd NE Ste 429E Albuquerque NM 87110-4290

ORTIZ, PAULINA PATRICIA, banker, research analyst; b. Panama City, Panama; came to U.S., 1964; d. Felix Alejandro Córdova and Esther (Burke) Blackburn; m. Philip Ortiz (dec. 1985); 1 child, Vanessa D. Grad. in bus. adminstrn., Excelsior Coll., Jamaica, 1962; student, Staten Island C.C., 1977-80, Bklyn. Coll., 1994, Pace U., 1980-85. Cert. data processor and computer programmer. Sec. Dr. Carlos Ibanez, Balboa, Panama, 1964; claims examiner Associated Hosp. Svcs. Greater N.Y., N.Y.C., 1965-66; comptometer operator Lerner Shops Exec. Office, N.Y.C., 1966-69; interect clk. examiner Citibank, N.A., N.Y.C., 1969-70, investigator, corr. clk., 1970-72, claims examiner, 1973, svc. asst., 1973-76, ombudsperson, 1976-79, couselor, 1979-84, customer svc. rep. for S.Am. and Carribean, 1984-86, rsch. investigator, 1986-93, rsch. analyst, 1993—. Former mem. East Bklyn. Chs. for devel. of Nehemiah Housing Project, 1984; mem. fin. com. Our Lady of Charity, former mem. alter guild, mem. ushers com., bd. trustees, sec. parish coun. on fund raiser com., v.p. and pres. Pastor's Aid Soc., 1986; campaign worker Howard Golden for Bklyn. Borough Pres., Congressman Adolphus Towns, 1986, Dist. Leader DaCosta Headley, 1994, Assemblyman Ed Griffith, 1988; candidate Sch. Bd. Dist. # 19, 1989; chairperson Linden Plz. Leaseholders, 1990-92; co-writer bylaws New Linden Plz. Tenants Assn., 1991-92, active, 1992—; charter mem. Day of Independence Com. of Panamanians in N.Y., 1993—; counselor St. Paul's Ch., 1994; active Divino Niño Jesus, 1994; treas., bd. dirs. Urban Bankers Coalition, 1995—, mem. Ea. regional com., 1997. Recipient Appreciation cert. as charter mem. Dem. Sen. task force Dem. Senatorial Campaign Com., 1994, Appreciation cert. Pres. Bill Clinton for support of Dem. Nat. Com., 1994, Outstanding Cmty. Svc. award Sen. Ada L. Smith, 1994, Third Degree, Grand Lady Carmela Rodriguez, 1993, Merit cert. Fourth Degree Georgiana Evans, Faithful Navigator, Ladies of Grace, 1993, Women's History Month Spl. Recognition award Congressman Adolphus Towns, 1989, Mother of Yr. award Jr. Daus. Ct. 229, 1990, Partner in Edn. award Adopt-a-Class Program N.Y. Bd. Edn., 1992-93, Hon. Trustee cert. Am. Indian Relief Coun., 1994, Citizenship cert. Boys Town, 1994, Silver Leader of Yr. cert. DAV Comdrs. Club, 1994, Cmty. award Office Black Ministry, Bklyn., 1995. Mem. Urban Bankers Coalition, Knights of Peter Claver & Ladies' Aux. Ct. (vice grand lady of ct. 229 in Bklyn. 1984, grand lady of ct. 229 in Bklyn. 1985, 86, 87, co-founder chpt. 33, established ct. 333 in Queens, N.Y., area dep. N.Y.C.). Avocations: dancing, cooking, mentoring, opera.

ORTIZ, RAPHAEL MONTAÑEZ, performance artist, educator; b. Bklyn., Jan. 30, 1934; s. Joseph H. and Eusabia (Velazquez) O. BS, Pratt Inst., 1964, MFA, 1964; MEd, Columbia U., 1974, EdD, 1982. Instr. grad. art faculty Tchr. Coll. Columbia U., N.Y.C., 1967; instr. art NYU, N.Y.C., 1968; adj. prof. art Fordham U., N.Y.C., 1971, C. W. Post Coll., L.I., N.Y., 1971; adj. prof. art Livingston Coll. Rutgers U., New Brunswick, N.J., 1971, assoc. prof. art Livingston Coll., 1972; assoc. prof. grad. and undergrad. faculty Mason Gross Sch. Arts Rutgers U., 1972, prof. I Mason Gross Sch. Arts, 1991—; lectr., panelist Sch. of Visual Arts 4th Ann. Nat. Conf. on Edn. of Artist, 1990, Internat. Exposition: Art Miami Art and Tech., 1995; panelist, moderator The Artist in Multiculturalism and Art History, Alternative Mus., Soho, N.Y.C., 1992, numerous others; The Robert Flaherty seminar spkr. Its All Digital, Wells Coll., Aurora, N.Y., 1993, The Mus. of Modern Art panelist the Artist as Activist, 1993, Cleve. Ctr. for Contemporary Art panelist: Performance is Dead Long Live Performance, 1994, others; presenter in field. Numerous one-man performances including Piano Destruction concert, BBC, London, 1966, Mother Father, Mercury Theater, London, 1966, Paper Bag and Piano Destruction concert, Fordham U., N.Y.C., 1967, Ecce Homo Gallery, N.Y.C., 1967, Piano Destruction concert, Bitter End Cafe, N.Y.C., 1967, Piano Destruction concert, Johnny Carson Show, 1968, Riverside Ch., N.Y.C., 1968, Theater Ritual, Middle Atlantic States regional meeting Am. Theater Assn., Temple U., Phila., 1970, Crossing, Mime Theater, N.Y.C., 1976, physio-psycho-alchemy San Francisco Art Inst., 1982, UCLA, 1985, Twin Palms Gallery, San Francisco, 1985, Museo del Barrio, N.Y.C., 1988, Piano Destruction duet Hommage to Huelsenback, Conz Archival Gallery, Verona, Italy, 1986, Atelier Sommering, Ko, 1990, Antiteatro U. P.R., Cleve. Ctr. Contemporary Art Performance-Installation, 1994, Snug Harbor Cultural Ctr., Performance-Installation, S.I., N.Y., 1995; co-exec. dir. and participant in Art and the Invisible Reality Internat. Symposium, Munich, 1988; organizer, participant Internat. Symposium of Art and the Invisible-Reality, U.S.A., Franklin-Furnace Mus., N.Y.C., Rutgers U., New Brunswick, N.J., 1989, Vision Quest Gallery Rem, Vienna, Austria, 1988, Vision Quest II Bloomfield Coll., N.J., 1989, Piano Destruction concert Hommage to Huelsenbeck, Soul Release project, Alternative Mus., N.Y.C., 1989, Exhbn. Kölnischer Kunstverein, Köln, computer-laser-video, Köln, Fed. Republic Germany, Soul Release-Ritual Kunst Müller Köln, 1989, Soul Release project Piano Sacrifice concert, Atelier Eva Ohlaw Bildskulpturenaktionmusik, Köln, 1990, Decade Show Dance Theater Workshop, N.Y.C., performance-ritual sponsored by the New Mus., N.Y.C., The Mus. of Contemporary Hispanic Art, N.Y.C., The Harlem Mus. of Contemporary Art, N.Y.C., 1990, Alternative Mus., Soho, N.Y.C., 1992, Mus. Modernerkunst, Stiftung Ludwig, 1992, performance-installation, Vienna, 1992, I.S.D.N. Video Conf. interactive audience participation between Kölin and Kassel Germany, The Electronic Cafe Gallery at Documenta, Kassel, 1993, Grand Prix, Regime Lomabdia, Prix Lago Maggiore XIV Festival Internat. de la video et des arts electroniques, Dance Number 22, computer-laser-video, Locarno, Switzerland, 1993, Cleve. Ctr. Contemporary Art, 1994, Museo del Barrio, N.Y.C., 1994, Whitney Biennial: Whitney Mus. of Am. Art, N.Y.C., 1995; one-person sculpture exhbn. Fordham U., N.Y.C., 1967, Museo del Barrio, N.Y.C., 1988, Francesco Conz Archival Gallery, Verona, Italy, 1986, DiMaggio Mus., Milan, Italy, 1989, Ateliér Sommering, Kô, 1990, (sculpture with text) Galerie David, Bielefeld, Germany, 1992, works Children of Treblinka in Memorium, Archaological Find No. 3, Estacion Plaza de Armas, Seville, Spain, 1992, Kunsthalle, Kôlin, 1993, Mus. Modern Art, N.Y.C., 1993, Johnson Mus. at Cornell U., Ithaca, N.Y., 1993, Whitney Mus. Am. Art, N.Y.C., 1993, 97; group shows include Whitney Mus. Am. Art, N.Y.C., 1965, 95, The Object Transformed, sculpture, Mus. Modern Art, N.Y.C., 1966, Franklin Furnace Mus., N.Y.C.; participated in Internat. Destruction in Art Symposium, London, 1966, Finch Coll. Mus. Art Destruction in Art Symposium Sculpture, 1968, sculpture, Everson Mus. Art, Syracuse, N.Y., 1973, sculpture, Chgo. Mus. Comtemporary Art, 1979, Ancient Roots New Visions, sculpture, Palacio de Mineria Mus., Mexico City, 1980, Rutgers Computer Art Group, Walters Gallery, Rutgers U., 1982, computer animation, Paul Robeson Gallery, Rutgers U., 1983, computer art, The Salem Syndrome, Tamasulo Gallery, N.J., 1985, computer graphics and sound, computer-laser-video, Bonnefanten Mus., Maastricht, Holland, 1986, computer-laser-video, De-Haag, Fed. Republic Germany, 1986, computer-laser-video Bridge Game, Mülheim Mus., Fed. Republic Germany, 1986, computer-laser-video, Berlin Internat. Video and Film Festival, Coll. of Art, Gwent, Wales, Eng., 1986, 87, computer-laser-video Techno-Bop 87, The Kitchen, N.Y.C., El Museo del Barrio, 1995; numerous one-man exhbns. including Rene Gallery Video Installation, Music Reconstruction, Amsterdam, Holland, 1988, computer-laser-video, Museo del Barrio, N.Y.C, 1988, Infermental 9, Internat., Video Mag., Dance No. 6, 1989, computer-laser-video, Barcelona Biennale, Spain, 1989, Beograd, Yugoslavia, 1989, Kriens Videodrom, Switzerland, 1989, computer-laser-video, Vienna, Austria, 1990, computer-laser-video, The Internat. Berlin Video and Film Festival, Berlin, 1990, computer-laser-video, Leningrad, Riga-Cine Fantom, USSR, 1990, Video Presentation Series I and II Median Werk Statt, Vienna, 1991, computer-laser-video, Stadtisches Kunstmus., Bonn, 1990, Median Operative, Juried Internat. Video Festival, Berlin, 1992, 6th Juried Internat. Video and TV Festival Montbeliard, France, 1992, Videonale 5 Juried Internat. Video Festival, Bonn, 1993, Video Arco 93 Juried Internat. Video Festival, Madrid, 1993, Mus. Modern Art, Video Works of Latin Am. Artists, Filmreferet Forum Stadpark, Graz, Austria, 1994, Berlin Internat. Film and Video Festival, 1994, Associazione Italiana Cinema d'Essai, 1995, Cinema Video Bienniale, De Lyon, France, 1996, Video Installation Performance, Trinity Video/Inter Access/V-Tape, Toronto, Canada, 1996; represented in mus. collections: sculpture Mattress de-structed by the artist, Mus. Modern Art, 1963, sculpture Disassembled Sofa, Whitney Mus. Am. Art, 1964, sculpture Shoe Construct-Destruct, Memorial to Buchenwald Holocaust Victims, Menil Mus., Houston, 1965, sculpture Disassembled Upholstered Chair, Chrysler Mus., Va., 1965, sculpture Disassembled Sofa, Everson Mus., Syracuse, N.Y., 1972, sculpture Feather Pyramids Museo del Barrio, 1982, computer-laser-video, Museo del Barrio, 1985, computer-laser-video, Everson Mus., Syracuse, N.Y., 1985, computer-laser-video, Friedricheshof Mus., Zurndorf, Austria, 1986, computer-laser-video, Mus. Modern Art, Brussels, 1987, Piano Destruction Fragments, Museo del Barrio, N.Y.C., 1988, Ludwig Mus., Cologne, Fed. Republic Germany, 1988, Centre Georges Pompidou, Paris, 1989, Stadishces Kunst Mus., Bonn, Germany, 1990, Neuer Belriner Kunstverein, Berlin, 1994, and numerous others. Recipient Cert. of Outstanding Achievement in Multicultural Edn., N.J. Dept. Higher Edn., 1993. Mem. Mus. Computer Art (founder, pres. 1984), Hispanic Assn. Higher Edn. (N.J.), Art Educators N.J., Coll. Art Assn., Assn. Rsch. and Enlightenment. Office: Mason Gross Sch Vis Arts New St & Livingston Ave New Brunswick NJ 08904

ORTIZ, SOLOMON P., congressman; b. Robstown, Tex., June 3, 1937; children: Yvette, Solomon P. Student, Del Mar Coll., Corpus Christi, Tex.; cert., Inst. Applied Sci., Chgo.; student, Nat. Sheriff's Tng. Inst., Los Angeles. Constable Neuces County, Tex., 1965-68, commr., 1969-76, sheriff, 1977-82; mem. 98th-105th Congresses from 27th Tex. dist., Washington, D.C., 1983—; mem. armed svcs. com., military installations and facilities subcom., readiness subcom., mcht. marine and fisheries com., subcoms.-environ. & natural resources, oceanography, Gulf of Mex., outer continental shelf, mcht. marine. Served with U.S. Army, 1960-62. Named Man of Yr., Internat. Order Foresters, 1981. Mem. Nat. Sheriff's Assn., Sheriff's Assn. Tex. Office: US Ho Reps 2136 Rayburn Bldg Washington DC 20515-4327*

ORTIZ-BUTTON, OLGA, social worker; b. Chgo., July 12, 1953; d. Luis Antonio and Pura (Acevedo) Ortiz; m. Dennis Vesley, Aug. 11, 1973 (div. 1976); m. Randall Russell Button, Nov. 3, 1984 (div. Oct. 1993); children: Joshua, Jordan, Elijah. BA, U. Ill., 1975; MSW, Western Mich. U., 1981. Cert. social worker, sch. social worker. Social svcs. dir. Champaign County Nursing Home, Urbana, Ill., 1976; social svcs. and activity dir. Lawton (Mich.) Nursing Home, 1977; job developer Southwestern Mich. Indian Ctr., Watervliet, 1977-78; staff asst. New Directions Alcohol Treatment Ctr., Kalamazoo, 1978; counselor, instr. Alcohol Hwy. Safety, Kalamazoo, 1978-79; clin. social worker Mecosta County Community Mental Health, Big Rapids, Mich., 1981-84; program dir. substance abuse Sr. Svcs., Inc., Kalamazoo, 1984-85; sch. social worker Martin (Mich.) Pub. Schs., 1985-96; owner, therapist Plainwell (Mich.) Counseling Ctr., 1989—; S.W. cons. Med. Pers. Pool, 1993-94. Vol. social worker Hospice-Wings of Hope, Plainwell, 1984-85, mem. CQI bd., 1993—; supporter Students Against Aparteid South Africa, Kalamazoo, 1979-81; mem. World Vision and Countertop Ptnr., 1984—, Christian Life Ctr., Kalamazoo, 1996; sponsor, vol. People for Ethical Treatment of Animals, 1986-91; vol. helper Sparkies for Awana Club Ch., 1989-95; consortium mem. Mich. Post Adoption Svc. System, 1994—. NIMH Rural Mental Health grantee, 1979-81. Mem. NASW, Mich. Assn. Sch. Social Workers, Am. Assn. Christian Counselors. Avocations: jogging, plants, cross country skiing. Office: Plainwell Counseling Ctr 211 E Bannister St Ste K Plainwell MI 49080-1372

ORTIZIO, DEBRA LOUISE, elementary education educator; b. Hoboken, N.J., Mar. 2, 1955; d. Louis Mario and Mary Evelyn (Borra) O. BA in Elem. Edn., Jersey City State Coll., 1977, MA in Reading, 1985, Reading Specialist, 1985, postgrad., 1986. Lic. elem. edn. tchr., reading specialist, N.J. Remedial reading tchr. St. Joseph Man Power Program, Union City, N.J., 1977-78; basic skills tchr. Gilmore Sch.-Union City (N.J.) Bd. Edn., 1978-86, 6th grade tchr., 1986—; coach advisor rifles and flag twirlers Emerson H.S., Union City, 1981-83; Students Awareness of Substance Abuse advisor Gilmore Sch., Union City, 1991-92, 93—, Earth Day coord., 1990, 91; fund raiser advisor Christmas Gifts for Christ Hosps., Gilmore Sch., Union City, 1989—, student coun. advisor, 1993-94. Recipient Tchr. Recognition award Hudson County, 1993, Tchr. Recognition award State of N.J., 1993. Roman Catholic. Home: 308 Passaic Ave Hasbrouck Heights NJ 07604-1704 Office: Gilmore Sch Union City NJ 07087

ORTIZ-QUIÑONES, CARLOS RUBEN, electronics engineer, educator; b. Bayamon, P.R.; s. Gregorio and Andrea (Quiñones) O. BSEE, U. P.R., 1986; MSEE, U. Dayton, 1990, PhD in Electronic Engring., 1994. Computer tech. instr. U. P.R., Mayaguez, 1986; electronics engr. USAF Wright-Patterson AFB, Dayton, Ohio, 1987-96; prof. electronics engring. Polytechnic U., P.R., 1996—. Contbr. articles to profl. jours. Mem. IEEE. Avocations: piano playing, reading, traveling.

ORTLEPP, BRUNO, marine navigation educator, master mariner; b. Nortorf, Germany, Apr. 3, 1935; s. Carl and Emilie (Strambovski) O; 1 child: Marie-Ann. 1 mate fgn. going, Fachhochschule Hamburg, 1958; master fgn. going, N.S. Nautical Inst., Halifax, Can., 1976; teacher diploma, N.S. Tchrs. Coll., Truro, 1984. O.s., a.b. various cos., Germany, 1951-56; 3rd officer German East Africa Line, Hamburg, 1958-60; from 2d officer to chief officer to master Irving Oil Ltd., Saint John, N.B., Can., 1960-76; chief officer Sanko Marine, Tokyo, Japan, 1976-81; marine educator, dept. edn. N.S. Nautical Inst., Halifax, 1982-92; pres. PELTRO Ltd., 1983-94. Author: Canadian Maritimes Sailing Aids, Vol. I, Tidal Streams for Bay of Fundy, 1965, 89, Vol. II, Tidal Streams for the River St. Lawrence, 1966, Vol. III, Distance Tables, 1966, 88, Vol. IV, Natural Squat, 1983, 89, Vol. V, The Deviascope, 1990; contbr. articles to profl. jours. Recipient 20th Century award, 1995. Mem. AAAS, FIBA, Nautical Inst. London. Home: Friedrichstrasse 19, 99894 Friedrichroda Thuringia, Germany Office: care Capt Walter S Franke, 12 Sycamore Ct, Lower Sackville, NS Canada B4C 1G1

ORTLIEB, ROBERT EUGENE, sculptor; b. San Diego, July 4, 1925; s. William Martin and Ruth Lina (Powers) O.; m. Donna Lynn Forman, Dec. 28, 1976. B.F.A., U. So. Calif., 1950, M.F.A., 1951. Instr. sculpture Riverside (Calif.) Art Center and Mus., 1960-85, Village Ctr. for the Arts, Palm Springs, Calif., 1966-90, U. So. Calif., Idyllwild Arts Found., 1964-76, Palos Verdes Community Arts Assn., 1970—, Instituto Professionale Stato Industria Artigianato, Marmo, Carrara, Italy, 1972; mem. art juries. Sculptor stone, plexiglas, wood, terra cotta, bronze, exhbns. in over 100 museums, galleries, including, Creative Galleries, N.Y.C., Cin. Art Mus., Denver Art Mus., Dallas Mus. Fine Arts, Oakland (Calif.) Art Mus., Santa Barbara (Calif.) Mus. Art, San Diego Fine Arts Gallery, Pasadena (Calif.) Art Mus., Los Angeles County Mus., San Francisco Mus. Art, Palm Springs Desert Mus.; represented in permanent collections, including, Met. Mus., N.Y.C., Achenbach Found. Graphic Arts Calif. Palace Legion Honor, San Francisco, Riverside Art Mus., Laguna Beach Art Mus., U. So. Calif., U. Calif. Riverside, Loma Linda (Calif.) U., Lawson Products, Inc., Chgo., City of Costa Mesa (Calif.) Community Center; represented by Miranda Galleries, Laguna Beach, Calif., Gallery La Jolla, Calif. Recipient numerous awards. Address: 2587 Thorman Pl Tustin Ranch CA 92782 *To create a totality of expression, sensitivity to dynamics and a comprehensive aliveness is indispensable to the nature of my work. In a broader sense, sculpture is life, disciplined, balancing on a knife edge between the emotional and intellectual forces. Art is like a religion, requiring a spiritual equilibrium from physical to etheric.*

ORTLIP, MARY KRUEGER, artist; b. Scranton, Pa.; d. John A. and Ida Mae (Phillips) Smale; m. Emmanuel Krueger, June, 1940 (dec. Nov. 1979); children: Diane, Keith; m. Paul D. Ortlip, June 26, 1981. Student, New Sch. Social Rsch., N.Y.C., 1957-59, Margarita Madrigal Langs., N.Y.C., Montclair (N.J.) Art Mus. Sch., 1978-79; Nomina Accademico Conferita, Academia Italia, Italy, 1986; DFA (hon.), Houghton Coll., 1988. Dancer, dance instr. Fleischer Dance Studio, Scranton, Pa., 1934-38. One-woman shows include Curzon Gallery of Boca Raton, Fla. and London, 1986-93, Galerie Les Amis des Arts, Aix-en-Provence, France, 1987; group exhbns.: Salmagundi Club, N.Y.C., 1980, James Hunt Barker Galleries, Nantucket, Mass. and N.Y.C., 1983, Salon Internationale Musée Parc Rochteau à Revin, France, 1985, 90, Accademia Italia, Milan, 1986, many others in Europe and Am.; permanent collections Musée de parc Rocheteau, Revin, France, Pinacothèque Arduinna, Charleville-Mezières, France. Named Invité d'Honneur, Le Salon des Nations a Retenu L'oeuvre, Paris, 1983, Artist of the Year, La Cote des Arts, France, 1986; recipient La Medaille d'Or, Du 13ème Salon Internationale al du Parc Rocheau au Revin, France, 1985, Medaille d' Honneur Ville de Marseille, France, 1987, Targo D'Oro, Accademia Italia Premio D'Italia, 1986; Trophy Arts Internationale Exposition de Peinture Marseille, Plaquette d' Honneur, Palais des Arts, 1987, Grand Prix Salon de Automne Club Internationale, 1987, Connaissance de Notre Europa Ardennes Eifel, Revin, France, 1990. Mem. Nat. Mus. Women in Arts, Accademia Italia (charter), Instituo D'Art Contemporanea Di Milano, Nat. Soc. Arts and Letters, Gov.'s Club, Salmagundi Club. Home (winter): 2917 S Ocean Blvd #703 Highland Beach FL 33487-1876 Home (summer): 588 Summit Ave Hackensack NJ 07601-1547 Office: The Curzon Gallery 501 E Camino Real Boca Raton FL 33432-6127

ORTLIP, PAUL DANIEL, artist; b. Englewood, N.J., May 21, 1926; s. Henry Willard and Aimee (Eschner) O.; m. Mary Louise Krueger, June 1981; children from previous marriage: Carol, Kathleen, Sharon (dec.), Danielle (dec.), Michelle. Diploma, Houghton Acad., 1944; student, Art Students League, 1947-49; diploma, Acad. la Grande Chaumiere, Paris, 1950; DFA (hon.), Houghton Coll., 1988. Tchr. Fairleigh Dickinson U., Teaneck, N.J., 1956-68; artist in residence, curator Fairleigh Dickinson U., Rutherford, N.J., 1968-72; official USN artist on assignment, Cuban missile crisis, Fla., 1963, Gemini 5 Recovery, Atlantic Ocean, 1965, Vietnam, 1967, Apollo 12 recovery, Pacific Ocean, 1969, Apollo 17 recovery, Pacific Ocean, 1972, Internat. Naval Rev., N.Y. harbor, 1976, USCG Sta., Key West, Fla., 1985; mem. USN Art Coop. and Liason Com. Exhbns. include Salonde L'Art Libre, Paris, 1950, Nat. Acad. Design, 1952, Allied Artists of Am., N.Y.C., Acad. Sci., Rundell Gallery, Rochester, N.Y., Monclair Art Mus., Hist. Mus, Lima, Ohio, Butler Art Inst., Youngstown, Ohio, Fine Arts Gallery, San Diego, State Capitol Bldg., Sacramento, Calif., Capitol Mus., Olympia, Wash., Mus. Gt. Plains, Lawton, Okla., Witte Meml. Mus., San Antonio, Nimitz Meml. Mus., Fredericksberg, Tex., Pentagon Collection of Fine Arts, James Hunt Barker Galleries, Palm Beach, Fla., Nantucket, Mass, N.Y.C., Smithsonian Inst., Gallerie Vollem Breuse, Biarritz, France, Galerie Mouffe, Paris, Guggenheim Gallery, London, Wickersham Gallery, N.Y.C., Soc. Illustrators, N.Y.C.; retrospective exhbn. Bergen Community Mus., Paramus, N.J. 1970, The Curzon Gallery, 1987, 88, 89, 93, Ardennes et de l'Eifel, Charleville Mézières, France, June-Sept. 1990; represented permanent collections including Salmagundi Club N.Y.C., Houghton (N.Y.) Coll., Portrait Meml. J.F. Kennedy Library, Fairleigh-Dickinson U., Nat. Air and Space Mus., Smithsonian Inst., Intrepid Sea-Air Space Mus., N.Y.C., Hist. Mural Visitors Ctr., Palisades Interstate Pk., Ft. Lee, N.J., Vets. Med. Ctr., East Orange, N.J., USN Exhbn. Ctr., Washington Navy Yard, Am. Coll. Clin. Pharmacology, N.Y.C., N.J. U. Dentistry & Medicine, Newark, Bergen County Ct. House, Hackensack, N.J., Dickinson Coll., Carlisle, Pa., George Washingtogn Meml Pk., Paramus, N.J., Marietta (Ohio) Coll., Mcpl. Bldg., Ft. Lee, N.J., Navy League U.S., Arlington, Va., Nat. Archives and Records Adminstrn., Washington, (mural) Pub. Libr., Fort Lee, N.J. Served to sgt. U.S. Army, 1944-47, ETO, PTO, 1946-47. Recipient 1st prize Am. Artists Profl. League State Exhibit N.J. chpt., Paramus, 1960, 1st prize U.S. Armed Forces Exhibit Far East, Seoul, Korea, Tokyo, 1946, Franklin Williams award, Salmagundi Club, N.Y., 1967, Outstanding Achievement award for oil painting, USN, 1968, Artist of Yr. award, Hudson Artists, Jersey City (N.J.) Mus., 1970, Statue of Victory World Culture prize, Academia Italia, Parma, 1982, Men of Achievement medal Cambridge, Eng., 1990, Connaissance de Notre Europe Gold medal Charleville-Mézières, France, 1990. Mem. Allied Artists Am. (art coop. and liaison com. with USN), Nat. Soc. Mural Painters, Nat. Soc. Arts and Letters, Bergen County Artists Guild (pres. 1960-62), Am. Portrait Soc., Artists Fellowship, Inc., U.S. Coast Guard Art Program, Art Students League N.Y. (life), Navy League U.S., VFW (life), Am. Legion. Clubs: Salmagundi (N.Y.C.) (art chmn. 1979-81); Gov.'s of the Palm Beaches (Fla.). Home: 588 Summit Ave Hackensack NJ 07601-1547 Office: care The Curzon Gallery 501 E Camino Real Boca Raton FL 33432-6127

ORTLOFF, GEORGE CHRISTIAN, SR. (CHRIS ORTLOFF), journalist, state legislator; b. Lake Placid, N.Y., Sept. 20, 1947; s. Carl Jacob and Lillian Grace (Travis) O.; m. Ruth Mary Hart, Jan. 28, 1978; children: George Christian Jr., Jonathan Hart. BS, Rensselaer Poly. Inst., 1969; MA, U. Mich., 1975. Reporter, producer Sta. WUOM-FM, Ann Arbor, Mich., 1973-75; reporter Nat. Pub. Radio, 1973-75, Adirondack Daily Enterprise, Saranac Lake, N.Y., 1976-77, Sta. WNBZ-Am, Saranac Lake, 1975-77; pub. rels. dir. Ctr. for Music, Drama and Art, Lake Placid, 1975-76; pres. Macromedia, Inc., Lake Placid, 1976-82; anchor, mng. editor Sta. WPTZ-TV, Plattsburgh, N.Y., 1981-85; mem. N.Y. State Assembly, Albany, 1986—, ranking minority mem. Legis. Commn. on Sci. and Tech., 1987—, chmn. Rep. program com., 1993—; mem. health and human svcs. task force Am. Legis. Exch. Coun., 1994—. Author: Lake Placid, The Olympic Years: 1932-80, 1976, A Lady in the Lake, 1985; reporter, producer (TV news series) "Special Segment", 1981-85 (N.Y. State Broadcasters Best Series award 1982, 83, 84, 85), (TV documentary) "A Time to Choose", 1985 (N.Y. State Broadcasters Best award 1986). Chief ceremonies 1980 Olympic Winter Games, Lake Placid, 1978-80; field asst. to congressman David O'B. Martin, Plattsburgh, 1981; chmn. Clinton County Rep. Com., 1995—; committeeman Essex County Rep. Com., 1980-81; trustee Lake Placid Village, 1977-81; lay reader Episcopal Ch., Lake Placid and Plattsburgh, 1976-92. Mem. VFW, AMVETS, Am. Legion, North Country Vietnam Vets. Assn., Elks, Kiwanis (pres. Lake Placid 1980-81). Avocations: skiing, piano, trumpet, painting, woodworking. Home: 23 Morrison Ave Plattsburgh NY 12901-1417 Office: NY State Assembly 450 Legislative Office Bldg Albany NY 12248

ORTMAN, ELDON E., entomologist, educator; b. Marion, S.D., Aug. 11, 1934; s. Emil and Kathryn (Tieszen) O.; m. Margene Adrian, June 27, 1957; children—Karen, Connie, Nancy. A.B., Tabor Coll., 1956; M.S., Kansas State U., 1957, Ph.D., 1963. Research entomologist USDA, No. Grain Insects Research Lab., Brookings, S.D., 1961-68; dir., leader investigations USDA, No. Grain Insects Research Lab., 1968-72; asst. prof. entomology S.D. State U., Brookings, 1961-63; asso. prof. S.D. State U., 1963-68, prof., 1968-72; asst. Entomology Research Div. Office, Beltsville, Md., 1971; prof. entomology Purdue U., West Lafayette, Ind., 1972-89; head dept. entomology Purdue U., 1972-89; assoc. dir. Ind. Agrl. Rsch. Programs, 1989—. Fellow AAAS; mem. Entomol. Soc. Am., Phi Kappa Phi, Gamma Sigma Delta, Sigma Xi. Research in plant resistance to insects and pest mgmt. Home: 3805 W Capilano Dr West Lafayette IN 47906-8881 Office: Purdue U Agrl Rsch AGAD West Lafayette IN 47907

ORTMAN, GEORGE EARL, artist; b. Oakland, Calif., Oct. 17, 1926; s. William Thomas and Anna Katherine (Noll) O.; m. Conni Whidden, Aug. 5, 1960 (dec.); 1 stepson, Roger Graham Whidden. Student, Calif. Coll. Arts and Crafts, 1947-49, Atelier Stanley William Hayter, 1949, Acad. Andre L'Hote, Paris, 1949-50, Hans Hoffman Sch. Art, 1949-50. Co-founder Tempo Playhouse, N.Y.C., 1954; Instr. painting and drawing NYU, 1962-65; co-chmn. fine arts Sch. Visual Arts N.Y.C., 1963-65; artist-in-residence Princeton U., 1966-69, Honolulu Acad. Art, 1969; head painting dept. Cranbrook Acad. Art, Bloomfield Hills, Mich., 1970-92. One-man exhbns. include Tanager Gallery, 1954, Wittenborn Gallery, 1955, Stable Gallery, 1957, 60, Howard Wise Gallery, 1962, 63, 64, 66, 69, Gimpel-Weitzenhoffer Gallery, 1972 (all N.Y.C.), Swetzoff Gallery, Boston, 1961-62, Fairleigh Dickinson U., 1962, Mirvish Gallery, Toronto, Can., 1964, Walker Art Center, Mpls., 1965, Milw. Art Center, 1966, Dallas Mus. Art, 1966, Portland Mus. Art, 1966, Akron Inst. Art, 1966, U. Chgo., 1967, Princeton U. Art Mus., 1967, Honolulu Acad. Art, 1969, Reed Coll., 1970, Cranbrook Acad. Art, 1970, 92, Indpls. Mus. Art, 1971, J.L. Hudson Gallery, Detroit, 1971, Gimpel-Weitzenhoffer, N.Y.C., 1972, 73, Gertrude Kasle Gallery, Detroit, 1976, Lee Hoffman Gallery, Detroit, 1977, Flint (Mich.) Mus. Art, 1977; other one-man exhbns. include Cranbrook Mus. Art, 1982; exhibited numerous group shows including Whitney Mus. Am. Art Annual, 1962, 63, 64, 65, 67, 73, Carnegie Internat., Pitts., 1964, 67, 70, Jewish Mus., N.Y.C., 1964, Corcoran Mus., Washington, 1964, others; represented permanent collections, Walker Art Center, Mpls., Mus. Modern Art, Whitney Mus. Am. Art, (both N.Y.C.), Guggenheim Mus., N.Y.C., Albright-Knox Mus., Buffalo, NYU, Christian Theol. Sem., Indpls., Indpls. Mus. Art, Cleve. Mus. Art, Mus. Am. Art, Washington, Honolulu Acad. Art, Newark Mus. Art, Container Corp. Am., Chgo. Ind. U. Music Bldg., Wausau (Wis.) Hosp. Center, Unitarian Ch., Princeton, Mfr. Hanover Trust Bldg., Albert Kahn & Assos., Detroit, Renaissance Center, Detroit, Mich. State Univ. Performing Arts Ctr., East Lansing, Detroit Inst. Arts. Guggenheim fellow, 1965-66; Ford Found. grantee, 1966; One of five Am. artists selected for 1965 Japanese Bi-ann.; recipient Gov. N.J.'s Purchase award 2d ann. exhbn. art, 1967; Best of Show Religion in Art Exhbn., Birmingham, Ala., 1966. Mem. Nat. Acad. of Design. Office: Tim Hill Gallery 163 Townsend St Birmingham MI 48009-6001

ORTNER, DONALD J., biological anthropologist, educator; b. Stoneham, Mass., Aug. 23, 1938; s. A.W. and Marie B. (Schweizer) O.; m. Joyce E. Walker, April 9, 1960; children: Donald J. Ortner Jr., Allison A. May, Karen L. Ortner. BA, Columbia Union Coll., 1960; MA, Syracuse U., 1967; PhD, U. Kans., 1970; DSc (hon.), U. Bradford, England, 1995. Asst. curator Smithsonian Instn., Washington, 1969-71, assoc. curator, 1971-76, curator, 1976—, chmn. anthropology, 1988-92; acting dir. Nat. Mus. Natural History, Washington, 1994-96; vis. prof. U. Bradford, 1988—; mem. editl. bd. Jour. Paleopathology, 1988—, Internat. Jour. Osteoarch., 1990—. Author: (book) Identification of Pathological Conditions in Human Skeletal Remain, 1981; editor: How Humans Adapt, 1983; co-editor: Human Paleopathology, 1991. Mem. Am. Assn. Phys. Anthropology (mem. exec. com. 1987-90), Internat. Skeletal Soc., Paleopathology Assn. Office: Smithsonian Inst Nat Mus Natural History 10th & Constitution Ave NW Washington DC 20560

ORTNER, EVERETT HOWARD, magazine editor, writer; b. Lowell, Mass., Aug. 25, 1919; s. Herman and Anne (Ehrenhaus) O.; m. Evelyn Francis Gelbman, Jan. 1, 1953. B.A., U. Ark., 1939. Editor Popular Publs., N.Y.C., 1946-52; assoc. editor Popular Sci., N.Y.C., 1953-56, copy chief, 1956-70, group editor, 1970-76, mng. editor, 1976-80, editor, 1980-85. Pres. Brownstone Revival Com. N.Y., 1968-76, chmn., 1986—; founder, pres. Back to the City, Inc., N.Y.C., 1974-83, chmn. bd., 1983—; v.p. L.I. Hist. Soc., Bklyn., 1979-83. Lt. U.S. Army, 1942-46, ETO. Recipient Cinderella award Bklyn. Union Gas Co., 1978, Honor citation Borough Pres. Bklyn., 1983, Disting. Citizen award City Louisville, 1979, Quality of Life award Kings County Hosp. Ctr., Bklyn., 1976, Spirit of Life award N.Y. Congl. Home, 1994. Mem. Overseas Press Club, Montauk Club, Ft. Hamilton Officers Club.

ORTOLANO, LEONARD, civil engineering educator, water resources planner; b. Bklyn., Sept. 26, 1941; s. Salvatore Thomas and Anna (Salerno) O. BSCE, Poly. Inst. Bklyn., 1963; MS in Engring., Harvard U., 1966, PhD, 1969. Sanitary engr. USPHS, Denver, 1963-65; rsch. scientist Ctr. for the Environment and Man, Hartford, Conn., 1969-70; prof. civil engring. Stanford (Calif.) U., 1970—, dir. program on urban studies, 1980—; vis. prof. Inst. Ricerca sulle Acqua, Rome, 1979, South China Environ. Inst. Sci., Guanzhou, 1987, Ecole Nat. des Ponts et Chaussées, Paris, 1987-88, Inst. Universitario Architecture Venice, Italy, 1996; vis. scholar Kyoto (Japan) U., 1992; vis. lectr. Nat. Sci. Coun. China, 1991. Author: Environmental Planning and Decision Making, 1984 (Chinese edit. 1989), Environmental Regulation and Impact Assessment, 1997; co-author: Implementing Environmental Policy in China, 1995. Resources for the Future Natural Resources fellow, 1968-69; Fulbright-Hays grantee, 1979, 87. Mem. ASCE, Internat. Water Resources Assn., Internat. Assn. for Impact Assessment. Office: Stanford Univ Dept Civil Engring Stanford CA 94305

ORTOLANO, RALPH J., engineering consultant; b. Phila., Apr. 12, 1931. BS in Marine Engring., U.S. Mcht. Marine Acad., 1954; MBA, Santa Clara U., 1969. Registered profl. engr., Calif. Engring. watch officer USN, 1954-56; sr. design engr. marine divsn. Westinghouse, Lester, Pa., 1956-64, Sunnyvale, Calif., 1964-69; mgr. project engring. corp. cost recovery dept. Litton Ship Systems, Inc., L.A., 1969-72; consulting engr., scientist So. Calif. Edison Co., Rosemead, Calif., 1972-92, chief cons., 1993—; formed Turbine RESCUE, 1984. Contbr. more than 100 articles to profl. jours.; holder 21 U.S. patents in field. Recipient William R. Gould award SCE, 1992. Mem. ASME (past dir. ASME-SCAC power chpt., past chmn. steam turbine com., past chmn. power divsn., mem. exec. com., co-chmn. steam turbine course 1984—, George Westinghouse Gold medal 1991).

ORTON, COLIN GEORGE, medical physicist; b. London, Essex, England, June 4, 1938; came to U.S., 1966; s. Frederick G. and Audrey V. (Sewell) O.; m. Barbara G. Scholes, July 25, 1964; children: Nigel, Susanne, Philip. BS in Physics with honors, Bristol U., 1959; MS in Radiation Physics, London U., 1961, PhD in Radiation Physics, 1965; MA (hon.), Brown U., 1976. ABR, ABMP. Instr. London U. St. Barts' Hosp., 1961-66; assoc. prof. NYU Med. Ctr., 1966-75, Brown U., R.I., 1975-81; prof., chief physicist Wayne State U., Harper Hosp., Detroit, 1981—; dir., grad program, Wayne State U., 1981—. Author: Radiation Physics Review Books I, 1971, II, 1978; editor: Electron Treatment Planning, 1978, Progress in Medical Physics I, 1982, II, 1985, Radiation Dosimetry, 1986; editor Med. Physics, 1997—. Marie Curie Gold Medal, Health Physics Soc., 1987. Fellow Am. Assn. Physicists in Am. (pres. 1981, William D. Coolidge award 1993), Am. Coll. Med. Physics (chmn. 1985), Inst. Physics London, Internat. Orgn. for Med. Physics (sec. gen. 1988-94, pres. 1997—), Am. Coll. Radiology. Avocations: golf, badminton, tennis, running, squash. Home: 8 Lakeside Ct Grosse Pointe MI 48230-1906 Office: Harper Hosp 3990 John R St Detroit MI 48201-2018

ORTON, GEORGE FREDERICK, aerospace engineer; b. Flushing, N.Y., Aug. 8, 1941; s. Harry and Evelyn (Brostrom) O.; m. Susan K., Dec. 21, 1962; children: Karen, Kevin, Kristen. BS in Aeron. Engring., U. Md., 1964; MS in Engring. Mechanics, St. Louis U., 1971. Engr. propulsion McDonnell Douglas, St. Louis, 1964-73, sr. engr. propulsion, 1973-77, unit chief propulsion, 1977-81, sect. chief propulsion, 1981-86, br. chief nat. aerospace plane, 1986-90, staff dir. nat. aerospace plane, 1990-92, dir. space programs, 1992-93, program mgr. Hypersonics Ctr. Excellence, 1993—. Contbr. articles to profl. jours. Advisor Explorer Post 9005, St. Louis, 1980-87; sci. advisor University City (Mo.) Schs. Fellow AIAA (assoc., mem. liquid propulsion tech. com. 1980-84, 91-96, Best Paper award 1986), St. Louis Head Injury Assn. Methodist. Achievements include patent for propellant acquisition device for zero-g engine starts, patent for propellant resupply system, NASA technology cash award for work on shuttle auxiliary propulsion. Office: McDonnell Douglas Corp PO Box 516 Mailcode S1067250 Saint Louis MO 63166-0516

ORTON, JOHN STEWART, lawyer; b. Cin., Nov. 25, 1949; s. Stewart and Hanni (S.) O.; m. Katharine Fleming Wilson, Aug. 8, 1975; children: Elizabeth Fleming, Virginia Stewart. BA in Polit. Sci., Trinity Coll., 1972; JD, Washington and Lee U., 1975. Bar: Tex. 1975, U.S. Dist. Ct. (so. dist.) Tex. 1976, Colo. 1990. Assoc. Rowland & Keim, Houston, 1976-77, Greenwood & Koby, Houston, 1977-80; assoc., ptnr. Barrow, Bland & Rehmet, Houston, 1980-85; ptnr. Brown, Parker & Leahy, L.L.P., Houston, 1985—. Bd. dirs. Planned Parenthood Houston and S.E. Tex., 1987-96, St. John's Sch. Alumni Assn., Houston, 1991-94, Glassell Sch. Art, Houston, 1988—. Mem. State Bar Tex. Assn., State Bar Colo., Houston Bar Assn., Briar Club, Houston Club, Galveston Country Club, Sugar Creek Country Club. Avocations: tennis, golf, skiing, hiking. Office: Brown Parker & Leahy LLP 1200 Smith St Ste 3600 Houston TX 77002-4502

ORTON, STEWART, retail company executive, merchant; b. Cin., Nov. 19, 1915; s. Henry S. and Helen (Block) O.; m. Hanni Stern, Nov. 16, 1946; children: Judith, John. BA, U. Mich., 1937. With Shillito's Dept. Store, Cin., 1937-57; v.p., gen. mdse. mgr. Shillito's Dept. Store, 1954-57; pres. J.N. Adam & Co. (dept. store), Buffalo, 1957-60; v.p. parent co. Associated Dry Goods Corp., N.Y.C., 1957-60; exec. v.p. Boston Store, Milw., 1960-63; v.p. Federated Dept. Stores, Cin., 1963; exec. v.p. Foley's, Houston, 1964-68, pres., 1968-78, chmn., CEO, 1979-82; exec. v.p. Federated Dept. Stores Inc. Found., 1982-88. Campaign chmn. Houston United Fund, 1968, pres., 1969; trustee U. Houston Found., Mus. Fine Arts, Houston, 1980-88; bd. dirs. Alley Theatre, Consumer Credit Conseling Svc., 1988—, chmn., 1990-92; bd. dirs. St. Joseph Hosp. Found., chmn., 1978-80; bd. dirs. Houston Com. for Pvt. Sector Initiatives, co-chmn., 1981-86; bd. dirs., v.p. Communities in Schs., 1986—; pres. Houston Econ. Devel. Coun., 1984-85; bd. dirs. Houston Symphony Orch., 1988—, chmn., 1990-91. Maj. Q.M.C., AUS, 1942-45. Mem. Houston C. of C. (dir., vice chmn. 1979-80, chmn. 1981-82). Clubs: Forum of Houston (pres. 1983, chmn. 1984); Plaza. Home: 3711 San Felipe St Apt 11J Houston TX 77027-4040 Office: 1200 Smith St Houston TX 77002-4313

ORTON, WILLIAM H. (BILL ORTON), former congressman, lawyer; b. North Ogden, Utah, Sept. 22, 1948. BS, Brigham Young U., 1973, JD, 1979. Adj. prof. Portland (Oreg.) State U./Portland C.C., 1974-76, Brigham Young. U., Provo, Utah, 1984-85; tax auditor IRS, 1976-77; corp. counsel WI Forest Products, Inc., Portland, Oreg., 1980-81; of counsel Merritt & Tenney, Atlanta, 1986-90; tax atty. pvt. practice, Utah, 1986-90, Washington, 1986-90; atty., 1980-90; mem. 102d-104th Congresses from 3f Utah dist., 1990-97; mem. budget com., mem. banking and fin. svcs. com.; pvt. practice Washington, 1997—. Democrat. Mormon. address: 411 Constitution Ave NE Washington DC 20002

ORTT, TERRY, hotel executive. Pres. Choice Hotels Can., Inc., Mississauga, Ont. Office: Choice Hotels Can Inc, 5090 Explorer Dr 6th Fl, Mississauga, ON Canada L4W 4T9

ORTTUNG, WILLIAM HERBERT, chemistry educator; b. Phila., June 16, 1934; s. Elmer Herbert and Rosalind Orttung; married; children: Robert W., Mark. H. SB, MIT, 1956; PhD, U. Calif., Berkeley, 1961. Asst. prof. chemistry Stanford (Calif.) U., 1960-63; asst. prof. chemistry U. Calif., Riverside, 1963-69, assoc. prof., 1969-79, prof., 1979-94; emeritus prof., 1994—. Mem. AAAS, Am. Chem. Soc., Am. Phys. Soc.

ORULLIAN, B. LARAE, bank executive; b. Salt Lake City, May 15, 1933; d. Alma and Bessie (Bacon) O.; cert. Am. Inst. Banking, 1961, 63, 67; grad. Nat. Real Estate Banking Sch., Ohio State U., 1969-71. With Tracy Collins Trust Co., Salt Lake City, 1951-54, Union Nat. Bank, Denver, 1954-57; exec. sec. Guaranty Bank, Denver, 1957-64, asst. cashier, 1964-67, asst. v.p., 1967-70, v.p., 1970-75, exec. v.p., 1975-77, also bd. dirs.; chair, CEO, dir. The Women's Bank N.A., Denver, 1989—, Colo. Bus. Bankshares, Inc., 1980—; vice chmn. Colo. Bus. Bank Littleton; chmn. bd., dir. Colo. Blue Cross/Blue Shield; bd. dirs. Rocky Mountain Life Ins. Co., Pro-Card, Inc., Holladay (Utah) Bank; chmn. bd. dirs. Frontier Airlines. Treas. Girl Scouts U.S.A., 1981-87, 1st. nat. v.p., chair exec. com., 1987-90, nat. pres., 1990-96; bd. dirs., chair Rocky Mountain Health Care Corp.; bd. dirs. Denver Improvement Assn; world bd. World Assn. Girl Guides Girl Scouts, London. Recipient Woman Who Made a Difference award Internat. Women's Forum, 1994; named to Colo. Women Hall of Fame, 1988, Colo. Entrepreneur of Yr., Inc. Mag. and Arthur Young and Co., 1989, Woman of the Yr., YWCA, 1989, EMC Lion Club (citizen of the year, 1995). Mem. Bus. and Profl. Women Colo. (3d Century award 1977), Colo. State Ethics Bd., Denver C. of C., Am. Inst. Banking, Am. Bankers Assn. (adv. bd. edn. found.), Internat. Women's Forum (Woman Who Makes a Difference award 1994), Com. of 200. Republican. Mormon. Home: 10 S Ammons St Lakewood CO 80226-1331

ORVICK, GEORGE MYRON, church denomination executive, minister; b. Hanlontown, Iowa, Jan. 9, 1929; s. George and Mabel Olina (Mandsager) O.; m. Ruth Elaine Hoel, Aug. 25, 1951; children: Daniel, Emily, Mark, Kirsten. AA, Bethany Luth. Coll., Mankato, Minn., 1948, candidate of theology, 1953; BA, Northwestern Coll., Watertown, Wis., 1950. Ordained to ministry Evang. Luth. Synod, 1953. Pastor Our Saviour Luth. Ch., Amherst Junction, Wis., 1953-54, Holy Cross Luth. Ch., Madison, Wis., 1954-86; cir. visitor Evang. Luth. Synod, Mankato, 1964-69, pres., 1970-76, 1980—. Author: Our Great Heritage, 1966; columnist: The Luth. Sentinel, 1982—. Home: 1117 Lori Ln Mankato MN 56001-4728 Office: Evang Luth Synod 6 Browns Ct Mankato MN 56001-6121

ORWOLL, GREGG S. K., lawyer; b. Austin, Minn., Mar. 23, 1926; s. Gilbert M. and Kleonora (Kleven) O.; m. Laverne M. Flentie, Sept. 15, 1951; children: Kimball G., Kent A., Vikki A., Tristen A., Erik G. BS, Northwestern U., 1950; JD, U. Minn., 1953. Bar: Minn. 1953, U.S. Supreme Ct. 1973. Assoc. Dorsey & Whitney, Mpls., 1953-59, ptnr., 1959-60; assoc. counsel Mayo Clinic, Rochester, Minn., 1960-63, gen. counsel, 1963-87, sr. legal counsel, 1987-91, sr. counsel, 1991-92; gen. counsel, dir. Rochester Airport Co., 1962-84, v.p., 1981-84; gen. counsel Mayo Med. Svcs., Ltd., 1972-90; bd. dirs., sec. and gen. counsel Mayo Found. for Med. Edn. and Rsch., 1984-90; gen. counsel Mid-Am. Orthopaedic Assn., 1984—, Minn. Orthopaedic Soc., 1985-95; asst. sec./sec. Mayo Found., Rochester, 1972-91; bd. dirs. Charter House, 1986-90; dir., officer Travelure Motel Corp., 1968-86; dir., v.p. Echo Too Ent., Inc.; dir., v.p. Oberhamer Inc.; bd. dirs. Am. Decal and Mfg. Co., 1989-93, sec., 1992-93; adj. prof. William Mitchell Coll. Law, 1978-84. Contbr. articles and chpts. to legal and medico-legal publs.; bd. editors HealthSpan, 1984-93; editorial bd. Minn. Law Rev., 1952-53. Trustee Minn. Coun. on Founds., 1977-82, Mayo Found., 1982-86; trustee William Mitchell Coll. Law, 1982-88, 89—, mem. exec. com. 1990—; bd. visitors U. Minn. Law Sch., 1974-76, 85-91; mem. U. Minn. Regent Candidate Adv. Coun., 1988—, Minn. State Compensation Coun., 1991-97. With USAF, 1944-45. Recipient Outstanding Svc. medal U.S. Govt., 1991. Mem. ABA, AMA (affiliate), Am. Corp. Counsel Assn., Minn. Soc. Hosp. Attys. (bd. dirs. 1981-86), Minn. State Bar Assn. (chmn. legal/med. com. 1977-81), Olmsted County Bar Assn. (v.p., pres. 1977-79), Rochester C. of C., U. Minn. Law Alumni Assn. (bd. dirs. 1973-76, 85-91), Rochester U. Club (pres. 1977), The Doctors Mayo Soc., Mid Am. Ortho. Assn. (hon.), Mayo Alumni Assn. (hon.), Phi Delta Phi, Phi Delta Theta. Republican. Home:

2233 5th Ave NE Rochester MN 55906-4017 Office: Mayo Clinic 200 1st St SW Rochester MN 55902-3008

ORWOLL, MARK PETER, magazine editor; b. Lynwood, Calif., Dec. 3, 1953; s. Sylfest Peter Jr. and Frances Patricia (Giffin) O.; m. Kathleen F. Fox, Aug. 6, 1983; children: Caitlin, Gillian, Rory. BA in Journalism, San Diego State U., 1978, MA in English, 1985. Reporter Star-News, Chula Vista, Calif., 1978-79; staff writer The Reader, San Diego, 1979-81; features editor Woman's World, Englewood, N.J., 1981; bus. editor American Salon, N.Y.C., 1981-83; editor Transfer, San Francisco, 1983-84; sr. editor USAir Mag., N.Y.C., 1985-87; mng. editor Travel & Leisure, N.Y.C., 1987—; lectr. Rice U. Pub. Program, Houston, 1994, Seabourn Cruise Line, India-Singapore, 1994; spkr. Am. Soc. Journalists and Authors, N.Y.C., 1991, New Sch. Social Rsch., N.Y.C., 1992. Ky. col. Hon. Order Ky. Cols., Frankfort, 1995. Mem. Am. Soc. Mag. Editors, 1990—. Office: Travel & Leisure 1120 Avenue Of The Americas New York NY 10036-6700

ORWOLL, ROBERT ARVID, chemistry educator; b. Mpls., Aug. 28, 1940; s. Arvid Lyder and Agnes Gertrude (Christiansen) O.; m. Betty Lou Magers, Feb. 24, 1972; children: Katherine Sonja, Karen Elizabeth. BA, St. Olaf Coll., Northfield, Minn., 1962; PhD, Stanford U., 1967. Postdoctoral fellow Dartmouth Coll., Hanover, N.H., 1966-67, rsch. instr., 1967-68; postdoctoral fellow U. Conn., Storrs, 1968-69; asst. prof. Coll. William and Mary, Williamsburg, Va., 1969-72, assoc. prof., 1972-82, prof., 1982, dir. applied sci., 1988-92, chair dept. of chemistry, 1995—. Bd. dirs. Williamsburg Hospice, 1989-94; bd. dirs. Wesley Found., 1974-84, 95—, treas., 1976-80. Recipient Alumni fellow teaching award Soc. Alumni William and Mary, 1985. Methodist. Home: 202 Buford Rd Williamsburg VA 23188-1509 Office: Coll William & Mary Dept Chemistry Williamsburg VA 23187

ORY, MARCIA GAIL, social science researcher; b. Dallas, Feb. 8, 1950; d. Marvin Gilbert and Esther (Levine) O.; m. Raymond James Carroll, Aug. 13, 1972. BA magna cum laude, U. Tex., 1971; MA, Ind. U., 1972; PhD, Purdue U., 1976; MPH, Johns Hopkins U., 1981. Rsch. asst. prof. U. N.C., Chapel Hill, 1976-77; from adj. asst. prof. to assoc. prof. sch. pub. health U. N.C., 1978-88; rsch. fellow U. Minn., Mpls., 1977-78; asst. prof. Sch. Pub. Health U. Ala., Bham, 1978-80; program dir. biosocial aging and health Nat. Inst. on Aging, Bethesda, Md., 1981-86; chief social sci. rsch. on aging Nat. Inst. on Aging, Bethesda, 1987—. Contbr. articles, editor vols. profl. jours. Mem. several nat. task forces on aging and health issues. Recipient Dept. of Health and Human Svcs. award, 1984, 85, 88, Am. Men and Women of Sci., 1989-90, Nat. Inst. of Health Dir.'s award, 1995; named Disting. Alumna by Purdue U. Fellow Gerontol. Soc. Am.; mem. APHA (gov. coun. 1986-88, program chmn. 1986, chmn.-elect 1989-91, chmn. 1992-93), Am. Sociol. Assn. (regional reporter 1984—, program com. 1986, nominations com. 1987, councilor-at-large 1992-93), Soc. Behavioral Medicine (program chmn. pub. health track 1988-89, program com. 1991-92), Phi Kappa Phi, Omicron Nu. Avocations: biking, birding, travel. Office: Nat Inst Aging Gateway Bldg Ste 533 7201 Wisconsin Ave # 9205 Bethesda MD 20814-4810

ORYSHKEVICH, ROMAN SVIATOSLAV, physician, physiatrist, dentist, educator; b. Olesko, Ukraine, Aug. 5, 1928; came to U.S., 1955, naturalized, 1960; s. Simeon and Caroline (Deneszczuk) O.; m. Oksana Lishchynsky, June 16, 1962; children: Marta, Mark, Alexandra. DDS, Ruperto-Carola U., Heidelberg, Ger., 1952, MD, 1953, PhD cum laude, 1955. Cert. Am. Assn. Electromyography and Electrodiagnosis, 1964; diplomate Am. Bd. Phys. Medicine and Rehab., 1966, Am. Bd. Electrodiagnostic Medicine, 1989. Research fellow in cancer Esptl. Cancer Inst., Rupert-Charles U., 1953-55; rotating intern Coney Island Hosp., Bklyn., 1955-56; resident in diagnostic radiology NYU Bellevue Med. Ctr.-Univ. Hosp., 1956-57; resident, fellow in phys. medicine and rehab. Western Res. U. Highland View Hosp., Cleve., 1958-60; orthopedic surgery Met. Gen. Hosp., Cleve., 1959; asst. chief rehab. medicine service VA West Side Med. Ctr., Chgo., 1961-74, acting chief, 1974-75, chief, 1975—; dir., coord. edn. U. Ill. Integrated Residency Program, Phys. Medicine & Rehab, 1974-89; clin. instr. U. Ill., 1962-65, asst. clin. prof., 1965-70, asst. prof., 1970-75, assoc. clin. prof., 1975-94, clin. prof., 1994—. Author, editor: Who and What in U.W.M.M., 1978; contbr. articles to profl. jours; splty. cons. in phys. medicine and rehab. to editorial bd. Chgo. Med. Jours., 1978-89. Founder, pres. Ukrainian World Med. Mus., Chgo., 1977; founder, 1st pres. Am. Mus. Phys. Medicine and Rehab., 1980-91. Fellow AAUP, Am. Acad. Phys. Medicine and Rehab.; mem. Assn. Acad. Physiatrists, Am. Assn. Electromyography and Electrodiagnosis, Ill. Soc. Phys. Medicine and Rehab. (pres., dir. 1979-80), Ukrainian Med. Assn. N.Am. (dir., pres. chpt. 1977-79, fin. mgr. 17th med. conv. and congress Chgo. 1977, adminstr. and conv. chmn. 1979), World Fedn. Ukrainian Med. Assns. (co-founder and 1st exec. sec. research and sci. 1977-79), Internat. Rehab. Medicine Assn., Rehab. Internat. U.S.A., Nat. Assn. VA Physicians, AAAS, Assn. Med. Rehab. Dirs. and Coordinators, Nat. Rehab. Assn., Nat. Assn. Disability Examiners, Am. Med. Writers Assn., Biofeedback Research Soc. Am., Chgo. Soc. Phys. Medicine and Rehab. (pres., founder 1978-79), Ill. Rehab. Assn., Ukrainian Acad. Med. Scis. (founder, pres. 1979-80), Gerontol. Soc., Internat. Soc. Electrophysiol. Kinesiology, Internat. Soc. Prosthetics and Orthotics, Fedn. Am. Scientists. Ukrainian Catholic. Major research interests: prosthetics, amputations, normal and pathological gaits, bracing-orthotics, strokes, rehabilitation. Home: 1819 N 78th Ct Elmwood Park IL 60707 Office: 820 S Damen Ave Chicago IL 60612-3728

ORZECHOWSKI, ALICE LOUISE, accountant; b. Washington, Jan. 14, 1952; d. Casimir T. and Frances (Zemaites) O.; m. Scott Mitchell Hoyman Jr. BS in Econs., U. Md., 1973, BS in Acctg., 1976; MS in Adminstrn. and Mgmt., Hood Coll., 1983. CPA, Md.; cert. mgmt. acct. Mgr. Gen. Bus. Svcs., Rockville, Md., 1972-78, Ross Assocs., Alexandria, Va., 1978-87; owner Alice L. Orzechowski, CPA, Cert. Mgmt. Acct., Frederick, Md., 1987—; adj. faculty Frederick (Md.) C.C., 1990-92, Montgomery Coll., Rockville, Md., 1992-97; spkr. in field. Named Outstanding Young Marylander, Md. Jaycees, 1991. Mem. AICPA, Am. Women's Soc. CPAs, Md. Assn. CPAs, Nat. Assn. Accts., Nat. Assn. Tax Practitioners, Downtowne Frederick Toastmasters (pres. 1991, Toastmaster of Yr. 1990), Frederick C. of C. (chair small bus. coun. 1990-91, dir. 1992-96, Entrepreneur of Yr. 1992). Office: 529 N Market St Frederick MD 21701-5242

OSBALDESTON, GORDON FRANCIS, business educator, former government official; b. Hamilton, Ont., Can., Apr. 29, 1930; s. John Edward and Margaret (Hanley) O.; m. Geraldine Keller, Oct. 3, 1953; children—Stephen, David, Robert, Catherine. B.Commerce, U. Toronto, Ont., Can., 1952; M.B.A., U. Western Ont., London, 1953, LL.D., 1984; LL.D., York U., Toronto, 1984, Dalhousie U., Halifax, N.S., 1985, Carleton U., Ottawa, Ont., Can., 1987. Fgn. service officer Dept. Trade and Commerce, Ottawa, 1953-54; vice consul, asst. trade commr. Dept. Trade and Commerce, Sao Paula, Brazil, 1954-57, Chgo., 1957-60; consul, trade commr. Dept. Trade and Commerce, Los Angeles, 1960-64; asst. dir., personnel trade commr. service Dept. Trade and Commerce, Ottawa, 1964-66, asst. dir. ops. trade commr. service, 1966-67, exec. dir. trade commr. service, 1967-68; asst. dep. minister Dept. Consumer and Corp. Affairs, Ottawa, 1968-70, dep. minister, 1972-73; dep. sec. Treasury Bd. Secretariat, Ottawa, 1970-72, sec., 1973-76; dep. minister Dept. Industry, Trade and Commerce, Ottawa, 1976-78; sec. Ministry of State for Econ. Devel., Ottawa, 1978-82; undersec. of state Dept. External Affairs, Ottawa, 1982; clk. privy council, sec. to cabinet Privy Council Office, Ottawa, 1982-86; mem. Queen's Privy Coun. for Can., 1986; prof. emeritus Western Bus. Sch. U. Western Ont., 1986—; bd. dirs. DuPont of Can. Inc., Nat. Bank of Can., Bell Can., NatCan Trust Co., Life Imaging Sci. Inc. Author: Keeping Deputy Ministers Accountable, 1989, Organizing to Govern, 1990. Decorated officer Order of Can.; recipient Outstanding Achievment award Can. Govt., 1981, Vanier medal Inst. Pub. Adminstrn., 1990. Mem. London Hunt and Country Club (bd. dirs.), Psi Upsilon. Roman Catholic. Avocations: philately; golf. Home: 1353 Corley Dr N, London, ON Canada N6G 4L4

OSBERG, TIMOTHY M., psychologist, educator, researcher; b. Buffalo, Aug. 11, 1955; s. John Carlton and Adeline Rose (Weichsel) O.; m. Debra A. Morreale, July 14, 1990; children: John Peter, Erika Evelyn. BA, SUNY, Buffalo, 1977, MA, 1980, PhD, 1982. Lic. psychologist, N.Y. Intern VA Med. Ctr., Buffalo, 1981-82; from asst. prof. to prof. Niagara U., N.Y., 1982—; pvt. practice Niagara Falls, N.Y., 1985—; psychologist Optifast Weight Loss Program, Niagara Falls, 1989-92; editorial bd. Jour. Personality and Social Psychology, 1988-92, Teaching of Psychology, 1991—, Jour. Correctional Edn., 1993—; instr. Attica Correctional Facility, 1980—; presenter in field. Contbr. articles to profl. jours. Vol. group leader prerelease program Attica (N.Y.) Correctional Facility, 1984-90, exec. com. Psychol. Assn. Western N.Y., Buffalo, 1982-87. Recipient Feldman-Cohen Meml. award SUNY, Buffalo, 1977. Fellow APA; mem. Am. Psychol. Soc., Eastern Psychol. Assn., Soc. for Personality Assessment, Assn. Advancement Behavior Therapy, Phi Beta Kappa. Democrat. Roman Catholic. Avocations: spectator sports, running, golf, tennis. Home: 2652 David Dr Niagara Falls NY 14304-4619 Office: Niagra U Dept Psychology Niagara University NY 14109

OSBORN, ANN GEORGE, retired chemist; b. Nowata, Okla., Aug. 1, 1933; d. David Thomas and Alice Audrey (Giles) George; m. Charles Wesley Osborn, Nov. 8, 1958 (dec. Dec. 1977); 1 child, Charles David. BA in Chemistry, Okla. Coll. Women, 1955. Rsch. chemist thermodynamics rsch. lab. Bartlesville (Okla.) Energy Rsch. Ctr., U.S. Dept. Energy, 1957—; ret., 1983. Contbr. articles to profl. jours. Mem. AAAS (emeritus), Am. Chem. Soc. Republican. Mem. Christian Ch. (Disciples of Christ). Home: 647 S Pecan St Nowata OK 74048-4015

OSBORN, DAVID LEE, engineer; b. Muscatine, Iowa, Feb. 10, 1953; s. Donald Dean and Emogene Faye (Strausbaugh) O.; m. Frances Marie Barnes, Apr. 11, 1981 (div. Feb. 1994); 1 child, Meredith Leigh. BSME, U. Iowa, 1978. Mech. engr. Stanley Cons., Muscatine, Iowa, 1978-82; gen. engr. Hdqrs. U.S. Army Armament, Munitions & Chem. Commd., Rock Island, Ill., 1982-89, Rock Island Arsenal, 1989—. Recipient Fed. Energy Mgmt. award Dept. Energy, 1993. Mem. Assn. Energy Engrs. Achievements include development of nationally recognized energy conservation program, development of over 29 million dollars in conservation projects including hydroelectric, heating plant modernization, lighting and heat/cooling system projects. Avocations: landscaping, home designs, golf, skiing, billiards. Office: Rock Island Arsenal Attn SIORI-PWE Rock Island IL 61299-5000

OSBORN, DEVERLE ROSS, insurance company executive; b. Leesburg, Ind., Sept. 29, 1925; s. Leland John and Beth (Bunnell) O.; m. Edith Helaine Germann, June 27, 1948 (dec. Mar. 1990); children: Bradford, Pamela, Andrea, Randall; m. Lillian C. Fellwock, Aug. 1990. Student, U. Notre Dame, 1944; BS in Air Transp. Engring., Purdue U., 1947. CLU. Spl. agt. FBI, Louisville, 1948, N.Y.C., 1948-53; life ins. agt. Conn. Mut. Life, N.Y.C., 1953-56; life ins. exec. Conn. Mutual Life, Hartford, 1956-65, Allentown, Penn., 1965-70; life ins. exec. Aid Assn. Luths., Appleton, Wis., 1970-78, Evansville, Ind., 1978-91; ret. Liaison State Legislators Justice Fellowship, Washington, 1982-85, chmn., 1989-92; fin. dir. Prescott, Ariz. Spl. Olympics, 1996—; bd. dirs. Habitat for Humanity, Evansville, Ind., 1991-92, Meals on Wheels, Prescott, 1997—. Naval Aviation cadet, 1943-45. Named Nat. Vol. Yr. Justice Fellowship, 1989. Mem. Soc. CLUs (v.p., pres. local chpts. 1968, 70), Gen. Agt. Mgr. Assn. (treas., v.p., pres. local chpts. 1966-68), Nat. Assn. Life Underwriters. Republican. Lutheran. Avocation: pilot. Home: 394 Sunny Cove Cir Prescott AZ 86303-5734

OSBORN, DONALD ROBERT, lawyer; b. N.Y.C., Oct. 9, 1929; s. Robert W. and Ruth C. (Compton) O.; m. Marcia Lontz, June 4, 1955; children: David, Judith, Robert; m. Marie A. Johnson, Sept. 11, 1986. BA, Cornell U., 1951; LLB, Columbia U., 1957. Bar: N.Y. 1957, U.S. Tax Ct. 1958, U.S. Ct. Claims 1961, U.S. Ct. Appeals (2d cir.) 1974, U.S. Ct. Appeals (8th cir.) 1974, U.S. Dist. Ct. (so. and ea. dists.) N.Y. 1975, U.S. Supreme Ct. 1975. Assoc. Sullivan & Cromwell, N.Y.C., 1957-64, ptnr., 1964-96, sr. counsel 1997—. Trustee Hamilton Coll., 1978-88, Mus. of Broadcasting, 1975-80; trustee, treas. Kirkland Coll., 1969-78; mem. coun. White Burkett Miller Ctr. Pub. Affairs, 1976-82; bd. dirs., pres. Stevens Kingsley Found., 1967—; sec., treas. Dunlevy Milbank Found., 1974—; bd. dirs. Spanel Found., 1978-88, CBS, Inc., 1975-80. Served with USN, 1951-54. Mem. ABA, N.Y. State Bar Assn., Assn. of Bar of City of N.Y., Am. Bar Found., Scarsdale Golf Club, India House, World Trade Ctr. Club (N.Y.C.), Regency Whist Club, Country Club of the Rockies. Presbyterian. Home: 1049 Park Ave New York NY 10128-1061 Office: Sullivan & Cromwell 125 Broad St New York NY 10004-2400

OSBORN, FREDERICK HENRY, III, church foundation executive; b. Phila., Dec. 31, 1946; s. Frederick Henry Osborn Jr. and Anne de Witt (Pell) O.; m. Anne Hampton de Peyster Todd, July 10, 1971; children: Frederick Henry IV, Elisabeth Van Cortlandt, Graham Livingston. Student in Econs., Princeton U., 1964-66; BA in Bus. Adminstrn., Colby Coll., 1971; postgrad., Nat. Planned Giving Inst., 1987, Philanthropy Tax Inst., 1988. Registered investment advisor. Pres. Call-Us, Inc., Edgartown, Mass., 1969-72; exec. v.p. Hall Labs., Boston, 1972-74; fin. officer Episcopal Diocese Mass., Boston, 1972-76; diocesan adminstr. Episcopal Diocese Maine, Portland, 1976-80; dir. adminstrn. Episcopal Diocese Conn., Hartford, 1980-86; dir. of devel. and planned giving Nat. Episcopal Ch., N.Y.C., 1987-94; dir. of devel. programs Episcopal Ch. Found., N.Y.C., 1995—; bd. dirs. Living Music, Inc., Ulysses Co., William O. Benson Co., FAN Trusts, Oslands, Inc., Boscobel Restoration, Inc., Garrison Sta. Plz., Inc., Garrison Landing Assn., Covenant Svcs., Inc.; prin. Cat Rock Counsel, Garrison, N.Y., 1990—. Coauthor: Planned Giving for the Episcopal Parish, 1989. Bd. dirs. The Giraffe Project, chmn. 1989-93, Alice Desmond & Hamilton Fish Libr.; chmn. bd. dirs. Hudson Highlands Land Trust; v.-chair., bd. dirs. Scenic Hudson, Berkeley Divinity Sch. Yale U., Nature Conservancy (lower Hudson chpt. chair 1994—); trustee Tabor Acad., Cathedral Ch. St. John the Divine, chair Hudson Highlands Music Festival, 1994-96. With U.S. Army, 1966-68, Vietnam. Mem. Nat. Assn. Fund Raising Execs., Nat. Planned Giving Assn., Nat. Environ. Leadership Coun., Planned Giving Group Greater N.Y., Social Investment Forum, Coun. Econ. Priorities, Social Venture Network, Century Assn., St. Andrews Soc. of N.Y., Highlands Country Club, N.Y. Yacht Club, Portland Yacht Club, Dauntless Club, Garrison Yacht Club, Princeton Club (N.Y.), Internat. Platform Assn. Avocations: sailing, music, photography. Home: PO Box 347 Cat Rock Rd Garrison NY 10524-0347 Office: Episcopal Ch Found 815 2nd Ave Rm 400 New York NY 10017-4503

OSBORN, JOHN EDWARD, lawyer, former government official, writer; b. Davenport, Iowa, Sept. 4, 1957; s. Edward Richard and Patricia Anne (O'Donovan) O.; m. Deborah Lynn Powell, Aug. 11, 1984; 1 child, Delaney Powell. Student, Coll. William and Mary, 1975-76; BA, U. Iowa, 1979; postgrad., Georgetown U., 1980; JD, U. Va., 1983; postgrad. Wadham Coll., Oxford U., 1987; MIPP, Johns Hopkins U., 1992; postgrad. Wharton Sch., U. Pa., 1994-95. Bar: Mass. 1985. Law clk. to Hon. Albert V. Bryan U.S. Ct. Appeals (4th cir.), Alexandria, Va., 1983-84; assoc. Hale and Dorr, Boston, 1984-88, Dechert Price & Rhoads, Phila., 1988-89; spl. asst. to legal adviser U.S. Dept. State, Washington, 1989-92; sr. counsel DuPont Merck Pharm. Co., Wilmington, Del., 1992-94, assoc. gen. counsel, 1994-96, v.p., assoc. gen. counsel, asst. sec., 1996-97; v.p. legal Cephalon, Inc., West Chester, Pa., 1997—; legal cons. Amnesty Internat. USA, 1987-88; vis. scholar East European studies, Woodrow Wilson Internat. Ctr. for Scholars; assoc. scholar Fgn. Policy Rsch. Inst., Phila., 1992—; rsch. assoc. William Davidson Inst., U. Mich., Ann Arbor, 1997—. Contbr. articles to profl. jours., newspapers and periodicals including NY Times, Wash. Post, Christian Sci. Monitor, Am. Jour. Internat. Law; articles editor: Va. Jour. Internat. Law, 1982-83. Mem. U. Va. Law Sch. Bus. Advisory Coun., Charlottesville, mem. nat. steering com. U. Iowa Endowment 2000 Campaign, Iowa City; rsch. aide, speechwriter George Bush for Pres. Com., 1979-80, 87-88, mem. Del. Rep. State Comm., 1995—, del. to Rep. Nat. Conv., 1996, mem., bd. dirs. Del. Ctr. for the Contemporary Arts, 1995—, ACLU Del., 1996—. Mem. ABA (bus. law, internat. law and practice sects.), Atlantic Coun. of the U.S., U. Iowa Pres.'s Club, Mortar Board, Phi Beta Kappa, Phi Delta Phi, Omicron Delta Kappa, Omicron Delta Epsilon, Sigma Delta Chi. Republican. Roman Catholic. Clubs: Capitol Hill. Home: 236 Stone Row Yorklyn DE 19736-0324 Office: 145 Brandywine Pkwy West Chester PA 19380-4245

OSBORN, JOHN SIMCOE, JR., lawyer; b. Louisville, Jan. 14, 1926; s. John S. and Ruby (Pinnell) O.; m. Mary Jo Fishback, Sept. 6, 1947; children—Robert, John, Donna. LL.B., U. Louisville, 1949. Bar: Ky. 1949, U.S. Dist. Ut. (ea. and we. dists.) Ky. 1952. Exec. v.p., gen. counsel Louisville Title Ins. Co., 1954-72; ptnr. Tarrant Combs & Bullitt (name changed to Wyatt Tarrant & Combs 1980), Louisville, 1972—; chmn. bd. Beargrass Corp. Served to capt. JAGC, U.S. Army, 1952-54. Fellow Am. Bar Found.; mem. Ky. Bar Assn., Louisville Bar Assn., ABA, Am. Land Title Assn., Am. Coll. Real Estate Lawyers. Democrat. Presbyterian. Lodge: Rotary (Louisville). Office: Wyatt Tarrant & Combs 2800 Citizens Plz Louisville KY 40202

OSBORN, JUNE ELAINE, pediatrician, microbiologist, educator; b. Endicott, N.Y., May 28, 1937; d. Leslie A. and Dora W. (Wright) O.; divorced; children: Philip I. Levy, Ellen D. and Laura A. Levy (twins). BA, Oberlin (Ohio) Coll., 1957; MD, Western Res. U., 1961; DSc (hon.), U. Med. Dental Sch. N.J., 1990; DMS (hon.), Yale U., 1992; DSc (hon.), Emory U., 1993, Oberlin Coll., 1993; LHD (hon.), Med. Coll. Pa., 1994; DSc (hon.), Rutgers U., 1994, Case Western Res. U., 1997. Intern, then resident in pediatrics Harvard U. Hosp., 1961-64; postdoctoral fellow Johns Hopkins, 1964-65, U. Pitts., 1965-66; mem. faculty, prof. med. microbiology and pediat. U. Wis. Med. Sch., Madison, Wis., 1966-84; prof. pediat. and microbiology U. Wis. Med. Sch., 1975-84, assoc. dean Grad. Sch., 1975-84; dean Sch. Pub. Health U. Mich., 1984-93; prof. epidemiology, pediat. and communicable diseases U. Mich., Sch. Pub. Health and Med. Sch., 1984-96, prof. emerita, 1997—; pres. Josiah Macy, Jr. Found., 1997—; mem. rev. panel viral vaccine efficacy FDA, 1973-79, mem. vaccines and related biol. products adv. com., 1981-85; mem. exptl. virology study sect. Divsn. Rsch. Grants, NIH, 1975-79; mem. med. affairs com. Yale U. Coun., 1981-86; chmn. life scis. associateships rev. panel NRC, 1981-84; mem. U.S. Army Med. R&D Adv. Com., 1983-85; chmn. working group on AIDS and the Nation's Blood Supply, NHLBI, 1984-89; chmn. WHO Planning Group on AIDS and the Internat. Blood Supply, 1985-86. Contbr. articles to med. jours. Mem. task force on AIDS, Inst. of Medicine, 1986; mem. adv. com. Robert Wood Johnson Found. Health Svcs. Program, 1986-91; mem. nat. adv. com. on health of pub. program Pew and Rockefeller Founds.; mem. health promotion and disease prevention bd. IOM, 1987-90, Global Commn. on AIDS, WHO, 1988-92; chmn. Nat. Commn. on AIDS, 1989-93; trustee Kaiser Found., 1990—; trustee Case Western Res. U., Cleve., 1993-97; mem. coun. Inst. Medicine, 1995—; mem. Nat. Vaccine Adv. Cte., HHS, 1995—; mem. adv. coun. Nat. Inst. on Drug Abuse, 1995—; bd. dirs. Corp. for Supportive Housing, 1994—. Grantee NIH, 1969, 72, 74-75, Nat. Multiple Sclerosis Soc., 1971; Scientific Freedom and Responsibility Award AAAS, 1994. Fellow Am. Acad. Arts and Scis., Am. Acad. Pediat., Am. Acad. Microbiology, Infectious Diseases Soc. Am.; mem. Am. Assn. Immunologists, Soc. Pediat. Rsch., Inst. Medicine. Office: Josiah Macy Jr Found Dept Epidemiology 44 E 64th St New York NY 10021-7306

OSBORN, LEN, business executive. Divsn. gen. mgr. JWK Internat. Corp., Annandale, Va. Office: JWK Internat Corp 7617 Little River Tpke Annandale VA 22003-2603

OSBORN, MARVIN GRIFFING, JR., educational consultant; b. Baton Rouge, Sept. 7, 1922; s. Marvin Griffing and Mamie (Hester) O.; m. Sarah Fleming, Aug. 3, 1945; children: Jane Fleming, Charles Porter. BA, La. State U., 1942, MA, 1946; LLD, St. Xavier U., 1971; DHum, Phillips U., 1977. Pub. relations counsel La. State U., 1945-47, acting dir. bur. pub. service, 1947; assoc. prof., chmn. dept. journalism and dir. pub. relations Howard Coll. (now Frank Samford U.), 1947-49; dir. pub. relations, lectr. journalism Miss. State Coll. (now Miss. State U.), 1949-53; dir. information Washington U., 1953-58, pub. relations adviser, 1955-58, dir. Devel. Funds, 1958-61; cons. coll. and univ. adminstrn., 1961—, including Drake, Duke, Phillips, Tampa, Tex. Christian univs., Atlantic Christian Coll. (now Barton Coll.), Bethany (W.Va.), Eckerd, Loretto Heights, St. Xavier U., Tenn. Wesleyan, Webster U., Hendrix, Mercy (Detroit), Bethel (Tenn.), McMurry U., St. Scholastica, Coker Coll., Christian Ch. Found., Nat. Meth. Found. Christian Higher Edn., Lexington Theol. Sem., Memphis Theol. Sem., Nat. Benevolent Assn. Christian Ch., Sisters of Loretto; interim pres. St. Xavier Coll., now St. Xavier U., 1968-69; mem. planning com. Conf. for Advancement Understanding and Support Higher Edn., White Sulphur Springs, W.Va., 1958; mem. exec. com. program and arrangements com. Gen. Assembly Christian Ch., 1977, 87-89. Bd. dirs. St. Louis Heart Assn., 1969-75, Fla. Christian Ctr., 1986-88; trustee Nat. City Christian Ch. Corp., 1981-85; mem. Christian Ch., bd. dirs., exec. com., sec. divsn. of higher edn., 1973-77, mem. panel to study fin. procedures of Christian Ch. (Disciples of Christ), 1987-89, Cypress Village Devel. Coun., Jacksonville, Fla., 1992—, chmn., 1995-97. Served from lt. to capt. 28th Inf. Divsn. AUS, 1942-45, ETO. Recipient Harry T. Ice disting. svc. award Christian Ch. Found., 1991. Mem. Am. Coll. Pub. Rels. Assn. (v.p. dists. 1951-52, v.p. membership 1952-53, sec.-treas. 1953-55, pres. 1959-60), Nat. Benevolent Assn. (amb. 1992—), Soc. Profl. Journalists, Omicron Delta Kappa, Sigma Chi. Home: 13655 Myrica Ct Jacksonville FL 32224-6626 also: PO Box 1639 Cashiers NC 28717-1639

OSBORN, MARY JANE MERTEN, biochemist; b. Colorado Springs, Colo., Sept. 24, 1927; d. Arthur John and Vivien Naomi (Morgan) Merten; m. Ralph Kenneth Osborn, Oct. 26, 1950. B.A., U. Calif., Berkeley, 1948; Ph.D., U. Wash., 1958. Postdoctoral fellow, dept. microbiology N.Y. U. Sch. Medicine, N.Y.C., 1959-61; instr. N.Y. U. Sch. Medicine, 1961-62, asst. prof., 1962-63; asst. prof. dept. molecular biology Albert Einstein Coll. Medicine, Bronx, N.Y., 1963-66; asso. prof. Albert Einstein Coll. Medicine, 1966-68; prof. dept. microbiology U. Conn. Health Center, Farmington, 1968—; dept. head U. Conn. Health Center, 1980—; mem. bd. sci. counselors Nat. Heart, Lung and Blood Inst., 1975-79; mem. Nat. Sci. Bd., 1980-86; adv. coun. Nat. Inst. Gen. Med. Sci., 1983-86, divsn. rsch. grants NIH, 1989-94, chair, 1992-94; trustee Biosci. Info. Systems, 1986-91; mem. German Am. Acad. Coun., 1994-97; mem. space scis. bd. NRC, 1994—, chair com. space biology and medicine, 1994—. Assoc. editor Jour. Biol. Chemistry, 1978-80; contbr. articles in field of biochemistry and molecular biology to profl. jours. Mem. rsch. com. Am. Heart Assn., 1972-77, chair, 1976-77. NIH fellow, 1959-61; NIH grantee, 1962-95 ; NSF grantee, 1965-68; Am. Heart Assn. grantee, 1968-71. Fellow Am. Acad. Arts and Scis. (coun. 1988-91), NAS (coun. 1990-93, com. sci. engring. and pub. policy 1993-96); mem. Am. Acad. Microbiology, Am. Fedn. Soc. Exptl. Biology (pres. 1982-83), Am. Soc. Biol. Chemists (pres. 1981-82), Am. Soc. Microbiology. Democrat. Office: U Conn Health Ctr Dept Microbiology Farmington CT 06030

OSBORN, RONALD EDWIN, minister, church history educator; b. Chgo., Sept. 5, 1917; s. George Edwin and Alma Edith (Lanterman) O.; m. Naomi Elizabeth Jackson, Sept. 10, 1940 (dec.); 1 dau., Virginia Elizabeth (dec.); m. Nola L. Neill, Aug. 29, 1986. Student, Lynchburg Coll., 1934-35, Union Theol. Sem. in Va., 1936; A.B., Philips U., 1938, M.A., 1939, B.D., 1942, Litt. D., 1969; postgrad., U. Okla., 1940-41; Ph.D., U. Oreg., 1955; D.D., Bethany Coll., 1989. Ordained to ministry Christian Ch. (Disciples of Christ), 1940. Min. Christian Ch., Lahoma, Okla., 1936-38, 1st Christian Ch., Geary, Okla., 1938-42, First Christian Ch., Jonesboro, Ark., 1942-43; editor youth publs. Christian Bd. Publ., St. Louis, 1943-45; prof. ch. history Northwest Christian Coll., Eugene, Oreg., 1946-50; min . Ch. of Christ, Creswell, Oreg., 1946-50; assoc. prof. ch. history Christian Theol. Sem. (formerly Butler U. Sch. Religion), Indpls., 1950-53, prof., 1953-73, dean, 1959-70; dir. ecumenical study Council Christian Unity, Disciples Christ, Indpls., 1954-57; vis. prof. ch. history and ecumenics Union Theol. Sem., Manila, Philippines, 1965; vis. prof. ch. history Sch. Theology, Claremont, Calif., 1970-71; prof. Sch. Theology, 1973-82; lectr. Grad. Sch. Ecumenical Studies, Chateau de Bossey, Switzerland, 1954-55; Del. World Conf. on Faith and Order, 1952, 63, 4th Assembly World Council Chs., Sweden, 1968; pres. Internat. Conv. Christian Chs., 1967-68; 1st moderator Christian Ch. (Disciples of Christ), 1968; staff Assembly World Council Chs., Evanston, Ill., 1954. Author: Toward the Christian Church, 1964, A Church for These Times, 1965, In Christ's Place, 1967, Experiment in Liberty, 1978, The Faith We Affirm, 1979, The Education of Ministers for the Coming Age, 1987, Creative Disarray: Models of Ministry in a Changing America, 1991; editor: Seeking God's Peace in a Nuclear Age, 1985, symposium The Reformation of Tradition, 1963, Encounter (formerly Shane Quar.), 1952-63. Mem. Disciples of Christ Hist. Soc. (trustee emeritus, past pres.), Am. Hist. Assn., Am. Soc. Ch. History, ACLU, Phi Kappa Phi, Theta Phi. Home: 85647 Bradbury Ln Eugene OR 97405-9683 *"A person who doesn't think is a slave; a person who won't imagine is a prisoner." — Daniel Dyer from "Imagine the world without imagination," Cleve. Plain Dealer, Jan. 3, 1986.*

OSBORN, TERRY WAYNE, biochemist, executive; b. Roswell, N.Mex., May 17, 1943; s. Woodrow Edward and Wilma Marie (Meador) O. AA, Ventura Coll., 1967; BS, U. Calif., Riverside, 1969; PhD, U. Calif.-Riverside, 1975; MBA, Pepperdine U., 1981. Research scientist McGaw Labs., Irvine, Calif., 1976, research scientist-project leader, 1976, research scientist, project team leader, 1976-79, group leader, sr. research scientist, 1978-79, mgr. clin. research, 1979-81, mktg. product mgr., 1981-82, mktg. group product mgr., 1982-83, dir. mktg., 1983-84; mktg. dir. IVAC Corp., San Diego, 1984-87; v.p. sales/mktg., officer Nichols Inst., Calif., 1987-89, v.p., asst. to chmn., 1990-91; v.p., gen. mgr. regional labs. Nichols Inst., 1991-93; pres., CEO Health Advance Inst., 1993—; 010 dirs. Med. Mktg. Assn., Peoria Med. Rsch. Corp.; mem. chemistry faculty Riverside City Coll., 1974-76, San Bernardino Valley Coll., 1974-76; asst. prof. clin. pharmacology U. Ill. Coll. Medicine. Served with U.S. Army, 1962-65. Recipient Agnes M. Toland Meml. Trust award, 1966; recipient Ventura Emblem Club award, 1967; Environ. Sci. fellow, 1970-73; Dean's Spl. fellow, 1974-75. Mem. Am. Chem. Soc., Am. Oil Chemists Soc., Med. Mktg. Assn. (bd. dirs.), Inst. Food Technologists, U.S. Ski Assn., One Mile Soc., Sigma Xi, Chi Gamma Iota, Alpha Gamma Sigma. Club: Tyrolean Ski (pres. 1972-73). Office: PO Box 1466 1 Illini Dr Peoria IL 61655-1466 *Nothing would be done at all if a man waited till he could do it so well that no one could find fault with it.*

OSBORN, WILLIAM A., trust company executive. Chmn. bd. dirs. No. Trust Corp., Chgo. Office: No Trust Corp 50 S La Salle St Chicago IL 60603-1003*

OSBORN, WILLIAM GEORGE, savings and loan executive; b. Alton, Ill., Dec. 9, 1925; s. Ralph A. and Pauline J. (Horn) O.; m. Hilda M. Alexander, Aug. 12, 1950; children: Barbara K., David A., Robert W., James A. B.S. in Math., Shurtleff Coll., 1947; certificate, Grad. Sch. Savs. and Loan, Ind. U., 1946-48; A.M. in Econs., St. Louis U., 1962. With Germania Fed. Savs. and Loan Assn., Alton, 1946-90; exec. officer Germania Fed. Savs. and Loan Assn., 1955-86, pres., 1964-86, chmn., 1981-86, chmn. trust com., 1982-86; pres. Fin. Service Assocs., Ft. Lauderdale, Fla., 1986—; pres. Germania Fin. Corp., 1970-86; owner Fin. Guidance, Alton, 1951—; mem. Opportunities Unltd., 1954-58; instr. Am. Savs. and Loan Inst.; bd. dirs. Nat. Coun. Savs. Instns., Washington, 1984-86. Author: Savings and Loan Operating Policies Manual, 1960, Economic Factors Influencing Savings and Loan Interest Rates, 1962. Pres. Alton Wood River Community Chest, 1959; bd. dirs. Piasa Bird coun. Boy Scouts Am., 1961-88, Mississippi Valley Jr. Achievement, Alton Area United Fund, 1961-63; founder, bd. dirs., treas. New Piasa Chautauqua Ch. Assembly, 1982-86; treas. Lewis and Clark Community Coll. Found., 1976-86; bd. dirs., sec. Riverbend Civic Progress, 1984-86. Served to lt. (j.g.) USNR, 1943-46, 50-51. Mem. Nat. Assn. Bus. Economists, Nat. Economists Club, St. Louis Economists Club, Am. Inst. Mgmt. Presbyterian (elder). Clubs: Masons (Alton); Shriners; Lockhaven Country (Alton); Chautauqua (Ill.) Yacht.

OSBORNE, BURL, newspaper publisher, editor; b. Jenkins, Ky., June 25, 1937; s. Oliver and Juanita (Smallwood) O.; m. Betty S. Wilder, Feb. 14, 1974; 1 son, Burl Jonathan. Student, U. Ky., 1955-57; B.A. in Journalism, Marshall U., 1960; M.B.A., L.I. U. Sch. Bus., 1984; A.M.P., Harvard Bus. Sch., 1984. Reporter Ashland (Ky.) Daily Ind., 1957-58; reporter, editor Sta. WHTN-TV, Huntington, W.Va., 1958-60; corr. AP, Bluefield, W.Va., 1960-62; statehouse corr. AP, Charleston, W.Va., 1963-64; corr. AP, Spokane, Wash., 1964-67; news editor AP, Denver, 1967-70; chief of bur. AP, Ky., 1970-72, Ohio, 1972-74; asst. chief of bur. AP, Washington, 1974-76; mng. editor AP, N.Y.C., 1977-80; exec. editor Dallas Morning News, 1980-83, v.p., 1981, sr. v.p., editor, 1983-84, pres., editor, 1985-90, pub., editor, 1991—; bd. dirs., pres. publ. divsn. A.H. Belo Corp., bd. dirs. AP, Pulitzer Prize, 1986-95, co-chair, 1994-95; bd. mem. adv. com. Nieman Found., Harvard U.; mem. journalism adv. com. Knight Found.; bd. dirs. Newspaper Assn. Am. Named Newspaper Exec. of Yr., Nat. Press Found., 1992; inducted to Ky. Journalism Hall of Fame, 1994; recipient Disting. Alumnus award Marshall U., 1997. Mem. Orgn. Profl. Journalists, Am. Soc. Newspaper Editors (bd. dirs. 1982-91, pres. 1990-91, 97—), Am. Press Inst. (chmn. 1988-93), Tex. Daily Newspaper Assn. (bd. dirs. 1982-92, pres. 1993), So. Newspaper Pub. Assn. (bd. dirs. 1995—). Home: 7609 Southwestern Blvd Dallas TX 75225-7927 Office: Dallas Morning News AH Belo Corp PO Box 655237 Dallas TX 75265-5237

OSBORNE, CHARLES WILLIAM (BILL OSBORNE), transportation executive; b. Dungannon, Va., Nov. 9, 1942; s. David Doyle and Lula Cordelia (Gillenwater) O.; m. Sandra Jean Elliot, Oct. 6, 1967; children: Jennifer, Michael, William. BS, Va. Tech., 1965; MA, West Ga. Coll., 1978. Mktg. planner Union Oil Co., Schaumburg, Ill., 1974-75, mgr. mktg. planning, 1981-82, mgr. purchasing, 1983-84, divsn. mktg. mgr., 1984-86; gen. mgr. mktg. Union Oil Co., Schaumburg, 1986-89; dist. sales mgr. Union Oil Co., Atlanta, 1975-78, mgr. divsn. svc., 1978-81; v.p. mktg. Uno-Ven Co., Arlington Heights, Ill., 1989-93; pres., CEO, bd. dirs. Nat. Auto/Truckstops, Inc., Nashville, 1992—; spl. asst. to chmn. U.S. Internat. Trade Commn., Washington, 1982-83. Bd. dirs. N.W. Comty. Hosp., Arlington Heights, 1989-94; active bus. adv. bd. Roosevelt U., Arlington Heights, 1989-96. 1st lt. U.S. Army, 1966-68. Mem. Am. Trucking Assn., Nat. Assn. Truckstop Operators, Petroleum Marketers Assn. Am., Petroleum Marketers Edn. Found. (bd. dirs.), Soc. Ind. Gasoline Marketers. Avocations: golf, racquetball, reading. Home: 6201 Belle Rive Dr Brentwood TN 37027-5613 Office: National Auto/Truckstops Inc 3100 W End Ave Ste 300 PO Box 76 Nashville TN 37202

OSBORNE, FREDERICK SPRING, JR., academic administrator, artist; b. Phila., Sept. 10, 1940; s. Frederick Spring and Katherine (Mitchell) O.; m. Deborah H. Cooper, June 30, 1964 (div. June 1979); children: Thomas, Sophia, Jessica; m. Judith K. M. Barbour, Feb. 15, 1986. BFA in Sculpture, Temple U., 1963; MFA in Sculpture, Yale U., 1965. From instr. to asst. prof. Grad. Sch. Fine Arts U. Pa., Phila., 1966-77; dir. continuing edn. Phila. Coll. Art, 1977-85; co-founder, dir., trustee Vt. Studio Ctr., Johnson, 1983—; dean, dir. Pa. Acad. Fine Arts, Phila., 1985—; lectr. Smith Coll., 1966, Phila. Coll. Art, 1976-85, U. Maine, 1980; cons. Inst. Internat. Edn., N.Y.C., 1984, Jury for Korean War Vet. Meml., Washington, 1989. Sculpture exhbns., 1962-82. Trustee Mantua-Powelton Edn. Fund, 1978-81, Assn. Ind. Coll. Art & Design, 1991—, Grass Roots Art and Comm. Effort, 1990—, Choral Arts Soc. Phila., 1997—; mem. Phila. Redevel. Authority Fine Arts Com.; co-chmn. Internat. Sculpture Conf., Phila., 1991. Mem. Nat. Assn. Sch. Art and Design (bd. dirs. 1989-96), Coll. Art. Assn., Nat. Art Edn. Assn., Nat. Assn. Art Administrs. Home: 3621 Hamilton St Philadelphia PA 19104-2327 Office: Pa Acad Fine Arts 118 N Broad St Philadelphia PA 19102-1510

OSBORNE, GEORGE DELANO, performing arts company director; b. Ft. Worth, Aug. 25, 1938; s. Hugh and Eula Catherine (Trent) O.; children from previous marriage: David Warren, Hugh Philip, George Douglas. B in Mus, Oklahoma City U., 1960; M in Mus, Ind. U., 1964; postgrad. in Arts Mgmt., Hartford Grad. Ctr., 1978. Mem. faculty Tex. Tech. U., Lubbock, 1962-64, S.W. Mo. State U., Springfield, 1964-66, Memphis State U., 1966-76, W.Va. U., Morgantown, 1976-78; gen. dir. Memphis Opera, Morgantown, 1971-76, Hartford (Conn.) Chamber Orch., Morgantown, 1978-79, Conn. Opera, Hartford, 1979—, Hartford Chamber Orch., 1979-88, Hartford Ballet, 1982-88; dir. opera prodns. Hartt Sch. Music, U. Hartford, 1993—. Mem. Hartford Cultural Affairs Commn., 1980. Fulbright scholar, Rome, 1960; Am. Leadership Forum fellow, 1986-87. Mem. Cen. Opera Svc. (regional dir.), Nat. Opera Assn. Home: 26 Riverview Avon CT 06001-2057 Office: Conn Opera Assn 226 Farmington Ave Hartford CT 06105-3501

OSBORNE, HAROLD WAYNE, sociology educator, consultant; b. Eldorado, Ark., Sept. 5, 1930; s. Carl Clinton and Mary Eunice (Peace) O.; m. Alice June Williams, Feb. 15, 1953; children—Michael, Van, Samuel. B.A. in History, Ouachita Bapt. Coll., 1952; M.A. in Sociology, La. State U., 1956, Ph.D. in Sociology, 1959. Research assoc. dept. rural sociology La. State U., 1954-56; social sci. analyst USDA, Baton Rouge, 1956-58; asst. prof. sociology Baylor U., Waco, 1958-60; assoc. prof. Baylor U., 1960-63, prof., 1963—, dir. grad. studies dept. sociology, 1963-87, chair dept. sociology, anthropology, social work and gerontology, 1988—; cons. in field; dir. workshops on crime and delinquency. Co-editor: Research Methods: Issues and Insights, 1971, Sociology: A Pragmatic Approach, 1996; co-author: Sociology: A Pragmatic Approach, 1981; assoc. editor for sociology Social Sci. Quar., 1965-75. Bd. dirs. Mclennan County Mental Health Assn., Tex., 1970-80. Served with inf. U.S. Army, 1952-54. Named Outstanding Baylor Prof., Baylor U., 1976, Master Tchr., 1993. Mem. Am. Sociol. Assn., Southwestern Sociol. Assn. (v.p. 1985-87, pres. 1987-88), Southwestern Social Sci. Assn., Population Assn. Am., Population Reference Bur., Am. Social Health Assn. (bd. dirs. Southwestern region). Democrat. Baptist. Home: 2717 Braemar St Waco TX 76710-2118 Office: Baylor U Dept Sociology Waco TX 76798

OSBORNE, HARRY ALAN, orthodontist; b. Youngstown, Ohio, Mar. 9, 1934; s. Kenneth L. and Marguerite (Filmer) O.; m. Carol June Williams, June 30, 1956 (dec. 1989); children: Elizabeth Ann, J. Scott, Linda J., Robert K.; m. Linda Sue Leister Simmons, May 9, 1993; stepchildren: William A. Simmons, John S. Simmons, Susan Jane Simmons. Student, Westminster Coll., New Wilmington, Pa., 1952-55; DDS, U. Pitts., 1959; MS, Northwestern U., 1962. Diplomate Am. Bd. Orthodontics. Intern Youngstown Hosp. Assn., 1959; practice dentistry specializing in orthodontics Canton, Ohio, 1964—. Supt. adv. com. North Canton Sch. Dist., 1960-87; mem. adv. com. Soc. Bank, Canton, 1962-89; chmn. bldg. com. Faith United Meth. Ch., 1975-80; chmn. cmty bd. YMCA, North Canton, 1986-96, charter mem. Heritage Club (Canton YMCA); v.p. Hills and Dales Homeowners Assn., 1993-96; mem. Christ Presbyn. Ch., Canton, Ohio. Recipient Disting. Service award, Jaycees, 1968. Mem. ADA, Pierre Fauchard Acad., Am. Assn. Orthodontists, Coll. of Diplomates of Am. Bd. Orthodontists (charter), Gt. Lakes Orthodontic Assn., Ohio Dental Assn., Cleve. Orthodontic Soc. (pres. 1983), Stark County Dental Soc. (pres. 1975-76), World Fedn. Orthodontists, Internat. Coll. Dentists, Shady Hollow Country Club (Massillon, Ohio) (bd. dirs. 1984-85, 87—), Brookside Country Club. Republican. Avocation: golf. Home: 2410 Strathmore Dr NW Canton OH 44708-1364 Office: 1021 Schneider St SE Canton OH 44720-3857

OSBORNE, JAMES ALFRED, religious organization administrator; b. Toledo, July 3, 1927; s. Alfred James and Gladys Irene (Gaugh) O.; m. Ruth Glenrose Campbell, Nov. 26, 1945; 1 child, Constance Jean (Mrs. Donald William Canning). Grad., Salvation Army Coll., 1947; student, U. Chattanooga, 1954-55; D of Pub. Svc. (hon.), Gordon Coll., 1991. Corps officer Salvation Army, Magness, Nashville, 1947, Southside, Memphis, 1948, Owensboro, Ky., 1949-54; comdg. officer Salvation Army, Chattanooga, 1954-61; city comdr. Salvation Army, Miami, Fla., 1961-65; divisional sec. Ky.-Tenn. Div. Salvation Army, 1965-68, gen. sec. N.C. and S.C. Div., 1968-70, pub. rels. sec. 15 so. states, D.C. and Mex., 1970-71, divisional comdr. Md. and No. W.Va. Div., 1971-73; divisional comdr. Nat. Capital and Virginias Div. Salvation Army, Washington, 1973-78; divisional comdr. Fla. Div. Salvation Army, 1978-80, chief sec. Western Ter., 1980-84; nat. chief sec. Salvation Army, Verona, N.J., 1984-86; territorial comdr. so. states Salvation Army, Atlanta, 1986-89; nat. comdr., Republic of Marshall Islands, Guam, P.R., Virgin Islands Salvation Army USA, 1989-93; chmn. Salvation Army Nat. Planning and Devel. Commn., 1974-76, 84-86; exec. bd. Vision Interfaith Satellite Network, Nat. Assn. Evangelicals, Christian Children's Fund Inc.; chmn. bd. Christian Mgmt. Assn., 1993-94; exec. com. religious alliance Against Pornography; rep. Salvation Army to numerous orgns. Bd. dirs. Nat. Law Ctr. for Children and Families; sec. Tenn. Conf. on Social Welfare, 1959, v.p., 1960; pres. Fla. Conf. on Social Welfare, 1965; pres. Ky. Welfare Assn., 1970. Mem. Chattanooga Pastors Assn. (pres. 1958), Va. and W. Va. Welfare Confs., Rotary.

OSBORNE, JAMES WILLIAM, radiation biologist; b. Pana, Ill., Jan. 17, 1928; s. Samuel Frederick and Ruby Clascena (Irel) O.; m. Marilyn Corrine Shaw, July 1, 1950; children—Walter, David. B.S., U. Ill., Champaign-Urbana, 1949, M.S., 1951, Ph.D., 1955. Research asst. dept. physics U. Ill., 1949-51; research asso. Control Systems Lab., 1951-55; asst. prof. Radiation Research Lab., U. Iowa, 1955-61, assoc. prof., 1961-67, prof., 1967—, dir. lab., 1978-93; dir. grad. program radiation biology U. Iowa, 1978—. Served with USAAF, 1946-47. Mem. Am. Soc. Therapeutic Radiology and Oncology, Radiation Rsch. Soc., Am. Physiol. Soc., Cell Kinetics Soc., Soc. Exptl. Biology and Medicine, Am. Assn. for Cancer Rsch. Methodist. Research, publs. on biol. effects of radiation and kinetics of cell populations. Home: 815 14th Ave Coralville IA 52241-1742 Office: Radiation Research Lab 77 Med Labs U Iowa Iowa City IA 52242

OSBORNE, JOHN WALTER, historian, educator, author; b. Bklyn., Aug. 19, 1927; s. Douglas Walter and Gertrude Ann (Purcell) O.; m. Frances Patricia Hannon, Aug. 2, 1958; 1 son, David. B.A., Rutgers U., 1957, M.A. (Louis Bevier fellow), 1959, Ph.D., 1961. Asst. prof. history Kean Coll. of N.J., 1961-63, N.J. Inst. Tech., 1963-64; asst. prof. Rutgers U., New Brunswick, N.J., 1964-66; assoc. prof. Rutgers U., 1966-69, prof., 1969-93, prof. emeritus, 1993—. Author: William Cobbett-His Thought and His Times, 1966, The Silent Revolution: The Industrial Revolution in England as a Source of Cultural Change, 1970, John Cartwright, 1972; co-author: Cobbett in His Times, 1990; editor: Jour. of Rutgers U. Libraries, 1975-80; co-editor: A Grammar of the English Language, 1983; contbr. articles to profl. jours. Recipient Henry Browne award for disting. teaching Rutgers U., 1988; Am. Philos. Soc. grantee, 1966, 75. Home: PO Box 426 Ivoryton CT 06442-1271

OSBORNE, MARY POPE, writer; b. Ft. Sill, Okla., May 20, 1949; d. William Perkins and Barnette (Dickens) Pope; m. William R. Osborne, May 16, 1976. BA in Religion, U. N.C., 1971. Author: Run, Run, As Fast As You Can, 1982, Love Always, Blue, 1983, Best Wishes, Joe Brady, 1984, Mo to the Rescue, 1985, Last One Home, 1986, Beauty and the Beast, 1987, Favorite Greek Myths, 1988, American Tall Tales, 1990, The Many Lives of Benjamin Franklin, 1990, Moon Horse, 1991, George Washington, Leader of a New Nation, 1991, Spider Kane Mystery Series, 1992, 93, Magic Tree House Series, 1992-97, Haunted Waters, 1994, Molly and the Prince, 1994, Favorite Norse Myths, 1996, One World, Many Religions, 1996, Rockinghorse Christmas, 1997. Recipient Disting. Alumna award U. N.C., Chapel Hill, 1994. Mem. PEN, Authors Guild (pres. 1993—, dir. found.), Authors League Fund (bd. dirs.), Author's Registry (founder). Office: Brandt & Brandt Lit Agy 1501 Broadway Ste 2310 New York NY 10036-5601

OSBORNE, MICHAEL JAMES, real estate executive, energy executive, author; b. Amarillo, Tex., Sept. 20, 1949; s. Jack Harold Osborne and Maxine Joan (Chambers) Novack; m. Dee Haws; children: Solomon, Hope; m. Layne Jackson, Dec. 22, 1991. Student, U. Tex., 1967-72. Owner Directions Co., Austin, Tex., 1971-74; mgr. Taylorvision, Taylor, Tex., 1974-76; owner/ptnr. Osborne Solar, Austin, 1977-94, Osborne Cos., Austin, 1988—, Catalina Investments and M&C Properties, Austin, 1984—, U.S. Renewables, Austin, 1991—, Virtual Conferencing, Austin, 1992—. Author: The Titanomachy, 1995; editor Spectra mag., 1981-83; inventor E.M.A.S.E.R., 1984, H.M.F. Power Plant, 1994. Trustee First Bapt. Ch., Elgin, 1980; bd. dirs. Kiwanis Club, Elgin, 1980; little league coach Optimist Club, Elgin, 1980; steering com. State of Tex. Energy Planning Partnership; chair Renewables; mem. Sustainable Energy Devel. Coun., State of Tex.; apptd. by Gov. Bush to Tex. Energy Coord. Coun., 1996. Recipient Disting. Svc. award Tex. Solar Energy Soc., 1985, Enlightened Leadership award Tex. Renewable Energy Industries Assn., 1993, Pres.'s award for Outstanding Contbns. in Renewable Energy, 1995. Mem. Tex. Renewable Energy Industries (pres. 1990-93), Solar Energy Soc., Internat. Solar Energy Soc., World Future Soc., Union of Concerned Scientists. Home: 909 W 23rd St Austin TX 78705-5007 Office: Osborne Energy PO Box 999 Elgin TX 78621-0999

OSBORNE, MICHAEL PIERS, surgeon, researcher, health facility administrator; b. Sutton, Surrey, Eng., Jan. 6, 1946; came to U.S., 1980; s. Arthur Frederick and Leonora Kate Hope (Miller) O.; m. Carolyn Patricia Malkinson, June 22, 1974; children: James, Simon, Andrew, Emma. MB, BS, London U., 1970, MS in Surgery, 1980. Diplomate Royal Coll. Surgeons of Eng., Am. Coll. Surgeons. Intern Charing Cross Group of Hosps., England, 1970-71; resident Brompton Hosp., London, St. James Hosp., London, West Herts Hosp., Eng.; hon. lectr. surgery Royal Marsden Hosp., London, 1977-81; fellow in surg. oncology Meml. Sloan-Kettering Cancer Ctr., N.Y.C., 1980-81, attending surgeon, 1981-91, head breast cancer rsch. lab., 1984-91; chief breast surgery N.Y. Hosp.-Cornell Med. Ctr., N.Y.C., 1991—; prof. surgery Cornell U. Med. Coll., N.Y.C., 1991—; dir., CEO Strang Cancer Prevention Ctr., N.Y.C., 1991-95, pres., CEO, 1995—; dir. Strang- Cornell Breast Ctr., N.Y.C., 1991—; mem. adj. faculty Rockefeller U. Hosp., N.Y.C., 1981-89, vis. physician, 1983—; mem. sci. adv. com. Am.-Italian Found., N.Y.C., 1991—; bd. trustees Nat. Consortium Breast Ctrs., 1992-95; cons. Meml. Sloan-Kettering Cancer Ctr., 1991-97; pres. N.Y. Met. Breast Group, 1995-97. Contbr. 12 chpts. to textbooks; contbr. over 100 articles to profl. jours. Recipient Gov.'s Clin. Gold medal Charing Cross Hosp. Med. Sch., 1970, Prize in Surgery, Charing Cross Hosp. Med. Sch., 1970, Raven prize British Assn. Surg. Oncology, 1978; Wellcome Trust fellow, 1975. Mem. Am. Surg. Assn., N.Y. Acad. Scis., N.Y. Surg. Soc., Brit. Assn. Surg. Oncology, Soc. Surg. Oncology, Royal Soc. Medicine, Am. Soc. Breast Disease (trustee 1993-95), Am. Assn. Cancer Rsch., Am. Soc. Clin. Oncology, Internat. Soc. for Cancer Chemoprevention (sec.-gen.). Office: Strang Cancer Prevention Ctr 428 E 72nd St Ofc 600 New York NY 10021-4635

OSBORNE, RICHARD DE JONGH, mining and metals company executive; b. Bronxville, N.Y., Mar. 19, 1934; s. Stanley de Jongh and M. Elizabeth (Ide) O.; m. Cheryl Anne Archibald, Dec. 14, 1957; children: Leslie Coleman, Lindsay Vogel, Nicholas de J., Stanley de J. A.B. in Econs., Princeton U., 1956. With Cuno Engring. Corp., Meriden, Conn., 1956-60; fin., planning and mktg. exec. IBM Corp., Armonk, N.Y., 1960-69; investment adviser Sherman M. Fairchild, N.Y.C., 1969-70; exec. v.p. fin. and bus. devel., dir. Fairchild Camera & Instrument Corp., Mountain View, Calif., 1970-74; v.p. fin. ASARCO Inc. (formerly Am. Smelting & Refining Co.), N.Y.C., 1975-77, exec. v.p., 1977-82, pres., 1982-85, chmn., pres., chief exec. officer, 1985—; bd. dirs. Schering-Plough Corp., BF Goodrich, The Tinker Found., So. Peru Copper Corp., Copper Devel. Assn. Mem. Nat. Mining Assn., Ams. Soc. (bd. dirs.), Coun. Fgn. Rels. (bd. dirs.), Am. Australian Assn. (bd. dirs.), Internat. Copper Assn. (bd. dirs.), Down Town Assn., Econs. Club, City Midday Club, Sakonnet Golf Club. Home: 40 E 94th St Apt 32B New York NY 10128-0759 Office: Asarco Inc 180 Maiden Ln New York NY 10038-4925

OSBORNE, RICHARD GEORGE, naval officer, cardiologist, educator; b. Rochester, N.Y., Feb. 10, 1946; s. Robert Edward and Ruth (Thomas) O.; m. Stephanie Leupp, May 21, 1966; children: Erica Michelle, Heather Kathryn, Nicholas Francis. BA Brown U., Brown U., 1968; MA, U. Wis., 1970; MD, U. Conn., 1975. Staff internist USN, Newport, R.I., 1978-80; fellow in cardiology USN Hosp., San Diego, 1980-82; staff cardiologist Great Lakes (Ill.) Naval Hosp., 1982-84; cardiologist Plymouth (New Hampshire) Internal Medicine, 1984-85; head dept. internal medicine Naval Aerospace Med. Instn., Pensacola, Fla., 1985-88; sr. med. officer USS Midway, Yokusuku, Japan, 1988-90; head of medicine USNS Mercy (TAH 19), Persian Gulf, 1990-91; head divsn. cardiology USN Hosp., Oakland, Calif., 1991-93; head divsn. cardiology Naval Med. Ctr., San Diego, 1993-95, chmn. dept. internal medicine, 1995—. Mem. San Diego Coun. Am. Heart Assn., 1997. Fellow ACP, Am. Coll. Cardiology; mem. Am. Heart Assn., Assn. Program Dirs. Internal Medicine. Home: 3040 Brant St San Diego CA 92103 Office: Naval Med Ctr 34800 Bob Wilson Dr San Diego CA 92134-5002

OSBORNE, RICHARD HAZELET, anthropology and medical genetics educator; b. Kennecott, Alaska, June 18, 1920; s. Clarence Edward and Margaret Jerenne (Hazelet) O.; m. Barbara White, Oct. 14, 1944; children: Susan, Richard, David; m. Barbara Teachman, Sept. 1, 1970. Student, U. Alaska, 1939-41; BS, BA, U. Wash., 1949; postgrad., Harvard U., 1949-50; PhD (Viking Fund Pre-doctoral fellow, Spl. fellow Inst. for Study Human Variation), Columbia, 1956; hon. doctor odontology, U. Oulu, Finland, 1994. Research asso. Columbia U., 1953-58; asst. Sloan-Kettering Inst., N.Y.C., 1958-60; asso. Sloan-Kettering Inst., 1960-62, asso. mem., head sect. human genetics, 1962-64; prof. anthropology and med. genetics U. Wis., Madison, 1964-86, prof. emeritus, 1986—; rsch. assoc. Quatenary Ctr. U. Alaska, Fairbanks, 1993—; asso. prof. preventive medicine Cornell Med. Coll., 1962-64; clin. geneticist Meml. Hosp. for Cancer, N.Y.C., 1963-65; vis. scientist Forsyth Dental Center, Boston, 1969-71; cons. human genetics Newington (Conn.) Childrens Hosp., 1971-73; Mem. com. on epidemiology and vets. follow-up studies NRC, 1969-73; mem. perinatal research com. Nat. Inst. Neurol. Diseases and Stroke, NIH, 1970-72; mem. cultural anthropology fellowship and rev. NIMH, 1969-73. Author: Genetic Basis of Morphological Variation, 1959, Biological and Social Meaning of Race, 1971; Editor: Social Biology, 1961-77, 81—; contbr. articles to profl. jours. Served to maj. USAAF, 1942-46. Decorated D.F.C., Air medal with 3 oak leaf clusters.; Named Health Research Council Career Scientist City N.Y., 1962-64. Fellow Explorers Club; Mem. Am. Assn. Phys. Anthropology (exec. com. 1965-67, v.p. 1968-70), Am. Soc. for Human Genetics (dir. 1960-61, 67-69), Behavior Genetics Assn. (pres. pro-tem 1970-71), Soc. for Study Social Biology (dir. 1981-83, 86—), Pioneers of Alaska (life), Sigma Xi. Office: PO Box 2349 Port Angeles WA 98362-0303

OSBORNE, RICHARD JAY, electric utility company executive; b. N.Y.C., Feb. 16, 1951; s. Victor and Evelyn Celia (Sweetbaum) O. B.A., Tufts U., 1973; M.B.A., U. N.C., 1975. Fin. analyst Duke Power Co., Charlotte, N.C., 1975-78, sr. fin. analyst, 1978-80, mgr. fin. rels., 1980-81, mgr. treasury activities, 1981, treas., 1981-88, v.p. fin., CFO, 1988-94, sr. v.p., CFO, 1994—. Pres. Charlotte Jewish Fedn.; mem. bd. Found. for the sch. of Pub. Health, U. N.C., Chapel Hill. Mem. Fin. Execs. Inst., Edison Electric Inst. (fin. & regulatory sect.), Found. for the Carolinas (chmn. investment com.), N.C. Coun. Edn. (chair). Democrat. Jewish. Office: Duke Power Co 422 S Church St Charlotte NC 28242-0001

OSBORNE, STANLEY DE JONGH, investment banker; b. San Jose, Costa Rica, Mar. 27, 1905; m. Elizabeth Ide, Oct. 28, 1929 (dec. Sept. 1984); children: Mary Ide (Mrs. John Witherbee), Richard de Jongh, Cynthia Adams (Mrs. Richard M. Hoskin). Student, Phillips Acad., Andover, Mass., 1918-22; AB cum laude, Harvard U., 1926, postgrad. bus. sch., 1926-27. Dir. publicity Harvard Athletic Assn., 1927-28; with Old Colony Corp., Boston, 1928-29; asst. to pres. Atlantic Coast Fisheries Co., 1929-30, treas., 1930-36, 39-43, asst. sec., 1932-42, v.p., 1936-43; spl. asst. to rubber dir. Washington, 1942-43; v.p. Eastern Airlines, Inc., 1944-50; fin. v.p. Mathieson Chem. Corp., Balt., 1950-54; exec. v.p. Olin Mathieson Chem. Corp., 1954-57, pres., chmn. dir., 1957-64; gen. ptnr. Lazard Freres & Co., N.Y.C., 1963-69, ltd. ptnr., 1970—; chmn. Pvt. Investment Corp. for Asia, Singapore, 1980-85. Spl. asst. to Pres., Am. Olympic Team, Gen. Douglas McArthur, Amsterdam, 1928; spl. adviser to Pres. John F. Kennedy, 1963-64; mem. Pres.'s Adv. Com. Supersonic Transport, 1964-67; spl. cons. to adminstr. NASA, 1966-68; bd. govs. Soc. N.Y. Hosp.-Cornell Med. Ctr., N.Y.C., 1957—, pres., 1975-80, chmn., 1980-85, hon. chmn., 1986—. Mem. Harvard Club, Brook Club, River Club. Episcopalian. Home: 1 E End Ave New York NY 10021-1102 Office: Lazard Freres & Co 30 Rockefeller Plz New York NY 10112

OSBORNE, THOMAS CRAMER, mineral industry consultant; b. Winnipeg, Man., Can., Mar. 21, 1927; s. Claude H. and Marguerite S. (Cramer) O.; m. Geraldine Smith, May 9, 1950; children—James, Michael. B.S. with honors, U. Man., 1948, M.S., 1949; postgrad., U. Ariz., 1949-50. Exploration geologist, mgr. Internat. Nickel Co., Asarco, and others, Can., U.S., Mex., Cuba, 1944-80; exec. v.p. Asarco Inc., 1980-92; chmn. Asarco Australia Ltd., 1986-92; mineral industry cons., 1992—. Mem. AIME, Can. Inst. Mining and Metallurgy. Home and Office: 7887 N La Cholla Blvd Apt 3168 Tucson AZ 85741-4359

OSBORNE, TOM, college football coach; b. Feb. 23, 1937; m. Nancy Tederman; children: Mike, Ann, Susie. B.A., Hastings Coll., 1959; M.A., U. Nebr., 1963, Ph.D. in Ednl. Psychology, 1965. Flankerback Washington Redskins, NFL, 1959-61, San Francisco 49ers, NFL, 1961-62; asst. football coach U. Nebr., 1962-73, head football coach, 1973—; coach team U. Nebr. (Cotton Bowl), 1974, U. Nebr. (Sugar Bowl), 1971, U. Nebr. (Astro-Bluebonnet Bowl), 1976, U. Nebr. (Liberty Bowl), 1977, U. Nebr. (Sun Bowl), 1980, U. Nebr. (Orange Bowl), 1979, 83, 84, 89, 92-95. Served in U.S. Army. Named Big Eight Coach of Yr., 1975, 78, 80; named Bobby Dodds Nat. Coach of Yr., 1978. Coached team to NCAA Divsn. IA Nat. Championship, 1994-95. Office: care Nebr Sports Info 116 South Stadium Lincoln NE 68588*

OSBORNE-POPP, GLENNA JEAN, health services administrator; b. East Rainelle, W.Va., Jan. 5, 1945; d. B.J. and Jean Ann (Haranac) Osborne; m. Thomas Joseph Ferrante Jr., June 11, 1966 (div. Nov. 1987); 1 child, Thomas Joseph Osborne; m. Brian Mark Popp, Aug. 13, 1988. BA cum laude, U. Tampa, 1966; MA, Fairleigh Dickinson U., 1982; cert., Kean Coll., 1983.

Cert. English, speech, dramatic arts tchr., prin./supr.; cert. nursing child assessment feeding scale and nursing child assessment tchg. scale, 1996. Tchr. Raritan High Sch., Hazlet, N.J., 1966; tchr. Keyport (N.J.) Pub. Schs., 1968-86, coord. elem. reading and lang. arts, 1980-84, supr. curriculum and instrn., 1984-86; prin. Weston Sch., Manville, N.J., 1986-88, The Bartle Sch., Highland Park, N.J., 1988-91, Orange Ave. Sch., Cranford, N.J., 1991-92; dir. The Open Door Youth Shelter, Binghamton, N.Y., 1992-94; child protective investigator supr. Dept. Health and Rehab. Svcs., Orlando, Fla., 1994-95; program supr. Children's Home Soc., Sanford, Fla., 1995; clin. supr. Healthy Families-Orange, Orlando, Fla., 1995—; regional trainer Individualized Lang. Arts, Weehawken, N.J., 1976-86; cons. McDougal/Little Pubs., Evanston, Ill., 1982-83; chair adv. bd. women's residential program Ctr. for Drug Free Living, Orlando, 1996. Contbr. chpt.: A Resource Guide of Differentiated Learning Experiences for Gifted Elementary Students, 1981. Sunday sch. tchr. Reformed Ch., Keyport, 1975-80, supt. Sunday sch., 1982-84. Mem. Order Ea. Star (Tampa, Fla.), Phi Delta Kappa. Republican. Methodist. Avocation: writing. Office: Healthy Families 623 S Texas Ave Orlando FL 32805-3064

OSBOURNE, OZZY (JOHN OSBOURNE), vocalist; b. Birmingham, Eng., Dec. 3, 1948. Vocalist Black Sabbath band, 1969-78, solo career, 1978—. Albums include Blizzard of Ozz, 1980, Diary of a Madman, 1981, Bark at the Moon, 1983, The Ultimate Sin, 1986, No Rest for the Wicked, 1989, Just Say Ozzy, 1990 (EP), No More Tears, 1991, Live & Loud, 1993, (with Black Sabbath) Black Sabbath, 1969, Paranoid, 1970, Master of Reality, 1971, Sabotage, 1975, Technical Ecstasy, 1976, Never Say Die, 1978; singles: So Tired, 1984, (with Black Sabbath) Paranoid, 1970. Grammy award, Best Heavy Metal Performance 1994 for "I Don't Want to Change the World". Address: Epic Records 550 Madison Ave New York NY 10019*

OSBY, LARISSA GEISS, artist; b. Artemowsk, Russia, June 7, 1928; came to U.S., 1951, naturalized, 1958; d. Andrew Frank and Valentine G. (Pogoreloff) Geiss; m. Howard M. Osby, June 7, 1952; children: Erik Andrew, Karin Marian. Student, U. Goettingen (Germany), 1947, 48, 49, Acad. Art, 1949-50, U. Munich, 1949-50; postgrad., U. Goettingen, Germany, 1951. BA in Philosophy U. Goettingen, Germany, 1950, MA in Philosophy, 1951; rsch. asst., translator, med. illustrator U. Pitts. Med. Sch., 1952-53; art instr. Pitts. Ctr. for Arts, 1961-64, 88-90; pvt. art tchr. Pitts., 1961-64; adv. artist Pitts. Bd. Edn., 1964-66; instr. anatomy, drawing and painting High Sch. for Creative and Performing Arts, Pitts., 1984—. One woman shows at, AAP Gallery, Pitts., 1960, Pitts. Plan for Art Gallery, 1961, 63, 65, 68, 71, 79, Carnegie Inst., Pitts., 1972, Pa. State U., 1973, Duquesne U., Pitts., 1980, Pitts. Ctr. for Arts, 1983, St. Vincent Coll., 1983, others; exhibited in group shows at, Butler Inst., Youngstown, Ohio, 1958, 59, 79, 86, Chautauqua Nat. Anns., 1964, 73, St. Paul Art Center, 1963, Marietta Coll., 1968, Walker Art Center, Mpls., 67, William Penn Meml. Mus., Harrisburg, Pa., 1971, also museums in Germany, France, Scotland, numerous others; represented in permanent collections at, Carnegie Inst., U. Pitts., Pitts. Bd. Edn., Am. Cancer Soc., Alcoa, U.S. Steel, Westinghouse, Koppers Co., others; commns. include, Koppers Co., First Fed. Savings & Loan Assn., Pitts., U.S. Steelworkers Am., others. Recipient Citation as Woman of Distinction, Gov. Pa., 1972; named Artists of Yr., Pitts. Ctr. for Arts, 1983, award Women in Art, 1995, 96, 20 Jury awards, others. Mem. Abstract Group Pitts. (pres. 1964-65), Associated Artists Pitts. (bd. dirs. 1965-68, 80-83), Pitts. Ctr. for Arts, Concept Gallery. Democrat. Address: 2665 Hunters Point Dr Franklin Park PA 15090

OSBY, ROBERT EDWARD, protective services official; b. San Diego, Oct. 29, 1937; s. Jesse William and Susie Lillian (Campbell) O.; m. Clydette Deloris Mullen, Apr. 11, 1961; children: Daryl Lawrence, Gayle Lorraine. AA in Fire Sci., San Diego Jr. Coll., 1970; BA in Mgmt., Redlands U., 1985. Recreation leader San Diego Parks and Recreation Dept., 1955-58; postal carrier U.S. Postal Service, San Diego, 1958-59; fire fighter San Diego Fire Dept., 1959-67, fire engr., 1967-71, fire capt., 1971-76, fire bn. chief, 1976-79; fire chief Inglewood (Calif.) Fire Dept., 1979-84, San Jose (Calif.) Fire Dept., 1985—. Served to 2d lt. Calif. NG, 1960-65. Mem. Calif. Met. Fire Chiefs (chmn. 1987—), Internat. Assn. Black Firefighters (regional dir. 1974-77), Brothers United (pres. 1972-75). Democrat. Avocations: fishing, jogging, landscaping. Home: 28203 Engelmann Oak Trl Escondido CA 92026-6960 Office: San Diego Fire Dept 1010 2nd Ave Ste 400 San Diego CA 92101-4912*

O'SCANNLAIN, DIARMUID FIONNTAIN, judge; b. N.Y.C., Mar. 28, 1937; s. Sean Leo and Moira (Hegarty) O'S.; m. Maura Nolan, Sept. 7, 1963; children: Sean, Jane, Brendan, Kevin, Megan, Christopher, Anne, Kate. BA, St. John's U., 1957; JD, Harvard U., 1963; LLM, U. Va., 1992. Bar: Oreg. 1965, N.Y. 1964. Tax atty. Standard Oil Co. (N.J.), N.Y.C., 1963-65; assoc. Davies, Biggs, Strayer, Stoel & Boley, Portland, Oreg., 1965-69; dep. atty. gen. Oreg., 1969-71; public utility commr. of Oreg., 1971-73; dir. Oreg. Dept. Environ. Quality, 1973-74; sr. ptnr. Ragen, Roberts, O'Scannlain, Robertson & Neill, Portland, 1978-86; judge, U.S. Ct. Appeals (9th cir.), San Francisco, 1986—, mem. exec. com., 1988-89, 1993-94, mem. Jud. Coun. 9th Cir., 1991-93; mem. U.S. Judicial Conf. Com. on Automation and Tech., 1990—; cons. Office of Pres.-Elect and mem. Dept. Energy Transition Team (Reagan transition), Washington, 1980-81; chmn. com. adminstrv. law Oreg. State Bar, 1980-81. Mem. council of legal advisers Rep. Nat. Com., 1981-83; mem. Rep. Nat. Com., 1983-86, chmn. Oreg. Rep. Party, 1983-86; del. Rep. Nat. Convs., 1976, 80, chmn. Oreg. del., 1984; Rep. nominee U.S. Ho. of Reps., First Congl. Dist., 1974; team leader Energy Task Force, Pres.'s Pvt. Sector Survey on Cost Control, 1982-83, trustee Jesuit High Sch.; mem. bd. visitors U. Oreg. Law Sch., 1988—; mem. citizens adv. bd. Providence Hosp., 1986-92. Maj. USAR, 1955-78. Mem. Fed. Bar Assn., ABA (sec. Apellate Judges Conf. 1989-90, exec. com. 1990—, chmn.-elect 1994—), Arlington Club, Multnomah Club. Roman Catholic. Office: US Ct Appeals 313 Pioneer Courthouse 555 SW Yamhill St Portland OR 97204-1336*

OSCARSON, KATHLEEN DALE, writing assessment coordinator, educator; b. Hollywood, Calif., Sept. 16, 1928; d. Chauncey Dale and Hermine Marie Rulison; m. David Knowles Leslie, June 16, 1957 (div. Aug. 1970); m. William Randolph Oscarson, Apr. 27, 1974. AB, UCLA, 1950, MA, 1952; Cert. Advanced Study, Harvard U., 1965; Diplomé Elementaire, Le Cordon Bleu U. Paris, 1972. Gen. secondary life credential, Calif. Cons. Advanced Placement English Calif. Dept. Edn., Sacramento, 1968-70; reader Calif. Assessment Program, Sacramento, 1989—; instr. individual study U. Calif. Extension, Berkeley, 1979-92; reader, leader Ednl. Testing Svc., Princeton, N.J. and Emeryville, Calif., 1967—; reader San Jose (Calif.) State U., 1991—; tchr. English, counselor Palo Alto (Calif.) Unified Sch. Dist., 1954-90, H.S. writing assessment coord., 1987—; adj. lectr. English Santa Clara (Calif.) U., 1990-91; commr. Curriculum Study Commn., San Francisco Bay Area, 1978—; chair tchrs. English Spring Asilomar Conf., Pacific Grove, Calif., 1992, Asilomar 44, Pacific Grove, 1994; presenter Conf. on English Leadership, Chgo., 1996. Mem. lang. arts assessment adv. com. Calif. State Dept. Edn., Sacramento, 1975-90; mem.-at-large exec. bd. Ctrl. Calif. Coun. Tchrs. English, Bay Area, 1969-71; mem. Medallion Soc. San Francisco Opera, 1984—; mem. ann. summer event com., membership com. Internat. Diplomacy Coun. Mem. MLA, Nat. Coun. Tchrs. English (group leader conf. San Francisco), Calif. Assn. Tchrs. English, Internat. Diplomacy Coun. San Francisco (membership and events coms. 1996), Harvard Club San Francisco, Christopher Marlowe Soc. Avocations: cuisine, voice, writing. Home: 230 Durazno Way Portola Valley CA 94028-7411

OSEGUERA, PALMA MARIE, marine corps officer, reservist; b. Kansas City, Mo., Dec. 29, 1946; d. Joseph Edmund and Palma Louise (Utke) O'Donnell; m. Alfonso Oseguera, Jan. 1, 1977; stepchildren: Kristie M. Daniels, Michelle L. Nielson, Lori A. Kelley. BA in Phys. Edn., Marycrest Coll., 1969. Commd. 2d lt. USMC, 1969, advanced through grades to col., 1991; asst. marine corps exch. officer Hdqs. and Hdqs. Squadron, Marine Corps Air Sta., Beaufort, S.C., 1969-71; classified material control officer Hdqs. and Svcs. Battalion, Camp S.D. Butler, Okinawa, 1971-73; adminstrv. officer, asst. Marine Corps exch. officer Marine Corps Air Sta., El Toro, Santa Ana, Calif., 1973-76; Marine Corps exch. officer Marine Corps Air Sta., Yuma, Ariz., 1976-77; asst. marine corps exch. officer Hdqrs. and Support Bat., Marine Corps Devel. & Edn. Command, Quantico, Va., 1977-79; marine corps exch. officer Hqrs. Marine Corps, Washington, 1979-80; adminstrv. officer Marine Air Base Squadon 46, Marine Air Group 46, Marine Corps Air Sta., El Toro, Santa Ana, 1981-83, Hdqs. and Maintanence Squadron 46, Marine Air Group 46, Marine Corps Air Sta., El Toro, Santa Ana, 1983-85, Mobilization Tng. Unit Calif. 53, Landing Force Tng. Command, Pacific, San Diego, 1985-89, 3d Civil Affairs Group, L.A., 1989; dep. asst. chief of staff G-1 I Marine Expeditionary Force, Individual Mobilization Augumentaee Detachment, Camp Pendleton, Calif., 1990-91; assoc. mem. Mobilization Tng. Unit Del. 01, Del., 1992-94; adminstrn. officer Mobilization Tng. Unit, CA-53, EWTG Pac, NAB, Coronado, San Diego, 1994-96; exch. officer MWRSPT ACT IMA Det MCB, Camp Pendleton, Calif., 1996—. Mem. choir St. Elizabeth Seaton, Woodbridge, Va., 1978-80, St. Patricks, Arroyo Grande, Calif., 1990-94; vol. Hospice, San Luis Obispo, 1995—; mem. Los Osos (Calif.) veteran's events com. Mem. AAUW (past libr.), Marine Corps Assn., Marine Corps Res. Officer Assn., Marine Corps Aviation Assn. (12 dist. dir. 1987), Women in Mil. Svc. for Am. Republican. Roman Catholic. Avocations: skiing, jogging, reading, pet care/sitting. Home: 728 Scenic Cir Arroyo Grande CA 93420-1617

OSEI, EDWARD KOFI, financial analyst, educator, strategic planner; b. Bibiani, Ghana, Jan. 3, 1959; came to U.S., 1975; s. Yaa Agnes (Bosuo) Osei. Student, U. Ghana, 1981; M in Internat. Mgmt., Baylor U., 1984; MA in Internat. Rels., Yale U., 1988; MBA, Stanford U., 1988. Gen. mgr. Express Messengers Ltd., Lagos, Nigeria, 1981-84; sr. fin. analyst Eastman Kodak Co., Rochester, N.Y., 1989-91, strategic planner, 1991-92; owner, pres. Ashanti Properties & Mgmt., Rochester, 1990-92; sr. bus. planner Pepsicola Internat., Somers, N.Y., 1992-95; sr. cons. Monitor Co., Boston, 1995-96; sr. mgr. Planning Bristol-Myers Squibb Co., 1996—; adj. prof. strategic mgmt. SUNY, Brockport, 1990-92; advisor Boy Scouts Am., Rochester, 1989—; dir. fin. Baiden Settlement Home, Rochester; bd. dirs. C.O.N.E.A., Rochester Nat. Treasures. Yale U. fellow, 1985, Stanford U. fellow, 1986; Baylor U. scholar, 1984. Mem. Nat. Black MBA Assn., AIESEC (project coord., Excellence award 1981), Stanford U. Alumni Assn., Yale U. Alumni Assn., Baylor U. Alumni Assn., Eastman Kodak Black Employees Assn., Toastmasters Internat. Home: 709 Kathy Dr Yardley PA 19067 Office: Bristol-Myers Squibb Box 4000 Princeton NJ 08543-4000

OSEN, GREGORY ALAN, water conditioning company executive; b. Beloit, Wis., Mar. 14, 1951; s. Vincent Darryl and Mavis Lucille (Lasher) O.; m. Deborah Ann Churchill Bladorn, Jan. 29, 1972 (div. Jan. 1987); m. Christine Adel Dauenbaugh Pulliam, Oct. 8, 1987; children: Leah Michelle, Felicia Ann. BA in Music Edn. with honors, Milton (Wis.) Coll., 1973; postgrad., Cardinal Stritch Coll., 1985. Machinist, assembler Nat. Detroit, Rockford, Ill., 1973-78; sales tech. Ill. Water Treatment, Rockford, 1978-79, sales engr., 1979-80, dist. sales engr., 1980-85; sales mgr. Glegg Water Conditioning Inc., Guelph, Ont., Can., 1985—. Pres. Seekers, Strawbridge Meth. Ch., 1995-96, mem. adminstrv. bd., 1996, mem. choir, 1995-96; trumpeter Harris County Big Band, 1993-95. Mem. Am. Water Works Assn. Avocation: video prodn., sports cars, auto racing. Home: 6002 Boulder Lake Ct Kingwood TX 77345 Office: Glegg Water Conditioning, 29 Royal Rd, Guelph, ON Canada N1H 1G2

OSENTON, THOMAS GEORGE, publisher; b. Boston, Apr. 9, 1953; s. George Thomas and Helen (Curran) O.; m. Mary Ellen Dalzell, Aug. 16, 1975; children: Curran Lynn, Matthew. BA, U. New Hampshire, 1976. Pub. relations dir. USA Hockey, Colorado Springs, Colo., 1976-78; exec. dir. Blue Line Club Wis., Madison, 1978-81; writer WCVB-TV Ch.5 ABC Affil., Boston, 1981-82; dir. olympic pub. ABC TV Network, N.Y.; dir. mktg. ABC Pub., N.Y., 1983-86; pub. Sports Mktg. News, Conn., 1986-88; pub. Am. Artist Billboard Publs. Inc., N.Y.C., 1988-89; pres., chief exec. officer Sporting News Pub. Co., St. Louis, 1989-93; pres. Courier New Media, Lowell, Mass., 1993—; chmn. Altered States, Inc., N.Y.C. Avocation: golf. Home: 55 Godfrey Rd W Weston CT 06883-1303 Office: 15 Wellman Ave North Chelmsford MA 01863-1334

OSEPCHUK, JOHN MOSES, engineering physicist, consultant; b. Peabody, Mass., Feb. 11, 1927; s. Moses Nicholas and Mary (Sukoff) O.; m. Shirley Greenwood Small; children: Jonathan Greenwood, Lauren Ann, Janet Miriam. AB, Harvard U., 1949, AM, 1950, PhD, 1957. Devel. engr. power tube div. Raytheon, Waltham, Mass., 1950-56, liaison engr. at CSF, 1956-57; devel. engr. microwave and power tube div. Raytheon Co., Burlington, Mass., 1957-62; prin. rsch. engr. rsch. div. Raytheon Co., Waltham, 1964-74; cons. scientist Raytheon Co., Lexington, Mass., 1974-95; chief microwave engr. Sage Labs., Natick, Mass., 1962-64; cons. in microwave heating and microwave safety Full Spectrum Cons., Concord, Mass., 1995—; mem. accredited standards com. C95 Am. Nat. Standards Inst., N.Y.C., 1968—. Editor: Biological Effects of Electromagnetic Radiation, 1983; contbr. over 80 articles to profl. jours.; patentee in field. Clk. Park St. Ch., Boston, 1958-65, trustee, 1965-72; mem. Rep. Town Com., Concord, Mass., 1974—. With U.S. Army, 1945-46. Fellow IEEE (chmn. com. on man and radiation, exec. sec. stds. coord. com. 1991-95, chmn. stds. coord. com. 1995—), Internat. Microwave Power Inst. (pres. 1992-95), Am. Sci. Affiliation; mem. Microwave Soc. of IEEE (nat. lectureship 1977-78), Electromagnetic Energy Policy Alliance (advisor to bd. dirs.), Bioelectromagnetics Soc., Sigma Xi, Phi Beta Kappa. Republican. Congregationalist. Avocations: tennis, music, tree work, writing. Home: 248 Deacon Haynes Rd Concord MA 01742-4759 Office: Full Spectrum Cons 248 Deacon Haynes Rd Concord MA 01742-4759

OSGOOD, CHRIS, professional hockey player; b. Peace River, Alta., Canada, Nov. 26, 1972. With Detroit Red Wings, 1991—. Named to WHL East All-Star Second Team, 1990-91, Sporting News All Star Team, 1996; recipient Bill Jennings Trophy NHL, 1996; played in NHL All-Star Game, 1996. Office: c/o Detroit Red Wings 600 Civic Center Dr Detroit MI 48226-4408

OSGOOD, FRANK WILLIAM, urban and economic planner, writer; b. Williamston, Mich., Sept. 3, 1931; s. Earle Victor and Blanche Mae (Eberley) O.; children: Ann Marie, Frank William Jr. BS, Mich. State U., 1953; M in City Planning, Ga. Inst. Tech., 1960. Prin. planner Tulsa Met. Area Plnning Commn., 1958-60; sr. assoc. Hammer & Co. Assocs., Washington, 1960-64; econ. cons. Marvin Springer & Assocs., Dallas, 1964-65; sr. assoc. Gladstone Assocs., Washington, 1965-67; prof. urban planning Iowa State U., Ames, 1967-73; pres. Frank Osgood Assoc./Osgood Urban Rsch., Dallas, 1973-84; dir. mktg. studies MPSI Americas Inc., Tulsa, 1984-85, Comarc Systems/Roulac & Co., San Francisco, 1985-86; pres. Osgood Urban Rsch., Millbrae, Calif., 1986-95; freelance writer Millbrae, Calif., 1994-95; VISTA vol. coord. Chrysalis, Santa Monica, Calif., 1995-96; pres. Osgood Urban Rsch., L.A., 1996—; adj. prof. U. Tulsa, 1974-76; lectr. U. Tex., Dallas, 1979, U. Tex., Arlington, 1983. Author: Control Land Uses Near Airports, 1960, Planning Small Business, 1967, Continuing Renewal Cities, 1970; contbr. articles to profl. jours. Chmn. awards Cub Scouts Am., Ames, 1971-73; deacon Calvary Presbyn. Ch., San Francisco, 1987-90. 1st lt. USAF, 1954-56. Recipient Community Leaders and Noteworthy Americans award 1976. Mem. Am. Planning Assn. (peninsula liaison 1987-89, dir. pro-tem 1990 No. Calif. sect., edn. coord. 1991-92, Calif., dir. N. Cen. Tex. sect., Tex. chpt. 1983), Am. Inst. Planners (v.p. Okla. chpt. 1975-77), Okla. Soc. Planning Cons. (sec., treas. 1976-79), Urban Land Inst., Le Club. Republican. Presbyterian. Home: Ter Trousdale 11400 National Blvd Los Angeles CA 90064-3729

OSGOOD, RICHARD MAGEE, JR., applied physics and electrical engineering educator, research administrator; b. Kansas City, Mo., Dec. 28, 1943; s. Richard Magee and Mary Neff (Russell) O.; m. Alice Rose Dyson, June 25, 1966; children—Richard Magee, III, Nathaniel David, Jennifer Anne. B.S. in Engring., U.S. Mil. Acad., 1965; M.S. in Physics, Ohio State U., 1968; Ph.D., MIT, 1973. Rsch. assoc. dept. physics MIT, Cambridge, 1969-72, mem. rsch. staff Lincoln Lab., 1973-80, project leader Lincoln Lab., 1980-81; assoc. prof. applied physics and elec. engring. Columbia U., N.Y.C., 1981-82, prof., 1982-91, Higgins prof., 1989—; dir. Microelectronics Sci. Labs., 1984-90; mem. Army Sci. and Tech. Basic Energy Scis. Adv. Com. Materials Rsch. Coun.-Advanced Rsch. Projects Agy.; cons. Los Alamos Nat. Lab.; mem. ad hoc com. Air Force Sci. Adv. Bd. Editor: Laser Diagnostics and Photochemical Processing of Semiconductor Devices, 1983; assoc. editor: Applied Physics; contbr. articles to profl. jours.; patentee in field. Served to capt. USAF, 1965-69. Recipient Samuel Burka award USAF Avionics Lab., 1968, Leos Travelling Lectr. award, 1986-87, Disting. Travelling Lectr. APS, R.W. Wood Prize, 1991, Optical Soc. Am.; John Simon Guggenheim fellowship, 1989. Fellow IEEE, Optical Soc. Am. (R.W. Wood award, 1991); mem. Am. Chem. Soc., Materials Rsch. Soc. (councillor 1983-86), Optical Device Assn. (Japanese hon. lectr. 1990), Am. Phys. Soc. (travelling lectureship 1992). Home: 345 Quaker Rd Chappaqua NY 10514-2615 Office: Columbia U Radiation Laboratory New York NY 10027

O'SHAUGHNESSY, ELLEN CASSELS, writer; b. Columbia, S.C., Oct. 1, 1937; d. Melvin O. and Grace Ellen (Cassels) Hemphill; m. John H. Sloan (dec.); children: John H., Anne H.; m. John F. O'Shaughnessy, Dec. 8, 1979 (div. Mar. 1990). BA, Internat. Coll., L.A., 1977; MA in Counseling Psychology, Fielding Inst., Santa Barbara, Calif., 1980. Tchr.'s aide, art instr. Monterey Peninsula (Calif.) Unified Sch. Dist., 1968-74; tchr. adult sch. Pacific Grove (Calif.) Unified Sch. Dist., 1974-82, spl. edn. cons., 1984-85; sustitute tchr. Monterey County Office Edn., Salinas, Calif., 1983-84; owner, writer, pub. Synthesis, Pacific Grove, Calif., 1984—. Author: Teaching Art to Children, 1974, Synthesis, 1981, You Love to Cook Book, 1983, I Could Ride on the Carousel Longer, 1989, Somebody Called Me A Retard Today...And My Heart Felt Sad, 1992, Walker & Co., N.Y.C. Episcopalian. Home: PO Box 51063 Pacific Grove CA 93950-6063

O'SHAUGHNESSY, GARY WILLIAM, military officer; b. N.Y.C., Feb. 6, 1939; s. William Eugene and Anne Elizibeth O'Shaughnessy; m. Diane Gertrude Gavin, May 8, 1971; children: Kim Gavin, Karen Anne. BA in English, Fordham U., 1960; MEd, Manhattan Coll., 1970. Commd. 2d lt. USAF, 1960, advanced through grades to maj. gen., 1989; adminstrv. officer Air Flight Test Ctr., Edwards AFB, Calif., 1960-62; student Communication Intelligence Officer Course, Goodfellow AFB, Tex., 1962-63; dir. ops. 6923RSM and OL, Vietnam, 1963; intelligence officer 6922ESG, Clark AB, P.I., 1963-65, Nat. Security Agy., Ft. Meade, Md., 1965-67; instr., comdt. of cadets Manhattan Coll., N.Y.C., 1967-70; intelligence officer Pacific Security Region, Wheeler AFB, Hawaii, 1970-72; asst. ops. officer 6921ESW, Misawa AB, Japan, 1972; intelligence officer USAF Security Svc., San Antonio, 1972-73; rep. to air staff Nat. Security Agy., Ft. Meade, 1974-77; comdr. 6903ESS, Korea, 1977-78, Electronic Security Command Units in Pacific, Hickam AFB, Hawaii, 1979-82, Electronic Security Command Units in Europe, Ramstein AB, Germany, 1982-85; assoc. dep. dir. for ops. Nat. Security Agy., Ft. Meade, 1985-87; dep. chief of staff, intelligence Hdqrs. U.S. Forces in Europe, Ramstein AB, Germany, 1987-88; dir. intelligence Hdqrs. U.S. European Command, Stuttgart-Vaihingen, Germany, 1988-89; comdr. Air Force Intelligence Command, San Antonio, 1989-93. Contbr. articles to profl. jours. Decorated Def. Superior Svc. medal, Legion of Merit, Bronze Star, Meritorious Svc. medal, Joint Svc. Commendation medal. Mem. Air Force Assn., USAF Security Svc./Electronic Security Command Assn. (pres. Potomac chpt.), Armed Force Comm. and Electronics Assn., Nat. Mil. Intelligence Assn., Assn. Old Crows, World Affairs Coun. Avocations: reading, carpentry, tennis, exercise. Home: 17808 Stoneridge Dr North Potomac MD 20878-1020 Office: Oracle Govt Corp 3 Bethesda Metro Ctr Bethesda MD 20814-5330

O'SHAUGHNESSY, JAMES PATRICK, lawyer; b. Rochester, N.Y., Mar. 3, 1947; s. John Andrew and Margaret May (Yaxley) O'S.; m. Terry Lee Wood. BS cum laude, Rensselaer Poly. Inst., 1972; JD, Georgetown U., 1977. Bar: Va. 1977, Ohio 1979, Wis. 1987. Assoc. Squire, Sanders & Dempsey, Cleve., 1978-81; ptnr. Hughes & Cassidy, Sumas, Wash., 1981-84; patent counsel Kimberly-Clark Corp., Neenah, Wis., 1984-85; ptnr. Foley & Lardner, Milw., 1986-96; v.p., chief intellectual property counsel Rockwell Internat. Corp., Seal Beach, Calif., 1996—; founder Innovatech Co., 1996—; mem. adv. bd. Licensing Econs. Rev.; mem. bd. visitors Georgetown U. Sch. Nursing; mem., bd. dir. Intellectual Property Owners; frequent lectr., chmn. seminars to legal and bus. groups. Contbg. author: Technology Licensing: Corporate Strategies for Maximizing Value, 1996; contbr. articles to profl. jours. Bd. dirs. Skylight Opera Theatre, 1991-92. With USN, 1964-68. Mem. CPR Inst. for Dispute Resolution (mediation/arbitration panel), Lic. Execs. Soc., Am. Intellectual Property Law Assn., Assn. Chief Patent Coun.; Disabled Am. Vets., Tau Beta Pi, Alpha Sigma Mu. Home: 3367 Crownview Dr Rancho Palos Verdes CA 90275 Office: Rockwell Internat Corp 2201 Seal Beach Blvd Seal Beach CA 90740-5603

O'SHAUGHNESSY, JOSEPH A., restaurant company executive. Sr. exec. v.p. Friendly Ice Cream Corp., Wilbraham, Mass., 1957—. Office: Friendly Ice Cream Corp 1855 Boston Rd Wilbraham MA 01095-1002

O'SHEA, CATHERINE LARGE, marketing and public relations consultant; b. Asheville, N.C., Feb. 27, 1944; d. Edwin Kirk Jr. and Mary Mitchell (Westall) Large; m. Roger Dean Lower, Dec. 19, 1970 (dec. Sept. 1977); children: Thaddeus Kirk Lower and David Alexander Lower (twins, dec.); m. Michael Joseph O'Shea, Dec. 29, 1980. BA in History magna cum laude, Emory U., 1966. Mktg. staff mem. Time Inc., N.Y.C., 1966-69; mktg. adminstr. Collier-Macmillan Internat., N.Y.C., 1970-71; circulation mgr. Coll. Entrance Exam. Bd., N.Y.C., 1971-73; spl. asst. to pres. Wayne Dressel Assocs. Exec. Search, N.Y.C., 1973-75; freelance writer, editor, pub. rels. Princeton, N.J., 1975-78; dir. constituency rels. Emory U., Atlanta, 1978-80; devel. assoc. U. Del., Newark, 1981-83; asst. to pres. Elizabethtown (Pa.) Coll., 1983-85; assoc. v.p. Beaver Coll., Glenside, Pa., 1985; cons. mktg. and pub. rels. Phila., S.C., 1985—. Co-author: 50 Secrets of Highly Successful Cats, 1994 (trans. German edit. Schnurrende Tyrannen by Manfred Sommer, 1996); editor Elizabethtown mag., 1983-85; contbr. articles to nat. mags. and profl. jours. Founder Helping Hands Internat.; trustee Large Found., Newberry Opera House Found. Mem. Pub. Rels. Soc. Am. (accredited), Mortar Bd., Phi Beta Kappa, Phi Mu.

O'SHEA, JOHN P., insurance executive; b. Poughkeepsie, N.Y., May 1, 1930; s. John P. and Mildred A. (Galbraith) O'S.; m. Nancy Ann Shaw; m. Michael, Patricia, Stephen, Sandra. BS, Fordham U., 1951. Various positions Marshall & Sterling Inc., Poughkeepsie, 1955-70, v.p., 1970-80, pres., 1980—; bd. dirs. Crabapple Ins. Co., vice chmn., 1992—, Bermuda, Riverside Bank, Poughkeepsie, 1987—, chmn. of bd., 1993—; chmn. bd. VBH Ins. Co., Barbados. Trustee Area Fund Dutchess County, Poughkeepsie, 1983-89, Marist Coll., 1994—, Mid-Hudson Med. Ctr., 1991—, Bardavon Opera House, 1990-94; chmn. bd. dirs. Vassar Bros. Hosp. and VBH Corp., Poughkeepsie, 1986-88; bd. dirs. Poughkeepsie Partnership, 1993—; nat. chmn. Marist Ann. Fund, 1995—; chmn. Alexis De Tocqueville Soc., United Way of Dutchess County. Lt. USNR, 1952-55, Korea; comdr., 1955-76. Mem. Poughkeepsie Area C. of C. (chmn. 1982-83), Dutchess Golf and Country Club, Rotary (pres. Poughkeepsie 1968-69). Avocation: golf. Office: 110 Main St Poughkeepsie NY 12601-3083

O'SHEA, LYNNE EDEEN, marketing executive, educator; b. Chgo., Oct. 18, 1945; d. Edward Fisk and Mildred (Lessner) O'S. B.A., B.J. in Polit. Sci. and Advt, U. Mo., 1968, M.A. in Communications and Mktg. Research, 1971; PhD in Consumer Cultures, Northwestern U., 1977; postgrad., Sch. Mgmt. and Strategic Studies, U. Calif., 1988. Pres. O'Shea Advt. Agy., Dallas, 1968-69; congl. asst. Washington, 1969-70; brand mgr. Procter & Gamble Co., Cin., 1971-73; v.p. Foote, Cone & Belding, Inc., Chgo., 1973-79; v.p. corp. communications Internat. Harvester Co., Chgo., 1979-82; dir. communications Arthur Andersen & Co., Chgo., 1983-86; v.p. strategic planning Campbell-Ewald, Detroit and Los Angeles, 1986; v.p. bus. devel. Gannett Co., Inc., Chgo., 1987-94; group strategic planning dir. DDB Needham Worldwide, Inc., Chgo., 1995-96; pres., chief oper. officer Shalit Place L.L.C., 1995—; exec. v.p. Mus. Broadcast Comm., Chgo., 1996—; prof. mktg. U. Chgo. Grad. Sch. Bus., 1979-80, Kellogg Grad. Sch. Mgmt., 1983-94; disting. vis. prof. Syracuse U., 1982—; vis. prof. Franklin Coll., Lugano, Switzerland, 1997—. Bd. dirs. Off-the-Street Club, Chgo., 1977-86; mem. adv. bd. U. Ill. Coll. Commerce, 1980-95, Girl Scouts Am., 1985—, Chgo. Crime Commn., 1987—, Stephenson Rsch. Ctr., 1987—, DePaul U., 1989—, Roosevelt U., 1994—. Recipient numerous Eagle Fin. Advt. awards, Silver medalist Am. Advt. Fedn., 1989; named Advt. Woman of Yr. Chgo. Advt. Club, 1989; named Glass Ceiling Commn., 1991-95, Com. 21st Century, 1992—. Mem. Internat. Women's Forum (v.p. devel., v.p. communications, exec. com., bd. dir.), Chgo. Network, Women's Forum Chgo., Women's Forum Mich., Tarrytown Group, Social Venture Network, Execs. Club Chgo., Mid-Am. Club (bd. govs. 1990—), Women's Athletic Club Chgo. Office: Nat Investment Svcs The John Hancock Ctr 60 E Chestnut St # 378 Chicago IL 60611-2012

O'SHEA, PATRICIA A., physician, educator; b. Syracuse, N.Y., June 14, 1944; d. John Daniel and Mildred (Olbeter) Allen; m. John S. O'Shea, July 5, 1969. BS summa cum laude, Le Moyne Coll., 1966; MD, Johns Hopkins U., 1970. Diplomate Am. Bd. Pathology, Am. Bd. Anatomic, Clin. and Pediat. Pathology. From intern to resident Duke U. Med. Ctr., Durham, N.C., 1970-74; from asst. to assoc. prof. pathology Brown U., Providence, 1974-90; assoc. prof. pathology Emory U., Atlanta, 1990—; mem. faculty Armed Forces Inst., Washington, 1989; short-course faculty U.S. and Can. Acad. Pathology, Augusta, Ga., 1992—. Contbr. articles to profl. jours. Fellow Am. Acad. Pediats., Coll. Am. Pathologists; m. Soc. Pediat. Pathology (mem. coun.). Avocations: tennis, opera, baseball, travel. Office: Egleston Children's Hosp Emory U 1405 Clifton Rd NE Atlanta GA 30322-1060

OSHEROFF, DOUGLAS DEAN, physicist, researcher; b. Aberdeen, Wash., Aug. 1, 1945; s. William and Bessie Anne (Ondov) O.; m. Phyllis S.K. Liu, Aug. 14, 1970. B.S. in Physics, Calif. Inst. Tech., 1967; M.S., Cornell U., 1969, Ph.D. in Physics, 1973. Mem. tech. staff Bell Labs., Murray Hill, N.Y., 1972-82, head solid state and low temperature physics research dept., 1982-87; prof. Stanford (Calif.) U., 1987—, J.G. Jackson and C.J. Wood prof. physics, 1992—; chair physics, 1993-96. Researcher on properties of matter near absolute zero of temperature; co-discoverer of superfluidity in liquid 3He, 1971, nuclear antiferromagnetic resonance in solid 3He, 1980. Co-recipient Simon Meml. prize Brit. Inst. Physics, 1976, Oliver E. Buckley Solid State Physics prize, 1981, Nobel prize in physics, 1996; John D. and Catherine T. MacArthur prize fellow, 1981. Fellow Am. Phys. Soc., Am. Acad. Arts and Scis., Nat. Acad. Scis. Office: Stanford U Dept Physics Stanford CA 94305-4060

O'SHIELDS, RICHARD LEE, retired natural gas company executive; b. Ozark, Ark., Aug. 12, 1926; s. Fay and Anna (Johnson) O'S.; m. Shirley Isabelle Washington, Nov. 8, 1947; children: Sharon Isabelle O'Shields Boles, Carolyn Jean, Richard Lee Jr. B.S. in Mech. Engring, U. Okla., 1949; M.S. in Petroleum Engring, La. State U., 1951. Registered profl. engr., Kans., Tex. Instr. petroleum engring. La. State U., 1949-51; prodn. engr. Pure Oil Co., 1951-53; sales engr., chief engr., v.p. Salt Water Control, Inc., Ft. Worth, 1953-59; cons. engr. Ralph H. Cummins Co., Ft. Worth, 1959-60; with Anadarko Prodn. Co. and parent co. Panhandle Eastern Pipe Line Co., 1960-88; pres. Anadarko Prodn. Co., 1966-68; exec. v.p. Panhandle Eastern Pipe Line Co., 1968-70, pres., chief exec. officer, 1970-79, chmn., chief exec. officer, 1979-83, chmn., 1983-88, also bd. dirs., 1969-93; pres., CEO Trunkline Gas Co., 1970-79, chmn., CEO, 1979-83, chmn., 1983-88. With USAAF, 1945. Mem. Am. Petroleum Inst., Soc. Petroleum Engrs., Ind. Natural Gas Assn. Am., Gas Research Inst., Ind. Petroleum Assn. Am., So. Gas Assn., Tau Beta Pi. Republican. Methodist. Lodge: Masons. Home: 3130 Camels Ridge Ln Colorado Springs CO 80904-1032

OSHIMA, MICHAEL W., lawyer; b. Big Rapids, Mich., Apr. 4, 1957; s. Walter W. and Mitsue (Marutani) O. AB, Brown U., 1979; MA, Harvard U., 1984; JD, NYU, 1987. Bar: N.Y. 1988, D.C. 1989. Sr. rsch. asst. John F. Kennedy Sch. Govt., Cambridge, Mass., 1981-84; assoc. Davis Polk & Wardwell, N.Y.C., 1987-90; assoc. Arnold & Porter, N.Y.C., 1990-96, ptnr., 1997—. Contbr. articles, reports to profl. publs. Mem. Am. Sociol. Assn., Law and Soc. Assn., N.Y. State Bar Assn., Assn. of Bar of City of N.Y. Office: Arnold & Porter 399 Park Ave New York NY 10022

O'SHONEY, GLENN, church administrator. Exec. dir. Mission Svcs. of Luth. Ch. Mo. Synod Internat. Ctr., St. Louis. Office: Luth Ch Mo Synod Inter Ctr 1333 S Kirkwood Rd Saint Louis MO 63122-7226*

OSIANDER, LOTHAR, soccer coach; came to U.S., 1958; children: Kurt, Erik. AA in Gen. Edn., San Francisco City Coll.; BA in Phys. Edn. and Modern Langs., U. San Francisco. coach Calif. Soccer Assn., 1972-89; head coach U.S. Nat. Team, U.S. Olympic Team. Named Coach of Yr., A-League, 1995. Office: LA Galaxy 1640 S Sepulveda Blvd Los Angeles CA 90025

OSIAS, RICHARD ALLEN, international financier, investor, real estate investment executive, corporate investor; b. N.Y.C., Nov. 13, 1938; s. Harry L. and Leah (Schenk) O.; m. Judy Delaine Bradford, Oct. 26, 1984; children: Kimberly, Alexandra Elizabeth. Grad., Columbia U., 1963; postgrad., David Lipscomb U., 1988—. Founder, chmn., CEO Osias Enterprises, Inc., numerous locations, 1953—; mem. bus. cabinet David Lipscomb U.; bd. dirs. Am. 21. Prin. works include city devel., residential and apt. units, founder City North Lauderdale, Fla., co-founder City of Lauderhill, Fla., complete residential housing communities, shopping centers, country clubs, golf courses, hotel chains, comprehensive housing communities; contributed Greystone Raquet and Tennis Club to Nolensville, Tenn.; owner, operator Coolsprings Exec. Plz., landmark office bldg., Internat. Common Market Shopping Complex and other office bldgs., shopping ctrs. in mid-southern region; co-author: South Florida Uniform Building Code. Mem. North Lauderdale City Coun., 1967—, mayor, 1968, police and fire commr., 1967—; mem. Gold Cir., Atlanta Ballet; benefactor Atlanta Symphony Soc.; founder Boys Clubs Broward County, Tower coun. Pine Crest Prep. Sch. (founder), v.p., bd. dirs. LaCiel Park Tower Condominium Assn. Recipient Best Am. House award Am. Home mag., 1962, Westinghouse award, 1968, Cert. of Merit for outstanding achievement and contbn. to City of Atlanta by Mayor Andrew Young, 1982; named Builder of Yr., Sunshine State Info. Bur., Fla. and Sunshine State Sr. Citizen, Fla., 1967-70, Builder of Month, Builder/Arch. Mag., 1992, Hon. Police Chief, Nashville, Tenn., 1995; profiles on nat. and internat. media, including NBC TV, CBS TV and Fuji Network (Japan). Mem. Ft. Lauderdale BBB, N.Y. BBB, Nashville BBB, Offshore Power Boat Racing Assn., Fraternal Order Police Assn. (pres.), U.S. C. of C., Fla. C. of C., Margate C. of C., Ft. Lauderdale C. of C., Smithsonian Instn., Soc. Founders U. Miami, Tower Coun., Columns Soc., Pinecrest Prep. Sch. (founder), Nat. Assn. Home Builders, Bankers Club (Miami, Fla.), Bankers Top of First Club, Quarter Deck Club (Galveston, Tex.), Boca Raton (Fla.) Yacht and Country Club, Maunalua Bay Club (Honolulu), Tryall Golf and Country Club (Jamaica), Top of the Home Club, Svc. Plus Club (France), Ensworth Red Gables Soc., Cannes Island Yacht Club, Canary Islands Yacht Club, Collier's Reserve Country Club (Naples, Fla.), Grey Oaks Country Club (Naples). Home: Club Le Ciel #1401 3991 Gulf Shore Blvd N Naples FL 34103-3693 also: The Hillsborough 505 Almonte Ct Nashville TN 37215-9006

OSIPOW, SAMUEL HERMAN, psychology educator; b. Allentown, Pa., Apr. 18, 1934; s. Louis Morris and Tillie (Wolfe) O.; m. Sondra Beverly Feinstein, Aug. 26, 1956; children: Randall A., Jay I., Reva S., David S. B.A., Lafayette Coll., Easton, Pa., 1954; M.A., Columbia U., 1955; Ph.D., Syracuse U., 1959. Lectr. U. Wis., Madison, 1961; psychologist, asst. prof. Pa. State U., 1961-67; mem. faculty Ohio State U., Columbus, 1967—; prof. psychology Ohio State U., 1969—, chmn. dept., 1973-86; vis. prof. Tel-Aviv U., 1972, U. Md., 1980-81; vis. research assoc. Harvard U., 1965; cons. to govt. Author: Strategies in Counseling for Behavior Change, 1970, Theories of Career Development, 1968, 4th edit. 1996, Handbook of Vocational Psychology, 2 vols., 1983, 2d edit. 1995, A Survey of Counseling Methods, 1984; editor: Jour. Vocat. Behavior, 1970-75, Jour. Counseling Psychology, 1975-81, Applied and Preventative Psychology, 1993—. Served to 1st lt. U.S. Army, 1959-61. Mem. APA (bd. dirs. 1985-88), Nat. Register Health Svc. Providers in Psychology (bd. dirs. 1982-89, chmn. 1986-89). Home: 330 Eastmoor Blvd Columbus OH 43209-2022 Office: Ohio State U Psychology Dept Columbus OH 43210

OSIYOYE, ADEKUNLE, obstetrician, attorney medical and legal consultant, gynecologist, educator; b. Lagos, Nigeria, Jan. 5, 1951; came to U.S., 1972; s. Alfred and Grace (Apena) Oshiyoye; m. Toyin Osinowo Oshiyoye, Dec. 28, 1991; children: Adekunle Jr., Adedayo Justice. Student, Howard U., 1972-73; BS, U. State of N.Y., 1974; postgrad., Columbia U., 1974-78; MD, Am. U., Montserrat, West Indies, 1979; JD, Thomas Cooley Law Sch., Lansing, Mich., 1997. Intern South Chgo. Community Hosp., 1980-81; intern dept. obstetrics-gynecology Cook County Hosp., Chgo., 1981-82, resident physician, 1982-84, chief resident physician dept. obstetrics-gynecology, 1984-85; assoc. prof. dept. obstetrics-gynecology Chgo. Osteo. Coll. Medicine, 1986—; health physician, cons. physician City of Chgo. Dept. Health, 1989—; attending physician St. Bernard Hosp., Chgo., 1985—, Hyde Park Hosp., Chgo., 1986—, Mercy Hosp., Chgo., 1987—, Roseland Hosp., Chgo., 1985—, Columbus Hosp., Chgo., 1985—, Jackson Park Hosp., Chgo., 1985—; coord. emergency rm. Cook County Hosp., 1983-85, cons. medical, legal residential care. Med. editor African Connections, 1990—; med. columnist Newsbreed Mag., 1990—; founding mem. Ob-Gyn Video Jour. Am. Organizer Harold Washington Coalition, Chgo., 1983-87; operation mem. Operation P.U.S.H., Chgo., 1987—; active Chgo. Urban League, 1989—, Cook County Dem. Party, 1988—; mem. Mayor's Commn. on Human Rels., Chgo., 1990—, State of Ill. Inaugural Com., 1991. Shell scholar, 1965-69; recipient Fed. Govt. scholarship award, 1972, Howard Univ. scholarship award, 1973, Fed. Govt. Nigeria grad. med. scholarship award, 1975-79, Cerebral Palsy rsch. award, 1977, Ob-gyn. Video Jour. award, 1989, Role Model award Chgo. Police Dept., 1991, 92, Chgo. Bd. Edn., 1991, Chgo. 100 Black Men, 1991, Gov.'s Recognition award, 1992; named one of Best Dressed Men in Chgo., Chgo. Defender, 1990, 91. Fellow Am. Coll. Internat. Physicians, Am. Coll. Obstetricians & Gynecologists; mem. AMA (physician recognition award 1986), Am. Coll. Glegal Medicine (edn. com.), Am. Soc. Law Medicine, Am. Pub. Heart Assn., Nat. Med. Assn., Ill. Med. Soc., Chgo. Med. Assn., Chgo. Gynecol. Soc., Cook County Physician Assn., Nigerian Am. Forum (chmn. health com., chmn. election com.), Cook County Hosp. Surg. Alumni Assn., Howard U. Alumni Assn. (regent, chmn. scholarship com. Chgo. chpt.), Eureka Lodge (investigating com.), Masons, Shriners, Order of Eastern Star, Alpha Phi Alpha (life mem., mem. Labor Day com., dir. edn1. programs Xi Lambda chpt. 1990—, co-chmn. courtesy Black & Gold com. 1989, 90, Recognition award 1991), Pan Hellenic Action Coun. (chmn. pub. rels. com.), Ill. Maternal and Child Health Coalition, Beta Kappa Chi. Apostolic. Avocations: ping pong, fishing, golf, basketball, swimming. Home: PO Box 15187 Lansing MI 48901-5187 Office: Dept Health 37 W 47th St Chicago IL 60609-4657

OSKOLKOFF, GRASSIM, Native American Indian tribal chief; b. Ninilchik, Alaska, Oct. 14, 1926; s. Michael and Zoya (Darien) O.; m. Marion Emma Encelewski, Oct. 30, 1952; children: Debra, Marla, Bruce, Gary, Becky. Student, Ninilchik Sch., Alaska. With Alaska R.R., Anchorage; comml. fisherman Ninilchik, Alaska; pres., dir. Ninilchik Native Assn., Inc., Alaska, 1971-82; chief, pres. Ninilchik Traditional Coun., Alaska, 1982—; former rep. Alaska Fedn. Natives, Anchorage; rep. Alaska Inter-Tribal Coun., Anchorage, Cook Inlet Treaty Tribes, Alaska; commr. Alaska Sea Otter Commn., Fairbanks. Bd. dirs. Russian Orthodox Ch., Ninilchik; environ. adv. Promotion of Peace Among People and Nations. With inf. AUS, WWII, PTO. Avocations: fishing, hunting. Office: Ninilchik Traditional Coun PO Box 39070 Ninilchik AK 99639-0070

OSLER, DOROTHY K., state legislator; b. Dayton, Ohio, Aug. 19, 1923; d. Carl M. and Pearl A. (Tobias) Karstaedt; BS cum laude in Bus. Adminstrn., Miami U., Oxford, Ohio, 1945; m. David K. Osler, Oct. 26, 1946; children: Scott C., David D. Mem. Conn. Ho. of Reps., 1973-92. Mem. Greenwich (Conn.) Rep. Town Meeting, 1968—, Eastern Greenwich Women's Rep. Club, 1970—; sec. Conn. Student Loan Found., 1973-83, v.p., 1983-84; mem. Spl. Edn. Cost Commn., 1976-77, Sch. Fin. Adv. Panel, 1977-78, Edn. Equity Study Com., 1980-81, Commn. on Goals for U. Conn. Health Ctr., 1975-76; bd. dirs. ARC, 1975. Mem. Nat. Order Women Legislators (sec. 1987-89), Conn. Order of Women Legislators (sec. 1983-84, pres. 1985-86), LWV (pres. Greenwich chpt. 1965-67, sec. Conn. chpt. 1967-72), AAUW (dir. 1971-73, 95-97), Mortar Board, Phi Beta Kappa, Alpha Omicron Pi. Republican. Christian Scientist. Bi-weekly columnist local newspaper, 1973-83.

OSLER, GORDON PETER, retired utility company executive; b. Winnipeg, Man., Can., June 19, 1922; s. Hugh Farquarson and Kathleen (Harty) O.; m. Nancy A. Riley, Aug. 20, 1948; children: Sanford L., Susan Osler Matthews, Gillian Osler Fortier. Student, Queen's U., Kingston, Ont., Can., 1940-41. Pres. Osler, Hammond & Nanton Ltd., Winnipeg, 1952-64, UNAS Investments Ltd., Toronto, Ont., Can., 1964-72; chmn. Slater Steel Industries, Hamilton, Ont., Can., 1972-86, N.Am. Life Assurance Co., Toronto, 1986-95; chmn. TransCan. Pipelines, Toronto, 1983-89, ret., 1993. Lt. Can. Army, 1942-45, ETO. Mem. Toronto Club, York Club (Toronto), Everglades Club (Palm Beach, Fla.). Avocation; golf. Home: 17 Lamport Ave, Toronto, ON Canada M4W 1S7 Office: TransCan Pipelines, 55 Yonge St 8th Flr, Toronto, ON Canada M5E 1J4

OSLER, HOWARD LLOYD, controller; b. Camden, N.J., Nov. 24, 1927; s. Howard B. and Miriam (Locke) O.; m. Barbara C. Skufca, 1987; children by previous marriage: Carol, Peter, Andrew, Bruce. B.A., Antioch Coll., 1951. CPA, D.C. Pub. acct. Peat, Marwick Mitchell & Co., Boston, 1949-55; staff asst. to corp. contr. Gillette Co., Boston, 1957-59; gen. mgr. Panamanian subs. Gillette Co., 1959-61; asst. to pres. Gillette Co. Argentine subs., 1961-63; asst. to corp. contr. Gillette Co., Boston, 1963-65; contr. mil. Far East div. Gillette Co., 1965-67; contr. U.S. div. Foxboro Co., Mass., 1967-68; corp. contr. Foxboro Co., 1968-87, sec., clk., 1976-86, v.p., contr., 1981-87, ret., 1987. Trustee Gilman Cemeteries, 1988—, Trust Funds, 1990-91, 94—; commr. Gilmanton Corner Precinct, 1989—; mem. Gilmanton Budget Com., 1990—, Sch. Bldg. Com., 1988, 90, Zoning Bd. Adjustment, 1990-91; mem. Gilmanton Bd. Selectmen, 1991-94. Home: PO Box 190 Gilmanton NH 03237-0190

OSLIN, K. T. (KAY TOINETTE OSLIN), country singer; b. Crossett, Ark.. Student, Lon Morris Jr. Coll. Sang in folk trio; professional singing debut at Purple Onion, 1962; mem. road co. Hello, Dolly, also N.Y.C.; mem. cast Promise, Promises, revival West Side Story; songwriter; songs include Do Ya?, Round the Clock Lovin, Where Is A Woman To Go, Come Next Monday, Younger Men, others; albums: 80's Ladies (Grammy 1987, Country-Best Vocal Perfomance, Female), Hold Me (Grammy 1988, Country-Best Song, Country-Best Vocal Performance, Female), This Woman, 1988, Love in a Small Town, 1990, Songs From An Aging Sex Bomb: K.T. Oslin's Greatest Hits, 1993, New Way Home, 1993, My Roots Are Showing, 1996. Recipient Top Female Vocalist award Acad. Country Music, 1988. Office: Moress Nanas c/o Stan Moress 1209 16th Ave S Nashville TN 37212-2901

OSMAN, EDITH GABRIELLA, lawyer; b. N.Y.C., Mar. 18, 1949; d. Arthur Abraham and Judith (Goldman) Udem; children: Jacqueline, Daniel. BA in Spanish, SUNY, Stony Brook, 1970; JD cum laude, U. Miami, 1983. Bar: Fla. 1983, U.S. Dist. Ct. (so. dist.) Fla. 1984, U.S. Dist. Ct. (mid. dist.) Fla. 1988, U.S. Ct. Appeals (11th cir.) 1985, U.S. Supreme Ct. 1987, U.S. Ct. Mil. Appeals 1990. Assoc. Kimbrell & Hamann, P.A., Miami, 1984-90, Dunn & Lodish, P.A., Miami, 1990-93; pvt. practice in law Miami, 1993—; spkr. in field. Mem. adv. com. for Implementation of the Victor Posner Judgement to Aid the Homeless, 1986-89; spkr. small firm and solo practitioner Town Hall Meetings, 1993; spkr. Bridge the Gap Seminar, Comml. Litigation, 1994. Mem. ABA (product liability com., corp. counsel com.), Fla. Bar Assn. (budget com. 1989-92, voluntary bar liaison com. 1989-90, spl. com. on formation of All-Bar Conf. 1988-89, chair mid-yr. conv. 1989, mem. long range planning com. 1988-90, bd. govs. 1991—, spl. commn. on delivery of legal svcs. to the indigent 1990-92, exec. com. 1992-93, bus. law cert. com. 1995-96, practice law mgmt. com. 1995-96, chair program evaluation com. bd. govs., 1996—, exec. com. 1992-93, 96—, rules and bylaws com. 1993-94, disciplinary rev. com. 1994—, investment com. 1994—, exec. com. 1996-97, vice-chair rules com. 1994—, Conf. chair 1997, Outstanding Past Voluntary Bar Pres. award 1996), Dade County Bar Assn. (fed. ct. rules com. 1985-86, chmn. program com. 1988-89, 90-91, exec. com. 1987-88), Fla. Assn. Women's Lawyers Assn. Pres. (Dade County chpt. bd. dirs. 1988-89, treas. 1989-90, v.p. 1990-91, pres. 1991-92), Fla. Assn. Women Lawyers (bd. dirs. 1985-86, v.p. Dade County chpt. 1986-87, pres. 1987-88, pres.-elect Fla. chpt. 1988-89, pres. 1989-90), Nat. Coun. Women's Bar Assn. (dir. nat. conf. 1990-91), Dade County Trial Lawyers Assn. Office: Edith G Osman PA Internat Place 100 SE 2nd St Ste 3920 Miami FL 33131-2148

OSMAN, MARY ELLA WILLIAMS, journal editor; b. Honea Path, S.C.; d. Humphrey Bates and Jennie Louise (Williams) Williams; student Coll. William and Mary, Ga. State Coll. for Women; A.B., Presbyn. Coll., 1939; B.S. in L.S., U. N.C., 1944; m. John Osman, Oct. 22, 1936. Asst. libr. Presbyn. Coll., Clinton, S.C., 1936-38, Union Theol. Sem., Richmond, Va., 1938-44; sr. cataloger, asst. libr. Rhodes Coll., Memphis, 1944-52; asst. test cities project Ford Found. Fund for Adult Edn., N.Y.C., 1952-57, assoc. dir. office of info., 1957-61, exec. asst. to pres., sec. to bd. dirs., 1960-61; asst. libr. AIA, Washington, 1962-68, asst. editor AIA Jour., 1969-72, assoc. editor, 1972-77, sr. editor, 1978-87. Mem. AIA (hon.), Chi Delta Phi, Kappa Delta. Presbyn. Contbr. to various mags. Home: 3600 Chateau Dr Apt 244 Columbia SC 29204-3971

OSMAN, STEPHEN EUGENE, historic site administrator; b. Berkeley, Calif., Aug. 8, 1949; s. Eugene Lee and June Elizabeth (Claus) O.; m. Wendy Kay Holmberg, June 21, 1975; children: Rachel Ann, Austin Thomas, Laurel Suzanne. BA in History and Edn. cum laude, St. Olaf Coll., 1971. Program mgr. Historic Ft. Snelling, St. Paul, 1971-85, dir., 1985—; program mgr. Legis. Commn. on Minn. Resources, 1985; mem. Coun. on Am.'s Mil. Past, Midwest Open Air Mus. Coord. Coun.; lectr. in field. Author: The Soldiers Handbook, 1825, 1972; contbr. articles to profl. jours. Fellow Co. Mil. Historians; mem. Assn. Living History Farms and Agrl. Mus., Living History Soc. Minn. Republican. Lutheran. Avocations: 19th Century military uniforms and equipment, historic crafts. Office: Minn Hist Soc Ft Snelling History Ctr Saint Paul MN 55111

OSMOND, DENNIS GORDON, medical educator, researcher; b. N.Y.C., Jan. 31, 1930; s. Ernest Gordon and Marjorie Bertha (Milton) O.; m. Anne Welsh, July 30, 1955; children: Roger Gordon, Martin Henry, David Richard. B.Sc. with first class honors, U. Bristol, Eng., 1951, M.B., Ch.B., 1954, D.Sc., 1975. House surgeon Royal Gwent Hosp., Newport, Eng., 1954-55; house physician Bristol Royal Infirmary, 1955; demonstrator, lectr. anatomy U. Bristol, 1957-60, 61-64; instr. anatomy U. Wash., Seattle, 1960-61; assoc. prof. anatomy McGill U., Montreal, Que., Can., 1965-67; prof. McGill U., 1967-74, Robert Reford prof. anatomy, 1974—, chmn. dept. anatomy and cell biology, 1985-95; vis. scientist Walter and Eliza Hall Inst. Med. Research, Melbourne, Australia, 1972-73; hon. sr. research fellow U. Birmingham, Eng., 1979; vis. scientist Basel Inst. Immunology, Switzerland, 1980, 96; Gaylord scholar Okla. Med. Rsch. Found., 1995. Contbr. numerous articles to profl. jours. Served with Royal Army Med. Corps, 1955-57. Fellow Royal Soc. Can.; mem. Am. Assn. Anatomists, Can. Assn. Anatomists, Anat. Soc. Gt. Britain and Ireland, Am., Can. assns. for immunology, Am. Assn. Immunology, Internat. Soc. for Exptl. Hematology. Home: 116 rue de Touraine, St Lambert, PQ Canada J4S 1H4 Office: Dept Anatomy McGill Univ, 3640 University St, Montreal, PQ Canada H3A 2B2

OSNES, LARRY G., academic administrator; b. Scottsbluff, Nebr., Oct. 30, 1941; s. Earl E. and Rose (DeRock) O.; m. Susan C.; 1 child, Justin. BA in History, Anderson Coll., 1963; MA in History, Wayne State Coll., 1965; PhD in History, U. Cin., 1970. Asst. prof. history and govt. U. Cin., 1967-69; dir. Am. studies Anderson (Ind.) Coll., 1970-75, chmn. dept. history, 1975-76, dean acadmeic devel., 1975-78, asst. corp. sec., dean academic devel. and pub. affairs, 1978-83; pres. Minn. Pvt. Coll. Coun., St. Paul, 1983-88, Hamline U., St. Paul, 1988—. Mem. Assoc. Colls. Twin Cities (chmn. 1988-90), Mpls. Club, St. Paul Athletic Club. Office: Hamline Univ 1536 Hewitt Ave Saint Paul MN 55104-1205*

OSNES, PAMELA GRACE, special education educator; b. Burke, S.D., Sept. 10, 1955; d. John Ruben and Dortha Grace (Wilson) O.; children: Jocelyn Fern, Logan John. BS in Spl. Edn., U. S.D., 1977, BS in Elem. Edn., 1977; MA in Clin. Psychology, W.Va. U., 1981; PhD in Spl. Edn., 1997. Spl. edn. tchr. Sioux Falls (S.D.) Sch. Dist., 1977-79; instr. psychology dept. W.Va. U., Morgantown, 1982-85; dir. Carousel Preschool Program, Morgantown, 1982-85; assoc. prof. U. South Fla., Tampa, 1986-93, adminstrv. coord. advanced grad. programs dept. spl. edn., 1994—. Mem. Assn. for Behavior Analysis, Coun. for Exceptional Children (div. early childhood, div. rsch., tchr. edn. div.), Coun. Adminstrs. Spl. Edn., Coun. for Children with Behavior Disorders.

OSNOS, DAVID MARVIN, lawyer; b. Detroit, Jan. 10, 1932; s. Max and Florence (Pollock) O.; m. Glenna DeWitt, Aug. 10, 1956; children: Matthew, Alison. A.B. summa cum laude, Harvard U., 1953, J.D. cum laude, 1956. Bar: D.C. 1956. Assoc. Arent, Fox, Kintner, Plotkin & Kahn, Washington, 1956-61, ptnr., 1962—, chmn. exec. com., 1978-97; bd. dirs. EastGroup Properties, Jackson, Miss., VSE Corp., Alexandria, Va., Washington Real Estate Investment Trust, Kensington, Md., Washington Wizards Basketball Club, Washington, Washington Capitals Hockey Club, Washington. Trustee Mt. St. Mary's Coll., Emmitsburg, Md., 1981-90; bd. dirs. Greater Washington Jewish Community Found., Rockville, Md., Jewish Community Ctr. Greater Washington, 1964-75. Avocations: tennis, music, enology. Office: Arent Fox Kintner 1050 Connecticut Ave NW Washington DC 20036

OSNOS, GILBERT CHARLES, management consultant; b. Detroit, Nov. 23, 1929; s. Herman Sol and Helen (Yudkoff) O.; m. Margaret N. Paysner, Aug. 18, 1957; children: Steven, Elisabeth. BA, U. Mich., 1951; MBA, Harvard U., 1953. Dept. mgr. Sams, Inc., Detroit, 1956-57, asst. buyer, 1957-58, dir. store ops., 1958, buyer, 1958-59, mdse. buyer, 1959-62; buyer Topps Divsn. Interstate Dept. Stores, N.Y.C., 1962-65; mdse. mgr. Arlans Dept. Stores, N.Y.C., 1965-68; pres. Nazareth Mills divsn. Kayser Roth, N.Y.C., 1968-73, Rosenau Bros., Phila., 1973-75, Warnaco Men's Sportswear, 1975-78; with Grisanti and Galef, 1979-81, ptnr., 1981—; pres. Grisanti, Galef & Osnos, N.Y.C., 1983—; chmn. Osnos & Co., Inc., 1986—; bd. dirs. Furrs Bishop, Am. Mirrex, Mrs. Field's, Turnaround Mgmt. Assn., chmn., 1990-91. Lt. j.g. USNR, 1953-56. Mem. Am. Apparel Assn. (consumer affairs com.), Am. Bankruptcy Inst., Bus. Execs. for Nat. Security, Harvard Club, Halloween Yacht Club. Avocations: sailing, opera, classical music, photography, reading. Office: Osnos & Company Inc 230 Park Ave Ste C-301 New York NY 10169

OSNOS, PETER LIONEL WINSTON, publishing executive; b. Bombay, India, Oct. 13, 1943; s. Joseph Lionel and Marta (Bychowski) O.; m. Susan R. Sherer, Aug. 18, 1973; children: Katherine Mason, Evan L.R. BA, Brandeis U., Waltham, Mass., 1964; MS in Journalism with honors, Columbia U., 1965. Editorial asst. I.F. Stone's Weekly, Washington, 1964-65; corr., editor The Washington Post, 1966-84; v.p. assoc. pub. Random House Trade Books and pub. Times Books, Random House, Inc., N.Y.C., 1984-96; cons. 20th Century Fund, 1996-97. Contbr. articles to profl. publs. Bd. dirs. Human Rights Watch, vice chmn., Helsinki. Fellow NEH, 1973-74. Mem. Assn. Am. Pubs. (vice chmn. gen. pub. divsn. 1993-96), Coun. on Fgn. Rels., Century Club. Office: Random House 201 E 50th St New York NY 10022-7703

OSOWIEC, DARLENE ANN, clinical psychologist, educator, consultant; b. Chgo., Feb. 16, 1951; d. Stephen Raymond and Estelle Marie Osowiec; m. Barry A. Leska. BS, Loyola U., Chgo., 1973; MA with honors, Roosevelt U., 1980; postgrad. in psychology, Saybrook Inst., San Francisco, 1985-88; PhD in Clin. Psychology, Calif. Inst. Integral Studies, 1992. Lic. clin. psychologist, Mo., Ill. Mental health therapist Ridgeway Hosp., Chgo., 1978; mem. faculty psychology dept. Coll. Lake County, Grayslake, Ill., 1981; counselor, supr. MA-level interns, chmn. pub. rels. com. Integral Counseling Ctr., San Francisco, 1983-84; clin. psychology intern Chgo.-Read Mental Health Ctr. Ill. Dept. Mental Health, 1985-86; mem. faculty dept. psychology Moraine Valley C.C., Palos Hills, Ill., 1988-89; lectr. psychology Daley Coll., Chgo., 1988-90; cons. Gordon & Assocs., Oak Lawn, Ill., 1989—; adolescent, child and family therapist Orland Twp. Youth Svcs., Orland Park, Ill., 1993; psychology fellow Sch. Medicine, St. Louis U., 1994-95; clin. psychologist in pvt. practice Chgo., 1996—; founder Maximum Potential, Chgo., 1996—. Ill. State scholar, 1969-73; Calif. Inst. Integral Studies scholar, 1983. Mem. APA, Am. Psychol. Soc., Am. Women in Psychology, Am. Statis. Assn., Ill. Psychol. Assn., Calif. Psychol. Assn., Mo. Psychol. Assn., Fla. Psychoo. Assn., Gerontol. Soc. Am., Am. Soc. Clin. Hypnosis, Internat. Platform Assn., Chgo. Soc. Clin. Hypnosis, NOW (chair legal adv. corps, Chgo. 1974-76). Avocations: playing piano, gardening, reading, backpacking, writing. Office: 2502 N Clark St Ste 215 Chicago IL 60614-1712

OSRIN, RAYMOND HAROLD, retired political cartoonist; b. Bklyn., Oct. 5, 1928; s. Elkan and Amelia (Boll) O.; divorced 1978; children: Caren, Glenn Elliot; m. Stephanie Hearshen, Aug. 23, 1981; stepchildren: Calanit, Orli. Student, Art Students League, 1945-47. Free-lance cartoonist, comic book illustrator, comic strip ghost artist and TV animator, W.R. Smith Inc., Pitts., 1957-58, staff artist, Pitts. Press, 1958-63, Cleve. Plain Dealer, 1963-66, polit. cartoonist, 1966-93. Vol. New Internat. Mus. of Cartooning, Boca Raton. Recipient Freedom award, 1966, 67, Nat. Headliners award, 1970, 3d pl. award Internat. Salon de Cartoon, Montreal, Que., Can., 1975, award for excellence in journalism Press Club Cleve., 1978, 82, Disting. Service award Sigma Delta Chi, 1983. Excellence in Journalism 1st pl. award Cleve. Press Club, 1991; inducted into Cleve. Press Club Hall of Fame, 1986.

OSSERMAN, ROBERT, mathematician, educator; b. N.Y.C., Dec. 19, 1926; s. Herman Aaron and Charlotte (Adler) O.; m. Maria Anderson, June 15, 1952; 1 son, Paul; m. Janet Adelman, July 21, 1976; children—Brian, Stephen. B.A., NYU, 1946; postgrad., U. Zurich, U. Paris; M.A., Harvard U., 1948, Ph.D., 1955. Tchg. fellow Harvard U., 1949-52, vis. lectr., rsch. assoc., 1961-62; instr. U. Colo., 1952-53; mem. faculty Stanford U., 1955-94, prof. emeritus, 1994—, prof. math., 1966—, chmn. dept. math., 1973-79, Mellon Prof. Interdisciplinary Studies, 1987-90; dep. dir. Math. Scis. Rsch. Inst., Berkeley, Calif., 1990-95, dir. spl. projects, 1995—; mem. NYU Inst. Math. Scis., 1957-58, Math. Scis. Rsch. Inst., Berkeley,., 1983-84, head math. br. Office Naval Rsch., 1960-61; researcher and author publs. on differential geometry, complex variables, differential equations, especially minimal surfaces, Laplace operator, isoperimetric inequalities, ergodic theory. Author: Two-Dimensional Calculus, 1968, A Survey of Minimal Surfaces, 1969, 2d edit., 1986, Poetry of the Universe, 1995. Fulbright lectr. U. Paris, 1965-66; Guggenheim fellow, 1976-77; vis. fellow U. Warwick, Imperial Coll., U. London. Fellow AAAS; mem. Am. Math. Soc., Math. Assn. Am. Office: Math Sci Rsch Inst 1000 Centennial Dr Berkeley CA 94720-5071

OSSOFF, ROBERT HENRY, otolaryngological surgeon; b. Beverly, Mass., Mar. 25, 1947; s. Michael Max and Eve Joan (Kladky) O.; m. Lynn Spilman, 1984; 1 child, Leslin; 1 child by previous marriage, Jacob. BA, Bowdoin Coll., 1969; DMD, Tufts U., 1973, MD, 1975; MS in Otolaryngology, Northwestern U., 1981. Intern Northwestern Meml. Hosp., Chgo., 1975-76; resident in otolaryngology Northwestern Med. Sch., Chgo., 1976-80, NIH Rsch. fellow dept. otolaryngology, 1977-78, Am. Cancer Soc. clin. fellow, 1980-81, jr. faculty clin. fellow, 1981-84; pvt. practice acad. medicine specializing in head and neck surgery, laryngology and care of the profl. voice, Chgo., 1975-86, Nashville, 1986—; chmn. dept. otolaryngology Vanderbilt U. Hosp., Nashville, 1986—, exec. med. dir. Vanderbilt Voice Ctr., 1991—; mem. staff Children's Meml. Hosp., Chgo., 1980-81, Nashville VA Hosp., 1986—; chmn. div. otolaryngology Evanston (Ill.) Hosp., 1983-86; chief div. otolaryngology VA Lakeside Hosp., Chgo., 1982-86; mem. staff Northwestern Meml. Hosp., Chgo., 1981-86, Children's Meml. Hosp., Chgo., 1981-84; asst. prof. Northwestern U. Dental Sch., 1980-86, asst. prof. Northwestern U. Med. Sch., 1980-85, assoc. prof., 1985-86; Guy M. Maness prof., chmn. dept. otolaryngology Vanderbilt U. Sch. Medicine, 1986—; assoc. dir. Vanderbilt Free-Electron Laser Ctr. Med. and Materials Rsch., 1992-95; assoc. vice-chancellor for health affairs and chief of staff, Vanderbilt U. Hosp., 1995—. Trustee Midwest Biolaser Inst., Chgo., 1981-86; bd. dirs. Laser Inst. Am., 1984-90, Am. Bd. Otolaryngology, 1995—. Recipient Lederer-Pierce award Chgo. Laryngol. and Otol. Soc., 1978. Fellow ACS, Am. Coll. Chest Physicians; mem. AMA, Am. Acad. Oral Medicine, Am. Acad. Oral Pathology, Am. Acad. Otolaryngology-Head and Neck Surgery (chmn. laser surgery com. 1983-89, chmn. self instl. package com. 1990-96, Cert. of Honor 1984, bd. dirs. 1992-95, disting. svc. award 1995), Am. Soc. Laser Medicine and Surgery (bd. dirs. 1985-88, pres.-elect 1988-89, pres. 1989-90, recipient William B. Mark award 1992), Am. Coll. Surgeons (bd. govs.), Soc. Head and Neck Surgeons, Am. Soc. Head and Neck Surgery (coun. 1991-94), Am. Broncho-esophagological Assn. (treas. 1980-84, pres.-elect 1994-95, pres. 1995-96), Soc. Ear, Nose and Throat Advances in Children, The Triological Soc. (coun. 1996—), Am. Laryngol. Assn. (coun. 1996—), Cartesian Soc. Mem. editl. rev. bd. Otolaryngology-Head and Neck Surgery, 1988—; sr. editor Lasers in Surgery and Medicine, 1987-94, editor in chief-elect, 1994-96, editor in chief 1995—; co-editor Complications in Head and Neck Surgery W.B. Saunders Co., 1993; mem. editl. bd. Clin. Laser Monthly, 1984—, Jour. of Voice, 1987—, The Laryngoscope, 1988—, Operative Techniques in Otolaryngology-Head and Neck Surgery, 1989—, Head and Neck Surgery, 1989—, Jour. of Laser Applications, 1989—; with edtl. adv. bd. Gen. Surgery News, 1990—; assoc. editor Diagnostic and Therapeutic Endoscopy, 1992—; contbr. chpts. to books, articles to profl. jours. Office: Vanderbilt U Med Ctr Dept Otolaryngology S-2100 Med Ctr N Nashville TN 37232-2559

OSTAR, ALLAN WILLIAM, academic administrator, higher education consultant; b. East Orange, N.J., Sept. 4, 1924; s. William and Rose (Mirmow) O.; m. Roberta Hutchison, Sept. 10, 1949; children: Karen, Rebecca, John. Cert. engring., U. Denver, 1943; B.A., Pa. State U., 1948; postgrad., U. Wis., 1949-55; LL.D., U. No. Colo., 1968, Eastern Ky. U., 1972, Whittier Coll., 1973; L.H.D., U. Maine, 1975; D.Letters, Central Mich. U., 1975; D.P.S., Bowling Green State U., 1975, R.I. Coll., 1983; D.Higher Edn., Morehead State U., 1977; L.H.D., Appalachian State U., 1977, No. Mich. U., 1978, Dickinson State Coll., N.D., 1979, Towson State U., 1980, Salem State Coll., 1980, Mont. Coll. Mineral Sci. and Tech., 1983, Ball State U., 1984; LL.D., U. Alaska, 1978, Ill. State U., 1983, Western Mich. U., 1984; D. Polit. Sci., Kyung Hee U., Korea, 1984; L.H.D., Fitchburg State Coll., 1986, Bridgwater State Coll., 1988, No. State Coll., 1988, Harris-Stowe State Coll., 1986; LLD, Edinboro U. Pa., 1987, Loch Haven U., Pa., 1989; LHD, No. Ariz. U., 1990, Shepherd (W.Va.) Coll., 1992, SUNY, 1993, Lincoln U., Mo., 1995. Dir. nat. pub. relations U.S. Nat. Student Assn., 1948-49; exec. asst. Commonwealth Fund, N.Y.C., 1952-53; asst. to dean extension div. U. Wis., 1949-52, dir. office communications services, 1954-58; dir. Joint Office Instnl. Research, Nat. Assn. State Univs. and Land Grant Colls., Washington, 1958-65; pres. Am. Assn. State Colls. and Univs., Washington, 1965-91; pres. emeritus Am. Assn. State Colls. and Univs., 1991—; sr. cons. Acad. Search Consultation Svc., 1991—; adj. prof. edn. Pa. State U., 1990—; mem. N.Y. Regents Commn. Libr. Bd., Pa. State U.; bd. advisors Bowie State U. Co-author: Colleges and Universities for Change, 1987; contbr. chpts. in books. Mem. 42d (Rainbow) div. U.S. Army, 1943-46. Decorated 2 Bronze Stars; recipient Centennial award for disting. svcs. to edn. U. Akron, 1970, Fogelsanger award Shippensburg (Pa.) State Coll., 1974, World Peace Through Edn. medal Internat. Assn. U. Pres., 1975, Disting. Achievement award, U. So. Colo., 1979, Chancellor's award U. Wis., 1985, Chancellor's medal CUNY, 1986, Disting. Alumnus award Pa. State U., 1989, svc. award Coun. on Internat. Ednl. Exch., 1990, Chancellor's medal Internat. Svc. U. Ark., Little Rock, 1990, Disting. Pub. Svc. medal Dept. of Def., 1991; Alumni fellow Pa. State U., 1975. Unitarian-Universalist. Home: 5500 Friendship Blvd Chevy Chase MD 20815-7219 Office: Acad Search Cons Svc 1818 R St NW Washington DC 20009-1604

OSTBERG, HENRY DEAN, corporate executive; b. Bocholt, Germany, July 21, 1928; came to U.S., 1939, naturalized, 1945; s. Fred and Lotte (Hertz) O.; m. Sydelle Burns, Dec. 13, 1987; 1 child, Neal; stepchildren: Elysa Bari, Brent Adam, Ross Jay. LLB, N.Y. Law Sch., 1950; MBA, Ohio State U., 1953, PhD, 1957. Pres. H.D. Ostberg Assocs., N.Y.C., 1950—; chmn. bd. Admar Research Co., Inc., N.Y.C., 1960; dir. Self-Instructional Devel. Corp., Amherst Group, Porter Industries, Inc.; pres. Eastman Enterprises, Inc.; assoc. prof. mktg. NYU, 1954-63. Trustee Ostberg Found. Capt. USAF, 1950-53. Jewish. Contbr. articles to profl. jours. Home: 278 Fountain Rd Englewood NJ 07631-4403 Office: Admar Rsch Inc 225 Park Ave S New York NY 10003-1604

OSTBY, FREDERICK PAUL, JR., meteorologist, retired government official; b. New Haven, Jan. 20, 1930; s. Frederick Paul and Edna Maria (Kruckenberg) O.; m. Joanne Bernice Sorvig, Jan. 1, 1955 (div. 1989); children: Paul, Neil, Karen, Lynn; m. Barbara Richards, Mar. 17, 1989. B.S. in Meteorology, NYU, 1951, M.S., 1960. Cert. Consulting Meteorologist. Meteorologist TWA, N.Y.C., 1953-54, Kansas City, Mo., 1955-56; Meteorologist N.E. Weather Service, Lexington, Mass., 1955, Travelers Weather Service, Hartford, Conn., 1956-60; research scientist Travelers Research Center, Hartford, 1960-70; meteorologist Nat. Weather Service, Silver Spring, Md., 1970-72; dep. dir. Nat. Severe Storms Forecast Center, Dept. Commerce, Kansas City, Mo., 1972-80; dir. Nat. Severe Storms Forecast Center, 1980-96; assoc. climatological Consulting Corp., 1997—; severe weather cons. The Weather Channel, 1997—. Contbr. papers to profl. lit. Served with USAF, 1951-53. Fellow Am. Meteorol. Soc. (council 1977-80, 84-87). Home: 12537 Broadmoor St Overland Park KS 66209-3234

OSTBY, RONALD, dairy and food products company executive; b. 1937. BS, U. S.D., 1959. With Pillsbury Co., 1961-84, v.p. fin. planning; v.p., chief fin. officer AG Processing, 1984-86; group v.p., chief fin. officer Land O'Lakes, 1986—. Office: Land O'Lakes Inc 4001 Lexington Ave N Saint Paul MN 55126-2934

OSTEEN, CAROLYN MCCUE, lawyer; b. Spartanburg, S.C., June 3, 1943; d. Howard McDowell Jr. and Carolyn Hartwell (Moore) McCue; m. Robert Tilden Osteen, Dec. 21, 1963; children: Carolyn Willingham Moore, Sarah Lloyd. Student, Wellesley Coll., 1960-63; LLB, Duke U., 1966, LLM, 1970. Bar: N.C. 1966, Mass. 1971. Assoc. Robinson O. Everett, Durham, N.C., 1967-68, Cox, Smith, Smith, Hale & Guenther, San Antonio, 1969-70; assoc. Ropes & Gray, Boston, 1970-79, ptnr., 1979—; tchr. taxes Tex. Asns. Realtors, 1969-70. Co-author: Harvard Manual-Tax Aspects of Charitable Giving, 7 edits., 1980—; contbr. articles to legal publs. Bd. dirs., clk. Historic Boston, Inc., 1978—, Trustees of Reservations, Boston, 1982—, John F. Kennedy Libr. Found., 1985. Fellow Am. Coll. Trusts and Estates Coun.; mem. ABA (chmn. exempt orgns. com. tax sect.), Boston Bar Assn. (vice-chmn. exempt orgns. com. 1987-92). Republican. Episcopalian. Office: Ropes & Gray 1 International Pl Boston MA 02110-2602

O'STEEN, SAM, film editor, director; b. Nov. 6, 1923. Asst. editor: (film) The Wrong Man, 1956; editor: (films) Youngblood Hawke, 1964, Kisses for My President, 1964, Robin and the Seven Hoods, 1964, Marriage on the Rocks, 1965, None But the Brave, 1965, Who's Afraid of Virginia Woolf?, 1966 (Academy award nomination best film editing 1966), Cool Hand Luke, 1967, The Graduate, 1967, Rosemary's Baby, 1968, The Sterile Cuckoo, 1969, Catch-22, 1970, Carnal Knowledge, 1971, Portnoy's Complaint, 1972, The Day of the Dolphin, 1973, Chinatown, 1974 (Academy award nomination best film editing 1974), (with Randy Roberts) Straight Time, 1978, Hurricane, 1979, Amityville II: The Possession, 1982, Silkwood, 1983 (Academy award nomination best film editing 1983), Heartburn, 1986, Nadine, 1987, Biloxi Blues, 1988, Frantic, 1988, Working Girl, 1988, (with Glenn Cunningham) A Dry White Season, 1989, Postcards from the Edge, 1990, Regarding Henry, 1991, Consenting Adults, 1992, Wolf, 1994; dir.: (films) Sparkle, 1976, (TV movies) A Brand New Life, 1973, I Love You, Goodbye, 1974, Queen of the Stardust Ballroom, 1975 (Emmy award nomination outstanding director of spl. program 1975), High Risk, 1976, Look What's Happened to Rosemary's Baby, 1976, The Best Little Girl in the World, 1981, Kids Don't Tell, 1985. Office: care Motion Picture Editors 7715 W Sunset Blvd Ste 220 Los Angeles CA 90046-3912*

O'STEEN, VAN, lawyer; b. Sweetwater, Tenn., Jan. 10, 1946; s. Bernard Van and Laura Emelyne (Robinson) O.; m. Deborah Ann Elias, May 18, 1974; children—Jonathan Van, Laura Ann. B.A., Calif. Western U., 1968; J.D. cum laude, Ariz. State U., 1972. Bar: Ariz. 1972, U.S. Dist. Ct. Ariz. 1972, U.S. Ct. Appeals (9th cir.) 1973, U.S. Supreme Ct. 1975. Staff atty. Maricopa Legal Aid Soc., Phoenix, 1972-74; atty. Bates & O'Steen, Legal Clinic, Phoenix, 1974-77; atty. O'Steen Legal Clinic, Phoenix, 1977-80; mng. ptnr. Van O'Steen and Ptnrs., Phoenix and Tucson, 1980—; pres. Van O'Steen Mktg. Group, Inc., Phoenix, 1985—. Author numerous self-help legal books. Founding dir. Ariz. Ctr. for Law in the Pub. Interest, 1974-80. Served with USNR, 1963-69. Mem. ABA (chmn. spl. com. delivery legal services 1982-85), Am. Legal Clinic Assn. (pres. 1979), Assn. Trial Lawyers Am. Democrat. Address: 3605 N 7th Ave Phoenix AZ 85013-3638

O'STEEN, WENDALL KEITH, neurobiology and anatomy educator; b. Meigs, Ga., July 3, 1928; s. Wellna Hubert and Lillian (Powell) O'S.; m. Sandra Lynn Kraeer, July 30, 1983; children: Lisa Diane, Kerry Keith, Buckley Powell. BA, Emory U., 1948, MS, 1950; PhD, Duke U., 1958. Asst. prof. Jr. Coll. Emory U., Valdosta, Ga., 1948-49; instr. Emory U., Atlanta, 1950-51, prof. Sch. Medicine, 1968-77; from asst. prof. to prof. med. br. U. Tex., 1958-67; asst. prof. Wofford Coll., Spartanburg, S.C., 1951-53; prof., chmn. dept. neurobiology and anatomy, Bowman Gray Sch. Med. Wake Forest U., Winston-Salem, N.C., 1977-93, prof. emeritus, 1993—; mem. anatomy com. Nat. Bd. Med. Examiners, Phila., 1982-87. Contbr. over 150 articles to books, nat. and internat. jours. Served to lt. col. USAR. Recipient Golden Apple teaching award Med. Br. U. Tex., Galveston, 1967, Outstanding Tchr. award Emory U., 1973, Williams Disting. Teaching award Emory U., 1974, award for teaching excellence Bowman Gray Sch. Medicine, Wake Forest U. Mem. Am. Assn. Anatomists (exec. com. 1980-84, v.p. 1990-92), Assn. Anatomy Chairmen (exec. com. 1982-84, pres. 1990-91), So. Soc. Anatomists (pres. 1975-76), Soc. for Neurosci., N.C. Soc. Neurosci. (pres. 1980-81), Western N.C. Soc. Neurosci. (pres. 1987-88), Assn. Rsch. in Vision and Ophthalmology, Alpha Omega Alpha. Republican. Methodist. Avocations: gardening, music. Office: Bowman Gray Sch of Medicine Wake Forest Univ Dept of Neurobiology & Anatomy Winston Salem NC 27157-1010

OSTEEN, WILLIAM L., SR., federal judge; b. 1931. BA, Guilford Coll., 1953; LLB, U. N.C., 1956. With Law Office of W.H. McElwee, Jr., North Wilkesboro, N.C., 1956-58; pvt. practive Greensboro, N.C., 1958-59; with Booth & Osteen, Greensboro, 1959-69; U.S. atty. U.S. Attys. Office, Greensboro, 1969-74; ptnr. Osteen, Adams & Osteen, Greensboro, 1974-91; fed. judge U.S. Dist. Ct. (mid. dist.) N.C., Greensboro, 1991—. With USAR, 1958-51. Fellow Am. Coll. Trial Lawyers; mem. ABA, N.C. State Bar, N.C. Bar Assn. (mem. and chair subcom. N.C. sentencing commn.), U. N.C. Law Alumni Assn. Office: US Dist Ct PO Box 3485 Greensboro NC 27402-3485*

OSTEN, MARGARET ESTHER, librarian; b. Mukacevo, Czechoslovakia; came to U.S., 1949; Profl. Diploma, Prague and Budapest, 1944, PhD, 1946; Indsl. Engr. Diploma, Vysoka Skola Obchodni, Prague, 1948; MS in Libr. Sci., Columbia U., 1952. Cert. pub. libr., N.Y. Prof. Prague Coll., Czechoslovakia, 1945-48; various to sr. cataloguer, libr. Columbia U., N.Y.C., 1952-59; sr. libr. Bklyn. Pub. Libr., 1959-62; libr., asst. prof. Manhattanville Coll., Purchase, N.Y., 1962-65; supr. libr., asst. sect. head; acting head of post 51 Nat. Union Catalog, 1965-69; head, cataloguing dept. CUNY Grad. Ctr., 1969-71; chief libr. Leo Baeck Inst., N.Y.C., 1971-72; libr.-in-charge, Engring. Libr. CUNY, 1972-75; tchr. St. John's Univ. Grad. Sch. Libr. Sci., 1972; lectr. 3rd World Congress of Czechoslovak Soc. Arts, Sci., Columbia U., 1966; curator of an exhibit, 50th anniversary of Czechoslovak Republic, 1968; Czechoslovakian del. to Coun. of European Women in Exile, pres., 1959; others. Contbr. articles to newspapers. Served on elections com. Morningside Heights Consumers Co-operative Columbia U. area, Manhattan, N.Y. Mem. ALA, SLA, N.Y. Libr. Club, AAUP, Nat. Coun. Women of Free Czechoslovakia (bd. dirs.), Nat. Coun. Women of U.S. Avocations: libr. sci., polit. econs., langs., skiing, tennis. Home: 80 La Salle St New York NY 10027-4711

OSTENDORF, LANCE STEPHEN, lawyer, investor, financial officer; b. New Orleans, Aug. 16, 1955. BBA summa cum laude, Loyola U., 1976, JD, 1980. Bar: La. 1980, U.S. Dist. Ct. (ea. dist.) La. 1981, U.S. Dist. Ct. La., U.S. Supreme Ct. 1980, U.S. Dist. Ct. (we. and mid. dists.) La. 1983. Ptnr. McGlinchey Stafford Lang, New Orleans, 1980-92; patent atty. Campbell McCranie, New Orleans, 1992—, treas., CFO; owner RCO Internat. Inc.; treas., CFO La. State U. Med. Found., New Orleans, 1992—. Mem. ABA, Fed. Bar Assn., Internat. Bar Assn., Metairie Bar Assn. Home: PO Box 8381 Metairie LA 70011

OSTER, JEFFREY WAYNE, marine corps officer; b. Milw., Nov. 11, 1941; s. Richard Alexander and Isabel Aagut (Jacobson) O.; m. Sherry Christine Holt, Feb. 1, 1969; children: Allison Brett, Jennifer Alexandria. BS in Geology, U. Wis., 1963, MBA, 1976; postgrad., Nat. War Coll., Washington, 1982-83. Commd. 2d lt. USMC, 1964, advanced through grades to major gen., 1992; various assignments USMC, U.S., Vietnam, Japan, 1964-81; exec. officer 4th marine rgt. 3d Marine Div., Okinawa, Japan, 1981-82; sec. gen. staff Hdqrs. USMC, Washington, 1983-86; ops. officer 1st Marine Div., Camp Pendleton, Calif., 1986-87, comdr. officer 7th marine rgt., 1987-89; comdg. gen. 9th Marine Expeditionary Brigade, Okinawa, 1989-90; comdr. Def. Electronics Supply Ctr., Dayton, Ohio, 1990-92; deputy chief of staff for Resources Hqrs. USMC, 1992—. Decorated Legion of Merit. Mem. Am. Def. Preparedness Assn. (bd. dirs. Tri-State chpt. 1990-92), Marine Corps Assn., Vietnam Vets. Am., U.S. Naval Inst., Dayton C. of C. (bd. dirs., vets. affairs com. 1990-92). Lutheran. Avocations: golf, running, computers. Office: DCS For Programs & Resorces HQ MC Washington DC 20380-0001 Address: 8923 Arley Dr Springfield VA 22153-1504

OSTER, LEWIS HENRY, manufacturing executive, engineering consultant; b. Mitchell, S.D., Jan. 18, 1923; s. Peter W. and Lucy (Goetsch) O.; m. Mary Mills, Aug. 17, 1948; children—David, Lewis, Nancy, Susan. B.S. in Engring., Iowa State U., 1948; M.B.A., Syracuse U., 1968. Registered profl. engr., Iowa. Mgr., Maytag Co., Newton, Iowa, 1953-59; sr. staff engr., mgr. Philco-Ford Corp., Phila., 1959-62; mgr. mech. and indsl. engring. Carrier Corp., Syracuse, N.Y., 1962-75; v.p. Superior Industries Internat., Van Nuys, Calif., 1981—; v.p., gen. mgr. Superior/Ideal, Inc., Oskaloosa, Iowa, 1975—; engring. cons., Louisville, 1951-53. Author: MTM Application Manual, 1957. Leader, Boy Scouts Am., Syracuse, 1965-73; fund chmn. United Fund, Syracuse, 1965-73. Served to lt. col. USAFR, 1942—; ETO. Decorated Purple Heart, Disting. Flying Cross, air medal with four oak leaf clusters. Mem. Am. Inst. Indsl. Engrs. (pres. 1951-53), Oskaloosa Country Club, Elks.

OSTER, LUDWIG FRIEDRICH, physicist; b. Konstanz, Germany, Mar. 8, 1931; came to U.S., 1958, naturalized, 1963; s. Ludwig Friedrich and Emma Josefine (Schwarz) O.; m. Cheryl M. Oroian, Oct. 10, 1987; children from previous marriage: Ulrika, Mattias. BS, U. Freiburg, Germany, 1951, MS, 1954; PhD, U. Kiel, Germany, 1956. German Sci. Coun. fellow U. Kiel, 1956-58; rsch. assoc. Yale U., 1958-60, asst. prof., then assoc. prof. physics, 1960-67; mem. faculty U. Colo., Boulder, 1967-83; prof. physics and astrophysics U. Colo., 70-83; program mgr. Nat. Radio Astronomy Obs., NSF, 1983-96; fellow Joint Inst. Astrophysics, Boulder, 1967-83; NRC Sr. assoc., 1981-82; vis. prof. U. Bonn, W.Ger., 1966, Johns Hopkins, 1981; cons. to govt. and industry. Author: Modern Astronomy, 1973 (also Spanish and Polish edits); editor: Scripta Technica, 1960-70; contbr. articles profl. jours. Recipient Humboldt Stiftung, 1974. Mem. Am. Phys. Soc., Am. Astron. Soc., Internat. Astron. Union, German Astron. Soc., Sigma Xi.

OSTER, ROSE MARIE GUNHILD, foreign language professional, educator; b. Stockholm, Feb. 26, 1934; came to U.S., 1958; d. Herbert Jonas and Emma Wilhelmina (Johnson) Hagetorn; m. Ludwig F. Oster, May 17, 1956; children: Ulrika, Mattias. Fil. mag., U. Stockholm, 1956; PhD, Kiel (Germany) U., 1958. Postdoctoral rsch. fellow linguistics Yale U., 1958-60, rsch. fellow Germanic langs., 1960-64, lectr. Swedish, 1964-66; mem. faculty U. Colo., Boulder, 1966-80, assoc. prof. Germanic langs. and lits., 1970-77, prof., 1977-80, chmn. dept., 1972-75, assoc. dean Grad. Sch., 1975-79, assoc. vice chancellor for grad. affairs Grad. Sch., 1979-80; dean for grad. studies and rsch. U. Md., College Park, 1980-83, prof. Germanic langs. and lits., 1980—; mem. Fulbright Nat. Screening Com., Scandinavia, 1973, 83-87, chair, 1986-87; mem. selection com. Scandinavia Internat. Exch. of Scholars, 1982-86; cons. panelist Nat. Endowment for Humanities, 1975—, mem. bd. cons., 1980—; state coord. Am. Coun. on Edn., Colo., 1978-80, Md., 1981-83, dir. dept. leadership program, 1986-91; mem. exec. com. Assn. Grad. Schs., 1980-83; mem. dean's exec. com. African-Am. Inst., 1981-85; interim dir. Washington Sch. Psychiatry, 1994-95; cons. in field. Contbr. articles and revs. to profl. publs. Bd. dirs. Washington Sch. Psychiatry, Am.-Swedish Hist. Mus., Phila., Open Theatre, Washington; mem. nat. fellowship com. Am.-Scandinavian Found., 1997—. Carnegie fellow, 1974; grantee Swedish Govt., Am. Scandinavian Found.; grantee German Acad. Exch. Svc. Mem. NOW, MLA (mem. Del. Assembly 1995—), AAUP, Soc. Advancement Scandinavian Studies (pres. 1979-80), Am. Scandinavian Assn. of Nat. Capital Area (pres. 1983-86, 96—), Am.-Scandinavian Found., Am. Assn. Higher Edn., Modern Lang. Assn. (mem. del. assembly). Home: 4977 Battery Ln Bethesda MD 20814-4931 Office: U Md Dept Germanic & Slavic College Park MD 20742

OSTERBERG, CHARLES LAMAR, marine radioecologist, oceanographer; b. Miami, Ariz., June 15, 1920; s. Arthur Edward and Grace Viola (Johnson) O.; m. Betty Peltier, Nov. 10, 1945; children: Cheryl Ann Osterberg Cheek, David Arthur, John Charles. BS, No. Ariz. U., 1948, MS, 1949; postgrad., Purdue U., 1958, U. Wash., 1960; PhD, Oreg. State U., 1962. Rsch. assoc. Lowell Obs., Flagstaff, Ariz., 1949-53; asst. scientist Atmospheric Rsch. Lab., No. Ariz. U., Flagstaff, 1953-56; tchr. high sch. Flagstaff, 1956-59; successively instr., asst. prof., assoc. prof., prof. oceanography Oreg. State U., 1962-67; asst. dir. vis. biomed. and environ. programs AEC, Washington, 1967-74; program mgr. environ. programs ERDA, Washington, 1974-76; dir. Internat. Lab. Marine Radioactivity, Mus. Océanographique, Monaco, 1976-79; marine scientist U.S. Dept. Energy, Washington, 1979-86, chmn. oceanography subcom., nuclear safety, Galileo and solar polar space project, ret., 1986; co-founder EnRad, Inc./Radon Testing and Engring., Inc., Gaithersburg, Md., 1986—; cons. Internat. Atomic Energy Agy., Vienna, Austria; participant NSF Acad. Yr. Inst., 1959-60. Contbr. numerous articles on radioecology to profl. jours. With AC, U.S. Army, 1940-45; PTO. Recipient Alumni Achievement award No. Ariz. U., 1983; USPHS fellow, 1962. Mem. Am. Soc. Limnology, Oceanography, Health Physics Soc., Am. Assn. Radon Scientists and Technologists (bd. dirs. 1988), Sigma Xi. Home: 14525 N Crown Point Dr Tucson AZ 85737-9322

OSTERBERG, JAMES NEWELL See POP, IGGY

OSTERBROCK, DONALD E(DWARD), astronomy educator; s. William Carl and Elsie (Wettlin) O.; m. Irene L. Hansen, Sept. 19. 1952; children: Carol Ann, William Carl, Laura Jane. PhB, U. Chgo., 1948, BS, 1948, SM, 1949, PhD, 1952; DSc (hon.), Ohio State U., 1986, U. Chgo., 1992, U. Wis., Madison, 1997. Postdoctoral fellow, mem. faculty Princeton, 1952-53; mem. faculty Calif. Inst. Tech., 1953-58; faculty U. Wis.-Madison, 1958-73, prof. astronomy, 1961-73, chmn. dept. astronomy, 1966-67, 69-72; prof. astronomy and astrophysics U. Calif., Santa Cruz, 1972-92, prof. emeritus, 1993—; dir. Lick Obs., 1972-81; mem. staff Mt. Wilson Obs., Palomar Obs., 1953-58; vis. prof. U. Chgo., 1963-64, Ohio State U., 1980, 86; Hill Family vis. prof. U. Minn., 1977-78. Author: Astrophysics of Gaseous Nebulae, 1974, James E. Keeler, Pioneer American Astrophysicist and the Early Development of American Astrophysics, 1984, Yerkes Observatory, 1892-1950: The Birth, Near Death and Resurrection of a Scientific Research Institution, 1997, (with John R. Gustafson and W.J. Shiloh Unruh) Eye on the Sky: Lick Observatory's First Century, 1988, Astrophysics of Gaseous Nebulae and Active Galactic Nuclei, 1989, Pauper and Prince: Ritchey, Hale, and Big American Telescopes, 1993; editor: (with C.R. O'Dell) Planetary Nebulae, 1968, (with Peter H. Raven) Origins and Extinctions, 1988, (with J.S. Miller) Active Galactic Nuclei, 1989; Stars and Galaxies: Citizens of the Universe, 1990; letters editor Astrophys. Jour., 1971-73. With USAAF, 1943-46. Recipient Profl. Achievement award U. Chgo. Alumni Assn., 1982, Antoinette de Vaucouleurs Meml. lecture and medal U. Tex., Austin, 1994; Guggenheim fellow Inst. Advanced Studies, Princeton, N.J., 1960-61, 82-83, Ambrose Monnell Found. fellow, 1989-90, NSF sr. postdoctoral rsch. fellow U. Coll., London, 1968-69. Mem. NAS (chmn. astronomy sect. 1971-74, sec. class math. and phys. sci. 1980-83, chmn. class math and phys. sci. 1983-85, councilor 1985-88), Am. Acad. Arts and Scis., Internat. Astron. Union (pres. commn. 34 1967-70), Royal Astron. Soc. (assoc., Gold medal 1997), Am. Astron. Soc. (councilor 1970-73, v.p. 1975-77, pres. 1988-90, vice chmn. hist. astronomy div. 1985-87, chmn. 1987-89, Henry Norris Russell lectr. 1991), Astron. Soc. Pacific (chmn. history com. 1982-86, Catherine Wolfe Bruce medal 1991, bd. dirs. 1992-95), Wis. Acad. Scis. Arts and Letters, Am. Philos. Soc. Congregationalist. Home: 120 Woodside Ave Santa Cruz CA 95060-3422

OSTERGARD, PAUL MICHAEL, bank executive; b. Akron, Ohio, Apr. 1, 1939; s. Paul and Janette Beryl (Laube) O.; m. Elizabeth K. McCombs, Jan. 1965 (div. Nov. 1971). AB magna cum laude, Case-Western Res. U., 1961; JD, U. Mich., 1964; MPA, Harvard U., 1969; student, U. Madrid, Spain, 1959-60. Bar: Ohio 1964. Atty. U.S. Steel Corp., Pitts., 1967-69; gen. atty. TWA Inc., N.Y.C., 1969-71; v.p. adminstrn., sec., counsel Pa. Co. (now Penn Ctrl. Corp.), 1971-74, and subs. Buckeye Pipe Line Co., N.Y.C., 1972-74; pub. affairs exec. GE, Fairfield, Conn., 1974-84; pres. GE Found., Fairfield, Conn., 1984-90; pres. Citicorp Found., N.Y.C., 1990—, also bd. dirs. Mem. Nat. Hispanic Scholarship Bd., Am. Coun. on the Arts Bd., Jr. Achievement of N.Y.; bd. dirs. ARC Greater Greater N.Y., Operation Smile; corp. adv. coun. ARC. Capt. USAF, 1965-68, Vietnam. Decorated Bronze Star, Legion of Merit (Vietnam); Univ. scholar, 1957-61; Littauer fellow, 1968-69. Mem. Ohio Bar Assn., Harvard Club, Atrium Club, Phi Beta Kappa, Omicron Delta Kappa. Episcopalian. Home: 12 Hillside View Rd Mahopac NY 10541 Office: Citibank 850 3rd Ave Fl 13 New York NY 10022-6222

OSTERGREN, GREGORY VICTOR, insurance company executive; b. Mpls., May 27, 1955; s. Theodora Carl and Donna Marie (Williams) O.; m. Diane Jane Schaller, Oct. 12, 1985; children: Patrick, Cynthia. BS in Math., BA in Econs., U. Minn., 1977. Actuarial analyst Allstate Ins. Co., Northbrook, Ill., 1977-79; actuary MSI Ins. Co., Arden Hills, Minn., 1979-84, dir.

actuarial dept., 1984-86, v.p. ops., 1986-90; pres., CEO Am. Nat. Property and Casualty Ins. Co., Springfield, Mo., 1990—, also bd. dirs.; mem. governing bd. Minn., S.D. and N.D. Auto Assigned Risk, Mpls., 1984-90. Bd. dirs. United Way of Ozarks, Springfield, 1990—, Springfield Pub. Sch. Found., 1994—; mem. cert. com. S.W. Mo. State U., Springfield, 1992-93; mem. steering com. Salvation Army, Springfield, 1992-93. Mem. Casualty Actuarial Soc., Am. Acad. Actuaries, Internat. Actuarial Assn., Midwest Actuarial Forum, Ins. Fraternity. Baptist. Avocations: golf, boating, scuba diving, reading, travel. Home: 1951 E Buena Vista St Springfield MO 65804-4326 Office: Am Nat Property Casualty 1949 E Sunshine St Springfield MO 65899-0001

OSTERHAUS, WILLIAM ERIC, television executive; b. N.Y.C., July 31, 1935; s. Eric Hugo and Helen (McAuliff) O.; m. Nancy Jean Heinemann, June 19, 1960 (dec.); children: Eric Frank, Marc Andrew; m. Annemarie Clark, Dec. 28, 1985. Student, Fordham U., 1953-54, Harvard U. Bus. Sch., summer 1970. Staff producer news and spl. events dept. Sta. WNBC-AM-TV, N.Y.C., 1956-61; exec. producer Sta. KYW-TV, Cleve., 1961-64; exec. producer Sta. KPIX, San Francisco, 1964-67, gen. mgr., 1969-73; program mgr. Sta. KYW-TV, Phila., 1967-69; pres., gen. mgr. Sta. KQED Inc., San Francisco, 1973-78; pres. SiteLine Comms., Inc., San Francisco, 1979—; chmn. bd. VariCom Inc., San Francisco, 1982-86; chmn. TV adv. com. Calif. Pub. Broadcasting Commn., 1977-78; mem. joint com. on film and broadcasting Indo-U.S. Subcommn. on Edn. and Culture., 1975-85; chmn. TV com. San Rafael Redevel. Agy., Calif., 1977-78; mem. citizens adv. com. CATV, San Rafael, 1976-77, Dominican Coll., San Rafael, 1972-80. Bd. dirs., chmn. advocacy com. The Ctr. for the Arts, San Francisco, 1985—; bd. dirs. Studio for Tech. and the Arts, 1995—. 1st lt. U.S. Army, 1958-60. Recipient Peabody award and Hillman award for One Nation Indivisible documentary, 1968. Office: 150 4th St Ste 295 San Francisco CA 94103-3048

OSTERHELD, R(OBERT) KEITH, chemistry educator; b. Bklyn., Apr. 19, 1925; s. Albert Henry and Hilda Pearl (Heatlie) O.; m. Jean Drake Evans, June 28, 1952; children: Robert Keith, Albert Laighton, James Evans, Thomas Heatlie. BS in Chemistry, Poly. Inst. Bklyn., 1945; PhD in Inorganic Chemistry, U. Ill., 1950. Instr. Cornell U., Ithaca, N.Y., 1950-54; asst. prof. chemistry U. Mont., Missoula, 1954-58, assoc. prof., 1958-65, prof., 1965-90; prof. emeritus U. Mont., 1990—; chmn. dept. U. Mont., Missoula, 1973-90. Contbr. articles to profl. jours. Mem. Florence (Mont.) Sch. Bd., 1969-75, chmn., 1972-73, 74-75; bd. dirs. Mont. Sch. Bd. Assn., Helena, 1973-75; council mem. Florence-Carlton Community Ch., 1965-90, treas., 1965-90. Served to sgt. USAAF, 1945-47. Mem. Am. Chem. Soc., N.Am. Thermal Analysis Soc., Sigma Xi. Home: 524 Larry Creek Loop Florence MT 59833-6705 Office: U of Montana Dept Of Chemistry Missoula MT 59812

OSTERHOFF, JAMES MARVIN, retired telecommunications company executive; b. Lafayette, Ind., May 18, 1936; s. Abel Lyman and Mildred Paulene (Post) O.; m. Marilyn Ann Morrison, Aug. 24, 1958; children—Anne Michelle Bitsie, Amy Louise Olmsted, Susan Marie. B.S.M.E., Purdue U., 1958; M.B.A., Stanford U., 1963. Staff asst. FMC Corp., San Jose, Calif., 1963-64; with Ford Motor Co., Dearborn, Mich., 1964-84; v.p. fin. Ford Motor Credit Co., Dearborn, 1973-75; controller car ops. N. Am. Automotive Ops., Ford Motor Co., Dearborn, 1975-76; asst. controller N. Am. Automotive Ops., Ford Motor Co., 1976-79; controller tractor ops. Ford Motor Co., Troy, Mich., 1979-84; v.p. fin., CFO Digital Equipment Corp., Maynard, Mass., 1985-91; exec. v.p., CFO U.S.West Inc., Englewood, Colo., 1991-95; bd. dirs. GenCorp, Inc., FSA Holdings, Ltd., Pvt. Sector Coun., Colo. Neurol. Inst., Goodwill Industries of Denver. Served to lt. (j.g.) USN, 1958-61. Recipient Disting. Engring. Alumnus award Purdue U.; named Outstanding Mech. Engring. Alumnus, Purdue U.

OSTERHOLM, J(OHN) ROGER, humanities educator; b. Worcester, Mass., Nov. 24, 1936; s. Walfred Anders and Ellen Olivia (Hendrickson) O.; m. Jo-Ann M. Doiron, Dec. 22, 1962 (div. 1981); children: Doreen, Jon R., Don J.; m. Diane Jane Ungerer, May 1, 1982. BA, Upsala Coll., 1959; MA, CCNY, 1966; PhD, U. Mass., 1978; postgrad., Tex. Tech U., 1961-62, Worcester (Mass.) State Coll., 1965-66, Clark U., 1972. Instr. Worcester Jr. Coll., 1962; supr. Aetna Life Ins. Co., N.Y.C., 1963-65; tchr. Wachusett Regional H.S., Holden, Mass., 1965-66; assoc. prof. Ctrl. N.E. Coll., Worcester, 1966-79, chmn. humanities, 1977-79; prof. Embry-Riddle Aero. U., Daytona Beach, Fla., 1979—; spkr. on journalism, aviation films and Bing Crosby; advisor to coll. student publs., 1969-94, adviser to student publs., 1967-78. Author: Literary Career of Isaiah Thomas, 1978, Bing Crosby: A Bio-bibliography, 1994; editor: The Riddle Reader, 1988; co-author: MiG-15 to Freedom, 1996; contbr. articles to profl. jours. Dirs. Daytona Playhouse, Daytona Beach, 1980-83; lector Grace Luth. Ch., Ormond Beach, Fla., 1989—. With USAF, 1960-62. Recipient Best Supporting Actor award Daytona Playhouse, 1981. Mem. Popular Culture Assn., Air Force Assn., Soc. Collegiate Journalists, Internat. Crosby Circle. Republican. Avocations: acting, airplane models, computer simulations. Office: Embry-Riddle Aero U Humanities Dept Daytona Beach FL 32114

OSTERHOUT, SUYDAM, physician, educator; b. Bklyn., Nov. 25, 1925; s. Howard and Edna Cornell (Davison) O.; m. Shirley Elizabeth Kirkman, Sept. 17, 1960; children—Mark, Martin, Ann. B.A., Princeton, 1945; M.D. (Hanes fellow), Duke, 1949; Ph.D., Rockefeller U., 1959. Diplomate: Am. Bd. Internal Medicine. Intern pathology Cleve. City Hosp., 1950; intern internal medicine Mass. Meml. Hosp., Boston, 1950-51; resident Duke Hosp., 1953-56; faculty Duke Med. Sch., Durham, N.C., 1959—; now prof. medicine, prof. microbiology, assoc. dean. Duke Med. Sch. Contbr. articles to profl. jours. Served with M.C. USAF, 1951-53. Recipient NIH Career Devel. award, 1960-65; Markle scholar in medicine, 1959-64. Fellow A.C.P.; mem. Am. Soc. Micro-Biology, Am. Fedn. Clin. Research, Sigma Xi, Alpha Omega Alpha. Home: 5133 N Willowhaven Dr Durham NC 27712-1956 Office: PO Box 3007 Durham NC 27715-3007

OSTERKAMP, DALENE MAY, psychology educator, artist; b. Davenport, Iowa, Dec. 1, 1932; d. James Hiram and Bernice Grace (La Grange) Simmons; m. Donald Edwin Osterkamp, Feb. 11, 1951 (dec. Sept. 1951). BA, San Jose State U., 1959, MA, 1962; PhD, Saybrook Inst., 1989. Lectr. San Jose (Calif.) State U., 1960-61, U. Santa Barbara (Calif.) Ext., 1970-76; prof. Bakersfield (Calif.) Coll., 1961-87, emeritus, 1987—; adj. faculty, counselor Calif. State U., Bakersfield, 1990—; gallery dir. Bakersfield Coll., 1964-72. Exhibited in group shows at Berkeley (Calif.) Art, Ctr., 1975, Libr. of Congress, 1961, Seattle Art Mus., 1962. Founder Kern Art Edn. Assn., Bakersfield, 1962, Bakersfield Printmakers, 1976. Staff sgt. USAF, 1952-55. Recipient 1st Ann. Svc. to Women award Am. Assn. Women in C.C., 1989. Mem. APA, Assn. for Women in Psychology, Assn. for Humanistic Psychology, Calif. Soc. Printmakers. Home: PO Box 387 Glennville CA 93226-0387 Office: Calif State Univ Stockdale Ave Bakersfield CA 93309

OSTERN, WILHELM CURT, retired holding company executive; b. Geisenheim am Rhein, Germany, Sept. 29, 1923; came to U.S., 1956, naturalized, 1970; s. Wilhelm A. and Margarete R. (Seul) O.; m. Beatrice Atkin, Jan. 3, 1992; children from previous marriage: Karen, Ellen, Wilhelm. Grad., Staatliches Realgymnasium, Geisenheim, 1941. With Bayer AG, and predecessor, 1941-88, officer and/or dir. subsidiaries and affiliates, 1956-89; vice chmn., chief fin. officer Mobay Corp., Pitts., 1974-86; vice chmn. Bayer USA, Inc., Pitts., 1986-88; bd. dirs. Schott Corp., Inc., Carl Zeiss, Inc., CDS Internat. Inc. With German Army, 1942-45. Hon. Consul Fed. Republic of Germany. Mem. Soc. Contemporary Crafts, Pitts. (bd. dirs.). Clubs: Brook (N.Y.C.); Duquesne (Pitts.). Home: Hartle Rd Sewickley PA 15143 Office: Bayer Corp 500 Grant St One Mellon Ctr Pittsburgh PA 15219-2502

OSTERTAG, ROBERT LOUIS, lawyer; b. N.Y.C., June 21, 1931; s. Frederick C. and Lillian (Bishop) O.; m. Ann Mary Flynn, Aug. 28, 1954; children—Thomas J., Daniel V., Debra A. B.A., Fordham U., 1953; LL.B., St. John's U., Bklyn., 1956; LL.M., Georgetown U., 1960. Bar: N.Y. 1957, U.S. Dist. Ct. (so. dist.) N.Y. 1969, U.S. Tax Ct. 1965, U.S. Ct. Mil. Appeals 1959, U.S. Supreme Ct. 1960. Atty. office chief counsel IRS, Washington, 1958-60; ptnr. Guernsey, Butts & Walsh, Poughkeepsie, N.Y., 1963-90, Guernsey, Butts, Ostertag & O'Leary, Poughkeepsie, N.Y., 1991-95, Ostertag & O'Leary, Poughkeepsie, 1995—; adj. prof. paralegal studies Marist Coll., Poughkeepsie, 1975-91; adj. prof. Fordham U. Sch. of Law, N.Y.C., 1993—; counsel Agr. Com., N.Y. State Assembly, 1967-68; mem. Gov.'s Jud. Screening Com., 1987-93; counsel to cons. and draftsman of proposed county charters and adminstrv. codes for Sullivan, Fulton, Orange and Onondaga Counties, N.Y., City of Poughkeepsie, N.Y.; mem. 9th Jud. Dist. Grievance Com., 1975-79, 9th Jud. Dist. Med. Malpractice Panel, 1975-91, mem. 9th Jud. Dist. Arbitration Panel, 1980—; mem. Chief Judges Com. on Pro Bono Legal Svc., 1992-93. Mem. adv. coun. Pace U. Sch. Law, 1975-84, paralegal adv. coun. Maris Coll., 1975—; bd. dirs. Com. for Modern Cts., 1975—; trustee Joseph F. Barnard Meml. Law Libr., Poughkeepsie, 1979—; mem. Dutchess County Charter Commn., N.Y., 1966-67, Dutchess County Bd. Health, 1964-70, pres., 1966-70; chmn. Dutchess County Charter Revision Task Force, 1979-88; dir. Hudson Valley Philharm. Soc., 1973-76; v.p., dir. High Tor Opera Co., 1967-70; dir. United Fund of Dutchess County, 1973-78, Dutchess County chpt. Am. Heart Assn., 1975-81, 84-89; trustee Sports Mus. Dutchess County, 1989-93, chmn., 1989-90; dir. Hudson Valley Stadium Corp., 1995—; dep. supr. Town of Poughkeepsie, 1976; dir. Standard Gage Co., 1972-88. Served to capt. JAGC, USAF, 1956-58. Recipient Recognition award Cen. Poughkeepsie Exch. Club, 1967, Marist Coll. Pres.'s award, 1991. Mem. Hudson Valley Estate Planning Council (pres. 1965-66, dir. 1969-74), ABA (chmn. conf. of state bar gen. practice leaders of gen. practice sect. 1980-87, mem. coun. 1982-86, chmn. by-laws com. 1988-89, chmn. litigation com. 1989-90, ho. of dels. 1985—, Gavel awards com. 1989—, standing com. on solo and small firm practitioners 1992-95), Am. Bar Found., N.Y. Bar Found., N.Y. State Bar Assn. (exec. com. 1983-85, 1986-93, ho. of dels. 1973-79, 80—, pres. 1991-92, chmn. unlawful practice of law com. 1977-81, chmn. com. on profl. econs. and efficiency rsch. 1982, chmn. sect. on gen. practice of law 1980-82, com. profl. ethics, 1986-90, 96—, chmn. long range planning com. 1992-95), Dutchess County Bar Assn. (sec. 1969-79, pres. 1984-85), Delta Theta Phi. Home: 5 Pat Dr Poughkeepsie NY 12603-5626 Office: 17 Collegeview Ave Poughkeepsie NY 12603-2406

OSTFELD, ADRIAN MICHAEL, physician; b. St. Louis, Sept. 2, 1926; s. Simon and Margaret (Fisman) O.; m. Ruth Vogel, Dec. 31, 1950; children: Barbara, Richard, Robin. Student, Washington U., St. Louis, 1943-44, 46-47, MD cum laude, 1951. Instr. Cornell U. Med. Coll., 1955-56; faculty U. Ill. Coll. Medicine Chgo., 1956-68, prof. preventive medicine, 1963-66, head dept., 1966-68; staff Research and Edn. Hosps., 1956-68; chmn. dept. epidemiology and pub. health Yale U., 1968-70, Anna Lauder prof. epidemiology and pub. health, 1970-94; prof. emeritus, 1994—; head div. chronic disease epidemiology Yale U., dir. med. student edn. Sch. Pub. Health, 1971-75; spl. cons. Surgeon Gen. USPHS, 1964—; chmn. ad hoc com. on life prolonging drugs NIH, 1973-76, mem. nat. adv. council on aging; cons. council on drugs AMA, 1964—; cons. human experimentation Nat. Inst. on Aging, 1977, cons., 1979, mem. overall program planning panel, 1981—; mem. Mayor's Com. on Elderly, New Haven, vice chmn., 1972, chmn., 1977-80; co-chmn. Nationwide Study Precursors of Stroke; dir. Conn. High Blood Pressure Program; cons. Am. Inst. Biol. Scis., Population Lab.; nat. cons. White House Conf. on Aging, 1981; mem. research rev. com. B Nat. Heart, Lung and Blood Inst., NIH, 1976—; mem. exec. com. Yale Center for Behavioral Medicine, 1977—; v.p. Conn. Heart Assn., 1978-80, pres., 1980-82; mem. nat. policy bd. on health and phys. fitness YMCA, 1979-81; chmn. Commrs. Council on Hypertension Conn.; mem. Interag. Planning Group on Coronary Heart Disease Prevention, 1981; cons. Robert Wood Johnson Found., Commonwealth Found; mem. cardiac adv. com. N.Y. State Health Dept., 1989; mem. com. on drug use in the workplace NRC, 1991. Author: The Common Headache Syndromes, 1962, Epidemiology of Aging, 1975, Psychosocial Variables in Epidemiological Studies of Cardiovascular Disease, 1985, Established Populations for Epidemiologic Studies of Elderly, 1986, Stress, Crowding and Blood Pressure in Prisons, 1987; assoc. editor The Black American Elderly, 1989; editor Am. Jour. Epidemiology, 1979-91; mem. editorial bd. 5 med. jours.; also numerous articles. Mem. panel on nat. health care survey Nat. Rsch. Coun., 1989. Recipient Wisdom Soc. award, 1970; fellow Morse Coll., Yale U.; named one of Conn.'s most Disting. Citizens, Hartford Courant, 1985. Fellow Royal Soc. Health, Soc. Clin. Investigation, Royal Soc. Medicine; mem. NAS (com. on rsch. in the prevention of addiction 1989), Inst. Medicine (com. to evaluate artificial heart program Nat. Heart, Lung and Blood Inst., coord. health promotion and disease prevention for the second fifty 1990, com. on epidemiology and vets. studies 1991), Am. Epidemol. Soc., Am. Coll. Epidemiology, Am. Heart Assn. (fellow couns. on stroke and epidemiology, chmn. com. risk edn. in heart attack and stroke, Disting. Vol. award 1976, C-E. A. Winslow award 1976, Ivy award 1987), Am. Soc. for Pharmacology and Exptl. Therapeutics, Am. Coll. Preventive Medicine, Gerontol. Soc., Internat. Platform Assn., Am. Pub. Health Assn., Am. Coll. Preventive Medicine, Inst. of Medicine (program com.), Conn. Acad. Sci. and Engring., Am. Soc. Clin. Investigation, AAUP, Sigma Xi, Alpha Omega Alpha. Research on relevant social and psychol. factors in cardiovascular disease and high blood pressure, risk factors for stroke, health and social problems of aging. Home: 17 Marlborough Rd North Haven CT 06473-2928 Office: Yale Univ 60 College St New Haven CT 06510-3210

OSTFELD, ALEXANDER MARION, advertising agency executive; b. St. Louis, Feb. 13, 1932; s. Simon and Margaret (Fishmann) O.; B.S., Washington U., St. Louis, 1953; postgrad. St. Louis U., 1953-56. Mktg. mgr. lighting div. Emerson Electric Co., St. Louis, 1955-59; dir. research and media Frank Block Assos., St. Louis, 1959-61; research and media supr. Compton Advt., Chgo., 1961-65; media and mktg. supr. Leo Burnett Advt., Chgo., 1965-68; dir. mktg. and account planning, v.p. McCann-Erickson, Chgo., 1968-72, Kenyon & Eckhardt, Chgo., 1972; dir. Canadian and internat. ops. A. Eicoff & Co., Chgo.; owner Alex Ostfeld Co. Advt. and Mktg., Woodbridge, Conn. and Can. Cons. Am. Assn. Advt. Agys., Yale/New Haven Sci. Park. Mem. Am. Mktg. Assn. (sec. St. Louis 1956-57), Internat. Platform Assn., Broadcast Advt. Club, Am. Research Found. Clubs: Chgo. Exec., Woodbridge Hunt (Conn.). Home: 4 Ledge Rd Woodbridge CT 06525-1802 Office: 6 Ledge Rd Woodbridge CT 06525-1802

OSTLING, RICHARD NEIL, journalist, author, broadcaster; b. Endicott, N.Y., July 14, 1940; s. Acton Eric Sr. and Christine Cathryn (Cumins) O.; m. Joan Elaine Kerns, July 8, 1967; children: Margaret Anne, Elizabeth Anne. BA, U. Mich., 1962; MS in Journalism, Northwestern U., 1963; MA in Religion, George Washington U., 1970; LittD (hon.), Gordon (Mass.) Coll., 1989. Reporter, copyreader Morning News and Evening Jour., Wilmington, Del., 1963-64; asst. news editor Christianity Today mag., Washington, 1965-67, news editor, 1967-69; staff corr. Time mag., N.Y.C., 1969-74, religion writer, 1975-94, sr. corr., 1994—; broadcaster Report on Religion, CBS Radio, Washington, 1979—; religion corr. Newshour with Jim Lehrer formerly MacNeil/Lehrer Newshour, 1991—; adv. bd. Ctr. for Religion and the News Media, Northwestern U., 1994—. Author: Secrecy in the Church, 1974; co-author: Aborting America, 1979. Served with USNG, 1964-70. McCormick Found. fellow, 1962-63; recipient Supple, Templeton and Wilbur awards for religion writing. Mem. Religion Newswriters Assn. (pres. 1974-76), Northwestern U. Alumni Hall of Achievement (charter), Phi Beta Kappa. Mem. Christian Reformed Ch. Home: 280 Hillcrest Rd Ridgewood NJ 07450-2400 Office: care Time Magazine 1271 Avenue Of The Americas New York NY 10020-1300

OSTLUND, H. GOTE, atmospheric and marine scientist, educator; b. Stockholm, June 26, 1923; came to U.S., 1963; s. Sven and Ruth (Lundin) O.; m. Doris Beck, Sept. 30, 1950; children: Stellan, Goran. Fil Kand., U. Stockholm, 1949, Fil Lic., 1958; hon. doctorate, U. Gothenburg, 1984. Research asst. U. Stockholm, 1944-46; tchr. Technol. Night Coll., Stockholm, 1946-51; research asst. Royal Inst. Tech., Stockholm, 1947; asst. instr. Royal Inst. Tech., 1948-52; head of lab. Swedish Nitrogen Fertilizer Works, Ltd., 1952-54, Radioactive Dating Lab., Stockholm, 1954-63; asst. instr. Royal Inst. Tech., Stockholm, 1956-57; vis. research asso. prof. Inst. Marine Scis., U. Miami (Fla.), 1960-61, asso. prof. geochemistry, 1963-67, prof. marine and atmospheric chemistry Rosenstiel Sch. Marine and Atmospheric Sci., 1967-97, chmn. div. chem. oceanography, 1970-72, coordinator Geochem. Oceans Sects., 1976-86, mem. exec. com. Geochem. Oceans Sects., 1973-86, coordinator Transient Tracers in Ocean, 1977-85, prof. emeritus, 1997—. Assoc. editor: Revs. of Geophysics and Space Physics, 1974-76; mem. editorial bd.: Marine Chemistry, 1974-93; mem. adv. bd.: Tellus B; contbr. articles to profl. jours. Served in Royal Swedish Air Force, 1943-44, 46. Mem. Am. Geophys. Union, Am. Meteorol. Soc., AAAS, Swedish Chem. Soc., Swedish Geophys. Soc., Fla. Acad. Scis. Office: U Miami 4600 Rickenbacker Cswy Miami FL 33149-1031

OSTMO, DAVID CHARLES, broadcasting executive; b. Mason City, Iowa, Jan. 16, 1959; s. Gene Charles and Charlene Lucille (Evans) O.; m. Beverly M. Cannon, May 10, 1997. Diploma, Brown Inst., 1979. Maintenance engr. Sta. KJRH-TV, Tulsa, 1981-84; chief news editor Sta. KOTV, Tulsa, 1984-86; chief engr. Sta. KXON-TV/Rogers State Coll., Claremore, Okla., 1986-90; dir. engring. Fairview AFX, Tulsa, 1990-92, Sta. KABB-TV, San Antonio, 1992-95; dir. ops. KABB-TV, San Antonio, 1995—; columnist TV Tech., Falls Church, Va., 1988-90. Producer, dir. (TV show) Theodore Kirby Show, 1988; dir. (TV show) Zebra Sports Review, 1987, RSC Spotlight, 1987; writer mag. News From the Back Porch, 1988-90, Tulsa TV Tidbits, 1988-91. Named Eagle Scout Boy Scouts Am., 1974. Mem. Soc. Broadcast Engrs. (sr. broadcast engr., chmn. Tulsa chpt. 1989-90, chmn. San Antonio chpt. 1993-95). Lutheran. Avocations: photography, genealogy, creative writing, computer science, golf. Home: 7419 Rainfall Park San Antonio TX 78249 Office: Sta KABB-TV 4335 NW Loop 410 San Antonio TX 78229-5136

OSTRACH, SIMON, engineering educator; b. Providence, Dec. 26, 1923; s. Samuel and Bella (Sackman) O.; m. Gloria Selma Ostrov, Dec. 31, 1944 (div. Jan. 1973); children: Stefan Alan, Louis Hayman, Naomi Ruth, David Jonathan, Judith Cele; m. Margaret E. Stern, Oct. 29, 1975. BS in Mech. Engring, U. R.I., 1944, ME, 1949; MS, Brown U., 1949, PhD in Applied Math, 1950; DS (h.c.) Technion, Israel Inst. Tech., 1986; D of Eng. (hon.), Fla. State U., 1994; DS (hon.), U. R.I., 1995. Rsch. scientist NACA, 1944-47; rsch. assoc. Brown U., 1947-50; chief fluid physics br. Lewis Rsch. Ctr. NASA, 1950-60; prof. engring., head div. fluid, thermal and aerospace scis. Case Western Res. U., Cleve., 1960-70; Wilbert J. Austin Distinguished prof. engring. Case Western Res. U., 1970—; home sec. Nat. Acad. Engring., 1992—; disting. vis. prof. City Coll. CUNY, 1966-67, Fla. A&M U., Fla. State U. Coll. Engring., 1990; Lady Davis fellow, vis. prof. Technion-Israel Inst. Tech., 1983-84; cons. to industry, 1960—; mem. rsch. adv. com. fluid mechanics NASA, 1963-68, mem. space applications adv. com., 1985—; hon. prof. Beijing U. Aeronautics and Astronautics, 1991; mem. space studies bd. Nat. Rsch. Coun., 1992, bd. govs., 1993—. Contbr. papers to profl. lit. Fellow Japan Soc. for the Promotion of Sci., 1987; recipient Conf. award for best paper Nat. Heat Transfer Conf., 1963, Richards Meml. award Pi Tau Sigma, 1964, Disting. Svc. award Cleve. Tech. Socs. Coun., 1987, Disting. pub. svc. medal NASA, 1993, Space Processing award Am. Inst. of Aeronautics and Astronautics, 1994. Fellow AIAA (Space Processing award 1993), ASME (hon., Heat Transfer Meml. award 1975, Freeman scholar 1982, Thurston lectr. 1987, Max Jacob meml. award 1983, Heat Transfer divsn. 50th Anniversary award 1988), Am. Acad. Mechanics; mem. NAE (chmn. com. on membership 1986, chmn. nominating com. 1989, chmn. awards com. 1990, sec., mem. space studies bd. 1992), Univs. Space Rsch. Assn. (trustee 1990), Soc. Natural Philosophy, Sigma Xi (nat. lectr. 1978-79), Tau Beta Pi. Home: 28176 Belcourt Rd Cleveland OH 44124-5618 Office: Case Western Res U Dept of Engineering Cleveland OH 44106

OSTRAGER, BARRY ROBERT, lawyer; b. N.Y.C., July 14, 1947; m. Pamela Goodman, Apr. 8, 1972; children: Anne Elizabeth, Katie, Jane. BA, CCNY, 1968, MA, 1973; JD, NYU, 1972. Bar: N.Y. 1973, Calif. 1996. Sr. ptnr., trial lawyer Simpson Thacher & Bartlett, N.Y.C., 1973—. Co-author: Handbook on Insurance Coverage Disputes, 8th edit., 1995, Modern Reinsurance Law and Practice, 1996. Mem. Am. Law Inst., Assn. of Bar of City of N.Y. Office: Simpson Thacher & Bartlett 425 Lexington Ave New York NY 10017-3903

OSTRANDER, THOMAS WILLIAM, investment banker; b. Detroit, July 20, 1950; s. Roland J. and Sybil (Swartout) O.; m. Mary Ellen Gallagher, Mar. 17, 1979; children: John Charles, Elizabeth Ann, Brian Thomas. AB, U. Mich., 1972; MBA, Harvard U., 1976. CPA, Mich. Staff acct. Ernst & Whinney, Detroit, 1972-74, sr. acct., 1974; sr. acct. Ernst & Whinney, Cleve., 1975; assoc. Kidder, Peabody & Co., N.Y.C., 1976-78, asst. v.p., 1978-80, v.p., 1980-86, mng. dir., 1986-89; mng. dir. Salomon Bros., Inc., N.Y.C., 1989—; bd. dirs. Westmoreland Coal Co.; mem. adv. bd. Paton Sch. Accountancy U. Mich., 1984-87, mem. vis. com. Lit., Sci. and Arts Sch., 1988-90, 95—. Mem. AICPA, Met. Club, Harvard Club, Hasty Pudding Club, The Creek, Bond Club, Beaver Dam Winter Sports Club, Theta Delta Chi. Home: 60 E End Ave Apt 25B New York NY 10028-7906 Office: Salomon Bros Inc 7 World Trade Ctr New York NY 10048-1102

OSTRIKER, ALICIA SUSKIN, poet; b. N.Y.C., Nov. 11, 1937; d. David and Beatrice (Linnick) Suskin; m. Jeremiah P. Ostriker, 1958; children: Rebecca, Eve, Gabriel. BA, Brandeis U., 1959; MA, U. Wis., 1961, PhD, 1964. Asst. prof. Rutgers U., New Brunswick, N.J., 1965-68, assoc. prof., 1968-72, prof. English, 1972—. Author: Vision and Verse in William Blake, 1965, Songs, 1969, Once More Out of Darkness, and Other Poems, 1974, A Dream of Springtime, 1979, The Mother/Child Papers, 1980, A Woman Under the Surface: Poems and Prose Poems, 1982, Writing Like a Woman, 1983, The Imaginary Lover, 1986 (William Carlos Williams prize Poetry Soc. Am. 1986), Stealing the Language: The Emergence of Women's Poetry in America, 1986, Green Age, 1989, Feminist Revision and the Bible, 1993, The Nakedness of the Fathers: Biblical Vision and Revisions, 1994, The Crack in Everything, 1996 (Nat. Book award finalist 1996); editor: William Blake: Complete Poems, 1977. Nat. Coun. on Humanities grantee, 1968; NEA fellow, 1976-77, N.J. Arts Coun. fellow, 1982, Guggenheim Found. fellow, 1984-85, faculty fellow Rutgers Ctr. for Hist. Analysis, 1995-96, Rockefeller Found. fellow, 1982; recipient Strousse Poetry prize Prairie Schooner, 1986, Edward Stanley award Prairie Schooner, 1994, Anna David Rosenberg Poetry award, 1994, Best American Poetry award, 1996. Office: Rutgers Univ Dept of English New Brunswick NJ 08903

OSTRIKER, JEREMIAH PAUL, astrophysicist, educator; b. N.Y.C., Apr. 13, 1937; s. Martin and Jeanne (Sumpf) O.; m. Alicia Suskin, Dec. 1, 1958; children—Rebecca, Eve, Gabriel. A.B., Harvard, 1959; Ph.D. (NSF fellow), U. Chgo., 1964; postgrad., U. Cambridge, Eng., 1964-65; hon. degree, U. Chgo., 1992. Rsch. assoc., lectr. astrophysics Princeton (N.J.) U., 1965-66, asst. prof., 1966-68, assoc. prof., 1968-71, prof., 1971—, chmn. dept. astronomy, dir. obs., 1979-95, Charles A. Young prof. astronomy, 1982—, provost, 1995—. Author: Development of Large-Scale Structure in the Univers, 1991; mem. editl. bd., trustee Princeton U. Press; contbr. articles to profl. jours. Alfred P. Sloan Found. fellow, 1970-72. Fellow AAAS; mem. NAS (bd. govs. 1993-95, counselor 1992-95), Am. Astron. Soc. (councilor 1978-80, Warner prize 1972, Russel prize 1980), Internat. Astron. Union, Am. Philos. Soc., Am. Acad. Arts and Scis., Royal Astron. Soc. (assoc.). Home: 33 Philip Dr Princeton NJ 08540-5409 Office: Princeton Univ Office of the Provost 3 Nassau St Princeton NJ 08542-4502

OSTROFF, ALLEN J., insurance company executive; b. Bklyn., Mar. 19, 1936; s. Irving and Sally (Cassoff) O; m. Lenore, Oct. 29, 1967; children: Bruce, Gary, Stephen. BS, NYU, 1957. Ops. analyst N.Y. Hilton, 1964-66, corp. asst/ v.p., 1967-68, gen. mgr., 1972; mgr. Statler Hilton, N.Y.C., 1969-71; group v.p. Americana Hotel, N.Y.C., 1974-75; v.p. The Prudential, Newark, 1976-93, mng. dir., 1993—; bd. dirs. Prime Hospitality Corp., Fairfield, N.J.; co-chair Am. Hotel Found., Inc., Washington; univ. lectr. in field. Mem. Cornell Soc. Hotelmen (chmn.), NYU Real Estate (chmn., inst. bd. exec. com.), Inst. Masters in Hospitality Program (chmn.), Am. Hotel and Motel Assn. Mgmt. (adv. com., co-chair Irefac, Washington). Avocations: teaching, boating. Office: The Prudential Realty Group 8 Campus Dr Parsippany NJ 07054-4401

OSTROFSKY, BENJAMIN, business and engineering management educator, industrial engineer; b. Phila., July 26, 1925; s. Eli and Edith (Segal) O.; m. Shirley Marcia Welcher, June 2, 1956; children: Keri Ellen Pearlson, Marc Howard. BSME, Drexel U., 1947; M in Engring., UCLA, 1962, PhD in Engring., 1968. Registered profl. engr., Tex., Calif. Lectr. Engring. Systems Design, UCLA, L.A., 1962-68; dir. ctr. mgmt. studies and analyses Coll. Bus. Adminstrn., Houston, 1970-72, prof. prodn. and logistics mgmt., 1969-73, chmn. dept., 1972-74; prof. indsl. engring. Cullen Coll. Engring., Houston, 1970—; prof. ops. mgmt. Coll. of Bus. Adminstrn., Houston, 1973—; lectr. Army Rsch. Inst. and various govt. and indsl. agys., also engring. industry, 1964-76; v.p. Tech. Soc. Logistics Engrs., 1974-76; nat. dir. Logistics Edn. Found., 1980—, acad. advisor, 1990—. Author: Design,

Planning and Development Methodology, 1977; co-author: Manned Systems Design: Methods, Equipment and Applications, 1981. Program mgr. USAF Office of Sci. Rsch. project, 1977-86. Lt. U.S. Army, 1943-45, USAF, 1950-53. Fellow AAAS, Soc. Logistics Engrs. (cert. profl. logistician, chmn. nat. edn. com. 1972-74, sr. editor Annals 1986—, mng. editor 1986—, Armitage medal 1978, Eccles medal 1988, Founders medal 1993); mem. NSPE, Inst. Indsl. Engrs., Ops. Rsch. Soc. Am., Decision Scis. Inst., Am. Soc. for Engring. Edn., IEEE Engring. Mgmt. Soc., Blue Key, Sigma Xi, Tau Beta Pi, Phi Kappa Phi, Alpha Iota Delta, Alpha Pi Mu. Home: 14611 Carolcrest Dr Houston TX 77079-6405

OSTROM, DON, political science educator; b. Chgo., Mar. 9, 1939; s. Irving and Margaret (Hedberg) O.; m. Florence Horan, Jan. 13, 1972; children: Erik, Rebecca, Katherine. BA, St. Olaf Coll., Northfield, Minn., 1960; MA, Washington U., 1970, PhD, 1972. Prof. polit. sci. Gustavus Adolphus Coll., St. Peter, Minn., 1972—; state rep. Minn. Ho. of Reps., St. Paul, 1988-96. Democrat. Home: 405 N 4th St Saint Peter MN 56082-1921

OSTROM, JOHN H., vertebrate paleontologist, educator, museum curator; b. N.Y.C., Feb. 18, 1928; s. William C. and Norma (Beebe) O.; m. Nancy Grace Hartman, June 14, 1952; children: Karen Ann Ostrom, Alicia Jane Linstead. BS in Geology, Union Coll., Schenectady, 1951, DSc (hon.), 1991; PhD in Vertebrate Paleontology, Columbia U., 1960. Lectr. Bklyn. Coll., 1955-56; instr. Beloit (Wis.) Coll., 1956-58, asst. prof. geology, 1958-61; asst. prof. geology Yale U., 1961-66; assoc. prof., 1966-71, prof., 1971-93; asst. curator vertebrate paleontology Peabody Mus. Natural History, 1961-66, assoc. curator, 1966-71, curator, 1971-93; research asst. vertebrate paleontology Am. Mus. Natural History, N.Y.C., 1951-56; research assoc. Am. Mus. Natural History, 1965—. Author: The Strange World of Dinosaurs, 1964, (with John McIntosh) Marsh's Dinosaurs: The Collections from Como Bluff, 1966; editor: Bull. Soc. Vertebrate Paleontology, 1962-74, Am. Jour. Sci., 1970—, Bull. Peabody Mus., 1993; co-editor: Tectonics and Mountain Ranges, 1975, The Beginnings of Birds, 1985, Proterozoic Evolution and Environments, 1990; contbr. articles on new fossil vertebrates, particularly Mesozoic reptiles to profl. jours. Recipient Alexander von Humboldt U.S. Sr. Scientist award, 1976-77, F.V. Hayden medal, 1986; Guggenheim fellow, 1966-67, Am. Acad. Arts & Scis. fellow, 1994. Mem. AAAS, Soc. Vertebrate Paleontology (pres. 1969-70, Romer-Simpson medal 1994), Soc. Study Evolution, Soc. Systematic Zoology (coun. 1975-78, 83-85), Paleontol. Soc., Soc. Earth Sci. Editors, Sigma Xi (pres. Yale chpt. 1972-73). Home: 198 Towpath Ln Cheshire CT 06410-3314 Office: Yale U Dept Geology & Geophysics New Haven CT 06520

OSTROM, MEREDITH EGGERS, retired geologist; b. Rock Island, Ill., Nov. 16, 1930; s. Meredith Louis Hult and Alma (Eggers) O.; m. Ann Carolyn Postels, Aug. 1, 1953; children—Michael Eric, Craig Alan, Terry Scott. B.S., Augustana Coll., Rock Island, Ill., 1952; M.S., U. Ill., 1954, Ph.D., 1959. Geologist Ill. Geol. Survey, Urbana, 1955-59; geologist Wis. Geol. and Natural History Survey, Madison, 1959-62; assoc. state geologist Wis. Geol. and Natural History Survey, 1962-72, state geologist, dir., 1972-90. Fellow Geol. Soc. Am.; mem. Am. Geol. Inst. (mem. governing bd. 1979-82), Am. Inst. Profl. Geologists (Pub. Svc. award 1991), Assn. Am. State Geologists (pres. 1982-83), Wis. Acad. Scis., Arts and Letters (pres. 1989), Masons. Unitarian. Home: 6802 Forest Glade Ct Middleton WI 53562-1711

OSTROM, PHILIP GARDNER, computer company executive; b. New Haven, Aug. 8, 1942; s. David McKellar and Barbara (Kingsbury) O.; m. Toni Hammons, Dec. 21, 1965; n. Nancy Jean Kahl, Apr. 2, 1983; children: Eric Craig, Paige Lynne. BS, U. Ariz., 1965; postgrad., U. Calif., 1992-94. Cert. sr. examiner quality control, Calif. Sales mgr. Procter & Gamble Co., Louisville, 1968-70, Dun & Bradstreet, L.A., 1970-71; internat. sales mgr. Memorex Corp., Santa Clara, Calif., 1971-82; dir. ops. Memtek Products, Campbell, Calif., 1982-86, Victor Techs., Scotts Valley, Calif., 1986-88; ops. mgr. Apple Computer, Cupertino, Calif., 1988-93; pres./CEO Ostrom & Assocs., San Jose, Calif., 1993—; ISO9000 lead assessor, 1992—. Spl. examiner CCQS, State of Calif., 1994—, presiding judge; examiner Malcolm Baldridge award, 1993—. Home: 1099 Maraschino Dr San Jose CA 95129-3317 Office: Ostrom & Assocs 1099 Maraschino Dr M/S07PG0 San Jose CA 95129-3317

OSTROM, VINCENT A(LFRED), political science educator; b. Nooksack, Wash., Sept. 25, 1919; s. Alfred and Alma (Knudson) O.; m. Isabell Bender, May 20, 1942 (div. 1963); m. Elinor Awan, Nov. 23, 1963. BA in Polit. Sci., UCLA, 1942, MA in Polit. Sci., 1945, PhD in Polit. Sci., 1950. Tchr. Chaffey Union H.S., Ontario, Calif., 1943-45; asst. prof. polit. sci. U. Wyo., Laramie, 1945-48; asst. prof. polit. sci. U. Oreg., Eugene, 1949-54, assoc. prof. polit. sci., 1954-58; assoc. prof. polit. sci. UCLA, 1958-64; prof. polit. sci. Ind. U., Bloomington, 1964-90, Arthur F. Bentley prof emeritus polit. sci., 1990—; Hooker disting. vis. scholar McMaster U., 1984-85; rsch. assoc. Bur. Mcpl. Rsch., 1950, Resources for Future, Inc., 1962-64; assoc. dir. Pacific NW Coop. Program in Ednl. Adminstrn., 1951-58; co-dir. Workshop in Polit. Theory and Policy Analysis, Ind. U., Bloomington, 1973—; cons. and lectr. in field. Author: Water and Politics, 1953, The Political Theory of a Compound Republic, 1971, 2nd rev. edit., 1987, The Intellectual Crisis in American Public Administration, 1974, 2nd edit., 1989, The Meaning of American Federalism, 1991, The Meaning of Democracy and the Vulnerability of Democracies, 1997; co-author: Understanding Urban Government, 1973, Local Government in the United States, 1988; author numerous monographs on polit. sci.; co-editor: Comparing Urban Service Delivery Systems, 1977, Guidance, Control and Evaluation in the Public Sector, 1986, Rethinking Institutional Analysis and Development, 1988, 2nd. edit. 1993; mem. bd. editors Publius, 1972—; mem. editl. bd. Constnl. Polit. Economy, 1989—; contbr. articles to profl. jours. Program coord. Wyo. Assessors' Sch., 1946-48, Budget Officer's Sch., 1947-48; exec. sec. Wyo. League of Municipalities, 1947-48; cons. Wyo. Legis. Interim Com., 1947-48, Nat. Resources, Alaska Constitutional Convention, 1955-56, Tenn. Water Policy Commn., 1956; mem. founding bd. Com. on Polit. Economy of the Good Soc., 1990—. Grantee and fellowships from numerous govt. and profl. agys. including Social Sci. Research Council, 1954-55, Ctr. Advanced Study in Behavioral Scis., 1955-56, Ctr. Interdisciplinary Rsch., 1981-82. Mem. AAAS, Am. Polit. Sci. Assn. (Spl. Achievement award for Significant Contbns. to Study of Federalism, 1991), Am. Econ. Assn., Am. Soc. Pub. Adminstrn., Pub. Choice Soc., Internat. Polit. Sci. Assn. Home: 5883 E Lampkins Ridge Rd Bloomington IN 47401-9726 Office: Ind U Workshop in Polit Theory 513 N Park Ave Bloomington IN 47408-3829

OSTROV, MELVYN R., physician; b. Bklyn., June 12, 1937; s. Alexander and Betty (Newman) O.; m. Irene Fishman, Dec. 24, 1959; children: Robert, David. BS, CUNY, 1959; MD, Chgo. Med. Sch., 1963. Diplomate Am. Bd. Internal Medicine, Am. Bd. Allergy and Immunology. Intern medicine and surgery Kings County Hosp., Bklyn., N.Y., 1963-64, resident in internal medicine, 1964-66; resident in allergy Jewish Hosp. of Bklyn., 1966-67; chief of allergy U.S. Army Hosp., Ft. Ord, Calif., 1967-69; ptnr. Allergy Assocs. of Waterbury, Conn., 1969—; chief allergy clinic St. Mary's Hosp., Waterbury, 1969—, attending physician, 1969—; attending physician Waterbury Hosp., 1969—. Contbr. articles to profl. jours. With. Travel grantee Am. Coll. Allergists, 1967. Fellow Am. Acad. Allergy (travel grantee 1967); mem. Conn. Soc. Allergy, New Haven County Med. Soc., Conn. State Med. Soc. Avocations: auto restoration, carpentry, art, guitar, jogging. Office: Allergy Assocs Waterbury 475 Chase Pkwy Waterbury CT 06708-3339

OSTROVSKY, LEV ARONOVICH, physicist, oceanographer, educator; b. Vologda, USSR, Dec. 10, 1934; s. Ahron L. Ostrovsky and Lidiya A. (Zaslavskaya) Khvilivitskaya; married, 1960; children: Svetlana, Alexander. Cert. rsch. physicist in radiophysics, U. Gorky, USSR, 1957; PhD, U. Gorky, 1964, Dr Sci, 1973. Asst. prof., then assoc. prof. physics Poly. Inst., Gorky, 1962-65; sr. researcher Radiophys. Rsch. Inst., Gorky, 1965-77; chief scientist and head lab. Inst. Applied Physics Russian Acad. Sci., Nizhni Novgorod (formerly Gorky), 1977—; assoc. prof to prof. U. Nizhni Novgorod, 1966-94. Co-author: Nonlinear Wave Processes in Acoustics, 1990, Modulated Waves, 1997; author or co-author 3 lectr. notes, numerous articles in profl. jours., patented various inventions; editor 3 book translations from English to Russian, 2 paper collection books, a topical dictionary; mem. editorial and bds. Internat. Jour. Nonlinear Mechanics, Chaos, Ultrasonics, various Russian sci. jours. Recipient State Prize of USSR, 1985, USSR State Discovery Cert., 1981. Fellow Acoustical Soc. Am.; mem. Acoustical Soc. Russia (mem. governing body), European Geophys. Soc., Am. Geophys. Union. Office: NOAA ERL ETL 325 Broadway St Boulder CO 80303-3337

OSTROW, JOSEPH W., advertising executive; b. N.Y.C., Feb. 22, 1933; s. Meyer H. and Helen (Small) O.; m. Francine Lee Goldberg, Sept. 4, 1955; children: Elizabeth Sara, Peter Mathew, William Nathan. B.S. in Mktg., NYU, 1955. Researcher W.R. Simmons, N.Y.C., 1954-55; with Young & Rubicam, N.Y.C., 1955-87; sr. v.p., dir. communication planning Young & Rubicam, 1972-73, exec. v.p., dir., dir. communications services, 1973-87, mem. N.Y. exec. com., U.S.A. bd. dirs.; pres., chief operating officer worldwide Direct Mktg. Group of Cos., 1983-84; exec. v.p., dir. media worldwide Foote, Cone & Belding Co., N.Y.C., 1987-94; pres., CEO Cabletelevision Advt. Bur., N.Y.C., 1994—; bd. dirs. Cabletelevision Advt. Bur., Multichannel Advt. Bur. Internat.; hon. chair bd. dirs. Cable Positive; past chmn. Traffic Audit Bur.; dir. Audit Bur. Circulations; bd. dirs., past mem. exec. com. Advt. Info. Svcs., Advt. Rsch. Found.; lectr. in field. Mem. nat. coun. Boy Scouts Am. Mem. Media Dirs. Coun. (past pres.), Am. Assn. Advt. Agys. (past vice chmn. media policy com.), Internat. Radio and TV Found. (bd. dirs.), Advt. Coun. (bd. dirs.), John Reisenbach Found. (bd. dirs.). Office: Cable TV Advt Bur 830 3rd Ave New York NY 10022-7522 *It is important that one continue to set goals that seem unachievable and at the same time live by standards that remain consistently high. The maintenance of integrity and adherence to principles which support it, are especially critical when dealing with consumer commercial persuasion. Anything less would be detrimental to the proper pursuit of both personal and business achievements.*

OSTROW, RONA LYNN, librarian, educator; b. N.Y.C., Oct. 21, 1948; d. Morty and Jeane Goldberg; m. Steven A. Ostrow, June 25, 1972; 1 child, Ciné Justine. BA, CCNY, 1969; MS in LS, Columbia U., 1970; MA, Hunter Coll., 1975; postgrad., Rutgers U., 1990—. Cert. libr., N.Y. Br. adult and reference libr. N.Y. Pub. Libr., N.Y.C., 1970-73, rsch. libr., 1973-78; asst. libr. Fashion Inst. Tech., N.Y.C., 1978-80; assoc. dir. Grad. Bus. Resource Ctr., Baruch Coll., CUNY, 1980-90, assoc. prof., 1980-90; assoc. dean of librs. for pub. svcs. Adelphi U., Garden City, N.Y., 1990-94; chief libr. Marymount Manhattan Coll., N.Y.C., 1994—. Author: Dictionary of Retailing, 1984, Dictionary of Marketing, 1987; co-author: Cross Reference Index, 1989. Mem. ALA, AAUW, Libr. Info. and Tech. Assn., Assn. Coll. and Rsch. Librs. (chair N.Y.C. sect.). Office: Shanahan Libr Marymount Manhattan Coll 221 E 71st St New York NY 10021-4501

OSTROW, STUART, theatrical producer, educator; b. N.Y.C.; m. Ann Elizabeth Gilbert; children: Julie Elizabeth, Katherine Ann, John Stuart. Cynthia Woods Mitchell chair, theatre prof. U. Houston; Pres. Stuart Ostrow Found., Inc., Musical Theatre Lab.; former mem. opera-musical theatre panel NEA; mem. bd. overseers com. to visit Loeb Drama Ctr., Harvard U. Producer: We Take the Town, 1961, The Apple Tree, 1966, 1776, 1969, Scratch, 1971, Pippin, 1972, The Moony Shapiro Songbook, 1981, American Passion, 1983, M. Butterly, 1988, La Bete, 1991, Face Value, 1993, Doll, 1995, Coyote Goes Salmon Fishing, 1996; producer, dir.: Here's Love, 1963, Swing, 1980; author, producer: Stages, 1978; assoc. dir.; Chicago, 1975. Served with USAF, 1952-55. Office: 10 S Briar Hollow Ln Apt 87 Houston TX 77027-2818

OSTRUM, DEAN GARDNER, actor, writer, calligrapher; b. Russell, Kans., Jan. 2, 1922; s. Oscar and Helen Mae (Gross) O.; m. Sarepta Pierpont, Dec. 25, 1943 (div. Sept. 1980); children: Karna Hanna, John Pierpont, Daniel Gross, Peter Gardner. A.B. with honors in Polit. Sci, U. Kans., 1947; J.D., Yale U., 1950. Bar: Kans. 1950, Mo. 1954, Tex. 1955, Oreg. 1958, Wash. 1961, Ohio 1964, N.Y. 1975. Ptnr. Ostrum & Ostrum, Russell, 1950-54; asst. atty. gen. Kan., 1953-54; atty. Southwestern Bell Telephone Co., St. Louis, 1954-55; asst. gen. atty. Southwestern Bell Telephone Co., Dallas, 1955-57; area. atty. Pacific Tel.&Tel. Co., Portland, Oreg., 1957-60; gen. atty. Pacific Tel.&Tel. Co., Seattle, 1960-61; v.p., gen. counsel Pacific N.W. Bell Telephone Co., Seattle, 1961-62, gen. comml. mgr., 1962-63; v.p., gen. counsel Ohio Bell Telephone Co., Cleve., 1963-74; v.p. regulatory matters Western Electric Co., Inc., N.Y.C., 1974-81; v.p., counsel AT&T Techs., Inc., 1981-85; dir. Nat. Corp. Theatre Fund, N.Y.C. Former trustee AT&T Found., Cleve. Playhouse, Cleve., Orch.; support care vol. St. Vincent's Hosp. Served with AUS, 1943-46, 50-52. Mem. AFTRA, SAG, SAG Book Pals, Actors Equity Assn., Actor's Fund Am. (life mem.), Amateur Comedy Club N.Y.C., Phi Beta Kappa, Sigma Nu. Episcopalian (past vestryman). Home and Office: 45 Christopher St Ph A New York NY 10014-3533

OSTRY, ADAM KNELMAN, public information office; b. London, Aug. 7, 1957; arrived in Can., 1960; s. Bernard and Sylvia Sarah (Knelman) O. BA with honors, U. Toronto, Can., 1979; MA, U. Laval, Quebec City, Can., 1983; postgrad., Ecole Nat. Adminstrn., Paris, 1987-89. Various policy analyst positions Govt. Can., Ottawa, 1982-87, mgr. telecom. policy planning dept. comm., 1989-90, dir. arts policy dept. comm., 1990-91, dir. gen. cultural industries policy dept. comm., 1991-94, dir. gen. sport Can. dept. Can. heritage, 1994—. Contbg. author: Les Cultures de Grande Consommation, 1992. Vol. AIDS Com. of Ottawa, 1995—. Mem. Assn. Profl. Execs. of the Pub. Svc. Can. Jewish. Avocations: literature, cinema, canoeing, traveling. Office: Dept Can Heritage, 15 Eddy St Ste 821, Hull, PQ Canada K1A OM5

OSTRY, SYLVIA, academic administrator, economist; b. Winnipeg, Man., Can.; d. Morris J. and B. (Stoller) Knelman; m. Bernard Ostry; children: Adam, Jonathan. BA in Econs., McGill U., 1948, MA, 1950; PhD, Cambridge U. and McGill U., 1954; also 17 hon. degrees. Lectr., asst. prof. econs. McGill U.; research officer Inst. Stats., U. Oxford, Eng.; assoc. prof. U. Montreal, Can.; with dept. stats. Econ. Coun. Can., Ottawa, 1964-72, chmn., 1978-79; chief statistician Stats. Can., Ottawa, 1972-75; dep. minister consumer and corp. affairs Govt. Can., Ottawa, 1975-78, dep. minister internat. trade, coordinator internat. econ. relations, 1984-85, ambassador for multilateral trade negotiations, personal rep. of Prime Minister for Econ. Summit, 1985-88; chancellor U. Waterloo, 1991-97; head dept. econs. and stats. OECD, Paris, 1979-83; chmn. Ctr. for Internat. Studies U. Toronto, Ont., Can., 1990—; lectr. Per Jacobssen Found., 1987; chmn. nat. coun. Can. Inst. Internat. Affairs, 1990-95; western co-chmn. Blue Ribbon Commn. for Hungary's Econ. Recovery, 1990-94; chmn. internat. adv. coun. Bank of Montreal; bd. dirs. Power Fin. Corp., mem. internat. adv. coun.; bd. dirs. UN U. World/World Inst. Devel. Econs. Rsch., Helsinki; expert adviser Commn. Transnat. Corps., UN, N.Y.C.; mem. internat. com. InterAm. Devel. Bank/Econ. Commn. L.A.-Carribbean Project; mem. internat. adv. coun. Ctr. for European Policy Studies, Brussels; mem. adv. bd. Inst. Internat. Econs., Washington; founding mem. Pacific Coun. on Internat. Policy; mem. acad. adv. bd. World Orgn. Rehab. through Tng., London; Volvo Disting. vis. fellow Coun. on Fgn. Rels., N.Y.C., 1989; bd. disting. advisors Ctr. for the Study of Ctrl. Banks. Author: Governments and Corporations in a Shrinking World: The Search for Stability, 1990, The Threat of Managed Trade to Transforming Economies, 1993; co-author: (with Richard Nelson) Technonationalism and Technoglobalism: Conflict and Cooperation, 1995; co-editor: (with Karen Knop, Richard Simeon, Katherine Swinton) Rethinking Federalism: Citizens, Markets and Governments in a Changing World, 1995; New Dimensions of Market Access, 1995, (with Gilbert R. Winham) The Halifax G-7 Summit: Issues on the Table, 1995, The Post-Cold War Trading System, 1997; contbr. articles on empirical and policy-analytic subjects to more than 90 profl. publs. Decorated companion Order of Can., 1990; recipient Outstanding Achievement award Govt. of Can., 1987, Hon. Assoc. award Conf. Bd. of Can., 1992; Disting. vis. fellow Volvo, 1989-90, U. Toronto fellow, 1989-90. Fellow Royal Soc. Can., Am. Statis. Assn.; mem. Am. Econ. Assn., Can. Econ. Assn., Royal Econ. Soc. (founding), Ctr. for European Policy Studies (internat. adv. coun.), Group of Thirty, Inst. for Internat. Econs. (adv. bd.). Avocations: films, theatre, contemporary reading. Office: U Toronto Ctr Internat Studies, 170 Bloor St W 5th Fl, Toronto, ON Canada M5S 1T9

OSTWALD, MARTIN, classics educator emeritus; b. Dortmund, Germany, Jan. 15, 1922; came to U.S., 1946, naturalized, 1956; s. Max and Hedwig (Strauss) O.; m. Lore Ursula Weinberg, Dec. 27, 1948; children: Mark F., David H. B.A., U. Toronto, 1946; A.M., U. Chgo., 1948; Ph.D., Columbia U., 1952; Dr. (hon.), Fribourg (Switzerland) U., 1995. Instr. classics and humanities Wesleyan U., Middletown, Conn., 1950-51; from lectr. to asst. prof. Greek and Latin, Columbia U., 1951-58; mem. faculty Swarthmore Coll., 1958—, prof. classics, 1966-92; prof. classical studies U. Pa., 1968-92, prof. emeritus, 1992—; vis. assoc. prof. Princeton, spring 1964; vis. prof. U. Calif. at Berkeley, summer 1969, Tel-Aviv U., 1996—; vis. fellow Balliol Coll., Oxford (Eng.) U., 1970-71, Wolfson Coll., Oxford, 1987, 91; dir. fellowships-in-residence in classics NEH, 1976-77, d'etudes, EHESS, Paris, 1991. Author: Autonomia, Its Genesis and Early History, 1982, From Popular Sovereignty to the Sovereignty of Law, 1987, Ananke in Thucydides, 1988, (with T.G. Rosenmeyer and J.W. Halporn) The Meters of Greek and Latin Poetry, 2d edit., 1980, Nomos and the Beginnings of the Athenian Democracy, 1969; translator with intro., notes and glossary Nicomachean Ethics (Aristotle), 1962; mem. editl. bd. Cambridge Ancient History, 1976-94; contbr. articles to profl. jours. Fulbright research fellow Greece, 1961-62; fellow Am. Council Learned Socs., 1965-66; fellow Nat. Endowment Humanities, 1970-71, 90-91; mem. Inst. for Advanced Study Princeton, 1974-75, 81-82, 90-91, Inst. Advanced Studies, Tel Aviv, 1994; Guggenheim fellow, 1977-78; Lang. fellow Swarthmore Coll., 1986-87. Fellow AAAS; mem. Am. Philos. Soc., Am. Philol. Assn. (pres. 1986-87), Classical Assn. Can., Soc. Promotion Hellenic Studies (hon.), Classical Assn. Atlantic States, Soc. Ancient Philosophy. Home: 408 Walnut Ln Swarthmore PA 19081-1137

O'SULLIVAN, BRENDAN PATRICK, lawyer; b. N.Y.C., May 26, 1930; s. Patrick Joseph and Rosaleen (McQuillan) O'S.; m. Maria Teresa Colonna, Sept. 8, 1957; children: Leslie, Laurie, James. Bar: N.Y. 1958, Fla. 1961, U.S. Dist. Ct. (so., mid. and no. dists.) Fla. 1961, U.S. Ct. Appeals (5th and 11th cirs.) 1961, U.S. Ct. Internat. Trade 1980, U.S. Supreme Ct. 1975, bd. cert. in admiralty and maritime law, 1996—. Staff atty. Maritime Adminstrn., Washington, 1958-60; assoc. Fowler, White, Gillen, Boggs, Villareal & Banker, P.A., Tampa, Fla., 1960-63, ptnr., 1963—. Coach, mgr. Tampa Bay Little League, Tampa, 1973-78. Lt. Comdr USNR-R, 1951-77. Mem. ABA, Fla. Bar Assn. (chmn. admiralty law com. 1979-80, admiralty and maritime law cert. com. 1995—), Hillsborough County Bar Assn., Maritime Law Assn. (bd. dirs. 1993-96), Fed. Bar Assn., Def. Rsch. Inst. (chmn. admiralty law com., 1988-91, editor newsletter, 1987-95), Civil Trial Lawyer (bd. cert.), Nat. Bd. Trial Advocates, Tampa Bay Mariners Club (skipper 1979-80, speakers trophy, 1976), Gray-Gables-Bon Air Civic Club (pres. 1964-65), Southeastern Admiralty Law Inst. (bd. govs. 1974-77), Tampa Cath. Lawyers Guild (v.p. 1996—), University Club, Centre Club. Democrat. Roman Catholic. Avocations: tennis, swimming, jogging. Office: Fowler White Gillen Boggs Villareal & Banker PA 501 E Kennedy Blvd Tampa FL 33602-5200

O'SULLIVAN, CHRIS, collegiate hockey player; b. May 15, 1974; s. Joahn and Ann O'S. Wing Boston U. Hockey Team, 1992—; player U.S. Nat. Team at World Championships, 1995 (team finished sixth); leading scorer for USA Select Team at Tampera Cup in Finland; played on gold-medal winning Team South, 1994 Summer Sports Festival; played for U.S. Team at World Jr. Championships, Czechoslovakia, 1990-91, numerous others. Named Second Team All-Am., MVP of NCAA Tournament, NCAA All-Tournament Team, First Team All-New England Hockey East All-Star Team, MVP of Mariucci Classic, all 1994-95. Office: Boston Univ Sports Info Office 285 Babcock St Boston MA 02215-1003*

O'SULLIVAN, CHRISTINE, executive director social service agency; b. Washington, July 5, 1947; d. George Albert and Mary Ruth (Stalcup) Markward; m. Donald Phillip O'Sullivan, June 27, 1985; 1 child: Kimberly Molly. Sec. Gas Distributors Info. Svc., Washington, 1966-70; adminstr. asst. Nat. Airlines, Washington, 1970-71; office mgr. Tire Industry Safety Coun., Washington, 1971-75; pres. Type-Right Exec. Sec. Svcs., Washington, Pitts., 1976-91; exec. dir. Eastside Cmty. Ministry, Zanesville, Ohio, 1991—; chair FEMA Emergency Bd., Muskingum, Morgan and Perry Counties, Ohio, 1994-96; chair United Way Exec. Dirs. Coun., 1994-97; v.p. Muskingum County Hunger Network, Zanesville, 1993-97. Author: Write a Good Resume, 1976. V.p. Muskingum County Women's Rep. Club, 1994, sec., 1995; bd. dirs. Muskingum County Women's Coalition, 1994-97; mem. Downtown Clergy Assn., 1992-97, pres., 1995-96; mem. bd. human care ministry, Ohio Dist., Lutheran Ch., Mo. Synod; task force mem. Literacy Coun., 1993-97, PRO-Muskingum, 1995-97; bd. dirs. Families and Children First Coun., 1995-97; commr. Mo. Synod Luths. to Commn. on Religion in Appalachia, 1996-98; mem. steering com. Muskingum County Operation Feed, 1992-97. Recipient Cert. of Achievement for Mil. Family Support, U.S. Army, 1991, Excellence in Cmty. Svc. award Aid Assn. Luths., 1993, Excellence in Cmty. Svc. award Muskingum County DAR, 1994, Positive Action award, NOW, 1997, YWCA Woman of Achievement award, 1997. Mem. Kiwanis, Richvale Grange. Avocations: creative writing, music. Home: 509 Van Horn Ave Zanesville OH 43701-2562 Office: Eastside Cmty Ministry 40 N 6th St Zanesville OH 43701-3656

O'SULLIVAN, EUGENE HENRY, retired advertising executive; b. Plainfield, N.J., June 8, 1942; s. Patrick J. and Helen (Callahan) O'S.; 1 child, Meredith. B.B.A., U. Notre Dame, 1964. Media buyer Foote Cone Belding, N.Y.C., 1967-68; account exec., mgmt. supr. Group Dtr, N.Y.C.; exec. v.p., dir. client svcs. Young & Rubicam, N.Y.C., 1968-84; sr. v.p., group dir. Ogilvy & Mather, N.Y.C., 1984-86, 87; exec. v.p. Hill, Holliday, Boston, 1986-87; exec. v.p., gen. mgr. McCann Erickson, N.Y.C., 1988-90; ret., 1990. Served to lt. (j.g.) USN, 1964-66. Mem. Lotos Club. Democrat. Home: 21 E 10th St New York NY 10003-5923

O'SULLIVAN, JOHN, editor; b. Liverpool, Eng., Apr. 25, 1942; s. Alfred and Margaret (Corner) O'S. B.A. (honors), London U., 1964. Jr. tutor Swinton (Eng.) Conservative Coll., 1965-67, sr. tutor, 1967-69; editor Swinton Jour., 1967-69; London corr. Irish Radio and TV, 1970-72; editorial writer, parliamentary sketchwriter London Daily Telegraph, 1972-79, asst. editor, polit. columnist, 1983-84; dir. studies Heritage Found., Washington, 1979-81; editor Policy Rev., Washington, 1979-83; columnist London Times, 1984-86, assoc. editor, 1986-87; editorial page editor N.Y. Post, 1984-86; spl. adv. Prime Min. Margaret Thatcher, London, 1987-88; editor Nat. Rev., N.Y.C., 1988—; founder, co-chmn. New Atlantic Inst., 1996—; mem. adv. coun. Social Affairs Unit, London; hon. bd. Civic Inst., Prague. Conservative candidate for Parliament, 1970; exec. adv. bd. Margaret Thatcher Found. Decorated comdr. Order British Empire, 1991; Harvard U. Inst. Politics fellow, 1983. Mem. Mont Pelerin Soc., Phil. Soc., Reform Club (London) Beefsteak Club (London). Avocations: theatre, films, reading, dining out. Office: Nat Review 215 Lexington Ave New York NY 10016-6023

O'SULLIVAN, JUDITH ROBERTA, lawyer, author; b. Pitts., Jan. 6, 1942; d. Robert Howard and Mary Olive (O'Donnell) Gallick; m. James Paul O'Sullivan, Feb. 1, 1964; children: Kathryn, James. BA, Carlow Coll., 1963; MA, U. Md., 1969, PhD, 1976; JD, Georgetown U., 1996. Editor Am. Film Inst., Washington, 1974-77; assoc. program coord. Smithsonian Resident Assocs., Washington, 1977-78; dir. instl. devel. Nat. Archives, Washington, 1978-79; exec. dir. Md. State Humanities Coun., Balt., 1979-81, 82-84, Ctr. for the Book, Libr. of Congress, Washington, 1981-82; dep. asst. dir. Nat. Mus. Am. Art, Washington, 1984-87, acting asst. dir., 1987-89; pres., CEO The Mus. at Stony Brook, N.Y., 1989-92; exec. dir. Nat. Assn. Women Judges, Washington, 1993; clk. Office Legal Adviser U.S. Dept. State, Washington, 1994-96; summer assoc. Piper & Marbury, Balt., 1995; atty.-advisor Atty. Gen.'s honors program U.S. Dept. Justice, 1996—; chair Smithsonian Women's Coun., Washington, 1988-89; mem. editorial advisory bd. Am. Film Inst., 1979—. Author: The Art of the Comic Strip, 1971 (Gen. Excellence award Printing Industry Am.), Workers and Allies, 1975, (with Alan Fern) The Complete Prints of Leonard Baskin, 1984, The Great American Comic Strip, 1991; editor Am. Film Inst. Catalogue: Feature Films, 1961-70, 1974-77. Trustee Child Life Ctr., U. Md., College Pk., 1971-74; chair Smithsonian Women's Coun., 1988-89. Univ. fellow U. Md., 1967-70, Mus. fellow, 1970-71; Smithsonian fellow Nat. Collection Fine Arts, Washington, 1972-73. Mem. Assn. Assn. Art Mus. Dirs., Am. Assn. Mus., Mid-Atlantic Mus. Conf., AAUW, Md. Bar Assn. Avocations: mystery writing. Home: 17 F Ridge Rd Greenbelt MD 20770-1749 Office: US Dept Justice Exec Office Immigration Rev Falls Church VA 22041

O'SULLIVAN, KEVIN PATRICK, foundation administrator; b. N.Y.C., Apr. 13, 1928; s. Patrick Joseph and Christina Nora (O'Sullivan) O'S.; m. Carole Evelyn Christensen, Apr. 19, 1958; 1 child, Erin Anne. BA in Polit. Sci., CUNY, 1950. Profl. singer and actor TV, theatre, night clubs, N.Y.C., 1951-55; mem. radio-TV promotion staff Ronson Corp., Newark, 1955-57; gen. sales mgr. Ind. TV Corp., N.Y.C., 1958-61; dir. program svcs. Harrington, Righter & Parsons, Inc., N.Y.C., 1961-67; v.p., gen. sales mgr. domestic sales div. ABC Films, Inc., N.Y.C., 1967-68, v.p., gen. mgr., 1969, pres., 1969-73; pres. ABC Internat. TV, N.Y.C., 1970-73; pres., CEO, Worldvision Enterprises, Inc., N.Y.C., 1973-80, chmn., CEO, 1981-87; pres. The O'Sullivan Children Found., Inc., Westbury, N.Y., 1981—; pres., CEO entertainment group Gt. Am. Broadcasting Co., N.Y.C., 1987-88. Bd. dirs. St. Francis Hosp., Roslyn, N.Y., Telicare, Uniondale, N.Y., Nat. Ethnic Coalition Orgns.; nat. bd. dirs. Boys Hope, St. Louis; former chmn. bd. trustees Old Westbury (N.Y.) Sch. of Holy Child. Fellow NATAS (life, founding bd. dirs., past chmn. bd. trustees found. of internat. coun., past treas., vice chmn.); mem. Internat. Radio and TV Soc., Am. Film Inst., Motion Picture Acad. Arts and Scis., 7th Rgt. Club (N.Y.C.), Brookville Country Club (L.I., N.Y.), Atlantis Golf Club (Palm Beach, Fla.). Avocations: golf, tennis, reading history. Home: 4 Bridle Path Dr Old Westbury NY 11568 Office: O'Sullivan Children Found 355 Post Ave Westbury NY 11590-2265

O'SULLIVAN, LAWRENCE JOSEPH, retired investment counselor; b. Curragh, Ireland, Jan. 12, 1924; s. Frank and Elizabeth (Heffernan) O'S.; m. Grace Ewart Logan, Feb. 24, 1947; children: Sharon, Lawrence, Maureen, James. BBA, St. John's U., Bklyn., 1953; postgrad., Coll. St. Rose Elmira U. Sr. investment analyst Lionel D. Edie, Inc., N.Y.C., 1953-57; asst. v.p., editor Forbes IAI, Inc., N.Y.C., 1957-62; asst. v.p., registered rep. N.Y. G.C. Haas, N.Y.C., 1962-63; rsch. dir. Fin. Investment Adv. Svc., N.Y.C., 1963-70; pres. Financialite Corp., N.Y.C., 1963-80; ret.; instr. world history N.Y. State Edn. Sys., Bethpage, Hernando County Schs., Fla. Author: W.S. Schley, Rogue Admiral, 1985, G.E. Graham, U.S. First Black International Spy, 1992. Econ. cons. Hernando County Health Authority, Fla., 1979-82, chmn., 1983-84; dir. Watervliet (N.Y.) Hist. Club, 1995—; founder Stage West Theater Group, Spring Hill, Fla., 1972; com. chmn. Boy Scouts Am., Bethpage, 1963. With USNR, 1942-46. Fellow Am. Fedn. Fin. Analysts (ret.); mem. N.Y. Soc. Security Analysts. Roman Catholic.

O'SULLIVAN, LYNDA TROUTMAN, lawyer; b. Oil City, Pa., Aug. 30, 1952; d. Perry John and Vivian Dorothy (Schreffler) Troutman; m. P. Kevin O'Sullivan, Dec. 15, 1979; children: John Perry, Michael Patrick. B.A., Am. U., 1974; J.D., Georgetown U., 1978, postgrad; Bar: D.C. 1978; assoc. firm Chapman, Duff & Paul, Washington, 1978-82, Gadsby & Hannah, Washington, 1983-85; ptnr. Perkins Coie, Washington, 1985-92, Fried, Frank, Harris, Shriver & Jacobson, Washington, 1993—; mem. adv. bd. Fed. Contracts Report; mem. faculty govt. contracts program George Washington U.; lectr. Contbr. articles to profl. jours. Mem. ABA (chair truth in negotiations com. 1991-94, chair acctg., cost and pricing com. 1996—, coun. sect. pub. contract law 1993-95, chair membership com. 1994—, budget and fin. officer 1995—). Office: Fried Frank Harris Shriver and Jacobson 1001 Pennsylvania Ave NW Washington DC 20004-2505

O'SULLIVAN, PAUL KEVIN, business executive, management and instructional systems consultant; b. Syracuse, N.Y., May 10, 1938; s. John Hugh and Helen Troy (Smith) O'S.; m. Lynda Troutman; children: Mary Kathleen and Karin Jennifer (twins), John Perry, Michael Patrick. A.B., Dartmouth Coll., 1960. Communications specialist Gen. Electric Co., Schenectady, N.Y., 1963-66; nat. inst. dir. Gen. Learning Corp., Washington, 1966-67; sr. con. ednl. systems. Aries Corp., McLean, Va., 1967-69; dir. profl. devel. Nat. Audio-Visual Assn., Fairfax, Va., 1969-74; exec. dir. Am. Soc. Tng. and Devel., Madison, Wis., 1974-80; sr. v.p. Sterling Inst., Washington, 1980-87, nat. account mgr. Orgnl. Dynamics, Inc., 1987-94; account exec. Zenger Miller, 1995-96, pres. The O'Sullivan Group, Inc., 1996—; staff dir. Nat. Audio-Visual Inst. for Effective Communications Ind. U., 1969-74; chief adminstr. Internat. Fedn. Tng. and Devel. Orgns., 1974-80; dir. Internat. Symposia for Tng. Communications in Switzerland, Australia and Middle East. Producer and dir. films and multi-media presentations; author communications and tng. courses, textbooks; contbr. articles to profl. jours. Served to lt. (j.g.), USNR, 1956-63. Recipient Honor medal for Literature Freedoms Found., 1963; Writers Gold Cup award Gen. Electric, 1966; Resolution for Outstanding Achievement Nat. Audio-Visual Assn., 1974, Pres.'s award for bus. achievement, 1989, 90, 91, 92, 93. Mem. Nat. Soc. for Performance and Instrn. (Presdl. citation 1977), Am. Soc. Assn. Execs. (Grand award for mgmt. achievement 1978), Am. Soc. Tng. and Devel. (hon. life).

O'SULLIVAN, THOMAS J., lawyer; b. New Haven, Apr. 7, 1940; s. Thomas J. and Marjorie (Hession) O'S.; m. Anita Brady, Aug. 10, 1968; children: Kathleen, Margaret, Mary Tess, Anne Elizabeth. BA in History, Yale U., 1961; LLB, Harvard U., 1966. Bar: Conn. 1966, U.S. Dist. Ct. Conn. 1967, N.Y. 1967, U.S. Dist. Ct. (so. and ea. dists.) N.Y. 1967, U.S. Ct. Appeals (2d cir.) 1971, U.S. Supreme Ct. 1971, U.S. Dist. Ct. (no. dist.) N.Y. 1976. Assoc. White & Case, N.Y.C., 1966-74, ptnr., 1974—. Served to 1st lt. U.S. Army, 1961-63. Mem. ABA, N.Y. State Bar Assn., Assn. of Bar of City of N.Y., Internat. Bar Assn. Clubs: Milbrook (Greenwich, Conn.); Yale (N.Y.C.). Home: 56 Hillside Rd Greenwich CT 06830-4835 Office: White & Case 1155 Avenue Of The Americas New York NY 10036-2711

OSVER, ARTHUR, artist; b. Chgo., July 26, 1912; s. Harry and Yetta (Woodrov) O.; m. Ernestine Betsberg, Aug. 12, 1940. Student, Northwestern U., 1930-31, Art Inst. Chgo., 1931-36. Instr. art Washington U., St. Louis, 1960-83. Works exhbtd., Art Inst. Chgo., Pa. Acad. Art, Carnegie Inst., Whitney Mus., St. Louis Art Mus., Nelson Gallery, Atkins Mus., Corcoran Art Gallery, U. Ill. Ann., Mus. Modern Art, Met. Mus., others, works in permanent collections, Whitney Mus., Toledo Mus., Isaac Delgado Mus., Peabody Mus., Rio de Janeiro Mus.; artist in residence, U. Fla., 1954-55; trustee emeritus Am. Acad Rome, 1993, artist in residence, 1957-58, one man shows, Wilson Gallery, Chgo., 1940, Grand Central Moderns, N.Y.C., 1947, 49, 51, 56, U. Tenn., 1948, Syracuse U., 1949, Hamline U., 1950, U. Fla., 1951, 55, Fairweather-Hardin Gallery, Chgo., 1953, 55, 69, others. Recipient John Barton Paine medal Va. Mus., 1944, purchase prize U. Ill., 1949, Temple gold medal and purchase prize Pa. Acad., Prix de Rome, 1952, 53, J. Henry Schiedt prize Pa. Acad. Fine Arts, award Am. Acad. and Inst. Arts and Letters, 1991, Arts & Edn. Excellence in Painting award, Arts and Edn. Coun. Greater St. Louis, 1994; James Nelson Raymond traveling fellow, 1936-38; Guggenheim fellow, 1950-51; sabbatical leave grantee Nat. Endowment Arts. Mem. Audubon Artists, Artists Equity. Address: 465 Foote Ave Webster Groves MO 63119

OSWALD, EVA SUE ADEN, insurance executive; b. Ft. Dodge, Iowa, Feb. 2, 1949; d. Warren Dale Aden and Alice Rae (Gingerich) Aspeslet; m. Bruce Elliott Oswald, Nov. 27, 1976. BBS, U. Iowa, 1972. With Great Am. Ins. Co., 1975—; v.p. mktg. div. Great Am. Ins. Co., Orange, Calif., 1987, v.p. profit ctr., 1988-90; pres. Garden of Eva, Inc., 1990—; mem. Snelling-Selby Bus. Coun. Mem. Nat. Assn. Ins. Women, State Guarantee Fund (bd. dirs. 1986-87), Exec. Women St. Paul, Midway C. of C., White Bear Lake C. of C. Methodist. Office: 1585 Marshall Ave Saint Paul MN 55104-6222

OSWALD, GEORGE CHARLES, advertising executive, management and marketing consultant; b. Springfield, Ill.; s. William A. and Lucille (Harrison) O.; m. Wanda Lillian Hartmann, Sept. 6, 1938; children: William Allan, Suzanne Mae, George Charles, Nanette Marie. B.S., U. Ill., 1936. Copywriter J. Stirling Getchell, Inc., 1936-37; Washington corr. Popular Sci., Picture Mag., 1937-38; copywriter, account exec. William Esty Co., Inc., 1942-50; v.p., account supr. Cecil & Presbrey, Inc., 1950-52; v.p., dir. regional offices and internat. div. Kenyon & Eckhardt, 1952-61; exec. v.p., dir. Geyer, Morey, Ballard, Inc., N.Y.C., 1961-65; pres., chief exec. officer Geyer, Morey, Ballard, Inc., 1965-67; pres., chief exec. officer Geyer-Oswald, Inc., 1967-69, chmn. bd., chief exec. officer, 1969-70; vice chmn. bd. Lennen & Newell, Inc., 1970-72; chief exec. officer, dir. Bailey-Oswald, Inc., Dannemora, N.Y., 1972-75; dir., mgmt. assoc. Quadrant Mktg. Counselors, Ltd., N.Y.C., 1976-80; chmn. Mgmt. Assocs., N.Y.C., 1980—; bd. dirs. Farm Products Labs., Matrix, Inc., Satellite Beach, Fla., Realtime Assocs., Inc., Satellite Beach, Fla., Technocraft, Inc., McElhattan, Pa., Ameratec Corp.; pres., dir. Realmar, Inc.; dir. Piper Indsl. Complex, Inc. Mem. Am. Assn. Advt. Agys. (gov. Eastern region 1964-66, nat. gov. 1966-69), Nat. Outdoor Advt. Bur. (dir.), Am. Arbitration Assn., Delta Chi. Clubs: N.Y. Athletic, Adirondack League, Camp Fire Am., Winged Foot Golf (N.Y.C.). Home: 38 Edgewood Rd Scarsdale NY 10583-6421

OSWALD, ROBERT BERNARD, science administrator, nuclear engineer; b. Detroit, May 25, 1932; s. Robert Bernard and Leona Virginia (LeFave) O.; m. Judith Ann Dick, Feb. 3, 1964; children: Robert Vernon, Susan Marie. BSME, U. Mich., 1957, BS in Math., 1957, MSME, 1958, PhD in Nuclear Engring., 1964. Rsch. physicist Harry Diamond Labs., U.S. Army, Washington, 1964-69, chief radiation, phys. br., 1970-72, chief rsch. lab., 1972-76; assoc. tech. dir. Harry Diamond Labs., U.S. Army, Adelphi, Md., 1976-79; asst. to dep. dir. sci. and tech. Def. Nuclear Agy., Alexandria, Va., 1979-81; tech. dir. Electronic R&D Command, U.S. Army, Adelphi, 1981-85; corp. v.p. Sci. Application Internat. Corp., McLean, Va., 1985-87; dir. R&D C.E. Washington, 1987-96; exec. dir. strategic environ. R&D program, 1992-94; vis. prof. dept. nuclear engring. U. Mich., Ann Arbor, 1969-70. Contbr. articles to profl. jours. With USAF, 1950-53. Recipient Louis J. Hamilton award U. Mich., 1973, Disting. Exec. award Pres. of U.S., 1983, Meritorious Exec. Pres. award, 1991; Meritorious Exec. Pres. award, 1996; Boeing fellow, 1957-58, Atomic Energy Spl. fellow, 1961-63. Fellow IEEE; mem. Am. Phys. Soc., Soc. Mil. Engrs., Cath. Acad. Scis., Cosmos Club. Republican. Roman Catholic. Avocations: sailing, woodworking, gardening.

OSWALD, RUDOLPH A., economist; b. Milw., Aug. 4, 1932; s. Carl J. and Anne O.; m. Mary Louise Hurney. B.A., Holy Cross Coll., 1954; postgrad. (Fulbright scholar), U. Munich, W. Ger., 1954-55; M.S., U. Wis., Madison, 1958; Ph.D. in Econs, Georgetown U., 1965. Research and edn. dir. Internat. Assn. Fire Fighters, Washington, 1959-63; economist research dept. AFL-CIO, Washington, 1963-72, asst. dir. edn. dept., 1975-76, dir. research dept., 1976-96, economist-in-residence George Meany Ctr for Labor Studies, 1996—; vis. prof. Cornell U., 1997; rsch. dir. Svc. Employees Internat. Union, Washington, 1972-75; adj. prof. econs. George Washington U.; mem. Fed. Employees Pay Coun., 1970-72, Sec. Navy's Adv. Bd. Edn. and Tng., 1975-78, Nat. Commn. Employment and Unemployment Stats., Fgn. Investment Adv. Com.; mem. adv. coun. Indsl. Labor Rels. Sch., Cornell U., 1981-85, 95, 96, Sch. Bus. U. S.C. 1992-96; mem. Consumer Adv. Com. Securities and Exchange Com., 1994-96, Labor Rsch. Adv. Coun. to Bur. Labor Stats., mem. adv. com. on trade, 1984-96; mem adv. com. Ex-Im Bank, 1989-92. Bd. dirs. Nat. Industries for the Blind, 1965-71. Served with U.S. Army, 1956-57. Mem. Am. Econ. Assn., Am. Statis. Assn., Indsl. Rels. Rsch. Assn. (past pres.), Nat. Bur. Econ. Rsch. (dir.), Nat. Planning Assn. (dir.), Joint Coun. on Econ. Edn. (dir.). Home: 11804 Devilwood Dr Rockville MD 20854-3407 Office: George Meany Labor Studies Ctr 10000 New Hampshire Ave Silver Spring MD 20903-1706

OSWALD, STANTON S., lawyer; b. Phila., Oct. 15, 1927; s. Sylvan J. and Myra (Steiger) O.; m. Bernice Boorstein, June 17, 1951; children: Jane Easley, Eve Robbins, David Oswald, Beth Oswald. BA, U. Pa., 1949; LLB magna cum laude, Harvard U., 1952. Bar: Pa., 1953. Law clk. to Judge William L. Hastie U.S. Ct. Appeals Third Circuit, Phila., 1952-53; assoc. Wolf, Block, Schorr & Solis-Cohen, Phila., 1953-63, ptnr., 1963-95, of counsel, 1995—. Trustee, hon. dir. Congregation Adath Jeshurun, Melrose Park; past chmn. bd. dirs. Pa. affiliate Am. Diabetes Assn., past chmn. bd. dirs. Phila. chpt. With USAF, 1946-47. Mem. ABA, Pa. Bar Assn., Phila. Bar Assn. Democrat. Jewish. Office: Wolf Block Schorr & Solis-Cohen 12th Fl Packard Bldg 15th and Chestnut St Philadelphia PA 19102-2625

OTA, TAKAO, American literature and studies educator; b. Minakuchi, Shiga, Japan, Mar. 25, 1942; s. Toshio and Chieko Ota; m. Reiko Arai, Feb. 26, 1946; children: Michiko, Takuo. BA in Math. and English, North Ctrl. Coll., Naperville, Ill., 1966; MA in Religion, Garrett-Evang. Theol. Sem., Evanston, Ill., 1975. Instr. English U. Hirosaki, Japan, 1975-78, assoc. prof., 1978-83; prof. English Niijima Gakuen Women's Jr. Coll., Takasaki, Japan, 1983—, dean of acad. affairs, 1983-86, 93—, dean of admissions, 1997—. Chief editor: Marty, 1986, Printer's Measure, 1980, Crime in the Streets, 1993, Introduction to Area Studies, 1997; editor periodicals Studies in Broadcasting Arts, Studies in Comparative Culture. Fulbright sr. rsch. fellow, 1981-82. Mem. United Ch. of Christ in Japan. Home: 3413-3 Saginomiya, Annaka 379-01, Japan Office: Niijima Gakuen Women's Jr Coll, 53 Showa-machi, Takasaki Japan

OTERO-SMART, INGRID AMARILLYS, advertising executive; b. Santurce, P.R., Jan. 9, 1959; d. Angel Miguel and Carmen (Prann) Otero; m. Dean Edward Smart, May 4, 1991; 1 child, Jordan. BA in Comm., U. P.R., 1981. Traffic mgr. McCann-Erickson Corp., San Juan, P.R., 1981-82, media analyst, 1982, asst. account exec., 1982-83, account exec., 1983-84, sr. account exec., 1984-85, account dir., 1985-87; account supr. Mendoza-Dillon & Assocs., Newport Beach, Calif., 1987-89, sr. v.p. client svcs., 1989-96, exec. v.p., dir. client svcs., 1996—. Mem. Youth Motivation Task Force, Santa Ana, Calif., 1989—; bd. dirs. Orange County Hispanic C. of C., Santa Ana, 1989-90, U.S. Hispanic Family of Yr.; mem. Santa Ana Project P.R.I.D.E., 1993. Avocations: reading, writing, antiques, music, theater. Office: Mendoza-Dillon & Assocs Ste 600 4100 Newport Place Dr Newport Beach CA 92660-2451

OTEY, ORLANDO, music executive, educator, pianist, theorist; b. Mexico City, Mexico, Feb. 1, 1925; s. Ponciano O. and Dolores (Olin) O.; D. Mus., U. Mexico, 1945; student Curtis Inst. Music, Phila., 1945-48; also studied with Luis Moctezuma, Vladimir Sokoloff, Walter Gieseking, Manuel M. Ponce, Gian-Carlo Menotti; m. Diane E. McAnney, Feb. 22, 1974; 1 son, Nathaniel; children by previous marriage—Olivia, Alexander. Pianist appearing in Mexico, U.S., recitals and with orchs., 1929—; mem. faculty Nat. Sch. Music, U. Mex., 1941-45, Jenkintown Music Sch.; faculty Wilmington (Del.) Mus. Sch., 1965-70, exec. dir., 1966-70; musical dir. Brandywine Pops Orch., 1969-74, Jewish Community Ctr. Orch., 1974-78; dir. Otey Music Sch., 1970—. Gen. mgr. Am. Trade Export Corp., 1960-63; tech. translator export dept. S.S. White Co. (Pennwalt), 1957-60; one of 3 U.S. pianists at Chopin Centennial Festival, Warsaw, Poland, 1949; organist, choirmaster St. John's Episcopal Ch., Bala-Cynwyd, Pa., 1962-64, Christ Episcopal Ch., Media, Pa., 1965-67, Mt. Salem United Meth. Ch., Wilmington, Del., 1973-84. Composer: Mexican Fantasy, 1941, Etudes for Piano, 1941, Sonata Tenochtitlan, 1948, Arabesque, 1950, (songs) Sinfonia Breve, 1956, Suite for Strings, 1957, Tzintzuntzan for strings, 1958, Poetica for Soprano and orch., 1958; Poetica for solo trumpet and orch., 1970; Sonata Adelita, 1982. Program chmn. Tri-County Concerts Assn., Wayne Pa., 1955-57; v.p. Main Line Symphony Orch., 1956-58; mem. steering com. Cultural Center Commn. Wilmington. Bd. dirs. Del. Symphony Orch. Mem. Nat. Assn. Composers U.S.A. (pres. Phila. chpt. 1959-61), Nat. Edn. Assn. Jazz Educators, Am. Guild Organists, Am. String Tchrs. Assn. (life), Pan-Am. Assn., Curtis Inst. Music Alumni Assn. (life), Nat. Music Tchrs. Assn. (Del. Music Tchr. of Yr. 1982), Phila. Music Tchrs. Assn., Del. Music Tchrs. Assn., Advancement Mus. Edn., Nat. Hist. Soc. (charter), Del. Classical Guitar Soc., Salem County (life), Valley Forge (life) hist. socs., Music Educators Nat. Conf., Rotary (pres. local club 1973). Author: Otey Music Teaching Method, 1973; discoverer formula of natural, exotic and non-septonic musical keys, 1978; rec. (albums) Sea of Galillee, Alacrán, 1992. Home and Office: 2391 Limestone Rd Wilmington DE 19808-4100

OTHERSEN, HENRY BIEMANN, JR., pediatric surgeon, physician, educator; b. Charleston, S.C., Aug. 26, 1930; s. Henry and Lydia Albertine (Smith) O.; m. Janelle Lester, Apr. 4, 1959; children: Megan, Mandy, Margaret, Henry Biemann III. B.S., Coll. Charleston, 1950; M.D., Med. Coll. S.C., 1953. Diplomate: Am. Bd. Surgery, Am. Bd. Thoracic Surgery, Am. Bd. Pediatric Surgery. Intern Phila. Gen. Hosp., 1953-54; postgrad. U. Pa., 1956-57; resident in gen. surgery Med. Coll. S.C., Charleston, 1957-62; resident in pediatric surgery Ohio State U. and Columbus Children's Hosp., 1962-64; research fellow Harvard U., Mass. Gen. Hosp., Boston, 1964-65; asst. prof. pediatric surgery Med. U. S.C., Charleston, 1965-68; assoc. prof. Med. U. S.C., 1968-72, prof., 1972—, chief pediatric surgery, 1972—; med. dir. Med. U. S.C. Hosp., 1981-85, Children's Hosp., 1985—. Editor The Pediatric Airway; mem. editorial bd. Jour. Pediatric Surgery, Jour. Parenteral and Enteral Nutrition; contbr. articles on pediatric oncology, esophageal, tracheal strictures to profl. jours. Bd. dirs., pres. S.C. div. Am. Cancer Soc., 1977-79. Served with USN, 1954-56, Korea. Fellow ACS, Am. Acad. Pediatrics; mem. Am. Pediatric Surg. Assn. (bd. govs. 1986-89, pres.-elect 1996, pres. 1997), Brit. Assn. Pediatric Surgeons (overseas coun.), Am. Surg. Assn., So. Surg. Assn., Am. Trauma Soc., Charleston County Med. Soc. (pres. 1980), Alpha Omega Alpha (councilor 1978-94). Home: 171 Ashley Ave Charleston SC 29425-0001 Office: MUSC Children's Hosp 171 Ashley Ave Charleston SC 29425-0001 *A man ought to do what he thinks is right.*

OTHMER, DAVID ARTMAN, television and radio station executive; b. West Medford, Mass., Mar. 18, 1941; s. Murray Eade and Mary (Artman) O.; m. Nancy Trumbull, Sept. 12, 1965 (div. Dec. 1982); 1 child, Rachel; m. Maureen Barden, June 4, 1983; 1 child, Matthew. BA, Harvard Coll., 1963; MBA, Harvard U., 1966. Asst. to pres. Sta. WNET, N.Y.C., 1974-75, dir. broadcasting, 1975-82, dir. telecommunications, 1982-83; v.p., sta. mgr. Sta. WHYY, Phila., 1983—. Exec. producer (TV show) Science Spots, 1985 (Ohio State award 1985); producer (TV show) Who is Red Grooms?, 1986 (Emmy 1986), various other TV shows, 1980— (Emmy nominations). Avocations: growing grapes and making wine. Home: 4220 Spruce St Philadelphia PA 19104-4040 Office: Sta WHYY 150 N 6th St Philadelphia PA 19106-1508

OTHS, RICHARD PHILIP, health systems administrator; b. N.Y.C., July 3, 1935; s. Philip John and Florence Violet (Kraus) O.; m. Eleanor Fuerst, May 11, 1957; children—Philip, Lisa, Eleanor, Richard. BS in Pharmacy, Fordham U., 1956; MBA in Health Care Adminstrn., CUNY, 1976. Field sales rep. E.R. Squibb & Sons, N.Y.C., 1960-63; hosp. rep. E.R. Squibb & Sons, 1963-65; div. mgr. E.R. Squibb & Sons, Manhattan, 1965-68; adminstr. operating room Mt. Sinai Hosp., N.Y.C., 1968-69, dir. admitting, 1969-71, asst. dir. hosp., 1971-76; v.p., mgr. Bethesda Hosp. Oak, Cin., 1976-84; pres. Am. Health Capital HIBI Mgmt., Inc., N.Y.C., 1984-88; pres., CEO Morristown (N.J.) Meml. Hosp., 1988-96, Atlantic Health System, Florham Park, N.J., 1996—; Goldwater fellow in hosp. adminstr. Mt. Sinai Hosp., N.Y.C., 1973; cons. Physicians Protective Trust Fund-Fla. Served with USAF, 1957-60. Recipient award E.R. Squibb-AMA, 1964. Mem. APHA, ACHA, Am. Hosp. Assn. Republican. Roman Catholic. Home: 26 Glen Gary Dr Mendham NJ 07945-3030 Office: 325 Columbia Tpke Florham Park NJ 07932

OTIS, ARTHUR BROOKS, physiologist, educator; b. Grafton, Maine, Sept. 11, 1913; s. Will Howe and Carrie (Brooks) O.; m. Eileen Macomber, Aug. 24, 1942; 1 son, Chandler Brooks. A.B., U. Maine, 1935; M.Ed., Springfield Coll., 1937; Sc.M., Brown U., 1939, Ph.D., 1941. Research assoc. cellular physiology State U. Iowa, 1941-42; instr. physiology U. Rochester Sch. Medicine, 1942-46, assoc. physiology, 1946-47, asst. prof. physiology, 1947-51; assoc. prof. physiology and surgery Johns Hopkins Sch. Medicine, 1952-56; prof. physiology U. Fla. Coll. Medicine, Gainesville, 1956-86; prof. emeritus U. Fla. Coll. Medicine, 1986—, head dept., 1956-80; civilian scientist OSRD, 1944; mem. physiology com. Nat. Bd. Med. Examiners, 1981-84. Author sci. papers; editor respiration sect.: Am. Jour. Physiology and Jour. Applied Physiology, 1962-64; editorial bd.: Respiration Physiology, 1970-81. Fulbright research scholar, 1950-51, 64-65. Mem. Am. Physiol. Soc., Soc. Gen. Physiologists, Phi Beta Kappa, Sigma Xi. Home: 2123 NW 4th Pl Gainesville FL 32603-1515 *I feel fortunate and grateful to have known so many fine people who, in one way or another, have given me so much help along the way.*

OTIS, DENISE MARIE, editor, writer; b. Detroit, July 25, 1927; d. J. Hawley and Florence Ruth O. AB cum laude, Radcliffe Coll., Cambridge, Mass., 1949. English tchr. Cambridge Sch., Weston, Mass., 1949-50; asst. to feature editor House and Garden, N.Y.C., 1952-53, assoc. decorating editor, 1953-56, editor, entertaining dept., 1956-66, assoc. editor, 1966-80, deputy editor, 1980-87; sr. editor and cons. Conde Nast Publs., N.Y.C., 1987-93; consulting editor Vogue Decoration, Paris, 1989-91. Author: Decorating with Flowers, 1978; contbr. articles to profl. jours. Fulbright scholar Inst. Internat. Edn., France, 1950-51. mem. Internat. Dendrology Soc., Decorators Club, Phi Beta Kappa. Episcopalian. Avocations: cooking, photography, gardening.

OTIS, GLENN KAY, retired army officer; b. Plattsburgh, N.Y., Mar. 15, 1929; s. Glenn Kirk and Violet Lucy (Hart) O.; m. Barbara Davies, June 6, 1953; children: Caren Otis, Nancee Otis Groh, Peter. BS, U.S. Mil. Acad., 1953; MS in Math., Rensselaer Poly. Inst., 1960; M in Mil. Sci., U.S. Army Command and Gen. Staff Coll., 1965. Commd. 2d lt. U.S. Army, 1953; gen.; dep. chief staff for ops. and plans Hdqrs. Dept. Army; comdg. gen. U.S. Army Tng. and Doctrine Command, Ft.Monroe, Va.; comdr. in chief U.S. Army Europe, Heidelberg, Federal Republic of Germany, 1983-88; ret. U.S. Army Europe, Heidelberg, 1988; exec. v.p. Coleman Rsch. Corp., 1989-95. Decorated D.S.C., Silver Star, Legion of Merit, Purple Heart. Roman Catholic. Home: 97 Normandy Ln Newport News VA 23606-1533

OTIS, JACK, social work educator; b. N.Y.C., Feb. 13, 1923; s. Abraham and Esther (Goldberg) O.; children: Elisabeth H., Erich R., Greta M., Marcus H., Alicia. A.B., Bklyn. Coll., 1946; M.S. in Social Work, U. Ill., 1948, M.Ed., 1955, Ph.D., 1957. Social worker Jewish Social Svc. Bur. Dade County, 1948-49; Psychiat. social worker Free Synagogue Social Service, N.Y. U., 1949-50; asso. prof. U. Ill., 1950-61; dep. dir. Office Juvenile Delinquency and Youth Devel., Dept. Health, Edn. and Welfare, 1961-65; dean Grad. Sch. Social Work U. Tex., 1965-77, prof. emeritus, 1993—; cons. to govt., 1961—; presenter Internat. Coun. on Social Welfare, Inter-Univ. Consortium for Internat. Social Devel., Internat. Assn. Schs. Social Work, 1994; mem. President's Com. Juvenile Delinquency and Youth Crime, 1961-65; spl. cons. for Am. social work edn. and rsch. European Ctr. for Social Welfare Tng. and Rsch., Vienna, Austria, 1976—. Author: (with George Barnett) Corporate Society and Education, 1961; contbr. article on child labor to Ency. Social Work, 1995. Bd. overseers Ctr. for Study Violence, Brandeis U., 1966-70. With AUS, 1943-46, PTO. Fulbright-Hays research fellow Austria, 1977-78. Mem. AAUP, Coun. on Social Work Edn. (commn. on accreditation), Philosophy of Edn. Soc., Nat. Assn. Social Workers, Am. Acad. Polit. and Social Sci., N.Y. Acad. Sci., Johannesburg Child Welfare Soc. (rsch. cons. South Africa chpt. 1990-91), Phi Kappa Phi (pres.). *The meaning of my life is whether I have added to the meaning of another's.*

OTIS, JAMES, JR., architect; b. Chgo., July 8, 1931; s. James and Edwina (Love) O.; m. Diane Cleveland, Apr. 9, 1955; children: James III, Julie C., David C. BArch cum laude, Princeton U., 1953; postgrad., U. Chgo., 1955-57. Registered architect, Ill., Ariz., Colo., Ind., Iowa, Wis. Designer Irvin A. Blietz Co., Wilmette, Ill., 1955-57; pres. Homefinders Constrn. Corp., Wilmette, 1957-59, O & F Constrn. Co., Northbrook, Ill., 1959-61; chmn. bd., chief exec. officer Otis Assocs., Inc., Northbrook, Ill., 1960-89; pres. Otis Co., 1981—; bd. dirs. Pioneer Bank, Chgo., So. Mineral Corp. Prin. works include GBC Corp. Hdqrs., Zurich Towers Office Complex, Schaumburg, Ill., AON Ins. Co. Corp. Hdqrs., Performing Arts Ctr., Northbrook, Ill., All State Regional Hdqrs., Skokie, Ill., Zurich Nat. Hdqrs.-Zurich Towers Schaumburg. Trustee Evanston (Ill.) Hosp., 1971-93, Better Govt. Assn., Chgo., Graham Found.; chmn. bd. trustees North Suburban YMCA, Northbrook, 1990—; governing mem. Shedd Aquarium; bd. govs. Chgo. Zool. Soc.; mem. adv. bd. Cook County Forest Preserve Dist.; mem. founder's coun. Field Mus., Chgo. Lt. USNR, 1953-55. Mem. AIA, Nat. Coun. Archtl. Registration Bds., Urban Land Inst., Northwestern U. Assocs., Chgo. Coun. Fgn. Rels. (assoc.), Internat. Wine and Food Soc., Princeton Club (pres. 1971-72), Econ. Club, Commonwealth Club, Chgo. Club, Comml. Club, Glen View Golf Club, Coleman Lake Club, Angler's Club. Republican. Episcopalian. Office: 310 Happ Rd Northfield IL 60093-3455

OTIS, JOHN JAMES, civil engineer; b. Syracuse, N.Y., Aug. 5, 1922; s. John Joseph and Anna (Dey) O.; m. Dorothy Fuller Otis, June 21, 1958; children: Mary Eileen Dawn, John Leon. BChemE, Syracuse U., 1943, MBA, 1950, postgrad., 1951-55. Registered profl. engr., Ala., Tex. Jr. process engr. GM, Syracuse, 1951-53, prodn. engr., 1954-58, process control engr., 1958-59, process engr., 1960-61; engr., writer GE, Syracuse, 1961-63; configuration control engr. GE, Phila., 1969; assoc. rsch. engr. Boeing Co., Huntsville, Ala., 1963-65; assoc. Planning Rsch. Corp., Huntsville, 1965-67; prin. engr. Brown Engring. Co. subs. Teledyne Co., Huntsville, 1967-69; mech. designer Drever Co., Beth Ayres, Pa., 1970-71; civil engr. U.S. Army Corps Engrs., Mobile, Ala., 1971-74, Galveston, Tex., 1974—. Lector, lay minister Roman Cath. Ch. Served with USNR, 1944-50. Mem. Am. Inst. Indsl. Engrs. (past v.p. Syracuse and Huntsville chpts.), Tex. Soc. Profl.

Engrs. (dir. Galveston County chpt. 1976-79, sec.-treas. 1979-80, v.p. 1980-81, pres. 1982-83), Am. Legion, Tau Beta Pi, Phi Kappa Tau, Alpha Chi Sigma, Chi Eta Sigma. Home: 2114 Yorktown Ct N League City TX 77573-5056 Office: US Army Corps Engrs Jadwin Bldg 2000 Fort Point Rd Galveston TX 77550-3038

OTIS, LEE LIBERMAN, lawyer, educator; b. N.Y.C., Aug. 19, 1956; d. James Benjamin and Deen (Freed) L.; m. William Graham Otis, Oct. 24, 1993. BA, Yale U., 1979; JD, U. Chgo., 1983. Bar: N.Y. 1985, D.C. 1994. Law clk. U.S. Ct. Appeals (D.C. cir.), Washington, 1983-84; spl. asst. to asst. atty. gen., civil div. U.S. Dept. Justice, Washington, 1984-86; dep. assoc. atty. gen. U.S. Dept. Justice, 1986, assoc. dep. atty. gen., 1986; law clk. to Justice Antonin Scalia U.S. Supreme Ct., Washington, 1986-87; asst. prof. law George Mason U., Arlington, Va., 1987-89; assoc. counsel to the Pres. Exec. Office of the Pres., Washington, 1989-92; assoc. Jones, Day, Reavis & Pogue, Washington, 1993-94; chief judiciary coun. U.S. Sen. Spence Abraham, 1995-96; chief counsel subcom. on immigration Com. on the Judiciary, U.S. Senate, 1997—; adj. prof. law Georgetown Law Sch., 1995, 96. Mem. Federalist Soc. for Law and Pub. Policy (founder). Republican. Jewish. Avocations: sailing, computers.

O'TOOLE, ALLAN THOMAS, electric utility executive; b. Waterloo, Iowa, Dec. 22, 1925; s. Delmar C. and Elsie M. (Winkelman) O'T.; m. Barbara Joyce Boyd, Sept. 2, 1947; children: Kathy Lynn, Timothy Allan. BA, Westminster Coll., Fulton, Mo., 1948; postgrad., U. Mich., 1965. With Pub. Svc. Co. Okla., 1953-88, asst. treas., 1967-70, treas., 1970-73, v.p., contr., 1973-76, v.p. adminstrn., 1976-80, v.p. materiel and property mgmt., 1980-85, v.p. corp. svcs., 1985-88; ret., 1988. Bd. dirs., chmn. bd., life mem. Tulsa Area chpt. ARC, 1975—, regional chmn. midwestern ops. hdqrs., 1989-92; bd. dirs., pres. Tulsa Sr. Svcs., Inc., 1990—; with Okla. State Svc. Coun., 1995—. Lt. USNR, 1943-46, 51-53. Mem. Tulsa C. of C., Adminstrv. Mgmt. Soc. (bd. dirs., pres.), Westminster Coll. Alumni Assn. (life, pres., bd. trustees), K.C., Cedar Ridge Country Club, Kappa Alpha. Roman Catholic. Home: 8442 S Florence Ave Tulsa OK 74137-1435

O'TOOLE, AUSTIN MARTIN, lawyer; b. New Bedford, Mass., Oct. 5, 1935; s. John Brian, Jr. and Helen Veronica O'T.; m. Kay Murphy, Nov. 27, 1982; children: Erin Ann, Austin Martin 2d. BBA, Coll. Holy Cross, 1957; JD, Georgetown U., 1963. Bar: N.Y. 1965, D.C. 1963, Tex. 1975. Law clk. to judge U.S. Ct. Appeals, Washington, 1962-63; assoc. White & Case, N.Y.C., 1963-74; sr. v.p., sr. counsel, sec. Coastal Corp., Houston, 1974—; bd. dirs. A.A. White Dispute Resolution Inst. Bd. editors Georgetown Law Jour., 1962-63. Bd. dirs., pres. Houston Coun. on Alcohol and Drug Abuse Found., 1995—; com. mem. Meth. Health Care Houston Marathon. Officer USMCR, 1957-60. Mem. ABA, Am. Soc. Corp. Secs. (bd. dirs. 1982-85), State Bar of Tex., Houston Bar Assn. (past chmn. corp. counsel sect. 1979-80), Am. Arbitration Assn. (comml. com.). Home: 2100 Welch (C-220) Houston TX 77019 Office: Coastal Corp 9 E Greenway Plz Houston TX 77046

O'TOOLE, DENNIS ALLEN, museum director; b. Scott AFB, Ill., Mar. 12, 1941; s. Roger Leslie and Emily May (Fisher) O'T.; m. Gertrude Lenore Probsting, July 10, 1965; children: Kara, Anne, Aaron. BA, Princeton U., 1963; MAT, Harvard U., 1965; PhD, Brown U., 1973; cert. exec. program, Dartmouth Coll., 1989. Tchr. Belmont (Mass.) H.S., 1965-67; curator of edn. Nat. Portrait Gallery, Washington, 1972-78; dir. group visits and ednl. programs Colonial Williamsburg (Va.), 1979; dep. dir. mus. ops. Colonial Williamsburg, Va., 1979-82, v.p. historic area programs and ops., 1982-88; v.p., chief edn. officer Colonial Williamsburg (Va.), 1988-92; pres. Strawbery Banke, Inc., Portsmouth, N.H., 1992—; at-large coun. mem. Am. Assn. Mus., Washington, 1988-91; mem. coun. Am. Assn. State and Local History, Nashville, 1992—; mem. coun., edn. com. Inst. Early Am. History and Culture, Williamsburg, 1988-92. House minority clk. R.I. Ho. of Reps., Providence, 1968; bd. dirs. Friends of Williamsburg Regional Libr., 1990-92; mem. Portsmouth Advocates, 1993—. Mem. Rotary. Avocations: tennis, hiking, cross-country skiing, biking, reading. Office: Strawbery Banke Mus PO Box 300 Portsmouth NH 03802-0300

O'TOOLE, FRANCIS J., lawyer; b. Dublin, Ireland, Feb. 10, 1944; came to U.S., 1960; s. Francis Herbert and Josephine (McCarthy) O'T.; m. Carole Ann Leland, Apr. 11, 1977; children: Kathleen, Kirra. AB, Harvard U., 1967; JD, U. Maine, 1970. Bar: Maine 1970, U.S. Supreme Ct. 1977, U.S. Dist. Ct. D.C., U.S. Dist. Ct. (ea. dist.) Va., U.S. Ct. Appeals (1st, 2d, 4th, 5th, 7th, 8th, 9th and 10th cirs.). Assoc. Fried, Frank, Harris, Shriver & Jacobsen, Washington, 1971-78, ptnr., 1978-92; ptnr. Sidley & Austin, Washington, 1992—. Editor-in-chief U. Maine Law Rev., 1969-70; contbr. articles to profl. jours. Reginald Heber Smith fellow Calif. Indian Legal Services, 1970-71. Mem. ABA. Avocations: horse breeding and racing. Home: 7700 Burford Dr Mc Lean VA 22102-1716 Office: Sidley & Austin 1722 I St NW Washington DC 20006-3705

O'TOOLE, JAMES JOSEPH, business educator; b. San Francisco, Apr. 15, 1945; s. James Joseph and Irene (Nagy) O'T.; m. Marilyn Louise Burrill, June 17, 1967; children: Erin Kathleen, Kerry Louise. BA, U. So. Calif., L.A., 1966; DPhil, Oxford (Eng.) U., (Eng.), 1970. Corr. Time-Life News Service, L.A., 1967-68, Nairobi, Kenya, 1967-68; mgmt. cons. McKinsey & Co., San Francisco, 1969-70; coordinator field investigations Pres.'s Comm. on Campus Unrest, Washington, 1970; spl. asst. to sec. HEW, Washington, 1970-73; prof. mgmt. U. So. Calif.-Los Angeles, 1973-93, Univ. Assocs. Chair of Bus., 1982-93; v.p. Aspen Inst., 1994-97; mng. dir. Booz-Allen & Hamilton Leadership Ctr., San Francisco, 1997—; chmn. sec.'s com. work in Am. HEW, Washington, 1971-72; exec. dir. The Leadership Inst., 1990-93; bd. dirs. Radica Games. Prin. author: Work in America, 1973, Energy and Social Change, 1976; author: Work, Learning and the American Future, 1977, Making America Work, 1982 (Phi Kappa Phi prize 1982), Vanguard Management, 1985, The Executive's Compass, 1993, Leading Change, 1995; bd. editors: Ency. Britannica, Chgo., 1981-87; editor: New Management, Los Angeles, 1983-89, The American Oxonian, 1996—. Mem. Project Paideia, Chgo., 1981-83. Rhodes scholar, 1966; recipient Mitchell prize Woodlands Conf., 1979. Mem. Phi Beta Kappa. Home: 23715 Malibu Rd # 552 Malibu CA 90265-4628 Office: Booz Allen Hamilton 101 California St San Francisco CA 94111-5802

O'TOOLE, JOHN DUDLEY, retired utility executive, consultant; b. N.Y.C., Sept. 16, 1921; s. Lawrence Patrick and Mary Gertrude (Casey) O'T.; m. Constance Telfair, Jan. 17, 1952; children: John D. Jr., Paul L., Mary C., Michelle E. Hair, Jane C. Keating. M.E. with honors, Stevens Inst. Tech., 1949; postgrad., Poly. Inst. Bklyn., 1949-51. Registered profl. engr., Conn. Engr. Gibbs & Cox Inc., N.Y.C., 1949-54; engring. mgr. Union Carbide Nuclear Co., Paducah, Ky., 1954-55, Combustion Engring. Inc., Windsor, Conn., 1955-62, Westinghouse Electric Co., Pitts., 1962-66; engring. mgr., v.p. United Nuclear Corp. and Gulf United Nuclear Corp., Elmsford, N.Y., 1966-72; asst. to v.p., then v.p. Consol. Edison Co. of N.Y., N.Y.C., 1973-86; cons. Power Mgmt. Assocs., 1986—; nuclear div. com. Electric Power Research Inst., Palo Alto, Calif., 1980-86; vice chmn. Welding Research Council, N.Y.C., 1984-86; mem. vis. com. Lehigh U., Bethlehem, Pa., 1982-86. Contbr. tech. papers and articles to profl. jours. Mgmt. com. Nature Preserve, Nature Conservancy, Katonah, N.Y., 1970; nominating com. Katonah-Lewisboro Sch. Bd., 1970. Served with USN, 1943-46. N.Y. State War Service scholar N.Y. Dept. Edn., 1949. Home: 7 Thomas St Barrington RI 02806-4824

O'TOOLE, MICHAEL DORAN, psychologist; b. N.Y.C., Dec. 22, 1947; s. Lawrence Aloysius and Edith Cordella (Fralick) O'T.; m. Regina Holliday, Sept. 12, 1987; 1 child, Meredith Doran. BA, Am. U., 1970, MA, 1974; tng. group therapy, U. N.C., 1978. Cert. adult correctional officer, N.C., 1975, police info. network ltd., N.C., 1980, youth correctional officer, Dept. Human Resources, 1981, advanced youth correctional, N.C., 1983, profl. lectr., N.C., 1984, criminal justice instr., N.C., 1987, sheriff's edn. ltd. lectr., N.C., 1989, health svc. provider-psychology assoc., N.C., 1994. From recreation staff to asst. dir. Program for Mentally Retarded and Physically Handicapped Ctr, Washington, 1970-74; staff psychologist N.C. Dept. Corrections, McLeansville, 1975-81; chief psychologist Stonewall Jackson Sch., Concord, 1981—; instr. Ctrl. Piedmont C.C., Charlotte, N.C., 1984-88, N.C. Justice Acad., Salemberg, 1989-91. Photojournalist in field. Singer Christ Ch., Charlotte, 1981—. Mem. Psi Chi. Avocations: photography, singing, foreign travel, motorcycle touring, golf. Home: 2432 Oak Leigh Dr Charlotte NC 28262 Office: Stonewall Jackson Sch Dept Human Resources 1484 Old Charlotte Rd Concord NC 28027-7026

O'TOOLE, ROBERT JOHN, II, telemarketing consultant; b. Binghamton, N.Y., Mar. 24, 1951; s. Robert John and Jean Ceclia (Martin) O'T.; m. Donna Sue Stevenson, Jan. 28, 1978 (div. 1984); 1 child, Irene Grace; m. Karen Irene Cady, Dec. 21, 1994. Student, Corning (N.Y.) C.C., 1969-71, SUNY, Brockport, 1970-71; BA, Wake Forest U., 1973; MBA, Southwestern Coll., 1986. Asst. dir. devel. Duvall Home for Children, DeLand, Fla., 1978-81; gen. mgr. Royale Art Advt., Odessa, Tex., 1981-82; v.p. Barnes Assocs. Advt., Odessa, 1982-84, Tex. Assn. for Blind Athletes, Austin, 1985-86; sales mgr. Los Amables Pub., Albuquerque, 1987-88; dir. devel. Albuquerque (N.Mex.) Help for the Homeless, 1988-91; chmn., CEO Advantage Ventures, Inc. (formerly Advantage Mktg., Inc.), Albuquerque, 1991—; CEO LaCourt, Medina & Sterling, Albuquerque, 1993—; cons. Nat. Child Safety Coun., Austin, 1985, Assn. Profl. Fire Fighters, Austin, 1985, Reynolds Aluminum, Austin, 1986, N.Mex. State Legis., 1990, Children's Charity Fund, 1996, N.Am. Found. for AIDS Rsch., 1992-93, N.Am. Pediatric AIDS Found., 1995. Author: Telemarketing Tickets, 1988, Fishing Secrets of the Florida Poachers, 1993; founder, editor: (newspaper) Albuquerque Street News, 1990; publisher: (newspaper) The New Mexican, 1991; contbr. articles to jours. Founder Permian Basin Rehab. Ctr., Odessa, 1983, Albuquerque (N.Mex.) Help for the Homeless, Inc., 1988. Recipient Cert. of Merit, Small Bus. Adminstrn., Odessa, 1984. Mem. Direct Mktg. Assn., Amnesty Internat. Avocations: restoration of historic bldgs., archeo-geomantics, travel. Home: Historic Coke House 1023 2nd St SW Albuquerque NM 87102-4124 Office: Advantage Ventures Inc 201 Pacific Ave SW Albuquerque NM 87102-4176

O'TOOLE, TARA J., federal official; d. Harold J. and Jeanne (Whalen) O'T. BA, Vassar Coll., 1974; MD, George Washington U., 1981; MPH, Johns Hopkins U., 1988. Diplomate Am. Bd. Internal Medicine, Am. Bd. Preventive/Occupational Medicine. Rsch. asst. Sloan-Kettering Cancer Inst., N.Y.C., 1974-77; resident in internal medicine Yale New Haven (Conn.) Hosp., 1981-84; physician Balt. Cmty. Health Ctrs., 1984-87; fellow in occupational medicine Johns Hopkins U., Balt., 1987-89; sr. analyst Office Tech. Assessment, Washington, 1989-93; asst. sec. energy for environ., safety and health Dept. Energy, Washington, 1993—. Democrat. Office: Dept of Energy Environ Safety & Health 1000 Independence Ave SW Washington DC 20585-0001*

O'TOOLE, TARA JEANNE, physician; b. Newton, Mass., May 3, 1951; d. Harold J. and Jeanne (Whalen) O'T. BA, Vassar Coll., 1974; MD, George Washington U., 1981; MPH, Johns Hopkins U., 1988. Rsch. tech. Sloan Kettering Cancer Inst., N.Y.C., 1974-77; gen. internist Balt. Cmty. Health Ctrs., 1984-88; sr. analyst Congl. Office of Tech. Assessment, Washington, 1989-93; asst. sec. energy for environment, safety and health U.S. Dept. Energy, Washington, 1993—. Democrat. Home: 1833 Old Annapolis Blvd Annapolis MD 21401 Office: US Dept Energy 2000 Independence Ave Washington DC 20585

OTOROWSKI, CHRISTOPHER LEE, lawyer; b. Teaneck, N.J., Nov. 20, 1953; s. Wladyslaw Jerzy and Betty Lee (Robbins) O.; m. Shawn Elizabeth McGovern, Aug. 4, 1978; children: Kirsten, Hilary. BSBA cum laude, U. Denver, 1974, MBA, 1977, JD, 1977. Bar: Wash. 1977, Colo. 1977, U.S. Dist Ct. (we. dist.) D.C. 1977, U.S. Dist. Ct. (we. dist.) Wash. 1978. Asst. atty. gen. Wash. State Atty. Gen., Spokane, 1978-79; atty. Bassett, Gemson & Morrison, Seattle, 1979-81; pvt. practice Seattle, 1981-88; atty. Sullivan, Golden & Otorowski, Seattle, 1988-91, Morrow & Otorowski, Bainbridge Island, 1996—; pvt. practice Morrow and Otorowski, Bainbridge Island, Wash., 1991-96. Contbr. articles to profl. jours. Bd. dirs. Bainbridge Edn. Support Team, Bainbridge Island, 1991—. Mem. Fed. Bar Assn. We. Dist. Wash. (sec. 1979-82, trustee 1990-93), Wash. State Trial Lawyers Assn. (bd. govs. 1991-93), Assn. Trial Lawyers Am., Seattle Tennis Club, Seattle Yacht Club. Avocations: photography, sailing. Office: 298 Winslow Way W Bainbridge Is WA 98110-2510

OTOSHI, TOM YASUO, electrical engineer, consultant; b. Seattle, Sept. 4, 1931; s. Jitsuo and Shina Otoshi; m. Haruko Shirley Yumiba, Oct. 13, 1963; children: John, Kathryn. BSEE, U. Wash., 1954, MSEE, 1957. Mem. tech. staff Hughes Aircraft Co., Culver City, Calif., 1956-61; sr. staff Jet Propulsion Lab., Calif. Inst. Tech., Pasadena, 1961—; cons. in field. Recipient NASA New Tech. awards, Exceptional Svc. medal NASA, 1994. Mem. Wagner Ensemble of Roger Wagner Choral Inst., L.A. Bach Festival Chorale. Fellow IEEE (life); mem. Sigma Xi, Tau Beta Pi. Contbr. articles to profl. jours; patentee in field. Home: 3551 Henrietta Ave La Crescenta CA 91214-1136 Office: Jet Propulsion Lab 4800 Oak Grove Dr Pasadena CA 91109-8001

OTSTOTT, CHARLES PADDOCK, company executive, retired army officer; b. Ft. Worth, June 2, 1937; s. Daniel Dushane and Sarah May (Paddock) O.; m. Candice Lee Curley, Nov. 6, 1982; 1 child, Kelley Ann; 1 child from previous marriage, James Boyd. BS, U.S. Mil. Acad., West Point, N.Y., 1960; MS, Purdue U., 1967. Commd. 2d lt. U.S. Army, 1960, advanced through grades to lt. gen., 1990; bn. advisor Republic of Vietnam, 1964-65; co. cmdr., S-3, 2d bn. 502 Inf. (Airborne) 101st Airborne Div., 1967-68; comdr. 1st bn. 46 Inf., 1st Armored Div., Erlangen, Fed. Republic Germany, 1976-78; student Nat. War Coll., Ft. McNair, D.C., 1978-79; comdr. 2d brigade 9th High Tech. Light Div., Ft. Lewis, Wash., 1979-82; chief of staff 9th High Tech. Light Div., Ft. Lewis, 1982-83; exec. to SACEUR Supreme Hdqrs. Allied Powers Europe, Belgium, 1983-85; asst. div. comdr. 1st Armored Div., Bamberg, Fed. Republic Germany, 1985-86; comdg. gen. Combined Arms Combat Devel. Activity, Ft. Leavenworth, Kans., 1986-88, 25th Inf. Div. (Light), Schofield Barracks, Hawaii, 1988-90; dep. chmn. NATO Mil. Com., Brussels, 1990-92; ret., 1992, pvt. cons. strategic planning, 1992-94; with Innovative Logistics Techniques (Innolog, Inc.), 1994-96; v.p. advanced program devel. Bolt, Beranek, and Newman (BBN), 1996—; instr., then asst. prof. dept. physics U.S. Mil. Acad., West Point, 1968-71. Chmn. adv. com. Brussels Am. Sch., 1990-92. Decorated Def. D.S.M., Army D.S.M., Def. Superior Svc. medal, Silver Star, Legion of Merit. Avocations: handball, jogging, picture framing, woodworking. Office: BBN Sys & Techs 1300 17th St N Ste 1200 Arlington VA 22209-3801

OTT, CARL NEIL, environmental engineer; b. Alton, Ill., Nov. 6, 1948; s. Seldon Temple and Ruth Maxine (Eisenreich) Schumaker; m. Joan Hamilton Ott, Dec. 20, 1969; children: Amy Elizabeth, Nancy Rebecca. BS in Biol. Engring., Rose-Hulman Inst. Tech., Terre Haute, 1970. Sanitary engr. sanitary engr., Ind. State Bd. Health, Indpls., 1970-74; dir. Divsn. Pub. Water Supply Ind. State Bd. Health, Indpls., 1975-84; design engr. R.E. Curry & Assoc., Plainfield, Ind., 1984-85; dir. Engring. Howard Consultants, Pittsboro, Ind., 1985-86; pres. Phoenix Consulting, Pittsboro, Ind., 1986-90; v.p. Capitol Engring., Indpls., 1990—; bd. mem. Ind. Chpt. Am. Backflow Prevention Assn., Indpls., 1985-92; chmn. Short Sch. Com. Am. Water Works Assn., Indpls., 1976-95. County surveyor Hendricks Co., Danville, Ind., 1991; mem. Rotary Internat. Brownsburg, Ind., 1987-93; pres. Jaycees N. Salem, Ind., 1976-77. Staff sgt. U.S. Army, 1970-76. Recipient Water Wheel award Am. Water Works Assn., Indpls., 1982, Bud Dale award Ind. Water Assn., Clarksville, 1987; named Honorary Life mem. Ind. Rural Water Assn., Nashville, Ind., 1984. Mem. NSPE, Am. Water Works Assn., Nat. Republican. Methodist. Avocations: nature activities, fossil hunting. Home: 7111 N State Road 236 North Salem IN 46165-9565 Office: Capitol Engring Inc 9100 Keystone Xing Fl 7 Indianapolis IN 46240-2154

OTT, DAVID MICHAEL, engineering company executive; b. Glendale, Calif., Feb. 24, 1952; s. Frank Michael and Roberta (Michie) O.; m. Cynthia Dianne Bunce. BSEE, U. Calif., Berkeley, 1974. Electronic engr. Teknekron Inc., Berkeley, 1974-79; chief engr. TCI, Berkeley, 1979-83; div. mgr. Integrated Automation Inc., Alameda, Calif., 1983-87, Litton Indsl. Automation, Alameda, 1987-92; founder, chmn. Picture Elements Inc., Berkeley, 1992—. Inventor method for verifying denomination of currency, method for processing digited images, automatic document image revision. Mem. IEEE, AAAS, Assn. Computing Machinery, Union of Concerned Scientists. Office: Picture Elements Inc 777 Panoramic Way Berkeley CA 94704-2538

OTT, GEORGE WILLIAM, JR., management consulting executive; b. Chgo., May 5, 1932; s. George William and Isabelle (Salkeld) O.; m. Joan Virginia Vasseur; June 20, 1954; children: Lisa Joan, George William III, Robert Alexander. BSBA, U. So. Calif., L.A., 1954, MBA, 1960. CPA, Tex. Engr. adminstr. Douglas Aircraft, El Segundo, Calif., 1956-59; adminstrv. engr. Lear Corp., Santa Monica, Calif., 1959-61; co. adminstr. Plasmadyne Corp., Santa Ana, Calif., 1961-63; ptnr. Peat Marwick Mitchell & Co., L.A. and Houston, 1963-71; v.p. Korn/Ferry Internat., L.A., 1971-76; founder, pres., chief exec. officer Ott and Hansen, Inc., Pasadena, Calif., 1976—; bd. dirs. Virco Mfg. Co.; mem. adv. bd. Compensation Resource Group Inc., 1988—. Past pres., bd. dirs. Career Encores, 1989—; chmn., bd. dirs. Salvation Army, L.A. Metro, 1989—. Lt. (j.g.) USN, 1954-56. Mem. Nat. Assn. Corp. Dirs. (pres. So. Calif. chpt.), Calif. Exec. Recruiters Assn. (pres. 1992), Jonathan Club (L.A.), Rotary. Avocations: golf, model railroading. Office: Ott & Hansen 136 S Oak Knolls Ave Ste 300 Pasadena CA 91101-2624

OTT, GILBERT RUSSELL, JR., lawyer; b. Bklyn., Apr. 15, 1943; s. Gilbert Russell Sr. and Bettina Rose (Ferrel) O.; m. Lisa S. Weatherford, Apr. 12, 1986; children: Gilbert R. III, Laura Elisabeth. BA, Yale U., 1965; JD, Columbia U., 1969, MBA, 1969. Bar: N.Y. 1970. Assoc. Chadbourne, Parke, Whiteside & Wolff, N.Y.C., 1969-72, LeBoeuf, Lamb, Leiby & MacRae, N.Y.C., 1972-78; assoc. gen. counsel Kidder, Peabody & Co., Inc., N.Y.C., 1978-96, asst. sec., 1978-91, asst. v.p., 1978-79, v.p., 1979-86, mng. dir., 1986-91, sr. v.p., sec., 1992-96; v.p. Kidder, Peabody Group Inc., N.Y.C., 1989-96, asst. sec., 1986-96; exec. v.p., gen. counsel, sec. Rodman & Renshaw Capital Group, Inc., Chgo. and N.Y.C., 1996—; bd. dirs. various subs. of Rodman and Renshaw Capital Group, Inc. Mem. Assn. of Bar of City of N.Y., Piping Rock Club, Univ. Club. Home: 260 Highwood Cir Oyster Bay NY 11771-3205 Office: Rodman & Renshaw Capital Group Sears Tower Ste 4500 233 S Wacker Dr Chicago IL 60606-6306 also: Rodman & Renshaw Capital Group Two World Fin Ctr Tower B 30th Fl New York NY 10281

OTT, JAMES FORGAN, financial executive; b. Chgo., Oct. 22, 1935; s. John Nash and Emily (Fentress) O.; m. Edna Cassinerio, July 8, 1961; children: Jeffery, Edna, Michael, Emily. A.B., Brown U., 1958; M.B.A., Northwestern U., 1961. C.P.A., Ill. Asso. investment banking White Weld & Co., Chgo., 1961-66; v.p. corp. fin. Eastman Dillon Union Securities & Co., Inc., Chgo., 1966-70; ptnr. Blunt Ellis & Simmons, Chgo., 1970-73; v.p., treas., CFO, The L.E. Myers Co., Chgo., 1973-83; sr. v.p., CFO, Chgo. Title and Trust Co., 1983-86; v.p. fin., CFO, sec., treas. Middleby Corp., Chgo., 1987-93; sr. account mgr. Fin. Rels. Bd., Inc., Chgo., 1994; v.p. corp. fin., sec. AmPro Corp., Melbourne, Fla., 1996—. Mem. Fin. Execs. Inst. Home: 525 John Rodes Blvd Melbourne FL 32934 Office: AmPro Corp Melbourne FL 32934

OTT, JOHN HARLOW, museum administrator; b. Ottawa, Ont., Can., Jan. 29, 1944; s. Thomas Gordon and Lois Elizabeth (Wright) O.; m. Lili Reineck, May 20, 1972; children—Jennie Elizabeth, Michael James Hutchins. B.A., Eastern Bapt. Coll., St. David's, Pa., 1966; M.A., SUNY-Oneonta, 1975; postgrad. Mus. Mgmt. Inst., U. Calif., Berkeley, 1987. Curator Hancock Shaker Village, Inc., Pittsfield, Mass., 1970-72, dir., 1972-83; exec. dir. Atlanta Hist. Soc., 1983-91, B&O R.R. Mus., Inc., Balt., 1991—; curator Ga. Hist. Soc., Savannah, 1983-87; mem. adv. bd. Concord (Mass.) Mus. Author: Hancock Shaker Village, 1976. Mem., chmn. arts com. Berkshire Hills Conf., Pittsfield, Mass., 1975-80; chmn. Pittsfield Civic Ctr. Commn., 1980-82; active Leadership Atlanta, 1984—; bd. dirs. Buckhead Bus. Assn., 1985-91, New Lebanon Shaker Heritage Found., N.Y.C., Hist. Ellicott City Restoration Found., 1992—; grad. 1993 Class of Leadership Balt.; mem. Mayor's Task Force on Greenways; mem. bd. dirs., chmn. Balt. City C. of C., 1994—; mem. Mayor's Adv. Com. on Tourism, Entertainment and Culture, 1995; reviewer hist. and cultural mus. assistance program Md. Dept. Housing & Cmty. Devel., 1996. Decorated Bronze Star; named mus. profl. of yr. in Ga., 1991, profl. of yr. Acad. for Travel, Hospitality and Tourism, 1996. Mem. Am. Assn. Mus. (accrediting officer 1982—), Am. Assn. for State and Local History, Mid-Atlantic Mus. Assn., Ga. Soc. Assn. Execs., Nat. Hist. Communal Socs. Assn. (pres. 1983-84), Nat. Soc. Fund Raising Execs. (bd. dirs. Ga. chpt. 1985-91, bd. dirs. Md. chpt. 1993), Balt. City C. of C. (chmn.), Md. Assn. History Mus. (bd. dirs. 1996). Republican. Episcopalian. Office: B&O Railroad Mus 901 W Pratt St Baltimore MD 21223-2644

OTT, KARL OTTO, nuclear engineering educator, consultant; b. Hanau, Germany, Dec. 24, 1925; came to U.S., 1967, naturalized, 1987; s. Johann Josef and Eva (Bergmann) O.; m. Gunhild G. Göring, Sept. 18, 1958 (div. 1986); children: Martina, Monika; m. Birgit Fehse, May 1, 1995. BS, J. W. von Goethe U., Frankfurt, Germany, 1948; MS, G. August U., Göttingen, Fed. Republic Germany, 1953, PhD, 1958. Physicist Nuclear Rsch. Ctr., Karlsruhe, Fed. Republic Germany, 1958-67, sect. head, 1962-67; prof. Sch. Nuclear Engring. Purdue U., West Lafayette, Ind., 1967—; cons. Argonne (Ill.) Nat. Lab., 1967—. Author: Nuclear Reactor Statics, 1983, 2nd edit., 1989, Nuclear Reactor Dynamics, 1985. Fellow Am. Nuclear Soc. Office: Sch Nuclear Engring Purdue U Lafayette IN 47907-1290

OTT, WALTER RICHARD, academic administrator; b. Bklyn., Jan. 20, 1943; s. Harold Vincent and Mary Elizabeth (Butler) O; children: Regina Winter Burrell, Christina W., Walter R. Jr. BS in Ceramic Engring., Va. Poly. Inst. and State U., 1965; MS in Ceramic Engring., U. Ill., 1967; PhD in Ceramic Engring., Rutgers U., 1969. Registered profl. engr., Pa. Process engr. Corning Inc., Buckhannon, W.Va., 1965-66; staff research engr. Champion Spark Plug Co., Detroit, 1969-70; prof. engring. Rutgers U., New Brunswick, N.J., 1970-80; dean, assoc. provost N.Y. State Coll. Ceramics, Alfred, 1980-88; provost, chief acad. officer Alfred U., Alfred, 1988—; rsch. assoc. Atomic Energy Commn.-E.I. duPont de Nemours, Aiken, S.C., 1971; cons. Haight & Hofeldt Inc., Chgo., 1984-88, Pillsbury, Mpls., 1977-79, Ctr. for Profl. Advancement, New Brunswick, 1971-79, Hammond (Ind.) Lead Products, 1970-80; bd. dirs. Victor (N.Y.) Insulator Inc., UNIPEG, 1987-88; chmn. bd. dirs. Alfred Tech. Resources N.Y. Contbr. articles to profl. jours.; patentee in field. Recipient Ralph Teetor award Soc. Automotive Engrs., 1973, PACE award Nat. Inst. Ceramic Engrs., 1975, Ann. award Ceramic Assn. N.J., 1980; named to Greaves Walker Roll, Keramos, 1991. Fellow Am. Ceramic Soc. (trustee 1980-83, v.p. 1988-89); mem. Ceramic Ednl. Coun. (pres. 1976-77), Ceramic Assn. N.Y. (treas. 1980-88, bd. dirs.), Ceramic Assn. N.J. (bd. dirs. 1974-80), Keramos (pres. 1982-84, Greaves-Walker Roll of Honor 1991), Tau Beta Pi. Avocations: tennis, reading. Home: 86 Maple Ave Wellsville NY 14895-1205 Office: Alfred U Provost Office Alfred NY 14802

OTT, WAYNE ROBERT, environmental engineer; b. San Mateo, Calif., Feb. 2, 1940; s. Florian Funstan and Evelyn Virginia (Smith) O.; m. Patricia Faustina Bertuzzi, June 28, 1967 (div. 1983). BA in Econs., Claremont McKenna Coll., 1962; BSEE, Stanford U., 1963, MS in Engring, 1965, MA in Comm., 1966, PhD in Environ. Engring., 1971. Commd. lt. USPHS, 1966, advanced to capt., 1986; chief lab. ops. br. U.S. EPA, Washington, 1971-73, sr. systems analyst, 1973-79, sr. rsch. engr., 1981-84, chief air toxics and radiation monitoring rsch. staff, 1984-90; vis. scientist dept. stats. Stanford (Calif.) U., 1979-81, 90—; vis. scholar Ctr. for Risk Analysis and dept. stats., civil engring., 1990-93; sr. environ. engr., EPA Atmospheric Rsch. and Exposure Assessment Lab, 1993-95; consulting prof. of civil engring. Stanford (Calif.) U., 1995—; dir. field studies Calif. Environ. Tobacco Smoke Study, 1993-95. Author: Environmental Indices: Theory and Practice, 1976, Environmental Statistics and Data Analysis, 1995; contbr. articles on indoor air pollution, total human exposure to chems., stochastic models of indoor exposure, motor vehicle exposures, personal monitoring instruments, and environ. tobacco smoke to profl. jours. Decorated Commendation medal USPHS, 1977; recipient Nat. Statistician award for outstanding contribution to environ. statistics EPA, 1995, Commendable Svc. Bronze medal for assessing human exposure from motor vehicle pollution, 1996. Mem. Internat. Soc. Exposure Analysis (v.p. 1989-90, Jerome J. Weselowski Internat. award for career achievement in exposure assessment 1995), Am. Statis. Assn., Am. Soc. for Quality Control, Air and Waste Mgmt. Assn., Internat. Soc. Indoor Air Quality and Climate, Phi Beta Kappa, Sigma Xi, Tau Beta Pi, Kappa Mu Epsilon. Democrat. Clubs: Theater, Jazz, Sierra. Avocations: hiking, photography, model trains, jazz recording. Developer nationally uniform air pollution index, first total human exposure activity pattern models. Home: 1008 Cardiff Ln Redwood City CA 94061-3678 Office: Stanford U Dept Stats Sequoia Hall Stanford CA 94305

OTT, WENDELL LORENZ, art museum director, artist; b. McCloud, Calif., Sept. 17, 1942; s. Wendell and Rose (Jacob) O. Student, San Francisco Art Inst., 1960-61, 62-63; B.A., Trinity U., San Antonio, 1968; M.F.A., U. Ariz., 1970; postgrad., Mus. Mgmt. Inst., U. Calif., 1984. Asst. dir. Roswell (N.Mex.) Mus. and Art Center, 1970-71, dir., 1971-86; dir. Tacoma (Wash.) Art Mus., 1986-92, Mus. of the Southwest, Tex., 1992-94, Tyler (Tex.) Mus. Art., 1995—; chmn. Roswell Humanities Series, 1972-73; instr. N.Mex. Mil. Inst., Roswell; mem. visual arts adv. com. Coll. of Santa Fe, 1985; grant reviewer Inst. Mus. Services, Washington, 1983. One man exhbns. include, Trinity U., 1967, 68, Men of Art Guild, San Antonio, 1967, 68, David Orr's Gallery, Roswell, 1976, G.W.V. Smith Art Mus., Springfield, Mass.; group exhbns. include Tex. Painting and Sculpture, Dallas Mus. Fine Arts, 1966, Witte Meml. Mus., San Antonio, 1967, 68, 1st ann. S.W. Arts Festival, Tucson, 1969, Graphics 69, Western N.Mex. U., 1969, 11th Ariz. ann. Phoenix Art Mus., 1969 (purchase awards), 9th ann., Security, Colo., 1969, 5th invitational Yuman Art Center, Yuma, Ariz., 1970, Juarez (Mexico) Mus. Art and History, 1973. Served with AUS, 1964-66. Mem. Am. Assn. Mus. (surveyor mus. assessment program 1984, pres. Washington arts consortium 1989—). Home: 5415 Old Bullard Rd # 108 Tyler TX 75703

OTTAWAY, JAMES HALLER, JR., newspaper publisher; b. Binghamton, N.Y., Mar. 24, 1938; s. James Haller and Ruth Blackburne (Hart) O.; m. Mary Warren Hyde, June 16, 1959; children—Alexandra, Christopher, Jay. Grad., Phillips Exeter Acad., 1955; B.A., Yale U., 1960; D.Journalism (hon.), Suffolk U., Boston, 1970; D.B.A. (hon.), Southeastern Mass. U., 1984. Reporter, mgmt. trainee New-Times, Danbury, Conn., 1960-62, Times Herald-Record, Middletown, N.Y., 1962-63; editor Pocono Record, Stroudsburg, Pa., 1963-65; publisher New Bedford (Mass.) Standard-Times, 1965-70; pres. Ottaway Newspapers, Inc., Campbell Hall, N.Y., 1970-85, chief exec. officer, 1976-88, chmn. bd., 1979—; v.p. Dow Jones & Co., 1980-86, sr. v.p., 1986—, also bd. dirs.; dir. Associated Press, 1982-91. Past. v.p. bd. trustees Phillips Exeter Acad.; trustee Am. Sch. Classical Studies at Athens, chmn., 1996—; trustee Storm King Art Ctr., Cornwall, N.Y., World Wildlife Fund USA, 1993—; chmn. World Press Freedom Com., 1996—; past pres., bd. dirs. Arden Hill Hosp. Found., Goshen, N.Y. Mem. Am. Newspaper Pubs. Assn., Am. Soc. Newspaper Editors. Episcopalian. Office: PO Box 401 Campbell Hall NY 10916-0401 also: Dow Jones & Co Inc 200 Liberty St New York NY 10281-1003

OTTAWAY, TERRI LOUISE, geologist, gemologist; b. Toronto, Ont., Can., Nov. 17, 1957; d. Donald Gordon and Dorothy Kay (Parsons) O.; m. John Kenny, Nov. 26, 1983 (div.); m. Gary LaRose, Apr. 15, 1994. BSc with honors, U. Toronto, 1981, MSc, 1991. Asst. curator, gemmologist Royal Ont. Mus., Toronto, 1980—. Rsch. featured in cover story Nature, 1994. Fellow Can. Gemmological Assn., Gemmological Assn. Gt. Britain (diploma 1981); mem. Mineral. Soc. Am., Mineral. Assn. Can. Achievements include analysis of gases and solutions trapped inside Colombian crystal emeralds; development of a model which explains formation of emeralds in Colombian black shales. Avocations: herpetoculture, windsurfing. Office: Royal Ont Mus Dept Earth Scis, 100 Queens Park, Toronto, ON Canada M5S 2C6

OTTE, PAUL JOHN, academic administrator, consultant, trainer; b. Detroit, July 10, 1943; s. Melvin John Otte and Anne Marie (Meyers) Hirsch; children: Deanna, John. BS, Wayne State U., 1968, MBA, 1969; EdD, Western Mich. U., 1983. With Detroit Bank and Trust Co., 1965-68; teaching fellow Wayne State U., Detroit, 1968-69; auditor, mgr. Arthur Young & Co., Detroit, 1969-75; contr., dir. Macomb Community Coll., Warren, Mich., 1975-79, v.p. bus., 1979-86; pres. Franklin U., Columbus, Ohio, 1986—; owner, mgmt. trainer Otte and Assocs., Hilliard, Ohio, 1976—; prof. undergrad. and grad. programs Franklin U., Columbus, 1986—. Author various tng. manuals, 1982. Bd. dirs. Ohio Found. Ind. Colls., Mt. Carmel Coll. Nursing. Cpl. USMC, 1961-65. Teaching fellow Wayne State U., 1968-69. Mem. AICPA, Mich. Assn. CPAs (chmn. continuing profl. edn. com. 1980-82, leadership com. 1981-83), Nat. Assn. Coll. and Univ. Bus. Officers (acctg. prins. com. 1986), Assn. Ind. Colls. and Univs. Ohio (bd. dirs.), Mich. Community Colls. Bus. Officers Assn., Greater Detroit C. of C. (leadership award 1983), Columbus C. of C. (info. svc. com.). Roman Catholic. Avocations: travel, speaking engagements. Office: Franklin U 201 S Grant Ave Columbus OH 43215-5301

OTTEN, ARTHUR EDWARD, JR., lawyer, corporate executive; b. Buffalo, Oct. 11, 1930; s. Arthur Edward Sr. and Margaret (Ambrusko) O.; m. Mary Therese Torri, Oct. 1, 1960; children: Margaret, Michael, Maureen Staley, Suzanne Hoodecheck, Jennifer. BA, Hamilton Coll., 1952; JD, Yale U., 1955. Bar: N.Y. 1955, Colo. 1959. Assoc. Hodges, Silverstein, Hodges & Harrington, Denver, 1959-64; ptnr. Hodges, Kerwin, Otten & Weeks (predecessor firms), Denver, 1964-73, Davis, Graham & Stubbs, Denver, 1973-86; gen. counsel Colo. Nat. Bankshares, Inc., 1973-93; pres., mem. Otten, Johnson, Robinson, Neff & Ragonetti, P.C., Denver, 1986—; rec. sec. Colo. Nat. Bankshares, Inc., Denver, 1983-93; gen. counsel Regis U., Denver, 1994—; com. bd. Centura Health, Denver, St. Anthony Hosps., Denver. Lt. USN, 1955-59. Mem. ABA, Colo. Bar Assn., Denver Bar Assn., Am. Arbitration Assn. (panel arbitrators, large complex case panel, mediator panel), Nat. Assn. Securities Dealers (bd. arbitrators), Law club, Univ. Club, Denver Mile High Rotary (pres. 1992-93), Phi Delta Phi. Republican. Roman Catholic. Avocations: hiking, biking, church activities. Home: 3774 S Niagara Way Denver CO 80237-1248 Office: Otten Johnson Robinson Neff & Ragonetti PC 1600 Colorado National Bldg 950 17th St Denver CO 80202-2828

OTTEN, JEFFREY, health facility administrator. CEO, pres. Brigham and Women's Hosp., Boston. Office: Brigham and Women's Hosp 75 Francis St Boston MA 02115-6110*

OTTEN, MICHAEL, data processing executive; b. N.Y.C., Apr. 19, 1942; s. Louis and Marjorie O.; BSE, Princeton U., 1963; M.S., Columbia U., 1965; MBA, Harvard U., 1967; PhD, Am. U., 1972; m. Evelyne Bonnem, Aug. 5, 1965; children—Sylvie, Daniel, Marc. Computer research engr. NIH, Bethesda, Md., 1967-69; with IBM, various locations, 1970—, dir. Channels Bus. Sys., IBM Corp. Hdqrs., North Tarrytown, N.Y., 1987—; adj. prof. Union Inst., Cin., 1987-90. Chmn. bd. trustees Green Chimneys Sch., Brewster, N.Y., 1979-88, trustee, 1977—; Scarsdale chmn. Princeton U. Alumni Schs. Com., 1978-95; mem. sch. bd., pres. Scarsdale Bd. Edn., 1993-94, trustee, 1988-94, nominating com., 1981-84; chair Scarsdale Schs. Cmty. Com. Info. Tech., 1997—; mem. Bd. of Scarsdale Sch. Pers. and Family Assistance Fund, Scarsdale Employee Assistance Program, Scarsdale Health Edn. Adv. Coun., 1988-90; active United Way (community service award Westchester and Putnam chpts., 1986), Scarsdale Youth Soccer Assn. (founding sec. 1982); mem. steering com. Scarsdale Japan Festival, 1993; mem. Scarsdale Human Rels. Coun., 1991-93, Village Youth Adv. Coun, 1990-91, Parks and Recreation Coun., 1992-94, Tchr. Ctr. Policy Bd., 1989-90, Princeton Nat. Schs. Com., 1992-95; chair Scarsdale Schs. Coun. for Info. Tech., 1996-97; hon. adv. Scarsdale Hist. Soc., 1993-94. Lt. comdr. USPHS, 1967-69. Recipient Penick award, 1993. Mem. IEEE, Assn. Computing Machinery. Clubs: Harvard U. Bus. Sch., Princeton Alumni of Westchester (founding officer). Office: IBM Corporate Hdqs Rockwood Rd North Tarrytown NY 10591

OTTENBERG, JAMES SIMON, hospital executive; b. N.Y.C., Feb. 28, 1918; s. Irving Simon and Madeleine (Hirsh) O.; m. Margaret Anne Davies, May 10, 1941; children: Jeffrey, Betsy (Mrs. Michael Cherkasky), Jill (Mrs. Joshua Muscat). A.B., Swarthmore Coll., 1939; J.D., Harvard, 1942; M.Pub. Adminstrn., N.Y. U., 1963, postgrad., 1963-65. Bar: N.Y. bar 1945. Pvt. practice N.Y.C.; sec. to judge Gen. Sessions Ct., N.Y.C., 1955-58; exec. asst. commr. Marine and Aviation, N.Y.C., 1958-62; dep. commr. Mental Health Dept., N.Y.C., 1962-67; grant adminstr. Addiction Services Agy., N.Y.C., 1967-68; asst. dir. Child Study Assn. Am., N.Y.C., 1968-69, exec. dir., 1969-72; exec. dir. Edn. and Research Found. Better Bus. Bur. Met. N.Y., 1973-77; adminstr. Crotona Park Community Mental Health Center, N.Y.C., 1977-89; dir. med. adminstrn. Bronx-Lebanon Hosp., N.Y.C., 1989-92, adminstr. alcohol programs, 1992—; lectr. sch. continuing edn. NYU, 1969. Author: (with Rachele Thomas) You, Your Child and Drugs, 1971; annotated bibliography Political Reform, Machines and Big City Politics 1950-62, 1962. Active campaigns N.Y. Citizens for Stevenson, 1956, Kennedy and Johnson, 1960, Wagner, 1961, Robert F. Kennedy, 1964; Bd. dirs. Lenox Hill Neighborhood Assn., N.Y.C., 1954-66, Union Settlement, 1968-70. Served with USAAC, 1942-45. Recipient Lepesqueur award for highest scholarship Grad. Sch. Pub. Adminstrn., N.Y. U., 1963. Fellow Am. Pub. Health Assn. Home: 145 E 92nd St New York NY 10128-2431 Office: 321 E Tremont Ave Bronx NY 10457-5304

OTTENSMEYER, DAVID JOSEPH, healthcare consultant, retired neurosurgeon; b. Nashville, Tenn., Jan. 29, 1930; s. Raymond Stanley and Glenda Jessie (Helpingstein) O.; m. Mary Jean Langley, June 30, 1954; children: Kathryn Joan, Martha Langley. BA, Wis. State U., Superior, 1951; MD, U. Wis., Madison, 1959; MS in Health Svcs. Adminstrn., Coll. St. Francis, 1985. Diplomate Am. Bd. Neurological Surgery. Intern then resident in gen. surgery Univ. Hosps., Madison, Wis., 1959-61; resident in neurol. surgery Univ. Hosps., 1962-65; staff neurosurgeon Marshfield Clinic, Wis., 1965-76; from instr. of neurol. surgery to clin. asst. prof. U. Wis. Med. Sch., Madison, 1964-77; CEO Lovelace Med. Ctr., Albuquerque, 1976-86, chmn., 1986-91; clin. prof. community medicine U. N.Mex., Albuquerque, 1977-79, clin. prof. neurol. surgery, 1979-92; exec. v.p., chief med. officer Equicor, 1986-90; part-time cons. pvt. practice, 1996; bd. dirs. Exogen Inc., Ultrasite Inc., United Clin. Rsch.; v.p. Marshfield Clinic, 1970-71, pres., CEO, 1972-75; pres., CEO The Lovelace Insts., 1991-96; sr. v.p., chief med. officer Travelers Ins. Co., 1990-91; served on numerous adv. and com. posts. Contbr. articles to profl. jours. Col. USAR, 1960-90. Fellow ACS, Am. Coll. Physician Execs. (pres. 1985-86); mem. Am. Group Practice Assn. (pres. 1983-84), Am. Bd. Med. Mgmt. (bd. dirs. 1989-95, chmn. 1995). Republican. Episcopalian. Avocations: flying; golf; travel. Home: 2815 Ridgecrest Dr SE Albuquerque NM 87108-5132

OTTENSTEIN, DONALD, psychiatrist; b. N.Y.C., Feb. 2, 1922; s. Morris Zachary and Sadelle (Fertig) O.; m. Leah May Helpern, Dec. 24, 1944; children: Paul, John, Beth, Daniel. BS, Harvard U., 1942; MD, Columbia U. Intern Boston City Hosp., 1948-49; resident Mass. Mental Health Ctr., Boston, 1950-53; fellow D.O. Thom Clinic, Boston, 1955-56; cons. Met. State Hosp., Waltham, Mass., 1955-58; dir. South Shore Mental Health Ctr., Quincy, Mass., 1959-67; asst. psychiatrist Beth Israel Hosp., Boston, 1959—; attending psychiatrist McLean Hosp., Belmont, Mass., 1970-85, Newton Wellesley Hosp., 1979-85; asst. clin. prof. Harvard U. Med. Sch., Boston, 1974-89. Contbr. articles to profl. jours. Served to capt. U.S. Army, 1953-55. Fellow Mass. Med. Soc., Am. Psychiat. Assn., Am. Orthopsychiat. Assn., Am. Acad. Child Psychiatry. Avocations: art collecting, tennis. Home and Office: 65 Gale Rd Belmont MA 02178-3945

OTTER, CLEMENT LEROY, lieutenant governor; b. Caldwell, Idaho, May 3, 1942; s. Joseph Bernard and Regina Mary (Buser) O.; m. Gay Corinne Simplot, Dec. 28, 1964; children: John Simplot, Carolyn Lee, Kimberly Dawn, Corinne Marie. BA in Polit. Sci., Coll. Idaho, 1967; PhD, Mindanao State U., 1980. Mgr. J.R. Simplot Co., Caldwell, Idaho, 1971-76, asst. to v.p. adminstrn., 1976-78, v.p. adminstrn., 1978-82, internat. pres., from 1982, now v.p.; lt. gov. State of Idaho, Boise, 1987—. Mem. Presdl. Task Force-AID, Washington, 1982-84; com. mem. invest tech. devel. State Adv. Council, Washington, 1983-84; mem. exec. council Bretton Woods Com., 1984—; mem. U.S. C. of C., Washington, 1983-84. Mem. Young Pres.' Orgn., Sales and Mktg. Execs., Idaho Assn. Commerce and Industry, Idaho Agrl. Leadership Council, Idaho Ctr. for Arts, Idaho Internat. Trade Council, Pacific N.W. Waterways Assn., N.W. Food Producers, Ducks Unltd. Republican. Roman Catholic. Clubs: Arid, Hillcrest Country. Lodge: Moose, Elks. Avocations: jogging, music, art collecting, horse training, fishing. Office: Office of the Lt Gov PO Box 83720 Boise ID 83720-0057*

OTTER, JOHN MARTIN, III, television advertising consultant, retired; b. Pottsville, Pa., Nov. 26, 1930; s. John Martin and Ruth A. (Knipe) O.; m. Susan Morgan Eaves, May 21, 1960; children—John Martin, IV, Robert Marshal. B.A., Cornell U., 1953. Comml. producer Arlene Frances Home Show, 1953-55; producer Dave Garroway Today Show, 1956-59; dir. spl. programs sales NBC-TV, 1959-61, v.p. nat. sales, 1962-64, v.p. charge sales, 1965-73; cons. sta. WNET-TV, Practising Law Inst., also Dragonwk Prodns., 1973-75; v.p., dir. network programming SSC&B Inc., 1975-78; sr. v.p., dir. network programming SSC&B Lintas Worldwide, N.Y.C., 1978-84; sr. v.p. dir. nat. broadcast McCann-Erickson U.S.A., N.Y.C., 1984-88; sr. v.p. spl. projects McCann-Erickson Worldwide, N.Y.C., 1988; pres. RETTO Internat. Inc., N.Y.C., 1989-94; retired, 1994. Mem. The Landings Club, The Landings Yacht Club. Republican. Episcopalian. Home: Four Seafarer's Cir Savannah GA 31411

OTTERBOURG, ROBERT KENNETH, public relations consultant, writer; b. N.Y.C., Jan. 26, 1930; s. Albert Marcus and Frances (Roset) O.; m. Susan Delman, Apr. 14, 1957; children—Laura Ann, Kenneth Douglas. BA, Colgate U., 1951; MS, Columbia U., 1954. Reporter, editor Fairchild Publs., N.Y.C., 1953-57; editor McGraw-Hill Pub. Co., 1957-59; v.p. pub. rels. Charles Mathieu & Co., 1959-61; pres. pub. rels. Otterbourg & Co., N.Y.C., 1962-69, 71—; sr. v.p. Daniel J. Edelman, 1970. Author: It's Never Too Late, 1993, Retire and Thrive, 1995; contbr. articles to profl. and consumer jours. Legis. asst. N.Y. State Senate, 1962-64; mem. exec. com. Columbia U. Sch. Journalism, N.Y.C., 1980-93, pres. exec. com., 1985-87; trustee Flat Rock Nature Ctr., pres., 1991-92; trustee Planned Parenthood Bergen County, 1985-88, v.p., 1986-88; trustee Urban League for Bergen County, 1988-93, Durham County Libr. Exec. Svc. Corps of the Greater Triangle; bd. dirs. Colgate U. Alumni Corp., 1969-93. 1st lt. USAF, 1951-53. Mem. Pub. Rels. Soc. Am., Columbia U. Grad. Sch. Journalism Alumni Assn. (pres. 1985-87). Democrat. Jewish. Home and Office: 68 Beverly Dr Durham NC 27707-2224

OTTERHOLT, BARRY L., technology management consultant; b. Richland, Wash., Aug. 15, 1953; s. Ernest D. and Jean T. Otterholt; m. Nancy L. Musgrave, Dec. 13, 1985; children: Casey J., Kris K., Cody M.E. BA in Computer Sci. Acctg., Western Wash. U., 1980; MBA in Bus. Administrn., Seattle Pacific U., 1982. Mgr. Robinson's, Wenatchee, Wash., 1971-75; purchasing agt. Sound Ctrs., Inc., Bellingham, Wash., 1975-79; chief oper. officer Speakerlab/Compulab, Seattle, 1979-82; mgmt. cons. Deloitte & Touche, Seattle, 1982-88; founder, prin. Solutions Consulting Group LLC, Bellevue, Wash., 1988—. Mem. Inst. Mgmt. Cons. (cert.). Office: Solutions Consulting Group 1400 112th Ave SE Bellevue WA 98004-6901

OTTERMAN, KENNETH JAMES, real estate investor, author, consultant; b. McKeesport, Pa., Jan. 21, 1949; s. Glenn Ewing Sr. and Beatrice May (Hill) O.; m. Deborah Jean Brown, Aug. 14, 1973; children: Kenneth J. Jr., Forrest G. BS in Bus., Pa. State U., 1973. exec. dir. Excel Telecomm. Prin., real estate investor Ken Otterman & Assocs., Reading, Pa., 1976; exec. dir. Excel Comms., Dallas, 1995—; bd. advisors D.I.G., Phila., R.E.I.A., Reading; org. mem, investor Berks County Bank, Reading, 1987—; exec. dir. Excel Telecomms. Author: Real Estate Investing for Cash Flow, 1986, Home Ownership Bargains From Your Government, 1986, Rules of the Game, 1984, (course) Become a Real Estate Investor, 1984. Club: R.E.I.A. (Reading) (pres. 1982-85). Avocations: skiing, travel. Office: Four Homestead Rd Leesport PA 19533

OTTESON, SCHUYLER FRANKLIN, former university dean, educator; b. Mondovi, Wis., July 17, 1917; s. Hans and Elizabeth (Meyer) O.; m. Marie Lila Rothering, 1940; children: Judith Marie, Martha Jean, Karn Wilma, John Christian. Student, Eau Claire State Tchrs. Coll., 1935-37; Ph.B., U. Wis., 1939; M.B.A., Northwestern U., 1940; Ph.D., Ohio State U., 1948. Research asst. exec. com. Fair Store, Chgo., 1940-42; asst. buyer Montgomery Ward & Co., 1942-43; instr. econs. and bus. adminstrn. Ohio Wesleyan U., 1943-44, asst. prof., 1944-46; asst. prof. mktg. Ind. U., 1946-48, assoc. prof., 1948-52, prof., 1952—, assoc. dir. Bur. Bus. Research, 1947-49, dir. Bur. Bus. Research, 1954-60, chmn. of mktg. dept., 1960-65, chmn. Dr. Bus. Adminstrn. Program, 1965-71, acting dean Sch. Bus., 1971-72, dean, 1972-82, also dir. Internat. Bus. Research Inst.; bd. dirs. Circle Income Shares, Inc.; mem. ednl. adv. com. Chgo. Bd. Trade, 1952-55, chmn. com., 1954-55; bd. dirs. Am. Assembly Coll. Schs. of Bus., 1978-82, pres., 1981; chmn. Ctr. for Leadership Devel., 1976—. Author: (with T.N. Beckman) Cases in Credits and Collections, 1949, (with William G. Panschar and James M. Patterson) Marketing: The Firm's Viewpoint, 1964; Editor: Marketing—Current Problems and Theories, 1952, Business Horizons, 1957-66; Contbr. articles profl. publs. Recipient leather medal Sigma Delta Chi, 1960; named Sagamore of Wabash, gov. Ind., 1956. Mem. Am., Midwest econs. assns., Ind. Acad. Social Scis. (pres. 1969-70), Am. Marketing Assn. (pres. 1965-66), Alpha Delta Sigma, Beta Gamma Sigma (bd. govs.). Home: 512 S Jordan Ave Bloomington IN 47401-5120

OTTINO, JULIO MARIO, chemical engineering educator, scientist; b. La Plata, Buenos Aires, Argentina, May 22, 1951; came to U.S., 1976; naturalized, 1990; s. Julio Francisco and Nydia Judith (Zufriategui) O.; m. Alicia I. Löffler, Aug. 20, 1976; children: Jules Alessandro, Bertrand Julien. Diploma in Chem. Engring., U. La Plata, 1974; PhD in Chem. Engring., U. Minn., 1979; exec. program Kellogg Sch. Mgmt., Northwestern U., 1995. Instr. in chem. engring. U. Minn., Mpls., 1978-79; asst. prof. U. Mass., Amherst, 1979-83, adj. prof. polymer sci., 1979-91, assoc. prof. chem. engring., 1983-86, prof., 1986-91; Chevron vis. prof. chem. engring. Calif. Inst. Tech., Pasadena, 1985-86; sr. rsch. fellow Ctr. for Turbulence Rsch. Stanford (Calif.) U., 1989-90; Walter P.Murphy prof. chem. engring. Northwestern U., Evanston, Ill., 1991—, chmn. dept. chem. engring., 1992—; cons. in field; Allan P. Colburn Meml. lectr. U. Del., 1987; Merck Sharp & Dohme lectr. U. P.R., 1989, Stanley Corrsin lectr. Johns Hopkins U., 1991; Centennial lectr. U. Md., 1994, William N. Lacey lectr. Calif. Inst. Tech., 1994. Author: The Kinematics of Mixing: Stretching, Chaos and Transport, 1989; contbr. articles to profl. jours.; assoc. editor Physics Fluids A, 1991—; mem. editl. bd. Internat. Jour. Bifurc. Chaos, 1991—; assoc. editor Am. Inst. Chem. Engring. Jour., 1991-95, assoc. editor., 1995—; one man art exhibit, La Plata, 1974. Recipient Presdl. Young Investigator award NSF, 1984; Univ. fellow U. Mass., 1988, Alpha Chi Sigma award AIChE, 1994. Fellow Am. Phys. Soc., AAAS; mem. Soc. for Natural Philosophy (selection com. 1993—), Am. Chem. Soc., Am. Phys. Soc., Soc. Rheology, Am. Soc. Engring. Edn., Nat. Acad. Engring., Sigma Xi (disting. lectr. 1997—), Pau Beta Pi. Achievements include research in fluid dynamics, chaos, mixing and turbulence, granular flows, polymer processing. Home: 1182 Asbury Ave Winnetka IL 60093-1402 Office: Northwestern U Dept Chem Engring 2145 Sheridan Rd Evanston IL 60208-0834

OTTLEY, JEROLD DON, choral conductor, educator; b. Salt Lake City, Apr. 7, 1934; s. Sidney James and Alice (Warren) O.; m. JoAnn South, June 22, 1956; children: Brent Kay, Allison. B.A., Brigham Young U., Provo, Utah, 1961; M.Mus., U. Utah, 1967; Fulbright study grantee, Fed. Republic Germany, 1968-69; D.M.A. (grad. teaching fellow), U. Oreg., 1972. Tchr. public schs. Salt Lake City area, 1961-65; mem. faculty U. Utah, Salt Lake City, 1967—, asst. prof. music, 1971-78, adj. assoc. prof. music, 1978-81, adj. prof. music, 1981—; assoc. conductor Salt Lake Mormon Tabernacle Choir, 1974-75, conductor, 1975—; also guest conductor throughout U.S. Conducted Mormon Tabernacle Choir in 13 concert tours U.S., 25 fgn. countries, Utah Phila. and Milw. Orchestra in performance; rec. artist CBS Masterworks, London/Decca Records, Bonneville Records and Laserlight; prepared choirs for Eugene Ormandy, Maurice Avravanel, Stanislaw Skrowaczewski, Michael Tilson Thomas, Robert Shaw, Julius Rudel, Sir David Willcocks, Ling Tung. Past mem. gen. music coms. Mormon Ch., cultural arts com. Salt Lake City C. of C. (Honors in the Arts award), past bd. advs. Barlow Endowment Music Composition; v.p., past bd. dirs., com. chair Chorus Am. Served with U.S. Army, 1957-59. Faculty Study grantee U. Utah, 1971-72; recipient Brigham Young U. Alumni Achievement award, 1990. Mem. Am. Choral Dirs. Assn., Am. Choral Found., Master Tchr. Inst. Arts (past trustee), Great Music West Festival. Office: Mormon Tabernacle Choir 50 E North Temple Fl 20 Salt Lake City UT 84150-0002

OTTLEY, WILLIAM HENRY, professional association director, consultant; b. N.Y.C., Mar. 7, 1929; s. James Henry and Margaret (Deeble) O. BA, Yale U., 1950; spl. cert., Georgetown U., 1953; D of Aero. Sci. (hon.), Embry Riddle Aero. U., 1979. Dir. pub. rels. Thomas A. Edison Co., West Orange, N.J., 1953-56; exec. v.p. Career Publs., Inc., N.Y.C., 1956-60; dir. spl. exhibits N.Y. World's Fair, 1960-65; exec. dir. Nat. Pilots Assn., Washington, 1965-77, U.S. Parachute Assn., Washington, 1978-92, Nat. Aero. Assn., Washington, 1992-93; pres. Internat. Gen. Aviation Commn., Paris, 1994—; v.p. Fedn. Aero. Internat., Paris, 1994—. 1st lt. USAF, 1951-53. Recipient Skydiving Lifetime Achievement award, 1994. Mem. Am. Mus. Sport Parachuting (pres.), Met. Club Washington, Soc. of Cin. Republican. Episcopalian. Avocations: skydiving (world record holder 1982), flying (world record holder 1985), scuba diving, waterskiing, snow skiing. Home and Office: 2627 Woodley Pl NW Washington DC 20008-1525

OTTMANN, PETER, choreologist, ballet master; b. Renfrew, Ont., Can., Apr. 15, 1957; m. Karen Cameron. Grad., Nat. Ballet Sch., 1975; postgrad., Benesh Inst., London, 1993. Mem. Nat. Ballet of Can., Toronto, Ont., 1976—, 1st soloist, 1983-93, resident choreologist, ballet master, 1993-96, asst. to artistic dir., 1996—; mem. dancer exch. program Australian Ballet Co. Created roles of Reginald Hargreaves and Caterpillar in Glen Tetley's Alice, La Ronde, Musings, The Second Detail, and for Café Dances, 1991; debuted as Lewis Carrol at Met. Opera House, N.Y.C., 1986; performed the lead role in The Nutcracker, Giseille, Romeo and Juliet, Don Juan, Don Quixote, The Miraculous Mandarin, La Ronde, 1987, Dream Dances, 1989, Forgottan Land, The Leaves Are Fading, 1990, the second detail, 1991, Steptext, The Strangeness of a Kiss, 1991, Musings, 1991, The Taming of the Shrew, 1992, The Merry Widow, 1992, (in films) Alice, 1989, La Ronde, 1989, (TV prodn.) A Moving Picture; guest appearances at Spoleto Festival, Italy, Toronto Symphony Orch., 1986, Houston Ballet, 1993, Paris Opera Ballet, 1997. Office: Nat Ballet Can W Carsen Ctr, 470 Queens Quay W, Toronto, ON Canada M5V 3K4

OTTO, CHARLES EDWARD, health care administrator; b. Somerville, N.J., Nov. 12, 1946; s. Hans and Virginia (Hegeman) O.; m. Wendy Ann Halsey; June 26, 1971; children: Eric, C. Halsey, Robert. BA, Hobart Coll., Geneva, N.Y., 1968; MBA, U. Pa., 1973. Adminstrv. asst. Mass. Gen. Hosp., Boston, 1970-71; adminstrv. resident Hosp. of U. of Pa., Phila., 1973; adminstrv. asst. Norwalk (Conn.) Hosp., 1974-76; exec. dir. Waveny Care Ctr., New Canaan, Conn., 1977-93; adminstr. Avery Heights Retirement Village, Hartford, Conn., 1994—; bd. chmn. Conn. Assn. of Non-Profit Facilities for the Aged, Wallingford, 1984-86; chmn. regional adv. group Conn. Community Care, Inc., Norwalk, 1983-85. Bd. chmn. S.W. Fairfield Am. Cancer Soc., Norwalk, 1985-87. Served to lt. (j.g.) USNR, 1968-70. Mem. Wharton Healthcare Alumni Assn. (bd. dirs. 1993-94), Rocky Point Club. Episcopalian. Home: 12 Lake Dr S Riverside CT 06878-2016

OTTO, DONALD R., museum director; b. North Loup, Nebr., Oct. 7, 1943; s. Leonard R. and Lorraine E. (Lindsay) O.; B.A., Hastings (Nebr.) Coll., 1967; m. Sylvia D. Cook, Aug. 7, 1965; 1 dau., Allison Lindsay. With Kans.-Nebr. Natural Gas Co., Hastings, 1967-68; exhibits dir. Hastings Museum, 1968-72; asst. dir. Kans. State Hist. Soc., 1972-75; program dir. Ft. Worth Mus. Sci. and History, 1975-77, exec. dir., 1977—; pres. Kans. Mus. Assn., 1974, 75; officer Mountain Plains Mus. Conf., 1976-79, pres., 1977-78; spl. cons. mus. curriculum planning Coll. Liberal Studies, U. Okla., 1980. Mem. adminstrv. bd. 1st Meth. Ch., 1978-80, 81-83, 84-86; bd. dirs. Sci. Mus. Exhibit Collaborative, 1983—, Ft. Worth Conv. and Visitors Bur., 1986—, Internat. Space Theater Consortium, 1981—, pres. 1984-86, exec. com. 1991-92; mem. Ft. Worth Cultural Dist. Com., 1979—, Ft. Worth Air Power Coun., 1985—, Leadership Ft. Worth, 1988—, Forum Ft. Worth, 1989—; mem. grants com. Cultural Arts Coun. of Houston, 1988-89; mem. adv. coun. Ft. Worth Sr. Citizen Ctrs., 1986-88; trustee Big Bros.-Big Sisters, 1988-89; chmn. Ft. Worth Tourism Coun., 1983. Mem. Am. Assn. Mus. (accreditation on site com. 1974—), Mt. Plains Mus. Assoc. Bd., 1975-78, pres., 1977, Am. Assn. State and Local History, Am. Assn. Sci. and Tech. Ctrs. (bd. dirs. 1984-88), Assn. Sci. Mus. Dirs., Tex. Assn. Mus. (coun. 1980-82, v.p. 1983-84), Ft. Worth Aviation Heritage Soc. (bd. dirs. 1988—), Methodist. Clubs: Ridglea Country, Rotary (Ft. Worth). Office: Ft Worth Mus Sci & History 1501 Montgomery St Fort Worth TX 76107-3017*

OTTO, FRED DOUGLAS, chemical engineering educator; b. Hardisty, Alta., Can., Jan. 12, 1935. BSc, U. Alta., 1957, MSc, 1959; BS in Chem. Engring., U. Mich., Ann Arbor, 1963. From asst. prof. to assoc. prof. U. Alta., Edmonton, 1962-70, chmn., 1975-84, prof. chem. engring., 19970—, dean engring., 1985-94; mem. governing coun. NRC, 1991-94. Fellow Can.

Acad. Engring.; mem. AIChE, Can. Soc. Chem. Engrs. (pres. 1986-87), Am. Soc. Engring. Edn., Assn. Profl. Engrs., Geologists and Geophysicsts of Alta. (1st v.p. 1995-96, Centennial award 1993). Office: U Alta, 5-18 Chem-Mineral Engr Bldg, Edmonton, AB Canada T6G 2G6

OTTO, INGOLF HELGI ELFRIED, banking institute fellow; b. Duesseldorf, Germany, May 7, 1920; s. Frederick C. and Josephine (Zisenis) O.; m. Carlyle Miller, 1943 (div. 1960); children: George Vincent Edward, Richard Arthur Frederick. A.B., U. Cin., 1941; M.A., George Washington U., 1950, Ph.D., 1959. CPCU. Assoc. prof. fin. NYU, N.Y.C., 1960-62; prof. fin. U. Nuevo Leon, Monterrey, Mexico, 1962-65, U. So. Miss., Hattiesburg, 1965-67, U. So. Ala., Mobile, 1967-81; sr. fellow Inst. Banking and Fin., Mexico City, 1981—. Contbr. articles on fin. to profl. jours. Served to col. U.S. Army, 1941-46. Decorated Legion of Merit, Meritorious Service medal, Purple Heart. Mem. Am. Econ. Assn., N.Am. Econ. and Fin. Assn.

OTTO, JEAN HAMMOND, journalist; b. Kenosha, Wis., Aug. 27, 1925; d. Laurence Cyril and Beatrice Jane (Slater) Hammond; m. John A. Otto, Aug. 22, 1946; children: Jane L. Rahman, Mary Ellen Takayama, Peter J. Otto; m. Lee W. Baker, Nov. 23, 1973. Student, Ripon Coll., 1944-46. Women's editor Appleton (Wis.) Post-Crescent, 1960-68; reporter Milw. Jour., 1968-72, editorial writer, 1972-77, editor Op Ed page, 1977-83; editorial page editor Rocky Mountain News, Denver, 1983-89, assoc. editor, 1989-92, reader rep., 1992—; Endowed chair U. Denver, 1992—. Founder, chmn. bd. trustees First Amendment Congress, 1979-85, chmn. exec. com., 1985-88, 89-91, pres. 1991—, mem. bd. trustees, 1979—; founding mem. Wis. Freedom of Info. Council. Recipient Headliner award Wis. Women in Communications, 1974; Outstanding Woman in Journalism award YWCA, Milw., 1977; Knight of Golden Quill Milw. Press Club, 1979; spl. citation in Journalism Ball State U., 1980; James Madison award Nat. Broadcast Editorial Assn., 1981; spl. citation for contbn. to journalism Nat. Press Photographers Assn., 1981; Ralph D. Casey award, 1984; U. Colo. Regents award, 1985; John Peter Zenger award U. Ariz., 1988; Paul Miller Medallion award Okla. State U., 1990; Colo. SPJ Lowell Thomas award, 1990, Disting. Alumna award Ripon Coll., 1992, Hugh M. Hefner First Amendment Lifetime Achievement award Playboy Found., 1994; named to Freedom of Info. Nat. Hall of Fame, 1996. Mem. Colo. Press Assn. (chmn. freedom of info. com. 1983-89), Assn. Edn. in Journalism and Mass Communications (Disting. Svc. award 1984), Am. Soc. Newspaper Editors (bd. dirs. 1987-92), Soc. Profl. Journalists (nat. treas. 1975, nat. sec. 1977, pres.-elect 1978, pres. 1979-80, First Amendment award 1981, Wells Key 1984, pres. Sigma Delta Chi Found. 1989-92, chair Found. 1992-94), Milw. Press Club (mem. Hall of Fame 1993). Office: Rocky Mountain News 400 W Colfax Ave Denver CO 80204-2607

OTTO, KLAUS, physicist, physical chemist; b. Friedrichroda, Germany, Sept. 18, 1929; came to U.S., 1960, naturalized, 1967; s. Theodor M.W.A. and Gertrud (Gohla) O.; m. Christa Thomsen, Nov. 16, 1962; children: Ina N., Peter N. Vordiplom, U. Hamburg, Fed. Republic of Germany, 1954, Diplom, 1957, D of Natural Scis., 1960. Rsch. asst. U. Hamburg, 1959-60; postdoctoral fellow Argonne (Ill.) Nat. Lab., 1960-62; sr. rsch. scientist Ford Motor Co., Dearborn, Mich., 1962-73, prin. rsch. scientist assoc., 1973-81, staff scientist, 1981-95; ret., 1995; adj. prof. Mich. State U., 1986-95. Contbr. articles to profl. jours. Recipient Parravano award for excellence in catalysis rsch. and devel., 1986. Mem. AAAS, Am. Chem. Soc., German Bunsen Soc. of Electrochemistry, Mich. Catalysis Soc. (pres. 1980-81), N.Y. Acad. Scis., Sigma Xi (pres. Ford chpt. 1985-86). Home: 201 E Tonto Dr Sedona AZ 86351-7323

OTTO, MARGARET AMELIA, librarian; b. Boston, Oct. 22, 1937; d. Henry Earlen and Mary (McLennan) O.; children—Christopher, Peter. A.B., Boston U., 1960; M.S., Simmons Coll., 1963, M.A., 1970; M.A. (hon.), Dartmouth Coll., 1981. Asst. sci. librarian M.I.T., Cambridge, 1963; Lindgren librarian M.I.T., 1964-67, acting sci. librarian, 1967-69, asst. dir., 1969-75, asso. dir., 1976-79; librarian of coll. Dartmouth Coll., Hanover, N.H., 1979—; pres., chmn. bd. Universal Serials and Book Exch., Inc., 1980-81; bd. dirs. Rsch. Libr. Group; trustee Howe Libr., Hanover, 1988—, chmn., 1992—; mem. Brown Libr. Com., rsch. lbirs. adv. com. OCLC, 1991—, ARL; editl. com. Univ. Press New Eng., 1993—. Council on Library Resources fellow, 1974; elected to Collegium of Disting. Alumnus Boston U., 1980. Mem. ALA (task force on assn. membership issues 1993—, ad hoc working group on copyright issues), Assn. Rsch. Librs. (chair preservation com. 1983-85, bd. dirs. 1985-88, mem. stats. com., chair membership com. 1992—), Coun. on Libr. Resources (proposal rev. com. 1992—), Dartmouth Club (N.Y.C.), St. Botolph Club (Boston), Sloane Club (London). Home: 2 Berrill Farms Ln Hanover NH 03755-3205 Office: Dartmouth Coll 115 Baker Meml Libr Hanover NH 03755

OTTOSON, HOWARD WARREN, agricultural economist, former university administrator; b. Detroit Lakes, Minn., Sept. 18, 1920; s. John Henry and Hilma Marie (Johnson) O.; m. Margaret Jane Featherstone, Oct. 22, 1944; children—Keith Richard, John Howard, David Thomas. B.S., U. Minn., 1942, M.S., 1950; Ph.D., Iowa State U., 1952. Chmn. dept. agrl. econs. U. Nebr., Lincoln, 1956-66, Bert Rodgers prof., 1965, dir., dean, 1966-79, asst. vice chancellor, 1979-81, vice chancellor, 1981-82, exec. v.p., provost, 1982-85, prof. agrl. econs. emeritus, 1985—; cons. USDA, Washington, 1961, 64, AID, Buenos Aires, Argentina, 1962, Colombian Inst. Agr., Bogota, 1970; mem. USDA Policy Adv. Com. on Feed Grains, Washington, 1966-68; chmn. Gt. Plains Agrl. Council, Lincoln, Nebr., 1971, 79; bd. dirs. Farm Found. Bd., Chgo., 1977-85. Sr. author: Land and People in the Northern Plains Tranition Area, 1966; sr. author Agrl. Land Tenure Research bull., 1962; editor: Land Use Problems and Policies in the U.S., 1963; co-editor: Transportation Problems and Policies in the Trans Missouri West, 1967. Pres. Lincoln Coun. Chs., Nebr., 1958-59, Nebr. divsn. UN Assn.-U.S.A., Lincoln, 1977-78; chmn. Mayor's Adv. Com. on Taxation, Lincoln, 1991; mem. Nebr. Commn. on Local Govt. Innovation and Restructuring, 1996—. Served to lt. USNR, 1944-46, PTO. Mem. LWV (bd. dirs. Nebr. 1993—), Am. Agrl. Econs. Assn., Internat. Assn. Agrl. Economists (travel fellow 1958, 64), Open Forum (pres. 1991-92), Fifty-Fifty Club, Norden Club (pres. 1985-87), Farm House, Sigma Xi, Phi Kappa Phi, Gamma Sigma Delta, Phi Delta Kappa. Democrat. Presbyterian. Avocations: golf; skiing; woodwork; Civil War history; gardening. Home: 5811 Margo Dr Lincoln NE 68510-5029

OTTWEIN, MERRILL WILLIAM GEORGE, real estate company executive, veterinarian; b. Troy, Ill., Apr. 24, 1929; s. Oscar J. and Hilda (Bardelmeier) O.; m. Grace Marie Schmidt, Jan. 22, 1932; children: Ann Marie, Amy Sue, Paul John, Emily Carol. BS with highest honors, U. Ill., 1951, MS in Agrl. Econs., 1952, BS in Vet. Medicine, 1954, DVM with honors, 1956. Lic. veterinarian, Ill., real estate broker, Ill. Pvt. practice Edwardsville, Ill., 1956-66; dir. Diakonia, Ch. World Svc., Honduras, 1967; mem. Ill. Senate, Springfield, 1968-70; real estate developer Cottonwood Sta. Corp., 1970-81; real estate broker Coldwell Banker, Edwardsville, 1981-91; exclusive buyer borker relocation svcs. Edwardsville, 1991—, O'Fallon, Ill., 1992—; mem. vet. med. adv. com. U. Ill., Urbana, 1960-64. Pres. Cahokia Mounds coun. Boy Scouts Am., 1969-71; mem. bd. for world ministries United Ch. of Christ, N.Y.C., 1970-74; active local Rep. politics. Mem. Nat. Assn. Exclusive Buyer Agts. (treas. 1995, 96, pres.-elect 1997), Ill. Assn. Realtors, Edwardsville-Glen Carbon C. of C., Edwardsville-Collinsville Bd. Realtors, Land of Goshen C. of C. (pres. 1974-75), U. Ill. Vet. Medicine Alumni Assn. (pres. 1960-61), Rotary (pres. Edwardsville 1976), Phi Kappa Phi, Alpha Zeta. Avocations: vocal and instrumental music, photography. Home: 34 Lilac St Edwardsville IL 62025-2706 Office: Home Buyers Relocation Svc 2888 S State Route 159 Edwardsville IL 62025-3107 also: 515 W Hwy 50 O'Fallon IL 62269

OTUS, SIMONE, public relations executive; b. Walnut Creek, Calif., Jan. 10, 1960; d. Mahmut and Alexa (Artemenko) O. BA, U. Calif., Berkeley, 1981. Account exec. Marx-David Advt., San Francisco, 1981-82; freelance writer Mpls. and San Francisco, 1982-83; account exec. D'Arcy, MacManus & Masius, San Francisco, 1983; account supr. Ralph Silver Assocs., San Francisco, 1984-85; ptnr., co-founder Blanc & Otus Pub. Relations, San Francisco, 1985—. Address: 135 Main St Ste 1200 San Francisco CA 94105-1816

OTVOS, LASZLO ISTVAN, JR., organic chemist; b. Szeged, Csongrad, Hungary, May 17, 1955; came to U.S., 1985; s. Laszlo and Ilona (Elekes) O.; m. Elisabeth Papp, Aug. 6, 1977; children: Balint, Judy. MS, Eotvos L. U., Budapest, 1979; PhD, Hungarian Acad. Sci., Budapest, 1985, DS, 1993. Assoc. scientist Chem. Works of Gedeon Richter, Budapest, 1979-82; assoc. scientist Wistar Inst., Phila., 1985-89, rsch. assoc., 1990-94, asst. prof., 1992—, assoc. prof., 1995—; asst. prof. pathology and lab. medicine U. Pa., Phila., 1992-95; cons., dir. peptide chemistry Symphony Pharms., Malvern, Pa., 1993—. Contbr. more than 120 articles to sci. jours. Recipient Weil award Am. Assn. Neuropathologists, 1988; grantee, NIH, NSF, AHAF, 1990—. Mem. Am. Chem. Soc., Am. Peptide Soc. (charter), Assn. Biomolecular Rsch. Facility, Soc. Neurosci. Home: 801 Mockingbird Ln Audubon PA 19403-1965 Office: Wistar Inst 3601 Spruce St Philadelphia PA 19104-4205

OTWELL, RALPH MAURICE, retired newspaper editor; b. Hot Springs, Ark., June 17, 1926; s. Walter Clement and Pearl Oda (Tisdale) O.; m. Janet Barbara Smith, July 18, 1953; children—Brian Thornton, Douglas Keith, David Smith. Student, U. Ark., 1947-48; B.S., Northwestern U., 1951; postgrad. (Nieman fellow), Harvard, 1959-60. Reporter, telegraph editor So. Newspapers, Inc., Hot Springs, 1943-44, 47; asst. city editor Chgo. Sun-Times, 1953-59, news editor, 1959-63, asst. mng. editor, 1963-65, asst. to editor, 1965-68, mng. editor, 1968-76, editor, 1976-80, exec. v.p., editor, 1980-84; Mgmt. bd. newspaper div. Field Enterprises, Inc., 1967-84; lectr. Medill Sch. Journalism, Northwestern U., 1955—; charter mem. Nat. News Council, 1973-80. Trustee Garrett-Evang. Theol. Sem., 1965-79; Mem. nat. bd. Christian Social Concerns, United Meth. Ch., 1968-72; mem. bd. Community Renewal Soc., 1987-90, Chgo. Reporter, 1987-90, student publs. Northwestern U., 1968-72. Served to 1st lt. AUS, 1944-47, 51-53. Recipient Page One award Chgo. Newspaper Guild, 1964; named Ill. Journalist of Year No. Ill. U., 1974. Mem. Am. Soc. Newspaper Editors (chmn. ethics com. 1976-77), AP Mng. Editors Assn., Soc. Profl. Journalists (dir. 1966-71, sec. 1971-72, v.p. 1972-73, pres. 1973-74), Northwestern U. Alumni Assn. (dir. 1965-68, 91-93, sec. 1993-94, Merit award 1969, Svc. award 1995), Sigma Delta Chi (pres. 1987-89), Kappa Tau Alpha, Econ. Club, Headline Club (pres. Chgo. chpt. 1965-66), Harvard Club Chgo., Chgo. Press Club (dir. 1968-77), Northwestern Club. Home: 2750 Hurd Ave Evanston IL 60201-1268

OUDENS, GERALD FRANCIS, architect, architectural firm executive; b. Manchester, N.H., May 18, 1934; s. John and Louise Esther (Wagner) O.; m. Monica Elizabeth Wohlfert, June 16, 1962; children: Elizabeth Marian, Matthew Thomas, Katherine Frances. BA in Architecture cum laude, Yale U., 1956, MArch, 1958. Registered arch., D.C., Va., Md., Pa., Ind., Nat. Coun. Archtl. Registration Bds. Intern architect Koehler & Isaak, Manchester, 1955-58; staff architect Office Surgeon Gen. USAF, Washington, 1958-61; assoc. Metcalf & Assocs., Washington, 1961-69; prin. Oudens & Knoop Architects, PC, Chevy Chase, Md., 1970—; vis. critic, thesis advisor dept. architecture Cath. U. Am., 1968-88; mem. adv. com. acad. med. ctr. study sch. architecture Rice U., 1975; mem. ambulatory care adv. panel U.S. VA, 1974-75; mem. adv. panel No. Ind. Health Systems Agy., 1977-81, AIA Rsch. Corp., 1978, Nat. Inst. Bldg. Scis., 1982-88; mem. design award juries Modern Healthcare Ann. Design Awards, 1992, Soc. for Critical Care Medicine/AACN/AIA ICU Design Awards, 1992-94, 96, AIA Health Facilities Rev. Jury, 1995; presenter in field. Principal works include NIH Master Plan, Bethesda, Md., Sibley Meml. Hosp., Washington, D.C., Washington Adventist Hosp., Takoma Park, Md., Martha Jefferson Hosp., Charlottesville, Va., Marion (Ind.) Gen. Hosp., Humana Lucerne Hosp., Orlando, Fla., Hosp. de Pedregal, Mexico City, Fairfax Hosp., Falls Church, Va., Humana Audubon Hosp. and Heart Inst., Louisville, Ky., Humana Greensboro (N.C.) Hosp., Centre Universitaire des Sciences de la Sante, Yaounde, Cameroon, Washington Home and Hospice, Washington, D.C., Stoddard Bapt. Home, Washington, D.C., Cuttington U. Coll., Suakoko, Liberia, Escuela Agricola Panamericana, El Zamorano, FM, Honduras, others; contbr. articles to profl. jours. Recipient Nat. Capital Architecture award D.C. Coun. Engring. and Archtl. Socs./Washington Acad. Scis., 1961. Mem. AIA (acad. on architecture for health 1971—, past pres. and dir., nat. healthcare policy task force 1993—, mem. adv. com. Am. Collegiate Schs. Architecture coun. on archtl. rsch. 1994—, Henry Adams award 1958, Honor award Ky. chpt., 1980, Outstanding Leadership and Commitment to Healthcare Design award 1987, Merit award Washington Met. chpt. 1989, Citations for Design Excellence 1988, 1990, Am. Hosp. Assn. Grad. Fellowship Rev. Panel), Am. Hosp. Assn. (mem. faculty continuing edn. insts. 1972-76, adv. panel 1978), Internat. Hosp. Fedn., Forum for Health Care Planing. Office: Oudens & Knoop Architects PC 2 Wisconsin Cir Chevy Chase MD 20815-7003

OUELLET, ANDRÉ, communication and distribution company executive; b. St. Pascal, Que., Canada, Apr. 6, 1939; s. Albert and Rita (Turgeon) O.; m. Edith Pagé, July 17, 1965; children: Sonia, Jean, Olga, Pierre. BA, U. Ottawa, Ont., Can., 1960, D (hon.), 1995; LLL, U. Sherbrooke, Can., 1963. Mem. Can. Parliament, Ottawa, 1967-93, min. consumer and corp. affairs, 1974-76, 80-83, min. state urban affairs, 1976-78, min. public works, 1978-79, min. labor, 1983-84; postmaster gen. Can., Ottawa, 1972-74, 80-81; min. fgn. affairs Can. Parliament, Ottawa, 1993-96; chmn. bd. Can. Post Corp., Ottawa, 1996—. Office: Canada Post Corp, 2701 Riverside Dr Ste N1250, Ottawa, ON Canada K1A 0B1

OUELLETTE, BERNARD CHARLES, pharmaceutical company executive; b. Windsor, Ont., Can., July 8, 1936; s. Edouard and Alice (Parent) O.; m. Mary Catherine Robert, Sept. 8, 1962; children: Timothy, Michelle, Maureen, Catherine, Suzanne. B.A., U. Windsor, 1964; M.B.A., Wayne State U., 1968; AMP, Harvard U., 1987. Pres. North York (Toronto) Cancer Soc., 1975-77; v.p. bus. devel. Connaught Biosciences Inc., 1975-78; exec. v.p. Winthrop Labs. Ltd., Toronto, Ont., Can., 1978-79; pres. Winthrop Labs. Ltd., 1979-80; exec. v.p. Winthrop Labs., N.Y.C., 1981-82, pres., 1982-83; pres. Pharm. Group Sterling Drug, Inc., N.Y.C., 1983-88, group v.p., 1984-88; pres., chief exec. officer Praxis Biologics Inc., Rochester, N.Y., 1988-89, also bd. dirs.; chief exec. officer Horus Therapeutics (formerly Biocare, Inc.), Rochester, 1989-90, chmn., pres., chief exec. officer, 1990—. Mem. Am. Mgmt. Assn. Roman Catholic. Home: 38 Yorkshire Dr Hilton Head Island SC 29928

OUREDNIK, PATRICIA ANN, accountant; b. Balt., Oct. 5, 1962; d. John Matthew and Patricia Ann (Ruzicka) O. BS in Acctg., U. Balt., 1984; MS in Mgmt. Info. Sys., Fla. Inst. Tech., 1991. CPA, Md. Acctg. clk. Cello Corp., Havre de Grace, Md., 1981-84; staff acct. KPMG Peat Marwick, Balt., 1984-85; audit supv. Coughlin & Mann, Chartered, Bel Air, Md., 1985-88, 89-92; CFO Kidde Sys., White Marsh, Md., 1988-89, FAMIC Corp., Columbia, Md., 1994-95, Top Tools Automation Sys., Timonium, Md., 1992-93; contr. CRMA, Balt., 1995—. Cons. Shepherd's Clinic, Balt., 1992—. Mem. Md. Assn. CPAs, Assn. Retarded Citizens. Republican. Methodist. Home: 1618 Bramble Ct Bel Air MD 21015-1560 Office: CRMA 100 E Pratt St Baltimore MD 21202-1009

OURIEFF, ARTHUR JACOB, psychiatrist; b. Boston, Jan. 20, 1924; s. James Leonard and Sigrid (Lewis) O.; m. Vernie Gusack, Aug. 17, 1947; children: Bruce, Martha, Sally. Student, Amherst Coll., 1941-43; MD, Harvard U., 1946. Intern Bellevue Hosp., N.Y.C., 1946-47; resident U. Ill., Chgo., 1947-51; psychoanalyst, psychiatrist L.A. Inst. Psychoanalysis with Adults and Children, 1953-59, pvt. practice, L.A., 1953—; asst. prof. psychiatry UCLA Med. Sch., L.A., 1970—. Lt (j.g.) USNR, 1949-51. Child Psychiatry fellow Inst. Juvenile Rsch., Chgo., 1951-53. Fellow Am. Psychoanalytic Assn.; mem. Am. Psychiat. Assn., So. Calif. Soc. Child Psychiatry. Democrat. Avocations: skiing, jogging, mountain climbing, Treking, travel. Home and Office: 320 N Cliffwood Ave Los Angeles CA 90049-2618

OURSLER, FULTON, JR., editor-in-chief, writer; b. West Falmouth, Mass., June 27, 1932; s. Fulton and Grace (Perkins) O.; m. Anne Noel Nevill, Nov. 29, 1954; children: Theresa Noel, Fulton III, Mark Nevill, James Randall, Carroll Grace. B.A., Georgetown U., 1954. With Reader's Digest, Pleasantville, N.Y., 1956-87, book editor, 1968-70, sr. staff editor, 1970-72, asst. mng. editor, 1973, mng. editor, 1974-82, exec. editor, 1982-85, dep. editor-in-chief, 1986-87; editor-in-chief Guideposts mag., 1992—; editor-in-chief, founding editor Angels on Earth mag., 1995—. Established: Fulton Oursler Meml. Collection, Georgetown U. Library.; editor: (commentary) Behold This Dreamer, 1964. Bd. dirs. Georgetown U. Library Assocs. Served with U.S. Army, 1954-56. Mem. Friends of the Nyacks, Cath. Actors Guild, Univ. Club. Home: 2 Laveta Pl Nyack NY 10960-1604 Office: Guide Post Mag 16 E 34th St New York NY 10016-4328 *Man makes two journeys in life: one in matter, the other in spirit. The first journey is outward and manifest; it leads to family, society, and career. The second journey is inward and invisible; it leads to the kingdom of God. The first journey is limited by logic, flesh, and time. The second is infinite, and its pathway is paradox. Self-preservation is the strongest instinct on the first journey; freedom, maturity, self-knowledge, power, and abundance seem to be important goals. But on the second journey, one learns that to find our truest selves, we must lose the sense of self; that to grow we must become as a child; that freedom is won by surrender, that the one counts for more than the many, that the meek are powerful, and the poor are rich. On both journeys, to gain life one must lose it, and be reborn.*

OUSSANI, JAMES JOHN, stapling company executive; b. Bklyn., Jan. 3, 1920; s. John Thomas and Clara (Tager) O.; m. Lorraine G. Tutundgy, Apr. 25, 1954; children: James J., Gregory P., Rita C. B.M.E., Pratt Inst., 1938-42; J.D. (hon.), Coll. Boca Raton, Lynn U.; LLD. Dir. research, mfg. Supertronic Co., N.Y.C., 1943-46; sr. partner Perl-Oussani Machine Mfg. Co., N.Y.C., 1946-49; founder The Staplex Co., Bklyn., 1949, pres., 1949—; exec. dir. Lourdes Realty Corp.; dir. Junios Corp.; producer air sampling equipment for radioactive fallout AEC, 1951—. Mem. Bur. Research Air Pollution Control, Pres.'s Council on Youth Opportunity, Cardinal's Com. for Edn.; trustee Ch. of Virgin Mary; bd. dirs. St. Joan Arc Found., Boca Raton; founding mem. Lumen Christi-Palm Beach Diocese; founder, bd. dirs. Oussani Found.; founder James J. & Lorraine G. Oussani Scholarship Fund, Coll. Boca Raton; mem. cardinal's com. of laity, bishop's com. of laity; mem. Lumen Christi Found.; bd. overseers Lynn U., Boca Raton. Recipient Blue Ribbon Mining award, Sch. Mgmt. award, Aerospace Pride Achievement award; installed Knight of Jerusalem. Mem. Adminstrv. Mgmt. Soc., Office Adminstrn. Assn., Nat. Stationery and Office Equipment AssOffice Equipment Assn., Office Execs. Assn., Nat. Office Machine Mfg. Assn., Nat. Office Machine Dealers Assn., Nat. Office Products Assn., Bus. Equipment Mfrs. Assn., Our Lady Perpetual Help Holy Name Soc., Knights of Holy Sepulchre, Knights of St. Gregory, Knights of Malta, Rotary, Salaam Club, Mahopac Golf Club (Lake Mahopac, N.Y.), Internat. Club of Boca Raton, Boca Raton Hotel and Resort Club. Inventor automatic electric stapling machine. Patentee in field. Office: 777 5th Ave Brooklyn NY 11232-1626

OUTCALT, DAVID LEWIS, academic administrator, mathematician, educator; b. Los Angeles, Jan. 30, 1935; s. Earl Kinyon and Alberta Estes Ferguson O.; m. Marcia Lee Beach, July 1, 1956; children—Jeffrey David, Kevin Douglas, Gregory Mark, Eric Matthew. B.A. in Math., Pomona Coll., 1956; M.A. in Math., Claremont Grad. Sch., 1958; Ph.D. in Math., Ohio State U., 1963; D.Pub. Adminstrn. (hon.), Kyung Hee U., Korea, 1984. Asst. prof. math. Claremont McKenna Coll., 1962-64; asst. prof. to prof. math. U. Calif.-Santa Barbara, 1964-80, chmn. dept. math., 1969-72, dean instrnl. devel., 1977-80; vice chancellor acad. affairs U. Alaska, Anchorage, 1980-81, prof. math., 1980-86, chancellor, 1981-86; prof. natural and applied sci. U. Wis., Green Bay, 1986-93, chancellor, 1986-93, Hendrickson prof. econ. devel., 1994—; pres. Mid-Continent athletic conf., 1990-91. Author math. textbooks; contbr. articles on math. and higher edn. to profl. jours. Moderator bd. trustees Humana Hosp. Anchorage, 1982-83; mem. exec. bd. Western Alaska coun. Boy Scouts Am., 1982-86, Bay-Lakes coun., 1987—, v.p. exploring, 1988-92, v.p. ops., 1992-93, pres., 1993-94; mem. Anchorage Symphony bd., 1986, Green Bay Symphony Bd., 1988—, mem. Weidner Ctr. Presents Bd., 1994—. Grantee USAF Office Sci. Research, 1964-71, U. Calif., 1975-78, NSF, 1976-79. Mem. Math. Assn. Am., Internat. Assn. Univ. Pres.'s (exec. com. 1988-96, internat. com. on tech. in higher edn. 1996—, exec. com. 1988—, vice chair, N.Am. coun. 1988-94, newsletter editor 1994-95), Greater Green Bay C. of C. (advance bd. 1987—, bd. dirs. 1991-94, 95-97), Brown County Indsl. Devel. (pres. bd. dirs. 1994—), Rotary, Sigma Xi. Mem. Congregational Ch. Home: PO Box 89 Athelstane WI 54104-0089

OUTKA, GENE HAROLD, philosophy and Christian ethics educator; b. Sioux Falls, S.D., Feb. 24, 1937; s. Harold Irvin and Gertrude Anne (Elliott) O.; m. Carole Lee DeVore, June 26, 1960 (div. 1982); children: Paul Harold, Elizabeth Noelle; m. Susan Jane Owen, Dec. 29, 1984; 1 child, Jacqueline Elliott. B.A., U. Redlands, 1959; B.D., Yale U., 1962, M.A., 1964, Ph.D., 1967; L.H.D., U. Redlands, 1978. Instr. Princeton U., N.J., 1965-66, lectr., 1966-67, asst. prof., 1967-73, assoc. prof., 1973-75; assoc. prof. Yale U., New Haven, 1975-81, Dwight prof. philosophy and Christian ethics, 1981—; chair dept. religious studies, 1992-95; dir. resdl. seminar for coll. tchrs. NEH, New Haven, 1977-78; Mary Farnum Brown lectr. Haverford Coll., Pa., 1977; mem. faculty workshop on teaching of ethics Hastings Inst. of Soc., Ethics and Life Scis., Princeton, N.J., 1979; Merrick lectr. Ohio Wesleyan U., Delaware, Ohio, 1983; Williamson Meml. lectr. Meth. Theol. Sch. in Ohio, 1986. Author: Agape: An Ethical Analysis, 1972; co-editor, contbr.: Norm and Context In Christian Ethics, 1968, Religion and Morality, 1973, Prospects for a Common Morality, 1992; editorial bd. Jour. Religious Ethics. Service fellow office of spl. projects Health Services and Mental Health Adminstrn., HEW, Washington, 1972-73; mem. adv. com. social ethics Inst. Medicine Nat. Acad. Scis., 1975-77. Fellow Am. Council Learned Socs., 1968-69; fellow NEH, 1979-80, Woodrow Wilson Internat. Ctr. for Scholars, 1983; vis. scholar Kennedy Inst. of Ethics, Georgetown U., 1972-73. Mem. Am. Acad. Religion, Soc. Christian Ethics (bd. dirs.). Office: Yale U Dept Religious Studies 320 Temple St New Haven CT 06511-6601

OUZTS, DALE KEITH, broadcast executive; b. Miami, Fla., Aug. 26, 1941; s. Jacob C. and Edna P. (Sloan) O.; m. Susan Ouzts; children: Dale Keith Jr., Karen, Ryan Keith. BJ, U. Ga., 1965, MA, 1966; postgrad. advanced mgmt. seminar, Harvard U., 1977. Mgr. Sta. WSJK-TV, Knoxville, Tenn., 1966-69; exec. v.p., gen. mgr. Sta. KPTS-TV, Wichita, Kans., 1969-72; gen. mgr. Sta. WSSR-FM, Springfield, Ill., 1972-77; sr. v.p. Nat. Pub. Radio, Washington, 1977-79; gen. mgr. Sta. WOSU-AM-FM and Sta. WOSU-TV Ohio State U., Columbus, Ohio, 1979—; gen. mgr. Sta. WPBO-TV, Portsmouth, Ohio, 1979—; Sta. WOSE-FM, Coshocton, 1996—; gen. mgr. Sta. WOSV-FM, Mansfield, Ohio, 1988—, Sta. WOSP-FM, Portsmouth, 1993—; assoc. prof. communications Ohio State U., Columbus, Ohio, 1979—, assoc. prof. journalism, 1983—; adminstrv. dir. Ohio State Awards, 1979-94; mem. Ohio Ednl. TV Stas., v.p., 1983-84, pres., 1988-90; pres. Ohio Pub. Radio, 1995—, Ohio Alliance for Pub. Telecom., 1996—; chmn. Nat. Pub. Radio, 1990-92; pres. Pub. Radio in Mid-Am., 1976-77, 85-87. Bd. dirs. Ctr. of Vocat. Alts. in Mental Health, 1985-93, 96—, sec.-treas., 1986-88, chmn., 1988-90, Pub. Radio Expansion Task Force, 1989-90; bd. dirs. Brule Conservation Trust, 1985-94, Columbus Zoo, 1984—, Mental Health Assn., Franklin County, 1987-93, Ohio China Coun., 1982-93, v.p., 1984-85, pres., 1987-89; advisor Chinese Student and Scholar Soc. at Ohio State U., 1987-91; program rev. panel Nat. Telecomms., 1988; mgmt. cons. Corp. for Pub. Broadcasting, 1975-95. Recipient Disting. Service award Nat. Pub. Radio, 1986, Disting. Service award Nat. Black Program Consortium, 1985, Disting. Service award PRIMA, 1977, 87, award for fundraising and promotion Corp. Pub. Broadcasting, 1971, Outstanding Broadcaster award Wichita (Kans.) Chpt. of Kappa Mu Psi, 1970, OEBIE award Ohio Ednl. Broadcasting Network Commn., 1987, Emmy award nomination Acad. TV Arts and Scis., 1987. Mem. Nat. Assn. Broadcasters, Ohio Alliance for Pub. Telecom. (pres. 1995-97), Ohio Assn. Broadcasters, Nat. Assn. State Univs. and Land Grant Colls. (mem. telecomms. com. 1980-93), Columbus Ducks Unltd. (bd. dirs. 1982-93), Scioto Valley Skeet Club (bd. dirs. 1982-92), Grand Hotel Hunt Club, Sawmill Athletic Club, Ohio-Rocky Mountain Elk Found., Rotary (Dublin-Worthington, v.p. 1988-89, pres. 1990-91). Avocations: racquetball, softball, golf, hunting, tennis. Home: 2038 Michelle Dr Grove City OH 43123-4019 Office: Sta WOSU 2400 Olentangy River Rd Columbus OH 43210-1027

OVADIAH, JANICE, cultural institute administrator; m. Isaac Ovidiah. BA, Washington U., St. Louis, 1965; MA, Columbia U., 1967, PhD, 1978. Dir. prof. study tours Am. Odysseys, Inc., 1973-84; escort, interpreter in French U.S. Dept. State, 1978-84; asst. to exec. dir. Meml. Found. for Jewish Culture, 1984-87; exec. dir. Congregation Shearith Israel/The Spanish & Portuguese Syn., N.Y.C., 1987-92, Sephardic House, N.Y.C., 1987—; instr. French Rutgers U., New Brunswick, N.J., 1972; asst. to dir. of The Maison Franclase, Columbia U., 1970-72; instr. French Columbia U., 1968-70; lectr. in field. Author: (books) Toward a Concept of Cinematic Literature: An Analysis of Hiroshima, Mon Amour, 1983, The Far Away Island of the Grey Lady, 1979, others; contbr. articles to profl. jours. Office: Sephardic House 2112 Broadway Rm 200 A New York NY 10023-2142

OVERALL, JAMES CARNEY, JR., pediatrics laboratory medicine educator; b. Nashville, Sept. 27, 1937; s. James Carney and Evelyn Byrd (Duncan) O.; m. Marie Kathryn Pauli, Aug. 14, 1965 (div. Jan. 2, 1996); children: David, Paul; m. Ilene Tueller McCleery, Sept. 26, 1996; children: Matthew, Bradley, Adrien. BS, Davidson Coll., 1959; MD, Vanderbilt U., 1963. Cert. pediat. infectious diseases. Intern Vanderbilt U. Hosp., Nashville, 1963-64; resident Columbia Presbyn. Med. Ctr., N.Y.C., 1964-66; rsch. assoc. Nat. Inst. Child Health, Bethesda, Md., 1966-68; instr. pediat. Rochester, N.Y., 1968-70; asst. prof. pediat., microbiology U. Utah Sch. Med., Salt Lake City, 1970-74, assoc. prof. pediat., microbiology, 1974-79, prof. pediat., 1979-97, prof. pathology, 1981-97; chief pediat. infectious diseases U. Utah Sch. Medicine, 1970-93, dir. virology course, 1980-97, vice chmn. dept. pediat., 1982-92, med. dir. diagnostic virology lab., 1981-97; mem. bd. govs. Primary Children's Med. Ctr., Salt Lake City, 1976-78. Contbr. chpts. to textbooks, articles to profl. jours. Vice moderator Holladay United Ch. Christ, Salt Lake City, 1982-85. Lt. comdr. USPHS, 1966-68. Recipient Investigator award Howard Hughes Med. Inst., 1974-80. Mem. Am. Pediat. Soc., Soc. Pediat. Rsch., Am. Soc. Virology, Infectious Diseases Soc. Am., Pan Am. Soc. for Clin. Virology (mem. coun.), Rapid Viral Diagnosis, Am. Bd. Pediat. (mem. sub-bd. for infectious diseases 1992-96), Am. Acad. Pediat. (mem. commn. on infectious diseases 1993-96). Mem. United Ch. of Christ. Home: 10 Hoyts Island General Delivery Kittery Point ME 03905 Office: Univ Utah Sch Med Dept Pediatrics Salt Lake City UT 84132

OVERBECK, GENE EDWARD, retired airline executive, lawyer; b. St. Louis, June 16, 1929; s. Harry C. and Edna (Kessler) O.; m. Patricia June Bay, Oct. 5, 1957; children: Richard, Thomas, Elizabeth, Katherine. B.A., U. Mich., 1951, J.D., 1953. Bar: Mich. 1953, Mo. 1954, N.Y. 1958, Tex. 1980. Asso. firm Sullivan & Cromwell, N.Y.C., 1957-59; gen. atty. Am. Airlines, 1959-67, v.p., gen. counsel, 1967-72, sr. v.p., 1972-90. Served with AUS, 1954-57. Home: 4634 Charleston Terrace NW Washington DC 20007-1900 also: 13606 Rex Terrace Rd Rapid City MI 49676

OVERBY, MONESSA MARY, clinical supervisor, counselor; b. Staples, Minn., Sept. 7, 1932; d. Joseph Melvin Overby and Marie Frances (Fellman) Vollstedt. BS, Coll. of St. Teresa, 1964; MS, Winona State U., 1978. Entered Franciscan Sisters, Roman Cath. Ch., 1953; nat. cert. counselor, Gestalt therapist, trainer. Elem. and jr. high tchr. Cath. Sch. System, Austin, Tracy, Lake City, Minn., 1955-67; sch. adminstr. McCahill Inst., Lake City, 1964-70; pastoral counselor and adult educator St. Edward's, Austin, Minn., 1970-76; adj. faculty and campus minister Winona (Minn.) State U., 1976-84; psychotherapist Family & Children's Ctr. and Human Devel. Assocs., La Crosse, Wis., 1978-84; family counselor Betty Ford Ctr., Rancho Mirage, Calif., 1987-89, dir. family and outpatient svcs., 1990—; workshop presenter in field. Mem. Am. Counseling Assn., Assn. for Specialists in Group Work, Minn. Assn. Specialists in Group Work (founding pres.). Democrat. Roman Catholic. Avocations: swimming, dog care, growing roses. Office: Betty Ford Ctr 39000 Bob Hope Dr Rancho Mirage CA 92270-3221

OVERBY, OSMUND RUDOLF, art historian, educator; b. Mpls., Nov. 8, 1931; s. Oscar Rudolph and Gertrude Christine (Boe) O.; m. Barbara Ruth Spande, Mar. 20, 1954; children: Paul, Katherine, Charlotte. B.A., St. Olaf Coll., 1953; B.Arch., U. Wash., 1958; M.A., Yale U., 1960, Ph.D., 1963. Asst. in instruction dept. of history of art Yale U., 1959-60, 61-62; architect Hist. Am. Bldgs. Survey, U.S. Nat. Park Service, 1960-61, summers 1959, 62, 63, 65, 68, 69, 70, 73, 85; lectr. dept. fine arts U. Toronto, Ont., Can., 1963-64; faculty dept. art history and archaeology U. Mo., Columbia, 1964—; dept. chmn. U. Mo., 1967-70, 75-77, prof. art history, 1979—, dir. Mus. of Art and Archaeology, 1977-83; vis. prof. dept. architecture U. Calif., Berkeley, 1980; Morgan prof. U. Louisville, 1989; vis. prof. dept. art history and archaeology Washington U., St. Louis, 1996; bd. advisors Nat. Trust for Hist. Preservation, 1974-83; cons., panelist Nat. Endowment for Humanities, 1974—; bd. Mo. Mansion Preservation Commn., 1974-87; advisor Heritage/St. Louis Survey, 1974-76; counsellor to St. Louis Landmarks Assn., 1977—; chmn. Task Force on Hist. Preservation City of Columbia, 1977-78; cons. on hist. preservation; active Mo. Adv. Council on Hist. Preservation, 1967-82; lectr., exhibitor profl. confs. in field. Author: Historic American Buildings Survey, Rhode Island Catalog, 1972; co-author: Laclede's Landing, a History and Architectural Guide, 1977, The Saint Louis Old Post Office, A History and Architectural Guide to the Building and Its Neighborhood, 1979; co-author, editor: Illustrated Museum Handbook, A Guide to the Collections in the Museum of Art and Archaeology, University of Missouri-Columbia, 1982; editor in chief Buildings of the United States series, 1990-96; contbr. sects. to books, articles to profl. publs. in field. Served with U.S. Army, 1953-55. Recipient various fellowships and grants in field. Mem. Soc. Archtl. Historians (bd. dirs. 1968-73, 78-81, Jour. editor 1968-73, dir. Mo. Valley chpt., session chmn. ann. meeting 1976, v.p. 1982-86, pres. 1986-88, chmn. coms.), Mid-Continent Am. Studies Assn. (editorial bd. American Studies 1965-70), Midwest Art History Soc. (bd. 1975-78, gen. chmn. annual meeting 1977), Mid-Am. Coll. Art Assn. (session chmn. annual meeting 1975), Mo. Heritage Trust (pres. 1976-79, 81-83, bd. dirs. 1979—), Coll. Art Assn., Landmarks Assn. St. Louis. Lutheran. Home: 1118 W Rollins Rd Columbia MO 65203-2221 Office: U Mo Dept Art History & Archaeology Columbia MO 65211

OVERFIELD, ROBERT EDWARD, physicist; b. Buffalo, Dec. 5, 1951; s. Russell Benton and Viola (Schavey) O.; m. Nancy Marie Dalesandro, Aug. 8, 1975; children: Brett Viola, Lindsay Grace, Anna Karina, Emily Patricia. BS in Physics, U. Rochester, 1974; PhD in Biophysics, U. Ill., 1979. Mech. engring. aide Xerox Corp., Webster, N.Y., 1974-75; grad. teaching and rsch. asst. U. Ill., Urbana, 1974-78, postdoctoral rsch. fellow, 1979-80; rsch. physicist Exxon Rsch. and Engring. Co., Linden, N.J., 1980-85; group leader hydrocarbon chemistry Exxon Rsch. and Engring. Co., Clinton, N.J., 1985-87; supr. analytical and materials Esso Resources Canada Ltd., Calgary, Alberta, 1987-91; mgr. oil sands R&D Imperial Oil Resources Ltd., Calgary, 1991-94; materials rsch. supr. Exxon Prodn. Rsch. Co., Houston, 1994-97; materials engring. supr. Esso Exploration and Prodn. Natuna, Inc., Houston, 1997—; chmn. organizing com. Canadian Oil Sands Network for R&D, Calgary, 1993-94. Contbr. articles to profl. jours. Eagle Scout Boy Scouts Am., Tonawanda, N.Y., 1966, asst. scoutmaster, 1970-74. Fellow NIH, 1975-78. Mem. Am. Chem. Soc. (divsn. petroleum chemistry). Achievements include several U.S. patents; development of innovation in molecular characterization used in heavy oil refining worldwide. Office: Esso E&P Natuna Inc PO Box 2180 Houston TX 77252-2180

OVERGAARD, MITCHELL JERSILD, lawyer; b. Chgo., Jan. 9, 1931; s. Kristen Mikkelsen and Rose Eunice (Jersild) O.; m. Joan Marquardt, Aug. 2, 1958; children: Wade, Kristin Bond, Neil. BA, U. Chgo., 1950, JD, 1953. Bar: Ill. 1957, U.S. Supreme Ct. 1975. Assoc. Dale, Haffner & Grow, Chgo., 1957-63; ptnr. Overgaard & Davis, Chgo., 1963—; Dir. Community Bank of Homewood-Flossmoor, Homewood, Ill., 1973-83. Trustee Village of Homewood, 1965-69, 85-95; commr. Homewood-Flossmoor Park Dist., 1969-77; past pres., bd. dirs. Family Svcs. and Mental Health Ctr. of South Cook County, Homewood Youth Coun.; bd. dirs. Ill. Philharm. Orch., 1992-95. With U.S. Army, 1953-56. Mem. Ill. Bar Assn., Chgo. Bar Assn. Mem. Reformed Ch. in America (elder). Home: 19137 Loomis Ave Homewood IL 60430-4431 Office: Overgaard & Davis 134 N La Salle St Chicago IL 60602-1086

OVERGAARD, ROBERT MILTON, religious organization administrator; b. Ashby, Minn., Nov. 6, 1929; s. Gust and Ella (Johnson) O.; m. Sally Lee Stephenson, Dec. 29, 1949; children: Catherine Jean Overgaard Thuleen, Robert Milton, Elizabeth Dianne Overgaard Almendinger, Barbara, Craig, David (dec.), Lori Overgaard Noack. Cert., Luth. Brethren Sem., 1954; BS, Mayville (N.D.) State U., 1959; MS, U. Oreg., 1970. Ordained to ministry Ch. Luth. Brethren Am., 1954. Pastor Elim Luth. Ch., Frontier, Sask., Can., 1954-57, Ebenezer Luth. Ch., Mayville, 1957-60, Immanuel Luth. Ch., Eugene, Oreg., 1960-63, 59th Street Luth. Ch., Bklyn., 1963-68, Immanuel Luth. Ch., Pasadena, Calif., 1969-73; exec. dir. world missions Ch. Luth. Brethren Am., Fergus Falls, Minn., 1973-86, pres., 1986—; Editor Faith and Fellowship, 1967-75. Home: 806 W Channing Ave Fergus Falls MN 56537-3221 Office: Ch Luth Brethren Am PO Box 655 Fergus Falls MN 56538-0655

OVERGAARD, WILLARD MICHELE, retired political scientist, jurisprudent; b. Montpelier, Idaho, Oct. 16, 1925; s. Elias Nielsen and Myrtle LaVerne (Humphrey) O.; m. Lucia Clare Cochrane, June 14, 1946; children: Eric Willard, Mark Fredrik, Alisa Claire. B.A., U. Oreg., 1949; Fulbright scholar, U. Oslo, 1949-50; M.A. (non-resident scholar 1954-55), U. Wis., Madison, 1955; Ph.D. in Polit. Sci. (adminstrv. fellow 1955-56, research fellow 1962-64), U. Minn., 1969. Instr., Soviet and internat. affairs Intelligence Sch., U.S. Army, Europe, 1956-62; dir. intelligence rsch. tng. program Intelligence Sch., U.S. Army, 1958-61; asst. prof. internat. affairs George Washington U., 1964-67; sr. staff polit. scientist Ops. Research Inst., U.S. Army Inst. Advanced Studies, Carlisle, Pa., 1967-70; assoc. prof. polit. sci., chmn. dept., dir. Internat. Studies Inst., Westminster Coll., New Wilmington, Pa., 1970-72; prof. polit. sci. and pub. law Boise (Idaho) State U., 1972-94, chmn. dept., 1972-87, acad. dir. M.P.A. degree program, personnel adminstr., mem. humanities council interdisciplinary studies in humanities, 1976-87, prof. of pub. law emeritus, 1994—, dir. Taft Inst. Seminars for Pub. Sch. Tchrs., 1985-87, coord. Legal Asst. Program, 1990-95; mem. comml. panel Am. Arbitration Assn., 1974—; mem. Consortium for Idaho's Future, 1974-75; adv. com. Idaho Statewide Tng. Program Local Govt. Ofcls., 1974-78; adv. group Gov. Idaho Task Force Local Govt., 1977; co-dir. Idaho State Exec. Inst., Office of Gov., 1979-83; grievance hearing officer City of Boise, 1981-85; arbitrator U.S. Postal Svc., 1988-90; cons. in field. Author: The Schematic System of Soviet Totalitarianism, 3 vols, 1961, Legal Norms and Normative Bases for the Progressive Development of International Law as Defined in Soviet Treaty Relations, 1945-64, 1969; co-author: The Communist Bloc in Europe, 1959; editor: Continuity and Change in International Politics, 1972; chief editor: Idaho Jour. Politics, 1974-76. Served with USAAF, 1943-45; with AUS, 1951-54; ret. maj. USAR. Named Disting. Citizen of Idaho Idaho Statesman, 1979; named Outstanding Prof. of Sch. Social Scis. and Pub. Affairs, Boise State U., 1988. Mem. ABA (assoc.), Res. Officers Assn. (life). Home: 2023 S Five Mile Rd Boise ID 83709-2316

OVERHAUSER, ALBERT WARNER, physicist; b. San Diego, Aug. 17, 1925; s. Clarence Albert and Gertrude Irene (Pehrson) O.; m. Margaret Mary Casey, Aug. 25, 1951; children—Teresa, Catherine, Joan, Paul, John, David, Susan, Steven. A.B., U. Calif. at Berkeley, 1948, Ph.D., 1951; D.Sc. (hon.), U. Chgo., 1979. Research asso. U. Ill., 1951-53; asst. prof. physics Cornell U., 1953-56, asso. prof., 1956-58; supr. solid state physics Ford Motor Co., Dearborn, Mich., 1958-62; mgr. theoret. scis. Ford Motor Co., 1962-69, asst. dir. phys. scis., 1969-72, dir. phys. scis., 1972-73; prof. physics Purdue U., West Lafayette, Ind., 1973-74; Stuart disting. prof. physics Purdue U., 1974—. With USNR, 1944-46. Recipient Alexander von Humboldt sr. U.S. scientist award, 1979, Nat. Medal of Sci., Pres. of U.S., 1994. Fellow Am. Phys. Soc. (Oliver E. Buckley Solid State Physics prize 1975), Am. Acad. Arts and Scis.; mem. NAS. Home: 236 Pawnee Dr West Lafayette IN 47906-2115 Office: Purdue U Dept Of Physics West Lafayette IN 47907

OVERHOLT, HUGH ROBERT, lawyer, retired army officer; b. Beebe, Ark., Oct. 29, 1933; s. Harold R. and Cuma E. (Hall) O.; m. Laura Annell Arnold, May 5, 1961; children: Sharon, Scott. Student, Coll. of Ozarks, 1951-53; B.A., U. Ark., 1955, LL.B., 1957. Bar: Ark. 1957. Commd. 1st lt. U.S. Army, 1957, advanced through grades to maj. gen., 1981; chief Criminal Law Div., JAG Sch., Charlottesville, Va., 1971-73; chief personnel, plans and tng. Office of JAG, U.S. Army, Washington, 1973-75; staff judge adv. XVIII Airborne Corps, Ft. Bragg, N.C., 1976-78; spl. asst. for legal and selected policy matters Office of Dep. Asst., 1978-79; asst. judge adv. gen. for mil. law Office of JAG, Washington, 1979-81; asst. judge adv. gen. Office of JAG, 1981-85, judge adv. gen., 1985-89; atty. Ward & Smith, New Bern, N.C., 1989—. Notes and comment editor Ark. Law Rev, 1956-57. Decorated Army Meritorious Service medal with oak leaf cluster, Army Commendation medal with 2 oak leaf clusters., Legion of Merit, Def. Meritorious Service medal, D.S.M. Mem. ABA, N.C. Bar Assn., Ark. Bar Assn., Assn. U.S. Army, Delta Theta Phi, Omicron Delta Kappa, Sigma Pi. Presbyterian. Office: Ward and Smith 1001 College Ct New Bern NC 28562-4972

OVERHOLT, MILES HARVARD, cable television consultant; b. Glendale, Calif., Sept. 30, 1921; s. Miles Harvard and Alma Overholt; A.B., Harvard Coll., 1943; m. Jessie Foster, Sept. 18, 1947; children: Miles Harvard, Keith Foster. Mktg. analyst Dun & Bradstreet, Phila., 1947-48; collection mgr. Standard Oil of Calif., L.A., 1948-53; br. mgr. RCA Svc. Co., Phila., 1953-63, ops. mgr. Classified Aerospace project RCA, Riverton, N.J., 1963; pres. CPS, Inc., Paoli, Pa., 1964-67; v.p. Gen. Time Corp.; mem. pres.'s exec. com. Gen. Time Corp., Mesa, Ariz., 1970-78; gen. mgr., dir. svc. Talley Industries, Mesa, 1967-78; v.p., gen. mgr. Northwest Entertainment Network, Inc., Seattle, 1979-81; v.p., dir. Cable Communication Cons., 1982—; mcpl. cable cons., 1981—; pub. The Mcpl. Cable Regulator. Served with USMCR, 1943-46. Decorated Bronze Star, Purple Heart (two). Mem. Nat. Assn. TV Officers and Advisors. Home: 8320 Frederick Pl Edmonds WA 98026-5033 Office: Cable Communication Cons 502 E Main St Auburn WA 98002-5502

OVERHOLT, MILES HARVARD, III, management consultant, family therapist; b. L.A., July 7, 1948; s. Miles Harvard and Jessie Louise (Foster) O.; m. Deborah Jean Robinson, Nov. 22, 1970; 1 child, Rebecca Robinson. BA, Lafayette Coll., 1970; MSW, U. Pa., 1976, D in Social Work, 1979. Cert. social worker; lic. marriage and family therapist, N.J.; cert. mgmt. cons.; cert. clin. hypnotherapist. Youth dir. Camden County YMCA, Haddonfield, N.J., 1970-71; dir. multi-service ctr. Community YMCA, Red Bank, N.J., 1972-74; indsl. cons. NE Community Mental Health/Mental Retardation, Phila., 1977; therapist Marriage and Family Therapy Assns., Wilingboro, Marlton, N.J., 1976-82; mgmt. cons., owner Ambler and Overholt Cons., Inc., Cherry Hill, N.J., 1979-85; therapist, ptnr. Affiliated Counseling and Therapy Assocs., Moorestown, N.J., 1982—; owner, cons. Applied Orgnl. Devel., Inc., Palmyra, N.J., 1985-90; instr. Burlington County Coll., Willingboro, 1978-80; mem. co-adj. faculty Rutgers U., 1978-80; prin. Riverton Mgmt. Cons. Group (formerly Comm. Link Co.), 1990—. Author: Building Flexible Organizations: A People Centered Approach, 1996; contbr. articles to profl. jours. Mem. Phila. Human Resource Planning Group Bd., 1996—. Mott scholar YMCA, 1974-75. Mem. NASW, Inst. Mgmt. Cons. (bd. dirs. Phila. chpt. 1987, nat. bd. dirs. 1988-91), Assn. Mgmt. Cons. (bd. dirs. 1985—, nat. conf. chmn. 1985, regional v.p. 1986-88, pres. 1988-90), Am. Assn. Marriage and Family Therapy (editor N.J. newsletter 1989), Coun. Cons. Orgns. (bd. dirs. 1989-93, sec., officer 1991-93), APICS (mem. nat. planning com. 1996—). Avocations: running, model trains. Office: Riverton Mgmt Cons Group 303 E Broad St Palmyra NJ 08065-1607

OVERMAN, DEAN LEE, lawyer, investor, author; b. Cook County, Ill., Oct. 9, 1943; s. Harold Levon and Violet Elsa (True) O.; m. Linda Jane Olsen, Sept. 6, 1969; children: Elisabeth True, Christiana Hart. BA, Hope Coll., 1965; student, Princeton Sem. and U., 1965-66; JD, U. Calif., Berkeley, 1969; postgrad. in bus., U. Chgo., 1974, U. Calif. Bar: Ill. 1969, D.C. 1977. Assoc. to ptnr. D'Ancona, Pflaum et al., Chgo., 1970-75; White House fellow, asst. to v.p. Nelson Rockefeller, Washington, 1975-76; assoc. dir. Domestic Council The White House, Washington, 1976-77; sr. ptnr. Winston & Strawn, Washington, 1977—; cons. White House; spl. counsel to Gov. James Thompson, Springfield, Ill.; adj. faculty in secured financing U. Va. Law Sch., Charlottesville; vice chmn. J.F. Forstmann Co.; chmn. Holland Investment Co.; adj. fellow Ctr. for Strategic and Internat. Studies, 1993-95; vis. scholar, officer Harvard U., 1994-95. Author: Toward a National Policy on State and Local Government Finance, 1976, Effective Writing Techniques, 1980, (with others) Financing Equipment, 1973, Sales and Financing Under the Revised UCC, 1975; monthly newspaper column Chgo. Daily Law Bull.; contbr. articles to profl. jours. Commencement spkr. Hope Coll., Holland, Mich., 1978; bd. dirs. Internat. Bus. Inst., White House Fellows Assn., Cmtys. in Schs., Inc.; adv. bd. The Beacon Group; former bd. dirs. U.S. Decathlon Assn. Reginald Heber Smith fellow U. Pa., 1969-70. Mme. Mensa, Intertel, ABA, Ill. Bar Assn., D.C. Bar Assn., Chgo. Bar Assn., Met. Club (D.C.), Internat. Philos. Enquiry, Triple Nine Soc., Burning Tree Club (Bethesda, Md.), Congl. Country Club (Bethesda), Harvard Club of N.Y.C., Macatawa (Mich.) Bay Yacht Club. Office: Winston & Strawn 1400 L St NW Washington DC 20005-3509

OVERMAN, DENNIS ORTON, anatomist, educator; b. Union City, Ind., Oct. 16, 1943; s. E. Orton and Marjorie J. (Mills) O.; m. Sue A. Sappenfield, June 4, 1966; children: Andrew D., Michael M., Amy S. BA, Bowling Green State U., 1965; MS, U. Mich., 1967, PhD, 1970. Tchr. Community Sch., Tehran, Iran, 1967-68; rsch. assoc. U. Colo., Boulder, 1970-71; from instr. to asst. prof. dept. anatomy W.Va. U., Morgantown, 1971-76; assoc. prof. U. W. Va., Morgantown, 1976—; vis. lectr. U. B.C., Vancouver, Can., 1979; vis. rschr. U. Turku, Finland, 1993, 96; clin. assoc. prof. dept. orthodontics, W.Va. U., Morgantown, 1985—. Author: (book chpt.) Bioethics and the Beginning of Life, 1990; editor: English transl. of Japanese textbook; mem. abstract com. Cleft Palate Jour., 1976—; contbr. articles to profl. jours. Mem. Soc. for Devel. Biology, Teratology Soc., Toastmasters Internat. (pres.). Democrat. Mem. Mennonite Ch. Avocations: woodcarving, pottery. Home: 461 Overhill St Morgantown WV 26505-4824 Office: U W Va Dept Anatomy Morgantown WV 26506

OVERMAN, GLENN DELBERT, college dean emeritus; b. Camden, Ark., Apr. 23, 1916; s. George D. and Mattie D. (Scott) O.; m. Roberta Marie Thomas, May 20, 1939; children—Priscilla Ann, George Dan. B.S., Central State U., Edmond, Okla., 1937; M.S., Okla. State U., 1946; D.B.A., Ind. U., 1954. Cert. for labor arbitration Fed. Mediation and Conciliation Service, also Am. Arbitration Assn. Tchr. bus. high sch. Fairfax, Okla., 1937-39; Okla. rep. South-Western Publishing Co., 1939-42; dir. Sch. Intensive Bus. Tng., Okla. State U. Coll. Bus., 1946-50; dean Oklahoma City U. Sch. Bus., 1952-56; dean Ariz. State U. Coll. Bus. Adminstrn., 1956-85, dean emeritus, 1985—; hon. prof. Autonomous U. Guadalajara, Mex., 1990—; mem. Dept. Navy, Naval Audit Svc. U.S.A., 1972-75. Author: Economics Concepts Everyone Should Know, 1956. Mem. law adv. bd. S.W. Found. Med. Rsch. and Edn.; mem. U.S. Office Edn. Appeal Bd., 1985-88. Served to lt. (s.g.), Supply Corps USNR, 1942-46. Mem. Soc. Advancement Mgmt., Financial Execs. Inst., Systems and Procedures Assn. Am., Am. Marketing Assn., Newcomen Soc. Am., Red Red Rose, Am. Right of Way Assn., Beta Gamma Sigma, Delta Sigma Pi, Pi Sigma Epsilon, Lambda Chi Alpha, Phi Kappa Phi, Delta Pi Epsilon, Phi Delta Kappa, Alpha Phi Sigma, Kappa Delta Pi, Delta Nu Alpha. Methodist. Home: 512 E Fairmont Dr Tempe AZ 85282-3723

OVERMAN, LARRY EUGENE, chemistry educator; b. Chgo., Mar. 9, 1943; s. Lemoine Emerson and Dorothy Jane Overman; m. Joanne Louise Dewey, June 5, 1966; children: Michael, Jackie. BA in Chemistry, Earlham Coll., 1965; PhD in Organic Chemistry, U. Wis., 1969. Asst. prof. chemistry U. Calif., Irvine, 1971-76, assoc. prof. chemistry, 1976-79, prof. chemistry, 1979—, chair dept. chemistry, 1990-93, disting. prof. chemistry, 1994—; mem. sci. adv. bd. Pharmacopeia, Inc., 1993—. Bd. editors Organic Reactions, 1984—, Organic Syntheses, 1986-94; mem. editl. adv. bd. Ann. Reports in Hetero Chem., 1989—, Synlett, 1989—, Jour. Am. Chem. Soc., 1996—, Chem. Revs., 1996—, Accounts Chem. Rsch., 1996—; mem. cons. editors Tetrahedron Publs., 1995—. NIH fellow, 1969-71, A.P. Sloan Found. fellow, 1975-77; Arthur C. Cope scholar, 1989; Guggenheim fellow, 1993-94; recipient Sr. Scientist award Alexander von Humboldt Found., 1985-87, Jacob Javits award Nat. Inst. Neurol. Sci., 1985-91, 92—. Fellow NAS, Am. Acad. Arts and Scis.; mem. Am. Chem. Soc. (exec. com. organic divsn., Cope Scholar award 1989, Creative Work in Synthetic Organic Chemistry award 1995), Royal Soc. Chemistry. Achievements include research in new methods for organic synthesis, natural products synthesis, medicinal chemistry. Office: U Calif Irvine Dept Chemistry 516 Physical Scis 1 Irvine CA 92697-2025

OVERMYER, DANIEL LEE, Asian studies educator; b. Columbus, Ohio, Aug. 20, 1935; s. Elmer Earl and Bernice Alma (Hesselbart) O.; m. Estella Velazquez, June 19, 1965; children—Rebecca Lynn, Mark Edward. B.A., Westmar Coll., LeMars, Iowa, 1957; B.D., Evang. Theol. Sem., Naperville, Ill., 1960; M.A., U. Chgo., 1966, Ph.D., 1971. Pastor Evangel. United Brethren Ch., Chgo., 1960-64; asst. prof. dept. religion Oberlin Coll., Ohio, 1970-73; prof. Asian studies U. B.C., Vancouver, Can., 1973—, acting head religious studies, 1984-85, head Asian studies, 1986-91; vis. prof. U. Heidelberg, 1993; prof. Chinese U. Hong Kong, 1996—. Author: Folk Buddhist Religion, 1976; Religions of China, 1986; (with David Jordan) The Flying Phoenix, 1986. Contbr. articles to encys. and profl. jours. Chmn. Sch. Consultative Com., Vancouver, 1976-77; coord. Vancouver Boys Soccer League, 1979-81; adult edn. coord. United Ch. Can., Vancouver, 1981-84; co-chmn. Endowment Lands Regional Park Com., 1987-90; co-chair China and Inner Asia Coun., Assn. Asian Studies, 1992—. With USNR, 1953-61. Recipient Killam faculty rsch. prize U. B.C., 1986; NEH fellow, 1978, 79, China Rsch. fellow, 1981, sr. fellow coun. humanities Princeton U., 1983, Wang Inst. Grad. Studies fellow, 1985-86. Fellow Royal Soc. Can.; mem. Am. Soc. Study Religion, Soc. Study Chinese Religions (pres. 1985-88), Assn. Asian Studies, Can. Asian Studies Assn. Democrat. Methodist. Avocations: photography, swimming, hiking, gardening. Home: 3393 W 26th Ave V, Vancouver, BC Canada V6S 1N4 Office: U BC, Dept Asian Studies, Vancouver, BC Canada V6T 1Z2

OVERSETH, OLIVER ENOCH, physicist, educator; b. N.Y.C., May 11, 1928; s. Oliver Enoch and Ione (Johnson) O.; m. Anneke deBruyn, Aug. 28, 1954 (divorced); children—Alison, Tenley. B.S., U. Chgo., 1953; Ph.D., Brown U., 1958. Instr. physics Princeton, 1957-60; mem. faculty U. Mich., Ann Arbor, 1961—; prof. physics U. Mich., 1968—; assoc. physicist Cern, Geneva, 1983—. Office: Cern PPE Div, CH-1211 Geneva Switzerland

OVERSTREET, HON. KAREN A., federal bankruptcy judge. BA cum laude, Univ. of Wash., 1977; JD, Univ. of Oregon, 1982. Assoc. Duane, Morris & Heckscher, Phila., 1983-86; ptnr. Davis Wright Tremaine, Seattle, 1986-93; bankruptcy judge U.S. Bankruptcy Ct. (we. dist.) Wash., Seattle, 1994—; assoc. editor Oregon Law Review; dir. People's Law Sch.; mem. advisory com. U.S. Bankruptcy Ct. (we. dist.) Wash. Mem. Nat. Conf. of Bankruptcy Judges, Wash. State Bar Assn. (creditor-debtor sec.), Seattle-King County Bar Assn. (bankruptcy sec.), Am. Bar Assn., Wash. Women Lawyers Assn. Office: US Bankruptcy Ct Park Place Bldg 1200 6th Ave Ste 424 Seattle WA 98101*

OVERSTREET, JIM, public relations executive; b. Savannah, Ga., Dec. 11, 1947. Reporter Atlanta Constitution, 1967-69; asst. sports editor Marietta Daily Jour., 1969-73; mktg. dir. Lake Lanier Islands Resorts, 1973-77; gen. mgr. Harlequin Theatre, 1977-78; acct. exec. Cohn & Wolfe, 1978-80, acct. supr., 1980-83, dir. acct. svc., 1983-84, exec. v.p., gen. mgr., 1984-92, vice chmn., gen. mgr., 1993—. Office: Cohn & Wolfe 225 Peachtree St NE Atlanta GA 30303-1701*

OVERTON, BENJAMIN FREDERICK, state supreme court justice; b. Green Bay, Wis., Dec. 15, 1926; s. Benjamin H. and Esther M. (Wiese) O.; m. Marilyn Louise Smith, June 9, 1951; children: William Hunter, Robert Murray, Catherine Louise. B.S. in Bus. Adminstrn., U. Fla., 1951, J.D., 1952; LL.D. (hon.), Stetson U., 1975, Nova U., 1977; LL.M., U. Va., 1984. Bar: Fla. 1952. With Office Fla. Atty. Gen., 1952; with firms in St. Petersburg, Fla., 1952-64; city atty. St. Petersburg Beach, Fla., 1954-57; circuit judge 6th Jud. Circuit Fla., 1964-74, chief judge, 1968-71; chmn. Fla. Conf. Circuit Judges, 1973; justice Supreme Ct. Fla., Tallahassee, 1974—; chief justice Supreme Ct. Fla., 1976-78; past adj. faculty Stetson U. Coll. Law and Fla. St. U. Coll. Law; bd. dirs. Nat. Jud. Coll., 1976-87; mem. Fla. Car Continuing Legal Edn. Com., 1963-74, chmn., 1971-74; 1st chmn. Fla. Inst. Judiciary, 1972; mem. exec. com. Appellate Judges Conf.; chmn. Appellate Structure Commn., 1978-79, Article Rev. Commn., 1983-84, Matrimonial Law Commn., 1982-85; chmn. Jud. Coun. Fla., 1985-89.; chmn. adv. com. for LLM program for appellate judges U. Va., 1985-94. Contbr. legal publs. Past reader, vestryman, sr. warden St. Albans Episcopal Ch., St. Petersburg; chmn. U.S. Constn. Bicentennial Commn. Fla. 1987-91; ch. Family Ct. Commn., 1990-91; ch. Death Case Postconviction Relief Proceeding 1990-91. Fellow Am. Bar Found.; mem. ABA (chmn. criminal justice task force to rev. trial and discovery standards 1991—), Fla. Bar Assn., Am. Judicature Soc. (dir., sec.). Democrat. Lodge: Rotary. Office: Fla Supreme Ct 500 S Duval St Tallahassee FL 32399-6556*

OVERTON, BRUCE, personnel executive, consultant; b. Caldwell, N.J., June 27, 1941; s. E.F. and V.B. Overton; m. Charlene Gayle Overton; children: Julie, Diane, Sharon. BS, Widener U., 1963. Personnel mgr. Xerox Corp., Rochester, N.Y., 1965-71; prin. cons. Sibson and Co., Princeton, N.J.,

1971-77; v.p. compensation RJR Nabisco, Inc., Atlanta, 1977-87, v.p. pers., 1987-89; ptnr. Ernst and Young, Atlanta, 1989-90; pres. Overton & Assocs., 1990-93; prnt. HR Mgmt. Inc., 1993—. Author articles on compensation and personnel mgmt., 1979—. Bd. dirs. Cobb County YMCA; bd. trustees Kennesaw Coll. Served to 1st lt. U.S. Army, 1963-65. Mem. Am. Compensation Assn. (chmn. bd. 1986-87). Republican. Presbyterian. Avocation: boating. Office: 3901 Roswell Rd Ste 330 Marietta GA 30062-6277

OVERTON, GEORGE WASHINGTON, lawyer; b. Hinsdale, Ill., Jan. 25, 1918; s. George Washington and Florence Mary (Darlington) O.; m. Jane Vincent Harper, Sept. 1, 1941; children—Samuel Harper, Peter Darlington, Ann Vincent. A.B., Harvard U., 1940; J.D., U. Chgo., 1946. Bar: Ill. 1947, U.S. Dist. Ct. (no. dist.) Ill. 1947, U.S. Supreme Ct. 1951. Assoc. Pope & Ballard, Chgo., 1946-48; ptnr. Overton & Babcock, Chgo., 1948-51, Taylor, Miller, Busch & Magner, Chgo., 1951-60; pvt. practice Chgo., 1960; sr. prin. Overton, Schwartz & Fritts and predecessor cos., Chgo., 1961-81; of counsel Wildman Harrold Allen & Dixon, Chgo., 1981—; bd. dirs. Ill. Inst. Continuing Legal Edn., 1974-81, chmn. 1980-81; mem. com. on profl. responsibility of Ill. Supreme Ct., 1986—, chmn., 1990-93. Contbr. articles to profl. jours. Bd. dirs. Open Lands Project, 1961—, pres., 1978-81; bd. dirs. Canal Corridor Assn., 1981—, chmn., 1981-84. 1st lt. U.S. Army, 1942-45. Mem. ABA (mem. com. on counsel responsibility 1985—, com. on nonprofit corps.), Ill. Bar Assn., Chgo. Bar Assn. (bd. mgrs. 1981-83), Assn. of Bar of City of N.Y., Am. Law Inst., Univ. Club. Office: Wildman Harrold Allen & Dixon 225 W Wacker Dr Chicago IL 60606-1224

OVERTON, JANE VINCENT HARPER, biology educator; b. Chgo., Jan. 17, 1919; d. Paul Vincent and Isabel (Vincent) Harper; m. George W. Overton, Jr., Sept. 1, 1941; children: Samuel, Peter, Ann. AB, Bryn Mawr Coll., 1941; PhD, U. Chgo., 1950. Rsch. asst. U. Chgo., 1950-52, mem. faculty, 1952-89, prof. biology, 1972-89; prof. emeritus, 1989. Author articles embryology, cell biology. NIH, NSF research grantee, 1965-87. Home: 1700 E 56th St Apt 2901 Chicago IL 60637-1935 Office: U Chgo 1103 E 57th St Chicago IL 60637-1503

OVERTON, MARCUS LEE, performing arts administrator, actor, writer; b. Calhoun, Ga., Aug. 13, 1943; s. Marcus Burl Jr. and Eva Mae (Greene) O. BS in Speech and Theatre, Northwestern U., 1965. Actor, tchr. Southeastern Shakespeare Festival, Atlanta, summer 1965; actor, co. mgr. Eagles Mere Assocs. Repertory Co., Chgo., 1966; prodn. stage mgr. Lyric Opera of Chgo., 1966-72; mgr. Ravinia Festival, Highland Park, Ill., 1973-77; performing arts program mgr. Smithsonian Instn., Washington, 1983-92; exec. dir., prod. dir. Spoleto Festival U.S.A., Charleston, S.C., 1992-94; program prodr., host Who Do You Know S.C. Pub. Radio, Charleston, 1994—; instr. in theatre and arts mgmt. Coll. Charleston, 1995—; narrator talking books Libr. Congress, Washington, 1982-83; adv. panelist Nat. Endowment for Arts, 1977-79, D.C. Commn. on Arts and Humanities, 1989, 90, 92; bd. dirs. Nat. Cultural Resources, 1989-90, Performing Arts Assistance Corp., 1992—; cons. in field. Prodr. Falstaff (L.A. Philharm.), 1981-82. Northwestern U. scholar, 1961-65. Avocations: travel, prehistoric cave art, motorcycle touring, linguistics, French culture. Office: 210 Little Oak Island Dr Folly Beach SC 29439-1486

OVERTON, SANTFORD VANCE, applications chemist; b. Rocky Mount, N.C., Sept. 15, 1949; s. Levy Lemuel and Irma Mae (Jenkins) O.; m. Joan Ann Lasota, Nov. 28, 1987. MS in Biology, East Carolina U., 1979; PhD in Plant Pathology, Va. Poly. Inst. and State U., 1986. Staff scientist Organogenesis, Inc., Cambridge, Mass., 1986-88; cons. Agri-Diagnostics Assocs., Cinnaminson, N.J., 1988-89; product mgr. Sci. Instrument Svcs., Ringoes, N.J., 1989—; adj. prof. dept. plant pathology, physiology and weed sci. Va. Poly. Inst. and State U., Blacksburg, 1994—. Contbr. articles to profl. publs. Mem. Am. Chem. Soc., Am. Soc. Mass Spectrometry, Am. Phytopathol. Soc., Sigma Xi, Gamma Sigma Delta, Phi Kappa Phi, Alpha Epsilon Delta. Achievements include patent for short-path thermal desorption apparatus for use in gas chromatography techniques, patent for injection assembly for transferring a component to be tested. Home: 8 Country Club Dr Ringoes NJ 08551-1901 Office: Sci Instrument Svcs 1027 Old York Rd Ringoes NJ 08551-1039

OVERTON, SARITA ROSA, psychologist; b. South Haven, Mich., June 7, 1954; d. Samuel Edward and Rosa Jane (McGuire) O. BA in Psychology with honors, Mich. State U., 1976, MA in Rehab. Counseling, 1978, MA in Counseling Psychology, 1987, PhD in Counseling Psychology, 1988. Lic. psychologist, Mich. Dir. Job Club, Capital Area Community Svcs., Lansing, Mich., 1978-84; instr. rehab. counseling master's program Mich. State U., East Lansing, 1981-82, program teaching asst., 1985-87, coord. career assistance project, 1984, 84-85, clin. trainee Counseling Ctr., 1986, rsch. asst. disability mgmt. project, 1985-87; clin. trainee St. Lawrence Hosp., Lansing, 1986-87, psychologist Psychol. Svcs. and Addictions Clinic, 1987-91; psychologist Comprehensive Psychol. Svcs., P.C., East Lansing, 1990-95; pvt. practice psychologist Meridian Health and Wellness Ctr., East Lansing, 1995—; conf. and clin. presenter in field. Contbr. articles to profl. publs. Recipient Presdl. recognition award Mich. Rehab. Assn., 1986; grantee Nat. Inst. Handicapped Rsch., 1985; dissertation rsch. fellow Mich. State U., 1985. Mem. APA. Democrat. Avocations: reading, aquarist, yoga, meditation, imagery, Tai Chi Chuan. Office: Meridian Health and Wellness 139 W Lake Lansing Rd Ste 200 East Lansing MI 48823-1433

OVERTON, STANLEY DIXON, banking executive; b. Dickson, Tenn., May 2, 1928; s. Dallas Stanley and Ova (Dixon) O.; m. Carolyn Ruane, Feb. 14, 1976; children—Stanley D. Jr., James Stanton; 1 stepchild, Cecelia Halter. Student Fall's Bus. Coll., Nashville, 1948-49; Acctg. degree Internat. Accts. Soc., 1952; student Savs. & Loan Grad. Sch. Ind. U., 1961-63. With Fidelity Fed. Bank, FSB, Nashville, 1950-92, exec. v.p., 1963-67, pres., 1967-74, chmn., pres., 1974-84, chmn., chief exec. officer, 1984-92; chmn., chief exec. officer, Union Planters Bank of Middle Tenn., 1992-94, chmn., 1994—, also bd. dirs. Union Planters Corp.; past bd. dirs. Fed. Home Loan Bank Bd., Cin. United Way, Nashville; bd. dirs. YMCA, Nashville, Fellowship of Christian Athletes, Nashville. Served with USNR, 1946-48. Mem. C. of C. (past bd. govs.), Tenn. League Savs. Assns. (pres. 1969-70), U.S. League Savs. Assns., Am. Savs. and Loan Inst. (past pres.), Found. for Savs. Instns. (trustee). Clubs: Hillwood Country,Nashville City. Lodges: Masons, Shriners, Kiwanis. Home: 7 Warwick Ln Nashville TN 37205-5012 Office: Union Planters Bank of Middle Tenn 401 Union St Nashville TN 37219-1708

OVERWEG, NORBERT IDO ALBERT, physician; b. Enschede, The Netherlands; s. Ido and Bella Theresa (Lievenboom) O.; MD, U. Amsterdam, 1957; m. Angelique de Gorter; children: Eleonore, Elizabeth, Harold. Intern, Univ. Amsterdam Hosp., 1958-60; resident Rochester (N.Y.) Gen. Hosp., 1961-62; postdoctoral fellow dept. pharmacology Columbia U. Coll. Physicians and Surgeons, 1962-65; instr. dept. public health Columbia U., 1965-66; rsch. assoc. dept. surgery Columbia U., 1967-71; rsch. collaborator, asst. attending physician Brookhaven Nat. Lab., 1966-67; asst. prof. dept. physiology and pharmacology N.Y. U., 1971-78; cons. Lung Rsch. Ctr., Yale U. Sch. Medicine, 1972-73; pvt. practice medicine specializing in internal medicine, N.Y.C., 1967—; attending staff St. Clare's Hosp. and Health Center, Cabrini Med. Ctr.; clin. investigator antihypertension, anti-depressant, anti-anxiety, Alzheimer's Disease, migraine headache, panick attack, and gastro-intestinal drugs. NIH fellow, 1964-65. Mem. Am. Soc. Pharmcology and Exptl. Therapeutics, Am. Physiol. Soc., Am. Soc. Hypertension, Am. Coll. Clin. Pharmacology, N.Y. Acad. Scis., AAAS, AAUP, Royal Dutch Soc. Advancement of Medicine, Harvey Soc., Netherlands Am. Med. Soc., Eastern Hypertension Soc., N.Y. County Med. Soc., Med. Soc. of N.Y., Sigma Xi. Club: Netherlands of N.Y., Inc. Contbr. articles to profl. jour. Office: 133 E 73rd St New York NY 10021-3556

OVESON, W(ILFORD) VAL, state official, accountant; b. Provo, Utah, Feb. 11, 1952; s. Wilford W. and LaVon Oveson; m. Emilee Nebeker, Sept. 1, 1973; children: Polly, Libby, Peter, Benjamin. Student, U. Utah, 1973-74; BS in Acctg., Brigham Young U., 1976. CPA, Utah. Acct. Squire and Co., Orem, Utah, 1975-79; pvt. practice acctg. Squire and Co., Orem, 1979-80; state auditor State of Utah, Salt Lake City, 1981-84, lt. gov., 1985-93; sr. mgr. KPMG Peat Marwick, 1993; chmn. Utah Tax Commn., Salt Lake City, 1993—; mem. dist. export coun. U.S. Dept. Commerce, 1985—, mem. bd. examiners, State of Utah, 1981-84; chmn. State Records Com., 1981-84. Bd. dirs., unit campaign dir. United Way of Greater Salt Lake, 1985-86; trustee Travis Found., 1985-88; treas. Utah County Rep. Party; mem. State Platform Com., 1982, 84; mem. exec. com. Utah State Rep. Party, 1981—. Mem. AICPA (mem. governing coun. 1986), Utah Assn. CPAs (Pub. Svc. award 1984). Republican. Mem. LDS Ch. Avocations: skiing, personal finance, computers, house plants, fishing. Home: 2125 S 900 E Bountiful UT 84010-3105*

OVITSKY, STEVEN ALAN, musician, symphony orchestra executive; b. Chgo., Oct. 12, 1947; s. Martin N. and Ruth (Katz) O.; m. Camille Levy; 1 child, David Isaac. MusB, U. Mich., 1968; MusM, No. Ill. U., 1975. Fine arts dir. Sta. WNIU-FM Pub. Radio, Dekalb, Ill., 1972-76; program mgr. Sta. WMHT-FM Pub. Radio, Schenectady, N.Y., 1976-79; gen. mgr., artistic dir. Grant Park Concerts, Chgo., 1979-90; v.p., gen. mgr. Minn. Orch., Mpls., 1990-95; v.p., exec. dir. Milw. Symphony Orch., 1995—; panelist Ill. Arts Coun., 1986, 87, 88, Chgo. Artists Abroad, 1987-91, Nat. Endowment for the Arts, 1987-89; bd. dirs. Ill. Arts Alliance, Chamber Music Chgo.; hon. dir. Chgo. Sinfonietta. With U.S. Army, 1968-71, Korea. Mem. NARAS, Am. Symphony Orch. League. Jewish. Avocations: audio, record collecting, softball. Office: Milw Symphony 330 E Kilbourn Ave Ste 900 Milwaukee WI 53202-3141

OVITZ, MICHAEL S., communications executive; b. 1946; m. Judy Reich, 1969; 3 children. Grad., UCLA, 1968. With William Morris Agy., 1968-75; co-founder, chmn. Creative Artists Agy., L.A., 1975-95; pres. Walt Disney Co., Burbank, Calif., 1995-97; mem. bd. advisors Med. Sch. UCLA, bd. dirs. Sch. Theatre, Film and TV. Trustee St. John's Hosp. and Health Ctr., Santa Monica, Calif., Mus. Modern Art, N.Y.C.; bd. govs. Cedars-Sinai Hosp., L.A.; mem. exec. adv. bd. Pediatric AIDS Found.; bd. dirs. Calif. Inst. Arts, Sundance Inst. Mem. Zeta Beta Tau. Avocations: contemporary art, African antiques, Chinese furniture. Office: Dreyer Edmonds & Assocs 355 S Grand Ave Ste 4150 Los Angeles CA 90071-3103*

OVSHINSKY, STANFORD ROBERT, physicist, inventor, energy and information company executive; b. Akron, Ohio, Nov. 24, 1922; s. Benjamin and Bertha T. (Munitz) O.; m. Iris L. Miroy, Nov. 24, 1959; children—Benjamin, Harvey, Dale, Robin Dibner, Steven Dibner. Student public schs., Akron; DSc (hon.), Lawrence Inst. Tech., 1980; DEng (hon.), Bowling Green State U., 1981; DSc (hon.), Jordan Coll., Cedar Springs, Mich., 1989. Pres. Stanford Roberts Mfg. Co., Akron, 1946-50; mgr. centre drive dept. New Britain Machine Co., Conn., 1950-52; dir. research Hupp Corp., Detroit, 1952-55; pres. Gen. Automation, Inc., Detroit, 1955-58, Ovitron Corp., Detroit, 1958-59; pres., chmn. bd. Energy Conversion Devices, Inc., Troy, Mich., 1960-78; pres., chief exec. officer, chief scientist Energy Conversion Devices, Inc., 1978—; adj. prof. engring. scis. Coll. Engring., Wayne State U.; hon. advisor for sci. and tech. Beijing (China) Inst. Aeronautics and Astronautics (name changed to Beijing U. Aeros. and Astronautics); chmn. Inst. for Amorphous Studies. Contbr. articles on physics of amorphous materials, neurophysiology and neuropsychiatry to profl. jours. Recipient Diesel Gold medal German Inventors Assn., 1968, Coors Am. Ingenuity award, 1988; named to Mich. Chem. Engring. Hall of Fame, 1983, Mich. Scientist of Yr., Impression 5 Sci. Mus., 1987. Fellow AAAS, Am. Phys. Soc.; mem. IEEE (sr.), Soc. Automotive Engrs., N.Y. Acad. Scis., Electrochem. Soc., Engring. Soc. Detroit, Cranbrook Inst. Sci. (bd. govs. 1981). Office: Energy Conversion Devices Inc 1675 W Maple Rd Troy MI 48084-7118

OWEISS, IBRAHIM MOHAMED, economist, educator; b. Egypt, Sept. 25, 1931; came to U.S., 1960; s. Mohamed Zaki and Warda (Zeiden) O.; m. Celine M. J. Lesuisse, July 19, 1975; children: Yasmeen, Kareem. B.Com., Alexandria U., Egypt, 1952; M.A., U. Minn., 1961, Ph.D., 1969. Tchr., 1953-55; econ. dir. indsl. projects Cairo, 1958-60; mem. faculty U. Minn., Mpls., 1961-67; mem. faculty Georgetown U., Washington, 1967—, prof. econs., 1973—; mem. faculty Johns Hopkins U., 1971-74; first undersec. state econ. affairs Govt. Egypt, Cairo, 1977; ambassador, 1977-79; chief Egyptian Econ. Mission to U.S., 1977-79; cons. econs., 1971—. Author: Pricing of Oil in World Trade, 1974, The Israeli Economy, 1974; editor: The Dynamics of U.S.-Arab Economic Relations, 1980, Economic Development of Egypt, 1982, Arab Civilization, Challenges and Responses, 1988, Political Economy of Contemporary Egypt, 1990. Pres. Assn. Egyptian-Am. Scholars, 1984-88; chmn. bd. dirs. Arab-Am. Bus. and Profl. Assn., Howard and Georgeanna Jones Inst. for Reproductive Medicine, 1984-90, Egyptian Am. Cultural Assn., 1975-77, Faith and Hope Project, 1975-77. Officer Egyptian Army, 1955-58. Decorated Egyptian Merit decoration 1st Order, Order of St. John, knight Order of Queen of Sheba, grand cordon Order Mohammed Ali Pasha; Ford Found. fellow, 1979-80. Mem. Am. Econ. Assn. Moslem. Club: University (N.Y.C.). Home: 4017 Glenridge St Kensington MD 20895-3708 Office: Georgetown University Dept Econs Washington DC 20057

OWEN, BRADLEY SCOTT, lieutenant governor; b. Tacoma, May 23, 1950; s. Laural Willis; m. Linda Owen; children: Shanie, Dana, Mark, Sherrie, Adam, Royce. Student pub. sch., Germany. State rep. Wash. Ho. Rep., Olympia, 1976-82; state senator Wash. State Senate, Olympia, 1983-96; lt. gov. State Wash., Olympia, 1997—. Mem. Wash. State substance abuse coun., 1997—. Mem. Elks, Kiwanis. Democrat. Office: Wash State Lt Gov PO Box 40400 Olympia WA 98504-0400

OWEN, CYNTHIA CAROL, sales executive; b. Ft. Worth, Oct. 16, 1943; d. Charlie Bounds and Bernice Vera (Nunley) Rhoads; m. Franklin Earl Owen, Oct. 20, 1961 (div. Jan. 1987); children: Jeffrey Wayne, Valeria Ann, Carol Darlena, Pamela Kay; m. John Edward White, Jan. 1, 1988 (div. Sept. 1991). Cert. Keypuncher, Comml. Coll., 1963; student, Tarrant County Jr. Coll., 1974-77; BBA in Mgmt., U. Tex., Arlington, 1981. Keypunch operator Can-Tex. Industries, Mineral-Wells, 1966-67; sec. Electro-Midland Corp., Mineral-Wells, 1967-68; exec. sec. to v.p. sales Pangburn Co., Inc., Ft. Worth, 1972-78; bookkeeper, sec. CB Svc., Ft. Worth, 1978-82; project mgr. Square D Co., Ft. Worth, 1982—. Mem. NAFE, NOW, AAUW. Baptist. Avocations: miniature golf, volleyball. Home: 816 Lee Dr Bedford TX 76022-7311 Office: Square D Co 860 Airport Fwy Ste 101 Hurst TX 76054-3249

OWEN, DUNCAN SHAW, JR., physician, medical educator; b. Fayetteville, N.C., Oct. 24, 1935; s. Duncan S. and Mary Gwyn (Hickerson) O.; m. Irene Lacy Rose, Oct. 22, 1966; children: Duncan Shaw III, Robert Burwell, Frances Gwyn. BS, U. N.C., 1957, MD, 1960. Diplomate Am. Bd. Internal Medicine (proctor 1977—). Intern Med. Coll. Va., Richmond, 1960-61; jr. asst. resident in medicine N.C. Meml. Hosp., Chapel Hill, 1961-62; asst. resident in medicine Med. Coll. Va., Richmond, 1964-65, fellow in rheumatic diseases, 1965-66; practice medicine specializing in internal medicine and rheumatology Richmond, Va., 1966—; instr. in medicine Med. Coll. Va., Richmond, 1966-67, asst. prof., 1967-71, assoc. prof., 1971-78, prof. dept. internal medicine, 1978—; Taliaferro/Scott Disting. prof. internal medicine Med. Coll. Va., Va. Commonwealth U., 1989—; dir. residency tng. Med. Coll. Va. Hosp.; dir. Rheumatology Clinics; mem. staff McGuire VA; dir. clin. tng. divsn. rheumatology, allergy, immunology, chmn. clin. activities comm., dept. internal mediine; chmn. med. adv. com. Richmond br. Arthritis Found., 1966-75, bd. dirs. 1966—, mem. nat. patient edn. com., 1979-80; med. advisor Social Security Adminstrn., HHS, 1967—; bd. dirs. Blue Shield Va., 1975-77, co-chmn. arthritis project Va. Regional Med. Program, 1975-76; bd. dirs. Univ. Internal Medicine Found., 1979—; prodr. Your Health TV series Va. Ednl. TV, 1978-79; prodr. Update in Medicine, Good Morning Virginia TV show, 1980; mem. various coms. in field. Contbr. numerous papers, chpts. in books, articles to profl. jours.; assoc. editor: Va. Med., 1978—; editorial reviewer Jour. AMA, 1979—, Arthritis Rheumatism, 1981—, Jour. Rheumatology, 1984—. Mem. usher's guild First Presbyn. Ch., Richmond, Va., 1966-70, deacon, 1974-77, chmn. of diaconate, 1976-77, elder, 1978—, chmn. witness com., 1978-80; co-chmn. physicians statewide capital funds campaign Va. Commn. U., 1986-87; bd. dirs. Mooreland Farms Assn., 1971-73, 77-81, Va. chpt. Arthitis Found., 1970-85; mem. Va. Mus., Richmond Symphony; bd. dirs. Richmond Area Health Care Coalition, 1980-84. Served to capt. MC, 1962-64. Recipient Army Commendation medal, 1964. Nat. Inst. Arthritis and Metabolic Diseases fellow, 1965-66; recipient Gerard B. Lambert award, 1974-75, Disting. Service award Arthritis Found., 1971. Fellow ACP (Laureate award 1997), Am. Coll. Rheumatology; mem. AMA (expert on diagnostic and therapeutic tech. assessment program), Am. Rheumatism Assn. (exec. com. 1979-80), Richmond Acad. Medicine (pres. 1982, chmn. bd. 1983, parliamentarian 1988—), Med. Soc. Va. (com. on aging 1980-89, v.p. 1973, 75, del. 1972—, scholarship com. 1980-89), Richmond Soc. Internal Medicine (bd. dirs. 1971-73), Met. Richmond C. of C. (bd. dirs. 1981-94), Jr. Clin. Club (emeritus), Country Club Va., Custis Hunting and Fishing Club, Alpha Omega Alpha. Avocations: hunting, fishing, photography, amateur radio. Home: 8910 Brieryle Rd Richmond VA 23229-7704 Office: Med Coll Va Ambulatory Care Ctr PO Box 980647 Richmond VA 23298-0647

OWEN, H. MARTYN, lawyer; b. Decatur, Ill., Oct. 23, 1929; s. Honore Martyn and Virginia (Hunt) O.; m. Candace Catlin Benjamin, June 21, 1952; children—Leslie W., Peter H., Douglas P. A.B., Princeton U., 1951; LL.B., Harvard U., 1954. Bar: Conn. 1954. Assoc. Shipman & Goodwin, Hartford, Conn., 1958-61, ptnr., 1961-94, of counsel, 1995—. Mem. Simsbury (Conn.) Zoning Bd. Appeals, 1961-67, Simsbury Zoning Commn., 1967-79; sec. Capitol Region Planning Agy., 1965-66; bd. dirs. Symphony Soc. Greater Hartford, 1967-73; trustee Renbrook Sch., West Hartford, Conn., 1963-72, treas., 1964-68, pres., 1968-72, hon. life trustee, 1972—; trustee Simsbury Free Library, 1970-84; pres. Hartford Grammar Sch., 1987—, trustee; corporator Hartford Hosp, 1990-96. Lt. USNR, 1954-57. Mem. ABA, Conn. Bar Assn., Hartford County Bar Assn., Am. Law Inst. Democrat. Episcopalian. Clubs: Princeton (N.Y.C.); Ivy (Princeton, N.J.). Home: 80 Matthew Dr Brunswick ME 04011-3275 Office: One American Row Hartford CT 06103-2819

OWEN, HENRY, former ambassador, consultant; b. N.Y.C., Aug. 26, 1920. A.B., Harvard U., 1941. Economist Dept. State, Washington, 1946-55, mem. policy planning staff, 1955-62, dep. counselor, vice chmn. policy planning coun., 1962-66, chmn. coun., 1966-69; dir. fgn. policy studies Brookings Instn., 1969-77; personal rep. of Pres. U.S. with rank of ambassador to participate in preparations for summit meetings, 1977-81; sr. adviser Salomon Bros., 1981—. Editor: Next Phase of U.S. Foreign Policy, 1971, (with Charles Schultze) Setting National Priorities, 1976. Served to lt. USN, 1942-46. Office: 1616 H St NW Washington DC 20006-4903

OWEN, HOWARD WAYNE, journalist, writer; b. Fayetteville, N.C., Mar. 1, 1949; s. E.F. and Roxie Geddie (Bulla) O.; m. Karen Lane Van Neste, Aug. 18, 1973. BA in Journalism, U. N.C., 1971; MA in English, Va. Commonwealth U., 1981. Sports writer Martinsville (Va.) Bulletin, 1971-73; sports editor Gastonia (N.C.) Gazette, 1973-74, Chapel Hill (N.C.) Newspaper, 1974-77; exec. sports editor Tallahassee Dem., 1977-78; asst. sports editor Richmond (Va.) Times-Dispatch, 1978-83, sports news editor, 1983-92, sports editor, 1992-95, dep. mng. editor, 1995—; founder Scholar/Athlete Awards, Richmond, 1986—. Author: Littlejohn, 1992, Fat Lightning, 1994, Answers to Lucky, 1996, The Measured Man, 1997; contbr.: Books of Passage, 1996. Bd. dirs. U. N.C. Alumni Assn., 1997—. Mem. AP Sports Editors (regional chmn. 1986-87), Va. Writers Club, PEN Am. Ctr., 2300 Club. Democrat. Avocations: travel, reading, cooking, sports, jogging. Home: 12836 Ashtree Rd Midlothian VA 23113-3095 Office: Richmond Newspapers Inc 333 E Grace St Richmond VA 23293-1000

OWEN, JACK WALDEN, retired hospital association administrator; b. Union City, Pa., Sept. 21, 1928; s. Wallace A. and Rosamond (Walden) O.; m. Charlotte Keller Owen, Sept. 14, 1957; children: Linda, Lisa, Jack II. BS, Western Mich. U., 1951, BA, 1953; MBA, U. Chgo., 1957. Chmn., CEO Princeton (N.J.) Ins. Co., 1975-83; pres. N.J. Hosp. Assn., Princeton, 1962-82; exec. v.p. Am. Hosp. Assn., Washington, 1982-89; pres. Am. Hosp. Assn., Chgo., 1991; pres. Am. Hosp. Assn. Svcs., Chgo., 1988-94, ret., 1994; bd. dirs. Robert W. Johnson Found., Princeton; chmn. Nat. Com. Prot. S.S., Washington, 1989—; assoc. trustee Suburban Hosp., Bethesda, Md., 1993—. Contbr. articles to profl. jours. Mem. Rocky Hill (N.J.) Sch. Bd., 1974-82. Cpl. U.S. Army, 1953-55. Recipient medal of honor U. Med. and Dentistry, Newark, 1980. Mem. City Tavern Club (Georgetown). Lutheran. Avocations: fishing, golf, woodworking. Home: 3249 Sandown Park Rd Keswick VA 22947

OWEN, JAMES CHURCHILL, JR., lawyer; b. Beverly, Mass., July 30, 1926; s. James Churchill and Alice Wright (Mann) O.; m. Garvene Hales, Feb. 3, 1950 (div. Feb. 1963); children: James Churchill III, Taylor Mann. Student, Yale U., 1944-47; BS, JD, U. Denver, 1956. Bar: Colo. 1957, U.S. Dist. Ct. Colo. 1957. Reporter Oklahoma City Times, 1947-50; writer Phila. Bull., 1951-54; assoc. Holme Roberts & Owen, Denver, 1957-60, prtn., 1961—; mem. faculty Colo. Grad. Sch. Banking, Boulder, 1975-86; cmty. bd. dirs. Norwest Bank Colo., N.A. Trustee Denver Pub. Libr. Friends Found., 1996—; trustee Denver Bot. Gardens, 1976-81, Denver Bot. Gardens Endowment, Inc., 1994—, Denver Zool. Found., 1992—; chmn. law alumni fund U. Denver Coll. Law, 1988-89, chmn. law alumni coun., 1989-91, mem. centennial planning com.; former mem. Colo. Gov.'s Coun. Advisors on Consumer Credit; bd. dirs. Rocky Mountain chpt. Juvenile Diabetes Found., 1993-96. Mem. ABA, Colo. Bar Assn. (past chmn. banking com. corp., banking and bus. law sect.), Denver Bar Assn., Colo. Bar Found., Econ. Club Colo. (co-founder, bd. dirs., sec.), Assn. Bank Holding Cos. (past chmn. lawyers' com.), Denver Country Club, Univ. Club, Law Club, Denver Club. Republican. Episcopalian. Avocation: classic cars. Office: Holme Roberts & Owen LLP 1700 Lincoln St Ste 4100 Denver CO 80203-4541

OWEN, JOE DAVID, editor; b. Abilene, Tex., Oct. 27, 1950; s. B. Pat and Emilie (Long) O.; m. Joni Leigh Collier, Aug. 6, 1977; children: Connor Clausell, Caitlin Collier, Austin Sciever. BFA, So. Meth. U., 1976. Assoc. editor Stephenville (Tex.) Empire-Tribune, 1977; editor DeSoto (Tex.) News-Advertiser, 1978; assoc. dir. editl. svc. Boy Scouts Am., 1982-89, mng. editor, 1989-94, dir., 1995; mng. editor Boys' Life Mag., Irving, Tex., 1995—. Editor: Boy Scout Handbook, 10th edit., 1988. Home: 9653 Crestedge Dr Dallas TX 75238-2526 Office: Boys Life Mag PO Box 152079 Irving TX 75015-2079

OWEN, JOHN, retired newspaper editor; b. Helena, Mont., June 10, 1929; s. John Earl and Ella Jean (McMillian) O.; m. Alice Winnifred Kesler, June 9, 1951; children—David Scott, Kathy Lynn. B.A. in Journalism, U. Mont., 1951. Sports editor Bismarck (N.D.) Tribune, 1953-55; wire editor Yakima (Wash.) Herald, 1956; with Seattle Post-Intelligencer, 1956-94, sports editor, 1968-80, assoc. editor, 1980-94, columnist, 1968-94. Author: Intermediate Eater Cookbook, 1974, Gourmand Gutbusters Cookbook, 1980, Seattle Cookbook, 1983, Great Grub Hunt Cookbook, 1989, Press Pass, 1994; also short stories. Served with AUS, 1951-52. Named Top Sports Writer in Wash. Nat. Sportswriters Orgn., 1966, 68, 69, 71, 74, 85, 88. Home: 611 Bell St Apt 4 Edmonds WA 98020-3065

OWEN, JOHN ATKINSON, JR., physician, educator; b. South Boston, Va., Sept. 24, 1924; s. John Atkinson and Mary Helen (Carrington) O.; m. Wanda Earle Reamy, Nov. 29, 1952; children—John Atkinson III, Ryland R. B.S., Hampden-Sydney Coll., 1944; M.D., U. Va., 1948. Intern Cin. Gen. Hosp., 1948-49; resident, fellow U. Va. Hosp., 1950-52; rsch. fellow Duke Med. Center, 1954-56; asst. prof. medicine Med. Coll. Ga., 1956-58, George Washington U. Med. Sch., 1958-60; mem. faculty U. Va. Sch. Medicine, 1960—, prof., 1970—, vice chmn. dept. internal medicine, 1972-74, James M. Moss prof. diabetes, sr. assoc. dean, 1995—; mem. Va. Vol. Formulary Bd.; mem. exec. com. U.S. Pharmacopeia, 1970-75, pres., 1975-80, trustee, 1975-85. Mem. editorial bd.: Jour. Clin. Pharmacology, 1971-84; editor-in-chief: Hosp. Formulary, 1974-83. Served with USNR, 1942-45, 48-50, 52-53; capt. M.C. Res. Recipient Raven award U. Va., 1948; co-recipient Horsley Research prize, 1962. Mem. AMA, Am. Fedn. Clin. Rsch., So. Soc. Clin. Investigation, Med. Soc. Va. (pres. 1990-91), Am. Diabetes Assn., Endocrine Soc. Presbyterian. (elder 1965—). Home: 106 Tally Ho Dr Charlottesville VA 22901-2034 Office: U Va Sch Medicine PO Box 242 Charlottesville VA 22908-0242

OWEN, LOYD EUGENE, JR., lawyer; b. Carthage, Mo., May 11, 1943; s. Loyd Eugene and Dorothy Marie (Eckhoff) O.; m. Linda S. Schaerrer, Sept. 5, 1965; 1 child, Patricia L. BBA, U. Mo., 1966, JD, 1968. Bar: Mo. 1968, U.S. Dist. Ct. Mo. 1968, U.S. Supreme Ct. 1979. Assoc. Lathrop & Gage (formerly Gage & Tucker), Kansas City, Mo., 1970—; mem. mgmt. com. Gage & Tucker, Kansas City, Mo., 1987-94; chmn. labor dept. Gage & Tucker, Kansas City, 1987-96; guest instr. health care law U. Kans., Lawrence; lectr. nat. and regional labor/health law. Author, contbg. editor

Employment Law in the 50 States, 1987, 89; contbg. editor: The Developing Labor Law, 1986, 88. Mem. ABA, Mo. Bar Assn., Kansas City Mo. Bar Assn. Avocations: sailing, scuba diving, hunting, fishing. Office: Lathrop & Gage 2345 Grand Blvd Ste 2800 Kansas City MO 64108-2625

OWEN, MICHAEL, ballet dancer; b. Carlisle, Pa.. Studied with Marcia Weary; student, Pa. Ballet Sch., Sch. Am. Ballet, Am. Ballet Theatre Sch. Mem. Ballet Reportory Co.; with Am. Ballet Theatre, 1974—, soloist, 1977-87, prin. dancer, 1987—. Appeared in ballets including La Bayadere, Coppelia, Fall River Legend, Giselle, Jardin aux Lilas, The Leaves are Fading, Manon, Pillar of Fire, Romeo and Juliet, The Sleeping Beauty, Swan Lake, Undertow. Office: Am Ballet Theatre 890 Broadway New York NY 10003-1211*

OWEN, MICHAEL LEE, lawyer; b. L.A., Aug. 17, 1942; s. Richard M. Owen and Betty Hamilton; m. Espy Bolivar. AB in Econ. with distinction, Stanford U., 1964; LLB, Harvard U., 1967. Bar: Calif., 1968, N.Y. 1968. Assoc. Reid & Priest, N.Y.C., 1967-69; mem. legal dept. Bank of Am. NT&SA, San Francisco, 1969-81; corp. sec. BRE Corp., San Francisco, 1970-75; v.p., assoc. gen. counsel Bank of Am. NT&SA, L.A., 1980-81; ptnr. & chair of Latin Amer. practice group Paul, Hastings, Janofsky & Walker, L.A., 1981—; mem. exec. com. Asia Pacific Dispute Resolution Ctr., NAFTA com. Am. Arbitration Assn.; mem. adv. bd. Southwestern Legal Found. Internat. and Comparative Law Ctr. Contbr. articles to profl. jours. regarding legal issues affecting financing and investment in Latin Amer. Mem. U.S.-Mex. Law Inst. (bd. dirs.), U.S.-Mex. C. of C. (bd. dirs. Pacific chpt.). Office: Paul Hastings Janofsky & Walker 555 S Flower St Fl 24 Los Angeles CA 90071-2300

OWEN, NATHAN RICHARD, manufacturing company executive; b. Burnt Hills, N.Y., May 3, 1919; s. George H. and Mildred T. (Sharpley) O.; m. Janet M. Smith, Sept. 26, 1942; children: Patricia O. Smith, David G., Lorinda O. Clauson. B.S. in Mech. Engring, Mass. Inst. Tech., 1941, M.S., 1942; D.Sc., Clarkson Coll., 1979. With Chase Brass & Copper Co., 1946-47; with J.H. Whitney & Co., N.Y.C., 1947-62, ptnr., 1951-62; chmn. bd. Gen. Signal Corp., 1962-84, chmn. exec. com., 1980-95; chmn. emeritus, 1995—; bd. dirs. TechnoServe, Inc., Braille Internat., Inc., Enabling Techs., Inc. Served to lt. USN, 1942-46. Home: 1100 SW Shoreline Dr Palm City FL 34990-4542 Office: PO Box 10351 Stamford CT 06904-2351

OWEN, PRISCILLA RICHMAN, judge. BA, Baylor U., JD, 1977. Bar: Tex. 1977, U.S. Ct. Appeals (4th, 8th and 11th cirs.). Former ptnr. Andrews & Kurth, L.L.P., Houston; justice Supreme Ct. Tex., Austin, 1995—; liaison to Tex. Legal Svcs. for Poor Spl. Supreme Ct. Tex., gender bias reform implementation com.; adv. com. Supreme Ct. on Ct.-Annexed Mediations. Named Young Lawyer of Yr., Outstanding Young Alumna, Baylor U. Office: Supreme Ct Tex PO Box 12248 Austin TX 78711

OWEN, RAY DAVID, biology educator; b. Genesee, Wis., Oct. 30, 1915; s. Dave and Ida (Hoeft) O.; m. June J. Weissenberg, June 24, 1939; 1 son, David G. BS, Carroll Coll., Wis., 1937, ScD, 1962; PhD, U. Wis., 1941, ScD, 1979; ScD, U. of Pacific, 1965. Asst. prof. genetics, zoology U. Wis., 1944-47; Gosney fellow Calif. Inst. Tech., Pasadena, 1946-47; assoc. prof. div. biology Calif. Inst. Tech., 1947-53, prof. biology, 1953-83, also chmn., v.p. for student affairs, dean of students, prof. emeritus, 1983—; research participant Oak Ridge Nat. Lab., 1957-58; Cons. Oak Ridge Inst. Nuclear Studies; mem. Pres.'s Cancer Panel. Author: (with A.M. Srb) General Genetics, 1952, 2d edit. (with A.M. Srb, R. Edgar), 1965; Contbr. articles to sci. jours. Recipient Gregor Mendel medal Czech Acad. Scis., 1965. Fellow AAAS; mem. Genetics Soc. Am. (pres., Thomas Hunt Morgan medal 1993), Am. Assn. Immunologists, Am. Soc. Human Genetics, Western Soc. Naturalists, Am. Soc. Zoologists, Am. Genetics Assn., Nat. Acad. Scis., Am. Acad. Arts and Scis., Am. Philos. Soc., Am. Acad. Allergy and Immunology (hon.), Internat. Soc. Animal Genetics (hon.), Sigma Xi. Home: 1583 Rose Villa St Pasadena CA 91106-3524 Office: Calif Inst Tech 156-29 Pasadena CA 91125

OWEN, RICHARD, federal judge; b. N.Y.C., Dec. 11, 1922; s. Carl Maynard and Shirley (Barnes) O.; m. Lynn Rasmussen, June 6, 1960; children: Carl R., David R., Richard. AB, Dartmouth Coll., 1947; LLB, Harvard U., 1950; MusD (hon.), Manhattan Sch. Music, 1989. Bar: N.Y. 1950. Practiced in N.Y.C., 1950-74; assoc. Willkie Owen Farr Gallagher & Walton, 1950-53, Willkie Farr Gallagher Walton & Fitzgibbon, 1958-60; pvt. practice, 1960-65; ptnr. Owen & Aarons, 1965-66, Owen & Turchin, 1966-74; asst. U.S. atty. So. Dist. N.Y., 1953-55; trial atty. antitrust div. U.S. Dept. Justice, 1955-58; U.S. dist. judge So. Dist. N.Y., 1974—; asst. prof. N.Y. Law Sch., 1951-53; adj. prof. law Fordham U. Sch. Law, 1966—. Composer, librettist operas A Moment of War, 1958, A Fisherman Called Peter, 1965, Mary Dyer, 1976, The Death of the Virgin, 1980, Abigail Adams, 1987, Tom Sawyer, 1989. Trustee Manhattan Sch. Music, N.Y.C.; founder, bd. dirs. Maine Opera Assn., 1975-85; pres., bd. dirs. N.Y. Lyric Opera Co. 1st lt. USAAF, 1942-45. Decorated D.F.C. with oak leaf cluster, Air medal with 3 oak leaf clusters. Mem. ASCAP, Century Assn., Chelsea Yacht Club. Republican. Mem. Soc. of Friends. Office: US Dist Ct US Courthouse Foley Sq New York NY 10007-1501

OWEN, ROBERT DEWIT, lawyer; b. St. Louis, Nov. 15, 1948; s. Kenneth Campbell Owen and Mary Elenor (Fish) Luebbers; m. Rebecca Roberts Baxter, June 4, 1977; children: Abigail Mary, James Roy, Charlotte Grace. BA, Northwestern U., 1970; JD cum laude, U. Pa., 1973. Assoc. Sullivan & Cromwell, N.Y.C., 1973-81; ptnr. Towne, Dolgin, Furlaud, Sawyier & Owen, N.Y.C., 1981-83, Owen & Fennell, N.Y.C., 1983-87, Owen & Davis, N.Y.C., 1987—; instr. Nat. Inst. Trial Advocacy, Boulder, Colo., 1988—; faculty mem. ABA Nat. Inst. 1992, 93. Bd. dirs. St. Christopher's-Jennie Clarkson Child Care Svcs., Dobbs Ferry, N.Y., 1991-97. Mem. Assn. Bar City N.Y., Fed. Bar Coun., Nat. Assn. Securities Dealers (bd. arbitrators 1985—), Colonial Springs Club (pres. 1986-94), India House. Episcopalian. Avocations: boating, running. Office: Owen & Davis 805 3rd Ave New York NY 10022-7513

OWEN, ROBERT HUBERT, lawyer, real estate broker; b. Birmingham, Ala., Aug. 3, 1928; s. Robert Clay and Mattie Lou (Hubert) O.; m. Mary Dane Hicks, Mar. 14, 1954; children: Mary Kathryn, Robert Hubert. B.S., U. Ala., 1950; J.D., Birmingham Sch. Law, 1956. Bar: Ala. 1957, Ga. 1965. Methods and procedures analyst, supr. Ala. Power Co., Birmingham, 1952-58; assoc. Martin, Vogtle, Balch & Bingham, Birmingham, 1958-63; asst. sec. So. Services, Atlanta, 1963-69; sec. Southern Co., Atlanta, 1969-71; sec., asst. treas. Southern Co., 1971-77; exec. v.p., sec., gen. counsel, dir. Proverbs 31 Corp., Atlanta, 1978-81, 90—; broker Bob Owen Realty, Atlanta, 1990—; pvt. practice law Marietta, 1978-85; v.p., gen. counsel Hubert Properties, 1985-86. Atlanta area rep. Inst. Basic Youth Conflicts, 1970-80. Served to maj. USAF, 1951-52, 61-62. Mem. Jasons, Delta Chi, Omicron Delta Kappa, Beta Gamma Sigma, Delta Sigma Pi, Phi Eta Sigma. Baptist. Home and Office: 6590 Bridgewood Valley Rd NW Atlanta GA 30328-2906

OWEN, ROBERT RANDOLPH, accountant; b. Ardmore, Okla., June 24, 1939; s. Buford Randolph and Ruth Marie (Cleeton) O.; m. Patra Malinda Randolph, June 20, 1958; children: Stacy Malinda Owen Hodges, Mindy Carol Owen Long. BBA with high honors, So. Meth. U., 1961; postgrad., Harvard U., 1985. CPA, Tex. Various positions Alford, Meroney & Co., Dallas, 1961-80, mgr., 1967-69, ptnr., 1969-73, mng. ptnr. Dallas office, 1975-78, firm mng. ptnr., 1978-80; dep. regional mng. ptnr. S.W. region Arthur Young & Co., Dallas, 1980-83, ptnr., nat. dir. entrepreneurial svcs., 1983-86, ptnr., nat. dir. indsl. specialization, 1986-89; ptnr., nat. dir. industry svcs. Ernst & Young, 1990—. Author, editor: The Arthur Young Guide to Financing for Growth, 1986, The Ernst & Young Guide to Raising Capital, 1991. Capt. USAF, 1961-64. Mem. Tex. Soc. CPAs (pres. 1994-95, pres. Dallas chpt. 1988-89, bd. dirs. 1986—), AICPA. Baptist. Office: Ernst & Young LLP 2121 San Jacinto St Ste 500 Dallas TX 75201-6714

OWEN, ROBERT ROY, retired manufacturing company executive; b. Somerton, Ariz., Aug. 29, 1921; s. Wilbur Parker and Flossye Bell (White) O.; m. Barbara Dean Burton, Apr. 3, 1943; children—Melinne, Claudia, Christina, Rebecca, Jennifer. B.S., U. Calif. at Davis, 1942. Plantation engr. Del Monte, Hawaii, 1946-49; tech. rep. E.I. duPont de Nemours & Co., 1949-50; head engring. Pineapple Research Inst. of Hawaii, 1950-56; farm implement planning mgr., product planning and programming mgr., asst. chief engr., gen. mgr. equipment operations Tractor and Implement div. Ford Motor Co., Birmingham, Mich., 1956-68; pres. Gt. Western Sugar Co., Denver, 1968-71, Gt. Western Producers Coop., Englewood, Colo., 1971-76, Eversman Mfg. Co., Denver, 1976-95; dir. Ivancie Cellars, Inc.; Gen. chmn. Birmingham Arts Festival, 1960; pres. Evergreen Homes Assn., 1969-71; mem. U.S. Dept. Agr. Joint Council Food and Agrl. Scis., 1983-86. Contbr. articles to profl. jours. Served with AUS, 1942-46; brig. gen. Res. Recipient Centennial citation U. Calif., 1968, Distinguished Service award Colo. State U., 1971. Fellow Am. Soc. Agrl. Engrs.; mem. Newcomen Soc., Internat. Wine and Food Soc., Denver Club, Hiwan Country Club. Patentee in field. Office: Eversman Mfg Co 7475 W 5th Ave Ste 214 Lakewood CO 80226-1674

OWEN, ROBERT VAUGHAN, financial company executive; b. No. Adams, Mass., June 2, 1920; s. William and Lucy Anne (Morgan) O.; m. Jean Ann Gebauer, Dec. 6, 1946; children: Robert, Nancy, Bruce, Elizabeth. BA cum laude, Dartmouth Coll., 1946; MBA, Amos Tuck Sch., 1947. Fin. mgr. Gen. Electric Co., various locations, 1950-62; sr. budget dir. Citibank, N.Y.C., 1962-68, v.p., 1968-78, mng. dir., 1978-83; pres., chief exec. officer Bob Owen Assocs., Inc., Darien, Conn., 1984—. Contbr. articles to profl. jours. With USNR, 1943-45. Mem. N.Y. Fin. Execs. Inst. (pres. 1976). Republican. Roman Catholic. Office: Bob Owen Assocs Inc 10 Haskell Ln Darien CT 06820-3301

OWEN, ROBERTS BISHOP, lawyer; b. Boston, Feb. 11, 1926; s. Roberts Bishop and Monica Benedict (Burrell) O.; m. Kathleen Comstock von Schrader, Aug. 27, 1966; children—David Roberts, Lucy Leffingwell, William Atreus. Student, Dartmouth Coll., 1943-44; A.B. cum laude, Harvard U., 1948, LL.B. cum laude, 1951; Dip.C.L.S., Cambridge U., Eng., 1952. Bar: D.C. 1952, U.S. Ct. Appeals (D.C. cir.) 1953, U.S. Supreme Ct. 1958. Assoc. Covington & Burling, Washington, 1952-60; ptnr. Covington & Burling, 1960-79, 81—; the legal advisor U.S. Dept. State, Washington, 1979-81; sr. advisor Sec. of State former Yugoslavia, 1995; arbitrator Fedn. Bosnia and Herzegovina, 1995; mem. Permanent Ct. Arbitration, The Hague, The Netherlands, 1980-86, 93—; mem. arbitration panel Internat. Ctr. for Settlement of Investment Disputes, 1995—. Served to ensign USN, 1943-46. Fulbright scholar, 1951-52; recipient Disting Honor award Dept. of State, 1981, Sec. of State Disting. Svc. award, 1996, Sec. of Defense's medal for outstanding pub. svc., 1996. Fellow Am. Coll. Trial Lawyers; mem. ABA, Council Fgn. Relations, Am. Soc. Internat. Law (exec. council 1981-85). Clubs: Royal Ocean Racing (London); Metropolitan, City (Washington). Office: Covington & Burling Po Box 7566 1201 Pennsylvania Ave NW Washington DC 20044

OWEN, STEPHEN LEE, lawyer; b. Danville, Va., Mar. 25, 1952; s. L. Davis and Ann (Brodie) O.; m. Catherine Bryan Mabry; children: Hillary Brodie, Stephen Grayson, Mary Bryan, Davis Hammond, Edward Bloxton. BA, Hampden-Sydney Coll., Va., 1974; JD, Coll. of William and Mary, Williamsburg, Va., 1977. Bar: Va. 1977, Md. 1977, U.S. Tax Ct. 1978, U.S. Dist. Ct. Md., D.C. 1990. Assoc. Venable, Baetjer & Howard, Balt., 1977-84, ptnr., 1985-93; ptnr. Piper & Marbury, Balt., 1993—. Co-author: Federal Taxation of Estates, Gifts & Trusts, 1988; co-author newsletter Real Estate Tax Ideas, 1985--; contbr. articles to profl. jours.; editorial bd. Jour. Partnership Taxation, 1984--, The Practical Tax Lawyer, 1985--. Bd. dirs. Balt. City Found., 1979-89. Mem. Am. Law Inst., Md. Bar Assn. (chmn. sect. of taxation 1989-90), Balt. Country Club, Caves Valley Golf Club. Avocation: golf. Office: Piper & Marbury 36 S Charles St Baltimore MD 21201-3020

OWEN, SUZANNE, retired savings and loan executive; b. Lincoln, Nebr., Oct. 6, 1926; d. Arthur C. and Hazel E. (Edwards) O. BSBA, U. Nebr., Lincoln, 1948. With G.F. Lessenhop & Sons, Inc., Lincoln, 1948-57; with First Fed. Lincoln, 1963-91; v.p., dir. personnel, 1975-81, 1st v.p., 1981-87, sr. v.p., 1987-91, ret., 1991; mem. pers. bd. City of Lincoln, 1989-96. Mem. Lincoln Human Resources Mgmt. Assn., Lincoln Mgmt. Soc., Phi Chi Theta. Republican. Christian Scientist. Clubs: Wooden Spoon, Exec. Women's Breakfast Group, Community Women's, Lincoln Symphony Guild. Lodges: Pi Beta Phi Alumnae, Order of Eastern Star (Lincoln).

OWEN, THOMAS BARRON, retired naval officer, space company executive; b. Seattle, Mar. 19, 1920; s. Thomas Barron and Ruth (Deane) O.; m. Rosemary Stolz, Dec. 24, 1944; children—Catherine Adams, Thomas Barron, James Rowell, Nancy Deane. B.S. cum laude, U. Wash., 1940; postgrad., U.S. Naval Postgrad. Sch., 1946-47; Ph.D. in Chemistry, Cornell U., 1950; postgrad., U. Amsterdam, 1950-51, Indsl. Coll. Armed Forces, 1961-62, Harvard Grad. Sch. Bus. Adminstrn., 1964. Commd. ensign U.S. Navy, 1940, advanced through grades to rear adm., 1967, combat duty with Pacific Fleet, 1940-45; officer distbn. div. Bur. Naval Personnel, 1945-46; with armaments br. and mil. operations br. Office Naval Research, 1951-53; asst. repair supt. (hull) and prodn. analysis supt. Long Beach (Calif.) Naval Shipyard, 1953-57; dir. applied scis. div., dir. research and devel. planning div. Navy Bur. Ships, 1957-61; mil. asst. to dep. dir. def. research and engring. engring. and chemistry, 1962-63; assigned Office Asst. Sec. Navy Research and Devel., 1963; dir. support services Naval Research Lab., 1963-65, dir., 1965-67; chief naval research, 1967-70, ret., 1970; asst. dir. nat. and internat. programs NSF, 1970-74; assoc. dean grad. affairs and rsch. Am. U., Washington, 1974-76; asst. provost Am. U., 1976-79; asst. adminstr. NOAA, Dept. Commerce, Rockville, Md., 1979-81; mgr. program planning Fairchild Space & Electronics Co., Germantown, Md., 1981-83; sr. dir. systems effectiveness Fairchild Space Co., Germantown, 1983-84, v.p. procurement, 1984-86. Author profl. papers. Decorated D.S.M., Silver Star, Bronze Star. Fellow AAAS; mem. Am. Chem. Soc., U.S. Naval Inst., Philos. Soc. Washington, Sigma Xi, Phi Kappa Phi, Phi Lambda Upsilon, Tau Beta Pi, Chi Psi. Club: Cosmos (Washington). Home: 8409 Magruder Mill Ct Bethesda MD 20817-2746 *Demand high standards of excellence for self and others. Achieve respect of others through own performance. Be direct; avoid circumspection. Develop empathy; listen; consider feelings and rights of others. Maintain philosophy of "Onward and Upward!".*

OWEN, THOMAS LLEWELLYN, investment executive; b. Patchogue, N.Y., June 24, 1928; s. Griffith Robert and Jeanette Roberts (Hatfield) O.; A.B. in Econs., Coll. William and Mary, 1951; postgrad. Columbia U., 1952, N.Y. Inst. Fin., 1960-62; M.B.A., N.Y. U., 1966. Exec. trainee Shell Oil Co., N.Y.C. and Indpls., 1951-59, supr., 1958-59; petroleum and chem. investment analyst Paine, Webber, Jackson & Curtis, N.Y.C., 1959-62; sr. oil investment analyst DuPont Investment Interests, Wilmington, Del., N.Y.C., 1962-66, dir. research, 1964-66; v.p., sr. investment officer, mem. policy, investment coms. Nat. Securities and Research Corp., N.Y.C., 1966-75; sr. investment exec., v.p., portfolio mgr. F. Eberstadt & Co. and Eberstadt Asset Mgmt., Inc., N.Y.C., 1975-85, mem. policy com., 1979-85, also dir. portfolio rev. com.; sr. investment exec., portfolio mgr. Brown Brothers Harriman, N.Y.C., 1985-89; pres., CEO Owen Capital Mgmt., N.Y.C., 1989—. Chmn. bd. trustees Congl. Ch. Patchogue, N.Y. Mem. N.Y. Soc. Security Analysts, Assn. of Investment Mgmt. and Rsch., Oil Analysts Group N.Y., Am. Econ. Assn., Investment Assn. N.Y., Am. Petroleum Inst., Nat. Assn. Petroleum Investment Analysts, Internat. Assn. Energy Economists. Contbr. chpt. "Oil and Gas Industries" to Financial Analysts Handbook, 1975. Home and Office: 251 E 32nd St New York NY 10016-6304 *Perseverance and hard work are essential. But intense desire and strong convictions in conjunction with ethical principles are the ingredients of an outstanding leader. When your peers recognize your abilities and accomplishments, you have reached the pinnacle of success. It can be lonely at the top ..... but so gratifying and rewarding.*

OWEN, THOMAS WALKER, banker, broker; b. Everett, Wash., June 7, 1925; s. Thomas Walker and Frances (Yantis) O.; m. Barbara May Neils, Oct. 20, 1951; children: Thomas W., Gerhard, Caroline, Jeffrey; m. Ingrid Lundgren, June 7, 1975. B.A., U. Wash., 1949, MA in Finance, 1953; postgrad., Pacific Coast Banking Sch., 1956. Adminstrv. trainee Seattle Trust & Savs. Bank, 1949-54, asst. br. mgr., 1954-56, trust investment officer, 1956-57, mgr. investment dept., chmn. investment com., 1957-59; v.p., mgr. investment dept. Pacific Nat. Bank Wash., Tacoma, 1959-66, vice chmn., 1967-71; exec. v.p. bank adminstrn. Pacific Nat. Bank Wash., 1971-73; v.p. Reeder, Owen & Co., Inc., 1975-92; pres., chmn. Owen, Reeder, Inc., Merrill Lynch, 1991-92; bd. dirs. West One Bank Wash., Tacoma, 1981-93. Served with AUS, 1943-45. Decorated Bronze Star, Purple Heart. Mem. N.W. Forum, Wash. Athletic Club, Tacoma Club (past pres.), Tacoma Country and Golf Club, Phi Gamma Delta. Home: 10819 Evergreen Ter SW Tacoma WA 98498-6701

OWEN, WADSWORTH, oceanographer, consultant; b. N.Y.C., Sept. 4, 1932; S. George Wadsworth and Helen (Hammett) O.; m. Elaine M. Brewster, Oct. 26, 1955 (div. 1973); children: Leslie Shore, Victoria Rand, Samantha; m. Margaret W. Emslie, May 31, 1975 (div. July 22, 1992); 1 child, Joanna W. BS in Physics and Math., U. Mass., 1961; MA in Phys. Oceanography, Johns Hopkins U., 1969. Asst. scientist Avco R&D, Wilmington, Mass., 1956-61; rsch. asst. Johns Hopkins U., Balt., 1961-64; engr. sonar devices Westinghouse-Undersea, Balt., 1964-66; sr. engr. Sikorski Aircraft, Stratford, Conn., 1966-67; mgr. marine tech. Raytheon Subsig, New London, Conn., 1967-69; divsn. mgr. marine sci. and v.p. underwater vehicles VAST, Inc., Waterford, Conn., 1969-73; divsn. dir. phys. sci. divsn. Normandeau Assocs., Bedford, N.H., 1973-77; dir. marine ops. Coll. Marine Studies, U. Del., Lewes, 1977-94. Contbr. articles to profl. jours.; patentee in field. Adv. bd. New Eng. Marine Rsch. Info. Program, R.I., 1970-73. Sgt. USMC, 1952-55, PTO. U. Mass. scholar, 1958-61; NDEA fellow, 1961-64. Mem. So. N.E. Marine Scis. Assn. (chmn. exec. bd. 1970-73), Am. Inst. Physics (pres. student sect. 1960-61), Lewes C. of C. (treas. 1990-91), Univ. Nat. Oceanography Lab. Sys. Assn., Rsch. Vessel Ops. Coun., Marine Tech. Soc., Acad. Model Aeronautics, Nat. Free Flight Soc. Avocations: model aircraft design and construction, art, history, boats, diving. Home: PO Box 268 Friendship ME 04547-0268

OWEN, WALTER SHEPHERD, materials science and engineering educator; b. Liverpool, Eng., Mar. 13, 1920; s. Walter L. and Dorothea (Lunt) O. B.Engring., U. Liverpool, 1940, M.Engring., 1942, Ph.D., 1950, D.Eng., 1972. Metallurgist English Electric Co., 1940-46; mem. research staff MIT, 1951-57; prof. metallurgy U. Liverpool, 1957-66; prof., dir. materials sci. and engring. Cornell U., 1966-70; dean Tech. Inst., 1970-71; v.p. sci. and research Northwestern U., Evanston, Ill., 1971-73; prof. and head materials sci. and engring. MIT, 1973-82, prof. phys. metallurgy, 1982-85, prof. emeritus, sr. lectr. materials sci. and engring., 1985—; Cons. to industry. Author research papers. Commonwealth Fund fellow, 1951. Fellow ASM; mem. NAE, AIME, Instn. Metallurgists, N.Y. Acad. Scis., Inst. Metals, Materials Rsch. Soc., Japan Inst. Metals (hon.). Home: 1 Marine Ter Porthmadog, Gwynedd LL49 9BL, Wales

OWEN, WILLIAM MICHAEL, real estate developer; b. Houston, Sept. 27, 1950; s. W. Frank and Lois Marie (Nelson) O.; m. Debra Ann Phillips, Jan. 9, 1971 (div.); 1 child, Heather Ann; m. Pamela C. Birkhead, Feb. 18, 1983; children: Sean Michael, Blane William. BA in Econs., U. North Tex., 1992, MBA in Fin., 1996. Pres. Owen Resource & Devel., Inc., Denton, Tex., 1992—; pub., editor The Profit Connection Fin. Newsletter, 1994—; v.p. Ivey & Owen Investments, Inc., Las Vegas, 1992—; pres. Owen Fin. Group, Dallas, 1978—. Office: Owen Resource & Develop Inc 309 Hollyhill Ln Denton TX 76205-7811

OWENBY, PHILLIP H., learning and communications consultant; b. Sevierville, Tenn., Nov. 25, 1951; s. H.W. and M.J. (Brewer) O.; m. Vicki Moore, Oct. 3, 1981; children: Johanna, Kristen. BA, Regents Coll., Albany, 1979; MA, Calif. State U., 1989; PhD, U. Tenn., 1996. Tng. & ops. officer Emergency Mgmt. Agy., Knoxville, 1979-81; from tng. officer to mgr. supervisory tng. TVA, Knoxville, 1981-88, mgr. exec. edn., 1995—; mgr. orgl. devel. & tng. Performance Devel. Corp., Oak Ridge, Tenn., 1988-91; sr. edn. & tng. cons. Sci. Applications Internat. Corp., Oak Ridge, 1991—; instr. adult devel. & tng. U. Tenn. Coll. Edn., Knoxville, 1994; instr. U. Tenn. Cmty. Edn. Programs, 1982-90; cons. TVA, 1993—. Cmty. HIV/AIDS educator ARC, Knoxville, 1995. Mem. APA, Am. Assn. Adult & Continuing Edn., Pi Lambda Theta. Episcopalian. Avocations: public speaking, great books, science fiction, regional history, rock and roll music. Office: TVA U 400 W Summit Hill Dr Knoxville TN 37902-1415

OWENS, ALEXANDRA CANTOR, professional society administrator; b. N.Y.C., Nov. 22, 1961; d. Murray A. and Lois (Van Arsdel) C.; m. Michael R. Owens. BA, William Smith Coll., 1983. Exec. sec. Nissel & Nissel, CPAs, N.Y.C., 1983-85, Am. Soc. Journalists and Authors Charitable Trust, N.Y.C., 1986—; exec. dir. Am. Soc. Journalists and Authors, N.Y.C., 1985—; dir. WriteSpeakers Referral Svc., N.Y.C., 1996—. Contbg. author: Tools of the Writer's Trade, 1990. Office: Am Soc of Journalists 1501 Broadway Ste 302 New York NY 10036-5501

OWENS, BARBARA ANN, English educator; b. Muskogee, Okla., Jan. 11, 1947; d. Carl Howard Fullbright and Iris Oleta (Staffan) Evans; m. David Warren Owens, Jr., Feb. 28, 1964; children: Shelia DeLynn, Katherine Elizabeth, David Warren III. BS, Northeastern Okla. State U., 1976; MEd, U. Okla., 1990. Cert. reading specialist. Tchr. Muldrow (Okla.) Pub. Schs., 1976-77, Stafford (Mo.) Pub. Schs., 1977-79, Oklahoma City C.C., 1991—, Moore (Okla.) Pub. Schs., 1979—; sponsor, state pres. Moore West Nat. Jr. Honor Soc., 1996-97. Bd. dirs. Moore Parks & Recreation, 1988-89. Mem. NEA, Oklahoma Edn. Assn., Okla. Reading Coun., Okla. Romance Writers Am. (v.p.), Romance Writers Am., Moore Assn. Classroom Tchrs. Avocations: travel, writing, reading. Office: Moore Pub Schs 9400 S Pennsylvania Ave Oklahoma City OK 73159-6903

OWENS, BUCK (ALVIS EDGAR, JR.), singer, musician, songwriter; b. Sherman, Tex., Aug. 12, 1929; s. Alvis Edgar and Maicie A.; m. Bonnie Owens, 1947 (div. 1955); children: Buddy, Mike; m. Phyllis Owens (div. 1972); 1 son, John; m. Jennifer, 1978. Attended pub. schs., Mesa, Ariz. Pres. Buck Owens Prodns., Buck Owens Crystal Palace; owner stas. KUZZ-FM, KCWR-AM, Bakersfield, Calif., stas. KCWW-AM, KNIX-FM, Phoenix, sta. KUZZ-TV, Bakersfield, Owens Enterprises, Bakersfield, Home Preview and Camera Ads Publs. Rec. artist, Capitol Records, 1958-76, 88—, Warner Bros. Records 1976-80; star syndicated TV shows Buck Owens Ranch Show; leader, Buck Owens' Buckaroos Band, 1960—; star of TV show Hee Haw, 1969-86. Records include Under Your Spell Again, Above and Beyond, Excuse Me, I Think I've Got a Heartache, Fooling Around, Under the Influence of Love, My Heart Skips a Beat, Act Naturally, Waitin' in the Welfare Line, Sam's Place, How Long Will My Baby Be Gone, Tall Dark Stranger, Too Old to Cut the Mustard, Rollin' in My Sweet Baby's Arms, The Kansas City Song, We're Gonna Get Together, albums include All Time Greatest Hits Vol. 1, 1990, vol. 2, 1992, vol. 3, 1993, The Buck Owens Collection (1959-90), 92, Half A Buck: Buck Owens' Greatest Duets, 1996, others. Recipient Instrumental Group of Year award Country Music Assn., 1967-68; named Artist of Decade Capitol Records, Country Artist of Year for 5 consecutive years Billboard, Cash Box and Record World; awarded 28 consecutive No. 1 records. Office: Buck Owens Prodns 3223 Sillect Ave Bakersfield CA 93308-6332*

OWENS, CHARLES VINCENT, JR., diagnostic company executive and consultant; b. Kansas City, Mo., May 15, 1927; s. Charles Vincent and Helen (Barrett) O.; m. Cheryl Kreighbaum, Feb. 12, 1955; children: Melody, Kevin, Michael, John, Barbara. B.S., U. Notre Dame, 1948; M.S. (Univ. fellow), U. N.C., 1949. Public health educator Richmond County (N.C.) Health Dept., 1949-51; with Miles Labs., Inc., Elkhart, Ind., 1951-82; pres. Ames Co. div. Miles Labs., Inc., 1967-71, group v.p. profl. products group, 1971-77, exec. v.p. internat. ops., 1977-82; chmn., chief exec. officer Kyoto Diagnostics, Inc., 1983-85; bd. dirs. Genesis Labs., Inc., St. Jude Med. Inc., Chronimed Inc.; chief exec. officer Genesis Inc., 1985-88, chmn., 1988—. Bd. dirs. Elkhart YWCA, 1972-76; vice chmn. Elkhart County Bd. Health, 1973-77; chmn. Child Abuse Task Force, Elkhart County, Ind., 1977-78. Served with M.C., USAAF, 1945-47. Mem. Am. Public Health Assn., Health Industry Mfg. Assn. (dir.), Pharm. Mfrs. Assn., Nat. Pharm. Council (pres. 1970-71, dir. 1965-73), Am. Mgmt. Assn., Am. Diabetes Assn., Am. Assn. Diabetes Educators, Internat. Diabetes Fedn., Am. Soc. Med. Tech. Republican. Roman Catholic.

OWENS, CHARLES WESLEY, university executive; b. Billings, Okla., Oct. 27, 1935; s. Fred Charles and Mary Isabel (Metheney) O.; m. Barbara Jeanne Williams, Dec. 18, 1955; children: Charles E., Wesley A., Michael L., Janet K. BS, Colo. Coll., 1957; PhD, U. Kans., 1963. Chemist Phillips Chem. Co., Borger, Tex., 1957-58; from asst. prof. to assoc. prof. to prof.

dept. chemistry U. N.H., 1963-89, chair dept. chemistry, 1979-82, assoc. v.p. for acad. affairs, 1983-87, interim v.p. for fin. and adminstrn., 1987-88, interim v.p. for acad. affairs, 1988-89; v.p. for acad. affairs, prof. chemistry Radford (Va.) U., 1989-96, acting pres., 1994-95; sr. assoc. Kaludis Cons. Group, 1996—; program chmn. New Eng. Assn. Chemistry Tchrs.; congl. sci. counselor to U.S. senators T. J. McIntyre and Gordon Humphrey; mem. NSF Rev. Panel for Coll. Tchr. Programs; NSF vis. scientist to New Eng. high schs.; mem., chair vis. teams Commn. on Colls., So. Assn. Colls. and Schs.; mem. task force on dependent benefits Joint Ops. Com., New Eng. Land Grant Univs.; bd. trustees N.H. Higher Edn. Assistance Found.; faculty fellow in acad. affairs U. N.H.; summer rsch. participant Oak Ridge Nat. Lab.; guest assoc. chemist Brookhaven Nat. Lab.; vis. prof. chemistry U. San Marcos, Lima, Peru; rsch. assoc. U. Kans.; cons. Boston Felt Co., Rochester, N.H., Random House, Inc., McGraw-Hill Book Co. Contbr. articles to profl. jours. Bd. trustees Sci. Mus. Western Va.; mem. Radford City Commn. on Arts and Events, 1995. 2d lt. U.S. Army, 1957-58. Mem. Am. Assn. Higher Edn., Am. Chem. Soc. (membership com. N.E. sect., com. on profl. tng.), Rotary Internat., Soc. for Coll. and Univ. Planning, Phi Beta Kappa, Delta Epsilon, Phi Kappa Phi, Phi Lambda Upsilon, Sigma Xi. Avocations: flying, hiking, tennis, painting, video production. Office: Radford U Box 6890 Preston Hall Radford VA 24142

OWENS, DANA (QUEEN LATIFA), recording artist, actress; b. N.J, Mar. 18, 1970; d. Lance and Rita O. Student, Borough of Manhattan C.C. CEO Flavor Unit Entertainment. TV appearances include Living Single, Fresh Prince of Bel Air, In Living Color, The Arsenio Hall Show; film appearances in Jungle Fever, 1991, Juice, 1992, House Party 2, 1992, Who's the Man, 1993, My Life, 1993, Sphere, 1997; albums include All Hail the Queen, 1990, The Nature of Sista, 1991, X-tra Naked, 1992, Black Reign, 1994. Named Best New Artist, New Music Seminar, 1990, Best Female Rapper, Rolling Stone Readers' Poll, 1990; recipient Grammy award nomination, 1990, Soul Train Music award, 1995, Sammy Davis Jr. award, 1995, Entertainer of Yr. award, 1995. *

OWENS, DEBRA ANN, chiropractor; b. Poplar Bluff, Mo., Dec. 21, 1953; d. James Alva and Veleta Frances (Pierce) Stutts; 1 child from previous marriage, Jacqueline. BS in Edn., S.E. Mo. State U., 1975; DC, Logan Coll. of Chiropractic, 1991; fellow, Internat. Acad. Clin. Acupunct, 1996. Chiropractor Albers Chiropractic, Washington, 1991-92, Owens Chiropractic Ctr., P.C., Dexter, Mo., 1992—. Mem. Am. Chiropractic Assn., Internat. Chiropractors Assn., Mo. Chiropractors Assn., World Congress of Women Chiropractors, Logan Coll. Alumni Assn. (alumni rsch. award 1991), Dexter C. of C. (2d v.p. 1993, 1st v.p. 1994, pres. 1995, sec. devel. corp. 1996, econ. devel. com. 1996), Kiwanis (bd. mem. 1994-97). Avocations: swimming, boating, patchwork quilting. Office: Owens Chiropractic Ctr PC 1013 Bus Hwy 60 W PO Box 678 Dexter MO 63841

OWENS, DONALD D., church officer; m. Adeline Owens; children: Donna Bean, Debbi Bohi, Darlene Conyers. MA in Religion, Bethany Nazarene Coll.; MA and PhD in Cultural Anthropology, U. Okla. Established Ch. of the Nazarene, Korea, 1954-66; tchr. Nazarene Theol. Sem., Kansas City, Mo., 1975-81, Bethany (Okla.) Nazarene Coll., 1966-74; founding pres. Asia Pacific Nazarene Theol. Sem., Manila, 1981-84; regional dir. Asia Pacific World Mission Divsn., Manila, 1981-85; pres. MidAm. Nazarene Coll., Olathe, 1985—; mem. bd. gen. supts. Ch. of the Nazarene, Indpls., 1989—; founder Korea Nazarene Theol. Coll. Author: Challenge in Korea, Church Behind the Bamboo Curtain, Revival Fires in Korea, Sing Ye Islands. Office: Church of Nazarene 6401 Paseo Blvd Kansas City MO 64131-1213*

OWENS, DORIS JERKINS, insurance underwriter; b. Range, Ala., June 16, 1940; d. Arthur Charles and Jennie (Lee) Jerkins; m. Gilbert Landers Owens, Jan. 29, 1959; 1 child, Alan Dale. Student Massey Draughon Bus. Coll., 1958-59, Auburn U., Montgomery, 1980, 81, 82. Cert. ins. counselor, profl. ins. woman. Exec. sec. Henry C. Barnet, Gen. Agt., Montgomery, Ala., 1959-66; sr. underwriter personal lines So. Guaranty Ins. Co., Montgomery, 1966—. Author: Bike Safety, 1976. Instr. Coop. State Dept. Defensive Driver Instr., 1975, 78; instr. ins. classes; v.p. Montgomery Citizens Fire Safety, 1981; panelist Gov.'s Safety Conf., Montgomery, 1975—; mem., panelist Women Annual Hwy. Safety Leaders, Montgomery, 1976, 78, 80; apptd. mem. Alliance Against Drugs, 1989. Recipient Able Toastmaster award Dist. 48 Toastmasters, 1979, Outstanding Lt. Gov. award, 1981, Outstanding Area Gov. award, 1980; named Ins. Woman of Year, 1979. Mem. Ins. Women Montgomery (pres. 1961, 85-86), Internat. Platform Assn., Blue-Gray Civitan Club. Office: So Guaranty Ins Co 2545 Taylor Rd Montgomery AL 36117-4706

OWENS, FLORA CONCEPCION, critical care nurse; b. Manila, Nov. 23, 1949; d. Felix and Marieta (Obsuna) Concepcion; m. George Owens, Feb. 13, 1976. Grad., San Juan de Dios Sch. Nursing, Pasay City, The Philippines, 1970; BSN, Concordia Coll., Manila, 1971. RN, Ill., Ark.; cert. in ACLS; CCRN. Staff nurse San Juan de Dios Hosp., 1970-71, Jefferson Meml. Hosp., Mt. Vernon, Ill., 1972, Russellville (Ark.) Nursing Home Ctr., 1973-76; staff nurse, relief supr. St. Mary's Regional Med. Ctr., Russellville, 1972-74, head nurse med. fl., 1975-76, insvc. coord. and unit mgr. med.-surg. ICU, 1976-90, staff nurse, charge nurse med.-surg. ICU, 1990—; instr. basic coronary care clas, 1979-90, basic arrythmia class, 1979-91, 94, 96, 97. Mem. AACN, CCRN, Ark. Tech. U. Nursing Honor Soc.

OWENS, HAROLD B., former state agency consultant; b. Knapp, Wis., Oct. 1, 1926; s. John Donald and Mabel Evelyn (Dunn) O.; m. Hazel Marie Allison, Aug. 23, 1927; children: Robert Bruce, Patrick Brian (dec.), Michael Shawn. Student, U. Mont., 1944, Rollins Coll., Winter Park, Fla., 1961-62, U. Hawaii, 1964-65. Field rep. Puget Sound Power & Light, Kirkland, Wash., 1946-48; machinist Boeing Co., Seattle, 1948; commd. officer and pilot USAF, 1949, advanced through grades to col., ret. 1979; exec. dir. Tex. Soc. Energy Auditors, College Station, 1979-80; v.p. ops. Entek Assocs., Inc., College Station, 1979-88; aviation cons. Tex. Aeronautics Commn., Austin, 1983-89; research assoc. Ctr. for Strategic Tech., Tex. A&M U. System, College Station, 1979-92; ret., 1992; aviation instr. Bryan, Tex., 1979—; ind. energy cons., 1988—. Contbr. articles to profl. jours. Commr. Bryan Hist. Landmark Commn., 1993-96; assoc. SOCV, 1992—. With U.S. Army, 1944-46, ETO. Decorated Legion of Merit, Bronze Star, Air Medal (7). Mem. Nat. Soc. Historic Preservation, Tex. Hist. Found., Nat. R.R. Hist. Soc. (nat. dir. 1988—), Air Force Assn. (chpt. pres. 1980-82, charter mem.), Nat. Aeronautics Assn., Order of Daedalians, Tex. A&M Assn. Former Students, Century Club, Faculty Club, The Ret. Officers Assn., Aircraft Owner's and Pilots Assn. Republican. Avocations: flying, music, sports, travel. Home: 3207 Wilderness Rd Bryan TX 77807-3222

OWENS, HELEN DAWN, elementary school educator, reading consultant; b. Eastman, Ga., Oct. 9, 1949; d. Eli B. and Irene (Harrell) Branch; m. Bobby Lee Owens, Dec. 9, 1967; children: Leslie Owens-McDonald, Monica Dawn. AA, Miami (Fla.) Dade Jr. Coll., 1969; BS, Fla. Internat. U., 1978; MEd, Mercer U., 1986, EdS, 1991. Cert. presch.-12th grade, reading specialist, early childhood edn. specialist, Ga. Youth ctr. dir. Dept. Def., Clark AFB, Philippines, 1969-70; English lang. instr. Chinese Mil. Acad., Feng Shan, Taiwan, 1973-75; tchr., music instr. ABC Presch., Miami, 1976-78; kindergarten and music tchr. Berkshire Sch., Homestead, Fla., 1978-79; tchr., reading specialist Perdue Elem. Sch. Houston County Bd. Edn., Warner Robins, Ga., 1979—; mem. nominating com. mem. Ga. picture book of yr. U. Ga., Athens, 1990-91; reading cons. for schs., county edn. bds., regional reading ctrs., Ctrl. Ga., 1990—. Author: With Loving Hands and Tender Hearts, 1975. Exec. bd. dirs. Ladies Ministries, Ch. of God., Warner Robins, 1990-94; dir. Internat. City Girls' Club, Warner Robins, 1990-96. Recipient 25-Yr. Bible Tchr. Svc. award Internat. City Ch. of God., 1991; named Fla. State Family Tng. Dir. of Yr., Fla. Ch. of God, 1979, Ga. Girls' Club Coord. of the Year, 1995. Mem. Internat. Reading Assn. (mem. Ga. coun. 1979-96, dir. mem. devel. 1993-96, v.p. 1996-97, pres. elect 1997—, past pres. HOPE coun. 1990-92), Profl. Assn. Ga. Edn. Republican. Avocations: reading, sewing, touring foreign countries, swimming, storytelling. Home: 111 Crestwood Rd Warner Robins GA 31093-6803 Office: Perdue Elem Sch 856 Highway 96 Warner Robins GA 31088-2222

OWENS, JACK BYRON, lawyer; b. Orange, Calif., Oct. 14, 1944; s. Jack Byron and Lenna Mildred (Gobar) O.; children: John Byron, David Harold, James Paul, Alexandra Grace. A.B., Stanford U., 1966, J.D., 1969. Bar: Calif. 1970, D.C. 1970. Law clk. U.S. Ct. Appeals 9th Circuit, 1969-70; asso. firm Wilmer, Cutler & Pickering, Washington, 1970-71, 74-75; atty. adv. Dept. Air Force, 1971-73; law clk. U.S. Supreme Ct., 1973-74; prof. law Boalt Law Sch., U. Calif., Berkeley, 1975-79; partner firm Orrick, Herrington & Sutcliffe, San Francisco, 1978-81; exec. v.p., gen. counsel E & J Gallo Winery, 1981—; adj. prof. Georgetown U. Law Sch. Contbr. articles legal publns. Served with USAF, 1971-73. Mem. Am. Law Inst., Am. Bar Assn., Phi Beta Kappa, Order of Coif. Office: E & J Gallo Winery PO Box 1130 600 Yosemite Blvd Modesto CA 95353

OWENS, JANA JAE, entertainer; b. Great Falls, Mont., Aug. 30, 1943; d. Jacob G. Meyer and Bette P. (Sprague) Hopper; m. Sidney Greif (div.); children: Matthew N., Sydni C.; m. Buck Owens. Student, Interlochen Music Camp, 1959, Internat. String Congress, 1960, Vienna (Austria) Acad. Music, 1963-64; BA magna cum laude, Colo. Womens Coll., 1965, MusB magna cum laude, 1965. Tchr. music Ontario (Oreg.) Pub. Schs., 1965-67, Redding (Calif.) Pub. Schs., 1969-74; entertainer Buck Owens Enterprises, Bakersfield, Calif., 1974-78, Tulsa, 1979—; concertmistress Boise (Idaho) Philharm., 1965-67, Shasta Symphony, Redding, 1969-74. Rec. artist (violinist, vocalist) Lark Records, 1978—. Avocations: skiing, tennis, swimming. Office: Jana Jae Enterprises Lake Record Prodns Inc PO Box 35726 Tulsa OK 74153

OWENS, JOHN MURRY, dean; b. Livermore, Calif., Feb. 13, 1942; s. John Stephen and Hazel Mae (Murry) O.; m. Diane Davis, June 12, 1971; children: John, Jennifer, Mark. AA, Orange Coast Coll., 1961; BSEE, U. Calif., Berkeley, 1963; MSEE, Stanford U., 1964, PhD, 1968. Registered profl. engr., Tex. Prof. elec. engring. U. Tex., Arlington, 1979-87, dir. bur. engring., 1983-85, asst. dean rsch. coll. engring., 1983-85, dir. ctr. for advanced electron devices, 1984-87; prof., chmn. elec. engring. dept. Santa Clara (Calif.) U., 1987-89; program dir. NSF, Washington, 1989-91; prof., dir. engring. exptl. sta., assoc. dean for rsch. Auburn (Ala.) U., 1991—; cons. Microwave and Electronic Systems Ltd., Edinburgh, United Kingdom, Ivory and Sime Ltd., Edinburgh, Herbies Foods, Fort Worth, Tex. Instruments, Dallas, Rockwell Internat., Anaheim, Calif., Westinghouse Electric, Pitts., E.W. Communication Inc., Palo Alto, Calif., Telsar, Inc., Campbell, Calif., ITT Aerospace and Optical, Ft. Wayne, Ind., SMA, Inc., Florence, Italy, many others. Patentee in field. Bd. dirs. Arlington Swim Club; dist. chmn. boy Scouts Am., Auburn; bd. dirs. Arlington Gifted and Talented Assn.; pres. Masters of Upper Tex. Swimmers. Fellow IEEE; mem. Am. Soc. Engring. Edn., Kiwanis (bd. dirs. Arlington club), Tau Beta Pi, Eta Kappa Nu, Sigma Xi. Avocations: swimming, water skiing, camping, hiking, airplanes. Office: Auburn U 108 Ramsay Hall Auburn AL 36849*

OWENS, JOSEPH, clergyman; b. Saint John, N.B., Can., Apr. 17, 1908; s. Louis Michael and Josephine (Quinn) O. Student, St. Mary's Coll., 1922-27, St. Anne's Coll., Montreal, Que. Can., 1928-30, St. Alphonsus Coll., Woodstock, Ont., Can., 1930-34; M.S.D., Pontifical Inst. Mediaeval Studies, Toronto, 1951. Ordained priest Roman Cath. Ch., 1933; parish asst. St. Joseph's Ch., Moose Jaw, Sask., Can., 1934-35, St. Patrick's Ch., Toronto, 1935-36, Maria-Hilf Ch., Tomslake, B.C., Can., 1940-44; instr. philosophy St. Alphonsus Sem., Woodstock, Ont., Can., 1936-40, 48-51, 53, Assumption U., Windsor, Ont., Can., 1954; with Pontifical Inst. of Mediaeval Studies, Toronto, 1954—; prof. Pontifical Inst. of Mediaeval Studies, 1960—; instr. mediaeval moral doctrine Accademia Alfonsiana, Rome, Italy, 1952-53; mem. faculty dept. philosophy Sch. Grad. Studies, U. Toronto. Mem. editorial bd.: The Monist, 1961—; Contbr. numerous articles to religious and profl. jours. Mem. Canadian Philos. Assn. (pres. 1981-82), Am. Catholic Philos. Assn. (pres. 1965-66), Metaphys. Soc. Am. (councillor 1965-67, pres. 1971-72), Soc. Ancient Greek Philosophy (pres. 1971-72), Catholic Commn. Intellectual and Cultural Affairs, Royal Soc. Can. Home: 141 McCaul St, Toronto, ON Canada M5T 1W3 Office: 59 Queen's Park Crescent, Toronto, ON Canada M5S 2C4

OWENS, JOSEPH FRANCIS, III, physics educator; b. Syracuse, N.Y., Sept. 23, 1946; s. Joseph Francis Jr. and Georgianna (Borst) O.; m. Linda S.; children: Jeffrey Forrest, Susan Melinda. BS, Worcester Polytechnic Inst., 1968; PhD, Tufts U., 1973. Rsch. assoc. Case Western Res. U., Cleve., 1973-76; rsch. assoc. Fla. State U., Tallahassee, 1976-79, rsch. asst. prof., 1979-80, asst. prof., 1980-82, assoc. prof., 1982-85, prof., 1985—, assoc. chmn. physics dept., 1988-91, chmn. physics dept., 1991—, disting. rsch. prof., 1995. Contbr. articles to profl. jours. Named Outstanding Jr. Investigator, U.S. Dept. Energy, 1979; recipient Developing Scholar award Fla. State U., 1982. Fellow Am. Phys. Soc.; mem. Acad. Model Aeronautics, Aircraft Owners and Pilots Assn., Exptl. Aircraft Assn. Achievements include rsch. in theoretical high energy physics using perturbation theory applied to quantum chromodynamics, scaling violations, structure functions, high-pt. processes, higher order calculations. Office: Fla State U Physics Dept B # 3106 Tallahassee FL 32306-3106

OWENS, MAJOR ROBERT ODELL, congressman; b. Memphis, June 28, 1936; m. Marie Cuprill; children: Christopher, Geoffrey, Millard, Carlos, Cecilia. Grad. with high honors, Morehouse Coll., 1956; M.S., Atlanta U., 1957. Mem. Internat. Commn. on Ways of Implementing Social Policy to Ensure Maximum Pub. Participation and Social Justice for Minorities, The Hague, Netherlands, 1972, 98th-105th Congresses from 12th (now 11th) N.Y. dist., 1983—; chmn. select edn. & civil rights subcom., edn. and labor com., 1987, ranking minority mem. econ. and ednl. opportunity subcom. on worker protections, mem. govt. reform and oversight com.; featured speaker White House Conf. on Librs., 1979. Pub. author and lectr. on library sci. Chmn. Bklyn. Congress Racial Equality; v.p. Met. Coun. on Housing, 1964; community coord. Bklyn. Pub. Library, 1964-66; exec. dir. Brownsville Community Coun., 1966-68; commr. N.Y.C. Community Devel. Agy., 1968-73; bd. dirs. community media program Columbia U., N.Y.C., 1973-75; mem. N.Y. State Senate, 1975-82, chmn. Dem. Ops. Com. Major R. Owens Day, named in his honor, City Bklyn., 1971. Office: US Ho of Reps 2305 Rayburn HOB Washington DC 20515-2311*

OWENS, MARILYN MAE, elementary school educator, secondary school educator; b. Poland, Ohio, Nov. 17, 1932; d. S. Reed and Vernice Mae (Flickinger) Johnson; m. J. Edward Owens, July 23, 1953; children: Charlene, Preston, Lorraine. BS in Art Edn., Millersville State U., 1970, elem. cert., 1983; MEd in Art, Towson U., 1975; elem. prin. cert., Western Md. U., 1984. Cert. elem. and secondary tchr. art, elem. tchr., Pa.; art supr. elem. and secondry, prin. elem., Md. Tchr art k-12 Northeastern Sch. Dist., Manchester, Pa., 1970—; adj. instr. humanities, art appreciation York Coll. of Pa., 1977-81; mem. long range planning com., Northeastern Sch. Dist., Manchester, 1988-90, supt.'s adv. bd., 1990-91, elem. adv. bd. Orendorf Sch., 1990-92, dist. budget com., 1991-92, elem. budget com. Conewago Elem. Sch., 1993-94, 94-95, 95-96, 96-97, computer tech. elem. com., 1993-94, 94-95, instrnl. and profl. devel. com., 1994-95, 95-96, 96-97, calligraphy tchr. Northeastern Adult Cmty. Edn., 1988-90. Leader Girl Scouts of U.S., Penn Laurel, York, Pa., 1963-67; mem. Northeastern Art Out-Reach program, Northeastern Edn. Assn. Comty. Rels. Com., Northeastern Sch. Dist.'s Portfolio Com. Recipient scholarship Ind. (Pa.) State Coll., 1950; grantee Northeastern Sch. Dist., Manchester, 1989-90. Mem. AAUW, Nat. Art Edn. Assn., Northeastern Edn. Assn. (v.p. 1987-88, pres. 1988-89, community rels. program 1993-95), Pa. Art Edn. Assn., Pa. Guild of Craftsmen (Yorktowne chpt.), Pa. Inst. CPA (Women's Aux. S. Ctrl. chpt.), York Art Assn., Phi Delta Kappa (scholarship com. 1990-94). Avocations: painting, crafts, hiking, camping, sewing. Home: 2505 Schoolhouse Ln York PA 17402-3918 Office: Northeastern Sch Dist 48 Harding St Manchester PA 17345-1100

OWENS, MARVIN FRANKLIN, JR., oil company executive; b. Oklahoma City, Feb. 20, 1916; s. Marvin Franklin and Levis (Coley) O.; m. Jessie Ruth Hay, June 15, 1941; children: Marvin Franklin III, William Earl, Jack Hay. B.S., U. Okla., 1937; postgrad., Stonier Grad. Sch. Banking Rutgers U., 1960-62. Petroleum engr. Brit. Am. Oil Producing Co., Oklahoma City, 1937-41; chief petroleum engr. Bay Petroleum Corp., Denver, 1946-54; sr. v.p. Cen. Bank of Denver, 1954-81. Elder Presbyn. Ch., Denver. With U.S. Army, 1941-46; col. Res. ret. Mem. Cherry Hills Country Club. Home: 3899 S Glencoe St Denver CO 80237-1024

OWENS, MERLE WAYNE, executive search consultant; b. Barnsdall, Okla., Mar. 30, 1933; s. Jesse Raymond and Beulah Juanita (Thompson) O.; m. Nettie Natalie Norris, June 6, 1953; children: Jesse Wayne, Jennifer Lee. BBA, U. Okla., 1955. Sales engr. Nat. Supply Co., Tulsa, 1956-60; underwriter Allstate Ins., Dallas, 1960-63; regional mgr. Blue Cross Blue Shield, Dallas, 1963-78; sr. v.p. Paul R. Ray & Co., Ft. worth, 1978-93; owner Merle Owens & Assocs., Ft. worth, 1993—. 1st lt. U.S. Army, 1955-56. Republican. Baptist. Avocations: hunting, fishing, woodworking. Home: 420 Blue Jay Ct Bedford TX 76021-3201 Office: Merle W Owens & Assocs 301 Commerce St Ste 1205 Fort Worth TX 76102-4112

OWENS, ROBIN MARIA, management consultant; b. Tulsa, Sept. 3, 1956; d. Robert Perry and Dorothy Cleo (Hopper) O. BA, Austin Coll., 1978; MBA, Harvard U., 1985. Systems rep. IBM, Tyler, Tex., 1978-83; area rep. IBM, Dallas, 1985-87; mktg. rep. IBM, Tyler, 1987-96; mgmt. cons. IBM, Dallas, 1997—. Treas. Hist. Tyler, Inc., 1990, bd. dirs., 1989; participant Leadership Tyler, 1988; Rep. treas. Grayson County, Sherman, Tex., 1977. Mem. Harvard Bus. Sch. Club Dallas, Harvard Club Dallas, Jr. League Dallas, Dallas Coun. World Affairs. Home: 8611 Labron Ave Dallas TX 74209-1703

OWENS, ROCHELLE, poet, playwright; b. Bklyn., Apr. 2, 1936; d. Max and Molly (Adler) Bass; m. George Economou, June 17, 1962. Fellow, Yale Sch. Drama, 1968. writer-in-residence, Brown U., 1989; tchr. U. Calif. 1982, U. Okla., 1985, 87, 88. Author: plays The String Game, 1965, Istanboul, 1965, Futz, 1967, Homo, 1966, Beclch, 1966, Futz and What Came After, 1968, He Wants Shih, 1969, Farmers Almanac, 1969, The Queen of Greece, 1969, Kontraption, 1970, The Karl Marx Play, 1971, O.K. Certaldo, 1975, Emma Instigated Me, 1976, The Widow and the Colonel, 1977, Mountain Rites, 1977, Who Do You Want, Peire Vidal, 1978, Chucky's Hunch, 1981, Who Do You Want, Peire Vidal, 1982; poetry Not be Essence That Cannot Be, 1961, Salt and Core, 1968, I am the Babe of Joseph Stalin's Daughter, Poems from Joe's Garage, The Joe 82 Creation Poems, The Karl Marx Play & Others, The Joe Chronicles, Part 2, Four Young Lady Poets, 1962, Shemuel, 1979, French Light, 1984, Constructs, 1985, Anthropologists at a Dinner Party, 1985, Who Do You Want Peire Vidal, 1986, W.C. Fields in French Light, 1986, How Much Paint Does the Painting Need, 1988, New and Selected Poems: 1961-1996, Black Chalk, 1992, Rubbed Stones: Poems from 1960-1992, 1994; (radio play) Sweet Potatoes, 1979 (Obie award 1982); (feature film) Futz, 1969; editor: (plays) Spontaneous Combustion; (Obie award 1967), Cimmarron Rev.; recs. include: From a Shaman's Notebook, 1968, The Karl Marx Play, 1974, Totally Corrupt, 1976, Black Box 17, 1979, (play) Three Front, 1990; (radio play) Guerre a'Trois, 1991; reading performances at St. Mark's Poetry Project, Mus. Modern Art, Guggenheim, Whitney Mus., Oxford U., Am. Coll., Paris; host of The Writer's Mind; producer radio show, U. Okla.; (video) Oklahoma Too, 1987, How Much Paint Does The Painting Need, 1992; translator Festival Franco-Anglais, 1991, The Passersby, 1993; (video) Black Chalk, 1994. Founding mem. N.Y. Theatre Strategy, Women's Theatre Council. Ford Found. grantee, 1965, Creative Arts Pub. Svc. grantee, 1973, Nat. Endowment for Arts grantee, 1974, Rockfeller Found. grantee, 1974; Guggenheim fellow, 1971; honors N.Y. Drama Critics Cir.; Rockefeller Found. Bellagio resident, 1993; recipient Nomination in poetry Okla. Ctr. for the Book, 1995. Mem. Dramatists Guild, ASCAP. Included in anthologies. Address: 1401 Magnolia St Norman OK 73072-6827 *Creativity, idealism and mental concentration have enabled me to pursue the world of ideas, transforming itself always into art.*

OWENS, RODNEY JOE, lawyer; b. Dallas, Mar. 7, 1950; s. Hubert L. and Billie Jo (Foust) O.; m. Sherry Lyn Bailey, June 10, 1972; 1 child, Jonathan Rockwell. BBA, So. Meth. U., 1972, JD, 1975. Bar: Tex. 1975, U.S. Dist. Ct. (no. dist.) Tex. 1975, U.S. Tax Ct. 1975, U.S. Ct. Appeals (5th cir.) 1975. Assoc. Durant & Mankoff, Dallas, 1975-78, ptnr., 1978-83; ptnr. Meadows, Owens, Collier, Reed, Cousins & Blau, Dallas, 1983—. Contbr. articles to profl. jours. Baptist. Home: 6919 N Jan Mar Dr Dallas TX 75230-3111 Office: Meadows Owens Collier Reed 901 Main St Ste 3700 Dallas TX 75202-3742

OWENS, STEPHEN J., lawyer; b. Kansas City, Mo., June 4, 1955. BSPA, U. Mo., 1977; JD, Wake Forest U., 1980. Bar: Mo. 1980, U.S. Dist. Ct. (we. dist.) Mo. 1980, U.S. Ct. Appeals (8th cir.) 1981, U.S. Ct. Appeals (10th cir.) 1982, U.S. Ct. Appeals (5th cir.) 1988, U.S. Ct. Appeals (4th cir.) 1992. Law clerk to Hon. William R. Collinson U.S. Dist. Ct. (we. dist.) Mo., 1980-81; lawyer Stinson, Mag & Fizzell, Kansas City, Mo. Mem. ABA (litigation and natural resources divsns.), Mo. Bar, Kansas City Met. Bar Assn. Office: Stinson Mag & Fizzell PO Box 419251 Ste 2800 Kansas City MO 64141-6251

OWENS, W. LARRY, hotel executive. Pres. Hospitality Internat. Inc., Tucker, Ga. Office: Hospitality Internat Inc 1726 Montreal Cir Tucker GA 30084

OWENS, WILBUR DAWSON, JR., federal judge; b. Albany, Ga., Feb. 1, 1930; s. Wilbur Dawson and Estelle (McKenzie) O.; m. Mary Elizabeth Glenn, June 21, 1958; children: Lindsey, Wilbur Dawson III, Estelle, John. Student, Emory U., 1947-48; JD, U. Ga., 1952. Bar: Ga. 1952. Mem. firm Smith, Gardner & Owens, Albany, 1954-55; v.p., trust officer Bank of Albany, 1955-59; sec.-treas. Southeastern Mortgage Co., Albany, 1959-65; asst. U.S. atty. Middle Dist. Ga., Macon, 1962-65; assoc., then ptnr. Bloch, Hall, Hawkins & Owens, Macon, 1965-72; judge U.S. Dist. Ct. for Mid. Dist. Ga., Macon, 1972—, now sr. U.S. dist. judge. Served to 1st lt., JAG USAF, 1952-54. Mem. State Bar Ga., Macon Bar Assn., Am. Judicature Soc., Phi Delta Theta, Phi Delta Phi. Republican. Presbyterian. Clubs: Rotarian, Idle Hour Golf and Country. Office: US Dist Ct PO Box 65 Macon GA 31202-0065*

OWENS, WILLIAM DON, anesthesiology educator; b. St. Louis, Dec. 12, 1939; s. Don and Caroline Wilhemena (Raaf) O.; m. Patricia Gail Brown, Dec. 12, 1964; children: Pamela, David, Susan. AB, Westminster Coll., 1961; MD, U. Mich., 1965. Diplomate Am. Bd. Anesthesiology. Resident and fellow Mass. Gen. Hosp. and Harvard Med. Sch., Boston, 1969-72; instr. Harvard Med. Sch., Boston, 1972-73; asst. prof. anesthesiology Washington U. Sch. Medicine, St. Louis, 1973-76, assoc. prof., 1976-82, prof., 1982—, chmn. dept., 1982-92; trustee Barnes Hosp., St. Louis, 1987-89; bd. dirs. Anesthesia Found.; sec.-treas. Am. Bd. Anesthesiology, 1991-94, pres., 1995-96. Assoc. editor Survey of Anesthesiology, 1977-92; contbr. 50 articles to profl. jours., 7 chpts. to books. Served to lt. comdr. USN, 1966-69. Fellow Am. Coll. Anesthesiology; mem. Am. Soc. Anesthesiologists (bd. dirs. 1989-95, 1st v.p. 1995-96, pres.-elect 1996—), Internat. Anesthesia Rsch. Soc., Acad. Anesthesiology, Assn. Univ. Anesthesiologists. Office: Washington U Sch Med Dept Anesthesiology 660 S Euclid Ave Saint Louis MO 63110-1010 also: Am Bd Anesthesiology The Summit Ste 510 4101 Lake Boone Trail Raleigh NC 27607-7506

OWEN-TOWLE, CAROLYN SHEETS, clergywoman; b. Upland, Calif., July 27, 1935; d. Millard Owen and Mary (Baskerville) Sheets; m. Charles Russell Chapman, June 29, 1957 (div. 1973); children: Christopher Charles, Jennifer Anne, Russell Owen; m. Thomas Allan Owen-Towle, Nov. 16, 1973. BS in Art and Art History, Scripps Coll., 1957; postgrad. in religion, U. Iowa, 1977; DD, Meadville/Lombard Theol. Sch., Chgo., 1994. Ordained to ministry Unitarian-Universalist Ch., 1978. Minister 1st Unitarian Universalist Ch., San Diego, 1978—; pres. Ministerial Sisterhood, Unitarian Universalist Ch., 1980-82; mem. Unitarian Universalist Svc. Com., 1979-85, pres., 1983-85. Bd. dirs. Planned Parenthood, San Diego, 1980-86; mem. clergy adv. com. to Hospice, San Diego, 1980-83; mem. U.S. Rep. Jim Bates Hunger Adv. Com., San Diego, 1983-87; chaplain Interfaith AIDS Task Force, San Diego, 1988—. Mem. Unitarian Universalist Ministers Assn. (exec. com. 1988, pres. 1989-91). Avocations: reading, walking, combating racism, promoting human rights, designing environments. Office: 1st Unitarian Universalist Ch 4190 Front St San Diego CA 92103-2030

OWINGS, DONALD HENRY, psychology educator; b. Atlanta, Dec. 7, 1943; s. Markley James and Loyce Erin (White) O.; m. Sharon Elizabeth Calhoun, Jan. 29, 1966; children: Ragon Matthew, Anna Rebekah. BA in Psychology, U. Tex., 1965; PhD, U. Wash., 1972. Asst. prof. psychology U. Calif., Davis, 1971-78, assoc. prof., 1978-83, prof., 1983—, chair dept., 1989-93. Contbr. articles to profl. jours., book chpts. NSF rsch. grantee, 1978-80, 82-84. Fellow Animal Behavior Soc.; mem. Internat. Soc. for Ecol.

Psychology, Internat. Soc. for Behavioral Ecology, Internat. Soc. for Comparative Psychology, Am. Psychol. Soc. Democrat. Avocations: hiking, music, bird watching, reading. Home: 815 Oeste Dr Davis CA 95616-1856 Office: U Calif Dept Psychology Davis CA 95616-8686

OWINGS, FRANCIS BARRE, surgeon; b. McColl, S.C., Mar. 9, 1941; s. Ralph Seer and Antoinette (Moore) O.; B.S., U. Miss., 1963, M.D., 1966; m. Judith Myers, Feb. 14, 1976; children—F. Patterson, Caroline C. Intern, San Francisco Gen. Hosp., 1966-67; resident in surgery U. Calif., San Francisco, 1969-74; surg. registrar Norfolk and Norwich Hosp., Norwich, Eng., 1971-72; practice medicine specializing in surgery, Atlanta, 1974—; mem. staff Crawford Long Hosp., pres. med. staff, 1981-82; mem. staff Piedmont Hosp.; clin. instr. surgery Emory U. Served to capt. USAF, 1967-69. Diplomate Am. Bd. Surgery. Fellow ACS, Southeastern Surg. Congress; mem. Med. Assn. Atlanta, Med. Assn. Ga., Naffziger Surg. Soc., Alpha Epsilon Delta, Sigma Chi, Phi Chi. Republican. Methodist. Home: 3400 Wood Valley Rd NW Atlanta GA 30327-1518 Office: 478 Peachtree St NE Atlanta GA 30308-3103

OWINGS, MALCOLM WILLIAM, retired management consultant; b. Cin., Feb. 5, 1925; s. William Malcolm and Margaret (Benvie) O.; m. Margie M. Gehiker, Sept. 4, 1948; children: Lynn A., Sandra S., Wendy K., Cheryl M. B.S. in Bus. Adminstrn., Miami U., Oxford, Ohio, 1950, LL.D., 1976; A.M.P., Harvard U., 1975. With Continental Can Co., 1950-83, corp. v.p., from 1971; v.p., gen. mgr. pub. affairs Continental Packaging Co (Continental Group, Inc.), 1982-83; owner, pres. Owings Assocs., Inc., Pinehurst, N.C., 1983-92; dir. First Bank, Pinehurst, N.C.; adviser to Am. del. Internat. Tin Council, 1978-82. Dean's assoc. exec. in residence Sch. Bus., Miami U., 1973, mem. alumni coun., 1958-65, mem. pres.'s devel. coun., 1965-69, meem. resource devel. bd., 1982; trustee Village of Thiensville, Wis., 1956-59; mem. N.C. Clean, 1985-94, chmn., 1986-93; bd. dirs. Barrington Area Devel. Coun., 1974-79, Sales Mgmt. Execs. Grad. Sch., Am. Soc. Environment, 1976, Keep Am. Beautiful, 1980-81, also chmn., 1990; chmn. Keep N.C. Beautiful Coun., Raleigh, 1988-92, Moore Meml. Hosp. Found., Pinehurse, N.C., 1986-89; mem. Moore Regional Hosp. Scroll Soc., 1991—, chmn., 1992-93; chmn. Moore County (N.C.) Rep. Party, 1986-88; co-founder Rep. Presdl. Task Force; mem. U.S. Senate Bus. Adv. Bd., 1981-91; commr. Moore County, 1988-96, Youth Svcs., 1993-95; apptd. to N.C. Watershed Protection Adv. Com. by N.C. Environ. Mgmt. Commn., 1990-92; bd. dirs. Pub. Edn. Found., 1994—, Ptnrs. for Children and Family, 1994—, Drug-Free Moore County Inc., 1995—, Dispute Settlement Ctr. of Moore County, 1995-97; mem. Moore County Bd. of Health, 1994-97. Recipient Cert. of Meritorious Svc. Miami U., 1967, Meritorious Svc. award Keep Moore County Beautiful, Inc., 1993-94; named Alumnus of Yr. Miami U., 1970; 1st Am. recipient Order of Apteryx Earth Awareness Found., 1971. Mem. Ill. C. of C. (bd. dirs. 1976-78), Miami U. Alumni Assn. (nat. pres. 1964-65), Omicron Delta Kappa, Sigma Chi, Delta Sigma Pi. Clubs: Pinehurst Country, Country of N.C. (Pinehurst). Home and Office: 805 Diamond Head Dr S Pinehurst NC 28374-9773 *The Golden Rule - "treating others as thyself" is not only a cornerstone for success, it is the foundation of personal happiness. However, it is well to remember that none of this is possible without political freedom and the contingent responsibilities that freedom requires.*

OWINGS, MARGARET WENTWORTH, conservationist, artist; b. Berkeley, Calif., Apr. 29, 1913; d. Frank W. and Jean (Pond) Wentworth; m. Malcolm Millard, 1937; 1 child, Wendy Millard Benjamin; m. Nathaniel Alexander Owings, Dec. 30, 1953. A.B., Mills Coll., 1934; postgrad., Radcliffe Coll., 1935; LHD (hon.), Mills Coll., 1993. One-woman shows include Santa Barbara (Calif.) Mus. Art, 1940, Stanford Art Gallery, 1951, stitchery exhbns. at M.H. De Young Mus., San Francisco, 1963, Internat. Folk Art Mus., Santa Fe, 1965. Commr. Calif. Parks, 1963-69, mem., Nat. Parks Found. Bd, 1968-69; bd. dirs. African Wildlife Leadership Found., 1968-80, Defenders of Wildlife, 1969-74; founder, pres. Friends of the Sea Otter, 1969-90; chair Calif. Mountain Lion Preservation Found., 1987; trustee Environmental Def. Fund, 1972-83; Regional trustee Mills Coll., 1962-68. Recipient Gold medal, Conservation Svc. award U.S. Dept. Interior, 1975, Convervation award Calif. Acad. Scis., 1979, Am. Motors Conservation award, 1980, Joseph Wood Krutch medal Humane Soc. U.S., Nat. Audubon Soc. medal, 1983, A. Starker Leopole award Calif. Nature Conservancy, 1986, Gold medal UN Environment Program, 1988, Conservation award DAR, 1990, Disting. Svc. award Sierra Club, 1991. Home: Grimes Point Big Sur CA 93920

OWNBY, CHARLOTTE LEDBETTER, anatomy educator; b. Amory, Miss., July 27, 1947; d. William Moss and Anna Faye (Long) Ledbetter; m. James Donald Ownby, Sept. 6, 1969; children: Holly Ruth, Mary Faye. BS in Zoology, U. Tenn., 1969, MS in Zoology, 1971; PhD in Anatomy, Colo. State U., 1975. Instr. Okla. State U., Stillwater, 1974-75, asst. prof., 1975-80, assoc. prof., 1980-84, prof., 1984—, regents prof., 1990—; dir. electron microscope lab. Okla. State U., Stillwater, 1977—, head dept., 1990-95. Editor Proc. 9th World Congress Internat. Soc. Toxicology, 1989; editorial bd. Toxion, 1984—. Recipient SmithKline-Beecham award for rsch. excellence, 1992; NIH, USPHS grantee, 1979-92. Mem. Okla. Soc. Electron Microscopy (pres. 1977-78), Pan Am. Soc. Toxinology (pres. 1984-96), Internat. Soc. of Toxinology (pres. 1994-97), Phi Beta Kappa, Sigma Xi, Phi Kappa Phi. Avocations: butterfly photography, bird watching, hiking, fishing. Office: Okla State U Anatomy Pathology and Pharmacology Dept Physiol Scis 264 Vet Medicine Stillwater OK 74078

OWNBY, DENNIS RANDALL, pediatrician, allergist, educator, researcher; b. Athens, Ohio, July 14, 1948; s. Dillard Ralph and Miriam (Lee) O.; m. Helen Louise Engelbrecht, May 24, 1970; children: David Randall, Kathryn Louise. BS, Ohio U., 1969; MD, Med. Coll. Ohio, 1972. Diplomate Am. Bd. Allergy and Immunology, Am. Bd. Pediatrics, Nat. Bd. Med. Examiners. Intern and resident Duke U. Sch. Medicine, Durham, N.C., 1972-74, asst. prof., 1977-80; staff physician Henry Ford Hosp., Detroit, 1980—, dir. Allergy Rsch. Lab., 1986—; clin. asst. prof. pediat. U. Mich., Ann Arbor, 1980-86, clin. assoc. prof., 1986-95. Contbr. articles to med. jours., chpts. to books. Recipient Young Investigator award Nat. Inst. Allergy and Infectious Disease, 1978. Fellow Am. Acad. Pediatrics, Am. Acad. Allergy. Office: Henry Ford Hosp Dept Allergy & Clin Immunology 2799 W Grand Blvd Detroit MI 48202-2608

OWNBY, JERE FRANKLIN, III, lawyer; b. Chicago Heights, Ill., Oct. 1, 1956; s. Jere Franklin Jr. and Emogene (Stephens) O.; m. Melissa Cooley, Mar. 17, 1990. BA, U. Tenn., 1986, JD, 1991. Bar: Tenn. 1991. Assoc. Law Offices of Peter G. Angelos, Knoxville, Tenn., 1991—. Mem. ABA, Assn. Trial Lawyers Am., Am. Inn of Ct., Tenn. Bar Assn., Knoxville Bar Assn., Tenn. Trial Lawyers Assn. Libertarian. Presbyterian. Avocation: gardening. Home: 3902 Glenfield Dr Knoxville TN 37919-6698 Office: Law Offices Peter G Angelos 2643 Kingston Pike Knoxville TN 37919-3399

OWNBY, JERRY STEVE, landscape architect, educator; b. Shawnee, Okla., Jan. 25, 1939; s. Hugh H. and N. Lorraine (Hopkins) O.; children by previous marriage: Gregory Steve, Mitchell Hugh; m. Arnola Colson, Dec. 19, 1971; 1 child, Steven Cory. BS, Okla. State U., 1961; MS in Landscape Architecture, Kans. State U., 1964, M in Landscape Architecture, 1970. Coun. Landscape Archtl. Registration Bds. cert. and registered landscape architect, Ariz., Kans., Okla., Mo., Tex. Extension landscape architect Kans. State U., Manhattan, 1963-64, instr., 1969-70; landscape architect Beardsley & Talley, Seattle, 1964-65; extension specialist Okla. State U., Stillwater, 1965-69, from asst. prof. to prof. landscape architecture and coordinator landscape architecture, 1970-85; pvt. practice, 1985—; chmn. Okla. Landscape Architect Registration Bd., 1980-85; mem. 1985 Expert Panel for Uniform Nat. Exam., 1984-85; gov.'s appointee Mo. Coun. Landscape Architects, 1991—. Designs include Las Laderas residence, 1978 (Merit award 1981), Student Union courtyard Okla. State U., 1981 (Honor award 1983). Chmn. Oklahomans for Landscape Architecture, 1979-80; chmn., vice chmn. Stillwater Park and Recreation Adv. Bd., Okla., 1971-79. Recipient Outstanding Prof. award Okla. State U. chpt. Alpha Zeta, 1975, svc. award Stillwater City Commn., 1980, design awards Springfield Planning and Zoning Commn., 1988, 89, 90, design award Springfield Environ. Adv. Bd., 1990, Gov.'s landscape design award for Andy Williams' Moon River Theatre, Branson, Mo., 1992, for Charley Pride Theater, Branson, 1995, design award Watershed Com., 1993; alumni fellow Kans. State U., 1995. Fellow Am. Soc. Landscape Architects (v.p. 1983-85, Okla. chpt. Svc. award 1980); mem. Nat. Coun. State Garden Clubs (accredited instr. 1964—), Nat. Coun. of Educators in Landscape Architecture, Mo. Assn. of Landscape Architects, Coun. Landscape Archtl. Registration Bds. (cert.), Phi Kappa Phi, Sigma Lambda Alpha. Republican. Baptist. Avocations: travel; photography; fishing. Home and Office: 1161 S Virginia Ave Springfield MO 65807-1727

OWSIA, NASRIN AKBARNIA, pediatrician; b. Babol, Iran, Dec. 5, 1940; came to U.S., 1968; d. Ahmad and Hoora O.; m. Behrooz A. Akbarnia, Mar. 19, 1968; children: Halleh, Ladan, Ramin. MD, Tehran (Iran) U., 1966. Intern in pediatrics Berkshire Med. Ctr. Hosp., Pittsfield, Mass., 1968-69; resident in pediatrics Albany (N.Y.) Med. Ctr. Hosp., 1969-72; pediatric gastroenterologist St. Christopher Hosp. for Children, Phila., 1972-73; asst. prof. Albany Med. Coll., 1973-76, Tehran U., 1976-80; asst. prof. St. Louis U. Med. Ctr., 1981-89, clin. assoc. prof., 1989-90; pvt. practice San Diego, 1990—. Bd. mem. Persian Cultural Ctr., San Diego, 1993—. Recipient award AMA. Fellow Am. Acad. Pediatrics; mem. Allergy and Asthma Found., Calif. Med. Soc., San Diego Med. Soc. Avocations: knitting, downhill skiing. Office: 8010 Frost St Ste 414 San Diego CA 92123-4284

OWSIANY, DAVID JAMES, lawyer, lobbyist; b. Livonia, Mich., Dec. 15, 1964; s. Thaddeus S. and Beatrice (DeBeul) O.; m. Kathryn Karoski, May 15, 1993. BA, U. Mich., 1987; JD, Washington U., St. Louis, 1991. Legal asst. U.S. Senate Jud. Com., Washington, 1991; jud. law clk. to Hon. Robert W. Cook Ill. Appellate Ct., Quincy, 1992-94; dir. legal and legis. affairs Ohio Dental Assn., Columbus, 1994—; legal editor Focus on Ohio Dentistry, Columbus, 1995—. Precinct del. Rep. Party, Redford, Mich., 1986-88; del. Mich. Rep. Convs., Lansing/Grand Rapids, 1986, 88; trustee Ohio Alliance for Civil Justice, Columbus, 1995—; cons. Ohio Citizens Against Lawsuit Abuse, 1995—. Mem. Mich. Bar Assn., Ohio Lobbying Assn., U. Mich. Alumni Assn., Federalist Soc. (Columbus lawyers chpt.), Century Club (mem. Ohio dental polit. action com.). Avocations: reading, writing. Home: 6924 Peachtree Cir Westerville OH 43082-4831 Office: Ohio Dental Assn 1370 Dublin Rd Columbus OH 43215-1009

OWSLEY, DAVID THOMAS, art consultant, appraiser, lecturer, author; b. Dallas, Aug. 20, 1929; s. Alvin Mansfield and Lucy (Ball) O. Grad., Phillips Andover Acad., 1947; A.B., Harvard, 1951; M.F.A., N.Y. U., 1964; fellow, Met. Mus. Am. Wing, 1964. Asst. curator dept. decorative arts and sculpture Boston Mus. Fine Arts, 1965-66; visitor Victoria and Albert Mus., London, Eng., 1966-68; curator antiquities, Oriental and decorative arts Mus. Art, Carnegie Inst., Pitts., 1968-78; mem. collections com. Dallas Mus. Art, 1994—. Served to 1st lt. USAF, 1952-54. Recipient Pres.' medal of Distinction Ball State U., 1989, Westmoreland Soc. Gold medal, 1991. Clubs: D.U. (Harvard Coll.); Leland Country (Mich.); Knickerbocker (N.Y.C.). Home: 116 E 68th St New York NY 10021-5905 *I have tried to pursue beautiful and significant works of art and to encourage others to share my love and respect for them.*

OWSLEY, WILLIAM CLINTON, JR., radiologist; b. Austin, Tex., Oct. 6, 1923; s. William Clinton and Lois (Lamar) O.; B.A., U. Tex., 1944; M.D., U. Pa., 1946; m. Betty Pinckard, 1949; 2 children. Intern, Hermann Hosp., Houston, 1946-47; resident Hosp. of U. Pa., Phila., 1949-52; instr. radiology U. Pa., 1950-52; practice medicine specializing in radiology, Houston, 1952—; mem. staff Hermann Hosp., Twelve Oaks Hosp., Bellville Hosp., St. Elizabeth Hosp., Brazos Valley Hosp.; assoc. clin. prof. radiology U. Tex. Served with USNR, 1947-48. Diplomate Am. Bd. Radiology. Fellow Royal Soc. Medicine (U.K.), Am. Coll. Radiology; mem. Am. Roentgen Ray Soc., Radiol. Soc. N.Am., Interam. Coll. Radiology, AMA. Republican. Baptist. Office: 4710 Greeley St Ste 230 Houston TX 77006-6254

OWYANG, CHUNG, gastroenterologist, researcher; b. Chung King, China, Nov. 20, 1945; arrived in Can., 1965; s. Chi and Ching-Ying (Fung) O.; m. Jeannette Lim; children: Stephanie, Christopher. BS with honors, McGill U., Montreal, Can., 1968, MD, 1972. Diplomate Am. Bd. Internal Medicine, Gastroenterology; lic. Gen. Med. Coun., U.K., Que., Can., Min. Med. lic., Mich. med. lic. Intern in internal medicine Montreal Gen. Hosp./McGill U., 1972-73, resident in internal medicine, 1973-75; clin. teaching fellow in internal medicine McGill U., 1974-75; fellow in gastroenterology Mayo Clinic and Found., Rochester, Minn., 1975-78; instr. internal medicine Mayo Med. Sch., Rochester, 1977-78; asst. prof. U. Mich., 1978-84, assoc. prof., 1984-88, assoc. chief divsn. gastroenterology, 1984-90, prof., 1988—, chief divsn. gastroenterology, 1991—, dir. med. procedures unit, 1992—, dir. Digestive Health Inst., 1992—; assoc. dir. Gastrointestinal Peptide Rsch. Ctr., U. Mich., 1984-95, dir. 1996—; cons. Rsch. Coun. Janssen Pharmaceutica Inc., 1985—, Ann Arbor VA Med. Ctr., 1978—, NIH, Bethesda, Md., 1989-94, FDA, Bethesda, 1995—; H. Marvin Pollard chair in gastroenterology, U. Mich., 1996—; speaker, presenter in field. Co-author: Textbook of Gastroenterology, 1991, 2d edit. 1995, Atlas of Gastroenterology, 1992; mem. edit. bd. Pancreas, 1986—, Am. Jour. Physiology, 1988—, Regulatory Peptide Letter, 1988—, Gastroenterology, 1990—, guest editor, 1991—, Digestive Diseases, 1993—; contbr. numerous chpts. to books, articles to profl. jours., jours. refereed. Grantee in field. Fellow ACP; mem. Am. Assn. Physicians, Am. Soc. Clin. Investigation, Am. Gastroenterological Assn., Am. Pancreatic Assn., Am. Diabetes Assn., Am. Fedn. Clin. Rsch., Am. Motility Soc., Ctrl. Soc. Clin. Rsch., Internat. Assn. Pancreatology, Midwest Gut Club. Office: U Mich Med Ctr 3912 Taubman Ctr Ann Arbor MI 48109

OWYOUNG, STEVEN DAVID, curator; b. San Francisco, Jan. 14, 1947; s. Fay and Ethel (Woo) O.; m. Diana Lee Wong, Aug. 29, 1971; children: Christopher Mark, Todd Alexander. BA, U. Hawaii, 1973; MA, U. Mich., 1977, postgrad., 1978. Lectr., editor Nat. Palace Mus., Taipei, Taiwan, 1971-72; curatorial assoc. Fogg Art Mus., Harvard U., Cambridge, Mass., 1980-82, asst. curator, 1982-83; curator Asian arts St. Louis Art Mus., 1983—; sec. commn. bd. commrs. St. Louis Art Mus., 1991-93; vis. Washington U., St. Louis, 1990—; cons. and contbr. Getty Art History Info. Program, 1993-96. Bd. dirs. World Affairs Coun. St. Louis, 1984-86, Nanjing-St. Louis Sister Cities, 1989-90; del. Chinese painting historians to People's Republic China, 1980. Charles L. Freer fellow Freer Gallery Art, 1976, 77, Horace H. Rackham predoctoral fellow, 1978, Louise W. Hackney fellow Am. Oriental Soc., 1978-79, Fulbright-Hays fellow, 1978-79, Social Sci. Rsch. Coun. and Am. Coun. Learned Socs. fellow, 1978-80; Samuel H. Kress Found. grantee, 1980, Horace H. Rackham grantee, 1980, Asian Cultural Coun. grantee, 1990. Mem. Asian Art Soc. Washington U. (bd. dirs. 1983—). Office: St Louis Art Mus Forest Pk Saint Louis MO 63110

OXELL, LOIE GWENDOLYN, fashion and beauty educator, consultant, columnist; b. Sioux City, Iowa, Nov. 17, 1917; d. Lyman Stanley and Loie Erma (Crill) Barton; m. Eugene Edwin Eschenbrenner, Aug. 8, 1936 (dec. 1954); children: Patricia Gene, Eugene Edward (dec. Feb. 1994); m. Henry J. Oxell, Nov. 3, 1956 (dec. July 1994). AS in Fashion Merchandising, Broward C.C., Davie, Fla., 1978. Fashion rep. Crestmoor Suit & Coat Co., St. Louis, 1951-56; with "To the Ladies" weekly TV show "To the Ladies" weekly TV show KSD-TV, St. Louis, 1950s; cons./instr. Miami-Herald Newspaper Glamor Clinic, Miami, Fla., 1957-71; pres./owner Loie's (Loy's) Inc., Miami, Fla., 1958-71; pres., owner West Coast East Talent Agy.; instr./lectr. Charron-Williams Coll., Miami, 1973-77; instr. Fashion Inst. Ft. Lauderdale, Fla., 1977-86; pres./owner Image Power Unltd., Plantation, Fla., 1992—; lectr. in field; columnist Sr. Life and Boomer Times, Fla., 1995—. Author: I'd Like You to Meet My Wife, 1964; author comedy skits, fashion segments, commentary, and TV commls. Del Russo Beauty Show, 1960s; actress Red Skelton TV show, Miami, Fla., also fashion show prodns., TV commls. Vol. The Work Force, lectr., instr. The AARP Sr. Cmty. Svc. Employment Program (SCSEP), Ft. Lauderdale and Hollywood, Fla., 1987—; keynote spkr. nat. conv. SCSEP Product Dirs., Charlestown, S.C., 1986; life mem. women's com. Miami Children's Hosp.; faculty advisor Nu Tau Sigma sorority Charron Williams Coll., 1973-77; pres. Venice of Am. chpt. Am. Bus. Women's Assn., 1975-76. Recipient Cert. of Appreciation Dade County Welfare Dept. Youth Hall, Miami, 1966, Community TV Found., Miami, 1966, 71, Woman of the Yr. award Am. Bus. Women's Assn. (Venice of Am. chpt.), 1976-77, Award for Svc. AARP Sr. Community Svc. Program, 1993. Mem. The Fashion Group Internat. Avocations: bridge, golf. Office: Image Power Unltd 1859 N Pine Island Rd # 339 Plantation FL 33322-5224

OXENBURY, HELEN, children's writer, illustrator; b. Suffolk, Eng., June 2, 1938; d. Thomas Bernard and Muriel (Taylor) O.; m. John Burningham, Aug. 15, 1965; children: Lucy, William Benedict, Emily Josephine. Stage designer Colchester, Eng., 1960, Tel-Aviv, 1961; TV designer London, 1963. Author, illustrator: Number of Things, 1967, ABC of Things, 1971, Pig Tale, 1973, The Queen and Rosie Randall, 1979, 729 Curious Creatures, 1980, 729 Merry Mix-ips, 1980, 729 Puzzle People, 1989, 729 Animal Allsorts, 1980, Crazy Creatures, 1980, Assorted Animals, 1980, Bill and Stanley, 1981, Bedtime, 1982, Monkey See, Monkey Do, 1982, Holidays, 1982, Helping, 1982, Mother's Helper, 1982, Animals, 1982, Bearch Day, 1982, Shopping Trip, 1982, Good Night, Good Morning, 1982, The Birthday Party, 1983, The Dancing Class, 1983, Eating Out, 1983, The Car Trip, 1983, The Drive, 1983, The Checkup, 1983, First Day of School, 1983, First Day at Playschool, 1983, Playschool, 1983, Grandma and Grandpa, 1984, Our Dog, 1984, The Important Visitor, 1984, Helen Oxenbury Nursery Story Book, 1985, Tom and Pippo Go Shopping, 1988, Tom and Pippo's Day, 1988, Tom and Pippo in the Garden, 1988, Tom and Pippo Go for a Walk, 1988, Tom and Pippo Make a Mess, 1988, Tom and Pippo Read a Story, 1988, Tom and Pippo See the Moon, 1988, Tom and Pippo and the Washing Machine, 1988, Pippo Gets Lost, 1989, Tom and Pippo and the Dog, 1989, Tom and Pippo in the Snow, 1989, Tom and Pippo Make a Friend, 1989, Tom and Pippo on the Beach, 1993, It's My Birthday, 1994, First Nursery Stories, 1994; (with Fay Maschler): A Child's Book of Manners: Verses, 1978; illustrator: The Great Big Enormous Turnip, 1968, The Quangle-Wangle's Hat, 1969, Letters of Thanks, 1969, The Dragon of an Ordinary Family, 1969, The Hunting of the Snark, 1970, Meal One, 1971, Cakes and Custard: Children's Rhymes, 1974, Balooky Klujypop, 1975, Animal House, 1976, Tiny Tim: Verses for Children, 1981, We're Going on a Bear Hunt, 1989, Farmer Duck, 1992, The Three Little Wolves and the Big Bad Pig, 1993, So Much, 1994. Office: care Greene and Heaton Ltd, 37 Goldhawk Rd, London W12 8QQ, England

OXENHANDLER, NEAL, language educator, writer; b. St. Louis, Feb. 3, 1926; s. Joseph and Billie (Lutsky) O.; m. Jean Romano (div. May 1976); children: Noelle, Daniel, Alicia; m. Judith I. Josel, Dec. 12, 1979; stepchildren: Rebecca, Marjorie Menza. AB, U. Chgo., 1948; MA, Columbia U., 1951; PhD, Yale U., 1955; MA (hon.), Dartmouth Coll., 1973. Lectr. French St. Louis U., 1951-52; asst. instr. Yale U., New Haven, Conn., 1952-54, instr., 1954-57; asst. prof. UCLA, 1957-60, assoc. prof., 1960-65; assoc. prof. U. Calif., Santa Cruz, 1965-66, prof., 1966-69; prof. Dartmouth Coll., Hanover, N.H., 1969—, Edward Tuck prof., 1987—, chmn. dept. French and Italian, 1987-91; dir. NEH Summer Seminar in Comparative Lit., 1981. Author: Scandal and Parade: Theater of Jean Cocteau, 1957, Aspects of French Literature, 1961, French Literary Criticism: The Basis of Judgment, 1966, Max Jacob and Les Feux de Paris, 1964, (novel) A Change of Gods, 1962, Looking for Heroes in Post-War France, 1995; adv. editor Film Quar., Berkeley, 1958-91; mem. editl. com. U. Calif. Press, Berkeley, 1966-69; asst. editor French Rev., 1969-73; contbr. articles, revs., poetry and translations to profl. jours. With U.S. Army, 1941-43, ETO, PTO. Fulbright scholar, Italy, 1953; Cross-Disciplinary fellow Soc. for Values in Higher Edn., France, 1966, Guggenheim fellow, France, 1962, Inst. for Shipboard Edn., 1995. Mem. MLA (adv. editor proc. 1977-80), Internat. Assn. Philosophy and Lit., Internat. Comparative Lit. Assn. Democrat. Roman Catholic. Avocations: skiing, fly-fishing. Home: 468 Monroe Dr Sarasota FL 34236-1715 Office: Dartmouth Coll Dept French Hanover NH 03755

OXENKRUG, GREGORY FAYVA, psychopharmacologist; b. St. Petersburg, Russia, Oct. 25, 1941; arrived in U.S., 1980; s. Faiva Moshe and Rose Gregory (Sherman) O.; m. Rachel Maria Izrina, May 3, 1972 (div. Feb. 1993); children: Alexander, Daniel. MD, St. Petersburg Med. Sch., 1965; PhD, Bekhterev Psyco. Rsch. Inst., 1970; MA, Brown U., 1990. Asst. to assoc. prof. Bekhterev Phychoneurol. Rsch. Inst., St. Petersburg, 1970-79; clin. assoc. prof. dept. psychiatry Boston U., 1980-82; assoc. to prof. dept. pharmacology and psychiatry Wayne State U., Detroit, 1982-87; prof. dept. psychiatry Brown U., Providence, 1987-94, Tufts U., Boston, 1995—; chmn. dept. psychiatry St. Elizabeth's Med. Ctr., Boston, 1994—; chief psychiatry svc. VA Ctrs., Providence, 1988-94; chief inpatient psychiatry Lafayette Clinic, Detroit, 1982-88; dir. Pineal Rsch. Lab., 1984—. Contbr. over 100 articles to profl. jours. Recipient merit Review grant Dept. Vet. Affairs, 1990—. Fellow Am. Coll. Neuropsychopharmacology (ethics com.), Am. Soc. Biol. Psychiatry. Jewish. Avocation: English history. Office: St Elizabeths Medical Ctr 736 Cambridge St # 3P Boston MA 02135-2907

OXER, JOHN PAUL DANIELL, civil engineer; b. Atlanta, Sept. 7, 1950; s. Robert B. Sr. and Leila Marie (Hammond) O.; m. Catherine Ann Stevens, Jan. 8, 1977. BCE, Ga. Inst. Tech., 1973; postgrad., U. Tex., Arlington, 1982-83. Lic. profl. engr. Ala., Ark., Ariz., Calif., Colo., Conn., Del., Fla., Ga., Hawaii, Idaho, Ill., Ind., Iowa, Kans., Ky., La., Maine, Mich., Minn., Miss., Mo., Mont., Nebr., Nev., N.H., N.J., N.Mex., N.C., N.D., Okla., Oreg., S.C., S.D., Tenn., Tex., Utah, Vt., Va., Wash., W.Va., Wis., Wyo.; diplomate Am. Acad. Environ. Engrs. Project engr. J.S. Ross & Assocs. Inc., Smyrna, Ga., 1973-75, Welker & Assocs. Inc., Marietta, Ga., 1976-78; sr. project. engr. Claude Terry & Assocs., Inc., Atlanta, 1978-79; chief environ. engr. Bernard Johnson Inc. (SE), Atlanta, 1979-80; chief civil engr. region VI Ecology & Environ., Inc., Dallas, 1981-84; S.E. regional mgr. Ecology & Environ., Inc., Tallahassee, Fla., 1984-88; dir. program devel. Ecology & Environ., Inc., Dallas, 1988-91, exec. asst. to the pres., 1991-92; exec. asst. to the pres. Ecology & Environ., Inc., Houston, 1992—; guest lectr. Fla. State U., U. Louisville, Fla. State U.; mem. Industry Functional Adv. Com. on Stds. for Trade Policy Matters, 1993—. Executive producer video documentary; writer, producer video documentary; co-author, dir. video prodn. Mem. indsl. bd. advisors Speed Sci. Sch. U. Louisville, 1991—. Named Young Engr. of Yr., Ga. Soc. Profl. Engrs., 1980. Mem. NSPE, ASCE, Am. Pub. Works Assn., Am. Soc. Landscape Archs., Am. Soc. Agrl. Engrs., Nat. Def. Exec. Res. (assigned to Fed. Emergency Mgmt. Agy.), Masons. Republican. Avocations: piano, biathlon, photography, gardening. Office: Ecology & Environ Inc 4801 Woodway Dr # 280-w Houston TX 77056-1805 also: Ecology & Environ Inc 1999 Bryan St Ste 2000 Dallas TX 75201-6811

OXFORD, CHARLES WILLIAM, university dean, chemical engineer; b. Texarkana, Tex., Nov. 16, 1921; s. Charles Edward and Ellen (Alphin) O.; m. Mary Rae Mauzy, Dec. 24, 1946; children—Constance Susan, Catherine Ellen. BS, U. Ark., 1944, LLD (hon.), 1992; postgrad., U. Minn., 1946-48; PhD, U. Okla., 1952; DSc (hon.), U. Ark., Little Rock. Asst. chemist Koppers Co., 1941; control chemist W.S. Dickey, 1942; asst. prof. chem. engrng. U. Ark., 1948-50, asso. prof., 1952-57, prof., 1957—; asso. dean U. Ark. (Coll. Engrng.), 1960—; asso. dir. U. Ark. (Engrng. Expt. Sta.), 1964—, adminstrv. v.p. univ., 1968-73, exec. v.p., 1973-79, v.p. acad. affairs, 1979-88, v.p. emeritus, 1987—; exec. dir. U. Ark. Found., Inc., 1989-91; research participant Union Carbide Co., 1952; research engr. Boeing Airplane Co., 1955; cons. to industry. Exec. dir. U. Ark. Found., 1988-91. Served with USNR, 1944-46. Mem. Am. Inst. Chem. Engrs., Am. Soc. Engring. Edn., Am. Soc. Profl. Engrs., Sigma Xi, Tau Beta Pi, Alpha Chi Sigma, Omicron Delta Kappa. Club: Lion. Home: 110 Cyndee St Fayetteville AR 72703-3987

OXFORD, SHARON M., insurance company executive; b. Ekalaka, Mont., Aug. 30, 1939; d. Price S. and Myrtle I. (Wilkoski) Purdum; m. James L. Oxford Jr., Sept. 7, 1958 (div. May 1973); children: James L. III, Dana Renee, Monica Lynn Oxford Jones; m. Ronald Butts, Jan. 1, 1990. Degree in bus. adminstrn., Nat. Coll. Bus., Rapid City, S.D., 1958; student, Mesa (Ariz.) Community Coll., 1979-80. CPCU; cert. ins. counselor. Office mgr. Foster Fritchle Ins. Co., Colorado Springs, Colo., 1968-71, Mikes Ives Ins./Profl. Ins. Exchange, Colorado Springs, 1971-73; asst. to pres. Tolley-Weidman Ins. Co., Colorado Springs, 1973-76; rater Home Ins. Co., Phoenix, 1976-78; mgr. adminstrn. Fred S. James & Co. Ariz., Phoenix and Tempe, 1978-84; v.p. Sedgwick James, Tempe, 1984-85; sr. v.p. Sedgwick James (formerly Fred S. James & Co. Ariz.), Tempe, 1985—. Vol. MADD, store monitor Red Ribbon campaign; corr. sec. Young Reps., Colo. Springs, 1967; v.p. Colorado Springs chpt. Parents Without Prtnrs., 1975; team mem. Red Cross DAT, Mass Care Com. Mem. Am. Inst. for Property and Liability Underwriters, Soc. Cert. Ins. Counselors, Jaycee Wives (pres. Colorado Springs chpt. 1970), Assoc. of Automated Mgmt. Republican. Avocations: dancing, square dancing. Office: Sedgwick 1600 W Broadway Rd Ste 300 Tempe AZ 85282-1137

OXHANDLER, MYRA, mental health nurse; b. Bklyn., June 14, 1948; d. Charles and Beatrice (Brown) Raye; m. David Oxhandler, Sept. 21, 1987; children: Bob, Seth. Cert. in Nursing, Cen. Fla. Community Coll., 1984; BS in Psychology, N.Y. Exteral Regents, 1989. Cert. psychiat./mental health nurse, tech. effective aggression mgmt. instr. Former dir. clin. nursing Lake Sumter Psychiat. Hosp., Leesburg, Fla., 1988-89, staff devel. crisis stabliza-tion nurse, inpatient counselor, 1990-91; mem. psychotic disorders team Shands Teaching Hosp./U. Fla., Gainesville, 1993—; mem. edn. com., 1996, 97; preceptor RN program Lake Sumter C.C., 1987-89; preceptor psychiat. RN Shands Tchg. Hosp., U. Fla., 1995; regional program coord. for mental health svcs. ABC Home Health, Ocala, Fla., 1992. Contbr.: Home Remedies—What Works, 1995. Mem. ANA (cert.), Alliance for the Mentally Ill, Am. Psychiat. Nurses Assn.

OXLEY, DWIGHT K(AHALA), pathologist; b. Wichita, Kans., Dec. 2, 1936; s. Dwight K. Jr. and Ruth Erdene (Warner) O.; m. Patricia Warren, June 18, 1961; children: Alice DeBloois, Thomas Oxley. AB, Harvard U., 1958; MD, U. Kans., 1962. Diplomate Am. Bd. Pathology (trustee 1992—), Am. Bd. Nuclear Medicine. Pathologist Wesley Med. Ctr., Wichita, 1969-74, Eisenhower Med. Ctr., Rancho Mirage, Calif., 1974-78, St. Joseph Health Ctr., Kansas City, Mo., 1978-88; chmn. dept. pathology Columbia-Wesley Med. Ctr., 1988—. Bd. editors Archives of Pathology and Lab. MEdicine, Chgo., 1984-95, Clinica Chimica Acta, Amsterdam, 1980-86, Am. Jour. Clin. Pathology, Chgo., 1974-80. Sr. warden St. Stephens Episcopal Ch., Wichita, 1994. Lt. commdr. USN, 1964-69. Fellow Am. Soc. Clin. Pathologists (various offices), Coll. Am. Pathologists (various offices); mem. Am. Pathology Found. (bd. dirs. 1979-89), Kans. Soc. Pathologists (pres. 1993-96). Republican. Avocations: music, athletics. Office: Wesley Med Ctr 550 N Hillside St Wichita KS 67214-4910

OXLEY, MARGARET CAROLYN STEWART, elementary education educator; b. Petaluma, Calif., Apr. 1, 1930; d. James Calhoun Stewart and Clara Thornton (Whiting) Bomboy; m. Joseph Hubbard Oxley, Aug. 25, 1951; children: Linda Margaret, Carolyn Blair Oxley Greiner, Joan Claire Oxley Willis, Joseph Stewart, James Harmon, Laura Marie Oxley Brechbill. Student, U. Calif., Berkeley, 1949-51; BS summa cum laude, Ohio State U., 1973, MA, 1984, postgrad., 1985, 88, 92. Cert. tchr., Ohio. 2d grade tchr. St. Paul Sch., Westerville, Ohio, 1973—; presenter in field. Editl. adv. bd. Reading Tchr., vol. 47-48, 1993—; editl. rev. bd. Children's Literature Jour., 1996—; co-author: Reading and Writing, Where it All Begins, 1991, Teaching with Children's Books: Path to Literature-Based Instruction, 1995. Active Akita Child Conservation League, Columbus, Ohio, 1968-70. Named Columbus Diocesan Tchr. of Yr., 1988; Phoebe A. Hearst scholar, 1951, Rose Sterheim Meml. scholar, 1951; recipient Mary Karrer award Ohio State U., 1994. Mem. Nat. Coun. Tchrs. English (Notable Trade Books in the Lang. Arts com. 1993-94, chair 1995-96, treas. Children's Literature Assembly bd. dirs. 1996—), Internat. Reading Assn. (Exemplary Svc. in Promotion of Literacy award 1991), Literacy Connection (pres.), Children's Lit. Assembly, Ohio Coun. Tchrs. English Lang. Arts (Outstanding Educator 1990), Phi Kappa Phi, Pi Lambda Theta (hon.). Democrat. Roman Catholic. Avocations: reading, writing, travel, gardening, working with children. Home: 298 Brevoort Rd Columbus OH 43214-3826

OXLEY, MICHAEL GARVER, congressman; b. Findlay, Ohio, Feb. 11, 1944; s. George Garver and Marilyn Maxine (Wolfe) O.; m. Patricia Ann Pluguez, Nov. 27, 1971; 1 child, Michael Chadd. BA, Miami U., Oxford, Ohio, 1966; JD, Ohio State U., 1969. Bar: Ohio 1969, U.S. Supreme Ct. 1985. Agt. FBI, 1969-71; mem. Ohio Ho. of Reps., 1973-81, 97th-103rd Congresses from 4th Ohio dist., Washington, D.C., 1981—; mem. commerce com., chmn. subcom. fin and hazardous materials, vice chmn. subcom. telecomm. trade and consumer affairs. Mem. ABA, Ohio Bar Assn., Findlay Bar Assn., Soc. Former Spl. Agts. FBI, Ohio Farm Bur., Sigma Chi. Lodges: Rotary, Elks. Office: US Ho Reps 2233 Rayburn House Bldg Washington DC 20515

OXMAN, DAVID CRAIG, lawyer; b. Summit, N.J., Mar. 10, 1941; s. Jacob H. and Kathryn (Grear) O.; m. Phyllis Statter; children—Elena, Lee. A.B., Princeton U., 1962; LL.B., Yale U., 1969. Bar: N.Y. 1970, N.J. 1974, U.S. Dist. Ct. (so. and ea. dists.) N.Y. 1974, U.S. Ct. Appeals (2d cir.) 1974, U.S. Tax Ct. 1977, U.S. Supreme Ct. 1974. Assoc. Davis Polk & Wardwell, N.Y.C., 1970-76, ptnr., 1977-95, sr. counsel, 1995—. Served with USN, 1962-66. Fellow Am. Coll. Trust and Estate Counsel; mem. ABA, N.Y. State Bar Assn., Assn. of Bar of City of N.Y., N.J. Bar Assn., N.Y. County Lawyers Assn. Office: Davis Polk & Wardwell 450 Lexington Ave New York NY 10017-3911

OXNARD, CHARLES ERNEST, anatomist, anthropologist, human biologist, educator; b. Durham, Eng., Sept. 9, 1933; arrived in Australia, 1987; s. Charles and Frances Ann (Golightly) O.; m. Eleanor Mary Arthur, Feb. 2, 1959; children: Hugh Charles Neville, David Charles Guy. BSc. with 1st class honors, U. Birmingham, Eng., 1955, MB, BChir in Medicine, 1958, PhD, 1962, D.Sc., 1975. Med. intern Queen Elizabeth Hosp., Birmingham, 1958-59; rsch. fellow U. Birmingham, 1959-62, lectr., 1962-65, sr. lectr., 1965-66, court govs., 1958-66; assoc. prof. anatomy, anthropology and evolutionary biology U. Chgo., 1966-70, prof., 1970-78, gov. biology collegiate div., 1970-78, dean coll., 1973-77; dean grad. sch. U. So. Calif., Los Angeles, 1978-83; univ. rsch. prof. biology and anatomy U. So. Calif., 1978-83, univ. prof., prof. anatomy and cell biology, prof. biol. scis., 1983-87; prof. anatomy and human biology, head dept. of anatomy and human biology U. Western Australia, 1987-90, 93-95, dir. ctr. for human biology, 1989—, head div. agr. and sci., 1990-92; rsch. assoc. Field Mus. Natural History, Chgo., 1967; overseas assoc. U. Birmingham, 1968—; Lo Yuk Tong lectr. U. Hong Kong, 1973, 94, hon. prof., 1978, Chan Shu Tzu lectr., 1980, Octagon lectr. U. Western Australia, 1987, Latta lectr. U. Nebr., Omaha, 1987; Stanley Wilkinson orator, 1991, Lo Yuk Tong Found. lectr., U. Hong Kong, 1994; rsch. assoc. L.A. County Natural History Mus., 1984—, George C. Page Mus., L.A., 1986; vis. scholar U. Hong Kong, 1995, Shaw Coll. Chinese U. of Hong Kong, 1995, U. of Hong Kong, 1996; bd. dirs. U. Western Australia Press, 1993-95; adv. on human biology World Sci. Pub. Co., 1993—. Author: Form and Pattern in Human Evolution, 1973, Uniqueness and Diversity in Human Evolution, 1973, Human Fossils: The New Revolution, 1977, The Order of Man, 1983, Humans, Apes, and Chinese Fossils, 1985, Anatomies and Lifestyles, 1990; series editor Recent Advances in Human Biology Series World Sci. Pub., Vol. I, The Origin and Past of Modern Humans, 1995, Vol. 2, Bone Structure and Remodeling, 1995, Perspectives in Human Biology, Vol. 1 Genes, Ethnicity and Aging, 1995, Vol. 2 Humans in the Australasian Region, 1996; mem. editl. bd. Annals of Human Biology; cons. editor: Am. Jour. Primatology, Jour. Human Biology, Jour. Human Evolution: Australia com. mem. Ency. Britannica, 1991—; bibliographic referee Britannica On-Line, 1994, 95; contbr articles to anat. and anthrop. jours. Mem. Pasteur Found., 1988; bd. dirs. West Australian Inst. for Child Health, 1991—; mem. electoral bd. Freemantle Hosp., 1991-94. Recipient Book award Hong Kong Coun., 1984, S.T. Chan Silver medal U. Hong Kong, 1980; grantee USPHS, 1960-71, NIH, 1974-87, NSF, 1971-87, Raine Found., 1988-91, Viertel Found., 1993-94, Australian Acad. Sci., 1995. Fellow N.Y. Acad. Sci., AAAS, So. Calif. Acad. Sci. (bd. dirs. 1985); mem. Chgo. Acad. Soc. (hon. life), Australasian Soc. for Human Biology (pres. 1987-90), Australia and New Zealand Anat. Soc. (pres. 1989-90), Anat. Soc. Gt. Britain and Ireland (councillor 1992-94), Nat. Health and Med. Rsch. Coun. (grantee 1988—), Australian Rsch. Coun. (grantee 1988—), Soc. for Study Human Biology (treas. 1962-66), Sigma Xi (pres., nat. lectr. 1990—), Phi Beta Kappa (pres. chpt.), Phi Kappa Phi (pres., Book award 1984). Office: U Western Australia, Ctr Human Biology, Nedlands WA 6009, Australia

OXTOBY, DAVID WILLIAM, chemistry educator; b. Bryn Mawr, Pa., Oct. 17, 1951; s. John Corning and Jean (Shaffer) O., m. Claire Bennett, Dec. 17, 1977; children: Mary-Christina, John, Laura. BA, Harvard, 1972; PhD, U. Calif., Berkeley, 1975. Asst. prof. U. Chgo., 1977-82, assoc. prof., 1982-86, prof., 1986—, Mellon prof., 1987-92, dir. James Franck Inst., 1992-95, dean physical scis. divsn., 1995—, William Rainey Harper prof., 1996—. Co-author: Principles of Modern Chemistry, 1986, Chemistry: Science of Change, 1990. Trustee Bryn Mawr Coll., 1989—; mem. bd. govs. Argonne Nat. Lab., 1996—. Recipient Quantrell award U. Chgo., 1986; Alfred P. Sloan Found. fellow, 1979, John Simon Guggenheim Found. fellow, 1987; Camille and Henry Dreyfus Found. tchr.-scholar, 1980. Fellow Am. Phys. Soc.; mem. Am. Chem. Soc., Royal Soc. Chemistry (Marlow medal 1983), Phi Beta Kappa. Office: James Franck Inst U Chgo 5640 S Ellis Ave Chicago IL 60637-1433

OXTOBY, ROBERT BOYNTON, lawyer; b. Huron, S.D., May 8, 1921; s. Frederic Breading and Frieda (Boynton) O.; m. Carolyn Bartholf; children: Michael, Thomas, Susan. Student, Ill. Coll.; B.A., Carleton Coll., 1943; J.D., Northwestern U., 1949. Bar: Ill. 1949. Mem. firm Van Meter, Oxtoby & Funk, 1949—; asst. U.S. atty., 1953-57, spl. asst. atty. gen., 1970—. Chmn. Ill Capital Devel. Bd., 1991-95; bd. dirs. Downtown Park, Inc., Springfield Bd. Edn. Served to 1st lt. USMCR, 1943-46, PTO. Home: 1933 Outer Park Dr Springfield IL 62704-3323 Office: First Am Ctr 1 Old Capitol Pla N Springfield IL 62701

OYE, KENNETH A., political scientist, educator; b. Phila., Oct. 20, 1949; s. George M. and Kazue Y. O.; Willa K. Michener; 1 child, Mari Katherine Michener Oye. BA in Polit. Sci. and Econs. with highest honors, Swarthmore Coll., 1971; PhD in Polit. Sci., Harvard U., 1983. Lectr. polit. sci. U. Calif., Davis, 1976-79; asst. prof. politics Princeton U., 1980-89; assoc. prof. polit. sci. Swarthmore Coll., 1989-90; assoc. prof. polit. sci. MIT, Cambridge, 1990—, dir. ctr. internat. studies, 1992—; lectr. summer program quantitative methods Kennedy Sch. Harvard U., 1974, 75; guest scholar The Brookings Instn., 1979-80; co-dir. seminar XXI program MIT, 1993—, mem. coun. global environment, 1994—; presenter in field. Author: Economic Discrimination and Political Exchange: World Political Economy in the 1930s and 1980s, 1993; editor: Cooperation under Anarchy, 1986, (with Robert J. Lieber and Donald Rothchild) Eagle Entangled: U.S. Foreign Policy in a Complex World, 1979, Eagle Defiant: United States Foreign Policy in the 1980s, 1983, Eagle Resurgent? The Reagan Era in United States Foreign Policy, 1987, Eagle in a New World: American Grand Strategy in the Post Cold War Era, 1992; mem. editl. com. World Politics, 1982-89, mem. editl. bd., 1989-95; contbr. chpts. in books and articles to profl. jours. Trustee World Peace Fedn., 1996, Boston World Affairs Coun., 1996. Econs. and Security grantee Pew Charitable Trusts, 1986; Grad. fellow Woodrow Wilson Found., 1971, NSF, 1971-74, MacArthur Found., 1995, Japan Found., 1996, Alliance for Global Sustaiability, 1997. Mem. Am. Econs. Assn., Am. Polit. Sci. Assn., Coun. Fgn. Rels., Phi Beta Kappa. Office: MIT Ctr Internat Studies 292 Main St # E38 648 Cambridge MA 02142-1014

OYEWOLE, GODWIN, lawyer; b. Lagos, Nigeria, Apr. 23, 1942; s. Benjamin Olufayo and Mabel Olubunkunola (Shokoya) O.; m. Saundra Elaine Herndon, Mar. 21, 1970; children: Ayodeji Babatunde Olusegun, Kolade Olufayo, Monisola Aramide. BA, SUNY, New Paltz, 1964; MBA, Loyola U., Chgo., 1970; Dr. in Communications, U. Mass., 1972; JD, Georgetown U., 1980, LLM, 1984. Bar: D.C. 1981, Va. 1982, U.S. Ct. Appeals (4th and D.C. cirs.) 1982; U.S. Ct. Military Appeals, 1988; U.S. Supreme Ct., 1990. Counsel Nat. Cable TV Assn., Washington, 1980-81; gen. mgr. Sta. WDCU-FM, Washington, 1981-86; mng. atty. Appellate Litigation Assocs., Washington, 1981-86; sole practice Washington, 1986—. Editor-in-chief Georgetown U. Law Weekly, 1979-80. Mem. ABA, Washington Bar Assn., Fed. Bar Assn., D.C. Bar Assn., Va. State Bar, Assn. Trial Lawyers Am. Democrat. Avocations: jazz, photography, flower arranging, African and Caribbean music. Home: 8206 Riverside Rd Alexandria VA 22308-1538 Office: 9th Fl 601 Pennsylvania Ave NW Ste 9 Washington DC 20004-2601

OYLER, GREGORY KENNETH, lawyer; b. Moses Lake, Wash., Sept. 16, 1953; s. Eugene Milton and Annetta Diane (Williams) O.; m. Evelyn Hartwell Wright, Oct. 18, 1986; 1 child, Elizabeth Atwood. AB, Princeton U., 1975; JD, Georgetown U., 1978; LLM, NYU, 1981. Bar: Pa. 1978, U.S. Tax Ct. 1978, U.S. Ct. Appeals (D.C. cir.) 1979, D.C. 1981, U.S. Supreme Ct. 1982, U.S. Ct. Fed. Claims 1983, U.S. Ct. Appeals (fed. cir.) 1987. Law clk. to judges U.S. Tax Ct., Washington, 1978-80; assoc. Hamel & Park, Washington, Washington, 1981-85; ptnr. Hopkins & Sutter, Washington, 1985-95, Scribner, Hall & Thompson, Washington, 1995—. Mem. adv. com. IRS Info. Reporting Program, 1993-94. Mem. ABA (tax sect., ins. and govt. submissions coms.), D.C. Bar Assn. (tax sect.), Fed. Bar Assn., Soc. Preservation Md. Antiquities (bd. dirs. 1991—). Office: Scribner, Hall & Thompson 1875 Eye St NW Ste 1050 Washington DC 20006

OZ, FRANK (FRANK RICHARD OZNOWICZ), puppeteer, film director; b. Hereford, Eng., May 25, 1944; s. Isidore and Frances Oznowicz. Student, Oakland City Coll., 1962. Puppeteer with the Muppets, N.Y.C., 1963—; characters performed include The Mighty Favag (Saturday Night Live 1975-76), Miss Piggy, Fozzie Bear, Animal, Sam the Eagle; now v.p. Jim Henson Prodns., N.Y.C.; creative cons. feature film The Great Muppet Caper; appeared in films The Blues Brothers, 1980, Trading Places, 1983, Labyrinth, 1986; voice of Yoda in films The Empire Strikes Back, 1980, Return of the Jedi, 1983; dir. films The Dark Crystal (with Jim Henson), 1982, The Muppets Take Manhattan, 1984, Little Shop of Horrors, 1986, Dirty Rotten Scoundrels, 1988, What About Bob?, 1991, Housesitter, 1992, The Indian in the Cupboard, 1995. Recipient 4 Emmy awards for outstanding performance. Mem. AFTRA, Dirs. Guild Am., Writers Guild Am., Screen Actors Guild, Acad. TV Arts and Scis. Office: Jim Henson Prodns 117 E 69th St New York NY 10021-5004*

OZAKI, NANCY JUNKO, performance artist, former educator; b. Denver, Feb. 14, 1951; d. Joe Motoichi and Tamiye (Saki) O.; m. Nathan Jeoffrey Inouye, May 25, 1980 (div. Aug. 1985); m. Gary Steven Tsujimoto, Nov. 12, 1989. BS in Edn., U. Colo., 1973; postgrad., U. Colo., Denver, 1977, Metro State Coll., 1982, Red Rocks C.C., 1982-83, U. No. Colo., 1982, U. N.Mex., 1985, U. No. Colo., 1988. Elem. tchr. Bur. Indian Affairs, Bloomfield, N.Mex., 1973-75, Aurora (Colo.) Pub. Schs., 1977-83, Albuquerque Pub. Schs., 1983-84, Denver Pub. Schs., 1984-87, Oak Grove Sch. Dist., San Jose, Calif., 1988-89, San Mateo (Calif.) City Elem. Dist., 1990-92; performing artist Japanese drums Young Audiences, San Francisco, 1992-93, Denver, 1994—; performing artist Japanese drums Walt Disney World, Epcot Ctr., Orlando, Fla., 1993—. Vol. worker with young Navajo children; co-sponsor girl's sewing and camping groups. Mem. Kappa Delta Pi (Theta chpt.). Avocations: reading, sewing, skiing, swimming, snorkeling. Home: 6713 W 53d Ave Arvada CO 80002 Office: One World Taiko 6713 W 53rd Ave Arvada CO 80002-3937

OZAKI, SATOSHI, physicist; b. Osaka, Japan, July 4, 1929; married, 1960; 2 children. BS, Osaka U., 1953, MS, 1955; PhD in Physics, MIT, 1959. Rsch. asst. physics MIT, 1956-59; rsch. assoc. Brookhaven Nat. Lab., 1959-61, asst. physicist, 1961-63, assoc. physicist, 1963-66, physicist, 1966-72, group co-leader physics, 1970-80, sr. physicist, 1972—; head Relativistic Heavy Iron Collider project Brookhaven Nat. Lab, Upton, N.Y., 1989—; dir. physics dept. Tristan Project Accelerator Dept. Nat. Lab. High Energy Physics, Japan, 1981-89; vis. prof. Osaka U., 1975-76. Fellow Am. Phys. Soc. Achievements include the study of high energy particle interactions, particle spectoscopy, high energy physics instrumentation, mgmt. of major accelerator constrn. projects. Office: Brookhaven Nat Lab Relativistic Heavy Ion Collider Upton NY 11973

OZAKI, YOSEHARU, English literature educator; b. Osaka-shi, Osaka-fu, Japan, May 24, 1932; s. Jintaro and Shizue (Okajima) O.; m. Kimiko Ozaki, May 27, 1962; children: Katsuyoshi, Megumi. BA, Kyoto U., Japan, 1955, MA, 1957. Lectr. Kyoto U., Japan, 1960-64, assoc. prof. English, 1964-69; assoc. prof. English Nara Women's U., Nara, Japan, 1969-77, prof. English, 1977-96; prof. English Seiwa Coll., Nishinomiya-shi, Japan, 1996—. Author: Shakespeare by the Riverside, 1994; co-author: (with others) A Shakespeare Handbook, 1969, Shakespeare's Dramatic Climate, 1975, Love and Death-Whereabouts of Eros, 1987. Mem. English Lit. Soc. Japan (councillor 1990-92), Shakespeare Soc. Japan (standing com. 1983-89, com. mem. 1989-93), Dramatic Soc. Japan, Internat. Shakespeare Assn. Avocations: theatre, opera, ballet, concerts, movies. Home: 1-14 Sujaku 4-chome, Nara-shi Nara-ken 631, Japan Office: Seiwa Coll, 7-54 Okadayama, Nishinomiya-shi Hyogo 662, Japan

OZAWA, MARTHA NAOKO, social work educator; b. Ashikaga, Tochigi, Japan, Sept. 30, 1933; came to U.S., 1963; d. Tokuichi and Fumi (Kawashima) O.; m. May 1959 (div. May 1966). BA in Econs., Aoyama Gakuin U., 1956; MS in Social Work, U. Wis., 1966, PhD in Social Welfare, 1969. Asst. prof. social work Portland (Oreg.) State U., 1969-70, assoc. prof. social work, 1970-72; assoc. rsch. prof. social work NYU, 1972-75; assoc. prof. social work Portland State U., 1975-76; prof. social work Washington U., St. Louis, 1976-85, Bettie Bofinger Brown prof. social policy, 1985—. Author: Income Maintenance and Work Incentives, 1982; editor: Women's Life Cycle: Japan-U.S. Comparison in Income Maintenance, 1989, Women's Life Cycle and Economic Insecurity: Problems and Proposals, 1989; editl. bd. Social Work, Silver Spring, Md., 1972-75, 85-88, New Eng. Jour. Human Svcs., Boston, 1987—, Ency. of Social Work, Silver Spring, 1974-77, 91-95, Jour. Social Svc. Rsch., 1977—, Children and Youth Svcs. Rev., 1991—, Social Work Rsch., 1994—, Jour. Poverty. Grantee Adminstrn. on Aging, Washington, 1979, 84, NIMH, 1990-93, Assn. for Pub. Policy Analysis and Mgmt. Mem. Nat. Assn. Social Workers, Nat. Acad. Social Ins., Nat. Conf. on Social Welfare (bd. dirs. 1981-87), The Gerontol. Soc. Am., Coun. Social Work Edn., Washington U. Faculty Club (bd. dirs. 1986-91), Soc. for Social Work and Rsch. Avocations: photography, tennis, swimming, gardening. Home: 13018 Tiger Lily Ct Saint Louis MO 63146-4339 Office: Washington U Campus PO Box 1196 Saint Louis MO 63130-4899

OZAWA, SEIJI, conductor, music director; b. Shenyang, China, Sept. 1, 1935; s. Kaisaku and Sakura Ozawa; m. Vera Motoki-Ilyin; children: Seira, Yukiyoshi. Student, Toho Sch. Music, Tokyo, Japan, 1953-59; studies with, Hideo Saito, Eugene Bigot, Herbert Von Karajan, Leonard Bernstein; student at the invitation of Charles Munch, Tanglewood, 1959; DMus (hon.), U. Mass., New England Conserv. Music, Wheaton Coll. Music dir. Boston Symphony Orch., 1973—. One of three asst. condrs., N.Y. Philharm., 1961-62 season, music dir. Ravinia Festival, 1964-68, music dir. Toronto Symphony Orch., 1965-69, San Francisco Symphony Orch., 1970-76, appointed artistic advisor Tanglewood Festival, 1970, condr. Boston Symphony Orch. Evening at Symphony (Emmy award); music advisor Boston Symphony Orch., 1972-73, Saito Kinen Orch., Japan, 1992, internat. tour and Dvorak Gala, Prague, 1993; guest condr. major orchs. Recipient 1st prize Internat. Competition Orch. Condrs., 1959, Koussevitzky prize Tanglewood Music Ctr., 1960, Inouye award for Lifetime Achievement, 1994; conducting fellow Tanglewood Music Ctr., summer 1959; named Laureate Fondation du Japon, 1988; Seiji Ozawa Hall named for him Tanglewood Music Ctr., 1994. Office: Columbia Artists Mgmt Inc care Ronald A Wilford 165 W 57th St New York NY 10019-2201*

OZELLI, TUNCH, economics educator, consultant; b. Ankara, Turkey, May 18, 1938; came to U.S., 1962; s. Sufyan and Saziye (Ozmorali) O.; m. Lale A. Baymur, Dec. 30, 1960 (div. Mar. 1972); children: Selva, Kerem; m. Nancy Ann Goldschlager, Feb. 3, 1974 (div. Dec. 1984); m. Meral Ozdemir, May 9, 1992. MBA, Fla. State U., 1963; PhD, Columbia U., 1968. Rsch. fellow Harvard U., Cambridge, Mass., 1969-70; econ. advisor Office Prime Minister, Ankara, 1970-72; prof. mgmt. N.Y. Inst. Tech., N.Y.C., 1972—; spl. advisor State Planning Orgn., Ankara, 1989-92. Contbr. articles to profl. jour. Ford Found. scholar, 1963-64, Found. for Econ. Edn. fellow, 1968. Mem. Am. Econ. Assn., Middle East Studies Assn., Turkish Mgmt. Assn., Delta Mu Delta. Avocation: equestrian activities. Office: Dept of Economics NY Inst Tech Old Westbury NY 11568

OZEREKO-DECOEN, MARY THERESE, therapeutic recreation specialist and therapist; b. Salem, Mass., Oct. 4, 1961; d. Domenic S. and Monica M. (Gesek) Ozereko; m. Jeffrey G. deCoen, Nov. 21, 1987. BS, U. Mass., 1982; MEd, Springfield Coll., 1987. Cert. therapeutic recreation specialist, Pa.; cert. golf club maker. Dir. promotions and ops. Wheat Thins mayors cup race Nabisco, Salem, 1984-86; conf. planner Pioneer Valley Conv. and Visitors Bur., Springfield, Mass., 1986-87; dir. tennis and recreation Village of Smugglers Notch, Vt., 1987-88; mental health profl., therapeutic recreation specialist Hoffman Homes for Youth, Gettysburg, Pa., 1988-89; therapeutic recreation aide Chambersburg (Pa.) Hosp., 1990; caseworker, therapeutic recreation specialist Tressler Wilderness Sch., Boiling Springs, Pa., 1989-92; intake dir. Mentor Clin. Care, Harrisburg, Pa., 1993—; owner GolfAugusta Pro Shops, Hershey, Pa., 1995—; cons. clin. seminars on recreational therapy for mental health profls. Mem. Hershey Partnership, 1995—, Pa. Children's Panel, Harrisburg, 1992—. Mem. NAFE, Nat. Recreation and Parks Assn., Pa. Mental Health Providers Assn., Pa. Parks and Recreation Assn., Ctrl. Pa. C. of C. (golf planner ea. amputee spl. olympics 1996—), U.S. Golf Assn., Cert. Golfmakers Assn., Nat. Coun. for Therapeutic Recreation Cert., U. Mass.-Keystone Alumni Assn. (pres. 1994—), Harrisburg Exec. Womens Com. Democrat. Roman Catholic. Avocations: sports, soccer, golf, collecting old toys and antiques, clubmaking. Office: 2090 Linglestown Rd Harrisburg PA 17110-9428

OZERO, BRIAN JOHN, chemical engineer; b. Winnipeg, Manitoba, Can., Dec. 14, 1932; came to U.S., 1963; s. Daniel and Mary Ozero; m. Ila Atlas, Dec. 14, 1985. BS in Chem. Engring., Queens U., Kingston, Ontario, Can., 1954; MS in Chem. Engring., NYU, 1968. Technologist Shell Oil Co., Montreal, Quebec, Can., 1954-60; design engr. Chem. Constrn. Co., London, 1960-63; sr. process engr. Sci. Design Co., N.Y.C., 1963-65, process mgr., 1965-75; tech. dir. Halcon SD Group Inc., N.Y.C., 1976-85; sr. process mgr. Tech. Evaluation and Devel. Assocs., Hoboken, N.J., 1986; pres., prin. cons. Scientech Assocs. Inc., N.Y.C., 1986—. Recognized expert in ethylene oxide/ethylene glycol, VCM, propylene oxide; contbr. articles and chpts. to tech. jours. and encyclopedias in field; patentee in field. Pres. Barrier Beach Preservation Assn., Westhampton, N.Y., 1985-88. Mem. Am. Inst. Chem. Engrs., Rotary. Republican. Roman Catholic. Avocations: reading, tennis, skiing. Home: PO Box 1524 Westhampton Beach NY 11978-7524 Office: Scientech Assocs Inc 225 E 36th St Apt 19A New York NY 10016-3628

OZI, ELIZABETH, private school administrator; b. São Paulo, Brazil, Aug. 5, 1959; d. Heni and Firmina O. BA in Psychology, U. Las Vegas, 1987; postgrad., NOVA U., Fla., 1989—; cert. of continuing profl. edn., U. Nev., 1988. Cert. tchr. Tchr. Clark County Sch. Dist., Las Vegas, Nev., 1990-94; owner, sch. dir. Parent's Choice, Las Vegas, Nev., 1993—; dir. Home Base Bus., Las Vegas, Nev., 1993—. Interviewer (Radio Show Series) Recognizing Signs to Prevent Suicide, 1990. Counselor Suicide Prevention, Nev., 1988-90. Recipient Cert. of Leadership award Nat. U., Las Vegas, 1990. Mem. Psi Chi. Avocation: writing. Home: 4646 Grasshopper Dr Las Vegas NV 89122

OZICK, CYNTHIA, author; b. N.Y.C., Apr. 17, 1928; d. William and Celia (Regelson) O.; m. Bernard Hallote, Sept. 7, 1952; 1 dau., Rachel Sarah. BA cum laude with honors in English, NYU, 1949; MA, Ohio State U., 1950; LHD (hon.), Yeshiva U., 1984, Hebrew Union Coll., 1984, Williams Coll., 1986, Hunter Coll., 1987, Jewish Theol. Sem. Am., 1988, Adelphi U., 1988, SUNY, 1989, Brandeis U., 1990, Bard Coll., 1991, Spertus Coll., 1991, Skidmore Coll., 1992. Author: Trust, 1966, The Pagan Rabbi and Other Stories, 1971, Bloodshed and Three Novellas, 1976, Levitation: Five Fictions, 1982, Art and Ardor: Essays, 1983, The Cannibal Galaxy, 1983, The Messiah of Stockholm, 1987, Metaphor and Memory: Essays, 1989, The Shawl, 1989, Epodes: First Poems, 1992, What Henry James Knew, and Other Essays on Writers, 1994, Portrait of the Artist as a Bad Character, 1996, The Cynthia Ozick Reader, 1996, Fame and Folly, 1996, The Puttermesser Papers, 1997; (plays) Blue Light, 1994, The Shawl, 1996; also poetry, criticism, revs., transls., essays and fictions in numerous periodicals and anthologies. Phi Beta Kappa orator, Harvard U., 1985. Recipient Mildred and Harold Strauss Living award Am. Acad. Arts and Letters, 1983, Rea award for short story, 1986, PEN/Spiegel-Diamonstein award for the Art of the Essay, 1997, Harold Washington Literary award City of Chgo., 1997; Lucy Martin Donnelly fellow, Bryn Mawr Coll., 1992, Guggenheim fellow, 1982. Mem. PEN, Authors League, Am. Acad. of Arts and Scis., Am. Acad. of Arts and Letters, Dramatists Guild, Académie Universelle des Cultures (Paris), Phi Beta Kappa. Office: care Alfred A Knopf Co 201 E 50th St New York NY 10022-7703

OZIER, IRVING, physicist, educator; b. Montreal, Que., Can., Sept. 7, 1938; s. Harry and Peppi (Schwartzwald) O.; m. Joyce Ruth Weinstein, July 4, 1963; children: Elizabeth, David, Douglas. B.A., U. Toronto, 1960; A.M., Harvard U., 1961, Ph.D., 1965. Research fellow Harvard U., Cambridge, Mass., 1965-67, MIT, Cambridge, Mass., 1966-67; mem. tech. staff Sci. Ctr. Rockwell Internat., Thousand Oaks, Calif., 1966-70; assoc. prof. physics U. B.C., Vancouver, B.C., Can., 1970-77, prof., 1977—; vis. rsch. fellow Katholieke Universiteit, Nijmegen, The Netherlands, 1976-77; vis. rsch. officer Nat. Rsch. Coun. Can., Ottawa, 1982-83; vis. prof. Eidgenossische

Technische Hochschule, Zurich, Switzerland, 1988-89. Author research articles in molecular spectroscopy. Alfred P. Sloan research fellow, 1972-74; Izaak Walton Killiam Meml. Sr. fellow U. B.C., 1982-83. Mem. Am. Phys. Soc., Can. Assn. Physicists. Office: Dept Physics Univ BC, 6224 Agriculture Rd, Vancouver, BC Canada V6T 1Z1

OZIO, DAVID, professional bowler. Winner Firestone Tournament of Champions, 1991; winner 10 Profl. Bowlers Assn. tournaments. Named to Profl. Bowlers Assn. Hall of Fame. Office: c/o Profl Bowlers Assn 1720 Merriman Rd Akron OH 44313-5252*

OZKAN, UMIT SIVRIOGLU, chemical engineering educator; b. Manisa, Turkey, Apr. 11, 1954; came to U.S., 1980; d. Alim and Emine (Ilgaz) Sivrioglu; m. H. Erdal Ozkan, Aug. 13, 1983. BS, Mid. East Tech. U., Ankara, Turkey, 1978, MS, 1980; PhD, Iowa State U., 1984. Registered profl. engr., Ohio. Grad. rsch. assoc. Ames Lab. U.S. Dept. Energy, 1980-84; asst. prof. Ohio State U., Columbus, 1985-90, assoc. prof. chem. engring., 1990-94, prof., 1994—. Contbr. articles to profl. jours. French Ctr. NAt. Rsch. Sci. fellow, 1994-95; recipient Women of Achievement award YWCA, Columbus, 1991, Outstanding Engring. Educator Ohio award Soc. Profl. Engrs., 1991, Union Carbide Innovation Recognition award, 1991-92, NSF Woman Faculty award in sci. and engring., 1991, Engring. Tchg. Excellence award Keck Found., 1994—, Ctrl. Ohio Outstanding Woman in Sci. & Tech., 1996. Fellow Am. Inst. Chemists; mem. NSPE, Am. Inst. Chem. Engring., Am. Soc. Engring. Edn., Am. Chem. Soc., Combustion Inst., Sigma Xi. Achievements include research in selective oxidation, catalytic incineration, NO reduction, hydrodesulfurization, hydrodenitrogenation, in-situ spectroscopy. Office: Ohio State U Chem Engring 140 W 19th Ave Columbus OH 43210-1110

OZMENT, STEVEN, historian, educator; b. McComb, Miss., Feb. 21, 1939; s. Lowell V. and Shirley M. (Edgar) O.; m. Andrea Todd Foster, Apr. 30, 1977; children: Amanda, Emma; children by previous marriage: Joel, Matthew, Katherine. B.A., Hendrix Coll., 1960; B.D., Drew Theol. Sch., 1964; Ph.D., Harvard U., 1967; M.A. (hon.), Yale U., 1975. Asst. prof. Inst. Late Medieval and Reformation Studies, U. Tübingen, Fed. Republic Germany, 1966-68; asst. prof. history and religious studies Yale U., New Haven, 1968-72; assoc. prof. Yale U., 1972-75, prof., 1975-79; prof. history Harvard U., 1979—, McLean prof. ancient and modern history, 1991—, assoc. dean undergrad. edn., 1984-87; Bonsall vis. prof. Stanford U., 1991. Author: Homo Spiritualis, 1969, The Reformation in Medieval Perspective, 1971, Mysticism and Dissent, 1973, The Reformation in the Cities, 1975, (with others) The Western Heritage, 1979, 5th edit., 1994, The Age of Reform, 1980 (winner Schaff prize, Nat. Book Award nominee 1980), Reformation Europe: A Guide to Research, 1982, When Fathers Ruled: Family Life in Reformation Europe, 1983, (with others) The Heritage of World Civilizations, 1985, 4th edit., 1996, Magdalena and Balthasar: An Intimate Portrait of Life in 16th Century Europe, 1986, Three Behaim Boys: Growing Up in Early Modern Germany, 1990, Protestants: The Birth of a Revolution, 1992, The Bürgermeister's Daughter: Scandal in a 16th Century German Town, 1996; mem. editl. bd. Archive for Reformation History, 1976-93, Sixteenth Century Jour., 1976—, Jour. Am. Acad. Religion, 1972-77, Jour. Hist. Ideas, 1986—, Netherlands Archive for Church History, 1987—. Morse fellow, 1970-71, Guggenheim fellow, 1978, Cabot fellow, 1992. Mem. Am. Soc. Reformation Rsch. (dir. 1979-83). Home: 69 High Rd Newbury MA 01951-1725 Office: Harvard Univ Robinson Hall Cambridge MA 02138

OZMON, KENNETH LAWRENCE, university president, educator; b. Portsmouth, Va., Sept. 4, 1931; emigrated to Can.; s. Howard Augustine and Anna Josephine (Lynch) O.; m. Elizabeth Ann Morrison, July 6, 1968; children: Angela Francene, Kendi Elizabeth. BA in Philosophy and History magna cum laude, St. Bernard Coll., Ala., 1955; MA in Psychology, Cath. U., 1963; PhD in Psychology, U. Maine, 1968. Lic. psychologist, N.S. Instr. U. Maine, Orono, 1966-68; vis. lectr. St. Dunstan's U., P.E.I., Can., 1967; asst. prof. Calif. State U., Chico, 1968-69; chmn. dept. psychology U. P.E.I., Charlottetown, 1969-72, dean of arts, 1972-79; pres. St. Mary's U., Halifax, N.S., 1979—; chmn. Pres.' Council N.S. U., 1982-85; chmn. Met. Halifax U. Pres.' Com., 1982-84, 86-87, 92—; co-chmn. coordinating com. Nat. U. Week, 1983, 86-87. Contbr. numerous articles to psychol. jours. Bd. dirs. United Way Halifax-Dartmouth, 1980-82, Friends N.S. Mus. Industry Soc., 1993—, Greater Halifax Econ. Devel. Partnership, 1995; bd. dirs. Interuniv. Svcs., Inc., 1987-94, chmn., 1992-94; provincial bd. dirs. Can. Assn. Mentally Retarded, 1980-82; co-chmn. Found. for Irish and Can. Studies, 1993; mem. nat. coun. Can. Human Rights Found., 1976; mem. selection com. J.H. Moore Awards for Excellence, Toronto, 1983-92; hon. chmn. ann. campaign N.S. div. Can. Paraplegic Assn., 1985-86; mem. fundraising com. Phoenix House, 1986-88, Charitable Irish Soc. Halifax; chmn. Human Rights Commn., 1990; mem. adv. coun. Order of Can., 1991-95; area chair for N.S. Internat. Coun. Psychologists, 1992-93. Recipient Gov. Gen. of Can. award, 1993; named hon. prof. U. Internat. Bus. and Econs., Beijing, People's Republic of China; trustee scholar U. Maine, 1965-67; NDEA fellow, 1967-68. Mem. Assn. Atlantic Univs. (vice chmn. 1983-85, chmn. 1985-87), Assn. Commonwealth Univs (governing coun. 1988-91), Assn. Univs. and Colls. Can. (exec. coun. 1985-89, vice chmn. 1990-91, chmn., 1991-93, mem. audit com. 1991—, chmn. exec. com. 1991—, vice-chmn. nominating com. 1990-91), Can. Psychol. Assn. (Nat. Univ. Week coordinating com. 1983, co-chmn. 1986-87, audit com. 1985—, co-chmn. steering com. Halifax Met. Econ. Summit II 1994), Halifax Bd. Trade (internat. trade com. 1985-91, bd. dirs. 1989-91), Halifax Press Club, Halifax Club, Ashburn Golf Club, Saraguay Club. Roman Catholic. Avocations: fishing, golf, running. Home: 5895 Gorsebrook Ave, Halifax, NS Canada B3H 1G3 Office: St Mary's U, Pres Office, Halifax, NS Canada B3H 3C3

OZNOWICZ, FRANK RICHARD See OZ, FRANK

OZOLEK, JOHN ANTHONY, pediatrician, neonatologist; b. Dubois, Pa., Feb. 24, 1963; s. Anthony John and Ann Elaine (Castrilla) O.; m. Jamie Lynn McCombe, Oct. 29, 1994. BS in Biology, Case Western Res. U., 1985; MD, U. Pitts., 1989. Diplomate Am. Bd. Pediatrics. Intern in pediatrics Children's Hosp., Pitts., 1989-90, resident in pediatrics, 1990-92; fellow in neonatology Magee Women's Hosp., Pitts., 1992-95; physician rep. medication rev. com. neonatal ICU Magee Women's Hosp., Pitts., 1994—. Contbr. articles to profl. jours. Fellow Soc. Pediatric Rsch., Am. Acad. Pediat.; mem. AMA, Nat. Perinatal Assn. Roman Catholic. Avocations: bowling, poetry. Home: 9501 Point Aux Chenes Rd Ocean Springs MS 39564-9596 Office: Dept Pediatrics Divsn Neonatology Keesler Med Ctr Biloxi MS 39534

PAAL, DOUGLAS H., educational association administrator. Student, Brown U., Harvard U. With U.S. Embassy, Singapore, Beijing; planning staff State Dept.; sr. analyst CIA; spl. asst. nat. security affairs Pres. Ronald Reagan, Pres. George Bush; sr. dir. Asian affairs Nat. Security Coun.; pres. Asia Pacific Policy Ctr. Contbr. articles to profl. publ. Office: Asia Pacific Policy Ctr Ste 1011 1730 Rhode Island Ave NW Washington DC 20036-3112

PAALZ, ANTHONY L., beverage company executive; b. Louisville, Apr. 18, 1924; s. Leon A. and Rose M. (Westendick) P.; m. Elaine Wolf, Feb. 11, 1956 (dec. Dec. 1981); children: Teresa Dawson, Eileen Baldwin, Anthony L. Jr.; m. Alison Kerr, May 3, 1986. BS, U. Ind., 1949. Chief acct. J.E. Seagram & Sons Inc., N.Y.C., 1959-69, asst. controller, 1969-72, dir. of taxes, 1972-84, v.p. taxes, 1984—. Served with USN, 1943-45, PTO. Decorated numerous battle stars. Mem. Tax Execs. Inst. Avocation: golf. Home: 29 Treeview Dr Melville NY 11747-2413 Office: Joseph E Seagram & Sons Inc 800 3rd Ave New York NY 10022-7604

PAANANEN, VICTOR NILES, English educator; b. Ashtabula, Ohio, Jan. 31, 1938; s. Niles Henry and Anni Margaret (Iloranta) P.; m. Donna Mae Jones, Aug. 15, 1964; children: Karl, Neil. AB magna cum laude, Harvard U., 1960; MA, U. Wis., 1964, PhD, 1967. Instr. English Wofford Coll., Spartanburg, S.C., 1962-63; asst. prof. Williams Coll., Williamstown, Mass., 1966-68; asst. prof. Mich. State U., East Lansing, 1968-73, assoc. prof., 1973-82, prof., 1982—, asst. dean Grad. Sch., 1977-82, chmn. dept. English, 1986-94; vis. prof. Roehampton Inst., London, 1982, 96, hon. fellow, 1992. Author: William Blake, 1982, 2d edit., 1996; contbr. articles to profl. and scholarly jours. Univ. fellow U. Wis., 1962, 63-64, Roehampton Inst. hon. fellow, London, 1992—; Harvard Nat. scholar, 1956-60. Mem. AAUP, Labor Party. Home: 152 Orchard St East Lansing MI 48823-4536 Office: Mich State Univ Dept of English Morrill Hall East Lansing MI 48824-1036

PAASWELL, ROBERT EMIL, civil engineer, educator; b. Red Wing, Minn., Jan. 15, 1937; s. George and Evelyn (Cohen) P.; m. Rosalind Snyder, May 31, 1958; children: Judith Marjorie, George Harold. B.A. (Ford Found. fellow), Columbia U., 1956, B.S., 1957, M.S., 1961; Ph.D., Rutgers U., 1965. Field engring. asst. Spencer White & Prentis, Washington, 1954-56; engr. Spencer White & Prentis, N.Y.C., 1957-59; rsch. scientist Davidson Lab., N.J., 1964; rsch. fellow Greater London Council, 1971-72; rsch. and teaching asst. Columbia U., 1959-62; asst. prof. civil engring. SUNY, Buffalo, 1964-68; chmn. bd. govs. Urban Studies Coll., 1973-76, assoc. prof., 1968-76, prof. civil engring., 1976-82; dir. Center for Transp. Studies and Research, 1979-82, chmn. dept. environ. design and planning, 1980-82; prof. transp. engring. U. Ill., Chgo., 1982-86, 89-90, dir. Urban Transp. Ctr., 1982-86; exec. dir. Chgo. Transit Authority, 1986-89; dir. transp. rsch. consortium, prof. civil engring. CCNY, 1990—, disting. prof., 1991—; faculty-on-leave Dept. Transp., 1976-77, cons., 1981—; v.p. Faculty Tech. Cons., Inc., Midwest Sys. Scis., Inc., 1982-86; dir. Urban Mass Transp. Adminstrn. Summer Faculty Workshop, 1980, 81; cons. transp. planning, energy and soil mechanics; spl. cons. to Congressman T. Tulski, 1973; vis. expert lectr. Jilin U. Tech., Changchun, Peoples Republic of China, 1985, hon. prof. transp., 1986—; bd. dirs. E'Escuto Archs. and Engrs., Chig, Hickling Co., Ottawa, Can., Transic Devel. Corp.; chmn. transp. steering adv. bd. Office of Tech. Assessment for Infrastructure and the Urban Core Project, 1994—; faculty Lincoln Inst. of Land Policy, 1994-95; vis. scholar Te. Aviv U., Israel, 1995—; arbitrator in productivity Met. Transp. Authority, N.Y.C., 1996—; mem. exec. com. Coun. on Transp., 1996—. Author: Problems of the Carless, 1977; editor: Site Traffic Impact Assessment, 1992; contbg. author: Decisions for the Great Lakes, 1982, World Book Encyclopedia, 1992, 93, 94, Transport and Urban Development, 1995; mem. bd. editors Jour. Environ. Systems, 1974—, Transp., 1978—, Jour. Urban Tech., 1992—; contbr. articles to profl. jours. Mem. Buffalo Environ. Mgmt. Commn., 1972-74; mem. Area Com. for Transit, Mayor's Energy Adv. Bd., 1974, Block Grant Rev. Com., City of Buffalo; chmn. com. on transp., mem. rev. adv. bd. Rsch. and Planning Coun. Western N.Y.; mem. transp. com. Chgo. 1992 Worlds Fair; mem. citizens' adv. bd. Chgo. Transit Authority, 1985—; mem. strategic planning com. Regional Transp. Authority, 1985; mem. steering com. Nat. Transit Coop. Rsch. Program, 1991—, Borough pres. (Manhattan) Trans. Adv. Bd., Bronx Ctr. Devel. Project; bd. dirs. Transit Devel. Corp., 1992—; exec. bd. Transp. Council, 1996—. Recipient Dept. Transp. award, 1977; SUNY faculty fellow, 1965-66. Fellow ASCE (past pres. Buffalo sect., chmn. steering com. 1992 specialty conf. traffic impact analysis); mem. AAAS, Transp. Rsch. Bd. (chmn. com. on transp. disadvantaged, mem. exec. com., peer rev. com. nat. transp. ctrs. 1988—), Inst. Transp. Engrs. (transit coun., exec. com., chmn. legis. policy com., rsch. com. surface transp. policy project 1995—), Coun. on Transportation (bd. dirs. 1996—), N.Y. Acad. Scis., Sigma Xi. Office: CCNY Inst Transp Systems Rm 220-Y 135th St and Convent Ave New York NY 10031

PABARCIUS, ALGIS, investment executive; b. Telsiai, Lithuania, May 1, 1932; came to U.S., 1950, naturalized, 1956; s. Vacius and Brone (Ziuryte) P.; B.S., U. Ill., 1955; M.S., Ill. Inst. Tech., 1958, Ph.D., 1964; postgrad. Technische Hochschule Muenchen, Germany, 1962; m. Eleanor A. Rakovic, Aug. 18, 1956; children—Nina, Lisa, Algis. Engr., Esso Research & Engring. Co., Linden, N.J., 1955-56; instr. U. Ill., Chgo., 1956-59, asst. prof., 1959-64; partner Zubkus, Zemaitis & Assocs., Architects and Engrs., Chgo., Washington, 1959-67; v.p. Garden Hotels Investment Co. and Whitecliff Corp., Lanham, Md., 1967-75; pres. Aras Investment Corp., 1975-79, Colony Funding Corp., Washington, 1979-92, Amtrust Corp., Alexandria, Va., 1992—. Registered profl. engr. Ill., D.C.; structural engr. Ill.; Danforth Found. grantee, 1960-61; NSF faculty fellow, 1961-62. Mem. ASCE, Sigma Xi, Tau Beta Pi, Sigma Tau, Chi Epsilon, Phi Kappa Phi. Home: 7620 Old Georgetown Rd Bethesda MD 20814 Office: Amtrust Corp 218 N Lee St Alexandria VA 22314-2631

PABST, EDMUND G., retired insurance company executive, lawyer; b. Chgo., Apr. 22, 1916. Student, U. Calif-Berkeley; LL.D., B.S.L., Northwestern U., 1940. Bar: Ill., D.C. Mem. firm Leonard & Leonard, Chgo., 1940-41; atty. FTC, Washington, 1941-42; civilian lawyer U.S. Army, 1942-43; trial atty. OPA, Chgo., 1946-47; atty. Combined Ins. Co. Am., Chgo., 1947, v.p., asst. gen. counsel, 1954-59, sec., 1959-62, exec. v.p. adminstrn., 1962-76, W.Ger. Ops., 1976-78, v.p., gen. counsel, 1978-81, dir., 1952-83, mem. exec. com., 1958-76; officer, dir., mem. exec. com. Combined Am. Ins. Co., 1960-76; officer, dir.,mem. exec. com. Combined Ins. Co. Wis., 1953-76; officer, dir., mem. exec. com. Combined Life Ins. Co. N.Y., 1971-76; pres. Combined Opportunities, 1972-76. Bd. dirs. Uptown Chgo. Commn., pres., 1959-61; pres. S.E. Evanston Assn., 1968-70, 87-88; founding mem. Dewey Community Orgn., Evanston; mem. Evanston Zoning Bd. Appeals, 1969-76; mem. Evanston Zoning Amendment Com., 1980-88; bd. dirs. St. Francis Hosp., Evanston, 1980-89; trustee Mundelein Coll., 1971-88; me. Commonwealth Edison Task Force City of Evanston, 1988-93; chmn. Foster Reading Ctr., 1992—. Mem. ABA, Ill. Bar Assn., Chgo. Bar Assn. (civil rights com. 1959-70, chmn. 1966-67, ins. law com. 1947-60, chmn. 1951-52), Health Ins. Assn. Am. (sec. bd. dirs. 1969-73), U.S. C. of C. (internat. ins. adv. council 1978-81), ACLU (dir. Ill. div., treas. 1969-76). Home: 425 Grove St Apt 7C Evanston IL 60201-4632

PACALA, LEON, retired association executive; b. Indpls., May 3, 1926; s. John and Anna (Ferician) P.; m. Janet Lefforge, Dec. 28, 1947 (dec. July 1987); children: Mark, Stephen, James; m. Virginia Strasenburgh, Mar. 10, 1990. AB, Franklin (Ind.) Coll., 1949; BD, Colgate Rochester Div. Sch., 1952; PhD, Yale U., 1960; LLD (hon.), Nazareth Coll., 1980; LHD (hon.), Franklin Coll., 1987. Ordained to ministry Baptist Ch., 1952. Asst. prof. philosophy and religion DePauw U., 1956-61; participant study religion undergrad. coll. Lilly Found., 1957-59; assoc. prof. religion Bucknell U., 1961-68, prof., 1968-73, chmn. dept., 1961-64, dean, 1962-73; pres. Colgate Rochester (N.Y.) Div. Sch.; also Bexley Hall, Crozer Theol. Sem., 1973-80; exec. dir. Assn. Theol. Schs. in U.S. and Can., 1980-91; cons. acad. adminstrn. Beirut Coll. Women, 1972. Contbr. articles to profl. jours. Exec. com. Christian Faith in Higher Edn. Projects, 1965-68; trustee Franklin Coll., 1967-73; bd. dirs. Rohesters Jobs, Inc., 1973-80; trustee Rochester Area Colls., 1973-80; dir. Nat. Housing Ministries, Am. Bapt. Chs., 1976-80. With USAAF, 1944-45. Internat. Rotary scholar, Louvain U., Belgium, 1952-53. Mem. Am. Conf. Acad. Deans (exec. com., treas., chmn., presiding officer 1973-74), Am. Assn. Higher Edn., Assn. Am. Colls. (commn. religion higher edn.), Assn. Theol. Schs. (com. accreditation), World Conf. Assns. Theol. Instns. (v.p. 1988—), Am. Bapt. Assn. Sem. Adminstrs. (chmn 1975-80). Home: 3515 Elmwood Ave Rochester NY 14610-3464

PACE, CHARLES ROBERT, psychologist, educator; b. St. Paul, Sept. 7, 1912; s. Charles N. and Lenore (Lee) P.; m. Rosella Gaarder, Dec. 18, 1937; children: Rosalind, Jenifer. B.A., De Pauw U., 1933; M.A., U. Minn., 1935, Ph.D., 1937. Instr. in gen. coll. U. Minn., 1937-40; research asso. Am. Council Edn., 1941-42; research psychologist Bur. Naval Personnel, Navy Dept., 1943-47; mem. faculty Syracuse U., 1947-61, asso. dir., then dir. evaluation service center, 1947-52, asst. to chancellor, 1948-52, prof. psychology, chmn. dept., dir. psychol. research center, 1952-61; prof. higher edn. UCLA, 1961-82, prof. emeritus, 1982—; Mem. adv. coms. Am. Council Edn., Coll. Entrance Exam. Bd., Social Sci. Research Council. Author: They Went to College, 1941, (with M. E. Troyer) Evaluation in Teacher Education, 1944, (with F.H. Bowles and J.C. Stone) How to Get Into College, 1968, College and University Environment Scales, 2d edit, 1969, Education and Evangelism, 1972, The Demise of Diversity?, 1974, Measuring Outcomes of College, 1979, Measuring the Quality of College Student Experiences, 1984, The Undergraduates, 1990. Post-doctoral fellow Rockefeller Found., 1940-41; fellow Center Advanced Study Behavioral Scis., 1959-60; recipient citation for meritorious civilian service Navy Dept., 1946, E.F. Lindquist award Am. Ednl. Research Assn. and Am. Coll. Testing Program, 1984, Suslow award for outstanding svc. Assn. for Instl. Rsch., 1989. Mem. Am. Psychol. Assn., Am. Ednl. Research Assn., Assn. for Study Higher Edn. (Disting. Career award 1989), Am. Assn. Pub. Opinion Research.

PACE, ERIC DWIGHT, journalist; b. N.Y.C., Oct. 13, 1936; s. Eric and Eleanor Robertson (Jones) Paepcke; m. Suzanne Monique Wiedel, June 12, 1976 (div. Jan. 1987); children: Christine, Lydia. Grad., Phillips Exeter Acad., 1953; student, U. Heidelberg, Germany, 1955-56; B.A. magna cum laude, Yale, 1957; M.A., Johns Hopkins, 1959. Reporter San Angelo (Tex.) Standard Times and Evening Standard, 1957-58; mem. staff Life mag., N.Y.C., 1959-61; assigned to Life mag., Bonn, 1961, Paris, 1961-62; corr. Time mag., Bonn., 1962-63, Hong Kong, 1963-65; mem. staff New York Times, N.Y.C., 1965-66; assigned to New York Times, Saigon, 1966, Cairo, 1966-69, Paris, 1969-70, Beirut, 1970-71, N.Y.C., 1971-74, Teheran, 1974-77, N.Y.C., 1977—. Author: novels Saberlegs, 1970, Any War Will Do, 1973, Nightingale, 1979; contbr. articles to Fgn. Affairs, also others. Served with AUS, 1957. Recipient George Polk Meml. award Overseas Press Club, 1968, Page One award N.Y.C. Newspaper Guild, 1968. Mem. Mystery Writers Am., Authors Guild, Crime Writers Assn. (Gt. Britain), Am. P.E.N. Unitarian. Clubs: Century (N.Y.C.), Squadron A (N.Y.C.). Office: New York Times 229 W 43rd St New York NY 10036-3913

PACE, JOHN EDWARD, III, chemical engineer; b. Ridgeway, Va., Apr. 6, 1948; s. John Edward Jr. and Retta Jean Stanley Sheppard; m. Carolyn Ann Gray, Aug. 31, 1969; children: Brian Edward, Kimberly Carol. BSChemE, Va. Poly. Inst. and State U., 1971, MS in Chem. Engring., 1972. Registered profl. engr., W.Va. Summer engr. Exxon, Baytown, Tex., 1971; devel. engr. Dow Badische, Anderson, S.C., 1972-76; process devel. engr. Borg Warner, Parkersburg, W.Va., 1976-88, GE Plastics, Parkersburg, 1988—. Contbr. articles to profl. jours. Pres. Bethel Place Homeowners Assn., Washington, W.Va., 1984. Mem. AIChE, Elfuns. Republican. Baptist. Achievements include 3 patents on ABS processes; development of bulk SAN and bulk ABS processes. Home: 51 Bethel Pl Washington WV 26181 Office: General Electric Plastics PO Box 68 Washington WV 26181

PACE, KAREN YVONNE, mathematics and computer science educator; b. Jefferson City, Mo., Dec. 29, 1957; d. William John and Georgia (Loesch) Sippel; m. Charles Edward Pace, Dec. 27, 1982. EdB, Mo. State U., 1980; EdM, Drury U., 1985. Cert. secondary tchr. Tchr. Salem (Mo.) Sch. Dist., 1980—, Southwest Bapt. U., Boliver, Mo., 1985—; dist. chair Career Ladder Com., Salem, 1991-92; treas. Cmty. Tchrs. Orgn., Salem, 1992-93; assessment expert Salem Sch. Dist., 1993-94; sr. leader Mo. Assessment Project 2000, 1994. Pres. Community Cause Club, Salem, 1994. Mem. Salem Tchrs. Assn. (budget com. chair 1992-94). Democrat. Avocation: music. Home: PO Box 795 Salem MO 65560-0795 Office: Salem Sch Dist 1400 W 3rd St Salem MO 65560

PACE, LEONARD, retired management consultant; b. Torrington, Conn., Oct. 24, 1924; s. Anthony and Maria G. P.; m. Maureen Therese Murphy, Sept. 15, 1956; children: Leonard Anthony, Susan Maria, Daniel Graham, Thomas William, Mary Macaire, Cathleen Anne. Student, Syracuse U., 1943; B.S.M.E., U. Conn., 1949; postgrad., N.Y. U., 1951-52, Wayne U., 1955. Cert. mgmt. cons. With GAF, 1949-57, asst. to div. controller, 1954-57; with Deloitte Haskins and Sells, N.Y.C., 1957—, head N.Y. mgmt. adv. services, 1965-67, head Eastern region, 1967-76, nat. dir. mgmt. adv. services, 1976-85, chmn. internat. mgmt. adv. svcs. com. Served as officer, pilot USAAF, 1943-45. Mem. Am. Mgmt. Assn., Inst. Mgmt. Cons. (dir., chmn. profl. standards com.). Clubs: Baltusrol Golf, Union League, Circumnavigators. Home: 35 Little Wolf Rd Summit NJ 07901-3112

PACE, STANLEY CARTER, retired aeronautical engineer; b. Waterview, Ky., Sept. 14, 1921; s: Stanley Dan and Pearl Eagle (Carter) P.; m. Elaine Marilyn Cutchall, Aug. 21, 1945; children: Stanley Dan, Lawrence Timothy, Richard Yost. Student, U. Ky., 1939-40; B.S., U.S. Mil. Acad., 1943; M.S. in Aero. Engring., Calif. Inst. Tech., 1949; LLD (hon.), Maryville Coll., 1987. Commd. 2d lt. USAAF, 1943, advanced through grades to col., 1953; pilot, flight leader B-24 Group, 15th Air Force, 1943-44; chief power plant br., procurement div. Hdqrs. Air Materiel Command Wright-Patterson AFB, Ohio, 1945-48; assignments, procurement div. Hdqrs. Air Materiel Command, 1949-53, dep. chief prodn. Hdqrs. Air Materiel Command, 1952-53, resigned, 1954; with TRW, Inc., Cleve., 1954-85, successively sales mgr., asst. mgr., mgr. West Coast plant; mgr. jet div. Tapco plant, Cleve.; asst. mgr. Tapco group, 1954-58, v.p., gen. mgr., 1958-65, exec. v.p., co., 1965-77, pres., 1977-85, vice chmn., 1985, dir., 1965-85; vice chmn., dir. Gen. Dynamics Corp., St. Louis, 1985, chmn., chief exec. officer, 1985-90, also bd. dirs. Head United Way drive, Cleve., 1984; former council commr., pres. Great Cleve. Council Boy Scouts Am.; former trustee Nat. Jr. Achievement, Denison U., Washington U., Judson Park; former chmn. Greater Cleve. Roundtable, Cleve. Found. Distbn. Com., Nat. Assn. Mfrs. Decorated Air medal with oak leaf clusters. Mem. AIAA, Aerospace Industries Assn. (chmn.), Soc. Automotive Engrs., Union Club, Country Club, Chagrin Valley Hunt Club, Pepper Pike Club, Eldorado Country Club, Rolling Rock Club, St. Louis Country Club, Delta Tau Delta. Home: 1709 Berkshire Rd Gates Mills OH 44040-9747

PACE, STEPHEN SHELL, artist, educator; b. Charleston, Mo., Dec. 12, 1918; s. John C. and Ora K. (Reeves) P.; m. Palmina Natalini, Feb. 26, 1949. Student, Inst. Fine Arts, San Miguel, 1945-46, Art Students League, N.Y.C., 1948-49, Grande Chaumiere, Paris, 1950, Inst. D'Arte Statale, Florence, Italy, 1951, Hans Hofmann Sch., N.Y.C., 1951-52. Artist in residence Washington U., 1959; instr. painting Pratt Inst., N.Y.C., 1961-69; artist in residence Des Moines Art Ctr., 1970; vis. artist U. Calif., 1968; asso. prof. Bard Coll., 1969-71, Am. U., 1975-83. One-man shows include Hendler Gallery, 1953, Artists Gallery, 1954, Poindexter Gallery, 1956, 57, Washington U., St. Louis, 1959, Holland-Goldowsky Gallery, Chgo., 1960, Howard Wise Gallery, Cleve., 1960, N.Y., 1960, 61, 63, 64, Dilexi Gallery, San Francisco, 1960, HCE Gallery, 1956-59, 61-63, 66, Dwan Gallery, Los Angeles, 1961, Hayden Gallery, Cambridge, Mass., 1961, Ridley Gallery, Evansville, Ind., 1966, U. Calif. at Berkeley, 1968, Graham Gallery, N.Y.C., 1969, Des Moines Art Center, 1970, U. Tex., Austin, 1970, Kansas City Art Inst., 1973, A.M. Sachs Gallery, N.Y.C., 1974, 76, 77, 78, 79, 81, 83, 85, Drew U., 1975, Bard Coll., 1975, Am. U., 1976, Roberto Polo Gallery, Washington, 1976, New Harmony (Ind.) Gallery, 1977, Farm Gallery, Far Hill, N.J., 1978, Barbara Fiedler Gallery, Washington, 1980, Chastenet Gallery, Washington, 1981, Katherina Rich Perlow Gallery, N.Y.C., 1987, 89, 91, 94, 97, Vanderwoude-Tananbaum Gallery, N.Y.C., 1991, U. N.C., Greensboro, 1991, Evansville Mus., 1992, Maine Coast Artists, Rockport, 1994, Bates Coll. Mus., Lewiston, Maine, 1994; exhibited in group shows in U.S., Europe, Japan, Middle East, India, Burma, Australia, N.Z., Hawaii, Central and S.Am.; represented in permanent collections, Whitney Mus., Chrysler Mus., Norfolk, Va., Provincetown (Mass.) Mus., Evansville (Ind.) Mus., U. So. Ill., Carbondale, Michener Found., Walker Art Center, U. Calif., CIBA-Geigy Collection, Hallmark Collection, Bundy Art Gallery, U. N.C., Greensboro, Chase Manhattan Bank, Munson-Williams-Procter Inst., Utica, N.Y., Des Moines Art Center, Boston Mus. Fine Arts, Met. Mus., N.Y.C., Phillips Collection, Washington, Am. U., Washington, Corcoran Gallery, Washington, J. Patrick Lannan Mus., Venice, Calif., Curie Inst., Paris, Hirshhorn Mus., Washington, Bristol Myers Collection, Indpls. Mus., Portland (Maine) Mus., Bowdoin Coll. Mus., Brown U., Providence, Oberlin (Ohio) Coll. Mus, Farmsworth Art Mus., Rockland, Maine, Bates Coll. Mus., Lewiston, Maine, Nat. Mus. Am. Art, Washington, Columbus Mus. Art, Yale U., New Haven. Served with AUS, 1941-45, ETO. Recipient Dolian Lorian award for promising Am. painters, 1954; Hallmark award, 1961; Guggenheim fellow, 1980; Creative Artists Pub. Service Program grantee, 1973. Mem. Nat. Acad. of Design (Benjamin Altman prize 1993). Address: RR 1 Box 40 Stonington ME 04681-9702

PACE, THOMAS M., lawyer; b. Mesa, Ariz., Feb. 5, 1952; s. Lemuel Max and Ann (Green) P.; m. Vi Garrett Pace, Jan. 24, 1981; children: Melanie, Brittany. BA, Stanford U., 1973; JD, U. Ariz., 1976. Bar: Ariz.; cert. real estate specialist. Assoc. Martin, Feldhacker & Freidl, Phoenix, 1976-77, Trew & Woodford, Phoenix, 1977-78; ptnr. Hecker, Phillips & Hooker, Tucson, 1978-88; sr. ptnr. O'Connor Cavanagh, Tucson, 1988-95. Mem. Mayor's Housing Task Force, Tucson, 1993; bd. dirs. Tucson Urban League, 1986—; chmn. So. Ariz. Homebuilders Polit. Action Com., 1995. Mem. So. Ariz. Homebuilders (tech. com), Stanford Club So. Ariz. Democrat. Office: 3443 N Campbell Ave Ste 145 Tucson AZ 85719-2379

PACE, WAYNE H., communications executive. V.p. fin., CFO Turner Broadcasting Sys., Atlanta. Office: Turner Broadcasting Sys 1 CNN Ctr Box 105366 Atlanta GA 30348-5366

PACELLA, BERNARD LEONARDO, psychiatrist; b. Toronto, Ont., Can., July 25, 1912; m. Theresa Rita Domalakes; children: Karen Pacella Oldham, Richard B., Madelyn Joyce Nichols, Bernard Leonard Jr. BS, U. Colo., 1931, MD, 1935; post doctoral, N.Y. Psychoanalytic Inst., 1946-51. Cert. child, adolescent, and adult psychoanalyst; Diplomate Am. Bd. Psychiatry and Neurology. Intern Kings County Hosp., Bklyn., 1935-37, resident in pediatrics, 1937-38; resident in psychiatry Dept. Psychiatry Columbia U. and N.Y. State Psychiat. Inst., N.Y.C., 1938-40; rsch. fellow in psychiatry Columbia Presbyn. Med. Ctr., N.Y.C., 1940-41, instr. mil. psychiatry, 1943-46; lectr. clin. psychiatry Coll. Physicians and Surgeons Columbia U., 1942-44, assoc. clin. psychiatry, 1944-45, instr., 1945-47, asst. clin. prof., 1947-55, assoc. clin. prof., 1955-72, clin. prof., 1972-84, spl. lectr., mem. faculty Ctr. Psychoanalytic Tng. and Rsch., 1984—, clin. prof. emeritus, 1990—. Contbr. articles to profl. jours.; reviewer Psychoanalytic Quar. Pres. Margaret S. Mahler Psychiat. Rsch. Found., 1970-88, bd. dirs.; sec.-treas., bd. dirs. Sigmund Freud Archives; pres. Psychoanalytic Assistance Fund, 1974-89, bd. dirs.; bd. dirs. Freud London Mus.; co-trustee Mary S. Sigourney award, 1990. With Colo. N.G., 1930-35, M.C. USAR, 1935-40. Decorated Cavaliere Officiale dell Ordine al Merito (Italy), 1958. Fellow Am. Coll. Psychoanalysis, Am. Acad. Child and Adolescent Psychiatry, N.Y. Acad. Medicine, Am. Psychiat. Assn.; mem. AMA, Am. Orthopsychiat. Assn., Am. Soc. Adolescent Psychiatry, Am. Psychoanalytic Assn. (reviewer jour., pres.-elect 1990, pres. 1992—, treas. 1983—), Assn. Child Psychoanalysis, Group Advancement Psychiatry, Assn. Psychoanalytic Medicine, N.Y. Psychoanalytic Soc. and Inst. (bd. dirs.), Internat. Psychoanalytic Assn., N.Y. Coun. Child and Adolescent Psychiatry, Alpha Omega Alpha. Home and Office: 115 E 61st St New York NY 10021-8172

PACH, PETER BARNARD, newspaper columnist and editor; b. Bklyn., Aug. 3, 1951; s. Stewart Warner and Constance (Barnard) P.; m. Kathleen Ann Megan, Sept. 7, 1985; children: Nell, Samuel. BA in English, Union Coll., 1973. Reporter Record Jour., Meriden, Conn., 1974-78, Wallingford bur. chief, 1978-83; Middletown bur. chief Hartford Courant, Conn., 1983-84, columnist, 1984-95; mem. editorial bd. Hartford (Conn.) Courant, 1992—; vis. instr. Wesleyan U., Middletown, Conn., 1985—. Recipient First Bus. and Econ. Reporting award New England Press Ass., 1977. Mem. Dedham County and Polo Club. Avocations: running, skiing, golf, gardening, reading. Home: PO Box 46 Middle Haddam CT 06456-0046 Office: Hartford Courant 285 Broad St Hartford CT 06115-2500

PACHECO, FELIPE RAMON, lawyer; b. Sagua la Grande, Las Villas, Cuba, Aug. 22, 1924; came to U.S., 1962; s. Felipe and Eugenia America (Rodriguez) P.; m. Maria Infiesta, Apr. 5, 1945; children: Carmen Pacheco Weber, Lilian C. Porter. D in philosophy and art, U. Havana, Cuba, 1947, D of laws, 1953; MS, Syracuse U., 1967; JD, U. Fla., 1975. Bar: Fla. 1975, U.S. Dist. Ct. (mid. dist.) Fla. 1976. Dir. librs. Ctrl. U. Las Villas, Santa Clara, Cuba, 1953-61; asst., assoc. catalog libr. Cornell U., Ithaca, N.Y., 1962-68, asst. law libr., 1969-70; law libr. Carlton, Fields, Tampa, Fla., 1971-75; pvt. practice Tampa, 1976—. Roman Catholic. Office: 4509 N Armenia Ave Tampa FL 33603-2703

PACHECO, MANUEL TRINIDAD, academic administrator; b. Rocky Ford, Colo., May 30, 1941; s. Manuel J. and Elizabeth (Lopez) P.; m. Karen M. King, Aug. 27, 1966; children: Daniel Mark, Andrew Charles, Sylvia Lois Elizabeth. BA, N.Mex. Highlands U., 1962; MA, Ohio State U., 1966, PhD, 1969. Prof. edn., univ. dean Tex. A&I U., Laredo, 1972-77, exec. dir. Bilingual Edn. Ctr., Kingsville, 1980-82; prof. multicultural edn., chmn. dept. San Diego State U., 1977-78; prof. Spanish and edn. Laredo State U., 1978-80, pres., 1984-88; assoc. dean Coll. Edn. U. Tex., El Paso, 1982-84, exec. dir. for planning, 1984; chief policy aide for edn. to gov. N.Mex., 1984; pres. U. Houston-Downtown, 1988-91, U. Ariz., Tucson, 1991—; cons. lang. div. Ency. Britannica, 1965-72; bd. dirs. Valley Nat. Bank Corp., Nat. Security Edn. Program; mem. exec. com. Bus.-Higher Edn. Forum. Co-editor: Handbook for Planning and Managing Instruction in Basic Skills for Limited English Proficient Students, 1983; producer: (videotapes) Teacher Training, 1976. Treas. adv. com. U.S. Commn. on Civil Rights, L.A., 1987-91; trustee United Way of Houston, 1988-91; chmn. pub. rels. Buffalo Bayou Partnership, Houston, 1988-91; bd. dirs. Ctr. for Addiction and Substance Abuse, Greater Tucson Econ. Coun., Ariz. Econ. Coun., Ariz. Town Hall. Recipient Disting. Alumnus award Ohio State U., Columbus, 1984; named Most Prominent Am.-Hispancis Spanish Today mag., 1984, one of 100 Outstanding Hispanics Hispanic bus., 1988, Man of Yr. Hispanic Profl. Action Com., 1991; Fulbright fellow U. de Montepellier, France, 1962. Mem. Am. Assn. State Colls. and Univs., Nat. Acad. of Pub. Adminstrn., Hispanic Assn. Colls. and Univs., Tex. Assn. of Chicanos in Higher Edn., Rotary, Phi Delta Kappa. Office: U Ariz Office of Pres Tucson AZ 85721*

PACHECO-RANSANZ, ARSENIO, Hispanic and Italian studies educator; b. Barcelona, Spain, Feb. 8, 1932; s. Arsenio Pacheco and Jacoba Ransanz-Alvarez; m. Mercedes Olivella-Sole, Sept. 1, 1956; children: Arsenio-Andrew, David-George. MA, U. Barcelona, 1954, PhD, 1958. Tutor Colegio Mayor Hispanoamericano Fray Junipero Serra, Barcelona, 1954-56; lectr. Hochschüle für Wirtschaft und Sozialwissenschaften, Nurnberg, 1956; asst. lectr. U. Glasgow, Scotland, 1957-59; lectr. U. St. Andrews, Scotland, 1960-70; vis. prof. U. Pitts., 1966; prof. Hispanic and Italian studies U. B.C., Vancouver, Can., 1970—. Editor: Historia de Xacob Xalabin, 1964, Testament de Bernat Serradell, 1971, Varia fortuna del soldado Pindaro, 1975; contbr. articles to profl. jours. Bd. dirs. Can. Fedn. Humanities, 1981-84. Fellow Royal Soc. Can.; mem. Can. Assn. Hispanists (pres. 1978-81), Asociacion Internacional de Hispanists, MLA, Assn. Hispanists Gt. Britain and Ireland, N.Am. Catalan Soc. (v.p. 1984-87, pres. 1987-90), Anglo Catalan Soc., Associacio Internacional de Llengua i Literaturea Catalana. Roman Catholic. Office: U BC, Hispanic and Italian Studies, Vancouver, BC Canada V6T 1Z1

PACHEPSKY, LUDMILA BAUDINOVNA, ecologist; b. Ukhta, Komi, Russia, Mar. 19, 1946; d. Baudin Nuraddin Islamov and Valentina Grigorievna (Tyrina) Islamova; m. Yakov Aronovich Pachepsky, June 8, 1978; children: Anna, Elizaveta. Diploma, Moscow State U., Russia, 1969, postgrad., 1969-72. Engr. Inst. Agrochemistry and Soil Sci. of Soviet Acad. Scis., Pushchino/Moscow, 1972-74, minor rsch. scientist, 1974-80, rsch. scientist, 1980-92; rsch. asst. U. Md., College Park, 1993-94; sr. rsch. scholar Duke U., Durham, N.C., 1994—; invited lectr. Moscow State U., 1990-91, U. Ekaterinburgh, Russia, 1990. Editor: Institute of Soil Science and Photosynthesis, 1983-86; author: Computer Modeling of Water and Salt Movement in Soils, 1973, Modeling of Soil Salinization and Alkalinization Processes, 1979, 86, Stable Characteristics and a Model of Ecosystems in Northern Prikaspy, 1982, Dynamic Model of the Tea Plantations Productivity, 1985, Photosynthetic Apparatus and Productivity of Triticale, 1991, Two-dimensional Model 2DLEAF of Plant Leaf Photosynthesis and Transpiration, 1996; contbr. articles to profl. jours. Recipient Spl. award for Efficient Sci. Govt. of Reg. of Georgia, USSR, 1985; rsch. grantee Terrestial Ecosystems Regional Rsch. and Analysis, USA, 1994, others. Mem. Am. Soc. Plant Physiologists, Am. Soc. for Gravitational and Space Biology, Am. Soc. Agronomy, Japanese Soc. Plant Physiologists, Nat. Geographic Soc. Russian Orthodox. Home: 10403 Snowden Rd Laurel MD 20708 Office: USDA:ARS:Remote Sensing and Model Lab Bldg 007 Rm 008 BARC-W 10300 Baltimore Ave Beltsville MD 20705-2325

PACHMAN, DANIEL J., physician, educator; b. N.Y.C., Dec. 20, 1911; s. Louis and Ann (Kleinman) P.; m. Vivian Allison Futter, Nov. 8, 1935; children—Lauren Merle, Grace Allison. A.B., U. N.C., 1931; M.D., Duke U., 1934. Diplomate Nat. Bd. Med. Examiners, Am. Bd. Pediatrics. Intern pediatrics U. Chgo., 1934-35, instr. pediatrics, 1937-40; intern pediatrics N.Y. Hosp., 1935-36; resident pediatrics, attending pediatrician Duke Hosp., Durham, N.C., 1936-37; instr. Duke U., 1936-37, Northwestern U., 1940-42; practice medicine specializing in pediatrics Chgo., 1940-96; ret., 1996; clin. asst. prof. pediatrics U. Ill., 1950-59, clin. assoc. prof., 1960-67, clin. prof., 1967-81, emeritus prof., 1981—; attending pediatrician Ill. Research and Edn. Hosp., 1950-81; cons. Presbyn.-St. Luke's Hosp., Chgo., 1971-81, South Shore Hosp., 1955-60, Ill. Central Hosp., 1970-72, chmn. dept. pediatrics, 1962-70; attending pediatrician Trinity Hosp., 1971—; prof. pediatrics Rush Med. Coll., 1971-81, emeritus prof., 1981—; staff Children's Meml. Hosp.; courtesy staff Chgo. Lying-in Hosp; Med. cons. Bd. Edn., S. Shore High Sch., 1954-56; mem. advisory com. on sch. health Chgo. Bd. Health, 1962—, Chgo. Bd. Edn., 1962-66; pediatric cons. Ill. Council for Mentally Retarded Children, 1960-66; chmn. subcom. on sch. health Chgo. Med. Sch., 1961-67; chmn. Ill. Pediatric Coordinating Council, 1969-76. Contbr. numerous articles to profl. jours. Mem. com. on rights of minors Ill. Commn. on Children, 1975-77; mem. Mayor's Com. on Sch. Bd. Nominations, 1965-68; mem., co-chmn. Ill. Bd. for Opinions on Profl. Nursing, 1980—. Served to lt. col. M.C. U.S. Army, 1942-46. Recipient Archibald L. Hoyne award Chgo. Pediatric Soc., 1977. Fellow Am. Acad. Pediatrics (mem. exec. com. Ill. 1961-69, rep. to adv. council on child health Nat. Congress Parents and Tchrs., chmn. sci. exhibits com. 1964-72), Am. Cancer Soc. (pub. edn. com. 1967-69), Chgo. Inst. Medicine (mem.-at-large jt. com. on sch. services 1961-64), Chgo. Med. Soc. (past chmn. child health com.), Chgo. Pediatric Soc., AMA (med./edn. com. on sch. and coll. health), Phi Beta Kappa, Sigma Xi. Club: Quadrangle (bd. dirs. 1969-72), Carlton. Home: 1212 N Lake Shore Dr Chicago IL 60610 *Knowledge, perception and an outlook of acceptance and encouragement make the life of a pediatrician an interesting and disciplined adventure.*

PACHMAN, FREDERIC CHARLES, library director; b. Paterson, N.J., Apr. 16, 1952; s. Morris J. and Barbara M. (Haagen) P.; m. Donna Kearns, May 2, 1982; children: Rick, Kristina. BA, Syracuse U., 1973; MLS, Columbia U., 1976; cert., Rutgers U., New Brunswick, N.J., 1996. Libr. dir. Hamilton Twp. (N.J.) Pub. Libr., 1981-83, Middletown Twp. (N.J.) Pub. Libr., 1983-85, Monmouth Med. Ctr., Long Branch, N.J., 1985—; mem. exec. bd. Hist. Soc. Ocean Grove, N.J., 1985-96, Interagy. Coun. on Info. Resources for Nursing, N.Y.C., 1985—; cons. Caucus Archival Program Evaluation Svc., N.J., 1990—; mem. adv. com. on preservation and access N.J. State Libr., 1992-95. Contbr. articles to profl. jours. Mem. ALA, N.J. Libr. Assn., Med. Libr. Assn., League Hist. Socs. N.J., Mid Atlantic Regional Archives Conf., Acad. of Health Info. Profls. (sr. mem. 1992-96, Disting. mem. 1996—). Avocations: backpacking, reading, historic preservation, archives. Office: Monmouth Med Ctr 300 2nd Ave Long Branch NJ 07740-6300

PACHOLSKI, RICHARD FRANCIS, retired securities company executive, financial advisor, consultant; b. Seattle, June 18, 1947; s. Theodore Francis and Nellie (Tarabochia) P.; m. Dorothy Irene Nelson, May 25, 1974; children: Nicolas, Tara. BA cum laude, U. Wash., 1969, MBA summa cum laude, 1970. CPA, Wash. Mgr. Arthur Andersen & Co., Seattle, 1970-76; v.p., contr. SNW Enterprises, Seattle, 1976-82; sr. v.p., treas., sec., dir. Seattle N.W. Securities, 1982-93; cons. Carl & Co., Portland, Oreg., 1984-88, Ellis & Carl Inc., Portland, 1979-83; pres. R. Pacholski, P.C., Redmond, Wash., 1979—; adj. prof. U. Wash., Seattle, 1976-80; bd. dirs. Seattle N.W. Securities. Mem. AICPA, Wash. Soc. CPAs, Nat. Assn. Securities Dealers (past bd. dirs. local dist.), Wash. Athletic Club, PacWest Club (Redmond, Wash.). Roman Catholic. Home and Office: 5060 164th Ct NE Redmond WA 98052-5294

PACHT, ERIC REED, pulmonary and critical care physician; b. Madison, Wis., Mar. 24, 1954; s. Asher Roger and Perle (Landau) P.; m. Karen Sue Dalpiaz, Aug. 7, 1982; children: Ben, Lora. BA summa cum laude, Lawrence U., 1976; MD cum laude, U. Wis., Madison, 1980. Diplomate Nat. Bd. Med. Examiners, Am. Bd. Internal Medicine. Intern, resident Ohio State U. Hosps., 1980-83, fellow in pulmonary and critical care medicine, 1983-86; asst. prof. Ohio State U., 1986-91, assoc. prof., 1991—; asst. dir. pulmonary and critical care Ohio State U., 1988-96, dir. pulmonary and critical care fellowship tng. program, 1988—, med. sch. rep. to Am. Fedn. for Clin. Rsch., 1990-94, med. dir. lung transplantation program, 1992-95, dir. clin. rsch., 1993—. Contbr. articles to profl. jours. Vol. Am. Lung Assn., Columbus, Ohio, Columbus Cancer Clinic. Recipient numerous rsch. awards. Fellow Am. Coll. Chest Physicians; mem. Am. Thoracic Soc., Ohio Thoracic Soc., Am. Fedn. Clin. Rsch., Phi Beta Kappa. Achievements include description of new form of respiratory failure and emphysema in patients with HIV. Home: 1224 Leicester Pl Columbus OH 43235-2181 Office: Ohio State U Divsn Pulmonary Medicine 1654 Upham Dr Columbus OH 43210-1250

PACHTER, IRWIN JACOB, pharmaceutical consultant; b. N.Y.C., July 15, 1925; s. Nathan and Ethel Lillian (Thomases) P.; m. Elaine Anna White, Aug. 23, 1953; children: Wendy, Jonathan. B.S., UCLA, 1947; M.S., U. N.Mex., 1949; Ph.D., U. So. Calif., 1951; postgrad., U. Ill., 1951-52, Harvard U., 1952-53. Research chemist Ethyl Corp., 1953-55; asso. research chemist Smith Kline & French, 1955-62, asst. sec. head, 1962; dir. medicinal chemistry Endo Labs., 1962-66; dir. research Endo div. du Pont Co., 1967-70; v.p. research and devel. Bristol Labs. div. Bristol-Myers Co., 1970-82; lectr. Adelphi U., 1963-69. Contbr. articles to profl. jours.; patentee in field. Trustee Gordon Research Conf., 1972-75; chmn. medicinal chemistry study group Walter Reed Inst. Research, 1975-77. Served with USN, 1944-46. Mem. Am. Chem. Soc. (chmn. div. medicinal chemistry 1974-76), Pharm. Mfrs. Assn. (chmn. research and devel. sect. 1975-76). Home: 101 Woodberry Ln Fayetteville NY 13066-1745

PACIFICO, ALBERT DOMINICK, cardiovascular surgeon; b. Bklyn., Sept. 24, 1940; s. Dominick Vincent and Amelia Catherine (Jannelli) P.; m. Vicki Lynne Overton, May 16, 1980; children: Albert D., Nicole M., Paul V. B.S., St. Johns U., 1960; M.D., N.J. Coll. Medicine, 1964. Diplomate Am. Bd. Surgery, Am. Bd. Thoracic Surgery. Med. intern Jersey City Med. Ctr., Seton Gall Coll. Medicine, 1964-65; asst. resident in surgery Mayo Clinic, Rochester, Minn., 1965-67; research fellow in surgery U. Ala., Birmingham, 1967-69, sr. resident, then chief resident surgery, resident in thoracic and cardiovascular surgery, 1968-72, mem. faculty dept. surgery, 1970—, prof. surgery, 1978-83, John W. Kirklin prof. cardiovascular surgery, 1983—, vice chmn. dept. surgery, 1990, dir. div. cardiothoracic surgery, 1984—, dir. Congenital Heart Disease Diagnosis and Treatment Ctr., 1985—; mem. staff gen., thoracic and cardiovascular surgery Univ. Hosp., Birmingham, 1972—, VA Hosp., Birmingham, 1972—; mem. staff Children's Hosp., Birmingham, 1971—, chief gen., thoracic and cardiovascular surgery, 1984—. Author: (with others) Pediatric Cardiac Surgery, 1985, Cardiology, 1985, Textbook of Surgery, 13th edit., 1986, The Treatment of Congenital Cardiac Anomalies, 1986, Perspectives in Pediatric Cardiology, 1988, Current Therapy in Cardiothoracic Surgery, 1989, Decision Making in Surgery of the Chest, 1989, Cardiac Surgery: Cyanotic Congential Heart Disease, 1989, Reoperation in Cardiac Surgery, 1989, others; mem. editorial bd. Am. Jour. Cardiology, 1983—, Heart and Vessel, 1985—, Jour. Cardiac Surgery, 1985—; cons. editorial referee Ala. Jour. Med. Scis., 1974-75; contbr. articles to med. jours. Fellow ACS, Am. Coll. Cardiology, Am. Surg. Assn.; mem. AMA, Ala. State Med. Soc., Jefferson County Med. Soc., Am. Heart Assn. (Paul Dudley White Internat. Svc. Citation 1977), Am. Assn. Thoracic Surgery, Soc. Thoracic Surgeons, Am. Surg. Soc., Internat. Coll. Pediatrics, John Kirklin Soc., Congentital Heart Surgeons Soc., Assn. Acad. Surgery, Ala. chpt. Mayo Clinic Alumni Assn., Panamanian Soc. Cardiology (hon.), Peruvian Soc. Thoracic and Cardiovascular Surgery (hon.), Soc. Nat. Inst. Cardiology Mex. (hon.), Cardiac Soc. Australia and New Zealand (corr.), Peruvian Soc. Cardiology (corr.), Alpha Omega Alpha. Republican. Roman Catholic. Office: Univ Ala UAB Station Dept Surgery Birmingham AL 35294

PACIFICO, DIANE ALANE, ophthalmic nurse; b. Bethlehem, Pa., Sept. 23, 1952; d. William Edward and Martha Lou (Bradford) Reichard; m. Ronald L. Pacificio, Sept. 25, 1982. Diploma, Abington (Pa.) Meml. Hosp., 1973. Cert. RN in ophthalmology. Med.-surg. nurse St. Luke's Hosp., Bethlehem, 1973-76; ophthalmic nurse physician's office, Pitts., 1976-77, Everett & Hurite Ophthalmic Assocs., Pitts., 1977-80; exec. dir. Assocs. in Ophthalmology, Inc., Pitts., 1980—; speaker in field. Contbr. articles to profl. jours. Mem. NAFE, Founders Soc., Am. Soc. Ophthalmic Registered Nurses, Abington Nurses Alumnae, Am. Soc. Ophthalmic Adminstrs. Office: 500 Lewis Run Rd Ste 218 Pittsburgh PA 15236 also: 125 Daugherty Dr Ste 320 Monroeville PA 15146 also: Town Centre Bldg 10475 Perry Hwy Ste 315 Wexford PA 15090 Address: 4140 Brownsville Rd Ste 237 Pittsburgh PA 15227

PACINO, AL (ALFREDO JAMES PACINO), actor; b. N.Y.C., Apr. 25, 1940; s. Salvatore and Rose P. Student, High Sch. of Performing Arts, N.Y.C., Actors Studio, from 1966. Formerly mail deliverer editorial offices Commentary Mag.; formerly messenger, movie theatre usher, bldg. supt.; co-artistic dir. The Actors Studio, Inc., N.Y.C., 1982-84. Served apprenticeship as actor, dir. and comedy writer in Off-Off Broadway theatres, Elaine Stewart's Cafe La Mama, Julian Beck & Judith Malina's Living Theatre; appeared in New Theatre Workshop prodn. of The Peace Creeps, Dec., 1966; joined Charles Playhouse, Boston, fall, 1967, and performed in New Theatre Workshop prodn. of America Hurrah and Awake and Sing; appeared in a one-act play Off Broadway The Indian Wants the Bronx, opened Astor Pl. Theater on Jan. 17, 1968 (Obie as best actor in Off-Broadway prodn. 1967-68); made Broadway debut in Does A Tiger Wear A Necktie?, 1969 (Tony award as best dramatic actor in a supporting role, named most promising new Broadway actor in a Variety poll of metropolitan drama critics); appeared in The Local Stigmatic at Actors Playhouse, N.Y.C., opening 1969; joined Repertory Theater of Lincoln Center, N.Y.C.; other plays include The Basic Training of Pavlo Hummel, Boston Repertory Theater, 1972, Camino Real, Richard III, 1973, 79, Jungle of Cities, 1979, The Connection, Hello Out There, Tiger at the Gates, American Buffalo, Julius Caesar, 1988, Salome, Chinese Coffee, Circle in the Square, 1992; (films) debut in Me, Natalie, 1969, Panic in Needle Park, 1971, The Godfather, 1972 (Best Actor award Nat. Soc. Film Critics, Acad. award nominee), Scarecrow, 1973, Serpico, 1973 (Acad. award nominee), The Godfather, Part II, 1974 (Acad. award nominee), Dog Day Afternoon (Acad. award nominee), 1975, Bobby Deerfield, 1977, And Justice for All, 1979 (Acad. Award nomination), Cruising, 1980, Author! Author!, 1982, Scarface, 1983, Revolution, 1985, Sea of Love, 1990, Dick Tracy, 1990 (Acad. award nominee), The Godfather Part III, 1990, Frankie and Johnny, 1991, Glengarry Glen Ross, 1992 (Acad. award nominee), Scent of a Woman, 1992 (Acad. award for Best Actor), Carlito's Way, 1993, Two Bits, 1994, Heat, 1995, City Hall, 1996, Donny Brasco, 1996, Devil's Advocate, 1997; actor, prodr., dir., writer Looking for Richard, 1996. Recipient Am. Comedy award film Dick Tracy, 1991. Office: CAA care Rick Nicita 9830 Wilshire Blvd Beverly Hills CA 90212*

PACK, ALLEN S., retired coal company executive; b. Bramwell, W.Va., Dec. 11, 1930; s. Paul Meador and Mable Blanche (Hale) P.; m. Glenna Rae Christian, June 21, 1952; children: Allen Scott Jr., David Christian, Mark Frederick, Andrew Ray. B.S., W.Va. U., 1952. Gen. mgr. Island Coal Co., Holden, W.Va., 1969-70, pres., 1970-73; v.p. adminstrn. Island Coal Co., Lexington, Ky., 1973-75; exec. v.p. Cannelton Holding Co., Charleston, W.Va., 1975-77, pres., chief ops. officer, 1977-80, pres., chief exec. officer, 1980-91; chmn., 1991-93, ret., 1993. Bd. dirs. Bucksin coun. Boy Scouts Am., Charleston, 1976—, pres., 1980, chmn., 1994, 95, 96; bd. dirs. W.Va. Univ. Found., Morgantown, 1978-96; trustee Davis and Elkins Coll., 1981. Capt. USMC, 1952-54. Recipient Silver Beaver award Boy Scouts Am., 1981. Presbyterian.

PACK, EMILY LLOYD See LLOYD, EMILY

PACK, LEONARD BRECHER, lawyer; b. Seattle, Feb. 7, 1944; s. Howard David and Vivian (Brecher) P.; m. Barbara-Jane Lunin (div. Sept. 1978); children: Jesse, Justin; m. Adele Susan Weisman, Jan. 7, 1979; 1 child, Anna Rae. BA, Columbia U., 1966, JD, 1970, MIA, 1970. Bar: N.Y. 1971. Law clk. to judge U.S. Ct. Appeals D.C. Circuit, 1970-71; assoc. Fried, Frank, Harris, Shriver & Jacobson, N.Y.C., 1971-78; sec., assoc. gen. counsel Metromedia, Inc., Secaucus, N.J., 1979-86; sr. v.p., gen. counsel Orion Pictures Corp., N.Y.C., 1986-90; ptnr. Berger Steingut & Stern, N.Y.C., 1990-93; pvt. practice N.Y.C., 1993—. Bd. dirs., v.p. Dance Theatre Workshop. Mem. ABA. Democrat. Jewish. Avocation: music. Office: 1500 Broadway 21st Flr New York NY 10036

PACK, RICHARD MORRIS, broadcasting executive; b. N.Y.C., Nov. 22, 1915; s. Charles and Bertha (Gross) P.; m. Laura Lipkin, June 27, 1940; children: Robert N., Judith (dec.). A.B., NYU, 1938. Dir. publicity and continuity Sta. WNYC, N.Y.C., 1938-40; dir. publicity Sta. WOR, N.Y.C., 1942-47; dir. programming Sta. WNEW, N.Y.C., 1949-52; dir. programming and ops. Sta. WNBC and WNBT-TV, N.Y.C., 1952-54; v.p. programming Westinghouse Broadcasting Co., Inc., N.Y.C., 1955-65, sr. v.p. programming and prodn., 1965-72; pres. Group W Films, 1966-72; exec. adviser to chmn. Westinghouse Broadcasting Co., 1972-76; creative cons. Post-Newsweek Stas., Washington, 1972-76; disting. vis. lectr. telecommunications and film San Diego State U., 1988. Exec. producer film: One Day in the Life of Ivan Denisovich; author: (with Jo Ranson) Opportunities in Radio, 1948, Opportunities in Television, 1950; editor TV Quar., 1981—. Mem. pres.'s coun. social work edn. NYU, 1963-73. With USAAF, 1943-46.

PACK, RUSSELL T., theoretical chemist; b. Grace, Idaho, Nov. 20, 1937; s. John Terrell and Mardean (Izatt) P.; m. Marion Myrth Hassell, Aug. 21, 1962; children: John R., Nathan H., Allen H., Miriam, Elizabeth, Quinn R., Howard H. BS, Brigham Young U., 1962; PhD, U. Wis., 1967. Postdoctoral fellow U. Minn., Mpls., 1966-67; asst. prof. Brigham Young U., Provo, 1967-71; assoc. prof. Brigham Young U., 1971-75, adj. prof., 1975-88; staff scientist Los Alamos (N.Mex.) Nat. Lab., 1975-83, fellow, 1983—, assoc. grp. leader, 1979-81; vis. prof. Max Planck Institut, Gottingen, 1981; chmn. Gordon Rsch. Conf., 1982; lectr. in field. Contbr. articles to profl. jours. Named Sr. U.S. Scientist, Alexander Vol Humboldt Found., 1981. Fellow Am. Phys. Soc. (sec.-treas. div. Chem. Physics 1990-93); mem. Am. Chem. Soc., Sigma Xi. Mem. Ch. of Jesus Christ of Latter Day Saints. Home: 240 Kimberly Ln Los Alamos NM 87544-3526 Office: Los Alamos National Lab T-12 Ms # B268 Los Alamos NM 87545

PACK, SUSAN JOAN, art consultant; b. N.Y.C., June 15, 1951; d. Howard Meade and Nancy (Buckley) P. BA summa cum laude, Princeton U., 1973. Copywriter Laurence Charles & Free, N.Y.C., 1978-83, Warwick Advt., N.Y.C., 1983-85; sr. copywriter Saatchi & Saatchi Compton, N.Y.C., 1985-88; pres. The Pack Collection, 1989—. Author: Film Posters of the Russian Avant-Garde, 1995. Mem. Princeton (N.J.) U. Libr. Coun., 1985-93; trustee Pack Found. for Med. Rsch., N.Y., 1983—; bd. dirs. The Poster Soc., N.Y., 1985-87. Recipient 4 Clio awards, 1981, 1 Clio award, 1982; named one of top art collectors under 40 Art and Antiques Mag., 1985, one of top 100 collectors in U.S., 1996. Mem. Phi Beta Kappa.

PACKARD, BONNIE BENNETT, former state legislator; b. Concord, N.H., Nov. 9, 1946; d. James Oliver and Caro Lucia (Arsenault) Bennett; m. David Bartlett Packard, Oct. 1, 1983. Mem. N.H. Ho. of Reps., Concord, 1981-82, 85-96, vice chair ho. econ. devel. com., 1992, chair ho. commerce com., 1993-96; v.p., treas. Dodd Ins. Agy., Contoocook, N.H., 1984-85; dir. govt. rels. Roussos & Hage, P.A., Attys. at Law, 1996—; bd. dirs. Bus. Fin. Authority, 1994-96. State pres. N.H. Fedn. Rep. Women, 1982-83; chmn. Merrimack County (N.H.) Rep. Com., 1979-80; mem. Hillsborough County Rep. Com., 1995, chair Hillsborough County Del., 1995-96; mem. Bd. Selectmen, New Ipswich, N.H., 1989-90; nat. del. trustee Nat. Kidney Found., 1990-91, 1st v.p. N.H. chpt., 1990-91. Recipient Spirit of Independence award N.H. Health Underwriter's Assn., 1996, Chmn.'s award Bus. Fin. Authority of State of N.J., 1996. Mem. New Ipswich Hist. Soc., Greenville Women's Club. Episcopalian. Avocations: sketching, antiques, political campaigns. Home: 6 Joy Ln New Ipswich NH 03071-3610 Office: One Eagle Sq Ste 505 Concord NH 03301 also: 1855 Elm St Manchester NH 03102

PACKARD, ELEANOR GOULD See GOULD, ELEANOR LOIS

PACKARD, GEORGE RANDOLPH, journalist, educator; b. Phila., May 27, 1932; s. George Randolph and Anita Porter (Clothier) P.; m. Mary Biddle Lloyd, June 26, 1954 (div. Aug. 1978); children: Frank Randolph, Mary Wingate, William Clothier, Andrew Lloyd, Benjamin Wood, Alexander Barnes, Kent Elizabeth Davis-Packard; m. Lavinia Fletcher Plumley, July 1990. A.B., Princeton U., 1954; Ph.D., Fletcher Sch. Law and Diplomacy, 1963; research scholar, Tokyo U., 1961-62. Spl. asst. to U.S. ambassador to Japan, 1963-65; chief diplomatic corr. Newsweek mag., Washington, 1965-67; mng. editor Phila. Bull., 1969-73, exec. editor, 1973-75; dep. dir. Woodrow Wilson Internat. Center for Scholars, Smithsonian Instn., Washington, 1976-79; prof. Sch. Advanced Internat. Studies Johns Hopkins U., 1967-68, 94—, dean Sch. Advanced Internat. Studies, 1979-93; vis. pres. Internat. U. Japan, 1994—. Author: Protest in Tokyo: The Security Treaty Crisis of 1960, 1966, Japan, Korea and China, 1979, also articles. Candidate for U.S. Senate from Pa., 1975-76; bd. dirs. Asia Found.,

San Francisco, Atlantic Council U.S. Served to 1st lt. AUS, 1956. Ford fellow, 1960-62. Mem. Assn. Asian Studies, Japan Soc. N.Y., Council Fgn. Relations N.Y., Phi Beta Kappa. Club: Metropolitan (Washington). Home: 4425 Garfield St NW Washington DC 20007-1143 Office: Johns Hopkins U Sch Advanced Internat Study 1619 Massachusetts Ave NW Washington DC 20036-2213

PACKARD, JOHN MALLORY, physician; b. Saranac Lake, N.Y., Sept. 25, 1920; s. Edward Newman and Mary Bissell (Betts) P.; m. Ann Maurine Schoonover, June 15, 1944; children: Michael David, John Mallory, Ann Maurine, Mary Betts, Charles Edward, Kris Asvananda, Frank Schoonover, Charlotte Mellen. B.A., Yale U., 1942; M.D., Harvard U., 1945. Diplomate Am. Bd. Internal Medicine. Intern Presbyn. Hosp., N.Y.C., 1945-46; resident in internal medicine Peter Bent Brigham Hosp., Boston, 1948-49; practice medicine specializing in internal medicine and cardiology Pensacola, Fla., 1954-68; prof. medicine, asso. dean Med. Sch. U. Ala., Birmingham, 1968-76; exec. dir. Ala. Regional Med. Program, Birmingham, 1968-73; corp. v.p. med. edn. Bapt. Med. Centers, Birmingham, 1976-92; ret. Contbr. articles to med. jours. Served with USN, 1946-54. Fellow ACP, Am. Coll. Cardiology, Council Clin. Cardiology; mem. Jefferson County Med. Soc., Med. Assn. Ala., AMA, Am. Soc. Internal Medicine, Ala. Soc. Internal Medicine (pres. 1981-82), Alpha Omega Alpha. Republican. Episcopalian.

PACKARD, MILDRED RUTH, middle school educator; b. Boulder, Colo., Sept. 8, 1947; d. Peter L.M. and Jane G. Packard. BA, Lynchburg Coll., 1969; MS, Va. Poly. Inst. and State U., 1973. Cert. phys. edn. tchr., Va. Tchr., basketball, gymnastics and track coach Osbourn High Sch., Manassas, Va., 1969-73; tchr., coach girls softball, basketball and volleyball Rippon Mid. Sch., Woodbridge, Va., 1973-89, athletic dir., 1982-89; tchr., athletic dir., volleyball coach Lake Ridge Mid. Sch., Woodbridge, 1989—. Mem. NEA, AAHPERD, Va. Edn. Assn., Prince William Edn. Assn., Va. Assn. Health, Phys. Edn., and Recreation. Avocations: volleyball, golf, reading. Office: Lake Ridge Mid Sch 12350 Mohican Rd Woodbridge VA 22192-1757

PACKARD, ROBERT CHARLES, lawyer; b. L.A., Sept. 21, 1919; s. Charles W. and Gertrude (Vern) P.; m. Nanette Taylor, Dec. 21, 1973 (dec.). B.S., U. So. Calif., 1941, J.D., 1947. Bar: Calif. 1948. Sr. ptnr. Kirtland & Packard, L.A., 1948-94, of counsel, 1994—. Fellow Am. Coll. Trial Lawyers; mem. ABA, L.A. Bar Assn. (substantive law com.), Intrenat. Bar Assn., Los Angeles County Bar Assn., Lawyer Pilots Bar Assn., Internat. Assn. Ins. Counsel (aviation com.), Am. Bd. Trial Advs., Am. Judicature Soc., Internat. Soc. Barristers, Calif. Club, Los Angeles Country Club, La Quinta Country Club, Phi Delta Phi. Home: 11445 Waterford St Los Angeles CA 90049-3438 Office: 1900 Avenue Of The Stars Los Angeles CA 90067-4301

PACKARD, ROCHELLE SYBIL, elementary school educator; b. June 25, 1951; d. Dave Wallace and Jeanette (Goddy) P. BA in Early Childhood Edn., Point Park Coll., 1973; MEd in Elem. Edn., U. Pitts., 1975. Instrnl. II permanent tchg. cert., Pa. Substitute tchr. Pitts. Pub. Bd. Edn., 1973-77, tchr. kindergarten, 1st grade, 2d grade, 1977—. Chair Israel Day Parade, Pitts., 1981; mem. Hadassah, Pitts., 1983—, Pioneer Women, Pitts., 1982—, ORT, Pitts., 1975—. Mem. Pitts. Fedn. Tchrs., Pitts. State Edn. Agy. Democrat. Jewish. Home: 4100 Lydia St Pittsburgh PA 15207

PACKARD, RONALD, congressman; b. Meridian, Idaho, Jan. 19, 1931; m. Jean Sorenson, 1952; children: Chris, Debbie, Jeff, Vicki, Scott, Lisa, Theresa. Student, Brigham Young U., 1948-50, Portland State U., 1952-53; D.M.D., U. Oreg., Portland, 1953-57. Gen. practice dentistry Carlsbad, Calif., 1959-82; mem. 98th-105th Congresses from 43rd (now 48th) Dist. Calif., 1983—; chmn. appropriations legis. subcom., former mem. pub. works and transp. com., sci., space, tech., also mem. appropriations fgn. ops. and transp. subcoms. Mem. Carlsbad Sch. Dist. Bd., 1962-74; bd. dirs. Carlsbad C. of C., 1972-76; mem. Carlsbad Planning Commn., 1974-76, Carlsbad City Coun., 1976-78; Carlsbad chmn. Boy Scouts Am., 1977-79; mayor City of Carlsbad, 1978-82; mem. North County Armed Svcs. YMCA, North County Transit Dist., San Diego Assn. Govts., Coastal Policy Com., Transp. Policy Com.; pres. San Diego div. Calif. League of Cities. Served with Dental Corps USN, 1957-59. Republican. Mem. Ch. LDS. Office: US Ho of Reps 2372 Rayburn HOB Washington DC 20515*

PACKARD, SANDRA PODOLIN, education educator, consultant; b. Buffalo, Sept. 13, 1942; d. Mathew and Ethel (Zolte) P.; m. Martin Packard, Aug. 2, 1964; children: Dawn Esther, Shana Fanny. B.F.A., Syracuse U., 1964; M.S.Ed., Ind. U., 1966, Ed.D., 1973. Cert. tchr. art K-12, N.Y. Asst. prof. art SUNY-Buffalo, 1972-74; assoc. prof. art Miami U., Oxford, Ohio, 1974-81, spl. asst. to provost, 1979-80, assoc. provost, spl. programs, 1980-81; dean Coll. Edn. Bowling Green State U., Ohio, 1981-85; provost and vice chancellor for acad. affairs U. Tenn., Chattanooga, 1985-92; pres. Oakland U., Rochester, Mich., 1992-95; prof. edn., 1995—; sr. fellow, dir. tech. in edn. Am. Assn. State Colls. and Univs., 1995; prof. Oakland U., Rochester, Mich., 1995—; cons. Butler County Health Ctr., Hamilton, Ohio, 1976-78; vis. prof. art therapy Simmons Coll., 1979, Mary Mount Coll., Milw., 1981; bd. dirs. SE Ctr. for Arts in Edn., 1994—; mem. corp. adv. com. Corp. Detroit Mag., 1994-95; cons. Univ. of the North, South Africa Project of the Am. Coun. on Edn., 1995; bd. mem. Fellows Coun. Am. Coun. on Edn., 1994-96. Sr. editor Studies in Art Edn. jour., 1979-81; editorial adv. bd. Jour. Aesthetic Edn., 1984-90; editor: The Leading Edge, 1986; contbr. articles to profl. jours., chpts. to conf. papers. Chmn. com. Commn. on Edn. Excellence, Ohio, 1982-83, Tenn. State Peformance Funding Task Force, 1988, Tenn. State Task Force on Minority Tchrs., 1988; reviewer art curriculum N.Y. Bd. Edn., 1985; mem. supt. search com. Chattanooga Pub. Schs., 1987-88; mem. Chattanooga Met. Coun., 1987-88, Chattanooga Ballet Bd., 1986-88, Fund for Excellence in Pub. Edn., 1986-90, Tenn. Aquarium Bd. Advisors, 1989-92, Team Evaluation Ctr. Bd., 1988-90; mem. Strategic Planning Action Team, Chattanooga City Schs., 1987-88, Siskin Hosp. Bd., 1989-92, Blue Ribbon Task Force Pontiac 2010: A New Reality, City of Pontiac Planning Divsn., 1992—; steering com., cultural action bd. Chattanooga, planning com United Way, 1987; Jewish Fedn. Bd., 1986-91; mem. coun. for policy studies Art Edn. Adv. Bd., 1982-91; ex-officio mem. Meadow Brook Theatre Guild, 1992-95; bd. chair Meadow Brook Performing Arts Co., 1992-95; chair World Cup Soccer Edn. Com./Mich. Host Com. 1993-95; bd. dirs. Ptnrs. for Preferred Future, Rochester Cmty. Schs., 1992-95, Traffic Improvement Assn. Oakland County, 1992-95, Oakland County Bus. Roundtable, 1993-95; Rochester C. of C. host com. chair on edn. World Cup, 1992-95; mem. fin. adv. com. Jewish Fedn. Detroit, 1995—; bd. dirs. United Way Southeastern Mich.: active United Way Oakland County, Pontiac 2010: A New Reality, mayor's transition team city/sch. rels. task force: team evaluation leader Dept. of State Am. Univ. Bulgaria, 1995; bd. trustees Cohn's & Colitis Found., 1996—. Am. Coun. on Edn. and Mellon fellow Miami U., 1978-79; recipient Cracking the Glass Ceiling award Pontiac Area Urban League, 1992. Fellow Nat. Art Edn. Assn. (disting.); mem. Am. Assn. Colls. for Tchr. Edn. (com. chair 1982-85), Am. Art Therapy Assn. (registered), Nat. Art Edn. Assn. Women's Caucus (founder, pres. 1976-78, McFee award 1986), Am. Assn. State Colls. and Univs. (com. profl. devel. 1993-95, state rep. 1994-95), Econ. Club Detroit (bd. dirs. 1992-95), Rotary Club, Great Lakes Yacht Club (social chmn. 1996-97), Phi Delta Kappa (Leadership award 1985). Avocation: sailing. Home: 5192 Mirror Lake Ct West Bloomfield MI 48323-1535 Office: Oakland U 536 O'Dowd Hall Rochester MI 48309

PACKENHAM, RICHARD DANIEL, lawyer; b. Newton, Pa., June 23, 1953; s. John Richard and Mary Margaret (Maroney) P.; m. Susan Patricia Smillie, Aug. 20, 1983. BA, Harvard U., 1975; JD, Boston Coll., 1978; LLM in Taxation, Boston U., 1985. Bar: Mass. 1978, Conn. 1979, U.S. Dist. Ct. Mass. 1979, U.S. Dist. Ct. Conn. 1979, U.S. Ct. Appeals (1st cir.) 1981, U.S. Supreme Ct. 1985. Staff atty. Conn. Superior Ct., 1978-79; ptnr. McGrath & Kane, Boston, 1979-94, Packenham, Schmidt & Federico, Boston, 1994—. Mem. ABA, Mass. Bar Assn., Conn. Bar Assn., Boston Bar Assn., Mass CLE (faculty). Democrat. Roman Catholic. Club: Harvard (Boston). Home: 1062 North St Walpole MA 02081-2307 Office: Packenham Schmidt & Federico 4 Longfellow Pl Boston MA 02114-2838

PACKER, BOYD K., church official. Acting pres. Quorum of the Twelve, Ch. of Jesus Christ of Latter-Day Saints. Office: LDS Church 47 E South Temple Salt Lake City UT 84150-1005

PACKER, KATHERINE HELEN, retired library educator; b. Toronto, Ont., Can., Mar. 20, 1918; d. Cleve Alexander and Rosa Ruel (Dibblee) Smith; m. William A. Packer, Sept. 27, 1941; 1 dau., Marianne Katherine. B.A., U. Toronto, 1941; A.M.L.S., U. Mich., 1953; Ph.D., U. Md., 1975. Cataloguer William L Clements Library, U. Mich., 1953-55, U. Man. (Can.) Library, Winnipeg, 1956-59; cataloguer U. Toronto Library, 1959-63; asst. prof. Faculty Library Sci., 1967-75, asso. prof., 1975-78, prof., dean, 1979-84, prof. emeritus, 1984—; head cataloguer York U. Library, Toronto, 1963-64; chief librarian Ont. Coll. Edn., Toronto, 1964-67. Author: Early American School Books, 1954. Mem. property tax working group Ont. Fair Tax Commn., 1991-92; mem. assessment reform working group City of Toronto, 1992-97. Recipient Disting. Alumnus award U. Mich., 1981. Mem. Can. Library Assn. (Howard Phalin award 1972), Phi Kappa Phi. Home: 53 Gormley Ave, Toronto, ON Canada M4V 1Y9 Office: U Toronto, Faculty Info Studies, 140 Saint George St, Toronto, ON Canada M5S 3G6

PACKER, MARK BARRY, lawyer, financial consultant, foundation official; b. Phila., Sept. 18, 1944; s. Samuel and Eve (Devine) P.; m. Donna Elizabeth Ferguson (div. 1994); children: Daniel Joshua, Benjamin Dov, David Johannes; m. Helen Margaret (Jones) Klinedinst, July, 1995. AB magna cum laude, Harvard U., 1965, LLB, 1968. Bar: Wash. 1969, Mass. 1971. Assoc. Ziontz, Pirtle & Fulle, Seattle, 1968-70; pvt. practice, Bellingham, Wash., 1972—; bd. dirs., corp. sec. BMJ Holdings (formerly No. Sales Co., Inc.), 1977—; trustee No. Sales Profit Sharing Plan, 1977—; bd. dirs. Whatcom State Bank, 1995—. Mem. Bellingham Planning and Devel. Commn., 1975-84, chmn., 1977-81, mem. shoreline subcom., 1976-82; mem. Bellingham Mcpl. Arts Commn., 1986-91, landmark rev. bd., 1987-91; chmn. Bellingham campaign United Jewish Appeal, 1979-90; bd. dirs. Whatcom Community Coll. Found., 1989-92; trustee, chmn. program com. Bellingham Pub. Sch. Found., 1991—; Heavy Culture classic lit. group, 1991—, Jewish studies group, 1993—; trustee Kenneth L. Kellar Found., 1995—; mng. trustee Bernard M. & Audrey Jaffe Found; trustee, treas. Congregation Eytz Chaim, Bellingham, 1995—. Recipient Blood Donor award ARC, 1979, 8-Gallon Pin, 1988, Mayor's Arts award City of Bellingham, 1993. Mem. Wash. State Bar Assn. (sec. environ. and land use law, sec. bus. law, sec. real property, probate and trust, com. law examiners 1992-94). Office: PO Box 1151 Bellingham WA 98227-1151

PACKER, REKHA DESAI, lawyer; b. N.Y.C., Apr. 20, 1955; d. Rajanikant C. and Santosh (Nagpaul) Desai; m. Michael Benjamin Packer, Aug. 11, 1979. AB magna cum laude, Harvard U., 1976, JD, 1979. Bar: Mass. 1979, U.S. Dist. Ct. Mass. 1979, U.S. Tax. Ct. 1980. Assoc. Gaston & Snow, Boston, 1979-87, ptnr., 1987-91; sr. ptnr. Hale and Dorr, Boston, 1991—; speaker Fed. Tax Inst., 1987—, World Trade Inst., 1986—. Mem. Internat. Bar Assn. (mem. com. on investment cos., funds and trusts 1989—), ABA (mem. com. on regulated investment cos., labor law sect. 1986—, com. on U.S. activities of foreigners 1988—), Boston Bar Assn. (labor law sect. 1987—, co-chmn. internat. tax. com. 1987-89), Phi Beta Kappa. Office: Hale and Dorr 60 State St Boston MA 02109-1800

PACKER, ROGER JOSEPH, neurologist, neuro-oncologist; b. Chgo., May 14, 1951; s. Harry and Mania (Kelmanowski) P.; m. Bernice Ruth Cizek, Mar. 28, 1976; children: Michael Joseph, Zehava Sarah. MB, Northwestern U., 1973, MD, 1976. Resident pediatrics Cin. (Ohio) Childrens Hosp., 1976-78; fellow child neurology Children's Hosp. Phila., Pa., 1978-81; attending neurologist Children's Hosp. Phila., 1981-89; prof. neurology and pediatrics U. Pa., Phila., 1981-89; chmn. neurology Childrens Nat. Med. Ctr., Washington, 1989—; prof. neurology and pediatrics George Washington U., Washington, 1989—; clin. prof. neurology Georgetown U., Washington, 1992—; clin. prof. neurosurgery U. Va., Charlottesville, Va., 1993—; chmn. brain tumor strategy group Childrens Cancer Group, Arcadia, Calif., 1989—. Author: New Trends in Neuro-Oncology, 1991; contbr. chpts. to books and articles to profl. jours. Grantee NIH, Am. Cancer Inst., others. Fellow Am. Acad. Pediatrics, Am. Acad. Neurology (chair sci. selection 1992—, chair neuro-oncology 1981), Child Neurology Soc. (chief liaison health plan reform 1991—). Avocation: sports. Office: Childrens Nat Med Ctr 111 Michigan Ave NW Washington DC 20010-2916

PACKER, RUSSELL HOWARD, business services company executive; b. Santa Fe, Sept. 8, 1951; s. Russell Howard Thorwaldsen and Florence (Bullis) Bryant; m. Melanie Lea Martell, Aug. 31. 1974; children: Lindsey Anne, Andrew Thomas. BS, U. So. Calif., 1973, MBA, 1975. Research analyst Automobile Club of So. Calif., Los Angeles, 1973-75, sr. fin. analyst, 1975-81, mgr. fin. and investment analysis, 1982-83; dir. planning and devel. Coca Cola Bottling Co. of Los Angeles, 1983-87; v.p. planning, adminstrn. Coca Cola Bottling Co. of San Diego, 1987-88; contr. Sunroad Capital Corp., San Diego, 1988-89; v.p., div. contr. Sunroad Enterprises, San Diego, 1989-90; v.p., treas., CFO Geometric Results Inc., Escondido, Calif., 1990—; lectr. fin. Calif. State U., Los Angeles, 1977-87, San Diego State U., 1988-90. Mem. Fin. Execs. Inst., Beta Gamma Sigma. Republican. Home: 12519 Shropshire Ln San Diego CA 92128-1016 Office: Geometric Results Inc 800 La Terraza Blvd Escondido CA 92025-3800

PACKERT, G(AYLA) BETH, lawyer; b. Corpus Christi, Tex., Sept. 25, 1953; d. Gilbert Norris and Virginia Elizabeth (Pearce) P.; m. James Michael Hall, Jan. 1, 1974 (div. 1985); m. Richard Christopher Burke, July 18, 1987; children: Christopher Geoffrey Makepeace Burke Packert, Jeremy Eliot Marvell Packert Burke. BA, La. Tech. U., 1973; MA, U. Ark., 1976; postgrad., U. Ill., 1975-81, JD, 1985. Bar: Ill. 1985, U.S. Dist. Ct. (no. dist.) Ill. 1985, U.S. Ct. Appeals (7th cir.) 1987, Va. 1988, U.S. Dist. Ct. (we. dist.) Va. 1989. Assoc. Jenner & Block, Chgo., 1985-88; law clk. U.S. Dist. Ct. Va. (we. dist.), Danville, 1988-89; asst. commonwealth atty. Commonwealth of Va., Lynchburg, Va., 1989-95; pvt. practice Lynchburg, 1995—. Notes and comments editor U. Ill. Law Rev., 1984-85. Mem. ABA, Phi Beta Kappa. Home: 3900 Faculty Dr Lynchburg VA 24501-3110 Office: 725 Church St Ste 15B PO Box 529 Lynchburg VA 24505

PACKHAM, MARIAN AITCHISON, biochemistry educator; b. Toronto, Ont., Can., Dec. 13, 1927; d. James and Clara Louise (Campbell) A.; m. James Lennox Packham, June 25, 1949; children: Neil Lennox, Janet Melissa. BA, U. Toronto, 1949, PhD, 1954. Sr. fellow dept. biochemistry U. Toronto, 1954-58, lectr. dept. biochemistry, 1958-63, 66-67; rsch. assoc. dept. physiol. scis. Ont. Vet. Coll., U. Guelph, 1963-65; rsch. assoc. blood and cardiovascular disease rsch. unit U. Toronto, 1965-66; asst. prof. U. Toronto dept. biochemistry, 1967-72, assoc. prof., 1972-75, prof., 1975-89, acting chmn. dept. biochemistry, 1983, univ. prof., 1989—. Contbr. articles to profl. jours. Royal Soc. Can. fellow, 1991; recipient Lt. Govs. Silver medal Victoria Coll., 1949; co-recipient J. Allyn Taylor Internat. prize in Medicine, 1988. Mem. Can. Biochem. Soc., Am. Soc. Hematology, Can. Soc. Hematology, Can. Soc. Clin. Investigation, Am. Soc. Investigative Pathology, Am. Heart Assn. (coun. on thrombosis), Internat. Soc. Thrombosis and Haemostasis, Can. Atherosclerosis. Avocation: skiing. Office: U Toronto, Dept Biochemistry, Toronto, ON Canada M5S 1A8

PACKWOOD, BOB, retired senator; b. Portland, Oreg., Sept. 11, 1932; s. Frederick William and Gladys (Taft) P.; children: William Henderson, Shyla. BA, Willamette U., 1954; LLB, NYU, 1957; LLB (hon.), Yeshiva U., 1982, Gallaudet Coll., 1983. Bar: Oreg. Law clerk to Justice Harold J. Warner Oreg. Supreme Ct., 1957-58; pvt. atty., 1958-68; chmn. Multnomah County Rep. Cen. Com., 1960-62; mem. Oreg. Legislature, 1963-69; U.S. senator from Oreg., 1969-95, chmn. small bus. com., 1981-84, chmn. commerce com., 1981-85, chmn. fin. com., 1985-86, ranking min. mem. fin. com., 1987-94, chmn. fin. com., 1995, resigned, 1995. Mem. Internat. Working Group of Parliamentarians on Population and Devel., 1977; mem. Pres.'s Commn. on Population Growth and the Am. Future, 1972; chmn. Nat. Rep. Senatorial Com., 1977-78, 81-82; bd. dirs. NYU, 1970; bd. overseers Lewis and Clark Coll., Portland, 1966. Named One of Three Outstanding Young Men of Oreg., 1967; Portland's Jr. 1st Citizen, 1966; Oreg. Speaker of Yr., 1968; recipient Arthur T. Vanderbilt award NYU Sch. Law, 1970; Anti-Defamation League Brotherhood award, 1971; Torch of Liberty award B'nai B'rith, 1971; Richard L. Neuberger award Oreg. Environ. Coun., 1972; Conservation award Omaha Woodmen Life Ins. Soc., 1974; Monongahela Forestry Leadership award, 1976; Solar Man of Yr., Solar Energy Industries Assn., 1980; Guardian of Small Bus. award Nat. Fedn. Ind. Bus., 1980; Forester of Yr., Western Forest Industries Assn., 1980; Am. Israel Friendship award B'nai Zion, 1982; Grover C. Cobb award Nat. Assn. Broadcasters, 1982; Religious Freedom award, Religious Coalition for Abortion Rights, 1983; 22d Ann. Conv. award, Oreg. State Bldg. and Constrn. Trade Council, 1983; United Cerebral Palsy Humanitarian award, 1984; Am. Heart Assn. Pub. Affairs award, 1985; Margaret Sanger award Planned Parenthood Assn., 1985; Worth his Wheat in Gold award for leadership on tax reform Gen. Mills., 1986; Am. Assn. Homes for the Aging for Outstanding Svc. in cause of elderly, 1987; NARAL award for congrl. leadership, 1987; James Madison award Nat. Broadcast Editorial Assn., 1987; Pub. Excellence award First Ann. Jacob K. Javits, 1987; Golden Bulldog award Watchdogs of Treasury, Inc., 1988, 90; Sound Dollar award, 1989; Golden Eagle award Nurse Anesthetists, 1990; John. F. Hogan Disting. Svc. award Radio-TV News Dirs. for def. of First Amendment, 1991; Nat. Conf. Soviet Jewry recognition, 1992, Space Shuttle Endeavor recognition, 1993, Spirit of Enterprise award U.S. C. of C., 1994, numerous others. Mem. Oreg. Bar Assn., D.C. Bar Assn., Beta Theta Pi. Office: Sunrise Rsch 2201 Wisconsin Ave NW Ste 120 Washington DC 20007-4112*

PACTER, PAUL ALLAN, accounting standards researcher; b. N.Y.C., Jan. 26, 1943; s. Bernard David and Hilda Libby (Margolies) P. B.S., Syracuse U., 1964; Ph.D., Mich. State U., 1967. C.P.A., N.Y. Asst. prof. N.Y.U., 1967-69; rsch. mgr. Peat Marwick, N.Y.C., 1969-73; exec. dir. Fin. Acctg. Standards Bd., Stamford, Conn., 1973-84; commr. fin. City of Stamford, 1984-90; prof. acctg., MBA program U. Conn., Stamford, 1990-96, adj. prof., 1982-84; adj. prof. NYU, 1982-84; project cons. Fin. Acctg. Standards Bd., 1990-96, fellow Internat. Acctg. Standards Com., London, 1993—. Consulting editor The Jour. of Accountancy, 1968-73. Chmn. Stamford Commn. on Human Rights, 1977-84, Stamford Film Commn., 1984-90; mem. Charter Revision Commn., Stamford, 1979-80, Gov.'s Tourism Coun., Conn., 1984-90, acctg. adv. coun. U. Conn., 1984-90; pres. N. Stamford Dem. Club, 1983-84, treas., 1987-95; dir. Stamford Coliseum Authority, 1984-90; vice chmn. govtl. acctg. stds. adv. coun., 1984-91; treas. Conn. Tourism Assn., 1987-90, North Stamford Assn., 1993-94; bd. dirs. Stamford Ctr. for the Arts, United Way Stamford, Stamford Theatre Works, Stamford Cmty. Fund, Housing Devel. Fund of Fairfield County. Earhart Found. fellow Mich. State U., 1966-67; U.S. Office of Edn. grantee, 1967. Mem. AICPA, Am. Acctg. Assn. (coun.), N.Y. State Soc. CPA's, Beta Gamma Sigma, Beta Alpha Psi. Jewish. Office: Internat Acctg Standards Com, 167 Fleet St, EC4A 2ES London England

PACUN, NORMAN, lawyer; b. Bklyn., Mar. 1, 1932; s. Joseph J. and Tillie (Demburg) P.; m. Carol Yvonne Anderson, June 8, 1957; children: Catherine Elizabeth, David Edward. A.B. magna cum laude, U. So. Calif., 1953; LL.B., Harvard U., 1958. Bar: N.Y. 1959. With firm Kirlin, Campbell & Keating, N.Y.C., 1958-61; with Crane Co., 1961-76, sec., gen. counsel, 1964-68, v.p., sec., gen. counsel, 1968-76; v.p., gen. counsel Ingersoll-Rand Co., Woodcliff Lake, N.J., 1977-82, cons., 1982-83; cons. corporate devel. Crane Co., 1985-86; dir. Huttig Sash and Door Co., 1971-76, CF&I Steel Corp., 1974-76. Sec.-treas. Mid-Atlantic Legal Found., 1977-81, bd. dirs., 1980-85, treas., vice-chmn., 1981-84; mem. com. Ctr. for Pub. Resources Legal Program, 1981-82; mem. Scarsdale Vol. Ambulance Corps, 1983-87, treas., 1985-87; emergency med. technician, N.Y., 1986-89; call firefighter and emergency med. technician Chatham Fire Assn., 1993—, v.p., 1995—; mem. Chatham Hist. Commn., 1989—, chmn., 1989-96; mem. Chatham Long-Range Planning Commn., 1993-94; mem. steering com. Barnstable County Juvenile Firesetters Intervention Program, 1997—. With AUS, 1953-55. Mem. ABA, Assn. Bar City N.Y., Am. Soc. Internat. Law, Harvard Club of Boston, Chatham Beach and Tennis Club (trustee 1994—), Chatham Platform Paddle Club (bd. govs. 1993-96, co-pres/ 1996—), Phi Beta Kappa. Home and Office: 14 Sunset Ln Chatham MA 02633-2461

PACUSKA, ALISON BRANDI, Russian studies professional; b. Falmouth, Mass., May 23, 1974; d. Stephen C. and Margaret Anne (Nightingale) P. BA in Internat. Studies, Am. U., 1996; postgrad., George Washington U., 1997—. Relocation asst. United Jewish Appeal Found., White Flint, Md., 1993-94; journalist First of Sept., Moscow, 1994; translator faculty of journalism Moscow State U., 1994; rsch. asst. Kennan Inst. for Advanced Russian Studies, Washington, 1995-96; mem. nat. staff United Cerebral Palsy Assn., 1996—. Contbr. articles to newspapers. Vol. Dem. Nat. Conv., Washington, 1993-94; participant CAAPS Peace Studies Student Conf., 1996. Presdl. scholar Am. U., 1992-94. Mem. Acad. Polit. Sci. Avocations: martial arts, music. Home: 1549 N Falkland Ln # 128 Silver Spring MD 20910

PADBERG, DANIEL IVAN, agricultural economics educator, researcher; b. Summersville, Mo., Nov. 9, 1931; s. Christopher Edward and Ruth (Badgley) P.; m. Mildred Frances True, Aug. 5, 1956; children: Susan Elizabeth, Jean Ellen, Carol Natalie. B.S., U. Mo., 1953, M.S., 1955; Ph.D., U. Calif.-Berkeley, 1961. Asst. prof. Ohio State U., Columbus, 1961-65; project leader Nat. Commn. on Food Mktg., Washington, 1965-66; prof. Cornell U., Ithaca, N.Y., 1966-75; head dept. agrl. econs. U. Ill., Urbana, 1975-81; dean U. Mass., Amherst, 1981-83, prof. agrl. econs., 1983; cons. Farm Credit System, 1983-84; head dept. agrl. econs. Tex. A&M U., College Station, 1984-90, prof., 1990-95, ret., 1995; Fulbright chair internat. econs. U. Tuscia, Viterbo, Italy, 1997; mem. White House Task Force on Farmer Bargaining, Washington, 1968; mem. food and nutrition bd. Nat. Acad. Sci., Washington, 1974-77; cons. Office Tech. Assessment, Washington, 1975-82; pres. Am. Agrl. Econs. Assn., 1987-88; exec. dir. Food and Agrl. Mktg. Consortium, 1993—; chmn. Nat. Adv. Com. on Concentration in Agrl., 1996. Author: Economics of Food Retailing, 1968, Todays Food Broker, 1971; editorial council: Am. Jour. Agrl. Econs., 1970-73, Jour. Consumer Affairs, 1974-76. Pres. council First Congregational Ch., Ithaca, 1971-72. Served to lt. (j.g.) USN, 1955-58, PTO. Consumer Research Inst. grantee, 1970; FDA grantee, 1971; USDA/NRI grantee, 1992; Simon research fellow U. Manchester, Eng., 1972-73. Mem. Am. Agrl. Econs. Assn. (Quality of Discovery award 1975, Quality of Communication in Research award 1977, chmn. awards 1979-80). Home: 90 S Highland Ave Apt 216 Tarpon Springs FL 34689-5344 *Not always right, but never in doubt.*

PADBERG, HARRIET ANN, mathematics educator; b. St. Louis, Nov. 13, 1922; d. Harry J. and Marie L. (Kilgen) P. AB with honors, Maryville Coll., St. Louis, 1943; MMus, U. Cin., 1949; MA, St. Louis U., 1956, PhD, 1964. Registered music therapist; cert. tchr. math. and music, La., Mo. Tchr. elem. math. and music Kenwood Acad., Albany, N.Y., 1944-46; tchr. secondary math. Acad. of Sacred Heart, Cin., 1946-47; instr. math. and music Acad. and Coll. of Sacred Heart, Grand Coteau, La., 1947-48; secondary tchr. music Acad. Sacred Heart, St. Charles, Mo., 1948-50; instr. math. and music Acad. and Coll. Sacred Heart, Grand Coteau, 1950-55, Maryville Coll., St. Louis, 1955-56; tchr. elem. and secondary math. and music Acad. Sacred Heart, St. Louis, 1956-57; asst. prof. Maryville Coll., St. Louis, 1957-64, assoc. prof., 1964-68, prof. math., 1968-92, prof. emeritus, 1992—; music therapist Emmaus Homes, Marthasville, Mo., 1992—. Recipient Alumni Centennial award Maryville Coll., St. Louis, 1986; grantee Danforth Found., Colorado Springs, 1970, Tallahassee, 1970, Edn. Devel. Ctr., Mass., 1975, U. Kans., 1980. Mem. Assn. Women in Math., Am. Math. Soc., Math. Assn. Am., Nat. Coun. Tchr. Math., Mo. Acad. Sci., Delta Epsilon Sigma (sec. local chpt. 1962), Pi Mu Epsilon (sec. local chpt. 1958), Sigma Xi. Avocations: computer music, organist, knitting.

PADBERG, MANFRED WILHELM, mathematics educator, researcher; b. Bottrop, North-Rhine, Westphalia, Fed. Republic Germany, Oct. 10, 1941; came to U.S., 1968; s. Fritz Georg and Franziska (Grosse-Wilde) P.; m. Brigitte Anna Trager, July 7, 1967 (div. 1980); children:Britta, Marc Oliver. Diploma in mathematics Westfalische Wilhelms U., 1967; M.S. in Industrial Adminstrn., Carnegie-Mellon U., 1971, Ph.D., 1971. Scientific asst. Universitat, Mannheim, Fed. Republic Germany, 1967-68; rsch. fellow IIM, Berlin, 1971-74; assoc. prof. NYU, N.Y.C., 1974-78, prof. ops. rsch., 1978—, rsch. prof. ops. rsch., 1988—; vis. prof. Bonn (Fed. Republic Germany) U., 1974, IBM Rsch., Yorktown Heights, N.Y., 1975-76, Westfälische Wilhelms U., Münster, Fed. Republic Germany, 1978, Inst. Nat. de Recherche en Informatique et d'Automatique, Rocquencourt, France, 1980-81, Univ. Cath. de Louvain, Belgium, 1981-82, Centro Nat. di Riccerche Roma, 1982, U. Scientifique et Med. de Grenoble, France, 1984, SUNY, Stony Brook, 1987, Cen. Nat. de la Recherche Sci., Paris, 1988, others; vis. dir. rsch. Ecole Poly., Paris, 1989-90; vis. disting. rsch. prof. George Mason U., 1990-95; vis. prof. Augsburg U., Germany, 1990-91, Cologne U., 1996, Centro Nat. di Riccerche Roma, 1997; cons. in field. Author: Linear Optimization and Extensions, 1995; co-author: Location, Scheduling Design and Integer Programming, 1996; editor: Combinatorial Optimization, 1980; co-editor: Polyhedra and Discrete Optimization, 1989, Algorithms and Discrete Optimization, 1989; contbr. numerous articles to profl. jours. Recipient Alexander-von-Humboldt Rsch. award, 1990-91. Mem. Ops. Research Soc. (Lanchester prize 1983), Math. Programming Soc. (G.B. Dantzig prize 1985). Avocation: traveling. Office: NYU Dept Math Washington Sq New York NY 10003

PADDISON, RICHARD MILTON, neurologist, educator; b. Rochester, N.Y., Aug. 20, 1919; s. Osborn Howard and Ruby (Rapp) P.; m. Josephine Butler Bowles, Dec. 18, 1943 (div. Nov. 1966); children: Richard Jr., Alice Jeannette, David Robert, Patricia Louise, Eileen Ruth, Wendy Ann; m. Vera Gay Davis, Nov. 20, 1966; children: Diane Bell, Stephen Matthew. AB, Duke U., 1943, MD, 1945. Diplomate Am. Bd. Psychiatry and Neurology. Intern Duke U. Hosp., Durham, N.C., 1945-46; instr. neurology and neuroanatomy U. Ga. Sch. Med., Augusta, 1948-49; resident in neurology Jefferson Med. Coll., Phila., 1949-51, instr. in neurology, 1952-53; resident in psychiatry Pa. Hosp., Phila., 1951-53; from asst. prof. to prof. La. State U. Med. Sch., New Orleans, 1964-84, head dept. neurology, 1965-79, med. dir. pvt. diagnostic clinics, 1979-82, dir. continuing med. edn. and alumni, 1982-84, prof. emeritus of neurology, 1984—; cons. Bur. Hearings and Appeals Soc. Security Adminstrn., New Orleans, 1972-95; med. dir. State of La. Office Preventive Medicine and Pub. Health, 1985-86; dir. Security Homestead, New Orleans, 1973-89. Contbr. to profl. books and jours., 1951-84; presenter lectures to profl. socs., 1952—. Regional rep. Duke Med. Sch., Durham, 1958-83; mem. Med. Adv. Bd. La. State Dept. Transp., Baton Rouge, 1976—; vol. tchr. La. State U. Med. Sch., 1984—. Served to capt. U.S. Army, 1946-48. Gitt Meml. vis. lectr., Washington U. Sch. Med., St. Louis, 1978; La. State U. Med. Sch. endowed lectureship named in his honor, 1979; endowed chair of neurology, La. State U. Sch. Med., 1989. Fellow Am. Acad. Neurology (com. chmn. 1958-70, disting. mem. 1987), ACP, Am. Electroencephalographic Soc., So. Electroencephalographic Soc. (past pres.);l mem. Soc. Clin. Neurologists (founder, past pres.), So. Yacht, Commanderie of Bordeaux (New Orleans). Methodist. Avocations: gardening, reading, travel, vol. teaching. Home: 1 Spinnaker Ln New Orleans LA 70124-1655

PADDOCK, ANTHONY CONAWAY, financial consultant; b. Paris, July 9, 1935; came to U.S., 1940; s. H. Watson and Mildred V. (Decker) P.; m. Wendy E. Brewer, Apr. 24, 1971. AB, Harvard U., 1957, JD, 1960; MBA, Columbia U., 1961. Bar: N.Y. 1961. Assoc. investment bank Merrill Lynch & Co., N.Y.C., 1961-69; v.p. Chase Manhattan Bank, N.Y.C., 1970-78, Standard Rsch. Cons., N.Y.C., 1978-84; mng. dir. Benchmark Valuation Cons., N.Y.C., 1978-84; prin. KPMG Peat Marwick, N.Y.C., 1984—; adj. prof. NYU, 1979-90. Mem. Assoc. for Corp. Growth, Inst. Mgmt. Cons. (cert.). Episcopalian. Home: 14 N Chatsworth Ave Larchmont NY 10538 Office: KPMG Peat Marwick 345 Park Ave New York NY 10154-0004

PADDOCK, AUSTIN JOSEPH, engineering executive; b. Washington Court House, Ohio, July 18, 1908; s. Leon A. and Nellie (Hare) P.; m. Janet Nevin, Aug. 3, 1934 (dec. Aug. 1964); children: Larry C. and Linda M. (twins), Jane M.; m. JoAnn Rourke, May 1966; 1 child, Jennifer Jo. BSCE, U. Mich., 1929. With Am. Bridge div. U.S. Steel Corp., 1929-61; from timekeeper constrn. dept., through ops. and sales to pres.; corp. adminstrv. v.p. fabrication and mfg. U.S. Steel Corp., 1961-69; chmn. bd., pres., chief exec. officer Blount, Inc., 1969-75; exec. v.p., chief oper. officer Pa. Engring. Corp., Pitts., 1975-78; vice chmn. bd., dir. Pa. Engring. Corp., 1978-87; dir., mem. exec. com. Pitts.-Des Moines Corp.; past dir. bldg. research adv. bd. Nat. Acad. Sci.; past dir. Am. Standards Inst., Steel Structures Paint Council; past dir. constrn. affairs com. U.S. C. of C.; past chmn. research tech. com. Am. Iron and Steel Inst. Past bd. dirs. Allegheny council Boy Scouts Am. Past dir. NAM. Clubs: Duquesne (Pitts.), Longue Vue Country (Pitts.); Montgomery Country, Men of Montgomery, Capital City. Home: 3875 Taylor Rd Montgomery AL 36116-6514

PADDOCK, JOHN, professional hockey team head coach; b. Oak River, Man., Can.; m. JIll Paddock; children: Jenny, Sally, Anna. Coach Maine Mariners, 1983-84, Hershey Bears, 1988-89; asst. gen. mgr. Phila. Flyers, 1989-90; coach Binghamton Rangers, 1990-91; head coach Winnipeg (Man.) Jets, 1991—, also gen. mgr.; gen. mgr. Phoenix Coyotes, 1996—. Twice named Am. League Coach of Yr. Office: Phoenix Coyotes One Renaissance Sq 2 N Ctrl Ste 1930 Phoenix AZ 85004*

PADEN, HARRY, municipal official; children: Shahara, Angela. Student, Am. U., 1971-73, Essex County (N.J.) Coll., 1981-83. Dir. social svcs. Unity Freedom Bapt. Ch., Newark, 1989-92; aide to freeholder pres. Essex County, 1992-96; code enforcement officer Township of Irvington, N.J., 1992-94, chief field rep. Office Neighorhood Preservation, 1994—. Host, prodr. (cable T.V. program) Parent to Parent; contbg. writer Jersey Girl mag.; columnist Irvington Herald. chmn. Irvington juvenile conf. com. Superior Ct.; v.p., former pres. PTA Irvington H.S.; exec. officer Essex County PTA; ednl. liaison mayor of Irvington; aide Irvington West Ward Council; celebrity reader Essex and Hudson County chpts. United Way; deacon, adminstrv. asst. to pastor Unity Freedom Bapt. Ch., Newark. Named Irvington African Am. Male of Yr., 1994, One of 100 Most Influential in State, City News, 1997; recipient Pinnacle award Being Single mag., 1995. Home: 49 Bross Pl # 23 Irvington NJ 07111-1848

PADEREWSKI, CLARENCE JOSEPH, architect; b. Cleve., July 23, 1908. BArch, U. Calif., 1932. Chief draftsman Sam W. Hamill, 1939-44; with Heitschmidt-Matcham-Blanchard-Gill & Hamill (architects), 1943; then practiced as C.J. Paderewski, 1944-48; pres. Paderewski, Dean & Asso., Inc. (and predecessor), San Diego, 1948-78; instr. adult edn. San Diego city schs., 1939-44, U. Calif. extension div., 1945, 56; Lectr. in field. Prin. works include Charactron Labs, Gen. Dynamics Corp., Convair, S.D., 1954, South Bay Elem. Schs., S.D., 1948-74; additions to El Cortez Hotel; including first passenger glass elevator in the world and New Travolator Motor Hotel, S.D., 1959, Palomar Coll., San Marcos, 1951-80, San Diego County U. Gen. Hosp., San Diego Internat. Airport Terminal Bldgs., Fallbrook Elem. Schs., 1948-74, Silver Strand Elem. Sch., Coronado, Tourmaline Terrace Apt. Bldg., San Diego Salvation Army Office Bldg. Mem. adv. bd. Bayside Social Service Center, 1953-75, San Diego Polonia Newspaper, 1994—; mem. San Diego Urban Design Com.; mem. adv. bd. Camp Oliver, 1963—, pres., 1975-76; bd. dirs. San Diego Symphony Orch. Assn., 1954-62, San Diego chpt. ARC, 1971-74; bd. dirs., chmn. coms., pres. San Diego Downtown Assn., 1963—; bd. dirs. Nat. Council Archtl. Registration Bds., 1958-66, bd. dirs. other offices, 1961-64, pres., 1965-66, chmn. internat. relations com., 1967-68, Salvation Army, vice chmn., 1989, life mem. adv. bd., 1993—, Copernicus Found., 1994—; mem. Calif. Bd. Archtl. Examiners, 1949-61, past pres., commr., 1961—; mem. Nat. Panel Arbitrators, 1953—, Nat. Council on Schoolhouse Constrn.; bd. dirs. Salvation Army, vice chmn., 1989, mem. coms., life mem. adv. bd., 1993—; hon. chmn. Ignacy Jan Paderewski Meml. Com., 1991; adv. bd. S.D. Balboa Park Cmty. Endowment Fund, 1995—. Decorated Knight Order Polonia Restituta, Polish govt. in exile, 1982; recipient Award of Merit for San Diego County Gen. Hosp., San Diego chpt., AIA, 1961, Honor award for San Diego Internat. Airport Terminal, Honor award Portland Cement Co., Golden Trowel award Plastering Inst., 1958-60, 4 awards Masonry Inst., 1961, award Prestressed Concrete Inst., 1976, Outstanding Community Leadership award San Diego Downtown Assn., 1963, 64, 65, 80. Fellow AIA (pres. San Diego chpt. 1948, 49, bd. dirs. 1947-53, chmn. several coms., spl. award 1977, Calif. Coun. Spl. award 1979, Calif. Coun. Disting. Svc. award 1992); mem. San Diego C. of C. (bd. dirs. 1959-62, 64-67), Am. Arbitration Assn. (San Diego adv. coun. 1969—), Sister City Soc. (bd. dirs.), Lions (past pres. Hillcrest Club, Lion of Yr. 1990, fellow internat. found. 1991), Father Serra Club (charter, past pres.), Outboard Boating Club San Diego, Chi Alpha Kappa, Delta Sigma Chi.*. Home: 2837 Kalmia Pl San Diego CA 92104-5418

PADGETT, GAIL BLANCHARD, lawyer; b. Douglasville, Ga., Aug. 20, 1949; d. William David and Dorothy Rose (Bennett) P. BA, Ga. State U., 1971, MD, 1974; JD, Georgetown U., 1981. Bar: Va., Ga., D.C., U.S. Supreme Ct. Tchr. Clayton Co. Bd. Edn., Jonesboro, Ga., 1971-77; spl. asst. to dir. Community Rels Svc., Chevy Chase, Md., 1977-81, gen. counsel, 1981-89, assoc. dir., 1989-96; asst. chief immigration judge U.S. Dept. Justice, Falls Church, Va., 1996—. chmn. community bd. Countryside, Va., 1983-85; chmn. adminstrn. bd. Galilee Methodist Ch., Sterling, Va., 1985-87. Recipient Disting. Svc. award Atty. Gen. of the U.S., 1992. Mem. Soc. Profls. in Dispute (officer 1988-90). Home: 12 Carrollton Rd Sterling VA 20165-5627

PADGETT, GREGORY LEE, lawyer; b. Greenfield, Ind., May 9, 1959; s. William Joseph and Anna Katherine (Hyre) P.; m. Ruth Anne Dorworth, June 5, 1982; children: Joshua David, William Joel. BA summa cum laude, DePauw U., 1981; JD, Northwestern U., 1984. Bar: Ill., U.S. Dist. Ct. (no. dist.) Ill. 1984, U.S. Ct. Appeals (7th cir.) 1986, Ind. 1988, U.S. Dist. Ct. (no. & so. dists.) Ind. 1988. Assoc. Kirkland & Ellis, Chgo., 1984-88, Baker & Daniels, Indpls., 1988-92; ptnr. Johnson, Lawhead and Padgett P.C., Indpls., 1992—; adj. prof. Butler U., 1989-90. Mem. Marion County Prosecutor's Rev. Task Force, Indpls., 1991; pres., bd. dirs. Theatre on the Square, Indpls., 1994-95; mem. coun. Hope Evang. Covenant Ch., 1992-96; bd. dirs. Meridian St. Found., 1994-96. Mem. Ind. State Bar Assn., Indpls. Bar Assn. (exec. com. alternative dispute resolution sect.), Pub. Investors Arbitration Bar Assn., Christian Legal Soc., Phi Beta Kappa. Avocations: theatre arts, vocal music, hiking, writing. Office: Johnson Lawhead and Padgett 8900 Keystone Xing Ste 940 Indianapolis IN 46240-2162

PADGETT, NANCY WEEKS, law librarian, consultant, lawyer; b. Newberry, S.C., June 3, 1932; d. Price John and Caroline (Weeks) P.; m. David Lazar, Aug. 6, 1953 (div. Feb. 1994). BS, Northwestern U., 1953; MLS, U. Md., 1972; JD, Georgetown U., 1977. Bar: D.C. 1977. Asst. law libr. U.S. Ct. Appeals for D.C. Dist., Washington, 1972-74, supervisory law libr., 1974-84, circuit libr., 1984—. Mem. ALA, D.C. Bar Assn., Am. Assn. Law Librs. (profl. law libr. cert.). Home: 5301 Duvall Dr Bethesda MD 20816-1873 Office: US Ct Appeals for DC Cir Judges' Libr 3518 US Court House Washington DC 20002-5618

PADILLA, ELSA NORMA, school system administrator; b. Guines, Havana, Cuba, Feb. 25, 1947; came to U.S., 1962; d. Regulo and Esther (Beato) Cuesta; m. Pedro Manuel Padilla, June 10, 1967; children: Jorge Alberto, Alejandro Manuel. BA, U. Ariz., 1970, MEd, 1972, cert. administration, 1982. Cert. elem. tchr. bilingual endorsement, spl. edn., adminstrn., Ariz. Spl. edn. tchr. Tucson Unified Sch. Dist., 1970, 1972-76, spl. edn. program specialist, 1976-78, spl. edn. tchr., 1978-81, bilingual diagnostician, 1981-84, asst dir. spl. edn., 1984-89; principal Ochoa Elem. Sch. Tucson Unified Sch. Dist., 1989-96, compliance coord., 1996—; part time instr. Ariz. Dept. Edn., 1980-87, No. Ariz. U., 1983-89, U. Ariz., Tucson, 1983-88; mem. Bilingual Diagnostic Team, Tucson Sch. Dist., 1978, author Bilingual Spl. Edn. Program, 1980; prin. in restructuring of sch. project funded by Charles Stewart Mott Found.; cons. in field. Co-author: Courage to Change. Bd. dirs. TETRA Corp., Tucson, 1988-94, Vista Adv. Coun., Tucson, 1990-93; mem. City of South Tucson Econ. Devel. Adv. Bd. Grantee: U.S. Dept. Edn., Tucson, 1984; recipient NEA Excellence award, 1994. Mem. ASCD, Tucson Assn. for Bilingual Edn., Tucson Adminstrs. Inc., Nat. Assn. for Bilingual Edn., Assn. Cubana de Tucson. Democrat. Avocations: cooking, swimming. Office: Morrow Edn Ctr 1010 E 10th St Tucson AZ 85719-5813

PADILLA, JAMES EARL, lawyer; b. Miami, Fla., Dec. 28, 1953; s. Earl George and Patricia (Bauer) P. BA, Northwestern U., 1975; JD, Duke U., 1978. Bar: Ill. 1978, U.S. Ct. Appeals (5th and 7th cir.) 1978, U.S. Supreme Ct. 1981, Colo. 1982, U.S. Ct. Appeals (10th cir.) 1982, D.C. 1985, N.Y. 1989. Assoc. Mayer, Brown & Platt, Chgo. and Denver, 1978-84; ptnr. Mayer, Brown & Platt, Denver, 1985-87, N.Y.C., 1988-96; private investor, 1996—. Contbg. author: Mineral Financing, 1982, Illinois Continuing Legal Education, 1993. Mem. ABA, Ill. Bar Assn., D.C. Bar Assn., Colo. Bar Assn., N.Y. State Bar Assn., Denver Bar Assn. Avocation: golf. Office: 1900 Summer St Apt 19 Stamford CT 06905-5024

PADOS, FRANK JOHN, JR., investment company executive; b. Easton, Pa., Feb. 9, 1944; s. Frank John and Mary Helen (Pokrifscak) P.; m. Barbara Janselwitz, July 6, 1968; children—Frank John (dec.), Kelly Ann, Kristin, Matthew John, Kaitlyn. B.A. cum laude in Econs, Boston Coll., 1966; M.B.A., U. Pa., 1968. Securities analyst Tchrs. Ins. and Annuity Assn., N.Y.C., 1971-74; investment officer Tchrs. Ins. and Annuity Assn., 1975-77, v.p., 1977-78, sr. v.p., mgr. securities div., 1978-83; mng. dir. Trust Co. of the West, 1983-95; exec. v.p. Desai Capital Mgmt., N.Y.C., 1995—; dir. Eyecare Ctrs. of Am. Served with U.S. Army, 1969-70. Decorated Bronze Star. Mem. Wharton Club, Sky Club. Roman Catholic. Home: 57 Thornley Dr Chatham NJ 07928-1360 Office: 540 Madison Ave New York NY 10022-3213

PADOVA, JOHN R., federal judge; b. 1935. AB, Villanova U., 1956; JD, Temple U., 1959. With Marcu & Marcu, 1960; ptnr. Solo, Bergman & Trommer, 1962-65, Solo, Abrams, Bergman, Trommer & Padova, 1965-71, Solo, Bergman, Trommer, Padova & Albert, 1971-74, Solo, Bergman & Padova, 1974-75, Solo & Padova, 1975-77, 84-86, Solo, Padova & Lisi, 1977-84, Padova & Hinman, 1986-91, Padova & Lisi, 1991-92; fed. judge U.S. Dist. Ct. (ea. dist.) Pa., 1992—. With USNGR, 1959-64, USAR, 1964-68. Mem. ABA, Am. Trial Lawyers Assn., Phila. Bar Assn., Nat. Bd. Trial Advocacy, Pa. Trial Lawyers Assn., Phila. Trial Lawyers Assn. Office: US Dist Ct 601 Market St Rm 7614 Philadelphia PA 19106-1713*

PADOVANO, ANTHONY THOMAS, theologian, educator; b. Harrison, N.J., Sept. 18, 1934; s. Thomas Henry and Mary Rose (Cierzo) P.; m. Theresa Lackamp, 1974; children—Mark, Andrew, Paul, Rosemarie. B.A. magna cum laude, Seton Hall U., 1956; S.T.B. magna cum laude, Pontifical Gregorian U., Rome, Italy, 1958, S.T.L. magna cum laude, 1960, S.T.D. magna cum laude, 1962; Ph.L. magna cum laude, St. Thomas Pontifical Internat. U., Rome, 1962; M.A., NYU, 1971; Ph.D., Fordham U., 1980. Ordained priest Roman Cath. Ch., 1959. Asst. chaplain Med. Center, Jersey City, 1960; asst. St. Paul of the Cross Ch., Jersey City, 1962, St. Catharine Ch., Glen Rock, N.J., 1963; prof. systematic theology Darlington Sem., Mahwah, N.J., 1962-74; prof. Am. lit. Ramapo Coll., N.J., 1971—; founding faculty mem., adj. prof. theology/religious studies Fordham U., 1973-93; mem. Archdiocesan Commn. Ecumenical and Interreligious Affairs, 1965, Commn. Instrn. Clergy in Documents Vatican II, 1966; del. dialogue group Luth.-Roman Cath. Theol. Conversations, 1969; del.-at-large senate of priests Archdiocese of Newark; Danforth assoc., 1975—; Cath. pastor Inclusive Cmty. World Coun. Chs., 1986—; lectr. in field, also appearances on radio and TV; parish min. St. Margaret of Scotland, Morristown, N.J. Author: The Cross of Christ, the Measure of the World, 1962, The Estranged God, 1966, Who is Christ, 1967, Belief in Human Life, 1969, American Culture and the Quest for Christ, 1970, Dawn Without Darkness, 1971, Free to be Faithful, 1972, Eden and Easter, 1974, A Case for Worship, 1975, America: Its People, Its Promise, 1975, Presence and Structure, 1975, The Human Journey, 1982, Trilogy, 1982, Contemplation and Compassion, 1984, Winter Rain: A Play, 1985, His Name is John: A Play, 1986, Christmas to Calvary, 1987, Love and Destiny, 1987, Summer Lightening: A Play, 1988, Conscience and Conflict, 1989, Reform and Renewal, 1990, A Celebration of Life, 1990, The Church Today: Belonging and Believing, 1990, Scripture in the Streets, 1992, A Retreat with Thomas Merton, 1996; editor: Centenary Issue Roman Echoes, 1959; editl. bd. The Advocate, 1966-73; contbr. articles to mags., Padovano Collection, personal and profl. papers, Archives, U. Notre Dame. Active Diocese Paterson Ecumenical Commn.; founding pres. Justice and Peace Commn., Diocese of Paterson, active Resigned Priests Com. Mem. Cath. Theol. Soc. Am., Mariological Soc. Am., Nat. Fedn. Priests Councils (ofcl. rep. to Constl. Conv., Chgo. 1968), Corpus (pres.), Fedn. Christian Ministries, Internat. Fedn. of Married Cath. Priests (v.p. for N.Am.). Home: 9 Millstone Dr Morris Plains NJ 07950-1536 Office: Dept of American Lit Ramapo Coll New Jersey Mahwah NJ 07430 *People rather than ideas have been most formative in my life. More accurately, people, as they embodied certain ideals have proved most decisive. There is nothing more persuasive than an idea which becomes so vital that it transforms the person who proclaims it.*

PADULA, FRED DAVID, filmmaker; b. Santa Barbara, Calif., Oct. 25, 1937; s. Fred and Mary (Adams) P.; married; 1 child. B.A. in Music, San Francisco State U., M.A. in Art, 1965. Adj. faculty U. Calif., San Francisco Art Inst., San Francisco State U.; artist-in-residence U. Minn., Mpls. Filmmaker: Ephesus, 1965 (1st pl. award San Francisco Internat. Film Festival, awards N.Y. Film Festival, Chgo. Internat. Film Festival, others), The Artist Speaks, Two Photographers: Wynn Bullock and Imogen Cunningham, Little Jesus (Hippy Hill), Anthology of Boats, David and My Porch, Salmon River Run, El Capitan (awards: Grand Prize Festival Internat. de Film D'Aventure Uecue, La Plagne, France, Grand Prize Film Festival Internat. Montagna Esplorazione, Trento, Italy, Grand Prize Banff Festival of Mountain Films, Can., Grand Prize Mountain Film, Telluride, Colo., Gold medal Festival Internat. du Film Alpine, Les Diablerets, Switzerland; electronic music compositions include: Barking Dogs, Charnet Loops, others; one-man shows (photography) include aerial photographic survey of Mayan Indian Ruins, Yucatan, Mex., 1989, San Francisco Internat. Airport, San Francisco Mus. Modern Art, Kalamazoo Inst. Arts, DeYoung Mus., San Francisco, San Fernando Valley State Coll., Bekersfield Coll., Wash. State U., George Eastman House, represented in permanent collections, Kalamazoo Inst. Arts, State of Calif., George Eastman House, San Francisco Internat. Airport, Crocker Art Mus., Oakland Mus. Art, 1004 Gallery, Port Towsend, Wash., New Horizons Nat. Bank Hdqs., San Rafael, Calif. Address: 47 Shell Rd Mill Valley CA 94941-1551

PADULO, LOUIS, university administrator; b. Athens, Ala., Dec. 14, 1936; s. Louis and Helen (Yarbrough) P.; m. Katharine Seamans, Jan. 28, 1963; children: Robert, Joseph. BSEE, Fairleigh Dickinson U., 1959; MSEE, Stanford U., 1962; PhD, Ga. Inst. Tech., 1966. Engr. design and devel. Radio Corp. Am., 1959-60; asst. prof. elec. engring. San Jose State Coll., 1962-63; asst. prof. math. Ga. State U., 1966-67; assoc. prof. Columbia U., summer 1969, Harvard U., summer 1970; asst. prof. Morehouse Coll., 1967-68, assoc. prof., chmn. dept. math., 1968-71; dir. exchange student program Stanford U., 1969-71, assoc. prof. elec. engring., 1971-75, assoc. prof. math., summers 1971-75, dir. MITE program, 1975; prof. elec. engring. and math., dean Coll. Engring. Boston U., 1975-88, assoc. v.p., 1986-87; pres. U. Ala., Huntsville, 1988-90; pres., chief exec. officer Univ. City Sci. Ctr., Phila., 1991—; vis. assoc. prof. Stanford U., 1969-71; vis. prof. U. Tokyo, 1986-88, MIT, 1987-88; program dir. Inst. on Computers, Logic and Automata Theory, NSF, 1969; founder, dir. dual degree program Atlanta U. Ctr. and Ga. Inst. Tech., 1968-70; numerical analyst Airesearch Corp., L.A., 1969; vis. scientist MIT, 1990-91; dir. Cmty of Sci., Inc., Nemawashi, Inc., Carver Fund, Tapelicator, Inc., Am. Dream Bus. Network. Author: System Theory, 1973, Minorities in Engineering, 1974; mem. editl. adv. bd. the Scientist, DiSyCom-Digital Sys. and Comm.; contbr. chpts. to books. Pres. Valley Found., Huntsville, Ala., 1988-89, Ala. Engring. Found., Huntsville, 1989; mem. task force Vision 2000, Huntsville, 1989; bd. dirs. North Ala. Internat. Trade Assn., 1989, Ala. Supercomputer Network, 1989, Vision 2000, Am. Poetry ctr., 1992, Benjamin Franklin Tech. Ctr., 1991; pres. Higher Edn. Congress, 1992—; bd. dirs. U.S. Japan Soc., 1990—; adv. com. United Negro Coll. Fund; trustee Fairleigh Dickinson U., 1989—, Presbyn. Found. Phila., 1993—, Phila. Fund for Edn., 1995—, Internat. House; vis. com. sch. engring. Tuskegee U., Coll. Engring. Drexel U., 1993—; mem. Huntsville Army Cmty. Rels. Com.; bd. vis. sch. bus. Temple U., 1993—. Recipient Excellence in Sci. and Engring. Edn. award Nat. Consortium for Black Profl. Devel., 1977, Reginald H. Jones Disting. Svc. award GE Found. and Nat. Action Coun. Minorities in Engring., 1983. Fellow IEEE, Am. Soc. Engring. Edn. (Western Electric Fund Excellence in Teaching award 1973, Vincent Bendix award 1984); mem. AAAS, ACM, Mass. Engrs. Coun., Math. Assn. Am., Union League of Phila., NAACP (life), Penn Club. Office: Univ City Sci Ctr 3624 Market St Philadelphia PA 19104-2614

PAFFENBARGER, RALPH SEAL, JR., epidemiologist, educator; b. Columbus, Ohio, Oct. 21, 1922; s. Ralph Seal and Viola Elizabeth (Link) P.; m. Mary Dale Higdon, Sept. 19, 1943 (dec.); children: Ralph, James (dec.), Ann, Charles, John (dec.), Timothy; m. Jo Ann Schroeder, July 20, 1991. A.B., Ohio State U., 1944; M.B., Northwestern U., 1946, M.D., 1947; M.P.H., Johns Hopkins U., 1952, Dr.P.H., 1954. Intern Evanston (Ill.) Hosp., 1946-47; research asst. pediatrics La. State U. and Charity Hosp., New Orleans, 1949-50; practice medicine, specializing in geriatrics Framingham, Mass., 1960-68; clin. asst. prof. preventive medicine U. Cin., 1955-60; lectr. biostatistics Sch. Pub. Health, Harvard U., 1961-62, clin. assoc. preventive medicine Med. Sch., 1963-65, lectr. epidemiology Sch. Pub. Health, 1965-68, vis. lectr., 1968-83, vis. prof. epidemiology, 1983-85, vis. lectr., 1986-88, adj. prof. epidemiology, 1988—; prof. epidemiology in-residence U. Calif. Sch. Pub. Health, Berkeley, 1968-69, adj. prof., 1969-80; prof. epidemiology Stanford U., 1977-93, prof. emeritus, 1993—; rsch. epidemiologist U. Calif., Berkeley, 1993—; commd. officer USPHS, 1947, med. dir., Atlanta, Ga., 1947-53, Bethesda, Md., 1953-55, Cin., 1955-60, Framingham, 1960-68, ret., 1968; mem. epidemiology and disease control study sect. NIH, 1972-76. Assoc. editor: Am. Jour. Epidemiology, 1972-75, 80—, editor, 1975-79; contbr. articles to profl. publs. Served with AUS, 1943-47. Recipient prize for Sports Scis. Internat. Olympic Com., 1996. Mem. AAAS, AMA, APHA, Am. Epidemiol. Soc., Am. Heart Assn., Internat. Epidemiol. Assn., Soc. Epidemiol. Rsch., Rsch. Soc. Am., Internat. Soc. Cardiology, Am. Assn. Suicidology, Marcé Soc., Am. Coll. Sports Medicine, Am. Acad. Sports Physicians, Nat. Fitness Leaders Assn., Royal Soc. Medicine, Phi Eta Sigma, Pi Kappa Epsilon, Delta Omega. Home: 892 Arlington Ave Berkeley CA 94707-1938 Office: Stanford U Sch Medicine Stanford CA 94305

PAGALA, MURALI KRISHNA, physiologist; b. Sri Kalahasti, Andhra, India, Oct. 2, 1942; came to U.S., 1970; s. Lakshmaiah and Radhamma (Bhimavaram) P.; m. Vijaya Bhimavaram, Dec. 12, 1969; children: Sobhan, Suresh. PhD in Zoology, S. V. Univ., Tirupati, A.P., India, 1969; MS in Computer Sci., Pratt Inst., N.Y., 1985. Postdoctoral fellow Inst. for Muscle Disease, N.Y.C., 1970-73, asst. mem., 1974; assoc. rsch. scientist NYU, N.Y.C., 1974-75; asst. to dir. Neuromus Disease Div. Maimonides Med. Ctr., Bklyn., 1975-89, dir. neuromuscular rsch., 1990—; vis. scientist II Physiol. Inst., U. Saarlandes, Hamburg, Germany, 1981, 82; sci. cons. UNDP/TOKTEN Program, Calcutta, India, 1990, NIGMS/FASEB MARC Program Grambling State U., La., 1992, 95; chair sci. confs., participated in Sci. Congress, Germany, 1990, Israel, 1992, Japan, 1994, 95. Reviewed and contbr. articles to profl. jours. Life mem. Telugu Assn. of North Am., 1989; sci. fair judge N.Y. Acad. Scis., N.Y.C., 1986—. Named Best speaker Zool. Soc. of S. V. Univ., 1964, Best Basic Rsch. paper Maimonides Med. Ctr., 1983, 88, 94; Fatigue Rsch. grantee Maimonides Rsch. Devel. Found., 1986—, Drug Rsch. grantee Maimonides Rsch. Devel. Found., 1989—, Aging Rsch. grantee Maimonides Rsch. Devel. Found., 1995—. Mem. N.Y. Acad. Scis., Am. Physiol. Soc., Assn. Scientists of Indian Origin in Am. (pres. 1993-94). Democrat. Hindu. Achievements include devel. in vitro electromyographic, electrocardiographic and multi-muscle chambers to evaluate the function of skeletal muscle, heart and smooth muscle preparations from experimental animals and human subjects; and development of consumer products. Home: 82 Pacific Ave Staten Island NY 10312-6212 Office: Maimonides Med Ctr 4802 10th Ave Brooklyn NY 11219-2916

PAGÁN, GILBERTO, JR., clinical psychologist; b. San Juan, P.R., Dec. 30, 1950; s. Gilberto Sr. and Juanita (Quiñones) P.; m. Grisselle Camacho, Aug. 6, 1972; children: Mariel, Lauren. Exch. student, SUNY, Albany, 1969-70; BA in Psychology magna cum laude, U. P.R., 1972; MS in Devel. Psychology, Rutgers U., 1974, PhD in Clin. Psychology, 1984. Lic. psychologist, N.J.; cert. sch. psychology. Psychometrician Well Baby Clinic of New Brunswick, N.J., 1972-73; staff psychologist Community Orgn. for Mental Health and Retardation, Inc., Phila., 1976-77; intern in clin. psychology Multimodal Therapy Inst., Kingston, N.J., 1979-80; sch. psychologist New Brunswick Pub. Sch. System, 1980-83; mental health clinician Community Mental Health Ctr. U. Medicine and Dentistry N.J., Piscataway, 1983-93; sch. psychologist Perth Amboy Pub. Sch. Sys., 1993-95; pvt. practice clin. psychology Newark, 1988—; sch. psychologist Jersey City Pub. Sch. Sys., 1995—; assoc. in psychiatry Univ. of Medicine and Dentistry of N.J., Piscataway, 1988—; field supr. Rutgers U., New Brunswick, N.J., 1988—; cons. in field to clients including Bloomfield Pub. Sch. System, Div. of Youth and Family Svcs. of State of N.J., Project Head Start, Plainfield, N.J. Columnist San Juan Star, 1990-93, El Hispano, Phila., 1977-78; contbr. profl. publs.; presenter in field. Pres. N.J. chpt. Nat. Com. for Puerto Rican Statehood, 1990-95. NIMH fellow, 1978-79; predoctoral rsch. fellow Inst. for Rsch. in Human Devel., Divsn. Psychol. Studies of Ednl. Testing Svc., Princeton, N.J., 1974-75; recipient P.R. Psychol. Assn. award, 1972, Puerto Rican Action Bds. Parents Assn. award 1985; inducted into Nat. Honor Soc. in Psychology, 1973. Mem. APA, NEA, N.J. Edn. Assn., N.J. Psychol. Assn., Jersey City Edn. Assn. Democrat. Roman Catholic. Home: 422 Johnstone St Perth Amboy NJ 08861-3330 Office: 467 Mount Prospect Ave Newark NJ 07104-2907

PAGAN, HARGOT OWENS, public relations executive; b. Lake Charles, La., Dec. 11, 1946; d. Thomas Llewellyn Owens and Doris Maire (Baumgardt) Owens-Wilson; m. Peter Mark van der Meulen, Mar. 17, 1972 (div.); 1 child, Dirk; m. Alexander M. Pagan, Apr. 4, 1992; children: Justin, Erik, Jessica. BA, Syracuse U. Gen. mgr. Via mag. Port authority of N.Y. and N.J., N.Y.C., 1995-96; dep. press sec. N.Y. State Atty. Gen., N.Y.C., 1996—. Recipient Hopper Citation, Hopper House Com., 1986. Mem. Nat. Pub. Rels. Soc., GAP, Overseas Press Club. Office: New York State Attorney Generals Office 120 Broadway New York NY 10271-0002

PAGANELLI, CHARLES VICTOR, physiologist; b. N.Y.C., Feb. 13, 1929; s. Charles Victor and Mary Barone (Spalla) P.; m. Barbara Harriet Slauson, Sept. 18, 1954; children: William, Kathryn, Peter, Robert, John. AB, Hamilton Coll., Clinton, N.Y., 1950; MA, Harvard U., 1952, PhD, 1957. Instr. physiology U. Buffalo, 1958-60, asst. prof., 1960-63; assoc. prof. SUNY, Buffalo, 1963-71, prof. physiology, 1971—; interim chair SUNY, Buffalo, 1991—. Editor: Physiological Function in Special Environments, 1990; contbr. articles to profl. jours. Recipient Elliott Coues award Am. Ornithologists Union, 1981. Mem. Am. Physiol. Soc., Undersea Hyperbaric Med. Soc., Alpha Omega Alpha, Sigma Xi, Phi Beta Kappa.

PAGANI, ALBERT LOUIS, aerospace system engineer; b. Jersey City, Feb. 19, 1936; s. Alexander C. and Anne (Salvati) P.; m. Beverly Cameron, Feb. 23, 1971; children: Penelope, Deborah, Michael. BSEE, U.S. Naval Acad., 1957; MBA, So. Ill. U., 1971. Commd. 2d lt. USAF, 1957, advanced through grades to col., 1978; navigator USAF, Lake Charles, La., 1957-63; pilot USAF, McGuire AFB, N.J., 1963-65; command pilot USAF, Anchorage, Alaska, 1965-68; mgr. airlift USAF, Saigon, Socialist Republic of Vietnam, 1968-69; chief spl. missions USAF, Scott AFB, Ill., 1969-74; commd. tactical airlift group USAF Europe, Mildenhall, Eng., 1974-76; dep. comdr. Rhein Main Air Base USAF Europe, Frankfurt, Fed. Republic Germany, 1976-78; chief airlift mgmt. USAF Military Airlift Command, Scott AFB, Ill., 1978-81, dir. tech. plans and concepts, 1981, dir. command and control, 1982-85; ret., 1985; program mgr. Lockheed Missile and Space Co., Sunnyvale, Calif., 1985-94; dir. data applications, dir. adv. programs PAR Govt. Systems Corp., New Hartford, NY, 1994—. V.p. Cath. Ch. Council, Mildenhall, 1974, pres., 1975. Decorated Legion of Merit, Bronze Star, Air medal, Vietnam Cross of Gallantry. Mem. Nat. Def. Transp. Assn., Soc. Logistics Engrs., Air Force Assn., Armed Forces Communication and Electronics Assn., Air Lift Assn., Inst. Noetic Scis., Daedalions, Mensa. Avocations: woodworking, neurolinguistics, volunteer senior executive consulting. Home: 8592 Red Hill Rd Clinton NY 13323

PAGAN MARTINEZ, JUAN, administrative corps officer; b. Cartagena, Murcia, Spain, Apr. 6, 1938; arrived in U.S., 1979; s. Juan and Rosa (Martinez) Pagan Lopez; m. Josefina Serrano Botella, Mar. 19, 1964; children: Rosa, Juan Carlos, Cristina. Degree, Escuela Pericial de Comercio, Cartagena, Spain, 1963. Warehouse, acctg. chief Almirante Bastarreche Profl. Sch., Cartagena, 1956-77; adminstrv. corps officer Spanish Navy, Cartagena, 1961-79, Embassy of Spain, Washington, 1979—. Contbr. articles to profl. jours. Centurion Franco's Youth Front, Cartagena, 1955; bandurria player Spanish Dance Soc., Washington, 1991—; sec. Sports and Phys. Edn. Coun., Cartagena, 1972-79. Recipient Golden Poet award World of Poetry, 1990, 91, Honorable mention, 1990, Blue Ribbon award So. Poetry Assn., 1990. Memb. Washington Spanish Club (sec. 1992-94, pres. 1994-96). Avocations: poetry, music composer, bandurria, lute, guitar, sax player. Home: 1009 1st St Rockville MD 20850-1451

PAGANO, ALICIA I., education educator; b. Sidney, N.Y., June 29, 1929; d. Neil Gadsby Leonard and Norma (Carr) Collins; m. LeRoy Pagano, Feb. 26, 1963 (div. Oct. 1985); children: Janice, Daniel. BA in Music, Barrington Coll., 1952; MAT in Music, Rollins Coll., 1964; EdD in Edn. Adminstrn., Am. U., 1972. Tchr. music Prince Georges County Pub. Schs., Beltsville, Md., 1966-69; asst. prof. Medgar Evers Coll., Bklyn., 1973-78; nat. program dir. Girl Scouts USA, N.Y.C., 1978-83; nat. dir. vol. development U.S. Com. UNICEF, N.Y.C., 1983-84; pres. Pagano Consulting Internat., Jersey City, 1984—; asst. prof. mgmt. Coll. Staten Island, CUNY, 1985-89; adj. prof. museum studies NYU, N.Y.C., 1986-91; assoc. exec. dir. Louis August Jonas Found., Red Hook, N.Y., 1988-89; asst. prof. edn. Jersey City State Coll., 1990—; chair Wingspread Nat. Conf./Nat. Collaboration for Youth, Washington, 1982; adv. bd. dirs. Early Childhood Ctr., Jersey City State Coll., 1994—. Author, editor: Social Studies in Early Childhood, 1979; author: The Future of American Business, 1985, (with others) Learning Opportunities Beyond School, 1987; contbr. articles to profl. jours. Judge annual awards Girls, Inc., N.Y.C., 1985-90; reader Jersey City Spelling Bee, 1991; vol. Girl Scouts USA, Essex/Hudson Counties, N.J., 1995—, Boys & Girls Clubs, Hudson County, N.J., 1995—. Mem. ASCD, AAUW, Am. Ednl. Rsch. Assn., Nat. Assn. Early Childhood Tchr. Edn. (bd. dirs. 1995—), N.J. Assn. Early Childhood Tchr. Educators (v.p. 1994—), Orgn. Mondiale pour l'Edn. Prescolaire (N.J. regional dir. 1996—). Avocations: hiking, swimming, international travel. Home: 169 Jefferson Dr Box 413 Mastic Beach NY 11951-4805

PAGANO, ANTHONY J., university dean; b. West New York, N.J., June 29, 1939; s. Louis Gerard and Lucy (Nicolosi) P.; m. Christine Catherine von Wiegandt, Sept. 7, 1963; children: Elizabeth, Micheline, Celeste. BS in Acctg., Fordham U., 1960; JD, U. Mich., 1963. Assoc. Morrison, Foerster, Holloway, Clinton & Clark, San Francisco, 1965-67; atty. legal dept. Crown Zellerbach, San Francisco, 1968-70; prof. law Golden Gate U., San Francisco, 1970-88, dean Sch. Law, 1988—; vis. prof. law U. Idaho, Moscow, 1974-75, U. San Diego, summer 1976, 79, U. San Francisco, 1981-82; mem. Law Sch. Coun.; mem. Fed. Bankruptcy Judge Screening Com. Author: (with others) California Attorney's Damages Guide, 1974, Valuation and Distribution of Marital Property, 1984, California Will Drafting, 1992; mem. editl. bd. Calif. Continuing Edn. of the Bar. Dir. Pub. Interest Clearinghouse, San Francisco, 1988—, Blum Found., San Francisco, 1988—. Mem. ABA, Am. Law Inst., Calif. Bar Assn., Law Sch. Coun., State Bar Calif. Democrat. Roman Catholic. Avocations: opera, classical music, art. Office: Golden Gate U Sch Law 536 Mission St San Francisco CA 94105-2921

PAGANO, FILIPPO FRANK, financial broker, commercial loan consultant; b. East Paterson, N.J., Feb. 4, 1939; s. Frank and Katherine (Tavano) P.; m. Rose Ann Melisi, June 10, 1960 (div. Dec. 1972); children: Paul, Cynthia Pagano Grube, Stefanie; m. Darlene Ann Coryea, Mar. 1987. BS in Pharmacy, Rutgers U., 1960. Registered pharmacist, profl. ski instr.; lic. capt. master USCG. System analyst Parke-Davis & Co., Detroit, 1964-72; sr. mktg. analyst internat. Schering-Plough Pharm. Co., Kenilworth, N.J., 1972-73; v.p. Robert S. First, N.Y.C., 1973-74; pres. M-P Consultations Inc., N.Y.C., 1974-75; chief exec. officer Nordic Inn, Landgrove, Vt., 1975-83; sea capt. Bahamas, 1983-85; food and beverage dir. Meredith Guest House, Durham, 1985-86, gen. mgr., 1986-88; pres. Flagship Yachts, Durham, N.C., 1988—; gen. mgr. Inter-Global Capital, Raleigh, N.C., 1989—. Co-author: Nordic Inn Book of Soups, 1979; contbr. articles on skiing to newspapers and mags. Mem. Vt. Ski Touring Operators Assn. (pres. 1979-81), Beaufort Off-Shore Sailing Soc., Boss Club (Beaufort), Kappa Psi. Republican. Roman Catholic. Avocations: sailing, snow skiing, culinary interests. Home and Office: 405 Hardscrabble Dr Hillsborough NC 27278-9766

PAGANO, JON ALAIN, data processing consultant; b. Kankakee, Ill., Dec. 26, 1958; s. Antoine and Agnes P.; m. Linda S. Gound, Dec. 22, 1983. BA in Philosophy, U. Ill., 1979; BA in Computer Sci., North Cen. Coll., 1989. Computer ops. staff Roper Inc., Kankakee, 1979-81; programmer Harris Bankcorp, Chgo., 1981-84; cons. Circle Cons., Kankakee, 1984; sr. programmer/analyst First Nat. Bank, Chgo., 1984-86; programmer/analyst Internet Systems Corp., Chgo., 1986-87; sr. systems analyst, mgr. Concord Computing Corp., Elk Grove, Ill., 1987-89; pres. Circle Cons., Naperville, Ill., 1989—. Ednl. lobbying U. Ill., Urbana, 1986—, alumni networking North Cen. Coll., 1991—, bd. advocate, 1996—. Mem. ACM, IEEE, U. Ill. Alumni Assn. (Pres.'s Coun. 1988—, Bronze Circle 1988), Pres. Club North Ctrl. Coll., Univ. Ill. Alumni Bd. (adv. 1996—). Avocations: running, camping, hiking, bouldering. Home: 344 Westbrook Cir Naperville IL 60565-3242 Office: Circle Cons 344 Westbrook Cir Naperville IL 60565-3242

PAGANO, JOSEPH STEPHEN, physician, researcher, educator; b. Rochester, N.Y., Dec. 29, 1931; s. Angelo Pagano and Marian (Vinci) Signorino; m. Anna Louise Reynolds, June 8, 1957; children: Stephen Reynolds, Christopher Joseph. A.B. with honors, U. Rochester, 1953; M.D., Yale U., 1957. Resident Peter Bent Brigham Hosp. Harvard U., Boston, 1960-61; fellow Karolinska Inst., Stockholm, 1961-62; mem. Wistar Inst., Phila., 1962-65; asst. prof., then assoc. prof. U. N.C., Chapel Hill, 1965-73, prof. medicine, 1974—, dir. div. infectious diseases, 1972-75; dir. U. N.C. Lineberger Comprehensive Cancer Ctr., Chapel Hill, 1974—; attending physician N.C. Meml. Hosp., Chapel Hill; vis. prof. Swiss Inst. Cancer Rsch., Lausanne, 1970-71, Lineberger prof. cancer rsch., 1986—; mem. virology study sect. NIH, Bethesda, Md., 1973-79; cons. Burroughs Wellcome Co., Research Triangle Park, N.C., 1978-95; mem. recombinant DNA adv. com. USPHS, 1986-90; mem. chancellor's adv. com. U. N.C., 1985-91, chair 1990-91; bd. dirs. Burroughs Wellcome Fund, 1993—; mem. adv. com. N.C. Cancer Coord. and Control, 1993—; Mclaughlin vis. prof. U. Tex. Med. Br., 1996. Mem. editorial bd. Jour. Virology, 1974-90; bd. assoc. editors Cancer Rsch., 1976-80; assoc. editor Jour. Gen. Virology, 1979-84, Antimicrobial Agts. and Chemotherapy, 1984-93; contbr. numerous articles to profl. publs., chpts. to books. Bd. dirs. Am. Cancer Soc., N.C., 1980—. Recipient Sinsheimer award, 1966-68, USPHS Research Career award NIH, 1968-73; named Harry F. Dowling lecturer, 1991. Mem. AAAS (Newcomb Anderson prize selection com. 1984-88), Assn. Am. Cancer Insts. (bd. dirs. 1992-95, v.p. 1995, pres. 1996-97), Infectious Disease Soc. Am., Am. Soc. Microbiology, Am. Soc. Clin. Investigation, Am. Soc. Virology, Am. Assn. Physicians, Internat. Assn. for Rsch. in Epstein-Barr Virus and Assocs. Diseases (pres. 1991-94, 1st Gertrude and Werner Henle lectr. on viral oncology 1990, N.C. award in sci. 1996), Chapel Hill Tennis Club (pres. 1980-82), Carolina Club, Baldhead Island Club. Episcopalian. Avocations: tennis, squash. Home: 114 Laurel Hill Rd Chapel Hill NC 27514-4323 Office: U NC Lineberger Comp Cancer Ctr Chapel Hill NC 27599-7295

PAGANUCCI, PAUL DONNELLY, banker, lawyer, former college official; b. Waterville, Maine, Apr. 18, 1931; s. Romeo J. and Martha (Donnelly) P.; m. Marilyn McLean, Sept. 10, 1966; children: Thomas Donnelly, Elizabeth Mary. A.B., Dartmouth Coll., 1953; M.B.A., Amos Tuck Sch. Bus. Adminstrn., 1954; J.D., Harvard U., 1957. Bar: N.Y. 1958, N.H. 1972. Staff asst. to pres. W.R. Grace & Co., N.Y.C., 1958-61, vice chmn., bd. dirs., 1986-89, chmn. exec. com., bd. dirs., 1989-91; pres., treas., bd. dirs. Lombard, Vitalis, Paganucci & Nelson, Inc., N.Y.C., 1961-72; prof. bus. adminstrn. Amos Tuck Sch. Dartmouth Coll., Hanover, N.H., 1972-77, assoc. dean, 1972-76, sr. investment officer, 1976-77, v.p., 1977-84, v.p. and treas., 1984-85; chmn. Ledyard Nat. Bank, Hanover, 1991—; bd. dirs. Grace Inst., N.Y.C., Filene's Basement, Inc., Allmerica Securities Trust, HRE Properties, Hypertherm, Inc., IGI, Inc.; allied mem. N.Y. Stock Exch., 1961-72. Chmn. bd. trustees Dartmouth Cath. Student Ctr., 1973-85, overseer, 1973—; trustee Colby Coll., 1975-85, 87—, Casque and Gauntlet; mem. Pres.'s Pvt. Sector Survey on Cost Control. Served with AUS, 1956-62. Mem. Inst. Chartered Fin. Analysts. Clubs: Dartmouth of N.Y. (dir., v.p., pres.); Union (Boston); Knights of Malta. Home: 33 Ropeferry Rd Hanover NH 03755-1404 Office: 38 S Main St Hanover NH 03755-2015

PAGE, ALAN CEDRIC, judge; b. Canton, Ohio, Aug. 7, 1945; s. Howard F. and Georgianna (Umbles) P.; m. Diane Sims, June 5, 1973; children: Nina, Georgianna, Justin, Khamsin. BA, U. Notre Dame, 1967; JD, U. Minn., 1978; LLD, U. Notre Dame, 1993; LLD (hon.), St. John's U., 1994, Westfield State Coll., 1994, Luther Coll., 1995. Bar: Minn. 1979, U.S. Dist. Ct. Minn. 1979, U.S. Supreme Ct. 1988. Profl. athlete Minn. Vikings, Mpls., 1967-78, Chgo. Bears, 1978-81; assoc. Lindquist & Vennum, Mpls., 1979-85; former atty. Minn. Atty. Gen.'s Office, Mpls., 1985-92; assoc. justice Minn. Supreme Ct., St. Paul, 1993—; cons. NFL Players Assn., Washington, 1979-84. Commentator Nat. Pub. Radio, 1982-83. Founder Page Edn. Found., 1988. Named NFL's Most Valuable Player, 1971, one of 10 Outstanding Young Men Am., U.S. Jaycees, 1981; named to NFL Hall of Fame, 1988, Coll. Football Hall of Fame, 1993. Mem. ABA, Minn. Bar Assn., Hennepin County Bar Assn., Minn. Minority Lawyers Assn. Avocations: running, biking. Office: 427 Minnesota Judicial Ctr 25 Constitution Ave Saint Paul MN 55155-1500

PAGE, ALBERT LEE, soil science educator, researcher; b. New Lenox, Ill., Mar. 19, 1927; s. Thomas E. and Hattie O. (Pease) Pugh; m. Shirley L. Jessmore, Sept. 14, 1952; children—Nancy, Thomas. BA in Chemistry, U. Calif.-Riverside, 1956; PhD in Soil Sci., U. Calif.-Davis, 1960. Prof. soil sci. U. Calif.-Riverside, 1960—; dir. Kearney Found., Univ. Calif.-Riverside, program of excellence in energy research. Editor: Methods of Soil Analysis, 1983, Utilization of Municipal Wastewater and Sludge on Land, 1983, Heavy Metals in the Environment, 1977. Served as QMQ1 USN, 1945-52. Recipient Environ. Quality Research award Am. Soc. Agronomy, 1984, Disting. Teaching award U. Calif., Riverside, 1976, Disting. Svc. award USDA, 1991; Fullbright scholar, 1966-67; Guggenheim Meml. Found. fellow, 1966-67. Fellow AAAS, Am. Soc. Agronomy, Soil Sci. Soc. Am.; mem. Internat. Soil Sci. Soc., Western Soil Sci. Soc., Soc. Environ. Geochemistry and Health, Sigma Xi. Home: 5555 Canyon Crest Dr Apt 1F Riverside CA 92507-6443 Office: Univ of Calif Dept Soil & Environ Sci Riverside CA 92521

PAGE, ANNE RUTH, gifted education educator, education specialist; b. Norfolk, Va., Apr. 13, 1949; d. Amos Purnell and Ruth Martin (Hill) Bailey; m. Peter Smith Page, Apr. 24, 1971; children: Edgar Bailey, Emmett McBrannon. BA, N.C. Wesleyan Coll.; student, Fgn. Lang. League; postgrad., N.C. State U.; student, Overseas Linguistic Studies, France, Spain, Eng., 1978, 85, 86. Cert. tchr., N.C. Tchr. Cary (N.C.) Sr. High Sch., 1971-72; tchr., head dept. Daniels Mid. Sch., Raleigh, N.C., 1978-83; chmn. fgn. lang. dept. Martin Mid. Gifted and Talented, Raleigh, N.C., 1983—; leadership team Senate Bill 2 Core co-chair; dir. student group Overseas Studies, Am. Coun. for Internat. Studies, France, Spain, Eng., 1982, 84, 86, 88; bd. dirs. N.T.H., Inc., Washington; cert. mentor tchr. Wake County Pub. Schs., 1989; dir. student exchs. between Martin Mid. Sch. and Sevigné Inst. of Compiegne, France. Sunday sch. tchr. Fairmont United Meth. Ch., Raleigh, 1983-85. Mem. Alpha Delta Kappa. Democrat. Home: 349 Wilmot Dr Raleigh NC 27606-1232 Office: Martin Mid Sch GT 1701 Ridge Rd Raleigh NC 27607-6737

PAGE, ANTHONY, film director; b. Bangalore, India, Sept. 21, 1935. Ed., U. Oxford. Dir.: (stage prodns.) Inadmissible Evidence, Waiting for Godot, A Patriot for Me, Look Back in Anger, Uncle Vanya, Cowardice, A Doll's House, 1996 (Tony award for Best Direction of a Play, 1997) others, (films) Inadmissible Evidence, 1968, Alpha Beta, 1976, F. Scott Fitzgerald in Hollywood, 1976, I Never Promised You a Rose Garden, 1977, Absolution, 1979, The Lady Vanishes, 1979, (TV films) The Patricia Neal Story, 1981, Bill, 1981, Johnny Belinda, 1982, Grace Kelly, 1983, Bill: On His Own, 1983, Murder by Reason of Insanity, 1985, Second Severe, 1986, Monte Carlo, 1986, Pack of Lies, (cable film) Forbidden, 1985. Mem. Dirs. Guild Am. *

PAGE, CLARENCE E., newspaper columnist; b. Dayton, Ohio, June 2, 1947; m. Lisa Johnson Cole, May 3, 1987. BS in Journalism, Ohio U., 1969. Reporter, asst. city editor Chgo. Tribune, 1969-80; dir. community affairs dept. Sta. WBBM-TV, 1980-82, reporter, planning editor, 1982-84; columnist, mem. editorial bd. Chgo. Tribune, 1984—, Tribune Media Svcs., Washington. Frequent guest Sta. WTTW-TV, Chicago Tonight, Chicago in Review; contbr. articles to profl. jours. Participant 1972 Chgo. Tribune Task Force Series on Vote Fraud which won the Pulitzer Prize. Recipient Community Svc. award Ill. UPI, 1980, James P. McGuire award CLU, 1987, Pulitzer Prize for commentary, 1989. Office: Tribune Media Svcs 1325 G St NW Washington DC 20005*

PAGE, CURTIS MATTHEWSON, minister; b. Columbus, Ohio, Oct. 24, 1946; s. Charles N. and Alice Matthewson P.; m. Martha Poitevin, Feb. 12, 1977; children: Allison, Charles, Abigail. BS, Ariz. State U., 1968; MDiv, San Francisco Theol. Sem., 1971, D Ministry, 1985. Ordained to ministry Presbyn. Ch., 1971. Pastor Ketchum (Idaho) Presbyn. Ch., 1972-80, Kirk O'The Valley Presbyn. Ch., Reseda, Calif., 1980-90; campaign dir. Kids 1st Edn. Reform Partnership, L.A., 1990-91; sr. pastor Orangewood Presbyn. Ch., Phoenix, 1991-93, First Meridian Heights Presbyn. Ch., Indpls., 1993—; mem. com. Ch. Devel., Ind., 1995—; bd. dirs. Express Pub., Ketchum. Bd. dirs. Mary Magdalene Home, Reseda; chmn. com. on preparation for the ministry, San Fernando, Calif., 1988-90; chmn. Ketchum City Zoning Commn., 1979-80; mem. Ketchum Master Planning Commn., 1974, L.A. Mayor's Citizen's Adv. Task Force on Ethics, 1990; co-chmn. Voice Cmty. Orgn. in San Fernando Valley, 1988-90; chair Family Cares, Indpls., 1995—. Avocations: amateur radio, tennis, snow skiing. Office: First Meridian Heights Pres 4701 Central Ave Indianapolis IN 46205-1828

PAGE, DOZZIE LYONS, vocational secondary school educator; b. Tiptonville, Tenn., Apr. 13, 1921; d. Lessie LeRoy and Carrie (Oldham) Lyons; children: Rita, Gerald. BS in Edn., Chgo. Tchrs. Coll., 1968; MS in Psychology, Counseling and Guidance Chgo. State U., 1976; MA in Bus. Edn., Govs. State U., 1979. Cashier receptionist Unity Mut. Life Ins. Co., Chgo., 1939-47; sec. United Transport Service Employees Union, Chgo., 1947-51; sec. to dir. West Side YWCA, Chgo., 1951-53; sec., office mgr. Joint Council Dining Car Employees AFL CIO, Chgo., 1957-59; sr. stenographer Chgo. Police Dept., 1962-65; tchr. office practice Manpower Devel. Tng. Act, Chgo. Bd. Edn., 1965-67; tchr. office occupations Dunbar Vocat. High Sch., Chgo., 1968-71, tchr., coord. distributive edn., 1971-90; mem. NAACP, DuSable Mus. African-Am. History. Mem. Office Occupations Club, Distributive Edn. Assn., Assn. for Supervision and Curriculum Devel., Chgo. Urban League, Chgo. Bus. Edn. Assn. (exec. bd. 1983—, Enos Perry award 1987, pres. 1991-92), Ill. Pers. and Guidance Assn., Am. Pers. and Guidance Assn., Am. Vocat. Assn., Chgo. Urban League, Nat. Bus. Edn. Assn., Ill. Bus. Edn. Assn., Chgo. Bus. Edn. Assn., Chgo. State U. Alumni Assn., Governor's State U. Alumni Assn., Phi Delta Kappa. Home: 6127 S Justine St Chicago IL 60636-2327

PAGE, ELLIS BATTEN, behavioral scientist, educator, corporate officer; b. San Diego; s. Frank Homer and Dorothy (Batten) P.; m. Elizabeth Latimer Thaxton, June 21, 1952; children: Ellis Batten (Tim), Elizabeth Page Sigman, Richard Leighton. A.B., Pomona Coll., 1947; M.A., San Diego State U., 1955; Ed.D., UCLA, 1958; postdoctoral (NSF fellow), U. Mich., 1959; postdoctoral (IBM fellow), MIT, 1966-67. Tchr. secondary schs. Calif., 1952-56; mem. psychology dept. San Diego City Coll., 1957-58; dir. guidance and testing Eastern Mich. U., 1958-60; dean Coll. Edn., prof. edn. and psychology Tex. Woman's U., 1960-62; dir. Bur. Ednl. Rsch. U. Conn., 1962-70, prof. ednl. psychology, 1962-79; prof. ednl. psychology and research Duke U., 1979—; vis. prof. U. Wis., 1960, 62, Stanford U., 1965, Harvard U., 1968-69, U. Javeriana, Bogotá, 1975; leader Ford Found. rsch. adv. team Venezuelan Ministry Edn., Caracas, 1969-70; vis. prof. Spanish Ministry Edn., 1972, 80, 82-85; rsch. cons. U.S. Office Edn., USN, Nat. Inst. Edn., Bur. Edn. Handicapped; chmn. nat. planning com. Nat. Ctr. Edn. Stats.; adviser Brazilian Ministry Edn., 1973, 80; chief Ministerial Commn. Edn., Bermuda, 1983-85; mem. Adv. Coun. for Edn. Stats., U.S. Dept. Edn., 1987-90; pres. TruJudge, Inc., 1993—. Author, editor in field. Capt. USMCR, 1943-46. Recipient Disting. Alumnus award San Diego State U., 1980. Fellow AAAS (life), APA (pres. ednl. psychology 1976-77), Am. Psychol. Soc., John Dewey Soc., Am. Assn. Applied and Preventive Psychology, Nat. Conf. Rsch. English, Philosophy Edn. Soc.; mem. Am. Coun. Assn., Am. Ednl. Rsch. Assn. (pres. 1979-80), Am. Statis. Assn. (officer N.C. chpt.), Assn. Computational Linguistics, Nat. Assn. Scholars, N.C. Assn. Rsch. Edn. (Disting. Rsch. award 1981, 91, pres. 1984-85), Rhetoric Soc. Am. (dir.), Psychometric Soc., Sociedad Espanola de Pedagogia (hon.), Sigma Xi, Phi Kappa Phi, Phi Gamma Delta, Psi Chi, Kappa Delta Pi, Phi Delta Kappa (life, svc. key). Anglican. Home: 110 Oakstone Dr Chapel Hill NC 27514-9585 Office: Duke U 213 W Duke Bldg Durham NC 27708

PAGE, ERNEST, medical educator; b. Cologne, Germany, May 30, 1927; came to U.S., 1936, naturalized, 1942; s. Max Ernest and Eleanor (Kohn) P.; m. Eva Veronica Gross, June 5, 1967; 1 son, Thomas J. A.B., Calif., Berkeley, 1949; M.D., Calif., San Francisco, 1952. Intern Peter Bent Brigham Hosp., Boston, 1952-53; resident Peter Bent Brigham Hosp., 1953-54, 57-58; research assoc. Harvard Med. Sch., 1957-65; assoc. prof. medicine and Physiology U. Chgo. Med. Sch., 1965-69, prof., 1969—. Editor: Am. Jour. Physiology: Heart and Circulatory Physiology, 1981-86. Served with AUS, 1945-46. Established investigator Am. Heart Assn., 1959-65. Mem. Am. Physiol. Soc., Biophys. Soc., Am. Soc. Cell Biology, Soc. Gen. Physiologists, Assn. Am. Physicians. Home: 5606 S Harper Ave Chicago IL 60637-1832 Office: U Chgo Med Sch 5841 S Maryland Ave Chicago IL 60637-1463

PAGE, FREDERICK WEST, business consultant; b. East Orange, N.J., Oct. 19, 1932; s. Frederick West and Dorothy (Donham) P.; m. Miriam Lowell Jones, Feb. 14, 1959; children: William, Janet, Thomas, James. A.B., Dartmouth Coll., 1954; postgrad., Wharton Grad. Sch. Bus., U. Pa., 1956-57; M.B.A., NYU, 1960. With Schering Corp. (now Schering-Plough), 1957-91, various mktg. positions, 1957-73, gen. mgr. animal health products, 1973-80, pres. U.S. Animal Health Products Div., 1980-83, v.p. pharm. ops., 1983-91; pres. Bus. Cons. Svcs., 1991—. Served with U.S. Army, 1954-56. Mem. Animal Health Inst. (exec. com. 1978-81, chmn. 1979-80). Republican. Club: Phi Kappa Psi. Home and Office: 22 Marin Rd West Caldwell NJ 07006-7419

PAGE, GEORGE KEITH, banker; b. Rolling Prairie, Ind., July 7, 1917; s. Glenn Keith and Ruth (Mansfield) P.; m. Carmen Bailey; children: Kay, Susan, John Michael. Ed., U. Ala. Coll. Commerce and Bus. Adminstrn. Asst. cashier Baldwin County Bank, Bay Minette, Ala., 1938-43; pres., dir. Baldwin County Savs. & Loan Assn., Robertsdale and Fairhope, Ala., 1943-58; chmn. bd., chief exec. officer United First Fed. Savs. & Loan Assn. (merger Barnett Bank S.W. Fla.), Sarasota, Fla., 1958-86; sr. chmn. Barnett Bank S.W. Fla., 1986-89; also bd. dirs. Barnett Bank S.W. Fla., Sarasota, Fla.; ret., 1989; trustees Found. for Savs. Instns., 1984-86. Pres. Ala. Savs. and Loan League, 1956; past pres., gen. campaign chmn., bd. dirs., mem. adv. coun. Sarasota United Way; past chmn. Sarasota Housing Authority; past bd. dirs. Met. YMCA Sarasota-Manatee Counties; past bd. dirs., treas. Sarasota County Libr. Bldg. Fund; trustee Sarasota Meml. Hosp. Found., 1986-92, 93-94, chmn. endowment com., 1987-92; bd. dirs. Sarasota Opera Assn., Inc., 1992—; past mem. adv. bd. Sunny Land coun. Boy Scouts Am.; past trustee Argus Found.; past bd. dirs. Indsl. Devel. Corp. Fla.; gen. chmn. capital campaign funds Sarasota YMCA, 1969. With USN, WWII. Recipient cert. of honor City Commn. and C. of C., Fairhope, 1958, Silver Beaver award Boy Scouts Am., Mobile, 1949, named Disting. Eagle Scout, 1982, Outstanding Citizen award Sarasota Jaycees, 1978, recipient Brotherhood award NCCJ, 1979. Mem. Fla. Savs. and Loan League (pres. 1970-71), Sarasota County C. of C. (past treas., bd. dirs.), Sarasota U. Club (past pres., bd. dirs.), Oaks Country Club, Field Club (bd. dirs. 1968-71), Masons (32d degree), Shriners. Avocation: golf. Office: 1800 2nd St Ste 808 Sarasota FL 34236-5904

PAGE, HARRY ROBERT, business administration educator; b. Milw., Mar. 22, 1915; s. Harry Allen and Lydia (Rosendahl) P.; m. Jeanne Tompkins, Apr. 1, 1945; children: Patricia Jeanne, Margaret Berenice. A.B., Mich. State U., 1941; postgrad., U.S. Army Command and Staff Coll., 1945-46, Indsl. Coll. Armed Forces, 1958-59; M.B.A., Harvard, 1950; Ph.D., Am. U., 1966. Served from 2d lt. to lt. col. U.S. Army, 1941-46; from lt. col. to col. USAF, 1947-61; exec. officer logistics directorate U.S. Joint Chiefs of Staff, Washington, 1959-61; asst. prof. bus. adminstrn. George Washington U., Washington, 1961-65; assoc. prof., chmn. dept. George Washington U., 1965-69, prof., chmn. dept. bus. adminstrn., 1970-74, assoc. dean, 1975-80, prof. emeritus, 1981—; cons. Advanced Study program Brookings Instn., Washington, 1966-70, Ednl. Svcs. Inst., U.S. Postal Svc., 1985-92. Author: Church Budget Development, 1964, An Analysis of the Defense Procurement Program Decision-Making Process, 1966, Public Purchasing and Materials Management, 1980, rev. edit., 1989; co-author: Federal Contributions to Management, 1972. Chmn. task force edn. and tng. Commn. Govt. Procurement, 1972-73; bd. dirs., treas. Coun. Chs., Greater Washington, 1963-68; bd. dirs. Hunter Assocs. Lab., Inc.; deacon Rock Spring Congregational Ch., 1994—. Decorated Air medal, Purple Heart, Legion of Merit. Fellow Nat. Contract Mgmt. Assn.; mem. Acad. mgmt., Nat. Assn. Purchasing Mgmt., Internat. Fedn. Purchasing and Materials Mgmt., Harvard Bus. Sch. Assn., Air Force Assn., Nat. Parks and Conservation Assn. (trustee), Air Force Sgts. Assn. (trustee, chmn. scholarship bd. 1971—), Harvard Bus. Club, Sch. of Wash. Club (dir., pres. 1980-81), Alpha Phi Omega, Lambda Chi Alpha Alpha Kappa Psi, Pi Sigma Alpha, Beta Gamma Sigma. Home: 3612 N Glebe Rd Arlington VA 22207-4317 Office: 710 21st St NE Washington DC 20002-4108

PAGE, JAKE (JAMES K. PAGE, JR.), writer, editor; b. Boston, Jan. 24, 1936; s. James Keena Page and Ellen Van Dyke (Gibson) Kunath; m. Aida de Alva Bound, Nov. 28, 1959 (div. 1974); children: Dana de Alva Page, Lea Gibson Page Kuntz, Brooke Bound Page; m. Susanne Calista Stone, Mar. 10, 1974; stepchildren: Lindsey Truitt, Sally Truitt, Kendall Barrett. BA, Princeton U., 1958; MA, NYU, 1959. Asst. sales promotion mgr. Doubleday & Co., 1959-60; editor Doubleday Anchor Books, 1960-62, Natural History Press, Doubleday, N.Y.C., 1962-69; editorial dir. Natural History Mag., N.Y.C., 1966-69; editor-in-chief Walker & Co., N.Y.C., 1969-70; sci. editor Smithsonian Mag., Washington, 1970-76; founder, dir. Smithsonian Books, Washington, 1976-80; start-up editor Smithsonian Air & Space Mag., Washington, 1985; pvt. practice as writer Waterford, Va., Corrales, N.Mex., 1980—; mag. cons. Denver Mus. Nat. History, 1989-90; contract text editor Doubleday, 1992. Author: (with Richard Saltonstall Jr.) Brown Out & Slow Down, 1972, (with Larry R. Collins) Ling-Ling & Hsing Hsing: Year of the Panda, 1973, Shoot the Moon, 1979, (with Wilson Clark) Energy, Vulnerability and War: Alternatives for America, 1981, Blood: River of Life, 1981, (with Susanne Page) Hopi, 1982, Forest, 1983, Arid Lands, 1984, Pastorale: A Natural History of Sorts, 1985, Demon State, 1985, (with Eugene S. Morton) Lords of the Air: The Smithsonian Book of Birds, 1989, Smithsonian's New Zoo, 1990, Zoo: The Modern Ark, 1990, Animal Talk: Science and the Voice of Nature, 1992, The Stolen Gods, 1993, Songs to Birds, 1993 (with Chalres B. Officer) Tales of the Earth, 1993, The Deadly Canyon, 1994 (with David Leeming) Goddess: Mythology of the Female Divine, 1994, The Knotted Strings, 1995, Smithsonian Guides to Natural America: Arizona and New Mexico, 1995, (with Susanne Page) Navajo, 1995, (with David Leeming) God: Mythology of the Male Divine, 1996, The Lethal Partner, 1996, (with Charles Officer) The Great Dinosaur Extinction Controversy, 1996, Operation Shatterhand, 1996; editor: (with Malcolm Baldwin) Law and the Environment, 1970; contbg. editorships Science Mag., 1980-86, Oceans Mag., 1987, Mother Earth News, 1990, National Geographic Traveler, 1990-93, TDC (Destination Discovery), 1991-95; contbg. author to numerous books and mags. Mem. nat. bd. advisors Futures for Children, Albuquerque, 1980—. Democrat. Avocation: Arab horses. Home and Office: PO Box 78 644 Dixon Rd Corrales NM 87048

PAGE, JOHN BOYD, physics educator; b. Columbus, Ohio, Sept. 4, 1938; s. John Boyd and Helen (Young) P.; m. Norma Kay Christensen, July 28, 1966; children: Rebecca, Elizabeth. BS, U. Utah, 1960, PhD, 1966. Rsch. assoc. Inst. for Theoretical Physics U. Frankfurt/Main, Fed. Republic of Germany, 1966-67; rsch. assoc. Cornell U., Ithaca, N.Y., 1968-69; asst. prof. physics Ariz. State U., 1969-75, assoc. prof., 1975-80, prof., 1980—; vis. prof. dept. physics Cornell U., 1989. Contbr. articles to profl. jours. Recipient Humboldt Rsch. award, 1991; NSF grantee, 1972-77, 77-80, 80-82, 82-86, 90-92, 91-94, 95—. Fellow Am. Phys. Soc.; mem. Am. Assn. Physics Tchrs., Phi Beta Kappa, Sigma Xi, Phi Kappa Phi, Phi Eta Sigma. Office: Ariz State U Physics Dept Tempe AZ 85287-1504

PAGE, JOHN GARDNER, research administrator, scientist; b. Milw., Sept. 14, 1940; s. Raymond G. and Leone B. (Churchill) P.; m. Joyce Ann Krueger, July 7, 1962; children: Teresa Ann, Kimberly Christine. B.S., U. Wis.-Madison, 1963, M.S., 1966, Ph.D., 1967. Diplomate Am. Bd. Toxicology. Sr. Scientist NIH, Bethesda, Md., 1967-69, Eli Lilly Co., Indpls., 1969-77; dir. toxicology and pathology Rhone Poulenc, Inc., Ashland, Ohio, 1977-79; dir. toxicology, Toxigenics, Inc., Decatur, Ill., 1979-83; sr. rsch. advisor Battelle Meml. Inst., Columbus, Ohio, 1983-87; head preclin. toxicology div. So. Rsch. Inst., Birmingham, Ala., 1987—; adj. prof. U. Ill., 1981-83, U. Ala., Birmingham, 1988—. Contbr. articles to profl. jours. Bd. dirs. Am. Cancer Soc., Greenfield, Ind., 1973-77. Recipient Rennebohm Outstanding Tchr's award U. Wis., 1964. Mem. AAAS, Fedn. Am. Socs. Exptl. Biology, Am. Soc. Pharm. Exptl. Therapeutics, Soc. Toxicology, Am. Coll. Toxicology, Internat. Soc. for Study Xenobiotics, Sigma Xi, Rho Chi. Avocations: photography; hiking, fishing. Home: 3601 Crosshill Rd Birmingham AL 35223-1546 Office: So Research Inst 2000 9th Ave S Birmingham AL 35205-2708

PAGE, JOHN HENRY, JR., artist, educator; b. Ann Arbor, Mich., Jan. 18, 1923; s. John Henry and Lucille (Bennett) P.; m. Mary Lou Franks, July 22, 1945; children: Jonathan, Marilyn, Jeremy. Student, Mpls. Sch. Art, 1940-42; B.Design, U. Mich., 1948; M.F.A., U. Iowa, 1950. Instr. Mankato (Minn.) State Coll., 1950-54; asst. prof. art U. No. Iowa, Cedar Falls, 1954-55; asst. prof. U. No. Iowa, 1955-59, assoc. prof., 1959-64, prof., 1964-87, acting head dept. art, 1984-85; head art dept. U. Omaha, 1959-60. One-man exhbns. include Luther Coll., Decorah, Iowa, 1981, Laura Musser Mus., Muscatine, Iowa, 1978, Coe Coll., Cedar Rapids, Iowa, 1975, Sheldon Gallery, Lincoln, Nebr., 1974, Creighton U., Omaha, 1969, Augustana Coll., Rock Island, Ill., 1964, Muskegon (Mich.) Mus. Art, 1983, retrospective (in three parts) Gallery of Art U. No. Iowa, Hearst Ctr. for the Arts, Cedar Falls, Iowa, Waterloo (Iowa) Mus. of Art, 1992; group exhbns. include 10th Nat. Print Show Bklyn. Mus., 1956, 9 Iowa Artists Gov. Exhbn., 1971-72, Walker Art Ctr., Mpls., 1973, Regional Invitational Exhbn., U. Omaha, 1978, Fragile Giants, Brunner Gallery, 1994-96; represented in permanent collections, Library of Congress, Walker Art Center, Des Moines Art Center, Joslyn Art Mus., Omaha, Carnegie Inst., Pitts. Served with U.S. Army, 1943-45. Nat. Endowment Arts grantee, 1975. Unitarian. Home: 114 E Los Arcos Green Valley AZ 85614-2429

PAGE, JONATHAN ROY, investment analyst; b. Harrisburg, Pa., Sept. 10, 1946; s. John and Ellen (Smith) P.; m. Patrice Marie Margerm, May 17, 1975; children: Elizabeth, Gregory, Richard, Brian. B.A., Dartmouth Coll., 1968; M.B.A., Tuck Sch. Dartmouth, 1969. Chartered fin. analyst. Investment officer Irving Trust Co., N.Y.C., 1970-75; sr. v.p., portfolio mgr. Dean Witter Intercapital Funds, N.Y.C., 1975—. Vestry person St. John's Ch., Ramsey, N.J., 1984-88. Mem. N.Y. Soc. Security Analysts, Fin. Analysts Fedn. Republican. Episcopalian. Avocations: tennis, golf, skiing, landscaping. Home: 36 Sturbridge Dr Saddle River NJ 07458-1742 Office: Dean Witter Intercapital Funds 2 World Trade Ctr Fl 72 New York NY 10048-0203

PAGE, JOSEPH ANTHONY, law educator; b. Boston, Apr. 13, 1934; s. Joseph E. and Eleanor M. (Santosuosso) P.; m. Martha Gil-Montero, May 18, 1984. AB, Harvard U., 1955, LLB, 1958, LLM, 1964. Asst. prof. coll. law U. Denver, 1964-67, assoc. prof., 1967-68; assoc. prof. law ctr. Georgetown U., 1968-73, prof., 1973—; bd. dirs. Pub. Citizen, Inc., Washington. Author: The Revolution That Never Was, 1972, The Law of Premises Liability, 1976, Peron: A Biography, 1984, The Brazilians, 1995; coauthor: Bitter Wages, 1973. Lt. USCGR, 1959-67. Office: Georgetown U Law Ctr 600 New Jersey Ave NW Washington DC 20001-2075

PAGE, LARRY KEITH, neurosurgeon, educator; b. Rayville, La., July 7, 1933; s. Ardie Lee and Edris Estelle (Chaney) P.; m. Joan Marie Doherty, Aug. 27, 1960; children: Matthew, Elizabeth, Jennifer. BS, La. State U., 1955, MD, 1958. Diplomate: Am. Bd. Neurol. Surgery. Intern Grad. Hosp., U. Pa., Phila., 1958-59; resident Children's Hosp. and Peter Bent Brigham Hosp., Boston, 1962-66; assoc. neurosurgeon Children's Hosp., assoc. surgeon Peter Bent Brigham Hosp., 1966-71; cons. Beverly Hosp., Mass., Robert Breck Brigham Hosp., Boston, Pondville Hosp., Boston, West Roxbury VA Hosp., Boston VA Hosp.; clin. instr. neurosurgery Harvard U., Boston, 1966-71; prof., vice chmn. dept. neurosurgery U. Miami, Fla., 1971-95, prof. emeritus, 1995—, chief div. pediatric neurosurgery, 1971-95; neurosurgeon VA Hosp., Miami, 1971-88; neurosurgeon Jackson Meml. Hosp., Miami, 1971-95, dir. neurosurgery, 1994-95; chief neurosurgery Mt. Sinai Hosp., Miami, 1990-94; neurosurg. cons. FDA; neurosurg. cons. NASA. Mem. editorial bds., contbr. articles to profl. jours. Served to lt. USN, 1959-62. Mem. ACS, Am. Acad. Pediatrics, Am. Assn. Neurol. Surgeons, Internat. Soc. Pediatric Neurosurgery, Am. Soc. Pediatric Neurosurgery, Congress Neurol. Surgeons, Fellowship of Acad. Neurosurgeons, Internat. Neurosurg. Forum, Royal Soc. Medicine, Soc. for Rsch. in Hydrocephalus and Spina Bifida, New Eng. Neurosurg. Soc., Fla. Neurosurg. Soc. (pres. 1989-90), Mass. Med. Soc., Dade County Med. Assn., Internat. Palm Soc., Alpha Omega Alpha. Roman Catholic. Home and Office: 13845 SW 73rd Ct Miami FL 33158-1213

PAGE, LESLIE ANDREW, disinfectant manufacturing company executive; b. Mpls., June 5, 1924; s. Henry R. and Amelia Kathryn (Steinmetz) P.; m. DeEtte Abernethy Griswold, July 6, 1952 (div. Sept. 1975); children: Randolph, Michael, Kathryn, Caroline; m. Mary Ellen Decker, Nov. 26, 1976. BA, U. Minn., 1949; MA, U. Calif., Berkeley, 1953; PhD, U. Calif., 1956. Asst. microbiologist, lectr. U. Calif., Davis, 1956-61; cons. San Diego Zoological Soc. Zoo Hosp., 1957-60; microbiologist, research leader Nat. Animal Disease Ctr., USDA, Ames, Iowa, 1961-79; ret., 1979, specialist in Chlamydial nomenclature and disease; med. text cons. Bay St. Louis, Miss., 1979-85; founder, pres., chmn. bd. Steri-Derm Corp., San Marcos, Calif., 1987—; cons. McCormick Distilling Co., Weston, Mo., 1994-95. Editor: Jour. Wildlife Diseases, 1965-68, Wildlife Diseases, 1976; contbr. chpts. to med. texts, over 70 articles to profl. jours.; patentee Liquid Antiseptic Composition, 1989. Pres. Garden Island Comty. Assn., Bay St. Louis, Miss., 1980-81; chief commr. East Hancock fire Protection Dist., Bay St. Louis, 1982-83; treas. Woodridge Escondido Property Owners Assn., 1986-88. Fellow Am. Acad. Microbiology (emeritus); mem. Wildlife Disease Assn. (pres. 1972-73, Disting. Svc. award 1980, Emeritus award 1984), Am. Soc. for Microbiology, Zool. Soc. San Diego, Sigma Xi, Phi Zeta (hon.). Home and Office: 1784 Deavers Dr San Marcos CA 92069-3359

PAGE, LEWIS WENDELL, JR., lawyer; b. Scottsboro, Ala., Nov. 6, 1947; s. Lewis Wendell and Maymie Elizabeth (Parks) P.; m. Dollie Lucretia Roberts, Dec. 24, 1977; children—Margaret Amelia, Katherine Elizabeth. B.A., Auburn U., 1970; J.D., U. Ala., 1973; LL.M., George Washington U., 1975. Bar: Ala. 1973, U.S. Dist. Ct. (no. dist.) Ala. 1974, U.S. Ct. Appeals (5th cir.) 1973, U.S. Ct. Appeals (11th cir.) 1978, U.S. Supreme Ct. 1982. Assoc. firm Sadler, Sadler, Sullivan & Sharp, Birmingham, Ala., 1973-74; assoc. firm Lange, Simpson, Robinson & Somerville, Birmingham, 1975-80, ptnr. 1980-93, Page Law Firm, 1993—; pres., CEO Control for Litig., L.L.C., 1997—. Served to 2d lt. U.S. Army, 1973. Mem. Ala. State Bar Assn. (chmn. antitrust sect. 1983-84, co-chmn. permanent code commn. 1986-88), Birmingham Bar Assn. (panel chmn. grievance com. 1983-84, chmn. fee arbitration com. 1984-85), ABA (antitrust sect., litigation sect., patent, copyright and trademark sect.), Auburn U. Bar Assn. (pres. 1993-94). Office: Morgan Keegan Ctr 2900 Hwy 280 Ste 200 Birmingham AL 35223

PAGE, LINDA KAY, banking executive; b. Wadsworth, Ohio, Oct. 4, 1943; s. Frederick Meredith and Martha Irene (Vance) P. Student Sch. Banking, Ohio U., 1976-77; cert. Nat. Pers. Sch., U. Md.-Am. Bankers Assn., 1981; grad. banking program U. Wis., Madison, 1982-84; BA Capital U. Asst. v.p., gen. mgr. Bancohio Corp., Columbus, Ohio, 1975-78, v.p., dist. mgr., 1979-80, v.p., mgr. employee rels., 1980-81, v.p., divsn. mgr., 1982-83; commr. of banks State of Ohio, Columbus, 1983-87, dir. dept. Commerce, 1988-90; pres., CEO Star Bank Cen. Ohio, Columbus, 1990-92; state dir. Rural Devel.-USDA, 1993—. Bd. dirs. Clark County Mental Health Bd., Springfield, Ohio, 1982-83, Springfield Met. Housing, 1982-83; bd. advisers Orgn. Indsl. Standards, Springfield, 1982-83; trustee League Against Child Abuse, 1986-90; treas. Ohio Housing Fin. Agy., 1988-90; vice chair Fed. Reserve Bd.-Consumer Adv. Coun., 1989-91. Bd. dirs. Pvt. Industry Coun. Franklin County, 1990—, Ohio Higher Edn. Facilities Commn., 1990-93, Ohio Devel. Corp., 1995—; trustee, treas. Columbus State Community Coll. Found., 1990—; bd. dirs. Columbus Urban League, 1992—. Recipient Leadership Columbus award Sta. WTVN and Columbus Leadership Program, 1975, 82, Outstanding Svc. award Clark County Mental Health Bd., 1983, Giles Mitchell Housing award, 1996. Mem. Nat. Assn. Bank Women (pres. 1980-81), Am. Bankers Assn. (govt. rels. coun. 1990-92), Women Execs. in State Govt., LWV (treas. edn. fund 1992—), Conf. State Bank Suprs. (bd. dirs., sec./treas. 1985-90), dist. chmn. 1984-85), Ohio Bankers Assn. (bd. dirs. 1982-83, 91-92), Internat. Womens Forum., Robert Morris Assocs. Democrat. Avocations: tennis, animal protection, reading, golf. Home: 641 Mirandy Pl Reynoldsburg OH 43068-1602 Office: 200 N High St Columbus OH 43215-2408

PAGE, LORNE ALBERT, physicist, educator; b. Buffalo, July 28, 1921; s. John Otway and Laura (Stewart) P.; m. Muriel Emily Jamieson, Sept. 7, 1946; children: J. Douglas, Kenneth L., James F., Donald S., David K. BSc, Queen's U., Can., 1944; PhD, Cornell U., 1950. Faculty U. Pitts., 1950—, prof. physics, 1958-86, prof. emeritus, 1987—. Contbr. articles to Phys. Rev., Rev. Modern Physics, Ann. Rev. Nuc. and Particle Sci. Served to lt. Royal Canadian Navy, 1944-45. Guggenheim fellow Upsala U., Sweden, 1957-58; Alfred P. Sloan research fellow, 1961-63. Fellow Am. Phys. Soc. Episcopalian. Achievements include early measurement of electron-electron scattering, measurement of the positron's mass, identification of positronium in condensed matter; development of method for analyzing circular polarization of high energy x-rays, first measurement of inherent polarization of positive beta particle. Home: 157 Lloyd Ave Pittsburgh PA 15218-1645

PAGE, LYMAN ALEXANDER, JR., physicist; b. San Francisco, Sept. 24, 1957; s. Lyman Alexander and Gillet (Thomas) P.; m. Elizabeth Olson, Feb. 12, 1990; children: William, James, Brent. BA with high honors, Bowdoin Coll., 1978; PhD, MIT, 1987. Rsch. technician Bartol Rsch. Found., Newark, Del., 1978-80; postdoctoral rsch. fellow MIT, 1989-90; instr. physics Princeton (N.J.) U., 1990-91, asst. prof. physics, 1991-95, assoc. prof., 1995—. Contbr. numerous sci. papers on cosmic microwave background Astrophys. Jour., 1979—. Surdna fellow Bowdoin Coll., 1978, NASA grad. student rschrs. program fellow MIT, 1987-89, David and Lucile Packard fellow Princeton U., 1994; Rsch. Corp. Cottrell scholar Princeton U., 1994. Mem. Am. Phys. Soc., Am. Astron. Soc. Achievements include measurement of tiny spatial variations in the temperature of the radiation thought to be the afterglow of the big-bang. Office: Princeton U Dept Physics Jadwin Hall Princeton NJ 08544-1019

PAGE, MARCUS WILLIAM, federal official; b. Washington, Sept. 20, 1937; s. Marcus William and Edna May (Horner) Pugh; m. Mary Jane Bitting, Dec. 10, 1989; 1 child from previous marriage, David Stephen. BA, Duke U., 1959; postgrad., George Washington U., 1961-65. Chief fin. svcs. FDA, Washington, 1965-68; chief fin. mgmt. br. Environ. Health Svc., Washington, 1968-70; chief acctg. ops. EPA, Washington, 1970-77, dir. fin. mgmt., 1977-81; dir. govt. acctg. systems Fin. Mgmt. Svc., Washington, 1981-83, dir. systems devel., 1983-84, dep. commr., 1984-87; dep. fiscal asst. sec. U.S. Treasury, Washington, 1987-95. Columnist Govt. Computer News, Washington, 1984-86; contbr. articles to various jours. Recipient Fin. Mgmt. Improvement award Joint Fin. Mgmt. Iprovement Program, Washington, 1980, Disting. Leadership award No. Va. Assn. Govt. Accts., 1986, Commrs. award Fin. Mgmt. Svc., 1987, Sec.'s Disting. Svc. award, 1995. Mem. Assn. Govt. Accts. (bd. dirs. 1981-85, pres. 1992-93), Planning Execs. Inst. (pres. 1973-74), Treasury Hist. Assn. (sec. 1990-92, chmn. bd. 1995—), Fed. Exec. Inst. Alumni Assn., C&O Canal Assn., Theta Chi. Avocations: hiking, science fiction, historic building restoration.

PAGE, MICHEL, biochemist; b. Quebec, Que., Can., Feb. 18, 1940; s. Hector and Alma (Dussault) P.; m. Marthe Boudreau, Dec. 17, 1966; children: Brigitte, Marie, Charles, Madeleine. B.A., Laval U., 1960; B.Sc., Ottawa U., 1965, Ph.D., 1969. Nat. Cancer Inst. postdoctoral fellow U. Colo., Boulder, 1968-70; research fellow Mt. Sinai Sch. Medicine, N.Y.C., 1970-71; clin. biochemist Hotel Dieu Hosp., Quebec, 1971-81; research scholar Nat. Cancer Inst. Can., 1975-81; prof. biochemistry U. Laval, Quebec City, 1982—; pres., founder BCM Biotech, Inc., 1988, BCM Développement Inc., 1993; mem. grant panels Med. Rsch. Coun., Nat. Cancer Inst.; pres. BCH Biotech Inc., BCH Devel. Inc. Author: La cuisine sans cholesterol, 1975, Cancer, 1983, Cancérologie expérimentale, 1993; contbr. over 125 articles to sci. publs. Mem. Ordre des Chimistes du Que., AAAS, Canadian Biochem. Soc., Canadian Immunol. Soc., Am. Soc. Cell Biology., Am. Assn. Clin. Research. Roman Catholic. Home: 9175 Pl Lavalliere, 125 Rue Dalhousie # 217, Quebec, PQ Canada G1K 4C5 Office: Faculty of Medicine, U Laval, Quebec, PQ Canada G1K 7P4

PAGE, OSCAR CLETICE, academic administrator; b. Bowling Green, Ky., Dec. 22, 1939; s. Elizabeth P.; m. Anna Laura Hood, June 12, 1965; children: Kristen, Matt. BA in Social Sci., Western Ky. U., 1962; MA in History, U. Ky., 1963, PhD in Early Modern European History, 1967. Instr. history Western Ky. U., Bowling Green, 1964; asst. prof., asst. chair history dept. U. Ga., Athens, 1967-71; dean Wesleyan Coll., Macon, Ga., 1971-78; v.p. acad. affairs Lander Coll., Greenwood, S.C., 1978-86, acting pres., 1985, provost, v.p. acad. affairs, 1986-88; pres. Austin Peay State U., Clarksville, Tenn., 1988-94, Austin Coll., Sherman, Tex., 1994—; mem. adv. com. Master of Mil. Art & Sci. Program, Leavenworth, Kans., 1994-96. Bd. dirs. United Way, Sherman, 1994—, Meml. Hosp., Clarksville, 1989-94, Nations Bank, Clarksville, 1988-94; mem. pres.'s commn. NCAA, 1990-94. Mem. Rotary, Sherman C. of C. Office: Austin Coll 900 N Grand Ave Sherman TX 75090-4440*

PAGE, RICHARD LEIGHTON, cardiologist, medical educator, researcher; b. San Diego, Mar. 8, 1958; s. Ellis Batten and Elizabeth Latimer (Thaxton) P.; m. Jean Reynolds, Oct. 12, 1985; children: Franklin Reynolds, Gillian Grace, Edward Batten. BS in Zoology magna cum laude, Duke U., 1980, MD, 1984. Diplomate Nat. Bd. Med. Examiners, Am. Bd. Internal Medicine, subspecialties cardiovascular disease and clin. cardiac electrophysiology; lic. physician, Tex. Rsch. fellow in pharmacology Columbia Presbyn. Med. Ctr., 1982-83; intern dept. medicine Mass. Gen. Hosp., Boston, 1984-85, resident dept. medicine, 1985-87; cardiology fellow clin. electrophysiology Duke U. Med. Ctr., Durham, N.C., 1987-89, clin. cardiology fellow, 1989, lectr. medicine divsn. cardiology, 1989-90, assoc. in medicine, 1990, asst. prof., dir. clin. electrophysiology lab., 1990-92; asst. prof. medicine U. Tex. Southwestern Med. Ctr., Dallas, 1992-95, assoc. prof., 1995—; dir. sect. clin. electrophysiology U. Tex. Southwestern Med. Ctr., Dallas, 1992—; dir. clin. electrophysiology lab., arrhythmia and pacemaker svc., Parkland Meml. Hosp., Dallas, 1992—; dir. Stanley J. Sarnoff Endowment for Rsch. in Cardiovasc. Sci., Inc., Bethesda, Md., 1990—, co-chmn., 1992. Mem. editl. bd. Cardiac Chronicle, 1993; author: (with others) Manual of Clinical Problems in Cardiology, 5th edit., 1995; contbr. articles to profl. jours., chpt. to book. Sarnoff Endowment fellow, 1982, Sarnoff scholar, 1987. Fellow Stanley J. Sarnoff Soc., Am. Heart Assn., Am. Coll. Cardiology; mem. N.Am. Soc. Pacing and Electrophysiology, Tex. Med. Assn., Dallas County Med. Soc., North Tex. Electrophysiology Soc. (trustee), Sigma Xi, Alpha Omega Alpha. Episcopalian. Avocations: tennis, sailing, gardening. Home: 1500 Ramsgate Cir Plano TX 75093-5044 Office: U Tex Southwestern Med Ctr 5323 Harry Hines Blvd Dallas TX 75235-7208

PAGE, ROBERT HENRY, engineer, educator, researcher; b. Phila., Nov. 5, 1927; s. Ernest Fraser and Marguerite (MacFarl) P.; m. Lola Marie Griffin, Nov. 12, 1948; children: Lola Linda, Patricia Jean, William Ernest, Nancy Lee, Martin Fraser. BS in Mech. Engring, Ohio U., 1949; MS, U. Ill., 1951, PhD, 1955. Instr., research assoc. U. Ill., 1949-55; research engr. fluid dynamics Esso Research & Engring. Co., 1955-57; vis. lectr. Stevens Inst. Tech., 1956-57, dir. fluid dynamics lab., prof. mech. engring., 1957-61; prof. mech. engring., chmn. dept. mech., indsl. and aerospace engring. Rutgers-The State U., 1961-76, prof., research cons., 1976-79; dean engring. Tex. A&M U., 1979-83, Forsyth prof., 1983-93, prof. emeritus mech. engring., 1994—; spl. research base pressure and heat transfer, wake flow and flow separation. Contbr. over 200 articles to profl. publs.; inventor impingement nozzles. Served with AUS, 1945-47, Pacific Theatre of Operations. Recipient Western Electric Fund award for excellence in engring. edn. Am. Soc. Engring Edn., 1968; Lindback Found. award for distinguished teaching, 1969; Disting. Alumnus award U. Ill., 1971; Disting. Service award, 1973; Life Quality Engring. award, 1974, James Harry Potter Gold medal, 1983, Ohio U. medal, 1983; named hon. prof. Ruhr U., Buchum, Fed. Republic Germany, 1984. Fellow AAAS, AIAA (assoc.), ABET, Am. Astron. Soc. (chmn. nat. space engring. com. 1969-70, 72-76), Am. Soc. Engring. Edn. (Centennial medal 1993); mem. ASME (hon. mem. award 1988), Am. Phys. Soc. Home: 1905 Comal Cir College Station TX 77840-4818

PAGE, ROBERT WESLEY, engineering and construction company executive, federal official; b. Dallas, Jan. 22, 1927; s. Arch Cleo and Zelma (Tyler) P.; m. Nancy Ann Eaton, Sept. 17, 1952; children: Robert W. Jr., David, Mark, Margaret. B.S. in Archtl. Engring., Tex. A&M U., 1950. Asst. prof. Am. Univ., Beirut, Lebanon, 1952-54; project mgr. Aramco, The Hague and Saudi Arabia, 1954-56; dir. constrn. and devel. Internat. Coll., Beirut, N.Y.C., 1956-58; internat. mgr. Bechtel Co., N.Y.C., 1958-64; v.p. Rockresorts Co., N.Y.C., 1964-71; pres., chief exec. officer George A. Fuller Co., N.Y.C., from 1971; corp. v.p. Northrop Corp., N.Y.C., from 1971; pres., chief exec. officer Rust Engring. Co., Birmingham, Ala., 1976-81; pres., chief exec. officer Kellogg Rust Inc., Houston, 1981-85, chmn., chief exec. officer, dir., 1985-86; pres., chief exec. officer PM Co., Houston, 1986; asst. sec. U.S. Dept. of Army, Washington, 1987-90; chmn. Panama Canal Commn., 1989-90; exec. v.p. McDermott Internat., Washington, 1990—; sr. lectr. MIT, 1993; chmn. Pegasus Cons., Inc., Cambridge, Mass., 1996—; adj. prof. Georgetown U.; bd. dirs. I.C.F./Kaiser Internat.; bd. dirs. Thormatrix, Inc., San Jose, Calif. Trustee Internat. Coll. Beirut; mem. Pres.'s Coun., U. Ala.; bd. dirs. Coll. Football Hall of Fame. With USNR, 1944-46, PTO. Trustee Am. U. in Cairo; trustee Wortham Theatre Ctr., Houston, Internat. Coll. Beirut; mem. Pres.'s Council, U. Ala.; mem. adv. bd. John E. Gray Inst., Lamar U.; bd. dirs. Coll. Football Hall of Fame. Served with USNR, 1944-46, PTO. Mem. ASME, ASCE, Rolling Rock Club (Ligoner, Pa.), Internat. Club (Washington), Army-Navy Club (Washington), Georgetown Club (Washington), Sakonnet Country Club (Little Compton, R.I.), Tau Beta Pi. Home: 3025 P St NW Washington DC 20007-3054 Office: 1850 K St NW Ste 950 Washington DC 20006-2213

PAGE, ROY CHRISTOPHER, periodontist, educator; b. Campobello, S.C., Feb. 7, 1932; s. Milton and Anny Mae (Eubanks) P. BA, Berea Coll., 1953; DDS, U. Md., 1957; PhD, U. Wash., 1967; ScD (hon.), Loyola U., Chgo., 1983. Cert. in periodontics. Pvt. practice periodontics Seattle, 1963—; asst. prof. U. Wash. Schs. Medicine and Dentistry, Seattle, 1967-70, prof., 1974—, dir. Ctr. Research in Oral Biology, 1976-96; dir. grad. edn. U. Wash. Sch. Dentistry, 1976-80; dir. rsch. U. Wash. Sch. Dentistry, Seattle, 1976-94, assoc. dean rsch., 1994—; vis. scientist MRC Labs., London, 1971-72; cons., lectr. in field; fellow Pierre Fauchard Acad. Author: Periodontal Disease, 1977, 2d edit., 1990, Periodontitis in Man and Other Animals, 1982. Recipient Gold Medal award U. Md., 1957; recipient Career Devel. award NIH, 1967-72. Fellow Internat. Coll. Dentists, Am. Coll. Dentists, Am. Acad. Periodontology (Gies award 1982, fellowship award 1989); mem. ADA, Am. Assn. Dental Rsch. (pres. 1982-83), Am. Soc. Exptl. Pathology, Internat. Assn. Dental Rsch. (pres. 1987, basic periodontal rsch. award 1977). Home: 8631 Inverness Dr NE Seattle WA 98115-3935

PAGE, SEAN EDWARD, emergency medical care provider, educator; b. York, Pa., May 27, 1966; s. William C. and Patricia (Huber) P. BS in Biochemistry, Elizabethtown Coll., 1988; BSN, York Coll. Pa., 1991. Cert. EMS instr. ARC; cert. BCLS, BTLS, EMT. Health and EMS dep. Manchester Twp. Emergency mgmt. Agy., 1983-90, officer, 1990—; mem. continuing edn. staff York Hosp., 1990-91, cln. nurse I, team leader transitional care unit, 1991-93, charge nurse, 1993; med. officer York County Hazardous Materials Emergency Response Team, 1992-95; instr. nursing Harrisburg Area C.C., 1994—; dep. coroner York County, 1991-93; key resource person hazardous materials med. response Internat. Assn. Fire Chiefs and Nat. Fire Protection Agy., 1994—. Mem. com. health and safety Boy Scouts Am., 1990—; disaster human resource system ARC, 1993—, disaster svcs. instr., 1994—. Pam Abel Nursing scholarship; recipient Outstanding Emergency Med. Svcs. Vol. York County, 1990. Mem. Emergency Health Svcs. Fedn. (edn. and cert. com. 1990-95), Pa. Nurses Assn. (Dist. 20 bd. dirs. 1992-94), Phi Sigma Pi, Sigma Theta Tau. Home: 207 E Locust Ln York PA 17402-1033

PAGE, THOMAS LESLIE, poet, writer; b. Wichita, Kans., Sept. 28, 1937; s. Thomas F. Page and Mary L. (O'Hara) Turner; m. Leslie Ellen Fox, Sept. 2, 1971; children: Thomas O., Mary C.E., Will A. BA, Wichita U., 1960; MA, Vanderbilt U., 1963; MFA, Wichita State U., 1985. Asst. prof. Latin Am. studies U. Fla., Gainesville, 1966-73; high sch. tchr. various, 1974-81; officer Wichita Police Dept., 1981-82; instr. Wichita State U., 1982-87; writer Wichita, 1987—. Author: ERA Vet, 1988, Name of the Place, 1989, The Fort Scott Poems, 1994; contbr. to literary jours. Com. mem. Fla. State McGovern Com., Orlando, 1970-72; organizer Vanderbilt Students for Kennedy, Nashville, 1960-63; ctrl. committeeman Dem. Party, 1984-86; sec., treas. The Forum, Wichita, 1973-78; dir. Mother Jones Found., 1988-91. With U.S. Army, 1964-65. NDEA fellowship Vanderbilt U., 1960-63, Ford Found. grant, 1961. Mem. Sons of Union Vets. of the Civil War, Soc. for the Study of Midwestern Lit., Associated Writing Programs, Sir John Falstaff Soc. Home and Office: PO Box 4446 Wichita KS 67204-0446

PAGE, TIM, music critic. Classical music critic Washington Post. Office: Washington Post 1150 15th St NW Washington DC 20071-0070*

PAGE, WILLIAM MARION, lawyer; b. Columbus, Ga., July 31, 1917; s. Roger McKeene and Louise Olivia (Seals) P.; m. Lucy Quillian Page, Feb. 8, 1941 (dec. 1982); children: John Roger, Jane Quillian Page McCamy, William Franklin (dec. Dec. 1996); m. Barbara Brown Waddell, May 10, 1985. LLB, U. Ga., 1939, JD. Bar: Ga. 1938, U.S. Supreme Ct. 1955. Ptnr. Page Scrantom Sprouse Tucker & Ford P.C., Columbus, Ga., 1939—. Bd. visitors U. Ga. Law Sch., 1969-74. With U.S. Army, 1941-46. Fellow Am. Coll. Trial Lawyers; mem. State Bar Ga. (bd. govs. 1964-71), ABA, Chattahoochee Circuit Bar Assn. (pres. 1948-49), Columbus Bar Assn. (pres. 1946-47), Am. Judicature Soc., Big Eddy Club, Chattahoochee River Club, Kiwanis. Home: 916 Overlook Dr Columbus GA 31906-3029 Office: PO Box 1199 Columbus GA 31902-1199

PAGE, WILLIS, conductor; b. Rochester, N.Y., Sept. 18, 1918. Grad. with distinction, Eastman. Sch. Music, Rochester., 1939. Mem. Rochester Philharm., 1937-40, Rochester Civic, 1939-40; prof. conducting Eastman Sch. Music, 1967-69; prof. conducting, dir. orchestral activities Drake U., Des Moines, 1969-71; guest condr. Sony concerts, Chiba, Japan, 1992. Mem. Boston Symphony Orch., 1940-55; prin. bass Boston Pops, 1947-55; condr. Cecilia Soc. Boston, 1952-54, New Orchestral Soc. Boston; assoc. condr. Buffalo Philharm., 1955-59; music dir./condr. Nashville Symphony Orch., 1959-67; music dir. Linwood Music Sch., 1955-59; 1st condr. Yomiuri Nippon Symphony, Tokyo, 1962-63; condr. Des Moines Symphony, 1969-71, Jacksonville (Fla.) Symphony Orch., 1971-83; founder, condr. St. John's River City Band, 1985-86; guest condr. Boston Pops, Toronto, Rochester Civic, Eastman-Rochester, Denver, Muncie, Jerusalem, St. Louis, Colorado Springs, Memphis, Hartford orchs., Yomiuri Nippon Symphony, 1988; founding condr., exec. dir. First Coast Pops Orch., 1989; condr. all-state orchs. of N.Y., Iowa, Ky., Tenn., Fla., also regional festivals; condr. 13 L.P. recordings including Symphony of the Air (Roger Williams soloist), Boston Festival Orch., Cook Labs., Nashville Symphony. Sgt. 95th inf. divsn. U.S. Army, 1943-45. Decorated Bronze Star; recipient Ford Found. European travel award, 1967.

PAGELS, JÜRGEN HEINRICH, balletmaster, dance educator, dancer, choreographer, author; b. Lübeck, Fed. Republic Germany, Apr. 16, 1925; came to U.S., 1955; s. Heinrich and Margret (Haas) P. Artists diploma, Hamburg (Fed. Republic Germany) State Exam Bd., 1947; advanced soloist exam. with honors, Assn. Russian Ballet, London, 1952, advanced tchrs. exam. with honors, 1961, sr. tchrs. exam. with honors, 1969; DFA, Pacific Western U., 1988. Ballet soloist Atlantic Theater, Lübeck, 1945-46, Stadt-Theater, Lübeck, 1946-47; prin. dancer Dortmund, Fed. Republic Germany, 1947-48, Operette and Stattl. Schauspielhaus Theater, Hamburg, 1949-50; ballet soloist Ballet Theater Co., Hamburg, 1950-51; prin. dancer Ballet Legat, London, 1951-52, Ballet Legat and Yugoslav Nat. Ballet, touring throughout Europe, 1952-53; guest ballet soloist Ballet Etoile, Paris Opera, Paris, 1954; dir., owner Pagels Legat Sch. Ballet, Dallas, 1955-62; guest tchr. ballet numerous dance acads. and ballet cos., worldwide, 1962-70; prof. dance Ind. Univ., Bloomington, 1970-90; prof. emeritus Ind. U., Bloomington, 1990—; guest tchr. ballet numerous orgns. including Vaganova Choreography Inst., Leningrad, USSR, Ballet do Rio de Janeiro, Egypt Nat. Ballet of Cairo, Ballet Intezet, Hungary, Nat. Ballet, Istanbul, Turkey, Royal Danish Ballet, Tex. Christian Univ., Ft. Worth, Nat. Ballet, Nicaragua; condr. master classes for Ballet Guatemala, Escuela Nacional de Danza, San Salvador, Academia de Danza Classica, Costa Rica, Nat. Ballet Venezuela, T.W. Univ., Nat. U. Costa Rica, Bellas Artes, Honduras, Ballet Nacional Nicaragua; co-founder, dir. Dallas Civic Ballet; art dir. Ballet Guatemala, 1978-79, Nat. Ballet Salvador, Ulm Theatre, Germany, Ballet Co., 1995, Artemis, Amsterdam, Holland; Internat. Ballet competition Managuq, Nicaraqua, 1995. Author of character dance books in English, German and Spanish, 1984, 85, and ballet dance books; collaborator and coach to Dame Margot Fonteyn. U.S. judge Internat. Ballet Competition, Trujillo, Peru, 1989, 90. Served as sgt. German Army, 1942-45. Research grantee Ind. Univ., 1977. Avocations: exhibited sculptor, tennis, deep-sea fishing. Home: 934 A Maxwell Ter Apt A Bloomington IN 47401-5278 Office: Ind U Sch Music Ballet Dept Bloomington IN 47405 also: Curtius Str 6, 23568 Luebeck Germany

PAGET, JOHN ARTHUR, mechanical engineer; b. Ft. Frances, Ont., Can., Sept. 15, 1922; s. John and Ethel (Bishop) P.; B. in Applied Sci., Toronto, 1946; m. Vicenta Herrera Nunez, Dec. 16, 1963; children: Cynthia Ellen, Kevin Arthur, Keith William. Chief draftsman Gutta Percha & Rubber, Ltd., Toronto, Ont., 1946-49; chief draftsman Viceroy Mfg. Co., Toronto, 1949-52; supr., design engr. C.D. Howe Co. Ltd., Montreal, Que., Can., 1952-58, sr. design engr. Combustion Engring., Montreal, 1958-59; sr. staff engr. Gen. Atomic, Inc., La Jolla, 1959-81. Mem. ASME, Soc. for History Tech., Inst. Mech. Engrs., Brit. Nuclear Energy Soc. Patentee in field. Home: 3183 Magellan St San Diego CA 92154-1515

PAGILLO, CARL ROBERT, elementary school educator; b. Bklyn., Apr. 11, 1950; s. Nicholas and Rachel (Rhyne) P.; m. Joanne Ferro, Aug. 1, 1992. BA, Queens Coll., 1973, MS in Elem. Edn., 1975; advanced in edn. adminstrn., Bklyn. Coll., 1993. Tchr. grade 3, 5, and 6 Pub. Sch. 207 Queens, Howard Beach, N.Y., 1983-93; tchr. multimedia PS 20 YQ, Howard Beach, N.Y., 1983-93; tchr. lang. arts PS 56 Q, Richmond Hill, N.Y., 1993—. Pres., founder Catherine St. Block Assn., Lynbrook, 1987-91; baseball coach, mgr. Little League, Pony League and Baby Ruth League, Nassau County, 1974-92; capt. Lynbrook 4.0. tennis team, 1984-93. Recipient Ely Trachtenberg award United Fedn. of Tchrs., 1986. Mem. Phi Delta Kappa. Avocation: tennis. Home: 17 Catherine St Lynbrook NY 11563-1207

PAGLIA, CAMILLE, writer, humanities educator; b. Endicott, N.Y., 1947; d. Pasquale John and Lydia (Colapietro) P. BA in English summa cum laude with highest honors, SUNY, Binghamton, 1968; MPhil, Yale U., 1971, PhD in English, 1974. Mem. faculty Bennington (Vt.) Coll., 1972-80; vis. lectr. Wesleyan U., 1980, Yale U., New Haven, 1980-84; prof. humanities U. Arts, Phila., 1984—. Author: Sexual Personae: Art and Decadence from Nefertiti to Emily Dickinson, 1990, Sex, Art, and American Culture, 1992, Vamps and Tramps: New Essays, 1994. Office: Univ Arts 320 S Broad St Philadelphia PA 19102-4901

PAGLIARINI, JAMES, broadcast executive. AB, Princeton U., 1975; MEd, Temple U., 1976. Asst. to gen. mgr. Sta. KTEH-TV, San Jose, Calif., 1976-80; co-founder Sta. KNPB-TV, Reno, Nev., 1980—, sta. mgr., 1982-83, gen. mgr., CEO, 1983—; bd. dirs. Agy. Instrnl. T.V., Pub. Broadcasting, Western Indsl. Nev.; chmn. bd. govs. Pacific Mountain network, 1987—; mem. Cable Access Bd., Reno, PBS assessment policy com., 1988-89, funding task force, 1991, task force on nat. prodns., 1992-93, exec. com., 1995-96, program pricing policy task force, 1995-96; mem. TV policy task force Corp. for Pub. Broadcasting, 1995-96. Chmn. community adv. com. U. Nev. Sch. Engring., Reno; past bd. dirs. Planned Parenthood No. Nev., Boy Scouts Am., We. Nev. Clean Cities Com. Mem. Nev. Pub. Broadcasting Assn. (pres.), Small Sta. Assn. (pres. 1991-92). Office: Station KNPB 1670 N Virginia St Reno NV 89503-1738

PAGLIARO, HAROLD EMIL, English language educator; b. N.Y.C., June 19, 1925; s. Harry E. and Linda (Ricci) P.; m. Judith Marie Egan, Sept. 16, 1966; children: Blake, Robert, Susanna, John. AB, Columbia U., 1947, MA, 1948, PhD, 1961. Instr. English, Columbia U., N.Y.C., 1956-60; asst. prof. Columbia U., 1961-63, faculty fellow, 1962, dir. honors sch. gen. studies, 1962-64; asst. prof. Swarthmore (Pa.) Coll., 1964-65, asso. prof., 1966-69, prof., 1970—, Alexander Griswold Cummins prof. English lit., 1982—, chmn. dept. English lit., 1970-74, 86-91, provost, 1974-79, Alexander Griswold Cummins prof. emeritus English, provost emeritus, 1992—; mem. sr. common room St. Edmund Hall, Oxford (Eng.) U., 1973-74, 79-80; assoc. Columbia U. Seminar 18th Century European Culture, 1982—. Author: Selfhood and Redemption in Blakes's "Songs", 1987, Naked Heart: A Soldier's Journey to the Front, 1996, Henry Fielding: A Literary Life, 1997; editor: Fielding's Journal of a Voyage to Lisbon, 1963, Major English Writers of the Eighteenth Century, 1969, Studies in Eighteenth Century Culture, Vol. 2, 1972, Vol. 3, 1973, Vol. 4, 1974; contbr. articles to profl. jours. Mem. coll. evaluation bd. Middle States Assn., 1966—. Served with AUS, 1943-45. Decorated Purple Heart; NEH sr. fellow, 1983-84; George Becker fellow, 1988-89. Mem. MLA, Am. Soc. for Eighteenth-Century Studies (editor Proc. 1971-75), Am. Soc. Eighteenth-Century Studies (mem. publs. com. 1974-76). Home: 536 Ogden Ave Swarthmore PA 19081-1129

PAGLIARO, JAMES DOMENIC, lawyer; b. Phila., Aug. 18, 1951; s. Domenic A. and Nancy I. (D'Amore) P.; m. Susan B. Boag, Aug. 25, 1973; children: Jamie C., Justin A. BA cum laude, LaSalle U., 1973; JD, Dickinson Law Sch., 1976. Bar: Pa. 1976, U.S. Dist. Ct. (ea. dist.) Pa. 1977, U.S. Ct. Appeals (3d, 8th, 9th and 10th cirs.) 1989, U.S. Supreme Ct. 1989. Regional atty. Gov. of Pa., Phila., 1976-79; sr. trial atty. office regional solicitor U.S. Dept. Labor, Phila., 1979-85; assoc. Morgan, Lewis & Bockius, LLP, Phila., 1985-88, ptnr. litigation, 1988—. Chmn. Home & Sch. Bd. Norwood Acad., Chestnut Hill, Pa., 1983-87; vestry Hist. St. Paul's Ch., Elkins Park, Pa., 1993-94. Mem. ABA, Pa. Bar Assn. (speaker continuing legal edn. 1987—), Phila. Bar Assn., Woolsach Honors Soc. Avocations: history, swimming, numismatics. Home: 404 Westview Rd Elkins Park PA 19027-2428 Office: Morgan Lewis & Bockius LLP 2000 One Logan Sq Philadelphia PA 19103

PAGLIARULO, MICHAEL ANTHONY, physical therapy educator; b. Amityville, N.Y., May 15, 1947; s. Anthony and Louise (Cipriani) P.; m. Patricia Marilyn Salm, Mar. 22, 1975; children: Michael, David, Elisa. BA in Biology, SUNY, Buffalo, 1969, BS in Phys. Therapy, 1970; MA in Phys. Therapy, U. So. Calif., 1974; EdD in Postsecondary Edn. Adminstrn., Syracuse U., 1988. Lic. phys. therapist, N.Y., Calif. Staff phys. therapist Brunswick Hosp. Ctr., Amityville, 1970; lectr. U. So. Calif., L.A., 1974-75, U. Calif., San Francisco, 1975-80; curriculum coord. Ithaca (N.Y.) Coll., 1980-82, asst. prof., 1982-84, acting dir., 1986-89, assoc. prof., dir., 1989-94, assoc. prof. phys. therapy, 1994-97; chair, 1997—. Author: Introduction to Physical Therapy, 1996. Bd. dirs. Marin/Roundtree Homeowners Assn., San Rafael, Calif., 1978-80; cubmaster Boy Scouts Am., Ithaca, 1989-91. Capt. U.S. Army, 1970-72. Mem. Am. Phys. Therapy Assn. (bd. dirs. Calif. chpt. 1979-80, treas. N.Y. chpt. 1989-91, Merit award 1988, 95, 97, Norma Chadwick award 1993, Outstanding Svc. award 1997). Congregationalist. Avocations: scuba diving, water and snow skiing, model trains. Office: Ithaca Coll Dept Phys Therapy Danby Rd Ithaca NY 14850

PAGLIO, LYDIA ELIZABETH, editor; b. Providence; d. Victor and Lydia Anne (DiPrete) P. BA, NYU. Researcher Young Pres. Orgn., 1970-71; editorial asst. Sport mag., N.Y.C., 1971-72; assoc. editor True Experience, also True Love mags., N.Y.C., 1972-73; editor True Experience mag., 1973-81; assoc. editor Dell Pub., N.Y.C., 1983; editor Dell Pub., 1983-84, sr. editor, 1984-87, dir. Candlelight Ecstasy Romances, 1984-87; sr. editor Zebra Books, Pinnacle Books, 1987-89; pres., owner Sutton Press, Inc., N.Y.C., 1991—; pub. cons., N.Y.C., 1989—; dir. publicity Dancer's World, Springfield, Mass., 1978-80. Author articles. Pres., sec., mem. exec. com. West Side Community Recycling Corp., 1979-81; pres. 41 W 82 St. Tenants, 1989—. Mem. Editl. Free-lance Assn. (bd. dirs. 1984).

PAGNI, PATRICK JOHN, mechanical and fire safety engineering science educator; b. Chgo., Nov. 28, 1942; s. Frank and Helen Boyle Pagni; m. Carol DeSantis, Dec. 26, 1970; children: Christina Marie, Catherine Ann, Patrick John Jr. B in Aeronautical Engring. magna cum laude, U. Detroit, 1965; SM, MIT, 1967, ME, 1969, PhD, 1970. Registered profl. mechanical engr., Calif., fire protection engr., Calif. Research asst. MIT, Cambridge, 1965-70; asst. prof. Mech. Engring. Dept. U. Calif., Berkeley, 1970-76, assoc. prof., 1976-81, prof., 1981—, vice chmn. grad. study, 1986-89; acting assoc. dean Coll. Engring. U. Calif., 1990; assoc. faculty scientist Lawrence Berkeley Lab., 1976—; vis. scientist Factory Mut. Research Corp., Norwood, Mass., 1980; cons. on fire safety sci. various orgns., 1972—. Editor: Fire Science for Fire Safety, 1984, Fire Safety Science--Procs. of the First Internat. Symposium, 1986, Procs. of the Second Internat. Symposium, 1989; contbr. articles to profl. jours. Grantee NSF, NASA, Nat. Bur. Standards, Nat. Inst. Standards and Tech., 1971—; Applied Mechanics fellow Harvard U., 1974, 77; Pullman Found. scholar, 1960. Mem. ASME, Am. Phys. Soc. (life), Combustion Inst., Soc. Fire Protection Engrs., Internat. Assn. Fire Safety Sci. (vice chmn., exec. com., chmn. awards com.), Tau Beta Pi, Pi Tau Sigma, Alpha Sigma Nu. Democrat. Roman Catholic. Home: 1901 Ascot Dr Moraga CA 94556-1412 Office: Univ of Calif Coll of Engring Mech Engring Dept Berkeley CA 94720-1740

PAGONIS, WILLIAM GUS, retired army general; b. Charleroi, Pa., Apr. 30, 1941; s. Constantinos V. and Jennie (Kontos) P.; m. Cheryl Elaine Miller, June 4, 1964; children: Gust, Robert. BS, Pa. State U., 1964, MBA in Bus. Logistics, 1970. Commd. 2d lt. U.S. Army, 1964, advanced through grades to lt. gen., 1991; comdr. 1097th Transp. Co., Vietnam, 1968; div. transp. officer, then exec. officer 2d bn., 501st inf., 101st Airborne Div., Vietnam, 1970-71; pers. staff officer U.S. Army Mil. Pers. Ctr., Alexandria, Va., 1973-75; staff officer Office Chief of Legis. Liaison, Washington, 1975-76; comdr. 10th transp. bn. 7th Transp. Group, Ft. Eustis, Va., 1977-78; dep. chief of staff, then ops. and rsch. systems analyst U.S. Army Transp. Sch. and Ctr., Ft. Eustis, 1978-79; dir. logistics, dir. indsl. ops., then chief of staff 193d Inf. Brigade, Panama, 1980-81, comdr. Logistics Support Command, 1981-82; comdr. Div. Support Command, 4th Inf. Div., Ft. Carson, Colo., 1982-85; spl. asst. to dep. comdg. gen. 21st Support Command, U.S. Army Europe, 1985-86, dep. comdg. gen., 1986-88; dir. plans and ops. Office Dep. Chief of Staff for Logistics, Washington, 1988-89, dir. transp., energy and troop support, 1989-90; comdg. gen. 22d Support Command, Dhahran, Saudi Arabia, 1990-91, U.S. Cen. Command/22d Support Command, Dhahran, 1991-92; comdr. 21st Theater Army Command, Germany, 1992-93; lt. gen., ret. U.S. Army, 1993; exec. v.p. logistics Sears & Roebuck Co., Hoffman Estates, Ill., 1993—. Author: Moving Mountains (Logistics Leadership and Management of the Gulf War), (one of top 30 best bus. books of 1992, top leadership book 1992 Soundview Exec. Book Summaries, 1992), 1992. Decorated D.S.M., Silver Star, Legion of Merit with oak leaf cluster, Bronze Star with 3 oak leaf clusters, Air medal with 2 oak leaf clusters, Meritorious Svc. medal with 4 oak leaf clusters, King Abdul Aziz 2d Class award Chief of Staff, Saudi Arabian Army, 1991, Kuwait Liberation medal Chief of Staff, Kuwait Army, 1992; recipient Merit and Honor award Govt. of Greece, 1991, Joseph C. Scheleen award Am. Soc. Transp. and Logistics, 1991, Man of Yr. award Modern Materials Handling, 1991, Grad. Man of Yr. award Alpha Chi Rho, 1991, AHEPA Man of Yr., 1992, Disting. Alumni award Pa. State U., 1994; named Hellenic Man of Yr., 1992; Pa. State U. fellow, 1992. Mem. Soc. Logistics Engrs. (hon.), Am. Legion, Am. Vets. Home: 25190 North Pawnee Rd Barrington IL 60010-1354 Office: Sears Roebuck & Co 3333 Beverly Rd Hoffman Estates IL 60192

PAGOTTO, LOUISE, English language educator; b. Montreal, June 22, 1950; came to U.S., 1980; d. Albert and Elena (Tibi) P. BA, Marianopolis Coll., Montreal, 1971; TESL Diploma, U. Papua New Guinea, 1975; MA, McGill U., 1980; PhD, U. Hawaii at Manoa, Honolulu, 1987. Tchr. Yarapos High Sch., Wewak, Papua New Guinea, 1971-73, Electricity Commn. Tng. Coll., Port Moresby, Papua New Guinea, 1975-76, Coll. of the Marshall Islands, Majuro, summers 1983-91, Leeward C.C., Pearl City, Hawaii, 1988-89, Kapiolani C.C., Honolulu, 1989—; presenter at confs. Contbr. articles to profl. jours. McConnell fellow McGill U., 1979, Can. Coun. fellow, 1980-83; recipient Excellence in Teaching award Bd. of Regents, 1993. Mem. AAUW, Linguistic Soc. Am., Nat. Coun. Tchrs. English, Hawaii Coun. Tchrs. English. Avocations: water sports (swimming, bodyboarding), walking. Office: Kapiolani CC 4303 Diamond Head Rd Honolulu HI 96816-4421

PAGTER, CARL RICHARD, lawyer; b. Balt., Feb. 13, 1934; s. Charles Ralph and Mina (Amelung) P.; m. Judith Elaine Cox, May 6, 1978; 1 child by previous marriage: Corbin Christopher. AA, Diablo Valley Coll., 1953; BA, San Jose State U., 1955; LLB, U. Calif., Berkeley, 1964. Bar:Calif. 1965, D.C. 1977, U.S. Supreme Ct. 1976. Law clk. Kaiser Industries Corp., Oakland, Calif., 1963-64, counsel, 1964-70; assoc. counsel Kaiser Industries Corp., Washington, 1970-73; counsel Kaiser Industries Corp., Oakland, Calif., 1973-75; dir. govt. affairs Kaiser Industries Corp., Washington, 1975-76; v.p., sec., gen. counsel Kaiser Cement Corp., Oakland, Calif., 1976-88; cons., gen. counsel Kaiser Cement Corp., San Ramon, 1988—. Author: (with A. Dundes) Urban Folklore from the Paperwork Empire, 1975, More Urban Folklore from the Paperwork Empire, 1987, Never Try to Teach a Pig to Sing, 1991, Sometimes the Dragon Wins, 1996. Served with USNR, 1957-61, to comdr., 1978. Mem. ABA, Contra Costa County Bar Assn., Am. Folklore Soc., Calif. Folklore Soc., Calif. Bluegrass Assn. (founder), Oakland Athletic Club, University Club. Republican. Home: 17 Julianne Ct Walnut Creek CA 94595-2610 Office: Kaiser Cement Corp 2680 Bishop Dr Ste 225 San Ramon CA 94583-4280

PAHNICHAPUTT, MOMLUANG ANANCHANOK, English and American literature educator; b. Bangkok, June 3, 1936; d. M.R. Boonarong Latavalya and Klia Amatyakul; m. Wanchai Pahnichaputt, Apr. 24, 1964; children: Anisa, Chayakorn. BA with honors, Chulalongkorn U., Bangkok, 1959, MA in English, 1961; MA in English, U. Denver, 1962, PhD in English, 1977. Prof. Faculty Arts Chulalongkorn U., Bangkok, 1986—, chair grad. com. for comprehensive examinations, 1977—, exec. com. mem. Grad. Sch., 1985-87, bd. mem. Grad. Sch., 1985-86; vis. fellow Amherst (Mass.) Coll., 1981-82, Yale U., New Haven, 1991, Harvard U., Cambridge, Mass., 1994. Author: American Literature: 1620-1858, 1982, Emily Dickinson's World, 1984, Imagery in Shakespeare's Tragedies, 1985, Modern American Novels, 1993, The Realm of Henry James, 1995. Fulbright grantee U.S. Govt., 1961-62; fellow Am. Coun. Learned Socs., 1981-82. Mem. MLA, Am. Studies Assn. in Thailand (charter mem. 1989—, bd. mem. 1989-92, founding editor Am. Studies jour. 1989), Am. Studies Assn., Mark Twain Circle. Avocations: oil painting, photography, music, reading. Office: Chulalongkorn Univ-English, Phyathai Rd, Bangkok 10330, Thailand

PAI, ANANTHA MANGALORE, electrical engineering educator, consultant; b. Mangalore, Karnataka, India, Oct. 5, 1931; came to U.S., 1979; s. Ramachandra M. and Janaki (Kamath) P.; m. Nandini Kamath, Nov. 25, 1956; children: Sunanda, Sujata, Shona, Gurudutt. BS, Madras U., India, 1953; MS, U. Calif., Berkeley, 1958, PhD, 1961. Elec. engr. Bombay Electric Supply Co., 1953-57; prof. Indian Inst. Tech., India, 1963-81, dean R&D, 1976-78; prof. U. Ill., Urbana, 1981—. Author: Computers in Power System, 1979, Power System Stability, 1981, Energy Functions, 1989. Recipient Bhatnagar award Govt. of India, 1974. Fellow IEEE, Indian Nat. Sci. Acad., NAE (India), Instn. Engrs. (India). Hindu. Office: U Ill Dept Elec Engring 1406 W Green St Urbana IL 61801-2918

PAI, SHIH I., Aeronautical engineer, educator; b. Tatung, Anhwei, China, Sept. 30, 1913; s. Hsi Chuan and Swe Lin (Cha) P.; BS in Elec. Engring., Nat. Central U. China, 1935; MS in Elec. Engring., MIT, 1938; PhD in Aeronautics and Math., Calif. Inst. Tech., 1940; D (hon.) Tech. U. Vienna, 1968; m. Alice Jen-Lan Wang, July 2, 1960; children: Stephen Ming Pai, Sue Pai Yang, Robert Yang Pai, Lou Lung Pai. Prof. aerodynamics Nat. Central U., China, 1940-47; vis. prof. Cornell U., 1947-49; rsch. prof. Inst. Phys. Sci. and Tech. (formerly, Inst. Fluid Dynamics and Applied Math.), U. Md., College Park, 1949-83, prof. emeritus, 1983-96; vis. prof. Tokyo U., 1966, Tech. U. Vienna, 1967, Tech. U. Denmark, 1974, U. Karlsruhe (Germany), 1980-81, U. Paris, 1981; hon. prof. Northwestern Poly. U., Peoples Republic China, 1980-96, Zhejiang U., Peoples Republic China, 1985-96; cons. Gen. Electric Co., N. Am. Aviation, Boeing Co., Martin Co. Served with Chinese Air Force, 1937-40. Guggenheim fellow, 1957-58, sr. scientist fellow NSF, 1966; recipient Alexander von Humboldt award, 1980, Centennial medal A. James Clark Sch. Engring. U. Md., 1994. Fellow Academia Sinica; mem. AIAA, Am. Phys. Soc., German Soc. Applied Math. and Mechanics, Internat. Acad. Astronautics (corr.). Author: 14 tech. books in fluid dynamics, latest being Two-Phase Flows, 1977; Modern Fluid Mechanics, 1981, (with Shijin Lu) The Theroetical and Computational Dynamics of a Compressible Flow, 1991; contbr. over 130 articles to profl. jours.; first to experimentally show the importance of coherent structure in turbulent flow, the authority of jet flow from low speed aerodynamics to hyperionic flow; contbr. modern fluid mechanics including magnetic fluid dynamics, radiation gas dynamics and two phase flows. Died May 23, 1996.

PAIDOUSSIS, MICHAEL PANDELI, mechanical engineering educator; b. Nicosia, Cyprus, Aug. 20, 1935; emigrated to Can., 1953, naturalized, 1976; s. Pandelis Aristeidis and Parthenope (Leptou) P. B in Engring., McGill U., 1958; PhD in Engring., U. Cambridge, 1963. Overseas fellow Gen. Electric Co., Erith, Kent, Eng., 1958-60; rsch. officer Atomic Energy of Can., Chalk River, Ont., 1963-67; with McGill U., Montreal, 1967—, prof., dept. mech. engring., 1976—, chmn., 1977-86, Thomas Workman prof., 1986—; cons. and rschr. in field. Editor Jour. Fluids and Structures; contbr. articles in field. Pres. Hellenic-Can. Solidarity Com. for Cyprus, 1974-80, Com. Pan-Can. de Solidarite pour Chypre, 1978-83; hon. consul gen. Republic of Cyprus, Montreal, 1983—. Recipient Brit. Assn. medal for high distinction in mech. engring., 1958, George Stephenson prize Inst. Mech. Engrs., 1976, commemorative medal for 125th ann. of Confederation of Can., 1993, medal Can. Congress Applied Mechs., 1995. Fellow Instn. of Mech. Engrs., ASME, Can. Soc. Mech. Engring., Royal Soc. Can., Am. Acad. Mechanics; mem. Internat. Assn. Hydraulic Rsch., Internat. Assn. Structural Mechanics in Reactor Tech., Order Engrs. Que. Home: 2930 Edouard Montpetit #PH2, Montreal, PQ Canada H3T 1J7 Office: 817 Ouest Rue Sherbrooke, Montreal, PQ Canada H3A 2K6

PAIER, ADOLF ARTHUR, computer software and services company executive; b. Branford, Conn., Oct. 27, 1938; s. Adolf Arthur and Margaret Mary (Almond) P.; m. Geraldine Shnakis, Sept. 17, 1966; children: Nathaniel Jason, Andrew Joseph, Alena Catherine. AA, Quinnipiac Coll., 1958; BS in Econs., U. Pa., 1960. Audit mgr. Touche Ross & Co., Phila., 1960-67; pres., dir. Safeguard Scientifics, Inc., Wayne, Pa., 1967-92; chmn., CEO, pres. Healthworks Alliance, Inc., Wayne, Pa., 1992—; pres., CEO Novus Corp., Radnor, Pa., 1992—; bd. dirs. Deltapaper, Croydon, Pa. Bd. dirs. Univ. of Arts, Phila., Lincoln Ctr. Family and Youth, Bridgeport, Pa.; mem. adv. bd. Analytical Graphics, Inc., King of Prussia, Pa. Mem. AICPA, Chief Execs. Orgn., Phila. Pres. Orgn. Office: Novus Corp 5 Radnor Corp Ctr 100 Matsonford Rd Ste 105 Radnor PA 19087

PAIGE, ANITA PARKER, retired English language educator; b. Valparaiso, Ind., Feb. 5, 1908; d. Eugene Mark and Grace Agnes (Noon) Parker; m. Robert Myron Paige, Aug. 12, 1933 (dec. 1965); children: Susan Marlowe Paige Morrison, Amy Woods Paige Dunker, Caroline Parker Paige McClennan. AB, Vassar Coll., 1929; MA, U. Chgo., 1930, postgrad., 1931-32. Instr. English Hillsdale (Mich.) Coll., 1930-31, asst. prof., 1931-33; bd. edn. Anglo-Am. Schs., Athens, Greece, 1948-51; tchr. secondary sch. Am. Sch., Teheran, Iran, 1957-58; instr. English Republic of China Mil. Cartographic Sec. group, Taipei, Taiwan, 1960-61; instr. dept. English Nat. Taiwan U., Taipei, 1961-62; intermittent lectr., 1988—; bd. dirs. Ginling Girls Mid. Sch., Taipei, 1960-62. Bd. dirs. (Presbyn.) Cmty. Ch., Teheran, 1957-58. Mem. LWV (chmn. Cook County, Ill. child welfare dept. 1933-36, mem. bd. Overseas Edn. Fund 1966-68), Diplomatic and Consular Officers Ret., Assn. Am. Fgn. Svc. Women, Asian Am. Forum (founding mem.), Friends of Soochow U., Phi Beta Kappa. Democrat.

PAIGE, GLENN DURLAND, political scientist, educator; b. Brockton, Mass., June 28, 1929; s. Lester Norman and Rita Irene (Marshall) P.; m. Betty Gail Grenier, Jan. 2, 1949 (div.); children: Gail, Jan, Donn, Sean, Sharon, Van; m. Glenda Hatsuko Naito, Sept. 1, 1973. Grad., Phillips Exeter Acad., 1947; A.B., Princeton U., 1955; M.A., Harvard U., 1957; Ph. D., Northwestern U., 1959; PhD (hon.), Soka U., 1992. Asst. prof. pub. adminstrn. Seoul Nat. U., 1959-61; asst. to assoc. prof. politics Princeton U., 1961-67; prof. polit. sci. U. Hawaii, Honolulu, 1967-92, prof. emeritus, 1992—; cons. Fla. Martin Luther King, Jr., Inst. for Nonviolence, 1997. Author: The Korean Decision, 1968, The Scientific Study of Political Leadership, 1977, To Nonviolent Political Science, 1993; editor: Political Leadership, 1972, (with George Chaplin) Hawaii 2000, 1973, (with Sarah Gilliatt) Nonviolence in Hawaii's Spiritual Traditions, 1991, Buddhism and Nonviolent Global Problem-Solving, 1991, (of Petra K. Kelly) Nonviolence Speaks to Power, 1993, (with Chaiwat Satha-Anand) Islam and Nonviolence, 1993; social sci. editor: Biography, 1977—. Program chmn. Hawaii Gov.'s Conf. on Yr. 2000, 1970; leader U.S. Group 103, Amnesty Internat., 1977-78; cons. UN Univ., 1980-86; faculty UN Univ. Internat. Leadership Acad., 1997; coord. planning project Ctr. for Global Nonviolence, U. Hawaii Spark M. Matsunaga Inst. for Peace, 1988-95; pres. Non-profit Ctr. for Global Nonviolence, 1994—; mem. nat. adv. group Martin Luther King Jr. Inst. for Nonviolence, State of N.Y., 1989-90. With U.S. Army, 1948-52. Decorated Commendation medal; recipient Seikyo Culture prize, 1982, Dr. G. Ramachandran award for internat. understanding, 1986, Anuvrat award for internat. peace, 1987, Jai Tulsi Anuvrat award, 1995; named Woodrow Wilson nat. fellow, 1955-56, Princeton U. Class of 1955 award, 1987, 3rd Gandhi Meml. lectr., New Delhi, 1990, Disting. life fellow Delhi Sch. Nonviolence,

1992. Mem. Internat. Peace Rsch. Assn. (co-convenor nonviolence study group 1989-91), Internat. Polit. Sci. Assn., World Future Studies Fedn., Phi Beta Kappa. Home: 3653 Tantalus Dr Honolulu HI 96822-5033 *Political science is a science that can liberate humankind from violence. To do so, it must first liberate itself. This will require five related transformations: normative, empirical, theoretical, institutional, and educational. The tasks of political scientists at the end of the 20th century are to begin these transformations. Twenty-first century successors must carry them forward, consolidate them, and extend their influence throughout global society.*

PAIGE, HILLIARD WEGNER, corporate director, consultant; b. Hartford, Conn., Oct. 2, 1919; s. Joseph Wegner and Ruth (Hill) P.; m. Dorothea Magner, Dec. 8, 1945; children: Elizabeth, Deborah, Hilliard, Jr. BSME, Worcester Poly. Inst., 1941, D Engring. (hon), 1971. Sr. v.p. for aerospace and computer ops. Gen. Electric, N.Y.C., 1941-71; pres. Gen. Dynamics, St. Louis, 1971-73; chmn., chief exec. officer Satellite Bus. Systems, Inc., Washington, 1973-76; vice chmn. bd. Internat. Energy Assocs., Ltd., Washington, 1976-85; chmn. bd. H.A. Knott, Ltd., Silver Spring, Md., 1984-89; dir. The Atlantic Coun. of U.S., 1987—, Computer Data Systems, Inc., Videoconferencing Systems, Inc., Gallager Marine Systems, Inc. Patentee in field; contbr. articles to profl. jours. Mem. Def. Sci. Bd. U.S. Dept. Def., Washington, 1973-78; trustee Worcester Poly. Inst., Mass., 1974—. Recipient Pub. Service award NASA, 1969, Order of Merit Italy, 1970, Engr. of Year award Greater Phila. Engring Council, 1960. Fellow AIAA, Explorers Club (nat.); mem. Nat. Acad. Engring. Republican. Congregationalist. Clubs: Metropolitan, Chevy Chase (Washington); Conquistadores del Cielo. Avocations: skiing, tennis, scuba diving, golf. Home: 905 Boca Raton Rd Boca Raton FL 33432 Office: 5163 Tilden St NW Washington DC 20016-1961

PAIGE, JEFFERY MAYLAND, sociologist, educator; b. Providence, June 15, 1942; s. Charles Warren and Dorothy Frances (Rice) P.; m. Karen Ericksen, Apr. 30, 1966 (div. 1980). AB summa cum laude, Harvard U., 1964; PhD, U. Mich., 1968. Asst. prof. U. Calif., Berkeley, 1968-76; assoc. prof. U. Mich., Ann Arbor, 1976-82, prof., 1982—, dir. ctr. for rsch. on social orgn., 1992—; vis. lectr. U. Ctrl. Am., San Salvador, El Salvador, 1990, Fla. Internat. U., Miami, 1992; internat. observer Nicaraguan Nat. Adv. Commn. on Atlantic Coast, Managua, 1986. Author: Agrarian Revolution, 1975 (Sorokin award 1976), Coffee and Power, 1997; co-author: The Politics of Reproductive Ritual, 1981. Fulbright fellow, 1990, Kellog fellow, 1991; rsch. grantee NSF, 1990-92. Mem. Am. Sociol. Assn. (coun. chair polit. econ. of world sys. sect. 1987-89), Latin Am. Studies Assn., Sociol. Rsch. Assn. Democrat. Avocations: hiking, Nordic and alpine skiing, sailing. Office: U Mich Dept Sociology Ann Arbor MI 48109

PAIGE, NORMA, lawyer, corporate executive; b. Lomza, Poland, Oct. 11, 1922; came to U.S., 1927; d. Morris and Edith (Kachourek) Zelaso; children: Holly Paige Russek, Madelyn Paige Givant. BA, NYU, 1944, JD, 1946; postgrad. in bus. adminstrn., CCNY, 1953, NYU, 1969. Bar: N.Y. 1946, U.S. Supreme Ct. 1951. Ptnr. Paige and Paige, N.Y.C., 1948—; v.p., bd. dirs. Astronautics Corp. Am., Milw., 1959—, chmn. bd., 1984—; exec. v.p., bd. dirs. Kearfott Guidance & Navigation Corp., Wayne, N.J., 1988—; bd. dirs. Astronautics C.A., Ltd., Israel. Recipient Jabotinsky Centennial medal Prime Minister of Israel, 1980, Tribute to Women in Indsl. Industry Twin II award YWCA, 1981, NYU Sch. Law Outstanding Alumnus of Yr. award, 1991, Judge Edward Weinfeld award, 1996. Mem. N.Y. Women's Bar Assn. (pres. 1958-59). Office: Astronautics Corp Am 4115 N Teutonia Ave Milwaukee WI 53209-6731

PAIGE, SUSANNE LYNN, financial consultant; b. Bklyn., Feb. 25, 1950; d. Abraham and Florence Roslyn (Rosenfeld) P.; divorced. BA cum laude, C.W. Post Coll., 1972, postgrad., 1975. Lic. mortgage broker, N.Y. Buyer B. Gertz and Sons, Inc., Jamaica, N.Y., 1973-76; nat. field sales mgr. LeVison Care Products, Inc., New City, N.Y., 1976-82, Am. Vitamin Products, Inc., Lakewood, N.J., 1984-85; prin. Paige & Assocs., Scarsdale, 1982-87; loan officer and fin. cons. Bayside Fed. Savs. and Loan, Jericho, N.Y., 1987-88; prin. Paige Capital Enterprises, Inc., Rye, N.Y., 1988—; mem. Comml. Investment Divsn./Westchester Bd. Realtors, White Plains, N.Y.; pub. spkr. and lectr. in field. Author: Closing the Deal in Today's Volatile Market, 1994; satarist/polit. cartoonist C.W. Post Coll. News and Editorial, Brookville, N.Y., 1968-72; contbr. articles to profl. jours. Recipient award for Best Original Essay, Newsday Harry F. Guggenheim award, Garden City, N.Y., 1967, Hon. Mention award C.W. Post Coll. Gallery, 1982, Hon. Mention (sculpture) Fresh Meadows (N.Y.) Merchant's Assn., 1971, meritorious notation Real Estate Weekly, 1991-93; selected as Comml. Deal-Maker of Yr., N.Y. Real Estate Jour., 1992, Real Estate Personality, 1993, Northeast Fin. Work-Out Specialist N.Y. and New Eng. Real Estate Jours., 1990-93, also meritorious notation, 1990-93. Mem. Alumni Assn. C.W. Post Coll., 60's East Realty Club, Westchester Bd. Realtors, White Plains, N.Y., Assn. Commercial Real Estate. Avocations: speaker for fin. seminars, writer, traveling. Office: Paige Capital Enterprises Inc PO Box 1234 Scarsdale NY 10583-9234

PAIGEN, KENNETH, geneticist, research director; b. N.Y.C., Nov. 14, 1927; s. Alexander and Ida (Kantor) P.; m. Beverly Vandermolen, June 14, 1970; children: Susan, Gina, Mark, David, Jennifer. A.B., Johns Hopkins U., Balt., 1946; Ph.D., Calif. Inst. Tech., Pasadena, 1950. Staff mem. Roswell Park Meml. Inst., Buffalo, 1955-72, dept. head, 1972-82; prof. dept. genetics U. Calif., Berkeley, 1982-89; dir., sr. staff scientist Jackson Lab., Bar Harbor, Maine, 1989—. Mem. AAAS, Am. Assn. for Cancer Rsch., Internat. Mammalian Genome Soc., Human Genome Orgn., Genetics Soc. Am., Am. Soc. for Biochemistry and Molecular Biology, Sigma Xi, Phi Beta Kappa. Democrat. Jewish. Avocation: sailing. Home: Old Farm Rd Bar Harbor ME 04609 Office: Jackson Lab 600 Main St Bar Harbor ME 04609-1523

PAIK, JOHN KEE, structural engineer; b. Seoul; came to U.S., 1955; s. Nam Suk and Kyong Ock (Yun) P.; m. Aine Fenoula Ievers, Feb. 20, 1970; 1 child, Brian Ievers Paik. BSCE, So. Meth. U., 1961; PhD, NYU, 1975. Lic. profl. engr. N.Y., N.J., Conn., Pa., Md., Mass., Vt., Ga., Fla., N.C. Chief engr. T.Y. Lin and Assocs., N.Y.C., 1960-67; chief structural engr. Soros Assocs., N.Y.C., 1967-68; sr. project engr. Stauffer Chem. Co., Dobbs Ferry, N.Y., 1975-77; prin., founder Paik and Assocs., Westchester County, N.Y., 1977—; chmn., founder The Future Home Tech. Inc., Port Jervis, N.Y., 1986—; chmn., pres. J.K.P. Constrn. Co. Inc., Mohegan Lake, N.Y., 1989—; adj. assoc. prof. Grad. Sch. Engring. Manhattan Coll., Bronx, 1985; lectr. Grad. Sch. Engring. Polytech. U., Bklyn., 1973-85, Cooper Union, N.Y.C., 1972. Mem. ASCE, NSPE, Am. Inst. Steel Constrn., Prestressed Concrete Inst., N.Y Acad. Scis., Am. Concrete Inst., Post Tensioning Inst., Constrn. Specifications Inst., Am. Arbitration Assn. (dispute arbitrator, constrn.), So. Meth. U. Alumni Club (pres. 1964), Chi Epsilon. Republican. Methodist. Achievements include the design of over 100 million sq. feet of comml., residential, indsl. and instnl. structures including several highrise bldgs. over 40 stories in N.Y.C. Home: Dyckman Dr Mohegan Lake NY 10547 Office: Paik and Assocs 115 E Stevens Ave Valhalla NY 10595-1252

PAIKOWSKY, SANDRA ROSLYN, art historian; b. St. John, N.B., Can., Dec. 29, 1945; d. Morton Ernest and Bessie Frances (Rabkin) P.; m. John Richard Fox, Dec. 11, 1982. B.A., Sir George Williams U., Montreal, Que., Can., 1967; M.A., U. Toronto, 1969. Curatorial asst. Royal Ont. Mus., Toronto, 1967-68; prof. art history Concordia U., Montreal, 1969—; curator Concordia Art Gallery, Montreal, 1981-92; Editor, publisher Jour. Can. Art History, 1972—; author exhbn. catalogues. Co-editor. Jour. Can. Art History, 1972-91, co-pub., 1981-91, editor, pub., 1991—; author exhbn. catalogues. Mem. Can. Mus. Assn., Univ. Art Assn. Can. Office: Coincordia U Fine Arts CB 204-4, 1455 de Maisonneuve Blvd W, Montreal, PQ Canada H3G 1M8

PAIN, BETSY M., lawyer; b. Albertville, Ala., Aug. 29, 1950; d. Charles Riley and Jean Faye (Rains) Stone; m. William F. Pain, Nov. 18, 1977; children: Taylor Holland, Emily Anne Pain. AA, Northeastern Okla. A&M, Miami, Okla., 1970; BA, U. Okla., 1974, JD, 1976. Bar: Okla. 1977; U.S. Dist. Ct. (we. dist.) 1979. Staff atty. Okla. Dept. Corrections, Oklahoma City, 1978-79; gen. counsel Okla. Pardon and Parole Bd., Oklahoma City, 1979-84, exec. dir., 1984-88; corp. counsel Roberts, Schornick & Assocs., Inc., Norman, Okla., 1990—. Editor: (newsletter) RSA Environmental Report, 1991—. With extended family program Juvenile Svcs., Inc. Cleveland County, Okla., 1983-91. Mem. Okla. Bar Assn. (environ. law sect. 1977—), Am. Corp. Counsel Assn. Democrat. Methodist. Avocations: reading, needlework, church activities. Office: Roberts Schornick & Assoc Inc 3700 W Robinson St Ste 200 Norman OK 73072-3639

PAIN, CHARLES LESLIE, lawyer; b. Austin, Tex., Apr. 26, 1913; s. William Francis and Ruby (Gates) P.; m. Roberta Wilmoth, Mar. 27, 1942; children—Charles Laurence, William Francis, Glenn David. B.A., LL.B., U. Okla., 1935. Bar: Okla. 1935. Asst. atty. Southwestern Light & Power Co., 1935-40; practice in Anadarko, 1956—; partner Pain & Garland, 1956—; Exec. sec. to Congressman Toby Morris, 1951-53; Mem. Okla. Bd. Bar Examiners, 1969-78. Pres. Black Beaver council Boy Scouts Am., 1971-72; bd. dirs. Okla. Baptist Found., Inc., 1984-85, vice chmn., 1985-87. Served with AUS, 1940-46; col. Res. (Ret.). Recipient Silver Beaver award Boy Scouts Am. Mem. Am., Okla., Caddo County bar assns., Am. Legion, Res. Officers Assn., Order of Coif, Phi Beta Kappa, Phi Eta Sigma, Phi Alpha Delta, Sigma Chi. Democrat. Baptist. Club: Lion (past dist. gov.). Office: 111 SW 2nd St Anadarko OK 73005-3401

PAINE, DAVID M., public relations executive; b. N.Y.C., Sept. 25, 1956. BA in Polit. Sci., Union Coll., 1979. Press advanceman The White House, Washington, 1980; with N.Y. State Assembly Judiciary Com.; acct. exec. Burson-Marsteller, N.Y.C.; founder, pres. Paine & Assocs., Costa Mesa, Calif., 1986—. Mem. Pub. Rels. Soc. Am. Office: Paine & Assocs 535 Anton Blvd Ste 450 Costa Mesa CA 92626-1977

PAINE, JAMES CARRIGER, federal judge; b. Valdosta, Ga., May 20, 1924; s. Leon Alexander and Josie Carriger (Jones) P.; m. Ruth Ellen Bailey, Sept. 8, 1950; children: James Carriger, Jonathan Jones, JoEllen. B.S., Columbia U., 1947; LL.B., U. Va., 1950, J.D., 1970. Bar: Fla. 1950. Mem. firm Earnest, Lewis, Smith & Jones, West Palm Beach, Fla., 1950-54, Jones Adams Paine & Foster, 1954-60, Jones Paine & Foster, 1960-79; judge U.S. Dist. Ct. (so. dist.) Fla., West Palm Beach, 1979—. Bd. dirs., pres. Children's Home Soc. Fla., 1978-80; mem. bd. Episcopal Diocese S.E. Fla. Served to lt. USNR, 1943-47. Mem. Greater West Palm Beach C. of C. (pres. 1973-74), Palm Beach County Bar Assn. Democrat. Office: US Dist Ct 701 Clematis St West Palm Beach FL 33401-5101

PAINE, ROBERT EDWARD, JR., internist; b. Roanoke, Va., Apr. 27, 1925; s. Robert Edward and Edith Emily (Davis) P.; m. Alice Frances Parson, May 1, 1946; children: Emily Anne, Robert Parson. Student, U. Richmond, 1942-43; MD, Med. Coll. Va., 1947. Lic. Va. Intern, asst. resident Norfolk (Va.) Gen. Hosp., 1947-49; resident Lewis Gale Hosp., Roanoke, 1949-51, 53; pvt. practice Salem, Va., 1953-68; med. officer, alcohol rehab. staff Vets. Care Ctr., Salem, 1968-80. Lt. USN, 1943-45, WWII, 1951-53, Korea. Decorated Mil. Order World Wars; named Father of Yr. Roanoke Valley, 1982; recipient Red Cross Svc. award Roanoke Red Cross chpt., 1992, Outstanding Svc. award Boy Scouts Am. Troop 54, 1967. Mem. Island Ford Hunt Club, Lakeland Masonic Lodge, Roanoke Scottish Rite Bodies, Kazim Temple Shrine, Mayflower Soc. (Va. state surgeon), Kappa Sigma (50 year plaque). Presbyterian. Avocations: tennis, hunting, fishing, travel, history museum.

PAINE, RUTH M., medical insurance company administrator; b. Washington; d. Hibbard A. and Ruth B. (Burrell) P.; m. Gerald R. Abbott, Dec. 5, 1981. BA, Am. U., 1974; MA, U. Northern Colo., 1975. Dir. emergency svcs. Guidance Ctr. of Camden County, Inc., 1982-83; adminstr. Biomed. Applications, Inc., 1983-85; sales mgr. Blue Cross & Blue Shield of N.J., 1985-86; from sales mgr. to gen. mgr. Delaware Valley HMO Independence Blue Cross, Phila., 1986-90; v.p. mktg. HealthInk, 1990-93; v.p. managed care Bay Life Svcs. Helix Health Sys., 1993-95; from dir. provider rels. to v.p. Mid-Atlantic ops. Prudential Health Care Plan Mid-Atlantic, 1995—. Home: 11913 Yellow Rush Pass Columbia MD 21044 Office: Prudential HealthCare 2800 N Charles St Baltimore MD 21218-4026

PAINTER, DIANA JEAN, urban designer, consultant; b. Seattle, Dec. 29, 1953; d. Robert Cook and Nancy Marie (Chivers) P.; m. John Hazen McKean, Aug. 10, 1973 (div. Feb. 1975). BA, Western Wash. U., 1977; MUP, U. Wash., 1984; postgrad., U. Pa., 1987; PhD, Sheffield U., England, 1990. Cert. planner. Designer Cope Linder Assn., Phila., 1987-88, Dagit-Saylor Architects, Phila., 1988; urban designer WRT, Phila., 1989; designer Edwin Schlossberg Inc., N.Y.C., 1989-90; urban designer The SWA Group, Laguna Beach, Calif., 1990-91; assoc. planner City of Tukwila, Wash., 1993—; cons. Diana J. Painter Archtl. & Cmty. History, Seattle, 1982—; instr. U. Wash., Seattle, 1986. Contbr. articles to profl. jours.; presenter in field. Mem. Allied Arts of Seattle Downtown Com., 1984-85; bd. dirs. Greystone Found., Pullman, Wash., 1992-93. Fellow Northwest Inst. Architecture & Urban Studies in Italy; mem. Am. Inst. Cert. Planners, Am. Assn. Planning (head mentoring program 1995—, vice-chmn. urban design divsn.), Am. Inst. Architects L.A. (mem. urban design com. 1990-91). Avocations: painting, rowing. Studio: 712 N 34th St Ste 205 Seattle WA 98103-8867

PAINTER, JACK TIMBERLAKE, civil engineer; b. Kincaid, W.Va., July 23, 1930; s. Troy Earl and Nannie Bell (Proffit) P. BSCE, W.Va. U., 1950, MSCE, 1955. Instr. civil engring. W.Va. U., 1950-51, 53-55; mem. faculty La. Tech U., Ruston, 1955—; prof. civil engring. La. Tech U., 1962-92, prof. emeritus, 1992—; Alumni Found. prof. La. Tech U., 1977-78; vis. lectr. Manhattan Coll., Coll. Forestry, SUNY, Syracuse, Cornell U., U. Wis., summers 1954-60. Nat. pres. Circus Fans Assn. Am., 1967; lic. layreader Episcopal Ch. Served with USNR, 1951-52. Faculty fellow NSF, 1958-59; named Man of Year Omicron Delta Kappa, 1972. Fellow ASCE (life); mem. Am. Congress Surveying and Mapping, La. Engring. Soc. (Charles M. Kerr Pub. Rels. award 1990), Am. Soc. Engring. Edn., Tau Beta Pi (outstanding Prof. award 1963, 68, 74, 78), Chi Epsilon (Excellent Tchg. award 19 85). Address: 1303 Hodges Ave Ruston LA 71270-5507

PAINTER, JOHN HOYT, electrical engineer; b. Winfield, Kans., Mar. 27, 1934; s. John Paul and Marjorie Marietta (Slack) P.; m. Joy Lou Vaughan, June 7, 1955; children—John Mark, Paul Burton, William Vaughan, Joy Lynn. B.S., U. Ill., Urbana, 1961; Gen. Electric Found. fellow, M.S., 1962; Ph.D., So. Meth. U., 1972; postgrad., Coll. William and Mary, 1967-69. Apollo comm. engr., tchr. astronauts NASA Manned Spacecraft Center, Houston, 1962-65; sr. engr. Motorola Govt. Electronics div., Scottsdale, Ariz., 1965-67; research engr. NASA Langley Research Center, Hampton, Va., 1967-74; asso. prof., elec. engring. Tex. A&M U., College Station, 1974-79, prof., 1979—; pres. ALTAIR Corps. cons., College Station, 1980—; tchr. Christian eschatology seminars. Served with USAF, 1953-58. Recipient Recognition cert. NASA, 1975. Mem. IEEE (sr.). Patentee digital communications processing. Home: 1119 Merry Oaks Dr College Station TX 77840-2606 Office: Tex A&M U Dept Elec Engring College Station TX 77843 *No matter how big one's thinking, there is always a concept bigger. Realizing that God is the ultimate upper bound brings relief from mental striving.*

PAINTER, LINDA ROBINSON, physics educator, dean; b. Lexington, Ky., May 4, 1940; d. J. Kenneth and Juanita Marie (Crosier) R.; m. Roy Allen Painter, May 6, 1967; children: Holly Suzanne, Brent Allen. BS in Physics, U. Louisville, 1962; MS in Physics, U. Tenn., 1963, PhD in Physics, 1968. Asst. prof. physics U. Tenn., Knoxville, 1968-75, assoc. prof. physics, 1975-82, prof. physics, 1982—, asst. dean, Grad. Sch., 1985-88; assoc. dean, 1988—; cons. Health Physics Div., Oak Ridge (Tenn.) Nat. Lab., 1967-77; adj. rsch. and devel. participant, Health and Safety Rsch. Div., Oak Ridge Nat. Lab., 1977-83, part-time employee, 1983-89; bd. dirs. Consultec Scientific, Inc. Contbr. numerous articles to profl. jours. Named Outstanding Young Woman of the Yr., Tenn., Outstanding Young Women of Am., 1974; recipient grants, U.S. Atomic Energy Commn., U.S. Energy Rsch. and Devel. Agy., U.S. Dept. Energy, 1968-89. Fellow Am. Phys. Soc.; mem. Tenn. Conf. Grad. Schs. (pres. 1990-91, editor 1985—), Radiation Rsch. Soc. (assoc. editor 1984-88), Coun. So. Grad. Schs. (publs. com. 1988-90, com. issues and planning 1991-96, exec. com. 1994-97). Baptist. Home: 7708 Devonshire Dr Knoxville TN 37919-8019

PAINTER, MARY E. (MARY PAINTER YARBROUGH), editor; b. Tulsa, July 15, 1920; d. Ernest Balf Parker and Maggie Mae (Renaud) P.; BA, Oklahoma City U., 1943; postgrad. Columbia U., 1944; m. Charles J. Yarbrough, Apr. 7, 1946; children: Kirby John, Kevin Lee. Editorial asst., feature writer Office War Info., 1943-46; feature writer, news editor Dept. State, 1946-53; with USIA, Washington, 1953-78, editor USIA World, 1967-78; with U.S. Internat. Communication Agy., 1978-80, editor USICA World, 1978-80; with Food Policy Center, Washington, 1981-84, World Hunger Yr., N.Y.C., 1981—; mng. editor Food Policy Center News/Views, 1981-84; assoc. editor Food Monitor, 1981-83, editor, 1986-88; editor WHY Mag., 1989-97. Editor USIAAA Newsletter, Washington, 1980-88, Reston (Va.) Interfaith Newsletter, 1982-90. Recipient Meritorious Service award USIA, 1964, Spl. Commendation, 1974; Dir.'s award for Outstanding Creativity, U.S. Internat. Communication Agy., 1980. Mem. NOW, ACLU, Women's Action Orgn., Assn. Am. Fgn. Svc. Women, Am. Fgn. Svc. Assn. Democrat. Baptist. Home: 12232 Quorn Ln Reston VA 20191-2635 Office: World Hunger Yr 505 8th Ave Rm 21 New York NY 10018-6505

PAINTER, PAUL WAIN, JR., lawyer; b. Cleveland, Tenn., Aug. 10, 1945; s. Paul Wain and Juanita (Davis) P.; m. Judith Ann Babine, Aug. 28, 1971; 1 child, Paul Wain III. BS, Ga. Tech., 1968; JD, U. Ga., 1974. Bar: Ga. 1974, U.S. Dist. Ct. (so. dist.) Ga., U.S. Ct. Appeals (11th cir.). Assoc. Bouhan, Williams & Levy, Savannah, Ga., 1974-79; ptnr. Karsman, Brooks, Painter & Callaway, Savannah, 1979-88, Ellis, Painter, Ratterree & Bart, Savannah, 1988—; faculty mem. Nat. Inst. Trial Advocacy, Emory U. Sch. Law, 1982-90; mem. com. on lawyer qualifications and conduct U.S. Ct. Appeals for 11th Cir., 1995—; mem. ct. adv. com. U.S. Dist. Ct. (so. dist.) Ga., 1992—; mem. Gov.'s Adv. Com. on Tort Reform, Atlanta, 1986. Trustee Ga. Inst. Continuing Legal Edn., Athens, 1992-95; pres. Savannah Arthritis Found., 1982-83; bd. dirs. Ga. Arthritis Found., Atlanta, 1983; grad. Leadership Savannah, 1986-88. Lt. (j.g.) USN, 1968-71. Fellow Am. Coll. Trial Lawyers; mem. ABA, State Bar Ga. (chair trial sect. 1992-93), Def. Rsch. Inst. (Ga. state chmn. 1988-91), Savannah Bar Assn. (pres. 93), Ga. Def. Lawyers Assn. (pres. 1986-87). Avocations: reading history and fiction, hunting, fishing. Office: Ellis Painter Ratterree Bart PO Box 9946 Savannah GA 31412-0146

PAINTER, ROBERT LOWELL, surgeon, educator; b. Winchester, Ind., Jan. 13, 1934; s. Lowell Walter and Lillian Genevieve (Pierson) P.; m. Esther Lillian Reece, Sept. 21, 1957 (div. Sept. 1977); children: Elizabeth Hains, Bradley, Robert R., Andrew, Jane Macy; m. Nancy Sue Macy, Feb. 10, 1980. BA, Earham Coll., Richmond, Ind., 1955; MD, Ind. U., 1959. Intern Hartford (Conn.) Hosp., 1959-65; resident Baylor U. Sch. Medicine, Houston, 1967-68; attending surgeon Day Kimball Hosp., Putnam, Conn., 1962-69; chmn., dir. surgery St. Francis Hosp., Hartford, 1991—; cons. Hartford Hosp., 1969—; assoc. prof. surgery U. Conn., 1991—. Capt. USAF, 1965-67. Fellow ACS, Am. Coll. Physician Execs.; mem. New Eng. Surg. Soc., New Eng. Vasc. Soc., Soc. Thoracic Surgery. Republican. Avocations: hiking, gardening, saxaphone. Office: Saint Francis Hosp Med Ctr 114 Woodland St Hartford CT 06105-1200

PAINTER, RUTH ROBBINS, retired environmental biochemist; b. Bethel, Conn., July 21, 1910; d. Bradford Hilton and Clara Mae (Davis) Robbins; m. Edgar Page Painter, July 4, 1940; children: Jane Painter Clapp, Page Robbins Painter. BS, U. Hawaii, 1931, MS, 1934. Cert. nutrition specialist. Nutrition investigator U. Hawaii, Honolulu, 1931-36; assoc. chemist USDA Bur. Home Econs., Washington, 1937; nutrition chemist Wash. State U., Pullman, 1937-40; asst. chemist agrl. toxicology pesticide residue rsch. U. Calif., Davis, 1960-66; assoc. specialist Environ. Toxicology, U. Calif., Davis, 1967-73, specialist, 1973-76; cons. Nutrition and Food Toxicology, Davis, 1940-60. Contbr. articles to profl. jours. and books. Pres. PTA Coun., Davis, 1959-60; chmn. UN Assn. Davis, 1963-65, chmn. Yolo County, Calif. chpt. ARC, 1988. Recipient Clara Barton medal Yolo County, Calif. ARC, U. Hawaii Gold medal, 1931. Mem. Am. Chem. Soc. (ret.), Inst. Food Technologists (profl.), Entomological Soc. Am. (emeritus, chmn. Yr. publs. 1973-75), Sigma Xi, Phi Kappa Phi. Home: 815 Miller Dr Davis CA 95616-3622

PAINTER, THEOPHILUS SHICKEL, JR., physician; b. Austin, Tex., Apr. 29, 1924; s. Theophilus Shickel and Anna Mary (Thomas) P.; m. Dorothy Bulkley, July 11, 1957; children: Dana Parkey, Amy Hur, Theophilus III. BA, U. Tex., 1944, MD, 1947. Diplomate Am. Bd. Internal Medicine, Am. Bd. Allergy and Immunology. Rotating intern Univ. Hosp., U. Mich., Ann Arbor, 1947-48, resident in internal medicine, 1948-51, fellow, jr. clin. instr., 1956-58; pvt. practice Austin, Tex., 1958-65; physician Allergy Assocs., Austin, 1965-87, Allergy Assocs. of Austin Diagnostic Clinic, Austin, 1987—. Capt. USAF, 1951-53. Fellow ACP, Am. Coll. Allergy and Immunology, Am. Acad. Allergy and Immunology. Avocations: fishing, carving, hunting, painting. Home: 3222 Tarry Hollow Dr Austin TX 78703-3026 Office: Allergy Assocs Austin Diagnostic Clinic 1510 W 34th St Austin TX 78703-1433

PAINTER, WILLIAM HALL, law educator; b. Pitts., May 2, 1927; s. John Littleton Dawson and Eleanor Cramer (Hall); m. Marion Symmes Homer, July 9, 1955; children: Richard William, Edward Homer. A.B., Princeton U., 1950; J.D., Harvard U., 1954. Bar: N.Y. 1955. Assoc. Debevoise, Plimpton & McLean, N.Y.C., 1954-58; teaching fellow Harvard U.Law Sch., Cambridge, Mass., 1958-59; prof. Villanova U. Law Sch., Phila., 1959-65; vis. prof. U. Mich. Law Sch., Ann Arbor, 1965; prof. U. Mo., Kansas City, 1965-71; spl. counsel, dir. study securities industry U.S. Ho. Reps., Washington, 1971-72; prof. U. Ill. Coll. Law, Champaign, 1972-81, Albert E. Jenner Jr. prof., 1981-87; Theodore Rinehart prof. law George Washington U., Washington, 1987—. Author: Federal Regulation of Insider Trading, 1968, Corporate and Tax Aspects of Closely Held Corporations, 1971, 2d edit., 1981, Problems and Materials in Business Planning, 1975, 3d edit., 1994, The Federal Securities Code and Corporate Disclosure, 1979, Painter on Close Corporations, 1991; contbr. articles to legal pubs. Mem. Ill. Bus. Corp. Act Revision Com., 1981-83. Mem. ABA (fed. securities commn. sect. corp., banking and bus. law, chmn. subcom. on legis. 1974-81), Assn. Am. Law Schs. (chmn. sect. bus. assn. 1976), Am. Law Inst., Phi Beta Kappa. Home: 6652 32nd St NW Washington DC 20015-2310 Office: George Washington U Nat Law Ctr 720 20th St NW Washington DC 20006-4306

PAINTON, IRA WAYNE, retired securities executive; b. Longdale, Okla., Nov. 3, 1917; s. Ira W. and Leatha (Ball) P.; m. Jane Tiffin, Apr. 9, 1941; children: Ann Painton Anderson, Scott W. A.B., Northwestern State U., Okla., 1940; postgrad., So. Meth. U., 1953. C.L.U. Mng. ptnr. Waynoka Motor Co., Okla., 1946-50; br. mgr. Am. Nat. Ins. Co., Omaha, 1953-57; dir. tng. Pacific Mut. Life Ins. Co., Los Angeles, 1957-61; dir. recruiting and tng. Fin. Programs, Inc., Denver, 1962-66; v.p. Securities Mgmt. & Research, Inc., Galveston, Tex., 1967; pres. Securities Mgmt. & Research, Inc., 1967-83; pres., dir. Am. Nat. Growth, Income and Bond Funds. Served to capt. Signal Corps, AUS, 1940-46, 50-52, Korea. Decorated Bronze Star. Mem. Am. Assn. CLUs, Northwestern Okla. State U. Alumni Assn. (Outstanding Bus./Profl. award 1992, chmn. foun. bd. 1993—). Home: 12004 Dahoon Dr Oklahoma City OK 73120-8131 *I believe real success, like beauty, is in the mind of the beholder. And as long as we persist in trying there can be no final failure, since success is usually a series of failures that turn out all right.*

PAINTON, RUSSELL ELLIOTT, lawyer, mechanical engineer; b. Port Arthur, Tex., Dec. 5, 1940; s. Clifford Elliott and Edith Virginia (McCutcheon) P.; m. Elizabeth Ann Mullins, July 2, 1965 (div. Dec. 1977); 1 child, Todd Elliott; m. Mary Lynn Weber, May 9, 1981. BS in Mech. Engring., U. Tex.-Austin, 1963, JD, 1972. Bar: Tex. 1972; registered profl. engr., Tex. Engr. Gulf States Utilities, Beaumont, Tex., 1963-66; engr. Tracor, Inc., Austin, Tex., 1966-70, corp. counsel, 1973-83, v.p., gen. counsel, 1983—, corp. sec., 1991—; atty. Brown, Maroney, Rose, Baker & Barber, Austin, 1972-73, Childs, Fortenbach, Beck & Guyton, Houston, 1973; corp. sec. Westmark Systems, Inc., Austin, 1990-91. Gen. counsel Paramount Theatre for Performing Arts, 1977-83, 2d vice chmn., 1978-80, 1st vice chmn., 1980-82, chmn. bd., 1982-84, retiring chmn., 1984-85; mem. Centex chpt. ARC; mem. adv. bd. Austin Sci. Acad., 1985-88, 93—; mem. adv. coun. Austin Transp., 1985-88; bd. dirs. Tex. Industries for the Blind and Handicapped, 1988-95, vice chmn., 1990-91. Named Boss of Yr. Austin Legal Secs. Assn., 1981. Mem. ABA, Tex. Bar Assn. (treas. corp. counsel sect. 1982-83), Travis County Bar Assn., Nat. Chamber Litigation Ctr., Better Bus. Bur. (arbitrator 1983—), Am. Electronics Assn. (chmn. Austin coun. 1985-86), Austin Yacht Club (race comdr. 1968-69, treas. 1970-71, sec. 1972, 75, vice commodore

1980, commodore 1981, fleet comdr. 1986), Order Blue Gavel, Houston Yacht Club, Delta Theta Phi. Republican. Episcopalian. Office: Tracor Inc 6500 Tracor Ln Austin TX 78725-2151

PAIS, ABRAHAM, physicist, educator; b. Amsterdam, Holland, May 19, 1918; s. Jesaja and Kaatje (van Kleeff) P.; m. Lila Atwill, Dec. 15, 1956 (div. 1962); 1 child, Joshua; m. Agnes Ida Benedicte Nicolaisen, Mar. 15, 1990. B.Sc., U. Amsterdam, 1938; M.Sc., U. Utrecht, 1940, Ph.D., 1941. Research fellow Inst. Theoretical Physics, Copenhagen, Denmark, 1946; prof. Inst. Advanced Study, Princeton, N.J., 1950-63; prof. physics Rockefeller U., N.Y.C., 1963-81, Detlev Bronk prof., 1981—, prof. emeritus, 1988—; Balfour prof. Weizmann Inst., Israel, 1977. Author: Subtle is the Lord (Am. Book award 1983, Am. Inst. Physics award 1983), Inward Bound, 1986, Niels Bohr's Times, 1991, Einstein Lived Here, 1994, A Tale of Two Continents, 1997. Decorated officer Order of Oranje Nassau (The Netherlands); recipient J.R. Oppenheimer Meml. prize, 1979, Physica prize The Netherlands, 1992, Gemant award Am. Inst. Physics, 1993, Lewis Thomas prize, 1995; Guggenheim fellow, 1960. Fellow Am. Phys. Soc.; mem. Royal Acad. Scis. Holland (corr., medal of sci. 1993), Royal Acad. Scis. and Letters, Denmark, Am. Acad. Arts and Scis., Am. Philos. Soc., Nat. Acad. Scis., Council on Fgn. Relations. Home: 1161 York Ave New York NY 10021-7940 Office: Rockefeller Univ Dept of Physics New York NY 10021

PAISLEY, KEITH WATKINS, state senator, small business owner; b. Mpls., Dec. 29, 1928; s. Manley G. and Maxine Alice (Watkins) P.; m. Jean Clare Robson, Sept. 23, 1950; children: Mark, Susan, Julie, Jeanne. BA, Hamline U., 1950. Rep. State of S.D., Pierre, 1981-84, senator, 1985—; owner Robson Hardware, Sioux Falls, S.D., 1972-93. Lutheran. Home: 2409 S Elmwood Ave Sioux Falls SD 57105-3315 Office: Robson Hardware 2322 W 12th St Sioux Falls SD 57104-3811

PAJAK, DAVID JOSEPH, lawyer, consultant; b. Buffalo, N.Y., June 19, 1956; s. William H. and Theresa A. (Granato) P.; m. Peggy J. Fisher, Aug. 1, 1981; children: Andrew J., Karl W. BA, State Coll. Buffalo, 1978; JD, U. Buffalo, 1982. Bar: N.Y. 1983, U.S. Dist. Ct. (we. dist.) N.Y., 1991. Social svcs. counsel Genesee County Dept. Social Svcs., Batavia, N.Y., 1984-93; pvt. practice Corfu, N.Y., 1983—, Buffalo, N.Y., 1993—; town justice Town of Pembroke, N.Y., 1994—; mem. legis. com. N.Y. Fed. on Child Abuse and Neglect, Albany, 1986—, bd. dirs., 1987-89; cons. N.Y. Pub. Welfare Assn., Inc., Albany, 1987-92; pres. Social Svcs. Attys. Assn. N.Y. State, 1990-91; instr. Klassic Karate Studios, Buffalo; cons. Cornell U. Family Life Devel. Ctr., 1993—. Contbr. articles to profl. jours. Mem. N.Y. State Bar Assn., N.Y. State Magistrate's Assn., Erie County Bar Assn., Genesee County Bar Assn., Genesee County Magistrate's and Peace Officers Assn., Corfu Area Bus. Assn. Republican. Avocations: karate, martial arts. Home: 17 E Main St Corfu NY 14036-9665 Office: 360 Statler Towers Buffalo NY 10420-2599

PAK, HYUNG WOONG, foundation executive; b. Ham-Hoong, Korea, Nov. 6, 1932; came to U.S., 1955, naturalized, 1968; s. Kyung-Koo and Myung-Sook (Lee) P.; m. Diana Lee Stenen Woodruff, 1975; children: Jonathan Tong-Hee, Michelle Hyun-Mi Lee. AB, U. Chgo., 1958. Editor and publisher Chgo. Rev., 1958-63, cons., 1963-65; assoc. editor Ency. Britannica Press, Chgo., 1963-64; sr. editor social scis. and humanities Ency. Britannica Press, 1964-66; ednl. dir. Bantam Books, Inc., N.Y.C., 1966-69; gen. mgr. sch. dept. Appleton-Century-Crofts/New Century, N.Y.C., 1970-72; v.p., editorial dir. D. Van Nostrand Co., N.Y.C., 1972-74; pres. D. Van Nostrand Co., 1974-76, Chatham Sq. Press, N.Y.C., 1976-83; pub. Urizen Books, Inc., N.Y.C., 1978-81; exec. v.p. Bus. Software Mag., Palo Alto, Calif., 1983-84; pub., editor Asian High-Tech. Report, 1984-90; exec. dir. The Philip Jaisohn Meml. Found., Inc., Phila., 1990—; fellow Hoover Instn., Stanford, Calif., 1984-85. Author: The Pacific Rim, 1990; columnist The Phila. Bus. Rev., 1993—. Mem. Bd. Sch. Dist. Cheltenham Twp., Pa., 1987-94; mem. Asian task force Phila. Sch. Dist., 1988-95; co-chmn. bus. adv. com. Montgomery County, Pa., 1991-93; del. Citizens' Assembly for a Greater Phila., 1991-95; chmn., mem. bd. Pan Asian Assn. Greater Phila., 1992-96, mem. bd. fellowship commn., 1992-95; mem.. Mem. ACLU (life), Phila. Mus. Art. Home: 1015 Sharpless Rd Philadelphia PA 19027-3040 also: Philip Jaisohn Meml Found 6705 Old York Rd Philadelphia PA 19126-2841

PAKE, GEORGE EDWARD, research executive, physicist; b. Jeffersonville, Ohio, Apr. 1, 1924; s. Edward Howe and Mary Mabel (Fry) P.; m. Marjorie Elizabeth Semon, May 31, 1947; children—Warren E., Catherine E., Stephen G., Bruce E. B.S., M.S., Carnegie Inst. Tech., 1945; Ph.D., Harvard U., 1948. Physicist Westinghouse Research Labs., 1945-46; mem. faculty Washington U., St. Louis, 1948-56, 62-70; prof. physics, provost Washington U., 1962-69, exec. vice chancellor, 1965-69, Edward Mallinckrodt prof. physics, 1969-70; v.p. Xerox Corp.; mgr. Xerox Palo Alto (Calif.) Research Center, 1970-78, v.p. corp. research, 1978-83, group v.p., 1983-86; dir. Inst. for Research on Learning, Palo Alto, Calif., 1987-91, dir. emeritus, 1991—; prof. physics Stanford U., 1956-62. Author: (with E. Feenberg) Quantum Theory of Angular Momentum, 1953, Paramagnetic Resonance, 1962, (with T. Estle) The Physical Principles of Electron Paramagnetic Resonance, 1973. Mem. gov. bd. Am. Inst. Physics, 1957-59; bd. dirs. St. Louis Research Council, 1964-70; mem. physics adv. panel NSF, 1958-60, 63- 66; chmn. physics survey com. Nat. Acad. Sci.-NRC, 1964-66; Mem. St. Louis County Bus. and Indl. Devel. Commn., 1963-66; chmn. bd. Regional Indsl. Devel. Corp., St. Louis, 1966-67, St. Louis Research Council, 1967-70; mem. President's Sci. Adv. Com., 1965-69; Bd. dirs. St. Louis Country Day Sch., 1964-70, Central Inst. for Deaf, 1965-70; trustee Washington U., 1970—, Danforth Found., 1971—, U. Rochester, 1982—; trustee Ctr. for Advanced Study in Behavioral Scis., Palo Alto, 1986-92, The Exploratorium, San Francisco, 1987—; bd. overseers Superconducting Super Collider, Univs. Rsch. Assn., 1984-89. Fellow Am. Phys. Soc. (pres. 1977); mem. Am. Assn. Physics Tchrs., AAUP, AAAS, Am. Acad. Arts and Scis., Nat. Acad. Scis., Sigma Xi, Tau Beta Pi. Home: 2 Yerba Buena Ave Los Altos CA 94022-2208 Office: Inst for Rsch on Learning 66 Willow Pl Menlo Park CA 94025-3601*

PAKISER, LOUIS CHARLES, JR., geophysicist; b. Denver, Feb. 8, 1919; s. Louis C. and Lila E. (Hanson) P.; m. Helen L. Meineke, Oct. 9, 1939. Geol. Engr., Colo. Sch. Mines, 1937-42; postgrad., U. Nancy, France, 1945, Stanford, U. Colo., 1958-60. Geophysicist Carter Oil Co., 1942-49; first nat. exec. dir. Am. Vets. Com., 1949-52; also mng. editor AVC Bull.; mem. nat. planning com.; geophysicist U.S. Geol. Survey, 1952-92; rep. geophysics br. U.S. Geol. Survey, Denver, 1958-60; chief maj. crustal studies U.S. Geol. Survey, 1960-61, chief br. crustal studies, 1961-65; acting chief Nat. Center Earthquake Research, 1965-67, chmn. exec. com. of center, 1967-68; chief Office Earthquake Research and Crustal Studies, 1967-70, research geophysicist, 1970-79, annuitant research geophysicist, 1979-92, chief br. seismicity and earth structure and nat. earthquake info. service, 1975-77; ad hoc panel on earthquake prediction OST, 1964-68; disting. lectr. Soc. Exploration Geophysicists, 1964; spl. lectr. U. New Orleans, 1982-83; chmn. interagy. staff group on minority participation in sci. and engring. U.S. Dept. Interior, 1972-74; adv. com. Am. Indian Ednl. Opportunity Program U. Colo., 1981-84; vis. com. geophysics dept. Colo. Sch. Mines, 1986-94. Chmn. land use adv. com. Douglas County, Colo., 1975-76, chmn. mineral extraction planning task force, 1989-90; mem. sci. stds. com. Douglas County Sch. Dist., 1992-94; bd. dirs. Nat. Consortium for Black Profl. Devel., 1976-79; mem. adv. coun. Am. Vets. Com., 1960-61; mem. steering com. Nat. Civil Liberties Clearing House, 1950-52; mem. Amnesty Internat.; assoc. charter mem. U.S. Holocaust Meml. Mus. Recipient Disting. Svc. award U.S. Dept. Interior, 1970. Mem. NAACP (exec. com. Tulsa br. 1949, co-chmn. membership com. 1949), AAAS, Anti-Defamation League, Am. Indian Sci. and Engring. Soc., Am. Geophys. Union, Soc. Advancement Chicanos and Native Ams. in Sci., Am. Geol. Inst. (chmn. adv. com. to minority participation program 1973-75), Geol. Soc. Am. (chmn. com. on minority participation in geol. scis. 1975-80, Disting. Svc. award 1996). Unitarian Universalist. Home: 111 Emerson St Apt 1142 Denver CO 80218

PAKTER, JEAN, medical consultant; b. N.Y.C.; d. David and Lillian (Kunitz) P.; m. Arnold L. Bachman, Sept. 17, 1939 (dec. Dec. 1992); children: Ellen Bachman Mendelson, Donald M. BS, NYU, 1931, MD, 1934; MPH, Coll. U. Sch. Pub. Health, 1955. Bd. cert. pediatrics. Intern Mt. Sinai Hosp., N.Y.C., 1934-36, resident, 1937-39; pediatrician pvt. practice, N.Y.C., 1939-43; dir. Bur. Dept. Health, Marernity, Newborn & Family Planning, N.Y.C., 1950-82; cons., lectr. maternity, child health Coll. U. Sch. Pub. Health, N.Y.C., 1984—; lectr. U. Sch. Pub. Health, N.Y.C. Contbr. articles to profl. jours. Advisor March of Dimes, N.Y.C., 1975—. Recipient Fund for City of N.Y. Pub. Svc. award, 1974, Martha May Eliot award, 1990. Fellow Am. Acad. Pediatrics, Am. Pub. Health Assn., N.Y. Acad. Medicine (trustee 1979-83), N.Y. Obs. Soc. (assoc.); mem. Pub. Health Assn. N.Y.C. (bd. dirs. 1992-96), Women's City Club, Alpha Omega Alpha. Avocations: concerts, opera, theatre, reading. Home: 1175 Park Ave New York NY 10128 Office: Coll U Sch Pub Health Ctr Population & Family 60 Haven Ave New York NY 10032-2604

PAKULA, ALAN J., producer, director; b. N.Y.C., Apr. 7, 1928; m. Hannah Cohn Boorstin, 1973. BA, Yale U., 1948. Prodr.'s apprentice Metro Goldwyn-Mayer, L.A., 1950; prodr.'s asst. Paramount Pictures, L.A., 1951; prodr. various studios, 1955—; founder, co-owner Pakula-Mulligan Prodns., Inc., L.A.; owner Pakula Prodns., Inc., N.Y.C. Prodr.: (play) There Must Be a Pony, (films) Fear Strikes Out, 1957, To Kill a Mockingbird, 1963, Love With the Proper Stranger, 1963, Baby, the Rain Must Fall, 1965, Inside Daisy Clover, 1965, Up the Down Staircase, 1967, The Stalking Moon, 1968; dir., prodr.: (films) The Sterile Cuckoo, 1969, Klute, 1971 (London Film Critics Best Dir. award), Love and Pain and the Whole Damned Thing, 1972, The Parallax View, 1974, (with James L. Brooks) Starting Over, 1979, (with Jon Boorstin) Dream Lover, 1986 (grand prize Avoriaz Film Festival), (with Susan Solt), Orphans, 1987; dir.: (films) All The President's Men, 1976 (Best Dir. award N.Y. Film Critics, Best Dir. award Nat. Bd. Rev.), Comes A Horseman, 1978, Rollover, 1981; dir., screenwriter, prodr.: (film) (with Keith Barish) Sophie's Choice, 1982, See You in the Morning, 1989, Presumed Innocent, 1990, The Pelican Brief, 1993, The Devil's Own, 1997. Office: Pakula Prodns Inc 330 W 58th St Ste 508 New York NY 10019-1819

PAL, PRABIR KUMAR, aluminium company executive; b. Chittagong, Bengal, India, Feb. 17, 1936; arrived in Can., 1969; s. Niranjan and Renuka (Mitter) P.; m. Nandinee Majumdar, Dec. 13, 1960; 1 child, Nobina. BA with honors in law, Cambridge U., 1958, MA, 1972; Diploma in Indsl. Mgmt., Geneva U., Geneva, 1964. Legal asst. Indian Aluminium Co. Ltd. (subs. Alcan), Calcutta, India, 1959-69, sec., 1972-76; fin. analyst Alcan Aluminium Ltd., Montreal, Que., Can., 1969-72, sr. legal and fin. officer, 1976-82, v.p., chief legal officer, 1987-88, v.p., chief legal officer, sec., 1988—; chief legal officer, treas. Alcan Europe, Geneva, 1982-84; chief legal and fin. officer Alcan Pacific, Vancouver, B.C., Can., 1984-86. Fellow Inst. Chartered Secs. and Adminstrs.; mem. Internat. Bar Assn., Univ. Club Montreal. Avocations: photography, rowing. Office: Alcan Aluminium Ltd. 1188 Sherbrooke St W, Montreal, PQ Canada H3A 3G2

PAL, PRATAPADITYA, museum curator; b. Bangladesh, Sept. 1, 1935; came to U.S., 1967; s. Gopesh Chandra and Bidyut Kana (Dam) P.; m. Chitralekha Bose, Apr. 20, 1968; children—Shalmali, Lopamudra. M.A., U. Calcutta, 1958, D.Phil., 1962; Ph.D. (U. K. Commonwealth Scholar), U. Cambridge, Eng., 1965. Research assoc. Am. Acad. of Benares, India, 1966-67; keeper Indian collections Mus. Fine Arts, Boston, 1967-69; sr. curator Indian and Southeast Asian art Los Angeles County Mus. Art, L.A., 1970-95, acting dir., 1979; vis. curator Indian and S.E. Asian art Art Inst. Chgo., 1995—; cons. curator Norton Simon Mus., Pasadena, Calif., 1995—; adj. prof. fine arts U. So. Calif., 1971-89; vis. prof. U. Calif., Santa Barbara, 1980, Irvine, 1994-95; William Cohn lectr. Oxford U., 1983; Catherine Mead meml. lectr. Pierpont Morgan Libr., N.Y.C., 1986; Ananda K. Coomaraswamy meml. lectr. Prince of Wales Mus., Bombay, 1987; D.J. Sibley prehistoric art lectr. U. Tex., Austin, 1989; Anthony Gardner meml. lectr. Victoria and Albert Mus., London, 1993, keynote spkr. 1st Internat. Conf. on Tibetan Art, 1994; mem. commr.'s art adv. panel IRS, Washington. Author: The Arts of Nepal, vol. 1, 1974, vol. 2, 1979, The Sensuous Immortals, 1977, The Ideal Image: Gupta Sculptures and its Influence, 1978, The Classical Tradition in Rajput Painting, 1978, Elephants and Ivories, 1981, A Buddhist Paradise: Murals of Alchi, 1982, Art of Tibet, 1983, Tibetan Painting, 1984, Art of Nepal, 1985, From Merchants to Emperors, 1986, Indian Sculpture, vol. 1, 1986, Icons of Piety, Images of Whimsey, 1987, Indian Sculpture, vol. 2, 1988, Buddhist Book Illuminations, 1988, Romance of the Taj Mahal, 1989, Art of the Himalayas, 1991, Pleasure Gardens of the Mind, 1993; Indian Painting, vol. 1, 1993, The Peaceful Liberators: Jain Art from India, 1994, On the Path to Void, 1996, A Collecting Odyssey, 1997; gen. editor: Marg mag., 1993—. Bd. dirs. Music Circle, Pasadena, Calif. John D. Rockefeller III Fund fellow, 1964, 69, fellow NEA, 1974; Getty scholar, 1995-96. Fellow Asia Soc. (Bombay, hon.); mem. Asiatic Soc. (Calcutta, B.C. Law gold medal 1993). *The guiding principles of my life have been hard work, total commitment to everything I do, whether work or play, fairness in all my dealings and treat everybody equally, whether a prince or a pauper.*

PALACIO, IRENE ELIZABETH, special education educator; b. Whitman AFB, Mo., Mar. 9, 1965; d. James Bartholomew Palacio and Martina Marlene (Vasquez) Brown, stepfather Gilbert Arthur Brown. BA, Oreg. State U., 1987; MS, Western Oreg. State Coll., 1989. Cert. tchr., Colo., Nev. Tchr. spl. edn. Kapa'a (Kauai, Hawaii) Elem. Sch., 1989-90, Kapa'a High Sch., 1990-91, Louisville (Colo.) Mid. Sch., 1991-96, Pau-Wa-Lu Mid Sch, Gardnerville, Nev., 1996—. Rural Cross cultural grantee for spl. edn. Western Oreg. State Coll., 1988-89. Mem. NEA, Alpha Omicron Pi. Avocations: travel, learning, outdoor activities, reading.

PALACIO, JUNE ROSE PAYNE, nutritional science educator; b. Hove, Sussex, Eng., June 14, 1940; came to U.S., 1949; d. Alfred and Doris Winifred (Blanch) P.; m. Moki Moses Palacio, Nov. 30, 1968. AA, Orange Coast Coll., Costa Mesa, Calif., 1960; BS, U. Calif., Berkeley, 1963; PhD, Kans. State U., 1984. Registered dietitian. Asst. dir. food svc. and res. halls Mills Coll., Oakland, Calif., 1964-66; staff dietitian Servomation Bay Cities, Oakland, 1966-67; commissary mgr. Host Internat., Inc., Honolulu, 1967-73; dir. dietetics Straub Clinic and Hosp., Honolulu, 1973-80; instr. Kans. State U., Manhattan, 1980-84; prof. and program dir. Calif. State U., L.A., 1984-85; prof., program dir. Pepperdine U., Malibu, Calif., 1985—; instr. Kapiolani Community Coll., Honolulu, 1973-79, U. Hawaii, Honolulu, 1975-80, Ctr. for Dietetic Edn., Woodland Hills, Calif., 1986—; cons. Clevenger Nutritional Svcs., Calabasas, Calif., 1985—, Calif. Mus. Sci. and Industry, L.A., 1989—, Calif. State Dept. Edn., Sacramento, Calif., 1985—. Author: Foodservice in Institutions, 1988, Introduction to Foodservice, 1992. Mem. Am. Dietetic Assn. (del. 1977-80, 86-89, reviewer 1986—), Calif. Dietetic Assn. (pres. 1992-93), L.A. Dist. Dietetic Assn., Foodsvc. Systems Mgmt. Edn. Coun., Dietetic Educators of Practitioners, Gamma Sigma Delta, Omicron Nu, Phi Upsilon Omicron. Republican. Episcopalian. Avocations: tennis, running, reading, traveling. Home: 24319 Baxter Dr Malibu CA 90265-4728 Office: Pepperdine U 24255 Pacific Coast Hwy Malibu CA 90263-0001

PALACIOS, ALANA SUE, computer programmer; b. Taylor, Tex., June 21, 1950; d. Alphonse T. and Doris Marie (Speegle) Hanzelka; m. Roberto C. Palacios, Mar. 10, 1956. BBA with honors, U. Tex., 1978; MPA, Calif. State U., 1993. Asst. staff mgr. Southwestern Bell Telephone, St. Louis, 1978-80; sr. analyst Mountain Bell Telephone, Denver, 1980-81; asst. staff mgr. Southwestern Bell Telephone, 1981-84; project leader Hughes Aircraft, Long Beach, Calif., 1984-86; programmer, analyst City of Long Beach, 1986—. Civil svc. commr. Signal Hill, Calif., 1994—. Mem. NAFE, Phi Kappa Phi, Pi Alpha Alpha. Democrat. Episcopalian. Avocation: the Internet. Office: City of Long Beach 333 W Ocean Blvd Fl 12 Long Beach CA 90802-4604

PALADE, GEORGE EMIL, biologist, educator; b. Jassy, Romania, Nov. 19, 1912; came to U.S., 1946, naturalized, 1952; s. Emil and Constanta (Cantemir) P.; m. Irina Malaxa, June 12, 1941 (dec. 1969); children—Georgia Teodora, Philip Theodore; m. Marilyn G. Farquhar, 1970. Bachelor, Hasdeu Lyceum, Buzau, Romania; M.D., U. Bucharest, Romania. Instr., asst. prof., then assoc. prof. anatomy Sch. Medicine, U. Bucharest, 1935-45; vis. investigator, asst. assoc., prof. cell biology Rockefeller U., 1946-73; prof. cell biology Yale U., New Haven, 1973-83; sr. research scientist Yale U., 1983-89; prof.-in-residence, dean sci. affairs Med. Sch., U. Calif., San Diego, 1990—. Author sci. papers. Recipient Albert Lasker Basic Research award, 1966, Gairdner Spl. award, 1967, Horwitz prize, 1970, Nobel prize in Physiology or Medicine, 1974, Nat. Medal Sci., 1986. Fellow Am. Acad. Arts and Scis.; mem. Nat. Acad. Sci., Pontifical Acad. Sci., Royal Soc. (London), Leopoldina Acad. (Halle), Romanian Acad., Royal Belgian Acad. Medicine. Research interests correlated biochem. and morphological analysis cell structures. *

PALADINO, DANIEL R., lawyer, beverage corporation executive; B.S., Fordham U., 1965; J.D., NYU, 1968. atty. Simpson Thacher & Bartlett, 1969-76; atty. Davis & Cox, 1976-79; exec. Office: Joseph Seagram & Sons Inc 375 Park Ave New York NY 10152-0002

PALADINO, JOSEPH ANTHONY, clinical pharmacist; b. Utica, N.Y., May 5, 1953; s. Paul Francis and Jacqueline Ann (Monaco) P.; m. Carol Ann Jenny, June 5, 1976; children: Nicholas Joseph, Matthew Jerome, Kathryn Elizabeth. BS in Biology, Siena Coll., Loudonville, N.Y., 1975; BS in Pharmacy, Mass. Coll. Pharmacy, 1977; D Pharmacy, Med. U. S.C., 1982. Acting dir. pharmacy Utica (N.Y.) Psychiat. Ctr., 1978-80; decentralized pharmacist Med. U. Hosp., Charleston, S.C., 1980-82; asst. dir. pharmacy Rochester (N.Y.) Gen. Hosp., 1982-87, adj. med. staff, 1986-87; clin. instr. pediatrics U. Rochester Sch. Medicine, 1985-87; clin. asst. prof. pharmacy SUNY, Buffalo, 1989-93, clin. assoc. prof., 1994—; dir. pharmacokinetics Millard Fillmore Suburban Hosp., Williamsville, N.Y., 1987—; dir. clin. outcomes and econs. rsch. Millard Fillmore Health System, Buffalo; editorial adv. bd. Jour. of Infectious Disease Pharmacotherapy, 1993—; mem. adv. bd. several major pharm. cos.; 1st vis. prof. pharmacy Tayside Health Bd., Dundee, Scotland, 1992. Author book chpts.; contbr. numerous articles to med., pharmacy, pharmacology, pharmacoecon. and infectious disease jours. Big Bro., Big Bros. and Big Sisters, Albany, N.Y., 1972-80; bd. mem., den leader Cub Scouts, Clarence, N.Y., 1989-91; founding bd., coach Clarence Little League Football, 1992-94. Fellow Am. Coll. Clin. Pharmacy (founder, 1st chmn. Outcomes and Econs. Practice and Rsch. Network); mem. Am. Soc. Microbiology, Soc. Infectious Diseases Pharmacists, N.Y. Acad. Scis. Achievements include pioneering a method of treating certain infectious diseases with an early switch from intravenous to oral antibiotics; co-development of a standardized format for dosing charts for critical intravenous medications; discovery of drug interaction between secobarbital and theophylline; integration of switch therapy with pharmacodynamics, outcomes therapy, and health care economics. Office: Millard Fillmore Suburban Hosp 1540 Maple Rd Williamsville NY 14221-3647 *Do not work at a job: it is far better to enjoy a career. Be persistent, take reasoned risks, and understand that what is obvious to you may not be apparent to others - what is easy for you may be arduous for others.*

PALAFOX, MARI LEE, private school educator; b. Des Moines, Sept. 22, 1952; d. Ronald Lester and Maxine Lucille (Miller) Watts; m. René Jose Palafox, July 13, 1974; 1 child, Rebecca Leigh. BA, U. Calif.-San Diego, La Jolla, 1975. Multiple subjects credential, Calif., Assn. Christian Schs. Internat. Teaching credential, 1990. Mid. sch. tchr. Santee (Calif.) Sch. Dist., 1975-80; tchr. math., softball coach Christian Jr. High Sch., El Cajon, Calif., 1980-89, Christian High Sch., El Cajon, 1989-95; math. specialist Christian Unified Schs. San Diego. Recipient cert. of recognition Ednl. Testing Svc., 1991; named Disting. Tchr., U. Calif., San Diego, 1996. Mem. Calif. Tchrs. Math., Greater San Diego Math. Coun. (pvt. sch. rep. 1982-83), Nat. Coun. Tchrs. Math. Avocations: softball, volleyball, basketball, cross-stitch. Home: PO Box 2067 El Cajon CA 92021-0067 Office: Christian High Sch 2100 Greenfield Dr El Cajon CA 92019-1161

PALAGI, ROBERT GENE, college administrator; b. Chgo., Aug. 20, 1948; s. Gene and Stella (Vasick) P.; m. Diane Joyce Sanderson, July 31, 1971; children: Melissa, Jason. AS, So. Ill. U., 1969, BS, 1972; MEd, DePaul U., 1975; MS, No. Ill. U., 1994. Cert. secondary tchr., cert. counselor. Educator Dept. Mental Health, Tinley Park, Ill., 1972-75; mental health specialist Dept. Mental Health, Tinley Park, 1975-77, grant coord., 1977-80; vocat. therapist Our Lady of Mercy Hosp., Dyer, Ind., 1980-81, mgr. edn. and tng., 1981-84; edn. cons. devel. St. Mary of Nazareth Hosp.; instr., counselor Chgo. City Colls., 1986-89, assoc. dir., 1989-90, coord. career devel., 1990-91, dir. acad. support, 1991-94; indsl. arts. specialist Ingalls Hosp., 1994—; cons. Chgo. Merc. Exch., Chgo., 1985-86; faculty Ind. U. N.W., Gary, Ind., 1981-82; mgr. evening svcs. Ind. Vocat. Tech. Coll., Hammond, Ind., 1990—. Chairperson pub. rels. Pullman Civic Orgn., Chgo., 1983, bd. dirs., 1993. Mem. Am. Vocat. Assn., Coop. Edn. Assn., Midwest Coop. Edn. Assn., Ill. Vocat. Assn., Ill. Coop. Edn. Assn. Home: 11316 S Langley Ave Chicago IL 60628-5126 Office: Ingalls Ctr for Otpt Rehab Dawson Tech Inst 1551 Huntington Dr Calumet City IL 60409-5440

PALAHNIUK, RICHARD JOHN, anesthesiology educator, researcher; b. Winnipeg, Man., Can., Dec. 5, 1944; s. George and Teenie (Lukinchuk) P.; m. Patricia June Smando, July 15, 1967; children: Christopher, Daniel, Andrew. BS in Medicine, U. Man., 1968, MD, 1968. Head obstetric anaesthesia Health Scis. Ctr., Winnipeg, 1973-79; prof. and chmn. of anaesthesia U. Man., Winnipeg, 1979-89; prof. anesthesiology, head dept. U. Minn., Mpls., 1989—. Contbr. papers and book chpts. to profl. publs.; mem. editorial bd. Can. Jour. Anaesthesia, Toronto, 1985-89. Fellow Med. Rsch. Coun. Can., 1972, rsch. grantee, 1974-79. Fellow Royal Coll. Physicians of Can.; mem. Can. Anaesthetists' Soc., Am. Soc. Anesthesiology, Internat. Anesthesia Rsch. Soc. (editorial bd. Cleve. chpt. 1987—). Roman Catholic. Avocations: running, fishing, carpentry. Office: U Minn Med Sch 420 Delaware St SE Minneapolis MN 55455-0374*

PALANCE, JACK, actor; b. Lattimer, Pa., Feb. 18; s. John and Anna (Gramiak) Palahnuik; m. Virginia Baker, Apr. 21, 1949 (div. 1969); children: Holly Kathleen, Brook Gabrielle, Cody John; m. Elaine Rochelle Rogers, May 6, 1987. Student, U. N.C., Stanford U. Appeared in stage plays The Big Two, 1947, Temporary Island, 1948, The Vigil, A Street Car Named Desire, 1948, The Silver Tassle, 1949, Darkness at Noon, 1950, Julius Caesar, The Tempest, 1955; motion pictures include Panic in the Streets, 1950, Halls of Montezuma, Sudden Fear (Acad. award nominee best supporting actor 1952), Shane (Acad. award nominee best supporting actor 1953), Arrowhead, Flight to Tangier, The Silver Chalice, Kiss of Fire, Attack!, Ten Seconds to Hell, The Big Knife, Man in the Attic, Warriors Five, Barabbas, I Died A 1000 Times, The Lonely Man, House of Numbers, Contempt, Torture Garden, Kill a Dragon, They Came to Rob Las Vegas, The Desperadoes, The Mercenary, Justine, Legion of the Damned, A Bullet for Rommel, The McMasters, The Professionals, Chato's Land, Companeros, Che, Oklahoma Crude, Craze, The Four Deuces, The Diamond, Hawk the Slayer, Gor, Bagdad Cafe, Young Guns, The Getaway, The Horsemen, The Shape of Things to Come, Hawk the Slayer, Without Warning, Tango & Cash, Batman 1989, Solar Crisis, 1990, City Slickers, 1991 (Acad. award for Best Supporting Actor 1991), Cops and Robbersons, 1994, City Slickers II: The Legend of Curley's Gold, 1994, Natural Born Killers, 1994, (voice) The Swan Princess, 1994, others; appeared on TV: Requiem for a Heavyweight (Sylvania award), Dr. Jekyll and Mr. Hyde, Dracula, (series) Bronk, 1975-76, (series host) Ripley's Believe It Or Not, (miniseries) Buffalo Girls, 1995. With AC, U.S. Army. Named Most Prominent Newcomer Theatre World, Best Screen Newcomer Look mag. Office: Martin Herwitz 427 N Canon Dr Ste 215 Beverly Hills CA 90210-4840*

PALANS, LLOYD ALEX, lawyer; b. St. Louis, Aug. 6, 1946; s. Hyman Robert and Mae (Sherman) P.; m. Deborah Regn, Aug. 5, 1972; children: Emily Rebecca, Samantha Jane. BS, Tulane U., 1968; JD, U. Mo., 1972. Bar: Mo. 1972, U.S. Dist. Ct. (ea. and we. dists.) Mo. 1972, U.S. Ct. Appeals (8th cir.) 1972, U.S. Ct. Appeals (5th cir.) 1974, U.S. Supreme Ct. 1975, U.S. Ct. Appeals (9th cir.) 1992. Ptnr. Kramer, Chused, Kramer, Shostak & Kohn, St. Louis, 1972-77, Blumenfeld, Marx & Tureen, P.C., St. Louis, 1978-81, Gallop, Johnson & Neuman, St. Louis, 1981-90, Bryan Cave, St. Louis, 1990—; adj. prof. Washington U. Sch. Law, St. Louis, 1989—. Bd. dirs. St. Louis Chpt. ARC, 1987—, St. Louis Chpt. Leukemia Soc., 1988—, Combined Health Appeal Greater St. Louis, 1988—, Combined Health Appeal of Am., 1990. Mem. ABA, Mo. Bar, St. Louis Met. Bar Assn. Office: Bryan Cave 1 Metro Sq 211 N Broadway Saint Louis MO 63102-2733

PALAST, GERI D., federal agency administrator. BA in Polit. Sci., Stanford U., 1972; JD, NYU, 1976. Atty., legis. program analyst Am. Fedn. State County and Mcpl. Employees, Washington, 1976-77; legal counsel, field rep. Nat. Treasury Employers Union, Washington, 1977-79; dir., supervising atty. Nat. Employment Law Project, Washington, 1979-81; dir. politics and legislation Svc. Employees Internat. Union, AFL-CIO, Washington, 1981-93; asst. sec. congrl. and intergovtl. affairs Dept. Labor, Washington, 1993—. Office: Dept Labor Congl & Intergovtl Affairs 200 Constitution Ave NW Washington DC 20210-0001

PALAST, GERI DEBORAH, government official, lawyer; b. L.A., Dec. 27, 1950; d. Gilbert Leon and Gladys Evelyn (Kaufman) P. BA in Polit. Sci. with honors, Stanford U., 1972; JD, NYU, 1976. Bar: Calif. 1976, D.C. 1978. Atty., legis. and program analyst Am. Fedn. State, County and Mcpl. Employees, Washington, 1976-77; legal counsel, field rep. Nat. Treasury Employees Union, Washington, 1977-79; dir. D.C. office, supervising atty. Nat. Employment Law Project, Washington, 1979-81; dir. politics and legislation Svc. Employees Internat. Union, AFL-CIO, Washington, 1981-83; asst. sec. labor congl. and intergovtl. affairs Dept. of Labor, Washington, 1993—; del. Labor Study Commn. to Sweden and Denmark, Comparative Labor Law and Labor Stds., 1978-82; commr. Washington Unemployment Compensation Bd., 1983-84; mem. calif. State Legislature's Task Force on Work and Family, 1988; chair senate marginal com. AFL-CIO, Oreg., 1991-93, Calif., 1986-93; lectr. in field. Co-founder, chair Eleanor Roosevelt Fund, Dem. Nat. Com., 1982-84, commr. compliance rev. commn., 1983-84, staff mem. platform drafting com., 1988, mng. trustee, co-chair healthcare task force, 1988-93; bd. dirs. Peace-Pac, 1992; mem. steering com. Emily's List, 1988-93; exec. com. Nat. Jewish Dem. Coun., 1991—; exec. com. Calif. State Dem. Party, 1988-93; Clinton del. (Calif.) 1992 Nat. Dem. Conv. Root-Tilden Pub. Svc. Law fellow, 1973-76; Law Student Civil Rights & Rsch. grantee, 1975. Avocation: dancing. Office: US Dept of Labor 200 Constitution Ave NW Washington DC 20210-0001

PALAUSI GALINAT, NICOLE, artist; b. Paris, Feb. 8, 1922; came to U.S. 1956; d. Henry and Marguerite (Pinel) P.; m. Edmund Galinat (dec.); children: Danuta, Beatrice. Student, Ecole des Beaux Arts, Paris; pupil of Othon Friesz. Artist: solo exhibits include Salon Pernod, Paris, 1955, Galerie du Font de Mer, Royan, France, 1955, Galerie Mouffe, Paris, 1975, Big Ben Gallery, Rouen, 1975, Casino de Cannes, France, 1976, 77, Alliance Francaise, Washington, 1976, Retrospective at Springfield (Ohio) Mus., 1976, Galerie Ben Lao, Paris, 1977, 78, Galerie La Mandragore Internationale, Paris, 1981, Paris Health Club, N.Y.c., 1996, 1st Unitarian Soc., Plainfield, N.J., 1997; over 50 group exhibits in Europe and U.S.; represented in permanent private and pub. collections including Springfield (Ohio) Art Mus. Decorated Knight Internat. Order of Arts and Letters, France, 1976; recipient 1st prize Internat. Festival, Lyon France, People's Choice, Michelangelo Found., France, 1977, Grand prize, Deauville, France, 1979, Targa D'Aurea, Oscar d'Oro, Napoli, Italy, 1980 (gold oscar to fgn. artist), Dio Pan Firenze, Italy, 1981 (art critics' award).

PALAY, SANFORD LOUIS, retired scientist, educator; b. Cleve., Sept. 23, 1918; s. Harry and Lena (Sugarman) P.; m. Victoria Chan Curtis, 1970 (div. Nov. 1990); children: Victoria Li-Mei, Rebecca Li-Ming. A.B., Oberlin Coll., 1940; M.D. (Hoover prize scholar 1943), Western Res. U., 1943. Teaching fellow medicine, rsch. assoc. anatomy Western Res. U., Cleve., 1945-46; NRC fellow med. scis. Rockefeller Inst., 1948, vis. investigator, 1953; from instr. anatomy to assoc. prof. anatomy Yale U., 1949-56; chief sect. neurocytology, lab. neuroanatomical scis. Nat. Inst. Neurol. Diseases and Blindness, NIH, Washington, 1956-61; chief lab. neuroanatomical scis. Nat. Inst. Neurol. Diseases and Blindness, NIH, 1960-61; Bullard prof. neuroanatomy Harvard, Boston, 1961-89, prof. emeritus, 1989—; Linnean Soc. lectr., London, 1959; vis. investigator Middlesex Hosp. (Bland-Sutton Inst.), London, Eng., 1961; Phillips lectr. Haverford Coll., 1959; Ramsay Henderson Trust lectr. U. Edinburgh, Scotland, 1962; George H. Bishop lectr.. Washington U., St. Louis, 1990; Disting. Scientist lectr. Tulane U. Sch. Medicine, 1969, 75; vis. prof. U. Wash., 1969; Rogowski Meml. lectr. Yale, 1973; Disting. lectr. biol. structure U. Miami, 1974; Disting. Scientist lectr. U. Ark., 1977; Disting. scholar-in-residence dept. biology Boston Coll., Chestnut Hill, Mass., 1994—; other Disting. lectureships; vis. prof. U. Osaka, Japan, 1978, Nat. U. Singapore, 1983; spl. vis. prof. U. Osaka, 1988; chmn. study sect. on behavioral and neural scis. NIH, 1984-86; mem. fellowship bd. NIH, 1958-61, cell biology study sect., 1959-65, adv. com. high voltage electron microscope resources, 1973-80, mem. rev. com. behavioral and neurol. scis. fellowships, 1979-86; chmn. Gordon Research Conf. Cell Structure and Metabolism, 1960; asso. Neurosci. Research Program, 1962-67, cons. assoc., 1975—; mem. anat. scis. tng. com. Nat. Inst. Gen. Med. Scis., 1968-72; mem. sci. adv. com. Oreg. Regional Primate Research Center, 1971-76. Author: The Fine Structure of the Nervous System, 1970, 3d edit., 1991, Cerebellar Cortex, Cytology and Organization, 1974; editor: Frontiers of Cytology, 1958, The Cerebellum, New Vistas, 1982; mem. sci. coun. Progress in Neuropharmacology and Jour. Neuropharmacology, 1961-66; mem. editorial bd. Exptl. Neurology, 1959-76, Jour. Cell Biology, 1962-67, Brain Research, 1965-71, Jour. Comparative Neurology, 1966—, Jour. Ultrastructure Research, 1966-86, Jour. of Neurocytology, 1972-87, Exptl. Brain Research, 1965-76, Neurosci, 1975-95, Anatomy and Embryology, 1968; co-mng. editor, 1978-88; editor in chief Jour. Comparative Neurology, 1981-93, editor emeritus, 1994—; mem. adv. bd. editors Jour. Neuropathology and Exptl. Neurology, 1963-82, Internat. Jour. Neurosci, 1969-74, Tissue and Cell, 1969-86; contbr. articles to profl. jours. Served to capt. M.C. AUS, 1946-47. Recipient 50 Best Books of 1974 award Internat. Book Fair, Frankfurt, Fed. Republic Germany, Best Book in Profl. Readership award Am. Med. Writers Assn., 1975, Biomed. Rsch. award Assn. Am. Med. Colls., 1989, Lashley award Am. Philos. Soc., 1991, Camillo Golgi award Fidia Rsch. Found., 1992; Guggenheim fellow, 1971-72; Fogarty scholar-in-residence NIH, Bethesda, 1980-81. Fellow Am. Acad. Arts and Scis.; mem. NAS, Am. Assn. Anatomists (chmn. nominating com. 1964, mem. exec. com. 1970-74, anat. nomenclature com. 1975-78, pres. 1980-81, Henry Gray award 1990), Histochem. Soc., Electron Microscope Soc. Am., AAAS, Am. Soc. Cell Biology (program com. 1975), Internat. Soc. Cell Biology, Soc. for Neurosci. (Gerard award 1990), Washington Soc. Electron Microscopy (organizing com., sec.-treas. 1956-58), Soc. Francaise de Microscopie Electronique (hon.), Royal Microscopical Soc. (hon.), Golgi Soc. (hon.), Anat. Soc. Gr. Britain and Ireland (hon.), Cajal Club (pres. 1973-74), Phi Beta Kappa, Sigma Xi, Alpha Omega Alpha. Home: 78 Temple Rd Concord MA 01742-1520

PALAZZI, JOSEPH L(AZARRO), manufacturing executive; b. New Haven, July 5, 1947; s. Joseph Anthony and Helen (Volosovich) P.; m. Lorna May Mickiewicz, May 27, 1978. BS, Quinnipiac Coll., 1969; MBA, U. New Haven, 1973. Mgr. budgets The Stanley Works, New Britian, Conn., 1972-76; mgr. planning Bangor Punta Corp., Greenwich, Conn., 1976-79; asst. corp. controller Pepperidge Farm, Norwalk, Conn., 1979-81, dir. fin. services, 1981-82, group controller, 1982-83; corp. controller Plessey, Inc., White Plains, N.Y., 1983-84, v.p. finance, 1984-86, chief fin. officer, 1986-89; v.p. fin., chief fin. officer BTR Inc., Stanford, Ct., 1990-92; pres. Fasco Industries Inc., Chesterfield, Mo., 1992—. Mem. Rep. Town Com., Newtown, Conn., 1981; bd. dirs. Danbury Hosp., 1987-92. Served with U.S. Army, 1969-76. Mem. AICPA, Nat. Assn. Accts., Sigma Six Flying Club. Episcopalian. Avocations: sailing, tennis, golf, flying. Home: 39 Villa Coublay Saint Louis MO 63131-2730 Office: Fasco Industries Inc 500 Chesterfield Ctr Ste 200 Chesterfield MO 63017-4823

PALAZZO, ROBERT P., lawyer, accountant; b. L.A., Apr. 14, 1952; s. Joseph Francis and Mickey Palazzo. BA in Econs., UCLA, 1973; MBA, U. So. Calif., 1976, JD, 1976; postgrad., U. Oxford, 1979. CPA Calif., Nev., Colo.; Bar: Calif. 1976, U.S. Dist. Ct. (so. dist.) Calif. 1977, U.S. Tax Ct. 1977, U.S. Ct. Appeals (9th cir.) 1978, U.S. Supreme Ct. 1980. Assoc. Graham & James, L.A., 1976-78; ptnr. Rader, Cornwall, Kessler & Palazzo CPAs, L.A., 1978-81, Palazzo & Kessler, attys at law, L.A., 1978-81; sole practice L.A., Darwin, Calif., 1981—; judge pro tem L.A. Mcpl. Ct., 1982—; bd. dirs. Cons. Am. Oil Co., Fin. Systems Internat. Inc., Adventures Prodns., Inc.; alumni advisor UCLA, 1977-81, mem. adv. and scholarship com., 1978-81; mem. profl. adv. com. West L.A. Coll., 1993—; lectr. U. Oxford, 1979, U. So. Calif., 1986; speaker 3rd Death Valley History Conf., 1992, 4th Death Valley History Conf., 1995; hist. cons. A&E Civil War Jour., Death Valley Memories (motion picture), A&E Biography; spkr. Calif. State U., Northridge, 1996, Death Valley 49ers Encampment, 1996; hist. cons. A&E Biography. Author: Darwin, California, 1996; contbg. editor: The Gun Report; prodr. (motion picture) L.A. Bounty; contbr. articles to profl. jours. Founder Ohio History Flight Mus.; bd. dirs. Calif. Cancer Found., L.A., 1978—, pres., 1979-80; bd. dirs. Friends of William S. Hart Park and Mus., 1990-93, v.p. Mus. Relations; chmn. dist. bd. dirs. Darwin Community Svcs., 1990-92. Mem. L.A. County Bar Assn. (arbitration com., fee dispute resolution program), Italian Am. Lawyers Assn. (bd. govs. 1980—, 1st v.p. 1984-88), Nat. Acad. Rec. Arts and Scis., Western Writers Assn., Century City Bar Assn. (vice-chmn. estate planning, trust and probate com. 1979-80), Am. Numismatic Assn. (dist. rep. Carson City 1981-82, L.A. 1982-83), Mensa, Omicron Delta Epsilon, Beta Alpha Psi (pres. 1972), Pi Gamma Mu, Phi Alpha Delta, Zeta Phi Eta. Office: 3002 Midvale Ave Ste 209 Los Angeles CA 90034-3418 also: 230 S Main St Darwin CA 93522

PALDUS, JOSEF, mathematics educator; b. Bzi, Czechoslovakia, Nov. 25, 1935; emigrated to Can., 1968; s. Josef and Ludmila (Danicek) P.; m. Eva Zdena Bajer, Jan. 26, 1961; 1 dau., Barbara Alice. MSc, Charles U., Prague, 1958, DrSc, 1995; PhD, Czechoslovak Acad. Sci., Prague, 1961. Research scientist Czechoslovak Acad. Scis., Prague, 1961-62, 64-68; postdoctoral fellow NRC, Ottawa, Can., 1962-64; assoc. prof. applied math. U. Waterloo, Ont., Can., 1968-75, prof., 1975—; assoc. dir. Fields Inst., 1992-95; vis. prof. U. Rheims, 1973, U. Louis Pasteur, Strasbourg, France, 1975-76, 82-83, Cath. U., Nijmegen, Holland, 1981, Technion, Haifa, Israel, 1983; vis. scientist NRC, Ottawa, 1966-68, Free U. Berlin, 1981; adj. prof. chemistry U. Fla., Gainesville, 1984—; fellow Inst. for Advanced Study, Berlin, 1986-87. Mem. editl. bd. Comtex Sci., 1981-83, Advances in Quantum Chemistry, 1986, Jour. Chem. Physics, 1987-89, Can. Jour. Chemistry, 1994-96, Internat. Jour. Quantum Chemistry, 1996; mem. adv. editl. bd. Internat. Jour. Quantum Chemistry, 1977-88, Theoretica Chimica Acta, 1988-94, Jour. Math. Chemistry, Switzerland, 1989; contbr. numerous articles to profl. jours., chpts. to books. Killam Rsch. fellow, 1987-89; recipient prize Chemistry divsn. Czechoslovak Acad. Scis., 1962, 67, J. Heyrovsky Gold medal Czechoslovak Acad. Sci., 1992, Gold medal Faculty of Math and Physics, Comenius U., Slovakia, 1994, Alexander von Humboldt Sr. Scientist award, 1996. Fellow Royal Soc. Can.; mem. Internat. Acad. Quantum Molecular Sci., Internat. Soc. Theoretical Chem. Physics (bd. dirs.), European Acad. Scis., Czech Learned Soc. (hon. mem.), Arts and Letters (corr.), Am. Inst. Physics, N.Y. Acad. Scis., Applied Math. Soc. Can., Can. Soc. for Chemistry, Chem. Inst. Can. Roman Catholic. Office: U Waterloo Dept Applied Math, University Ave, Waterloo, ON Canada N2L 3G1

PALECEK, SANDRA MARIE, reading education specialist; b. Ashland, Wis., Oct. 31, 1940; d. Francis Joseph and Martha Evelyn (Verville) Bonneville; m. John Allan Palecek, Oct. 3, 1964; children: Stephanie Lynn, Michael John. BS in Elem. Edn., U. River Falls, 1971; MS in Reading, U. Superior, 1981. Tchr. grades 2 and 3 Spring Valley (Wis.) Sch., 1959-62; tchr. grade 2 Pleasant Hill Sch., Waukesha, Wis., 1962-64; tchr. grades 2 and 3 Glidden (Wis.) Sch., 1964-65; Chpt. I tchr. Butternut (Wis.) Sch., 1966-68; Chpt. I reading specialist Glidden Schs., 1968—; amb. of reading People to People to China, 1993. Pres. Chequmegon Reading Coun., Park Falls, Wis., 1981. Herb Kohl fellow, 1994; recipient Outstanding Svc. award Title I Program, Glidden, 1980, Significant Contbns. award Chpt. I Program, Madison, Wis., 1990; named Dist. Tchr. of Yr., Dept. Pub. Instrn., Madison, 1980, 94, Exemplary Remedial Reading award, 1989, 30 Yr. Svc. award Chpt. I, New Orleans, 1996. Mem. Internat. Reading Assn., Wis. State Reading Assn., Glidden Fedn. Tchrs. Union (v.p., then pres.). Avocations: reading, hiking, cross-country skiing, bowling. Home: N15517 Town Hall Rd Park Falls WI 54552-8069 Office: Glidden Sch Glidden WI 54527

PALERMO, ANTHONY ROBERT, lawyer; b. Rochester, N.Y., Sept. 30, 1929; s. Anthony C. and Mary (Palvino) P.; m. Mary Ann Coyne, Jan. 2, 1960; children: Mark Henry, Christopher Coyne, Peter Stuart, Elisabeth Megan McCarthy, Julie Coyne Lawther, Gregg Anthony. BA, U. Mich., 1951; JD, Georgetown U., 1956. Bar: D.C. 1956, N.Y. 1957, U.S. Supreme Ct. 1961. Trial atty. U.S. Dept. Justice, Washington, 1956-58; asst. atty. U.S. Dept. Justice, N.Y.C., 1958-60; asst. U.S. atty. in charge U.S. Dept. Justice, Rochester, N.Y., 1960-61; ptnr. Brennan, Centner, Palermo & Blauvelt, Rochester, 1962-81, Harter, Secrest & Emery, Rochester, 1981-94, Hodgson, Russ, Andrews, Woods & Goodyear, Rochester, 1994—. Note editor Georgetown Law Jour., 1956. Bd. dirs. McQuaid Jesuit H.S., Rochester, 1978-84, St. Ann's Home for Aged, Rochester, 1974—; bd. dirs., sec. St. Ann's Home Found., Rochester, 1989—; trustee, charter chmn. Clients' Security Fund N.Y., 1981-90; chmn. Govs. Jud. Screening Com. 4th Jud. Dept., mem. statewide com., 1987-89; chair magistrate selection com. U.S. Dist. Ct. (we. dist.) N.Y., 1995. Fellow Am. Bar Found., N.Y. State Bar Found. (bd. dirs. 1978-91), Am. Coll. Trial Lawyers; mem. ABA (ho. dels. 1980—, state del. 1982-85, bd. govs. 1985-88, 1989-93, sec. 1990-93), N.Y. State Bar Assn. (pres. 1979-80, ho. dels. 1973-75, 77—), Monroe County Bar Assn. (pres. 1973), Oak Hill Country Club. Roman Catholic. Avocation: golf. Home: 38 Huntington Meadow Rochester NY 14625

PALERMO, DAVID STUART, retired psychology educator and administrator. BS in Psychology and Edn., Lynchburg Coll., 1951; MS in Psychology, U. Mass., 1953; PhD, U. Iowa, 1955. Rsch. assoc. Iowa Child Welfare Rsch. Sta. U. Iowa, 1955; asst. prof. psychology So. Ill. U., Carbondale, 1955-58; asst. prof. Inst. Child Devel. U. Minn., Mpls., 1958-63; vis. prof. dept. psychology U. Edinburgh, Scotland, 1969-70; sr. Fulbright scholar dept. psychology U. Sydney, Australia, 1975; prof. Inst. Advanced Psychol. Studies Adelphi U., Garden City, L.I., N.Y., 1978-79; assoc. prof. Pa. State U., University Park, 1963-66, prof., 1966—, assoc. dir. Ctr. for the Study of Child, Adolescent Devel., 1984-88, assoc. dean for rsch. and grad. studies, Coll. Liberal Arts, 1988-92; prof. emeritus, 1992—; assoc. The Behavioral and Brain Scis., 1982—; vis. prof. SUNY Purchase, 1995-97. Editor Child Development Abstracts and Bibliography, 1971-74; editor Jour. Exptl. Child Psychology, 1973-83, mem. editorial bd., 1966—; mem. editorial bd. Jour. Verbal Learning and Verbal Behavior, 1964-77, Metaphor and Symbolic Activity, 1983—, Cognitive Devel., 1990-93; contbr. numerous articles to profl. jours. Recipient Career Devel. award Nat. Inst. of Child Health and Human Devel. award, 1965-70. Fellow APA; mem. Soc. for Rsch. in Child Devel., Ea. Psychol. Assn., Jean Piaget Soc., Sigma Xi,.

PALERMO, GREGORY SEBASTIAN, architect; b. Westfield, N.Y., Oct. 28, 1946; s. Sebastian and Frances Joan (Ciminella) P.; divorced; children: Mark Sebastian, Christopher Anthony. BArch, Carnegie Mellon U., 1969; MArch in Urban Design, Wash. U., 1976. Registered architect, Mo., Calif., N.Y., Iowa. Architect PGAV Inc., St. Louis, 1976-79; sr. v.p. HOK, Inc., St. Louis, 1980-87; sr. assoc. Mackey Assocs., St. Louis, 1987-89; v.p., prin. Stone Marraccini Patterson, St. Louis, 1989-91; affiliate asst. prof. Washington U. Sch. Arch., 1984-90; vis. assoc. prof. Iowa State U. Dept. Arch., 1992-95, assoc. prof., 1995—; chair Des Moines Archtl. Adv. Com., 1996; mem. Des Moines Gateway Planning Com., 1996. Editorial bd. Iowa Architect mag., 1992—, assoc. ed., 1995—. Mem. Light Rail Transit Rev. Com., 1985, St. Louis Mayoral Task Force, 1986; exec/coun. Arts in Transit Com., St. Louis, 1987—; chmn. design rev. com.,St. Louis Metrolink Transit System, 1989-91; chair Nat. AIA Edn. Task Force, 1990; mem. Leadership St. Louis, 1990-91, Archtl. Adv. Commn. city of Des Moines, 1992—. Fellow AIA (bd. dirs., nat. v.p.); mem. Nat. Archtl. Accreditation Bd (pres. 1993-94). Office: Iowa State Univ Dept Architecture Rm 156 Ames IA 50011-3093

PALERMO, PETER M., JR., photography equipment company executive; b. Rochester, N.Y., Aug. 21, 1941; s. Peter M. and Adeline M. (Bruno) P.; m. Marcia G. Hendershott, Aug. 25, 1962; children; Peter M., Lisa M., Michelle A. B.A., Bowling Green U., 1963; M.B.A., U. Rochester, 1973. Mgr. mktg. Kodak Caribbean, Ltd., San Juan, P.R., 1976-79; gen. mgr. Kodak Philippines Ltd., Manila, 1979-81; gen. mgr. Mexican Ops. Eastman Kodak Co. Internat. Photo div., Mexico City, 1983-84; corp. v.p., gen. mgr. Eastman Kodak Co. Health Scis. div., Rochester, N.Y., 1984-86; corp. v.p., gen. mgr. consumer products div. Eastman Kodak Co., Rochester, 1986—, corp. v.p., gen. mgr. consumer imaging, 1991-93, v.p., dir. mktg., sr. v.p. imaging, 1993—; pres., CEO The Jason Found. for Edn., Pittsford, N.Y., 1993—; pres. Ultra Techs. div. Eastman Tech., Inc. (subs. Eastman Kodak Co.), 1989—; adj. faculty mem. Rochester Inst. of Tech., 1965-69. Contbr. articles to profl. jours. Bd. dirs. Spl. Olympics, 1990. Recipient Catholic Media award Pope John Paul II, Manila, 1981; named one of Outstanding Young Men of Am., 1973. Fellow Profl. Photog. Soc. of Philippines; mem. Health Industry Mfrs. Assn. (corp. mem., trustee 4-H com. 1990), Internat. Mgmt. Assn. (corp. mem.), Photo Mktg. Assn. Internat. (corp. mem.), Assn. Photog. Mfrs. Mex. Republican. Roman Catholic. Clubs: Manila Polo, Dorado Beach Country P.R. Lodge: Rotary (dir. Manila, 1979-81). Avocations: scuba diving; writing; photography; tennis. Office: Pres/CEO The Jason Fund for Edn 40A Grove St Pittsford NY 14534-1326

PALERMO, ROBERT JAMES, architect, consultant, inventor; b. N.Y.C., Mar. 25, 1949; s. Vitorio and Simone (DiFlorio) P.; m. Lore Bernadette Bilbao, July 22, 1972 (dec. Feb. 1977); m. Patricia Dolores Ward, June 14, 1981; children: Jaime, Justin, Kristen Leigh. BS, CCNY, 1971, BArch, 1972; MBA, Baruch Grad. Ctr., 1974; postgrad., Nat. Asbestos Tng. Inst., 1987. Lic. asbestos investigator; registered architect, N.Y., N.J. Architect Rongved, Wilcox, Erickson, N.Y.C., 1972-73, Welton Becket Assocs., N.Y.C., 1973-75; architect, prin. Jaime Lore Design, Bklyn., 1976—; bd. dir. Nat. Meddlex Med. Constrn. Corp., Hicksville, N.Y., 1981-85; pres. Corp. Design of Am., P.C., 1989—. Mem. Am. Inst. Archs., Soc. Am. Registered Archs., Cert. Interior Decorators Assn., Phi Sigma Kappa. Republican. Roman Catholic. Avocations: rare coin collecting, philatelics, Beaux Art prints. Home: 160 Pelican Rd Middletown NJ 07748-3042 Office: Corp Design of Am PC 461 Park Ave S New York NY 10016-6822

PALERMO, STEVE, sportscaster, color analyst, former umpire; b. Worcester, Mass., Oct. 9, 1949; m. Debbie, 1991. Attended, Norwich U., Worcester State Coll. Umpire N.Y. Penn League, 1972; umpire winter baseball P.R., Fla., and, Dominican Republic, 1972-74; umpire, single A baseball Carolina League, 1973; umpire, double A baseball Ea. League, 1973-74; umpire, triple A baseball Am. Assn., 1975-76; umpire Am. League Baseball, 1977-91; sports caster Seattle Mariners, 1992-94; sports caster MSG Network, 1994—, back-up color analyst, 1994—; sports analyst The Baseball Network, 1994—; umpire Am. League Championships, 1980, 82, 84, 89, World Series, 1983, Baseball All-Star Game, 1986; spl. asst. Major League Baseball Exec. Coun., 1994—. Co-founder Steve Palermo Found. for Spinal Cord Injuries, Overland Park, Kans. Recipient over 25 awards for courage and dedication, Arthur Ashe Courage award, 1994; named Sporting News # 1 Rated Am. League Umpire, 1991. Office: MSG Network 2 Penn Plz Fl 14 New York NY 10121-1499*

PALESKY, CAROL EAST, tax accountant; b. Orange, N.J., May 13, 1940; d. Neil Norell and Marie R. Reiss; m. Jacob Palesky; children: Donna, Lewis. AB, Am. Inst., Pleasantville, N.J., 1973; postgrad., Am. Inst., Portland, Maine, 1980; student, Atlantic C.C., Mays Landing, N.J., 1971-73. With mgmt. First Nat. Bank of South Jersey (now First Fidelity), Pleasantville, N.J., 1967-74; loan officer Maine Savs. Bank, Portland, 1980-81; acct., owner East Assocs., Topsham, Maine, 1985—. Treas., bd. dirs. Congl. Term Limits Coalition, Topsham, 1993—; bd. dirs. Maine Citizens Rev. Bd., Portland, 1993—. Scholar Nat. Taxpayer Union, 1992, 94; recipient United to Serve Am. award, 1992. Mem. Nat. Assn. Small Business Owners, Maine Taxpayers Action Network (pres. 1990—), Topsham Taxpayer Assn. (pres. 1991—). Roman Catholic. Home and Office: 24 Sokokis Cir Topsham ME 04086-1615

PALEWICZ, RICHARD ALFRED, judge; b. Chgo., June 26, 1927; s. Emil FRanz Witold and Alfreds (Pold) P.; m. Shirley Ann Bauman, July 10, 1954 (dec. Apr. 1993). BA in Econs. and Speech, U. Ill., 1950; JD, Loyola U., Chgo., 1958; diploma, U.S. Army War Coll., Carlisle, Pa., 1979, U.S. Army Command & Staff Coll, Ft. Riley, Kans., 1976. Merchandise sect. head Montgomery Ward & Co., Chgo., 1954-56; oper. mgr. Allied Radio Co., Chgo., 1956-58; gen. office mgr. Win-Chek Products Corp., Addison, Ill., 1959; legal editor labor law Commerce Clearing House, Chgo., 1960-62; sr. ptnr. Bamberger & Palewicz, Chgo., 1959-62; atty. trade regulations FTC, Chgo., 1962-65, sr. trial atty., 1966-74, supervising atty. trade regulations, 1975-80; U.S. adminstrv. law judge Office Hearing & Appeals Health & Human Svcs., Chgo., 1980-81; hearing office chief adminstrv. law judge Office Hearing & Appeals Health & Human Svcs. (HHS), Chgo., 1981-88; U.S. adminstrv. law judge Office Hearings & Appeals HHS & Social Sec. Adminstrn., Chgo., 1989—. Bd. dirs. Jane Adams Hull House-Uptown Ctr., Chgo., 1972—; pres. Truman Coll. Coun., Chgo., 1978-80; chmn. presdl. selection com. Truman Coll., Chgo., 1978, mem. coll. coun., 1979—. Col. Inf., U.S. Army, 1951-54; active res. 1954-80. Recipient Honoree Night award Cook County Vets. Assistance Commn., Chgo. Mem. ABA, FBA, Ill. State Bar Assn., Chgo. Bar Assn., Res. Officers Assn. U.S. (nat. judge advocate 1992-94, pres. Ill. dept. 1988, pres. Cook County chpt. 1986. Eagle award 1993, Brigade of Vols. 1990), Mil. Order World Wars (comdr. Ill. State 1976, chgo. chpt. comdr. 1975, vice-comdr. in chief 1991-93, sr. vice comdr. 1993-94, comdr. in chief 1994-95, Youth Leadership award 1995), Advocate Soc., Chgo. Soc. PNA SARCOM (Sr. Army Res. Comdrs. - Col. & Generals). Roman Catholic. Home: 501 Skyline Dr Algonquin IL 60102 Office: Office Hearings & Appeals 55 W Monroe St Ste 700 Chicago IL 60603-5003

PALEY, ALAN H., lawyer; b. Apr. 28, 1950. BA, Case Western Res. U., 1972; JD, NYU, 1975, LLM, 1976. Bar: N.Y. 1976. Fellow securities inst. sch. law NYU, 1975-76; mem. Debevoise & Plimpton, N.Y.C. Mem. Phi Beta Kappa. Office: Debevoise & Plimpton 875 3rd Ave New York NY 10022-6225

PALEY, ALFRED IRVING, value engineering and consulting company executive, lecturer; b. Monticello, N.Y., Apr. 12, 1927; s. Max and Dora (Gutkin) P.; m. Sylvia Tiffel, June 26, 1949; children: Maureen, Howard, Doreen. BEE, Poly. Inst. Bklyn., 1949. Sr. engr. W.L. Maxson Corp., N.Y.C., 1950-58; chief engr. Acoustica Assocs., Mineola, N.Y., 1958-60; staff scientist in acoustics Am. Bosch Arma Corp., Garden City, N.Y., 1960-62; chief engr. in elec. acoustics Janus Products, Syosset, N.Y., 1962-63; mgr. Anti-Submarine Warfare systems Gyrodyne Co. of Am., St. James, N.Y., 1963-67; mgr. cost and value control Loral Electronic Systems, Yonkers, N.Y., 1967-80; v.p. program mgmt. FEL Corp., Farmingdale, N.J., 1980-84; pres. NRI Assocs., Ltd., 1984—; value engring. program mgr. CECOM, U.S. Army, Ft. Monmouth, N.J., 1985-95, ret. 1995; assoc. prof. Poly. Inst. Bklyn., 1955-65, Hofstra U., Hempstead, N.Y., 1974-79; lectr. Am. Mgmt. Assn., N.Y.C., 1973-80. Contbr. articles to profl. jours. Patentee in field. Bd. dirs. Suburban Temple, Wantagh, N.Y., 1964-80, Monmouth Reform Temple, Tinton Falls, N.J., 1983-91; bd. dirs. Miles Value Found., sec., 1996—. Served with USN, 1945-46. Recipient Outstanding Achivement Through Value Engring. award Dept. Def., 1995. Mem. Project Mgmt. Inst., Soc. Info. Display (sec. 1978), Nat. Mgmt. Assn. (pres. chpt. 1975-76), SAVE Internat. (Value Engr. of Yr. 1985-86, 88-89, Disting. Svc. award 1991). Democrat. Jewish. Home and Office: 5442 N Whitethorn Pl Tucson AZ 85704-2634

PALEY, GERALD LARRY, lawyer; b. Albany, N.Y., Sept. 11, 1939; s. Arthur and Mary (Peckner) P.; m. Joyce R., June 25, 1961 (div. June 1985); children: Jonathan, Eric, Suzanne; m. Sheryl Gae, Aug. 14, 1985. BA, Union Coll., 1961; JD with distinction, Cornell U., 1964. Bar: N.Y. 1964. Assoc. Nixon, Hargrave, Devans & Doyle, Rochester, N.Y., 1964-69; assoc. solicitor Dept. Labor, Washington, 1969-71; ptnr. Nixon, Hargrave, Devans & Doyle, Rochester, 1971-87, Phillips, Lytle, Hitchcock, Blaine & Huber, Rochester, 1987—. Author: Handbook of Federal Labor Relations Laws, 1981, Understand Employee Regulations, 1984. Mem. ABA. Republican. Jewish. Office: Phillips Lytle Hitchcock et al 1400 First Federal Pla Rochester NY 14614

PALEY, GRACE, author, educator; b. N.Y.C., Dec. 11, 1922; d. Isaac and Mary (Ridnyik) Goodside; m. Jess Paley, June 20, 1942; children: Nora, Dan.; m. Robert Nichols, 1972. Ed., Hunter Coll., NYU. Formerly tchr. Columbia, Syracuse U.; ret. mem. lit. faculty Sarah Lawrence Coll., Stanford, Johns Hopkins, Dartmouth, CUNY. Author: The Little Disturbances of Man, 1959, Enormous Changes at the Last Minute, 1974, Leaning Forward, 1985, Later the Same Day, 1985, Long Walks and Intimate Talks, 1991, New and Collected Poems, 1992, The Collected Stories, 1994 (Nat. Book award nomination 1994); stories published in Atlantic, Esquire, Ikon, Genesis West, Accent, others. Sec. N.Y. Greenwich Village Peace Center. Recipient Literary award for short story writing Nat. Inst. Arts and Letters, 1970, Edith Wharton award N.Y. State, 1988, 89, Rea award for short story, 1993, Vt. Gov.'s award for Excellence in the Arts, 1993, award for contbn. to Jewish culture Nat. Found. Jewish Culture; Guggenheim fellow. Mem. Am. Acad. and Inst. Arts and Letters. Office: PO Box 620 Thetford VT 05074-0620

PALEY, NORMAN, advertising executive. Print buyer collateral prodn. dept. Ogilvy & Mather, Inc., 1964-68, prodn. mgr., 1968-73, with direct response group, 1973-76; ptnr. Ogilvy & Mather Direct Response, 1976-85, sr. ptnr., 1985—. Office: Ogilvy & Mather Direct 309 W 49th St New York NY 10019-7316

PALIA, ASPY PHIROZE, marketing educator, researcher, consultant; b. Bombay, Nov. 27, 1944; came to U.S., 1973; s. Phiroze E. and Homai P. (Irani) P. BE in Mech. Engring., U. Bangalore, 1966; MBA, U. Hawaii at Manoa, 1976; DBA, Kent State U., 1985. Sales engr. Larsen & Toubro Ltd., 1966-72, export sales engr., 1972-73; teaching fellow Coll. Bus. Adminstrn. Kent State U., 1977-80, instr. Coll. Bus. Adminstrn., 1982-84; asst. prof. Coll. Bus. Adminstrn. U. Hawaii, Manoa, 1984-89, assoc. prof., 1990-95, prof., 1996—, pres. faculty coun., 1995-96; senator U. Hawaii Manoa Faculty Congress, 1996—; vis. prof. Coll. Mgmt. Nat. Sun Yat-sen U., Kaohsiung, Taiwan, 1992, Chulalongkorn U., Bangkok, Thailand, 1992, 93, U. Otago, New Zealand, 1995, Adminstrv. Staff Coll. India, Hyderabad, 1992; mem. U. Hawaii Manoa Ctr. for Teaching Excellence Faculty Adv. Group, 1991; mem. mktg. plan adv. com. U. Hawaii, Manoa, 1994, mem. honors and awards com., 1990-91, pres. faculty coun. 1995-96; vis. scholar faculty bus. adminstrn. Nat. U. Singapore, 1991, Mktg. Inst. Singapore Exec. Devel. Seminars, 1991, 94-95, Hong Kong Inst. Mktg. Exec. Devel. Seminar, 1996, others; affiliate faculty Japan Am. Inst. Mgmt. Sci., Honolulu, 1989—; vis. prof. Grad. Sch. Internat. Mgmt., Internat. U. Japan, Uhrasa, Yamatomachi, 1991, U. Internat. Bus. and Econs., Beijing, 1991, U. Kebangsaan Malaysia, Bangi-Selangor, Kuala Lumpur, Malaysia, 1991, 92; lectr., cons., presenter in field. Editor: (with Dennis A. Rondinelli) Project Planning and Implementation in Developing Countries, 1976; contbr. conf. procs. and articles to profl. jours. and books, including Indsl. Mktg. Mgmt., Internat. Bus. Jour., Asia-Pacific Jour. Mgmt., Internat. Mktg. Rev., Fgn. Trade Rev., Internat. Rev. Econs. & Bus., others; contbr. to numerous confs. and symposia in field; developer various mktg. decision support systems and decision-making tools for use in strategic market planning and in marketing simulations. Mem. various program rev. coms. Pacific and Asian Mgmt. Inst., Acad. Internat. Bus., Assn. Bus. Simulation and Exptl. Learning, others; bd. examiners Nat. U. Singapore Sch. Postgrad. Mgmt. Studies, 1991; mem. adv. bd. Soc. Coll. of Bus. Adminstrn. Alumni and Friends Exec. Com., 1991-93; adv. bd. Salvation Army Resdl. Treatment Facilities for Children and Youth Adv. Coun., 1989-96, vice chair, 1987-89; chair Salvation Army Family Treatment Svcs. Adv. Coun., 1997—; mem. Salvation Army Honolulu Adv. Bd., 1997—; treas., bd. dirs. Kings Gate Homeowners Assn., 1994-96. Univ. fellow Kent State U., 1983; East-West Ctr. scholar East-West Ctr., 1973-75; Ednl. Improvement Fund grantee, 1989, Instrl. Travel and Devel. Fund grantee Office Faculty Devel. and Acad. Support, 1991, 95, joint rsch. grants U. Kebangsaan Malaysia, Nat. U. Singapore, U. So. Queensland, Australia, U. Otago, New Zealand; recipient Internat. Agreements Fund award Office Internat. Programs and Svcs., 1990-91, 91-92, ORA travel award U. Rsch. Coun., 1986, 88, 89, 91, 92, 94, 95, 96, 97. Mem. Am. Mktg. Assn. (academia editor Honolulu chpt. 1986-87), Acad. Internat. Bus. (chair Pacific Basin Region 1995, chair Pacific Basin chpt. 1996—, co-chair Asia Pacific Conf. 1997), Pacific Asian Consortium for Internat. Bus. Edn. and Rsch., Assn. for Bus. Simulation and Exptl. Learning, Pan-Pacific Bus. Assn. (charter), Mortar Bd. (Outstanding Educator award 1993, Mentor award 1995), East-West Ctr. Alumni Assn. U.S. (v.p. Hawaii chpt. 1987-89, ad campaign com. 1987-88), Beta Gamma Sigma (faculty advisor, sec.-treas. Alpha of Hawaii chpt. 1990—, Outstanding Svc. award 1992-93, Bd. Govs. Commitment to Excellence award 1997), Mu Kappa Tau, Pi Sigma Epsilon. Avocations: music, photography, swimming, reading, hiking. Home: 2724 Kahoaloha Ln Apt 1605 Honolulu HI 96826-3337 Office: U Hawaii Manoa Dept Mktg 2404 Maile Way Honolulu HI 96822-2223

PALIHNICH, NICHOLAS JOSEPH, JR., retail chain executive; b. Montclair, N.J., Nov. 9, 1939; s. Nicholas Joseph and Lucille (Pflugh) P.; m. Diane Lorraine Parise, Nov. 12, 1966; children: Nicholas, Kristin, Danielle. B.B.A., U. Notre Dame, 1961. Retail buyer R.H. Macy, N.Y.C., 1961-66, Korvettes, Inc., N.Y.C., 1966-69; retail v.p., gen. mdse. mgr. Mangurians Inc., Ft. Lauderdale, Fla., 1970-72; sr. v.p. retail mgmt. Korvettes Inc., N.Y.C., 1973-79; pres. Korvettes Inc., 1979-81; sr. v.p. retail mgmt. Lane Bryant, 1981-83; pres. retail mgmt. Dan Inc., 1984-86; exec. v.p. retail Bally U.S.A, 1987-93; gen. mgr. retail, dir. The Rockport Co., Marlborough, Mass., 1994—. Served with U.S. Army, 1962. Republican. Roman Catholic. Office: 220 Donald Lynch Blvd Marlborough MA 01752-4708

PALIK, ROBERT RICHARD, mechanical engineer; b. Iowa City, Iowa, Mar. 10, 1923; s. Frank and Maria (Pavco) P.; m. Wanita Slaughter, Dec. 19, 1945; children: Andrea Denise, Stephen Brett, Robert Neil. BSME, State U. Iowa, 1949, MSME, 1950. Registered profl. engr. Va. Lab. tech. State U. Iowa Physics Dept., Iowa City, 1941-42; chief engr. Keokuk (Iowa) Steel Casting Co., 1950-54; mgr. rsch. engring. Reynolds Aluminuim Co., Richmond, Va., 1954-70; v.p. Crown Aluminium Inds., Roxboro, N.C., 1970-75; div. chief City of Richmond, 1975-79; gen. engr. U.S. Dept. Housing and Urban Devel., Richmond, 1979-94. Pres. West Wistar Civic Assn., Richmond, 1957; legis. chmn., treas. PTA, Richmond, 1957. Lt. Col. USAF, 1942-45. Fellow ASME; mem. Pi Tau Sigma. Achievements include method of treating metal patent. Home and Office: 9318 Westmoor Dr Richmond VA 23229-6247

PALIN, MICHAEL EDWARD, actor, screenwriter, author; b. May 5, 1943; s. Edward and Mary P.; m. Helen M. Gibbons, 1966; 3 children. BA, U. Oxford, Eng., 1965. Writer, performer BBC Corp., 1965-69. Actor, writer: (TV shows) Monty Python's Flying Circus, 1969-74, Ripping Yarns, 1976-80; (films) And Now for Something Completely Different, 1970, Monty Python and the Holy Grail, 1974, Monty Python's Life of Brian, 1978, Time Bandits, 1980, Monty Python's The Meaning of Life, 1982, American Friends, 1991; TV presenter, writer Great Railway Journeys of the World, 1980, Around the World in 80 Days, 1989, Pole to Pole, 1993, Palin's Column, 1994, Great Railway Journeys of the World, 1994, Full Circle, 1997; actor: (TV shows) Three Men in a Boat, 1975, GBH, 1991; (films) Jabberwocky, 1976, A Private Function, 1984, Brazil, 1985, A Fish Called Wanda (Best Supporting Actor Brit. Acad. Film and TV Arts, 1989), Fierce Creatures, 1997; actor, writer and co-producer: The Missionary, 1982; writer (stage play) The Weekend, 1994; author: Monty Python's Brand New Book, 1973, Dr. Fegg's Encyclopaedia of All World Knowledge, 1984, Limericks, 1985, Around the World in 80 Days, 1989, Pole to Pole, 1993, Pole to Pole: The Photographs, 1994, Hemingway's Chair 1995, Full Circle, 1997, Full Circle: The Photographs, 1997; (children's books) Small Harry and the Toothache Pills, 1981, The Mirrorstone, 1986, The Cyril Stories, 1986. Co-recipient (with Monty Python) Michael Balcon award for outstanding contribution to cinema British Academy of Film and TV Arts, 1987. Avocations: reading, running, railways. Office: 68 A Delancey St, London NW1 7RY, England

PALINSKY, CONSTANCE GENEVIEVE, hypnotherapist, educator; b. Flint, Mich., May 31, 1927; d. George and Genevieve Treasa (Pisarski) Ignace; m. Joseph Palinsky, July 3, 1947; children: Joseph II, Mark Robert. Art student, Flint Inst. Arts, Oriental Artists Sch., others; numerous hypnosis studies including, Ethical Tng. Hypnosis Ctr., N.J. and Fla., Mid-West Inst., Hypnodye Found, Ill. and Fla.; tng., Nat. Guild Hypnotherapists. Cert NLP practitioner, neuro linguistics programmer. Owner, operator Palinsky Gallery of Art and Antiques, Flint, 1970-80; art lectr. Genesee County Grade Sch. System Flint Inst. Arts, 1972-74; owner, hypnosis cons. Hypno-Tech. Ctr., Flint, 1975-80; asst. mgr. Wethered-Rice Fine Jewelry, Flint, 1982-83; hypnotherapist, sr. cons. Dailey Life Ctr., Flint, 1985-96; mem. Am. Bd. Hypnotherapy, Calif.; numerous radio and TV shows and guest appearances, Flint, 1957—, ABC Nat. Network, 1959, Flint Calbe TV, 1972, others. Author: Constructive Personality Development, 1987, Secrets Revealed for Hypnosis Scripting, 1989, Designing Hypnosis Scripts for Relief of Multiple Sclerosis, 1994, Substance Abuse Issues Revealed of Effective Hypnosis Interventions, 1994, Light Touch Therapy for Pain Relief of Stress-Headache and Back Pain Relief--A Form of Hypno-Acupressure, 1995; one-woman show Dell's Artcraft Gallery, 1958; group shows at Flint Inst. Arts, U. Mich., Purdue U., Lafayette, Inc., Flint Artist Market, Saginaw, Detroit and Grand Rapids, Mich., Japan, others; contbr. articles to profl. jours.; author scripts and software in hypnosis field. Bd. dirs. The Chapel of The Angles Bldg. Fund for Lapeer County, 1974-75; pub. speaker various civic orgns. Named Oil Colorist of Yr. Profl. Photographers of Mich., 1959; recipient Pub. Svc. award Genesee County Sheriff's Dept., 1974. Mem. Internat. Soc. Profl. Hypnosis (regional v.p. 1977-79), Internat. Soc. Profl. Hypnotists and Counselors, Internat. Med. and Dental Hypnotherapist Assn., Nat. Guild Hypnotherapists, Nat. Guild Hypnotists (rsch. award for hypnosis for relief of multiple sclerosis 1991), Questers Antique Study Group (various offices including pres. 1972-90), Internat. Psychic Arts Rsch. (founder, pres. 1974-75), Flint Artist Market Group (program dir., treas.), Flint Soc. Arts and Crafts (v.p., pres. 1958-59), Quota Club, others. Republican. Roman Catholic. Avocations: writing, painting, sculpting, travel, water skiing. Home: 2362 Nolen Dr Flint MI 48504-5201

PALISCA, CLAUDE VICTOR, musicologist, educator; b. Rijeka, Croatia, Nov. 24, 1921; came to U.S., 1930; s. Matthew and Gisella (Fleischhacker) P.; m. Jane Agnes Pyne, June 12, 1960 (div. Feb. 1987); children: Carl Pyne, Madeline Grace; m. Elizabeth Ann Keitel, Apr. 4, 1987. B.A., Queens Coll., 1943; M.A., Harvard U., 1948, Ph.D., 1954; M.A. (hon.), Yale U., 1964. Instr., then asst. prof. music U. Ill. at Urbana, 1953-59; asso. prof. history music Yale U., New Haven, 1959—, prof., 1964-80, Henry L. and Lucy G. Moses prof. music, 1980-92, emeritus, 1992—, dir. grad. studies music, 1967-69, 87-92, chmn. music dept., 1969-75, chmn., dir. grad. studies in Renaissance studies, 1977-80; chmn. council on humanities Yale U., 1977-79, fellow Silliman Coll., 1963—; sr. fellow council humanities Princeton U., 1961; cons. U.S. Office Edn., 1963—, NEH, 1967—; dir. Nat. Seminar Music Edn., 1963. Author: Girolamo Mei: Letters on Ancient and Modern Music, 1960, 2d edit., 1977, (with others) Musicology, 1963, Baroque Music, 1968, 3d edit., 1991, (with Donald Grout) History of Western Music, 5th edit., 1996, Humanism in Italian Renaissance Musical Thought, 1985 (Internat. Musicol. Soc. award 1987), The Florentine Camerata, 1989, Studies in the History of Italian Music and Music Theory, 1994; translator: (with Guy Marco) Zarlino, The Art of Counterpoint, 1968; editor: Hucbald, Guido and John on Music: Three Medieval Treatises, 1978, Norton Anthology of Western Music, 1980, 3rd edit., 1996, (with D. Kern Holloman) Musicology in the 1980's, 1982, Zarlino, On the Modes, 1983, Yale Music Theory Translation Series, Boethius, Fundamentals of Music, 1989, The Theory of Music (Franchino Gaffurio) 1993; mem. editorial and adv. bds. Studies in Music (Western Australia); mem. exec. com.: New Grove Dictionary, Jour. History of Ideas, Jour. Music Theory; contbr. articles to publs. Bd. dirs., exec. com. Arts Council Greater New Haven, 1964-77, Neighborhood Music Sch., 1966-69; mem. exec. com. Ednl. Center for Arts, New Haven, 1973-83, chmn., 1979-80; bd. dirs., chmn. edn. com. New Haven Symphony Soc., 1966-72, v.p., 1968-72; mem. ednl. adv. bd. J.S. Guggenheim Meml. Found., 1983-92. Served with AUS, 1943-46. John Knowles Paine traveling fellow, 1949-50; Fulbright fellow, 1950-52; Guggenheim fellow, 1959-60, 81-82; Nat. Endowment for the Humanities sr. fellow, 1972-73; Misha Strassberg sr. fellow in creative arts U. Western Australia, summer, 1984. Fellow AAAS, Am. Coun. Arts in Edn. (pres. 1967-69); mem. Internat. Musicol. Soc. (dir., v.p. 1977-82), Am. Musicol. Soc. (hon., pres. 1970-72), Coll. Music Soc. (coun.), Renaissance Soc. (coun. 1973-74, exec. com. 1978-87), ACLS-Soviet Union of Composers Commn. on Music Composition and Musicology (co-chmn. 1986-90). Office: Yale Univ PO Box 208310 New Haven CT 06520-8310

PALISI, ANTHONY THOMAS, psychologist, educator; b. Rahway, N.J., Mar. 8, 1930; s. Anthony Francis and Marianne Catherine (Picone) P.; m. Dyane Cassidy, Apr. 19, 1954; children: Jane, Anthony Francis II, Phyllis, Damian-Marie. BS, Seton Hall U., 1951, MA, 1958; EdD, Temple U., 1973. Cert. secondary tchr., elem. prin., psychologist, rehab. counselor, N.J.; mem. Nat. Register Health Care Profls. in Psychology. Tchr., coach pub. schs. Rahway, 1953-60; sports editor Rahway News-Record, 1950-60; prin. elem. pub. sch. Franklin Twp., N.J., 1960-65; asst. prof. edn. Seton Hall U., 1965-73, assoc. prof., 1974-77, prof., 1977-82, acting grad. dean, 1976-77, dir., 1969-80, indsl. cons. group dynamics, 1967—. Contbr. articles and short stories to profl. jours. and popular periodicals. Mem. Rahway Bd. Edn. 1961-62; trustee Rahway Libr., 1961-68, pres. 1967-68. Recipient award N.J. Sportswriters' Assn., 1953. Mem. APA, ACA, Am. Mgmt. Assn. (co-author video tng. program), N.J. Psychol. Assn., Assn. for Specialists in Group Work (mem. rsch. com. 1980-82), N.Y. Acad. Scis., Nat. Acad. Counselors and Family Therapists (chmn., exec. dir. 1988-93, co-editor Family Letter 1985-93), Nat. Register of Health Svc. Providers in Psychology, Am. Coll. Counselors. Roman Catholic.

PALITZ, BERNARD G., finance company executive; b. N.Y.C., Aug. 21, 1924; s. Clarence Y. and Ruth (Krummas) P.; m. Louise Beringer; children: Bernard G. Jr., Anne L. BS, MIT, 1947. Chmn. bd. Comml. Alliance Corp., N.Y.C., 1963-88, Credit Alliance Corp., N.Y.C., 1963-88, Leasing Svc. Corp., N.Y.C., 1963-88, Fin. Guaranty Ins. Co., Wilmington, Del., 1975—, Colonial Surety Co., Pitts., 1976—, Fin. Fed. Corp., 1989—; pres. Gregory Capital Corp., N.Y.C., 1996—; pres. Am. Credit Mgmt., Inc., N.Y.C., 1996. Trustee Coun. for Arts, MIT, 1979—, Haverford Coll., Pa., 1979-82, Rockefeller U. Coun.; incorporator Worcester (Mass.) Art Mus. Mem. Harmonie Club (N.Y.C.), Quaker Ridge Club (Scarsdale, N.Y.), Beach Point Club (Mamaroneck, N.Y.), Econ. Club of N.Y. Home: PO Box 287 221 E 70th St New York NY 10021-5203 Office: Gregory Capital Corp 445 Park Ave New York NY 10022-2606

PALITZ, CLARENCE YALE, JR., commercial finance executive; b. N.Y.C., Jan. 21, 1931; s. Clarence Yale and Ruth (Kromnes) P.; m. Muriel Dobson (div. Nov., 1988), children: Michael, Suzanne; m. Anka Kriser. B.A., Dartmouth Coll., 1952; M.B.A., NYU, 1953. With Bankers Trust Co., N.Y.C., 1952-53; v.p., dir. Credit Am. Corp., N.Y.C., 1956-58; asst. sec. James Talcott, Inc., N.Y.C., 1958-60; v.p., mng. dir. Shopper's Park-Westmount, Ltd., Edmonton, Alta., Can., 1958-74; pres., dir. 140 E 72d St. Corp., N.Y.C., 1962-65, Comml. Alliance Corp., N.Y.C., 1963-88, Credit Alliance Corp., N.Y.C., 1963-88, Leasing Service Corp., N.Y.C., 1963-88, Colonial Surety Co., Pitts., 1976—, Fin. Guaranty Ins. Co., Wilmington, Del., 1976—, Kidde Credit Corp., N.Y.C., 1976-80, First Interstate Comml. Alliance Corp., 1984-88, Fin. Fed. Corp., 1989—; pres., chmn. bd. dirs. First Land Devel. Inc., Allamuchy, N.J., 1987—; chmn. bd. Fin. Fed. Credit Inc., Houston; bd. dirs. City & Suburban Fin. Corp. Served to lt. (j.g.) USN, 1953-56. Office: Fin Fed Credit Inc 300 Frank W Burr Blvd Teaneck NJ 07666-6703

PALLADINO, NUNZIO JOSEPH, retired nuclear engineer; b. Allentown, Pa., Nov. 10, 1916; s. Joseph and Angelina (Trentalange) P.; m. Virginia Marchetto, June 16, 1945; children: Linda Susan, Lisa Anne, Cynthia Madaline. B.S., Lehigh U., 1938, M.S., 1939, D.Eng. (hon.), 1964. Registered profl. engr., Pa. Engr. Westinghouse Electric Co., Phila., 1939-42; nuclear reactor designer Oak Ridge Nat. Lab., 1946-48; staff asst. to div. mgr. Argonne Nat. Lab., Lemont, Ill., 1948-50; mgr. PWR reactor design subdiv. Westinghouse Electric Corp., Pitts., 1950-59; head nuclear engring. dept. Pa. State U., University Park, 1959-66, dean Coll. Engring., 1966-81; chmn. Nuclear Regulatory Commn., Washington, 1981-86; past mem. Pa. Gov.'s Sci. Adv. Com., Gov.'s Energy Coun., Pa.'s Commn. To Investigate Three Mile Island; mem. Nat. Nuclear Accrediting Bd., 1989-92. Contbr. tech. articles to profl. jours. Served to capt. AUS, 1942-45. Recipient Order of Merit Westinghouse Electric Corp. Fellow ASME (Prime Movers award), Am. Nuclear Soc. (past pres., A.H. Compton award, W. Zinn award), Am. Soc. Engring. Edn.; mem. NAE, NSPE, Argonne Univs. Assn. (past interim pres., past bd. dirs.). Roman Catholic. Club: Rotary. *Do it right the first time.*

PALLADINO, VINCENT NEIL, lawyer; b. Phila., Dec. 5, 1950; s. Vincent Salvatore and Agnes (Ludwig) P.; m. Laurel Ruth Tanner, Apr. 15, 1984; children: Alissa Kathryn, Samantha Leigh. BA, Yale U., 1972; JD, Columbia U., 1975. Bar: N.Y. 1976. Atty. Nims, Howes, Collison & Isner, N.Y.C., 1975-77; atty. Fish & Neave, N.Y.C., 1977—, ptnr., 1987—. Editor-in-chief The Trademark Reporter, N.Y.C., 1986-88, mem. adv. bd., 1988—. Mem. ABA, Assn. Bar City of N.Y., N.Y. Intellectual Property Law Assn., Internat. Trademark Assn., Copyright Soc. U.S.A. Avocations: reading, running. Office: Fish & Neave 1251 6th Ave New York NY 10020-1104

PALLADINO-CRAIG, ALLYS, museum director; b. Pontiac, Mich., Mar. 23, 1947; d. Stephan Vincent and Mary (Anderson) Palladino; m. Malcolm Arnold Craig, Aug. 20, 1967; children—Ansel, Reed, Nicholas. BA in English, Fla. State U., 1967; grad., U. Toronto, Ont., Can., 1969; MFA, Fla. State U., 1978, PhD in Humanities, 1996. Editorial asst. project U. Va. Press, Charlottesville, 1970-76; instr. English Inst. Franco American, Rennes, France, 1974; adj. instr. Fla. State U., Tallahassee, 1978-79, dir. Four Arts Ctr., 1979-82, dir. U. Mus. of Fine Arts, 1982—. Curator, contbg. editor various articles and exhbn. catalogues, 1982—, including Nocturnes and Nightmares, Monochrome/Polychrome, Chroma, The Gun as Image; guest curator, author: Mark Messersmith: New Mythologies; gen. editor Athanor XVI, 1980—; represented in permanent collections Fla. Ho. of Reps., Barnett Bank, IBM. Individual artist fellow Fla. Arts Coun., 1979. Mem. Am. Assn. Mus., Fla. Art Mus. Dirs. Assn. (sec. 1989-91), Phi Beta Kappa. Democrat. Avocation: antique American fountain pen collecting. Home: 1410 Grape St Tallahassee FL 32303-5636 Office: Fla State U Mus of Fine Arts 250 Fine Arts Bldg Tallahassee FL 32306-2055

PALLAM, JOHN JAMES, lawyer; b. Cleve., May 19, 1940; s. James John and Coralia (Gatsos) P.; m. Evanthia Venizelos, Nov. 29, 1969; 1 child, Alethea. BA, Case Western Res. U., 1962; JD, Ohio State U., 1965. Bar: Ohio 1965, U.S. Ct. Claims 1969, U.S. Ct. Mil. Appeals 1969, U.S. Supreme Ct. 1970. Law clk. to presiding justice Cuyahoga County Ct., Cleve., 1965-66; assoc. Burke, Habor & Berick, Cleve., 1970-73; corp. atty. Midland Ross Corp., Cleve., 1973-80, corp. counsel, 1980-87; v.p., gen. counsel Brush Wellman Corp., Cleve., 1987—; guest lectr. Nat. Foundry Assn., Chgo., 1986—. Contbr. articles on labor and environ. matters to jours. Legal advisor Am. Hellenic and Prog. Assn., Cleve., 1966—. Served to capt. JAGC U.S. Army, 1966-70, Vietnam. Decorated Bronze Star with oak leaf cluster. Mem. Ohio Bar Assn. (committeeman 1984—), Cleve. Bar Assn. (merit svc. award 1972), Hellenic Bar Assn., Hellenic Univ. Club, Rowfant. Greek Orthodox. Avocations: history, antiques, golfing, rare books, railroading. Office: 17876 Saint Clair Ave Cleveland OH 44110-2602

PALLASCH, B. MICHAEL, lawyer; b. Chgo., Mar. 30, 1933; s. Bernhard Michael and Magdalena Helena (Fixari) P.; m. Josephine Catherine O'Leary, Aug. 15, 1981; children: Bernhard Michael III and Madeleine Josephine (twins). B.S.S., Georgetown U., 1954; J.D., Harvard U., 1957; postgrad., John Marshall Law Sch., 1974. Bar: Ill. 1957, U.S. Dist. Ct. (no. dist.) Ill. 1958, U.S. Tax Ct. 1961, U.S. Ct. Claims 1961, U.S. Ct. Appeals (7th cir.) 1962. Assoc. Winston & Strawn, Chgo., 1958-66; resident mgr. br. office Winston & Strawn, Paris, 1963-65; ptnr. Winston & Strawn, Chgo., 1966-70, sr. capital ptnr., 1971-91; sr. ptnr. B. Michael Pallasch & Assocs.; 1991—; dir., corp. sec. Tanis, Inc., Calumet, Mich., 1972—, Greenbank Engring. Corp., Dover, Del., 1976-91, C.B.P. Engring. Corp., Chgo., 1976-91, Chgo. Cutting Svcs. Corp., 1977-88; corp. sec. Arthur Andersen Assocs., Inc., Chgo., 1976—, L'hotel de France of Ill., Inc., Chgo., 1980-85, Water & Effluent Screening Co., Chgo., 1988-91; dir. Bosch Devel. Co., Longview, Tex., 1977-87, Lor Inc., Houghton, Mich., 1977-87, Rana Inc., Madison, Wis., 1978-87, Woodlak Co., Houghton, 1977-87, Zipatone, Inc., Hillside, Ill., 1975-82, Keco Inc., Madison, 1977-81. Bd. dirs. Martin D'Arcy Mus. Medieval and Renaissance Art, Chgo., 1975—; bd. dirs. Katherine M. Bosch Found., 1978—; asst. sec. Hundred Club of Cook County, Chgo., 1966-73, bd. dirs., sec., 1974—. Served with USAFR, 1957-63. Knight of Merit Sacred Mil. Constantinian Order of St. George of Royal House of Bourbon of Two Sicilies, knight comdr. with star Sovereign Mil. Order of Temple of Jerusalem; named youth mayor City of Chgo., 1950; recipient Outstanding Woodland Mgmt. Forestry award Monroe County (Wis.) Soil and Water Conservation Dist., 1975. Mem. Ill. Bar Assn. (tax lectr. 1961), Advs. Soc., Field Mus. Natural History (life), Max McGraw Wildlife Found., English Speaking Union. Roman Catholic. Clubs: Travellers (Paris); Saddle and Cycle (Chgo.). Home: 737 W Hutchinson St Chicago IL 60613-1519 Office: 35 W Wacker Dr Ste 4700 Chicago IL 60601-1614 *Personal philosophy: We define and measure success in various ways: achievement, position, wealth: and attribute it to the application of various attributes but is there any degree of success that we can achieve that is worthier than the knowledge that we have faithfully served those who depend upon and trust in us?.*

PALLASCH, MAGDALENA HELENA (MRS. BERNHARD MICHAEL PALLASCH), artist; b. Chgo., Sept. 6, 1908; d. Frank and Anna (Meier) Fixari; m. Bernhard Pallasch, Nov. 26, 1931 (dec. Nov. 1977); children: Bernhard Michael, Diana Pallasch Miller. Student, Chgo. Acad. Fine Arts, 1922-26, Am. Acad. Fine Arts, 1926-30, U. Chgo., 1960, Art Inst. Chgo.; pvt. study with Joseph Allworthy, 1935-38, hon. doctorate, 1985. Contbr. two murals and ten life size figures for Woman's World Fair, Chgo., 1928, Century of Progress Exhbn., Chgo., 1933-34; portrait artist, subjects include Cardinal Cody, Chgo., 1958—, mural St. Mary of the Lake Ch., Chgo., 1987; exhbn. at Montifiori Estate, 1992, 93, 94, Hinsdale Art Ctr., 1995, 96, 97; represented in pvt. and pub. collections Loyola U., Chgo., Barat Coll., Lake Forest, Ill., Internat. Coll. Surgeons, Chgo., Med. Library, Columbus Hosp. Recipient first award for still life Arts Club, N.Y.C., 1960; First award Nat. League Am. Pen Women, 1972; 1st place and best of show State Exhibit, Springfield, Ill., 1973; 1st award Chgo. Woman's Club, 1978; hon. mention for portrait Italian Cultural Ctr.; hon. alumna award Loyola U., Chgo., 1983; award of excellence for portrait of author Gail Brook Burket, Wheaton Hist. Mus., 1987; Gold Medal of Honor for disting. lifelong achievements, 1987; award of honor for portrait of sculptor Lisa Gengler, 1989; named Dame, Sovereign Mil. Order Temple of Jerusalem, 1995. Mem. Presentation Ball Aux.; mem. President's Club, Loyola U., also mem. women's bd. Nat. League Am. Pen Women (v.p. Chgo. br. 1966-68, art chmn. 1978-80, Margaret Dingle Meml. award 1979), Mcpl. Art League Chgo., Nat. Soc. Arts and Letters (art chmn. chgo. chpt. 1982—, apptd. nat. chmn. 1997—), Friends of Austria, Friends of D'Arcy Gallery of Medieval and Renaissance Art., Ill. Cath. Women Club (gov. 1979—), Cuneo Mus. (Vernon Hills, Ill.). Home and Studio: 723 W Junior Ter Chicago IL 60613-1512

PALLIN, IRVING M., anesthesiologist; b. Boston, Feb. 11, 1910; s. Abraham and Lillian (Stoler) P.; m. Ann Gertrude Lear, 1940; children: Samuel Lear, Mary Jane, Carol Sue, Jonathan Jacob. B.S., Tufts U., 1932, M.D., 1937. Diplomate: Am. Bd. Anesthesiology. Intern W.W. Backus Hosp., 1937-39; resident anesthesiology N.Y. Postgrad. Med. Sch. and Hosp., 1939-41; practice medicine specializing in anesthesiology N.Y.C., 1941-70, Sun City, Ariz., 1970-80; attending anesthesiologist Jewish Hosp. Bklyn., 1942-54, sec. med. bd., 1951-70, pres. med. bd., 1962-63, dir. dept. anesthesiology, 1954-70; cons. anesthesiologist VA Hosp., Bklyn., 1950-65; dir. anesthesiology Cumberland Hosp., 1948-55; dir. dept. anesthesiology Queens Gen. Hosp., 1955-66; former prof. clin. anesthesiology SUNY Coll. Medicine, Bklyn.; chief anesthesia Boswell Meml. Hosp., Sun City, Ariz., 1970-77; dir. Asso. Hosp. Service (Blue Cross) Greater N.Y.; chmn. advisers of AMA to Am. Assn. Med. Assts., 1968-70. Contbr. articles to profl. publs. Co-chmn. Bklyn. physicians div. United Jewish Appeal, 1953-56; pres. Sun City unit Am. Cancer Soc., 1981-85, bd. dirs. Ariz. div., 1982—; pres. Beth Shalom Congregation of Sun City, 1976-78, Brotherhood, 1980, 81, pres. 1982-83; bd. dirs. Ariz. Endowment of Jewish Welfare, 1982-85. Recipient Heritage award State of Israel Bonds, 1983. Fellow Am. Coll. Anesthesiologists, N.Y. Acad. Medicine, N.Y. Acad. Scis.; mem. AMA (del. 1964—), Kings County Med. Soc. (pres. 1960-61, hon.), N.Y. Med. Soc. (ho. dels. 1952-54, sec. sect. anesthesiology 1952057), Acad. Medicine Bklyn. (pres. 1961), Am. Soc. Anesthesiologists (pres. 1957), N.Y. Soc. Anesthesiologists (pres. 1949-50, chmn. jud. com. 1951-56, hon.), Tam O'Shanter Golf Club (pres. 1960-63, Union Hills Country Club. Home: 10358 Highwood Ln Sun City AZ 85373

PALLIN, SAMUEL LEAR, ophthalmologist; b. N.Y., May 8, 1941; s. Irving and Gertrude (Lear) P.; divorced; children: Daniel Jay, Marla Jean, Laura Jane. BA, Hofstra U., 1963; MD, SUNY, Bklyn., 1968. Diplomate Nat. Bd. Med. Examiners, Am. Bd. Ophthalmology. Intern L.I. Jewish Med. Ctr., 1968-69; resident Bklyn. Eye and Ear Hosp., 1972-75; prin. The Lear Eye Clinic, Ltd., Sun City, Ariz., 1975—; mem. staff Walter O. Boswell Meml. Hosp., Del E. Webb Meml. Hosp., Scottsdale Meml. Hosp., St. Luke's Med. Ctr., Thunderbird Samaritan Hosp.; presenter in field. Patentee in method of making self-sealing episcleral incision. Trustee Congr. Beth El Endowment Fund, 1987; mem. exec. bd. Ariz. chpt. Israel Bonds, 1988. With USAF, 1969-71. Mem. AMA, ACS, Am. Soc. Cataract and Refractive Surgery, Am. Acad. Ophthalmology, Ariz. Med. Assn., Ariz. Easter Seal Soc. (bd. dirs. 1989, life dir.), Maricopa County Med. Assn., Outpatient Ophthalmic Surgery Soc., Lions; hon. mem. Mex. Ophthalmology Soc. N.E., Mex. Intraocular Implant Soc., Ctrl. Mex. Ophthalmol. Soc. Office: The Lear Eye Clinic Ltd Bldg A-100 10615 W Thunderbird Blvd Sun City AZ 85351-3033

PALLISER, CHARLES, writer, educator; b. Holyoke, Mass., Dec. 11, 1947. BA, Oxford U., 1970, BLitt, 1975. Lectr. Strathclyde U., Scotland,

1974-90. Author: The Quincunx, 1989, The Sensationist, 1991, Betrayals, 1995. Recipient Sue Kaufman 1st fiction prize Am. Acad. & Inst. Arts and Letters, N.Y.C., 1991.

PALLMEYER, REBECCA RUTH, federal judge; b. Tokyo, Sept. 13, 1954; came to U.S., 1957; d. Paul Henry and Ruth (Schrieber) P.; m. Dan P. McAdams, Aug. 20, 1977; children: Ruth, Amanda. BA, Valparaiso (Ind.) U., 1976; JD, U. Chgo., 1979. Bar: Ill. 1980, U.S. Ct. Appeals (7th cir.) 1980, U.S. Ct. Appeals 11th and 5th cirs.) 1982. Jud. clk. Minn. Supreme Ct., St. Paul, 1979-80; assoc. Hopkins & Sutter, Chgo., 1980-85; judge administrv. law Ill. Human Rights Commn., Chgo., 1985-91; magistrate judge U.S. Dist. Ct., Chgo., 1991—; mem. jud. resources com. Jud. Conf. of U.S., 1994—. Bd. govs. Augustana Ctr., 1990-91. Mem. Fed. Bar Assn. (bd. mgrs. Chgo. chpt. 1995-96), Womens Bar Assn. Ill. (bd. mgrs. 1995—), Nat. Assn. Women Judges, Fed. Magistrate Judges Assn. (bd. dirs. 1994—), Chgo. Bar Assn. (chair devel. law com. 1992-93, David C. Hilliard award 1990-91), Valparaiso U. Alumni Assn. (bd. dirs. 1992-94). Lutheran. Avocations: choral music, sewing, running. Office: US Dist Ct 219 S Dearborn St Rm 2578 Chicago IL 60604-1802

PALLONE, ADRIAN JOSEPH, research scientist; b. Lille, France, Apr. 8, 1928; came to US., 1946; s. Giovanni and Laurina (Caccia) P.; m. Teresa Maria Violino, June 12, 1954; children—John M., Anne Marie, Janet M., Joan L. B.S. in Aero. Engring., Poly Inst. Bklyn., 1952, M.S. in Aero. Engring., 1953, Ph.D. in Applied Mechanics, 1959; cert., Sloan Sch. Mgmt., MIT, 1984. Research assoc. Poly. Inst. Bklyn., 1955-59; mgr. Avco Systems Div., Wilmington, Mass., 1959-63; mem. faculty NYU, N.Y.C., 1963-67; dir. Avco Systems Div., Wilmington, 1967-78; chief scientist Avco Systems Div., 1978-87; aerospace cons. Textron Def. Systems, Wilmington, 1987-91; pres. Aerophysics Systems & Tech., Inc., Silver Lake, N.H., 1992—. Patentee in field. Contbr. articles to sci. jours. Fellow AIAA; mem. N.Y. Acad. Scis., Sigma Xi, Sigma Gamma Tau. Roman Catholic. Avocations: skiing; sailing; hiking. Office: Aerophysics Systems & Tech Inc PO Box 189 Silver Lake NH 03875-0189

PALLONE, FRANK, JR., congressman; b. Long Branch, N.J., Oct. 30, 1951. Grad. cum. laude, Middlebury Coll., 1973; MA, Tufts U., 1974; JD, Rutgers U., 1978. Councilman City of Long Branch, 1982-88; mem. N.J. Senate, 1984-88, 101st-104th Congresses from 3d (now 6th) N.J. dist., 1988—; commerce subcom. on energy and power. Democrat. Roman Catholic. Office: US Ho of Reps 420 Condon Ter SE Washington DC 20032-3710 Address: 504 Broadway Ste 118 Long Branch NJ 07740-5965

PALLONE, NATHANIEL JOHN, psychologist, educator; b. Chgo., Oct. 30, 1935; s. Louis T. and Adeline (Tenkach) P.; m. Letitia Clarke, Sept. 19, 1983; children: Andrea, Angela. AB, Cath. U. Am., 1951, MA, 1960; PhD, NYU, 1963. Cert. psychologist, N.J. Psychologist St. Francis Coll., Bklyn., 1960-63; asst. prof. U. Notre Dame, South Bend, Ind., 1963-66; dept. chair NYU, N.Y.C., 1966-72; assoc. dean U. Hartford, Conn., 1972-73; dean Rutgers U., New Brunswick, N.J., 1973-79, acad. v.p., 1979-87, univ. disting. prof. psychology, 1987—; vis. prof. Harvard U., Cambridge, Mass., 1987-88; case cons. Office of Pub. Defender, New Brunswic, 1987-91; cons. social svc. agys., criminal justice agys., 1963—; chair classification rev. bd. for sex offenders N.J. Dept. Corrections, 1975—. Editor: Jour. Offender Rehab., 1989—; exec. editor Current Psychology, 1989—; sr. editor Society, 1992—; author books; contbr. articles to profl. publs. Fellow Am. Psychol. Assn., Am. Coll. Forensic Psychology, Am. Psychol. Soc.; mem. Am. Bd. Profl. Psychology (diplomate), Phi Beta Kappa. Office: Rutgers Univ 213 Smithers Hall New Brunswick NJ 08903

PALLOT, JOSEPH WEDELES, lawyer; b. Coral Gables, Fla., Dec. 23, 1959; s. Richard Allen Pallot and Rosalind Brown (Wedeles) Spak; m. Linda Fried, Oct. 12, 1956; children: Richard Allen, Maxwell Ross. BS, Jacksonville U., 1981; JD cum laude, U. Miami, Coral Gables, Fla., 1986. Bar: Fla. 1986. Comml. lending officer S.E. Bank, N.A., Miami, 1981-83; ptnr. Steel Hector & Davis, Miami, 1986—. Bd. dirs. MOSAIC: Jewish Mus. of Fla., Miami Beach, 1993—; gov. Fla. Philharm. Orch., Coral Gables, 1994—; dir. Fla. Grand Opera, 1996—. Mem. Miami City Club. Avocations: golf, tennis. Office: 200 S Biscayne Blvd Miami FL 33131-2310

PALLOTTI, MARIANNE MARGUERITE, foundation administrator; b. Hartford, Conn., Apr. 23, 1937; d. Rocco D. and Marguerite (Long) P. BA, NYU, 1968, MA, 1972. Asst. to pres. Wilson, Haight & Welch, Hartford, 1964-65; exec. asst. Ford Found., N.Y.C., 1965-77; corp. sec. Hewlett Found., Menlo Park, Calif., 1977-84, v.p., 1985—; bd. dirs. Overseas Devel. Network. Bd. dirs. N.Y. Theatre Ballet, N.Y.C., 1986—, Consortium for Global Devel., 1992, Miramonte Mental Health Svcs., Palo Alto, Calif., 1989, Austin Montessori Sch., 1993. Mem. Women in Founds., No. Calif. Grantmakers, Peninsula Grantmakers. Avocations: running, skiing, hiking. Home: 532 Marine World Pky # 6203 Redwood Shores CA 94065 Office: William & Flora Hewlett Found 525 Middlefield Rd Ste 200 Menlo Park CA 94025-3448

PALM, CHARLES GILMAN, university official; b. Havre, Mont., Apr. 25, 1944; s. Victor F. and Laura (McKinnie) P.; m. Miriam Willits, Sept. 15, 1968. AB, Stanford U., 1966; MA, U. Wyo., 1967; MLS, U. Oreg., 1970. Asst. archivist Hoover Instn., Stanford (Calif.) U., 1971-74, dep. archivist, 1974-84, archivist, 1984-87, head libr., 1986-87, assoc. dir., 1987-90, dep. dir., 1990—. Co-author: Guide to Hoover Institution Archives, 1980, Herbert Hoover, Register of His Papers in the Hoover Institution Archives, 1983. Mem. Calif. Heritage Preservation Commn., Sacramento, 1988—, vice chmn., 1993-97, chmn., 1997—; mem. Nat. Hist. Records and Publs. Commn., Washington, 1990-96. Fellow Soc. Am. Archivists; mem. Am. Hist. Assn., Soc. Calif. Archivists (pres. 1983-84), Bohemian Club. Republican. Office: Hoover Instn Stanford CA 94305

PALM, GARY HOWARD, lawyer, educator; b. Toledo, Sept. 2, 1942; s. Clarence William, Jr. and Emily Marie (Braunschweiger) P. AB, Wittenberg U., 1964; JD, U. Chgo., 1967. Bar: Ill. 1967, U.S. Dist. Ct. (no. dist.) Ill. 1967, U.S. Ct. Appeals (7th cir.) 1970, U.S. Supreme Ct. 1974. Assoc. Schiff Hardin & Waite, Chgo., 1967-70; dir. Edwin F. Mandel Legal Aid Clinic, Chgo., 1970-91, atty., 1991—; asst. prof. law U. Chgo., 1970-75, assoc. prof., 1975-83, prof., 1983-91, clin. prof., 1991—; peer rev. reader, clin. edn. grants U.S. Dept. Edn., Washington, 1980, 81, 83, 84, 86, 87, Legal Svcs. Corp., 1986-87; chairperson-elect, chairperson sect. clin. legal edn. Assn. Am. Law Schs., 1985, 86. Vol. ACLU, Chgo., 1968-75. Mem. ABA (clin. edn. com. 1974-80, membership com. 1984-85, skills tng. com. 1985-90, accreditation for Law Schs., 1987-94, mem. coun. sect. on legal edn. and admissions to the bar 1994—), Chgo. Bar Assn., Chgo. Council Lawyers, Ill. State Bar Assn. (legal edn., admission and competence com. 1985-91, 93—, vice chair 1995-96, chair 1996—), ATLA, Assn. Am. Law Sch. (clin. tchg. confs. 1985, 86, 87, 89, recipient Award for Outstanding Contbn. to Clin. Edn., sect on clin. legal edn., 1989, co-recipient of the award, 1994), Clin. Legal Edn. Assn. (ad hoc com. on accreditation 1996, Clin. All Star 1996). Democrat. Home: 2800 N Lake Shore Dr Apt 3706 Chicago IL 60657-6254 Office: Mandel Legal Aid Clinic 6020 S University Ave Chicago IL 60637-2704 *Notable cases include: Logan vs. Zimmerman Brush Co.; Buckhalter vs. Pepsi-Cola Gen. Bottlers, Inc.; Scott vs. Ill.; Slate vs. McFetridge.*

PALM, GERALD ALBERT, lawyer; b. Seattle, Nov. 4, 1942; s. Albert Nels and Gladys Elizabeth (Danberg) P.; m. Nancy Lee Himes, Dec. 6, 1969; children: Jason E., Kimberly A. BA, Dartmouth Coll., 1964; LLB, Harvard U., 1967. Bar: Wash. 1967, U.S. Dist. Ct. (we. dist.) Wash. 1967, U.S. Ct. Appeals (9th cir.) 1981, U.S. Dist. Ct. (ea. dist.) Wash. 1982. Assoc. Jones, Grey, Bayley, Kehoe, Hooper & Olsen, Seattle, 1967-68; assoc. Williams, Kastner and Gibbs, Seattle, 1968-74, ptnr., 1974-95; sole practitioner Seattle, 1995—. Youth basketball coach Jewish Community Ctr., Mercer Island, Wash., 1984-88; deacon, youth commn. Mercer Island Covenant Ch., 1988-95. Mem. FBA, Am. Bd. Trial Advocates (pres. Wash. chpt. 1989), Def. Rsch. Inst., Wash. Def. Trial Lawyers Assn. (trustee 1971), Wash. State Bar Assn., King County Bar Assn., Dartmouth Lawyers Assn., Mercer Island Country Club (trustee 1991-94, pres. 1993-94), Wash. Athletic Club. Republican. Mem. Covenant Ch. Avocations: tennis, water skiing, snow skiing, running, attending musicals and theatre. Home: 7400 E Mercer Way Mercer Island WA 98040-5819 Office: Law Office of Gerald A Palm Washington Mut Tower 1201 3rd Ave Ste 2830 Seattle WA 98101-3000

PALM, MARY EGDAHL, mycologist; b. Mpls., Jan. 27, 1954; d. Lauren and Mary E.; children: Natalie Elizabeth, Christopher Steven. BA in Biology, St. Olaf Coll., 1976; MSc in Plant Pathology (mycology), U. Minn., 1979, PhD in Plant Pathology (mycology), 1983. Lab. asst. St. Olaf Coll. Biology Dept., Northfield, Minn., 1974; tchg. asst. St. Olaf Coll. Biology Dept., Northfield, 1975-76; rsch. asst. U. Minn. plant pathology dept., Mpls., 1976-83, post doctoral rsch. assoc., 1983-84; mycologist (botanist GS12) USDA/APHIS biol. assessment and support staff, Beltsville, Md., 1984-91; mycologist (botanist GS13) biol. assessment and taxonomic support USDA/Animal and Plant Health Inspection Svc., Beltsville, 1991—; instr., coord. seminars and tng. sessions for USDA and ednl. sci. group, 1982—; adj. assoc. prof. plant pathology Pa. State U., State College, 1995. Co-author: Deuteromycetes and Selected Ascomycetes That Occur On or In Wood: An Indexed Bibliography, 1979, An Indexed Bibliography and Guide to Taxonomic Literature, 1988, A Literature Guide for the Identification of Plant Pathogenic Fungi, 1987, Fungi on Rhododendron: A World Reference, 1996, Mycology in Sustainable Development: Expanding concepts, Vanishing Borders, 1997; contbr. articles to profl. jours. including Mycologia, Plant Disease, Can. Jour. Botany, Mycotaxon. Recipient St. Olaf Coll. Hon. Biology scholarship, 1976; grantee U. Minn. Computer Ctr. 1979, 80, 81, 82. Mem. Am. Phytopathol. Soc. (chairperson mycology com. 1988, 89, vice chairperson 1987, mem. 1985, 86, regulatory plant pathology com. 1993—, organizer, moderator colloquim on systematics of plant pathogenic fungi 1987), Mycol. Soc. Am. (sec. 1991-94, Am. Inst. Biol. Scis. rep. 1994—, v.p. 1995-96, pres.-elect 1996-97, pres. 1997-98, other coms.), L.Am. Mycol. Assn. (U.S. liaison), Internat. Assn. Plant Taxonomy (subcom. C of com. on fungi and lichens 1986, 87, 88). Office: USDA Rm 329 B-011A 10300 Baltimore Ave Beltsville MD 20705-2325

PALMA, DOLORES PATRICIA, urban planner, consultant, lecturer, author; b. Bklyn.; d. Anthony Michael Resse and Eleanor Dorothea (Palma) Graffeo; m. Doyle G. Hyett. BA, CUNY, Bklyn., 1972; M of Urban Planning, U. Mich., 1974. Intern Mich. Mcpl. League, Ann Arbor, 1973-74; park planner Metro Bd. Parks and Recreation, Nashville, 1975; preservation planner Metro. Hist. Commn., Nashville, 1976; sr. community planner Metro Planning Commn., Nashville, 1977-79; exec. dir. Metro Hist. Zoning Commn., Nashville, 1980-82; asst. dir. Mid-Atlantic Regional Office, Nat. Trust for Hist. Preservation, Washington, 1983, dir. Office of Neighborhood Conservation, 1984, project dir. Urban Demonstration Program Nat. Main St. Ctr., 1985-87; pres. HyettPalma Inc. 1985—, HyettPalma Publs. 1988—; del. Nat. Assn. Neighborhoods Platform Conv., 1979. Founder Neighborhood Reinvestment Corp., Nashville, 1978; mayoral appointee Neighborhood Housing Services, Nashville, 1979-82; dir. Restore the U.S. Capitol Campaign, 1983. Author: Salaries, Wages and Fringe Benefits in Michigan Cities and Villages, 1973; Nashville: Conserving a Heritage, 1977; Neighborhood Commercial Buildings: A Survey and Analysis of Metropolitan Nashville, 1983; Business Enhancement Plan for Downtown Poughkeepsie, N.Y., 1987; Future Directions for Seward, Alaska, 1987; Action Agenda for Gay Street, Knoxville, 1987; Agenda for Economic Enhancement of Haymarket Lincoln, Nebraska, 1987; Management of Downtown Palmer, Alaska, 1988; Successful Business Recruitment Strategies in the U.S., 1988, Business Plans for Business Districts, 1988, Office Tenant Recruitment for Pittsfield, Mass., 1989, Business Plan for the Heart of Corpus Christi, Tex., 1989, Retail Recruitment Strategies for Reading, Pa., 1989, Seward 2000: Comprehensive Plan, Seward, Alaska, 1989, Business Plan for Downtown Rocky Mount, N.C., 1990, Retail and Restaurant Audit for Rosslyn, Va., 1990, Market Analysis and Enhancement Strategies for Liberal, Kans., 1990, Market Analysis and Enhancement Strategies for Geneva, N.Y., 1990, Building the Vision: Washington Street Corridor, Falls Church, Va., 1990, The Magnetic Mile Vision, Glendale, Ariz., 1990, Downtown Hopkinsville (Ky.) Business Plan, 1990, Downtown Denton (Md.) Devel. Plan, 1991. East Downtown Dearborn (Mich.) Bus. Plan, 1991, Leavenworth/Lansing Market Analysis, 1991; (with Nat. League of Cities) City Commercial Centers Reborn: Building Commercial District Dynamism, 1990, Downtown Visions, 1992, Focus Groups for Downtown, 1992, Business Retention and Expansion, 1993, Winning Ways, 1993, Downtowns and Utilities, 1994, Downtown Safety: Addressing the Myths and the Realities, 1994, Downtown Parking Management, 1995, Downtown Public Space Maintenance, 1995, Accepting the Challenge: The Rebirth of America's Downtown, 1995, Enhancing Downtown's Curb Appeal, 1996, Downtown Revitalization: A Survey of Public Power Utility Programs, 1997; project dir.: A Market and Design Study for the Broadway National Register Historic District, 1982; author studies, pamphlet, articles; contbr. newsletters; editor Edgefield News, Nashville, 1979-80. Publicity dir. Hist. Edgefield, Inc., 1979; ptnr. Nat. League of Cities The Rebirth of Am's. Downtowns Pilot Program, 1993-94, Nat. League of Cities Am. Downtown: New Thinking New Life, 1995—; hon. mem. Tenn. State Legislature, 1980. Woodlawn scholar Nat. Trust for Hist. Preservation, 1976; named one of Outstanding Young Women of Am., 1985, award of excellence Va. Downtown Devel. Assn., 1990, Am. Planning Assn., 1991. Office: HyettPalma Inc 1600 Prince St Ste 110 Alexandria VA 22314-2836

PALMEIRO, RAFAEL CORRALES, professional baseball player; b. Havana, Cuba, Oct. 24, 1964. Degree in Comml. Art, Miss. State U. With Chgo. Cubs, 1986-88, Tex. Rangers, 1988-93; first baseman Balt. Orioles, 1994—. Named to Coll. All-Am. Team, 1985, to Nat. League All-Star Team, 1988, 95, to Am. League All-Star Team, 1991; named Eastern League Most Valuable Player, 1986. Office: Balt Orioles 333 W Camden St Baltimore MD 21201-2435*

PALMER, ALICE EUGENIA, retired physician, educator; b. Chgo., Sept. 17, 1910; d. Charles Grover and Eugenia Marie (Sundquist) P.; m. Lawrence A. Pratt, 1935; m. Clyde K. Bowles, 1973; children: Lawrene Alice, Dorothy Jane Pratt (Mrs. John D. Shilling). BSc, U. Chgo., 1932, MS in Physiology, 1937; MD, Wayne State U., 1938. Diplomate Am. Bd. Dermatology (preceptor 1956—). Resident pathology Detroit Receiving Hosp., 1938, resident physician dermatology, 1939-42; practice medicine specializing in dermatology Detroit, 1942-61, 65-71, Sun City, Ariz., 1971-90; instr. pathology Sch. Medicine, Wayne State U., Detroit, 1938, assoc. clin. prof. medicine, 1946-61, 65-68, adj. clin. prof., 1968-71; chmn. dept. dermatology Grace Hosp., Detroit, 1956-61, 68-71; sr. cons. dermatology Jennings Hosp., Detroit, 1954-71; med. educator U.S. AID, 1961, chief med. edn. project, Vietnam, 1961-65, med. cons., Vietnam and East Asia, 1965-68; mem. 3-man team for Survey S.E. Asian Med. Rsch. Instns., 1966; vis. prof. dermatology faculty medicine U. Saigon, 1961, 62, 63, 64, 71-73; mem. Nat. Program Dermatology, 1969-75; served Clinica Adelante, Surprise, Ariz. Assoc. editor Detroit Med. News, 1959-60. Bd. dirs., exec. bd. YWCA, Detroit, 1965-70. Recipient Disting. Alumni award Wayne State U., 1987, Disting. Svc. award Sch. Medicine, Key to the City of Detroit, 1959, U.S. Civilia Svc. medal Vietnam; named one of 10 Top Women in Detroit, 1959; Julius Stieglitz fellow in chemistry U. Chgo., 1932. Mem. AMA, Ariz. Med. Soc., Mich. Med. Soc. (chmn. dermatology 1959), Pacific Dermatol. Soc., Detroit Dermatol. Soc. (pres. 1959), Phoenix Dermatol. Soc. (v.p. 1977), Am. Acad. Dermatology (mem. internat. com., mem. internat. task force 1971-75), Maricopa County Med. Soc., Internat. Soc. Tropical Dermatology, Am. Soc. Dermatologic Surgery, Am. Geriatric Soc., Am. Acad. Cosmetic Surgery, Am. Soc. Lipo-Suction Surgery, Am. Acad. Facial Plastic and Reconstructive Surgery, S.W. Derm. Soc. (sec.-treas. 1978—, pres. 1980-81), Women's Econ. Club Detroit (bd. dirs.), Pilot Club (pres.), Sigma Xi, Alpha Omega Alpha. Home and Office: 18170 N 91st Ave Apt 1155 Peoria AZ 85382-0868

PALMER, ANN THERESE DARIN, lawyer; b. Detroit, Apr. 25, 1951; d. Americo and Theresa (Del Favero) Darin; m. Robert Towne Palmer, Nov. 9, 1974; children: Justin Darin, Christian Darin. BA, U. Notre Dame, 1973, MBA, 1975; JD, Loyola U., Chgo., 1978. Bar: Ill. 1978, U.S. Supreme Ct. 1981. Reporter Wall Street Jour., Detroit, 1974; freelancer Time Inc. Fin. Publs., Chgo., 1975-77, extern, Midwest regional solicitor U.S. Dept. Labor, 1976-78; tax atty. Esmark Inc., 1978; counsel Chgo. United, 1978-81; ind. contractor Legal Tax Rsch., 1981-89; fin. and legal news contbr. The Chgo. Tribune, 1991—, Bus. Week Chgo. Bur., 1991—, Automotive News, 1993—, Crain's Chgo. Bus., 1994—. Mem. Saddle and Cycle Club of Chgo., Detroit Golf Club. Roman Catholic. Home: 873 Forest Hill Rd Lake Forest IL 60045-3905

PALMER, ARNOLD DANIEL, professional golfer; b. Youngstown, Pa., Sept. 10, 1929; s. Milfred Jerome and Doris M. Palmer; m. Winnie Walzer, Dec. 20, 1954; children: Peggy Palmer Wears, Amy Palmer Saunders. Student, Wake Forest Coll., LLD, 1970. Profl. golfer, 1954—, businessman, entrepreneur, 1960—; nat. spokesman Pennzoil Petroleum Products, Sears Can., Rolex, Lofts Seed, Cadillac Motor Car, GTE, Golf mag., Rayovac, Textron, 84 Lumber, Lexington Furniture, Office Depot, Cooper Tires, Arnold Palmer Golf Co.; designer numerous golf courses. Author: Arnold Palmer's Golf Book, 1961, Portrait of a Professional Golfer, 1964, My Game and Yours, 1965, rev. edit., 1983, Situation Golf, 1970, Go for Broke, 1973, Arnold Palmer's Best 54 Holes of Golf, 1977, Arnold Palmer's Complete Book of Putting, 1986, Play Great Golf, 1987, (with Thomas Hauser) A Personal Journey, 1994. With USCG, 1951-54. Winner over 90 major golf tournaments, 1955—, including Masters Championship, 1958, 60, 62, 64, U.S. Open, 1960, U.S. Amateur, 1954, Brit. Open, 1961, 62; recipient numerous golf awards including Bob Jones award U.S. Golf Assn., William D. Richardson award Golf Writers Assn. Am., Herb Graffis award Nat. Golf Found.; named Athlete of Decade PA, 1969, Sportsman of Yr. Sports Illustrated mag., 1960, Player of Yr. Profl. Golfers Assn., 1960, 62; Profl. Golfers Assn. Tour Money Leader, 1958, 60, 62, 63; elected to World Golf Hall of Fame, Profl. Golfers Assn. Hall of Fame. Mem. Latrobe (Pa.) Country Club, Laurel Valley Golf Club, Rolling Rock Club (Ligonier, Pa.), Bay Hill Club, Duquesne Club (Pitts.). Avocation: aviation. Home and Office: PO Box 52 Youngstown PA 15696-0052

PALMER, BRENT DAVID, environmental physiology educator, biologist; b. Burbank, Calif., May 13, 1959; s. Warren Thayer and Yvonne Lita (McKelvey) P.; m. Sylvia Irena Karalius, June 26, 1982. BA, Calif. State U., Northridge, 1985; MS, U. Fla., 1987, PhD, 1990. Grad. asst. U. Fla., Gainesville, 1985-90; asst. prof. Wichita (Kans.) State U., 1990-91, Ohio U., Athens, 1991-97; asst. prof. environ. physiology U. Ky., Louisville, 1997—; cons. U.S. EPA, 1992—, Environment Can., 1995-96. Contbr. chpts. to books, articles on vertebrate reproductive biology and toxicology to profl. jours.; reviewer Biology of Reproduction, Champaign, Ill., Harper Collins pubs., N.Y.C., Reproduction, Fertility and Devel., Australia, Comments on Toxicology, Ind. Press, Jour. Morphology, N.Y.C., Environ. Health Perspective,s Biology of Reproduction, Gen. and Comparative Endocrinology, Am. Jour. Anatomy. Coord. Sci. Olympiad, Wichita, 1991, So. Ohio Dist. Sci. Day, 1992-94, Sci. and Engring. Fair, 1992-94. Rsch. grantee NIH, 1995—; recipient Best Student Paper award Herpetologists League, 1988, Stoye award Am. Soc. of Ichthyologists & Herpetologists, 1988, Student Rsch. award Soc. Study of Amphibian & Reptiles, 1989, Grants-in-aid of Rsch., Sigma Xi, 1989. Mem. AAAS, Am. Soc. Zoologists, Soc. Study Reproduction, Phi Beta Kappa. Achievements include description of functional morphology, physiology, and biochemistry of reptilian and amphibian oviducts; establishment of the evolution of an archosaurian reproductive system that may have implications for dinosaur reproduction; description of the effects of environmental endocrine disrupters on wildlife and humans. Office: Ohio U Dept Biol Scis Athens OH 45701-2979

PALMER, BRIAN EUGENE, lawyer; b. Mpls., May 16, 1948; s. Eugene Philip and Virginia Breeze (Rolfshus) P.; m. Julia Washburn Morrison, Dec. 29, 1972; 1 child, Julia Hunter. AB, Brown U., 1970; JD, William Mitchell Coll. of Law, 1974. Bar: Minn. 1974, U.S. Dist. Ct. Minn. 1975, U.S. Ct. Appeals (8th cir.) 1980, U.S. Ct. Fed. Claims 1984, U.S. Supreme Ct. 1980. Asst. pub. defender Hennepin County Pub. Defender, Mpls., 1974-78; assoc. Dorsey & Whitney LLP, Mpls., 1978-82, ptnr., 1983—. Home: 1190 Lyman Ave Wayzata MN 55391-9671 Office: Dorsey & Whitney LLP Pillsbury Ctr S 220 S 6th St Minneapolis MN 55402-4502

PALMER, BRUCE HARRISON, college director; b. Hartford, Conn., Apr. 13, 1955; s. David Alan and Marilyn Elaine (Shelburne) P. BA, Gordon Coll., 1977; MA, Gordon-Conwell Sem., 1979; MEd, Harvard U., 1982. Mng. publs. editor, asst. to fin. aid dir. Gordon-Conwell Sem., South Hamilton, Mass., 1979-81; dir. student fin. aid Roberts Wesleyan Coll., Rochester, N.Y., 1982-86; v.p. staff Roberts Wesleyan Coll., Rochester, 1983-84; assoc. dir. student fin. aid, coord. Info. and Data Svcs., lectr., gen. faculty U. Va., Charlottesville, 1986-94; dir. fin. aid Ea. Coll., St. Davids, Pa., 1994-95, Franklin Pierce Coll., Rindge, N.H., 1995—; deacon Congl. Ch. Temple, N.H., 1997—. Contbr. articles to newspapers. Program devel. Cmty. Outreach Park Street Ch., Boston, 1981; student pastor Park Street Bapt. Ch., Framingham, Mass., 1982; mem. Ivy Creek Found., Charlottesville, 1988—; vol. John Heinz Nat. Wildlife Refuge, Phila., 1994. Mem. Nat. Assn. Student Pers. Adminstrs., Nat. Assn. Student Fin. Aid Adminstrs. (editor jour.), Va. Assn. Student Fin. Aid Adminstrs. (tng. com., instr., automated svcs.), N.H. Assn. Student Fin. Aid Adminstrs., Phi Delta Kappa. Democrat. Home: RR 2 Box 459 Temple NH 03084-9759 Office: Franklin Pierce Coll College Rd Rindge NH 03461

PALMER, CHRISTINE (CLELIA ROSE VENDITTI), operatic singer, performer, pianist, vocal instructor; b. Hartford, Conn., Apr. 2; d. John Marion and Immacolata (Morcaldo) Venditti; m. Raymond Smith, Oct. 5, 1949 (div. June 1950); m. Arthur James Whitlock, Feb. 25, 1953. Student Mt. Holyoke Coll., 1937-38, student New Eng. Conservatory of Music, 1941-42, pvt. studies in Boston, Hartford, N.Y.C., Florence and Naples, Italy; RN with honors, Hartford Hosp. Sch. Nursing, 1941. Leading operatic soprano N.Y.C. Opera, Chgo., San Francisco, San Carlo, other cities, 1944-62; presented concert N.Y. Town Hall, 1951; soloist with symphony orchs. maj. U.S. cities, 1948-62; soloist Marble Collegiate Ch., Holy Trinity Ch.; coast-to-coast concert tour, 1948; numerous appearances including St. Louis Mcpl. Opera, Indpls. Starlight Theatre, Lambertville Music Circus; soloist Holiday on Ice, 1949-50; rec. artist; TV performer including Home Show on NBC, Telephone Hour on NBC, Holiday Hotel; performer at various supper clubs, N.Y.C., Atlanta, Bermuda, Catskills, others including Number One Fifth Avenue, The Embers, The Carriage Club, Viennese Lantern; artist-in-residence El Centro Coll., Dallas, 1966-71; pvt. vocal instr.-coach, specializing in vocal technique for opera, mus. comedy, supper club acts, auditions, Dallas, 1962-94; voice adjudicator San Francisco Opera Co., 1969-72, Tex. Music Tchrs. Assn., 1964-75, others; lectr. in field; appearances with S.M. Chartocks' Gilbert and Sullivan Co.; now performing lecture/entertainment circuit. Hon. mem. women's bd. Dallas Opera Assn.; mem. adv. bd. Tex. Opera News; mem. Tex. Music Tchrs. Cert. Bd., Collegiate Chorale, Don Craig Singers, The Vikings; mem. women's bd. Dallas Bapt. Univ. Oliver Ditson scholar, 1942; recipient Phi Xi Delta prize in Italian, 1937; named Victor Herbert Girl, ASCAP; Spl. Recognition Gold book of Dallas Soc. Mem. Nat. Assn. Tchrs. of Singing (pres. Dallas chpt. 1972-74), Nat. Fedn. Music Clubs, Tex. Fedn. Music Clubs, Dallas Fedn. Music Clubs (pres. 1972-74), Dallas Symphony League, Dallas Music Tchrs. Assn. (pres. 1971-72, Tchr. of Yr. 1974), Thesaurus (pres. 1990-91, 97-98), Friday Forum (Dallas, bd. dirs.), Dallas Women's C. of C., Eagle Forum, Pub. Affairs Luncheon Club, Dallas Fedn. Music Club, Pro Am., Wednesday Morning Choral Club, Dallas Knife and Fork Club, Prestoncrest Rep. Club. Presbyterian. Home: 6232 Pemberton Dr Dallas TX 75230-4036

PALMER, CRUISE, newspaper editor; b. Kansas City, Kans., Apr. 9, 1917; s. Thomas Potter and Margaret Scroggs (McFadden) P.; m. Dorraine Humphreys, Sept. 7, 1946; children: Thomas Cruise, Martha D. Sprague. B.S. in Journalism, Kans. State U., 1938. With Kansas City (Mo.) Star, 1938—, news editor, 1963-64, mng. editor, 1965-66; exec. editor and bd. Star and Times, 1967-77, cons., 1978—; dir. Purtec Systems, Inc. Mem. bd. govs. Am. Royal Live Stock and Horse Show Assn., 1967-91; bd. dirs. ARC, 1978-91, Kansas City Mayor's Corps Progress, 1978-91; found. trustee Kans. State U.; trustee Kansas City Sister Cities Commn., 1978-91. Served to lt. (j.g.) USNR, 1943-46. Recipient Distinguished Service award Kans. State U., 1967; First Place award Pro-Am. Southgate Open Golf Tournament, 1973; Second Place award Pro-Am. Hawaiian Open, 1973, 85; Third Place, 1981; First Place award Jim Colbert Celebrity Tournament, 1981, First Place Team award Kansas City area Am. Cancer Soc. Golf Tournament, 1986. Mem. Am. Soc. Newspaper Editors, Soc. Profl. Journalists, Kansas City Sr. Golf Assn., Mo. Sr. Golf Assn., Kansas City Press Club (pres. 1953-54, 64-65, permanent trustee, pres. scholarship found. 1989), Kansas City Club, Chiefs Red Coat Club, Milburn Golf and Country Club, Beta Theta Pi (Greater Kansas City Beta of Yr. 1980). Episcopalian (former vestryman and lay reader). Home: 4900 W 64th Ter Shawnee Mission KS 66208-1340 Office: 1729 Grand Ave Kansas City MO 64108-1413

PALMER, DAVE RICHARD, retired military officer, academic administrator; b. Ada, Okla., May 31, 1934; s. David Furman and Lorena Marie

(Clardy) P.; m. LuDelia Clemmer, Apr. 13, 1957; children: Allison, J. Kersten. BS, U.S. Military Acad., 1956; MA in History, Duke U., 1966; postgrad., Army War Coll., 1972-73; PhD (hon.), Duke U., 1990. Commd. U.S. Army, 1956, advanced through grades to lt. gen.; mem. faculty dept. history U.S. Mil. Acad., 1966-69; mem. staff (Pentagon), 1973-76, Joint Chiefs of Staff, 1979-81; comdr. Baumholder Mil. Community, W. Ger., 1981-83; dep. comdt. Command and Gen. Staff Coll., Ft. Leavenworth, Kans., 1983-85; comdg. gen. 1st Armored Div., W.Ger., 1985-86; supt. U.S. Mil. Acad., 1986-91, ret., 1991; pres. Walden U., 1995—. Author: The River and the Rock, 1969, The Way of the Fox, 1975, Summons of the Trumpet, 1978, 1794-America, Its Army, and The Birth of the Nation, 1994. Bd. dirs. Walden U., 1992-94. Decorated Legion of Merit (3); Bronze Star (2), D.S.M.(2). Mem. Assn. U.S. Army, Armor Assn., Mil. History, Soc. Cin.

PALMER, DAVID, dancer; b. Cairns, Australia. Attended, Saill Acad. of Dance, Sydney, Australia; studied with Janice Breen. Dancer Australian Ballet, Joffrey Ballet, Miami City Ballet, Royal Ballet of Flanders; prin. dancer San Francisco Ballet, 1994—; guest artist Sydney Dance Co., Ballet du Nord, France, Pact Ballet of South Africa, Queensland Ballet, Australian Ballet, Ballet Theatre of Miami. Dance performances include Prodigal Son, Apollo, Scotch Symphony, Rubies, Donizetti Variations, La Source, Bugaku, Diverimento No. 15, Tchaikovsky Pas de Deux, Minkus Pas de Trois, Sylvia Pas de Deux, Stars and Stripes, Diana and Acteon, Taming of the Shrew, Romeo & Juliet, Jeu Des Cartes, Lady and the Fool, La Fille mal gardée, Illuminations, Valentine, Jamboree, Kettantanz, Suite Saint-Säens, Trinity, Light Rain, Forgotten Land, Return to a Strange Land, Dream Dances, Arden Court, Aureole, Cloven Kingdom, Reus, Transtangos, Movillisimanoble, Caoticos, Contropical, Concerto for La Donna, The Moor's Pavane, Threshold, Rosalinda, La Bayadere, Nutcracker, Beyond Twelve, Surfacing, Aerial, The Huntchback of Notre Dame, Le Corsaire Pas de Deux, The Three Muscateers, Valses Poeticos, Maestrom, In the Night, The Concert, Company B, Rodeo, others; (film) To Dream of Roses, 1990; choreographer Aerial, Memories, Beauty and the Beast, Intimacy Pas de Deux, Collage. Office: San Francisco Ballet 455 Franklin St San Francisco CA 94102-4438*

PALMER, DAVID GILBERT, lawyer; b. Lakewood, N.J., Jan. 10, 1945; s. Robert Dayton and Lois (Gilbert) P.; m. Susan Edmundson Walsh, Aug. 17, 1968; children: Jonathan, Megan. AB, Johns Hopkins U., 1967; JD, U. Colo., 1970. Bar: Colo. 1970, U.S. Dist. Ct. Colo. 1970, U.S. Ct. Appeals (9th and 10th cirs.) 1970, U.S. Supreme Ct. 1970. Ptnr., chmn. litigation dept. Holland & Hart, Denver, 1970-87, Gibson, Dunn & Crutcher, Denver, 1987—. Chmn. N.W. region Am. Heart Assn., Dallas, 1986—, bd. dirs., 1986—, sec., 1990—, chmn. elect, 1991-92, chmn., 1992-93; pres., bd. dirs. Colo. Heart Assn., Denver, 1974; bd. dirs. C. H. Kempe Nat. Ctr. for Prevention of Child Abuse, Denver, 1984-90, pres., 1989-90; bd. dirs. Goodwill Industries, Denver, 1981-84. Mem. ABA, Colo. Bar Assn., Denver Law Club. Clubs: University, Mile High (Denver). Home: 3120 Ramshorn Dr Castle Rock CO 80104-9073 Office: Gibson Dunn & Crutcher 1801 California St Ste 4100 Denver CO 80202-2641

PALMER, DAVID SCOTT, political scientist, educator; b. Boston, July 16, 1937; s. Walter S. and Jean (Stuart) P.; m. Sarah Crawford, 1966 (dec. Nov. 1985); children: Walter Scott, Henry Crawford, Asa MacAdam. BA in Internat. Rels. cum laude, Dartmouth Coll., 1959; MA in Hispanic Am. Studies, Stanford U., 1962; PhD in Comparative Govt., Cornell U., 1973. Vol. leader Peace Corps, Peru, 1962-64; asst. dean freshmen, asst. to dir. admissions Dartmouth Coll., Hanover, N.H., 1964-68; from instr. to asst. prof. dept. govt. Bowdoin Coll., 1972-76; professorial lectr. Sch. Advanced Internat. Studies Johns Hopkins U., Washington, 1977-88; assoc. dean for programs Fgn. Svc. Inst., Dept. State, 1984-88, chair Latin Am. and Caribbean studies, 1976-88; prof. polit. sci. Boston U., 1988—, prof. internat. rels., 1990—, dir. Latin Am. studies, 1991-94; vis. lectr. Princeton U., 1978-79, Georgetown U., 1985. Author: Peru: The Authoritarian Tradition, 1980, (with Kevin Middlebrook) Military Government and Political Development: Lessons from Peru, 1975 (with Robert Wesson and others) The Latin American Military Institution, 1985; editor, contbr.: Shining Path of Peru, 1992, 2d edit., 1994; contbr. chpts. to books, articles and revs. to profl. jours. Recipient Meritorious Honor award U.S. Dept. of State, 1981; Daniel Webster nat. scholar, 1955-59; Edward John Noble Found. leadership grantee 1959-62. Mem. Latin Am. Studies Assn. (exec. com. 1983-86), New Eng. Coun. Latin Am. Studies (exec. com. 1989—, pres. 1993-94), Interam. Coun. of Washington (pres. 1978-79), Phi Beta Delta, Phi Kappa Phi, Sigma Delta Pi. Home: 69 Waverley St Belmont MA 02178-1958 Office: Boston U 152 Bay State Rd Boston MA 02215-1501

PALMER, DEBORAH JEAN, lawyer; b. Williston, N.D., Oct. 25, 1947; d. Everett Edwin and Doris Irene (Harberg) P.; m. Kenneth L. Rich, Mar. 29, 1980; children: Andrew, Stephanie. BA, Carleton Coll., 1969; JD cum laude, Northwestern U., 1973. Bar: Minn. 1973, U.S. Dist. Ct. Minn. 1973, U.S. Ct. Appeals (8th cir.) 1975, U.S. Supreme Ct. 1978. Econ. analyst Harris Trust & Savs. Bank, Chgo., 1969-70; assoc. Robins, Kaplan, Miller & Ciresi, LLP, Mpls., 1973-79, ptnr., 1979—. Trustee Carleton Coll., 1984-88; mem. bd. religious edn. Plymouth Congl. Ch., 1992-95; bd. dirs. Mpls. YWCA, 1996—. Mem. ABA, Minn. Bar Assn., Minn. Women Lawyers Assn. (sec. 1976-78), Hennepin County Bar Assn., Hennepin County Bar Found. (bd. dirs. 1978-81), Carleton Coll. Alumni Assn. (bd. dirs. 1978-82, sec. 1980-82), Women's Assn. of Minn. Orch. (bd. dirs. 1980-85, treas. 1981-83). Home: 1787 Colfax Ave S Minneapolis MN 55403-3008 Office: Robins Kaplan Miller & Ciresi LLP 800 Lasalle Ave Minneapolis MN 55402-2006

PALMER, DENNIS DALE, lawyer; b. Alliance, Nebr., Apr. 30, 1945; s. Vernon D. Palmer and Marie E. (Nelson) Fellers; m. Rebecca Ann Turner, Mar. 23, 1979; children: Lisa Marie, Jonathan Paul. BA, U. Mo., 1967, JD, 1970. Bar: Mo. 1970, U.S. Dist. Ct. (we. dist.) Mo. 1970, U.S. Ct. Appeals (8th and 10th cirs.) 1973, U.S. Supreme Ct. 1980. Staff atty. Legal Aid Soc. Western Mo., Kansas City, 1970-73; assoc. Shughart, Thomson & Kilroy, P.C., Kansas City, 1973-76, ptnr., bd. dirs., 1976—. Contbr. articles on franchise and employment law to legal jours. Bd. dirs., chmn. legal assts. adv. bd. Avila Coll., Kansas City, 1984-87. 2d lt. U.S. Army, 1970. Mem. ABA (litigation com. 1980, forum com. on franchising 1987), Mo. Bar Assn. (antitrust com. 1975—, civil practice com. 1975—), Kansas City Bar Assn. (chmn. franchise law com. 1987—), Univ. Club. Avocations: jogging, golf, tennis, outdoor activities, reading. Home: 13100 Canterbury Rd Leawood KS 66209-1700 Office: Shughart Thomson & Kilroy 12 Wyandotte Plz 120 W 12th St Fl 16 Kansas City MO 64105-1917

PALMER, DONALD CURTIS, interdenominational missionary society executive; b. Nelson, Minn., Oct. 8, 1934; s. Roy August Adn Cora (Bergner) P.; m. Dorothy Mae Nordquist, Mar. 16, 1962; children: Jean Marie, John Eric. Student, U. Minn., 1952-55; BS in Bible, Briercrest Bible Coll., Caronport, Can., 1958; MA in Missions, Trinity Divinity Sch., Deerfield, Ill., 1967; D in Ministry, Trinity Divinity Sch., 1989. Missionary Colombia GMU Internat., Kansas City, Mo., 1959-71; dir. evangelism GMU Internat., 1969-71, field sec. Latin Am., 1971-73, v.p. field ministries for Latin Am., 1973-85, v.p. research and strategy, 1985-92; gen. dir. Am. Missionary Fellowship, Villanova, Pa., 1992—; bd. dirs. Am. Missionary Fellowship, Villanova, 1978-92; vis. prof. Grace Coll. of the Bible, Omaha, 1982-92; mem. Frontier People's Com., 1985-92, Evang. Missiological Soc., 1991—. Author: Explosion of People Evangelism, 1974; (with others) Dynamic Religious Movements, 1978, Managing Conflict Creatively, 1990. Republican. Baptist. Avocations: golf, tennis, hiking. Home: 200 Cohasset Ln West Chester PA 19380-6504 Office: Am Missionary Fellowship 672 Conestoga Rd Villanova PA 19085-1428 *The greatest inner quality that a person can possess is a thankful, grateful spirit.*

PALMER, DORA DEEN POPE, English and French language educator; b. Jackson, Miss., June 26, 1946; d. Melvin Sr. and Gladys (Wolfe) Pope; m. Carey Palmer Jr.; 1 child, Cawandra V. AA, Utica Jr. Coll., 1966; BS in Edn., Jackson State U., 1968, MA in Edn., 1976. Cert. English and French tchr. Tchr. English and French McCullough H. S., Monticello, Miss., 1968-69, Topeka-Tilton H.S., Monticello, 1969-70, Crystal Springs (Miss.) H.S., 1971-93; tchr. French Jackson (Miss.) Pub. Sch. Dist., 1993—; chair English Dept., Crystal Springs, 1983-93; lectr. Jackson State Upward Bound, Jackson, 1984—; chair Crystal Springs H.S. steering and editing com. So. Assn. Colls. and Schs.; prodr., sponsor black history projects. Drama coach N.W. Mid. Sch., Jackson, 1993—; sponsor Beta Club, Crystal Springs, 1979; sec. Expo-Social & Civic Club, Jackson, 1988—; pianist Mount Wade Missionary Bapt. Ch., 1965-80, Terry Mission Missionary Bapt. Ch., 1979-87. Named Tchr. of Month, Tiger Pause newspaper, 1989, Star Tchr. Jackson State Upward Bound, 1992, Tchr. of Yr. Crystal Springs H.S., 1993; recipient Tchr. Appreciation award The Tiger ann., 1987, Outstanding Svc. award Terry Mission Bapt. Ch., 1983. Mem. ASCD, Nat. Assn. Edn., Miss. Assn. Edn. Democrat. Avocations: playing piano, reading, cooking Southern dishes, sewing. Home: 316 S Denver St Jackson MS 39209-6303 Office: Jackson Pub Schs N W Jackson 7020 Hwy 49 N Jackson MS 39213

PALMER, DOUGLAS S., JR., lawyer; b. Peoria, Ill., Mar. 15, 1945. AB cum laude, Yale U., 1966; JD cum laude, Harvard U., 1969. Bar: Wash. 1969. Mem. Foster Pepper & Shefelman, Seattle. Office: Foster Pepper & Shefelman 1111 3rd Ave Fl 34 Seattle WA 98101-3207

PALMER, EARL A., ophthalmologist, educator; b. Winchester, Ohio, July 2, 1940; m. Carolyn Mary Clark, June 13, 1963; children: Andrea, Aaron, Genevieve. BA, Ohio State U., 1962; MD, Duke U., 1966. Diplomate Am. Bd. Pediatrics, Am. Bd. Ophthalmology. Resident in pediatrics U. Colo. Med. Ctr., Denver, 1966-68; resident in ophthalmology Oreg. Health Scis. U., Portland, 1971-74; fellow Baylor Coll. Medicine, Houston, 1974-75; asst. prof. Pa. State U., Hershey, 1975-79; prof. Oreg. Health Scis. U., 1979—; chmn. Multicenter Outcome Study of Retinopathy of Prematurity. Contbr. articles to profl. jours. Fellow Am. Acad. Pediatrics, Am. Acad. Ophthalmology (Honor award); mem. Am. Assn. Pediatric Ophthalmology and Strabismus (pres. 1996-97). Avocation: golf. Office: Casey Eye Inst 3375 SW Terwilliger Blvd Portland OR 97201-4146

PALMER, EDWARD L., social psychology educator, television researcher, writer; b. Hagerstown, Md., Aug. 11, 1938; s. Ralph Leon and Eva Irene (Brandenburg) P.; children: Edward Lee, Jennifer Lynn. BA, Gettysburg Coll., 1960; BD, Luth. Theol. Sem., Gettysburg, 1964; MS, Ohio U., 1967, PhD, 1970. Asst. prof. Western Md. Coll., Westminster, 1968-70; asst. prof. Davidson Coll., N.C., 1970-77, assoc. prof., 1977-86, chair, 1985—, prof., 1986—, Watson prof., 1991—; guest rschr. Harvard U., Cambridge, Mass., 1977; vis. scholar UCLA, 1984; cons. Council on Children, Media, Merchandising, 1978-79, 1st Union Bank Corp., Charlotte, N.C., 1975-79; NSF proposal reviewer, 1978—. Editl. reviewer Jour. Broadcasting and Electronic Media, 1978—; editor: Children and the Faces of TV, 1980; author: (book) Children in the Cradle of TV, 1987; contbr. to Wiley Ency. of Psychology, 1984, Lawrence Erlbaum Assocs., 1991, Sage Pub., 1993, 96; author jour. articles and book chpts. Sec. A. Mecklenburg Child Devel. Assn., Davidson and Cornelius, N.C., 1974-78; bd. mem. pub. radio sta. WDAV, 1970-90. Telecommunications task force Rutgers U., 1981. Recipient Thomas Jefferson Teaching award Robert Earl McConnell Found., 1993. Mem. APA, Soc. Rsch. in Child Devel., Am. Psychol. Soc., Assn. Heads Depts. Psychology (chair 1994-96), Southeastern Psychol. Assn., Southeastern Soc. Social Psychologists, So. Assn. Pub. Opinion Rsch., Phi Beta Kappa (pres. Davidson chpt. 1985-86). Avocations: sunrise and sunset walks, writing poetry, bird watching, music composition and performance. Office: Davidson Coll PO Box 1719 Davidson NC 28036-1719

PALMER, EDWARD LEWIS, banker; b. N.Y.C., Aug. 12, 1917; s. William and Cecelia (Tierney) P.; m. Margaret Preston, Jan. 5, 1940; children: Edward Preston, Jane Lewis. A.B., Brown U., 1938. With N.Y. Trust Co., 1941-59, v.p., 1952-59; with Citibank, N.A., N.Y.C., 1959-82; sr. v.p. Citibank, N.A., 1962-65, exec. v.p., 1965-70, dir., chmn. exec. com., 1970-82; pres. Mill Neck Group, Inc., 1982; bd. dirs. Devon Group, Inc., SunResorts Ltd., Holmes Protection Group Inc.; dir. emeritus Cornign Inc.; trustee emeritus Mut. N.Y. Trustee emeritus Met. Mus. Art, Brown U. Served to lt. comdr. USNR, 1942-46. Mem. Phi Gamma Delta. Home: Horseshoe Rd Mill Neck NY 11765 Office: 399 Park Ave New York NY 10022

PALMER, FORREST CHARLES, librarian, educator; b. Burlington, Wis., Oct. 17, 1924; s. Forrest Blaire and Marie Florence (Rubach) P.; m. Lois Mae Davis, June 12, 1946; children: Forrest Charles, Beth Elaine, Janet Lorrayne. Student, U. Pitts., 1943-44; B.A., Valparaiso U., 1948; B.S. in L.S, George Peabody Coll., 1949, M.S. in L.S, 1953. Head catalog dept. Janesville (Wis.) Pub. Library, 1949-50; serials cataloger N.C. State U., Raleigh, 1950-51; head serials dept. N.C. State U., 1951-55; dir. libraries Miss. State U., State College, 1955-62; librarian, head dept. library sci. James Madison U., Harrisonburg, Va., 1962-70, head librarian, 1970-74, prof. library sci., documents librarian, 1973-89, ret., 1989, prof. emeritus, 1990—, mem. faculty senate, 1982-86, faculty marshall, 1983-85, treas. senate, 1985-86; mem. library com. Va. Higher Edn. Study Commn.; sec. joint law library com. Laird L. Conrad Meml. Library, Harrisonburg, 1974-89; adv. com. Va. Council Higher Edn.; Madison Coll. rep. Library Affairs Va. U. Center. Editor: Virginia Librarian, 1963-65. Contbr. articles and book revs. to profl. publs. Mem. edn. com. Starkville (Miss.) Youth Ctr., 1956; chmn. adv. bd. YMCA, State College, Miss., 1957-59; vice-chmn. Rep. city com., Harrisonburg, 1979-81; mem. land use adv. com. Ctrl. Shenandoah Planning Dist. Commn., 1979; mem. Bd. Zoning Appeals, Harrisonburg, 1981-91, vice chmn., 1983-85, chmn., 1985-91; ruling elder Presbyn. Ch. U.S., clk. of session, 1982-84; mem. task force on maintenance Synod of Mid-Atlantic, Presbyn. Ch., Massanetta Springs, 1991; mem. Ft. Delaware Soc., 1992, life mem., 1995—; mem. LaPorte County Hist. Steam Soc., Inc., 1996—. With Signal Corps AUS, PTO, 1943-46. Recipient Golden Triangle award YMCA. Mem. ALA (liaison com. Library Instrn. Round Table 1978-80, com. on instrn. in use of libraries 1977-79, mem. Govt. Documents Round Table 1983-89), Southeastern Library Assn. (chmn. coll. sect. 1960-62, treas., mem. exec. bd. 1975-76, budget com. 1974-80, hdqrts. liason com., 1987-91), Miss. Library Assn. (chmn. standards and planning com. 1958-59, chmn. coll. sect. 1959-60), Va. Library Assn. (activities com. 1962-65, chmn. publs. com. 1963-65, 1st v.p. 1968, pres. 1969-70), Pi Gamma Mu, Alpha Beta Alpha (adviser 1962-70), Beta Phi Mu. Republican. Presbyterian. Home: 60 E Weaver Ave Harrisonburg VA 22801-3041 *Long-lasting and meaningful contributions to society are those made out of consideration for others, not those where another individual is harmed.*

PALMER, GARY ANDREW, portfolio manager; b. Stamford, Conn., Dec. 30, 1953; s. Andrew and Edna Balz (Brogan) P.; m. Suzanne Branyon, Oct. 10, 1981; children: Gregory Allen, Kimberly Lynn. BS in Bus. Adminstrn.; U. Vt., 1977; MBA, U. N.C., 1979. Sr. fin. analyst Carolina Power and Light Co., Raleigh, N.C., 1979-80; dir. fin. planning and analysis Fed. Home Loan Mortgage Corp., Washington, 1980-85; sr. v.p. capital markets Imperial Corp. of Am., San Diego, 1985-90; sr. v.p., treas. Pacific 1st Fin. Corp., Seattle, 1990-92, Gentral Capital Corp., Seattle, 1993-95; CFO So. Pacific Funding Corp., Lake Oswego, Oreg., 1995-97.

PALMER, GARY STEPHEN, health services administrator; b. Murphy, N.C., Jan. 19, 1949; s. Bruce and Mary Frances (Patterson) P.; m. Kathleen Hart Middleton, June 12, 1976; children: Eric S., Brian S. BS in Bus. Adminstrn., U. N.C., 1971; MHA, Baylor U., 1982. Commd. U.S. Army, 1972, advanced through grades to lt. col., 1990; dir. program budget Letterman Army Med. Ctr., San Francisco, 1979-80; adminstrv. resident Womack Community Hosp., Fayetteville, N.C., 1981-82, ambulatory healthcare adminstr., 1982-83, asst. adminstr. profl. svcs., 1983-85; ambulatory healthcare adminstr. USA Health Svcs., San Antonio, 1985-88; COO U.S. Army Den Rl Activity, Killeen, Tex., 1988-91; dir. managed care Tripler Army Med. Ctr., Honolulu, 1991-93; inspector gen. Womack Army Med. Ctr., Ft. Bragg, N.C., 1993-94; assoc. dir. exec. master's program Sch. Pub. Health U. N.C., Chapel Hill, 1994—, dir. network devel. and external affairs, 1996—. Fellow Am. Coll. Healthcare Execs. (army regent's adv. coun. 1988-92, Elua Alii chpt. Honolulu 1991-93); mem. Med. Group Mgmt. Assn. Home: 103 William White Ct Carrboro NC 27510-4120 Office: U NC Sch Pub Health CB 7400 Dept Health Policy/Adminstn Chapel Hill NC 27599-7400

PALMER, HARVEY JOHN, chemical engineering educator, consultant; b. N.Y.C., Apr. 3, 1946; s. Harvey Anthony and Pearl Edna (Weber) P.; m. Donna Mary Partigan, July 11, 1966; children—Harvey D., Angeline, Thomas. B.S.C.E., U. Rochester, 1967; Ph.D. in Chem. Engring., U. Wash., 1971. Lic. profl. engr., N.Y. Asst. prof. chem. engring. U. Rochester, N.Y., 1971-77, assoc. prof., 1977-84, prof., 1984—, assoc. dean for grad. studies, 1983-89, chair dept. chem. engring., 1990—; cons. Pfaudler Co., Rochester, 1978-79, Eastman Kodak Co., Rochester, 1982-92, Helios Corp., Mumford, N.Y., 1983-91, Boehringer Mannheim Corp., Indpls., 1993; bd. dirs. Transmation Inc., Rochester. Contbr. articles to profl. jours. Mem. sch. bd. Honeoye Falls-Lima Central Schs., N.Y., 1983-92, pres., 1988-90. Recipient Undergrad. Teaching award Coll. Engring., U. Rochester, 1979, 82. Mem. Am. Inst. Chem. Engrs. (sec. Rochester sect. 1976-77), Sigma Xi. Office: Univ Rochester Dept Chem Engring Rochester NY 14627

PALMER, IRENE SABELBERG, university dean and educator emeritus, nurse, researcher, historian; b. Franklin, N.J., May 28, 1923; d. John Joseph and May (Heiser) Sabelberg; 1 son, Andrew C. B.S., N.J. State Tchrs. Coll., 1945; diploma, Jersey City Med. Center Sch. Nursing, 1945; M.A., N.Y. U., 1951, Ph.D., 1963. Edn. dir. Diploma Schs. Nursing, N.J., Mass., 1948-52; ednl. dir. Glenn Dale (Md.) Hosp., D.C. Dept. Pub. Health, 1956, dir. nursing svc. and edn., 1956-61; assoc. clin. prof. nursing Georgetown U., 1960-61; USPHS trainee, 1961-62; assoc. chief nursing svc. for rsch. VA Hosp., San Francisco, 1963-64; rsch. nurse cons. HEW, USPHS, Div. Nursing, Nursing Rsch. Field Center, San Francisco, 1964-66; asst. dean, assoc. prof. nursing U. Colo. Sch. Nursing, Denver, 1966-68; dean, prof. nursing Boston U. Sch. Nursing, 1968-74; prof. Hahn Sch. Nursing, U. San Diego, 1974-91, prof. emeritus, 1991—, dean, 1974-87, dean emeritus, 1988—; lectr. Clasical Alliance of the western States, Uskudar, Turkey, 1994, Italy, 1995. Editor: Nursing Clinics of North America, 1970; Contbr. articles to profl. jours. Served to capt. Nurse Corps U.S. Army, 1953-56. Internat. Nightingale scholar; Nat. Health Svc. fellow; recipient Excellence in Nursing Scholarship award Orgn. Nurse Execs., 1993. Fellow Nat. League Nursing (bd. visitors 1977-87), Am Acad. Nursing; mem. ANA, Am. Assn. History Nursing, Am. Assn. Colls. Nursing (hon.), Boston U. Nursing Archives, German Rsch. Assn. (pres. 1995), Sigma Theta Tau (Leadership award Zeta Mu chpt. 1986, Excellence in Nursing award 1991).

PALMER, JAMES ALVIN, baseball commentator; b. N.Y.C., Oct. 15, 1945; children: Jamie, Kelly. Student, Ariz. State U., Towson (Md.) State Coll. Pitcher Balt. Orioles, 1966-84; commentator ABC Sports, 1984—, Home Team Sports, Bethesda, Md.; also appears in TV and print advertisements. Author: (with Jack Clary) Jim Palmer's Way to Fitness, 1985, (with Jim Dale) Together We Were Eleven Foot Nine: The Twenty-Four Year Friendship of Hall of Fame Pitcher Jim Palmer and Orioles Manager Earl Weaver, 1996. Recipient Cy Young Meml. award Am. League, 1973, 75, 76; named Am. League Pitcher of Year The Sporting News, 1973, 75, 76; elected to Baseball Hall of Fame, 1990. Played All-Star Game, 1970, 71, 72, 77, 78. Office: care Home Team Sports 7700 Wisconsin Ave Bethesda MD 20814*

PALMER, JAMES DANIEL, information technology educator; b. Washington, Mar. 8, 1930; s. Martin Lyle and Sarah Elizabeth (Hall) P.; m. Margret Kupka, June 21, 1952; children: Stephen Robert, Daniel Lee, John Keith. AA, Fullerton Jr. Coll., 1953; BS (Alumni scholar), U. Calif., Berkeley, 1955, MS, 1957; PhD, U. Okla., 1963; DPS (hon.), Regis Coll., Denver, 1977. Chief engr. Motor vehicle and Illumination Lab. U. Calif., Berkeley, 1955-57; assoc. prof. U. Okla., Norman, 1957-63; prof. U. Okla., 1963-66, asst. to dir. Rsch. Inst., 1960-63, cons. Rsch. Inst., 1966-69, dir. Sch. Elec. Engring., 1963-66, dir. Systems Rsch. Center, 1964-66; dean sci. and engring., prof. elec. engring. Union Coll., Schenectady, 1966-71; pres. Met. State Coll., Denver, 1971-78; rsch. and spl. programs adminstr. Dept. Transp., Washington, 1978-79; v.p., gen. mgr. rsch. and devel. div. Mech. Tech., Inc., Latham, N.Y., 1979-82; exec. v.p. J.J. Henry Co., Inc., Moorestown, N.J., 1982-85; BDM internat. prof. info. tech. George Mason U., Fairfax, Va., 1985—; bd. dirs. J.J. Henry Co., Inc.; cons. Sym Mgmt. Co., Boston, Higher Edn. Exec. Assocs., Denver, PERI, Princeton; adj. prof. U. Colo. Co-author: (with A.P. Sage) Software Systems Engineering, (with Aseltine, Beam and Sage) Introduction to Computer Systems, Analysis, Design and Application. Bd. dirs., exec. v.p. adv. com. U.S.A. Vols. for Internat. Tech. Assistance, 1967-83, exec. v.p., 1970-71, chmn. exec. com.; trustee, vice chmn. Nat. Commn. on Coop. Edn.; mem. exec. policy bd. Alaska Natural Gas Pipeline, 1978-79; trustee Auraria Higher Edn. Program, Denver; mem. Fulbright fellow Selection Com., Colo.; bd. mgrs., mem. exec. com. Hudson-Mohawk Assn. Colls. and Univs., trustee, chmn. bd., 1970-71; adv. com. USCG Acad., 1972-82, chmn. adv. com., 1979-82; mem. Colo. Gov.'s Sci. and Tech. Adv. Council; pres. Denver Cath. Community Services Bd.; mem. Archdiocesan Catholic Charities and Community Services; mem. bd. U. Okla. Rsch. Inst.; mem. adv. com. Mile-Hi Red Cross. With USMC, 1950-51. Case-Western Res. Centennial scholar, 1981; recipient U.S. Coast Guard award and medal for meritorious pub. service, 1983. Fellow IEEE (exec. and adminstrv. coms., v.p. long-range planning and finance, chmn. com. on large scale systems, Joseph E. Wahl Outstanding Career Achievement award 1993); mem. Systems, Man and Cybernetics Soc. (pres., Outstanding Contbns. award 1981), alumni assns. U. Calif. and U. Okla., Inst. Internat. Edn. (bd. dir. Rocky Mt. sect.), Soc. Naval Architects and Marine Engrs., Am. Soc. Engring. Edn., Am. Mil. Engrs., N.Y. Acad. Sci., Navy League, Sigma Xi, Eta Kappa Nu, Pi Mu Epsilon, Alpha Gamma Sigma. Home: 860 Cashew Way Fremont CA 94536 Office: George Mason U Sch of Info Tech & Engring Fairfax VA 22030

PALMER, JAMES DANIEL, inspector; b. Oklahoma City, Okla., Aug. 11, 1936; s. Athol Ford and Marjorie Lorraine (Ward) P.; m. Gail Dorothy Myers, June 1954 (div. Sept. 1956); 1 child, James Douglas; m. Gloria Jean West, Dec. 14, 1963; children: Diana Lorraine, Elana Louise, Sheri Francis. AB in Police Sci. with honors, San Jose (Calif.) State U., 1963, AB in Psychology, 1964; MPA, Golden Gate U., 1972. Cert. Calif. police officers standards and tng. Asst. foreman Hunts Foods, Inc., Hayward, Calif., 1959-64; spl. investigator Dept. A.B.C. State of Calif., Oakland, 1964-67; criminal inspector Contra Costa County Dist. Atty., Martinez, Calif., 1967-72, lt. of inspectors, 1972-92; ret., 1992; pres. Contra Costa County Peace Officers, Richmond, 1974-75; past v.p. Contra Costa County Dist. Atty's Inv. Assn., Martinez, 1971, tng. officer, 1990-92. Contbr. articles to profl. jours. Past pres. South Hayward (Calif.) Dem. Club, 1976, 77, San Leandro (Calif.) Dems., 1975; mem. Gov's Law Enforcement Adv. Commn., Sacramento, Calif., 1972-76, Calif. Dem. Coun., 1972-73; rev. Am. Fellowship Protestant Ch., 1990—, min., 1990—. With USAF, 1955-58. Avocations: stocks, bonds, real estate, family, church. Home: 2788 Sydney Way Castro Valley CA 94546-2738

PALMER, JAMES EDWARD, public relations executive; b. Evansville, Ind., July 30, 1935; s. James Edward and Verble (Hearin) P. B.A. in English, N.Y.U., 1955. Reporter Evansville Courier, 1955-59; non-fiction editor Cosmopolitan mag., N.Y.C., 1959-61; exec. editor Cosmopolitan mag., 1961-65; editor Mag. Mgmt. Co., Inc., 1971-72; editor-in-chief Liberty mag., N.Y.C., 1972-73; dir. mag. and book dept. Carl Byoir & Assos., N.Y.C., 1973-76; corp. public relations dir. Macmillan, Inc., N.Y.C., 1977-80; pres. James Palmer Assos., N.Y.C., 1980-88, The Palmer Group, Houston, 1988—. Mem. Sigma Chi. Office: PO Box 90422 Houston TX 77290-0422

PALMER, JEFFRESS GARY, hematologist, educator; b. Bklyn., Oct. 7, 1921; s. William Ware and Margaret Lee (Boswell) P.; m. Jane Ann Cartwright, Feb. 2, 1951; children: Kristin Cartwright, Julie Mitchell. BS, Emory U., 1942, MD, 1944. Intern N.C. Bapt. Hosp., 1944-45; resident in medicine Emory U., Atlanta, 1947-49; fellow hematology U. Utah, Salt Lake City, 1949-52; from asst. prof. to prof. medicine U. N.C., Chapel Hill, 1952—. Capt. M.C. AUS, 1945-47. Mem. AAAS, AAUP, AMA, Am. Fedn. for Clin. Rsch., So. Soc. for Clin. Investigation, N.Y. Acad. Scis., Am. Soc. Hematology. Home: Morgan Creek Rd Chapel Hill NC 27514

PALMER, JOHN BERNARD, III, lawyer; b. Ft. Wayne, Ind., May 18, 1952; s. John Bernard and Dorothy Alma (Lauer) P. B.A., Mich. State U., 1974, J.D. U. Mich., 1977. Bar: Ill. 1977, U.S. Dist. Ct. (no. dist.) Ill. 1977, U.S. Tax Ct. 1979. Assoc. Mayer Brown & Platt, Chgo., 1977-80; assoc. Hopkins & Sutter, Chgo., 1980-83, ptnr., 1983—; adj. prof. Ill. Inst. Tech.-Kent Coll. of Law, Chgo., 1984—. Mem. ABA. Office: Hopkins & Sutter Three First Nat Plaza Chicago IL 60602

PALMER, JOHN L., social sciences researcher, educator; b. Upper Darby, Pa., Apr. 10, 1943; s. Richard Sidwell and Helen (Logan) P.; m. Nancy Hetenyi, June 29, 1968 (div. Dec. 1984); 1 child, Georgina; m. Stephanie Graham Gould, June 21, 1986; 1 child, Joanna. BA in Math., Williams Coll., 1965; PhD in Econs., Stanford U., 1970. Asst. prof. econs. Stanford U., Calif., 1969-71; dir. office income security policy HEW, Washington,

1971-75; asst. sec. HHS, Washington, 1979-81; sr. fellow The Brookings Instn., Washington, 1975-79, The Urban Inst., Washington, 1981-88; dean Maxwell Sch. Syracuse U., 1988—; adj. faculty Harvard U., Cambridge, Mass., 1982-84; cons. numerous govt. agys. and pvt. founds., 1975-79, 81—. Author, editor 12 books; contbr. numerous articles on econs., social and budgetary concerns and policies. Woodrow Wilson fellow, 1965, NDEA scholar, Stanford U. Fellow Nat. Acad. Pub. Adminstrn.; mem. Am. Econ. Assn., Assn. Pub. Policy Analysis and Mgmt., NAS (various coms.), Nat. Acad. Social Ins. (pres. 1997—). Home: 6980 Woodchuck Hill Rd Fayetteville NY 13066-9760 Office: Syracuse U 200 Eggers Hall Syracuse NY 13244-1090

PALMER, JOHN N., communications executive. BA, U. Miss., MBA. Founder, pres. Mobile Comm. Corp. Am., Jackson, Miss., 1973-89; chmn., CEO Mobile Telecomm. Techs. Corp., Jackson, 1989—. Bd. dirs. Entergy Corp., Deposit Guaranty Nat. Bank, Inst. Tech. Devel. and Found. for Mid-South, U. Miss. Found.; bd. trustees Nat. Symphony Orch., EastGroup Properties, Millsaps Coll. Office: Mobile Telecomm Techs PO Box 2469 Jackson MS 39225

PALMER, LANGDON, banker; b. Montclair, N.J., Mar. 4, 1928; s. Lubin and Marjorie (Maxfield) P.; m. Millicent M. Lott, June 27, 1954; children—Jennifer Leigh, Langdon Jr., Christopher Lott. B. in Comml. Sci., Dartmouth Coll., 1951; M.B.A., NYU, 1959; postgrad. in advanced mgmt., Harvard Bus. Sch., 1968. Sr. v.p. Chase Manhattan Bank, N.Y.C., 1953-83; chmn., chief exec. officer Horizon Bank, Morristown, N.J., 1984-89; ret., 1989; bd. dirs. Chem. Bank N.J., N.A., 1989-92, now mem. adv. bd., 1992-95. Exec. v.p. Greater N.Y. coun. Boy Scouts Am., unitl 1983, Morris Sussex coun., 1984—; bd. dirs. N.J. Conservation Found., Morris County Agrl. Devel. Bd., until 1993, Morris County Park Commn.; bd. dirs. Nature Conservancy, chmn. N.J. chpt.; trustee Morris County Parks and Conservation Found.; chmn. bd. Morris 2000, until 1994. Decorated Bronze Star; named Knight Great Commander of Liberian Humane Order of African Redemption, 1983; Ordre National Republic of Guinee, 1982; recipient Silver Beaver award Boy Scouts Am., 1977, Disting. Eagle award, 1989. Mem. Morris County C. of C. (bd. dirs. 1984—, vice chmn. 1987—, chmn. 1988). Republican. Episcopalian. Clubs: Morristown (N.J.); Anglers (N.Y.C.). Avocation: fly fishing.

PALMER, LARRY ISAAC, lawyer, educator; b. 1944. AB, Harvard U., 1966; LLB, Yale U., 1969. Bar: Calif. 1970. Asst. prof. Rutgers U., Camden, N.J., 1970-73, assoc. prof., 1973-75; assoc. prof. Cornell U., Ithaca, N.Y., 1975-79, prof. of law, 1979—, vice provost, 1979-84, v.p. acad. programs, 1987-91, v.p. acad. program and campus affairs, 1991-94; vis. fellow Cambridge U., 1984-85. Mem. Am. Law Inst. Office: Cornell U Law Sch 120 Myron Taylor Hall Ithaca NY 14853-4901

PALMER, LESLIE HOWARD, literature educator; b. Memphis, Jan. 25, 1941; s. Milton Howard and Janie Lee (Weaver) P.; m. Joyce Arline Cornette, Aug. 27, 1965; children: David Leslie, Rachel Joyce. BA, Memphis State U., 1962; MA, U. Tenn., 1963, PhD, 1966. Instr. U. Tenn., Knoxville, 1966-67; prof. English U. North Tex., Denton, 1967—; mem. athletic coun. U. North Tex., 1975-82, scholarship com., 1988-94; presenter poetry readings and guest lectrs. in field. Author: (poetry books) A Red Sox Flag, 1983, Ode to a Frozen Dog: and Other Poems, 1992, Artemis' Bow, 1993, The Devil Sells Ice Cream, 1994; asst. editor: Studies in the Novel, 1973-86; contbr. articles to profl. jours. Faculty sponsor Amnesty Internat., U. North Tex., 1984-86, North Tex. Chess Club, Denton, 1978-90; sch. vol. Denton Ind. Sch. Dist., 1977—. Recipient Beaudoin Gemstone award, Memphis, 1963, 64, Mid-South Free Verse award, Memphis, 1965, Outstanding Poet mention Pushcart Press, 1981. Mem. MLA, Modern Humanities Rsch. Assn., PEN, Denton C. of C. (cons.), Mensa, Phi Kappa Phi. Office: Univ North Tex Denton TX 76203

PALMER, MADELYN STEWART SILVER, family practice physician; b. Denver, July 18, 1964; d. Barnard Stewart and Cherry (Bushman) Silver; m. James Michael Palmer, Sept. 26, 1992; children: Adoniram Jacob, Benjamin Kern. BA cum laude, Wellesley (Mass.) Coll., 1986; MD, U. Utah, 1990. Family practice resident Mercy Med. Ctr., Denver, 1990-93; physician South Fed. Family Practice, Denver, 1993-95, South West Family Pracice, Littleton, Colo., 1995, Family Medicine Clinic, P.C., 1996—; staff St. Anthony Ctrl. Hosp., Denver, Porter Hosp., Denver, Swedish Hosp., Littleton Hosp. Ward Young Women's pres. LDS Ch., Littleton, ward primary sec., choir dir., Englewood. Mem. Am. Acad. Family Practice, Colo. Acad. Family Practice, Colo. Med. Soc. Achievements include research on physician practices and underimmunization of children. Home: 543 E Maplewood Dr Littleton CO 80121 Office: 6169 S Balsam Way Ste 220 Littleton CO 80123-3063

PALMER, MARCIA STIBAL, food and wine retailer, interior designer, real estate investor; b. Berea, Ky., Mar. 31, 1948; d. Earl and Marie (Gabbard) Harrison; m. George E. Palmer; children: Anthony Craig, Everrett Todd, Melony Brook. Grad. high sch., Richmond, Ky., 1967. Prin. Hanna Hardware, Ft. Lauderdale, Fla., 1971-81, J-Mar-J-Design, Ft. Lauderdale and L.A., 1980—, Fernando's Internat. Market & Vintage Winery, Ft. Lauderdale, 1995; pvt. practice real estate investing Ft. Lauderdale, 1971—. Mgr. campaign Rocky Rodriguez for City Commr., Ft. Lauderdale, 1987-88; del. Rep. State Conv., 1985—, Rep. Nat. Com., Washington, 1985—; active on Holy Cross Hosp. Aux., Ft. Lauderdale, 1984—. Mem. Nat. Safety Coun., Police Benevolent Assn., Hon. Order of Ky. Cols. (Frankfort), Ft. Lauderdale C. of C., Lauderdale-by-the-Sea. Baptist. Avocations: photography, sketching, art, antique collecting. Home and Office: 340 Sunset Dr Apt 1510 Fort Lauderdale FL 33301-2649

PALMER, MARTHA H., counseling educator; b. Chgo., Jan. 10, 1954; d. Thomas Manuel Sr. and Marie Louise (Cranford-Crawford) P.; m. Lewis A. Boahene, Mar. 1992; 1 child, Kwasi A. BA in Psychology, Ea. Ill. U., 1976, MS, 1977; cert. in cmty. law, John Marshall Law Sch., Chgo., 1981; student, U. Ill., Chgo., 1992; postgrad., No. Ill. U., 1995—. Med. asst. health svcs. Ea. Ill. U., Charleston, 1976-77; dir. sch. age and sr. citizen programs YMCA, Chgo., 1978-80; site dir., facilities mgr. Ctrs. for New Horizons, Chgo., 1980-85; counselor No. Ill. U., DeKalb, 1985-89; lectr. Malcolm X Coll., Chgo., 1989, recruitment coord., 1989-90; dir. Bethel Self Sufficiency Program, Chgo., 1989-90; asst. prof. counseling Harold Washington Coll. City Colls. Chgo., 1990—; developer Harold Washington Coll. Sisters Academic Scholarship Program, 1997. Creator of character Marty The Clown; author poems; contbr. articles to profl. jours. Coord. Afrikan Cultural Pageant, Ea. Ill. U., Charleston and No. Ill. U., DeKalb, 1972-86; mem. polit. com. Chgo. Black United Comtys. and Black Ind. Polit. Orgns., Chgo., 1981—; program chair 500 Black Men and Women, Chgo., 1989-92; pres., mem. Sojourners United Polit. Action Commn., Chgo., 1993—; founder Harold Washington Coll., Black Women's Caucus, Chgo., 1991—; edn. rep. Task Force for Black Polit. Empowerment, Chgo., 1994—; coord. Coll. Support Groups for Self Help, 1991; co-founder Black Maleness Program, 1991; vol. La Rida Hosp., Chgo.; co-convenor Rainbow PUSH Coalition City Coll. Chgo. divsn. Recipient Sharps and Flats Music Club Adv. award, 1994, BSU award, 1996. Mem. NOW, Nat. Assn. Black Psycholigist, Ill. Assn. Black Psychologist, Delta Sigma Theta. Democrat. Roman Catholic. Avocations: singing, dancing, designing, drawing. Office: City Coll Chgo Harold Washington Campus 30 E Lake St Chicago IL 60601-2403

PALMER, PATRICK EDWARD, radio astronomer, educator; b. St. Johns, Mich., Dec. 6, 1940; s. Don Edward and Nina Louise (Kyes) P.; m. Joan Claire Merlin, June 9, 1963; children—Laura Katherine, Aidan Edward, David Elijah. S.B., U. Chgo., 1963; M.A., Harvard U., 1965, Ph.D., 1968. Radio astronomer Harvard U., Cambridge, Mass., 1968; asst. prof. astronomy and astrophysics U. Chgo., 1968-70, asso. prof., 1970-75, prof., 1975—; vis. assoc. prof. astronomy Calif. Inst. Tech., Pasadena, 1972; vis. radio astronomer Cambridge (Eng.) U., 1973; vis. rsch. astronomer U. Calif., Berkeley, 1977, 86; vis. scientist Nat. Radio Astronomer Obs., 1980-96. Contbr. articles on radio astron. investigations of comets and interstellar medium to tech. jours. Recipient Bart J. Bok prize for contbns. to galactic astronomy, 1969, Alfred P. Sloan Found. fellow, 1970-72, Helen B. Warner prize, 1975. Fellow AAAS (Chmn. sect. D astronomy 1984); mem. Am. Astron. Soc. (chmn. nominating com. 1981, publs. bd. 1985-86, Warner Prize selection com. 1977-78), Royal Astron. Soc., Internat. Astron. Union, AAUP. Club: U. Chgo. Track. Home: 5549 S Dorchester Ave Chicago IL 60637-1720 Office: Univ Chgo Astronomy & Astrophysics Ctr 5640 S Ellis Ave Chicago IL 60637-1433

PALMER, PAUL EDWARD, communications executive; b. York, Pa., Nov. 18, 1942; s. Daniel Isaih Palmer and Eleanor (Beard) Wolff; m. Margaret Ann Strong, Oct. 2, 1965; children: Paul Joseph, Wendy Suzanne, Caroline Marie. BA in Speech Radio/TV, U. Md., 1964. With Sta. WBAL Radio, Balt., 1964-65; account exec. Sta. KDKA Radio, Pitts., 1965-68, RAR, Chgo., 1968-70; sales mgr. Sta. WIND Radio, Chgo., 1970-72; v.p., gen. mgr. Sta. KFMB AM-FM, San Diego, 1972—; pres. Sun Mountain Broadcasting, Inc., San Diego, 1985—. Mem. Assn. Ind. Met. Stas. Home: 2915 Woodford Dr La Jolla CA 92037-3545 Office: Sta KFMB AM 2915 Woodford Dr La Jolla CA 92037-3545

PALMER, PAUL RICHARD, librarian, archivist; b. Cin., Jan. 21, 1917; s. Gardiner O. and Sarah Ellen (Christy) P. BA, U. Cin., 1949; MS, Columbia U., 1950, MA, 1955. Asst. br. libr. Bklyn. Pub. Library, 1950-51; libr. Columbia U., N.Y.C., 1951-67, libr. sch. libr. svc., 1968, libr. and curator Brander Matthews Dramatic Mus., 1969-73, bibliographer Avery Archtl. Libr., 1974, curator Columbiana Collection, 1974—; cons. Am. Libr. Assn., Chgo. and N.Y.C., 1954-59. Contbr. articles to profl. jurs. With U.S. Army, 1942-45, ETO and NATOUSA. Fellow The Pierpont Morgan Libr.; mem. Theatre Libr. Assn. (exec. coun. 1970-74), Mus. Modern Art, Metro. Mus. Art, Am. Film Inst., Am. Mus. Britain, French Inst., Soc. Hist. Preservation, Lincoln Ctr. Film Soc., Manuscript Soc., Grolier Club, Church Club N.Y., St. George's Soc. N.Y., VFW, Phi Beta Kappa. Episcopalian. Home: 560 Riverside Dr Apt 21-b New York NY 10027-3236

PALMER, PHILIP EDWARD STEPHEN, radiologist; b. London, Apr. 26, 1921. Ed., Kelly Coll., Tavistock, Eng., 1938; M.B., B.S., U. London, 1944, D.M.R., 1946, D.M.R.T., 1947. Intern, then resident Westminster Hosp.; cons. radiologist West Cornwall (Eng.) Hosp. Group, 1947-54; sr. govt. radiologist Matabeleland, Rhodesia-Zimbabwe, 1954-64; prof. radiology U. Cape Town, South Africa, 1964-68; prof. U. Pa., 1968-70; prof. diagnostic radiology and vet. radiology U. Calif., Davis, 1970—; WHO cons. in field. Author: The Radiology of Tropical Diseases, 1980; contbr. articles to profl. publs. Recipient German Röentgen award, 1993, 1st Béclère medal Internat. Soc. Radiology, 1996, 1st Antoine Béclère lectr. Internat. Soc. Radiology, 1996. Fellow Calif. Radiol. Assn., Royal Coll. Physicians (Edinburgh), Royal Coll. Radiologists (Eng.), Romanian Soc. Radiol. and Nuclear Med.; mem. Brit. Inst. Radiology, Brit. Med. Assn., Calif. Med. Assn., Internat. Skeletal Soc., Assn. Univ. Radiologists, Radiol. Soc. N. Am., Kenya Radiol. Soc., South African Coll. Medicine, Egyptian Soc. Radiology and Nuclear Medicine, Yugoslav Assn. for Ultrasound, West African Assn. Radiologists. Address: 821 Miller Dr Davis CA 95616-3622

PALMER, RAYMOND A., administrator, librarian; b. Louisville, May 8, 1939. BA in Biology, U. Louisville, 1961; MLS, U. Ky., 1966. Adminstrv. asst. Johns Hopkins Med. Libr., Balt., 1966-69; asst. librarian Harvard Med. Libr., Boston, 1969-74; health scis. librarian Wright State U., Dayton, Ohio, 1974-82, assoc. prof. library adminstrn., 1974-82; exec. dir. Med. Libr. Assn., Chgo., 1982-92, Am. Assn. Immunologists, Bethesda, Md., 1992-95; dir. info.-edn. svcs. Nat. Ctr. Edn. Maternal-Child Health Georgetown U., Arlington, Va., 1995—; cons. Acad. Mil. Med. Scis. Libr., Beijing, 1990, Alzheimer's Assn., Chgo., 1991. Author: Management of Library Associations; mng. editor: Jour. Immunology, 1992-95; contbr. articles to profl. jours. Mem. ALA, Am. Soc. Assn. Execs., Greater Washington Soc. Assn. Execs., Spl. Librs. Assn., Biomed. Communication Network (chmn. 1980-82), Am. Mgmt. Assn. (strategic planning adv. coun. 1987-91), Coun. Biology Editors, Friends of Nat. Libr. Medicine (bd. dirs. 1989-92, 94—), Internat. Fedn. Libr. Assns. and Instns. (exec. com. Round Table for Mgmt. of Libr. Orgns. 1989-92), Med. Libr. Assn., Spl. Libr. Assn.

PALMER, RICHARD JOSEPH, communications director; b. Mpls., June 23, 1929; s. Charles Henry and Josephine (Shimek) P.; m. Bernice Arvilla Schumacher, Sept. 18, 1954; children: Howard, Penny Rae, Pamela, Randall, Roger. Diploma in Journalism, U. Minn., 1957. Reporter/photographer Fairmont Daily Sentinel, Minn., 1953-54, 57-59; newsman, capitol corrs. AP, Mpls., Fargo and Bismarck, N.D., 1959-67; comms. dir. N.D. Education Assn., Bismarck, 1967-93; comms. cons. NEA, Washington, 1993—; pres., State Edn. Editors of NEA, 1974, sec./treas. Pub. Rels. Coun., 1977-79, chmn. Sml. States Printing Consortium, 1977-88. Editor/photographer: (video) Come In, Please, To My World, 1990 (Best of Show in NEA Pub. Rels. Coun. 1991); contbr. publs. in field. Coun. mem. Trinity Luth. Ch., Bismarck, 1994-96. Ssgt. U.S. Army, 1950-52, Korea. Named Outstanding Male Grad. in Journalism, Sigma Delta Chi, 1957; recipient Friend of Edn. award N.D. Edn. Assn., Bismarck, 1993. Mem. N.D. Wildlife Fedn. (Conservation Comms. award 1971), Soc. for Profl. Journalists, Lions (3d to 1st v.p. Bismarck club 1994-96). Avocations: photography, hunting, fishing, travel, woodcarving. Home: 1801 Marian Dr Bismarck ND 58501-1552 Office: Palmer Comms 1801 Marian Dr Bismarck ND 58501-1552

PALMER, RICHARD N., judge; b. Hartford, Conn., May 27, 1950. BA, Trinity Coll., 1972; JD with high honors, U. Conn., 1977. Bar: Conn. 1977, U.S. Dist. Ct. Conn. 1978, D.C. 1980, U.S. Ct. Appeals (2nd cir.) 1981. Law clk. to Hon. Jon O. Newman U.S. Ct. Appeals (2nd cir.), 1977-78; assoc. Shipman & Goodwin, 1978-80; asst. U.S. atty. Office U.S. Atty. Conn., 1980-83, 87-90, U.S. atty. dist. Conn., 1991, chief state's atty. Conn., 1991-93; ptnr. Chatigny and Palmer, 1984-86; assoc. justice Conn. Supreme Ct., Hartford, 1993—. Mem. Phi Beta Kappa. Office: 231 Capitol Ave Hartford CT 06106-1548

PALMER, RICHARD WARE, lawyer; b. Boston, Oct. 20, 1919; s. George Ware and Ruth French (Judkins) P.; m. Nancy Fernald Shaw, July 8, 1950; children: Richard Ware Jr., John Wentworth, Anne Fernald. AB, Harvard U., 1942, JD, 1948. Bar: N.Y. State 1950, Pa. 1959. Sec., dir. N.Am. Mfg. Co., Natick, Mass., 1946-48; assoc. Burlingham, Veeder, Clark & Hupper, Burlingham, Hupper & Kennedy, N.Y.C., 1949-57; ptnr. Rawle & Henderson, Phila., 1958-79; ptnr. Palmer, Biezup & Henderson, Phila., 1979-95, of counsel, 1996—; sec., bd. dirs. Underwater Technics, Inc., Camden, N.J., 1967-85; adv. on admiralty law to U.S. del. Inter-Govtl. Maritime Consultative Orgn., London, 1967; mem. U.S. Shipping Coordinating Com., Washington legal sub com., 1967—; U.S. del. 30th-34th internat. confs. Titular mem. Comité Maritime International; v.p., sec., bd. dirs. Phila. Belt Line R.R.; bd. dirs. Mather (Bermuda) Ltd. Editor: Maritime Law Reporter. Mem., permanent adv. bd. Tulane Admiralty Law Inst., Tulane U. Law Sch., New Orleans, 1975—; trustee Seamen's Ch. Inst., Phila., 1967—, pres., 1972-84; Harvard Law Sch. Assn., Phila., Pa. (exec. com. 1986—); bd. dirs. Havrford (Pa.) Civic Assn., 1972-85, pres., 1976-79; consul for Denmark in State of Pa., 1980-91, consul emeritus,1 992—. Lt. comdr. USNR, 1942-46. Fellow World Acad. Art and Sci. (treas. 1986—); mem. ABA (former chmn. stdg. com. on admiralty and maritime law 1978-79), N.Y.C. Bar Assn., Phila. Bar Assn., Am. Judicature Soc., Maritime Law Assn. (chmn. limitation liability com. 1977-83, 2d v.p. 1984-86, 1st v.p. 1986-88, pres. 1988-90, immediate past pres. 1990-92), Internat. Bar Assn., Internat. Assn. Def. Counsel, Assn. Average Adjusters USA and Gt. Britain, Port of Phila. Maritime Soc., Harvard Law Sch. Assn. of Phila. (exec. com. 1986—), Fgn. Consul assn. of Phila., Danish Order of Dannebrog, Phila. Club, Rittenhouse Club, India House, Harvard Club of N.Y.C. and Phila. (v.p., mem. exec. com. 1983-86, 94—). Republican. Episcopalian. Home: 318 Grays Ln Haverford PA 19041-1907 Office: Palmer Biezup & Henderson Pub Ledger Bldg 620 Chestnut St Philadelphia PA 19106-3413

PALMER, ROBERT B., computer company executive; b. 1940. BS, Tex. Tech U., MS. V.p. semiconductor ops. Digital Equipment Corp., v.p. mfg., pres., CEO, 1992—, now also chmn., 1995—. Office: Digital Equipment Corp 111 Powder Mill Rd Maynard MA 01754-1482 Office: Digital Equipment Corp 111 Powder Mill Rd Maynard MA 01754-1482

PALMER, ROBERT BAYLIS, librarian; b. Rockville Centre, N.Y., Apr. 5, 1938; s. John Frederick and Marion (Baylis) P.; divorced; 1 child, Michele Palmer Fracasso. A.B., Kenyon Coll., Gambier, Ohio, 1960; M.S. in L.S, Simmons Coll., Boston, 1965; M.A. in English, Middlebury (Vt.) Coll., 1965. Tchr. Brooks Sch., North Andover, Mass., 1960-65; librarian Brooks Sch., 1961-65; acting librarian Columbia Coll., 1965-66; asst. to dir. libraries Columbia U., 1965-67; dir. Barnard Coll. Library, 1967-81; Fulbright lectr. Tribhuvan U. Library, Kathmandu, Nepal, 1972-73, Kathmandu, 1980; vol. lectr. USIS, library cons., Asia, 1976; Fulbright lectr. Wuhan, Peoples Republic China, 1984-85; library cons., advisor, Peoples Republic China, 1986-87, Zanzibar, Tanzania, 1988; lectr., cons. Kenya, Ethiopia, Zimbabwe, 1988; English lang. escort officer U.S. Dept. State, 1989—. Mem. ALA. Address: 190 Riverside Dr New York NY 10024-1008 *Low overhead, a ready laugh, and a love of reading make for a good life.*

PALMER, ROBERT BLUNDEN, newspaper, printing executive; b. Port Huron, Mich., Nov. 25, 1917; s. Joseph Frank and Hazel Quinn (Blunden) P.; m. Mary Bellatti (dec.), Feb. 11, 1946; children: Robert L. Palmer, Frances Lobpries, Barbara Caldwell. Office mgr. Palmer Circulation Co., Midwest, 1933-41; reporter, bus. mgr. Titus County Tribune, Mt. Pleasant, Tex., 1941-42, editor, 1946-57; pub., editor Daily Tribune, Mt. Pleasant, Tex., 1957-88; pres. Palmer Media, Inc., Mt. Pleasant, Tex., 1972—, NorTex Press, Inc., Mt. Pleasant, Tex., 1973—, F.V.P. Network, Inc., Mt. Pleasant, Tex., 1989; owner Palmer Real Estate, 1968—. Capt. U.S. Army, 1942-46, ETO. Presbyterian. Avocations: reading, golf, travel, music. Office: Palmer Media Inc. 1705 Industrial Rd Mount Pleasant TX 75455-2235

PALMER, ROBERT JEFFREY, special education educator; b. Clarksburg, W.Va., June 25, 1961; s. Robert Edward and Katherine Elizabeth (Snopps) P. BS in Phys. Edn., W.Va. U., 1984, MA in Spl. Edn., 1994. Cert. tchr. phys. edn. 7-12, safety edn. 7-12, spl. edn. K-12. Tchr. Berkeley County Schs., Martinsburg, W.Va., 1988-89; tchr. spl. edn. Morgan County Schs., Berkeley Springs, W.Va., 1989—; mem. staff devel. coun. Morgan County Schs., 1994—. Mem. Coun. for Exceptional Children, W.Va. Edn. Assn., Moos, Lions. Democrat. Disciples of Christ. Avocations: motorcycles, music, reading, golf, baseball. Home: PO Box 455 435 Moser Ave Paw Paw WV 25434 Office: Paw Paw High Sch 422 Moser Ave Paw Paw WV 25434-9501

PALMER, ROBERT ROSWELL, historian, educator; b. Chgo., Jan. 11, 1909; s. Roswell Roy and Blanche (Steere) P.; m. Esther Howard, Dec. 19, 1942; children: Stanley, Richard, Emily. Ph.B., U. Chgo., 1931, LL.D., 1963; Ph.D., Cornell U., 1934; Litt.D., Washington U., St. Louis, 1962; L.H.D., Kenyon Coll., 1963, U. New Haven, 1980; Dr. honoris causa, U. Toulouse, France, 1965, U. Uppsala, Sweden, 1977. Mem. faculty Princeton U., 1936-63, 66-69, prof. history, 1946-63, Dodge prof. history, 1952-63; dean faculty arts and sci., prof. history Washington U., St. Louis, 1963-66; prof. history Yale U., 1969-77, emeritus, 1977; adj. prof. U. Mich., 1977-80; vis. prof. U. Chgo., summer 1947, U. Colo., summer 1951, U. Calif. at Berkeley, summer 1962, U. Mich., 1969, 75. Author: Catholics and Unbelievers in 18th Century France, 1939, Twelve Who Ruled, 1941, A History of the Modern World, 1950, (with Joel Colton) A History of the Modern World, 2d edit., 1955, 8th edit. 1994, also in Swedish, Italian, Finnish, Spanish and Chinese, The Age of the Democratic Revolution, 1959, vol. II, 1964, also German, Italian edits., World of the French Revolution, 1971, also in French, School of the French Revolution, 1975, The Improvement of Humanity: Education and the French Revolution, 1985, From Jacobin to Liberal, Marc-Antoine Jullien 1775-1848, 1993, J.b. Say Economist in Troubled Times, 1997; editor, translator: The Two Tocquevilles, Father and Son on the Coming of the French Revolution, 1987; co-author: Organization of Ground Combat Troops, 1947, Procurement and Training of Ground Combat Troops, 1948; editor: Rand McNally Atlas of World History, 1957. Served hist. div. U.S. Army, 1943-45. Recipient of ACLS Spl. prize, 1960, Bancroft prize, 1960, Antonio Feltrinelli Internat. prize, Rome, 1990. Mem. Am. Acad. Arts and Scis., Mass. Hist. Soc., Am. Philos. Soc., Am. Hist. Assn. (pres. 1970), Soc. French Hist. Studies (pres. 1961), Acad. Naz. dei Lincei. Home: Pennswood Village # K205 Newtown PA 18940-2401

PALMER, ROBERT TOWNE, lawyer; b. Chgo., May 25, 1947; s. Adrian Bernhardt and Gladys (Towne) P.; m. Ann Therese Darin, Nov. 9, 1974; children: Justin Darin, Christian Darin. BA, Colgate U., 1969; JD, U. Notre Dame, 1974. Bar: Ill. 1974, D.C. 1978, U.S. Supreme Ct. 1978. Law clk. Hon. Walter V. Schaefer, Ill. Supreme Ct., 1974-75; assoc. McDermott, Will & Emery, Chgo., 1975-81, ptnr., 1982-86; ptnr. Chadwell & Kayser, Ltd., 1987-88, Connelly, Mustes, Palmer & Schroeder, 1988-89; of counsel Garfield & Merel Ltd., 1990—; mem. adj. faculty Chgo. Kent Law Sch., 1975-77, Loyola U., 1976-78; mem. adv. com. Fed. Home Loan Mortgage Corp., 1988-89; bd. dir. Chgo. Bldg. Svcs., Lincoln Legal Found., Cen. Fed. Savs. & Loan Assn. of Chgo.; mem. Chgo. Ctr. Adv. Bd. Voyageur Outward Bound Sch., 1988-91. Mem. ABA, Ill. State Bar Assn. (Lincoln award 1983), Chgo. Bar Assn., Internat. Assn. Def. Counsel, Chgo. Club, Dairymen's Country Club, Lambda Alpha. Contbr. articles to legal jours. and textbooks. Office: Garfield & Merel Ltd 211 W Wacker Dr Ste 1500 Chicago IL 60606-1217

PALMER, R(OBIE MARCUS HOOKER) MARK, banker; b. Ann Arbor, Mich., July 14, 1941; s. Robie Ellis and Katherine (Hooker) P.; m. Sushma Palmer. BA, Yale U., 1963. Copy asst. N.Y. Times, N.Y.C., 1963; asst. to producer WNDT-TV, N.Y.C., 1963-64; entered U.S. Fgn. Service, 1964; third sec. U.S. Embassy, New Delhi, India, 1964-66; internat. relations officer NATO affairs, Dept State, Washington, 1966-68; second sec. U.S. Embassy, Moscow, 1968-71; prin. speechwriter Sec. of State Rogers, Kissinger, Washington, 1971-75; counselor for polit. affairs U.S. Embassy, Belgrade, Yugoslavia, 1975-78; dir. office disarmament and control of arms Bur. of Polit.-Mil. Affairs Dept. State, Washington, 1978-81, dep. to undersec. for polit. affairs, 1981-82, dep. asst. sec. state for European affairs, 1982-86; amb. U.S. Embassy, Budapest, Hungary, 1986-90; pres., chief exec. officer Cen. European Devel. Corp., 1990—; chmn. bd. Berlin-Brandenburg TV; pres., CEO Television Devel. Ptnrs., Inc., 1996—. Author: speeches for five Secs. of State and three Presidents. Recipient Superior Honor award Dept. State, 1980, Presdl. Meritorious Service award, 1984. Mem. Council Fgn. Relations, Am. Fgn. Service Assn., Phi Beta Kappa. Episcopalian. Avocation: tennis. Home and Office: 4437 Resevoir Rd NW Washington DC 20007

PALMER, ROGER CAIN, information scientist; b. Corning, N.Y., Oct. 14, 1943; s. Wilbur Clarence and Eleanor Louise (Cain) P. AA, Corning (N.Y.) C.C., 1964; BA, Hartwick Coll., 1966; MLS, SUNY, Albany, 1972; PhD, U. Mich., 1978. Tchr. Penn Yan (N.Y.) Acad., 1966-68, 70-71; dep. head, grad. libr. SUNY, Buffalo, 1972-75; asst. prof. UCLA, 1978-83; sr. tech. writer Quotron Sys., Culver City, 1984; sr. sys. analyst Getty Art History Info., Santa Monica, Calif., 1984-90, mgr. tech. devel., 1990-93; mgr. internal cons. group The J. Paul Getty Trust, Santa Monica, 1993-96; mgr. ITS Infrastructure Ops. The J. Paul Getty Trust, L.A., 1996—; gen. ptnr. Liu-Palmer, L.A., 1989—. Author: Online Reference and Information Retrieval, 1987, dBase II and dBase III: An Introduction, 1984, Introduction to Computer Programming, 1983. With U.S. Army, 1968-70. Mem. IEEE Computer Soc., ALA, Am. Soc. for Info. Scis., Spl. Librs. Assn., Art Librs. Soc. of N.Am., Assn. for Computing Machinery, Pi Delta Epsilon, Beta Phi Mu. Home: 1045 N Kings Rd Apt 310 West Hollywood CA 90069-6027 Office: The J Paul Getty Trust 1200 Getty Center Dr Ste 200 Los Angeles CA 90049-1657

PALMER, ROGER FARLEY, pharmacology educator; b. Albany, N.Y., Sept. 23, 1931; m. Nelida Santiago, Apr. 1994. B.S. in Chemistry, St. Louis U., 1953; postgrad., Fla. State U., 1955-56, Woods Hole Marine Biology Lab., 1956; M.D., U. Fla., 1960. Intern Johns Hopkins Hosp., 1960-61, resident in medicine, 1961-62; asst. dept. biochemistry U. Fla., Gainesville, 1957; asst. medicine Osler Med. Service, 1960-62; instr. pharmacology and therapeutics U. Fla., 1962, asst. prof. pharmacology, therapeutics and medicine, 1964-67, assoc. prof. pharmacology and medicine, 1967-69, prof. medicine, chief div. clin. pharmacology, 1969-70, 81-82; prof., chmn. dept. pharmacology, prof. medicine U. Miami, Fla., 1970-81; clin. prof. medicine U. Miami, 1982—; chmn. pharmacology sect. Nat. Bd. Med Examiners, 1977-81; cons. Nat. Acad. Scis.; chmn. pharmacology sect. Nat. Bd. Med. Examiners, 1977-81. Editorial bd. Pharmacol. Revs.; assoc. editor Advances in Molecular Pharmacology; ad hoc editor Am. Heart Jour.; editor Horizons in Clinical Pharmacology, 1976; author abstracts; contbr. articles to profl. jours. Served with USAR. Mosby scholar, 1957-60; Markle scholar in acad. medicine, 1965-70; recipient Basic Sci. Teaching award U. Miami, 1975-76; Meritorious Service medal Am. Heart Assn., 1972; citation for meritorious

Service So. Region Am. Heart Assn., 1979; Visitante Distinguido award, Costa Rica, 1979; Outstanding Tchr. award U. Miami, 1982. Mem. Am. Coll. Clin. Pharmacology, Am. Fedn. Clin. Rsch., Am. Therapeutic Soc. (prize essay award 1970), Am. Soc. Pharmacology and Exptl. Therapeutics, N.Y. Acad. Scis., So. Soc. Clin. Investigation, U.S. Pharmacopeia Revision Com., Internat. Study Group Rsch. Cardiac Metabolism, Am. Soc. Internal Medicine, Royal Soc. Health, Key Biscayne Yacht Club (bd. govs. 1994—), Sigma Xi. Office: 24 W Enid Dr Key Biscayne FL 33149-2009

PALMER, ROGER RAYMOND, accounting educator; b. N.Y.C., Dec. 31, 1926; s. Archibald and Sophie (Jarnow) P.; m. Martha West Hopkins, June 7, 1986; children by previous marriage: Kathryn Sue, Daniel Stephen, Susan Jo. BS, U. Wis., 1949; MBA, Cornell U., 1951; postgrad., NYU, 1951-54. Auditor, Ernst and Ernst, CPA's, N.Y.C., 1953-54; auditor Gen. Dynamics Corp., 1956-60; mgr. corp. audits Tex. Instruments, 1960-64; auditor 1st Nat. Bank, St. Paul, 1964-68, v.p. planning, 1968-69, v.p., comptr., 1969-75, sr. v.p., contr., 1975-82; chmn. dept. fin. Coll. of St. Thomas (now U. St. Thomas), St. Paul, 1982—; dir. First Met. Travel, Inc.; guest lectr. U. Minn., 1966; conf. leader, speaker, 1959—. Contbr. articles to publs. Bd. dirs. Waterford (Conn.) Civic Assn., 1959-60, Friends of St. Paul Pub. Library, 1967, Mpls. Citizens League; chmn. bd. dirs. Film in the Cities, 1983-85; mem. acctg. adv. council U. Minn.; trustee, chmn. fin. com. Hazelton Found. With U.S. Maritime Svc., 1945-47; with U.S. Army, 1954-56. Mem. Inst. Internal Auditors (pres. So. New Eng chpt. 1957-60, edn. chmn. Dallas 1961, Twin City chpt. 1965-66), Nat. Assn. Accts. (dir. Norwich, Conn. chpt. 1958-60), Nat. Assn. Accountants (St. Paul chpt. 1967), Assn. Bank Audit, Control and Operation, Am. Inst. Banking, Fin. Execs. Inst., Planning Forum (pres. Twin Cities chpt. 1984-85), Univ. Club (St. Paul). Club: St. Paul Athletic. Home: 1411 Lincoln Ave Saint Paul MN 55105-2217 Office: U St Thomas Dept Fin and Acctg Saint Paul MN 55105

PALMER, RON, police chief. Chief Tulsa Police Dept. Office: Office of the Police Chief 600 Civic Ctr Tulsa OK 74103-3829

PALMER, RONALD DEWAYNE FAISAL, retired diplomat, educator, consultant; b. Uniontown, Pa., May 22, 1932; s. Wilbur Fortune and Ethel Danya (Roberts) P.; m. Tengku Intan Badariah Abubakar; children: Derek Ronald, Alyson Cecily, Natasha Elina, Nadiah Raha. BA, Howard U., 1954; MA in Internat. Studies, Johns Hopkins U., 1957. Assigned to U.S. Mil. Acad., Indonesia, Denmark, Malaysia, The Philippines, prior to 1976; amb. to Togo, 1976-78; dep. dir. gen. Fgn. Service State Dept., 1978-81; amb. to Malaysia Kuala Lumpur, 1981-83; sr. scholar, mem. adv. bd. Ctr. Strategic and Internat. Studies, Washington, 1983-86; amb. to Mauritius Port Louis, 1986-89; ret., 1989; prof., diplomatic con. internat. studies George Washington U., 1990—. Author: Building Cooperation - 20 Years of ASEAN, 1987. Decorated Order of Mono, Togo, Most Hon. Order of Johor Sultan of Johor Bahru, Malaysia; recipient Sr. Fgn. Svc. Performance award U.S. Dept. State, 1985. Mem. Am. Fgn. Svc. Assn., Coun. on Fgn. Rels., Inst. Strategic Studies, Assn. Black Am. Ambs., Malaysia-Am. Soc. (pres.), U.S. Indonesia Soc. (mem. adv. bd.), Royal Asia Soc., Wash. Inst. Fgn. Affairs, Asia Soc., Mauritius-U.S. Bus. Soc., UNA/DC. Office: George Washington U Elliott Sch Internat Affair 2013 G St NW # 4600 Washington DC 20006-4205 also: care State Dept Fgn Svc Mailroom 2201 C St NW Washington DC 20520-0001

PALMER, RUSSELL EUGENE, investment executive; b. Jackson, Mich., Aug. 13, 1934; s. Russell E. and Margarite M. (Briles) P.; m. Phyllis Anne Hartung, Sept. 8, 1956; children: Bradley Carl, Stephen Russell, Russell Eugene, III, Karen Jean. BA with honors, Mich. State U., 1956; D in Comml. Sci. (hon.), Drexel U., 1980; MA (hon.), U. Pa., 1984; PhD (hon.), Chulalongkorn U., 1988, Free U. Brussels, 1989, York Coll., 1989. With Touche Ross & Co., N.Y.C., 1956-83, mng. ptnr., CEO, 1972-82, also bd. dirs., exec. coms.; mng. dir., CEO Touche Ross Internat., 1974-83; dean, Reliance prof. mgmt. and pvt. enterprise Wharton Sch. U. Pa., 1983-90, CEO; bd. dirs. GTE Corp., The May Dept. Stores Co., Bankers Trust Co., Allied-Signal, Inc.; corp. bd. Safeguard Scientifics, Inc., Fed. Home Loan Mortgage Corp.; adv. bd. Cassidy & Assocs. Mem. pub. bds. Dirs. & Bds., Mergers & Aquisitions, Directory Corp. Affiliations, Directory Leading Pvt. Cos. Pres. Fin. Acctg. Found., 1979-82; trustee Acctg. Hall of Fame; bd. dirs. Joint Coun. Econ. Edn., 1978-83, United Fund Greater N.Y., 1980-83, UN Assn. U.S.A.; mem. Bus. Com. Arts, 1977-83; mem. Pres.'s Mgmt. Improvement Coun., 1979-80; mem. N.Y. adv. bd. Salvation Army, past mem. nat. adv. bd.; former mem. adv. coun. Sch. Internat. and Pub. Affairs Columbia U., Grad. Sch. Bus. Stanford U., Womens Way; mem. assocs. coun. Bus. Sch. Oxford U.; mem. adv. panel Comptr. Gen. U.S.; mem. U.S. Sec. Labor's Commn. on Workforce Quality and Labor Market Efficiency; pub. mem. Hudson Inst., mem. adv. bd. Radnor Venture Ptnrs.; bd. dirs. SEI Ctr. for Advanced Studies in Mgmt. Recipient Gavin Meml. award Beta Theta Pi, 1956, Disting. Community Svc. award Brandeis U., 1974, Outstanding Alumnus award Mich. State U., 1978, Humanitarian award Fedn. Jewish Philanthropies, 1979, Disting. Aux. Svc. award Salvation Army, 1979, LEAD Bus. award, 1984, Good Scout award Phila. coun. Boy Scouts Am., 1987. Mem. Cts. of Phila. Club, Merion Cricket Club, Merion Golf Club, Round Hill Club, Lost Tree Country Club, Conf. Bd. (bd. dirs.), Beta Gamma Sigma (mem. bd. govs.). Presbyterian. Office: The Palmer Group 3600 Market St Ste 530 Philadelphia PA 19104-2649

PALMER, SAMUEL COPELAND, III, lawyer; b. Phila., June 9, 1934; s. Samuel Copeland Jr. and Vivian Gertrude (Plumb) P.; divorced; children: Samuel C. IV, Sarah Anne, Bryan Douglas. Grad., Harvard Sch., Los Angeles, 1952; student, Yale U., 1953; A.B., Stanford U., 1955; JD, Loyola-Marymount U., Marymount, 1958. Bar: Calif. 1959, U.S. Dist. Ct. (cen., ea. and so. dists. Calif.) 1959, U.S. Ct. Appeals (9th cir.) 1970, U.S. Supreme Ct. 1971. Dep. city atty. Los Angeles, 1959-60; assoc. firm Pollock & Deutz, Los Angeles, 1960-63; ptnr. firm Pollock & Palmer, Los Angeles, 1963-70, Palmer & Bartenetti, Los Angeles, 1970-81, Samuel C. Palmer III, P.C., 1981-85; ptnr. Thomas, Snell, Jamison, Russell & Asperger, 1985—; adj. prof. Calif. State U., Fresno, 1993. Trustee Western Ctr. Law and Poverty; bd. dirs. Big Bros./Big Sisters, Fresno, Lively Arts Found., Nat. Sleep Found., Vols. in Parole; pres., bd. dirs. Poverello House; founder, pres. Fresno Crime Stoppers. Mem. ABA, State Bar Calif. (disciplinary subcom., bar examiners subcom.), Fresno County Bar Assn. (pres., bd. dirs. 1988-93), Pickwick Soc., Am. Bd. Trial Advocates, Chancery Club, Downtown Club, Calif. Club, Fig Garden Tennis Club, Rotary, Delta Upsilon, Phi Delta Phi. Home: 4607 N Wilson Ave Fresno CA 93704-3038 Office: 2445 Capitol St Fresno CA 93721-2224

PALMER, STACY ELLA, periodical editor; b. Middletown, Conn., Oct. 25, 1960; d. Marvin Jerome Palmer and Eileen Sondra (Cohen) Palmer Burke. B in Liberal Arts and Internat. Rels., Brown U., 1982. Asst. editor Chronicle of Higher Edn., Washington, 1982-86, sr. editor, 1986-88; news editor Chronicle of Philanthropy, Washington, 1988-93, mng. editor, 1993—. Bd. dirs. Brown Alumni Monthly, Providence, 1988-91, vice chmn., 1991-93, mem. 1996—. Mem. Comm. Network in Philanthropy, Investigative Reporters and Editors, Brown Club Washington (bd. dirs. 1993—, pres. 1994—). Avocations: swimming, bicycling, travel. Home: 2301 Connecticut Ave NW #7C Washington DC 20008 Office: Chronicle of Philanthropy 1255 23rd St NW Washington DC 20037-1125

PALMER, STEPHEN EUGENE, JR., government official; b. Superior, Wis., July 31, 1923; s. Stephen Eugene Sr. and Katharine (Greenslade) P.; m. Nancy Jane Swan, July 26, 1947 (div. 1986); children: Katharine Caldwell, Susan Greenslade, Stephen Eugene III; m. Patsy Elaine Simmons Lee, Sept. 7, 1989. A.B., Princeton U., 1944; postgrad., Columbia U., 1947-48, M.A., 1971; postgrad. Serbo-Croatian lang. and Balkan area, Ind. U., 1953-54; postgrad. in French Fgn. Service Inst., 1982-83. Tchr. Am. Community Sch., Tehran, Iran, 1946-47; with U.S. Govt., 1949-51; joined U.S. Fgn. Service, 1951; vice consul Nicosia, Cyprus, 1951-53; 3d sec., vice consul Belgrade, Yugoslavia, 1954; 2d sec., 1954-56, consul, 1956-57; consul, prin. officer Sarajevo, Yugoslavia, 1957-59; fgn. affairs officer Office UN Polit. Affairs, State Dept., 1959-63; 1st sec., chief polit. sect. Tel Aviv, Israel, 1963-66; 1st sec. polit. div. Middle Eastern and North African affairs Am. embassy, London, 1966-68; counselor for polit. affairs Am. embassy, Rawalpindi, Islamabad, Pakistan, 1968-71; consul gen. Madras, India, 1971-73; fellow Center for Internat. Affairs, Harvard, 1973-74; dir. Office Near Eastern and South Asian Regional Affairs, Dept. State, 1974-78; also staff dir. interdepartmental group for Near East and South Asia NSC, 1974-78; project dir. country reports on human rights and practices Dept. State, 1978; minister-counselor for refugee and humanitarian affairs U.S. Mission to Geneva, 1979, prin. dep. asst. sec. of state for human rights and humanitarian affairs, 1980-81, acting asst. sec., 1981; Dept. State mem. Congl. Commn. on Security and Cooperation in Europe, 1981-82; chmn. Fgn. Service Selection Bd., 1983, Project for Dissemination of the Laws of Armed Conflict, 1983-84; sr. advisor mgmt. systems and programs Dept. State, 1984-88, sr. cons., 1988-91, insp., 1991-93; mem. editorial team for country reports on human rights practices, 1993-94. Co-author: Yugoslav Communism and the Macedonian Question, 1971. Mem. Fairfax County Dem. Com. Served to 1st lt. USMCR, 1943-46. Recipient Superior Svc. awards U.S. Dept. of State, 1966, 82, Meritorious Honor award, 1971, John Jacobs Rogers award, 1988. Mem. Fgn. Svc. Res. Corps. Home: 10202 Tamarack Dr Vienna VA 22182-1844

PALMER, STEVEN O., federal official; b. Bowdle, S.D., Feb. 1, 1956; s. Richard James and Beverly Ann (Barlund) P.; m. Laurel Beach, July 17, 1982; children: Kristin Michelle, Lindsay Ann. BA in Polit. Sci., Kalamazoo Coll., 1978; MPA, U. Tex., Austin, 1980. Rschr. U. Tex., Austin, 1979-80; presdl. mgmt. intern Dept. Transp., 1980-82; mem. profl. staf com. budget U.S. Senate, Washington, 1982-83, sr. mem. staff subcom. on aviation, 1983-90, sr. mem. profl. staff subcom. sci., tech. and space, com. commerce, sci. and transp., 1990-93; asst. sec. govtl. affairs U.S. Dept. Transp., Washington, 1993—; team leader Clinton-Gore Presdl. Transition, 1992. Office: Dept Transp Govtl Affairs 400 7th St SW Rm 10408 Washington DC 20590-0001

PALMER, STUART HUNTER, sociology educator; b. N.Y.C., Apr. 29, 1924; s. Herman G. and Beatrice (Hunter) P.; m. Anne Barbara Scarborough, June 22, 1946; 1 dau., Catherine. BA, Yale U., 1949, MA, 1951, PhD, 1955. Asst. to dean Yale Coll., New Haven, 1949-51; instr. sociology New Haven Coll., 1949-51, 53-55; faculty U. N.H., Durham, 1955—; prof. U. N.H., 1964—, chmn. dept. sociology and anthropology, 1964-69, 79-82, dean Coll. Liberal Arts, 1982-95, dir. London program, 1995—; disting. vis. prof. SUNY, Albany, 1970-71; vis. behavioral scientist N.H. Div. Mental Health; vis. prof. U. Sussex, Eng., 1976, U. Ga., 1977; cons. U.S. Office Edn., USPHS, U.S. Office Delinquency and Youth Devel., Dept. Justice; mem. adv. com. for sociology Com. on Internat. Exchange of Persons; mem. exec. com. N.H. Gov.'s Commn. on Crime and Delinquency; co-chmn. Internat. Symposium on Univs. in Twenty-First Century; co-chmn. Internat. Confs. on Stress Rsch., Nat. Commn. Arts and Scis. Author: Understanding Other People, 1955, A Study of Murder, 1960, (with Brian R. Kay) The Challenge of Supervision, 1961, Deviance and Conformity, 1970, (with Arnold S. Linsky) Rebellion and Retreat, 1972, The Violent Society, 1972, The Prevention of Crime, 1973, (with John A. Humphrey) Deviant Behavior, 1980, Role Stress, 1981, Deviant Behavior: Patterns, Sources, and Controls, 1990; also articles. Chmn. bd. trustees Daniel Webster Coll., New Eng. Aero. Inst. Served to lt. AC AUS, 1942-45; Served to lt. AC USAF, 1951-53. Decorated Air medal with 3 oak leaf clusters; Henry Page fellow, 1953-55. Mem. Am. Sociol. Assn., Eastern Sociol. Soc., Internat. Sociol. Soc., Internat. Soc. Criminology, Internat. Soc. Forecasters, Am. Assn. Colls., Council for Liberal Learning, Am. Assn. Higher Edn., Council Colls. Arts and Scis., Nat. Assn. State Univs. and Land-Grant Colls., AAAS, Am. Acad. Polit. and Social Scis., N.Y. Acad. Scis., Am. Assn. Suicidology, Soc. Cross-Cultural Research, Am. Soc. Criminology, Assn. Gov. Bds. Univs. and Colls., Phi Beta Kappa (hon.), Sigma Xi, Alpha Kappa Delta. Home: PO Box 904 Durham NH 03824-3304 *Be honest with yourself.*

PALMER, STUART MICHAEL, microbiologist; b. Orange, N.J., Dec. 26, 1958; s. Victor Bernard and Adelaide Amy (Brothers) P.; m. Becky Elizabeth Buckley, Sept. 29, 1984; children: Jessica, Christopher, Kelly. BS in Microbiology and Biochemistry, Rutgers U., 1981, MS in Microbiology, 1984, PhD in Microbiology, 1986. Scientist in infectious diseases Abbott Diagnostics, Abbott Park, Ill., 1986-88, head sect. hepatitis tech. support, 1988-89, mgr. reagent process devel., 1989-90, mgr. TDxR tech. support, 1990-92; dir. therapeutic drug monitoring Roche Diagnostics, Somerville, N.J., 1992-96, dir. diagnostic rsch. and process devel., 1996—; mem. tech. adv. bd. Abbott Diagnostics, 1991-92; del. rep. Nat. Com. on Clin. Lab. Stds., Somerville, 1994—; mem. Roche patent coord. com. Hoffmann-La Roche, Nutley, N.J., 1994—. Mem. United Way adv. bd. Roche Diagnostic Sys., Somerville, 1994; vol. Am. Heart Assn., Milburn, N.J., 1995; mem. Roche action com. Hoffmann-La Roche, 1994—. Charles and Joanna Busch Meml. Fund predoctoral fellow Rutgers U., 1985; recipient Student Presentation award Theobald Smith Soc. of Am. Soc. for Microbiology, New Brunswick, N.J., 1985. Fellow Assn. Clin. Scientists; mem. AAAS, Am. Assn. Clin. Chemistry, Am. Soc. Clin. Lab. Sci., Clin. Lab. Mgmt. Assn., N.Y. Acad. Scis. Achievements include development of large-scale bioreactor processes for Rubella virsu and Toxoplasma gondii production; development of multiple fluorescence polarization assays for therapeutic drug monitoring tests on COBAS Integra chemistry system. Avocations: skiing, gardening. Home: 9 Pine Way Long Valley NJ 07854 Office: Roche Diagnostics 1080 Us Highway 202 S Somerville NJ 08876-3733

PALMER, WILLIAM D., lawyer. BS in Mgmt. with honors, Rensselaer Poly. Inst., 1973; JD cum laude, Boston Coll., 1976. Bar: Fla. 1976, U.S. Dist. Ct. (no., mid. and so. dists.) Fla. 1976; cert. civil mediator, family mediator, Fla. Assoc. Carlton, Fields, Ward, Emmanuel, Smith & Cutler, Orlando, Fla., 1976-82, ptnr., 1982—; arbitrator Am. Arbitration Assn., Ct. Annexed Arbitration Program of the U.S. Dist. Ct. (mid. dist) Fla., Orange County Bar Assn's. Fee Arbitration Com. Bd. dirs. Fla. Hosp. Found.; past chmn. bd. dirs. Ctrl. Fla. Helpline. Mem. ABA (mem. litigation sect., mem. antitrust sect.), Fla. Def. Lawyers Assn., Def. Rsch. Inst., Fla. Bar (mem. litigation, appellate law and family law sects.), Orange County Bar Assn. (chmn. various coms.). Office: Carlton Fields Ward Emmanuel Smith & Cutler PA 255 S Orange Ave Orlando FL 32801-3445

PALMER, WILLIAM JOSEPH, accountant; b. Lansing, Mich., Sept. 3, 1934; s. Joseph Flammin Lacchia and Henrietta (Yagerman) P.; m. Judith Pollock, Aug. 20, 1960 (div. Nov. 1980); children: William W., Kathryn E., Leslie A., Emily J.; m. Kathleen Francis Booth, June 30, 1990. BS, U. Calif., Berkeley, 1963; stepchildren: Blair T. Manwell, Lindsay A. Manwell. CPA. With Coopers and Lybrand, 1963-80, mng. ptnr., Sacramento, 1976-80; ptnr. Arthur Young & Co., San Francisco, 1980-89; ptnr. Ernst & Young, San Francisco, 1989-94; guest lectr. Stanford U. Engring. Sch., 1976; lectr. Golden Gate Coll., 1975; prof. U. Calif., Berkeley, 1994—. Author: (books) Businessman's Guide to Construction, 1981, Construction Management Book, 1984, Construction Accounting & Financial Management 5th Edition, 1994, Construction Litigation-Representing The Contractor, 1992, Construction Insurance, Bonding and Risk Management, 1996. Bd. dirs. Sacramento Met. YMCA, 1976-82, v.p., 1979-82; bd. dirs. Sacramento Symphony Found., 1977-80; asst. state fin. chmn. Calif. Reagan for Pres., 1980. Served to Lt. USN, 1953-59. Mem. AICPA (vice chmn. com. constrn. industry, 1975-81), Nat. Assn. Accts. (pres. Oakland/East Bay chpt. 1972, Man of Yr. 1968), Calif. Soc. CPAs., Assn. Gen. Contractors Calif. (bd. dirs. 1971-74), World Trade Club, Commonwealth Club (San Francisco), Del Paso Country Club, Sutter Club, Lambda Chi Alpha. Presbyterian. Avocations: antique boats, sailing, tennis, book collecting, pipe collecting. Home: 6 Heather Ln Orinda CA 94563-3508 Office: Ernst & Young 555 California St San Francisco CA 94104

PALMER-HASS, LISA MICHELLE, state official; b. Nashville, Sept. 4, 1953; d. Raymond Alonzo Palmer and Anne Michelle (Jones) Davies; m. Joseph Monroe Hass, Jr. BSBA, Belmont Coll., 1975; AA in Interior Design, Internat. Fine Arts Coll., 1977; postgrad., Tenn. State U., 1991—. Interior designer Lisa Palmer Interior Designs, Nashville, 1977-84; sec. to pres. Hermitage Elect. Supply Corp., Nashville, 1981-83; sec. to dir. Tenn. Dept. Mental Health and Mental Retardation, Nashville, 1984-86; transp. planner Tenn. Dept. Transp., Nashville, 1986—. Mem. Nat. Arbor Day Found. Recipient cert. of appreciation Tenn. Dept. Mental Health and Mental Retardation, 1986; named Hon. Mem. Tenn. Ho. of Reps., 1990. Mem. NAFE, Nat. Wildlife Fedn., Profl. Secs. Internat. (cert.), Nashville Striders Club, The Music City Bop Club, Music City Bop Club Dance and Exhibn. Team, Mensa. Republican. Mem. Disciples of Christ Ch. Office: Tenn Dept Transp Environ Planning Office 505 Deaderick St Ste 900 Nashville TN 37219-1402

PALMERI, MARLAINA, principal; b. Rochester, N.Y., Feb. 20, 1950; d. Joseph Michael and Eleanor Louise (Polisseni) P. BA, SUNY, Plattsburgh, 1971; MA, SUNY, Brockport, 1984; EdD, U. Rochester, 1993; student, U. Matlock, England, U. Copenhagen, Denmark, U. Moscow, Russia. Cert. Sch. Dist. Adminstr., Sch. Adminstr. Supr., N-6, N.Y. Tchr. Rochester (N.Y.) City Schs., 1972-86, supr. elem. magnet schs., 1986-88, vice prin., 1988-92, prin., 1992—. Mem. Assn. Supervision, Curriculum and Devel., Nat. Assn. Elem. Sch. Prins., Phi Delta Kappa. Avocations: tennis, golf. Home: 254 Mendon Ionia Rd Honeoye Falls NY 14472-9742 Office: Charles Carroll Sch # 46 250 Newcastle Rd Rochester NY 14610-1350

PALMERI, SHARON ELIZABETH, freelance writer, community educator; b. Gary, Ind., July 23, 1948; d. Theodore and Eugena (Bias) Wozniak; m. John James Palmeri, Apr. 9, 1969; 1 child, Renee Suzanne. BS in Edn. English/Journalism with honor, Ind. U. NW, 1991. Health columnist Lake County Star, Crown Point, Ind., 1989-92; corr. Post Tribune, Gary, 1992-93; feature corr. The Munster (Ind.) Times, 1993—; educator creative and news writing Merrillville (Ind.) Adult Edn., 1989—; educator writer's workshop Purdue U. Calumet, Hammond, Ind., 1990—; educator creative writing Purdue U. N. Ctrl., Westville, Ind., 1995—; bd. dirs. N.W. Ind. Arts and Humaniteis Consortium, Gary, 1994; dir. Write-On Hoosiers, Inc., Crown Point, 1989—; educator news & creative writing Bethlehem Steel Career Devel. Ctr., 1996—; educator news class Forest Ridge Acad., 1996—; book doctor, publicity agt., local book and mag. promoter The Creative Connection; educator New Class Forest Ridge Acad., 1996, News and Creative Writing Bethlehem Steel Career Devel. Ctr., 1996—, No. Ind. Arts Assn., 1997—; educator, book dr., publicity agent, local book, mag. promoter. Exec. editor: Hoosier Horizon, 1991—; co-editor: Hoosier Horizon Children's Mag., 1993—; contbr. short stories and essays to Spirits Mag., 1990, 91. Recipient Best of Show award Southlake Camera Club, Crown Point, 1975, Focal Point Camera Club, Portage, 1982. Mem. Nat. Coun. Tchrs. English, Soc. Profl. Journalists, N.W. Ind. Arts Assn. (educator 1997—), Communicators N.W. Ind., Ind. U. Alumni Assn., Kappa Delta Pi (newsletter editor 1991-94). Avocations: sailing, photography. Home and Office: 3605 Kingsway Dr Crown Point IN 46307-8934

PALMIERI, VICTOR HENRY, lawyer, business executive; b. Chgo., Feb. 16, 1930; s. Mario and Maria (Losacco) P.; children: Victor Henry, Matthew B., John W.; m. Cathryn Connors, July 6, 1990. AB in History, Stanford U., 1951, JD, 1954. Bar: Calif. 1954. Assoc. O'Melveny & Myers, L.A., 1955-59; exec. v.p. Janss Investment Corp., L.A., 1959-63, pres., 1963-68; chmn. Pa. Co. and its subs. Great S.W. Corp., 1969-77; chmn. bd. Palmieri Co., N.Y.C., 1969—; chmn. PHL Corp., Inc. (formerly Baldwin-United Inc.), Phila., 1983-87; trustee, CEO Colo.-Ute Electric Assn. Inc., 1990-92; spl. dep. rehabilitator Confederation Life Ins. Co., 1994—; dep. rehabilitator, CEO Mut. Benefit Life Ins. Co., 1991-94; pres., CEO MBL Life Assurance Corp., 1994-95; dir. William Carter Corp., 1992-95, Outlet Comms., Inc., 1993-95, Broadcasting Ptnrs. Inc., 1994-95, Mullin Cos. Inc., 1990—. Chmn. Am. Learning Corp., 1970-85; dep., exec. dir. Nat. Adv. Commn. on Civil Disorders, 1967-68; ambassador-at-large, U.S. coord. Refugee Affairs, Dept. State, 1979-81; trustee Rockefeller Found., 1979-89; pres., bd. dirs. Lincoln Ctr. Theater, 1985-89; chmn. Overseas Devel. Coun., 1985-91; mem. Coun. on Fgn. Rels.; bd. dirs. The Police Found., 1996—. Office: Palmieri Co 245 Park Ave Fl 35 New York NY 10167-0002

PALMINTERI, CHAZZ, actor; b. Bronx, N.Y., May 15, 1951. Actor: (theatre) The Guy in the Truck, 1982, Broadway, 1983, The King's Men, 22 Years, The Flatbush Faithful, 1985, (TV movies) Peter Gunn, 1990, (films) Oscar, 1991, Bullets Over Broadway, 1994 (Academy award nomination best supporting actor 1994), The Perez Family, 1994, The Usual Suspects, 1995, Jade, 1995, Faithful, 1996, Diabolique, 1996, Mulholland Falls, 1996, Dante and the Debutante, 1996; playwright, actor: (theatre) A Bronx Tale, 1989; screenwriter, actor: (film) A Bronx Tale, 1993. Office: ICM 8942 Wilshire Blvd Beverly Hills CA 90211*

PALMORE, CAROL M., state official; b. Owensboro, Ky., Jan. 13, 1949; d. P.J. and Carrie Alice (Leonard) Pate; m. John Stanley Palmore Jr., Jan. 1, 1982. BS in History and Polit. Sci., Murray State U., 1971; JD, U. Ky., 1977. Social worker Dept. Human Resources, Frankfort, Ky., 1971-74; assoc. atty. Rummage, Kamuf, Yewell & Pace, Owensboro, 1977-81; hearing officer Ky. Bd. Claims, Frankfort, 1980-81; gen. counsel Ky. Labor Cabinet, Frankfort, 1982-83, dep. sec. labor, 1984, 1986-87, sec. labor, 1987-90, 91-94; ptnr. Palmore & Sheffer Attys., Henderson, Ky., 1984-86; dep. sec. Ky. Pers. Cabinet, Frankfort, 1996—; chmn. Ky. Safety & Health Stds. Bd., Frankfort, 1987-90, 91-94; co-chmn. Ky. Labor Mgmt. Adv. Coun., Frankfort, 1987-90, 91-94; bd. dirs. Ky. Workers' Comp Funding Commn., Frankfort, 1987-90, 91-94, Community Svc. Commn., Frankfort, 1993-94, Ky. Info. Resources Mgmt. Commn., Frankfort, 1994, Sch.-to-Work Partnership Coun., Frankfort, 1994; ex-officio bd. dirs. Pub. Employees Collective Bargaining Task Force, Frankfort, 1994, Ky. Workforce Partnership Coun., Frankfort, 1994. Labor liaison Jones for Gov., Lexington, 1990-91; del. Dem. Nat. Conv., N.Y.C., 1992; mem. inaugural class Ky. Women's Leadership Network, Frankfort, 1993; bd. dirs. Alliant Health Systems Adult Oper. Bd., Louisville, 1992-96, Ky. Commn. Homeless, Frankfort, 1993-94; candidate for Sec. State Commonwealth Ky., 1995; chair Dem. Women's Think Tank, 1995. Mem. Ky. Bar Assn. (del. ho. dels. 1985-86, chair law day/spkr. bur. 1985-86, mem. 1986-90), Ky. Bar Found. (bd. dirs. 1985-92, sec. 1986-89, pres. elect 1989-90, pres. 1990-91), Rotary (program chair Frankfort chpt. 1993-94). Episcopalian. Avocations: antiques, reading, vintage jewelry, walking. Home: 2310 Peaks Mill Rd Frankfort KY 40601-9437 Office: Personnel Cabinet 200 Fair Oaks Ln Frankfort KY 40601-1134

PALMORE, FRED WHARTON, III, lawyer; b. Richmond, Va., May 22, 1945; s. Fred W. Jr. and Elizabeth (Taylor) P.; m. Pamela Goodrich, July 13, 1968; children: Michael G., Elizabeth C. AB, Coll. William & Mary, 1967; JD, U. Richmond, 1973. Bar: Va. 1973, U.S. Dist. Ct. (ea. dist.) Va. 1975, U.S. Ct. Appeals (4th crct.) 1978, U.S. Supreme Ct. 1989. From assoc. to ptnr. Mays & Valentine, Richmond, 1973—; gen. counsel Va. Bankers Assn., Richmond, 1991—; lectr. Va. Banker's Sch. Bank Mgmt., U. Va., 1992, 93, Mid-Atlantic Inst. on Bankruptcy & Reorgn., Charlottesville, 1990. Author: (newsletter) Ann. Survey of Bus. Law Decisions; co-author: Foreclosure and Repossession in Virginia, 1985, (periodical) The Problem of Insider Guarantees, 1990. Lt. USN, 1968-72, Vietnam. Mem. Va. Bar Assn. (bd. dirs. bus. law sect., chmn. bus. law sect. 1991-92, chmn. bankruptcy law sect. 1990-91), Richmond Bar Assn. (former chmn. bankruptcy coun. sect.). Home: 4324 Croatan Rd Richmond VA 23235-1118 Office: Mays & Valentine 1111 E Main St Richmond VA 23219-3500

PALMORE, JOHN STANLEY, JR., retired lawyer; b. Ancon, C.Z., Aug. 6, 1917; s. John Stanley and Antoinette Louise (Gonzalez) P.; m. Eleanor Anderson, July 31, 1938 (dec. 1980); 1 child, John Worsham (dec.); m. Carol Pate, Jan. 1, 1982. Student, Western Ky. State Coll., 1934-36; LL.B. cum laude, U. Louisville, 1939. Bar: Ky. 1938. Practice law Henderson, 1939-42, 47-59; judge Ct. Appeals Ky. (name changed to Supreme Ct. Ky. 1975), 1959-82, chief justice, 1966, 73, 77-82; practice law Frankfort, Ky., 1983-84; ptnr. Palmore & Sheffer, Henderson, 1984-86; sr. counsel Jackson & Kelly, Lexington, Ky., 1986-92; ret., 1992; city pros. atty., Henderson, 1949-53, city atty., 1953-55; commonwealth's atty. 5th Circuit Ct. Dist. Ky., 1955-59. Served to lt. USNR, 1942-46, 51-52. Mem. Ky. Bar Assn., Am. Legion, Ky. Hist. Soc., Frankfort Country Club, Lexington Club, Frankfort Rotary Club (pres. 1993-94), Masons, Shriners, Elks, Phi Alpha Delta. Episcopalian (past vestryman, sr. warden). Home: 2310 Peaks Mill Rd Frankfort KY 40601-9437

PALMREUTER, KENNETH RICHARD LOUIS, principal; b. Vassar, Mich., Feb. 8, 1939; s. Clarence L. and Louise M. (Koch) P.; m. Martha Marie Zoellick, June 16, 1962; children: Pauline, Karen, Joel. BS in Edn., Concordia Tchrs. Coll., 1962; MA in Elem. Sch. Adminstrn., U. Mich., 1967; postgrad., Wayne State U., 1976-78, U. Colo., 1988-89; LLD, Concordia Tchrs. Coll., Seward, Nebr., 1993. Tchr. Grace Luth. Sch., River Forest, Ill., 1960-61; tchr. Calvary Luth. Sch., Lincoln Park, Mich., 1962-63, prin., tchr. jr. high, 1963-76; asst. prin. Luth. High Sch. West, Detroit, 1976-78, prin., 1978-87; exec. dir., prin. Luth. High Sch., Denver, 1987—, mem. Commn. on Theology and Ch. Rels., Luth. Ch.-Mo. Synod, 1995—, mem. planning coun. for mission and ministry, 1988-90; adv. team Luth. High Schs., 1984-88, 94—, Concordia Centennial adv. com., 1992; day sch. com.

Rocky Mountain Dist., 1990-94, tchrs. conf. chmn., 1990-94, dist. conv. com., 1988, 91; nominations com. Mich. Dist., 1987, bd. social ministry, 1980-84, dist. conv. com., 1972, student aid com., 1974-78; conf. program com. Mich. Assn. Non-Pub. Schs., 1984-85; adv. coun. Wayne County Cmty. Coll., 1986-87. Named Outstanding Young Educator, Lincoln Park Jaycees, 1973; nominated Nat. Disting. Luth. Prin., 1992. Mem. NASSP, ASCD, Assn. Luth. Secondary Schs., Luth. Edn. Assn. Lutheran. Home: 2783 S Depew St Denver CO 80227-4106 Office: Lutheran High Sch 3201 W Arizona Ave Denver CO 80219-3941*

PALMS, JOHN MICHAEL, academic administrator, physicist; b. Rijswijk, The Netherlands, June 6, 1935; naturalized, 1956; s. Peter Joannes and Mimi Adele (DeYong) P.; m. Norma Lee Cannon, June 2, 1958; children: John Michael, Daniele Maria, Lee Cannon. BS in Physics, The Citadel, 1958, DSc (hon.), 1980; MS in Physics, Emory U., 1959; PhD, U. N.Mex., 1966. Commd. 2d lt. USAF, 1958, retired capt. Res., 1970; lectr. physics dept. U. N.Mex., 1959-62; instr. physics dept. USAF Acad., 1961-62; staff mem. Western Electric Sandia Lab., 1961-62, U. Calif. Los Alamos Sci. Lab., 1962-66, Oak Ridge Nat. Lab., 1966; asst. prof. Emory U., Atlanta, 1966-69; assoc. prof. Emory U., 1969-73, chmn., assoc. prof. dept. physics, assoc. prof. radiology dept. Med. Sch., 1973-74, prof., chmn. dept. physics, 1973-74, dean Coll. Arts. and Scis., 1974-80, acting chmn. dept. math. and computer sci., 1976-77, v.p. arts and scis., 1979-82, acting dean Emory Coll., 1979-80, acting dir. Emory U. Computing Ctr., 1980-82, v.p. acad. affairs, 1982-88, interim dean Grad. Sch., 1985-86, Charles Howard Candler prof. nuclear, radiation and environ. physics, 1988-90; pres., prof. physics Ga. State U., Atlanta, 1989-91, U. S.C., Columbia, 1991—; bd. dirs. Peco Energy Co., Fortis, Inc., N.Y.C., Policy Mgmt. Sys. Corp., Columbia; adv. com. Oak Ridge Nat. Lab., 1984-89; mem. Nat. nuclear accrediting bd. Inst. Nuclear Power Ops., 1985-91, Inst., adv. coun., 1995; nat. adv. coun. Inst. Nuclear Power Ops.; mem. panel for semiconductor detectors NAS/NRC, 1963-74; cons. Acad. Natural Scis., Phila., EG&G, INc., Santa Barbara, Calif., Tennelec, Inc., radiology dept. U. So. Calif. Med. Sch., Three Mile Island Environ. Study, Phila. Health Funds, ORTEC, Inc., Oak Ridge, Allied-Gulf Nuclear Svcs., Barnwell, S.C., TRW Space Sys. Divsn., L.A., AEC, Harshaw Chem. Co., Canberra Industries, dept. radiol. health Ga. Dept. Human Resources, Nat. Cancer Inst.; mem. high tech. task force Atlanta C. of C. Contbr. articles on nuclear, atomic, med. and environ. physics to profl. jours. Mem. adv. be. The Citadel, Oak Ridge Nat. Lab.; mem. exec. bd. Atlanta Area Coun. Boy Scouts of Am., 1989-90; mem. cmty. rels. bd. U.S. Penitentiary, Atlanta; trustee, vice-chmn. Inst. Def. Analysses, Wesleyan Coll., 1984-89, Pace Acad., 1984-89, St. Joseph's Hosp., Atlanta, 1987-89, Ga. Rsch. Alliance, 1988-89; mem. S.C. Univs. Rsch. and Ednl. Found. Bd., S.C. Rsch. Authority Bd.; bd. dirs. Civic-Atlanta Partnership Bus. and Edn., Inc., 1988-90, United Way; chair Rhodes scholar selective com., 1989, S.C., 1995-96, 97. Mem. AAAS, Am. Phys. Soc., Am. Assn. Physics Tchrs., IEEE (Nuclear Sci. Group), Am. Nuclear Soc., Am. Coun. Edn., Coun. Provosts and Acad. V.P.s, Am. Conf. Acad. Deans, Soc. Nuclear Medicine, Health Physics Soc., Columbia C. of C. (bd. dirs.), Rotary, Columbia C. of C., Phi Beta Kappa, Sigma Xi, Phi Kappa Phi, Omicron Delta Kappa, Sigma Pi Sigma. Home and Office: U SC House of the President Columbia SC 29208

PALMS, ROGER CURTIS, religious magazine editor, clergyman; b. Detroit, Sept. 13, 1936; s. Nelson Curtis and Winifred Jessie (Bennett) P.; m. Andrea Sisson, Aug. 22, 1959; children—Grant Curtis, Andrea Jane. B.A., Wayne State U., 1958; B.D., Eastern Baptist Sem., Phila, 1961, M.Div., 1971, D.D., 1977; M.A., Mich. State U., 1971. Ordained to ministry Am. Bapt. Chs., 1961. Pastor Ronceverte Bapt. Ch., W.Va., 1961-64; pastor 1st Bapt. Ch., Highland Park, N.J., 1964-67; chaplain Am. Bapt. Student Found., Mich. State U., East Lansing, 1967-73; assoc. editor Decision mag. Billy Graham Evang. Assn., Mpls., 1973-76, editor, 1976—; guest lectr. at schs of evangelism and writers' confs. Author over 13 books including Living on the Mountain, 1985, Enjoying the Closeness of God, 1989, Let God Help You Choose, 1989, Celebrate Life After 50, 1995; spkr. nationally syndicated radio program Something for You. Trustee No. Bapt. Theol. Sem., 1973—. Mem. Evang. Press Assn. (pres. 1991-93). Office: Decision Mag Billy Graham Evang Assn 1300 Harmon Pl Minneapolis MN 55403-1925 *Investing in people's spiritual lives, giving time and counsel, will bring multiplied results for generations. It is one of the most far-reaching ways I can put faith to work.**

PALO, NICHOLAS EDWIN, professional society administrator; b. Waukegan, Ill., Nov. 18, 1945; s. Edwin Arnold and Eevi Kustaava (Hukkala) P.; m. Lauren M. Reynolds, Aug. 18, 1990 (dec.). BA, U. Wis., Eau Claire, 1971; MS, U. Mo., 1975. Instr., coordinator U. Mo. Extension, Columbia, 1974-85; exec. officer Am. Bd. Profl. Psychology, Columbia, 1984—. Pres. Columbia Community Band, 1987; chmn. Arts Resources Coun., Columbia, 1988; adv. bd. Columbia Art League. Mem. Am. Soc. Assn. Execs., Psychology Execs. Roundtable, Mensa, Windjammers Unltd. Club, Am. Assn. Concert Bands Club, Internat. Trombone Assn., N.Am. Brass Band Assn., Phi Delta Kappa (hon.), Phi Mu Alpha (hon.). Democrat. Lutheran. Avocation: music. Home: 608 Spring Valley Rd Columbia MO 65203-2261 Office: Am Board of Profl Psychology 2100 E Broadway Ste 313 Columbia MO 65201-6082

PALOCHKO, ELEANOR LARIVERE, retired secondary education educator; b. Woonsocket, R.I., May 8, 1924; d. Albert E. and Rosella (Hernan) LaRivere; m. Raymond Francis Palochko, June 26, 1948; children: Ellen, David, Gary, Peggy. BS, U. Conn., 1945; postgrad., Columbia U., 1946, U. Conn., 1982, Cen. Conn. State U. Tchr. bus. Morgan High Sch., Clinton, Conn., 1945-46, Bassick High Sch., Bridgeport, Conn., 1947-49, Jonathan Law High Sch., Milford, Conn., 1961-92; ret., 1992. Former leader Girl Scouts U.S.A., Brownie Scouts; former treas., sec., v.p., pres. PTA, Milford; advisor Keyettes; vol. Milford Hosp. Aux., Bloodmobile drives ARC; sec. Friends of Counted Embroidery, Milford Sr. Ctr.; treas. Milford Hosp. Aux. Mem. NEA, AAUW (exec. bd., past v.p., sec., treas., Ednl. Found. gift in her name 1984-85), Conn. Edn. Assn., Milford Edn. Assn. (bldg rep.), New Eng. Bus. Educators Assn. (rep. profl. devel. com.), Conn. Bus. Educators Assn., Ret. Tchrs. of Bridgeport and New Haven, U. Conn. Alumni Assn., Ret. Profl. Women's Club (sec.), Conn. State Ret. Tchrs. Roman Catholic. Avocations: counted cross-stitch, reading, golf, Elderhostels travel. Home: 134 Corona Dr Milford CT 06460-3514

PALOR, JOHN, media group executive. Pres. Gannett News Media Group, Arlington, Va. Office: Gannett Co Inc 1100 Wilson Blvd Arlington VA 22209-2297

PALOVCIK, REINHARD ANTON, research neurophysiologist; b. Dornheim, Hessen, Germany, June 30, 1950; came to U.S. 1956; s. Anton and Elfriede (Lankus) P. BS, U. Mich., 1973; MA, Wayne State U., Detroit, 1979, PhD, 1982. Rsch. asst. E.B. Ford Inst. Med. Rsch., Detroit, 1973-78; teaching asst. Dept. Psychology, Wayne State U., Detroit, 1978-79, grad. trainee, 1979-81, grad. asst., 1981-82; postdoctoral assoc. dept. physiology U. Fla., Gainesville, 1982-86, postdoctoral assoc. dept. neurosci., 1986-89, postdoctoral assoc. dept. neurosurgery, 1989-90, postdoctoral assoc. neurology dept., 1991, rsch. cons.; rsch. health scientist rsch. svc. VA Med. Ctr., Gainesville, 1990-95, clin. rsch. cons., 1995—. U. Mich. Regents Alumni scholar, 1969; NIMH predoctoral tng. grantee, 1979; NIH Nat. Rsch. Svc. awardee, 1983; Epilepsy Rsch. Found. Fla. postdoctoral grantee, 1990. Mem. AAAS, IEEE, APA, Soc. for Neurosci., Am. Statis. Assn., Internat. Neural Network Soc. Avocations: classical and modern music, Japanese culture, Korean karate, creative photography, paleontology. Home: 2209 NE 15th Ter Gainesville FL 32609-8918

PALOVICH, MARILYN LEE, elementary education educator; b. Trinidad, Colo., Apr. 24, 1943; d. Raymond Leon and Mary (Swigle) Swift; m. Joseph Lawrence Palovich, June 6, 1964; children: Milena Jo, Chad Michael. AA, Trinidad State Jr. Coll., 1963; BA, Adams State Coll., Alamosa, Colo., 1966. Cert. elem. edn. Tchr. grades 1-2-3-4 North Garcia Sch. Dist. No. 5, Trinidad, 1963-65; tchr. kindergarten Trinidad Sch. Dist. No. 1, 1965-68, tchrs. grades 3 and 5, 1970—; mem. adv. bd. Louden/Henritze Archaeology Mus., Trinidad, 1993—. Author: (poetry) Treasured Poems of America, 1994. Pres. Assn. Retarded Citizens, Trinidad, 1987-89; pres., v.p. So. Colo. Assn. to Aid the Handicapped, Trinidad, 1989—; mem. adv. bd., treas. So. Colo. Devel. Disability Svcs., Trinidad, 1987-89. Recipient Outstanding Elem. Tchr. award, 1974, 1st Pl. Nat. 5th Grade award Weekly Reader Editors, Middletown, 1994, Grand Prize Nat. 5th Grade award, 1995. Mem. NRA, Western Slavonic Assn., Colo. Fedn. Tchrs., Trinidad Fedn. Tchrs. Avocations: leather sewing and tooling, gun engraving, reading, writing poetry, handcrafts. Home: 733 Pine St Trinidad CO 81082-2314

PALOYAN, EDWARD, physician, educator, researcher; b. Paris, Mar. 19, 1932; s. Michael and Renee (Palaian) P.; m. Geraldine Richveis, July 7, 1957; children—Vivian, Regina, Edmund, Grace. M.D., U. Chgo., 1956. Intern U. Chgo. hosps. and clinics, 1956-57; resident in surgery, 1957-58, 1960-65, asst. prof. surgery, 1965-68; assoc. prof. surgery U. Chgo. Hosps. and Clinics, Pirtzker Sch. Medicine, 1968-73; prof. surgery Loyola U. Stritch Sch. Medicine, Maywood, Ill., 1973-94; chief endocrine surgery Loyola and Hines, Ill., 1980-94; assoc. chief of staff for rsch. VA Hosp., Hines, 1973-94; assoc. staff Hinsdale (Ill.) Hosp., 1991—. Author: (with A.M. Lawrence) Endocrine Surgery, 1976, (with A.M. Lawrence, F.H. Straus) Hyperparathyroidism, 1973. Served with USN, 1958-60. Recipient McClintock award U. Chgo. Med. Sch., 1971. Mem. Am. Surg. Assn., Soc. Univ. Surgeons, Endocrine Soc., Central Surg. Assn., Am. Assn. Endocrine Surgeons (pres. 1987). Home: 827 Taft Rd Hinsdale IL 60521-4836 also: 40 S Clay St Ste 217W Hinsdale IL 60521-3257

PALSER, BARBARA F., botany researcher, retired educator; b. Worcester, Mass., June 2, 1916; d. G. Norman and Cora A. (Munson) P. A.B., Mt. Holyoke Coll., 1938, A.M., 1940, D.Sc. (hon.), 1978; Ph.D., U. Chgo., 1942. From instr. to prof. botany U. Chgo., 1942-65; from assoc. prof. to prof. botany Rutgers U., New Brunswick, N.J., 1965-83, dir. grad. program in botany, 1973-80; adj. prof. botany U. Mass., Amherst, 1991—; Erskine fellow U. Canterbury, Christchurch, N.Z. 1969; vis. prof. Duke U., Durham, N.C., fall 1962; vis. research fellow U. Melbourne, Australia, fall 1984-85. Author lab. manual Principles of Botany, 1973, also numerous research papers in bot. jours.; bot. adviser Ency. Brit., Chgo., 1958-59; editor Bot. Gazette, Chgo., 1960-65. Named Outstanding Tchr., Rutgers Coll., 1977. Mem. Bot. Soc. Am. (sec. 1970-74, v.p. 1975, pres. 1976, Merit award 1985), Torrey Bot. Club (pres. 1968), Internat. Soc. Plant Morphologists, N.J. Acad. Scis. (pres. elect 1987-88, pres. 1988-89, Outstanding Svc. award 1985, 90), Am. Inst. Biol. Scis. Avocations: mountain hiking and climbing; stamp collecting; photography. Home: 330 Spencer Dr Amherst MA 01002-3367 Office: U Mass Dept Biology Morrill (South) PO Box 35810 Amherst MA 01003-5810

PALTER, ROBERT MONROE, philosophy and history educator; b. N.Y.C., June 19, 1924; s. Meyer and Mildred (Gilder) P.; m. Ruth Rappeport, July 15, 1945; 1 child, Alixe Daphne Cielo; m. Toni Ann Inmam, Apr. 5, 1955; children: Geoffrey Meyer, Jennifer Thorn Allan, Nicholas Trask, Adam Finch; m. Annette B. Weiner, May 21, 1979 (div. 1982). AB, Columbia U., 1943; PhD, U. Chgo., 1952. From instr. to asso. prof. phys. scis. and philosophy U. Chgo., 1949-64; prof. philosophy and history U. Tex., Austin, 1964-82; Dana prof. history of sci. Trinity Coll., Hartford, Conn., 1983-91, prof. emeritus, 1991—. Author: Whitehead's Philosophy of Science, 1960; editor: Toward Modern Science, 1961, The Annus Mirabilis of Sir Isaac Newton, 1971. Served with AUS, 1944-46. Mem. Phi Beta Kappa.

PALUMBO, BENJAMIN LEWIS, public affairs consulting company executive; b. Boston, Mar. 4, 1937; s. Guido Americo and Stella Marie (Lombardo) P.; m. Magdalene Julia Palinczar, Nov. 18, 1961; children: Matthew, Jason, Guy. BA, Rutgers U., 1959, MA, 1961. Adminstrv. asst. to Gov. Richard J. Hughes, N.J., 1963-65; dir. rsch. N.J. Dem. Com., Trenton, 1965-66; asst. to commr. N.J. Dept. Transp., Trenton, 1966-70; asst. dean Woodrow Wilsonn Sch., Princeton (N.J.) U., 1970-71; adminstrv. asst. to Senator Harrison Williams, U.S. Senate, Washington, 1971-73, staff dir. Dem. caucus, 1975-77, subcom. on govt. activities and transp., 1977-78; nat. campaign dir. Bentsen for Pres., Washington, 1973-75; dir. fed. govt. rels. Phillip Morris, Inc., Washington, 1978-83; pres. Palumbo & Cerrell, Inc., Washington, 1983—. Bd. dirs. Washington Performing Arts Soc., Arlington County Commn. on the Arts. Mem. Nat. Press Club, Rutgers Club Washington, Am. League Lobbyists, KC, Nat. Dem. Club. Democrat. Roman Catholic. Office: Palumbo & Cerrell Inc 1717 K St NW Ste 500 Washington DC 20006-1501

PALUMBO, FRANCIS XAVIER BERNARD, pharmacy educator; b. Scranton, Pa., June 19, 1945; s. Frank Bernard and Marcia DeSales (Fidati) P.; m. Karen Ann Setterlund, June 26, 1971; 1 child, Janice Lynn. BS in Pharmacy, Med. U. S.C., 1968; MS, U. Miss., 1973, PhD in Health Care Adminstrn., 1974; JD, U. Balt., 1982. Bar: Md. 1983, D.C. 1990; lic. pharmacist S.C., Md. Asst. prof. pharmacy U. Md., Balt., 1974-79, assoc. prof., 1979-91, assoc. dir. Ctr. on Drugs and Pub. Policy, 1988—, prof., 1991—, chmn. dept. pharmacy practice and adminstrv. sci., 1991-93; atty. Hyman, Phelps & McNamara, P.C., Washington, 1988-89; mem. study sect. NIH, Bethesda, Md., 1984-88; cons. in field. Co-author: Containing Costs in Third Party Drug Programs, 1979. Bd. govs. Rodgers Forge Cmty. Assn., Balt., 1987-95; bd. dirs. Luth. Health Care Corp., Balt., 1988-93, Edenwald Continuing Care Retirement Cmty., 1996—. With U.S. Army, 1969-71. Mem. Am. Pharm. Assn. (chair econ., social and adminstrn. sci. 1992-93), Acad. Pharm. Rsch. and Sci. (pres. 1994-95), Am. Assn. Coll. Pharmacy, Md. State Bar Assn., Am. Assn. Pharm. Scientists, Am. Soc. Pharmacy Law. Home: 318 Overbrook Rd Baltimore MD 21212-1801 Office: U Md Sch Pharmacy 100 Penn St Baltimore MD 21201-1083

PALUMBO, MATTHEW ALOYSIUS, marketing executive; b. Queens, N.Y., Sept. 17, 1961; s. John Christopher and Seiko (Murakami) P. BS, Cornell U., 1986; MBA in Mktg. Mgmt., St. John's U., 1990. Mortgage clk. Salomon Bros., Inc., N.Y.C., 1986; mut. fund adminstr. Bank of N.Y. Co., Inc., N.Y.C., 1986-88; copywriter Pierce Assocs., N.Y.C., 1988-90; dir. mktg. cons. Palumbo Assocs., S.I., 1989-90; adj. prof. St. John's U., S.I., 1990; mktg. dir., copy dir. Flaghouse Inc., Mt. Vernon, N.Y., 1990-93; spl. projects mgr., group product mgr. Global Computer Supplies, Port Washington, N.Y., 1993—; guest lectr. Am. direct mktg. techniques Sheffield Halleron U. (Eng.), 1993; guest lectr. designed and acquired funding Cornell U., Ithaca, 1992—. N.Y. State Regents scholar, 1979, Annette Brodsky scholar, 1988. Mem. Am. Assn. MBA Execs., Hudson Valley Direct Mktg. Assn., Cornell Asian Alumni Assn. (v.p. alumni affairs 1993-95), Cornell ILR Alumni, Direct Mktg. Club N.Y., Cornell Club N.Y., Cornell Club Fairfield County, Cornell U. Quadrangle Club, 1995—, Beta Gamma Sigma. Avocations: reading, sports, music. Home: 17 Willowbrook Ct Stamford CT 06902-6228

PALVINO, JACK ANTHONY, broadcasting executive; b. Rochester, N.Y., May 28, 1934; s. John Charles and Mary Aurelia P.; m. Joyce Ann Vilkaitis, Oct. 8, 1960; children: John Charles, Jill Marie, Jason Allen. B.S., St. John Fisher Coll., 1955. Broadcaster, program dir. Sta. WGVA, Geneva, N.Y., 1958-60; radio personality Sta. WBBF, Rochester, N.Y., 1958-78; pres. Sports and Spls. TV, 1970-73; co-owner, exec. v.p. Lincoln Group Ltd., 1978—; gen. mgr. Stas. WHAM, WVOR, WHTK, WPXY, Rochester, 1978—. Chmn. bd. trustees St. John Fisher Coll. Served with U.S. Army, 1957-58. Mem. St. John Fisher Alumni Assn., Nat. Assn. Broadcaster, Rochester Radio Broadcasters Assn. (pres. 1987—), N.Y. State Broadcasters Assn., Rochester C. of C. Roman Catholic. Clubs: University, Rochester Press Radio (pres. 1974), Rotary. Office: 207 Midtown Plz Rochester NY 14604-2016

PALVINO, NANCY MANGIN, librarian; b. Rochester, N.Y., Nov. 22, 1937; d. John Bernard and Miriam Lucille (Fox) Mangin; m. Lawrence Robert Palvino, July 2, 1960; children: Mark, Laurie, Lisa, Katharine, Thomas. BS, SUNY, Geneseo, 1959; MLS, U. Buffalo, 1993. Cert. libr., N.Y. Libr. Spencerport (N.Y.) Elem. Sch., 1959-60; tchr. East Greenbush (N.Y.) Elem. Sch., 1960-63; libr. # 41 Sch., Rochester, 1993—. Author: (bibliography) Autism, 1991. Fundraiser Rochester Philharm. Orgn., 1970; mem. women's bd. dirs. St. Mary's Hosp., Rochester, 1980—, giftshop chairperson, 1989-92, exec. coun., 1989-92, chmn. of ball, 1985, Imperial Ball Meml. Art Gallery, 1987, Holiday Open House, 1988; v.p. women's coun. Meml. Art Gallery, Rochester, 1989-91. Grantee DeWitt Wallace Reader's Digest Fund, 1994. Mem. N.Y. Libr. Assn. (scholarship 1992), Greater Rochester Areas Media Specialists (chmn. scholarship com. 1994-95, scholarship 1992). Avocations: golf, reading, walking, knitting. Home: 345 Kilbourn Rd Rochester NY 14618 Office: # 41 Sch 279 Ridge Rd W Rochester NY 14615-2927

PAMPLIN, ROBERT BOISSEAU, SR., textile manufacturing executive, retired; b. Sutherland, Va., Nov. 25, 1911; s. John R. and Pauline (Beville) P.; m. Mary K. Reese, June 15, 1940; 1 child, Robert Boisseau Jr. BBA, Va. Poly. Inst. & State U., 1933; postgrad., Northwestern U., 1933-34; LLD (hon.), U. Portland (Oreg.), 1972; LHD (hon.), Warner Pacific Coll., 1976. With Ga.-Pacific Corp., Portland, 1934-76, sec., from 1936, adminstrv. v.p., 1952-55, exec. v.p., 1955-57, pres., 1957-67, chmn. bd., chief exec. officer, from 1967; ret., 1976; with R.B. Pamplin Corp., 1957—, chmn. bd., CEO, to 1996; chmn. bd., CEO Mt. Vernon Mills Inc. (subs. R.B. Pamplin Corp.), Greenville, S.C., retired, 1996. Office: R B Pamplin Corp 900 SW 5th Ave Ste 1800 Portland OR 97204-1227

PAMPLIN, ROBERT BOISSEAU, JR., agricultural company executive, minister, writer; b. Augusta, Ga., Sept. 3, 1941; s. Robert Boisseau and Mary Katherine (Reese) P.; m. Marilyn Joan Hooper; children: Amy Louise, Anne Boisseau. Student Va. Poly. Inst., 1960-62; BSBA Lewis and Clark Coll., 1964, BS in Acctg., 1965, BS in Econs., 1966, LHD (hon.), 1995, DHL (hon.), 1995; MBA U. Portland, 1968, MEd, 1975, LLD (hon.), 1972, Western Bapt. Coll., 1989; MCL Western Conservative Bapt. Sem., 1978, DMin, 1982, PhD Calif. Coast U., DHL (hon.) Warner Pacific Coll., 1988, LLD (hon.) Western Bapt. Coll., 1989; cert. in wholesale mgmt. Ohio State U., 1970; cert. in labor mgmt. U. Portland, 1972; cert. in advanced mgmt. U. Hawaii, 1975; DD (hon.) Judson Bapt. Coll., 1984; DBA (hon.) Marquis Giuseppe Scicluna Internat. U. Found., 1986; LittD (hon.) Va. Tech. Inst. and State U., 1987, LHD (hon.); D of Sacred Letter (hon.) Western Conservation Bapt. Sem., 1991; DD Western Evang. Sem., 1994; DBA (hon.) U. S.C., 1996. Pres., COO R.B. Pamplin Corp., Portland, Oreg., 1964—; chmn., CEO Columbia Empire Farms, Inc., Lake Oswego, Oreg., 1976—, United Tile Co., Pamplin Comms., Oreg. Wilbert Vault; chmn., CEO Mt. Vernon Mills Inc.; lectr. bus. adminstrn. Lewis and Clark Coll., 1968-69, trustee, 1989—; adj. asst. prof. bus. adminstrn., U. Portland, 1973-76; pastor Christ Cmty. Ch., Lake Oswego; lectr. in bus. adminstrn. and econs. U. Costa Rica, 1968, Va. Tech. Found., 1986; chmn. bd. dirs. United Tile Co., Christian Supply Ctrs., Inc. Author: Everything is Just Great, 1985, The Gift, 1986, Another Virginian: A Study of the Life and Beliefs of Robert Boisseau Pamplin, 1986, (with others): A Portrait of Colorado, 1976, Three in One, 1974, The Storybook Primer on Managing, 1974, One Who Believed, Vol. I, 1988, Vol. II, 1991, Climbing the Centuries, 1993, Heritage The Making of an American Family, 1994, American Heroes, 1995, Prelude to Surrender, 1995; editor Oreg. Mus. Sci. and Industry Press, 1973, trustee, 1971, 74—; editor Portrait of Oregon, 1973, (with others) Oregon Underfoot, 1975; hon. life pres. Western Conservative Bapt. Seminary; chmn. regents Western Sem., 1994. Mem. Nat. Adv. Coun. Vocat. Edn., 1975—; mem. Western Interstate Com. Higher Edn., 1981-84; co-chmn. Va. Tech. $50 million Campaign for Excellence, 1984-87, Va. Tech. Found., 1986—, Va.-Oreg. State Scholarship Commn., 1974—, chmn., 1976-78; mem. Portland dist. adv. coun. SBA, 1973-77; mem. rewards rev. com., City of Portland, 1973-78, chmn., 1973-78; bd. regents U. Portland, 1971-79, chmn. bd., 1975-79, regent emeritus, 1979—; trustee Oreg. Episc. Schs., 1979, Linfield Coll., U. Puget Sound, 1989—; chmn. bd. trustees Lewis and Clark Coll., 1991. Recipient Disting. Alumnus award Lewis and Clark Coll., 1974, ROTC Disting. Svc. award USAF, 1974, Albert Einstein Acad. Bronze medal, 1986, Disting. Leadership medal Freedoms Found., Disting. Bus. Alumnus award U. Portland, 1990, Nat. Caring award Caring Inst., 1991, Pride of Portland award Portland Lions Club, Hero Athlete award, 1994, Herman Lay Entrepreneurship award 1995; Va. Tech Coll. Bus. Adminstrn. renamed R.B. Pamplin Coll. Bus. Adminstrn. in his honor; Western Conservative Bapt. Sem. Lay Inst. for Leadership, Edn., Devel. and Rsch. named for R.B. Pamplin, Jr., 1988. Mem. Acad. Mgmt., Delta Epsilon Sigma, Beta Gamma Sigma, Sigma Phi Epsilon, Waverley Country Club, Arlington, Multnomah Athletic Club, Capitol Hill Club, Greenville Country Club, Poinsett Club, Eldorado Country Club, Thunderbird Country Club, Rotary. Republican. Episcopalian. Office: R B Pamplin Corp Inc 900 SW 5th Ave Portland OR 97204-1235

PAMPUSCH, ANITA MARIE, academic administrator; b. St. Paul, Aug. 28, 1938; d. Robert William and Lucille Elizabeth (Whaley) P. BA, Coll. of St. Catherine, St. Paul, 1962; MA, U. Notre Dame, 1970, PhD, 1972. Tchr. St. Joseph's Acad., St. Paul, 1962-66; instr. philosophy Coll. of St. Catherine, St. Paul, 1970-76, assoc. acad. dean, 1979, acad. dean, 1979-84, pres., 1984—; Am. Council Edn. fellow Goucher Coll., Balt., 1976-77; bd. dirs. St. Paul Cos.; head Women's Coll. Coalition, 1988-91. Author: (book rev.) Philological Quarterly, 1976; contbr. articles to profl. jours. Mem. adv. com. Instl. Leadership project, Columbia U., 1986—; dist. chmn. Rhodes Scholarship Selection com., Mo., Neb., Minn., Kans., N.D., S.D., 1987—; exec. com. Women's Coll. Coalition, Washington, 1985—. Mem. Coun. for Ind. Colls. (bd. dirs. 1987—, chair 1991—), Am. Philos. Assn., St. Paul C. of C. (bd. dirs. 1986—), St. Paul's Athletic Club, Mpls. Club, Phi Beta Kappa. Roman Catholic. Avocations: swimming, camping, reading, music. Office: Coll of St Catherine Office of the President 2004 Randolph Ave Saint Paul MN 55105-1750

PAN, CODA H. T., mechanical engineering educator, consultant, researcher; b. Shanghai, China, Feb. 10, 1929; came to U.S., 1948; s. Ming H. Pai and Chih S. Ling; m. Vivian Y.C. Chang, June 2, 1951; children—Lydia Codetta, Philip Daniel. Student, Tsing Hwa U., Beijing, China, 1946-48; B.S. in Mech. Engring., Ill. Inst. Tech., 1950; M.S. in Aero. Engring., Rensselaer Poly. Inst., 1958, Ph.D., 1961. Engr. Gen. Electric Co., Schenectady, 1950-61; dir. research Mech. Tech. Inc., Latham, N.Y., 1961-73; tech. dir. Shaker Research Corp., Ballston Lake, N.Y., 1973-81; prof. mech. engring. Columbia U., N.Y.C., 1981-87; sr. cons. engr. Digital Equipment Corp., Shrewsbury, Mass., 1987-92; adj. prof. Rensselaer Poly. Inst., 1961-81; vis. prof. Tech. U. Denmark, Copenhagen, 1971, U. Poitiers, France, 1987; mem. adv. panel rand Corp., 1974; engring. cons., 1992—, v.p. Indsl. Tribology Inst., Troy, N.Y., 1982—; co-prin. investigator Spacelab I, 1984. Contbg. author: Tribology, 1980, Structural Mechanical Software Series 3, 1980; contbr. articles to profl. jours.; patentee in field. Recipient IR-100 award, 1967; NIH fellow, 1972. Fellow ASME, Soc. Tribologists and Lubrication Engrs.; mem. AAAS, Am. Phys. Soc., Am. Acad. Mechanics. Home and Office: 6 Pinehurst Cir Millbury MA 01527-3361*

PAN, HENRY YUE-MING, clinical pharmacologist; b. Shanghai, China, Dec. 27, 1946; came to U.S. 1969; s. Chia-Liu and Siu-Ging (Sung) P.; m. Mary Agnes Tse; children: Lincoln Jonathan, Gregory Kingsley. BSc (hon.), McGill U., Montreal, 1969; MS in Toxicology, U. Hawaii, 1973, PhD in Pharmacology, 1974; MD, U. Hong Kong, 1979. Rsch. asst. U. Hawaii, Honolulu, 1969-74, teaching asst., 1970-74; med. officer Queen Mary Hosp., Hong Kong, 1979-81; asst. prof. medicine U. Hong Kong, 1981-85; vis. asst. prof. Stanford (Calif.) U., 1983-85; asst. clin. pharmacology dir. Squibb Inst. Med. Rsch., Princeton, N.J., 1985-87, assoc. clin. pharmacology dir., 1987-88, clin. pharmacology dir., 1988-89, exec. dir. clin. rsch., 1989-91; v.p. clin. rsch. Bristol-Myers Squibb Pharm. Rsch. Inst., Princeton, 1991-92; v.p. clin. rsch. and devel. DuPont Merck Pharm. Co., Wilmington, Del., 1992-93, sr. v.p. drug devel., 1993-96; exec. v.p. R & D DuPont Merck Pharm. Co., 1997—. Contbr. articles to profl. jours. Stanford Asian Med. Fund grantee, 1983-85. Fellow Am. Coll. Clin. Pharmacology, Am. Heart Assn. Coun., Am. Coll. Cardiology; mem. AAAS, Am. Soc. Clin. Pharmacology and Therapeutics, Am. Soc. for Pharmacology and Exptl. Therapeutics, Am. Fedn. Clin. Rsch. Roman Catholic. Avocations: tennis, golf, distance running, cycling, baseball, classical music, plays. Office: DuPont Merck Pharm Co DuPont Merck Plz Centre Rd Wilmington DE 19805

PAN, HUO-HSI, mechanical engineer, educator; b. Fuzhou, Peoples Republic of China, Nov. 11, 1918; came to the U.S., 1948; s. Bai-ming and Won-ching (Chen) P.; m. Chao Pan, June 4, 1960; children: Lillian, Nina. BS in Mech. Engring., Nat. S.W. Associated U., Kunming, Peoples Republic of China, 1943; MS in Mech. Engring., Tex. A&M U., 1949; MS in Applied Mechanics, Kans. State Coll., 1950; PhD, U. Calif., Berkeley, 1954. Asst. engr. Yunnan Smelting Plant, Peoples Republic of China, 1942-43; from mem. tech. staff to head inspection dept. 21st Arsenal, Peoples Republic of China, 1943-47; from teaching asst. to assoc. mech. engring. U. Calif., Berkeley, 1950-53; rsch. engr. Portland Cement Assn., 1954; asst. prof. U. Toledo, 1954-55, U. Ill., Champaign, 1955-57; asst. prof. engring. mechanics NYU, 1957-59, from asst. prof. to prof. applied mechanics, 1957-73; prof. applied mechanics, mech. engring. Poly. U., 1973-90, prof. emeritus, 1990—; cons. Frankford Arsenal, Picatinny Arsenal, Petro-Chem Devel. Co.; referee Jour. Applied Mechanics, AIAA Jour., Internat. Jour. Mech. Sci.,

Internat. Jour. Solid and Structures, NSF; reviewer Applied Mechanics Revs.; sect. chmn. Internat. Modal Analysis Confs.; lectr. Kunming Inst. Tech., Tsinghua U., Jilin U. Tech., Jilin U., 1984. Contbr. numerous articles to Jour. Applied Mechanics, AIAA Jour., Jour. Mecanique, Jour. Engring. Mechanics, Jour. Applied Math. and Physics, Quar. Jour. Mechanics and Applied Math., Quar. Applied Math., Internat. Jour. Mech. Sci., Bull. Acad. Polonaise des Scis., Jour. Sound and Vibration, many others. Grantee NSF, 1964-67, NASA, 1966-68. Mem. ASME, AIAA, Am. Acad. Mechanics, Soc. Engring. Sci., Soc. for Indsl. and Applied Math., U.S. Assn. for Computational Mechanics, Internat. Assn. for Computational Mechanics, Phi Kappa Phi, Sigma Xi, Tau Beta Pi, Pi Tau Sigma, Pi Mu Epsilon. Achievements include development of method for reduction of vibrational systems, general method of modal analysis, solution for ordinary differential equation containing symbolic functions, eigenfunction expansion method in vibration problems of viscoelestic bodies. Home: 76 Edgars Ln Hastings On Hudson NY 10706-1122 Office: Poly U Dept Mech Engring 6 Metrotech Ctr Brooklyn NY 11201-3840

PAN, LORETTA REN-QIU, retired educator; b. Changzhou, China, Oct. 1, 1917, came to U.S., 1951, naturalized, 1965; d. Ke-jun and Mei-ying (Xue) P.; B.A. in English Lit., Ginling Coll., 1940; cert. English Lit., Mt. Holyoke Coll., 1952. Instr. English, Nanking U., 1940-41; instr. English and Chinese, St. Mary's Girls Sch., Shanghai, 1941-44; instr. English, Ginling Coll., 1944-45; sr. translator info. dept. Brit. Embassy, Shanghai, 1945-48; Chinese editor U.S. Consulate Gen., Hong Kong, 1949-51; researcher, editorial asst. modern China project Columbia U., 1955-60, lectr. Chinese, 1960-67, sr. lectr., 1968-87. Methodist. Contbr. to various profl. publs. Home: 600 W 111th St New York NY 10025-1813

PANAGIDES, JOHN, pharmacologist; b. N.Y.C., Aug. 15, 1944; s. Chris and Sophie (Marmar) P.; m. Kathleen Ann Heimann, July 9, 1967; children: Christopher, Melissa, Adrienne. BS, CCNY, N.Y.C., 1966; MS, U. N.C., 1968; PhD, SUNY, Buffalo, 1972. Rsch. assoc. Rockefeller U., N.Y.C., 1972-73; sr. scientist Lederle Labs., Pearle River, N.Y., 1973-83; sr. clin. monitor Ayerst Labs., N.Y.C., 1983-87; dir. clin. projects, CNS Organon Inc., West Orange, N.J., 1987—. Contbr. articles to profl. jours. NDEA Title IV fellow, Chapel Hill, 1966-68. Mem. AAAS, Am. Soc. Pharmacology and Exptl. Therapeutics. Achievements include development of haemophilus influenza vaccine, 23-valent pneumococcal vaccine, fenbufen, lodine, cotazym, cotazym-S, zymase, remeron. Home: 7 Catawba Dr West Nyack NY 10994-2304 Office: Organon Inc 375 Mount Pleasant Ave West Orange NJ 07052-2724

PANARESE, WILLIAM C., civil engineer; b. Framingham, Mass., Mar. 6, 1929; s. Angelo and Stephanie (De Profilo) P. BSCE, Purdue U., 1952. Structural research engr. Assn. Am. Railroads, Chgo., 1952-55; with Portland Cement Assn., Chgo. and Skokie, Ill., 1957-76, 80-94; mgr. concrete tech. sect. Portland Cement Assn., 1973-76, assoc. mgr. bldg. constrn. sect., 1980-83, mgr. bldg. tech. dept., 1983-86, mgr. constrn. info. services dept., 1987-94. Author, editor Design and Control of Concrete Mixtures, Concrete Masonry Handbook for Architects, Engineers, Builders, High Strength Concrete, Concrete Floors on Ground, Fiber Reinforced Concrete, Cement Mason's Guide, other bldg. guides and handbooks; editor Concrete Constrn. mag., 1976-80, Concrete Tech. Today newsletter, 1980-94. Served with C.E. U.S. Army, 1955-57. Fellow Am. Concrete Inst. (coms. 302 on constrn. of concrete floors, 332 on residential concrete work, chmn. 332 1984-88). Roman Catholic. Home: 942 Washington St Glenview IL 60025-4273

PANARETOS, JOHN, mathematics and statistics educator; b. Kythera, Lianianika, Greece, Feb. 23, 1948; s. Victor and Fotini (Kominu) P.; m. Evdokia Xekalaki; 1 child, Victor. First degree, U. Athens, 1972; MSc, U. Sheffield, Eng., 1974; PhD, U. Bradford, Eng., 1977. Lectr. U. Dublin, Ireland, 1979-80; asst. prof. U. Mo., Columbia, U.S, 1980-82; assoc. prof. U. Iowa, Iowa City, U.S., 1982-83, U. Crete, Iraklio, Greece, 1983-84; assoc. prof. div. applied math., Sch. Engring. U. Patras, Greece, 1984-87, prof., 1987-91, assoc. dean sch. engring., chmn. div. applied math., 1986-87, vice-rector, 1988-91; prof. Athens U. Econs., 1991—, chair dept. stats., 1993-96; pres. Nat. Coun. Edn. of Greece, 1996—; sec.-gen. Ministry Edn. and Religious Affairs, Greece, 1988-89, 95-96. Contbr. articles to profl. jours. Mem. Sci. Coun. of Greek Parliament, 1987—; mem. ednl. com. OECD, 1994-97; mem. governing bd. CERI of OECD, 1994-97; chmn. rsch. com., pers. com. U. Patras, 1988-91. Mem. N.Y. Acad. Sci., Am. Statis. Assn., Inst. Math. Stats., Bernoulli Soc. for Probability and Math. Stats., Greek Math. Soc., Greek Statis. Inst., Internat. Statis. Inst. Office: Athens U Econs, 76 Patision St, 10034 Athens Greece

PANARO, JOSEPH, financial services company executive; b. Stamford, Conn., May 15, 1950; s. Anthony and Ruth (Scharf) P.; m. Janet Lyn Lucas, June 17, 1972; children: Jennifer, Alyson. BS, N.H. Coll., 1972; MBA, U. Bridgeport, 1976; postgrad., U. Pa., 1987, 89. Asst. v.p. Western region Jos. E. Seagram and Sons, N.Y.C., 1976-81; region mktg. mgr. Coca-Cola Co., Atlanta, 1981-86; divsn. sales mgr. RJR Nabisco, East Hanover, N.J., 1986-92; region v.p. Western Union, Paramus, N.J., 1992-94; v.p. Info. Resources, Chgo., 1994-95, MasterCard Internat., Purchase, N.Y., 1995—. Team leader Emmaus, New Canaan, Conn., 1991-93. Mem. New Canaan Field Club (bd. dirs. 1993-95), K.C. (advocate 1994-95). Republican. Roman Catholic. Avocations: tennis, paddle tennis. Home: 76 Glen Dr New Canaan CT 06840-3636 Office: MasterCard Internat 2000 Purchase St Purchase NY 10577-2507

PANARO, VICTOR ANTHONY, radiologist; b. Buffalo, Aug. 7, 1928; s. Anthony and Teresa P.; m. Virginia Spann, Dec. 4, 1954; children: Denise, Lynn, Stephen. BA summa cum laude, U. Buffalo, 1948, MD, 1952. Diplomate Am. Bd. Radiology, Am. Bd. Nuclear Medicine, Am. Bd. Med. Examiners. Intern E. J. Meyer Meml. Hosp., Buffalo, 1952-53; resident E. J. Meyer Meml. Hosp., 1953-54, 56-58, Roswell Park Meml. Hosp. Cancer Inst., Buffalo, 1956-57; practice medicine specializing in radiology and nuclear medicine Buffalo, 1961—; mem. staff Erie County Med. Center, Buffalo, 1961—; assoc. dir. radiology dept. Erie County Med. Center, 1972—; mem. staff Westfield (N.Y.) Meml. Hosp., 1959-81, dir. radiology dept., 1959-81; mem. staff Buffalo Psychiat. Inst., 1974—, dir. radiology dept., 1974—; cons. nuclear medicine and radiology Brooks Meml. Hosp., 1970—; cons. VA Hosp., Buffalo; prof. radiology and nuclear medicine SUNY, Buffalo. Served as capt. M.C. U.S. Army, 1954-56. Fellow Am. Coll. Radiology; mem. AMA, N.Y. State Med. Soc., Erie County Med. Soc., Radiol. Soc. N.Am., Assn. Univ. Radiologists, Buffalo Radiol. Soc., Radiologists Bus. Mgrs. Assn., N.Y. State Radiol. Soc., Gibson Anatomical Soc., Gross Med. Soc., Cath. Physicians Guild Western N.Y., Phi Beta Kappa, Phi Chi. Republican. Roman Catholic. Clubs: Baccelli Med, Holy Name Soc, Romulus, Dante Allegiehri Soc. Home: 25 Elmhurst Rd Buffalo NY 14226-3539 Office: Erie County Med Center 462 Grider St Buffalo NY 14215-3021

PANAYIOTOU, GERGIOS KYRIAKOU See MICHAEL, GEORGE

PANAYIRCI, SHARON LORRAINE, textiles executive, design engineer; b. San Diego, Nov. 11, 1957; d. Robert Vernon and Edna Ruth (Bayless) Reed; m. Mehmet Vefki Panayirci, Mar. 1, 1985; 1 child, Ruth Naile. AAS cum laude, Sinclair Coll., 1981; B in Tech. cum laude, U. Dayton, 1984. Designer Dayton (Ohio) Progress Corp., 1981-85; design engr. Hartzell Propeller Inc., Piqua, Ohio, 1987-88; v.p. Patex Exim Inc., Dayton, 1986-93, Aegean Apparel, Dayton, 1993—; cons. Cepateks A.S. Indsl. Engr., Denizli, Turkey, 1985-86; fin. cons. Aegean Apparel Inc., Dayton, 1991-93. Mem. NAFE, AAUW. Democrat. Avocations: horseback riding, auto repair and restoration. Office: Aegean Apparel Inc 4365 Lisa Dr Tipp City OH 45371-9463

PANCAKE, JOHN, newspaper editor. State news editor, environ. editor Miami Herald; arts editor Washington Post. Office: Washington Post 1150 15th St NW Washington DC 20071-0070*

PANCHERI, EUGENE JOSEPH, chemical engineer; b. South Bend, Ind., Jan. 23, 1947; s. Raymond Albert and Dora Lugenia (Martin) P.; m. Janice Edwina Sutton, Mar. 9, 1986; children: Brent Jason, Ayrie Ann, Joseph Sutton. BSChE, Purdue U., 1969. Staff mem. Procter & Gamble, Cin., 1969-74, group leader, 1974-92, prin. engr., 1993-95, rsch. fellow, 1995—. Mem. AIChE, Am. Oil Chemists Soc., Nat. Geneal. Soc., Trentini nel Mondo, Phi Eta Sigma, Alpha Tau Omega. Achievements include 17 U.S. patents and 18 foreign patents for dishwashing and laundry cleaning products. Office: Procter & Gamble ITC 5299 Spring Grove Ave Cincinnati OH 45217-1025

PANCOAST, EDWIN C., retired senior foreign service officer, writer, researcher; b. Stratford, N.J., Aug. 20, 1925; m. Eunice Billings, June 12, 1948; children: Laurence E., Karen L., Joanne L. B.A., Maryville Coll., 1949; M.S., George Washington U., 1971; grad., Nat. War Coll., Washington, 1971. Served U.S. Fgn. Svc., Dept. State, 1949-53, USIA, 1953-86; sr. policy officer USIA, Washington, 1984-86; chief of policy Voice of Am., 1975-79; U.S. consul, dir. Amerika Haus, Munich, 1979-84; ret., 1986. 1st lt. AUS, 1943-46, ETO. Address: 4813 Drummond Ave Chevy Chase MD 20815-5428

PANDAK, CAROL ANN, fraternal organization administrator; b. Park Ridge, Ill., Feb. 27, 1960; d. Theodore J. and Bette J. (Brune) P. BA, U. Ill., 1982; MA, Northeastern Ill., 1986; EdD, No. Ill. U., 1997. Customer svc. rep. Baxter, Inc., Deerfield, Ill., 1984-87; sales mgr. Parke DeWatt Labs., Chgo., 1987-90; program. mgr. Soc. Actuaries, Schaumburg, Ill., 1990-92; coord. found. tng. Rotary Internat., Evanston, Ill., 1992-95, asst. mgr., 1995-96, supr. polio eradication program, 1996—. Recipient Achievement certs. Am. Soc. Assn. Execs., 1992; Paul Harris fellow Rotary Internat., 1993, Dissertation Completion fellow No. Ill. U., 1995-96. Mem. Literacy Vols. Am., Am. Assn. Adult & Continuing Edn., Assn. Rsch. on Nonprofit Orgns. and Vol. Action, Internat. Soc. Third Sector Rsch., Rotary, Kappa Delta Pi. Avocations: reading, cycling, theater, walking. Home: 1926 Prairie Sq Apt 131 Schaumburg IL 60173-4129

PANDEY, DHIRENDRA KUMAR, mechanical engineer,scientist; b. Jaunpur, India, July 1, 1951; came to U.S., 1978; s. Ram Raj and Ram Patti Pandey; m. Snehlata Pandey, Jan. 27, 1981; children: Nirnimesh, Nisheeth, Niket. BS, Banaras Hindu U., Varanasi, India, 1972, MS, 1974; PhD, U. Ill., Chgo., 1982. Asst. prof. H.B. Technol. Inst., Kanpur, India, 1976-78, Banaras Hindu U., 1975-76; tchg. and rsch. asst. U. Ill., 1978-82; rsch. asst. prof. Old Dominion U., Norfolk, Va., 1982-85; rsch. scientist Info. & Control Sys., Hampton, Va., 1986-89; prin. scientist Hughes STX Corp., Hampton, 1989-92; atmospheric scientist Sci. Applications Internat. Corp., Hampton, 1992—. Contbr. articles to profl. jours.; patentee high temperature directional emissivity measurement system. Mem. Am. Meteorol. Soc., Am. Geophys. Union. Avocations: reading, writing. Home: 1 Carlisle Ct Hampton VA 23666-6024 Office: SAIC One Enterprise Pky Ste 250 Hampton VA 23666

PANDEY, RAMESH CHANDRA, chemist; b. Naugaon, India, Nov. 5, 1938; came to U.S., 1967; s. Gauri Dutt and Jivanti Pandey. B.Sc., U. Allahabad (India), 1958; M.Sc., U. Gorakhpur (India), 1960; Ph.D., U. Poona (India), 1965. Jr. research fellow C.S.I.R. Nat. Chem. Lab., Poona, India, 1960-64, research officer, 1965-67, scientist organic div., 1970-72; research assoc. dept. chemistry U. Ill., Urbana, 1967-70, vis. scientist, 1972-77; sr. scientist fermentation program Nat. Cancer Inst. Frederick (Md.) Cancer Research Facility, 1977-82, head chem. sect., 1982-83; sr. scientist Abbott Labs., North Chicago, Ill., 1983-84; pres. Xechem, Inc., Melrose Park, Ill., 1984-90, pres., CEO, dir. tech. devel., New Brunswick, N.J., 1990—; chmn., CEO, pres. Xechem Internat. Inc., 1994—; cons. Washington U. Sch. Medicine, St. Louis, 1976-85, LyphoMed, Inc., Melrose Park, 1984-85; vis. prof. Waksman Inst. Rutgers U., Piscataway, N.J., 1984-86. Mem. editorial bd. Internat. Jour. Antibiotics, 1986—; patentee graft thin layer chromatography. Fellow Am. Inst. Chemists; mem. Am. Chem. Soc., Am. Soc. Microbiology, Am. Soc. Mass Spectrometry, Am. Assn. Cancer Rsch., Am. Soc. Hosp. Pharmacists, Am. Soc. Pharmacognosy, Soc. Indsl. Microbiology, N.Y. Acad. Scis., Indian Sci. Congress Assn. Office: Xechem Inc Ste 310 100 Jersey Ave Bldg B New Brunswick NJ 08901-3200

PANDEYA, NIRMALENDU KUMAR, plastic surgeon, flight surgeon, military officer; b. Bihar, India, Feb. 9, 1940; came to U.S., 1958, naturalized, 1965; s. Balbhadra and Ramasawari (Tewari) P.; children: by previous wife Alok, Kiran; m. Haripriya Pradhan, June 15, 1988; 1 stepchild, Bibek. BSc, MS Coll., Bihar U.-Motihari, 1958; MS, U. Nebr., 1962; postgrad. U. Minn., 1959, Ft. Hays State Coll., 1961, D.O., Coll. Osteo. Medicine and Surgery, Des Moines, 1969, Hamilton Co. Pub. Hosp.; grad. Sch. Aerospace Medicine, U.S. Air Force, 1979. Diplomate Nat. Bd. Osteo. Med. Examiners. USPHS fellow dept. ob-gyn Coll. Medicine, U. Nebr., Omaha, 1963-65; intern Doctors Hosp., Columbus, Ohio, 1969-70; resident in gen. surgery Des Moines Gen. Hosp., 1970-72, Richmond Heights Gen. Hosp. (Ohio), 1972-73; fellow in plastic surgery Umea U. Hosp. (Sweden), 1973, Karolinska Hosp., Stockholm, 1974-75; mil. cons. in plastic surgery, USAF surgeon gen.; clin. prof. scis. Coll. Osteo. Medicine and Surgery, Des Moines, 1975-76, also adj. clin. prof. plastic and reconstructive surgery; chief flight surgeon Iowa Air Nat. Guard; practice in reconstructive and plastic surgery, Des Moines, 1975—; mem. staff Des Moines Gen. Hosp., Mercy Hosp. Med. Ctr., Charter Cmty. Hosp., Davenport Osteo. Hosp., Franklin Gen. Hosp., Ringgold County Hosp., Madison County Meml. Hosp., Winterset, Iowa, Mt. Ayr Surgery Ctr. of Des Moines, Hamilton County Hosp., Webster City Decatur County Hosp., Leon, Story County Hosp., Nev., Kirksville Osteopathic Med. Ctr., Grim Smith Hosp., Kirksville, St. Anthony's Hosp., Carroll, Iowa Meth. Hosp., Des Moines. Served to col. M.C., USAF; chief flight surgeon Iowa Air N.G. Regents fellow U. Nebr., Lincoln, 1961-62. Fellow Internat. Coll. Surgeons, Assn. Surgeons of India (life), Interam. Coll. Surgeons, Assn. Physicians India; mem. Assn. Plastic Surgeons of India (life), Assn. Mil. Surgeons of U.S. (life), Assn. Mil. Plastic Surgeons, AMA, Am. Osteo. Assn., Polk County Med. Soc., Iowa Soc. Osteo. Physicians and Surgeons, Polk County Soc. Osteo. Physicians and Surgeons (pres. 1978), Soc. U.S. Air Force Clin. Surgeons, Aerospace Med. Assn., Air N.G. Alliance of Flight Surgeons, AAUP, Am. Coll. Osteo. Surgeons, Am. Acad. Osteo. Surgeons (cert.), Soc. U.S. Air Force Flight surgeons. Hindu. Club: Army Navy. Contbr. numerous articles to profl. jours. Home: 4405 Mary Ann Cir West Des Moines IA 50265-5328

PANDINA, ROBERT JOHN, neuropsychologist; b. Rochester, N.Y., July 19, 1945; s. Jack and Jane (Prezzevento) P.; 1 child, Gahan. BA in Psychology, Hartwick Coll., 1967; MA in Psychology, U. Vt., 1969, PhD in Psychology, 1973. Assoc. prof. Ctr. of Alcohol Studies Rutgers U., Piscataway, 1976-90, grad. faculty clin. psychology and neuroscis., 1976—, sci. dir. Ctr. Alcohol Studies, 1983—, prof. clin. psychology grad. sch. applied & profl. psych., 1990—, prof. psychology Ctr. Alcohol Studies, 1990—, dir. Ctr. Alcohol Studies, 1992—; lectr. Rutgers/Prudential Alcohol Edn. Workshops, Rutgers U., 1984—; cons. in field; mem. adv. bd. N.J. Collegiate Consortium for Health in Edn., 1991—; mem. sci. adv. bd. Ctr. for Edn. and Drug Abuse Rsch., Western Psychiat. Inst. and Clinic, Pitts., 1991—. Reviewer, mem. editl. bd. Am. Jour. Drug and Alcohol Abuse, Jour. Studies on Alcohol; reviewer Psychol. Bull., Jour. Abnormal Psychology, Am. Psychologist, Alcoholism: Clin. and Exptl. Rsch.; contbr. articles to profl. publs., chpts. to books. Trustee Alcohol Rsch. Documentation, Inc., Piscataway, 1982—, v.p., 1982-91, pres., 1982, 92—. William James fellow; Nat. Inst. Drug Abuse grantee, 1982-83, 83-86, 86-88, 89-91, 91-97, Nat. Inst. Alcohol Abuse and Alcoholism grantee, 1983-86, 86-88, 88-91, Dept. Health, Human Svcs. Pub. Health Svc. grantee, 1978-81, Nat. Inst. Justice grantee, 1981-83. Mem. APA, Rsch. Soc. on Alcoholism, Soc. Psychologists in Addictive Behavior. Achievements include research on animal and human psychopharmacology, physiological and behavioral mechanisms in alcohol/drug related problems, experimental and clinical neuropsychology, neuropsychological models of mental disorders. Office: Rutgers U Ctr Alcohol Studies Busch Campus-Smithers Hall Piscataway NJ 08855-0969

PANDYA, DEANNA MEARS, mental health counselor; b. Norfolk, Va., Aug. 11, 1937; d. James Gordon Jr. and Sarah Talmadge (Johnson) Mears; m. David Luther Brinkley Jr. (div.); children: Kim Brinkley Hebebrand, David III, Jeffrey Lawrence Brinkley; m. Shirish Ramachandra Pandya, June 7, 1978 (dec.). AA, U. Akron, 1980; BA, Va. Wesleyan, 1983, MA, Antioch U., 1994. Dir. edn. svcs. Va. Coun. on Alcoholism, Drugs, Norfolk, 1985-87, exec. dir., 1990-93; outpatient program specialist Maryview Psychiat. Hosp., Portsmouth, Va., 1988-89; clin. therapist City of Portsmouth, 1988-89; educator, therapist City of Va. Beach, 1984-86, 93-95; mental health counselor Glasgow High Wellness Ctr., Newark, Del., 1995; family counselor, addiction specialist Williamsburg (Va.) Pl., 1997; founder Survivors of Suicide, Virginia Beach, 1982-86, vol. educator AARP Bear, Del., 1995. Contbr. articles to profl. jours., various presentations. Bd. dirs. Hospice of Virginia Beach, 1983-85, Safe Place, 1988-90, Civitan Internat., 1990-92, comty. adv. coun. for curriculum Coll. of Edn., Old Dominion U., Norfolk, 1991-92. Named Rookie of Yr., Civitan Internat., 1991; recipient Disting. Svc. award Va. Alcohol and Drug Abuse Counselors, 1992. Mem. AAUW, Nat. Coun. Sexual Addiction and Compulsivity, Nat. Assn. Alcohol and Drug Abuse Counselors, Am. Christian Counselors Assn., Obsessive Compulsive Disorders Found., Am. Counselors Assn., Nat. Assn. Cognitive Behavioral Therapists, Parents and Friends of Lesbians and Gays, Lions Club Internat. Avocations: reading, bird watching, walking, writing, vol. work.

PANE, REMIGIO UGO, Romance languages educator; b. Scigliano, Italy, Feb. 5, 1912; s. Michele Antonio and Carmela (Gigliotti) P.; m. Philomena Pascale, Apr. 13, 1941 (dec. Aug. 14, 1959); children: Michael A., Elissa A.; m. Josephine R. Bruno, Aug. 15, 1964. B.A., Rutgers U., 1938, M.A., 1939; student, Middlebury Spanish Sch., Italian Sch., summers 1937-38, Columbia U., 1939-41. From instr. to assoc. prof. Romance langs. Rutgers U., 1939-57, prof., 1957-81, chmn. dept., 1952-71; dir., founder Rutgers Jr. Year in Italy, 1971-73; assoc. dean Rutgers Coll., 1977-80, prof. emeritus, 1981—; State coord. Am. Assn. Tchrs. Spanish and Portuguese, also Am. Assn. Tchrs. Italian, 1958; chmn. N.E. Conf. Teaching Fgn. Langs., 1960; chmn. examining com. Italian achievement test Coll. Entrance Exam. Bd., 1964-71; mem. selection com. Center 20th Century Studies, U. Wis.-Milw., 1970-71; v.p. Nat. Fedn. Modern Lang. Tchrs. Assns., 1969, pres., 1970, exec. coun., 1976-87; mem. nat. scholarship com. Internat. Ladies Garment Workers Union, 1964-94; dir. NDEA Fgn. Lang. Inst., Rutgers U., summers, 1963, 64, 65, 66, 67; cons. fgn. langs. U.S. Office Edn.; chmn. evaluating bd. Italian program Def. Lang. Inst. Author: English Translations from the Spanish, 1484-1943, A Bibliography, 1944, (with J.G. Fucilla) Annual Bibliography of Italian Language and Literature, 1961-70; editor: Italian Americans in the Professions, 1983; Asst. editor: Modern Lang. jour., 1965-71; Contbr. to: The Literatures of the World in Translation, 1970, The Italian Americans, 1987; Contbr. articles to profl. jours. Mem. Italian contbrn. sect. nat. com. U.S.A. Bicentennial; mem. Italian heritage com. 41st Internat. Eucharistic Congress, 1976; mem. Middlesex County Cultural and Heritage Commn., 1984-94, chmn., 1990-93; vice chmn. N.J. Christopher Columbus Quincentennial Observance Commn., 1989-93; chair Friends of the Rutgers Librs. Adv. Coun., 1989—; mem. N.J. Hist. Commn., 1991-97. Decorated Latern Cross Vatican, 1954, Commendatore, 1955, Grande Ufficiale, 1970, dell'Ordine della Stella della Solidarieta Italiana, 1976, Sovereign Order St. John of Jerusalem Knights Malta; named Man. of Yr. Columbus Civic League, Trenton, 1962, Italian Am. Club, N. Brunswick, N.J., 1963; recipient award Leonardo da Vinci Soc., Ft. Lee, N.J., 1966, Presdl. plaque Am. Inst. Italian Culture, 1970, Disting. Svc. plaque Unico Nat., 1981, Immigrant of Yr. award Italians Found. of Miami, 1982, meritorous svc. award Alumni Fedn., 1996; Grand Marshall N. Brunswick, N.J., Columbus Day Parade, 1984; inducted into Italian Am. Hall of Fame, 1985, Rutgers U. Hall of Disting. Alumni, 1992. Mem. MLA (life), AAUP, Am. Assn. Tchrs. Italian (life, pres. 1968-72, exec. coun. 1976—, hon. life pres., Leonard Covello Educator of Yr. award Italian Tchrs. chpt. 1991), Am. Assn. Tchrs. Spanish and Portuguese (life), Am. Coun. Teaching Fgn. Langs., N.J. Modern Lang. Tchrs. Assn. (life, pres. 1962-64, award 1979), Am. Italian Hist. Assn. (exec. coun. 1978-93, coord. nat. conf. 1979), Deputazione di Storia Patria per la Calabria (hon.). Home: 69 Lincoln Ave Highland Park NJ 08904-1823 *When I was leaving home at the age of seventeen to emigrate to the United States I asked my mother if she had any advice to give me and she replied, "The world will teach you, but be sure to always associate with people who are better than you, even if you have to pay their meals." Upon arrival in the United States I found that indeed I had a great deal to learn from the world, but associating with people 'better' than myself made the learning easier.*

PANEK, JAN, electrical power engineer, consultant; b. Benesov, Czechoslovakia, Aug. 10, 1930; came to U.S., 1971; s. Ludvik and Marie (Holzerova) P.; m. Eva Soukupova, Aug. 16, 1957; children: Hana, Paul. BSEE, Czech U. Engring., Prague, 1953, MSEE, 1956; PhD in Elec. Engring. Sci., Czechoslovak Acad. Scis., Prague. Rsch. engr. Rsch. Inst. Elec. Engring., Prague, 1953-65; elec. engring. expert UNESCO, Paris, 1965-71; chief tech. advisor UNESCO, Mexico City, 1969-71; cons. engr. GE, Phila., 1971-72, mgr. High Power Lab. switchgear div., 1972-74, cons. elec. power group tech. resources, 1975-78; mgr. transmission studies, elec. utility systems div. GE, Schenectady, 1978-85, mgr. transmission and distbn. studies system devel. engring. dept., 1985-87, sr. cons. dept. power systems engring., 1987-94; adj. prof. Rensselear Poly. Inst., Troy, N.Y., 1994—; Pres. Electric Power Cons. Group, Inc., 1995—. Contbr. over 40 articles to profl. jours. Bd. dirs. Mental Health Orgn., Schenectady, 1985-92. Fellow Nat. Poly. Inst., Mexico City, 1971. Fellow IEEE (various offices 1971—, prize paper awards 1984, 85, 92), Conf. Internat. Grands Reseaux Electriques. Office: 711 Plank Rd Clifton Park NY 12065-2016

PANELLI, EDWARD ALEXANDER, retired state supreme court justice; b. Santa Clara, Calif., Nov. 23, 1931; s. Pilade and Natalina (Della Maggiora) P.; m. Lorna Christine Mondora, Oct. 27, 1956; children: Thomas E., Jeffrey J., Michael P. BA cum laude, Santa Clara U., 1953, JD cum laude, 1955, LLD (hon.), 1986; LLD (hon.), Southwestern U., L.A., 1988. Bar: Calif. 1955. Ptnr. Pasquinelli and Panelli, San Jose, Calif., 1955-72; judge Santa Clara County Superior Ct., 1972-83; assoc. justice 1st Dist. Ct. of Appeals, San Francisco, 1983-84; presiding justice 6th Dist. Ct. of Appeals, San Jose, 1984-85; assoc. justice Calif. Supreme Ct., San Francisco, 1985-94; chief judicial officer JAMS/Endispute, 1995—; instr. Continuing Legal Edn., Santa Clara, 1976-78. Trustee West Valley Community Coll., 1963-72; trustee Santa Clara U., 1963—, chmn. bd. trustees, 1984—. Recipient Citation, Am. Com. Italian Migration, 1969, Community Legal Svcs. award, 1979, 84, Edwin J. Owens Lawyers of Yr. award Santa Clara Law Sch. Alumni, 1982, Merit award Republic of Italy, 1984, Gold medal in recognition of Italians who have honored Italy, Lucca, Italy, 1990, St Thomas More award, San Francisco, 1991, Filippo Mazzei Internat. award, Florence, Italy, 1992; Justice Edward A. Panelli Moot Courtroom named in his honor Santa Clara U., 1989. Mem. ABA, Nat. Italian Bar Assn. (inspiration award 1986), Calif. Trial Lawyers Assn. (Trial Judge of Yr. award Santa Clara County chpt. 1981), Calif. Judges Assn. (bd. dirs. 1982), Jud. Coun. Calif. (vice-chair 1989-93), Alpha Sigma Nu, Phi Alpha Delta Law Found. (hon. mem. Douglas Edmonds chpt.). Republican. Roman Catholic. Avocations: golf, jogging, sailing. Office: JAMS/Endispute Inc 111 N Market St San Jose CA 95113-1112

PANENKA, JAMES BRIAN JOSEPH, financial company executive; b. Milw., July 13, 1942; s. Alois J. and Jeanette (Buettner) P.; m. Kimberly A., Kerry A., Kristine A. BA, Marquette U., 1965. Sales rep. Pillsbury Corp., Milw., 1965-71; investment broker Marshall Co., Milw., 1971-72, E.F. Hutton, Milw., 1972-77; v.p. investments Dean Witter Inc., Milw., 1977-81; sr. v.p. investments Blunt Ellis & Loewi Inc./Kemper Securities, Inc./Everen Securities, Inc., Milw., 1981—; mem. Pres.'s Coun., Kemper Securities Group, Inc., 1981—. Bd. dirs. Mental Health Assn. of Wis., Milw., 1981-91, Sherri Steinhauer LPGA Mental Health Golf Tournament, Madison, Wis., 1991—; life mem. Marquette U. Pres.'s Coun., Milw., 1985—. Mem. Western Racquet Club (Elm Grove, Wis.), Geneva Nat. Golf Club (Lake Geneva, Wis.), Milw. Yacht Club. Roman Catholic. Avocations: tennis, golf, yachting. Office: Blunt Ellis & Loewi Kemper Securities Everen Securities 815 N Water St Milwaukee WI 53202-3526

PANES, JACK SAMUEL, publishing company executive; b. N.Y.C., Apr. 6, 1925; s. Max S. and Sophie (Levine) P.; m. Pearl Shaine, Dec. 25, 1949; children—Stephanie Jill, Michael Jonathan. B.A., Bklyn. Coll., 1947; M.S. in Journalism, Northwestern U., 1949. Editor, pub. The Howe Service, Inc., N.Y.C., 1949-54; founder, pub. Publs. for Industry, N.Y.C., 1955—, Panes Publs., Inc., N.Y.C., 1959—; owner Drug Products Display Service Advt. Co., N.Y.C., 1955—, Supplies for Industry Co., N.Y.C., 1956—; pres. Senap Devel. Corp., Great Neck, N.Y., 1972—. Pres. Russsell Woods Civic Assn., Great Neck. Served with inf. AUS, 1942-45, ETO. Decorated Silver Star medal, Bronze Star medal. Mem. Deadline Club, Sigma Delta Chi. Home: 21 Russell Woods Rd Great Neck NY 11021-4644 Office: Panes Publications Inc Great Neck NY 11021

PANETH, DONALD JOSEPH, editor, writer; b. N.Y.C., Feb. 28, 1927; s. Irving and Maud (Kramer) P.; m. Elma Olans, Apr. 10, 1949 (dec. 1987); children: Thea, Ira. BBA, CCNY, 1948; postgrad., Columbia U., 1949-50. Reporter N.Y. Times, 1947-49; free-lance journalist N.Y.C., 1950-56, 73-75, 77-83, 94—; rewriteman Daily Mirror, N.Y.C., 1956-63; copy editor The Morning Telegraph, N.Y.C., 1964-65; staff writer Med. Tribune, N.Y.C., 1966-72; copy editor L.I. Press, Queens, N.Y., 1975-77; editor-in-chief News Dictionary: People, Places and Events, 1977-80; editor, writer Yearbook of the UN, N.Y.C., 1986-93; documents editor UN Office Conf. Svcs., N.Y.C., 1993-94; adj. lectr. English York Coll., CUNY, 1983-86; cons. study of lit. of far right extremist groups in U.S. Anti-Defamation League, N.Y., 1995-96. Author: William Baziotes: A Literary Portrait, 1961, Current Affairs Atlas, 1979, The Ency. of American Journalism, 1983; contbr. articles to Commentary mag., The Nation, Village Voice, Peacework, WorldPaper, others; work included in anthologies Commentary on the American Scene, 1953, New York City Folklore, 1956. Mem. The Authors Guild, Willa Cather Pioneer Meml., Am.-Scandinavian Found. Avocation: reading. Home and Office: 240 Cabrini Blvd Apt 1E New York NY 10033-1116

PANETTI, RAMON STANLEY, investment company executive, consultant, lawyer; b. Akron, Ohio, Sept. 18, 1931; s. Augustine and Margaret Ruth (Sirdefield) P.; m. Bernadette S. Browne, Oct. 21, 1967; 1 child, Robert Lincoln. BBA, John Carroll U., 1954; MBA, U. Pa., 1958; JD, Cleve. State U., 1964. Bar: Ohio 1964. Fin. exec. Standard Oil Co. (Ohio), Cleve., 1957-65; mgmt. cons. Alspaugh & Co., Cleve., 1965-66; CEO, bd. dirs. Intersvc. Corp., Cleve., 1966-73; fin. cons., Cleve., 1973-77; CEO, investment cons. Capital Res. Advisors Inc., Newport Beach, Calif., 1978—; lectr. econs., fin. and bus. policy John Carroll U., Cleve., 1965-67. 1st lt. U.S. Army, 1954-56. Mem. Chancellor's Club (U. Calif., Irvine), Univ. Athletic Club, Univ. Club. Office: Capital Res Advisors Inc 1500 Quail St Ste 210 Newport Beach CA 92660-2734

PANG, DARREN, hockey analyst; b. Ottawa, Ont., Can., Feb. 17, 1964; came to U.S., 1990; Post-game show host Chgo. Blackhawks Sta. WBBM-AM, 1990-92; dir., prodr. Blackhawk Hotline Phone Svc., 1990-92; color analyst, studio analyst, reporter Ctrl. Collegiate Hockey Assn. (CCHA) SportsChannel, Chgo., 1989-94; analyst Internat. Hockey League games Prime Network, 1989-93; guest analyst Norris Divsn. playoffs ESPN, 1988; goaltender Chgo. Blackhawks, 1985, hockey player, 1987-88, ret., 1990; NHL game analyst ESPN2, 1993—; goalie coach U. Ill.-Chgo. Flames, Ctrl. Collegiate Hockey Assn. Named to NHL All-Rookie team, 1987. Office: care ESPN ESPN Pla Bristol CT 06010

PANG, HERBERT GEORGE, ophthalmologist; b. Honolulu, Dec. 23, 1922; s. See Hung and Hong Jim (Chuu) P.; student St. Louis Coll., 1941; BS, Northwestern U., 1944, MD, 1947; m. Dorothea Lopez, Dec. 27, 1953. Intern Queen's Hosp., Honolulu, 1947-48; postgraduate course ophthalmology N.Y.U., Med. Sch., 1948-49; resident ophthalmology Jersey City Med. Ctr., 1949-50, Manhattan Eye, Ear, & Throat Hosp., N.Y.C., 1950-52; practice medicine specializing in ophthalmology, Honolulu, 1952-54, 56—; mem. staffs Kuakini Hosp., Children's Hosp., Castle Meml. Hosp., Queen's Hosp., St. Francis Hosp.; asst. clin. prof. ophthalmology U. Hawaii Sch. Medicine, 1966-73, now asso. clin. prof. Cons. Bur. Crippled Children, 1952-73, Kapiolani Maternity Hosp., 1952-73, Leahi Tb. Hosp., 1952-62. Capt. M.C., AUS, 1954-56, Diplomate Am. Bd. Ophthalmology. Mem. AMA, Am. Acad. Ophthalmology and Otolaryngology, Assn. for Rsch. Ophthalmology, ACS, Hawaii Med. Soc. (gov. med. practice com. 1958-62, chmn. med. speakers com. 1957-58), Hawaii Eye, Ear, Nose and Throat Soc. (pres. 1960), Pacific Coast Oto-Ophthalmological Soc., Pan Am. Assn. Ophthalmology, Mason, Shriner, Eye Study Club (pres. 1972—). Home: 346 Lewers St Honolulu HI 96815-2345

PANG, JOSHUA KEUN-UK, trade company executive; b. Chinnampo, Korea, Sept. 17, 1924; s. Ne-Too and Soon-Hei (Kim) P.; came to U.S., 1951, naturalized, 1968; m. He-Young Yoon, May 30, 1963; children: Ruth, Pauline, Grace. BS, Roosevelt U., 1959. Chemist, Realemon Co. Am., Chgo., 1957-61; chief-chemist chem. div. Bell & Gossett Co., Chgo., 1961-63, Fatty Acid Inc., div. Ziegler Chem. & Mineral Corp., Chgo., 1963-64; sr. chemist-supr. Gen. Mills Chems. Inc., Kankakee, Ill., 1964-70; pres., owner UJU Industries Inc., Broadview, Ill., 1971—, also dir. Bd. dirs. Dist. 92, Lindop Sch., Broadview, 1976-87; chmn. Proviso Area Sch. Bd. Assn., Proviso Twp., Cook County, Ill., 1976-77; bd. dirs. Korean Am. Community Svcs., Chgo., 1979-80; mem. governing bd. Proviso Area Exceptional Children, Spl. Edn. Joint Agreement, 1981-84, 85-87; alumni bd. govs. Roosevelt U., 1983-89; pres. Korean Am. Sr. Ctr., 1991-92; pres. Korean Am. Srs. Assn. Chicagoland, 1992—. Mem. Am. Chem. Soc., Am. Assn. Arts and Science, Am. Inst. Parliamentarians (region 2 treas. 1979-81, region 2 gov. 1981-82), Internat. Platform Assn., Ill. Sch. Bd. Assn., Nat. Assn. Sch. Bds., Chgo. Area Parliamentarians, Parliamentary Leaders in Action (pres. 1980-81), Nat. Speakers Assn. (dir. Ill. chpt. 1981-82, nat. parliamentarian 1982-84, 2d v.p. chpt. 1983-84), Toastmasters (dist. gov. 1969-1970), DADS Assn. U. Ill. (chmn. Cook County 1985—, bd. dirs. 1987-95, treas. 1990-91, v.p. 1991-92), Korean Am. Assn. of Chgo. (exec. dir. 1990), World Future Soc. (Chgo. area chpt. coord. 1988—, pres. Greater Chicagoland Futurists 1991-95), Chicagoland C. of C. (edn!., environ. and Pacific-Rim coms., internat. divsn.). Home: 2532 S 9th Ave Broadview IL 60153-4804 Office: UJU Industries Inc PO Box 6351 Broadview IL 60153-6351

PANGILINAN, DANILO MANALESE, internist; b. Lubao, Pampanga, Philippines, Nov. 18, 1954; came to U.S., 1984; s. Bernardo Cruz and Magdalena M. (Manalese) P.; m. Erlinda Culling, July 18, 1981; children: Karla Ann, Karelle Grace. BS in Psychology, U. Santo Tomas, Manila, Philippines, 1976; MD, Virgen Milagrosa Inst., San Carlos City, Philippines, 1981. Diplomate Philippine Med. Bd., Fed. Lic. Exam. (U.S.) 1991. Rotating internship Jose Reyes Meml. Hosp., Philippines, 1981-82; rural health physician Escolastica Romero Dist. Hosp., Philippines, 1981; resident physician Romana Pangan Dist. Hosp., Philippines, 1983-84; psych. asst. The Inst. of Living, Hartford, 1985-89; intern Mt. Sinai Hosp., Hartford, Conn., 1989-90; resident U. Conn. Health Ctr., Farmington, 1990-92; physician pvt. practice, Hartford, Conn., 1992—; med. dir. Mack Geriatric Clinic, Immanuel House Geriatric Clinic, Hartford, Conn., 1992—; attending physician St. Francis Hosp. and Med. Ctr./Mt. Sinai Hosp., Hartford, 1992—; clin. instr. U. Conn. Sch. Medicine, Farmington, 1993— (recipient Cmty. Faculty award for Excellence in Tchg., 1997);. Governing bd. Seabury Retirement Community, Bloomfield, Conn., 1992—. Mem. AMA, Conn. State Med. Soc., Hartford County Med. Assn., Conn. Assn. Filipino Physicians. Roman Catholic. Avocations: photography, golf. Office: Danilo M Pangilinan MD 21 Woodland St Ste 311 Hartford CT 06105-4318

PANICCIA, PATRICIA LYNN, television news reporter, lawyer; b. Glendale, Calif., Sept. 19, 1952; d. Valentino and Mary (Napoleon) P.; m. Jeffrey McDowell Mailes, Oct. 5, 1985; children: Alana Christine, Malia Noel. BA in Communication, U. Hawaii, Honolulu, 1977; JD, Pepperdine U., Malibu, Calif., 1981. Bar: Hawaii 1981, Calif. 1982, U.S. Dist. Ct. Hawaii 1981. Extern law clk. Hon. Samuel P. King U.S. Dist. Ct., Honolulu, 1980; reporter, anchor woman Sta. KEYT-TV, Santa Barbara, Calif., 1983-84; reporter Sta. KCOP-TV, Los Angeles, 1984-88; reporter CNN L.A., 1989-93; instr. communications law Pepperdine Sch. Law, 1987, 94—, adj. prof.; profl. surfer, 1977-81. Recipient Clarion award Women In Communication, Inc., 1988. Mem. ABA (chair of law and media com. young lawyers div., 1987-88, nat. conf. com. lawyers and reps. of media, 1987-91), Calif. State Bar (mem. com. on fair trial and free press 1983-84, pub. affairs com. 1985-87), Hawaii Bar Assn., Phi Delta Phi (historian 1980-81). Avocations: surfing, skiing, piano, guitar. Office: 1313 Foothill Blvd Ste 11 La Canada CA 91011-2146

PANICH, DANUTA BEMBENISTA, lawyer; b. East Chicago, Ind., Apr. 9, 1954; d. Fred and Ann Stephanie (Grabowski) B.; m. Nikola Panich, July 30, 1977; children: Jennifer Anne, Michael Alexei. A.B., Ind. U., 1975, J.D., 1978. Bar: Ill. 1978, U.S. Dist. Ct. (no. dist.) Ill. 1978, U.S. Dist. Ct. (cen. dist.) Ill. 1987, U.S. Ct. Appeals, 1987. Assoc. Mayer Brown & Platt, Chgo., 1978-86, ptnr., 1986—. Mem. ABA, Ill. State Bar Assn. Republican. Roman Catholic. Office: Mayer Brown & Platt 190 S La Salle St Chicago IL 60603-3410

PANICHAS, GEORGE ANDREW, English language educator, critic, editor; b. Springfield, Mass., May 21, 1930; s. Andrew and Fotini (Dracouli) P. BA, Am. Internat. Coll., 1951, LittD (hon.), 1984; AM, Trinity Coll., Conn., 1952; PhD, Nottingham (Eng.) U., 1962. Instr., English and comparative lit. U. Md., College Park, 1962-63; asst. prof. U. Md., 1963-66, assoc. prof., 1966-68, prof., 1968-92; mem. Richard M. Weaver fellowship awards com., 1984-88, Ingersoll Prizes Jury Panel, 1986; co-chmn. Conf. on Irving Babbitt: Fifty Years Later, 1983. Author: Adventure in Consciousness: The Meaning of D.H. Lawrence's Religious Quest, 1964, Epicurus, 1967, The Reverent Discipline: Essays in Literary Criticism and Culture, 1974, The Burden of Vision: Dostoevsky's Spiritual Art, 1977, The Courage of Judgment: Essays in Criticism, Culture and Society, 1982, The Critic as Conservator: Essays in Literature, Society, and Culture, 1992; Editor: (with G.R. Hibbard and A. Rodway) Renaissance and Modern Essays: Presented to Vivian de Sola Pinto in Celebration of His Seventieth Birthday, 1966, Mansions of the Spirit: Essays in Literature and Religion, 1967, Promise of Greatness: The War of 1914-1918, 1968, The Politics of Twentieth-Century Novelists, 1971, The Simone Weil Reader, 1977, Irving Babbitt: Representative Writings, 1981, (with C. G. Ryn) Irving Babbitt in our Time, 1986; Modern Age: The First Twenty-Five Years, A Selection, 1988, In Continuity: The Last Essays of Austin Warren, 1996; editorial advisor Modern Age: A Quar. Rev., 1971-77; assoc. editor, 1978-83, editor, 1984—; adv. bd. Continuity: A Jour. of History, 1984-88, Humanitas, 1993—; contbr. articles and revs. to profl. jours. Mem. Acad. Bd. Nat. Humanities Inst., 1985—; trustee Found. for Faith in Search of Understanding, 1987. Grantee Earhart Found., 1982. Fellow Royal Soc. Arts (U.K.). Eastern Orthodox. Home and Office: PO Box Ab College Park MD 20741-3025 *In a profane age of unrest and breakdown, it is not enough for the critic to be purely and simply critical. He must work to conserve what is timeless, time-tested, time-honored. He must fight for causes he believes in, even if they appear to be lost causes. The critic's burden of responsibilty is also his vision of order.*

PANISH, MORTON B., physical chemist, consultant; b. N.Y.C., Apr. 8, 1929; s. Isidore and Fanny (Glasser) P.; m. Evelyn Wally Chaim, Aug. 20, 1951; children: Steven, Paul, Deborah. Student, Bklyn. Coll., 1946-48; BS in Chemistry, Denver U., 1950; MS in Chemistry, Mich. State U., 1951, PhD in Phys. Chemistry, 1954. Chemist Oak Ridge (Tenn.) Nat. Lab., 1954-57; mem. tech. staff RAD div. AVCO Corp., Wilmington, Mass., 1957-61, sect. chief, 1961-64; mem. tech. staff Bell Telephone Labs. (now Bell Labs.), Murray Hill, N.J., 1964-69, dept. head, 1969-86, disting. mem. tech. staff, 1986-92; cons., 1992—; mem. com. on microgravity rsch. NRC, 1991-96, mem. com. on future of space sci. rsch. priorities, 1994-95, space studies bd.; mem. com. on human rights NAS, 1996—. Co-author: Heterostructure Lasers, 1978, Gas Source Molecular Beam Epitaxy, 1993; contbr. numerous articles to profl. jours.; patentee in field. Mem. dean's adv. bd. Coll. Natural Sci., Mich. State U., 1990-95. Recipient Electrochem Soc. Electronics Divsn. award, 1972, Solid state medal, 1979, C&C Found. prize, Japan, 1986, Internat. Crystal Growth award Am. Assn. Crystal Growth, 1990, John Bardeen award The Minerals, Metals and Materials Soc., 1994. Fellow IEEE (Morris N. Liebmann Meml. award 1991); mem. Nat. Acad. Engring., Nat. Acad. Scis. Avocation: photography. Home and Office: 9 Persimmon Way Springfield NJ 07081-3605

PANITZ, LAWRENCE HERBERT, lawyer; b. N.Y.C., Feb. 3, 1941; s. Abraham Alexander and Anita Rosyln (Zuckerberg) P.; m. Karin Blaschke, May 27, 1965. AB, Princeton U., 1962; JD, Columbia U., 1965. Bar: N.Y. 1965. Assoc., Wolf, Haldenstein, Adler, Freeman & Herz, N.Y.C., 1965-69; asst. chief fgn. counsel W.R. Grace & Co., N.Y.C., 1969-74; v.p., chief internat. counsel Revlon, Inc., N.Y.C., 1974-84; exec. v.p., chief adminstrv. officer ICN Pharms., Inc., Costa Mesa, Calif., 1985-87; ptnr. Myerson & Kuhn, N.Y.C., 1988-89, Frere Cholmeley, London, Brussels, Milan, Monte Carlo, Berlin, Paris, Rome, Barcelona, 1990-92; sr. v.p. corp. devel. Trefisco AG, Zürich, Switzerland, 1993; exec. v.p. corp. devel. Quantum Economic Devel., Ltd., Zürich, 1994-97; group v.p., gen. counsel sulzer Medica U.S.A., Inc., Angleton, Tex., 1997—; arbitrator Am. Arbitration Assn., 1966—. Founder Park Ave. Malls Planting Project, 1984; patron Met. Opera, N.Y.C., 1987—. Princeton U. fellow, 1961. Mem. Assn. of Bar of City of N.Y., Presdl. Roundtable, Heritage Found. (assoc., inst. for econ. studies, adv. com.), Rep. Senatorial Inner Circle (U.S. senate bus. adv. bd.), Rep. Eagles, Knight of Malta, Order of St. John of Jerusalem. Republican. Home: 5110 San Felipe Houston TX 77053 Office: Sulzer Medica USA Inc 4000 Technology Dr Angleton TX 77515

PANKEN, PETER MICHAEL, lawyer; b. N.Y.C., Dec. 30, 1936; s. Harold Ira and Sylvia Rita (Haimes) P.; m. Beverly Muriel Goldner, June 19, 1960; children: Aaron, Melinda. BA cum laude, Haverford Coll., 1957; LLB magna cum laude, Harvard U., 1962. Bar: N.Y. 1962, U.S. Dist. Ct. N.Y. 1962, U.S. Ct. Appeals (2d cir.) 1969, 3d cir. 1988, (10th cir.) 1989, U.S. Supreme Ct. 1989. Assoc. Paul Weiss Rifkind Wharton Garrison, N.Y.C., 1962-66, Poletti Freiden Prashker Feldman & Gartner, N.Y.C., 1966-67; assoc. Parker Chapin Flattau & Klimpl, N.Y.C., 1967-72, ptnr., 1973—, chair employment and labor law dept., 1986—. Editor: Harvard Law Rev., 1961-62; editor-in-chief: ALI-ABA Resource Materials on Labor and Employment Law (1st to 8th edits.), 1982—; contbr. articles on law and bus. to profl. jours. Pres., bd. dirs. Fedn. of Handicapped, N.Y.C., 1984-92; bd. dirs. Fedcap Rehab. Svcs., 1993—; pres. metro N.Y. chpt. Soc. for Human Resource Mgmt., 1990-92. Mem. ABA (labor and employment sect., com. on NLRB law), N.Y. State Bar Assn. (labor and employment law sect., continuing legal edn. com.), Am. Law Inst.-ABA (chmn. employment law programs), Am. Law Inst. (com. on restatement of agy.), SHRM (com. on employment practices). Office: Parker Chapin Flattau & Klimpl 1211 Avenue Of The Americas New York NY 10036-8701

PANKEY, DEBORAH SUE, critical care nurse; b. Wichita, Kans., Jan. 5, 1965; d. Bobby Frank and Barbara Alice (Brown) Benson; m. Donald Russell Pankey, Aug. 3, 1985 (div. Oct. 1991); m. Nov. 27, 1992. BSN, St. Mary of the Plains, 1989. RN, Kans.; cert. ACLS affiliate faculty, TNCC instr., ENPC instr., BLS, ENA. Nurse technician Via Christi Regional Med. Ctr./St. Joseph Campus, Wichita, 1988-90, staff nurse, relief charge nurse, chest pain ctr. coord., 1990-96; specialist in critical care in the home Caritas Home Care, 1996-97; dir. clin. svcs. specializing in critical care in the home Prime Health Home Care, Wichita, Kans., 1997—; presenter in field. Mem. Emergency Nurses Assn. (sec. local chpt. 1994). Avocations: reading, biking, fishing, camping, computers. Home: 172 Champion St Haysville KS 67060-1901 Office: Prime Health 1120 S Clifton Ave Wichita KS 67218-2913

PANKEY, EDGAR EDWARD, rancher; b. Irvine, Calif., May 22, 1916; s. John Henry and Emma (Bercaw) P.; m. Elizabeth Searles, Feb. 4, 1939; children—Victor Searles, James Henry, Peter Searles, Roberta Pankey Hurst. B.A., Pomona Coll., 1938. Owner Pankey Ranches, Inc., Tustin, Calif., 1949-64; owner Edgar E. Pankey Ranches, Tustin, 1945-80, Pankey Consolidated, Tustin, 1980—; grower agrl. crops, cattle in So. and Central Calif., Ariz., South Australia; owner, dir. Pankey-Blower Investment Corp., Riverside, Calif., 1963-74, Tustin East Corp., 1967-82; vice chmn. Bank of Irvine, 1973-77, chmn., 1977-83; vice chmn. Valley Irrigation Co., 1963-78; pres. Lake Woodmoor Assos., Colorado Springs, 1980-91, Sunwood, Carson City, 1992—; bd. dirs. Sunkist, Pyrotronics, Inc., Lilac; cons., fgn. agrl. visitors U.S. State Dept., 1961-75; mem. Fed. Orange Mktg. Com., 1968-74, Calif. Citrus Adv. Com., 1959-89; mem. study mission to European Common Market, 1963; v.p. Maricopa Mining Co., 1977-81. Mem. Tustin Sch. Bd., 1951-59, pres., 1957-59; pres. Orange County Sch. Bd. Assn., 1958-59, Calif. Lemon Men's Club, 1964-66; bd. dirs. Bowers Mus., NCCJ, Orange County Grand Jury Assn.; bd. dirs. Pioneer Coun., pres., 1990-93; pres. bd. dirs. Children's Hosp., Orange County; assoc. bd. dirs. Cmty. Hosp., Santa Ana; pres. World Affairs Coun., Orange, 1977-79, chmn., 1979-80; delegate Labor Policy, London, 1983, People to People Citriculture, China, 1986; bd. dirs. Chapman U., 1980-95, treas., 1987-95; fin. chmn. Children's Hosp., 1969-80, pres., 1981-82. Capt. USAAF, World War II. Mem. Assn. Farmers Orange County (pres. 1954), Calif. Farm Bur. (governing body 1957-58), Orange County Farm Bur. (pres. 1956-57), Orange County C. of C., Aircraft Owners and Pilots Assn., Naui Scuba. Presbyterian (trustee, pres. 1955-58). Lodge: Elks. Pioneered non-cultivation for citriculture; avocado variety expts. comml. users. Office: Pankey & Co 4800 Legray Rd Arvin CA 93203-9773

PANKEY, GEORGE ATKINSON, physician, educator; b. Shreveport, La., Aug. 11, 1933; s. George Edward and Annabel (Atkinson) P.; m. Patricia Ann Carreras, Sept. 22, 1972; children: Susan Margaret, Stephen Charles, Laura Atkinson, Edward Atkinson. Student, La. Poly. Inst., 1950-51; B.S., Tulane U., 1954, M.D., 1957; M.S., U. Minn., 1961. Diplomate Am. Bd. Internal Medicine, Am. Bd. Infectious Diseases. Intern U. Minn. Hosps., 1957-58, resident in internal medicine, 1958-60; resident in internal medicine Mpls. VA Hosp., Mpls. Gen. Hosp., 1960-61; practice medicine New Orleans, 1961—; partner Ochsner Clinic, New Orleans, 1968—; asst. vis. physician Charity Hosp. La., New Orleans, 1961-62; vis. physician Charity Hosp. La., 1962-75, sr. vis. physician, 1975-95; cons. infectious diseases Ochsner Clinic and Found. Hosp., 1963—, head sect. infectious diseases, 1972-94; instr. dept. medicine, div. infectious diseases Tulane U. Sch. Medicine, New Orleans, 1961-63; clin. instr. Tulane U. Sch. Medicine, 1963-65, clin. asst. prof. medicine, 1965-68, clin. asso. prof., 1968-73, clin. prof., 1973—; clin. prof. dept. medicine La. State U. Sch. Medicine, 1979—; clin. prof. oral diagnosis, medicine and radiology La. State U. Sch. Dentistry, 1983—; cons. World Health Info. Services Inc., 1974—; dir., founder Century Nat. Bank, New Orleans; mem. medicine test com. Nat. Bd. Med. Examiners, 1979-83; mem. infectious diseases adv. bd. Hoffman-LaRoche, 1982—; cons. Federal Air Surgeon, 1997—. Author: A Manual of Antimicrobial Therapy, 1969; editor: (with Geoffrey A. Kalish) Outpatient Antimicrobial Therapy - Recent Advances, 1989, Infectious Diseases Digest, 1983-95, So. Med. Assn. Program for Infectious Diseases Dial-Access, 1983-92, Ochsner Clinic Reports on Serious Hosp. Infections, 1985—, Ochsner Clinic Reports on Geriatric Infectious Diseases, 1990-93, Ochsner Clinic Reports on the Management of Sepsis, 1991-93; bd. editors: Patient Care, 1969-75, Today in Medicine, 1990—; mem. editl. bd. Nat. Infectious Disease Info. Network, 1983—; mem. editl. adv. bd. Compendium Continuing Edn. in Dentistry, 1984—, Quinolones Bull., 1985-93; contbr. numerous articles to profl. jours. Dir. Camp Fire Inc.; Pres. New Orleans Young Republican Club, 1969-71; adv. bd. Angie Nall Sch. Hosp., Beaumont, Tex.; trustee Nall Found. for Children, Beaumont. Recipient cert. merit Am. Acad. Gen. Practice, 1969, 70. Fellow ACP (laureate award La.-Miss. chpt. 1997), Am. Coll. Preventive Medicine, Infectious Disease Soc. Am. (clinician award 1996), Am. Coll. Chest Physicians, Royal Soc. Medicine; mem. Am. Assn. Contamination Control (chpt. pres. 1968-70), Am. Fedn. Clin. Research, So. Med. Assn. (certificate of award 1970), Am. Soc. Internal Medicine (del. ann. meeting 1971-72), Am. Soc. Microbiology, Am. Thoracic Soc., New Orleans Acad. Internal Medicine (pres. 1977-78, 96-97), AMA, Aerospace Med. Assn., Am. Soc. Tropical Medicine and Hygiene, Am. Venereal Disease Assn., Am. Soc. Parasitologists, Interactive Travel Medicine Soc., La. Soc. Internal Medicine (pres. 1972-73), La. Med. Soc., La. Thoracic Soc. (chmn. program com. 1968, governing council 1976-80), Surg. Infection Soc., Immunocompromised Host Soc., Musser Burch Soc., Orleans Parish Med. Soc., N.Y. Acad. Scis., Pan Am. Med. Assn. (diplomate mem. sect. internal medicine 1971, sect. pres. infectious diseases and virology 1978-85), SAR, Huguenot Soc. Founders Manakin in Colony of Va, Aviation Medical Examiner. Clubs: Masons (32 deg), Shriners. Home: 5910 Prytania St New Orleans LA 70115-4348 Office: Ochsner Clinic & Hosp 1514 Jefferson Hwy New Orleans LA 70121-2429

PANKO, JESSIE SYMINGTON, education educator; b. Jan. 19, 1935. Student, Hunter Coll., N.Y., 1959-62; BA, SUNY, 1969, MS, 1969; PhD, Syracuse U., 1974. Tchr. Anderson Elem. Sch., Mariana Islands, Guam, 1964-65; tchr. Herman Ave. Elem. Sch., Auburn, N.Y., 1969-71; asst. prof. edn. dept. SUNY, Cortland, N.Y., 1971-76, Utica, Rome, N.Y., 1974-76; asst. prof. applied scis. dept. Loop Coll., Chgo., 1976-77; assoc. prof. social scis. dept. Truman Coll., Chgo., 1977-81; dir. student teaching St. Xavier Coll., Chgo., 1976—, dir. undergrad. edn., 1977-79, dir. grad. edn., 1979-81, prof. edn. ctr., 1981-83, dir. grad. prog. in edn., 1983-86, dir. edn. ctr., 1986-89, dean sch. edn., 1989-92; bd. dirs. Queen of Peace, Acad. of Our Lady; mem. com. grad. programs St. Xavier Coll., 1986-89, tchr. edn. coun., 1976—, early childhood adv. bd., 1976-92. Moffett SUNY scholar, 1969. Mem. AAUP, ASCD, Am. Assn. Colls. of Tchr. Edn. (instnl. rep. 1987-92), Assn. Ind. Liberal Arts Colls. of Tchr. Edn. (instl. rep. 1986-92), Ill. Assn. of Tchr. Edn. in Pvt. Colls. (instnl. rep. 1985-96), Ill. Assn. Colls. Tchr. Edn. (coll. rep. 1981-96, sec. 1990-92), Assn. Tchr. Educators, Nat. Assn. Educatos Young Children, Ill. Dirs. Student Tchg., Chgo. Consortium Dirs. Student Tchg. (chairperson 1976-79), Ill. Assn. Tchr. Educators, Pi Lambda Theta, Kappa Delta Pi. Office: St Xavier Coll 3700 W 103rd St Chicago IL 60655-3105

PANKOPF, ARTHUR, JR., lawyer; b. Malden, Mass., Feb. 1, 1931. BS in Marine Transp., Mass. Maritime Acad., 1951; BS in Fgn. Svc. and Internat. Transp., Georgetown U., 1957, JD, 1965. Bar: Md. 1965, D.C. 1966, U.S. Supreme Ct. 1977. Ea. area mgr. Trans Ocean Van Service of Consol. Freightway, 1958-61; with U.S. Maritime Adminstrn., 1961-65; assoc. firm Preston, Thorgrimson, Ellis & Holman, Washington, 1976-77; minority chief counsel Com. on Mcht. Marine & Fisheries U.S. Ho. of Reps., Washington, 1965-69; minority chief counsel, staff dir. Com. on Commerce, U.S. Senate, 1969-76; mng. dir. Fed. Maritime Commn., 1977-81; pvt. practice Washington, 1981-84; dir. legis. affairs Corp. Pub. Broadcasting, 1984-86, v.p., gen. counsel, sec., 1986-88; pvt. practice Washington, 1988-90, 96—; dir. fed. affairs Matson Navigation Co. Inc., Washington, 1990-96. Mem. Maritime Adminstrv. Bar Assn. (pres. 1995-96). Home: 7819 Hampden Ln Bethesda MD 20814-1108

PANKOVE, JACQUES ISAAC, physicist; b. Chernigov, Russia, Nov. 23, 1922; came to U.S., 1942, naturalized, 1944; s. Evsey Leib and Miriam (Simkine) Pantchechnikoff; m. Ethel Wasserman, Nov. 24, 1950; children: Martin, Simon. BSEE, U. Calif., Berkeley, 1944, MSEE, 1948; PhD in Physics, U. Paris, 1960. Mem. tech. staff RCA Labs., Princeton, N.J., 1948-70; physicist, fellow RCA Labs., 1970-85; prof. U. Colo., Boulder, 1985-93, prof. emeritus, 1993—, Hudson Moore Jr. Univ. prof., 1989-93, program mgr. materials and devices Ctr. for Optoelectronic Computing Systems, 1986-89; Disting. Rsch. fellow Nat. Renewal Energy Lab. (formerly Solar Energy Rsch. Inst.), 1985-93; v.p. for rsch. and tech. Astralux, Inc., 1993—; vis. McKay lectr. U. Calif., Berkeley, 1968-69; vis. prof. U. Campinas, Brazil, 1975; Disting. vis. prof. U. Mo., Rolla, 1984; participant NAS sci. exch. program with Romania, 1970, Hungary, 1972, Yugoslavia, 1976. Mem. hon. editl. bd. Solid State Electronics, 1970-94, Solar Energy Materials, 1984—, Optoelectronics, 1986-95; regional editor Crystal Lattice Defects and Amorphous Materials, 1984-90; author: Optical Processes in Semiconductors, 1971, 75, (ednl. film) Energy Gap and Recombination Radiation, 1962; editor: Electroluminescence, 1977, Display Devices, 1980, Hydrogenated Amorphous Silicon, 1984; co-editor: Hydrogen in Semiconductors, 1991, Wide Bandgap Semiconductors, 1992, III-Nitrides, 1997; designer: laser sculpture, Bklyn. Mus., 1968; contbr. articles to profl. jours.; patentee in field. Trustee Princeton Art Assn., 1970-82; mem. Experiment-in-Arts-and-Tech., Berkeley, 1968-69. Served with U.S. Army, 1944-46. Recipient RCA achievement awards, 1952, 53, 63; David Sarnoff scholar, 1956. Fellow IEEE (J. J. Ebers award 1975, assoc. editor Jour. Quantum Electronics 1968-77, mem-at-large IEEE awards bd. 1992-95), Am. Phys. Soc.; mem. AAAS, NAE (hon.), Materials Rsch. Soc., Internat. Soc. for Optical Engring., Sigma Xi. Home: 2386 Vassar Dr Boulder CO 80303-5763 Office: U Colo Dept Elec Engring Boulder CO 80309-0425 also: Astralux Inc 2500 Central Ave Boulder CO 80301

PANLILIO, ADELISA LORNA, public health physician; b. Manila, Jan. 23, 1949; came to U.S., 1955; d. Filadelfo and Elsie Belle (Nessia) P. AB, Radcliffe Coll., 1969; MD, SUNY Downstate Med. Coll., Bklyn., 1973; MPH, Harvard Sch. Pub. Health, 1988. Intern in pediatrics Babies Hosp., Columbia-Presbyn., N.Y.C., 1973-74, resident in pediatrics, 1974-75; pediatric hematology fellow Downstate/Kings County Hosp. Med. Ctr., Bklyn., 1975-76, blood banking fellow, 1976-77; asst. med. dir. ARC Blood Services, Nashville, 1977-80, med. dir., 1980-84, acting dir., 1984-85, med. dir., 1985-87; epidemic intelligence service officer Ctrs. Disease Control & Prevention, USPHS, Atlanta, 1988-90; med. epidemiologist Ctrs. for Disease Control and Prevention, Atlanta, 1990—; asst. clin. prof. pathology Vanderbilt U. Sch. Medicine, Nashville, 1977-87. Contbr. articles to med. jours. V.p., bd. dirs. Nashville CARES, 1986-87. Mem. Alpha Omega Alpha. Office: Ctr Disease Control 1600 Clifton Rd NE # 68 Atlanta GA 30329-4018

PANNEBAKER, JAMES BOYD, lawyer; b. Middletown, Pa., Mar. 9, 1936; s. Boyd Alton and Kathryn Kennedy (Brindle) P.; divorced; children: Jeffery B., Renee E. Pannebaker Bench, Traci Lee Pannebaker. BS, Elizabethtown Coll., 1958; JD, U. Mich., 1961. Bar: Pa. 1962, U.S. Dist. Ct. (mid. dist.) Pa., U.S. Ct. Appeals (3d cir.), U.S. Supreme Ct. 1969. Pvt.

practice, Harrisburg, 1965-86; pres. Pannebaker & Jones, P.C., Middletown, 1986—; mem. regional adv. bd. Mellon Bank, Harrisburg, 1980—. Bd. dirs. Cmty. Gen. Osteo. Hosp., Harrisburg, 1970—; trustee Elizabethtown (Pa.) Coll., 1972-78; mem. adv. bd. Villa Teresa Nursing Home, Harrisburg, 1985—; chmn. Middletown chpt. ARC. Capt. U.S. Army, 1962-65. Mem. Am. Legion, Masons, Shriners, Elks. Republican. Methodist. Avocations: skiing, sailing, horseback riding, outdoor activities. Office: Pannebaker & Jones PC 4000 Vine St Middletown PA 17057-3565

PANNELL, ROBERT D., lawyer; b. Thomson, Ga., June 27, 1942. BBA, Emory U., 1964; LLB, U. Va., 1968. Bar: Ga. 1968. Writing dir. Va. Legal Rsch. Group, 1967-68; contbr. articles to profl. jours. Mem. Nat. Assn. Bond Lawyers, Atlanta Bar Assn, Delta Theta Phi. Office: Nelson Mullins Riley & Scarborough 999 Peachtree St NE Ste 1400 Atlanta GA 30309-3964

PANNER, BERNARD J., pathologist, educator; b. Youngstown, Ohio, Oct. 9, 1928; s. Morris W. and Matilda (Giber) P.; m. Molly R. Seidenberg, Feb. 11, 1962; children—Morris J., Aaron M., Daniel Z. A.B., Western Res. U., 1949, M.D., 1953. Diplomate Am. Bd. Pathology. Intern in internal medicine Kings County Hosp., Bklyn., 1953-54; resident in pathology Boston City Hosp., 1954-55, Strong Meml. Hosp., Rochester, N.Y., 1958-60; asst. prof. pathology Sch. Medicine, U. Rochester, 1960-67, assoc. prof., 1967-72, prof., 1972-96, emeritus prof., 1996—; pathologist Strong Meml. Hosp., Rochester, 1972—; cons. Genesee Hosp., Rochester, 1974—. Contbr. articles to profl. jours. Served with USNR, 1955-57. Recipient Mapstone Teaching prize Sch. Medicine, U. Rochester, 1981. Mem. Internat. Acad. Pathology, Am. Assn. Pathologists, Internat. Soc. Nephrology, Am. Soc. Nephrology, Sigma Xi. Democrat. Jewish. Home: 330 Wilmot Rd Rochester NY 14618-2947 Office: U Rochester Sch Medicine Dept Pathology 601 Elmwood Ave Rochester NY 14642-0001

PANNER, JEANNIE HARRIGAN, electrical engineer; b. Malone, N.Y., Jan. 4, 1948; d. Martin Thomas and Marjorie (Boyea) Harrigan; m. John Charles Panner, Aug. 17, 1974. BS summa cum laude, SUNY, Plattsburgh, 1970; MA in Math., U. Vt., 1974, MSEE, 1993. Programmer Microelectronics Divsn. IBM, Burlington, Vt., 1970-71, assoc. programmer, 1971-74, sr. assoc. programmer, 1974-79, staff engr., 1979-85, adv. engr., 1985-90, sr. engr., 1990—. Contbr. articles to engring. jours.; patentee in field. Mem. IEEE, ACM. Avocations: golf, travel, gardening. Home: RR 1 Box 1310 Underhill VT 05489-9405

PANNER, OWEN M., federal judge; b. 1924. Student, U. Okla., 1941-43, LL.B., 1949. Atty. Panner, Johnson, Marceau, Karnopp, Kennedy & Nash, 1950-80; judge, now sr. judge U.S. Dist. Ct. Oreg., Portland, 1980—. Office: US Dist Ct 335 US Courthouse 620 SW Main St Portland OR 97205-3037

PANNETON, JACQUES, librarian; b. Trois-Rivières, Que., Can., May 7, 1943; s. Marcel and Bernadette (Page) P.; married; children—Anne-Marie, Luce. B.L.S., U. Montréal, 1964. Cataloguer Bibliothèque de Trois-Rivières, 1964-65; dep. librarian, then head librarian Bibliothèque Centrale de Pret de la Mauricie, Trois-Rivières, 1965-74; head librarian Bibliothèque de la Ville de Montréal, 1974—; prof. pub. libraries U. Montréal Library Sch., 1974-75; mem. Com. Cons. du Livre, Govt. Que., 1976; mem. adv. bd. Nat. Library Can., 1978—; mem. com. d'étude sur bibliothèques publiques Govt. Qué., 1987; invited guest German libraries, German Fed. Republic, summer 1976, Brit. libraries, spring 1978. Contbr. articles to profl. jours. Mem. Canadian, Am., Que. library assns., Corp. Profl. Librarians Que. (past pres.), Assn. pour l'avancement des sci. et des techniques de la documentation, Council Adminstrs. Large Urban Pub. Libraries, Internat. Fedn. Library Assns., Internat. Assn. Met. City Libraries. Office: Bibliothèque de Montreal, 5650 d'Iberville St Ste 400, Montreal, PQ Canada H2G 3E4

PANNIER, CHERYL JANE, radio broadcast executive; b. Springfield, Ill., Sept. 9, 1961; d. Clarence W. and Marian Elaine (Winter) P. AA, Iowa Ctr. C.C., Ft. Dodge, 1981. On air work/sports host KIDA, Ida Grove, Iowa, 1981-86; air personality KASI/KCCQ, Ames, Iowa, 1986-93; area dir. Am. Cancer Soc., Des Moines, 1993-95; ops. supr. 1040 WHO Radio, Des Moines, 1995—. Mem. women's adv. bd. Iowa State U./Margaret Sloss Women's Ctr., Ames, 1990-93; bd. sec. Ames/Story County Cyclone Club, 1994—. Mem. Ames C. of C. (Leadership Ames 1992-93, amb. 1989-93), Ames Jaycees. Lutheran. Avocations: golf, running, softball, woodwork. Home: 2810 Grand Ave #4 Ames IA 50010 Office: WHO Radio 1801 Grand Ave Des Moines IA 50309-3309

PANNKE, PEGGY M., long term care insurance agency executive; b. Chgo., Oct. 26; d. Victor E. and Leona (O'Leary) Stich; children: Thomas Scott, David Savonne, Heidi Mireille, Peter Helmut. Office mgr. DeHaan & Richter P.C., Chgo. and Des Plaines, Ill., 1983-86; v.p. long term care ins. Sales & Seminars, Des Plaines, 1986-90; pres., founder Nat. Consumer Oriented Agy., Des Plaines, 1990—; cons. on long-term care ins. The Travelers, Tchrs. Ins. & Annuity Assocs., and numerous other ins. cos., N.Y.C., Hartford, Conn. and throughout U.S.; speaker Exec. Enterprises, N.Y.C., 1988-93. Contbr. articles on long-term care ins. to profl. jours.; columnist Senior News. Sponsor Ill. Alliance for Aging, Chgo., 1990—, Ill. Assn. Homes for Aging, 1990-91; bd. govs. St. Matthew Luth. Home, Park Ridge, Ill., 1993-95. Recipient Speakers awards Health Ins. Assn. Am., Washington, 1990, Retired Officers Assn., Glenview, Ill., 1991, 93, Nat. Assn. Sr. Living Industries, Denver, 1992, Exec. Enterprises, N.Y.C., 1993, Gov.'s Conf. on Aging, Chgo., 1996. Mem. Nat. Assn. Sr. Living Industries, Nat. Assn. Long Term Care Profls. (charter), Ctr. for Applied Gerontology, Nat. Coun. on Aging, Mature Ams. (ad hoc com.), Am. Mensa of Ill. (program dir. 1983-85), Kiwanis (bd. dirs. Park Ridge 1992—, pres. 1996-97), Am. Soc. on Aging, Internat. Soc. for Retirement Planning, Park Ridge C. of C., Boulder C. of C. Avocations: songwriting, travel, sketching wildflowers, reading. Office: Nat Consumer Oriented Agy 2200 E Devon Ave Ste 359 Des Plaines IL 60018-4505 Branch Office: 4450 Arapahoe Ave Boulder CO 80303

PANOFSKY, WOLFGANG KURT HERMANN, physicist, educator; b. Berlin, Germany, Apr. 24, 1919; came to U.S., 1934, naturalized, 1942; s. Erwin and Dorothea (Mosse) P.; m. Adele Du Mond, July 21, 1942; children: Richard, Margaret, Edward, Carol, Steven. A.B., Princeton U., 1938, DSc (hon.), 1983; Ph.D., Calif. Inst. Tech., 1942; D.Sc. (hon.), Case Inst. Tech., 1963, U. Sask., 1964, Columbia U., 1977, U. Hamburg, Fed. Republic Germany, 1984, Yale U., 1985; hon. degree, U. Beijing, Peoples Republic China, 1987; DSc (hon.), U. Rome, 1988; hon. degree, Uppsala U., Sweden, 1991. Mem. staff mem. radiation lab. U. Calif., 1945-51, asst. prof., 1946-48, asso. prof., 1948-51; prof. physics Stanford U., 1951-62, prof. Stanford Linear Accelerator Ctr., 1962-89, prof. emeritus, 1989—; dir. Stanford (High Energy Physics Lab., Stanford Linear Accelerator Center), 1962-84, dir. emeritus, 1984—; Am. del. Conf. Cessation Nuclear Tests, Geneva, 1959; mem. President's Sci. Adv. Com., 1960-65; cons. Office Sci. and Tech., Exec. Office Pres., 1965-73, U.S. ACDA, 1968-81; mem. gen. adv. com. to White House, 1977-81; mem. panel Office of Sci. and Tech. Policy, 1977; with nat. def. rsch. Calif. Inst. Tech. and Los Alamos, 1942-45; mem. JASON, 1965—; chmn. bd. overseers Superconducting Supercollider Univs. Rsch. Assn., 1984-93; mem. com. to provide interim oversight DOE nuc. weapons complex NAS, 1988-89, mem. DOE panel on nuc. warhead dismantlement and spl. nuc. materials control, 1991-92; active Commn. Particles and Field of Internat. Union of Pure and Applied Physics, 1985-93. Decorated officer Legion of Honor; recipient Lawrence prize AEC, 1961, Nat. Medal Sci., 1969, Franklin medal, 1970, Ann. Pub. Service award Fedn. Am. Scientists, 1973, Enrico Fermi award Dept. Energy, 1979, Shoong Found. award for sci., 1983, Hilliard Roderick prize Sci. AAAS, 1991, Matteucei medal, 1997; named Calif. Scientist Yr., 1966. Fellow Am. Phys. Soc. (pres. 1974); mem. NAS (chmn. com. on internat. security and arms control 1985-93, CISAC mem. 1985—, mem. scis. com. on scholarly comm. with People's Republic of China 1987-92), AAAS, Am. Phys. Soc. (v.p., pres. 1974), Am. Philosophical Soc., Academie des Scis. (France, fgn. mem.), Russian Acad. Scis., Academia Nazionale deo Lincei (Italy), Phi Beta Kappa, Sigma Xi. Home: 25671 Chapin Rd Los Altos CA 94022-3413 Office: Stanford Linear Accelerator Ctr PO Box 4349 Palo Alto CA 94309-4349

PANSINI, MICHAEL SAMUEL, tax and financial consultant; b. Molfetta, Italy, July 12, 1928; came to U.S., 1935; s. Ralph and Isabel (Cirilli) P.; m. Anna D'Angelo, June 5, 1949 (div. 1970); children: Elizabeth, Valerie, Michael; m. Elizabeth Bischoff, Oct. 3, 1970 (div. Feb. 1992); 1 child, Elissa Michelle. B.S., NYU, 1950, M.B.A., 1952, LL.M., 1960; LL.D., Fordham U., 1956. Bar: N.Y. 1956, U.S. Tax Ct. Tax mgr. Pfizer Corp., N.Y.C., 1951-64; asst. treas. Hooker Chem. Corp., N.Y.C., 1964-69; treas., dir. United Indsl. Corp., N.Y.C., 1969-72; sr. v.p., gen. counsel Beker Industries Corp., Greenwich, Conn., 1972-87; pres., dir. Panmer, Inc., 1987—; tax, fin. cons., 1988—; v.p., corp. counsel Champion Energy Corp. and affiliates, 1991-93, Champion Holdings Co. and affiliates, 1993-96; v.p., chmn. various coms. Tax Exec. Inst., N.Y.C., 1963-72; pres., dir. Fed. Tax Forum, Inc., N.Y.C., 1961-72; dir. Intelligent Bus. Communications Corp. Mem. Rep. Town Com. 19th Dist., Stamford, Conn., 1993—; commr. Econ. Devel. Commn., Stamford, 1994—. Republican. Home and Office: 76 Lawrence Hill Rd Stamford CT 06903-2120

PANTAGES, LOUIS JAMES, lawyer; b. Plainfield, N.J., Apr. 29, 1916; s. Dimitrios Louis and Bessie (Massas) P.; m. Dorothea Carol Adams, Dec. 16, 1950; children: James, Peter, Elaine Marie. A.B., Rutgers U., 1938, LL.B., 1940. Bar: N.J. 1941, U.S. Dist. Ct. N.J. 1941, U.S. Dist. Ct. (so. dist.) N.Y. 1955, U.S. Supreme Ct. 1960, U.S. Ct. Appeals (3d cir.) 1967. Since practiced in Newark; with firm Cox & Walburg, 1938-54; partner Mead, Gleeson, Hansen & Pantages, 1954-68, Gleeson, Hansen & Pantages, 1968-72, Hansen, Pantages, Sellar & Zavesky, 1972-77, Pantages Sellar Richardson & Stuart, 1977-82, Stein, Bliablias, McGuire, Pantages & Gigl, 1982—; trial lawyer in cts. of N.J., U.S. Dist. cts. of N.J., U.S. Dist. Ct., So. Dist. N.Y., U.S. Supreme Ct., others. Capt. C.W.S., AUS, 1942-46; Capt. M.I., U.S. Army, 1950-52. Fellow Am. Coll. Trial Lawyers, Internat. Acad. Law and Sci.; mem. ABA, N.J. Bar Assn., Essex County Bar Assn., Am. Judicature Soc., Trial Attys. N.J., N.J. Def. Assn., Internat. Assn. Def. Counsel, Fedn. Ins. and Corp. Counsel, Def. Rsch. Inst., Am. Arbitration Assn., Arbitration Forums, Inc., Rutgers Law Sch. Alumni Assn., Essex Fells Country Club, Hellenic Univ. Club N.Y. Republican. Greek Orthodox. Avocations: art, antiques, music. Home: 36 Windemere Rd Upper Montclair NJ 07043-2544 Office: 354 Eisenhower Pky Livingston NJ 07039-1023

PANTAZELOS, PETER GEORGE, financial executive; b. Cambridge, Mass., Dec. 8, 1930; s. George P. and Marion (Nichols) P.; m. Hytho Haseotes, May 26, 1963; children—George, Marion. BSEE, Northeastern U., 1953; MSEE, MIT, 1955; Acctg. Cert., Bentley Corp., Waltham, Mass., 1975. Mgr. engring. dept. Thermo Electron Engring. Corp., Waltham, Mass., 1960-68; v.p. corp. planning Thermo Electron Corp., Waltham, Mass., 1968-72, v.p. ops. fin., 1972-80, exec. v.p., 1980—. Mem. IEEE, Am. Mgmt. Assn., Fin. Execs. Inst., Eta Kappa Nu, Tau Beta Pi, Sigma Xi. Mem. Greek Orthodox Ch. Club: Brae Burn (Newton, Mass.). Avocations: golfing; gardening. Office: Thermo Electron Corp 81 Wyman St Waltham MA 02154-1223

PANTEL, GLENN STEVEN, lawyer; b. Plainfield, N.J., Sept. 25, 1953; s. Donald and Sarah Libby (Pearlman) P.; m. Lisa Pamela Krop, June 28, 1981; 1 child, Adam Scott. AB, Johns Hopkins U., 1975; JD, U. Pa., 1978. Bar: N.J. 1978, U.S. Dist. Ct. N.J. 1978, Pa. 1978, Fla. 1980, U.S. Ct. Appeals (3d cir.) 1982. Law clk. to presiding judge U.S. Dist. Ct. (so. dist.), Miami, Fla., 1978-79; from assoc. to ptnr. Shanley & Fisher P.C., Morristown, N.J., 1979—, also bd. dirs. Trustee Friday Evening Club Cultural Presenters, Morristown, 1984—, Integrity, Inc., Drug and Alcohol Abuse Program, Newark; trustee, mem. scholarship com. 200 Club of Somerset County. Mem. ABA, Fla. Bar Assn., N.J. Bar Assn., Morris County Bar Assn., Phi Beta Kappa. Avocations: skiing, sailing. Home: 3 Cross Way Mendham NJ 07945-3120 Office: Shanley & Fisher PC 131 Madison Ave Morristown NJ 07960-6086

PANTENBURG, MICHEL, hospital administrator, health educator, holistic health coordinator; b. Denver, Oct. 6, 1926; d. Arthur Robert and Alice (McKenna) P. Diploma, Providence Nursing Sch., Kansas City, Kans., 1951; B.S. in Nursing Edn., St. Mary Coll., Leavenworth, Kans., 1958; M. in Nursing, Cath. U. Am., 1960. Joined Sisters of Charity, Roman Catholic Ch., 1945; lic. amateur radio operator. Dir. nursing Providence Hosp., Kansas City, Kans., 1958-62; nursing coordinator Sisters of Charity, Leavenworth, 1962-67; hosp. adminstr. St. Mary Hosp., Grand Junction, Colo., 1967-73, St. Vincent Hosp., Billings, Mont., 1973-84; dir. focus on leadership program Gonzaga U., Spokane, Wash., 1985-92; chaplain pastoral care dept. St. Marys Hosp. and Med. Ctr., Grand Junction, Colo., 1994—; dir. Norwest Bank, Billings. Co-author, editor: Management of Nursing (CHA award 1969), 1967. Bd. dirs. De Paul Hosp., Cheyenne, Wyo., 1980-96, Ronald McDonald House, Billings, 1982-85, St. Joseph Hosp., Denver, 1994-97. Named Woman of Yr., Bus. and Profl. Women, Billings, 1979. Mem. Cath. Hosp. Assn. (bd. dirs., sec.), Am. Hosp. Assn. (regional del. 1975-80), Am. Coll. Hosp. Adminstrn., Mont. Hosp. Assn. (pres.), Billings C. of C. (v.p. 1977-78). Avocations: hiking; skiing. Office: Pastoral Care Dept St Marys Hosp & Med Ctr Grand Junction CO 81501

PANTUSO, VINCENT JOSEPH, food service consultant; b. Charleston, W.Va., Aug. 13, 1940; s. Fortunato F. Pantuso and Josephine Malcom (Ginestra) Pantuso Messer; m. Carol Barber, Dec. 10, 1964 (div. 1976); children: Lisa, Barbara, Tina; m. Nancy Josephine Chellman, Sept. 30, 1978 (div. 1995). Student, Drexel U.; BSBA, St. Joseph's U., 1968; postgrad., Rollins Coll., 1984-85. Asst. mgr. Marriott Hotels, Inc., Bethesda, Md., 1962-64; v.p. sales mktg. ARA Services, Inc., Phila., 1964-72; sr. v.p. Inter-state United Corp., Chgo., 1972-84; pres. V.J. Pantuso Services, Inc., Orlando, Fla., 1984—, New Vista Services, Inc., 1988—. Mem. Nat. Assn. Concessionaires (bd. dirs. 1982—, pres. 1989-91, chmn. 1991-94, Master Concessionaire, Chgo. 1985), Nat. Assn. Food Equipment Mfrs. (doctorate 1989). Republican. Episcopalian. Club: Citrus (Orlando). Avocation: fishing. Home: 9325 Bay Vista Estate Blvd Orlando FL 32836-6304

PANUSKA, JOSEPH ALLAN, academic administrator; b. Balt., July 3, 1927; s. Joseph William and Barbara Agnes (Preller) P. BS, Loyola Coll., Balt., 1948; PhD, St. Louis U., 1958; STL, Woodstock Coll., 1961; LLD (hon.), U. Scranton, 1974; degree (hon.), Trnava (Slovakia) U., 1997. Joined S.J., 1948; ordained priest Roman Cath. Ch., 1960. Instr. dept. physiology Emory U. Sch. Medicine, 1962-63; asst. prof. biology Georgetown U., 1963-66, assoc. prof., 1966-72, prof., 1973; provincial, bd. dirs. Jesuit Conf. Md. Province (S.J.), 1973-79; acad. v.p., dean faculties, prof. biology Boston Coll., 1979-82; pres. U. Scranton, Pa., 1982—; mem. Pa. Commn. Ind. Colls. and Univs., 1982—, mem. exec. com., treas., 1987-91, vice chmn., 1988-89, chmn., 1990-91; mem. President's Commn., NCAA, 1989-90. Mem. editl. bd. Cryobiology, 1968-88, editor-in-chief, 1971-74; contbr. chpts. to books, articles to sci. rsch. jours. Mem. corp. Am. Found. Biol. Rsch., 1967-85, pres. bd. dirs., 1974-79, v.p., 1979-83; trustee Loyola Coll., 1979-85, St. Joseph's U., 1979-84, U. Scranton, 1970-73, St. Peter's Coll., 1971-72, Woodstock Coll., 1973-76, Fordham U., 1982-88, Cambridge Ctr. for Social Studies, 1973-79 (pres. 1973-79), Corp. Roman Cath. Clergymen, 1973-79 (pres. 1973-79); rector Jesuit Community at Georgetown U., 1970-73; bd. dirs. United Way Pa., 1985-87, Scranton Preparatory Sch., 1984-90, Scranton Area Found., 1997—; chmn. Pa. Commn. for Ind. Colls. and Univs., 1990-91; bd. dirs. John Carroll U., 1992—, Nat. Inst. Environ. Renewal, 1992—. NIH postdoctoral trainee, 1962-63; recipient Danforth Found. Harbison prize for disting. teaching, 1969, B'nai B'rith Americanism award, 1997; vis. fellow St. Edmunds Coll., Cambridge U., 1969. Mem. Am. Physiol. Soc., Soc. for Cryobiology, Soc. Exptl. Biology and Medicine, Assn. Jesuit Colls. and Univs. (bd. dirs. 1982—, treas. 1993—), Pa. Assn. Colls. and Univs. (exec. com., adv. com. to State Bd. Edn. 1990-91), Scranton C. of C. Home and Office: U Scranton Office of Pres Scranton PA 18510 *In order to be happy in a leadership role and to succeed in it, I have to possess a sense of coherence with my life values. I also need to recognize that my own activity makes a real difference in the empowerment of others so that there is a multiplier effect which extends me beyond my own person and activity.*

PANVINI, ROBERT S., physics researcher/educator; b. Bklyn., Apr. 22, 1937; m. Doria J. Bacigalupi, Aug. 16, 1959; 3 children. BS in Physics, Rensselaer Poly. Inst., 1958; postgrad., Brown U., 1958-60; PhD, Brandeis U., 1965. Research assoc. Brookhaven Nat. Lab., Upton, L.I., N.Y., 1965-67, asst. physicist, 1967-69, assoc. physicist, 1969-71; assoc. prof. physics Vanderbilt U., Nashville, 1971-80, prof., 1980—; organizer of 8 Vanderbilt High Energy Physics Confs., 1973-87; vis. staff physicist U.S. Dept. Energy, 1990-92. Contbr. over 100 articles to profl. jours. NSF research grantee, 1971—. Fellow Am. Phys. Soc. (divsn. particles and fields). Avocations: classical music, opera, travel, hiking, photography. Home: 200 Stokesboro Ct Nashville TN 37215-1572 Office: Vanderbilt U Dept Physics and Astronomy Nashville TN 37235

PANY, KURT JOSEPH, accounting educator, consultant; b. St. Louis, Mar. 31, 1946; s. Joseph Francis and Ruth Elizabeth (Westerman) P.; m. Darlene Dee Zabish, June 3, 1971; children: Jeffrey, Michael. BSBA, U. Ariz., 1968; MBA in Mgmt., U. Minn., 1971; PhD in Accountancy, U. Ill., 1977. CPA, Ariz., cert. fraud examiner. Staff auditor Arthur Andersen & Co., Mpls., 1968-69, Touche Ross & Co., Phoenix, 1971-73; teaching asst. U. Minn., Mpls., 1969-71; teaching asst. auditing and acctg. U. Ill., Urbana, 1972-76; asst. prof. acctg. Ariz. State U., Tempe, 1977-81, assoc. prof., 1981-85, Arthur Andersen/Don Dupont prof. acctg., 1985-91; mem. acctg. and auditing standards com. State of Ariz., Phoenix, 1989—; reviewer Jour. Acctg. and Pub. Policy, 1983—. Contbg. author: CPA Exam. Rev., 1983—; co-author: Principles of Auditing, 1988—, Auditing, 1993—; co-editor Auditing: A Jour. Practice and Theory, 1984-88; mem. editl. bd. Advances in Acctg., 1982—, Jour. Acctg. Edn., 1983—; reviewer Acctg. Rev., 1984—, ad hoc editor, 1989—; contbr. numerous articles to profl. jours. Active various child-related orgns. Peat, Marwick, Mitchell & Co. Found. grantee, 1985. Fellow AICPA (auditing stds. divsn. 1989-90, acctg. lit. selection com. 1989-90, acctg. lit. awards com. 1979-83, mem. auditing stds. bd. 1995—); mem. Am. Acctg. Assn. (tech. program com. 1980-81, chairperson Western region auditing sect. 1981-83, acctg. lit. nominating com. 1982-84, 88-89, acctg. lit. selection com. 1989-90, dir. auditing stds., chmn. auditing stds. com. 1989-90), Ariz. Soc. CPA's (auditing stds. com. 1978-81, ethics com. 1981-84). Avocation: baseball. Office: Ariz State U Sch of Accountancy Tempe AZ 85287

PANZARINO, SAVERIO JOSEPH, physician; b. East Orange, N.J., Nov. 29, 1930; s. Joseph Saverio and Pasqua (Binetti) P.; m. Suzanne Laico, Apr. 24, 1934; children: Laura, Kathleen. BA, Columbia Coll., 1952; MD, U. Rome, 1957. Diplomate Am. Bd. Surgery, Am. Bd. Pediat. Surgery. Intern St. Vincent's Hosp., N.Y.C., 1957-58; resident in gen. surgery Manhattan VA Hosp., N.Y.C., 1958-62; fellow in pediat. surgery Hosp. for Sick Children, London, 1962-63; pvt. practice, 1963-90; ret.; clin. assoc. surgery Columbia Coll. Physicians and Surgeons, N.Y.C., 1980-90; part-time med. legal cons., 1990—. Recipient Bowen Brooks scholarship N.Y. Acad. Medicine, 1962. Fellow ACS; mem. AMA, Am. Acad. Pediats. Home and Office: 10 Kenneth Ct Summit NJ 07901-2021

PANZER, MARY CAROLINE, museum curator; b. Flint, Mich., May 29, 1955; d. Milton and Caroline Alice (Weis) P. BA, Yale U.; MA, Columbia U., 1980; PhD, Boston U., 1990. Asst. prof. U. Kans., Lawrence, 1989-91; curator photographs Spencer Mus. Art, Lawrence, 1989-91; asst. dir. SMART Mus. Art, Chgo., 1991; curator photographs Nat. Portrait Gallery Smithsonian Instn., Washington, 1992—. Mem. Am. Studies Assn., Coll. Art Assn., Oracle, Mid-Atlantic Radical Historians Orgn., Orgn. Am. Historians. Office: Nat Portrait Gallery Smithsonian Instn Mrc # 213 Washington DC 20560

PANZER, MARY E., state legislator; b. Waupun, Wis., Sept. 19, 1951; d. Frank E. and Verna L. P.; 1 adopted child, Melissa. BA, U. Wis., 1974; mem., Wis. State Ho. Reps. from 53rd dist. Rep. State of Wis., Madison, 1980-93, senator, 1993—. Home: 635 W Tamarack Dr West Bend WI 53095-3653 Office: Wis State Senate State Capital Madison WI 53702

PANZER, MITCHELL EMANUEL, lawyer; b. Phila., Aug. 2, 1917; s. Max and Cecelia P.; m. Edith Budin, Apr. 13, 1943; children: Marcy C., Leslie S. Katz. AB with distinction and 1st honors, Temple U., 1937; JD magna cum laude, U. Pa., 1940; LLD honoris causa, Gratz Coll., 1972. Bar: Pa. 1942, U.S. Dist. Ct. (ea. dist.) Pa. 1948, U.S. Ct. Appeals (3d cir.) 1949, U.S. Supreme Ct. 1961. Gowen Meml. fellow U. Pa. Law Sch., 1940-41; law clk. Phila. Ct. Common Pleas, No. 7, 1941-42; assoc. Wolf, Block, Schorr and Solis-Cohen, Phila., 1946-54, ptnr., 1954-88, of counsel, 1988—; spl. adv. counsel Fed. Home Loan Mortgage Corp., Fed. Nat. Mortgage Assn., 1972-82; dir. emeritus, former counsel St. Edmond's Savs. and Loan Assn.; former dir. State Chartered Group, Pa. Bldg. and Loan Assn. Treas., Jewish Fedn. Greater Phila., 1981-82, v.p., 1982-86, trustee, 1963—, mem. exec. com., 1981-86, hon. life trustee, 1992—; trustee emeritus Pa. Land Title Inst., 1992—; bd. overseers Gratz Coll., 1958—, pres., 1962-68. Served to capt. USAF, 1942-46. Decorated Bronze Star medal; recipient Man of Year award Gratz Coll. Alumni Assn., 1964. Mem. Am. Coll. Real Estate Lawyers, ABA (chmn. spl. com. on residential real estate transactions 1972-73), Pa. Bar Assn. (mem. spl. com. on land titles), Phila. Bar Assn. (chmn. com. censors 1966, chmn. bd. govs. 1971, parliamentarian 1965-67, 71, chmn. charter and by-laws com. 1972), Jewish Pub. Soc. (trustee 1966-81, 85-88, v.p. 1972-75, sec. 1975-78), Order of Coif (pres. 1961-63, exec. com.). Jewish. Clubs: 21 Jewel Square (Phila.); Masons. Patentee in field. Home: 505 Oak Ter Merion Station PA 19066-1340 Office: Wolf Block Schorr & Solis-Cohen 12th Fl Packard Bldg 15th And Chestnut St Philadelphia PA 19102-2625

PAOLANTONIO, SAL, sports correspondent; b. Queens, N.Y.. BA in History, SUNY, Oneonta, 1977; M in Journalism, NYU, 1978. Reporter Albany Times Union; host Sat. Morning Sports Page Sta. WIP-AM, Phila., 1993-95; reporter Inquirer News Tonight Sta. WPHL-TV, Phila., 1994-95; polit. reporter Phila. Eagles Phila. Inquirer, 1985-93, beat reporter Phila. Eagles, 1993-95; NFL SportsCenter corr. ESPN, 1995—. Author: The Last Big Man in Big City America, 1993. With USN, 1979-83. Recipient Mng. Editor's award for enterprise reporting AP, 1985, Sports Editor award for Reporting, 1994. Office: care ESPN ESPN Pla Bristol CT 06010-8005

PAOLINI, GILBERTO, literature and science educator; b. L'Aquila, Italy; naturalized citizen, 1954; s. John and Assunta A. (Turavani) P.; m. Claire Jacqueline Landro; children: Angela Janet, John Frank. B.A., U. Buffalo, 1957, M.A., 1959; postgrad., Middlebury Coll., summer 1960, 61; Ph.D., U. Minn., 1965. Lectr. Spanish Rosary Hill Coll., Buffalo, 1957-58; instr. Italian and Latin lit. U. Mass., Amherst, 1958-60; instr. Spanish and Italian Syracuse U., 1962-65, asst. prof., 1965-67; assoc. prof. Spanish lit. Tulane U., New Orleans, 1967-76, prof., 1976—; dir. Tulane scholars and honors program Tulane U., 1981-83, chmn. colloquia dept., 1981-83; originator Spanish Culture Week, New Orleans, 1977, 79; chmn. adv. com. Jambalaya program Nat. Endowment Humanities, New Orleans, 1975-80; Spanish essay reader Ednl. Testing Svc., Princeton, 1979-85; co-founder, gen. chmn. La. Conf. on Hispanic Langs. and Lits., 1981, 83, 85, 87, 89, 93, 95. Author: Bartolome Soler: novelista: Procedimientos estilísticos, 1963; An Aspect of Spiritualistic Naturalism in the Novel of B.P. Galdos: Charity, 1969; mem. editorial bd.: Forum Italicum, 1967-71, Critica Hispanica, 1979—, Discurso Literario, 1985—, Letras Peninsulares, 1987—; assoc. editor: South Central MLA Bull, 1978-80; editor: La Chispa'81: Selected Procs., 1981, Papers on Romance Literary Relations, 1983, La Chispa '83: Selected Procs., 1983, La Chispa '85: Selected Procs., 1985, La Chispa '87: Selected Procs. 1987, La Chispa '89: Selected Procs., 1989, La Chispa '93: Selected Procs. 1993; cons. editor South Central Rec., 1988-92; contbr. articles to profl. jours. With AUS, 1952-54, USAFRES, 1954-57. Recipient Disting. Service award Sociedad Espanola, 1979, Knight Cross of Order of Isabel the Catholic, 1984. Mem. MLA, AAUP, Am. Assn. Tchrs. Spanish and Portuguese (chmn. pub. rels. com. 1981-86, pres. La. chpt. 1979-81, 88-89), Am. Assn. Tchrs. Italian, Am. Assn. Advancement Humanities, Soc. for Lit. and Sci., Asociacion Internacional de Hispanistas, Southeastern Am. Soc. 18th Century Studies (exec. v.p.), Asociacion Internacional de Galdosistas, Sociedad de Literature Española del Siglo XIX, Phi Sigma Iota, Sigma Delta Pi (v.p. for S.W. 1989-92). Office: Tulane Univ 304 Newcomb Hall New Orleans LA 70118

PAOLINO, RICHARD FRANCIS, manufacturing company executive; b. Fall River, Mass., Feb. 16, 1945; s. Emelio and Sylvia (Fasciani) P.; m. Elizabeth Jane Maloney, Sept. 9, 1973; children: Christopher Matthew, Kathryn Elizabeth. AB in Engring. Sci., Dartmouth Coll., 1967; MBA in Mktg. and Fin., U. Chgo., 1973. Plant engr. Polaroid Corp., Cambridge, Mass., 1967; from salesman to asst. br. mgr., Fed. Products Corp., Chgo., 1967-74; area mgr., nat. accounts mgr., Husky Injection Molding Systems, Chgo. and Toronto, Can., 1974-76; v.p. mktg. Quality Measurement Systems Inc., Penfield, N.Y., 1976-78; dir. mktg. Automation and Measurement div. Bendix Corp., Dayton, Ohio, 1978-82; gen. mgr. Boice div. MTI, Latham, N.Y., 1982-85; v.p., gen. mgr. coordinate Measuring Sys. Divsn., Brown &

Sharpe Mfg. Co., North Kingstown, R.I., 1985-94; v.p., gen. mgr. comml. ops. Measuring Sys. Group Worldwide, 1995-97; pres., CEO DEA SpA, Turin, Italy, 1995-96; CEO Dynisco, Inc., Sharon, Mass., 1997—; pres., mng. dir. DEA Iberica, Barcelona, Spain, DEA France, Villebon Sur Yvette, France, Brown and Sharpe Cos.; condr. seminars, lectr. in field. Bd. dirs. Automation Software, Inc., Providence, R.I., Leitz Messtechnik GmbH, Wetzlar, Germany, Brown & Sharpe-Precizika, Vilinus, Lithuania. 1st lt. USMCR, 1967-69. Mem. Soc. Mfg. Engrs. (past chmn. quality assurance tech. coun.), Am. Soc. Quality Control, Machinery and Allied Products Mktg. Coun., Mfr.'s Alliance for Productivity and Innovation (gen. mgrs. coun.), Assn. Mfg. Tech. Address: 16 Quincy Adams Rd Barrington RI 02806-5024 Office: Dynisco Inc Four Commercial St Sharon MA 02067

PAOLINO, RONALD MARIO, clinical psychologist, consultant, psychopharmacologist, pharmacist; b. Providence, Mar. 15, 1938; s. Lawrence and Mary Corinne (Guglielmi) P.; m. Eileen Frances Quimby, June 18, 1960; children: Lisa Katherine, David Lawrence. Student, Providence Coll., 1955-56; BS in Pharmacy, U. R.I., 1959; PhD in Pharmacology/Toxicology, Purdue U., 1963; postdoctoral studies Exptl. Psychology, Yale U., 1963-65; postdoctoral studies in clin. psychology, Purdue U., 1972-74; postdoctoral studies in existential analytic psychotherapy, Okla. Inst. Existential Analysis and Psychotherapy, 1974-75; Hostage Negotiation, FBI, 1991, Advanced Hostage Negotiation, 1995; Crisis Negotaition, FBI Acad., 1994; MA (hon.), Brown U., 1977. Lic. psychologist, R.I., pharmacist R.I.; nat. registered health svc. provider in psychology; cert. arbitrator; cert. nat. registered group psycho-therapists; cert. edn. provider N.Y.; Diplomate Am. Coll. Forensic Examiners, Am. Bd. Forensic Examiners, Am. Bd. Forensic Medicine. Intern dept. psychiatry and behavioral scis. U. Okla. Health Scis. Ctr., 1974-75; David Ross predoctoral fellow dept. pharmacology/toxicology Purdue U., 1961-63; NIMH postdoctoral fellow in psychology dept. psychology Yale U., 1963-65; asst. prof. pharmacology U. Conn. Sch. Pharmacy, 1965-67; assoc. prof. psychopharmacology Purdue U., 1967-74; NIMH fellow in clin. psychology U. Okla. Health Scis. Ctr., 1974-75; coord. group psychotherapy tng. program Brown U. Program in Medicine, 1983-85, assoc. prof. psychiatry and human behavior, 1976-90; pvt. practice; chief drug dependency treatment program VA Med. Ctr., Providence, 1975-87, dir. biofeedback clinic, 1977-87, primary hostage negotiator, 1991—; primary hostage negotiator, 1991, Psychiatric Cons. VA Police alternate Dispute Resolution Mediator, New Eng. Veterans Integrated Svc. Network, 1996—; mem. Pharmacology and Therapeutic Agts. Com., 1979-87, VA Med. Ctr., coord. VA Contracted Half-Way Project for Substance Dependent Vets., 1981-85, chmn. Pain Mgmt. Task Force, 1984-85, mem. Supervisory Level Pharmacy Profl. Standards Bd., 1990—, mem. Mgmt. Suicidal and Violent Patient Task Force, 1990-91, chmn. Com. Prevention & Mgmt. of Disturbed Behaviors, 1991—, chief crisis mgmt. program, 1993-96, advisor FBI Hostage Negotiations, 1991—, Instr. R.I. State Police Acad., 1994, Instr., Drug Recognition Experts Recert PRGM, R.I. Dept Health, 1995, Faculty, Law Enforcement Mgmt. Command Sch. U.R.I., 1991—, Va. Nat. Law Enforcement Tng. Ctr., 1997; chmn. Outpatient Psychiatry Svcs. Reorganization Task Force, 1991, mem. VA-Dept. Def. Desert Storm Emergency Plan Com., 1991; advisor OSHA Dept. Labor for Violence in the Work Place, 1994—; mem. E. Prov. Clergy & Mental Health Providers Alliance, 1995—; mem. substance abuse and prevention grant application rev. com. R.I. Adv. Coun. on Substance Abuse, 1982—, prevention, edn. and tng. com. on substance abuse, 1981—, chmn. 1981-82; adj. assoc. prof. psychology, U. R.I., 1982—; mem. planning com. State Conf. on Substance Abuse in the Hispanic Community, 1986; mem. alcohol awareness commn. Episc. Diocese of R.I., 1983-85; gubernatorial appointee Gov.'s Permanent Coun. on Drug Abuse Control, 1978-82; mem. rev. com. for funding of state drug abuse programs R.I. Single State Agy. on Drug Abuse, R.I. Dept. Mental Health Retardation and Hosps., 1978-82; cons. Nurses Renewal Com., 1980-81, substance abuse prevention edn. for elem. sch. children R.I. chpt. ARC, 1977, mem. suicide prevention steering com., 1977; mem.Interagy. Drug Abuse Steering Com., Lafayette, Ind. 1969-72; bd. dirs. Providence VA Med. Ctr. Credit Union; mem. bd. cert. for alcoholism counselors R.I. Assn. Alcohol Counselors, 1979-81; mem. Gov.'s Task Force on Substance Abuse at Adult Correctional Instn., 1977-78, Gov.'s Task Force on Mental Health Svcs. at Adult Correctional Instn., 1977-78, chmn. reclassification of inmates com., 1977-78; chmn. com. on edn. and cert. biofeedback practioners Conn. Biofeedback Soc., 1977-78; summer faculty fellow U. Conn., 1967; vis. scientist lectr. Assn. Am. Colls. Pharmacy, 1972-73; cons. to bus., unions, law enforcement. Author: (2 chpts.) Drug Testing: Issues and Options, 1991; contbr. 37 articles to profl. jours. Bd. dirs. R.I. chpt. Samaritans Internat. Suicide Prevention Orgn., 1978-84; v.p. Experience Jesus Inc.; mem. cmty adv. bd. Cpina Bifida Assn. R.I., 1980-83; mem. R.I. East Bay Clergy and Mental Health Profls. Coun.; congressman appointee (Patrick J. Kennedy); mem. veterans adv. commn., 1995—. Recipient Citation award for svc. and contbns. to formulation of state policy for treatment and prevention of drug abuse Gov. R.I., 1983, Letter of Commendation, Gov.'s R.I. Adv. Coun. on Substance Abuse, 1986, vc. Recognition award DAV, 1990, Spl. Contbn. award Providence VA Med Ctr., 1990. Mem. APA, Am. Coll. Forensic Examiners, Am. Psychotherapy Assn., Am. Soc. Pharmacology Exptl. Therapeutics, Internat. Brain Rsch. Orgn., Internat. Narcotic Enforcement Officers Assn., R.I. Group Psychotherapy Soc. (pres. 1991-93, continuing edn. dir. psychologists 1990—, exec. bd. 1986—, tng. faculty 1985—, co-dir. tng. 1986-87, tng. adv. bd. 1985-86), R.I. Psychol. Assn. (chmn. substance abuse ins. subcom. 1986-87, rep. Gov.'s Coun. on Mental Health State Plan Com. 1982-84), Hostage Negotiators of Am., R.I. East Bay Clergy and Mental Health Providers Alliance. Office: Mental Health Providers Alliance PO Box 159 Barrington RI 02806-0159

PAOLUCCI, ANNE ATTURA, playwright, poet, English and comparative literature educator; b. Rome; d. Joseph and Lucy (Guidoni) Attura; m. Henry Paolucci. BA, Barnard Coll; MA, Columbia U., PhD, 1963; hon. degree, Lehman Coll., CUNY, 1995. Mem. faculty English dept. Brearley Sch., N.Y.C., 1957-59; asst. prof. English and comparative lit. CCNY, 1959-69; univ. research prof. St. John's U., Jamaica, N.Y., 1969—; prof. English St. John's U., 1975—, acting head dept. English, 1973-74, chmn. dept. English, 1982-91, dir. doctor of arts degree program in English, 1982—; Fulbright lectr. in Am. drama U. Naples, Italy, 1965-67; spl. lectr. U. Urbino, summers 1966-67, U. Bari, 1967, univs. Bologna, Catania, Messina, Palermo, Milan, Pisa, 1965-67; disting. adj. vis. prof. Queens Coll., CUNY; bd. dirs. World Centre for Shakespeare Studies, 1972—; spl. guest Yugoslavia Ministry of Culture, 1972; rep. U.S. at Internat. Poetry Festival, Yugoslavia, 1981; founder, exec. dir. Council on Nat. Lits., 1974—; mem. exec. com. Conf. Editors Learned Jours.-MLA, 1975—; del. to Fgn. Lang. Jours., 1977—; mem. adv. bd. Commn. on Tech. and Cultural Transformation, UNESCO, 1978—; vis. fellow Humanities Research Centre, Australian Nat. U., 1979; rep. U.S. woman playwright Inter-Am. Women Writers Congress, Ottawa, Ont., Can., 1978; organizer, chmn. profl. symposia, meetings; TV appearances; hostess Mags. in Focus, Channel 31, N.Y.C., 1971-72; mem. N.Am. Adv. Council Shakespeare Globe Theatre Center, 1981—; mem. Nat. Grad. Fellows Program Fellowship Bd., 1985—; mem. Garibaldi Centennial Com., 1981; mem. Nat. Grad. Fellows Program, 1985—; trustee Edn. Scholarship, Grants Com. of NIAF, 1990—; guest speaker with E. Albee Ohio No. State U., 1990. Author (with H. Paolucci) books, including: Hegel On Tragedy, 1962, From Tension to Tonic: The Plays of Edward Albee, 1972, Pirandello's Theater: The Recovery of the Modern Stage for Dramatic Art, 1974, Poems Written for Sbek's Mummies, Marie Menken, and Other Important Persons, Places, and Things, 1977, Eight Short Stories, 1977, Sepia Prints, 1985, 2nd edit., 1986; plays include: Minions of the Race (Medieval and Renaissance Conf. of Western Mich. U. Drama award 1972), Cipango!, 1985, pub. as book, 1985, 86, videotape excerpts, 1986, revision, 1990; performed N.Y.C. and Washington, 1987-88, Winterthur Mus., U. Del., 1990; The Actor in Search of His Mask, 1987, Italian translation and prodn., Genoa, 1987, The Short Season, Naples, 1967, Cubiculo, N.Y., 1973, German translation, Vienna, 1996, Three Short Plays, 1995; poems Riding the Mast Where It Swings, 1980, Gorbachev in Concert, 1991, Queensboro Bridge (and other Poems), 1995 (Pulitzer prize nominee 1995-96), Terminal Degrees, 1997; contbr. numerous articles, rev. to profl. jours.; editor, author introduction to: Dante's Influence on American Writers, 1977; gen. editor ...pe-cassette series China, 1977, 78; founder Coun. on Nat. Lit.; gen. editor ...ies Rev. Nat. Lits., 1970—, CNL/Quar. World Report, 1974-76, semi..., 1977-84, ann., 1985—; full-length TV tape of play Cipango! for pub. ...V and ednl. TV with original music by Henry Paolucci, 1990. Bd. dirs. Italian Heritage and Culture City-wide com., 1986—; Pres. Reagan appointee Nat. Grad. Fellows Program Fellowship Bd., 1985-86, Nat. Coun. Humanities, 1986—, Ann. award, FIERI, 1990; pres. Columbus: Countdown, 1992 Fedn.; mem. Gov. Cuomo's Heritage Legacy Project for Schs., 1989—; bd. dirs. Am. Soc. Italian Legions of Merit (chmn. cultural com. 1990—); trustee CUNY, 1996—, chairwoman bd. trustees, 1997—; mem. adv. com. on edn. N.Y. State Senate, 1996—. Named one of 10 Outstanding Italian Ams. in Washington, awarded medal by Amb. Rinaldo Petrignani, 1986; named Cavaliere Italian Republic, 1986, "Commendatore" of the Italian Republic Order of Merit, 1992; recipient Notable Rating for Mags. in Focus series N.Y. Times, 1972, Woman of Yr. award Dr. Herman Henry Scholarship Found., 1973, Amita award, 1970, award Women's Press Club N.Y., 1974, Order Merit, Italian Republic, 1986, Gold medal for Quincentenary Can. trustee NIAF, 1990, ann. awards Consortium of Italian-Am. Assns., 1991, Am.-Italian Hist. Assn., 1991, 1st Columbus award Cath. Charities, 1991, Leone di San Marco award Italian Heritage Coun. of Bronx and Westchester Counties, 1992, Children of Columbus award Order of Sons of Italy in Am., 1993, 1st Nat. Elena Cornaro award Order of Sons of Italy, 1993, Golden Lion award OSIA, 1997, Ann. award Am. Italian Cultural Roundtable, 1997, Am. Italian Tchrs. Lifetime Achievement award, 1997, Italian-Am. Legislator's award, Albany, 1997, N.Y. State Italian-Am. Legis. Lifetime Achievement award, 1997; Columbia U. Woodbridge hon. fellow, 1961-62; Am. Council Learned Socs. grantee Internat. Pirandello Congress, Agrigento, Italy, 1978. Mem. Internat. Shakespeare Assn., Shakespeare Assn. Am., Renaissance Soc. Am., Renaissance Inst. Japan, Internat. Comparative Lit. Assn., Am. Comparative Lit. Assn., MLA, Am. PEN, Hegel Soc. Am., Dante Soc. Am. (v.p. 1976-77), Am. Found. Italian Arts and Letters (founder, pres.), Pirandello Soc. (pres. 1978—), Nat. Soc. Lit. and Arts, Nat. Book Critics Circle, Am. Soc. Italian Legions of Merit (bd. dirs. 1990—). Office: St Johns U Dept English Jamaica NY 11439 *My own first practical premise has been to organize every task (even routine chores) so that there is always time and energy for whatever important projects come up. There is enough room in the day for doing a number of things—and for creating "space" every so often to do one's own special work (writing fiction or poetry or plays, in my case). Organization is all-important; but perhaps the basic premise in intellectual things is organic growth, letting "in" those things that are meaningful because they already suggest an intrinsic pattern. In my case, I discovered long after the projects and books themselves had taken shape and had been published, that I had been tending for a number of years more and more exclusively toward drama and dramatic criticism and theory. Well, that, obviously, was my own potential "law" organizing from within my various interests. One must continue to allow for new interests to revitalize those already familiar.*

PAONE, PETER, artist; b. Phila., Oct. 2, 1936; s. George and Angelina (Vitrella) P.; m. Alma Alabilikian, 1976. B.A., Phila. Mus. Coll. Art, 1958. Instr. Phila. Mus. Coll. Art, Pratt Inst., others; head graphics dept. Fleisher Art Meml., 1959-62; tchr. Pa. Acad. Fine Arts, 1978—, also chmn. graphics dept.; instr. Positano Art Sch., Italy, 1961. One man shows include Ft. Worth Mus., 1963, Grippi Gallery, 1959, 60, 61, Phila. Print Club, 1961-64, 83, Robinson Gallery, Houston, 1978-79, Pa. Acad. Fine Arts, 1983, Ryder Coll., Pa., 1991, Merlin Verlag, Hamburg, Germany, 1996; exhibited in group shows at Phila. Mus. Art, 1960, 61, 63, Contemporary Am., 1961, Lehigh (Pa.) U., Bklyn. Mus., 1962, Paris Biennial, 1963, Dallas Mus., Otis Art Inst., L.A., Syracuse U., 1964, La Escuela Nacional, Mexico City, Vanderbilt U., N.Y. World's Fair, Exhbn. Pakistan, 1967, Clydie Jessop Gallery, London, 1968, David Gallery, Houston, Kennedy Gallery, N.Y.C., 1970-72, Hooks-Epstein Gallery, 1978, 80, 81, 82, 83, 85, 87, 88, 90, Rider Coll. N.J., 1991, Merlin Verlag, 1996, Dresden, Germany, 1996; represented in permanent collections of Libr. of Congress, Phila. Mus. Art, Sumner Found., N.Y. Mus. Modern Art, Princeton Libr., Phila. Libr., Gen. Mills, Phila. Print Club, Rosenwald Collection, Carl Sandburg Meml. Libr., Syracuse U., Ft. Worth Mus., Victoria and Albert Mus., Brit. Mus., Art Inst. Chgo., Yale U. Recipient award of merit Phila. Print Club, 1983; Tiffany Found. grantee, 1962, 64; John Simon Guggenheim fellow, 1965-66; grantee Penn Council for the Arts, 1985. Mem. NAD (assoc.). Home: 1027 W Westview St Philadelphia PA 19119-3718 *Somewhere between the world of realism and surrealism, there is a world that deals with the reality of relationships, favoring the substance of the imagination rather than the substance of everyday vision. Objects that seemingly have no real relationship to each other in their existence are juxtaposed in the life of the artist. They have touched each other and have become part of the vision, and in turn have become his iconography. There is no urgency in this vision. The private reality has always been there and always will be. The viewer is allowed to question his knowledge of it, and in doing so, he often is uneasy and bewildered before the assemblage. This, at first, implies fantasy; this is not true. Instead, this is a reconstruction of reality, not an escape from it.*

PAP, BEATRIZ DÍAZ, secondary education educator; b. Arequipa, Peru, Dec. 2, 1948; came to U.S., 1977; d. Jésus Heradio Díaz Vargas and Elisa (Huamán) Díaz Peralta; m. Federico Vera Ponce de León, May 22, 1965 (div. 1977); 1 child, Edson Giovanni; m. Leo Pap Dorn, Oct. 27, 1977. BS in Spanish, San Agustin U., 1974; MS in Gen. Edn., SUNY, New Paltz, 1978-81, postgrad. Cert. elementary and secontary tchr., French and Spanish lang. tchr., N.Y. Tchr. Spanish Huguenot Nursery Sch., New Paltz, N.Y., 1983; tchr. elem. bilingual Ellenville (N.Y.) Sch. Dist., 1984-85; tchr. Spanish Poughkeepsie (N.Y.) Sch. Dist., 1985-86, Liberty (N.Y.) Sch. Dist., 1986-88, Fla. Unified Sch. Dist., Fla., N.Y., 1988-89; tchr. Spanish-French Hyde Park (N.Y.) Sch. Dist., 1989-91; tchr. Spanish Greenburgh Eleven Unified Sch. Dist., Dobbs Ferry, N.Y., 1991—, Copake-Taconic Hills Sch., Hillsdale, N.Y., 1995-96, FDR Sch., Bristol Twp., Pa., 1996-97; substitue tchr. Newburgh, Wallkill, Onteora Sch. Dists., Poughkeepsie, N.Y., 1982-83; exec. sec. Hotels & Restaurants Assn., Arequipa, Peru, 1972-73; mem. asst. Radio Club Dr. Oscar Guillen, Arequipa, 1971. Chair woman fund Dem. Com., New Paltz, 1991-92; mem. fundraising com. Multicultural Edn., New Paltz, 1992; mem. Mid. Sch. Steering Com., 1989-91, Multicultural Edn. Com., 1991—, steering com. Maurice Hinchey Nat. Bilingual Edn., 1980—. Fulbright Hays fellow to Dominican Rep., 1991; faculty grantee SUNY, 1978, 83-84. Mem. NAFE, Am. Assn. Tchrs. Spanish, N.Y. Fgn. Lang. Tchrs. Assn. (pres.), N.Y. Union Tchrs., Faculty Wives and Women (pres. 1989-92). Avocations: photography, video production, handicrafts, reading, golf. Home: 1 Rita St New Paltz NY 12561-2117 Office: Greenburgh Eleven Unified Sch Dist PO Box 501 Dobbs Ferry NY 10522-0501

PAPA, VINCENT T., financial insurance company executive; b. Bklyn., Dec. 11, 1946; s. Frank R. and Carmela (Farruggia) P.; m. Karen Ann Conroy, July 4, 1969; children: Kimberly, Jennifer, Kristen. BBA, Hofstra U., 1969; AAS, Nassau Community Coll., 1967; CPA, N.Y. Staff acct. Arthur Andersen & Co., N.Y.C., 1969-72; comptroller Finserv Corp., N.Y.C., 1972-80; sr. v.p. Orion Capital Corp., N.Y.C., 1980—; chmn. bd. dirs. William H. McGee & Co., Inc., N.Y.C. Mem. AICPA, Nat. Assn. Corp. Treas., Am. Mgmt. Assn. (mem. ins. and risk mgmt. coun.), N.Y. State Soc. CPAs, Ins. Soc. N.Y. Office: Wm H McGee Co Inc Two World Trade Ctr New York NY 10048

PAPADAKIS, CONSTANTINE N., university executive; b. Athens, Greece, Feb. 2, 1946; came to U.S., 1969; s. Nicholas and Rita (Masciotti) P.; m. Eliana Apostolides, Aug. 28, 1971; 1 child, Maria. Diploma in Civil Engring., Nat. Tech. U. Athens, 1969; MS in Civil Engring., U. Cin., 1970; PhD in Civil Engring., U. Mich., 1973. Registered profl. engr., Ohio, Greece. Engring. specialist, geotechnical group Bechtel, Inc., Gaithersburg, Md., 1974-76; supr. and asst. chief engr. geotechnical group Bechtel, Inc., Ann Arbor, Mich., 1976-81; v.p., bd. dirs. water resources div. STS Cons. Ltd., Ann Arbor, 1981-84; v.p. water and environ. resources dept. Tetra Tech-Honeywell, Pasadena, Calif., 1984; head dept. civil engring. Colo. State U., Ft. Collins, 1984-86; dean Coll. Engring. U. Cin., 1986-95, dir. Groundwater Rsch. Ctr., 1986-95; dir. Ctr. Hill Solid and Hazardous Waste Rsch. Ctr. EPA, Cin., 1986-93; pres. Drexel U., Phila., 1995—; adj. prof. civil engring. U. Mich., 1976-83; cons. Gaines & Stern Co., Cleve., 1983-84, Honeywell Europe, Maintal, Fed. Republic of Germany, 1984-85, Arthur D. Little, Boston, 1984-85, Camargo Assocs., Ltd., Cin., 1986, King Fahd U. Rsch. Inst., Dhahran, Saudi Arabia, 1987, King Abdulaziz City for Sci. and Tech., Riyadh, Saudi Arabia, 1991, Henderson & Bodwell Cons. Engrs. Inc., 1991, Cin. Met. Sewer Dist., 1992, Ohio River Valley Water Sanitation Commn., 1994; acting pres. Ohio Aerospace Inst., 1988-90; interim pres. Inst. Advanced Mfg. Scis. Ohio Edison Tech. Ctr., 1989-90; bd. govs. Edison Materials Tech. Ctr., 1988-95; adv. bd., founding mem. Hamilton County Bus. Incubator, 1988-95; bd. dirs. Nat. Commn. for Coop. Edn., U. City Sci. Ctr., Ben Franklin Tech. Ctr., WHYY Inc., Fidelity Fed. Bank, Opera Co. of Phila., Corcell, Inc., Greater Phila. First, Hellenic Coll./Holy Cross Acad. Author: Problems on Strength of Materials, 1968, Sewer Systems Design, 1969; editor: Fluid Transients and Acoustics, 1978, Pump-Turbine Schemes, 1979, Small Hydro Power Fluid Machinery, 1982; Megatrends in Hydraulics, 1987; contbr. more than 65 articles to profl. jours. Mem. Greater Cin. C. of C. Blue Chip Campaign for Econ. Devel. Task Force, 1988-93, bd. dirs. Bus. Assistance Ctr., 1989-95; mem. Ohio Coun. on Rsch. and Econ. Devel., 1988, Ohio Sci. and Tech. Commn. Adv. Group, 1989-90, 92-95; coun. mem. St. Nicholas Ch. Parish, Ann Arbor, 1981-84; mem. City of Ft. Collins Drainage Bd., 1984-86; bd. dirs. Dan Beard coun. Boy Scouts Am., 1995, Intelligent Vehicle Hwy. Soc. Ohio, 1994-95; bd. dirs. Liberty Bell Coun. of the Boy Scouts of Am., 1996—. Recipient Horace W. King scholarship civil engring. dept. U. Mich., 1971-73, 6 Bechtel Merit awards, 1974-79, Young Engr. of Yr. award Mich. Soc. Profl. Engrs., Ann Arbor, Mich., 1982, Disting. Engr. award Engrs. and Scientists Cin. Tech. Socs. Coun., 1989, Acad. of Achievement in Edn. award Am. Hellenic Ednl. Progressive Assn., 1995, Hellenic Univ. Club of Phila. Achievement award, 1996, Krikos Disting. Hellene Leader award, 1996. Fellow ASCE (pres. Ann Arbor br. 1980-81, pres.-elect Mich. sect. 1983-84, hydraulics divsn. publ. com. 1980-83), ASME (chmn. fluid transients com. 1978-80, mem. fluids engring. divsn. awards com. 1981-84), Am. Soc. Engring. Edn.; mem. NSPE (legis. and govt. affairs com. 1994-95, chair profl. engrs. in edn. divsn. 1995), Order of the Engr., Internat. Assn. for Hydraulic Rsch., Ohio Engring. Dean's Coun. (chmn.-elect 1989-91), Rotary, Sigma Xi, Chi Epsilon, Tau Beta Pi. Greek Orthodox. Avocations: photography, classical music, travel, swimming, racquetball. Home: 103 Airedale Rd Bryn Mawr PA 19010 Office: Drexel Univ 3141 Chestnut St Philadelphia PA 19104-2816

PAPADAKIS, EMMANUEL PHILIPPOS, physicist, consultant; b. N.Y.C., Dec. 25, 1934; s. Philippos E. and Helen (Eastman) P.; m. Stella Christopher, Sept. 4, 1960; children: Susan H., Philip E., Christopher E., Nicholas E. S.B. in Physics, M.I.T., 1956, Ph.D. in Physics, 1962; M.M. in Mgmt, U. Mich., 1979. Mem. tech. staff Bell Telephone Labs., Allentown, Pa., 1962-69; dept. head Panametrics, Inc., Waltham, Mass., 1969-73; prin. staff engr. Ford Motor Co., Detroit, 1973-75, supr., 1975-87; ptnr. E&S Antiques, Ames, Iowa, 1978—, pres. Quality Systems Concepts Inc., 1991—; assoc. dir. Ctr. for Nondestructive Evaluation, Iowa State U., Ames, 1988-95; adj. prof. Northeastern U. ext., Waltham, 1970-73, elec. engring. and computer engring. Iowa State U., 1988-95; cons. quality, NDT, TQM, ISO-9000, acoustics and ultrasonic testing sys., 1969-73, 88—. Contbr. numerous articles on electronics, ultrasonics, acoustics, nondestructive testing, crystallography and quality to profl. jours.; assoc. editor IEEE Transactions on Ultras, Ferroelectrics and Frequency Control, 1972-92; assoc. tech. editor Materials Evaluation, 1975-87, rsch. coord., 1980-86, quality concepts coord., 1986-88, tech. editor, 1988—; reviewer various jours. in physics, testing materials and sci. instrumentation; reviewer proposals to various govtl. agencies. Fellow IEEE, Acoustical Soc. Am. (Biennial award 1968), Am. Soc. for Nondestructive Testing (Mehl honor lectr. 1979, tutorial award 1993); mem. ASTM, Am. Phys. Soc., Soc. Mfg. Engrs., Am. Soc. Metals, Am. Soc. Quality Control, Soc. Automotive Engrs., Soc. Engring. Mechanics, Sigma Xi. Patentee in field; developer method and instrument for measuring ultrasonic velocity, method for bonding thin slabs to substrates, instrument for sheet metal texture determination, method using DSSS in ultrasonic flaw detection. Office: QSC Inc PO Box 1229 379 Diem Woods Dr New Holland PA 17557-8800

PAPADAKIS, MYRON PHILIP, lawyer, educator, pilot; b. N.Y.C., Dec. 11, 1940; s. Philip E. and Helen (Eastman) P.; m. Ann Hall, Sept. 1968; children: Wade, Nicholas. BS in Mech. Engring., U. Nebr., 1963; JD, South Tex. Coll. Law, 1974. Bar: Tex. 1975. Pilot, capt. Delta Airlines, Houston, 1970—; pvt. practice Papadakis et al, Houston, 1975-90; of counsel Slack & Davis, Austin, Tex., 1994—; adj. prof. South Tex. Coll. Law, Houston, 1980—. Co-author: Best of Trial-Products Liability, 1991, Aviation Accident Reconstruction and Litigation, 1995; contbr. articles to profl. jours. Lt. USN, 1963-69. Fellow Internat. Soc. Air Safety Investigators (chmn. ethics com. 1986-92); mem. Million Dollar Advocates Forum, ATLA (vice chmn. aviation sect.). Avocations: flying, test flying, photography, fishing. Home: 5214 Buckman Mtn Austin TX 78746 Office: Slack and Davis Ste 2110 8911 N Capital of Tex Hwy Austin TX 78759-7247

PAPADAKOS, DOROTHY JEAN, composer, organist; b. Coral Gables, Fla., Oct. 22, 1960; d. Peter James Papadakos and Dorothy Mae Johnson. BA, Barnard Coll., 1982; MM, Juilliard Sch., 1986. Organist, choirmaster St. Mark's Ch., Islip, N.Y., 1980-85; asst. organist Cathedral of St. John the Divine, N.Y.C., 1987-89, cathedral organist, 1990—; artistic dir. Vespers Improvisation Series, Cathedral St. John the Divine, N.Y.C., 1995; mem. Paul Winter Consort, Litchfield, Conn., 1984—; project dir. Gt. Organ Restoration Fund, Cathedral St. John the Divine, N.Y.C., 1990—. Composer: (orch. works for ballet) Triantafilia, 1992, Overture and Variation in E flat, 1991; improviser, performer: (CD rec.) Dorothy Over the Rainbow, 1996, (commd. mass) Missa Divinum Mysterium, 1996; incidental music for Mona 7, 1997. Mem. adv. bd. AIDS Action, Internat., N.Y.C., 1994—. Composition grantee Meet the Composer, 1991, 92. Mem. ASCAP, Am. Guild Organists (1st prize N.Y.C. chpt. 1983). Democrat. Episcopalian. Avocations: travel, astronomy, mythology, antique furniture. Home and Office: Cathedral St John Divine 1047 Amsterdam Ave New York NY 10025

PAPADAKOS, NICHOLAS PETER, retired state supreme court justice; b. Hoboken, N.J., Jan. 24, 1925; s. Petros and Olga (Christopoulou) P.; m. Roula Sakellariou, 1950; children: Peter, James, Thomas. LL.B., Columbus Law Sch., Washington, 1952; B.A., Dickinson Coll., 1949. Bar: D.C. 1952, Pa. 1957, U.S. Supreme Ct. 1975. Atty. Dept. Labor, Washington, 1950-55; office mgr. Pa. Dept. Labor, McKeesport, 1955-57; pvt. practice McKeesport, Pa., 1957-75; judge Ct. of Common Pleas, Pitts., 1976-84; justice Pa. Supreme Ct., 1984-95; solicitor Versailles Sch. Dist., McKeesport, Pa., 1964-65, Port Vue Borough, Pa., 1969-75, City of McKeesport, 1974-75; instr. in bus. law Pa. State U.-McKeesport, 1960-75; mem. nat. panel arbitrators Am. Arbitration Assn., 1986. Laic chmn. Greek Orthodox Diocese of Pitts.; past mem., past chmn. U.S. Selective Service Bd., McKeesport, Pa., early 1970s; bd. dirs. Mendelssohn Choir, Pitts. Served to sgt. A.C., U.S. Army, 1943-46; PTO. Mem. Pa. State Trial Judges Conf., Greek-Am. Progressive Assn., Am. Hellenic Ednl. Progressive Assn., Tall Cedars Club, Optimists Club, Lions, Elks, Masons. Democrat.

PAPADIMITRIOU, DIMITRI BASIL, economist, college administrator; b. Salonica, Greece, June 9, 1946; came to U.S., 1965, naturalized, 1974; s. Basil John and Ellen (Tacas) P.; m. Viki Fokas, Aug. 26, 1967; children: Jennifer E., Elizabeth R. BA, Columbia U., 1970; PhD, New Sch. Social Rsch., 1986. V.p., asst. sec. ITT Life Ins. Co. N.Y., N.Y.C., 1970-73; exec. v.p., sec., treas. William Penn Life Ins. Co. N.Y., N.Y.C., 1973-78, also dir.; exec. v.p., provost Bard Coll., 1978—, Jerome Levy prof. econs., 1978—, exec. dir. Bard Ctr., 1980—, Jerome Levy Econs. Inst., 1988—; adj. lectr. econs. New Sch. Social Rsch., 1975-76; fellow Ctr. for Advanced Econ. Studies, 1983; Wye fellow Aspen Inst.; bd. dirs. William Penn Life Ins. Co. N.Y.; mem. adv. com. Hudsonia, Inc.; bd. govs. Jerome Levy Econs. Inst., 1986—; mem. subcoun. capital allocation Competitiveness Policy Coun.; mem. adv. com. Women's World Banking; radio econs. commentator Sta. WAMC, Monitor Radio, NPR, Money Radio. Co-author: Community Development Banking, 1993, A Path to Community Development, 1993, An Alternative in Small Business Finance, 1994, Monetary Policy Uncovered: The Federal Reserve's Experiment with Unobservables, 1994, Targeting Inflation: The Effects of Monetary Policy on the CPI and Its Housing Component, 1996; editor and contbr.: Profits, Deficits and Instability, 1992, Aspects of Distribution of Wealth and Income, 1994, Stability in the Financial System, 1996; co-editor and contbr.: Poverty and Prosperity in the USA in the Late Twentieth Century, 1993, Financial Conditions and Macroeconomic Performance, 1992; bd. editors Ea. Econ. Jour.; book reviewer Econ. Jour. Bd. dirs. Catskill Ballet Theatre; trustee ACHAEA Found., Am. Symphony Orch. Mem. Am. Econ. Assn., Am.-Hellenic Banker Assn., Royal Econ. Soc., Am. Fin. Assn., European Econ. Assn., Eastern Econ. Assn., Econ. Sci. Chamber of Greece, Assn. for Evolutionary Econs. Home and Office: Bard Coll Annandale On Hudson NY 12504

PAPAGEORGE, TOD, photographer, educator; b. Portsmouth, N.H., Aug. 1, 1940; s. Theodore and Eileen Elizabeth (Flanigan) P.; m. Pauline Whitcomb, Feb. 3, 1962 (div. 1970); m. Deborah Flomenhaft, June 21, 1987; 1 child, Theo. BA in English Lit., U. N.H., 1962; MA, Yale U., 1979.

Lectr. in photography MIT, Cambridge, Mass., 1974-75; lectr. in visual studies Harvard U., Cambridge, 1975-76; Walker Evans prof. of photography Yale U., New Haven, 1978—; vis. instr. in photography The Parsons Sch. Design, N.Y.C., 1969-72, The Pratt Inst. of Art, N.Y.C., 1971-74, The Cooper Union Sch. Art, N.Y.C., 1971-74; adj. lectr. in photography Queens Coll., N.Y.C., 1972-74. Guest dir. exhbn., Mus. Modern Art, N.Y.C., 1977, Yale Art Gallery, 1981; one-man shows include Light Gallery, N.Y.C., 1973, 79, Cronin Gallery, Houston, 1977, Art Inst. Chgo., 1978, Galerie Zabriskie, Paris, 1979, Stills Photography Group, Edinburgh, Scotland, 1980, Daniel Wolf Gallery, N.Y.C., 1981, 85, Akron (Ohio) Art Mus., 1981, Sheldon Meml. Art Gallery, Lincoln, Nebr., 1981, Franklin Parrasch Gallery, N.Y.C., 1991; group shows include Mus. Modern Art, N.Y.C., 1971, 73, 74, 76, 77, 78, 79, 91, Lowe Art Mus., Coral Gables, Fla., 1974, Balt. Mus. Art, 1975, Mus. Fine Arts, Boston, 1976, 91, Thomas Gibson Gallery, London, 1976, Galerie Zabriskie, Paris, 1977, 87, U. Colo., 1977, Houston Mus. Fine Arts, 1977, Art Inst. Chgo., 1979, Corcoran Gallery Art, Washington, 1980, Fraenkel Gallery, San Francisco, 1981, Daniel Wolf Gallery, N.Y.C., 1982, 83, 86, Albright-Knox Mus., Buffalo, 1983, The Whitney Mus. Art, N.Y.C., 1983, The Photographer's Gallery, London, 1983, Nat. Mus. Am. Art, Washington, 1984, The Dog Mus., N.Y.C., 1984, The Barbican Nat. Gallery, London, 1985, Light Gallery, N.Y.C., 1985, Centro Reina Sophia, Madrid, Spain, 1987, N.Y. State Mus., Albany, 1987, Worcester (Mass.) Art Mus., 1990, 94, Jewish Mus. Art, Wellesley, Mass., 1990, Musee De La Photographie, Mont-Sur-Marchienne, Belgium, 1991, Franklin Parrasch Gallery, N.Y.C., 1992, others; represented in permanent collections Mus. Modern Art, Art Inst. Chgo., Boston Mus. Fine Arts, Yale U. Art Gallery, Bibliothéque Nationale, Paris, Mus. Fine Arts, Houston, Dallas Mus. Fine Arts, Nat. Mus. Am. Art, Washington, J.B. Speed Mus., Louisville, Seattle Art Mus., Kunsthaus, Zurich, Switzerland, others; commd. by Seagrams Corp., 1975, Mus. Modern Art, N.Y., 1977, AT&T, 1978, Yale U. Art Gallery, 1981, Warner Comm., 1983; author: Walker Evans and Robert Frank: An Essay on Influence, 1981; editor: Public Relations: The Photographs of Garry Winogrand, 1977. Guggenheim fellow, 1970, 77; Nat. Endowment Arts fellow, 1973, 76. Subject of numerous articles and publs. Home: 122 Cottage St New Haven CT 06511-2406 Office: Yale U Sch Art PO Box 208270 New Haven CT 06520-8270

PAPAGEORGIOU, JOHN CONSTANTINE, management science educator; b. Kallithea, Greece, Nov. 22, 1935; came to U.S., 1969, naturalized, 1975; m. Thalia Christidou, 1969; children: Constantine, Elena, Demetrios, Antigone. B.Sc., Athens (Greece) Sch. Econs. and Bus. Scis., 1957; diploma tech. sci., U. Manchester, Eng., 1963, Ph.D. in Mgmt. Scis, 1965. Lectr. Athens Sch. Econs. and Bus. Scis.; also postgrad. Inst. Bus. Adminstrn., Athens, 1966-68; asst. prof. Faculty Adminstrv. Studies, York U., Toronto, Ont., Can., 1968-69; asst. prof. mgmt. Wayne State U., 1969-71; assoc. prof. mgmt. scis. St. Louis U., 1971-72; vis. prof. ops. rsch. Athens Sch. Econs. and Bus. Scis., 1972-73; assoc. prof. ops. analysis U. Toledo, 1974-76; assoc. prof. mgmt. sci. and coord. Coll. Profl. Studies, U. Mass., Boston, 1976-78; prof., coord. Coll. Profl. Studies, U. Mass., 1978-80; prof. mgmt. scis. dept. Coll. Mgmt. U. Mass., 1980—, chmn. mgmt. scis. dept., 1980-85; assoc. dean Coll. Mgmt. U. Mass., 1995; head dept. econ. research Agrl. Bank Greece, 1966-67; ops. analyst Esso-Pappas Indsl. Co., Greece, 1967-68; spl. adv. Center Planning and Econ. Research, Greece, 1972-73; cons. in field; condr. seminars. Author: Introduction to Operations Research (in Greek), 1973, Fundamentals of Operations Research, 1973, Management Science and Environmental Problems, 1980; co-author: Data on the Greek Economy, 1966; assoc. editor technos: Ops. Mgmt. Newsletter; spl. issues editor: Interfaces; guest editor: Internat. Jour. Tech. Mgmt.; mem. editorial bd. Jour. Managerial Issues, Southwestern Bus. Rev.; editor: TIMS COLIME Newsletter; contbr. articles to profl. jours. Served to 2d lt. Greek Army, 1958-60. Greek Govt. scholar, 1962-65; NATO postdoctoral fellow, 1965; Air Force Office Sci. Research fellow, summer 1980. Fellow AAAS; mem. INFORMS (1985 nat. meeting program com., 1994 joint nat. meeting program chmn., chmn. nat. meeting com. 1985, faculty-in-residence com., coll. officer, chpt. officer, activities com.), Am. Inst. Decision Scis. (nat. innovative edn. com. 1981, programs and meetings com. 1983), Sigma Xi. Address: 14 Putney Rd Wellesley MA 02181-5315 *Our achievements are a function of our goals. I usually set ambitious but achievable goals and I try to achieve them through hard work, persistence, and belief in God's help. I believe that there is always room for improvement in the status-quo and that a continuous search for improvements is the major factor for continuous progress.*

PAPAGEORGIOU, PANAGIOTIS, medical educator; b. Thessaloniki, Greece, Dec. 23, 1959. MD, Aristotelian U., Thessaloniki, 1984; PhD in Physiology, Harvard U., 1990. Cert. Ednl. Com. for Fgn. Med. Grads., FLEX; diplomate Am. Bd. Internal Medicine, subspecialty in cardiovasc. disease; lic. physician, Mass. Rsch. fellow Am. Heart Assn., Mass. affiliate, 1989-90; intern in medicine Beth Israel Hosp., Harvard Med. Sch., Boston, 1990-91, jr. asst. resident internal medicine, 1991-92, clin. cardiology fellow cardiovascular divsn., 1992-94, clin. electrophysiology fellow cardiovascular divsn., 1994-96, staff electrophysiologist, 1996—; tchg. fellow dept. cellular and molecular physiology Harvard U., 1985-90, clin. fellow medicine, 1990-95, instr., 1995—. Contbr. articles to profl. jours., chpts. to books. Greek Nat. scholar, 1977-84, Albert J. Ryan scholar Harvard Med. Sch., 1987-90; recipient clinician-investigator devel. award NIH, 1995, Clinician Scientist awrd AHA, Nat. Ctr., 1995. Mem. ACP, AMA, Tessaloniki Med. Soc., Am. Heart Assn., Mass. Med. Soc., Biophys. Soc., Am. Heart Assn. Basic Rsch. Coun., Am. Coll. Cardiology. Office: Beth Israel Hosp 330 Brookline Ave Boston MA 02215-5400

PAPAI, BEVERLY DAFFERN, library director; b. Amarillo, Tex., Aug. 31, 1949; d. Clarence Wilbur and Dora Mae (Henderson) Daffern; m. Joseph Andrew Papai, Apr. 3, 1976. BS in Polit. Sci., West Tex. State U., Canyon, 1972; MSLS, Wayne State U., 1973. Head extension dept. and Oakland County Subregional Libr. The Farmington Cmty. Libr., Farmington Hills, Mich., 1973-79, coord. adult svcs., br. head, 1980-83, asst. dir., 1983-85, dir., 1985—; cons. U.S. Office of Edn., 1978, Battelle Meml. Inst., Columbis, Ohio, 1980; presenter in field. Contbr. articles to profl. jours. Bd. dirs. Mich. Consortium, 1987-91; trustee Libr. of Mich., 1989-92, vice chair, 1991, 97—, chair, 1992; del. White House Conf. on Librs. and Info. Svcs., 1991; founder, treas., fiscal agt. METRO NET Libr. Consortium, 1993—. Recipient Athena award Farmington/Farmington Hills C. of C. and Gen. Motors, 1994; Amarillo Pub. Libr. Friends Group fellow, 1972, Wayne State U. Inst. of Gerontology fellow, 1972. Mem. ALA (officer), Mich. Libr. Assn. (chair specialized libr. svcs. roundtable 1975, chair conf. program 1982, chair pub. policy com. 1988-89, chair devel. com. 1994-95, chair ann. conf. and program coms. 1995-96, pres. 1996—, Loleta D. Fyan award 1975), LWV of Mich., Farmington Exch. Club, Coun. on Resource Devel. Democrat. Roman Catholic. Home: 6805 Wing Lake Rd Bloomfield Hills MI 48301-2959 Office: The Farmington Cmty Libr 32737 W 12 Mile Rd Farmington Hills MI 48334-3302

PAPALEO, ANTHONY See FRANCIOSA, ANTHONY

PAPALIA, DIANE ELLEN, human development educator; b. Englewood, N.J., Apr. 26, 1947; d. Edward Peter and Madeline (Borrin) P.; m. Jonathan Finlay, June 19, 1976; 1 child, Anna Victoria Finlay. A.B., Vassar Coll., 1968; M.S., W.Va. U., 1970, Ph.D. (NSF fellow), 1971. Asst. prof. child and family studies U. Wis., Madison, 1971-75; assoc. prof. U. Wis., 1975-78, prof., 1978-87, coordinator child and family studies, 1977-79; adj. prof. psychology in pediatrics U. Pa. Sch. Medicine, 1987-89. Co-author: (with Sally W. Olds) A Child's World: Infancy Through Adolescence, 1975, 7th edit., 1996, Human Development, 1978, 6th edit., 1995, Psychology, 1985, 2d edit., 1988, (with Cameron J. Camp and Ruth Duskin Feldman) Adult Development and Aging, 1996; contbr. articles to profl. jours. Am. Council on Edn. fellow, 1979-80; U. Wis. grantee. Fellow Gerontol. Soc.; mem. Am. Psychol. Assn., Soc. Research in Child Devel., Nat. Council Family Relations, Psi Chi. Home: 316 E 18th St New York NY 10003-2803

PAPALIOLIOS, COSTAS DEMETRIOS, physics educator; b. Brooklyn, N.Y., May 15, 1931; s. Demetrios K. and Helen (Georgiou) P.; m. Alice Wochele, Sept. 7, 1963; children—Andreas, Dimitri. B.S., Rensselaer Poly. Inst., 1953; A.M., Harvard, 1960, Ph.D., 1965. Mem. tech. staff Bell Telephone Labs., 1953-55; prof. physics Harvard, 1966—; physicist Smithsonian Astrophys. Obs., 1965. Served with AUS, 1955-57. Home: 40 Long Ridge Rd Carlisle MA 01741-1837 Office: Harvard U Dept. Physics Cambridge MA 02138

PAPANEK, GUSTAV FRITZ, economist, educator; b. Vienna, Austria, July 12, 1926; s. Ernst and Helene P.; m. Hanna Kaiser, June 13, 1947; children: Thomas H., Joanne R. Papanek Orlando. BA in Agrl. Econs, Cornell U., 1947; MA in Econs, Harvard U., 1949, PhD, 1951. Economist, dep. dir. program planning for Asia, tech. coop. adminstrn. Dept. State, 1951-53; econ. adv., then dir. adv. group to planning commn. Harvard U., Pakistan, 1954-58; dep. dir., then dir. Devel. Adv. Svc. Harvard U., 1958-70; dir. adv. group to planning commn. Harvard U., Indonesia, 1971-73; prof. econs. Boston U., 1974-92, prof. emeritus, 1992—, chmn. dept., 1974-83, interim dir., 1977-80, dir. Ctr. for Asian Devel. Studies, 1983-90, dir. Asian program, 1991-92; dir., cons. team devel. studies to planning commn. Govt. of Indonesia, 1987-89; pres. Boston Inst. for Developing Econs., Ltd. (BIDE), 1987—; dir. policy adv. team to Federated States of Micronesia, 1995—; cons. in field. Author: Pakistan's Development: Social Goals and Private Incentives, 1967, The Indonesian Economy, 1980, Development Strategy, Growth Equity and the Political process in Southern Asia, 1986; co-author: Decision Making for Economic Development, 1971, The Indian Economy, 1988; several other books; contbr. articles to profls. jours. With AUS, 1944-46. Grantee Ford Found., AID, World Bank, UN Devel. Program, UN Univ., HEW, Asian Devel. Bank. Mem. Am. Econs. Assn., Am. Agrl. Econs. Assn., Soc. Internat. Devel. (past mem. exec. com.), Assn. Comparative Econ. Studies (pres. 1982), Assn. Asian Studies (pres. New Eng. conf. 1975-77), Pakistan Econ. Assn. Home and Office: 2 Mason St Lexington MA 02173-6315

PAPANEK, VICTOR, designer, educator, writer; b. Vienna, Austria, Nov. 22, 1926; came to U.S., 1939; s. Richard Franz Josef and Helene (Von Spitz) P.; m. Winifred Nelson, 1951 (div. 1957); 1 child, Nicolette; m. Harlanne Herdman, July 29, 1966 (div. 1989); 1 child, Jennifer Satu. BArch, BFA in Design, Cooper Union, 1950; student with, Frank Lloyd Wright, 1949; cert., Inst. Gen. Semantics, Chgo., 1956; M.S., MIT, 1955; D.H.L. (hon.), Marycrest Coll., 1983; Ph.D. (hon.), U. Victoria, 1984, U. Zagreb, Yugoslavia, 1986. Head Ind. Design and Product Devel. Office, 1964—; instr. Ont. Coll. Art U. Toronto, 1954-59; vis. guest prof. creative engring. R.I. Sch. Design, Providence, 1959; assoc. prof. art and design SUNY-Buffalo, 1959-62; head dept. product design and assoc. prof. design N.C. State Coll., 1962-64; vis. guest critic Penland Sch. Crafts, N.C., summers 1963-67; assoc. prof. art and design Purdue U., Lafayette, Ind., 1964-68, prof., 1968-70, chmn. environ. and indsl. design dept., 1968-70; prof. Calif. Inst. Arts, Valencia, Calif., 1970-71, dean, 1971-72; vis. guest prof. Kunstakademiets Arkitekskole, Copenhagen, Denmark, 1972-73; vis. prin. lectr. Faculty of Art and Design Manchester Poly. Inst., 1973-75; vis. guest prof. architecture and indsl. design Carleton U., Ottawa, Ont., Can., 1975-76; prof., chmn. dept. design Kansas City Art Inst., 1976-81; J.L. Constant Disting. prof. design U. Kans., Lawrence, 1981—; scholar in residence Schumacher Coll., Dartington, Eng., 1991-93; design cons. WHO, Geneva, 1969—, Planet Products Pty. Australia, 1979—, Dartington Industries, South Devon, Eng., 1980-83, Croatia Products, Zagreb, Yugoslavia, 1984—. Author: Creative Engineering: Students Workbook, 1961, Creative Engineering: Instructor's Handbook, 1961, Miljon Och Miljonerna: Design Som Tjanst Eller Fortjanst, 1970, Design for the Real World: Human Ecology and Social Change, 1971, Big Character Poster No. 1: Work Chart for Designers, 1973, (with Jim Hennessey) Nomadic Furniture: Where to Buy and How to Build Furniture that Folds, Stacks, Inflates, Is Light-Weight for Moving, or Can Be Thrown Away and Recycled, 1973, Nomadic Furniture 2: More About Where to Buy and How to Build Furniture that Folds, Stacks, Inflates, Is Light-Weight for Moving, or Can Be Thrown Away and Be Recycled, 1974, (with Jim Hennessey) How Things Don't Work, 1977, Viewing the World Whole, 1983, Design for Human Scale, 1984, Design for the Real World, revised edit., 1985, The Green Imperative: Ecology and Ethics in Design and Architecture, 1995; contbr. chpts. to books, articles to profl. jours.; exhibitions: Mus. of Modern Art, N.Y.C., 1962, Internat. Design Ctr., West Berlin, 1973, Gallery Grada Zagreb, 1974. Recipient Design award UNESCO, 1963, Gold medal Art Dirs. Club Am., 1968, Honours award Internat. Coun. Socs. Indsl. Design, 1981, Augustus St. Gaudens medal Cooper Union, 1987, IKEA Internat. award Sweden and Holland, 1989, Lewis Mumford award for environment Architects, Designers & Planners for Social Responsibility, 1995. Fellow Chartered Soc. Designers, Am. Scandinavian Found. (hon.), Design Student Coun. New Zealand, Soc. Designers in Ireland, Design Soc. Mex. (diplomat), Creative Edn. Found.; mem. Internat. Congress Socs. of Indsl. Design, Developing Countries Design Info. Group (co-founder), Industrielle Designere Danmark, Indsl. Design Inst. Australia, Indsl. Designers Soc. Am., Soc. Designers Ireland (hon. life), Croatian Designers Soc., Gliding Assn. Australia, Am. Soaring Soc., Grafik Design Austria. Anglican. Avocations: flying gliders and soaring planes; cookery; writing science fiction. Office: U Kans Sch Architecture Marvin Hall 417 Lawrence KS 66045

PAPARELLA, MICHAEL M., otolaryngologist; b. Detroit, Feb. 13, 1933; s. Vincent Paparella and Angela Creat; m. Treva Buzard, Oct. 2, 1992; children: Mark, Steven, Lisa. BS, U. Mich., 1953, MD, 1957. Diplomate Am. Bd. Otolaryngology (guest examiner 1967-75, bd. dirs. 1976, mem. standards and residencies com. 1976, fgn. med. grads. com. 1978, credentials com. 1984-85, examiner 1976—); lic. physician, Mich., Mass., Ohio, Minn. Rotating intern Emanuel Hosp., Portland, Oreg., 1957-58; resident in otolaryngology Henry Ford Hosp., Detroit, 1958-61, jr. mem. staff, 1960-61; mem. geographic staff, asst. Mass. Eye and Ear Infirmary, Boston, 1963-64; instr. Harvard U. Med. Sch., Boston, 1963-64; asst. prof. otolaryngology, dir. otological research lab. Ohio State U., Columbus, 1964-67; mem. staff dept. otolaryngology Ohio State U. Hosps., 1964-67; prof., chmn. dept. otolaryngology U. Minn., Mpls., 1967-84, dir. otopathology lab., 1967—, clin. prof., 1984—; mem. staff U. Minn. Hosps., 1967-84; pres. Minn. Ear, Head and Neck Clinic, Mpls., 1984—; dir. Nat. Temporal Bone Bank Program Midwestern Ctr., Mpls., 1979—; cons. VA Hosp., Dayton, Ohio, 1964-67. Mem. editl. bd. Minn. Med. Assn. Medicine, The Laryngoscope, Modern Medicine, Am. Jour. Clin. Rsch, Am. Jour. Otolaryngology, Annals Otology, Rhinology & Larynology, Acta Oto-Laryngologica; editor: (films) Surgical Techniques and Auditory Rsch., Surgical Treatment for Intractable External Otitis, Tympanoplasty, parts 1 and 2, Endolymphatic Sac, Canalplasty; (books) Atlas of Ear Surgery, 1968, 2d ed., 1971, 3d ed., 1980, Biochemical Mechanisms in Hearing and Deafness, 1970, Clinical Otology: An International Symposium, 1971, Year Book of the Ear, Nose and Throat, 1972-75, Otolaryngology: Basic Sciences and Related Disciplines, 1973, 2d ed. vol I, 1980, Otolaryngology: Ear, vol. II, 1973, 2d ed., 1980, Otolayrnology: Head and Neck, vol. III, 1973, 2d ed., 1980, Year Book of Otolarynology, 1976—, Boies's Fundamentals of Otolaryngology: A Textbook of Ear, Nose and Throat Diseases, 5th ed., 1978, Ear Clinics International, vols. I-III. 1982, Medicassette Otolaryngology, 1986; also contbr. numerous article to profl. pubs. Founder, sec., bd. dirs. Internat. Hearing Found., 1984—; mem. Presch. Med. Survey Vision and Hearing. Grantee NIH, Am. Otological Soc., Deafness Research Found., Hartford Found., Guggenheim Found., Bodman Found.; recipient Kobrak Research award, 1960, Amicitiae Sacrum honor Collegium Oto-Rhino-Laryngologicum, 1976; named Brinkman lectr. U. Nijmegen, Holland, 1986, Guest of Honor 5th Asia-Oceanic Meeting, Korea, 1983. Fellow ACS, Am. Acad. Ophthalmology and Otolaryngology (assoc. sec. continuing edn., assoc. sec., chmn. undergrad. edn. subcom., chmn. otorhinolaryngology self-improvement com., chmn. subcom. on evaluation new info. and edn. of hearing and equilibrium com., head and neck surgery equilibrium subcom. 1984-86, Merit award 1975); mem. Acad. Medicine Columbus County, Acad. Medicine Franklin County, Am. Assn. for Lab. Animal Scis., AMA, Am. Neurotology Soc. (audiology study com. 1976), Am. Otological Soc. (trustee research fund, pres.), Assn. Acad. Depts. Otolaryngology (pres. pro tem, organizer 1971-72, sec.-treas. 1972-74, pres. elect 1974-76, pres. 1976-78), Barany Soc., Better Hearing Inst. (adv. bd.), Deafness Research Found. (trustee, Centurion Club), Collegium Oto-Rhino-Laryngologicum Amicitiae Sacrum, Columbus Ophthalmology and Otolaryngological Soc., Hennepin County Med. Soc., Mpls. Hearing Soc. (bd. dirs.), Minn. Acad. Medicine, Minn. Acad. Ophthalmology and Otolaryngology (council), Minn. Coll. Surgeons, New England Otolaryngological Soc., Ohio State Med. Soc., Pan Am. Med. Assn., Soc. Univ. Otolaryngologists (exec. council 1969-71), Triological Soc. (v.p. middle sect. 1976, council mem. 1976, asst. editor), Alpha Kappa Kappa, Sigma Xi. Lodge: Lions (dir. hearing ctr., adv. council hearing ctr.). Office: 701 25th Ave S # 200 Minneapolis MN 55454-1443

PAPAS, IRENE KALANDROS, English language educator, writer, poet; b. Balt., Mar. 16, 1931; d. Louis and Kounia (Stamatakis) Kalandros; m. Steve S. Papas, Sept. 10, 1952; children: Fotene Stephenie Tina, Barbara Counia. AA with highest honors, Balt. C.C.; BA magna cum laude, Goucher Coll., 1968; MA in English Lang. and Lit., U. Md., 1974, postgrad., 1980—. Lic. theology profl. Tchr./tutor various schs., Balt., 1965—; tchr. theology U. Md. Free Univ., College Park, 1979—; author/pub. Ledger Publs., Silver Spring, Md., 1982—; TV producer Arts and Humanities Prodns., Silver Spring, 1991—; lectr. in English, philosophy, Montgomery Coll., Goucher Coll.; instr. English Composition, World Literature, U. Md., College Park, 1968—; adj. faculty various colls.; White House duty, 1997—. Author: Irene's Ledger Songs of Deliverance, 1982, Irene's Ledger Song at Sabbatyon, 1986, Small Meditations, Leaves for Healing, 1996; prodr./dir. tv. progs. Election judge, Montgomery County (Md.) Suprs. Bd. of Elections, 1980's, 90's; tutor in literacy, 1989. Recipient First Prize Arts and Culture Category Smithsonian Inst., 1991; honored 6th Annual Awards Ceremony Montgomery Community, 1991. Mem. AAUP, Internat. Platform Assn., Nat. Poetry Assn., Phi Beta Kappa. Democrat. Greek Orthodox. Avocations: art/iconography, calligraphy, music, needlepoint. Office: PO Box 10303 Silver Spring MD 20914-0303

PAPAZIAN, DENNIS RICHARD, history educator, political commentator; b. Augusta, Ga., Dec. 15, 1931; s. Nahabed Charles and Armanouhe Marie (Pehlevanian) P.; m. Mary Arshagouni. BA, Wayne State U., 1954; MA, U. Mich., 1958; NDG, Moscow State U., 1962; PhD, U. Mich., 1966. Head dept. social and behavioral scis. U. Mich., Dearborn, 1966-69, head div. lit., sci. and the arts, 1969-73, assoc. dean acad. affairs, 1973-74; dir. Armenian Assembly Am., Washington, 1975-79; dir. grad. studies U. Mich., Dearborn, 1979-85, prof. history, dir. Armenian Rsch. Ctr., 1985—; fellow Ctr. for Russian and East-European Studies, U. Mich., Ann Arbor, 1982-92; chmn. bd. dirs. Mich. Ethnic Heritage Studies Ctr., U. Mich., 1987-92. Author: St. John's Armenian Church, 1974; editor: The Armenian Church, 1983, Out of Turkey, 1994; editor Jour. of Soc. Armenian Studies, 1995—. Bd. dirs. Armenian Apostolic Soc., Southfield, Mich., 1968-78; chmn. bd. dirs. Alex Manoogian Found., Taylor, Mich., 1969-77; mem. evaluation team Ind. Schs. Assn. Ctrl. States, Chgo., 1985; polit. commentator WXYZ-TV, ABC, Detroit, Southfield, 1984—, WWJ-Radio, Detroit, 1984—; bd. dirs. Southeastern Mich. chpt. ARC, 1988—, chmn. internat. svcs. com., 1988—, disaster and mil. family svcs. com., 1988—. Scholar/diplomat U.S. Dept. State, Washington, 1976; grantee NEH, Washington, 1977, AID, Washington, 1978, Knights of Vartan, 1984; recipient Dadian Armenian Heritage award, 1993. Mem. AAUP (chpt. pres. 1962-65), Nat. Assn. Armenian Studies and Rsch. (bd. dirs. 1961-91), Nat. Ethnic Studies Assn. (bd. dirs. 1976-85), Am. Hist. Assn., Soc. Armenian Studies (pres. exec. com. 1988-91, 97—, sec./treas. exec. com. 1991-97), Am. Assn. Advancement of Slavic Studies, Am. Acad. Polit. Sci., Armenian Students Assn. (Arthur S. Dadian Armenian Heritage award 1993), Knights of Vartan. Armenian Orthodox. Avocations: reading; travel. Home: 1935 Bluff Ct Troy MI 48098-6616 Office: U Mich 4901 Evergreen Rd Southfield MI 48075

PAPE, WILLIAM JAMES, II, newspaper publisher; b. Waterbury, Conn., Aug. 14, 1931; s. William B. and Helen (Cronan) P.; m. Patricia Moran, Oct. 15, 1959; children: William B. II, Andrew J. BS, U.S. Naval Acad., 1953; MBA, Harvard U., 1959; LHD (hon.), Teikyo Post U., 1991. Commd. ensign USN, 1953, advanced through grades to lt., 1955, resigned, 1957; asst. treas. Ea. Color Printing Co., Waterbury, 1959-63; pres., treas. Ea. Color Printing Co., Avon, Conn., 1977-87; v.p., asst. treas. Am.-Republican Inc., Waterbury, 1963-64, asst. publisher, comptroller, v.p., treas., 1964-72, pres., treas., 1972—; pub. Waterbury Republican-Am., 1972—, editor, 1988—; also bd. dirs.; v.p., asst. treas. & dir. Paper Delivery, Inc., 1972—; bd. dirs. Platt Bros., Waterbury. Bd. dirs. Conn. Coun. Freedom of Info., 1968-88, Conn. Bus. and Industry Assn., 1980-83, Naugatuck Valley Devel. Corp., Regional Action Coun., Waterbury, 1991; bd. dirs. Conn. Citizens for Jud. Modernization, pres., 1973-75; bd. dirs. Waterbury YMCA, 1970-78, trustee, 1972—, chmn. trustees, 1976-85; trustee Northeast Utilities, 1974—, Greater Waterbury Health Network Inc., 1993-95; mem. Conn. Pub. Expenditure Coun. Inc., 1974-77, dir. Conn. policy and econ. coun., 1994—; trustee Teikyo Post U., 1976-96; grants com. Waterbury Found., 1980-87; pub. affairs com. Waterbury Hosp., 1984-90, past trustee; incorporator Conn. Found. for Open Govt. Inc.; active Conn. Legislature Commn. to Study Modernization and Unification of Cts., 1973-75, Citizens for Better Govt. Through Reorganization, 1977. Mem. Am. Judicature Soc. (assoc. dir. 1975-76), New England Newspaper Assn. (Conn. bd. govs. 1983-87), Conn. Bar Assn. (task force conflict of interest 1979), Conn. Daily Newspaper Assn. (pres. 1970, exec. com. 1971-91), Waterbury C. of C. (exec. com., v.p. 1975, chmn. 1977-79, dir. 1980-83, vice-chmn. transp. 1981—), Navy League U.S. (communications bd. 1982), Waterbury Club, Madison Beach Club, Highfield. Republican. Roman Catholic. Avocations: sailing, firearms, walking, carpentry. Home: Old Sherman Hill Rd Woodbury CT 06798 Office: Waterbury Rep-Am PO Box 2090 389 Meadow St Waterbury CT 06722-2090

PAPENFUSE, EDWARD CARL, JR., archivist, state official; b. Toledo, Oct. 15, 1943; m. Sallie Fisher; children: Eric, David. BA in Polit. Sci., Am. U., 1965; MA in History, U. Colo., 1967; PhD, Johns Hopkins U., 1973. Assoc. editor Am. Hist. Rev., Washington, 1970-73; asst. archivist Md. Hall of Records, Annapolis, 1973-75, archivist, 1975—, commr. land patents, 1975—. Author: In Pursuit of Profit: The Annapolis Merchants in the Era of the American Revolution, 1975, (with others) Directory of Maryland Legislators, 1635-1789, 1974, (with others) Maryland: A New Guide to the Old Line State, 1976, The Hammond-Harwood House Atlas of Historical Maps of Maryland, 1608-1908, 1982, Doing Good to Posterity, 1995; also articles and revs. Mem. Johns Hopkins U. Med. Archives. NEH grantee; recipient Disting. Svc. award to State Govt. Nat. Gov.'s Assn., 1985, Marylander of Yr. award Md. Colonial Soc., 1985. Fellow Soc. Am. Archivists, Md. Hist. Soc., Am. Antiquarian Soc. Home: 206 Oakdale Rd Baltimore MD 21210-2520 Office: Md State Archives 350 Rowe Blvd Annapolis MD 21401-1685

PAPENTHIEN, RUTH MARY, fiber artist, retired educator; b. Milw., Aug. 30, 1924; d. Roy Oliver and Hazel Mary (Heyer) P. BA, U. Wis., 1946; student, The Konstfackskolan, Stockholm, 1959-60; MFA, Cranbrook Acad. Art, Bloomfield Hills, Mich., 1965. Elem. sch. tchr. Milw. Pub. Schs., 1948-63; instr. fiber art Alverno Coll., Milw., 1966-67; vis. instr. fiber art Sch. Fine Arts Ohio State U., Columbus, 1967-72; fiber art instr. Arrowmont Sch. Arts and Crafts, Gatlinburg, Tenn., summer 1970; vis. artist fiber art Ball State U., Muncie, Ind., 1972; asst. prof. fiber art Tyler Sch. Art Temple U., Phila., summer 1973; tchr. Cheley Colo. Camps, Estes Park, 1959, 64, 65. One-woman shows include Alverno Coll., Milw., 1967, Ohio State U. Union, Columbus, 1968, The Liturgical Arts, St. Luke's Meth. Ch., Oklahoma City, 1974; exhibited in group shows in Wis. Designer Craftsmen exhbns. at Milw. Arts Ctr. (Anonymous Donor award 1963, 64, Court of Honor 1965, 66, 70, 71), Miss. River Craft Exhbn., Brooks Meml. Art Gallery, Memphis, 1963, Detroit Art Inst., 1964, Rockford (Ill.) Art Assn. Burpee Gallery of Art, 1964, 65 (1st pl. and hon. mention 1966), Rochester (Minn.) Art Ctr., 1967, Capital U., Columbus, Ohio (Liturgical Art award 1967, 71, 73), Coll. of Wooster, Ohio, 1970, Midland (Mich.) Art Ctr., 1972, Ball State U., Muncie, Ind., 1972, S.C. Johnson Collection Contemporary Crafts, 1970-72, Ohio State U., 1972, Huntington Nat. Bank and Trust Co., Columbus, 1972, Ozaukee Art Ctr., Cedarburg, Wis., 1976, West Bend (Wis.) Gallery Fine Arts, 1978, Peninsula Mus. Art, Newport News, Va., 1995, Blue Skies Gallery, Hampton, Va., 1997; represented in permanent collections Alverno Coll., Milw., Ohio Hist. Ctr., Columbus, Ohio Med. Indemnity Inc., Columbus, Karlsberger and Assoc. AIA, Columbus, U. Rochester (N.Y.) Meml. Gallery, IBM Bldg., Columbus, The Prairie Archives, Milw. Art Ctr.; represented in pvt. collections in Ohio, Wis., Fla., La., Calif., Va.; contbr. artwork to jours. Home: 208 Woodmere Dr Williamsburg VA 23185

PAPER, LEWIS J., lawyer, educator; b. Newark, Oct. 13, 1946; s. Sidney and Dorothy (Neiman) P.; m. Jan Clachko, Sept. 4, 1972; children—Lindsay, Brett. B.A., U. Mich., 1968; J.D., Harvard U., 1971; LL.M., Georgetown U., 1972. Bar: D.C. 1971, N.J. 1975, Md. 1984. Fellow, Inst. Pub. Interest Representation, Georgetown U. Law Sch., Washington, 1971-72; staff atty. Citizens Communications Ctr., Washington, 1972-73; legis. counsel to Sen. Gaylord Nelson, U.S. Senate, 1973-75; assoc. atty. Lowenstein, Sandler, Brochin, Kohl & Fisher, Newark, 1975-78; asst. gen. counsel Fed. Communications Commn., Washington, 1978-79, assoc. gen. counsel, 1979-81;

ptnr. Grove, Engelberg & Gross, Washington, 1981-86, Keck, Mahin & Cate, 1986-95, Dickstein, Shapiro, Morin & Ushinsky LLP, Washington, 1995—; adj. prof. law Georgetown U. Law Sch., Washington, 1983-86. Author: John F. Kennedy: The Promise and the Performance, 1975, 79, Brandeis: An Intimate Biography, 1983, Empire: William S. Paley and the Making of CBS, 1987. Contbr. articles to newspapers, mags., and profl. jours. Office: Dickstein Shapiro Morin & Oshinsky LLP 2101 L St NW Washington DC 20037

PAPERNIK, JOEL IRA, lawyer; b. N.Y.C., May 4, 1944; s. Herman and Ida (Titefsky) P.; m. Barbara Ann Barker, July 28, 1972; children: Deborah, Ilana. BA, Yale U., 1965; JD cum laude, Columbia U., 1968. Bar: N.Y. 1969. Assoc. Shea & Gould, N.Y.C., 1968-76, ptnr., 1976-91; sr. ptnr., chmn. corp. and securities dept., mem. exec. com. Squadron, Ellenoff, Plesent & Sheinfeld, N.Y.C., 1991—; lectr. various panels. Author: Risks of Private Foreign Investments in the U.S. Served with USAR, 1967-73. Mem. ABA (sect. on corp. law, mem. forum on sports and entertainment law), N.Y. Sate Bar Assn. (lectr. various panels, mem. securities law com.), Assn. of Bar of City of N.Y. (chmn., lectr., mem. corp. law com., mem. securities regulation com. 1992-95(, N.Y. Tri-Bar Opinion Com., Yale Club. Office: Squadron Ellenoff Plesent & Sheinfeld 551 Fifth Ave New York NY 10176

PAPET, LOUIS M., retired federal official, civil engineer; b. White Castle, La., June 14, 1933; s. Leonce A. and Corrine C. (Comedux) P.; m. Lee Anna Blanchard, May 30, 1959; children: Louis M. Papet Jr., Benjamin J. Papet. BSCE, La. State U., 1954-57. Registered profl. civil engr. La.; land surveyer La. Project engr. La. Dept Hwys., Baton Rouge, La., 1957-61; hwy. engr. U.S. Bur. Pub. Roads, Ala., N.C., Ga., Md., 1963-81; divsn. adminstr. U.S. Fed. Hwy. Adminstrn., Harrisburg, Pa., 1981-85, Atlanta, Ga., 1985-88; chief, pavement divsn. U.S. Fed. Hwy. Adminstrn., Washington, 1989—. With Army Civil Engrs., 1952-54.

PAPI, LIZA, artist, writer, educator; b. Malacacheta, Minas Gerais, Brazil, Jan. 19, 1949; came to U.S., 1978; d. Rivadavia and Lair Bronzon Papi; 1 child. BA, Inst. Fine Arts Rio de Janeiro, 1974; MFA, CUNY, 1992. Art instr. CUNY, Henry St. Settlement, N.Y.C., Third St. Music; illustrator Studio T. Graphics; artist in residence Mus. del Barrio, N.Y.C.; dir. publicity Art Sphere Cultural Ctr., N.Y.C., 1990-91; coord. Americanos, N.Y.C., 1990-94. Author: The Vanishing Beetles, 1991, Carnavalia, African Brazilian Folklore and Crafts, 1994. Residency planning grantee N.Y. Found. Arts, 1994. Mem. Soka Gakkai Internat., Coll. Art Assn., The Fgn. Press. Buddhist. Avocations: contemprary dance, biking. Office: Papi Studio 231 W 25th St Apt 3D New York NY 10001-7113

PAPIANO, NEIL LEO, lawyer; b. Salt Lake City, Nov. 25, 1933; s. Leo and Ruth Ida (Cotten) P. B.A., Stanford, 1956, M.A. in Polit. Sci, 1957; J.D., Vanderbilt U., 1961. Bar: Calif. bar 1961. Partner Iverson, Yoakum, Papiano & Hatch (and predecessor firm), Los Angeles, 1961—; bd. dirs. Nederlander Orgn. and related cos., SCOA Industries, Inc., Ocean Tech., Inc., King Nutronics, Inc. V.p. Los Angeles County Welfare Planning Coun., 1966-71; chmn. L.A. Forward, 1970-71; vice chmn. Cal. Com. for Welfare Reform, 1972; mem. Calif. Jud. Selection Com., 1972-74; co-finance chmn. Rep. State Central Com., 1975; treas. L.A. Opera Co., 1964, bd. dirs., 1965; treas. So. Calif. Choral Music Assn., 1964, bd. dirs., 1964-73; bd. dirs. Citizens Adv. Coun. on Pub. Transp., Orthopedic Hosp., Stanford U. Athletic Bd., Nat. Athletic Health Inst., L.A. Music Ctr. Operating Co., L.A. Light Opera; bd. govs. USO, 1967-71, Performing Arts Coun. L.A. Music Ctr., 1981-87, Greater L.A. Homeless Partnership, 1985—, L.A. Olympic Com., 1986-88; bd. trustees The Am. U., 1980—. Mem. Am., Calif. bar assns., Los Angeles Area C. of C. (pres. 1966, dir. 1964-67, 72-75), California Club, Los Angeles Country Club, Rotary, Phi Delta Theta. Office: Iverson Yoakum Papiano & Hatch One Wilshire Bldg 27th Floor 624 S Grand Ave Ste 2700 Los Angeles CA 90017-3328

PAPIKE, JAMES JOSEPH, geology educator, science institute director; b. Virginia, Minn., Feb. 11, 1937; s. Joseph John and Sistine Marie (Tassi) P.; m. Pauline Grace Maras, Sept. 6, 1958; children: Coleen, Coreen, Jimmy, Heather. BS in Geol. Engring. with high honors, S.D. Sch. Mines and Tech., 1959; PhD, U. Minn., 1964. Rsch. geologist U.S. Geol. Survey, Washington, 1964-69; assoc. prof. dept. earth and space scis. SUNY, Stony Brook, 1969-71, prof., 1971-82, chmn. dept., 1971-74; prof. dept. geology and geol. engring. S.D. Sch. Mines and Tech., Rapid City, 1982-87, Disting. prof., 1987-90, dir. Inst. for Study Mineral Deposits, 1982-90, dir. Engring. and Mining Expt. Sta., 1984-90; Regents' prof. dept. geology, dir. Inst. Meteoritics, U. N.Mex., Albuquerque, 1990—; mem. adv. com. for earth scis. NSF, 1985-89, Continental Sci. Drilling Rev. Group, Dept. Energy, 1986-87, Lunar and Planetary Sample Team, 1990—, Lunar Outpost Site Selection Com., 1990-91, organizing com. for FORUM for Continental Sci. Drilling, 1990—, adv. com. Inst. Geophysics and Planetary Physics, Los Alamos Nat. Lab., 1991—. Assoc. editor procs. 4th Lunar Sci. Conf., 1973, Jour. Geophys. Rsch., 1975-77, 82-84; editor procs. Internat. Conf.: The Nature of Oceanic Crust, 1976, Luna 24 Conf., 1977, Conf. on Lunar Highlands Crust, 1980; guest editor spl. issue Geophys. Rsch. Letters, 1991; mem. editorial bd. Procs. Lunar and Planetary Sci. Confs., 1987; contbr. numerous articles to profl. jours. Recipient NASA medal, 1973, Centennial Alumni award S.D. Sch. Mines and Tech., 1985; grantee NSF, NASA, Dept. Energy, 1969—. Fellow Geol. Soc. Am., Mineral. Soc. Am. (life, MSA medal 1974, past mem. coun.), Soc. Econ. Geologists (mem. coun.); mem. Am. Geophys. Union (past sec.), Geochem. Soc. (v.p. 1988-89, pres. 1989-91), Meteoritical Soc., Mineral. Assn. Can. Roman Catholic. Office: U NMex Inst Meteoritics Northrop Hall Rm 313 Albuquerque NM 87131-1126

PAPIN, NANCY SUE, educational computer coordinator; b. Long Beach, Calif., Apr. 5, 1951; d. Emil Richard and Marjorie (Wright) DeSmet; m. Robert N. Papin, Oct. 5, 1971; children: Karina L., Brianne M. Student, Apple Computer Co., 1987-91. Sec. Sebring Products, Inc., L.A., 1970-74, bus. owner, 1970—; bus. owner Sebring Internat. of Hollywood, Calif., 1971-74; computer coord. Centralia Sch. Dist., Buena Park, Calif., 1986-95; Apple edn. advisor Apple Computer Co., 1993—; mem. edn. tech. com. Centralia Sch. Dist., Buena Park, 1991-95; mem. sch. site coun. Los Coyotes Sch., La Palma, Calif., 1986-92, San Marino Sch., Buena Park, 1991-94; mem. grant writing com. Kennedy H.S., La Palma, 1991; mem. Vision 21 coordinating counsel Centralia Sch. Dist.; mem. sch. site coun. Walker Jr. H.S., 1994-95; mem. tech. com. J.F. Kennedy H.S., 1996—. Author: History/Social Science Frameworks Correlation, 1991. Republican. Roman Catholic. Avocations: computers, sewing, needlepoint, reading. Office: San Marino Sch 6215 San Rolando Way Buena Park CA 90620-3635

PAPKIN, ROBERT DAVID, lawyer; b. New Bedford, Mass., Feb. 26, 1933; s. Barney and Rose (Shuster) P.; m. Rachel Friedberg, Aug. 29, 1965; children: Steven C., Daniel M. AB, Harvard U., 1954, LLB, 1957. Bar: Mass. 1957, D.C. 1964. Legal asst. NRLB, Washington, 1958-61; assoc. Cox, Langford & Brown, Washington, 1963-66, ptnr., 1966-73; ptnr. Squire, Sanders & Dempsey, Washington, 1973—. Trustee Art Svcs. Internat., 1990—. Served with U.S. Army, 1957-58, 61-62. Mem. ABA, D.C. Bar Assn., Fed. Bar Assn., Internat. Bar Assn., Met. Club Washington D.C., Cosmos Club. Democrat. Jewish. Home: 9702 Leeds Landing Cir Easton MD 21601 Office: Squire Sanders & Dempsey PO Box 407 1201 Pennsylvania Ave NW Washington DC 20004-2401

PAPP, LASZLO GEORGE, architect; b. Debrecen, Hungary, Apr. 28, 1929; came to U.S., 1956; m. Judith Liptak, Apr. 12, 1952; children: Andrea, Laszlo-Mark (dec. 1978). Archtl. Engr., Poly. U. Budapest, 1955; MArch, Pratt Inst., 1960. Designer Harrison & Abramovitz, Architects, N.Y.C., 1958-63; ptnr. Whiteside & Papp, Architects, White Plains, N.Y., 1963-67; pres. Papp Architects, P.C., White Plains, N.Y., 1967-96, chmn., 1996—. Mem. Pres.'s Adv. Com. on Pvt. Sector Initiatives, 1980-85; mem. adv. com. Westchester C.C., 1971-75, Iona Coll., New Rochelle, N.Y., 1982-87, Norwalk State Tech. Coll., 1983—; v.p. Clearview Sch., 1985-89, pres., 1990-91; mem. Town Coun. New Canaan, Conn., 1993—. Fellow AIA (reg. dir. 1983-85); mem. Internat. Union Architects (rep. habitat com. 1986-90), N.Y. State Assn. Architects (v.p. 1977-80, pres. 1981), Am.-Hungarian Engrs. Assn. (bd. dirs. 1978-90), Am. Coun. World Fedn. Hungarians (pres. 1993—), Hungarian Univ. Assn. (pres. 1958-60), Westchester County C. of C. (bd. dirs. 1968-71, vice chmn. bd. for area devel. 1983-89, chmn. bd. dirs. 1989-90), Am.-Hungarian C. of C. (charter 1989—). Home: 1197 Valley Rd New Canaan CT 06840-2428 Office: Papp Architects PC 7-11 S Broadway White Plains NY 10601-3531

PAPP, LEANN ILSE KLINE, respiratory therapy educator; b. Niles, Ohio, June 18, 1944; d. Lee Andrew and Mildred Alice (Vaughan) Kline; m. Roger John Papp, July 11, 1964; 1 child, Lisa Marie. AAS in Respiratory Therapy, Sinclair C.C., Dayton, Ohio, 1975; ASN, Manatee Jr. Coll., Bradenton, Fla., 1983; B in Allied Health Edn., Ottawa U. of Kansas City, Overland Park, Kans., 1988; MS in Health and Wellness, Calif. Coll. Health Scis., 1995. RN, Fla., Ark.; cert. respiratory therapy technologist, registered respiratory therapist, BCLS instr., Am. Heart Assn., cert. hypnotherapist. Staff therapist Childrens' Med. Ctr., Dayton, 1975-79; staff therapist L.W. Blake Hosp., Bradenton, Fla., 1979; chief therapist The Breath Ctr., Sarasota, Fla., 1979-83; mem. clin. faculty Sarasota Meml. Hosp., 1983-84; spl. procedures therapist, mem. clin. faculty North Little Rock (Ark.) Meml. Hosp., 1984-85; clin. edn. coord. St. Vincent Infirmary, Little Rock, 1985-86; dir. clin. edn. for respiratory therapy tech. Pulaski Vo-Tech, North Little Rock, 1986-88; staff therapist Cobb Gen. Hosp., Austell, Ga., 1988-89; program dir. respiratory therapy tech. Coosa Valley Tech. Inst., Rome, Ga., 1989—; cons. Applied Measurement Profls., Lenexa, Kans, 1991-92, 93-94; faculty Am. Heart Assn., Marietta, Ga., 1989—; advisor Ga. Coun. on Vocat. Edn., Atlanta, 1991-94; mem. ednl. commn. Author: Nosocomial Infection and Control, 1993; co-author: Georgia State Standards-Respiratory Therapy Technology, 1989-90, 93-94. Co-chairperson Cystic Fibrosis Found., Atlanta, 1990; mem. Am. Lung Assn. (Ga. chpt.), 1995, bd. dirs., 1995. Recipient Commr.'s award of Excellence Ga. Dept. Tech. and Adult Edn., 1994. Mem. Am. Assn. Respiratory Care, Ga. Soc. Respiratory Care (mem. edn. com. 1993—, mem. health care reform com. 1995), Ga. Vocat. Assn., Health Occupations Educators (Outstanding New Tchr. award 1992, election com. chair 1996, 97), Lambda Beta Soc. Office: Coosa Valley Tech Inst 785 Cedar Ave Rome GA 30161-6757

PAPPAGIANIS, DEMOSTHENES, microbiology educator, physician; b. San Diego, Mar. 31, 1928; s. George John and Mary (Terzakis) P.; m. Alice Ertel, Jan. 28, 1956; children: Michele, Marika. A.B., U. Calif.-Berkeley, 1949, M.A., 1951, Ph.D., 1956; M.D., Stanford U., 1962. Diplomate Am. Bd. Microbiology. Rotating intern Walter Reed Gen. Hosp., Washington, 1962-63; asso. prof. Sch. Public Health, U. Calif., Berkeley, 1963-67; prof. med. microbiology Sch. Medicine, U. Calif., Davis, 1967—; chmn. dept. med. microbiology Sch. Medicine, U. Calif., 1968-85; asso. mem. Armed Forces Epidemiol. Bd. Contbr. to profl. jours. and books. Served from 1st lt. to capt. M.C. U.S. Army, 1962-63. Recipient Meridian award Med. Mycol. Soc. Ams., 1986, Calif. medal Am. Lung Assn. Calif., 1988, Rhoda Benham award Med. Mycol. Soc. Am., 1992, Charles E. Smith Meml. award Coccidioidomycosis Study Group, 1994. Fellow Infectious Disease Soc. Am.; mem. Am. Soc. Microbiology, Am. Thoracic Soc., Calif. Thoracic Soc., Internat. Soc. Human and Animal Mycology, Sigma Xi, Alpha Omega Alpha. Home: 1523 Orange Ln Davis CA 95616-0912 Office: U Calif Sch Medicine Dept Med Microbiology Davis CA 95616

PAPPANO, ROBERT DANIEL, financial company executive; b. Chgo., Apr. 8, 1942; s. John Robert and Lucille Carmelita (Metallo) P.; m. Karen Marie Muellner, July 2, 1966; children: John, Kimberly, Robert, William. BS in Commerce, DePaul U., Chgo., 1964; MBA, Roosevelt U., Chgo., 1982. CPA, Ill. Audit supr. Alexander Grant & Co., Chgo., 1964-73; with W.W. Grainger, Inc., Skokie, Ill., 1973—, asst. to contr., 1973-75, contr., corp. acct., 1975-78, contr., asst. treas., 1978-84, v.p., contr., asst. treas., 1984-85, v.p., treas., asst sec., 1985-95; v.p. financial reporting and investor rels., 1995—. 1st lt. U.S. Army, 1965-67. Mem. AICPA, Ill. CPA Soc., Fin. Execs. Inst. Roman Catholic. Office: W W Grainger Inc 455 Knightsbridge Pkwy Lincolnshire IL 60069-3614

PAPPAS, ALCESTE THETIS, consulting company executive, educator; b. Dix Hills, N.Y., May 5, 1945; d. Costas Ernest and Thetis (Hero) P.; m. Sylvan V. Endich, Sept. 13, 1987. AB, U. Calif.-Berkeley, 1967, PhD, 1978; EdM, Harvard U., 1969. Cert. guidance counselor, Mass., secondary sch. tchr., Mass. Dir. student-young alumni affairs Calif. Alumni Assn., Berkeley, 1969-71; dir. residential programs U. Calif., Berkeley, 1971-73, dir. housing and childcare, 1973-79; sr. cons., mgr. Peat, Marwick, Mitchell & Co., N.Y.C., 1979-80, 80-82, sr. mgr., 1982-84; ptnr. in charge edn., other instns. Peat, Marwick, Main & Co., N.Y.C., 1984-93; pres. Pappas Cons. Group, Inc., Greenwich, Conn., 1993—; spkr. in field. Author: Reengineering Your Non-Profit Organization: A Guide to Strategic Transformation, 1996; contbr. articles to profl. jours., author monographs. Mem. Merola Opera Bd., San Francisco, 1978-80, Calif. Alumni Council, 1976-79; bd. overseers Regents Coll., 1986-89; bd. dirs., mem. fin. com. Hellenic Coll. and Holy Cross Sch. Theology, Brookline, Mass., 1983-87, Seabury Western Theol. Sem., Evanston, Ill., 1983-89; bd. dirs. N.Y. Chiropractic Coll., 1986-88, Com. on Econ. Devel., 1986-88, Greek Orthodox Archdiocese Council, N.Y.C., 1985-89; bd. dirs., vice chmn. St. Basil Acad., 1983-87; bd. dirs., mem. exec. com. YWCA, N.Y.C., 1985-90, Catalyst, 1988-90; chairperson capital campaign com. U. Calif., Berkeley, exec. v.p. exec. coun. Coll. Letters and Sci.; trustee Clark U., 1993-95, U. Calif. Found., 1993—; bd. dirs. Nat. Coun. for Rsch. on Women, 1996—. Named mem. Acad. Women Achievers, YWCA, N.Y.C., 1984; recipient award Nat. Mgmt. Assn., 1997. Mem. Mid. States Assn. Schs. and Colls. (bd. dirs., fin. com. 1984-89, planning com. 1988-89), Mortar Bd., Pi Lambda, Lambda Theat, Prytanean. Avocations: opera; gourmet cooking; travel. Office: Pappas Cons Group Inc 2 Greenwich Plz Ste 100 Greenwich CT 06830-6353

PAPPAS, BARBARA E., Biblical studies educator, author; b. Chgo., July 26, 1941; m. George G. Pappas, Sept. 20, 1964; children: Dheanna Pappas Fikaris, Michele Pappas Glavanovits, Laina Pappas Krabbe. Lay asst. Holy Apostles Ch., Westchester, Ill., 1976—; sec., lectr. Diocese of Chgo. Religious Edn. Commn., 1982—; founder, dir. Holy Apostles Resource Ctr., Westchester, 1984—. Author: Are You Saved?, The Orthodox Christian Process of Salvation, 1984, 4th edit., 1997, The Christian Life in the Early Church and Today, Commentaries on Paul's Epistles to the Corinthians, Vol. I, 1989, Vol. II, 1997. Mem. ASCD. Greek Orthodox. Home: 379 Arboretum Cir Wheaton IL 60187

PAPPAS, CHARLES ENGELOS, plastic surgeon; b. Phila., May 20, 1946; s.Engelos George and Angelina (Biniaris) P.; m. Marilyn Ann Pappas; children: Evan, Angela, Chrysten. BA, BS, U. Pa., 1968; MD, Temple U., 1972. Intern, then resident in gen. surgery Johns Hopkins Hosp., Balt., 1972-75; resident in gen. surgery Temple U. Hosp., Phila., 1975-76, resident in plastic surgery, 1976-78, chmn. dept. plastic surgery, 1978-81, clin. assoc. prof. surgery, 1981—; chief dept. plastic surgery Meml. Hosp., Phila., 1986—; clin. assoc. plastic surgery Chestnut Hill Hosp., Phila., 1979—, chief/dir. dept. plastic surgery, 1994—; med. dir. Ft. Washington Surgery Ctr., 1994—; dir. Inst. for Aesthetic Plastic Surgery, Ft. Washington, Pa., 1985—; med. dir. Cosmeticare 2000 Internat., Ft. Lauderdale, Fla., 1997—; chmn. bd. Am. Gaming Industries, 1984—; dir., ptnr. Tristate Quicklube Co., 1982-91, Medars; pres., dir. two carwash cos., Phila., 1989—; med. dir. Fort Washington Surgery Ctr., 1995—, dir., trustee, 1996—. Contbr. articles to profl. jours. Trustee Germantown Acad., Ft. Washington, 1986—, Commonwealth Nat. Country Club, Horsham, 1988—, Patrons' Charity Found. Fellow ACS, Royal Coll. Surgeons; mem. Am. Soc. Plastic Reconstructive Surgeons (diplomate), Am. Soc. Aesthetic Plastic Surgeons (diplomate), Phila. Soc. Plastic Surgeons (pres. 1990-92). Greek Orthodox. Avocations: golf, tennis, investing, skiing. Office: Inst Aesthetic Plastic Surgery 467 Pennsylvania Ave Ste 202 Fort Washington PA 19034-3420

PAPPAS, EDWARD HARVEY, lawyer; b. Midland, Mich., Nov. 24, 1947; s. Charles and Sydell (Sheinberg) P.; m. Laurie Weston, Aug. 6, 1972; children: Gregory Alan, Steven Michael. BBA, U. Mich., 1969, JD, 1973. Bar: Mich. 1973, U.S. Dist. Ct. (ea. dist.) Mich. 1973, U.S. Dist. Ct. (we. dist.) Mich. 1980, U.S. Ct. Appeals (6th cir.) 1983, U.S. Supreme Ct. 1983. Ptnr. firm Dickinson, Wright, Moon, Van Dusen & Freeman, Detroit and Bloomfield Hills, Mich., 1973—; mediator Oakland County Cir. Ct., Pontiac, Mich., 1983—; hearing panelist Mich. Atty. Discipline Bd., Detroit, 1983—, chmn., 1987—; mem. bus. tort subcom. Mich. Supreme Ct. Com. Standard Jury Instructions, 1992-94. Trustee Oakland Community Coll., Mich., 1982-90, Oakland-Livingston Legal Aid, 1982-90, v.p., 1982-85, pres., 1985-87; trustee, adv. bd. Mich. Regional Anti-Defamation League of B'nai B'rith, Detroit, 1983-90; planning commr. Village of Franklin, Mich., 1987-91, chmn. 1989-91, councilman, 1991-92, chmn. charter com., 1993-94; chmn. State Bar Mich. Long Range Planning com.; pres.-elect Oakland County Bar Assn., 1996-97, chmn. Jud. Selection Task Force, 1997; bd. dirs. Franklin Found., 1989-92; trustee The Oakland Medication Ctr., 1992-96. Fellow Mich. State Bar Found., Oakland Bar-Adams Pratt Found., ABA Found.; mem. ABA, Fed. Bar Assn., State Bar Mich. (co-chmn. nat. moot ct. competition com. 1974, 76, com. on legal aid, chmn. standing com. on atty. grievances 1989-92, comml. litigation com., civil procedure com. 1992-94), Oakland County Bar Assn. (vice-chmn. continuing legal edn. com., chmn. continuing legal edn. com. 1985-86, mediation com. 1989-90, chmn. mediation com. 1990-91, bd. dirs. 1990—, chmn. select com. Oakland County cir. ct. settlement week 1991, chmn. strategic planning com. 1992-93, editor Laches monthly mag. 1986-88, co-chair task force to improve justice systems in Oakland County 1993—, pres.-elect, bd. dirs. 1996—), Am. Judicature Soc., Mich. Def. Trial Lawyers, Def. Rsch. and Trial Lawyers Assn., (com. practice and procedure), B'nai B'rith Barristers. Home: 32223 Scenic Ln Franklin MI 48025-1702 Office: Dickinson Wright Moon Van Dusen & Freeman 525 N Woodward Ave Bloomfield Hills MI 48304-2971

PAPPAS, EFFIE VAMIS, English and business educator, writer; b. Cleve., Dec. 26, 1924; d. James Jacob and Helen Joy (Nicholson) Vamis; m. Leonard G. Pappas, Nov. 3, 1945; children: Karen Pappas Morabito, Leonard J., Ellen Pappas Daniels, David James. BBA, Western Res. U., 1948; MA in Edn., Case Western Res. U., 1964; MA in English Lit., Cleve. State U., 1986; postgrad., Indiana U. Pa., 1979-80, 81-86. Cert. elem. and secondary tchr., Ohio. Tchr. elem. schs., Ohio, 1963-70; office mgr. Cleve. State U., 1970-72, adminstr. pub. relations, 1972-73; med. adminstr. Brecksville (Ohio) VA Hosp., 1974-78; lectr. English, econs./bus. mgmt., math., comm., composition Cuyahoga C.C., Cleve., 1978-92; tchg. asst. Case Western Reserve U., 1979-80; lectr. bus. comms. Cleve. State U., 1980; participant in Sci. and Cultural Exch. dels. Am. Inst. Chemists, to Peoples Republic of China, 1984 and to Soviet Union, 1989. Feature writer The Voice, 1970-78; editor, writer Cleve. State U. newsletter and mag., 1970-73. Cub scout den mother Boy Scouts Am., Brecksville, 1960; mem. local coun. PTA, 1965-70; sec. St. Paul's Coun., 1990-91; Sunday Sch. tchr., mem. choir Brecksville United Ch. of Christ, 1975-76, mem. bd. missions, 1966-67, membership com. 1993, St. Paul Ladies Philoptohos, 1990-97; mem. Women's Equity Action League. Recipient Editor's Choice award for outstanding achievement in poetry, Nat. Libr. of Poetry, 1995; grantee Cuyahoga C.C., 1982; named to Nat. Women's Hall of Fame. Mem. NEA, NAFE, AAUW (legis. chair, del. Ohio meetings 1993, 94, del. Ohio Coalition for Change, 1993, 94, mem. Ohio and Cleve. br. del. Gt. Lakes regional meeting 1994, internat. co-chair Clev. br. 1994, 96-97, del. to Internat. Fedn. Univ. Women triennial meeting Stanford U. 1992), AARP, Ohio Edn. Assn. (rep. assembly Columbus 1994), Nat. Mus. Women in Arts (hon. roll mem.), Nat. Trust for Hist. Preservation, Case Western Res. U. Planning Com. for Edn. Forum, Greater Cleve. Learning Project, Nature Conservancy, Smithsonian Instn., Internat. Soc. Poets. Avocations: travel, art, legal studies, theater, correspondence with national and international friends. Home: 8681 Brecksville Rd Cleveland OH 44141-1912

PAPPAS, GEORGE DEMETRIOS, anatomy and cell biology educator, scientist; b. Portland, Maine, Nov. 26, 1926; James and Anna (Dracopoulos) Pappatheodoros; m. Bernice Levine, Jan. 14, 1952; children: Zoe Alexandra, Clio Nicollette. BA, Bowdoin Coll., 1947; MS, Ohio State U., 1948, PhD, 1952; DSc (hon.), U. Athens, Greece, 1988. Vis. investigator Rockefeller Inst., N.Y.C., 1952-54; assoc. in anatomy Coll. Physicians and Surgeons, Columbia U., N.Y.C., 1956-57, asst. prof. anatomy, 1957-63, assoc. prof., 1963-66; prof. anatomy Albert Einstein Coll. Medicine, Yeshiva U., N.Y.C., 1967-77, prof. neurosci., 1974-77, vis. prof. neurosci., 1977—; prof., head dept. anatomy and cell biology U. Ill. Coll. Medicine, Chgo., 1977-96, prof. cell biology and psychiatry, 1996—; trustee Marine Biol. Lab., Woods Hole, Mass., 1975-81. Author: (with others) The Structure of the Eye, 1961, Growth and Maturation of the Brain, vol. IV, 1964, Nerve as a Tissue, 1966, The Thalmus, 1966, Pathology of the Nervous System, vol. 1, 1968, Structure and Function of Synapses, 1972, Methodological Approaches to the Study of Brain Maturation and Its Abnormalities, 1974, Advances in Neurology, vol.12, 1975, The Nervous System, vol. 1 The Basic Neurosciences, 1975, Cellular and Molecular Basis of Synaptic Transmission, 1988, also author many conf. procs.; contbr. over 200 articles to profl. jours.; former mem. editorial bd. Anatomical Record, Biol. Bull., Brain Rsch., Jour. Neurocytology, Microstructure, Neurol. Rsch.; patentee method inducing analgesia by implantation of cells releasing neuroactive substances. Arthritis and Rheumatism Found. fellow, 1954-56; recipient career devel. award Columbia U., 1964-66; rsch. grantee NIH. Fellow AAAS, N.Y. Acad. Scis., Inst. Medicine Chgo.; mem. Am. Soc. Cell Biology (pres. 1974-75), Am. Assn. Anatomists (chmn. pub. policy com. 1981-82), Assn. Anatomy Chmn. (exec. com. 1978-80, pres. 1981-82), Electron Microscopy Soc. Am. (program chmn. 1984-85), N.Y. Soc. Electron Microscopy (pres. 1967-68), Soc. for Neurosci. (pres. Chgo. chpt. 1985-86), Harvey Soc., Internat. Brain Rsch. Orgn., Cajal Club, Sigma Xi. Home: 506 W Roscoe St Chicago IL 60657-3535 Office: U Ill Coll Medicine Dept Anatomy & Cell Biology 808 S Wood St Chicago IL 60612-7300

PAPPAS, GEORGE FRANK, lawyer; b. Washington, Oct. 5, 1950; s. Frank George and Lora Marie (Stauber) P.; m. Susan Elizabeth Bradshaw, Apr. 25, 1980; children: Christine Bradshaw, Alexandra Stauber. BA, U. Md., 1972, JD, 1975. Bar: Md. 1976, D.C. 1991, U.S. Dist. Ct. Md. 1976, U.S. Dist. Ct. (D.C. cir.) 1986, U.S. Dist. Ct. (we. dist.) Tex. 1993, U.S. Ct. Appeals (4th cir.) 1976, U.S. Ct. Appeals (D.C. cir.) 1984, U.S. Ct. Appeals (fed. cir.) 1991, U.S. Ct. Appeals (2d cir.) 1993, U.S. Ct. Appeals (6th and 7th cirs.) 1994, U.S. Supreme Ct. 1984, U.S. Ct. of Fed. Claims, 1995. Assoc. H. Russell Smouse, Balt., 1976-81; assoc. Melnicove, Kaufman, Wiener & Smouse, Balt., 1981-83, prin., 1983-88; ptnr. Venable, Baetjer and Howard, Balt., 1988—; lectr. Wash. Coll. Law, Am. U., Washington, 1980-84; mem. moot ct. bd., 1974-75; Master of the Bench , Inn XIII, Am. Inns of Ct., 1989. Founding editor-in-chief Internat. Trade Law Jour., 1974-75. 1st lt. USAF, 1972-76. Mem. ABA, Nat. Assn. R.R. Trial Counsel, Internat. Assn. Def. Counsel, Md. Bar Assn. (chmn. internat. coml. law sect., 1980-81), Am. Intellectual Property Law Assn., U.S. Trademark Assn., Omicron Delta Kappa, Phi Kappa Phi, Phi Beta Kappa. Republican. Greek Orthodox. Club: L'Hirondelle. Home: 9 Roland Ct Baltimore MD 21204-3550 Office: Venable Baetjer & Howard 2 Hopkins Plz Baltimore MD 21201-2930 also: 1201 New York Ave NW Ste 1000 Washington DC 20005-3917

PAPPAS, JAMES PETE, university administrator; b. Price, Utah, June 30, 1939; s. Pete S. and Dia P. (Metrakis) P.; m. Peggy Ann Kunz, Aug. 30, 1964; children: C. Jennifer, Peter T. AS in Psychology, Coll. Eastern Utah, 1959; BA in Psychology, U. Utah, 1961; MS in Counseling Psychology, Ohio U., 1964; PhD in Clin. Psychology, Purdue U., 1968; cert. in Mgmt., Stanford U., 1979; cert. in adminstrn., Harvard U., 1985. Supervising clin. psychologist U. Utah, Salt Lake City, 1967-69, asst. dir. counseling ctr., 1969-72, dir. ctr. for acad. advising, 1972-75, prof. ednl. psychology, 1972-87, assoc. dean liberal edn., 1975-78, assoc. dean divsn. of continuing edn., 1978-87; prof. ednl. psychology and liberal studies U. Okla., Norman, 1987—, vice provost continuing edn., adj. prof. adult, higher edn., 1987—; group therapist Utah State Prisons, Salt Lake City, Utah, 1980-84; bd. dirs. Hermes Real Estate Devel., Salt Lake City, 1980-87; bd. rep. Instl. Mgmt. Lifelong Learning, Cambridge, Mass., 1985; adv. bd. S.W. Ctr. for Human Rels., Norman, Okla., 1988-95; cons. Nat. Assn. Home Care, Washington, 1995. Author: (case study) Harvard Case Study Series, 1983; (book) Windows of Opportunity: Preparing University Based Residential Continuing Education for the Twenty-First Century, 1992; co-author: (workbook) Promotional Techniques, 1987; author: (with others) The Learning Sanctuary, 1990. Mem. Holladay-Cottonwood Coun., Salt Lake City County, 1978; state chmn. Utah Endowment for Humanities, 1985-88; bd. dirs. ARC Coun., Cleveland County, Okla., 1989-93; pres. Norman Arts and Humanities Coun., 1994-95. Nat. Adminstrv. Orgn. award Nat. U. Continuing Edn., Washington, 1982, 93, Regional Innovations award, 1992; St. Paul award Greek Orthodox Ch. of N. Am., Denver, 1990. Mem. Am. Assn. Counseling and Devel. (nat. senator 1975-77), Assn. Acad. Affairs Adminstr. (bd. dirs. 1977-78), Adult Edn. Assn. Utah (bd. dirs. 1979-82), Utah Assn. Counseling and Devel. (pres. 1974-75), Nat. Univ. Continuing Edn. Assn. (pres. 1996—; treas. 1993-95), Nat. Assn. State Univs. and Land Grant Colls. (bd. dirs. 1994-97). Mem. Greek Orthodox Ch. Avocations: reading, cmty. svc., writing, sports, travel. Office: Coll Continuing Edn 1700 Asp Ave Rm 111 Norman OK 73072-6407

PAPPAS, JOHN GEORGE, secondary school educator; b. Munich, Germany, May 8, 1962; parents U.S. citizens; s. Michael Thomas and Sophie Athens (Stambolis) P. BS in Bus. Adminstrn. and Mgmt., La Roche Coll., 1985; math./secondary education cert., California U. Pa., 1993. Acct., bookkeeper South Hills Anesthesia Assocs., Pitts., 1986-87; personal fitness instr. and sales profl. Prince's Gym, Canonsburg, Pa., 1988-92; math. tchr. Baldwin-Whitehall Sch. Dist., Pitts., 1993—; sponsor Freshmen Class, Pitts., 1993—. Asst. coord. Spl. Olympics, Baldwin H.S., 1994. Mem. Nat. Coun. Tchrs. Math., Baldwin Transition Team. Home: 2009 Clearfork Rd Bridgeville PA 15017-1605

PAPPAS, MARIA ELENI, nurse; b. Encino, Calif., Oct. 1, 1960; d. Nicholas Constantine and Helen Cleo (Tannors) P. BSN, U. San Francisco, 1985; M in Nursing, UCLA, 1991. Cert. critical care nurse, pub. health nurse. Staff med./surg. nurse VA Med. Ctr., West L.A., 1985-87; staff nurse ICU VA Med. Ctr., San Francisco, 1987-88; staff nurse SICU St. Mary's Hosp., San Francisco, 1988-89; staff nurse ICU St. Joseph's Hosp., Burbank, Calif., 1989-91; clin. nurse specialist Northridge (Calif.) Hosp. Med. Ctr., 1991-95; asst. clin. prof. Sch. Nursing, UCLA, 1993—. Co-author: (manual) Brain Death Policy Manual, 1993. VA scholar U. San Francisco, 1984, Reynolds Estate scholar UCLA, 1991. Mem. Sigma Theta Tau (Outstanding Contbn. award 1989). Greek Orthodox. Avocations: tennis, cross-stitch, swimming, pistol range, skiing. Home: 8012 Comanche Ave Winnetka CA 91306-1832 Office: Raytel Heart Ctr 10445 Balboa Blvd Granada Hills CA 91344-7323

PAPPAS, MICHAEL, financial services company executive; b. N.Y.C., Sept. 10, 1940; s. Michael Alexander Papadopoulos and Despina (Vrioni) Kokindo; m. Eileen McGovern, Jan. 25, 1969. BBA in Acctg. and Data Processing, Pace U., N.Y.C., 1973. Mgr. acctg. E.F. Hutton, N.Y.C., 1972-75, bus. unit mgr., 1976-77; mgr. payroll and commn. acctg. Drexel Burnham Lambert, N.Y.C., 1977-81, v.p., project mgr., 1981-83, v.p., mgr. gen. acctg., 1983-85, v.p., mgr. fin. info. systems, 1985-86, v.p., govt. reporting coord., 1986-89; dir. compensation Gruntal & Co., Inc., N.Y.C., 1989—. Sgt. U.S. Army, 1963-65. Mem. Securities Industry Assn. (tech. tax com. 1986-88), Hellenic Am. Bankers Assn. (bd. dirs. 1991-92, v.p. 1992-94, pres. 1995—). Greek Orthodox. Avocations: golf, bowling, collecting award winning movies. Office: Gruntal & Co Inc 14 Wall St New York NY 10005-2101

PAPPAS, MICHAEL, congressman; b. New Brunswick, N.J., Dec. 29, 1960. Mem. U.S. House of Reps., Washington; mem. Nat Security com., Small Bus. com., Govt. Reform and Oversight Com.; vice chmn. Civil Svc. subcom. Govt. Reform and Oversight com.; mem. Caucus on Hellenic Issues; freeholder Somerset County, dep. dir. 1986, 87, 92, 96, freeholder dir., 1998, 93; chmn. Somerset County Bd. Social Svcs., 1986-96; past liaison Somerset County Agriculture Devel. Bd.; mem. Franklin Township Coun., 1982-87, mayor, 1983-84. Trustee Somerset Med. Ctr. Recipient Disting. Svc. award Somerville Area Jaycees, 1992; named Outstanding Young Citizen, N.J. Jr. C. of C., 1993. Mem. Somerset County 4-H Assn. (Outstanding Svc. award 1994), Franklin Township Lions Club (Citizen of Yr. 1988), Ctrl. Jersey Club of the Deaf, Inc., Order AHEPA. Office: 1710 Longworth Washington DC 20515-3012*

PAPPAS, PETER WILLIAM, zoology educator; b. Pasadena, Calif., Dec. 9, 1944; s. William and Rosalie (Ashton) P.; m. Carolyn Ann Clague, Jan. 25, 1966; children: Allyson Rosalie Pappas Horsley, Nicholas W. BA, Humboldt State U., Arcata, Calif., 1966, MA, 1968; PhD, U. Okla., 1971. NIH postdoctoral fellow Rice U., Houston, 1971-73; asst. prof. zoology Ohio State U., Columbus, 1973-77, assoc. prof., 1977-82, prof., 1982-89, chairperson, prof., 1989—. Editor: Biology of Eucestoda, 1983; contbr. articles to profl. jours. Mem. Am. Soc. Parasitologists (H.B. Ward medal 1984), Ann. Midwestern Conf. Parasitologists. Home: 1709 Andover Rd Columbus OH 43212-2302 Office: Ohio State U Zoology Dept 1735 Neil Ave Columbus OH 43210-1220

PAPPAS, PHILIP JAMES, real estate company executive; b. Chgo., Sept. 29, 1954; s. Nicholas James and Ann (Nicholson) P.; m. Ana Lucia Sant'Anna; children: Tiago, Marcelo, Amanda. BA, Shimer Coll., 1975. Mgr. Cook County Hosp., Chgo., 1975-77, purchasing agt., 1977-81; pres. L.G. Properties, Chgo., 1980—, Tiamar Real Estate, 1990—; docent Chgo. Archictecture Found., 1976-78. Life mem. OSA Boy Scouts Am.; pres. Lincoln Park Builders Assn., Lake View Developers, pres., 1988-89; mem. Shimer Coll. Bldg. com., 1996-97, trustee. Recipient 1st pl. award for best interior restoration Nat. Hist. Trust for Preservation, 1991, Good Neighbor award for exceptional property restoration Northwide Real Estate Bd. Chgo. and Nat. Assn. Realtors, 1992, 95. Mem. Oxford Union Soc. (life), Chgo. Assn. Realtors. Greek Orthodox. Office: L G Properties 3654 N Lincoln Ave Chicago IL 60613-3536

PAPPE, STUART H., film editor. Editor: (films) The Killers, 1964, The Loved One, 1965, The President's Analyst, 1967, Bob & Carol & Ted & Alice, 1969, Alex in Wonderland, 1970, (with Gordon Scott and Maury Winetrobe) The Gumball Rally, 1976, An Unmarried Woman, 1978, Oliver's Story, 1978, (with Ronald Roose) The Wanderers, 1979, Carny, 1980, Class, 1983, Songwriter, 1984, (with Robert Lawrence) 8 Million Ways to Die, 1986, The Big Town, 1987, Moon Over Parador, 1988, Enemies, A Love Story, 1989, Scenes from a Mall, 1991, What's Love Got to Do with It?, 1993, (with John Carter and Pembroke Herring) Sister Act 2: Back in the Habit, 1993. Office: care Motion Picture Editors 7715 W Sunset Blvd Ste 220 Los Angeles CA 90046-3912*

PAPPER, EMANUEL MARTIN, anesthesiologist; b. N.Y.C., July 12, 1915; s. Max and Lillian (Weitzner) P.; m. Patricia Meyer, Nov. 30, 1975; children: Richard Nelson Papper, Patrick Goldstein, Amy Goldstein. AB, Columbia U., 1935; MD, NYU, 1938; MD (hon.), Univ. Uppsala, Sweden, 1964, U. Turin, Italy, 1969, U. Vienna, Austria, 1977; DSc (hon.), Columbia U., 1988; PhD, U. Miami, 1990. Diplomate Am. Bd. Anesthesiology (dir. 1956-65, pres. 1964-65). Fellow medicine NYU, 1938-39, fellow physiology, 1940, asst. prof., 1946-49, assoc. prof., 1949; intern Bellevue Hosp., 1939-40, resident in anesthesiology, 1940-42; prof. anesthesiology, chmn. dept. Columbia U.; also dir. anesthesiology service Presbyn. Hosp., 1949- 69; dir. anesthesiology, vis. anesthesiologst Francis Delafield Hosp., 1951-69; v.p. med affairs, dean, prof. anesthesiology U. Miami, 1969-81, prof. pharmacology, 1972-81; dir. Abbott Labs., No. Trust Bank of Fla., Miami; cons. div. med. scis. NRC, 1954-69, Huntington (N.Y.) Hosp., 1949-69; nat. cons. surgeon gen. USAF, 1963-70; mem. surgery study sect. NIH, 1958-62; civilian cons. First Army, USN; prin. cons. Nat. Inst. Gen. Med. Scis., 1965-66, chmn. project com. gen. med. research program, 1966-70; mem. nat. heart council NIH, 1962-66; hon. cons. Royal Prince Alfred Hosp., Sydney, Australia. Author 300 sci. papers pub. in various med. jours., 3 textbooks, 1 non-fiction book. Bd. dirs. PBS-Channel 2, Miami, 1984—. Served from 1st lt. to maj. M.C. U.S. Army, 1942-46; chief anesthesiology sect. Torney, Dibble and Walter Reed hosps. Recipient Silver medal City of Paris, 1972; established E.M. Papper chair in anesthesiology Columbia U. Coll. Physicians and Surgeons, 1984, E.M. Papper lectures in anesthesiology Columbia U. and UCLA, 1978. Hon. fellow Royal Coll. Anaesthetists (England), Royal Coll. Surgeons (Ireland, faculty anaesthetists), Royal Soc. Medicine (England), Australian and New Zealand Coll. Anesthesiologists ; mem. N.Y. Acad. Medicine (1st pres. sect. anesthesiology), Am. Surg. Assn., Am. Soc. Anesthesiologists (pres. 1967-68), N.Y. State Soc. Anesthesiologists (past pres.), NRC (chmn. com. anesthesia 1962-67), Am. Coll. Anesthesiologists, World Fedn. Soc. Anesthesiologists (v.p.), Am. Soc. Pharmacology and Exptl. Therapeutics, AMA, N.Y. Acad. Scis., N.Y. Co. Med. Soc., Am., N.Y. socs. anesthesiologists, AAAS, Am. Assn. Thoracic Surgery, Harvey Soc, Am. Soc. Clin. Investigation, Am. Thoracic Soc., Assn. Univ. Anesthetists (co-founder, 1st pres.), Pan Am. Med. Assn., Assn. Anaesthetists Gt. Britain and Ireland (hon.), Swedish Soc. Anesthesiologists (hon. mem.), Finnish Soc. Anesthesiologists (hon. mem.), Israeli Soc. Anesthesiologists (hon. mem.), Australian Soc. Anaesthesiologists (hon. mem.), N.Y. State Soc. Anesthesiologists (hon. mem.), D.C. Soc. Anesthesiologists (hon. mem.), Calif. Soc. Anesthesiologists (hon. mem.), German Soc. Anesthesiologists (hon. mem.), Halsted Soc., Japan Soc. Anesthesiologists (hon.), Am. Soc. Anesthesiologists (pres. 1969), European Acad. Anesthesiology (hon., Gold medal), Phi Beta Kappa, Sigma Xi, Alpha Omega Alpha. Clubs: Cosmos (Washington); Century Assn. (N.Y.C.). Home: 1 Grove Isle Dr Miami FL 33133 Office: PO Box 016370 Miami FL 33101-6370

PAPROCKI, THOMAS JOHN, lawyer, priest; b. Chgo., Aug. 5, 1952; s. John Henry and Veronica Mary (Bonat) P. BA, Loyola U., Chgo., 1974; student Spanish lang. study, Middlebury Coll., 1976, student Italian lang. study, 1987; M in Divinity, St. Mary of the Lake Sem., 1978; student Spanish lang. study, Instituto Cuannahuac, 1978; Licentiate in Sacred Theology, St. Mary of the Lake Sem., 1979; JD, DePaul U., 1981; JCD, Gregorian U., Rome, 1991. Bar: Ill. 1981, U.S. Dist. Ct. (no. dist.) Ill. 1981, U.S. Supreme Ct. 1994. Assoc. pastor St. Michael Ch., Chgo., 1978-83; pres. Chgo. Legal Clinic, 1981-87, 91—; exec. dir. South Chgo. Legal Clinic, 1981-85, bd. dirs., 1987—; adminstr. St. Joseph Ch., Chgo., 1983-86; vice-chancellor Archdiocese of Chgo., 1985-92, chancellor, 1992—; senator Presbyteral senate Archdiocese of Chgo., 1985-87, mem. Presbyteral coun., 1992—, mem. Cardinal's cabinet, 1992—, sec. coll. consultors, 1992—; chmn. incardination com., 1991—; bd. dirs. Cath. Conf. Ill., 1985-87. Editorial Adv. Bd. Chicago Catholic Newspaper, 1984-85; contbr. articles to profl. jours. Bd. dirs. United Neighborhood Orgn., Chgo., 1982-85, S.E. Community Youth Svc. Bd., Chgo., 1985, Ctr. for Neighborhood Tech., Chgo., 1986-87, Chgo. Area Found. for Legal Svcs., 1994—; active Chgo. Cmty. Trust Com. on Children, Youth and Families, 1991—, Ill. Family Violence Coordinating Coun., 1994—. Fellow Leadership Greater Chgo.; mem. Ill. Bar Assn., Chgo. Bar Assn. (Maurice Weigle award 1985), Advs. Soc. Lawyers, Cath. Lawyers Guild, The Chgo. Jr. Assn. Commerce and Industry (Ten Outstanding Young Citizens award 1986), Union League Club of Chgo., Pi Sigma Alpha, DePaul U. Alumni Assn. Avocations: hockey, running, reading. Home: 730 N Wabash Ave Chicago IL 60611-2514 Office: Archdiocese of Chgo PO Box 1979 155 E Superior Chicago IL 60690-1979

PAPSIDERO, JOSEPH ANTHONY, social scientist, educator; b. Niagara Falls, N.Y., Nov. 7, 1929; s. Vincent and Mary Angela (Gallo) P.; m. Wilma Alice Toye, Aug. 26, 1950; children: Michael J., John A., Mary J., Mark V. EdB, U. Buffalo, 1953, EdM, 1956; MPH, U. N.C., 1961; EdD, Case Western Res. U., 1970. Health educator North Tonawanda (N.Y.) Dept. Pub. Health, 1953-56; health educator, asst. exec. dir. Tb and Heart Assn. of Montgomery County, Md., 1956-61; USPHS trainee, 1960-61; program dir. Tb and Respiratory Disease Assn. of Cleve., 1961-67; planning assoc. Health Planning and Devel. Commn., Health and Welfare Fedn. of Cleve., 1967-69; planning cons. Met. Health Planning Corp., Cleve., 1969-71; sr. instr. dept. cmty. health Sch. Medicine, Case Western Res. U., Cleve., 1969-71; asst. prof. human medicine Mich. State U., East Lansing, 1971-73, assoc. prof., 1973-77, prof., 1977-78, prof. community health scis. Coll. Human Medicine and Coll. Osteo. Medicine, 1978-85, assoc. dir. Office Health Services, Edn. and Research, Coll. Human Medicine, 1973-78, chmn. dept. cmty. health sci., 1983-93, dir. divsn. geriatrics and long term care dept. physical medicine and rehab., 1993—, dir. cmty. integrated med. programs and studies Coll. Osteo. Medicine, 1993—, co-dir. Ctr. for Aging Studies, Geriat. Edn. Ctr., 1988-90, dir. Ctr. for Policy Analysis in Aging and Long-Term Care, 1987—; dir. Geriat. Edn. Ctr. Mich.; cons. to pub. and pvt. orgns. and agys.; pres. Active Life Sys. Inc.; vis. prof. U. Rome, 1992—. Editor, contbg. author: (with others) Chance for Change: Implications of the Chronic Disease Module Study, 1979; mem. editorial bd. Aging: Clin. and Exptl. Rsch.; contbr. articles to profl. jours. Mem. APA, APHA, Assn. Tchrs. of Preventive Medicine, Am. Coll. Epidemiology, Gerontol. Soc. Am., Am. Geriat. Soc. Roman Catholic. Research gerontology/geriatrics, long-term care, epidemiology, health services and policy. Office: Mich State U B215 W Fee Hall East Lansing MI 48824

PAQUETTE, DEAN RICHARD, retired computer company executive, consultant; b. Detroit, July 15, 1930; s. William Roy and Neta Norine (Hadder) P.; B.A., U. Md., 1970; M.S., George Washington U., 1971; grad. Nat. War Coll.; m. Emma Shirley Jones, July 2, 1952; children—Neta E., Diane R., Kingsley W. Joined U.S. Army, 1946, Commd. 2d lt. U.S. Army, 1952, advanced through grades to col., 1972; mil. advisor to Indonesian Army, Djakarta, 1963-64; action officer army aviation directorate, The Pentagon, 1965-68, dep. dir. facilities engring. Chief of Engrs., 1975-76; div. chief, support requirements, 1973-75, divsn. chief, dep. chief ops. hdqs., 1973-75; sr. Army rep. in Australia, 1971-73; sr. Army liasion Internat. Civil Aviation Orgn., FAA, 1965-68; chief, research and devel. facilities constrn., 1969-71; chief of ops., mem. faculty Army Engr. Sch., 1958-61; ret., 1976; mgr. def. and space planning Control Data Corp., Alexandria, Va., 1977—. Vice pres. Waynewood (Va.) PTA, 1967. Decorated D.F.C., Purple Heart, Legion of Merit with 2 oak leaf clusters, Air medal with 8 oak leaf clusters. Mem. Army Engr. Assn. C.E.'s (disting., Hall of Fame), Order of Purple Heart, Daedalions, Order of Carabao, Assn. U.S. Army, Army Aviation Assn., Quiet Birdmen, Pinewild Country Club. Home: 23 Lasswade Dr Pinehurst NC 28374-6703

PAQUETTE, ELISE GOOSSEN, rehabilitation nurse; b. Mt. Kisco, N.Y., Nov. 20, 1956; d. Frederick Lawrence and Angela Rita (Menichelli) Goossen; m. J. Steven Paquette, Aug. 20, 1977; children: Justin, Gregory, Courtney. Diploma in Nursing, Albany Med. Ctr. Sch. Nursing, N.Y., 1977. CRRN. Staff nurse orthopedics Hahnemann Hosp., Phila., 1977-78; staff nurse rehab. Thomas Jefferson U. Hosp., Phila., 1978-79; staff nurse orthopedics, day charge arthritis unit Presbyn. U. Hosp., Pitts., 1979-82; orthopedic nurse to pvt. phys. practice Oakland Orthopedic Assocs., Pitts., 1982-84; sr. rehab. staff nurse George Washington U. Hosp., Washington, 1984-89, asst. head nurse, 1989-90; cons. Comprehensive Rehab. Assocs., Vienna, Va.; unit coord. (head nurse) New Medico Head Injury, Lynn, Mass., 1991; dir. orthopedic rehab. program Reconditioning Program Northeast Rehab. Hosp., Salem, N.H., 1992-94, cons. to clin. programs, 1994—, facilitator cmty. amputee support group, 1992; mem. arthritis subcom. Presbyn. U. Hosp., Pitts., 1987. Mem. com. Boy Scouts Am., Boxford, Mass., 1990-94; bd. dirs. Topsfield/Boxford Newcomers Club, 1991-92. Mem. AMFAR (cert. cmty. AIDS educator), Assn. Rehab. Nurses, Inst. Children's Lit. Avocations: drama, reading, gardening, writing children's literature.

PAQUETTE, JACK KENNETH, management consultant, antiques dealer; b. Toledo, Ohio, Aug. 14, 1925; s. Hector J. and Nellie (McCormick) P.; m. Jane Russell, Sept. 13, 1947; children: Jan Eriksen, Mark Russell, Mary Beth, John Eric. Student, Baldwin-Wallace Coll., 1943-44, Marquette U., 1944; B.A., Ohio State U., 1949, M.A., 1951; postgrad., Wayne State U., 1966. Editor monthly pub. Bur. Motor Vehicles, State of Ohio, 1947-49; asst. city editor, copy editor Ohio State Jour., 1949-51; copywriter Owens-Ill., Inc., Toledo, 1951-53; copy chief mktg. dept. Owens-Ill., Inc., 1953-55, asst. advt. mgr. mktg. dept., 1955-59; advt. mgr. Owens-Ill., Inc. (Libbey div.), 1959-61; mgr. advt. and sales promotion Owens-Ill., Inc. (Libbey products), 1961-64, mgr. customer mktg. services glass container div., 1964-67, dir. corporate orgn. planning, 1967-69, v.p. adminstrv. div., dir. corp. relations, 1969-70, corporate v.p., dir. corp. relations, 1970-80, corp. v.p., asst. to chmn. bd., 1980-84, cons., 1984-86; pres. Paquette Enterprises, 1984—; owner The Trumpeting Angel, antiques, 1985—; mem. adv. bd. Cresset Chem. Co., 1987—. Author: A History of Owens-Illinois Inc., (1818-1984), 1985, The Glassmakers, 1994. Bd. dirs. Toledo YMCA, 1970-74, Vis. Nurse Svc., 1970-73, Children's Services Bd., 1973-80, Toledo council Boy Scouts Am., trustee, v.p. fin., 1978-84; trustee Owens Tech. Coll. Fund, 1978-81; mem. Advt. Club Toledo, 1951-75, trustee, 1960-62; hon. bd. dirs. Greater Toledo area chpt. ARC, 1970—; mem. adv. bd. Mercy Hosp., Toledo, 1981-84, Mary's Adult Day Care Ctr., 1989-93, St. Anthony's Children's Ctr., 1993; mem. pub. rels. com. Catholic U. Am., 1979-82; chmn. U.S. Savs. Bonds, Lucas County, 1977-79; trustee Bowling Green State U. Found., 1976-83, pres., 1980-82; mem. Nat. Commn. on a Free and Responsible Press, 1980-83; v.p. trustee Toledo Repertoire Theatre, 1984-88; trustee Crosby Gardens, 1983-89, chmn. 1987-88; trustee Toledo Botanical Gardens, 1989-90, chmn. emeritus and hon. lifetime trustee, 1990—; mem. pres.'s council Toledo Mus. Art, Bowling Green State U.; trustee Riverside Hosp. Found., 1984-94, chmn. 1986-89; mem. Juvenile Justice Adv. Bd., 1986-87; advisor R.B. Hayes Presdl. Ctr., 1990-92. With USNR, 1943-46, PTO. Recipient Gold Key award Pub. Rel. News, 1970, Silver Anvil award Pub. Rel. Soc., 1971, 72; named to Toledo Clean Hall of Fame, 1983. Mem. Ohio Mfrs. Assn. (v.p., trustee 1969-84), Keep Am. Beautiful, Inc. (nat. chmn., exec. com., 1978-84, chmn. emeritus, mem. nat. adv. coun. 1984—), Bus. Com. for the Arts (corp. liason 1980-84), Pub. Affairs Council, Glass Packaging Inst. (chmn. com. govtl. relations 1973-80), NAM, U.S. C. of C., Toledo C. of C. (cons. affairs com.), Martin County (Fla.) Hist. Soc., Western Great Lakes Hist. Soc., Maine Maritime Mus., Toy Soldier Collectors of Am. Soc., Glass Collectors Club Toledo, USN Armed Guard Assn., Sampson WWII Navy Vets. Assn., OSU Alumni Assn. (life), Am. Legion (Toledo post), Pi Sigma Alpha. Clubs: Toledo Press (founding trustee), Toledo, Torch, Rotary. Home and Office: 2355 Parliament Sq Toledo OH 43617-1256

PAQUETTE, RICHARD, airport executive. V.p. airport devel. Calgary Airport, AB, Can. Mem. Calgary Conv. and Visitors Bureau, Alta. Aviation Coun. Mem. Am. Assn. Airport Execs., Calgary C. of C., Calgary Rotary Club. Avocations: golf, skiing, bike riding, photography, hockey. Office: Calgary International Airport, 2000 Airport Rd NE, Calgary, AB Canada T2E 6W5*

PAQUIN, ANNA, actress; b. Canada, 1982; d. Mary P. Appeared in (film) The Piano, 1993 (Academy Award best supporting actress 1993, Golden Globe nomination best supporting actress 1993), Jane Eyre, 1995, Fly Away Home, 1996. Office: William Morris Agency 151 S El Camino Dr Beverly Hills CA 90212-2704

PAQUIN, EDWARD H., JR., state legislator; b. Bennington, Vt., Feb. 2, 1953; s. Edward H. Sr. and Alice Marie (Tremblay) P.; m. Patricia LaRose, July 4, 1981; 1 child, Katherine Marie. BA, U. Vt., 1975. Various positions including silversmith and factory worker; rep. Vt. Gen. Assembly, Montpelier, 1991—; dir. Vt. Ctr. for Ind. Living Franklin Grand-Isle Mental Health Svcs. Inc. Dir. summer camp for low-income rural children CAMP!. Recipient Victory award Nat. Rehab. Hosp., 1991. Democrat. Baptist. Home: PO Box 219 Fairfax VT 05454-0219 Office: Vt Gen Assembly 133 State St Montpelier VT 05633-0001

PAQUIN, PAUL PETER, corporate finance executive; b. Marlboro, Mass., Aug. 20, 1943; s. Adolph Phileous and Hazel Ann (Duplessis) P.; m. Lorraine Theresa Belliveau, June 26, 1965; children: Renée, Michele, Kenneth, Raymond. BSBA, Clark U., 1968, MBA, 1971; PhD, ABD, Cath. U., 1982. Fin. analyst Honeywell Inc., Framingham, Mass., 1963-67, Sprague Electric Co., Worcester, Mass., 1969-72; sr. analyst Fed. Nat. Mortgage Assn., Washington, 1972-76, dir. investor rels., 1976-85, v.p. investor rels., 1985-89, sr. v.p. investor rels., 1989-94; v.p. investor rels. Capital One Fin. Corp., Falls Church, Va., 1995—. Mem. Nat. Investor Rels. Inst. (pres. capitol area chpt., 1979, officer 1978-80).

PAQUIN, THOMAS CHRISTOPHER, lawyer; b. Quincy, Mass., Feb. 12, 1947; s. Henry Frederick and Rita Marie (St. Louis) P.; m. Jean Jacqueline O'Neill, Aug. 5, 1972; children: Martha, Edward. BS in Acctg., Bentley Coll., 1969; JD, U. Notre Dame, 1974. Bar: Mass. 1974, U.S. Dist. Ct. Mass. 1976. Tax atty. Coopers and Lybrand, Boston, 1974-76; assoc. Cargill, Masterman & Cahill, Boston, 1976, Wilson, Curran & Malkasian, Wellesley, Mass., 1976-77; ptnr. Bianchi and Paquin, Hyannis, Mass., 1977—; bd. dirs., chmn. nominating com. Elder Svcs. Cape Cod and Islands, Inc., Dennis, Mass., 1986-91; bd. dirs., corporator Vis. Nurse Assn. Cape Cod Found., Inc., Dennis, 1988-97; pres. Life Svcs. Inc., 1991-95. Mem. Bass River Golf Commn., Yarmouth, Mass., 1980-83, chmn., 1982-83; chmn. Yarmouth Golf Course Bldg. Com., 1985-89; mem. hearing com. bd. Bar Overseers of the Supreme Jud. Ct., 1989-95; bd. dirs. Project Coach, Inc., 1990—; conciliator Barnstable Superior Ct., 1992—. Fellow Mass. Bar Found.; mem. ABA, Mass. Bar Assn. (del. 1986-87, mem. com. on bicentennial U.S. Constn. 1986-88, fee arbitration bd. 1985-86, chmn. spkrs. and writers subcom. 1986-88), Barnstable County Bar Assn. (chmn. seminar com. 1979-83, mem. exec. com. 1981-84, v.p. 1984-86, pres. 1986-87), Estate Planning Coun. Cape Cod (exec. com. 1985—, sec. 1991-93, pres.-elect 1993-95, pres. 1995-97), Mass. Conveyancers Assn., Mid-Cape Men's Club (v.p. 1992, pres. 1993), Cummaquid Golf Club. Office: Bianchi and Paquin 55 Sea Street Ext Hyannis MA 02601-5109

PARADIS, ANDRE, librarian; b. Quebec City, Que., Can., June 26, 1938; s. Theodule and Marcelle (Letarte) P.; m. Helene Legare, July 1, 1968. B.A., Seminaire de Quebec, 1960; diplome bibliotheconomie, U. Laval, 1963; baccalaureat en bibliotheconomie, U. Montreal, 1966. With Bibliotheque Municipale de Quebec, Quebec City, 1962-76; head br. office Bibliotheque Municipale de Quebec, 1963-65, chief librarian, 1966-75, chief tech. services, 1975-76; with Que. Pub. Libraries Service, 1976-96; ret., 1996. Mem. Corporation des Bibliothecaires Professionnels du Quebec. Home: 8580 De Marseille St, Charlesbourg, PQ Canada G1G 3S6

PARADIS, JAMES GARDINER, historian; b. Walker, Minn., Oct. 3, 1942; s. Louis Adelard and Rosalie Jane (Gardiner) P.; m. Judith Ellen Schmuckler, July 3, 1970; children: Emily, Rosalind. BS in Natural Sci., St. John's U., 1964; AM in English, NYU, 1971; PhD in English, U. Wash., 1976. Chemistry instr. Harar Tchr. Tng. Inst., Harar, Ethiopia, 1964-66; sci. tchr. Pub. Sch. 143, N.Y.C., 1966-71; English instr. Univ. Wash., Seattle, 1974-76; asst. prof. sci. and tech. communication MIT, Cambridge, Mass., 1977-79, assoc. prof., 1980-89, chmn. program in writing & humanistic studies, 1982-85, 97—, prof., 1990—; communications cons. Exxon Chemicals Corp., Baton Rouge, La., 1982-83, U.S. Dept. of Interior, Anchorage, Alaska, 1983, Brookhaven Nat. Lab., L.I., N.Y., 1978-90. Author: Thomas Henry Huxley, 1978; co-editor: Victorian Science and Values, 1981, Evolution and Ethics, 1989, Textual Dynamics of the Professions, 1991; editorial cons. MIT Press/Harvard U./U. Chgo., 1980-97. Adv. com. Driscoll Elem. Sch., Brookline, Mass., 1990-91. Recipient devel. grant Internat. Bus. Machines, 1986-87, rsch. grant NEH, 1979-80, Am. Philos. Soc., 1976-77. Mem. Modern Lang. Assn., History of Sci. Soc., Soc. for Tech. Communications, British Soc. for History of Sci. Avocations: rock and ice climbing, cycling, winter mountaineering. Home: 26 Salisbury Rd Brookline MA 02146-2105 Office: MIT 77 Massachusetts Ave Cambridge MA 02139-4301

PARADIS, RICHARD ROBERT, engineering executive; b. Fall River, Mass., Oct. 17, 1956; s. Arthur A. and Joan M. (Kuttner) P.; m. Katherine A. MacKie, Feb. 26, 1983; children: Jason Ryan, Kyle Richard, Eric James. BA in Geography/Geology, Clark U., 1978. Cert. energy mgr. Energy conservation coord. Norwood (Mass.) Mcpl. Light Dept., 1978-79; analyst Shooshanian Engrins. & Assoc., Boston, 1979-84; facility mgr. Cooperative Corp., Waltham, Mass., 1984-89; energy conservation specialist R.W. Beck & Assocs., Waltham, 1989; group mgr. Energy Investment, Inc., Boston, 1989-93; energy engring. mgr. for sys. and svcs. N.Am. Mgmt. Team, Johnson Controls, Inc., Lynnfield, Mass., 1993—; panelist Illuminating Engring. Soc. Award Com., N.Y.C., 1992, 93. Co-author: Conservation & Load Management Program Design for Fall River Gas Company, 1991, Evaluation of Natural Gas C&LM Program for Residential New Construction, 1992. Coach Franklin (Mass.) Youth Soccer Assn., 1990-93; musical minister Paulist Ctr., Boston, 1982-92. Recipient Region 1 award NASA Skylab Project, 1970, Quality Improvement Showcase award, 1995, Peoples Choice award, 1995, Merit award, 1995, Chmn.'s award, 1995, Johnson Controls. Mem. AAAS, Assn. Energy Engrs., Illuminating Engring. Soc. (bd. mgrs. New Englan sect., Internat. Illuminating Design award com. chmn. 1994-97). Democrat. Roman Catholic. Home: 51 Dale St Franklin MA 02038-2223 Office: Johnson Ctrls Inc 39 Salem St Lynnfield MA 01940-2621

PARADISE, LOUIS VINCENT, educational psychology educator, university official; b. Scranton, Pa., Apr. 19, 1946; s. Louis Benjamin and Lucille (Bochicchio) P.; children: Christopher, Gabrielle,Victoria. BS, Pa. State U., 1968; MS, Bucknell U., 1974; PhD, U. Va., 1976. Lic. psychologist, profl. counselor; cert. sch. psychologist. Assoc. prof. Cath. U. Am., Washington, 1976-83; prof. edn., chmn. edn. leadership U. New Orleans, 1983-90, dean Coll. Edn., 1990-92, univ. exec. vice chancellor and provost, 1992-94, exec. vice chancellor for acad. affairs, 1994—. Author: Ethics in Counseling and Psychotherapy, 1979, Questioning: Skills for the Helping Process, 1979, Counseling in Community College, 1982. 1st lt. U.S. Army, 1968-72. DuPont scholar U. Va., 1974. Mem. APA, ACA (ethics com. 1986-89), Am. Edn. Rsch. Assn., So. Assn. Counselor Edn. (chmn. ethics com. 1988-89), Chi Sigma Iota (founding chpt. pres. 1985-87). Roman Catholic. Avocations: running, cycling. Office: U New Orleans Office Acad Affairs New Orleans LA 70148

PARADISE, ROBERT RICHARD, publishing executive; b. Bklyn., Nov. 29, 1934; s. Vincent James and Marie (Sangermano) P.; m. Camille Teresa Cosenza, July 11, 1964; children: Christine, Caren M., Robert V., Steven C. BA, St. Bonaventure U., 1956; MBA, NYU, 1972. Advt. sales rep. The Wall Street Jour., N.Y.C., 1961-63, retail advt. sales mgr., 1963-66, fin. advt. sales mgr., 1966-70, assoc. advt. sales mgr., 1970-74, ea. advt. sales mgr., 1974-80, nat. dir. advt. svc., 1980-85; v.p. adminstrn., mag. & internat. group Dow Jones & Co., Inc., N.Y.C., 1985—; bd. dirs. Am. Demographics, Ithaca, N.Y., 1986, Dow Jones So. Holding Co., Inc., 1988; assoc. pub. Barron's Nat. Bus. and Fin. Weekly, V.P. mag. group, 1988, pub., 1989—. Mem. bd. edn. Scarsdale (N.Y.) Schs., 1986-92. Served to lt. USNR, 1956-61. Mem. Advt. Club of N.Y., Fin. Com. Soc., Nat. Investors Rels. Inst. Roman Catholic. Club: Coveleigh (Rye, N.Y.) (bd. govs. 1987). Avocations: tennis, boating. Home: 8 Woods Ln Scarsdale NY 10583-6408 Office: Dow Jones & Co Inc Barron's Nat Bus 200 Liberty St New York NY 10281-1003*

PARADY, JOHN EDWARD, information systems executive, consultant; b. Inglewood, Calif., Sept. 26, 1939; s. Raymond Oliver and Ella Louise (Timm) P.; m. Barbara Lyn Pettit, Aug. 13, 1966; children: John, Renee, Stacy. BS, Calif. State U., Los Angeles, 1966; MS, U. So. Calif., 1968. Cert. data processing. Dir. info. systems Weyerhauser Co., Tacoma, Wash., 1975-82; exec. dir. McKenna, Conner & Cuneo, Los Angeles, 1982-83; sr. v.p. Bank of Am., San Francisco, 1983-85; pvt. practice cons. L.A., 1986-88; exec. v.p. Pacific Stock Exchange, Los Angeles, 1988-93; chief info. officer Coldwell Banker Corp., Mission Viejo, 1994-96; exec. v.p., chief info. officer CB Comml. Real Estate Group, L.A., 1996—; mem. The Rsch. Bd., N.Y.C., 1983—; bd. dirs. The Ctr. for Info. Systems Rsch., Cambridge, Mass., 1977-85; bd. dirs. The Molding Corp., Am., Cal-Air, Inc. Served to 2d lt., U.S. Army, 1959-64. Republican. Mormon. Avocations: fishing, camping, woodworking. Home: 1004 Vista Del Valley Rd La Canada Flintridge CA 91011-1805 Office: 970 W 190th St Torrance CA 90502-1000

PARAGAS, ROLANDO G., physician; b. Philippines, Apr. 15, 1935; came to U.S., 1959; s. Epifanio Y. and Ester (Guiang) P.; m. Liwayway Galvey, May 5, 1963; children: Suzanne, Richard, Esther, Dawn. AA, U. Philippines, 1953; MD, Far Eastern U., 1958. Physician pvt. practice, Burlington, Iowa, 1968—. Fellow Am. Acad. Pediatrics; mem. AMA, Assn. Philippine Physicians in Am., Iowa Med. Soc. Office: 828 N 7th PO Box 249 Burlington IA 52601

PARALEZ, LINDA LEE, technology management consultant; b. Raton, N.Mex., Oct. 29, 1955. AS, Amarillo Coll., 1975; student West Tex. State U., 1975-77, BBA, Century U., Beverly Hills, Calif., 1984, MBA, 1987, PhD in Bus. Mgmt. and Econ. Century U. Teaching asst. Amarillo (Tex.) Coll., 1974-75; drafter natural gas div. Pioneer Corp., Amarillo, 1975-76, sr. drafter exploration div. Amarillo Oil Co. 1976-77; drafting supr., engrng. svcs. supr., dir. speakers' bur. Thunder Basin Coal Co., Atlantic Richfield Co., Wright, Wyo., 1977-86; ptnr., tech. and adminstrv. cons. Rose Enterprises, Inc., 1986—; prof. tech. mgmt. U. Phoenix, Utah, 1995-96; adj. prof. Weber State U., Ogden, Utah; tech. writer Eaton Corp., Riverton, Wyo., 1986-88; cons. State Wyo. Office on Family Violence and Sexual Assault, Cheyenne, 1986-89; Diamond L Industries, Inc., Gillette, Wyo., 1986-88; tech. writer, pubs. cons. Thiokol Corp., Brigham City, Utah, 1987-89, design specialist space ops., 1989-90, mgr. total quality mgmt. ctr. space ops., 1990—, cons. organizational effectiveness and quality mgmt. principles; cons. incident investigation team NASA Solid Rocket Booster Program, Huntsville, Ala.; cons. process improvement Puget Power, Seattle, Wash., Pub. Svc. Co. of Colo., W.R. White Co.; cons. process design Microsoft Corp., Seattle. Author: (poetry) God was Here, But He Left Early, 1976, Gift of Wings, 1980, 89; columnist Wytech Digest; contbr. numerous articles to profl. jours. Vol. NASA Young Astronauts Program Adv. Com., 1991—; bd. dirs. Campbell County Drafting Adv. Coun., 1984-85; sec. bd. dir. exec. com. Am. Inst. Design and Drafting, 1984-85, tech. publ. chairperson, 1984-85; vol. educator, data specialist child abuse prevention coun. Ogden. Named Most Outstanding Woman, Beta Sigma Phi, 1980, 81; recipient Woman in the Industry recognition Internat. Reprographics Assn., 1980; grand prize winner Wyo. Art Show with painting titled Energy, 1976. Mem. AAUW, NAFE, NOW, Am. Soc. Quality Control, Am. Productivity and Quality Coun., Am. Legion Aux., Ocean Rsch. Edn. Soc., Gloucester, Mass. (grant proposal writer, 1984), Soc. Tech. Communications, 4-H Club. Home: 2888 N 1300 E Ogden UT 84414-2607

PARAMEKANTHI, SRINIVASAN MANDAYAM, software services executive; b. Mysore City, India, July 1, 1940; s. Appalacharya Paramekanthi and Singamma Budugan; came to U.S., 1970, naturalized 1991; B.S., U. Mysore, 1959, B.E. in Mech. Engring., 1963; M.S. in Ops. Research, Poly. Inst. N.Y., 1974, M.S. in Computer Sci., 1983; m. Ranganayaki Srirangapatnam, June 18, 1967; children: Srikala, Srilatha, Sriharsha. Costing engr. Heavy Engring. Corp., Ranchi, Bihar, India, 1963-70; inventory analyst Ideal Corp., Bklyn., 1970-75; systems analyst Electronic Calculus, Inc., N.Y.C., 1975-76; cons. in software, project leader Computer Horizons Corp., N.Y.C., 1976-85; pres. Compmusic, Bellerose, N.Y., 1985—; tchr., cons. in-house tng. Founding mem. governing council Vishwa Hindu Parishad of U.S.A., 1973—, pres. N.Y. State chpt., 1977-86; chmn. Indian/South Asian Cmty. Orgn. of Eastern Queens, N.Y.C., 1996—. Mem. IEEE, Assn. for Computing Machinery, Inst. Engrs. (India). Republican. Hindu. Office: Compmusic Inc 8229 251st St Bellerose NY 11426-2527

PARAN, MARK LLOYD, lawyer; b. Cleve., Feb. 1, 1953; s. Edward Walter and Margaret Gertrude (Ebert) P. AB cum laude in Sociology, Harvard U., 1977, JD, 1980. Bar: Ill. 1980, Mass. 1986, Tex. 1993. Assoc. Wilson & McIlvaine, Chgo., 1980-83, Lurie Sklar & Simon, Ltd., Chgo., 1983-85, Sullivan & Worcester, Boston, 1985-92; pvt. practice, Boston, 1992; pvt. practice, Euless, Tex., 1992—. Mem. ABA, State Bar Tex. Avocations: tornado hunting, observation of severe thunderstorms, photography. Home and Office: 1050 W Ash Ln Apt 1015 Euless TX 76039-2161

PARASCOS, EDWARD THEMISTOCLES, utilities executive; b. N.Y.C., Oct. 20, 1931; s. Christos and Nina (Demitrovich) P.; BSME, CCNY, 1956, MSME, 1958; postgrad. ops. rsch. N.Y.U., 1964; m. Jenny Morris, July 14, 1978; children: Jennifer Melissa, Edward Themistocles. Design engr. Ford Instrument, 1957-61; reliability engring. supr. Kearfott div. Gen. Precision Inc., 1961-63; staff cons. Am. Power Jet, 1963-64; reliability mgr. Perkin Elmer Corp., 1964-66; dir. system effectiveness CBS Labs., Stamford, Conn., 1966-72; pres. Dipar Cons. Svcs. Ltd., East Elmhurst, N.Y., Lapa Trading Corp.; gen. mgr., prin. reliability engr. engring., mgr. transp. and stores environ. affairs Consol. Edison Co., N.Y.C., 1972—; pres., chmn. bd. RAM Cons. Assocs.; pres., 1978-80; chmn. 1st Reliability Engring. Conf. Electric Power Industry, 1974, also 4th and 18th confs.; chmn. bd. Inter-Ram Q Conf. for electric power industry; gen. chmn. 18th Inter-Ramq Conf. for electric power industry; lectr. in field. Registered profl. engr., Calif. Fellow Am. Soc. Quality Control (vice chmn. Reliability div. 1968-70, sr. mem.); mem. ASME, Soc. Reliabilty Engrs., Edison Engring. Soc. Home: 30-02 83rd St Flushing NY 11370-1919 Office: 31-01 20th Ave Astoria NY 11105-2014

PARCELLS, BILL (DUANE CHARLES PARCELLS), professional football coach; b. Englewood, N.J., Aug. 22, 1941; m. Judith Parcells; children: Suzy, Jill, Dallas. B.A., Wichita State U., 1964. Asst. coach Hastings Coll. (Nebr.), 1964, Wichita State U. (Kans.), 1969, U.S. Mil. Acad., 1966-69, Fla. State U., Tallahassee, 1970-72, Vanderbilt U., Nashville, 1973-74, Tex. Tech U., Lubbock, 1975-77; head coach U.S. Air Force Acad., Colorado Springs, Colo., 1978; asst. coach New Eng. Patriots, NFL, 1980; asst. coach N.Y. Giants, NFL, 1981-82, head coach, 1983-91; NFL studio analyst NBC Sports, 1991-92; head coach New England Patriots, NFL, 1993-97, NY Jets, 1997—. Coach NFL championship team N.Y. Giants, 1986. Address: NY Jets 1000 Fulton Ave Hempstead NY 11550*

PARCELLS, FREDERICK R., product management; b. Chgo., May 14, 1957; s. Charles Hubbard and Winifred Elaine (Summer) P. AA, Barton County C.C., Great Bend, Kans., 1977; BA in Fin., U. Ill., 1980; MBA, Ind. U., 1985. CFP, CPCU; assoc. in risk mgmt., assoc. in reinsurance/Ins. Inst. Am. Actuarial trainee CNA Ins., Chgo., 1980-81; actuarial technician Sentry Ins., Stevens Point, Wis., 1982-83; scouting intern The Buffalo Bills, Orchard Park, Fredonia, N.Y., 1984; underwriting trainee Kemper Group, Chgo., 1986-87; casualty underwriter Kemper Group, Chgo. and St. Louis, 1987-88; acct. underwriter Northbrook P&C Ins. (subs. Allstate), Chgo., 1988-91; sr. account underwriter Northbrook Property and Casualty Ins., Chgo./Rolling Meadows, 1991; sr. underwriter Allstate Ins., South Barrington, Ill., 1991-95; product analyst CNA Ins. Cos., Chgo., 1995—. Asst. chmn. civic affairs com., Cambridge Forest Assn., Lincolnshire, Ill., 1980-81; treas. Santa Claus Anonymous, Chgo., 1990-91, 91-92, pres., 1992-93; vol. duplex constrn. Habitat for Humanity, Chgo., 1988, 89. Mem. CPCU Soc. (sec. Chgo. chpt. 1994-95, bd. dirs./pub. rels. chmn. 1993-94, mem. nat. underwriting sect. com. 1994—, treas. Chgo. chpt. 1995-96, v.p. Chgo. chpt. 1996—). Presbyterian. Home: 1330 N LaSalle St Chicago IL 60610-1925 Office: CNA Ins Cos CNA Plz 38 South Chicago IL 60685

PARCH, GRACE DOLORES, librarian; b. Cleve., May ; d. Joseph Charles and Josephine Dorothy (Kumel) P. B.A., Case Western Res. U., 1946, postgrad., 1947-50; B.L.S., McGill U., 1951; M.L.S., Kent State U., 1983; postgrad., Newspaper Library Workshop, Kent State U., 1970, Cooper Sch. Art, 1971-72, API Newspaper Library Seminar, Columbia U., 1971, Coll. Librarianship, U. Wales, 1984, 85. Cert. literacy instr., Ohio. Publicity librarian Spl. Services U.S. Army, Germany, 1951; post librarian Spl. Services U.S. Army, Italy, 1952; USAF base librarian, 1953-54; br. librarian Cleveland Heights (Ohio) Pub. Library, 1954-63; asst. head reference div. Va. State Library, Richmond, 1964; dir. Twinsburg (Ohio) Pub. Library, 1965-70; dir. newspaper library Cleve. Plain Dealer, 1970-83; county librarian N.C., 1987-92; cons. Cath. Library Assn., 1961-64; mem. home econs. adv. com., Summit County, 1969, books/job com., 1968; mem. adv. com. Guide to Ohio Newspapers, 1793-1973, 1971-74; appointed to del. spl. librs. for People-to-People Program in Russia, 1995. Exhibited oil paintings at Cuyahoga Cmty. Coll., 1996, 97; contbr. articles to Plain Dealer, N. Summit Times, Twinsburg Bull., Sun Press; author: Where In The World But in the Plain Dealer Library, 1971; Editor: Directory of Newspaper Libraries in the U.S. and Canada, 1976. Donor coll. scholarship grants at Hayesville, H.S., N.C., 1997. Recipient MacArthur Found. award, 1988, Libr. of Am. award, 1988. Mem. McGill U. Alumnae Assn. (sec. 1973), Kent State U. Alumni Assn., ALA (rep. on joint com. with Cath. Library Assn. 1967-70), John Cotton Dana award 1967, Library Pub. Rels. Coun. award 1972), Cath. Library Assn. (co-chmn. 1960-63), Spl. Libraries Assn. (chmn. newspaper library directory com. 1974-76, chmn. pub. relations Cleve. chpt. 1973, chmn. edn. com. newspaper div. 1982-83, mem. edn. com. nominating com. 1984), Ohio Library Assn., Western Res. Hist. Soc., Am. Soc. Indexers, Cleve. Mus. Art Assn., Coll. and Research Librarians, Nat. Micrographic Assn., Women Space, Women's Nat. Book Com., Nat. Trust Hist. Preservation. Roman Catholic. Clubs: Cleve. Athletic, Cleve. Women's City. Home: 688 Jefferson St Bedford OH 44146-3711 *Greatness results in adapting aspects or ideas in other disciplines to one's own specialty.*

PARDE, DUANE ARTHUR, insurance company executive. BA in Polit. Sci., History, U. Kans. Legis. rsch. asst. Atty. Gen. Office, Topeka, 1986-87; dir. state legis. rsch. Am. Legis. Exchange Coun., Washington, 1989-92; dir. state affairs Coun. Affordable Health Ins., Alexandria, Va., 1992-95, chief of staff, 1995-96, exec. dir., 1996—; bd. adv. Kans. Pub. Policy Inst. Mem. Am. Soc. Assn. Exec. Office: Am Legis Exchange Coun 910 17th St NW Fl 5 Washington DC 20006

PARDEE, ARTHUR BECK, biochemist, educator; b. Chgo., July 13, 1921; s. Charles A. and Elizabeth B. (Beck) P.; m. Ruth Sager; children by previous marriage: Michael, Richard, Thomas. B.S., U. Calif. at Berkeley, 1942; M.S., Calif. Inst. Tech., 1943, Ph.D., 1947; D (hon.), U. Paris, 1993. Merck postdoctoral fellow U. Wis., 1947-49; mem. faculty U. Calif. at Berkeley, 1949-61, assoc. prof., 1957-61; NSF fellow Pasteur Inst., 1957-58; prof. biology, chmn. dept. biochem. scis. Princeton, 1961-67; prof. biochemistry Princeton U., 1961-75; Donner prof. sci. Princeton, 1966; prof. Dana Farber Cancer Inst. and biochem. pharmacology dept. Harvard Med. Sch., Boston, 1975—; Mem. research adv. council Am. Cancer Soc., 1967-71. Co-author: Experiments in Biochemical Research Techniques, 1957; editor: Biochemica et Biophysica Acta, 1962-68. Trustee Cold Spring Harbor Lab. Quantitative Biology, 1963-69. Recipient Young Biochemists travel award NSF, 1952, Krebs Medal Fedn. European Biochem. Socs., 1973, Rosenstiel award Brandeis U., 1975, 3M award Fedn. Am. Socs., Exptl. Biology, 1980, CIIT Prize, 1993; Princess Takamatu lectr., 1990. Fellow AAAS; mem. NAS (editl. bd. proc. 1971-73, com. on scis. and pub. policy 1973-76), Am. Chem. Soc. (Paul Lewis award 1960), Am. Soc. Biol. Chemists (treas. 1964-70, pres. 1980-81), Am. Assn. Cancer Rsch. (pres. 1985-86), Am. Soc. Microbiologists, Japanese Biochem. Soc., Ludwig Inst. Cancer Rsch. (sci. com. 1988—), Chem. Industry Inst. Toxicology (Founders award), D. Home: 30 Codman Rd Brookline MA 02146-7555 Office: Dana-Farber Cancer Inst 375 Longwood Ave Boston MA 02215-5328

PARDEE, MARGARET ROSS, violinist, violist, educator; b. Valdosta, Ga., May 10, 1920; d. William Augustus and Frances Ross (Burton) P.; diploma Inst. Mus. Art, Juilliard Sch. Music, 1940, grad. diploma, 1942, diploma Juilliard Grad. Sch., 1945; m. Daniel Rogers Butterly, July 5, 1944. Instr. violin and viola Manhattanville Coll. Sacred Heart, N.Y.C., 1942-54, Juilliard Sch., N.Y.C., 1942—, Meadowmount Sch. Music, Westport, N.Y., 1956-84, 88-92, Bowdoin Coll. Music Festival and Sch., Maine, summer 1987; mem. faculty Estherwood Sch. and Summer Festival, 1984-86, Killington (Vt.) Music Festival, 1993—, Mannes Coll. of Music, 1996—; concert master Great Neck (L.I.) Symphony, 1954-85; adj. assoc. prof. Aaron Copland Sch. Music, Queens Coll., Flushing, N.Y., 1978—; adj. assoc. prof. Adelphi U., Garden City, N.Y., 1979-83; adj. prof. SUNY, Purchase, 1980-93; vis. prof. Simon Bolivar Youth Orch. and Conservatory, Caracas and Barquisimeto, Venezuela, 1988, 89, Conservatoria de la Orch. Nat. Juvenil, Caracas, Venezuela, 1988, 89; debut N.Y. Town Hall, 1952; toured U.S. as soloist and in chamber music groups; soloed with symphony orchs. in Miss., N.J., D.C. and N.Y.; mem. jury for internat. competitions; guest artist prof. 1st Internat. Festival for Young Violinists, Caracas, 1988, guest vis. prof. Orch. Filarmónica Nacional & Municipal Sinfonica de Caracas, Venezuela, 1991—. Recipient Merit award and citation for exceptional leadership Am. String Tchrs. Assn, 1990, Andres Bello award Minister Edn. of Venezuela, 1993. Bd. dirs. Meadowmount Sch. Music. Mem. Soc. for Strings (dir. 1965-92), Associated Music Tchrs. League N.Y. (cert.), N.Y. State Music Tchrs. Assn. (cert., citation 1989), Music Tchrs. Nat. Assn., Am. String Tchrs. Assn. (Citation award 1990), Am. Fedn. Musicians, Viola Rsch. Soc. Office: care Juilliard Sch Lincoln Ctr Plz New York NY 10023

PARDEE, OTWAY O'MEARA, computer science educator; b. Seattle, June 26, 1920; s. Otway and Mary Gertrude (O'Meara) P.; m. Marilynn Lowrie, Aug. 9, 1946; children—Irene, Loraine, Suzanne. B.S. in Elec. Engring., U. Wash., 1941; Ph.D. in Elec. Engring., Stanford U., 1948. Instr. math. Syracuse U., N.Y., 1948-52, asst. to assoc. prof., 1952-69, dir. Computing Ctr., 1962-69, prof. computer sci., 1969-86; prof. emeritus Syracuse U., 1986—. Served with U.S. Navy (USNR) 1944-46. Mem. AAUP (pres. Syracuse U. chpt. 1960), Assn. Computing Machinery (chmn. Syracuse chpt. 1963), Am. Math. Soc., Math. Assn. Am., Am. Phys. Soc., IEEE, Sigma Xi, Tau Beta Pi. Avocations: camping; photography. Home: 843 Maryland Ave Syracuse NY 13210-2502 Office: Syracuse U Ctr for Sci and Tech Ste 2-120 Syracuse NY 13244-4100

PARDEE, SCOTT EDWARD, securities dealer; b. New Haven, Oct. 11, 1936; s. William Durley and Catherine (Eames) P.; m. Aida Milagros Fuentes Tavarez, Jan. 29, 1966; 1 child, Alan Alexander. B.A., Dartmouth Coll., 1958; Ph.D., MIT, 1962. Research asst. Fed. Res. Bank, Boston, 1959-62; teaching asst. in econs. MIT, Cambridge, Mass., 1961-62; research economist Fed. Res. Bank N.Y., N.Y.C., 1962-66, mgr. fgn. dept., 1967-70, asst. v.p. fgn. dept., 1970-74, v.p. fgn. dept., 1974-79; tchr. banking and fin. NYU, 1965-67, Am. Inst. Banking, 1969-72; adj. prof. Grad. Sch. Bus. Columbia U., N.Y.C., 1972-75; dep. mgr. fgn. ops. Fed. Res. System Open Market Account, 1975-79, mgr. fgn. ops., 1979-81; exec. v.p., dir. Discount Corp. N.Y., N.Y.C., 1981-86; dir. Am. Internat. Group, 1982-86; vice chmn. Yamaichi Internat. Am. Inc., N.Y.C., 1986-88, chmn., 1988-95, sr. advisor, 1995—. Author: A Study of Inter-City Wage Differentials, 1962. Trustee Geonomics Inst., 1994—, Woodrow Wilson Fellowship Found., 1994—; mem. coun. Rockefeller U., 1994—; mem. Coun. on Fgn. Rels., 1995—. Woodrow Wilson fellow MIT, 1958-59; recipient Dr. Louis M. Spadaro award Fordham U., 1980. Mem. Coun. on Fgn. Rels., Phi Beta Kappa. Home: 250 South End Ave New York NY 10280-1074 Office: Yamaichi Internat Am Inc 2 World Trade Ctr Ste 9650 New York NY 10048-0203

PARDEN, ROBERT JAMES, engineering educator, management consultant; b. Mason City, Iowa, Apr. 17, 1922; s. James Ambrose and Mary Ellen (Fahey) P.; m. Elizabeth Jane Taylor, June 15, 1955; children—Patricia Gale, James A., John R., Nancy Ann. B.S. in Mech. Engring, State U. Iowa, 1947, M.S., 1951, Ph.D., 1953. Reg. profl. engr. Iowa, Calif.; lic. gen. contractor Calif. Indsl. engr. LaCrosse Rubber Mills, 1947-50; asso. dir. Iowa Mgmt. Course, 1951-53; asso. prof. indsl. engring. Ill. Inst. Tech., 1953-54; prof. engring. mgmt. Santa Clara U., 1955—, dean Sch. Engring., 1955-82; prin. Saratoga Cons. Group (Calif.), 1982—; Mem. Sec. Navy's Survey Bd. Grad. Edn., 1964. Mem. Saratoga Planning Commn., 1959-61. Served to 1st lt., Q.M.C. AUS, 1943-46. Named to Silicon Valley Engring. Hall of Fame Silicon Valley Engring. Coun., 1993. Mem. ASME (chmn. Santa Clara Valley sect. 1958), Am. Soc. Engring. Edn. (chmn. Pacific N.W. sect. 1960), Am. Inst. Indsl. Engrs. (edn. chmn. 1958-63, dir. ASEE-ECPD affairs 1963-68), Nat. Soc. Profl. Engrs., Engrs. Council Profl. Devel. (dir. 1964-65, 66-69), Soc. Advancement Mgmt., ASEM, Sigma Xi, Tau Beta Pi. Roman Catholic. Home: 19832 Bonnie Ridge Way Saratoga CA 95070-5010 Office: Santa Clara U Sch Engring Santa Clara CA 95053

PARDES, HERBERT, psychiatrist, educator; b. Bronx, N.Y., July 7, 1934; s. Louis and Frances (Bergman) P.; m. Judith Ellen Silber, June 9, 1957; children: Stephen, Lawrence, James. BS, Rutgers U., 1956, MD, SUNY, Bklyn., 1960; DSc (hon.) SUNY, 1990. Straight med. intern Kings County Hosp., 1960-61, resident in psychiatry, 1961-62, 64-66; asst. prof. psychiatry Downstate Med. Ctr., Bklyn., 1968-72, prof., chmn. dept., 1972-75; dir. psychiat. services Kings County Hosp., Bklyn., 1972-75; prof., chmn. dept. psychiatry U. Colo. Med. Sch., 1975-78; dir. psychiat. services Colo. Psychiat. Hosp., Denver, 1975-78; dir. NIMH, Rockville, Md., 1978-84; asst. surgeon gen. USPHS, 1978-84; prof. psychiatry Columbia U., N.Y.C., 1984—, chmn. dept., 1984—, dir. Psychiat. Inst., 1984-89, v.p. for health scis. and dean faculty of medicine, 1989—. Committeeman, Kings County Dem. Com., 1972-75; pres. sci. bd. Nat. Alliance for Research on Schizophrenia and Depression. Capt. M.C., AUS, 1962-64. Decorated Army Commendation medal; ann. hon. lectr. Downstate Med. Ctr. Alumni Assn., 1972, recipient Alumni Achievement medal, 1980, William Menninger award ACP, 1992, Dorothy Dix award Mental Illness Fedn., 1992, Vester Mark award, 1993, Salmon award, 1996. Mem. Assn. Am. Med. Colls. (chair-elect 1994-95, chair 1995-96), Am. Psychiat. Assn. (v.p. 1986-88, pres. 1989-90, Disting. Svc. award 1993), Inst. Medicine, Am. Psychoanalytic Assn., Coun. of Deans (adminstrv. bd., chair-elect 1993-94, chair 1994-95), Assoc. Med. Schs. N.Y. (pres. 1995—), Phi Beta Kappa, Alpha Omega Alpha. Contbr. articles to med. jours. Home: 15 Claremont Ave Apt 93 New York NY 10027-6814 Office: Columbia U Coll Phys & Surgeons Dept Psychiatry 630 W 168th St New York NY 10032-3702 also: NY State Psychiat Inst 722 W 168th St New York NY 10032-2603

PARDO, DOMINICK GEORGE (DON PARDO), broadcasting announcer; b. Westfield, Mass., Feb. 22, 1918; s. Dominik J. and Waleria (Romaniak) P.; m. Catherine A. Lyons, Aug. 22, 1939; children: Paula Kay, Dona Marie, Michael D., David J., Katherine A. Student, Emerson Coll., 1942. Announcer Sta. WJAR, 1942-44. Actor, 20th Century Players, Sta. WJAR, Providence, 1938-40; announcer radio and TV, NBC, N.Y.C., 1944—; announcer for radio shows Pepper Young's Family, The Doctors; announcer TV shows Ford 50th Anniversary Show, 1953 (Sylvania TV award), Fred Allen's Judge for Yourself, Martha Raye Shows, 1953-58, Arthur Murray Party, Four Star Revue, Colgate Comedy Hour, Kate Smith Hour, Show of Shows, Caesar's Hour, Jonathan Winters Show; TV game shows Winner Take All, 1950, Price is Right (original), 1956-83, Jeopardy, 1964-75, Saturday Night Live, 1975-81, 83—; numerous other shows, including, Bill Stern's Sports, Magnificent Montague; others; newscaster, 1944-54. *

PARDO, MARIAN URSULA, investment management company executive; b. Rockville Centre, N.Y., Sept. 23, 1946; d. Francis V. and Dorothy E. (Bellidora) P.; BA, Barnard Coll., 1968; m. Michael S. Toonkel. With J.P. Morgan Cos., N.Y.C., 1968—, v.p. investment group, 1980-95, mng. dir., 1995—. Former chmn. bd. dirs. Opportunity Resources for Arts. Mem. Columbus Citizens Found., Bank & Fin. Analysts Assn. Office: JP Morgan Investment 522 5th Ave New York NY 10036-7601

PARDOLL, PETER MICHAEL, gastroenterologist; b. Bklyn., Oct. 24, 1946; s. Abraham Jacob and Lee (Nyfield) P.; m. Lois, June 29, 1969; children: Todd, Missy, Mindy. MD, Med. Coll. Va., 1971. Intern U. Miami Affiliated Hosps., 1971-72, resident, 1972-74; fellow gastroenterology U. South Fla., 1974-76; gastroenterologist pvt. practice, St. Petersburg, Fla., 1978-92; pres. Ctr. Digestive Diseases, St. Petersburg, Fla., 1992—; bd. dirs. Palms of Pasadena Hosp., v.p. Founder, bd. dirs. Menorah Manor Home for Living, St. Petersburg. Maj. USAF, 1976-78. Gastroenterology fellow U. South Fla., 1974-76. Fellow Coll. Gastroenterology (chmn. com. practice affairs), Am. Coll. Gastroenterology; mem. HCFA (gastroenterology rep., carrier adv. com.), Fla. Gastroenterology Soc. (sec., pres.-elect), Fla. Ind. Physicians Assn. (bd. dirs. region 5), North Fla. Am. Coll. Gastroenterology (gov.). Avocations: cycling, health care activism. Office: Ctr Digestive Diseases 1609 Pasadena Ave S Ste 3-m Saint Petersburg FL 33707-4565

PARDUE, DWIGHT EDWARD, venture capitalist; b. North Wilkesboro, N.C., Aug. 3, 1928; s. Gilbert F. and Nina (Glass) P.; m. Annie Eller, Mar. 24, 1951; children: Richard S., Dwight E. Cert., Clevenger Bus. Coll., 1956. Dir. warehousing Lowe's Co., Inc., North Wilkesboro, 1956-57; store mgr. Lowe's Co., Inc., Sparta, N.C., 1957-59, Richmond, Va., 1959-70; regional v.p. Lowe's Co., Inc., North Wilkesboro, 1970-75, sr. v.p. store ops., 1975-78, exec. v.p. sales and store ops., 1978-86, sr. exec. v.p., 1986-90; pres., investor D. Pardue & Assocs., Wilkesboro, N.C., 1990—; mem. steering com. Home Ctr. Leadership Coun., Nat. Home Ctr. Home Improvement Congress and Exposition, 1983-86; bd. dirs. Wilkes Nat. Bank, North Wilkesboro, N.C.; chmn. bd. Community Bancshares, Inc., Wilkesboro, 1992—. Served with U.S. Army, 1950-52. Mem. Oakwoods Country Club, Jefferson Landing Golf Club, Masons. Office: D Pardue & Assocs PO Box 791 North Wilkesboro NC 28659-0791

PARDUE, LARRY G., botanical garden administrator, educator; b. Glasgow, Ky., Dec. 6, 1944; s. Samuel Robert and Etta Belle (Napier) P.; children: James, Robert, Mathew. BA, U. South Fla., 1967, MA, 1970. Plant info. officer N.Y. Botanical Garden, N.Y.C., 1969-75; v.p. Wild Flower Preservation Soc., N.Y.C., 1970-73; exec. dir. Hort. Soc. N.Y., N.Y.C., 1975-88, Marie Selby Botanical Garden, Sarasota, Fla., 1988-93, Crosby Arboretum, Picayune, Miss., 1994—. Office: Crosby Arboretum PO Box 190 370 Ridge Rd Picayune MS 39466

PARDUE, MARY LOU, biology educator; b. Lexington, Ky., Sept. 15, 1933; d. Louis Arthur and Mary Allie (Marshall) P. B.S., William and Mary Coll., 1955; M.S., U. Tenn., 1959; Ph.D., Yale U., 1970; D.Sc. (hon.), Bard Coll., 1985. Postdoctoral fellow Inst. Animal Genetics, Edinburgh, Scotland, 1970-72; assoc. prof. biology MIT, Cambridge, 1972-80; prof. MIT, 1980—, Boris Magasanik prof. biology, 1995—; summer course organizer Cold Spring Harbor Lab., N.Y., 1971-80; mem. rev. com. NIH, 1974-78, 80-84, nat. adv. gen. med. scis. coun., 1984-86, sci. adv. com. Wistar Inst., Phila, 1976—; mem. health and environ. rsch. adv. com. U.S. Dept. Energy, 1987-94; bd. trustees Associated Universities, Inc., 1995—; Burroughs Wellcome Adv. Com. on Career Awards in Biomed. Scis., 1996—. Mem. editorial bd. Chromsoma, Molecular and Cellular Biology, Biochemistry; contbr. articles to profl. jours. Mem. rev. com. Am. Cancer Soc., 1990-93, Howard Hughes Med. Inst. Adv. Bd., 1993—. Recipient Esther Langer award Langer Cancer Rsch. Found., 1977, Lucius Wilbur Cross medal Yale Grad. Sch., 1989; grantee NIH, NSF, Am. Cancer Soc. Fellow AAAS, NAS (chmn. genetics sect. 1991-94, coun. 1995—), Am. Acad. Arts and Sci. (coun. mem. 1992-96); mem. NRC (bd. on biology 1989-95), Genetics Soc. Am. (pres. 1982-83), Am. Soc. Cell Biology (coun. 1977-80, pres. 1985-86), Phi Beta Kappa, Phi Kappa Phi. Office: MIT Dept Biology 68-670 77 Massachusetts Ave Cambridge MA 02139-4301

PARDUS, DONALD GENE, utility executive; b. Stafford Springs, Conn., Aug. 1, 1940; s. William L. and Marion (Wondrasck) P.; m. Marilyn L. Riquier, June 10, 1961; children: David J., Susan L., Linda M. BS in Bus. Adminstrn, U. Hartford, Conn., 1966; grad., Harvard Bus. Sch., 1977. Internal auditor Conn. Light and Power Co., Berlin, 1958-67; fin. asst., then asst. treas. N.E. Utilities Svc. Co., Berlin, 1967-79; v.p., CFO, treas. Eastern Utilities, Boston, 1979-85, pres., CFO, 1985-87, pres., COO, trustee, 1987-89, pres., CEO, trustee, 1989-90, chmn., CEO, trustee, 1990—; chmn., dir. Blackstone Valley Electric Co., Newport Electric Corp., Eastern Edison Co., Montaup Electric Co., EUA Svc. Corp., EUA Investment Corp., EUA Ocean State Corp., EUA Cogenex Corp.; bd. dirs. Yankee Atomic Elec. Co., Conn. Yankee, Maine Yankee and Vt. Yankee. Office: Eastern Utilities Assocs PO Box 2333 1 Liberty Sq Boston MA 02107

PAREDES, AMERICO, English language educator; b. Brownsville, Tex., Sept. 3, 1915; s. Justo and Clotilde (Manzano-Vidal) Paredes-Cisneros; m. Amelia Sidzu Nagamine, May 28, 1948; children: Julia, Americo, Alan, Vicente. B.A., U. Tex., Austin, 1951, M.A., 1953, Ph.D., 1956. Journalist, 1936-50; mem. faculty U. Tex., Austin, 1951—; Ashbel Smith prof. English and anthropology U. Tex., 1981-83, Dickson, Allen and Anderson Centennial prof., 1983—, Dickson, Allen and Anderson Centennial prof. emeritus, 1985—. Author: With His Pistol in His Hand, 1958, Folktales of Mexico, 1970, A Texas-Mexican Cancionero, 1976, George Washington Gomez, 1990, Between Two Worlds, 1991, Uncle Remus Con Chile, 1993, Folklore and Culture on the Tex.-Mex. Border, 1993, The Hammon and the Beans and Other Stories, 1994; editor: Jour. Am. Folklore, 1968-1973. With AUS, 1944-46. Decorated Order of Aztec Eagle (Mex.), 1990, Order of José de Escandón (Mex.), 1991; recipient Charles Frankel prize NEH, 1989, award for lifetime achievement Tex. Inst. Letters, 1995; Guggenheim fellow, 1962. Mem. Am. Folklore Soc. (award 1990), Acad. Norteamericana de la Lengua Espanola, Mex. Acad. History. Office: Univ Tex Dept English Austin TX 78712

PAREDES, JAMES ANTHONY, anthropologist, educator; b. N.Y.C., Sept. 29, 1939; s. Antonio P. Piñero and Mildred Olene (Brown) P.; m. Anna Hamilton, Nov. 25, 1959 (div. 1984); children: J. Anthony Jr., Anna Teresa P. Lesinski, Sara Caroline P. Campbell; m. Elizabeth Dixon Purdum, Aug. 10, 1985 (div. 1994); 1 stepchild, David Joseph Plante. BA, Oglethorpe U., 1961; MA, U. N.Mex., 1964, PhD, 1969. Rsch. coord. Upper Miss. Mental Health Ctr., Bemidji, Minn., 1964-67; asst. prof., acting dir. Am. Ind. Studies Bemidji State Coll., 1967-68; community devel. specialist U. Minn. Agrl. Extension Svc., Bemidji, 1967-68; asst. prof. dept. anthropology Fla. State U., Tallahassee, 1969-74, assoc. prof., 1974-78, prof., 1979—, chmn. dept., 1974-77, 84-90; adj. prof. dept. anthropology U. Fla., Gainesville, 1979—; cons. Nat. Marine Fisheries Svc., Galveston, Tex., 1987-88, Bur. Indian Affairs, Washington, 1985, 92, Fed. Recognition Panel, Assn. on Am. Indian Affairs, N.Y.C., 1987-88. Author: Indios de los Estados Unidos Anglosajones, 1992; editor: Anishinabe: Six Studies of Modern Chippewa, 1980, Indians of the Southeastern United States in the Late 20th Century, 1992; author or co-author numerous articles, chpts. in books, revs. Mem. Sci. and Statis. Com., Gulf of Mex. Fishery Mgmt. Coun., Tampa, Fla., 1978-88. Recipient svc. award Poarch Creek Indians, 1990, Woodrow Wilson Found. fellow U. N.Mex., 1961-62; Nat. Inst. Mental Health predoctoral fellow U. N.Mex., 1968-69; Rockefeller Ctr. for Study of So. Culture and Religion fellow, Fla. State U., 1978. Fellow Am. Anthrop. Assn., Soc. for Applied Anthropology (assoc. editor 1983-88, pres. 1993-95); mem. So. Anthrop. Soc. (pres. 1988-89), Fla. Acad. Scis. (sect. chair 1984-85), Sigma Xi (Fla. State U. chpt. pres. 1977-78). Democrat. Avocation: walking. Office: Fla State U Dept Anthropology Tallahassee FL 32306

PARELL, MARY LITTLE, federal judge, former banking commissioner; b. Fond du Lac, Wis., Aug. 13, 1946; d. Ashley Jewell and Gertrude (McCoy) Little; m. John Francis Parell, May 28, 1972 (div. 1990); children: Christie, Morgan, Shawn, John Brady. AB in Polit. Sci. cum laude, Bryn Mawr Coll., 1968; JD, Villanova U., 1972; LLD (hon.), Georgian Ct. Coll., 1987. Bar. N.J. 1972. Assoc. McCarter & English, Newark, 1972-80, ptnr., 1980-84; commr. N.J. Dept. Banking, Trenton, 1984-90; assoc. gen. counsel Prudential Property & Casualty Ins. Co., Holmdel, N.J., 1991-92; judge U.S. Dist. Ct. N.J., 1992—; chmn. bd. Pinelands Devel. Credt Bank. Bd. trustees Exec. Commn. Ethical Standards, Trenton, 1984-90, Corp. Bus. Assistance, Trenton, 1984-91, N.J. Housing & Mortgage Fin. Agy., Trenton, 1984-90, N.J. Cemetery Bd. Assn., 1984-90, N.J. Hist. Soc., 1976-79., YMCA of Greater Newark, 1973-76, Diocesan Investment; mem. Supreme Ct. N.J. Civil Practice Com., 1982-84, Supreme Ct. N.J. Dist. Ethics Com., 1982-84; lay assesor Ecclesiastical Ct. Episc. Diocese Newark, 1980-84. Fellow Am. Bar Found.; mem. ABA, N.J. Bar Assn., Princeton Bar Assn. Office: US Courthouse 402 E State St Ste 5000 Trenton NJ 08608-1507*

PARENT, ANDRÉ, neurobiology educator, researcher; b. Montreal, Que., Can., Oct. 3, 1944; s. Lucien and Yvette (Gagné) P.; m. Doris Côté, July 8, 1970; children: Geneviève, Philippe, Martin. BSc, U. Montreal, 1967; PhD in Neurobiology, U. Laval, Quebec City, Que., 1970; postgrad., Max-Planck Inst., Frankfurt, Germany, 1971. Asst. prof. anatomy Laval U. Med. Sch., 1971-76, assoc. prof., 1976-81, prof., 1981—, sci. dir. Neurobiology Rsch. Ctr., 1985-92. Author: Comparative Neurobiology of the Basal Ganglia, 1986, Human Neuroanatomy, 9th edit., 1996. Studentship Med. Rsch. Coun. Can., 1967-70, fellow, Frankfurt, 1970-71, scholar, 1973-78. Mem. Royal Soc. Can., Internat. Brain Rsch. Orgn. Avocations: music, reading. Office: Ctr Rsch Univ Laval Robert-Giffard, 2601 de la Canardiere, Beauport, PQ Canada G1J 2G3

PARENT, DAVID HILL, investment company executive; b. Salem, Oreg., Apr. 13, 1940; s. Donald Allan and Pauline Louise (Lyons) P.; m. Christine Hedwige Marie Theérèse Wielezynski, Sept. 25, 1976; children: Marc Alexander Lair Thompson, Nathalie Jacqueline Marie Pauline. BS, U. Calif. Berkeley, 1963; MBA, Columbia U., 1965. Internat. fellow Columbia U., N.Y.C., 1963; dir. mktg. Europe Vendo Internat., Brussels, 1965-69; exec. v.p. T.S.I., Hempstead, N.Y., 1969-70; v.p. mktg. Gateway-Globus, Forest Hills, N.Y., 1970-72; mgr. Ctrl. Africa, Leon Tempelsman & Son, N.Y.C., 1972-79; pres. The Parent Co., Plano, Tex., 1979—; advisor to pres. of Gabon, Libreville, 1976-79. Mem. Rockwall Citizens's Counc. (exec. com.), Rockwall C. of C., Plano C. of C. Republican. Roman Catholic. Avocations: travel, skiing, scuba diving. Home and Office: 6410 Meadowcreek Dr Dallas TX 75240

PARENT, GILBERT, member Canadian House of Commons; b. Mattawa, Ont., Can., July 25, 1935; m. Joan Davis, Aug. 23, 1958; children: Michèle Hundertmark, Monique Finley, Madeleine Thomas, Thérèse Perruzza. BSc, St. Joseph's Coll., LLD (hon.), 1995; MA, Niagara U.; MEd, U. N.Y.; LLD (hon.), Niagara U., 1995, Brock U., 1996. M.P. Ho. of Commons, Ottawa, Ont., Can., 1974; re-elected, 1979, 88; Parliamentary Sec.to Min. Veterans Affairs Ottawa, Ont., Can., 1977-79, Parliamentary Sec. to Min. of Labour, 1979-81, Parliamentary Sec. to Min. of Fitness and Amateur Sports, 1981-83; Speaker of the House Ho. of Commons, Ottawa, Ont., Can., 1994; appted. Critic for Youth, 1989, Labour, 1992; assoc. critic CIDA, 1989, Industry, 1992. Mem. Parliament for Niagara Ctr. (formerly the Riding of Welland - St. Catharines - Thorold). Mem. Can.-U.S. Parliamentary Assn. (vice-chair). Office: House of Commons, Rm 328-N Centre Block, Ottawa, ON Canada K1A 0A6

PARENT, RODOLPHE JEAN, Canadian air force official, pilot; b. Thurso, Que., Can., June 16, 1937; s. Eugène Jean and Eliane Marie (Raby) P.; m. Michelle Marie Masse, Aug. 10, 1963; children—Stéphane, Nathalie, Cynthia. Student, Coll. Militaire Royal de St-Jean, 1958-61; B.Sc., Royal Mil. Coll. Can., Kingston, Ont., 1963. Commd. Royal Can. Air Force, 1958; advanced through grades to brig.-gen., 1984; joined 425 Squadron for ops. on CF-101 aircraft Bagotville, Que., 1964-69; worked for Directorate of Recruiting and Selection at Nat. Def. Hdqrs., Ottawa, Ont., Can., 1969-71; chief of ops. 433 Tactical Fighter Squadron, Bagotville, 1972-75, Can. Forces Base Bagotville, 1975-76; comdg. officer 433 Tactical Fighter Squadron, 1976-80; asst. dir. personnel careers Nat. Def. Hdqrs., Ottawa, 1980-81; base comdr. Can. Forces Base Lahr, Federal Republic Germany, 1981-83; commandant Coll. Militaire Royal de Saint-Jean, Que., 1983-86; dir. gen. personnel careers other ranks Nat. Def. Hdqrs., Ottawa, 1986-89; def. attaché Paris, 1989-92; ret., 1992. Decorated Order of Mil. Merit, Order of St. John of Jerusalem. Roman Catholic. Avocations: hockey; tennis; windsurfing.

PARENTE, WILLIAM JOSEPH, political science educator; b. Chgo., July 7, 1937; s. Salvatore S. and Genevieve (Rooney) P.; m. Diane Alpern, Nov. 30, 1963; children: Elizabeth, Margaret, William Joseph, Caroline, Rebecca, Catherine, Abigail, Christopher, Natalya. A.B. cum laude, Xavier U., Ohio, 1961; Ph.D. (Woodrow Wilson fellow, Woodrow Wilson dissertation fellow), Georgetown U., 1970. Woodrow Wilson intern Wilberforce (Ohio) U., 1965-66; asst. prof., chmn. polit. sci. dept. Antioch Coll., 1966-69, assoc. dean faculty, 1969-70; dean Coll. Arts and Scis., U. Scranton, Pa., 1970-85; assoc. prof. polit. sci. Coll. Arts and Scis., U. Scranton, 1970-73, prof., 1973—; Fulbright scholar Chulalongkorn U., Bangkok, Thailand, 1985-86, Inst. for Policy Studies, Washington, 1986-87; mem. nat. Fulbright screening com. for East Asia, Southeast Asia; mem. adv. com. Inst. Internat. Edn.; cons. on world affairs to Peace Corps. Author articles in field. Fellow Inst. Acad. Deans, 1971, Inst. Ednl. Mgmt., Harvard Bus. Sch., 1972, Fulbright fellow, Korea, 1974, Indonesia, 1978, Germany, 1980, Thailand, 1985-86, fellow NEH Seminar, U. Va., 1976, Harvard U., 1985, Columbia U., 1988, George Mason U., Va., 1990, UCLA, 1991, U. Mich., 1992, William and Mary, 1993, U. Iowa, 1994, U. Accra, Ghana, 1996; scholar-diplomat program State Dept., 1970, 73; vis. scholar in humanities NYU, 1989. Fellow Union Experimenting Colls. and Univs., Inst. for Policy Studies, Soc. for Religion in Higher Edn.; mem. Am. Polit. Sci. Assn., Assn. Jesuit Colls. and Univs. (chmn. conf. on internat. edn. 1981-85), Alpha Sigma Nu (nat. sec.-treas. 1979-82, nat. pres. 1983-85), Pi Sigma Alpha, Eta Sigma Phi, Alpha Sigma Lambda, Tau Kappa Alpha, Phi Alpha Theta. Roman Catholic. Home: 1608 Summit Pointe Scranton PA 18508 Office: U Scranton Coll Arts & Sciences Scranton PA 18510

PARESKY, DAVID S., travel company executive; b. Boston, Sept. 27, 1938; s. Paul and Ada (Rudnick) P.; m. Linda Kotzen, Aug. 18, 1963; children: Pamela, Laura, Mark. BA, Williams Coll., 1960; JD, Harvard U., 1963, MBA, 1965. Bar: Mass. Pres., chmn. bd. Crimson Travel Service, Inc., Cambridge, Mass., 1965-89; pres., CEO Thomas Cook Travel, Cambridge, 1989-94, also chmn. bd. dirs. Dir., Gov.'s Mgmt. Task Force, Boston, 1979-83, Mass. Port Authority, Boston, 1980-83; mem. Bd. Higher Edn., Boston, 1980; trustee New Eng. Med. Ctr., 1982-83; mem. Bd. Regents of Higher Edn., Boston, 1980-86. Mem. Mass. Bar Assn., Am. Soc. Travel Agts., Travel Trust Internat., Greater Boston C. of C., Young Pres. Orgn. (chmn. New Eng. chpt. 1985), Chief Execs. Orgn., Phi Beta Kappa. Home: 231 Winter St Weston MA 02193-1034

PARET, DOMINIQUE, petroleum company executive; b. Boulogne, Billancourt, France, Jan. 11, 1948; came to U.S. 1994; m. Laure de Monts de Savasse; children: Astrid, Daphne. MA in Econs, MA in Mgmt., Paris U.; PMD, Harvard. Asst. treas. corp. desk Banque Francaise Du Commerce Exterieur, 1972-74; asst. treas. internat. dept. Elf Aquitane, Paris, 1975-78, asst. to chmn. and CEO, 1979-81, head U.S. desk, 1982-85; CFO finance Elf Gabon, Libreville, Gabon, 1986-90; mgng. dir. Elf Petroleum Asia, Brunei Darussalam, 1991-93; exec. v.p., COO Elf Aquitane, Inc., New York, 1994—; v.p. USA Northeast Conseillers du Commercer Exterieur de la France, French Am. C. of C. in U.S. (dir. N.Y. chapt.), bd. dirs. NYU Maison Francaise;. Mem. Internat. Hockey Assn. (adv. to pres.), Stade Francais (v.p. finance), French Field Hockey Assoc. (sr. v.p.), Internat. Olympic Acad. French Commn. (v.p., pres.), Haut Comite de la Jeunesse, des Sports, et des Loisirs. Office: Elf Aquitaine Inc 280 Park Ave New York NY 10017-1216

PARET, PETER, historian; b. Berlin, Apr. 13, 1924; s. Hans and Suzanne Aimée (Cassirer) P.; m. Isabel Harris, Sept. 23, 1961; children: Suzanne Aimée, Paul Louis Michel. BA, U. Calif., Berkeley, 1949; Ph.D., U. London, 1960, DLitt, 1992; LittD, U. S.C., 1995; HHD, Coll. of Wooster, 1996. Resident tutor, delegacy of extramural studies Oxford U., 1959-60; research assoc. Center of Internat. Studies, Princeton U., 1960-62, 63; vis. asst. prof. U. Calif., Davis, 1962-63; assoc. prof. U. Calif., 1963-66, prof., 1966-69; prof. history Stanford U., 1969-77, Raymond A. Spruance prof. internat. history, 1977-86; Andrew W. Mellon Prof. in humanities Inst. Advanced Study, Princeton, N.J., 1986—; mem. Inst. for Advanced Study, Princeton, 1966-67; fellow Ctr. for Advanced Study in Behavioral Scis., Stanford, Calif., 1968-69; vis. fellow London Sch. Econs., 1972-73; NEH fellow, 1979-80; sr. fellow Hoover Instn., Stanford U., 1988-93. Author: (with John Shy) Guerrillas in the 1960's, 1962, French Revolutionary Warfare from Indochina to Algeria, 1964, Yorck and the Era of Prussian Reform, 1966, Clausewitz and the State, 1976, rev. edit., 1985; The Berlin Secession, 1980, Art as History, 1988, (with Beth Irwin Lewis and Paul Paret) Persuasive Images, 1992, Understanding War, 1992, Imagined Battles, 1997; editor, translator: (with Michael Howard) On War (C. v. Clausewitz), 1976, (with Daniel Moran) Historical and Political Writings (C. v. Clausewitz), 1992; editor: Frederick the Great, 1968, Frederick the Great—A Historical Profile, 1972, Sisyphus or the Limits of Education, 1973, The Age of German Liberation, 1977, Berliner Secession, 1981, Makers of Modern Strategy, 1986, (with Ekkehard Mai) Sammler, Stifter & Museen, 1993. Served with inf. U.S. Army, 1943-46. Fellow AAAS, Royal Hist. Soc., Hist. Kom zu Berlin, Leo Baeck Inst., London Sch. Econs. (hon.); mem. Am. Philos. Soc. (Jefferson medal), Soc. for Mil. History (Samuel Eliot Morison medal). Office: Sch Hist Studies Inst Advanced Study Princeton NJ 08540

PARETSKY, SARA N., writer; b. Ames, Iowa, June 8, 1947; d. David Paretsky and Mary E. Edwards; m. S. Courtenay Wright, June 19, 1976; children: Kimball Courtenay, Timothy Charles, Philip William. BA, U. Kans., 1967; MBA, PhD, U. Chgo., 1977. Mgr. Urban Rsch Ctr., Chgo., 1971-74, CNA Ins. Co., Chgo., 1977-85; writer, 1985—. Author: (novels) Indemnity Only, 1982, Deadlock, 1984 (Friends of Am. Writers award 1985), Killing Orders, 1985, Bitter Medicine, 1987, Blood Shot, 1988 (Silver Dagger award Crime Writers Assn., 1988), Burn Marks, 1990, Guardian Angel, 1992, Tunnel Vision, 1994, also numerous articles and short stories. Pres. Sisters in Crime, Chgo., 1986-88; dir. Nat. Abortion Rights Action League Ill., 1987—. Named Woman of Yr. Ms mag., N.Y.C., 1987. Mem. Crime Writers Assn. (Silver Dagger award 1988), Mystery Writers Am. (v.p. 1989), Authors Guild, Chgo. Network. Avocations: baseball, opera. Address: 1507 E 53rd St # 223 Chicago IL 60615*

PARHAM, CAROL SHEFFEY, school system administrator; b. Balt.; m. William N. Parham, Jr.; children: William N. III, Julie T. BA in Social Studies Edn., U. Md.; M in Edn. Guidance and Counseling, Johns Hopkins U., postgrad. studies; EdD, U. Md. Social studies tchr. Balt. City Schs., personnel specialist, acting staff specialist, personnel assoc.; supr. office personnel Howard County Pub. Schs., 1985-89; dir. personnel Anne Arundel County Pub. Schs., 1989—. Bd. dirs. Anne Arundel Trade Coun., United Way Ctrl. Md.; mem. task force Md. State Dept. Edn.; mem. edn. adv. com. Johns Hopkins U. Sch. Continuing Studies; mem. adv. bd. Leadership Anne Arundel; trustee Western Md. Coll. Recipient Outstanding Achievement in Leadership award Md. State Tchrs. Assn., Outstanding Leadership in Edn. award St. John United Meth. Women; Good Scout award Baltimore Area Coun. Boy Scouts Am.; named Woman of Yr., Glen Burnie Chpt. Nat. Fedn. Bus. Profl. Women, Md. Supt. of Yr., 1995. Mem. Pub. Sch. Supts. Assn. Md. (pres.), Assn. Sch. Bus. Officials Md. and DC (past pres.), Md. Pers. Assn. (past pres.), Coalition 100 Black Women, Rotary, Delta Sigma Theta. Office: Office of Supt 2644 Riva Rd Annapolis MD 21401-7305

PARHAM, ELLEN SPEIDEN, nutrition educator; b. Mitchells, Va., July 15, 1938; d. Marion Coote and Rebecca Virgrinia (McNiel) Speiden; m. Arthur Robert Parham, Jr., Dec. 16, 1961; children: Katharine Alma, Cordelia Alyx. BS in Nutrition, Va. Poly. Inst., 1960; PhD in Nutrition, U. Tenn., 1967; MSEd in Counseling, No. Ill. U., 1994. Registered dietitian; lec. profl. counselor. Asst. prof. to prof. No. Ill. U., DeKalb, Ill., 1966—; coord. programs in dietetics No. Ill. U., DeKalb, 1981-86, 90—, coord. grad. faculty sch. family, consumer, nutrition scis., 1985-87; cons. on nutrition various hosps., clins. and bus., Ill., 1980—; founder, dir. Horizons Weight Control Program, DeKalb, 1983-91; founder, leader "Escaping the Tyranny of the Scale" Group, 1994—; co-chair Nutrition Coalition for Ill., 1989-90; pres., mgr. Design on Fabric, 1986—; adj. counselor Ctr. for Counsel, Family Svc. Agy. of DeKalb County. Bd. editors Jour. Nutrition Edn., 1985-90, Jour. Am. Dietetic Assn., 1991—; contbr. articles to profl. jours. Mem. Am. Inst. Nutrition, Soc. Nutrition Edn., Am. Dietetic Assn., Soc. Nutrition Edn. (treas. 1991-94, chair divsn. nutrition and weight realities 1995-96), N.Am. Assn. Study Obesity. Avocations: painting in watercolor, gardening, reading.

PARHAM, JAMES ROBERT, lawyer; b. East St. Louis, Ill., June 3, 1921; s. James Elbert and Edith Virginia (May) P.; m. Caroline Short, Nov. 4, 1950 (dec.); m. Elizabeth Joan Rinck, June 29, 1957; children: James R., Jr., Joseph R., J. Randolph. A.B., Princeton U., 1943; J.D. with honors, U. Ill., 1948. Bar: Ill. 1948, U.S. Dist. Ct. (so. dist.) Ill. 1948, U.S. Supreme Ct. 1968. Assoc., Pope & Driemeyer, East St. Louis, 1948-59, ptnr., Belleville, Ill., 1960-84, Thompson & Mitchell, 1985-95, Thompson Coburn, 1996—; mem. adv. coun. Ill. Inst. for Continuing Legal Edn., Springfield, Ill., 1965-74. Contbr. articles to profl. jours. Sec., YMCA of S.W. Ill., Belleville, 1979-84. Served with U.S. Air Corps, 1943, 45, USAFR, 1950-53. Recipient Man of Yr. award Bicounty YMCA, Belleville, 1973; Disting. Service award Ill. Inst. Continuing Edn., 1974. Fellow Am. Bar Found., Ill. State Bar Found.; mem. Ill. State Bar Assn. (chmn. state tax sect. 1974), ABA, Met. St. Louis Bar Assn., Res. Officers Assn., Order of Coif. Republican. Methodist. Clubs: St. Clair Country (Belleville, v.p. 1955-56); Grey Oaks Country Club (Naples, Fla.). Lodge: Rotary (pres. East St. Louis club 1976-77). Home: 7535 Claymont Ct # 3 Belleville IL 62223-2218 Office: Thompson Coburn 525 W Main St PO Box 750 Belleville IL 62222

PARINS, ROBERT JAMES, professional football team executive, judge; b. Green Bay, Wis., Aug. 23, 1918; s. Frank and Nettie (Denissen) P.; m. Elizabeth L. Carroll, Feb. 8, 1941; children: Claire, Andrée, Richard, Teresa, Lu Ann. B.A., U. Wis., 1940, LL.B., 1942. Bar: Wis. Supreme Ct. 1942. Pvt. practice Green Bay, Wis., 1942-68; dist. atty. Brown County, Wis., 1949-50, cir. judge, 1968-82, res. judge, 1982—; pres. Green Bay Packers, Inc., 1982-90, chmn. bd., 1990-92; hon. chmn. bd., 1992-94. Mem. Wis. State Bar Assn. Roman Catholic.

PARIS, DEMETRIUS THEODORE, electrical engineering educator; b. Stavroupolis, Thrace, Greece, Sept. 27, 1928; came to U.S., 1947, naturalized, 1954; s. Theodore P. and Aspasia (Yannakis) Paraskevopoulos; m. Elsie Edwards, Jan. 5, 1952. B.S., Miss. State U., 1951; M.S., Ga. Inst. Tech., 1958, Ph.D., 1962. With Westinghouse Electric Corp., 1952-58, Lockheed-Ga. Co., 1958-59; asst. prof. elec. engring. Ga. Inst. Tech., 1959-63, assoc. prof., 1963-66, prof., 1966—, asst. dir. elec. engring., 1966-69, dir., 1969-89, v.p for rsch. and grad. programs, 1989-95; cons.Sci.-Atlanta, Inc., Lockheed-Ga. Co., U.S. Army Ltd. War Lab., Aberdeen, Md.; chair internat. activities com. Accreditation Bd. for Engring. and Tech., 1991—. Author: Basic Electromagnetic Theory, 1969. Recipient Sigma Xi award for best research paper by a mem. Ga. Inst. Tech. faculty, 1965. Fellow IEEE (editor trans. on edn. 1976-79, Centennial medal 1984, ednl. activities bd. meritorious svc. citation 1989, IEEE rep. to Accreditation Bd. for Engring. and Tech. bd. dirs. 1990-95), Accreditation Bd. for Engring. and Tech.; mem. IEEE Edn. Soc. (Achievement award 1980, pres. 1986), Am. Soc. Engring. Edn., Sigma Xi, Kappa Mu Epsilon, Tau Beta Pi, Eta Kappa Nu, Phi Kappa Phi. Home: 2797 Alpine Rd NE Atlanta GA 30305-3401

PARIS, STEVEN MARK, software engineer; b. Boston, May 26, 1956; s. Julius Louis and Frances (Keleishik) P. BS, Rensselaer Poly. Inst., 1978; MS, Boston U., 1980, postgrad., 1980-84. Sr. software engr. Prime Computer Inc., Framingham, Mass., 1978-82; sr. analyst Computervision Corp., Bedford, Mass., 1982-84; prin. engr. Lotus Devel., Inc., Cambridge, Mass., 1984-88; pres. Tri-Millennium Corp., 1988-91; sr. researcher Tech. Edn. Rsch. Ctr., Cambridge, Mass., 1990-93; prin. engr. Beyond, Inc., Burlington, Mass., 1993, Bus. Matters Inc., Waltham, Mass., 1994-96; v.p. engr. Ambit, Inc., Brighton, Mass., 1996—. Lt. Mass. Civil Def. Recipient Boston Sci. Fair 1st prize, 1973, 74, State of Mass. Sci. Fair 3d prize, 1973, 2d prize, 1974. Mem. Assn. for Computing Machinery, IEEE, Boston Computer Soc., Planetary Soc. Jewish. Office: Watermill Ctr 800 South St Waltham MA 02154-1439

PARIS, VIRGINIA HALL (GINGER PARIS), elementary school educator; b. Talladega, Ala., Sept. 25, 1962; d. Robert Dorch and Bonnie (Green) Hall; m. Walter Kevin Paris, June 8, 1985; children: Taylor Ray, Tyger Jean. AS, Jefferson State Jr. Coll., 1982; BS, Auburn U., 1984; MS, Jacksonville State U., 1991, U. Ala., Birmingham, 1994. Cert. ednl. leadership. Tchr. gifted program Talladega County Schs., 1984-85, tchr. learning disabled program, 1988-89; tchr. Big Bend C.C., Vicenza, Italy, 1986-87; tchr., dir. Villagio Child Devel. Ctr., Vicenza, 1987-88; tchr. social studies Dixon Mid. Sch., Talladega, 1989-91, tchr. sci., 1991—; insvc. edn. cons. U. Montevallo, 1994—; acad. pep squad sponsor, 1995—, sch. news reporter, 1989-93, 95—, ann. photographer, 1991-94, student coun. adv., 1989—, sponsor Trail Blazer/Ecology Club, 1992-96, mem. staff devel. accreditation com. chairperson, comm. com. sec.; tchr. rep. spl. edn. screening com. Talladega City Schs., 1989-93; vis. com. So. Assn. Colls. and Schs., Montgomery, Ala., 1992. Vol. instr. ARC, Vicenza, 1986, Talladega, 1988; coord. Adopt-a-Grandparent program Talladega Health Care, 1991-96; mem. Friends of Libr., Talladega, 1992; coord., sponsor March for Parks, Talladega, 1994, 95, 96, 97; bd. dirs. Talladega Parks and Recreation, chairperson, 1994—; mem. planning com. Talladega 2000, mem. steering com., 1996. Recipient Tchr. of Yr. award Dixon Rep. Ala., 1991-92, Pilot Club Tchr. of Yr 1995, Tchr. of Yr. award Dixon Rep. Jacksonville State U., 1992-93; Tchr. of the Yr. Jaycees 1994-95. Mem. NEA, Ala. Edn. Assn., Nat. Sci. Tchrs. Assn., Talladega City Edn. Assn., Anniston Mus. Natural History, Ala. Cattlewomen's Assn., Environ. Edn. Assn., Nat. Pks. and Conservation Assn., Nat. Audubon Soc., Nat. Arbor Day Found., Nat. Wildlife Assn., Auburn U. Alumni Assn., Ala. Middle Sch. Assn. (program dir. region VI 1995-96),S Kappa Delta Pi, Delta Zeta Alumni. Republican. Baptist. Avocations: softball, volleyball, swimming, aerobics, animals. Home: 620 Cherry St Talladega AL 35160-2716 Office: Dixon Mid Sch 415 Elm St Talladega AL 35160-2704

PARISER, RUDOLPH, chemicals company executive, consultant; b. Harbin, China, Dec. 8, 1923; came to U.S., 1941, naturalized, 1944; s. Ludwig Jacob and Lia (Rubinstein) P.; m. Margaret Louise Marsh, July 31, 1972. BS in Chemistry, U. Calif., Berkeley, 1944; PhD in Phys. Chemistry, U. Minn., 1950. With E.I. du Pont de Nemours & Co., Wilmington, Del., 1950-89, with elastomer chems. dept., 1967-79, dir. pioneering rsch., 1974-79, rsch. dir. polymer products dept., 1980-81, dir. polymer sci. cen. R & D dept., 1981-86, dir. advanced materials sci. cen. R & D dept., 1986-89; cons., pres. R. Pariser & Co., Inc., Hockessin, Del., 1989—; mem. materials rsch. adv. com. Nat. Sci. Found., 1986-89. Assoc. editor Jour. Chem. Physics, 1966-69, Chem. Physics Letters, 1967-70, Du Pont Innnovation, 1969-75; mem. adv. bd. Jour. Polymer Sci., 1980-89; mem. editorial bd. New Polymeric Materials, 1985-92; patentee in field; contbr. articles to profl. jours. With U.S. Army, 1944-46. Mem. AAAS, Am. Chem. Soc., Am. Phys. Soc., Internat. Union Pure and Applied Chemistry, Phila. Interlocuters (pres. 1972-76), Sigma Xi, Phi Lambda Upsilon, Du Pont Country Club, Rodney Sq. Club, Univ. and Whist Club Wilmington. Avocations: skiing, tennis, golf, sailing, gardening.

PARISH, J. MICHAEL, lawyer, writer; b. Decatur, Ill., Nov. 9, 1943; s. John Mitchell and Gladys Margaret (Daulton) P.; m. Susan Lee Sgarlat, July 24, 1976 (div.); m. Ellen R. Harnett, Dec. 3, 1991; children: Margaret Ruth, William Walter. AB cum laude, Princeton U., 1965; LLB, Yale U., 1968. Assoc. LeBoeuf Lamb et al, N.Y.C., 1968-73, ptnr., 1974-89; ptnr. Winthrop Stimson Putnam & Roberts, N.Y.C., 1989-95, Reid & Priest, N.Y.C., N.Y.C., 1995—; bd. dirs. Forum Funds, Portland, Maine, Core Trust. Contbr. poetry to mags. Dir. PBS Am. Poetry Project, 1985-90; coord. Yale Law Sch. Clinton Election com.; class sec. Princeton Class of 1965. Univ. scholar Princeton U., 1965. Mem. Princeton Club N.Y. Avocations: soccer referee, coach Little League, poetry, fiction, nonfiction. Home: 100 Riverside Dr New York NY 10024-4822 Office: Reid & Priest 40 W 57th St New York NY 10019-4001

PARISH, JAMES ROBERT, author, cinema historian; b. Cambridge, Mass., Apr. 21, 1944; s. Fred Arthur and Ann Lois (Magilevy) P. BA, U. Pa., 1964, LLB, 1967. Pres. Entertainment Copyright Rsch.Co. Inc., N.Y.C., 1967-68; film reporter, reviewer, interviewer Variety, Motion Picture Daily, 1968-69; entertainment publicist Harold Rand & Co., 1969-70; freelance writer, publicist, film book cons., film reviewer, novelist, 1970—; acquisition editor Renaissance Books, 1996—. Author: (with P. Michael) The Emmy Awards: A Pictorial History, 1970, The Fox Girls, 1971, The Great Movie Series, 1971 (with A.H. Marill) The Cinema of Edward G. Robinson, 1972, The Slapstick Queens, 1972, The Paramount Pretties, 1972, (with R. Bowers) The MGM Stock Company, 1973, Actors TV Credits, 1950-72, 73, Good Dames, 1973, (with M.R. Pitts) The Great Spy Pictures, 1973, The RKO Gals, 1973, (with S. Whitney), The George Raft File, 1973, (with M.R. Pitts) Film Directors: A Guide to Their American Pictures, 1974, Hollywood's Great Love Teams, 1974, (with S. Whitney) Vincent Price Unmasked, 1974, The Great Movie Heroes, 1975, (with D. Stanke), The Glamour Girls, 1975, The Debonairs, 1975, (with L. DeCarl) Hollywood Players: The Forties, 1975, (with J. Ano) Liza! (The Liza Minnelli Story), 1975, (with M.R. Pitts) The Great Gangster Pictures, 1975, The Elvis Presley Scrapbook, 1975, (with W. Leonard) Hollywood Players: The Thirties, 1976, (with D. Stanke) The All Americans, 1976, Film Directors: A Guide for Western Europe, 1976, Great Child Stars, 1976, The Jeanette McDonald Story, 1976, (with D. Stanke) The Leading Ladies, 1977, (with M.R. Pitts) The Great Science Fiction Pictures, 1977, Film Actors Guide: Western Europe, 1977, The Elvis Presley Scrapbook (update), 1977, (with M. Trost) Actors TV Credits: Supplement One, 1977, (with M.R. Pitts) Hollywood on Hollywood, 1978, (with R. Braff et al.) Hollywood Character Actors, 1978, (with G. Mank and D. Stanke) The Hollywood Beauties, 1978, (with W. Leonard) The Funsters, 1979, (with D. Stanke) The Forties Gals, 1980, (with G. Mank) The Hollywood Reliables, 1980, The Great American Movies Book, 1980, (with G. Mank) The Best of MGM, 1981, (with M.R. Pitts) The Great Spy Pictures II, 1986, (with M.R. Pitts) The Great Gangster Pictures II, 1987, (with M.R. Pitts) The Great Western Pictures II, 1988, Black Action Pictures from Hollywood, 1989, (with M.R. Pitts) The Great Science Fiction Pictures II, 1990, (with V. Terrace) Complete Actors TV Credits, 1990, (with M.R. Pitts) Hollywood Songsters, 1990, The Great Cop Pictures, 1990, Prison Pictures from Hollywood, 1991, (with M.R. Pitts) Hollywood's Great Musicals, 1992, (with D. Stanke) Hollywood Baby Boomers, 1992, Prostitution in Hollywood Film, 1992, The Hollywood Death Book, 1992; Let's Talk: America's Favorite Talk Show Hosts, 1993, Gays and Lesbians in Mainstream Cinema, 1993, Hollywood's Celebrity Death Book, updated and expanded, 1994, Ghosts and Angels on the Hollywood Screen, 1995, Today's Black Hollywood, 1995, Pirates and Seafaring Swashbucklers, 1995, The Great Child Stars, 1996, The Unofficial "Murder She Wrote" Casebook, 1997, Rosie: The Rosie O'Donnell Story, 1997, Whoopi Goldberg, 1997; assoc. editor: The American Movies Reference Book, 1969, TV Movies, 1969, The Great American Movie Book, 1980. Mem. Phi Beta Kappa. Avocations: docent, reading, writing. Address: 4338 Gentry Ave Unit 1 Studio City CA 91604-1764 *To succeed in one's ambitions requires an unyielding avoidance of other people's skepticisms.*

PARISH, JOHN COOK, insurance executive; b. Montezuma, Iowa, Mar. 26, 1910; s. Ariel Robert and Mary Ora (Cook) P.; m. Elizabeth Myers, Sept. 2, 1936; children: John C., Michael Myers, Judith, Robert S. Student, UCLA; B.A., Dartmouth Coll., 1936. Officer Dollar S.S. Lines, Seattle, 1930-31; with Ginn & Co. (pubs.), Manila, 1933-34; sec. to U.S. rep. Warsaw, Poland, 1934; with St. Paul Fire & Marine Ins. Co., 1936—, exec. spl. agt., 1943-44, asst. mgr. Pacific dept., 1947-48, asst. sec., 1948-50, sec., 1950-68, v.p., 1968—; also dir.; sec. St. Paul Mercury Ins. Co., 1950-68, v.p., 1968—; also dir.; v.p. St. Paul Ins. Co., 1968—. Mem. Bishop's council Minn. Espiscopal Diocese; past pres. treas. Summit Sch. for Girls, St. Paul; past pres. Indianhead council Boy Scouts Am., past regional chmn. and mem. nat. exec. bd., internat. commr., v.p., 1972-78; hon. v.p. U.S. Found. for Internat. Scouting; chmn. St. Paul United Fund, 1963, pres., 1966; trustee Endowment Fund, Seabury Western Theol. Sem., Am. Humanics Found.; v.p. U.S. Found. Internat. Scouting, Salem Found.; bd. dirs. Inst. Ecumenical and Cultural Research, St. John's Coll.; mem. World Scout Com.; bd. trustees Naples (Fla.) Community Hosp.; sr. warden Trinity By the Cove Episcopal Ch., Naples, 1981-82; dir. Mooring Pk. Found. Decorated Cross of St. George Colombia; recipient Silver Tamaraw award Philippine Islands, Inter-Am. award Svc. to Youth, Silver Beaver, Silver Antelope, Silver Buffalo and Disting. Eagle award Boy Scouts Am., Bronze Wolf award for svc. to youth of world, Emerald Flower award Republic of China; Baden Powell fellow World Scout Found., 1982. Mem. St. Paul C. of C. (dir. 1973—), Somerset Country Club (St. Paul, dir. 1968), Royal Poinciana Club (Naples, Fla., past pres. and dir.), Collier Athletic Club, Beta Theta Pi. Home: Apt G-601 122 Moorings Park Dr Naples FL 34105-2169

PARISH, LAWRENCE CHARLES, physician, editor; b. Cambridge, Mass., Oct. 12, 1938; s. Fred A. and Ann Lois (Magilavy) P.; m. Sheila Gail Rovner, July 31, 1966; children: Daniel Howard, Jennifer Leigh. Student, U. Mich., 1955-56; AB, U. Pa., 1959; MD, Tufts U., 1963. Diplomate Am. Bd. Dermatology, 1969. Asst. prof. dermatology U. Pa., Phila., 1969-73, clin. assoc. prof., 1973-80, adj. assoc. prof. comparative dermatology Sch. Vet. Medicine, 1973-87, prof. comparative dermatology, 1987—; clin. assoc. prof. Jefferson Med. Coll., Phila., 1980-84, clin. prof., 1984—; dir. Jefferson Ctr. for Internat. Dermatology, 1987—; vis. prof. Yonsei U., Seoul, Korea, 1983—, Zagazig U., Egypt, 1990—. Author: Louis A. Duhring, Pathfinder for Dermatology, 1967, (with John Crissey) The Dermatology and Syphilology of the 19th Century, 1981, (with others) Cutaneous Infestations of Man and Animal, 1983, Practical Management of the Dermatologic Patient, 1986, (with John Pettit) Manual of Tropical Dermatology, 1984, (with F.G. Gschnait) Manual of Sexually Transmitted Diseases, 1989, (with others) Pediatric Dermatology, 1989, (with Gary P. Lask) Aesthetic Dermatology, 1991, (with others) Color Atlas of Sexually Transmitted Diseases, 1991, Color Atlas of Difficult Diagnoses in Dermatology, 1994, Global Dermatology, 1994, Manual of Medical Mycology, 1995, Color Atlas of Cutaneous Infections, 1995, The Decubitus Ulcer in Clinical Practice, 1997; editor-in-chief Internat. Jour. Dermatology, 1981, Clinics in Dermatology, 1983—; editl. bd. Cutis, P&T, Clin. Therapeutics Chronical Dermatologica, Annali Italiani di Dermatologia, Jour. European Acad. Dermatology and Venereology, Drug Therapy, Medicina Cutanea Ibero-Latino-Am., Advances in Therapeutics, Gulf Jour. Dermatology; assoc. editor Concepts, 1994—. Served to maj. U.S. Army, 1967-69; Korea. Recipient Andreus Bello award First Order of Venezuela. Fellow ACP, Coll. Physicians Phila. (chair sect. med. history 1975-78, founding chair sect. dermatology 1982-85); mem. Polish Acad. Dermatology (hon.), Brit. Assn. Dermatologists, Am. Acad. Vet. Dermatology, Venezuela Soc. Dermatology, Bulgarian Soc. Dermatology, French Soc. Dermatology and Venereology (corr. mem.), Italian Soc. Dermatology and Venereology (corr.), Israeli Soc. Dermatology, Istanbul Dermatol. Soc., Am. Dermatol. Assn., Can. Dermatology Assn., Internat. Soc. Dermatology, Internat. Acad. Cosmetic Dermatology (founding pres. 1995—), History of Dermatology Soc. (founding pres. 1972—), Masons, B'nai Brith. Jewish. Avocations: gardening, travel, history of medicine, genealogy, collecting majollica and bargeware. Home: 941 Bryn Mawr Ave Penn Valley PA 19072-1524 Office: 1819 John F Kennedy Blvd Philadelphia PA 19103-1733

PARISH, RICHARD LEE, engineer, consultant; b. Kansas City, Mo., May 31, 1945; s. Charles Lee and Ruth (Duncan) P.; m. Patricia Ann Erickson, June 2, 1968; children: Christie Lynn White, Kerry Anne Parish-Philp. BS in Agrl. Engring., U. Mo., 1967, MS in Agrl. Engring., 1968, PhD, 1970. Registered profl. engr., Ohio. Asst., then assoc. prof. engring. Univ. Ark., Fayetteville, 1969-74; mgr. mech. research and devel. O.M. Scott & Sons Co., Marysville, Ohio, 1974-83; assoc. prof., then prof. La. State U., Baton Rouge, 1983—; pvt. practice engring. cons. Baton Rouge and Hammond, La., 1984—; prof. Hammond Rsch. Sta., 1995—; cons. in equipment design and evaluation, expert witness testimony in agrl. and hort. equipment, 1984—. Contbr. over 100 articles to profl. jours. and trade pubs.; patentee in field (3). Bd. dirs. Agrl. Missions Found. Recipient Quality award ITT, 1979, Rsch. Dirs. award O.M. Scott Co., 1978; NSF fellow, 1967-69; rsch. grantee Cotton Inc., Raleigh, N.C., 1970-74, 91-93, 95-96, La. Dept. Natural Resources, 1985-87, Italian Trade Commn., 1988-90. Mem. Am. Soc. Agrl. Engrs. (chmn. agrl. chem. application com. 1982-83, power and machinery div. program com. 1986-87), La. Vegetable Growers Assn., Am. Soc. Hort. Sci. Republican. Baptist. Avocations: gardening, woodwork, bicycling. Home: 21135 Hwy 16 Amite LA 70422 Office: Hammond Rsch Sta 21549 Old Covington Hwy Hammond LA 70403-0533

PARISH, ROBERT LEE (CHIEF PARISH), professional basketball player; b. Shreveport, La., Aug. 30, 1953; m. Nancy Parish; 1 child, Justin. Student, Centenary Coll., 1972-76. Center Golden State Warriors, San Francisco, 1976-80, Boston Celtics, 1980-94; with Charlotte Hornets, 1994-96, Chgo. Bulls, 1996—; player NBA Championship Teams, 1981, 84. Named to Sporting News All-Am. First Team, 1976, NBA All-Star Team, 1981-87, 90-91. Office: Chgo Bulls 1901 W Madison St Chicago IL 60612*

PARISH, THOMAS SCANLAN, human development educator; b. Oak Park, Ill., Jan. 24, 1944; s. Robert S. and Florence Catherine (Fleming) P.; children: Robert V., Kimberly E., David G., Thomas P., Kathryn E.; m. Tatyana Gridneva, Jan. 3, 1997. BA, No. Ill. U., 1968; MA, Ill. State U., 1969; PhD, U. Ill., 1972. Instr. psychology Parkland Coll., Champaign, Ill., 1971-72; asst. prof. Okla. State U., Stillwater, 1972-76; assoc. prof. Kans. State U., Manhattan, 1976-80, prof., 1980—, asst. to dean of edn., 1992-97; ctrl. Kan. area coord. adult edn. program Kans. State U., 1997—; assoc. dir. ARIOS-Kan., 1994-96; rsch. coord. for Midwest Desegration Asst. Ct., 1994—. Assoc. editor: Jour. of Social Studies Rsch., 1994—; cons. editor Jour. Genetic Psychology, 1984—, Jour. Reality Therapy, 1992—, The Genetic, Social and General Psychology Monographs, 1984—; contbr. articles to profl. jours. Bd. dirs. Friendship Tutoring Program, Manhattan, 1982-91, Stillwater Awareness Coun., 1973-74; co-founder, bd. dirs. Youth Alternatives, Inc., Champaign, 1971-72; pres.-elect Mid-Western Edn. Rsch. Assn., 1997—. Fellow Am. Psychol. Soc.; mem. Am. Ednl. Rsch. Assn., APA, Assn. Reality Therapists, Soc. for Rsch. in Child Devel., Phi Delta Kappa, Phi Kappa Phi. Home: 2047 College View Rd Manhattan KS 66502-3509 Office: Kans State U Coll of Edn Bluemont Hall Manhattan KS 66506

PARISI, JOSEPH (ANTHONY), magazine editor, writer-consultant, educator; b. Duluth, Minn., Nov. 18, 1944; s. Joseph Carl Parisi and Phyllis Susan (Quaranta) Schlecht. B.A. with honors, Coll. St. Thomas, 1966; M.A., U. Chgo., 1967, Ph.D. with honors, 1973. Asst. prof. Roosevelt U., Chgo., 1969-78; assoc. editor POETRY Mag., Chgo., 1976-83; acting editor POETRY Mag., 1983-85, editor, 1985—; vis. prof. U. Ill., Chgo., 1978-87; cons., writer ALA, Chgo., 1980—; cons. NEH, 1983—. Author: The Poetry Anthology, 1912-1977, 1978, Voices and Visions Reader's Guide, 1987, Marianne Moore: The Art of a Modernist, 1990, (listener's guide) Poets in Person, 1992; contbr. articles and reviews to profl. jours.; producer, dir. (audio series on NPR) Poets in Person, 1991. Recipient Alvin Bentley award Duns Scotus Coll., 1963; fellow U. Chgo., 1966-69. Mem. Delta Epsilon Sigma. Club: Cliff Dwellers. Avocations: piano, photography, book and record collecting. Office: Poetry Mag 60 W Walton St Chicago IL 60610-3305

PARIZA, MICHAEL WILLARD, research institute executive, microbiology and toxicology educator; b. Waukesha, Wis., Mar. 10, 1943; married; 3 children. BSc in Bacteriology, U. Wis., 1967; MSc in Microbiology, Kans. State U., 1969, PhD in Microbiology, 1973. Postdoctoral trainee McArdle Lab. for Cancer Rsch. U. Wis., Madison, 1973-76, asst. prof. Food Rsch. Inst. dept. Food Microbiology and Toxicology, 1976-81, assoc. prof., 1981-84, prof., 1984—, assoc. dept. chmn., 1981-82, dept. chmn. food microbiology and toxicology, 1982—, dir. Food Rsch. Inst., 1986—, disting. prof., 1993—; with Wis. Clin. Cancer Ctr., Environ. Toxicology Ctr., Dept. Nutritional Scis., Dept. Food Sci.; mem. Inst. Medicine's Food Forum; mem. com. on comparative toxicity naturally occurring carcinogens NAS; trustee Internat. Life Scis. Inst.-N.Am., 1986—. With U.S. Army, 1969-71. Fellow Inst. Food Technologists. Office: U Wis Food Rsch Inst 1925 Willow Dr Madison WI 53706-1103

PARIZEAU, JACQUES, former Canadian government official; b. Montréal, Aug. 9, 1930; s. Gérard and Germaine (Biron) P.; m. Alicja Poznanska, Apr. 12, 1956 (dec. 1990); children: Bernard, Isabelle; m. Lisette LaPointe, Dec. 12, 1992. Degree, Inst. d'études politiques, Paris, 1952; PhD in Econs., London Sch. Econs., 1955. Prof. École des Hautes Études commerciales, Montréal, 1955-65, 67-70, 85-89; chmn. Inst. Applied Econs., Montréal, 1970-73; mem. Can. Nat. Assembly, Que., 1976-84, 89—; pres. Parti Québécois Can. Nat. Assembly, 1988—; min. fin. Québec Govt., 1976-84, min. revenue, 1976-84, pres. treasury bd., 1976-81, min. fin. instns., 1981-82, chmn. ministerial econ. devel. com., 1981-82, prime min., 1994-95; econ. and fin. adviser Premiers of Québec: Lesage, Johnson, Bertrand, Que., 1961-69; pres. Que. Fin. Instns. Task Force, 1970-73; chmn. Comm. of Enquiry on Future of Municipalities, Que., 1985. Editor L'Actualité économique, Montréal, 1955-61; chmn. bd. dirs. Daily Le Jour, Montréal, 1974-75; bd. dirs. Daily Le Devoir, Montréal, 1985-87. Bd. dirs. U. Montréal, 1969-74; bd. dirs., bd. govs. Théâtre du Nouveau-Monde, Montréal, 1988-92; pres. No com. Referendum on Charlottetown Accord, Que., 1992. Mem. Club de la Garnison (Que.), Knowlton Golf and Country Club (Lac Brome). Roman Catholic. Avocations: reading, music, gardening. Office: 88 S, Grand Alle est, Quebec, PQ Canada G1A 1A2

PARIZEK, ELDON JOSEPH, geologist, college dean; b. Iowa City, Apr. 30, 1920; s. William Joseph and Libbie S. P.; m. Mildred Marie Burger, Aug. 9, 1944; children—Richard, Marianne, Elizabeth, Amy. B.S., U. Iowa, 1942, M.S., 1946, Ph.D., 1949. Instr. U. Iowa, 1947-49; asst. prof. geology U. Ga., 1949-54, assoc. prof., 1954-56; assoc. prof. U. Kansas City, 1956-63; prof. U. Mo., Kansas City, 1963—; chmn. dept. geoscis. U. Mo., 1968-78; dean U. Mo. (Coll. Arts and Scis.), 1979-86. Served with USN, 1942-45. Fellow Geol. Soc. Am.; mem. AAUP, Assn. Mo. Geologists, AAAS, Sigma Xi. Roman Catholic. Research, numerous publs. on mass wasting, slope failure, underground space, geology of West Mo. Home: 6913 W 100th Shawnee Mission KS 66212 Office: 5100 Rockhill Rd Kansas City MO 64110-2446

PARK, ALICE MARY CRANDALL, genealogist; b. Loda, Ill., Oct. 4, 1901; d. Frederick Adam and Sarah Elizabeth (Clemens) Crandall; m. Lee I. Park, Aug. 29, 1925 (dec. Aug. 24, 1978); children: Lee Crandall, Nancy Park Kern. BS, U. Chgo., 1924. Tchr. U. Chgo. Lab. Sch., 1924-25; genealogy rschr. Washington, 1925—. Author: Park/e/s and Bunch on the Trail West, 1974, rev. edit., 1982, Schenck and Related Families in New Netherlands, 1992, One Crandall Family 1651-1995, 1996. Pres. Falls Church (Va.) PTA, 1941-42, LWV, Fairfax County, Va., 1947-48. Mem. Chevy Chase Club, Met. Club Washington. Avocations: gardening, travel, cooking, music. Home: 4200 Cathedral Ave NW Washington DC 20016-4931

PARK, BEVERLY GOODMAN, public relations professional; b. Boston, Nov. 10, 1937; d. Morris and Mary (Keller) Goodman; divorced; children: Glynis Forcht, Seth, Elyse. BS, Simmons Coll., 1959; MS, Ea. Conn. State U., 1968; postgrad., Western N.E. Coll. Law, 1994—. Asst. dir. comty. svc. Hartford (Conn.) Courant, 1976-79; mayor Borough of Colchester, Conn., 1979-83; lifestyle editor Chronicle, Willimantic, Conn., 1980-82, suburban editor, 1982-84; officer mktg. & comm. U. Conn. Health Ctr., Farmington, 1984—; selected team mem. radiation exposure info. study Belorussia, 1993; mem. adv. bd. Hosp. News; mem. women's affairs com. U. Conn. Health Ctr. Women's Networking Task Force; mem. Univ. Adminstrv. Staff Coun.; mem. minority awards com. U. Conn. Health Ctr., mem. John N. Dempsey hosp. disaster plan com. Designer: (libr. studies curriculum) Classroom Instruction on the Use of Books and Libraries, 1972; pub.: (ednl. booklets) Have You Made Plans for the Future?, 1977-78; editor of edn. holiday and bridal supplements The Chronicle, 1980-84; editor: U. Conn. Health Ctr. Anniversary Mag., 1986, U. Conn. Health Ctr. Med. Catalog, 1986—, (ann. pub.) Salute, 1988—, U. Conn. Health Ctr. 30th Anniversary Supplement, 1991. Bd. dirs. Ea. Conn. Found. for Pub. Giving, Norwich, 1990—; women's club officer Dem. Town Com., Colchester, Conn., 1963-90; active Hadassah, Northampton/Amherst, 1996—, Women's League for Conservative Judaism. Recipient Lifestyle Page award New England Press Assn., 1980, Media Excellence in Covering Human Svcs. award Conn. chpt. NASW, 1982, Ragan Report Arnold's Admirables award for excellence in graphics and typography, 1985, Gold award Healthcare Mktg. Report, 1987, award for video ACS, 1990. Mem. NOW (membership com. Southea. chpt., mem. legis. task force, Meritorious Svc. award Southea. Conn. chpt. 1985), Am. Soc. for Hosp. Mktg. and Pub. Rels., Am. Mktg. Assn., Assn. Am. Med. Colls. (mem. group on pub. affairs), Conn. Hosp. Assn. (participant hosp. pub. rels. conf.), State of Conn. Pub. Info. Coun. (mem. steering com.), New England Hosp. Pub. Rels. and Mktg. Assn. (bd. dirs. 1987, 88). Avocations: swimming, hiking, spending time with grandchildren. Home: 111 Rick Dr Florence MA 01060-1047

PARK, CHARLES DONALD, SR., financial executive; b. N.Y.C., Aug. 1, 1945; s. Charles and Madeline (Springer) P.; m. Pauline De Meo; children: Paula, Madeline. BA, Pace U., 1968, MBA, 1970. Coord. fin. reports Gen. Telephone & Electronics, N.Y.C., 1968-70; mgr. fin. analysis Mobil Corp., N.Y.C., 1970-73; mgr. corp. bus. planning and analysis Gen. Instrument, N.Y.C., 1973-74; controller Microelectronics Group Gen. Instrument, Hicksville, N.Y., 1974-77, chief fin. officer, 1977-81; corp. dir., fin. analysis Bendix, Southfield, Mich., 1981-82; v.p. fin. and adminstrn. MCI Internat., Inc., Rye Brook, N.Y., 1982-86; sr. v.p. fin. Sprague Techs., Inc., Stamford, Conn., 1987-89; exec. v.p., CFO Briggs Industries, Tampa, Fla., 1989—.

PARK, CHUNG IL, librarian; b. Chang-won, Korea, Aug. 25, 1938; s. Zung S. and Bong-y (Choo) P.; m. Jung Yoo, Aug. 30, 1969; children: Charlotte, Sue, Andrew. BA, Yonsei U., 1961; MLS, U. So. Calif., L.A., 1971; postgrad., U. Ill., 1975. Libr., mem. faculty Malcolm X Coll., Chgo., 1971—. Compiler, editor: (books) Best Sellers and Best Choices 1980-83, Best Books by Consensus 1984-88, Advertisement Digest: Library and Information Services, 1979; editor COINT, 1980-88; contbr. articles to profl. jours. Mem. ALA, Am. Fedn. Tchrs. Avocation: automobile travel. Home: 9302 Parkside Ave Morton Grove IL 60053-1570 Office: Malcolm X Coll 1900 W Van Buren St Chicago IL 60612-3145

PARK, DAVID ALLEN, physicist, educator; b. N.Y.C., Oct. 13, 1919; s. Edwin Avery and Frances (Paine) P.; m. Clara Justine Claiborne, Aug. 18, 1945; children: Katharine, Rachel, Paul, Jessica. A.B., Harvard, 1941; Ph.D., U. Mich., 1950. Instr. Williams Coll., 1941-44; ops. research on radar countermeasures Harvard U. and Eng., 1944-45; instr. U. Mich., 1950; mem. Inst. Advanced Study, Princeton, 1950-51; mem. faculty Williams Coll., 1952-88, prof. physics, 1960-88, emeritus, 1988—; sr. vis. Cambridge (Eng.) U., 1962-63; vis. lectr. U. Ceylon, 1955-56, 72, Mass. Inst. Tech., 1966; vis. prof. U. N.C., 1964. Author: Quantum Theory, 1964, 3d edit., 1991, Contemporary Physics, 1964, Strong Interactions, 1966, Classical Dynamics and Its Quantum Analogues, 1979, 2d edit., 1990, The Image of Eternity, 1980, (with P.J. Davis) No Way, 1987, The How and the Why, 1988, The Fire Within the Eye, 1997. Fellow Am. Phys. Soc.; mem. Internat. Soc. for Study Time (pres. 1973-76). Office: Williams Coll Dept Physics Williamstown MA 01267

PARK, FRANCES MIHEI, food products executive, author; b. Cambridge, Mass., Apr. 3, 1955; d. Sei-Young and Heisook Hong Park. BS in Psychology, Va. Poly. Inst. and State U., 1977. Supr. masters programs Sch. Govt. and Bus. Adminstrn. George Washington U., Washington, 1978-81; founder, co-owner Park Ltd. T/A Chocolate Chocolate, Washington, 1982—. Contbr. stories, poems to profl. publs. Bus. subject of various mag. and newspaper articles, including Kiplinger Mag., Washington Dossier, N.Y. Times, Victoria Mag., Washington Post, Gault Millau Guide, Washington Mag., also featured on local, nat. and internat. cable TV, BBC and NPR; recipient Best Candy Store award Washington Mag., 1986, 2d prize for fiction award Willow Rev., 1993, Rosebud Mag. award for contemporary writing for short story "Premonition," 1995. Avocations: tennis, reading. Office: Chocolate Chocolate 1050 Connecticut Ave NW Washington DC 20036

PARK, JAMES THEODORE, microbiologist, educator; b. Palo Alto, Calif., Aug. 3, 1922; s. Charles V. and Frances (Odenheimer) P.; m. Helen Sternberg, Dec. 13, 1952; children: Jane Frances, David Franklin, Elizabeth Ann. A.B., Central Mich. U., 1943, D.Sc., 1963; M.S., U. Wis., 1944, Ph.D., 1949. Biochemist Ft. Detrick, Md., 1949-53; germ-free animal research unit Walter Reed Army Med. Center, 1953-57; asso. prof., then prof. microbiology Vanderbilt U. Sch. Medicine, 1958-62; chmn. dept. Tufts U. Sch. Medicine, 1962-70, prof., 1962-93, prof. emeritus microbiology, 1993—; mem. study sect. biochem. microbiology Nat. Inst. Allergy and Infectious Diseases, 1964-68; microbiology tng. com. Nat. Inst. Gen. Med. Scis., 1971-73; chmn. microbial physiology and genetics study sect. NIH, 1985-88; vis. scientist Karolinska Inst. Stockholm, 1995. Editorial bd.: Jour. Bacteriology, 1964-69, Antimicrobial Agts. and Chemotherapy, 1983-86. NSF sr. postdoctoral research fellow Cambridge (Eng.) U., 1957-58; NIH spl. fellow U. Umea, Sweden, 1969-70. Mem. Am. Acad. Arts and Scis., Am. Soc. Biol. Chemists, Am. Soc. Microbiology, Soc. Gen. Microbiology. Home: 11 Bradford Rd Weston MA 02193-2104 Office: 136 Harrison Ave Boston MA 02111-1817

PARK, JOHN THORNTON, academic administrator; b. Phillipsburg, N.J., Jan. 3, 1935; s. Dawson J. and Margaret M. (Thornton) P.; m. Dorcas M Marshall; June 1, 1956; children: Janet Ernst, Karen Daily. BA in Physics with distinction, Nebr. Wesleyan U., 1956; PhD, U. Nebr., 1963. NSF postdoctoral fellow Univ. Coll., London, 1963-64; asst. prof. physics U. Mo., Rolla, 1964-68, assoc. prof. physics, 1968-71, prof., 1971—, chmn. dept. physics, 1977-83, vice chancellor acad. affairs, 1983-85, 86-91, interim chancellor, 1985-86, 91-92, chancellor, 1992—; vis. assoc. prof. NYU, 1970-71; pres. Talema Electronics, Inc., St. James, Mo., 1983—; prin. investigator NSF Rsch. Grants, 1966—; bd. dirs. Mo. Tech. Corp., Jefferson City, Mo., 1994—. Contbr. articles to profl. jours. Recipient Most Disting. Scientist award Mo. Acad. Sci., 1994. Fellow Am. Phys. Soc. (mem. divsn. elec. and atomic physics); mem. Am. Assn. Physics Tchrs., Rotary. Methodist.

PARK, JOSEPH CHUL HUI, computer scientist; b. Seoul, Korea, Aug. 6, 1937; s. Don Gil and Eui Kyung (Shin) P.; m. Young Ja Yoon, Aug. 17, 1968; children: Esther Y.J., Maria Y.S., David Y.W., Jonathan Y.S. BA, Coll of Wooster, Ohio, 1959; BS, MIT, 1959; MS, U. Ill., 1961, PhD, 1967. Mem. rsch. staff Stanford Linear Accelerator Ctr Stanford U., 1969-72, 73-75; assoc. prof., then prof. computer sci. Korea Advanced Inst. of Sci., Seoul, 1975-82; head Computer Sci. Rsch. Ctr. Korea Advanced Inst. Sci., Seoul, Korea, 1980-82; mem. tech. staff Braegen Corp., Milpitas, Calif., 1982-86, Hewlett-Packard Labs., Palo Alto, Calif., 1986-92; tech mgr. compiler Advanced Processor div. Intergraph Corp., Palo Alto, 1992-93; sr. staff engr. Sun Microelectronics, Sun Microsystems Compter Corp., Mountain View, Calif., 1993—; lectr. in computer engring. Santa Clara (Calif.) U., 1987-94. Mem. IEEE, Assn. Computing Machinery. Baptist. Home: 14800 Masson Ct Saratoga CA 95070-9715

PARK, LEE CRANDALL, psychiatrist; b. Washington, July 15, 1926; s. Lee I. and Alice (Crandall) P.; m. Barbara Ann Merrick, July 1, 1953; children: Thomas Joseph, Jeffrey Rawson; m. Mary Woodfill Banerjee, Apr. 27, 1985; stepchildren: Stephen Kumar, Scott Kumar. Grad., Putney Prep. Sch., Vt.; B.S. in Zoology, Yale, 1948; M.D., Johns Hopkins, 1952. Diplomate Nat. Bd. Med. Examiners, Am. Bd. Psychiatry and Neurology. Intern medicine Johns Hopkins Hosp., Osler Clinic, Balt., 1952-53; resident psychiatry USN Hosp., Oakland, Calif., 1954, Henry Phipps Psychiat. Clinic, Johns Hopkins Hosp., Balt., 1955-59; asst. psychiatrist Henry Phipps Psychiat. Clinic, Johns Hopkins Hosp., 1955-59, staff psychiatrist, 1959—, staff dept. medicine, 1970—, dir. psychiat. outpatient svcs. and community psychiatry program, 1972-74, asst. dir. clin. svcs. dept. psychiatry, 1973-74, mem. departmental coun., 1974-76; fellow psychiatry Johns Hopkins U., 1955-59, faculty in psychiatry, 1959—, assoc. prof., 1971—, physician charge psychiat. svcs. student health svc., 1961-73; vis. psychiatrist Balt. City Hosp., 1960-61; co-prin., prin. investigator NIMH Psychopharmacology Rsch. Br. Outpatient Study of Drug-Set Interaction, 1960-68, co-dir. (with Eugene Meyer) Time-Limited Psychotherapy Rsch. Grant, 1969-73; pvt. practice psychiatry, 1964—; cons. Met. Balt. Assn. Mental Health, 1961-63, Bur. Disability Ins., Social Security Adminstrn., 1964-81; attending staff Seton Psychiat. Inst., 1966-73, exec. bd., 1970-73; staff Sheppard and Enoch Pratt Hosp., 1974—; rsch. includes borderline and narcissistic conditions, long-term effects of childhood emotional abuse, interrelationships of psychotherapy and pharmacotherapy, time ltd. psychotherapy, ethical considerations in clin. rsch. Contbr. articles and chpts. to profl. jours. and books. Served to lt. M.C., USNR, 1953-55, div. psychiatrist 1st Marine Div., Korea, staff psychiatrist USN Hosp., Camp Pendelton, Calif., 1954-55. Fellow AAAS, Am. Psychiat. Assn. (life mem. assembly 1983-93); mem. AMA, AAUP, SAR, Am. Psychosomatic Soc., Internat. Soc. Study of Personality Disorders, Am. Soc. Adolescent Psychiatry, Am. Coll. Neuropsychopharmacology, Am. Assn. Pvt. Practicing Psychiatrists, Md. Psychiat. Soc. (pres. 1978-79), Soc. Psychotherapy Rsch., N.Y. Acad. Scis., Group Therapy Network, Md. Interdisciplinary Coun. Children and Adolescents (treas. 1980-87), Med. and Chirurg. Faculty Md., Baltimore City Med. Soc., Baltimore County Med. Soc., Johns Hopkins Med. and Surg. Assn., Am. Assn. Pvt. Practicing Psychiatrists, Md. Assn. Pvt. Practicing Psychiatrists, Avery Assn., Denison Soc., Crandall Soc., Van Kouwenhoven-Conover Assn., Van Vorhees Soc., Parke Soc., Nat. Soc. of the Sons and Daus. of the Pilgrims, Gen. Soc. of War of 1812 (bd. dirs. State of Md. 1997-99), Descendants of Mexican War Vets., Sons of Union Vets. of Civil War, Johns Hopkins Club (Balt.), Met. Club (Washington), Farmington Country Club (Charlottesville, Va.), Chevy Chase (Md.) Country Club, Phi Beta Pi. Episcopalian. Home: 308 Tunbridge Rd Baltimore MD 21212-3803 Office: 1205 York Rd Ste 35 Lutherville Timonium MD 21093-6211

PARK, LELAND MADISON, librarian; b. Alexandria, La., Oct. 21, 1941; s. Arthur Harris and Jane Rebecca (Leland) P. Student, McCallie Sch., 1957-59; A.B., Davidson Coll., 1963; M.L.S., Emory U., 1964; postgrad., Simmons Coll., 1968; Adv.M. in L.S., Fla. State U., 1973, Ph.D., 1974. Reference librarian Pub. Library of Charlotte and Mecklenburg County, N.C., 1964-65; head reference and student personnel Davidson (N.C.) Coll. Library, 1967-70, asst. dir., 1970-75, dir., 1975—; cons. coll. cons. network So. Assn. Colls and Schs.; vis. lectr. Emory U., summer 1972; temporary instr. Fla. State U., 1973; libr. cons.; conf. spkr.; chmn. state adv. com. Libr. Svcs. and Constrn. Act, 1975-79; mem. N.C. State Libr. Commn., 1983-85, 87-92, chmn., 1989-92; mem. Dividson (N.C.) Town Appearance Commn., 1986-93, Hist. Preservation Commn., 1994-96. Editor Southeastern Librarian, 1976-78; acad. sect. editor N.C. Libraries, 1972-77; contbr. articles to profl. jours. Mem. Wake County Citizens for Better Librs., N.C., 1965-67; sec. com. libr. affairs Piedmont U. Ctr., 1969-70, chmn., 1970-72; mem. nat. bd. cons. NEH, 1976—; clk. mission com. St. Alban's Episcopal Mission, Davidson, N.C., 1969-72, layreader, 1970-75, treas., 1975-86. Recipient H.W. Wilson library periodical award, 1979, Alumni Achievement award The McCallie Sch., 1989, Order of Long Leaf Pine presented by N.C. Gov. James G. Martin, 1993. Mem. ALA, Southeastern Libr. Assn. (chmn. coll. and univ. sect. 1976-78, exec. bd. 1976-78), N.C. Libr. Assn. (2d v.p. 1975-77, 1st v.p. 1981-83, pres. 1983-85), Metrolina Libr. Assn. (pres. 1969-71), Mecklenburg County Libr. Assn. (treas. 1969-70), Soc. of Cin. (2d v.p. Ga. Soc. 1982-83), SAR, Mil. Order World Wars, Raleigh Jaycees (chmn. libr. com. 1965-67), Res. Officer Assn., SCV, Soc. Colonial Wars, S.C. Huguenot Soc., Beta Phi Mu, Sigma Nu, Omicron Delta Kappa. Lodge: Rotary. Home: PO Box 777 235 Ney Circle Davidson NC 28036 Office: Davidson Coll E H Little Libr PO Box 1837 Davidson NC 28036-1837

PARK, MARY WOODFILL, information consultant; b. Nevada, Mo., Nov. 20, 1944; d. John Prossor and Elizabeth (Devine) Woodfill; m. Salil Kumar Banerjee, Dec. 29, 1967 (div. 1983); children: Stephen Kumar, Scott Kumar; m. Lee Crandall Park, Apr. 27, 1985; stepchildren: Thomas Joseph, Jeffrey Rawson. BA, Marywood Coll., 1966; postgrad., Johns Hopkins U., 1983, Goucher Coll., 1986. Asst. to dir. U. Pa. Librs., Phila., 1968-69; investment libr. Del. Funds, Phila., 1969-71; investment officer Investment Counselors Md., Balt., 1980-84, 1st Nat. Bank Md., Balt., 1984-85; founder Info. Consultancy, Balt., 1985—; lectr. Villa Julie Coll., Balt., 1989, Loyola Coll., Balt., 1991-92, Cath. U., 1993. Author: InfoThink—Practical Strategies for Using Information in Business, 1998; editor, contbr. to profl. publs. Vol. Internat. Visitors' Ctr., Balt., 1979-80, 91; del. White House Conf. on Librs.; v.p. bd. dirs. Friends of Goucher Libr., 1988-90; mem. industry applications com. Info. Tech. Bd., State of Md., 1993—; mem. info. tech. com. of the Tech. Coun., Greater Balt. Com., 1993—. Named One of Md.'s Top 100 Women, Warfield's Bus. Publn., 1996. Mem. Spl. Librs. Assn. (pres. Balt. chpt. 1991-92, mem. network coord. coun. Sailor project 1993-95), Am. Soc. Info. Sci., Assn. Ind. Info. Profls., Md. Libr. Assn., Info. Futures Inst., Hamilton St. Club (bd. dirs. 1989-92), Soc. Competetive Intelligence Profls. Office: The Info Consultancy 308 Tunbridge Rd Baltimore MD 21212-3803

PARK, ROBERT MCILWRAITH, science and engineering educator; b. Glasgow, Scotland, July 28, 1957; came to U.S., 1988; s. Robert McIlwraith and Elsie (Black) P.; m. Katherine Jean Angers, Dec. 21, 1985. BSc with honors, U. Glasgow, 1978, PhD, 1982. Sr. rsch. scientist 3M Can., Inc., Toronto, 1982-86, rsch. specialist, 1986-88; assoc. prof. dept. materials sci. and engring. U. Fla., Gainesville, 1988-93, prof., 1993—. Contbr. chpts. to books, over 60 articles to profl. jours. Recipient 3M Circle of Tech. Excellence award 1986, Rsch. Initiation awrd NSF, 1989, Rank prize for Optoelectronics, 1993. Achievements include patent for invention of a P-type doping process for the semiconductor zinc selenide. Office: U Fla Dept Materials Sci and Engring Gainesville FL 32611

PARK, RODERIC BRUCE, academic administrator; b. Cannes, France, Jan. 7, 1932; came to U.S., 1932; s. Malcolm Sewell and Dorothea (Turner) P.; m. Marijke DeJong, Aug. 29, 1953; children: Barbara, Marina, Malcolm. AB, Harvard U., 1953; PhD, Calif. Inst. Tech., 1958. Postdoctoral fellow Calif. Inst. Tech., 1958, Lawrence Radiation Lab., Berkeley, Calif., 1958-60; prof. botany U. Calif., Berkeley, 1960-89, prof. plant biology, 1989-93, prof. emeritus, 1993—; chmn. dept. instrn. in biology U. Calif., 1965-68; provost, dean U. Calif. (Coll. Letters and Sci.), 1972-80, vice chancellor, 1980-90; chancellor U. Colo., Boulder, 1994-97; pres. Brickyard Cove Harbors, Inc., 1975-77; dir. William Kaufmann, Inc., 1976-86; mem. corp. Woods Hole Oceanographic Instn., 1974-80; mem. Harvard Vis. Com. on Biochemistry and Molecular Biology, 1990-93. Co-author: Cell Ultrastructure, 51967, Papers on Biological Membrane Structure, 1968; Biology editor, W.H. Freeman & Co., 1966-74; Contbr. articles to profl. jours. Trustee Athenian Sch., 1980—, U. Calif.-Berkeley Found., 1986-90; pres. Jepson Endowment, 1992—, pres., 1994—; bd. dirs. Assoc. Harvard Alumni, 1976-79; bd. overseers Harvard U., 1981-87; mem. exec. com. Coun. Acad. Affairs, 1986-90, chmn., 1988-89; mem. exec. com. Nat. Assn. State Univs. and Land Grant Colls., 1988-90; mem. vis. com. Arnold Arboretum, 1981-88, chmn., 1986-88; acting dir. Univ. and Jepson Herbaria, 1991-93; co-chair Colo. Combined Campaign, 1996-97. Recipient New York Bot. Gardens award, 1962. Fellow AAAS; mem. Am. Soc. Plant Physiologists, Am. Bot. Soc., Am. Soc. Photobiology, Danforth Assn. (pres. San Francisco chpt. 1972), Richmond Yacht Club (commodore 1972, dir. found. 1992—), Transpacific Yacht Club, Pacific Cup Yacht Club, Explorers Club. Home: 531 Cliffside Ct Port Richmond CA 94801 Office: U Colo Office of the Chancellor Boulder CO 80309-0017

PARK, ROGER COOK, law educator; b. Atlanta, Jan. 4, 1942; s. Hugh and Alice (Cook) P.; m. Rosemarie J. Lilliker, June 14, 1967 (div. 1979); 1 child, Matthew; m. Suzanne Nicole Howard, Feb. 18, 1984; stepchildren: Sophie Currier, Nicolas Currier. BA cum laude, Harvard U., 1964, JD magna cum laude, 1969. Bar: Mass. 1969, Minn. 1973. Law clk. to Hon. Bailey Aldrich U.S. Ct. Appeals (1st Cir.), Boston, 1969-70; with Zalkind & Silverglate, Boston, 1970-73; prof. Law Sch. U. Minn., Mpls., 1973-95, Fredrikson and Byron profl. Law Sch., 1990-95; Disting. prof. law U. Calif./Hastings Coll. Law, San Francisco, 1995—; vis. prof. Law Sch. Stanford U., Palo Alto, Calif., summer 1977, Sch. Law Boston U., 1981-82, Law Sch. U. Mich., Ann Arbor, fall 1984; bd. dirs. Ctr. for Computer-Aided Legal Instrn., 1982-96; reporter adv. group civil Justice Reform Act, Dist. of Minn.; mem. evidence adv. com. Minn. Supreme Ct., 1988-95. Author: Computer Aided Exercises in Civil Procedure, 1979, 4th edit., 1995, (with McFarland) Trial Objections Handbook, 1991, Waltz and Park Casebook on Evidence, 8th edit., 1994; contbr. articles to profl. jours. Lt. U.S. Army, 1964-66, Vietnam. Mem. ABA (mem. subcom. on fed. rules of evidence, mem. rules of criminal procedure adn evidence com. criminal justice sect. 1988—), Am. Law Inst., Am. Assn. Law Schs. (chairperson evidence sect. 1994). Office: Hastings Coll of Law 200 Mcallister St San Francisco CA 94102-4707

PARK, ROY HAMPTON, JR., advertising executive; b. Raleigh N.C., July 23, 1938; s. Roy Hampton and Dorothy Goodwin (Dent) P.; m. Elizabeth Tetlow Parham, July 29, 1961; children: Elizabeth P. Fowler, Roy H., III. BA in Journalism, U. N.C., 1961; MBA, Cornell U., 1963. Sr. account exec., rev. bd. exec., advt. planning dir., awards chmn., pers. group head J. Walter Thompson Co., N.Y.C., and Miami, Fla., 1963-70; v.p. mktg. and account mgmt. Kincaid Advt. Agy., div. First Union Nat. BanCorp, Inc., Charlotte, N.C., 1970-71; v.p. Park Outdoor Advt., Ithaca, N.Y., 1971-75; v.p. advt. and promotion Park Broadcasting, Inc., Ithaca, 1976-81; mng. editor Park Communications Newsletter, 1976-81; mng. dir. Ag Rsch. Advt. Agy., Ithaca, 1976-84; v.p. and gen. mgr. Park Outdoor Advt., 1981-84; pres., chief exec. officer, dir. Park Outdoor Advt. of N.Y., Inc., 1984—; pres. Outdoor Advt. Coun. N.Y., Inc., 1986-91, chmn., dir., 1992-95; dir. Park Comm., Inc., 1993-95; dir., sr. v.p. RHP, Inc., 1994-96, RHP Properties, Inc., 1994-96; dir. Boyce Thompson Inst. for Plant Rsch., Inc., 1995—; trustee Park Found., Inc., 1995—. Mem. region I plans bd. Inst. Outdoor Advt., 1984-86; mem. adv. coun., founding mem. alumni exec. com. Cornell U. Johnson Grad. Sch. Mgmt., 1984-88, mem. adv. coun., 1996—; bd. vis. U. N.C. Sch. Journalism & Mass. Comm., 1994—; mem. N.C. Soc. of N.Y., 1994—; chmn. Ithaca Assembly Cotillion, 1979-81; dir. pub. rels. Tompkins County Conf. and Tourist Coun., 1976; exec. com. Tompkins County Rep. Fin. Com. 1983-84; chmn. Fin. Com. MacNeil for Assembly, 1984-86, co-chmn., 1978-82; bd. dirs. Tompkins County Coun. Arts, 1976; chmn. pub. relations com. United Way Tompkins County, 1973-74, loaned publicity exec. 1977; bd. chmn., publicity dir. Junior Olympics 1973-74; dir. pub. rels. United Fund Raleigh, N.C., 1971; fin. com. Special Children's Ctr., 1979. Recipient Project of Yr. award, 1974. Mem. Tompkins County C. of C. (chmn. legis. action com. 1976, acting chmn. nominating com. 1976, chmn. sign ordinance com. 1975-76, pub. rels. coun. 1976, chmn. sign ordinance com. recognition award 1975), Charlotte (N.C.) C. of C. (pub. rels. com. 1970-71), adv. Beach Preservation Assn. Pine Knoll Shores, N.C., Ithaca Yacht Club, Ithaca Country Club, Boca Bay Pass Club. Republican. Presbyterian. Office: Park Outdoor Advt PO Box 6477 Ithaca NY 14851-6477

PARK, SAM-KOO, transportation executive. BA in Econs., Yonsei U., 1967. Exec. dir. internat. trading Samyang Tire Indsl. Co., 1967-68; mng. dir. Korea Synthetic Rubber Indusl. Co., 1968-73; mng. dir. Kumho & Co., 1973-74, pres. L.A. br., 1974-79, v.p., 1979-80, pres., 1980-91; pres., CEO Asiana Airlines, Inc., 1991—. Office: Asiana Airlines Inc 3530 Wilshire Blvd Ste 1450 Los Angeles CA 90010-2342*

PARK, SOONG-KOOK, internist, researcher; b. Pyung-Yang, Korea, Aug. 9, 1938; s. Tae-Soo and Wha-Sil (Lee) P.; m. Sine-Ja, Oct. 9, 1965; children: Han-Kil, See-Nae, Han-Sol. BA, MD, Kyung-Pook Nat. U., Taegu, Korea, 1963. Med. diplomate. Surgeon gen. Republic of Korea, 1963-67; hosp. intern Bklyn. Jewish Hosp., 1968-69; resident in internal medicine Grassland Hosp., Valhalla, N.Y., 1969-72; fellow in gastroenterology Lahey Clinic, Boston, 1972-74; chief internal medicine Dongsan Presbyn. Hosp., Taegu, Korea, 1974-76; cons. in internal medicine, chief staff Mariana Med. Ctr., Guam, 1977-78; chief internal medicine Bak Hosp., Seoul, Korea, 1978, Dongsan Presbyn. Hosp., Taegu, 1978-90; prof. Keimyung U. Med. Sch., Taegu, 1980—; supt. Dongsan Med. Ctr., Taegu, 1990-94, Kyungju Dongsan Hosp., Kyungju, Korea, 1994-96; v.p. for med. affairs Keimyung U., 1996—; dir. Dongsan Med. Ctr., 1996—. Elder Sungji Presbyn. Ch., Taegu, 1976—; bd. dirs. YMCA, Taegu, 1980—; dist. gov. Y's Men's Internat., Taegu, 1987-88; comdt. Med. Drs. Soccer Team, Taegu, 1990-94, 96—; pres. Korea Christian Hosp. Assn., 1997—. Recipient Elmar Crown, Y's Men's Club Internat., 1988. Mem. Korean Assn. Internal Medicine (councilor 1980), Korean Assn. Gastroenterology (councilor 1980—), Korean Soc. Gastrointestinal Endoscopy (coun. 1988—, pres. 1996), Korean Soc. Gastrointestinal Motility Study (pres. 1993), Am. Coll. Gastroenterology (internat.) N.Y. Acad. Scis. Presbyterian. Avocations: tennis, soccer, choir. Home: 424 Dongsan-Dong, Taegu 700-712, Republic of Korea Office: Dongsan Med Ctr, 194 Dongsan-Dong, Taegu 700-712, Republic of Korea

PARK, THOMAS JOSEPH, biology researcher, educator; b. Balt., June 8, 1958; s. Lee Crandall and Barbara Ann (Merrick) P.; m. Stephanie Suzanne Reynolds, June 22, 1985; 1 child, Nicholas Timothy. BA, Johns Hopkins U., 1982; PhD, U. Md., 1988. Vis. scientist Coll. of France, Paris, 1988-89; rsch. fellow U. Tex., Austin, 1989-94; Alexander von Humboldt rsch. fellow U. Munich, 1994-95; with U. Ill. dept biol. scis., Chgo., 1995—. Contbr. chpt. to book, articles to Jour. Neurosci., Jour. Comparative Psychology, Hearing Rsch., Jour. Neurophysiol. Grantee NIMH, 1986, Nat. Ctr. Sci. Rsch., Paris, 1988, NIH. Mem. AAAS, Soc. for Neurosci., Assn. for Rsch. in Otolaryngology. Office: U Ill at Chgo Dept Biol Scis Chicago IL 60607

PARK, U. YOUNG, nuclear engineer; b. Seoul, Republic of Korea, Oct. 12, 1940; came to U.S., 1968; s. Myung W. and Duk-Jo (Chang) P.; children: Tara Lynne, Thomas Robert, Kyung Gi. BS, Seoul Nat. U., 1963; MS, U. Cin., 1970. Registered profl. engr., Ohio, Calif. Nuclear engr. State of Ohio, Columbus, 1975-78, Batelle Columbus (Ohio) Labs., 1978-81, Bechtel, San Francisco, 1981-88; program mgr. Savannah River Site U.S. Dept. Energy, Aiken, S.C., 1988-95; Bechtel nuclear project advisor Korea Electric Power Corp, Seoul, 1993—. Mem. Am. Nuclear Soc. Office: care Bechtel Korea 50 Beale St San Francisco CA 94105-1813

PARK, WILLIAM H(ERRON), financial executive; b. Monongahela, Pa. Sept. 19, 1947; s. William M. and Marjorie (Herron) P.; m. Mary Cornell, June 25, 1977; children: William H., Douglas C. BS in Indsl. Engring. with distinction Cornell U., 1969, MBA, 1970. Engr. True Temper Corp., Geneva, Ohio, 1970-72; with Price Waterhouse & Co., Boston, 1972-82; exec. v.p., CFO United Asset Mgmt. Corp., Boston, 1982—; v.p. The UAM Funds, 1992—; dir. No. Light Asset Mgmt., 1992—; bd. dirs. The Chautauqua Found., Inc., 1992—, v.p., treas., 1996—. Treas., trustee Tower Sch. in Marblehead, 1982-92. Home: 3 Fort Sewall Ter Marblehead MA 01945-3505 Office: United Asset Mgmt Corp One Internat Pl Boston MA 02110

PARK, WILLIAM WYNNEWOOD, law educator; b. Philadelphia, Pa., July 2, 1947; s. Oliver William and Christine (Lindes) P. BA, Yale U., 1969; JD, Columbia U., 1972; MA, Cambridge U., 1975. Bar: Mass. 1972, D.C. 1980. Assoc. Coudert Frères, Paris, 1972-75; fellow Selwyn Coll., U. Cambridge, Eng., 1975-77; assoc. Hughes, Hubbard & Reed, Paris, 1977-79; prof. law Boston U., 1979—; counsel Ropes & Gray, Boston; v.p. London Ct. Internat. Arbitration; dir. Boston U. Ctr. Banking Law Studies, 1990-93; adj. prof. Fletcher Sch. Tufts U., Medford, Mass., 1980-86; vis. prof. U. Dijon, France, 1983-84, Inst. Univ. de Hautes Etudes Internat., Geneva, 1983. Author: International Chamber of Commerce Arbitration, 1984, 2nd edit., 1990, International Forum Selection, 1995, International Commercial Arbitration, 1997; contbr. articles and book revs. to profl. jours. Trustee Mass. Bible Soc. Fellow Chartered Inst. Arbitrators. Home: 36 King St Cohasset MA 02025 Office: Boston U Law Sch 765 Commonwealth Ave Boston MA 02215-1401 also: Ropes and Gray 1 International Pl Boston MA 02110

PARKANY, JOHN, business educator, international financial consultant; b. Budapest, Hungary, Jan. 28, 1921; came to U.S., 1947; s. Sandor and Renee (Linksz) P.; m. Betty Ruth Baird, Oct. 30, 1954; children: John Stephen, Ann Emily, Nancy. J.D., U. Budapest (Hungary), 1945; M.A., Georgetown U., 1949; Ph.D., Columbia U., 1955. Mktg. research mgr. Formica Corp., Cin., 1956-61; assoc. prof. Xavier U., Cin., 1961-62; mgr. econ. research Weyerhaeuser Co., Tacoma, Wash., 1962-73; v.p., sr. internat. economist Wells Fargo Bank N.A., San Francisco, 1973-80; Richard S. Reynolds Jr. prof. bus. adminstrn. Coll. of William and Mary, Williamsburg, Va., 1980-91; prof. emeritus Coll. of William and Mary, Williamsburg, 1991—. Mem. council econ. advisors Gov. Wash. State, Olympia, 1967-73; pres. Council Fgn. Affairs, Tacoma, Wash., 1968-69. Mem. Nat. Assn. Bus. Economists (v.p. San Francisco chpt. 1973-74), Am. Econ. Assn. Home: 151 Ridings Cv Williamsburg VA 23185-3903

PARKE, DAVID WILKIN, II, ophthalmologist, educator, healthcare executive; b. Columbus, Ohio, May 19, 1951; s. David William Parke and Eunice Joyce Erikson; m. Julie Diane Thorne, Sept. 15, 1975; children: David W. III, Laura Thorne, Lindsey Diane. AB, Stanford U., 1973; MD, Baylor U., 1977. Diplomate Am. Bd. Ophthalmology. Resident in internal medicine Baylor Coll. Medicine, Houston, 1977-78, resident in ophthalmology, 1978-81, fellow in med. retina, 1981-82, asst. prof., 1983-90, assoc. prof., 1990-92; fellow diseases and surgery of the retina and vitreous Med. Coll. of Wis., 1982-83; prof., chair dept. ophthalmology U. Okla., Oklahoma City, 1992—; pres., CEO McGee Eye Inst., Oklahoma City, 1992—. Active Okla. Econ. Devel. Found., 1992, Okla. Health Ctr. Found., 1992; trustee Presbyn. Health Found., 1995—, Casady Sch., 1997—; mng. dir. Stephenson Laser Ctr., 1996—; bd. mgrs. Okla. Health Alliance, 1995—. Fellow Am. Acad. Ophthalmology (assoc. sec. 1983-92, Honor award 1980); mem. Assn. Univ. Profs. Ophthalmology (trustee 1997—), Retina Soc., Vitreous Soc., Alpha Omega Alpha. Office: Dean A McGee Eye Institute 608 Stanton L Young Blvd Oklahoma City OK 73104-5014

PARKE, ROBERT LEON, communications executive; b. Jersey City, Aug. 28, 1940; s. Edwin Gager and Alice Elizabeth (Servis) P.; m. Geraldine R. Pavlick, Sept. 2, 1967; children: Cheryl Lynn, Tracy Ann, David Scott. Grad. high sch., Jersey City. Asst. bookkeeper Snow-Kist Frozen Foods, Jersey City, 1964-67; supr. accounts receivable Swift Line Transfer Co., Inc., North Bergen, N.J., 1967-69; contr. Imperial Cartage Co., Inc., Jersey City, 1969-79; supr. inventory mgmt. Vista United Telecommunications, Lake Buena Vista, Fla., 1980—; corp. sec. Imperial Warehouse Co., Inc., Jersey City, 1968-79, Arbe Transfer Co. Inc., 1968-79; v.p. Cole Foods, Inc., Jersey City, 1968-79;. Spl. min. of the eucharist Diocese Orlando, Fla., 1992; vol. Gave Kids The World, Kissimmee, Fla.; mem. Pemberton Twp. Zoning Bd., Browns Mills, N.J., 1977-79; trustee, bd. dirs. Browns Mills Improvement Assn., 1974-79; trustee Rebecca Worf Meml. Fund Browns Mills, N.J., Parke Soc., S.E. Milw.; hon. trustee Am. Indian Relief Coun. Recipient Cert. Appreciation Am. Indian Relief Coun., 1996, hon. trustee; recipient spl. recognition award masters degree program in Nat. Security Studies, Grad. Sch. of Georgetown U., 1996; Bob Parke day proclaimed by Twp. of Pemberton, 1979. Mem. Nat. Notary Assn., Fla. Notary Assn., Am. Soc. Notaries, Nat. Assn. Purchasing Mgmt. Ctrl. Fla. (named scholar), Nat. Assn. Purchasing Mgmt. (scholarship for continued edn., Ctrl. Fla. Most Supportive Mem. 1994), Fla. Sheriffs Assn. (life, hon.). Office: Vista United Telecommunications 3100 Bonnet Creek Rd Lake Buena Vista FL 32830 *Everyone can have a dream, but only those that care and show perseverance will achieve success.*

PARKER, ADRIENNE NATALIE, art educator, art historian; b. N.Y., May 23, 1925; d. Benjamin and Bertha (Levine) Lefkowitz; m. Norman Richard Parker, July 22, 1945; children: Dennis, Jonathan W., Steven L. BA cum laude, Hunter Coll., 1945; MFA, Montclair Coll., 1975; postgrad., Instituto Des Artes, San Miguel, Mex., 1987. Instr. art, English Granby High Sch., Norfolk, Va., 1945-46; instr. art Mahwah (N.J.) Bd. Edn., 1970-75, Daus. of Miriam Home for the Aged, Clifton, N.J., Fedn. Home, Paterson, N.J.; instr. art, history Bergen C.C., Paramus, N.J., 1980—. One-woman show Bergen C.C.; exhibited in group shows N.J. Art Educators, Bergen County Art Educators, N.J. Tercentenary (1st place), Pine Libr., Sara Delano Roosevelt House, Hunter Coll., Woodstock Art Assn., 1990-95, Fair Lawn Art Assn., 1991 (award), Palisade Guild Spinners and Weavers, 1994, Bergen C.C., 1994, 95. Editor Fairlawn H.S. PTA, Thomas Jefferson Jr. H.S.; pres. The Comty. Sch., Fairlawn, 1983-86, bd. dirs.; mem. art adv. exhbn. com. Pine Libr., 1992, 93, 94, 95, 96. Mem. N.J. Art Educators, Bergen County Art Educators, Wood Stock Art Assn., Fairlaw Art Assn., Hunter Coll. Alumni Assn. (bd. dirs. no. N.J. chpt. 1970—, pres. 1977-79, program chmn./v.p. 1993-94), Palisade Guild Spinners and Weavers (founder, editor, charter) Phi Beta Kappa. Avocations: hiking, cross country skiing, travel, archeology, study of primitive cultures. Home: 3827 Fair Lawn Ave Fair Lawn NJ 07410-4325

PARKER, ALAN JOHN, veterinary neurologist, educator, researcher; b. Portsmouth, Eng., Oct. 28, 1944; came to U.S., 1969; s. William Barton and Emily (Begley) P.; m. Heather Margaret Nicholson, Oct. 30, 1971; children: Alyxander John, Robert William. B.Sc. with honors, Bristol U., 1966, B.V.Sc. with honors, 1968; M.S., U. Ill., 1973, Ph.D., 1976. Diplomate Am. Coll. Vet. Internal Medicine-Neurology, European Coll. Vet. Neurology. Intern Vet. Coll., U. Calif.-Davis, 1969-70; instr. vet. clin. medicine U. Ill., Urbana, 1970-71, 72-76, asst. prof., 1976-77, assoc. prof., 1977-82, prof., 1982—; cons. pharm. cos., seminar presenter; cons. in neurology Berwyn Vet. Hosp., Chgo., 1973—, Lake Shore Animal Hosp., Chgo., 1978—. Contbr. numerous articles to sci. jours., chpts. to books. Active Boy Scouts Am., Champaign, Ill., 1982—; active Presbyn. Ch., Monticello, Ill., 1979—. Recipient Vigil Honor and Founder's award Order of the Arrow, Boy Scouts Am.; sci. grantee various orgns., 1972—. Mem. AVMA, Am. Animal Hosp. Assn., Brit. Vet. Assn., Ill. State Vet. Assn. Republican. Office: U Ill Coll Vet Medicine 1008 W Hazelwood Dr Urbana IL 61802-4714

PARKER, ALAN WILLIAM, film director, writer; b. London, Feb. 14, 1944; s. William Leslie and Elsie Ellen P.; m. Annie Inglis, July 30, 1966; children: Lucy Kate, Alexander James, Jake William, Nathan Charles. Student Brit. schs. Advt. copywriter, 1966-69, dir. TV commls. Author: screenplay Melody, 1968; novel Bugsy Malone, 1975, Puddles in the Lane, 1977; author, dir.: No Hard Feelings, 1972, Our Cissy, 1973, Footsteps, 1973, Bugsy Malone, 1975 (5 Brit. Acad. awards), Come See the Paradise, 1990; dir.: The Evacuees (Brit. Acad. award, Internat. Emmy award, Press Guild U.K. award), Midnight Express (6 Golden Globe awards, 3 Brit. Acad. awards, 2 Oscar awards), Fame, 1980 (Brit. Acad. award, Golden Globe award, 2 Oscar awards), Shoot the Moon, 1982, Pink Floyd-The Wall, 1982, Birdy, 1984 (Grand Prix Spl. du Jury, Cannes Film Festival), A Turnip Head's Guide to the British Cinema, 1986 (British Press Guild award), Angel Heart, 1987, Mississippi Burning, 1988 (Oscar award), The Commitments, 1991 (4 BAFTA awards), The Road to Wellville, 1994, Evita, 1996 (2 Golden Globe awards). Recipient 4 Brit. Acad. awards. Mem. Brit. Acad. Film and TV Arts, Dirs. Guild Am., Writers Guild G.B., Writers Guild Am., Dirs. Guild G.B., Acad. Motion Pictures Arts and Scis. Office: care Michael Wimer Creative Artists Agy 9830 Wilshire Blvd Beverly Hills CA 90212-1804

PARKER, ALICE, composer, conductor; b. Boston, Dec. 16, 1925; d. Gordon and Mary (Stuart) P.; widowed; children: David, Timothy, Katharine, Mary, Elizabeth. BA, Smith Coll., Northampton, Mass., 1947; MS, Julliard Sch., N.Y.C., 1949; MusD (hon.), Hamilton U., Clinton, N.Y., Macalester Coll., St. Paul, Bluffton (Ohio) Coll., Westminster Choir Coll., Princeton, N.J. Arranger Robert Shaw Chorale, N.Y.C., 1948-66; freelance composer, condr. N.Y.C., 1960—; tchr., workshop leader Westminster Choir Coll., Princeton, N.J., summers 1972—; artistic dir. Melodious Accord, N.Y.C., 1985—. Composer 4 operas, 30 cantatas, 8 song cycles and numerous anthems and suites. Recipient composer's award ASCAP, 1968—, Barlow Endowment, 1992, spl. award Nat. Endowment Arts, 1976. Mem. Am. Choral Dirs. Assn., Am. Condrs. Guild, Chorus Am. (Founders award 1994), Am. Music ctr., Hymn Soc. Am., Sigma Alpha Iota. Office: Melodious Accord Inc Park West Fin Sta PO Box 20801 New York NY 10025

PARKER, ANGELO PAN, lawyer; b. Detroit, Feb. 10, 1945; s. Pan A. and Clementine (Kaplanis) P.; m. Dena Apostle, Mar. 9, 1975; children: Denise, Alyssa. BBA, St. Mary's U., San Antonio, Tex., 1967, JD, 1970. Bar: Tex. 1970, Nebr. 1973. Ptnr. Kutak Rock, Omaha, 1973-80, McCall, Parkhurst & Horton, Dallas, 1980-85, Strasburger & Price, L.L.P., Dallas, 1986—. 1st lt. U.S. Army, 1970-73. Office: Strasburger & Price LLP 4200 Nations Bank Plz 901 Main St Dallas TX 75202-3714

PARKER, ANN (ANN PARKER NEAL), photographer, graphic artist; b. London, Mar. 6, 1934; d. Russell Johnston and Mildred Grace (Best) P.; m. Avon Neal, Oct. 31, 1964. Student, R.I. Sch. Design, 1952-54; B.F.A., Yale U., 1956. V.p. Thistle Hill Press, North Brookfield, Mass., 1979—; artist-in-residence Altos de Chavon, Dominican Republic, 1983, 84; panel mem. Fulbright Hays Com. for Photography, Film and Video, 1983, 85, 86. Freelance photographer and graphic artist, 1956—; exhbns. include Santa Fe Ctr. Photography, 1982, Focus Gallery, San Francisco, 1983, Altos de Chavon, Dominican Republic, 1984, 86, 87, Nat. Mus. Art, La Paz, Bolivia, 1985, Princeton U. Libr., 1986, Instituto Dominicano de Cultura Hispanica, Santa Domingo, Dominican Republic, 1987, Gallery of Graphic Arts, N.Y.C., 1987, Maxwell Mus. Anthropology, U. N.Mex., Albuquerque, 1988, Gallery Twerenbold, Luzern, Switzerland, 1991, San Antonio Mus. Assns., 1992, Worcester (Mass.) Art Mus., 1993, Gallery of Graphic Arts, N.Y.C., 1994, Lumina Gallery, Taos, N.Mex., 1995, Gallery of Graphic Arts, N.Y.C., 1995, U. Conn., 1996, U. Mass. Med. Ctr., 1996, Ute Stebich Gallery, Lenox (Mass.), 1996, Sony Gallery A.U.C., Cairo, 1997; work pub. in Smithsonian mag., Am. Heritage Life, Americana, Aperture, Natural History, others; works in permanent collections N.Y. Pub. Libr., George Eastman House, Rochester, N.Y., Met. Mus. Art, N.Y.C., Mus. Modern Art, N.Y.C., Mus. Fine Arts, Boston, Ctr. Creative Photography, Tucson, MIT, Libr. of Congress, Smithsonian Instn., Rosenwald Collection, Mellon Collection, Whitney Mus., others; art books Ephemeral Folk Figures, 1969, Molas, 1977, Scarecrows, 1978, Early American Stone Sculpture, 1982, Los Ambulantes, 1982, Hajj Paintings 1995, Folk Art of the Great Pilgrimage, 1995. Recipient 1st pl. award Mass. Open Photography, 1978, Am. Inst. Graphic Design awards, 1956, 77, 79, Mass. Arts Coun. award, 1988, 96; Ford Found. grantee, 1962-63, 63-64; Fund Four Directions grantee, 1995. Address: Thistle Hill North Brookfield MA 01535

PARKER, BOBBY EUGENE, SR., college president; b. Wortham, Tex., May 28, 1925; s. Thomas W. and Stacy (Beasley) P.; m. Marietta Vickrey, Sept. 1, 1946; children: Bobby Eugene Jr., Mark. AA, Westminster Jr. Coll., 1948; BS, Sam Houston State Coll., 1951; MS, Baylor U., 1954, EdD, 1964; LLD (hon.), Houston Bapt. U., 1990; HHD (hon.), U. Mary Hardin-Baylor, 1996. Prin., counselor pub. schs. Richland and Mexia, Tex., 1948-57; dean students Howard Payne Coll., Brownwood, Tex., 1957-59; mem. faculty Baylor U., Waco, Tex., 1960-69; v.p. Mary Hardin-Baylor Coll., Belton, Tex., 1969-71; pres. U. Mary Hardin-Baylro, 1971-91, chancellor, 1991—; pres. emeritus U. Mary Hardin-Baylor, 1996—; hon. chancellor Ebino (Japan) Kohgen Internat. Coll., 1994; hon. pres. Allen Jr. Coll., Kuji Iwate Japan, 1992. Mem. King's Daus. Hosp. Assn., Heart O' Tex. coun. nat. Boy Scouts Am., pres. 1995; trustee Bell County Mus. History and Art; bd. dirs.

Greater Waco Safety Coun., 1963-67, Waco Girl's Club, 1967-69, Tex. Safety Assn., 1963; pres. coun. Heart of Tex. Athletic Conf. With USNR, 1943-46. Recipient Spl. Safety award Tex. Safety Assn., 1965, Exemplary medal San Marcos Bapt. Acad., 1991, Good Shepherd award Boy Scouts Am., 1996; named Man of Yr. Belton Area C. of C., 1978, Outstanding Christian Educator Mexican Bapt. Conv.; fellow Paul Harris. Mem. Internat. Platform Assn., Tex. Baptist Sch. Adminstrs. Assn., Tex. Found. Vol. Supported Colls. and Univs. (former chmn. bd.), Assn. Am. Colls., Am. Council Edn., Ind. Colls. and Univs. of Tex. (former mem. exec. bd.), Nat. Assn. Intercollegiate Athletics (former pres. adv. com.), Belton C. of C. (past bd. dirs.), East Tex. C. of C., Killeen C. of C., Temple C. of C., Friends of Scott and White. Lodge: Rotary Internat. (Gov. 1984, Dist. Gov.'s Role of Fame; Gov. Dist. 587. 1986-87). Home: 2506 River Oaks Dr Belton TX 76513-1654 Office: U Mary Hardin Baylor PO Box 8440 Belton TX 76513-0999

PARKER, BRENT MERSHON, retired medical educator, internist, cardiologist; b. St. Louis, July 3, 1927; s. William Bahlmann and Florence (Mershon) P.; m. Martha Shelton, Aug. 1, 1953; children: Martha Parker Burgess, Elizabeth, Margaret. MD cum laude, Wash. U., St. Louis, 1952. Diplomate Am. Bd. Internal Medicine. Intern and asst. resident N.Y. Hosp.-Cornell, N.Y.C., 1952-54; asst. resident, fellow Barnes Hosp., Wash. U., St. Louis, 1954-57; cardiology sect. chief VA Hosp., U. Oreg., Portland, 1957-59; asst. prof. to assoc. prof., co-dir. cardiovascular div., chief adult cardiac catherization Wash. U. Sch. Medicine, St. Louis, 1959-73; prof. medicine U. Mo., Columbia, 1973-89, prof. emeritus, 1989-94, chief of staff, assoc. dean, 1976-82, chief of cardiology, 1983-89; mem. colloquium faculty Merck, Sharp and Dohme, West Point, Pa., 1980-86. Author or co-author 58 papers in referred jours., 6 book chpts., teaching papers, others. Bd. dirs. St. Louis Heart Assn., 1962-73, v.p. 1972-73; bd. dirs. Mo. Heart Assn., 1965-75, pres. 1970-71. Served with USN, 1945-46. Recipient Arthur Strauss award St. Louis Heart Assn., 1973, 3 teaching awards U. Mo. Sch. Medicine, 1974, 75, 86, Preventive Cardiology Acad. award, Nat. Heart Lung and Blood Inst., 1982-87, Alumni Achievement award Washington Univ. Sch. Medicine, 1992; Brent Mershon Parker professorship estab. in honor U. Mo., 1989. Fellow ACP, Am. Coll. Cardiology (Mo., Kans. council rep. 1973-77), Clin. Cardiology Soc. Am. Heart Assn.; mem. Am. Fedn. Clin. Research, Cen. Soc. for Clin. Research, Alpha Omega Alpha, Sigma Xi. Episcopalian. Avocations: choral singing, jogging, camping, back packing.

PARKER, BRIAN PRESCOTT, forensic scientist; b. Norfolk, Va., Aug. 31, 1929; s. Milton Ellsworth and Louise Randall (Smith) P.; BS in Quantitative Biology, M.I.T., 1953; JD, Northwestern U., 1957; M.Criminology, U. Calif., Berkeley, 1961, D.Criminology, 1967; m. Sonia Garcia Rosario, Dec. 23, 1960; children: Robin Marie, Augustin Keith. Research asst. U. P.R. Med. Sch., 1961; cons. P.R. Justice Dept., 1961-63; spl. asst. FDA, Washington, 1964; lectr., then asst. prof. criminology U. Calif., Berkeley, 1964-70; sr. criminalist, then sr. forensic scientist Stanford Research Inst., Menlo Park, Calif., 1971-73; prof. forensic sci. and criminal justice Calif. State U., Sacramento, 1973-92; prof. emeritus, 1988—; project dir. phys. evidence Dept. Justice, 1969-70; vis. fellow Nat. Police Research Unit, Australia, 1985; vis. prof. Elton Mayo Sch. Mgmt., South Australia Inst. Tech., 1985. Mem. Am. Chem. Soc. Co-author: Physical Evidence in the Administration of Criminal Justice, 1970, The Role of Criminalistics in the World of the Future, 1972; asso. editor Law, Medicine, Science—and Justice, 1964; contbr. to Ency. Crime and Justice, 1983. Home: 5117 Ridgegate Way Fair Oaks CA 95628-3603

PARKER, CAMILLE KILLIAN, physician, surgeon; b. Columbus, Ohio, June 28, 1918; d. John Vincent and Myrtle (Kagy) Hill; m. E.W. Killian, Apr. 25, 1943 (dec.); children—Paul Wesley, Clyde Bernard; m. Francis W. Parker, Dec. 7, 1958. Student, U. Chgo., 1942-43; B.S., U. Ill., 1945; M.D., 1946; postgrad. in ophthalmology, Northwestern U., 1947-48. Diplomate Am. Bd. Ophthalmology. Intern Wesley Meml. Hosp., Chgo., 1946-47; resident in ophthalmology Ill. Eye and Ear Infirmary, Chgo., 1949-51; practice medicine specializing in med. and surg. ophthalmology Logansport, Ind., 1951—; sec. staff Meml. Hosp., Logansport, 1959; pres. med. staff St. Joseph Hosp., Logansport, 1965. Pres., Logansport Council for Pub. Schs., 1961,62; mem. Lake Maxinkuckee Mgmt. Com., Culver, Ind., 1981—; chmn. social concern Meth. Ch., 1963-65, ofcl. bd., 1961-65. Recipient Service award Culver Mil. Acad., 1969. Fellow Am. Acad. Ophthalmology and Otolaryngology; mem. AMA (physicians recognition award 1971, 75, 79, 82, 85, 88, 93, 94), Soc. Eye Surgeons (charter), Logansport C. of C., Cass County Med. Soc. (pres. 1971), Ind. State Med. Assn., Ind. Acad. Ophthalmology and Otolaryngology (pres. 1979-80). Republican. Clubs: Altrusa (v.p. 1967-69), Culver Mothers (pres. 1968-69). Home and Office: 2500 E Broadway Logansport IN 46947-2002

PARKER, CAROL JEAN, psychotherapist, consultant; b. Plant City, Fla., Sept. 4, 1946; d. Fennimore Blaine and Verna Melissa (Robinson) Bowman; m. Charles Bridges, June 1, 1968 (div. 1979); children: James, Nova. AA, Hillsborough C.C., Tampa, Fla., 1979; BA, Internat. Coll., L.A., 1981, MA, 1983. Asst. Dr. Clarke Weeks, Plant City, 1964-65; med. transcriber Tampa Gen. Hosp., 1965-71, St. Joseph's Hosp., Tampa, 1976-80; psychotherapist Discovery Inst., Tampa, 1980-85; owner, dir. Ananda Counseling Ctr., Tampa, 1985—; clinician Human Devel. Ctr., New Port Richey, Fla., 1979-81; exec. dir. women's program, The Manors Hosp., Tarpon Springs, Fla., 1992—; program dir. stress related disorders Daylight Corp., Tampa, 1996—. Participant Task Force on Prostitution and Female Offender Diversion Program, Tampa, 1988. Mem. ACA, Am. Assn. on Mental Health, Am. Assn. Clin. Hypnotists, Internat. Soc. for Study Multiple Personality Disorders and Disassociation (pres. 1996-97), Tampa Bay Assn. Women Therapists (bd. dirs.), Tampa Bay Study Group on Multiple Personality Disorders and Dissociation (chmn. bd. 1990—, Outstanding Mem. award 1991), Tampa Bay Assn. Women Psychotherapists (pres. 1996-97), Fla. Guardian Assn. Office: Ananda Counseling Ctr 420 W Platt St Tampa FL 33606-2244

PARKER, CAROL TOMMIE, psychotherapist, educator; b. Birmingham, Ala.; d. Estes Carter and Anny May (Skinner) Thompson; m. John W. Hill; children: Patrick, Laurie, Annette (dec.), Timothy, Gail, Daniel. BSW, U. Nebr., Omaha, 1977; MSW, U. Nebr., Lincoln, 1978. Diplomate Am. Bd. Med. Psychotherapists; cert. master social worker. Practice psychotherapy specializing in individual and family therapy Omaha, 1980—; family therapist Med. Coll. U. Nebr., Omaha, 1978-94; asst prof., adj. faculty sch. social work U. Nebr., Omaha, 1987-94, asst. prof. courtesy faculty Coll. Medicine Dept. Psychiatry, Dept. Family Practice U. Nebr. Med. Ctr., 1988—; practicum instr. sch. social work U. Nebr., Omaha, 1980-94. Bd. dirs. Advocacy Office Children and Youth, Omaha, 1984-85. Fellow Nat. Assn. Social Workers; mem. Acad. Cert. Social Workers, Internat. Acad. Behavioral Medicine, Counseling and Psychotherapy, Inc. (diplomate), Am. Assn. Marriage and Family Therapy (clin., approved supr.), Omaha Club., Omaha Press Club. Democrat. Office: MRI SR WK 600 S 42nd St Omaha NE 68198-1002

PARKER, CHARLES WALTER, JR., consultant, retired equipment company executive; b. nr. Ahoskie, N.C., Nov. 22, 1922; s. Charles Walter and Minnie Louise (Williamson) P.; m. Sophie Nash Riddick, Nov. 26, 1949; children: Mary Parker Hutto, Caroline Parker Robertson, Charles Walter III, Thomas Williamson. B.S. in Elec. Engring, Va. Mil. Inst., 1947; Dr. Engring. (hon.), Milw. Sch. Engring., 1980. With Allis-Chalmers Corp., 1947-87; dist. mgr. Allis-Chalmers Corp., Richmond, Va., 1955-57, Phila., 1957-58; dir. sales promotion industries group Allis-Chalmers Corp., Milw., 1958-61; gen. mktg. mgr. new products Allis-Chalmers Corp., 1961-62, mgr. mktg. services, 1962-66, v.p. mktg. and public relations services, 1966-70, v.p., dep. group exec., 1970-72, staff group exec. communications and public affairs, 1972-87, ret., 1987; prin. Charles Parker & Assocs., Ltd., Milw., 1987—; retired chmn. bd. dirs. Associated Dental Svc. Inc., Milw., 1989-93; founding mem. World Mktg. Contact Group, London; bd. dirs. Internat. Gen. Ins. Corp., Dinermite Corp. Gen. chmn. United Fund Greater Milw. Area, 1975; trustee Boy Scouts Am. Trust Fund, Milw.; bd. dirs. Jr. Achievement; pres. bd. trustees Univ. Sch. Milw., 1978-80; trustee Carroll Coll., Waukesha, Wis.; bd. dirs. Milw. Children's Hosp.; bd. regents Milw. Sch. Engring.; mem. Greater Milw. Com.; chmn. bd. dirs. Milw. Found., 1987-89. Served to capt. AUS, 1943-46, ETO. Decorated Bronze Star. Mem. NAM (dir.), IEEE (assoc.), Wis. C. of C. (pres. 1974-76), Sales and Mktg. Execs. Internat. (pres., CEO 1974, 75, Eduardo Rihan Internat. Mktg. Exec. of Yr. award 1979), Wis. Mfrs. and Commerce Assn. (exec. com.), Pi Sigma Epsilon (pres. 1976-77, trustee and chmn. nat. edn. found. 1979-86), Kappa Alpha. Home: 4973 N Newhall St Milwaukee WI 53217-6049 Office: PO Box 92398 828 N Broadway Milwaukee WI 53202-3611

PARKER, CHERYL JEAN, small business owner; b. Kansas City, Kans., Feb. 3, 1948; d. Mildred Eileen (Mayer) Ross; m. Jack W. Parker, June 25, 1977; children: Brian Scott, Kimberly Michelle. BS, Kans. State U., 1970; MA, U. Mo., Kansas City, 1975; postgrad., Dept. Def. Info. Sch., 1984. Cert. tchr. Mo., Kans. Migrant tchr. Piper Unified Schs. 203, Kansas City, Kans., 1970-72; tchr. North Kansas City Pub. Schs., Kansas City, 1970-75; elem. guidance counselor Excelsior (Mo.) Springs Pub. Schs., 1975-77; rsch. asst. foster parent rsch. project Coll. Human Ecology, Manhattan, Kans., 1977-78; test examiner 1st Inf. Div., Fort Riley, Kans., 1980-82; pub. affairs specialist 1st Inf. Div., Fort Riley, 1983-85; pers. clerk 3rd ROTC Div. Hdqrs., Fort Riley, 1982-83; tchr. Living Word Christian Sch., Manhattan, 1985-86; program mgr., career counselor Army Community Svcs., Army War Coll., Carlisle, Pa., 1987-90; elem. guidance counselor Shawnee Mission (Kans.) Pub. Schs., 1990-96; small bus. owner, 1996—; recording sec. Career Edn. Com., Excelsior Springs, 1975-77; career counselor personal contacts and referrals, Carlisle, 1986-90; career counselor relocation/outplacement, U.S. Army, Carlisle, 1987-90; job fair coord. Army Community Svcs., Carlisle, 1989-90; guest speaker various clubs, confs., Carlisle, Excelsior Springs. Author: (with others, catalog) Foster Parent Resources, 1977-78; contbr. articles to profl. jours. Violinist Christ Community Ch. Orch., Camp Hill, Pa., 1986-89, Full Faith Ch. Psalm 150 Orch., 1993; mem. hospitality com. PTA, Carlisle, 1987-88; mem. Suggestion Awards Rev. Com., Fort Riley, 1983-85. Hollis Award scholar Kans. State U., 1968, Kansas City Star scholar Kansas City Star Newspaper, 1966-70. Mem. Kans. NEA, Kans. Assn. Counseling and Devel. (Spurs Acad. hon. mem.), Carlisle Area Pers. Assn., Federally Employed Women (nomination chmn. 1989—), Federal Women's Program (program mgr. 1988-89, certificate 1989), Alpha Lambda Delta. Mem. Christian Ch. Avocations: Christian and classical music, reading, needlework, travel, swimming. Home: 9824 W 132nd Ter Overland Park KS 66213-3319

PARKER, CHRISTOPHER WILLIAM, lawyer; b. Evanston, Ill., Oct. 26, 1947; s. Robert H. and Dorothy Boynton P.; m. Mary Ann P., Dec. 28, 1984. BA, Tufts U., 1969; JD, Northeastern U., 1976. Bar: Mass. 1977, U.S. Dist. Ct. Mass. 1977, U.S. Dist. Ct. (we. dist.) Tex. 1986, U.S. Ct. Appeals (1st cir.) 1988, U.S. Supreme Ct. 1988. Law clk. to judge U.S. Bankruptcy Ct. Mass. dist., Boston, 1976-77; assoc. Fletcher, Tilton & Whipple, Worcester, Mass., 1977-79; counsel U.S. Trustee, Boston, 1979-81; assoc. Craig and Macauley P.C., Boston, 1982-84, ptnr., 1984-87; counsel Hinckley, Allen, Snyder & Comen, Boston, 1987-88, ptnr., 1989-91; ptnr. McDermott, Will & Emery, Boston, 1991—. Mem. ABA, Mass. Bar Assn., Am. Bankruptcy Inst. Boston Bar Assn., Comml. Law League. Club: Union Boat (Boston). Home: 45 Walnut St Lynnfield MA 01940-2009 Office: McDermott Will & Emery 75 State St Boston MA 02109

PARKER, CLEA EDWARD, retired university president; b. Talisheek, La., Apr. 2, 1927; s. William A. and Lutritia (Davis) P.; m. Peggy Ann Faciane, June 21, 1953; children—Brian, Stephen, Karen, Robin. B.A., Southeastern La. U., 1948; M.Ed., La. State U., 1952, Ed.D., 1965. Coach, tchr. Rugby Acad., New Orleans, 1948-50; tchr., prin., supr. instr., dir. curriculum and instrn. St. Tammany Parish Sch. Bd., 1950-67; prof. edn., head dept. student teaching Nicholls State Coll., Thibodaux, La., 1967-68; acting pres. Southeastern La. U., Hammond, 1968; pres. Southeastern La. U., 1968-80, pres. emeritus, 1980—; liaison La. State Dept. Edn., Higher Edn. and Bds. for Edn. in La., 1986; vis. lectr. La. State U., 1965-69; Past pres. St. Tammany Parish Tchrs. Assn., La. Assn. Supervision and Curriculum Devel.; past pres. elementary dept. La. Tchrs. Assn.; chmn. Pres.'s Council La. Bd. Edn., 1972-73; v.p. Conf. La. Colls. and Univs., 1973-74, pres., 1974-75; pres. elect Gulf South Conf., 1974-75, pres., 1975-76; mem. Steering Com. on Curriculum Devel. and Revision for Career Edn. for State La., 1973; mem. adv. council for State Plan for Career Edn., 1973. Mem. planning com. Gov.'s Conf. on Aging, 1976; v.p. chpt. 15 La. Good Samaritans, 1987-88; bd. dirs. Assn. for Retarded Citizens, pres.-elect, 1981; mem. Zemurray Park Recreation Commn., Hammond, 1992-95; chmn. bd. dirs. Lallie Kemp Meml. Hosp., 1993-94; bd. dirs. Lallie Kemp Med. Ctr., 1994—, chmn., 1994-95. With USCGR, 1945, 93-94. Named Hon. State Farmer La., 1970; Distinguished Alumnus of Yr. Southeastern La. U. Alumni Assn., 1977, 91, 92. Mem. Am. Assn. State Colls. and Univs. (com. on nat. svc. 1972-73, task force on aging 1975-76, 78-79, nominating com. 1977—, state Rep. for La. 1979—, com. agr. renewable resources and rural devel. 1979-80, Svc. to Edn. award 1980), Hammond C. of C., La. Assn. for Sch. Execs., Ozone Ramblers Camping Club (pres. 1988), KC (lectr. 1982, 85, 90-91, chancellor 1983-84, 87—, dep. grand knight 1995-96), Rotary (bd. dirs. Hammond, internat. svc. dir. 1972), Phi Delta Kappa, Kappa Delta Pi. Home: 10 Golden Dr Hammond LA 70401-1010

PARKER, DAVID FORSTER, real estate development consultant; b. Sarnia, Ont., Can., July 4, 1934; s. George William and Bessie Havergal (Forster) P.; m. Marilynn Catherine McFadden, Oct. 15, 1960; children: John Christopher, Stephen, David, Daniel. Student, U. Toronto, Ont., Can., 1954-57; BS, Mich. State U., 1964, M in Urban Planning, 1965; D in Pub. Adminstrn., SUNY, Albany, 1980. Prin. Tricon Ltd. Builders, Sarnia, Ont., 1957-62; urban planner N.Y. State Dept. Transp., Albany, 1965-66; asst. to dir. N.Y. State Budget, Albany, 1967-69; pres. Audubon Devel. Corp., Buffalo, 1969-76; dep. dir. Sadat City, Cairo, Egypt, 1976-79; cons. Milton Keynes (Eng.), 1979-80; v.p. Bos Corp., Jacksonville, Fla., 1980-82; prin. Clark Parker Assocs., Jacksonville, 1982-90, Parker Assocs., Jacksonville, 1990—, Clark Parker Realty, Jacksonville, 1982-92; pres. Fla. Real Estate Clinic, Inc., 1991-94; real estate broker, 1992—; pres. PFE, Inc., 1994—. Author: Marketing New Homes, 1990 (recognition 1990), Selling New Homes, 1990 (recognition 1990); contbr. articles to profl. jours. Chmn. Albany Citizens Against Poverty, 1966-67, Ctrl. Jacksonville Residential Task Force, 1986-88, Mayor's Housing Com., Jacksonville, 1990-95. Mem. Inst. Residential Mktg., Nat. Assn. Home Builders, Jacksonville C. of C., S.E. Resort Real Estate Coun., Urban Land Inst., Comty. Devel. Coun., Am. Inst. Cert. Planners, Soc. for Preservation and Encouragement of Barbershop Quartet Singing in America (greater Jacksonville chpt. pres. 1990-92, sunshine dist. dir. 1993—, v.p. 1995-97), Selva Marina Country Club, Phi Kappa Phi, Beta Alpha Sigma, Phi Sigma Alpha. Home: 1739 Live Oak Ln Jacksonville FL 32233-5605 Office: Parker Assocs 14500 Beach Blvd Jacksonville FL 32250-2302

PARKER, DENNIS GENE, former sheriff, karate instructor; b. Kansas City, Kans., Jan. 5, 1956; s. Billy Gene and Lola Ruth (Martens) P.; m. Rebecca Shepherd, Nov. 1, 1994; children: Heatheryn Ruth, Jessica Elise. Student, U. Kans., 1984. Martial arts instr. Northland Tai-Ryuku, Kansas City, Mo., 1974-84; police cpl. Atchison (Kans.) Dept. Police, 1984-90; estate investigator Am. Rsch. Bur., L.A., 1990; sheriff Atchison County, Kans., 1990-94; bd. dirs. Atchison County Community Corrections; team mem. Atchison County Multidisciplinary Child Protection Team, 1992—; bd. dirs. N.E. Kans. Drug Task Force, Oskaloosa, 1990-91. Bd. dirs. N.E. Kans. Community Action Program, Atchison, 1991—, Atchison Area Drug Task Force, 1993—. Recipient Silver Star for Bravery Am. Police Hall of Fame, 1992, Honor award, 1992, John Edgar Hoover Meml. award Nat. Assn. Chiefs of Police and Police Hall of Fame, 1993, State of Kans. medals of valor, 1992, 93, Pres.'s Nat. medal of patriotism, 1993. Mem. World Black Belt Bur., Sandan-3d Level Black Shito-Ryu Okinawa Te. Baptist. Home and Office: 5125 NW Parkdale Rd Kansas City MO 64151-3205

PARKER, DIANA LYNNE, restaurant manager, special events director; b. Eureka, Calif., June 21, 1957; d. Carol Dean and Lynne Diane (Havemann) P. BA in English, Humboldt U., 1981, postgrad., 1982-84. Lic. real estate agent, Calif. Retail clk. Safeway, Inc., Eureka, 1977-84; caterer, owner TD Catering, Eureka, 1982-84; asst. buyer Macy's Calif., San Francisco, 1984-85; realtor Mason-McDuffie, Alameda, Calif., 1985-87; host, Rotunda Neiman Marcus, San Francisco, 1987-89, asst. mgr., rotunda, 1989—, dir. spl. events, 1989—. Mem. Mus. Modern Art, Calif. Restaurant Assn., San Francisco Visitor and Conv. Bur., Common Wealth Club Calif. Republican. Avocations: gourmet chef, artist, antique collecting. Office: Rotunda at Neiman Marcus 150 Stockton St San Francisco CA 94108-5807

PARKER, DONALD FRED, college dean, human resources management educator; b. Oilton, Okla., Nov. 7, 1934; s. Robert Fred Parker and Georgia Marie (Culley) Meek; m. Jo Ellen Dunfee, Apr. 6, 1963; children: Margaret Elizabeth, Emily Lyle. BA in Sociology, U. Okla., 1957; MS in Personnel Adminstrn., George Washington U., 1966; PhD in Human Resource Mgmt., Cornell U., 1975. Commd. ensign USN, 1957, advanced through grades to capt., 1977; staff officer with chief naval ops. USN, Washington, 1969-71; comdg. officer, exec. officer, Patrol Squadron Ten USN, Brunswick, Maine, 1974-76; prof. Naval War Coll. USN, Newport, R.I., 1976-78; comdg. officer Navy Personnel Research & Devel. Ctr. USN, San Diego, 1978-80; ret. USN, 1980; asst. prof. Grad. Sch. Bus., U. Mich., Ann Arbor, 1980-84; prof. human resources mgmt., dean Coll. Commerce and Industry U. Wyo., Laramie, 1984-91; Sara Hart Kimball dean bus., prof. human resources mgmt. Oreg. State U., Corvallis, 1991—; advisor U.S. West Wyo. State Bd. Advisors, Cheyenne, 1986-91; bd. dirs. Unicover Corp., Rocky Mountain FSB; ex-officio dir. Wyo. Indsl. Devel. Corp., Casper, 1987; vis. prof. Acad. Internat. Econ. Affairs, Hsinchu, Taiwan, 1986-91. Author numerous articles, book chpts., case studies. Mem. Acad. of Mgmt. (human resource mgmt. divsn. dir. 1983-85), Midwest Assn. Deans and Dept. Chairs in Bus. (pres.), Western Assn. Collegiate Schs. Bus. (bd. dirs., sec./treas. 1997), Phi Kappa Phi, Beta Gamma Sigma (pres.-elect 1996-97). Avocations: jogging, skiing, hiking. Home: 4400 NW Honeysuckle Dr Corvallis OR 97330-3355 Office: Oreg State U Coll Bus Bexell Hall # 200 Corvallis OR 97331-2603

PARKER, DONALD HENRY, psychologist, author; b. Syracuse, N.Y., Apr. 18, 1912; s. Henry Melvin and Ethel (Madden) P.; m. Fritzi Taylor; 1 child, Dona Jean (Mrs. Roger Sell). B.A. cum laude, U. Fla., 1950, M.A. in Psychology, 1952; Ed.D. in Guidance, Columbia U., 1957. With Sears, Roebuck & Co., 1930-43; propr. Personnel Research Counselors (psychol. testing and guidance), Jacksonville, Fla., 1946-50; psychologist Childrens Home Soc. Fla., 1948-50; psychologist, reading cons. Bradford County schs., Fla., 1950-51; lectr., dir. Reading Lab., U. N.C., 1951-53; dir. Reading Center, Charlotte pub. schs., also Charlotte Coll., N.C., 1954-55; reading cons. Westchester County pub. schs., N.Y.; also instr. reading Columbia U., 1955-57; prof. edn., dir. Reading Lab., U. Bridgeport, Conn., 1957-58; multilevel cons. Sci. Research Assos., Chgo., 1957-64; dir. Inst. for Multilevel Learning Internat., 1964—, Biofeedback Counseling Center, Monterey, Calif., 1976-79; lectr. on multilevel philosophy (application of psychology of individual differences, devel. psychology and psychology of learning to theory that schooling consists of tng. and edn.), 1950—; cons. U.S. AID, Venezuela, 1965-67; participant, lectr. photopsychography, body-mind harmony and health 1st World Congress Parapsychology and Psychotronics, Prague, Czechoslovakia, 1973, 2d world congress, Monte Carlo, 1975; lectr. in Europe, 1960, 63, 71, 78, S.E. Asia, Australia, N.Z., 1969, Africa, India, Thailand, Hong Kong, Philippines, 1971; ednl. cons. to China, 1980, U.S.S.R., 1985. Author: SRA Reading Labs., 1957— (used by over 61,000, 000 students in 62 countries), Schooling for Individual Excellence, 1961, Schooling for What?, 1970, Photopsychography: New Image of Man, 1974, The New American Pioneer Community, 1988, SRA Reading Power for Home Schooling, 1991, Into the 21st Century With Goddess Power, 1996; founder (with Sean Shanahan, Patricia Larkin), Gateway Literacy Project, 1992, The New American Community School, 1992, Failing Schools! Why?, 1993; contbr. articles to profl. jours. Served with USN, 1943-46. Mem. Am. Psychol. Assn., Internat Reading Assn., Assn. Supervision and Curriculum Devel., Internat. Assn. Psychotronics Research, Am. Personnel and Guidance Assn., Phi Delta Kappa. Address: Heartsong House 148 San Remo Rd Carmel CA 93923-9763 *Increasingly, during the last few years of my eighty-two on Planet Earth, I have been influenced by the ancient Oriental philosophy of Yin-Yang, the dynamism and, yes, the continuum of possibility between good-bad, black-white, day-night, man-woman, and so on. While we may decry the one and cherish the other, we cannot have the one without the other. Still further, the truth usually lies somewhere along a line between the two. When I discover that truth, I act upon it to the best of my ability.*

PARKER, DONALD HOWARD, landscape architect; b. Boston, July 27, 1922; s. Glennes Arthur Sheldon and Vida Mary (Kendrew) P.; m. Ella Mae Stinson, Sept. 8, 1945 (dec. 1983); children—Randall Tebow, Sheldon Kendrew, Susan Bowen, Elizabeth Stinson; m. Helen Jackson Anthony, June 19, 1987; 1 stepson, Scott Douglas Paul. B.S., U. Mass., Amherst, 1946, B. in Landscape Architecture, 1947. Registered landscape architect Va., N.C., N.Y., Mass. Landscape draftsman L.E. Moore, C.E., Boston, 1947-48, Leo A. Novick, L.A., N.Y.C., 1948-49; asst. landscape architect Colonial Williamsburg (Va.) Found., 1949-60, chief landscape architect, 1960-85; pvt. practice landscape architecture Williamsburg, 1949—; adv. com. Hist. Am. Bldg. Survey, 1969-71, Smithsonian Instn., 1977-80. Contbr. chpts. to books, articles to profl. jours. Active, Boy Scouts Am., 1958-84. Served to 2d lt. U.S. Army, 1942-45. Recipient Dist. Grad. award Dept. Land Architecture, U. Mass., 1984; Paul Harris fellow Rotary Found., 1981. Fellow Am. Soc. Landscape Architects (trustee Potomac chpt. 1977, Va. chpt. 1978-83, treas. Va. chpt. 1984-86, Disting. Svc. award Va. chpt. 1994); mem. Assn. Preservation Va. Antiquities (corr. sec., bd. dirs. 1995—), 20th Century Art Gallery (bd. dirs. 1980-84, treas. 1992-96), Williamsburg Inn Lawn Bowling Club (pres. 1985-90, sec.-treas. 1991-93, treas. 1994—, tournament dir. 1985-94), Rotary (pres. Williamsburg club 1979-80). Avocations: sports, gardening, canoeing, traveling, lawn bowling. Home and Office: 108 Archers Hope Rd Williamsburg VA 23185-4406

PARKER, DONN BLANCHARD, retired information security consultant; b. San Jose, Calif., Oct. 9, 1929; s. Donald William and Miriam Estelle (Blanchard) P.; m. Lorna Ruth Schroeder, Aug. 16, 1952; children: Diane Parker Wisdom, David. B.A., U. Calif, Berkeley, 1952, M.A., 1954. Sr. engr. Gen. Dynamics Co., San Diego, 1954-62; staff cons. Control Data Corp., Palo Alto, Calif., 1962-69; sr. mgmt. systems cons. SRI Internat., Menlo Park, Calif., 1969-97; speaker San Francisco Commonwealth Club, 1991. Author: Crime by Computer, 1976, Ethical Conflicts in Computer Technology, 1977, 89, Computer Security Management, 1982, Fighting Computer Crime, 1983, Fighting Crime in Cyberspace, 1997. Rsch. grantee NSF, 1971-79, U.S. Dept. Justice, 1979—; recipient Individual Achievement award Info. Systems Security Assn., 1991-92, Nat. Computer System Security award, 1994, Disting. Lectr. award Aerospace Computer Security Assocs., 1994. Mem. Assn. Computing Machinery (sec. 1969-75), Am. Fedn. Info. Processing Socs. (bd. dirs. 1974-76), Am. Soc. Indsl. Security. Republican. Lutheran. Office: SRI Internat Menlo Park CA 94025

PARKER, DOUGLAS MARTIN, writer, retired lawyer; b. Chgo., Mar. 6, 1935; s. Lewis Wallace and Elaine (Schulz) P.; m. Angela Macintosh, June 5, 1965; children: Heather Louise, Melissa Meredith. A.B., Cornell U., 1956, LL.B., 1958. Bar: N.Y. 1959, U.S. Supreme Ct. 1966, D.C. 1969. Assoc. Mudge Rose Guthrie Alexander & Ferdon, N.Y.C., 1958-59, 62-69, ptnr., 1977-94, of counsel, 1995; ptnr, Lankler & Parker, Washington, 1969-73; with Office of Counsel to Pres., 1973; dep. gen. counsel HUD, 1974-77. Bd. dirs. Acad. Performing Arts, Orleans, Mass. Served to capt. U.S. Army, 1959-62. Mem. Am. Arbitration Assn., CPR Inst. for Dispute Resolution (mem. regional panel of neutrals.). Republican. Congregationalist. Home: 7 Highwood Rd South Orleans MA 02662

PARKER, ELLIS D., retired career officer, electronics executive; b. Adams, Tenn., Nov. 1, 1932; s. Ellis A. and Lorene (Qualls) P.; m. Judy C. Matthews, Dec. 24, 1952; children: Donald S., Phillip R., David B. BS in Psychology, U. Nebr., 1972; MPA, Shippensburg U., 1979; LLD (hon.), Miles U., 1989. Rated aviator FAA. Commd. 2d lt. U.S. Army, Korea, 1957; advanced through ranks to lt. gen. U.S. Army, 1992; aviation officer, comdr. 17th aviation brigade U.S. Army, Korea, 1978-80; asst. divsn. commdr. 101st airborne divsn. U.S. Army, Fort Campbell, Ky., 1983-84; cmmdg. gen. Army Aviation County Sch. U.S. Army, Fort Rucker, Ala., 1984-89; dir. requirements army staff Pentagon, Washington, 1980-83, dir. army staff, 1989-92; bd. dirs. Canadian Electronics, Toronto and Binghamton, N.Y., 1993—; bd. dirs. Cobro Corp., St. Louis; v.p. aviation Lear Siegler, Oklahoma City, 1992-94. Contbr. articles to profl. jours. Chmn. Fort Rucker Mus. Found., 1995—; mem. presdl. search com. Enterprise (Ala.0 Jr. Coll.; adv. bd. Troy State U., Dotham, 1992—; chair retiree coun. for chief of staff U.S. Army. Decorated D.S.M. with oak leaf cluster, D.F.C., Legion of Merit, Bronze Star with two oak leaf clusters, Meritorious Svc. medals, 23 Air medals; named to Hall of Honor Gov. Ala., 1993—. Mem. Army Aviation Assn. Am. (Order of St. Michel, Gold 1992), Assn. U.S. Army (mem. exec. com. Fort Rucker chpt. 1994, named to Army

Aviation Hall of Fame 1994), Enterprise (Ala.) C. of C. (dir. 1995—), Enterprise Rotary Club (chmn. allocations com. 1993—). Republican. Avocations: flying, hunting, fishing, volunteering in community. Home and Office: 128 Deer Run Strut Enterprise AL 36330-7812

PARKER, EUGENE NEWMAN, retired physicist, educator; b. Houghton, Mich., June 10, 1927; s. Glenn H. and Helen (MacNair) P.; m. Niesje Meuter, 1954; children—Joyce, Eric. BS, Mich. State U., 1948; PhD, Calif. Inst. Tech., 1951; DSc, Mich. State U., 1975; Doctor Honoris Causa in Physics and Math., Univ. Utrecht, The Netherlands, 1986; Doctor of Philosophy Honoris Causa in Theoretical Physics, U. Oslo, 1991. Instr. math. and astronomy U. Utah, 1951-53, asst. prof. physics, 1953-55; mem. faculty physics U. Chgo., 1955-95, prof. dept. physics, 1962-95, prof. dept. astronomy and astrophysics, 1967-95, prof. emeritus, 1995—. Author: Interplanetary Dynamical Processes, 1963, Cosmical Magnetic Fields, 1979, Spontaneous Current Sheets in Magnetic Fields, 1994. Recipient Space Sci. award AIAA, 1964, Chapman medal Royal Astron. Soc., 1979, Gold medal, 1992, Disting. Alumni award Calif. Inst. Tech., 1980, Karl Schwarzschild award Astronomische Gesselschaft, 1990, Bruce medal Astron. Soc. Pacific, 1997, medal Assn. Internat. Devel. Nice (France) Observatory, 1997. Mem. AAAS, NAS (H. K. Arctowski award 1969, U.S. Nat. Medal of Sci. award 1989), Am. Astron. Soc. (Henry Norris Russell lectr. 1969, George Ellery Hale award 1978), Am. Geophys. Union (John Adam Fleming award 1968, William Bowie medal 1990), Norwegian Acad. Sci. and Letters. Achievements include development of theory of the origin of the dipole magnetic field of Earth; of prediction and theory of the solar wind and heliosphere; of theoretical basis for the X-ray emission from the Sun and stars. Home: 1323 Evergreen Rd Homewood IL 60430-3410

PARKER, EVERETT CARLTON, clergyman; b. Chgo., Jan. 17, 1913; s. Harry Everett and Lillian (Stern) P.; m. Geneva M. Jones, May 5, 1939; children: Ruth A. (Mrs. Peter Weiss), Eunice L. (Mrs. George Kolczun, Jr.), Truman E. AB, U. Chgo., 1935; BD magna cum laude, Chgo. Theol. Sem., 1943, Blatchford fellow, 1944-45, DD, 1964; DD, Catawba Coll., Salisbury, N.C., 1958; L.H.D., Fordham U., 1978, Tougaloo Coll., 1987. Pastor Waveland Ave. Congl. Christian Ch., 1943; asst. pub. service and war program mgr. NBC, 1943-45; founder-dir. Protestant Radio Commn., 1945-50; lectr. communication Yale Div. Sch., 1946-58, dir. communications research project, 1950-54; dir. Office Communication United Ch. Christ, 1954-83; sr. research assoc., adj. prof. Fordham U., 1983—; founder citizen movement to protect minority rights in media, 1963—; chmn. broadcasting and film commn. Nat. Coun. Chs., 1969-72, mem. gen. bd., 1966-72; chair Study Commn. on Theology, Edn. and Electronic Media, 1985-87; founder Found. for Minority Interests in Media, 1985—, treas., 1985—, Hispanic Telecommunications Network, 1986—; mem. adv. com. on advanced TV svcs., Consumer Adv. Group FCC, 1988-92. Producer-dir.: nat. TV programs including series Off to Adventure, 1956, Tangled World, 1965; originator: series Six American Families, PBS-TV, 1977; Author: Religious Radio, 1948, Film Use in the Church, 1953, The Television-Radio Audience and Religion, 1955, Religious Television, 1961, (with others) Television, Radio, Film for Churchmen, 1969, Fiber Optics to the Home: The Changing Future of Cable, TV and The Telephone, 1989, Social Responsibility of Television in the United States, 1994. Recipient Human Relations award Am. Jewish Com., 1966, Faith and Freedom award Religious Heritage Found., 1966, 77, Alfred I. DuPont-Columbia U. award pub. service in broadcasting, 1969; Roman Cath. Broadcasters Gabriel award pub. service, 1970; Lincoln U. award significant contbn. human relations, 1971; Racial Justice award Com. for Racial Justice, United Ch. Christ, 1973; Ch. Leadership award Council for Christian Social Action, 1973; Public Service award Black Citizens for a Fair Media, 1979, Pioneer award World Assn. for Christian Communication, 1988; Congl. citation, 1993. Club: Yale (N.Y.C.). Home: 11 Midland Ave White Plains NY 10606-2828 Office: Fordham University Dept Communications Bronx NY 10458

PARKER, FRANK LEON, environmental engineering educator, consultant; b. Somerville, Mass., Mar. 23, 1926; s. Benjamin James and Bertha (Cohen) P.; m. Elaine Marilyn Goldman, Aug. 22, 1954; children: Nina Madeline, Aaron Bennet, Stephan Alexander, David Seth. BS, MIT, 1948; MS, Harvard U., 1950, PhD, 1955. Registered profl. engr., N.Y. Engr. U.S. Bur. Reclamation, Riverton, Wyo., 1948; field engr. Rockland Light & Power Co., Nyack, N.Y., 1949-50; cons. Howard M. Turner, Boston, 1955; sect. chief IAEA, Vienna, Austria, 1960-61; chief radioactive waste disposal research sect. Oak Ridge Nat. Lab., 1956-66; prof. environ. engring. Vanderbilt U., Nashville, 1967-89, Disting. prof. environ. and water resources engring., 1989—, Alexander Heard Disting. prof., 1988; Westinghouse Savannah River Disting. Sci. prof. Clemson (S.C.) U., 1991-96, emininent scientist prof., 1997—; Harvie Branscomb Disting. prof., 1994-95; sr. rschr. Beijer Inst., 1983-87, Internat. Inst. Applied Sys. Analysis, 1995—; chmn. bd. radioactive waste mgmt. NAS, 1985-91; commr. Monitored Retrievable Storage Rev. Commn., 1988-89. Mem. Port Authority Nashville, 1979-90; mem. Nashville Appeals Bd., 1979-88; mem. Jewish Community Rels. Coun., Nashville, 1981-87. With U.S. Army, 1943-46. Mem. NAE, Soc. Risk Analysis, AAAS, Am. Nuclear Soc., Am. Geophys. Union, Health Physics Soc., Nat. Coun. Radiation Protection and Measurements (consociate). Co-author: Physical and Engineering Aspects of Thermal Pollution, 1970; Engineering Aspects of Thermal Pollution, 1969; Biological Aspects of Thermal Pollution, 1969. Home: 4400 Iroquois Ave Nashville TN 37205-3832 Office: PO Box 1596 Nashville TN 37202-1596

PARKER, FRANKLIN, writer, educator; b. N.Y.C., June 2, 1921; m. Betty June Parker, June 12, 1950. BA, Berea Coll., 1949; MS, U. Ill., 1950; EdD, Peabody Coll. of Vanderbilt U., 1956. Librarian, speech tchr. Ferrum (Va.) Coll., 1950-52; librarian Belmont Coll., Nashville, 1952-54; circulation librarian George Peabody Coll. Tchrs. Vanderbilt U., Nashville, 1955-56; assoc. prof. edn. SUNY, New Paltz, 1956-57, U. Tex., Austin, 1957-64; prof. edn. U. Okla., Norman, 1964-68; Benedum prof. edn. emeritus W. Va. U., Morgantown, 1968-86; prof. emeritus, 1986; disting. vis. prof. Ctr. for Excellence in Edn. No. Ariz. U., 1986-89; disting. vis. prof. Coll. Edn. and Psychology Western Carolina U., 1989-94; research fellow U. Coll. Rhodesia, Africa, 1957-58, Rhodes-Livingstone Inst. Social Research, Africa, 1961-62; vis. prof. edn. U. Calgary, Alta., Can., summer 1969, U. Alta., Edmonton, summer 1970, No. Ariz. U., Flagstaff, summer 1971, U. Lethbridge, Can., (summers) 1971-73, Meml. U., Nfld., summer 1974; mem. Internat. Conf. African Adminstrn., Cambridge, (Eng.) U., 1957, European Bur. Adult Edn., Finland and Fed. Republic of Germany, 1966, nat. conf. White House Conf. on Edn., 1965, Nat. Fgn. Policy Conf. of Educators Dept. State, 1966; cons. Office Edn. HEW, 1970-75, NSF, 1980-86; cons. pubs. Macmillan, Merrill, Tchrs. Coll. Press, Wm. C. Brown, 1988—. Author: African Development and Education in Southern Rhodesia, 1960, 74, Africa South of the Sahara, 1966, George Peabody, A Biography, 1971, rev. edit., 1995, The Battle of the Books: Kanawha Country, 1975, What Can We Learn from the Schools of China?, 1977, British Schools and Ours, 1979; co-author: John Dewey: Master Educator, 2d rev. edit., 1961, Government Policy and International Education, 1965, Church and State in Education, 1966, Strategies for Curriculum Change: Cases from 13 Nations, 1968, Dimensions of Physical Education, 1969, International Education: Understandings and Misunderstandings, 1969, Understanding the American Public High School, 1969, Education in Southern Africa, 1970, Curriculum for Man in an International World, 1971, Administrative Dimensions of Health and Physical Education Programs, Including Athletics, 1971, Education and the Many Faces of the Disadvantaged, 1972, The Saber-Tooth Curriculum, meml. edit., 1972, Accelerated Development in Southern Africa, 1974, Myth and Reality: A Reader in Education, 1975, Six Questions: Controversy and Conflict in Education, 1975, Crucial Issues in Education, 6th rev. edit., 1977, Censorship and Education, 1981, Academic Profiles in Higher Education, 1993; series compiler and editor American Dissertations on Foreign Education, A Bibliography with Abstracts, vol. I Can., 1971, vol. II India, 1972, vol III Japan, 1972, vol. IV Africa, 1973, vol. V Scandinavia, 1974, vol. VI China, 1975, vol. VII Korea, 1976, vol. VIII Mex., 1976, vol. IX South Am., 1977, vol. X Cen. Am., 1978, vol. XI Pakistan, Bangladesh, 1979, Vol. XII Iran and Iraq, 1980, vol. XIII Israel, 1980, vol. XIV Middle East, 1981, vol. XV Thailand, 1983, vol. XVI Asia, 1985, vol. XVII Pacific, 1986, vol. XVIII Philippines, 1986, vol. XIX Australia and New Zealand, 1988, vol. XX Great Britain, 1990; (with Betty June Parker) Education in Puerto Rico and of Puerto Ricans in the U.S.A., vol. I, 1978, vol. II, 1984; Women's Education--A World View: Annotated Bibliography of Doctoral Dissertations vol. I, 1979; U.S. Higher Education: A Guide to Information Sources, 1980; Women's Education--A World View: Annotated Bibliography of Books and Reports, vol. II, 1981, Education in the People's Republic of China, Past and Present: Annotated Bibliography, 1986, Education in England and Wales: An Annotated Bibliography, 1991; spl. cons. U.S. and internat. edn. terms The Random House Dictionary of the English Language, 2d edit., 1987; mem. editorial bd. Jour. of Thought, 1965-80, Western Carolina U. Jour. Edn., 1969-76, W. Va. U. Mag., 1969-78, Ednl. Studies, 1975-77, Rev. Edn., 1977-86, Core (Collected Original Resources in Edn.), 1977—, Internat. Jour African Hist. Studies, 1977-86 Edn. Digest, 1976-80, U.S.A. Today, 1981—, Collier's Yearbook, 1965-72, Compton's Yearbook, 1965-66, Dictionary of Am. Biography, supplement 5, 1951-55, 77, Dictionary of Scientific Biography, vol. 8, 1973, vol. 10, 1974, vol. 14, 1976, McGraw-Hill Ency. of World Biography, 1973, Acad. Am. Ency., 1979, Reader's Digest Almanac and Yearbook, 1968-73, others; mem. editorial bd., regular contbr. Americana Ann., 1961-89. Served with USAAF, 1942-46. Sr. Fulbright research scholar, 1961-62. Mem. African Studies Assn., S.W. Philosophy Edn. Soc. (pres. 1960), Am. Acad. Polit. and Social Sci., Am. Ednl. Research Assn., US Comparative and Internat. Edn. Soc. (feature writer 1963-68, v.p. 1963-64, internat. sec. 1965-68), Can. Comparative and Internat. Edn. Soc., Comparative Edn. Soc. Europe, History Edn. Soc. (pres. 1963-64), Appalachian Writers Assn., Kappa Delta Pi (life mem., Harold R.W. Benjamin fellow internat. edn. 1957-58, sec. com. on internat. edn. 1968-70), Phi Delta Kappa (life, research award chmn. commn. on internat. relations in edn. 1963-67), Phi Gamma Mu, Phi Kappa Phi (life).

PARKER, FRED I., federal judge; b. 1938. BA, U. Mass., 1962; LLB, Georgetown U., 1965. With Lyne, Woodworth & Everts, Boston, 1965-66, Office Atty. Gen., Montpelier, Vt., 1969-72, Langrock and Sperry, Middlebury, Vt., 1972-75; ptnr. Langrock, Sperry, Parker & Stahl, Middlebury, 1975-82, Langrock, Sperry, Parker & Wool, Middlebury, 1982-90; fed. judge U.S. Dist. Ct. (Vt. dist.), 1990-91, chief judge, 1991-94; fed. judge U.S. Ct. Appeals (2d cir.), 1994—; mem. conduct bd. Vt. Supreme Ct., 1975-79, jud. conduct bd., 1982-88. Active Vt. Lawyers Project. Mem. Vt. Bar Assn. (chair spl. com. reform of judiciary 1988-89), Chittenden County Bar Assn. Office: US Dist Ct 11 Elmwood Ave Fl 5 Burlington VT 05401-4366*

PARKER, GARRY OTIS, mission executive, missiologist; b. Ft. Smith, Ark., Sept. 13, 1942; s. Garry Cecil and Louise Elizabeth (Boring) P.; m. Sarah Merrick Whittum, June 10, 1967; children: Elizabeth Louise Parker-Sloat, Rebekah Lynne. AB, Taylor U., 1964; MDiv, Asbury Theol. Sem., 1968; postgrad., Cornell U., 1972, Princeton Theol. Sem., 1982-85, Johns Hopkins U., 1984. Ordained clergy United Meth. Ch., 1967. Missionary supr. OMS Internat., Malang, Indonesia, 1972-78; missionary, pastor The Union Ch., San Salvador, El Salvador, 1979-81; pastor Cmty. United Meth. Ch., Royal Oak, Md., 1981-84, Wesley United Meth., Elkton, Md., 1984-87; exec. cons. Gen. Bd. Global Ministry/United Meth. Ch., N.Y.C., 1987-89; pastor Tilghman (Md.) United Meth. Ch., 1989-91; pres., CEO The Mustard Seed, Pasadena, Calif., 1991—; corp. pres. The Mustard Seed, Pasadena, 1993—; Am. sch. bd. mem. Am. Sch. in El Salvador, San Salvador, 1980-81; global min. Peninsula Conf. Bd. United Meth. Ch., Dover, Del., 1982-88; bd. mem. Mission Compassion, San Francisco, 1995. Contbr. chpt. to book and articles to profl. jours. Chaplain Vol. Fire Dept., Tilghman, 1988-91. John Wesley fellow A Fund for Theol. Edn., Lexington, 1982. Mem. Christian Mgmt. Assn. Office: The Mustard Seed 1539 E Howard St Pasadena CA 91104-2635

PARKER, GEORGE, retired pen manufacturing company executive; b. Janesville, Wis., Nov. 9, 1929; s. Russell C. and Eleanor (Jackson) P.; m. Nancy E. Bauhan, Aug. 11, 1951; children: George Safford III, Elizabeth, Martha, Patricia. B.A., Brown U., 1951, LL.D. (hon.), 1986; M.A., U. Mich., 1952; LL.D. (hon.), Milton Coll., 1974. With Parker Pen Co., Janesville, 1952-86; beginning as asst. to gen. mgr. Gilman Engring. Co. subs. Parker Pen Co., successively asst. domestic advt. mgr., fgn. advt. mgr., dir. fgn. sales, dir. domestic sales, v.p., gen. mgr., 1958-60, exec. v.p., 1960-66, pres., 1966-77, 81-82, chief exec. officer, 1966-80, 81-82, chmn. bd., 1976-86; chmn. bd. Manpower Inc., 1976-86; pres., chmn. Caxambas Assocs. of Fla., Inc., 1986—; chmn. bd. BANCWIS Corp., 1971-84, dir. emeritus, chmn. bd. 1971-84; bd. dirs. Bank of Wis.; chmn. bd. Moebius Printing Co., Milw., 1992-93. Chmn. Wis. Rep. Fin. Com., 1971-73, state chmn., 1974-76; mem. Nat. Rep. Fin. Com., 1971-73; mem. Rep. Nat. Com., 1974-76; chmn. bd. dirs., chief exec. officer Janesville Found.; bd. dirs., pres. Marco Island Taxpayers Assn., 1993-94; fellow Lake Forest Acad.; trustee emeritus Brown U., Beloit Coll.; chmn. emeritus bd. fellows Beloit Coll.; dir. Wis. Acad. Found., 1994—, v.p., 1996, pres., 1997.

PARKER, GEORGE EDWARD, III, lawyer; b. Detroit, Sept. 26, 1934; s. George Edward and Lucia Helen (Muir) P.; m. Margaret G. Koehler; children—George, David, Benjamin. AB, Princeton U., 1956; JD, U. Mich., 1959. Bar: Mich. 1959, D.C. 1981, Fla. 1982. Assoc. Miller, Canfield, Paddock & Stone, Detroit, 1959-68; ptnr. Miller, Canfield, Paddock & Stone, 1968—. Bd. dirs. Detroit Econ. Growth Corp.; ctrl. allocations com. United Way; trustee David Whitney Fund, Grayling Fund. Republican. Office: Miller Canfield Paddock et al 150 W Jefferson Ave Ste 2500 Detroit MI 48226-4432

PARKER, GERALD WILLIAM, physician, medical center administrator, retired air force officer; b. Susquehanna, Pa., Oct. 22, 1929; m. Susan Emerson, May 4, 1985. BS, Union Coll., Schenectady, 1951; MD, N.Y. Med. Coll., 1955. Diplomate Nat. Bd. Med. Examiners, Am. Bd. Internal Medicine; lic. physician, N.Y., Tex., D.C. Intern Ellis Hosp., Schenectady, 1955-56; resident internal medicine Wilford Hall, USAF Med. Ctr., San Antonio, 1958-61; resident in gastroenterology Water Reed Army Med. Ctr., Washington, 1965-66; commd. capt. U.S. Air Force, 1956, advanced through grades to brig. gen., 1980, retired, 1986; chair dept. medicine USAF Hosp., Clark AFB, Philippines, 1967-69; chief internal medicine Malcolm Grow USAF Med. Ctr., Andrews AFB, Washington, 1969-70; chair dept. medicine Malcolm Grow USAF Med. Ctr., 1970-72, Wilford Hall USAF Med. Ctr., Lackland AFB, Tex., 1972-75; dir. hosp. services Wilford Hall USAF Med. Ctr., 1975-77; comdr USAF Hosp., Torrejon Air Base, Spain, 1977-78; dep. dir. med. plans and resources Office of Surgeon Gen. USAF, Washington, 1978-80; dir. med. plans and resources Office of Surgeon Gen. USAF, 1980-81; dir. med. inspection AF Inspection and Safety Ctr., Norton AFB, Calif., 1981-83; dep. surgeon gen. for ops. AF Med. Service Ctr., Brooks AFB, Tex., 1983-85; dir. profl. affairs and quality assurance Office of Surg. Gen., USAF, Washington, 1985-86; dep. dir., chief profl. services King Health Ctr., U.S. Soldiers and Airmens Home, Washington, 1986—; adj. prof. Health Care Scis., George Washington Univ., 1987—; clinical prof. medicine Uniformed Svcs. Univ. of Health Scis., 1988—. Decorated Air Force D.S.M. with oak leaf cluster, Legion of Merit with oak leaf cluster, Bronze Star, Air Medal with oak leaf cluster, ACP Laureate award, 1996. Fellow ACP; mem. AMA, Soc. AF Physicians, D.C. Med. Soc., Am. Geriatric Soc., ACP Execs., Alpha Omega Alpha. Office: King Health Ctr USSAH 3700 N Capitol St NW Washington DC 20317-0001

PARKER, GRACE PATRICE, insurance specialist; b. Phila., July 11, 1958; d. Patrick Henry and Doris Clara (Mason) P. BS, Temple U., 1980. 4th grade tchr. Clara Muhammad Sch., Phila., 1980; policy svc. clk. Dept. Vet. Affairs, Phila., 1981-85, ins. specialist, 1985—, total quality mgmt. instr., 1990—. Pres. bd. dirs. Acad. for Early Learning, Phila., 1992-95, bd. dirs., 1995—; bd. dirs. VA Employees Assn., 1996—. Mem. NAFE, Fed. Women's Exec. Leadership Program (diploma 1994). Baptist. Avocations: jazz music, reading. Home: 8244 Forrest Ave Philadelphia PA 19150 Office: Dept Vets Affairs 5000 Wissahickon Ave Philadelphia PA 19144-4867

PARKER, H. LAWRENCE, investor, rancher, retired investment banker; b. Portchester, N.Y., June 16, 1926; s. Raeburn H. and Alice (Lawrence) P.; m. Eleanor Sage, Mar. 3, 1951 (div. 1967); children: Katherine, Richard, Michael, Douglas (dec.); m. Regine Hawes, Nov. 15, 1994. B.A., Yale U., 1949. With Morgan Stanley & Co., N.Y.C., 1950—; ptnr. Morgan Stanley & Co., 1959-75, mng. dir., 1975-83, adv. dir., 1984—; pres. Morgan Stanley Can. Ltd., 1976-79, chmn., 1979-84; mem. adv. bd. on edn. and tng. Sec. Navy, 1985-87. Trustee Green Mountain Valley Sch., Waitsfield, Vt., 1981-91. Served with USMCR, 1944-46. Mem. Investment Bankers Assn. Am. (bd. govs. 1966-70, pres. 1969), Nat. Assn. Securities Dealers (gov. 1981-84), Sublette County Hist. Soc. (trustee 1987-91). Clubs: Nat. Golf Links Am., Links (N.Y.C.), Blind Brook, Augusta Nat. Golf (Ga.), Bedford Golf and Tennis, Jupiter Island, Seminole Golf. Home: One Angas Trail Hobe Sound FL 33455

PARKER, HAROLD ALLEN, lawyer, real estate executive; b. Denver, Sept. 14, 1924; s. Hyman and Sophia P.; m. Gertrud Parker; children: David, Rodney, Diana, Jesse, Jonathan. JD, Golden Gate U., 1971. Bar: Calif. 1972. Pvt. practice San Francisco; gen. ptnr. Harold Parker Properties, San Francisco; legal cons. San Francisco Craft and Folk Art Mus.; past mem. Bay Area Lawyers for the Arts; spkr. in field; prime developer Union St. Comml. Corridor, San Francisco, 1963—. Pub.: Wolfgang Paalen, His Art and His Writings, 1980, Richard Bowman, Forty Years of Abstract Painting, 1986. Chmn. Fine Arts Commn., Tiburon, Calif., 1976-78. Mem. Family Club (San Francisco). Avocations: music, art, tennis. Office: 1844 Union St San Francisco CA 94123-4308

PARKER, HAROLD TALBOT, history educator; b. Cin., Dec. 26, 1907; s. Samuel Chester and Lucile (Jones) P.; m. Louise Salley, July 9, 1980. PhB, U. Chgo., 1928, PhD, 1934; postgrad., Cornell U., 1929-30. Mem. faculty Duke U., Durham, N.C., 1939—, assoc. prof., 1950-57, prof. history, 1957-77, emeritus, 1977—; adj. prof. U. Ala., Huntsville, 1978-81; faculty U. N.C., Chapel Hill, 1984. Author: The Cult of Antiquity and the French Revolutionaries, 1937, Three Napoleonic Battles, 1944, 83, (with Marvin Brown) Major Themes in Modern European History, 3 vols., 1974, Bureau of Commerce in 1781, 1979, An Administrative Bureau During the Old Regime, 1993, History of St. Philip's Episcopal Church (Durham, N.C.) 1978-1994, 1997; editor: (with Richard Herr) Ideas in History, 1965, Problems in European History, 1979, (with Georg Iggers) International Handbook of Historical Studies, 1979, Theory and Social History, 1980, (with L.S. Parker) Proc. Consortium of Revolutionary Europe, 1981, 84, 85, 86; assoc. editor Historical Dictionary of Napoleonic France, 1985; regional editor, contbg. author: Great Historians of the Modern Age, 1991; contbr. articles to profl. jours. With USAAF, 1942-45. Recipient Disting. Svc. award Consortium on Revolutionary Europe, 1993, Disting Svc. award So. Hist. Assn. European History Sect., 1993. Mem. Soc. for French Hist. Studies (pres. 1957, Disting. Svc. award 1989), AAUP (pres. Duke U. chpt. 1960), Phi Beta Kappa (pres. Duke chpt. 1961). Episcopalian. Home: 5-A Exum Dr West Columbia SC 29169

PARKER, HARRY JOHN, retired psychologist, educator; b. Sioux City, Iowa, Jan. 18, 1923. A.B., Elmhurst Coll., 1947; M.A., Northwestern U., 1953, Ph.D., 1956, postgrad., 1958; postgrad., Roosevelt U., 1957-58; LittD, Elmhurst Coll., 1990. Lic. psychologist, Okla. Tex. Counselor Northwestern U. Counseling Ctr., Chgo., 1952-56; counseling psychologist Northwestern U. Counseling Ctr., 1956-59, asst. dir., 1957-58, dir., 1958-59; pvt. practice counseling psychologist Chgo., 1956-59, Okla., 1959-69, Tex., 1969—; prof. edn. U. Okla., 1959-69; dir. manpower planning, regional med. program and Sch. Health Related Professions U. Okla. Med. Ctr., Oklahoma City, 1967-69; prof. preventive medicine and pub. health U. Okla. Med. Ctr., 1966-69, prof. human ecology, 1969; assoc. dean Sch. Allied Health Scis. U. Tex. Southwestern Med. Ctr., Dallas, 1969-74; prof. phys. medicine and rehab. U. Tex. Southwestern Med. Ctr., 1969-90; prof. psychiatry U. Tex. Southwestern Med. Ctr., 1969-90, prof. rehab. sci., 1970-90; adj. prof. rehab. U. N. Tex., 1990; adj. prof. psychology Ill. Inst. Tech., 1990-96, Tex. Woman's U., 1991—; adj. prof. allied health edn. U. Tex. Southwestern Med. Ctr., Dallas, 1990—. Contbr. articles to profl. jours. Served with U.S. Army, 1943-46. Fellow Am. Psychol. Assn.; mem. Southwestern Psychol. Assn., Dallas Psychol. Assn., Tex. Psychol. Assn., Sigma Xi, Phi Delta Phi, Alpha Eta.

PARKER, HARRY LAMBERT, university rowing coach; b. Fitchburg, Mass., Oct. 28, 1935; s. Lambert Achilles and Ruth Margaret (Burnham) P.; m. Kathryn E. Keeler, Aug. 10, 1985; children: George Franklin, David Lambert, Abigail Keeler. A.B., U. Pa., 1957. Rowing coach Harvard U., 1960—; coach U.S. Olympic team, 1964, 68, 72, 80, 84; mem. U.S. Olympic Rowing com., 1964-68, 72-84; head coach U.S. Women's Olympic rowing team, 1976. Mem. town meeting, Winchester (Mass.), 1971-73. Served with USNR, 1957-60. Mem. Rowing Hall of Fame., U.S. Rowing Assn. (dir. 1966-85). Coach U.S. eight-oared crew, silver medalist 1972 Olympics, nat. intercollegiate championship crews Harvard U., 1983, 85, 87, 88, 89, 92; coach Harvard U. crew winners Grand Challenge Cup, Henley Royal Regatta, 1985, Ladies Challenge Plate, 1973, 90, Brittania Challenge Cup, 1993. Home: 26 Hancock St Winchester MA 01890-2002 Office: Harvard Univ 60 John Fitzgerald Kennedy St Cambridge MA 02138-4933

PARKER, HARRY LEE, retired military officer, counselor; b. Birmingham, Ala., Feb. 20, 1944; s. Guy Milburn and Grace (Lee) P.; m. Sheri Lynn Pogue (div. Oct. 1973); children: John Lee, Suzanne Grace, Stephen Scott; m. Melanie Louise Cox, Apr. 20, 1979; 1 child, Christopher Robert. BA, Miss. State U., 1966; MS, Johns Hopkins U., 1980; postgrad., U.S. Army Command & Staff Coll, 1982. Commd. 2d lt. U.S. Army, 1966, advanced through grades to lt. col.; maintenance officer 85th Maintenance Bn., Hanau, Fed. Republic of Germany, 1967-69; commanding officer 143d Engr. Co. and A Co. 34th Engr. Bn., Long Binh, Vietnam, 1969-70; chief plans and ops. div. Dir. of Logistics, Ft. Rucker, Ala., 1971-73; supply and maintenance officer 97th Signal Bn. NATO, Mannehim, Fed. Republic of Germany, 1973-76; asst. materiel officer 8th Maintenance Battalion, Grossalheim, Fed. Republic Germany, 1977; tng. evaluator HQ 1st US Army, Ft. Meade, Md., 1978-81; logistics coord. Cuban Task Force, Ft. Indiantown Gap, Pa., 1980; project officer Dept. Def., Project Office, Mobile Electric Power, Washington, 1982-85; exec. officer 193d Spt. BN Ft. Clayton, Panama, 1986-88; chief of maintenance U.S. Army South, Ft. Corozol, Panama, 1986-88; prof. mil. Sci. Army ROTC, Miss. State U., Starkville, Miss., 1988-90; ops. officer 101st area support group, Guardian City, Saudia Arabia, logistics officer, 1st Corps Support Command, XVIII Airborne Corps., Damman, Saudi Arabia (Desert Shield and Desert Storm), 1990-91; career/coop. edn. counselor Cen. Fla. C.C., Ocala, Fla., 1992-95. Presbyn. elder. Decorated 2 Bronze Stars, 3 Meritorious Svc. medals, 5 Army Commendation medals. Mem. Ret. Officers Asn., Am. Legion, Miss. State U. Alumni Assn., Sigma Chi (life). Avocations: woodworking, pilot, scuba diving, boating, computers. Home: 7514 NW 42nd Ave Gainesville FL 32606

PARKER, HERBERT GERALD, state official; b. Fayetteville, Ark., May 13, 1929; s. Otis James and Anna Berthina (Fisher) P.; m. Florida Lucylle Fisher, June 27, 1959; 1 child, Christie Lynne. BS, U. Nebr., Omaha, 1962; MS, N.C. A&T State U., Greensboro, 1970; PhD, Fla. State U., Tallahassee, 1982. Commd. 2d. lt. U.S. Army, 1947, advanced through grades to col., 1969; served advisor mil. assistance advisory group Republic of China, Taiwan, 1962-65; prof. mil. sci. N.C. A&T State U., Greensboro, 1965-68; comdr. all U.S. Spl. Forces units the Delta, S. Vietnam, 1968-69; dir. non-resident instrn. U.S. Army Civil Affairs Sch., Ft. Gordon, Ga., 1969-71, commandant and dir., Ft. Bragg, N.C., 1971-73; prof. mil. sci., dept. head Fla. A&M U., Tallahassee, 1973-77; ret., 1977; chief Crimes Compensation Bur., State of Fla., 1979-87, chief internal auditor Fla. Dept. Edn., 1988-91, dir. of adminstrn. Fla. dept. edn., 1991-94. Bd. dirs. Opportunities Industrialization Centers, Leon County United Way, 1977-81, Fla. Victim/Witness Network, 1985-87; bd. dirs. Nat. Assn. Crime Victims Compensation Bds., 1981-87 (pres. 1984-86); mem. Nat. Urban League; pres. Fla. A&M U Boosters Club, 1983-85; bd. dirs. Tallahassee Urban League, 1982—, pres., 1985-87; bd. dirs. Tallahassee Cmty. Rels., 1993—, Tallahassee Sr. Citizens Found., 1994—, Tallahassee Sr. Citizens Adv. Bd., 1994—, pres., 1996—, adv. bd. Tallahassee Cmty. Justice Ctr., 1995—. Decorated Silver Star, Legion of Merit (2), Bronze Star (3), Purple Heart, Air Medal (3); recipient disting. service award Boy Scouts Am., 1969, James A. Fogarty award Fla. Victim/Witness Network, 1990, Barbershop Ann. Man of Yr. award SPEBSQSA, 1996. Mem. Nat. Assn. Social Scientists, U.S. Army Civil Affairs Assn. (Disting. Service award, 1973), Assn. Parents and Teachers, Tallahassee C. of C., Fla. State U. Coll. Edn. Alumni Assn. (sec. 1991-93), Mil. Order of the World Wars, 555th Parachute Infantry Assn., Inc., Capital Chordsmen (treas. 1991-94, 96—), Capital Rotary Club (Paul Harris fellow), Sigma Pi Phi (Sire Archon/pres. 1992-94), Kappa Alpha Psi, Phi Kappa Phi. Democrat. Methodist. Clubs: Jack and Jill of Am., Am. Bowling Congress, Univ. Men's League (pres.), Fla. A&M Credit Union Bowling League (pres.), Champion Chevrolet Men's Classic Bowling League, Hilaman Park Men's Golf Assn., Bass Anglers Sportsman Soc., Winewood Men's Golf Assn. (v.p.), Toastmasters Internat. (assn. v.p., pres. Ft. Bragg chpt. 1971-73), Nat.

Geog. Soc. Home: 3510 Tullamore Ln Tallahassee FL 32308-3127 Office: Dir of Adminstrn Fla Dept Edn The Capitol Tallahassee FL 32399

PARKER, ISRAEL FRANK, national association consultant; b. Sylvania, Ga., Oct. 29, 1917; s. Cornelius Dean and Mary Eunice (Lewis) P.; m. Mary Alice, Dec. 26, 1938; 1 dau., Rebecca Gaye. Student, Ga. So. U., 1935-36, U. Ala., Birmingham, 1942-43, 49-50. Bus. mgr. United Bakery Workers Local 441, Birmingham, 1941-42; internat. rep. Retail, Wholesale and Dept. Store Union, AFL-CIO, Birmingham, 1942-52, asst. regional dir. So. area, 1957-60; regional dir. So. area Retail, Wholesale and Dept. Store Union, AFL-CIO, 1970-76; internat. sec.-treas. Retail, Wholesale and Dept. Store Union, AFL-CIO, N.Y.C., 1976-80; bd. govs. Nat. Assn. of Unemployment Ins. Appellate Bds., 1989-90; mem. bd. appeals Ala. Unemployment Compensation; trustee Retail, Wholesale and Dept. Store Internat. Union and Industry Health and Benefit Fund and Pension Fund; past chmn. Internat. Found. Employee Benefit Plans; chmn. Ala. Trade Union Coun. for Histadrut, 1970; bd. dirs. Found. for Internat. Meetings. Treas. Canterbury Meth. Men., 1993. Served with USN, 1944-46. Named Man of Yr. Birmingham Frat. Order Police, 1972. Mem. Altadena Valley Golf and Country Club. Home: 745 Bentley Dr Birmingham AL 35213-2543

PARKER, JACK, collegiate athletic coach; b. Somerville, Mass., Mar. 11, 1945; m. Jacqueline Gibson; children: Allison, Jacqueline. Head hockey coach Boston U., 1973—. Winner two NCAA titles, four consecutive Eastern crowns, others; recipient Spencer Penrose Meml. trophy as NCAA Coach of Yr., 1975, 1978; named New Eng. Coach of Yr., 1978, 84, 86, Hockey East Coach of Yr., 1986, 92, Gridiron Club Co-Coach of Yr., 1992; inducted into B.U. Athletic Hall of Fame, 1994; recipient Disting. Alum award Boston U., 1992. Mem. Am. Hockey Coaches Assn. (past pres.). Achievements include being the Terrier's all-time winningest coach with a 493-241-37 record, coaching the team to 13 NCAA Tournament appearances. Office: Boston Univ Sports Info 285 Babcock St Boston MA 02215-1003*

PARKER, JACK STEELE, retired manufacturing company executive; b. Palo Alto, Calif., July 6, 1918; s. William Leonard and Mary Isabel (Steele) P.; m. Elaine Elizabeth Simons; 1 child, Kaaren Parker Gray. BSME, Stanford U., 1939; DBA (hon.), Southeastern Mass. U., 1970; LLD (hon.), Clark U., 1972, Renssalaer Poly. Inst., 1986. Engr. Western Pipe & Steel Co., San Francisco, 1939-40; marine surveyor Am. Bur. Shipping, Seattle, 1940-42; supt. steel constrn. Todd Shipyards, Houston, 1942-44; supt. outfitting Todd Shipyards, L.A., 1944-46; asst. chief engr. Am. Potash & Chem., Trona, Calif., 1946-50; mgr. separations div. GE, Hanford Works, Wash., 1950-52; div. mgr., v.p. aircraft gas turbines GE, Cin., 1952-57; v.p. corp. rels. GE, N.Y.C., 1957-61, v.p., group exec. aerospace and electronics, 1961-68, vice chmn., exec. officer, dir., 1968-80, dir. emeritus, 1980—; bd. dirs. L.A. Whitehall Corp. Overseer Hoover Instn., Stanford U., chmn. 1974-76; trustee Monterey Bay Aquarium Found., Heard Mus., Phoenix, Ariz.; hon. trustee Renssalaer Poly. Inst., Troy, N.Y.; bd. dirs. Smithsonian Instn., 1985-91; mem. bd. advisors Stanford Rsch. Inst. Fellow AIAA, ASME; mem. NAE, NAS (Pres.'s Circle), The Conf. Bd. (councilor for life, chmn. 1971-73), Aerospace Industries Assn. (chmn. 1966-68, hon. dir.), Augusta (Ga.) Nat. Golf Club, Desert Forest Golf Club, Desert Mountain Club, Bohemian Club, Boone & Crocket Club, Conquistadores del Cielo, Forest Highlands Club. Avocations: fishing, shooting, golf. Home: 6972 Stage Coach Pass Carefree AZ 85377 Office: GE 260 Long Ridge Rd Stamford CT 06927-1600

PARKER, JAMES, retired curator; b. Boston, Jan. 22, 1924; s. Cortlandt and Elizabeth (Gray) P. A.B., Harvard U., 1946. Fellow in European decorative arts, 16th-19th centuries Met. Mus. Art, N.Y.C., 1951; asst. Met. Mus. Art, 1952-54, asst. curator, 1954-62, assoc. curator, 1962-68, curator, 1968-93; adj. prof. Inst. Fine Arts, NYU, 1968-69, 71-72, 80. Author: (with others) Decorative Art from the Samuel H. Kress Collection at the Metropolitan Museum of Art, 1964; Contbr. articles to museum bulls. Trustee French Inst.-Alliance Francaise, N.Y.C. Served with F.A. AUS, 1944-45, PTO. Club: Union (N.Y.C.). Home: 17 E 89th St New York NY 10128-0615 Office: Met Mus Art Fifth Ave # 82nd St New York NY 10028

PARKER, JAMES AUBREY, federal judge; b. Houston, Jan. 8, 1937; s. Lewis Almeron and Emily Helen (Stuessy) P.; m. Florence Fisher, Aug. 26, 1960; children: Roger Alan, Pamela Elizabeth. BA, Rice U., 1959; LLB, U. Tex., 1962. Bar: Tex. 1962, N.Mex. 1963. With Modrall, Sperling, Roehl, Harris & Sisk, Albuquerque, 1962-87; judge U.S. Dist. Ct. N.Mex., Albuquerque, 1987—; mem. Standing Commn. on Rules of Practice and Procedures of U.S. Cts., N.Mex. Commn. on Professionalism, 1986—. Articles editor Tex. Law Rev., 1961-62. Mem. ABA, Fed. Judges Assn., Am. Judicature Soc., Am. Bd. Trial Advocates, Tex. Bar Assn., N.Mex. Bar Assn., Albuquerque Bar Assn., Order of Coif, Chancellors, Phi Delta Phi. Avocations: ranching, fly fishing, running, skiing. Office: US Dist Ct PO Box 566 Albuquerque NM 87103-0566

PARKER, JAMES FLETCHER, middle school educator; b. Washington, Aug. 13, 1951; s. Clifford Marion and Martha Lois (McPhail) P. Student, Shenandoah Coll., 1969-71; BS, Old Dominion U., 1973. Cert. tech. edn., Va. Tchr. Spratley Jr. High Sch., Hampton, Va., 1974, Lindsey Jr. High Sch., Hampton, 1974, East Suffolk (Va.) Mid. Sch., 1974-79, Driver Intermediate Sch., Suffolk, 1979-90, John Yeates Mid. Sch., Suffolk, 1990—. Contbr.: (state curriculum guide) Introduction to Technology, 1988. Vol. Suffolk Young Dems., 1976-78; mem. Driver Intermediate Sch. PTA, 1979-90, John Yeates Mid. Sch. PTA, Suffolk, 1990—. Mem. ASCD, NEA, Va. Edn. Assn., Edn. Assn. of Suffolk (v.p. 1997—), Am. Vocat. Assn., Va. Vocat. Assn., Internat. Tech. Edn. Assn., Va. Tech. Edn. Assn., Suffolk Tech. Edn. Assn., Edn. Assn. Suffolk (exec. bd. 1996-97), Tech. Student Assn. (chpt. adv. 1979—), Tidewater Tech. Tchrs., Va. Mid. Sch. Assn., Coun. Tech. Tchr. Edn. Avocations: golf, reading, computers. Home: 95 Bolling Rd Portsmouth VA 23701-2061 Office: John Yeates Mid Sch 4901 Bennetts Pasture Rd Suffolk VA 23435-1405

PARKER, JAMES FRANCIS, lawyer, airline executive; b. San Antonio, Jan. 1, 1947; s. Raymond Francis and Libbie Olivia (Dusek) P.; m. Patricia Elaine Lorang, May 15, 1971; children: James, Jennifer. BA with hons., U. Tex., 1969, JD with hons., 1971. Bar: Tex., U.S. Dist. Ct. (ea., we., so. no. dists.) Tex., U.S. Ct. Appeals (5th and 11th cirs.), U.S. Supreme Ct. Law clk. to presiding judge U.S. Dist. Ct., Austin, Tex., 1972-76; asst. atty. gen. State of Tex., Austin, 1976-79; atty. Oppenheimer, Rosenberg, Kelleher & Wheatley, San Antonio, 1979-86; v.p., gen. counsel SW Airlines Co., Dallas, 1986—. Mem. ABA, Tex. Bar Assn. Democrat. Lutheran. Office: SW Airlines Co 2702 Love Field Dr Dallas TX 75235-1908

PARKER, JAMES ROGER, chemist; b. L.A., July 19, 1936. BS, Pomona Coll., 1958; PhD, Iowa State U., 1964. Lab. asst. Ames (Iowa) Lab Atomic Energy Commn., 1958-64; analytical supr. PPG Industries, Natrium, W.Va., 1964-73, Corpus Christi, Tex., 1973-82; agrl. chemist PPG Industries, Barberton, Ohio, 1982-89; infrared spectroscopist PPG Industries, Monroeville, Pa., 1989-96, scientist, 1996—. Contbr. articles to profl. jours. Mem. Am. Chem. Soc., Soc. for Applied Spectroscopy, Spectroscopy Soc. Pitts., Soc. for Analytical Chemists Pitts., Phi Lambda Upsilon. Achievements include research in analytical chemistry of metal halides, iodine compounds, alkali metal oxides, coordination chemistry of phosphine oxides, qualitative identifications with proton magnetic resonance spectroscopy and polymer analyses with photoacoustic infrared spectroscopy. Office: PPG Industries 440 College Park Dr Monroeville PA 15146-1536

PARKER, JEFFREY SCOTT, law educator, university official; b. Alexandria, Va., Sept. 6, 1952; s. Clarence Franklin and Mary Florence (Partlow) P. B in Indsl. Engring., Ga. Inst. Tech., 1975; JD, U. Va., 1978. Bar: N.Y. 1979, U.S. Dist. Ct. (ea. and so. dists.) N.Y. 1979, U.S. Ct. Appeals (3d cir.) 1981, U.S. Ct. Appeals (2d cir.) 1984, U.S. Supreme Ct. 1984, U.S. Ct. Appeals (fed. cir.) 1985, U.S. Ct. Appeals (4th cir.) 1992. Assoc. Sullivan & Cromwell, N.Y.C., 1978-86, Sacks Montgomery, N.Y.C., 1986-87; dep. chief counsel U.S. Sentencing Commn., Washington, 1987-88; of counsel Sacks Montgomery, N.Y.C., 1988-90; assoc. prof. of law George Mason U., Arlington, Va., 1990-94; prof. law, assoc. dean acad. affairs George Mason U. Sch. Law, 1994-96, prof. law, 1996—; cons. counsel U.S. Sentencing Commn., Washington, 1988-89. Contbr. articles to law revs.; mem. editorial bd. Va. Law Rev., 1976-78. Mem. ABA, Assn. of Bar of City of N.Y., N.Y. State Bar Assn., Am. Law and Econs. Assn., Am. Econs. Assn. Office: George Mason U Sch of Law 3401 Fairfax Dr Arlington VA 22201-4411

PARKER, JENNIFER WARE, chemical engineer, researcher; b. Berkeley, Calif., Apr. 18, 1959; d. Raymond Paul and Maureen Christina (Trehearne) Ware; m. Henrik Davidson Parker, July 30, 1983; children: Katherine Joyce, Nathaniel Henrikson. BSChemE, Princeton U., 1980; MSChemE, UCLA, 1983, PhDCHemE, 1986. Devel. engr. Am. Pharmaseal, Glendale, Calif., 1980-81; rsch. engr. Crump Inst. Med. Engring, UCLA, 1986-87; sr. engr. The BOC Group, Murray Hill, N.J., 1987-90, lead engr., 1990-92; sr. rsch. engr. CFM Techs., Inc., West Chester, Pa., 1993—. Contbr. articles to profl. jours. Mem. Am. Inst. Chem. Engrs., N.Y. Acad. Scis. Avocations: sports, music, gardening. Home: 201 W Country Club Ln Wallingford PA 19086-6507

PARKER, JOHN MALCOLM, management and financial consultant; b. Halifax, N.S., Can., June 13, 1920; s. Charles Fisher and Mabel (Hennigar) P.; came to U.S., 1936, naturalized, 1942; m. Irene Wilson Davis, Oct. 11, 1942 (dec. Nov. 1987); 1 child, Elane Parker Jones; m. Kathryn Harvey Smithey, Apr. 22, 1989. Cert. internal auditor. With Standard Oil Co. N.J., Charlotte, N.C., 1941, Duke Power Co., Charlotte, 1941-42, So. Bell Tel. & Tel. Co., Charlotte, 1946-50, Atlanta, 1950-68, with South Central Bell Telephone Co., Birmingham, Ala., 1968-83, asst. v.p., gen. internal auditor; pres. Omega Assocs., Inc., 1983—; commr. gen. assembly Presbyn. Ch. of U.S., 1968, 81. Served with AUS, 1942-46. Mem. Inst. Mgmt. Accts. (pres. local chpt. 1972-73, nat. dir.), Am. Mgmt. Assn., Inst. Internal Auditors (pres. chpt. 1978-79, dist. dir. 1979-81, regional dir. 1981-83, internat. vice chmn. 1983-84, internat. bd. dirs. 1979-87, v.p. found. 1984-85). Internat. Platform Assn. Republican. Home: 4509 Clairmont Ave S Birmingham AL 35222-4438 Office: Omega Assocs Inc PO Box 530452 Birmingham AL 35253-0452

PARKER, JOHN MARCHBANK, consulting geologist; b. Manhattan, Kans., Sept. 13, 1920; s. John Huntington and Marjorie Elizabeth (Marchbank) P.; m. Agnes Elizabeth Potts, Mar. 17, 1978; m. Jan Goble, July 18, 1941 (div. 1968); children—Susan Kelly, Elizabeth Douglass, Deirdre Parker, John Eric; m. Nancy Booth, Jan. 24, 1970 (div. 1974). Student U. Minn., 1937, U. Wyo., 1938; B.S., Kans. State U., 1941. Cert. petroleum geologist Am. Inst. Profl. Geologists. Geologist, U.S. Pub. Roads Adminstrn., Alaska Hwy., Can., 1942-43; Field geologist Imperial Oil Ltd., Northwest Ter., Can., 1943-44; dist. geologist Stanolind Oil & Gas Co., Casper, Wyo., 1944-52; v.p. exploration Kirby Petroleum Co., Houston, 1952-74; v.p. exploration Northwest Exploration Co., Denver, 1974-75; cons. geologist Denver, 1975—. Contbr. articles to profl. jours. Recipient Disting. Service in Geology award Kans. State U., 1983. Fellow AAAS, Geol. Soc. Am.; mem. Am. Assn. Petroleum Geologists (pres. 1982-83, adv. council Tulsa 1983-84, Hon. Mem. award), Rocky Mountain Assn. Geologists (explorer of yr. 1979; pres. 1980-81). Home: 2615 Oak Dr No 32 Lakewood CO 80215

PARKER, JOHN VICTOR, federal judge; b. Baton Rouge, La., Oct. 14, 1928; m. Mary Elizabeth Fridge, Sept. 3, 1949; children: John Michael, Robert Fridge, Linda Anne. B.A., La. State U., 1949, J.D., 1952. Bar: La. 1952. Atty. Parker & Parker, Baton Rouge, 1954-66; asst. parish atty. City of Baton Rouge, Parish of East Baton Rouge, 1956-66; atty. Sanders, Downing, Kean & Cazedessus, Baton Rouge, 1966-79; chief judge U.S. Dist. Ct., Middle Dist. La., Baton Rouge, 1979—; vis. lectr. law La. State U. Law Sch. Served with Judge Adv. Gen.'s Corps U.S. Army, 1952-54. Mem. ABA, Am. Judicature Soc., Am. Arbitration Assn., La. State Bar Assn. (past mem. bd. govs.), Baton Rouge Bar Assn. (past pres.), Order of Coif, Phi Delta Phi. Democrat. Club: Baton Rouge Country. Lodges: Masons (32 deg.); Kiwanis (past pres.). Office: Russell B Long Fed Bldg & Courthouse 777 Florida St Ste 355 Baton Rouge LA 70801-1717

PARKER, JOHN WILLIAM, pathology educator, investigator; b. Clifton, Ariz., Jan. 5, 1931; m. Barbara A. Atkinson; children: Ann Elizabeth, Joy Noelle, John David, Heidi Susan. BS, U. Ariz., 1953; MD, Harvard U., 1957. Diplomate Am. Bd. Pathology. Clin. instr. pathology U. Calif. Sch. Medicine, San Francisco, 1962-64; asst. prof. U. So. Calif. Sch. Medicine, L.A., 1964-68, assoc. prof., 1968-75, prof., 1975—, dir. clin. labs., 1974-94, vice chmn. dept. pathology, 1985—, dir. pathology reference labs., 1991-94; assoc. dean sci. affairs U. So. Calif., 1987-89; co-chmn. 15th Internat. Leucocyte Culture Conf., Asilomar, Calif., 1982; chmn. 2d Internat. Lymphoma Conf., Athens, Greece, 1981; v.p. faculty senate U. So. Calif., 1991-92; bd. dirs. ann. meeting Clin. Applications of Cytometry, Charleston, S.C., 1988—. Founding editor (jour.) Hematological Oncology, 1982-93; assoc. editor Jour. Clin. Lab. Analysis, 1985—; co-editor: Intercellular Communication in Leucocyte Function, 1983; founding co-editor (jour.) Communications in Clin. Cytometry, 1993—; contbr. over 175 articles to profl. jours., chpts. to books. Named sr. oncology fellow Am. Cancer Soc., U. So. Calif. Sch. Medicine, 1964-69, Nat. Cancer Inst. vis. fellow Walter and Eliza Hall Inst. for Med. Research, Melbourne, Australia, 1972-73. Fellow Coll. Am. Pathologists, Am. Soc. Clin. Pathologists; mem. Am. Assn. Pathologists, Am. Soc. Hematology, Internat. Acad. Pathology, Clin. Cytometry Soc. (v.p. 1994-95, pres. 1995-97), Phi Beta Kappa, Phi Kappa Phi. Avocations: gardening, reading, hiking. Office: U So Calif Sch Medicine CSC 108 2250 Alcazar St Los Angeles CA 90033-4523

PARKER, JOSEPH B., JR., psychiatrist, educator; b. Knox County, Tenn., July 8, 1916; s. Joseph B. and Sue (York) P.; m. Phyllis Maxine Foster, May 25, 1946; children: Suzanna Margaret, Joseph B. III. B.S., U. Tenn., 1939, M.D., 1941. Diplomate: Am. Bd. Psychiatry and Neurology. Intern Knoxville Gen. Hosp., 1941-42; resident Duke U. Hosp., Durham, N.C., 1946-48; resident in psychiatry St. Elizabeth Hosp., Washington, 1944-45; practice medicine specializing in psychiatry Durham, 1948-49, 53-59, Memphis, 1949-53, Lexington, Ky., 1959-70; instr. psychiatry Duke U., 1948-49, assoc. prof., 1953-59; assoc. prof. psychiatry, dir. Child Guidance Clinic U. Tenn. Coll. Medicine, 1949-53; chief psychiatry VA Hosp., Durham, 1953-59; prof., chmn. dept. psychiatry U. Ky. Med. Ctr., 1959-69; prof. psychiatry Duke Med. Ctr., 1970-83, prof. emeritus, 1983—; vis. faculty U. Pitts., 1967, Harvard, 1968-69; cons. USPHS Hosp., VA Hosp., Lexington. Editor: Psychotherapeutics, 1979. Mem. prof. adv. com. Cerebral Palsy; mem. prof. adv. com. Jr. League Opportunity Workshop; mem. Gov. Ky. Adv. Council Mental Health, 1962—, Gov. Ky. Manpower Commn., 1963—; exec. com., trustee Central Ky. Mental Health Bd. Served to lt. comdr., M.C. USNR, 1942-46. Fellow Am. Psychiat. Assn. (cons. continuing edn. project 1971—), Am. Coll. Psychiatrists, So. Psychiat. Assn. (regent, pres. 1972), Ky. Psychiat. Assn. (past pres.); mem. Am. Psychopath. Assn., Soc. Biol. Psychiatry, Delta Tau Delta, Phi Chi, Delta Phi Alpha, Alpha Omega Alpha. Address: 24 Stoneridge Cir Durham NC 27705-5510

PARKER, JOSEPH CORBIN, JR., pathologist; b. Richmond, Va., Aug. 1, 1937; s. Joseph Corbin and Alice Cabell (Horsley) P.; m. Patricia Singleton, June 24, 1961; children: John Randolph, Nancy Jordan. BA, Va. Mil. Inst., 1958; MD, Med. Coll. Va., 1962; MS in Pathology, U. Minn., 1968. Fellow Mayo Clinic, Rochester, Minn., 1963-68; asst. prof. Duke U., Durham, N.C., 1969-70, Harvard U., Boston, 1970-71; assoc. prof. U. Ky., Lexington, 1971-75; prof. U. Miami, Fla., 1975-81; assoc. dean, prof. U. Tenn., Knoxville, 1981-86; prof. pathology, chmn. U. Mo., Kansas City, 1986-92; prof., chair dept. pathology U. Louisville Sch. Medicine, 1992-96, A.J. Miller prof., chair dept. pathology, 1996—; bd. dirs. Truman Med. Ctr., Kansas City, Mo., Hosp. Hill Health Svc., Kansas City. Author 4 chpts. in books; contbr. 100 articles to profl. jours. Bd. dirs. Multiple Sclerosis Soc., Knoxville, Tenn., 1985, Alzheimers Assn., Kansas City, 1988-91, U. Louisville Med. Sch. Fund. 1st lt. USAR, 1958-67. Recipient 1st Jackson -Hope medal Va. Mil. Inst., 1958; Caldwell award Alzheimers Assn., 1986. Fellow Am. Assn. Neuropathology, Am. Soc. Clin. Pathology, Coll. Am. Pathology, Assn. Clin. Scientists; mem. So. Med. Assn., Am. Acad. Neurology, Am. Soc. Neurol. Surgeons, Univ. Pathologists (pres.). Democrat. Unitarian. Achievements include discovery of autosomal recessive neonatal adrenal leuko-distrophy. Home: 4606 Wolf Creek Pky Louisville KY 40241-5502 Office: U Louisville Sch Medicine Dept Pathology Louisville KY 40292

PARKER, JOSEPH MAYON, printing and publishing executive; b. Washington, N.C., Oct. 11, 1931; s. James Mayon and Mildred (Poe) P.; m. Lauretta Owen Dyer, Mar. 23, 1957; children: Katherine Suzanne, Joseph Wilbur. Student, Davidson Coll., 1949-51; BA, U. N.C., 1953, MPA, 1992; postgrad., Carnegie Inst. Tech., 1955-56. Mgr. print div. Parker Bros., Inc., Ahoskie, N.C., 1956-71, chief editorialist, 1961-77, gen. mgr., 1971-77, pres., chief exec. officer, 1977—; dir. Governor's Hwy. Safety Program, 1993—; treas. Chowan Graphic Arts Found., Murfreesboro, N.C., 1971-90, pres. 1990-92. Editor, columnist five community newspapers, N.C.; panelist: (TV talk show) North Carolina This Week, 1986-89. Mem. Ind. Devel. Commn., 1974-86; vice chmn. N.C. Goals and Policy Bd., Raleigh, 1977-84; trustee Pitt County Meml. Hosp., 1980-88; pres. Com. of 100, Winton, N.C., 1984-87; chmn. Northeastern N.C. Tomorrow, Elizabeth City, 1981-84, sec., 1984-90; del. Dem. Nat. Conv., N.Y.C., 1980, platform com., 1988; dist. chmn. N.C. Dem. Ctrl. Com., 1980-82. With U.S. Army, 1953-54, col. USAR, 1954-88. Mem. Soc. Profl. Journalists, East N.C. Press Assn. (past pres.), N.C. Press Assn., Nat. Newspaper Assn. (state chmn. 1976-83), Roanoke Island Hist. Assn. (vice-chmn. 1987-89), Ea. C. of C. (past chmn.), Rotary, Raleigh Exec. Club. Democrat. Methodist. Avocations: golf, reading. Home: 4500 Connell Dr Raleigh NC 27612-5600 Office: 215 E Lane St Raleigh NC 27601-1035

PARKER, KEVIN JAMES, electrical engineer educator. BS in Engring. Sci. summa cum laude, SUNY, Buffalo, 1976; MSEE, MIT, 1978, PhD, 1981. Rsch. assoc. lab. for med. ultrasound MIT, Cambridge, 1977-81; asst. prof. dept. electrical engring. U. Rochester, N.Y., 1981-85, assoc. prof., 1985-91, prof., chair, 1992—, assoc. prof. dept. radiology, 1989-91, prof., 1992—; dir. Rochester Ctr. Biomedical Ultrasound, 1990—; com. mem. Internat. Symposium on Ultrasound Imaging, 1989—. Editorial bd. Ultras. Med. Biology, 1989—; contbr. numerous articles to profl. jours., chpts. to books. Fellow NIH, 1979, Lilly Teaching fellow, 1982; named IBM Supercomputing Contest Finalist, 1989; recipient Ultrasound in Medicine and Biology prize World Fed., 1991, Outstanding Innovation award Eastman Kodak Co., 1991. Mem. IEEE (sr. mem., Ultrasound Symposium Tech. Com. 1985—), Acoustical Soc. Am., Am. Inst. Ultrasound in Medicine (ethics com. 1987—, standards com. 1990—). Achievements include three patents in field. Office: Univ of Rochester Ctr for Biomedical Ultrasound 203 Hopeman Engineering Bldg Rochester NY 14627*

PARKER, KIMBERLY JANE, nonprofit association executive, paralegal; b. Ann Arbor, Mich., Sept. 24, 1958; d. John Richard and Jane Eleanor (Twichell) P. BA in Polit. Sci., U. Redlands, 1980; Cert. in Legal Assistantship, U. Calif. Irvine, 1983, Cert. in Non-Profit Exec. Mgmt., 1990; Cert. in Adminstrn. Non-Profit Programs, Calif. State U. Long Beach, 1991; MA in Psychol. Studies, Trinity Coll. Grad. Studies, 1996. Hostess Disneyland, Anaheim, Calif., 1976-80; legal sec., asst. John R. Parker Law Corp., Orange, Calif., 1976-81; legal asst. C.D. Daly Law Corp., Newport Beach, Calif., 1981-83; exec. dir. Christian Conciliation Svc., Anaheim, 1983—. Editor: Peacemaker's Handbook; contbr. articles to profl. jours. Grad. Leadership Orange, 1993. Recipient Cert. of Appreciation, County of Orange, 1992; grantee Christian Conciliation, 1985. Mem. Calif. Assn. Marriage & Family Therapists, Christian Legal Soc., Christian Ministry Mgmt., So. Calif. Mediation Assn., County Assn. Dispute Resolution, Christian Conciliation Svc. (bd. dirs. 1983—), Assn. Christian Therapists, Christian Assn. Psychol. Studies, Vol. Ctr. of Orange County, Christian Arbitrator and Mediation Svcs., Inc. Republican. Presbyterian. Avocations: theology, snow skiing, reading, hiking. Office: Christian Arbitration & Mediation Svcs Inc 18002 Irvine Blvd Ste 170 Tustin CA 92780-3321

PARKER, LEONARD S., architect, educator; b. Warsaw, Poland, Jan. 16, 1923; came to U.S. 1923; s. Rueben and Sarah (Kollica) Popuch; m. Betty Mae Buegen, Sept. 1, 1948 (dec. 1983); children—Bruce Aaron, Jonathan Arthur, Nancy Anne, Andrew David. BArch., U. Minn., 1948; MArch., MIT, 1950. Sr. designer Eero Saarinen Assocs., Bloomfield Hills, Mich., 1950-56; CEO, chmn. bd., pres., dir. design The Leonard Parker Assocs., Mpls., 1957—; pres., dir. design The Alliance Southwest, Phoenix, 1981-91; prof. grad. program Sch. Architecture, U. Minn., Mpls., 1959—; pres. Minn. Archtl. Found., 1991. Author: Abandoning the Catalogs, 1979, Rivers of Modernism, 1986, Collaboration-Same Bed, Different Dream?. Panel mem. Mpls. City Hall Restoration Com., Am. Arbitration Assn., USAF bd. visitors (chmn.). Served with U.S. Army, 1943-46; ETO. Firm has received 84 nat. and regional awards for design excellence. Fellow AIA; mem. Minn. Soc. Architects (pres. 1981, Gold medal 1986, pres. Mpls. chpt. 1979), Tau Sigma Delta. Home: 3936 Willmatt Hl Hopkins MN 55305-5142 Office: The Leonard Parker Assocs 430 Oak Grove St Ste 300 Minneapolis MN 55403-3234*

PARKER, LYNDA MICHELE, psychiatrist; b. Phila., Sept. 28, 1947; d. Albert Francis and Dorothy Thomasinia (Herriott) P.; B.A., C. W. Post Coll., 1968; M.A. (Martin Luther King Jr. scholar 1968-70), N.Y.U., 1970; M.D., Cornell U., 1974; postgrad. N.Y. Psychoanalytic Inst., 1977-82. Diplomate Am. Coll. Forensic Examiners. Intern, N.Y. Hosp., N.Y.C., 1975; resident in psychiatry Payne Whitney Clinic, N.Y.C., 1975-78; psychiatrist in charge day program Cabrini Med. Center, N.Y.C., 1978-79, attending psychiatrist, 1978-96; admitting psychiatrist inpatient psychiat. treatment Payne Whitney Clinic, N.Y.C., 1978-96, supr. psychiatry residents, 1978-96, supr. long-term psychotherapy, 1980-82; attending psychiatrist N.Y. Hosp., Cornell Med. Center, 1979-96; practice medicine specializing in psychiatry, N.Y.C., 1979-96; instr. psychiatry Cornell U. Med. Coll., 1979-86, asst. prof., 1986-96; instr. psychiatry, N.Y. Med. Coll., 1978-96; regional chair dept. psychiatry Tex. Tech. U. Health Scis. Ctr., Amarillo, 1996—; psychiat. cons. Bldg. Service 32BJ Health Fund, 1983-89, Inwood House, N.Y.C., 1983-86, Time-Life Inc., 1986-96, Ind. Med. Examiners, 1986-96, Epilepsy Inst., 1986-87, asst. med. dir., 1987-88, med. dir., 1988; ind. med. examiner Rep. Health Care Rev. Sys. Mem. adv. bd. St. Bartholomew Community Presch., N.Y.C., 1990-96. Mem. Am. Psychiat. Assn., Am. Womens Med. Assn. Episcopalian. Office: Tex Tech U Health Scis 1400 Wallace Blvd Amarillo TX 79106-1708

PARKER, MACEO, jazz musician, alto saxophone; b. Kinston, N.C.. Student, Agrl. and Tech. Coll. N.C. (now N.C. Agrl. and Tech. U.). Musician James Brown, 1964-84, Own Group, 1984—. Albums include: Roots Revisited, 1990, Mo' Roots, 1991, 92, Live on Planet Groove, 1992, Southern Exposure, 1994. Office: Verve Digital Records 825 8th Ave New York NY 10019-7416*

PARKER, MARY ALTHEA, painter, art educator; b. Oxford, N.C., Nov. 20, 1906; d. Richard Joseph and Lottie Lee (Barnes) P. BA, Rhodes Coll., 1928; MA, Case Western Res. U., 1944; postgrad., Cleve. Sch. Art, 1942-44, Hans Hofmann Sch. Art, 1950, 54. RN, 1931. Psychiat. and occupational therapy nurse Highland Hosp., Asheville, N.C., 1931-42; prof. art history Colby-Sawyer Coll., New London, N.H., 1944-72; tchr. art Kingswood-Cranbrook Summer Inst., Bloomfield Hills, Mich., summers 1948-49, Transylvania Music Camp, Brevard, N.C., summers 1951-55; prof. art, art history Claflin Coll., Orangeburg, S.C., 1973-77; prof. sr. grad. faculty workshop Western Carolina U., Cullowhee, N.C., summer 1991, prof. sr. grad. faculty in painting, 1991-93; ret., 1993; represented by Art Gallery Ltd., New Bern, N.C.; bd. dirs. Black Mountain (N.C.) Coll. Mus. Arts Ctr. One-woman retrospective show at World Gallery, Asheville, N.C., 1990; exhibited in group shows at Art Gallery Ltd., Zone One Contemporary, Asheville. Mem. Sister City Pairing Project-Russia, Black Mountain, 1989—. Fellow Va. Ctr. for Creative Arts, The McDowell Colony; mem. LWV, Women's Internat. League for Peace and Freedom. Democrat. Mem. Religious Soc. of Friends. Avocations: music, reading. Home: 21 Wagon Trl Black Mountain NC 28711-2557

PARKER, MARY EVELYN, former state treasurer; b. Fullerton, La., Nov. 8, 1920; d. Racia E. and Addie (Graham) Dickerson; m. W. Bryant Parker, Oct. 31, 1954; children: Mary Bryant, Ann Graham. BA, Northwestern State U., La., 1941, hon. doctorate, 1987; diploma in social welfare, La. State U., 1943. Social worker Allen Parish, La., 1941-42; pers. adminstr. War Dept., Camp Claiborne, La., 1943-47; editor Oakdale, La., 1947-48; exec. dir. La. Dept. Commerce and Industry, Baton Rouge, 1948-52; with Mut. of N.Y., Baton Rouge, 1952-56; chmn. La. Bd. Pub. Welfare, Baton Rouge, 1950-51; commr. La. Dept. Pub. Welfare, Baton Rouge, 1956-63; sec. Am. Pub. Welfare Assn., 1962-64; commr. La. Divsn. Adminstrn., 1964-67; treas. State of La., 1968-87. Chmn. White House Conf. on Children and Youth, 1960; pres. La. Conf. on Social Welfare, 1959-61; mem. Dem. Nat. Com.,

1948-52; bd. dirs. Woman's Hosp., Baton Rouge; trustee Episcopal H.S., Baton Rouge Gen. Hosp. Found.; mem. adv. coun. Coll. Bus., Tulane U., New Orleans. Named Baton Rouge Woman of Yr., 1976. Baptist. Home: 141 Duster Dr Natchez MS 39120-5263

PARKER, MARY PATRICE, management consultant; b. Offenbach, Germany, May 19, 1952; came to U.S., 1953; d. Charles Arthur and Helen Louise (Maguire) P. BA in Psychology, U. Fla., 1974. Edn. coord. Clark County Head Start, Clarksville, Ind., 1974-77; pub. rels. Brevard County Sch. Bd., Rockledge, Fla., 1978-79; customer svc. rep. Am. Bank of the South, Merritt Island, Fla., 1980-82, mktg. officer, 1982-85, v.p., 1985-96, v.p., cashier, 1992-96; pres. Computer Mgmt. Corp. of South, Cocoa, Fla., 1996—; instr. Am. Inst. Banking, Brevard County, 1985-87, advisor, 1987-88, mem. exec. mgmt. com., 1993-96. Mem. Mortar Bd. Republican. Office: Computer Mgmt Corp of South 2436 Kathi Kim St Cocoa FL 32926-5347

PARKER, MAYNARD MICHAEL, journalist, magazine executive; b. L.A., July 28, 1940; s. Clarence Newton and Virginia Esther (Boyce) P.; m. Judith Karen Seaborg, Dec. 11, 1965 (div.); 1 child, Francesca Lynn; m. Susan Fraker, Sept. 15, 1985; children: Nicholas Maynard, Hugh Fraker. B.A., Stanford U., 1962; M.A., Columbia U., 1963. Reporter Life mag., 1963-64, corr. Hong Kong Bur., 1966-67; corr. Hong Kong Bur. Newsweek, 1967-69; Saigon bur. chief Newsweek, Vietnam, 1969-70; chief Hong Kong Bur. Newsweek, 1969-73, sr. nat. affairs editor, 1975-77, asst. mng. editor, 1977-80, exec. editor, 1980-82, editor, 1982—; mng. editor Newsweek Internat. Newsweek, N.Y.C., 1973-75. Contbr. articles to Fgn. Affairs, Fgn. Policy, Reporter, Atlantic. Past chmn. Stanford Alumni Bd. 1st lt. inf. U.S. Army, 1964-66. Mem. Am. Soc. Mag. Editors, Coun. on Fgn. Rels., Stanford U. Alumni Bd. (chmn. emeritus), Overseas Press Club. Episcopalian. Avocations: reading, skiing, tennis, fly-fishing. Office: Newsweek Mag 251 W 57th St New York NY 10019-1802

PARKER, MEL, editor; b. N.Y.C., Feb. 11, 1949; s. David Parker and Mollie (Kantorowicz) Lederman; m. Diane Nancy Goldberg, June 27, 1971; children: Emily, David. AB, Rutgers U., 1971; AM in English, N.Y.U., 1973. Editorial researcher Esquire Mag., N.Y.C., 1973; grad. asst. NYU, 1974-77; adj. lectr. CUNY, 1977-78; editor Leisure Books, N.Y.C., 1978-81; sr. editor Playboy Paperbacks, N.Y.C., 1981-82; sr. editor Berkley Pub. Group, N.Y.C., 1982-85, exec. editor, 1985-86, editor-in-chief, 1986-87; v.p., editor in chief Warner Paperbacks, N.Y.C., 1987-90, pub., 1990-96; sr. v.p. Warner Books Pub., Warner Paperbacks, 1996—. Mem. exec. pub. com. UJA Fedn., Anti-Defamation League, N.Y. Book Fair for the Homeless, HArlem RBI. Mem. Assn. Am. Publs. (mem. exec. coun. trade divsn.). Office: Warner Books Inc Time-Life 1271 Avenue Of The Americas New York NY 10020-1300

PARKER, MICHAEL (MIKE PARKER), congressman; b. Laurel, Miss., Oct. 31, 1949; m. Rosemary Prather; children: Adrian, Marisa, Thomas. BA, William Carey Coll., 1970. Operator various businesses; mem. House Budget Com., textile caucus, sunbelt caucus, arts caucus 101st-104th Congresses from 4th Miss. dist., 1989—, mem. appropriations com., Energy, Water and Military Construction Subcom., 1989—. Presbyterian. Office: US Ho of Reps 2445 Rayburn Bldg Washington DC 20515-2404

PARKER, NANCY WINSLOW, artist, writer; b. Maplewood, N.J., Oct. 18, 1930; d. Winslow Aurelius and Beatrice (Gaunt) P. B.A., Mills Coll., 1952; student, Sch. Visual Art, N.Y.C., Art Students League. Pub. relations exec. N.Y. Soccer Club, N.Y.C., 1961-63; with RCA, N.Y.C., 1964-67; art dir. Appleton-Century-Crofts, N.Y.C., 1968-70; staff designer Holt Reinhart & Winston, N.Y.C., 1970-73; free lance writer, illustrator, 1974—. Author, illustrator: The Man with The Take-Apart Head, 1974, The Party at the Old Farm, 1975, Mrs. Wilson Wanders Off, 1976, Love from Uncle Clyde, 1977, The Crocodile Under Louis Finneberg's Bed, 1978, The President's Cabinet, 1978, rev. edit., 1991, The Ordeal of Byron B. Blackbear, 1979, Puddums, The Cathcarts' Orange Cat, 1980, Poofy Loves Company, 1980 (ALA Notable Book 1980), The Spotted Dog, 1980, The President's Car, 1981, Cooper, The McNallys' Big Black Dog, 1981, Love from Aunt Betty, 1983, The Christmas Camel, 1983, The United Nations from A to Z, 1985; co-author: Bugs, 1987, Frogs, Toads, Lizards and Salamanders, 1990, Working Frog, 1992, Money, Money, Money, 1995, Locks, Crocs and Skeeters, The Story of the Panama Canal, 1996; illustrator: Oh, A Hunting We Will Go!, 1974, Warm as Wool, Cool as Cotton, The Story of Natural Fibers, 1975, The Goat in the Rug, 1976, Willy Bear, 1976 (Christopher award 1976), Sweetly Sings the Donkey, 1976, The Substitute, 1977, Hot Cross Buns and Other Old Street Cries, 1978, No Bath Tonight, 1978, My Mom Travels a Lot, 1981 (Christopher 1981), Paul Revere's Ride, 1985, General Store, 1988, Aren't You Coming Too?, 1988, Peter's Pockets, 1988, the Jacket I Wear in the Snow, 1989, At Grammy's House, 1990, Black Crow, Black Crow, 1991, When The Rooster Crowed, 1991, Barbara Frietchie, 1992, The Dress I'll Wear to the Party, 1992, Sheridan's Ride, 1993, Here Comes Henny, 1994, The Bag I'm Taking to Grandma's, 1995, We're Making Breakfast for Mother, 1996, The House I'll Build for the Wrens, 1997. Sec. East 74th St. Block Assn., 1974-83. Recipient various awards, 1974—; Jane Tinkham Broughton fellow, 1975. Mem. Author's Guild, Mills Coll. Club of N.Y., Mantoloking Yacht Club. Home: 51 E 74th St New York NY 10021-2716

PARKER, NORMAN NEIL, JR., software systems analyst, mathematics educator; b. Chgo., June 23, 1949; s. Norman Neil and Sarah Anne Parker; m. Rowena Robles, June 27, 1987. BS with honors, Iowa State U., 1971, MS with honors, 1974. Cert. secondary math. tchr., Ill. Grad. teaching asst. math. dept. Iowa State U., Ames, 1971-72; tchr. math. dept. Thornwood High Sch., South Holland, Ill., 1972-81; software system analyst, space shuttle software IBM, Houston, 1981-94; software system analyst Loral Space Info. Systems, Houston, 1994-96; chmn. software architecture rev. bd. onbd. shuttle Lockheed Martin Space Mission Systems & Svcs., Houston, 1994—, software sys. analyst onbd. shuttle, 1996—; cons. Atomic Energy Commn., Iowa State U., Ames, 1970-72; Iowa State U. rep. NSF Regional Conf., Northfield, Minn., 1972. Contbr. articles to profl. jours. Life mem. Order of Demolay, 1963—; gymnastic judge Ill. High Sch. Assn., Nat. Gymnastics Judges Assn., Internat. Gymnastics Fedn., 1971-81; gymnastics coach Thornwood High Sch., South Holland, Ill., 1972-80; gymnastics program dir. South Holland Park Dist., 1976-80; devel. coord Spaceweek Corp., Houston, 1983-87; officer Filipino-Internat. Families Tex., Houston, 1989-93; mem. retreat team Christ Renews His Parish, 1993-97. Mem. AIAA (sr.), Clear Lake Area Spl. Interest Group Ada, Space Ctr. Object-oriented Projects and Engring. (charter), Johnson Space Ctr. Employees Activities Assn. (assoc.), Gong Yuen Chuan Fa Fedn. (sr.). Republican. Roman Catholic. Home: 4307 Alysheba Ln Friendswood TX 77546 Office: Lockheed Martin 1812 Space Park Dr Rm 102-23A Houston TX 77058-3508

PARKER, NORMAN W., scientist; b. Brewster, Ohio, Nov. 3, 1922; s. Norman W. Sr. and Blanche (Rexford) P.; m. Margaret Marsh Parker, Mar. 15, 1947; children: Norman William Parker III, Margaret Ann Cooper. Cert. profl. engr. Ill. Engr. Brush Devel. Co., Cleve., 1941-42, 45-48, AVCO, Cin., 1948-50; v.p. Motorola, Inc., Schaumberg, Ill., 1950—. Inventor, over 50 U.S. patents. Mem. bd. dirs. Erie Neighborhood House, Chgo. With USN, 1941-45. Recipient Inventor of the Yr. award Chgo. Bar Assn. Fellow IEEE (life). Office: Motorola Inc 1303 E Algonquin Rd Schaumburg IL 60196-4041

PARKER, OLIVIA, photographer; b. Boston, June 10, 1941; d. Harvey Perley and Barbara Ellen (Churchill) Hood; m. John Otis Parker, Apr. 4, 1964; children: John Otis, Helen Elizabeth. B.A., Wellesley Coll., 1963. Tchr. photog. workshops, 1975—; trustee Friends of Photography, 1981-92, 95—, v.p., 1985-89. Photographer, 1969—; Author: (monographs) Signs of Life, 1978, Under the Looking Glass, 1983, Weighing the Planets, 1987; portfolios of black and white photographs Ephemera, 1977, Lost Objects, 1980; one-woman shows include, Vision Gallery, Boston, 1976, 77, 79, 82, 83, 86, 87, Friends of Photography, Carmel, Calif., 1979, 81, Marcuse Pfeifer, N.Y.C., 1980, 83, George Eastman House, Rochester, N.Y., 1981, Art Inst. Chgo., 1982, Photo Gallery Internat., Tokyo, 1983, 84, 87, Fotografie Forum Gallery, Frankfurt, Germany, 1985, Lieberman and Saul, N.Y.C., 1988, Mus. Photographic Arts, San Diego, 1988, Photographers' Gallery, London, 1990, Brent Sikkema, N.Y.C., 1990, 91, Parco, Tokyo, 1991, ICAC/Weston, Tokyo, 1992, Vision, San Francisco, 1993, Robert Klein, Boston, 1993, 96, Wooster Gardens, N.Y.C., 1996; group shows include, Mus. Fine Arts, Boston, 1978, 92, 93, 96. Chgo. Art Inst., 1978, Internat. Ctr. Photography, N.Y.C., 1985, 87, Fogg Art Mus. Harvard U., 1989; represented in permanent collections, Mus. Modern Art, N.Y.C., Art Inst. Chgo., Boston Mus. Fine Arts, Victoria and Albert Mus., London. Bd. dirs. MacDowell Colony, 1988—; trustee Art Inst. Boston, 1992—. Artists Found. fellow, 1978; recipient Wellesley College Alumnae Achievement award, 1996. Mem. Soc. for Photog. Edn. Club: Chilton. Office: Robert Klein 4th Fl 38 Newbury St Fl 4 Boston MA 02116-3210 *I am interested in the way people think about the unknown. New ideas form, the old are shattered, and sometimes old ideas pop up among the new like graffiti on a wall. All is uncertainty and change, but optimists and bingo players are on the look out for moments of perfect knowledge and perfect cards.*

PARKER, OMAR SIGMUND, JR., lawyer; b. Jacksonville, Fla., Apr. 10, 1945; s. Omar Sigmund and Dorothea (Heath) P.; children: Omar Sigmund, Christopher Michael, Julie Anne, Melissa Suzanne, Amy Kathleen. BA, U. Wash., 1968; JD, U. Oreg., 1971. Bar: Wash. 1971, U.S. Dist. Ct. (we. dist.) Wash. 1971, U.S. Ct. Appeals, 1972. Ptnr. Perkins Coie, Seattle, 1971—. Contbr. articles to profl. jours. Bd. dirs. YMCA Youth and Govt. Program, Seattle, 1973-75. Mem. ABA, Wash. State Bar Assn., King County Bar Assn., Am. Coll. Real Estate Lawyers, Am. Coll. Mortgage Attys., Overlake Golf and Country Club, Order of Coif. Avocations: golf, youth coaching. Office: Perkins Coie 1201 3rd Ave Fl 40 Seattle WA 98101-3099

PARKER, PATRICK STREETER, manufacturing executive; b. Cleve., 1929. BA, Williams Coll., 1951; MBA, Harvard U., 1953. With Parker-Hannifin Corp. and predecessor, Cleve., 1953—, sales mgr. fittings div., 1957-63, mgr. aerospace products div., 1963-65, pres. Parker Seal Co. div., 1965-67, corp. v.p., 1967-69, pres., 1969-71, pres. and chief exec. officer, 1971-77, chmn. bd. and chief exec. officer, 1977-84, chmn. bd., 1984—, pres., 1982-84, also bd. dirs., 1982—. Bd. trustees Case Western Res. U.; With USN, 1954-57. Mem. Union Club, Country Club, Pepper Pike Club. Office: Parker Hannifin Corp 17325 Euclid Ave Cleveland OH 44112-1209

PARKER, R. JOSEPH, lawyer; b. St. Louis, June 29, 1944; s. George Joseph and Ann Rosalie (VanVactor) P.; m. Theresa Gaynor, Aug. 26, 1967; children: Christa Michele, Kevin Blake. AB, Georgetown U., 1966; JD, Boston Coll., 1969. Bar: Ohio 1969. Law clk. to judge U.S. Ct. Appeals (6th Cir.), Akron, Ohio, 1969-70; assoc. Taft, Stettinius & Hollister, Cin., 1970-78; ptnr. Taft, Stettinius & Hollister, Cin., 1978—; arbitrator Am. Arbitration Assn., Cin., 1980—; faculty Nat. Inst. for Trial Advocacy, 1990—; faculty advanced trial advocacy program IRS, 1993. Editor Law Rev. Ann. Survey Mass. Law, 1967-69; contbg. author: Fed. Civil Procedure Before Trial-6th Circuit. Bd. dirs. West End Health Ctr., Inc., Cin., 1972-76, Legal Aid Soc. Cin., 1982-85; chmn. bd. dirs. Vol. Lawyers for Poor Found., Cin., 1986-88; master Am. Inn of Court, 1984—. Fellow Am. Coll. Trial Lawyers; mem. Ohio State Bar Assn., Cin. Bar Assn., Cin. Country Club, Order of Coif. Democrat. Roman Catholic. Avocations: golf, squash. Office: 1800 Star Bank Bldg 425 Walnut St Cincinnati OH 45202

PARKER, RICHARD E., building products manufacturing company executive. Exec. v.p. interior products group ABTco, Troy, Mich. Office: ABTco Inc 3250 W Big Beaver Rd Ste 200 Troy MI 48084-2902

PARKER, ROBERT ALLAN RIDLEY, government administrator, astronaut; b. N.Y.C., Dec. 14, 1936; s. Allan Elwood and Alice (Heywood) P.; m. Joan Audrey Capers, June 14, 1958 (div. 1980); children: Kimberly Ellen, Brian David Capers; m. Judith S. Woodruff, Apr. 2, 1981. A.B., Amherst Coll., 1958; Ph.D., Calif. Inst. Tech., 1962. NSF postdoctoral fellow U. Wis., 1962-63, asst. prof., then assoc. prof. astronomy, 1963-74; astronaut NASA, Johnson Space Ctr., 1967-91; dir. policy plan Office Space Flight, NASA Hdqs., Washington, 1991, dir. space ops. utilization program, 1992—; mem. support crew Apollo XV and XVII, mission scientist Apollo XVII, program scientist Skylab program, mission specialist for Spacelab 1, 1983, ASTRO-1, 1990. Mem. Am. Astron. Soc., Phi Beta Kappa. Office: Code MO NASA-HQ Washington DC 20546

PARKER, ROBERT BROWN, novelist; b. Springfield, Mass., Sept. 17, 1932; s. Carroll Snow and Mary Pauline (Murphy) P.; m. Joan Hall, Aug. 26, 1956; children: David, Daniel. BA, Colby Coll., 1954; MA, Boston U., 1957, PhD, 1971; LittD (hon.), Northeastern U., 1987. Various bus. and advt. positions N.Y.C. and Boston, 1956-62; lectr. Boston U., 1962-64; mem. faculty Lowell (Mass.) State Coll., 1964-66, Bridgewater State Coll., 1966-68; asst. prof. English Northeastern U., Boston, 1968-73, assoc. prof., 1973-76, prof., 1976-79; lectr. Suffolk U., 1965-66; co-chmn. Parker-Farman Co., 1960-62. Author: (with others) The Personal Response to Literature, 1970, (with Peter L. Sandberg) Order and Diversity: The Craft of Prose, 1973, Godwulf Manuscript, 1974, God Save the Child, 1974, (with John R. Marsh) Sports Illustrated Weight Training, 1974, Mortal Stakes, 1975, Promised Land, 1976 (Edgar Allan Poe award for best novel Mystery Writers Am. 1976), The Judas Goat, 1978, (with Joan Parker) Three Weeks in Spring, 1978, Wilderness, 1979, Looking for Rachel Wallace, 1980, Early Autumn, 1981, A Savage Place, 1981, Surrogate: A Spenser Short Story, 1982, Ceremony, 1982, The Widening Gyre, 1983, Love and Glory, 1983, Valediction, 1984, The Private Eye in Hammett and Chandler, 1984, A Catskill Eagle, 1985, Parker on Writing, 1985, Taming a Seahorse, 1986, Pale Kings and Princes, 1987, Crimson Joy, 1988, Playmates, 1989, (with Raymond Chandler) Poodle Springs, 1989, Stardust, 1990, Perchance to Dream, 1990, A Year at the Races, 1990, Pastime, 1991, Double Deuce, 1992, Paper Doll, 1993, Walking Shadow, 1994, All Our Yesterdays, 1994, Spenser's Boston, 1994, Thin Air, 1995, Chance, 1996, Small Vices, 1997, Night Passage, 1997; screenwriter with Joan Parker: (TV movies) Blues for Buder, 1988, High Rise, 1988, Spenser: Ceremony, 1993, Spenser: Pale Kings and Princes, 1993; contbr., cons.: (TV series) Spenser: For Hire, 1985-88, A Man Called Hawk, 1989-90. Served with U.S. Army, 1954-56. Mem. Writers Guild Am. Avocations: jogging, weightlifting.

PARKER, ROBERT FREDERIC, university dean emeritus; b. St. Louis, Oct. 29, 1907; s. Charles T. and Lydia (Gronemeyer) P.; m. Mary L. Warner, June 20, 1934; children: David Frederic, Jane Eleanor (Mrs. Howard H. Hush, Jr.). B.S., Washington U., St. Louis, 1925, M.D., 1929. Diplomate: Am. Bd. Microbiology. Asst. radiology Washington U. Med. Sch., 1929-30, instr. medicine, 1932-33; asst. Rockefeller Inst., 1933-36; mem. faculty Case Western Res. U., 1936—, prof. microbiology, 1954-77, prof. emeritus, 1977—, assoc. dean, 1965-73, dean, 1973-76, dean emeritus, 1976—. Mem. Cleve. Acad. Medicine (past bd. dirs.), Am. Soc. Clin. Investigation, Central Soc. Clin. Research, Am. Acad. Microbiology, Sigma Xi, Alpha Omega Alpha. Spl. research virus immunology, quantitative aspects virus infection, tissue culture, action of antibiotics. Home: 1890 E 107th St Apt 436 Cleveland OH 44106-2243 Office: 2085 Adelbert Rd Cleveland OH 44106-2622

PARKER, ROBERT GEORGE, radiation oncology educator, academic administrator; b. Detroit, Mich., Jan. 29, 1925; s. Clifford Robert and Velma (Ashman) P.; m. Diana Davis, June 30, 1977; children by previous marriage: Thomas Clifford, James Richardson. BS, U. Wis., 1946, MD., 1948. Diplomate Am. Bd. Radiology (trustee 1978-90, pres. 1988-90). Intern U. Nebr. Hosp., Omaha, 1948-49; resident in pathology Western Res. U., Cleve., 1949-50; resident in radiology U. Mich., Ann Arbor, 1950, 52-54, instr. in radiology, 1954-55; staff radiotherapist Swedish Hosp. Tumor Inst., Seattle, 1955-58; prof. radiology U. Wash., Seattle, 1958-77; prof. radiation oncology UCLA, 1977—. Lt. USNR, 1950-52. Fellow Am. Coll. Radiology; mem. AMA (radiology residence rev. com.), Am. Soc. Therapeutic Radiologists (pres. 1975-76), Radiol. Soc. N.Am. (bd. dirs. 1984-90, pres. 1991-92), Am. Radium Soc. (bd. dirs. 1988-92, pres. 1992). Office: UCLA Ste B265 200 UCLA Medicine Plz Los Angeles CA 90095-6951

PARKER, ROBERT LEE, SR., petroleum engineer, drilling company executive; b. Tulsa, July 16, 1923; s. Gifford Clevel and Gladys Carolyn (Baker) P.; m. Catherine Mae McDaniel, Dec. 16, 1944; children: Robert Lee, Carolyn Louise, Debra Ann. B.S., U. Tex., 1944; LL.D. (hon.), John Brown U., 1967, Oral Roberts U., 1977. With Parker Drilling Co., 1947—, owner, mgr., 1953—, pres., 1954-92, chmn. bd., 1967—; bd. dirs. CWI, Inc.; dir. Bank Okla., Enterra Corp., Mapco Inc.; chmn. Nat. Energy Task Force, 1981-82. Chmn. St. Francis Hosp., Tulsa, U. Tex. Engring. Found.; trustee U. Tulsa, 1st Methodist Ch., Tulsa; bd. dirs. Tulsa YMCA, Jr. Achievement, So. Meth. U.; active Boy Scouts Am. Served with U.S. Army, 1945-47. Named Distinguished Engring. Grad. U. Tex., 1969. Mem. Am. Petroleum Inst., Internat. Assn. Drilling Contractors, Okla. Ind. Petroleum Assn., Soc. Profl. Engrs. Republican. Clubs: So. Hills Country, Tulsa, Houston, Odessa Country. Office: Parker Drilling Co 8 E 3rd St Tulsa OK 74103-3610 *A discipline of character and work, an enthusiasm for life and an awareness of God's constant help have all had positive impacts on my life.*

PARKER, ROBERT LEE, JR., drilling company executive; b. Midland, Tex., Nov. 9, 1948; s. Robert Lee and Catherine Mae (McDaniel) P.; m. Carolyn Diane Daniel, June 1971 (div. 1974); 1 dau., Christy Diane; m. 2d, Patricia Ann Dollarhite, Oct. 21, 1977 (div. 1984); children—Robert Lee III, Austin Leeann; m. Risa Elaine Blackman, Nov. 24, 1986. Student Okla. State U., 1967-68; M.B.A., U. Tex., 1972. Contract rep. Parker Drilling Co., Tulsa, 1972-73, mgr. U.S. ops., 1973-74, v.p., 1974-76, exec. v.p., 1976-77, pres., chief operating officer, 1977-91, pres., chief exec. officer, 1991—, also dir.; bd. dirs. Alaska Air Group Inc. Bd. dirs. United Way, Tulsa, 1983-88, ARC, Tulsa chpt., 1985—. Recipient 3d place award Tex. Trophy Hunters Assn., 1983. Republican. Methodist. Office: Parker Drilling Co 8 E 3rd St Tulsa OK 74103-3610

PARKER, ROBERT M., federal judge; b. 1937. BBA, U. Tex., 1961, JD, 1964. Bar: Tex. 1964. Ptnr. Parish & Parker, Gilmer, Tex., 1964-65, Kenley & Boyland, Longview, Tex., 1965, Roberts, Smith & Parker, Longview, 1966-71, Rutledge & Parker, Ft. Worth, 1971-72, Nichols & Parker, Longview, 1972-79; judge U.S. Dist. Ct. (ea. dist.) Tex., 1979-94, chief judge, 1991-94; judge U.S. Ct. Appeals (5th Cir.), Tyler, Tex. Mem. Tex. Bar Assn. Office: 221 W Ferguson St Ste 400 Tyler TX 75702-7200*

PARKER, ROY DENVER, JR., entomologist; b. San Diego, Jan. 18, 1943; s. Roy Denver and Helen Crowder (Connor) P.; m. E. Yvonne Wright, Sept. 2, 1967; children: John Michael, Preston Scott, Christopher Todd. AS, Kilgore Coll., 1963; BS, Tex. A&M U., 1966, MS with honors, 1968, PhD, 1979. Cotton field scout Tex. Agrl. Extension Svc., Knox City, 1965; leader cotton field scouts Tex. Agrl. Extension Svc., Lubbock, 1966; svc. mgr. Hunter Extermination Corp., San Antonio, 1971-72; county extension entomologist Tex. Agrl. Extension Svc., Weslaco, 1972-75; extension entomologist Tex. Agrl. Extension Svc., Corpus Christi, 1978—. Editor: (handbook) Cotton Demonstration Results in the Coastal Bend of Texas, 1983; editor procs. in field. Capt. Med. Svc. Corps, U.S. Army, 1968-71, Vietnam. Decorated Army Commendation medal, Bronze Star medal. Mem. Tex. Agrl. Extension Svc. Specialist Assn., Entomol. Soc. Am., Southwestern Entomol. Soc., Am. Registry of Profl. Entomologists, Alpha Zeta. Mem. Ch. of Christ. Home: 10713 Rockwood St Corpus Christi TX 78410-2715 Office: Tex Agrl Extension Svc RR 2 Box 589 Corpus Christi TX 78406-9704

PARKER, SARA ANN, librarian; b. Cassville, Mo., Feb. 19, 1939; d. Howard Franklin and Vera Irene (Thomas) P. B.A., Okla. State U., 1961; M.L.S., Emporia State U., Kans., 1968. Adult svcs. librarian Springfield Pub. Libr., Mo., 1972-75, bookmobile dir., 1975-76; coord. S.W. Mo. Libr. Network, Springfield, 1976-78; libr. developer Colo. State Libr., Denver, 1978-82; state librarian Mont. State Libr., Helena, 1982-88, State Libr. Pa., Harrisburg, 1988-90; Pa. commr. librs., dep. sec. edn. State of Pa., Harrisburg, 1990-95; state libr. State of Mo., Jefferson City, 1995—; cons. and lectr. in field. Author, editor, compiler in field; contbr. articles to profl. jours. Sec., Western Coun. State Librs., Reno, 1984-88, mem. Mont. State Data Adv. Coun., 1983-88, Mont. Telecommunications Coun., 1985-88, WLN Network Coun., 1984-87, Kellogg ICLIS Project Mgmt. Bd., 1986-88. Recipient President's award Nature Conservancy, 1989, Friends award Pa. Assn. Ednl. Communications and Techs., 1989; fellow Inst. Ednl. Leadership, 1982. Mem. ALA, Chief Officers State Libr. Agys. (pres. 1996-98), Mont. Libr. Assn. (bd. dirs. 1982-88), Mountain Plains Libr. Assn. (sec. chmn. 1980, pres. 1987-88). Home: PO Box 554 Jefferson City MO 65102-0554 Office: Mo State Libr PO Box 387 600 W Main St Jefferson City MO 65102

PARKER, SARAH JESSICA, actress; b. Nelsonville, Ohio, Mar. 25, 1965; m. Matthew Broderick May, 1997. Actress: (theatre) The Innocents, 1976, The Sound of Music, 1977, Annie, 1978, The War Brides, 1981, The Death of a Miner, 1982, To Gillian on Her 37th Birthday, 1983, 84, Terry Neal's Future, 1986, The Heidi Chronicles, 1989, (films) Rich Kids, 1979, Somewhere Tomorrow, 1983, Firstborn, 1984, Footloose, 1984, Girls Just Want to Have Fun, 1985, Flight of the Navigator, 1986, L.A. Story, 1991, Honeymoon in Vegas, 1992, Hocus Pocus, 1993, Striking Distance, 1993, Ed Wood, 1994, Miami Rhapsody, 1995, If Lucy Fell, 1996, Mars Attacks!, 1996; (TV movies) My Body, My Child, 1982, Going for the Gold: The Bill Johnson Story, 1985, A Year in the Life, 1986, The Room Upstairs, 1987, Dadah Is Death, 1988, The Ryan White Story, 1989, Twist of Fate, 1989, In the Best Interest of the Children, 1992, (TV series) Square Pegs, 1982-83, A Year in the Life, 1987-88, Equal Justice, 1990-91, (TV pilots) The Alan King Show, 1986. Office: CAA 9830 Wilshire Blvd Beverly Hills CA 90212-1804

PARKER, SCOTT JACKSON, theatre manager; b. Ft. Bragg, N.C., July 28, 1945; s. John William and Darice Lee (Jackson) P. MA, U. N.C., 1971; MFA, U. Va., 1978. Mng. dir. Duke U. Theatre, Durham, N.C., 1970-76; gen. mgr. East Carolina U. Theatre, Greenville, 1980-85; producer The Lost Colony Outdoor Drama, Manteo, N.C., 1986-89; dir. Inst. of Outdoor Drama U. N.C., Chapel Hill, N.C., 1990—; v.p. Paul Green Found., nationwide, 1989—. Producer, mgr., dir., scene designer. With U.S. Army, 1969-70. Mem. Nat. Theatre Conf. (v.p. 1997—), Assn. for Theatre in Higher Edn. (founding mem. 1987), Southeastern Theatre Conf. (pres. 1982), Arts Advs. of N.C. (pres. 1993-94), The Players Club N.Y.C. Democrat. Baptist. Avocations: white water Kayaking, camping, hiking. Office: U NC Inst Outdoor Drama Cb # 3240 Chapel Hill NC 27599

PARKER, SCOTT LANE, management consultant; b. Phila., Feb. 23, 1946; s. Waldo G. and Nettie M. (Fulton) P.; m. Irene H. Lewis (div. Sept. 1969); m. Claudia E. Nebel, June 14, 1948; children: Adam Michael, Jay Maxwell, Zachary Scott. BA in Econs., U. Va., 1969, MBA, 1971. Mgmt. cons. The MAC Group, 1971-88, co-mng. dir., 1988-90; sr. v.p. operational support Gemini Consulting, 1991-92; sr. v.p. global strategic initiatives Gemini Consulting, Morristown, N.J., 1993-94; adj. prof. strategic mgmt. U. Md., College Park, 1994—; pres. Parker & Co., Bethesda, Md., 1995—. William Michael Shermet scholar U. Va., 1970; U.S. Steel fellow, U. Va., 1970.

PARKER, SUSAN BROOKS, healthcare executive; b. Newport, N.H., Nov. 7, 1945; d. Ronald Elliott and Elizabeth Louise (Wiggins) P.; married; children: Jeffrey Roberts Avery, Mark Brooks Avery. BS in English and French, U. Vt., 1968; MSW in Social Planning, Boston Coll., 1978. Activities dir. Avery Vt. Inns, Fairlee, 1968-71, retail buyer, 1969-75, mgr., 1972-74; aftercare worker Orange County Mental Health, Bradford, Vt., 1974-76; adminstrn. asst. Mass. Assn. for Mental Health, Boston, 1976-77; mental health planner Tri-City Area Office, Malden, Mass., 1977-78; exec. dir. Grafton County Human Services Commn., Lebanon, N.H., 1978-80, N.H. Developmental Disabilities Council, Concord, N.H., 1980-87; commr. Dept. of Mental Health, Augusta, Maine, 1987-89; assoc. commr. U.S. Social Security Adminstrn., Balt., 1989-93; sec. gen. Rehab. Internat., N.Y.C., 1994—; cons. Nat. Gov.'s Assn., Washington, 1985-86, Office of Health and Developmental Services, Washington, 1987; directorship Nat. Assn. of Devel. Disabilities, Washington, 1983-87, Cen. N.H. Mental Health Ctr., Concord, 1985-87; cons. in field. Author: poetry collection Scheme, 1965; contbr. articles to newspapers and profl. jours. Pres. PTO, Fairlee, Vt., 1972-73; dir. Ford Sayre Ski Program, Fairlee, 1972-76, United Way, Concord, 1983-86; bd. dirs. PTO Rundlett Jr. H.S., Concord, 1982-85; pres. U.S. Coun. for Internat. Rehab., 1993. Recipient Assn. Retarded Citizens Children's Disability Pub. Policy award, 1992, Kathryn C. Arneson award People to People, 1992, Commr.'s citation for outstanding efforts in developing policy Social Security Adminstrn., 1992, Dep. Commn.'s citation for outstanding exec. leadership, 1993; named Outstanding Alumnus Boston Coll., 1991, Adminstrn. Devel. Disabilities prin. investigator grantee, 1986. Mem. Am. Assn. Mental Retardation, Nat. Assn. State Mental Health Program Dirs., Nat. Assn. Retarded Citizens, Concord Luncheon Club. Avocations: skiing, canoeing, mountain climbing, reading, travel. Office: Rehab Internat 25 E 21st St New York NY 10010-6207

PARKER, THERESA ANN, special education educator; b. Spencer, W.Va., Jan. 16, 1947; d. Harry Clay and Betty Jean (Richards) Boggs; m. Larry Glen Parker, Apr. 29, 1967; children: Carey Ann, Jill Renee, Timothy Preston, Jeremy David, Leanna Michelle. AA in sec. studies, Glenville (W.Va.) State Coll., 1967, BA in music edn., 1970; MA in spl. edn., Coll. of Grad. Studies, 1991; EDS in ednl. leadership, W.Va. Grad. Coll., 1996. Cert. tchr. Pvt. practice piano teacher Spencer, 1967-95; sub. tchr. Roane County Schs., Spencer, 1970-71; tchr. spl. edn. Roane County Schs., 1987—, educator team mem.-parent/educator resource ctr., 1989—; sub. tchr. Marietta (Ohio) City Schs., 1986; administrator Sand Hill Day Care Ctr., Reno, Ohio, 1986-87; spl. edn. rep. W.Va. Dept. Edn., Charleston, 1995—; dir. Safetytown Roane County, Spencer, 1989-93. Author: (with others) Selected Teaching Models Integrated with West Virginia's Academic Model for Gifted Education, 1991. Chmn. Cub Scout Pack Boy Scouts Am., Reno, 1983-87, dist. trainer, Parkersburg, W.Va., 1986-87, chmn. Boy Scout Troop, Spencer, 1987-91; organizer First Bapt. Ch. Diabetes Sup. Group, 1995—. Safetytown grantee W.Va. Dept. Edn., Roane County, 1989, W.Va. Edn. Fund, Roane County, 1992; Dental Health grantee W.Va. Edn. Fund, Clover Sch., 1992; Diabetes Support Group grantee Benedium Found., Roane and Calhoun/Jackson Counties, 1995. Mem. Assn. for Supervision and Curriculum Develop., W.Va. Profl. Educators, Inc., Lions Club Internat. (program chmn.), Blue Grass Riding Club. Democrat. Baptist. Avocations: reading, sewing, playing piano, attending children's activities. Home: 749 Parkersburg Rd Spencer WV 25276 Office: Roane County Schs 102 Chapman Ave Spencer WV 25276-1310

PARKER, THOMAS LEE, business executive; b. Ft. Worth, Aug. 23, 1921; s. J.T. Parker and Frances Gertrude (Rogers) Heer; m. Frances N. Newlon, Dec. 14, 1943 (dec. 1981); children: Richard T. (dec.), Pamela Parker Gartin. BSBA, Ohio State U., 1943. Sales rep. Frozen Drumstick Sales Co., Columbus, Ohio, 1946-47; sec.-treas., gen. mgr. Cream Cone Machine Co., Columbus, 1948-57; pres. Drumstick Inc., Columbus, 1958-62; pres. Big Drum, Inc., Columbus, 1962-83, chmn. bd., 1983-86; dir. Ohio Semitronics. Mem. nat. adv. coun. Boy Scouts Am., Dallas. Maj. U.S. Army, 1943-46, ETO. Decorated Bronze Star; recipient Service to Mankind Columbus Sertoma Club, 1975, Silver Beaver Boy Scouts Am., 1975, Silver Antelope Boy Scouts Am., 1977, Silver Buffalo Boy Scouts Am., 1986; Baden Powell fellow World Scouts, Geneva, 1982. Mem. Scioto Country Club (pres. 1977), Athletic Club (pres. 1971), Masons, Delta Tau Delta. Republican.

PARKER, WILLIAM ELBRIDGE, consulting civil engineer; b. Seattle, Mar. 18, 1913; s. Charles Elbridge and Florence E. (Plumb) P.; m. Dorris Laurie Freeman, June 15, 1935; children—Dorris Laurie, Jane Elizabeth. B.S., U.S. Naval Acad., 1935. Party chief King County Engrs., 1935-39; exec. sec., cons. engr. State Wash., 1946-49; city engr., chmn. Bd. Pub. Works, City of Seattle, 1953-57; cons. City of San Diego, 1957; ptnr. Parker-Fisher & Assocs., 1958-66; cons. engr. Minish & Webb Engrs., Seattle, 1966-70; city engr. City of Bremerton (Wash.), 1970-76; owner Parker & Assocs., Seattle, 1976—. Served to capt. C.E.C., USNR, 1939-45, 51-53. Named to Broadway Hall of Fame. Registered profl. engr., Wash. Mem. Am. Pub. Works Assn., U.S. Naval Inst., Pioneers of State Wash. (pres.), U.S. Naval Acad. Alumni Assn. (chpt. pres.), College Club (Seattle). Lodges: Masons, Shriners.

PARKER, WILLIAM H., III, federal official; b. Westbrook, Maine, May 4, 1937; s. William H. II and Anne Marney (Delaney) P.; m. Joan Moody Currier, June 17, 1959; children: Laurie Jean, Michael Currier, Suzan Elizabeth, Julie Ann. BS, U. Maine, 1960; MS, Northeastern U., 1966; MEM, U. Detroit, 1981, MBA, 1982; postgrad., Nova U. Diplomate Am. Acad. Environ. Engrs. Project engr. Camp Dresser & McKee, Boston, 1962-72, v.p., 1972-75; v.p. E.C. Jordan, Portland, Maine, 1975-77; sr. v.p., reg. mgr. Camp Dresser & McKee, Detroit, 1977-87, bd. dirs., 1982-87; sr. v.p. CDM Fed. Programs Corp., Washington, 1987-88, bd. dirs., 1987-88; dep. asst. sec. Dept. of Def., Washington, 1988-90; dir. environ. health and safety programs, dir. chem programs EG&G Inc., Wellesley, Mass., 1990—; bd. dirs. Parker Currier Inc., Brunswick, Maine; fin. cons. VMI, treas., pres., 1993—, White River Junction, Vt., 1987-90; presenter Congl. test, 1988-90; keynote speaker tech. and profl. socs., 1988—. Contbr. articles to profl. jours. Mem., chmn. planning bd. Town of Reading, Maine, 1968-73; mem. Town Meeting, Reading, 1969-75, Mcpl. Light Bd., Reading, 1974-75. 1st lt. U.S. Army, 1960-62. Recipient Outstanding Pub. Svc. medal Sec. of Def., 1989. Fellow ASCE; mem. NSPE, Mass. Soc. Profl. Engrs (Young Engr. of Yr. award 1971), Am. Def. Preparedness Assn., Engring. Socs. New Eng. (New Eng. award 1990), Soc. Am. Mil. Engrs., Nat. Security Industries Assn. (hon.), Water Pollution Control Fedn., Am. Water Works Assn., Mass. Jaycees (Reading) (local pres., state v.p. 1970-72, Econ. Club Detroit, Detroit Club, Sigma Xi, Tau Beta Pi, Alpha Kappa Psi, Beta Gamma Sigma, Phi Kappa Phi, Chi Epsilon. Republican. Roman Catholic. Avocations: reading, writing, traveling. Home: 15 Montclair Rd West Newbury MA 01985-2216 Office: EG&G Inc 45 William St Wellesley MA 02181-4004

PARKER, WILLIAM NELSON, economics educator; b. Columbus, Ohio, June 14, 1919; s. Murray Nelson and Evalyn Mae (Gares) P.; m. Josephine Yvonne Forbus, Sept. 20, 1948; children: Yvonne Victoria, Jarrett Nelson. A.B. magna cum laude, Harvard, 1939, M.A., 1941, Ph.D., 1951; M.A., Yale, 1962. Economist atomic energy com. U.S. Senate, 1946, Dept. State, 1947-48; cons. President's Materials Policy Commn., 1951; asst. prof. econs. Williams Coll., 1951-56; assoc. prof., then prof. econs. U. N.C. at Chapel Hill, 1956-62; prof. econs. Yale, 1962-89, emeritus, 1989—, dir. grad. studies in econs., 1968-72, 74-78; Del. to Am. Coun. Learned Socs., 1975-78; chmn. Coun. on West European Studies, 1985-89; dir. Mellon West European Project, 1987-92. Co-author: Coal and Steel in Western Europe, 1957; Editor, contbr.: Trends in the American Economy in the Nineteenth Century, 1958, The Structure of the Cotton Economy of the Antebellum South, 1970, American Economic Growth, 1972, European Peasants and Their Markets, 1976; Economic History and the Modern Economist, 1986; co-editor: Jour. Econ. History, 1960-66; author: Europe, America, and the Wider World, Vol. I, 1984, Vol. II, 1990. Served to maj. AUS, 1941-45. Nat. fellow Harvard U., 1935-41, Social Sci. Rsch. Coun. fellow, 1948-51, 62-63, Ford Faculty fellow, 1958-59, Resources for Future rsch. fellow, 1955-57, Guggenheim fellow, 1966-67, St. Anthony's Coll. fellow, 1972-73, Australian Nat. U. vis. fellow, 1983, 89. Mem. Am. Philos. Soc., Econ. History Assn. (pres. 1969-70, Hughes prize for excellence in tchg. 1995), Agrl. History Assn. (pres. 1979-80), Am. Econ. Assn. (rep. adv. com. U.S. Archives 1978-81), Am. Acad. Arts and Scis. Contbr. 1st Internat. Conf. Econ. History, Stockholm, Sweden, 1960, 3d conf., Munich, Germany, 1965, 7th conf., Edinburgh, 1978; U.S./USSR Historians Conf., Moscow, 1978, Tallinn, 1987; Sapporo Am. Studies Conf., Japan, 1981; French-Am. Fedn. prof. Ecole Des Hautes Etudes, Paris, 1984-85. Home: 144 Edgehill Rd Hamden CT 06517-4011

PARKERSON, HARDY MARTELL, lawyer; b. Longview, Tex., Aug. 22, 1942; s. Winifred Lenore (Robertson) P.; m. Janice Carol Johnson, Aug. 3, 1968; children: James Blaine Parkerson, Stanley Andrew Parkerson, Paul Hardy Parkerson. BA, McNeese State U., Lake Charles, La.; JD, Tulane U., 1966. Bar: La. 1966, U.S. Supreme Ct. 1971. Assoc. Rogers, McHale & St. Romain, Lake Charles, 1967-69; pvt. practice Lake Charles, 1969—; chmn. 7th Congl. Dist. Crime and Justice Task Force, La. Priorities for the Future, 1980; asst. prof. criminal justice La. State U., 1986. Bd. dirs. 1st Assembly of God Ch., Lake Charles, 1980—; bd. regents So. Christian U., Lake Charles, 1993—; mem. La. Dem. State Ctrl. Com., 1992-96, Calcasieu Parish Dem. Com., 1988— (sec.-treas., exec. com., 1988—); former mem. Gulf Assistance Program, Lake Charles; 7th Congl. Dist. La. mem. Imports and Exports Trust Authority, Baton Rouge, 1984-88. Mem. Pi Kappa Housing Corp. of Lake Charles (bd. dirs., sec.-treas. 1985—), Optimists, Pi Kappa Phi (Beta Mu chpt.). Democrat. Mem. Assembly of God Ch. Avocations: political activist, television talk show host. Home: 127 Greenway St Lake Charles LA 70605-6821 Office: The Parkerson Law Firm 807 Alamo St Lake Charles LA 70601-8665

PARKES, KENNETH CARROLL, ornithologist; b. Hackensack, N.J., Aug. 8, 1922; s. Walter Carroll and Lillian Carolyn (Capelle) P.; m. Ellen Pierce Stone, Sept. 6, 1953. B.S., Cornell U., 1943, M.S., 1948, Ph.D., 1952. Curator birds Cornell U., 1947-52; mem. staff Carnegie Mus. of Natural History, Pitts., 1953—; curator birds Carnegie Mus., 1962-86, chief curator life scis., 1975-85, sr. curator birds, 1986-96, curator emeritus birds, 1997—; research fellow epidemiology and microbiology U. Pitts., 1956, vis. lectr. Pymatuning Field Lab., 1957, adj. mem. grad. faculty, 1963—; mem. adminstrv. bd. Lab. Ornithology, Cornell U., 1962-68, 70-75; bd. trustees Del. Mus. Natural History, 1976-90. Taxonomic editor: Avian Biology, 1971-75; co-editor, 1977-93; cons. on bird art to artists, pubs.; contbr. articles to profl. jours., encys. Served with AUS, 1943-46. Fellow Am. Ornithologists Union (2d v.p. 1975-76); mem. Audubon Soc. Western Pa. (trustee 1982-91), Wilson Ornithol. Soc. (pres. 1973-75), numerous other profl. socs. Democrat. Unitarian. Office: Carnegie Museum Natural History 4400 Forbes Ave Pittsburgh PA 15213-4007

PARKEY, ROBERT WAYNE, radiology and nuclear medicine educator, research radiologist; b. Dallas, July 17, 1938; s. Jack and Gloria Alfreda (Perry) P.; m. Nancy June Knox, Aug. 9, 1958; children: Wendell Wade, Robert Todd, Amy Elizabeth. BS in Physics, U. Tex., 1960; MD, S.W. Med. Sch., U. Tex., Dallas, 1965. Diplomate Am. Bd. Radiology, Am. Bd. Nuclear Medicine. Intern St. Paul Hosp., Dallas, 1965-66; resident in radiology U. Tex. Health Sci. Ctr., Dallas, 1966-69, asst. prof. radiology, 1970-74, assoc. prof., 1974-77, prof., chmn. dept. radiology, 1977—, Effie and Wofford Cain Disting. chair in diagnostic imaging, 1994—; chief nuc. medicine Parkland Meml. Hosp., Dallas, 1974-79, chief dept. radiology, 1977—. Contbr. numerous chpts., articles and abstracts to profl. publs. Served as capt. M.C., Army N.G., 1965-72. NIH fellow Nat. Inst. Gen. Med. Sci., U. Mo., Columbia, 1969-70; Nat. Acad. Scis.-NRC scholar in radiol. research James Picker Found., 1971-74. Fellow Am. Coll. Cardiology, Am. Coll. Radiology; mem. Am. Coll. Nuclear Physicians (charter, ho. of dels. 1974—), Council on Cardiovascular Radiology of Am. Heart Assn., AMA, Assn. Univ. Radiologists, Dallas County Med. Assn., Dallas Ft. Worth Radiol. Soc., Radiol. Soc. N.Am., Soc. Chairmen of Acad. Radiology Depts., Soc. Nuclear Medicine (acad. council), Tex. Med. Assn., Tex. Radiol. Soc., Sigma Xi, Alpha Omega Alpha. Avocations: gardening, golf, tennis. Academic research interests: nuclear cardiology, development of new imaging technologies, medical education. Office: U Tex Southwestern Med Ctr Dallas Dept Radiology 5323 Harry Hines Blvd Dallas TX 75235-7208

PARKHILL, HAROLD LOYAL, artist; b. Fresno, Ohio, Feb. 16, 1928; s. Jesse Blair and Ella (Buser) P.; m. Rosalee Lavonne Croup, Aug. 5, 1950 (div. Nov. 1969); children: Lorie Cathrine, Scott Thomas, Cynthia Anne, Carrie Sue. Grad. high sch., Keene, Ohio. Farmer Fresno, 1947-52, 1964-80; bus driver Western Greyhound Lines, Calif., Ariz., N.Mex. and Tex., 1952-61; dispatcher Ea. Greyhound Lines, Cin., 1963; artist Coshocton, Ohio, 1980—. Represented in permanent collections Zanesville Art Ctr., Pomerene Fine Art Ctr.; represented in various corp. collections; works included in Modern Maturity's Seasoned Eye 3 Show, 1990-91; works shown in 4th, 5th, 6th and 8th edits. of Ency. of Living Artists; represented in group show at Kennedy Ctr., 1991. Past trustee Coshocton Pomerene Fine Art Ctr. With USNR, 1945-46, PTO. Recipient numerous best of show awards in oil and watercolor art, incl. award, 25th anniversary art show Internat. Platform Assn., Washington, 1989, 1st Pl. Painting, Internat. Platform Assn. 26th ann. art show, 1990. Mem. VFW, Internat. Platform Assn., Am. Legion, Ohio Realist Group, Am. Artists Profl. League, Elks. Republican. Methodist. Avocations: travel, gun collecting. Home: PO Box 85 Coshocton OH 43812-0085

PARKHURST, CHARLES, retired museum director, art historian; b. Columbus, Ohio, Jan. 23, 1913; s. Charles Percy and Isabella (Woodbridge) P.; m. Elizabeth Huntington Rusling, June 15, 1938 (div. 1962); children: Andrew, Christopher, Bruce; m. Rima Zevin Julyan, Sept. 1, 1962 (div. 1972); 1 child, Brooke; stepchildren: Candace, David, Mark; m. Carol Canda Clark, July 18, 1986. BA, Williams Coll., 1935; AM, Oberlin Coll., 1938; MFA, Princeton U., 1941. Rd. and bridge constrn. worker Danali Park Alaska Rd. Commn.; tchr. music, coach basketball Wasilla, Alaska, 1935-37; asst. curator (registrar) Nat. Gallery of Art, Washington, 1942-43; dep. chief, monuments, fine arts and archives sect. Allied Mil. Govt. in both U.S. Zones, Germany, 1945-46; asst. curator Albright Art Gallery, Buffalo, 1946-47; asst. prof. art and archaeology Princeton (N.J.) U.; asst. dir. Princeton (N.J.) Art Mus., 1947-49; head dept. fine arts, dir. Art Mus., prof. history and appreciation of art Oberlin (Ohio) Coll., 1949-62; dir. Balt. Mus. Art, 1962-70; asst. dir., chief curator Nat. Gallery Art, Washington, 1971-83, ret., 1983; co-dir. Mus. Art Williams Coll., 1983-84, mem. vis. faculty, 1980, Clark vis. prof., 1985-86, acting dir. grad. program in art history, 1986-87, dir. M.B. Prendergrast Systematic Catalogue project, 1983-87; interim dir. Smith Coll. Mus. Art, 1991-92, emeritus dir., 1992; faculty fellow Fund for Advancement Edn., 1952-53; Fulbright rsch. scholar U. Utrecht, Netherlands, 1956-57; vis. faculty U. Minn., 1953, UCLA, 1964, Johns Hopkins U., 1971, U. Wis., 1979, Williams Coll., 1980-92; lectr. on art, color theory and Giotto and vernacular Italian drama ca. 1300; chmn. Md. Arts Coun., 1967-68; chmn. Md. Revolutionary War Bicentennial Commn., 1968-70, Gov.'s Coun. on Arts in Md., 1966-68; trustee, officer Williamstown Regional Art Conservation Lab., 1983-90; ind. cons. Asian Art Mus., 1993-94. Contbr. articles to profl. jours. Commr. Nat. Mus. Am. Art, 1983-93; overseer Case Western Res. U., Cleve., 1982-86; trustee Amon Carter Mus., 1977-85, Hill-Stead Mus., Farmington, Conn., 1994-96. With USNR, 1943-62. Decorated chevalier Legion d'Honneur de la République Française, 1947; recipient research grants Am. Council Learned Socs. and Am. Philos. Soc., 1961. Mem. Coll. Art Assn. (pres. 1958-60, bd. dirs.), Intermus. Conservation Assn. (co-founder), Assn. Art Mus. Dirs., Am. Assn. Mus. (pres. 1966-68, founder, mem. mus. accreditation com. 1970-76). Office: 33 Dana Pl Amherst MA 01002-2212

PARKHURST, CHARLES LLOYD, electronics company executive; b. Nashville, Aug. 13, 1943; s. Charles Albert Parkhurst and Dorothy Elizabeth (Ballou) Parkhurst Crutchfield; m. Dolores Ann Oakley, June 6, 1970; children: Charles Thomas, Deborah Lynn, Jere Loy. Student, Hume-Fogg Tech. Coll., 1959-61; AA, Mesa Community Coll., 1973; student, Ariz. State U., 1973-76. Mem. design staff Tex. Instruments, Dallas, 1967-68; mgr. design Motorola, Inc., Phoenix, 1968-76; pres. LSI Cons., Inc., Tempe, Ariz., 1976-85, LSI Photomasks, Inc., Tempe, 1985-94, Charles Parkhurst Books, Inc., Prescott, Ariz., 1994—. Designer 1st digital watch chip, 1973. Mem. Rep. Congl. Leadership Coun., Washington, 1988; life mem. Rep. Presdl. Task Force, 1990. Served as cpl. USMC, 1961-64. Mem. Ariz. State U. Alumni Assn. (life), Antiquarian Booksellers Assn. of Am. Baptist. Achievements include design of the world's first digital watch chip. Avocations: genealogy, coin collecting, scuba diving, book collecting. Office: Charles Parkhurst Books Inc PO Box 10850 Prescott AZ 86304-0850

PARKIN, GERARD FRANCIS RALPH, chemistry educator, researcher; b. Middlesbrough, Cleveland, Eng., Feb. 15, 1959; s. Ralph and Clementine (Gill) P.; m. Rita K. Upmacis. BA with honors, Oxford (Eng.) U., 1981, MA, 1984, PhD, 1985. NATO/SERC (U.K.) postdoctoral rsch. fellow Calif. Inst. Tech., 1985-88; asst. prof. Columbia U., N.Y.C., 1988-91, assoc. prof., 1991-94; prof., 1994—. Contbr. more than 90 articles to profl. jours. Recipient Camille and Henry Dreyfus Tchr.-Scholar award, 1991, award in pure chemistry Am. Chem. Soc., 1994, Corday Morgan medal Royal Soc. Chemistry, 1995; A.P. Sloan rsch. fellow; NSF Presdl. faculty fellow, 1992—. Roman Catholic. Achievements include discovery that bond stretch isomerism in an artifact. Office: Columbia U 116th St And Broadway New York NY 10027

PARKIN, STUART S. P., materials scientist. Rsch. staff mem. IBM Almaden Rsch. Ctr., San Jose, Calif. Recipient Internat. prize for new materials Am. Phys. Soc., 1994, C.V. Boys prize Inst. Physics, London, 1991, Inaugural Outstanding Young Investigator award Materials Rsch. Soc., 1991, Europhysics prize Hewlett-Packard, 1997. Office: IBM Almaden Rsch Ctr K11/D2 650 Harry Rd San Jose CA 95120-6001

PARKINS, FREDERICK MILTON, dental educator, university dean; b. Princeton, N.J., Sept. 8, 1935; s. William Milton and Phyllis Virginia (Plyler) P.; m. Carolyn V. Rude; children: Bradford, Christopher, Eric. Student, Carleton Coll., 1953-56; D.D.S., U. Pa., 1960; M.S.D. in Pedodontics, U. N.C., Chapel Hill, 1965; Ph.D. in Physiology, 1969. Instr. pedodontics U. N.C., 1965-67; asst. prof. pedodontics U. Pa., 1967-68, dir. Dental Aux. Utilization program, chmn. pedodontics, 1968-69; assoc. prof., head pedodontics U. Iowa, Iowa City, 1969-72; prof., head pedodontics U. Iowa, 1972-75; asst. dean acad. affairs U. Iowa (Coll. Dentistry), 1974-75, asso. dean acad. affairs, 1975-79, dir. continuing edn., 1975-77; prof. pedodontics, dean Sch. Dentistry, U. Louisville, 1979-85, prof. pediatric dentistry, 1985—; mem. Hillenbrand Fellowship adv. com. Am. Fund Dental Health, 1980-85; cons. Div. Dental Health USPHS, 1969-72; dental cons., med. staff Children's Hosp. Phila., 1968-71; med. staff Kosair Children's Hosp. Louisville, 1983—; cons., mem. pedodontic adv. com. Council Dental Edn., 1974-80, chmn. pedodontic adv. com., 1978-80, cons. council on legislation, 1978-79; dental cons. Aux. Utilization VA, 1968-69; cons. Bur. Health Resources Devel., 1974-76, Dept. Army, 1980—, numerous others. Assoc. editor: Jour. Preventive Dentistry, 1973-79; editorial bd., 1980-83; editorial reviewer: Jour. Pediatrics, 1969—, Jour. Dental Edn, 1978—, Jour. AMA, 1979—; asso. editor: Jour. Clin. Preventive Dentistry, 1979-84; Contbr. chpts. to textbooks, articles to profl. publs. Bd. govs. Youth Performing Arts Coun., Louisville-Jefferson County Sch. Dist., 1980-89, pres., 1986-88; bd. govs. Regional Cancer Ctr., U. Louisville, 1979-84, Univ. Hosp., 1979-84; mem. human studies com. U. Louisville, 1988-90. Robert Wood Johnson Congl. fellow Inst. of Medicine, 1977-78; USPHS postdoctoral fellow, 1963-67; NIH grantee, 1971-75; Recipient Earle Banks Hoyt Teaching award, 1969. Fellow AAAS, Am. Acad. Pediat. Dentistry (chmn. rsch. com. 1972-73, Ann. Rsch. award 1968, chmn. advanced edn. com. 1974-75, chmn. dental care programs com. 1978-80); mem. ADA, Am. Coll. Dentistry, Am. Soc. Dentistry for Children (exec. bd. Iowa unit 1969-75, award com. 1973-76, edn. com. 1974-77, chmn. rsch. adv. com. 1973-76), Biophys. Soc., Internat. Assn. Dental Rsch., N.Y. Acad. Dentistry, Ky. Dental Assn. (exec. bd. 1979-84), Am. Assn. Dental Schs. (coun. deans 1979-85, chmn. pedodontics sect. 1976, chmn. continuing edn. sect. 1979, legis. com. 1978-83), Louisville Dental Alumni Assn. (bd. govs. 1979-84), Am. Assn. Dental Rsch. (nat. affairs com. 1978-85), Acad. Laser Dentistry (co-chmn. rsch. and edn. 1997, bd. dirs. 1997—, cert. com.), Southeastern Soc. Pediat. Dentistry, U.S. Power Squadron (bd. govs. 1987-93, sec. 1989, adminstrv. officer 1990, exec. officer 1991, comdr. 1992), Aircraft Owners and Pilots Assn., Omicron Kappa Upsilon (pres. Wa. chpt. 1991-92), Louisville Boat Club, Rotary. Unitarian. Home: 6424 Marina Dr Prospect KY 40059-8846 Office: U Louisville Sch Dentistry Dept Orth Pediatric & Geriatric Dent Rm 306 Louisville KY 40292

PARKINSON, BRADFORD WELLS, astronautical engineer, educator; b. Madison, Wis., Feb. 16, 1935; s. Herbert and Metta Tisdale (Smith) P.; m. Virginia Pinkham Wier, Nov. 26, 1977; children: Leslie, Bradford II, Eric, Ian, Bruce, Jared Bradford. BS, U.S. Naval Acad., 1957; MS, MIT, 1961; PhD, Stanford U., 1966. Commd. 2d lt. USAF, 1957, advanced through grades to col., 1972; divsn. chief AF Test Pilot Sch., 1966-68; chair dept. astronautics and computer sci. USAF Acad., 1969-71; dir. engring. ABRES, 1972; program mgr. NAVSTAR GFS, 1972-78; ret. USAF, 1978; prof. mech. engring. Colo. State U., Ft. Collins, 1978-79; v.p. advanced engring. Rockwell Internat., Downey, Calif., 1979-80; gen. mgr., v.p. Intermetrics, Inc., Cambridge, Mass., 1980-84; prof., dir. gravity probe-B Stanford (Calif.) U., 1984—; chair adv. coun. NASA; dir. Trimble Navigation Ltd., Sunnyvale, Calif., Draper Lab., Cambridge, Integrinautics, Palo Alto, Calif., Aerospace Corp., El Segundo, Calif. Decorated Def. Superior Svc. medal, AF Commendation medal with oak leaf cluster, Meritorius Svc. medal, Presdl. Unit citation, Bronze Star, Legion of Merit, Air medal with oak leaf cluster; recipient Thurlow award Inst. Navigation, 1986, Kepler award, 1991, von Karman Lectureship Am. Inst. of Aeronautics and Astronautics, 1996. Fellow AIAA, Royal Inst. Navigation (Gold medal 1983); mem. IEEE (Pioneer award 1994), AAS, NAE, Sigma Xi, Tau Beta Pi. Avocations: hiking, skiing, running. Home: 817 Santa Rita Rd Los Altos CA 94022-1131 Office: HEPL Stanford U Stanford CA 94305

PARKINSON, ETHELYN MINERVA, author; b. nr. Oconto, Wis., Sept. 13, 1906; d. James Nelson and Ethel Mabelle (Bigelow) P. Teaching certificate, County Normal Sch., Oconto Falls, Wis., 1923; R.N., Bellin Meml. Sch. Nursing, 1928. Author: Double Trouble for Rupert, 1958, Triple Trouble for Rupert, 1960, Good Old Archibald, 1960, The Merry Mad Bachelors, 1961, The Terrible Troubles of Rupert Piper, 1963, The Operation that Happened to Rupert Piper, 1966, Today I Am a Ham, 1968, Higgins of the Railroad Museum, 1970, Elf King Joe, 1970, Never Go Anywhere with Digby, 1971, Rupert Piper and Megan, the Valuable Girl, 1972, Rupert Piper and the Dear, Dear Birds, 1976 (Jr. Lit. Guild selection), Rupert Piper and the Boy Who Could Knit, 1979. Recipient Wis. Dramatic Soc. 1st place for playwriting, 1933; 1st place children's fiction Scholastic Book Services, 1957; Abingdon award, 1970; award of merit Wis. Hist. Soc., 1971. Republican. Presbyn. Address: 1031 Anderson Dr Green Bay WI 54304-5000 *I look at any success I may have had most humbly and most thankfully. I'm humble because I have a feeling that I haven't done things, but rather that things have happened to me. Perhaps that's because people have inspired and so helped me, all the way, children especially. I'm dedicated to giving as much happiness as I can to children, through my writing, and other ways. Childhood seems shorter now than ever, and when one of my stories makes children happy, makes them laugh, I am happy, too, and grateful.*

PARKINSON, GEORGINA, ballet mistress; b. Brighton, Eng., Aug. 20, 1938. Studied with Royal Ballet Sch. Mem. Royal Ballet, London, from 1955, soloist, from 1959, then prin.; ballet mistress Am. Ballet Theatre, N.Y.C., 1978—. Created roles in: La Belle Dame Sans Merci (Andree Howard), The Invitation (Kenneth MacMillan), Romeo and Juliet (Kenneth MacMillan), Mayerling (Kenneth MacMillan), The Concert (Jerome Robbins), Enigma Variations (Sir Frederick Ashton), Daphnis and Chloe (John Cranko), Everlast (Twyla Tharp). Office: care Am Ballet Theatre 890 Broadway New York NY 10003-1211*

PARKINSON, JAMES THOMAS, III, investment consultant; b. Richmond, Va., July 10, 1940; s. James Thomas and Elizabeth (Hopkins) P.; m. Molly O Owens, June 16, 1962; children: James Thomas, Glenn Walser. BA, U. Va., 1962; MBA, U. Pa., 1964. Trainee Chem. Bank, N.Y.C., 1964-66; assoc., corp. fin. dept. Blyth & Co., Inc., N.Y.C., 1968-69; v.p., corp. fin. dept. Clark Dodge & Co., Inc., N.Y.C., 1969-74; pvt. practice investment mgmt., N.Y.C., 1974-85, 87—; v.p. Pleasantville Advisors, Inc., N.Y.C., 1986-87; instr. corp. fin. Ind. U., 1966-68. Sr. warden Ch. of Holy Trinity, N.Y.C., 1978-79; trustee Am. Bible Soc. With AUS, 1966-68. Republican. Episcopalian. Clubs: Univ., (N.Y.C.); Va. Country (Richmond). Office: 575 Madison Ave Ste 1006 New York NY 10022-2511

PARKINSON, MARK VINCENT, state legislator, lawyer; b. Wichita, Kans., June 24, 1957; s. Henry Filson and Barbara Ann (Gilbert) Horton; m. Stacy Abbott, Mar. 7, 1983; children: Alex Atticus, Sam Filson, Kit Harlan. BA in Edn., Wichita State U., 1980; JD, Kans. U., 1984. Assoc. Payne and Jones Law Firm, Olathe, Kans., 1984-86; ptnr. Parkinson, Foth & Reynolds, Lenexa, Kans., 1986—; mem. Kans. Ho. Reps., 1990-92, Kans. Senate, 1993—. Mem. ABA, Johnson County Bar Found. (pres. 1993—), Kans. Bar Assn. Republican. Avocations: travel, running, movies. Office: Parkinson Foth & Reynolds 13628 W 95th St Lenexa KS 66215-3304

PARKINSON, WILLIAM CHARLES, physicist, educator; b. Jarvis, Ont., Can., Feb. 11, 1918; came to U.S., 1925, naturalized, 1941; s. Charles Franklin and Euphemia Alice (Johnston) P.; m. Martha Bennett Capron, Aug. 2, 1944; children: Martha Reed, William Reid. B.S.E., U. Mich., Ann Arbor, 1940, M.S., 1941, Ph.D., 1948. Physicist Applied Physics Lab., Johns Hopkins U., 1942-46, OSRD, 1943-44; mem. faculty U. Mich., 1947—, prof. physics, 1958-88, prof. emeritus physics, 1988—, dir. cyclotron lab., 1962-77; mem. subcom. nuclear structure NRC, 1959-68; mem. nuclear physics sub panel mgmt. and costs nuclear program, 1969-70; adv. panel physics NSF, 1966-69; cons. grad. sci. facilities, 1968, chmn. postdoctoral fellowship evaluation panel, 1969, cons. to govt. and industry, 1955—. Quondam mem. Trinity Coll., Cambridge, Eng. Recipient Ordnance Devel. award Navy Dept., 1946; Fulbright research scholar Cavendish Lab., Cambridge U., 1952-53. Fellow Am. Phys. Soc.; mem. N.Y. Acad. Scis., Biophys. Soc., Grad. "M" Club (awarded hon. "M" 1991), Sigma Xi, Phi Kappa Phi, Kappa Kappa Psi. Patentee in field. Home: 1600 Sheridan Dr Ann Arbor MI 48104-4052 Office: Univ Mich Dept Physics Ann Arbor MI 48109

PARKO, EDITH MARGARET, special education educator; b. Sanford, Fla., Sept. 1, 1943; d. Clarence Robert Jones and Domarious (LeCroy) Varn; m. Joseph Edward Parko Jr., Apr. 16, 1966; 1 child, Kimberly Graham. AA, U. Fla., 1963; BA, Stetson U., 1965; MA, Atlanta U., 1970; PhD, Ga. State U., 1984. Lic. tchr., sch. counselor, instrnl. leadership, Ga.

Tchr. sci. Seminole County Bd. Edn., Sanford, Fla., 1965-66; tchr. sci./math. Atlanta City Schs., 1966-68; tchr. emotionally disturbed Ga. Mental Health Inst., Atlanta, 1972-79; tchr. learning disabilities The Howard Sch., Atlanta, 1983-87; cons. Ga. Dept. Edn., Atlanta, 1987-88; tchr. emotionally disturbed Atlanta City Schs., 1988-90, researcher, 1990-91, coord. learning disabilities, 1991-94, coord. youth svcs., 1994—. Author children's lit. Named Outstanding Adminstrn. Met. Atlanta Coun. Exceptional Children, 1995. Mem. Coun. Exceptional Children (outstanding adminstr. Ga. Fedn. 1995-96), Learning Disabilitis Assn., PAGE. Avocations: golf, writing, reading, trout fishing, travel. Home: 325 Elmira Pl NE Atlanta GA 30307-2039

PARKS, BEATRICE GRIFFIN, elementary school educator; b. Columbus, Miss., Jan. 3; d. James D. and Jimmie (McCottrell) Griffin; m. Orbia Ray Parks, Aug. 12, 1956 (div. May 1987); children: Donna Raye, Monica Lynn, David Griffin. BS in Edn., Lincoln U., Jefferson City, Mo., 1954. Elem. tchr. Cape Girardeau (Mo.) Pub. Schs., 1954-55, East St. Louis (Ill.) Bd. Edn., 1955-56; tchr. U.S. Army, Germany, 1956-57; elem. tchr. St. Louis Bd. Edn., 1960—, art specialist, 1980-94; floral designer Silk Expressions by Bea, St. Louis, 1991—; interior decorator Trans Designs, St. Louis, 1987-89. Arts chairperson Visual/Performing Arts Ctr., St. Louis, 1985-90; mem. Phyllis Wheatley YWCA. Recipient Svc. award Visual and Performing Arts Ctr., St. Louis, 1983-84, Art Excellence award, 1985-86. Mem. Nat. Art Edn. Assn., Mo. Art Edn. Assn., St. Louis Tchrs. Assn., Nat. Lincoln U. Alumni Assn., Greater St. Louis Lincoln U. Alumni Assn., Alpha Kappa Alpha (Founders award 1985, Arts and Heritage award 1988-89, Soror of Yr. 1992). United Ch. of Christ. Avocations: music, theater, writing. Home: 7192 White Oak Ln Saint Louis MO 63130-1816 Office: Silk Expressions by Bea PO Box 3087 Saint Louis MO 63130-0487

PARKS, DONALD LEE, mechanical engineer, human factors engineer; b. Delphos, Kans., Feb. 23, 1931; s. George Delbert and Erma Josephine (Boucek) P.; student Kans. Wesleyan U., 1948-50; BSME, Kans. State U., 1957, BS in Bus. Adminstrn., 1957, MS in Psychology, 1959; cert. profl. Ergonomist; m. Bessie Lou Schur, Dec. 24, 1952; children: Elizabeth Parks Anderson, Patricia Parks-Holbrook, Donna, Charles, Sandra. Elem. tchr., 1950-51; with Kans. State U. Placement Svc., 1957-59; human factors engr., systems engr. Boeing Co., Seattle, 1959-90, sr. specialist engr., 1972-74, sr. engring. supr., 1974-90; pres. D-Square Assocs. Engring. Cons., 1990-95; pres. Venture Worlds, 1995—; adj. lectr. UCLA Engring. Extension, 1989—; cons., lectr. in field; participant workshops on guidelines in profl. areas, NATO, NSF, Nat. Acad. Sci., NRC. Mem. Derby (Kans.) Planning Commn., 1961-62, chmn., 1962; del. King County (Wash.) Republican Conv., 1972. With AUS, 1952-54. Mem. Human Factors Soc. (Puget Sound Pres.'s award 1969), ASME, Am. Psychol. Assn., Elks. Presbyterian. Contbr. over 80 articles to publs., chpts. to 8 books. Home: 6232 127th Ave SE Bellevue WA 98006-3943

PARKS, GEORGE RICHARD, librarian; b. Boston, Apr. 11, 1935; m. Carol A. Richmond; children: Elizabeth, Jennifer, Geoffrey. A.B. summa cum laude, U. N.H., 1959; M.A.L.S., U. Mich., 1962; postgrad., Johns Hopkins, 1959-65; EFM cert. Sch. Theology, U. of the South, 1985. Preprofl. young adult librarian Enoch Pratt Free Library, Balt., 1960-61; ctrl., br. librarian Enoch Pratt Free Library, 1962-65, asst. to asst. dir., 1965-66; asst. dir. for adminstrn., libraries U. Rochester, 1966-68, chief adminstrv. officer, 1968-69; dean of libraries U. R.I., 1969-80; univ. librarian Colgate U., 1980-85, U. So. Maine, Portland, 1985—; lectr. in field, cons. libr. bldg.; cons. antique map collection; mem. exec. bd. Greater Portland Theol. Libr., 1986-88, Maine Community Cultural Alliance, 1992—; mem. exec. bd. So. Maine Libr. Dist., 1990-97, chmn., 1993. Apptd. Maine State Libr. Commn., 1994—. Recipient Margaret Mann award U. Mich., 1962; Phillips Exeter Acad. scholar, 1952-54; U. N.H. scholar, 1955-59; Johns Hopkins U. scholar, 1959-60; Enoch Pratt Free Library scholar, 1961-62. Mem. ALA, Assn. Coll. Rsch. Librs. (pres. New Eng. chpt. 1975, chmn. nat. conf. 1978, coll. librs. sect. planning com. 1994—), Consortium R.I. Acad. Rsch. Librs. (chmn. 1972-73), Maine Libr. Assn., New Eng. Libr. Assn. (chmn. planning com. 1992—, v.p./pres. elect 1995-96, pres. 1996-97), Libr. Adminstrn. and Mgmt. Assn. (exec. bd. bldgs. and equipment sect., libr. bldg. awards com. 1983-85), Phi Beta Kappa, Phi Kappa Phi, Beta Phi Mu. Home: 4 Pierce St Westbrook ME 04092-2331 Office: U So Maine Libr PO Box 9301 314 Forest Ave Portland ME 04104-9301

PARKS, GORDON ROGER ALEXANDER BUCHANAN, film director, author, photographer, composer; b. Ft. Scott, Kans., Nov. 30, 1912; s. Jackson and Sarah (Ross) P.; m. Sally Alvis, 1933 (div. 1961); m. Elizabeth Campbell, 1962 (div. 1973); m. Genevieve Young, Aug. 26, 1973 (div. 1979); children by previous marriage: Gordon (dec.), Toni Parks Parsons, David, Leslie. Student pub. schs., Fort Scott, St. Paul; DFA (hon.), Md. Inst., 1968, Fairfield U., 1969; D (hon.), Boston U., 1969; LittD (hon.), Kans. State U., 1970; LHD (hon.), St. Olaf Coll., 1973; DFA (hon.), Colby Coll., 1974; DLit (hon.), MacAlester Coll., 1974; D (hon.), Lincoln U., 1975; HHD (hon.), Thiel Coll., 1976; DA (hon.), Columbia Coll., 1977; DFA (hon.), Rutgers U., 1980, Pratt Inst., 1981; LHD (hon.), Suffolk U., 1982; DFA (hon.), Kansas City Art Inst., 1984; LHD (hon.), Art Ctr. Coll. Design, 1986; DA (hon.), Hamline U., 1987; DFA (hon.), Am. Internat. Coll., 1988; HHD (hon.), Savannah Coll. Art and Design, 1988; D (hon.), U. Bradford, Eng., 1989; DFA (hon.), Rochester Inst. Tech., 1989, SUNY, 1990, R.I. Coll., 1990, Parsons Sch. Design, 1991, Manhattanville Coll., 1992, Coll. New Rochelle, 1992, Skidmore Coll., 1993; LittD (hon.), Montclair State U., 1994. Freelance fashion photographer Mpls., 1937-42; photographer Farm Security Adminstrn., 1942-43, OWI, 1944, Standard Oil Co., N.J., 1945-48, Life mag., 1948-68; ind. photographer, film maker, 1954—; color and black and white cons. various motion picture prodns., U.S. and Europe, 1954—. Writer, producer, dir.: The Learning Tree, 1969; dir.: (films) Shaft, 1972, Shaft's Big Score, 1972, The Super Cops, 1974, Leadbelly, 1976, Odyssey of Solomon Northup, 1984, Moments Without Proper Names, 1986 (Silver medal Internat. Film Festival 1989); creator, composer, dir. Martin, 1990; TV documentary: Diary of a Harlem Family, 1968 (Emmy award); author: Flash Photography, 1947, Camera Portraits: The Techniques and Principals of Documentary Portraiture, 1948, The Learning Tree, 1963, A Choice of Weapons, 1966 (Notable Book award ALA 1966), A Poet and His Camera, 1968, Whispers of Intimate Things, 1971, Born Black, 1971, In Love, 1971, (poetry) Moments Without Proper Names, 1975, Flavio, 1977 (Christopher award 1978), To Smile in Autumn, 1979, (novel) Shannon, 1981, Voices in the Mirror, 1990, (photography, paint and poetry) Arias in Silence, 1994; founder, editorial dir. Essence mag., 1970-73; composer Piano Concerto, 1953, Tree Symphony, 1967, 3 piano sonatas, 1956, 58, 60, modern works for piano and wind instruments, (film scores) The Learning Tree (Libr. Congress Nat. Film Registry Classics film honor, 1989), Shaft's Big Score, The Odyssey of Solomon Northup, Moments Without Proper Names; dir., composer (film) Ballet for Martin Luther King, 1991; poetry: Gordon Parks: A Poet and His Camera, Gordon Parks: Whispers of Intimate Things, In Love, Moments Without Proper Names; traveling exhibits in U.S. and abroad, 1990. Bd. dirs. Schomburg Ctr. for Research in Black Culture, Am. Arts. Alliance, W. Eugene Smith Meml. Fund, Black Tennis and Sports Found., Rondo Ave. Inc., St. Paul; Harlem Symphony Orch., N.Y.C.; mem. adv. com. Kans. Ctr. for the Book; bd. advocates Planned Parenthood Fedn. Am. Inc.; patron N.Y. City Housing Authority Symphony; supporter Apple Corps Theatre, N.Y.C., Quindaro Project, Kans., numerous other civic activities. Decorated Comdr. de l'Ordre des Arts et des Lettres (Republique Francaise); recipient Julius Rosenwald award for photography, 1942, award NCCJ, 1964, awards Syracuse U. Sch. Journalism, 1961, Newhouse citation Syracuse U., 1963, awards Phila. Mus. Art, 1964, awards N.Y. Art Dirs. Club, 1964, 68, Frederic W. Brehm award, 1962, Carr Van Anda Journalism award Ohio U., 1970, Carr Van Anda Journalism award U. Miami, 1964, Pres.'s fellow award R.I. Sch. Design, 1984, Am. Soc. Mag. Photographers award, 1985, Nat. Medal Arts award Commonwealth Mass. Communications, 1988, Kans. Gov.'s medal, 1986, Nat. medal of Arts, 1988, World Press Photo award, 1988, N.Y.C. Mayor's award, 1989, Artist of Merit Josef Sudek medal, 1989, award Internat. Ctr. Photography, 1990; named Kansan of Yr. Sons and Daus. Kans., 1985. Mem. Urban League N.Y., ASCAP, Writers Guild, NAACP (Spingarn award 1972, Hall of Fame 1984), Acad. Motion Pictures Arts and Scis., AFTRA, Am. Inst. Pub. Service, Nat. Urban League Guild, Internat. Mark Twain Soc. (hon.), Newspaper Guild, Assn. Composers and Dirs., Dirs. Guild (nat. dir.), Dirs. Guild N.Y., Am. Soc. Mag. Photographers (Photographer of Yr. award 1960, 85), Nat. Assn. for Am. Composers and Condrs., Stylus Soc. (hon.), U.S. Tennis Assn. Inc., Am. film Inst.Kappa Alpha Mu. Clubs: Pen; Black Tennis and Sports Found. (bd. dirs.). Home: 860 United Nations Plz New York NY 10017-1810*

PARKS, HAROLD FRANCIS, anatomist, educator; b. Anna, Ill., Sept. 28, 1920; s. Guy Clay and Margaret (McCumiskey) P.; m. Margaret Bryner, Sept. 11, 1948; children—Edwin Thomas, Margaret Caroline. B.Ed., So. Ill. U., 1942; Ph.D., Cornell U., 1950. Tchr. music Martinsville (Ill.) High Sch., 1942; asst. band dir. Cornell U., 1942-43, dir. bands, 1943-46, teaching asst. comparative anatomy and histology and embryology, 1945-50, prof. zoology, 1961-64; instr., then asst. prof. anatomy U. N.C. Med. Sch., 1950-54; asst. prof., then assoc. prof. anatomy U. Rochester Sch. Medicine and Dentistry, 1954-61; prof. anatomy U. Ky. Med. Center, 1964-91, chmn. dept., 1964-79; vis. scientist Karolinska Inst., 1956; Exec. com. Ky.-Mich.-Ohio Regional Med. Library Program. Mem. AAAS, Am. Inst. Biol. Scis., Am. Assn. Anatomists (com. on status of women in anatomy 1978-80), Am. Soc. Cell Biology, Electron Microscopy Soc. Am., Am. Soc. Zoologists, So. Soc. Anatomists (council 1968-69), Assn. Anatomy Chmn. (council 1971-72), Sigma Xi, Omicron Kappa Upsilon (hon.), Phi Kappa Phi. Home: 837 Cahaba Rd Lexington KY 40502-3318

PARKS, HAROLD RAYMOND, mathematician, educator; b. Wilmington, Del., May 22, 1949; s. Lytle Raymond Jr. and Marjorie Ruth (Chambers) P.; m. Paula Sue Beaulieu, Aug. 21, 1971 (div. 1984); children: Paul Raymond, David Austin; m. Susan Irene Taylor, June 6, 1985; 1 stepchild, Kathryn McLaughlin. AB, Dartmouth Coll., 1971; PhD, Princeton U., 1974. Tamarkin instr. Brown U., Providence, 1974-77; asst. prof. Oreg. State U., Corvallis, 1977-82, assoc. prof., 1982-89, prof. math., 1989—; vis. assoc. prof. Ind. U., Bloomington, 1982-83. Author: Explicit Determination of Area Minimizing Hypersurfaces, vol. II, 1986, (with Steven G. Krantz) A Primer of Real Analytic Functions, 1992, (with G. Musser, R. Burton, W. Siebler) Mathematics in Life, Society and the World, 1997; contbr. articles to profl. publs. Cubmaster Oregon Trail Coun. Boy Scouts Am., 1990-92. NSF fellow, 1971-74. Mem. Am. Math. Soc., Math. Assn. Am., Soc. Indsl. and Applied Math., Phi Beta Kappa. Republican. Mem. Soc. of Friends. Home: 33194 Dorset Ln Philomath OR 97370-9555 Office: Oreg State U Dept Math Corvallis OR 97331-4605

PARKS, JAMES WILLIAM, II, public facilities executive, lawyer; b. Wabash, Ind., July 30, 1956; s. James William and Joyce Arlene (Lillibridge) P.; m. Neil Ann Armstrong, Aug. 21, 1982; children: Elizabeth Joyce, Helen Frances, James William III. BS, Ball State U., 1978; JD, U. Miami, 1981. Bar: La. 1981, Fla. 1982, U.S. Dist. Ct. (ea. dist.) La. 1981, U.S. Dist. Ct. (mid. dist.) La. 1982, U.S. Ct. Appeals (5th cir. and 11th cir.) 1981. Atty. Jones, Walker, Waechter, Poitevent, Carrere et al., New Orleans, 1981-83, Foley & Judell, New Orleans, 1983-88, McCollister & McCleary, pc, Baton Rouge, 1988-95; exec. dir. La. Pub. Facilities Authority, Baton Rouge, 1995—. Mem. AICPA, Nat. Assn. Bond Lawyers, La. State Bar Assn., Fla. Bar Assn., Assn. for Gifted and Talented Students, Baton Rouge (treas. 1994-96, pres.-elect 1996-97, pres. 1997—), Soc. La. CPA (govt. acctg. and auditing com. 1994-95), Nat. Assn. Higher Edn. Facilities Authorities 1996—). Avocations: travel, computers. Home: 5966 Tennyson Dr Baton Rouge LA 70817-2933 Office: La Pub Facilities Authority 2237 S Acadian Thruway Ste 650 Baton Rouge LA 70808-2371

PARKS, JOE BENJAMIN, state legislator; b. McAlester, Okla., Dec. 17, 1915; s. James Allen and Mary Florence (Youngblood) P.; m. Florence M. Evans, Oct. 25, 1941; children: Anne, Kathryn. BS in Pub. Adminstrn., Okla. State U., 1939. Div. dir. U.S. VA, Washington, 1946-56; spl. asst., cons. U.S. GSA, Washington, 1957-58; mgr. dist. EDP div. RCA Corp., Washington, 1959-65; mgr. Ea. region Dashew Bus. Machines, Arlington, Va., 1966-68; assoc. adminstr. social and rehab. svc. U.S. Dept. Health, Edn. & Welfare, Washington, 1969-73; dir. mktg. govt. systems div. Booz, Allen & Hamilton, Washington, 1974-75; ptnr. Forbes & Parks, Dover, N.H., 1976—; mem. N.H. State Legislature, Concord, 1985-92, chmn. joint com. on elderly affairs, 1987-92; mem. com. on health, human svcs. and elderly N.H. State Legislature, 1987-90; chmn. subcom. mileage and electronic roll call, 1989-90, vice chmn. legis. adminstrn. com., 1990-91, mem. appropriations com., 1991-92; proprietor Portsmouth (N.H.) Athenaeum, 1992—; corporator Wentworth Douglas Hosp., Dover, 1980-89; pres. Berr Par, Inc., 1994—. Columnist Nat. Antiques Rev., 1975-77, Boston Globe N.H. Weekly 1987-88, Foster's Daily Democrat (Dover, N.H.), 1988-90; freelance writer, 1990—. Vice chmn. N.H. State Rep. Com., 1987-88; chmn. Strafford County Reps., 1988. Decorated Bronze Star; recipient Lawmakers award for disting. environ. svc. Sierra Club, 1990. Congregationalist. Avocation: rhododendron hybridizing. Home and Office: 195 Long Hill Rd Dover NH 03820-6108

PARKS, JOHN MORRIS, metallurgist; b. Lafayette, Ind., July 16, 1917; s. Morris Randlette and Ruby Mildred (Beeker) P.; m. Martha Mac Elhose, June 8, 1944 (dec. Mar. 1978); children: Lorinda Ruth Parks Wiggins, Sarah Ann, Victoria Parks Nice, Daniel Sandford. B Chem. Engring. with distinction, Purdue U., 1939; M Metall. Engring., Rensselaer Poly. Inst., 1941, PhD, 1942. Registered profl. engr., Ohio. Instr. metallurgy Rensselaer Poly. Inst., Troy, N.Y., 1939-45; editor Am. Soc. Metals, Cleve., 1945-46; supr. welding rsch. Armour Rsch. Found., Chgo., 1946-53; mgr. materials rsch. Air Reduction Co., Murray Hill, N.J., 1953-56; head sci. dept. Lincoln Electric Co., Euclid, Ohio, 1956—. Achievements include 99.98% ductile rod for making welding electrode, innershield welding electrode; computer programs for solidification temperatures of cast and weld metal; thermodynamic calculations (precision to 7 significant figures); metallographic and impact properties of weld metal and its relationship to solidification structure of steel; surface tension transfer welder. Home: 5151 SOM Center Rd Solon OH 44139-1455 Office: Lincoln Electric Co 22801 Saint Clair Ave Euclid OH 44117-2524

PARKS, JOHN SCOTT, pediatric endocrinologist; s. John Louis and Mary Dean (Scott) P.; m. Georgia Bigley, May 7, 1959; children: Stephanie Dean, Paige Wallace Parks Adams, John Thurston. AB in Am. Studies magna cum laude, Amherst Coll., 1961; MD, U. Pa., 1966, PhD in Biochemistry, 1971. Diplomate Nat. Bd. Med. Examiners, Am. Bd. Pediat. Intern in pediat. Children's Hosp. Phila., 1967-68, resident in pediat., 1968-69; clin. assoc. endocrinology br. Nat. Cancer Inst. NIH, Bethesda, Md., 1969-71; endocrinology fellow Children's Hosp. Phila., 1971-73; from instr. pediat. to assoc. prof. pediat. U. Pa., 1971-83; asst. physician, asst. endocrinologist Children's Hosp. Phila., 1972-74, assoc. physician, assoc. dir. endocrinology, 1974-82, assoc. endocrinologist, 1974-82, dir. hypothyroidism program, 1978-81, sr. physician, dir. adolescent medicine, 1980-82; from assoc. prof. pediat. to prof. pediat. Emory U., Atlanta, 1982—, assoc. prof. biochemistry, 1983—, dir. pediat. endocrinology, 1982—; pediat. endocrinologist Henrietta Egleston Hosp., 1982—, Grady Meml. Hosp., 1982—; lectr. in field. Author books; contbg. author over 50 book chpts.; contbr. over 65 articles to profl. jours. Bd. dirs. Spruce Hill Cmty. Assn., 1967-69, Hill Top Prep. Sch., 1977-81. Recipient fellowship NIH, 1963-64, 66-67, 75-80, GM Nat. scholarship, 1957-61, Ford Found. fellowship, 1960-61, Am. Cancer Soc. fellow, 1962-63, Morton McCutcheon award, 1963, Merck award, 1966, numerous rsch. awards, 1964—. Mem. Am. Pediat. Soc., Endocrine Soc. (organizing com. 1990), Soc. for Pediat. Rsch., Coll. Physicians and Surgeons of Phila., Lawson Wilkins Pediat. Endocrine Soc. (program com. chair 1983-87, bd. dirs. 1990-93, pres. 1996-97), Spinx Soc., Scarab Soc., Phi Beta Kappa, Psi Upsilon. Office: Emory Univ Sch Medicine Div Pediat Endocrinology 2040 Ridgewood Dr NE Atlanta GA 30322-1028

PARKS, LLOYD LEE, oil company executive; b. Kiefer, Okla., Dec. 9, 1929; s. Homer Harrison and Avis Pearl (Motes) P.; m. Mary Ellen Scott, Aug. 20, 1948; children: Connie Jo, Karyn Ann, Rebecca Lee. Student, Okla. State U., 1948-50, Tulsa U., 1950-51, Harvard U. Bus. Sch., 1965. Acct. Deep Rock Oil Corp., 1951-54; chief acct. Blackwell Oil & Gas Co., Tulsa, 1954-60; sec. treas. Blackwell Oil & Gas Co., 1960-62; v.p., controller Amax Oil & Gas Inc., Houston, 1962-67, pres., CEO, 1968—92; v.p. Amax, Inc., 1975-92; pvt. practice oil and gas and real estate imvestment Salado, Tex., 1992—. Served with AUS, 1946-48, 50-51. Mem. Ind. Petroleum Assn. Am. (dir.), Mill Creek Country Club, Wildflower Country Club (Temple, Tex.), Lions Club. Republican. Office: PO Box 1021 Salado TX 76571-1021 *Work hard, work smart and believe in yourself. You can and will be successful; if you want to be.*

PARKS, MADELYN N., nurse, retired army officer, university official; b. Jordan, Okla.. Diploma, Corpus Christi (Tex.) Sch. Nursing, 1943; B.S.N., Incarnate Word Coll., San Antonio, 1961; M.H.A. in Health Care Adminstrn, Baylor U., 1965. Commd. 2d lt. Army Nurse Corps, 1943, advanced through grades to brig. gen., 1975; basic tng. Fort Meade, Md., 1944; staff nurse eye ward Valley Forge (Pa.) Gen. Hosp., 1944; served in India, Iran, Italy, 1944-45; gen. duty staff nurse Fort Polk, La., 1951; nurse eye clinic Tripler Army Med. Center, Hawaii, 1951-54; staff nurse eye, ear, nose and throat ward Brooke Army Med. Center, San Antonio, 1954-57; ednl. coordinator Fort Dix, N.J., 1957-58; instr., supr. enlisted med. tng. U.S. Army Med. Tng. Center, Fort Sam Houston, Tex., 1959-61; chief nurse surg. field hosp. 62d Med. Group, Germany, 1961-62, sr. nurse coordinator, 1962-63; adminstrn. resident Letterman Gen. Hosp., San Francisco, 1964-65; dir. clin. specialist course Letterman Gen. Hosp., 1965-67; chief nurse 85th Evacuation Hosp., Qui Nhon, Vietnam, 1967-68; asst. chief nursing sci. div., asst. prof. Med. Field Service Sch., U.S. Army-Baylor U. Program in Health Care Adminstrn., 1968-72; chief nurse surgeons office Hdqrs. Continental Army Command, Fort Monroe, Va., 1972-73; chief dept. nursing Walter Reed Army Med. Center, Washington, 1973-75; chief Army Nurse Corps, Office of Surgeon Gen., Dept. Army, Washington, 1975-79; ret. Army Nurse Corps, Office of Surgeon Gen., Dept. Army, 1979; faculty assoc. adminstr. U. Md., 1974-78. Decorated D.S.M., Army Commendation medal with 2 oak leaf clusters, Legion of Merit, Meritorious Service medal; recipient Alumna of Distinction award Incarnate Word Coll., 1981. Mem. Ret. Officers Assn., AMEDD Mus. Found. Address: 5211 Metcalf San Antonio TX 78239-1933

PARKS, MICHAEL CHRISTOPHER, journalist; b. Detroit, Nov. 17, 1943; s. Robert James and Rosalind (Smith) P.; m. Linda Katherine Durocher, Dec. 26, 1964; children: Danielle Anne, Christopher, Matthew. AB, U. Windsor, Ont., Can., 1965. Reporter Detroit News, 1962-65; corr. Time-Life News Service, N.Y.C., 1965-66; asst. city editor Suffolk Sun, Long Island, N.Y., 1966-68; polit. reporter, foreign corr. The Balt. Sun, Saigon, Singapore, Moscow, Cairo, Hong Kong, Peking, 1968-80; fgn. corr. L.A. Times, L.A., Peking, Johannesburg, Moscow, Jerusalem, 1980-95, dpty. fgn. editor, 1995-96; mng. editor, 1996—; v.p. L.A. Times, 1996-97, sr. v.p., 1997—. Recipient Pulitzer Prize, 1987. Mem. Royal Commonwealth Soc. London, Soc. Profl. Journalists, Fgn. Corr. Club (Hong Kong). Office: L A Times Times Mirror Sq Los Angeles CA 90012

PARKS, PATRICIA JEAN, lawyer; b. Portland, Oreg., Apr. 2, 1945; d. Robert and Marion (Crosby) P.; m. David F. Jurca, Oct. 17, 1971 (div. 1976). BA in History, Stanford U., 1963-67; JD, U. Penn., Phila., 1967-70. Bar: N.Y. 1971, Wash. 1974. Assoc. Milbank, Tweed, Hadley & McCoy, N.Y.C., 1970-73; assoc. Shidler, McBroom, Gates & Lucas, Seattle, 1974-81, ptnr., 1981-90; ptnr. Preston, Thorgrimson, Shidler, Gates & Ellis, Seattle, 1990-93; pvt. practice Seattle, 1993—. Active Vashon Allied Arts, Mountaineers, N.W. Women's Law Ctr., Wash. State Women's Polit. Caucus. Mem. NOW, ABA, Wash. State Bar Assn. (past pres. tax sect., past chair gift and estate tax com.), Washington Women in Tax, Washington Women Lawyers, Seattle-King County Bar Assn., Employee Stock Ownership Plan Assn., Western Pension Conf., Pension Roundtable, Wash. Athletic Club. Avocations: kayaking, hiking, Contra dancing, bird watching, karate. Office: 1301 5th Ave Ste 3800 Seattle WA 98101-2635

PARKS, PAUL, corporate executive; b. Indpls., May 7, 1923; s. Cleab Jiles and Hazel (Crenshaw) P.; m. Virginia Loftman, Sept. 18, 1971; children: Paul, Pamela, Stacey. BS in Civil Engring., Purdue U., 1949; postgrad., MIT, 1958, U. Mass.; DEng, Northeastern U., 1994. Registered profl. engr., Mass. With Ind. State Hwy. Commn., Indpls., 1949-51; designer Stone & Webster Engring., Boston, 1951, Fay, Spofford & Thorndike, Boston, 1951-52; missile designer Chance Vought Aircraft, Boston, 1952-53; nuclear engr. Pratt & Whitney Aircraft, Boston, 1953-57; pntr. architecture and engring. firm, Boston, 1957-67; adminstr. Boston Model City Adminstrn., 1968-76; sec. ednl. affairs Commonwealth of Mass., Boston, 1976—; pres. Paul Parks and Assocs. Inc., Boston, 1979—; lectr. Tufts U. Sch. Civil Engring., 1968—; mem. northeastern regional bd. Fannie Mae, 1994—; corp. mem. Ptnrs. Healthcare Coop. Cons. gen. acctg. office Mayor's Com. Adminstrn. Justice; mem. Atty. Gen.'s Adv. Com. Civil Rights, 1969-71; mem. health task force Boston Fed. Exec. Bd.; adviser Boston Mothers for Adequate Welfare, 1966-68; speech therapist Vets. Lang. Clinic, Mass. Gen. Hosp., 1964-66; mem. Mass. Adv. Coun. on Edn., 1968-71, Mass. Com. Children and Youth, 1962-67; chmn. Mass. adv. com. to U.S. Civil Rights Commn., 1961-73; chmn. urban affairs com. Mass. Fedn. Fair Housing and Equal Rights, 1961-67; mem. Community Ednl. Coun., 1961-73; pres. Com. for Community Ednl. Devel. Inc., 1968-74; presdl. adv. commn. Nat. Coun. Ednl. Programs for Women, 1976-81; pres. Boston Pub. Libr.; mem. zoning bd. appeals City of Boston; adult leader youth programs Roxbury YMCA, 1951-58; trustee Brigham Hosp., Women's Hosp.; bd. dirs. Mass. Planned Parenthood Assn., Mass. Mental Health Assn., Mass. Soc. Prevention Blindness, Boston Coll. Upward Bound Program; corp. bd. Ptnrs. Healthcare; chmn. sch. com. City of Boston, 1992—; mem. regional adv. coun. Fannie Mae. Served with AUS, 1943-46, ETO, PTO. Mem. ASCE, NSPE, NAACP (co-chmn. edn. com. 1960-68, v.p. Boston br. 1965-70), Nat. Acad. Pub. Adminstrn., Ams. Dem. Action (nat. bd. 1971-74, state bd. 1970-74), Greater Boston C. of C. (edn. com.). Mem. United Ch. of Christ (mem. nat. social action bd. 1963-68). Home: 78 Woodhaven St Mattapan MA 02126-1730 Office: 100 Boylston St Ste 815 Boston MA 02116-4610

PARKS, ROBERT EMMETT, JR., medical science educator; b. Glendale, N.Y., July 29, 1921; s. Robert Emmett and Carolyn M. (Heinemann) P.; m. Margaret Ellen Ward, June 15, 1945; children: Robert Emmett III, Walter Ward, Christopher Carr. AB, Brown U., 1944; MD, Harvard U., 1945; PhD, U. Wis., 1954. Intern Boston's Children's Hosp., 1945-46; rsch. assoc. Amherst (Mass.) Coll., 1948-51; postdoctoral fellow Enzyme Inst., Madison, Wis., 1951-54; mem. faculty U. Wis. Med. Sch., 1954-63, prof. pharmacology, 1961-63; prof. med. sci. Brown U., Providence, 1963-91, prof. emeritus, 1991—, dir. grad. program in pharmacology and exptl. pathology, 1978-81, chmn. sect. biochem. pharmacology, 1963-78, 83-91; cons. in field. Contbr. articles to profl. jours. With AUS, 1943-45, 46-48. Acad. medicine scholar John and Mary Markle Found., 1956-61. Mem. Am. Soc. Pharmacology and Exptl. Therapeutics, Am. Soc. Biol. Chemists, Am. Assn. Cancer Rsch. (bd. dirs. 1982-86), Sigma Xi. Home: 62 Alumni Ave Providence RI 02906-2310 Office: Brown U 429 Biomed Ctr Providence RI 02912

PARKS, ROBERT HENRY, consulting economist, educator; b. New Orleans, Sept. 20, 1924; s. Charles Samuel and Amelia (England) P.; m. Inta Kondrats, Sept. 20, 1958; children: Karen E., Robert R., Alison J.; m. Annette Fiechter, Dec. 10, 1982 (div.). A.B. in Econs., Swarthmore Coll., 1949; M.A., Ph.D. in Econs., U. Pa., 1958. Economist Econ. Forecasting div. Gen. Electric Co., 1958-61; dir. econ. research Life Ins. Assn. Am., 1961-68; chief economist Maj. Wall St. Investment Firms, 1968-80; pres. Robert H. Parks & Assocs., Inc., N.Y.C., 1980—; cons. to instnl. investment officers; prof. fin., dir. Inst. Internat. Fin. Pace U., Wharton Sch. (U. Pa.), Baruch (CUNY); prof. fin. Lehigh U. Author: The Witch Doctor of Wall Street, 1996, Prometheus; contbr. articles to profl. jours. Democrat. Home and Office: 31 Sherwood Rd Short Hills NJ 07078-2038

PARKS, R(OBERT) KEITH, missionary, religious organization administrator; b. Memphis, Tex., Oct. 23, 1927; s. Robert Crews and Allie Myrtle (Cowger) P.; m. Helen Jean Bond, May 24, 1952; children: Randall, Kent, Eloise, Stanley. BA, U. North Tex., 1948; BD, Southwestern Bapt. Theol. Sem., 1951, ThD, 1955; LittD (hon.), Hardin-Simmons U., 1976; D Missions (hon.), Calif. Bapt. Coll., 1980; STD (hon.), S.W. Bapt. Coll., Bolivar, Mo., 1981; DD (hon.), U. Richmond, 1987; HHD (hon.), Mercer U., 1992. Ordained to ministry So. Bapt. Conv., 1950. Pastor Red Springs (Tex.) Bapt. Ch., 1950-54; instr. Bible Hardin-Simmons U., Abilene, Tex., 1953-54; missionary Fgn. Mission Bd., So. Bapt. Conv., Indonesia, 1954-68; area dir. S.E. Asia Fgn. Mission Bd., So. Bapt. Conv., Richmond, Va., 1968-75, dir. div. mission support, 1975-79, pres., 1980-92; global missions coord. Coop. Bapt. Fellowship, Atlanta, 1993—; mem., past chmn. Inter-Agy. Coun., So. Bapt. Conv., 1980-92; trustee Bapt. Joint Com. on Pub. Affairs, Washington, 1980-91. Author: Crosscurrents, 1966, World in View, 1987; also numerous articles. Recipient Disting. Alumnus award Southwestern Bapt. Theol. Sem., 1980, U. North Tex., 1991, E.Y. Mullins Denominational Svc. award So.

Bapt. Theol. Sem., 1989. Office: Coop Bapt Fellowship PO Box 450329 Atlanta GA 31145-0329

PARKS, ROBERT MYERS, appliance manufacturing company executive; b. Nevada, Mo., July 18, 1927; s. Cecil R. and Marcella (Myers) P.; m. Audrey Lenora Jones, June 18, 1955; children—John Robert, Janet M. Parks Huston. B.S., U. Mo., 1949; M.B.A., Harvard, 1952. Asst. dept. mgr. Jewett & Sherman Co., Kansas City, Mo., 1949-50; staff cons. Harbridge House, Inc., Boston, 1952; v.p. Electronic Splty. Co., Inc., Los Angeles, 1952-57; founder, chmn. bd. Parks Products, Inc., Hollywood, Calif., 1957—; pres. Generalist Industries, Inc., Hollywood, 1960-73; chmn. bd. Shaver Corp. Am., Los Angeles, 1965—; lectr. mktg. UCLA Extension div., 1960-61. Contbr. articles on mktg. and bus. mgmt. to profl. publs.; patentee in field. Active YMCA; bd. dirs. Hollywood Presbyn. Med. Center Found., Presbyn. Homes Found.; mem. dean's adv. council U. Mo. Bus. Sch., mayor's task force on L.A. River Cahuenga Pass Coalition. Served with USNR, 1944-45. Mem. Sales and Marketing Execs. Assn., C. of C., Navy League, World Affairs Council, Calif. Caballeros, Rangers, Vaqueros del Desierto, Los Caballeros, Rancheros Visitadores, E Clampus Vitus, Delta Sigma Pi, Sigma Chi. Presbyn. Clubs: Mason (Shriner), Los Angeles Breakfast, Braemar Country, Saddle and Sirloin. Home: 7421 Woodrow Wilson Dr Los Angeles CA 90046-1322 Office: 3611 Cahuenga Blvd W Hollywood CA 90068-1205

PARKS, STEPHEN ROBERT, curator; b. Columbus, Ohio, July 18, 1940. BA, Yale U., 1961; PhD, Cambridge U., U.K., 1964. Assoc. curator, curator James Marshall and Marie-Louise Osborn Collection, 1967—; libr. Elizabethan Club Yale U., New Haven, Conn., 1972—. Author: Sale Catalogues of Libraries of Eminent Persons, 1972, John Dunton and the English Book Trade: A Study of his Career with a Checklist of his Publications, 1975, The Elizabethan Club of Yale University and its Library, 1986, (with P.J. Croft) English Literary Autographs, 1984; editor Yale U.L. Gazette, 1980—; wine columnist The New Haven Register, 1979-89; contbr. articles to profl. jours. Postdoctoral fellow U. Edinburgh, 1964-67. Home: 248 Bradley St New Haven CT 06510-1103 Office: Beinecke Libr Yale U PO Box 208240 New Haven CT 06520

PARKYN, JOHN WILLIAM, editor, writer; b. London, Dec. 7, 1931; came to U.S., 1967; citizen, 1973; s. James R. and Eva M. (Dix) P.; m. Sybil (Judy) Hetherington; 1 child, Elaine. Student, Dulwich Coll., 1943-48. Staff writer Bus. Mag., London, 1954-56, Amalgamated Press, London, 1956-58; features editor Woman's Illustrated mag., London, 1958-60; staff writer Internat. Pub. Corp., London, 1960-61; editor Westward mag. Daily News Ltd., London, 1961-64; assoc. editor Daily Telegraph mag., London, 1964-66; features editor King mag. Europress, Ltd., London, 1966-67; assoc. editor Tropic mag. Miami (Fla.) Herald, 1967-69; editor Tropic mag., 1969-77; editor Calif. Today mag. San Jose (Calif.) Mercury News, 1977-83; editor Sunshine: The Mag. of South Fla. Sun-Sentinel Co. (subs. Tribune Co.), Ft. Lauderdale, Fla., 1983-96; freelance writer/editor, 1996—; cons. Het Parool newspaper, Amsterdam, 1965; freelance writer/editor, 1996—. Contbr. numerous articles to Am. and European mags. Chmn. Sunday Mag. Editors Conf., Louisville, 1973. With RAF, 1950-52. Recipient Outstanding Use of Editl. Color award Editor & Pub. mag., 1974, 75, 77, Nat. Headliner award, 1976, 79; named Editor Best Weekly Mag. in State Fla. Press Club, 1985-93, 95. Office: 505 Beachland Blvd Ste 1-275 Vero Beach FL 32963-1710

PARLER, ANNE HEMENWAY, elementary education educator, horse trainer; b. Rochelle, Ill., July 15, 1931; d. William Merwin and Edith Florence (Ranger) Hemenway; m. William Carlos Parler, Aug. 13, 1955; children: William Jr., Blair Hemenway, Bethanie Parler Detar, B. Carolyn. BS in Edn., No. Ill. U., 1953; postgrad., Long Beach State U., U. S.C., U. Md. Cert. tchr. Music (K-12), Md. Tchr. Long Beach (Calif.) Sch. Dist., 1953-54, West Covina (Calif.) Sch. Dist., 1954-55, Columbia (S.C.) Sch. Sys., 1955-58, U. Md., College Park, 1970-71, St. Patrick's Episcopal Sch., Washington, 1971-73, Montgomery County Pub. Schs., Rockville, Md., 1973-95; ret., 1995; owner Sunny Meadows Horse Farm, Frankford, Del., 1994—; pvt. voice and piano tchr., Rockville, 1960-90. Contralto soloist Faith Meth. Ch., Rockville, 1968-90, dir. handbell choirs, 1985—; Dem. election judge, Rockville. Mem. NEA, MCEA (union rep.), Music Educators Nat. Conf., Met. Opera Guild, Nat. Women in the Arts Mus., Am. Guild English Handbell Ringers, Malice Domestic Mystery Writers Conv., Am. Quarter Horse Assn., Ill. State Soc., Harvard Law Wives, Navy Wives Club, Sigma Sigma Sigma, Sigma Alpha Iota. Democrat. Methodist. Home: 7005 Old Stage Rd Rockville MD 20852 Office: Sunny Meadows Horse Farm RFD 1, Box 204 Ocean View DE 19970

PARLIN, CHARLES C., JR., retired lawyer; b. Trenton, Feb. 12, 1928; s. Charles C. and Miriam (Boyd) P.; m. Joan Bona, June 28, 1948; children: C. Christopher, Robert B., Timothy B. B.A., U. Chgo., 1946; LL.B., U. Pa., 1949. Bar: N.Y. 1951. Assoc. firm. Shearman & Sterling, N.Y.C., 1950-59, ptnr., 1959-90, of counsel, 1990-92, ret., 1992. Home: Pudding Ln Silver Bay NY 12874

PARMELEE, ARTHUR HAWLEY, JR., pediatric medical educator; b. Chgo., Oct. 29, 1917; s. Arthur Hawley and Ruth Frances (Brown) P.; m. Jean Kern Rheinfrank, Nov. 11, 1939; children: Arthur Hawley III, Ann (Mrs. John C. Minahan Jr.), Timothy, Ruth Ellen. BS, U. Chgo., 1940, MD, 1943. Diplomate Am. Bd. Pediatrics (examiner 1966—). Intern U.S. Naval Hosp., Bethesda, Md., 1943-44; extern Yale Inst. Child Devel., 1947, New Haven Hosp., 1947-48, L.A. Children's Hosp., 1948-49; mem. faculty UCLA Med. Sch., 1951—, prof. pediat., 1967-88, prof. emeritus, 1988, dir. divsn. child devel., 1964-88; mem. Brain Rsch. Inst., 1966-88, Mental Retardation Rsch. Ctr., 1970-88; rsch. prof. pediat. U. Göttingen, Germany, 1967-68; mem. com. child devel. rsch. and pub. policy NRC, 1977-81; cons. Nat. Inst. Child Health and Human Devel., 1963-70, Holy Family Adoption Svc., 1949-80. Author articles, chpts. in books. Trustee Los Angeles Children's Mus., 1979. Served with USN, 1943-47. Recipient C. Anderson Aldrich award in child devel., 1975; Commonwealth fellow Centre de Recherches Biologiques Neonatales, Clinique Obstetricale Baudelocque, Paris, 1959-60; fellow Ctr. Advanced Study in Behavioral Scis., Stanford U., 1984-85; hon. lectr. Soc. for Developmental and Behavioral Pediat., 1996. Mem. AMA, Am. Pediat. Soc., Soc. Pediat. Rsch., Western Soc. Pediat. Rsch., Am. Acad. Pediat. (chmn. com. sect. child devel. 1966), Assn. Ambulatory Pediat. (mem. coun. 1966-69), Soc. Rsch. in Child Devel. (pres. 1983-85, Disting. Sci. Contbns. to Child Devel. award 1993), Assn. Psychophysiol. Study of Sleep, Los Angeles County Med. Soc., Phi Beta Kappa. Home: 764 Iliff St Pacific Palisades CA 90272-3927 Office: Univ Calif Dept Pediatrics Los Angeles CA 90024

PARMELEE, DAVID FREELAND, biologist, educator; b. Oshkosh, Wis., June 20, 1924; s. Gale Freeland and Helen Dale (MacNaughton) P.; m. Jean Marie Peterson, Dec. 4, 1943; 1 dau., Helen Gale. BA, Lawrence U., Appleton, Wis., 1950; MS, U. Mich., 1952; PhD, U. Okla., 1957. Grad. asst., then instr. U. Okla., 1952-58; from asst. prof. to prof. biology Kans. State U., Emporia, 1958-70; prof. ecology and behavioral biology U. Minn., Mpls., 1970-92, chmn. field biology program, 1970-84; curator birds Bell Mus. U. Minn., 1985-92; rsch. curator ornithology U. Nev., Las Vegas, 1992—; dir. field ops. bird virus and parasite rsch. studies U. Okla. Med. Ctr., 1963-65; program dir. U. Minn. Forestry and Biol. Sta., Lake Itasca, 1970-86, Cedar Creek Natrual History Area, 1970-84; lectr. on cruise vessels to Arctic and Antarctic for Travel Dynamics, N.Y.C., 1988—, Space Expedition, Inc., Seattle, 1993—, Cheesemans' Ecology Safaris, 1994—. Served with USMCR, 1943-46. Recipient Native Son award Rotary Internat., 1982; grantee NSF-U.S. Antarctic Research Program, 1972-90, Canadian Arctic Research Programs-NSF-Arctic Inst. N.Am.-Nat. Museum Can., 1953-71; recipient Conservation Edn. award Kans. Wildlife Fedn., Conservation Edn. award Sears-Roebuck Found., 1965; Antarctic site named Parmelee Massif in his honor. Fellow Explorers Club: mem. Orgn. Biol. Field Stas. (pres. 1984-85), Brit. Ornithol. Union, Cooper Ornithol. Soc., Wilson Ornithol. Soc., Nature Conservancy, Brit. Ornithologists' Club.

PARMENTER, CHARLES STEDMAN, chemistry educator; b. Phila., Oct. 12, 1933; s. Charles Leroy and Hazeltene Lois (Stedman) P.; m. Patricia Jean Patton, Mar. 31, 1956; children: Tighe Stedman, Kyle Kirkland, Leigh Patton. BA, U. Pa., 1955; PhD in Phys. Chemistry, U. Rochester, 1963. Tech. rep. photo products E.I. du Pont de Nemours & Co., 1958; NSF fellow chemistry Harvard U., Boston, 1962-63, NIH rsch. fellow, 1963-64, from asst. prof. to prof., 1964-88; Disting. prof. chemistry Ind. U., Bloomington, 1988—; Simon H. Guggenheim fellow U. Cambridge, 1971-72; vis. fellow Joint Inst. Lab. Astrophysics, Nat. Bur. Standards and U. Colo., 1977-78, 92. Lt. USAF, 1956-58. Recipient Humboldt Sr. Scientist award Tech. U. Munchen, 1986; Fulbright Sr. Scholar Griffith U., Australia, 1980. Earle K. Plyler Prize, Am. Physical Soc., 1996. Fellow AAAS, Am. Phys. Soc. (Earle K. Plyler prize 1996); mem. NAS, Am. Acad. Arts and Scis., Am. Chem. Soc. (chmn. div. phys. chemistry 1986-87). Research in photochemistry, laser spectroscopy, energy transfer. Office: Ind U Dept of Chemistry Bloomington IN 47405

PARMENTER, ROBERT HALEY, physics educator; b. Portland, Maine, Sept. 19, 1925; s. LeClare Fall and Esther (Haley) P.; m. Elizabeth Kinnecom, Oct. 27, 1951; children: David Alan, Douglas Ian. B.S., U. Maine, 1947; Ph.D., Mass. Inst. Tech., 1952. Mem. staff solid state and molecular theory group Mass. Inst. Tech., 1951-54; guest scientist Brookhaven Nat. Lab., 1951-52; mem. staff Lincoln Lab., 1952-54, RCA Labs., 1954-66; vis. scientists RCA Labs., Zurich, Switzerland, 1958; acting head solid state research group RCA Labs., 1962-65; prof. physics U. Ariz., 1966-96, chmn. dept., 1977-83, prof. emeritus, 1996—; mem. NASA rsch. adv. com. electrophysics, 1964-68, chmn., 1966-68, mem. rsch. and tech. adv. com. basic rsch., 1966-68; vis. lectr. Princeton (N.J.) U., 1960-61. Served with USNR, 1944-46. Fellow AAAS, Am. Phys. Soc. (chmn. div. condensed matter physics 1967-68); mem. Sigma Xi, Tau Beta Pi. Achievements include predicting the existence of the acoustoelectric effect, the enhancement of the transition temperature of a superconductor by means of tunneling extraction; demonstration of the conditions under which deterministic chaos occurs in quantum mechanical systems. Home: 1440 E Ina Rd Tucson AZ 85718-1175 Office: U Ariz Physics Dept Tucson AZ 85721

PARMENTIER, E. M. (MARC), geophysics educator; b. Waynesburg, Pa., Oct. 29, 1945. BS, W.Va. U., 1968; M in Engring., Cornell U., 1969, PhD, 1975. Rsch. scientist/engr. AVCO-Everett Rsch. Lab., 1969-72; rsch. fellow geol. scis. Oxford U., 1975-77; from asst. prof. to prof. geol. scis. Brown U., Providence, 1977—. Fellow Am. Geophys. Union; mem. Sigma Xi. Office: Brown U Dept Geological Sciences Providence RI 02912-9100

PARMER, DAN GERALD, veterinarian; b. Wetumpka, Ala., July 3, 1926; s. James Lonnie and Virginia Gertrude (Guy) P.; 1 child by previous marriage, Linda Leigh; m. Donna Louise Kesler, June 7, 1980; 1 child, Dan Gerald. Student L.A. City Coll., 1945-46; DVM, Auburn U., 1950. Gen. practice vet. medicine, Galveston, Tex., 1950-54, Chgo., 1959-83; vet. in charge Chgo. Commn. Animal Care and Control, 1974-88; med. dir. food protection divsn. Chgo. Dept. Health, 1988-93; ret. 1993; chmn. Ill. Impaired Vets. Com.; mem. Ala. Impaired Vets. Com.; tchr. Highlands U., 1959; humane officer Elmore County, 1994—; dir. sales for south, southeast and lower midwest Am. Vet. Identification Devices, Norco, Calif., 1993—, nat. dir. companion animal divsn, 1996—. Pres. Elmore County Humane Soc. Served with USNR, 1943-45, PTO; served as staff vet. and 2d and 5th Air Force vet. chief USAF, 1954-59. Decorated 9 Battle Stars; recipient Vet. Appreciation award U. Ill., 1971, Commendation, Chgo. Commn. Animal Care and Control, 1987. Mem. VFW, AVMA (nat. com. for impaired vets., coun. pub. health and regulatory medicine 1990—), Ill. Vet. Medicine Assn. (chmn. civil def. and package disaster hosps. 1968-71, Pres.' award 1986), Chgo. Vet. Medicine Assn. (bd. govs. 1969-72, 74-81, pres. 1982), South Chgo. Vet. Medicine Assn. (pres. 1965-66), Am. Animal Hosp. Assn. (dir.), Ill. Acad. Vet. Practice (pres. 1993), Nat. Assn. of Professions, Am. Assn. Zoo Vets., Am. Assn. Zool. Parks and Aquariums, Elmore County Humane Soc. (pres. 1994-95), Midlothian Country Club, Valley Internat. Country Club, Masons, Shriners, Kiwanis. Democrat. Discoverer Bartonellosis in cattle in N.Am. and Western Hemisphere, 1951; co-developer bite-size high altitude in-flight feeding program USAF, 1954-56. Address: 6720 Post Oak Ln Montgomery AL 36117-2424 Office: Am Vet Identification Devices 3179 Hamner Ave Norco CA 91760-1983

PARMER, JESS NORMAN, university official, educator; b. Elkhart, Ind., Nov. 23, 1925; s. Jess Noah and Zayda Irene (Tressler) P.; m. Bessie Norma Peterson, September 12, 1948; children: Thomas Norman, Sarah Irene. B.A., Ind. U., 1949; M.A., U. Conn., 1951; Ph.D., Cornell U., 1957. Resident in Malaya, Southeast Asia program, Cornell U., 1952-55; instr., then asst. prof. history U. Md., 1956-59; mem. faculty No. Ill. U., 1959-67, prof. history, 1960-67, chmn. dept., 1959-63; assoc. dean Coll. Arts and Scis. Ohio U., also dir. Center Internat. Studies, 1967-69, asst. dean faculties for internat. studies, 1969-75; v.p. acad. affairs Trinity U., San Antonio, 1975-82, prof. history, 1975-92; scholar in residence and dir. of special projects Ohio U., Athens, 1993-96; cons. business, govt., edn.; Peace Corps rep. in Malaya, 1961-63, Tanzania, summer 1965, Malawi, summer, 1966, Korea, 1967; lectr. Fgn. Service Inst., 1958, 61, 65; vis. prof. history Nat. U. Malaysia, 1984; cons. social scis. com. Ill. Curriculum Program, 1961; cons. various corps.; vis. fellow Cornell U., 1987-88, vis. prof. 1989; luce scholar in res. Ohio U., 1990-91. Author: Governments and Politics of Southeast Asia, 2d edit., 1964, Colonial Labor Policy and Administration, 1960, Southeast Asia: Documents of Political Development and Change, 1974, People and Progress: A Global History, 1977; contbr. chpts. The World of Asia, 1995. Served with inf. AUS, 1944-46, ETO. Mem. AAUP, ACLU, Assn. Asian Studies (chmn. S.E. Asia regional coun. 1968-72, dir. 1969-72), Midwest Conf. Asian Affairs (chmn. library com. 1960-61), Southwest Conf. Asian Studies (pres. 1982-83), Am. Hist. Assn., Sons of the Am. Revolution, Torch Internat., Soc. of Ind. Pioneers, Tex. Soc. War of 1812. Office: Ohio U Ctr Internat Studies 7 Banbury Dr Athens OH 45701-3337 *I find my life full of opportunity, excitement and satisfaction. Satisfaction comes from seeing ideas find institutional or behavioral expression and influencing people in positive ways. Self-fulfillment, hard work, respect for others, and honesty have been guiding principles and I have found them compatible and rewarding.*

PARMET, HERBERT SAMUEL, historian, educator; b. N.Y.C., Sept. 28, 1929; s. Isaac and Fanny (Scharf) P.; m. Joan Kronish, Sept. 12, 1948; 1 child, Wendy. BS, SUNY, Oswego, 1951; MA, Queens Coll., 1957; postgrad., Columbia U., 1958-62. Prof. history Grad. Sch. CUNY, 1968-95, disting. prof. history, 1983-95, prof. emeritus, 1995—; cons. ABC-TV, N.Y.C., 1983, KERA-TV, Dallas, 1986-91, WGBH-TV, Boston, 1988-91. Author: Aaron Burr: Portrait of an Ambitious Man, 1967, Never Again: President Runs for a Third Term, 1968, Eisenhower and the American Crusades, 1972, The Democrats, 1976, Jack: The Struggles of John F. Kennedy, 1980, JFK: The Presidency of John F. Kennedy, 1983, Richard Nixon and His America, 1990, George Bush: The Life of a Lone Star Yankee, 1997; editorial bd. Presdl. Studies Quar. Cpl. U.S. Army, 1952-54. Grantee, NEH, 1987. Fellow Soc. Am. Historians; mem. Am. Hist. Assn., Orgn. Am. Historians, Authors Guild. Avocation: photography. Home: 36 Marsten Ln Hillsdale NY 12529-5816

PARMITER, JAMES DARLIN, retired safety engineer; b. McKeesport, Pa., Apr. 5, 1934; s. James Harry and Ruth Adeline (Ulm) P.; student Pa. State U., 1952-56; m. Nancy Jane Light, Aug. 24, 1954; children: James Victor, David Baird. With Gen. Motors Co., Wilmington, Del., 1962-65; with Boeing Helicopter Co., Ridley Park, Pa., 1965-84, mgr. safety and indsl. hygiene, 1967-84; occupational safety and health mgr. Phila. Naval Shipyard, 1984-94, dir. occupational safety, health, and environ., 1994-96; mem. faculty Pa. State U., Cheyney State Coll., West Chester U., Del. County Community Coll.; also cons. Mem. Gov.'s Adv. Com. on Occupational Safety and Health for Pa., 1967-84, Adv. Com. on Occupational Safety and Health Pa. State U., 1967-83; mem. Springfield Sch. Bd., 1969-75, Delaware County Sch. Bd., 1969-75; vol. curator staff Ind. Seaport Mus., Penn's Landing, Phila. With USN, 1953-63, comdr. res. (ret.). Recipient Ben Franklin award Greater Phila. Safety Coun., 1981; Phila. Vision award Phila. Optometric Soc., 1972, Meritorious Civilian Svc. medal Dept. of Navy, 1996. Mem. Nat. Safety Coun. (aerospace sect. gen. chmn. 1974-76), Am. Soc. Safety Engrs. (pres. Phila. 1980-82, Safety Profl. of Yr. for region XII, 1982), Phila. Safety Coun. (chmn. bd. 1974-75), Am. Helicopter Soc., Am. Indsl. Hygiene Assn., Assn. Fed. Safety and Health Profls., Fed. Mgrs. Assn., Am. Philatelic Assn., Pa. State U. Alumni Assn., Masons., Shriners. Republican. Methodist. Home: 242 Brock Rd Springfield PA 19064-3116 also: 5525 Bay Ave Ocean City NJ 08226-1241

PARMLEY, LOREN FRANCIS, JR., medical educator; b. El Paso, Tex., Sept. 19, 1921; s. Loren Francis and Hope (Bartholomew) P.; m. Dorothy Louise Turner, Apr. 4, 1942; children—Richard Turner, Robert James, Kathryn Louise. B.A., U. Va., 1941, M.D., 1943. Diplomate Am. Bd. Internal Medicine, Am. Bd. Internal Medicine-Cardiovascular Disease. Commd. 1st lt. U.S. Army, 1944; advanced through grades to col., 1968; intern Med. Coll. Va., 1944; resident in internal medicine Brooke Gen. Hosp., San Antonio, 1948-49, U. Wis. Gen. Hosp., Madison, 1949-51; asst. prof. mil. med. sci. Med. Coll. U. Wis., Madison, 1949-51; asst. attache (med.) U.S. Embassy, New Delhi, 1953-55; fellow in cardiovascular disease Walter Reed Gen. Hosp., Washington, 1956-57; chief medicine and cardiology Letterman Gen. Hosp., San Francisco, 1958-63; med. and cardiology cons. U.S. Army Europe, Heidelberg, Germany, 1963-64; chief medicine Walter Reed Gen. Hosp., Washington, 1965-68; prof. medicine, asst. dean Med. U. S.C., Spartanburg, 1968-75; dir. med. edn. Spartanburg Gen. Hosp., Spartanburg, 1968-75; prof. medicine U. South Ala., Mobile, 1975-87, chief div. cardiology, 1980-87, prof. emeritus medicine, 1988—; lectr. medicine U. Calif.-San Francisco, 1959-63; clin. assoc. prof. medicine Georgetown U., Washington, 1967-68; clin. prof. medicine Med. Coll. Ga., Augusta, 1969-75; cons. internal medicine Surgeon Gen. U.S. Army, Washington, 1966-68. Contbg. author: The Heart, 1966, 70, 74, 78 Cardiac Diagnosis and Treatment, 1976, 80, The Heart in Industry, 1960, 70. Recipient Gold award sci. exhibit Am. Soc. Clin. Pathologists and Coll. Am. Pathologists, 1959; Certificate of Achievement in cardio-vascular disease Surgeon Gen. U.S.A., Washington, 1962; Bronze Medallion Meritorious Service, Am. Heart Assn., S.C., Columbia, 1969, 73; decorated Legion of Merit. Fellow ACP, Am. Coll. Cardiology (bd. govs. U.S. Army 1967, S.C. 1969-73), Am. Coll. Chest Physicians; mem. Am. Heart Assn. (fellow coun. on clin. cardiology), Soc. Med. Cons. to Armed Forces, Kiwanis. Republican. Episcopalian. Avocations: golf, swimming. Home: 549 Fairway Dr Kerrville TX 78028-6440 also: 5862 Falls Church Rd E Mobile AL 36608-2961 Office: U South Ala Coll Medicine Dept Medicine Mastin Bldg 2451 Fillingim St Rm 414 Mobile AL 36617-2238

PARNAS, DAVID LORGE, computer scientist, engineer, educator; b. Plattsburgh, N.Y., Feb. 10, 1941; s. Jacob M. and Hildegarde Marienne (Lorge) P.; m. Lillian Lai Ngan Chik, Nov. 7, 1979; children: Jacob McNeil, Henrietta Heng Li. BS, Carnegie Inst. Tech., 1961, MS, 1964, PhD, 1965; Dr. honoris causa, Eidgenössische Technische Hochshule, Zürich, Switzerland, 1986, Cath. U. Louvain, Belgium, 1996. Mem. faculty Carnegie Mellon U., 1965-73, U. Md., 1965; vis. advisor Philips-Electrologica, Apeldoorn, Netherlands, 1969-70; prof. Technische Hochschule Darmstadt, W. Ger., 1973-76; prof. computer sci. U. N.C., Chapel Hill, 1976-82; vis. scientist IBM, Bethesda, Md., 1980-82; computer scientist Naval Rsch. Lab., Washington, 1972-86; prof. computer sci. U. Victoria, B.C., Can., 1982-86; mem. faculty McMaster U., Hamilton, Ont., Can., 1991—; cons. Bell Labs., TRW, Inc., DEC, BNR. Recipient Norbert Wiener award, 1987. Fellow Royal Soc. Can., Assn. Computing Machinery; mem. IEEE (sr.), Gesellschaft fur Informatik. Home: 551 Old Dundas Rd, Ancaster, ON Canada L9G 3J3 Office: McMaster U Comm Rsch Lab Dept Elec Computer Engring, 1280 Main St W, Hamilton, ON Canada L8S 4K1 *Only the truth allows us to be free. Science is a search for the truth.*

PARNELL, CHARLES L., speechwriter; b. Myrtis, La., Feb. 13, 1938; s. Forrest L. and Dorothy D. (Jones) P. BA, Rice U., 1960; M Bus. and Pub. Adminstrn., Southeastern U., 1977. Commd. ens. USN, 1960, advanced through grades to comdr., 1975, ret., 1987; speechwriter Mead Data Cen., Dayton, Ohio, 1987-89, Nationwide Ins. Co., Columbus, Ohio, 1989-90; exec. speechwriter Miller Brewing Co., Milw., 1990-96; speech writer Milw., 1996—. Contbr. articles to profl. pubs. Mem. U.S. Naval Inst., Ret. Officers Assn., World Future Soc. Avocations: reading, writing, travel.

PARNELL, FRANCIS WILLIAM, JR., physician; b. Woonsocket, R.I., May 22, 1940; s. Francis W. and Dorothy V. (Lalor) P.; m. Diana DeAngelis, Feb. 27, 1965; children: Cheryl Lynn, John Francis, Kathleen Diana, Alison Anne, Thomas William. Student, Coll. Holy Cross, 1957-58; AB, Clark U., 1961; MD, Georgetown U., 1965. Diplomate: Nat. Bd. Med. Examiners, Am. Bd. Otolaryngology. Intern Univ. Hosps., Madison, Wis., 1965-66; resident in gen. surgery Univ. Hosps., Madison, 1966-67, otolaryngology, 1967-70; pvt. practice medicine specializing in otolaryngology San Rafael, Calif., 1972-75, Greenbrae, Calif., 1972-75, 78—; chmn., pres., CEO Parnell Pharms., Larkspur, Calif., 1982—; cons. corp. med. affairs, 1978-82; corp. med. dir. Becton, Dickinson & Co., Rutherford, N.J., 1976-78; clin. instr. U. Calif. at San Francisco, 1972-75, asst. clin. prof., 1975-76; Alt. del., U.S. Del. 27th World Health Assembly WHO, Geneva, 1974. Contbr. articles to profl. jours. Candidate Calif. State Assembly, 1988; bd. dirs. Marin Coalition, 1980-96, chmn., 1986-87; trustee Ross (Calif.) Sch. Dist., 1981-89; mem. governing bd. Marin Cmty. Coll. Dist., 1995—. Maj. M.C. AUS, 1970-72, lt. col. M.C., USAR, 1985-94. Fellow ACS (gov. 1988-94), Am. Acad. Otolaryngology. Home: PO Box 998 Ross CA 94957-0998 Office: 1100 S Eliseo Dr Greenbrae CA 94904-2017

PARNELL, THOMAS ALFRED, physicist; b. Lumberton, N.C., Nov. 24, 1931; s. Johnathan Alfred and Lula Beale (Lashley) P.; m. Elizabeth G. Brite, June 4, 1955; children: Marc Thomas, Gina Ann. B.S. in Physics, U. N.C., 1954, M.S. in Physics, 1962, Ph.D. in Physics, 1965. Rsch. adj., dept. physics U. N.C., Chapel Hill, 1962-65; ops. analyst U.S. Air Force Europe, Wiesbaden, W. Ger., 1965-66; asst. prof. physics Marshall U., Huntington, W.Va., 1966-67; physicist NASA-Marshall Space Flight Center, Huntsville, Ala., 1967—; chief astrophysics br. NASA-Marshall Space Flight Center, 1969—; mem. grad. faculty U. Ala., Huntsville. Mem. editorial bd. Radiation Measurements; contbr. articles to profl. jours. Served to capt. USNR, 1975-91. Recipient Exceptional Sci. Achievement medal, Outstanding Leadership medal NASA, U.S. Antartica Svc. medal. Mem. Am. Phys. Soc., Sigma Xi. Club: Monte Sano (Huntsville). Home: 907 Corinth Cir SE Huntsville AL 35801-2064 Office: Marshall Space Flight Ctr ES 84 Huntsville AL 35812

PARODE, ANN, lawyer; b. L.A., Mar. 3, 1947; d. Lowell Carr and Sabine (Phelps) P. BA, Pomona Coll., 1968; JD, UCLA, 1971. Bar: Calif. 1972, U.S. Dist. Ct. (so. dist.) Calif. 1972, U.S. Ct. Appeals (9th cir.) 1975. Assoc. Luce, Forward et al, San Diego, 1971-75; gen. counsel, exec. v.p., sec. San Diego Trust & Savings, 1975-94; judge pro tem San Diego Mcpl. Ct., 1978-84; campus counsel U. Calif., San Diego, 1997—. Bd. dirs. San Diego Cmty. Found., 1989—, chmn., 1994-96; bd. dirs. The Burnham Inst., 1995—. Mem. Calif. Bar Assn. (corp. law com. 1980-83, client trust fund commn. 1986-90, chmn. 1989-90), San Diego County Bar Found. (founder, bd. dirs., pres. 1980-83), San Diego Bar Assn. (bd. dirs. 1977-81, v.p. 1977-78, 80-81, treas. 1979-80), Law Libr. Justice Found. (pres. 1994).

PARR, CAROLYN MILLER, federal court judge; b. Palatka, Fla., Apr. 17, 1937; d. Arthur Charles and Audrey Ellen (Dunklin) Miller; m. Jerry Studstill Parr, Oct. 12, 1959; children: Kimberly Parr Trapasso, Jennifer Parr Turek, Patricia Audrey. BA, Stetson U., 1959; MA, Vanderbilt U., 1960; JD, Georgetown U., 1977; LLD (hon.), Stetson U., 1986. Bar: Md. 1977, U.S. Tax Ct. 1977, D.C. 1979, U.S. Supreme Ct. 1983. Gen. trial atty. IRS, Washington, 1977-81, sr. trial atty. office of chief counsel, 1982; spl. counsel to asst. atty. gen. tax divsn. U.S. Dept. Justice, Washington, 1982-85; judge U.S. Tax Ct., Washington, 1985—. Nat. Def. fellow Vanderbilt U., 1959-60; fellow Georgetown U., 1975-76; recipient Spl. Achievement award U.S. Treasury, 1979. Mem. ABA, Md. Bar Assn., Nat. Assn. Women Judges, D.C. Bar Assn., Am. Judges Assn., Exec. Women in Govt. Office: US Tax Ct 400 2nd St NW Washington DC 20217-0001

PARR, GRANT VAN SICLEN, surgeon; b. N.Y.C., Dec. 30, 1942; s. Ferdinand Van Siclen and Helene H. P.; m. Helen Mushat Frye, July 1, 1967; children: Kathleen Gage, Helen Johnston. A.B. with honors, Wesleyan U., 1965; M.D., Cornell U., 1969. Diplomate: Am. Bd. Thoracic Surgery, Am. Bd. Surgery. Intern, resident U. Hosps. of Cleve., 1969-71; resident in surgery U. Ala. Hosps., Birmingham, 1971-74; chief resident in surgery U. Ala. Hosps., 1974-75, resident in cardiovascular and thoracic surgery, 1975-77; practice medicine specializing in thoracic surgery Hershey, Pa., 1978-82; mem. staff Presbyn.-U. Pa. Med. Ctr., Phila., 1982-88, chief div. Thoracic surgery, 1984-88, acting chmn. Dept. Surgery, 1988; chief cardiovascular surgery Presbyn.-U. Pa. Med. Ctr., 1984-88; asst. prof. cardiothoracic surgery M.S. Hershey Med. Center, Hershey, Pa., 1987-88; chief cardiovascular surgery Morristown (N.J.) Meml. Hosp., 1988-97, co-chmn. dept. cardiovascular scis., 1997—; asst. prof. Pa. State U., 1978-82; clin. assoc. prof. surgery U. Pa., 1982-89; assoc. prof. clin. surgery Columbia U., 1992—; chief cardiovascular surgery Overlook Hosp., 1988—, Atlantic Health Systems, 1988—. Contbr. articles on thoracic surgery to med. jours. Fellow Am. Coll. Cardiology, ACS, Am. Coll. Chest Physicians, Phila. Coll. Physicians; mem. AMA, Internat. Cardiovascular Soc., Assn. of Acad. Surgeons, Am. Assn. Thoracic Surgery, Phila. County Med. Soc., Soc. Thoracic Surgeons, Soc. Critical Care Medicine Pa., Thoracic Surg. Soc., John W. Kirklin Soc., Pa. Med. Assn., N.J. Soc. Thoracic Surgery, N.Y. Soc. Thoracic Surgery, Morris County Golf Club, NYU Club, Beverkill Trout Club. Office: Morristown Meml Hosp 100 Madison Ave Morristown NJ 07960-6013

PARR, HARRY EDWARD, JR., financial executive; b. Dayton, Ohio, Sept. 2, 1928; s. Harry Edward and Naomi Theresa (Oesbeck) P.; m. Michelle Brooks, Mar. 16, 1996; children from previous marriage: Constance, Cynthia, Claudia, Brian, Patrick. BSBA, U. Dayton, 1951. With Chrysler Corp., Detroit, 1953-66; v.p., controller Diebold, Inc., Canton, Ohio, 1966-78, v.p., treas., 1978-82, sr. v.p. fin., treas., 1982-91, also bd. dirs., ret., 1992. Bd. dirs. Jr. Achievement Stark County, Canton United Way; trustee Walsh Coll., Canton, Canton Cultural Ctr. for Arts; trustee, mem. devel. bd. Stark County; bd. dirs. Aultman Health Found. Served to 1st lt. U.S. Army, 1951-53. Mem. Fin. Execs. Inst., Nat. Assn. Accts., Planning Execs. Inst., Canton C. of C. (former trustee). Club: Brookside Country (Canton).

PARR, JAMES GORDON, writer; b. Peterborough, Eng., May 26, 1927; went to Can., 1953; s. Reuben Scotney and Edith Grace (Rollings) P.; children: Mark Anthony, Katharine Elizabeth, Daniel John; m. Carole Elizabeth Vaughan, Dec. 1975. BSc, U. Leeds, Eng., 1947; PhD, U. Liverpool, Eng., 1953; LLD (hon.), U. Windsor, 1984. Registered profl. engr., Ont. Lectr. U. Liverpool, 1948-53; research assoc., lectr. U. B.C., Vancouver, 1953-55; assoc. prof., then prof. U. Alta., Edmonton, 1955-64; dean applied sci. U. Windsor, Ont., Can., 1964-72; chmn. com. univ. affairs Govt. Ont., Toronto, 1972; dep. minister Ministry Colls. and Univs., Govt. Ont., 1973-79; chmn., chief exec. officer TVOnt., Toronto, 1979-85; dir. gen. Ont. Sci. Ctr., Don Mills, 1985-88; founding pres. Indsl. Research Inst., U. Windsor, 1967-72. Author: Man, Metals and Modern Magic, 1958, (with A. Hanson) An Introduction to Stainless Steel, 1965, (with A. Hanson) The Engineer's Guide to Steel, 1965, Any Other Business, 1977, Is There Anybody There? Collected Verse, 1979, Megafart, a novel, 1990, Essays, 1992. Recipient Centennial medal Can., 1967, Jubilee medal, 1977. Fellow Royal Soc. Can., Am. Soc. Materials Internat., Ryerson Polytech. Inst., Ont. Inst. for Studies in Edn. Home: 10 Governor's Rd, Toronto, ON Canada M4W 2G1

PARR, LLOYD BYRON, state official; b. Arvada, Colo., Oct. 27, 1931; s. Earle Ruly and Leva Corinne (Livengood) P.; m. Fransess Clyde Durham, Dec. 30, 1951; children: Russell Owen, Christopher Lee, Ryan Whitney. Diploma, Compton (Calif.) Jr. Coll., 1950; student, No. Mont. State U., 1964-65, U. Ark., Little Rock, 1969-70. Lic. civil engring. technician. Enlisted USN, 1950, aviation machinist mate, 1950-54; surveyor Denver Water Bd., 1955-56; enlisted USAF, 1957, advanced through grades to master sgt., 1971; site developer USAF, Korea, Okinawa, Turkey, Vietnam, 1957-73; ret. USAF, 1973; airport engr. State of Mo., Jefferson City, 1974-80, adminstr. aviation, 1981—. Sunday sch. tchr. Ch. of Christ, Eldon, Mo., 1973—. Decorated Bronze Star. Mem. Nat. Assn. State Aviation Ofcls. (bd. dirs. 1991-92, fin. com. 1988-93, treas. 1993-94, 2d v.p. 1994-95, 1st v.p. 1995-96, pres. 1996-97, chmn. bd. dirs. 1997), Am. Assn. State Hwy. and Transp. Ofcls. (aviation com. 1986-95). Office: Mo Dept Transp Capital and Jefferson Sts PO Box 270 Jefferson City MO 65102-0270 *Few of we mortals have the opportunity to contribute something truly unique to our world. Most of us can either add a few bricks to the wall of life or, if we choose to, we can tear down what others have built. I can only hope that the few bricks I add during my life will lend strength and color to the wall.*

PARR, ROBERT GHORMLEY, chemistry educator; b. Chgo., Sept. 22, 1921; s. Leland Wilbur and Grace (Ghormley) P.; m. Jane Bolstad, May 28, 1944; children: Steven Robert, Jeanne Karen, Carol Jane. AB magna cum laude with high honors in Chemistry, Brown U., 1942; PhD in Phys. Chemistry, U. Minn., 1947; D (hon.), U. Leuven, 1986, Jagiellonian U., 1996. Asst. prof. chemistry U. Minn., 1947-48; mem. faculty Carnegie Inst. Tech., 1948-62, prof. chemistry, 1957-62; prof. chemistry Johns Hopkins U., 1962-74, chmn. dept., 1969-72; William R. Kenan, Jr. prof. theoretical chemistry U. N.C., Chapel Hill, 1974-90, Wassily Hoeffding prof. chem. physics, 1990—; vis. prof. chemistry, mem. Ctr. Advanced Study, U. Ill., 1962; disting. vis. prof. SUNY, Buffalo, Pa. State U., 1967; vis. prof. Japan Soc. Promotion Sci., 1968, 79, U. Haifa, 1977, Free U., Berlin, 1977, Duke U., 1996-97; Firth prof. U. Sheffield, 1976; Coochbehar prof. Indian Assn. Cultivation of Sci., 1990; Sandoval Vallarta prof. UAM-Iztapalapa, 1992; chmn. com. postdoctoral fellowships in chemistry NAS-NRC, 1961-63; chmn. panel theoretical chemistry Westheimer com. survey chemistry NAS, 1964; mem. coun. Gordon Rsch. Conf., 1974-76; mem. Commn. on Human Resources, NRC, 1979-82; mem. coun. Inst. for Molecular Sci., Okazaki, Japan, 1986-88; bd. trustees Inst. for Fundamental Chemistry, Kyoto, Japan, 1988—. Author: Quantum Theory of Molecular Electronic Structure, 1963, Density-Functional Theory of Atoms and Molecules, 1989, also numerous articles.; Asso. editor: Jour. Chem. Physics, 1956-58, Chem. Revs, 1961-63, Jour. Phys. Chemistry, 1963-67, 77-79, Am. Chem. Soc. Monographs, 1966-71, Theoretica Chimica Acta, 1966-69, 92-96; bd. editors: Jour. Am. Chem. Soc, 1969-77; adv. editorial bd.: Internat. Jour. Quantum Chemistry, 1967—, Chem. Physics Letters, 1967-79. Recipient Outstanding Achievement award U. Minn., 1968, N.C. Disting. Chemist award, 1982; fellow U. Chgo., 1949; research asso., 1957; Fulbright scholar U. Cambridge, Eng., 1953-54; Guggenheim fellow, 1953-54; NSF sr. postdoctoral fellow U. Oxford (Eng.) and Commonwealth Sci. and Indsl. Research Orgn., Melbourne, Australia, 1967-68; Sloan fellow, 1956-60. Fellow AAAS, Am. Phys. Soc. (chmn. divsn. chem. physics 1963-64); mem. NAS, AAUP, Am. Chem. Soc. (chmn. divsn. phys. chemistry 1978, Irving Langmuir award in chem. physics 1994), Am. Acad. Arts and Sci., Indian Nat. Sci. Acad., Internat. Acad. Quantum Molecular Sci. (pres. 1991-97), Phi Beta Kappa, Sigma Xi, Phi Lambda Upsilon, Pi Mu Epsilon. Home: 701 Kenmore Rd Chapel Hill NC 27514-2019 Office: U NC Dept Chemistry Chapel Hill NC 27599-3290

PARR, SANDRA HARDY, government affairs administrator; b. Atlanta, Dec. 30, 1952; d. Raymond William Hardy and Ruth (Berry) Yancey; m. James Parr Jr., Apr. 14, 1978; 1 child, James Andrew Parr III. Student, Lurleen B. Wallace Jr. Coll., 1972. Sales adminstr. Etec Corp., Hayward, Calif., 1976-77; adminstrv. sec. Cities Svc. Co., Atlanta, 1977-82; sales and planning coord. Intermodal Transp. Co., Norcross, Ga., 1982-83; freelance temp. sec. Atlanta met. area, 1983-86; freelance word processor, cons. Amoco Container Co., Norcross, 1986-88; psychiat. rev. asst. Am. Psychiat. Assn., Atlanta, 1988-89; support svcs. mgr. Parkside Health Mgmt. Corp., Atlanta, 1989-90; med. staff coord. C.P.C. Parkwood Hosp., Atlanta, 1991—; health svcs. asst. Ciba Vision Corp., 1991-93. Del. internat. nursing conf., citizen amb. program to People's Republic China, Seattle Washington People to People, Beijing, 1989; part-time exercise instr. Mem. NAFE. Avocations: creative writing, reading, exercising, calenetics instructing, ceramics. Home: 1301 Eugenia Ter Lawrenceville GA 30245-7437 Office: CPC Parkwood Hosp 1999 Cliff Valley Way NE Atlanta GA 30329-2420 Address: Philip Morris Mgmt Corp Govt Affairs 3 Ravinia Dr Ste 1560 Atlanta GA 30346-2118

PARRA, PAMELA ANN, physician, educator; b. New Orleans, La., Nov. 24, 1949; d. Morris Louis and Mary Elizabeth (Monaghan) P.; m. Garrett John Beadle, May 7, 1983; children: Erin Elizabeth, Ryan Garrett. BS, Loyola U., 1971; MD, Tulane U., 1975. Diplomate Am. Bd. Emergency Medicine. Emergency physician Lakewood Hosp., Morgan City, La., 1975-76, 81-86; resident Charity Hosp., New Orleans, 1976-79, staff physician, 1979-81; staff physician Baton Rouge (La.) Gen. Med. Ctr., 1986—; asst. prof. medicine La. State U., Med. Sch., New Orleans, 1989—. Fellow Am. Coll. Emergency Physicians (sec.-treas. La. chpt. 1993—). Mem. La. State Med. Soc. Republican. Roman Catholic. Avocation: photography. Home: 1020 Pastureview Dr Baton Rouge LA 70810-4725 Office: Baton Rouge Gen Med Ctr 3600 Florida Blvd Baton Rouge LA 70806-3842

PARRAGUIRRE, RONALD DAVID, judge; b. Reno, July 8, 1959; s. Paul Charles and Iris Mae (Bleick) P. BBA, San Diego State U., 1982; JD, U. San Diego, 1985. Bar: Pa. 1986, Nev. 1986, D.C. 1987. Legis. asst. U.S. Senator Paul Laxalt, Washington, 1985-86; counsel subcom. on criminal law, judiciary com. U.S. Senate, Washington, 1986-87; lawyer Parraguirre & Parraguirre, Las Vegas, Nev., 1987-91; mcpl. ct. judge Dept. 6 City of Las Vegas, 1991—. Mem. ABA, ATLA, Am. Judges Assn., Nev. Judges Assn., Clark County Bar Assn. (exec. bd. dirs.). Republican. Lutheran. Avocations: skiing, racquetball, hunting, fishing. Office: Las Vegas Mcpl Ct 400 Stewart Ave Las Vegas NV 89101-2927

PARRAMORE, BARBARA MITCHELL, education educator; b. Guilford County, N.C., Aug. 29, 1932; d. Samuel Spencer and Nellie Gray (Glosson) Mitchell; m. Lyman Griffis Worthington, Dec. 23, 1956 (div. 1961); m. Thomas Custis Parramore, Jan. 22, 1966; children: Lisa Gray, Lynn Stuart. AB, U. N.C., Greensboro, 1954; MEd, N.C. State U., 1959; EdD, Duke U., 1968. Counselor, thcr. Raleigh City Schs., 1954-59, sch. prin., 1959-65; prof. dept. of curriculum and instrn. N.C. State U., 1970-96, prof. emeritus, 1996—; acad. specialist Office Internat. Edn., U.S. Info. Svcs., sec. sch. initative program, The Philippines, 1987. Author: The People of North Carolina, 1972, 3rd edit. 1983. Japan Inst. Social and Econ. Affairs fellow, 1980; N.C. AAUW award for juvenile lit., 1973, Holladay medal for excellence N.C. State U., 1994. Mem. ASCD, N.C. ASCD (pres. 1994-96), N.C. Coun. for Social Studies (pres. 1985-87), Assn. Tchr. Educators, Delta Kappa Gamma, Kappa Delta Pi. Home: 5012 Tanglewood Dr Raleigh NC 27612-3135

PARRAVANO, AMELIA ELIZABETH (AMY BETH), recording industry executive; b. Providence, Apr. 5, 1951; d. Olindo Luigi and Violet Carmella (Russo) Izzo; m. Grimaldo Antonio Parravano, July 4, 1979; children: Peter Paul, Paula Elizabeth. AA, Roger Williams Coll., 1972; postgrad., R.I. Coll., 1972-73. Owner, operator Aura Arts & Crafts, Cranston, R.I., 1985-88; pres. Peridot and Caprice Rec. Artist, Cranston, 1990—; freelance artist Artist Letters League, Cranston, 1992—; singer, songwriter, musician. Active PTA, Cranston, 1991-92; artist mem. R.I. State Coun. on Arts, Providence, 1986-92; active Pawtucket (R.I.) Arts Coun., 1986-92. Mem. Am. Soc. Composers, Authors and Pubs., Songwriters Guild Am., Gospel Music Assn., County Music Assn., Country Music Showcase Internat., Broadcast Music Inc. (pub.), Retirement Entertainment Orgn., Internat. Fan Club Assn., Greater So. Country Music Assn. (state rep. for R.I.). Avocations: golf, bicycling, entertaining at children's parties, painting, poetry. Home: 17 Woodbine St Cranston RI 02910-1916

PARREIRA, CARLOS ALBERTO, soccer coach; b. Rio de Janeiro, Mar. 25, 1943; m. Leila Parreira; children: Vanessa, Danielle. Diploma in phys. edn., Fed. U., Rio de Janeiro, 1966. Coach Novo Mexico, Brazil, 1965, Sao Cristovao, Brazil, 1966-67, Nat. Team, Ghana, 1967, Kotoko, Ghana, 1968; phys. preparation mgr. Vasco, Brazil, 1969, Flumenise and Brazil's Nat. Team, 1970-74; coach Flumenise, 1974, 84, coach, phys. preparation mgr., 1975; coach Nat. Team, Kuwait, 1976-83, Brazil, 1983, 91-94, United Arab Emirates, 1984-88, 90, Saudi Arabia, 1988-89; coach Bragantino, Brazil, 1991, Valencia, Spain, 1994-95, Fenerbahce, Turkey, 1995-96, Sao Paulo, Brazil, 1996, N.Y./N.J. Metro Stars, Secaucus, N.J., 1996—. Avocations: painting, rug collecting. Office: Metro Stars 1 Harmon Plz 8th Fl Secaucus NJ 07094

PARREIRA, HELIO CORREA, physical chemist; b. Rio de Janeiro, Brazil, July 12, 1926, came to U.S., 1960; s. Francisco Correa and Maria Faria Parreira; m. Dulcinea M. Moreira, Jan. 2, 1953; children: Rogerio M., Regina M. BS in Chemistry, U. Brazil, Rio de Janeiro, 1949, tchrs. diploma, 1950; PhD, U. Cambridge, 1958. Asst. prof. U. Rio de Janeiro, 1950-52; phys. chemist Brazilian Atomic Commn., 1958-67; rsch. assoc. Columbia U., N.Y.C., 1960-62, dir. instrn. in chemistry Joint Program for Tech. Edn. N.S.F., 1960-64, asst. prof., 1963-65; group leader and prin. sci. Inmont Corp., Clifton, N.J., 1965-69; asst. dir. rsch. Johnson & Johnson, Brazil, 1969-70, exec. dir. rsch., mem. exec. com., 1970-72, sr. rsch. assoc., New Brunswick, N.J., 1972-84, sr. scientist, 1984-90; mem. bd. examiners Med. Sch. U. Brazil, 1953, 55, Faculdade Fluminense de Medicina, Niteroi R.J., Brazil, 1953. Contbr. articles to profl. jours.; contbg. editor Chemistry A to Z, 1964. Brit. Coun. scholar U. Cambridge , 1954; Oliver Gatty Scholar U. Cambridge, 1956-58. Mem. Am. Chem. Soc., Math. Assn. Am., Sigma Xi. Achievements include in surface and colloid science; transcutaneous drug delivery.

PARRETT, SHERMAN O., lawyer; b. Cin., Jan. 8, 1943; s. Earl and Ruby (Angel) P.; m. Rosalind K. Brooks, Sept. 21, 1985; children: Laura, Samantha. BSEE, U. Cin., 1965; JD with honors, George Washington U., 1969. Bar: Calif. 1970, D.C. 1975, Ariz. 1992. Assoc. Flehr, Hohbach et al., San Francisco, 1970-73; ptnr. Cushman, Darby & Cushman, Washington, 1973-86, Irell & Manella, L.A., 1986-91, Streich Lang, Phoenix, 1991-94, Snell & Wilmer, Phoenix, 1994—. Office: Snell & Wilmer One Arizonia Ctr Phoenix AZ 85004-0001

PARRIGIN, ELIZABETH ELLINGTON, lawyer; b. Colon, Panama, May 23, 1932; d. Jesse Cox and Elizabeth (Roark) Ellington; m. Perry G. Parrigin, Oct. 8, 1975. BA, Agnes Scott Coll., 1954; JD, U. Va., 1959. Bar: Tex. 1959, Mo. 1980. Atty. San Antonio, 1960-69; law libr. U. Mo., Columbia, 1969-77, rsch. assoc., 1977-82; atty. pvt. practice, Columbia, 1982—. Elder, clk. of session First Presbyn. Ch., Columbia; mem. permanent jud. commn. Presbyn. Ch. U.S., 1977-83, mem. advisory com. on constitution, 1983-90. Mem. ABA, Mo. Bar Assn. (chmn. sub-com. revision of Mo. trsut law 1988-92). Democrat. Presbyterian. Avocations: music, gardening, reading. Home: 400 Conley Ave Columbia MO 65201-4219 Office: 224 N 8th St Columbia MO 65201-4844

PARRINO, CHERYL LYNN, state agency administrator; b. Wisconsin Rapids, Wis., Jan. 21, 1954; m. Jack J. Parrino, Sept. 1, 1990; 1 child, George. BBA in Acctg., U. Wis., 1976. Auditor Pub. Svc. Commn. Wis., Madison, 1976-82, dir. utility audits, 1982-86, exec. asst. to chmn., 1986-91, commr., 1991—, chmn., 1992—; mem. adv. bd. Bellcore, 1991; vice chmn. bd. dirs. Wis. Ctr. Demand Side Rsch., Madison, 1991-92; chmn. bd. dirs. Wis. Pub. Utility Inst., Madison, 1992-95. Mem. Gov.'s Task Force Gross Receipts Tax, Madison, 1991-92, Gov.'s Task Force Alternative Fuels, Madison, 1992—, Gov.'s Task Force Clean Air, Madison, 1992—, Gov.'s Task Force Telecom., Madison, 1993-94. Mem. Nat. Assn. Pub. Utility Commrs. (exec. com. 1991, chmn. comm. com. 1992—, pres. 1995-96, pres. Gt. Lakes conf. 1996). Republican. Lutheran. Avocations: snow skiing, tennis, traveling. Office: Pub Svc Commn Wis PO Box 7854 Madison WI 53707-7854

PARRIOTT, JAMES DEFORIS, retired oil company executive, consultant; b. Moundsville, W. Va., Aug. 21, 1923; s. James D. and Bessie (Sadler) P.; m. Marynette Sonneland, Aug. 3, 1946; children—James Deforis III, Sara Graham. Student, Ohio Wesleyan U., 1941-43; LL.B., U. Colo., 1949. Bar: Colo. bar 1949, practice in Denver 1949-53. Asst. city atty. Denver, 1950-51; asst. atty. gen. Colo., 1952-53; chief counsel Bur. Land Mgmt., Dept. Interior, 1953, assoc. solicitor lands and minerals, 1954-56; atty. Ohio Oil Co., Washington, 1956-60, Findlay, Ohio, 1960-62; mgr. employee relations Marathon Oil Co., 1962-69, dir. pub. affairs, 1969-74, dir. pub. and govt. affairs, 1974-85; sr. cons. Hill and Knowton, Inc., Los Angeles. Pilot, USAAF, 1943-46. Mem. ABA, Fed. Bar Assn., Pacific Corinthian Yacht Club, Phi Alpha Delta, Phi Gamma Delta. Epsicopalian. Home: 1802 Emerald Isle Way Oxnard CA 93035

PARRIS, DONNA SANDS, secondary school educator; b. Winter Haven, Fla., July 30, 1951; d. Maxwell Lloyd and Thelma Desmond (Darby) Sands; 1 child, Brad; m. Jack Andy Parris, June 5, 1992; 1 stepchild, Andy. BS in Edn., Western Carolina U., 1973. Cert. tchr., N.C. Mgr. Alfredo's Restaurant, Maggie, N.C., 1981-85; tchr. health, phys. edn. Haywood County Schs., Waynesville, N.C., 1973-81, 89—, tchr. dropout prevention, 1985-88, mentor, trainer, 1989—, mem. staff devel. cadre, 1991—; health, phys. edn. and 7-8 lang. arts tchr. Ctrl. Haywood H.S., 1994—. Co-author: (textbook) Making Life Choices; editor ednl. handbooks and teaching resources. Named N.C. Health Tchr. Yr., N.C. Assn. Health Edn., 1992. Mem. AAHPERD, ASCD, N.C. Assn. Educators (officer various coms. including polit. action com. for edn. 1974-81), Waynesville Bus. and Profl. Women. Democrat. Methodist. Avocations: camping, water sports, reading, textile painting, horseback riding. Office: Haywood Ctrl HS PO Box 249 Clyde NC 28721-0249

PARRIS, MARK, federal agency official; b. Mpls.; m. Joan Elizabeth Gardner; 2 children. BS magna cum laude, Georgetown U., 1974. With Fgn. Svc., 1972-77; polit. counselor Fgn. Svc., Moscow, 1982-85, dir. Office Soviet Union Affairs, 1985-88; dep. chief mission U.S. Embassy, Tel Aviv, 1989-92; spl. asst. pres., sr. dir. Nat. Security Coun., Washington, 1995—. Mem. policy bd. Una Chapman Cox Found., U.S.-Israel Edn. Found. Phi Beta Kappa. Office: Nat Security Council Near East & S Asian Affairs 1600 Pennsylvania Ave NW Washington DC 20500-0005*

PARRIS, NINA GUMPERT, curator, writer, researcher, photographer; b. Berlin, Ger., Sept. 11, 1927; came to U.S., 1937, naturalized, 1944; d. Martin and Charlotte (Blaschko) Gumpert; m. Arthur Parris, Feb. 13, 1949 (div. 1974); children: Carl Joseph, Thomas Martin. BA, Bryn Mawr Coll., 1968; MA, U. Pa., 1969, PhD, 1979. Teaching fellow U. Mich., Ann Arbor, 1969-70; lectr. Phila. Coll. Art, 1970-71; research asst. Phila. Mus. Art, 1970-71; curator, lectr. U. Vt. Robert Hall Fleming Mus., Burlington, 1971-79; chief curator Columbia Mus., S.C., 1979-89; resident faculty visual arts Vt. Coll. Norwich Univ., 1991—; visual arts chair Burlington Coll., 1996—. Author: Prints, Paintings and Drawings in Collection of Robert Hall Fleming Mus., 1979, (exhibition catalogue) Through a Master Printer, 1985, The South Carolina Collection of the Columbia Museum, 1987; columnist State newspaper, Columbia, 1984-88; one person show at Living Learning Ctr., U. Vt., 1994, Meteor Gallery, Columbia, S.C., 1994, St. Michael's Coll. McArthur Arts Ctr., Colburn Gallery, U. Vt. Bd. dirs. Photography Cooperative, Montpelier, Vt., 1977-79, Chittenden Arts Coun., Burlington, Vt., 1976-78. Woodrow Wilson fellow, 1968, Univ. fellow Ford Found., 1968-72; grantee NEA, NEH, S.C. Com. Humanities, Vt. Coun. Arts. Mem. Am. Assn. Museums (pres. curator's com. 1985-87, v.p. 1983-85).

PARRIS, ROBERT, composer; b. Phila., May 21, 1924; s. Louis and Rae (Oettinger) P. B.S. in Music Edn, U. Pa., 1945, M.S., 1946; B.S., Juilliard Sch. Music, 1948; student, Ecole Normale de Musique, Paris, Frnace, 1952-53. Mem. faculty Wash. State Coll., 1948-49, Juilliard Summer Sch., 1948; pvt. tchr., 1949-63; prof. music George Washington U., 1963—; mem. Broadcast Music, Inc. Composer: Concerto for Five Kettledrums and Orchestra, 1955, Fantasy and Fugue for Solo Cello; Lamentations and Praises, 1966, Sonata for Solo Violin, 1964, The Messengers for Orchestra, 1974; rec. artist: (albums) Concerto for Trombone and Orchestral Book of Imaginary Beings; Symphonic variations commd. by Nat. Endowment for Arts, Rostropovich and Nat. Symphony Orch., 1987, Parabolae Salomonis, 1995; solo recitals on harpsichord and piano, also in chamber music. Home: 3307 Cummings Ln Bethesda MD 20815-3239 Office: George Washington U Acad Ctr 21st And I St NW Washington DC 20052

PARRIS, THOMAS GODFREY, JR., medical facility administrator; b. Phila., Jan. 30, 1937; married. BS, Pa. State U., 1958; M Health Care Adminstrn., U. Pitts., 1965. Adminstrv. resident Homestead (Pa.) Hosp., 1964-65; exec. assoc. to v.p. Assocs. Hosp. Svcs. of N.Y., N.Y.C., 1965-67; asst. adminstr. Hackensack (N.J.) Med. Ctr., 1967-68; assoc. exec. dir. Met. Hosp. Ctr., N.Y.C., 1968-73; adminstr., CEO Women and Infants Hosp. of R.I., Providence, 1973-76, exec. v.p., CEO, 1976-79, pres., CEO, 1979—. Contbr. articles to prof. publs. Active various cmty. orgns. Fellow Am. Coll. Health Care Execs. (regent R.I. 1984-90); mem. Am. Hosp. Assn. (mem. com., del., trustee 1985-88), R.I. Hosp. Assn. (bd. dirs. 1973—, exec. com. 1974-79, chair 1978-79, del. 1979-80). Office: Women & Infants Hosp RI 45 Willard Ave Providence RI 02905-3218*

PARRISH, ALMA ELLIS, elementary school educator; b. Peoria, Ill., Mar. 28, 1929; d. William Edward and Marie (Allton) Ellis; m. Clyde R. Parrish, Jr., Nov. 20, 1949; children: Clyde R. III, Charles, Donald, Royce, Christopher. BS, Bradley U., Peoria. Cert. elem. tchr., S.C., Ill. Tchr. Community Consol. Sch. Dist. 59, Elk Grove Village, Ill., Sipp Sch. Dist., Peoria, Kershaw County Sch. Dist., Camden, S.C. Mem. DAR, NOW, ACLU, UUA, AARP, S.C. Ret. Edn. Assn., Tchrs. Coun. Dist. 59 (pres., com.), Kershaw County Edn. Assn. (sec., PACE com.), Ill. Ret. Tchr.'s Assn., S.I. Coun.

PARRISH, BENJAMIN EMMITT, II, insurance executive; b. Statesboro, Ga., Dec. 20, 1945; s. Benjamin E. and Ouida L. (Anderson) P.; m. Sandra Dianne Bragg, July 26, 1964; children: Michelle, Benjamin III, Sonya. Student, Atlanta Art Inst., 1963-65. Cert. ins. agt., Ga., Fla., S.C., N.C., Ala., Va. Art dir. Macy's, Atlanta, 1965-66; sales mgr. Clearbrook Realty, Atlanta, 1966-72; pres., comml. pilot, flight instr. Parrish Enterprises, Statesboro, 1972-77; v.p. Design Concepts, Statesboro, 1977-85; cons., pres. Parrish Assocs., Statesboro, 1985-87; ind. ins. agy. Statesboro, Ga., 1987—; dist. coord. Am. Family Life Assurance Corp., Ga., 1987-92, regional coord., 1993—. Author: Captive Management, 1972; writer/dir. (video) Tax Savings 125, 1991. Bd. dirs. Statesboro-Bulloch County C. of C., Chamber Connection, 1992-93; chmn. Statesboro Main Street Action Commn., 1993-94. Featured in Life & Health Ins. Sales mag., Apr. 1992. Republican. Baptist. Avocations: travel, painting, photography, golf. Home: 5633 Ga Hwy 46 Statesboro GA 30458-8515 Office: Parrish and Assocs 18 S Main St Statesboro GA 30458-5245

PARRISH, CARMELITA, secondary school educator; b. Varina, N.C., Mar. 19, 1934; d. James Robert and Nita Mae (Webb) Beal; m. John J. Parrish, July 24, 1953 (dec.); children: Deborah Joy Parrish White, Toni Lynne Parrish Altenburg. AA, Mid. Ga. Coll., 1979; BS in Edn. Ga. So. U., 1981; MEd, Valdosta State U., 1988, U. Ga., 1993. Secondary tchr. English, graphic arts, Spanish Ware County Bd. Edn., Waycross, Ga., 1981-91; tchr. Spanish, English Telfair County Bd. Edn., McRae, Ga., 1991-92, Pickens County H.S., Jasper, Ga., 1992—; co-advisor Spanish Club; advisor yearbook; tchr. Spanish, journalism. Former leader Girl Scouts U.S., Spain; tchr. area Sunday sch.; band chaperone; tour leader student travel in Europe, 1985—. Recipient Star Tchr. award, Waycross-Ware County C. of C., 1987. Mem. ASCD, NEA, Nat. Coun. Tchrs. of English, Ga. Assn. Educators (local assoc. pres., legislator contact team, Ga. Assn. Educators-Polit. Action Com.), So. Assn. Colls. and Schs. (mem. evaluation com.), Phi Kappa Phi. Home: 124 Navaho Trl Jasper GA 30143-1207 Office: 339 W Church St Jasper GA 30143-1401

PARRISH, DAVID WALKER, JR., legal publishing company executive; b. Bristol, Tenn., Feb. 8, 1923. BA, Emory & Henry Coll., 1948, LLD, 1978; BS, U.S. Merchant Marine Acad., 1950; LLB, U. Va., 1951. Pres. The Michie Co., Charlottesville, Va., 1969-89, vice chmn., 1989-96; pub. cons., 1996—. Home: 114 Falcon Dr Charlottesville VA 22901-2013 Office: 300 Preston Ave Ste 103 Charlottesville VA 22902-5044

PARRISH, EDGAR LEE, financial services executive; b. Washington, Apr. 11, 1948; s. Frank Jennings Parrish and Lorene (Lomax) Parrish.; m. Katherine Ellen MacLachlan, Sept. 12, 1987; children: Robert Alexander Wilson, Stephen Edgar MacLachlan. BS in Commerce, U. Va., 1970. Sr. v.p. Wheat, First Securities, Inc., Washington, 1971-79; v.p. Merrill Lynch, Pierce, Fenner & Smith, Inc., Washington, 1979-82, Phila., 1982-85; sr. v.p., fin. cons. Shearson Lehman Bros., Inc., Phila., 1985-87; sr. v.p., fin. cons., mem. chmn.'s coun. Shearson Lehman Bros., Inc., Washington, 1987-93, mem. dirs. coun., 1986; sr. v.p. investments PaineWebber, Inc., Washington, 1993—; pres. HESCO Corp., Manassas, Va., 1989—, also bd. dirs.; mem. Pacesetter Coun., 1994-96. Capt. USAFR, 1970-76. Mem. U. Va. Club (Washington), U. Va. Alumni Assn., Investment Mgmt. Cons. Assn. Democrat. Episcopalian. Home: 4502 Wetherill Rd Bethesda MD 20816-1813 also: PO Box 282 Washington VA 22747 Office: PaineWebber Inc Franklin Sq 1300 I St NW Washington DC 20005-3314

PARRISH, EDWARD ALTON, JR., electrical and computer engineering educator, academic administrator; b. Newport News, Va., Jan. 7, 1937; s. Edward Alton and Molly Wren (Vaughan) P.; m. Shirley Maxine Johnson, Oct. 26, 1963; children: Troy Alton, Gregory Sinton. B.E.E., U. Va., 1964, M.E.E., 1966, D.Sc. in Elec. Engring., 1968. Registered profl. engr., Tenn., Va. Group leader Amerad Corp., Charlottesville, Va., 1961-64; asst. prof. elec. engring. U. Va., Charlottesville, 1968-71, assoc. prof. elec. engring.,

1971-77, prof. elec. engring., 1977-86, chmn. dept. elec. engring., 1978-86; dean, centennial prof. electrical engring. Vanderbilt U., Nashville, 1987-95; pres., prof. elec. and computer engring. Worcester Poly. U., 1995—; cons. U.S. Army, Charlottesville, Va., 1971-77, ORS, Inc., Princeton, N.J., 1973-74, Sperry Marine Systems, Charlottesville, 1975-76, Hajime Industries Ltd., Tokyo, 1978-84. Contbr. numerous articles to profl. jours. Served with USAF, 1954-58. Recipient numerous grants, contracts from industry, govt. agys. Fellow IEEE (bd. dirs. 1990-91, v.p. ednl. activities 1992-93, mem. accreditation bd. engring. tech. commn. 1989—, exec. com. 1991—, officer 1993—, chair elect 1994-95, chair 1995-96, chmn. 1996-97, editor-in-chief IEEE Computer 1995—), IEEE Computer Soc. (sec. 1977, v.p. 1978-81, pres. 1988), Pattern Recognition Soc., Sigma Xi, Eta Kappa Nu, Tau Beta Pi. Baptist. Avocations: music; woodworking. Office: Office of Pres 100 Institute Rd Worcester MA 01609-2247

PARRISH, FRANK JENNINGS, food company executive; b. Manassas, Va., Dec. 29, 1923; s. Edgar Goodloe and Alverda (Jennings) P.; m. Lorene Lomax, Feb. 11, 1944 (div. Apr. 1984); children: Edgar Lee, Julia Lorene; m. Mary Jane Biser, Aug. 25, 1984. Student, Va. Poly. Inst., 1942-43; grad., Indsl. Coll. Armed Forces, 1972. Pres. Manassas Frozen Foods, Inc., 1946—; pres., mgr. Certified Food Buyers Service, Inc., 1953—; pres. First Nat. Acceptance Co., 1966—; v.p. Manassas Ice & Fuel Co. Mem. bus. adminstrn. adv. com. No. Va. Community Coll.; chmn. bd. North Va. coun. Am. Heart Assn., 1987-88; mem. inaugural com., 1961, vice-chmn. inaugural parade com. Maj. USAAF, 1943-46, CBI; ret. brig. gen. comdr. 909th TAC Airlift Group 1969-73, USAF; moblzn. asst. DCS plans and ops. Hdqrs., 1973-79. Decorated Legion of Merit, Air medal. Mem. Nat. Inst. Locker and Freezer Provisioners Am. (past pres., Industry Leadership award 1968), Va. Frozen Foods Assn. (past pres., dir.), Hump Pilots Assn., Va. Assn. Meat Processors (pres. 1986-90), Kiwanis. Methodist (chmn. bd. trustees 1958-66). Home: 9107 Park Ave Manassas VA 20110-4350 Office: 9414 Main St Manassas VA 20110-5424 *Do unto others as you would have them do unto you.*

PARRISH, JAY See PIFER, ALAN

PARRISH, JEANNE ELAINE, former mayor, city councilwoman, former health services administrator, nurse; b. Great Falls, Mont., Sept. 7, 1921; d. Robert Edwin and Golda Mae (Jones) Cunningham; m. Charles Edward Parrish, Nov. 9, 1940; children: Charles Edwin, Carol Jean Parrish Wixted. BA, Calif. State Coll., San Diego, 1957, MA, 1959; MPH, U. Calif., Berkeley, 1962. RN, Calif. Staff nurse Rsch. Hosp., Kansas City, Mo., 1945, VNA, 1946; office nurse Rsch. Hosp., San Diego, 1947-50, pub. health nurse, 1950-52; supr. pediatrics San Diego County Hosp., 1952-54, clin. instr. pediatrics, 1955-58; dir. vocat. nurse program Grossmont, Calif., 1958-59; adminstrv. resident Cedars Sinai Hosp., L.A., 1962; exec. asst. nursing L.A. County Hosp., 1962-65; sr. asst. adminstr. Hollywood Presbyn. Hosp., L.A., 1965-75; med./legal analyst Farmers Ins., L.A., 1975-77; mental health cons. Calif. State Dept. of Mental Health, L.A., 1977-78, pub. health cons., 1978-84, med. area mgr., 1984-87; ret., 1987; elected city councilwoman City of Rancho Mirage, Calif., 1992-93; mayor City of Rancho Mirage, Calif., 1993-96; dir. pub. affairs Inst. Critical Care Medicine, Palm Springs, Calif., 1996—. Mem. Womens Club of Rancho Mirage, 1992; mem. Rep. Womens Fedn., Rancho Mirage, 1991; bd. dirs., past pres. Desert Coun. for Aging, Riverside, 1990; bd. dirs., sec. Retired Sr. Vol. Program, Palm Desert, 1992; bd. dirs. Coachella Valley ARC, 1990, Joslyn Sr. Ctr., Palm Desert Pres., Assistance League of Palm Springs Desert Area; mem. Riverside County Bd. Mental Health. Republican. Avocations: volunteering, consulting, teaching. Home: 65 Colgate Dr Rancho Mirage CA 92270-3703 Office: Inst Critical Care Medicine 1695 N Sunrise Way Palm Springs CA 92262-5309

PARRISH, JOHN BRETT, manufacturing executive; b. Clinton, Ill., Sept. 9, 1934; s. John Craig and Mary Lucille (Brett) P.; m. Lori Ann Burge, Mar. 15, 1990; children from previous marriage: Michael, Douglas, Lynn, Scott. AB in Econs., U. Ill., 1960. With GE Co., 1960-81; vice pres. fin. GE do Brazil S.A., Sao Paulo, 1976-79, v.p. and gen. mgr. consumer products, 1979-81; v.p. fin. services Burlington No. Inc., Seattle, 1981-82, v.p. and treas., 1982, sr. v.p. and chief fin. officer, 1982-83; chmn. and chief exec. officer Glacier Park Co. affiliate Burlington No., Inc., Seattle, 1983-85; exec. v.p. CEM Assocs., Inc., Bellevue, Wash., 1985-86; pres. Parrish, Inc., Seattle, 1986—. Woodrow Wilson fellow, 1960. Mem. Phi Beta Kappa. Home: 16742 45th Ave NE Seattle WA 98155-5616

PARRISH, MATTHEW DENWOOD, psychiatrist; b. Washington, Apr. 1, 1918; s. Forrest Denwood and Alice Lorena (Flynn) P.; m. Virginia John Bennet, Sept. 24, 1944 (div.); children: Denwood, John, Stephen; m. Marilyn Kay Arney, May 30, 1978; children: Megan, Maxwell. BA, U. Va., 1939; MD, George Washington U., 1950. Diplomate Am. Bd. Psychiatry. Intern Letterman Hosp., San Francisco, 1950-51; resident in psychiatry Walter Reed Hosp., Washingotn, 1951-54; commd. 2d lt. U.S. Army, 1941, advanced through grades to col., 1967, ret., 1971; chief tng. Ill. Dept. Mental Health, Chgo., 1972-74; supt. Singer Mental Health Ctr., Rockford, Ill., 1974-85, med. dir., 1985-93; child and adolescent psychiatrist, 1986-95, ret., 1996; clin. prof. psychiatry U. Ill., Chgo., 1972-76; clin. asst. prof. psychiatry Coll. Med., Rockford, 1976—. Editor in chief: U.S. Army Vietnam Medical Journal, 1967-68. Decorated Legion of Merit (2). Fellow Am. Psychiat. Assn. (life); mem. Soc. Med. Cons. in Armed Forces, Assn. Mil. Surgeons U.S. Avocations: writing, photography, painting, linguistics, electronics.

PARRISH, MAURICE DRUE, museum executive; b. Chgo., Mar. 5, 1950; s. Maurice and Ione Yvonne (Culumns) P.; m. Gail Marie Sims, Sept. 2, 1978; children: Theodore, Andrew, Brandon, Cara. BA in Arch., U. Pa., 1972; MArch, Yale U., 1975. City planner City of Chgo., 1975-81; architect John Hiltscher & Assocs., Chgo., 1981-83, Barnett, Jones & Smith, Chgo., 1983-84; zoning adminstr. City of Chgo., 1984-87, bldg. commr., 1987-89; dep. dir. Detroit Inst. of Arts, 1989—. Bd. dirs. Arts League of Mich., Detroit, 1994—; co-chmn. Mayor's Affordable Housing Task Force, Chgo., 1984-89; chmn. Chgo. Elec. Commn., 1988-89; mem. Chgo. Econ. devel. Commn., 1987-89; pres. St. Philip Neri Sch. Bd., Chgo., 1981-85, South Shore Commn., Chgo., 1982-84. King Chavez Parks fellow U. Mich., 1991, H.I. Feldman fellow Yale U., 1972; Franklin W. Gregory scholar Yale U., 1974, Nat. Achievement scholar U. Pa., 1968. Mem. Am. Assn. Mus., Am. Assn. Mus. Adminstrs., Constrn. Specifications Inst., Lambda Alpha. Avocations: golf, chess, reading, astronomy. Office: Detroit Inst of Arts 5200 Woodward Ave Detroit MI 48202-4008

PARRISH, OVERTON BURGIN, JR., pharmaceutical corporation executive; b. Cin., May 26, 1933; s. Overton Burgin and Geneva Opal (Shinn) P. B.S., Lawrence U., 1955; M.B.A., U. Chgo., 1959. With Pfizer Inc., 1959-74; salesman Pfizer Labs., Chgo., 1959-62; asst. mktg. product mgr. Pfizer Labs., N.Y.C., 1962-63; product mgr. Pfizer Labs., 1964-66, group product mgr., 1966-67, mktg. mgr., 1967-68, v.p. mktg., 1969-70, v.p., dir. ops., 1970-71; exec. v.p. domestic pharm. div. Pfizer Pharms., 1971-72; exec. v.p., dir. Pfizer Internat. Divsn., 1972-74; pres., chief operating officer G.D. Searle Internat., Skokie, Ill., 1974-75, pres., chief exec. officer, 1975-77; pres. Worldwide Pharm./Consumer Products Group, 1977-86; pres., chief exec. officer Phoenix Health Care, Chgo., 1987—; chmn., CEO, bd. dirs. Wis. Pharmiacal Co., Inc., 1990-96; co-chmn. Inhalon Pharms., 1991-95, also bd. dirs.; chmn. ViatiCare Ltd., 1993—, also bd. dirs.; chmn., CEO, bd. dirs. The Female Health Co., 1996—; bd. dirs. Microbyx Corp., 1997—. Author: The Future Pharmaceutical Marketing; International Drug Pricing, 1971. Trustee Mktg. Sci. Inst.; trustee Food and Drug Law Inst., 1979—, Lawrence U., 1983—. Served to 1st lt. USAF, 1955-57. Mem. Am. Mktg. Assn., Am. Mgmt. Assn., Beta Gamma Sigma, Phi Kappa Tau. Home: 505 N Lake Shore Dr Chicago IL 60611-3427 Office: Phoenix Health Care 919 N Michigan Ave Chicago IL 60611-1681

PARRISH, ROBERT ALTON, retired pediatric surgeon, educator; b. Augusta, Ga., Sept. 10, 1930; s. Robert Alton and Thelma Elizabeth (Roney) P.; children: Joyce Ann, Cynthia Ann. A.B., Mercer U., 1951; M.S., U. Ga., 1953; M.D., Med. Coll. Ga., 1956. Diplomate: Am. Bd. Surgery. Intern Bapt. Meml. Hosp., Memphis, 1956-57; resident in surgery U. Tenn., Memphis, 1957-62; gen. surgeon Med. Coll. Ga., Aususta, 1962-64; asst. prof. surgery Med. Coll. Ga., Augusta, 1964-67, assoc. prof., 1967-70, prof. pediatric surgery, chief pediatric surgery, 1970-93, prof. emeritus pediatric surgery, 1993—; cons. to hosps. Named Outstanding Tchr. of Yr. Med. Found. Ga., Med. Coll. Ga., 1966. Fellow ACS; mem. Am Assn. Surgery of Trauma, So. Surg. Assn., Am. Acad. Pediatrics, Alpha Omega Alpha, Phi Sigma, Alpha Epsilon Delta. Methodist. Home: 433 Scott Way Augusta GA 30909-9591

PARRISH, SHERRY DYE, elementary school educator; b. Birmingham, Ala., Oct. 18, 1957; d. Charles Max and Peggy Gail (Doss) Dye; m. James Wiley Parrish, June 13, 1987; 1 child, Taylor Austin Shaw. BS in Elem. Edn., Samford U., 1979; MS in Elem. Edn., U. Ala., 1995. Cert. tchr. Rank I, Class A., Ala. Tchr. Franklin Acad., Birmingham, Ala., 1979-83, Shades Cahaba Elem. Sch., Homewood, Ala., 1986-94, Trace Crossings Sch., Hoover, Ala., 1994-95, South Shades Crest Sch., Hoover, Ala., 1995—; chairperson sci. fair Shades Cahaba Elem. Sch., Homewood, 1990-94; mem. accreditation team, Warrior (Ala.) Sch., 1990; presenter Homewood City Schs., 1988, Constructivist Conf., Birmingham, 1994, 95, co-presenter NCTM regional conf., 1995, presenter Mid-South Whole Lang. Conf., Birmingham, 1995. Rsch. participant (book) Theme Immersion: Inquiry Based Curriculum in Elementary and Middle Schools, 1994. Founder, tchr. Women in Transition, Shades Mt. Baptist Ch., Birmingham, 1993—; presenter Festival of Marriage, Ridgecrest N.C, 1994, Dayspring Women's Conf., Birmingham, 1994. Mem. Nat. Coun. Teachers of Math., Am. Edn. Rsch. Assn., Educator's Forum. Avocations: reading, tennis, travel. Office: South Shades Crest Elem 3770 S Shades Crest Rd Hoover AL 35244-4123

PARRISH, THOMAS KIRKPATRICK, III, marketing consultant; b. Richmond, Va., May 18, 1930; s. Thomas Kirkpatrick and Sally Cary (Friend) P.; divorced: children: Linn Cary, Wayne Elizabeth, Susan Scott, Thomas Kirkpatrick IV. A.B., Princeton U., 1952. Product mgr. Vick Chem. Co., N.Y.C., 1955-58; v.p. Benton & Bowles Advt. Agy., N.Y.C., 1958-65; pres. Am. Chicle Co. div. Warner-Lambert Co., Morris Plains, N.J., 1965-70, Life Savers Inc. div. Squibb Corp., N.Y.C., 1970-73, Lanvin-Charles of Ritz Inc. subs. Squibb Corp., N.Y.C., 1974-76; dir. parent co. Squibb Corp., 1974-77; group dir. new bus. devel. Gillette Co., Boston, 1977-78; exec. v.p. SSC & B, Inc., N.Y.C., 1978-81; sr. assoc. Am. Cons. Corp., 1982-86; prin. The Parrish Co., N.Y.C., 1986—. Mem. N.Y. State Republican Com., 1962-63; bd. dirs. YMCA Ctr. for Internat. Mgmt. Studies, N.Y.C., 1970-85. Served to lt., jr. grade USN, 1952-55. Home: 215 E 73rd St New York NY 10021-3653

PARRISH, WILLIAM EARL, history educator; b. Garden City, Kans., Apr. 7, 1931; s. Earl Milton and Anna Maye (Stoker) P.; m. Ellen Kaye Vickers, June 14, 1959 (div. 1971); m. Helen Sue Lewis Stoppel, June 2, 1972; children: Elizabeth Ann, William Lewis. BS with honors, Kans. State U., 1952; MA, U. Mo., 1953, PhD, 1955. Asst. prof. to Harry S. Truman prof. in Am. history Westminster Coll., Fulton, Mo., 1955-78, dean of coll., 1973-75; prof. history Miss. State U., Mississippi State, 1978-96, head dept. history, 1978-85, prof. emeritus, 1996—. Author: David Rice Atchison of Missouri, 1961, Turbulent Partnership, Missouri and the Union, 1963, Missouri Under Radical Rule, 1865-1870, 1965, A History of Missouri, Vol. III, 1860-1875, 1973, (with Charles T. Jones, Jr. and Lawrence Christensen) Missouri: The Heart of the Nation, 1992; gen. editor Sesquicentennial History of Missouri, 5 vols., 1971-97. Mem. Mo. Adv. Coun. on Hist. Preservation, 1967-78; chmn. Mo. Am. Revolution Bicentennial Com., 1974-77; nat. adv. bd. Soc. of Civil War Historians, 1986-97; mem. State Hist. Records Adv. Bd., 1980-95. Recipient proclamation for quarter century of svc. Gov. of Mo., 1978, award of merit Am. Assn. State and Local History, 1974. Mem. Orgn. Am. Historians, Western History Assn., So. Hist. Assn., Nat. Trust Hist. Preservation, Miss. Hist. Soc. (pres. 1995-96), State Hist. Soc. Mo. (life), Rotary, Phi Alpha Theta (internat. pres. 1985-87), Phi Gamma Delta (historian 1989—). Presbyterian. Avocation: deltiology. Office: Miss State U Dept History Drawer H Mississippi State MS 39762 Home: 703 Bonnie Rd Starkville MS 39759-2104

PARR-JOHNSTON, ELIZABETH, academic administrator; b. N.Y.C., Aug. 15, 1939; d. Ferdinand Van Siclen and Helene Elizabeth (Ham) Parr; m. David E. Bond, Dec. 28, 1962 (div. July 1975); children: Peter V.S., Kristina Aline; m. Archibald F. Johnston, Mar. 6, 1982; children: James, Heather, Alexandra, Margaret. BA, Wellesley Coll., 1961; MA, Yale U., 1962, PhD, 1973; postgrad., Harvard U., 1986. Various positions Govt. of Can., Ottawa, Ont., 1973-76, INCO Ltd., Toronto, 1976-79; chief of staff, sr. policy advisor Ministry of Employment and Immigration, Govt. of Can., 1979-80; various positions Shell Can. Ltd., Calgary, Alta., 1980-90; pres. Parr-Johnston & Assocs., Calgary, 1990-91; pres., vice chancellor Mt. St. Vincent U., Halifax, Nova Scotia, N.S., 1991-96; pres., vice-chancellor The U. New Brunswick, Fredericton, Can., 1996—; instr. U. Western Ont., London, Ont., 1964-67, U. B.C., Vancouver, 1967-71; vis. scholar Wesleyan U., Middletown, Conn., 1971-72; acad. rsch. assoc. Carleton U., Ottawa, 1972-73; bd. dirs. Nova Scotia Power, Bank of Nova Scotia, Fishery Products Internat., The Empire Co.; spkr. and presenter in field. Mem. editorial bd. Can. Econ. Jour., 1980-83; contbr. articles to profl. jours. Bd. dirs. Dellcrest Home, 1980-84, Calgary S.W. Fed. Riding Assn., 1985-91, The Learning Ctr., Calgary, 1989-91, Halifax United Way, 1991-92, North/South Inst., 1992-96, Coun. for Can. Unity, 1993—, Vol. Planning N.S., 1992-93; planning chmn. John Howard Soc., 1980-84; mem. policy adv. com. C.D. Howe, 1980-85; mem. Ont. Econ. Coun., 1981-84. Woodrow Wilson fellow, 1962. Mem. Assn. Atlantic Univs. (chair 1994-96), Assn. Univs. and Colls. in Can. (bd. dirs., mem. exec. com. 1994-96), Coun. for Can. Unity (bd. dirs.), Women in Acad. Adminstrn. (adv. bd. 1991-96), Calgary Coun. Advanced Tech. (exec. 1990-91), Can. Econs. Assn., Inst. Pub. Adminstrn. Can., Sr. Women Acad. Adminstrs. Can., Phi Beta Kappa. Anglican. Avocations: skiing, golf, sailing. Office: U NB Office of Pres, PO Box 4400, Fredericton, NB Canada E3B 5A3

PARROTT, CHARLES NORMAN, bank executive; b. West Chester, Pa., June 5, 1947; s. Charles Orrin and Dorothy Emma (Rissel) P.; m. Karol Ellen Gress, Sept. 6, 1986. BS in Psychology, U. Cin., 1972, BS in Econs., 1975; postgrad., Stonier Grad. Sch. Banking, Rutgers, N.J., 1982. Cert: CLU, CFP, ChFC, CMFC, cert. trust and fin. adv. Asst. br. mgr. Cen. Trust Co., Cin., 1967-76; trust officer Bank of Pa., Reading, 1976-83; v.p. Lebanon Valley Nat. Bank, Lebanon, Pa., 1983—. Past pres. Sertoma, Lebanon, 1987; chmn. Mid Atlantic Air Mus., 1994; pres. The Salvation Army, Lebanon, 1994; vice chmn. The Am. Red Cross, 1994. Recipient Presdl. citation Am. Banking Assn., 1984; scholar Rotary Found., 1980. Mem. Lebanon Valley Sertoma Club (pres.), Annville Rotary Club (pres. 1997). Avocations: photography, tennis, rail fan. Home: 1650 Robin Rd Lebanon PA 17042-6433 Office: Lebanon Valley Nat Bank 555 Willow St Lebanon PA 17046-4869

PARROTT, ROBERT HAROLD, pediatrician, educator; b. Jackson Heights, N.Y., Dec. 29, 1923; s. Harold Leslie and Ruth Mabel (Hargrove) P.; m. Paula McDonough, June 2, 1951; children: Timothy, Maureen, Daniel, Theresa, Christopher, Edward. Student, Fordham U.; M.D., Georgetown U., 1949. Intern Hosp. of St. Raphael, New Haven, Conn., 1949-50; resident Children's Hosp. of D.C., 1950-52; staff pediatrician, chief Pediatric Unit, Lab. of Clin. Investigation, Nat. Inst. Allergy and Infectious Diseases, NIH, Bethesda, Md., 1952-56; physician-in-chief, dir. Research Found., Children's Hosp. of D.C., Washington, 1956-62, dir., 1962-85, dir. emeritus, 1985—; prof. pediatrics George Washington U., Washington. Mem. AMA, Am. Acad. Pediatrics, Am. Pediatric Soc., Am. Acad. Med. Dirs., Am. Coll. Physician Execs., D.C. Med. Soc., Infectious Diseases Soc. Club: Cosmos (Washington). Home: 13064 Deanmar Dr Highland MD 20777-9519 Office: Children's Nat Med Ctr 111 Michigan Ave NW Washington DC 20010-2916

PARROTT, SHARON LEE, elementary educator; b. Ostrander, Ohio, Oct. 15, 1949; d. Fay Llewellyn and Thelma Irene (Reed) P. BS in Elem. Edn., Ind. Wesleyan U., 1975. From kindergarten assoc. tchr. to assoc. tchr. Columbus (Ohio) Children's Coll., 1975; 1st grade tchr. Kayenta (Ariz.) Unified Sch. Dist. 27, 1975-84, presch. tchr., 1986-95, 1st grade tchr., 1995—; substitute tchr. Delaware and Union County Schs., Ohio, 1984-86. Tchr. Kayenta Bible Ch., 1981—, recorder, 1991-93. Mem. ASCD, Internat. Reading Assn., Nat. Coun. Tchrs. English, Assn. for Childhood Edn. Internat. Avocations: cooking, reading, outdoor activities. Home: PO Box 2172 Kayenta AZ 86033-2172 Office: Kayenta Unified Sch Dist 27 PO Box 337 Kayenta AZ 86033-0337

PARROTT-FONSECA, JOAN, federal agency administrator. BA in History, Howard U.; MA in Human Resource Mgmt., Georgetown U., JD. Acting dir., dep. dir. D.C.'s Dept. Consumer and Regulatory Affairs; former assoc. adminstr. Office of Enterprise Devel./U.S. Gen. Svcs. Adminstrn.; dir. Minority Bus. Devel. Agy./U.S. Dept. Commerce, 1995—. Office: US Dept of Commerce Minority Bus Devel Agy 14th & Constitution Ave NW Washington DC 20230

PARRUCK, BIDYUT, electrical engineer; b. Calcutta, W. Bengal, India, Oct. 31, 1958; came to U.S., 1981; s. Birendra Singh and Jyotsna (Kothari) P. B in Tech., Indian Inst. Tech., Kharagpur, 1981; MS in Elec. Engring., Va. Poly. Inst., 1983. Mem. tech. staff ITT Advanced Tech. Ctr., Shelton, Conn., 1983-86; R & D engr. Contel Fin. Systems, Stamford, Conn., 1987-89; sr. design engr. TranSwitch Corp., Shelton, 1989-93; sect. head II Farinon divsn. Harris Corp., San carlos, Calif., 1993; prin. engr. Network Equipment Techs., Redwood City, Calif., 1993-94; v.p. asynchronous transfer mode sonet CorEl MicroSystems, Fremont, Calif., 1994—, also bd. dirs.; founder, advisor Next Generation Systems, Matawan, N.J., 1986—; advisor, cons. OSS Corp., Shelton, Conn., 1988—. Contbr. articles to profl. jours.; patentee in field. Vol. Ourhouse-North, Daly City, Calif., 1993-94, Holiday Project, San Francisco, 1995-96. Mem. IEEE. Avocaitons: ballroom dancing, sculpting, sailing, hiking, photography. Home: 1325 Buckthorne Way San Jose CA 95129

PARRY, ATWELL J., JR., state senator, retailer; b. Ogden, Utah, June 14, 1925; s. John Atwell and Nina Virginia (McEntire) P.; m. Elaine Hughes, Feb. 6, 1946; children—Bonnie, Michael, Jay, Donald, David, Delbert, Kent. Student pub. schs., Nampa, Idaho. Salesman, King's Packing Co., Nampa, 1947-54, credit mgr., 1954-55; plant mgr. Stone Poultry Co., Nampa, 1955-56; salesman Nestle Chocolate Co., 1956-64; owner, mgr. Melba Foods, Idaho, 1964-82; mem. Idaho Senate, 1981—; bd. dirs. Western Idaho Tng. Ctr., 1987-90; chmn. Senate Finance Com. and co-chmn. Joint Fin. and Appropriations Com., 1987—; chmn. Idaho State Bd. for Nat. Ctr. for Constl. Studies, 1988-90. Bd dirs. Alcohol Treatment Ctr., Nampa, 1978-82; mem. adv. bd. Mercy Med. Ctr., Nampa, 1976-81; mem. Melba City Council, 1971-74. Recipient Silver Beaver award Boy Scouts Am., 1959, Service award Mercy Med. Ctr., Outstanding Rep. Legislator in Idaho State award, 1993, Friend of Agr. award, 1989-90, 91-92, 94-95, Melba Citizen of Yr. award, 1996. Republican. Mormon.

PARRY, BARBARA DREPPERD, educational administrator; b. Coral Gables, Fla., Sept. 6, 1935; d. Clarence Hartsel and Mildred (Orme) Drepperd; m. William J. Parry, Nov. 3, 1978; children: William H. Glassford Jr., Robert K. Glassford. BEd, U. Miami, 1957; MS in Ednl. Leadership, Nova U., 1993. State Cert. POP Observer, Fla. Tchr. Dade County Pub. Schs., Miami, Fla., Montpelier (Vt.) Pub. Schs., Longmeadow (Mass.) Pub. Schs.; prin. Lower Sch. Gulliver Acad., Coral Gables. Mem. ASCD, NAESP, Nat. Coun. Tchrs. Math., AAUW, Delta Kappa Gamma. Office: Gulliver Acad 12595 Red Rd Coral Gables FL 33156-6397

PARRY, DALE D., newspaper editor. BS in Journalism cum laude, Ball State U., Muncie, Ind., 1981. Feature writer, editor and columnist Richmond (Ind.) Palladium-Item, 1981-84; feature writer Cin. Enquirer, 1984-86, asst. editor Today sect., 1986-87; editor Today section The Dallas Morning News, 1987-90; assignment editor The Way We Live sect. Detroit Free Press, 1990-92, dep. features editor, 1992-94, features editor, 1993—. Mem. Am. Assn. Sun. and Feature Editors. Office: Detroit Free Press 321 W Lafayette Blvd Detroit MI 48226

PARRY, LANCE AARON, newspaper executive; b. Allentown, Pa., Sept. 4, 1947; s. Harwood Clayton Bachman and Iola Mary (Johnson) P.; m. Virginia Eleanor Ford, Apr. 24, 1971; children: Halloran Lee, Christine Ford. BS in Edn., Kutztown U., 1969; postgrad., W.Va. U., 1970. With Call-Chronicle Newspapers, Allentown, 1970-81, mng. editor, 1979-81; asst. news editor The Phila. Inquirer, 1981-82, systems editor, 1982-84, night news editor, 1984-86, news editor daily edit., 1986-87, news editor Sunday edit., 1987-89, sr. editor/systems and tech., 1989-93, page design dir., 1993-94, features news editor, 1994-96; news editor Sunday edit., 1996—. Recipient 1st Place award for front page design Pa. Newspaper Pubs. Assn./Pa. Soc. Newspaper Editors, 1985, 87, 88, Disting. Alumnus award Kutztown U., 1992; Sigma Delta Chi scholar, 1969. Mem. Soc. Profl. Journalists, Pen and Pencil Club. Democrat. Presbyterian. Home: 16 Salisbury Ln Malvern PA 19355-2836 Office: The Phila Inquirer 400 N Broad St Philadelphia PA 19130-4015

PARRY, ROBERT WALTER, chemistry educator; b. Ogden, Utah, Oct. 1, 1917; s. Walter and Jeanette (Petterson) P.; m. Marjorie J. Nelson, July 6, 1945; children: Robert Bryce, Mark Nelson. BS, Utah State Agr. Coll., 1940; MS, Cornell U., 1942; PhD, U. Ill., 1946; DSc (hon.), Utah State U., 1985. Research asst. NDRC Munitions Devel. Lab., U. Ill. at Urbana, 1943-45, teaching fellow 1945-46; mem. faculty U. Mich., 1946-69, prof. chemistry, 1958-69; Distinguished prof. chemistry U. Utah, 1969-97, prof. emeritus, 1997; indsl. cons., 1952—; chmn. bd. trustees Gordon Rsch. Conf., 1967-68. Chmn. com. teaching chemistry Internat. Union Pure and Applied Chemistry 1968-74. Recipient Mfg. Chemists award for coll. teaching, 1972, Sr. U.S. Scientist award Alexander Von Humboldt-Stiftung (W. Ger.), 1980, First Govs. medal of Sci. State Utah, 1987. Mem. Am. Chem. Soc. (Utah award Utah Sect. 1978, past chmn. inorganic div. and div. chem. edn., award for distinguished service to inorganic chemistry 1965, for chem. edn., 1977, dir. 1973-83, bd. editors jour. 1969-80, pres.-elect 1981-82, pres. 1982-83, Priestly medal 1993), Internat. Union Pure and Applied Chemistry (chmn. U.S. nat. com.), AAAS, Sigma Xi. Founding editor Inorganic Chemistry, 1960-63. Research, publs. on some structural problems of inorganic chemistry, and incorporation results into theoretical models; chemistry of phosphorus, boron and fluorine. Home: 5002 Fairbrook Ln Salt Lake City UT 84117-6205 Office: U Utah Dept Chemistry Henry Eyring Bldg Salt Lake City UT 84112-1194

PARRY, SCOTT BRINK, psychologist; b. Reading, Pa., Sept. 4, 1932; s. George Raymond and Claire (Blackburne) P.; m. Joan SantAntonio; 1 child, Christiana Claire Parry. BA, Princeton U., 1954; MS, Boston U., 1960; PhD, NYU, 1969. Account exec. Hill & Knowlton, Inc., N.Y.C., 1960-62; editor Harcourt, Brace, Jovanovich, N.Y.C., 1962-64; ptnr. Parry & Robinson, Inc., N.Y.C., 1964-66; mgr. N.Y.C. office Sterling Inst., 1966-71; v.p., pres., chmn. Tng. House, Inc., N.Y.C., Princeton, 1971—; edn. cons. UNESCO, Paris, Nigeria, Ghana, 1963, 64; mem. adv. bd. Tng. mag., Lakewood Publs., Mpls., 1988-92; adj. prof. NYU, 1968-74; spkr. at convs. and profl. meetings in 17 countries on 6 continents; cons. to more than 50 Fortune 500 cos. Author: The Story of Handbells, 1957, (book, musical arrangements) A Handbell Handbill, 1963, From Managing to Empowering, 1993, The Managerial Mirror, 2 vols., 1997, 46 tng. books; contbr. over 30 articles to profl. jours. and newspapers. Lt. U.S. Army, 1957-59. Recipient Best Tng. Product award Human Resource Exec., 1990, 94; named hon. chmn. 25th anniversary Am. Guild English Handbell Ringers, Orlando, Fla., 1979. Mem. ASTD (bd. dirs. N.Y.C. chpt. 1972-74, adv. bd. 1992—), Internat. Fedn. Tng. and Devel. Orgns., Internat. Soc. for Performance Improvement, Instructional Sys. Assn. Republican. Presbyterian. Avocations: music (harpsichord, organ), collecting and restoring antiques, renovating bldgs. Office: Training House Box 3090 Princeton NJ 08540

PARRY, THOMAS HERBERT, JR., school system administrator, educational consultant; b. Detroit, June 28, 1928; s. Thomas Herbert Sr. and Isabel Constance (Brinsmead) P.; m. Frances Ellen Coley, Aug. 15, 1956; children: Virginia Gilkeson, William Thomas, Robert Brinsmead. BA in Edn., U. Fla., 1950; MEd, U. Va., 1958, EdD, 1967. Lic. profl. supr. of counselors; nat. cert. counselor. Tchr. Broward County Pub. Schs., Ft. Lauderdale, Fla., 1950-51, 54-62; instr. Mary Baldwin Coll., Staunton, Va., 1965-66; psychologist McGuffey Reading Ctr., Charlottesville, Va., 1966-67; prof. Clemson (S.C.) U., 1967-86; pres. Ednl. Horizons, Inc., Clemson, 1986-89, Poquoson, Va., 1989—; cons. Sch. Desegregation Ctr., Columbia, 1970; cons., counselor Advocacy Bd. S.C., 1980-82; exec. sec. S.C. Pers. and Guidance Assn., Columbia, 1980-81; founder S.C. Assn. Measurement and Evaluation in Guidance, 1974-75. Co-author: Developing a Leisure Learning Program, 1980, Beyond the Book: Activities to Correlate with the Virginia Young Readers, 1990-91, Bibliocounseling with Contemporary Children's Literature: A Resource Book for the Clinical Setting, 1996; editor S.C. Pers. and Guidance Newsletter and Jour., 1969-74; founder, editor S.C. Pers. and

Guidance Assn. Jour., 1972-74; contbr. articles to profl. jours. Bd. dirs. Peninsula Agy. on Aging, Inc., 1994—. Recipient Svc. award S.C. Pers. and Guidance, 1968-81, Nat. Award for Excellence State Publs. and Guidance Assn., 1971, Meritorious Svc. award Am. Pers. and Guidance Assn., 1973, Award of Merit for Svc. to Youth Boy Scouts Am., 1975. Mem. APA, Am. Counseling Assn., S.C. Counseling Assn., Kiwanis (bd. dirs., chmn. community svc. com. 1991—, disting. sec. 1994-96, Kiwanian of Yr. 1995-96, life capital dist. Kiwanis Found., Inc. 1995), Ft. Benning Lodge # 579, Kappa Delta Pi, Phi Delta Kappa. Presbyterian. Avocations: walking, gardening, photography. Home and Office: 1 Ebb Tide Lndg Poquoson VA 23662-1334

PARRY, WILLIAM DEWITT, lawyer; b. Hartford, Conn., June 4, 1941; s. William Brown and Mary Elizabeth (Caton) p.; m. Andrea Hannah Lewis, June 30, 1973; children: Sara, Jessica. BA, U. Mass., 1963; JD, U. Pa., 1966. Bar: N.J. 1987, Pa. 1967, U.S. Dist. Ct. (ea. dist.) Pa. 1974, U.S. Ct. Appeals (3d cir.) 1980, U.S. Supreme Ct. 1980. Assoc. Shapiro, Cook & Bressler, Phila., 1966-67; asst. dir. ABA joint com on continuing egal edn. Am. Law Inst., Phila., 1967-73; assoc. Lowenschuss Assocs., Phila., 1973-85; of counsel Weiss, Golden & Pierson, Phila., 1985-88; pvt. practice Phila., 1988—; ptnr. Rubin, Quinn, Moss & Patterson, Phila., 1989-93; pvt. practice Phila., 1993—. Author: Understanding and Controlling Stuttering: A Comprehensive New Approach Based on the Valsalva Hypothesis, 1994; editor U. Pa. Law Rev., 1964-66, The Practical Lawyer, 1967-73. Founder Phila. area chpt. Nat. Stuttering Project, 1985—, dir. Nat. Stuttering Project, 1996—; trustee Unitarian Soc. Germantown, Phila., 1983-86. Mem. ABA, Assn. Trial Lawyers Am., Pa. Bar Assn., Phila. Bar Assn., Pa. Trial Lawyers Assn. Democrat. Avocations: writing, lecturing. Home: 520 Baird Rd Merion Station PA 19066-1302 Office: 1608 Walnut St Ste 900 Philadelphia PA 19103-5451

PARSEGHIAN, GENE, talent agent; b. Oneonta, N.Y., Dec. 11, 1944; s. Richard and Leona (Spickerman) P.; life ptnr. Michael D. Colberg; 1 child, Rachel Colberg-Parseghian. BA, Antioch Coll., 1967; MFA, Stanford U., 1970. Owner Parseghian Assocs., Inc., N.Y.C., 1977-78; founding ptnr., owner Kimble/Parseghian, Inc., N.Y.C., 1978-81, DHKPR, N.Y.C., 1981-84, Triad Artists, Inc., N.Y.C., 1984-92; sr. v.p. William Morris Agy., Inc., N.Y.C., 1992—; bd. dirs. Artsgenesis, N.Y.C. Mem. Creative Coalition, N.Y.C., 1991—. Democrat. Office: William Morris Agy Inc 1325 Avenue Of The Americas New York NY 10019-6026

PARSHALL, GEORGE WILLIAM, research chemist; b. Hackensack, Minn., Sept. 19, 1929; s. George Clarence and Frances (Virnig) P.; m. Naomi B. Simpson, Oct. 9, 1954; children: William, Jonathan, David. B.S., U. Minn., 1951; Ph.D., U. Ill., 1954. Research chemist E.I. duPont de Nemours & Co., Wilmington, Del., 1954-65, research supr., 1965-79, dir. chem. sci., 1979-92, cons., 1992—, mem. com. on environ. mgmt. techs., 1994-97; mem. chem. stockpile disposal com. NRC, Washington, 1992—; bd. chem. sci. NRC, Washington, 1983-86; Reilly lectr. Notre Dame U., 1980; Ipatieff lectr. Northwestern U., 1994. Author: Homogeneous Catalysis, 1980, 2d rev. edit. 1992; editor: Inorganic Syntheses, 1974, Jour. Molecular Catalysis, 1977-80. Recipient Ballar Inorganic Chemistry medal U. Ill., 1976. Mem. NAS, Inst. Chemists (Chem. Pioneer award 1992, Gold medal award 1995), Am. Chem. Soc. (award in inorganic chemistry 1983, award for leadership in chem. rsch. mgmt. 1989), Am. Acad. Arts Scis., Guild Episcopal Scholars (treas. 1994—). Episcopalian. Home: 2504 Delaware Ave Wilmington DE 19806-1220

PARSHALL, GERALD, journalist; b. St. Paul, Apr. 24, 1941; s. William Elmer and Evelyn (Steckling) P.; m. Sandra Grant, Dec. 20, 1970. B.A., U. Minn., 1963; M.A., U. Mich., 1964; grad. fellow, U. Chgo., 1966-67. Reporter York (Pa.) Gazette and Daily, 1968, Balt. Evening Sun, 1968-71; Capitol Hill staff U.S. News & World Report, Washington, 1971-77; sr. editor U.S. News & World Report, 1977-79, asst. mng. editor, 1979-90, sr. writer, 1990—; mem. Exec. Com. of Periodical Corrs., U.S. Congress, 1974-80, chmn., 1979-80. Served to 1st lt. U.S. Army, 1964-66. Recipient Front Page award Washington-Balt. Newspaper Guild, 1971, Silver Gavel award ABA, 1983. Home: 1004 Congress Ln McLean VA 22101-2116 Office: 2400 N St NW Washington DC 20037-1153

PARSKY, GERALD LAWRENCE, lawyer; b. West Hartford, Conn., Oct. 18, 1942; s. Isadore and Nettie (Sanders) P.; m. Susan Haas, June 26, 1966; children: Laura, David; m. Robin Cleary, Jan. 27, 1980. A.B., Princeton U., 1964; J.D., U. Va., 1968. Bar: N.Y. 1969, D.C. 1974, Calif. 1983. Assoc. Mudge Rose Guthrie & Alexander, N.Y.C., 1968-71; spl. asst. to under sec. U.S. Treasury Dept., Washington, 1971-73; exec. asst. to dep. sec. Fed. Energy Office U.S. Treasury Dept., 1973-74, asst. sec. internat. affairs, 1974-77; sr. ptnr. Gibson, Dunn & Crutcher, Los Angeles, 1977-90; of counsel Gibson, Dunn & Cruther, L.A., 1990-92; chmn. Aurora Capital Ptnrs., L.A., 1990—. Bd. govs. Performing Arts Council, Los Angeles Music Ctr. Recipient Alexander Hamilton award U.S. Treasury, 1976. Mem. ABA, Coun. Fgn. Rels., N.Y. Princeton Club, Calif. Club, Racquet Club, Anandale Club, Beach Club. Office: Aurora Capital Ptnrs 1800 Century Park E Los Angeles CA 90067-1501

PARSONS, A. PETER, lawyer; b. Norwood, Mass., May 29, 1945; s. Charles A.A. and Elizabeth P. (Coombs) P.; children—A. Peter, Christopher P.; m. Elizabeth A. Lee, Aug. 24, 1991; 1 child Alex W. A.A., Palm Beach Jr. Coll., 1968; B.S., Fla. Atlantic U., 1969; J.D., Duke U., 1973. Bar: Wash. 1973, U.S. Dist. Ct. (ea. and we. dists.) Wash. 1974, U.S. Ct. Appeals (9th cir.) 1974; C.P.A., Fla., Wash. Acct., Haskins & Sells, Ft. Lauderdale, 1969-70; tax cons. Arthur, Young & Co., Portland, Oreg., 1972; law clk. Wash. Supreme Ct., 1973-74; atty. Perkins, Coie, Seattle, 1974-77; mem., mng. dir. Weinrich, Gilmore & Adolph, Seattle, 1978-87; ptnr. Davis Wright Tremaine LLP, 1988—; adj. prof. U. Puget Sound, 1974-75; lectr. U. Wash., 1978-81. Mem. editorial bd. Duke U. Law Jour., 1971-73. Contbr. articles to legal jours. Chmn. bd. dirs. PIVOT, non-profit corp., Seattle, 1975-78; Group Theater, Seattle, 1984-86; chmn. bd. dirs. MIT Enterprise Forum, Seattle, 1984-92 ; founder, bd. dirs. Rainier Found., Seattle, 1983—, Wash. State Biotechnology Assn. 1991-94, Washington Software & Digital Media Alliance, Bellevue, 1996—, Midisoft Corp., Issaquah, 1996—. Served with USAF, 1963-67. Mem. ABA, Wash. Bar Assn., Am. Intellectual Property Law Assn., Computer Law Soc., Am. Inst. CPAs, Wash. Soc. CPAs, Seattle-King County Bar Assn., Am. Coll. of Mediators. Clubs: Rainier, Seattle Yacht. Home: 1864 Broadmoor Dr E Seattle WA 98112-2312 Office: Davis Wright & Tremaine 2600 Century Sq 1501 4th Ave Seattle WA 98101-1662

PARSONS, ANDREW JOHN, management consultant; b. Kingston, Surrey, Eng., July 22, 1943; came to U.S., 1968; s. S. John and Hylda P. (Wili) P.; m. Carol Ann Iannucci, June 6, 1970; children: Alexandra, Katherine. BA, MA, Oxford U., 1965; MBA, Harvard U., 1970. Account exec. Leo Burnett, London, 1965-68; from strategic planning dir. to v.p. mktg. Prestige Group Ltd. div. Am. Home Products, N.Y.C. and London, 1970-76; v.p. mktg. Kurzweil Computer Products div. Xerox Corp., Cambridge, Mass., 1979-80; assoc. McKinsey & Co., Inc., N.Y.C., 1976-82, prin., 1982-88, dir. consumer industries sector, mktg. ctr., sr. ptnr., 1988—; underwriting mem. Lloyds of London, 1986—. Contbr. articles to profl. jours. Chmn. adv. bd. Salvation Army, Greater N.Y., 1983—; bd. dirs. United Way, N.Y.C., 1988—; trustee Sarah Lawrence Coll., Bronxville, N.Y., 1993—. Baker scholar Harvard Bus. Sch., 1970. Mem. Siwanoy Country Club, Watch Hill Yacht Club. Home: 56 Hereford Rd Bronxville NY 10708-5408 Office: McKinsey & Co Inc 55 E 52nd St New York NY 10055-0002

PARSONS, BENNY, auto racing commentator. Auto racer NASCAR cir., 1963-88; NASCAR commentator ESPN, 1988—; analyst Winston Cup Race, Busch Grand Nat. Race. Winner Daytona 500, 1963, 75, NASCAR series championship, 1973; recipient CableACE award for best sports analyst, 1989. Office: c/o ESPN ESPN Plaza Bristol CT 06010

PARSONS, CHARLES ALLAN, JR., lawyer; b. Mpls., July 16, 1943; s. Charles Allan and Grace Adelaide (Covert) P.; m. JoAnne Ruth Russell, Oct. 16, 1965; children: Charles, Daniel, Nancy. BS, U. Minn., 1965, JD cum laude, 1972. Bar: Minn. 1972, U.S. Dist. Ct. Minn. 1972, U.S. Supreme Ct. 1995. Ptnr. Moss & Barnett, P.A., 1972—. Bd. dirs. Legal Advice Clinics Ltd., Mpls., 1975-93; chair steering com. S.E. Asian Legal Assn. Assistance Project, Mpls., 1988-93. Named Vol. Atty. of Yr., Legal Advice Clinics, Ltd., Mpls., 1990. Mem. ABA, Am. Coll. Real Estate Lawyers, Minn. State Bar Assn. (co-chair legis. com. real property sec. 1986—, coun. mem. 1986—, chair real property sect. 1993-94), Hennepin County Bar Assn. (chair real property sect. 1988-89). Roman Catholic. Avocations: reading, walking, biking, running, hiking. Office: Moss & Barnett PA 4800 Norwest Ctr 90 S 7th Minneapolis MN 55402-4119

PARSONS, DANIEL LANKESTER, pharmaceutics educator; b. Biscoe, N.C., Sept. 10, 1953; s. Solomon Lankester and Doris Eva (Bost) P. BS in Pharmacy, U. Ga., 1975, PhD, 1979. Asst. prof. pharmaceutics U. Ariz., Tucson, 1979-82; asst. prof. Auburn (Ala.) U., 1982-86, assoc. prof., 1986-91, prof., 1991—, chmn. divsn., 1990—; cons. Wyeth-Ayerst, Phila., 1989-93, Technomics, Ardsley, N.Y., 1990-93, Murty Pharm., Lexington, Ky., 1996—; presenter in field. Author: (with G.V. Betageri and S.A. Jenkins) Liposome Drug Delivery Systems, 1993. Named Disting. Alumni Sandhills Coll., 1990, Tchr. of Yr., Pharmacy Student Coun., 1987, Grad. Faculty Mem. of Yr., Grad. Student Orgn., 1994. Mem. Am. Pharm. Assn., Am. Assn. Pharm. Scientists, Am. Coll. Clin. Pharmacology (scoun. 1990-93), Phi Kappa Phi, Kappa Psi (advisor 1990-95, Svc. award 1990, 95, Advisor award 1992, nat. grad. devel. com. 1993-95, nat. scholarship com. 1995—). Achievements include research on plasma protein binding of drugs and effects of perfluorochemical blood substitutes on such binding. Office: Auburn U Sch Pharmacy Auburn AL 36849

PARSONS, DAVID, artistic director, choreographer. Dancer Paul Taylor Dance Co.,, 1978-87; founder, artistic dir. Parsons Dance Co., 1987—. Choreographer The Envelope, 1984, Sleep Study, 1987, Caught, 1987, Elysian Fields, 1988, Reflections of Four, 1991, A Hairy Night on Bald Mountain, 1991, Bachiana, 1993, Destines, 1993, Ring Around the Rosie, 1993; performed with N.Y.C. Ballet, Berlin Opera, White Oak Dancer Project. Choreography fellow Nat. Endowment for the Arts, 1988-89, 95. Office: Parsons Dance Co c/o Sheldon Soffer Mgt Inc 130 W 56th St New York NY 10019-3803*

PARSONS, DONALD D., bishop. Bishop of Alaska Evang. Luth. Ch. in Am., Anchorage. Office: Synod of Alaska 1847 W Northern Lights Blvd # 2 Anchorage AK 99517-3343*

PARSONS, DONALD JAMES, retired bishop; b. Phila., Mar. 28, 1922; s. Earl and Helen (Drabble) P.; m. Mary Russell, Sept. 17, 1955; children—Mary, Rebecca, Bradford. B.A., Temple U., 1943; M.Div., Phila. Div. Sch., 1946, Th.D., 1951, D.D. (hon.), 1964; postgrad., U. Nottingham, Eng., 1968; D.C.L., Nashotah (Wis.) House, 1973. Ordained priest Episcopal Ch., 1946, consecrated bishop, 1973; curate Immanual Ch., Wilmington, Del., 1946-49; rector St. Peter's Ch., Smyrna, Del., 1949-50; prof. N.T., Nashotah House, 1950-73, pres., dean, 1963-73; bishop Diocese of Quincy, Ill., 1973-88. Author: A Life-time Road to God, 1966, In Time with Jesus, 1973, Holy Eucharist: Rite Two, 1976. Home: 308 W Edgevale Pl Peoria IL 61604-1607

PARSONS, EDMUND MORRIS, investment company executive; b. Houston, Oct. 19, 1936; s. Alfred Morris and Virgina (Hanna) P. AB, Harvard U., 1958; MBA, U. Pa., 1961; MS, MIT, 1970. Pres. Fredonia Enterprises, Inc., Houston, Tex., 1990—; fgn. service officer U.S. Dept. State, Washington, 1965-90; 1st sec. Am. Embassy, Mexico City, 1973-76; economist Fed. Res. Bank N.Y., N.Y.C., 1976-77; chief food aid div. U.S. Dept. State, Washington, 1977-80, dir. office devel., 1981-82, dir. office econ. policy, 1983-84; dep. chief mission U.S. Mission to FAO, Rome, 1985-86; dir. Office Ecology and Natural Resources U.S. Dept. State, Washington, 1986-88; dir. Office of Internat. Narcotics Control Programs, 1988-89; min.-counselor for econ. affairs Am. Embassy, Mexico City, 1989-90; pres. Fredonia Enterprises, Inc., Houston, 1990—; co-chmn. Tropical Forest Task Force, Washington, 1986-88; dep. U.S. rep. UN FAO, Rome, 1985-86; alt. U.S. rep. to environ. program U.S. Del. Nairobi, Kenya, 1987. Capt. USAF, 1962-72. Mem. Am. Fgn. Svc. Assn., Houston Restaurant Assn. (bd. dirs. 1992—), Houston World Affairs Coun. (bd. dirs. 1995—), Consular Corps of Houston (hon.), Houston Hispanic C. of C., Coun. Fgn. Rels. (Houston com.), Univ. Club (Houston). Republican. Methodist. Avocation: genealogy. Office: 2727 Fondren Rd Ste 2A Houston TX 77063-4114

PARSONS, EDWIN SPENCER, clergyman, educator; b. Brockton, Mass., Feb. 16, 1919; s. Edwin Webber and Ethel Faunce (Marsh) P.; m. Eleanor Millard, Nov. 3, 1944; children: William Spencer, Ellen, James Millard, Bradford Delano. A.B., Denison U., 1941, D.D., 1967; B.D., Andover Newton Theol. Sch., 1945; D.D., Kalamazoo Coll., 1966; L.H.D., Chgo. Coll. Osteo. Medicine, 1978. Ordained to ministry Am. Baptist Ch., 1944; asst. minister First Bapt. Ch., Newton Centre, Mass., 1945-47; exec. dir. Bapt. Student Found., Inc., Cambridge, Mass., 1947-59; pastor Hyde Park Union Ch., Chgo., 1959-65; assoc. prof. ethics U. Chgo. Div. Sch., 1965-78, prof., 1978-81; dir. ministerial field edn., 1977-79, asst. to dean, 1981-88; dean Rockefeller Meml. Chapel, 1965-79; v.p., dir. New Eng. office Health Resources Ltd., Kansas City, Mo., 1979-89; cons. dept. ch. and soc. Am. Bapt. Chs. of Mass., 1979-86, also editor Mass. Bapt. News, 1983-85; chmn. strategy and action com., bd. dirs. Mass. Council Chs., 1983-85; adj. prof. Andover Newton Theol. Sch., 1981-85. Author: The Christian Yes or No, 1964; contbr.: Belief and Ethics, 1978. Pres. Council Hyde Park-Kenwood Chs. and Synagogues, 1963; chmn. Abortion Rights Assn. Ill., 1974-79; founder, chmn. Ill. Religious Coalition for Abortion Rights, 1975, Ill. Clergy Consultation Services on Problem Pregnancies, 1971-79; bd. dirs., chmn. clergy adv. com. Planned Parenthood Assn., Chgo., 1977-79; bd. dirs. Hyde Park YMCA, Facing History and Ourselves Nat. Found., 1983-87; bd. govs. Internat. House, Chgo., 1969-79; trustee Packard Manse (Mass.), Bapt. Theol. Union, U. Chgo., 1960-70, 81-96, hon. trustee, 1996—; pres., bd. mgrs. Ministers and Missionaries Benefit Bd., 1975-81; mem. policy council Religious Coalition for Abortion Rights of Mass., 1980-86; sec., treas. Bolton Inst. for Sustainable Future, 1983-87; mem. gen. bd., mem. exec. com., mem. commn. on Christian unity Am. Bapt. Chs., 1963-72, 74-81; bd. dirs. Planned Parenthood League of Mass., 1984-92; interim assoc. dir. Mass Coun. Chs., 1988-89. Democrat. Home: 82 Briarwood Cir Worcester MA 01606

PARSONS, ELMER EARL, retired clergyman; b. Cloverland, Wash., Oct. 4, 1919; s. Claud Solomon and Bessie Lillian (Campbell) P.; m. Marjorie Emma Carlson, Aug. 29, 1942; children—Karl Elmer, James Myron, Helen Joy, Ann Elizabeth, Lois Marie, Louise Melba. B.A., Seattle Pacific U., 1942; S.T.B., N.Y. Theol. Sem., 1945; S.T.M., Asbury Theol. Sem., Wilmore, Ky., 1955; D.D. (hon.), Greenville (Ill.) Coll., 1958. Ordained to ministry Free Methodist Ch., 1944; acad. dean Wessington Springs (S.D.) Coll., 1945-47; missionary to China, 1947-49, missionary to Japan, 1949-54; supt. Japan Free Meth. Mission, 1950-54; pres. Central Coll., McPherson, Kans., 1955-64, Osaka (Japan) Christian Coll., 1964-74; Asia area sec., Free Meth. Ch., 1964-74; bishop Free Meth. Ch. N.Am., 1974-85. Author: Witness to the Resurrection, 1967. Chmn. Free Meth. Study Commn. on Doctrine, 1990-95. Named Alumnus of Year Seattle Pacific U., 1976. Mem. Wesleyan Theol. Soc.

PARSONS, ESTELLE, actress; b. Lynn, Mass., Nov. 20, 1927; d. Eben and Elinor (Mattson) P.; m. Richard Gehman, Dec. 19, 1953 (div. Aug. 1958); children: Martha and Abbie (twins); m. Peter L. Zimroth, Jan. 2, 1983; 1 child, Abraham. B.A. in Polit. Sci., Conn. Coll. Women, 1949; student, Boston U. Law Sch., 1949-50. Stage appearances include: Happy Hunting, 1957, Whoop Up, 1958, Beg, Borrow or Steal, 1960, Threepenny Opera, 1960, Mrs. Dally Has a Lover, 1962, Ready When You Are C.B, 1964, Malcolm, 1965, Seven Descents of Myrtle, 1968, And Miss Reardon Drinks a Little, 1971, Mert and Phil, 1974, The Norman Conquests, 1975-76, Ladies of the Alamo, 1977, Miss Margarida's Way, 1977-78, The Pirates of Penzance, 1981, The Shadow Box, 1994; adapted, dir., performer Orgasmo Adulto Escapes from the Zoo, 1983, The Unguided Missile, Baba Goya, 1989, Shimada, 1992, Grace & Glory, 1996; film appearances include: Bonnie and Clyde, 1966; Rachel, Rachel, 1967, I Never Sang for My Father, 1969, Dick Tracy, 1990, Boys On The Side, 1995, Looking for Richard, 1996, That Darn Cat, 1997; TV appearances include: Roseanne, 1990—; artistic dir. N.Y. Shakespeare Festival Players, 1986. Recipient Theatre World award, 1962-63, Obie award, 1964; recipient award Motion Picture Acad. Arts and Scis., 1967; Recipient Medal of Honor, Conn. Coll., 1969. Home: 924 West End Ave T5 New York NY 10025-3543 *It's in attempting all, that one succeeds.*

PARSONS, GEORGE RAYMOND, JR., lawyer; b. N.Y.C., May 5, 1938; s. George Raymond and Gertrude (Blackburn) P.; m. Katharine P. Sook, Oct. 16, 1982; children: Timothy, Geoffrey, Amy, Julia, Elizabeth. BA with distinction, Wesleyan U., 1959; LLB with honors, Cornell U., 1962. Bar: N.Y. 1962, U.S. Dist. Ct. (we. and no. dists.) N.Y. 1962, Fla. 1974. Assoc. Nixon, Hargrave, Davans & Doyle LLP, Rochester, N.Y., 1962-69, ptnr., 1970—; lectr. continuing legal edn. programs. Editor-in-chief, contbr. articles to Cornell Law Rev., 1961-62, New Republic; contbr. John Updike Newsletter. Officer, bd. dirs. Rochester Philharm. Orch., 1976-83; pres. Friends of Rochester Pub. Libr., 1972-75; trustee Monroe County Libr. Sys., 1986-87, 94-96, Reynolds Libr., 1987— (pres. 1996—), Rochester Regional Libr. Coun., 1988—, pres. 1994—; bd. dirs. Rundel Libr. Found., Inc., 1989—; pres. Friends of U. Rochester Librs., 1989-91; trustee Rochester Pub. Libr., 1978-81, 83—, pres. 1986-87, 94-96; bd. dirs. Writers and Books, 1991—; del. N.Y. State Gov.'s Conf. on Librs. and Info. Svcs., 1990; mem. trustee's vis. com. on librs. U. Rochester, 1991-95; trustee Halycon Hill Found., 1992—; trustee Rochester Grantmakers Forum, 1997—. Mem. N.Y. Bar Assn., Monroe County Bar Assn., Am. Coll. of Trust and Estate Counsel, Estate Planning Council Rochester. Democrat. Office: Nixon Hargrave et al Clinton Sq PO Box 1051 Rochester NY 14603-1051

PARSONS, GEORGE WILLIAMS, retired medical center administrator, cattle rancher; b. Natural Bridge, Va., Jan. 21, 1918; s. George Washington and Mary Elizabeth (Williams) P.; m. Miriam Rebecca Boyer, May 2, 1942; children: Mary Locke Parsons Black, Anne Boyer Parsons Talkington, George Russell. Student, Washington and Lee U., 1935-37; B.S. in Edn., U. Va., 1941; grad., USNR Tng. Sch., 1942, USNR Officer Candidate Sch., 1944, USNR Command Sch., 1944, Ind. Coll. Armed Forces, 1963, Fed. Health Care Inst., 1966. Tchr. Winchester, Va., 1941-42; asst. phys. dir. VA Hosp., Roanoke, Va., 1946-47; asst. chief spl. services VA Hosp., 1947-51; chief spl. services VA Hosp., Lyons, N.J., 1951-58; spl. asst. to hosp. mgr. VA Hosp., Pitts., 1958-62; asst. dir. VA Hosp., Clarksburg, W.Va., 1962-67, Erie, Pa., 1967-69, Marion, Ind., 1969-72, Bklyn., 1972-75; dir. VA Outpatient Clinic, Lubbock, Tex., 1975-76; dir. VA Med. Center, Bklyn., 1976-82, Alexandria, La., 1982-86; faculty, preceptor M.P.H./M.B.A. Program in Health Adminstrn., Columbia U.; faculty NYU; mem. dean's com. Tulane U. Sch. Medicine, New Orleans, 1982-86; chmn. Fed. Exec. Bd., N.Y.C., 1982; cluster leader Presdl. Mgmt. Intern Program, Nat. Inst. Public Affairs, 1980-82; mem. dist. bd. Health Systems Agy., Bklyn.; chmn. Combined Fed. Campaign for all VA Med. Facilities in N.Y.C., all fed. agys. in Rapides Parish (La.), 1984; mem. Rockbridge County (Va.) Farm Bur., Natural Bridge Ruritan Club; aide de camp Gov. David Treen, State of La., 1982, Gov. Edwin Edwards, State of La., 1985. Lt. comdr. USNR, 1942-46; PTO. Decorated 11 decorations and awards including two Presdl. Unit Commendations; recipient Outstanding Achievement award Am. Legion, 1975, Disting. Svc. award, 1975, Recognition award, 1978, Recognition award VFW, 1975, 83, United Vets. Assn. award Queens, N.Y., 1979; 9 citations and awards, 1980; 7 awards and citations, 1982; Outstanding Career award VA, 1986; also numerous other awards and commendations from VA, vets., civic orgns., 1946-86. Fellow Am. Coll. Healthcare Execs. (oral examiner), Royal Soc. Health; mem. Assn. Mil. Surgeons U.S. (pres. N.Y. chpt. 1979-80), Am. Hosp. Assn., La. Hosp. Assn. (pres. Central Dist. 1983-84), Sr. Exec. Service U.S. Govt., Fed. Hosp. Inst. Alumni Assn., N.Y. Acad. Scis., Res. Officers Assn. U.S.A. (pres. W.Va. chpt. 1967), Greater Alexandria/Pineville C. of C. (mil. affairs com. 1982-86), VFW (comdr Post 484 1949-50). Club: Rotary (pres. 1958, 71). Home: 1905 Canterbury Ln Apt 20 Sun City Center FL 33573-5641

PARSONS, HARRY GLENWOOD, retired surgeon; b. San Bernardino, Calif., Mar. 5, 1919; s. Harry Glenwood and Evelen May (Peris) P.; m. Rubyann Kattenhorn, Sept. 28, 1986. AB, Stanford (Calif.) U., 1942, MD, 1946. Diplomate Am. Bd. Surgery, Am. Bd. Thoracic Cardio-Vascular Surgery. Intern Stanford Hosp., San Francisco, 1941-42, Rockor fellow in surg. rsch., 1944-45, asst. resident in surgery, 1945-52, chief resident in surgery, 1952-53, Boyd fellow in thoracic cardiovasc. surgery, 1953-54; asst. clin. prof. surgery Stanford Med. Sch., 1955-65; med. dir., faculty head Weimar (Calif.) Med. Ctr., 1955-72; ret. Capt. M.C. U.S. Army, 1940-44. Fellow ACS; mem. AMA, Western Thoracic Surg. Soc., Placer Nevada County Med. Assn. (pres. 1979), Calif. Med. Assn. (del.), Alpha Omega Alpha. Avocation: flying.

PARSONS, HELGA LUND, writer; b. Seattle, Sept. 5, 1906; d. Gunnar and Marie Pauline (Vognild) Lund; m. Durwin David Algyer, June 6, 1937 (dec. 1971); children: Deanne Algyer Mathisen, Marilyn A. McIntosh; m. James Stewart Parsons, Sept. 30, 1972 (dec. 1988). Grad., Columbia Coll. Expression, Chgo., 1926. Lead actress Repertory Playhouse, Seattle, 1929-34; assoc. prof. drama U. Wash., 1931-32; dir. apprentice group Repertory Playhouse, Seattle 1932-34; writer, anchor radio programs Bon Marche Dept. Store, Seattle 1933-35; v.p. creative dir. Norwegian Am. Mus., Decorah, Iowa 1960-66. Author: Norway Travel Newspaper Series, Seattle, 1930, Concert Touring, Monodramas, 1936, (novelized version) Blondie and Dagwood King Features, 1946; script writer serials for WOR, CBS, NBC, N.Y.C.; appeared in Solid Gold Cadillac, I Remember Mama; editor Surfsedge Newsletter. Activities chmn. Glenview, Naples. Mem. Norwegian Am. Mus. (life), MIT (hon.). Republican. Avocations: family, fitness, writing.

PARSONS, HENRY MCILVAINE, psychologist; b. Lenox, Mass., Aug. 31, 1911; s. Herbert and Elsie Worthington (Clews) P.; m. Renee Oakman, 1938 (div. 1945); 1 son, Jack; m. Marina Svetlova, 1949 (div. 1957); m. Marjorie Thorson, 1957. BA, Yale U., 1933; MA, Columbia U., 1947; PhD, U. Calif., Los Angeles, 1963. Reporter N.Y. Herald Tribune, 1935-42; organizer N.Y. Newspaper Guild, 1942; asst., then lectr. psychology Columbia U., 1947-52; research asso. N.Y. U., 1951-52; supr. Electronics Research Labs., Columbia U., 1952-58; mem. human factors staff Douglas Aircraft Co., Long Beach and Santa Monica, Calif., 1956-58; sr. human factors scientist, br. head System Devel. Corp., Santa Monica and Falls Church, Va., 1958-68; self-employed cons., 1968-69; 70-73; v.p. research Riverside Research Inst., N.Y.C., 1969-70; exec. dir. Inst. Behavioral Research Inc., Silver Spring, Md., 1974-79; pres. Exptl. Coll. of Inst. Behavioral Research, Silver Spring, 1974-80; mgr. human factors projects Human Resources Research Orgn., Alexandria, Va., 1980-83; sr. staff scientist Essex Corp., Alexandria, Va., 1983-90; mgr. Ctr. for Human Factors Rsch. Human Resources Rsch. Orgn., Alexandria, 1990—; adj. prof. Lehigh U., 1983-84. Author: Man-Machine System Experiments, 1972; also chpts. in books, articles in jours. Served with USNR, 1942-45. Fellow AAAS, APA (pres. divsn. 21 1975-76, Franklin V. Taylor award 1992), Human Factors and Ergonomics Soc. (pres. 1968-69, Pres.'s Disting. Svc. award 1993), Washington Acad. Scis., Am. Psychol. Soc.; mem. N.Y. Acad. Scis., Ergonomics Soc., Sigma Xi. Clubs: Century (N.Y.C.); Cosmos (Washington). Home: 1600 S Eads St Apt 1223 N Arlington VA 22202-2924 Office: Human Resources Rsch Orgn 66 Canal Center Plz Alexandria VA 22314-1591

PARSONS, IRENE, management consultant; b. North Wilkesboro, N.C.; d. Everett T. and Martha (Minton) P. B.S. in Bus. Edn. and Adminstrn, U. N.C., 1941, LL.D. (hon.), 1967; M.S. in Pub. Adminstrn, George Washington U., 1965. Tchr. Roanoake Rapids (N.C.) High Sch., 1941-42; rep. U.S. Civil Service Commn., 1942-43; with VA, 1946-74, asst. adminstr. vets. affairs, dir. personnel, dir. equal employment opportunity, 1965-74; mgmt. cons., 1974—; Exec. com. Pres.'s Study Group Careers for Women. Served to lt. USCGR, 1943-46. Recipient Fed. Woman's Outstanding Achievement award, 1966, Silver Helmet award Amvets, 1971, Career Svc. award Nat. Civil Svc. League, 1972, Disting. Alumni Achievement award George Washington U., 1973; named to Brevard Coll. Hall of Fame, 1984. Mem. Assn. Fed. Woman's Award Recipients (chmn. 1972-76). Address: PO Box 2046 North Wilkesboro NC 28659

PARSONS, JEFFREY ROBINSON, anthropologist, educator; b. Washington, Oct. 9, 1939; s. Merton Stanley and Elisabeth (Oldenburg) P.; m. Mary Thomson Hrones, Apr. 27, 1968; 1 child, Apphia Hrones. B.S., Pa. State U., 1961; Ph.D., U. Mich., 1966. Asst. prof. anthropology U. Mich., Ann Arbor, 1966-71; assoc. prof. U. Mich., 1971-76, prof., 1976—, dir. mus.

anthropology, 1983-86; vis. prof. Universidad Nacional Autonoma de Mexico, 1987; vis. prof. Universidad Buenos Aires, 1994, Univ. Nac de Catamarca, Argentina, 1996, Univ. Nac de Tucuman, Argentina, 1996. Author: Prehistoric Settlement Patterns in the Texcoco Region, Mexico, 1971; (with William T. Sanders and Robert Stanley) The Basin of Mexico: The Cultural Ecology of a Civilization, 1979, (with E. Brumfiel) Prehispanic Settlement Patterns in the Southern Valley of Mexico, 1982, (with M. Parsons) Chinampa Agriculture and Aztec Urbanization in the Valley of Mexico, 1985, (with Mary H. Parsons) Maguey Utilization in Highland Central Mexico, 1990, The Production of Consumption of Salt During Postclassic Times in the Valley of Mexico, 1994, (with E. Brumfiel and M. Hodge) The Developmental Implications of Earlier Dates for Early Aztec in the Basin of Mexico, 1996. Research grantee NSF, 1967, 70, 72-73, 75-76, 81, Nat. Geog. Soc., 1984, 86, 88. Mem. Am. Anthrop. Assn., Soc. Am. Archaeology, AAAS, Inst. Andean Rsch., Inst. Andean Studies, Sociedad Mexicana de Antropologia, Sociedad Argentina de Antropologia. Office: Museum of Anthropology U Mich Ann Arbor MI 48109

PARSONS, JUDSON ASPINWALL, JR., lawyer; b. Rochester, N.Y., Dec. 15, 1929; s. Judson A. and Frances (Holsopple) P.; m. Chesley Kahmann, Aug. 8, 1959; children: Ames, Brockett. BA, Amherst Coll., 1951; LLB, Harvard U., 1954. Bar: N.Y. 1954, N.J. 1973. Asst. U.S. atty. So. Dist. N.Y., N.Y.C., 1954-55; assoc. Dewey, Ballantine, Bushby, Palmer & Wood, N.Y.C., 1958-65, ptnr., 1966-82; pres. Orbiting Clef Prodns., Inc., Summit, N.J., 1982-86; spl. counsel Laughlin, Markensohn, Lagani & Pegg, P.C., Morristown, N.J., 1986-90, Parsons & Pegg, Morristown, 1990-91; sole practice, 1991—. Served to 1st lt. U.S. Army, 1955-58. Office: 108 Woodland Ave Summit NJ 07901-2003

PARSONS, LEONARD JON, marketing educator, consultant; b. Pitts., Sept. 1, 1942; s. Leonard J. and Marion Jane (Williams) P.; m. Julia Grieve, Jan. 23, 1965; children: Lorelei, Leonard Jon Jr. BSChemE, MIT, 1964; MS in Indsl. Adminstrn., Purdue U., 1965, PhD in Indsl. Adminstrn., 1968. Asst. prof. Ind. U., Bloomington, 1968-70; assoc. prof. Claremont (Calif.) Grad. Sch., 1970-77; prof. marketing Ga. Inst. Tech., 1977—; vis. scholar MIT, Cambridge, fall 1973; Fulbright-Hays sr. scholar Cath. U. Leuven, Belgium, spring 1977; vis. prof. INSEAD, France, fall 1984, Norwegian Sch. Mktg., Oslo, fall 1989, UCLA, spring 1990, Advt. Edn. Found., Anheuser Busch, St. Louis, summer 1993, CREER/FUCAM, Belgium, Fall 1995; mem. rsch. and test devel. com. Grad. Mgmt. Admissions Coun., 1988-90. Author: Using Microcomputers in Marketing, 1986; co-author: Market Response Models, 1990, Marketing Management, 1995, others; edtl. bd. Jour. Mktg. Rsch., 1970-80, 83-85, Jour. Bus. Rsch., 1973-79, Jour. Mktg., 1978-80; assoc. editor: Decision Scis., 1976-79; mktg. dept. editor: Mgmt. Sci., 1980-82; contbr. numerous chpts. to books, articles to profl. jours. Recipient first prize rsch. design contest Am. Mktg. Assn., 1971-72. Mem. Am. Statis. Assn. (chmn. stats. in mktg. sect. 1995), European Mktg. Acad. (mem. exec. com. 1981-84), Theta Delta Chi, Beta Gamma Sigma, Phi Kappa Phi. Office: Ga Inst Tech Dupree Sch Mgmt Atlanta GA 30332-0520

PARSONS, MARCIA PHILLIPS, judge. Bankruptcy judge U.S. Bankruptcy Ct. (Tenn. ea. dist.), 6th circuit, Greeneville, 1993—. Office: US Courthouse 101 W Summer St Greeneville TN 37743-4944

PARSONS, MARK FREDERICK, college development officer; b. Mpls., Nov. 18, 1950; s. Frederick A. and Margaret C. (Anderson) P. BA, U. Minn., 1972; MDiv, United Theol. Sem., New Brighton, Minn., 1976; JD magna cum laude, William Mitchell Coll. Law, St. Paul, 1987; PhD, U. Minn., 1993. Bar: Minn. 1987; ordained deacon Meth. Ch., 1975, elder, 1978. Assoc. min. First United Meth. Ch., Worthington, Minn., 1976-77; min. Fairfax (Minn.) United Meth. Ch., 1977-78, Gethsemane United Meth. Ch., Lino Lakes, Minn., 1979-83; sr. min. Edgewater Emmanuel United Meth. Ch., Mpls., 1983-92; dir. gift planning Hamline U., St. Paul, 1992—; assoc. atty. Lange & Anderson, P.A., Bloomington, Minn., 1988-91. Merrill fellow Harvard Div. Sch., Cambridge, Mass., 1992. Mem. Minn. State Bar, Minn. Planned Giving Coun., Phi Kappa Phi. Avocations: hiking, reading, golf, volunteering, travel. Office: Hamline U 1536 Hewitt Ave Saint Paul MN 55104-1205

PARSONS, MERRIBELL MADDUX, museum administrator; b. San Antonio. BFA, Newcomb Coll., 1964; MA, M.Phil., Inst. Fine Arts, NYU, 1968. Curator of sculpture and decorative arts Mpls. Inst. Arts, 1969-74, chief curator, 1974-79; vice-dir. for edn. Met. Mus. Art, N.Y.C., 1979-87; dir. Columbus Mus. Art, Ohio, 1987-95; exec. dir. Julian Wood Glass Jr. Mus. Inc., Winchester, Va., 1995—. Author: Sculpture: David Daniels Collection; editor, author exhbn. catalogues and articles. Mem. pub. art com. Greater Columbus Arts Coun., 1989, Downtown Planning Group, Columbus, 1989. Clawson Mills fellow Met. Mus. Art, 1967; NEA professional grantee, Washington, 1972. Mem. Assn. Art Mus. Dirs., Am. Assn. Mus., Columbus C. of C. (bd. dirs. 1990-92). Office: 467 E Olmos Dr San Antonio TX 78212-2035

PARSONS, ROBERT EUGENE, transportation consultant; b. Cin., Apr. 19, 1931; s. Charles Eugene and Samantha Ellen (Snider) P.; m. Beverly Greenhalgh, Dec. 30, 1949; children: Brian Scott, Barry Lawrence, Robert Stephen, Kimberly Ann. ME, U. Cinn., 1954; MSME, Drexel Inst. Tech., 1959. Registered profl. engr., Calif., Nev., Md., Ohio. Asst. project engr. The Martin Co., Balt., 1956-62, sect. mgr., 1962-64; dep. dir. Supersonic Transp. Office FAA, Washington, 1964-71; dir. rsch. and devel. plans U.S. Dept. Transp., Washington, 1971; assoc. adminstr. Fed. RR Adminstrn., Washington, 1975-80; dir. ctr. field methods Nat. Bur. Standards, Gaithersburg, Md., 1980-81; dir. RR rsch. and devel. program U. Calif., Berkeley, 1981-84; cons. Walnut Creek, Calif., 1986-90; dir. program on advanced technology for hwy. U. Calif. Berkeley, 1984-93; prin. Parsons Transp. Assocs., Midlothian, Va., 1993—; ons. Assn. Am. R.R.s, Washington, U. Calif., Calif. Dept. Transp., U.S. Dept. T ransp., Radar Control Sys., Rand, Sys. Control Tech., Intelligent Vehicle Hwy. Soc. Techs., Inc., Lawrence Livermore Nat. Lab., French Inst. Transp. Safety, Intelligent Vehicle Hwy. Soc. Am., chmn. sys. arch. com.; cons. IMRA Am., Inc. JKH & Assocs., Sci. Atlanta, Va. Tech., Va. Dept. Transp. Contbr. articles to profl. jours. Mem. SAE, Intelligent Transp. Soc. Am. (chair system arch. com), Intelligent Transp. Sys. of Va. (bd. mem., chmn. strategic planning com.), ITS World (editorial bd.). Methodist. Avocations: computer work, woodworking. Home: 3106 Cove Ridge Rd Midlothian VA 23112-4354

PARSONS, RODNEY HUNTER, lawyer; b. Pasadena, Calif., Feb. 4, 1947; s. Clarence Eugene and Agnes Prentice (Hunter) P.; m. Deneise Renee Trebotich, Aug. 2, 1980; children: Shannon, Justin, Ryan, Renee, Morgan. BA, UCLA, 1968, JD, 1975. Bar: Calif. 1975, U.S. Dist. Ct. (cen. dist.) Calif. 1980. Assoc. Law Offices Manley Freid, L.A., 1975-78, Robert P. Lawton Inc., Brea, Calif., 1978-79; ptnr. Lether & Parsons, Brea, Calif., 1979-84; owner, pres. Rodney H. Parsons Inc., Fullerton, Calif., 1984—; judge pro tem Superior Ct., 1989—. Bd. dirs. Brea C. of C., 1979-88, pres., 1980-82; bd. dirs. Brea Found., 1990. Mem. Orange County Bar Assn. (family law sect.), Rotary (bd. dirs. 1979-81). Avocations: golf, youth sports, model trains, writing. Office: 285 Imperial Hwy Fullerton CA 92835-1048

PARSONS, VINSON ADAIR, retired computer software company executive; b. Frankfort, Ky., Oct. 22, 1932; s. Richard Adair and Nina (Mefford) P.; m. Elizabeth Ann Peltier, June 2, 1956. A.S., Mitchell Coll., 1959; B.S., U. Conn., 1960; AMP, Harvard U., 1985. Auditor, Price Waterhouse & Co. (C.P.A.s), Hartford, Conn., 1960-65; controller Pervel Industries Inc., Plainfield, Conn., 1965-70; v.p., controller Akzo Am. Inc., Asheville, N.C., 1970-71, 73-83, v.p., chief fin. officer, 1983-86; v.p., chief fin. officer System Software Assocs. Inc., Chgo., 1986-89, also bd. dirs.; ret., 1990; dir. Am. Tape Co., BRIntec Co., Control Tech. Corp. Elected commr. Town of Weaverville Bd. Commrs., 1994—. With USN, 1953-57. Mem. Am. Mgmt. Assn., Fin. Execs. Inst., Inst. Mgmt. Accts. (pres. local chpt. 1969-70). Clubs: Asheville Country; University (N.Y.C.); Reems Creek Golf. Home and Office: 15 Preston Ct Weaverville NC 28787-8907

PARTAIN, CLARENCE LEON, radiologist, nuclear medicine physician, educator, administrator; b. Memphis, July 12, 1940; s. Archie Leon and Vergie (Young) P.; m. Judith Stafford, Jan., 1964; children: David Blane, Teri Ellyn, Amy Leigh. B.S.N.E., U. Tenn., 1963; M.S.N.E., Purdue U., 1965, Ph.D. in Nuclear Engring., 1967; M.D., Washington U., St. Louis, 1975. Diplomate: Am. Bd. Nuclear Medicine, Am. Bd. Radiology; registered profl. engr., Mo. Asst. prof. nuclear engring. U. Mo.-Columbia, 1968-71, assoc. prof., 1971-75; resident N.C. Meml. Hosp., Chapel Hill, 1975-79; assoc. prof. radiology U. N.C.-Chapel Hill, 1978-79; assoc. prof. Vanderbilt U., Nashville, 1980-85; prof. radiology and biomed. engring. Vanderbilt U., 1985—, vice chmn. radiology, 1989-92, dir. nuclear medicine, 1981-85, dir. magnetic resonance imaging, 1983-92, chmn. radiology, radiologist in chief, 1992—; cons. NIH, Bethesda, Md., 1980—. Author: Nuclear Magnetic Resonance (NMR) Imaging, 1983, NMR Imaging: Clinical Utility and Correlation, 1984, Thyroid and Parathyroid Imaging, 1986, Magnetic Resonance Imaging, 2d edit., 1988, Correlative Image: Nuclear Medicine, Magnetic Resonance, Computer Tomography, Ultrasound, 1988; editl. bd. Acad. Radiology, Magnetic Resonance Imaging, Jour. Magnetic Resonance Imaging, Jour. Nuclear Medicine. AEC Spl. fellow, 1964-66; grantee Nat. Inst. Neurosci., Communicative Diseases and Stroke, 1977-78. Fellow Am. Coll. Nuclear Physicians, Am. Coll. Radiology, Soc. Magnetic Resonance Imaging (bd. dirs.); mem. AMA, IEEE, Radiol. Soc. N.Am., Assn. Univ. Radiologists (exec. com.), Soc. Nuclear Medicine (trustee, Benedict Casson lectr. 1981), Am. Roentgen Ray Soc. (exec. coun.), Soc. Magnetic Resonance in Medicine (trustee), Internat. Soc. of Magnetic Resonance in Medicine (governance coun.), Sigma Phi Epsilon. Baptist. Home: 5471 Pinewood Rd Franklin TN 37064-9235 Office: Vanderbilt U Med Ctr 1611 21st Ave S Nashville TN 37212-3103

PARTAIN, EUGENE GARTLY, lawyer; b. Memphis, Oct. 4, 1930; s. Eugene Gardner and Zoe (Allen) P.; m. Ute Agnes Reinsch, July 8, 1952; children—Gia Michele, Matthew Reinsch. B.A., Duke U., 1952, LL.B., 1958; M.A., Northwestern U., 1959. Bar: Ga. 1961, U.S. Supreme Ct. 1980. Sr. ptnr. King & Spalding, Atlanta. Served to capt. USAF, 1952-54. Fellow Am. Coll. Trial Lawyers, Internat. Acad. Trial Lawyers, Internat. Soc. Barristers, Am. Bd. Trial Advocates; mem. ABA, Atlanta Bar Assn. (exec. com.), Ga. Def. Lawyers Assn. (pres. 1982-83), Best Lawyers in Am., Old War Horse Lawyers Club, Lawyers Club of Atlanta. Presbyterian. Office: King & Spalding 191 Peachtree St NE Ste 4900 Atlanta GA 30303-1740

PARTAIN, LARRY DEAN, solar research engineer; b. McKinney, Tex., Apr. 27, 1942; s. Archie Leon and Vergie Ann (Young) P.; m. Deborah Patton, July 1986; children: Lauren Elizabeth, Catherine Ann. BSEE, U. Tenn., 1965; PhD, Johns Hopkins U., 1971. Assoc. prof. elec. engring. U. Del., Newark, 1971-78; engr. Engring. Research div. Lawrence Livermore Nat. Lab., Calif., 1978-80; sr. research engr. Chevron Research Co., Richmond, Calif., 1980-87; sr. scientist, mktg. mgr. Varian Ginzton Research Ctr., Palo Alto, Calif., 1987—. Co-author/editor: Solar Cells and Their Applications, 1995; contbr. articles to tech. jours.; patentee microwave sensor, solar cells, solar arrays, optical switch. Solar Energy Rsch. Inst. grantee, 1978-79, 84-86; duPont rsch. grantee, 1974-75; grantee USAF Wright Aero. Lab., 1984-85, 88-90, 91-93, Sandia Nat. Labs., 1985-86, Naval Surface Warfare Ctr., 1994, 95. Mem. IEEE. Office: Varian Rsch Ctr 3075 Hansen Way Palo Alto CA 94304-1025 *Technical advances are keyed to the pragmatic scientists' search for simple, accurate, and predictive physical models. This contrasts with the search for truth—a seductive and distracting abstraction better left to philosophers and theologians.*

PARTAN, DANIEL GORDON, lawyer, educator; b. Gardner, Mass., Aug. 2, 1933; s. Toivo Antero and Lempi Sivia (Adamson) P.; m. Doris Liepmann, June 8, 1957; children: Andrew Stewart, Matthew Alexander, Sarah Ruth, Iliana Maria, Juan Carlos. AB, Cornell U., 1955; LLB, Harvard U., 1958, LLM, 1961. Bar: Mass. 1959. Rsch. assoc. Harvard Law Sch., 1961, Rule of Law Ctr., Duke U. Law Sch., 1962-65; assoc. prof. U. N.D., 1964-65; assoc. prof. law Boston U., 1965-68, prof., 1968—; mem. NAFTA dispute settlement roster and binat. dispute panel U.S.-Can. Free Trade Agreement; cons. Dept. State, UN Devel. Program, Am. Acad. Arts and Sci.; pres., chmn. Bd. dirs. UN Assn. Greater Boston, 1969-71, 76-77; chmn. Brookline Selectmen's Com. on Harvard Energy Plant, 1976—; vis. scholar Harvard Law Sch., 1977-78; vis. fellow Cambridge (Eng.) U., 1972. Author: Population in the United Nations System, 1973, Documentary Study of the Politicization of UNESCO, 2 vols., 1975, The International Law Process, 1992; co-author: Legal Problems of International Administration, 1968, The United States and the International Labor Organization, 1980; co-editor: Corporate Disclosure of Environmental Risks: U.S. and European Law, 1990; contbr. articles to books and jours. Mem. ABA, Boston Bar Assn., Bretton Woods Com., Commn. to Study the Orgn. Peace, Am. Law Inst., Acad. Coun. UN System, Am. Soc. Internat. Law, Internat. Law Assn., European Communities Studies Assn., UN Assn., Coalition for a Strong UN. Office: 765 Commonwealth Ave Boston MA 02215-1401

PARTANEN, CARL RICHARD, biology educator; b. Portland, Oreg., Nov. 23, 1921; s. Emil and Ellen (Engstrom) P.; m. Jane Nelson, June 24, 1961; children: Karen, Kirsten, Richard (dec.). Student, Multnomah Jr. Coll., 1946-48; B.A., Lewis and Clark Coll., 1950; M.A., Harvard, 1951, Ph.D., 1954. Am. Cancer Soc. postdoctoral research fellow Columbia, 1954-55, Harvard, 1955-57; research asso. Childrens Cancer Research Found., Boston, 1957-61; asso. prof. biology U. Pitts., 1961-64, prof. biology, 1964-86, chmn. biology, 1964-70, prof. emeritus, 1987—; Research fellow U. Edinburgh, Scotland, 1971-72, U. Nottingham, Eng., 1978-79. Contbr. articles to profl. jours. Served with AUS, 1942-45, ETO. Recipient Distinguished Achievement award Lewis and Clark Coll., 1968. Mem. Am. Genetic Assn., Bot. Soc. Am., Soc. for Devel. Biology, Soc. for In Vitro Biology, Am. Inst. Biol. Sci. Home: 1112 Farragut St Pittsburgh PA 15206-1746 Office: U Pitts Dept Biol Scis Pittsburgh PA 15260

PARTCH, KENNETH PAUL, editor, consultant; b. Mt. Vernon, N.Y., June 22, 1925; s. Edward Augustus and Grace Jane (Crabb) P.; m. Dorothy Sophia Iversen, July 16, 1953; children—Marjorie, Stephen, Jessica. A.B., Bklyn. Coll., 1949. Mng. editor Moore Publishing Co., 1955, Chain Store Age mag., 1955-59, Sales Mgmt. mag., 1961; editor Food Topics mag., 1961-68; dir. mktg. Grocery Mfrs. Am., 1969-70; editor Chain Store Age-Supermarket Group, N.Y.C., 1970-77; cons. to supermarket industry, 1977-80; editor-in-chief Supermarket Bus. mag., 1980-93, editor-at-large, 1993—. Contbr. to Wharton Mag. Served with USAAF, 1943-46. Decorated Air medal; recipient Jesse Neal award Assoc. Bus. Press, 1968, Grand award ABP Points of Light Award, 1991. Mem. Sigma Delta Chi. Home: 20 Devils Gardens Rd Norwalk CT 06854-3315

PARTEE, BARBARA HALL, linguist, educator; b. Englewood, N.J., June 23, 1940; d. David B. and Helen M. Hall; m. Morriss Henry Partee, 1966 (div. 1971); children: Morriss M., David M., Joel T.; m. Emmon Werner Bach, 1973 (div. 1996); m. Vladimir B. Borschev, 1997. BA with high honors in Math., Swarthmore Coll., 1961; PhD in Linguistics, MIT, 1965; DSc (hon.), Swarthmore Coll., 1989, Charles U., Prague, Czechoslovakia, 1992. Asst. prof. UCLA, 1965-69, assoc. prof., 1969-73; assoc. prof. linguistics and philosophy U. Mass., Amherst, 1972-73, prof., 1973-90, Disting. Univ. prof., 1990—, head dept. linguistics, 1987-93; fellow Ctr. for Advanced Study in Behavior Scis., 1976-77; mem. bd. mgrs. Swarthmore Coll., 1990—. Author: (with Stockwell and Schachter) The Major Syntactic Structures of English, 1972, Fundamentals of Mathematics for Linguists, 1979, (with ter Meulen and Wall) Mathematical Methods in Linguistics, 1990; editor: Montague Grammar, 1976; co-editor: (with Chierchia and Turner) Properties, Types and Meaning, Vol. I: Foundational Issues, Vol. II: Semantic Issues, 1989, (with Bach, Jelinek and Kratzer) Quantification in Natural Languages, 1995; mem. editoral bd: Language, 1967-73, Linguistic Inquiry, 1972-79, Theoretical Linguistics, 1974—, Linguistics and Philosophy, 1977—. Recipient Chancellor's medal U. Mass., 1977; NEH fellow, 1982-83; Internat. Rsch. and Exchanges Bd. fellow, 1989-90, 95. Fellow AAAS; mem. NAS (chair anthropology sect. 1993-96), Linguistic Soc. Am. (pres. 1986), Am. Philos. Assn., Assn. Computational Linguistics, Am. Acad. Arts and Scis., Sigma Xi. Home: 50 Hobart Ln Amherst MA 01002-1321 Office: U Mass Dept Linguistics Amherst MA 01003 *I had the good fortune to have loving and encouraging parents and stimulating teachers, to find a field of inquiry which I love and can contribute to, and to have the constant inspiration of wonderful collegues, wonderful students and wonderful family.*

PARTHASARATHY, RAJAGOPAL, writer, literature educator; b. Tirupparaittrai, India, Aug. 20, 1934; came to U.S., 1982; s. Krishnaswamy and Ambujam Rajagopal; m. Shobhan Koppikar, Oct. 26, 1969; children: Gautam, Arjun. BA, Bombay U., 1957, MA, 1959; Diploma in English Studies, Leeds (Eng.) U., 1964; PhD, U. Tex., 1987. Lectr. in English Ismail Yusuf Coll., Bombay, 1959-62, Mithibai Coll., Bombay, 1962-63, 64-65; lectr. in English lang. teaching Brit. Coun., Bombay, 1965-66; asst. prof. English Presidency Coll., Madras, 1966-67; lectr. in English South Indian Edn. Soc. Coll., Bombay, 1967-71; regional editor Oxford U. Press, Madras, 1971-78; editor Oxford U. Press, Delhi, 1978-82; asst. prof. English Skidmore Coll., Saratoga Springs, N.Y., 1986-92, assoc. prof., 1992—, dir. program in Asian studies, 1994—; dir. poetry workshop Stella Maris Coll., Madras, 1972-75; part-time lectr. in book pub. Coll. Vocat. Guidance, Delhi U., New Delhi, 1979-81. Author: (verse) Rough Passage, 1977; editor (verse) Ten Twentieth-Century Indian Poets, 1976, (with J.J. Healy) Poetry from Leeds, 1968; translator: (verse and prose) The Tale of an Anklet: An Epic of South India (The Cilappatikaram of Ilanko Atikal), 1993. Brit. Coun. scholar, 1963; recipient Ulka Poetry prize Poetry India, 1966, PEN/Book-of-the-Month Club Translation citation, 1994, Translation prize Sahitya Akademi (Nat. Acad. Letters India), 1995, Assn. for Asian Studies A.K. Ramamjan Book, 1996; U.S. Dept. State exch. visitor, 1978. Mem. MLA, PEN, Am. Comparative Literature Assn., Am. Lit. Translators Assn., Assn. for Asian Studies (A.K. Ramanujan Book prize for transl. 1996), Phi Kappa Phi. Avocations: travel, classical music, gardening. Home: 8 Salem Dr Saratoga Springs NY 12866-3726 Office: Skidmore Coll Dept English 815 N Broadway Saratoga Springs NY 12866-1631

PARTHEMORE, JACQUELINE G., physician, educator; b. Harrisburg, Pa., Dec. 21, 1940; d. Philip Mark and Emily (Buvit) Parthemore; m. Alan Morton Blank, Jan. 8, 1967; children: Stephen Eliot, Laura Elise. BA, Wellesley Coll., 1962; MD, Cornell U., 1966. Rsch. edn. assoc. VA Hosp., San Diego, 1974-78; staff physician VA Med. Ctr., San Diego, 1978-79, asst. chief, med. svc., 1979-80, acting chief, med. svc., 1980-81, chief of staff, 1984—; asst. prof. medicine U. Calif. Sch. Medicine, San Diego, 1974-80, assoc. prof. medicine, 1980-85, prof. medicine, assoc. dean, 1985—; mem. nat. rsch. resources coun. NIH, Bethesda, Md., 1990-94. Contbr. articles to profl. jours., chpts. to books. Bd. dirs. San Diego Vets. Med. Rsch. Found.; mem. adv. bd. San Diego Opera. Recipient Bullock's 1st Annual Portfolio award, 1985, San Diego Pres.'s Coun. Woman of Yr. award, 1985, YWCA Tribute to Women in Industry award, 1987. Fellow ACP; mem. Endocrine Soc., Am. Fedn. Clin. Rsch., Nat. Assn. VA Chiefs Staff (pres. 1989-91), Am. Assn. Clin. Endocrinologists, Wellesley Coll. Alumnae Assn. (1st v.p. 1992-95). Avocations: gardening, reading, sailing, cooking, travel. Office: VA Med Ctr 3350 La Jolla Village Dr San Diego CA 92161-0002

PARTHUM, CHARLES ALBERT, civil engineer; b. Lawrence, Mass., Sept. 26, 1929; s. Albert and Elsie Ida (Eichner) P.; m. Mary Catherine Wiggin, Oct. 20, 1956; children: Stephen Charles, Julie Elizabeth. BSCE, Northeastern U., 1951. With Camp Dresser & McKee, Inc., Boston, 1951—; ptnr. Camp Dresser & McKee, Inc., 1967—, sr. v.p., dir., 1971-92; cons., 1992-97; cons. EPA, 1980. Treas., deacon, moderator, clk. Tabernacle Ch., Salem, Mass.; chmn. Engr.-Joint Contacts Documents Com., 1980. Recipient Outstanding Civil Engring. Alumnus award Northeastern U., 1989. Mem. NSPE, ASCE (bd. dirs. 1987-90, pres. 1995-96, William H. Wisely Am. Civil Engr. award 1993), Am. Acad. Environ. Engrs. (diplomate), Boston Soc. Civil Engrs. (hon., pres. 1975-76), Water Pollution Control Fedn. (chmn. constrn. and bylaws com. 1972-77), Am. Water Resources Assn., Mass. Soc. Profl. Engrs., Am. Water Works Assn., New England Water Works Assn., New England Water Pollution Control Assn., Chi Epsilon (hon.). Office: One Cambridge Ctr Cambridge MA 02142

PARTIDA, GILBERT A., chamber of commerce executive; b. Nogales, Ariz., July 27, 1962; s. Enrique Gilberto and Mary Lou (Flores) P.; m. Soncee Ray Brown, July 30, 1992. BA with distinction, U. Ariz., 1984; JD cum laude, Pepperdine U., 1987; LLD (hon.), Calif. Western Sch Law, San Diego, 1993. V.p., bd. mem. Partida Brokerage, Inc., Nogales, 1983-91; law clk. Office of Ariz. Atty. Gen., Tucson, 1985; assoc. Gray, Cary, Ames & Frye, San Diego, 1986-89, sr. assoc., 1990-92; chmn. Mex. Practice Group Gray, Cary, Ames & Frye, 1992; pres. Greater San Diego C. of C., 1993—; corp. counsel San Diego Incubator Corp., 1990—. Contbr. articles to profl. jours. Mem. United Way Latino Future Scan Com., 1990; mentor Puente, 1991; leadership tng. mentor Chicano Fedn., 1992; dinner com. Young at Art, 1991; mem. Children's Initiative, 1993, Superbowl Task Force, 1993, San Diego Dialogue, 1993; hon. mem. Sister City, 1993, LEAD, 1993; hon. chair Easter Seals Telethon, 1994; vice chmn. Border Trade Alliance, 1989-91; mem. nat. gala com. HDI Ednl. Svcs., 1990; Calif. state del. U.S.-Mexico Border Govs.' Conf., 1990, 92; exec. com. San Diego Conv. and Visitors Bur. Mem. San Diego County Hispanic C. of C. (chmn. 1991, pres. 1990-91, v.p. 1989-90, internat. com. chair 1989-90, sec. 1989, founding bd. mem. 1988), Consejo Nacional de Maquiladoras, Calif. Hispanic C. of C. (state conv. joint venture com. 1991, spl. projects chair 1991), San Diego/Tijuana Sister Cities Soc. (adv. coun. 1993—), San Diego County Bar Assn. (U.S./Mexico liaison com.), ABA (U.S./Mexico bar liaison com.), Hispanic Alliance for Free Trade, Rotary Club San Diego. Avocations: tennis, running, creative writing. Office: Greater San Diego C of C 402 W Broadway Ste 1000 San Diego CA 92101-8507

PARTINGTON, JAMES WOOD, naval officer; b. Omaha, Jan. 16, 1939; s. Lee Edward and Carol Virginia (Wood) P.; m. Barbara Jean Arline, July 15, 1961; children: Jennifer, Kathleen, Mary Elizabeth. BA, U. R.I., 1970; grad., Naval War Coll., 1971. Commd. ensign USN, 1961, advanced through grades to rear adm., 1989; ops. officer Attack Squadron 122, Lemoore, Calif., 1974-77; comdg. officer Attack Squadron 27, Lemoore, 1977-80, Strike Fighter Squadron 125, Lemoore, 1980-82; coord. F/A 18 program Chief Naval Ops., Washington, 1982-84; comdg. officer Naval Air Sta., Lemoore, 1984-86; chief of staff Cruiser Destroyer Group 5, San Diego, 1986-87; dir. Naval Aviation Officer Assignments, Washington, 1987-88; comdr. Strike Fighter Wings Atlantic, Jacksonville, Fla., 1988-90, Naval Tng. Ctr., Great Lakes, Ill., 1990-92; v.p., dir. corp. planning Sr. Technologies Inc., 1992-94; pres. Partington and Associates, Lincoln, 1994—. Decorated Legion of Merit (5), DFC, Air medal (28), Meritorious Svc. medal. Mem. U.S. Naval Inst., Assn. Naval Aviation, Naval Order of U.S. Roman Catholic. Avocations: sailing, tennis, scuba diving.

PARTLETT, DAVID F., law educator; b. 1947. LLB, Sydney U., 1970; LLM, Mich. U., 1972, 74; SJD, U. Va., 1980. Bar: New South Wales 1971, Australian Cap. Terr. 1978. Vis. asst. prof. U. Ala., 1972-73; legis. officer Australia A-GOffice, 1974-76; dir, rsch. Australian Law Reform Commn., 1976-78; lectr. Australian Nat. U., 1978-80, sr. lectr., 1980-87; vis. prof. Vanderbilt U., Nashville, 1987-88, prof. law, 1988—, acting dean, 1996-97; Sparkman Dist. vis. prof. Ala. U., 1986-87. Office: Vanderbilt U Sch Law 21st Ave S Nashville TN 37240

PARTNOY, RONALD ALLEN, lawyer; b. Norwalk, Conn., Dec. 23, 1933; s. Maurice and Ethel Marguerite (Roselle) P.; m. Diane Catherine Keenan, Sept. 18, 1965. B.A., Yale U., 1956; LL.B., Harvard U., 1961; LL.M., Boston U., 1965. Bar: Mass. 1962, Conn. 1966. Atty. Liberty Mut. Ins. Co., Boston, 1961-65; assoc. counsel Remington Arms Co., Bridgeport, Conn., 1965-70; gen. counsel Remington Arms Co., 1970-88, sec., 1983-93; sr. counsel E.I. du Pont de Nemours & Co., Wilmington, Del., 1985-95. Served with USN, 1956-58; to capt. USNR (ret.). Mem. ABA, Sporting Arms and Ammunition Mfrs. Inst. (chmn. legis. and legal affairs com. 1971-86), Am. Judicature Soc., U.S. Navy League (pres. Bridgeport coun. 1975-77, nat. dir., Conn. pres. 1977-80, v.p. Empire region 1980-85), Naval Res. Assn. (3d dist. pres., nat. exec. com. 1981-85), Chancery Club, Harvard Club of Boston, Harvard Club of Phila., Yale Club of N.Y.C. Home: 616 Bayard Rd Kennett Square PA 19348-2504

PARTON, DOLLY REBECCA, singer, composer, actress; b. Sevier County, Tenn., Jan. 19, 1946; d. Robert Lee and Avie Lee (Owens) P.; m. Carl Dean, May 30, 1966. Country music singer, rec. artist, composer, actress, radio and TV personality; entrepreneur, owner entertainment park Dollywood, established 1985. Radio appearances include Grand Ole Opry, WSM Radio, Nashville, Cass Walker program, Knoxville; TV appearances include Porter Wagoner Show, from 1967, Cass Walker program, Bill Anderson Show, Wilburn Bros. Show, Barbara Mandrell Show; rec. artist, Mercury, Monument, RCA , CBS record cos.; star movie Nine to Five, 1980, The Best Little Whorehouse in Texas, 1982, Rhinestone, 1984, Steel Magnolias, 1989, Straight Talk, 1991; albums include Here You Come Again (Grammy award 1978), Real Love, 1985, Just the Way I Am, 1986, Portrait, 1986, Think

About Love, 1986, Trio (with Emmylou Harris, Linda Ronstadt) (Grammy award 1988), 1987, Heartbreaker, Great Balls of Fire, Rainbow, 1988, White Limozeen, 1989, Home for Christmas, 1990, Eagle When She Flies, 1991, Slow Dancing with the Moon, 1993 (Grammy nomination, Best Country Vocal Collaboration for Romeo (with Tanya Tucker, Billy Ray Cyrus, Kathy Mattea, Pam Tillis, & Mary-Chapin Carpenter), (with Tammy Wynette and Loretta Lynn) Honky Tonk Angels, 1994, The Essential Dolly Parton, 1995, Just the Way I Am, 1996, Super Hits, 1996, (with others) I Will Always Love You & Other Greatest Hits, 1996; composer numerous songs including Nine to Five (Grammy award 1981, Acad. award nominee and Golden Globe award nominee 1981); author: Dolly, 1994. Recipient (with Porter Wagoner) Vocal Group of Yr. award, 1968; Vocal Duo of Yr. award All Country Music Assn., 1970, 71; Nashville Metronome award, 1979; Am. Music award for best duo performance (with Kenny Rogers), 1984; named Female Vocalist of Yr., 1975, 76; Country Star of Yr., Sullivan Prodns., 1977; Entertainer of Yr., Country Music Assn., 1978; People's Choice award, 1980, 88; Female Vocalist of Yr., Acad. Country Music, 1980; Dolly Parton Day proclaimed, Sevier County, Tenn., designated Oct. 7, 1967, Los Angeles, Sept. 20, 1979; recipient Grammy awards for best female country vocalist, 1978, 81, for best country song, 1981, for best country vocal performance with group, 1987; co-recipient (with Emmylou Harris and Linda Ronstadt) Acad. Country Music award for album of the yr., 1987; named to Small Town of Am. Hall of Fame, 1988, East Tenn. Hall of Fame, 1988. Address: RCA 6 W 57th St New York NY 10019*

PARTON, JAMES, historian; b. Newburyport, Mass., Dec. 10, 1912; s. Hugo and Agnes (Leach) P.; m. Jane Audra Bourne, Dec. 9, 1950 (dec. 1962); children: James III, Dana (dec.), Sara. A.B., Harvard U., 1934. Asst. E.L. Bernays, N.Y.C., 1934-35; aviation editor Time Mag., 1935-36, bus. and financial editor, 1937-39, asst. gen. mgr., 1940, bus. mgr. air express edit., 1941; promotion mgr. Time-Life Internat., 1945; editorial dir. Pacific Coast news burs. Time, Inc., 1947; editor and pub. Los Angeles Ind., 1948-49; cons. U.S. Dept. State, 1949; promotion dir. N.Y. Herald Tribune, 1950; asst. to pres., chmn. Herald Tribune Forum and dir. N.Y. Herald Tribune, Inc., 1951-53; v.p., treas. Thorndike, Jensen & Parton, Inc., 1953-57; founder, pres. Am. Heritage Pub. Co., Inc., 1954-70; pres. Ency. Brit. Ednl. Corp., Chgo., 1970-72; chmn. exec. com. Ency. Brit. Ednl. Corp., 1973; pres. James Parton & Co., N.Y.C., 1973-81, Parton Enterprises, Inc., 1981-84; dir. planning study Custom House Inst., N.Y.C., 1973; chmn. Nat. Advt. Rev. Bd., 1974-76; asst. librarian for pub. edn. Library of Congress, 1976-77; chmn. exec. com. Hist. Times, Inc., 1979-81; chmn. U.S. Army com. which produced ofcl. Eighth Air Force book Target-Germany, 1943. Author: "Air Force Spoken Here", General Ira Eaker and the Command of the Air, 1986. Editor, pub. Impact, The Army Air Forces Confidential Picture History of World War II, 8 vols. 1980. Trustee Loomis Inst., 1952—, pres., 1964-66, chmn., 1967-70; trustee USAF Hist. Found., 1955—; bd. visitors Air U., 1988-91. Commd. 2d lt. in USAAF, 1942; advanced through grades to lt. col. 1944. Decorated Legion of Merit, Bronze Star, European Theater ribbon with 4 battle stars. Mem. Army and Navy Club (Washington). Home: PO Box 796 Hanover NH 03755-0796

PARTRIDGE, BRUCE JAMES, lawyer, educator; b. June 4, 1926, Syracuse, N.Y.; came to Can., 1969; s. Bert James and Lida Marion (Rice) P.; m. Mary Janice Smith, June 13, 1948 (dec. 1986); children: Heather Leigh, Eric James, Brian Lloyd, Bonnie Joyce; m. May S. Archer, May 28, 1988; stepchildren: Sheila Archer, Laurel Archer. AB cum laude, Oberlin Coll., Ohio, 1946; LLB, Blackstone Coll., Chgo., 1950, JD, 1952; LLB, U. B.C., 1974. Bar: B.C. 1976, N.W.T. 1980. Rsch. physicist Am. Gas Assn., Cleve., 1946-48; bus. adminstr. Rochester Inst. Tech., N.Y., 1953-58, Baldwin-Wallace Coll., Berea, Ohio, 1951-53, Cazenovia (N.Y.) Coll., 1948-51; v.p. bus. and mgmt., U. Del., Newark, Del., 1958-63; v.p. adminstrn. Johns Hopkins U., Balt., 1963-69; pres. U. Victoria, B.C., Can., 1969-72; assoc. Clark, Wilson & Co., Vancouver, B.C., 1975-78; successively solicitor, mng. solicitor, gen. solicitor, v.p. law and gen. counsel, sec. Cominco Ltd., Vancouver, 1978-88; exec. dir. Baker & McKenzie, Hong Kong, 1988-90; v.p. Pacific Creations Inc., 1990-92; faculty Camosun Coll., 1992—. Co-author: College and University Business Administration, 1968. Chmn. editorial com. Purchasing for Higher Education, 1962. Contbr. numerous articles to profl. jours. Chmn. commn. on adminstrv. affairs Am. Council on Edn., Washington, 1966-69; mem. Pres.'s Com. on Employment of Handicapped, Washington, 1967-69; mem. adv. council Ctr. for Resource Studies, Queen's U.; bd. dirs. L'Arche in the Americas; mem. adv. council Westwater Research Centre, U. B.C. Mem. Law Soc. B.C., Law Soc. of N.W. Ters., Assn. Can. Gen. Counsel, Fedn. Ins. and Corp. Counsel, Def. Research Inst. (product liability com.), Am. Corp. Counsel Assn., Vancouver Club, Aberdeen Marine Club, Hong Kong Football Club. Unitarian. Office: Camosun Coll, 4461 Interurban Rd, Victoria, BC Canada V8X 3X1

PARTRIDGE, MARK VAN BUREN, lawyer; b. Rochester, Minn., Oct. 16, 1954; s. John V.B. and Constance (Brainerd) P.; m. Mary Roberta Moffitt, Apr. 30, 1983; children: Caitlin, Lindsay, Christopher. BA, U. Nebr., 1978; JD, Harvard U., 1981. Bar: Ill. 1981, U.S. Dist. Ct. (no. dist.) Ill. 1981, U.S. Dist. Ct. (ea. dist.) Mich. 1983, U.S. Ct. Appeals (fed. cir.) 1983, U.S. Ct. Appeals (4th cir.) 1986, U.S. Ct. Appeals (5th cir.) 1993. Assoc. Pattishall, McAuliffe, Newbury, Hilliard & Geraldson, Chgo., 1981-88, ptnr., 1988—; adj. prof. John Marshall Law Sch., Chgo., 1990—; arbitrator Cook County Mandatory Arbitration Program, 1989—; v.p. Harvard Legal Aid Bur., 1980-81. Contbr. articles to profl. law reviews; mem. editl. bd. The Trademark Reporter, 1994-97; adv. bd. IP Litigator, 1995—. Vol. Chgo. Vol. Legal Svcs., 1983—. Mem. ABA (com. chmn. 1989-91, 94—), Internat. Trademark Assn. (com. vice chair 1996p), Am. Intellectual Property Law Assn. (com. chmn. 1989-91, 96—), Intellectual Property Law Assn. Chgo. (com. chmn. 1993-96, Brand Names Ednl. Found., moot ct. regional chmn. 1994-96, nat. vice chair 1997—), Legal Club, Executives' Club, Union League Club. Avocations: writing, genealogy, travel, computers. Office: Pattishall McAuliffe Newbury Hilliard & Geraldso 311 S Wacker Dr Ste 5000 Chicago IL 60606-6622

PARTRIDGE, WILLIAM RUSSELL, retired federal executive; b. Torrance, Calif., Jan. 9, 1927; s. Frederick Walter and Dorothy (Keller) P.; m. Phyllis Ruth Squires, Feb. 6, 1949; children: William M., Carol C., Mark F. Student, U. Idaho, W. Va. U., 1944-45; BA, Pomona Coll., 1949; MPA, Syracuse U., 1950; MBA, UCLA, 1963. Various mgmt. positions U.S. AEC, Oak Ridge, 1950-55; staff asst., adminstr. mgmt. devel., ops. analyst Gen. Offices and Rocketdyne div./N.Am. Aviation Co., L.A., 1955-61; mgr. mgmt. systems Gen. Offices, N.Am. Aviation Co., L.A., 1961-65; project engr. info. sys. divsn. autonetics N.Am. Aviation Co., Anaheim, Calif., 1965-69; ops. rsch. scientist System Devel. Corp., Santa Monica, Calif., 1961; various govt. positions to asst. inspector gen. DOE, 1975-87; staff mem. House Appropriations Com., 1987-90; dep. inspector gen., sr. exec. svc. Fed. Emergency Mgmt. Agy., Washington, 1990-95. With AUS, 1944-46. Mem. Am. Soc. Pub. Adminstrn., Ops. Rsch. Soc. Am. Address: 1604 E Crown Ridge Way Tucson AZ 85737-7101

PARTRIDGE, WILLIAM SCHAUBEL, retired physicist, research company executive; b. Ranchester, Wyo., Jan. 20, 1922; s. William Clayton and Elsie (Schaubel) P.; m. Jeannette Noble, Mar. 21, 1942; children—Nancy, Dianne, William Noble, Carol, Murray Noble (dec.). B.A., U. Wyo., 1946, M.A., 1948; Ph.D., U. Utah, 1951. Staff scientist U. Calif., Los Alamos, 1951-52; asst. dir. explosives research group U. Utah, Salt Lake City, 1952-55; assoc. research prof., dir. high velocity research lab. U. Utah, 1955-58, v.p. for research, 1966-79; pres. U. Utah Rsch. Inst., 1972-83, Utah Bioresearch, 1983-89, ret.; chmn. bd. Tech. Rsch. Assocs., Inc., 1983-89; pres., gen. mgr. Utah R & D Co., Salt Lake City, 1958-64; staff scientist Jet Propulsion Lab., Pasadena, Calif., 1964-66; mem. exec. com. Nat. Coun. Univ. Rsch. Adminstrs., 1969-71; pres., gen. mgr. U. Utah Rsch. Inst., 1972-83; mem. nat. adv. com. on planning and instl. affairs NSF, 1971-73; nat. adv. rsch. resources coun. NIH, 1974-78, mem. adv. com. to dir. NIH, 1981-84. Contbr. articles to profl. jours. Served to capt. USAAF, World War II. Patentee in field. Home: 11843 S Pond Ridge Dr Draper UT 84020

PARVER, JANE W., lawyer. AB summa cum laude, Tufts U.; MA, Fletcher Sch. Law and Diplomacy; JD, Columbia U., 1972. Bar: N.Y. 1973. Law clk. so. dist. N.Y. U.S. Dist. Ct., 1972-73; asst U.S. atty. so. dist. N.Y. criminal divsn. U.S. Atty's. Office, 1976-81; chief Major Crimes Unit, 1981-84; exec. asst. U.S. Atty., chief Pub. Corruption Unit, 1984-85; ptnr. Kaye, Scholer, Fierman, Hays & Handler, N.Y.C. Office: Kaye Scholer Fierman Hayes & Handler 425 Park Ave New York NY 10022-3506

PARVIN, PHILIP E., retired agricultural researcher and educator; b. Manatee, Fla., July 3, 1927; s. Clinton Fisk and Beatrice (Ward) P. MS, Miss. State U., Starkeville, 1950; PhD, Mich. State U., 1965. Asst. prof. U. Fla., Gainesville, 1952-55; extension specialist U. Calif., Davis, 1963-66; gen. mgr. Rod McLellan Co., San Francisco, 1966-68; horticulturist Maui Agrl. Rsch. Ctr. U. Hawaii, Kula, 1968-93. Contbr. over 100 articles to profl. jours. With U.S. Army, 1945-46. Fellow Am. Soc. for Hort. Sci.; mem. Am. Acad. Floriculture (hon.), South African Protea Prodrs. and Exporters (hon. life), Internat. Protea Assn. (hon. life, chmn. rsch. com. 1983-89), Protea Growers Assn. Hawaii (hon. life), Rotary (pres. Maui chpt. 1981-82). Republican. Methodist. Achievements include development of Hawaii protea industry. Home: 2395 Nuremberg Blvd Punta Gorda FL 33983-2626

PARYANI, SHYAM BHOJRAJ, radiologist; b. Bhavnagar, Gujarat, India, July 18, 1956; came to U.S., 1966; s. Bhojraj Thakurdas and Sarswati (Shewarkanani) P.; m. Sharon Dale Goldman, May 12, 1979; children: Lisa Ann, Jason Bhojraj, Gregory Shyam. BSEE, U. Fla., 1975, MSEE, 1979, MD, 1979. Diplomate Am. Bd. of Radiology. Intern U. Tex., M.D. Anderson Hosp., Houston, 1979-80; resident Stanford (Calif.) U. Hosp., 1980-83, chief resident, 1983; dir. Williams Cancer Ctr., Bapt. Med. Ctr., Jacksonville, Fla., 1983—, Fla. Cancer Ctr., Jacksonville, Fla., 1985—; bd. dirs. Bapt. Med. Ctr., Jacksonville, 1986—, Meml. Med. Ctr., Jacksonville, 1987—, Meth. Hosp., Jacksonville, 1988—. Contbr. articles to profl. jours. Pres. Am. Cancer Soc., Jacksonville, 1992; bd. dirs. Jacksonville C. of C., 1991; adv. bd. Boy Scouts, 1990—. Mem. Am. Cancer Soc. (pres. 1992), Rotary Club. Republican. Hindu. Achievements include patent in Scott-Paryani Quick Implanter. Office: Fla Cancer Ctr 3599 University Blvd S Ste 1500 Jacksonville FL 32216-7400

PARZEN, EMANUEL, statistical scientist; b. N.Y.C., Apr. 21, 1929; s. Samuel and Sarah (Getzel) P.; m. Carol Tenowitz, July 12, 1959; children: Sara Leah, Michael Isaac. AB in Math., Harvard U., 1949; MA, U. Calif., Berkeley, 1951, PhD, 1953. Research scientist Columbia, 1953-56, asst. prof. math. statistics, 1955-56; faculty Stanford, 1956-70, asso. prof. statistics, 1959-64, prof., 1964-70; prof. statistics State U. N.Y. at Buffalo, 1970-73, prof. statis. sci., 1973-78; distinguished prof. statistics Tex. A and M U., College Station, 1978—; guest prof. IMperial Coll., London, 1961-62; vis. prof. MIT, 1964-65, Harvard U., 1976, 88, Ctr. for Advanced Study in Behavioral Scis., 1983-84. Author: Stochastic Processes, 1962, Modern Probability Theory and its Applications, 1960, Time Series Analysis Papers, 1967, also articles. Fellow AAAS, Internat. Statis. Inst., Am. Statis. Assn., Royal Statis. Soc., Inst. Math. Statistics; mem. Am. Math. Soc., Soc. Indsl. and Applied Math., Bernoulli Soc., N.Y. Acad. Scis., Phi Beta Kappa, Sigma Xi. Research in time series analysis, non-parametric statistical data modeling, change analysis. Office: Tex A&M U Dept Stats College Station TX 77843-3143

PASACHOFF, JAY MYRON, astronomer, educator; b. N.Y.C., July 1, 1943; s. Samuel S. and Anne (Traub) P.; m. Naomi Schwartz, Mar. 31, 1974; children: Eloise Hilary, Deborah Donna. A.B., Harvard U., 1963, A.M. (NSF fellow), 1965, Ph.D. (NSF fellow, N.Y. State Regents fellow for advanced grad. study), 1969. Research physicist Air Force Cambridge Research Labs., Bedford, Mass., 1968-69; Menzel research fellow Harvard Coll. Obs., Cambridge, Mass., 1969-70; research fellow Hale Obs., Carnegie Instn., Washington, and Calif. Inst. Tech., Pasadena, 1970-72; dir. Hopkins Obs. Williams Coll., Williamstown, Mass., 1972—; chmn. astronomy dept. Williams Coll., 1972-77, 91-92, asst. prof. astronomy, 1972-77, assoc. prof., 1977-84, prof., 1984, Field Meml. prof. of astronomy, 1984—; adj. asst. prof. astronomy U. Mass., Amherst, 1975-77, adj. assoc. prof., 1977-83, adj. prof., 1986—; vis. colleague and vis. assoc. prof. astronomy Inst. for Astronomy, U. Hawaii, 1980-81; vis. scientist Inst. d'Astrophysique, Paris, 1988; mem. Inst. Advanced Study, Princeton, 1989-90, Harvard-Smithsonian Ctr. for Astrophysics, 1993-94; total and other solar eclipse expdns., Mass., 1959, Que., Can., 1963, Mex., 1970, asst. dir. Harvard-Smithsonian-Nat. Geog. Expdn., P.E.I., Can., 1972, NSF expdn., Harvard-Smithsonian-Williams Expdn., Kenya, 1973; NSF expdn., Colombia, 1973 (annular eclipse), Australia, 1974, Pacific Ocean, 1977, Man., Can., 1979, NSF expdn., India, 1980, Pacific Ocean, 1981, Java, Indonesia, 1983, Miss., 1984 (annular eclipse), Papua, New Guinea, 1984, Sumatra, Indonesia, 1988, Hawaii 1989 (partial), Finland, 1990, Hawaii, 1991, Calif., 1992 (annular eclipse), Pacific near Africa, 1992, N.H., 1994 (annular eclipse), Chile, 1994, India, 1995, Israel, 1996, Mongolia, 1997; rsch. fellow Owens Valley Radio Obs., 1974; guest investigator NASA Orbiting Solar Obs.-8, 1975-79. Author: Contemporary Astronomy, 1977, 4th edit., 1989, Astronomy Now, 1978, Astronomy: From Earth to the Universe, 1979, A Brief View of Astronomy, 1986, First Guide to Astronomy, 1988, First Guide to the Solar System, 1990, Journey Through the Universe, 1992; co-author: (with Marc L. Kutner, Naomi Pasachoff) Student Study Guide to Contemporary Astronomy, 1977, (with Kutner, Pasachoff and N.P. Kutner) Student Study Guide to Astronomy Now, 1978; (with M.L. Kutner) University Astronomy, 1978, Invitation to Physics, 1981; (with N. Pasachoff, T. Cooney) Physical Science, 1983, 2d edit., 1990, Earth Science, 1983, 2d edit., 1990; (with D.H. Menzel) A Field Guide to the Stars and Planets, 2d edit., 1983, 3d edit., 1992; (with R. Wolfson) Physics, 1987, 2nd edit., 1995, (Extended with Modern Physics, 1989, 2nd edit. 1995), (with N. Pasachoff, R.W. Clark, M.H. Westermann) Physical Science Today, 1987; (with N. Pasachoff and others) Discover Science, 7 vols., 1989; (with Michael Covington) Cambridge Eclipse Photography Guide, 1993; (with Len Holder and James DeFranza) Calculus, 1994, Single Variable Calculus, 1994, Multivariable Calculus, 1995; (with Edward Cheng, Patrick Osmer and Hyron Spinrad) The Farthest Things in the Universe, 1994; editor (with J. Percy) The Teaching of Astronomy, 1990, (with Leon Golub) The Solar Corona, 1997; assoc. editor: Jour. Irreproducible Results, 1972-94, Annals of Improbable Rsch., 1994—; abstractor from Am. jours. for Solar Physics, 1968-78; cons. editor McGraw-Hill Ency. Sci. and Tech., 1983—; co-editor-in-chief (with S.P. Parker), McGraw-Hill Ency. of Astronomy, 1993; cons. Random House Dictionary, 1983-86, Nat. Geographic Atlas, 5th edit., 1981, 6th edit., 1990; phys. sci. com. World Book Encyclopedia, 1989-95, cons., 1996—; contbr. articles to profl. jours. and encys., articles and photographs to non-tech. publs. Recipient Bronze medal Nikon Photo Contest Internat., 1971, photograph aboard NASA Voyagers, 1977, Dudley award Dudley Obs., 1985; grantee: NSF, 1973-75, 79-83, 88—, Nat. Geog. Soc., 1973-86, 91— Rsch. Corp., 1973-74, 75-78, 82-88, Getty Found., 1994-95. Fellow AAAS (chair sect. D 1987-88, 97—), Royal Astron. Soc., Am. Phys. Soc. (mem.-at-large Am. Phys. Soc./Am. Assn. Physics Tchrs. Forum on Edn. 1995—), N.Y. Acad. Sci., Internat. Planetarium Soc.; mem. AAUP (chpt. pres. 1977-80), Internat. Astron. Union (U.S. nat. rep. Commn. on Tchg. Astronomy 1976—, chair Eclipse Working Group 1991—, rep. to Com. on Tchg. Sci. of Internat. Coun. Sci. Unions 1991-93), Am. Astron. Soc. (astronomy edn. adv. bd. 1990—, astronomy news com. 1991—), Astron. Soc. Pacific, Union Radio Sci., Am. Assn. Physics Tchrs. (astronomy com. 1983-87), Sigma Xi (chpt. pres. 1973-74, 95—, nat. lectr. 1993-97). Home: 1305 Main St Williamstown MA 01267-2630 Office: Hopkins Obs Williams Coll Williamstown MA 01267-2565

PASAHOW, LYNN H(AROLD), lawyer; b. Ft. Eutiss, Va., Mar. 13, 1947; s. Samuel and Cecelia (Newman) P.; m. Leslie Aileen Cobb, June 11, 1969; 1 child, Michael Alexander. AB, Stanford U., 1969; JD, U. Calif., Berkeley, 1972. Bar: Calif. 1972, U.S. Ct. Appeals (9th cir.) 1972, U.S. Dist. Ct. (no. dist.) Calif. 1973, U.S. Dist. Ct. (cen. dist.) Calif. 1974, U.S. Supreme Ct. 1976, U.S. Dist. Ct. (ea. dist.) Calif. 1977, U.S. Ct. Appeals (fed. cir.) 1990. Law clk. judge U.S. Dist. Ct. (no. dist.) Calif., San Francisco, 1972-73; assoc. McCutchen, Doyle, Brown & Enersen, San Francisco, 1973-79, ptnr., 1979—; dir. Copyright Soc. No. Calif., San Francisco; mem. lawyer's com. Bay Area Biosci. Ctr., 1993—, attys. adv. panel, 1993—; moderator Lexis Counsel Connect Nat. Patent Forum, 1996—. Author: Pretrial and Settlement Conferences in Federal Court, 1983; co-author: Civil Discovery and Mandatory Disclosure: A Guide to Effective Practice, 1994; contbr. articles to profl. jours. Mem. ABA, Calif. Bar Assn., Am. Intellectual Property Law Assn. Democrat. Office: Doyle Brown & Enersen 1 Embarcadero Pl 2100 Geng Rd Palo Alto CA 94303-3307 *Notable cases include: duPont vs. Cetus, PCR patent litigation, nicotine patch patent litigation.*

PASANELLA, GIOVANNI, architect, architectural educator; b. N.Y.C., Jan. 13, 1931; children: Marco, Nicolas. Student, Cooper Union, 1949-53, Yale U., 1953-58. Registered architect, N.Y. Designer Edward L. Barnes, N.Y.C., 1959-64; prin. Giovanni Pasanella, N.Y.C., 1964-76; co-owner Pasanella & Klein, N.Y.C., 1976—; critic architecture U. Ky., Lexington, 1963, Yale U., New Haven, 1964; adj. prof. architecture Columbia U., N.Y.C., 1965-87; vis. fellow urban studies Inst. of Architecture, 1975. Project dir. Inst. of Urban Environ. Columbia U., N.Y.C., 1965-68; cons. architecture to chmn. N.Y.C. Planning Commn., 1967; cons. urban design City of Lucca, Italy, 1985; bd. trustees Il Piccolo Teatro dell' Opera, Bklyn., 1986. Yale U. traveling fellow, 1958-59; Architecture award Archtl. Record, 1974, 75. Fellow AIA (Residential award N.Y. Soc. 1971); mem. Soc. of Archtl. Historians, Mcpl. Arts Soc. Office: Pasanella & Klein Architects 330 W 42nd St New York NY 10036-6902 Home: Cannizzaro, Via Fondi CAmaiore, Lucca Italy*

PASCAL, AMY, film company executive. Pres. Columbia Pictures, Culver City, Calif. Office: Columbia Pictures 10202 W Washington Blvd Culver City CA 90232*

PASCAL, C(ECIL) BENNETT, classics educator; b. Chgo., May 4, 1926; s. Jack and Goldie (Zeff) P.; m. Ilene Joy Shulman, Feb. 1, 1959; 1 child, Keith Irwin. BA, UCLA, 1949, MA, 1950; MA, Harvard U., 1953, PhD, 1956. Instr. U. Ill., Champaign, 1955-56, Cornell U., Ithaca, N.Y., 1957-60; asst. prof. U. Oreg., Eugene, 1960-75, prof. classics, 1975-96, prof. emeritus, 1996—, head dept., various years - 1965-85. Author: Cults of Cisalpine Gaul, 1964; contbr. articles to profl. jours. Mem. Eugene Bicycle Com., 1971-83. Served with USN, 1944-46. Traveling fellow, Italy, Harvard U., 1956-57, Fulbright-Hays fellow, Rome, 1967-68. Mem. Am. Philol. Assn., Classical Assn. Pacific N.W. (pres. 1965-66), AAUP, Archeol. Inst. of Am. (past pres., sec. Eugene Soc.). Democrat. Jewish. Avocations: skiing, fishing, novel writing. Home: 330 Ful Vue Dr Eugene OR 97405-2788 Office: U of Oreg Dept Classics Eugene OR 97403

PASCAL, DAVID, artist; b. N.Y.C., Aug. 16, 1918; s. Boucour and Carolina (Finor) P.; m. Theresa Auerbach, Aug. 24, 1962; 1 child, Jeffrey B. Student, Am. Artists Sch., 1936-38; M Practioner, N.Y. Tng. Inst. Neuro-Linguistic Programming, 1992. Instr. Sch. Visual Arts, N.Y.C., 1955-58; lectr. mus., schs., congresses N.Y., Paris, Italy, Sao Paulo, Buenos Aires, Argentina; organizer 1st Am. Internat. Congress Comics, N.Y.C., 1972; artistic counselor to bd. dirs. Lucca Internat. Comics Congresses, 1976—; participant overseas tours for Def. Dept., 1957, 58, 61; Auditor Coll. de Pataphysique, Paris. One-man show Librairie Le Kiosque, Paris, 1965, Museu de Arte, Sao Paulo, Brazil, Graham Gallery, N.Y.C., 1973, Museude Arte Moderna Rio de Janeiro, Brazil, 1973, Man and His World, Montreal, 1974, 75, World Gallery, N.Y.C., 1977, Musee d'Angouleme, France, 1983, 1st Cartoon Biennale Invitational, Davos, Switzerland, 1986, group show, Musee des Arts Decoratifs, 1967, Pinocchio/Graphis Invitational Exhbn., Venice, 1987, École Nat. Supérieure des Beaux-Arts, Paris, 1989 ; drawings appeared in Paris-Match; others; 73 1971); author, illustrator: The Art of Inferior Decorating, 1963, 15 Fables of Krylov, 1965 (in permanent exhibit at Congl. Library), The Silly Knight, 1967, Perspectives, 1985; also publ.: comics An American Expressionism (in archives Mus. of Art, Sao Paulo); editor "An American in Paris" issue Pilote Mag., Paris, 1988; co-editor spl. internat. comics issues Graphis mag, Zurich, Switzerland, Goofus, Paris, 1975; regular contbr. to The New Yorker. Served with U.S. Mcht. Marine, 1940-45. Recipient Dattero d'Oro Salone Intdelle Umorismo, Italy 1963, Illustrator's award Nat. Cartoonists Soc. 1969, 77, Phenix award, Paris 1971. Mem. Nat. Cartoonists Soc. (fgn. affairs sec. 1963—), Internat. Comics Orgn. (Am. rep. 1970—), Association des Auteurs de Comics et de Cartoons (Am. rep.). Home and Studio: 133 Wooster St New York NY 10012-3176 *Work is adult play. Knowing what you really want to do and finding the best ways to do it are the keys to joy of life.*

PASCAL, FRANCINE, writer; b. N.Y.C., May 13, 1937; d. William and Kate (Dunitz) Rubin; m. Jerome Offenberg, Sept. 9, 1958; children: Jamie, Laurie, Susan; m. John Robert Pascal, Aug. 18, 1964 (dec. 1981). BS, NYU, 1958. Author: Hanging Out With Cici, 1977, My First Love and Other Disasters, 1979, Hand Me Down, Kid, 1980 (Dorothy Canfield Fisher award, 1982, Meml. Childrens Book award, Bernard Versele award, Brussels, Milner award 1988), Save Johanna!, 1981, Love and Betrayal, 1985, Hold the Mayo, 1985, If Wishes Were Horses, 1994; collaborator on book of musical George M!, 1968; creator young adult book series Sweet Valley High, 1983, Sweet Valley Twins, 1986, Sweet Valley Kids, 1989, Sweet Valley University, 1993. Mem. PEN, NOW, Dramatist's Guild, Writer's League, Screen Writer's Guild.

PASCAL, ROGER, lawyer; b. Chgo., Mar. 16, 1941; s. Samuel A. and Harriet E. (Hartman) P.; m. Martha Hecht, June 16, 1963; children: Deborah, Diane, David. AB with distinction, U. Mich, 1962; JD cum laude, Harvard U., 1965. Bar: Ill. 1965, U.S. Dist. Ct. (no. dist.) Ill. 1965, U.S. Ct. Appeals (7th cir.) 1969, U.S. Supreme Ct. 1976, Wis. 1985, U.S. Ct. Appeals (2d and 9th cirs.) 1986. Assoc. Schiff Hardin & Waite, Chgo., 1965-71, ptnr., 1972—; adj. prof. law Northwestern U. Law Sch., 1994—. Bd. dirs., mem. exec. com. Chgo. Law Enforcement Study Group, 1975-80, pres., 1978-80; pres. Harvard Law Soc. Ill., 1976-78; bd. dirs. ACLU of Ill., 1984—, gen. counsel, 1986—. Mem. ABA (antitrust and litigation sects.), Pub. Interest Law Initiative (bd. dirs. 1989—, v.p. 1995—), Fund for Justice (v.p., bd. dirs. 1986—), Chgo. Coun. Lawyers (bd. dirs. 1970-74, 80-84), Chgo. Legal Assistance Found. (bd. dirs. 1985-88), Phi Beta Kappa, Univ. Club, Met. Club. Office: Schiff Hardin & Waite 7200 Sears Tower Chicago IL 60606-6327

PASCALE, DANIEL RICHARD, circuit judge; b. Racine, Wis., Mar. 22, 1940; s. Domenic and Fannie Colette (Julian) P.; m. Mary Sara McDonald, June 28, 1986; 1 child, Alexander. AB cum laude, Harvard U., 1962; JD, U. Chgo., 1965. Bar: Ill. 1966, U.S. Ct. Appeals (7th cir.) 1967, U.S. Dist. Ct. (no. dist.) Ill. 1969, U.S. Supreme Ct. 1972. Asst. corp. counsel City of Chgo., 1966-72, chief appellate atty., 1972-79, 1st dep. corp. counsel, 1979-84; assoc. Rudnick & Wolfe, Chgo., 1984-87, ptnr., 1987-90; judge Circuit Ct. of Cook County, Ill., 1990-94, 96—; adminstrv. dir. Adminstrv. Office of Ill. Cts., Chgo., 1995-96. Bd. dirs. DeKoven Found., Racine, 1986—; adv. bd. Art Resources in Teaching, Chgo., 1987-94; v.p. Episcopal Homes Mgmt., Inc., Milw., 1988-94. Mem. ABA, Ill. Bar Assn., Chgo. Bar Assn., Chgo. Coun. Lawyers, Woman's Bar Assn., Justinian Soc., Union League Club Chgo., English-Speaking Union. Democrat. Episcopalian. Office: 160 N La Salle St Chicago IL 60601-3103

PASCARELLA, HENRY WILLIAM, lawyer; b. New Haven, Conn., Aug. 15, 1933; s. John Manlio and Mary (Iannotti) P.; m. Tessa Peruzzi, Jan. 28, 1967; children: Averardo, Leonora, Cassandra. B.S. in Econs., U. Pa., 1955; LL.B., Yale U., 1958. Bar: Conn. 1958, U.S. Sup. Ct. 1963. Ptnr. Badger, Fisher, Cohen & Barnett and predecessors, Greenwich, Conn., 1959-73; sr. counsel to Tyler, Cooper & Alcorn, Greenwich, 1978—; pres., dir. The Timber Trails Corp. Sherman, Conn.; dir. Nine West Group, Inc. Dir. Planned Parenthood League of Conn., Greenwich coun. Boy Scouts Am., 1990-96; mem. Greenwich Democratic Town Com. 1968-70. Served to lt. (j.g.) USCG, 1959. Mem. ABA, Greenwich Bar Assn. (pres. 1967), Conn. Bar Assn. Club: Yale (N.Y.C.), Belle Haven Club (Greenwich). Author column, theater critic Greenwich Times, 1964-67. Home: 675 Steamboat Rd Greenwich CT 06830 Office: 675 Steamboat Rd Greenwich CT 06830-7140

PASCARELLA, PERRY JAMES, author, editor, speaker; b. Bradford, Pa., Apr. 11, 1934; s. James and Lucille Margaret (Monti) P.; m. Carol Ruth Taylor, May 4, 1957; children: Cynthia, Elizabeth. AB, Kenyon Coll., 1956; Coll. William and Mary, William and Mary Coll., 1957; postgrad., George Washington U., 1958. Credit reporter Dun & Bradstreet, Cleve., 1956, 60; asst. editor Steel mag., Cleve., 1961-63, asso. editor, 1963-67, bus. editor, 1968-69, mng. editor, 1969; mng. editor Industry Week mag., Cleve., 1970-71, exec. editor, 1971-86, editor-in-chief, 1986-89; v.p. editorial Penton Pub. Inc., 1989-96; lectr. in field. Author: Technology-Fire in a Dark World, 1979, Humanagement in the Future Corporation, 1981, The New Achievers, 1984, The Purpose-Driven Organization, 1989, The Ten Commandments of the Workplace, 1996; contbg. author: Optimistic Outlooks, 1982, Creating a Global Agenda, 1984, Leadership in a New Era, 1994, The New Bottom Line, 1996. Lt. comdr. USNR, 1957-60. Recipient Disting. Service award

Kenyon Coll., 1975, 81, Am. Bus. Press Crain award, 1992; Carnegie scholar, 1952-56. Mem. World Future Soc., U. Akron Inst. for Future Studies (bd. advisors). Presbyterian (elder). Home: 30413 Winsor Dr Cleveland OH 44140-1143

PASCH, ALAN, philosopher, educator; b. Cleve., Dec. 1, 1925; s. P. Jerome and Esther (Broverman) P.; m. Eleanor Kudlich Berna, Dec. 27, 1950; 1 child, Rachel. B.A., U. Mich., 1949; M.A., New Sch. Social Research, 1952; Ph.D., Princeton U., 1955; Bamford fellow, 1955-56. Instr. philosophy Ohio State U., 1956-59, asst. prof., 1959-60; assoc. prof. philosophy U. Md., College Park, 1960-67, prof., 1967—. Author: Experience and the Analytic, 1958; also articles, revs. Active ACLU. Served with AUS, 1944-46, PTO. Mem. AAUP, Am. Philos. Assn. (exec. dir. 1969-72, sec.-treas. Eastern div. 1965-68), Metaphys. Soc. Am., Washington Philosophy Club (pres. 1978-79), Washington Rare Book Group. Office: U Md Dept Philosophy College Park MD 20742

PASCHALL, LEE MCQUERTER, retired communications consultant; b. Sterling, Colo., Jan. 21, 1922; s. Lee McQuerter and Agnes (Woldridge) P.; m. Bonnie Jean Edwards, Oct. 24, 1942; children: Patricia Ann Grillos, Stephen Lee, David Edward. B.A., U. Ala., 1957; M.A., George Washington U., 1964. Served with U.S. Army, 1940-46; communications engr. Colo. Air N.G., Denver, 1946-51; commd. maj. U.S. Air Force, 1951, advanced through grades to lt. gen., 1974, ret., 1978; ind. cons. Springfield, Va., 1978-81; pres., chief exec. officer Am. Satellite Co., Rockville, Md., 1981-84, chmn., 1984-85; dir. Gen. Data Comm. Industries. Contbr. numerous articles to profl. publs. Mem. com. rev. nat. communications system initiatives NRC, 1982-88. Decorated Legion of Merit with oak leaf cluster; decorated disting. service medals; recipient Eascon IEEE, 1979. Mem. Armed Forces Comms.-Electronics Assn. (chpt. pres., nat. bd. dirs. Disting. Svc.), Air Force Assn., Phi Beta Kappa. Mem. Disciples of Christ. Home and Office: 1513 Hampton Hills Cir Mc Lean VA 22101-6018

PASCHALL, ROD, writer; b. San Antonio, Sept. 1, 1935; s. Samuel and Helen (Roddy) P.; m. Patricia Diane Greenwalt, May 17, 1969; children: Christen, Karen Elizabeth. BA, U.S. Mil. Acad., 1959; MS, George Washington U., 1970; MA, Duke U., 1971. Asst. prof. U.S. Mil. Acad., West Point, N.Y., 1971-74; officer U.S. Embassy, Cambodia, 1974; comdr. 3rd Battalion 5th Spl. Force, Ft. Bragg, N.C., 1975-80; plans officer Office Joint Chiefs of Staff, Washington, 1979-80; comdr. Delta Force, Ft. Bragg, 1980-82; dir. Spl. Warfare Devels., Ft. Bragg, 1983-84, Mil. History Inst., Carlisle Barracks, Pa., 1984-89; cons. Office of Internat. Criminal Justice, Chgo., 1989—; book author, cons. Carlisle, 1989—. Author: Defeat of Imperial Germany, 1989, Low Intensity Conflict, 2010, 1990, Critical Incident Management, 1992, Witness To War: Korea, 1995; TV scriptwriter, A&E History Channels. Decorated with Silver Star, 1967, Purple Heart, 1966.

PASCHANG, JOHN LINUS, retired bishop; b. Hemingford, Nebr., Oct. 5, 1895; s. Casper Paschang and Gertrude Fischer. D of Canon Law, Cath. U. Am., Washington, 1925, MA, 1926, PhD, 1927; JD (hon.), Creighton U., 1960. Pastor St. Rose Ch., Hooper, Nebr., 1921-23, Holy Cross Ch., Omaha, 1927-51; bishop Grand Island, Nebr., 1951-72; ret., 1972. Author: The Sacramentals, 1925, The Popes and Revival of Learning, 1927. Mem. KC (state chaplain 1938-42). Republican. Roman Catholic. Avocation: missionary work. Home: St Josephs Home 320 E Decatur St West Point NE 68788

PASCHKE, DONALD VERNON, music educator; b. Menominee, Mich., Oct. 22, 1929; s. Leo Carl Ferdinand and Augusta O. (Fritz) P.; m. Helen Inez Burton, Feb. 17, 1951; children: David Vernon, Celeste Eileen. MusB, BS in Choral Music Edn., U. Ill., 1957, MusM in Voice, 1958; D Mus. Arts, U. Colo., 1972. Instr. music Berea (Ky.) Coll., 1958-62; asst. prof. music Eastern N.Mex. U., Portales, 1962-71, assoc. prof., 1971-76, prof., 1976-94; prof. emeritus, 1994. Translator, editor: A Complete Treatise on the Art of Singing, Part Two (Manuel Garcia II), 1975; Part One, 1984. Songleader Portales Christian Breakfast, 1976—, pres., 1975-76, 90-91, v.p. 1974-75, 89-90; chancel choir dir. 1st Presbyn. Ch., Clovis, N.Mex., 1976-95. With U.S. Army, 1951-53. Mem. Nat. Assn. Tchrs. Singing (lt. gov. N.Mex. 1968-72, v.p. Gt. Plains chpt. 1972-74, chpt. pres. 1974-78), Pi Kappa Lambda, Phi Kappa Phi. Republican. Presbyterian. Avocations: photography, do-it-yourself projects. Home: 228 Kansas Dr Portales NM 88130-7121

PASCO, HANSELL MERRILL, retired lawyer; b. Thomasville, Ga., Oct. 7, 1915; s. John and Katherine (Merrill) P.; m. Williamine Carrington Lancaster, June 28, 1941; children: Hansell Merrill, Dabney, Robert, Elizabeth, Carrington. B.A., Va. Mil. Inst., 1937; LL.B., U. Va., 1940. Bar: Va. bar 1939. Ptnr. Hunton & Williams, Richmond, Va., 1948-81, sr. counsel, 1981—; mng. partner Hunton & Williams, 1968-76. Chmn. State Counsel Higher Edn. for Va., 1978-80; trustee Protestant Episcopal Sem., Alexandria, Va., 1980-85. Served with U.S. Army, 1940-45. Office: Hunton & Williams Riverfront Plz E Tower 951 E Byrd St Richmond VA 23219-4040

PASCOE, PATRICIA HILL, state senator, writer; b. Sparta, Wis., June 1, 1935; d. Fred Kirk and Edith (Kilpatrick) Hill; m. D. Monte Pascoe, Aug. 3, 1957; children: Sarah, Ted, Will. BA, U. Colo., 1957; MA, U. Denver, 1968, PhD, 1982. Tchr. Sequoia Union High Sch. Dist., Redwood City, Calif. and Hayward (Calif.) Union High Sch. Dist., 1957-60; instr. Met. State Coll., Denver, 1969-75; instr. Denver U., 1975-77, 81, research asst. bur. ednl. research, 1981-82; tchr. Kent Denver Country Day, Englewood, Colo., 1982-84; freelance writer Denver, 1985—; mem. Colo. Senate, Denver, 1989-93, 95—; commr. Edn. Commn. of the States, Denver, 1975-82. Contbr. articles to numerous publs. and jours. Bd. dirs. Samaritan House, 1990-94, Cystic Fibrosis Found., 1989-93; pres. East H.S. Parent Tchr. and Student Assn., Denver, 1984-85; mem. Moore Budget Adv. Com., Denver, 1966-72; legis. chmn. alumni bd. U. Colo., Boulder, 1987-89; del. Dem. Nat. Conv., San Francisco, 1984, N.Y.C., 1992; mem. Denver Woman's Press Club, 1986—, Colo. Arts Coalition, 1988-97; bd. dirs. Opera Colo., 1996—. Mem. Soc. Profl. Journalists, Common Cause (bd. dirs. Denver chpt. 1986-88), Colo. Endowment for Humanities, Phi Beta Kappa. Presbyterian.

PASCRELL, WILLIAM J., JR., congressman; b. Paterson, N.J., Jan. 25, 1937; s. William J. Sr. and Roffie (Loffredo) P.; m. Elsie Marie Botto; children: William III, David, Glenn. BS, Fordham U., 1959; MA, Montclair State Coll., 1961; postgrad., Fairleigh Dickinson U. Tchr. Jr. High Sch., Clifton, N.J., 1962, Paramus (N.J.) High Sch., 1962-74; adult sch. tchr. Dwight Morrow High Sch., Englewood, N.J., 1969-70; prof. Fairleigh Dickinson U., Madison, N.J., 1963-68; dir. Dept. Pub. Works City of Paterson, 1974-77, dir. Dept. Policy Planning and Mgmt., 1977-87; mem. N.J. Gen. Assembly, 1988—, chmn. higher edn. com., 1988—, vice chmn. edn. com., 1988—, mem. appropriations com., 1988—; mayor City of Paterson, 1990-97; mem. 105th Congress from 8th N.J. dist., 1997—. Pres. Paterson Bd. Edn., 1979-82; campaign coord. Robert A. Roe for Gov., N.J., 1977; regional coord. James Florio for Gov., Hudson County, N.J., 1981; active County Chairmen for Sen. Frank Lautenberg, N.J., 1982—; chmn. Passaic County Democrats, N.J., 1982—. With U.S. Army, 1961-67. Named Man of Yr., Mother Cabrini Soc., 1978, Am. Legion (John Road Post), 1983, St. Gerard's Parish, 1988, Assn. Retarded Citizens, 1991. Mem. N.J. Math. Coalition (bd. govs. 1991—), UNICO (Paterson chpt. Man of Yr., 1981), Italian Sport Club. Roman Catholic. Office: 1722 Longworth Washington DC 20515-3008*

PASEORNEK, HELENE, public relations executive. BA in Journalism, BS in Econs., George Washington U. V.p. Burson-Marsteller, N.Y.C.; exec. v.p., COO Wang Assocs. Health Comm., N.Y.C., 1995—. Office: Wang Assocs Health Comm 373 Park Ave S New York NY 10016-8805

PASEWARK, WILLIAM ROBERT, author, management consultant; b. Mt. Vernon, N.Y., Sept. 9, 1924; s. William and Barbara (Hermann) P.; m. M. Jean McHarg, Mar. 17, 1956; children: William Robert, Lisabeth Jean, Jan Alison, Carolyn Ann, Scott Graham, Susan Gayle. B.S., NYU, 1949, M.A., 1950, Ph.D., 1956. Instr. NYU, 1949-51; assoc. prof. Meredith Coll., Raleigh, N.C., 1951-52; asst. prof. Mich. State U., 1952-56; prof. Tex. Tech. U., Lubbock, 1956-82; author, owner Office Mgmt. Cons., 1982—; cons. bus. and ednl. agys., lectr. in field, 1955—; field reader rsch. div. U.S. Office Edn., 1966—; mem. commn. to revise curricula Tex. Edn. Agy., 1974—; mem. adv. com. Lubbock Vocat. Office Edn.; mem. regional bd. examiners Am. Assn. Bus. Colls.; vis. prof. Calif. State U., Fresno, 1959, No. Ariz. State U., 1969, Ctrl. Conn. State Coll., 1974. Author: Individualized Instruction in Business and Office Education, 1973, Electronic and Mechanical Printing Calculator Course, 1974, Electronic Display Calculator Course, 1975, 2d edit., 1984, Clerical Office Procedures, 6th edit., 1978, Rotary Calculator Course, 1962, Ten-Key Listing Machine, 5th edit., 1981, Key-Driven Calculator Course, 1962, Full-Keyboard Adding Listing Machine Course, 3d edit, 1963, Secretarial Office Procedures, 10th edit., 1982, Duplicating Machine Processes, 1971, 2d edit., 1975, Office Machines Course, 1971, 5th edit., 1979, Curso de Máquinas de Oficina, 1977, Técnicas Secretariales y Procedimientos de Oficina, 1978, Machine Transcription Word Processing, 1979, 2d edit., 1987, Electronic Printing Calculator Course, Canadian edit., 1980, Electronic Printing Calculator, 3d edit., 1990, Electronic Calculating Machines Simulation, 4th edit., 1991, Procedures for the Modern Office, 7th edit., 1983, Electronic Display-Printing Calculator, 1983, Reprographics, 1983, Super Calc 3 Learning, Using, and Mastering, 1986, Electronic Office Machines, 6th edit., 1987, The Office: Procedures and Technology, 1987, 2nd edit., 1993 (Textbook Excellence award in bus. Text and Acad. Authors Assn. 1994, William Holmes McGuffy award for textbook excellence and longevity Text and Acad. Authors Assn. 1994), Working With SuperCalc 4, 1987 (Danish transl. 1987), Machine Transcription, Dictation, and Proofreading: An Introduction, 1987, Danish Translation of Supercalc 4, 1987, Microsoft Works: Tutorial and Applications IBM Version, 1991, Calculating Machines Simulation, A Short Course, 1991, Electronic Calculators: Display, Print, Display-Print, 2d edit., 1992, Microsoft Works: Tutorial and Applications Macintosh Version, 1992, Calculator Math for Job and Personal Use, 1992, Ten-Key Skill Builder, 1992, PFS: First Publisher: Tutorial and Applications, IBM 3.0, 4.0, 1993, Publish It!: Tutorial and Applications, IBM version 2.0, 1993, Publish It! Apple version, 1993, Microsoft Works for Windows, 1994, Microsoft Works 3.0 Macintosh, 1994 (Textbook Excellence award in computer text Text & Acad. Authors Assn. 1994), Microsoft Works for Windows 3.0 Tutorial and Applications, Express Publisher Tutorial and Applications, 1994, Microsoft Works DOS 3.0 Quick Course, 1994, Microsoft Works for Windows 3.0 Quick Course, 1995, Microsoft Works Macintosh 4.0 Quick Course, 1995, Microsoft Works 2.0/3.0 DOS: Applications for Reinforcement, 1995, Microsoft Works 2.0/3/0 for Windows: Applications for Reinforcement, 1995, Microsoft Works 4.0 for Macintosh: Tutorial and Applications, 1995, Microsoft Works 4.0 for Windows 95: Tutorial and Applications, 1996, Microsoft Office for Windows 95: Tutorial and Applications, 1996, ClarisWorks 4.0 for Macintosh: Tutorial and Applications, 1996, Pagemaker 5.0 for Windows and Macintosh: QuickTorial, 1996, Microsoft Works 95: QuickTorial, 1996, Microsoft Office 4.3 for Windows: Tutorial and Applications, 1996, Microcomputer Applications: Business, Career, Personal, and School, 1997, Microsoft Office 97: Tutorial and Applications, 1997 and numerous others; assoc. editor: Am. Bus. Edn. Yearbook, 1953; contbr. articles to profl. jours. Adviser Lubbock Opportunities Industrialization Center; mem. Tex. Bus. Tchr. Edn. Council; v.p. Lubbock Econ. Council, 1983, pres., 1984; pres. Lubbock Area Presbyn. Council, 1969; chmn. Lubbock City-County Child Welfare Bd., 1973-74; active local Boy Scouts Am., United Fund. Served with USMCR, 1943-46. Recipient Founders Day award N.Y.U., 1956; Outstanding Educator of Am. award, 1970; citation Tex. Ho. of Reps., 1973; Tex. Bus. Tchr. of Year award, 1973. Mem. Nat. Bus. Edn. Assn., Nat. Assn. Bus. Tchr. Edn., Mountain-Plains Bus. Edn. Assn., Tex. Bus. Edn. Assn. (chmn. legislative com. 1973-80), Nat. Assn. Tchr. Edn. for Bus. and Office Edn., Edn. for Bus. Coordinating Council, Bus. Edn. State Suprs. and Tchr. Educators (nat. planning com.), W. Tex. Bus. Edn. Assn. (pres. 1958), Better Bus. Bur. (edn. com.), Am. Vocat. Assn. (pres. bus. and office div. 1976-77, dir. 1976-77, nat. adv. council 1976-84, award of merit 1978), Office Systems Research Assn., Text and Acad. Authors Assn., Authors Guild, Internat. Platform Assn., Lubbock Execs. Assn. (bd. dirs.), Lubbock C. of C., PTA (local pres. 1972), Delta Pi Epsilon, Phi Delta Kappa, Kappa Phi Kappa, Pi Omega Pi, Alpha Kappa Psi, Kappa Delta Pi. Clubs: Lion (past dir.), Lubbock Country. Research in office adminstrn. and ednl. systems. Home: 4403 11th St Lubbock TX 79416-4814 Office: 1901 University Ave Ste 504A Lubbock TX 79410-1556

PASHAYEV, HAFIZ MIR JALAL, diplomat, physics educator; b. Baku, Azerbaijan, May 2, 1941; s. Mirjalal Ali and Pusta (Kazymova) P.; m. Rena Musa Aliyeva, Apr. 8, 1967; children: Mirjamal, Jamila. M Physics, Baku (Azerbaijan) State U., 1963; PhD in Physics, Inst. Atomic Energy, Moscow, 1971; DSc, Acad. Scis., Baku, 1984. Researcher Inst. Physics, Baku, 1963-75; PhD fellow Inst. Atomic Energy, Moscow, 1967-71; postdoctoral fellow U. Calif., Irvine, 1975-76; head metall. physics lab. Acad. Scis., Baku, 1976-92; amb. to U.S.A. from Azerbaijan Washington, 1993—. Author 3 books in physics; co-author 2 dictionaries, 1991-92; contrb. articles to phys. jours. and mass media. Avocations: drawing, sports. Office: Embassy of Azerbaijan 927 15th St NW Ste 700 Washington DC 20005-2304*

PASHEK, ROBERT DONALD, economics educator emeritus; b. The Dalles, Oreg., Feb. 27, 1921; s. Gregory and Mary M. (Bonomi) P.; children: William J., Nicole M. A.B., Central Wash. Coll., 1949; M.A., State U. Iowa, 1950; Ph.D., U. Ill., 1955; postgrad., Columbia U., 1947, Inst. Minerva, Zurich, 1947-48. Asst. prof. U. Wichita, 1953-55; asst. prof. Pa. State U., 1956-58, prof., 1960—, head dept. bus. logistics, 1964-73; assoc. dean Pa. State U. (Coll. Bus. Adminstrn.), 1973-87, dir. internat. programs, 1987-89, prof. emeritus, 1989; vis. prof. San Francisco State U., 1963-64; cons. Commonwealth of Pa., U.S. AID, U.S. Dept. Commerce. Served with AUS, 1944-46. Named Transp. Man of Year Delta Nu Alpha, 1964. Mem. Coun. Transp. Rsch. Ctrs. (pres. 1981-82), Am. Soc. Transp. and Logistics (past pres., dir. Joseph C. Scholeen award for excellence 1985), Am. Econ. Assn. (Disting. Mem. award Pub. Utilities Group 1985), Transp. Rsch. Forum, Beta Gamma Sigma, Alpha Kappa Psi. Research on econ. and social impact hwys., transport systems planning, logistic systems design and planning. Home: 512 Wallingford Ave N Seattle WA 98103-6143 Office: Bus Adminstrn Bldg Pa State Univ University Park PA 16802

PASHGIAN, MARGARET HELEN, artist; b. Pasadena, Calif., Nov. 7, 1934; d. Aram John and Margaret (Howell) P. BA, Pomona Coll., 1956; MA in Fine Arts, Boston Univ., 1958; student, Columbia U., 1957. Art instr. Harvard-Newton Program Occidental Coll., Newton, Mass., 1959-62, instr. art, 1977-78; artist in residence Calif. Inst. Tech., 1970-71; grants panelist Calif. Arts Coun., Sacramento, 1993. Artist: solo shows include Rex Evans Gallery, L.A., 1965, 67, Occidental Coll., 1967, Kornblee Gallery, N.Y.C., 1969-72, U. Calif., Irvine, 1975, U. Calif. Santa Barbara, 1976, Stella Polaries Gallery, L.A., 1981, 82, Kaufman Galleries, Houston, 1982, Modernism Gallery, San Francisco, 1983, Works Gallery, Long Beach, Costa Mesa, Calif., 1986, 87, 88, 89, 90, 91, 92, Malka Gallery, L.A., 1997; group exhibitions include Pasadena Art Mus., 1965, Carson Pirie Scott, Chgo., 1965, Calif. Palace of Legion of Honor, San Francisco, 1967, Esther Bear Gallery, Santa Barbara, 1967, 69, Lytton Ctr. of the Visual Arts, L.A., 1968, Salt Lake Art Inst., Salt Lake City, 1968, Mus. Contemporary Crafts, Internat. Plastics Exhibition, 1969, Second Flint (Mich.) Invitational, 1969, Milw. Art Ctr., 1969, U.S.I.S. Mus., N.Y.C., Mus. Contemporary Art, Chgo., 1970, Studio Merconi, Milan, 1970, Calif. Inst. Tech., Baxter Art Galley, 1971, 1980, Calif. Innovations, Palm Springs Dessert Mus., 1981, Calif. Internat. Arts Found. Mus. of Modern Art, Paris, 1982, L.A. Artists in Seoul, Donsangbang Gallery, 1982, An Artistic Conversation, 1931-82, Poland, USA, Ulster Mus., Belfast, Ireland, 1983, Madison (Wis.) Art Ctr., 1994, Calif. State U., Fullerton, 1995, Oakland (Calif.) Mus., 1995; represented in pub. collections at River Forest (Ill.) State Bank, Atlantic Richfield Co., Dallas, Frederic Weisman Collection, L.A., Security Pacific Bank, L.A., Singapore, Andrew Dickson White Mus. of Art, Cornell U., Ithaca, N.Y., L.A. County Mus. of Art, Santa Barbara Art Mus., Laguna Beach Mus. of Art. Trustee, Pomona Coll, Claremont, Calif., 1987—; parade judge Tournament of RosesCentennial Parade, Pasadena, 1987; bd. dirs. L.A. Master Chorale, 1992—. NEA grantee, 1986. Home and Studio: 731 S Grand Ave Pasadena CA 91105-2424

PASICH, KIRK ALAN, lawyer; b. La Jolla, Calif., May 26, 1955; s. Chris Nick and Iva Mae (Tormey) P.; m. Pamela Mary Woods, July 30, 1983; children: Christopher Thomas, Kelly Elizabeth, Connor Woods. BA in Polit. Sci., UCLA, 1977; JD, Loyola Law Sch., L.A., 1980. Bar: Calif. 1980, U.S. Dist. Ct. (no., so., ea. and cen. dists.) Calif. 1981, U.S. Ct. Appeals (9th cir.) 1982, U.S. Ct. Appeals (1st cir.) 1992. Assoc. Paul, Hastings, Janofsky & Walker, L.A., 1980-88, ptnr., 1988-89; ptnr. Troop Meisinger Steuber & Pasich (formerly Hill Wynne Troop & Meisinger), L.A., 1989—. Author: Casualty and Liability Insurance, 1990, 96; co-author: Officers and Directors: Liabilities and Protections, 1996; contbg. editor: West's California Litigation Forms: Civil Procedure Before Trial, 1996; entertainment law columnist, ins. law columnist L.A. and San Francisco Daily Jour., 1989—; contbr. articles to profl. jours. Active bd. dirs. Nat. Acad. Jazz, L.A., 1988-89, chmn. bd. dirs. Woody Herman Found., L.A., 1989-92, active L.A. City Atty's. Task Force for Econ. Recovery, 1992-93. Named to Calif's. Legal Dream Team as 1 of state's top 25 litigators, Calif. Law Bus., 1992, as one of the nation's top 45 lawyers under age 45, The Am. Lawyer, 1995. Mem. ABA (mem. Task Force on Complex Insurance Coverage Litigation). Office: 10940 Wilshire Blvd Los Angeles CA 90024-3915

PASINETTI, PIER MARIA, author; b. Venice, Italy, June 24, 1913; came to U.S., 1946, naturalized, 1952; s. Carlo and Maria (Ciardi) P. Dottore in Lettere, U. Padua, Italy, 1935; Ph.D. in Comparative Lit., Yale U., 1949. Fellow La. State U., 1935-36, U. Calif. at Berkeley, 1936-37; lectr. U. Stockholm, 1942-46; prof. Italian and comparative lit. UCLA, 1949—. Author: L'ira di Dio, 1942, Venetian Red, 1960, The Smile on the Face of the Lion, 1965, From the Academy Bridge, 1970, Suddenly Tomorrow, 1971, Dall' Estrema America, 1975, Il Centro, 1979, Dorsoduro, 1983, Life for Art's Sake: Studies in the Literary Myth of the Romantic Artist, 1985, Melodramma, 1993, Piccole Veneziane Complicate, 1996; also articles, revs., film scripts. Recipient Fiction award Nat. Inst. Arts and Letters, 1965. Mem. Authors Guild. Club: Elizabethan Yale. Office: 1259 Dorsoduro, Venice Italy 30123

PASK, JOSEPH ADAM, ceramic engineering educator; b. Chgo., Feb. 14, 1913; s. Adam Poskozcem and Catherine (Ramanauskas) P.; m. Margaret J. Gault, June 11, 1938; children: Thomas Joseph, Kathryn Edyth. B.S., U. Ill., 1934, Ph.D., 1941; M.S., U. Wash., 1935. Ceramic engr. Willamina Clay Products Co., Oreg., 1935-36; teaching asst. ceramic engring. U. Ill., 1938, instr., 1938-41; asst. ceramic engr. electrotech. lab. U.S. Bur. Mines, 1941; assoc. ceramic engr. N.W. Exptl. Sta., 1942-43; asst. prof. ceramic engring., head dept. Coll. of Mines, U. Wash., Seattle, 1941-43; research ceramist, lamp div. Westinghouse Electric Corp., N.J., 1943-46; research engr. ceramic sect. Westinghouse Electric Corp., 1946-48; assoc. prof. ceramic engring., head ceramic group div. materials sci. and engring. U. Calif. at Berkeley, 1948-53, founder program ceramic engring. and sci., 1948, prof., 1953-80, prof. emeritus, 1980—, vice chmn. div., 1956-57, chmn. dept., 1957-61; assoc. dean grad. student affairs U. Calif. at Berkeley (Coll. Engring.), 1969-80; sr. faculty scientist Lawrence Berkeley Lab.; John Dorn Meml. lectr. Northwestern U., 1977; mem. clay mineral com. NRC; mem. materials adv. bd., chmn. ad hoc com. ceramic processing, adv. commn. metallurgy div. U.S. Bur. Standards; chmn. NSF study objective criteria in ceramic engring. edn., U.S.-China Seminar on Basic Sci. of Ceramics, Shanghai, 1983. Recipient John F. Bergeron Meml. Svc. award Ceramic Engring. div. U. Wash., Seattle, 1969, gold medal for research and devel. French Soc. for Research and Devel., 1979, Berkeley citation U. Calif., 1980, Alumni honor award for disting. service in engring. U. Ill. Coll. Engring., 1982, Outstanding Achievement in Edn. award Com. of Confucius, 1982, Internat. Prize Japan Fine Ceramics Assn., 1988, Engring. Alumni Achievement award U. Wash. Coll. Engring., 1991. Fellow AAAS, Am. Ceramic Soc. (disting. life mem., v.p. 1953-54, pres. ednl. coun. 1954-55, trustee 1959-62, chmn. electronics div. 1959-60, John Jeppson award 1967, Ross Coffin Purdy award 1979), Mineral Soc., Acad. Dental Materials; mem. NAE, Nat. Inst. Ceramics Engrs., N.Y. Acad. Scis., Am. Soc. Matls, Brit. Ceramic Soc., Internat. Acad. Ceramics,, Am. Soc. Engring. Edn. (chmn. materials com. 1961-63, Centennial Cert. 1993), Clay Minerals Soc., Ceramics Soc. Japan (hon., Centennial medal 1991), Materials Rsch. Soc. Japan (hon.), Keramos, Sigma XI, Tau Bet Pi, Alpha Sigma Mu. Home: 994 Euclid Ave Berkeley CA 94708-1437 Office: U Calif Dept Ceramic Engring Berkeley CA 94720 *Whatever success I have had can be attributed to hard work generated by a desire for success and recognition by my peers. This attitude was generated by my mother who came to this country, a land of opportunities, as an immigrant from Lithuania at the age of 16 without any knowledge of English. There was no question in her mind—and consequently mine—that I would get an education and be successful.*

PASMANICK, KENNETH, bassoonist; b. Rochester, N.Y., Aug. 23, 1924; s. Philip and Rose (Levitt) P.; m. Frances Virginia Cohen, Dec. 22, 1946; children: Philip, Anne. Student, Eastman Sch. Music, 1942-43, Juilliard Sch. Music, 1946-47; BA, Am. U., 1962. Am. specialist abroad for Dept. State, El Salvador and Costa Rica, 1966-67; instr. bassoon Am. U., Washington; prof. U. Md. Performed with Martha Graham Ballet tour and at Ziegfield Theater, 1946; prin. bassoonist Nat. Symphony Orch., 1947—, Washington Opera Soc.; performed (world premiere) Serenata for Bassoon and Chamber Orch. (Gian Francesca Malipiero), 1962, The Windhover (Robert Evett); performed (world premiere) Bassoon Concerto (David Amram), 1972, (N.Y. premiere), 1993; performed Concerto for Bassoon and Orch., 1971; performed (U.S. premiere) Concerto for Bassoon and Orch. (Gunther Schuller), 1985; performed (European premiere) Radio Orch. of Saarbrücken, Germany, 1992; rec. with Newport Classics Recs., Saarbrücken Radio Orch. for GM Recs., 1992; rec. (CD) Air for Bassoon and Strings (Alec Wilder) with Manhattan Chamber Orch., 1994; performed (World premiere) Concerto for Bassoon and Orchestra/Moscow Philharmonic, Tchaikovsky Hall, Moscow, 1997. Served in USAAF, 1943-46. Recipient Gold medal for cultural contbn. in Costa Rica. Mem. Nat. Symphony Wind Soloists (founder). Home: 5227 Chevy Chase Pky NW Washington DC 20015-1747 *Irrational culturally induced ideas aside, I see no limits on the creative capacities of humans to forge a just and rational world for all its inhabitants.*

PASNICK, RAYMOND WALLACE, labor union official, editor; b. New Kensington, Pa., Apr. 29, 1916; s. Stanley and Mary Ann Pasnick; m. Margaret Solberg, Mar. 3, 1937; children: Victor Keith, Raymond Gene. Ed. pub. schs. Editor Aluminum Workers Jour., New Kensington, 1936-37; publicity dir. Aluminum Workers Am., Pitts., 1937-44; asst. editor Steel Labor, Pitts., 1944-46; editor Steel Labor, 1962-78; Midwest editor, also Midwest dir. edn. United Steelworkers Am., Chgo., 1946-62; nat. editor, dir. comm. United Steelworkers Am., 1962-65; dir. pub. rels. United Steelworker Am., Pitts., 1965-78; editor OLDTIMER quar., 1978-86; vol. editor Steelworker Oldtimer, 1986—. Pub. mem. Chgo. Bd. Edn., 1955-66. Recipient of Civil Rights award Jewish Labor Com. Chgo., 1962, Man of Year award Chgo. unit Nat. Frontiersmen, 1963. Mem. Internat. Labor Press Assn. (pres. 1972-74), Am. Fedn. Tchrs., Chgo. Newspaper Guild (treas. 1948-56, v.p. 1957). Democrat. Roman Catholic. Home and Office: 2248 Country Club Dr Pittsburgh PA 15241-2335 *Living for one's self alone can be self-defeating. I have learned that the right way to live is to find others with common goals and work together with them. This is the most effective way to confront mutual challenges and make genuine social and economic progress.*

PASQUA, THOMAS MARIO, JR., journalism educator; b. L.A., Aug. 13, 1938; s. Thomas Mario and Ann Ione (Anderson) P.; m. Sandra Mae Liddell; children: Bruce Burks, Julie Burks, Geoffrey, Alexis. BA, Whittier (Calif.) Coll., 1960; MA, UCLA, 1961; PhD, U. Tex., 1973. Cert. secondary tchr. Reporter, photographer Whittier Daily News, 1954-65; tchr. LaSerna High Sch., Whittier, 1961-63, 64-65; lectr. Calif. State U., Fullerton, 1973-75, Mesa Coll., San Diego, 1978-83, U. San Diego, 1979-80, San Diego State U., 1985; prof. Southwestern Coll., Chula Vista, Calif., 1965—; staff writer San Diego Mag., 1997. Co-author: Excellence in College Journalism, 1983, Mass Media in the Information Age, 1990, Historical Perspectives in Popular Music, 1993; editor C.C. Journalist, 1983—; bibliographer Journalism Quar., 1974-92; contbr. articles to profl. jours. Mem. ch. coun. St. Andrew Luth. Ch., Whittier, 1965; mem. Chula Vista Bd. of Ethics, 1978-86; mem. Chula Vista Charter Rev. Com., 1969; mem. adv. bd. Bay Gen. Hosp., Chula Vista, 1985-87; mem. ch. coun. Victory Luth. Ch., Chula Vista, 1989-90; adv. com. Otay Valley Regional Park, 1990—. Wall St. Jour. Newspaper Fund fellow U. Wash., 1962; recipient Nat. Teaching award Poynter Inst. Media Studies, 1987. Mem. C.C. Journalism Assn. (archivist 1989—, charter inductee Hall of Fame, 1994), Journalism Assn. C.C.'s (exec. sec. 1975-81), Assn. for Edn. in Journalism and Mass Comm. (Markham prize 1974), Internat. Comm. Assn., Coll. Media Advisers, Am. Fedn. Tchrs. (pres. Southwestern Coll. 1977-78, 81-87), Phi Kappa Phi, Kappa Tau Alpha, Pi Sigma Alpha. Democrat. Avocations: gardening, cats, reading mysteries. Home: 760 Monterey Ave Chula Vista CA 91910-6318 Office: Southwestern Coll 900 Otay Lakes Rd Chula Vista CA 91910-7223

PASQUARELLI, JOSEPH J., real estate, engineering and construction executive; b. N.Y.C., Mar. 5, 1927; s. Joseph and Helen (Casabona) P.; B.C.E. cum laude, Manhattan Coll., 1949; m. JoAnne Brienza, June 20, 1964; children: Ronald, Richard, June, Joy. Engr., Madigan-Hyland, N.Y.C. and Burns & Roe Inc., N.Y.C., 1949-56; sr. engr., asst. to exec. dir. Office of Sch. Bldgs., N.Y.C. Bd. Edn., 1956-67; dir. design and constrn. mgmt. City U. N.Y., 1967-72; dir. constrn. mgmt. Morse/Diesel Inc., N.Y.C., 1972-76; dir. projects and proposals Burns & Roe Indsl. Svcs. Corp., Oradell, N.J., 1976-80, dir. facilities and infrastructure, 1980-86; dir. design engring, constrn., devel. mgmt. Xerox Realty Corp., Stamford, Ct., 1986-89; exec. v.p. The Galvin Group N.Y.C., 1989-90; assoc. prin. Pei/Galvin Holdings, Ltd., N.Y.C., 1990-93; sr. v.p. Pei Group Holdings, Ltd., N.Y.C., 1993-96; exec. dir. archtl. svcs. and space planning Pace U., Briarcliff Manor, N.Y., 1996—. Served with U.S. Army, 1944-46. Licensed profl. engr., N.Y., N.J. Fellow ASCE; mem. N.Y. Bldg. Congress (past gov., chmn. legis. com.), NSPE, Mcpl. Engrs., Am. Arbitration Assn., Chi Epsilon. Contbr. articles to profl. jours. Home: 38 Oak Pl North Caldwell NJ 07006 Office: Pace U Dow Hall 235 Elm Rd Briarcliff Manor NY 10510-2207

PASQUIER, JOËL, music educator; b. Montmorency, France, Sept. 25, 1943; arrived in Can., 1967; s. Jean and Raymonde (Gourdin) P.; m. Anne Vachon, Nov. 28, 1970; 1 child, Ariane. Grad. in piano and chamber music, Conservatoire Nat. Superieur de Musique, Paris, 1962. Prof. Conservatoire de Musique de St. Germain-en-Laye, France, 1964-65; grad. asst. Sch. Music, Ind. U., Bloomington, 1965-67; tchr. piano Ecole de Musique, U. Laval, Quebec, Can., 1967—; dir. Ecole de Musique, U. Laval, Quebec, 1988-91. Appeared as solo pianist concert halls, radio, TV, with chamber and symphony orchs. in France, U.S., Can., The Netherlands. Fulbright scholar Ind. U., 1965. Mem. Que. Yacht Club. Office: U Laval Sch Music, Pavillon Casault, Sainte Foy, PQ Canada G1K 7P4

PASS, BOBBY CLIFTON, entomology educator; b. Cleveland, Ala., Nov. 4, 1931; s. Rufus Clifton and Alma Antoinette (Payne) P.; m. Annie Ruth Rutherford, Aug. 17, 1955; 1 child, Kevin Clifton. Student, Snead Jr. Coll., 1949-50; BS in Agr. Edn., Auburn U., 1952, MS in Entomology, 1960; PhD in Entomology, Clemson U., 1962. Rsch. asst. Auburn (Ala.) U., 1958-60, Clemson (S.C.) U., 1960-62; asst. prof. U. Ky., Lexington, 1962-67, assoc. prof., 1967-68, assoc. prof., chair, 1968, prof., chmn., 1969—; cons. USAID/Indonesia, 1985—, UK/Shandong Agr. U., People's Republic China, 1986—. Contbr. articles on insect mgmt. to profl. jours. Mem. Entomological Soc. Am. (pres. 1986-87, governing bd. 1983-88), Am. Registry Profl. Entomologists (cert., pres. 1979-80), Can. Entomological Soc., Internat. Orgn. for Biol. Control, S.C. Entomological Soc., Kans. Entomological Soc., Ky. Acad. Sci., Soc. Sigma Xi, Gamma Sigma Delta, Phi Kappa Phi. Democrat. Methodist. Home: 3234 Pepperhill Rd Lexington KY 40502-3545 Office: U Ky Dept Entomology Lexington KY 40546-0091

PASSAGE, DAVID, diplomat; b. Charlotte, N.C., June 16, 1942; s. John T. and Virginia (Beam) P. BA in Internat. Rels., U. Denver, 1964; MS in Internat. Econs., Georgetown U., 1966; student, Nat. War Coll., Ft. Mcnair, Washington, 1981-82. With U.S. Dept. State, 1966—; politico-mil. affairs officer Am. Embassy, London, 1966; pacification program analyst U.S. Mil. Command, Siagon, Vietnam, 1968; with U.S. State Dept. Ops. Ctr., 1970; officer Secretariat Staff, 1971; special asst. to Asst. Sec. State Politico-Mil. Affairs, 1972-74; pol. officer Quito, Ecuador, 1974-76; spl. asst. to Sec. of State Henry Kissinger U.S. State Dept., Washington, 1976; polit. counselor Am. Embassy, Canberra, Australia, 1977-79; dir. Press Office and Assoc., 1979; from. dep. to acting spokesman U.S. Dept. State, dep. dir. So. African Affairs, 1982-84; dep. chief mission/charge d'affairs Am. Embassy, San Salvador, 1984-86; dir. Office Regional Affairs Africa Bur., 1986; dir. Nat. Security Coun. Africa The White House, Washington, 1989; U.S. amb. to Botswana, 1990-93; polit. adviser to U.S. Spl. Opers. Command MacDill AFB, Fla., 1993-96; dir. Andean affairs Dept. State, Washington, 1996—; lectr. Nat. War Coll., John F. Kennedy Spl. Warfare Ctr., USAF Spl. Ops. Sch., others. Contbr. chpt.: Managing Contemporary Conflict, 1996; contbr. articles to profl. jours. Recipient Chuong My BoiTinh medal (Vietnam), Def. Disting. Civilian Svc. medal Dept. Def. Centennial scholar U. Denver. Avocations: environment and conservation. Home: 2416 Chain Bridge Rd NW Washington DC 20016 Office: US Dept State 2201 C St NW Washington DC 20520-0001

PASSAGE, STEPHEN SCOTT, energy company executive; b. Miami, Oct. 10, 1946; s. John Thompson and Virginia Frances (Beam) P.; m. Ellen Shapiro, Aug. 21, 1988. BS in Civil Engring., Pol. Sci., MIT, 1969; MA in Pol. Sci., New Sch. Soc. Rsch., 1972, MA in Econs., 1975. Cer. Profl. Engr. Mem. engring. dept. Port Authority N.Y. and N.J., 1969-86; pres. Montenay Power Corp., N.Y., 1986—; chmn. IWSA. Contbr. articles to profl. jours. Chmn. 607 West End Ave Corp., 1991—. Mem. ASME, NSPE. Avocations: chess, hiking, tennis, canoeing, reading. Office: Montenay Power Corp 800 3rd Ave New York NY 10022-7604

PASSAGLIA, CANDACE V., special education educator; b. Woodstock, Ill., Nov. 17, 1951; d. Vaughn D. and Phyllis (Higgins) Heidenreich; m. Roger Michael Passaglia, Dec. 29, 1973; children: Ryan James, Shannon Marie. BS in Edn./Spl. Edn., No. Ill. U., 1973, MS in Spl. Edn. Adminstrn., 1995; learning disabilities/physically handicapped cert., U. Calif., Irvine, 1986. Cert. elem. edn., Ill., Calif.; cert. spl. edn. K-12. Tchr. grade 4 Woodstock (Ill.) Cmty. Sch. Dist. 200, 1973; exec. sec. various cos., 1974-83; instrnl. aide, substitute tchr. various sch. dists., Calif., 1984-87; resource specialist Irvine Unified Sch. Dist., 1987-89; learning disabilities tchr. Cary (Ill.) Elem. Sch. Dist. # 26, 1989-95; learning disabilities specialist Wilmette (Ill.) Sch. Dist. 39, 1995-96; tchr. grade 5 Cary Elem. Sch. Dist. 26, 1996—; instr. No. Ill. U. Grad. Sch., 1996—; tech. com., sys. operator computer network, mem. sch. improvement com. Cary (Ill.) Sch. Dist. # 26, 1990—; lectr. No. Ill. U., DeKalb, 1993, 94; keynote spkr. Kans. State U., Manhattan, 1994, 95. Author, editor: (nat. newsletter) Co-Teaching Network News, 1992—. Bd. dirs. Mission Viejo (Calif.) Little League Assn., 1985-87; mem. Cary (Ill.)-Grove H.S. Baseball Parent's Assn., 1990-94; oboist Crystal Lake Cmty. Band, 1989-91; 1st soprano The New Oratorio Singers, 1991-92; mem. Cary Cmty. Theatre, 1995—. Mem. ASCD, United Learning Disabilities Assn. Avocations: computers, writing, gardening, family time, reading. Office: Three Oaks Sch Cary Elem Sch Dist 26 15 S 2nd St Cary IL 60013-2810

PASSANO, E. MAGRUDER, JR., publishing executive; b. Balt., Oct. 2, 1942; s. Edward M. and Mildred P. (Nelson) P.; m. Helen C. Marikle, Sept. 4, 1971; children: Catherine, Tammy, Sarah. BS, Johns Hopkins U., 1967, MLA, 1969. With Waverly, Inc., Balt., 1965—, salesman, 1970-73, v.p., 1973-75, v.p. adminstrn., sec., 1975-90. vice chmn., sec., 1990—. Pres., Passano Found., Balt., 1982—, Am. Lung Assn. Md., 1982-84; mem. exec. com. Vol. Coun. Equal Opportunity, Balt., 1978—, chmn., 1995—; bd. dirs. Combined Health Appeal Am.; pres. (CHA) Combined Health Agys., Md., 1985-87, chmn. exec. com., 1987-95; pres. 12:30 Club Balt., 1981-83; mem. exec. com. Balt. City Life Museums, 1982-93, v.p. 1987-93, trustee emeritus, 1993—; mem. adv. coun. Johns Hopkins U. Sch. Continuing Studies, 1984—, exec. chair alumni chpt., 1986-89, chair edn. cmty. devel. iniative, 1995—; mem. Md. Gov.'s Commn. on High Blood Pressure and Related Cardiovascular Risk Factors, 1986—; bd. govs. Md. New Directions, Inc., 1987-94; bd. dirs., mem. exec. com. YMCA Ctrl. Md., 1988-96; bd. dirs., chair edn. com. Pride of Balt., 1990—; bd. dirs. Independent Coll. Fund Md., 1994—; bd. vis. Towson State U., 1994—, Sch. Medicine U. Md., 1995—; mem. planning com. Md. Bus. Responsive Govt., 1994—. Served with USN, 1963-65. Recipient Prince Hall Bicentennial award Masons, 1975; citations Mayor of Balt., 1976, City of Balt., 1977, Vol. of Yr. award for outstanding svc. to CICHA, 1984-85, Presdl. award for outstanding svc. to Am. Lung Assn. Md., 1985, Outstanding Vol., 1988, Disting. Svc. award Soc. Profl. Journalists, 1987, Outstanding Svc. award Am. Heart Assn., 1988, Outstanding Vol. Svc. award Balt. Assn. Retarded Citizens, 1990, Vol. of Yr./Outstanding Leadership and Dedication award Combined Health Agys., 1991-92. Mem. Purchasing Mgmt. Assn. Md. (chmn. com. 1968-70), Balt. Jaycees (v.p. 1974-76, internat. senator 1975), Greater Balt. Minority Purchasing Coun. (Service award 1978), Soc. Colonial Wars (chpt. gov., 1989-91), Johns Hopkins U. Alumni Assn. (pres. Balt. 1984-86, Univ. Heritage award 1987). Democrat. Episcopalian. Home: 3925 Linkwood Rd Baltimore MD 21210-3001 Office: Waverly Inc 351 W Camden St Baltimore MD 21201-2435

PASSANO, EDWARD MAGRUDER, printing company executive; b. Towson, Md., Dec. 22, 1904; s. Edward Boetler and Eleanor (Isaac) P.; m. Mary Troy Fleming, Apr. 2, 1982; 1 son, Edward Magruder. B.S. in Econs., Johns Hopkins U., 1927. With Waverly Press, Inc. (name changed to Waverly Inc. 1988), Balt., 1927-82, treas., 1946-68, pres., 1963-71, chmn. exec. com., 1971-75, also bd. dirs., ret., 1982. Bd. dirs., treas. Passano Found., Inc., 1970—. Mem. Soc. Colonial Wars (life, gen. coun.). Republican. Episcopalian. Home: 6873 Travelers Rest Pt Easton MD 21601-7631 Office: Waverly Inc 351 W Camden St Baltimore MD 21201-2435

PASSANTINO, BENJAMIN ARTHUR, marketing executive; b. Bklyn., Feb. 26, 1956; s. Anthony Frank and Ann Marie (Ruggerio) P.; m. Jane Ellen Collins, Nov. 26, 1983; children: Blythe Ann, Paige Ellen. BA, Drew U., 1978; BSBA, Pace U., 1979. Mgr. pub. rels. AT&T, N.Y.C., 1978-82, mgr. mktg. communications, new techs., 1982-84; pres. B. Arthur Communications, Morristown, N.J., 1984-89; sr. v.p. bus. devel. IMEDIA Creative Corp. Mktg., Morristown, 1989-94, also dir.; mng. ptnr., CEO, Tribeca Global, Inc., Hackettstown, N.J., 1994—; bd. dirs. Dieknowlogist, Inc., N.Y.C., One World Botanicals, Inc., Red Bank, N.J., Lasercomb Am., Inc., N.Y.C. Co-author: One with the Flame, 1985, NFL Quarterbacks, 1987; contbr. articles to mags. Bd. dirs. Am. Cancer Soc., Morristown, 1986—, Jr. Achievement, Basking Ridge, N.J., 1979—; mem. Washington Twp. (Morris County) Planning Bd., chairperson econ. devel. com.; trustee Drakestown United Meth. Ch. Mem. Internat. Assn. Bus. Communicators, Am. Mktg. Assn., Bus. Profls. of Advt. Assn., Conf. Bd. Home: 235 Flocktown Rd Long Valley NJ 07853-3827 Office: 108 High St 2d Fl Hackettstown NJ 07840

PASSANTINO, RICHARD J., architect; b. N.Y.C., Apr. 4, 1934; s. Charles V. and Ruth M. (Defina) P.; m. Erika F. Dethlefs, Sept. 1, 1962; children: Stefan C., Fiona R. BS in Architecture, U. Cin., 1957. Registered arch., D.C., Md., Va., Ga., Miss., Fla., Ky., Mo., N.J., S.C.; cert. Nat. Coun. Archtl. Registration Bds. Rsch. assoc. McLeod, Ferrara, Ensign, Washington, 1960-70; founding prin. Richard J. Passantino, AIA Architects, Bethesda, Md., 1970-80; pres. SAIC Architects, McLean, Va., 1980-90, LEA/Passantino & Bavier, Arlington, Va., 1990-94, Passantino & Bavier subs. Facility Holding Corp. Smyrna, Ga., Bethesda, Md., 1995—; spkr. to various ednl. instn. in U.S., AIA rep. Union Internat. Archs., 1985-88; mem. nat. archtl. juries throughout U.S., 1975—. Co-author: Urban Schools in Europe, 1963; contbr. numerous articles to profl. jours.; designer 7 earthquake resistant schs. in So. Italy, 1985-88, Project Dir., for design of multiple U.S. Navy projects in Greece, 11 locations, 1985-89, Early Childhood Ctr., Buffalo, 1995, psychiat. hosp., Leesburg, Va., 1979, Haile Selassie U., Addis Ababa, Ethiopia; designer modifications Am. Consulate Gen., Ecuador, Am. embassies, Papua-New Guinea, The Philippines, Liberia, Ghana, others. Bd. dirs. Nat. Child Rsch. Ctr., Washington, 1969-74. 1st lt. USAF, 1958-60; capt. USAFR, 1960-62. Recipient award for sch. architecture exhbn. Am. Assn. Sch. Bd. Adminstrs., 1984. Mem. v.p. chmn., architecture for edn. 1994), Coun. for Ednl. Facilities Planners (co-recipient Projects of Distinction award 1993), recipient of Coun. of Ednl. Facility Planners Internat., 1996, recipient of the James D, MacConnell award for Ednl. Facility Planning Excellence, Assn. for Childhood Edn. Internat., Assn. Sch. Bus. Ofcls. Internat. (award of excellence 1986), Nat. Hist. Trust, Soc. Am. Mil. Engrs. Avocations: tennis, photography, travel. Office: Passantino & Bavier Archs 2233 Lake Park Dr SE Ste 450 Smyrna GA 30080-8813

PASSARO, EDWARD, JR., surgeon, educator; b. Newark, Apr. 12, 1930; s. Edward and Elvira (Troina) P.; m. Geng Wang, Dec. 15, 1985; children: Dario, Cristoforo, Pamella, Nai-Kang Kuan, Nai-Ling Kuan. BA, NYU, 1951; MD, U. Rochester, 1955; M Med. Sci., Ohio State U., 1960. Diplomate Am. Bd. Surgery. Chief surg. svc. Wadsworth Hosp., L.A., 1971-96; prof. surgery UCLA, 1978—; mem. surg. field adv. com. VA, Washington, 1986—. Capt. USAF, 1956-58. Avocations: sailing, farming. Home: 12304 5th Helena Dr Los Angeles CA 90049 Office: West LA VA Med Ctr 11301 Wilshire Blvd Los Angeles CA 90073-1003

PASSEY, GEORGE EDWARD, psychology educator; b. Stratford, Conn., Sept. 28, 1920; s. Henry Richard and Elizabeth (Angus) P.; m. Algie Aldridge Ashe, Nov. 18, 1950; children—Richard Ashe, Elizabeth Aldridge, Mary Louise. B.S., Springfield Coll., 1942; M.A., Clark U., 1947; Ph.D., Tulane U., 1950. Asst. prof. U. Ala., Tuscaloosa, 1952-55; assoc. prof. U. Ala., 1955-56, 57-59, prof., 1959-63; prof. psychology, chmn. div. social and behavioral scis. U. Ala., Birmingham, 1967-73; prof. engring. U. Ala., 1969-84, Disting. Service prof. psychology, 1984-85, Disting Service prof. emeritus, 1985—; dean U. Ala. (Sch. Social and Behavioral Scis.), 1973-84; research scientist Lockheed Ga. Co., Marietta, Ga., 1956-57, 63-65, cons., 1965-67; prof. Ga. Inst. Tech., 1965-67. Served with USNR, 1942-46, PTO; with USAF, 1951-52. Fellow Am. Psychol. Assn.; mem. So. Soc. for Philosophy and Psychology, Southeastern Psychol. Assn., Ala. Psychol. Assn., Pine Harbor Golf and Racquet Club, Coosa Pines Golf Club, Sigma Xi. Home: 7141 Skyline Dr Pell City AL 35125-6936 *Whatever success I have enjoyed ought to be attributed to the attempt I have made to carry out the admonitions of my parents to make choices only after having appraised the alternatives in terms of their consequences, to weigh ethical considerations above all others, never to demand of others what one is unwilling to give of himself, and to work untiringly for those causes to which one is committed.*

PASSI, BETH, school administrator. Dir. Blake Lower Sch., Hopkins, Minn., 1982—. Recipient elem. sch. recognition award U.S. Dept. Edn., 1989-90, 93-94, Bush prin. leadership fellow, 1993-94. Office: Blake Lower Sch 110 Blake Rd Hopkins MN 55343

PASSMORE, HOWARD CLINTON, JR., geneticist, biological sciences educator; b. Drexel Hill, Pa., Sept. 12, 1942; s. Howard Clinton and Thelma (Walter) P.; m. Irene Grace Wrigley, Aug. 22, 1964; children: Lisa, Heather. AB, Franklin and Marshall Coll., 1964; PhD, U. Mich., 1970. Asst. prof. genetics Rutgers U., New Brunswick, N.J., 1971-77, assoc. prof., 1977-88, prof., 1988—, dir. grad. program in microbiology and molecular genetics, 1995—; assoc. dir. Bur. Biol. Rsch., 1982-85; mem. mammalian genetics study sect. NIH, 1988-92. Rsch. grantee NIH, 1978—. Mem. Am. Assn. Immunologists, Genetics Soc. Am., Am. Soc. Human Genetics. Home: 21 W Mill Rd Long Valley NJ 07853-3435 Office: Rutgers U Bur of Biol Rsch PO Box 1059 Piscataway NJ 08855-1059

PASSMORE, JAN WILLIAM, private investor; b. Winchester, Ind., Nov. 5, 1940; s. Gale Orth and Helen Louise (Hoskinson) P.; m. Pamela Boa, Feb. 14, 1964. Student Nebr. State U., 1959-61; BS, Ball State U., 1963. With Aetna Life & Casualty, 1964-75, Western region dir., San Jose, Calif., 1972-75; broker, Sanders & Sullivan, San Jose, 1975-78, partner, 1978-80, pres., 1979-81; pres., CEO Corroon & Black, San Jose, 1981-88, chmn. 1988-90; pres. First Richmond Corp., First Richmond Realtors, 1991-93; v.p. Prestwick, Inc. 1991-93; pres. Industries, Inc., 1990-96, pres. The Wellesley Group., 1993—, pres. econ. devel. commn., Richmond, 1996— ; chmn. nat. adv. council INA Marketdyne, 1980-82; chmn. bd. Econ. Devel. Corp. Wayne County, Ind., 1993; chmn. Nat. Adv. Coun. Cigna Corp., 1983-86; chmn. Aetna Life & Casualty Regional Adv. Council, 1982-84, 87-89. Chmn. bd. Goodwill Industries, 1978-80, 86-89; pres. Boy Scouts Am., 1981-83; bd. dirs. Music and Arts Found., 1980-85, Alexian Bros. Hosp. Found., 1978-85, Small Bus. Devel. Ctr. Region # 9, 1993-95, chmn., 1994; chmn. bd. Hope Rehab., 1985-87; chmn. bd. dirs. Santa Clara County United Way; mem. San Jose Trolley Commn.; past pres. bd. trustees Alum Rock United Meth. Ch.; past pres. bd. trustees 1st Meth. Ch. San Jose; nat. council rep. Boy Scouts Am., 1985-90; chmn. bd. Mayor's Blue Ribbon Commn. Fin. City of Richmond, Ind., 1993.; chmn. fin. 1st Meth. Ch., Richmond. Recipient Silver Beaver award, Benefactors award Boy Scouts Am., Mayoral Proclamation City of San Jose, Suprs. Proclamation County of Santa Clara, Proclamation from Calif. State Assembly; named Citizen of Yr., Aetna Life & Casualty Co., 1975, Disting. Citizen of Yr. Santa Clara County, 1985; INA-Marketdyne Golden Circle, 1977-82, 87; named hon. Ky. Col. Mem. Western Assn. Ins. Brokers (trustee 1987-90), Nat. Assn. Ind. Ins. Agts., Richmond-Wayne County C. of C. (chmn. 1993, bd. dirs. 1990-95, disting. svc. award 1996). Republican. Clubs: San Jose Country Club (treas., bd. dirs.), Scotts Boys Club (pres. 1994-96, trustee 1992—), Kiwanis Club. of Richmond (chmn. bd., 1996-97), Sainte Claire, Spartan Found., Pres.'s Council San Jose State U., Aetna Life and Casualty Gt. Performers, Forest Hills Country Club, Columbia Club, Masons, Shriners, Kiwanis (pres. Mechanicsburg, Pa. chpt. 1969, lt. gov. Pa. 1970-72, pres. San Jose chpt. 1986, mem. Richmond club 1990—, bd. dirs. 1991-93, Hero award 1995, MVP award 1991-96), Kiwanis Internat. (legion of honor 30 years). Home: 729 Toddsbury Ln Richmond IN 47374-7152 Office: PO Box 1441 Richmond IN 47375-1441 *A lot of people have provided opportunities for me - I have tried to recognize them as a trust and give each a 100% effort.*

PASSMORE, MICHAEL FORREST, environmental research administrator; b. Oroville, Calif., July 9, 1947; s. Audley Forrest and Betty Beryle (Elkin) P.; m. Laura Ann Travis, Sept. 7, 1968 (div. 1985); children: Travis Forrest, Robert Bryan; m. Elise Jean Bechtold, Nov. 9, 1985; 1 child, Heather Elise. BS, Oreg. State U.,, 1974, MS, 1977; PhD, Tex. A&M U., 1981. Research asst. Oreg. State U., Corvallis, 1974-77, research assoc., 1977; grad. fellow Rob and Bessie Welder Wildlife Found., Sinton, Tex., 1977-80; wildlife biologist Environ. Resources Br. U.S. Army Corps Engrs., Walla Walla, Wash., 1980-87; asst. chief Environ. Resources Br. U.S. Army Corps Engrs., Walla Walla, 1986-87, chief, 1987-96; chief stewardship br. waterways experiment sta. Vicksburg, Miss., 1996—; master bird bander Fish and Wildlife Svc., 1981-90; citizen ambassador, wildlife biology del. People-to-People Internat., China, 1987; cert. wildlife biologist, 1987—. Co-author: Raptors on COE Lands, 1986, Ecology of Band-tailed Pigeons in Oregon, 1992; contbr. articles to profl. publs. Coach youth sports, 1984-92; vol. Boy Scouts Am., Walla Walla, 1986-95. Mem. The Wildlife Soc. (mem. spl. award com. 1987-88, assoc. editor Bulletin 1997—), Nat. Mil. Fish and Wildlife Assn. Methodist. Avocations: hunting, wildlife photography, camping.

PASSON, RICHARD HENRY, academic administrator; b. Hazleton, Pa., Aug. 18, 1939; s. Henry Richard and Grace Miriam (Bernstein) P.; m. Margaret Rose Ferdinand, Aug. 14, 1965; children—Michael, Rebecca, Christopher. B.A. (Bishop Hafey scholar), King's Coll., Pa., 1961; M.A., U. Notre Dame, 1963, Ph.D. (NDEA fellow), 1965. From instr. to prof. English U. Scranton, 1964-73, chmn. English dept., 1970-73, fgn. student adviser, 1965-67; dean Coll. Arts and Scis., Creighton U., Omaha, 1973-77; acad. v.p. St. Joseph's U., Phila., 1977-84; provost U. Scranton, Pa., 1984—. Contbr. articles profl. jours. Recipient grant Nat. Assn. Fgn. Students, 1966. Mem. Modern Lang. Assn., Am. Assn. Higher Edn., Am. Assn. Acad. Deans. Democrat. Roman Catholic. Office: U Scranton Office of Provost Scranton PA 18510

PASSWATER, BARBARA GAYHART, real estate broker; b. Phila., July 10, 1945; d. Clarence Leonard and Margaret Jamison; m. Richard Albert Passwater, June 2, 1964; children: Richard Alan, Michael Eric. AA, Goldey-Beacom Coll., 1963; BA, Salisbury State U., 1981. Notary pub., Md. Sec. DuPont, Wilmington, Del., 1963-65, Nuclear-Chgo., Silver Spring, Md., 1965-67; office mgr. Montgomery County Sch. System, Wheaton, Md., 1977-79; adminstrv. asst. Solgar Nutritional Rsch. Ctr., Berlin, Md., 1979-94, asst. to dir. rsch., 1995—; assoc. broker Prudential-Groff Realty, Berlin, Md., 1983-87, ReMax, Inc., Berlin, Md., 1987-88; broker, mgr., developers rep. River Run Sales Ctr., Berlin, Md., 1988-96; broker Solager Realty LLC, Berlin, Md., 1997—. Treas. Ocean Pines (Md.) Vol. Fire Dept. Aux., 1981-84; emergency med. tech. Ocean Pines Vol. Fire Dept., 1983-95, life mem., 1996—; sec. Ocean Pines Fire Dept., 1990-95; mem. Foster Care Review Bd., Snow Hill, Md., 1984-97. Mem. Beta Sigma Phi, Phi Kappa Phi. Avocations: photography, golf, grandchildren. Office: Solgar Nutritional Rsch Ctr 11017 Manklin Meadows Ln Berlin MD 21811-9340

PASSWATER, RICHARD ALBERT, biochemist, author; b. Wilmington, Del., Oct. 13, 1937; s. Stanley Leroy and Mabel Rosetta (King) P. BS, U. Del., 1959; PhD, Bernadean U., 1976. Cert. firefighter; m. Barbara Sarah Gayhart, June 2, 1964; children: Richard Alan, Michael Eric. Supr. instrumental analysis lab. Allied Chem. Corp., Marcus Hook, Pa., 1959-64; tech. svcs. rep. F&M Sci. Corp., Avondale, Pa., 1965; dir. applications lab. Am. Instrument Co., Silver Spring, Md., 1965-77; dir. Am. Gen. Enterprises, Minn.; former daily broadcaster Sta. WMCA, N.Y.C., 1980-88; former daily broadcaster Sta. WRNG, Atlanta, 1982-85; rsch. dir. Solgar Nutritional Rsch. Ctr., 1978—, corp. v.p. Solgar Co., Inc.; chmn. Worcester County Emergency Planning Com., 1985-96; bd. dirs. Worcester Meml. Hosp., Atlantic Gen. Hosp., River Run Assn; pres. 1989-92, Subaqueous Exploration and Archeology Ltd. Author: Guide to Fluorescence Literature, vol. 1, 1967, vol. 2 1970, vol. 3, 1974, Supernutrition, 1975, Supernutrition For Healthy Hearts, 1977, Super Calorie, Carbohydrate Counter, 1978, Cancer and Its Nutritional Therapies, 1978, 83, 93, The Easy No-Flab Diet, 1979, Selenium As Food and Medicine, 1980, The Slendernow Diet, 1982, (with Dr. E. Cranton) Trace Elements, Hair Analysis and Nutrition, 1983, The New Supernutrition, 1991, The Longevity Factor, 1993, Cancer Prevention and Nutritional Therapy, 1993, (with Ben Friedrich and Hans Kugler) Heart Health, 1994, Pycnogenol: The Super Protector Nutrient, 1994, Lipoic Acid: The Metabolic Antioxidant, 1995; contbg. author: Fire Protection Guide to Hazardous Materials, 1991; editor Fluorescence News, 1966-77, Jour. Applied Health Scis., 1982-83; mem. editorial bd. Nutritional Perspectives, 1978-96, The Body Forum, 1979-80, Jour. Holistic Medicine, 1981-88, VIM Newsletter, 1979—; contbg. editor Firehouse Mag., 1988-94, Jour Applied Nutrition; contbr. over 400 health articles to mags.; co-editor booklet series Your Good Health; sci. adv. and columnist Whole Foods mag.; patentee in field. bd. dirs. Sci. Documentation Ctr., Dunfermline, Eng.; Am. Found. Firefighter Health and Safety; chief Ocean Pines Vol. Fire Dept., 1984-93; active Emergency Med. Tech.; adviser Nat. Inst. Nutrition Edn.; past adv. bd. Stephen Decatur High Sch., Worcester County Dept. Edn. Cubmaster, 1975-79. Named Citizen of Yr. Ocean Pines, Md., 1987, 5th Ann. Achievement award, 1989, VFW Cert. of Commendation, 1988, Industry award Nat. Inst. Nutritional Edn., 1991; inducted into Delmarva Fireman's Hall of Fame, 1993. Fellow Internat. Acad. Preventive Medicine, Am. Inst. Chemists; mem. ASTM, AAAS, Am. Chem. Soc., Gerontology Soc., Am. Geriatric Soc., Am. Aging Assn., Soc. Applied Spectroscopy, Internat. Found. Preventive Medicine (v.p.), Internat. Union Pure and Applied Chemistry, Royal Soc. Chemistry (London), Internat. Acad. Holistic Health and Medicine, Capital Chem. Soc., Nutrition Today Soc., Am. Acad. Applied Health Scis. (pres., bd. dir.), Internat. Found. Preventive Medicine (v.p., dir.), Inst. Nutritional Rsch., Internat. Platform Assn., N.Y. Acad. Scis., Nat. Fire Protection Assn. (cert. firefighter level III, com. on properties of hazardous chemicals), Pi Kappa Alpha. Office: 11017 Manklin Meadows Ln Berlin MD 21811-9340

PASSY, CHARLES, arts critic; b. N.Y., Jan. 9, 1964; s. Victor and Beverly (Green) P.; m. Leslie M. Olsen, Dec. 15, 1989; 1 child, Jacob E. BA, Columbia U., 1985. Assoc. Jay K. Hoffman and Assocs., N.Y., 1983-87; sr. editor, mng. editor Ovation Mag., N.Y., 1988-89; editor Classical Mag., N.Y., 1989-91; editor-in-chief Musical Am. Pub., N.Y., 1991-92; staff writer The Palm Beach Post, West Palm Beach, 1992—; announcer, prodr. WNYC FM, N.Y., 1984-85; entertainment stringer N.Y. Newsday, 1987-92. Author: (with others) New Voices: Selected University and College Prize Winning Poems, 1989, The New Grove Dictionary of Jazz, The New Grove Dictionary of Music and Musicians in the United States, 1989; editor: (with others) The Letters of Virgil Thomson, 1988; contbr. numerous articles to jours. in field. Recipient Poetry award Acad. Am. Poets Columbia U., 1985, Criticism awards Soc. Profl. Journalists, 1995, 97, Fla. Press Club, 1993, Fla. Soc. Newspaper Editors, 1993; fellow Knight Ctr. for Specialized Journalism, 1993. Mem. Music Critics Assn., Louis August Jonas Found. Avocations: poetry, baseball, theater, collecting sports memorabilia, reading. Home: 5481 Eagle Lake Dr Palm Bch Gdns FL 33418-1546 Office: Palm Beach Newspapers Inc 2751 S Dixie Hwy West Palm Beach FL 33405-1233

PASTAN, LINDA OLENIK, poet; b. N.Y.C., May 27, 1932; d. Jacob L. and Bess (Schwartz) Olenik; m. Ira Pastan, 1953; children: Stephen, Peter, Rachel. BA, Radcliffe Coll., 1954; MLS, Simmons Coll., 1955; MA, Brandeis U., 1957. Author: (poetry) A Perfect Circle of Sun, 1971, On the Way to the Zoo, 1975, Aspects of Eve, 1975, The Five Stages of Grief, 1978 (Alice Fay di Castagnola award Poetry Soc. Am. 1978), Setting the Table, 1980, Waiting for My Life, 1981, PM/AM: New and Selected Poems, 1982 (Am. Book award nomination 1982), A Fraction of Darkness: Poems, 1985, The Imperfect Paradise, 1988, Heroes in Disguise, 1991, An Early Afterlife, 1995. Recipient Dylan Thomas Poetry award Mademoiselle, 1958, Virginia Faulkner award Prarie Schooner, 1992, Charity Randall citation Internat. Poetry Forum, 1996; NEA fellow; grantee Md. Arts Coun. Jewish. Office: 11710 Beall Mountain Rd Potomac MD 20854-1105

PASTER, BENJAMIN G., lawyer; b. St. Louis, July 8, 1947. Student, London Sch. Econs.; BS magna cum laude in Econs., U. Pa., 1970; LLM, U. Cambridge, 1972; postgrad., Academie De Droit Internat. de la Haye, The Hague, The Netherlands; JD, Yale U., 1974. Bar: N.Y. 1975, U.S. Tax Ct. 1975, R.I. 1976. With Adler Pollock & Sheehan Inc., Providence; asst. instr. law Yale U., 1973-74; adj. prof. Bryant Coll., 1980-81; vis. mem. faculty U. Cambridge, 1984. Contbr. articles to profl. jours. Recipient Gregson-Benn award; Trinity Hall scholar. Fellow Am. Coll Trust and Estate Counsel; mem. ABA (real property, probate and trust com., taxation sect.) R.I. Bar Assn. Office: Paster & Harpooton Ltd One Plaza Providence RI 02903

PASTER, HOWARD G., public relations, public affairs company executive; b. N.Y.C., Dec. 23, 1944. BA with honors, Alfred U., 1966; MS in Journalism, Columbia U., 1967. Legis. dir. UAW, 1977-80; exec. v.p. Timmons & Co., 1980-92; asst. to pres. and dir. Office Legis. Affairs White House, Washington, 1993; chmn., CEO Hill and Knowlton, Inc., N.Y.C., 1994—; bd. dirs. Ctr. Nat. Policy. Bd. dirs. Christmas-in-April. Office: Hill and Knowlton Inc 466 Lexington Ave Lbby 3 New York NY 10017-3140

PASTER, JANICE D., lawyer, former state legislator; b. St. Louis, Aug. 4, 1942. BA, Northwestern U., 1964; MA, Tufts U., 1967; JD, U. N.Mex., 1984. Atty. in pvt. practice, 1984—; mem. N.Mex. State Senate from 10th dist., 1988-96. Democrat. Home: 5553 Eakes Rd NW Albuquerque NM 87107-5529 Address: 824 Gold SW Albuquerque NM 87102

PASTERNACK, FRED L., cardiologist; b. Bklyn., July 12, 1945; s. Jack and Lillian (Illions) P.; m. Susan Schoenfeld, Dec. 23, 1967 (div. 1975); m. Barbara Horan Landreth, May 28, 1982; children: Alexander, Gregory. AB, Dartmouth Coll., 1966; MD, Albert Einstein Coll. Medicine, Bronx, N.Y., 1970. Commd. capt. USAF, 1971, advanced through grades to col.; flight surgeon USAF, Otis AFB, Westover AFB, Mass., 1971-74; flight surgeon, chief aerospace medicine 104th Tactical Fighter Group Mass. Air Nat. Guard, Westfield, Mass., 1974-81; flight surgeon, chief aerospace medicine 106th Med. Squadron N.Y. Air Nat. Guard, Westhampton Beach, N.Y., 1990-93, cmdr., 1993—; assoc. attending physician Beth Israel Med. Ctr., N.Y.C.; pvt. practice, N.Y.C., 1979—; adj. physician Lenox Hill Hosp., N.Y.C., 1979—; sr. aviation med. examiner, ind. med. sponsor FAA; cardiology cons. Am. Mayflower Life Ins. Co.; pres. Medair Leasing Ltd., Frebar Devel. Corp.; ptnr. Northeastern Aviation; pilot Skytypers. Fellow Alliance Air Nat. Guard Flight Surgeons (bd. govs.), Aerospace Med. Flight Surgeons Assn.; mem. Am. Coll. Cardiology, Am. Heart Assn., N.Y. Cardiol. Soc., Soc. USAF Flight Surgeons, Aerospace Med. Assn. (aviation safety com.). Avocations: flying, skiing, scuba diving, motor racing, sky diving. Home and Office: 29 E 63d St New York NY 10021

PASTERNACK, ROBERT FRANCIS, chemistry educator; b. N.Y.C., Sept. 20, 1936; 2 children. B.A., Cornell U., 1957, Ph.D. in Chemistry, 1962. Research assoc. in chemistry U. Ill., Champaign, 1962-63; from asst. to prof. chemistry Ithaca Coll., N.Y., 1963-66, Charles A. Dana Endowed prof. chemistry, 1976-82; Edmund Allen prof. chemistry Swarthmore Coll., Pa., 1984—; invited speaker seminars, colls., univs., nat., internat. meetings, confs. including Bioinorganic Chem., Italy, Portugal, Gordon Rsch. Confs., Spanish Royal Soc. Chem., many others; lectr. series Nankai U., China, U. Messina, Italy; mem. adv. com. Rsch. Corp.; mem. sci. & art com. Franklin Inst.; co-organizer, chmn. workshop on rsch. at undergrad. instn. NSF, mem. undergrad. curriculm chem.; vis. prof., vis. rschr. U Messina, U. Paris, Nakai, Rome, King's Coll., London, Fritz Haber Inst., Berlin; co-developer A Unified Lab. Program; initiator, chmn. C.P. Snow Lectr. Series. Author, co-author more than 100 sci. publs. Mem. com. on sci. and the arts Franklin Inst., 1992—. Grantee NSF, 1965-66, 69-72, 77-78, 83-84, 86-94, 95—, Petroleum Rsch. Fund, 1967-74, 86-88, NIH, 1971-89, Monsanto Corp., 1986-92, Rsch. Corp., 1974-75, 78-79, 84-85, Danforth Assocs., 1978-84, Camille and Henry Dreyfus Found., 1981, 95, NATO, 1979, 88-89, 95-96; recipient Camille and Henry Dreyfus Tchg./Scholar award, 1987-89, NSF Manpower Improvement award, King's Coll., U. London, 1977-78; NSF sci. faculty fellow U. Rome, 1968-70. Mem. AAAS. Am. Chem. Soc., N.Y. Acad. Sci., Sigma Xi. Office: Swarthmore Coll Dept Chemistry Swarthmore PA 19081

PASTERNACK, ROBERT HARRY, school psychologist; b. Bklyn., Nov. 30, 1949; s. William and Lillian Ruth (Levine) P.; m. Jeanelle Livingston, Apr. 10, 1980; children: Shayla, Rachel. BA, U. South Fla., 1970; MA, N.Mex. Highlands U., 1972; PhD, U. N.Mex., 1980. Dir. Eddy County Drug Abuse Program, Carlsbad, N.Mex., 1972-73; adminstrv. intern U.S. Office Edn., Washington, 1975-76; exec. dir. Villa Santa maria, Cedar Crest, N.Mex., 1976-78; clin. dir. Ranchos Treatment Ctr., Taos, N.Mex., 1978-79; sch. psychologist N.Mex. Boys Sch., Springer, 1980—, supt., 1991; pres. Ensenar Health svcs., Inc., Taos, 1980—; exec. dir. Casa de Corazon, Taos, N.Mex., 1994—; instr. N.Mex. Highlands U., Las Vegas, 1980—, U. N.Mex., Albuquerque, 1980—; cons. N.Mex. Youth Authority, Santa Fe, 1988—, N.Mex. Devel. Disabilities Bur., Santa Fe, 1986—, various sch. dists. Author: Growing Up: The First Five Years, 1986; contbr. articles to profl. publs. Pres., bd. dirs. Children's Lobby, N.Mex., 1978, N.Mex. Spl. Olympics, 1986-88, Child-Rite, Inc., Taos, 1990; mem. Gov.'s Mental Health Task Force, Albuquerque, 1988—. Mem. Nat. Assn. Sch. Psychologists, Correctional Edn. Assn., Nat. Alliance Mentally Ill, N.Mex. Coun. on Crime and Delinquency. Avocations: tennis, racquetball, skiing, cooking. Home and Office: Enseñar Inc PO Box 3126 Taos NM 87571-3126 Office: Casa de Corazon PO Box 73 Taos NM 87571-0073

PASTERNAK, JOANNA MURRAY, special education and gifted and talented educator; b. Houston, Feb. 9, 1953; d. Lee Roy and Evelyn Mary (Kirmss) Murray; children: Sheila Ann Tanner, Lawrence Ross Tanner IV; m. Allen Pasternak, Jan. 9, 1993. BA in Liberal Arts with honors, Our Lady of the Lake, San Antonio, 1990. Acctg. clk. Houston Post, 1981-85; owner, art cons. Tanner Fine Art, Houston, 1985-92; spl. edn. tchr. Houston Ind. Sch. Dist., 1991-94, dept. chmn., 1994—; art cons. Plz. Gallery, Houston, 1985; mem. benefits com. Houston Ind. Sch. Dist., 1992—; presenter Am. Fedn. Tchrs. Nat. Edn. Conf., 1994. Contrb. articles to profl. jours. Vol. legis com. nat. health care campaign AFL-CIO; bd. dirs. PTA, SDMC; mem., pres. Westlawn Terrace Civic Club; Dem. campaign worker, 1993—; precinct and state del. Dem. Senate, 1994-96; sec. Dist. 13 Dem. Com., 1996. Recipient Vick Driscoll award Tex. Commerce Bank, 1996. Mem. Am. Assn. Children with Learning Disabilities, Tex. Fedn. Tchrs. (bd. dirs. quality ednl. stds. in tchg. 1993, legis. com., chairperson 1993—), Houston Fedn. Tchrs. (chair legis. liaison com. 1993—, v.p. 1992—), Westlawn Terr. Civic Club (pres.), Delta Mu Delta. Democrat. Avocations: civic and political activities. Home: 2141 Colquitt St Houston TX 77098-3310 Office: Houston Fedn Tchrs 3202 Weslayan St Ste 102 Houston TX 77027-5748

PASTIN, MARK JOSEPH, executive consultant, association executive; b. Ellwood City, Pa., July 6, 1949; s. Joseph and Patricia Jean (Camenite) P.; m. Joanne Marie Reagle, May 30, 1970 (div. Mar. 1982); m. Carrie Patricia Class, Dec. 22, 1984 (div. June 1990); m. Christina M. Brecto, June 15, 1991. BA summa cum laude, U. Pitts., 1970; MA, Harvard U., 1972, PhD, 1973. Asst. prof. Ind. U., Bloomington, 1973-78, assoc. prof., 1978-80; founder, bd. Compliance Resource Group, Inc., 1983—; chmn., CEO, pres. Coun. Ethical Orgns., Alexandria, Va., 1986—; prof. mgmt., dir. Ariz. State U., Tempe, 1988-92, prof. emeritus, 1996—; prof. emeritus, 1996—; chair Health Ethics Trust, 1995—; adv. bd. Aberdeen Holdings, San Diego, 1988-90; dir. Sandpiper Group, Inc., N.Y.C., 1987—, S.W. Projects, Inc., San Diego, 1988-90, Learned Nicholson, Ltd., 1990-91; bd. Japan Am. Soc. Phoenix, Found. for Ethical Orgns.; cons. GTE, Southwestern Bell, 1987-89, Tex. Instruments, MicroAge Computers, Med-Tronic, Blood Sys., Inc., Opus Corp., GTE, NyNex, Am. Express Bank, Kaiko Bussan Co., Japan, Arex Co., Japan, Century Audit Co., Japan, Scottsdale Meml. Hosp., Consanti Found., Lincoln Electric Co., Tenet Healthcare Corp., The Williams Co.; vis. faculty Harvard U., 1980; invited presenter Australian Inst. Mgmt., Nippon Tel. & Tel., Hong Kong Commn. Against Corruption, 1984, Young Pres.'s Orgn. Internat. U., 1990, Nat. Assn. Indsl. & Office Parks, 1990, ABA, 1991, Govt. of Brazil, 1991, Tzuzuki Edn. Sys., 1995. Author: Hard Problems of Management, 1986 (Book of Yr. award Armed Forces Mil. Comtrs. 1986, Japanese edit. 1994), Power by Association, 1991, The Hotline Handbook, 1996, The State of Ethics in Arizona, 1991, Planning Forum, 1992; editor: Public-Private Sector Ethics, 1979; columnist Bus. Jour. Founding bd. mem. Tempe Leadership, 1985-89; bd. mem. Ctr. for Behavioral Health, Phoenix, 1986-89, Tempe YMCA, 1986—, Valley Leadership Alumni Assn., 1989—; mem. Clean Air Com., Phoenix, 1987-90. Nat. Sci. Found. fellow, Cambridge, Mass., 1971-73; Nat. Endowment for the Humanities fellow, 1975; Exxon Edn. Found. grant, 1982-83. Mem. Strategic Mgmt. Soc. (invited presenter 1985), Am. Soc. Assn. Execs. (invited presenter 1987-95), Bus. Ethics Soc. (founding bd. dirs. 1983), Found. Ethical Orgns. (chmn. 1988, pres.), Pres.'s Assn., Am. Mgmt. Assn., Golden Key, Harvard Club D.C., Phi Beta Kappa. Avocations: golf, running. Home: 7206 Park Terrace Dr Alexandria VA 22307-2035 Office: 1216 King St Ste 300 Alexandria VA 22314-2927

PASTINE, MAUREEN DIANE, university librarian; b. Hays, Kans., Nov. 21, 1944; d. Gerhard Walter and Ada Marie (Hillman) Hillman; m. Jerry Joel Pastine, Feb. 5, 1966. AB, in English, Ft. Hays State U., 1967; MLS, Emporia State U., 1970. Reference librarian U. Nebr.-Omaha, 1971-77; undergrad. libr. U. Ill., Urbana, 1977-79; reference librarian, 1979-80; univ. libr. San Jose State U.-Calif., 1980-85; dir. librs. Wash. State U., Pullman, 1985-89; ctrl. univ. libr. So. Meth. U., 1989—; mem. adv. bd. Foothill Coll. Libr. 1983-85; leader ednl. del. librs. to People's Republic of China, 1985, Australia/New Zealand, 1986, Soviet Union, 1988, East & West Germany, Czechoslovakia, Hungary, Austria, 1991, Brazil, 1993. Co-author: Library and Library Related Publications: A Directory of Publishing Opportunities, 1973; asst. compiler: Women's Work and Women's Studies, 1973-74, 1975; compiler procs. Teaching Bibliographic Instruction in Graduate Schools of Library Science, 1981; editor: Integrating Library Use Skills into the General Education Curriculum, 1989, Collection Development: Present and Future in Collection Management, 1996; co-editor: In the Spirit of 1991: Access to Western European Libraries and Literature, 1992; contbr. articles to profl. publs. Recipient Disting. Alumni Grad. award Emporia State U., 1986, Dudley Bibliog. Instruction Libr. of Yr. award, 1989. Mem. ALA (chmn. World Book-ALA Goal awards jury 1984-85), Assn. Coll. and Rsch. Librs. (editorial adv. bd. BIS Think Tank 1982-85, chmn. bibliographic instrn. sect. 1983-84, editorial bd. Choice 1983-85, chmn. Miriam Dudley Bibliographic Instrn. Libr. of Yr. award com. 1984-85, mem. task force on librarians as instrs. 1986-88, chair task force internat. rels. 1987-89, BIS Libr. of Yr. 1989, rep. to AAAS/CAIP, 1989—, chair internat. rels. com. 1990-94, ALA pay equity com. 1994—, chmn. rsch. libr. of yr. award's com. 1995-96, acad. status com. 1996—), Libr. Adminstrn. and Mgmt. Assn. (chmn. stats. sect. com. on devel., orgn., planning and programming 1982-83, sec. stats. sect. exec. com. 1982-83, mem. at large 1986-88), ALA Library Instrn. Round Table (long range planning com. 1986-94), ALA Libr. Rsch. Round Table, Wash. Libr. Assn., Assn. Libr. Collections & Tech. Svcs. Divsn., Sr. Fellows Inst. (mem. info. resources com. in cause 1996—), Libr. and Info. Tech. Assn., Assn. Specialized and Coop. Libr. Agencies (chair multi-lincs internat. networking discussion group 1990-92), Libr. Rsch. Roundtable, Women's Studies Sect., Eng. and Am. Lit. Studies Discussion Group, Tex. Libr. Assn. (mentor Tall Texans Leadership Inst., 1995-96), Pacific N.W. Libr. Assn., Phi Kappa Phi, Beta Phi Mu. Home: 8720 Hanford Dr Dallas TX 75243-6416 Office: So Meth U Cen Univ Librs PO Box 750135 Dallas TX 75275-0135

PASTOR, ED, congressman; b. June 28, 1943. Mem. Maricopa County Bd. Suprs., Phoenix, Ariz., 1976-91; mem. 102nd-105th Congresses from Ariz. 2nd dist., 1991—; mem. appropriations com. Office: House of Reps 2465 Rayburn Bldg Washington DC 20515-0302

PASTORE, THOMAS MICHAEL, telecommunications sales executive; b. Bronx, N.Y., Jan. 25, 1959; s. Philip J. and Olga E. (DeGenito) P.; m. Kimberly A. Coppersmith, Dec. 13, 1986; children: Gabriela Maria, Thomas John. BA in Bus., Western State Coll., 1981. Sales rep. Victor Technologies Inc., Denver, 1981-84; account mgr. No. Telecom Inc., Denver, 1984-87, v.p. sales coun., 1985—, sales engr., 1987-92, dist. sales mgr., 1992—. Mem. Better Air Campaign, 1990—; sec. Warren Sq. Homeowners Assn., Denver, 1987-92; player, contbr. Dale Tooley Tennis Tournament, 1991-92; fundraiser Am. Cancer Soc., Denver, 1991—; mem. Denver Art Mus., 1991-92. Republican. Roman Catholic. Avocations: skiing, tennis, biking. Home and Office: No Telecom Inc 16095 Quarry Hill Dr Parker CO 80134-9553

PASTORELLE, PETER JOHN, film company executive, radiological services and waste management company executive; b. White Plains, N.Y., Jan. 23, 1933; s. Dominic John and Marguerite Delphine (Xavier) P.; m. Maria Rita Delcampo, Oct. 10, 1970; children: Betchie, Jomar. B.S., Fordham U., 1955; M.A., NYU, 1961; B.D., SUNY-Maryknoll, 1963. Radio news writer Western Conn. Broadcasting, Stamford, 1964-65; producer, dir. United Nations TV, N.Y.C., 1965-70; pres. The NDL Orgn., Inc., Peekskill, N.Y., 1965—, now chief exec. officer; pres. Peter Pastorelle Prodns., Mount Kisco, N.Y., 1970—, NDL Transport, Inc., 1984—, NDL Radon Services, Inc., 1988—; lectr. Am. Inst. Plant Engrs., Phila., 1981, Am. Chem. Soc., Phila., 1981, Low Level Radioactive Waste Mgmt. Decision Makers Forum, Fla., 1993; Blue Ribbon panelist NATAS, N.Y.C., 1980—; mem. Maxey Flats Steering Com.; mem. exec. com. N.Y. State Low Level Waste Group. Producer, writer films; Face of Hunger, 1976 (Dept. Commerce award), Samoa: Culture in Crisis, 1982 (Gold award), Water, 1978 (Silver award), composer film scores for UN including Faces of My Brother, Face of Hunger, Messengers of Peace; contbg. writer Radwaste Mag., 1994—. Mem. del. Citizen Amb. Program Nuclear Fuels Mgmt., Russia, Ukraine; mem. chmn.'s adv. bd. Rep. Nat. Com., 1994—; mem. Eisenhower Commn., 1995—. Served with U.S. Army, 1956-58. Recipient Editor's Choice award Nat. Libr. Poetry. Mem. Health Physics Soc., Am. Nuclear Soc., Radiation Research Soc., N.Y. Acad. Sci., Pres.'s Club Fordham U. Republican. Roman Catholic. Home: PO Box 318 Mount Kisco NY 10549-0318 Office: The NDL Orgn Inc PO Box 791 Mount Kisco NY 10549-0791

PASTORES, GREGORY MCCARTHY, physician, researcher; b. Bklyn., Sept. 4, 1959; s. Jovito Camara and Annie Harrington (McCarthy) P. MD, U. St. Thomas, 1983. Diplomate Am. Bd. Pediatrics, Am. Bd. Med. Genetics in Clin. Genetics and Clin. Molecular Genetics. Pediatric resident Mt. Sinai Med. Ctr., N.Y., 1986-89; fellow med. genetics Mayo Clinic Found., Rochester, Minn., 1989-91; med. and molecular genetics Mt. Sinai Sch. Medicine, N.Y., 1991-92, instr., pediatrics, genetics, 1992-93, asst. prof. pediatrics, human genetics, 1993—. Roman Catholic. Home: 345 E 93rd St Apt 9H New York NY 10128-5518 Office: Mt Sinai Med Ctr Fifth Ave # 100th St New York NY 10029

PASTRANA, RONALD RAY, Christian ministry counselor, theology and biblical studies educator, former school system administrator; b. N.Y.C., Sept. 5, 1939; s. Anthony and Mildred Pastrana; m. Josephine Pastrana; children: Christine, Therese. BA in History/Sci. Edn., Queens Coll., 1963; advanced sci. cert., Pace U., 1964-68; MS in Counseling Edn., St. John's U., 1967; diploma, U.S. Acad. of Health Sci., 1975, U.S. Army Command and Gen. Staff Coll., 1979; D Ministry, Sch. Bible Theology Sem., 1996. Tchr. sci. Marie Curie Jr. High Sch., Bayside, N.Y., 1963-68; guidance counselor Half Hollow Hills High Sch., Dix Hills, N.Y., 1969-71; guidance counselor Walt Whitman High Sch., Huntington Station, N.Y., 1968-69, coord. occupational svcs., 1971-74; guidance coord. Dutchess County Bd. Coop. Ednl. Svcs. Tech. Edn. Ctr., Poughkeepsie, N.Y., 1974-86; coord. guidance and related acads. Dutchess County BOCES Tech. Edn. Ctr., Poughkeepsie, N.Y., 1986-96; asst. dir. Reach Out Sch. of Ministry, Hyde Park, N.Y., 1996—; retired lt. col. U.S. Army Res., 1992; ednl. cons. N.Y. State Edn. Dept., Albany, 1975-83, Armed Forces Vocat. Testing Group, Dept. of Def., Washington, 1975-77; cert. educator Lunar Edn. Project NASA, 1986-87. Author: Career Guidance in the Classroom, 1974, A Curriculum Guide to the Study of the Seven Dispensations and Eight Covenants, 1996. Lt. col. USAR, ret. 1992. NSF sci. study grantee, 1964-68; recipient: Dutchess County Counselor of the Year award, 1995; decorated Joint Svc. Commendation medal, Army achievement medal, Selective Svc. Meritorious medal, Army Res. Components Achievement medal, Nat. Def. Svc. medal, N.Y.S. medal for Meritorious Svc. Mem. Am. Counselors Assn., Am. Mental Health Counselors Assn., Nat. Career Devel. Assn., Am. Assn. Christian Counselors, N.Y. Acad. Scis., N.Y. State Assn. for Counseling and Devel., Sch. Adminstrs. Assn. N.Y. State, Dutchess County Counseling Assn. (exec. bd. 1989-96), Phi Delta Kappa. Avocations: rock and mineral collecting, fitness activities, canoeing, hiking. Home: 26 Greentree Dr S Hyde Park NY 12538-2132 Office: Reach Out Sch of Ministry PO Box 2035 251 Crum Elbow Rd Hyde Park NY 12538

PASTREICH, PETER, orchestra executive director; b. Bklyn., Sept. 13, 1938; s. Ben and Hortense (Davis) P.; m. Jamie Garrard Whittington; children by previous marriages: Anna, Milena, Emanuel, Michael. A.B. magna cum laude, Yale Coll., 1959; postgrad., N.Y. U. Sch. Medicine, 1959-60; studied trumpet, with Robert Nagle at Yale U., with Raymond Sabarich, Paris. Asst. mgr. Denver Symphony, Balt. Symphony; mgr. Greenwich Village Symphony, N.Y.C., 1960-63; gen. mgr. Nashville Symphony, 1963-65, Kansas City Philharmonic, 1965-66; asst. mgr., mgr. St. Louis Symphony, 1966-78, exec. dir., 1966-78; exec. dir. San Francisco Symphony, 1978—; instr. orch. mgmt. Am. Symphony Orch. League; bd. dirs. Nat. Com. for Symphony Orch. Support; founder San Francisco Youth Orch.; rep. planning and constrn. Davies Symphony Hall, San Francisco Symphony, 1980. Author: TV comml., 1969 (CLIO award); contbr. articles to various newspapers. Mem. recommendation bd. of the Avery Fisher Artist Program, Yale U. Council com. on music; past mem. adv. panel Nat. Endowment for the Arts, co-chmn. music panel, 1985; founding mem. bd. dirs. St. Louis Conservatory, mem. policy com. Maj. Orch. Mgrs. Conf., chmn., 1980; bd. dirs. Laumeier Sculpture Park, St. Louis, Stern Grove Festival, San Francisco Conv. and Visitors Bur.; chmn. fund campaign French-Am. Internat. Sch., San Francisco. Served with U.S. Army, 1960. Recipient First Disting. Alumnus award Yale U. Band, 1977, cert. Merit Yale Sch. Music, 1984. Mem. Am. Symphony Orch. League (dir., chmn., former chmn. task force on mgmt. tng.; mem. exec. and long-range planning com., chmn. standing com. on adminstrv. policy), Assn. Calif. Symphony Orchs. (dir.), Bankers Club of San Francisco. Club: Yale (N.Y.C.). Office: San Francisco Symphony Davies Symphony Hall San Francisco CA 94102*

PASTRICK, HAROLD LEE, aeronautical engineer; b. Ambridge, Pa., June 28, 1936; s. Samuel and Mary (Makara) P.; m. Vivienne Lee Nusser Heinricher, June 3, 1961; children: Tracy Lee, Gregory Harold, Michael Joseph Samuel. BSEE, Carnegie-Mellon U., 1958; postgrad., Rutgers U., 1959-61, CCNY, 1961-63, U. Ala. Huntsville, 1964-66, 68-73; student, MIT, summers 1961-63; MS in Aeronautics & Astronautics, Stanford U., 1967, engr. in Aeronautics & Astronautics, 1972; PhD in Engring., Calif. Western U., 1977. Registered prof. engr., Ala. Metallurgical engring. aide Jones & Laughlin Steel Corp., Aliquippa, Pa., 1955-56; asst. engr., designer Am. Bridge Divsn., U.S. Steel Corp., Ambridge, 1957; electronics engr. Avionics Divsn., U.S. Army Signal R&D Labs., Ft. Monmouth, N.J., 1958-63; aerospace engr., Inertial Systems Team Missile R&D Labs., Redstone Arsenal, Ala., 1963-64; tech. dir. Army Inertial Guidance & Tech. Ctr., Redstone Arsenal, 1964-66; project engr. Inertial Guidance Br., Redstone Arsenal, 1967-71; rsch. aerospace engr. Guidance & Control Br., Redstone Arsenal, 1971-73; group leader Terminal Homing Missile Analysis, Redstone Arsenal, 1973-79; staff specialist, asst. to dir., land warfare Office of Under Sec. Def., Rsch. and Engring., Washington, 1979-80; chief, guidance and control analysis U.S. Army Missile Command, Redstone Arsenal, Ala., 1980-81; v.p. engring. Control Dynamics Co., Huntsville, 1981-83; asst. v.p., engring. analysis divsn. Sci. Applications Internat. Corp., Huntsville, 1983-86; v.p. theater missile def. and system analysis operation, 1986-91; corp. v.p., gen. mgr. SRS Technologies, Huntsville, 1991—; acting pres. and COO SRS Techs., 1994, mem. corp. exec. mgmt. com., 1991—, mem. profit sharing and 401(k) com., 1993—; lectr. Sch. of Sci. and Engring., U. Ala., Huntsville, 1967-83; lectr. dept. continuing edn. George Washington U., 1985-87; engring. seminar dir. Applied Tech. Inst., Frankfurt, Germany, 1984, Singapore, 1986; tech. tng. dir. Tech. Tng. Corp., Tel Aviv, 1988; lectr. Advanced Tech. Internat., Ltd., London, 1985; guidance and control cons. various labs Dept. of Def., Washington, 1971-96; lectr., rsch. advisor Southeastern Inst. Tech., Huntsville, 1978-84; lectr., seminar leader Guidance and Control Technologies, U.S., Europe, Asia, Mex., 1980-94. Contbr. over 120 articles to profl. jours. Chmn. combined fed. campaign ARDEC, United Way, Redstone Arsenal, 1976; mem. Huntsville Econ. Devel. Com., 1994; chmn. indsl. contbns. C. of C., Armed Forces Week, Huntsville-Madison County, 1993-96, vice chmn. mil. affairs com., 1994-95, chmn., 1996; program chmn. tech. and bus. symposium and exhbn., Huntsville, 1994-95, gen. chmn., 1995-96; pres. Greek Orthodox Ch., 1967, 73, chmn. planning com., 1993—. Capt. U.S. Army, 1958-64. Fellow AIAA (assoc. missile tech. com. 1989-91, guest editor Jour. Guidance and Control 1981, vice-chmn. Huntsville chpt. 1979); mem. IEEE (sr., chpt. program chmn. 1972-73), Am. Def. Preparedness Assn. (vice-chmn. Huntsville chpt. 1974-75), Soc. for Computer Simulation, Assn. of U.S. Army, Inst. of Navigation, Ala. Acad. Sci. (vice chmn. 1978-79, engring. chmn. 1979-81), Rotary (dir. internat. svc. Greater Huntsville Club 1992-94, sec. 1994-95, pres.-elect 1995-96, pres. 1996-97), Heritage Club (Huntsville), Greenwhyche Club (v.p. 1979), Redstone Golf Club. Achievements include pioneering hardware in the loop simulations for testing laser semi-active guided missiles. Avocations: golf, weight tng., choral music, reading, running. Home: 2624 Trailway Rd SE Huntsville AL 35801-1474 Office: SRS Technologies 500 Discovery Dr NW Huntsville AL 35806-2810

PASVOLSKY, RICHARD LLOYD, parks, recreation, and environment educator; b. Englewood, N.J., Feb. 16, 1924; s. Valentine and Ellen Isabel (Stoughton) P.; m. Jo Anne Evans, June 16, 1968. BEd, Panzer Coll., 1950; MA in Edn., NYU, 1955; D in Recreation, Ind. U., 1973. Asst. supt. recreation City of Rutland, Vt., 1951-53; supt. recreation City of Montpelier, Vt., 1953-55; dir. parks and recreation Twp. of Parsippany-Troy Hills, N.J., 1955-62; asst. prof. outdoor and environ. edn. N.J. State Sch. Conservation, Branchville, 1962-71; assoc. prof. edn. Ramapo Coll. N.J., Mahwah, 1972-84, coach archery, 1973-84; adj. prof. Kean Coll. N.J., Union, 1985—; instr. archery, dir. dance and recreation World Archery Ctr., Pomfret, Conn., 1964-92; dir. N.J. State Coll. divsn. Nat. Archery Asns., 1978-84. Advisor to choreographer, cons. prodn. office closing ceremonies Statue of Liberty Centennial Celebration, 1986; rec. artist: Square Dances, 1961, 91, mag. articles, 1954-66; columnist Lines About Squares, 1983—. Instr. dance camp staff Lloyd Shaw Found., 1981—, bd. dirs., 1982-88; bd. trustees Sussex County Sr. Legal Resources Ctr., 1992-94. With U.S. Army, 1943-46, ETO. Recipient Alumni award Panzer Coll. N.J., 1979, Spl. Alumni award, 1987; named to Ramapo Coll. Athletic Hall of Fame, 1993. Mem. AAHPERD (Recreator of Yr. Ea. Dist. 1977), N.J. Alliance Health, Phys. Edn., Recreation and Dance, Callers Coun. N.J., Callerlab, Phi Delta Kappa. Avocations: calling square dances, ballroom dancing, skiing, golf, tennis. Home: 31 Newton Ave Branchville NJ 07826-4203 Office: Kean Coll NJ Phys Edn Dept Union NJ 07083

PATAKI, GEORGE E., governor; b. Peekskill, N.Y., June 24, 1945; m. Elizabeth (Libby) Rowland; children: Emily, Teddy, Allison, George Owen. BA, Yale U., 1967; JD, Columbia U. Sch. Law, 1970. Mayor City of Peekskill, Westchester, N.Y., 1982-84; elected mem. State Assembly, N.Y., 1985-92, State Senate, N.Y., 1993—; assoc. Law Firm of Dewey, Ballantine, Bushby, Palmer & Wood, 1970-74; ptnr. Law Firm Plunckett & Jaffe, P.C., N.Y.C., White Plains,, Albany and Peekskill, 1974-89; co-proprietor Pataki Farm, Peekskill, N.Y.; governor State of New York, 1996—. Advanceman Friends of Rockefeller Team, 1970; upstate campaign coord. Com. to Elect Gov. Wilson, 1974; mem. Peekskill Rep. City Com., 1974—, chmn. 1977-83; mem. N.Y. State Rep. Com., 1980-85. Address: Office of the Gov State Capitol Albany NY 12224*

PATAKY, PAUL ERIC, ophthalmologist; b. Phila., May 19, 1945; s. Andrew and Helen (Koffler) P.; m. Aimee Janet Margoles, June 13, 1971; Meryl Corinne, Lisa Ann. BS, Trinity Coll., 1966; MD, Pa. State Univ., 1971. Diplomate Am. Bd. Ophthalmology. Resident ophthalmology Mass. Eye & Ear Infirm, Boston, 1972-76; asst. in ophthalmology Harvard Medical Sch., Boston, 1976-79; ophthalmologist Dedham (Mass.) Medical Assocs., 1976-79, Paul E. Pataky M.D. P.A., Boynton Beach, Fla., 1979—; chmn. dept. of surgery Bethesda Meml. Hosp., Boynton Beach, 1988-89; pres. medical staff, 1990-91, chmn. credentials chmn., 1992-93, chmn. surgical care com., 1993—. Fellow Am. Acad. Ophthalmology; mem. Fla. Soc. Ophthalmology, AMA, Pan-Am. Assn. Ophthalmology, Palm Beach County Medical Soc., Fla. Medical Assn. Avocations: cycling, travel. Office: 2623 S Seacrest Blvd Ste 102 Boynton Beach FL 33435-7531

PATARCA, ROBERTO, immunologist, molecular biologist, physician; b. Caracas, Venezuela, Feb. 12, 1958; came to U.S., 1981; s. Umberto Jose and Ivonne Noemi (Montero) P. MS, Ctrl. U. Venezuela, Caracas, 1981; PhD, Harvard U., 1987; MD, U. Miami, 1994. Cert. high-complexity clin. lab. dir., Am. Bd. Bioanalysis, cert. clin. cons., tech. cons. Computer programmer, systems analyst Centro Medico Docente La Trinidad, Caracas, 1978-81; rsch. fellow Mt. Sinai Sch. Medicine and Columbia U., N.Y.C.,

1981-82, MIT-NASA Program, Boston, 1982; from rsch. fellow to asst. prof. pathology Harvard Med. Sch., Boston, 1982-90; asst. prof. medicine/immunology/microbiology U. Miami, 1994—; sci. dir. E.M. Papper lab. clin. immunology U. Miami, Fla., 1994—; teaching asst. Ctr. and Met. U., Caracas, 1977-80; lectr. and presenter in field. Co-editor Jour. Chronic Fatigue Syndrome and Critical Reviews in Oncogenesis/Clin. Mgmt. Chronic Fatigue Syndrome, 1994—; contbr. articles to profl. jours. Sub-guide Boy Scouts Am., Caracas, 1971-73; stake missionary Ch. of Jesus Christ of Latter Day Sts., Boston, 1985. Decorated Order of Merit (Venezuela); recipient Licha Lopez award Harvard Med. Sch., 1984, Richard A. Smith Rsch. award Dana-Farber Cancer Inst., 1989, Rsch. Distinction in Immunology U. Miami, 1994; Conicit and Gran Mariscal de Ayacucho Found. scholar, 1976-87, Am. Found. AIDS Rsch. scholar, 1990-93. Mem. AAAS, ACP, AMA, Fla. and Dade County Med. Assn., Clin. Immunology Soc., N.Y. Acad. Scis., Peruvian Soc. Immunology and Allergy, Alpha Omega Alpha. Avocations: classical guitar, tap dancing, swimming. Home: 16445 Collins Ave Apt 328 Miami FL 33160-4562 Office: U Miami Sch Medicine PO Box 016960 Miami FL 33138

PATCH, LAUREN NELSON, insurance company, chief executive officer; b. Lexington, Ky., Apr. 14, 1951; s. Nathaniel M. and Gertrude (Lasseter) P.; m. Helen Sloneker, June 30, 1973; children: Henry L., John Stewart. BS, U. Ky., 1973; attended exec. program, U. Mich., 1990. With Ohio Casualty Ins. Co., Hamilton, 1973—, pres., 1991, also bd. dirs., 1987—; pres., CEO Ohio Casualty Corp.; bd. dirs. Ins. Svcs. Office; dir. First Fin. Bancorp. Bd. dirs. Hamilton-Fairfield Arts Coun., 1990—, Dan Beard Coun. Boy Scouts. Mem. Young Pres. Assn. (Cin. chpt.), Wyoming Golf Club (bd. dirs. 1989—). Republican. Episcopalian. Avocations: golf, reading. Office: Ohio Casualty Ins Co 136 N 3rd St Hamilton OH 45011-2726

PATCHAN, JOSEPH, lawyer; b. Bklyn., June 29, 1922; m. Nancy Joy Letaw, Jan. 7, 1951 (dec.); children: Reed, Judith, David. B.S., Miami U., Oxford, Ohio, 1943; J.D., Cleve. State U., 1952. Bar: Ohio 1952, D.C. 1977. Pvt. practice law, 1955-69; judge U.S. Bankruptcy Ct., No. Dist. Ohio, 1969-75; ptnr. Baker & Hostetler, Cleve., 1975-91; dep. gen. counsel Resolution Trust Corp., Washington, 1991-94; dir. exec. Office for U.S. Trustees, U.S. Dept. Justice, Washington, 1994—; mem. adj. faculty Cleve. State U. Law Sch., 1959-74; mem. faculty Nat. Bankruptcy Seminar, Fed. Jud. Ctr., Washington, 1971-77; mem. adv. com. bankruptcy rules U.S. Jud. Conf., 1978-91; lectr. bankruptcy law seminars. Author: Practice Comments to Rules of Bankruptcy Procedure, 1973-91; contbr. articles on bankruptcy law to profl. publs. Served with USN, 1943-46. Fellow Am. Coll. Bankruptcy; mem. ABA (rep. nat. conf. lawyers and collection agys., chmn. 1985-88), Ohio Bar Assn., Cleve. Bar Assn. (chmn. bankruptcy and comml. law sect. 1984-86), D.C. Bar Assn., Nat. Conf. Bankruptcy Judges (assoc.), Am. Judicature Soc., Am. Bankruptcy Inst., Army and Navy Club (Washington). Jewish. Office: 901 E St NW # 700 Washington DC 20004-2037

PATCHETT, ARTHUR ALLAN, medicinal chemist, pharmaceutical executive; b. Middletown, N.Y., May 28, 1929; s. Arthur Allan and Anna Gertrude (Vossler) P.; m. Lois Rhoda Mc Neil, Aug. 18, 1962; Thomas John, Steven Edward. BA, Princeton U., 1951; PhD, Harvard U., 1955. Rsch. assoc. NIH, Bethesda, Md., 1955-57; rsch. chemist Merck Rsch. Labs., Rahway, N.J., 1957-62, dir. synthetic chem. rsch., 1962-69, sr. dir. synthetic chem. rsch., 1969-71, sr. dir. new lead discovery, 1971-76, exec. dir. new lead discovery, 1976-88, v.p. exploratory chemistry, 1988-95, v.p. medicinal chemistry, 1995—. Contbr. 135 papers to profl. jours., sci. confs. Elected N.J. Inventors Hall of Fame, N.J. Inst. Tech., 1990; recipient Discoverers award Pharm. Mfrs. Assn., 1992. Fellow AAAS; mem. Am. Chem. Soc. (chmn. div. medicinal chemistry 1971, E.B. Hershberg Important Discoveries in Medicinally Active Substances award 1993). Achievements include 155 U.S. patents (co-holder); co-inventor antihypertensive drug Vasotec; key contbr. to discovery of cholesterol lowering drug Mevacor. Home: 1090 Minisink Way Westfield NJ 07090-3727 Office: Merck Rsch Labs PO Box 2000 Rahway NJ 07065-0900

PATE, FRANCES VALERIE, psychotherapist, clinical social worker; b. Passaic, N.J., Aug. 2, 1939; d. Frank and Sadie Vizzi; m. Fred L. Pate, Mar. 28, 1969; 1 child, Valerie. BS, NYU, 1961, MSW, 1985. Lic. ind. social worker, profl. counselor, S.C.; diplomate Am. Bd. Social Work Examiners. Clin. social worker Cath. Charities Counseling Svc., Bronx, N.Y., 1985-86, Patrick B. Harris Psychiatric Hosp., Anderson, S.C., 1986-87, Perry Correctional Inst., Pelzer, S.C., 1987-88; pvt. practice Greenville, S.C., 1986—; psychotherapist, dir. numerous support groups for people with AIDS and family members, Greenville, 1988—. Founder Upstate Area AIDS Network, Greenville, 1988—. Mem. NASW (accredited cert.), Am. Group Psychotherapy Assn., S.C. Soc. for Clin. Social Workers (editor newsletter 1988-89). Democrat. Avocations: reading, gardening, music, swimming. Office: Psychotherapy Svcs 250 S Pleasantburg Dr Ste 103 Greenville SC 29607-2522

PATE, JACQUELINE HAIL, retired data processing company manager; b. Amarillo, Tex., Apr. 7, 1930; d. Ewen and Virginia Smith (Crosland) Hail; student Southwestern U., Georgetown, Tex., 1947-48; children: Charles (dec.), John Durst, Virginia Pate Edgecomb, Christopher. Exec. sec. Western Gear Corp., Houston, 1974-76; adminstr., treas., dir. Aberrant Behavior Ctr., Personality Profiles, Inc., Corp. Procedures, Inc., Dallas, 1976-79; mgr. regional site svcs programs Digital Equipment Corp., Dallas, 1979-92, ret. 1992; realtor Keller Williams Realty, Austin, Tex., 1996—; mem. Austin Bd. Realtors. Active PTA, Dallas, 1958-73. Mem. Daus. Republic Tex. (treas. French legation state com. 1996). Methodist. Home: 5505-B Buffalo Pass Austin TX 78745

PATE, JAMES LEONARD, oil company executive; b. Mt. Sterling, Ill., Sept. 6, 1935; s. Virgil Leonard and Mammie Elizabeth (Taylor) P.; m. Donna Charlene Pate, Oct. 23, 1955; children: David Charles, Gary Leonard, Jennifer Elizabeth. Prof. econs. Monmouth (Ill.) Coll., 1965-68; sr. economist Fed. Res. Bank Cleve., 1968-72; chief economist B.F. Goodrich Co., Akron, Ohio, 1972-74; asst. sec. Dept. Commerce, Washington, Ohio, 1974-76, spl. adviser to White House, 1976, sr. v.p. fin., 1976; v.p. fin. Pennzoil Co., Houston, Ohio, 1976-89, exec. v.p., 1989, exec. v.p., chief oper. officer, 1990, pres., chief exec. officer, 1990—, also chmn. bd., 1994—. Contbr. articles to profl. jours. and text books. Bd. govs. Rice U.; mem. Senate Monmouth Coll.; bd. dirs. Am. Petroleum Inst., Nat. Petroleum Coun. Fellow Royal Econ. Soc.; mem. Pi Gamma Mu. Republican. Office: Pennzoil Co PO Box 2967 Houston TX 77252-2967*

PATE, MICHAEL LYNN, lawyer; b. Ft. Worth, Tex., July 9, 1951; s. J.B. and Mary Anna (Hable) P.; m. Barbara Ann Linch, May 28, 1977. AA, Schreiner Coll., 1971; BS, Tex. Wesleyan Coll., 1973; JD, U. Tex., 1975. Bar: Tex. 1976, D.C. 1983, U.S. Tax Ct. 1986, U.S. Supreme Ct. 1987. Adminstrv. asst. to Senator Sherman, counsel natural resources com. Tex. Senate, 1976-77; adminstrv. asst. to Lt. Gov. Bill Hobby, Austin, Tex., 1977-79; legis. asst. Senator Bentsen, Washington, 1979-81, legis. dir., 1981-86; ptnr. Bracewell & Patterson, Washington, 1986—. Mem. ABA, Tex. Bar Assn., D.C. Bar Assn. Democrat. Methodist. Avocations: basketball, tennis, golf. Office: Bracewell & Patterson 2000 K St NW Ste 500 Washington DC 20006-1809

PATE, PAUL DANNY, state senator, business executive, entrepreneur; b. Ottumwa, Iowa, May 1, 1958; s. Paul Devern and Velma Marie (McConnell) P.; m. Jane Ann Wacker, July 15, 1978; children: Jennifer Ann, Paul Daniel III, Amber Lynn. AA in Bus., Kirkwood Coll., 1978; grad. in fin. mgmt., U. Pa., 1990. Exec. dir. Jr. Achievement, Cedar Rapids, Iowa, 1978-82; pres. PM Systems Corp., Cedar Rapids, 1982—; pres., pub. DAVCO Inc., Cedar Rapids, 1985—; senator Iowa State Senate, Des Moines, 1989—; Sec. of State State of Iowa. Chmn. Iowa Young Reps., Des Moines, 1989—, Rep. Senate Campaign Com., 1990; co-chmn. Young Rep. Nat. Platform Com., Miami, Fla., 1991; bd. dirs. Iowa Right to Work Com., Linn County Hist. Soc. Recipient Guardian Small Bus. award Nat. Fedn. Independent Bus., 1990; named Young Entrepreneur of Yr. U.S. Small Bus. Adminstrn., Iowa, 1988, Alumnus of Yr. Kirkwood Coll., Cedar Rapids, 1990. Methodist. Avocations: private pilot, water skiing. Home: 2670 27th Ave Marion IA 52302-1240 Office: Off of State Senate Capitol Bldg Des Moines IA 50319*

PATE, ROBERT HEWITT, JR., counselor educator; b. Abingdon, Va., Apr. 5, 1938; s. Robert Hewitt and Esther Frances (Kirk) P.; m. Ellen O'Neal Pope, Dec. 11, 1960; children: Robert Hewitt III, Mary Ellen Pate Barton. AB, Davidson Coll., 1960; MEd, U. Va., 1965; PhD, U. N.C., 1968. Lic. prof. counselor, Va. Marketer Sinclair Refining Co., Abingdon, Va., 1960-61, 63-64; counselor St. Andrews Presbyn. Coll., Laurinburg, N.C., 1965-66; prof. counselor edn. U. Va., Charlottesville, 1968—, interim dean, 1994-95, sr. assoc. dean, 1995—; mem. adj. faculty Fed. Exec. Inst., Charlottesville, 1978—. Author: Being A Counselor, 1983. Elder local Presbyn. ch. 1st lt. U.S. Army 1961-63. Mem. Am. Counseling Assn., Va. Counselors Assn. (pres. 1983-84), Nat. Bd. Cert. Counselors (chair 1996-97). Avocation: reading. Home: 552 Dryden Pl Charlottesville VA 22903-4666 Office: U Va Ruffner Hall 405 Emmet St S Charlottesville VA 22903-2424

PATE, STEPHEN PATRICK, lawyer; b. Beaumont, Tex., May 6, 1958; s. Gordon Ralph and Shirley Jean (Riley) P.; m. Jean Janssen; 1 child, Teddy. BA, Vanderbilt U., 1980, JD, 1983. Bar: Tex. 1984, U.S. Dist. Ct. (ea. dist.) Tex. 1984, U.S. Dist. Ct. (so. dist.) Tex. 1985. Law clk. to judge Joe J. Fisher U.S. Dist. Ct. Tex., Beaumont, 1983-84; ptnr. Fulbright & Jaworski, Houston. Contbr. articles to profl. jours. Fellow Houston Bar Found., Tex. Bar Found.; mem. ABA (vice chmn. property ins. com. tort and ins. practice sect. 1994—), Tex. Bar Assn., Tex. Young Lawyers Assn. (bd. dirs. 1992-94), Houston Young Lawyers Assn. (bd. dirs. 1990-92, sec. 1992-93, chmn. professionalism com., mem. sunset rev. com. 1990), Manitoba Master Angler, Billfish Found. (Top Angler 1993), Knight of Momus, The Briar Club, Phi Beta Kappa. Republican. Roman Catholic. Avocations: hunting, fishing. Home: 2740 Arbuckle St Houston TX 77005 Office: Fulbright & Jaworski 1301 Mckinney St Houston TX 77010-3031

PATÉ-CORNELL, MARIE-ELISABETH LUCIENNE, industrial engineering educator; b. Dakar, Senegal, Aug. 17, 1948; came to U.S., 1971; d. Edouard Pierre Lucien and Madeleine (Tournissa) Paté; m. C. Allin Cornell, Jan. 3, 1981; children: Phillip, Ariane. Eng. Degree, Inst. Polytechnique de Grenoble (France), 1971; MS in Ops. Rsch., Stanford U., 1972, PhD in Engring.-Econ. Systems, 1978. Asst. prof. in civil engring. MIT, 1978-81; asst. prof. indsl. engring. Stanford (Calif.) U., 1981-84, assoc. prof. indsl. engring., 1984-91, prof. indsl. engring., 1991—; cons. U.S. Water Resource Coun., 1979, EPA, 1980, Electric Power Rsch. Inst., 1985, WHO, 1988, Shell Oil, 1990, Texaco, 1992, Electric Power Rsch. Inst., 1995, SRI Internat. 1993, Atty. Gen. of N.Mex., 1995; mem. NASA Adv. Coun., 1995—, Marine Bd. of the NRC, 1995-97, Army Sci. Bd., 1995-97. Contbr. numerous articles to profl. jours. Numerous rsch. grants. Mem. Soc. for Risk Analysis (councilor 1985-86, pres. 1995), Ops. Rsch. Soc. Am., Inst. for Mgmt. Scis., Nat. Acad. Engring. Avocations: tennis, swimming, chess, music. Home: 110 Coquito Way Menlo Park CA 94028-7404 Office: Stanford U Dept Indsl Engring Stanford CA 94305

PATEL, CHANDRA KUMAR NARANBHAI, communications company executive, educator, researcher; b. Baramati, India, July 2, 1938; came to U.S., 1958, naturalized, 1970; s. Naranbhai Chaturbhai and Maniben P.; m. Shela Dixit, Aug. 20, 1961; children: Neela, Meena. B.Engring., Poona U., 1958; M.S., Stanford U., 1959, Ph.D., 1961. Mem. tech. staff Bell Telephone Labs., Murray Hill, N.J., 1961-93, head infrared physics and electronics rsch. dept., 1967-70, dir. electronics rsch. dept., 1970-76, dir. phys. rsch. lab., 1976-81, exec. dir. rsch. physics and acad. affairs div., 1981-87, exec. dir. rsch., materials sci., engring. and acad. affairs div., 1987-93; trustee Aerospace Corp., L.A., 1979-88; vice chancellor rsch. UCLA, 1993—; mem. governing bd. NRC, 1990-91; bd. dirs. Accuwave Corp., Santa Monica, Calif., chmn. bd. Contbr. articles to tech. jours. Chmn. Calif. Biomed. Found., 1994—; mem. exec. bd. Calif. Healthcare Inst., 1995—. Recipient Ballantine medal Franklin Inst., 1968, Coblentz award Am. Chem. Soc., 1974, Honor award Assn. Indians in Am., 1975, Founders prize Tex. Instruments Found., 1978, award N.Y. sect. Soc. Applied Spectroscopy, 1982, Schawlow medal Laser Inst. Am., 1984, Thomas Alva Edison Sci. award N.J. Gov., 1987, William T. Ennor Manufacturing Technology award ASME, 1995, Nat. Medal of Sci., 1996. Fellow AAAS, IEEE (Lamme medal 1976, medal of honor 1989), Am. Acad. Arts and Scis., Am. Phys. Soc. (coun. 1987-91, exec. com. 1987-90, George E. Pake prize 1988, pres. 1995), Optical Soc. Am. (Adolph Lomb medal 1966, Townes medal 1982, Ives medal 1989), Indian Nat. Sci. Acad. (fng.); mem. NAS (coun. 1988-91, exec. com. 1989-91), NAE (Zworykin award 1976), Gynecol. Laser Surgery Soc. (hon.), Am. Soc. for Laser Medicine and Surgery (hon.), Third World Acad. Scis. (assoc.), Calif. Biomed. Found. (pres. 1994—), Calif. Healthcare Inst. (exec. com. 1995—), Sigma Xi (pres. 1994-96). Home: 1171 Roberto Ln Los Angeles CA 90077-2302 Office: UCLA Vice Chancellor Rsch PO Box 951405 Los Angeles CA 90095-1415

PATEL, HOMI BURJOR, apparel company executive; b. Bombay, June 28, 1949; s. Burjor Ratan and Roshen Burjor (Marfatia) P.; married; children: Neville H., Cyrus H., Natasha E. BS in Stats., U. Bombay, 1973; MBA in Fin. and Mktg., Columbia U., 1975. Exec. asst. to pres. Corbin Ltd., N.Y.C., 1976, dir. mktg., 1978; with subs. Hartmarx Corp., Chgo., 1979—; v.p., gen. mgr. Fashionaire Apparel Inc., Chgo., 1979-81; exec. v.p. Austin Reed of Regent St., Chgo., 1981-82, M. Wile and Co., Buffalo, 1982-84; pres., chief exec. officer M. Wile & Co., Johnny Carson Apparel, Intercontinental Apparel, Buffalo, 1984—; group exec. v.p. Hartmarx Mens Apparel Group Corp., Buffalo, 1987-91; chmn., ceo Hartmarx Mens Apparel Group Corp., Chgo., 1991-92; pres., COO Hartmarx Corp., Chgo., 1992—; bd. dirs., 1994—. Mem. Clothing Mfrs. Assn. Am. (bd. dirs. 1984—, chmn. mills rels. com. 1986—, exec. v.p. 1989—, pres. 1991, chief labor negotiator for U.S. tailored clothing industry), Univ. Club N.Y., Chgo. Club. Office: Hartmarx Corp 101 N Wacker Dr Fl 23 Chicago IL 60606-1718

PATEL, MARILYN HALL, federal judge; b. Amsterdam, N.Y., Sept. 2, 1938; d. Lloyd Manning and Nina J. (Thorpe) Hall; m. Magan C. Patel, Sept. 2, 1966; children: Brian, Gian. B.A., Wheaton Coll., 1959; J.D., Fordham U., 1963. Bar: N.Y. 1963, Calif. 1970. Mng. atty. Benson & Morris, Esq., N.Y.C., 1962-64; sole practice N.Y.C., 1964-67; atty. U.S. Immigration and Naturalization Svc., San Francisco, 1967-71; sole practice San Francisco, 1971-76; judge Alameda County Mcpl. Ct., Oakland, Calif., 1976-80, U.S. Dist. Ct. (no. dist.) Calif., San Francisco, 1980—; adj. prof. law Hastings Coll. of Law, San Francisco, 1974-76. Author: Immigration and Nationality Law, 1974; also numerous articles. Mem. bd. visitors Fordham U. Sch. Law. Mem. ABA (litigation sect., jud. adminstrn. sect.), ACLU (former bd. dirs.), NOW (former bd. dirs.), Am. law Inst., Am. Judicature Soc. (bd. dirs.), Calif Conf. Judges, Nat. Assn. Women Judges (founding mem.), Internat. Inst. (bd. dirs.), Advs. for Women (co-founder), Assn. Bus. Trial Lawyers (bd. dirs.). Democrat. Avocations: piano playing; travel. Office: US Dist Ct PO Box 36060 450 Golden Gate Ave Rm 19-5356 San Francisco CA 94102

PATEL, MUKUND RANCHHODLAL, electrical engineer, researcher; b. Bavla, India, Apr. 21, 1942; came to U.S., 1966; s. Ranchhodlal N. and Shakariben M. Patel; m. Sarla Shantilal, Nov. 4, 1967; children: Ketan, Bina, Vijal. BEng, Sardar U., Vidyanagar, India; MEng with honors, Gujarat U., Ahmedabad, India; PhD in Engring., Rensselaer Poly. Inst., 1972. Registered profl. engr., Pa.; chartered mech. engr., U.K. Lectr. elec. engring. Sardar U., Vidyanagar, India, 1965-66; sr. devel. engr. GE, Pittsfield, Mass., 1967-76; mgr. R & D, Bharat Bijlee (Siemens) Ltd., Bombay, 1976-80; fellow engr. Westinghouse R & D Ctr., Churchill, Pa., 1980-84, mem. senate, 1982-84; pres. Induction Gen., Inc., Pitts., 1984-86; prin. engr. rsch. and devel. Space Divsn. GE, Princeton, Pa., 1986-96; disting. vis. prof. elec. power systems U. Minn., Duluth, 1996—; cons. Nat. Productivity Coun., New Delhi, 1976-80. Assoc. editor IEEE Insulation Mag.; contbr. articles to nat. and internat. profl. jours. Fellow Instn. Mech. Engrs.; mem. IEEE (sr.), Am. Soc. Sci. Rsch., Elfun Soc. Vols., Tau Beta Pi, Eta Kappa Nu, Omega Rho. Achievements include patents and invention awards on electromechanical design of superconducting generators; NASA award for research on space power systems; international authority in the area of electromechanical design of large power. Home: 1199 Cobblestone Ct Yardley PA 19067-4751 Office: Power Systems Engring 1199 Cobblestone Ct Yardley PA 19067-4751

PATEL, MULCHAND SHAMBHUBHAI, biochemist, researcher; b. Sipor, India, Sept. 9, 1939; came to U.S., 1965; s. Shambhubhai J. and Puriben (Patel) P.; m. Kankuben M. Patel; children: Sumitra, Yashomati, Mayank. BS, Gujarat U., 1961; MS, U. Baroda, 1964; PhD, U. Ill., 1968. Asst. prof. pediatric rsch. Sch. Medicine Temple U., Phila., 1970-72, rsch. asst. prof. medicine, 1972-75, rsch. asst. prof. biochemistry, 1970-75, rsch. assoc. prof. biochem. medicine, 1975-78; assoc. prof. biochemistry Case Western Res. U. Sch. Medicine, Cleve., 1978-86, prof., 1986-93; prof., chmn. biochemistry SUNY, Buffalo, 1993—; mem. NIH biochem. study sect. 2, 1984-88; mem. editl. bd. Jour. Biol. Chem., 1991—. Author, co-author research articles. Recipient Gold Medal in Biochemistry, U. Baroda, 1973, Fulbright Research Scholar award to India, 1987; prin. investigator, research grantee NIH. Mem. Am. Soc. for Biochemistry and Molecular Biology, Am. Inst. Nutrition, Biochem. Soc. London, Am. Soc. Neurochemists, Internat. Soc. Neurochemistry. Office: SUNY-Dept Biochemistry Sch Medicine 140 Farber Hall 3435 Main St Buffalo NY 14214-3001

PATEL, RONALD ANTHONY, newspaper editor; b. Detroit, Oct. 7, 1947; s. Chhotalal Ukabhai and Joan (Kaczynski) P.; m. Jane Elizabeth Douglas-Willan, Sept. 5, 1974; 1 child, Wendy Elizabeth; m. Susan Florence Winters, Nov. 16, 1982. Student, Wayne State U., 1965-69. Asst. city editor Royal Oak (Mich.) Daily Tribune, 1967-69; rewriteman, copyeditor Detroit News, 1969-70; asst. news editor Newsday, Garden City, N.Y., 1970-73; news editor Phila. Inquirer, 1973-80, asst. mng. editor, 1980-86, assoc. mng. editor for features, 1986-95, Sunday editor, 1995—; cons. New Century Network, 1997. Contbr. to Elements of Newspaper Design (Steven Ames), 1989, Your Career in the Comics (Andrews and McNeal), 1995. Mem. Am. Assn. Sunday and Feature Editors (sec. 1979, pres. 1982), Newspaper Features Coun. (bd. dirs. 1990, meeting chmn. 1991, sec.-treas. 1992, pres. 1993-95, Jester award 1996), Pen and Pencil Club (pres. 1990—), Sigma Delta Chi. Office: Phila Inquirer 400 N Broad St Philadelphia PA 19130-4015

PATEL, VIRENDRA CHATURBHAI, mechanical engineering educator; b. Mombasa, Kenya, Nov. 9, 1938; came to U.S., 1969, naturalized, 1975; s. Chaturbhai S. and Kantaben N. (Rai) P.; m. Manjula Patel, May 29, 1966; children: Sanjay, Bindiya. BSc with honors, Imperial Coll., London, 1962; PhD, Cambridge (Eng.) U., 1965; Doctor honoris causa, Tech. U. Civil Engring., Bucharest, Romania, 1994. Sr. asst. in research Cambridge U., 1965-69; vis. prof. Indian Inst. Tech., Kharagpur, 1966; cons. Lockheed Ga. Co., Marietta, 1969-70; mem. faculty U. Iowa, Iowa City, 1971—; prof. mech. engring. U. Iowa, 1975—, chmn. div., 1976-82, chmn. mech. engring., 1978-82, U. Iowa Found. Disting. prof., 1990—; research engr. Iowa Inst. Hydraulic Research, 1971—, dir., 1994—; mem. Iowa Gov. Sci. Advisory Council, 1977-83; mem. resistance com. Internat. Towing Tank Conf., 1978-87; vis. prof. U. Karlsruhe, W. Ger., 1980-81, Ecole Nationale Superieure de Mechanique, Nantes, France, 1984, 96; jubilee prof. Chalmers Inst. Tech., Goteborg, Sweden, 1988; cons. in field. Author: Three Dimensional Turbulent Boundary Layers, 1972, also articles; assoc. editor AIAA Jour., 1987-90. Recipient Sr. Scientist award Alexander von Humboldt Found., 1980, 93. Fellow ASME, AIAA (assoc.); mem. Am. Soc. Engring. Edn., Soc. Naval Archtl. Marine Engrs., Sigma Xi, Pi Tau Sigma. Home: 60 Kennedy Dr Iowa City IA 52246-2780 Office: Inst Hydraulic Research U Iowa 404 Hydraulics Lab Iowa City IA 52242-1585

PATENT, DOROTHY HINSHAW, author, photographer; b. Rochester, Minn., Apr. 30, 1940; d. Horton Corwin and Dorothy Kate (Youmans) Hinshaw; m. Gregory Joseph Patent, Mar. 21, 1964; children: David Gregory, Jason Daniel. BS, Stanford U., 1962; MA, U. Calif., Berkeley, 1965, PhD, 1968; postgrad., U. Wash., 1965-67. Postdoctoral fellow Sinai Hosp., Detroit, 1968-69, Stazione Zoologica, Naples, Italy, 1969-70; acting asst. prof. U. Mont., Missoula, 1977. Author: Buffalo: The American Bison Today, 1986, The Way of the Grizzly, 1987, Christmas Trees, 1987 (Jr. Lit. Guild selection 1987), The Whooping Crane: A Comeback Story, 1988, Babies!, 1988, A Horse of a Different Color, 1988, Looking at Dolphins and Porpoises, 1989, Where the Wild Horses Roam, 1989, How Smart Are Animals?, 1990, Places of Refuge, 1992, Feathers, 1992, Nutrition: What's in the Food We Eat?, 1992, Dogs: The Wolf Within, 1993, Horses: Understanding Animals, 1994, What Good is a Tail?, 1994, Deer and Elk, 1994, Alligators, 1994, The Vanishing Feast, 1994, Return of the Wolf, 1995, West by Covered Wagon, 1995, Biodiversity, 1996, Children Save the Rain Forest, 1996, Prairies, 1996, Quetzal: Sacred Bird of the Cloud Forest, 1996, Flashy Fantastic Rain Forest Frogs, 1997, Pigeons, 1997, Back to the Wild, 1997. Recipient Eva L. Gordon award Am. Nature Study Soc., 1986. Mem. Am. Inst. Biol. Scis., Soc. Children's Book Writers and Illustrators, Authors Guild. Avocations: gardening, racquetball, travel.

PATERMASTER, JOHN JOSEPH, inventor, consultant; b. Newport, Pa., June 29, 1932; s. Ernest Wilford and Margaret (Barsauskas) P.; m. Hebé Colon, May 10, 1954 (div. Aug. 10, 1962); children: Mara, Karen, Vivian; m. Elizabeth Sharon Kenyon, Jan. 4, 1964; children: Lisa, John Jr., Robert. BS in Bus. and Pub. Adminstrn., U. Md., 1959. CPA, P.R. Asst. treas. Double Day-Hill, Inc., Washington, 1959-60; jr. acct. Price Waterhouse & Co., San Juan, P.R., 1960-61; auditor/contr. P.R. Express Co., San Juan, 1961-62; audit mgr. Def. Supply Agy., Alexandria, Va., 1962-68, NSF, Washington, 1968-71, Inter-Am. Found., Rosslyn, Va., 1971-88; cons. Devel. Assistance Corp., Washington, 1989-92; inventor West River, Md., 1993—; instr. Inter-Agy. Auditor Tng. Ctr., Washington, 1968-71; part-time cons. Capital Consulting Corp., Fairfax, Va., 1992-95. Patentee in simplified checkbook balancing computer sys. Bd. dirs. South County Cultural Arts, Inc., Shadyside, Md., 1992-93. With USN, 1951-55. Recipient Spl. Recognition award Dept. Commerce, 1973. Avocations: big band trombone player, boating, gardening. Home: 4910 West Chalk Point Rd West River MD 20778

PATERNO, JOSEPH VINCENT, college football coach; b. Bklyn., Dec. 21, 1926; s. Angelo Lafayette and Florence (de LaSalle) P.; m. Suzanne Pohland, May 12, 1962; children: Diana Lynne, Mary Kathryn, David, Joseph Vincent, George Scott. B.A., Brown U., 1950, LL.D., 1975. Asst. football coach Pa. State U., 1950-66, head football coach, 1966—. Author (with Bernard Asbell): The Paterno Principle, 1989; Paterno: By the Book, 1989. Served with AUS, 1945-46. Named Coach of Yr. Walter Camp Football Found., 1972, Coach of Yr. Washington Touchdown Club, 1973, 86, Coach of Yr. Football Writers Assn. Am., 1978, 82, 86; coached Nat. Collegiate Champions, 1982, 86, Named Sports Illustrated's 1986 Sportsman of the Yr. Mem. Am. Football Coaches Assn. (dir., Coach of Yr. awards 1968, 78, 82, 86). Ranked 4th in All-Time Divsn. IA Coaching Victories, 1st among active coaches. Office: Pa State U Dept Athletics University Park PA 16802*

PATERSON, BASIL ALEXANDER, lawyer; b. N.Y.C., Apr. 27, 1926; s. Leonard J. and Evangeline (Rondon) P.; m. Portia Hairston, 1953; children: Daniel, David. BS, St. John's Coll., 1948; JD, St. John's U., 1951. Bar: N.Y. 1952. Ptnr. Paterson, Michael, Jones and Cherot, N.Y.C., 1956-77, Meyer, Suozzi, English & Klein, P.C., Mineola, N.Y., 1983—; mem. N.Y. State Senate, 1965-70; dep. mayor for labor rels. City of N.Y., 1978; sec. of state State of N.Y., 1979-82; pres. Inst. Mediation and Conflict Resolution, 1971-77; chmn. 2d Jud. Screening Com., 1985-95; assoc. chmn. N.Y. State Sentencing Guidelines Com.; commr. Port Authority N.Y. and N.J., 1989-95. vice chmn. Dem. Nat. Com., 1972-78, mem., 1972-78. Recipient Eagleton Inst. Politics award, Disting. Svc. award Guardians Assn. N.Y. Police Dept., City Club N.Y. award, Black Expo award, Excellence medal St. John's U., Kibbe award CUNY. Roman Catholic. Office: Meyer Suozzi English & Klein PC 1505 Kellum Pl Mineola NY 11501-4811

PATERSON, EILEEN, radiation oncologist, educator; b. Bklyn., Oct. 16, 1939; d. John Alexander and Frances (Rabito) P.; m. Bruce Leroy Benedict, Jan. 2, 1981. BA, Wilson Coll., Chambersburg, Pa., 1961; MD, Woman's Med. Coll. Pa., 1965. Diplomate Am. Bd. Radiation Oncology, Am. Bd. Nuclear Medicine. Intern Highland Hosp., Rochester, N.Y., 1965-66; resident radiology (radiation therapy) U. Rochester, 1966-69; asst. prof. radiation oncology U. Rochester, N.Y., 1970-83, assoc. prof., 1983—; chief dept. radiation oncology Rochester Gen. Hosp., 1983—; cons. Arnot Ogden Hosp., Elmira, N.Y., 1970-74, Genesee Hosp., Rochester, 1983—. Contbr. articles to med. jours. Mem. Am. Coll. Radiology, Am. Soc. Therapeutic Radiology and Oncology. Avocations: raising and showing German shepherds and Missouri fox trotting horses. Office: Rochester Gen Hosp 1425 Portland Ave Rochester NY 14621-3001

PATERSON, KATHERINE WOMELDORF, writer; b. Qing Jiang, China, Oct. 31, 1932; came to U.S., 1940; d. George Raymond and Mary Elizabeth

(Goetchius) Womeldorf; m. John Barstow Paterson, July 14, 1962; children: Elizabeth Polin, John Barstow, David Lord, Mary Katherine Nah-he-sah-pe-che-a. A.B., King Coll., Bristol, Tenn., 1954, Litt.D. (hon.), 1978; M.A., Presbyn. Sch. Christian Edn., 1957; postgrad., Kobe Sch. of Japanese Lang., 1957-60; M.R.E., Union Theol. Sem., 1962; LHD (hon.), Otterbein Coll., 1979; Litt.D. (hon.), U. Md., 1982, St. Mary's of the Woods, 1981, Shenandoah Coll., 1982; hon. degree, Washington and Lee U.; hon. LHD, Norwich U., 1990, Mount St. Vincent U., Halifax, N.S., Can., 1994. Tchr. Lovettsville (Va.) Elementary Sch., 1954-55; missionary Presbyn. Ch., Japan, 1957-61; master sacred studies and English Pennington (N.J.) Sch. for Boys, 1963-65. Author: The Sign of the Chrysanthemum, 1973, Of Nightingales That Weep, 1974, The Master Puppeteer, 1976, Bridge to Terabithia, 1977, The Great Gilly Hopkins, 1978, Angels and Other Strangers, 1979, Jacob Have I Loved, 1980, Rebels of the Heavenly Kingdom, 1983, Come Sing, Jimmy Jo, 1985, (with John Paterson) Consider the Lilies, 1986, Park's Quest, 1988, The Tale of the Mandarin Ducks, 1990, The Smallest Cow in the World, 1991, Lyddie, 1991, The King's Equal, 1992, Who Am I?, 1992, Flip-Flop Girl, 1994, A Midnight Clear: Stories for the Christmas Season, 1995, A Sense of Wonder, 1995, The Angel and the Donkey, 1996, Jip: His Story, 1996; translator: The Crane Wife, 1981, The Tongue-Cut Sparrow, 1987. U.S. nominee for Hans Christian Andersen award, 1979, 89; recipient Nat. Book award, 1977, 79, Newbery medal, 1978, 91, Newbery honor, 1979, New Eng. Book award New Eng. Booksellers Assn., 1982, Union medal Union Theol. Sem., 1992, Scott O'Dell award for hist. fiction, 1997, May Hill Arbuthnot Lectr. award, 1997. Mem. Authors Guild, PEN, Children's Book Guild Washington. Democrat. Office: Lodestar/Dutton 375 Hudson St New York NY 10014-3658

PATERSON, RICHARD DENIS, financial executive; b. Ottawa, Ont., Can., Oct. 13, 1942; m. Antoinette Paterson; children: Christopher, Russell, Kathlyn, Victoria, Connor. B in Commerce, Concordia U., Montreal, Que., Can., 1964. Auditor Coopers & Lybrand, Montreal, 1964-67; acct. Genstar Corp., Montreal, 1967-69; dir. fin. and adminstrn. Indussa Corp. (subs. Genstar Corp.), N.Y.C., 1969-73; v.p., comptroller Genstar Corp., Montreal and San Francisco, 1973-83; sr. v.p., CFO Genstar Corp., San Francisco, 1983-87; exec. v.p. Genstar Investment Corp., San Francisco, 1987-95; mng. dir. Genstar Capital LLC, Foster City, 1996—; bd. dirs. Gentek Bldg. Products, Inc., Panolam Industries Inc.; chmn. bd. dirs. Prestolite Electric Inc., Andros Inc. Mem. Order Chartered Accts. Que. Office: Genstar Investment Corp Metro Tower Ste 1170 950 Tower Ln Foster City CA 94404-2121

PATERSON, ROBERT E., trading stamp company executive; b. Kearny, N.J., Nov. 30, 1926; s. Robert McKinley and Ethel (Brookes) P.; m. Eileen Josephine Connolly; children: Carol, Joan, Robert, Richard, Donald, Jeffrey. MBA, Columbia U., 1971. Cert. fin. planner. Sr. v.p. fin., treas. The Sperry & Hutchinson Co., Inc., N.Y.C., 1952-87, also bd. dirs.; mem. Nat. Assn. Accts., 1954-89, nat. treas., 1985-88; bd. dirs. Govt. Obligations Fund, 1986-87. Elected mem. Borough Coun., 1991—, coun. pres., 1995-97. Served with U.S. Army, 1944-45, PTO.

PATHAK, SUNIT RAWLY, business owner, consultant, journalist; b. Calcutta, India, Feb. 14, 1953; came to U.S., 1973.; s. Santosh K. and Bira (Laharry) P.; m. Koruna Dutt; 1 child, Adrit. BA, Calcutta U., 1972; BBA, U. Ga., 1975; MBA, U. Ark., 1978. Sr. analyst Norton-Christensen, Oklahoma City, 1981-84; bus. cons. Cactus Feeders, Inc., Dumas, Tex., 1984-85; analyst, controller Grindwell-Norton, Calcutta, 1985-87; prin. Tech. Venture Cons., Inc., Amarillo, Tex., 1985-93, Venture Mktg. Cons., Inc., Santa Barbara, Calif., 1985—; journalist Morris Communications, Amarillo, 1987-92; ptnr. Internat. Mktg. Inc./Venture Mktg. Cons., Inc., Amarillo, 1989-93; assoc. N.W. Environ. Tng. Inst., Amarillo, 1992-93; mng. editor Claude (Tex.) News, 1992-93; adj. faculty econs. and acctg. Allan Hancock Coll., Santa Maria, Calif.; assoc. Dameron Petroleum, Midland, Tex., Cease Fire, Inc., Southfield, Mich.; sys. educator Brittania, Inc., Arroyo Grande, Calif., Eco-Adventures, USA, Santa Maria; assoc. Pre-Med, Inc., Santa Monica, Calif. Fundraiser United Way, Oklahoma City, 1983; patron Nitish Laharry Children's Libr., Calcutta, 1984—. Recipient English Lit. prize Brit. Coun., 1969; Rotary Dist. 690 scholar, 1973. Mem. Inst. Mgmt. Accts. (v.p. membership Amarillo chpt. 1989-90), Meeting Planners Internat., Tex. Press Assn., Santa Barbara C. of C., Petroleum Club (Bakersfield, Calif.), Calcutta Cricket Club, Indian Polo Assn., Dalhart Country Club, Calcutta Club, Santa Barbara Polo & Racquet Club. Hindu. Avocations: polo, tennis, international air travel. Office: TVC Inc-Pathak PO Box 8363 Fort Wayne IN 46898-8363

PATIN, MICHAEL JAMES, oil company executive; b. Orange, Tex., Jan. 2, 1957; s. Lee Roy Julius and Theresa Estelle (Bonsall) P. BS in Petroleum Engring., U. Southwestern La., 1980. Registered profl. engr., Tex. Ops. engr. Getty Oil Co., Mobile, Ala., 1980-83; sr. petroleum engr. Kerr-McGee Corp., Calgary, Alta., Can., 1983-86; supr. joint ventures Kerr-McGee Corp., Oklahoma City, 1987-89; mgr. Dallas dist. Headington Oil Co., Dallas, 1990-92; pres. Michael J. Patin and Assocs., Houston, 1992-97; owner Patin Oil and Gas Co., Inc., Houston, 1997—. Mem. Soc. Petroleum Engrs. (bd. dirs. Mobile/Pensacola chpt. 1981-83, Dallas chpt. 1983—), Am. Assn. Drilling Engrs., Soc. Petroleum Evaluation Engrs., Can. Joint Venture Assn., Toastmasters Internat. (regional spkrs. award 1989), Am. Assn. Profl. Landman, Stratford Pl. Home Owners Assn. (bd. dirs.1987-90, 92-95). Avocations: tennis, fishing, music, French/Cajun culture. Office: 3000 Wilcrest #115 Houston TX 77042

PATINKIN, TERRY ALLAN, physician; b. Oak Park, Ill., Feb. 1, 1950; s. Lester D. and Marcella Jaqueline (Steinburg) P.; m. Sandra Lee Friedman, Apr. 21, 1985; children: Jonathan, Zachary. BS, U. Ill., 1971; MD, U. Calif., San Francisco, 1975; MPH in health care mgmt., Harvard U., 1996. Diplomate Am. Bd. Emergency Medicine, Am. Bd. Family Medicine. Intern, resident in family practice U. Calif. San Francisco/Natividad Med. Ctr., Salinas, Calif., 1975-78; assoc. dir. family medicine residency program U. Calif. San Francisco/Natividad Med. Ctr., Salinas, 1978-90; dir. emergency dept. Natividad Med. Ctr., Salinas, 1985-91, dir. continuing med. edn., 1978-91, dir. undergrad. edn., 1978-90, emergency physician, 1979-91; emergency physician Sturdy Meml. Hosp., Attleboro, Mass., 1991-94; dir. emergency dept. Roger Williams Hosp., Providence, 1994—; asst. clin. prof. U. Calif., San Francisco, 1981-88, assoc. clin. prof., 1988-91; clin. asst. prof. Stanford U., 1990-93; asst. clin. prof. Brown U., Providence, 1995—. Fellow Am. Coll. Emergency Physicians; mem. Am. Coll. Physician Execs., U. Ill. Alumni Assn. (life), U. Calif. San Francisco Alumni Faculty Assn. Office: Roger Williams Med Ctr 825 Chalkstone Ave Providence RI 02908-4728

PATINO, DOUGLAS XAVIER, foundation and university administrator; b. Calexico, Calif., Apr. 11, 1939; s. Jose Luis and Maria Teresa (Seymour) P.; m. Barbel Wilma Hoyer, Aug. 13, 1970; 1 child, Viktor Xavier. AA, Imperial Valley Coll., 1960; BA, Calif. State U., San Diego, 1962, MA, 1966; PhD, U.S. Internat. U., 1972. Deputy dir. Sacramento (Calif.) Concilio, Inc., 1968-69; v.p. student affairs U. So. Colo., Pueblo, 1973-75; dep. dir. for planning and rev. svc. br. to dir. Calif. Employment Devel. Dept., dir.; sec. Calif. Health & Welfare Agy., 1975-83; dir. Ariz. Dept. of Econ. Security, Phoenix, 1983-87; pres., chief exec. officer Marin Community Found., Larkspur, Calif., 1987-91; pres. New Partnership Found. and Patino Group, San Rafael, Calif., 1991-93; vice chancellor Calif. State U., Long Beach, 1993—; commr. Wm. T. Grand Found., 1986-88, Enterprize for the Ams., Washington, 1994—; trustee C.S. Mott Found., Flint, Mich., 1995—. Mem. Sec. of U.S. Dept. of Labor Task Force, Ariz., 1985-86, Staff Adv. Com. of the Human Resource Com., Nat. Gov. Assn., Washington, 1983-86; bd. dirs. Calif. Leadership, Santa Cruz, Calif., 1985-95, No. Calif. Grantmakers, 1990-91, Ariz. Assn. Bus., 1984; chair U.S. Savs. Bond Dr. for State of Calif., 1982; trustee Nat. Hispanic U., Oakland, Calif., 1987-90, Hispanic Community Fund, San Francisco, 1989-95, C.S. Mott Found., 1995—; bd. dirs. Calif. Sch. Profl. Psychology, 1989-94, Coun. on Found., Washington, 1990—, Found. Ctr., N.Y., 1993. Recipient The Monty Disting. Alumni award San Diego State U., 1997, Simon Bolivar award for cmty. leadership award Hispanic Cmty. Found. and Bay Area United Way, 1996, Azteca award Human Devel. Corp., 1991, Leadership award Nat. Concilors of Am. and United Way of Bay Area, 1990, Disting. Performance award, Nat. Alliance of Bus., Washington, 1985, Superior Svc. Mgmt. award, Am. Soc. Pub. Adminstrn., 1985, Humanitarian award, Los Padrinos, Inc., 1981, Small and Minority Bus. award for the State of Calif. 1982, Disting. Alumni award, Calif. Jr. Community Coll. Assn., Sacramento, 1982, Silver Spur award, Nat. Fedn. of Charros in Guadalajaro, Jalisco, Mex., 1974, Calif. Community Svc. award, Former Gov. Ronald Reagan, Sacramento, 1973. Mem. chair, Hispanics in Philanthropy, Am. Pub. Welfare Assn. (bd. dirs., Leadership award 1987), Rotary, 1987-93. Office: Calif State U 400 Golden Shore St Ste 116 Long Beach CA 90802-4209

PATINO, HUGO, food science research engineer; b. Monterey, Nuevo Leon, Mex., Oct. 1, 1952; came to U.S., 1982; s. Francisco De Paula and Aurora (Leal) P.; m. Leslie Ellen Nickels, May. 20, 1978; children: Erica, Laura Elizabeth. B of Engring., Monterrey Inst. Tech., 1974; PhD, U. Waterloo, 1979. Asst. prof. Monterrey (Mex.) Inst. Tech., 1975-76; mgr. brewing product engring. Cuauhtemoc Breweries, Monterey, 1979-82; asst. prof. U. Calif., Davis, 1982-84; dept. head rsch. Coors Brewing Co., Golden, Colo., 1984-91, dir. rsch. & devel., 1991-93, v.p., R & D, 1993—; bd. govs. Colo. Alliance for Sci., Boulder. Co-author: Quality Control in Commercial Vegetable Processing, 1989; contbr. articles to profl. jours. Recipient Profl. Achievement award Nat. Hispanic Employers Assn., 1997. Mem. Am. Soc. Brewing Chemists (edit. bd. mem. 1991—), Master Brewers Assn. Am. (tech. com. mem. 1991—, Presdl. award Best Paper 1990), Am. Inst. Chem. Engring., Inst. Food Technologists. Roman Catholic. Achievements include patents for the use of freeze concentration to prepare malt liquers and for the production of a clear malt beverage. Office: Coors Brewing Co BC600 Golden CO 80401

PATINO, ISIDRO FRANK, law enforcement educator; b. San Antonio, Mar. 10, 1943; s. Isidro F. and Maria (Narro) P.; children: Michael, Rebecca, Karleen. BS, Calif. State U., L.A., 1973; MBA, U. Redlands, 1995. Records comdr. Placentia (Calif.) Police Dept., 1980-85; asst. dean Criminal Justice Tng. Ctr. Golden West Coll., Huntington Beach, Calif., 1986-89, assoc. dean instrn., 1989-92; divsn. dean dept. pub. svc. Rio Hondo Coll., Whittier, Calif., 1992—; pres., mem. State Chancellors Adv. Com. Pub. Safety Edn., 1991—; chmn. So. Calif. Pub. Safety Tng. Consortium, 1994—, active, 1993—; bd. suprs. L.A. County Spl. Task Force on Pub. Safety Tng., 1995—; mem. Hispanic male adv. com. Dept. Edn. Connections Project. Kellogg C.C. Diversity Leadership fellow, 1996-97. Mem. Calif. Law Enforcement Assn. Records Suprs. (pres. so. chpt. 1985-87, state pres. 1986-87), Calif. Acad. Dirs. Assn. (chmn. 1988-89), Am. Soc. Criminologists, Acad. Criminal Justice Scis., Western and Pacific Assn. Criminal Justice Educators, Calif. Assn. Adminstrn. of Justice Educators (v.p. 1996-97, state pres. 1997—), Calif. Peace Officers Stds. and Tng. Basic Course Consortium (chmn. instrn. com. 1987-88),World Future Soc. (pres. Orange County-Long Beach chpt. 1988- 92), Nat. Assn. Field Tng. Officers (nat. pres. 1992-93), Nat. Assn. Chiefs of Police, Internat. Assn. Chiefs of Police, Soc. Law Enforcement Trainers. Roman Catholic.

PATKAU, JOHN, architect; b. Winnipeg, Man., Can., Aug. 18, 1947; s. Abe John and Bertha (Klassen) P.; m. Patricia Frances Gargett, Aug. 10, 1974. BA, U. Manitoba, 1969, BA in Environ. Studies, 1969, MArch, 1972. Registered architect, B.C., Ont. Prin. John Patkau Architect Ltd., Edmonton, Can., 1977-83; ptnr. Patkau Archs. Inc., Vancouver, B.C., Can., 1984—; chmn. edn. com. Alta. Assn. Architects, 1981; vis. critic U. Calgary, 1981, 92, U. Waterloo, 1987, 89, U. Pa., 1987, Tech. U. N.S., 1987, U. B.C., 1988, 89, UCLA, 1989; design critic U. B.C., 1985-86; urban design panel Vancouver, 1990-92; vis. prof. William Lyon Somerville Lectureship U. Calgary, 1994; Eliot Noyes vis. design critic Harvard U., 1995. Recipient Progressive Architecture citation, 1981, Progressive Architecture award, 1993, 95, Can. Architects award, 1983, 86, 87, 89, 90, 92, 94, Wood Coun. First award, 1984, Gov. Gen. medal, 1986, 90, 92, 94, 97, Gov. Gen. award, 1990, 97, Lt. Gov. Archtl. medal, 1992, Honor award, 1992. Fellow Royal Archtl. Inst. Can. (chmn. design com. 1987); mem. Archtl. Inst. B.C., Royal Can. Coll. Art, Ont. Assn. Architects. Office: Patkau Archs, 560 Beatty St Ste L110, Vancouver, BC Canada V6B 2L3

PATKAU, PATRICIA, architect, architecture educator; b. Winnipeg, Manitoba, Can., Feb. 25, 1950; d. John Frederick and Aileen Constance (Emmett) Gargett; m. John Robert Patkau, Aug. 10, 1974. BA in Interior Design, U. Manitoba, 1973; MA in Architecture, Yale, New Haven, Conn., 1978. Ptnr. Patkau Archs., Vancouver, B.C., Can., 1983—; asst. prof. Sch. Architecture UCLA, U.S.A., 1988-90; assoc. prof. Sch. Architecture U. B.C., Can., 1992—; vis. critic U. Calgary, 1981, 87, U. Waterloo, 1987, U. Pa., U.S.A., 1987, U. Toronto, 1988, Southern Calif. Inst. Architecture, U.S.A., 1990, UCLA, 1991, U. Oreg., U.S.A., 1992, MIT, U.S.A., 1993, Yale U., 1993; design critic U. B.C., 1984-87; vis. prof. Harvard U., U.S.A., 1993, U. Calgary, 1994. Ctrl. Mortgage and Housing fellow, 1977, 78; recipient Manitoba Gold medal, 1973, Progressive Architecture citation, 1981, 93, Can. Architect Excellence award, 1983, 86, 87, 89, 90, 92, 94, Can. Wood Coun. First award, 1984, Honor award, 1992, Gov. Gen. Architecture medal, 1986, 90, 92, 94, 97, Gov. Gen. Architecture award, 1990, 97, Lt. Gov. Architecture medal, 1992, Can. Wood Coun. award, 1991. Fellow Royal Archtl. Inst. Can.; mem. Archtl. Inst. B.C. (Honor award 1988). Office: Patkau Archs, 560 Beatty St Ste L110, Vancouver, BC Canada V6B 2L3

PATMAN, JEAN ELIZABETH, journalist; b. Lincolnshire, Eng., Dec. 12, 1946; came to U.S., 1955, naturalized, 1967; d. Donald Geoffrey and Regina (Iwanir) P. BA in English, CCNY, 1967. Stringer Newsweek mag., 1966-67; copygirl, then asst. to entertainment editor N.Y. Post, 1964-70; successively copy editor, spl. sects. editor, night city editor Reporter-Dispatch, White Plains, N.Y., 1970-74; assoc. editor United Feature Syndicate, 1974-75; successively copy editor, asst. news editor, news editor, Sunday editor, exec. news editor, fgn. editor Newsday, L.I., 1975-85; asst. view editor, view editor L.A. Times, 1985-89; owner, pub. Keystone Gazette Weekly, Bellefonte, Pa., 1989-92; asst. mng. editor Fla. Today, 1992-95; writing coach Gannett, 1996—. Dir. team that won 1985 Pulitzer prize for international reporting. Office: Gannett Suburban Newspapers 1 Gannett Dr White Plains NY 10604

PATMOS, ADRIAN EDWARD, university dean emeritus; b. Paterson, N.J., June 29, 1914; s. Adrian and Myra (Van Splinter) P.; m. Pearl Van Den Heuvel, Apr. 25, 1942; children: Adrian Edward III, Bruce Douglas. A.B. magna cum laude, N.Y.U., 1935, A.M., 1936; LLD, Wittenberg U., 1996; Penfield scholar, 1937-38; grad. study, Am. U., 1936-37. Asst. prof. econs. Wittenberg U., 1938-47, assoc. prof., head dept., 1947-50, prof. econs., 1950—, head dept., 1950-64, dir. mgmt. devel. program, 1952-79, eve. sessions, 1952-78; dean Wittenberg U. (Sch. Community Edn.), 1955-79, dean emeritus, 1979—; jr. accountant Def. Plant Corp., Curtiss-Wright Corp., summer 1943; vis. instr. Ohio Wesleyan U., summer 1944; spl. field rep. NLRB, 1946; vis. lectr. econs. N.Y.U., 1946-47, summer 1948; vis. prof. econs. USAF Inst. Tech., 1949, 50; cons. Clark C.C., 1982-84, Urbana U., 1983-94. Chmn. Clark County Health Facilities Planning Com., 1965-66, City commr., Springfield, Ohio, 1958-62, mayor, 1960-62; Trustee United Way, Springfield and Clark County, 1960-74; trustee Clark Tech. Coll., 1965-78, chmn., 1969-71; trustee Springfield Community Hosp., 1975-84, Elderly United, 1979-92. Recipient Wittenberg award for meritorious svc. to univ., 1964, Silver Knight award Nat. Mgmt. Assn., Sta. WIZE award for outstanding cmty. svc., Cmty. Svc. award C. of C., 1979, award of distinction Bd. of Realtors, Outstanding Svc. in Cmty. Labor-Mgmt. Relationships award Fed. Mediation Svc., citation as one of Ohio's foremost educators Ohio Senate, Medal of Honor for leadership in liberal arts edn., 1987; named Jr. Achievement Hall of Fame laureate, 1996. Mem. Ohio Coll. Assn. (pres. adult edn. sect. 1959-60), Am. Econs. Assn., Kiwanis (Disting. Svc. to Cmty. award), Phi Beta Kappa, Phi Gamma Delta, Blue Key. Baptist.

PATNAUDE, WILLIAM E., architect; b. Sanger, Calif., Sept. 24, 1937; s. Eugene Joseph Patnaude and Vera Mae (Giles) Patnaude Fagan; m. Mary Esther Simerly, Aug. 22, 1971 (div. 1987); children—Nathaniel, Matthew. B.Arch., U. Calif., Berkeley, 1961; postgrad., Calif. State U.-Fresno, 1968-72. Registered architect, Calif., Oreg., Wash., Idaho, Nev., N.Mex., Colo., Utah, Ariz., Mont., Ind., Iowa, Nebr., Ohio. Draftsman, architect Robert Stevens Assoc., Santa Cruz, Calif., 1963-66; architect Llewelyn Davies, Weeks & Ptnrs., London, 1966; architect Allen Y. Lew, Fresno, Calif., 1967-69, assoc., 1969-74; v.p., architect Lew & Patnaude, Inc., Fresno, Calif., 1978-84; pres. Lew & Patnaude, Inc., 1985—; instr. Calif. State U., Fresno, 1968-81. Constn. arbitrator Am. Arbitration Assn., 1976—; chair ctrl. area plan citizen's adv. com. City of Fresno, 1991-93, chair gen. plan update com., 1994-97; bd. dirs. Fresno Arts Ctr., 1971-74, Fresno County Alliance for the Arts, 1986-88, 91-94. With USNR, 1961-63. Recipient Award of Merit, Calif. Hist. Preservation Conf., Orange County, 1983; Award of Excellence Woodwork Inst. Calif., 1982. Fellow AIA (nat. dir. 1983-85, pres. Calif. coun. 1982, San Joaquin chpt. 1978, Awards of Excellence, 1972-95; mem. Constrn. Specifications Inst. (pres. Fresno chpt. 1977). Democrat. Avocations: photography; fine wines. Home: 4190 N Van Ness Blvd Fresno CA 93704-4213 Office: Lew & Patnaude Inc 1050 S St Fresno CA 93721-1407

PATON, LELAND B., investment banker; b. Worcester, Mass., Nov. 30, 1943; s. Andrew John and Anne Louise (Kehoe) P.; m. Nancy Carlon Nation, May 13, 1978;children: Scott Bartlett, Mark Grosvenor, Elisabeth Anne. Asst. sec. New England Mcht. Nat. Bank, Boston, 1965-69; with Prudential Bache Securities Inc. Prudential Securities Inc., 1969—; mgr. N.Y. instl. sales, N.Y.C., 1976-77; dir.mktg., 1977-82; pres. Capital Markets Group, 1986—; also bd. dirs.; mem. operating com. Prudential Securities Inc.; exchange ofcl. Am. Stock Exchange; bd. dirs. Chgo. Bd. of Options Exchange. Bd. dirs. Riverdale Country Sch. Mem. N.Y. Stock Exchange, Securities Industry Assn. (chmn. mktg. com. 1981, bd. dirs.), Securities Ind. Inst. (bd. dirs.), Am.Mktg. Assn., Bond Club, N.Y., Apawamis Club, Harvard Club, Mid-Ocean Club, Long Cove Club. Office: Prudential Securities Inc One New York Plz New York NY 10292-2015

PATON WALSH, JILL, author; b. London, England, Apr. 29, 1937; d. John Llewelyn and Patricia (Dubern) Buss; m. Antony Edmund Paton Walsh, Aug. 5, 1961; Children: Edmund, Margaret, Clare. Author: Hengest's Tale, 1966, The Dolphin Crossing, 1967, Fireweed, 1969, (with Kevin Crossley-Holland, World Book Festival award 1970), Wordhoard, 1969, Goldengrove 1972, Farewell Great King, 1972, Toolmaker, 1973, The Dawnstone, 1973, The Emporer's Winding Sheet, 1974 (Whitbread prize 1974), The Huffler, 1975, The Island Sunrise: Preshistoric Culture in the British Isles, 1975, Unleaving, 1976 (Boston Globe, Horn Book award 1976), Children of the Fox: Crossing to Salamis, 1977, The Walls of Athens, 1978, Persian Gold, 1978, A Chance Child, 1978, The Green Book, 1981, Babylon, 1982, Parcell of Patterns, 1983 (Universe prize 1984), Lost and Found, 1984, Gaffer Samson's Luck, 1984 (Smarties Grand prix 1984), Lapsing, 1985, A School for Lovers, 1989, Birdy and the Ghosties, 1990, "Grace", 1991, Matthew and the Sea Singers, 1992, When Grandma Came, 1992, The Wydham Case, 1993, Knowledge of Angels, 1994, A Piece of Justice, 1995, Connie Came to Play, 1995, Thomas and the Tinners, 1995, The Serpentine Cave, 1997. Fellow Royal Soc. of Lit. (CBE award 1996). Addres: care David Higham Assocs, 5-8 Lower John St, Golden Sq London W1R 3PE, England

PATRIC, JASON, actor; s. Jason and Linda Gleason Miller. Appeared in films The Lost Boys, 1987, The Beast, 1988, After Dark, My Sweet, 1990, Denial Loon, 1991, Rush, 1991, Geronimo-An American Legend, 1993, The Journey of August King, 1995, Sleepers, 1996, Incognito, 1997, Speed 2, 1997, (tv movie) Toughlove, 1985, (tv episode) Teach 109. Office: United Talent Agy 9560 Wilshire Blvd 5th Fl Beverly Hills CA 90212*

PATRICK, BILL, sports network host; b. Nov. 12, 1955. BA in Broadcast/Film, U. Maine, 1979. Sports anchor, reporter WABI-TV, Bangor, Maine, 1977-80; sports dir. WOWK-TV, Huntington, W.Va., 1980; sports anchor, reporter WFSB-TV, Hartford, Conn., 1981-88; anchor/reporter SportsCenter ESPN, 1988-93, freelance anchor/reporter, 1993—; owner Patrick Media Prodns., Hartford, 1993—. Co-creator Future Earth. Office: c/o ESPN ESPN Plaza Bristol CT 06010

PATRICK, BRENDA JEAN, educational consultant; b. Dallas, Aug. 24, 1955; d. Gene Everett and Peggy Rose (Tanzy) P.; children: Michael Everett, Tray Riley. BS in Elem. Edn., Tex. A&M U, Commerce, 1981, MS, 1984, postgrad., 1989—. Cert. profl. supr., mid-mgmt. adminstr. Tchr. Garland Ind. Sch. Dist., 1982-87, acad. coach, 1983-86; with Austin Acad. for Excellence, 1987-88; sr. cons. Region 10 Edn. Svc. Ctr., 1988—; coord. Tchr. Expectation Student Achievement; trainer Devel. Capable People, Tex. A&M-Commerce/Profl. Devel. Ctr. Project; developer, presenter workshops and seminars in field; mem. adv. bd. Network for Effective Schs. Recipient Tex. History Tchr. award Daus. of Republic of Tex., Am. History Tchr. award Daus. of Am. Revolution; named Vol. with a Heart, YWCA. Mem. Tex. PTA (hon. life), Tex. Staff Devel. Coun., Phi Delta Kappa.

PATRICK, CARL LLOYD, theatre executive; b. Honaker, Va., Dec. 6, 1918; s. Deward and Virginia Mae (McGraw) P.; m. Frances Estelle Wynn, Feb. 14, 1943; children: Carl Lloyd Jr., Michael Wynn. Ed. high sch., Dublin, Md. Gen. mgr. Martin Theatres, Columbus, Ga., 1945-69, pres., 1969-70; pres. Fuqua Industries, Inc., Atlanta, 1970-78, vice chmn., 1978-82; chmn. Carmike Cinemas, Inc., Columbus, 1982—; bd. dirs. Columbus Bank & Trust Co. Trustee Columbus Mus., 1983—, Ga. Southwestern Coll., Americus, 1984—, Columbus Coll., 1985—; bd. dirs. Columbus Tech. Inst., 1988—. Maj. U.S. Army, 1941-45. Mem. Nat. Assn. Theatre Owners (Sherrill Corwin award 1984, Hassanein Humanitarian award 1996, Exhibitor of the Decade award 1990). Methodist. Avocation: golf. Home: 2701 Lynda Ln Columbus GA 31906-1248 Office: Carmike Cinemas 1301 1st Ave Columbus GA 31901-2109

PATRICK, CHARLES WILLIAM, JR., lawyer; b. Monroe, N.C., Oct. 9, 1954; s. Charles William and Louise (Nisbet) P.; m. Celeste Hunt, June 5, 1976; children: Laura Elizabeth, Charles William III. BA magna cum laude, Furman U., 1976; JD, U. S.C., 1979. Bar: S.C. 1979, U.S. Dist. Ct. S.C. 1981, U.S. Ct. Appeals (11th cir.) 1981, U.S. Ct. Appeals (10th cir.) 1983, U.S. Ct. Appeals (4th cir.) 1986. Law clk. to presiding judge 9th Cir. Ct. State of S.C., Charleston, 1979-80; assoc. Ness, Motley, Loadholt, Richardson and Poole and predecessor firm Blatt and Fales, Charleston, 1980—; assoc. Motley, Loadholt, Richardson and Poole and predecessor firm Blatt and Fales, Charleston, 1980-84, ptnr., 1984—. Exec. editor S.C. Law Review, 1978; contbr. articles to profl. jours. Mem. ABA, Assn. Trial Lawyers Am., S.C. Assn. Trial Lawyers, Trial Lawyers for Pub. Justice, Phi Beta Kappa. Democrat. Presbyterian. Avocations: boating, skiing, fishing. Home: 38 Church St Charleston SC 29401-2742 Office: Ness Motley Loadholt Richardson & Poole 151 Meeting St Box 1137 Charleston SC 29402

PATRICK, CRAIG, professional hockey team executive; b. Detroit, May 20, 1946; s. Lynn P.; m. Sue Patrick; children—Erin, Cory, Ryan. M.B.A., U. Denver. Hockey player Calif. Golden Seals, 1971-74; hockey player St. Louis Blues, 1974-75, Kansas City, 1975-76, World Hockey Assn., Minn., 1976-77, Washington Capitals, 1977-79; v.p., gen. mgr. N.Y. Rangers, N.Y.C., 1981-86; dir. athletics and recreation Univ. Denver, 1987-89; gen. mgr., exec. v.p. Pitts. Penguins, 1989—. Capt., U.S. Nat. Team, World Championships, Moscow, 1979; asst. mgr. and asst. coach U.S. Olympic Hockey Team, 1980. Office: Pitts Penguins Civic Arena Gate # 9 Pittsburgh PA 15219*

PATRICK, DAN, sportscaster; b. May 15, 1957; married; 2 children. BA in Broadcasting, U. Dayton, 1979. Morning sports and news reporter WTUE-Radio, Dayton, Ohio, 1979-81; weekend sports anchor, reporter WDTN-TV, Dayton, Ohio, 1981-83, CNN, 1983-89; sports dir. WKLS-AM, Atlanta, 1987-91; reporter weekday sports Laser 103, Milw., WLVQ-AM, Columbus, 1989-91; anchor, reporter SportsCenter ESPN, Bristol, Conn., 1989—; reporter weekday sports KSEG-AM, Sacramento, 1991. Office: ESPN Inc Comms Dept ESPN Plz 935 Middle St Bristol CT 06010-1000*

PATRICK, DANE HERMAN, lawyer; b. San Antonio, Oct. 18, 1960; s. Kae Thomas and Joyce Lynn (von Scheele) P.; m. Kelly Marie Carlson, May 17, 1986. BA in Econs. with honors, U. Tex., 1983; JD, So. Meth. U., 1987. Assoc. Law Office of Earl Luna, Dallas, 1987-88, Veitch & Davis, San Antonio, 1988-91; pvt. practice San Antonio, 1991—. Mem. Assn. Trial Lawyers Am., Tex. Trial Lawyers Assn., San Antonio United Shareholder Assn. (chmn. 1988-92). Democrat. Methodist. Avocations: weight lifting, hunting, martial arts. Office: 111 Soledad St Ste 300 San Antonio TX 78205-2298

PATRICK, DEVAL LAURDINE, lawyer; b. Chgo., July 31, 1956; s. Laurdine Kenneth and Emily Mae (Wintersmith) P.; m. Diane Louise Bemus, May 5, 1984; children: Sarah Baker, Katherine Wintersmith. AB cum laude, Harvard Coll., 1978, JD, 1982; JD (hon.), Dist. Columbia Law Sch., 1994, Morris Brown Coll., 1996. Bar: Calif. 1983, D.C. 1985, Mass. 1987, U.S. Dist. Ct. Mass. 1987, U.S. Dist. Ct. (cen. dist.) Calif. 1983, U.S. Ct. Appeals (1st and 5th cirs.) 1984, U.S. Ct. Appeals (9th and 11th cirs.) 1984, U.S. Supreme Ct. 1988. Law clk. to Hon. Stephen Reinhardt U.S. Ct. Appeals (9th cir.), L.A., 1982-83; asst. counsel NAACP Legal Def. Fund, N.Y.C., 1983-86; ptnr. Hill & Barlow, Boston, 1986-94; asst. atty. gen. civil rights divsn. U.S. Dept. Justice, Washington, 1994-97; ptnr. Day, Berry & Howard, Boston, 1997—; Herman Phleger disting. vis. prof. Stanford Law Sch., 1997; lectr. Boston Coll. Sch. Law, 1997, Harvard Law Sch., 1997. Dir., mem. exec. com., chmn. New Eng. steering com. NAACP Legal Def. and Edn. Fund., Inc., 1991-94, vice chmn. Mass. Jud. Nominating Coun., 1991-93; trustee, mem. exec. com. Milton Acad., 1985-97; overseer WGBH, 1993-94; corporator Milton Hosp., 1991-94. Recipient George Leisure award Harvard Law Sch., 1981; Rockefeller Traveling fellow, 1978. Mem. ABA (numerous bds. and coms.), Mass. Bar Assn., Mass. Black Lawyers Assn., Boston Bar Assn. (coun. mem. 1993), Harvard Club of Boston, Harvard Alumni Assn. (dir. 1993-96). Avocations: squash, cooking, gardening.

PATRICK, H. HUNTER, lawyer, judge; b. Gasville, Ark., Aug. 19, 1939; s. H. Hunter Sr. and Nelle Frances (Robinson) P.; m. Charlotte Anne Wilson, July 9, 1966; children: Michael Hunter, Colleen Annette. BA, U. Wyo., 1961, JD, 1966. Bar: Wyo. 1966, U.S. Dist. Ct. Wyo. 1966, Colo. 1967, U.S. Supreme Ct. 1975. Mcpl. judge City of Powell (Wyo.), 1967-68; sole practice law Powell, 1966-88; atty. City of Powell, 1969-88; justice of the peace County of Park, Wyo., 1971-88; bus. law instr. Northwest Community Coll., Powell, 1968—; dist. judge State of Wyo. 5th Jud. Dist., 1988—; mem. Wyo. Dist. Judges Conf., sec.-treas., 1993-94, vice chair, 1994-95, chair, 1995-96. Editor: Bench Book for Judges of Courts of Limited Jurisdiction in the State of Wyoming, 1980-90. Dir. cts. Wyo. Girls State, Powell, 1982-85, 89-96; elder, deacon, moderator of deacons Powell Presbyn. Ch., 1997. Recipient Wyo. Crime Victims Compensation Commn. Judicial award, 1995. Fellow Am. Bar Found., Wyo. Jud. Adv. Coun.; mem. ABA (Wyo. state del. to ho. of dels. 1994—, Wyo. del. judicial adminstrn. divsn., Pub. Svc. award for ct.-sponsored Law Day programs 1990, 92), Wyo. Bar Assn., Colo. Bar Assn., Park County Bar Assn. (sec. 1969-70, pres. 1970-71), Wyo. Assn. Cts. Ltd. Jurisdiction (pres. 1973-80), Am. Judicature Soc., Nat. Coun. Juvenile and Family Ct. Judges. Avocations: photography, travel, fishing, camping, bicycling. Home: PO Box 941 Powell WY 82435-0941 Office: PO Box 1868 Cody WY 82414-1868

PATRICK, HUGH TALBOT, economist, educator; b. Goldsboro, N.C., Feb. 22, 1930; s. Talbot and Paula (Miller) P.; B.A., Yale U., 1951; M.A. in Far Eastern Studies, U. Mich., 1955, M.A. in Econs., 1957; Ph.D. in Econs., 1960; M.A. (hon.), Yale U., 1968; children—Stephen, Matthew, Catherine. Econ. analyst U.S. Govt., 1951-52; lectr. econs. U. Mich., 1958-60; asst. prof. econs. Yale U., New Haven, 1960-64, assoc. prof., 1964-68, prof. Far Eastern econs., 1968-84, dir. Yale Econ. Growth Center 1976-79, 80-83; R.D. Calkins prof. internat. bus. Columbia U., 1984—; vis. prof. U. Bombay, 1961-62; mem. Japan-U.S. Econ. Relations Group, 1978-81, Nat. Com. for Pacific Econ. Coop.; dir. Ctr. on Japanese Econ. and Bus., Columbia U., 1986—. Ford Found. fellow, 1957-58; Am. Council Learned Socs. grantee, 1962; Guggenheim fellow, 1964-65; Fulbright research prof., 1964-65; Fulbright-Hays NDEA fellow, 1968-69; Assn. Asian Studies Disting. lectr., 1977. Mem. Japan Soc. (dir. 1973-79, 81—), Social Sci. Research Council (dir., chmn. 1985-88), Pacific Trade and Devel. Confs. (chmn.). Democrat. Editor: Japanese Industrialization and Its Social Consequences, 1976, Japanese High Technology Industries-Lessons and Limitations of Industrial Policy, 1986; co-author, co-editor: Asia's New Giant-How the Japanese Economy Works, 1976; chapter author: (co-editor with Masahiko Aoki) The Japanese Finance Main Bank System: Its Relevance for Developing and Transforming Economies, 1994, (co-editor with Larry Meissner) Pacific Basin Industries in Distress: Structural Adjustment and Trade Policy in Nine Industrialized Economies, 1991 (Masayoshi Ohira Meml. prize, 1992); co-editor: (with Yung Chul Park) The Financial Development of Japan, Korea, and Taiwan: Growth, Repression and Liberalization, 1994. Office: Columbia U 522 Uris Hall 3022 Broadway New York NY 10027-6902

PATRICK, JAMES DUVALL, JR., lawyer; b. Griffin, Ga., Dec. 28, 1947; s. James Duvall and Marion Wilson (Ragsdale) P.; m. Cynthia Hill, Jan. 19, 1991. BS in Indsl. Mgmt., Ga. Inst. Tech., 1970; JD, U. Ga., 1973. Bar: Ga. 1973, U.S. Dist. Ct. (mid. dist.) Ga. 1973, U.S. Dist. Ct. (so. dist.) Ga. 1983, U.S. Ct. Appeals (5th cir.) 1974, U.S. Supreme Ct., U.S. Ct. Appeals (11th Cir.) 1981, U.S. Tax Ct. 1985. Assoc. Cartledge, Cartledge & Posey, Columbus, Ga., 1973-74; ptnr. Falkenstrom, Hawkins & Patrick, Columbus, 1975, Falkenstrom & Patrick, Columbus, 1975-77; sole practice, Columbus, 1977—; instr. bus. law Chattahoochee Valley C.C., Phenix City, Ala., 1975-77; instr. paralegal course Columbus Coll., 1979, 84; del. U.S./China Joint Session on Trade, Investment, and Econ. Law, Beijing, 1987, Moscow Conf. on Law and Bilateral Econ. Rels., Moscow, 1990. Mem. Hist. Columbus Found., Mayor's Com. for the Handicapped, 1987-88; local organizer, worker Joe Frank Harris for Gov. Campaign, Columbus, 1982; bd. dirs. Columbus Symphony Orchestra, 1988-94. Mem. ATLA, ABA, State Bar Ga., Ga. Trial Lawyers Assn., Columbus Young Lawyers Club, Columbus Lawyers Club, Columbus Kappa Alpha Alumni Assn. (sec.), Phi Delta Phi, Kappa Alpha. Methodist. Clubs: Civitan (bd. dirs. 1975-77), Country of Columbus, Georgian (Atlanta), Buckhead. Office: 831 2nd Ave Columbus GA 31901-2703

PATRICK, JANE AUSTIN, association executive; b. Memphis, May 27, 1930; d. Wilfred Jack and Evelyn Eudora (Branch) Austin; m. William Thomas Spencer, Sept. 11, 1952 (dec Apr. 1970); children: Duke Anthony-Spencer Austin, ToniLee Candice Spencer Hughes; m. George Milton Patrick, Oct. 1, 1971. Student Memphis State U., 1946-47; BSBA, Ohio State U., 1979. Svc. rep. So. Bell Tel. and Tel., Memphis, 1947-52; placement dir. Mgmt. Pers., Memphis, 1965-66; pers. dir. E & E Ins. Co., Columbus, Ohio, 1966-69; Ohio exec. dir. Nat. Soc. for Prevention of Blindness, Columbus, 1969-73; regional dir. Ohio and Ky. CARE and MEDICO, Columbus, 1979-87; v.p. Career Execs. of Columbus, 1987-91; owner, pres. Patrick Distribution, 1994—; lectr., cons. in field. Mem. choir 1st Cmty. Ch., Columbus, Ohio State Univ. Svc. Bd.; bd. dirs. Columbus Coun. on World Affairs, 1980-92, sec., 1983-91, chmn. devel. com.; chmn. pers. com. Ohio Hunger Task Force, 1989-90. Recipient commendations Nat. Soc. Prevention Blindness and Ctrl. Ohio Lions Eye Bank, 1973. Plaques for Svc. award Upper Arlington Pub. Schs., 1986. Mem. Non-Profit Orgn. Mgmt. Inst. (pres.), Nat. Soc. Fund-Raising Execs. (cert., nat. dir.), Pub. Rels. Soc. Am. (cert., membership com. chairperson), Ins. Inst. Am. (cert.), Mensa Internat., Columbus Dental Soc. Aux. (historian and publicity chair), Alpha Gamma Delta, Epsilon Sigma Alpha (pres.). Home: 2620 Love Dr Columbus OH 43221-2645

PATRICK, JANET CLINE, personnel company executive; b. San Francisco, June 30, 1934; d. John Wesley and Edith Bertha (Corde) Cline; m. Robert John Patrick Jr., June 13, 1959 (div. 1988); children: John McKinnon, Stewart McLellan, William Robert. BA with distinction, Stanford U., 1955; postgrad. U. Calif.-Berkeley, 1957, George Washington U., 1978-82. English tchr. George Washington H.S., San Francisco, 1957, K.D. Burke Sch., San Francisco, 1957-59, Berkeley Inst., Bklyn., 1959-63; placement counselor Washington Sch. Secs., Washington, 1976-78, asst. dir. placement, 1978-81; mgr. med. personnel service Med. Soc. D.C., 1981-89, pres. Med. Pers. Svcs. Inc., 1989—. Chmn. area 2 planning com. Montgomery County Pub. Schs. (Md.), 1974-75; mem. vestry, corr. sec., Christ Ch., Kensington, Md., 1982-84, vestry, sr. warden, 1984-85, vestry, chmn. ann. giving com., 1986-89; chmn. long-range planning com., 1989-92, sec., 1992-93, jr. warden, 1994, co-chair capital campaign, 1996; fin. com. Montgomery County Pvt. Industry Coun., 1994. Mem. Met. D.C. Med. Group Mgmt. Assn., Phi Beta Kappa. Republican. Episcopalian. Club: Jr. League (Washington). Home: 5206 Carlton St Bethesda MD 20816-2306 Office: Med Personnel Svcs Inc 1707 L St NW Ste 250 Washington DC 20036-4215

PATRICK, JOHN FRANKLIN, education educator; b. Washington, Nov. 17, 1933; s. Clifford Walker and Dorothy (Knoblauch) P.; m. Barbara Florence Sanders, Apr. 3, 1965; children: Susan Lynn, Robert Franklin. BS, U. Va., 1955; MA, George Washington U., 1961; PhD, U. Md., 1977. Commd. 2nd lt. USAF, 1957, advanced to col., 1981; med. forces advisor Office of Surgeon Gen. USAF, Bolling AFB, Washington, 1981-85; mgmt. trainer Dept. Def., Ft. Meade, Md., 1969; chief, mgr. level program Dept. Def., Ft. Meade, 1969-71, exec. Jr. Officer Career Program, 1971-74, instr. course dir., 1974-77, chief Gen. Edn. Div., 1977-81, sr. edn. and tng. officer, 1985-88, sr. ops. staff officer, 1988-90; adj. assoc. prof. George Washington U., Washington, 1990-95; asst. profl. lectr. George Washington U., 1981-85, assoc. profl. lectr., 1985-90. Contbr. articles and reports to profl. jours. and mags. mem. Am. Soc. Pub. Adminstrn., Assn. Mil. Surgeons of U.S., Howard County Alumni Club U. Md. (1st v.p. 1983-87). Methodist.

PATRICK, JOHN JOSEPH, social sciences educator; b. East Chicago, Ind., Apr. 14, 1935; s. John W. and Elizabeth (Lazar) P.; m. Patricia Grant, Aug. 17, 1963; children—Rebecca, Barbara. A.B., Dartmouth Coll., 1957; Ed.D., Ind. U., 1969. Social studies tchr. Roosevelt High Sch., East Chicago, 1957-62; social studies tchr. Lab. High Sch., U. Chgo., 1962-65; research assoc. Sch. Edn., Ind. U., Bloomington, 1965-69, asst. prof., 1969-74, assoc. prof., 1974-77, prof. edn., 1977—, dir. social studies devel. ctr., 1986—, dir. ERIC clearinghouse for social studies, social sci. edn., 1986—; bd. dirs. Biol. Scis. Curriculum Study, 1980-83; ednl. cons. Author: Progress of the Afro-American, 1968, The Young Voter, 1974; (with L. Ehman, Howard Mehlinger) Toward Effective Instruction in Secondary Social Studies, 1974, Lessons on the Northwest Ordinance, 1987; (with R. Remy) Civics for Americans, 1980, rev. edit. 1986; (with Mehlinger) American Political Behavior, 1972, rev. edit. 1980, (with C. Keller) Lessons on the Federalist Papers, 1987; America Past and Present, 1983; (with Carol Berkin) History of the American Nation, 1984, rev. edit., 1987; Lessons on the Constitution, 1985, James Madison and the Federalist Papers, 1990, How to Teach the Bill of Rights, 1991, Ideas of the Founders on Constitutional Government: Resources for Teachers of History and Government, 1991, Young Oxford Companion to the Supreme Court of the United States, 1994, Founding the Republic: A Documentary History, 1995. Bd. dirs. Law in Am. Soc. Found., 1984-88, Social Sci. Edn. consortium, 1984—; mem. Gov.'s Task Force on Citizenship Edn., Ind., 1982-87; active Ind. Commn. on Bicentennial of U.S. Constn., 1986-92; bd. dirs. Coun. for the Advancement of Citizenship, Nat. History Edn. Network, 1994-96; mem. Natr. Coun. for History Standards, 1991-94. Mem. ASCD, Nat. Coun. Social Studies, Social Sci. Edn. Consortium (v.p. 1985-87), Coun. for Basic Edn., Am. Polit. Sci. Assn., Am. Hist. Assn., Orgn. Am. Historians, Phi Delta Kappa. Home: 1209 E University St Bloomington IN 47401-5045 Office: Ind U 2805 E 10th St Bloomington IN 47408-2601

PATRICK, LYNN ALLEN, lawyer, construction and land development company executive; b. Stettler, Alta., Can., Dec. 7, 1935; s. Allen Russell and Florence Lorene (Lynn) P.; m. Roberta Colleen Hughes, May 9, 1959; children: Diane Elizabeth, Ross Gordon. B.Sc., U. Alta., Edmonton, Can., 1957, LL.B., 1960. Bar: Alta. 1961. Ptnr. Cormie Kennedy, Edmonton, Alta., 1961-83; sr. v.p., gen. counsel Mutual Fund Group, Edmonton, 1983-88; pres. Stuart Olson Constrn., Inc., Edmonton, 1989-92; v.p., corp. counsel, sec. The Churchill Corp., 1992—. Past pres., trustee Minerva Found., Edmonton; adv. council mem. Minster of Edn., Alta.; gov. Banff Ctr. Mem. Can. Bar Assn., Edmonton Bar Assn., Law Soc. Alta., Royal Glenora Club (Edmonton). Progessive. Home: 64 Quesnell Rd, Edmonton, AB Canada T5R 5N2 Office: The Churchill Corp, 10180 101st St Ste 2280, Edmonton, AB Canada T5J 3S4

PATRICK, MICHAEL WYNN, theatre executive; b. Columbus, Ga., May 17, 1950; m. Jayne Johnston, Mar. 26, 1976; 1 child, Michael W. II. BS, Columbus Coll., 1972. Successively dist. mgr., v.p. film, v.p. spl. projects Martin Theatres, Columbus, 1972-81; pres., chief exec. officer Carmike Cinemas, Columbus, 1981—; bd. dirs. Columbus Bank and Trust Co. Mem. Will Rogers Inst. (dir.), Variety Internat. (dir.), Motion Picture Pioneers (dir.), Green Island Country Club, Country Club of Columbus. Methodist. Avocations: golf, fishing. Office: Carmike Cinemas Inc 1301 1st Ave Columbus GA 31901-2109

PATRICK, MIKE, sports commentator; b. Clarksburg, W.Va.. BA in Speech, George Washington U., 1966. Broadcaster WVSC-Radio, Somerset, Pa., 1966-70; sports dir. WJXT-TV, Jacksonville, Fla., 1970-75; sports reporter, weekend anchor WJLA-TV, Washington, 1975-87; play-by-play NFL commentator ESPN, 1987—; commentator Jefferson Pilot football telecasts, 1984-85, ACC basketball; owner Patrick Prodns. Office: c/o ESPN ESPN Plaza Bristol CT 06010

PATRICK, UEAL EUGENE, oil company executive; b. Ky., Mar. 10, 1929; s. Clevel and Maxine (Hackworth) P.; m. Nancy Sparrow, Mar. 7, 1953; children: Steve, Rick, Sherry, Mark. BA, Mich. State U., 1955. Acct. Bond and Co., Jackson, Mich., 1955-57; contr., then exec. v.p., mgr. Midway Supply Co., Jackson, 1957-62; pres., chief exec. officer, bd. dirs. Patrick Petroleum Co., Mich., Jackson, 1969-95, Patrick Petroleum Corp., Jackson, 1962-95, Patrick Racing Team, Inc., 1971—; pres., chief exec. officer, sec., bd. dirs. Fayette Corp., 1966-78; pres., chief exec. officer, treas., Patrick Oil and Gas Corp., 1968-90; chmn. bd. Mark Aviation, Inc., 1971-81; chmn. bd., chief exec. officer Jet Way, Inc., 1971-81; chief exec. officer, bd. dirs. K & C Corp., 1974-81, Western Stamping Corp., 1972-79; pres., chief exec. officer Patrick Energy Co., 1980-90, Patrick Properties, Inc., 1980—; pres., bd. dirs. Patrick Petroleum Internat., Inc., 1972-90, Patrick Petroleum Internat. Australia, Inc., 1972-80, Patrick Petroleum Internat. Indonesia, Inc., 1972-80, Patrick Petroleum U.K. Ltd., 1974-80, Patrick Petroleum Italiana, Inc. (S.P.A.), 1974-80; chmn. bd. Championship Auto Racing Teams, Inc., 1978-82; chmn. bd., chief exec. officer, bd. dirs. Belibe Coal Corp., 1978-84, Black Nugget Coal Co., Inc., 1978-84, Patrick Coal Corp., 1978-84; sec.-treas. Jackson Towing Co., 1972-84; bd. dirs. Vermillion Bay Land Co., Jackson Found. With USAF, 1948-52. Mem. Am. Petroleum Inst., Ind. Petroleum Assn. Am. (bd. dirs. 1968-80), Oil Investment Inst. (gov. 1970-81), Mich. Oil and Gas Assocs., Detroit Athletic Club, Detroit Renaissance Club, Jackson Country Club. Republican. Office: 301 W Michigan Ave Jackson MI 49201-1316

PATRICK, WENDY LYNN, lawyer; b. Orange, Calif., Oct. 19, 1968. BA, UCLA, 1990; JD, Calif. Western Sch. of Law, 1994. Bar: Calif. 1994, U.S. Dist. Ct. (so. dist.) Calif. 1994, U.S. Ct. Appeals (9th cir.) 1995. Lawyer San Diego Pub. Defender's Office, 1994-97, San Diego Dist. Atty.'s Office, 1997—. Mem. Law Review Calif. Western Law Sch. Mem. San Diego County Bar Assn. Roman Catholic. Avocations: skiing, concert violinist, travel, karate. Office: San Diego Dist Atty 410 S Melrose Dr Ste 200 Vista CA 92083-6623

PATRICK, WILLIAM BRADSHAW, lawyer; b. Indpls., Nov. 29, 1923; s. Fae William and Mary (Bradshaw) P.; m. Ursula Lantzsch, Dec. 28, 1956; children: William Bradshaw, Ursula, Nancy. AB, The Principia, 1947; LLB, Harvard U., 1950. Bar: Ind. Supreme ct. 1950, U.S. Dist. Ct. (so. dist.) Ind. 1950, U.S. Ct. Apls. (7th cir.) 1961. Ptnr., Patrick & Patrick, Indpls., 1950-53; sole practice, Indpls., 1953—; gen. counsel Met. Planning Commn. Marion County and Indpls., 1955-66; dep. prosecutor Marion County, Ind., 1960-62; past pres., dir. The Cemetery Co., operating Meml. Park Cemetery, Indpls.; sec., dir. Rogers Typesetting Co., Indpls., 1966-85. Pres. Indpls. Legal Aid Soc., 1963. Lt. (j.g.) USNR, 1942-46. Recipient DeMolay Legion of Honor. Mem. ABA, Ind. Bar Assn., Indpls. Bar Assn., Lawyers Assn. Indpls., Indpls. Estate Planning Coun., Am. Legion, SAR (sec. Ind. Soc. 1953-59), Svc. Club Indpls., U.S. Navy League, Mil. Order Loyal Legion (comdr. Ind. soc.), Mason (33 degree), Shriners. Address: 7 N Meridian St Indianapolis IN 46204-3053

PATRICK, WILLIAM HARDY, JR., wetland biogeochemist, educator, laboratory director; b. Johns, Miss., Nov. 9, 1925; s. William Hardy and Alma (Webb) P.; m. Ruth Martin, Dec. 21, 1951; children: Terry Lynn, William Hardy, Carol Ann, Henry Carr. B.S., La. State U., 1950, M.S., 1951; Ph.D., La State U., 1954; D.Honoris Causa, U. Ghent (Belgium), 1979. Asst. prof. agronomy dept. La. State U., Baton Rouge, 1953-56, assoc. prof., 1956-61, prof., 1961-76, prof. marine scis., 1977-78, Boyd prof. marine scis., 1978—; dir. Wetland Biogeochemistry Inst., Baton Rouge; Moore lectr. in ecology U. Va., 1985, York lectr. U. Fla., 1989; cons. numerous govt., indsl. orgns. Contbr. articles to sci. jours. Organizer, dir. La. Methodist World Hunger Scholarship Program, Baton Rouge, 1979—. Served with AUS, 1944-46. grantee numerous research orgns., 1963—. Fellow AAAS, Am. Soc. Agronomy, Soil Sci. Soc. Am. (Internat. award 1992, Rsch. award 1993); mem. Sigma Xi, Phi Kappa Phi. Republican. Methodist. Home: 888 Dubois Dr Baton Rouge LA 70808-5008 Office: Louisiana St Univ Wetland Biogeochemistry Baton Rouge LA 70803

PATRICKS, EDWARD J, elementary education educator; b. Chgo., Jan. 19, 1958; s. John Anthony and Marion Nora (Kinnavy) P. Ed, Ill. Benedictine, Lisle, Ill., 1981. Cert. tchr., Ill. Sci. tchr. St. Pius X, Stickney, Ill., 1981-84; dept. chair, sci. tchr. St. Giles Junior High, Oak Park, Ill., 1984—. Commr. City of Berwyn, 1991—, North Berwyn Pk. Dist., 1995—; past commr. St. Mary of Celle Little League; sponsor Berwyn Playground and Recreation Commn., Berwyn Blazers Taveling Soccer; bd. dirs. Dem. Orgn. Berwyn, St. Mary of Celle, St. Vincent De Paul Conf. Mem. ASCD, NSTA, Nat. Cath. Educators Assn., Ill. Assn. Pk. Dists., Ill. Sheriffs Assn., Suburban Pks. and Recreation Divsn., Nat. Recreation and Pk. Assn., Berwyn Devel. Corp., KC (4 degree). Home: 1809 Euclid Ave Berwyn IL 60402-1845 Office: Saint Giles 1030 Linden Ave Oak Park IL 60302-1351

PATRIE, PETER HUGO, gaming control board investigator; b. Dayton, Ohio, Dec. 19, 1946; s. C. Hugo and Margaret (Penny) P.; m. Janis Lee Yates, Feb. 5, 1968; children: Peter Todd, Brent, Ryan. BSBA, Miami U., Oxford, Ohio, 1968; postgrad., U. Fla., 1968-69. Mgr. credit dept. Atlantic Nat. Bank, Jacksonville, Fla., 1970-72; regional credit mgr. Kaiser Cement & Gypsum, Long Beach, Calif., 1972-73; dist. mgr. ITT Consumer Fin., Denver, 1973-80; sr. v.p. Nev. First Bank, Reno, 1981-89, Bank of Am. Nev., Reno, 1989-90; gen. mgr. Silver State Thrift & Loan, Reno, 1990-94; investigator State of Nev. Gaming Control Bd., Carson City, 1995—; grad. asst. U. Fla. Grad. Sch., Gainesville, 1968; prof. Reno Bus. Coll., 1991. Mem. Western Indsl. Nev., Reno, 1989-91; tchr. Jr. Achievement-Bus. Alliance, Reno, 1990. Recipient Grad. Fellowship U. Fla. Grad. Sch., Gainesville, 1969. Mem. Sparks C. of C., Greenbrae Lions. Republican. Avocations: baseball cards, coins, artwork, real estate rentals. Office: 1150 E William St Carson City NV 89701-3109

PATRIKIS, ERNEST T., lawyer, banker; b. Lynn, Mass., Dec. 1, 1943; s. Theodore A. and Ethel (Stasinopolous) P.; m. Emily Herrick Trueblood, Mar. 18, 1972. BA, U. Mass., 1965; JD, Cornell U., 1968. Bar: N.Y. 1969. Exec. v.p., gen. counsel Fed. Res. Bank N.Y., 1968-95 1st v.p., 1995—; dep. gen. counsel Fed. Open Market Com., 1988-95. Contbr. articles to legal jours. Fellow Fgn. Policy Assn., 1995—. Fellow Fgn. Policy Assn.; mem. Assn. of Bar of City of N.Y. (banking law com. 1982-84, 90—, futures regulation com. 1986-89); N.Y. State Bar Assn. (chmn. com. internat. banking, securities and fin. transaction 1987-91, banking law com. 1986—, vice chmn. internat. practice sect. 1991—), ABA (subcom. on gen. banking matters 1986), Coun. on Fgn. Rels. Home: 20 E 9th St New York NY 10003-5944 Office: Fed Reserve Bank NY 33 Liberty St New York NY 10045-1003

PATRON, JUNE EILEEN, former government official; b. N.Y.C., May 15; d. Irving B. and Mollie Patron; B.A. in Govt. with honors, Clark U., Worcester, Mass., 1965; M.A., Am. U., 1967. With U.S. Dept. of Labor, 1966-95, dir. Black Lung benefits program, 1976-79, asst. adminstr. pension and welfare benefit programs, 1979-84, assoc. dir. pension and welfare benefit programs, 1984-88, dir. program svcs., 1988-95, ret., 1995; mem. Sr. Exec. Svc. Recipient various awards Dept. Labor. Home: 3001 Veazey Ter NW Washington DC 20008-5454

PATRON, NICHOLAS VICTOR, special education educator; b. Canton, Ohio, Mar. 26, 1951; s. Nicholas Victor and Mary Josephine (Ottavio) P. BA, Walsh U., Canton, Ohio, 1973. Elem. tchr. Diocese of Youngstown Schs., Canton, 1973-87; spl. edn. tchr. Plain Local Schs., Canton, 1987—; bus. dir. Head of the Class, Canton, 1992—. Libr. substitute Stark County Libr., Canton, 1990—. Named Canton's Best Tchr., City of Canton, 1983; recipient Nat. Honor Soc. award Glen Oak H.S., 1994. Fellow NEA, Ohio Tchr.'s Retirement Assn. Avocations: art, reading, crafts, gardening, walking.

PATRON, SUSAN HALL, librarian, writer; b. San Gabriel, Calif., Mar. 18, 1948; d. George Thomas and Rubye Denver (Brewer) H.; m. René Albert Patron, July 27, 1969. BA, Pitzer Coll., 1969; MLS, Immaculate Heart Coll., 1972. Children's libr. LA Pub. Libr., 1972-79, sr. children's libr., 1980-92; reviewer Sch. Libr. Jour., 1980—, Pubs. Weekly, 1986-91, The Five Owls, 1987-95. Author: (with Christopher Weiman) Marbled Papers, 1979, Burgoo Stew, 1991, Five Bad Boys, Billy Que, and the Dustdobbin, 1992, Maybe Yes, Maybe No, Maybe Maybe, 1993 (ALA Notable Book 1994), Bobbin Dustdobbin, 1993, Dark Cloud Strong Breeze, 1994. Mem. ALA (Caldecott award com. 1988), PEN (mem. West Lit. awards jury 1997), Calif. Libr. Assn. (Patricia Beatty award com. 1987-89, 91-92), Internat. Bd. on Books for Young Children, Soc. Children's Book Writers and Illustrators, So. Calif. Coun. on Lit. for Children and Young People (awards com. 1985), Authors Guild, Friends of Children and Lit. (mem. award com. 1984). Office: LA Pub Libr Childrens Svcs 630 W 5th St Los Angeles CA 90071-2002

PATRONELLI, RAYMOND, church administrator. Asst. gen. overseer, minister Christian Ch. of N. Am., Christian Assembly Tampa. Office: Christian Church of North Am 6203 Kelly Rd Plant City FL 33565-3567*

PATTEN, BEBE HARRISON, minister, chancellor; b. Waverly, Tenn., Sept. 3, 1913; d. Newton Felix and Mattie Priscilla (Whitson) Harrison; m. Carl Thomas Patten, Oct. 23, 1935; children: Priscilla Carla and Bebe Rebecca (twins), Carl Thomas. D.D., McKinley-Roosevelt Coll., 1941; D.Litt., Temple Hall Coll. and Sem., 1943. Ordained to ministry Ministerial Assn. of Evangelism, 1935; evangelist in various cities of U.S., 1933-50; founder, pres. Christian Evang. Chs. Am., Inc., Oakland, Calif., 1944—, Patten Acad. Christian Edn., Oakland, 1944—, Patten Bible Coll., Oakland, 1944-83; chancellor Patten Coll., Oakland, 1983—; founder, pastor Christian Cathedral of Oakland, 1950—; held pvt. interviews with David Ben-Gurion, 1972, Menachim Begin, 1977, Yitzhak Shamir, 1991; condr. Sta. KUSW world-wide radio ministry, 70 countries around the world, 1989-90, Stas. WHRI and WWCR world coverage short wave, 1990—. Founder, condr.: radio program The Shepherd Hour, 1934—; daily TV, 1976—, nationwide telecast, 1979—; Author: Give Me Back My Soul, 1973; Editor: Trumpet Call, 1953—; composer 20 gospel and religious songs, 1945—. Mem. exec. bd. Bar-Ilan U. Assn., Israel, 1983; mem. global bd. trustees Bar-Ilan U., 1991. Recipient numerous awards including medallion Ministry of Religious Affairs, Israel, 1969; medal Govt. Press Office, Jerusalem, 1971; Christian honoree of yr. Jewish Nat. Fund of No. Calif., 1975; Hidden Heroine award San Francisco Bay coun. Girl Scouts U.S.A., 1976, Golden State award Who's Who Hist. Soc., 1988; Ben-Gurion medallion Ben-Gurion Rsch. Inst., 1977; Resolutions of Commendation, Calif. Senate Rules Com., 1978, 94, Disting. Leadership award Ch. of God Sch. of Theology, 1996; hon. fellow Bar-Ilan U., Israel, 1981; Dr. Bebe Patten Social Action chair established Bar-Ilan U., 1982. Mem. Am. Assn. for Higher Edn., Religious Edn. Assn., Am. Acad. Religion and Soc. Bibl. Lit., Zionist Orgn. Am., Am. Assn. Pres. of Ind. Colls. and Univs., Am. Jewish Hist. Soc., Am.-Isreal Pub. Affairs Com. Address: 2433 Coolidge Ave Oakland CA 94601-2630 *He that labors in any great or laudable undertaking has his fatigues first supported by hope, and afterwards rewarded by joy. To strive with difficulties, and to conquer them, is the highest human felicity. I am not afraid of tomorrow for I have seen yesterday and I love today.*

PATTEN, BERNARD MICHAEL, neurologist, writer, educator; b. N.Y.C., Mar. 23, 1941; s. Bernard M. and Olga (Vaccaro) P.; m. Ethel Doudine, June 18, 1964; children: Allegra, Craig. AB summa cum laude, Columbia Coll., 1962; MD, Columbia U., 1966. Med. intern N.Y. Hosp. Cornell Med. Ctr., N.Y.C., 1966-67; resident neurologist Columbia Presbyn. Med. Ctr., N.Y.C., 1967-69, chief resident neurologist, 1969-70; assoc. prof. neurology Baylor Coll. Medicine, Houston, 1973-95; ret., 1995; asst. chief med. neurology NIH, Bethesda, Md., 1970-73; mem. med. bd. Nat. Myasthenia Gravis Found., 1973—, Nat. AmyoTrophic Lateral Sclerosis Found., 1982—, Nat. Myositis Assn., 1995—. Contbr. more than 200 articles to profl. jours. With USPHS, 1970-73. Rsch. grantee NIH, pvt. founds., nat. health orgns. Fellow ACP, Royal Coll. Physicians. Roman Catholic. Achievements include discoverer (with others) L-Dopa for Parkinson's disease; pioneered use of immune suppression for myasthenia gravis, diagnosis and treatment of medical and neurologcal complications of breast implants. Home: 1019 Baronridge Dr Seabrook TX 77586-4001

PATTEN, CHARLES ANTHONY, management consultant, retired manufacturing company executive, author; b. Allentown, Pa., May 12, 1920; s. Charles Henerie and Mae (Doyle) P.; m. Kathleen Marie Breene, Jan. 6, 1951; children: Charles Anthony Jr., Amy Elizabeth Goddard, Nancy Kathleen Hansen. B.S.M.E., Lehigh U., 1942. With Joy Mfg. Co., 1947-63, works mgr., 1956-63; v.p. mfg. White Motor Corp., 1963-68, Colt Industries, 1968-69; With Dravo Corp., Pitts., 1942-47, 69-85; gen. mgr. engring. works div. Dravo Corp., 1970-71, corp. v.p., gen. mgr. engring. works div., 1971-75, corp. group v.p., chief exec. officer Dravo Mfg. Group, 1975-81, corp. sr. v.p., mem. corp. policy com., chief exec. officer Dravo Mfg. Group, 1981-83, corp. sr. v.p., asst. to pres. and chief exec. officer, mem. exec. com., 1984-85; pres. C.A. Patten Enterprises, 1985—; bd. dirs., v.p. Dravo (Can.) Ltd., 1975-85; dir., pres. Dravo-Okura Co. Ltd., 1974-79; dir. Dravo Mfg. (Can.) Ltd., 1975-83, Tru Weld Grating Inc., 1983-85; v.p. Dravo Internat., Inc., 1974-85. Trustee Ohio Valley Gen. Hosp., McKees Rocks, Pa., 1975-82, Marietta (Ohio) Coll., 1979-89, emeritus trustee, 1989—; bd. dirs. Vocat. Rehab. Center of Allegheny County, 1972-79, Jr. Achievement of S.W. Pa., 1975-80. Mem. ASME, Neville Island Mfrs. Assn. (pres. 1975-85), Am. Arbitration Assn. (panel of arbitrators, 1989-95), Duquesne Club. Republican. Roman Catholic. Home and Office: 2304 Clearvue Rd Pittsburgh PA 15237-1632 *The successful manager is a time-oriented goal setter. Without waiting for others to ask him, he envisions things that should happen and thinks through possible paths to reach the goals. When the goals are reached, he is quick to laud and praise his people for their accomplishment.*

PATTEN, DUNCAN THEUNISSEN, ecologist educator; b. Detroit, Oct. 13, 1934; s. Marc T. and Doris (Miller) P.; m. Eva Chittenden, July 27, 1957; children: Michael, Marc, Robin, Scott. BA, Amherst Coll., 1956; MS, U. Mass., Amherst, 1959; PhD, Duke U., 1962. Asst. prof. ecology Va. Poly. Inst., Blacksburg, 1962-65; asst. prof. ecology Ariz. State U., Tempe, 1965-67, assoc. prof., 1967-73, prof., 1973-95, prof. emeritus, 1995—, dir. ctr. environ. studies, 1980-95. Contbr. articles to profl. jours. Fellow AAAS, Ariz.-Nev. Acad. Sci.; mem. Ecol. Soc. Am. (bus. mgr. 1979-95), Brit. Ecol. Soc., Soc. Range Mgmt., Am. Inst. Biol. Scis., Soc. Wetland Scientists (pres. 1996-97), Am. Water Resource Assn., Am. Geophys. Union, Soc. Conservation Biology, Sigma Xi. Office: Arizona State Univ Ctr for Environ Studies Box 873211 Tempe AZ 85287-3211

PATTEN, LANNY RAY, industrial gas industry executive; b. St. Joseph, Mo., July 31, 1934; s. E.L. and Sarah Catherine (Langner) P.; m. Ann Rogers Hall, Oct. 26, 1957; children: David, John, Jeffrey, Mark. BS in Engring., Iowa State U., 1956; AMP, Harvard U., 1976. Field engr. Carrier Corp., Kansas City, Mo., 1957; sales engr. Air Products and Chems., Inc., Allentown, Pitts., Chgo., 1960-63; dist. mgr. Air Products and Chems., Inc., Cleve., 1964-66; region mgr. Air Products and Chems., Inc., Pitts., 1966-68; div. gen. sales mgr. Air Products and Chems., Inc., Allentown, Pa., 1969-75; v.p., div. gen. mgr. Air Products and Chems., Inc., Allentown, 1975-88, sr. v.p., gases and equipment, 1988-90; pres., COO Airgas Inc., Radnor, Pa., 1990-91; pres., chief exec. officer CylServ, Inc., West Choshohocken, Pa., 1992—. Chmn. Lehigh U. Parents Assn., Bethlehem, Pa., 1977-90; campaign com. chmn. Good Shepherd Home, Allentown, 1989-90; mem. Boy Scouts Am., Allentown, 1978-90; pres., coach Youth Baseball Assn., Allentown, 1970-83. USAF Officer, 1957-60. Recipient PACE award for Engring. Achievement Iowa State U., 1990, Friend of Lehigh award, 1991. Mem. Compressed Gas Assn. (exec. bd. dirs. 1977-91), Internat. Oxygen Mfg. Assn. Allentown C. of C. (exec. bd. dirs. 1978-82), Kappa Sigma. Republican. Episcopalian. Avocations: baseball, golf, reading. Home: 1306 Club House Rd Gladwyne PA 19035-1006

PATTEN, ROBERT LOWRY, English language educator; b. Oklahoma City, Apr. 26, 1939; s. Charles H. and Helen (Lowry) P.; m. Faith L. Harris, June 12, 1960 (div. 1974); children: Jocelyn S., Christina S. BA, Swarthmore Coll., 1960; MA, Princeton U., 1963, PhD, 1965. Lectr. Bryn Mawr (Pa.) Coll., 1964-66, asst. prof. English, 1966-69; asst. prof. Rice U., Houston, 1969-71, assoc. prof., 1971-76, prof. English, 1976—, chair, dept. of English, 1991-92, master Grad. House, 1992-95; pres. PEN S.W., Houston, 1989-92. Author: Charles Dickens and His Publishers, 1978, George Cruikshank's Life, Times and Art, vol. 1, 1992, vol. 2, 1996; editor: (book by Charles Dickens) Pickwick Papers, 1972, George Cruikshank: A Revaluation, 1974, 2d edit., 1992, (with John O. Jordan) Literature in the Marketplace, 1995; editor SEL: Studies in English Lit., 1978-84, 90—. Bd. dirs. Cultural Arts Coun., Houston, 1979-80, Tex.Com. for the Humanities, 1979-80; pres., bd. dirs. Houston Ctr. for the Humanities, 1976-84. NEH fellow, 1968-69, 77-78, 87-88; Guggenheim fellow, 1980-81; Nat. Humanities Ctr. fellow, 1987-88; Nat. Gallery of Art Assoc., 1988-89. Mem. AAUP, MLA, PEN Am. Ctr., Dickens Fellowship, Dickens Soc., Phi Beta Kappa (pres. Beta chpt. Tex. 1991-94, 97—). Episcopalian. Avocations: travel, opera. Office: Rice U Dept English MS 30 6100 Main St Houston TX 77005-1827

PATTEN, RONALD JAMES, university dean; b. Iron Mountain, Mich., July 17, 1935; s. Rudolph Joseph and Cecelia (Fuse) Pataconi; m. Shirley Ann Bierman, Sept. 5, 1959; children: Christine Marie, Cheryl Ann, Charlene Denise. BA, Mich. State U., 1957, MA, 1959; PhD, U. Ala., 1963. Acct. Price Waterhouse & Co., Detroit, 1958; instr. No. Ill. U., 1959-60; asst. prof. U. Colo., 1963-65; assoc. prof. Va. Poly. Inst. and State U., 1965-67, prof., 1967-73, head dept. accounting, 1966-73; dir. research Financial Accounting Standards Bd., Conn., 1973-74; dean Sch. Bus. Adminstrn., U. Conn., Storrs, 1974-88; chief of party-Eastern Caribbean Arthur D. Little Internat., 1988-89; dean Coll. Commerce and Kellstadt Grad. Sch. Bus. De Paul U., Chgo., 1989—; cons. to industry; bd. dirs. Transco Inc.; mem. individual investors adv. com. N.Y. Stock Exch., 1993—. Contbr. articles to profl. jours., chpts. to books. Bd. dirs. U.S. com. UNICEF, Chgo. 2d lt. F.A. AUS, 1958. Recipient Nat. Quartermaster award Nat. Quartermaster, Assn., 1956. Mem. AICPA, Am. Acctg. Assn., Inst. Mgmt. Accts., Acad. Internat. Bus. (Dean of Yr. award 1987), Internat. Assn. for Acctg. Edn. and Rsch., Chgo. Coun. Fgn. Rels., Ill. Coun. Econ. Edn. (Chgo., trustee 1989—), Execs. Club Chgo., Econ. Club Chgo., Pacioli Soc., Heidelberg Club, Internat., Scabbard and Blade, Golden Key, Beta Gamma Sigma (mem. bd. govs. 1975-90, nat. sec.-treas. 1980-82, nat. v.p. 1982-84, nat. pres. 1984-86), Beta Alpha Psi (bd. dirs. 1992-94), Delta Sigma Pi, Phi Kappa Phi, Delta Mu Delta. Avocations: hiking, skiing, walking, golf, travel. Home: 334 N Montclair Ave Glen Ellyn IL 60137-5253

PATTEN, THOMAS HENRY, JR., management, human resources educator; b. Cambridge, Mass., Mar. 24, 1929; s. Thomas Henry and Lydia Mildred (Lindgren) P.; m. Jule Ann Miller, Aug. 27, 1972; children—Laurie Kathryn, Rhonda Josephine, Jenny Lydia. A.B., Brown U., 1953; M.S., Cornell U., 1955, Ph.D., 1959. Dir. program planning Ford Motor Co., Dearborn, Mich., 1957-65; prof. mgmt. and sociology U. Detroit, 1965-67; prof. orgnl. behavior and personnel mgmt. Sch. Labor and Indsl. Relations, Mich. State U., E. Lansing, 1967-84; prof. mgmt. and human resources Calif. State Poly. U., Pomona, 1984—; cons. in field. Author: The Foreman: The Forgotten Man of Management, 1968, Manpower Planning and the Development of Human Resources, 1971, OD-Emerging Dimensions and Concepts, 1973, A Bibliography of Compensation Planning and Administration, 1960-1974, 2d rev. edit., 1981, 3d rev. edit., 1987, Pay: Employee Compensation and Incentive Plans, 1977, Classics of Personnel Management, 1979, Organizational Development Through Teambuilding, 1981, A Manager's Guide to Performance Appraisal, 1982, Fair Pay: The Managerial Challenge of Comparable Job Worth and Job Evaluation, 1988, Exercises for Developing Human Resources Management Skills, 1996. Served with USMC, 1946-51. Mem. ASTD (chmn. orgn. devel. div. 1972), Indsl. Rels. Rsch. Assn. (chpt. pres. 1970-71), Am. Sociol. Assn., Internat. Pers. Mgmt. Assn., Internat. Indsl. Rels. Assn., Inst. Applied Behavioral Sic., Am. Compensation Assn. Home: 353 Independence Dr Claremont CA 91711-1954 Office: Calif State Poly U Dept Mgmt & Human Resources 3801 W Temple Ave Pomona CA 91768-2557 *Human values come first.*

PATTEN, THOMAS LOUIS, lawyer; b. Mo., Oct. 3, 1945; m. Sherry V. Patten; children: Elizabeth, Caroline, Brooke. BS, U. Mo., 1967, JD, 1969. Bar: Mo. 1969, D.C. 1972, U.S. Dist. Ct. D.C. 1972, U.S. Claims Ct. 1972, U.S. Ct. Appeals (fed. cir.) 1972, U.S. Supreme Ct. 1972, U.S. Ct. Appeals (9th cir.) 1974, U.S. Ct. Appeals (4th cir.) 1981, Va. 1983, U.S. Dist. Ct. (ea. and we. dists.) Va. 1983. Ptnr Latham & Watkins, Washington. Fellow Am. Coll. Trial Lawyers. Office: Latham & Watkins Ste 1300 1001 Pennsylvania Ave NW Washington DC 20004-2505

PATTENAUDE, RICHARD LOUIS, university administrator; b. Seattle, Feb. 22, 1946; s. Joseph Arthur and Alice June (Vrooman) P.; m. Michele Arlen Stevenson, May 31, 1975; children: Lauren, Lisa, Dylan, Joshua. BA with honors in Econs., Calif. State U.-San Jose, 1968; PhD in Polit. Sci., U. Colo., 1974. Assoc. prof. Drake U., Des Moines, 1974-80, assoc. dean liberal arts, 1976-80; asst. v.p. acad. affairs SUNY-Binghamton, 1980-82, assoc. v.p., 1982-86; v.p. acad. affairs, prof. polit. sci. Cen. Conn. State U., New Britain, 1986-91; pres. U. So. Maine, Portland, 1991—; cons. in field; panelist, presenter various nat. higher edn. meetings. Contbr. numerous articles to profl. jours., also chpts. to books in field. Commnr. Occupational and Licensing Commn., Iowa, 1978-80; mem. Gov's Com. Efficiency, 1979; mem. adv. council planning dept. City of Binghamton, 1984—; bd. dirs. Broome County United Way, 1985, Greater Hartford Red Cross, 1991-93, Mercy Hosp., Portland, 1992—, Portland Symphony Orch., Maine Devel. Found., Maine Sci. and Tech. Found, Porland Mus. Art, Blue Cross/Blue Shield of Maine, Inst. Civic Leadership, 1992-94. Served with U.S. Army, 1969-71, Vietnam. Fanny W. Ames scholar, 1965; Title II fellow, 1970. Mem. ASPA, AAUP, Assn. Instl. Research and Planning Officers (v.p. 1983-84, pres. 1984-85), Am. Assn. State Colls. and Univs. (state rep. 1995—), Greater Portland C. of C. Office: U So Maine Office of the Pres Portland ME 04103

PATTERSON, ALBERT LOVE III, career military officer; b. Columbus, Ga., Sept. 18, 1949; s. John Malcolm and Mary Joe (McGowin) P.; m. Kathryn Stuart Prillaman, June 26, 1976; children: David, Benjamin, Timothy. BS, U.S. Mil. Acad., West Point, N.Y., 1971, Ga. Inst. Technology, Atlanta, 1982; MS, Ga. Inst. Technology, Atlanta, 1982. Enlisted U.S. Army, 1971, advanced through grades to col.; ops. officer, cmdr. C Troop 2d Infantry Divsn. U.S. Army, Camp Stanley, Korea, 1983-84; asst. prof. aerospace engring. U.S. Mil. Acad. U.S. Army, 1984-87; exec. officer aviation brigade 1st Infantry Divsn. U.S. Army, Ft. Riley, Kans., 1987-89; cmdr. 4/501 aviation 17th Aviation Brigade U.S. Army, Camp Page, Korea, 1989-91; dep. dir. combat devel., cmdr. 1st Aviation Brigade U.S. Army Aviation Ctr. and Sch., Ft. Rucker, Ala., 1992-95; chief aviation divsn. force devel. Office Chief of Staff U.S. Dept. Army, Pentagon, 1995—. Coun. exec. bd. Boy Scouts Am., 1992-95. Mem. Assn. U.S. Army, Army Aviation Assn. Am., Assn. Grads. U.S. Army War Coll., Assn. Grads. U.S. Army War Coll., Am. Legion. Methodist. Avocations: hiking, camping, running, woodworking. Home: 9611 Oakington Dr Fairfax Station VA 22039-2640 Office: Aviation Divsn HQDA ODCSOPS 400 Army Pentagon Washington DC 20310-0400

PATTERSON, AUBREY BURNS, JR., banker; b. Grenada, Miss., Sept. 25, 1942; s. Aubrey Burns and Elizabeth (Staten) P.; m. Ruby Kathryn Clegg, Dec. 12, 1964; children: Aubrey B. III, Clayton H., Jennifer L. BBA, U. Miss., 1964; MBA, Mich. State U., 1969; student, Grad. Sch. Banking, U. Wis. With Bank of Miss., Tupelo, 1972—, pres., 1983—, chmn., chief exec. officer, 1990—; chmn., CEO BancorpSouth, Inc.; bd. dirs. Vol. Bank, Jackson, Tenn. Former chmn. bd. dirs. Salvation Army, Tupelo, 1978—; bd. dirs. Cmty. Devel. Found., chmn. bd., 1994-95; bd. dirs. Columbia Theol. Sem., Decatur, Ga., Miss. Univ. for Women Found., Presbyn. Ch. U.S.A. Found., Miss. Econ. Coun., Jackson, 1986—, chmn., 1994; bd. dirs. North Miss. Health Svcs. Inc., 1987—, also exec. com.; moderator St. Andrews Presbytery Presbyn. Ch. USA; pres., bd. dirs. U. Miss. Found. Capt. USAF, 1965-72. Decorated Air Force Commendation medal, Meritorious Svc. medal. Mem. ABA (govt. rels. coun.), Am. Bankers Assn., Miss. Bankers Assn. (pres. 1995—), Soc. Internat. Bus. Fellows, Bankers Adv. Coun., Tupelo Country Club, Univ. Club, Kiwanis (pres. Tupelo 1987), Beta Gamma Sigma, Beta Alpha Psi. Presbyterian. Home: 1 Overdale Dr Tupelo MS 38801-1237 Office: Bancorp Miss PO Box 789 Tupelo MS 38802

PATTERSON, BEVERLY ANN GROSS, fund raising consultant, grant writer, federal grants administrator, social services administrator, poet; b. Pauls Valley, Okla., Aug. 5, 1938; d. Wilburn G. Jack and Mildred E. (Steward) Gross; m. Kenneth Dean Patterson, June 18, 1960 (div. 1976); children: Tracy Dean, Nancy Ann Patterson-McArthur, Beverly Jeanne Patterson-Wertman. AA, Modesto (Calif.) Jr. Coll., 1958; BA in Social Sci., Fresno (Calif.) State U., 1960; M in Community Counseling, Coll. Idaho; postgrad., Stanislaus State Coll., Turlock, Calif., U. Idaho, Boise (Idaho) State U. Cert. secondary tchr., Calif., Idaho, lic. real estate agt., Idaho. Secondary tchr. Ceres and Modesto Calif., Payette and Weiser Idaho, Ontario Oreg., 1960-67; dir. vol. svcs. mental retardation and child devel. State of Idaho, 1967-70, cons. dir. vol. svcs. health and welfare, 1970-72; dir. Ret. Sr. Vol. Program, Boise, 1972-74; exec. dir. Idaho Nurses Assn., Boise, 1974-76; community svcs. adminstr. City of Davis, Calif., 1976-78; dir. devel. and fundraising Mercy Med. Ctr., Nampa, Idaho, 1978-85; exec. dir. St. Alphonsus Med. Ctr. Found., Boise, 1985-87; dir. devel. and gift planning Idaho Youth Ranch, Boise, 1989-94; fund devel. cons. Mercy Housing, Nampa, Idaho, 1994-96, Pratt Ranch Boys Home, Emmett, Idaho, 1994-96, Northwest Childrens Home, Lewiston, Idaho, 1994-96, Idaho Spl. Olympics, Boise, 1994-95, Idaho Found. for Parks and Lands, Boise, 1994-95, St. Vincent de Paul, Inc., Boise, 1995-96, Nampa Shelter Found., Inc., 1994-95, Turning Point Inc., Nampa, 1994-95, Port of Hope Treatment Ctr. Inc., Boise, 1994-97, Idaho Theater for Youth, Inc., Boise, 1995-96, Boise Tennis Coalition, Inc., 1995—, El Ada Cmty. Action Ctr., Boise, 1995, Hemophilia Found. Idaho, 1995-96, Boise YWCA, 1996, Marsing (Idaho) Sch. Dist., 1996—; and many more; founder Fellowship Christian Adult Singles, Boise, 1974; cons., exec. dir. Boise Hotline, 1988-90; co-dir. ACOA workshop leader Child Within Concepts, Inc., Boise, 1987—; cons. coord. Rural Hosp. Edn. Consortium, 1988; cons. hosp. fund devel. and cmty. resources Gritman Meml. Hosp., Moscow, Idaho, 1987-88; cons., conf. coord. State of Idaho, 1987-88; counsel Adult Children of Alcoholics, 1991; pres. Nonprofit Solutions, Inc., Boise, 1995—; co-dir. Child Within Concepts, Inc., Meridian, 1996—; pres. Q&A Distbg. and Cons., Meridian, Idaho, 1994-95; 501 coord. CellNet of Idaho, Boise, 1996-97; cmty. resource devel. specialist Idaho Dept. Hwy., 1997—. Contbr. articles to profl. jours. Coord. Idaho Golf Angels Open Pro-Am Tournament, Boise, 1989-91; founding exec. v.p. Coll. Fund for Students Surviving Cancer, 1993-96; bd. dirs. Arthritis Found., Idaho, 1984-86, Idaho Mental Health Assn., 1978-97; founder Ctrl. Vol. Bur., Boise, 1971. Named Idaho Statesman Disting. Citizen, 1985. Mem. Nat. Assn. for Hosp. Devel. (accredited, treas. 1980, accreditation chmn. 1984-86, conf. chmn. 1982, 85), Assn. Healthcare in Philanthrophy (accredited), Nat. Soc. Fund Raising Execs., Idaho Devel. Network, Choices in Giving, Inc., Nationwide Auto Club (fleet dir. 1997—). Mem. Community Christian Ch. Avocations: golf, family activities. Office: PO Box 213 Meridian ID 83680-0213 Home and Office: Child Within Concepts Rt 1 Box 1277A Homedale ID 83628

PATTERSON, CHARLES DAROLD, librarian, educator; b. Wahpeton, N.D., Aug. 8, 1928; s. Charles Irwin and Inez Fern (Slagg) P. B.Sc., Bemidji State U., 1950; M.A., U. Minn., 1956; M.Music, W.Va. U., 1964; advanced cert., U. Pitts., 1968, Ph.D., 1971. Tchr. music Fargo (N.D.) public schs., 1950; jr. reference librarian U. Minn. Libraries, 1954-55; head librarian Bemidji (Minn.) State U., 1955-58; dir. libraries, asst. prof. Glenville (W.Va.) State Coll., 1958-62; asst. prof. W.Va. U., 1962-66; instr. Grad. Sch. Library and Info. Scis. U. Pitts., 1966-71, asst. prof., 1971-72; assoc. prof. Sch. Library and Info. Sci. La. State U., Baton Rouge, 1972-78; prof. Sch. Library and Info. Sci. La. State U., 1978-93; prof. emeritus, 1993; Del. La. Gov.'s Conf. on Library and Info. Services, 1978. Author: Analysis of Library of Congress Music Subject Headings, 1971, JEL Cumulative Index, 1979, supplement, 1982, (with D.G. Davis) ARBA Guide to Library Science Literature, 1987; editor: W.Va. Libraries, 1963-66; mem. editorial bd.; Jour. of Edn. for Librarianship, 1975-79, editor, 1980-84; editor: Jour. Edn. for Library and Info. Sci., 1984-88; asst. editor Reference Services Review, 1986-93; contbr. articles to profl. jours. Served with U.S. Army, 1950-52. Recipient La. State U. Faculty Excellence award, 1984, ALA/Beta Phi Mu award, 1989. Mem. ALA (chmn. scholarship jury 1972-73), W.Va. Library Assn. (chmn. coll. and univ. library sect. 1960-61, exec. bd. 1960-61, 64-66), Assn. Coll. and Research Libraries (pres. Tri-state chpt. 1972), Assn. Am. Library Schs. (exec. bd. 1980-88), La. Library Assn., Southeastern Library Assn., AAUP (pres. chpt. 1985-86), Am. Guild Organists (dean chpt. 1985-86), Pitts. Bibliophiles, Univ. Chamber Music Soc. (pres., dir. 1979-80), Beta Phi Mu. (dir.-at-large 1982-85). Methodist. Home: 1480 Kenmore Ave Baton Rouge LA 70808-1130 also: Birchmont Beach Bemidji MN 56601 Office: La State U Sch Libr and Info Sci Baton Rouge LA 70803 *When one is confident in his own mind that he has, with given abilities, done his very best, then perhaps he has paid for his niche in eternity.*

PATTERSON, CHRISTOPHER NIDA, lawyer; b. Washington Courthouse, Ohio, Apr. 17, 1960; s. Donis Dean and JoAnne (Nida) O.; children: Travis, Kirsten. BA, Clemson U., 1982; JD, Nova U., 1985. Bar: Fla. 1985, U.S. Dist. Ct. (mid. dist.) Fla. 1985, U.S. Ct. Mil. Rev. 1986, U.S. Ct. Mil. Appeals 1987, U.S. Dist. Ct. (ea. dist.) Va. 1987, U.S. Supreme Ct. 1990, U.S. Ct. Appeals (11th cir.) 1992, U.S. Dist. Ct. (no. dist.) Fla. 1992, U.S. Dist. Ct. (so. dist.) Tex. 1995; cert. criminal trial lawyer Fla. Bar. and Nat. Bd. Trial Advocacy. Prosecutor Fla. State Attys. Office, Orlando, Fla., 1985; spl. asst. U.S. Atty. U.S. Dist. Ct. (ea. dist.) Va., 1987-90; ptnr. Patterson, Hauversburk and Cassidy, Panama City, Fla., 1992—; adj. prof. law Gulf Coast Coll. Author: Queen's Pawn, 1996, Treasure Trove, 1997. Capt. JAGC, U.S. Army, 1986-92, Desert Storm. Mem. Nat. Assn. Criminal Def. Lawyers, Fla. Assn. Criminal Def. Lawyers, Acad. Fla. Trial Lawyers, Fla. Bar (criminal law sect., mil. law standing com., Pro Bono Svc. award), Bay County Bar Assn. Episcopalian. Avocations: athletics, triathlons. Office: PO Box 1368 303 Magnolia Ave Panama City FL 32401-3124

PATTERSON, CLAIRE ANN, vocational educator; b. Cin., Dec. 28, 1950; d. Lloyd E. and Ruth T. (Flaherty) Lachtrupp; m. Calvin Stanley Patterson, Jr., July 14, 1973; children: Christopher, Alicia. BS, U. Cin., 1973, MEd, 1980. Cert. elem. tchr., elem. supr., secondary math, secondary prin., asst. supt., Ohio, Va., P.R. Third grade tchr. Acadamia de Aguidilla, P.R., 1973-74; fifth grade tchr. Our Lady of the Rosary, Norfolk, Va., 1974-76; jr. high math and sci. tchr. Yavneh Hebrew Day Sch., Cin., 1976-79; math tchr. Winton Woods City Schs., Cin., 1979-80; math. coord. Great Oaks Inst. of Tech. and Career Devel., Cin., 1980-86, benefits coord./personnel profl., 1986-88, career devel. mgr., 1987-93, asst. dir., 1993—; ednl. cons. schs. in Ohio, 1988—. Author: Let's Celebrate Math, 1991; contbr. articles to profl. jours. Mem. Ohio Career Devel. Task Frce, 1991-93. Recipient Career Coord. award State of Ohio, 1993. Mem. Ohio Vocat. Assn. (com. chmn. 1990-93, OVA Pacesetter award 1991, 92, 93), Career Edn. Assn. (pres. 1992-93), Nat. Coun. Local Adminstrs., S.W. Career Coun. (pres. 1991-92), Ohio Vocat. Edn. Leadership Inst. (grad. 1993). Republican. Roman Catholic. Avocations: writing murder-mystery plays, travel, reading. Office: Great Oaks Inst Tech and Career Devel 3254 E Kemper Rd Cincinnati OH 45241-1540

PATTERSON, DAVID ANDREW, computer scientist, educator, consultant; b. Evergreen Park, Ill., Nov. 16, 1947; s. David Dwight and Lucie Jeanette (Ekstrom) P.; m. Linda Ann Crandall, Sept. 4, 1967; children: David Adam, Michael Andrew. BS in Math., UCLA, 1969, MS in Computer Sci., 1970, PhD, 1976. Mem. tech. staff Hughes Aircraft Co., L.A., 1972-76, Thinking Machines Corp., Cambridge, Mass., 1979; prof. computer sci. div. U. Calif., Berkeley, 1977—, chmn., 1990-93, Pardee chair, 1992—; cons. Sun Microsystems, Inc., Mountain View, Calif., 1984—; com. to study scope and role of computer sci. NAS, Washington, 1990-92; chmn. program com. 4th Symposium on Archtl. Support for Operation Systems and Computer Architecture, Santa Clara, Calif., 1991; mem. Mgmt. Ops. Working Group NASA, 1992—; co-chair program com. Hot Chips Symposium IV, Stanford, Calif., 1992. Author: A Taste of Smalltalk, 1986, Computing Unbound, 1989, Computer Architecture: A Quantative Approach, 2nd edit., 1996, Computer Organization & Design: The Hardware/Software Interface, 2nd edit., 1998. Recipient Disting. Teaching award U. Calif., Berkeley, 1982, Outstanding Alumnus award UCLA Computer Sci. Dept. Fellow IEEE (undergrad. tchg. award 1996, tech. achievement award 1996), ACM (Karl V. Karlstrom Outstanding Educator award 1991); mem. NAE, Computing Rsch. Assn. (bd. dirs. Washington 1991—, chair 1993-95), Spl. Interest Group on Computer Architecture of ACM (bd. dirs. 1987-90, chair 1993—). Avocations: biking, soccer, weight lifting, body surfing. Office: U Calif Computer Sci 635 Sodahall Berkeley CA 94720

PATTERSON, DAWN MARIE, dean, consultant, writer; b. Gloversville, N.Y., July 30; d. Robert Morris and Dora Margaret (Perham) P.; m. Robert Henry Hollenbeck, Aug. 3, 1958 (div. 1976); children: Adrienne Lyn, Nathaniel Conrad. BS in Edn., SUNY, Geneseo, 1962; MA, Mich. State U., 1973, PhD, 1977; postgrad., U. So. Calif. and Inst. Ednl. Leadership. Librarian Brighton (N.Y.) Cen. Schs., 1962-67; asst. to regional dir. Mich. State U. Ctr., Bloomfield Hills, 1973-74; grad. asst. Mich. State U., East Lansing, 1975-77; cons. Mich. Efficiency Task Force, 1977; asst. dean Coll. Continuing Edn., U. So. Calif., L.A., 1978-84; dean, assoc. prof. continuing edn. Calif. State U., L.A., 1985-96; v.p. external affairs West Coast U., 1996-97; CEO Acclaims Enterprises Internat.; pres. Co-Pro Assocs. Mem. Air Univ. Bd. Visitors, 1986-90, Commn. on Extended Edn. Calif. State U. Calif., 1988-91; Hist. Soc., Los Angeles Town Hall, Los Angeles World Affairs Council. Dora Louden scholar, 1958-61; Langworthy fellow, 1961-62; Edn. Professions Devel. fellow, 1974-75; Ednl. Leadership Policy fellow, 1982-83; Leadership Calif., 1992, Leadership Am., 1994. Mem. AAUW (pres. Pasadena br. 1985-86), Am. Assn. Adult and Continuing Edn. (charter), Nat. Univ. Continuing Edn. Assn., Internat. Assn. Continuing Edn. and Tng. (bd. dirs. 1990—), Calif. Coll. and Mil. Educators Assn. (pres.), Los Angeles Airport Area Edn. Industry Assn. (pres. 1984), Rotary Club of Alhambra (bd. dirs.), Fine Arts (Pasadena), Zonta (pres. 1994-96), Women in Internat. Trade, Kappa Delta Pi, Phi Delta Kappa, Phi Beta Delta, Phi Kappa Phi. Republican. Unitarian. Office: PO Box 86 South Pasadena CA 91031-0086

PATTERSON, DENNIS JOSEPH, management consultant; b. Honolulu, Apr. 13, 1948; s. Joseph John and Dorothy Elizabeth (Snajkowski) P.; m. Susan Tyra Pedlow, Dec. 31, 1981; children: Valerie Jean, Christina Elizabeth. BA, Elmhurst (Ill.) Coll., 1970; MA, George Washington U., 1973. Asst. dir. Vancouver (B.C.) Gen. Hosp., 1973-76, dir., 1975-76; v.p. Shaugnessy Hosp., Vancouver, 1976-79; pres. Westcare, Vancouver, 1979-84; mgr. Ernst & Whinney, Chgo., 1984-86, sr. mgr., 1986-88, ptnr., 1988-93; pres. FHP Internat. Cons. Group, Inc., Fountain Valley, Calif., 1993-95; ptnr. KPMG Peat Marwick, 1996-97; sr. cons. Hoy Group, 1997—. Contbr. articles to profl. jours. fin. mgr. Electoral Action Movement, Vancouver, 1978; trustee George Washington U., 1992-96, Calif. Sch. Profl. Psychology, 1993-96. Fellow Am. Coll. Healthcare Execs.; mem. Royal Vancouver Yacht Club, Va. Country Club, Manhattan Beach C.C., Phi Gamma Mu. Republican. Anglican. Avocation: sailboat racing, golf.

PATTERSON, DONALD EUGENE, research scientist; b. El Paso, Tex., Feb. 7, 1958; s. Donald M. Patterson and Beverly Lee (Viles) McElroy; m. Mary Jane Ingram, May 6, 1989. BS, U. Tex., 1982, MS, 1984; MA, Rice U., 1987, PhD, 1989. Rsch. scientist Rice U., Houston, 1989-91; sr. rsch. scientist Houston Advanced Rsch. Ctr., The Woodlands, Tex., 1989-93; sr. scientist SI Diamond Tech. Inc., Houston, 1991-95; sr. rsch. scientist TSA, Inc., The Woodlands, 1991-95; dir. R & D SI Diamond Tech. Inc., Houston, 1995-96; edn. supr. ITT Tech. Inst., Houston, 1996—. Contrb. articles to profl. jours. Recipient Harry B. Wieser award Rice U., 1988; Rice U. Graduate fello, 1984; UTEP Grad. scholar, 1983, Davis and Bertha Green scholar, 1982, VFW Voice Democracy scholar, 1974. Mem. AAAS, Materials Rsch. Soc., Am. Chem. Soc., N.Y. Acad. Sci., Phi Kappa Phi, Sigma Xi. Achievements include 3 patents in field. Home: 3622 Hansford Pl Pearland TX 77584 Office: ITT Tech Inst 2950 S Gessner Rd Houston TX 77063-3751

PATTERSON, DONALD FLOYD, human, medical and veterinary genetics educator; b. Maracaibo, Venezuela, Feb. 2, 1931; came to U.S., 1932; s. Carl Earl and Dayne (Murphy) P.; children: Russell H., Wade D. DVM, Okla. State U., 1954; DSc, U. Pa., 1967. Diplomate Am. Coll. Vet. Internal Medicine, Am. Bd. Vet. Internal Medicine, Am. Bd. Vet. Cardiology. Intern Angell Meml. Hosp., Boston, 1954-56; instr. Okla. State U., Stillwater, 1956; instr., asst. prof. Vet. Sch. U. Pa., Phila., 1958-64, from assoc. prof. to prof. Vet. Sch., 1966-73, chief sect. med. genetics, 1966-95, Sheppard prof. med. genetics Vet. Sch., 1973—, prof. human genetics Med. Sch., 1974—; NIH spl. fellow divsn. med. genetics Johns Hopkins U., Balt., 1964-66; dir. Ctr. for Comparative Med. Genetics U. Pa., Phila., 1995—. Author computer program for canine genetic diseases; contbr. over 300 papers to sci. and med. jours. Capt. USAF, 1956-58. Recipient Merit award Am. Animal Hosp.

Assn., 1982, NIH Merit award, 1989, 91, Med. Rsch. award World Congress Vet. Medicine, 1992. Fellow Am. Coll. Cardiology, Phila. Coll. Physicians; mem. AVMA (Gaines Rsch. award 1972, Career Rsch. Achievement award 1995), Am. Soc. Human Genetics. Democrat. Avocations: canoeing, poetry, literature. Office: U Pa Sch Vet Medicine 3900 Delancey St Philadelphia PA 19104-4107

PATTERSON, DONALD LEE, music educator; b. Colorado Springs, Colo., Aug. 14, 1947; s. Thurman Alvin and Bernice Eileen (May) P.; m. Janet Louise Andrews, Feb. 19, 1971. MusB, U. Denver, 1969; MusM, Manhattan Sch. Music, 1972; MusD, U. North Tex., 1977. Staff accompanist Harlem Sch. Arts, N.Y.C., 1970-72, Manhattan Sch. Music, N.Y.C., 1970-72; music instr. Angelo State U., San Angelo, Tex., 1972-74; teaching fellow U. North Tex., Denton, 1974-76; music prof. U. Wis., Eau Claire, 1976—. Co-author: Vincent Persichetti: A Bio-bibliography, 1989; author (sound rec.) EDUCO, Inc., Contemporary Recording Soc. Mem. Am. Liszt Soc., Sonneck Soc., Music Tchrs. Nat. Assn. (cert.), Recs. for Contemporary Rec. Soc., Educo, Inc., Kappa Kappa Psi, Phi Mu Alpha Sinfonia, Pi Kappa Lambda. Home: 2130 15th St Eau Claire WI 54703-2655 Office: U Wis Music Dept Eau Claire WI 54702

PATTERSON, DONIS DEAN, bishop; b. Holmesville, Ohio, Apr. 27, 1930; s. Raymond J. and Louella Faye (Glasgo) P.; m. JoAnne Nida, Dec. 22, 1951; children: Christoper Nida, Andrew Joseph. BS, Ohio State U., 1952; STB, Episcopal Theol. Sch., 1957; M Div, Episcopal Divinity Sch., 1972; DD (hon.), Nashotah House Sem., 1984, U. of South, 1986. Rector St. Andrews Ch., Washington Court House, Ohio, 1957-63, St. Marks Ch., Venice, Fla., 1963-70, All Sts. Ch., Winter Park, Fla., 1970-83; bishop Episcopal Diocese Dallas, 1983-92; assisting bishop Episcopal Diocese of Ctrl. Gulf Coast, 1992-96; trustee Seabury Western Theol. Sem., Evanston, Ill., 1981-82, U. of South, 1983-92, Episcopal Theol. Sem. S.W., 1983-92. Chmn. Episcopal Ch. House of Bishops Armed Forces Com., 1989-93. Col., chaplain U.S. Army, 1952-54, Korea.

PATTERSON, EDWIN, minister; b. Andalusia, Ala., Sept. 6, 1921; s. Walter Levi and Kate Edline (Aughtman) P.; m. Margaret Alice Hall, May 14, 1966. Degree, Brennan Bus. Sch., 1940; postgrad., Samford U., 1950-57. Ordained to ministry So. Bapt. Conv., 1947. Pastor various chs. Ala., 1947—; including Hopwell, 1949-67, Harmony Bapt. Ch., Andalusia, 1967-80, Searight Bapt. Ch., Dozier, Ala., 1980—; acct. C.G. Tomberlin, M.D., Andalusia, 1985—. Mem. bd. regents Liberty U., Lynchburg, Va. Home: 407 Lakeview Dr Andalusia AL 36420-3542 Office: PO Box 486 Andalusia AL 36420-0486 *In Him, we live and move and have our being. Therefore, my heart's desire is to honor Christ in all things, for He is the way, the truth, and the life.*

PATTERSON, ELIZABETH JOHNSTON, former congresswoman; b. Columbia, SC, Nov. 18, 1939; d. Olin DeWitt and Gladys (Atkinson) Johnston; m. Dwight Fleming Patterson, Jr., Apr. 15, 1967; children: Dwight Fleming, Olin DeWitt, Catherine Leigh. BA, Columbia Coll., 1961; postgrad. in polit. sci., U. S.C., 1961, 62, 64; LLD (hon.), Columbia Coll., 1987; D Pub. Svc. (hon.), Converse Coll., 1989. Pub. affairs officer Peace Corps, Washington, 1962-64; postgrad. VISTA, OEO, Washington, 1965-66; D Pub. Svc. Head Start and VISTA, OEO, Columbia, 1966-67; tri-county dir. Head Start, Piedmont Community Actions, Spartanburg, S.C., 1967-68; mem. Spartanburg County Coun., 1975-76, S.C. State Senate, 1979-86, 100th-102nd Congresss from 4th S.C. dist., 1987-93. Trustee Wofford Coll., 1975-81; bd. dirs. Charles Lea Ctr., 1978-90, Spartanburg Coun. on Aging; pres. Spartanburg Dem. Women, 1968; v.p. Spartanburg County Dem. party, 1968-70, sec., 1970-75; trustee Columbia Coll., 1991—. Mem. Bus. and Profl. Women's Club, Alpha Kappa Gamma. Methodist. Office: PO Box 5564 Spartanburg SC 29304-5564

PATTERSON, ELLMORE CLARK, banker; b. Western Springs, Ill., Nov. 29, 1913; s. Ellmore Clark and Harriet Emma (Wales) P.; m. Anne Hyde Choate, Sept. 28, 1940; children: Michael Ellmore, Arthur Choate, Robert Ellmore, David Choate, Thomas Hyde Choate. Grad., Lake Forest Acad., 1931; B.S., U. Chgo., 1935. With J. P. Morgan & Co., Inc., N.Y.C., 1935-39, 39-41, 46-59; v.p. J. P. Morgan & Co., Inc., 1951-59; exec. v.p. Morgan Guaranty Trust Co. N.Y. (merger J.P. Morgan and Guaranty Trust Co.), 1959-65, dir., chmn. exec. com., 1967-68, pres., 1969-71, chmn., 1971-77, chmn. exec. com., 1978; with Morgan Stanley & Co., 1939; dir. comml. Union Corp., Engelhard Hanovia, Inc.; chmn. dirs. adv. coun. Morgan Guaranty Trust Co.; mem. Presdl. Com. on Fin. Structure and Regulation, 1970-72. Bd. mgrs. Meml. Hosp. Cancer and Allied Diseases, N.Y.C.; Sloan-Kettering Inst. Cancer Center, N.Y.C., U. Chgo., Mass. Inst. Tech. Served from ensign to lt. comdr. USNR, 1941-46. Mem. Psi Upsilon. Episcopalian. Clubs: Links (N.Y.C.); Bedford (N.Y.); Golf and Tennis; Jupiter Island (Hobe Sound, Fla.); Fishers Island Country; Seminole Golf (Palm Beach, Pla.). Office: 23 Wall St New York NY 10260-1000

PATTERSON, EUGENE CORBETT, retired editor, publisher; b. Valdosta, Ga., Oct. 15, 1923; s. William C. and Annabel (Corbett) P.; m. Mary Sue Carter, Aug. 19, 1950; 1 child, Mary Patterson Fausch. Student, North Ga. Coll., Dahlonega, 1940-42; AB in Journalism, U. Ga., 1943; LL.D., Tusculum Coll., 1965, Harvard U., 1969, Duke U., 1978, Stetson U., 1984, Ind. U., 1990; Litt.D., Emory U., 1966, Oglethorpe Coll., 1966, Tuskegee U., 1966, Roanoke Coll., 1968, Mercer U., 1968, Eckerd Coll., 1977, U. South Fla., 1986, Dillard U., 1992; Colby Coll., 1994. Reporter Temple (Tex.) Daily Telegram and Macon (Ga.) Telegraph, 1947-48; mgr. for S.C. United Press, 1948-49; night bur. mgr. United Press, N.Y.C., 1949-53; mgr. London bur. United Press, also chief corr. U.K., 1953-56; v.p., exec. editor Atlanta Journal-Constitution, 1956-60; editor Atlanta Constitution, 1960-68; mng. editor Washington Post, 1968-71; prof. polit. sci. Duke U., 1971-72; editor, pres. St. Petersburg (Fla.) Times, 1972-84, chmn., chief exec. officer, 1978-88, editor emeritus, 1988—; editor, pres. Congl. Quar., Washington, 1972-86; chmn., chief exec. officer Congl. Quar., 1978-88; chmn. bd., chief exec. officer Fla. Trend mag., 1980-88, Ga. Trend mag., 1984-88, Ariz. Trend mag., 1986-88, Governing mag., 1987-88, Modern Graphic Arts, Inc., 1978-88, Poynter Inst. Media Studies, 1978-88, Poynter Fund, 1978-88. Vice chmn. U.S. Civil Rights Commn., 1964-68; mem. Pulitzer Prize Bd., 1973-84; trustee ASNE Found., 1981-84, U. Ga. Found., 1982-88, North Ga. Coll. Found., 1991-93, Am. Press Inst., Reston, Va., 1983-88, Duke U., 1988-94, Fla. Bar Found., 1992-93, LeRoy Collins Ctr. for Pub. Policy, 1990-93. Decorated Silver Star, Bronze Star with oak leaf cluster in 10th Armored Divsn., Gen. Patton's 3rd Army; recipient Pulitzer prize for editl. writing Columbia U., 1966, William Allen White Nat. Citation award U. Kans., 1980, Elijah Parish Lovejoy award Colby Coll., 1994; inducted into Fla. Newspaper Hall of Fame Fla. Press Assn., 1997. Fellow Soc. Profl. Journalists; mem. Am. Soc. Newspaper Editors (pres. 1977-78), St. Petersburg Yacht Club. Home: Snell Isle 1967 Brightwaters Blvd NE Saint Petersburg FL 33704-3007

PATTERSON, GLENN WAYNE, botany educator; b. China Grove, N.C., Mar. 9, 1938; s. Simpson Wayne and Alice (Fisher) P.; m. Nancy Ann deLesdernier, Sept. 2, 1961; children: Steven, Eric, Alan. B.S., N.C. State U., 1960; M.S., U. Md., 1963, Ph.D., 1964. Asst. prof. dept. botany U. Md., College Park, 1964-69, assoc. prof., 1969-73, prof. botany, 1973—, chmn. dept., 1977-87, acting assoc. dean Colls. Agriculture and Life Scis., 1986-89. Recipient Biol. Scis. award Washington Acad. Scis., 1971. Mem. Am. Soc. Plant Physiologists, Am. Oil Chemists Soc. Office: Dept Botany Univ Md College Park MD 20742

PATTERSON, GRACE LIMERICK, library director; b. N.Y.C., Nov. 21, 1938; d. Robert and Frieda (Zeiontz) Limerick; m. Joseph Nathaniel Patterson (dec.); children: Lorrayne Carole, Joseph Nathaniel Jr. BA in Sociology, Edn., CUNY, 1971; MLS, Columbia U., 1975; MS in Comm., Coll. New Rochelle, 1989. Cert. libr. N.J. Exec. dir. Manhattanville Community Outreach, N.Y.C., 1971-74; br. and outreach svcs. Paterson (N.J.) Pub. Libr., 1975-79; media specialist II Passaic County C.C., Paterson, 1979-81; coord. outreach svcs. Irvington (N.J.) Pub. Libr., 1981-84; assoc. prof. libr. Rockland C.C., Suffern, N.Y., 1984-89; libr. dir. Hudson County C.C., Jersey City, 1989—. Editor jours. in field. Exec. bd. dirs. IFLA/CPRT, sec.-treas., 1996—; vol. Ridgewood (N.J.) Schs., 1981-83; Ridgewood Centennial Com. First Night, 1993. U.S. Dept. Edn. fellow, 1974-75. Mem. ALA (com., chairperson Black Caucus pub. rels. 1990-92), N.J. Libr. Assn. Avocations: photography, oral history, travel, geneology, public speaking. Office: Hudson County CC 25 Journal Sq Jersey City NJ 07306-4012

PATTERSON, GRADY LESLIE, JR., financial advisor; b. Abbeville, S.C., Jan. 13, 1924; s. Grady Leslie and Claudia (McClain) P.; m. Marjorie Harrison Faucett, Dec. 22, 1951; children—Grady Leslie III, Steven G., M. Lynne, Laura A., Amy S., M. Beth. LLB, U. S.C., 1950, BS, 1975, LLD (hon.), 1980; LLD (hon.), The Citadel, 1985, Lander Coll., 1990, U. Charleston, S.C., 1992, Clemson U., 1992. Bar: S.C. 1950. County service officer Abbeville County, S.C., 1950; ops. officer S.C. Air N.G., Columbia, 1952-59; asst. atty. gen. State of S.C., Columbia, 1959-66, treas., 1967-95; fin. advisor, 1995—. Served with USAAF, 1943-46; maj. USAF, 1950-52, 61-61, ret. Maj. Gen. Decorated D.S.M. USAF. Mem. S.C. Bar Assn. Democrat. Presbyterian. Avocations: golf; jogging. Home: 3016 Petigru St Columbia SC 29204-3618 Office: 914 Richland St Ste C Columbia SC 29201-2357

PATTERSON, HARLAN RAY, finance educator; b. Camden, Ohio, June 27, 1931; s. Ernest Newton and Beulah Irene (Hedrick) P.; children by previous marriage: Kristan Lee, Elizabeth Jane, Nolan Gene. BS cum laude, Miami U., Oxford, Ohio, 1953, MBA, 1959; PhD, Mich. State U., 1963. Asst. prof. fin. U. Ill., Champaign-Urbana, 1962-66; mem. faculty Ohio U., Athens, 1966—; prof. fin. Ohio U., 1977-94, prof. emeritus fin., 1994—; vis. prof., fellow Chgo. Merc. Exc., 1971; fin. cons., researcher projects for industry. Contbr. articles to acad. and profl. jours. Chmn. City of Athens Rainbow Adv. Bd., 1972-77; state chmn. scholarship com. for Ohio Rainbow Girls, 1975-87. Commd. officer USN, 1953-56. Recipient Fred Astaire Bronze I Achievement level; named Congressional Alternate to West Point, 1949; won competitive appointment U.S. Naval Acad., 1950; NROTC scholar, 1950; Stonier fellow, 1961, Mortgage Banking fellow, 1974, Found. Econ. Edn. fellow, 1965, 67, 69, 71. Mem. Internat. Platform Assn., Rotary Internat. (Paul Harris fellow), Masons, Shriners, Order Eastern Star (worthy patron 1989, 92), Phi Beta Kappa (pres. faculty chpt. 1975), Beta Gamma Sigma (faculty adviser), Phi Eta Sigma, Alpha Kappa Psi, Delta Sigma Pi, Sigma Tau Alpha (adviser), Omicron Delta Epsilon, Pi Kappa Alpha. Republican. Avocations: dance classes, gentleman host. Home: 9B Station St Athens OH 45701-2763

PATTERSON, HAROLD DEAN, superintendent of schools; b. Alexander City, Ala., May 29, 1932; s. Obed Howard and Sara Bell (Joiner) P.; m. Shirley Bryant, May 31, 1958; children: Lisa Jane, Anne Leslie, Harold Dean Jr. BS, Auburn U., 1954; MA, Vanderbilt U., 1957, EdD, 1964. Cert. sch. adminstr., Ala., S.C., Ill. Tchr. Bessemer (Ala.) High Sch., 1957-63, asst. prin., 1959-62; prin. North Hall, Evanston (Ill.) Twp. High Sch., 1964-66; prin. Mountain Brook (Ala.) High Sch., 1966-71; assoc. supt. Greenville County Schs., Greenville, S.C., 1971-74; supt. Sumter County Sch. Dist. 17, Sumter, S.C., 1974-82, Spartanburg County Sch. Dist. 7, Spartanburg, S.C., 1982-88; supt. Guntersville (Ala.) City Schs., 1988-95, legis. liaison, 1995—. Mem. S.C. Gov.'s Com. on Financing Edn., Columbia, 1983, S.C. Pvt. Industry Coun., Columbia, 1984-88, S.C. Legis. Oversight Com., Columbia, 1984; pres. Peabody alumni bd. Vanderbilt U., Nashville, 1989-90. 2d lt. U.S. Army, 1954-56. Recipient Outstanding Educator award Florence chpt. Phi Delta Kappa, 1981, The Exec. Educator 100 award The Exec. Educator mag., 1987. Mem. Am. Assn. Sch. Adminstrs. (chmn. legis. corp. 1985-95, mem. exec. com. 1988-91, James R. Kirkpatrick award 1987), Ala. Assn. Sch. Adminstrs., Nat. Assn. Secondary Sch. Prins., Rotary (dist. 6860 gov. 1995-96). Methodist. Avocation: golf. Home: 5020 Neely Ave Guntersville AL 35976-8102

PATTERSON, HELEN CROSBY, clinical psychologist; b. Jackson, Miss., Nov. 12, 1947; d. Thomas Atkinson and Helen Elizabeth (Crosby) Patterson; m. Fred C. Craig, July 7, 1967 (div. July 1970); 1 child, Erin Crosby. BA in Psychology, Millsaps Coll., 1972; MS in Clin. Psychology, U. Wyo., 1976, PhD in Clin. Psychology, 1978. Lic. clin. psychologist, Miss., N.Mex., Del. Coord., supervision and internships Antioch N.E. Grad. Sch., Keene, N.H., 1979-80; sr. clinician Jackson (Miss.) Mental Health Ctr., 1980-82; pvt. practice Miss. and, N.Mex., 1981—; psychol. cons. Disability Determination Svcs., Jackson, 1983—, Albuquerque, 1988-90, 91-93, Wilmington, Del., 1993-95; EAP cons., So. Beverage Co., Jackson, 1986-91, clin. dir. Pain Mgmt. Ctr., St. Vincent Hosp., Santa Fe, 1990-91. Mem. Hinds County Assn. for Children with Learning Disabilities, Jackson, 1985-88, Hinds County Mental Health Assn., Jackson, 1980-83. Mem. APA. Avocations: wholistic health studies, jyotish astrology, horses, ice skating, skiing. Office: 11 Northtown Dr Ste 205 Jackson MS 39211-3059

PATTERSON, JAMEE JORDAN, lawyer; b. L.A., Sept. 28, 1955; d. James Joseph Jr. and Marie Antanette (Kunz) Jordan; m. Timothy Raymond, Aug. 6, 1983; 1 child, Joseph Thomas. BA, UCLA, 1977; JD, Loyola U., L.A., 1981. Bar: Calif. 1981, U.S. Dist. Ct. (ctrl. dist.) Calif. 1981, U.S. Dist. Ct. (so. dist.) Calif. 1982, U.S. Supreme Ct. 1986, U.S. Ct. Appeals (9th cir.) 1991. Dep. atty. gen. Atty. Gen.'s Office, L.A., 1981-83, San Diego, 1983—; liaison to Calif. Coastal Com. Co-chair Women Employees Adv. Com., San Diego, 1986-87. Regents scholar UCLA, 1973-77, regents fellow, 1977-78; recipient Disting. Legal Svc. award Assn. of Calif. State Attys, 1996. Mem. Assn. Deps. Atty. Gen. (pres. 1987, 94), San Diego County Bar, Lawyers Club San Diego (co-chair reproductive rights com. 1990). Avocations: reading, running, skiing, cross country skiing, cooking. Office: Calif Atty Gen PO Box 85266 110 W A St Ste 1100 San Diego CA 92186-5266

PATTERSON, JAMES, mayor; b. San Mateo, Calif., Feb. 18, 1948; m. Sharon LeTourneau, 1968; children: B.J., Jason, Lindsay. BA in Polit. Sci. summa cum laude, Calif. State U., Fresno, 1992. Radio broadcasting exec. Sta. KIRV-AM, Fresno, Calif., 1968—; mayor City of Fresno, 1993—. Chair San Joaquin River Conservancy; vice chair Fresno County Transp. Authority; bd. mem. Fresno City-County Consortium Agy.; chmn. NO on Measure H Com., 1989, Criminal Justice and Law Enforcement Commn., 1990-91; vice chmn. YES on Measure E Com., 1988; mem. Human Rels. Commn., City of Fresno, 1987-91; bd. dirs. Leadership Fresno Alumni Assn., 1989-91, Fresno County YFC/Campus Life, 1984-88. Mem. Fresno City and County C. of C. (chmn. local govt. affairs com. 1990-91, bd. dirs. FRESPAC 1990-91, city budget rev. com. 1989-91, privatization task force 1988-89, charter sect. 809 rev. task force 1987-88). Office: Office of the Mayor City Coun City Hall 2600 Fresno St Fresno CA 93721-3620*

PATTERSON, JAMES MILTON, marketing specialist, educator; b. DeQueen, Ark., Oct. 15, 1927; s. Charles Edward and Phoebe Allene (Steel) P.; m. Della Jeanne Hays, July 3, 1964; children—J. Marshall, Julia M.; children by previous marriage—Robert T., Donald A. B.S., U.S. Mcht. Marine Acad., 1948; M.B.A. (Teagle Found. fellow), Cornell U., 1954, Ph.D. (Ford Found. dissertation fellow), 1961. Third mate Esso Shipping Co., 1948-52; instr. in bus. adminstrn. Northwestern U., 1957-60; lectr. Center for Programs in Govt. Adminstrn., U. Chgo., 1959; asst. prof. mktg. Ind. U., 1960-63, assoc. prof., 1963-69, prof., 1969—, chmn. dept. mktg., 1972-78, asso. dir. Poynter Ctr., 1980, acting dir., 1981, co-sec. U. Faculty Coun., pres. Bloomington Faculty Coun.; dir. Ind. U. Inst. for Advanced Study, 1994—; bd. dirs. Inst. Advanced Study; cons. petroleum mktg.; expert witness on antitrust and mktg. Author: Marketing: The Firm's Viewpoint, 1964, Highway Robbery: An Analysis of the Gasoline Crisis, 1974, Competition Ltd.: The Marketing of Gasoline, 1972. Served with USNR, 1945-48. Mem. Assn. for Practical & Profl. Ethics. Democrat. Home: 2431 N Dunn St Bloomington IN 47408-1117 Office: Ind U Inst Advanced Study Bloomington IN 47405

PATTERSON, JAMES RANDOLPH, physician; b. Lancaster, Pa., Jan. 30, 1942; m. Linda Lewis Patterson, Nov. 22, 1969. AB, U. Pa., 1964; MD, Columbia U., 1968. Diplomate Nat. Bd. Med. Examiners, Am. Bd. Internal Medicine, Subspecialty of Pulmonary Disease. Pulmonary and critical care specialist The Oregon Clinic, Portland, 1975—; clin. prof. medicine Oreg. health Scis. U., Portland, 1978—; mem. Am. Bd. Internal Medicine, Phila., 1995—; trustee Collins Med. Trust, Portland, Oreg., 1992—. Contbr. numerous articles to profl. jours. Recipient Class of 1964 award U. Pa., Van Loan award Am. Lung Assn. Oreg., 1990, Meritorious Achievement award Oreg. Health Scis. U., 1991; named Class Pres. Coll. Physicians and Surgeons of Columbia U., 1968, Tchr. of Yr. Providence Med. Ctr., Portland, Oreg., 1976, Internist of Yr., 1983, Best Doctors in Am., 1992-95. Mem. AMA, Am. Thoracic Soc., Am. Coll. Chest Physicians, Oreg. Lung Assn., North Pacific Soc. of Internal Medicine, Pacific Interurban Clin. Club, Multnomah County Med. Soc., Oreg. Med. Assn., Oreg. Soc. Ctirical Care Medicine. Office: The Oregon Clinic 507 NE 47th Ave Portland OR 97213-2236

PATTERSON, JAMES WILLIS, pathology and dermatology educator; b. Takoma Park, Md., Dec. 29, 1946; s. James Clark and Helen (Hendricks) P.; m. Julie Wyatt, Dec. 30, 1989; 1 child, James Wyatt. BA, Johns Hopkins U., 1968; MD, Med. Coll. Va., 1972. Diplomate Am. Bd. Dermatology, Am. Bd. Dermatopathology, Nat. Bd. Med. Examiners. Fellow dermatopathology Armed Forces Inst. Pathology, Washington, 1979-80; rotating intern in medicine Med. Coll. Va., Richmond, 1972-73, resident in dermatology, 1973-76, assoc. prof. pathology and dermatology, 1982-89, prof., 1989-92, dir. dermatopathology, 1982-92; clin. prof. dermatology and pathology Med. Coll. of Va., 1992-96; with Dermatology Assocs. of Va., 1992-96, Va. Dermatopathology Svcs., Richmond, 1992-96; prof. pathology and dermatology U. Va., 1996—; clin. instr. dermatology U. Colo. Med. Ctr., Denver, 1980-82; cons. in pathology McGuire VA Hosp., Richmond, 1982-92; cons. in pathology and dermatology Kenner Army Hosp., Ft. Lee, Va., 1982-95. Author: Dermatology: A Concise Textbook, 1987; contbr. over 100 articles on dermatology and pathology to med. jours.; asst. editor Jour. Cutaneous Pathology, 1989-94. Mem. nat. alumni schs. com. Johns Hopkins U., 1986—. With M.C., U.S. Army, 1976-82, col. Res. Recipient Stuart McEwen award Assn. Mil. Dermatologists, 1980, 82. Fellow ACP, Am. Acad. Dermatology, Am. Soc. Dermatopathology; mem. Va. Dermatol. Soc. (sec.-treas. 1984-88, v.p. 1988-89, pres. 1989-90), Johns Hopkins U. Alumni Assn. (pres. cen. Va. chpt. 1989), Tau Epsilon Phi (life). Republican. Presbyterian. Avocations: American history, baseball, golf.

PATTERSON, JERRY EUGENE, author; b. Ft. Worth, May 2, 1931; s. Charles Edward and Lois (Pruitt) P. B.A., U. Tex., 1952, M.A., 1955; postgrad., Yale U., 1955-57, Columbia U., 1958-60. Asst. editor Hispanic Am. Hist. Rev., 1954; manuscript. div. librarian Yale U. Library, 1955-57; cataloguer Edward Eberstadt & Sons, N.Y.C., 1958-61; with Parke-Bernet Galleries, N.Y.C., 1962-68; asst. v.p. Parke-Bernet Galleries, 1964-65, v.p., 1965-68; U.S. rep. Christie, Manson & Woods, N.Y.C., 1968-71; sr. v.p. Sotheby Parke Bernet Inc., 1980-83; Cons. Library of Congress, 1964-67. Author: Autographs, a Collectors Guide, 1973, A Collector's Guide to Relics and Memorabilia, 1974, Antiques of Sport, 1975, The City of New York, 1978, Porcelain, 1979, Living It Up: A Guide to the Named Apartment Houses of New York, 1984, The Vanderbilts, 1989, The Best Families: The Town & Country Social Directory, 1846-1996, 1996; mng. editor: Artnewsletter, 1975-78; contbr. to Auction Antiques Ann, 1971, also articles on rare books, manuscripts and art market to Am. and fgn. periodicals. Republican. Episcopalian. Home: 176 E 77th St New York NY 10021-1908

PATTERSON, JOHN C., clinical psychology researcher; b. Asheville, N.C.. BS in Psychology, Stephen F. Austin State U., MS in Psychology; PhD in Psychology, Tex. A&M U., 1981. Resident in psychology Wilford Hall USAF Med. Ctr., San Antonio, 1981; staff psychologist, maximum security unit Rusk State Psychiatric Hosp., Tex.; unit dir. USAF Sch. Aerospace Medicine; chief, aerospace clin. psychology function USAF Aeromed. Consultation Svc., 1985—; faculty mem. USAF Sch. Aerospace Medicine and U. Tex. Health Sci. Ctr., San Antonio (Psychiatry); internat. vis. lectr. in aeromed. neuropsychiatry; cons. in aerospace clin. psychology and neuropsychology evaluation; mem. NASA In-House Working Group on Astronaut Selection; cons. NASA. Contbr. over 30 articles to profl. jours.; rschr. in psychological factors associated with heart disease, aircrew and astronaut selection, spatial disorientation, aviator cognitive funcitoning, and airsickness; presenter in field. Recipient Armstrong Lab. Dirs. award for Rsch. 1993. Mem. APA, Aerospace Med. Assn. (Raymond F. Longacre award 1995), Am. Soc. Clin. Hypnosis, Internat. Neuropsychology Soc., AF Soc. for Clin. Psychologists, Bexar County Psychol. Assn. Office: USAF Aeromed Consultation AL-AOCN 2507 KEnnedy Cir Brooks AFB TX 78235*

PATTERSON, JOHN DE LA ROCHE, JR., lawyer; b. Schenectady, N.Y., July 8, 1941; s. John de la Roche Sr. and Jane C. (Clay) P.; m. Michele F. Demarest, Nov. 28, 1987; children: Daniel C., Sara R., Amy C. BA, Johns Hopkins U., 1963; LLB, Harvard U., 1966. Bar: Mass. 1968. Vol. Peace Corps, Chad, 1966-67; assoc. Foley, Hoag & Eliot, Boston, 1967-73, ptnr., 1974—, exec. com., 1989—. Chmn. Kodaly Ctr. Am. Inc., Newton, Mass., 1977-87. Mem. ABA, Boston Bar Assn. Democrat. Avocations: sailing, tennis, travel, reading. Office: Foley Hoag & Eliot 1 Post Office Sq Boston MA 02109

PATTERSON, JOHN MALCOLM, judge; b. Goldville, Ala., Sept. 27, 1921; s. Albert Love and Agnes Louise (Benson) P.; m. Florentine M. Sawyers, Oct. 17, 1975; children—Albert L., Barbara Louise. J.D., U. Ala., 1949. Bar: Ala. bar 1949. Practiced in Phenix City, 1949-51, 53-55; atty. gen., securities commr. State of Ala., 1955-59; gov. of Ala., 1959-63; practice law Montgomery, Ala., 1963-84; judge Ala. Ct. Criminal Appeals, 1984-97, part-time judge, 1997—; chief judge Ct. of the Judiciary, 1989-97; cattle farmer. Bd. editors: Ala. Law Review, 1948-49. Chmn. bd. Lyman WArd Mil. Acad. Served to maj., F.A. AUS, 1940-45; maj. 1951-53. Nominated one of 10 outstanding young men of U.S., 1956, one of four outstanding young men of Ala. Jr. C. of C. Mem. ABA, Ala. Bar Assn., VFW, Am. Legion. Farrar Order of Jurisprudence, Ala. Acad. Honor, Alpha Tau Omega, Phi Alpha Delta, Sigma Delta Kappa, Phi Eta Sigma, Omicron Delta Kappa. Office: PO Box 301555 Montgomery AL 36130-1555

PATTERSON, JOSEPH CROMWELL, financial company executive; b. Detroit, Nov. 21, 1928; s. Walter Rodney and Mildred Lona (Cromwell) P.; student Ohio State U., 1953; BA, Ohio Wesleyan U., 1954; m. Anne Elizabeth Ferrall, Jan. 19, 1952; children: J. Sean, Kevin B., Michael B., Mary A., Kathleen M., Julia M., Susan E., Margaret A., Patrick D., Jane M. Pres., Med. Mgmt. Inc., Dayton, Ohio, 1954-60; exec. staff Rsch. Inst. Am., N.Y.C., 1960-62, 62-64; cons. E.F. MacDonald Co., Dayton, 6 mos.; pres. Fin. Mgmt. Inst., Dayton, 1964-72, Fiscal Concepts Inc., Newport Beach, Calif., 1972-90; pres., CEO Tessa Fin. Group, Inc., Costa Mesa, Calif., 1991—; cons. in field. Served with USAAF, 1946-49, 51-52. Mem. Am. Mgmt. Assn., Am. Soc. Mgmt. Cons., Am. Profl. Practice Assn. (editor ofcl. jour. 1966-68), Internat. Assn. Fin. Planners. Republican. Roman Catholic. Editorial adviser Med. Econs. mag., 1956-60. Office: Tessa Fin Group Inc 2910 Red Hill Ave Costa Mesa CA 92626-5993

PATTERSON, JOSEPH REDWINE, lawyer; b. Corsicana, Tex., Apr. 16, 1927; s. Joseph Isham and Caroline Anderson (White) P.; m. Ann Louise Cumber, Mar. 9, 1956; children—Joseph Redwine, Amy Cumber. B.A. in Philosophy, So. Methodist U., 1948, M.A. in Govt, 1951, J.D., 1954. Bar: Tex. 1954. Asst. dist. atty. Dallas County, 1955-56; assoc. gen. counsel Traders and Gen. Ins. Co., Dallas, 1957; ptnr. firm Patterson, Lamberty, Stanford & Walls, Dallas, 1957—; ptnr. PLS Properties (real estate), Dallas, 1971—. Contbr. legal jours. Founding dir. Dallas chpt. Action on Smoking and Health; mem. chancel choir University Park United Meth. Ch., Dallas. Served with USN, 1945-46. Fellow Tex. Bar Found., Dallas Bar Found.; mem. ABA, Tex. Bar Assn., Dallas Bar Assn., Cross Country Club Dallas. Democrat. Home: 6131 Meadow Rd Dallas TX 75230-5058 Office: 2011 Cedar Springs Rd Dallas TX 75201-1808

PATTERSON, LLOYD CLIFFORD, psychiatrist; b. Toronto, Ont., Can., Jan. 16, 1917; came to U.S., 1942; s. William Henry and Florence May (Sonley) P.; m. Gloria May Patterson, Nov. 12, 1943; children: Diane Meisenheimer, Pamela DeBarr. MD, U. Western Ont., London, 1942. Diplomate Am. Bd. Psychiatry; cert. Am. Psychoanalytic Assn. Intern Hollywood Presybn. Hosp., L.A., 1942-43; fellow in intern medicine U. Calif. Hosp., San Francisco, 1943-44; resident in psychiatry Langley Porter Neuropsychiat. Inst., San Francisco, 1944-48; cons. psychiatrist student health U. Calif., Berkeley, 1960-70; assoc. clin. prof. U. Calif. Med. Sch., San Francisco, 1972—; dir. med. edn. Alta Bates Med. Ctr., Berkeley, 1988—; program chair Western Divisional Psychoanalytic meetings, San Francisco, 1966. Mem. East Bay Psychiat. Assn. (pres. 1962), No. Calif. Psychiat. Assn. (pres. 1968-69), San Francisco Psychoanalytic Soc. (pres. 1972-73), Am. Psychiat. Soc., Am. Psychoanalytic Soc., Calif. Med. Assn. (hosp. surveyor, mem. continuing med. edn. com. 1985-91, cons. CME com. 1992), Alameda Contra Costa Med. Assn. Avocations: tennis, golf. Home: 409

Cola Ballena Alameda CA 94501-3608 Office: 3021 Telegraph Ave Berkeley CA 94705-2013

PATTERSON, LYDIA ROSS, industrial relations specialist, consulting company executive; b. Carrabelle, Fla., Sept. 3, 1936; d. Richard D. Ross and Johnnie Mae (Thomas) Kelley; m. Edgar A. Corley, Aug. 1, 1964 (div.); 1 child, Derek Kelley; m. Berman W. Patterson, Dec. 18, 1981. BA, Hunter Coll., 1958. Indsl. rels. specialist U.S. Dept. Energy, N.Y.C., 1966-68; regional dir./mgr. Div. Human Rights State of N.Y., N.Y.C., 1962-66, 68-76; v.p. Bankers Trust Co., N.Y.C., 1976-87; pres., CEO Lydia Patterson Comm., N.Y.C., 1985-95; CEO Lydia Patterson Comms., 1996—; v.p., mgr. Merrill Lynch and Co. Inc., N.Y.C., 1987-90; seminar speaker Columbia U., Wharton Sch. Bus., Harvard U., Duke U., Cornell U., 1976-85; mem. conf. bd. Cornell U., Bus. Policy Rev. Coun., Exec. Leadership Coun. Bd. dirs. Project Discovery Columbia U., 1988, CUNY, Vocat. Edn. Adv. Coun., 1990-91, Gulfstream Goodwill Industries, 1997. Mem. Nat. Urban League, Fin. Women's Assn. (govt. and cmty. affairs com. 1986-87), Women's Forum, Wellington Cmty. Edn. Found. (bd. dirs. 1992-94), Leadership Palm Beach County. Office: 12689 Coral Breeze Dr Wellington FL 33414-8070

PATTERSON, MADGE LENORE, elementary education educator; b. Vandergrift, Pa., Nov. 9, 1925; d. Paul Warren and Lucy Mae (Lemmon) Schaeffer; m. Stanley Clair Patterson, June 19, 1948 (dec.); 1 child, Stanley Kent. BS in Edn., Indiana State Tchrs. Coll., Pa., 1946, MEd, 1971. Elem. tchr. New Kensington (Pa.) Pub. Schs., 1946-49; elem. tchr. Armstrong Sch. Dist. Schs., Ford City, Pa., 1951-52, kindergarten tchr., 1967-93; kindergarten tchr. Rural Valley (Pa.) Presbyn. Ch., 1957-67; vol. tutor Adult Lit., Kittanning, Pa., 1993—; co-owner dairy farm. Sunday sch. tchr., choir mem., 1949—; sec. Rural Valley Presbyn. Ch. Women's Assn., 1988-92. Mem. NEA, Pa. Assn. Sch. Retirees, Clara Cockerille Reading Coun. (treas. 1994-97), Pa. State Edn. Assn., Internat. Reading Assn., Keystone Reading Assn., Assn. Early Childhood Edn., Rural Valley Bus. and Profl. Club, Women's Civic Club (Woman of Yr. 1994), Am. Assn. Ret. Persons, Rural Valley Grange (former lectr.). Democrat. Avocations: dancing (line, square, ballroom), reading, camping, music, travel. Home: RR 2 Box 182 Dayton PA 16222-8813

PATTERSON, MARIA JEVITZ, microbiology-pediatric infectious disease educator; b. Berwyn, Ill., Oct. 23, 1944; d. Frank Jacob and Edna Frances (Costabile) Jevitz; m. Ronald James Patterson, Aug. 22, 1970; children: Kristin Lara, Kier Nicole. BS in Med. Tech. summa cum laude, Coll. St. Francis, Joliet, Ill., 1966; PhD in Microbiology, Northwestern U., Chgo., 1970; MD, Mich. State U., 1984. Diplomate Am. Bd. Med. Examiners, Am. Bd. Pediatrics Gen. Pediatrics, Am. Bd. Pediatrics Infectious Diseases. Lab. asst., instr. med. microbiology for student nurses Med. Sch. Northwestern U., Chgo., 1966-70; postdoctoral fellow in clin. microbiology affiliated hosps. U. Wash., Seattle, 1971-72; asst. prof. microbiology and pub. health Mich. State U., East Lansing, 1972-77, assoc. prof., 1977-82, assoc. prof. pathology, 1979-82, lectr. dept. microbiology and pub. health, 1982-87, resident in pediatrics affiliated hosps., 1984-85, 86-87, clin. instr. dept. pediatrics and human devel., 1984-87, assoc. prof. microbiology-pub. health-pediatrics-human devel., 1987-90, prof., 1990—; staff microbiologist dept. pathology Lansing Gen. Hosp., 1972-75; dir. clin. microbiology grad. program. Mich. State U., 1974-81, staff microbiologist, 1978-81; postdoctoral fellow in infectious diseases U. Mass. Med. Ctr., Worcester, 1985-86; asst. dir. pediatrics residency Grad. Med. Edn. Inc., Lansing, 1987-90; med. dir. Pediatrics Health Ctr. St. Lawrence Hosp., Lansing, Mich., 1987-90, Ingham Med. Ctr., 1990-94; cons. clin. microbiology Lansing Gen. Hosp., 1972-75, Mich. State U., 1976-82, Mich. Dept. Pub. Health, 1976—, Ingham County Health Dept., 1988—, Mich. Dept. Pub. Health, 1976—, Am. Health Cons., 1993; cons. to editorial bd. Infection and Immunity, 1977; presenter seminars. Contbg. author: Microbiology: Principles and Concepts, 1982, 4th edit., 1995, Pediatric Emergency Medicine, 1992, Principles and Practice of Emergency Medicine, 1997; item writer certifying bd. examination Bd. Am. Acad. Pediats., 1990—, Am. Bd. Osteopathy, 1997—; contbr. articles to profl. jours. and publs. Mem. hon. com. Lansing AIDS Meml. Quilt, 1993. Recipient award for teaching excellence Mich. State U. Coll. Osteo. Medicine, 1977, 78, 79, 80, 83, Disting. Faculty award Mich. State U., 1980, Woman Achiever award, 1985, excellence in pediatric residency teaching award, 1988, Alumni Profl. Achievement award Coll. of St. Francis, 1991; grantee renal disease divsn. Mich. Dept. Pub. Health 1976-82. Fellow Pediatric Infectious Diseases Soc., Infectious Diseases Soc. Am., Am. Acad. Pediatrics; mem. Am. Coll. Physician Execs., Am. Soc. Microbiology, Am. Soc. Clin. Pathologists (affiliate, bd. registrant), South Ctrl. Assn. Clin. Microbiology, Mich. Soc. Infectious Diseases, N.Y. Acad. Scis., Kappa Gamma Pi, Lambda Iota Tau. Roman Catholic. Home: 1520 River Ter East Lansing MI 48823-5314 Office: Mich State Univ Microbiology/Pub Health East Lansing MI 48824-1101

PATTERSON, MARION LOUISE, photographer, educator; b. San Francisco, Apr. 24, 1933; d. Morrie Leslie and Esther Elizabeth (Parker) P. BA, Stanford U., 1955; MA, Calif. State U., San Francisco, 1970. Clk. Best's Studio (Ansel Adams Gallery), Yosemite, Calif., 1958-61; asst. to photography editor Sunset mag., Menlo Park, Calif., 1961-64; freelance photographer, Oaxaca, Mex., 1964-66; comm. cons. Projects to Advance Creative in Edn., San Mateo, Calif., 1966-68; instr. photography, chmn. dept. Foothill Coll., Los Altos Hills, Calif., 1968—; instr. U. Calif., Santa Cruz, 1984—. One woman shows include West German Embassy in the Hague, Bayreuth, Republic of Germany, Kasteel Hoensbroeck, Netherlands, Oaxaca, Mex., San Francisco Mus. of Modern Art, Focus Gallery, San Francisco, Oakland Mus., Monterey County Mus., Stanford U., Ansel Adams Gallery, Yosemite, and others; exhibited in group shows MIT, George Eastman House, Polaroid Corp., Art in the Embassies, Ind. U., U. of Ala., Critics Choice Traveling Exhibit, New Light, New Directions, Reclaiming Paradise, and others; contbr. photographs and articles in books and magazines. Mem. Soc. for Photographic Edn.

PATTERSON, MARK JEROME, computer software designer; b. Inglewood, Calif., July 23, 1960; s. Jerry Lee Patterson and Robin Helen McCracken Steely; m. Jenny Anne Lynn, Dec. 31, 1995. Programmer Green & Assocs., L.A., 1985-87; systems analyst The Software Works, Glendale, Calif., 1987-90; programmer Snow Software, Clearwater, Fla., 1990; pres. Atomic Software, Altadena, Calif., 1990-94; mgr. KPMG Peat Marwick, Palo Alto, Calif., 1994—; design cons. Prestige Station, Inc., 1990-93, Petro-Can., Inc., Calgary, Alta., 1988-90. Author computer programs: Set of Dataflex Macros, 1990, Ultimate File Viewer, 1992, Data Communications and Client/Server Systems, 1993-97. Libertarian. Scientologist. Achievements include 1 patent pending for data reporting technology; rschr. Worldwide Web based sales automation and retail franchise applications and electronic software distribution technology. Avocations: running, bicycling. Home: 814 N Mentor Ave Pasadena CA 91104

PATTERSON, MARTHA ELLEN, artist, art educator; b. Anderson, Ind., Mar. 12, 1914; d. Clarence and Corrine Ringwald; m. John Downey, Nov. 27, 1935 (div. 1946); 1 child, Linda Carol; m. Raymond George Patterson, May 6, 1947; children: Albert Handell, John Pike, Valfred Thelin, Don Dennis, Marilyn Hughey Phillis. Student, Dayton Art Inst., Bendell Art Sch., Bradenton, Fla. Beauty operator WRENS, Springfield, Ohio, 1932-40; co-owner Park Ave. Gallery, Dayton; window decorator, art tchr.; tchr. art; judge art shows. One-woman shows include N.C.R. Country Club, Bill Turner Interiors, U. Dayton, High Street Gallery, Trails End Club, The Designerie, Riverbend Park, Statesman Club, State Fidelity Bank, Wegerzyn Hort. Ctr., Pebble Springs, Backstreet, First City Fed. Bank, Bradenton, Fla., Alley Gallery, Merrill Lynch, Miami U., Gem. City Bank, Dayton, Ohio, Winters Bank, Dayton, Sherwin Williams, Howard Johnsons, Dayton Woman's Club, Bergamo, Dayton Meml. Hall, Bob and Arts, Del Park Med. Soc., The Dayton Country Club, Christ Methodist Ch., Unitarian Ch., The Metropolitan, Rikes, Dr. Pavey's, Dr. Chaney's, Dayton Convention Ctr., The Yum Yum, Jan Strunk Interiors, Park Avenue Gallery; artist: (water colors, oils, acylics, inks and pastels) group exhbns. include: Dayton Art Inst., Meml. Hall of Dayton, Dayton Country Club, Bergamo, Women's Club of Dayton, Am. Watercolor Soc., Sarasota Art Ctr., Art League of Manatee County, Butler Inst., Riverbend Park, First City Fed., NCR Country Club, Springfield (Ohio) Mus., Longboat Key Art Ctr., others; represented in permanent collections of Mr. and Mrs. Richard Nixon, Virginia Graham, Les Brown, Paul Lynde, Air Force Mus. at Wright Patterson, Mr. and Mrs. Charles Lange of NCR, U. Dayton-Ohio, Dr. Stephen House, Doug Yeager and others. Vol. Christian Woman's Soc. of Am., Twig Children's Hosp., Dayton, The Utopians; mem. Tri Art Dayton, Long Boat Key Art Ctr., Fla., Dr. Stephen House Twigs of Childrens. Recipient first prize Dayton Soc. Painters and Sculptors Show Rikes, First Prize, 1976, 77, First Prize, Best in Show, 1978, Beavercreek Art Assn. First Place, Best in Show, Artist and Sculpture Yearly Show, 1966, 68 2d place, Dayton Art Inst. 2d prize, Tri County Hon. Mention, Walker Motor Sales 2d place, Bendell Art Gallery 2d and 3d, Montgomery County Fair Best in Show. Mem. Art League of Manatee County (Fla.), Nat. Mus. Women in Art, Am. Watercolor Soc., Springfield Mus. Art, Dayton Soc. Painters, N.Y. Watercolor Soc., Long Boat Key Art League, Tri Art. Republican. Methodist. Avocations: art mus., books, music, travel, gourmet cooking. Home: 3853 Lawrenceville Dr Springfield OH 45504-4459 Winter Address: 5920 7th Ave W Bradenton FL 34209-3519

PATTERSON, MARY-MARGARET SHARP, writer, editor, media strategist; b. Fairmont, W.Va., July 12, 1944; d. H. Sutton Sharp and Columbia Strock; m. David Sands, June 15, 1968; 1 child, Scott Sutton. BA cum laude, Ohio State U., 1966, MA, 1967. Media coordinator Am. Hosp. Assn., Chgo., 1969; feature and mag. writer Chgo. Today newspaper, 1969-70; reporter Houston Chronicle, 1971-73; instr. journalism U. Houston, 1974-76; asst. prof. Utica (N.Y.) Coll. U. Syracuse, 1976-78; dir. undergrad. studies coll. journalism U. Md., College Park, 1978-82, editor, 1982; dir. information and devel. Audubon Naturalist Soc. Cen. Atlantic States, Inc., Chevy Chase, Md., 1982-89; dir. media rels. Defenders of Wildlife, Washington, 1989-90; resident Johns Hopkins-Nanjing U. Ctr. for Chinese and Am. Studies, Nanjing, China, 1990-91; writer, editor Am. Assn. Retired Persons, Washington, 1993-95; prin. Mary Margaret Patterson Writer, Editor, Media Cons., 1996—; cons. project Africa Carnegie Mellon U. Pitts., 1969; newspaper div. head summer journalism inst. Trinity U., San Antonio, 1979-81; columnist San Antonio Mag., 1976-79; cons. Callahan & Assoc., Washington, 1992—. Editor: Credit Unions On-Line, 1996—; contbr. numerous articles and book revs. to newspapers and mags. Recipient Reporting Excellence award The Newspaper Fund, Cleve., 1966; Univ. Grad. fellow Ohio State U., 1966, Nat. Grad. fellow Women in Communications, 1967. Mem. Soc. Profl. Journalists, Mortar Bd., Washington Ind. Writers, Inc., Nat.Press CLub Libr., Kappa Tau Alpha.

PATTERSON, MELISSA, elementary education educator; b. Grand Island, Nebr., Nov. 24, 1956; d. John Abbott and Mabel Edith (Schimmer) P. BA, So. Calif. Coll., Costa Mesa, 1979; postgrad., San Diego State U., Imperial (Calif.) Valley Coll. Cert. multiple subject tchr., learning handicapped specialist, Calif., life sci. tchr., resource specialist. Dir., tchr. It's a Small World Presch., Imperial, Calif., 1980-82; prin., tchr. Faith Acad. Christian Sch., Imperial, 1982-87; tchr. 2d grade Imperial Unified Sch. Dist., 1988-90, secondary tchr. biology and chemistry, elem. reading specialist, 1990-91, reading, resource specialist, 1991-96; resource specialist, spl. edn. tchr. Calexico (Calif.) Unified Sch. Dist., 1996—. Mem. NEA, Coun. for Exceptional Children, Nat. Assn. Biology Tchrs., Calif. Sci. Tchrs. Assn., Calif. Edn. Assn., Southwest Marine Educators Assn. Home: 514 S F St Imperial CA 92251-1530 Office: Blanche Charles Elem Sch 1201 Kloke Ave Calexico CA 92231-3491

PATTERSON, MILDRED LUCAS, teaching specialist; b. Winston-Salem, N.C., Jan. 24, 1937; d. James Arthur and Lula Mae (Smith) Lucas; m. James Harrison Patterson Jr., Mar. 31, 1961; children: James Harrison III, Roger Lindsay. BA, Talladega Coll., 1958; MEd, St. Louis U., 1969; postgrad., Webster U., 1970. Classroom tchr. Winston-Salem (N.C.) Pub. Schs., 1959-61; classroom tchr. St. Louis Bd. Edn., 1961-72, reading specialist, 1972-88, co-host radio reading show, 1988-91; tchr. specialist Reading to Achieve Motivational Program, St. Louis, 1991—; bd. dirs. Supt.'s Adv. Com., University City, Mo., 1994—; presenter Chpt. I Regional Conf. Co-author: Wearing Purple, 1996. Bd. dirs. Gateway Homes, St. Louis, 1989-93; mem. com. University City Sch. Bond Issue, 1994. Recipient Letter of Commendation, Chpt. I. Regional Conf., 1991, Founders' award Gamma Omega chpt. Alpha Kappa Alpha, 1985. Mem. Internat. Reading Assn. (Broadcast Media award for radio 1990, Bldg. Rep. award St. Louis chpt. 1990), St. Louis Alliance of Black Educators. Avocations: reading, arts and crafts, storytelling, motivational speaking.

PATTERSON, ORLANDO, sociologist; b. Jamaica, June 5, 1940; came to U.S., 1970.; s. Charles A. Patterson and Almina Morris; m. Nerys Wyn Thomas, Sept. 5, 1965 (div. 1994); children: Rhiannon, Barbara; m. Anita Haya Goldman, Aug. 12, 1995. BS, U. of the West Indies, 1962; PhD, London Sch. of Econs., 1965; MA, Harvard U., Harvard, 1971; LHD (hon.), Trinity Coll., Conn., 1992. Asst. lectr. U. of London, London Sch. Econs. and Polit. Sci., 1965-67; lectr. U. of West Indies, 1967-70; vis. lectr. Harvard U., Cambridge, Mass., 1970-71, Allston Burr sr. tutor, 1971-73, prof. sociology, 1971-93, John Cowles prof. sociology, 1993—; vis. mem. Inst. Advanced Study, Princeton, N.J., 1975-76; vis. fellow, Wolfson Coll., Cambridge U., 1978-79; Phi Beta Kappa vis. scholar, 1988-89; mem. tech. advisory com. to prime min. and govt. of Jamaica, 1972-74; sp. advisor to prime min. of Jamaica, 1973-80. Author: (novels) The Children of Sisyphus, 1964 (1st prize Dakar Festival Negro Arts 1966), An Absence of Ruins, 1967, Die the Long Day, 1972, (nonfiction) The Sociology of Slavery, 1967, Ethnic Chauvinism, 1977, Slavery and Social Death, 1982 (co-winner Ralph Bunche award Am. Polit. Sci. Assn. 1983), Freedom; vol. 1, Freedom in the Making of Western Cluture, 1991 (Nat. Book award Nat Book Found. 1991), The Ordeal of Integration: Progress and Resentment in America's Racial Crisis, 1997; contbr. Stories from the Caribbean, 1965. Recipient UCLA medal, 1992; Guggenheim fellow, 1978-79. Mem. Am. Acad. Arts and Scis., Am. Sociol. Assn. (citation for disting. contbn. to scholarship 1983). Office: Harvard Univ Dept of Sociology William James 520 Cambridge MA 02138

PATTERSON, PAUL M., school administrator; b. Aberdeen, S.D., Sept. 29, 1946; s. Robert M. and Esther M. (Wellman) P.; 1 child, Jennifer K. BS, No. State U., 1964; MS, U. Ill., 1976, EdD, 1994. Tchr. Rapid City (S.D.) Pub. Schs., 1968-75, Rock Island (Ill.) Pub. Schs., 1975-76; tchr. Sch. Dist. U-46, Elgin, Ill., 1976-85, coord. fine arts, 1985-92, dir. instructional programs, 1992—; cons. Chgo. Pub. Schs., 1990, North Palos Dist. 117, North Palos Hills, Ill., 1993. Contbr. articles to profl. jours. Adv. bd. Ill. Arts Coun., Chgo., 1994—, Ill. Alliance for Arts Edn., Chgo., 1987—, Ill. State Bd. Edn. Fine Arts Com., Springfield, 1986-94; mem. Heritage Commn., Elgin, 1985-88. Ill. Administr. scholar Ill. Bd. Edn. and Nat. Gallery of Art, Washington, 1991. Mem. ASCD, Ill. ASCD, Am. Assn. Sch. Adminstr., Phi Delta Kappa, Kappa Delta Pi. Home: # 202 1371 Todd Farm Dr Elgin IL 60123-2302 Office: School District 46 355 E Chicago St Elgin IL 60120-6543

PATTERSON, PERRY WILLIAM, economist, publishing company executive; b. Lancaster, Pa., Nov. 18, 1949; s. William and Helen (Bergmark) P.; m. A. Kimball Harrill, Mar. 3, 1984; children: Reed W., Amy M. BS in Econs., U. Hartford, 1972; MA, U. Mass., 1974; MBA, Rutgers U., 1983. From econ. analyst to dir. econs. Cahners Pub. Co., 1974-81; economist, asst. dir. Ctr. Internat. Bus. Cycle Rsch., Rutgers U., 1981-83; dir. corp. rsch. and devel. Gordon Publs., Inc., 1984-88; dir. prod. dev. Faulkner & Gray, 1988-89; group pub., dir. confs. Inst. Mgmt. and Adminstrn., N.Y.C., 1989—; founder, pres. IBC, 1988—. Designer aerospace products mag., 1986—, newsletters; contbg. editor: Bus. Mktg., 1982-91; contbr. articles to profl. jours. Mem. Am. Econ. Assn., Nat. Assn. Bus. Economists, Bus. Profl. Advt. Assn., Am. Bus. Press (rsch. com.). Home: 259 Forest Ave Glen Ridge NJ 07028-1728 Office: Inst Mgmt and Adminstrn 29 W 35th St New York NY 10001-2299

PATTERSON, RICHARD NORTH, writer, lawyer; b. Berkeley, Calif., Feb. 22, 1947; s. Richard Wallace and Marjorie Frances (North) P.; m. Laurie Anderson, Apr. 13, 1993; children: Shannon Heath, Brooke North, Adam Chandler, Chase Kenyon, Katherine Jeanne Blunt, Stephen Thomas Blunt. BA History, Ohio Wesleyan U., 1968; JD, Case Western Reserve, 1971. Bar: Ohio, 1971, D.C., 1973, Ala., 1975, Calif., 1984. Asst. atty. gen. State of Ohio, 1971-73; with divsn. enforcement SEC, Washington, 1973-75, San Francisco, Calif., 1878-81; assoc. atty. Berkowitz, Lefkovits & Patrick, Birmingham, Ala., 1975-77, ptnr., 1978; assoc. McCutchen, Doyle, Brown & Enerson, San Francisco, Calif., 1985-87, ptnr., 1987-93, of counsel, 1993-94; mem. dean's nat. adv. com. Case Western Res. Sch. Law. Author: The Lasko Tangent, 1979, The Outside Man, 1981, Escape the Night, 1983, Private Screening, 1985, Degree of Guilt, 1993, Eyes of a Child, 1995, The Final Judgement, 1995, Silent Witness, 1997. Mem. bd. trustees Ohio Wesleyan U.; mem. regional panel for the selection of WhiteHouse Fellows, 1997; mem. dean's nat. adv. com. Case Western Res. Sch. Law. Recipient Edgar Allen Poe award for best 1st novel Mystery Writers Am., 1979, Grand Prix de Literateur Policiere, 1995, Pres.'s award for disting. Alumni, Case Western Res. U., 1997. Mem. PEN (bd. dirs., President's award for disting. alumni, 1997). Home: 2609 Fillmore St San Francisco CA 94115-1235

PATTERSON, ROBERT ARTHUR, physician, health care consultant, retired health care company executive, retired air force officer; b. Palestine, Ill., Sept. 3, 1915; s. Robert Bruce and Nera (McColpin) P.; m. Judith Scheirer, May 15, 1961; children: Mary Kay, Elaine Alice Mills, Robert Arthur II, Victoria Patterson Goodrum. Student, U. Ill., 1933-35; M.D., U. Louisville, 1939. Diplomate: aerospace medicine Am. Bd. Preventive Medicine. Intern Detroit Receiving Hosp., 1939-40; joined Mich. N.G., 1940; commd. USAAF, 1946; advanced through grades to lt. gen. USAF, 1972; rated chief flight surgeon and command pilot; assigned U.S. and ETO, 1940-45; assigned U.S., Spain, Japan, Philippines, 1945-63; dep. dir. plans and hospitalization Office Surgeon Gen., USAF, Washington, 1963-65; dir. plans and hospitalization Office Surgeon Gen., USAF, 1965-68; surgeon Hdqrs. USAFE, Lindsey Air Sta., Germany, 1968-71, Hdqrs. SAC, Offutt AFB, 1971-72; surgeon gen. USAF, 1972-75, ret., 1975; health care cons. Arlington, Va., 1975; sr. v.p. sci. affairs Baxter Travenol Labs., Inc., Deerfield, Ill., 1976-86, health care cons., 1987—. Decorated D.S.M. with oak leaf cluster, Legion of Merit with oak leaf cluster, Air Force Commendation medal; recipient citation of honor Air Force Assn., citation of distinction Fed. Hosp. Execs., citation of distinction Am. Hosp. Assn. Fellow Am. Coll. Preventive Medicine, Aerospace Medicine Assn., Am. Coll. Physician Execs. (founder); mem. Assn. Mil. Surgeons (pres. 1972), AMA, Am. Acad. Med. Dirs., Ret. Officers Assn., Soc. Mil. Cons. to Armed Forces, Soc. Armed Forces Med. Labs. Scis., NIH Alumni, U. Ill. Alumni Assn., Aircraft Owners and Pilots Assn., Order Daedalians, Assn. for Advancement of Med. Instrumentation, Exptl. Aircraft Assn., Deutsch Kurzhaar Verband, N.A. Versatile Hunting Dog Assn., Uniformed Services U. Health Scis. Alumni Assn., Air Safety Found. Clubs: Mid-America (Chgo.), Cen. Fla. Conservation and Hunt (Lake Wales, Fla.), Yacht and Country (bd. govs., pres., 1996-97, Stuart, Fla.), Sunshine Gun, Yacht (Stuart), Willoughby Golf Club (Stuart). Home and office: Yacht & Coutry Club 3474 SE Fairway East Stuart FL 34997

PATTERSON, ROBERT EDWARD, lawyer; b. Los Angeles, Sept. 14, 1942; s. Ellis Elwood and Helen (Hjelte) P.; m. Christina Balboni, Oct. 2, 1971; 1 child, Victor Ellis. BA, UCLA, 1964; JD, Stanford U., 1972, grad. bus. exec. program, 1986. Bar: Calif. 1972. Ptnr. Graham & James, Palo Alto, Calif., 1972—; bd. dirs. Procyte Corp., Thompson Clive (Venture Capital). Served to lt. comdr. USN, 1964-69. Mem. Am. Arbitration Assn. (panelist), Rotary, Palo Alto Club, Menlo Circus Club, Bohemian Club. Democrat. Office: Graham & James LLP 600 Hansen Way Palo Alto CA 94304-1024

PATTERSON, ROBERT HUDSON, library director; b. Alexandria, La., Dec. 11, 1936; s. Hubert Hudson and Beth (Jones) P.; 1 child, Jennifer Bookhart. B.A., Millsaps Coll., Jackson, Miss., 1958; M.A., Tulane U., 1963; M.L.S., U. Calif., Berkeley, 1965. Mem. profl. staff Tulane U. Libr., New Orleans, 1965-69, 73-76, asst. dir. collection devel., 1973-76; head spl. collections cataloging U. Tex., Austin, 1970-73; dir. librs. U. Wyo., Laramie, 1976-81, U. Tulsa, 1981—; chmn. exec. bd. Wyo. State Libr. Adv. Com., 1976-81; mem. bd. Okla. State Libr. Adv. Com., 1981-84; mem. adv. coun. Bibliog. Ctr. for Rsch., Denver, 1978-81; past mem. exec. bd. S.E. La. Libr. Network; bd. dirs. Amigos Bibliog. Coun., 1983-86; cons. NEH, Harry Ransom Humanities Rsch. Ctr., U. Tex., Austin. Editor Conservation Adminstrn. News, 1979-93; contbr. articles to profl. jours. Pres. Western Conservation Congress, 1981-82. Sr. fellow CLR/UCLA, 1989. Fellow Internat. Boswell Inst.; mem ALA (various offices), Okla. Libr. Assn. (various offices).

PATTERSON, ROBERT PORTER, JR., federal judge; b. N.Y.C., July 11, 1923; s. Robert Porter and Margaret (Winchester) P.; m. Bevin C. Daly, Sept. 15, 1956; children: Anne, Robert, Margaret, Paul, Katherine. AB, Harvard U., 1947; LLB, Columbia U., 1950. Bar: N.Y. 1951, D.C. 1966. Law clk. Donovan, Leisure, Newton & Lumbard, N.Y.C., 1950-51; asst. counsel N.Y. State Crime Commn. Waterfront Investigation, 1952-53; asst. U.S. atty. Chief of Narcotics Prosecutions and Investigations, 1953-56; asst. counsel Senate Banking and Currency Com., 1954; assoc. Patterson, Belknap, Webb & Tyler, N.Y.C., 1956-60, ptnr., 1960-88; judge U.S. Dist. Ct. (so. dist.) N.Y., 1988—; counsel to minority select com. pursuant to house resolution no. 1, Washington, 1967; mem. Senator's Jud. Screening Panel, 1974-88, Gov.'s Jud. Screening Panel, 1975-82, Gov.'s Sentencing Com., 1978-79. Contbr. articles to profl. jours. Chmn. Wm. T. Grant Found., 1974-94, Prisoners' Legal Services N.Y., 1976-88; dir. Legal Aid Soc., 1961-88, pres., 1967-71; chmn. Nat. Citizens for Eisenhower, 1959-60, Scranton for Pres., N.Y. State, 1964; bd. mgrs. Havens Relief Fun Soc., 1994—, Millbrook Sch., 1966-78, Vera Inst. Justice, 1981—, New Sch. for Social Rsch., 1986-94, George C. Marshall Found., 1987-93; mem. exec. com. Lawyers Com. for Civil Rights Under Law, 1968-88; mem. Goldman Panel for Attica Disturbance, 1972, Temporary Commn. on State Ct. System, 1971-73, Rockefeller U. Council, 1986-88, exec. com. N.Y. Vietnam Vets. Meml. Commn., 1982-85, Mayor's Police Adv. Com., 1985-87. Served to capt. USAAF, 1942-46. Decorated D.F.C. with cluster, Air medal with clusters. Mem. ABA (ho. of dels. 1976-80), N.Y. State Bar Assn. (pres. 1978-79), Assn. Bar City N.Y. (v.p. 1974-75), N.Y. County Lawyers Assn., Am. Law Inst., Am. Judicature Soc. (bd. dirs. 1979). Republican. Episcopalian. Home: Fair Oaks Farm Cold Spring NY 10516 Office: US Court House 500 Pearl St New York NY 10007-1316

PATTERSON, RODNEY LEE, foreign language and literature educator, translator; b. Sutherland, Nebr., Sept. 1, 1935; s. Milo Thomas Patterson and Ethel Marie Cochran; m. Marilyn Ruth Devereaux, March 22, 1968 (div. 1976); m. Sally Beth Hankwitz, Oct. 2, 1982; 1 child, Caitlin Clara. BA, UCLA, 1962, MA, 1964, PhD, 1969. Interpreter U.S. Army, 1958-61; asst. prof. U. Calif., Davis, 1967-73; assoc. SUNY, Albany, 1973—. Summer Slavic assoc., U. Ill., 1975; Fulbright Fellow, USSR, 1979-80. Mem. Am. Assn. Tchrs. Slavic and East European Lang. Avocation: writing poetry. Home: 5 Miller Rd Canaan NY 12029 Office: SUNY 1400 Washington Ave Albany NY 12222-0100

PATTERSON, RONALD PAUL, publishing company executive, clergyman; b. Ashland, Ohio, Dec. 4, 1941; s. Donald Edward and Mildred (Niswender) P.; m. Marlene Pfahler, Sept. 1, 1962; children: Paul Edward, Mark Loren. BA, Malone Coll., 1963; MDiv, United Theol. Sem., Dayton, Ohio, 1967; MA, Syracuse U., 1970; DD, Cen. Meth. Coll., 1988. Ordained to ministry United Methodist Ch., 1967. Editor youth publs. Otterbein Press, Dayton, 1964-68; assoc. editor The Upper Room, Nashville, 1970-74; editor Word Books, Waco, Tex., 1974-77; editorial dir. Abingdon Press, Nashville, 1977-88; book editor United Meth. Ch. Pub. House, 1977-88, v.p., 1984-88, sr. editor Ch. Resources, 1988-92; pub., CEO United Methodist Reporter, Dallas, 1992—; v.p. Religious Pub. Rels. Coun. Nashville, 1970-74; jr. coll. instr. creative writing, Waco; leader writers' workshops. Author: (with others) The Kyle Rote Story, 1975; editor: Come On, Let's Pray, 1972; compiler: The Coming of Easter, 1973; founding editor Alive Now! devotional publ.; editorial dir. Quar. Rev., 1980-87; contbr. articles to mags. Tchr. Tenn. State Prison, Nashville, 1984-88; vice chmn. pastor-parish com., Hermitage, Tenn., 1984-86; mem. bd. dirs. Perkins Sch. Theology, 1996—. Recipient George Washington Honor medal Nat. Freedom Found., Valley Forge, Pa., 1960, Paul M. Hinkhouse award Religious Pub. Relations Council, N.Y.C., 1973; named one of Outstanding Young Men Am., 1972. Mem. Am. Acad. Religion, Religion Pub. Group, Christian Publs. Assn., Southeastern Pubs. Assn. (exec. com. 1985-88), Pubs. Assn. of South (treas.), Evang. Christian Pubs. Assn. (bd. dirs. 1987-88), Protestant Ch.-owned Pubs. Assn. (bd. dirs.), Internat. Pubs. Assn. World Meth. Coun., Downtown Rotary Club (Dallas). Democrat. United Methodist. Avocations: boating, refinishing furniture, golf. Home: 1563 Waterside Ct Dallas TX 75218-4488 Office: 2400 Lone Star Dr Dallas TX 75212-6309

PATTERSON, RONALD R(OY), health care systems executive; b. Baton Rouge, Mar. 4, 1942. BS, U. Houston, 1965; MS, Trinity U., San Antonio, 1973. Asst. adminstr. Med. Br. Tex. U., Galveston, 1972-75; asst. v.p. Hosp. Affiliates Internat., Nashville, 1975-81; chief oper. officer Affiliated Hosp. Systems, Houston, 1981-82; sr. v.p. Republic Health Corp., Dallas, 1982-88; pres. Miller Patterson Inc., Plano, Tex., 1988-89; ind. healthcare mgmt. cons. Plano, 1989-90; sr. v.p. Harris Meth. Health System, Ft. Worth, Tex., 1990-91; exec. v.p., COO Champion Healthcare Corp., Houston, Tex., 1991-96; exec. v.p., pres. healthcare ops. Paracelsus Healthcare Corp., Houston, 1996—. Fellow Am. Coll. Healthcare Execs.; mem. Tex. Hosp. Assn. (vice chmn. multi-hosp. constituency 1987), Fedn. Am. Health Sys. (bd. govs. 1996-97, bd. dirs. 1997—). Avocation: photography. Office: Paracelsus Healthcare Corp 515 W Greens Rd Ste 800 Houston TX 77067-4511

PATTERSON, ROY, physician, educator; b. Ironwood, Mich., Apr. 26, 1926; s. Donald I. and Helmi (Lantta) P. M.D., U. Mich., 1953. Diplomate: Am. Bd. Internal Medicine, Am. Bd. Allergy and Immunology. Intern U. Mich. Hosp., Ann Arbor, 1953-54; med. asst. research U. Mich. Hosp., 1954-55, med. resident, 1955-57, instr. dept. medicine, 1957-59; attending physician VA Research Hosp., Chgo., Northwestern Meml. Hosp.; mem. faculty Northwestern U. Med. Sch., Chgo., 1959—; prof. medicine Northwestern U. Med. Sch., 1964—, Ernest S. Bazley prof. medicine, chief sect. allergy-immunology dept. medicine. Editor: Jour. Allergy and Clin. Immunology, 1973-78. Served with USNR, 1944-46. Fellow Am. Acad. Allergy (pres. 1976), A.C.P.; mem. Central Soc. for Clin. Research (pres. 1978-79). Office: Northwestern U Med Sch Dept Medicine 303 E Chicago Ave Chicago IL 60611-3008*

PATTERSON, RUSSELL, conductor, opera executive; b. Greenville, Miss., Aug. 31, 1930; s. Dudley Russell and Elizabeth (Taylor) P.; m. Teresa Gutierrez de Celis, Aug. 28, 1979; children: Richard Russell, Christopher Leonard. B.A., B.Mus., S.E. La. U., 1950; M.Mus., Kansas City Conservatory of Music, 1952; D.M.A., U. Mo. at Kansas City. Prof. music Kansas City Conservatory of Music, 1960-68; mem. profl. com. Met. Opera, 1962—; condr. Kansas City Symphony, 1982-83, artistic dir., 1982-86, condr. emeritus, 1986—; cons. Ford Found. Musician with Baton Rouge Symphony, 1948-50, Brevard Music Festival, 1947-49, Kansas City Philharmonic Orch., 1951-59, Bayrische Staatsoper, Munich, Germany, 1952-53; condr. Kansas City Philharmonic Orch., 1965-66, Point Lookout (Mo.) Festival, 1967—, Kansas City Ballet, 1965-66, Am. Ballet Co., European tour, 1958; gen. dir., Lyric Opera of Kansas City, 1958—, artistic dir., Missouri River Festival, 1976—; dir. Sunflower Music Festival, 1978—. Mem. opera com. Mo. Council Arts, 1965-69; mem. music panel Nat. Endowment Arts, 1970-72; mem. Univ. Assocs. U. Mo. at Kansas City, 1970—. Recipient Alice M. Ditson condrs. award Columbia U., 1982, W.F. Yates medalion William Jewell Coll.; named Disting. Alumni Southeast La. U. Mem. Friends of Art, Opera America (v.p. 1971-73), Phi Mu Alpha Sinfonia, Pi Kappa Lambda, Mensa. Home: 4618 Warwick Blvd Apt 1A Kansas City MO 64112-1751 Office: Lyric Opera Lyric Theater 1029 Central St Kansas City MO 64105-1619*

PATTERSON, SAMUEL CHARLES, political science educator; b. Omaha, Nov. 29, 1931; s. Robert Foster and Garnet Marie (Jorgensen) P.; m. Suzanne Louise Dean, June 21, 1956; children—Polly Ann, Dean Foster, Grier Edmund. B.A., U. S.D., 1953; M.S., U. Wis., 1956, Ph.D., 1959. Asst. prof. polit. sci. Okla. State U., Stillwater, 1959-61; asst. prof. U. Iowa, Iowa City, 1961-64, assoc. prof., 1964-67, prof., 1967-85, Roy J. Carver prof., 1985-86; prof. Ohio State U., Columbus, 1986—; vis. prof. U. Wis., 1962, U. Okla., 1968-78, U. Essex, Colchester, Eng., 1969-70. Author: (with others) Representatives and Represented, 1975, A More Perfect Union, 4th edit., 1989; co-author: The Legislative Process in the United States, 4th edit., 1986, Comparing Legislatures, 1979; editor: American Legislative Behavior, 1968; co-editor: Comparative Legislative Behavior: Frontiers of Research, 1972, Parliaments in the Modern World, 1994, Handbook of Legislative Research, 1985, Political Leadership in Democratic Societies, 1991; editor Am. Jour. Polit. Sci., 1970-73; co-editor Legis Studies Quar., 1981-85; mng. editor Am. Polit. Sci. Rev., 1985-91. Served with U.S. Army, 1953-55. Recipient Disting. Scholar award Ohio State U., 1990; fellow social Sci. Rsch. Coun., 1961, 67, Guggenheim, 1984-85; vis. fellow Brookings Instn., 1984-85, Ctr. Advanced Study in Behavioral Scis., 1993-94; Fulbright Bologna chair, 1995. Mem. Internat. Polit. Sci. Assn., So. Polit. Sci. Assn., Can. Polit. Sci. Assn., Am. Polit. Sci. Assn., Midwest Polit. Sci. Assn. (pres. 1980-81), Phi Beta Kappa, Phi Kappa Phi, Pi Sigma Alpha. Office: Ohio State U Dept Polit Sci 2140 Derby Hall 154 N Oval Mall Columbus OH 43210-1330

PATTERSON, STEVE, professional hockey team executive; b. Beaver Dam, Wis., Sept. 21, 1957. BBA with honors, U. Tex., 1980, JD, 1984. Bar: Tex. 1984. Gen. mgr., profl. basketball team counsel Houston Rockets, 1984-89, profl. basketball mktg. exec. group ticket sales, mgr., bus. ops. exec., gen. mgr., 1989-94; pres. profl. hockey team Houston Aeros, 1994—; pres. Arena Oper. Co., Houston, 1995—. Office: Houston Aeros 24 E Greenway Plz Ste 800 Houston TX 77046-2409

PATTERSON, VEDA MALIA, equal opportunity specialist; b. Greensboro, N.C., Nov. 9, 1954; d. Walter and Dorothy Martelle (Dusenbury) P. BA, Howard U., 1976; MS, Am. U., 1987. Claims svc. rep. State Farm Ins. Co., Alexandria, Va., 1978-83; substitute tchr. Fairfax County, Arlington County and Alexandria City Schs., 1983-88; cons. pub. rels. United Black Fund, Washington, 1985-87; equal opportunity specialist U.S. Dept. Agriculture, Washington, 1988—; participant U.S. Dept. Agriculture Mgmt. Devel. Program, Washington, 1993-94; cons. in field. Co-founder No. Va. chpt. Nat. Polit. Congress of Black Women. Mem. Continental Socs., Inc. (No. Va. chpt. v.p. 1993—), Jr. League No. Va., Howard U. Alumni Assn. (No. Va. chpt. charter mem., past sec., past v.p., pres.), Alpha Kappa Alpha. Democrat. Presbyterian. Avocations: photography, travel, cultural activities, political trivia, writing. Home: 8671 Maple Glen Ct Springfield VA 22153

PATTERSON, W. MORGAN, college president; b. New Orleans, Oct. 1, 1925; s. E. Palmer and Jess Margaret (Wood) P.; m. Ernestine North, June 10, 1948; children—W. Morgan, II, Jay North. B.A., Stetson U., 1950, D.D. (hon.), 1979; M.Div., New Orleans Baptist Theol. Sem., 1953, Th.D., 1956; postdoctoral, Oxford U., 1965-66, 72-73. Prof. ch. history New Orleans Bapt. Theol. Sem., 1956-59; prof. ch. history, David T. Porter prof. ch. history, dir. grad. studies So. Baptist Theol. Sem., Louisville, Ky., 1959-76; dean acad. affairs Golden Gate Bapt. Theol. Sem., Mill Valley, Calif., 1976-84; pres. Georgetown Coll., Ky., 1984-91; vis. prof. Midwestern Bapt. Theol. Sem., Kansas City, Mo., La. Coll., Pineville, 1991-92, Golden Gate Bapt. Theol. Sem., Mill Valley, Calif., 1992-94, New Orleans Bapt. Theol. Sem., 1995, 96; chmn. hist. commn. So. Bapt. Conv., Nashville, 1969-72; honored guest 2d Vatican Coun., Rome, 1965. Author: Baptist Successionism: A Critical View, 1969; co-editor: Professor in the Pulpit, 1963; contbr., editor: Ency. Southern Baptists; book rev. editor Review and Expositor, 1965-70. Served as flight officer USAAF, 1943-46. Recipient Disting. Alumnus award Stetson U., 1992, Disting. Svc. award for outstanding contbn. to Bapt. history Hist. Commn., So. Bapt. Conv., 1993; Am. Assn. Theol. Schs. fellow, 1965-66. Mem. Am. Soc. Ch. History, So. Bapt. Hist. Soc. (pres. 1979-80), William H. Whitsitt Bapt. Heritage Soc., Conf. on Faith and History, Commn. on Bapt. Heritage of Bapt. World Alliance. Avocations: travel; philately; collecting books. Home: 7 Pierce Dr Novato CA 94947-4450

PATTERSON, WILLIAM BRADFORD, surgical oncologist; b. New Rochelle, N.Y., June 25, 1921; s. Arthur Henry and Gertrude Claire (Hough) P.; m. Helen Russell Ross, May 17, 1943; children: William Bradford, Rebecca H. Bruns, Linda Stevens, Stuart Ross. A.B., Harvard U., 1943, M.D., 1950. Diplomate: Am. Bd. Surgery. Chemist E.I. DuPont Co., 1942-44; intern Peter Bent Brigham Hosp., Boston, 1950-51; resident in surgery, 1951-56; surgeon Boston City Hosp., 1956-59; practice medicine specializing in surgery Boston, 1963-70; chief Pondville Hosp., 1959-63; prof. surgery U. Rochester, N.Y., 1970-78; assoc. dir. for cancer control Dana Farber Cancer Inst., Boston, 1978-91; vis. prof. surgery Harvard Med. Sch., 1978-89; cons. Nat. Cancer Inst. Contbr. chpts. to books, articles to med. jours. Served with USNR, 1944-46. Fellow ACS; mem. Mass. Med. Soc., Boston Surg. Soc., New Eng. Surg. Soc., New Eng. Cancer Soc. Democrat. Congregationalist. Home: RR 1 Box 59 Middlebury VT 05753-9505

PATTERSON, WILLIAM BROWN, university dean, history educator; b. Charlotte, N.C., Apr. 8, 1930; s. William Brown and Eleanor Selden (Miller) P.; m. Evelyn Byrd Hawkins, Nov. 27, 1959; children: William Brown Patterson, Evelyn Byrd Donatelli, Lucy Patterson Murray, Emily Patterson Higgs. BA, U. South, 1952; MA, Harvard U., 1954, PhD, 1966, cert. ednl. mgmt., 1982; BA, Oxford (Eng.) U., 1955, MA, 1959; MDiv, Episc. Div. Sch., Cambridge, Mass., 1958. Ordained to ministry Episcopal Ch. as deacon, 1958, as priest, 1959. Asst. prof. history Davidson (N.C.) Coll., 1963-66, assoc. prof., 1966-76, prof. history, 1976-80; dean Coll. Arts and Scis. U. South, Sewanee, Tenn., 1980-91, prof. of history, 1980—. Author: (with others) Discord, Dialogue, and Concord, 1977; mem. bd. editors St. Luke's Jour. Theology, Sewanee, 1982-90; contbr. numerous articles to profl. jours. Trustee U. South, 1968-71; mem. internat. adv. com. U. Buckingham, Eng., 1977—; pres. So. Coll. and Univ. Union; organizer Associated Colls. of South, 1988-89. Danforth Found. grad. fellow, 1952, Mellon Appalachian fellow U. Va., 1992-93, rsch. fellow NEH, 1967, Folger Shakespeare Libr., Washington, 1975, Inst. for Rsch. in Humanities, U. Wis., Madison, 1976, Newberry Libr., Chgo., 1979; Rhodes scholar, 1953. Mem. Am. Hist. Assn., Am. Soc. Ch. History, N.Am. Conf. on Brit. Studies, Eccles. History Soc. Eng., Renaissance Soc. Am., So. Hist. Assn., Soc. for Values in Higher Edn., Episcopal Div. Sch. Alumni/ae Assn. (mem. exec. com. 1984-87), Phi Beta Kappa, Beta Theta Pi. Avocations: gardening, tennis. Home: 195 N Carolina Ave Sewanee TN 37375-2040 Office: U of the South Dept History Sewanee TN 37383-1000

PATTERSON, WILLIAM ROBERT, lawyer; b. Wathena, Kans., Feb. 25, 1924; s. George Richard and Jessie (Broadbent) P.; m. Lee Rhyne, Aug. 16, 1947; children: Martha, Robert, Elizabeth. Student, U. Rochester, 1943-44; A.B., Lenoir-Rhyne Coll., 1947; LL.B. with distinction, Duke U., 1950. Bar: Ga. 1951, D.C. 1962. Asso. firm Sutherland, Asbill & Brennan, Atlanta, 1950-58; partner Sutherland, Asbill & Brennan, 1958—; trustee Ga. Tax Conf., 1980-83, pres., 1980-82; lectr. in field. Mem. bd. visitors Duke U. Law Sch., 1973-87, chmn., 1977-87, life mem., 1987—; trustee Pace Acad., Atlanta, 1958-89, trustee emeritus, 1989—; mem. devel. bd. Lenoir-Rhyne Coll., 1976-79, trustee, 1980-89; elder Trinity Presbyterian Ch., Atlanta. With USN, 1942-46. Fellow Am. Coll. Mortgage Attys. (bd. regents 1993—, pres.-elect 1996—); mem. ABA, Ga. State Bar, Atlanta Bar Assn., D.C. Bar Assn., Am. Coll. Real Estate Lawyers (bd. govs. 1987-90), Am. Law Inst., So. Fed. Tax Inst. (trustee 1957-90, adv. trustee 1990—, pres. 1974-75, chmn. 1975-76), Atlanta Tax Forum (trustee 1977-83, pres. 1981-82), Order of Coif, Cherokee Town and Country Club, Commerce Club, Peachtree Club. Home: 2939 Rivermeade Dr NW Atlanta GA 30327-2039 Office: Sutherland Asbill & Brennan First Union Pla 23d Fl 999 Peachtree St NE Atlanta GA 30309-3964

PATTESON, ROY KINNEER, JR., clergyman, administrator; b. Richmond, Va., Oct. 27, 1928; s. Roy Kinneer and Mary (Anderson) P.; m. Edna Pauline Cox, Apr. 15, 1950; children: Stephen, David. B.A., U. Richmond, 1957; B.D., Union Theol. Sem., 1961; Th.M., Duke U., 1964, Ph.D., 1967. Ordained to ministry Presbyterian Ch. in U.S.A., 1961. Fellow Duke U. Inst. Medieval and Renaissance Studies, 1968; pres. So. Sem. Jr. Coll., 1970-72; v.p. Mary Baldwin Coll., 1972-77; pres. King Coll., Bristol, Tenn., 1977-79; asst. to pres. Va. Wesleyan Coll., 1979-81, v.p., 1981-85; v.p. Westminster-Canterbury of Hampton Rds., Inc., Virginia Beach, Va., 1985-88; asst. sec. bd. trustees Westminster-Canterbury of Hampton Rds., Inc., 1986-88; dir. Norfolk (Va.) Sr. Ctr., 1987-88; cons. Marts & Lundy Inc., Rockbridge Baths, Va., 1988-92; trustee, treas. Beverley St. Studio Sch., Staunton, Va., 1996—; pastor Pittsboro and Mt. Vernon Springs Presbyn. chs., Pittsboro, N.C., 1962-65; mem. mission council and chmn. budget com. Shenandoah Presbytery, 1973-77; chmn. com. on higher edn. Norfolk Presbytery, 1980-82; mem. community adv. bd. Madison Coll., 1975-77; bd. dirs. Tenn. Ind. Coll. Fund; v.p. Mid-Appalachian Coll. Council, 1978-79. Vice pres. Rockbridge Hist. Soc., Lexington, Va., 1970-77; chmn. edn. com. Staunton-Augusta C. of C. Served with U.S. Army, 1948-49; with U.S. N.G., 1949-52. Recipient Grad. Scholar award Duke U., 1966. Office: 342 Bellevue Ln Rockbridge Baths VA 24473-2134

PATTI, SISTER JOSEPHINE MARIE, health science facility administrator; b. Buffalo, July 5, 1934; d. Joseph John and Caroline Mary (Mayer) P. BS, D'Youville Coll., Buffalo, 1964; MHA, Xavier U., Cin., 1974. Joined Grey Nuns of Sacred Heart, Roman Cath. Ch., 1954. Med. technologist Griffin Meml. Hosp., Kodiak, Alaska, 1964-70; asst. supr., sr. med. tech. A.B. Hepburn Hosp., Ogdensburg, NY, 1970-72; adminstrv. res. St. Joseph's Infirmary, Atlanta, 1973-74; adminstr. Kodiak (Alaska) Island Hosp., 1974-78; adminstrv. asst. St. Joseph's Hosp. Inc., Atlanta, 1978-79; asst. adminstr. St. Joseph's Hosp., 1979-80; dir., misson effective St. Joseph's Hosp., Atlanta, 1986-88, asst. v.p., 1988-90, v.p. misc. effect, 1990-95; adminstr. Motherhouse, Grey Nuns of the Sacred Heart, Yardley, Pa., 1980-85; dir. St. Joseph's Mercy Care Corp., Atlanta, 1988-95; v.p. Mission St. Joseph Healthcare, Nashua, N.H., 1995-97; v.p. mission integration Optima Healthcare, Manchester, N.H., 1997—; chairperson bd. dirs. Atlanta Cmty. Health Program for the Homeless, 1988-91; vice chairperson bd. dirs. Mercy Mobile Health Program, 1991-94; dir. South Ctrl. Health Planning and Devel., Inc., Anchorage, 1976-77. Mem. adv. bd. Lifelink Ga., 1988-91; mem. instnl. rev. bd. AIDS Rsch. Consortium, Atlanta, 1988-95; dir. North Atlanta Sr. Svcs., 1988-93; bd. dirs. Mercy Sr. Care, 1991-95, sec., 1991-93; mem. Hispanic Svcs. Adv. Bd., 1991-94; bd. dirs. Cath. Social Svcs., Inc., 1992-95. Fellow Am. Coll. Health Care Execs.; mem. Sohegan Nursing Assn., Inc. (bd. dirs. 1996—). Office: Optima Healthcare One Executive Park Dr Bedford NH 03110

PATTILLO, MANNING MASON, JR., academic administrator; b. Charlottesville, Va., Oct. 11, 1919; s. Manning Mason and Margaret (Camblos) P.; m. Martha A. Crawford, June 8, 1946; children: Manning Mason III (dec.), Martha Crawford, John Landrum. Student, Johns Hopkins U., 1937-38; BA with highest honors, U. of South, 1941, DCL, 1993; student, U. Calif. at Berkeley, 1941-42; AM, U. Chgo., 1947, PhD, 1949; LLD, LeMoyne Coll., 1967, St. John's U., 1968, Oglethorpe U., 1994; LHD, U. Detroit, 1968, Coll. New Rochelle, 1967, Park Coll., 1973; LittD, St. Norbert Coll., 1967. From instr. to assoc. prof. higher edn. U. Chgo., 1949-56; assoc. dir. Lilly Endowment, Inc., Indpls., 1956-60; exec. dir. for edn. Lilly Endowment, Inc., 1961-62; dir. Danforth commn. on ch. colls. and univs., 1962-66; assoc. dir. The Danforth Found., 1964-66, v.p., 1966-67; pres. The Found. Center, N.Y.C., 1967-71; adj. prof. N.Y. U., 1968-71; dir. spl. projects U. Rochester, 1972-75; pres. Oglethorpe U., Atlanta, 1975-88, chancellor, 1988—; cons. in field; tech. asst., then assoc. sec. commn. on colls. and univs. North en. Assn. Colls. and Secondary Schs., 1948-56; cons. USAF Acad., 1952, Phillips Exeter Acad., 1974; chmn. IBM Incentive awards com., 1970-75; adv. com. Brookings Instn., 1970-71; vis. prof. Inst. Higher Edn., U. Ga., 1988—; bd. dirs. Fidelity Nat. Bank. Author: (with D.M. Mackenzie) Church Sponsored Higher Education in the United States, 1966, (with D.M. Mackenzie) Eight Hundred Colleges Face the Future, 1965, Private Higher Education in the United States, 1990, The Episcopal Church: Diagnosis and Reform, 1989; contbr. articles to profl. jours. Mem. pres.'s adv. coun. Wellesley Coll., 1969-72; trustee Seabury Press, Japan Internat. Christian U., 1970-72, Le Moyne Coll., 1970-83, Sacred Heart U., 1968-75, U. of South, 1984-88, St. Martin's Episc. Sch.; bd. dirs., chmn. Atlanta Coll. Art, 1984-95, Howard Sch.; trustee Greater Rochester Community Found., 1973-75, pres., 1975; trustee, chmn. Nat. Coun. on Philanthropy, 1968-80; trustee, chmn. bd. trustees Park Coll., 1967-74; provost St. Mary's Coll. of Md., 1975; bd. visitors Kanuga Confs., Inc.; pres., life trustee Ga. Found. for Ind. Colls., 1977-79; chmn. Univ. Center in Ga., 1978-79; pres. Assn. Pvt. Colls. and Univs. of Ga., 1980-81; trustee, chmn. Ga. Spl. Olympics; trustee, mem. exec. com. Nat. Assn. Ind. Colls. and Univs., Ind. Coll. Funds of Am., 1982-86; co-dir. Coll. Cons. Network, So. Assn. Colls. and Schs., 1988-96; mem. De Kalb Community e lations Commn.; chmn. De Kalb Community Coun. on the Aging; mem. commn. on colls. and steering com. on revision accrediting procedures So. Assn. Colls. and Schs.; vice-chmn bd. and life trustee, Woodruff Arts Ctr.; mem. adv. coun. ARC. Witth AUS, 1942-46. Mem. Nat. Assn. Scholars, Assn. for Higher Edn., Nat. Assn. Ind. Schs. (bd. dirs.), Guild of Scholars, English Speaking Union (dir., pres. br., nat. bd. dirs.), Country Day Sch. Headmasters Assn. U.S. (hon.), Phi Beta Kappa Assn. of Atlanta (pres., chmn.), Atlanta Hist. Soc., Dekalb C. of C. (dir., chmn.), Phi Beta Kappa, Omicron Delta Kappa, Kappa Sigma. Episcopalian (vestryman, sr. warden, mem. cathedral chpt., diocesan council, standing com.). Clubs: Century (N.Y.C.); Commerce, Capital City. Lodge: Rotary. Office: Office of Chancellor Oglethorpe Univ 4484 Peachtree Rd NE Atlanta GA 30319-2737

PATTIS, S. WILLIAM, publisher; b. Chgo., July 3, 1925; s. William Robert and Rose (Quint) P.; m. Bette Z. Levin, July 16, 1950; children: Mark Robert, Robin Quint Himovitz. BS, U. Ill., 1949; postgrad., Northwestern U., 1949-50. Exec. v.p., pub. United Bus. Publs., 1949-59; chmn., CEO 3M/Pattis, 1959-88; pres. NTC Pub. Group, Lincolnwood, Ill., 1961-96, Next Chapter Holdings, L.P., Highland Park, Ill., 1996—; dir. P-B Comm., Winnetka, Ill., 1978—; bd. dirs. 1st Colonial/Highwood; mem. book and libr. com. USIA, Washington, 1986-89, chmn., 1989-93; mem. exec. com. Pub. Hall of Fame, 1987—; chmn. U.S.-USSR Bilateral Info. Talks, Moscow, 1990. Mem. Pres.'s Coun. Youth Opportunity, 1968-70; bd. dirs. Photography Youth Found., 1970-73, Expt. in Internat. Living, 1970, Inst. Human Creativity, 1983—, Fund for Am.'s Libraries, 1996—; vice chmn. bd. dirs. Annenberg Ctr. for Health Scis., 1991-96, vice chmn., 1996—; trustee Eisenhower Med. Ctr., Rancho Mirage, Calif., 1989—, exec. com. mem., 1996—; trustee Am. Coun. Tchrs. Russian, 1992-96; bd. dirs. Nat. Security Edn. Act, Washington, 1993-94; lord of manor, Kirkbride, Eng., 1989—. Recipient Human Rels. award Am. Jewish Com., 1971, Paul Simon award Cen. States Conf. on Tchg. Fgn. Langs., 1992. Mem. Standard Club (Chgo.), Northmoor Country Club (Highland Park, Ill.), Tamarisk Country Club (Rancho Mirage). Home: 195 Elder Ln Highland Park IL 60035-5368 Office: Next Chpt Holdings Port Clinton Sq 600 Central Ave Highland Park IL 60035-3211

PATTISHALL, BEVERLY WYCKLIFFE, lawyer; b. Atlanta, May 23, 1916; s. Leon Jackson and Margaret Simkins (Woodfin) P.; children by previous marriage: Margaret Ann Arthur, Leslie Hansen, Beverly Wyckliffe, Paige Terhune Pattishall Watt, Woodfin Underwood; m. Dorothy Daniels Mashek, June 24, 1977; 1 stepchild, Lyssa Mashek Piette. BS, Northwestern U., 1938; JD, U. Va., 1941. Bar: Ill. 1941, D.C. 1971. Pvt. practice law Chgo., 1946—; ptnr. Pattishall, McAuliffe, Newbury, Hilliard & Geraldson and predecessor firms, Chgo.; dir. Juvenile Protective Assn. Chgo., 1946-79, pres., 1961-63, hon. dir., 1979—; dir. Vol. Interagy. Assn., 1975-78, sec., 1977-78; U.S. del. Diplomatic Confs. on Internat. Trademark Registration Treaty, Geneva, Vienna, 1970-73, Diplomatic Conf. on Revision of Paris Conv., Nairobi, 1981; mem. U.S. del. Geneva Conf. on Indsl. Property and Consumer Protection, 1978; adj. prof. trademark, trade identity and unfair trade practices law Northwestern U. Sch. Law, Chgo. Author: (with David C. Hilliard) Trademarks, Trade Identity and Unfair Trade Practices, 1974, Unfair Competition and Unfair Trade Practices, 1985, Trademarks, 1987, Trademarks and Unfair Competition, 1994, 2d edit., 1996; contbr. articles to profl. jours. Bd. dirs. Constl. Rights Found. Chgo., 1996—. Lt. comdr. USNR, WWII, ETO, PTO, ATO, ret. comdr. Award after Beverly Wyckliffe Pattishall Brand Nams Found. Fellow Am. Coll. Trial Lawyers (bd. regents 1979-83); mem. ABA (chmn. sect. patent, trademark copyright law 1963-64), Internat. Patent and Trademark Assn. (pres. 1955-57, exec. com. 1955—), Assn. Internat. Pour La Protection Propriete Indsl. (mem. of honor), Ill. Bar Assn., Chgo. Bar Assn., D.C. Bar Assn., Chgo. Bar Found. (dir. 1977-83), U.S. Trademark Assn. (dir. 1963-65), Legal Club, Law Club (pres. 1982-83), Econ. Club, Chikaming Country Club, Univ. Club, Mid-Am. Club, U. Va. Lile Law Soc. (sr. counselor), Selden Soc. (London, Ill. rep.). Office: Pattishall McAuliffe Newbury Hilliard & Geraldson 311 S Wacker Dr Ste 5000 Chicago IL 60606-6622

PATTISON, ABBOTT LAWRENCE, sculptor; b. Chgo., May 15, 1916; s. William L. and Bonnie (Abbott) P.; m. Mary Grant, June 2, 1945; children: William G., Grant A., Harry A., Jean G. BA, Yale, 1937, BFA, 1939. Tchr. Chgo. Art Inst., 1946-51; instr. Skowhegan Art Sch., 1955-56. Sculptor in residence U. Ga., 1953-54; affiliated Feingarten Gallery, Los Angeles, Fairweather Hardin Gallery, Chgo., Alwin Gallery, London; major commns. include Mayo Clinic, Rochester, Minn., Cen. Nat. Bank, Cleve., U. Chgo., Chgo. State U., Ill. Capitol Bldg., Lincoln Library, Springfield, Ill., Northbrook (Ill.) Library, New Trier West High Sch., Northfield Ill., Culligan Internat. & Commerce Plaza, Oak Brook, Ill.; 1st Logan prize and purchase Art Inst. Chgo. 1942, Eisendrath prize 1946, 1st Pauline Palmer prize for sculpture 1950, prize 1953, 3d prize contemporary sculpture show Met. Mus. Art 1951, 1st prize Chgo. Sculptor Show, Art Cen. 1955, 1st prize McCormick Pl. Art Show 1962, prize Bundy Mus., Waitsfield, Vt. 1963; work in China and Japan, 1940, Europe, 1950-51, 55-56, 58, 60-61, Italy, 1955-96, 58, 60-61; represented in collections Art Inst. Chgo., Corcoran Gallery, Washington, Phoenix Museum, Calif. Palace Legion of Honor, others; represented permanent collections at Whitney Mus., N.Y.C., Israel State Mus. Jerusalem, San Francisco Mus., Buckingham Palace, London, Eng., Yorkshire (England) Sculpture Park, U.S. State Dept., St. Louis Mus., Palm Springs Desert Mus., Portland (Maine) Mus., Addison Gallery Am. Art., Davenport Mus., Evansville Mus., Ravinia Pk., Highland Pk., Ill. Capt. USN, 1942-45. Recipient of Yale U.'s 1st traveling fellowship, 1939, 1st Logan prize Art Inst. Chgo., 1942, medal of merit City of Florence, Italy, 1994. Address: RR 2 Box 12 Lincolnville ME 04849-9601

PATTISON, JON ALLEN, computer scientist, consultant; b. Sturgis, Mich., July 18, 1960; s. Jerome and Karen Pattison; m. Nandini Pattison, July 14, 1990; 1 child, Nisha Lynn. Student, Glen Oaks C.C., 1978-79, U. Tex., Arlington, 1987. Mgr. Magic City Hardware, 1978-79; engring. technician Quazon Corp., 1983-84, Sci. Machines Corp., 1984; design engr. Tex. Arrays, 1984-86, EMS Group, Inc., 1986-89; hardware project leader Vortech Data, 1990; systems engr. Computer Task Group, 1991; cons. Decision Cons. Inc., 1992; self-employed cons., 1989, 91-92, 93; cons. Oxford and Assocs., Inc., 1992-94, R.S. Internat., 1993-94; product mgr. Teknekron InfoSwitch, Fort Worth, 1994—. Author design papers and system design documents. Served to sgt. USMC, 1979-83. Avocations: woodworking, scuba diving.

PATTISON, ROBERT MAYNICKE, architect; b. Colonia, N.J., Feb. 22, 1923; s. Maynicke Munn Pattison and Lillian Cornelia (Garretson) Pattison Fox; divorced; children: Jeannine (Mrs. D. Harper), Darrel Keith, Michael Shaun. Lic. architect, Ohio. Project coord. Walker & Weeks, Cleve., 1948-60; project architect Shaefer, Flynn & Williams, Cleve., 1960-62; v.p. Williams-Pattison Assoc., Inc., Cleve., 1962-74; prin. Robert M. Pattison, Architect, Berea, Ohio, 1974-85, 90—; architect, plan examiner City of Cleve. Bldg Dept., 1985-90; project architect Dalton-Dalton-Newport A/E, Shaker Heights, Ohio, 1977-78; asst. supr. Turner Constrn., Inc., Cleve., 1980; architect Lawson Co., Cuyahoga Falls, Ohio, 1980-81. Co-author: IEEE White Book, 1979. With USN, 1943-45. Mem. Kiwanis (pres. Middleburg Heights club 1991-92). Republican. Home and Office: 444 Woodlawn Cir Berea OH 44017-1231

PATTON, ALTON DEWITT, electrical engineering educator, consultant, research administrator; b. Corpus Christi, Tex., Feb. 1, 1935; s. Alton G. and Civilia Louise (Taylor) P.; m. Nancy Jo Elder, Mar. 1, 1959; children: Elizabeth, Carolyn. BEE, U. Tex., Austin, 1957; MEE, U. Pitts., 1961; PhD in Elec. Engring., Tex. A&M U., 1972. Registered profl. engr., Tex. Engr. Westinghouse Electric Corp., Pitts., 1957-65; prof. elec. engring. dept. Tex. A&M U., College Station, 1965-79, 82—, head elec. engring. dept., 1992-96, Brockett prof., 1986, Dresser prof., 1987, dir. Electric Power Inst., 1976-79, 85-92; rsch. fellow Tex. Engring. Expt. Sta., College Station, 1985; dir. Ctr. for Space Power Tex. Engring. Expt. Sta., 1987-92; pres. Associated Power Analysts Inc., College Station, Tex., 1973—. Contbr. articles to elec. engring. jours., 1960—. Fellow IEEE (tech. com., aerospace policy com., prize paper award 1975, 94); mem. NSPE, Internat. Conf. on Large High Voltage Electric Systems. Republican. Presbyterian. Avocations: fishing, hunting, photography, stamp and coin collecting. Home: 1217 Merry Oaks Dr College Station TX 77840-2608 Office: Tex A&M U Elec Engring Dept College Station TX 77843

PATTON, BOB J., oil industry executive; b. Whitt, Tex., Nov. 5, 1925; s. John Elmer and Dora Althia (Davis) P.; m. Glenda Nell Colbert, May 30, 1950; children: Eva Diane, Elaine Gay, John Carl. BS in Physics, U. North Tex., 1949, MS in Physics, 1950. Instr. U. North Tex., Denton, 1950-51; rschr. Gulf R & D, Pitts., 1951-53; rsch. assoc. Mobil R & D, Dallas, 1953-80; mwd mgr. Gearhart Industries, Ft. Worth, 1980-82; pres. Patton Cons., Inc., Dallas, 1982—. Patentee in field. With USN, 1945-46. Mem. Soc.

Petroleum Engrs., Aircraft Owners & Pilots Assn., Sigma Pi Sigma. Republican. Avocations: inventing, woodworking, flying. Home and Office: 2436 Monaco Ln Dallas TX 75233-2826

PATTON, CARL ELLIOTT, physics educator; b. San Antonio, Sept. 14, 1941; s. Carl Elliott and Geraldine Barnett (Perry) P. BS, MIT, 1963; MS, Calif. Inst. Tech., 1964, PhD, 1967. Sr. scientist Raytheon Co., Waltham, Mass., 1967-71; assoc. prof. physics Colo. State U., Ft. Collins, 1971-75, prof., 1975—; IEEE Magnetics Soc. Disting. lectr., 1993; chair-elect Am. Phys. Soc. Topical Group on Magnetism and its Applications. editor-in-chief IEEE Transactions on Magnetics, 1987-91. Fellow IEEE, Am. Phys. Soc. Office: Colo State Univ Dept Physics Fort Collins CO 80523

PATTON, CARL VERNON, academic administrator, educator; b. Coral Gables, Fla., Oct. 22, 1944; s. Carl V. and Helen Eleanor (Benkert) P.; m. Gretchen West, July 29, 1967. BS in Community Planning, U. Cin., 1967; MS in Urban Planning U. Ill.-Urbana, 1969, MS in Pub. Adminstrn., 1970; MS in Pub. Policy, U. Calif.-Berkeley, 1975, PhD in Pub. Policy, 1976. Instr. to prof. U. Ill., 1968-83, dir. Bureau of Urban and Regional Planning Rsch., 1977-79, prof., chmn. dept., 1979-83; prof., dean Sch. Architecture and Urban Planning, U. Wis., Milw., 1983-89; v.p. acad. affairs, prof. polit. sci., geography and urban planning U. Toledo, 1989-92; pres. Ga. State U., Atlanta, 1992—. Author: Academia in Transition, 1979; (with others) The Metropolitan Midwest, 1985; (with David Sawicki) Basic Methods of Policy Analysis and Planning, 1986, rev. 2d edit., 1993; (with Kathleen Reed) Guide to Graduate Education in Urban and Regional Planning, 1986, 88; editor: Spontaneous Shelter: International Perspectives and Prospects, 1988, (with G. William Page) Quick Answers to Quantitative Problems: A Pocket Primer, 1991; assoc. editor Jour. of Planning Edn. and Rsch., 1983-87, mem. editl. bd., 1987-89; mem. editl. bd. Habitat International, 1993—, Atlanta International Magazine, 1993—; contbr. articles to profl. jours. Chmn. Community Devel. Commn., Urbana, 1978-82; mem. Civic Design Ctr., Milw., 1983-87; mem. City of Milw. Art Commn., 1988-89, ToledoVision, 1989-92, Toledo Art Ctr. Bd., 1989-92, City of Toledo Bd. Cmty. Rels., 1990-92; bd. dirs. The Atlanta Downtown Partnership, pres., 1997, Ctrl. Atlanta Progress, Ga. Rsch. Alliance, Ctrl. Atlanta Hospitality Childcare, Inc., Atlanta Convention and Vis. Bur., Atlanta United Way, Woodruff Art Ctr., Fox Theatre; chair Grady (Hosp.) Healthcare, Inc.; mem. exec. com. The Fairlie-Poplar Task Force, Grady Healthcare Inc., The Univ. Ctr. in Ga.; mem. Ga. Coun. on Econ. Edn., Atlanta Neighborhood Devel. Ptnrship. Fellow NIMH, 1973-75, U. Ill. Center for Advanced Studies, 1973-74. Mem. Am. Planning Assn., Am. Inst. Cert. Planners, Assn. Collegiate Schs of Planning (v.p. 1985-87, pres. 1989-91), Atlanta C. of C. Avocations: racquetball, photography, travel. Home: 3807 Tuxedo Rd NW Atlanta GA 30305-1042 Office: Ga State U Office of Pres University Plz Atlanta GA 30303-3083

PATTON, DAVID WAYNE, health care executive; b. Utica, N.Y., June 15, 1942; s. Dale Willard and Eleanor (Miller) P.; BS, Ariz. State U., 1964; MHA, U. Minn., 1966; MA, Claremont U., 1989, MBA, 1991, PhD, 1997; m. Barbara Jean; children: Jodi Lynn, Steven Wayne. Asst. adminstr. Maricopa County Gen. Hosp., Phoenix, 1969-71; adminstr. Holy Rosary Hosp., Miles City, Mont., 1971-74; exec. dir. St. Luke's Hosp., Aberdeen, S.D., 1974-79; pres., CEO Parkview Episcopal Med. Ctr., Pueblo, Colo., 1979-84; pres. Cmty. Health Corp. and Riverside (Calif.) Cmty. Hosp., 1984-92; pres. DevelopMed Inc., Fullerton, Calif., 1993-95; adminstr., CEO Kona Cmty. Hosp., Kealakekua, Hawaii, 1995—; Bd. dirs. San Louis Valley Health Maintenance Orgn., 1982-84, World Pres. Orgn., Riverside C. of C., 1986-91, pres. 1988-89; campaign chmn. United Way of the Inland Valleys, 1989-90; founder Leadership Pueblo, 1982; founder, chmn. Leadership Riverside, 1987-89. Capt. USAF, 1966-69. Fellow Am. Coll. Healthcare Execs. (regent 1976-79). Republican. Home: PO Box 2268 Kealakekua HI 96750

PATTON, DIANA LEE WILKOC, artist; b. New Rochelle, N.Y., June 28, 1940; d. August E. and Meta Diane (Neuburg) Wilkoc; m. Gardner C. Patton, Aug. 10, 1963; children: Michael, Talryn, Shawn. AB cum laude Brown U., 1962; postgrad. Pan-Am. Art Inst., 1962-63. Svc. mgr. Lord and Taylor, N.Y.C., 1962-63; tchr. adult edn., Mountain Lakes, N.J., 1972-74, Somerville, N.J., 1978-82, Bound Brook Adult Sch., 1982—; artist in watercolors, pen and ink, acrylics, jewelry created; one-woman and group shows N.E. U.S., Perth, Australia, 1977, spl. bicentennial exhibit, Trenton, 1976, Rutgers U., 1980, Brookdale Coll., 1982, Camden County Coll., 1986, Morris County Coll., 1988, Bergen Mus. Arts and Scis., 1987, 88, 90, 91, North Gallery, Far Hills, 1982, 86, Clarence Dillon Gallery, 1989, 91, Princeton Med. Ctr. 1993, 94, 96; work represented pvt. and public collections in U.S., Australia, N.Z., Germany, Luxembourg, Japan, Eng.; designer ofcl. poster N.J. Festival of Ballooning, 1990, Arc Challenge Races, 1993, 94; instr. in field; developer art appreciation courses for children and adults; toymaker, 1973-76. Winner bronze medal in watercolor Nat. Mystic (Conn.) Outdoor Art Festival, 1977; Mayor's Purchase prize Franklin Twp., 1976; Tri-State Watercolor award Somerset County Coll., 1978; Best in Show Raritan Valley Art Assn., 1978, 94; award Garden State Watercolor Soc., 1979, 1984, 95; 1st and 2d and Best in Show awards Somerset and Westfield Art Assns. shows; 1st place for profl. watercolor Plainfield Tri-State Arts Festival, 1983, 85, 87, 96, N.E. Art Festival Caldwell Coll., 1990, 95; Tewksbury award, 1990; 2d place in watercolor Internat. Miniature Art Show, Washington, 1983; best in show and Grumbacher award Caldwell State show, 1984; 1st place Carrier Clinic Tri-State 1984; Grumbacher Bronze award, 1984, Grumbacher Silver award, 1985, 88, 94, Watercolor award Artists League Cen. N.J. show Cornelious Lowe Mus., 1986, Winsor-Newton award Am. Artists Proleague, 1987, Robert Simmons award, 1989, Basking Ridge Environmental Ctr. award, 1994; Best in Show N.J. State Juried, Piscataway, 1988; 2d place N.J. Miniature Art Soc., 1989; 1st pro Raritan Valley, 1992, 93, 1st mixed media B.R. Environ. Ctr., 1994; artist-in-residence grant Middlesex Librs., 1983-92, watercolor demonstrator, 1983—; TV appearances, State of the Arts-N.J., 1986, Midday (pvt. art shows), 1986, TKR, 1995. Elisha Benjamin scholar Brown U., 1960. Mem. Garden State Watercolor Soc. (writer, editor 1994—), Miniature Art Socs., Fla., Washington, AAUW (life, various offices 1963-73), art assns. Raritan Valley (pres. 1980-82, writer, editor newsletter 1993—), Somerset, Westfield, North Haven (Maine), Essex Watercolor Club, Am. Artists Profl. League. Presbyterian. Clubs: Hanover Squares (co-pres. 1972-73), Morris County Folk Dancers (co-pres. 1963). Home and Studio: 497 Stony Brook Dr Bridgewater NJ 08807-1945 *Be your own unique self (especially helpful in the arts!). Strive to be better, and measure up to your best standards, not others! But also be kind to yourself (and others), and fully enjoy exploring who you are and what you can do.*

PATTON, GEORGE SMITH, military officer; b. Boston, Dec. 24, 1923; s. George Smith, Jr. and Beatrice Banning (Ayer) P.; m. Joanne Holbrook, June 14, 1952; children: Margaret, George, Robert, Helen, Benjamin. BS, U.S. Mil. Acad., 1946; MPS, George Washington U., 1965. Commd. 2d lt. U.S. Army, 1946, advanced through grades to maj. gen., 1973; parachutist Germany, 1947-51; assigned Armor Br., 1949; instr. tank offense sect. Armored Sch. Fort Knox, Ky., 1952-53; comdr. Co. A, 140th Tank Bn. Korea, 1953, exec. officer I, Corps Reconnaissance Bn., 1953-54; co. tactical officer dept. tactics U.S. Mil. Acad., 1954-56; officer exec. dept. U.S. Naval Acad., 1956-57; assigned Command and Gen. Staff Coll., Fort Leavenworth, Kans., 1957-58; a.d.c. comdg. gen. 7th Army and comdr. in chief U.S. Army, Europe, 1958-60; exec. officer 1st squadron 11th Armored Cav. Regt. Straubing, Germany, 1960-61; assigned Armed Forces Staff Coll. Norfolk, Va., 1961-62; assigned U.S. Army War Coll. Carlisle Barracks, Pa., 1964-65; spl. forces ops. officer Mil. Assistance Command Vietnam, 1962-63; comdr. 2/81 Armor, 1st Armored Div. Fort Hood, Tex., 1963-64; chief Mainland S.E. Asia br. Far East-Pacific div. Office Dep. Chief Staff for Mil. Ops., Dept. Army, 1965-67; chief force devel. div. U.S. Army, Vietnam, 1967-68; comdg. officer 11th Armored Cav. Regt. Vietnam, 1968-69; assigned U.S. Army Primary Helicopter Ctr., Ft. Wolters, Tex., 1969-70, Ft. Rucker, Ala., 1969-70; asst. div. comdr. for support 4th Armored div. Hdqrs. U.S. Army, Europe, 1970-71; comdt. U.S. Army Armor Sch. Fort Knox, 1971-73; dir. security assistance Hdqrs. U.S. European Command, 1973-74, comdr. Army Readiness Region, 1974-75; comdr. 2d Armored Div. Fort Hood, 1975-77; dep. comdg. gen. U.S. VII Corps, 1977-79; dir. readiness Hdqrs. Dept. Army Materiel Devel. and Readiness Command Alexandria, Va., 1979-80; ret., 1980; instr. history U. Md., 1960-61. Mem. West Point Fund, Alexandria, Va.; trustee Essex Agrl. and Tech. Inst., Hathorne, Mass. Decorated D.S.C. with oak leaf cluster, Silver Star with oak leaf cluster, Legion of Merit with two oak leaf clusters, D.F.C., Bronze Star with oak leaf cluster, Purple Heart; Cross of Gallantry with gold, silver and bronze stars Vietnam; Army Forces Honor medal 1st class. Mem. Assn. U.S. Army, Armor Assn., Blackhorse Assn., Ducks Unltd., N.E. Farm Bur., Legion of Valor, Am. Legion. Home: 650 Asbury St South Hamilton MA 01982-1321

PATTON, JACK THOMAS, family practice physician; b. Rogers, Ark., Feb. 18, 1941; s. Jack Marcus and Jewell Selah (Pense) P.; m. Lynette Anne Carr, Sept. 2, 1960; children: Robert, John, Mark, Christopher. BA in History, Calif. State U., 1963; MD in Medicine, U. So. Calif., L.A., 1967; MA in Bib. Studies, Mennonite Brethren Bib. Sem., Fresno, Calif., 1980; MA in History, Calif. State U., Fresno, 1993. Cert. Bd. Med. Examiners, Calif., Hawaii. Intern Tripler Army Med. Ctr., Honolulu, 1967-68; resident in gen. practice Walson Army Hosp., Ft. Dix, N.J., 1968-70; med. supt. Nazarene Hosp., Papua New Guinea, 1973-80; chmn. family practice dept. Sharp Rees-Stealy, San Diego, 1981-86; chmn. occupational medicine Kaiser Permanente, Fresno, 1986-87; assoc. med. dir. Sharp Rees-Stealy, San Diego, 1987-92; med. dir. Summer Inst. Linguistics, Papua New Guinea, 1993-94; with family practice dept. Sharp Rees-Stealy Med. Group, San Diego, 1994-97, Northwest Med. Group, Fresno, Calif., 1997—; family practice residency liaison Tripler Army Med. Ctr., Honolulu, 1972-73; chief medicine, dep. commr. Schofield Army Med. Clinics, Waihiwa, Hawaii, 1970-72; lectr. San Jose Christian Coll., 1997—. Mem. med. sch. support Salerni Collegium, U. So. Calif. Sch. Medicine, 1967-85; lectr. Ch.-Mission Inst., Mennonite Brethren Bib. Sem., 1984-92; sec. S.E. Asian task force Mennonite Brethren Ch. Fresno, 1990-93. Maj. U.S. Army, 1966-73. Mackenzie scholar U. So. Calif. Sch. Medicine, 1966-67. Fellow Am. Acad. Family Physicians; mem. Am. Bd. Family Practice (diplomate), Calif. Acad. Family Physiciians, Royal Soc. Medicine (assoc., London). Avocations: history, travel, hiking. Home: 1566 S Adler Ave Fresno CA 93727-5101 Office: 4770 W Herndon Ave Fresno CA 93722-8401

PATTON, JAMES LEELAND, JR., lawyer; b. Wilmington, Del., Sept. 28, 1956; s. James L. Patton and Eleanor Phillips Crawford Brown; m. Kathleen Long Patton, May 29, 1981; children: Kathryn Stuart, Diana Lantz. BA in Philosophy, Davidson (N.C.) Coll., 1979; JD, Dickinson Sch. Law, Carlisle, Pa., 1983. Bar: Del. 1983, U.S. Dist. Ct. Del. 1983, U.S. Ct. Appeals (3rd cir.) 1988, U.S. Supreme Ct. 1991. Ptnr., chair Bankruptcy Dept. Young Conaway Stargatt & Taylor, Wilmington, 1983—; trustee Pvt. Panel Bankruptcy Trustees, 1985-88. Contbr. (ref. ency.): Fletcher Corporate Bankruptcy, Reorganization and Dissolution, 1992. Mem. ABA, Del. State Bar Assn. (bankruptcy law subcom. chmn. 1986—). Avocation: photography, sailing. Office: Young Conaway et al PO Box 391 11th & Market Wilmington DE 19899

PATTON, JAMES RICHARD, JR., lawyer; b. Durham, N.C., Oct. 27, 1928; s. James Ralph and Bertha (Moye) P.; m. Mary Margot Maughan, Dec. 29, 1950; children: James Macon, Lindsay Fairfield. AB cum laude, U. N.C., 1948; postgrad., Yale U., 1948; JD, Harvard U., 1951. Bar: D.C. bar 1951, U.S. Supreme Ct. 1963. Attache of Embassy; spl. asst. to Am. ambassador to Indochina, 1952-54; with Office Nat. Estimates, Washington, 1954-55; atty. Covington & Burling, Washington, 1956-61; founding ptnr., chmn. exec. com. Patton Boggs, LLP, Washington, 1962—; Lectr. internat. law Cornell Law Sch., 1963-64, U.S. Army Command and Gen. Staff Coll., 1967-68; Mem. Nat. Security Forum, U.S. Air War Coll., 1965, Nat. Strategy Seminar, U.S. Army War Coll., 1967-70, Global Strategy Discussions, U.S. Naval War Coll., 1968, Def. Orientation Conf., 1972; mem. Com. of 100 on Fed. City, Washington; mem. adv. council on nat. security and internat. affairs Nat. Republican Com., 1977-81; bd. dirs. Madeira Sch., Greenway, Va., 1975-81, Lawyers Com. for Civil Rights Under Law, Washington, Legal Aid Soc. Washington; mem. Industry Policy Adv. Com. for Trade Policy Matters, 1984-87; councillor of Atlantic Council of U.S., 1987-90; mem. visiting com. Ackland Art Mus. U. N.C., 1987—, Nat. Coun. Anderson Ranch Arts Ctr., 1987—. Adv. coun. mem. Johns Hopkins U. Sch. Advanced Internat. Studies, 1989-92; nat. bd. dirs. Aspen Mus., 1987-90; nat. coun. mem. Whitney Mus., 1992—; bd. dirs., exec. com. Nat. Mus. Natural History, Smithsonian, 1992—; trustee Aspen Music Assocs., 1993—. Mem. ABA (past com. chmn.), Inter-Am. Bar Assn. (past del.), Internat. Law Assn. (past com. chmn.), Am. Soc. Internat. Law (treas., exec. coun.), Washington Inst. Fgn. Affairs, Nat. Gallery (collectors com. 1988-91), Gerrard Soc., Met. Club (Washington), Phi Beta Kappa, Alpha Epsilon Delta.

PATTON, JOANNA, advertising agency owner; b. Quincy, Ill., Dec. 20, 1946; d. John H. and Jane Vandike P.; m. Bill Persky, 1995. Student Stetson U., 1964-66, Fla. State U., 1966-67. Para legal, Miami, Fla., 1968-74; exec. asst. Louis Nizer, Atty., N.Y.C., 1974-77; adminstrv. asst. to pres. Cosmair, N.Y.C., 1977-78, mgr. pub. rels., 1978, dir. pub. rels., 1978-79, mktg. dir., 1980-81; owner Joanna Patton Advt., N.Y.C., 1982-83; ptnr. Levinger & Patton, N.Y.C., 1983-86, Lotas Minard Patton McIver, Inc. 1986—. Hon. co-chair Cannes Advt. Film Festival Gala. Mem. Fashion Group, Advt. Women N.Y. Office: Lotas Minard Patton McIver 152 W 57th St New York NY 10019-3301

PATTON, JOSEPH DONALD, JR., management consultant; b. Washington, Pa., Jan. 4, 1938; s. Joseph Donald and Priscilla Ann (Johnson) P.; BS in Phys. Scis. and Math. Edn., Pa. State U., 1959; MBA in Mktg., U. Rochester (N.Y.), 1970; m. Susan Oertel, June 3, 1967; children: Jennifer Ann, Joseph Donald, III. Tchr., Aschaffenburg (W.Ger.) Am. Sch., 1963-64; with Xerox Corp., Rochester, 1964-75, mgr. field engring., 1973-75; chmn., CEO Patton Cons., Inc., Rochester, 1975-93, Hilton Head, S.C., 1993—, chmn., CEO Mgmt. Metrics Svcs., Inc., 1996—; mem. adj. faculty Rochester Inst. Tech., SUNY, Geneseo. Served as capt. U.S. Army, 1959-63. Registered profl. quality engr., Calif.; cert. profl. logistician; cert. quality engr., cert. reliability engr.; cert. service exec. Fellow Am. Soc. Quality Control (reliability and maintainability tech. award 1982), Soc. Logistics Engrs. (Sole Armitage medal 1980, 82); sr. mem. Instrument Soc. Am.; mem. Assn. Field Service Mgrs. (publs. award 1981), Nat. Assn. Service Mgrs. (life cert. svc. exec.), Am. Prodn. and Inventory Control Soc. Republican. Presbyterian. Author 7 texts in field; contbr. over 100 articles to profl. jours. Office: Patton Consultants Inc 36 Blue Heron Pt Hilton Head Island SC 29926-1209

PATTON, NANCY MATTHEWS, elementary education educator; b. Pitts., Apr. 7, 1942; d. Thomas Joseph and Sara Theresa (Jocunskas) Matthews; m. Jack E. Patton, July 20, 1974; children: Susan, Steven. BS in Edn., Ind. U. of Pa., 1963; grad. student, U. Pitts. 4th grade tchr. Elroy Sch., Pitts., 1980-91; 6th grade tchr. Brentwood Middle Sch., Pitts., 1991—; sponsor Brentwood Middle Sch. newspaper; coach Brentwood Varsity Cheerleaders, 1981-93. Councilperson Brentwood Borough Coun., 1988—, v.p., 1994—; sec. Brentwood Dem. Com., 1989-95; bd. trustees Brentwood Libr. Bd., 1988—; mem. Brentwood Econ. Devel. Corp., 1995—. Mem. NEA, AAUW, Nat. Sci. Tchrs. Assn., Pa. State Edn. Assn., Brentwood Century Club, Lithuanian Citizens' Soc. Democrat. Roman Catholic. Avocations: reading, community service. Home: 105 Hillson Ave Pittsburgh PA 15227-2941

PATTON, PAUL E., governor; b. Fallsburg, KY. Grad. in mech. engring., U. Ky., 1959. With coal bus., until 1979, dep. sec. transp.; judge-exec. Pike County, 1981; lt. gov., sec. econ. devel., pres. senate State of KY, Frankfort, KY, 1991—; governor State of Kentucky, 1995—; served on Ky. Crime Commn., Ky. Tourism Commn., Task Force for Workplace Literacy; former mem. Prichard Com. for Acad. Excellence. Mem. bd. overseers Bellarmine Coll., bd. trustees Pikeville Coll.; chmn. Ky. Dems., 1981-83; del. Dem. Nat. Conv.; served numerous terms Pike County Dem. Exec. Com. Office: Office the Governor The Capitol 700 Capitol Ave Frankfort KY 40601-3410

PATTON, RICHARD WESTON, retired mortgage company executive; b. Evanston, Ill., Sept. 26, 1931; s. Robert Ferry and Sue Buckley P.; m. Lynda A. Kruse, Feb. 2, 1971; 1 child, Robert Weston. B.A., Amherst Coll., 1954. Sales engr. Thermo Fax Sales Corp., Chgo., 1958-60; account exec. Nat. Mortgage Investors, Inc., Chgo., 1960-61; sales mgr. Nat. Mortgage Investors, Inc., Pasadena, Calif., 1962-66; asst. v.p. Nat. Mortgage Investors, Inc., 1966-67, v.p., 1967-69, exec. v.p., 1969-73, pres., chief exec. officer, dir., 1973-84, vice-chmn. bd., 1984-90; pres. Richard W. Patton Enterprises, Pasadena, 1990—; pres., chmn. exec. com., dir. Ocean Park Restaurant Corp., Santa Monica, Calif., 1977-88; dir. Cenfed Bank, Cenfed Fin. Corp. Bd. dirs. Pasadena Boys' Club, 1963-66, Opera Assocs., 1984-90; mem. steering com. Amherst Coll. Capital Fund Drive, 1963-66. With USMCR, 1955-58. Mem. Amherst Coll. Alumni Assn. (bd. dirs. 1963—, pres. 1977-79, 86-89), Overland Club (sec., bd. dirs.), Kroenstadt Ski Club (past pres.). Office: Rich W Patton Enterprises 3644 San Pasqual St Pasadena CA 91107-5419

PATTON, ROBERT FREDERICK, lawyer, banker; b. New Castle, Pa., Dec. 9, 1927; s. Wylie E. and Lena Francis (Gardner) P.; m. Virginia Lee Reehl, Aug. 15, 1952; children: Thomas E., Barbara L., Susan G., Laura L. A.B., Westminster Coll., New Wilmington, Pa., 1950; J.D., Harvard U., 1953. Bar: Pa. 1954. Assoc. Buchanan, Ingersoll, Rodewald, Kyle & Buerger, Pitts., 1953-60, ptnr., 1960-83; chmn. Union Nat. Corp., 1983-89; vice chmn. Integra Fin. Corp., Pitts., 1989, now bd. dirs., 1989-96; chmn. Bank Cons. Assocs., Pitts., 1990—; adj. prof. U. Pitts. Law Sch., 1978. Trustee Westminster Coll., 1976-91, sec., 1978-93, chmn., 1988-91; vice moderator Pitts. Presbytery, 1987; chmn. Allegheny County Mental Health/Mental Retardation Bd., 1977-80; trustee Montefiore Hosp., 1985-90, Jewish Healthcare Found., 1990-94. Mem. Am. Law Inst., Am. Bar Found., Allegheny Bar Assn., Duquesne Club, Chartiers Country Club, Nauset Beach Club. Republican. Home: 293 Dixon Ave Pittsburgh PA 15216-1207 Office: Bank Cons Assocs 5800 Usx Tower Pittsburgh PA 15219

PATTON, SHARLENE DARLAGE, nurse; b. Seymour, Ind., July 20, 1933; d. Alfred J. and Viora E. (Elkins) Darlage; children: Raye Ellen, Scott, Susan, Martha, Elise. RN, Sch. Nursing Michael Reese Hosp., 1953; BA, Gov.'s State U., 1985. Head nurse Drug Abuse Program, Chgo.; nurse Tinley Park (Ill.) Mental Hosp. Mem. ANA. Address: 593 8th St Chicago Heights IL 60411-1926

PATTON, STUART, biochemist, educator; b. Ebenezer, N.Y., Nov. 2, 1920; s. George and Ina (Neher) P.; m. Colleen Cecelia Lavelle, May 17, 1945; children—John, Richard, Gail, Thomas, Mary Catherine, Patricia, Joseph. B.S., Pa. State U., 1943; M.S., Ohio State U., 1947, Ph.D., 1948. Chemist Borden Co., 1943-44; research fellow Ohio State U., Columbus, 1946-48; mem. faculty Pa. State U., University Park, 1949-80, prof., 1959-80; Evan Pugh rsch. prof. agr. Pa. State U., 1966-80; adj. prof. neurosci. Sch. Medicine U. Calif., San Diego, 1981—; vis. scientist Scripps Instn. Oceanography; cons. in field, 1950—. Author: (with Robert Jenness) Principles of Dairy Chemistry, 1959, (with Robert G. Jensen) Biomedical Aspects of Lactation, 1975. Served to lt. (j.g.) USNR, 1944-46. Recipient Borden award chemistry milk Am. Chem. Soc., 1957, Agrl. and Food Chemistry award, 1975; Alexander von Humboldt sr. scientist award, 1981, Macy-Gyorgy award Internat. Soc. for Rsch. on Human Milk and Lactation, 1997. Mem. Am. Chem. Soc., Am. Dairy Assn., Am. Soc. Biochemistry and Molecular Biology, Am. Soc. Cell Biology. Home: 6208 Avenida Cresta La Jolla CA 92037-6510 Office: U Calif San Diego Ctr Molecular Genetics 0634-J La Jolla CA 92093

PATTON, SUSAN OERTEL, clinical social worker, educator; b. Syracuse, N.Y., May 18, 1946; d. Robert William and Jane (VanWormer) Oertel; m. Joseph D. Patton, Jr., June 3, 1967; children: Jennifer, Joseph D. III. BA, SUNY, Geneseo, 1984; MSW, SUNY, Buffalo, 1987. Cert. social worker, N.Y.; lic. ind. social worker, S.C.; cert. employee assistance profl.; qualified clin. social worker; bd. cert. fellow in managed mental health care; diplomate in clin. social work. Counselor Profl. Counseling Svc., Gowanda, N.Y., 1987-88, Mental Health Mgmt., Rochester, N.Y., 1988-93; counselor The Health Assn., Rochester, 1988-89, sr. counselor, 1989-90, asst. dir. mktg. and tng., 1990-92; pvt. practice Rochester, 1988-93; employee assistance program dir. Recovery Ctr. EAP, Hilton Head, S.C., 1993-95; pres., dir. Employee Assistance Program, Inc., Hilton Head Island, S.C., 1995—; instr. Medaille Coll., Buffalo, 1990-93. Co-author: Treating Perpetrators of Sexual Abuse, 1990. Mem. NASW, Acad. Cert. Social Workers, Am. Bd. Cert. Managed Care Providers, S.C. Counselors Assn., Employee Assistance Soc. N.Am., Employee Assistance Profls. Assn. Office: Employee Assistance Program 10 Office Park Rd Hilton Head Island SC 29928-7535

PATTON, THOMAS EARL, lawyer; b. Nov. 25, 1940; s. Thomas E. and Alice F. (Rodarmel) P.; m. Patricia Mann, Aug. 12, 1965 (dec.); m. Barbara Wood, Sept. 21, 1974; 1 child, David Earl. A.B., Cath. U. Am., 1962, J.D. summa cum laude, 1965. Bar: N.Y. 1966, D.C. 1966, Va. 1982. Assoc. Sullivan & Cromwell, N.Y.C., 1965-69; mem. Williams Connolly & Califano, Washington, 1970-75; asst. gen. counsel U.S. Dept. Energy, Washington, 1977-78; ptnr. Schnader, Harrison, Segal & Lewis, Washington, 1979-94; disting. lectr. Cath. U. Am., 1970-90, 95—, bd. regents; nat. arbitrator Am. Arbitration Assn.; bd. dirs. Elcotel, Inc., Info. Exch., Inc. Author: Securities Litigation, 1989, Federal Procedure Casebook, 1990; contbr. articles to profl. jours.; editor in chief Cath. U. Am. Law Rev. Mem. Washington World Affairs Coun., 1980—. Mem. ABA, D.C. Bar (founder and chair litigation sect.), Cosmos Club. Roman Catholic. Office: Tighe Patton Tabackman & Babbin 1750 Pennsylvania Ave NW Washington DC 20006-4502

PATTON, THOMAS F., academic administrator, pharmaceutical chemist; b. McKeesport, Pa., Aug. 14, 1948; s. Floyd E. and Alberta I. (Trager) P.; m. Denise Pretzer, Mar. 1, 1986; 1 child, William Patrick. BS, U. Wis., 1971, MS, 1973, PhD, 1975. Prof. U. Kansas, Lawrence, 1975-86, assoc. vice chancellor, 1981-85; assoc. dir. The Upjohn Co., Kalamazoo, Mich., 1986-88; v.p. ops. Oread Labs., Lawrence, Kans., 1988-89; sr. dir. pharm. R&D Merck, Rahway, N.J., 1990-93; v.p. pharm. R&D Dupont-Merck, Wilmington, Del., 1993-94; pres. St. Louis Coll. Pharm., 1994—. Fellow AAAS Acad. Pharm. Scis., Am. Assn. Pharm. Scis., Sigma Xi, Rho Chi. Office: St Louis Coll Pharmacy 4588 Parkview Pl Saint Louis MO 63110-1029

PATTON, THOMAS JAMES, sales and marketing executive; b. Cleve., Nov. 2, 1948; s. Michael Anthony and Delores (Bammerlin) P.; m. Thomasina Bernadette Cavallaro, Aug. 9, 1969; children: Thomasina, Thera V. A in Transp., Cleve. State U., 1971, BA in Mktg., 1973; BA, SUNY, Empire State, 1994. CLU; ChFC; registered health underwriter; registered employee benefit cons. Ins. salesman Manulife, Cleve., 1972-75, Mass. Mut., Cleve., 1976-80, Patton Ins. Assn., Inc., Avon Lake, Ohio, 1976—; ins. cons. Diversified Benefit Plans, Inc., Avon Lake, 1978-93, dir. sales and mktg., 1993—; pres. commerce Benefits Group, Inc. and Ins. Mktg. Group, Inc., 1995; prin. Cmty. Health Ptnrs., Ltd., Ill., 1994; pres. Commerce Benefits Group, Inc.; cons. Regional Sch. Consortium, Lorain County, Ohio, 1986—, County of Lorain, 1984—, City of Lorain, 1986—, County of Lorain, 1984—, City of Lorain, 1984—; prin. Comty. Health Ptnrs. Ltd.; bd. Italian Cultural Found. Pres. Lake Erie Rate Coun., Cleve., 1970-71; mem. Lorain County Dem. Ctrl. Com., Avon Lake, Ohio, 1986—; mem. com. Cleve. Leukemia Soc., 1985; bd. dirs. Villa Serena Sr. Housing, St. Francis Soc., Italian Cultural Found. Mem. Nat. Assn. Life Underwriters, Profl. Ins. Agts. Assn., Cert. Profl. Ins. Agts. Soc., Soc. Benefit Plan Adminstrn., Lorain County Life Underwriters, Irish Heritage, Order Italian Sons and Daus., Profl. Assn. Dive Instrs./Nat. Assn. Underwater Instrs. (SCUBA diving instr.). Roman Catholic. Avocations: fishing, skin and scuba diving, soccer, photography. Office: Diversified Benefit Plan Inc PO Box 900 Elyria OH 44036-0900

PATTON, WARREN ANDRE, non-commissioned officer, journalist; b. Chgo., Oct. 15, 1954; s. Willie Roosevelt and Adriana Ultima (Rhodes) P.; m. Annie Yolanda Thomas, Nov. 19, 1981 (div. May 1988); 1 child, Thomas; m. Olga Enid Ostalaza, July 31, 1993 (div. May 1996); children: Rafaela, Jennifer, Christopher, Michael. B in Criminal Justice, Chaminade U., 1986; MBA, Chadwick U., 1992; MPA, Troy State U., 1993. Enlisted USN, 1978, advanced through grades to chief, 1991; journalist USN, 1978—. Fundraiser Combined Fed. Campaign, Pensacola, Fla., 1991, Waterfront Mission, Pensacola, 1993. Mem. ASPA, Nat. Assn. Black Journalists, Conf. of Minority Pub. Adminstrs., Fleet Res. Assn., Hannibal Masonic Lodge No. 1. Avocations: reading, bowling, chess, poetry, judging. Office: Navy Recruiting Area Eight 1301 Clay St Oakland CA 94612-5217

PATTY, ANNA CHRISTINE, middle school educator; b. Atlanta, Aug. 25, 1937; d. Henry Richard and Gertrude (Smith) Johnson; children: Robert E., C. Wayne Jr., Christine E. BS in Math., U. Ga., 1959; MA in Edn., Va. Poly. Inst. and State U., 1991. Cert. tchr., Va. Mgr. Steak and Ale Restaurants, Inc., Dallas, 1982-84; bus. mgr. Nova Plaza Corp., Charlotte, N.C., 1984-86; asst. mgr. WoodLo, Inc., Charlotte, 1986-87; food activity mgr. Army and Air Force Exch. Svc., Schweinfurt, Fed. Republic Germany, 1987-89; substitute tchr. Montgomery County Schs., Christiansburg, Va., 1989-91; rsch. asst. Va. Poly. Inst. and State U., Blacksburg, 1990-91; math. and sci. middle sch. tchr. Hampton (Va.) City Schs., 1991—; mem. NSTA/APST Summer Inst., U.Md., 1992, NSTA Summer Inst., Sci. and Tech., SUNY, Stoney Brook, N.Y., 1995; EXCEL coach Christopher Newport U., 1993-95. With Operation Path Finders, Sandy Hook, N.J., 1994. Mem. NEA, Va. Educators Assn., Nat. Sci. Tchrs. Assn. (summer inst. participant 1992), Va. Middle Sch. Assn., Va. Sci. Tchrs., Nat. Coun. Tchrs. Math. Republican. Unitarian. Avocations: hiking, camping, herbs, wine tasting, cooking. Home: 811 Player Ln Newport News VA 23602

PATTY, CLAIBOURNE WATKINS, JR., lawyer; b. Cleve., Feb. 19, 1934; s. Claibourne Watkins and Eleanor (Todd) P.; m. Barbara Benton, May 4, 1968; children—Claibourne Watkins III, William Jordan. B.A., U. of South, 1955; J.D., U. Ark., 1961. Bar: Ark. 1961. Law clk. U.S. dist. judge, Ft. Smith, 1961-63; pvt. practice Little Rock, 1963-68; asst. ins. commr. State of Ark., 1968-69; trust officer Union Nat. Bank of Little Rock, 1969-77; asst. dean U. Ark. Sch. Law, Little Rock; also exec. dir. Ark. Inst. for Continuing Legal Edn., 1977-86; law clk. 2d Div. Chancery Ct., Pulaski County, 1986-89; of counsel Gruber Law Firm, Little Rock, 1989—; lectr. law Ark. Sch. Law, 1965; bd. dirs., chmn. Pulaski County Legal Aid Bur., 1966-69. Bd. dirs., pres. Family Svc. Agy. of Ctrl. Ark., 1976-81, 86-93; bd. dirs., pres. Good Shepherd Ecumenical Retirement Ctr., 1975—; bd. dirs. Am. Diabetes Assn., Ark. Affil., 1996—, Ark. Gerontol. Soc. 1996—; mem. Ark. adv. com. U.S. Commn. on Civil Rights, 1985-89. With AUS, 1955-57. Mem. Beta Theta Pi, Phi Alpha Delta. Office: Gruber Law Firm 315 N Broadway St North Little Rock AR 72114-5379

PATTY, R. BRUCE, architect; b. Kansas City, Mo., Jan. 25, 1935; s. Charles Everett and Sarah Louise (Pendleton) P.; m. Donna Jean Watts, June 1, 1958; children—Kristen, Jennifer, Scott. B.S. in Architecture, U. Kans., 1958. Cert. Nat. Council Archtl. Registration Bds. V.p. Kivett & Myers (architects), Kansas City, Mo., 1959-70; prin. Patty Berkebile Nelson Immenschuh Architects Inc., Kansas City, Mo., 1970-90; pres. Patty/Archer/Architects/Engrs., Kansas City, 1991-94; v.p. mktg., dir. arch. design Burns & McDonnell, Kansas City, MO, 1994—; Mem. chancellors assos. U. Kans., 1980—; bd. dirs. Downtown, Inc., 1972—, v.p., 1978-79, U. Kans. Alumni Assn., 1990—. Prin. works include Kansas City Internat. Airport, 1968 (Design award Kans. chpt. AIA 1974), Truman Office Bldg, Jefferson City, Mo., 1975 (Design award State of Mo. 1976), Kansas City Police Sta, 1976 (Design award Central States AIA 1980). Recipient Disting. Alumni award U. Kans., 1983. Fellow AIA (pres. Kansas City chpt. 1974, nat. dir. 1980-82, nat. v.p. 1983, nat. pres. 1985), Royal Archtl. Inst. Can. (hon.); mem. Greater Kansas City C. of C. (bd. dirs.), Fedn. Collegicos Architects, Mex. (hon.), University Club (bd. dirs., pres. 1990), Indian Hills Country Club (bd. dirs.), Rotary (bd. dirs.). Presbyterian. Home: 3840 W 56th St Shawnee Mission KS 66205-2784 Office: Burns and McDonnell 9400 Ward Pkwy Kansas City MO 64114-3319

PATUREAU, ARTHUR MITCHELL, chemical engineer, consultant; b. Beaumont, Tex., Nov. 22, 1913; s. Arthur M. Sr. and Gertrude Helen (Brammer) P.; m. Clara Davis, Dec. 24, 1934. BSChemE, U. Tex., 1943, postgrad.; postgrad., Pa. State U., 1946. Chief process engr. Gasoline Plant Constrn. Co., Corpus Christi, Tex., 1944-46, McCarthy Chem. Co., Houston, 1946-48; chief application engr. Fisher & Porter Co., Hatboro, Pa., 1948-50; cons. reactor coolant controls Nautilus nuc. submarine Westinghouse Atomic Power Divsn., Pitts., 1950-53; chief application engr. chem. industry Brown Instrument Divsn., Phila., 1953-55; western sales mgr. Barksdale Valves, L.A., 1955-56; western divisional mgr. Pa. Indsl. Chem. Co., L.A., 1956-73; divisional mgr. Hercules, Inc., L.A., 1973-75; cons. to chem. industry McQueeney, Tex., 1975—; pres. Artgraphics, Inc., 1975—. Editor: (tech. book) Resins in Rubber, 1975; contbg. author to Ency. Chem. Engring.; contbr. articles to profl. jours. mem. engring. found. adv. coun. U. Tex. Coll. Engring., 1970-75. Mem. AIChE, L.A. Rubber Group, River Art Group, Elks. Episcopalian. Avocations: flying, art work, camping, travel, computer work. Home and Office: 4312 S 31st St Apt 55 Temple TX 76502-3359

PATY, DONALD WINSTON, neurologist; b. Peking, China, Sept. 25, 1936; s. Robert Morris and Katherine (Behenna) P.; m. Jo Anne Haymore, Dec. 28, 1958; children: Morris Britten, Beverly Behenna, Breay Winston, Donald Blake. B.A., Emory U., 1958, M.D., 1962. Intern Duke U., 1962-63; resident in medicine and neurology Emory U., 1965-70; fellow in immunology MRC Demyelinating Diseases Unit, U. Newcastle-upon-Tyne, Eng., 1970-72; asst. prof., then prof. neurology U. Western Ont. (Can.) Med. Sch., 1972-80; prof. neurology, head div. U. B.C. Med. Sch., Vancouver, 1980—; sec.-gen. XV World Congress of Neurology, Vancouver, B.C., 1993; advisor London (Ont.) chpt. Multiple Sclerosis Soc. Can., 1972-80; sec. exec. com., med. adv. bd. Internat. Fedn. Multiple Sclerosis Socs. Author articles in field.; Mem. editorial bds. profl. jours. Bd. dirs. London Symphony, 1978-80; chmn. grants rev. com. Multiple Sclerosis Soc. of Can.; mem. exec. com. med. adv. bd., chmn. med. mgmt. com. Internat. Fed. Multiple Sclerosis Soc. With USPHS, 1963-65. Fellow Can. Life Ins. Assn., 1972-77; grantee Multiple Sclerosis Soc. Can.; grantee Med. Rsch. Coun. Can.; recipient John Dystel Rsch. award Multiple Sclerosis Soc./Am. Acad. Neurology, 1995, Sir Richard Cave award Multiple Sclerosis Soc. Gt. Britain and No. Ireland, 1995, Charcot award Internat. Fedn. of Multiple Sclerosis Socs., 1995. Fellow ACP, Royal Coll. Physicians and Surgeons Can. (chmn. com. in neurology 1982-86), Am. Acad. Neurology; mem. Can. Neurol. Soc. (pres. 1989-90), Am. Neurol. Assn., Brit. Assn. Neurologists (hon.), World Fedn. Neurology (chmn. multiple sclerosis rsch. group), Alpha Omega Alpha. Unitarian. Home: 3657 W 24th Ave, Vancouver, BC Canada V6S 1L7

PATZ, ARNALL, physician; b. Elberton, Ga., June 14, 1920; s. Samuel and Sarah (Berman) P.; m. Ellen B. Levy, Mar. 12, 1950; children: William, Susan, David, Jonathan. BS, Emory U., 1942, MD, 1945. Pvt. practice ophthalmology Balt., 1951-70; faculty ophthalmology Johns Hopkins Sch. Medicine, 1955—, prof., 1973—; William Holland Wilmer prof., chmn. dept. ophthalmology, dir. Wilmer Ophthal. Inst., 1979-89; mem. Nat. Diabetes Adv. Bd., 1977-80. First recipient Edward Lorenzo Holmes award Inst. Medicine Chgo., 1954, Helen Keller Prize for Vision Rsch. Helen Keller Rsch. Found., 1994; Sight-Saving award D.C. Soc. Prevention Blindness, 1954; E. Mead Johnson award Am. Acad. Pediatrics, 1956; Albert Lasker award Am. Pub. Health Assn., 1956; 1st Seeing Eye Research Prof. Ophthalmology award, 1970; Derrick Vail medal Ill. Soc. Prevention of Blindness, 1981; Jules Stein award for Disting. Ophthalmic Achievement, Research to Prevent Blindness, 1981; David Rumbough Sci. award Juvenile Diabetes Found. Internat., 1983; 1st Issac C. Michaelson award Israel Acad. Scis. and Humanities, 1986; 1st Paul Henkind lectureship The Macula Soc., 1989. Mem. AMA (Billings silver medal 1973), Am. Acad. Ophthalmology (honor award 1973, sr. honor award 1981, pres.-elect 1986, pres. 1987), Assn. for Rsch. in Vision and Ophthalmology (Friedenwald Meml. award 1980, Weisenfeld award 1993), Nat. Soc. Prevention of Blindness (v.p. 1981—, 1st Disting. Scientist award), Am. Ophthal. Soc. (Howe medal 1991), Balt. City Med. Soc., Md. Soc. Prevention Blindness (past pres.), Pan-Am. Assn. Ophthalmology, Md. Soc. Eye Physicians and Surgeons. Home: 2A Slade Ave Baltimore MD 21208-5214 Office: Johns Hopkins Med Insts 600 N Wolfe St Baltimore MD 21205-2110

PATZ, EDWARD FRANK, retired lawyer; b. Balt., Aug. 25, 1932; s. Maurice A. and Violet (Furman) P.; m. Betty Seldner Levi, Nov. 18, 1956; children—Evelyn Anne, Edward Frank, Thomas L. B.S., U. Md., 1954, LL.B., 1959. Bar: Md. 1959. Ptnr. Weinberg and Green and predecessor firms, Balt., 1959-97; ret., 1997. Bd. dirs. Jewish Family and Children's Service, 1965-71; mem. regional bd. dirs. NCCJ. Mem. ABA, Md. Bar Assn., Balt. Bar Assn., Comml. Law League Am., Am. Bankruptcy Inst., Ctr. Club, Suburban of Balt. Country Club (bd. govs., pres.), Caves Valley Golf Club, Hammock Dunes Club. Home: 39 Island Estates Pkwy Palm Coast FL 32137

PAUL, ANDREW MITCHELL, venture capitalist; b. N.Y.C., Feb. 10, 1956; s. John William and Bobba Lorraine (Ice) P.; m. Margaret Rae Batchelor, Sept. 19, 1987. BA, Cornell U., 1978; MBA, Harvard U., 1983. Mktg. rep. IBM Corp., N.Y.C., 1978-81; assoc. Hambrecht & Quist Venture Capital Co., San Francisco, 1983-84; gen. ptnr. Welsh, Carson, Anderson & Stowe, N.Y.C., 1984—; bd. dirs. Lincare Inc., St. Petersburg, Fla., Medcath, Inc., Charlotte, N.C., Am. Oncology Inc., EmCare Holdings Inc., Housecall Inc. Mem. Nat. Venture Capital Assn., N.Y. Venture Capital Assn., Bronxville Field Club, Siwanoy Country Club, Hudson Nat. Golf Club., Roaring Fork Club, Aspen. Avocations: tennis, golf, skiing, biking, traveling. Home: 283 Pondfield Rd Bronxville NY 10708-4936 Office: Welsh Carson Anderson & Stowe One World Fin Ctr 320 Park Ave New York NY 10022-6815

PAUL, ANDREW ROBERT, trade association executive; b. N.Y.C., Aug. 14, 1938; s. Andrew B. and Maria (Filotas) P.; m. Britt-Marie Hagelbrant, Feb. 6, 1988. AB in French, Dartmouth Coll., 1960; MS in Fgn. Svc., Georgetown U., 1967. Dir. govt. rels. Motorola, Inc., Washington, 1968-75, Paramount Communications, Washington, 1975-90; sr. v.p. Satellite Broadcasting and Communications Assn., Alexandria, Va., 1990—; mem. Gatt adv. com. on Intellectual Property, Washington, 1988-94; advisor MS in Fgn. Svc. program Georgetown U., Washington, 1981—. Presdl. campaign advance man Rep. Nat. Com., 1964; pres. chpt. XI Spl. Forces Assn., Washington, 1981-82; chmn. Alternative House Crisis Intervention Ctr., Vienna, Va., 1983-84. Capt. U.S. Army, 1960-65. Roman Catholic. Home: 1013 Heather Hill Ct Mc Lean VA 22101-2024 Office: Satellite Broadcasting & Comm Assn 225 Reinekers Ln Alexandria VA 22314-2875

PAUL, ARA GARO, university dean; b. New Castle, Pa., Mar. 1, 1929; s. John Hagop and Mary (Injejikian) P.; m. Shirley Elaine Waterman, Dec. 21, 1962; children: John Bartlett, Richard Goyan. BS in Pharmacy, Idaho State U., 1950; MS, U. Conn., 1953, PhD in Pharmacognosy, 1956. Cons. plant physiology Argonne (Ill.) Nat. Lab., 1955; asst. prof. pharmacognosy Butler U., Indpls., 1956-57; faculty U. Mich., Ann Arbor, 1957—; prof. pharmacognosy U. Mich., 1969—; dean U. Mich. Coll. Pharmacy, 1975-95; dean emeritus, prof. pharmacognosy; vis. prof. microbiology Tokyo U., 1965-66; mem. vis. chemistry faculty U. Calif., Berkeley, 1972-73; del. U.S. Pharmacopeial Conv., 1980, 90; scholar-in-residence Am. Assn. Colls. Pharmacy, 1996. Contbr. articles to profl. jours. Recipient Outstanding Tchr. award Coll. Pharmacy, U. Mich., 1969, Outstanding Alumnus award Idaho State U., 1976, Profl. Achievement award Coll. Pharmacy, Idaho State U., 1990; G. Pfeiffer Meml. fellow Am. Found. Pharm. Edn., 1965-66, Disting. Svc. Profile award Am. Found. Pharm. Edn., 1992; fellow Eli Lily Found., 1951-53, Am. Found. Pharm. Edn., 1954-56, NIH, 1972-73. Fellow AAAS; mem. Am. Pharm. Assn., Mich. Pharm. Assn., Am. Soc. Pharmacognosy, Acad. Pharm. Scis., Am. Assn. Colls. Pharmacy, Washtenaw County Pharm. Soc., Am. Assn. Pharm. Scientists, Phi Lambda Upsilon, Sigma Xi, Phi Delta Chi, Phi Sigma Kappa, Rho Chi. Home: 1415 Brooklyn Ave Ann Arbor MI 48104-4496 Office: U Mich Coll Pharmacy Ann Arbor MI 48109-1065

PAUL, ARTHUR, artist, graphic designer, illustrator, art and design consultant; b. Chgo., Jan. 18, 1925; m. Beatrice Miller, Dec. 24, 1949 (div. 1973); children: William Warren, Fredric; m. Suzanne Seed, Mar. 8, 1975; 1 dau., Nina. Student, Inst. Design, 1947-51. Vice-pres., art dir. HMH Pub. Co., Playboy, Chgo., 1962-82; also sr. art dir., corp. art dir. Playboy mag.; pres. Art Paul Design; freelance artist Chgo., 1984—; lectr. in field. Free lance illustrator, designer, 1951-53; designer 1st issue: Playboy mag, 1953, Playboy Rabbit symbol, 1953; exhibited in one man shows at, Etc. Gallery, 1949, 500D Gallery, 1965, U. Ill., 1965; organizer, exhibitor: travelling exhbn. Beyond Illustration-The Art of Playboy; museums, Europe, Asia, U.S., 1971-73, Can., 1976-77; author: Vision-Art Paul, 1983, Art of Playboy, 1986; designer PBS-TV title for humorous feature film presentations on American Playhouse; prodn. design cons. (PBS-TV movie) Who Am I This Time?. Trustee Chgo. Mus. Contemporary Art, 1970-86; apptd. trustee by Gov. of Ill. to Ill. Summer Sch. of Arts, 1987—. Served with USAAF, 1943-46. Recipient numerous art awards, 1951 including Polycube award Art Dirs. Club Phila., 1975, Art Direction Mag. award, 1975, Gold medal for Chgo. Film Festival poster Art Dirs. Club N.Y., 1980, Top Midwest Mktg. award Playboy TV Subscription Ad, 1979, 82, Gold medal for exhbn. Beyond Illustration City of Milan, 1971, Profl. Achievement award IIT Inst. Design Alumni Assn., 1983; Art Inst. scholar, 1943; named to Art Dirs. Hall of Fame, 1986. Mem. 27 Designers Chgo. (hon.), Alliance Graphique Internationale. Home: 175 E Delaware Pl #7511 Chicago IL 60611-1756 *Design is more than a sense of order for me. It is beauty and common sense. To draw, to paint and to look at art is in the fabric of my life. I enjoy working with ideas and seeing them develop into a reality, after which I am fortunate enough to learn whether they have performed as intended.*

PAUL, BENJAMIN DAVID, anthropologist, educator; b. N.Y.C., Jan. 25, 1911; s. Phillip and Esther (Kranz) P.; m. Lois Fleischman, Jan. 4, 1936; children: Robert Allen, Janice Carol. Student, U. Wis., 1928-29; AB, U. Chgo., 1938, PhD in Anthropology, 1942. Lectr., rsch. dir. Yale U., 1942-44; community orgn. expert Inter-Am. Ednl. Found., 1946; from lectr. to assoc. prof. anthropology Harvard U., 1946-62, dir. social sci. program Sch. Pub. Health, 1951-62; prof. anthropology Stanford (Calif.) U., 1963—, chmn. dept., 1967-71, dir. program in medicine and behavioral sci., 1963-70; cons. NIH, 1957—. Editor: Health, Culture and Community: Case Studies of Public Reactions to Health Programs, 1955, Changing Marriage Patterns in a Highland Guatemalan Community, 1963, The Maya Midwife as Sacred Professional, 1975, Mayan Migrants in Guatemala City, 1981, The Operation of a Death Squad in San Pedro la Laguna, 1988. 2d lt. AUS, 1944-46. Travelling fellow Social Sci. Rsch. Coun., 1940-41, Ctr. Advanced Study Behavioral Scis. fellow, 1962-63. Mem. Am. Anthropol. Assn. (Disting. Svc. award 1994), Phi Beta Kappa, Sigma Xi. Ethnographic field rsch. in Guatemala, 1941, 62, 64-65, 68-69, 73-79, 83-95. Home: 622 Salvatierra St Palo Alto CA 94305-8538 Office: Stanford U Dept Anthropology Stanford CA 94305

PAUL, CARL FREDERICK, lawyer, former judge; b. N.Y.C., June 10, 1910; s. Carl Frederick and Kate (Wagner) P.; m. Lilian Iris O'Neill, Apr. 18, 1953; children: Julie S., Carl F., Cynthia Marie, Celeste Wagner, Paul (dec. June 1982). AB magna cum laude, U. Rochester, 1932; LLB, Harvard U., 1935. Bar: N.Y. 1935, D.C. 1949, U.S. Supreme Ct. 1941. Assoc. Nixon, Hargrave, Devans & Doyle, Rochester, N.Y., 1935-41, 46-48; atty. Office Gen. Counsel HEW, Washington, 1958-59; commd. officer USN, 1941, advanced through grades to capt., ret., 1958; chief trial counsel NASA, Washington, 1959-74, judge Bd. Contract Appeals, 1974-79; assoc. Burch & Bennett, P.C., Washington, 1979—. Mem. ABA, Fed. Bar Assn. (pres. D.C. chpt., plaque 1995, 96), Inter-Am. Bar Assn., D.C. Bar Assn., Monroe County (N.Y.) Bar Assn., Washington Fgn. Law Soc. (pres.), Phi Beta Kappa, Theta Delta Chi. Clubs: Univ. (Rochester, N.Y.); Nat. Aviation (Washington). Home: 5702 Warwick Pl Chevy Chase MD 20815-5502

PAUL, CAROL ANN, academic administrator, biology educator; b. Brockton, Mass., Dec. 17, 1936; d. Joseph W. and Mary M. (DeMeulenaer) Bjork; m. Robert D. Paul, Dec. 21, 1957; children: Christine, Dana, Stephanie, Robert. BS, U. Mass., 1958; MAT, R.I. Coll., 1968, Brown U., 1970; EdD, Boston U., 1978. Tchr. biology Attleboro (Mass.) High Sch., 1965-68; asst. dean., mem. faculty biology North Shore Community Coll., Beverly, Mass., 1969-78; master planner N.J. Dept. for Higher Edn., Trenton, 1978-80; assoc. v.p. Fairleigh Dickinson U., Rutherford, N.J., 1980-86; v.p. acad. affairs Suffolk Community Coll., Selden, N.Y., 1986-94, assoc. prof. biology, 1994—; faculty devel. cons. various colls., 1979—, title III evaluator, 1985—. Author: (lab. manual and workbook) Minicourses and Labs for Biological Science, 1972 (rev. edit., 1975); (with others) Strategies and Attitudes, 1986; book reviewer, 1973-77. V.p. League of Women Voters, Beverly, 1970-74, Cranford, N.J., 1982-83; alumni rep. Brown U., Cranford, 1972—. Commonwealth Mass. scholar, 1958; recipient Acad. Yr. award NSF, 1968-69, Proclamation for Leadership award Suffolk County Exec., 1989. Mem. AAHE, AAWCC, Profls. and Orgn. Developers (planning com. 1977-79, nat. exec. bd. 1979-80), Nat. Coun. for Staff, Phi Theta Kappa, Pi Lambda Theta. Roman Catholic. Avocation: swimming. Address: 75 Fairview Cir Middle Island NY 11953-2340 Office: Suffolk Community Coll 533 College Rd Selden NY 11784-2851

PAUL, CHARLES S., motion picture and television company executive; b. 1949. BA, Stanford U., 1971; JD, U. Santa Clara, 1975. Law clk. U.S. Supreme Ct., 1975-76; with Cooley Castro Huddleson & Tatum, 1976-79; with Atari Inc., 1979-85, sr. v.p., gen. counsel, pres. coin-operated games div., 1983-85; with MCA, Inc., Universal City, Calif., 1985—, v.p., pres. MCA Enterprises div., 1986-89, exec. v.p., 1989, also bd. dirs. Office: MCA 100 Universal City Plz Universal Cty CA 91608-1002*

PAUL, CHARLOTTE P., nursing educator; b. Clarendon, Tex., Jan. 13, 1941; d. William Clyde Peggram and Sibyl (Rattan) Jones; m. Robert M. Paul, Apr. 4, 1964; children: Peter, Lauraine. Diploma, St. Anthony's Hosp. Sch. Nursing, Amarillo, Tex., 1961; student, Amarillo Coll., 1958-65; BS, Syracuse U., 1972, MS, 1973, PhD in Edn. Adminstrn., 1979; postgrad., Wright State U., 1977-79, U. Tex., El Paso, 1983-86, U. Pitts., 1992-94. Nurse St. Anthony's Hosp., Amarillo, Tex., 1961-65; evening charge nurse Upstate Med. Ctr. SUNY, Syracuse, 1966-68, VA Hosp. Gen. Hosp., Syracuse, 1965-66; asst. to head nurse Meml. Hosp., Syracuse, 1966-68; nurse IV therapy Community-Gen. Hosp., Syracuse, 1968-72; instr. Syracuse Cen. Sch. System, 1972; asst. dir. insvc. edn. House of Good Samaritan Hosp., Watertown, N.Y., 1973-74; instr. SUNY Sch. Nursing, Syracuse, 1974-75, Syracuse U. Sch. Nursing, 1975-76; asst. dean Wright State U., Dayton, Ohio, 1977-79; assoc. prof. Edinboro U. Pa., 1979-86, prof., 1986—, chairperson dept. grad. studies, 1980-82, chairperson dept. nursing, 1987-89; coord. quality assurance William Beaumont Army Med. Ctr., Ft. Bliss, Tex., 1982-85; adj. assoc. prof. U. Tex., El Paso, 1982-85; cons. in field. Contbr. articles to profl. jours., papers in field. Bd. dirs. ARC, Syracuse, 1970-77, Erie County Emergency Mgmt. Agy.; chairperson Lake Erie Higher Edn. Coun., 1972-74, cons., 1987—; mem. Coun. on Aging Com. on Long Term Care, Dayton, 1977-78. Lt. col. USAR. Recipient Unit Citation award CAP, 1968, Excellence in Nursing Edn. award, 1992, Commdr.'s Commendation award, 1995, Leadership and Svc. award Lake Area Health Edn. Ctr., 1994; Gladys Post scholar, 1958-61, Rodney Horle scholar, 1971-72, Nellie Hurly scholar, 1971-72; grantee HEW, 1977, Wright State U., 1977-78, William Beaumont Army Med. Ctr., 1986, Edinboro (Pa.) U., 1979-80, 91; Nightingale Soc. fellow, 1988; named to Internat. Profl. and Bus. Women's Hall of Fame, 1994. Mem. APHA, St. Anthony's Hosp. Sch. Nursing Alumni Assn., Syracuse U. Alumni Assn., N.Y. Acad. Sci., Assn. Mil. Surgeons, U.S. Nightengale Soc., Nat. Ski Patrol (life), Kiwwanis (bd. dirs. Edinboro club 1987-95, pres. 1988-89, v.p. 1987-88), Sigma Theta Tau (advisor 1987-94), Pi Lambda Theta (life, pres. local chpt. 1973-75). Republican. Office: Edinboro U Pa 139 Centennial Hall Edinboro PA 16412

PAUL, COURTLAND PRICE, landscape architect, planner; b. Pasadena, Calif., Mar. 11, 1927; s. Charles Price and Ethyle Louisa (Stanyer) P.; m. Kathryn Nadine Knauss, July 5, 1947; children: Pamela Kathryn, Courtland Scott, Kimberly Carol, Robyn Annette, Sanford Elliott. AA, John Muir Coll., 1948; student, Calif. Poly. U., 1948-49. Lic. landscape architect Ariz., Nebr., Nev., Calif. Founder, sr. prin., landscape architect Peridian Group, P.C., Pasadena, 1951-96; ret., 1996; apptd. Calif. State Bd. Landscape Architects, 1960, 1964, pres., 1964; lectr. Calif. Poly. U., Pomona, Tex. A&M U., UCLA, Orange Coast Coll. Bd. dirs. Landscape Architecture Found., 1981-85 (pres. 1983). Served with USN, 1944-46. Recipient Achievement award Calif. Landscape Contractors Assn., 1963, citation award Pasadena Beautiful Found., 1969, Landscape Architecture award of merit Calif. Garden Clubs, 1970, commendation resolution Calif. State Senate Rules Com.,1 986, Profl. of Yr. Life Mem. award, 1986, 1st outstanding svc. to industry and environ. award Long Beach/O.C., Meridian award Landscape Contractors Assn., Max Tipton Meml. award, 1993; named Man of Yr. Landscape and Irrigation mag., 1987. Fellow Am. Soc. Landscape Archs. (at-large coun. fellows); mem. Calif. Coun. Landscape Archs. (pres. 1958, Outstanding Svc. citation 1984). Office and Home: 27605 Avenida Larga San Juan Capistrano CA 92675-3805 *People!! A career must be based on people - family, friends, friends of friends, friends of your clientele. They have shaped and made my career!! Always be there for them! Be on time, produce more than is expected and always, ALWAYS be fair!!!.*

PAUL, DONALD ROSS, chemical engineer, educator; b. Yeatesville, N.C., Mar. 20, 1939; s. Edgar R. and Mary E. (Cox) P.; m. Sally Annette Cochran, Mar. 28, 1964 (wid. Jan. 1995); children: Mark Allen, Ann Elizabeth. B.S., N.C. State Coll., 1961; M.S., U. Wis., 1963, Ph.D., 1965. Research chem. engr. E.I. DuPont de Nemours & Co., Richmond, Va., 1960-61; instr. chem. engring. dept. U. Wis., Madison, 1963-65; research chem. engr. Chemstrand Research Center, Durham, N.C., 1965-67; asst. prof. chem. engring. U. Tex., Austin, 1967-70; assoc. prof. U. Tex., 1970-73, prof., 1973—, T. Brockett Hudson prof., 1978-85, Melvin H. Gertz Regents chmn. chem. engring., 1985—, chmn. dept. chem. engring., 1977-85, dir. Center for Polymer Research, 1981—; Turner Alfrey vis. prof. Mich. Molecular Inst., 1990-91; cons. in field. Author: (with F.W. Harris) Controlled Release Polymeric Formulations, 1976, (with S. Newman) Polymer Blends, 2 vols., 1978, (with Y.P. Yampolskii) Polymeric Gas Separation Membranes. Recipient award Engring. News Record, 1975, Ednl. Svc. award Plastics Inst. Am., 1975, awards U. Tex. Student Engring. Coun., 1972, 75, 76, award for engring. teaching Gen. Dynamics Corp., 1977, Joe J. King Profl. Engring. Achievement award, 1981, Holcott Engring. Rsch. award, 1994, Disting. Engring. Alumnus award N.C. State U., 1994, Outstanding Grad. Teaching award U. Tex., 1994. Fellow AIChE (South Tex. best fundamental paper award 1984, Materials Engring. and Scis. Divsn. award 1985); mem. Am. Chem. Soc. (Doolittle award 1973, Phillips award in applied polymer sci. 1984), Soc. Plastics Engrs. (Outstanding Achievement in Rsch. award 1982, Internat. Edn. award 1989, Internat. award 1993), Fiber Soc., Nat. Acad. Engring., Nat. Materials Adv. Bd., Phi Eta Sigma, Tau Beta Pi, Phi Kappa Phi, Sigma Xi. Home: 7001 Valburn Dr Austin TX 78731-1818 Office: U Tex Dept Chem Engring Ctr Polymer Rsch EPS 206 Austin TX 78712

PAUL, DONALD W., therapist, audiologist; b. Lincoln, R.I., Apr. 11, 1947; m. Leslie Christine Paul, June 8, 1968; children: Geoffrey, Jon. BS, Boston U., 1973, MS, 1975. Cert. audiologist. Instr. Bridgewater (Mass.) State Coll., 1979-81, Northeastern U., Boston, 1977-82; dir. speech hearing Beltone Hearing Ctr., Boston, 1977-92; pvt. practice North Easton, Mass., 1992—. Fellow Am. Acad. Audiology; mem. Am. Speech Lang. Hearing Assn., Coun. on Accreditation of Occupational Hearing Conservationists, Mass. Hearing Aid Soc. Home: PO Box 312 44 Baltic Ave North Easton MA 02356

PAUL, DOUGLAS ALLAN, insurance executive; b. Chgo., Feb. 9, 1949; s. Eugene Frank and Flo Sinclair (Broomhead) P.; m. Pamela DeGroot, Oct. 20, 1984. BS, Rensselaer Polytechnic Inst., Troy, N.Y., 1971; MBA, U. Pa., 1976. Asst. dir. admissions and alumni affairs Rensselaer Polytechnic Inst., 1971-74; sr. mgr. McKinsey and Co. Inc., N.Y.C., 1977-82; v.p. strategic planning Am. Internat. Group, N.Y.C., 1983—; chmn. bd. dirs. AIG Designs Holdings, Inc.; bd. dirs. Fischbach Corp.; trustee St. Vincents Hosp. and Med. Ctr., 1996—; mem. adv. com. Mgmt. Dept. Bklyn. Poly. U., 1996—. Mem. Wall St. Planning Group (exec. dir. 1984—). Home: 284 W 11th St New York NY 10014-2413 Office: Am Internat Group Inc 70 Pine St New York NY 10270-0002

PAUL, ELDOR ALVIN, agriculture, ecology educator; b. Lamont, Alta., Can., Nov. 23, 1931; s. Reinhold and Ida (Mohr) P.; m. Phyllis Ellen Furhop, Aug. 3, 1955; children: Lynette, Linda. BSc, U. Alta., 1954, MSc, 1956; PhD, U. Minn., 1958. Asst. prof. U. Saskatchewan, Saskatoon, Can., 1959-64, assoc. prof., 1964-70, prof., 1970-80; mem. faculty, chmn. dept. plant and soil biology U. Calif., Berkeley, 1980-85; mem. faculty, chairperson dept. of crop and soil sciences Mich. State U., East Lansing, 1985-94; prof. crop and soil sci., 1994—; vis. prof. U. Ga., Athens, 1972-73, USDA, Ft. Collins, 1992-93. Author: Soil Microbiology and Biochemistry, 1988, 1996; editor: Soil Biochemistry, vols. 3-5, 1973-81; Soil Organic Matter in Temperate Agro Ecosystems, 1997; contbr. over 200 articles on microbial ecology and soil microbiology to sci. publs. Fellow AAAS, Soil Sci. Soc. Am., Can. Soc. Soil Sci., Am. Soc. Agronomy (Soil Sci. Rsch. award 1995); mem. Internat. Soc. Soil Sci. Soil Biology (chmn. 1978-82), Am. Soc. Microbiology, Am. Ecol. Soc. Home: 4232 Sugar Maple Ln Okemos MI 48864-3225 Office: Mich State U Dept Crop & Soil Scis East Lansing MI 48824

PAUL, ELIAS, food company consultant; b. Michigan City, Ind., Nov. 16, 1919; s. Phillip P. and Esther (Kranz) P.; m. Gloria Payne, Aug. 24, 1942; children—Nancy E., Janet L. B.S., U. Ill., 1947. Exec., div. mgr. Swift & Co., Chgo., 1947-64; exec. operating com. Hygrade Food Products, Detroit, 1965; v.p., gen. mgr. meat div. Cudahy Co., Phoenix, 1966; pres. Cudahy Co., 1966-71; also chief exec. officer, dir.; chmn. bd. Am. Salt Co., Kansas

City, Mo., 1966-71, Milk Specialties Co., Dundee, Ill.; ret. pres., chief exec. officer, dir. John Morrell & Co., Chgo.; chmn. bd. Golden Sun Feed Co., John Morrell & Co. Ltd.; dir. United Brands, Foster Grant, Baskin Robbins; cons. United Brands, Boston.; Vice chmn., dir. Am. Meat Inst., ret. Mem. Ariz. Retirement System Bd.; chmn. Investment Adv. Council. Served to maj. Chem. Corps, AUS, 1941-46. Mem. Chgo. Bd. Trade, Chgo. Merc. Exchange, Internat. Monetary Market, Phoenix Country Club, Forest Highlands Country Club, Gamma Sigma Delta, Phi Kappa Phi. Home: 140 E San Miguel Ave Phoenix AZ 85012-1339

PAUL, EVE W., lawyer; b. N.Y.C., June 16, 1930; d. Leo I. and Tamara (Sogolow) Weinschenker; m. Robert D. Paul, Apr. 9, 1952; children: Jeremy Ralph, Sarah Elizabeth. BA, Cornell U., 1950; JD, Columbia U., 1952. Bar: N.Y. 1952, Conn. 1960, U.S. Ct. Appeals (2nd cir.) 1975, U.S. Supreme Ct. 1977. Assoc. Botein, Hays, Sklar & Herzberg, N.Y.C., 1952-54; pvt. practice Stamford, Conn., 1960-70; staff atty. Legal Aid Soc., N.Y.C., 1970-71; assoc. Greenbaum, Wolff & Ernst, N.Y.C., 1972-78; v.p. legal affairs Planned Parenthood Fedn. Am., N.Y.C., 1979—, v.p., gen. counsel, 1991—; bd. dirs. Ctr. for Gender Equality, Inc. Contbr. articles to legal and health publs. Trustee Cornell U., Ithaca, N.Y., 1979-84; mem. Stamford Planning Bd., Conn., 1967-70; bd. dirs. Stamford League Women Voters, 1960-62, Ctr. for Gender Equality, 1995—. Harlan Fiske Stone scholar Columbia Law Sch., 1952. Mem. ABA, Conn. Bar Assn., Assn. of Bar of City of N.Y., Stamford/Norwalk Regional Bar Assn., U.S. Trademark Assn. (chairperson dictionary listings com. 1988-90), Phi Beta Kappa, Phi Kappa Phi. Office: Planned Parenthood Fedn 810 7th Ave New York NY 10019-5818 *The ability to plan the number and timing of my children has made it possible for me to enjoy career, marriage and family.*

PAUL, EVELYN ROSE, critical care nurse; b. New Bern, N.C., May 10, 1953; d. Robert Austin and Sadie Marie (Simpson) P. BSN, U. N.C., 1975. Cert. critical care nurse, ACLS. Staff nurse Beaufort County Hosp., Washington, N.C., 1975-79; chief nurse, nurse clinician, staff nurse surg. ICU Med. U. S.C., Charleston, 1979-85; staff/charge nurse cardiac surgery Pitt County Meml. Hosp., Greenville, N.C., 1985-89, asst. nurse mgr. cardiac surgery, 1989-95, RN IV, 1995-96, asst. nurse mgr. cardiac surgery ICU, 1996—. Mem. AACN (pres. elect Heart of the East chpt. 1991-92).

PAUL, FRANK, retired consulting company executive; b. Germany, Apr. 13, 1924; came to U.S., 1947, naturalized, 1953; s. Georg and Hedwig (Muenz) P.; m. Trudy Maier, Apr. 9, 1947; 1 son, Robert. B.B.A. summa cum laude, Baruch Coll., CCNY, 1960. Acctg. supr. S. Augstein Co., College Point, N.Y.C., 1953-58; controller Werner Mgmt. Cons., N.Y.C., 1958-61; v.p. fin. adminstrn. Werner Mgmt. Cons., 1961-67; exec. v.p. Werner Assocs., N.Y.C., 1968-84; also dir.; pres. ORU Group Inc., N.Y.C., 1973-84; bd. dirs. Treasurer Reliance Cons. Group Inc; cons., 1983-84.

PAUL, FRANK ALLEN, physician; b. Joshua Tree, Calif., Oct. 30, 1958; s. Louis Marion and Vivian Ann Paul. AA in Pharmacy and Marine Biology, Fullerton Coll., Calif., 1979; BA in Biochemistry and Biology, Calif. State U., Fullerton, 1982; DO, U. New Eng., 1990. Bd. cert. physician emergency medicine. Store mgr. Alpha Beta Markets, La Habra and Industry, Calif., 1977-81; constrn. supr. Louis M. Paul Constrn. Co., La Habra, 1977-82; co-owner Finecraft of Calif., Mfr./Jeweler, Claremont, Calif., 1978—; teaching fellow U. New Eng., Biddeford, Maine, 1988-89; intern Mt. Clemens (Mich.) Gen. Hosp., 1990-91, resident in emergency medicine, cons. staff, 1991-94; rsch. dir. Herpetol. and Ichthyol. Infectious Disease Rsch. Assocs.; clin. faculty mem. U. New England Coll. Osteo. Medicine, 1994—; dir. edn. and rsch. staff St. Johns Hosp., Springfield, Ill., 1997—. Contbr. publs. to Jour. Am. Osteo. Assn., Procs. of 3d Internat. Aquarium Congress, Handbook of Antimicrobial Therapy for Reptiles and Amphibians. Mem. AMA, Am. Osteo. Assn., Am. Acad. Osteopathy, Am. Coll. Emergency Physicians, Am. Coll. Osteopathic Emergency Physicians. Republican. Roman Catholic.

PAUL, FRANK WATERS, mechanical engineer, educator, consultant; b. Jersey Shore, Pa., Aug. 28, 1938. BSME, Pa. State U., 1960, MSME, 1964; PhD in Mechanical Engring., Lehigh U., 1968. Registered profl. control engr., Calif. Control engr. Hamilton Standard div. United Techs. Corp., 1961-64; instr. mechanical engring. Lehigh U., Bethlehem, Pa., 1964-68; asst. prof. mechanical engring. Carnegie-Mellon U., Pitts., 1968-73, assoc. prof., 1973-77; assoc. prof. Clemson (S.C.) U., 1977-79, prof., 1979-83, McQueen Quattlebaum prof., 1983—; cons. numerous cos. including Westinghouse Electric, 1969, 82-83, Alcoa Rsch. Labs., 1976-80, State of N.J., Dept. Higher Edn., 1986, Dunlop Sports, Inc., 1988, BPM Tech.; hon. prof. engring. Hull U. Eng., 1990-93; Dora Jones vis. prof. of electronic engring., 1993; dir. Ctr. for Advanced Mfg., 1982; lectr. to colls. and univs., U.S. and abroad. Author: (book, with others) Progress in Heat and Mass Transfer, Vol. 6, 1972, Metals: Processing and Fabrication, Encyclopedia of Materials Science and Engineering, 1986; contbr. articles to IEEE Control Systems mag., Jour. of Engring. for Industry (ASME), Jour. of Dynamic Systems Measurement and Control (ASME), and other scholarly publs. Sabbatical United Techs. Rsch. Ctr., 1985-86, Hull U., 1993. Mem. ASME (participant and paper reviewer Dynamic Systems and Control divsn. 1968—, chmn. panel on robotics 1985-87), Am. Soc. Engring. Educators, Soc. Mech. Engrs. (charter mem. Robotics Internat.), Pi Tau Sigma, Tau Beta Pi, Sigma Tau, Sigma Xi. Achievements include patents related to manufacturing automation. Office: Clemson U Fluor Daniel Bldg Rm 100 Clemson SC 29634-0921

PAUL, GORDON LEE, behavioral scientist, psychologist; b. Marshalltown, Iowa, Sept. 2, 1935; s. Leon Dale and Ione Hickman (Perry) P.; m. Joan Marie Wyatt, Dec. 24, 1954; children: Dennis Leon, Dana Lee, Joni Lynn. Student, Marshalltown Community Coll., 1953-54, San Diego City Coll., 1955-57; B.A., U. Iowa, 1960; M.A., U. Ill., 1962, Ph.D., 1964. Social sci. analyst VA Hosp., Danville, Ill., 1962; counseling psychologist U. Ill., Urbana, 1963; clin. psychologist VA Hosp., Palo Alto, Calif., 1964-65; pvt. practice clin. psychology, 1964-65; asst. prof. psychology U. Ill., Champaign-Urbana, 1965-67; assoc. prof. U. Ill., 1967-70, prof., 1970-80; Cullen disting. prof. psychology U. Houston, 1980—; pvt. practice psychology Champaign, 1965-80, Houston, 1980—; psychotherapy rsch. cons., Palo Alto, 1964-65; cons. Ill. Dept. Mental Health, 1965-73, 78-82, NIMH, 1968-78; adviser Ont. (Can.) Mental Health Found., 1968-69, NSF, 1968-69, Can. Coun., 1969-75, VA, 1972, 80—, APA, 1970—, UCLA/VA Med. Ctr./Camarillo Schizophrenia Rsch. Ctr., 1978-93, Alliance for Mentally Ill, 1980—. Author: Insight vs. Desensitization in Psychotherapy, An Experiment in Anxiety Reduction, 1966, Anxiety and Clinical Problems, 1973, Psychosocial Treatment of Chronic Mental Patients, 1977, Assessment in Residential Treatment Settings, Part 1, 1986, Observational Assessment Instrumentation for Service and Research, Part 2, 1987, Part 3, 1988; mem. editl. bd. Behavior Therapy, 1969-75, Behavior Therapy and Exptl. Psychiatry, 1969—, Schizophrenia Bull., 1971—, Jour. Abnormal Psychology, 1972-76, Jour. Residential Treatment, 1983—, Jour. Psychopathology and Behavioral Assessment, 1985—; cons. editor Jour. Applied Behavior Analysis, 1966-77, 81—, Psychol. Bull., 1967—, Jour. Abnormal Psychology, 1970-72, 76—, Psychosomatic Medicine, 1971-77, Psychophysiology, 1972—, Archives Gen. Psychiatry, 1973-74, Behavior Therapy, 1976-87, Profl. Psychologist, 1977-87, Hosp. Community Psychiatry, 1980-94, Biobehavioral Revs., 1980-84, Jour. Cmty. Psychology, 1983, Am. Psychologist, 1983—, Brit. Jour. Clin. Psychology, 1985-87, Nervous and Mental Disease, 1992, Current Directions in Psychol. Sci., 1992—; contbr. articles to profl. jours. Served with USN, 1954-58. Recipient Creative Talent award Am. Inst. Rsch., 1964, Teaching award U. Ill., 1968, 75; rsch. award Mental Health Assn., 1985; listed among 353 best mental health experts in nation Good Housekeeping, 1994; NIMH fellow, 1963-64. Fellow Am. Psychol. Assn. (corr. com. 1965-70, pres. sect. III, div. 12 1972-73, exec. com. div. 12 1974-77, Disting. Scientist award sect. III, div. 12 1977), Am. Psychol. Soc., Assn. Clin. Psychosocial Rsch., Am. Assn. Applied and Preventive Psychology; mem. Midwestern Psychol. Assn., Tex. Psychol. Assn., Houston Psychol. Assn., Assn. for Advancement Psychology, Phi Beta Kappa, Chi Gamma Iota. Subject of NIMH sci. report monograph, 1981: Treating and Assessing the Chronically Mentally Ill: The Pioneering Research of Gordon L. Paul. Home: 6239 S Braeswood Blvd Houston TX 77096-3715 Office: Psychology Dept U Houston Houston TX 77004

PAUL, GORDON WILBUR, marketing educator; b. Muskegon, Mich., Aug. 12, 1933; s. Wilbur M. and Ruth Hansen P.; m. Gloria W (Borns), Apr. 29, 1961; children: Christopher G., Bradley A. BS, Tulsa U., 1955; MBA, U. Tex., 1962; PhD, Mich. State U., 1966. Material controller Brunswick Corp., Muskegon, Mich., 1959-61; pres. Paul Bros., Inc., 1965—; assoc. prof. La. State U., Baton Rouge, 1965-69; prof., chmn. U. Mass., Amherst, 1969-77; prof. U. Cen. Fla., Orlando, 1977—; lectr. in field; Fulbright lectr., Portugal, 1985, 90, Athens, Greece, 1974. Author: (with others): Consumer Behavior: An Integrated Approach, 1975, Marketing Management, 1994, Marketing Management Strategy and Programs, 1997. Served to capt. USAF, 1955-58. Mem. Am. Mktg. Assn., Am. Inst. Decision Scis., Sales and Mktg. Execs., So. Mktg. Assn. (v.p. 1987). Methodist. Avocation: boating.

PAUL, HERBERT MORTON, lawyer, accountant, taxation educator; b. N.Y.C.; s. Julius and Gussie Paul; m. Judith Paul; children: Leslie Beth, Andrea Lynn. BBA, Baruch Coll.; MBA, NYU, LLM; JD, Harvard U. Ptnr. Touche Ross & Co., N.Y.C.; assoc. dir.-tax Touche Ross & Co., dir. fin counseling; mng. ptnr. Herbert Paul, P.C., N.Y.C., 1983—; prof. taxation, trustee NYU. Author: Ordinary and Necessary Expenses; editor: Taxation of Banks; adv. tax editor The Practical Acct.; mem. adv. bd. Financial and Estate Planning, Tax Shelter Insider, Financial Planning Strategist, Tax Shelter Litigation Report; bd. dirs. Partnership Strategist, The Business Strategist; cons. Profl. Practice Mgmt. Mag.; mem. panel The Hot Line; advisor The Partnership Letter, The Wealth Formula; cons. The Insider's Report for Physicians; mem. tax bd. Business Profit Digest; cons. editor physician's Tax Advisor; bd. fin. cons. Tax Strategies for Physicians; tax and bus. advisor Prentice Hall; contbg. editor. Jour. of Accountancy; mem. editl. bd. Family Bus. Advisor. Trustee NYU, mem. bd. overseers Grad. Sch. Bus.; mem. com. on trusts and estates Rockefeller U.; trustee Alvin Ailey Am. Dance Theatre, Associated Y's of N.Y.; chmn. NYU Alumni Assn., bd. dirs.; co-chmn. accts. divsn. Fedn. Philanthropies. Mem. Inst. Fed. Taxation (adv. com. chmn.), Internat. Inst. on Tax and Bus. Planning (adv. bd.), Assn. of Bar of City of N.Y., NYU Tax Soc. (pres.), Bur. Nat. Affairs-Tax Mgmt. (adv. com. on exec. compensation), Am. Inst. CPAs (com. on corp. taxation), Tax Study Group, ABA (tax sect.), N.Y. County Lawyers Assn., N.Y. State Soc. CPAs Dir. (chmn. tax div. com. on fed. taxation, gen. tax com., furtherance com., com. on rels. with IRS, bd. dirs.), Nat. Assn. Accts., Assn. of Bar of City of N.Y., Accts. Club of Am., Pension Club, Nat. Assn. Estate Planners (bd. dirs.), N.Y. Estate Planning Coun. (bd. dirs.), N.Y. C. of C. (tax com.), Grad. Sch. Bus. of NYU Alumni Assn. (pres.), Pres. Council (NYU), NYU Alumni Assn. (chmn.). Clubs: Wall St., City Athletic (N.Y.C.), Inwood Country.

PAUL, HERMAN LOUIS, JR., valve manufacturing company executive; b. N.Y.C., Dec. 30, 1912; s. Herman Louis and Louise Emilie (Markert) P.; student Duke, 1931-32, Lehigh U., 1932-33; m. Janath Powers (dec. Jan. 1996); children—Robert E., Charles Thomas, Herman Louis III. Power plant engr. Paul's Machine Shop, N.Y.C., 1935-43; pres., chief engr. Paul's Machine Shop, N.Y.C., 1943-48; v.p., chief engr. Paul Valve Corp., East Orange, N.J., 1948-54; pres., chief engr. P-K Industries, Inc., North Arlington, N.J., 1954-59; v.p., dir. research Gen. Kinetics, Englewood, N.J., 1959-62; engring. cons., N.Y.C., 1962-65; v.p., dir. Hydromatics, Inc., Bloomfield, N.J., 1965-67; with P.J. Hydraulics, Inc., Myerstown, Pa., 1967—, pres., chief engr., 1968-80, dir. and stockholder, 1980-81; pres. Flomega Industries, Inc., Cornwall, Pa., 1982—; cons. to Metal Industries Devel. Center, Taiwan, 1979; engring. cons. valves and complimentary equipment, 1980—; valve cons. Continental Disc Corp., Kansas City, Mo., 1980—. Vice chmn. Nat. UN Day Com., 1977, 78, 79, 80. Mem. ASME, Instrument Soc. Am., Am. Soc. Naval Engrs., Internat. Platform Assn., The Navy League, The Naval Inst. Club: Heidelberg Country (Bernville, Pa.), Quentin (Pa.) Riding. Patentee in field. Home: RD 5 370 Dogwood Ln Lebanon PA 17042

PAUL, JAMES CAVERLY NEWLIN, law educator, former university dean; b. Chestnut Hill, Pa., Apr. 30, 1926; s. William Allen Butler and Adelaide Sims (Newlin) P.; m. Margaret Morris Clausen, June 25, 1948; children: Nicholas Newlin, Martha Morris, Adelaide Sims. B.A., Princeton U., 1948; J.D., U. Pa., 1951. Bar: Pa. bar 1952. Legal sec. to Chief Justice U.S., 1951-53; prof. U. N.C., 1953-55; asst. dir. Inst. Govt., U. N.C., 1953-55; prof. law, dir. Inst. Legal Research, U. Pa., 1955-63; prof. law, dean and founder of faculty of law Haile Selassie U., Ethiopia, 1963-67; v.p. acad. affairs Haile Selassie U., 1967-69; exec. v.p. Ednl. and World Affairs, N.Y.C., 1969-70; dean Sch. Law, Rutgers U., Newark, 1970-74, prof. law, 1970-96, Newhouse scholar in law, 1984-88, William J. Brennan prof., 1988-96; exec. sec., trustee Internat. Ctr. for Law in Devel., N.Y.C., 1974—; founding mem., sec.-treas. Internat. Third World Legal Studies Assn., N.Y.C., 1980-96; adj. prof. Columbia U., 1973-95; cons. Constl. Commn. of Transitional Govt. of Ethiopia, 1992-93, UN Devel. Programme, 1994-96. Author: Rift in the Democracy, 1951, (with others) Federal Censorship, 1961, Ethiopian Constitutional Development, 1969, Lawyers in the Third World, 1981, The International Context of Rural Poverty in the Third World, 1986, Incorporating Human Rights Into the World Summit for Social Development, 1995. Candidate for U.S. Congress from 9th Dist. Pa., 1958; del. Dem. Nat. Conv., 1960. Served with USNR, 1943-46, PTO. Recipient spl. medal for distinguished service to univ. edn. in Ethiopia, 1969. Mem. Am., N.J., Pa. bar assns., Internat. Third World Legal Studies Assn. (sec.-treas. 1980—), Order of Coif. Club: Princeton (N.Y.C.). Home: 1352 Chancellor Pl Trappe MD 21673 Office: 15 Washington St Newark NJ 07102-3105 *My life in law and teaching about law gives satisfaction because it enables me to direct my energies towards thinking about social justice, individual dignity, and the possibilities of attaining more of the conditions enabling these ideals. But that satisfaction is tempered by constant realization of my own frailities and the failure everywhere of people, particularly those most fortunately endowed, to be guided by principled thinking.*

PAUL, JAMES WILLIAM, lawyer; b. Davenport, Iowa, May 3, 1945; s. Walter Henry and Margaret Helene (Hillers) P.; m. Sandra Kay Schmid, June 15, 1968; children: James William, Joseph Hillers. BA, Valparaiso U., 1967; JD, U. Chgo., 1970. Bar: N.Y. 1971, U.S. Ct. Appeals (2d cir.) 1971, U.S. Dist. Ct. (so. and ea. dists.) N.Y. 1972, U.S. Supreme Ct. 1977, U.S. Ct. Appeals (6th cir.) 1981, Ind. 1982, U.S. Dist. Ct. (no. dist.) Ind. 1982, U.S. Claims Ct. 1989, U.S. Dist. Ct. (ea. dist.) Mich. 1989, U.S. Ct. Appeals (fed. cir.) 1991. Assoc. Rogers & Wells, N.Y.C., 1970-78, ptnr., 1978—; dir., officer Musica Sacra, Inc., 1972-81. Bd. dirs. Turtle Bay Music Sch., Am. Lutheran Publicity Bur. Recipient Disting. Alumnus award Valparaiso U., 1994. Mem. ABA (antitrust sect. ins. com.), Assn. Bar City N.Y. (civil ct. com.), Fed. Bar Council (young lawyers com.). Democrat. Clubs: Yale (N.Y.C.), Sky (N.Y.C.); Quaker Hill Country (Pauling, N.Y.). Home: 360 East 72nd St Apt A-710 New York NY 10021 also: 5 Curtis Dr Sherman CT 06784-1220 Office: Rogers & Wells 200 Park Ave Ste 5200 New York NY 10166-0005

PAUL, JOHN JOSEPH, bishop; b. La Crosse, Wis., Aug. 17, 1918; s. Roland Philip and Louise (Gilles) P. B.A., Loras Coll., Dubuque, Iowa, 1939; S.T.B., St. Mary's Sem., Balt., 1943; M.Ed., Marquette U., 1956. Ordained priest Roman Catholic Ch., 1943; prin. Regis High Sch., Eau Claire, Wis., 1948-55; rector Holy Cross Sem., La Crosse, 1955-66, St. Joseph's Cathedral, La Crosse, 1966-77; aux. bishop Diocese of La Crosse, 1977-83, bishop, 1983—. Office: PO Box 4004 La Crosse WI 54602-4004*

PAUL, JOSEPH B., information technology executive; b. Bklyn., Jan. 21, 1961; s. Samuel and Ruth (Bassin) P.; m. Rose Jacklyn Futterman, Apr. 1, 1984. BS in Computer Sci., CUNY, S.I., 1983; MBA, Nova U., 1988; postgrad., Calif. Coast U. Computer programmer Office of Mgmt. and Budget, N.Y.C., 1981-83; programmer, analyst Harris Corp., Melbourne, Fla., 1983-84; sr. analyst AT&T, Maitland, Fla., 1984-85; project leader Fla. Power and Light, Miami, 1985-90; project mgr. S.E. Toyota Distbr., Deerfield Beach, Fla., 1990-93; dir. customer svcs. Data Net Corp., Miramar, Fla., 1993-95; v.p. PC support Citizens Fed. Bank, Ft. Lauderdale, Fla., 1995-96; v.p. info. tech., CIO Compass Health Sys., North Miami, Fla., 1996—; pres. S.E. Area Focus Users Group, Miami, 1986-89, Co-Log Users Group, Miramar, 1993-94. Mem. agy. rels. sub-com. United Way South Fla., Miami, 1988-90; pres. Archtl. Control Com., Sunrise, Fla., 1991-93. Mem. Health Info. Mgmt. Systems Soc., Am. Mgmt. Assn., Am. Mktg. Assn., Coll. Healthcare Info. Mgmt. Execs., Toastmasters, Tau Alpha Pi (pres. 1982-83). Republican. Jewish. Avocations: photography, woodworking, dog breeding, computers. Home: 13120 NW 11th Dr Sunrise FL 33323-2951 Office: Compass Health Sys PA 4th Fl 1065 NE 125th St Fl 4 North Miami FL 33161-5821

PAUL, JUSTUS FREDRICK, historian, educator; b. Boonville, Mo., May 27, 1938; s. Firdel W. and Emma L. (Frankenfeld) P.; m. Barbara Jane Dotts, Sept. 10, 1960; children: Justus, Rebecca, Ellen. A.B., Doane Coll., Crete, Nebr., 1959; M.A., U. Wis., 1960; Ph.D., U. Nebr., 1966. Tchr. Wausau High Sch., Wis., 1960-62; instr. history U. Nebr., 1963-66; mem. faculty U. Wis., Stevens Point, 1966—; prof. history U. Wis., 1973—, chmn. dept., 1969-86, chmn. faculty senate, 1977-79, 83-85, dean Coll. Letters and Scis., 1986—. Author: Senator Hugh Butler and Nebraska Republicanism, 1976, The World is Ours: The History of the University of Wisconsin-Stevens Point, 1894-1994, 1994; editor: Selected Writings of Rhys W. Hays, 1977; co-editor: The Badger State: A Documentary History of Wisconsin, 1979; contbr. articles to profl. jours. Chmn. Portage County (Wis.) Bd. Adjustment, 1976-90; moderator 1st Congl. United Ch. of Christ, 1988-90; bd. dirs. Monteverdi Master Chorale, 1988-90, sec., 1988-89, pres., 1989-90, bd. govs., 1994—, sec. 1996—; bd. dirs. United Ch. Family Svcs., 1992—, sec., 1994, treas., 1995-97. Grantee State of Wis., 1974-80, Am. Assn. State and Local History, 1968-69; recipient Paul Kersenbrock Humanitarian award Doane Coll., 1996, Rothman award for local history, 1996. Mem. Am. Hist. Assn., Orgn. Am. Historians, Hist. Soc. Wis., Nebr. Hist. Soc. Mem. United Ch. Christ. Home: 2001 Country Club Dr Stevens Point WI 54481-7009 Office: Coll Letters and Scis U Wis 130 CCC Stevens Point WI 54481

PAUL, LES, entertainer, inventor; b. Waukesha, Wis., June 9, 1915; s. George and Evelyn (Stutz) Polfuss; m. Mary Ford (dec. 1977); children: Lester, Gene, Colleen, Robert, Mary. Student pub. schs., Waukesha. Appeared on numerous radio programs throughout Midwest, in 1920's and 1930's; formed Les Paul Trio, 1936-37, and appeared with Fred Waring, N.Y.C.; appeared on first television broadcast with an orch. from NBC, N.Y.C., 1939; mus. dir., WJJD and WIND, Chgo., 1941; appeared with Mary Ford on own television show, Mahwah, N.J., 1953-57; host: Edison 100th Anniversary of invention of phonograph at Edison Home, West Orange, N.J., 1977; numerous TV, club appearances, especially Fat Tuesday's, N.Y.C.; recs. include: Lover and Brazil, 1948, Nola, 1949, Goofus, 1950, Tennessee Waltz, 1950, Little Rock Getaway, 1950, Mockin' Bird Hill, 1951, Just One More Chance, 1951, Walkin' and Whistlin' Blues, 1951, How High The Moon, 1951 (Hall of Fame award 1979), Smoke Rings, 1952, The World's Waiting For The Sunrise, 1952, Tiger Rag, 1953, Meet Mr. Callaghan, 1953, Jazz Me Blues, 1952, Vaya Con Dios, 1954, Chester and Lester, 1976 (Grammy award), Guitar Monsters, 1977 (Grammy nominee), The Legend and the Legacy, 1991, The Best of the Capitol Masters with Mary Ford, 1992, The Guitar Artistry of Les Paul, Greatest Hits!, 1994. Served with Armed Forces Radio Service, World War II. Les Paul and Mary Ford named to Grammy Hall of Fame, 1977; Grammy Achievement award for contbns. to rec., musical instruments industry; named to Rock 'N' Roll Hall of Fame, 1988; named to Wis. Performing Artists Hall of Fame, 1990. Mem. AFTRA, ASCAP, SAG, Audio Engring. Soc., Am. Fedn. Musicians. Pioneer multi-track tape recorder; inventor 1st 8-track tape recorder; inventor sound-on-sound recording; creator Les Paul electric solid body guitars; consultant, Gibson Guitar Corp., Nashville. Address: Columbia Records 550 Madison Ave New York NY 10022 *To be successful requires hard work, determination, a positive attitude, believing in one's self, a God given talent and luck.**

PAUL, LINDA BAUM, geriatrics nurse, toy business owner; b. Syracuse, N.Y., Aug. 18, 1946; d. LeRoy Stanley and Evelyn Lucille (Miller) Baum; m. James Frederick Paul, Mar. 2, 1974; children: Patricia Ann, Sharon Joy, Sarah Leigh. LPN, Ctrl. Tech. Adult LPN Program, Syracuse, 1970; postgrad. in RN, Human Svc., Onondaga C.C., 1990-92, postgrad. in MSW/Counseling, 1996—. LPN, charge nurse Maple Lawn Nursing Home, Manlius, N.Y., 1970-73; nurse, foster parent, personal care provider Ofc. Mental Retardation & Devel. Disabilities/Sequin Cmty., Syracuse, 1974-87; LPN, charge nurse Cmty. Gen. Hosp., Syracuse, 1989-96; owner Wood-You Crafts, Manlius, 1987-92. Election insp. Dem. Com. Bd. Elections, Dewitt/Fayetteville, N.Y., 1986-87; mem. Jamesville-DeWitt PTG, 1974—; mem. ch. missions and outreach Manlius Meth. Ch., 1995—, choir dir., 1993; choir dir. Bridgeport Meth. Ch., 1974-76; soloist Syracuse Chorale; mem. ENABLE/United Cerebbral Palsy Ctr. Avocations: singing, piano, bowling. Home: 219 Hobson Ave Fayetteville NY 13066-1616

PAUL, MAURICE M., federal judge; b. 1932. BSBA, U. Fla., 1954, LLB, 1960. Bar: Fla. 1960. Assoc. Sanders, McEwan, Mims & MacDonald, Orlando, Fla., 1960-64; ptnr. Akerman, Senterfitt, Eidson, Mesmer & Robinson, Orlando, 1965-66, Pitts, Eubanks, Ross & Paul, Orlando, 1968-69; judge U.S. Cir. Ct. (9th cir.) Fla., 1973-82; judge, now chief judge U.S. Dist. Ct. (no. dist.) Fla., 1982—. Office: US Dist Ct 401 SE 1st Ave Gainesville FL 32601-6851*

PAUL, NANCY ELIZABETH, psychiatric-mental health nurse; b. Summit, N.J., Mar. 5, 1943; d. Victor Carl and Lois Emily (Procter) Bonardel; m. Richard Edward Paul, Apr. 8, 1967; children: Deborah, Michael, Kimberly. BSN, Skidmore Coll., 1965; MA in Counseling, Framingham State Coll., 1991. RN, Mass.; ANA cert. psychiat.-mental health nurse, clin. specialist; lic. mental health counselor. Head nurse Mass. Mental Health Ctr., Boston, 1965-68; nurse Cushing Hosp., Framingham, Mass., Charles River Hosp., Wellesley, Mass., 1969-72; staff nurse Leonard Morse Hosp., Natick, Mass., 1979-94, charge nurse, 1994-95; therapist Psychol. Svcs. Counseling Ctr., Natick, 1993—; clin. nurse, specialist in partial hosp. Columbia Metro West Hosp., 1996—. Mem. Mass. Nurses Assn. Home: 933 Old Connecticut Path Framingham MA 01701-7750

PAUL, NANCY HAWORTH, educator; b. New Brunswick, N.J., Sept. 11, 1939; d. James Alfred and Rose Catherine (Kull) Haworth; m. Charles William Paul, Aug. 13, 1966; children: Ellen Elizabeth, William Charles. BS, Georgian Ct. Coll., 1962; MS in Edn., Rutgers U., 1964; postgrad., L.I. U., 1988, Coll. New Rochelle, 1988-89. Tchr. Joyce Kilmer Sch., Milltown, N.J., 1962-64, Rutgers Prep. Sch., Somerset, N.J., 1964-66, North St. Sch., White Plains, N.Y., 1966-71; substitute tchr. White Plains Pub. Schs., 1976-84, 84-88; tchr. English as 2d lang. George Washington Sch., White Plains, 1988—; del. Curriculum Coun., White Plains, 1967-69; dir. Christian Doctrine Convent, Greenwich, Conn., 1982-83, 88-90; mem. sch. base Mgmt. Coun., White Plains, 1990-92; planner & host staff devel. day George Washington Sch., 1995. Del. Parent Tchr. Coun. Harrison (N.Y.) Pub. Schs., 1981-84, v.p., 1983-84; treas. W. Harrison (N.Y.) Boy Scout Coun., 1981-85; leader Girl Scouts U.S., West Harrison, 1979-90; vol. Meals on Wheels, West Harrison, 1980-84. Mem. Assn. Tchrs. of English to Speakers Other Langs., Nat. Curriculum Devel. Coun., N.Y. State Tchrs. of English to Speakers Other Langs., PTA. Roman Catholic. Avocations: piano, crafts. Home: 15 White Plains Ave West Harrison NY 10604-2813

PAUL, NORMAN LEO, psychiatrist, educator; b. Buffalo, N.Y., July 5, 1926; s. Samuel Joseph and Tannie (Goncharsky) P.; m. Betty Ann Byfield, June 6, 1951 (dec. May 1994); children: Marilyn, David Alexander. MD, U. Buffalo, 1948. Fellow pharmacology Coll. Medicine, U. Cin., Ohio, 1949-50; resident psychiatry Mass. Mental Health Ctr., Boston, 1952-55; fellow child psychiatry James Jackson Putnam Children's Ctr., Boston, 1957-58, 59, Mass. Gen. Hosp., Boston, 1958-59; chief psychiatrist Day Hosp. Mass. Mental Health Ctr., Boston, 1960-64; dir. conjoint family therapy Boston (Mass.) State Hosp., 1964-65, cons. in family psychiatry, 1965-70; assoc. clin. prof. dept. neurology Boston (Mass.) U. Sch. Medicine, 1977—; cons. Mental Health Ctr., Alaska Native Hosp., Anchorage, 1967, 68; cons. in family psychiatry Boston (Mass.) VA Hosp., 1967-71, Mass. Soc. for the Prevention of Cruelty to Children, Boston, 1993—; lectr. in psychiatry Harvard Med. Sch., Boston, 1976—; faculty assoc. Mgmt. Analysis Corp., Cambridge, Mass., 1979-82; vis. family therapist St. George's Med. Sch., London, 1996-97. Family therapist: (tv documentary) PBS-Trouble in the Family, 1965 (George Foster Peabody award 1965); co-author A Marital Puzzle, 1977, 86, German edit., 1987, French edit., 1995, Chinese edit., 1996. Sponsor Mass. Orgn. to Repeal Abortion Laws, Boston, 1965-70; chair Audio Unit of Child Devel. and Mass Media, White House Conf. on Children and Youth, Washington, 1970; bd. trustees Cambridge (Mass.) Coll., 1977-89. Capt. USAF, 1950-52. Recipient Edward A. Strecker, M.D. award for young psychiatrist of yr., 1966, Cert. of Merit, Mass. Coun. on Family Life, Boston, 1967, Cert. of Commendation, Mass. Assn. for Mental Health, Boston, 1967, Disting. Achievement award Soc. for Family Therapy and Rsch., Boston, 1973. Fellow Royal Soc. Medicine, Am. Psychiat. Assn. (life); mem. Am. Assn. Marriage and Family Therapy (bd. dirs. 1983-86), Am. Family Therapy

Assn. (v.p. 1982-83, Disting. Contbn. award 1984), Assn. for Rsch. in Nervous and Mental Disorders, Group for the Advancement Psychiatry (chair com. on the family 1982-84). Avocations: study of codes, travelling. Office: 394 Lowell St Ste 6 Lexington MA 02173-2575

PAUL, OGLESBY, cardiologist; b. Villanova, Pa., May 3, 1916; s. Oglesby and Laura Little (Wilson) P.; m. Marquerite Black, May 29, 1943 (dec. Jan. 1979); children: Rodman, Marquerite; m. Jean Lithgow, Jan. 17, 1981. AB, Harvard Coll., 1938; MD, Harvard Med. Sch., 1942. Intern Mass. Gen. Hosp., Boston, 1942-43, resident, 1946-48; prof. medicine Northwestern U., Evanston, Ill., 1963-77; sr. physician emeritus Brigham & Womens Hosp., Boston, 1977—; prof. medicine emeritus Harvard Med. Sch., Boston, 1977—; v.p. health scis. Northwestern U., Evanston, 1974-75; dir. admissions Harvard Med. Sch., Boston, 1977-82. Author: Take Heart, 1986, The Caring Physician, 1991. Pres. Am. Heart Assn., Dallas, 1960-61. Lt. USNR. Home: 10 Longwood Dr Apt 322 Westwood MA 02090-1142 Office: Harvard Med Sch Countway Libr 10 Shattuck St Boston MA 02115-6011

PAUL, RHONDA ELIZABETH, university program director, career development counselor; d. John and Vivian (Griffin) P. BA, Mich. State U., 1977; MA, Atlanta U., 1979; postgrad., Wayne State U., 1982—. Cert. counselor, Mich.; nat. cert. career counelor; lic. profl. counselor. Counselor, student affairs dept. Spelman Coll., Atlanta, 1978-79; life/career devel. specialist Wayne State U., Detroit, 1979-81, minority devel. counselor, 1981-83; prog. dir. recruitment dept. Wayne State Sch. of Medicine, Detroit, 1983—; cons./proprietor RP Career Assocs., Detroit, 1990—. Recipient Award of Pride, Mich. State U., Lansing, 1977, Spl. Recognition award Nat. Bd. for Cert. Counselors, 1993. Mem. NAACP, Am. Counseling Assn., Mich. Counseling Assn., Assn. Multicultural Counseling and Devel. (nat. stds. and cert. com.), Nat. Career Devel. Assn., Nat. Coalition of 100 Black Women (bd. dirs.), Alpha Kappa Alpha. Avocation: aerobic dancing. Home: 4068 Cortland St Detroit MI 48204-1506 Office: Wayne State U Dept Recruitment Detroit MI 48202

PAUL, RICHARD STANLEY, lawyer; b. Whitefish, Mont., Apr. 26, 1941; s. Richard C. and Esther (Shenefelt) P.; m. Elizabeth Headley, May 28, 1966; children: Christopher, Matthew. BA in History, U. Mont., 1963; MA in Am. History, U. Minn., 1964; JD, U. Pa., 1969. Bar: Del. 1969, Conn. 1988. Assoc. gen. counsel Xerox Corp., Stamford, Conn., 1980-88; dep. gen counsel Xerox Corp., Stamford, 1988-89, v.p., gen. counsel, 1989—, sr. v.p., gen counsel, 1992—. Mem. exec. com. Ctr. for Pub. Resources. Mem. ABA, Del. Bar Assn., Conn. Bar Assn., Am. Corp. Cousnel Assn., Assn. Gen. Counsel. Republican. Lutheran. Office: Xerox Corp 800 Long Ridge Rd Stamford CT 06902-1227

PAUL, RICHARD WRIGHT, lawyer; b. Washington, May 23, 1953; s. Robert Henry Jr. and Betty (Carey) P.; m. Paula Ann Coolsaet, July 25, 1981; children: Richard Haven, Timothy Carey, Brian Davis. AB magna cum laude, Dartmouth Coll., 1975; JD, Boston Coll., 1978. Bar: Mich. 1978, U.S. Dist. Ct. (ea. dist.) Mich. 1978, U.S. Ct. Appeals (6th cir.) 1982, U.S. Supreme Ct. 1989, U.S. Dist. Ct. (we. dist.) Mich. 1991. Assoc. Dickinson, Wright, Moon, Van Dusen & Freeman, Detroit, 1978-85, ptnr., 1985—; mediator Wayne County cir. Ct. Co-author, Barbarians At The Gate: Daubert Two Years Later, 1995. Mem. ABA, Def. Rsch. Inst., Detroit Bar Assn., Mich. Def. Trial Counsel, Dartmouth Lawyers Assn., Oakland County Bar Assn., Assn. Def. Trial Counsel, Alumni Coun. Dartmouth Coll., Dartmouth Detroit Club (pres. 1980—). Avocations: tennis, cycling. Office: Dickinson Wright Moon Van Dusen & Freeman 525 N Woodward Ave Ste 2000 Bloomfield Hills MI 48304-2970 Office: Dickinson Wright Moon Van Dusen and Freeman 525 N Woodward Ave Ste 2000 Bloomfield Hills MI 48304-2970

PAUL, ROBERT, lawyer; b. N.Y.C., Nov. 22, 1931; s. Gregory and Sonia (Rijock) P.; m. Christa Holz, Apr. 6, 1975; 1 child, Gina. BA, NYU, 1953; JD, Columbia U., 1958. Bar: Fla. 1958, N.Y. 1959. From assoc. to ptnr. Paul, Landy, Beiley & Harper, P.A., Miami, 1964-94; counsel Republic Nat. Bank Miami, 1967—. Past pres. Fla. Philharm., Inc., 1978-79; trustee U. Miami. Mem. ABA, N.Y. Bar Assn., Fla. Bar Assn., Fla. Zool. Soc., French-Am. C. of C. of Miami (pres. 1986-87). Home: 700 Alhambra Cir Miami FL 33134-4808

PAUL, ROBERT ARTHUR, steel company executive; b. N.Y.C., Oct. 28, 1937; s. Isadore and Ruth (Goldstein) P.; m. Donna Rae Berkman, July 29, 1962; children: Laurence Edward, Stephen Eric, Karen Rachel. AB, Cornell U., 1959; JD, Harvard U., 1962, MBA, 1964. With Ampco-Pitts. Corp. (formerly Screw & Bolt Corp. Am.), 1964—, v.p., 1969-71, treas., 1973-79, exec. v.p., 1972-79, pres., COO, 1979-94, pres., CEO, 1994—, dir., 1969—; exec. v.p., bd. dirs. Louis Berkman Co.; bd. dirs. Nat. City Corp.,; gen. ptnr. Romar Trading Co.; instr. Grad. Sch. Indsl. Adminstrn. Carnegie Mellon U., 1966-69; trustee Cornell U. Trustee H.L. and Louis Berkman Found., Presbyn. Univ. Hosp.; trustee, pres. Fair Oaks Found.; treas. Jewish Health-care Found. Pitts. Mem. ABA, Mass. Bar Assn., Harvard Club (N.Y.), Concordia Club, Pitts. Athletic Club, Duquesne Club. Republican. Jewish. Office: Ampco-Pitts Corp 600 Grant St Pittsburgh PA 15219-2702

PAUL, ROBERT CAREY, lawyer; b. Washington, May 7, 1950; s. Robert Henry and Betty Jane (Carey) P. AB, Dartmouth Coll., 1972; JD, Georgetown U., 1978. Assoc. Milbank Tweed Hadley & McCloy, N.Y.C., 1978-85; ptnr. Dechert Price & Rhoads, N.Y.C., 1986-89, Kelley, Drye & Warren, Brussels, 1989-93; counsel Rockefeller & Co., Inc., N.Y.C., 1995—. Home: 310 E 46th St Apt 9B New York NY 10017-3023 Office: Rockefeller & Co Inc 30 Rockefeller Plz New York NY 10112

PAUL, ROBERT DAVID, management consultant; b. N.Y.C., Nov. 1, 1928; s. Joseph Wolf and Freda (Sturm) P.; m. Eve Weinschenker, Apr. 9, 1952; children: Jeremy Ralph, Sarah Elizabeth. BS in Engring., U. Mich., 1950. Administrv. asst. Martin E. Segal Co., N.Y.C., 1950; naval architect Gibbs & Cox, N.Y.C., 1951; with The Segal Co., N.Y.C., 1953—, pres., 1967-76, vice chmn., 1977-91, chmn., 1991-94; dir., cons. Segal Co., N.Y.C., 1994—; trustee Employee Benefit Rsch. Inst., Washington, 1978-94, chair fellow com., 1994; bd. dirs. Wiss, Janney, Elstner Assocs., Northbrook, Ill., Empire Blue Cross Blue Shield. Contbr. articles to profl. jours. Cpl. U.S. Army, 1951-53. Mem. Soc. Human Resources Mgmt., Am. Compensation Assn., Am. Benefits Conf., Internat. Found. Employee Benefit Plans (past chmn. corp. com.), Univ. Club. Avocations: naval and mil. history, jazz piano. Office: The Segal Co 1 Park Ave New York NY 10016-5802

PAUL, ROLAND ARTHUR, lawyer; b. Memphis, Jan. 19, 1937; s. Rol and Hattye (Mincer) P.; m. Barbara Schlesinger, June 10, 1962; children: Deborah Lynn, Arthur Eliot. B.A. summa cum laude, Yale U., 1958; LL.B. magna cum laude, Harvard U., 1961. Bar: N.Y. 1962, Mich. 1978, Conn. 1989. Law clk. to judge U.S. Ct. Appeals, 1961-62; fgn. affairs officer, spl. asst. to gen. counsel Dept. Def., 1962-64; assoc. firm Cravath, Swaine & Moore, N.Y.C., 1964-69; counsel fgn. relations subcom. security commitments U.S. Senate, 1969-71; assoc. firm Simpson Thacher Bartlett, N.Y.C., 1971-73; v.p., gen. counsel Howmet Corp., Greenwich, Conn., 1976—; v.p., gen. counsel, dir. Pechiney Corp., Greenwich, Conn., 1984-95. Author: American Military Commitments Abroad. Mem. Council Fgn. Relations, Am. Bar Assn., Mich. Bar Assn. Home: 8 Ellery Ln Westport CT 06880-5202 Office: Pechiney Corp 475 Steamboat Rd Greenwich CT 06830-7144

PAUL, RON, congressman; b. Pitts.; m. Carol Paul; five children. Grad., Gettysburg Coll., Duke U. Sch. Medicine. Mem. 94th-98th, 105th Congresses from 14th Tex. dist., 1976-84, 96—; mem. banking and fin. svcs. com., com. edn. and workforce. Author: Challenge to Liberty, The Case for Gold, others. With USAF. Recipient Taxpayer's Best Friend award, National Taxpayers Union, Mises Inst. Groseclose Prize and Leadership award, Leadership award Coalition for Peace Through Strength, Disting. Svc. award Am. Constl. Action, Torch Freedom award Young Conservatives Tex., Guardian Freedom award Young Am. Freedom.

PAUL, RONALD NEALE, management consultant; b. Chgo., July 22, 1934; s. David Edward and Frances (Kusel) P.; m. Nona Maria Moore, Dec. 27, 1964 (div. Oct. 1981); children: Lisa, Karen, Brenda; m. Georgeann Elizabeth Lapkoff, Apr. 10, 1982. BS in Indsl. Engring., Northwestern U., 1957, MBA, 1958. Asst. to pres. Victor Comptometer Co., Chgo., 1958-64; cons. Corplan, Chgo., 1964-66; pres. Technomic Inc., Chgo., 1966—; mng. ptnr. L/P Ptnrs., Chgo., 1978-84; bd. dirs. Summit Restaurants, Salt Lake City, 1990-96. Co-author: The 101 Best Performing Companies in America, 1986, Winning the Chain Restaurant Game, 1994. Mem. Am. Mktg. Assn., Am. Mgmt. Assn., Planners Forum, Pres.'s Assn., Product Devel. Mgmt. Assn., Beta Gamma Sigma. Avocations: reading, racquetball. Office: Technomic Inc 300 S Riverside Plz Ste 1940 Chicago IL 60606-6613

PAUL, RONALD STANLEY, research institute executive; b. Olympia, Wash., Jan. 19, 1923; s. Adolph and Olga (Klapstein) P.; m. Margery Jean Pengra, June 5, 1944; children: Kathleen Paul Crosby, Robert S., James N. Student, Linfield Coll., 1940-41, Reed Coll., 1943-44, Harvard U., 1945; BS, U. Oreg., 1947, MS, 1949, PhD, 1951. Physicist, research mgr. Gen. Electric Co., Richland, Wash., 1951-64; asso. dir. Battelle N.W. Labs., Richland, 1965-68; dir. Battelle N.W. Labs., 1971-72, Battelle Seattle Research Ctr., 1969-70; v.p. ops. Battelle Meml. Inst., Columbus, Ohio, 1973-76, sr. v.p., 1976-78, exec. v.p., 1978-81, pres., 1981-87, chief exec. officer, 1984-87, assoc. trustee, 1986-92; lectr. modern physics Ctr. for Grad. Studies, Richland, 1951-62; IAEA cons. to, Japan, 1962; bd. dirs. LifeSpan Biosciences, 1995—. Contbr. articles to profl. jours. Trustee Linfield Coll., 1970-73, Denison U., 1982-88, Oreg. Mus. Sci. and Industry, 1971-72, Columbus Ctr. Sci. and Industry, 1973-87, Columbus Cancer Clinic, 1974-87, Columbus Children's Hosp. Research Found., 1975-87, Franklin U., 1987; trustee Pacific Sci. Ctr., 1969-74, Found. assoc., 1989—; v.p. exec. bd. Cen. Ohio council Boy Scouts Am., 1976-87; mem. exec. bd. of fellows Seattle-Pacific Coll., 1970-73; bd. overseers Acad. for Contemporary Problems, 1971-75; mem. nat. adv. bd. Am. U., 1982-86, Ohio State U. Found., 1985-87; bd. dirs. Edward Lowe Found., 1985—. Served with USAAF, 1943-46. Recipient Silver Beaver award Boy Scouts Am., 1986. Mem. Am. Phys. Soc., Am. Nuclear Soc., Sigma Xi, Sigma Pi Sigma, Pi Mu Epsilon. Republican. Presbyterian. Home: 7706 173rd St SW Edmonds WA 98026-5018

PAUL, STEPHEN HOWARD, lawyer; b. Indpls., June 28, 1947; s. Alfred and Sophia (Nahmias) P.; m. Deborah Lynn Dorman, Jan. 22, 1969; children: Gabriel, Jonathan. AB, Ind. U., 1969, JD, 1972. Bar: Ind. 1972, U.S. Dist. Ct. (so. dist.) Ind. 1972. Assoc. Baker & Daniels, Indpls., 1972-78, ptnr., 1979—. Editor in chief Ind. U. Law Jour., 1971. Pres. Belle Meade Neighborhood Assn., Indpls., 1974-78; v.p., counsel Brentwood Neighborhood Assn., Carmel, Ind., 1985-88, pres., 1988-91. Mem. ABA (state and local tax com. 1985—, sports and entertainment law com.), Am. Property Tax Counsel (founding mem.), Ind. State Bar Assn., Order of Coif. Office: Baker & Daniels 300 N Meridian St Indianapolis IN 46204-1755

PAUL, THOMAS A., book publisher. Pres. Gale Rsch. Co., Detroit, Mich., 1987-90; pres., CEO Internat. Thomson Pub., Stamford, Conn., 1990—. Office: Internat Thomson Pub 1 Station Pl Stamford CT 06902-6800

PAUL, THOMAS DANIEL, lawyer; b. Butte, Mont., June 10, 1948; s. Thomas Anthony and Helen (O'Brien) P.; m. Carolyn Hicks, Dec. 20, 1976; children: Thomas Richard, Jennifer Ann. AB, Carroll Coll., 1970; MS, Ind. U., 1975, PhD, 1977; JD, U. Houston, 1987. Diplomate Am. Bd. Med. Genetics. Asst. prof. SUNY, Buffalo, 1977-84; assoc. Fulbright & Jaworski, Houston, 1987-90, participating assoc., 1990-94, ptnr., 1994—; staff cons. N.Y. State Dept. Mental Hygeine, Perrysburg, 1978-84. Contbr. articles to profl. jours. Named to Order of Coif U. Houston, 1987. Mem. Tex. Bar Assn., Houston Bar Assn., Am. Intellectual Property Law Assn., Houston Intellectual Property Law Assn. Home: 11803 Fidelia Ct Houston TX 77024-7112 Office: Fulbright & Jaworski 1301 Mckinney St Ste 5100 Houston TX 77010-3095

PAUL, THOMAS FRANK, lawyer; b. Aberdeen, Wash., Sept. 23, 1925; s. Thomas and Loretta (Ounstead) P.; m. Dolores Marion Zaugg, Apr. 1, 1950; chilren: Pamela, Peggy, Thomas Frank. BS in Psychology, Wash. State U., 1951; JD, U. Wash., 1957. Bar: Wash. 1958, U.S. Dist. Ct. (no. and so. dists.) Wash. 1958, U.S. Ct. Appeals (9th cir.) 1958, U.S. Supreme Ct. 1970. Ptnr., shareholder, dir. LeGros, Buchanan & Paul, Seattle, 1958—; lectr. on admiralty and maritime law. Mem. ABA (chmn. com. on admiralty and maritime litigation 1982-86), Wash. State Bar Assn., Maritime Law Assn. U.S.A. (com. on nav. and C.G. matters 1981-82, com. on U.S. Mcht. Marine program 1981-82, com. on practice and procedure 1982-86, com. on limitation of liability 1982-86, com. on maritime legislation 1982—), Asia Pacific Lawyers Assn., Rainier Club, Columbia Tower Club. Republican. Home: 1323 Willard Ave W Seattle WA 98119-3460 Office: LeGros Buchanan & Paul 701 5th Ave Seattle WA 98104-7016

PAUL, WILLIAM, physicist, educator; b. Deskford, Scotland, Mar. 31, 1926; came to U.S., 1952; s. William and Jean (Watson) P.; m. Barbara Anderson Forbes, Mar. 28, 1952; children—David, Fiona. M.A., Aberdeen U., Scotland, 1946; Ph.D., Aberdeen U., 1951; A.M. (hon.), Harvard U., 1960; D Honoris Causa, Paris, 1994. Asst. lectr., then lectr. Aberdeen U., 1946-52; mem. faculty Harvard U., 1953—, Gordon McKay prof. applied physics, 1963-91, Mallinckrodt prof. applied physics, 1991—, prof. physics, 1980—; professeur associé U. Paris, 1966-67; cons. solid state physics, 1954—; Ripon prof., Calcutta, 1984. Author: Handbook on Semiconductors: Band Theory and Transport Properties, 1982; co-editor: Solids Under Pressure, 1963, Amorphous and Liquid Semiconductors, 1980. Carnegie fellow, 1952-53; Guggenheim fellow, 1959-60; Humboldt awardee, 1990; fellow Clare Hall Cambridge U., 1974-75. Fellow Am. Phys. Soc., Brit. Inst. Physics, N.Y. Acad. Scis., Royal Soc. Edinburgh; mem. AAUP, Sigma Xi. Home: 2 Eustis St Lexington MA 02173-5612 Office: Harvard U Pierce Hall Cambridge MA 02138

PAUL, WILLIAM DEWITT, JR., artist, educator, photographer, museum director; b. Wadley, Ga., Sept. 26, 1934; s. William DeWitt and Sonoma Elizabeth (Tinley) P.; m. Dorothy Hefling, Sept. 2, 1962; children: Sarah Elizabeth, Barbara Susan, Dorothy Ann. Student, Emory U., summer 1952, U. Rome, summer 1953, Ga. State Coll. Bus. Adminstrn., Atlanta, 1953—, summer 1956; B.F.A., Atlanta Art Inst., 1955; A.B., U. Ga., 1958, M.F.A., 1959. Instr. art and art history Park Coll., Parkville, Mo., 1960-61; dir. exhbns., instr. art history Kansas City (Mo.) Art Inst., 1959-64, curator study collections, asst. prof. art, 1964-65; coordinator basic courses dept. art, asst. prof. art U. Ga., Athens, 1965-67; curator Ga. Mus. Art, asso. prof. art, 1967-69, dir., asso. prof., 1969-80, prof., 1997—; chmn. visual arts rev. panel Ga. Council for Arts and Humanities, 1976-77; v.p. Arts Festival Atlanta, 1982, 84, 85, trustee, 1982-93; guest artist Arts Festival Atlanta, 1987; mem. parents council Randolph-Macon Woman's Coll., Lynchburg, Va., 1986-87. Exhibited in one man shows at Ga. Mus. Art, 1959, Atlanta Art Assn., 1959, Unitarian Gallery, Kansas City, 1960, Palmer Gallery, Kansas City, 1965, Heath Gallery, Atlanta, 1976, Hunter Mus. Art, Chattanooga, 1976, Forum Gallery, N.Y.C., 1977, Madison (Ga.) Morgan Cultural Ctr., 1980, Columbus (Ga.) Mus. Arts and Scis., 1980, Macon (Ga.) Mus. Arts and Sci., 1980, Banks Haley Gallery, Albany, Ga., 1980, Augusta Richmond County (Ga.) Mus., 1980, Heath Gallery 1982, Moon Gallery, Berry Coll., Rome, Ga., 1983, Bathhouse Gallery, Atlanta, 1987, MIA Gallery, Seattle, 1988, Valencia C.C., Orlando, Fla., 1991, Gasperi Gallery, New Orleans, 1993, Contemporary Arts Ctr., New Orleans, 1994; numerous site-specific installations, 1986-97; exhibited group shows, New Arts Gallery, Atlanta, 1961, Kansas City Art Inst., 1960-64, Park Coll., 1960, Mulvane Art Ctr., Topeka, 1965, Palazzo Venezia, Rome, 1984, Elaine Benson Gallery, Bridgehampton, L.I., N.Y., 1986, Dulin Gallery Art, Knoxville, Tenn., 1986, 1987 Atlanta Biennale, Nexus Contemporary Art Ctr., Atlanta, Valencia C.C., Orlando, 1988, Greg Kucera Gallery, Seattle, 1992, King Plow Arts Ctr., Atlanta, 1994, Leslie-Lohman Found., N.Y.C., 1995, others; represented in permanent collections Gen. Mills, Inc., Mpls., Hallmark Cards, Kansas City, Little Rock Arts Ctr., Ga. Mus. Art, U. Ga. Ford Found. faculty enrichment grantee, 1978; recipient numerous awards for paintings. Mem. Am. Fedn. Arts (trustee 1969-81), Coll. Art Assn., Am. Assn. Museums (council 1981), Lovis Corinth Meml. Found., Ga. Alliance Arts Edn. (dir. 1975-77), Phi Kappa Phi. Home: 150 Bar H Ct Athens GA 30605-4702

PAUL, WILLIAM ERWIN, immunologist, researcher; b. Bklyn., June 12, 1936; s. Jack and Sylvia (Gleicher) P.; m. Marilyn Heller, Dec. 25, 1958; children: Jonathan M., Matthew E. AB summa cum laude, Bklyn. Coll., 1956; MD cum laude, SUNY-Downstate Med. Ctr., 1960, DSc (hon.), 1991. Intern, then asst. resident Mass. Meml. Hosp., Boston, 1960-62; clin. assoc. Nat. Cancer Inst. NIH, Bethesda, Md., 1962-64; postdoctoral fellow, instr. NYU Sch. Medicine, N.Y.C., 1964-68; sr. investigator Lab. Immunology Nat. Inst. Allergy and Infectious Diseases, NIH, Bethesda, 1968-70, chief Lab. Immunology, 1970—; dir. Office of AIDS Rsch. NIH, Bethesda, assoc. NIH dir., 1994—; mem. bd. sci. advisors Jane Coffin Childs Meml. Fund for Med. Research, 1982-90; G. Burroughs Mider lectr. NIH, 1982; mem. sci. rev. bd. Howard Hughes Med. Inst., 1979-85, 87-91, mem. med. adv. bd., 1992-96; mem. bd. sci. couns. Meml. Sloan-Kettering Cancer Ctr., N.Y.C., 1984-92; chmn. adv. com. Harold C. Simmons Arthritis Rsch. Ctr., 1984-90; bd. dirs. Fed. Am. Soc. Experimental Biology, 1985-88; mem. bd. basic biology NRC, 1986-89; mem. select com. Alfred P. Sloan Jr. Prize, Gen. Motors Cancer Res. Fedn., 1986-87; mem. awards assembly, 1995—; sci. adv. coun. Cancer Rsch. Inst., 1985-94; mem. com. to visit div. med. sci., bd. overseers Harvard Coll., 1987-93; Jonathan Lax lectr., Westar Inst., 1997, Solomon Berson lectr. Mount Sinai Sch. of Medicine, 1997; Carl Moore lectr. Sch. Medicine, Washington U., St. Louis, 1986; mem. adv. com. Pew Scholars Program in Biomed. Scis., 1988-91; Richard Gershon lectr. Yale U. Sch. Medicine, 1986; Nelson Med. lectr., U. Calif., Davis, 1988; Disting. Alumnus lectr., Univ. Hosp., Boston, 1989; Anderson med. lectr. U. Va., 1990, La Jolla sci. lectr., 1991, Wellcome vis. prof. Wayne State U., 1991, mem. Adv. Com. dept. of Molecular Bio., Princeton U., 1993-94, ann. lectr., Dutch Soc. for Immunology, 1992, Yamamura Meml. lectr. Osaka U., 1992, Kunkel lectr., Johns Hopkins U. Sch. of Medicine, 1993; Welcome vis. prof. SUNY Stony Brook, 1993; Benacerraf lectr. Harvard Med. Sch., 1993; Sulkin lectr. U. Tex. Southwestern Med. Ctr., 1995. Editor: Fundamental Immunology, 1984, 3rd edit., 1993, Ann. Rev. Immunology, Vols. 1-15, 1983—; adv. editor Jour. Exptl. Medicine, 1974—; assoc. editor Cell, 1985-96; transmitting editor Internat. Immunology, 1989-96; corr. editor Procs. Royal Soc. Series B, 1989-93; mem. editl. bd. Molecular Biology of Cell, 1990-92; contbg. editor Procs. NAS U.S.A., 1992-94; contbr. numerous articles to sci. jours. With USPHS, 1962-64, 75-96. Recipient Founders' prize Tex. Instruments Found., 1979, Alumni medal SUNY Downstate Med. Ctr., 1981, Disting. Svc. medal USPHS, 1985, 3M Life Scis. award, 1988, Tovi Comet-Wallerstein prize CAIR Inst., Bar-Ilan U., 1992, 6th ann. award for excellence in immunologic rsch. Duke U., 1993, Alumni honors Bklyn. Coll., 1994. Fellow Am. Acad. Arts and Scis.; mem. NAS, Inst. Medicine NAS, Am. Soc. Clin. Investigation (pres. 1980-81), Am. Assn. Immunologists (pres. 1986-87), Assn. Am. Physicians, Scandinavian Soc. Immunology (hon.). Office: NIH Bldg 31 Rm 4C02 31 Center Dr MSC 2340 Bethesda MD 20892-2340

PAUL, WILLIAM GEORGE, lawyer; b. Pauls Valley, Okla., Nov. 25, 1930; s. Homer and Helen (Lafferty) P.; m. Barbara Elaine Brite, Sept. 27, 1963; children—George Lynn, Alison Elise, Laura Elaine, William Stephen. B.A., U. Okla., 1952, LL.B., 1956. Bar: Okla. bar 1956. Pvt. practice law Norman, 1956; ptnr. Oklahoma City, 1957-84; with Crowe & Dunlevy, 1962-84, 96—; sr. v.p., gen. counsel Phillips Petroleum Co., Bartlesville, Okla., 1984-95; ptnr. Crowe & Dunlevy, Oklahoma City, 1996—; assoc. prof. law Oklahoma City U., 1964-68; adv. bd. Martindale Hubbell, 1990—. Author: (with Earl Sneed) Vernon's Oklahoma Practice, 1965. Bd. dirs. Nat. Ctr. for State Cts., 1993—, Am. Bar Endowment, 1986—. 1st lt. USMCR, 1952-54. Named Outstanding Young Man Oklahoma City, 1965, Outstanding Young Oklahoman, 1966. Fellow Am. Bar Found. (chmn. 1991), Am. Coll. Trial Lawyers; mem. ABA (bd. govs. 1995—), Okla. Bar Assn. (pres. 1976), Oklahoma County Bar Assn. (past pres.), Nat. Conf. Bar Pres. (pres. 1986), U. Okla. Alumni Assn. (pres. 1973), Order of Coif, Phi Beta Kappa, Phi Delta Phi, Delta Sigma Rho. Democrat. Presbyterian. Home: 13017 Burnt Oak Rd Oklahoma City OK 73120-8919 Office: Crowe & Dunlevy 1800 Mid-Am Tower 20 N Broadway Ave Oklahoma City OK 73102-8202

PAUL, WILLIAM MCCANN, lawyer; b. Cambridge, Mass., Feb. 9, 1951; s. Kenneth William and Mary Jean (Lamson) P.; m. Janet Anne Forest, Feb. 25, 1984; children: Emily L'Engle, Andrew Angwin, Elizabeth Seton. Student, U. Freiburg, Fed. Republic of Germany, 1971-72; BA, Johns Hopkins U., 1973; JD, U. Mich., 1977. Bar: D.C. 1978, U.S. Dist. Ct. D.C. 1978, U.S. Ct. Claims 1984, U.S. Ct. Appeals (4th cir.) 1980, U.S. Ct. Appeals (fed. cir.) 1983, U.S. Tax Ct. 1990. Law clk. to judge U.S. Ct. Appeals (5th cir.), Austin, Tex., 1977-78; assoc. Covington & Burling, Washington, 1978-87, ptnr., 1987-88, 89—; dep. tax legis. counsel U.S. Treasury Dept., 1988-89. Mem. ABA, D.C. Bar Assn., Am. coll. Tax Counsel, Order of Coif. Presbyterian. Home: 5604 Chevy Chase Pky NW Washington DC 20015-2520 Office: Covington & Burling PO Box 7566 1201 Pennsylvania Ave NW Washington DC 20004-2401

PAULAUSKAS, EDMUND WALTER, real estate broker, retired; b. Lowell, Mass., Nov. 16, 1937; s. Vladas and Barbara (Antonavicius) P.; m. Joyce Wagenhauser, Feb. 5, 1977. BS in Bus., Boston U., 1959; M Div., Oblate Coll. of SW, 1976; PhD in Psychology, Sussex U., Brighton, Eng., 1979. Lic. real estate broker, lic. mortgage broker, Fla.; ordained priest Roman Cath. Ch., 1970. Priest Diocese of Beaumont, Tex., 1970-77; psychotherapist Houston Dept. Pub. Health, 1979-84; pres., broker Vets. Realty, Ft. Lauderdale, Fla., from 1984. Producer TV program Catholic Church Today, 1975. Mem. Ft. Lauderdale Bd. Realtors. Home: 4250 Galt Ocean Dr Unit 1N Fort Lauderdale FL 33308

PAULEY, JANE, television journalist; b. Indpls., Oct. 31, 1950; m. Garry Trudeau; 3 children. BA in Polit. Sci, Ind. U., 1971; D. Journalism (hon.), DePauw U., 1978. Reporter Sta. WISH-TV, Indpls., 1972-75; co-anchor WMAQ-TV News, Chgo., 1975-76, The Today Show, NBC, N.Y.C., 1976-90; corr. NBC News, N.Y.C., 1976—; prin. writer, reporter NBC Nightly News, 1980-82, substitute anchor, 1990—; co-anchor Early Today, NBC, 1982-83; prin. corr. Real Life With Jane Pauley, NBC, 1990; co-anchor Dateline NBC, 1992—. Office: NBC News 30 Rockefeller Plz New York NY 10112*

PAULEY, ROBERT REINHOLD, broadcasting executive, financial executive; b. New Canaan, Conn., Oct. 17, 1923; s. Edward Matthew and Grace Amanda (Smith) P.; m. Barbara Anne Cotton, June 22, 1946; children: Lucinda Teed, Nicholas Andrew, Robert Reinhold Jr., John Adams. Student, Harvard U., 1946, MBA, 1951; DSc (hon.), Curry Coll., 1966. With radio sta. WOR, 1951-52, NBC, 1953-56, CBS, 1956-57; account exec. ABC, 1957-59, sales mgr., 1959-60, v.p. in charge, 1960-61, pres., 1961-67; pres. Mutual Broadcasting System, N.Y.C., 1967-69; v.p. corp. fin. E.F. Hutton & Co., Inc., 1971-81; founder, chmn. TV News Inc., N.Y.C.; founder Nat. Black Network, N.Y.C.; founder, pres. Cablenet Internat. Corp. and Cablenet News, N.Y.C.; disting. lectr. U. S.C., Spartanburg. Trustee Curry Coll.; bd. dirs. Found. to Improve TV. Mem. Radio-TV Execs. Soc., SAR, St. Nicholas Soc. Clubs: Harvard (Boston, N.Y.C.), Myopia Hunt, Tryon Hounds. Home: PO Box 217 Landrum SC 29356-0217

PAULEY, STANLEY FRANK, manufacturing company executive; b. Winnipeg, Man., Can., Sept. 19, 1927; came to U.S., 1954, naturalized, 1961; s. Daniel and Anna (Tache) P.; m. Dorothy Ann Ruppel, Aug. 21, 1949; children: Katharine Ann, Lorna Jane. B.E.E., U. Man., 1949. With Canadian Industries Ltd., Kingston, Ont., 1949-53; sr. engring. asst. Canadian Industries Ltd., 1952-53; controls designer Standard Machine and Tool Co. Ltd., Windsor, Ont., 1953-54; prodn. supt. E.R. Carpenter Co., Richmond, Va., 1954-57, pres., 1957-83, chmn., CEO, 1983-94; chmn., CEO, Carpenter Co. (formerly E.R. Carpenter Co.), Richmond, 1994—, also bd. dirs.; bd. dirs. Carpenter Co. of Can., Carpenter de Mexico, Carpenter Plc., Carpenter S.a., Am. Filtrona Corp., Carpenter Gmbh, Mentor Portfolio Fund. Trustee U. Richmond, Hampden-Sydney Coll., Va. Mus. Found., Va. Mus. Fine Arts, Va. Higher Edn. Tuition Trust Fund. Mem. Commonwealth Club, Forum Club, Country Club of Va. Republican. Presbyterian. Home: 314 St Davids Ln Richmond VA 23221-3708 Office: Carpenter Co 5016 Monument Ave Richmond VA 23230-3620

PAULIKAS, GEORGE ALGIS, physicist; b. Pagegiai, Lithuania, May 14, 1936; came to U.S., 1949, naturalized, 1955; s. George and Olga (Pacas) P.; m. Joan Marie Gross, Sept. 7, 1957; 1 child, Nancy Marie. B.S. in Engring. Physics, U. Ill., Chgo. and Urbana, 1957, M.S. (univ. fellow 1957-58), 1958; Ph.D. in Physics (NSF fellow 1958-61), U. Calif., Berkeley, 1961. With Aerospace Corp., El Segundo, Calif., 1961—, head space particles and fields dept., 1968, dir. space sics. lab., 1968-81, v.p. labs., 1981-85, group v.p.

devel., 1985-89, group v.p. programs, 1989-94, exec. v.p., 1992—; mem. various ad hoc coms. NAS, 1970, 73, 79, 80, ann., 1984-87, 91-92, mem. com. solar and space physics, 1977-80; mem. adv. coun. geophysics U. Calif., 1973-75, exec. com. space scis. lab., Berkeley, 1978-81; mem. sci. adv. bd. USAF, 1975-82, 91-95; cons. Lawrence Berkeley Lab., 1961-66, Office Space Scis., NASA, 1975-82, Los Alamos phys. divsn. adv. com., 1983-96, Naval Rsch. Adv. Com., 1984-86, Naval Studies Bd., 1989-95; mem. def. space tech. com. NRC, 1987-92. Author papers in field; asso. editor: Jour. Geophys. Research, 1972-75. Trustee Calif. Mus. of Sci. and Industry, 1994—. Recipient Aerospace Corp. Trustees Disting. Achievement award, 1980, Meritorious Civilian Svc. award USAF, 1982, 95, U. Ill. Alumni Disting. Engring. award, 1992; named U. Ill. (Navy Pier) Hall of Fame, 1996. Fellow AIAA (chmn. tech. com. space sci. and astronomy 1976-77), Am. Phys. Soc.; mem. Am. Geophys. Union, Sigma Xi. Home: 1537 Addison Rd Pls Vrds Est CA 90274-1808 Office: Aerospace Corporation 2350 E El Segundo Blvd El Segundo CA 90245-4609

PAULIN, AMY RUTH, civic activist, consultant; b. Bklyn., Nov. 29, 1955; d. Ben and Alice Lois (Roth) P.; m. Ira Schuman, May 25, 1980; children: Beth, Sarah, Joseph. BA, SUNY, Albany, 1977, MA, 1978, postgrad., 1979—. Instr. SUNY, Albany, 1978, Queens (N.Y.) House of Detention, 1979; fundraiser United Jewish Appeal Fedn., N.Y.C., 1979-83; dir. devel. Altro Health & Rehab., Bronx, N.Y., 1983-86; fundraising cons. N.Y.C., 1986-88; pres. LWV, Scarsdale, N.Y., 1990-92, Westchester, N.Y., 1992-95; trustee Scarsdale (N.Y.) Village, 1995—. Mem. adv. coun. Family Ct.; co-chair woman Westchester Womens Agenda; mem. adv. com. Fund for Women & Girls; bd. dirs. Mid. Sch. PTA, Westchester Coalition for Legal Abortion, Scarsdale Open Soc. Assn., 1992-95, United Jewish Appeal Fedn. Scarsdale Women's Campaign; v.p. Westchester Children's Assn.; troop leader Girl Scouts U.S.; mem. Town Club Edn. Com., 1983-89; mem. Scarsdale Bowl com., 1992-95, chair, 1994-95; mem. Scarsdale Japanese Festival, 1992-93; mem. Westchester Women's Equality Day, 1987-92; mem. nominating com. Heathcote Neighborhood Assn., 1991-92; bd. dirs. Westchester County Found., 1994-95; mem. Scarsdale Village Youth Bd., 1992-95; mem. legislators task force on women and youth at risk Westchester County Bd., 1994—; mem. Updating Voting Equipment Com., 1994; chair Countys Tobacco Free Westchester, 1993-95, chair 1995—; co-chair Parent Tchr. Coun. Sch. Budget Study, 1991-94; future planning chair Kids Base Bd., 1992-95, dir. 1992-94, chair future planning com. 1994-95; chair parking and traffic subcom. Village Downtown Devel. Com., 1994-95; mem. Westchester Commn. Campaign Fin. Reform, Westchester Commn. Child Abuse; exec. com. Westchester Mcpl. Offcls. Assn., 1996—; adv. com. Jr. League, 1996—. Mem. LWV (bd. dirs. women and children's issues Westchester chpt., issues specialist N.Y. state), N.Y. State Pub. Health Assn. (bd. dirs. Lower Hudson Valley chpt.). Avocations: swimming, dancing. Home: 12 Burgess Rd Scarsdale NY 10583-4410

PAULIN, HENRY SYLVESTER, antiques dealer, emeritus educator; b. Cleve., Nov. 8, 1927; s. Sylvester and Mary (Zimmerman) P.; m. Florence Caroline Schwegman, Aug. 30, 1952. B.S. in Edn, Kent (Ohio) State U., 1951; M.A., Ohio State U., 1958, Ph.D., 1964. Tchr. indsl. arts Brimfield Jr.-Sr. High Sch., Kent, 1954-55, Zanesville (Ohio) High Sch., 1955-57; instr. ceramics Art Inst., Zanesville, 1956-57; asst. prof., then asso. prof. indsl. arts State U. Coll., Oswego, N.Y., 1956-63; instr. Ohio State U., 1961-63; assoc. prof., coordinator Indsl. Arts Div., Kent State U., 1963-67; prof. and chmn. dept. design and industry San Francisco State U., 1967-80, prof. emeritus, 1980—; propr. Paulin Place (Fine Antiques and Paintings), Oxford, Ohio, 1980—; vis. prof. No. Ill. U., summer 1965. Served with AUS, 1946-48. Mem. Calif. Tchrs. Assn., Oxford C. of C., Oxford Retail Mchts. Assn., Epsilon Pi Tau, Phi Delta Kappa. Home: 6294 Fairfield Rd Oxford OH 45056-1555

PAULINA, DIANA, alternative school educator; b. Detroit; d. Walter and Marie (Hrit) P.; m. Kevin Crawley, Aug. 23, 1981. BA in German and English Edn., U. Mich., 1969; MA in Edn. Alternative Sch., Ind. U., 1979. Cert. tchr., German, English and reading. Various tchg. positions USAF/ Lang. Inst., Germany, 1970-74; instr. Marshalltown (Iowa) C.C., 1974-79; dir., counselor Unbound, Inc., Iowa City, Iowa, 1980-90; instr. Cmty. Edn. Ctr. Alternative Schs., Iowa City, 1984—; sponsor Iowa City (Iowa) Student Computer Club, 1993—; internet cons. Iowa City Cmty. schs., 1991—; v.p., bd. dirs. Response TV, Inc., Iowa City, 1992—; policy bd. chair Iowa Student Computer Assn. bull. Bd. Svc., 1992—. Mem. ASCD, ALA, AAUW, NEA, Iowa State Edn. Assn. (internet cons. 1992—, Mem. of Yr. East Ctrl. Uniserve unit 1996), Iowa City Edn. Assn. (pres., v.p., tech. chair, Mem. of Yr. 1996), Internat. Reading Assn., Nat. Coun. Tchrs. English, Iowa Coun. Tchrs. Lang. Arts, Iowa Assn. Alternative Educators (Educator of Yr. award 1996), Iowa City Edn. Cable Consortium, Iowa City Pub. Access (cmty. cable prodr. 1983—), Iowa Student Computer Assn., Assn. Computing Machinery, U. Mich. Alumni Assn., Ind. U. Alumni Assn. Avocations: reading, bowling, Internet exploration, handcrafts, wallyball. Home: PO Box 1963 Iowa City IA 52244-1963 Office: CEC Alternative Schs 509 S Dubuque St Iowa City IA 52240-4228

PAULING, LINUS CARL, JR., health science administrator. Pres., chmn. Linus Pauling Inst. of Sci. and Medicine, Palo Alto, Calif. Recipient. Office: Linus Pauling Inst of Sci & Med 440 Page Mill Rd Palo Alto CA 94306-2025

PAULINO, SISTER MARY MCAULEY, principal; b. Inarajan, Guam, Aug. 24, 1934; d. Mariano Torres Paulino. BA in Edn., U. Guam, 1974; M in Pvt. Sch. Adminstrn., U. S.F., 1992; postgrad., U. Guam. tchr. religious edn., Guam. V.p. Archdiocese of Agana, Guam; prin. Santa Barbara Sch., Dededo, Guam, 1978-81, Cathedral Grade Sch., 1986-90, 92-95, Baumgartner Meml. Sch., 1995—; coach math Olympiad and spelling bee; mem. peace and justice com. Agana Cathedral Parish Coun. Recipient Appreciation award for support of Guam historic preservation, faithful and valuable svc. to edn., commendation and congratulatory resolution 20th Guam Legis., Gov.'s Art award 1989. Mem. Nat. Cath. Educators Assn., ASCD, Internat. Reading Assn., Civic Ctr. Guam Found., Phi Delta Kappa.

PAULISSEN, JAMES PETER, physician, county official; b. Chgo., Aug. 14, 1928; s. Joseph Edward and Louise Catherine (Muno) P.; m. Lorraine Antoinette Polly, Sept. 11, 1954; children—Linda, Steven, Mark, Daniel. Student Loyola U., 1946-49, M.D. cum laude, 1953; M.P.H., Johns Hopkins U., 1966. Diplomate Am. Bd. Pediatrics. Intern Milw. County Hosp., 1953-54; resident Milw. Children's Hosp., 1957-59; practice medicine specializing in pediatrics Wauwatosa Children's Clinic, Wis., 1959-65; chief Bur. Maternal and Child Health, Ill. Dept. Pub. Health, Springfield, 1966-70, chief Div. Family Health, 1970-76; exec. dir. DuPage County Health Dept., Wheaton, Ill., 1976-93; bd. dirs., mem. exec. com. Suburban Cook-DuPage Health Systems Agy., Oak Park, Ill., 1976-82; bd. dirs., past pres. Comprehensive Health Council Met. Chgo., 1977-87; dir. Sr. Home Sharing, Inc., Wheaton, 1981-83. Mem. Ill. Commn. on Children, 1971-85 , vice chmn., 1983-85 , chmn. Ill. Perinatal Adv. Com., 1981-84, mem. 1981-92; mem. Ill. Sch. Health Adv. Com., 1982-93, Gov.'s Adv. Council on Devel. Disabilities, 1973-76, Ill. Med. Determinations Bd., 1985-93; vice-chmn. Ill. Bd. Pub. Health Advisors, 1988-91; mem. adv. bd. div. Svcs. Crippled Children U. Ill., 1986-94; trustee DuPage County Med. Found., 1976-82, 86-92; bd. dirs DuPage Cmty. Clinic, 1993—, Cmty. Nursing Svc. of DuPage, 1993—; mem. cmty. health com. Ctrl. DuPage Health Sys., 1993—; del. White House Conf. for Children, 1970. Served to capt. USAF, 1954-56. Recipient Dir.'s award for Sustained Excellence Ill. Dept. Pub. Health, 1988, Ill. Pediatrician of Yr. award, 1992. Fellow Am. Acad. Pediatrics, Am. Pub. Health Assn., Am. Coll. Preventive Medicine; mem. Am. Acad. Pediatrics (mem. exec. com. Ill. chpt. 1978-81), Ill. Pub. Health Assn. (pres. 1977-78; Disting. Service award 1983, sec. 1988-92), Ill. Assn. Maternal and Child Health (pres. 1975-76). Avocation: model railroading. Home: 28w660 Hawthorne Ln West Chicago IL 60185-2472

PAULK, ANNA MARIE, office manager; b. Columbia, Tenn., Feb. 5, 1959; d. Earl Gaston Woodard, Sr. and Anna Genette (McCuin) Woodard Tison; m. John Eason Paulk III, June 6, 1982 (div. June 1992); children: Erica Marie, Aimee Renae, Janna Elizabeth. AAS, Abraham Baldwin Coll., 1988; BBA cum laude, Ga. Southwestern U., 1992; MBA magna cum laude, Albany State U., 1997. Office mgr. E.J. Tison, D.D.S., P.C., Ashburn, Ga., 1979—. Pres. PTO/Tiftarea Acad., 1993-95. Mem. Gamma Beta Phi, Delta Mu Delta. Republican. Mem. Ch. of Christ. Avocations: canvas painting, weight lifting, bicycling, Atlanta Braves. Home: 792 Cedar Dr Ashburn GA 31714 Office: EJ Tison DDS PC 372 E College Ave Ashburn GA 31714-5232

PAULL, LAWRENCE G., production designer; b. Chgo., Apr. 13, 1946; s. Albert and Sally (Miller) P.; m. Marcy Bolotin, Oct. 23, 1983; 1 child, Michael. BA, Univ. of Ariz., 1968. Prodn. designer: (films) Little Fauss and Big Halsey, 1970, Chandler, 1971, The Hired Hand, 1971, A Tattered Web, 1971, Star Spangled Girl, 1971, They Only Kill Their Masters, 1972, Murder Once Removed, 1972, She Waits, 1972, Second Chance, 1972, Heat of Anger, 1972, The Naked Ape, 1973, The Last American Hero, 1973, The Nickel Ride, 1974, Terror on the Fortieth Floor, 1974, The Stranger Who Looks Like Me, 1974, W. W. and the Dixie Dance Kings, 1975, The Bingo Long Traveling All-Stars and Motor Kings, 1976, Sherlock Holmes in New York, 1976, Which Way Is Up?, 1977, Tail Gunner Joe, 1977, The Storyteller, 1977, A Circle of Children, 1977, Blue Collar, 1978, FM, 1978, Friendly Fire, 1979, How to Beat the High Cost of Living, 1980, In God We Trust, 1980, Doctor Detroit, 1982, Rehearsal for Murder, 1982, Blade Runner, 1982 (Academy award nomination best art direction 1982, British Academy award best art direction 1983), (with Augustin Huarte) Romancing the Stone, 1984, American Flyers, 1985, (with Todd Hallowell) Back to the Future, 1985, (with Bill Elliot) Cross My Heart, 1987, Project X, 1987, License to Drive, 1988, Cocoon: The Return, 1988, Harlem Nights, 1989, (with Geoff Hubbard) The Last of the Finest, 1990, (with Hubbard) Predator 2, 1990, City Slickers, 1991, Unlawful Entry, 1992, Memoirs of an Invisible Man, 1992, Born Yesterday, 1993, (with Richard Hudolin) Another Stakeout, 1993, The Naked Gun 33 1/3: The Final Insult, 1994. Office: care Craig Jacobsen Hansen Jacobson & Teller 450 N Roxbury Dr Fl 8 Beverly Hills CA 90210-4222*

PAULL, RICHARD ALLEN, geologist, educator; b. Madison, Wis., May 20, 1930; s. Ethra Harold and Martha (Schaller) P.; m. Rachel Kay Krebs, Mar. 6, 1954; children: Kay Marie, Lynn Ellen, Judith Anne. B.S., U. Wis., 1952, M.S., 1953, Ph.D., 1957. Party chief Pan Am. Petroleum Co., 1955-57; research group leader Jersey Prodn. Research Co., 1957-62; mem. faculty U. Wis.-Milw., 1962—, chmn. dept. geol. scis., 1962-66, prof., 1966—; cons. in field, 1966—. Author books, papers in field. Served with USAF, 1953-55. Hon. curator Milw. Museum; recipient Amoco Distinguished Teaching award, 1975. Fellow Geol. Soc. Am. (chmn. ann. meeting 1970, tech. program com. 1970, 77, membership com. 1977-80, chmn. 1980); mem. AAAS, Am. Assn. Petroleum Geologists (chmn. sci. fair award com. 1980, membership com. 1981-87, vis. petroleum geologists com. 1982-87, pub. affairs com. 1982-85), Soc. Econ. Paleontologists and Mineralogists, Nat. Assn. Geology Tchrs. (v.p. 1976-77, pres. 1977-78), Am. Geol. Inst. (governing bd. 1977-79, sec. and exec. com. 1986-88), Nature Conservancy, Sigma Xi. Home: 722 E Carlisle Ave Milwaukee WI 53217-4834 Office: U Wis Dept Geoscis Milwaukee WI 53201

PAULSEN, FRANK ROBERT, college dean emeritus; b. Logan, Utah, July 5, 1922; s. Frank and Ella (Ownby) P.; m. Marye Lucile Harris, July 31, 1942; 1 son, Robert Keith; m. Lydia Ransier Lowry, Nov. 1, 1969. B.S., Utah State U., 1947; M.S., U. Utah, 1948, Ed.D., 1956; Kellogg Found. postdoctoral fellow, U. Oreg., 1958; Carnegie Found. postdoctoral fellow, U. Mich., 1959-60. High sch. prin. Mt. Emmons, Utah, 1948-51; supt. schs. Cokeville, Wyo., 1951-55; from asst. prof. to assoc. prof. edn. U. Utah, 1955-61; prof. edn., dean Sch. Edn. U. Conn., 1961-64; dean Coll. Edn. U. Ariz., Tucson, 1964-84, dean emeritus, prof. emeritus higher edn., 1984—; scholar-in-residence Fed. Exec. Inst., Charlottesville, Va., 1970; Disting. prof. edn. U. Bridgeport, summer 1972; dir. Am. Jour. Nursing Pub. Co., N.Y.C., Am. Capital Growth Fund, Am. Series Portfolio Stock Co., Houston, Am. Gen. Equity Fund, Am. Capital Bond Fund, Am. Capital Convertible Securities Fund, Am. Capital Exchange Fund, Am. Series Portfolio Co., Am. Capital Income Trust; exec. com. New Eng. Council Advancement Sch. Adminstrn., 1962-64; trustee Common Sense Trust Co., Houston. Author: The Administration of Public Education in Utah, 1958, Contemporary Issues in American Education, 1966, American Education: Challenges and Images, 1967, Changing Dimensions in International Education, 1968, Higher Education: Dimensions and Directions, 1969, also numerous articles. Trustee Joint Council Econ. Edn., 1962-70; v.p., dir. Southwestern Coop. Ednl. Lab., 1965-67; bd. dirs. Nat. League for Nursing, 1967-69, mem. com. on perspectives, 1966-72; dir., chmn. exec. com. ERIC Clearinghouse on Tchr. Edn., 1968-70; bd. dirs. Tucson Mental Health Center, 1968-70. Served with AUS, 1942-46, PTO. Mem. Aerospace Med. Assn., NEA, Assn. Higher Edn., Am. Assn. Sch. Adminstrs., Am. Acad. Polit. and Social Sci., John Dewey Soc., Utah Acad. Letters, Arts and Scis., Ariz. Acad., Am. Assn. Colls. Tchrs. Edn. (Conn. liaison officer 1962-64, mem. studies com. 1962-68, dir.), Ariz. Assn. Colls. Tchr. Edn. (pres. 1972-80), AAAS, Am. Ednl. Research Assn., Kappa Delta Pi, Pi Sigma Alpha, Pi Gamma Mu., Phi Delta Kappa. Lodge: Rotary.

PAULSEN, SERENUS GLEN, architect, educator; b. Spooner, Wis., July 27, 1917; s. Serenus Justin and Edna Anne (Dalton) P.; m. Virginia C. Habel, Jan. 26, 1944; children: Thomas J., Nancy Lee (Mrs. John Marshall). Student, U. Ill., 1938-42; B.Arch. cum laude, U. Pa., 1947; Diploma in Architecture and City Planning, Royal Acad. Art, Stockholm, 1948. With Carroll, Grisdale & Van Alan (Architects), Phila., 1946-47, Eero Saarinen & Assos., Bloomfield Hills, Mich., 1949-51, 53-57; chief designer Reisner & Urbahn (Architects), N.Y.C., 1951-52; archtl. coordinator Knoll Assos., N.Y.C., 1952-53; prin. Glen Paulsen Assos., Birmingham, Mich., 1958-69; prin., v.p. Tarapata-MacMahon-Paulsen Assos., Inc. (Architects), Bloomfield Hills, 1969-77; pres. Cranbrook Acad. Art, head dept. architecture, 1966-70; prof., chmn. Masters Program in Architecture U. Mich., 1976-78, Emil Lorch prof. architecture, 1982-85, prof. emeritus, 1985—; Mem. Nat. Com. on Urban Planning and Design, 1971-72; archtl. commn. U. Wash., Seattle, 1968-76. (Recipient 3d prize Bi-Nat. Competition for Design Rainbow Center Plaza, Niagara Falls, N.Y. 1972). Gov. emeritus Cranbrook Acad. Art. Served with C.E. USAAF, 1942-46. Fellow AIA (honor awards Detroit chpt. for Shapero Hall of Pharmacy 1965, Our Shepherd Lutheran Ch. 1966, Ford Life Sci. Bldg. 1967, Birney Elementary Sch., Detroit 1971, Fed. Bldg., Ann Arbor, Mich. 1978, gold medal for 1980 Detroit chpt.); mem. Mich. Soc. Architects, (Robert F. Hastings award 1985). Home: 3 Southwick Ct Ann Arbor MI 48105-1409 Office: U Mich Coll Architecture and Urban Planning Ann Arbor MI 48109

PAULSON, BELDEN HENRY, political scientist; b. Oak Park, Ill., June 29, 1927; s. Henry Thomas and Evelina (Belden) P.; m. Louise D. Hill, Jan. 9, 1954; children: Eric, Steven. AB, Oberlin (Ohio) Coll., 1950; MA, U. Chgo., 1955, PhD, 1962. With Italian service mission Naples, 1950-53; organizer Homeless European Land Program, Sardinia, 1957-59; with UN High Commn. Refugees, Rome, 1960-61; mem. faculty U. Wis., Milw., also; U. Wis. extension, 1962—, prof. polit. sci., 1969—; chmn. Center Urban Community Devel., 1967-90; co-founder High Wind Assn. for Modeling an Alternative Cmty., 1980; co-founder, pres. Plymouth Inst. for Sustainable Devel., 1992—; hon. rsch. prof. Internat. Tech. and Economy Inst, Inst. for Sci. of Scis., Shanghai, China, 1990—. Author: The Searchers, 1966; also articles. Served with USNR, 1945-46. Findhorn Found. fellow; grantee Social Sci. Rsch. Coun., 1967-68. Mem. Am. Polit. Sci. Assn., World Future Soc., Internat. Ctr. Integrative Studies, Soc. Sustainable Futures. Home: W7122 County Rd U Plymouth WI 53073-4538 Office: U Wis Dept Urban Community Devel 161 W Wisconsin Ave Fl 6 Milwaukee WI 53203-2602

PAULSON, BERNARD ARTHUR, oil company executive, consultant; b. Lakeview, Mich., July 12, 1928; s. Arthur Bernard and Genevieve Talbard (Bushley) P.; m. Joan Lee Curtiss, Dec. 4, 1954; children: James, Joseph (dec.), Ann, Thomas (dec.), Bernadette, Patricia, Steven. B.S. in Chem. Engring., Mich. State U.-East Lansing, 1949. Registered profl. engr., Tex. Process engr. Mid-West Refineries Inc., Alma, Mich., 1949-57; plant mgr. Kerr-McGee Corp., Cleve. and Wynnewood, Okla., 1957-66; v.p. Coastal States Petrochemical, Corpus Christi, Tex., 1966-71, Koch Industries Inc., St. Paul and Wichita, 1971-88; cons. Koch Industries Inc., Corpus Christi, Tex., 1988-94; pres. Koch Refining Co., Wichita, 1981-88; chmn. bd. dirs. The Automation Group Inc.; chmn., CEO The Inspection Group Inc.; bd. dirs. Hitox Corp. Am. Chmn., pres. Cleve. Area Hosp. Corp., 1962; dir. Ada Wilson Hosp. Found.; pres. Corpus Christ Bd. Trade. 1st lt. USAF, 1955-57. Recipient Claud R. Erickson Disting. Alumnus award Mich. State U., 1994. Mem. AIChE (fuels and petrochem. award 1989), Nat. Petroleum Refiners Assn., Refining Am. Petroleum Inst., Wichita Area C. of C. (bd. dirs.), Bd. Trade, Corpus Christi Town Club (bd. dirs.), Elks. Home: 5310 Greenbriar Dr Corpus Christi TX 78413-2827 Office: The Inspection Group PO Box 10432 Corpus Christi TX 78410

PAULSON, DONALD ROBERT, chemistry educator; b. Oak Park, Ill., Sept. 6, 1943; s. Robert Smith and Florence Teresa (Beese) P.; m. Elizabeth Anne Goodwin, Aug. 20, 1966; children: Matthew, Andrew. BA, Monmouth Coll., 1965; PhD, Ind. U., 1968. Asst. prof. chemistry Calif. State U., Los Angeles, 1970-74, assoc. prof., 1974-78, prof., 1979—, chmn. dept., 1982-90; vis. prof. U. B.C., Vancouver, Can., 1977-78, U. Sussex, Brighton, Eng., 1984-85. Author: Alicyclic Chemistry, 1976; contbr. articles to profl. jours. Named Outstanding Prof., Calif. State U., Los Angeles, 1978, 84, 96. Mem. Am. Chem. Soc., Chem. Soc. (London), InterAm. Photochem. Soc., Nat. Assn. Sci. Tchrs., Sigma Xi. Democrat. Episcopalian. Avocations: photography, hiking, soccer. Home: 1627 Laurel St South Pasadena CA 91030-4710 Office: Calif State U Dept Chemistry 5151 State University Dr Los Angeles CA 90032-4226

PAULSON, GLENN, environmental scientist; b. Sycamore, Ill., Sept. 14, 1941; s. Orville Madison and Clarice Hope (Lewis) P.; m. Linda Joyce Cooper, May 17, 1985. BA with honors, Northwestern U., 1963; PhD, Rockefeller U., 1971; ScD (hon.), L.I. U., 1972. Dir. sci. for citizen program New Sch. for Social Rsch., N.Y.C., 1967-69; exec. dir. Scientists' Com. for Pub. Info., N.Y.C., 1971-72; staff scientist, adminstr. sci. support prog. Natural Resources Def. Coun., N.Y.C., 1971-74; asst. commr. N.J. Dept. Environ. Protection, Trenton, 1974-79; v.p. Nat. Audubon Soc., N.Y.C., 1979-82, sr. v.p., 1982-84; v.p. Clean Sites, Inc., Alexandria, Va., 1984-88; dir. Ctr. for Hazardous Waste Mgmt. Ill. Inst. Tech., Chgo., 1988-90, rsch. prof. dept. environ. engring., 1988-95; pres. Paulson and Cooper, Inc., 1992—; chmn. environ. mgmt. adv. bd. Dept. Energy, 1992-94, mem., 1992—; adj. prof. environ. health scis. Med. U. S.C., 1995—. Editor, author: Environment, USA, 1974; contbr. articles to profl. jours. Bd. dirs. Citizens for Clean Air, N.Y.C., 1965-74, Rene Dubos Ctr., N.Y.C., 1981-90. NSF grantee, 1976, A.W. Mellon Found. grantee, 1979-84; Rockefeller Univ. fellow, 1963-71. Fellow AAAS, Am. Inst. Chemists; mem. Am. Chem. Soc., Soc. for Environ. Toxicology and Chemistry, Coun. for Advancement Sci. Writing (bd. dirs. 1968-95), Soc. Risk Assessment, Sec. Energy Adv. Bd. (charter mem. 1990-93). Avocation: outdoor activities. Office: Paulson and Cooper Inc PO Box 1541 Jackson Hole WY 83001

PAULSON, JAMES MARVIN, engineering educator; b. Wausau, Wis., Jan. 1, 1923; s. Gustav Victor and Susanna (Dracy) P.; m. Marjorie Beulah Burton, May 11, 1946; children—Vicki Rae, Michael James. B.S. in Civil Engring, The Citadel, 1947; M.S. in Civil Engring, Ill. Inst. Tech., 1949; Ph.D., U. Mich., 1958. Registered profl. engr., Mich. Draftsman Wausau Iron Works, 1946; engr. Charles Whitney Cons. Engr., Milw., 1948-49; faculty Wayne State U., Detroit, 1949—, prof., 1961-85, chmn. dept. civil engring., 1967-72, assoc. dean Coll. Engring., 1973-83, prof. emeritus, 1985—; v.p. Civil Engrs., Inc., 1954—; cons. in field. Served with AUS, 1943; Served with USMCR, 1943-46. Mem. ASCE (life), Mich. Soc. Profl. Engrs. (life), Am. Soc. for Engring. Edn., Sigma Xi, Tau Beta Pi, Chi Epsilon. Presbyterian. Home: PO Box 23 Greenbush MI 48738-0023

PAULSON, JEROME AVROM, pediatrician; b. Balt., July 31, 1949; s. Robert R. and Edna (Brenner) P.; m. Susan Miller, 1973 (div. 1986); m. Gwen Victor Gampel, July 2, 1989. BS in Biochemistry, U. Md., 1971; MD, Duke U., 1974. Diplomate Am. Bd. Pediatrics, Nat. Bd. Med. Examiners. Resident in pediatrics Johns Hopkins Hosp., Balt., 1974-76; resident in pediatrics Sinai Hosp., Balt., 1976-77, fellow in ambulatory pediatrics, 1977-78; asst. prof. pediatrics Case Western Res. U., Cleve., 1978-86; dir. sci. rsch. and pub. policy devel. Joseph P. Kennedy Jr. Found., Washington, 1986-87; dir. pediatrics Regional Inst. for Children and Adolescents, Rockville, Md., 1987-89; clin. assoc. prof. pediatrics Georgetown U., Washington, 1987—; exec. dir. Research!America, Alexandria, Va., 1989-90; assoc. prof. health care scis. and pediatrics George Washington U., Washington, 1990—, fellow Ctr. Health Policy Rsch., 1991—; mem. conf. on methodology/std. definitions for childhood injury rsch. Nat. Inst. Children and Human Devel., 1989; mem. health adv. com. Congressman James Moran, 8th Congl. Dist., Va., 1992-94; advisor Health Pages, 1994—. Contbr. articles to profl. jours., chpts. to books. Profl. adv. bd. Nat. Safety Town Ctr., Cleve., 1981-85; bd. dirs., pres. James Renwick Alliance, Washington, 1986-93, 95—. Recipient Cert. for Ednl. and Pub. Policy Activity, Ohio State Senate/Ho. of Reps., 1985; Robert Wood Johnson Health Policy fellow, 1985-86. Fellow Am. Acad. Pediatrics; mem. Ambulatory Pediatric Assn. Jewish. Avocation: collecting contemporary American crafts. Office: George Washington Univ 2150 Pennsylvania Ave NW Washington DC 20037-3201

PAULSON, JOHN DORAN, newspaper editor, retired; b. Grand Forks, N.D., Oct. 1, 1915; s. Holger D. and Irene E. (Finkle) P.; m. Zoe Y. Bean Hensley, July 6, 1946 (dec. Aug. 1993); children: James L., Michael D., Christine R., David E., Patrick R. Student, U.N.D., 1932-34; B.S., U. Minn., 1936. Copy editor Mpls. Star, 1936; reporter The Forum, Fargo, N.D.-Moorhead, Minn., 1937-39; polit. writer The Forum, 1939-51, mng. editor, 1951-56, editor, 1957-80; v.p. Dakota Photographics Inc., Fargo, 1963-93. Del. N.D. Constl. Conv., 1971-72. Served with AUS, 1942-46. Mem. Am. Soc. Newspaper Editors. Home: 1362 2nd St N Fargo ND 58102-2725

PAULSON, KENNETH ALAN, journalist, lawyer, business executive; b. Chgo., Dec. 3, 1953; s. Knut Norman and Helen Elizabeth (Beardsley) P.; m. Peggy Jean Foot, June 12, 1976; children: Carrie Ann, David. BA in Journalism, U. Mo., Columbia, 1975; JD, U. Ill., Champaign, 1978. Bar: Ill., 1978, Fla. 1979. Exec. editor, v.p. news Gannett Suburban Newspapers, White Plains, N.Y., 1992-97; exec. dir. 1st. Amendment Ctr. Vanderbilt U., Nashville; sr. v.p. Freedom Forum, Arlington, Va. Co-author: (book) Truly One Nation, 1988, Profiles of Power, 1988.

PAULSON, LORETTA NANCY, psychoanalyst; b. L.A., Nov. 5, 1943; d. Frank Morris and Rose (Kaufman) Fargo; m. Maurice Krasnow; 1 child, Kira. BA, U. So. Calif., 1966; MS in Social Work, Columbia U., 1969; cert. psychoanalyst, C.G. Jung Inst., N.Y.C. Cert. clin. social worker, N.Y., Conn., N.J. Pvt. practice psychoanalysis N.Y.C. and Wilton, Conn., 1976—; faculty, supr., past vice chmn. Inst. Tng. Bd. Mem. NASW (diplomate in clin. social work), Internat. Assn. for Analytical Psychology (del., bd. dirs.), N.Y. Assn. for Analytic Psychology (pres., program com.), Conn. Soc. Clin. Social Work (com. on psychoanalysis). Democrat. Office: 6 Turtleback Rd Wilton CT 06897-1223 Office: 334 W 86th St Apt 1A New York NY 10024-3130

PAULSON, PAUL JOSEPH, advertising executive; b. White Plains, N.Y., Sept. 25, 1932; s. Paul and Ann (Loughlin) P.; m. Kathryn P. Keeler, June 30, 1962; children: Thomas, Mark, Kathryn, John, Clifford. BSBA, Ohio State U., 1954; MBA, U. Pa., 1959. With Compton Advt. Inc., N.Y.C., 1959-78; mgmt. supr. Compton Advt. Inc., 1965-78, sr. v.p., 1968-78, also dir.; pres., dir. Doyle Dane Bernbach Inc., N.Y.C., 1978-83; pres., chief exec. officer Isidore & Paulson, Inc., N.Y.C., 1983-93; chmn., pres., CEO Paulson & Co. Mktg. Svcs., Greenwich, 1993—; mem. Ohio State U. Alumni Adv. Coun., 1982—; pres. coun. mem. Ohio State U., 1993—. Author: Fundamentals of Consumer Goods Marketing, 1966. Chmn. Christmas for Underprivileged Children, N.Y.C., 1963—. Served to lt. (j.g.) USNR, 1955-58, MTO, ETO. Mem. Wharton Grad. Bus. Sch. Alumni Assn. (pres. N.Y.C. club 1963-65, dir. 1972—), Ohio State U. Alumni Assn., Wharton Grad. Bus. Sch. Roman Catholic. Clubs: N.Y. (dir.), Milbrook, Sigma Chi. Home: 45 W Brother Dr Greenwich CT 06830-6726

PAULSON, PETER JOHN, librarian, publishing company executive; b. N.Y.C., Jan. 30, 1928; s. Peter John and Lillian Agnes Elaine (Neuman) P.; m. Josephine C. Bowen, Dec. 5, 1953; children: David, Debora. B.Social Scis. cum laude, CCNY, 1949; M.A. in History, Columbia, 1950; M.A. in L.S, SUNY, Albany, 1955. Library asst. N.Y. State Library, Albany, 1952-55; head, gift and exchange sect. N.Y. State Library, 1955-65, head catalog sect., 1965-66, prin. librarian tech. services, 1966-71, dir., 1972-85; exec. dir. OCLC Forest Press, 1985—; adj. asst. prof. library sci. State U. N.Y. at Albany, 1960-71; Adv. com. Ohio Coll. Library Center, 1970-71; adv.

council to pub. printer depository libraries, 1972-77, chmn., 1975-77; com. fed. depository library service N.Y. State, 1960-70, chairperson, 1960-70; bd. dirs. Capital Dist. Libr. Coun., Nat. Info. Standards Orgn., N.E. Document Conservation Ctr. Mem. ALA (chmn. com. on legislation 1980-82, pres. state library agy. sect. 1982-83), N.Y. Library Assn. (pres. 1975), Hudson-Mohawk Library Assn. (v.p. 1964), SUNY-OCLC Network (governing bd. 1980-82), Phi Beta Kappa. Home: 24 Tillinghast Ave Albany NY 12204-2312 Office: OCLC Forest Press 85 Watervliet Ave Albany NY 12206-2023

PAULSON, RONALD HOWARD, English and humanities educator; b. Bottineau, N.D., May 27, 1930; s. Howard Clarence and Ethel (Tvete) P.; m. Barbara Lee Appleton, May 25, 1957 (div. 1982); children: Andrew Meredith, Melissa Katherine. BA, Yale U., 1952, PhD, 1958. Instr. U. Ill., 1958-59, from asst. to assoc. prof., 1959-63; prof. English Rice U., Houston, 1963-67; prof. English Johns Hopkins U., Balt., 1967-75, chmn. dept., 1968-75, Andrew W. Mellon prof. humanities, 1973-75, Mayer prof. humanities, 1984—, chmn. dept., 1985-91; prof. English Yale U., New Haven, Conn., 1975-84, Thomas E. Donnelly prof., 1980-84, Ward Phillips lectr., 1978, Alexander lectr., 1979, Brown and Haley lectr., 1979, Hodges lectr., 1980. Author: Theme and Structure in Swift's Tale of a Tub, 1960, Fielding, 1962, Hogarth's Graphic Works, 1965, rev. edits., 1970, 89, Fictions of Satire, 1967, Satire and the Novel, 1967, (with Thomas F. Lockwood) Fielding: The Critical Heritage, 1969, Satire: Modern Essays in Criticism, 1971, Hogarth: His Life, Art and Times, 1971, Rowlandson: A New Interpretation, 1972, Emblem and Expression: Meaning in Eighteenth Century English Art, 1975, The Art of Hogarth, 1975, Popular and Polite Art in the Age of Hogarth and Fielding, 1979, Literary Landscape: Turner and Constable, 1982, Book and Painting: Shakespeare, Milton and the Bible, 1983, Representations of Revolution, 1983, Breaking and Remaking, 1989, Figure and Abstraction in Contemporary Painting, 1990, Hogarth Vol. 1: The Making of the Modern Moral Subject, 1991, Hogarth Vol. 2: High Art and Low, 1991, Hogarth Vol. 3: Art and Politics, 1993, The Beautiful, Novel, and Strange: Aesthetics and Heterodoxy, 1996, Don Quixote in England: The Aesthetics of Laughter, 1997. 1st lt. AUS, 1952-54. Sterling fellow 1957-85, Guggenheim fellow 1965-66, 1986-87, NEH fellow 1977-78. Fellow Am. Acad. Arts and Scis.; mem. Am. Soc. for 18th Century Studies (pres. 1986-87). Home: 2722 St Paul St Baltimore MD 21218-4332 Office: Johns Hopkins U Dept English Baltimore MD 21218

PAULSON, STANLEY FAY, educational association administrator; b. Atwater, Minn., Mar. 5, 1920; s. Adolph and Ida May (Fay) P.; m. Margaret Nan Appelquist, Sept. 8, 1944; children—Richard Stanley, Lynn Edith. B.A. in Philosophy, U. Minn., 1942, M.A., 1949, Ph.D., 1952; B.D., Bethel Theol. Sem., 1944. Instr. U. Minn., 1948-53; research asso. studies in lang. and behavior Bur. Naval Research, 1952-53; overseas instr. U. Md. Program in, Germany and Eng., 1953-54; asst. prof. U. Minn., 1954-56; mem. faculty San Francisco State U., 1956-66, prof. speech, chmn. dept., 1959-62, v.p. acad. affairs, 1963-65, acting pres., 1965-66; prof., chmn. dept. speech Pa. State U., 1966-69, dean Coll. Liberal Arts, 1969-84; bd. dirs. Assn. Am. Colls., 1978-85, chmn. bd., 1983-84, v.p., 1985-87; presdl. search cons. Assn. Governing Bd. Univs. and Colls., Washington, 1987-88; sr. cons., chair bd. dirs. Acad. Cons. Service, Washington, 1988—. Author: (with Bystrom, Ramsland) Communicating Through Speech, 1951; also articles. Served to lt. (j.g.) USNR, 1945-46. Fulbright lectr. Kanazawa (Japan) U., 1962-63. Mem. Speech Communication Assn. (vice chmn. group methods sect. 1961-62), Western Speech Assn. (counselor pub. address 1961—), AAUP, Internat. Communication Assn., Council Colls. Arts and Scis. (dir. 1971-75, v.p. 1972, pres. 1973). Home: 5500 Friendship Blvd Apt 2403N Bethesda MD 20815-7218 Office: Acad Search Consultation Svc 1818 R St NW Washington DC 20009-1604

PAULSTON, CHRISTINA BRATT, linguistics educator; b. Stockholm, Sweden, Dec. 30, 1932; came to U.S., 1951; d. Lennart and Elsa (Facht) Bratt; m. Rolland G. Paulston, July 26, 1963; children: Christopher-Rolland, Ian Rollandsson. B.A., Carleton Coll., 1953; M.A. in English and Comparative Lit., U. Minn., 1955; Ed.D., Columbia U., 1966. Cert. tchr., Minn. Tchr. Clara City and Pine Island High Schs., Minn., 1955-60, Am. Sch. of Tangier, Morocco, 1960-62, Katrineholm Allmanna Laroverk, Katrineholm, Sweden, 1962-63, East Asian Library, Columbia U., N.Y.C., 1963-64; asst. instr. Tchrs. Coll., Columbia U., 1964-66; instr. U. Punjab, Chandigarh, India, summer 1966, Pontificia Universidad Catolica Del Peru, Lima, 1966-67; cons. Instituto Linguistico de Verano, Lima, 1967-68; asst. prof. linguistics U. Pitts., 1969-75, prof., 1975—, asst. dir. English Lang. Inst., 1969-70, dir. English Lang. Inst., 1970—, acting dir. Lang. Acquistion Inst., fall 1971, acting chmn. dept. gen. linguistics, 1974-75, chmn., 1975-89. Author numerous books and articles on linguistics. Recipient research award Am. Ednl. Research Assn., 1980; Fulbright-Hays grantee, Uruguay, 1985. Mem. Assn. Tchrs. of English to Speakers of Other Langs. (2d v.p., conv., chmn. 1972, exec. com. 1972-75, rsch. com. 1973-75, 78-80, chmn. 1973-75, 1st v.p. 1975, pres. 1976), Linguistics Soc. Am. (com. linguistics and pub. interest 1973-77), Internat. Assn. of Tchrs. of English as a Fgn. Lang., Am. Council on Teaching of Fgn. Langs., MLA (exec. com. lang. and soc. 1975-76), Ctr. Applied Linguistics (trustee 1976-81, exec. com. 1980, publs. com. 1981, research com. 1981), Eastern Competitive Trailriding Assn. Democrat. Episcopalian. Office: U Pitts Linguistics Pittsburgh PA 15260

PAULUS, ELEANOR BOCK, professional speaker, author; b. N.Y.C., Mar. 12, 1933; d. Charles William Bock and Borghild (Nelson) Garrick; m. Chester William Paulus Jr., Sept. 6, 1952; children: Chester W. III, Karl Derrick, Diane Paulus Henricks. Student, Smith Coll., 1952-53. Owner, founder Khan-Du Chinese Shar-Pei, Somerset, N.J., 1980—; dir. Pet Net, Santa Fe, N.Mex., 1992—; co-owner, CFO Am. Dream TV Prodns., Washington, 1993—; co-owner, exec. prodr. Capitol Ideas, 1995—, Pierre Salinger's Round Table, 1997; lectr., cons. on Chinese Shar-Pei and canine health, 1980—; internat. con., lectr. on pet care and health. Author: Health Care Handbook for Cats, Dogs and Birds, The Proper Care of Chinese Shar-Pei; contbr. articles to mags. and jours., chpts. to books; creator, prodr. World of Dogs. Dir. bd. trustees Rutgers Prep. Sch., Somerset, 1970-76, v.p. bd. trustees, 1976-81, pres. PTA, 1966-76; chmn. Raritan River Festival, New Brunswick, N.J., 1980-91. Named Woman of Yr., City of New Brunswick, 1982. Mem. Dog Writers Am. Assn., Dog Fanciers N.Y.C., Bonzai Clubs Internat., Koi Club N.Y., Raritan Valley Country Club, Chinese Shar-Pei Club of Am. (v.p. 1982-86, bd. dirs. east sect. 1980-82, Humanitarian award 1986). Avocations: travel, dog related activities, gardening. Home: 321 Skillmans Ln Somerset NJ 08873-5325 Office: E B Paulus 20 Sutton Pl S # 5A New York NY 10022-4165

PAULUS, NORMA JEAN PETERSEN, lawyer, state school system administrator; b. Belgrade, Nebr., Mar. 13, 1933; d. Paul Emil and Ella Marie (Hellbusch) Petersen; LL.B., Willamette Law Sch., 1962; LL.D., Linfield Coll., 1985; LittD (hon.), Whitman Coll., 1990; LHD (hon.), Lewis & Clark Coll., 1996; m. William G. Paulus, Aug. 16, 1958; children: Elizabeth, William Frederick. Sec. to Harney County Dist. Atty., 1950-53; legal sec., Salem, Oreg., 1953-55; sec. to chief justice Oreg. Supreme Ct., 1955-61; admitted to Oreg. bar, 1962; of counsel Paulus and Callaghan, Salem, mem. Oreg. Ho. of Reps., 1971-77; sec. state State of Oreg., Salem, 1977-85; of counsel firm Paulus, Rhoten & Lien, 1985-86; supt. pub. instrn. State of Oreg., 1990—; Oreg. exec. bd. US West, 1985—; adj. prof. Willamette U. Grad. Sch, 1985; mem. N.W. Power Planning Com., 1986-89. Fellow Eagleton Inst. Politics, 1971; mem. Pacific NW Power Planning Council, 1987-89; adv. com. Defense Adv. Com. for Women in the Service, 1986, Nat. Trust for Hist. Preservation, 1988—; trustee Willamette U., 1978—; bd. dirs. Benedictine Found. of Oreg., 1980—, Oreg. Grade. Instn. Sci. and Tech., 1985—, Mid Willamette Valley coun. Camp Fire Girls, 1985-87, Edn. Commn. States, 1991—, Coun. Chief State Sch. Officers, 1995—, Nat. Assessment Governing Bd., 1996—; overseer Whitman Coll., 1985—; bd. cons. Goodwill Industries of Oreg.; mem. Salem Human Relations Commn., 1967-70, Marion-Polk Boundary Commn., 1970-71; mem. Presdl. Commn. to Monitor Philippines Election, 1986, Nat. Assessment Governing Bd. .Recipient Distinguished Service award City of Salem, 1971, LWV, 1995; Path Breaker award Oreg. Women's Polit. Caucus, 1976; named One of 10 Women of Future, Ladies Home Jour., 1979. Woman of Yr., Oreg. Inst Managerial and Profl. Women, 1982, Oreg. Women Lawyers, 1982, Woman Who Made a Difference award Nat. Women's Forum, 1985. Mem. Oreg. State Bar, Nat. Order Women Legislators, Women Execs. in State Govt., Women's Polit. Caucus Bus. and Profl. Women's Club (Golden Torch award 1971), Zonta Internat., Delta Kappa Gamma.

PAULUS, STEPHEN HARRISON, composer; b. Summit, N.J., Aug. 24, 1949; s. Harrison Child and Patricia Jean (Clark) P.; m. Patricia Ann, July 18, 1975; children: Gregory Stephen, Andrew Christopher. Student, Macalester Coll., 1967-69; B.A., U. Minn., 1969-71, M.A., 1972-74, Ph.D., 1974-78. Co-founder, fundraiser Minn. Composers Forum, St. Paul, 1973-84; Exxon/Rockefeller composer in residence Minn. Orch., Mpls., 1983-87; composer in residence Santa Fe Chamber Music Festival, summer 1986; Regent's lectr. U. Calif., Santa Barbara, Nov. 1986; composer in residence Atlanta Symphony Orch., 1988-92, Dale Warland Singers, 1991-92; composer in residence Aspen Festival, summer, 1992. Performances with Tanglewood Festival, 1980, Edinburgh Festival, 1983, Aldeburgh Festival, 1985; composer (orchestral works) Sinfonietta, Concertante, Ordway Overture, Concerto for Orchestra, Seven Short Pieces for Orchestra, Translucent Landscapes, Spectra, Reflections: Four Movements on a Theme of Wallace Stevens, Divertimento for Harp and Chamber Orchestra, Trumpet Concerto, Suite from Harmoonia, Suite from The Postman Always Rings Twice, Ground Breaker--An Overture for Constrn. Instruments and Orch., Symphony in Three Movements, Street Music, Manhattan Sinfonietta, Violin Concerto, Symphony for Strings, Concerto for Violin, Cello & Orch., Organ Concerto, Violin Concerto No. 2, (recordings) Violin Concerto, Concertante and Symphony for Strings, Songs: Bittersuite, All My Pretty Ones, Artsongs, (for orch.) Violin Concerto (Kennedy Ctr. Friedheim award for 3d pl. Am. Works for Orch., 1988), Symphony for Strings, Street Music, Echoes Between the Silent Peaks, (operas) The Woodlanders, The Postman Always Rings Twice, The Woman At Otowi Crossing, The Village Singer, Harmoonia, The Woman at Otowi Crossing, The Three Hermits; (for chorus and orch.), So Hallow'd Is the Time, (5 carols for chorus and strings) Christmas Tidings, Letters for the Times, North Shore, Canticles: Songs and Rituals for the Easter and the May, Voices, (chamber work) Seven for the Flowers Near the River, Seven Miniatures, Fantasy in Three Parts, Quartessence, Dramatic Suite, others, also numerous works for chamber groups including Partita for Violin and Piano, Music for Contrasts (string Quartet), String Quartet No.2, Quartessence, (for soprano voice, piano, percussion and string quartet) Letters From Colette, American Vignettes (for cello and piano); (for solo voice) All My Pretty Ones, Artsongs, Mad Book, Shadow Book: Michael Morley's Songs, Elizabethan Songs, Bittersuite for baritone and piano, (solo voice/bass-baritone and vn, vc. pf.) The Long Shadow of Lincoln; (for solo instruments) Two Moments for Guitar, (piano) Translucent Landscapes; (for chorus) Madrigali di Michelangelo, Four Preludes on Playthings of The Wind, Peace, Personals, Marginalia, Echoes Between the Silent Peaks, Jesu Carols, Meditations of Li Po, Love's Philosophy, Three Songs for Mixed Chorus, The Earth Sines, The Elixir, God be With Us, Songs from the Japanese, (narrative and chamber orch.) Voices from the Gallery, (chamber) Music of the Night (for violin, voice and percussion), (choral) Visions from Hildegard, Part I (for flute, oboe, timpany, percussion, organ and chorus), Part Two (for brass quintet, percussion and chorus), (for narrator and chamber orch.) Voices from the Gallery, (vocal) Songs of Love and Longing, (chamber/instrumental) Air on Seurat, (chorus) Three Songs for Mixed Chorus, Christ Our Passover, (piano) Preludes, (organ duet) The Triumph of the Saint, Toccata, (chorus and chamber ensemble) Whitman's Dream. Recipient Outstanding Achievement award U. Minn., 1991, Disting. Alumni award, 1991, Lancaster Symphony Orch. Composer's award, 1994; Guggenheim fellow, 1982-83, NEA fellow, 1978; NEA Consortium grantee, 1987. Mem. ASCAP (bd. dirs. 1990), Am. Music Ctr., Minn. Composers Forum (v.p. 1984-87, bd. dirs.). Avocations: tennis, reading. Home and Office: 1719 Summit Ave Saint Paul MN 55105-1833

PAULY, BRUCE HENRY, engineering consultant; b. Washington, Nov. 11, 1920; s. Elmer George and Charlotte May (Weck) P.; m. Dorothy Buhrman Rollins, June 20, 1945; 1 child, Margaret MacKenzie Pauly Price. B.S. in Mech. Engring., Va. Poly. Inst., 1941; M.S. in Engring. Adminstrn., Case Inst. Tech., 1965. Registered profl. engr., Pa. lic. pvt. pilot. Sect. mgr. Aviation Gas Turbine div., Westinghouse Electric Corp., Lester, Pa., 1945-52; sales mgr. aircraft (Pesco) Borg-Warner Corp., Bedford, Ohio, 1952-55; v.p. research and engring. Weatherhead Co., Cleve., 1955-69; v.p. engring. Eaton Corp., Cleve., 1969-82; co-owner, dir. Crystaloid Electronics Co., Hudson, Ohio, 1983-85; mem. vis. com. Fenn Coll. Engring., Cleve. State U., 1973-85; mem. engring. adv. com. Cuyahoga Community Coll., Cleve., 1979—; exec. com. Coll. Engring. Va. Poly Inst. and State U., Blacksburg, 1980—; mem. com. Transp. Research Bd. NRC, Washington, 1982-84. Patentee turbojet control, hydraulic pump, gas regulator, hose crimper. Mem. task force Pres.' Pvt. Sector Survey, Washington, 1982; mem. Cleve. Sr. Council, 1983—. Served to lt. col. USAAF, 1941-45, ETO; USAF Ret. Res., 1986—. Decorated Legion of Merit; decorated Bronze Star, Croix de Guerre (France). Mem. AIAA (co-chmn. nat. aerospace propulsion conf. Cleve 1982), Soc. Automotive Engrs. (chmn. motor vehicle council 1981-82), Nat. Conf. on Fluid Power (gen. chmn. 1977), Cleve. Engring. Soc. (bd. govs. 1979-81), Chagrin Valley C. of C., Mil. Order World Wars (comdr. Cleve. 1984-85), Res. Officers Assn., Cheshire Cheese Club (Cleve), Pi Tau Sigma, Pi Delta Epsilon. Republican. Episcopalian. Home: 143 Kenton Rd Chagrin Falls OH 44022-2503

PAULY, JOHN EDWARD, anatomist; b. Elgin, Ill., Sept. 17, 1927; s. Edward John and Gladys (Myhre) P.; m. Margaret Mary Oberle, Sept. 3, 1949; children: Stephen John, Susan Elizabeth, Kathleen Ann, Mark Edward. B.S., Northwestern U., 1950; M.S., Loyola U., Chgo., 1952, Ph.D., 1955. Grad. asst. gross anatomy Stritch Sch. Medicine, Loyola U., Chgo., 1953-54; rsch. asst. anatomy Chgo. Med. Sch., 1952-54, research instr., 1954-55, instr. in gross anatomy, 1955-57, assoc. in gross anatomy, 1957-59, asst. prof. anatomy, 1959-63, asst. to pres., 1960-62; assoc. prof. anatomy Tulane U. Sch. Medicine, 1963-67; prof., head dept. anatomy U. Ark. for Med. Scis., Little Rock, 1967-83; prof., head dept. physiology and biophysics U. Ark. for Med. Scis., 1978-80, vice chancellor for acad. affairs and sponsored rsch., 1983-92, assoc. dean Grad. Sch., 1983-92, prof. anatomy, 1992-95, prof. emeritus, 1995—; tech. adviser Ency. Brit. Films, 1956; mem. safety and occupational health study sect. Nat. Inst. Occupational Safety and Health, Ctr. for Disease Control, 1975-79; vis. prof. faculty medicine Kuwait U., 1993, 94, vis. prof. anatomy U. Nev., 1996. Author: (with Hans Elias) Human Microanatomy, 1960, 3d edit. 1966, (with Elias and E. Robert Burns) Histology and Human Microanatomy, 1978; editor: (with Lawrence E. Scheving and Franz Halberg) Chronobiology, 1974, (with Heinz von Mayersbach and Lawrence E. Scheving) Biological Rhythms in Structure and Function, 1981, The American Association of Anatomists, 1888-1987. Essays on the History of Anatomy in America and a Report on the Membership-Past and Present, 1987, (with Lawrence E. Scheving) Advances in Chronobiology, 1987, (with Dora K. Hayes and Russel J. Reiter) Chronobiology: Its Role in Clinical Medicine, General Biology and Agriculture, 1990; editor Am. Jour. Anatomy, 1980-92; co-mng. editor Advances in Anatomy, Embryology and Cell Biology, 1980-95; mem. adv. editorial bd. Internat. Jour. Chronobiology, 1973-83; contbr. articles to profl. jours. Served with USNR, 1945-47. Recipient merit certificates AMA, 1953, 59; Bronze award Ill. Med. Soc., 1959; Lederle Med. Faculty award, 1966. Fellow AAAS; mem. Am. Assn. Anatomists (sec.-treas. 1972-80, pres. 1982-83, Centennial award 1987, Henry Gray award 1995), So. Soc. Anatomists (pres. 1971-72), Assn. Anatomy Chmn. (sec.-treas. 1969-71), Am. Physiol. Soc., Internat. Soc. Chronobiology, Pan-Am. Assn. Anatomy, Internat. Soc. Electrophysiol. Kinesiology, Internat. Soc. Steriology, Consejo Nacional de Profesores de Ciencias Morfologicas (hon.), Sigma Xi, Sigma Alpha Epsilon. Roman Catholic.

PAUNOV, CATHERINE PENNINGTON, legal technology consultant; b. Washington, Jan. 4, 1950; d. William Carter and Marcia Moss (Lewis) Pennington; m. Zlatko Paunov, Mar. 6, 1996. BS, U. Md., 1975; MS, Am. U., 1977; MLS, Brigham Young U., 1980, JD, 1980. Bar: Tex. 1981. Acquisitions asst. Am. U., Washington, 1976-77; libr. asst. Brigham Young U., Provo, Utah, 1977-80; sr. reference libr. So. Meth. U., Dallas, 1980-81; law libr. Johnson & Swanson, Dallas, 1981-85; cons., sr. libr. N.Y. Pub. Libr., N.Y.C., 1985-86; assoc. law libr. St. John's U., Jamaica, N.Y., 1986-89, asst. prof. div. libr. and info. sci., 1987-89, adj. prof. law, 1988-89; dir. libr. svcs. Chadbourne & Parke, N.Y.C., 1989-94; prin. Pennington Consulting, 1994—. Author: Microcomputer Software Selection for Law Libraries, 1987-93, (with others) videotape Organizing a Small Law Firm Library, 1985, Planning the Small Law Office Library, 1994, Microsoft Word for Windows in One Hour for Lawyers, 1995. Dem. precinct chair Dallas County, Tex., 1983-85; sec. St. George Civic Assn., S.I., N.Y., 1988-90, v.p., 1990-92. Fellow Am. Bar Found., ABA (chair libr. com. 1987-90, chair rsch. skills 1990-92, law practice mgmt. sect. 1992, editor-in-chief network 2d 1992-94, coun. 1994—); mem. Am. Assn. Law Librs. (chair pvt. law libr. sect. 1985-86, Bender grantee 1981). Mormon. Avocations: quilting, swimming, skiing. Office: 17 Carroll Pl Staten Island NY 10301-1503

PAUP, BRYCE ERIC, professional football player; b. Scranton, Iowa, Feb. 29, 1968. Degree in Bus., U. No. Iowa. With Green Bay Packers, 1990-94; linebacker Buffalo Bills, 1995—. Selected to Pro Bowl, 1994-95, AFC MVP by NFL Players Assn, AP All-Pro First Team, Assoc. Press Defensive Player of the Year, United Press Internat. Defensive Player of the Year, Pro Football Weekley Defensive Player of the Year, College and Pro Football Newsweekley Defensive Player of the Year, All-Pro First Team, Newspaper Enterprise Assns. George Halas awd.-NFL Defensive Player of the Year, Football Digest All-Pro First Team, Pro Football Weekley All-Pro Team, Sports Illustrated All-Pro First Team, USA Today All-Pro First Team, NFL Alumni's Linebacker of the Year, Pro Bowl Starter. Office: Buffalo Bills 1 Bills Dr Orchard Park NY 14127-2237*

PAUSTENBACH, DENNIS JAMES, environmental toxicologist; b. Pitts., Oct. 29, 1952; s. Albert Paustenbach and Patricia Jean Iseman; m. Louise Dunning, Feb. 23, 1985; children: Mark Douglas, Anna Louise. BSChemE, Rose-Hulman Inst. Tech., 1974; MS in Indsl. Hygiene, U. Mich., 1977; MS in Indsl. Psychology, Ind. State U., 1978; PhD in Environ. Toxicology, Purdue U., 1982. Diplomate Am. Bd. Toxicology, Am. Bd. Indsl. Hygiene, Bd. Cert. Safety Profls.; cert. indsl. hygienist, safety profl., environ. assessor. Chem. process engr. Eli Lilly & Co., Clinton, Ind., 1974-76; indsl. hygiene engr. Eli Lilly & Co., Lafayette, Ind., 1977-80; prof. toxicology and indsl. hygiene Purdue U., West Lafayette, Ind., 1979-82; risk assessment scientist Stauffer Chem. Co., Westport, Conn., 1982-84; mgr. indsl. and environ. toxicology Syntex Corp., Palo Alto, Calif., 1984-87; v.p. McLaren/Hart Environ. Engring., Alameda, Calif., 1987-95, chief tech. officer, 1991-96, pres., CEO, 1996—; cons. IBM, Kodak, Hercules, Exxon, GE, Ft. Wayne, Ind., 1980-82, Weyerhauser, 1980-82, 95, Maxus Energy Corp., 1980-82, 87-95, Hewlett-Packard, San Diego, 1984-86, Semicondr. Indsl. Assn., San Jose, Calif., 1984-86, Hughes Aircraft, L.A., 1987-92; com. mem. nat. coun. on radiol. protection and sci. adv. bd. U.S. EPA; vis. prof. Harvard Sch. Pub. Health, 1996-97. Contbr. over 130 articles to profl. jours., 10 chpts. to books; author coll. textbook on environ. risk assessment. Recipient Kusnetz award in Indsl. Hygiene. Fellow Am. Acad. Toxicological Scis.; mem. AICE, Am. Indsl. Hygiene Assn., Soc. Toxicology, Soc. Risk Analysis, Soc. Environ. Toxicology and Chemistry, Soc. Exposure Assessment, Am. Conf. Govtl. Indsl. Hygienists, N.Y. Acad. Scis., Sigma Xi. Roman Catholic. Avocations: antique furniture, jogging, golf, baseball. Home: 65 Roan Pl Woodside CA 94062-4229 Office: McLaren/Hart Environ Engrng 1135 Atlantic Ave Alameda CA 94501-1145

PAUSTIAN, BONITA JOYCE, school health administrator; b. Duluth, Minn., Apr. 17, 1935; d. Theodore Herald Oliver and Olga Magdalene (Bongey) Oliver-Spaulding; m. E. Earl Paustian, June 30 1956; children: Caprice, Lori, Leisa, Jodi, Jena. Diploma, Mercy Hosp. Sch. Nursing, 1956; BS, Colombia Pacific U., 1985. RN, Mich., Ind.; cert. Nat. Bd. for Cert. Sch. Nurses. Staff nurse Mercy Hosp., Benton Harbor, Mich., 1956-60; charge nurse rehab. unit Berrien Gen. Hosp., Berrien Center, Mich., 1960-61; charge nurse newborn nursery Meml. Hosp., St. Joseph, Mich., 1965-70; sch. nurse Berrien Springs Pub. Schs., 1970-88; in-svc. dir. Medco, South Bend, Ind., 1989; ins. examination nurse Exam Mgmt. Svcs., Kalamazoo, Mich., 1989—; health educator, 1989; supr. sch. health Buchanan (Mich.) Cmty. Schs., 1990—; ctr. nurse Berrin County Juvenile Detention Ctr., Mich., 1996—; lectr., presenter various programs in field; nurse cons., Mich., 1992—; OSHA/MIOSHA trainer, Mich., 1992—; pres. Sch. Nurse Consulting Svcs. Author: School Nurse Brochures, 1994; prodr., photographer slide show The Michigan School Nurse, 1988. Mem. choir Berrien Center Bible Ch., 1985—. Recipient Golden Nugget award Mich. Coun. for Exceptional Children, 1994, cert. of appreciation Optimist Club, Berrien County Day Program for Hearing Impaired Children, Ottawa Elem. Sch., Moccasin Elem. Sch. cert. of honor Am. Heart Assn.; named Mich. Sch. Nurse of Yr., 1987, One of Top 10 Nurses in Mich., Wayne State U. and Met. Woman's Mag., 1994. Mem. Mich. Assn. Sch. Nurses (pub. rels. chair 1993—, exec. bd., Pres. award 1993, Sch. Nurse of Yr. 1987), Nat. Assn. Sch. Nurses (exec. dir., state bd. dirs. 1994—, cert. recognition, 1995). Avocations: travel, reading, cross-stitch, freelance writing, vocal music. Home: 5703 Windy Acres Ln Berrien Springs MI 49103-1524 Office: Buchanan Cmty Schs 401 W Chicago St Buchanan MI 49107-1044

PAVA, ESTHER SHUB, artist, educator; b. Hartford, Conn., June 29, 1921; d. Jacob H. and Rose (Rietkop) Shub; m. Jacob Pava, June 16, 1946; children: David Lauren, Jonathan Michael, Daniel Seth, Nathaniel Alexander. BFA, R.I. Sch. of Design, 1944; MA, San Francisco State U., 1971. Artist New Eng. Roto Engraving Co., Holyoke, Mass., 1944-46, Wyckoff Advt. Agy., San Francisco, 1947-48; tchr. San Francisco Unified Sch. Dist., 1963-66, Laguna Salada Sch. Dist., Pacifica, Calif., 1966-83; artist, educator Belmont, Calif., 1983—; tchr. pvt. students Manor House, Belmont, Caif. Recipient numerous awards for artwork. Mem. Nat. League Am. Pen Women, Burlingame Art Soc. (pres. 1983-84), Thirty and One Artists (pres. 1992-93), Soc. Western Artists (signature mem. and juror), Calif. Watercolor Assn., Nat. League Am. Pen Women, others. Avocations: world travel, book discussion groups, sketching. Home: 2318 Hastings Dr Belmont CA 94002-3318 Studio: Manor House 1219 Ralston Ave Belmont CA 94002-1902

PAVALON, EUGENE IRVING, lawyer; b. Chgo., Jan. 5, 1933; m. Lois M. Frenzel, Jan. 15, 1961; children: Betsy, Bruce, Lynn. BSL, Northwestern U., 1954, JD, 1956. Bar: Ill. 1956. Sr. ptnr. Pavalon & Gifford, Chgo., 1970—; mem. com. on discovery rules Ill. Supreme Ct., 1981—; lectr., mem. faculty various law schs.; bd. dirs. ATLA Mut. Ins. Co. Former mem. state bd. dirs. Ind. Voters Ill; bd. overseers Inst. Civil Justice, Rand Corp., 1993—; mem. vis. com. Northwestern U. Law Sch., 1990-96. Capt., USAF, 1956-59. Fellow Am. Coll. Trial Lawyers, Internat. Soc. Barristers, Internat. Acad. Trial Lawyers, Roscoe Pound Found. (life fellow, pres. 1988-90); mem. ABA, Chgo. Bar Assn. (bd. mgrs. 1978-79), Ill. Bar Assn., Ill. Trial Lawyers Assn. (pres. 1980-81), Trial Lawyers for Pub. Justice (founding mem., v.p. 1991-92, pres.-elect 1992-93, pres. 1993-94), Assn. Trial Lawyers Am. (parlimentarian 1983-84, sec. 1984-85, v.p. 1985-86, pres. elect 1986-87, pres. 1987-88), Am. Bd. of Profl. Liability Attys. (diplomate), Chgo. Athletic Assn., Standard Club. Author: Human Rights and Health Care Law, 1980, Your Medical Rights, 1990; contbr. articles to profl. jours., chpts. in books. Home: 1540 N Lake Shore Dr Chicago IL 60610-1607 Office: Pavalon & Gifford 2 N La Salle St Chicago IL 60602-3702

PAVAROTTI, LUCIANO, lyric tenor; b. Modena, Italy, Oct. 12, 1935; s. Fernando and Adele (Venturi) P.; m. Adua Veroni, Sept. 30, 1961; children—Lorenza, Cristina, Giuliana. Diploma magistrale, Istituto Magistrale Carlo Sigonio, 1955; studies with, Arrigo Pola, Ettore Campogalliani. Formerly tchr. elem. schs.; salesman ins. Debut as Rodolfo in La Bohème, Reggio Emilia, Italy, 1961; roles include Edgardo in debut Lucia di Lammermoor, Amsterdam, 1963, the Duke in debut Rigoletto,Carpi, 1961, Rodolfo in La Bohème, Covent Garden, 1963, Tonio in debut The Daughter of the Regiment, Covent Garden, 1966, appeared in Lucia di Lammermoor, Australia, 1965, Am. debut, Miami, Fla., 1965; numerous European performances including Italy, Vienna Staatsoper, Paris; performed with San Francisco Opera, 1967, debut, Met. Opera, N.Y.C., 1968; appeared in The Daughter of the Regiment, Met. Opera, 1971, Elisir d'Amore, Met. Opera, 1973, La Bohème, Chgo. Opera, 1973, La Favorita, San Francisco Opera, 1973, Il Trovatore, San Francisco Opera, 1975, Bellini I Puritani, Met. Opera, 1976, Ponchielli La Gioconda, San Francisco Opera, 1979, Aida, San Francisco Opera, 1981, Mozart, Idomeneo, Met. Opera, 1982, Verdi, Ernani, Met. Opera, 1983, Tosca, Met. Opera, 1995; numerous internat. performances including La Scala, Milan, Hamburg, Teatro Colon, Buenos Aires, Australian Opera, Sydney; concert series of Am. and internat. cities, including Carnegie Hall, 1973, Buenos Aires, Moscow, Beijing, Hong Kong, Tokyo, including arena concerts, Madison Square Garden, 1984, and major cities in America, Europe, South America; appeared in film Yes, Giorgio, 1983; established Opera Co. of Philadelphia/Luciano Pavarotti Vocal Competition, 1980; rec. artist on Winner Concorso Internationale, Reggio Emilia, 1961, Amore, 1992, Pavarotti and Friends, 1993, Ti Amo-Puccini's Greatest Love Songs, 1993, Pavarotti and Friends 2, 1995; appeared in PBS TV spl. (with Placido Domingo & Jose Carreras) The Three Tenors, 1994. Named

Artist of Yr. Gramophone, 1992; recipient Grammy award, 1981, 1988. Office: care Herbert Breslin 119 W 57th St New York NY 10019

PAVILANIS, VYTAUTAS, microbiology educator, physician; b. Kaunas, Lithuania, June 7, 1920; s. Kazys and Antonina (Eimontas) P.; m. Irene Stencelis, Mar. 8, 1947; children: Alain, Christine Gaputis, Marina Pavilanis Branigan, Ingrid. MD, U. Kaunas, 1942; diploma in microbiology, Institut Pasteur, Paris, 1947, diploma in serology and hematology, 1948; hon. doctorate, U. Que., 1988, 89. Asst. prof. pathology U. Kaunas, 1942-44; resident physician Siegburg, Germany, 1944-45; asst. Institut Pasteur, Paris, 1945-48; asst. prof. U. Montreal, Can., 1948; head virus dept. Institut Armand-Frappier, Ville de Laval, Que., Can., 1948-75; sci. dir. Institut Armand-Frappier, 1970-75, research coordinator, 1975-78, dir. quality control, 1976-79, asst. dir. teaching and research, 1978-82; assoc. prof. U. Montreal, 1956-85, prof. emeritus, 1985—; prof. U. Que., 1974-85, prof. emeritus, 1985—; cons. in field. Contbr. articles to profl. jours. Recipient Queen's Jubilee medal Can., 1977, Prix d'excellence Province of Que., 1993. Fellow Royal Soc. Can., Royal Coll. Physicians (Can.); mem. Can. Soc. Microbiology (2d v.p. 1966, award 1984), Can. Public Health Assn. (chmn. lab. sect. 1969), Virology Club Montreal (pres. 1969), Coll. Physicians and Surgeons P.Q., Can. Med. Assn., Can. Assn. Med. Microbiologists, Soc. Microbiology P.Q., N.Y. Acad. Sci. Home: 4742 The Boulevard, Westmount, PQ Canada H3Y 1V3 Office: PO Box 100, Laval, PQ Canada H7N 4Z3

PAVIN, COREY, professional golfer. Winner Mastercard Colonial, 1996; mem. Ryder Cup Team, 1993. PGA Tour top U.S. golfer, leading money winner, 1991, 6th on PGA Tour 1992; Tour Wins include: Honda Classic, 1992, L.A. Open, 1994, Nissan Open, 1995, U.S. Open, 1995. Address: care PGA Tour 112 Tpc Blvd Ponte Vedra Beach FL 32082-3046*

PAVLATH, ATTILA ENDRE, research chemist; b. Budapest, Hungary, Mar. 11, 1930; came to U.S., 1958; s. Eugene Rudolph and Yolanda Elizabeth (Hortobagyi) P.; m. Katalin Wappel, July 27, 1951; children: George, Grace. Diploma in chem. engring., Tech. U., Budapest, 1952; D in Chemistry, Hungarian Acad. of Sci., Budapest, 1955. Asst. prof. Tech. U., Budapest, 1952-56; group leader Cen. Chem. Rsch. Inst., Budapest, 1954-56; rsch. fellow McGill U., Montreal, Can., 1957-58; sr. group leader Stauffer Chem. Co., Richmond, Calif., 1958-67; project leader Western regional rsch. ctr. USDA, Albany, Calif., 1967-78, rsch. leader Western regional rsch. ctr., 1979—. Author three books; contbr. articles to profl. jours; patentee in field. Fellow Am. Inst. Chemists (councilor 1985-95, dir. 1993-95); mem. Am. Chem. Soc. (councilor 1973-90, dir. 1991—), Royal Chem. Soc. Great Britain, N.Am. Thermonalysis Soc., Internat. Union of Pure and Applied Chemistry. Avocations: flying, tournament bridge, tennis, table tennis, computers. Office: USDA Western Regional Rsch Ctr 800 Buchanan St Berkeley CA 94710-1105

PAVLICK, CHARLES RALEIGH, architect, engineer, retired air force officer; b. Chgo., Mar. 28, 1918; s. Charles Harry and Myrtle Mildred (von Meyenberg) P.; m. Hilda Fay vanDeinse, Feb. 8, 1945; children: Ann, Charles, Elizabeth, James. Student, Deforrests Electronics Sch., Chgo. Art Inst., Chgo. Acad. Fine Arts, Air War Coll., Ohio State U. Commd. 2nd lt. USAAF, 1937; advanced through grades to col. USAF, 1968; served in WWII, Korea, Vietnam, USAAF and USAF; supervising arch.-engr. D.C. Dept. Pub. Works, Washington, 1968-93; owner, pres. Pavlick-Restordance, Alexandria, Va., 1993—; ret., 1968; cons. Met. Washington rea. Decorated Bronze Star, Air medal. mem. NRA, Mil. Order Purple Heart, Ret. Officers Assn., Navy Tailhook Assn., Air Force Assn., Am. Legion, Navy League, U.s. Naval Sailing Assn., Inst. Legis. Affairs, Naval Inst., USCG Aux., Brotherood of St. Andrew. Republican. Episcopalian. Avocations: collecting military memorabilia, antiques, hunting, fishing, political history. Home and Office: 326 N Royal St Alexandria VA 22314

PAVLIK, JAMES WILLIAM, chemistry educator; b. Chgo., Sept. 22, 1937; s. Victor William and Rose (Jaros) P.; m. children—Claire, David, Anne. A.B., Carthage Coll., 1959; M.S., Va. Poly. Inst. and State U., 1961; Ph.D., George Washington U., 1970. Asst. prof. chemistry Haile Sellasie I U., Addis Ababa, Ethiopia, 1967-69; research scientist George Washington U., Washington, 1969-70; from asst. prof. to assoc. prof. chemistry U. Wis., River Falls, 1970-74; prof. chemistry Worcester Poly. Inst., Mass., 1974—; cons. in field. Contbr. articles to profl. jours. Recipient Award for Outstanding Teaching, Worcester Poly. Inst., 1981. Mem. Am. Chem. Soc., Inter-Am. Photochem. Soc., Sigma Xi. Home: 11 Sawyer Rd Northborough MA 01532-1353 Office: Dept Chemistry Worcester Poly Inst Institute Rd Worcester MA 01609-2706

PAVLIK, NANCY, convention services executive; b. Hamtramck, Mich., July 18, 1935; d. Frank and Helen (Vorobojoff) Phillips; m. G. Edward Pavlik, June 30, 1956; children: Kathleen, Christine, Laureen, Michael, Bonnie Jean. Student, U. Ariz., 1956-80. Exec. sec. Mich. Bell, Detroit, 1951-56, RCA, Camden, N.J., 1956-58; owner, pres. S.W. Events Etc., Scottsdale, Ariz., 1969-77. Chmn. hospitality industry com. Scottsdale City Coun., 1989-95; bd. dirs. Scottsdale Curatorial Bd., 1987-89. Mem. Soc. Incentive Travel Execs., Meeting Planners Internat., Am. Soc. Assn. Execs., Indian Arts and Crafts Assn., Scottsdale C. of C. (bd. dirs., tourism steering com. 1984-88), Contemporary Watercolorists Club. Democrat. Roman Catholic. Avocations: watercoloring, Indian arts, crafts. Home: 15417 Richwood Fountain Hills AZ 85268 Office: SW Events Etc 3200 N Hayden Rd Ste 100 Scottsdale AZ 85251-6653

PAVLIK, ROGER ALLEN, professional baseball player; b. Houston, Oct. 4, 1967. Selected Tex. Rangers, 1987, pitcher, 1992, 93, 94—; selected Am. League All-Star Team, 1996. Office: c/o Texas Rangers 1000 Ballpark Way Arlington TX 76011-5168

PAVLIK, WILLIAM BRUCE, psychologist, educator; b. Cleve., Feb. 29, 1932; s. William Frank and Mary (Maco) P.; m. Mary Katherine Findley, May 22, 1979; children by previous marriage: William James, Heather Ann, Russell Matthew, James Clark; 1 child, Amelia Katherine. B.S., Western Res. U., 1953; M.A., Ohio State U., 1955, Ph.D., 1956. Asst. prof. psychology Western Mich. U., 1956-60; asst. prof., then asso. prof. Rutgers U., 1960-68; prof. psychology Va. Poly. Inst. and State U., 1968-77, chmn. dept., 1968-72; prof. psychology U. Ga., Athens, 1977-94; ret., head dept., 1977-84. Author articles in field. Mem. Eastern Psychol. Assn., Southeastern Psychol. Assn. (pres. 1985-86), Psychonomic Soc. Home: 555 Forest Rd Athens GA 30605-3823

PAVLOVICH, DONALD, educator, support person; b. Euclid, Ohio, Mar. 25, 1957; s. Paul George and Carroll Rose (McDonald) P. BS, Cleve. State Univ., 1981. Tech. writer, instr. Cleve. (Ohio) Inst. Electronics, 1982-85; instr. Lorain (Ohio) County Community Coll., 1985-86; tech. writer Picker Internat.-Gov. systems, Highland Heights, Ohio, 1986-87; sr. tech. writer Picker Internat.-MRI, Highland Heights, Ohio, 1987-94; tech. support specialist Rockwell Software, 1997—; part-time regulatory specialist Picker Internat., 1994-95; part-time instr. Sawyer Coll. Bus. Author (lesson books): ROMS, PROMs, and PLAs, 1983; co-author (lesson books): Karnaugh Maps, 1984, One-Shots, Astables and Schmitt Triggers, 1983; editor: Microprocessor Course, 1985; book reviewer. Vol. Cleve. Mus. of Art, 1991. Named Jr. Tech. Student of Yr. Cleve. State Engring. Alumni Assn., 1980. Mem. IEEE (reviewer Microprocessor and Microcomputer stds. subcom., 1990—), Alpha Beta Kappa. Home: 19015 Van Aken Blvd Apt 404 Shaker Heights OH 44122 Office: Rockwell Software 6680 Beta Dr Mayfield Village OH 44143-2327

PAVONY, WILLIAM H., retail executive; b. Bklyn., Mar. 1, 1940; s. Harry and Mollie (Leibell) P.; m. Geraldine Rice, June 10, 1961; 1 child, Sheryl. BBA cum laude, Hofstra U., 1960. CPA, N.Y., Tex. Mgr. Arthur Andersen & Co. Inc., N.Y.C., 1960-73; group sr. v.p. Purolator Svcs. Inc., New Hyde Park, N.Y., 1973-75; v.p., contr. Purolator Inc., Piscataway, N.J., 1975-78; sr. v.p. Zale Corp., Dallas, 1978-85; sr. v.p. fin., chief fin. officer Alexander's Inc., N.Y.C., 1985-88, exec. v.p., chief fin officer, 1988-89; exec. v.p. adminstrn. The Kobacker Co., Columbus, Ohio, 1989-93; also bd. dirs.; exec. v.p. Arthur Rutenberg Homes, Clearwater, Fla., 1993-94; CFO Color Tile, Inc., Ft. Worth, 1994-95; pres. Pavony Assocs., 1995—. Treas., bd. dirs. Tex. Vis. Nurses Assn., Dallas, 1984-85. Mem AICPA, Fin. Execs. Inst. (past bd. dirs. North Tex. chpt., sec. Columbus chpts.), N.Y. Soc. CPAs, Inst. Mgmt. Accts. Home: 7308 Monticello Pky Colleyville TX 76034-6856

PAVSEK, DANIEL ALLAN, banker, educator; b. Cleve., Jan. 18, 1945; s. Daniel L. and Helen A. (Femec) P. AB, Maryknoll Coll., Glen Ellyn, Ill., 1966; MA, Maryknoll Sch. Theology, Ossining, N.Y., 1971, Cleve. State U., 1972; PhD, Case Western Res. U., 1981. Pres. Coun. Richmond Heights, Ohio, 1972-75; lectr. econs. Cleve. State U., 1972-75; asst. prof. Baldwin-Wallace Coll., Berea, Ohio, 1975-81; v.p., economist Ameritrust Co., Cleve., 1981-91; dean, prof. econs. Harry F. Byrd Jr. Sch. Bus. Shenandoah U., Winchester, Va., 1992—; adj. prof. bus. adminstrn. Baldwin-Wallace Coll., Berea, Ohio, 1981-91. Mem. Am. Econ. Assn., Nat. Tax Assn., Pub. Choice Soc., Nat. Assn. Bus. Econs. Democrat. Home: 231 Woodberry Ln Apt 119 Winchester VA 22601-3592

PAWELEC, WILLIAM JOHN, retired electronics company executive; b. Hammond, Ind., Feb. 15, 1917; s. John and Julia (Durnas) P.; BS in Acctg., Ind. U., 1939; m. Alice E. Brown, May 30, 1941 (dec. Dec. 1970); children: William John, Betty Jane Pawelec Conover; m. 2d, June A. Shepard, Nov. 27, 1976 (div. June 1980). Statistician, Ind. State Bd. Accounts, 1939-41; with RCA, 1941—, mgr. acctg. and budgets internat. div., 1957-61, controller internat. div., 1961-68, corp. mgr. internat. fin. ops. and controls, 1968-75, mgr. corp. acctg., 1975-77, dir. internat. acctg., 1977-81, ret., 1981; controller RCA Internat., Ltd., Electron Ins. Co., 1977, RCA Credit Corp., 1979; ret., 1981. Active Westfield United Fund, 1967—. Mem. Nat. Assn. Accts. (past nat. v.p.), Watchung Power Squadron, N.J. State C. of C., Commerce and Industry Assn. N.Y., Stuart Cameron McLeod Soc., Ind. U. Alumni Assn. (pres. N.J. chpt.), Beta Gamma Sigma, Sigma Epsilon Theta, Echo Lake Country Club. Home: 86 New England Ave Summit NJ 07901-1828

PAWLEY, RAY LYNN, zoological park herpetology curator; b. Midland, Mich., Nov. 7, 1935; s. Lynn Richard and Alice Marie (Skelton) P.; m. Ethel Marie Condon, Feb. 19, 1955 (div. 1974); children: Ray Allyn, Shanna Sue, Cynthia Ann, Dawn Marie, Brandon Earl, Dareen Joy; m. Hedda P. Saltz, Mar. 16, 1997. Student in zoo adminstrn., Mich. State U., 1954-57. Asst. curator/lectr. Black Hills Reptile Gardens, Rapid City, S.D., summers 1952-53; owner, adminstr. Reptile Exhibit, St. Ignace, Mich., 1957-59; animal coord. Marlin Perkin's Wild Kingdom (Don Meier Prodns.), Chgo., 1961-62; zoologist Lincoln Park Zool. Gardens, Chgo., 1961-64; curator Brookfield (Ill.) Zoo, 1964—; assoc. dept. zoology Field Mus. Natural History, Chgo.; internat. zoo and conservation cons., Russia, Latvia, Mex., Kenya, China, Ecuador, Czechoslovakia; past instr. herpetology Field Mus., Coll. of DuPage, Triton Coll.; info. resource for fed. and state wildlife agys.; lectr., cons. in field. Contbr. oer 50 articles to profl. jours. and popular mags.; co-creator money bench Chgo. Children's Mus. Immediate past v.p. Ill. Endangered Species Protection Bd., Springfield; liaison Endangered Species Tech. Adv. Com., Springfield. Mem. Am. Zoo Assn. (3d Outstanding Svc. awards), Internat. Herpetological Alliance (officer), Chgo. Acad. Scis. (life), Chgo. Herpetologoical Soc. (life, cons.), Mensa. Avocations: hiking, archaeology, art, mechanics, paleontology. Home: PO Box 218 Hinsdale IL 60522-0218 Office: Chicago Zool Park Brookfield IL 60513

PAWLICZKO, GEORGE IHOR, academic administrator; b. Rochester, N.Y., Oct. 26, 1950; s. Roman and Irene Olha (Zubryckyj) P.; m. Ann Maria Lencyk, June 10, 1978. BA, St. John Fisher Coll., 1972; MA, Fordham U., 1974, MBA, 1986, PhD, 1989. Admissions counselor Fordham U., Bronx, N.Y., 1977-78; asst. dean Grad. Sch. of Bus. Fordham U., N.Y.C., 1978-81; asst. to pres., dir. mgmt. info. systems Marymount Coll., Tarrytown, N.Y., 1981-82; exec. dir. N.Y. Inst. Credit, N.Y.C., 1982-94, Am. Inst. Banking of Greater N.Y., N.Y.C., 1994—. Trustee St. Andrew's Ch., Hamptonburgh, N.Y., 1986—. Mem. Shevchenko Scientific Soc., Beta Gamma Sigma, Phi Alpha Theta. Office: Am Inst Banking of Greater NY 80 Maiden Ln New York NY 10038-4811

PAWLSON, LEONARD GREGORY, physician; b. Victoria, Tex., 1943. MD, U. Pitts., 1969; MPH, U. Wash., 1976. Diplomate Am. Bd. Internal Medicine. Intern, affiliate hosps. Stanford U., 1969-70, resident in medicine, 1970-71; fellow in endocrinology U. Wash., 1973-75, Robert Wood Johnson clin. scholar, 1975-76; asst. prof. medicine and health care scis. George Washington U., Washington, 1976-80, assoc. prof. med. and health care scis., 1980-85, prof. health care scis., medicine, and health svcs. mgmt. and policy, 1985—, assoc. chmn. dept. health care scis., 1978-90, Mudoch head prof. preventive medicine, 1995—, acting chmn., 1987-90, chmn., 1990—; attending physician George Washington Hosp., 1976—. Robert Wood Johnson health policy fellow, 1986-87; bd. dirs. Bon Secours Hosp. System, 1993—, U.S. Soliders and Airmans Home, 1992—, Med. Faculty Assocs., 1990—. Mem. ACP, Am. Geriatrics Soc. (past pres. and chmn. bd., editor law and pub. policy sect. Jour. Am. Geriatrics Soc.); mem. Soc. Gen. Internal Medicine (past bd. dirs.), Assn. Tchrs. Preventive Medicine (chair pub. policy com.). Office: George Washington U Med Ctr Dept Health Care Scis 2150 Pennsylvania Ave NW Washington DC 20037-3201

PAWSON, ANTHONY J., molecular biologist. Sr. scientist Samuel Lunenfeld Rsch. Inst., Toronto, Ont., Can. Recipient Internat. award Gairdner Found., 1994. Fellow Royal Soc. London, Royal Soc. Can. Office: Samuel Lunenfeld Rsch Inst, 600 University Ave, Toronto, ON Canada M5G 1X5

PAXON, L. WILLIAM, congressman; b. Buffalo, Apr. 29, 1954; s. Leon W. and Mary P. (Sellers) P.; m. Susan Molinari, July 3, 1994; 1 child, Susan Ruby. BA, Canisius Coll., 1977. Mem. Erie County Legis., N.Y., 1978-82, N.Y. State Assembly, 1983-89, 101st-105th Congresses from 31st (now 27th) N.Y. dist., 1989—; chair Nat. Rep. Congrl. Com.; mem. com. on commerce. Mem. Buffalo C. of C., Lions. Roman Catholic. Youngest mem. in history of Erie County Legislature. Office: US Ho of Reps 2412 Rayburn HOB Washington DC 20515-3227 also: 5500 Main St Williamsville NY 14221-6737*

PAXSON, RICHARD, newspaper editor. Editor Va. news desk, Va. weeklies The Washington Post. Office: The Washington Post 1150 15th St NW Washington DC 20071-0001

PAXTON, ALICE ADAMS, artist, architect and interior designer; b. Hagerstown, Md., May 19, 1914; d. William Albert and Josephine (Adams) Rosenberger; m. James Love Paxton Jr., June 26, 1942 (div.); 1 child, William Allen III (dec.). Student, Peabody Inst. Music, Balt., 1937-38; grad., Parson's Sch. Design, N.Y., 1940; studies with J. Laurie Wallace, 1944-46; studies with Augustus Dunbier, 1947-48, Sylvia Curtis, 1949, Milton Wolsky, 1950, Frank Sapousek, 1951. Freelance work archtl. rendering and interior design, N.Y., 1937-40; interior designer, designer spl. furnishings, muralist Orchard and Wilhelm, Omaha, 1940-42; tchr. art classes Alice Paxton Studio, Omaha, 1957-64; tchr. mech. drawing, archtl. rendering and mech. perspective Parson's Sch. Design, N.Y., 1937-40. Designer (interior) Chapel Boys' Town, Nebr., 1942; one-woman show of archtl. renderings Washington County Mus. Fine Arts, Hagerstown, 1944; exhibited group shows at Joslyn Mus., Omaha, 1943-44 (1st place), Ann. Exhbn. Cumberland Valley Artists, Hagerstown, 1945; represented in permanent collections at No. Natural Gas Co. Bldg., Omaha, Swanson Found., Omaha; also pvt. collections; vol. designer, decorator: recreation room Omaha Blood Bank, ARC, 1943, recreation room Creighton U., 1943, lounge psychiat. ward Lincoln (Nebr.) Army Hosp., 1944; planner, color coordinator Children's Hosp., Omaha, 1947, painted murals, 1948, decorated dental room, 1950; designed Candy Stripers' uniforms; painted and decorated straw elephant bag presented to Mrs. Richard Nixon, 1960; contbr. articles and photographs to Popular Home mag., 1958. Co-chair camp and hosp. coms. ARC, 1943-45, mem. county com. to select and send gifts to servicemen, 1943-46; mem. Ak-Sar-Ben Ball Com., Omaha, 1946-48, Nat. Mus. Women in the Arts, The Md. Hist. Soc.; judge select Easter Seal design, Joslyn Mus., 1946; mem. council Girl Scouts U.S., Omaha, 1943-47; spl. drs. chmn. Jr. League, Omaha, 1947-48, chair Jr. League Red Cross fund dr., 1947-48; bd. dirs., vol. worker Creche, Omaha, 1954-56; mem. Omaha Jr. League; chmn. Jr. League Community Chest Fund Dr., 1948-50; co-chair Infantile Paralysis Appeal, 1944; numerous vol. profl. activities for civic orgns., hosps., clubs, chs., community playhouse, and for establishing wildlife sanctuary. Recipient three teaching scholarships Parson's Sch. Design, 1937-40, presdl. citation ARC activities, 1946, 1st prize Ann. Midwest Show Joslyn Mus., 1943. Mem. Associated Artists Omaha (charter), Internat. Platform Assn., U.S. Hist. Soc., Nat. Mus. Women in Arts (charter), Md. Hist. Soc., Fountain Head Country Club. Republican. Episcopalian. Home: 19614 Meadowbrook Rd Hagerstown MD 21742-2519

PAXTON, BILL, actor, writer, director; b. Ft. Worth, May 17, 1955; s. John Lane and Mary Lou (Gray) P; m. Louise Newbury. Student, NYU; studies with Stella Adler, Vincent Chase. Actor: (feature films) Mortuary, 1981, The Lords of Discipline, 1982, Streets of Fire, 1983, Impulse, 1983, Weird Science, 1984, Terminator, 1984, Commando, 1985, Aliens, 1985 (Saturn award Acad. of Sci. Fiction, Fantasy, and Horror Films 1986), Near Dark, 1986, Pass the Ammo, 1987, Next of Kin, 1989, The Last of the Finest, 1990, Navy Seals, 1990, Predator 2, 1990, One False Move, 1992, Hurricane, 1992, The Vagrant, 1992, Indian Summer, 1993, Boxing Helena, 1993, Tombstone, 1993, True Lies, 1994, Frank and Jesse, 1994, Apollo 13, 1995, Twister, 1995, Evening Star, 1996, The Last Supper, 1996, Traveler, 1996 (also prodr.), Titanic, 1997, (TV movies) Deadly Lessons, 1983, The Atlanta Child Murders, 1985, An Early Frost, 1985, (TV mini-series) Fresno, 1986, (TV series) The Hitch-Hiker, 1986; dir. (theatrical short) Fish Heads, 1982 (Spl. Award Melbourne Film Festival 1982); prodr., co-author (theatrical short) Scoop, 1983. Mem. Screen Actors Guild. Address: Banner Entertainment 3d Fl 8000 Sunset Blvd Los Angeles CA 90046

PAXTON, J. WILLENE, retired university counseling director; b. Birmingham, Ala., Oct. 30, 1930; d. Will and Elizabeth (Davis) P. AB, Birmingham So. Coll., 1950; MA, Mich. State U., 1951; EdD, Ind. U., 1971. Nat. cert. counselor, lic. profl. counselor, Tenn. Dormitory dir. Tex. Tech U., Lubbock, 1951-53; counselor Mich. State U., East Lansing, summer 1951, 52; dir. univ. ctr. and housing SUNY, Fredonia, 1953-56, assoc. dean of students, 1956-57; asst. dean of women U. N.Mex., Albuquerque, 1957-63; dean of women East Tenn. State U., Johnson City, 1963-68, 70-78, dir. counseling ctr., 1978-93; ret., 1993. Sec. adminstrv. bd. Meth. Ch., 1983-86, vice chmn., 1993, chmn., 1994—, chmn. social concerns com., 1991-93, program chmn. Good Timers fellowship, 1994-95, pres. Sunday Sch. class, 1994, chmn. fin. campaign, 1995, chair promotion and publicity, bldg. com., 1996—, chair scholarship com.; tng. dir. Contact Teleministries, Inc., 1983-87, chmn., 1988, 95, vice chmn., 1993-95; bd. dirs. Asbury Cts., 1990—, policy com., 1991—, chmn. policy com., 1995—, mem. fin. com., 1996. Mem. APA, AAUW (br. pres., mem. nominating com. 1993-96, fin. com. 1996), Am. Counseling Assn., Tenn. Psychol. Assn., Assn. Univ. and Coll. Counseling Ctr. Dirs. (conv. planning com. 1991), Am. Coll. Pers. Assn. (media bd., newsletter editor), Nat. Assn. Women Deans, Adminstrs. and Counselors, Tenn. Assn. Women Deans and Counselors (state pres., v.p., program chmn.), East Tenn. Edn. Assn. (chmn. guidance divsn.), East Tenn. State U. Retirees Assn. (bd. dirs. 1993—, program com. 1993—, chair program com. 1996, pres.-elect 1996, pres. 1997), Gen. Federated Woman's Club (pres. 1980-81, 88-89, 95-96, 2d v.p. 1991-95, advisor 1995-97), Univ. Women's Club (v.p. 1993-94, pres. 1994, 95, chair excursions com. 1997—), Delta Kappa Gamma (chpt. pres. 1974-76, state rec. sec. 1977-79, v.p. 1979-81, chmn. nominating com. 1981-83, internat. rsch. com. 1982-84, chmn. leadership devel. com. 1983-85, chmn. self-study com. 1985-87, com. to study exec. sec. 1987-89, state pres. 1989-91, parliamentarian 1991-93, internat. constn. com. 1992-94, awards com. 1993-95, chmn. internat. conv. meal functions com. 1994, state pers. com. 1995—, state achievement award 1987). Avocations: reading, bridge, travel, needlework. Home: 1203 Lester Harris Rd Johnson City TN 37601-3335

PAXTON, ROBERT OWEN, historian, educator; b. Lexington, Va., June 15, 1932; s. Matthew W. and Nell B. (Owen) P.; m. Sarah Plimpton, Dec. 9, 1983. B.A., Washington and Lee U., 1954, LittD (hon.), 1974; B.A., Oxford (Eng.) U., 1956, M.A., 1961; Ph.D., Harvard U., 1963; DHL (hon.), SUNY, Stony Brook, 1994; DL (hon.), U. Caen, France, 1994. Instr. history U. Calif., Berkeley, 1961-63, asst. prof., 1963-67; asso. prof. SUNY, Stony Brook, 1967-69; prof. history Columbia U., 1969—, chmn. dept., 1980-82, dir. Inst. on West Europe, 1991-95. Author: Parades and Politics at Vichy, 1966, Vichy France: Old Guard and New Order, 1940-44, 1972, Europe in the Twentieth Century, 1975, 3d edit., 1997; co-author: Vichy France and the Jews, 1981; co-editor: De Gaulle and the U.S., 1995. Served with USNR, 1956-58. Decorated chevalier Ordre National des Arts et des Lettres (France), officer Ordre National du Mérite (France); Rhodes scholar, 1954-56; Am. Coun. Learned Socs. fellow, 1974-75; Rockefeller Found. fellow, 1978-79; German Marshall Fund fellow, 1986. Fellow Am. Acad. Arts and Letters; mem. Am. Hist. Assn., Soc. d'histoire moderne, Linnaean Soc. N.Y. (pres. 1978-80). Home: 460 Riverside Dr Apt 72 New York NY 10027-6820 Office: Columbia U Dept History New York NY 10027

PAXTON, TOM, songwriter, entertainer, author; b. Chgo., Oct. 31, 1937; s. George Burton and Esther Hildegard (Peterson) P.; m. Margaret Ann Cummings, Aug. 5, 1963; children: Jennifer Ann, Katherine Claire. BFA, U. Okla., 1959. Rec. artist with Elektra, Flying Fish, Hogeye, Reprise, Vanguard, Mountain Railroad, Pax Records, Sugar Hill, 1962—; owner Pax Records. Folk artist, U.S., Can., Gt. Brit., Scandanavia, France, Germany, Australia, N.Z., Italy, Spain, 1960—; albums include Ramblin' Boy, 1964, Ain't That News, 1965, Outward Bound, 1966, Morning Again, 1968, The Things I Notice Now, 1969, Number 6, 1970, The Complete Tom Paxton, 1971, How Come the Sun, 1971, Peace Will Come, 1972, New Songs for Old Friends, 1973, Something in My Life, 1975, New Songs from the Briar Patch, 1977, Heroes, 1978, Up and Up, 1980, The Paxton Report, 1980, One Million Lawyers...and Other Disasters, 1986, The Marvelous Toy and Other Gallimaufry, 1987, Even a Gray Day, And Loving You, 1987, Politics, 1989, The Authentic Guitar of Tom Paxton Song Book, 1989, It Ain't Easy, 1991, Wearing the Time, 1995, Live for the Record, 1996; author: (children's books) Jennifer's Rabbit, 1988, Belling The Cat, 1990, Englebert the Elephant, 1990, Aesop's Fables Retold in Verse, 1988, Androcles and The Lion, 1991, Birds of a Feather, 1992, The Animals' Lullaby, 1993, Where's the Baby, 1993, The Story of Santa Claus, 1995, The Story of the Tooth Fairy, 1996, The Marvelous Toy, 1996, Goin' to the Zoo, 1996, Engelbert Joins the Circus, 1997. Bd. dirs. Kerrville Folk Festival, 1990. Recipoent Lifetime Achievement award Swannanoa Gathering, Warren Wilson Coll., N.C., 1996; named to Kerrville Folk Festival Hall of Fame, 1996. Mem. ASCAP, AFTRA, Am. Fedn. Musicians, Screen Actors Guild.

PAYCHECK, JOHNNY, country western musician; b. Greenfield, Ohio, May 31, 1941. Played with Faron Young, George Jones, Ray Price; songs include A-11, 1965, Heartbreak Tennessee, 1966, The Lovin' Machine, 1966, Apartment No. 9, Touch My Heart, She's All I Got, Someone to Give My Love to, 1972, Love is a Good Thing, 1972, Something About You I Love, 1973, Mr. Lovemaker, 1973, Song and Dance Man, 1973, Slide Off Your Satin Sheets, 1974, I'm the Only Hell Mama Ever Raised, 1974, Take This Job and Shove It, 1974, Maybellene, 1978, You Can Have Her, 1979, You Better Move On, 1980, I Can't Hold Myself in Line, 1981, I Never Got Over You, 1983; albums include Double Trouble (with George Jones), Greatest Hits, Take This Job and Shove It, Armed and Crazy, Everybody's Got a Family, Back On The Job, Mr. Lovemaker, Johnny Paycheck Sings George Jones, 1996. *

PAYMER, DAVID, actor. Appeared in films The In-Laws, 1979, Airplane II: The Sequel, 1982, Irreconcilable Differences, 1984, Perfect, 1985, Love Mary, 1985, Pleasures, 1986, No Way Out, 1987, Crazy People, 1990, City Slickers, 1991, Mr. Saturday Night, 1992, Heart and Souls, 1993, Searching For Bobby Fischer, 1993, City Slickers II: The Legend of Curly's Gold, 1994, Quiz Show, 1994, Cagney & Lacey: The Return, 1994, Cagney & Lacey: Together Again, 1995, Get Shorty, 1995, The American President, 1995, Nixon, 1995, City Hall, 1996, Carpool, 1996, The Sixth Man, 1997, Gang Related, 1997, (tv series) Boston Common, 1996-97. Office: Susan Smith & Assocs 121 N San Vicente Blvd Beverly Hills CA 90211*

PAYN, CLYDE FRANCIS, technology company executive, consultant; b. Auckland, New Zealand, Jan. 17, 1952; came to U.S., 1973; s. Phillip Francis and Ngaire Eunice P.; m. Betsy Ann Dannels, June 17, 1978; children: Tamara, Brittany, Erik. Cert., Auckland Inst. Tech., 1971; MBA, Vanderbilt U., 1980. Tech. mgr. Carborundum (N.Z.) Ltd., Auckland, 1968-73; mem. product application tech. staff Carborundum Co., Niagara Falls, N.Y., 1973-78; mgr. product mktg. Universal Abrasives, Phila., 1978-80; bus.

mgr., catalyst advocate Johnson Matthey, Inc., Phila., 1980-84; pres. Catalyst Cons., Inc., Phila., 1984—; CEO Catalyst Group, Phila., 1988—. Pres. Hideaway Hill Civic Assn., Maple Glen, Pa., 1988, 89. Mem. AIChE, Am. Chem. Soc., Catalysis Soc., Comml. Devel. Assn., Chem. Mktg. Rsch. Assn., Polymer Mfg. Engrs. Assn. Achievements include development of new process technology, catalyst and product development for petroleum, petrochemical, chemical, polymer and environ. industries. Office: The Catalyst Group Inc PO Box 637 Spring House PA 19477-0637

PAYNE, ALMA JEANETTE, English language educator, author; b. Highland Park, Ill., Oct. 28, 1918; d. Frederick Hutton and Ruth Ann (Colle) P. BA, Wooster (Ohio) Coll., 1940; MA, Case Western Res. U., 1941, PhD, 1956. Tchr. English, history, Latin Ohio Pub. Schs., Bucyrus and Canton, 1941-46; from instr. to prof. English and Am. studies Bowling Green (Ohio) State U., 1946-79, dir. Am. studies program, 1957-79, chair Am. culture PhD program, 1978-79, prof. emerita English, Am. studies, 1979—; adj. prof. Am. studies U. South Fla., 1982—. Author: Critical Bibliography of Louisa May Alcott, 1980, Discovering the American Nations, 1981; contbr. articles to profl. jours.; editor Nat. Am. Studies Assn. Newsletter; contbr. articles to profl. jours. Nat. Coun. for Innovation in Edn. grantee, Norway, U.S. Embassy and Norwegian Dept. Ch. and State, 1978-79; recipient MAry Turpie award in Am. studies, 1996. Mem. AAUW (pres. 1982-84), Soc. Mayflower Descs in Fla. (state treas. 1985), Nat. Am. Studies Assn. (v.p. 1977-79), Zonta, Phi Beta Kappa, Phi Kappa Phi, Kappa Delta Pi, Alpha Lambda Delta. Republican. Presbyterian. Avocations: travel, gardening, baseball, photography, reading. Home and Office: 11077 Orangewood Dr Bonita Springs FL 34135-5720

PAYNE, ANCIL HORACE, retired broadcasting executive; b. Mitchell, Oreg., Sept. 5, 1921; s. Leslie L. and Pearl A. (Brown) P.; m. Valerie Dorrance Davies, Apr. 6, 1959; children: Anne Sparrow, Alison Louise, Lucinda Catherine. Student, Willamette U., 1939-41, U. Oreg., 1941, U. Notre Dame, Ohio State U., 1943; B.A., U. Wash., 1947; postgrad., Am. U., 1950-51; hon. PhD, Willamette Univ., 1991. Adminstrv. asst. to congressman, Washington, 1949-52; gen. mgr. Martin Van Lines, Anchorage, 1952-56; mgr. Frontiers-Oreg. Ltd., Portland, Oreg., 1956-59; asst. v.p. bus. div. King Broadcasting Co., Seattle, 1959-63, v.p., 1963-70, exec. v.p., 1970-71, pres., 1971-87; chmn. bd. affiliates NBC, 1975-80. Mem. Oreg. Bd. Higher Edn., 1966-70; bd. trustees Whitman Coll., 1985-90; bd. dirs. Centrum Found., Film Com, Inc. Lt. (j.g.) USNR, 1942-45, PTO. Mem. Monday Club, Rainier Club, Columbia Tower Club, Phi Beta Kappa Assocs., Alpha Delta Sigma. Episcopalian. Home: 1107 1st Ave Apt 2001 Seattle WA 98101-2948 Office: Ancil H Payne & Assocs 1107 1st Ave Apt 606 Seattle WA 98101-2944

PAYNE, ANITA HART, reproductive endocrinologist, researcher; b. Karlsruhe, Baden, Germany, Nov. 24, 1926; came to U.S., 1938; d. Frederick Michael and Erna Rose (Hirsch) Hart; widowed; children: Gregory Steven, Teresa Payne-Lyons. BA, U. Calif., Berkeley, 1949, PhD, 1952. Rsch. assoc. U. Mich., Ann Arbor, 1961-71, asst. prof., 1971-76, assoc. prof., 1976-81, prof., 1981—, assoc. dir. Ctr. for Study Reprodn., 1989-94; vis. scholar Stanford U., 1987-88; mem. reproductive biology study sect. NIH, Bethesda, Md., 1978-79, biochem. endocrinology study sect., 1979-83, population rsch. com. Nat. Inst. Child Health and Human Devel., 1989-93. Assoc. editor Steroids, 1987-93; contbr. book chpts., articles to profl. jours. Recipient award for cancer rsch. Calif. Inst. for Cancer Rsch., 1953, Acad. Women's Caucus award U. Mich., 1986. Mem. Endocrine Soc. (chmn. awards com. 1983-84, mem. nominating com. 1985-87, coun. 1988-91), Am. Soc. Andrology (exec. coun. 1980-83), Soc. for Study of Reprodn. (bd. dirs. 1982-85, sec. 1986-89, pres. 1990-91). Office: Stanford U Med Ctr Dept Gynecology/ Obstetrics Div Reproductive Biology Stanford CA 94305-5317

PAYNE, ARLIE JEAN, parent education administrator; b. Priest River, Idaho, Oct. 9, 1920; d. Charles Ross and Novella (Person) Randall; m. Edgar E. Payne, July 18, 1942; children: Randy, Nancy, Kathleen, Charles, Stacy. BA, East Washington U., 1942, MEd, 1968. Tchr. Rainier (Wash.) Pub. Schs., 1941-42; tchr. phys. edn. George Dewey Jr. High Sch., Bremerton, Wash., 1946; coll. dir. nursery sch. Farragut, Idaho, 1946-47; tchr. kindergarten West Valley Pub. Schs., Dishman, Washington, 1951-52; tchr. kindergarten Mercer Island, Washington, 1952-53, active devel. and op. pvt. child care ctr., 1957-63; tchr. pvt. nursery sch. Community Colls. of Spokane, Mercer Island, Washington, 1964-65; developer 1st program for presch. age handicapped children Lake Washington Spl. Edn. Ctr., Kirkland, Washington, 1965-67; cons. parent edn. Lake Wash. Sch. Dist., Kirkland, Washington, 1967-68; legis. chairperson A.H.E., 1970-72; coord. family life Shoreline Community Coll., Seattle, 1968-72; dir. parent cooperative program Community Colls. of Spokane, 1973-85; mem. Gov.'s Commn. for Child Care, 1985; owner Whimisical Jean's Books. Author: Kids Crazy, 1993; editor, publisher Lake Spokane News Forum. Recipient Crystal Apple award for Support for Edn. Wash. State Pub. Rels. Assn., 1995. Home: 16094 N Saddlebrook Rd Nine Mile Falls WA 99026-9352

PAYNE, DONALD M., congressman; b. Newark, July 16, 1934. BA, Seton Hall U. Freeholder Essex County, 1973-78; ins. co. exec., prior to 1989, former v.p. computer forms mfr.; mem. Newark Mcpl. Coun., 1982-89, 101st-105th Congresses from 10th N.J. dist., 1989—; mem. econ. and ednl. opportunity com., mem. internat. rels. com. Chmn. World YMCA Refugee and Rehab. Com., 1973-81; pres YMCA's of USA. Democrat. Office: US Ho of Reps 2244 Rayburn HOB Washington DC 20515-3010 also: 50 Walnut St # 1016 Newark NJ 07102-3506*

PAYNE, DOUGLAS DEFREES, cardiothoracic surgeon, educator; b. Dayton, Ohio, Feb. 13, 1940; s. William Gebhart and Elizabeth (Defrees) P.; m. Geraldine Rupp, June 10, 1966. BA, Harvard U., 1962, MD, 1966. Diplomate Am. Bd. Surgery, Am. Bd. Thoracic Surgery. Cardiothoracic surgeon New England Med. Ctr., Boston, 1975—, vice chmn. dept. cardiothoracic surgery, 1985-93, acting chmn. dept. cardiothoracic surgery, 1993-94, chief divsn. cardiothoracic surgery, 1994—, acting chmn. surgery, 1996—; assoc. prof. surgery Tufts U., Boston, 1982-90, prof. surgery, 1990—. Lt. col. U.S. Army, 1973-75, Korea. Fellow ACS; mem. Am. Heart Assn., Am. Coll. Chest Physicians. Soc. Thoracic Surgeons, Internat. Soc. for Heart Transplantation, Internat. Cardiovascular Soc. Office: New Eng Med Ctr 750 Washington St Boston MA 02111-1526

PAYNE, ELIZABETH ELEANORE, surgeon, otolaryngologist; b. Detroit, Mar. 17, 1945; d. Richard Franklin and Eleanore Grace (Dieterich) P.; 1 child from previous marriage, Julia Elizabeth Komanecky. Student, St. Olaf Coll., 1962-64; MD, U. Iowa, 1968. Cert. Am. Bd. Otolaryngology, Am. Acad. Otolaryngic Allergy; lic. in medicine, Minn., Iowa. Intern Phila. Gen. Hosp., 1968-69; resident gen. surgery U. Minn., Mpls., 1969-70; resident otolaryngology U. Minn., 1970-74, clin. asst. prof. dept. otolaryngology, asst. clin. prof. dept. family practice and community health; pvt. practice, Mpls., 1974—; mem. med. staff North Meml. Med. Ctr., Mpls., Children's Med. Ctr., AbbottNorthwestern Hosp. Contbr. articles to profl. jours. Mem. AMA, Am. Acad. Otolaryngology Head and Neck Surgery, Am. Acad. Otolaryngic Allergy, Minn. State Med. Assn., Minn. Acad. Otolaryngology Head and Neck Surgery (coun. mem.), Minn. Acad. Medicine, Hennepin County Med. Assn. Office: Affiliated Otolaryngologists 3366 Oakdale Ave N Ste 307 Minneapolis MN 55422-2977

PAYNE, EUGENE EDGAR, insurance company executive; b. San Antonio, Aug. 9, 1942; s. Eugene Edgar and Louise (Speer) P.; m. Karen S. James, June 10, 1978; children: Kelly Lynn, Katherine Louise, Mary Patricia, Kerry Erin, Kimberley Ann, Thomas Julius. B.S., Tex. A&M U., 1964, M.S., 1965; Ph.D. (research fellow 1968-70), U. Okla., 1970. Mgmt. cons. E.I. DuPont de Nemours Co., Del., 1965-68; dir. mgmt. info. systems, spl. cons. Electronic Data Systems Corp., Dallas, 1970-71; dir. planning and mgmt. systems U. Tex., Dallas, 1971-74; v.p. fin. and mgmt. S.W. Tex. State U., San Marcos, 1974-81; v.p. fin. and adminstrn. Tex. Tech U., 1981-88, Tex. Tech Health Ctr., Lubbock, 1981-88; treas. Tex. Tech U. Found., 1981-88; exec. v.p. Investors Life Ins. of N.Am., Austin, Tex., 1988—, Investors Life of Calif., 1988—, Standard Life Ins. of Miss., 1988—, InterContintental Life of N.J., 1988—; exec. v.p. Family Life Ins. Co., 1991—, Fin. Industries Corp., Austin, Tex., 1991—; cons. in field. Contbr. articles to profl. jours. Vestry, fin. com. St. Christopher's Episc. Ch., 1983-86; chmn. bd. trustees All Saints Episc. Sch., Lubbock, 1985-89, Episc. Sem. of Southwest, Austin, Tex., 1985-89. NDEA fellow, 1969. Mem. Am. Inst. Indsl. Engrs. (Sr.), Inst. Mgmt. Scis., Ops. Research Soc. Am., Assn. Computing Machinery, Assn. Instl. Research, Soc. Coll. and Univ. Planning, Nat. Assn. Coll. and Univ. Bus. Officers, Rotary. Home: 1300 Circle Ridge Dr West Lake Hls TX 78746-3402 Office: FIC Ins Group 701 Brazos St Ste 1400 Austin TX 78701-3232

PAYNE, FLORA FERN, retired social service administrator; b. Carrollton, Mo., Sept. 25, 1932; d. George Earnest and Bernadine Alice (Schaefer) Chrisman; m. H.D. Mattícks, Oct. 20, 1950 (div. Oct. 1959); children: Dennis Don, Kathi D.; m. S.L. Freeman, Nov. 25, 1960 (div. Jan. 1973); 1 child, Gary Mark; m. Vernon Ray Payne, Mar. 18, 1988. Student, S.E. C.C., Burlington, Iowa, 1976-77; cert. stenographer, Corr. Sch., Chgo., 1960-61. Social svc. designee Mo. League Nursing, 1991. Sec. to v.p. Moore Co., Marceline, Mo., 1973-75; steno to trainmaster A.T. & S.F. Rlwy. Co., Fort Madison, Iowa, 1975-88; with social svc. Brookfield (Mo.) Nursing Ctr., 1990-95; candidate for Linn County Pub. Adminstr., 1996. Mem. NAFE, Mo. Orgn. Social Svcs. Republican. Avocations: writing poetry, dancing, interior decorating. Home: 603 Hickory St Bucklin MO 64631-9097

PAYNE, FRANCES ANNE, literature educator, researcher; b. Harrisonburg, Va., Aug. 28, 1932; d. Charles Franklin and Willie (Tarvin) P. B.A., Shorter Coll, 1953, B.Mus., 1953; M.A., Yale U., 1954, Ph.D., 1960. adj. fellow St. Anne's Coll., Oxford Eng. Instr. Conn. Coll., New London, 1955-56; instr. U. Buffalo, 1958-60, lectr., 1960, asst. prof., 1960-67; assoc. prof. SUNY, Buffalo, 1967-75; prof. English and medieval lit. SUNY, 1975—; adj. fellow St. Anne's Coll., Oxford, Eng., 1966—. Author: King Alfred and Boethius, 1968; Chaucer and Menippean Satire, 1981. Contbr. articles to scholarly publs. AAUW fellow, Oxford, 1966-67; Research Found. grantee SUNY Central, Oxford, 1967, 68, 71, 72; recipient Julian Park award SUNY-Buffalo, 1979. Mem. Medieval Acad. Am., Internat. Arthurian Soc., New Chaucer Soc., Internat. Soc. Anglo-Saxonists, Pi Kappa Lambda. Office: SUNY-Buffalo 306 Clemens Hall Buffalo NY 14260

PAYNE, FRED J., physician; b. Grand Forks, N.D., Oct. 14, 1922; s. Fred J. and Olive (Johnson) P.; m. Dorothy J. Peck, Dec. 20, 1948; children: Chris Ann Payne Graebner, Roy S., William F., Thomas A. Student U. N.D., 1940-42; BS, U. Pitts., 1948, MD, 1949; MPH, U. Calif., Berkeley, 1958. Diplomate Am. Bd. Preventive Medicine. Intern, St. Joseph's Hosp., Pitts., 1949-50; resident Charity Hosp., New Orleans, 1952-53; med. epidemiologist Ctr. Disease Control, Atlanta, 1953-60; prof. tropical medicine La. State U. Med. Ctr., New Orleans, 1961-66; dir. La. State U. Internat. Ctr. for Med. Rsch. and Tng., San Jose, Costa Rica, 1963-66; exec. sec. 3d Nat. Conf. on Pub. Health Tng., Washington, 1966-67; epidemiologist Nat. Nutrition Survey, Bethesda, Md., 1967-68; chief pub. health professions br. NIH, Bethesda, 1971-74, med. officer, sr. rsch. epidemiologist Nat. Inst. Allergy and Infectious Diseases, 1974-78; asst. health dir. Fairfax County (Va.) Health Dept., 1978-94, dir. HIV/AIDS case mgmt. program, 1988-94, cons. epidemiologist 1994—; med. advisor Ams. for Sound AIDS Policy, 1996—; clin. prof. La. State U., 1966-79; cons. NIH, 1979-81; leader WHO diarrheal disease adv. team, 1960. Contbr. articles to profl. jours. Served with AUS, 1942-46, 49-52. Decorated Combat Medic Badge. Fellow Am. Coll. Preventive Medicine, Am. Coll. Epidemiology; mem. AAAS, AMA, Am. Soc. Microbiology, Internat. Epidemiology Assn., Soc. Epidemiologic Rsch., USPHS Commd. Officers Assn., Sigma Xi. Home: 2945 Ft Lee St Herndon VA 20171-1813 Office: 102 Elden St Herndon VA 20170-4809

PAYNE, FRED R(AY), aerospace engineering educator, researcher; b. Mayfield, Ky., Jan. 26, 1931; s. Joe L. and Bonnie (Vincent) P.; m. Marilyn Maassen, Oct. 12, 1957; children: John P., Kevin R., Joel F. BS in Physics, U. Ky., 1952; MS Aero. Engring., Pa. State U., State College, 1964, PhD, 1966. Registered profl. engr., Tex. Commd. 2d lt. USAF, 1952, advanced through grades to maj., 1966, resigned, 1966; prof. Pa. State U., State Coll., 1966-68; design specialist Gen. Dynamics, Ft. Worth, 1968-69; prof. U. Tex., Arlington, 1969—, aero. engring. grad. advisor, 1973-82, 92-96; bd. dirs. TRL-Aero. Engring., U. Tex., 1972—; organizer profl. confs. Editor Integral Methods in Sci. Engring., 1986-91; editor newsletter Ft. Worth Chess Club, 1973-78, Tex. Chess Assn., 1977-78; contbr. articles to profl. jours. Chess instr. Dan Danciger Community Ctr., Ft. Worth, 1973-77; youth dir. Ft. Worth Chess Club, 1973-78. Rsch. grantee USN, NSF, NASA, 1963-67, 75-91, Orgn. Rsch. Fund, 1975-89; faculty fellow NASA Ames Rsch. Ctr., 1988, 89. Mem. Am. Math. Soc., Am. Phys. Soc., Am. Acad. Mechanics, Soc. for Indsl. and Applied Math., Ky. Chess Club, Tex. Chess Club (pres. 1950-52, 73-75), Sigma Xi (pres. U. Tex.-Arlington chpt. 1990-92). Avocations: chess master (postal), classical music, gardening. Office: U Tex Aerospace Engring Arlington TX 76019

PAYNE, GARELD GENE, vocal music educator, medical transcriptionist; b. Colony, Okla., Aug. 27, 1931; s. Eugene A. and Agnes D. (Chastain) P.; children: Gareld, S. Raymond, Lynn Dita, Jana Lee. MusB, Oklahoma City U., 1965; MusM in Edn., North Tex. State U. (name change to U. North Tex.), 1969; ednl. specialist, Pitts. State U., 1989; postgrad., Okla. State U. Ind. organist, pianist numerous nightclubs, nationwide, 1956-64; instr. vocal, instrumental music Muenster (Tex.) Ind. Sch. Dist., 1965-69; tchr. vocal music Dallas Ind. Sch. Dist., 1966-74, Carrizo Springs (Tex.) Ind. Sch. Dist., 1976-79, Coffeyville (Kans.) Unified Sch. Dist., 1979-91; tchr. elem. vocal music Oklahoma City Pub. Schs., 1996—. Rec. artist (album) Evening With Gareld, 1984; composer publ. anthems. With USAF, 1950-53. Scholar Oklahoma City U., 1949. Mem. Am. Fedn. Musicians, NEA, Am. Orff-Schulwerk Assn., Am. Recorder Soc., Am. Theater Organ Soc., Am. Guild Organist Orgns. of Am. Kodaly Educators, Phi Mu Alpha Sinfonia Frat., Phi Delta Kappa. Republican. Methodist. Avocations: astrology, oil and water color painting, cooking, reading, computers. Home: 3627 NW 15th St Oklahoma City OK 73107-4423

PAYNE, GERALD LEW, physics educator; b. Columbus, Ohio, Mar. 11, 1938; s. Harry Moses and Lucy Loretta (Frabott) P.; m. Candia Walker Draves, Dec. 31, 1963; children: Tracy, Lucy, Karen. BS in Engring., MS in Physics, Ohio State U., 1961; PhD in Physics, U. Calif., San Diego, 1967. Rsch. assoc. U. Md., College Park, 1967-69; asst. prof. physics U. Iowa, Iowa City, 1969-74, assoc. prof., 1974-80, prof., 1980—, chmn. dept. physics and astronomy, 1991—; cons. Los Alamos (N.Mex.) Nat. Lab., 1975—, Lockheed Rsch. Lab., Palo Alto, Calif., 1977-86. Contbr. over 100 articles to profl. jours. Lt. comdr. USN, 1961-64. Fellow NSF, 1965. Fellow Am. Phys. Soc.; mem. AAAS, AAUP, Am. Assn. Physics Tchrs. Democrat. Office: U Iowa 305 Van Dept Physics Iowa City IA 52242

PAYNE, GERALD OLIVER, retired elementary education educator; b. East St. Louis, Ill., July 17, 1930; s. Amos Oliver and Suzanne Louise (Goussery) P.; m. Nancy Louise Ecklund, Aug. 8, 1959; children: Paul Clifton, Christopher Amos, Scott Eric, Miriam Louise, Susan Jeannette. BA, Yale U., 1953; MusB, U. Dubuque, Iowa, 1957; PhD, U. Wis., 1969. Tchr. pub. schs. Aspen, Colo., 1959-61; tchr. pub. schs. Madison, 1961-65; coord. fgn. langs., 1964-69, asst. dir. curriculum, 1967-69; assoc. prof. edn. SUNY, Buffalo, 1969-71, prof. edn., 1971-86, chmn. dept. curriculum and supervision, 1975-78, coord. advanced studies in adminstrn. and supervision, 1969-75, 78-86, assoc. chmn. dept. elem. edn. and reading, 1985-86; chmn. dept. edn. and psychology Warren Wilson Coll., N.C., 1986-90, chmn. div. social sci. and profl. studies, 1987-90; tchr. Hendersonville (N.C.) County Schs., Hendersonville, N.C., 1990-96. Contbr. articles to profl. jours. Chmn. troop com. Greater Niagara Frontier coun. Boy Scouts Am., Lewiston, N.Y., 1974-76, scoutmaster, 1976-79; advisor Explorer Post, 1979-83, Order of Arrow, 1978-83; elder 1st Presbyn. Ch., Lewiston, 1978-83, 1st Presbyn. Ch., Hendersonville, N.C., 1991-94; leader Stephen Ministries. Mem. NEA (life), Western N.Y. Yale Alumni Assn. (mem. schs. com. 1972-83, dir. 1977-83), Nat. Middle Sch. Assn., Assn. for Supervision and Curriculum Devel., Phi Delta Kappa (exec. com. 1978-81, sec. 1985-86, pres.-elect 1986). Republican. Lodge: Masons. Home: RR 4 Box 287 Hendersonville NC 28739 also: 1119 Periwinkle Way 141 Sanibel Island FL 33957-4710

PAYNE, GLORIA MARQUETTE, business educator; b. Elkins, W.Va., Dec. 21, 1923; d. Anthony and Roselyn Marquette; m. Carl Wesley Payne, Mar. 6, 1950; 1 child, Mary Debra Payne Moore. BA, Davis and Elkins Coll., MHL (hon.); MA, W.Va. U.; PhD, U. Pitts., 1975; postgrad., NYU Fashion Inst. Tech. Cert. designed appearance cons. Sec. Equitable Ins. Co., Elkins, 1943-44; tchr., dept. head Spencer (W.Va.) High Sch., 1944-45; prof. bus. Davis & Elkins Coll., Elkins, 1945-93; image cons. Elkins, 1988-93, bus. cons., 1970-93; mgr. Elkins Wallpaper Shop, 1945-65; owner Merle Norman Cosmetic Studio, Elkins, 1950-56; dir. tchr. workshops W.Va. U., Marshall U., State Dept. Edn., Charleston, W.Va., summers; dir. machine shorthand workshops for tchrs. throughout the U.S.; dir. designer appearance World Modeling Assn., N.Y.C., 1989—; instr. modeling Davis & Elkins Coll., 1980-93. Author: A Methods Class is Interesting and Challenging, 1970, The Oak or the Pumpkin; mem. editl. bd. Nat. Assn. of Business Teachers Edn. Pub., 1993, 94; contbr. articles to profl. jours. Chair Bi-Centennial, City of Elkins; dir. Elkins Fair, City of Elkins; pres. St. Brendans Parish; judge Mountain State Forest Festival Parades, 1988-94; rep. Region I at Dallas Nat. Conv., 1994 (one of five nat. finalists); div. chair bus., econs., and tourism. Recipient Outstanding Prof. award Sears-Roebuck Co., Lois Latham award for Excelence in Teaching, Community Svc. award Elkins C. of C., 1992, award for Outstanding Educator W.Va. Vocat. Assn., 1994, Region I award for Outstanding Vocational Educator; 1st recipient James S. McDonnell Found. Fully Endowed Acad. Chair in Bus. and Econs.; named Educator of Yr., W.Va. Women's Club, Outstanding Educator AAUW. Mem. Am. Bus. Writers Assn., W.Va. Edn. Assn. (past pres., Outstanding Prof., Outstanding Svc. award, Outstanding Bus. Educator award), Tri-State Bus. Edn. Assn. (historian, outstanding svc. award, Tchr.-Educator of the South award 1991), World Modeling Assn. (v.p. 1988-90, modeling award 1989), Designed Appearance U.S. (dir. 1990-95), W.Va. C. of C., The Fashion Club (advisor), Beta Sigma Phi (advisor), Beta Alpha Beta (advisor), Pi Beta Phi, Phi Beta Lambda (advisor). Democrat. Roman Catholic. Avocations: flower arranging, modeling. Home: 301 Davis St Elkins WV 26241-4030 Office: Davis & Elkins Coll 100 Sycamore St Elkins WV 26241-3996

PAYNE, HARRY CHARLES, historian, educator; b. Worcester, Mass., Mar. 25, 1947. BA, Yale U., 1969, MA, 1969; PhD, 1973; MPhil, Yale U., 1970; hon. degree, Hamilton Coll., 1988, Colgate U., 1989, Williams Coll., 1993, Amherst Coll., 1994. Mem. faculty Colgate U., Hamilton, N.Y., 1973-85, prof. history, 1982-85; provost, acting pres. Haverford (Pa.) Coll., 1985-88; pres. Hamilton Coll., Clinton, N.Y., 1988-93, Williams Coll., Williamstown, Mass., 1994—. Contbr. numerous articles and revs. to scholarly publs. Bd. dirs. Clark Art Inst., Williamstown Theatre Festival, Barnard Coll., Nat. Assn. Ind. Colls. and Univs. (chair 1997), Mass. Mus. Contemporary Art. Overseas fellow Churchill Coll., Cambridge U., Eng., 1977. Mem. Am. Soc. 18th-Century Studies (Article prize 1977, pres. 1984-85). Office: Williams Coll Office of Pres Williamstown MA 01267

PAYNE, HARRY EUGENE, JR., state labor commissioner; b. Wilmington, Sept. 11, 1952; s. Harry E. and Margaret G. (Tucker) P.; m. Ruth Ann Sheehan, May 28, 1994; 1 child, Harry E., III. AB in Psychology and Polit. Sci., U. N.C., 1974; JD, Wake Forest U., 1977. Pvt. practice as lawyer; with Scott, Payne, Boyle & Swart, Wilmington; mem. N.C. Gen. Assembly, 1980-92; commr. labor N.C. Dept. Labor; co-chmn. adminstrv. rules rev. com. N.C. Gen. Assembly, 1983, chmn. mfrs. and labor com. 1985, chmn. constl. amendments com. 1987, chmn. rules, appointments and the calendar com. 1989, co-chmn. appropriations com. 1989, mem. subcom. edn.; adv. coun. constrn. safety U.S. Dept. Labor. Active N.C. Small Bus. Adv. Coun.; mem. indsl. tech. adv. bd. East Carolina U.; mem. adv. bd. Z. Smith Reynolds Found., Shaw-Speaks Ctr.; chmn. credentials com. 7th dist. Dem. Conv., 1980; mem. State Dem. Exec. Com., 1993—, N.C. Commn. Indian Affairs, 1993—; chmn. literacy task force Gov.'s Commn.. Workforce Preparedness, 1993—; bd. dirs. N.C. Pub. Sch. Forum, Cmty. Penalties, N.C. Ctr. Pub. Policy Rsch. Recipient Right-To-Know award N.C. Occupl. Safety and Health, 1985, Award of Appreciation, Southeastern Sickle Cell Assn., 1985, Award of Appreciation, Wilmington C. of C., 1987, Friends of Labor award Am. Fedn. Labor-Congress Indsl. Orgns., 1987, Award of Appreciation, N.C. Speech & Hearing Assn., 1987-88, Cert. of Appreciation, Boys Club Am., 1988, Susan B. Anthony award New Hanover chpt. NOW, 1987, Legis. award N.C. chpt. Am. Planning Assn., 1988, Disting. Svc. award N.C. Pub. Health Assn., 1990; named Consumer Adv. of Yr., N.C. Consumer Coun., 1985, Outstanding Govt. Ofcl., Wilmington Jaycees, 1986, Boss of Yr. Battleship chpt. Am. Bus. Womens' Assn., 1988, Legislator of Yr., N.C. Acad. Trial Lawyers, 1989, Legislator of Yr., N.C. Assn. Deaf, 1989. Mem. Nat. Assn. Govtl. Labor Ofcls. (1st v.p.), N.C. Bar Assn. (mem. dispute resolution com.), Southeastern Strategic Coun. Office: Labor Dept 4 W Edenton St Raleigh NC 27601-2805

PAYNE, HARRY MORSE, JR., architect; b. Norwood, Mass., Nov. 3, 1922; s. Harry Morse and Edna May (Beardsley) P.; m. Helen Marion Beasley, Aug. 29, 1946; children: Harry Morse, Thomas Beasley, Amelia Morse. Student, Boston Archtl. Center, 1946-49, MIT, 1949-50. Draftsman William G. Upham, Norwood, 1946-47; designer William Riseman Assos., Boston, 1947-49, Harry J. Korslund, Norwood, 1949-51, William Hoskins Brown, Boston, 1951-52; designer, prin. dir. The Architects Collaborative, Cambridge, Mass., 1952-86; pres. The Architects Collaborative, 1975-77, emeritus, 1986—; emeritus Boston Archtl. Center, 1963-65, 71-73; asst. prof. Harvard U. Grad. Sch. Design, 1954-63. Prin. works include U.S. Embassy, Athens, Greece, U. Baghdad, Iraq, Temple Israel, Boston, Quincy Sch., Boston; author: The Survey System of the Old Colony, 1985, Name Change—Paine to Payne, 1992, Cape Code Land Strategy, 1994. Served with USN, 1943-46. Fellow AIA; mem. Boston Soc. Architects, Mass. State Assn. Architects, New Eng. Hist. and Geneal. Soc., The Colonial Soc. Mass., Mass. Soc. Genealogists (pres. 1986-88), Lincoln Hist. Soc. (pres. 1990-92). Home: 245 Aspen Cir Lincoln MA 01773-4922

PAYNE, HOWARD JAMES, insurance company executive; b. Des Moines, Iowa, Oct. 22, 1940; s. James W. and Wilma F. (Kever) P.; m. Mary J. Kellam, June 8, 1963; children: Scott D., Steven M. MBA, U. Iowa, 1986. CPCU; assoc. in underwriting, assoc. in mgmt. Underwiter Allied Ins. Co., Des Moines, 1963-70; br. underwriting mgr. Allied Ins. Co., Phoenix, 1973-75; asst. br. mgr. Allied Ins. Co., Santa Rosa, Calif., 1975-77; casualty underwriting mgr. Am. States Ins. Co., Indpls., 1970-73; asst. v.p. underwriting Lumberman's Mut. Ins. Co., Mansfield, Ohio, 1977-80; asst. v.p., underwriting mgr. Hastings (Mich.) Mutual Ins. Co., 1980-82; v.p. underwriting John Deere Ins. Co., Moline, Ill., 1982-86, v.p., regional mgr., 1986-90; v.p. credit ins. mgr. John Deere Ins. Co, Des Moines, 1990-93; v.p., spl. program mgr. John Deere Transp., Brookfield, Wis., 1993—; ins. instr. Am. States Ins. Co., Indpls., 1971-73, CPCU chpt., Phoenix, 1973-75; ins. instr. and adviser C.C. Mansfield, Ohio, 1978-80; pres. Am. States Credit Union, Indpls., 1973. Mem. CPCU Soc., West Des Moines C. of C. Republican. Avocations: tennis, physical fitness, reading. Home: 1641A S Coachlight Dr New Berlin WI 53151 Office: John Deere Transp 350 N Sunny Slope Rd Brookfield WI 53005-4846

PAYNE, JOHN ROSS, rare books and archives appraisal consulting company executive, library science educator; b. Clarksville, Tex., Dec. 4, 1941. BA, Tex. Christian U., 1963; MLS, North Tex. State U., 1967. Successively acting dir., asst. to dir., assoc. libr. for acquisitions, assoc. libr. for ops., rsch. assoc. Harry Ransom Humanities Rsch. Ctr. U. Tex., Austin, 1969-85, prof. Grad. Sch. Libr. and Info. Sci., 1988-89, 91—, prof. grad. course in rare books and lit. manuscripts, 1989—; dir. Payne Assocs., 1978—. Author: A Bibliography of W. H. Hudson, 1977, Modern British Fiction: An Exhibit, 1972; co-author: (with Elizabeth Johnson) Katherine Mansfield: An Exhibit, 1973, (with Adrian Goldstone) A Bibliographical Catalogue of John Steinbeck, 1975; contbr. articles to profl. jours. Lilly fellow Ind. U., 1967-68. Mem. ALA, Am. Soc. Appraisers (state dep. dir.), Appraisers Assn. Am., Soc. Am. Archivists (hon., speaker at Atlanta meeting 1988), Manuscripts Soc., Tex. Libr. Assn., Tex. State Hist. Assn., Book Club of Tex., Grolier Club, Book Collectors of L.A. Home: 2309 Camino Alto Austin TX 78746-2404

PAYNE, KENNETH EUGENE, lawyer; b. Kansas City, Kans., Jan. 12, 1936; s. Felton T. and Irene Elizabeth (Snyder) P.; m. Deidre Lee Hood, Aug. 11, 1957; children: Steven Scott, Kendra Ann. BS, U. Kans., 1959; JD, Am. U., 1965. Bar: Mo. 1965, D.C. 1967. Assoc., Irons, Birch, Swindler & McKie, Washington, 1966-69; ptnr. Irons, Stockman, Sears & Santorelli, 1969-71; asst. gen. counsel U.S. Dept. Commerce, Washington, 1971-73; ptnr. Finnegan, Henderson, Farabow, Garrett & Dunner, Washington, 1973-96, mng. ptnr., 1990-96; del. Inter-Am. Commn. on Sci. and Tech. Transfer, U.S. Dept. State; cons. UN Indsl. Devel. Orgn.; lectr. Practicing Law Inst., Licensing Law and Bus. Inst. Capt. U.S. Army, 1960-68. Mem. Licensing

Execs. Soc. Internat. (treas. 1986-87, pres.-elect 1988, pres. 1989), Licensing Execs. Soc. U.S. and Can. (pres.-elect 1982-83, pres. 1983-84), ABA, Am. Patent Law Assn., Assn. Trial Lawyers Am. Republican. Methodist. Contbr. articles to profl. jours. Home: 4415 33rd St N Arlington VA 22207-4465 Office: Finnegan Henderson Farabow et al 1300 I St NW Ste 700 Washington DC 20005-3314

PAYNE, KEVIN JOSEPH, association executive; b. Yonkers, N.Y., Mar. 5, 1953; s. Joseph F. and Maureen L. (Delahanty) P.; m. Pamela Jane Groves, Oct. 18, 1980; children: Ashley Marie, Rebecca Fields. Student, LeMoyne Coll., Syracuse, N.Y., 1971-73, SUNY, Purchase, 1975-76. Asst. news dir. Radio Sta. WLNA-WHUD, Peekskill, N.Y., 1975-83; news corr. Radio Sta. WOR-AM, N.Y.C., 1980-83; news anchor Radio Sta. WCBS-FM, N.Y.C., 1982-83; news dir. Radio Sta. KVMT-FM, Vail, Colo., 1983-84; dir. chamber services Vail Resort Assn., 1984-85; exec. dir. Avon Beaver Creek (Colo.) Resort Assn., 1985-89; nat. adminstr. U.S. Soccer, 1989-90, dept. exec. dir., dir. mktg., 1990-91; exec. v.p. sales and mktg., then CEO Soccer USA Ptnrs. (now API Soccer), 1991—; pres./CEO D.C. United soccer team, Herndon, Va., 1994—; bd. dirs. World Ski Championships Organizing Com., Am. Ski Classic, Vail, 1984—; mem. mgmt., mktg. and competition coms. Major League Soccer; bd. dirs. Soccer 94 Found., Washington. Bd. dirs. Bravo! Colo. Performing Arts Found., Vail, 1987—, Internat. Sculpture Arts Ctr., Avon/Beaver Creek, 1986—, Eagle County Transit Commn., 1987—, Vail Soccer Club Inc., 1983—, Vail/Eagle Valley Arts Council, 1986. Recipient Regents scholarship N.Y. State, 1971,. Mem. Rocky Mountain Ski Writers (assoc.). Clubs: Homestead Ct., Singletree Golf (Edwards, Colo.). Lodge: Vail/Eagle Valley Rotary (bd. dirs. 1986-87). Home: 2580 Himalaya Ct Colorado Springs CO 80919-3832

PAYNE, LADELL, college president; b. Birmingham, Ala., Dec. 6, 1933; s. Clyde Ladell and Martha Gerusia (McBrayer) P.; m. Mary Jean Taylor, Aug. 23, 1954; children: Lisa, Jennifer. BA with honors, Samford U., 1955; MA in English, La. State U., 1956; PhD in English, Stanford U., 1966; LttD, Samford U., 1996. From instr. to prof. English, chmn. dept. lit. and presdl. asst. Claremont McKenna Coll., Calif., 1960-79; pres. Randolph-Macon Coll., Ashland, Va., 1979—; Fulbright lectr. U. Vienna, Austria, 1971-72; nat. cons. Ctr. for Study So. Culture, U. Miss., Oxford, 1980—; adminstrv. assoc. Am. Coun. on Edn., Washington, 1979, mem. nat. panel, commn. on women in higher edn., 1981—; founding mem. pres.'s commn. Nat. Collegiate Athletic Assn., 1984—. Author: Thomas Wolfe, 1969, Black Novelists and the Southern Literary Tradition, 1981; contbr. articles on William Faulkner, Robert Penn Warren, Thomas Wolfe, and Ellen Glasgow to profl. jours. Mem. Va. bd. dirs. NCCJ, 1980-92, chmn. Va. region, Richmond, 1982-85; trustee, mem. exec. com. The Collegiate Schs., Richmond, 1986-89. NEH fellow, 1973. Mem. Nat. Assn. Ind. Colls. and Univs. (bd. dirs. 1990-93), Coun. on Postsecondary Accreditation (bd. dirs. 1991-93), Phi Kappa Phi, Phi Beta Kappa. Methodist. Avocation: classical music. Office: Randolph-Macon Coll Office of the President PO Box 5005 Ashland VA 23005

PAYNE, LAWRENCE EDWARD, mathematics educator; b. Enfield, Ill., Oct. 2, 1923; s. Robert Ulysses and Harriet (Lasher) P.; m. Ruth Marian Winterstein, Dec. 27, 1948; children: Steven L., John E., Marcia G., Christopher J., Michele T. Student, Miami U., Oxford, Ohio, 1943-44; B.S. in Mech. Engring, Iowa State U., 1946, M.S. in Applied Math, 1948, Ph.D., 1950; DSc (hon.), Nat. U. Ireland, 1990. Jr. engr. Linde Air Products, North Tonawanda, N.Y., 1946-47; asst. prof. math. U. Ariz., 1950-51; research assoc. U. Md., 1951-52, asst. prof., 1952-55, asso. prof., 1955-60, prof., 1960-65; prof. Cornell U., Ithaca, N.Y., 1965-94; prof. emeritus Cornell U., Ithaca, N.Y., 1994—; dir. Center for Applied Math. Cornell U., 1967-71, 76-77, 80-81; Lectr. in field; cons. Nat. Bur. Standards, 1958-65. Mem. editorial bd. Jour. of Elasticity, Applicable Analysis, Math. Methods in the Applied Sciences, Stability and Applied Analysis of Continuous Media; contbr. articles to profl. jours. Served with USNR, 1943-46. Recipient Sci. Achievement Math. award Washington Acad. Scis., 1962, Citation of Merit Iowa State U., 1992; NSF sr. postdoctoral fellow, 1958-59. Mem. Am. Math. Soc. (Steele prize in math. 1972), Soc. Indsl. Applied Math., Am. Acad. Mechanics, Soc. Engring. Sci., Soc. Natural Philosophy, Internat. Soc. for the Interaction Mechanics and Math., Royal Soc. of Edinburgh (elected hon. fellow. 1991), Sigma Xi. Office: Cornell U Dept Math Ithaca NY 14853

PAYNE, LESLIE, newspaper editor, columnist, journalist, author; b. Tuscaloosa, Ala., July 12, 1941; m. Violet S. Cameron; children—Tamara Olympia, Jamal Kenyatta, Haile K. B.A., U. Conn., 1964. Reporter Newsday, L.I., N.Y., 1969-73, copy editor, mag. editor, 1973, minority affairs specialist, 1974-77, nat. corr., 1977-81, syndicated columnist, 1980—, nat. editor, 1981-85, asst. mng. editor, 1985—; judge Pulitzer Prize Selection Com., 1983, 84, Emmy Blue-Ribbon Panel, Acad. TV Arts and Scis., 1981, 83. Author: Life and Death of the Symbionese Liberation Army, 1976; co-author: Heroin Trail, 1974. Served to capt. U.S. Army, 1963-69. Decorated Bronze Star; recipient Pulitzer prize, 1974, Tobenkin award Columbia U., 1978, World Hunger Media award UN, 1983, Unity award Lincoln U., Journalism prize Howard U., AP and UPI awards (commentary), 1984, numerous other awards. Mem. Nat. Assn. Black Journalists (pres. 1981-83), Com. to Protect Journalists, Internat. Press Inst. Avocations: painting; softball; mountain climbing. Office: Newsday Inc 235 Pinelawn Rd Melville NY 11747-4226*

PAYNE, LEWIS FRANKLIN, JR. (L.F. PAYNE), former congressman; b. Amherst, Va., July 9, 1945; m. Susan King; children: Graham, Hunter, Sara, Anna. BA, Va. Mil. Inst., 1967; MBA, U. Va. Mem. 100th-104th Congresses from 5th Va. dist., Washington, 1988-96. Democrat. Presbyterian. Office: PO Box 767 Charlottesville VA 22902*

PAYNE, MARY ALICE MCGILL, mental health quality consultant; b. Centreville, Miss., Jan. 2, 1936; d. Robert Malcolm and Alice (Brannon) McGill; m. Donald Ray Payne, Aug. 8, 1958; children: Patricia Alice, Margaret Jean, Donald Paul. Diploma, So. Bapt. Hosp. Sch. Nursing, New Orleans, 1958; BSN, Northwestern State U., 1962, postgrad. Psychiat. nursing instr. McNeese U., Lake Charles, La., 1964-67; drug rsch. nurse dept. psychiatry Med. Sch., Tulane U., New Orleans, 1969-79; psychiat. nurse East La. State Hosp., Jackson, 1959-80; acting CEO Feliciana Forensic Facility, Jackson, 1989, quality assurance dir., 1984-91. Mem. ANA, NAFE, Am. Psychiat. Nurses Assn., Am. Coll. Healthcare Execs. (assoc.), La. State Nurses Assn., Nat. Assn. Healthcare Quality, La. Assn. Healthcare Quality, Bapt. Nursing Fellowship, Feliciana Dist. Nurses Assn., Am. Soc. Quality Control, Nat. League for Nursing. Home: PO Box 144 3226 E College St Jackson LA 70748-0144

PAYNE, MARY LIBBY, judge; b. Gulfport, Miss., Mar. 27, 1932; d. Reece O. and Emily Augusta (Cook) Bickerstaff; m. Bobby R. Payne; children: Reece Allen, Glenn Russell. Student, Miss. Univ. Women, 1950-52; BA in Polit. Sci. with distinction, U. Miss., 1954, LLB, 1955. Bar: Miss. 1955. Ptnr. Bickerstaff & Bickerstaff, Gulfport, 1955-56; sec. Guaranty Title Co., Jackson, Miss., 1957; assoc. Henley, Jones, & Henley, Jackson, Miss., 1958-61; freelance rschr. Pearl, Miss., 1961-63; solo practitioner Brandon, Miss., 1963-68; exec. dir. Miss. Judiciary Commn., Jackson, 1968-70; chief drafting & rsch. Miss. Ho. Reps., Jackson, 1970-72; asst. atty. gen. State Atty. Gen. Office, Jackson, 1972-75; founding dean, assoc. prof. Sch. Law Miss. Coll., Jackson, 1975-78, prof., 1978-94; judge Miss. Ct. Appeals, Jackson, 1995—; adv. bd. Sarah Ison Ctr. Women Studies U. Miss., 1988-97; bd. disting. alumnae Miss. U. Women, 1988-97. Contbr. articles to profl. jours. Founder, bd. dirs. Christian Conciliation Svc., Jackson, 1983-93; counsel Christian Action Com. Rankin Bapt. Assn., Pearl, 1968-92. Recipient Book of Golden Deeds award Pearl Exch. Club, 1989, Excellence medallion Miss. U. Women, 1990; named Woman of Yr. Miss. Assn. Women Higher Edn., 1989, Miss. Woman '96 Miss. Gov.'s Conf., 1996. Fellow Am. Bar Found.; mem. Christian Legal Soc. (nat. bd. dirs., regional membership coord.). Baptist. Avocations: public speaking, travel, needlepoint, sewing, reading. Office: Ct Appeals PO Box 22847 Jackson MS 39225

PAYNE, MAXWELL CARR, JR., retired psychology educator; b. Nashville, Feb. 9, 1927; s. Carr and Mary Evans (Tarpley) P.; m. Juanita Campbell, Oct. 17, 1958; children: Maxwell Carr III, Elizabeth Campbell McKinney, Mary Allison Klausner. AB, Vanderbilt U., 1949; AM, Princeton U., 1950, PhD, 1951. Rsch. assoc. U. Ill., Urbana, 1951-54; asst. prof. psychology Ga. Inst. Tech., Atlanta, 1954-60, assoc. prof., 1961-65, prof., 1965-90, ret., 1991; cons. Lockheed-Ga. Co., Marietta, 1963; testing dir. Aircrew Ctr., Am. Insts. Rsch., Atlanta, 1960-75; faculty Atlanta Sch. Art, 1970; mem. Ga. State Bd. Examiners of Psychologists, 1970-74. Contbr. articles to profl. jours. Sunday Sch. tchr. Northside United Meth. Ch., Atlanta, 1989—. With USNR, 1944-46. Recipient Disting. Tchr. award Ga. Inst. Tech., 1970. Fellow AAAS; mem. Am. Psychol. Assn., Ga. Psychol. Assn. (Cert. of Merit), Southeastern Psychol. Assn., So. Soc. Philosophy and Psychology (treas. 1971-74, pres. 1985-86), Ga. Inst. Tech. Faculty Club (pres. 1970), Phi Beta Kappa, Sigma Xi, Phi Kappa Phi, Omicron Delta Kappa, Beta Theta Pi. Avocation: gardening. Home: 3035 Farmington Dr NW Atlanta GA 30339-4704

PAYNE, MEREDITH JORSTAD, physician; b. St. Louis, Feb. 7, 1927; d. Louis Helmar and Cleone Gladys (Branian) Jorstad; m. Spencer Payne, 1948 (div. 1959); m. James McGarity, 1965 (div. 1977); children: Maureen Meredith, James Louis. AB, Washington U., St. Louis, 1947, MD, 1950. Diplomate Am. Bd. Surgery, Am. Bd. Plastic Surgery. Intern gen. surgery St. Louis City Hosp., 1950-51, asst. resident surgery, 1951-54; chief surg. resident Roswell Park Meml. Hosp., Buffalo, 1954-55; chief plastic surgery resident Allentown (Pa.) Gen. Hosp., 1955-57; clin. instr. surgery Washington U. Med. Sch., 1957-70; vis. surgeon Homer G. Phillips Hosp., St. Louis, 1957-70; staff St. Luke's, St. Louis and Bethesda, 1957—, St. Mary's, 1988—, Vets. Hosp., 1986—; assoc. prof. plastic surgery (clin.) St. Louis U. Sch. Medicine, St. Louis, 1986—; bd. dirs. Blue Cross and Blue Shield, St. Louis, 1985-89; med. dir. St. Luke's Cleft Palate Clinic. Contbr. articles to profl. jours. Fellow ACS; mem. AMA, Am. Soc. Plastic and Reconstructive Surgery, Mo. Med. Assn. (del., councillor 1988—), St. Louis Met. Med. Soc. (councillor 1983-86), Am. Cleft Palate Assn., Roswell Park Surgery Assn., So. Med. Assn., Washington U. Med. Alumni Assn., Am. Geriatrics Soc., Midwestern Assn. Plastic Surgeons, Pan Am. Med. Assn., City Hosp. Alumni Assn., Soc. Head and Neck Surgeons, St. Louis Area Soc. Plastic Surgeons (pres. 1990-93), City Hosp. Alumni Assn. (v.p. 1995), Mo. Assn. Plastic and Reconstructive Surgery (treas. 1995—), AMWA (treas. St. Louis chpt. 1995), Order Eastern Star, Zonta (St. Louis pres. 1968-69), College Club (bd. dirs. St. Louis 1983-85). Avocations: skiing, tennis, sewing, knitting, gardening. Home: 7314 Westmoreland Dr Saint Louis MO 63130-4240 Office: 224 S Woods Mill Rd Ste 320 Chesterfield MO 63017-3451

PAYNE, MICHAEL CLARENCE, gastroenterologist; b. Chgo., June 30, 1955; s. Clarence H. and Mary P.; m. Cynthia Dillon, June 25, 1983; children: Morgan, Tyler, Dillon, Slater. AB in Biochem. cum laude, Harvard U., 1977, MD, 1982, MPH, 1982. Diplomate Am. Bd. Internal Medicine, Gastroenterology. Intern Beth Israel Hosp., Boston, 1982-85, resident; fellowship New England Med. Ctr.; pvt. practice in gastroenterology Williamstown (Mass.) Med. Assocs., 1988—. Fellow Am. Coll. Gastroenterology; mem. ACP, AGA, ASGE, AMA, ACG. Office: Williamstown Med Assocs 197 Adams Rd Williamstown MA 01267-2930

PAYNE, MICHAEL DAVID, English language educator; b. Dallas, Jan. 17, 1941; s. Fred G. Payne and Jocie Marie (Kirkham) Lundberg; children: Jeffrey, Jennifer, Albert, Edward. Student, U. Calif.-Berkeley, 1958-59, 61; B.A., So. Oreg. Coll., 1962; Ph.D., U. Oreg., 1969. Tchr. English, Medford (Oreg.) Sr. High Sch., 1962-63; instr. English, U. Oreg., Eugene, 1963-69; asst. prof. to prof. English, Bucknell U., Lewisburg, Pa., 1969—, chmn. dept. history, 1980-82, chmn. dept. English, 1982-88, 92-94, Presdl. prof., 1982-86, John P. Crozer prof. English lit., 1986—; dir. Bucknell Univ. Press, 1972-76; assoc. editor Bucknell Rev., 1970-85, editor, 1985-88. Author: Irony in Shakespeare's Roman Plays, 1974, Reading Theory, 1993, Reading Knowledge, 1997; editor: Contemporary Essays on Style, 1969, Shakespeare: Contemporary Critical Approaches, 1979, Text, Interpretation, Theory, 1985, Perspective, 1986, Criticism, History and Intertextuality, 1987, The Senses of Stanley Cavell, 1988, Blackwell Dictionary of Cultural and Critical Theory, 1996; gen. editor Bucknell Lectures in Lit. Theory, 1990-95. Recipient Lindback award for disting. teaching, 1976, Disting. Svc. award CEA, 1988, Profl. Achievement award, 1993; Folger Shakespeare Libr. fellow, 1973, NEH fellow, 1974, Bucknell Alumni fellow, 1978-79. Mem. Johnson Soc. London, Inst. for Romance Studies (U. London), MLA, Coll. English Assn., Phi Beta Kappa (hon.). Home: 9 Market St Apt A Lewisburg PA 17837-1632

PAYNE, MICHAEL LEE, association management executive; b. Monroe, N.C., Aug. 6, 1948; s. Robert H. and Martha (Brooks) P. BA in History, U. S.C., 1970, BA in Journalism, 1971; BA in Polit. Sci., 1972. Program dir. Coastal Plains Reg. Commn., Washington, 1972-75; dir. fed. rels. Office Coastal Zone Mgmt. NOAA, Washington, 1975-80; investment specialist Econ. Dirs. Adminstrn. U.S. Dept. Commerce, Washington, 1980-82; dep. to asst. sec. for congl. affairs Office of Sec. U.S. Dept. Commerce, Washington, 1982-84; sr. v.p. Smith-Bucklin Assoc., Washington, 1984—; bd. dirs. Smith-Bucklin Assoc.; presenter to hospitality industry. Author: Complete Guide to Non-Profit Management, 1993; contbr. numerous articles to profl. publs. Mem. Am. Soc. Assn. Execs., Profl. Convention Mgrs. Assn., Meeting Profls. Internat. Avocations: travel, tennis, fishing, handball, biking. Office: Smith-Bucklin Assoc 1200 19th St NW Washington DC 20036-2412

PAYNE, NANCY SLOAN, visual arts educator; b. Johnstown, Pa., Aug. 5, 1937; d. Arthur J. and Esther Jenkins (Ashcom) Sloan; m. Randolph Allen Payne, Nov. 19, 1970; 1 child, Anna Sloan. BS in Art Edn., Pa. State U., 1959; MFA in Sculpture, George Washington U., 1981. Visual arts tchr. Alexandria (Va.) Schs., 1960-61; art tchr. sch. program Corcoran Gallery of Art, Washington, 1962; visual arts tchr. Montgomery County Schs., Rockville, Md., 1965-67; instr. No. Va. C.C., Alexandria, 1971-73, Mt. Vernon Coll., Washington, 1971-73; visual arts tchr. Arlington (Va.) County Schs., 1967-79; edn. coord. The Textile Mus., Washington, 1982-87; mid. sch. visual arts tchr., K-12 dept. chair St. Stephen's and St. Agnes Sch., Alexandria, 1988—; co-founder Fiber Art Study Group, Washington, 1988—; co-owner Art Gallery, Chincoteague Island, Va., 1989—. Exhibited in group shows at Craftsmen's Biennial Va. Commonwealth U. (Excellence in Textiles award), 1973, Va. Craftsmen Biennial The Va. Mus., 1980, Creative Crafts Coun. 15th Biennial, 1982, Alexandria's Sculpture Festival, 1983, 84, 13 Fiber Artists Exhbn. Foundry Gallery, Washington, 1985. Founding mem. Alexandria Soc. for Preservation Black Heritage, Alexandria, 1982—. Mem. Nat. Art Edn. Assn. Democrat. Avocations: growing flowers, collecting hub caps, McDonald toys, and polit./campaign items. Home: 600 Johnston Pl Alexandria VA 22301-2512 Office: 4401 W Braddock Rd Alexandria VA 22304-1009

PAYNE, PAULA MARIE, minister; b. Waukegan, Ill., Jan. 13, 1952; d. Percy Howard and Annie Maude (Canady) P. BA, U. Ill., 1980; MA, U. San Francisco, 1986; MDiv, Wesley Theol. Sem., 1991, student, 1995—. Ordained to ministry United Meth. Ch., 1990. Chaplain for minority affairs Am. U., Washington, 1988-89; chaplain, intern NIH, Bethesda, Md., 1989-90; pastor Asbury United Meth. Ch., Charles Town, W.Va., 1990—; supt. ch. sch. United Meth. Ch., Oxon Hill, Md., 1989-90; mem. AIDS task force Wesley Theol. Sem., Washington, 1988-89; mem. retreat. com. Balt. Conf., 1990—; chair scholarship com. Asbury United Meth. Ch., 1990—. Bd. dirs. AIDS Task Force Jefferson County, Charles Town, 1991—, Cmty. Ministries, Charles Town, 1991—. Tech. sgt. USAF, 1984-88; chaplain Army N.G., Md., 1994-96; chaplain USAFR, 1997. Recipient Cert. of Recognition, Ill. Ho. of Reps., 1988, 20th Century award of Achievement Internat. Biog. Ctr., Cambridge, Eng., 1993, 1st Five Hundred, Cambridge, 1994, Citizen's citation, City of Balt., 1994, others; Ethnic Minority scholar United Meth. Ch., 1988-89, Brandenburg scholar, 1988-89, Tadlock scholar, 1989-90, Calvary Fellow scholar Calvary United Meth. ch., 1989-90. Mem. U. Ill. Alumni Assn. (bd. dirs. 1987-88), Alpha Kappa Alpha (pres. local chpt. 1974-76, v.p. 1973). Democrat. Home: 8005 Richard Dr Forestville MD 20747 *What good is excellence in scholarship, if one cannot lead souls to Christ.*

PAYNE, ROBERT E., federal judge; b. 1941. BA in Polit. Sci., Washington and Lee U., 1963; LLB magna cum laude, Washington & Lee U., 1967. Assoc., ptnr. McGuire, Woods, Battle & Boothe, Richmond, Va., 1971-92; fed. judge U.S. Dist. Ct. (ea. dist.) Va., 1992—. Notes editor Wash. & Lee U. Law Rev. Capt. U.S. Army, 1967-71. Mem. ABA, Va. Bar Assn., Va. State Bar Assn., Va. Assn. Def. Attys. (chmn. comml. litigation sect. 1989-91), Richmond Bar Assn., Order of Coif. Episcopalian. Office: Lewis F Powell Jr US Courthouse 1000 E Main St Ste 334 Richmond VA 23219-3525

PAYNE, ROBERT WALTER, psychologist, educator; b. Calgary, Alta., Can., Nov. 5, 1925; s. Reginald William and Nora (Cowdery) P.; m. Helen June Mayer, Dec. 1948 (div. 1972); children: Raymond William, Barbara Joan, Margaret June; m. Josephine Mary Riley Adams, Mar. 1977 (div. 1982); children: George Reginald Alexander, Robin Charles; m. Jean Isobel Dawson, Aug., 1983. B.A., U. Alta., 1949; Ph.D., U. London, Eng., 1954. Lectr. psychology Inst. Psychiatry U. London, 1952-59; prof. psychology Queens U., Kingston, Ont., 1959-65; prof. psychology, chmn. dept. behavioral sci. Temple U. Med. Sch., Phila., 1965-73; prof. dept. psychiatry Temple U. Med. Sch., 1973-78; med. research scientist III Eastern Pa. Psychiat. Inst., Phila., 1965-78; prof. psychology U. Victoria, B.C., Can., 1978-91, prof. emeritus, 1991—, dean Faculty Human and Social Devel., 1978-83. Contbr. articles to profl. jours. Recipient Stratton Research award, 1964. Fellow Am. Psychol. Assn., Brit. Psychol. Soc., Canadian Psychol. Assn., Am. Psychopath. Assn. Home: 2513 Sinclair Rd, Victoria, BC Canada V8N 1B5

PAYNE, ROGER LEE, geographer; b. Winston-Salem, N.C., Oct. 26, 1946; s. Irvin Lee and Gladys Odel (Binkley) P.; m. Sara Lucinda Parker, Aug. 16, 1970 (div. Feb. 1992); 1 child, Jennifer Nicole; m. Anne F. Remen, June 11, 1995. BA, East Carolina U., 1969, MA, 1972. Geographer, chief geog. names U.S. Geol. Survey, Reston, Va., 1974—; instr. geography and history Pan Am. Inst./U.S. Geog. Survey, 1989—; exec. sec. U.S. Bd. Names, U.S. Geol. Survey, Washington, 1990—; part-time instr. East Caroline U., Greenville, N.C., 1979-81, George Washington U., Washington, 1977-90, George Mason U., Fairfax, Va., 1979-83, Benjamin Franklin U., Washington, 1985-87; del. UN, N.Y.C., 1987—, instr., 1995—; mem. scientist exch. Geol. Survey, Beijing, 1989; instr. Nat. Black Colls., Howard U., 1985. Author: Urban Development in South Africa, 1972, Place Names of Outer Banks, 1985, Manuals on Auto Names, 1987, 89; coord., editor: (book series) National Gazetter U.S., 1982—; contbr. articles, revs. to profl. jours. Chmn. E. Carolina Blood Dr., Greenville, 1969. Lt. USAF, 1970-72. Recipient Guy Buzzard award Gamma Theta Upsilon, 1970; Superior Svc. award Geol. Survey, 1988. Fellow Explorers Club; mem. Assn. Am. Geographers (various coms. 1969-95, pres. mid-Atlantic divsn. 1981-82, treas., sec.), Am. Name Soc. (pres. 1989), Am. Nat. Std. Inst. (rep. 1986), Cosmos Club. Avocations: hiking, volleyball. Home: 47762 Hammerstone Way Sterling VA 20165-4769 Office: US Geol Survey 523 National Ctr 12201 Sunrise Valley Dr Reston VA 20191-3401

PAYNE, ROGER S., conservation organization executive; b. N.Y.C., Jan. 29, 1935; m. Katy Boynton, 1960 (div. 1985); chilren: John, Holly, Laura Sam; m. Lisa Harrow. AB in Aminal Behavior, Harvard U., 1957; PhD, Cornell U. Rsch. zoologist Inst. for Rsch. in Animal Behavior N.Y. Zool. Inst., N.Y.C., 1968-71; asst. prof. biology Rockefeller U., N.Y.C., 1968-71; founder, pres. Whale Conservation Inst., Lincoln, Mass., 1971—. Author: Among Whales, 1995; host (TV documentary) In the Company of Whales, 1992 (series) Ocean Planet, 1994-95. Co-recipient Albert Schweitzer medal Animal Welfare Inst., 1980; recipient Joseph Wood Krutch medal Humane Soc. U.S., 1989, Lyndhurst prize Lyndhurst Found., 1994; genius grantee John D. and Catherine T. MacArthur Found., 1984. Office: World Wildlife Fund Depr Ecology Conservat 191 Weston Rd Lincoln MA 01773-4516*

PAYNE, ROY STEVEN, judge; b. New Orleans, Aug. 30, 1952; s. Fred J. and Dorothy Julia (Peck) P.; m. Laureen Fuller, Sept. 8, 1973; children: Julie Elizabeth, Kelly Kathryn, Alex Steven, Michael Lawrence. BA with distinction, U. Va., 1974; JD, La. State U., 1977; LLM, Harvard U., 1980. Bar: La. 1977, U.S. Dist. Ct. (we. dist.) La. 1980, U.S. Ct. Appeals (5th cir.) 1980, U.S. Supreme Ct. 1983. Law clk. to judge U.S. Dist. Ct., Shreveport, La., 1977-79; assoc. Blanchard, Walker, O'Quin & Roberts, Shreveport, 1980-83, ptnr., 1984-87; U.S. Magistrate judge, We. Dist. La., Shreveport, 1987—; instr. New Eng. Sch. Law, Boston, 1979-80. Contbr. articles to profl. jours. Chmn. Northwest La. Legal Svcs. Assn., Shreveport, 1984-85. Mem. 5th Cir. Bar Assn., 5th Cir. Jud. Coun. (magistrate judges com. 1992—), La. State Bar Assn. (editorial bd. Forum jour., 1983-87, legal aid com.), Fed. Magistrate Judges Assn., Shreveport Bar Assn., La. Assn. Def. Counsel (bd. dirs. 1987), Harry V. Booth Am. Inn of Ct. (pres. elect 1994-95, pres. 1996—), Order of Coif, Rotary, Phi Kappa Phi, Phi Delta Phi. Methodist. Home: 12494 Harts Island Rd Shreveport LA 71115-8505 Office: US Courthouse 300 Fannin St Ste 4300 Shreveport LA 71101-3121

PAYNE, R.W., JR., lawyer; b. Norfolk, Va., Mar. 16, 1936; s. Roland William and Margaret (Sawyer) P.; m. Gail Willingham, Sept. 16, 1961; children: Darrell, Preston, Darby, Clinton. BA in English, U. N.C., 1958, LLB, 1961; LLB, Stetson U., 1962. Bar: Fla. 1963, U.S. Dist. Ct. (so. dist.) 1964, U.S. Ct. Appeals (11th cir.) 1965, U.S. Supreme Ct. 1970. Assoc. Roney & Beach, St. Petersburg, Fla., 1963-64, Nichols, Giather, Beckham, Miami, Fla., 1964-67; ptnr. Spence, Payne, Masington, Miami, 1967-95, Payne, Leeds, Colby & Robinson, P.A., Miami, 1995—; presenter numerous profl. convs. and seminars. Contbr. articles to legal jours., legal edn. books. Mem. Ottawa Roughriders, Can. Football League, fall 1958; capt. football team U. N.C., 1957, bd. dirs., v.p. alumni bd., 1984-92, bd. dirs. ednl. found., 1988-92; bd. dirs. Chem. Dependency Tng. Inst.; past pres. Coral Gables (Fla.) Sr. H.S. Athletic Boosters Club; past bd. dirs. Coral Gables War Meml. Youth Ctr., 1st United Meth. Ch. Coral Gables; past mem. gov.'s coun. on phys. fitness and sports, Fla.; past assoc. mem. Jr. Orange Bowl Com. With USMC, 1959. Fellow Am. Coll. Trial Lawyers, Internat. Acad. Trial Lawyers; mem. ABA, Fla. Bar Assn., Acad. Fla. Trial Lawyers (past mem. bd. govs.), Dade County Bar Assn. (past bd. dirs.), Dade County Trial Lawyers Assn. (founder, past pres.), Bankers Club, Miami Club, Univ. Club, Coral Reef Yacht Club, Order of Golden Fleece, Order of Old Well, Sigma Chi, Phi Delta Phi. Avocations: boating, golf, diving. Office: Payne Leeds Colby Robinson 2950 SW 27th Ave Ste 300 Miami FL 33133-3765

PAYNE, SIDNEY STEWART, archbishop; b. Fogo, Nfld., Can., June 6, 1932; m. Selma Carlson, 1962; children: Carla Ann, Christopher Stewart, Robert Clement, Angela Marie Louise. BA, Meml. U., St. John's, Nfld., 1958; lic. of theology, Queen's Coll., St. John's, 1958; BDiv, Gen. Synod, 1968; DDiv (hon.), King's Coll., Halifax, N.S., Can., 1981. Ordained priest Anglican Ch., 1958, bishop, 1978, archbishop, 1990. Deacon Mission of Happy Valley, Goose Bay, Labrador, Nfld., Can., 1957-65; rector Parish of Bay Roberts, Nfld., Can., 1965-70, Parish of St. Anthony, Nfld., 1970-76, 1976-78; bishop Diocese of Western Nfld., 1978-90, archbishop of Western Nfld. and Met. Eccles. Province of Can., 1990—; pres. Diocesan Synod, chmn. exec. com., mem. ex-officio diocesan coms.; pres. Provincial Synod, Provincial Coun.; chair Provincial House of Bishops; mem. long range planning com., ministry com., mem. nat. exec. coun. Partners in World Mission, Stewardship and Fin. Devel. Com.; mem. Anglican/Roman Cath. Bishops' Dialogue, Can.; active Provincial and Nat. House of Bishops. Mem. Internat. Grenfell Assn. (past bd. dirs.). Avocations: reading, walking, gardening, cross-country skiing. Home: 13 Cobb Ln, Corner Brook, NF Canada A2H 1C2 Office: Anglican Diocesan Ctr, 25 Main St, Corner Brook, NF Canada A2H 1C2

PAYNE, THOMAS L., university official; b. Bakersfield, Calif., Oct. 17, 1941; s. Harry LeRoy and Opal Irene (Ansel) P.; m. S. Alice Lewis, Feb. 1, 1963; children: Jacob, Joanna. AA in Liberal Arts, Bakersfield (Calif.) Jr. Coll., 1962; BA in Zoology, U. Calif., Riverside, 1965, MS in Entomology, 1967, PhD in Entomology, 1969. Asst. prof. entomology and forest sci. Tex. A&M U., College Station, 1969-73, assoc. prof., 1973-78, prof., 1978-87, rsch. coord. USDA so. pine beetle program, 1974-78; prof. entomology, head dept. Va. Poly. and State U., Blacksburg, 1987-92; dir. Ohio Agrl. R & D Ctr., assoc. dean for rsch. Ohio State U. Coll. Agr., Wooster, 1993—; sec. protection sect. Nat. Planning Conf. for Rsch. in Forestry and assoc. Rangelands, 1977; bd. dirs. Urban Pest Control Rsch. Ctr. Endowment Fund, 1988—; dean's rep., ex officio mem. Va. Pesticide Control Bd., 1989—; vis. prof. Forest Zoology Inst., U. Freiburg, Germany, 1978. Editor: (with Birch and Kennedy) Mechanisms in Insect Olfaction, 1986; mem. editorial bd. Jour. Ga. Entomol. Soc., 1979-83; co-editor Jour. Insect Behavior, 1987—; contbr. chpts. to books. Pres., co-founder Brazos County Firefighters Assn., 1979-81; v.p., co-founder Precinct 2 Vol. Fire Dept., 1979-80, pres., 1982-86; author grant to build Edge Tex. Sr. Citizens Ctr., 1979; mem. Friends of Blacksburg Master Chorale. Recipient numerous awards, 1976—, including cert. of appreciation for svc. as rsch. coord. expanded so. pine beetle rsch. USDA, 1976, 78, 80, rsch. award Tex. Forestry Assn., 1977, awards Am. Registry Profl. Entomologists, 1979, Alexander von Humboldt Stiftung sr. U.S. scientist award, 1982, Faculty Disting. Achievement award in rsch. Assn. Former Students Tex. A&M U., 1985, A.D. Hopkins award for outstanding rsch.-adminstrn. in forest entomology, 1991; Volkswagenwerk fellow U. Freiburg, 1978. Mem. AAAS, Entomol. Soc. Am. (CIBA-GEIGY agrl. recognition award 1982), Internat. Soc. Chem. Ecology, Internat. Chemoreception Workshop on Insects, Internat. Union Forest Rsch. Orgns., Nat. Corn Growers Assn., So. Forest Insect Work Conf., Va. Agribus. Coun., Va. Agrl. Chem. and Soil Fertility Assn., Va. Hort. Soc. (exec. coun. 1989), Va. Corn Growers Assn., Va. Soybean Assn., Va. Pest Control Assn, Western Forest Insect Work Conf., Coll. Agr. and Life Scis. Agr. Faculty Assn., Sigma Xi, Gamma Sigma Delta. Office: Ohio State U Ohio Agrl R & D Ctr 1680 Madison Ave Wooster OH 44691-4114*

PAYNE, TIMOTHY E., management consultant; b. Valdosta, Ga., Oct. 12, 1948; s. Ernest Elbert and Lorraine (Tomlinson) P. BS, Valdosta State U., 1971. Profl. safety cert. Nat. Safety Coun.; cert. assoc. in risk mgmt. Ins. Inst. Am. Sr. cons. Kent Watkins & Assocs., Miami, Fla., 1975-80; mgmt. engrng. coord. U. Fla., Gainesville, 1980-86; adminstrv. sys. mgr. Amelia Island (Fla.) Co., 1986-89; CEO, pres. Payne & Assocs., Gainesville, Fla., 1989—; cons. Grace Com., Gainesville, 1991; teaching asst. La. State U., New Orleans, 1971. Author: Industrial Location Survey, 1971, (workbook) Bonus Calculation Procedures, 1977; contbr. articles to Indsl. Mgmt. Jour., Compete, Jour. Competitive Techs. Internat. Gov.'s intern State Ga., Atlanta, 1971. Mem. Am. Soc. Safety Engrs., Nat. Safety Mgmt. Soc. (state v.p. 1994—). Avocations: golf, tennis.

PAYNE, TYSON ELLIOTT, JR., retired insurance executive; b. Dallas, May 25, 1927; s. Tyson Elliott and Winnie Claris (Denman) P.; m. Billie Jane Spears, Aug. 28, 1948; children: David Tyson, Sally Jane. B.J., U. Tex., 1949. CLU, ChFC. Sports editor Lufkin (Tex.) News, 1949-51, Tyler (Tex.) Courier Times, 1951-53; with Am. Nat. Ins. Co., Galveston, Tex., 1953-88; v.p. health ins. ops. Am. Nat. Ins. Co., St. Louis, 1965-1970; v.p. mktg. Am. Nat. Ins. Co., Galveston, 1970-86; pvt. practice ins. agt. Austin, Tex., 1987-88; exec. v. p., dir. Sch. of Ins. & Fin. Svcs. at U. Houston, 1988-92; ret., 1992. Elder Presbyn. Ch. With USNR, 1945-46. Home: 8110 Cardin Dr Austin TX 78759-8704

PAYNE, WILLIAM HAYDON, broadcasting executive; b. Washington, July 3, 1939; s. William Howard and LoRena Elizabeth (Haydon) P.; m. Gail Ann Curtis, July 3, 1960; children—Anne Marguerite, Kelly Gail, Haydon Michelle, William Haydon, II. B of Indsl. Arts in Electronic Engrng., Oklahoma City U., 1961. Announcer Sta. KOMA, Oklahoma City, 1959-61; electronic technician FAA, Oklahoma City, 1961-62; owner, gen. mgr. Sta. KWHP, Edmond, Okla., 1962-79; owner, pub. Graphic Newspaper, Oklahoma City, 1973-77; owner, pres. also morning drive air personality for country music radio Sta. KTFX, Tulsa, 1977-95; pres. Central Broadcast Co., 1977—; exec. dir. Internat. Idea Bank, 1987—; operator KTFX-FM and KTOW-AM radio stas. in Sand Springs, Okla., KRQZ in Wagoner and KITX in Hugo; owner Caney Ridge Heights Mobile Home Park and Cabins, Tenkiller Lake, Okla. Pub. Edmond Map, 1964-81. Deacon 1st Presbyn. Ch., Edmond, 1962-65. Recipient numerous service and appreciation awards. Mem. Nat. Assn. of Broadcasters, Radio Advt. Bur., Okla. Broadcasters Assn., Oklahoma City Advt. Club, various chambers including those in Tulsa, Wagoner and Hugo (Okla.), Edmond C. of C. (medal of merit 1979), Paris (Tex.) C. of C., Lions (Hugo club). Democrat. Club: Edmond Kiwanis (past pres.). Pioneer Time of Day machine. Office: KTFX (FM) 8107 E Admiral Pl Tulsa OK 74115-8116

PAYNE, WILLIAM JACKSON, microbiologist, educator; b. Chattanooga, Aug. 30, 1925; s. Henry Frederick and Maude (Fonda) P.; m. Jane Lindsey Marshall, June 16, 1949; children: William Jackson, Marshall, Lindsey. BS, Coll. William and Mary, 1950, DSc (hon.), 1996; MS, U. Tenn., 1952, PhD, 1955. Instr. bacteriology U. Tenn., 1953-54; mem. faculty U. Ga., 1955-95, prof. microbiology, head dept., 1962-77, Alumni Found. Disting. prof., 1982-95, acting dean Franklin Coll. Arts and Scis., 1977-78, dean Franklin Coll. Arts and Scis., 1978-88; vis. professorial fellow U. Wales, Cardiff, 1975, hon. professorial fellow, 1977-87; cons. U. Ala., 1959, 68, 70, 85, Philip Morris Co., 1981, Iowa State U., 1988, Howard U., 1989, U. Ctrl. Fla., 1992, U. Tenn., 1994—, Auburn U., 1995; summer rsch. participant Oak Ridge Nat. Lab., 1960; chmn. Com. Nat. Registry Microbiologists, 1966-72; cons. U.S. EPA, 1971; mem. biol. oceanography panel NSF, 1976-77; mem. nitrogen-fixation panel CRGO U.S. dept. Agr., 1982; mem. vis. com. So. Assn. Colls., Miss. State U., 1983; vis. lectr. Ctr. for Environ. Biotech., Danish univs.-Copenhagen, Aarhus, Aalborg, 1989; co-chair 1st Gordon Rsch. Conf. on nitric oxide in biochemsitry and biology, 1995. Author: (with D.R. Brown) Microbiology: A Programmed Presentation, 1968, 2d edit., 1972, (transl. to Spanish, 1975), Denitrification, 1981, also articles; mem. editl. bd. Applied and Environ. Microbiology, 1974-79, Environ. Ethics, 1982-95, U. Ga. Press, 1975-78, 88-91. Trustee Athens Acad., 1967-72. Served with USNR, 1943-46. Recipient M.G. Michael award 1960, creative rsch. award U. Ga., 1982, Alumni Achievement award McCallie Sch., 1993. Fellow Am. Acad. Microbiology; mem. Am. Soc. Microbiology (pres. southeastern br. 1963, found. lectr. 1972-73, dir. found. 1973-76, chmn. found. com. 1977-82, com. undergrad. and grad. edn. 1974-77, steering com. undergrad. faculty-mentor enhancement program 1988-90, P.R. Edwards award southeastern br. 1972, R.G. Eagon award 1995), Ga. Acad. Sci., Athens City Club, Sigma Xi (pres. U. Ga. chpt. 1963, rsch. award U. Ga. chpt. 1973), Phi Kappa Phi (pres. U. Ga. chpt. 1983), Sigma Alpha Epsilon. Episcopalian. Home: 111 Alpine Way Athens GA 30606-4002

PAYNE, W(ILLIAM) SPENCER, retired surgeon; b. St. Louis, Mar. 22, 1926; s. Richard Johnson and Mary (Matthews) P.; m. Maureen J.S. Divertie, Oct. 3, 1959; children: Susan Mary, William Spencer, Sarah Elspeth. Student, DePauw U., Greencastle, Ind., 1944-45, Haverford (Pa.) Coll., 1945-46; MD, Washington U., St. Louis, 1950; MS, U. Minn., 1960. Intern, then resident in internal medicine St. Louis City Hosp., 1950-52, resident in gen. surgery, 1954-55; resident in gen. surgery, then resident in thoracic surgery Mayo Grad. Sch., Rochester, Minn., 1955-61; practice medicine specializing in surgery Rochester, 1962-90, ret., 1990; cons. thoracic and cardiovascular surgery Mayo Clinic and Mayo Found., 1962—; prof. surgery Mayo Med. Sch., 1974—, James C. Masson prof. surgery, 1982-87; head sect. gen. thoracic surgery Mayo Clinic, 1987-90; mem. staff Rochester Meth., St. Mary's, Rochester State hosps.; bd. dirs. Am. Bd. Thoracic Surgery, 1985-89. Author: The Esophagus, 1974, Manual of Upper Gastrointestinal Surgery, 1985; contbr. 274 articles to profl. jours.; mem. editl. bd. Annals of Thoracic Surgery, 1987-89. Lt. M.C., USNR, 1952-54, Korea. Recipient Howard K. Gray award Mayo Assn., 1959; named James C. Masson prof. Mayo Found. Mem. ACS, Am. Surg. Assn., Am. Assn. Thoracic Surgery, Soc. Thoracic Surgeons, Am. Coll. Chest Physicians, Central Surg. Assn., Minn. Surg. Soc., Internat. Assn. Study Lung Cancer, Mayo Alumni Soc. Thoracic Surgery, Priestly Soc., Internat. Soc. Diseases of the Esophagus (hon.), Esophageal Surg. Club (hon.), Soc. of Thoracic and Cardiovascular Surgeons of Great Britain and Ireland (hon.), U. Club (Rochester), Madeline Island Yacht Club (LaPointe, Wis.). Presbyterian. Office: Mayo Clinics 200 1st St SW Rochester MN 55902-3008

PAYNE, WINFIELD SCOTT, national security policy research executive; b. Denver, Jan. 20, 1917; s. Winfield Scott and Mildred (Hulse) P.; m. Barbara P. Reid, Nov. 18, 1945; children: Judith P. Beland, Patricia P. Dominguez. AB, U. Colo., 1939, MA (grad. scholar), 1941; postgrad. (fellow) Syracuse U., 1942; MPA, Harvard U., 1948, PhD, 1955. Economist, Bur. Budget, Washington, 1944-46; staff Inter-Univ. Case Program, Washington, 1948-50; indsl. analyst Pres.'s Materials Policy Commn., Washington, 1950-52; project leader Ops. Research Office, Johns Hopkins U., Bethesda, Md., 1952-63; sr. research staff, panel dir. Inst. for Def. Analyses, Arlington, Va., 1963-72; asst. to pres. System Planning Corp., Arlington, 1972-86; cons. 1986-88; adj. rsch. staff Inst. Def. Analyses, 1989—; assoc. prof., lectr. George Washington U., Washington, 1963-65; cons. Def. Advanced Research Project Agy., 1972-76; guest lectr., various univs. Mem. Cabin John (Md.) Fire Bd., 1955-65. Served with USMC, 1942. Littauer fellow, 1946-48. Mem. AAAS, Cosmos Club, Phi Gamma Delta, Pi Gamma Mu. Contbr. articles to profl. jours.; contbr.: Public Administration and Policy Development: A Case Book, 1951. Home: 8820 Walther Blvd # 1304 Parkville MD 21234-9023

PAYNTER, HARRY ALVIN, retired trade association executive; b. Miami, Ariz., July 22, 1923; s. Harry and Mabel Vera (Moore) P.; m. Betty Clarice Wilkins, Dec. 3, 1944; children: Harry Alvin, Steven Wilkins, Barbara Elizabeth, Susan Moore. B.S., Okla. State U., 1948; M.B.A., Harvard U., 1954; postgrad., Air Command and Staff Coll., 1957, Armed Forces Staff Coll., 1961, Nat. War Coll., 1969. Commd. 2d lt. AC U.S. Army, 1943; advanced through grades to col. USAF, 1968; service as flight comdr. 8th Air Force, World War II and Berlin airlift; asst. air attache (Am. embassy), Karachi, Pakistan, 1958-60; air attache (Am. embassy), Quito, Ecuador, 1965-67, Vietnam, 1969; prof. aerospace studies Dartmouth, 1967-68; ret., 1970; mng. dir. Gas Appliance Mfrs. Assn., Inc., N.Y.C., 1970-73; pres. Gas Appliance Mfrs. Assn., Inc., Arlington, Va., 1973-88. Decorated D.F.C., Air medal with 3 oak leaf clusters, Purple Heart, Joint Services Commendation medal with oak leaf cluster U.S.; Abdon Calderon Ecuador; recipient Am. Bankers award, 1947; named Ecuador Hon. Command Pilot. Mem. Can. Gas Assn. (life), Guild Ancient Supplers (hon.), Am. Soc. Gas Engrs. (hon.), Air Force Assn., Ret. Officers Assn., Am. Soc. Assn. Execs., Nat. Press Club. Phi Kappa Phi. Presbyterian. Home: 1416 N Inglewood St Arlington VA 22205-2735

PAYNTER, VESTA LUCAS, pharmacist; b. Aiken County, S.C., May 29, 1922; d. James Redmond and Annie Lurline (Stroman) Lucas; m. Maurice Alden Paynter, Dec. 23, 1945 (dec. 1971); children: Sharon Lucinda, Maurice A. Jr., Doyle Gregg. BS in Pharmacy, U. S.C., 1943. Lic. pharmacist. Owner, pharmacist Cayce Drug Store, S.C., 1944-52, Dutch Fork Drug Store, Columbia, S.C., 1955-60, The Drug Ctr., Cayce, 1963-81; pharmacist Lane-Rexall, Columbia, 1952-55; dist. pharmacist S.C. Dept. Health and Environ. Control, Columbia, 1983-90, ret., 1990. Named Preceptor of Yr., Syntex Co., student body U. S.C., 1981. Fellow, 5th Dist. Pharm. Assn., S.C. Pharm. Assn., S.C. Pub. Health Assn., Alpha Epsilon Delta; mem. China, India, Burma VA Assn. (assoc.), 14th Air Force Assn. (assoc.). Baptist. Lodges: Order of Eastern Star, Order of Amaranth, Sinclair Lodge, White Shrine of Jerusalem, Columbia Shrine #6. Avocations: travel, tennis, golf, art. Home: 2351 Vine St Cayce SC 29033-3000

PAYSON, MARTIN FRED, lawyer; b. Bklyn., Dec. 25, 1940; m. Rhoda Shapiro, Oct. 8, 1961; children: Jacqueline, Marla. BBA, CCNY, 1961; JD, Bklyn. Law Sch., 1966. Bar: N.Y. 1967, Pa. 1989, U.S. Ct. Appeals (1st cir.) 1971, U.S. Ct. Appeals (2d and 3d cirs.) 1968, U.S. Ct. Appeals (4th cir.) 1969, U.S. Supreme Ct. 1970. Gen. ptnr. Jackson, Lewis, Schnitzler & Krupman, White Plains, N.Y., 1967—; lectr. in field. Contbr. articles to various publs. With U.S. Army, 1961-62. Mem. N.Y. State Bar Assn. (labor and employee rels. sects.), Soc. for Human Resource Mgmt. Avocations: photography, cycling. Office: Jackson Lewis Schnitzler & Krupman One N Broadway White Plains NY 10601

PAYSON, RONALD SEARS, biology educator; b. Springfield, Mass., Oct. 17, 1938; s. Peter Martin and Beatrice Thelma (Sears) Farrell; m. Cynthia Myrtle Henderson Smith, July 17, 1965 (div. Jan. 1977); children: Melinda Martha Payson-English, Ronald Sears Payson Jr., Angelique Payson-Bernstein, Marcus A. AASN, U. of the State of N.Y.; BS, U. Mass., MAT in Biology/Ecology. R.N. Prof. biol. scis. Columbia-Greene C.C., 1970-94, prof. emeritus; cons. Spinrut Hill Assocs., Craryville, N.Y., 1994—; dir. Ctr. for Effective Teaching, coord. distance edn. Hudson Valley (N.Y.) C.C., 1995—. Sec. bd. dirs. N.E. Marine Environ. Inst.; bd. dirs. Hudson River Sloop Clearwater; treas. Vol. Fire Co. Home: RR 1 Box 242 Coxsackie NY 12192

PAYTON, BENJAMIN FRANKLIN, college president; b. Orangeburg, S.C., Dec. 27, 1932; s. Leroy Ralph and Sarah (Mack) P.; m. Thelma Louise Plane, Nov. 28, 1959; children: Mark Steven, Deborah Elizabeth. BA, S.C. State Coll., 1955; BD (Danforth grad. fellow 1955-63), Harvard U., 1958; MA, Columbia U., 1960; PhD, Yale U., 1963; LLD (hon.), Eastern Mich. U., 1972; LHD (hon.), Benedict Coll., 1972; LittD (hon.), Morgan State U., 1974, U. Md., 1987; LLD, Morris Brown Coll., Lehigh U., 1990. Asst. prof. sociology of religion and social ethics Howard U., Washington; also dir. Howard U. (Community Rsch.-Svc. Project, 1963-65; exec. dir. dept. social justice and Commn. on Religion and Race Nat. Coun. Chs. of Christ in U.S.A., 1966-67; pres. Benedict Coll., Columbia, S.C., 1967-72; program officer higher edn. and rsch. Ford Found., 1972-81; pres. Tuskegee (Ala.) U., 1981—; mem. nat. rev. bd. (Ctr. for Cultural and Tech. Exch. between U.S. and Asia); mem. commn. on Pre-Coll. Edn. in Math., Sci. and Tech. NSF; ednl. advisor to V.P. George Bush during Seven-Nation Tour of Africa, 1982; team leader U.S. Presdl. Task Force on Agrl. and Econ. Devel. to Zaire; bd. dirs. AmSouth Bancorp., ITT Corp., Libr. Corp., Praxair, Inc., Sonat, Inc.; mem. vis. com. Dept. Humanities MIT, 1988-90; vis. com. bd. overseers Harvard U., 1989-95. Author: (with Dr. Seymour Melman) A Strategy for the Next Stage in Civil Rights: Metropolitan-Rural Development for Equal Opportunity, 1966. Mem. nat. commn. on higher edn. issues Am. Coun. Edn.; bd. dirs. Ala. Shakespeare Festival. Recipient Billings Prize, 1st Pl., Harvard U., 1957, Gold medal award Napoleon Hill Found., 1987, Benjamin E. Mays award, 1988, Centennial Alumnus award S.C. State Coll., 1988; named South Carolinian of Yr. by statewide TV-Radio, 1972. Mem. NAACP, Am. Soc. Scholars, Soc. for Religion, Higher Edn. (dir.), Assn. Governing Bds. (pres.'s adv. coun.), Phi Beta Kappa, Alpha Phi Alpha, Alpha Kappa Mu, Sigma Pi Phi. Home: Grey Columns 399 Montgomery Rd Tuskegee AL 36083 Office: Office of the Pres Tuskegee Univ Tuskegee AL 36088*

PAYTON, GARY DWAYNE, professional basketball player; b. Oakland, Calif., July 23, 1968; m. Monique Payton; children: Raquel, Gary Dwayne. Grad., Oreg. State U., 1990. Drafted NBA, 1990; guard Seattle Supersonics, 1990—. Named mem. All-Am. First Team, The Sporting News, 1990, Pacific-10 Conf. Player of Yr., 1990, NBA All-Star, 1994, 95, NBA Player of the Week; named to NBA All-Def. 1st Team, 1994, 95. Office: Seattle Supersonics 190 Queen Anne Ave N Ste 200 Seattle WA 98109-4926*

PAYTON, THOMAS WILLIAM, corporate finance consultant executive; b. Toronto, Ont., Can., Sept. 7, 1946. With Can. Imperial Bank of Commerce, Toronto; dir. Bramalea Ltd., Toronto, 1981-82, v.p., 1982-88, sr. v.p., 1988-90, sr. v.p., treas., 1991-93; pres. DelLyn Advisors Inc., 1993—; dir. Cadillac Fairview, Inc., 1994-95. Office: DelLyn Advisors Inc, 8 King St E Ste 810, Toronto, ON Canada M5C 1B5

PAYTON, WALTER (SWEETNESS PAYTON), professional race car driver, former professional football player; b. Columbia, Miss., July 25, 1954; s. Peter Edward and Alyne Payton; m. Connie Payton; children: Jarrett, Brittney. BA in Communications, Jackson State U. Running back Chgo. Bears, 1975-88; played Pro Bowl, 1976-86; mem. NFL Championship team, 1985; professional race car driver, 1993; owner Walter Payton, Inc., Hoffman Estates, Ill., 1996—; co-owner Am.'s Bar, Chgo., Studebaker's, Schaumburg, Ill.; part-owner Payton-Coyne Racing Team; owner Walter Payton's Roundhouse, Aurora, Ill., 1996—. Representative for Food for Thought Program, Bryan Foods, 1993—. Named NFC Player of Yr., The Sporting News, 1976-77, to NFC All-Star Team, 1976-78, NFC Player of Yr., UPI, 1977, NFL Most Valuable Player, Profl. Football Writers Am., 1978, played in nine Pro Bowls, inducted into Pro Football Hall of Fame, 1993, Coll. Football Hall of Fame, South Bend, Ind., 1996; Black Athlete of the Year, Gordon's Gin, 1985. NFL all-time rushing leader. *

PAYUK, EDWARD WILLIAM, elementary education educator; b. St. Louis, July 19, 1948; s. Stanley Eli and Lillian (Bluestein) P.; m. Pamela Karen Miller, Sept. 5, 1970 (div. Oct. 1986); children: Stacy Lynne, Lori Michelle; m. Judith Ann Cohen, Dec. 4, 1986; stepchildren: Jeffrey Alan Kieffer, Kimberly Beth Kieffer. AA, Meramec C.C., St. Louis, 1969; BS, U. Mo., St. Louis, 1971; MA, Webster U., 1973, postgrad., 1976. Educator Ferguson (Mo.) Florissant Sch. Dist., 1971—; tutor, St. Louis, 1984-91; tchr. mentor Ferguson-Florissant Sch. Dist., St. Louis, 1986—, mem. sci. Cadre, 1988—. Contbr. articles to profl. jours. Sci. literacy com. St. Louis Sci. Acad., 1991—; rep. Tchrs., Industry & Environment Conf., Jefferson City, Mo., 1995; mem. Little Creek Nature Study Adv. Com., 1997, mem. curriculum adv. com. dist. level, 1997. With U.S. Army, 1969-70. Mem. NEA, Mo. Edn. Assn., Ferguson-Florissant Edn. Assn. Jewish. Avocation: collector of Einsteinia. Home: 13660 Amiot Dr Saint Louis MO 63146-3608 Office: Ferguson-Florissant Sch Dist 1005 Waterford Dr Florissant MO 63033-3649

PAZ, HAROLD LOUIS, internist and educator; b. N.Y.C., Jan. 3, 1955. BA in Biology and Psychology, U. Rochester, 1977, MD, 1982; MS in Life Sci. Engring., Tufts U., 1979. Diplomate Am. Bd. Internal Medicine, subspecialty in Pulmonary Medicine, Critical Care Medicine. Intern internal medicine Northwestern U. Med. Ctr., Chgo., 1982-83, resident internal medicine, 1983-85, chief medical resident, 1985-86; instr. clin. medicine Northwestern U., Chgo., 1985-86; fellow pulmonary and critical care John Hopkins U., Balt., 1986-88, fellow environ. health scis., 1986-88; asst. prof. medicine Hahnemann U., Phila., 1988-94, asst. prof. anesthesia, 1989-94, assoc. dean grad. med. edn., 1992—; assoc. prof. medicine Hahnemann U., 1992-94, dir. med. intensive care unit, 1988-94; assoc. hosp. med. dir. Ctr. for Clin. Outcomes, Hahnemann U., Phila., 1983-94; med. dir., assoc. dean for clin. affairs, assoc. prof. of clin. medicine UMDNJ, Robert Wood Johnson Med. Sch., New Brunswick, N.J., 1994-95; dean, CEO, assoc. prof. medicine U. Med. Group, 1995—. Editor Jour. Undergrad. Rsch., 1976, Med. Staff News newsletter, 1992—; cons. Annals Internal Medicine, Clin. Immunology and Immunopathology. Endowood fellow Johns Hopkins U., 1987-88; U. Rochester scholar, 1979. Fellow ACP, Am. Coll. Chest Physicians; mem. AMA, Am. Coll. Physician Execs., Am. Fedn. Clin. Rsch., Am. Thoracic Soc., Philip Drinker Soc. for Critical Care (pres. 1992-94). Office: UMDNJ Robert Wood Johnson Med Sch 125 Paterson St New Brunswick NJ 08901-1962

PAZ, OCTAVIO, poet, Mexican diplomat; b. Mex., Mar. 31, 1914; s. Octavio Paz and Josephina Lozano; m. Elena Garro, 1937 (div.); m. Marie José Tramini, 1964. Student, U. Mex.; D (hon.), New Sch. Social Rsch. Sec. Mex. Embassy, Paris, 1945; chargé d'affaires Mex. Embassy, Tokyo, 1951, secretariat external affairs, 1953-58; extraordinary and plenipotentiary minister Mex. Embassy, Paris, 1959-62; Mex. amb. to India, 1962-68; vis. prof. U. Tex., Austin, U. Pitts., 1968-70; Simón Bolívar prof. Latin Am. studies, 1970; fellow Churchill Coll., Cambridge U., 1970-71; Charles Eliot Norton prof. poetry Harvard U., 1971-72; Regent's fellow U. Calif., San Diego; now dir. Revista Vuelta, Mexico City; founder literary rev. Barandal, 1931; mem. editorial bd., columnist El Popular; co-founder Taller, 1938; co-founder, editor El Hijo Prodigo, 1943-46; editor Plural, 1971-75; founder, editor Vuelta, 1976—. Author: (poetry) Luna Silvestre, 1933, No pasarán!, 1936, Raíz del hombre, 1937, Bajo tu clara sombra y otros poemas sobre España, 1937, Entre la piedra y la flor, 1941, A la orilla del mundo y primer dia, 1942, Libertad bajo palabra, 1949, Aguila o sol?, 1951 (pub. as Eagle or Sun?, 1970), Semillas para un himno, 1954, Piedra de sol, 1957 (pub. as Sun Stone, 1963), La estación violenta, 1958, Agua y viento, 1959, Libertad bajo palabra: obra poética 1935-1958, 1960, Salamandra 1958-1961, 1962, Selected Poems, 1935-1957, 1963, Viento entero, 1965, Vrindaban, Madurai, 1965, Blanco, 1967, Disco visuales, 1968, Ladera este (1962-1968), 1969, La centana: poemas 1935-1968, 1969, Configurations, 1958-1969, 1971, Renga, 1971, Topoemas, 1971, Early Poems 1935-1955, 1973, Pasado en claro, 1975, Vuelta, 1976, A Draft of Shadows and Other Poems, 1979, Selected Poems, 1979, Airborn/Hijos del aire, 1981, Poemas 1935-1975, 1981, Poemas recientes, 1981, Instante y revelación, 1982, Selected Poems, 1984, Cuatro chopos/The Four Poplars, 1985, Arbol adentro, 1987 (pub. as A Tree Within, 1988), Nineteen Ways of Looking at Wang Wei, 1987, The Collected Poems of Octavio Paz 1957-1987, 1988, Lo mejor de Octavio Paz: el fuego de cada día, A Tale of Two Gardens: Poems from India 1952-95, 1997; (prose) El laberinto de la soledad, 1950 (pub. as The Labyrinth of Solitude: Life and Thought in Mexico, 1961), Aguila o Sole, 1951, El arco y la lira: el poema, la revelación poética, poesía e historia, 1956 (pub. as The Bow and the Lyre: The Poem, the Poetic Revelation, Poetry and History, 1973), Las peras del olmo, 1957, Tamayo en la pintura mexicana, 1959, Cuadrivio, 1965, Los signos en rotación, 1965, Puertas al campo, 1966, Claude Lévi-Strauss; o, El nuevo festín de Esopo, 1967 (pub. as Claude Lévi-Strauss: An Introduction, 1970), Corriente alterna, 1967 (pub. as Alternating Current, 1973), Marcel Duchamp; o, El castillo de la pureza, 1968 (pub. as Marcel Duchamp; or, The Castle of Purity, 1970), México: la última década, 1969, Conjunciones y disyunciones, 1969 (pub. as Conjunctions and Disjunctions, 1974), Posdata, 1970 (Pub. as The Other Mexico: Critique of the Pyramid, 1972), Las cosas en su sitio: sobre la literatura española del siglo XX, 1971, Los signos en rotación y otros ensayos, 1971, Traducción: literatura y literalidad, 1971, Apariencia desnuda: la obra de Marcel Duchamp, 1973 (pub. as Marcel Duchamp: Appearance Stripped Bare, 1979), El signo y el garabato, 1973, Solo a dos voces, 1973, Teatro de signos/transparencias, 1974, Versiones y diversiones, 1974, Los hijos del limo: del romanticismo a la vanguardia, 1974 (pub. as Children of the Mire: Modern Poetry from Romanticism to the Avant-Garde, 1974), El mono gramético, 1974 (pub. as The Monkey Grammarian, 1981), La búsqueda del comienzo: escritos sobre el surrealismo, 1974, The Siren and the Seashells and Other Essays on Poets and Poetry, 1976, Xavier Villaurrutia en persona y en obra, 1978, El ogro filantrópico: historia y política 1971-1978, 1979, Rufino Tamayo: Myth and Magic, 1979, México en la obra de Octavio Paz, 1979, Rufino Tamayo, 1982, Sor Juana Inés de la Cruz, o, Las trampas de la fe, 1982 (pub. as Sor Juana, or, The Traps of Faith, 1988), Tiempo nublado, 1983 (pub. as One Earth, Four or Five Worlds: Reflections on Contemporary History, 1985), Sombras de obras: arte y literatura, 1983, Günter Gerzo, 1983, Hombres en su siglo y otros ensayos, 1984 (pub. as On Poets and Others, 1986), Pasión crítica: conversaciones con Octavio Paz, 1985, Convergences: Essays on Art and Literature, 1987, Generaciones y semblanzas: escritores y letras de México, 1987, El pelegrino en su patria: historia y política de México, 1987, Los privilegios de la vista: arte de México, 1987, Primeras letras, 1931-1943, 1988, One World or the Other, 1989, Poesía, mito, revolución, 1989, La otra voz: poesía y fin de siglo, 1990 (pub. as The Other Voice, 1992), Essays on Mexican Art, 1993, My Life With the Wave, 1994, The Double Flame, 1995, In Light of India: Essays, 1997; adapter: (plays) La hija de Rappaccini, 1956; editor: Voces de España, 1938, Laurel: antología de la poésia moderna en lengua española, 1941, Anthologie de la poésie mexicaine, 1952, Anthología poética, 1956, Anthology of Mexican Poetry, 1958, Tamayo el la pintura mexicana, 1959, Magia de la risa, 1962, Antología by Fernando Pessoa, 1962, Cuatro poetas contemporáneos de Suecia: Martinson, Lundkvist, Ekelöf, y Lindegren, 1963, Poesía en movimiento: Mexico 1915-1966, 1966, Remedios varo, 1966, Antología by Xavier Villaurrutia, 1980; translator: Sendas de Oku by Basho, 1957, Veinte poemas by William Carlos Williams, 1973, 15 poemas by Guillaume Appollinaire, 1979; writer (film) Yo, la Peor de Todas, 1990. Guggenheim fellow, U.S., 1944; recipient Grand Prix Internat. de Poesie (Belgium), 1963, Jerusalem prize, 1977, Critics prize (Spain), 1977, Nat. prize for letters (Mex.), 1977, Grand Golden Eagle Internat. Festival (Paris) 1979, Grand Aigle d'Or (Nice), 1979, Premio Ollin Yoliztli (Mex.), 1980, Miguel de Cervantes prize (Spain), 1982, Neustadt Internat. prize for literature, 1982, Wilhelm Heinse medal (Germany), 1984, Fedn. German Book Trade Peace prize, 1984, Gran Cruz de Alfonso X el Sabrio, 1986, T.S. Eliot award for creative writing Ingersoll Found., 1987, Alexis de Toqueville prize Inst. France, 1988, Nobel Prize in literature, 1990. Mem. AAAL (hon.). Office: Revista Vuelta Amigos del Arte AC, Presidente Canonza 210, 4000 Coyoacan Mexico Mexico also: care Churchill Coll, Cambridge England*

PAZANDAK, CAROL HENDRICKSON, liberal arts educator; b. Mpls.; d. Norman Everard and Ruth (Buckley) Hendrickson; m. Bruce B. Pazandak (dec. 1986); children: David, Bradford, Christopher, Eric, Paul, Ann; m. Joseph P. O'Shaughnessy, May 1991. PhD, U. Minn., 1970. Asst. dir. admissions U. Minn., Mpls., 1970-72, asst. dean liberal arts, 1972-79, asst. to pres., 1979-85, office of internat. edn., acting dir., 1985-87, asst. prof. to assoc. to prof. liberal arts, 1970-96, prof. emerita, 1996—; vis. prof. U. Iceland, Reykjavik, 1984, periods in 1983, 86, 87, 88, 89, 90-92, 93, 94, 96; vis. rsch. prof. U. Oulu, Finland, 1993; exec. sec. Minn.-Iceland Adv. Com., U. Minn., 1984—; cons. U. Iceland, 1983—; co-chair Reunion of Sisters-Minn. and Finland Confs., 1986—; sec. Icelandic Assn. of Minn., 1995—. Editor: Improving Undergraduate Education in Large Universities, 1989. Past pres. Minn. Mrs. Jaycees, Mpls. Mrs. Jaycees; formerly bd. govs. St. John's Preparatory Sch., Collegeville, Minn.; former bd. trustees Coll. of St. Teresa, Winona, Minn. Recipient Partnership award for contbn. to advancing shared interests of Iceland and Am., 1994; named to Order of the Falcon, Govt. of Iceland, 1990, Coll. Liberal Arts Alumna Notable Achievement, 1995, Pres.'s Club, U. Minn., 1996. Mem. Am. Psychol. Assn., Soc. Advancement of Scandinavian Studies, Soc. for Disability Studies. Home: 1361 Prior Ave S Saint Paul MN 55116-2656 Office: U Minn N 218 Elliott Hall 75 E River Rd Minneapolis MN 55455-0280

PAZICKY, EDWARD PAUL, human resources executive; b. Jersey City, Oct. 15, 1946; s. Edward P. Sr. and Marie M. (Loporto) P.; m. Diana Loercher, Sept. 25, 1976; 1 chld, Luke A.E. BA, Wittenberg U., Springfield, Ohio, 1968; M in Govt. Adminstrn., U. Pa., 1970. Trainee, staff pers. rep., sr. pers. rep. Port Authority of N.Y. and N.J., N.Y.C., 1970-78; asst. dir. mgmt. pers. Consol. Rail Corp., Phila., 1978-80; v.p. Marsh & McLennan Inc., N.Y.C., 1980-82, mng. dir., 1982—. Trustee Chapin Sch., Princeton, N.J., v.p., 1989-91; trustee Parkinsons Disease Found., 1996—; elder First Presbyn. Ch., Morrisville, Pa., 1991—. Mem. Soc. for Human Resources Mgmt. (mem. Exec. Forum, bd. dirs. N.Y. chpt. 1989), Human Resources Policy Inst., Human Resource Planning Soc. Republican. Avocations: horticulture, running, tennis, scuba diving, politics. Office: Marsh & McLennan Inc 1166 Avenue Of The Americas New York NY 10036-2708

PAZIENZA, VINNY, professional boxer; b. Cranston, R.I., Dec. 16, 1962. Profl. boxer, 1983—; winner IBF Lightweight Title, 1987-88, WBA Jr. Middleweight Title, 1991. Office: c/o IBF 134 Evergreen Pl Ste 9 East Orange NJ 07018-2012

PAZIRANDEH, MAHMOOD, rheumatologist, consultant; b. Hamadan, Iran, Jan. 1, 1932; came to U.S., 1966; naturalized U.S. Citizen, 1977; s. Rahim and Zahra (Shoushtar) P.; m. Parvin Danesh, Apr. 19, 1961; children: Bruce, Justin, Navid. MD, U. Tehran, 1958; postgrad., Eng., 1959-64, Pitts. U., 1967-68. Diplomate Am. Bd. Internal Medicine and Rheumatology. Asst. prof. Tehran U., Iran, 1964-67; clin. assoc. Cleve. Clinic Found., 1969-70; clin. instr. Case Western Res. U., Cleve., 1970-72, sr. clin. instr., 1972-78, clin. asst. prof., 1979-93, clin. assoc. prof., 1993—; dir. med. edn. Lake Hosp., Cleve., 1984-97, pres. med. staff, 1990-93; mem. CME com. Case Western Res. U. Sch. Medicine, 1994-97; dir. med. edn. Euclid Hosp., Cleve., 1971-73, dir. quality assurance, 1989-93. Contbr. articles to profl. jours. Speaker pub. edn. radio, TV and seminars, Cleve., 1984—; chmn. pub. forums Arthritis Found., Cleve., 1985—, trustee, 1986-97, chmn. pub. edn. com., 1987—; vol. physician Lake County Free Med. Clinic, 1993-97. Recipient recognition svc. award Arthritis Found., 1976, Robert Stecher Vol. award, 1988, Nat. Vols. Svc. citation, 1989; Eng. and Iranian Govt. scholar, 1959-63. Fellow ACP, Am. Coll. Rheumatology; mem. Am. Soc. Internal Medicine, Ohio State Med. Assn. (del. 1989-96, State Ohio accreditation com. on continuing med. edn. 1996-97), Lake County Med. Soc. (pres. 1988—), Cleve. Rheumatism Soc. (pres. 1974). Republican. Avocations: arts, antiques. Home: 124 Pheasant Ln Hunting Valley OH 44022-4043 Office: Case Western Res U 36100 Euclid Ave Willoughby OH 44094-4456

PAZMIÑO, PATRICIO AUGUSTO, physician, scientist, consultant; b. Quito, Ecuador, Nov. 7, 1943; came to U.S., 1967; s. Manuel Eduardo and Angela Alicia (Narvaez) P.; m. Lydia Zulema Bohorquez, 1970; children: Patricio, Pablo, Carlos, Katherine. BS, Gonzaga U., 1968; PhD, U. Ill., 1971; D of Medicine & Surgery, Ctrl. U. Ecuador, 1974. Diplomate Am. Bd. Internal Medicine, Am. Bd. Nephrology. Asst. prof. pharmacology Ctrl. U. Sch. Medicine, Quito, Ecuador, 1971-74; staff nephrologist, internist Nat. Naval Med. Ctr., Bethesda, 1979-84; asst. prof. medicine Uniformed Svcs. U. Health Scis., Bethesda, Md., 1980-83; head nephrology divsn. Nat. Naval Med. Ctr., Bethesda, 1983-84; med. dir. El Paso (Tex.) Dialysis Ctr., 1986-89, Nephrology, Internal Medicine & Hypertension Ctr., El Paso, 1987—; asst. prof. medicine Tex. Tech. Sch. Medicine, El Paso, 1989—; med. dir. BMA Dialysis Ctr., El Paso, 1989-95; dir. Total Renal Care, 1995—; staff internist, nephrologist Columbia Med. Ctrs., Sierra Med. Ctr., Southwestern Gen. Hosp., R.E. Thomason Gen. Hosp., Rio Vista Rehab. Ctr., Providence Meml. Hosp., William Beaumont Army Med. Ctr. Author: Farmacologia Hormonal, 1974; contbr. articles to profl. jours. and books. Served with USN, 1979-84. Fellow ACP, Interam. Coll. Physicians and Surgeons; mem. Am. Soc. Nephrology, Mayo Clinic Alumni (del.), El Paso County Med. Assn., 1993-97, Am. Heart Assn. (pres. 1996-97, bd. dirs. El Paso divsn. 1994—), S.W. Renal Soc. (pres. 1991-92), S.W. Assn. Hispanic Am. Physicians (pres. 1993, Outstanding Pres. award 1993), Ecuadorean Acad. Medicine. Mem. ACP, AMA, Interam. Coll. Physicians and Surgeons, Nat. Kidney Found., Tex. Med. Assn., El Paso County Med. Assn., Am. Heart Assn., S.W. Renal Soc., S.W. Assn. Hispanic Am. Physicians, Ecuadorean Acad. Medicine, Mayo Clinic Alumni Assn. Avocations: photography, scientific research, travel, chess, sports cars. Office: NIH Ctr 1701 N Mesa St Ste 101 El Paso TX 79902-3503

PAZUR, JOHN HOWARD, biochemist, educator; b. Zubne, Czechoslovakia, Jan. 17, 1922; came to U.S., 1946, naturalized, 1961; s. John and Mary (Bonko) P.; m. Jean Josephine Glabais, Nov. 22, 1950; children—Robert Leslie, Barbara Jean, Beverly Ann, Carolyn Jo. B.S., U. Guelph, 1944; M.S., McGill U., 1946; Ph.D., Iowa State U., 1950. Instr. chemistry Iowa State U., 1950-51; asst. prof. biol. chemistry U. Ill., 1951-52; mem. faculty U. Nebr., 1952-66, prof. biochemistry, 1959-66, chmn. dept., 1960-66; prof. biochemistry Pa. State U., 1966—, chmn. dept., 1966-74. Mem. Am. Chem. Soc., Am. Soc. Biol. Chemists. Home: Unit 306 403 S Allen St State College PA 16801-5252 Office: Penn State U 108 Althouse Lab University Park PA 16802-4500

PEABODY, DEBBIE KAY, elementary school educator; b. Wooster, Ohio, Apr. 9, 1954; d. Walter L. and Carolyn E. (Lee) Mussatto; m. David Leslie Peabody, Jan. 6, 1973; children: Dawn Kathleen, Lesli Kay. BS in Elem. Edn., Southwestern Adventist Coll., Keene, Tex., 1986. Cert. tchr. K-8, Ariz. Head tchr. SDA Elem. Sch., Camp Verde, Ariz., 1986-89; tchr. 6th grade Roosevelt Sch. Dist., Phoenix, 1989-93, jr. high reading tchr., 1993-94, collaborative peer tchr., 1994—; dist. assessment plan co-chair Roosevelt Sch. Dist., 1993—; mem. Greater Phoenix Curriculum Coun. Dist. Assessment Plan Writing Team, 1994—; CHAMPS coord. Sunland Elem. Sch., Phoenix, 1991-94. Co-author: (activity book) Explosion of ASAP Activities, 1994. Recipient Edn. of Merit award Southwestern Union Coll., 1985, 86. Mem. ASCD, NEA, Ariz. Edn. Assn., Roosevelt Edn. Assn., Nat. Coun. Tchrs. Math. Avocations: quilting, embroidery, biking, hiking, canoeing. Office: Southwest School 1111 W Dobson Phoenix AZ 85041

PEABODY, WILLIAM TYLER, JR., retired paper manufacturing company executive; b. Melrose, Mass., Mar. 17, 1921; s. William Tyler and Dorothy (Atkinson) P.; m. Florence Marshall Peabody, July 27, 1946 (dec.); children: Carol Peabody Moomey, William Tyler III, Janet Peabody Barrow, Marshall R. A.B. cum laude, Harvard U., 1942, postgrad. Grad. Sch. Arts and Scis., 1946-47, LL.B., 1949. Bar: N.Y. 1950. Asso. firm Root, Ballantine, Harlan, Bushby & Palmer, N.Y.C., 1949-54; with law div. Scott Paper Co., Phila., 1954-62, 67-85; asst. to gen. mgr. Scott Paper Co., Everett, Wash., 1962-67; asst. sec. Scott Paper Co., 1965-71, corp. sec., 1971-83, asst. sec., 1983-84, ret. Pres. Knollwood Terrace Civic Assn., Carle Place, N.Y., 1952-53; pres. Carle Place Taxpayers Assn., 1953-54; bd. dirs. Nether Providence Cmty. Assocs., Inc., Wallingford, Pa., 1969-75, pres., 1969-70; bd. dirs. Ethel Mason Day Care Ctr., Wallingford, 1976-81, pres., 1979-80; vestryman St. Mary's Episc. Ch., Carle Place, N.Y., 1953-54; vestryman, jr. warden Trinity Episc. Ch., Everett, Wash., 1965-67; chmn. Rose Valley Folk, 1977-78; bd. dirs. Helen Kate Furness Free Libr., Wallingford, 1984-87, v.p., 1986-87; bd. dirs. Chester-Wallingford chpt. ARC, 1991—, exec. com., 1992—, 1st vice chmn., 1994-95, chmn., 1995—; bd. dirs. Everett, Wash. Area C. of C., 1965-67; Snohomish County Family Counseling Svc., Everett, 1962-67, pres., 1965; pres. Wallingford, Pa. Swim Club, 1960-61. Lt. USNR, 1942-46. Mem. ABA, Am. Soc. Corp. Secs. (dir. 1977-81, pres. Middle Atlantic group 1976-77), Harvard Club (Phila., sch. com. 1959-62, 76-90). Home: 15 Rose Valley Rd Moylan PA 19063-4217

PEACE, H. W., II, oil company executive; b. Clinton, Okla., May 21, 1935; s. Herman Wilbern and Bernice (Mitchell) P.; m. Norma June Williams; children: Hugh William, Susannah Lee. BS in Geology, U. Okla., 1959, MS in Geology, 1964; postgrad., U. S.W. La., 1968. Jr. geologist Union Oil Co. Calif., Houston, 1964-65; area geologist Union Oil Co. Calif., Lafayette, La., 1965-70; geologist dist. exploration Union Oil Co. Calif., Oklahoma City, 1970-77; mgr. Rocky Mountain exploration Union Oil Co. Calif., Casper, Wyo., 1977-80; mgr. div. exploration Cotton Petroleum Corp., Tulsa, 1980-83; v.p. exploration Hadson Petroleum Corp., Oklahoma City, 1983-85, exec. v.p., chief operating officer, 1985-88, also bd. dirs.; exec. v.p., chief ops. officer Mosswood Oil and Gas Co., Oklahoma City, 1985-88; exec. v.p., chief ops. officer Anadarko Supply Co., Oklahoma City, 1986-88, also bd. dirs.; mng. ptnr. EXAD, Oklahoma City, 1988-91; pres., chief exec. officer, dir. Panhandle Royalty Co., Oklahoma City, 1991—; mem. mgmt. com. PLC Energy Data, LLC, 1994—. Dir. sch. geology adv. com. U. Okla., Norman, 1984—, vice chmn. 1988-89, chmn. 1989-90, exec. com. 1990—. Lt. USN 1959-63, capt. USNR, 1963-82, retired list 1995. Mem. Am. Assn. Petroleum Geology (rep. del. or alt. 1984—), Soc. Exploration Geophysicists, Soc. Econ. Paleontologists and Mineralogists, Petroleum Assn. Wyo. (v.p. 1979-80), Tulsa Geol. Soc., Oklahoma City Geol. Soc. (chmn. profl. affairs 1976-77), Naval Res. Assn., Cherokee Hills Homeowners Assn. (pres. 1971-73), Fieldstone Homeowners Assn. (pres. 1983), Navy League. Republican. Lodge: Civitan. Avocations: golf, swimming, hiking. Office: Panhandle Royalty Co 5400 N Grand Blvd Ste 210 Oklahoma City OK 73112-5654

PEACH, PAUL E., physician, medical facility administrator; b. Owensboro, Ky., June 2, 1943; s. Elbert B. and Ermal M. (Bennett) P. Student, So. Meth. U., 1961-63; BS, Ind. U., 1965, JD, 1969; student, U. New Orleans, 1977-79; MD, La. State U., 1983. Bar: Ind., 1970; diplomate Am. Bd. Phys. Medicine and Rehab. Atty. pvt. practice Indpls., 1970-72; staff atty La. Dept. Health & Human Svcs., New Orleans, 1972-77; resident La. State U. Charity Hosp., New Orleans, 1983-84, Wadsworth VA Hosp., Cedars-Sinai Hosp., L.A., 1984-86; med. dir. Roosevelt Warm Springs (Ga.) Inst. for Rehab., 1986—; pvt. practice atty., New Orleans, 1972-77; clin. assoc. prof. Ctr. for Rehab. Medicine Emory U., Atlanta, 1987—. Author: (with others) Late Effects of Poliomyelitis, 1991, Effect of Compliance in Treatment Outcomes in Patients with Post-Polio Syndrome, 1991. Fellow Am. Acad. Phys. Medicine and Rehab.; mem. Med. Assn. Ga., Tri-County Med. Assn. Ga. (pres. 1990-91, 93-96), Ga. Soc. Phys. Medicine and Rehab. (pres. 1989-90, 95-96), Am. Acad. Electrodiagnostic Medicine (assoc.), Am. Hosp. Assn. (governing bd. 1988-91, del. rehab. sect. 1990). Avocations: photography, music. Home: Roosvelt Inst Box 336 Warm Springs GA 31830 Office: Roosevelt Inst for Rehab Box 1000 Warm Springs GA 31830-0268

PEACHEY, LEE DEBORDE, biology educator; b. Rochester, N.Y., Apr. 14, 1932; s. Clarence Henry and Eunice (DeBorde) P.; m. Helen Pauline Fuchs, June 7, 1958; children: Michael Stephen, Sarah Elizabeth Keating, Anne Palmer Lorenz. BS, Lehigh U., 1953; postgrad., U. Rochester, 1953-56; Ph.D. (Leitz fellow), Rockefeller U., 1959; MA (hon.), U. Pa., 1971. Research asso. Rockefeller U., 1959-60; asst. prof. zoology Columbia U., 1960-63, asso. prof., 1963-65; asso. prof. biochemistry and biophysics U. Pa., Phila., 1965-70; prof. biology U. Pa., 1970—; adj. prof. molecular, cellular and developmental biology U. Colo., 1969-84; mem. molecular biology study sect. NIH, 1969-73; internat. vis. prof. Ministry Edn., Sci. and Culture Gunma (Japan) U. Med. Sch., Maebashi, 1992-95; mem. Biomed. Rsch. Tech. Rev. Com., NIH, 1994—; mem. Mayor's Sci. and Tech. Adv. Coun., Phila., 1972—; chmn. Gordon Rsch. Conf. on Muscle, 1983; mem. ext. evaluation com. Nat. Inst. Physiol. Sci., Okazaki, Japan, 1997—. Editor: Third and Fourth Conferences on Cellular Dynamics, N.Y. Acad. Scis., 1967, First and Second Confs. on Cellular Dynamics, 1968, Am. Physiol. Soc. Handbook on Skeletal Muscle, 1983; mem. editorial bd. Tissue and Cell, 1969—, Jour. Cell Biology, 1970-73, Pitman Series in Cellular and Development Biology, 1977—, Microscopy Rsch. and Technique, 1982-93, Advances in Optical and Electron Microscopy, 1983—, Neuroimage, 1991—, Jour. Microscopy, 1992-96, Bioimages, 1993—; contbr. articles to sci. jours. Trustee Keith R. Porter Endowment for Cell Biology, Narberth, Pa., 1981—. Guggenheim and Fulbright-Hays fellow, 1967-68, Overseas fellow Churchill Coll., Cambridge, Eng., 1967-68, Fogarty Sr. Internat. fellow, 1979-80, hon. rsch. fellow U. Coll., London, 1979-80; Royal Soc. (London) guest rsch. fellow, Cambridge, 1986; grantee NSF, 1960-72, NIH, 1973—, Muscular Dystrophy Assn. Am., Inc. 1973-91. Fellow AAAS, Electron Microscopy Soc. Am. (council 1975-78, pres. 1982), Am. Soc. Cell Biology (program chmn. 1965, coun. 1966-69), Biophys. Soc. (program chmn. 1976, coun. 1976-80, exec. com. 1976-82, pres. 1981-82), Internat. Union Pure and Applied Biophysics (coun. 1978-84, v.p. 1984-87, pres. 1987-90, chmn. commn. on cell and membrane biophysics 1981-84, hon. v.p. 1990-93), Physiol. Soc. (Eng.); mem. Internat. Soc. Stereology (internat. stereology software com. 1982-94), Soc. Gen. Physiologists. Achievements include research in mechanisms of muscle cell contraction; development of methods in light and electron microscopy; development of computer graphic methods for three-dimensional image analysis and reconstruction. Home: 606 Old Gulph Rd Narberth PA 19072-1622 Office: U Pa Dept Biology Philadelphia PA 19104-6018

PEACOCK, A(LVIN) WARD, textile company executive; b. Durham, N.C., June 17, 1929; s. Erle Ewart and Vera Louise (Ward) P.; m. Barbara Sheppard White, July 2, 1955; children: Alvin Ward, Stephen White, Nancy Lay. B.S. in Commerce, U. N.C., 1950; M.B.A., Harvard U., 1952. Asst. to v.p. Erwin Mills, Inc., Durham, 1953-55, sec., 1957-62, sec.-treas., 1962-64; v.p. Dixie Yarns, Inc., Chattanooga, 1964-76, sr. v.p., 1976-81; sr. v.p. Springs Industries, Fort Mill, S.C., 1981-86; exec. v.p. Springs Industries, Fort Mill, 1986-92; bd. dirs. Palmetto Seed Capital Corp.; regional dir. First Wachovia Corp., Charlotte, N.C., 1988-92. Trustee Holston Conf. Colls., Tenn., 1968-79, Sci. Mus. Charlotte, 1990-94; bd. dirs. Chattanooga Meml. Hosp., 1979-81, Charlotte Symphony, 1990-94, Greater Carolinas chpt. ARC, 1988-94; dir. Allied Arts Fund, 1978-81, Metrolina Food Bank, 1994—; mem. Chattanooga Wastewater Regulation Bd., 1978-81. 1st lt. USAF, 1955-57. Mem. Tenn. Mfrs. Assn. (chmn. bd. dirs. 1980-81), Chattanooga Mfrs. Assn. (pres. 1968-69), Am. Textile Mfrs. Inst., Univ. Club, River Hills Club, Phi Beta Kappa, Alpha Kappa Psi, Sigma Nu. Republican. Methodist. Home: 22 Wood Hollow Rd River Hills SC 29710

PEACOCK, ERLE EWART, JR., surgeon, lawyer, educator; b. Durham, N.C., Sept. 10, 1926; s. Erle Ewart and Vera Louise (Ward) P.; m. Mary Louise Lowrey, Apr. 17, 1954; children: James Lowrey, Susan Louise, Virginia Gayle. Cert. in medicine, U. N.C., 1947, BS, 1990; MD, Harvard U., 1949; JD, U.N.C., 1993. Bar: N.C. 1993. Intern, asst. resident surgery Roosevelt Hosp., N.Y.C., 1949-51; from asst. resident gen. surgery U. N.C. Hosps., Chapel Hill, 1953-54, chief resident gen. surgery, 1954-55; resident in plastic surgery Barnes Hosp., St. Louis, 1955-56; mem. faculty dept. surgery U. N.C., Chapel Hill, 1956-69; prof. surgery, head div. plastic surgery U. N.C., 1965-69; prof., chmn. dept. surgery U. Ariz., Tucson, 1969-77; prof. surgery Tulane U., New Orleans, 1977-82; pvt. practice surgery Chapel Hill, N.C., 1982-93; vis. prof. surgery U. Va., Charlottesville, 1988-97; clin. prof. surgery U. N.C., Chapel Hill, 1996—; chief hand surgery Valley Forge Army Hosp., Phoenixville, Pa., 1951-53; pres. Am. Bd. Plastic Surgery, 1975. Author: Wound Repair, 1977, 3d edit., 1982; assoc. editor: Am. Jour. Surgery, 1967—, Surgery Yearbook, 1970-89, Plastic and Reconstructive Surgery, 1972-78; asst. editor: Jour. Surg. Rsch., 1970-76. With USN, 1945-46; capt. M.C., U.S. Army, 1951-53. Served with U.S. Navy, 1945-46; served to capt. M.C. U.S. Army, 1951-53. Recipient Yandell medal Louisville Surg. Soc., 1972, McGraw medal Detroit Surg. Soc., 1973, Disting. Svc. award U. N.C., 1979, Jacob Markowitz award Acad. Surg. Rsch., 1993, Lifetime Achievement award Wound Healing Soc., 1994. Mem. AAAS, ACS, ABA, Womack Sur. Soc. (pres. 1979-80), Soc. U. Surgeons (treas. 1965-68), Plastic Surgery Rsch. Coun. (pres. 1966), Am. Surg. Assn., Am. Bd. Plastic Surgery (pres. 1976), Am. Bd. Gen. Surgery, Am. Assn. Plastic Surgeons (Clinician of Yr. 1985), Am. Soc. Surgery Hand, Internat. Soc. Surgeons, So. Surg. Assn., Rotary, Alpha Omega Alpha. Republican. Methodist. Home: 645 Rock Creek Rd Chapel Hill NC 27514-6714 Office: Hollowell Peacock & Meyer PO Box 31208 Raleigh NC 27622

PEACOCK, GEORGE ROWATT, retired life insurance company executive; b. Lakeland, Fla., Aug. 27, 1923; s. Robert and Annie Keane (Rowatt) P.; m. Virginia Jenkins, June 7, 1952; 1 child, Robert George. B.A., U. Fla., 1948, postgrad., 1948-49; postgrad., U. N.C., 1949-50, 51, Ind. U., summers 1966, 67. With Equitable Life Assurance Soc. U.S., 1952-88; v.p., head real estate dept. Equitable Life Assurance Soc. U.S., N.Y.C., 1974-77; sr. v.p., head equities sector Equitable Life Assurance Soc. U.S., 1977-80, sr. v.p., head real estate sector, 1980-84; chmn., chief exec. Equitable Real Estate Investment Mgmt., Inc., 1984-88; pres., chief exec. officer Carluke Inc., 1988—; past pres. Planters Redevel. Corp., St. Louis, 1984-87; trustee Equitable Life Mortgage & Realty Investors, 1981-83; bd. dirs. E.Q.K. Realty Investors, Arbor Properties Trust (formerly E.Q.K. Green Acres); emeritus mem. adv. bd. govs. Wharton Real Estate Ctr., U. Pa., 1985—. Author papers in field. Trustee Urban Land Inst., 1982-88; bd. dirs. Urban Land Found., 1994—; bd. govs. Ctrl. Atlanta Progress, 1984-86. With USAAF, 1942-45, with USAF, 1950-51. Decorated Purple Heart. Mem. Am. Soc. Real Estate Counselors, Urban Land Inst., Brit. Am. Property Investment Council, Am. Inst. Real Estate Appraisers, Real Estate Bd. N.Y. (past gov.), Phi Beta Kappa, Phi Kappa Phi, Phi Gamma Delta. Democrat. Office: 3414 Peachtree Rd NE Atlanta GA 30326-1113

PEACOCK, HUGH ANTHONY, agricultural research director; b. Cairo, Ga., May 30, 1928; s. Leslie Hugh and Annie John (Aldredge) P.; m. Mary Helen Willis, Oct. 8, 1949; children: Ramon Anthony, Elizabeth Ann, Mary Evelyn. BS in Agronomy, U. Fla., 1952, MS in Agronomy, 1953; PhD, Iowa State U., 1956. Rsch. assoc. Iowa State U., Ames, 1955-56; asst. agronomist U. Fla., Leesburg, 1957-58; rsch. agronomist Ga. Exptl. Sta. USDA, Experiment, 1959-73; dir. Agrl. Rsch. & Edn. Ctr., prof. U. Fla., Jay, 1973-97, prof. emeritus, 1997—. Contbr. articles to Agronomy Jour., Crop Sci., Plant Disease, Jour. Nematology. Director Hist. Soc. Santa Rosa County, Milton, Fla., 1979-80, Kiwanis Club of Milton, 1974—, chmn. agrl. com., 1987-89. Cpl. U.S. ARmy, 1946-47, CBI. John D. Rockefeller Inst. scholar, 1953. Mem. Environ. Enhancement Assn. West Fla. (bd. dirs. Pensacola chpt. 1976-96), Am. Soc. Agronomy (assoc. editor 1980-83), Am. Genetic Assn., Crop Sci. Soc. Am. (assoc. editor 1976-80), Alpha Zeta, Phi Kappa Phi, Sigma Xi, Gamma Sigma Delta. Methodist. Achievements include research in number of genes controlling defoliation vs. non-defoliation in cotton; effect of heterosis and combining ability on yield of cotton, effect of nitrogen fertilization on yield; effect of skip-row culture on fiber characteristics of cotton; yield response of cotton to spacing, effect of seed source on seedling vigor, yield and lint of upland cotton; a cone-type planter for experimental plots; subsurface sweep for applying herbicides; yield responses of soybean cultivars to Meloidogyne incognita; cotton responses to nitrogen fertilization. Office: U Fla Agr Rsch Ctr West Fla 4253 Experiment Dr Hwy 182 Jay FL 32565-8926

PEACOCK, JAMES DANIEL, lawyer; b. Moorestown, N.J., Dec. 19, 1930; s. L. Lawrence and Esther H. Peacock; m. Joan Peacock, June 14, 1953; children: Elizabeth Levine, Martha McLaughlin, Margaret Mae Daly, Mary Anne Freidman. AB, Duke U., 1952; LLB, U. Md., 1957. Bar: M. 1957, U.S. Ct. Appeals (4th cir.) 1959, U.S. Dist. Ct. Md. 1957, U.S. Supreme Ct. 1976. Of counsel Semmes Bowen & Semmes, Balt., 1957-97. Trustee Sheppard & Enoch Pratt Hosp., Towson, Md., 1964— (chair 1993—). Fellow Am. Coll. Trial Lawyers (state chair 1985-86, adj. state chair 1992-93), Am. Bar Found., Md. Bar Found.; mem. Wednesday Law Club (pres. 1987-88). Home: 105 Bonnie Hill Rd Baltimore MD 21204-4209

PEACOCK, JUDITH ANN See ERWIN, JUDITH ANN

PEACOCK, LAMAR BATTS, retired physician; b. Albany, Ga., Sept. 21, 1920; s. Herbert A. and Helen Marian (LeVan) P.; m. Jane Bonner, June 7, 1947; children: Helen Lee (Mrs. Richard Paul Wade), Linda Jane (Mrs. Mathew Gossage), Lamar Bonner. BA, Emory U., 1941; MD, Med. Coll. Ga., 1946. Diplomate: Am. Bd. Internal Medicine. Intern Univ. Hosp., Augusta, 1946-47; resident Univ. Hosp., 1947-48; fellow internal medicine U. Va. Hosp., Charlottesville, 1948-49; resident Univ. Hosp., Augusta, 1949-50; practice medicine specializing in internal medicine and allergy Atlanta, 1950-91; mem. staff St. Joseph's Infirmary, Crawford Long Hosp., Piedmont Hosp., Grady Meml. Hosp., Hughes Spalding Pavilion, Northside Hosp., West Paces Ferry Hosp., all Atlanta, Cobb Gen. Hosp., Austell, Ga., Douglasville (Ga.) Hosp.; instr. internal medicine Ga. Bapt. Hosp., Atlanta, 1950-58, chief medicine, 1958-72; mem. faculty Emory U. Sch. Medicine, Atlanta, 1950—, asst. clin. prof. medicine, 1962—; instr. internal medicine Sch. Dentistry, 1958—. Chief med. br., health services Atlanta Met. Area Civil Def., 1960-63; mem. Ga. Pub. Health Assn., 1967-69, Ga. Bd. Health, 1966-72, Ga. Vocational Rehab. Council, 1973—; Pres. trustees Med. Coll. Ga. Found., 1963. Fellow ACP, Am. Coll. Allergy, Asthma and Immunology (nat. pres. 1972-73), Am. Acad. Allergy and Immunology; mem. AMA, Am. Heart Assn., Ga. Heart Assn., Am. Soc. Internal Medicine, Ga. Soc. Internal Medicine, 5th Dist. Med. Soc., Ga. Thoracic Soc., Med. Assn. Atlanta (prs. 1965), Med. Assn. Ga. (1st v.p. 1966-67), Southeastern Allergy Assn. (pres. 1963-64), So. Med. Assn., Cherokee Town and Country Club. Episcopalian. Home: 3120 Verdun Dr NW Atlanta GA 30305-1940

PEACOCK, LELON JAMES, psychologist, educator; b. Brevard, N.C., May 25, 1928; s. L.J. and Dorothy (Barrett) P.; m. Marian Davis, June 8, 1945; children: Lynn Barrett, Janice Davis, Timothy Lee. Student, Emory U., 1945-47; A.B., Berea Coll., 1950; M.S., U. Ky., 1952, Ph.D., 1956. Psychophysiologist U.S. Army Med. Research Lab., Ft. Knox, Ky., 1954-56; rsch. assoc., acting dir. Yerkes Labs. of Primate Biology, Inc., Orange Park, Fla., 1956-59; assoc. prof. psychology U. Ga., Athens, 1959-65; prof. U. Ga., 1966-90, prof. emeritus, 1990—. Author: (with R.V. Heckel) Textbook of General Psychology, 1966; Contbr. articles profl. jours. Recipient U. Ga. M.G. Michael Research award, 1964. Fellow AAAS; mem. APA, So. Soc. Philosophy and Psychology (pres. 1973-74), Soc. Neurosci., Sigma Xi, Phi Kappa Phi. Home: 145 Woodland Way Athens GA 30606-4349

PEACOCK, MARKHAM LOVICK, JR., English educator; b. Shaw, Miss., Sept. 19, 1903; s. Markham Lovick and Mary (Patton) P.; m. Dora Greenlaw, Dec. 29, 1928. Grad., Webb Sch., 1921; B.A., Washington and Lee U., 1924, M.A., 1926; Ph.D., Johns Hopkins, 1942. Mem. faculty Va. Polytech. Inst., 1926—, prof. English, 1945—, chmn. dept., 1960-66. Author: The Critical Opinions of William Wordsworth, 1949, also critical, ednl. and lit. articles. Mem. Am. Assn. U. Profs., Nat. Council of Tchrs. English, Modern Lang. Assn., Internat. Fedn. of Modern Langs. and Lits., Modern Humanities Research Assn., Acad. Polit. Sci., N.E.A., Guild of Scholars, Omicron Delta Kappa, Lambda Chi Alpha, Sigma Upsilon, Phi Kappa Phi, Gold Triangle. Episcopalian. Clubs: Shenandoah; Tudor and Stuart (Balt.), Johns Hopkins (Balt.); Princeton. Home: 801 Draper Rd SW Blacksburg VA 24060-5117

PEACOCK, MARY WILLA, magazine editor; b. Evanston, Ill., Oct. 23, 1942; d. William Gilbert and Mary Willa (Young) P. B.A., Vassar Coll., 1964. Assoc. lit. editor Harper's Bazaar mag., N.Y.C., 1964-69; staff editor Innovation mag., N.Y.C., 1969-70; editor in chief, co-founder, sec.-treas., pres. Rags mag., N.Y.C., San Francisco, 1970-71; co-founder, features editor Ms. mag., N.Y.C., 1971-77; pub., pres. Rags mag., N.Y.C., 1977-80; sr. editor Village Voice, N.Y.C., 1980-85, style editor, 1985-89; editor-in-chief Model mag., N.Y.C., 1989—, editorial cons., 1991—; fashion dir. Lear's Mag., N.Y.C., 1992-93; dep. editor In Style Mag., 1993-94, Mirabella mag., 1994-95; cons., 1995—; writer in field.

PEACOCK, MOLLY, poet; b. Buffalo, June 30, 1947; d. Edward Frank and Pauline Ruth (Wright) P. BA magna cum laude, Harpur Coll., Binghamton, N.Y., 1969; MA with honors, Johns Hopkins U., 1977. Adminstr., lectr. in English, SUNY-Binghamton, 1970-76; lectr. Johns Hopkins U., Balt., 1977-78, Barnard Coll., 1989-93; instr. English, Friends Sem., N.Y.C., 1981-92; poet-in-residence Bucknell U., NYU, Sarah Lawrence Coll., U. Western Ontario, 199-96—. Author: And Live Apart, 1980; Raw Heaven, 1984, Take Heart, 1989, Original Love, 1995; contbg. writer House and Garden mag., 1996 contbr. poems to The New Yorker, The New Republic, The Nation. Danforth Found. fellow, 1976; Yaddo fellow, 1980, 82, 89, Ingram Merrill Found., 1981, 86, New Va. Rev., 1983; grantee Creative Artists Pub. Svc. Program, 1977, N.Y. Found. for Arts, 1985, NEA, 1991; Lila Wallace/Woodrow Wilson fellow, 1994, 95, 96. Mem. PEN, Poetry Soc. Am. (governing bd. 1988—, pres. emeritus). Home: 505 E 14th St Apt 3G New York NY 10009-2903 also: 229 Emery St E, London, ON Canada N6C 2E3

PEAGLER, OWEN F., college administrator; b. New Milford, Conn., Nov. 28, 1936; s. Robert James and Myrtle (Gary) P.; m. Joyce Hancock (div. 1983); children: Catherine, Robert; m. Teresa Boone, Mar. 20, 1985; 1 child, Kirin. BS, Western Conn. State U., 1956; MA, NYU, 1959, profl. diploma, 1964. Tchr. New Milford Pub. Schs., 1955-56; dir. guidance White Plains (N.Y.) Pub. Schs., 1957-69; dean sch. continuing edn. Pace U., N.Y.C., 1969-78, Ea. Conn. State U., Willimantic, 1978—; chmn. bd. WAVE, Inc., Washington, 1976—; cons., V.I., 1970-73. Sec. dept. community affairs State of Del., Wilmington, 1982-83; asst. to N.Y. Rep. State Chmn. N.Y. Rep. State Com., Albany, 1970-78; chmn. Pres'. Adv. Coun. on Edn. Disadvantaged Children, Washington, 1973-78. Named N.Y. State Young Man of Yr. N.Y. Jr. C. of C., 1964; recipient Outstanding Coll. Programs award Conn. Nat. Guard, 1988. Home: 57 Boughton Rd Old Lyme CT 06371-1321 Office: Ea Conn State U Office of Dean Cont Edn 83 Windham St Willimantic CT 06226-2211

PEAKE, FRANK, middle school educator; b. Elgin, S.C., Oct. 25, 1939; s. Barney and Elrie (Branham) P. AA, Anderson Coll., 1966; BS, U. S.C., 1968; MA in Teaching, The Citadel, 1976. Cert. tchr., S.C. Classroom tchr. Berkeley Jr. High, Moncks Corner, S.C., 1968-70; classroom tchr. Berkeley Middle Sch., Moncks Corner, 1970-85, 90-95, ret., 1995; classroom tchr. Macedonia Middle Sch., Moncks Corner, 1986-88, North Ctrl. High, Kershaw, S.C., 1988-89. With S.C. Air Nat. Guard, 1959-65. Mem. Nat. Coun. Tchrs. Math., Mensa. Republican. Baptist. Avocations: reading. Home: 195 Peake Rd Elgin SC 29045

PEAL, CHRISTOPHER JOHN, educational administrator; b. Moline, Ill., Dec. 17, 1963; s. Gerald J. and Annette M. Peal. BA, Olivet Nazarene U., 1986; MA, U. Mich., 1989; PhD, Loyola U., 1996. Cert. supt., adminstr., tchr., Ill., Mich., Wis. English, lang. arts, speech, journalism tchr., newspaper advisor Plymouth-Canton High Sch., Mich., 1986-90; asst. prin. Muskegon Catholic Ctrl. Jr./High Sch., Mich., 1990-91; dean students Canton Mid. Sch., Streamwood, Ill., 1991-94; prin. North Elem. Sch., Watervliet, Mich., 1994—; mem. Watervliet Sch. Improvement Team, 1994—; mem. Elgin (Ill.) Sch. Dist. U-46 Mid. Sch. Task Force, 1991-94; advisor to student newspaper, adj. instr. Lake Mich. Coll., 1997—. Mem. Watervliet PTO, 1994—. Recipient Spl. Tribute award State of Mich., 1987, Gold Apple Teaching Excellence award Wayne County (Mich.) Intermediate Sch. Dist., 1987, 88, 89; dean's merit fellow U. Mich., 1987, 88, Dow Jones Newspaper Fund fellow, 1988. Mem. ASCD, Mich. Elem. and Mid. Sch. Prins. Assn., Nat. Assn. Elem. Sch. Prins., Mich. Interscholastic Press Assn. (judge 1988-90), Columbia Scholastic Press Assn. (bd. judges 1987-90, conv. speaker), Gt. Lakes Interscholastic Press Assn. (judge 1988-90), Journalism Edn. Assn. Avocations: antiquing, computers, golf. Office: North Sch 287 Baldwin Ave Watervliet MI 49098

PEALE, RUTH STAFFORD (MRS. NORMAN VINCENT PEALE), religious leader; b. Fonda, Iowa, Sept. 10, 1906; d. Frank Burton and Anna Loretta (Crosby) Stafford; m. Norman Vincent Peale, June 20, 1930; children: Margaret Ann (Mrs. Paul F. Everett), John Stafford, Elizabeth Ruth (Mrs. John M. Allen). AB, Syracuse U., 1928, LLD, 1953; LittD, Hope Coll., 1962; LHD (hon.), Milw. Sch. Engring., 1985, Judson Coll., 1988; LHD, Milw. Sch. Engring., 1985. Tchr. math. Cen. High Sch., Syracuse, N.Y., 1928-31; nat. pres. women's bd. domestic missions Ref. Ch. Am., 1936-46; sec. Protestant Film Commn., 1946-51; chmn. Am. Mother's Com., 1948-49; pres., editor-in-chief, gen. sec., CEO, chmn. bd. dirs. Peale Ctr. for Christian Living, 1940—; nat. pres. bd. domestic missions Ref. Ch. in Am., 1955-56; mem. bd. N Am. Missions, 1963-69, pres., 1967-69; mem. gen. program council Ref. Ch. in Am., 1968—; mem. com. of 24 for merger Ref. Ch. in Am. and Presbyn. Ch. U.S., 1966-69; v.p. Protestant Council N.Y.C., 1964-66; hon. chancellor Webber Coll., 1972—; co-founder, pub. Guideposts, N.Y.C., 1945—, pres., 1985-92, chmn. bd., 1992—; pres. Fleming H. Revell, Tarrytown, N.Y., 1985-92; founder Ruth Stafford Peale Ctr., Syracuse, 1989—. Appeared on: nat. TV program What's Your Trouble, 1952-68; Author: I Married a Minister, 1942, The Adventure of Being a Wife, 1971, Secrets of Staying in Love, 1984; founder, pub. (with Dr. Peale) Guidepost mag., 1957—; co-subject with husband: film One Man's Way, 1963. Trustee Hope Coll., Holland, Mich., Champlain Coll., Burlington, Vt., Stratford Coll., Danville, Va., Lenox Sch., N.Y.C., Interchurch Center Syracuse U., 1955-61; bd. dirs. Cook Christian Tng. Sch., Lord's Day Alliance U.S.; mem. bd. and exec. com. N.Y. Theol. Sem., N.Y.C.; sponsor Spafford Children's Convalescent Hosp., 1966—; bd. govs. Help Line Telephone Center, 1970—, Norman Vincent Peale Telephone Center, 1977; mem. nat. women's bd. Northwood Inst., 1981. Named N.Y. State Mother of Yr., 1963, Disting. Woman of Yr., Nat. Art Assn., Religious Heritage Am. Ch. Woman of Yr., 1969; recipient Cum Laude award Syracuse U. Alumni Assn. N.Y., 1965, Honor Iowans award Buena Vista Coll., 1966, Am. Mother's com. award for religion, 1970, Disting. Svc. award Coun. Chs., N.Y.C., 1973, Disting. Citizen award Champlain Coll., 1976, Disting. Svc. to Cmty. and Nation award Gen. Fedn. Women's Clubs, 1977, Horatio Alger award, 1977, Religious Heritage award, 1979, joint medallion with husband Soc. for Family of Man, 1981, Soc. Family of Man award, 1981, Alderson-Broaddus award, 1982, Marriage Achievement award Bride's mag., 1984, Gold Angel award Religion in Media, 1987, Adela Rogers St. John Roundtable award, 1987, Disting. Achievement award Am. Aging, 1987, Paul Harris award N.Y. Rotary, 1989, Leader's award Arthritis Found. Dutchess County, 1992, Dave Thomas Well Done! award, 1994, Norman Vincent Peale award for positive thinking, 1994, Master of Influence award Nat. Speakers Assn., 1995. Mem. Insts. Religion and Health (bd. exec. com.), Am. Bible Soc. (trustee 1948-93, hon. trustee 1993—), United Bible Soc. (v.p.), Interch. Ctr. (bd. dirs. 1957-92, chmn. 1982-90), Nat. Coun. Chs. (v.p. 1952-54, gen. bd.; treas. gen. dept. Uniteed Ch. Women, vice chmn. broadcasting and film commn. 1951-55, program chmn. gen. assembly 1966), N.Y. Fedn. Women's Clubs (chmn. religion 1951-53, 57-58), Home Missions Coun. N.A. (nat. pres. 1942-44, nat. chmn. migrant com. 1948-51), Internat. Platform Orgn. (bd. govs. 1994—, Norman Vincent Peale award 1994), PEO, Alpha Phi (Frances W. Willard award 1976). Republican. Office: Peale Ctr Christian Living 66 E Main St Pawling NY 12564-1409

PEALE, STANTON JERROLD, physics educator; b. Indpls., Jan. 23, 1937; s. Robert Frederick and Edith May (Murphy) P.; m. Priscilla Laing Cobb; June 25, 1960; children: Robert Edwin, Douglas Andrew. BSE, Purdue U., 1959; MS in Engring. Physics, Cornell U., 1962, PhD in Engring. Physics, 1965. Research asst. Cornell U., Ithaca, N.Y., 1962-64, research assoc., 1964-65; asst. research geophysicist, asst. prof. astronomy UCLA, 1965-68; asst. prof. physics U. Calif., Santa Barbara, 1968-70, assoc. prof., 1970-76, prof., 1976-94, prof. emeritus, rsch. prof., 1994—; mem. com. lunar and planetary exploration NAS-NRC, Washington, 1980-84, lunar and planetary geosci. rev. panel, 1979-80, 86-89, 94-96, Planetary Sys. Sci. Working Group, 1988-93, Lunar and Planetary Sci. Coun., 1984-87; lunar sci. adv. group NASA-JPL, Pasadena, Calif., 1970-72; mem. Keck time allocation com. NASA, 1996—. Assoc. editor: Jour. Geophys. Research, 1987; contbr. articles to profl. jours. Recipient Exceptional Scientific Achievement medal NASA, 1980, James Craig Watson award Nat. Acad. Scis., 1982; vis. fellowships U. Colo., Boulder, 1972-73, 1979-80. Fellow AAAS (Newcomb Cleveland prize 1979), Am. Geophys. Union; mem. Am. Astron. Soc. (divsns. planet sci. and dynamic astronomy, Dirk Brouwer award 1992), Internat. Astron. Union. Avocation: gardening. Office: U Calif Santa Barbara Dept Physics Santa Barbara CA 93106

PEAPPLES, GEORGE ALAN, automotive executive; b. Benton Harbor, Mich., Nov. 6, 1940; s. Arthur L. and Kathleen C. (Peters) P.; m. Rebecca Dean Sowers, June 27, 1962; children: Lucia Christine, Sarah Bouton. BA in Econs., U. Mich., 1962, MBA in Fin., 1963. Fin. analyst GM Corp., Detroit, 1964-68; dir. capital analysis and investment N.Y.C., 1968-73; asst. divsn. comptr. Delco Moraine divsn. Dayton, Ohio, 1973-75; asst. treas. bank rels. Detroit, 1975-77, asst. comptr., 1980-82; v.p. fin. mgr. Can., Ltd. Oshawa, Ont., 1982-84; group dir. strategic bus. planning Chevrolet-Pontiac-Canada group Warren, Mich., 1984-86; v.p., gen. mgr. Detroit, 1986-94; v.p. corp. affairs Washington, 1994—; asst. sec. of Navy U.S. Dept. Def., 1977-80; bd. dirs. Am. Coalition for Traffic Safety and Fed. City Coun.; mem. vis. com. U. Mich.; mem. nat. fgn. trade coun. Congl. Mgmt. Found.; mem. bd. govs. Nat. Ctr. for Asia-Pacific Econ. Cooperation; mem. task force on U.S.-China policy Ctr. strategic Internat. Studies; mem. Bus.-Govt. Rels. Coun. Chmn. bd. dirs. Coalition for Vehicle Choice; bd. dirs. Shakespeare Theatre. Recipient Disting. Pub. Svc. award Washington, 1980. Mem. Nat. Assn. Mfrs. (bd. dirs.), Mich. Mfrs. Assn. (mem. nat. com. on U.S.-China rels.), Econ. Club. Washington. Office: GM Corp 1660 L St NW Ste 401 Washington DC 20036 also: GM Bldg 3044 W Grand Blvd Detroit MI 48202-3037

PEARCE, COLMAN CORMAC, conductor, pianist, composer; b. Dublin, Leinster, Ireland, Sept. 22, 1938; came to U.S., 1987; s. Charles Edward and Elizabeth Mary (Byrne) P.; m. Eithne McGrath, Jan. 25, 1964 (div. 1991); 1 child, Deborah. BMus, Nat. U. Ireland, Dublin, 1960; studied with Franco Ferrara, 1965, pvt. pupil of Hans Swarowsky, 1969. From staff condr. to prin. condr. Radio TV Ireland (RTE), Dublin, 1965-83; prin. condr., music dir. Miss. Symphony Orch., Jackson, 1987—; dir. orch. studies, Royal Irish Acad. Music, Dublin, 1970-78; music examiner, Dept. Edn., Dublin, 1965-87; choral arranger, Castle Tours, Limerick, Ireland, 1974—. Recordings on CD include Contemporary Irish Composers, The Memory is a Living Thing. Avocations: art collecting, reading, theatre, travel. Home: 5045 Meadow Oaks Park Dr Jackson MS 39211-4816 Office: Miss Symphony Orch PO Box 2052 201 E Pascagoula St Jackson MS 39225

PEARCE, DAVID HARRY, biomedical engineer; b. Newport News, Va., July 20, 1943. BSEE, Va. Poly. Tech. and State U., 1966; PhD, U. Va., 1972. Registered profl. engr., Miss. Asst. prof. dept. physiology U. Miss. Med. Sch., Jackson, Miss., 1972-74, E. Tenn. State U. Sch. Medicine, JohnsonCity, Tenn., 1974-75; biomed. engr. Miss. Meth. Rehab. Ctr., Jackson, Miss., 1975-82, dir. biomedical engring., 1987—; v.p. Bobby J. Hall & Assocs., McComb, Miss., 1982-87; grant adminstr. HUD Block Grant, Magnolia, Miss., 1985-87. Contbr. articles to profl. jours. Young Investigator Pulmonary award NIH, 1973. Mem. IEEE, Am. Soc. Hosp. Engrs., Assn. Advancement of Med. Instrumentation, Jackson Photo Soc. (pres. 1980), Miss. Writers Assn. (treas. 1992). Avocations: photography, woodworking, writing. Address: PO Box 5336 Brandon MS 39047-5336 Office: Miss Meth Rehab Ctr 1350 E Woodrow Wilson Ave Jackson MS 39216-5112

PEARCE, DONALD JOSLIN, retired librarian; b. Southampton, Eng., May 31, 1924; came to U.S., 1949, naturalized, 1952; s. Alfred Ernest and Constance May (Jeffrey) P.; m. June Inez Bond, Dec. 7, 1946; children—Kristin, Kim. Student, Sch. Oriental and African Studies, U. London, 1942-43; A.B., George Washington U., 1953; M.S. in L.S, Cath. U. Am., 1954. Part-time library asst. U.S. Dept. Agr., 1949-54; student asst. George Washington U. Library, 1950-53; circulation librarian Denison U., 1954-56; staff Ohio State U. Library, 1956-59, asst. acquisition librarian, 1958-59; head librarian, asst. prof. U. N.D., 1959-69, chief bibliographer, 1969-73, asst. dir. libraries, 1973-75, asst. prof. Oriental philosophy, 1969-75; library dir., asst. prof. philosophy U. Minn., Duluth, 1975-88, ret., 1988; Chmn. staff orgn. round table Ohio Library Assn., 1958-59. Served with Brit. Army, 1943-47. Mem. ALA, N.D. Library Assn. (pres. 1965-67), Minn. Library Assn. (sec. 1978-80, v.p. 1985, pres. 1986), Assn. Coll. Reference Librarians, Mountain Plains Library Assn. (v.p. 1968-69), Buddhist Assn., Phi Beta Kappa, Beta Phi Mu. Home: 1804 Vermilion Rd Duluth MN 55803-2509

PEARCE, DRUE, state legislator; b. Fairfield, Ill., Apr. 2, 1951; d. H. Phil and Julia Detroy (Bannister) P.; m. Michael F.G. Williams; 1 child, Tate Hanna Pearce-Williams. BA in Biol. Scis., Ind. U., 1973; MPA, Harvard U., 1984; cert. exec. program Darden Sch. Bus., U. Va., 1989. Sch. tchr. Clark County, Ind., 1973-74; curator of edn. Louisville Zoo, 1974-77; dir. Summerscene, Louisville, 1974-77; asst. v.p., br. mgr. Ala. Nat. Bank N., 1977-82; legis. aide to Rep. John Ringstad Ala. Ho. of Reps., Juneau, 1983; mem. Ala. Ho. of Reps., 1984-88, minority whip, 1986; state senator State of Ala., 1988—, chmn. com. oil and gas, mem. exec. com. energy coun., 1989-90, chmn. com. labor and commerce, mem. exec. coms. western state conf., coun. state govts., energy coun., 1991-92, co-chmn. senate fin., chmn. energy coun., vice chmn. com. energy, nat. coun. state govts., 1993-94, mem. select com. legis. ethics and legis. coun., 1993—, pres. senate, mem. exec. com. energy coun., vice chmn. senate coms. resources and rules, 1995-96, co-chmn. com. senate fin., mem. exec. com. energy coun., vice chmn. com. senate judiciary, 1997—; fin. cons. Bowman and Miller, Anchorage, 1983; ptnr. 4150 Co., Anchorage and Kotzebue, Ala., 1983—, Cloverland N., Anchorage, 1993—; investor, bd. dirs. Wave Energy Corp., Anchorage; resources cons. Artic Slope Regional Corp., Anchorage, 1987-91, 95-96. Bd. dirs. Ala. Women's Aid in Crisis, Anchorage Econ. Devel. Coun., Ala. Aerospace Devel. Corp., Ala. Spl. Olympics, Gov.'s Bd.; mem. Ala. Resource Devel. Coun., Ala. Women's Polit. Caucus. Mem. DAR, Alaska C. of C. Republican. Home: 716 W 4th Ave Ste 500 Anchorage AK 99501-2107 Office: Office of the State Senate State Capitol Juneau AK 99801

PEARCE, ELI M., chemistry educator, administrator; b. Bklyn., May 1, 1929; s. Samuel and Sarah (Reitzen) Perlmutter; m. Maxine I. Horowitz, Feb. 21, 1951 (div. 1978); children:Russell Gane, Debra Nore; m. Judith Handler, May 29, 1980. BS, Bklyn. Coll., 1949; MS, NYU, 1951; PhD, Poly. Inst. Bklyn, 1958. Research chemist NYU-Bellevue Med. Ctr., N.Y.C., 1949-53, DuPont, Wilmington, Del., 1958-62; sec. mgr. J.T. Baker, Phillipsburg, N.J., 1962-68; tech. supr. Allied Corp., Morristown, N.J., 1968-72, research cons., 1972-73; dir. Dreyfus Lab. Research Triangle Inst., Research Triangle Park, N.C., 1973-74; prof. polymer chemistry and chem. engring. Poly. Inst. N.Y., Bklyn., 1974—, dir. Polymer Research Inst., 1981-96, Univ. prof., 1990—, head dept. chemistry, 1976-82, dean arts and scis., 1982-90; cons. AMP, Inc., Harrisburg, Pa., Arco, Newton Square, Pa., Colgate, Piscataway, N.J., Dupont, Richmond, Va., Texaco, Beacon, N.Y. Co-author: Laboratory Experiments in Polymer Synthesis and Characterization, 1982, High Performance Thermosets; editor: Macromolecular Synthesis, Vol. 1, 1982; co-editor: Fiber Chemistry, 1983, Contemporary Topics in Polymer Science, vol. 2, 1977, Flame Retardance of Polymeric Materials, vols. 1-3, Jour. Polymer Sci.; mem. editl. bd. Ency. Materials Sci., 1983; contbr. over 230 articles on polymers to profl. jours. Bd. dirs. Petroleum Research Fund, 1982-84; bd. dirs. Nat. Materials Adv. Bd., 1975-77. Served with U.S. Army, 1953-55. Recipient Edn. Service award Plastics Inst. Am., 1973; recipient Disting. Faculty citation Poly. Inst. N.Y., 1980, Paul J. Flory Polymer Edn. award, 1992, Kaufman Lectr. award Ramapo Coll., 1992, Gold Medal award N.Y. Inst. Chemists, 1992, Reed-Lignin Lectr. award U. Wis., 1987. Fellow AAAS, Am. Inst. Chemists, N.Am. Thermal Analysis Soc., N.Y. Acad. Scis. (chmn. polymer sect. 1972-73), Soc. Plastics Engrs. (Internat. Edn. award 1988); mem. Am. Chem. Soc. (councilor 1978—, chmn. polymer divsn. 1980, coun. policy com. on coms., chmn. com. sci.), Sigma Xi. Home: 2 Fifth Ave New York NY 10011 Office: Polytech U Polymer Rsch Inst 6 Metrotech Ctr Brooklyn NY 11201-3840

PEARCE, GEORGE HAMILTON, archbishop; b. Boston, Jan. 9, 1921; s. George Hamilton and Marie Louise (Duval) P. BA, Marist Coll. and Sem., Framingham, Mass., 1943. Tchr. Marist Coll. & Sem., Bedford, Mass., 1947-48, St. Mary's High Sch., Van Buren, Maine, 1948-49; missionary Roman Catholic Vicariate of Samoa, 1949-67, vicar apostolic of Samoa, 1956-66; bishop Diocese of Samoa, 1966-67; archbishop Archdiocese of Suva, Suva, Fiji, 1967-76; apostolic adminstr. Diocese of Agana, Guam, 1969; pres. Episcopal Conf. of the Pacific, 1969-71; staff mem. Bethany House of Intercession, Hastings-on-Hudson, N.Y., 1977-83; asst. to bishop Diocese of Providence, 1983—. Home: 30 Fenner St Providence RI 02903-3603*

PEARCE, HARRY JONATHAN, lawyer; b. Bismarck, N.D., Aug. 20, 1942; s. William R. and Jean Katherine (Murray) P.; m. Katherine B. Bruk, June 19, 1967; children: Shannon Pearce Baker, Susan J., Harry M. BS, USAF Acad., Colorado Springs, Colo., 1964; JD, Northwestern U., 1967. Bar: N.D. 1967, Mich. 1986. Mcpl. judge City of Bismarck, 1970-76, U.S. magistrate, 1970-76, police commr., 1976-80; sr. ptnr. Pearce & Durick, Bismarck, 1970-85; assoc. gen. counsel GM, Detroit, 1985-87, v.p., gen. counsel, 1987-92, exec. v.p., gen. counsel, 1992-94, exec. v.p., 1994-95, vice chmn., 1996—; bd. dirs. GM Corp., Hughes Electronics Corp., GM Acceptance Corp., Am. Automobile Mfrs. Assn., Marriott Internat. Inc., Econ. Strategy Inst., United Way for Southeastern Mich., Theodore Roosevelt Medora Found., MDU Resources Group, Inc., Na Def. Univ. Found., Detroit Investment Fund. Mem. vis. com., dean's adv. coun. Sch. Law, Northwestern U.; mem. bd. visitors U.S. Air Force Acad.; chmn. Product Liability Adv. Coun. Found.; founding mem. minority counsel demonstration program Commn. on Opportunities for Minorities in the Profession, ABA; chmn. The Sabre Soc., USAF Acad.; trustee Howard U., U.S. Coun. for Internat. Bus., New Detroit, Inc.; mem. The Mentor's Group Forum for U.S.-European Union Legal-Econ. Affairs, The Conf. Bd., Network of Employers for Traffic Safety's Leadership Coun., Pres.'s Coun. on Sustainable Devel., World Bus. Coun. for Sustainable Devel. Capt. USAF, 1964-70. Hardy scholar Northwestern U., Chgo., 1964-67, recipient Alumni Merit award, 1991. Fellow Am. Coll. Trial Lawyers, Internat. Soc. Barristers; mem. Am. Law Inst. Avocations: amateur radio, woodworking, sailing. Office: GM Corp Mail Code 482-A-39-H03 100 Renaissance Center PO Box 431301 Detroit MI 48243-7301

PEARCE, HERBERT HENRY, real estate company executive. Student, New Haven Coll.; LLD (hon.), U. New Haven, 1980; LHD (hon.), Albertus Magnus Coll., 1988. Various mgmt. positions A.C. Gilbert Co., New Haven, Conn., 1935-57; chmn., CEO H. Pearce Real Estate Co., North Haven, Conn., 1958—. Hon. chmn. YMCA Fund Raising Project; mem. Yale New Haven Hosp. Devel. Com.; nominations com. U. New Haven; bd. dirs. Nation Conf. Christians and Jews; mem. adv. bd. South Ctrl. Jr. Achievement; chmn. United Way Loaned Exec. Com.; chmn. mktg. and rsch. Conn. Regional Econ. Devel. Coun.; advisor Eli Whitney Mus. on A.C. Gilbert Project. Recipient Cmty. Leadership award Greater New Haven C. of C., Greater New Haven Realtor of Yr. award, Outstanding Achievement award Nat. Jr. Achievement Orgn., Humanitarian award Hunger Relief and Devel., Inc., YMCA Cmty. Leadership award; inducted into Jr. Achievement Free Enterprise Hall of Fame. Fellow Berkeley Coll. (assoc.), Yale U. (assoc.); mem. Conn. Assn. Realtors (past pres.), Greater New Haven Bd. Realtors (past pres.), Quinnipiack Club, New Haven Country Club, Mory's Assn., Kiwanis. Office: H Pearce Real Estate Co 393 State St North Haven CT 06473-3115

PEARCE, JOSEPH HUSKE, industrial engineer; b. Sarasota, Fla., Mar. 7, 1941; s. Joseph Huske and Lola (Smelcer) P.; m. Victoria Lee Georgie (div. Aug. 1976); children: Sherri Lynn, Lara Ann. BSEE, U. Fla., 1968. Elec. engr. trainee guided missiles range div. Pan Am. World Airways, Patrick AFB, Fla., 1964-65; asst. base ops. mgr. trainee Pan Am. World Airways, Freeport, The Bahamas, 1965-66; installation engr. safeguard anti ballistic missile project Western Electric Co., Winston-Salem, N.C., 1968-73; design and test engr. Western Electric Co., Madison, N.J., 1973-74; indsl. engr. AT&T, Rolling Meadows, Ill., 1974-91; cons. engr. Cen. Office Equipment, 1991—. Petty officer 2d class USN, 1959-63. Republican. Lutheran. Avocations: American and Civil War history, fishing, hunting, classic literature. Office: AT&T PO BOx 140335 Gainesville FL 32614

PEARCE, MARGARET TRANNE, law librarian; b. San Bernadino, Calif., Mar. 20, 1946; d. Paul Nelson and Margaret (Buchanan) Gregory; m. Ronald Wayne Pearce, Jan. 13, 1973; 1 child, Alice. BA in Edn., U. Kans., 1968; MLS, Emporia State U., 1969; postgrad., Washington U., 1982-83. Asst. libr. Kans. State U., Manhattan, 1969-73; assoc. law libr. Washington U., St. Louis, 1974-80; ct. libr. Mo. Ct. Appeals (ea. dist.), St. Louis, 1981-83; libr. 8th Cir. Libr., Kansas City, Mo., 1983—. Guardian ad litem Ct. Appointed Spl. Advocates, Johnson County, Kans., 1984-88. Mem. Am. Assn. Law Libr., Mid-Am. Assn. Law Libr., Kansas City Assn. Law Librs. (bd. dirs. 1992-93, sec. 1995—). Home: 8408 W 113th St Overland Park KS 66210-2438 Office: US Cts Libr 811 Grand Blvd Kansas City MO 64106-1909

PEARCE, PAUL FRANCIS, retired aerospace electronics company executive; b. Boston, Sept. 17, 1928; s. George Hamilton and Marie Louise (Duval) P.; m. Gilda Troisi, Apr. 11, 1953; children: Janet, Theresa, Diane. BSEE (Edwards scholar), MIT, 1950; M.S., Mass. Inst. Tech., L.A., 1952; postgrad. (Hughes fellow), U. Calif., Los Angeles, 1957-58, U. So. Calif., 1958-59, Inst. Mgmt. Northwestern U., 1966. Project engr. Trans-Sonics, Inc., Burlington, Mass., 1952-55; sect. head application engring., strategic systems Hughes Aircraft Co., Culver City, Calif., 1955-59; with Lockheed Electronics Co., Plainfield, N.J., 1959-67; gen. mgr. div. mil. systems Lockheed Electronics Co., 1964-65, v.p., gen. mgr., 1965-67; v.p., div. mgr. Tele-Dynamics div. AMBAC Industries, Inc., Ft. Washington, Pa, 1967-74; group v.p. comml. and aerospace electronics group AMBAC Industries, Inc., Carle Place, N.Y., 1973-80; pres. James G. Biddle Co., Blue Bell, Pa., 1980-93, ret.; bd. dirs. AVO Internat. Ltd., 1987-91. Mem. Armed Forces Communications and Electronics Assn. (pres. 1969-71), Inst. Nav., Delaware Valley Mfrs. Assn. (sr. vice chmn. 1987-89, chmn. 1990-92—), Greater Phila. C. of C., Ft. Washington Indsl. Park Mgmt. Assn. (gov. 1973-74), Sigma Xi. Clubs: Mfrs'. Golf and Country (Oreland, Pa.) (handicap chmn. 1987-90), St. David's Golf Club (Wayne, Pa.).

PEARCE, RONALD, retired cosmetic company executive; b. Whitstable, County of Kent, Eng., Apr. 29, 1920; came to U.S., 1949; s. Fernley Charles and Medora Kate (Lissenden) P.; m. Olive Stacey, Apr. 4, 1942; children: David Fernley, Jane Ryding Robertson. Cambridge matriculation, Lindisfarne Coll., Ruabon, North Wales, U.K., 1937. Chief cashier Westminster Bank, Croydon, Eng., 1947-48; comml. officer Brit. Consulate, Dallas, 1949-52; v.p. World Gift Co., Dallas, 1953-63, Nelson Electronics, Dallas, 1963-68; stockbroker Walston & Co., Dallas, 1968-73; dir. purchasing Mary Kay Cosmetics, Inc., Dallas, 1973-85; pres. Global Water Techs., Inc., 1992-95, Alpha Aqua Tech., 1996—. Chmn. bd. Dallas Lighthouse for the Blind, 1987. Served to flight lt. RAF, 1940-46. Republican. Episcopalian. Home: 6918 Lloyd Valley Ln Dallas TX 75230-3129

PEARCE, WILLIAM JOSEPH, retired public broadcasting executive, consultant; b. Ponca City, Okla., Jan. 15, 1925; s. William Thomas and Mary Madeline (Fitzgerald) P.; m. Michaele Evelyn Mitchell, Aug. 1, 1958 (div. June 1962); m. Mary Simmen, June 6, 1964 (div. Mar. 31, 1982); children: Margaret Wickens, Daniel Ethan; m. Noel Knille, Sept. 1, 1983 (div. Dec. 1988); children: Ryder Fitzgerald and Tyler Lightsinger (twins); stepchildren: Laura Rutherford Stone, Alexandra Garret Stone. B.A., U. Miami, 1950; postgrad., U. Conn., 1952-53; M.S., Syracuse U., 1959; grad. Advanced Mgmt. Program, Harvard U., 1976, Wharton Sch., U. Pa. Tchr. public schs. East Lyme, Conn., 1953-56; tchr. Dept. Air Force, Japan, 1956-58; exec. producer TV N.Y. State Edn. Dept., Albany, 1959-60; dir. radio-TV Brown U., 1960-65; cons. ETV, Rochester (N.Y.) City Sch. Dist., 1966-68; gen. mgr. Sta. WLIW-TV, Plainview, N.Y., 1968-69; pres., gen. mgr. Sta. WXXI-TV-AM-FM, Rochester, 1969-96; pres. Media Cons., Rochester, 1996—; bd. dirs. Native Am. Pub. Telecommunications, Rochester Philharm. Orch., Am. Program Svc., Rochester Sch. Arts; chmn. Brookings Inst. Ctr. Advanced Study, Rochester. Mem. bd. mgmt. Rochester YMCA Camps; dir. Hunt Hollow Devel. Corp.; v.p. fin. Urbanarium, Rochester Devel. Cmty.; dir. Friends of Ganondogan. Recipient George Foster Peabody award, numerous other spl. radio and TV programming and prodn. awards for public affairs and performance programs, Civic medal for edn. City of Rochester. Mem. Nat. Assn. Pub. TV Stas., Nat. Pub. Radio, Nat. Assn. Broadcasters, N.Y. State Broadcasters Assn. (bd. dirs.), Rochester Radio Reading Svc., Rochester C. of C., VFW, Univ. Club of Rochester (bd. dirs.), Tennis Club of Rochester, Rotary. Roman Catholic. Office: 35 Berkeley St Rochester NY 14607-2207 *I never had an idea I didn't get from reading. There is no substitute for reading.*

PEARCE, WILLIAM MARTIN, history educator; b. Plainview, Tex., Mar. 11, 1913; s. Will Martin and Annie Eugenia (Bates) P.; m. Frances Elizabeth Campbell, Sept. 6, 1939; children—William Martin III, Richard Campbell. A.A., Kemper Mil. Sch., 1932; A.B., So. Meth. U., 1935; M.A., Tex. Tech U., 1937; Ph.D., U. Tex., 1952; LL.D., Tex. Wesleyan Coll., 1978. Instr. history Tex. Tech Coll., 1938-42, 46-47, asst. prof. history, 1949-53, asso. prof. history, 1953-55, prof., head dept. history, 1955-60, v.p. coll., 1960-68; dir. Tex. Tech Coll. (Archeol. Field Sch.), Glorieta, N.Mex., 1948, Tex. Tech Coll. (Valley of Mexico), 1949; pres. Tex. Wesleyan Coll., 1968-78; ret., 1978. Author: The Matador Land and Cattle Company, 1964. Served as lt. AUS, 1942-45. Decorated Bronze Star, Purple Heart; recipient Distinguished Alumnus award Tex. Tech U., 1975. Mem. Panhandle-Plains Hist. Soc. (dir.), Phi Alpha Theta, Pi Kappa Alpha, Phi Kappa Phi. Methodist. Home: 101 N Troy Ave #D Lubbock TX 79416-3029

PEARL, HARVEY, rehabilitation psychologist; b. N.Y.C., July 11, 1930; s. Louis and Blanche (Birnbaum) P.; B.S., N.Y. U., 1953, M.A., 1957; Ph.D., Syracuse U., 1970; m. Dorothy Morrison, June 20, 1953; children—Stuart Ray, Lesley, Andrea. Tchr. indsl. arts Public Schs. Elizabeth (N.J.), 1955-56; workshop supr. United Cerebral Palsy Assn., Roosevelt, N.Y., 1956-58; workshop dir. Jewish Vocat. Service, Cin., 1958-61; dir. work tng. center Assn. Retarded Children, Rochester, N.Y., 1961-63; asst. exec. dir. Consol. Industries Greater Syracuse (N.Y.) 1965—; instr. Cornell U., Ithaca, N.Y., 1970—; cons. Social Security Adminstrn., 1962—. Pres., Jewish Family Service Bur., 1974-82; adv. council Cazenovia Coll., 1977—, Occupational Edn., Syracuse City Sch. Dist., 1971—. Served with U.S. Army, 1953-55. Recipient citation of merit Syracuse U. Sch. Social Work, 1972; cert. rehab. counselor. Mem. Nat. Rehab. Assn., Am. Counseling Assn., Am. Rehab. Counseling Assn., Nat. Vocat. Guidance Assn., Am. Psychol. Assn., Am. Wine Soc. Author: (with A. Speiser, A. Staniec) Bibliography of Work Evaluation in Vocational Rehabilitation, 1966; Comparison of Personal Values and Worker Assessments of Work Evaluators in Rehabilitation and Industrial Settings, 1970. Home: 227 Wellington Rd De Witt NY 13214-2225 Office: 100 W Court St Syracuse NY 13204-1318

PEARL, HELEN ZALKAN, lawyer; b. Washington, Sept. 12, 1938; d. George and Harriet (Libman) Zalkan; m. Jason E. Pearl, June 27, 1959; children: Gary M., Esther H., Lawrence J. BA with hons., Vassar Coll., 1959; JD, U. Conn., 1978. Bar: Conn. 1978, U.S. Dist. Ct. Conn. 1978. Mkt. rsch. analyst Landers, Frary & Clark, New Britain, Conn., 1960-61; managerial statistician Landers, Frary & Clark, 1961-62; real estate salesperson Denuzze Co., New Britain, 1966-70; property mgr. self-employed New Britain, 1970-75; legal asst. Atty. Gen. Office, State of Conn., Hartford, 1978; assoc. Weber & Marshall, New Britain, 1978-83; ptnr. Weber & Marshall, 1983—; hearing officer Commn. on Human Rights & Opportunities, State of Conn., 1980—; spl. master State of Conn. Judicial Dept., 1986—. New Britain rep. to Cen. Conn. Regional Planning Agy., 1973-75, 84—, chmn., 1990-92; mem. New Britain Bd. Fin. and Taxation, 1973-77; founder, mem. Conn. Permanent Commn. on Status of Women, 1975-82; also others. Recipient Women in Leadership award, YWCA of New Britain, 1988, Book award for torts, Am. Jurisprudence, 1976, Econs. prize, Vassar Coll., 1959. Mem. AAUW (pres. 1970-72), Conn. Bar Assn., New Britain Bar Assn., LWV (Conn. specialist 1987—, local pres. 1995—), Hartford Vassar Club, Phi Beta Kappa. Democrat. Jewish. Avocations: travel, theater, reading, cooking. Home: 206 Hickory Hill Rd New Britain CT 06052-1010 Office: Weber & Marshall PO Box 1568 New Britain CT 06050-1568

PEARL, JUDEA, computer scientist, educator; b. Tel-Aviv, Sept. 4, 1936; U.S. citizen; married; 3 children. BSc, Israel Inst. Tech., 1960; MSc, Newark Coll. Engring., 1961; PhD in Elec. Engring., Poly. Inst. Bklyn., 1965. Rsch. engr. Dental Sch., NYU, 1960-61; mem. tech. staff RCA Rsch. Labs., 1961-65; dir. advanced memory devices Electronic Memories, Inc., Calif., 1966-69; prof. engring. sys. and computer scis. UCLA, 1969—; instr. Newark Coll. Engring., 1961; cons. Rand Corp., 1972, Integrated Sci. Corp., 1975, Hughes Aircraft, 1989. Recipient Outstanding Achievement award RCA Labs., 1965. Fellow IEEE, Am. Assn. Artificial Intelligence; mem. Nat. Acad. Engring. Office: UCLA Dept Computer Sci 4731 Boelter Hall Los Angeles CA 90024

PEARL, WILLIAM RICHARD EMDEN, pediatric cardiologist; b. N.Y.C., Nov. 1, 1944; s. William Emden and Sara (Gilston) P.; m. Karlyn Katsumoto, July 9, 1978; children: Jeffrey, Kristine. BA, Queens Coll., 1966; MD, SUNY, Bklyn., 1970. Diplomate Am. Bd. Pediatrics, Am. Bd. Pediatric Cardiology. Intern Roosevelt Hosp., N.Y.C., 1970-71; resident N.Y. Hosp.-Cornell Med. Ctr., N.Y.C., 1971-72; fellow Albert Einstein Coll. Medicine, N.Y.C., 1972-74; asst. prof. U. Hawaii, Honolulu, 1974-76; asst. prof. Tex. Tech. Med. Sch., El Paso, 1976-82, assoc. prof., 1982-92; chief pediatric cardiology William Beaumont Army Med. Ctr., El Paso, 1976-94; assoc. prof. med. branch U. Tex. Med. Br., Galveston, 1994—; cons. Miami (Fla.) Children's Hosp., 1988, Driscol Children's Hosp., Corpus Christi, Tex., 1992, Thomason Hosp., El Paso, 1976-92. Contbr. articles to profl. jours. Col. USAR, 1974-92. N.Y. State Bd. Regents scholar, 1962-66, Fed. Health Careers scholar, 1967-70; NIH fellow, 1972-73; recipient Dept. of Army Commendation for outstanding sci. achievement, 1984. Fellow Am. Acad. Pediatrics, Am. Coll. Cardiology; mem. Am. Heart Assn. (coun. on cardiovascular disease in the young 1982). Office: U Tex Med Br Children's Hosp 301 University Blvd Galveston TX 77550-2708

PEARLMAN, BARBARA, artist, educator; b. N.Y.C., Apr. 25, 1938; d. Henry and Edith (Stein) P.; 1 child, Alexandre Yulish. BA, Parsons Sch. Design, 1960. Illustrator Neiman Marcus, Dallas, 1960-61, Vogue, Marie Claire, France, Eng., Germany, 1961-65, Galey & Lord, N.Y.C., 1965-78, Vogue, Harpers, N.Y. Mag., Glamour, N.Y. Art, N.Y.C., 1965-78; tchr. Parsons Sch. Design, N.Y.C., 1975-79, Fashion Inst. Tech., N.Y.C., 1979-95, Nassau Fine Arts Mus., 1980-81; Spkr. NYU Phenomenology in the Arts. Exhbns. N.Y.C., Germany, 1978-95; featured in Russian and Polish mags.; works featured in History of Fashion (Eunic Sloane), numerous others; contbr. articles to Gebracht Graphic mag. Recipient award Soc. Illustrators, 1976, 69, 70. Mem. Nat. Orgn. Women Artists. Home: 2259 Edsall Ave Bronx NY 10463

PEARLMAN, DAVID SAMUEL, allergist; b. Syracuse, N.Y., Jan. 20, 1934; s. Benjamin Norman and Sylvia Rene (Karp) P.; m. Doris Ann Greenberg, Apr. 16, 1966; children—Michael, Melanie. Student, Cornell U., 1951-54; M.D., SUNY, Syracuse, 1958. Diplomate Am. Bd. Allergy and Immunology (dir. 1973-78). Intern, then asst. resident in pediatrics Univ. Hosps., Cleve., 1958-60; chief resident in pediatrics U. Colo. Med. Center, Denver, 1960-61; mem. faculty U. Colo. Med. Center, 1962—, clin. prof. pediatrics, 1978—, dir. pediatric allergy tng. program, 1964-66, co-dir., 1966-73; practice medicine specializing in allergy Denver, 1972—; assoc. Colo. Allergy and Asthma Clinic, 1972—; acting chief dept. pediatric allergy Nat. Jewish Hosp. and Rsch. Ctr., 1972-73, sr. staff physician pediatrics allergy, 1973-92; mem. allergy and infectious disease tng. grant com. NIH, 1970-72. Contbr. articles to med. jours. Served to maj. M.C. AUS, 1967-69. Fellow U. Colo. Med. Center, 1961-62; Fellow NIH, 1963-66, 69-72. Fellow Am. Acad. Pediatrics (chmn. sect. on allergy and Clin. Immunology, 1992-94), Am. Acad. Allergy (exec. com. 1978-81), Am. Coll. Allergists; mem. AAAS, Am. Soc. Cert. Allergists, Am. Thoracic Soc., Am. Coll. Chest Physicians, Colo. Allergy Soc., Joint Council Allergy and Immunology (bd. dirs. 1985-92, pres. 1988-90), Colo. Med. Soc., Denver Med. Soc., Adams-Aurora County Med. Soc., Friends of Chamber Music (dir. 1965-81). Jewish. Address: 6029 E Prentice Pl Englewood CO 80111-1415

PEARLMAN, JERRY KENT, electronics company executive; b. Des Moines, Mar. 27, 1939; s. Leo R. Pearlman; married; children: Gregory, Neal. BA cum laude, Princeton U., 1960; MBA, Harvard U., 1962. With Ford Motor Co., 1962-70; v.p. fin. dir. Behring Corp., 1970-71; from contr. to chmn. Zenith Electronics Corp., Glenview, Ill., 1971-95, also dir.; bd. dirs. Stone Container Corp., Am. Nat. Bank, Current Assets LLC. Bd. dirs. Evanston (Ill.) Hosp., Ctrl. Asia-Am. Enterprise Fund, Northwestern U. Office: 21 Linden Ave Wilmette IL 60091-2837

PEARLMAN, LOUIS JAY, aviation and promotion company executive; b. Flushing, N.Y., June 19, 1954; s. Herman and Reenie (Nevler) P. BA, Queens Coll., 1976; MBA, Century U., 1980; Degree in Sales Mgmt., SUNY, Buffalo, 1980; PhD in Bus. Adminstrn., Century U., 1983. Pres. Commuter Helicopter Corp., N.Y.C., 1974-75; pres., chief operating officer Trans Continental Airlines, Inc., N.Y.C., 1975—; gen. mgr. U.S. Westdeutsche Luftwerbung GmbH, N.Y.C., 1976-85; chmn., pres., CEO Airship Internat. Ltd., N.Y.C., 1982—, bd. dirs., 1985—; pres., CEO Trans Continental Records, Inc., 1992—; pres. Backstreet Boys, Inc., 1993—; CEO Chippendales, Inc., 1996—; cons. Queens Coll., CUNY, 1977—. Author: Survey and Analysis of the Airline Industry, 1983; song writer. Active Mitchell-Linden Civic Assn., Flushing, 1980-82, Kissimmee (Fla.) Mcpl. Airport, 1985—. Mem. U.S. Power Squadron, Wings Club (disting., recipient Lighter-than-Air award 1987), Lighter-than-Air Soc. (hon.), Young Entrepreneurs Am., Young Millionaires Club, Internat. Air Transport Assn., Blimp Port U.S.A. (pres. 1987—), Friar's Club (N.Y.C.). Avocations: flying airplanes, helicopters and blimps, swimming, bowling, music, boating. Office: Airship Internat Ltd Trans Continental Airlines 7380 Sand Lake Rd Ste 350 Orlando FL 32819-5257

PEARLMAN, MITZI ANN, elementary education educator; b. Houston, July 21, 1951; d. Bernard Joseph and Annie Mae (Gollob) P. BA in Sociology, U. Colo., Boulder, 1975; MA in Elem. Edn., U. Colo., Denver, 1988. Cert. elem. tchr., Colo. Tchr. 2d grade Cherry Creek Schs., Englewood, Colo., 1987-88; tchr. 2d, 3rd grades Douglas County Schs., Castle Rock, Colo., 1988—. Vol. Denver Zoo. Recipient Douglas County NOVA awards for Creative Excellence in Teaching, 1988, 89, 90, 91, 92, Innovative Instrn. award Bus. Week mag., 1990, Douglas County Edn. Found. grants, 1993, Pub. Svc. Intergenerational grant, 1993, Classroom Connection Disseminator grants, 1992, 93, Classroom Connection Adaptor grants, 1992, 93, 94, 95, 96, 97, Douglas County mini grant, 1989; named Channel 7 Tchr. of the Week, 1993. Mem. ASCD, Internat. Reading Assn., Douglas County Reading Assn. (treas. 1992-94), Colo. Assn. Sci. Tchrs., Phi Delta Kappa. Avocations: reading, pets, relaxing. Office: Acres Green Elem Sch 13524 Acres Green Dr Littleton CO 80124-2701

PEARLMAN, RONALD ALAN, lawyer; b. Hamilton, Ohio, July 10, 1940. A.B. with honors, Northwestern U., 1962, J.D. cum laude, 1965; LL.M. in Taxation, Georgetown U., 1967. Bar: D.C. 1991, U.S. Tax Ct. 1969, U.S. Supreme Ct. 1968. Atty. office chief counsel IRS, Washington, 1965-69; assoc. Thompson & Mitchell, St. Louis, 1969-70, ptnr., 1970-83; dep. asst. sec. for tax policy Dept. Treasury, Washington, 1983-84, asst. sec. tax policy, 1984-85; ptnr. Bryan, Cave, McPheeters & McRoberts, St. Louis, 1986-88; chief of staff joint com. on taxation U.S. Congress, Washington, 1988-90; ptnr. Covington & Burling, Washington, 1991—; adj. prof. Sch. Law Wash. U., St. Louis, 1972-83; vis. instr. Sch. Law U. Va., Charlottesville, 1995—; mem. BNA Tax Mgmt. Adv. Bd., 1986-88, 93—; participant ednl. seminars. Mem. bd. editors Northwestern U. Law Rev.; contbr. articles to various publs. Fellow Am. Coll. Tax Counsel; mem. ABA (chair govt. rels. com., mem. coun., tax sect. 1986-88), FBA (tax sect.), Am. Law Inst. (tax adv. group, cons. pass-through entities project and tax integration project), D.C. Bar (tax sect.), Order of Coif. Office: Covington & Burling PO Box 7566 1201 Pennsylvania Ave NW Washington DC 20044-7566

PEARLMAN, SAMUEL SEGEL, lawyer; b. Pitts., May 28, 1942; s. Merle Maurice and Bernice Florence (Segel) P.; m. Cathy Schwartz, Aug. 16, 1964; children: Linda P. Kraner, Caren E. AB, U. Pa., 1963, LLB magna cum laude, 1966. Bar: Pa. 1966, Ohio, 1967, U.S. Ct. Appeals (3d cir.) 1967. Law clk. U.S. Dist. Ct. (Ea. dist.) Pa., 1966-67; assoc. Burke, Haber & Berick, Cleve., 1967-72, prin., 1973-86, prin. Berick, Pearlman & Mills, 1986—; lectr. law Case Western Res. U. Sch. Law, 1978-82; mem. registration com. Ohio Div. Securities, 1979-89; adv. dir. Midland Title Security, Inc. Trustee Realty ReFund Trust (NYSE). Mem. ABA, Ohio State Bar Assn., Greater Cleve. Bar Assn. (chmn. securities law sect. 1985-86), Order of Coif. Republican. Jewish. Author: Cases, Forms and Materials for Modern Real Estate Transactions, 1978, 82. Office: 1111 Superior Ave 1350 Eaton Ctr Cleveland OH 44114

PEARLMAN, SETH LEONARD, civil engineer; b. Steubenville, Ohio, Aug. 6, 1956; s. Abraham and Rita Joy (Morov) P.; m. Pamela Diane Bretton, Mar. 29, 1987; children: Isaac Joseph, Julian Brett. BSCE, Carnegie Mellon U., 1978, MSCE, 1979. Registered profl. engr., Pa., Va. Sr. engr. GAI Cons., Pitts., 1979-82; v.p. mktg. Belot Concrete Industries, Tiltonsville, Ohio, 1982-86; chief design engr. Nicholson Constrn. Co., Bridgeville, Pa., 1986-93, regional mktg. mgr., 1993-95; dir. bus. devel. Nicholson Constrn. Co., Bridgeville, 1995—; speaker, lectr. in field. Author conf. publs. Fundraiser United Jewish Fedn., Pitts., 1988—; bd. dirs. Beth El Congregation of the South Hills, Pitts., 1991—. Mem. ASCE (mem. geotech. sect. com. Pitts. chpt. 1990-94), NSPE (pres. Wheeling W.Va. chpt. 1986), Am. Concrete Inst. (fiber reinforced concrete com. 1982-96, co-chmn. state of art report, mem. concrete piling com. 1989-95, bd. dirs. Pitts. chpt. 1984-87), Deep Founds. Inst. (mini piles com. 1996—), ADSC Internat. Assn. Found. Drilling (earth retention com. 1991-96). Democrat. Home: 266 Twin Hills Dr Pittsburgh PA 15216-1108 Office: Nicholson Constrn PO Box 98 Bridgeville PA 15017-0098

PEARLMUTTER, FLORENCE NICHOLS, psychologist, therapist; b. Bklyn., Mar. 17, 1914; d. William and Marie Elizabeth (Rugamer) Griebe; m. Wilbur Francis Nichols, Aug. 17, 1940 (dec. 1967); 1 child, Roger F.; m. F. Bernard Pearlmutter, June 27, 1969. BS, NYU, 1934, postgrad., 1965-75; MS, Yeshiva U., 1960. Psychologist P.P.P. Counseling Ctr., Northport, N.Y., 1967-69; hypno-therapist Robert E. Peck, M.D., Syosset, N.Y., 1969-75; therapist Arthur J. Gross, M.D., Hicksville, N.Y., 1975—; rsch. asst. and prof. rsch. in field. Mem. NEA, AAUW, Nassau County Psychol. Assn., N.Y. State Psychol. Assn. (assoc.), Nat. Women's Hall of Fame, Kappa Delta Pi. Avocations: cooking, phototgraphy, travel, fishing.

PEARLSTEIN, PHILIP, artist; b. Pitts., May 24, 1924; s. David and Libbie (Kalser) P.; m. Dorothy Cantor, Aug. 20, 1950; children: William, Julia, Ellen. BFA, Carnegie Inst. Tech., 1949; MA, NYU, 1955. Instr. Pratt Inst., 1959-63; vis. critic Yale U., 1962-63; from asst. prof. to prof. art dept. Bklyn. Coll., 1963-88, now Disting. prof. emeritus. Shows include Tanager Gallery, N.Y.C., 1955, 59, Peridot Gallery, N.Y.C., 1956, 57, 59, Allan Frumkin Gallery, N.Y.C., 1962, 63, 65, 67, 69, 72, 74, 76, 78, 80, 83, Frumkin Gallery, Chgo., 1960, 65, 69, 73, 75, 80, 81, Hirschl & Adler Mod., N.Y.C., 1985, 88, 91, 92, 93, Robert Miller Gallery, N.Y.C., 1995, 96, 97, Kansas City Art Inst., 1962, Ceeje Gallery, 1965, 66, Reed Coll., 1965, 79, Galerie Thelen, Cologne, Germany, 1972, Galleri Ostergren, Malmo, Sweden, 1972, Galerie Kornfeld, Zurich, Switzerland, 1972, Staatliche Museen-Kupferstichkabinett, Berlin, 1972, Kunstverein, Hamburg, Germany, 1972, Editions La Tortue, Paris, 1973, Donald Morris Gallery, Detroit, 1973, 76, 80, 94, Gimpel Fils Ltd., London, 1975, 79, Marianne Friedland Gallery, Toronto, Ont., Can., 1975, 81, Springfield (Mo.) Art Mus., 1978, 95, Harkus Krakow Gallery, Boston, 1978-79, Myers Fine Arts Gallery, SUNY, Plattsburg, 1979, Galerie Jöllenbach, Cologne, Germany, 1979, 89, Carnegie-Mellon U., Pitts., 1979, Assoc. Am. Artists, 1980, FIAC, Paris, 1980, Brooke Alexander Gallery, 1980, 81, Ringling Mus. Art, Sarasota, Fla., 1981, San Antonio Mus. Art, 1981, (Retrospective) Milw. Art Mus., The Bklyn. Mus., The Pa. Acad. Fine Arts, Phila., The Toledo Mus. Art, 1983-84, Carnegie Inst. Mus. Art, Pitts., 1982, Brody's Gallery, Washington, 1983, Images Gallery, Toledo, 1984, Galerie Rudolph Zwirner, Cologne, Germany, 1989, 91, Compass Rose Gallery, Chgo, 1991, Printworks Gallery, Chgo., 1990, Condeso Lawler Gallery, N.Y.C., 1991, P.S. 1, N.Y., 1992, Butler Art Inst, Youngstown, Ohio, 1992; group shows at Carnegie Internat., 1955, 64, 67, Whitney Mus. Am. Art, 1955, 56, 58, 62, 65, 67, 70, 72, 73, 74, 79, 91, U. Ill., 1965, 67, 68, Providence Art Club, 1965, U. Mich. Mus., 1965, Corcoran Gallery, 1967, Vassar Coll., 1968, Milw. Art, 1969, Pa. Acad. Fine Arts, 1971-72, Indpls. Mus. Art, 1972, Galerie Lowenadler, Stockholm, Sweden, 1973, Nat. Acad. Arts and Letters, N.Y.C., 1973 (award), Yale U., 1973, 74, Hofstra U., 1973, Helsinki (Finland) Mus. Art, 1974, Art Inst. Chgo., 1974, Cleve. Mus. Art, 1974, America 1976 Bicentennial Exhbn., U.S. Dept. Interior, 1976, Wildenstein Gallery, N.Y.C., 1976, Tokashima Art Mus., Japan, 1992, many others, retrospective exhbns., Finch Coll., 1974, U. Tex., Austin, 1974, Cranbrook Acad. Art, Mich., 1974, Notre Dame U., 1975, Grand Rapids (Mich.) Art Mus., 1975, Kalamazoo Inst. Arts, Tampa Bay Art, 1975, Miami Art, 1975, Philbrook Art, 1980, Chryler Mus., 1980, Akron Art Mus., 1981, San Antonio Mus., 1981, Honolulu Acad. of Art, 1994; represented in permanent collections, Phila. Mus. Art, San Antonio Mus. Assn., Pa. State U., Whitney Mus., Mus. Modern Art, N.Y., Met. Mus. of Art, Bklyn Mus., Carnegie Mus., Syracuse U., James A. Michener Found., Hirshhorn Mus., Corcoran Gallery, Art Inst. Chgo., Milw. Art Ctr., Ludwig Collection, Aachen, Germany, Sydney and Frances Lewis Found., Richmond, Va., Cleve. Mus. Art, Milw. Mus., others. Fulbright fellow to Italy, 1958-59; Guggenheim fellow, 1971-72; Nat. Endowment for the Arts grantee, 1968, grantee Am. Acad. Arts and Letters, 1992; NAD assoc., 1983. Mem. Am. Acad. Arts and Letters.

PEARLSTEIN, SEYMOUR, artist; b. Bklyn., Oct. 14, 1923; s. Morris Lazarus and Anna (Bassiur) P.; m. Toby Tessie Rubinstein, Mar. 21, 1943; children: Judith Helene, Lawrence Jonathan. Cert., Pratt Inst., Bklyn., 1950, Art Students League N.Y., 1954; student of Jack Potter. Owner, illustrator, designer Sy Pearlstein Advt. Art Studio, N.Y.C., 1946-71; artist-painter rep. by Far Gallery, N.Y.C., 1969-81; prof. N.Y.C. Tech. Coll., CUNY, Bklyn., 1971-94, prof. emeritus, 1994—, chmn. art and advt. design dept., 1985-88. One-man shows Silvermine Guild of Artists, New Canaan, Conn., 1973, Far Gallery, 1973, 75, 78, Klitgord Ctr., N.Y.C., C.C., 1974, De Mers Gallery, Hilton Head, S.C., 1975, Adelphi U., Garden City, N.Y., 1979, Grace Gallery, N.Y.C. Tech. Coll., 1992; group shows A.M. Sachs Gallery, N.Y.C., 1971, Springfield (Mo.) Art Mus., 1971, Am. Acad. Arts and Letters, N.Y.C., 1975, 76, 77, NAD, N.Y.C., 1986, 87, 89, 91, 92, Butler Inst. Art, Ohio, 1975, Ball State U., Queens Mus., N.Y.C., 1978, 81, Dept. State Art in Embassies Program, N.Y. Hist. Soc., 1981, Colo. Heritage Mus., Denver, 1981, 82, 86, Am. Watercolor Soc., N.Y.C., Ingber Gallery, N.Y.C., 1985, Audubon Artists, N.Y.C., 1990, 91, 92, Allied Artists Am., N.Y.C., 1990, 91, 95, Phila. Mus. Sales and Loan Gallery, Nat. Arts Club, N.Y.C., 1989, Grace Gallery, N.Y.C. Tech. Coll., CUNY, 1995, 96, 97, others; represented in permanent collections Mus. N.Mex., Santa Fe, Mint Mus. Art, Charlotte, N.C., NAD, N.Y.C., Fine Arts Gallery, San Diego, Adelphi U., Queens Mus., N.Y.C., Munson-Williams-Proctor Inst., Utica, N.Y., N.Y.C. Tech. Coll., Bklyn. Served with AUS, 1942-46. Recipient Gold medal Nat. Acad. Design, 1969, Hassam Fund Purchase award Am. Acad. Arts and Letters, 1969, 77, Gold medal of honor Nat. Arts Club, 1970, Ranger Fund Purchase award NAD, 1971, 82, Gold medal Soc. Illustrators, 1972, Nat. Inst.-Am. Acad. Arts and Letters grant, 1975. Mem. NAD (sec. coun.) 1980-84, W.H. Leavin prize 1985), Am. Watercolor Soc. (bd. dirs. 1979-80, Watercolor U.S.A. award 1971), Art Students League of N.Y. (life), Allied Artists Am. (bd. dirs. 1976-79, E. Lowe award 1969, gold medal 1980, George Tweed Meml. award 1989, 92), Audubon Artists (bd. dirs. 1986-89, 91-93, Grumbacher award 1971, Fabri medal 1980), Alliance Figurative Artists (c0chmn. 1976-77), Profl. Staff Congress. Home: 52 Dartmouth St Forest Hills NY 11375-5142 Office: NYC Tech Coll CUNY 300 Jay St Brooklyn NY 11201-1909

PEARLSTINE, NORMAN, editor; b. Phila., Oct. 4, 1942; s. Raymond and Gladys (Cohen) P.; m. Nancy Colbert Friday, 1988. A.B., Haverford Coll., 1964; LL.B., U. Pa., 1967. Staff reporter Wall Street Jour., Dallas, Detroit, L.A., 1968-73; Tokyo bur. chief Wall Street Jour., 1973-76; mng. editor Asian Wall Street Jour., Hong Kong, 1976-78; exec. editor Forbes Mag., Los Angeles, 1978-80; nat. news editor Wall Street Jour., N.Y.C., 1980-82; editor, pub. Wall Street Jour./Europe, Brussels, 1982-83; mng. editor, v.p. Wall Street Jour., N.Y.C., 1983-91, exec. editor, 1991-92; pres., chief exec. officer Friday Holdings, L.P., N.Y.C., 1993-94; editor-in-chief Time Warner, Inc., N.Y.C., 1994—. Pres. Atsuko Chiba Found.; bd. dirs. Am. Woman's Econ. Devel. Recipient Editor of Yr. award Nat. Press Found., 1989. Mem. ABA, D.C. Bar Assn. (trustee), N.Y. Hist. Soc. (former chmn.), Coun. Fgn. Rels. Office: Time Warner Inc 1271 Avenue Of The Americas New York NY 10020-1300

PEARSALL, GEORGE WILBUR, materials scientist, mechanical engineer, educator, consultant; b. Brentwood, N.Y., July 13, 1933; s. Milo Dickerson and Margaret Elizabeth (White) P.; m. Patricia Louise Stevens, Oct. 11, 1962. B. Metall. Engring., Rensselaer Poly. Inst., 1955; Sc.D. (Am. Soc. Metals fellow), MIT, 1961. Registered profl. engr., N.C. Research engr. Dow Chem. Co., Midland, Mich., 1955-57; research asst. MIT, 1959-60, asst. prof. metallurgy, 1960-64; assoc. prof. mech. engring. Duke U., 1964-66, prof., 1966-81, prof. mech. engring. and materials sci., 1981—, prof. pub. policy studies, 1982—, acting dean Sch. Engring., 1969-71, dean, 1971-74, 82-83; trustee Triangle Univs. Ctr. for Advanced Studies, 1976-92, chmn. exec. com., 1983-88; dir. Duke-IBM Product Safety Inst., 1979-90. Author: (with W.G. Moffatt and J. Wulff) The Structure and Properties of Materials, 1964; mem. editl. bd. Jour. Products Liability, 1977-96, Proceedings of the IEEE, 1994-96; contbr. articles to profl. jours. Served with AUS, 1957. Mem. AAAS, ASME, ASTM, Soc. Risk Analysis, Am. Soc. Metals (life), Soc. Plastics Engrs., Sigma Xi, Phi Lambda Upsilon, Tau Beta Pi, Pi Tau Sigma. Home: 2941 Welcome Dr Durham NC 27705-5555

PEARSALL, GREGORY HOWARD, naval officer; b. Riverhead, N.Y., Nov. 2, 1951; s. Smith Gregory and Betty Irene (Tuthill) P.; m. Barbara Jean Hesler, June 28, 1970; children: Christopher, Andrew, Kevin. BS in Mgmt., U.S. Naval Acad., Annapolis, Md., 1974; MS in Bus., Naval Postgrad. Sch., Monterey, Calif., 1986; MA in Fgn. Affairs, Naval War Coll., Newport, R.I., 1994. Supply officer USS Hermitage, Virginia Beach, Va., 1978-80, Naval Ordnance Sta., Indian Head, Md., 1980-83; asst. supply officer USS Shenandoah, Norfolk, Va., 1983-85; ADP project officer, comptroller Navy Fleet Material Support Office, Mechanicsburg, Pa., 1987-90; comptroller U.S. Naval Acad., Annapolis, 1990-92; supply officer USS Sierra, Charleston, S.C., 1992-93; dir. fleet/indsl. support group Navy Ships Parts Control Ctr., Mechanicsburg, 1994-95; exec. officer Navy Fleet Material Support Office, Mechanicsburg, 1995—; dir. Charles County Econ. Devel. Commn., Waldorf, Md., 1980-83; mem. Capital Region Econ. Devel. Corp., Camp Hill, Pa., 1995—. Coach St. Andrews Little League, Charleston, 1993, King Phillip Little League, Bristol, R.I., 1994, Bristol Youth Soccer Assn., 1994, Hampden Youth Soccer Assn., Mechanicsburg, 1995, 96, 97. Recipient Meritorious Svc. medal Pres. of the U.S., 1983, 90, 92, 93, Hammer award Nat. Performance Review, 1995, Mil. Outstanding Vol. Svc. medal, 1996. Avocations: gardening/landscaping, woodworking, coin/card collecting, sports. Office: Navy Fleet Material Support Office 5450 Carlisle Pike Box 2010 Mechanicsburg PA 17055

PEARSALL, SAMUEL HAFF, III, landscape ecologist, geographer, foundation administrator; b. Nashville, Sept. 2, 1949; s. Sam H. Jr. and Margaret Isabelle (Ikard) P.; m. Patricia Davenport, July 1973 (div. 1978); 1 child, Rachel Claire; m. Linda Louise Parrish, Sept. 4, 1982; 1 child, Paul Samuel. BS, U. Tenn., 1972; M. Prof. Studies, Cornell U., 1982; PhD, U. Hawaii, 1993. Exec. dir. Coastal Resources Ctr., Bar Harbor, Maine, 1975-77; program dir. Natural Areas and Natural Heritage Survey Tenn. Dept. Conservation, Nashville, 1978-81, dir. Ecol. Svcs. divsn., 1982-85; dir. Pacific Sci. The Nature Conservancy, Honolulu, 1989-91; dir. sci. and stewardship The Nature Conservancy, Durham, N.C., 1992—; adj. faculty geography U. N.C., 1993—; founder Pacific Sci. program The Nature Conservancy, 1989, founding mem. conservation com., 1994—, Ecoregions working group, 1996-97; adj. faculty Nicholas Sch. Environment Duke U., 1997—; mem. So. Blue Ridge Ecoregional Planning Team, 1996—; leader Mid-Atlantic Coastal Plain Ecoregional Planning Team, 1997—. Author: Terrestrial Coastal Environments and Tourism in Western Samoa, 1993, (with others) Wildlife Conservation Evaluation Methods in U.S., 1985; contbr. more than 30 nature conservation articles to profl. jours.; sole author conservation databases on 10 Pacific island countries, 1988—. Bd. dirs. Tenn. Environ. Coun., Nashville, 1980-85, Natural Areas Assn., Rockford, 1984-87; counselor Conservation Trust for N.C., 1993—; founder Tenn. Protection Planning Com.; student fellow East-West Ctr., 1985-90. Recipient Hodgson award Assn. Am. Geographers, 1988, Wiens award U. Hawaii, 1993. Achievements include research in nature conservation and landscape ecology in Western Samoa and North Carolina. Home: 1307 Chaney Rd Raleigh NC 27606-2736 Office: Nature Conservancy 4011 University Dr Ste 201 Durham NC 27707-2549

PEARSE, WARREN HARLAND, association executive, obstetrician and gynecologist; b. Detroit, Sept. 28, 1927; s. Harry Albridge and Frances (Wressell) P.; m. Jacqueline Anne Langan, June 15, 1950; children: Kathryn, Susan, Laurie, Martha. B.S., Mich. State U., 1948; M.B., M.D., Northwestern U., 1950. Intern. Univ. Hosp., Ann Arbor, Mich., 1950-51; resident obstetrics and gynecology, 1951-53, 55-56; practice medicine specializing obstetrics and gynecology Detroit, 1956-58; mem. faculty U. Nebr. Med. Center Omaha, 1959-71, Found. prof., chmn. dept. obstetrics and gynecology, 1962-71; asst. dean U. Nebr. Med. Center Omaha (Med. Coll.), 1963-71, mem. residency rev. com. obstetrics and gynecology, 1968-93; dean Med. Coll. Va., Richmond, 1971-75; exec. dir. Am. Coll. Obstetrics and Gynecology, 1975-93; cons., 1993—; editor Women's Health Issues, Washington, 1993—; chmn. rsch. adv. group Maternal Child Health Svc., Health Scis. Mental Health Adminstrn., HEW, 1967—; cons. family planning Office Econ. Opportunity, 1970—. Author: (with R.W. Stander) Obstetrics and Gynecology at the University of Michigan, 1969; Contbr. chpts., articles tech. lit. Served from 1st lt. to capt. AUS, 1953-55. Mem. Am. Coll. Obstetrics and Gynecology (dist. sec., treas. 1964-68, vice chmn. 1968-71), Am. Gynecology Soc., Soc. Gynecology Investigation, Assn. Profs. Gynecology and Obstetrics (sec., treas. 1969—), Alpha Omega Alpha. Home: 350 S River Landing Rd Edgewater MD 21037-1549 Office: American College of Obs & Gyns 409 12th St SW Washington DC 20024-2125

PEARSON, ALBERT MARCHANT, food science and nutrition educator; b. Oakley, Utah, Sept. 3, 1916; s. Levi and Mary (Marchant) P.; m. Harriet Eilenberger, Nov. 16, 1946; children—Richard A., Carol Jane, Marian Beth, Donna Gay, David C. B.S., Utah State U., 1940; M.S., Iowa State U., 1941; Ph.D., Cornell U., 1949. Grad. asst. Iowa State U., 1940-41, Cornell U., 1946-49; asst. prof., then assoc. prof. U. Fla., 1949-54; mem. faculty Mich. State U., 1954-89, prof. food sci. and human nutrition, 1961-89; adj. prof. animal sci. Brigham Young U., 1989-90; courtesy prof. anima sci. Oreg. State U., 1991—. Served with USMCR, 1942-45, PTO. Mem. Am. Soc. Animal Sci. (sec.-treas. 1965-68, pres. 1969-70), Reciprocal Meat Conf. (chmn. 1956), Sigma Xi, Phi Kappa Phi. Spl. research body composition, muscle proteins, flavor components in meat. Home: 7765 Bates Rd S Salem OR 97306-9419 Office: Oreg State U Dept Animal Sci Corvallis OR 97331

PEARSON, APRIL VIRGINIA, lawyer; b. Martinsville, Ind., Aug. 11, 1960; d. Clare Grill and Sheila Rosemary (Finch) Rayner; m. Randall Keith Pearson, Dec. 10, 1988; children: Randall Kyle, Austin Finch, Autumn Virginia. BA, Calif. State U., Long Beach, 1982; JD, Pepperdine U., 1987. Bar: Calif. 1987, Idaho 1993, D.C. 1989. Assoc. counsel Union Oil of Calif., L.A., 1988—; v.p. Pa's Bier, Long Beach, Calif., 1988—; bd. dirs. Unocal Chems. Internat., The Hague, The Netherlands, 1993-95, Ammonia Safety Tng. Inst., 1995—, sec., 1997—. Mem. Women Lawyers of Long Beach (v.p.

1990-93), Orange County Bar Assn., Chem. Industry Coun. Calif. (chair regulatory affairs com. 1995, cert. indsl. fire brigade and HAZWOPER team mem.). Avocations: bicycling, tae kwon do. Office: Union Oil Co care Unocal 376 Valencia Ave Brea CA 92823-6345

PEARSON, CHARLES THOMAS, JR., lawyer; b. Fayetteville, Ark., Oct. 14, 1929; s. Charles Thomas and Doris (Pinkerton) P.; m. Wyma Lee Hampton, Sept. 9, 1988; children: Linda Sue, John Paddock. B.S., U. Ark., 1953, J.D., 1954; postgrad., U.S. Naval Postgrad. Sch., 1959; A.M., Boston U., 1963. Bar: Ark. bar 1954. Practice in Fayetteville, 1963—; dir. officer N.W. Comms., Inc., Dixieland Devel., Inc., Jonlin Investments, Inc., World Wide Travel Svc., Inc., Oklania Farms, Inc., N.W. Arl. Land & Devel., Inc., Garden Plaza Inns, Inc. Word Data, Inc., M.P.C. Farms, Inc., Fayetteville Enterprises, Inc., NWA Devel.Co., Delta Comm., Inc.; past. dir., organizer N.W. Nat. Bank. Adviser Explorer Scouts, 1968—; past pres. Washington County Draft Bd.; past pres. bd. Salvation Army. Served to comdr. Judge Adv. Gen. Corps USNR, 1955-63. Mem. ABA, Ark. Bar Assn., Washington County Bar Assn., Judge Advs. Assn., N.W. Ark. Ret. Officers Assn. (past pres.), Methodist Men (past pres), U. Ark. Alumni Assn. (past dir.), Sigma Chi (past pres. N.W. Ark. alumni, past chmn. house corp.), Alpha Kappa Psi, Phi Eta Sigma, Delta Theta Phi. Republican. Methodist. Clubs: Mason (32 deg., K.T., Shriner), Moose, Elk, Lion, Metropolitan. Office: 36 E Center St Fayetteville AR 72701-5301

PEARSON, CLARENCE EDWARD, management consultant; b. Chgo., Apr. 22, 1925; s. Edward and Irene (Silander) P.; m. June Waldhe, Apr. 21, 1951 (dec. 1967); 1 child, Scott; m. Laurie Norris, Apr. 25, 1995. BS, No. Ill. U., 1950; MPH, U. N.C., 1952. Instr. Mt. Prospect (Ill.) Pub. Schs., 1950-51; dir. health edn. DuPage County Health Dept., Wheaton, Ill., 1952-55; chief health edn. St. Louis Health Dept., 1955-57; dir. health and hosps. Health and Welfare Council, St. Louis, 1957-61; dir. health and safety Met. Life Ins. Co., N.Y.C., 1961-87; prof. edn. Columbia Tchrs. Coll., 1975—; prof. pub. health U. N.C., 1987—; pres. Universal Health Concepts, N.Y.C., 1984-87; Coun. Internat. Health, Washington, 1981-84; bd. dirs. Health Info. Co., Nat. Coun. Internat. Health, Washington, 1981-84; chmn. Profl. Exam. Svc., N.Y.C., 1996—; v.p. Peter Drucker Found. for Nonprofit Mgmt., 1994-96; mem. adv. bd. C. Everett Koop Inst.; bd. overseers Dartmouth Med. Sch., 1992-96; pres., CEO Nat. Ctr. for Health Edn., 1997—. Co-author: Managing Health Promotion, 1982; contbr. chpts. to books in field. Co-chmn. Scandinavian-Ams. for Rockefeller presdl. campaign, N.Y., 1968. Served as staff sgt. U.S. Army, 1943-46. Recipient Disting. Career award Am. Pub. Health Assn., Washington, 1981, Gold Medal for Achievement, Columbia U., N.Y.C., 1984, Internat. Health award Asia Pacific Consortium, Honolulu, 1984, Porter Prize, Pitts. Health Ctr., 1986. Fellow Am. Pub. Health Assn. (governing council 1970-78), The Univ. Club (N.Y.C.). Home: 530 E 23rd St New York NY 10010-5022 Office: Nat Ctr for Health Edn 72 Spring St New York NY 10012-4019

PEARSON, DANIEL S., lawyer; b. N.Y.C., Oct. 9, 1930; children: Elizabeth Oster, William M., Charles M.; m. Fredricka G. Smith, June 19, 1982; 1 child, Deardre Smith. BA, Amherst Coll., 1952; JD, Yale U., 1958. Bar: Fla. 1959, U.S. Supreme Ct. 1967, N.Y. 1982, U.S. Ct. Appeals (1st, 5th, 9th and 11th, DC cirs.). Asst. U.S. atty., Miami, 1961-63, pvt. practice, 1963-67; ptnr. Pearson, Josefsberg & Tarre, P.A., Miami, 1967-80; judge Dist. Ct. Appeal (3rd dist.), Miami, 1980-89; ptnr. Holland & Knight, Miami, 1989—; ind. counsel for investigation of Ron Brown, Sec. of Commerce, 1995—; adj. prof. U. Miami Sch. Law; lectr. Practicing Law Inst., Fla. Bar; mem. Am. Bd. Trial Advs. Served with USCG, 1951-54. Mem. ABA, Am. Law Inst., Am. Coll. Trial Lawyers, Am. Acad. Appellate Lawyers, Am. Bd. Trial Advocates, Order of Barristers, Dade County Bar Assn. Home: 7580 Erwin Rd Miami FL 33143-6273 Office: Holland & Knight 701 Brickell Ave Miami FL 33131-2813

PEARSON, DAVID PETRI, chemist; b. Portland, Oreg., Oct. 24, 1926; s. Brewer Petri and Laura Alvine (Johnson) P.; m. Patricia Margaret Cowan, June 4, 1949; children—Kathryn A., James P., Rebecca L., Kristine R., Judith G. B.A. in Chemistry, Reed Coll., 1949; M.S. in Phys. Chemistry, Oreg. State U., 1953; Ph.D. in Phys. Chemistry, U. So. Calif., 1960. Research chemist Phillips Petroleum Co. (AEC), Idaho Falls, Idaho, 1957-62, Bartlesville, Okla., 1962-69; lectr. in chemistry, Portland State U., 1969-71; asst. prof. chemistry So. Oreg. State Coll., Ashland, 1971-72; research assoc. Oreg. Grad. Ctr., Beaverton, 1972-74; sr. chemist Portland Gen. Electric Co., 1975-87; ret., 1987. Patentee in field. Served to cpl. USAAF, 1946-47. Mem. Am. Chem. Soc. (treas. Portland sect. 1979-82, chmn. 1983), Electrochem. Soc. Clubs: Am. Alpine, Idaho Alpine (sec. Idaho Falls 1961, pres. 1962). Republican. Presbyterian. Home: 6324 SW Radcliffe St Portland OR 97219-5749

PEARSON, DENNIS LEE, optometrist; b. Portland, Oreg., June 21, 1951; s. Alvin Wesley and Pharaby Iva (Barnett) P.; m. Corinne Elaine Boggs, Aug. 27, 1972; children: Kathleen Erin, Erik Edward. BS in Chemistry, Portland State U., 1974; OD, Pacific U., Forest Grove, Oreg., 1978. Optometrist Drs. Diederich & Pearson, St. Helens, Oreg., 1979-83; pvt. practice Lebanon, Oreg., 1983—; adv. panel mem. managed care Vision Svc. Plan, Rancho Cucamunga, Calif., 1995—; adv. panel mem. laser refraction Laser Vision Ctr. at Pacific U., Portland, 1995—. Sch. bd. mem. Sodaville Sch. Dist., Oreg., 1989-93; bd. dirs. Lebanon Boys & Girls Club, 1989-91, 93-94; elder Lebanon Presbyn. Ch., 1992—. Mem. Am. Optometric Assn., Oreg. Optometric Assn. (bd. dirs. 1988—, past pres.), Kiwanis Club of Lebanon, Lebanon C. of C. Avocations: skiing, sailing, kayaking, reading, mountain biking. Office: 90 Market St Ste 20 Lebanon OR 97355-2328

PEARSON, DONALD EMANUAL, chemist, educator; b. Madison, Wis., June 21, 1914; s. Gustav E. and Clara (Bjelde) P.; m. Gwen Smiseth, June 5, 1950; children: Donald T., Jeanah C., Sam S. Grad., U. Wis., 1936, U. Ill., 1940. Chemist Pitts. Plate Glass Co., Milw., 1940-42; tech. aide OSRD, 1942-45; chemist MIT, 1945-46; faculty Vanderbilt U., Nashville, 1946-79; prof. chemistry Vanderbilt U., 1954-79, prof. emeritus, 1979—; pvt. practice as cons., chem. rschr. Nashville; cons. in chem. and environ. problems, arson cases; rsch. dir Reclamation Svcs., Madisonville, Ky.; mem. Com. for Re-orgn. of Tenn. Dept. Health.; NSF resident to Tenn. Toxics Program. Author: (with R.C. Elderfield) Phenazines, 1956, (with C.A. Buehler) Survey of Organic Syntheses, 1970, Vol. II, 1977; also numerous articles. Mem. Am. Chem. Soc. Discoverer new method of substitution in aromatic compounds, new rearrangement hydrazone; research on mechanisms of Beckmann rearrangement, reactions in polyphosphoric acid; structure of diuretic mercuhydrin; synthesis of barbiturates, anti-malarials, plant regulatory substances and spin labels.

PEARSON, GERALD LEON, food company executive; b. Mpls., June 24, 1925; s. Perry and Lillian (Peterson) P.; m. Beverly Mary Schultz, Nov. 10, 1946; children: Steven, Perry, Liecia. Grad., Trimont (Minn.) High Sch., 1943. Treas. Trimont Packing Co., 1946-52; v.p. Spencer Foods, Iowa, 1952-68, pres., chief exec. officer, 1969-80, chmn. bd., chief exec. officer, 1972-80; chmn. Beef Specialists of Iowa Inc., 1983-94; bd. dirs. Graffaloy, Inc., El Cajon, Calif., dir. applied mem. tech., Minnetonka, Minn.; chmn., CEO World Champions of Golf Inc.; owner Brooks Golf Club, Okoboji, Iowa. Pres. Pearson Art Found.; bd. dirs. Bethany Coll., Lindsborg; commr. Nat. Mus. Am. Art-Smithsonian Instn., 1995; founder Internat. Ctr. for Jazz Found. With USN, 1943-46. Mem. Swedish Royal Roundtable, Swedish Council Am. (bd. dirs.). Home: 7224 E Stagecoach Pass Carefree AZ 85262-5003 Office: World Champions of Golf& D PO Box 195 Spencer IA 51301-0195

PEARSON, HENRY CHARLES, artist; b. Kinston, N.C., Oct. 8, 1914; s. A. Louis and Estelle P. BA, U. N.C., 1935; MFA, Yale U., 1938; postgrad., Art Students League, 1953-56. Stage scene designer, 1937-42; instr. art New Sch. Social Research, N.Y.C., 1965—, Pa. Acad. Fine Arts, Phila., 1973-88. Exhbns. include Workshop Gallery, N.Y.C., 1958, Stephen Radich Gallery, N.Y.C., 1960-70, The Responsive Eye, Mus. Modern Art, 1965, 29th Biennial Exhbn., Corcoran Gallery Art, Washington, 1965, Retrospective N.C. Mus. Art, Raleigh, N.C., 1968, Drawings USA, Minn. Mus. Art, St. Paul, 1971-73, Betty Parsons Gallery, N.Y.C., 1971-76, Art Students League Centennial, 1975, Truman Gallery, N.Y.C., 1976-79, Marilyn Pearl Gallery, N.Y.C., 1980—; retrospective Columbia (S.C.) Mus. Art, 1988, Henry Pearson and Friends Arts Ctr., Kinston, N.C., 1993, Seamus Heaney & Henry Pearson, Gordon College, Wenham, Ma., 1996; represented in permanent collections Mus. Modern Art, N.Y.C., Met. Mus. Art, N.Y.C., Whitney Mus. Am. Art, N.Y.C., Albright-Knox Gallery, Buffalo, N.C. Mus. Art, Raleigh; represented in commd. works include List Art Posters, 1965, N.Y. Film Festival poster, 1968; illustrator: Rime of the Ancient Mariner, 1964, Five Psalms, 1969, Seamus Heaney's Sweeney Praises the Trees, 1981, Seamus Heaney's Poems and a Memoir, 1982, Seamus Heaney's Three Short Poems, 1993-94. With AUS, 1942-48, USAF, 1948-53. Ford Found. fellow, 1964; Recipient gold medal for achievement in the fine arts N.C. Gov., 1970. Mem. Am. Abstract Artists, Century Assn. Studio: 58 W 58th St New York NY 10019-2502

PEARSON, HENRY CLYDE, judge; b. Ocoonita, Lee County, Va., Mar. 12, 1925; s. Henry James and Nancy Elizabeth (Seals) P.; m. Jean Calton, July 26, 1956; children—Elizabeth, Frances, Timothy Clyde. Student Union Coll., 1947-49; LL.B., U. Richmond, 1952. Bar: Va. 1952, U.S. Ct. Appeals (4th cir.) 1957, U.S. Supreme Ct. 1958. Sole practice, Jonesville, Va., 1952-56; asst. U.S. atty. Western Dist. Va., Roanoke, 1956-61; ptnr. Hopkins, Pearson & Engleby, Roanoke, 1961-70; judge U.S. Bankruptcy Ct. Western Dist. Va., Roanoke, 1970—; participant Va. Continuing Edn. Seminars; mem. adv. com. fed. rules bankruptcy procedure. Mem. Va. Ho. of Reps., 1954-56, Va. Senate, 1968-70; Republican nominee Gov. of Va., 1961. Served with USN, 1943-46; PTO. Mem. Va. State Bar, ABA, Va. Trial Lawyers Assn., Assn. Trial Lawyers Am., Am. Judicature Soc., Am. Judges Assn., Fed. Bar Assn., Delta Theta Phi, Tribune Jefferson Senate, Am. Legion, VFW. Methodist. Clubs: Masons, Shriners. Editorial bd. Am. Survey Bankruptcy Law, 1979. Office: US Courthouse PO Box 2389 Roanoke VA 24010-2389

PEARSON, JAMES BOYD, JR., electrical engineering educator; b. McGehee, Ark., June 3, 1930; s. James Boyd and Lydia Frances (Lacey) P.; m. Marian Scarborough, Feb. 16, 1957; children: Sarah, Jane, Carol, Catherine, Susan, Joanne. BSEE, U. Ark., 1958, MSEE, 1959; PhD, Purdue U., 1962. Asst. prof. electrical engring. Purdue U., Lafayette, Ind., 1962-65; assoc. prof. Rice U., Houston, 1965-70, prof., 1970-79, J.S. Abercrombie prof., 1979—. Served to capt. USAR, 1952-55. Fellow IEEE. Office: Rice Univ Dept Elec and Computer Engring Houston TX 77251

PEARSON, JOHN, mechanical engineer; b. Leyburn, Yorkshire, U.K., Apr. 24, 1923; came to U.S., 1930, naturalized, 1944; s. William and Nellie Pearson; m. Ruth Ann Billhardt, July 10, 1944 (wid. Nov. 1984); children: John, Armin, Roger; m. Sharoll L. Chisolm, Sept. 8, 1993. B.S.M.E., Northwestern U., 1949, M.S., 1951. Registered profl. engr., Calif. Rsch. engr. Naval Ordnance Test Sta., China Lake, Calif., 1951-55, head warhead rsch. br., 1955-58, head solid dynamics br., 1958-59, head detonation physics group, 1959-67; head detonation physics div. Naval Weapons Ctr., China Lake, Calif., 1967-83, sr. rsch. scientist, 1983—; cons., lectr. in field; founding mem. adv. bd. Ctr. for High Energy Forming, U. Denver; mem. bd. examiners Sambalpur U., India, 1982-83. Author: Explosive Working of Metals, 1963; Behavior of Metals Under Impulsive Loads, 1954; contbr. articles to profl. publs; patentee impulsive loading, explosives applications. Charter mem. Sr. Exec. Svc. U.S., 1979. With C.E., U.S. Army, 1943-46, ETO. Recipient L.T.E. Thompson medal, 1965, William B. McLean medal, 1979, Superior Civilian Svc. medal USN, 1984, Haskell G. Wilson award, 1985, cert. of recognition Sec. Navy, 1975, merit award Dept. Navy, 1979, cert. of commendation Sec. Navy, 1981, Career Svcs. award Sec. Navy, 1988, John A. Ulrich award Am. Def. Preparedness Assn., 1991; 1st disting. fellow award Naval Weapons Ctr., 1989. Fellow ASME; mem. Am. Soc. Metals, Am. Phys. Soc., AIME, Fed. Exec. League, Sigma Xi, Tau Beta Pi, Pi Tau Sigma, Triangle. Home and Office: PO Box 1390 858 N Primavera St Ridgecrest CA 93555-7907

PEARSON, JOHN DAVIS, retired naval officer; b. Pinetops, N.C., June 22, 1939; s. Hugh Oliver Sr. and Lillian Marie (Williams) P.; m. Georgeanne Spalding, Dec. 29, 1962; children: Brian Davis, Elizabeth Ann. BS in Naval Sci., U.S. Naval Acad., Annapolis, Md., 1961; MS in Underwater Acoustics, U.S. Naval Postgrad. Sch., Monterey, Calif., 1970. Commd. ensign USN, 1961, advanced through ranks to rear adm., 1989; engr. officer USS California, Norfolk, Va., 1971-76; exec. officer USS Richmond K. Turner, Norfolk, 1976-77; instr. Prospective Engr. Officer Course, Idaho Falls, Idaho, 1977-79; comdg. officer USS Thomas C. Hart, Norfolk, 1979-81, USS Truxtun, San Diego, 1981-84; officer in charge Sr. Officer Ship Material Readiness Course, Idaho Falls, 1984-86; div. dir. Office Chief of Naval Ops., Washington, 1987-89; dep. commdr. Joint Task Force Four, Key West, Fla., 1989-91; commdr. Mine Warfare Command, Corpus Christi, Tex., 1991—. Decorated Legion of Merit, Disting. Svc. medal. Avocations: golf, fishing, skiing.

PEARSON, JOHN EDWARD, lawyer; b. Jamaica, N.Y., Aug. 20, 1946; s. Stanley Charles and Rose Margaret (Manning) P.; m. Laura Marie Johannes, Dec. 28, 1968; children: Laura Rose, Jack. BA, Manhattan Coll., 1968; JD, St. John's U., 1972. Bar: N.Y. 1973, Fla. 1981, U.S. Dist. Ct. (so. dist.) N.Y. 1977, U.S. Dist. Ct. (so. dist.) Fla. 1982, U.S. Ct. Appeals (11th cir.) 1982, U.S. Ct. Appeals (5th cir.) 1982. Assoc. Sage, Gray, Todd & Sims, N.Y.C., 1972-78, ptnr., 1979; ptnr. Sage, Gray, Todd & Sims, Miami, Fla., 1980-87; ptnr. Hughes, Hubbard & Reed, Miami, 1987-91, 94—, N.Y.C., 1992-93. Author jour. article (Best Article award 1971). With USMCR, 1968-69. Mem. ABA, Fla. Bar Assn., N.Y. State Bar Assn., Assn. Bar City N.Y., Dade County Bar Assn., N.Y. County Lawyers Assn., Greater Miami C. of C. (trustee). Republican. Roman Catholic. Avocations: sailing, running. Home: 276 Sea View Dr Key Biscayne FL 33149-2504 Office: Hughes Hubbard & Reed Miami Ctr Ste 2500 201 S Biscayne Blvd Ste Miami FL 33131-4332

PEARSON, JOHN KING, judge; b. St. Paul, Nov. 15, 1945; s. John S. Pearson and Jacqueline H. (Anderson) Pearson Purkey; m. Sue M. Stordahl, June 22, 1968; children: Linnea E., Kaaren M. BA in German and History, U. Wis., 1968; student Ludwig Albert U., Freiburg, Germany, 1965-66; J.D., Hastings Coll. Law, 1973. Bar: Kans. 1974, Calif., 1974, U.S. Supreme Ct., 1980, U.S. Ct. Appeals (9th and 10th cirs.) 1974, U.S. Dist. Ct. (no. dist.) Calif. 1982, U.S. Dist. Ct. (cen. dist.) Calif. 1982, U.S. Dist. Ct. Kans. 1974. Asst. U.S. trustee Dept. Justice, Wichita, Kans., 1979-82; mng. atty. McDowell, Rice & Smith, Chartered, Wichita, 1982-86; judge U.S. Bankruptcy Ct. Dist Kans., Wichita, 1986—; adj. prof. law Wichita State U., 1978-84. Author/editor: A Bank's Rights in Bankruptcy, 1982, Kansas Bankruptcy Handbook, 1986, Drafting Reorganization Plans, 1988, 2nd edit., 1993, Kansas Secured Transactions Handbook, 1988, 2nd edit., 1993. Recipient Spl. Achievement award U.S. Dept. Justice, Wichita, 1980. Office: US Banker Ct 104 US Courthouse 401 N Market St Wichita KS 67202-2000

PEARSON, JOHN Y., JR., lawyer; b. Norfolk, Va., July 23, 1942. AB, Washington & Lee U., 1964; JD, U. Va., 1971. Bar: Va. 1971. Atty. Willcox & Savage P.C., Norfolk, Va. Bd. editors: Va. Law Rev., 1969-71. Fellow Am. Coll. Trial Lawyers; mem. ABA (mem. litigation, tort and ins. practice sects.), Va. Assn. Def. Attys., Order of Coif. Office: Willcox & Savage PC 1800 NationsBank Ctr Norfolk VA 23510-2197

PEARSON, LARRY LESTER, journalism educator, internet presence provider; b. Sioux Falls, S.D., Sept. 27, 1942; s. Lester Loren and Lois Ursula (Cochran) P.; m. Alice Marie Simons, Sept. 15, 1979; children: Gregory Eric, Hillary Yvette, Andrew Todd. BA cum laude, U. Minn., 1964, PhD, 1990; MA, U. Wis., 1969. Newsman UPI, Mpls., 1962-63; newsman Daily American, Rome, Italy, 1964-65; instr. Journalism Sch., U. Wis., 1965-67; with Mpls. Tribune, 1967-85, wire editor, 1970-72, news editor, 1972-82; news editor Mpls. Star & Tribune, 1982; asst. prof. U. Alaska, Anchorage, 1985-92, assoc. prof., 1992—, dir. Ctr. for Info. Tech., 1990-92; spl. cons. to Alaska Ho. Com. on Telecomm., 1985-90; proprieter Online Design, 1995—. Mem. Internat. Communication Assn., Am. Soc. Newspaper Design, Assn. Edn. in Journalism and Mass Communication. Lutheran. Home: 2410 E 16th Ave Anchorage AK 99508-2906 Office: U Alaska 3211 Providence Dr Anchorage AK 99508-4614

PEARSON, MARGARET DONOVAN, former mayor; b. Nashville, Oct. 29, 1921; d. Timothy Graham and Nelle Ligon (Schmidt) Donovan; m. Jimmie Wilson Pearson, Aug. 2, 1946 (dec. Oct. 1978). BS, Vanderbilt U., 1944, MA, 1950; MS, U. Tenn., 1954. Cryptanalyst Army Signal Corps, Washington, 1944-45; phys. edn. tchr. Nashville Bd. Edn., 1945-46; tchr. English, phys. edn. White County Bd. Edn., Sparta, Tenn., 1946-57; spl. edn. supr. Tenn. Dept. Edn., Cookeville, 1957-65; staff devel. dir. Tenn. Dept. Edn., Nashville, 1965-84; ret., 1984; 1st woman alderman City of Sparta, 1987-91, 1st woman mayor, 1991-95. Mem. U.S. Ret. Sr. Vol. Program, 1985—; dist. dir. Tenn. Mcpl. League, 1987-94, 1st woman elected as v.p.; mem. Tenn. Gov.'s Com. Employment of Disabled, 1989—. Recipient Cmty. Leader award Wal-Mart; Am. Speech, Lang. and Hearing Assn. fellow, 1971; Ky. Col.; Tenn. Col. Mem. Sparta C. of C., Rotary (1st woman elected pres.). Methodist. Avocations: reading, knitting, needlepoint. Home: 114 Highland Dr PO Box 22 Sparta TN 38583-0022

PEARSON, MARGIT LINNEA, development company executive; b. Weymouth, Mass., Nov. 6, 1950; d. Eric Gustav and Evelyn (Forest) P. BA, Simmons Coll., 1972; MBA, Harvard U., 1975. Sr. mgr. McKinsey & Co., Inc., N.Y.C., 1975-83; pres. Berkey, Inc., Greenwich, Conn., 1987-89, APC Corp., Hawthorne, N.J., 1990-91; mng. dir. Renaissance, N.Y.C., 1992-93; pres. Sunset Point Devel., Charleston, S.C., 1993—. Bd. dirs. Ctr. for Contemporary Art, Desert Chorale, Santa Fe, 1994—, Tchrs. Network, N.Y.C., 1996—. Avocations: art, skiing, travel. Home: 9 E 96th St New York NY 10128-0778 Office: 1590 Canyon Rd Santa Fe NM 87501-6136

PEARSON, MICHAEL P., lawyer; b. Houston, June 9, 1953. BA, U. Tex., 1975, JD, 1978. Bar: Tex. 1978, U.S. Ct. Appeals (5th cir.) 1981. Atty. Jackson & Walker L.L.P., Houston. Assoc. editor: Tex. Law Rev., 1977-78; contbr. articles to profl. jours. Mem. ABA, Internat. Bar Assn., Phi Beta Kappa, Phi Kappa Phi. Office: Jackson & Walker LLP PO Box 4771 1100 Louisiana Ste 4200 Houston TX 77210-4771

PEARSON, NATHAN WILLIAMS, investment management executive; b. N.Y.C., Nov. 26, 1911; s. James A. and Elizabeth (Williams) P.; m. Kathleen P. McMurtry, Apr. 9, 1947; children: James S. (dec.), Nathan Williams. A.B., Dartmouth Coll., 1932; M.B.A., Harvard, 1934; LLD (hon.), Thiel Coll., 1972. With U.S. Steel Corp., 1939-42; mgr. research Matson Navigation Co., 1946-47; controller Carborundum Co., 1947-48; with T. Mellon and Sons, Pitts., 1948-70; v.p., gov. T. Mellon and Sons, 1957-70; chmn., chief exec. officer, chmn. emeritus Mellon Bank N.A. & Mellon Bank Corp., Pitts., 1987—; fin. exec. for Paul Mellon, 1948—. Chmn. Pitts. Theol. Sem., 1987. Served from lt. (j.g.) to comdr. USNR, 1942-46. Mem. Allegheny Country Club, Harvard-Yale Princeton Club, Duquesne Club, Laurel Valley Golf Club, Edgeworth Club, Rolling Rock Club (Ligonier, Pa.), Racquet and Tennis Club. Republican. Presbyterian. Home: 10 Woodland Rd Sewickley PA 15143-1123 Office: Mellon Bank Corp 525 William Penn Pl Pittsburgh PA 15219-1707

PEARSON, NATHAN WILLIAMS, broadcast executive; b. Sewickley, Pa., Aug. 1, 1951; s. Nathan Williams Sr. and Kathleen Patricia (McMurtry) P.; m. Jane Ruth Wallace, Oct. 12, 1985; children: Nathan McMurtry, Howe Quinn, Henry Wallace. BA and MA in Music, Conn. Wesleyan U., 1974; MBA, Columbia U., 1982. Pvt. practice cons. N.Y.C. and Washington, 1974-82; with McKinsey & Co., N.Y.C. and L.A., 1982-88; exec. v.p., chief fin. officer, mng. prin., sec., treas. Broadcasting Ptnrs., Inc., N.Y.C., 1988-95; chmn. Broadcasting Ptnrs., L.L.C., Rye, N.Y., 1995—; vice chmn. Icelandic Broadcasting Corp., Reykjavik; mng. dir. Commonwealth Holdings, Inc., N.Y.C., 1996—. Author: "Goin' to Kansas City," 1987; producer LP records, TV and radio programs; contbr. articles to profl. jours. Sec., bd. dirs. CityLore, Inc., N.Y.C., 1986—; bd. dirs. Young Audiences, N.Y., 1987—, pres., 1995-96; bd. dirs. Young Audiences, Inc., 1995—. Mem. Soc. for Ethnomusicology, Am. Folklore Soc., Wadawanuck Club, Nat. Assn. Broadcasting, Beta Gamma Sigma. Avocations: boardsailing, river running, hiking. Home: 3 Holly Ln Rye NY 10580-3953 Office: Broadcasting Ptnrs LLC 3 Holly Ln Rye NY 10580-3953

PEARSON, NORMAN, urban and regional planner, administrator, academic and planning consultant, writer; b. Stanley, County Durham, Eng., Oct. 24, 1928; arrived in Can., 1954; s. Joseph and Mary (Pearson) P.; m. Gerda Maria Josefine Riedl, July 25, 1972. BA in Fine Arts with honors in Town and Country Planning, U. Durham (Eng.), 1951; PhD in Land Economy and Ecol. Planning, Internat. Inst. Advanced Studies, 1979; MBA, Pacific Western U., Colo., 1980, DBA, 1982; PhD In Mgmt., Calif. U. for Advanced Studies, 1986; PhD (hon.) in Environ. Planning, Internat. U. Found., 1987. Cons. Stanley Urban Dist. Coun., U.K., 1946-47; planning asst. Accrington Town Plan and Bedford County Planning Survey, U. Durham Planning Team, U.K., 1947-49, Allen and Mattocks, cons. planners and landscape designers, Newcastle upon Tyne, U.K., 1949-51; adminstrv. asst. Scottish Div., Nat. Coal Bd., Edinburgh, Scotland, 1951-52; planning asst. London County Coun., Westminster, U.K., 1953-54; planner Ctrl. Mortgage and Housing Corp., Ottawa, Ont., Can., 1954-55; planning analyst City of Toronto (Ont.) Planning Bd., 1955-56; dir. planning Hamilton Wentworth Planning Area Bd., Hamilton, Ont., 1956-59, Burlington (Ont.) and Suburban Area Planning Bd., Can., 1959-62; commr. planning City of Burlington, Ont., 1959-62; pres. Tanfield Enterprises Ltd., London, Ont., Can., 1962—, Norman Pearson & Assocs. Ltd., London, Ont., Can., 1962—, Internat. Planning Mgmt. Cons., London, Ont., Can., 1962—, Leahy, Pearson, Toll & Assocs. Ltd., London, Ont., Can., 1993-95; chmn., CEO The Tanfield Group, 1995—; pres. Greenleaf Collaborative, Inc., 1997—; cons. in urban, rural and regional planning, 1962—; life mem. U.S. Com. for Monetary Research and Edn., 1976—; spl. lectr. in planning McMaster U., Hamilton, 1956-64, Waterloo (Ont.) Luth. U., 1961-63; asst. prof. geography and planning U. Waterloo (Ont.), 1963-67; assoc. prof. geography U. Guelph (Ont.), 1967-72, chmn., dir. Ctr. for Resources Devel.; prof. polit. sci. U. Western Ont., London, 1972-78; chmn. bd. dirs. Alma Coll., St. Thomas, Ont., 1990-96; adj. prof. of ecological planning and land econs. Internat. Inst. for Advanced Studies, Clayton, Mo., 1980-89; core faculty Doctoral Program in Adminstrn/Mgmt. Walden U., Mpls., 1985-96, chair adminstrn.-mgmt., 1989-96, mem. acad. coun., 1992-96; prof. bus. adminstrn. and mgmt. Greenwich U., Hawaii, 1995—; mem. bd. regents Calif. U. for Advanced Studies, Petaluma, 1987-94; assoc. faculty bus. and orgn. Grad. Sch. Am., 1996—; prof. 21st century studies Green Leaf U., St. Louis, 1996—, bd. govs., 1996—; prof. orgn. and mgmt. Greenwich U., Hawaii, 1996—; mem. Social Scis., Econ. and Legal Aspects Com. of Rsch. Adv. Bd. Internat. Joint Commn., 1972-76; cons. to City of Waterloo, 1973-76, Province of Ont., 1969-70; advisor to Georgian Bay Regional Devel. Coun., 1968-72; real estate appraiser, province of Ont., 1976—; pres., chmn. bd. govs. Pacific Western U., Canada, 1983-84. Author: Administration Management: New Needs and New Opportunities, 1992, Franchise & Partnership: A New Concept of Urban Development, 1995, Pipelines & Farming, 1995, Resources Development Policies in Canada, 1995, Planning for Eastern Georgian Bay, 1996; (with others) An Inventory of Joint Programmes and Agreements Affecting Canada's Renewable Resources, 1964, An Emerald Light, 1994, Light Beyond the Craft in Canada, 1994; editor, co-author: Regional and Resource Planning in Canda, 1963, rev. edit., 1970; editor (with others): The Pollution Reader, 1968; contbr. numerous articles on town planning to profl. jours., chpts. to books. Pres. Unitarian Ch. of Hamilton, 1960-61. With RAF, 1951-53, RAFVR, 1953-68. Decorated knight of grace Sovereign Order St. John of Jerusalem, 1979, knight Order St. Lazarus of Jerusalem, 1991, Internat. Order of Merit, 1991, Order Internat. Fellowship, 1995, knight of the Order of the Temple of Jerusalem, 1996; recipient Friend of the Escarpment award Province of Ont., 1992. Fellow Royal Town Planning Inst. (Bronze medal 1957), Royal Econ. Soc., Lambda Alpha Internat.; mem. Am. Inst. Planners, Can. Inst. Planners, Can. Polit. Sci. Assn., Internat. Soc. City and Regional Planners, Internat. Assn. Engrs. and Drs. Indsl. Applied Scis., Bruce Trail Assn. (founding pres., chmn., hon. mem., Founder's Plaque 1995), Ont. Club, Empire Club, Univ. Club (London), Baconian Club. Office: PO Box 5362, Station A, London, ON Canada N6A 4L6

PEARSON, OSCAR HARRIS, plant breeder, geneticist; b. Stratham, N.H., Jan. 17, 1902; s. Frank Harris and Grace Eunice (Gowen) P.; m. Helen Ruth Monosmith, Dec. 15, 1929; children: Robert, David, Ann, Charles, George, Sandra. BS, U. N.H., 1923, MS, 1925; PhD, U. Calif., Berkeley, 1928. Jr. olericulturist U. Calif., Davis, 1928-33; head seed R & D Ea. States Farmers Exch., West Springfield, Mass., 1934-59; dir. seed R & D Seed Rsch. Specialists, Hollister, Calif., 1959-63, Niagara Seed, San Juan Bautista, Calif., 1963-67; sr. rsch. assoc. plant breeding dept. Cornell U., Ithaca, N.Y., 1967-70; cons. Bud Senegal, Dakar, 1970-75. Contbr. articles to profl. jours. Fellow AAAS, Am. Soc. Hort. Sci. (Asgrow award 1969). Achievements include basic program of hybrid cabbage seed production; development of Pearson tomato cultivar, the Butter and Sugar high quality bicolor hybrid sweet corn, other cultivars; isolation of a "n" male sterile cabbage for use in hybrid seed production. Office: 62 Reise Ter Portsmouth RI 02871-2710

PEARSON, PATRICIA KELLEY, marketing representative; b. Carrollton, Ga., Jan. 21, 1953; d. Ben and Edith (Kelley) Rhudy; m. Ray S. Pearson, June 4, 1976; children: Chad, Jonathan, Kelly. BA in Journalism, Ga. State U., 1974; BSN, West Ga. Coll., 1990. RN Fla. Pub. rels. asst. Grady Meml. Hosp., Atlanta, 1974-77; editorial asst. Childers & Sullivan, Huntsville, Ala., 1977-78; sales rep. AAA Employment Agy., Huntsville, 1978-80; editor Wright Pub. Co., Atlanta, 1980-82; elect./electronic drafter PRC Cons., Atlanta, 1980-87; researcher Dept. Nursing at West Ga. Coll., Carrollton, 1989-90; med./surg. nurse Tanner Med. Ctr., Carrollton, Ga., 1989-90, Delray Community Hosp., Delray Beach, Fla., 1990-91; sales rep. Innovative Med. Svcs., 1991-94; with staff devel., employee rels. Beverly Oaks Rehab. and Nursing Ctr., 1994-95; sales rep./pub. rels. rep. Columbia HCA, Melbourne, Fla., 1996—. Vol. Project Response, Brevard County Sexual Assault Victim Svcs. All-Am. scholar U.S. Achievement Acad., 1990, recipient Nat. Coll. Nursing award, 1989. Mem. NOW, Space Coast Bus. Writer's Guild, Omicron Delta Kappa. Democrat. Home: 139 Jamaica Dr Cocoa Beach FL 32931-2825

PEARSON, PAUL DAVID, lawyer, mediator; b. Boston, Jan. 22, 1940; s. Bernard J. and Ruth (Bayla) Horblit; m. Carol A. Munschauer; children—David Todd, Lisa Kari. AB, Bucknell U., 1961; LLB, U. Pa., 1964. Bar: Mass. 1966, N.Y. 1987. Staff atty., tech. assoc. lab. of community psychiatry, dept. psychiatry Harvard Med. Sch., Boston, 1966-68; assoc. Snyder Tepper & Berlin, Boston, 1968-71, ptnr., 1971-77; with Hill & Barlow, Boston, 1977-87, ptnr., chmn. family law dept.; with Hodgson, Russ, Andrews, Woods and Goodyear, Buffalo, 1987-96, ptnr. chmn family law dept., lectr. Mass. Continuing Legal Edn., New Eng. Law Inst.; of counsel Sullivan & Oliverio, 1996—; instr. law and mental health Boston Psychoanalytic Soc. and Inst., 1975-87; lectr. in field. Founding mem. Alliance for Dispute Resolution; trustee, v.p., legal counsel Boston Ballet Soc.; trustee, chmn., legal counsel Wayland (Mass.) Townhouse; trustee Family Counseling Service (region West); mem., chmn., clk. Wayland Zoning Bd. Appeals; v.p., counsel, Arts Wayland Found., 1982-87; vis. fellow Woodrow Wilson Found., 1985-87; with Mass. Gov.'s Spl. Commn. on Divorce, 1985-87; lectr. dept. psychiatry SUNY-Buffalo Med. Sch., 1989—; bd. dirs. Jewish Community Ctr. Greater Buffalo and Buffalo chpt., Am. Jewish Com., 1991—, pres., 1995—, Arts Coun. Buffalo and Erie County, 1992—. Served to capt. Mil. Police Corps, USAR. Fellow Am. Acad. Matrimonial Lawyers (pres., bd. mgrs. Mass.); mem. ABA (family law and ADR coms.), Mass. Bar Assn. (chmn. family law sect.), Acad. Family Mediators, N.Y. State Coun. on Divorce Mediation, Assn. Family and Conciliation Cts., Boston Bar Assn. (family law com., legis. chmn.), N.Y. Bar Assn. (family law com.), Erie County Bar Assn. (chmn. alternative dispute resolution com., family law com.). Contbr. articles to profl. jours. Home: 605 Lebrun Rd Buffalo NY 14226-4232 Office: 600 Main Place Tower Buffalo NY 14202-3706

PEARSON, PAUL GUY, academic administrator emeritus; b. Lake Worth, Fla., Dec. 5, 1926; s. Eric Conrad and Dora Wilma (Capen) P.; m. Winifred Clowe, June 30, 1951; children: Thomas, Jean, Andrew. Student, Palm Beach Jr. Coll., 1946-47; B.S. with honors, U. Fla., 1949, M.S., 1951, Ph.D., 1954; Litt.D. (hon.), Rutgers U., 1982; LL.D. (hon.), Juniata Coll., 1983; commandeu de L'ordre de merite, Grand Duchy of Luxembourg, 1988. Asst. prof. U. Tulsa, 1954-55; asst. prof. Rutgers U., New Brunswick, N.J., 1955-60; assoc. prof. Rutgers U., 1960-64, prof., 1964-81, assoc. provost, 1972-77, exec. v.p., 1977-81, acting pres., 1978; pres., prof. Miami U., Oxford, Ohio, 1981-92; bd. dirs. Union Ctrl. Life Ins., Cin., S.W. Ohio Sr. Svcs., Cin., Nat. Conservancy, Ohio. Mem. U.S. Army Sci. Bd., 1984-86. Served with USNR, 1944-46. Fellow AAAS; mem. Am. Inst. Biol. Scis. (governing bd. 1968-79, v.p. 1977, pres. 1978), Rotary Internat. (Paul Harris fellow), Phi Beta Kappa (assoc.). Home: 5110 Bonham Rd Oxford OH 45056-3606

PEARSON, PAUL HAMMOND, physician; b. Bolenge, Belgian Congo; s. Ernest B. and Evelyn (Utter) P. B.S., Northwestern, 1944, B.Medicine, 1946, M.D., 1947; M.P.H., UCLA, 1963. Diplomate: Am. Bd. Pediatrics. Intern Los Angeles County Gen. Hosp., 1946-47; resident Cin. Children's Hosp., 1949-51; fellow convulsive disorders and electroencephalography Johns Hopkins Hosp., Balt., 1951-53; resident in child psychiatry U. B.C., Can., Vancouver, 1976-77; practice medicine specializing in pediatrics L.A., 1953-62; chief mental retardation br. USPHS div. chronic disease, 1963-65; asst. dir. mental retardation program Nat. Inst. Child Health and Human Devel., NIH, 1965-66; spl. asst. to surgeon gen. USPHS, 1966-67; C.L. Meyer prof. child health, prof. pub. health and preventive medicine, dir. Meyer Children's Rehab. Inst., 1967-81, McGaw prof. adolescent medicine, dir. adolescent medicine, 1982-89, prof. emeritus dept. pediatrics, 1989—; mem. grad. faculty U. Nebr. Coll. Medicine, Omaha, 1967—; med. dir. Univ. Hosp. Eating Disorder Program U. Nebr. Coll. Medicine, 1983-89, sr. cons. Univ. Hosp. Eating Disorder Program, 1989—; from instr. to asst. clin. prof. U. So. Calif. Med. Sch., 1953-62; from assoc. clin. prof. pediatrics to clin. prof. pediatrics Georgetown U. Sch. Medicine, Washington, 1963-67; Cons., mem. profl. services program com. United Cerebral Palsy Assn., 1969-72, mem. nat. awards com., 1971; Am. Acad. Pediatrics liaison rep. to Am. Acad. Orthopedic Surgery, 1969-73; apptd. to Nat. Adv. Council Services and Facilities for Developmentally Disabled Dept. Health. Edn. and Welfare, 1971-75; councilor Accreditation Council Facilities for Mentally Retarded, Joint Commn. on Accreditation Hosps., 1973-74; fellow adolescent medicine Boston Children's Hosp. Med. Center, 1981. Cons. editor: Am. Jour. Mental Deficiency, 1970-72; Contbr. articles to profl. jours. Mem. com. on accessible environments Nat. Acad. Scis., 1974-77. Served to capt. MC AUS, 1947-49. Mem. Am. Acad. Pediatrcs (com. on children with handicaps 1969-75, com. sect. on child devel. 1974—), Am. Assn. Mental Deficiency, Nat. Assn. for Retarded Children, Greater Omaha Assn. for Retarded Children (dir.), Am. Pub. Health Assn., Am. Acad. Cerebral Palsy and Developmental Medicine (exec. com. 1971-76, chmn. sci. program com. 1972-74, sci. sec. 1974-77, mem. research and awards com. 1977-78, pres. 1981-82, bd. dirs. 1982-84), Assn. Univ.-Affiliated Facilities (exec. com. 1973—, v.p. 1974-75, pres. 1975-76, dir. 1971-78), Soc. Adolescent MedicineAlpha Omega Alpha. Home: 1123 N 122nd St Omaha NE 68154-1411 Office: U Nebr Med Ctr Dept Pediatrics Omaha NE 68198

PEARSON, PAUL HOLDING, insurance company executive; b. Worcester, Mass., Feb. 14, 1940; s. Malcolm D. and Myra L. (Holding) P.; m. Judith N. Howe, July 13, 1958 (div. June 1974); children: Scott D., Todd E.; m. Anne Beck, July 26, 1974. BA in Bus. and Econs., U. Maine, 1961. C.L.U., 1971. Jr. life underwriter State Mut. Am., Worcester, 1961-63, life underwriter, 1963-67, sr. life underwriter, 1967-69; dir. life underwriting Security Mut. Life Ins. Co., Binghamton, N.Y., 1969, 2d v.p. underwriting, 1970, v.p., 1971-75, sr. v.p. ins. services div., 1975-79, exec. v.p., 1979-81, pres., 1981-96, chief exec. officer, 1987-97; chmn. Security Mutual Life Ins. Co. of N.Y., Binghamton, 1996-97; chmn., CEO, bd. dirs. SML Properties corp., Binghamton, Security Equity Life Ins. Co., Binghamton, 1987-93; vice-chmn. Generalife, 1997—. Trustee, treas. Lourdes Meml. Hosp., Binghamton, 1978-92; mem. SUNY Found., Binghamton, 1982-89; trustee, chmn. fin. com. Elmira Coll., 1983-87; bd. dirs. Broome C.C. Found., 1982-91, pres. 1985-86; pres. New Industries for Broome, Binghamton, 1985-95, N.Y. State Bus. Devel. Coun., 1987-96; bd. dirs. Valley Devel. Found., 1987-91, Bus. Coun. N.Y., 1988-97, Am. Coun. Life Ins., 1990-96. Mem. Assn. for Advanced Life Underwriting, Nat. Assn. Life Underwriters, Broome County C. of C. (bd. dirs. 1980-88, chmn. 1986), Binghamton C/C Live Wire Club. Office: PHP Consultants Court House Sq 2 Reflection Dr Sandwich MA 02563-3110

PEARSON, PHILLIP THEODORE, veterinary clinical sciences and biomedical engineering educator; b. Ames, Iowa, Nov. 21, 1932; s. Theodore B. and Hazel C. (Christianson) P.; m. Mary Jane Barlow, Aug. 28, 1954; children: Jane Catherine, Bryan Theodore, Todd Wallace, Julie Ann. DVM, Iowa State U., 1956, PhD, 1962. Intern Angell Meml. Animal Hosp., Boston, 1956-57; instr. Coll. Vet. Medicine Iowa State U., 1957-59, asst. prof., 1959-63, assoc. prof., 1963-64, prof. vet. clin. scis. and biomed. engring., 1965-72, 89-96, dean, 1972-89; dir. Vet. Med. Rsch. Inst., 1972-89; prof. Sch. Vet. Medicine, U. Mo., 1964-65. Bd. dirs. Iowa Sate Meml. Union, 1970-84; v.p. Iowa State Meml. Union, 1975; chmn. coun. of deans Assn. Am. Vet. Medicine Colls., 1978-79. Recipient Riser award, 1956; distinguished Tchr. award Norden Labs., 1962; Gaines award Gen. Foods Corp., 1966; Outstanding Tchr. award Iowa State U., 1968; Faculty citation, 1974; named Iowa Vet. of the Yr., 1988. Mem. AVMA, Iowa Vet. Medicine Assn., Am. Animal Hosp. Assn., Am. Assn. Vet. Clinicians, Am. Coll. Vet. Surgeons (bd. regents 1972, pres. 1977), Nat. Acad. Practice, Kiwanis (bd. dirs., pres. Ames 1966—), Sigma Xi, Phi Kappa Phi, Phi Zeta, Alpha Zeta, Gamma Sigma Delta (Alumni award of merit 1991). Home: 1610 Maxwell Ave Ames IA 50010-5536

PEARSON, RALPH GOTTFRID, chemistry educator; b. Chgo., Jan. 12, 1919; s. Gottfrid and Kerstin (Larson) P.; m. Lenore Olivia Johnson, June 15, 1941 (dec. June 1982); children—John Ralph, Barry Lee, Christie Ann. B.S., Lewis Inst., 1940; Ph.D., Northwestern U., 1943. Faculty Northwestern U., 1946-76, prof. chemistry, 1957-76; prof. chemistry U. Calif., Santa Barbara, 1976-89, prof. emeritus, 1989—; Cons. to industry and govt., 1951—. Co-author 5 books. Served to 1st lt. USAAF, 1944-46. Recipient Chemical Pioneer award Am. Inst. Chemists, 1995; Guggenheim fellow, 1951. Mem. Am. Chem. Soc. (Midwest award 1966, Inorganic Chemistry award 1969), Nat. Acad. Sci., Phi Beta Kappa, Sigma Xi, Phi Lambda Upsilon (hon.). Lutheran. Achievements include being originator prin. of hard and soft acids and bases.

PEARSON, RICHARD JOSEPH, archaeologist, educator; b. Kitchener, Ont., Can., May 2, 1938; s. John Cecil and Henrietta Anne (Wallwin) P.; m. Kazue Miyazaki, Dec. 12, 1964; 1 child, Sarina Riye. B.A. in Anthropology with honours, U. Toronto, 1960; Ph.D., Yale U., 1966. Asst. prof., then assoc. prof. archaeology U. Hawaii, 1966-71; mem. faculty U. B.C., Vancouver, 1971—; now prof. archaeology U. B.C. Author: The Archaeology of the Ryukyu Islands, 1969, Higashi Ajia no Kodai Shakai to Kokogaku, 1984, Windows on the Japanese Past, Studies in Archaeology and Prehistory, 1986, Ancient Japan, 1992; contbr. articles to profl. jours. Guggenheim fellow. Mem. Am. Anthrop. Assn., Soc. Am. Archaeology, Indo-Pacific Prehistory Assn., Assn. Asian Studies. Office: U BC, Dept Anthropology-Sociology, Vancouver, BC Canada V6T 1Z1

PEARSON, RICHARD L., lawyer; b. La Rochelle, France, Jan. 14, 1955. AB, U. N.C., 1977; JD, U. Ala., 1980. Bar: Ala. 1980. Mem. Balch & Bingham, Birmingham, Ala. Ala. editor: Ala. Law Rev., 1979-80. Hugo C. Black scholar. Mem. ABA (mem. uniform comml. code subcom.), Ala. State Bar, Birmingham Bar Assn., Order of Coif, Omicron Delta Kappa. Office: Balch & Bingham PO Box 306 1710 6th Ave N Birmingham AL 35201

PEARSON, ROBERT ALLEN, optometrist; b. Scottsbluff, Nebr., Dec. 8, 1946; s. William Franklin and Hope Jacqueline (Williams) P.; m. Sue Ione Parmelee, Sept. 6, 1969. BS, BA, U. Wyo., 1970; OD, So. Calif. Coll. Optometry, 1986. Microbiologist State of Nev., Las Vegas, 1970-82; optometrist S.W. Vision, Las Vegas, 1986—. Mem. LIGA Internat., Inc., Santa Ana, Calif., Vision U.S.A., St. Louis, VOSH-Calif. Mem. APHA, Nev. Pub. Health Assn., Am. Optometric Assn., Nev. Optometric Assn. (Optometrist of Yr. 1988), Nev. State Bd. Optometry. Avocations: physical fitness, auto racing, travel. Home: 3404 El Cortez Ave Las Vegas NV 89102-3925 Office: SW Vision PO Box 15645 Las Vegas NV 89114-5645

PEARSON, ROBERT GREENLEES, writing services company executive; b. Kansas City, Mo., Feb. 19, 1917; s. Ridley Stillson and Agnes (Greenlees) P.; m. Laura Gray Betsy Dodge, Jan. 3, 1945; children—Bradbury, Wendy, Robert Ridley. A.B. with honors, U. Kans., 1938. Mgr. corporate public relations Shell Oil Co. (N.Y. Head Office), 1938-71; v.p. public relations Council Better Bus. Bur. (N.Y. Hdqrs.), 1971-73; writer public affairs dept. Mobil Oil Corp., N.Y.C., 1973-74; sr. advisor Alcoholics Anonymous World Services, Inc., N.Y.C., 1974-85; pres. Robert Pearson Assocs., Writing Svcs., Riverside, Conn., 1985—; Bd. dirs. Nat. Safety Council; pres. Fairfield County (Conn.) Council on Alcoholism, 1962. Author: Oil for Victory, 1946, The J.C. Nichols Chronicle, 1994; contbr. articles to profl. jours. Served to lt. comdr. USNR, 1941-45. Congregationalist. Clubs: Riverside (Conn.); Yacht, Dutch Treat. Home: 17 Jones Park Dr Riverside CT 06878-2205 Office: PO Box 671 Riverside CT 06878-0671

PEARSON, ROGER, organization executive; b. London, Aug. 21, 1927; s. Edwin and Beatrice May (Woodbine) P.; m. Marion Primrose Simms, June 3, 1959; children: Edwin, Sigrid, Emma, Rupert. BS with honors, U. London, 1951, MS, 1954, PhD, 1969. Chmn. Pakistan Tea Assn., 1964; mng. dir. Octavius Steel & Co. of Pakistan Ltd., Chittagong, East Pakistan, 1959-65; chmn. Plummer Bros., Ltd., Chittagong, East Pakistan, 1959-65, Chittagong Warehouses, Ltd., Chittagong, East Pakistan, 1960-65; chmn. dept. sociology and anthropology Queens Coll., Charlotte, N.C., 1970-71; chmn. dept. anthropology U. So. Miss., Hattiesburg, 1971-74; dean acad. affairs, dir. research Mont. Coll. Mineral Sci. Tech., Butte, 1974-75; exec. dir. Council for Econ. and Social Studies, Washington, 1975—. Author: Eastern Interlude, 1954, Introduction to Anthropology, 1978, Anthropological Glossary, 1985, Race, Intelligence and Bias in Academe, 1991, Shockley on Eugenics and Race, 1992, Heredity and Humanity, 1996; editor: Ecology and Evolution, 1982; editor, pub. Jour. Indo-European Studies, 1973—, Jour. Social Polit. and Econ. Studies, 1976—. Trustee, Benjamin Franklin U., Washington, 1984-87. Served to lt. Brit. Indian Army, 1945-48. Fellow Inst. Chartered Secs. Adminstrs. (London), Oriental Club, Reform Club (London), Army and Navy Club (Washington). Office: Coun Econ and Social Studies 1133 13th St NW Apt C-2 Washington DC 20005-4203

PEARSON, ROGER LEE, library director; b. Galesburg, Ill., Dec. 7, 1940; s. Clifford Emmanuel and Lillian Louise (Fisher) P. B.A., Knox Coll., 1963; M.A. in Sociology, U. Nebr.-Omaha, 1968; M.A. in Library Sci., Rosary Coll., 1974. Vol. U.S. Peace Corps, Brazil, 1964-66; extension service supr. Brown County Libr., Green Bay, Wis., 1974-75; system adminstr. Nicolet Libr. System, Green Bay, 1976-77; exec. dir. South Central Libr. System, Madison, Wis., 1977-81; dir. Corpus Christi Pub. Librs., Tex., 1981-84, Naperville (Ill.) Pub. Librs., 1984-95, Sonoma County Libr., Santa Rosa, Calif., 1996—; lectr. Grad. Sch. Libr. and Info. Sci., Rosary Coll., River Forest, Ill., 1991-95. Mem. ALA, TRAC, Am. Assn. Ret. People, Calif. Libr. Assn. Avocations: walking, travel research, train travel. Home: 5225 Old Redwood Hwy Apt 1 Santa Rosa CA 95403 Office: Sonoma County Libr 3d and E Sts Santa Rosa CA 95404

PEARSON, RONALD DALE, retail food stores corporation executive; b. Des Moines, 1940; married. B.S. in Bus. Adminstrn., Drake U., 1962. With Hy-Vee Food Stores, Inc. (name changed to Hy-Vee, Inc in 1996), Chariton, Iowa, 1962—; pres. Hy-Vee, Inc., Chariton, Iowa, 1983—; chmn., pres., & CEO Hy-Vee, Inc., 1989—; dir. Beverage Mfrs., Inc., Civic Ctr. Cts., Inc. Office: Hy-Vee Inc 5820 Westown Pkwy West Des Moines IA 50266-8223*

PEARSON, SCOTT ROBERTS, economics educator; b. Madison, Wis., Mar. 13, 1938; s. Carlyle Roberts and Edith Hope (Smith) P.; m. Sandra Carol Anderson, Sept. 12, 1962; children—Sarah Roberts, Elizabeth Hovden. BS, U. Wis.-Madison, 1961; MA, Johns Hopkins U., 1965; PhD, Harvard U., 1969. Asst. prof. Stanford U., Calif., 1968-74, assoc. prof., 1974-80, assoc. dir. Food Research Inst., 1977-84, dir., 1992-96, prof. food econs., 1980—. Cons. AID, World Bank, Washington, 1965—; staff economist Commn. Internat. Trade, Washington, 1970-71. Author: Petroleum and the Nigerian Economy, 1970; (with others) Commodity Exports and African Economic Development, 1974, (with others) Rice in West Africa, Policy and Economics, 1981, (with others) Food Policy Analysis, 1983, (with others) The Cassava Economy of Java, 1984, (with others) Portuguese Agriculture in Transition, 1987, (with Eric Monke) The Policy Analysis Matrix, 1989, (with others) Rice Policy in Indonesia, 1991, (with others) Structural Change and Small-Farm Agriculture in Northwest Portugal, 1993, (with others) Agricultural Policy in Kenya, 1995. Mem. Am. Agrl. Econs. Assn., Am. Econ. Assn. Home: 691 Mirada Ave Stanford CA 94305-8477 Office: Stanford U Food Rsch Institute Stanford CA 94305

PEARSON, SUSAN ROSE, psychotherapist, fine arts educator, artist; b. Elmhurst, Ill., June 14, 1950; d. Ernest Elliott and Helen Julia (Drogoi) P. BA in Psychology, Calif. State U., 1992, MS in Ednl. Psychology & Counseling, 1995. Cert. pupil pers. svcs., cert. hypnotherapists. Art tchr., master artist Susan Rose Fine Art Gallery, Reseda, Calif., 1979—; therapist Lifestyle with Dignity, Canoga Park, Calif., 1985-93; author, speaker, cons., inventor. Mem. Am. Counseling Assn., Am. Sch. Counselor Assn., Calif. Assn. Marriage & Family Therapists, Nat. Honor Soc. in Psychology (life), Nat. Bd. for Cert. Clin. Hypnotherapists (cert. hypnotherapist), Internat. Soc. Speakers, Authors and Cons., Am. Hypnosis Assn. Home: 8105 Garden Grove Ave Reseda CA 91335

PEARSON, THOMAS ARTHUR, epidemiologist, educator; b. Berlin, Wis., Oct. 21, 1950; married; 2 children. BA, Johns Hopkins U., 1973, MD, 1976, MPH, 1976, PhD in Epidemiology, 1983. Fellow cardiology Johns Hopkins Sch. Medicine, 1981-83, from asst. prof. to assoc. prof. medicine, epidemiology, 1983-88; prof. epidemiology Columbia U., 1988—, prof. medicine, 1995—; dir. Mary Imogene Bassett Rsch. Inst., 1988-97; prof. medicine, Jane Forbes Clark chair in health rsch. Columbia U., N.Y.C., 1995-97; Kaiser prof., chair Sch. Medicine U. Rochester, N.Y., 1997—; chmn. monitoring bd. CARDIA project Nat. Heart, Lung and Blood Inst., 1987—; mem. rsch. com. Md. Heart Assn., 1986-88; chmn. data safety monitoring bd. HIT trial VA, 1994—; commr. Md. Coun. Phys. Fitness, 1985-88; mem. clin. applications and prevention commn. NIH, 1987-91, chmn., 1990-91. Mem. ACP, Am. Heart Assn. (nat. rsch. com. 1987-92, coun. epidemiology 1987—, vice chmn. 1994-95, chmn. 1996-98), Am. Fedn. Clin. Rsch., Am. Coll. Epidemiology, Am. Coll. Preventive Medicine, Am. Coll. Cardiology (prevention com.), Soc. Epidemiol. Rsch. (rsch. prize 1978). Achievements include research in the etiology and pathogenesis of atherosclerosis. Office: Dept Cmty Preventitive Medicine 601 Elmwood Ave Rochester NY 14642-0001

PEARSON, WALTER DONALD, editor, columnist; b. Pittsfield, Mass., Feb. 5, 1916; s. Edgar C. and Edna (Scott) P.; divorced; children: Florence, Donald, Sharon; m. Elsa Swanson; 1 child, Richard Scott. Student, Dartmouth Coll., 1941-43. Advt. salesman, 1935-41; securities broker Charles A. Day Co., Boston, 1947-55; founder, owner, mgr. First New Eng. Securities Co., Inc., Southbridge, Mass., 1955-71; now owner, editor Pearson Investment Letter, Dover, Fla.; ptnr. Pearson Capital Mgmt.; fin. columnist World Intelligence Rev.; free-lance columnist various publications; fin. advisor, investment mgr. Author: Investing for the Millions, 1990. With inf. U.S. Army, 1943-45, ETO. Decorated Bronze star, Croix de Guerre (France), Combat Infantry badge. Home: 1628 White Arrow Dr Dover FL 33527-5741

PEARSON, WILLIAM ROWLAND, nuclear engineer; b. New Bedford, Mass., Sept. 30, 1923; s. Rowland and Nellie (Hilton) P.; BS, Northeastern U., 1953; postgrad. U. Ohio, 1960; m. Arlene Cole Loveys, June 14, 1953; children: Denise, Robert, Rowland, Nancy. Engr., Goodyear Atomic Corp., Portsmouth, Ohio, 1953-63, Cabot Titania Corp., Ashtabula, Ohio, 1963-64; supr. United Nuclear, Wood River, R.I., 1964-72; sr. engr. Nuclear Materials and Equipment Co., Apollo, Pa., 1972-74; engr. U.S. Nuclear Regulatory Commn., Rockville, Md., 1974-90, ret., 1990. Served with USNR, 1942-45. Decorated Air medal. Mem. AAAS, Am. Nuclear Soc., Am. Inst. Chem. Engrs. (chmn. 1966-67). Republican. Baptist. Clubs: Masons, Elks. Home: 60 Meeting Hill Rd Hillsboro NH 03244-4856

PEARTON, STEPHEN JOHN, materials science and engineering educator; b. Hobart, Tasmania, Australia, Jan. 15, 1957; came to U.S., 1982; s. Dennis Gregory and Margaret Faye (Godfrey) P.; m. Cammy R. Abernathy, June 28, 1993. BS with honors, U. Tasmania, Australia, 1979, PhD, 1983. Exptl. officer Australian Atomic Energy Commn., Sydney, 1981-82; postdoctoral fellow U. Calif., Berkeley, 1982-83; mem. tech. staff AT&T Bell Labs., Murray Hill, N.J., 1984-94; prof. materials sci. and engring. U. Fla., Gainesville, 1994—. Author: Hydrogen in Crystalline Semiconductors, 1991, Topics in Growth and Device Processing of III-V Semiconductors, 1996; editor: (conf. proceedings) O.C.H&N in Crystalline Silicon, 1986, Defects in Electronic Materials, 1988, Ion Implanatation for Compound Semiconductors, 1990, Degredation Mechanisms in Compound Semiconductor Devices and Structures, 1990, Advanced III-V Compound Semiconductor Growth, Processing and Devices, 1992, III-V Electronic and Photonic Device Fabrication and Performance, 1993, Hydrogen in III-V Semiconductors, 1994, Topics in Growth and Device Processing of III-V Semiconductors, 1996, III-V Nitride Materials and Devices, 1996, High Speed Electronics for Wireless Applications, 1996, Wide Band Gap Semiconductors and Devices, 1995, Stake of the Art Propery on Compound Semiconductors, 1996, Gan and Realted Materials, 1997. Recipient scholarship Australian Inst. Nuclear Sci. and Engring., 1979-81. Fellow Electrochemical Soc.; mem. Am. Physical Soc. (life), Materials Rsch. Soc., Am. Vacuum Soc., IEEE. Republican. Achievements include several patents involving use of ion implantation and dry etching to fabricate semiconductor devices; contributions in areas of hydrogen in semiconductors, dry etching and ion implantation of semiconductors. Home: 4830 NW 43rd St Gainesville FL 32606-4401 Office: U Fla Dept Materials Sci & Engr Rhines Hall Gainesville FL 32611

PEASBACK, DAVID R., recruiting company executive; 1 child, Jennifer. B.A., Colgate U., 1955; LL.B., U. Va., 1961. Mgmt. trainee Proctor & Gamble, N.Y.C., 1955-56; assoc. Covington & Burling, Washington, 1961-64; litigation counsel Litton Industries, Inc., Beverly Hills, Calif., 1965-67; v.p. Bangor Punta Ops., Greenwich, Conn., 1968-71; assoc. Heidrick and Struggles, N.Y.C., 1972-76, ptnr., 1976-88, pres., chief exec. officer, 1983-87; vice-chmn., chief exec. officer Canny, Bowen, Inc., N.Y.C., 1988—. Served as sgt. USMC, 1956-58. Office: Canny Bowen Inc 200 Park Ave Fl 49 New York NY 10166-0005

PEASE, DAVID GORDON, artist, educator; b. Bloomington, Ill., June 2, 1932; s. Gordon A. and June (Stephens) P.; m. Julie Jensen, Mar. 29, 1956; children: Lisa Kay, Kerry Susan. B.S., U. Wis., 1954, M.S., 1955, M.F.A., 1958. Instr. art Mich. State U., 1958-60; mem. faculty Tyler Sch. Art, Temple U., Phila., 1960-83; prof. Tyler Sch. Art, Temple U., 1970-83, chmn. painting dept., 1968-77, dean, 1977-83; prof. of painting Yale U. Sch. Art, New Haven, 1983—, dean, 1983-96, dir. grad. studies/painting, 1997—; vis. faculty mem. Yale U. Summer Sch. Music and Art, 1970-72. One-man shows include Baylor U., 1972, U. Wis., 1972, Pa. Acad. Fine Arts, 1977, Terry Dintenfass Inc., N.Y.C., 1969, 71, 76, Phila. Art Alliance, 1961, 70; group exhbns. include Carnegie Internat., Pitts., 1961, Corcoran Biennial, Washington, 1961, 63, Whitney Annual, N.Y.C., 1963; represented in permanent collections Whitney Mus. Am. Art, Phila. Mus. Art, Pa. Acad. Fine Arts, Des Moines Art Center, Pa. State U., U. Wis., Temple U., Hallmark Cards Inc., Columbia Pictures, others. Trustee Louis Comfort Tiffany Found., 1988-97. With U.S. Army, 1955-57. Recipient William A. Clark award Corcoran Biennial, 1963, Lindbeck Found. Disting. Teaching award, 1968, Disting. Alumni award U. Wis., 1991; Guggenheim Found. fellow, 1965-66; Tiffany Found. grantee, 1975-76. Mem. Coll. Art Assn. Am., Nat. Assn. Schs. Art, Nat. Coun. Art Adminstrs., Alliance Ind. Colls. of Art (bd. dirs. 1988-91), Assn. Ind. Colls. Art and Design (trustee 1992-96). Home: 95 Thankful Stow Rd Guilford CT 06437-2529 Office: Yale U Sch Art 180 York St New Haven CT 06511-4804

PEASE, EDWARD ALLAN, lawyer, former state senator, university official; b. Terre Haute, Ind., May 22, 1951; s. Robert Richard and Joanna Rose (Pilant) P.; A.B. with distinction (Wendell Willkie scholar), Ind. U., Bloomington, 1973, J.D. cum laude, Indpls., 1977; postgrad. Memphis State U., 1975-76, Ind. State U., 1978-85. Gen. law clk. appellate and contracts div. Office Ind. Atty. Gen., Indpls., 1974-75; nat. dir. alumni affairs Pi Kappa Alpha Frat., Memphis, 1975-76; admitted to Ind. bar, 1977; partner firm Thomas, Thomas & Pease, Brazil, Ind., 1977-84; of counsel firm Thomas & Thomas, Brazil, 1984-96; v.p. Ind. State U., 1993-96; mem. Ind. Senate, 1980-92, chmn. Judiciary Com.; chmn. Ind. Commn. Trial Cts., 1987-89; mem. Ho. of Reps. from 7th dist. Ind., 1996—; mem. adv. bd. 1st Bank & Trust Co. Clay County; mem. exec. bd. Wabash Valley council Boy Scouts Am., 1972—, exec. bd. east cen. region, 1986-88, v.p., 1977-84, pres., 1984-88, mem. nat. Order of Arrow com., 1984—, nat. vice chmn., 1990-93, nat. chmn., 1993—; mem. exec. bd. Nat. Intrafrat. Conf., 1994—; mem. Ind. Senate, 1980-92. Recipient Silver Beaver award Boy Scouts Am., 1975, Silver Antelope, 1992, Disting. Eagle Scout award, 1995. Mem. Ind. Bar Assn., Phi Beta Kappa, Pi Kappa Alpha (nat. pres. 1988-90). Republican. Methodist. Club: Columbia (Indpls.). Office: 226 Cannon HOB Washington DC 20515-1407

PEASE, ELLA LOUISE, elementary education educator; b. Kokomo, Ind., May 31, 1928; d. James E. and Carrie Alice (Ringer) Earnest; m. Harold Edwin Pease, Aug. 10, 1985; children: Charles Miller, James Miller, Ricky Ensley, Wanda Cisna. BS, Ball State U., 1956, MA, 1959; postgrad., Ind. U., Ft. Wayne. Tchr. 1st grade Union Twp. (Ind.) Pub. Schs., 1953-56, Wells City (Ind.) Pub. Schs., Forest Park Sch., Ft. Wayne, Ind., 1956-93. Docent Ft. Wayne Art Mus.; libr. Simpson United Meth. Ch., Ft. Wayne, bd. dirs., mem. child care bd. Mem. NEA-Ret., Internat. Reading Assn., Ret. Ind. Tchrs. Assn., Ft. Wayne Ret. Tchrs. Assn. Home: 5108 E State Blvd Fort Wayne IN 46815-7467

PEASE, ROGER FABIAN WEDGWOOD, electrical engineering educator; b. Cambridge, Eng., Oct. 24, 1936; came to U.S., 1964; s. Michael Stewart and Helen Bowen (Wedgwood) P.; m. Caroline Ann Bowring, Sept. 17, 1960; children: Emma Ruth, Joseph Henry Bowring, James Edward. BA, Cambridge U., Eng., 1960, MA, 1964, PhD, 1964. Rsch. fellow Trinity Coll., Cambridge, 1963-64; asst. prof. U. Calif., Berkeley, 1964-67; mem. tech. staff AT&T Bell Labs., Murray Hill, N.J., 1967-78; prof. elec. engring. Stanford (Calif.) U., 1978—; cons. IBM, San Jose, Calif., 1964-67, Xerox Corp., Palo Alto, Calif., 1978-84, Perkin Elmer Co., Hayward, Calif., 1979-90, Lawrence Livermore (Calif.) Labs., 1984-92, Affymax Rsch. Inst., 1989-93, Affymetrix, 1993—; mem. tech. adv. bd. Ultratech. Stepper, 1993—. Contbr. more than 200 articles to profl. jours. Patentee (8) in field. Scoutmaster Boy Scouts Am., Holmdel, N.J., 1977-78. Pilot officer RAF, 1955-57. Fellow IEEE (Rappaport award 1982), San Jose Sailing Club. Avocations: sailboat racing, windsurfing. Home: 570 Fremont St Menlo Park CA 94025-5127 Office: Stanford U Dept Elec Engring Stanford CA 94305

PEASE-PRETTY ON TOP, JANINE B., community college administrator; b. Nespelern, Wash., Sept. 17, 1949; d. Benjamin and Margery Louise (Jordan) Pease; m. Sam Vernon Windy Boy, July 30, 1975 (div. Jan. 1983); children: Rosella L. Windy Boy, Sam Vernon Windy Boy; m. John Joseph Pretty On Top, Sept. 15, 1991. BA in Sociology, Anthropology, Ctrl. Wash. U., 1970; MEd, Mont. State U., 1987, EdD, 1994; HHD (hon.), Hood Coll., 1990; LLD (hon.), Gonzaga U., 1991; EdD (hon.), Whitman Coll., 1993. Dep. dir. Wash. State Youth Commn., Olympia, 1971; tutor student svcs. Big Bend C.C., Moses Lake, Wash., 1971-72, upward bound dir., 1972-75; women's counselor Navajo C.C., Many Farms, Ariz., 1972; dir. adult & continuing edn. Crow Ctrl. Edn. Commn., Crow Agy., Mont., 1975-79; ednl. cons. Box Elder, Mont., 1979-81; dir. Indian career svc. Ea. Mont. Coll., Billings, 1981-82; pres. Little Big Horn Coll., Crow Agency, 1982—; exec. com. Am. Indian Higher Ednl. Consortium, Washington, 1983—; bd. dirs. Am. Indian Coll. Fund, N.Y.C., 1988—; sec. Indian Nations at Risk U.S. Dept. Edn., Washington, 1990-91, collaborator task force, 1990-91; 2d vice chmn. Nat. Adv. Coun. Indian Edn., Washington, 1994—. Chmn. Bighorn County Dem. Ctrl. Com., Hardin, Mont., 1983-88; mem. coun. First Crow Indian Bapt. Ch., 1989—. MacArthur fellow John D. & Catharine MacArthur Found., 1994. Mem. Nat. Indian Edn. Assn. (Indian educator of yr. 1990), Crow Tribe Nighthawk Dance Soc. Office: Little Big Horn Coll PO Box 370 Crow Agency MT 59022

PEASLAND, BRUCE RANDALL, financial executive; b. Buffalo, N.Y., Mar. 24, 1945; s. Kenneth Arthur and Edith Grace (Bristow) P.; m. Debra Myers Peasland, June 13, 1981; children: Michael John, Timothy Scott, Amanda Jean. BS, U. So. Calif., 1971, MBA in Fin., 1978; JD, Western St. U., 1983. Price and cost analyst McDonnell Douglas Corp., Long Beach, Calif., 1966-70; cost mgr. The Gillette Co., Santa Monica, Calif., 1971-78; controller Lear Siegler Inc., Santa Ana, Calif., 1978-85, British Petroleum, Hitco, Newport Beach, Calif., 1986-87; v.p. fin., dir. Control Components Inc., Rancho Santa Margarita, Calif., 1987-90; chief fin. officer MacGillivray Freeman Films, Laguna Beach, Calif., 1990-91; exec. v.p., chief fin. officer Intervest Industries Inc, Carlsbad, Calif., 1992—. Youth advisor YMCA, Dana Point, Calif., 1985—. With USMC, 1963-69. Recipient of Mgr. of Yr. award Nat. Mgmt. Assn., 1984. Fellow U. So. Calif. MBA Assn.; mem. Nat. Assn. of Accts., Nat. Mgmt. Assn. (dir. 1978-85), U. So. Calif. Trojan Club, U. So. Calif. Alumni Club. Republican. Episcopalian. Avocations: sailing, snow skiing. Home: 25211 Yacht Dr Dana Point CA 92629-1439 Office: Intervest Industries Inc 7720B El Camino Real Ste 201 Carlsbad CA 92009-8506

PEASLEE, JAMES M., lawyer; b. Scranton, Pa., Sept. 1, 1952; s. Robert Victor and Jean (Mark) P. BA, Yale U., 1973, MA, 1973; JD, Harvard U., 1976; LLM in Taxation, NYU, 1979. Bar: N.Y. 1977. Assoc. Cleary, Gottlieb, Steen & Hamilton, N.Y.C., 1976-84, ptnr., 1984—. Office: Cleary Gottlieb Steen & Hamilton 1 Liberty Plz New York NY 10006-1404

PEASLEE, MARGARET MAE HERMANEK, zoology educator; b. Chgo., June 15, 1935; d. Emil Frank and Magdalena Bessie (Cechota) Hermanek; m. David Raymond Peaslee, Dec. 6, 1957; 1 dau., Martha Magdelena Peaslee-Levine. A.A., Palm Beach Jr. Coll., 1956; B.S., Fla. So. Coll., 1959; med. technologist, Northwestern U., 1958, M.S., 1964, Ph.D., 1966. Med. technologist Passavant Hosp., Chgo., 1958-59; med. technologist St. James Hosp., Chicago Heights, Ill., 1960-63; asst. prof. biology Fla. So. Coll., Lakeland, 1966-68, U. S.D., Vermillion, 1968-71; assoc. prof. U. S.D., 1971-76, prof., 1976, acad. opportunity liaison, 1974-76; prof., head dept. zoology La. Tech. U., Ruston, 1976-90, assoc. dean, dir. grad. studies and rsch., prof. biol. scis. Coll. Life Scis., 1990-93; v.p. for acad. affairs U. Pitts. at Titusville, Pa., 1993—. Contbr. articles to profl. jours. Fellow AAAS; mem. AAUP, Am. Inst. Biol. Scis., Am. Soc. Zoologists, S.D. Acad. Sci. (sec.-treas. 1972-76), N.Y. Acad. Scis., Pa. Acad. Sci., La. Acad. Sci. (sec. 1979-81, pres. 1983), Sigma Xi, Phi Theta Kappa, Phi Rho Pi, Phi Sigma, Alpha Epsilon Delta. Office: U Pitts Office of Acad Affairs Titusville PA 16354-0287

PEAT, RANDALL DEAN, defense analysis company executive, retired air force officer; b. Chicago, July 6, 1935; s. Thomas R. and Lulu M. (Ray) P.; m. Joyce Enid Hunter, Sept. 15, 1956; children—Brian James, Sondra Lee Peat Gadell. B.S. in Journalism, Medill Sch. Journalism Northwestern U., Evanston, Ill., 1956, M.S. in Journalism Mgmt., 1957. Commd. officer U.S. Air Force, 1957, advanced through ranks to maj. gen.; pilot, instr. Strategic Air Command, Westover AFB and Clinton-Sherman, Okla., 1958-66; asst. air attache Am. Embassy, Djakarta, Indonesia, 1967; pilot Pacific Command Airborne Command Post, Hickam AFB, Hawaii, 1968-70; staff officer 7th Air Force, Saigon, Vietnam, 1971, Hdqrs. U.S. Air Force, Pentagon, D.C., 1972-75, SHAPE, Belgium, 1976-79, Hdqrs. U.S. Air Force, Pentagon, D.C., 1980-81; dep. dir. plans Office Joint Chief of Staff, Pentagon, D.C., 1982-84; asst. chief of staff ops. Supreme Hdqrs. Allied Powers Europe, Belgium, 1984-87; chief of staff Strategic Air Command, Offutt AFB, Nebr., 1987-89; v.p. R&D Assocs., Europe, 1989—. Decorated Air medal, Bronze Star, Meritorious Service medal, Def. Superior Service medal, Def. Disting. Service medal; Republic of Vietnam Cross of Gallantry with Palm, Republic of Vietnam Campaign medal. Mem. Daedalians (vice flight capt. 1976), Air Force Assn., Pi Alpha Mu. Avocations: cooking; hiking; painting; British mystery writers. Home: Rue des Allies 43, B-7870 Lens Belgium also: LOGICON RDA 6053 W Century Blvd Los Angeles CA 90045-6430

PEATTIE, LISA REDFIELD, urban anthropology educator; b. Chgo., Mar. 1, 1924; d. Robert and Margaret (Park) Redfield; m. Roderick Peattie, June 26, 1943 (dec. 1962); children: Christopher, Sara, Miranda, Julia; m. William A. Doebele, 1973 (div.). M.A., U. Chgo., 1950, Ph.D., 1968. Faculty mem. dept. urban studies MIT, Cambridge, 1965—, prof. urban anthropology, 1968-85; now prof. emeritus, sr. lectr. MIT; cons. World Bank, 1975, 76, 81, UN, 1980. Author: The View from the Barrio, 1968, Thinking About Development, 1982, (with W. Ronco) Making Work, 1983, (with Martin Rein) Women's Claims, 1983, Planning: Rethinking Ciudad Guayana, 1987. Recipient Paul Davidoff award Am. Soc. Collegiate Schs. of Planning, 1989. Mem. Am. Anthrop. Assn., Soc. Applied Anthropology. Office: Dept Urban Studies MIT Cambridge MA 02139

PEAVLER, NANCY JEAN, editor; b. Kansas City, Mo., Dec. 19, 1951; d. Elmer Alfred and Ruth Lenoris (Peterson) Zimmerli; m. Craig Eugene Peavler, Dec. 6, 1975; 1 child, Matthew Dean. Assoc., Kansas City (Kans.) Community Coll., 1976; BS in Human Resources Mgmt., Friends U., Wichita, Kans., 1995. Staff writer The Kansas City Kansan, 1972-73; assoc. editor Capper's Stauffer Communications, Topeka, 1976-87, editor, 1987—. Precinct com.-woman Shawnee County Rep. Party, Topeka, 1985-87. Mem. Women in Communications, Soc. Profl. Journalists. United Methodist. Office: Cappers 1503 SW 42nd St Topeka KS 66609-1214

PEAVY, HOMER LOUIS, JR., real estate executive, accountant; b. Okmulgee, Okla., Sept. 4, 1924; s. Homer Louis and Hattie Lee (Walker) P.; children: Homer Martin, Daryl Mark. Student Kent State U., 1944-49; grad. Hammel-Actual Coll., 1962. Sales supr. Kirby Sales, Akron, Ohio, 1948-49; sales mgr. Williams-Kirby Co., Detroit, 1949-50; area distributor Peavy-Kirby Co., Phila., 1953-54; salesman James L. Peavy Realty Co., Akron, 1954-65; owner Homer Louis Peavy, Jr., Real Estate Broker, Akron, 1965—; pvt. practice acctg., Akron, 1962—; fin. aid officer Buckeye Coll., Akron, 1982. Author: Watt Watts, 1969; poet: Magic of the Muse, 1978, P.S. I Love You, 1982; contbr. poetry to Am. Poetry Anthology, 1983, New Worlds Unlimited, 1984, Treasures of the Precious Moments, 1985, Our World's Most Cherished Poems, 1985; songs: Sh...Sh, Sheree, Sheree, 1976, In Akron O, 1979; teleplay: Revenge, 1980. Bd. dirs. Internat. Elvis Gold Soc., 1978—; charter mem. Statue of Liberty-Ellis Island Found., 1984, Nat. Mus. of Women in Arts, 1986, Nat. Mus. Am. Indian, U.S. Holocaust Meml. Mus.; mem. Nat. Trust for Hist. Preservation, Ohio Hist. Soc., Preservation/N.C., Japanese Am. Nat. Mus.; charter mem. USS Constn., Libr. Congress Nat. Assocs. Mus. Recipient Am. Film Inst. Cert. Recognition, 1982, Award of Merit cert. World of Poetry 10th ann. contest, 1985, Golden Poet award World of Poetry, 1985, 87, 88, 89. Mem. NAACP (mem.-at-large), Ohioana Library Assn., Internat. Black Writers Conf., Acad. Am. Poets, Poetry Soc. Am., Smithsonian Nat. Assocs., Manuscript Club Akron, Internat. Platform Assn., Ohio Theatre Alliance, Kent State U. Alumni Assn. Democrat. Home and Office: 1160 Cadillac Blvd Akron OH 44320-2858

PEAVY, SALLY HUDGINS, special education educator, diagnostician, school psychologist; b. Macon, Ga., Nov. 30, 1948; d. Jack W. and Lillian T. (Bloodworth) Jenkins; m. Luke L. Hudgins, Sept. 5, 1970 (dec. Apr. 13, 1978); 1 child, Emily W.; m. Donald P. Peavy, Nov. 18, 1970; 1 child, Dallas L. BS in Elem. Edn. and Mental Retardation, Auburn U., 1970; MEd in Learning Disabilities and Behaviour Disorders, Ga. State U., 1972, postgrad., 1990—. Cert. tchr. T-5 in spl. edn., T-4 in mental retardation, T-6 in sch. psychology, Ga. Spl. edn. instr. Smith Station (Ala.) Elem. Sch., 1970-71; spl. edn. instr., resource tchr. Sagamore Hills and Montclair Elem. Schs. De Kalb County Schs, Atlanta, 1972-75; spl. edn. instr. Panola Way Elem. Sch., Atlanta, 1987-90; spl. edn. instr. Gwinnet County Summerour Middle Sch., Lawrenceville, Ga., 1990-92, sch. psychologist, 1994—. Leader Girl Scouts Am., Dekalb County, Ga., 1983-88; guide Mus. of Art, Atlanta, 1983; bd. dirs. PTA, Dekalb County, 1984; chmn. tutorial reading program, Jr. League of Dekalb County, 1986-87; team parent Tucker Baseball Assn.; nursery tchr. Mt. Carmel Christian Ch.; Specific Learning Disabilities vol. DeKalb County, Jolly Elem. Recipient Bob Clarke Meml. scholarship Gwinnet County Sch. System, 1992; grantee U.S. Govt., Auburn U., 1969-70, Ga. State U., 1971-72. Mem. Nat. Assn. Sch. Psychologists, Ga. Assn. Sch. Psychologists, Coun. Exceptional Children (diagnostic div.), Kappa Delta Pi.

PEAY, J.H. BINFORD, III, career officer; b. Richmond, Va., May 10, 1940; m. Pamela Jane Pritchett; children: James, Ryan. BS, Va. Mil. Inst., 1962; MA, George Washington U.; grad., U.S. Army Command and Gen. Staff Coll., U.S. Army War Coll. Second lt. U.S. Army, 1962, advanced through grades to comdr. in chief, U.S. ctrl. command, 1994—. Decorated Silver Star, Legion of Merit, Purple Heart, Bronze Star Medal with three oak leaf clusters, Air medal, others. Office: Headquarters US Ctrl Command MacDill AFB Tampa FL 33621*

PECANO, DONALD CARL, truck trailer manufacturing executive; b. L.A., Dec. 2, 1948; s. Domenick Lawrence and Carlotta Noble (Martello) P.; m. Sandra Ann Tuminello, Apr. 26, 1969; children: Julia Ann, Melissa Ann, Donald Carl. BS in Acctg, Pa. State U., 1970; MBA in Mktg., Youngstown State U., 1981; postgrad., Case Western Res. U., 1995. CPA, Pa. Contr. Atlas Guard Svc. subs. SERVISCO, East Orange, N.J., 1974-76; asst. to pres. SERVISCO, Hillside, N.J., 1976-77; v.p. fin. Columbus Svcs., Inc. subs. SERVISCO, New Castle, Pa., 1977-82; dir. fin. East Mfg. Corp. and subs. cos., 1982-88, v.p. fin. and adminstrn., 1988—, also mem. exec. com.; v.p. fin. Intermodal Techs. Inc., 1991—; bd. dirs. Intermodal Techs. Inc.; Weatherhead profl. fellow Case Western Res. U., 1995. Republican. Roman Catholic. Office: 1871 State Route 44 Randolph OH 44265 *Placing the best interests of the company ahead of your own is ultimately in your own best interest.*

PECCARELLI, ANTHONY MARANDO, lawyer, conflict resolutions company executive; b. Newark, Apr. 12, 1928; s. Adolph and Mary (Marano) P.; m. Mary Dearborn Hutchison, Dec. 23, 1953; children: Andrew Louis, David Anthony, Laura Elizabeth. BS, Beloit Coll., 1953; JD, John Marshall Law Sch., 1959; M in Jud. Studies, U. Nev., 1990. Bar: Ill. 1961, U.S. Dist. Ct. (no. dist.) Ill., U.S. Supreme Ct. Supr. real estate and claims Gulf Oil Corp., Chgo., 1956-61; asst. state's atty. DuPage County, Wheaton, Ill., 1961-65; first asst. state's atty. DuPage County State's Atty., Wheaton, Ill., 1965-69; mem.-del. Ill. Constnl. Conv., Springfield, 1969-70; exec. dir. Ill. State's Atty. Assn., Elgin, 1970-71; ptnr. Barclay, Damisch & Sinson, Chgo., 1971-79; assoc. cir. judge 18th Jud. Cir. Ct., Wheaton, 1979-82; cir. judge, 1982-93; chief judge 18th Jud. Cir. Ct., Wheaton, 1989-93; presiding judge domestic rels. divsn., 1982-83, presiding judge law divsn., 1987-89; chief judge 18th Judicial Cir., 1989-93; justice 2nd dist. Ill. Appellate Ct., Wheaton, 1993-94; state's atty. DuPage County, Wheaton, Ill., 1995-96; assoc., of counsel Ottosen Sinson Trevarthen Britz & Dooley, Ltd., Wheaton, Ill., 1996—; chair Ill. Jud. Conf. Ill. Supreme Ct., Springfield, 1987-89. Contbr. articles to profl. jours. Bd. dirs., treas. DuPage Coun. for Child Devel.; bd. dirs. Ctrl. DuPage Pastoral Counseling Ctr.; chair Wheaton Com. for Jud. Reform, 1962; trustee Midwestern U., 1993—, vice chmn., bd. trustees 1997—. Cpl. USMC, 1946-48. Mem. DuPage County Bar Assn. (pres. 1972-73), DuPage County Legal Assistance Fedn. (pres. 1973-74), DuPage County Lawyer Referral Svc. (pres. 1972),. Congregationalist.

PECHILIS, WILLIAM JOHN, lawyer; b. Brockton, Mass., May 13, 1924; s. John and Kaleroe (Karmeris) P.; m. Kay Dillon, June 7, 1958; children: Julie W., Karen P., John D. BA, Harvard U., 1946, LLB, 1951. Bar: Mass. 1951. Law clk. to assoc. justice Supreme Judicial Ct., Boston, 1951-52; assoc. Goodwin, Procter and Hoar, Boston, 1952-61, ptnr., 1961-94, of counsel, 1995—. Trustee Concord (Mass.) Acad., 1978-80, Wang Inst. Grad. Studies, Tyngsboro, Mass., 1979-87, Wang Ctr. for Performing Arts, 1983—, Anatolia Coll., Boston, 1984-91; mem. fin. com. Weston, Mass., 1972-74. With USNR, 1943-46, PTO. Fellow Am. Coll. Trust and Estate Counsel; mem. ABA, Mass. Bar Assn., Boston Bar Assn., Harvard Club, Weston Golf Club, Woods Hole Golf Club, Phi Beta Kappa. Avocation: golf. Home: 59 Jericho Rd Weston MA 02193-1409 Office: Goodwin Procter and Hoar Exchange Pl Boston MA 02109-2808

PECHUKAS, PHILIP, chemistry educator; b. Akron, Ohio, Oct. 30, 1942; s. Alphonse and Evelyn (Grebenak) P.; children: Rolf Birkhoff, Maria Berenson, Sarah Landau, Fiona Veronese, Amy Hayes. BS, Yale U., 1963; PhD, U. Chgo., 1966. Asst. prof. chemistry Columbia U., N.Y.C., 1967-72, assoc. prof., 1972-78, prof., 1978—, chmn. dept. chemistry, 1984-87. Contbr. articles to profl. jours. Fellow Nat. Bur. Standards, 1966-67, Alfred P. Sloan Found., 1970-74, J.S. Guggenheim Found., 1975, Haverford Coll., 1985. Fellow Am. Phys. Soc.; mem. Am. Chem. Soc. (chmn. theoretical chemistry subdivision 1985-86), Humboldt Sen. Scientist, 1993-94. Office: Columbia Univ Dept Chemistry 3000 Broadway MC 3116 New York NY 10027

PECK, ABRAHAM, editor, writer, educator, magazine consultant; b. N.Y.C., Jan. 18, 1945; s. Jacob and Lottie (Bell) Peckolick; m. Suzanne Wexler, Mar. 19, 1977; children: Douglas Benjamin, Robert Wexler. B.A., N.Y. U., 1965; postgrad., CUNY, 1965-67. Engaged in community organizing and tutoring, 1962-64; with N.Y.C. Welfare Dept., 1965-67; freelance writer, 1967—; writer, organizer Chgo. Action Youth Internat. Party, 1968; editor Chgo. Seed, 1968-70; treas. Seed Pub., Inc., 1968-70; mem. coordinating com. Underground Press Syndicate, 1969; assoc. editor Rolling Stone mag., San Francisco, 1975, contbg. editor, 1976—; cons. various mags., 1984—; ednl. cons. Asian Sources Media Group, Hong Kong, Manila, 1989—; feature writer Chgo. Daily News, 1977-78; with features dept. Chgo. Sun-Times, 1978-81; from asst. prof. to assoc. prof. Medill Sch. Journalism, Northwestern U., 1981-92, prof., 1992—, dir. M.S.J. mag. pub. program, 1982—, chmn. mag. program, 1988—, mem. sch. ops. com., 1990—, dir. Nat. Arts Journalism Program, 1993-97, mem. adv. bd., 1997—; critic at large Sta. WBBM, 1979-82; editor, co-founder Sidetracks, alt. newspaper supplement, Chgo. Daily News, 1977-78; mem. exec. com. Assn. for Edn. in Journalism and Mass Communication, mag. divsn., 1987-89, 92—, pres., 1994-95; mem. adv. bd. Academe mag., Am. Assn. Univ. Profs., 1990—, Heartland Jour., 1990—, Technos, 1992—. Editor: Dancing Madness, 1976; author: Uncovering the Sixties: The Life and Times of the Underground Press, 1985, 91; cons. editor, contbr.: The Sixties, 1977; contbr.: The Eighties: A Look Back, 1979, Voices From the Underground, 1993. Served with AUS, 1967. Office: Northwestern U Medill Sch Journalism 1845 Sheridan Rd Evanston IL 60201-5004

PECK, ABRAHAM JOSEPH, historian; b. Landsberg, Fed. Republic of Germany, May 4, 1946; came to U.S., 1949; s. Shalom W. and Anna (Koltun) P.; m. Jean Marcus, June 21, 1969; children: Abby, Joel. BA, Am. U., 1968, MA, 1970; PhD, U. East Anglia, Eng., 1977; postgrad., U. Hamburg, Fed. Republic Germany, 1973-74. Adminstrv. dir. Am. Jewish Archives, Cin., 1976—; exec. dir. Holocaust Mus., Houston, 1997—; lectr. in Judaic studies U. Cin., 1980—; mem. internat. adv. bd. Internat. Ctr. for Holocaust Studies, 1986—; mem. adv. bd. Nat. Cath. Inst. for Holocaust Studies, 1988—; founding mem. Greater Cin. Interfaith Holocaust Found., 1986—. Author: Radicals and Reactionaries, 1978; editor Jews and Christians After the Holocaust, 1982; co-editor Am. Rabbinate: A Century of Continuity and Change 1883-1983, 1985, Studies in the American Jewish Experience II, 1984, Queen City Refuge: An Oral History of Cincinnati's Jewish Refugees from Nazism, 1989, Sephardim in the Americas: Studies in Culture and History, 1993; editor: The German-Jewish Legacy in America: From Bildung to the Bill of Rights, 1989, Selected Documents of World Jewish Congress, 1936-50, 2 vols., 1991; contbr. articles to profl. jours. Spl. advisor U.S. Holocaust Meml. Coun., Washington, 1982-86; bd. dirs. Am. Jewish Com., Cin., 1978-84, Anti-Defamation League of Ohio, Ind. and Ken., Columbus, 1982-86, Jewish Community Rels. Coun., Cin., 1980-86; mem. Am. Hist. Found., Orgn. Am. Historians. Fullbright Found. fellow, 1973-74; Ohio Program in the Humanities grantee, 1980, 83, 85. Mem. Assn. Jewish Studies, Soc. Scholarly Pub., Soc. Am. Archivists, Internat. P.E.N. Centre of German-Speaking Writers Abroad. Avocations: travel, raising dogs. Office: Am Jewish Archives 3101 Clifton Ave Cincinnati OH 45220-2404

PECK, ARTHUR JOHN, JR., diversified manufacturing executive, lawyer; b. Trenton, N.J., Mar. 2, 1940; s. Arthur John and Mary Ellen (Kelly) P.; m. Susan Williams Lodge, July 18, 1970; children: David A., Margaret E. BA in Hist., Yale U., 1962; LLB, Washington & Lee U., 1968. Admissions officer Lawrenceville Sch., N.J., 1962-65; atty. Shearman & Sterling, N.Y.C., 1968-72; asst., assoc. counsel Corning (N.Y.), Inc., 1972-81, asst. sec., 1981-88, sec., 1988—; sec. Teddington Co., Ltd., 1989—, Corning Inc. Found. 1981—, Corning Europe, Inc., 1989—, Corning Inc., 1988—, Corning Internat. Corp., 1991—; dir., sec. Corning Inc. Fgn. Sales Corp., 1992—, Watkins Glen Internat., Inc., 1983-97, Corning Classic Charities, Inc., 1978—; asst. sec. Corning Enterprises, Inc., 1974—, Corning Mus. Glass, 1981—, Market St. Restoration Corp., 1974—; trustee, sec. The Rockwell Mus., 1983—; bd. dirs. Wisland, S.A. Office: Corning Inc Riverfront Plaza Corning NY 14831

PECK, AUSTIN H., JR., lawyer; b. Pomona, Calif., Dec. 25, 1913; s. Austin H. and Helen (Templeton) P.; m. Jean Albertson, Nov. 9, 1939; children: Julie, Francesca, Lisa. A.B. with distinction, Stanford, 1935, J.D., 1938. Bar: Calif. 1938. Since practiced in Los Angeles; mem. firm Latham & Watkins, 1946-76, of counsel, 1976-92. Mem. nat. coun. House Ear Inst. Mem. Am., Calif., Los Angeles bar assns., Zeta Psi, Phi Delta Phi. Clubs: California (L.A.), L.A. Country, Birnam Wood (Montecito, Calif.), Valley (Montecito), Cypress Point. Home: 770 San Ysidro Ln Santa Barbara CA 93108-1323 Office: 633 W 5th St Los Angeles CA 90071-2005

PECK, BERNARD SIDNEY, lawyer; b. Bridgeport, Conn., July 26, 1915; s. James and Sadie P.; m. Marjorie Eloise Dean, Apr. 10, 1943; children: Daniel Dean, Constance Lynn. B.A., Yale U., 1936, LL.B., 1939. Bar: Conn. 1939, Fla. 1979, N.Y. 1982. Pvt. practice Bridgeport, 1939-84; ptnr. Goldstein and Peck, 1946-84; judge Mcpl. Ct., Westport, Conn., 1951-55; ptnr. Peck & Peck, Naples, Fla., 1983-87, Porter, Wright, Morris & Arthur, Naples, 1987-90, Peck, Peck & Volpe, Naples, 1990-92, Peck, Volpe & Sullivan, Naples, 1992-94, Peck & Faga, Naples, 1994—. Moderator town meeting, Westport, 1950-51; mem. Westport Republican Town Com., 1951-79; pres. Westport YMCA, 1957, trustee, 1964-84; pres. endowment bd. YMCA Naples, 1987-88. Capt. AUS, 1942-46. Fellow Am. Coll. Trial Lawyers, Internat. Acad. Trial Lawyers; mem. ABA, Collier County Bar Assn., Phi Beta Kappa. Clubs: Linville (N.C.) Ridge Country; Royal Poinciana Golf (dir. 1983-90, pres. 1987-89), Yale (trustee 1985—) (Naples, Fla.). Home: 4951 Gulf Shore Blvd N Apt 202 Naples FL 34103-2696 Office: Peck & Faga 5801 Pelican Bay Blvd Ste 103 Naples FL 34108-2709 also: 821 Crest Trl Linville Ridge NC

PECK, CAROL FAULKNER, poet, writer, publisher, educator; b. Detroit, June 20, 1934; d. Edward Carroll and Barbara Ann (Fite) Faulkner; m. Lawrence David Peck, Dec. 18, 1954; children: David Edward Peck, Wendy Carol Peck Webster. BA in English, U. Mich., 1958; MA in English, U. Md., 1964; postgrad. in Teaching Creative Writing, U. Denver, 1977. Artist-in-edn. Md. State Arts Coun., Balt., 1971—; lectr. in English U. Md. Univ. Coll., Coll. Park, Md., 1971—; writer in residence Sidwell Friends Sch., Washington, D.C., 1978-91; poetry workshop leader Montgomery County Pub. Schs. Alternative Programs, Rockville, Md., 1978—; leader numerous poetry and writing workshops for ednl. and other audiences, 1971—; editl. bd. Md. English Jour., 1968-84, 95—; editor novels and dissertations for writers of same; owner carolpeck prodns., pacem Press. Author: From Deep Within, 1989; contbr. numerous articles to ednl. jours., poems to poetry and literary mags. Vol. poetry workshop leader Bethesda Retirement and Nursing Ctr., Chevy Chase, Md., 1978-91; judge numerous sch. and lit. groups poetry and writing contests; vol. Hospice Caring, Inc., 1994—. Assembly scholar U. Mich., 1953; recipient Hopwood award, 1953, first prize sonnet div. Alexandria Br., Nat. League of Am. PEN Women, 1984, Disting. Achievement award Ednl. Press Assn. Am., 1989, Excellence in Teaching award U. Md./U. Coll., 1993. Mem. Writers Ctr., Nat. Coun. Tchrs. English, Md. Coun. Tchrs. of English Lang. Arts, Internat. Women's Writing Guild, Alpha Lambda Delta, Phi Beta Kappa, Phi Kappa Phi. Home and Office: 14910 Brownstone Dr Burtonsville MD 20866-1849

PECK, CHARLES EDWARD, retired construction and mortgage executive; b. Newark, Dec. 1, 1925; s. Hubert Raymond and Helen (White) P.; m. Delphine Murphy, Oct. 15, 1949; children: Margaret Peck Iovino, Charles Edward, Katherine Peck Koustmer, Perry Anne Peck Flanagan. Grad., Phillips Acad., 1943; student, MIT, 1944; BS, U. Pa., 1949; PhD in Pub. Svc. (hon.), Univ. Coll., 1995. With Owens-Corning Fiberglas Corp., 1949-61; from sales mgr. home bldg. products to exec. v.p. Owens-Corning Fiberglas Corp., Toledo, 1961-81; bd. dir. Owens-Corning Fiberglas Corp.; co-chmn. The Ryland Group, Columbia, Md., 1981-82; chmn., CEO The Ryland Group, Columbia, 1982-90; dir. The Delaware Group of Funds, 1991—; sec. Enterprise Homes, Inc., 1992—; mem. statutory vis. com. U.S. Nat. Bur. Standards, 1972-77; mem. adv. com. Fed. Nat. Mortgage Assn., 1977-78, 85-86; mem. vis. com. MIT-Harvard Joint Ctr. for Urban Studies; chmn. Prodrs. Adv. Forum, 1977-81; mem. pres.'s adv. coun. Washington Coll., 1997—. Vis. com. Harvard U. Grad. Sch. Design, 1981-86; chmn. Howard County United Way Campaign, Md., 1987, chmn. Cmty. Partnerships, 1991-94; bd. dirs. Nat. Inst. for Urban Wildlife, 1986-90, United Way Ctrl. Md., 1987-91, Howard County Gen. Hosp., 1988-94, Columbia Festival, Inc., 1988-91, NAHB Rsch. Found., 1989-92, Alliance to End Childhood Lead Poisoning, 1990-93; adv. bd. U. Md. Engring. Sch., 1990—, Continuing Edn. Johns Hopkins U., 1988-91; policy adv. bd. Harvard Joint Ctr. Housing Studies, 1984-94; chmn. Chancellor's Adv. Comm. U. Md. Sys., 1988—; chmn. Univ. Md. Found., 1990-94, bd. dirs., 1990—; exec. fellow Kennedy Sch., Harvard U., 1990-92; chmn. Affordable Housing Initiative, Columbia, Md., 1990-92; bd. overseers U. Md., College Park, 1994—; bd. visitors Sch. Law U. Md., Balt., 1996—; bd. dirs. Ctr. for Grant Devel., 1994—, Victory '94 com. Md. State Rep. party, chmn. election inquiry funding com., 1994-

95; chmn. Children of Separation and Divorce Ctr., 1995—; pres. advisory coun. Washington Coll., Chestertown, Md., 1997—. 2d lt. USAAF, 1944-46. Mem. U.S. C. of C. (bd. dirs. 1975-81), Ohio C. of C. (bd. dirs. 1975-81), Depression and Related Affective Disorders Assn. (pres. 1986-89, bd. dirs. 1986—, pres. 1993-94), Rotary, Talbot Country Club, City Club, Ctr. Club, Caves Valley Golf Club, Phi Gamma Delta. Home: 7649 Woodstream Way Laurel MD 20723-1163 Office: PO Box 1108 Columbia MD 21044-0108

PECK, DALLAS LYNN, retired geologist; b. Cheney, Wash., Mar. 28, 1929; s. Lynn Averill and Mary Hazel (Carlyle) P.; m. Tevis Sue Lewis, Mar. 28, 1951 (dec.); children: Ann, Stephen, Gerritt; m. Carmella M. Peck, Apr. 29, 1995. B.S., Calif. Inst. Tech., 1951, M.S., 1953; Ph.D., Harvard U., 1960. With U.S. Geol. Survey, 1954-95; asst. chief geologist, office of geochemistry and geophysics U.S. Geol. Survey, Washington, 1967-72, geologist, geologic div., 1972-77, chief geologist, 1977-81, dir., 1981-93, geologist, 1993-95, emeritus scientist, 1995—; mem. Lunar Sample Rev. Bd., 1970-71; chmn. earth scis. adv. com. NSF, 1970-72; vis. com. dept. geol. scis. Harvard U., 1972-78; mem. Earthscis. Adv. Bd., Stanford U., 1982-93; chmn. com. earth scis. Fed. Coord. Coun. Sci., Enring. and Tech., 1987-92; mem. sci., tech. com. UN Decade for Nat. Disaster Reduction, 1992-94. Recipient Meritorious Svc. award Dept. Interior, 1971, Disting. Svc. award, 1979; Presdl. Meritorious Exec. award, 1980, Disting. Alumni award Calif. Inst. Tech., 1985, Ian Campbell medal Am. Geol. Inst., 1994. Fellow AAAS (pres. sect. E. 1996-97), Geol. Soc. Am., Am. Geophys. Union (pres. sect. volcanology, geochemistry and petrology 1976-78). Home: 2524 Heathcliff Ln Reston VA 22091-4225

PECK, DANIEL FARNUM, chemical company executive; b. Port Jervis, N.Y., Aug. 6, 1927; s. John Flint and Frances Ann (Farnum) P.; m. Ardyce Chase Hoover, July 14, 1951 (dec. July 1979); children: Cheryl H. Gerber, Daniel Farnum Jr., Laurie A. Peck Perry; m. Barbara Ann Gunning Gillinder, Sept. 5, 1980. BSChemE, Clarkson U., 1950. Field engr. Rsch. Corp., Bound Brook, N.J., 1950-51; process devel. engring. supr. Nat. Starch and Chem. Corp., Plainfield, N.J., 1951-55, prodn. dept. head, 1955-60; divsn. supt. Nat. Starch and Chem. Corp., Indpls., 1960-67; plant and mfg. mgr. Nat. Starch and Chem. Corp., Meredosia, Ill., 1967-72, dir. mfg., 1972-76, divsn. v.p., 1976-80, corp. v.p., 1980-84, group v.p., 1984-89, ret., 1989; also bd. dirs. Nat. Starch and Chem. Corp., Bridgewater, N.J. Mem. Envelope Mfrs. Assn., Soc. Chem. Industry, Adhesive Mfrs. Assn., Adhesive Sealant Coun. (pres. edn. found., bd. dirs.). Avocations: boating, golf, bridge, hunting, fishing.

PECK, DAVID BLACKMAN, electrical engineer; b. Whitewater, Wis.; s. Clarence Neil and Jean Briese (Blackman) P. BSEE, San Diego State U., 1976. Engring. specialist Litton Systems, Woodland Hills, Calif., 1977-89; engr., proprietor Cockpit Devices, Edgerton, Wis., 1989—. Mem. NSPE, IEEE. Avocations: private pilot, jazz trumpeter. Home and Office: Cockpit Devices 913 Bliven Rd Edgerton WI 53534-9543

PECK, DIANNE KAWECKI, architect; b. Jersey City, June 13, 1945; d. Thaddeus Walter and Harriet Ann (Zlotkowski) Kawecki; m. Gerald Paul Peck, Sept. 1, 1968; children: Samantha Gillian Gildersleeve, Alexis Hilary. BArch, Carnegie-Mellon U., 1968. Architect, P.O.D. R & D , 1968, Kohler-Daniels & Assos., Vienna, Va., 1969-71, Beery-Rio & Assocs., Annandale, Va., 1971-73; ptnr. Peck & Peck Architects, Occoquan, Va., 1973-74, Peck, Peck & Williams, Occoquan, 1974-81; corp. officer Peck Peck & Assoc., Inc., Woodbridge, Va., 1981—; CEO, interior design group Peck Peck & Assoc., 1988—. Work pub. in Am. Architecture, 1985. Vice pres. Vocat. Edn. Found., 1976; chairwoman architects and engrs. United Way; mem. Health Systems Agy. of No. Va., commendations, 1977; mem. Washington Profl. Women's Coop.; chairwoman Indsl. Devel. Authority of Prince William, 1976, vice chair, 1977, mem., 1975-79; mem. archtl. rev. bd. Prince William County, 1996—; developer research project Architecture for Adolescents, 1987-88; mem. inaugural class Leadership Am., 1988, Leadership Greater Washington; mem. D.C. Coun. Metrication, 1992—, D.C. Hist. Preservation League, Rep. Nat. Com. Recipient commendation Prince William Bd. Suprs., 1976, State of Art award for Contel Hdqrs. design, 1985, Best Middle Sch. award Coun. of Ednl. Facilities Planners Internat., 1989, Creativity award Masonry Inst. Md., 1990, First award, 1990, Detailing award, 1990, Govt. Workplace award for renovations of Dept. of Labor Bldg., 1990, Creative Use of Materials award Inst. of Bus. Designers, 1991, 1st award Brick Inst. Md., 1993, award Brick Inst. Va., 1994, Bull Elephant award Prince William County Young Reps., 1995; named Best Instl. Project Nat. Comml. Builders Coun.; subject of PBS spl.: A Success in Howard Co. Mem. Soc. Am. Mil. Engrs., Prince William C. of C. (bd. dir.). Roman Catholic. Club: Soroptimist. Research on inner-city rehab., adolescents and the ednl. environ. Office: 2050 Old Bridge Rd Woodbridge VA 22192-2447

PECK, DONALD VINCENT, musician; b. Yakima, Wash., Jan. 26, 1930; s. Clarence Leon and Bertha A. (Compin) P. Diploma in Music, Curtis Inst. Music, 1951; student, Seattle U., 1948-49. With Seattle Symphony Orch., 1947-49, Nat. Symphony Orch., Washington, 1951-52; prin. flutist Kansas City Philharmonic Orch., 1955-57, Chgo. Symphony Orch., 1957—; instr. flute and woodwind ensemble DePaul U., Chgo.; guest soloist with various orchs. Served with USMCR, 1952-55. Office: care Chgo Symphony Orch 220 S Michigan Ave Chicago IL 60604-2501 also: Parsons Artists Mgmt PO Box 160 Highland Park IL 60035-0160*

PECK, EDWARD LIONEL, retired foreign service officer, corporate executive; b. Los Angeles, Mar. 6, 1929; s. Alexander George and Rae (Lee) P.; m. Heather Dianne Hicks-Beach, Jan. 20, 1957 (div. July 1971); m. Ann Day Slevin, May 5, 1974; children—Heather Anne, Brian Michael, Thomas William, Julia Katherine. B.S., UCLA, 1956; M.B.A., George Washington U., 1973. Joined Fgn. Service Dept. State, Washington, 1957, intelligence specialist, 1968-71, spl. asst., 1971-74; econ. counselor U.S. Embassy, Cairo, 1974-77; chief of mission U.S. Interests Sect., Baghdad, Iraq, 1977-80; dir. Office of Egyptian affairs Washington, 1980-82; ambassador U.S. Embassy, Nouakchott, Mauritania, 1983-85; dep. dir. Vice Pres.' Task Force on Combatting Terrorism, 1985-86; dir. Office of Career Transition, 1986-88; ret., 1989; pres. Fgn. Svcs. Internat., 1989—; exec. sec. Am. Acad. Diplomacy, 1989-92; trainer, lectr., cons. on fgn. affairs, internat. bus., 1990—; dir. polit. tradecraft program Nat. Fgn. Affairs Tng. Ctr., Arlington, Va., 1991-96; sr. assoc. Global Bus. Access Ltd., Washington, 1991—; Woodrow Wilson vis. fellow, 1993—. Served to capt. U.S. Army, 1946-49, 50-52. Recipient Meritorious Honor award Dept. State, 1967, 73, 77, 79, Superior Honor award Dept. State, 1974, 88, Wilbur J. Carr award, 1989; Rivkin award Am. Fgn. Svc. Assn., 1973. Home and Office: 106 Grafton St Bethesda MD 20815-3426

PECK, EDWIN RUSSELL, real estate management executive; b. Akron, Ohio, Aug. 19, 1931; s. Roy Zola and Mary Susan (Snyder) P.; m. Lou Ellen Smith, Oct. 28, 1949; children—Edwin Russell, Lori Rae. B.S. in Gen. Bus., San Diego State U., 1957. Mortgage trainee South Pacific Corp., San Diego, 1957-58; asst. sec., loan officer Southland Savs., Lamesa, Calif., 1958-60; supr. Phoenix Mut. Life Ins. Co., Hartford, Conn., 1960-63; v.p. comml. loan T.J. Bettes Co., Houston, 1963-68; sr. v.p. comml. loan Am. Mortgage Co., Houston, 1968-72; sr. v.p. real estate S.C.I., Houston, 1972-87, cons., 1987-97, retired, 1997. Served with USN, 1949-52; Japan/Korea. Republican. Presbyterian. Home: 11738 Oak Valley Dr Houston TX 77065-2937 Office: Service Corp Internat 1929 Allen Pky Houston TX 77019-2507

PECK, ELDRED GREGORY, actor; b. La Jolla, Calif., Apr. 5, 1916; m. Greta Rice, 1942 (div. 1949); m. Veronique Passani; 5 children. Ed., U. Calif., Neighborhood Playhouse Sch. Dramatics. Mem. Nat. Council on Arts, 1965—. Actor: (plays) including Sons and Soldiers, (films) including: Keys of the Kingdom, 1945, Valley of Decision, 1945, Spellbound, 1945, The Yearling, 1946, Duel in the Sun, 1947, The Macomber Affair, 1947, Gentlemen's Agreement, 1947, The Paradine Case, Yellow Sky, The Great Sinner, 1948, Twelve O'Clock High, 1949, The Gunfighter, 1950, Captain Horatio Hornblower, 1951, Only the Valiant, 1951, David and Bathsheba, 1951, Snows of Kilamanjaro, 1952, Roman Holiday, 1953, Night People, Man With a Million, Purple Plains, Moby Dick, 1954, Man in the Grey Flannel Suit, 1956, The Designing Woman, 1956, The Bravados, 1958, Pork Chop Hill, 1959, Beloved Infidel, 1959, On The Beach, 1959, Guns of Navarone, 1961, To Kill a Mockingbird (Acad. award as best actor 1962), Cape Fear, 1962, How the West Was Won, 1963, Captain Newman, M.D, 1963, Behold a Pale Horse, 1964, Mirage, 1965, Arabesque, 1966, Mackenna's Gold, 1967, The Chairman, 1968, The Stalking Moon, 1968, Marooned, 1969, I Walk the Line, 1970, Shootout, 1971, Billy Two-Hats, 1972, Amazing Grace and Chuck, 1987, Old Gringo, 1989, Cape Fear, 1991, Other People's Money, 1991; co-producer, star: (films) The Big Country, 1958; producer, star: (films) The Omen, 1976, MacArthur, 1977, The Boys from Brazil, 1978, The Sea Wolves, 1981, The Scarlet and Black, 1983, (TV miniseries) The Blue and the Gray, 1982, The Portrait, 1993, Sinatra: 80 Years My Way, 1995, A Salute to Martin Scorsese, 1997; voice: (TV miniseries) Baseball, 1994; rec.: (audio cassette) The New Testament, 1985-86. Nat. chmn. Am. Cancer Soc., 1966; founder, prodr. La Jolla Playhouse, 1947-52. Recipient Presdl. Medal of Freedom, Jean Hersholt Humanitarian award, 1968, Life Achievement award Am. Film Inst., 1989, Career award Cannes Film Festival, 1989, Kennedy Ctr. Honors, 1991, Lifetime Achievements award Lincoln Ctr., N.Y.C., 1992, Legion d'Honneur, France, 1993. Mem. Acad. Motion Picture Arts and Scis. (gov.; pres. 1967-70), Am. Film Inst. (founding chmn. bd. trustees 1967-69). Office: care Academy of Motion Picture Arts & Sciences 8949 Wilshire Blvd Beverly Hills CA 90211-1907*

PECK, ELLIE ENRIQUEZ, retired state administrator; b. Sacramento, Oct. 21, 1934; d. Rafael Enriquez and Eloisa Garcia Rivera; m. Raymond Charles Peck, Sept. 5, 1957; children: Reginaldo, Enrico, Francisca Guerrero, Teresa, Linda, Margaret, Raymond Charles, Christina. Student polit. sci. Sacramento State U., 1974. Tng. services coord. Calif. Div. Hwys., Sacramento, 1963-67; tech. and mgmt. cons., Sacramento, 1968-78; expert examiner Calif. Pers. Bd., 1976-78; tng. cons. Calif. Pers. Devel. Ctr., Sacramento, 1978; spl. cons. Calif. Commn. on Fair Employment and Housing, 1978; cmty. svcs. rep. U.S. Bur. of Census, No. Calif. counties, 1978-80; spl. cons. Calif. Dept. Consumer Affairs, Sacramento, 1980-83, project dir. Golden State Sr. Discount Program, 1980-83; dir. spl. programs for Calif. Lt. Gov., 1983-90, ret., 1990; pvt. cons., 1990—; cons., project dir. nat. sr. health issues summit Congress Calif. Srs. Edn. and Rsch. Fund, 1995; project dir. various post-White House Conf. on Aging seminars and roundtables, 1995—; coord. Calif. Sr. LEgis., 1995—; project dir. SSI/QMB Outreach Project, 1993-94. Author Calif. Dept. Consumer Affairs publ., 1981, U.S. Office Consumer Edn. publ., 1982. Bd. dirs Sacramento/Sierra Am. Diabetes Assn., 1989-90. Author: Diabetes and Ethnic Minorities: A Community at Risk. Trustee, Stanford Settlement, Inc., Sacramento, 1975-79; bd. dirs. Sacramento Emergency Housing Ctr., 1974-77, Sacramento Cmty. Svcs. Planning Coun., 1987-90, Calif. Advs. for Nursing Home Reform, 1990—, Calif. Human Devel. Corp., 1995—; campaign workshop dir. Chicano/Latino Youth Leadership Conf., 1982-95; v.p. Comision Femenil Nacional, Inc., 1987-90; del. Dem. Nat. Conv., 1976; mem. exec. bd. Calif. Dem. Cen. Com., 1977-89; chairperson ethnic minority task force Am. Diabetes Assn., 1988-90; steering com. Calif. Self-Esteem Minority Task Force, 1990-93; del. White House Conf. Aging, 1995. Recipient numerous awards including Outstanding Cmty. Svc. award Comuicaciones Unidos de Norte Atzlan, 1975, 77, Outstanding Svc. award, Chicano/Hispanic Dem. Caucus, 1979, Vol. Svc. award Calif. Human Devel. Corp., 1981, Dem. of Yr. award Sacramento County Dem. Com., 1987, Outstanding Advocate award Calif. Sr. Legis., 1988, 89, Calif. Assn. of Homes for Aging, Advocacy award, 1989, Resolution of Advocacy award, League Latin-Ams. Citizens, 1989, Meritorious Svc. to Hispanic Cmty. award Comite Patriotico, 1989, Meritorious Svc. Resolution award Lt. Gov. of Calif., 1989, Cert. Recognition award Sacramento County Human Rights Commn., 1991, Tish Sommers award Older Women's League/Joint Resolution Calif. Legislature, 1993, Latino Eagle award in govt. Tomas Lopez Meml. Found., 1994. Mem. Hispanic C. of C., Older Women's League, CongressCalif. Srs., Sacramento Gray Panthers, Latino Dem. Club Sacramento County (v.p. 1982-83). Home and Office: 2667 Coleman Way Sacramento CA 95818-4459

PECK, ERNEST JAMES, JR., academic administrator; b. Port Arthur, Tex., July 26, 1941; s. Ernest James and Karlton Maudean (Luttrell) P.; children from previous marriage: David Karl, John Walter; m. Frances R. Taylor; 1 stepchild, Michael R. Peck. BA in Biology with honors, Rice U., 1963, PhD in Biochemistry, 1966. Rsch. assoc. Purdue U., West Lafayette, Ind., 1966-68, asst. prof., 1968-73; asst. prof. Baylor Coll. Medicine, Houston, 1973-74, assoc. prof., 1974-80, prof., 1980-82; prof., chmn. biochemistry Sch. Med. Sci., U. Ark., Little Rock, 1982-89; dean sci. and math. U. Nev., Las Vegas, 1989-95; vice chancellor acad. affairs U. Nebr., Omaha, 1995—; adj. prof. U. Ark., Pine Bluff, 1986-88; program dir. NSF, Washington, 1988-89; mem. editl. bd. Jour. Neurosci. Rsch., N.Y.C., 1982-92. Co-author: Female Sex Steroids, 1979, Brain Peptides, 1979. Recipient Rsch. Career award NIH, Nat. Inst. of Child Health and Human Devel., 1975-80; NIH fellow, 1964-66. Fellow AAAS; mem. Am. Chem. Soc., Am. Soc. Biochemistry and Molecular Biology, Am. Soc. Neurochemistry, Endocrine Soc., Sigma Xi. Avocations: fishing, hunting. Office: U Nebr-Omaha Vice Chancellor Acad Affair 60th and Dodge Sts Omaha NE 68182-0001

PECK, FRED NEIL, economist, educator; b. Bklyn., Oct. 17, 1945; s. Abraham Lincoln and Beatrice (Pikholtz) P.; m. Jean Claire Ginsberg, Aug. 14, 1971; children: Ron Evan, Jordan Shefer, Ethan David. BA, SUNY, Binghamton, 1966; MA, SUNY, Albany, 1969; PhM, NYU, 1984; PhD, Pacific Western U., 1984; MS in Edn., Coll. New Rochelle, 1993. Lectr. SUNY, Albany, 1969-70; research asst. N.Y. State Legislature, Albany, 1970; sales and research staff Pan Am. Trade Devel. Corp., N.Y.C., 1971; v.p., economist The First Boston Corp., N.Y.C., 1971-88; mng. dir. Sharpe's Capital Mkt. Assocs. Inc., N.Y.C., 1988-89; pres., chief economist Hillcrest Econs. Group, N.Y.C., 1989-93; dir. edn. The Ednl. Advantage, Inc., New City, N.Y., 1990-95; adj. prof. Hofstra U., Hempstead, N.Y., 1975; lectr. NYU, 1982; mem. faculty New Sch. for Social Rsch., N.Y.C., 1974-94; coord. computer aided instrn. N.Y.C. Bd. of Edn., 1990—. Author, editor: (biennial publ.) Handbook of Securities of U.S. Government, 1972-86. Mem. ASCD, Am. Econ. Assn., Ea. Econ. Assn., Econometric Soc., Nat. Assn. Bus. Economists, Am. Statis. Assn., Doctorate Assn. of N.Y. Educators, Beta Gamma Sigma (hon. soc.), Phi Delta Kappa. Democrat. Jewish. Lodges: Knights Pythias, Knights Khorassan. Office: PS 169 at JHS 60 420 E 12th St New York NY 10009-4019 *March in one place long enough and eventually you will wind up leading the parade of progress...No one grows old. When you tire of learning, of experiencing new things your are old.*

PECK, GARNET EDWARD, pharmacist, educator; b. Windsor, Ont., Can., Feb. 4, 1930; s. William Crozier and Dorothy (Marentette) P.; m. Mary Ellen Hoffman, Aug. 24, 1957; children: Monique Elizabeth, Denise Anne, Philip Warren, John Edward. B.S. in Pharmacy with Distinction, Ohio No. U., 1957; M.S. in Indsl. Pharmacy, Purdue U., 1959, Ph.D., 1962. Sr. scientist Mead Johnson Research Center, 1962-65, group leader, 1965-67; assoc. prof. indsl. and phys. pharmacy Purdue U., West Lafayette, 1967-73; prof. Purdue U., 1973—, dir. indsl. pharmacy lab., 1975—, assoc. dept. head, 1989-96; cons. in field. Contbr. articles to profl. jours. Mem. West Lafayette Mayor's Advisory Com. on Community Devel., 1973—; mem. West Lafayette Citizen's Safety Com., 1974-81; mem. West Lafayette Park Bd., 1981—, pres., 1983-96. Served with U.S. Army, 1951-53. Recipient Lederle Faculty award Purdue U., 1976. Fellow APHA, AAAS, Am. Inst. Chem., Am. Assn. Pharmaceutical Scientists; mem. Am. Chem. Soc., Acad. of Rsch. and Sci. (Sidney Riegelman award 1994), Am. Assn. Colls. of Pharmacy, Cath. Acad. Sci. (founding mem.), KC, Rho Chi, Phi Lambda Upsilon, Phi Kappa Phi, Phi Sigma Lambda. Roman Catholic. Office: Purdue U Sch Pharmacy & Pharm Scis Dept Industrial & Physical Pharm West Lafayette IN 47907

PECK, JOAN KAY, systems engineer; b. Cedar Rapids, Iowa, Sept. 22, 1959; d. Leonard Allen and Mildred Jane (Keller) P. BS in Indsl. Engring., Iowa State U., 1983; MS in Space Tech., Fla. Inst. Tech., 1986. Student intern Rockwell-Collins, Cedar Rapids, 1979; coop. student Amana (Iowa) Refrigeration, 1981; sr. engr. Harris Govt. Aerospace Systems, Palm Bay, Fla., 1983-88; sr. systems engr. McDonnell Douglas Space Systems Co., Kennedy Space Ctr., Fla., 1988-94; clergy intern River City Met. Cmty. Ch., Sacramento, 1993—. Editor: Imago Dei. V.p. programming Inst. Indsl. Engrs., Ames, 1982-83; victim advocate Sexual Assault Victims Svcs., Fla. State Attys. Office, Brevard County, 1991-92. Recipient Outstanding Achievement award NASA, 1991.

PECK, MARYLY VANLEER, college president, chemical engineer; b. Washington, June 29, 1930; d. Blake Ragsdale and Ella Lillian (Wall) VanLeer; m. Jordan B. Peck, Jr., June 15, 1951; children: Jordan B. III, Blake VanLeer, James Tarleton VanLeer, Virginia Ellaine.; m. 2d, Walter G. Ebert, Sept. 3, 1983 (dec. June 1990); m. 3d Edwin L. Carey, Apr. 13, 1991. Student, Ga. Inst. Tech., 1948, 55-58, Duke U., 1947-48; B.Ch.E., Vanderbilt U., 1951; M.S.E., U. Fla., 1955, Ph.D., 1963. Chem. engr. Naval Research Lab., Washington, 1951-52; chem. engr. Med. Field Research Lab., Camp LeJeune, N.C., 1952; asso. research and instr. U. Fla., Gainesville, 1953-55; chem. engr., research asso. Ga. Tech. Expt. Sta., Atlanta, 1956-58; lectr. Ga. State Coll., Atlanta, 1957-58; lectr. math. East Carolina Extension, Camp Lejeune, 1959; sr. research engr. Rocketdyne div. N.Am. Aviation Co., 1961-63; self-employed as lectr., 1963; assoc. prof. Campbell Coll., Buie's Creek, N.C., 1963-66; prof. Campbell Coll., 1966; acad. dir. St. John's Episcopal Sch., Upper Tumon, Guam, 1966-68; chmn., prof. phys. scis. U. Guam, Agana, 1968-73; dean Coll. Bus. and Applied Tech. U. Guam, 1973-74, dean Community Career Coll., 1974-77; pres. Cochise Coll., Douglas, Ariz., 1977-78; systems planning analyst Urban Pathfinders, Inc., Balt., 1978-79; dean undergrad. studies U. Md. Univ. Coll., College Park, 1979-82; pres. Polk Community Coll., Winter Haven, Fla., 1982—. Founder, pres. Guam Acad. Found., 1972-77; bd. dirs. Cochise Coll. Found., 1977-78; charter bd. dirs. Turnaround Inc., 1987-91, chmn. 1990—; bd. dirs. United Way Cen. Fla., 1986—, bd. dirs. All Saints Acad., 1994—, vice chmn., 1992, chair-elect, 1993, chmn. 1994; founding mem. Prince George's Ednl. TV Cable Coalition; mem. Prince George's Cable TV Ednl. Adv. Group, 1980-82, Polk County Coun. Econ. Edn., 1982; sec. Polk Community Coll. Found., 1982—; mem. Polk County Coordinating Coun. Vocat. Edn., 1982-91, PRIDE Adv. Coun.; vice chmn. Fla. Job Tng. Coordinating Coun., 1983-87, Fla. Edn. Fund Bd., 1988-93. Named Disting. Alumnus U. Fla., 1992, Woman of Distinction Girls Scouts U.S.A., 1994; fellow NSF, 1961-63; recipient She Knows Where She's Going award Girls Inc. of Winter Haven, 1995. Fellow Soc. Women Engrs. (nat. v.p. 1962-63); mem. AAUW, Am. Inst. Chem. Engrs., Am. Chem. Soc., NSPE, Am. Assn. for Higher Edn., Am. Assn. Community and Jr. Colls., Am. Assn. Univ. Adminstrs., Rotary, Sigma Xi, Tau Beta Pi, Chi Omicron Gamma, Phi Kappa Phi, Delta Kappa Gamma. Episcopalian. Home: 1290 Howard Ter NW Winter Haven FL 33881-3158 Office: Polk Community Coll 999 Avenue H NE Winter Haven FL 33881-4256

PECK, MERTON JOSEPH, economist, educator; b. Cleve., Dec. 17, 1925; s. Kenneth Richard and Charlotte (Hart) P.; m. Mary McClure Bosworth, June 13, 1949; children—Richard, Katherine, Sarah, David. AB, Oberlin Coll., 1949; AM, Harvard U., 1951, PhD, 1954; AM (hon.), Yale U., 1963. Teaching fellow, instr. econs. Harvard U., Boston, 1951-55, asst., then assoc. prof. bus. adminstrn., 1956-61; asst. prof. econs. U. Mich., Ann Arbor, 1955-56; dir. systems analysis Office Sec. Def., Washington, 1961-63; prof. econs. Yale U., New Haven, Conn., 1963—; chmn. dept. Yale U., New Haven, 1967-74, 77-84, acting dean sch. of orgn. and mgmt., 1987-88; Mem. Council Econ. Advisers, Exec. Office of Pres., 1968-69; cons. in field, 1954—. Author: (with others) The Economics of Competition in the Transportation Industries, 1959, Competition in the Aluminum Industry, 1945-58, 1961, (with F. Scherer) The Weapons Aquisition Process, An Economic Analysis, 1962, (with others) Technological Change, Economic Growth and Public Policy, 1967, Federal Regulation of Television, 1973; editor The World Aluminum Industry in a Changing Energy Era, 1988; co-editor: What Is To Be Done? Proposals for the Soviet Transition to the Market, 1991, Competitiveness, The Impact of Public Policy, 1992; contbr. (with others) articles to profl. jours. With AUS, 1944-46. Mem. Am. Econ. Assn., Am. Assn. U. Profs., Lawn Club, Yale Club. Home: 27 Temple Ct New Haven CT 06511-6820

PECK, MIRA PASZKO, lawyer; b. Minsk, USSR, Mar. 31, 1946; d. Wolf and Zofia (Wlaznik) Paszko; m. David O. Peck, May 15, 1971. BSChemE, Melbourne U. Tech., Australia, 1972; MS in Indsl. Adminstrn., Union Coll., 1976; JD, Rutgers U., 1984. Bar: N.J. 1984, U.S. Dist. Ct. N.J. 1984. Tchr. sci. Victoria Edn. Dept., 1971-72; process engr. GAF Corp., Rensselaer, N.Y., 1974-77; design engr. BASF Corp., Parsippany, N.J., 1977-80, product mgr., 1980-86, mgr. corp. strategic planning, 1986-92; pvt. practice Denville, N.J., 1984—. Mem. counsel Protect Wildlife Water and Woods, Denville, 1987—; mem. Mus. Modern Art, N.Y.C. Mem. ABA, N.J. Bar Assn., Am Inst. Chem. Engrs., Am. Humanist Assn., Amnesty Internat., Planning Forum, NOW. Democrat. Avocations: art, reading, music, hiking, bicycling. Office: BASF Corp 3000 Continental Dr N Budd Lake NJ 07828-1202

PECK, RALPH BRAZELTON, civil engineering educator, consultant; b. Winnipeg, Man., Can., June 23, 1912; (parents Am. citizens); s. Orwin K. and Ethel Indie (Huyck) P.; m. Marjorie Elizabeth Truby, June 14, 1937; children: Nancy Jeanne Peck Young, James Leroy. D in Civil Engring., Rensselaer Poly. Inst., 1937; postgrad., Harvard U., 1938; D Eng. (hon.), Rensselaer Poly. Inst., 1974; DSc (hon.), Laval U., 1987. Registered profl. engr., Ill., civil engr., Calif. Structural detailer Am. Bridge Co., Ambridge, Pa., 1937; asst. subway engr. City of Chgo., 1939-43; chief engr. testing Holabird & Root, Scioto Ordnance Plant, Marion, Ohio, 1943; research asst. prof. soil mechanics U. Ill., Champaign-Urbana, 1943-48, research prof. found. engring., 1948-57, prof. found. engring., 1957-74, prof. emeritus, 1974—; cons. founds., tunnels, earth dams, landslides, throughout U.S. and various fgn. countries, 1943—. Author: (with K. Terzaghi and G. Mesri) Soil Mechanics in Engineering Practice, 1948, 3d edit., 1996, (with T.H. Thornburn and W.E. Hanson) Foundation Engineering, 1953, 2d edit., 1973, Judgment in Geotechnical Engineering: The Professional Legacy of Ralph B. Peck, 1984; author more than 200 tech. papers. Recipient Disting. Civilian Svc. award Dept. of Army, 1973, Moles Non-mem. award, 1973, Nat. Medal Sci. Pres. Gerald Ford, 1974, Golden Beaver award, 1983, Disting. Svc. award Deep Founds Inst., 1984, award of merit Am. Cons. Engrs. Coun., 1988. Fellow Geol. Soc. Am. (sr.); mem. NAE, ASCE (hon.; nat. dir. 1962-65; Norman medal 1944, Wellington prize 1965, Terzaghi award 1969, Washington award 1976, Pres.'s award 1986, John Fritz medal 1987, Rickey medal 1988), Am. Acad. Arts and Scis., Internat. Soc. Soil Mechanics and Found. Engring. (pres. 1969-73), Southeast Asian, Japanese, Mexican Socs. Soil Mechanics (hon.), NSPE (award 1972), Sigma Xi, Chi Epsilon, Tau Beta Pi, Phi Kappa Phi. Home: 1101 Warm Sands Dr SE Albuquerque NM 87123-4328

PECK, RICHARD EARL, academic administrator, playwright, novelist; b. Milw., Aug. 3, 1936; s. Earl Mason and Mary Amanda (Fry) P.; m. Donna Joy Krippner, Aug. 13, 1960; children: Mason, Laura. AB magna cum laude, Carroll Coll., Waukesha, Wis., 1961; MS, U. Wis., 1962, PhD, 1964. Asst. prof. U. Va., Charlottesville, 1964-67; assoc. dean, prof. Temple U., Phila., 1967-84; dean arts and scis. U. Ala., 1984-88; provost, v.p. academic affairs Ariz. State U., Tempe, 1988-89, interim pres., 1989-90; pres. U. N.Mex., Albuquerque, 1990—. Editor: Poems/Nathaniel Hawthorne, 1967, Poems/Floyd Stovall, 1967; author: (books) Final Solution, 1973 (nominated for John W. Campbell award as Best Sci. Fiction Novel of 1973 by Sci. Fiction Rsch. Assn.), Something for Joey, 1978, Passing Through, 1982, (plays) Sarah Bernhardt and the Bank, 1972, Don't Trip over the Money Pail, 1976, The Cubs Are in fourth Place and Fading, 1977, Phonecall, 1978, Bathnight, 1978, Prodigal Father, 1978, Lovers, Wives and Tennis Players, 1979, Curtains, 1980, A Party for Wally Pruett, 1982, Allergy Tests, 1982, Your Place or Mine, 1987, (films) Starting over Again, 1982, What Tangled Webs, 1974, Tutte le Strade Portanno a Roma, 1974, Il Diritto, 1974; contr. numerous scholarly articles to lit. jours., book revs., travel articles and humor columns to newspapers and mags., papers to univ. orgns. and witers' confs. Bd. dirs. East Valley Partnership (Econ. Devel. Orgn.), Sci. and Tech., Samaritan Health Svcs.; gubernatorial appointee, bd. dirs. Ala. Humanities Found.; mem. Nat. Found. for Post-Secondary Edn.; bd. dirs. Phila. Alliance for Teaching Humanities in the Schs., Dela. Valley Faculty Exch.; adv. bd. Ea. Pa. Theater Coun.; chmn. Temple U. Bicentennial Festival of Am. Arts, 1976; mem. Univ. Negotiating Team in re: Temple-AAUP faculty contract. Capt. USMC, 1954-59. Recipient Whitman Pub. scholarship, 1959-63, Woodrow Wilson fellowship, 1961-62, Knapp Found. fellowship, 1962-63, C. Brooks Fry award Theater Americana, Altadena, Calif., 1979. Mem. MLA, Northeast MLA. Conf. Univs. and Colls. Arts, Letters and Scis., Coun. Colls. Arts and Scis., Nat. Assn. State Univs. and Land-Grant Colls. Home: 1901 Roma Ave NE Albuquerque NM 87106-3824 Office: U NMex Office of Pres Scholes Hall Rm 160 Albuquerque NM 87131*

PECK, RICHARD WAYNE, novelist; b. Decatur, Ill., Apr. 5, 1934; s. Wayne Morris and Virginia (Gray) P. Student, Exeter (Eng.) U., 1954-55;

B.A., DePauw U., 1956; M.A., So. Ill. U., 1959. Mem. faculty Sch. Edn., Hunter Coll., 1965-71; lectr. in field; adj. prof. libr. sci. La. State U., 1996—. Author: books for adolescents, including Are You in the House Alone?, 1977 (Edgar Allen Poe award 1977), Father Figure, 1978, Secrets of the Shopping Mall, 1979; (poetry anthology) Sounds and Silences, 1970; (novels for adults) New York Time; Contbr. articles on architecture and local history to N.Y. Times. Asst. dir. Council Basic Edn., Washington, 1969-70. Served with U.S. Army, 1956-58. English-Speaking Union fellow Jesus Coll., Oxford (Eng.) U., 1973; winner Nat. Prize for Young People's Lit. ALA, 1990. Mem. Authors Guild, Authors League, Delta Chi. Republican. Methodist. Home: 155 E 72nd St New York NY 10021-4371

PECK, ROBERT A., newspaper publisher; b. Riverton, Wyo., Oct. 7, 1924; s. LeRoy E. and Elvira Eugenia (Sostrom) P.; m. Cordelia S. Peck, Oct. 5, 1949; children: Christopher, George, Steven. BA, U. Wyo., 1949. Pub. The Riverton Ranger, 1949—; mem. Wyoming State Senate, 1991—. Pres. Central Wyo. Coll. Bd., Riverton, 1966-81; sec. CWC Found., Riverton, 1968—. Staff sgt. U.S. Army, 1943-45, ETO. Mem. Soc. Profl. Journalists, Masons, Phi Beta Kappa. Republican. United Methodist. Office: The Riverton Ranger 421 E Main PO Box 993 Riverton WY 82501-0993

PECK, ROBERT DAVID, educational foundation administrator; b. Devil's Lake, N.D., June 1, 1929; s. Lester David and Bernice Marie (Peterson) P.; m. Lylia June Smith, Sept. 6, 1953; children: David Allan, Kathleen Marie. BA, Whitworth Coll., 1951; MDiv, Berkeley (Calif.) Bapt. Div. Sch., 1958; ThD, Pacific Sch. Religion, 1964; postgrad., U. Calif., Berkeley, 1959-60, 62-63, Wadham Coll., Oxford U., Eng., 1963. Music tchr. pub. schs. Bridgeport, Wash., 1954-55; prof., registrar Linfield Coll., McMinnville, Oreg., 1963-69; asst. dir. Ednl. Coordinating Coun., Salem, Oreg., 1969-75; assoc. prof. Pacific Luth. U., Tacoma, 1976-79, U. Puget Sound, Tacoma, 1977; v.p. John Minter Assocs., Boulder, Colo., 1979-81, Coun. Ind. Colls., Washington, 1981-84; adminstrv. v.p. Alaska Pacific U., Anchorage, 1984-88; pres. Phillips U., Enid, Okla., 1988-94, chancellor, 1994-95; chmn. The Pres. Found. for Support of Higher Edn., Washington, 1995—; pres. Phillips U. Ednl. Enterprises Inc., 1994-95; cons. Higher Edn. Exec. Assocs., Denver, 1984—; owner Tyee Marina, Tacoma, 1975-77; yacht broker Seattle, 1977-79. Author: Future Focusing: An Alternative to Strategic Planning, 1983, also articles. Dem. county chmn., McMinnville, 1968, Dem. candidate for state Ho. of Reps., McMinnville, 1969; pres. McMinnville Kiwanis, 1965-69. Cpl. Signal Corps, U.S. Army, 1952-54. Carnegie Corp. grantee, 1982, 84. Mem. Okla. Ind. Coll. Assn. (sec. 1989—). Mem. Christian Ch. Avocation: sailing, sculpting.

PECK, ROBERT MCCRACKEN, naturalist, science historian, writer; b. Phila., Dec. 15, 1952; s. Frederick William Gunster and Matilda (McCracken) P. BA in Art History, Princeton U., 1974; MA, U. Del., 1976. Dir. Pocono Lake (Pa.) Preserve Nature Ctr., 1971, 72; asst. to dir. Natural History Mus. Acad. Natural Scis., Phila., 1976-77; tech. dir. Bartram Heritage Study U.S. Dept. Interior and Bartram Trail Conf., Atlanta and Montgomery, Ala., 1977-78; spl. asst. to pres. Acad. Natural Scis., Phila., 1977-82, acting v.p. Nat. History Mus., 1982-83, fellow, 1983—; cons. BBC, Eng., 1987-92; bd. dirs. Phila. Conservationists, Natural Lands Trust, Phila., Libr. Co. of Phila., Phila. City Inst.; mng. editor Frontiers, 1979-82; lectr. in field. Author: A Celebration of Birds: The Life and Art of Louis Agassiz Fuertes, 1982, Headhunters and Hummingbirds: An Expedition Into Ecuador, 1987, Wild Birds of America: The Art of Basil Ede, 1991, Land of the Eagle: A Natural History of North America, 1991, German edit., 1992; author: (with others) William Bartram's Travels, 1980, John Cassin's Illustrations of the Birds of California, Texas, Oregon, British and Russian America, 1991; author: (foward) The Birds of America by John James Audubon, 1985; editor: Bartram Heritage Report, 1978; author (with others), editor: Philadelphia Wildfowl Exposition Catalog, 1979; contbr. chpts. to books, articles to mags. and newspapers including The New York Times. Trustee Chestnut Hill Acad., Phila.; bd. dirs. RARE Ctr. Tropical Bird Conservation, Mus. Coun. of Phila. Recipient Richard Hopper Day Meml. award Acad. Natural Scis. of Phila., 1991; Eleanor Garvey fellow in printing and graphic arts Houghton Libr., Harvard U., 1995. Fellow Royal Geographic Soc., Explorers Club (various coms. 1983—, Explorers award 1988); mem. Soc. History of Natural History, Sigma Xi. Achievements include discovery of a new species of frog, Eleutherodactylus pecki; rsch. on orthoptera indigenous to the Caribbean, status of invasive African Desert Locust in the West Indies, the Orinoco River and its tributaries, botanical, entomological, ichthyological, herpetological and malacological specimens for the Smithsonian Instn. and the Acad. of Natural Scis.; participation in expeditions which discovered several new species of fish in Guyana Shield, Venezuela, discovered several new species of amphibians and insects as well as two new races of birds in Ecuador, investigated the ecological, economic and political impact of instream-flow legislation on the Yellowstone River Basin, current projects include biological and cultural research in Mongolia. Office: Academy of Natural Sciences 1900 Benjamin Franklin Pky Philadelphia PA 19103-1101

PECK, ROBERT STEPHEN, lawyer, educator; b. Bklyn., Dec. 11, 1953; s. Irwin and Edith Rose (Welt) P.; m. Terre Garcia; 1 child, Zachary Madison. BA in Polit. Sci., George Washington U., 1975; JD, Cleve.-Marshall Law Sch., 1978; postgrad., NYU, 1978; LLM, Yale U., 1990. Bar: N.Y. 1979, U.S. Dist. Ct. (so. and ea. dists.) N.Y. 1979, D.C. 1989. Congl. aide U.S. Ho. of Reps., Washington, 1972-74; div. dir. Automated Correspondence, Washington, 1974-75; law clk. to presiding justice Cleve. Mcpl. Ct., 1976; editor Matthew Bender & Co., N.Y.C., 1977-78; legal dir. Pub. Edn. Assn., N.Y.C., 1978-82; staff dir. ABA, Chgo., 1982-87, Washington, 1987-89; jud. fellow U.S. Supreme Ct., 1990-91; legis. counsel ACLU, 1991-95; adj. prof. American U., Washington, 1991—; dir. legal affairs Assn. Trial Lawyers Am., 1995—; legal advisor Freedom to Read Found., Chgo., 1986—, exec. com. bd. trustees, 1987-90, 93—, pres., 1988-90, v.p., trustee, 1993—; bd. dirs. Nat. Constl. Ctr., 1990-93; lectr. on constl. law, legal ethics. Author: We the People, 1987, The Bill of Rights and the Politics of Interpretation, 1991; co-author: Speaking and Writing Truth, 1985; editor: Understanding the Law, 1983, Blessings of Liberty, 1986, To Govern A Changing Society, 1990; contbr. numerous articles on constl. law to law revs. Mem. N.Y. State Edn. Adv. Bd., Albany, N.Y., 1979-81; bd. dirs. Nat. Com. on Pub. Edn. and Religious Liberty, 1995—, Ams. for Religious Liberty, 1995—; nat. chair Lawyers for Librs., 1996—; chair legal adv. com. Nat. Ctr. for Sci. Edn., 1996—; mem. first amendment adv. coun. Media Inst., 1996—. NEH grantee 1983, 85. Mem. ABA (chmn. pub. election law com. 1983-85, 87-90). Democrat. Jewish. Avocations: tennis, music, travel. Office: Assn Trial Lawyers Am 1050 31st St NW Washington DC 20007-4409

PECK, THOMAS, newspaper publishing executive. BS in Acctg., U. Conn.; MS Wharton Sch. Bus., U. Pa. CPA. Audit mgr. and computer audit specialist Ernst & Young, 1969-75; v.p. fin. and adminstrn. Orba Corp., 1975-83; controller and chief acctg. officer Esprit Systems, 1983-85; v.p. PRD Property Devel., 1985-89; asst. v.p. Mac Andrews & Forbes, 1989-90; CFO Daily News, L.P., 1990—. Office: NY Daily News Office of the CFO 450 W 33rd St Fl 3 New York NY 10001-2603*

PECK, WILLIAM ARNO, physician, educator, university official and dean; b. New Britain, Conn., Sept. 28, 1933; s. Bernard Carl and Molla (Nair) P.; m. Patricia Hearn, July 10, 1982; children by previous marriage: Catherine, Edward Pershall, David Nathaniel; stepchildren: Andrea, Elizabeth, Katherine. A.B., Harvard U., 1955; M.D., U. Rochester, N.Y., 1960. Intern, then resident in internal medicine Barnes Hosp., St. Louis, 1960-62; fellow in metabolism Washington U. Sch. Medicine, St. Louis, 1963; mem. faculty U. Rochester Med. Sch., 1965-76, prof. medicine and biochemistry, 1973-76, head div. endocrinology and metabolism, 1969-76; John E. and Adaline Simon prof. medicine, co-chmn. dept. medicine Washington U. Sch. Medicine, St. Louis, 1976-89; physician in chief Jewish Hosp., St. Louis, 1976-89; prof. medicine and exec. vice chancellor med. affairs, dean sch. medicine, pres. univ. med. ctr. Washington U., St. Louis, 1989—; chmn. endocrinology and metabolism adv. com. FDA, 1976-78; chmn. gen. medicine study sect. NIH, 1979-81; chmn. Gordon Conf. Chemistry, PHysiology and Structure of Bones and Teeth, 1977; chmn. Consensus Devel. Conf. on Osteoporosis, NIH, 1984; co-chmn. Workshop on Future Directions in Osteoporosis, 1987; chmn. Spl. Topic Conf. on Osteoporosis, U.S. FDA, 1987; dir. Angelica Corp., Boatman's Trust Co., Allied Healthcare Products, Hologic, Reinsurance Group of Am. Editor Bone and Mineral Rsch. Anns., 1982-88; mem. editorial adv. bd. Osteoporosis Internat., other jours.; contbr. to med. jours. Pres. Nat. Osteoporosis Found., 1985-90. Served as med. officer USPHS, 1963-65. Recipient Lederle Med. Faculty award, 1967, career program award NIH, 1970-75, commr.'s spl. citation FDA, 1988, Humanitarian award Arthritis Found. Ea. Mo., 1995, Founders award Nat. Osteoporosis Found., 1996. Home: 2 Apple Tree Ln Saint Louis MO 63124-1601 Office: Washington U Sch Medicine 600 S Euclid Ave Saint Louis MO 63110-1010

PECK, WILLIAM HENRY, museum curator, art historian, archaeologist, author, lecturer; b. Savannah, Ga., Oct. 2, 1932; s. William Henry Peck and Mildred (Bass) Peck Tuten; m. Ann Amelia Keller, Feb. 2, 1957 (dec. 1965); children: Alice Ann, Sarah Louise; m. Elsie Holmes, July 8, 1967; 1 child, William Henry IV. Student Ohio State U., 1950-53; BFA, Wayne State U., 1960, MA, 1961. Jr. curator Detroit Inst. Arts, 1960-62, asst. curator, 1962-64, assoc. curator, 1964-68, curator ancient art, 1968—, acting chief curator, 1984-88, sr. curator, 1988—; lectr. art history Cranbrook Acad. Art, Bloomfield Hills, Mich., 1963-65; vis. lectr. U. Mich., Ann Arbor, 1970; adj. prof. art history Wayne State U., Detroit, 1966—; excavations in Egypt, Mendes, 1964-66, Precinct of Mut, Karnak, 1978—. Author: Drawings from Ancient Egypt, 1978, The Detroit Institute of Arts: A Brief History, 1991; co-author: Ancient Egypt: Discovering its Splendors, 1978; Mummies, Diseases and Ancient Cultures, 1980; also articles. With U.S. Army, 1953-55. Ford Motor Co. travel grantee, 1962; Am. Research Ctr. Egypt fellow, 1971; Smithsonian Instn. travel grantee, 1975; recipient Award in the Arts Wayne State U., 1985. Mem. Archaeol. Inst. Am., Am. Research Ctr. Egypt, Internat. Assn. Egyptologists, Soc. Study Egyptian Antiquities, Am. Assn. Mus., Oriental Inst.-U. Chgo. Democrat. Episcopalian. Avocations: origami, performance of early music, collecting T.E. Lawrence material. Office: Inst Arts 5200 Woodward Ave Detroit MI 48202-4008

PECKER, DAVID J., magazine publishing company executive; b. N.Y.C., Sept. 24, 1951; m. Karen Balan, Oct. 31, 1987. BBA, Pace U., postgrad. CPA, N.Y. Sr. auditor Price Waterhouse & Co.; mgr. fin. reporting Diamandis Communications, Inc., N.Y.C., 1979; dir. fin. reporting Diamandis Communications, Inc., dir. acctg., asst. contr., 1983; COO, CFO, exec. v.p. pub. Hachette Mags., Inc., N.Y.C., 1990-91, pres., COO, 1991-92, pres. and CEO, 1992—; mem. Fashion Group's Internat. Adv. Bd., The N.Y. City Partnership Com.; mem. bd. dirs. The Madison Square Boys & Girls Club. Bd. dirs. Pace U., N.Y.C., Drug Enforcement Agents Found., 1995—. Mem. Am. Mgmt. Assn. Office: Hachette Mags Inc 1633 Broadway Fl 45 New York NY 10019-6708

PECKHAM, DONALD EUGENE, retired utilities company executive; b. Willis, Kans., Nov. 28, 1922; s. Rolland Claude and Winona Maude (Lewis) P.; m. Evelynn Darlene Dodson, Dec. 20, 1949 (dec.). B.A. cum laude in Acctg, Eastern N.Mex. U., 1953; M.B.A., U. Ariz., 1954. Acct. Ill. Power Co., Decatur, Ill., 1954-57; with Public Service Co. of N.Mex., Albuquerque, from 1957, sec., 1968-70; sec., asst. treas. Public Service Co. of N.Mex., 1970-74, sec., treas., 1974-79, sec., asst. treas., from 1979; sec. Paragon Resources, Inc., 1972-75, sec., asst. treas., from 1975; sec. Sunbelt Mining Co., Inc., 1980-81, sec., asst. treas., from 1981; sec. Meadows Resources, Inc., from 1981; now ret. Served with USMC, 1943-46. Republican. Lodge: Elks.

PECKHAM, JOHN MUNROE, III, investment executive, author, lecturer; b. Abington, Mass., July 25, 1933; s. John Munroe and Mildred (Davis) P.; m. Ann M. Murphy, Apr. 30, 1995; children: Lisa, Holly, John M. IV. AB, Tufts U., 1955; postgrad., Columbia U., 1955-56. Pres. Peckham Boston Adv. Co., 1964—; pres., chmn. Boston Hall Corp., Boston, 1987—; pres. Boston Hall Pub. Co., 1988—. Founder Realtors Concerned for Realtors, Chgo., 1986—; mem. bd. advisors Kids Stop, Boston, 1988-89; bd. dirs. Am. Fedn. for Children and Youth, L.A., 1988-89. Lt. comdr. USN, 1956-62. Mem. Nat. Assn. Realtors (v.p.), Realtors Nat. Mktg. Inst. (v.p. 1988), Internat. Fedn. Realtors, Inst. Real Estate Mgmt., Ten Club (pres. Boston chpt. 1974-79), Friends of Bill W. Republican. Baptist. Avocations: bicycling, swimming, cribbage, speaking, reading. Office: Peckham Boston Advisory Co. 4 Longfellow Pl Ste 2003 Boston MA 02114-2817

PECKOL, JAMES KENNETH, consulting engineer; b. Cleve., Oct. 24, 1944; s. William John and Elinor Elizabeth (Bustard) P.; children: Erin, Robyn. BS Engring., Case Inst. Tech., 1966; MSEE, U. Wash., 1975, PhDEE, 1985. Cons. GE, Raytheon, Ling Temco Vought, RCA, Boeing Co., 1966-72; sr. staff engr. indsl. products bus. unit John Fluke Mfg. Co., Seattle, 1972-83, sr. staff engr. automated systems bus. unit, 1983-86, sr. staff engr. MR&D Bus. unit, 1986-93; founder Oxford Cons., Edmonds, Wash., 1987—; affiliate asst. prof. dept. elec. engring., affiliate asst. prof. dept. computers and software sys. U. Wash., Seattle, 1984-87, 95—, prof. dept. elec. engring., 1997—; sr. lectr., assoc. prof. dept. elec. engring. U. Aberdeen, Scotland, 1987; lectr. dept. math. and sci. Shoreline C.C., Seattle, 1989—; lectr. dept. computer sci. Edmonds (Wash.) C.C., 1992—; assoc. prof. dept. engring./computer sci. U. Nantes, Frances, 1993, 96; mem. computer sci. and elec. engring. curriculum adv. bd. Wash. State U., 1990—; lectr. various confs. and univs. Contbr. articles to profl. jours.; patentee in field. Mem. IEEE, Am. Assn. Artificial Intelligence, Assn. Computing Machinery, Tau Beta Pi. Home and Office: Oxford Cons Ltd 859 14th St SW Edmonds WA 98020-6611

PECKOLICK, ALAN, graphic designer; b. N.Y.C., Oct. 3, 1940; s. Charles and Belle (Binenbaum) P.; m. Jessica Margot Weber, June 3, 1984. AAS, Pratt Inst., Bklyn., 1968. Art dir. McCann-Erickson, 1964-68; graphic designer Herb Lubalin, 1968-72; v.p., creative dir. Lubalin, Smith, Carnase, Inc., N.Y.C., 1972-74, LCS & P Design Group, Inc., N.Y.C., 1974-76; pres. Lubalin Peckolick Assoc., N.Y.C., 1976-81, Pushpin, Lubalin, Peckolick, N.Y.C., 1981-86, Peckolick and Ptnrs., N.Y.C., 1986-89; design dir. Addison Design Cons., N.Y.C., 1989-91; chmn. Peckolick Inc., N.Y.C., 1991—; bd. advisors Designworld mag., Victoria, Australia, 1983—, Herb Lubalin Study Ctr., N.Y.C.; lectr. Pratt Inst., Parsons Sch. Design, Sch. Visual Arts, also various orgns. Co-author, designer: Herb Lubalin Graphic Designer, 1986; exhibited at Sony Gallery, Tokyo, 1989. Bd. dirs. Glaucoma Found., 1993, Whale Conservation Inst., 1994. Recipient awards AIGA, Art Directors Club awards. Mem. N.Y. Art Dirs. Club (6 gold medals, over 50 awards), N.Y. Type Dirs. Club (bd. dirs.), Alliance Graphique Internationale, Art Dirs.Club Bergen (Norway) (hon.). Avocations: automobile racing, sculpting, collecting art and prints, cooking, travel. Home: 30 E 10th St New York NY 10003-6202 Office: Peckolick Inc 30 E 21st St New York NY 10010

PECORA, ROBERT, chemistry educator; b. Bklyn., Aug. 6, 1938; s. Alfonso Edward and Helen (Buscavage) P. A.B., Columbia U., 1959, A.M., 1960, Ph.D., 1962. Asst. prof. chemistry Stanford U., 1964-71, assoc. prof., 1971-78, prof., 1978—; chmn. chemistry, 1992—; vis. prof. U. Manchester, (Eng.), 1970-71, U. Nice, (France), 1978; cons. chemistry to maj. corps. Coauthor: Dynamic Light Scattering, 1976; contbr. articles to profl. jours. Recipient Sr. Scientist award Alexander von Humboldt Found., 1985; NSF fellow, 1960-62, Am. Acad. Scis. postdoctoral fellow U. libre de Bruxelles, Belgium, 1963. Fellow AAAS, Am. Phys. Soc.; mem. Am. Chem. Soc. Home: 707 Continental Cir Mountain View CA 94040-3366 Office: Stanford U Dept Chemistry Stanford CA 94305

PECORINO, LAUREN TERESA, biologist; b. Bronx, N.Y., June 17, 1962; d. Joseph Salvatore and Raffaela (Rapillo) P. BS in Biology, SUNY, Stony Brook, 1984, PhD, 1990. Postdoctoral fellow Ludwig Inst. for Cancer Rsch., London, 1991-96; lectr. U. Greenwich, 1996—. Contbr. articles to profl. jours. Postdoctoral fellow European Molecular Biology Orgn., 1991-93, NATO, 1993-95. Mem. AAAS, N.Y. Acad. Scis., Brit. Sub-Aqua Club, Sigma Xi. Home: 1422 San Meteo Ave Lady Lake FL 32159 Office: U Greenwich, Woolwich Campus, Wellington St, Woolwich London SE18 6PF, England

PECSOK, ROBERT LOUIS, chemist, educator; b. Cleve., Dec. 18, 1918; s. Michael C. and Katherine (Richter) P.; m. Mary Bodell, Oct. 12, 1940 (dec. Apr. 1996); children: Helen Pecsok Wong, Katherine, Jean Pecsok Nagle, Michael, Ruth Pecsok Hughes, Alice Pecsok Tominaga, Sara Pecsok Lima; m. Marcella Beeman, Apr. 23, 1997. S.B. summa cum laude, Harvard, 1940, Ph.D., 1948. Prodn. foreman Procter & Gamble Co., Balt., 1940-43; instr. chemistry Harvard, 1948; asst. prof. chemistry U. Calif. at Los Angeles, 1948-55, asso. prof., 1955-61, prof., 1961-71, vice chmn. dept., 1965-70; prof., chmn. dept. U. Hawaii, Honolulu, 1971-80; dean natural scis. U. Hawaii, 1981-89; sci. adviser FDA, 1966-69. Author: Principles and Practice of Gas Chromatography, 1959, Analytical Methods of Organic and Biochemistry, 1966, Modern Methods of Chemical Analysis, 1968, 2d edit., 1976, Modern Chemical Technology, 1970, rev. edit. 1989, Physicochemical Applications of Gas Chromatography, 1978. Served as lt. USNR, 1943-46. Recipient Tolman medal, 1971; Guggenheim fellow, 1956-57; Petroleum Research Fund Internat. fellow, 1963-64. Mem. Am. Chem. Soc., Am. Inst. Chemists, Phi Beta Kappa, Alpha Chi Sigma, Phi Lambda Upsilon. Home: 13855 Riverhead Ct San Diego CA 92129-3222

PEDDICORD, ROLAND DALE, lawyer; b. Van Meter, Iowa, Mar. 29, 1936; s. Clifford Elwood and Juanitas Irene (Brittain) P.; m. Teri Linn O'Dell; children: Erin Sue, Robert Sean. BSBA with honors, Drake U., 1961, JD with honors, 1962. Bar: Iowa 1962; cert. civil trial specialist Nat. Bd. Trial Advs. Asst. atty. gen. State of Iowa, 1962-63; assoc. Steward, Crouch & Hopkins, Des Moines, 1962-65; ptnr. Peddicord, Wharton, Thune & Spencer, Des Moines, 1968—; lectr. in law Drake U., 1962-68; lectr. law Coll. Osteo. Medicine, Des Moines, 1965-72. Editor and chief Drake Law Rev., 1961-62. Past mem. nat. bd. dirs., nat. coun. YMCA of U.S.A., past vice chmn. nat. bd.; bd. dirs., past chmn. Greater Des Moines YMCA, 1968-89. With USMC, 1954-57. Mem. ABA, ATLA, Iowa Bar Assn., Polk County Bar Assn., Iowa Trial Lawyers Assn., Iowa Acad. Trial Lawyers, Am. Bd. Trial Advs. (past pres. Iowa chpt.). Republican. Methodist. Office: 405 6th Ave Ste 700 Des Moines IA 50309-2415 Office: Peddicord Wharton Thune Spencer PO Box 9130 Des Moines IA 50306-9130

PEDEN, KATHERINE GRAHAM, industrial consultant; b. Hopkinsville, Ky., Jan. 2, 1926; d. William E. and Mary (Gorin) P. Student pub. schs. Vice pres. radio sta. WHOP-CBS, Hopkinsville, 1944-68; owner sta. WNVL, Nicholsville, Ky., 1961-71; commr. commerce Ky., 1963-67; mem. Gov. Ky. Cabinet, Frankfort, 1963-67; pres., cons. Katherine G. Peden & Assos. Inc., Louisville; indsl. and community developers Katherine G. Peden & Assos. Inc.; bd. dirs. Westvaco Corp.; mem. adv. bd. Norfolk So. Corp. Chmn. Louisville and Jefferson County Riverport Authority, 1975-80; civilian aide to Sec. of Army, 1978-82; mem. com. Pres.'s Commn. on Status of Women, 1961-62; mem. Pres.'s Commn. on Civil Disorders, 1967; pres. Ky. Derby Festival, 1979-80; Dem. nominee U.S. Senate, 1968; mem. adv. coun. U. Ky. Coll. Bus.; trustee Spalding U., 1980-86. Named Woman of Year Hopkinsville, 1952. Mem. Fedn. Bus., Profl. Women's Clubs (pres. state 1955-56, 1st nat. v.p. 1960-61, nat. pres. 1961-62). Mem. Christian Ch. (deaconess 1956-59, 60-63). Home: 3818 Washington Sq Louisville KY 40207-1954 Office: PO Box 6268 Louisville KY 40206-0268

PEDERSEN, DARLENE DELCOURT, health science publishing consultant; b. Westbrook, Maine; 1 child, Jorgen David. BSN, U. Conn., 1967; postgrad., U. B.C., 1974-75; MSN, U. Pa., 1997. RN, Pa. Various nursing positions, psychiat.-comty health, 1967-79; assoc. editor JB Lippincott Co., Phila., 1979-84; acquisition editor WB Saunders Co., Phila., 1984-88, v.p., editor in chief, 1988-91, sr. v.p., editorial dir. books divsn., liaison to London office, 1991-95; domestic and internat. cons. in pvt. practice Phila., 1995—. Author: (with others) Canadian Nurse, 1976; contbr. Basic Nursing Skills, 1977; oil painter. Mem. ANA, Am. Psychiat. Nurses Assn., Am. Med. Pubs. Assn., Assn. Am. Pubs., Internat. Soc. Psychiat. Consultation Liaison Nurses, Forum Exec. Women, The Manuscript Soc., Assn. Profl. Comm. Cons., Internat. Platform Assn., Psychiatric Advanced Practice Nurses Pa., Soc. for Edn. and Rsch. in Psychiat. Mental Health Nursing, Emily's List, Am. Orthopsychiat. Assn., U.S. Dressage Fedn., Inc., Internat. Soc. Traumatic Stress Studies. Avocations: autograph and art collection, travel, francophile, French music, reading. Office: 516 Gordon Ave Ste 200 Narberth PA 19072-1531

PEDERSEN, GEORGE J., engineering company executive, computer support company executive; b. 1935. Student, Rutgers U., 1952-53. Contracts mgr. VitroLabs, West Orange, N.J., 1953-68; with Mantech Internat. Corp., Fairfax, Va., 1968—; now chmn. bd., CEO., pres. ManTech Internat. Corp. Office: ManTech Internat Corp 12015 Lee Jackson Hwy Fairfax VA 22033-3300

PEDERSEN, KAREN SUE, electrical engineer; b. Indianola, Iowa, Apr. 27, 1942; d. Donald Cecil and Dorothy Darlene (Frazier) Kading; m. Wendell Dean Pedersen, May 6, 1961; children: Debra Ann Pedersen Schwickerath, Michael Dean. AA, Grand View Coll., Des Moines, 1975; BSEE, Iowa State U., 1977; MBA, Bentley Coll., Waltham, Mass., 1989. Registered profl. engr., Mass. Engr. Iowa Power & Light Co., Des Moines, 1978-80, rate engr., 1980-84; sr. rsch. engr. Boston Edison Co., Boston, 1984-87, sr. engr., 1987-94, prin. rsch. analyst, 1994—. Ops. chmn. Old South Ch., Boston, 1989—. Mem. IEEE (chmn. Iowa ctrl. chpt. 1983-84), NSPE, Mass. Soc. Profl. Engrs. (pres. 1992-93, NSPE/PEI vice chair northeast region 1995-97, sec. 1997-98), Eta Kappa Nu. Republican. Congregationalist. Office: Boston Edison Co 800 Boylston St # P1706 Boston MA 02199

PEDERSEN, KEN, recording industry executive. CFO Virgin Records Am. Inc., Beverly Hills, Calif. Office: Virgin Records Am Inc 338 N Foothill Rd Beverly Hills CA 90210-3608*

PEDERSEN, KNUD GEORGE, economics educator, university president; b. Three Creeks, Alta., Can., June 13, 1931; s. Hjalmar Neilsen and Anna Marie (Jensen) P.; m. Joan Elaine Vanderwarker, Aug. 15, 1953 (dec. 1988); children: Greg, Lisa; m. Penny Ann Jones, Dec. 31, 1988. Diploma in Edn., Provincial Normal U., 1952; BA, U. B.C., 1959; MA, U. Wash., 1964; PhD, U. Chgo., 1969; LLD (hon.), McMaster U., 1996. Asst. prof. econs. of edn. U. Toronto; asst. prof. econs. of edn., assoc. dir. U. Chgo., 1970-72; dean, assoc. prof., then prof. U. Victoria, B.C., 1972-75; acad. v.p., prof. U. Victoria, 1975-79; pres., prof. Simon Fraser U., Vancouver, B.C., 1979-83, U. B.C., Vancouver, 1983-85; pres., vice-chancellor U. Western Ont., London, Can., 1985-94, prof. econs. of edn., 1985-96; interim pres. U. No. B.C., 1995; pres. Royal Roads U., 1995-96; bd. dirs. Assn. Univs. and Colls., Can., 1979-84, chmn., 1989-91; bd. dirs. Vancouver Bd. Trade, 1983-85; pres. Can. Club Vancouver, 1983-84; mem. coun. trustees Inst. for Rsch. on Pub. Policy, Ottawa, Ont., Can., 1983-89; chmn. Coun. Ont. Univs., 1989-91. Author: The Itinerant Schoolmaster, 1972; contbr. chpts. to books. Decorated officer Order of Can., Order of Ont.; recipient 125th Anniversary of Confedn. of Can. medal; fellow Ford Found., 1965-68, Can. Coll. Tchrs., 1977, Royal Soc. for Encouragement of Arts, 1984; also 11 major scholarships. Mem. Semiahmoo Golf and Country Club. Avocations: golf, fishing, gardening.

PEDERSEN, NORMAN A., lawyer; b. Modesto, Calif., Dec. 29, 1946; s. Melvin R. and Hilda R. (Akenhead) P. BA, U. Calif., Berkeley, 1970, MA, 1972; JD, UCLA, 1975. Bar: Calif., D.C. Trial atty. Fed. Power Commn., Washington, 1975-77; asst. to commr. Fed. Regulatory Commn., Washington, 1977-79; ptnr. Kadison, Pfaelzer, Woodard, Quinn & Rossi, Washington, 1979-87, Graham & James, Washington, 1987-88, Jones, Day, Reavis & Pogue, Washington, 1988—. Office: Jones Day Reavis & Pogue 555 W 5th St Los Angeles CA 90013-1010

PEDERSEN, NORMAN ARNO, JR., retired headmaster, literary club director; b. Harvey, Ill., May 27, 1927; s. Norman Arno and Helen Baker (Reeves) P.; m. Isabel Whitla Braham, June 24, 1950; children: Selina, Norman A. III, Laura. AB, Princeton U., 1949; MA, U. Buffalo, 1958. Tchr., coach Nichols Sch., Buffalo, N.Y., 1954-69; headmaster Brunswick Sch., Greenwich, Conn., 1969-88; interim headmaster Erie (Pa.) Day Sch., 1988-89, ret., 1989; dir. Chautauqua (N.Y.) Lit. and Sci. Cir., 1992—; mem. adv. bd. Braitmeyer Found., Boston, 1987-91. Cmty. divsn. chair United Way Campaign, Greenwich, Conn., 1986-87; bd. dirs. Greenwich Coun. on Youth and Drugs, 1979-88; elder First Presbyn. Ch., Greenwich, 1971-74. Fulbright summer grantee, 1961. Mem. Country Day Sch. Headmasters Assn., Acad. Sr. Profls. at Eckerd Coll., Exec. Svc. Corp. of Manasota. Avocations: reading, fly-fishing, golf, swimming, bicycle riding. Home: 3702 Sun Eagle Ln Bradenton FL 34210-4236

PEDERSEN, PAUL BODHOLDT, psychologist, educator; b. Ringsted, Iowa, May 19, 1936. BA in History and Philosophy, U. Minn., 1958, MA in Am. Studies, 1959; ThM, Luth. Sch. Theology, Chgo., 1962; MA in Ednl. Psychology, U. Minn., 1966; PhD in Asian Studies, Claremont (Calif.) Grad. Sch., 1968. Asst. prof. dept. psychoednl. studies, psychologist U. Minn., Mpls., 1971-75; sr. fellow Culture Learning Inst. East-West Ctr., Honolulu, 1975-76, sr. fellow coord., 1975-76; assoc. prof. dept. psychoednl. studies, psychologist U. Minn., 1975-78, higher edn. coord., 1976-77; sr. fellow Culture Learning Inst. East-West Ctr., 1979-81; prof., chmn. dept. counselor edn. Syracuse (N.Y.) U., 1982-90, prof. edn. dept. counseling and human svcs., 1989—, adj. prof. dept. internat. rels., 1993—; prof. counseling edn. U. Ala., Birmingham, 1996—; vis. lectr. Nommensen U., Medan, Sumatra, Indonesi, 1962-65, U. Malaya, 1969-71; vis. prof. dept. psychology U. Hawaii, 1978-81; spkr. in field. Author numerous books, chpts. to books, articles to profl. jours.; mem. editl. bd. Am. Jour. Multicultural Counseling and Devel.; editl. advisor Jour. Profl. Psychology, Jour. Simulation and Games, Internat. Jour. Intercultural Rels. Mem. APA, Am. Assn. Counseling and Devel. Internat. (mem. rels. com., editl. bd. Jour. Counseling and Devel., editor Internationally Speaking newsletter, mentor media com.), Internat. Assn. for Cros Cultural Psychology, Internat. Coun. Psychologists, Soc. Intercultural Tng. and Rsch. (exec. com. mem., program chairperson 1977, chairperson Pacific Com. 1977, pres. 1978-80, editl. bd. Jour. Intercultural Rels.). Office: U Ala Dept Human Studies 157 Edn Bldg 901 S 13th St Birmingham AL 35294-1250*

PEDERSEN, PAUL RICHARD, composer, educator; b. Camrose, Alta., Can., Aug. 28, 1935; s. Richard and Anna (Rasmussen) P.; m. Jean Frances Stollery, Aug. 6, 1956; children: Rebecca, David (dec.), Katherine, Andrew. B.A., U. Sask., 1957; Mus.M., U. Toronto, 1961, Ph.D., 1970. Music dir. Camrose Lutheran Coll., 1962-64; prof. McGill U., Montreal, Que., 1966-90, chmn. dept. theory, 1970-74, dir. Electronic Music Studio, 1971-74, assoc. dean faculty of music, 1974-76, dean faculty of music, 1976-86, dir. McGill records, 1976-90; dean Faculty Music, U. Toronto, Ont., Can., 1990-95. Contbr. articles to music jours.; Composer: chamber music Woodwind Trio No. 1, 1956, Woodwind Trio No. 2, 1957, Chorale Prelude No. 2, 1958, Lament, 1958, Ricercare, 1958, Woodwind Quintet (commd. Saskatoon Summer Festival), 1959, Come Away, 1959, Fugue, 1959, Sonata for Violin and Piano (commd. Andrew Dawes), 1960, Serial Composition, 1965, An Old Song of the Sun and the Moon and the Fear of Loneliness, 1973, Wind Quintet No. 2, 1975, 6 Chorale Preludes for Organ, 1996; choral works Ecclesiastes XII, 1958, Psalm 117, 1959, All praise to Thee, 1960, Built on a Rock, 1961, Passion Oratorio, 1961, rev., 1990, God Himself is Present, 1961, O Darkest Woe, 1961, Psalm 134, 1961, On the Nativity of Christ, 1963; 12 Chorales, SAB Choir, 1974, chorale mass, SAB Choir, 1983, De Profundis Choir and Orch., 1987; electronic music The Lone Tree, 1964, Themes from the Old Testament, 1966, Fantasie, 1967, Origins, 1967, For Margaret, Motherhood and Mendellssohn, 1971, Elegy for cello and tape, 1996—; orchestral music Concerto for Orchestra, 1961, Lament, 1962. Recipient Can. Council awards, 1958, 59, 73; Queen Elizabeth II Ont. scholar, 1965; Province of Ont. grad. fellow, 1964-65. Mem. Candian League Composers. Home: 70 Indian Grove, Toronto, ON Canada M6R 2Y4 Office: U Toronto, Faculty Music, Toronto, ON Canada M5S 1A1

PEDERSEN, RICHARD FOOTE, diplomat and academic administrator; b. Miami, Ariz., Feb. 21, 1925; s. Ralph Martin and Gertrude May (Foote) P.; m. Nelda Newell Napier, May 9, 1953; children: Paige Elizabeth, Jonathan Foote, Kendra Gayle. BA summa cum laude, Coll. of Pacific, 1946; MA, Stanford U., 1947; PhD, Harvard U., 1950; LLD (hon.), George Williams Coll., 1964, U. of Pacific, 1966, Am. U., Cairo, 1997. Teaching fellow, tutor Harvard U., Cambridge, Mass., 1949-50; with UN econ. and social affairs Dept. State, Washington, 1950-53; adviser econs. and social affairs U.S. Mission to UN, N.Y.C., 1953-55, adviser polit. and security affairs, 1956-59, sr. advisor polit. and security affairs, 1959-64, minister, counselor, 1964-66, ambassador, sr. adviser to U.S. rep., 1966-67; ambassador, dep. U.S. rep. UN security coun., N.Y.C., 1967-69; counselor Dept. State, 1969-73; ambassador to Hungary, 1973-75; sr. v.p. internat. U.S. Trust Co., 1975-78; pres. Am. U., Cairo, 1978-90; dir. internat. programs Calif. Poly Pomona U., 1990-95; mem. adv. bd. Nat. Coun. U.S.-Arab Rels., 1985—; trustee Consortium for Internat. Devel., 1990-95; mem. adv. bd. Ctr. New Eastern Studies UCLA, 1996—; chair adv. bd. internat. studies U. Pacific, 1997—. Mem. Nat. Coun. YMCAs, 1961-73; bd. dirs. Ctr. for Civic Edn., 1995—, Physicians for Peace, 1988-90; mem. Fulbright bd., Egypt, 1980-82, adv. bd. Fulbright Cultural Enrichment Program, So. Calif., 1991—. With AUS, 1943-45 ETO. Recipient Sumner Peace prize Harvard U., 1950, Outstanding Alumnus award U. Pacific, 1962, Order of Sacred Treasure, Gold and Silver Star, Govt. of Japan, 1987; named One of 10 Outstanding Young Men, U.S. Jr. C. of C., 1956; awarded Order of Scis. and Arts, first class Govt. of Egypt, 1990. Mem. Royal Inst. Internat. Affairs, Coun. Fgn. Rels., Am. Soc. Internat. Law, L.A. World Affairs Coun., Am. Fgn. Svc. Assn., Middle East Inst., UN Assn. Am., Internat. Assn. Univ. Pres., Pacific Coun. Internat. Policy. Democrat. Congregationalist. Clubs: Harvard (N.Y.); Cosmos (Washington). Avocations: swimming, tennis, Egyptology, local history. Home: 2503 N Mountain Ave Claremont CA 91711-1545

PEDERSEN, WESLEY NIELS, public relations and public affairs executive; b. South Sioux City, Nebr., July 10, 1922; s. Peder Westergaard and Marie Gertrude (Sorensen) P.; m. Angela Kathryn Vavra, Oct. 17, 1948; 1 son, Eric Wesley. Student, Tri-State Coll., Sioux City, Iowa, 1940-41; BA summa cum laude, Upper Iowa U.; postgrad., George Washington U., 1958-59. Editor, writer Sioux City Jour., 1941-50; corr. N.Y. Times, Life, Time, Fortune, 1948-50; editor Dept. State, 1950-53; fgn. svc. officer Dept. State, Hong Kong, 1960-63; fgn. affairs columnist, roving corr., counselor summit meetings and fgn. ministers confs. USIA, 1953-60, chief, worldwide spl. publs. and graphics programs, 1963-69; chief Office Spl. Projects, Washington, 1969-78, Office Spl. Projects, Internat. Comm. Agy., 1978-79; v.p. Fraser Assocs., pub. rels., Washington, 1979-80; dir. comm. and pub. rels. Pub. Affairs Coun., Washington, 1980—; lectr. creative comm. Upper Iowa U., 1975; chmn., Europe, Ambassadorial Internat. Affairs Seminar, Fgn. Svc. Inst., 1975; lectr. internat. pub. rels. Pub. Rels. Inst., Am. U., 1976; lectr. bus. and mgmt. divsn. NYU, 1976, 77, 78; cons. pub. rels., editl. and design; del. founding sessions 1st Amendment Congress, Phila. and Williamsburg, Va., 1980, mem. exec. com., 1980. Columnist Pub. Rels. Jour., 1980-85; author: Mr. President: Lyndon B. Johnson, 1964, Legacy of a President, 1964, Mr. President: Richard M. Nixon, 1969; American Heroes of Asian Wars, 1969; co-author: Effective Government Public Affairs, 1981; editor: Escape At Midnight and Other Stories (Pearl S. Buck), 1962, Exodus From China (Harry Redl), 1962, Macao, 1962, China's Men of Letters (K.E. Priestley), 1963, The Chinese Model (Werner Klatt), 1963, Children of China (Pearl S. Buck and Margaret Wylie), 1963, Destination the Moon (William Howard), 1964, Man on the Moon, 1964, Bounty From the Land, 1965, The Americans and the Arts (Howard Taubman), 1969, The Dance in America (Agnes de Mille), 1969, Getting the Most From Grassroots Public Affairs Programs, 1980, Computer Applications in Public Affairs, 1984, Cost-Effective Management for Today's Public Affairs, 1984, Making Community Relations Pay Off: Tools and Strategies, 1988, Winning at the Grassroots: How to Succeed in the Legislative Arena by Mobilizing Employees and Other Allies, 1989, Leveraging State Government Relations, 1990, Managing the Business-Employee PAC, 1992, Adding Value to the Public Affairs Function, 1994, Pub. Affairs Rev. mag., 1980-86, Impact newsletter on nat. and internat. pub. affairs, 1980—; contbr. to The Commissar, 1972, Informing the People: A Public Affairs Handbook, 1981, The Practice of Public Relations, 1984; mem. editl. bd. Pub. Rels. Quar., 1975—, Fgn. Svc. Jour., 1975-81; mem. adv. bd. Pub. Rels. News, 1991—; contr. articles to profl. jours. Founding chmn. bd. dirs. Nat. Inst. for Govt. Pub. Info. Rsch., Am. U., 1977-80. Served with USAAF, 1943-46. Recipient 2 awards A.P. Mng. Editors Assn., Iowa, 1949, Meritorious Svc. award USIA, 1963, Presdl. commendation, 1964, 1st prizes Fed. Editors Assn., 1970, 74-75, Dirs.' citation USIA, 1974, 1st prizes Soc. Tech. Comm., 1974, 75-76, Gold award Internat. Newsletter Conf., 1982, Silver award, 1985, Eddi award for design excellence Editor's Workshop, 1983, Gold Circle award for outstanding comm. Am. Soc. Assn. Execs., 1983-89, 97, Editors' Forum award, 1988-90, 94, 95, 96, Assn. Trends award, 1989-97, Grand prize Internat. Ann. Report Conf., 1989, Gold award 1997, Comm. Concepts awards, 1989-97, Grand prize, 1992, MerComm awards, 1990-97, Nat. Media Conf. award, 1989, 90, Internat. Acad. Comm. Arts and Scis. award, 1994, 95, 96, 97, Grand prize, 1995, awards Printing and Graphic Assn., 1987, 91, 96; named Most Outstanding Info. Officer in Exec. Br. Govt. Info. Orgn., 1975, Ky. Col. and Adm. Nebr. Navy, 1984. Mem. Am. Fgn. Svc. Assn., Internat. Assn. Bus. Communicators (Communicator of Yr. Washington chpt. 1978, various awards 1973, 76-78, 84, 90, 94, 95, 96, 97), Nat. Assn. Govt. Communicators (pres. 1978-79, Communicator of Yr. 1977, Disting. Svc. award 1978), Pub. Rels. Soc. Am. (mem. Counselor's Acad. 1980—, chmn. 1st Amendment task force 1980-81, co-recipient Thoth award 1980, 81, 94, recipient Thoth awards 1995, 96, 97), World Affairs Coun., Soc. of Profl. Journalists, Fgn. Svc. Club, Nat. Press Club, Overseas Press Club. Episcopalian. Home: 4701 Willard Ave Apt 1007 Chevy Chase MD 20815 Office: Pub Affairs Coun 1019 19th St NW Ste 200 Washington DC 20036-5105 *Keenness of mind and an abundance of luck, it is said, are the key ingredients of personal success. The truth be told, however, I've performed only one act of brilliance in my lifetime: the selection of my parents. But I've had an enormous amount of good fortune, a fact manifestly clear to anyone who has ever met my wife and son. They, thank goodness, chose me.*

PEDERSEN, WILLIAM FRANCIS, JR., lawyer; b. N.Y.C., Apr. 4, 1943; s. William F. and Priscilla S. (Auchincloss) P.; m. Ellen L. Frost, Feb. 2, 1974; children: Mark Francis, Claire Ellen. BA, Harvard U., 1965, LLB, 1968. Bar: Mass. 1969, D.C. 1978. Assoc. Ropes & Gray, Boston, 1969-72; staff atty. EPA, Washington, 1972-75; dep. gen. counsel, then assoc. gen. counsel EPA, 1976-85; staff counsel Senate Com. on Govt. Ops., Washington, 1975-76; lectr. Harvard Law Sch., 1985-86; of counsel Perkins Coie, Washington, 1987—, ptnr., 1989-94; ptnr. Shaw, Pittman, Potts & Trowbridge, Washington, 1994—. Contbr. articles to profl. jours. Mem. ABA (standing com. on environ. law 1987-89). Republican. Episcopalian. Office: Shaw Pittman Potts & Trowbridge 2300 N St NW Washington DC 20037-1122

PEDERSON, CON, animator. Grad., UCLA. Former writer, animator Walt Disney; animator Graphic Films Corp.; co-founder Abel & Assocs.; sr. animator MetroLight Studios, L.A., 1987—; animator for Redstone rocket project, also Explorer Satellite program, 1958. Spl. effects supr., animated models designer (film) 2001: A Space Odyssey. Office: MetroLight Studios 5724 W 3rd St Ste 400 Los Angeles CA 90036-3078

PEDERSON, GORDON ROY, state legislator, retired military officer; b. Gayville, S.D., Aug. 8, 1927; s. Roy E. and Gladys F. (Masker) P.; m. Betty L. Ballard, Mar. 8, 1955; children: James D., Carol A. Pederson Niemann, Nancy G. Pederson Holub, Gary W. Student, Yankton Coll., 1948-50, Fla. State U., 1963; advanced course, Infantry Sch., 1958-59. Drafted U.S. Army, 1945-47, commd. 2nd lt., 1952, advanced through grades to lt. col., 1967, served Korean War, 1950-54; served CONUS World War II, platoon leader 17th infantry regiment, 7th infantry divsn. U.S. Army, Korea, 1953-54; rifle co. commdr. 10th mountain divsn. U.S. Army, Germany, 1955-58; instr., dir. instrn. U.S. Army Jungle Warfare Tng. Ctr. U.S. Army, Ft. Sherman, Canal Zone, 1961-63, comdr. post, 1963-64; 1st brig., 1st infantry divsn. U.S. Army, Vietnam, 1965-66; dir. tng. hdqs. U.S. Army, Ft. Leonard Wood, 1966-68; advisor Ministry of Nat. Def., Rep. China on Taiwan, 1969-70; retired U.S. Army, 1970; rep. S.D. Ho. Reps., Pierre, 1977—; operator Dairy Queen, Wall, S.D., 1990-95; chmn. transp. com. S.D. Ho. Reps., 1979-93. Del. S.D. Rep. Conv., 1974-78, 80, 82, 84, 86, 88, 90, 92, 94, 96, Rep. Conv. S.D., 1994, Nat. Rep. Conv., 1976, 80, 84, 88, 92, 96; bd. dirs. Legis. Rsch. Coun., 1988, 90, 92, 96. Decorated Bronze Star, Medal of Merit, U.S. Presdl. Unit Citation, Rep. Korea Presdl. Unit Citation, Rep. Vietnam Presdl. Unit Citation, Combat Infantry Badge with Star, Legion of Merit, Air Medal with 2 Oak Leaf Clusters, Army Accomodation medal with 2 oak leaf clusters, Cross of Gallantry with Palm, Republic Vietnam. Mem. VFW, DAV, Am. Legion, Retired Officers Assn., Wall C. of C., Internat. Lions Club. Lutheran. Home: PO Box 312 116 W 7th St Wall SD 57790 Office: SD Ho of Reps State Capitol Bldg Pierre SD 57501

PEDERSON, RENA, newspaper editor. Editorial page editor Dallas Morning News. Office: The Dallas Morning News 508 Young St Dallas TX 75202-4808

PEDERSON, TONY WELDON, newspaper editor; b. Waco, Tex., Oct. 27, 1950; s. Lloyd Moody and Ida Frances (Walker) P.; m. Julianne Kennedy, Mar. 21, 1974. B.A., Baylor U., 1973; M.A., Ohio State U., 1976. Sports writer Waco (Tex.) Tribune, Tex., 1970-73; sports writer Houston Chronicle, 1974-75, copy editor, 1976-80, sports editor, 1980-83, mng. editor, 1983—; adj. faculty U. Houston, 1977-79. Mem. Houston Com. Fgn. Rels. Mem. Nat. AP Mng. Editors Assn., Tex. AP Mng. Editors Assn. Methodist. Avocations: golf; reading. Office: Houston Chronicle Pub Co 801 Texas St Houston TX 77002-2906

PEDERSON, WILLIAM DAVID, political scientist, educator; b. Eugene, Oreg., Mar. 17, 1946; s. Jon Moritz and Rose Marie (Ryan) P. BS in Polit. Sci., U. Oreg., 1967, MA in Polit. Sci., 1972, PhD in Polit. Sci., 1979. Teaching asst. polit. sci. dept. U. Oreg., Eugene, 1975-77; instr. govt. dept. Lamar U., Beaumont, Tex., 1977-79; asst. prof. polit. sci. dept. Westminster Coll., Fulton, Mo., 1979-80; asst. prof., head polit. sci. and pre-law Yankton Coll. U. S.D., 1980-81; prof. polit. sci. dept. La. State U., Shreveport, 1981—; program analyst NIH, Bethesda, Md., summer 1973; assoc. prof. jr. state program Am. U., Washington, summer 1984; rsch. assoc. Russian and East European Ctr. U. Ill., Urbana, summers 1982—; founding dir. Washington semester La. State U., Shreveport, 1982-91, 96—, Presdl. Conf. Series, 1992—, Am. Studies program, 1982—; editorial staff writer The Times, Shreveport, 1990. Author: The Rating Game in American Politics, 1987; editor: The Barberian Presidency, 1989; Congressional-Presidential Relations: Governmental Gridlock, 1991; co-editor: Grassroots Constitutionalism, 1988; Morality and Conviction in American Politics, 1990, Great Justices of the U.S. Supreme Court: Ratings and Case Studies, 1993, 2d edit., 1994, Lincoln and Leadership: A Model for a Summer Teachers Institute, 1993; Abraham Lincoln: Sources and Style of Leadership, 1994, Abraham Lincoln: Contemporary, 1995, 2d printing, 96; guest editor Quarterly Jour. Ideology, 1994, FDR and the Modern Presidency: Leadership and Legacy, 1997; editor: The Polit. Sci. Educator, 1996—; contbr. articles to profl. jours.; founder La. Lincolnator, 1994. Mem. Mayor's Comm. on the Bicentennial U.S. Constn., 1987; active Barnwell Ctr., Shreveport, 1984, Am. Rose Soc., Shreveport, 1982. Served with U.S. Army, 1968-70. Recipient Tng. award NIH 1973, Outstanding Prof. award Westminster Coll. 1980, La. State U., 1984, Cultural Olympiad award, 1995, Page Shreveport rose Shreveport Times Jour., 1995; grantee La. State U., 1982, La. Endowment for Humanities, 1987, 93, 95, 96, 97; fellow NEH, 1981-85. Fellow Am. Polit. Sci. Assn., Am. Judicature Soc.; mem. Abraham Lincoln Assn. (mem. bd. dirs. 1994, dir. conf. in the south, 1992, dir. 1st summer Inst. on Abraham Lincoln, 1993, grantee 1992, 93, Achievement award 1994), Ctr. Study Presidency, Internat. Soc. Polit. Psychology, Am. Studies Assn, Internat. Lincoln Assn. (bd. dirs. 1994-95, pres. 1990-93), Lincoln Forum (bd. dirs. 1996—). Office: La State U Dept Polit Sci & Am Studies 1 University Pl # 148 Bh Shreveport LA 71115-2301

PEDESKY, GERALDINE GOLICK, design project professional; b. Hayward, Calif., Oct. 27, 1935; d. Charles Anthony and Dolores Irene (Lemon) Golick; m. Charles Francis Pedesky, Nov. 10, 1960. BA, San Jose State Coll., 1957. Flight attendant Trans Continental Airlines, Burbank, Calif., 1958-62; office mgr. The Hertz Corp., L.A., 1964-77; v.p. adminstr. Vitousek Real Estate Sch., Honolulu, 1977-94; project mgr. Philpotts & Assoc., Honolulu, 1994—; mem. sec. Hawaii Assn. Real Estate Schs., Honolulu, 1977-93. Trustee Bernice Pauahi Bishop Mus., Honolulu, 1988-94, mem. exec. com., 1994; mem. Bishop Mus. Assn., Honolulu, 1983-87 (past pres.), Bishop Mus. Svc. League, Honolulu, 1977-83 (pres. 1982); bd. dirs. Outrigger Duke Kahanamoku Found., Honolulu, 1986-94 (pres.1989). Mem. Outrigger Canoe Club (bd. dirs., sec.-treas., v.p. ops.), Honolulu Acad. Arts, Contemporary Mus. Art, Nature Conservancy, Bishop Mus. Assn. Avocations: outrigger canoe paddling (state champion, 1980, 83, 85-91, 93), hiking, runnning. Office: Philpotts & Assocs 925 Bethel St Ste 200 Honolulu HI 96813-4307

PEDINI, KENNETH, radiologist; b. Hartford, Conn., Mar. 19, 1940; s. Daniel Victor and Elizabeth Catherine Pedini; m. Egle Damijonaitis; children: David D., Julian A. AB in Philosophy, Trinity Coll., 1962; MD, Boston U., 1966. Diplomate Nat. Bd. Med. Examiners, Am. Bd. Radiology. Resident radiology Boston City Hosp., 1967-70, chief resident radiology, 1969-70, jr. staff radiologist, 1970-71; jr. staff radiologist U. Hosp., Boston, 1970-71; ptnr. Shawsheen Radiology, Andover, Mass., 1971—; sr. radiologist Lawrence (Mass.) Gen. Hosp., 1971-75, dir. radiology, 1976-87; sr. radiologist Melrose (Mass.)-Wakefield Hosp., 1971-93, chief radiologist, 1993—; pres. L & M Radiology Inc, Andover, Mass., 1994—; bd. trustees Lawrence Gen. Hosp., 1984-89, mem. fin. com., 1986-96, mem. fin. com. regional health system, 1996—. Trustee Lawrence Gen. Hosp. Health Enterprises, Inc., 1990-93; mem. fin. com. Lawrence Gen. Hosp., 1986-96, Lawrence Gen. Regional Health Sys., 1996—; co-founder Andover Sch. of Montessori, 1975—; mem. alumni adv. com. Trinity Coll., 1995. Fellow Am. Coll. Radiology (councilor 1979-81); mem. New England Roentgen Ray Soc., Mass. Radiol. Soc. (pres. 1985-86, pres.-elect 1984-85, v.p. 1983-84, exec. com. 1977-87), Mass. Med. Soc., Stonehorse Yatch Club. Office: L&M Radiology Inc 100 Burtt Rd Andover MA 01810-5920

PEDLEY, JOHN GRIFFITHS, archaeologist, educator; b. Burnley, Eng., July 19, 1931; came to U.S., 1959; s. George and Anne (Whitaker) P.; m. Mary Grace Sponberg, Aug. 30, 1969. BA, Cambridge (Eng.) U., 1953, MA, 1959; postgrad. (Norton fellow), Am. Sch. Classical Studies, Athens, Greece, 1963-64; PhD, Harvard U., 1965. Loeb research fellow in classical archaeology Harvard U., 1969-70; asst. prof. classical archaeology and Greek U. Mich., Ann Arbor, 1965-68; assoc. prof. U. Mich., 1968-74, acting chmn. dept. classical studies, 1971-72, 75-76; dir. Kelsey Mus. Archaeology, 1973-86, prof., 1974—; guest scholar J. Paul Getty Mus., vis. scholar UCLA, 1989; resident in archaeology Am. Acad. in Rome, 1990; mem. staff excavations, Sardis, Turkey, 1962-64, Pylos, Greece, 1964, co-dir. excavations, Apollonia, Libya, 1966-68; field dir. Corpus Ancient Mosaics, Tunisia, Thysdrus, 1972-73; co-prin. investigator excavations, Carthage, N.Africa, 1975-79, dir. excavations, Paestum, Italy, 1982-85. Author: Sardis in the Age of Croesus, 1968, Ancient Literary Sources on Sardis, 1972, Greek Sculpture of the Archaic Period: The Island Workshops, 1976, Paestum: Greeks and Romans in Southern Italy, 1990, Greek Art and Archaeology, 1992, 2d edit., 1997, The Sanctuary of Santa Venera at Paestum, Vol. 1, 1993, Corpus des Mosaiques de Tunisie vol. III, 1996; co-author: Apollonia, the Port of Cyrene, 1977; editor: New Light on Ancient Carthage, 1980; co-editor: Studies Presented to GMA Hanfmann, 1971. Am. Coun. Learned Socs. fellow, 1972-73; grantee Am. Philol. Soc., 1979, Nat. Endowment Arts Mus., 1974, 77, 79, 80, NEH, 1967, 75, 77, 83, 84; NEH fellow, 1986; vis. scholar Am. Acad. Rome, 1995. Home: 1233 Baldwin Ave Ann Arbor MI 48104-3623 Office: Kelsey Mus U Mich Ann Arbor MI 48109

PEDLEY, TIMOTHY ASBURY, IV, neurologist, educator, researcher; b. Phoenix, Aug. 31, 1943; s. Timothy Asbury Pedley III and Mary Adele (Newcomer) Melis; m. Barbara S. Koppel, Mar. 17, 1984. BA, Pomona Coll., 1965; MD, Yale U., 1969. Cert. neurology, 1975, electroencephalography, 1975, clin. neurophysiology, 1993. Intern Stanford U. Hosp., 1967-70, resident in neurology, 1970-73, post-doctoral fellow in neurophysiology, 1973-75, asst. prof. neurology, 1975-79; assoc. prof. neurology Columbia U., 1979-83, prof., vice chmn. dept. neurology, 1983—; dir. comprehensive epilepsy ctr. Columbia-Presbyterian Med. Ctr., N.Y.C., 1983—. Contbr. articles to profl. jours. Bd. dirs. Epilepsy Found Am., 1984—, chmn. profl. adv. bd., 1985-87, pres., 1991-93, chmn. 1993-95. mem. rev. com. NIH Nat. Inst. Neurol. and Chronic Diseases and Strokes, 1985-89; vis. fellow in exptl. neurology Inst. Psychiatry, London, 1978; mem. merit review bd. neurobiology rsch., VA, 1992-96, chmn., 1995-96, Editor-in-chief Epilepsia, 1994—. Fellow Am. Acad. Neurology, Am. Electroencephalographic Soc. (pres. 1989-90, bd. dirs. 1981, 85); mem. Am. Neurol. Assn. (coun. 1992-94, treas. 1995—), Am. Epilepsy Soc. (treas. 1980-83, pres. 1991-92), Soc. for Neurosci., Internat. League Against Epilepsy (mem. exec. com. 1994—), Alpha Omega Alpha. Clubs: Yale (N.Y.C.), Met. Opera (N.Y.C.), Shenorock Shore (Rye, N.Y.). Office: The Neurological Inst 710 W 168th St New York NY 10032-2603

PEDOE, DANIEL, mathematician, writer, artist; b. London, Eng., Oct. 29, 1910; came to U.S., 1962, naturalized, 1972; B.Sc., U. London, 1930; B.A., Magdalene Coll., Cambridge, Eng., 1933, Ph.D., 1937; postgrad., Princeton U., 1935-36. Instr. Southampton U., Birmingham U., Eng., 1936-47; Leverhulme rsch. fellow Cambridge (Eng.) U., 1947-48; reader U. London, 1948-52; prof. U. Khartoum, 1952-59, U. Singapore, 1959-62, Purdue U., 1962-64; prof. math. U. Minn., Mpls., 1964-81. Author: Circles, 1957, Gentle Art of Mathematics, 1958, Projective Geometry, 1963, A Course in Geometry, 1970, Geometry and the Liberal Arts, 1976; co-author: Methods of Algebraic Geometry, 3 vols., 1947-53, Japanese Temple Geometry Problems, 1990. Recipient Lester R. Ford award for expository writing Math. Assn. Am., 1968. Mem. Am. Math. Assn. Home: 704 14th Ave SE Minneapolis MN 55414-1595

PEDONE, JOSEPH LAWRENCE, advertising executive; b. Teaneck, N.J., Dec. 13, 1947; s. Richard and Frances (Maenza) P.; m. Nancy Ann Tolve, June 19, 1982; children: Jill Marie, Leigh Ann. AA, Rockland Community Coll., 1968; BSBA, Youngstown State U., 1970. Asst. prodn. mgr. Pace Advt., N.Y.C., 1972-77; prodn. mgr. Doubleday Advt., N.Y.C., 1977-78, Smith Greenland, N.Y.C., 1978-79; assoc. promotion dir. Edwin Bird Wilson, N.Y.C., 1979-80; print/traffic dir. Bozell & Jacobs, Union, N.J., 1980-81; print, art svcs. dir. Saatchi & Saatchi Advt. Inc., N.Y.C., 1981—. Contbr. articles to profl. jours. Recipient Good Scout award Greater N.Y. Coun. Boy Scouts Am., 1988, Fellowship award N.Y. Club Printing House Craftsmen, 1989, Luminaire award Women in Prodn., 1991, Electronic Integration Pioneer award Lasers in Graphics Conf., 1992; inducted Pub. and Prodn. Exec.'s Hall of Fame, 1992. Mem. Am. Assn. Advt. Agys. (chmn. 1990-93), Gravure Advt. Coun. (vice chmn. 1990—), Pub. and Prodn. Execs. (editorial advisor 1989—), Specification for WEB Offset Pubs. (bd. dirs. 1991-96), NYU Bd. Graphic comms. Mgmt. and Tech. Ctr., Digital Distribution of Advtsg. for Pubs. Assn. (chmn.). Republican. Roman Catholic. Office: Prudential Advt 213 Washington St Newark NJ 07102-2917

PEDRAM, MARILYN BETH, reference librarian; b. Brewster, Kans., Apr. 3, 1937; d. Edgar Roy and Elizabeth Catherine (Doubt) Crist; m. Manouchehr Pedram, Jan. 27, 1962 (Oct. 28, 1984); children: Jaleh Denise, Cyrus Andre. BS in Edn., Kans. State U., 1958; MLS, U. Denver, 1961. Cert secondary educator, Mo. 7th grade tchr. Clay Ctr. (Kans.) Pub. Schs., 1958-59, Colby (Kans.) Pub. Sch. System, 1959-60; reference libr. Topeka (Kans.) Pub. Libr., 1961-62, extension dept. head, 1963-64, reference libr., 1964-65; br. libr. asst. Denver Pub. Libr., 1965-67; reference libr. Kansas City (Mo.) Pub. Libr., Plaza Br., 1974-79, Kansas City (Mo.) Main Libr., 1979—. Mem. AARP, ALA, NAFE, Mo. Libr. Assn., Pub. Libr. Assn., Kansas City Assn. Law Librs., Gluten Intolerance Group N.Am., Celiac Sprue Assn., Kans. State U. Alumni Assn., Kansas City Online Users Group, Nat. Parks and Conservation Assn. Avocations: flower gardening, gourmet cooking, travel, reading, walking. Office: Kansas City Pub Libr 311 E 12th St Kansas City MO 64106-2412

PEDRAZA, PEDRO, research director; b. N.Y.C., Sept. 30, 1946; s. Pedro Pedraza Algarin and Catherine (Martinez) Pedraza; m. Irza Ortiz, Sept. 3, 1964 (div. 1980); children: Pedro III, Andre; m. Enercida Guerrero, June 14, 1985; children: Lucas, Xiomara, Roxanne. BA, Occidental Coll., 1968; MS, Columbia U., 1973. Rsch. dir. Ctr. for Puerto Rican Studies CUNY, N.Y.C., 1973—, acting dir. Ctr. for Puerto Rican Studies, 1994. Bd. dirs. Educators for Social Responsibility, N.Y.C., 1990-94, Advs. for Children, N.Y.C., 1987-94, Youth Action Program, El Barrio Popular Edn. Program, P.R./Latino Edn. Roundtable. Home and Office: Hunter Coll Ctr Puerto Rican Studies 160 E 107th St # 1 New York NY 10029

PEDROTTI, LENO STEPHANO, physics educator; b. Zeigler, Ill., May 21, 1927; s. Celeste Louis and Dolores (Galeaz) P.; m. Wilma Jean Sullivan, June 23, 1951; children—Daro Stephano, Michael Louis, Sandra Maria, Laura Jean, Catherine Ann, Leno Matthew, Mary Ann, John Owen. B.S. in Edn, Ill. State U., 1949; M.S. in Physics, U. Ill., 1951; Ph.D., U. Cin., 1961. Teaching asst. U. Ill., Urbana, 1949-51; prof. physics, chmn. dept. Air Force Inst. Tech., Wright-Patterson AFB, Ohio, 1951-82, prof. emeritus, 1982—; cons., editor Ctr. Occupational Rsch. & Devel., Waco, Tex., 1975-82, sr. v.p., 1982—; presenter in field, 1982—; author, editor, lectr. laser and electro-optics Engrng. Tech., Inc., Waco, 1978—; mem. indsl. adv. com. laser electro-optics program Cin. Tech. Coll., 1981-82; tech. cons. Univ. Eye Surgeons, Inc., Ohio State U., 1979-82; mem. exec. com. joint svcs. optical program Optical Scis. Ctr., U. Ariz., 1975-82. Author: Principles of

Technology, 1986, Introduction to Optics, 1987, rev. edit., 1993, Applied Mathematics, 1988; contbg. author: Technical Prep Associate Degree: A Win/Win Experience, 1991, The Science Technology, Society Movement, 1993; contbr. articles to profl. jours. Faculty fellow NSF, 1959. Mem. Am. Nuclear Soc., Am. Phys. Soc. (vice chmn. then chmn. So. Ohio sect. 1974-76), Laser Inst. Am. (bd. dirs. 1974-84), Am. Assn. Physics Tchrs., Am. Soc. Engring. Edn., Optical Soc. Am., Am. Vocat. Assn. (Outstanding Mem. award 1988 vocat. instrnl. materials affiliate Ednl. Exhibitor Assn.-SHIP citation for outstanding commitment to vocat.-tech. edn. 1994), Nat. Coun. Tchrs. Math., Sigma Xi, Tau Beta Pi (Outstanding Tchr. award 1961, 62, 63, 68), Sigma Pi Sigma. Home: 11006 Trailwood Dr Waco TX 76712-3131 Office: Cord 601 Lake Air Dr Waco TX 76710-5841

PEEBLER, CHARLES DAVID, JR., advertising executive; b. Waterloo, June 8, 1936; s. Charles David and Mary E. (Barnett) P.; student Drake U., 1954-56; m. Susie Jacobs, June 5, 1958 (div. 1977); children: David Jacobs, Mark Walter; m. Tonita Worley, Nov. 12, 1979; 1 son, Todd Whitney. Asst. to exec. v.p. J.L. Brandeis & Sons, Omaha, 1956-58; with Bozell, Jacobs, Kenyon & Eckhardt (formerly Bozell & Jacobs), 1958—, v.p., mem. plans. bd. 1960-65, pres. mid-continent ops., Omaha, 1965-67, pres., CEO, 1967-86, CEO, 1986—. Hon. chmn. bd. dirs. Am. Craft Mus.; bd. dirs. Nat. Jr. Achievement of Am. Mem. Drake U., Southampton Hosp., Gtr. N.Y. Coun. Boy Scouts Am., Madison Square Boys and Girls Club, Nat. Ctr. Learning Disabilities, Juvenile Diabetes Found. Internat., N.Y.C. Partnership; partnership corp. com. Central Park Conservancy; campaign steering com. Morehouse Sch. Medicine. Mem. Nat. Golf Links Am., CEO Orgn., Blind Brook Club (Purchase), Eldorado Country Club (Indian Wells), Old Baldy Club, Mill Reef Club, Meadow Club (Southampton), Lyford Cay Club (Bahamas). Home: 166 E 64th St New York NY 10021-7478 Office: Bozell, Jacobs, Kenyon& Eckhardt 40 W 23rd St New York NY 10010-5200

PEEBLES, CARTER DAVID, lawyer; b. Chgo., July 9, 1934; s. Carter Davis and Vera Virginia (Howd) P.; m. Donna Ruth Hostetter, Aug. 3, 1957; children: John Carter, Mary Elizabeth, Sarah Anne. A.B., DePauw U., 1956; M.A., U. Stockholm, Sweden, 1955; J.D., U. Chgo., 1959. Bar: Ind. 1959, Ill. 1960. Ptnr. Peebles, Thompson, Rogers & Skekloff and predecessor firms, Ft. Wayne, Ind., 1976-91; pvt. practice law Ft. Wayne, 1991—; faculty labor relations Purdue U. Regional Campus; U.S. commr., 1961-71, U.S. magistrate, 1971-84. Author: (with others) Model Business Corporation Act, 3 vols, 1960, Indiana Bankruptcy Handbook, 2d edit, 1976, Business Practice Under the UCC, 1970, (with Daniel E. Johnson) Indiana Legal Business Forms, 2 vols, 1967, Forms and Comment, 2 vols, 1970, (with James A. Knauer) Indiana Collection Law, 1981, (with Jerald I. Ancel) Farm Foreclosure Prevention, 1983, (with Thomas L. Ryan) The Farmer in Financial Distress, 1985, (with David H. Kleiman) Farmers and Lenders - The Financial Dilemma, 1986, (with Daniel J. Skekoff) Basic Bankruptcy in Indiana, 1987, (with J.T. Massey) Farm Foreclosure Defense, 1990; contbr. articles to profl. jours. Bd. dirs. Antioch Found., Religious Instrn. Assn., Religious Heritage of Am. Mem. ABA, Ill., Ind., Allen County Bar Assns., Am. Bankruptcy Inst., Am. Agrl. Law Assn., Phi Delta Phi. Lodges: Masons, Shriners, Jesters. Home: 6737 Blue Mist Rd Fort Wayne IN 46819-1503 Office: 1325 Spy Run Ave Fort Wayne IN 46805-4027 *As a young man, I was passionate, and later compassionate. Now, cynicism has me. Men used to do business on a handshake; now, a lengthy contract seems made only to be broken. People seem to seek the unfair advantage, forgetting that the only "good deal" is the deal fair to both sides. Fortunately, most people don't want something for nothing, will recognize a moral obligation and, many times, possess deep moral courage. If there is revolution in this country, it will not be black against white or have against have-not, but care against care-not. It appears that compassion wins after all.*

PEEBLES, CHRISTOPHER SPALDING, anthropologist, dean, academic administrator; b. Clearwater, Fla., May 26, 1939; s. Frederick Thomas and Corinne deGarmendia (Stephens) P.; m. Laura Ann Wisen, Oct. 6, 1993. AB, U. Chgo., 1963; PhD, U. Calif., Santa Barbara, 1974. Asst. prof. U. Windsor, Ont., Can., 1970-74; asst. curator U. Mich., Ann Arbor, 1974-81; prof. prehistory U. Amsterdam, The Netherlands, 1981-82; prof. Ind. U., Bloomington, 1983—, dean acad. computing, acting assoc. v.p., 1992—. Author: Excavations at Moundville, 1974, Representations in Archaeology, 1992. With USAF, 1956-60. Mem. Cosmos Club. Avocation: flying. Office: Ind U Franklin Hall 116 Bloomington IN 47405

PEEBLES, PEYTON ZIMMERMAN, JR., electrical engineer, educator; b. Columbus, Ga., Sept. 10, 1934; s. Peyton Zimmerman Peebles Sr. and Maida Erlene (Denton) Dials; m. Barbara Ann Suydam, Sept. 6, 1969; children: Peyton Zimmerman III, Edward Arlen. BSEE, Evansville Coll., 1957; MSEE, Drexel Inst., 1963; PhD, U. Pa., 1967. Design engr. RCA, Moorestown, N.J., 1958-64, systems engr., 1966-69; prof. U. Tenn., Knoxville, 1969-75, 76-81; vis. prof. U. Hawaii, Honolulu, 1975-76; prof. U. Fla., Gainesville, 1981-84, 90-96, assoc. chmn., 1984-90, prof. emeritus, 1996—; cons. in field. Author: Communication System Principles, 1976, Probability, Random Variables and Random Signal Principles, 1980, 3d edit., 1993, Digital Communication Systems, 1987; prin. author: Principles of Electrical Engineering, 1991; contbr. articles to profl. jours.; patentee in field. Capt. USAFR, 1957-61. David Sarnoff fellow, 1964-66. Fellow IEEE; mem. Sigma Xi, Eta Kappa Nu, Tau Beta Pi, Sigma Pi Sigma, Phi Beta Chi. Methodist. Avocations: fishing, painting, woodworking. Office: U Fla Elec Engring Dept Gainesville FL 32611

PEEBLES, RUTH ADDELLE, secondary education educator; b. Livingston, Tex., Dec. 9, 1929; d. Andrew Wiley and Addelle (Green) P. BA, East. Tex. Baptist Coll., 1951; M of Religious Edn., Southwestern Baptist Seminary, Ft. Worth, 1955; MA, Sam Houston State U., 1968. Instr. of religion and Baptist student dir. Ea. N.Mex. U., Portales, 1955-58; Baptist student dir. Madison Coll., Harrisonburg, Va., 1958-60; youth dir. Garden Oaks Baptist Ch., Houston, 1960-62; history tchr. Livingston Ind. Sch. Dist., 1962-84. Editor: Pictorial History of Polk County, Texas, 1976; author: There Never Were Such Men Before, 1987. Bd. dirs. Polk County Libr. and Mus., Livingston, 1980-83, Polk County Heritage Soc., 1987-89. Recipient Cmty. Svc. award Polk County C. of C., 1980, Hist. Preservation awards Polk County Heritage Soc., 1987, Tex. State Hist. Commn., 1989, SCV Cert. of Appreciation, 1993, Ladies Appreciation medal SCV, 1994. Mem. Daughters of the Republic of Tex., Tex. State Hist. Assn., Tex. State Hist. Found., Hood's Tex. Brigade Assn., Polk County Heritage Soc., Atascosito Hist. Assn., Fort Delaware Soc. Baptist. Avocations: hist. rsch., wood carving.

PEECHATKA, WALTER NORMAN, government official; b. East Stroudsburg, Pa., Sept. 3, 1939; s. Walter Clinton and Lillian Mae (Post) P.; m. Bonita Louise Umholtz, Apr. 20, 1968; children—Troy, Trent. B.S. in Forestry, Pa. State U., University Park, 1961. Asst. supt. coop. for mgmt. Dept. Forests and Waters, Harrisburg, Pa., 1967-69; program specialist State Soil and Water Conservation Commn., Harrisburg, 1969-71; dir. Bur. Soil and Water Conservation, Harrisburg, 1971-82; exec. vice. pres. Soil Conservation Soc. Am., Ankeny, Iowa, 1982-87; dir. Bur. Plant Industry Pa. Dept. Agr., Harrisburg, 1987-91, dep. sec. for regulatory programs, 1991-95, exec. dep. sec., 1995—. Served to capt. USAR, 1962-64. Recipient Pres.'s Citation, Soil Conservation Soc. Am., 1983, Disting. Svc. award Nat. Assn. Conservation Dists., 1986. Mem. Assn. Soil Conservation Adminstrv. Officers (pres. 1978), Pa. Forestry Assn. (pres. 1973-74). Lutheran. Office: Pa Dept Agr Exec Dep Sec Exec Office 2301 N Cameron St Harrisburg PA 17110-9405

PEEK, ROBIN PATRICIA, library and information science educator; b. San Francisco, Jan. 10, 1958; d. Duane Edwin and Geneve Ellen (Purvis) Geer; m. Gerald Paul Miller, Sept. 15, 1992. BS, U. Oreg., 1980; MS, Syracuse U., 1988, PhD, 1997. Indexer, abstracter ERIC Clearinghouse, 1987; asst. prof. Simmons Coll., Boston, 1992—; lectr. Syracuse (N.Y.) U., 1988, 89, grad. asst. 1988, 89-91; vis. prof. SUNY, Albany, 1989. Author, editor: Scholarly Publishing: The Electronic Frontier, 1996; columnist Info. Today, 1997. Mem. Am. Soc. Info. Sci. (mem. edtl. bd. Jour. Am. Soc. Info. Sci.), Assn. Libr. and Info. Sci. Educators. Office: Simmons Coll Grad Sch Libr and Info Sci 300 Fenway Boston MA 02115-5820

PEELE, ROGER, hospital administrator; b. Elizabeth City, N.C., Dec. 24, 1930; s. Joseph Emmett and Catherine (Groves) P.; m. Diana Egan, June 15, 1963 (dec.); children: Amy, Rodney, Holly; m. Gail Nelson Oct. 15, 1992. A.B., U. N.C., 1955; M.D., U. Tenn., 1960. Cert. adminstrv. psychiatry, 1970 cert. forensic psychiatry, 1982. Intern St. Elizabeths Hosp., Washington, 1960-61; resident in psychiatry St. Elizabeths Hosp., 1961-64, tng. officer, 1964-67, chief of service William A. White div., 1967-69; dir. Area D Community Mental Health Center, 1969-73, asst. supt., 1974-75, 77-79, acting supt., 1975-77, chmn. dept. psychiatry, 1979-95; clin. prof. George Washington U., 1979—; asst. dir. NIMH, 1978-79; chief clin. officer D.C. Commn. on Mental Health, 1987-91; med. dir. Northern Va. Mental Health Ctr. Contbr. articles on clin., forensic and adminstrv. issues in Am. psychiatry to profl. jours. Served with USAF, 1950-53. Superior Service award HEW, 1967. Fellow Am. Coll. Psychiatry, Am. Psychiat. Assn. (speaker 1986-87, Adminstr. of Yr. 1989); mem. AMA, D.C. Med. Soc., Am. Assn. Psychiat. Adminstrs. (past pres.), Group for Advancement Psychiatry, Med. Soc. St. Elizabeth's Hosp. (past pres.), Fed. Physicians Assn. (past pres.). Episcopalian. Home: 5302 41st St NW Washington DC 20015-1904 Office: PO Box 39249 Washington DC 20016-9249 *A key to effective treatment is not to allow the seductiveness of logic to narrow one's observations.*

PEELER, BOB, state official; b. Gaffney, S.C., 1952; s. Smith and Sally (Bratton) P.; m. Bett Carter; children: Caroline, Robert, Jr. V.p. Peeler's Milk; former chmn. Cherokee County Sch. Bd., S.C. State Bd. Edn.; now lt. gov. State of S.C.; founding mem. advancement bd. Coll. Commerce, Clemson U. Mem. S.C. Dairy Assn. (past pres.), Cherokee County C. of C. (past pres.), Sertoma Internat. (life), Rotary (Gaffney chpt.), Masons, York Rite. Republican. Methodist. Office: Office Lt Gov Box 142 Columbia SC 29202-0142

PEELER, SCOTT LOOMIS, JR., foreign language educator; b. Rome, Ga., Aug. 25, 1947; s. Scott Loomis Sr. and Emily Willis P. BA in Spanish and French, U. South Fla., 1969, MA in Spanish and Edn., 1974; EdD candidate, Ariz. State U., 1982-91. Cert. tchr., Fla. Tchr. Spanish Polk County Schs., Lakeland, Fla., 1969—; tchr. Brandon (Fla.) Adult and Community Sch., 1978-79, Hillborough C.C., Fla., 1986; grad. rsch. asst. Ctr. Indian Edn., Ariz. State U., Tmpe, 1983-84; bi-lingual census worker U.S. Dept. Census, Tampa, 1980; part-time tchr. tribal mgmt. program Scottsdale (Ariz.) C.C., 1988; lect. in field; part-time tour guide. Author: Historical Markers and Monuments in Tampa and Hillsborough County, Florida, 1994; contbr. articles to profl. jours. Donor Peeler Am. Indian Scholarship U. South Fla., 1986; active Ptnrs. of Ams., Sister Cities Internat., Tampa, 1972—, chair edn. com., bd. dirs., 1990—; mem. Tampa Hist. Soc., 1972—, bd. dirs., 1994—, Mus. Cherokee Indian (life), Ybor City Mus. (charter); started ptnr. city relationship between Lakeland, Fla. and Valledupar, Cesar, Colombia, 1977; co-chair Ariz. Indian Edn./Native Am. Lang. Issues Conf., 1984; mem. pres.'s coun. U. South Fla.; mem. Sister Cities Com., Lakeland, Fla., del. on ofcl. visit to Japan, 1993; mem. minority task force Tampa Bay Area Blood Marrow Donor Program; vol. Tampa/Hillsborough County Conv. and Visitors Ctr. Recipient Teaching Incentive award Carnation Milk Corp., Phoenix, 1984, named one of Outstanding Young Men of Am., Montgomery, Ala., 1984; Am. Indian Leadership prog. grantee Ariz. State U., 1982-84; Newberry Library fellow Am. Indian Ctr. History, Chgo., 1981. Mem. Nat. Indian Edn. Assn. (Ariz. steering com. 1984), Huguenot Soc. S.C. (life), Fla. Geneal. Soc., U. South Fla. Alumni Assn., Christian Hope Indian Eskimo Fellowship, Cajun Connection, Alliance Francaise, L'Unione Italiana, Tampa Bay History Ctr. (charter), Ybor City Mus. (charter), Nat. Congress Am. Indians, Tampa Trolley Soc., Krewe of the Knights of Sant 'Yago, Tampa Bay Area Camellia Soc., Nat. Mus. Am. Indians (charter), Nat. Indian Adult Edn. Assn. (planned conf. in Tampa 1995), Sons of Confederate Vets. Home: 433 Summit Chase Dr Valrico FL 33594-3841 Office: George Jenkins High Sch 6000 Lakeland Highlands Rd Lakeland FL 33813-3877

PEELER, STUART THORNE, petroleum industry executive and independent oil operator; b. Los Angeles, Oct. 28, 1929; s. Joseph David and Elizabeth Fiske (Boggess) P.; m. Sylvia Frances Townley, Nov. 5, 1985. B.A., Stanford U., 1950, J.D., 1953. Bar: Calif. 1953. Ptnr. Musick, Peeler & Garrett, Los Angeles, 1958-73; with Santa Fe Internat. Corp., Orange, Calif., 1973-81; v.p., sec., assoc. gen. counsel Santa Fe Internat. Corp., 1973-74, sr. v.p., gen. counsel, dir., 1975-81; vice-chmn. bd., chmn. exec. com. Supron Energy Corp., 1978-82; chmn. bd., chief exec. officer Statex Petroleum, Inc., 1982-89; chmn., pres. and chief exec. officer Putumayo Prodn. Co., 1989—; bd. dirs. Cal Mat Co., Homestake Mining Co., Chieftain Internat. Inc. Trustee J. Paul Getty Trust; mem. U.S. Tuna Team, 1957-67, capt., 1966. Served with U.S. Army, 1953-55. Decorated Army Commendation medal. Mem. AIME, State Bar Calif., Am. Judicature Soc., Theta Chi, Phi Delta Phi, Tucson Country Club, Skyline Country Club. Republican. Congregationalist. Office: PO Box 35852 Tucson AZ 85740-5852

PEENO, LARRY NOYLE, state agency administrator, consultant; b. Evansville, Ind., Dec. 24, 1941; s. Paul Albert and Marcella (Imogene) Franz; m. Margaret Marie Graf, June 8, 1973. AB, Western Ky. U., 1968, MA, 1969; EdD, U. Mo., 1977. Cert. tchr. Mo. Art tchr. Normandy Sr. High Sch., St. Louis, 1974-90, chmn. art dept., 1976-89; dist. art coord. Normandy Sch. Dist., St. Louis, 1983-88; fine arts cons. Dept. Elem. and Secondary Edn., Jefferson City, Mo., 1990—; mem. adv. bd. St. Louis Art Mus., 1988—. Contbg. author: Supervision and Administration: Programs, Positions, Perspectives, 1991, Nat. Standards For Arts Edn.: What Every Young American SHould Know and Be Able To Do in The Arts, 1994, Nat. Visual Arts Standards, 1994; editor Show-Me-Art newsletter, 1983-84. With USAF, 1959-62. Mem. ASCD, Nat. Art Edn. Assn. (nat. program coord. 1993, bd. dirs. 1995-97, Nat. Newsletter award 1983-84, Award of Excellence 1983-84), Nat. Assn. State Dirs. Art Edn., Mo. Art Edn. Assn. (Secondary Art Tchr. of Yr. 1987-88, Outstanding Art Educator award 1983-84), Music Educators Nat. Conf., Mo. Music Educators Assn. Office: Dept Elem and Secondary Edn 205 Jefferson State Ofc Jefferson City MO 65102

PEEPLES, RUFUS RODERICK, JR. (RODDY PEEPLES), farm and ranch news radio broadcaster; b. Tehuacana, Tex., July 3, 1932; s. Rufus Roderick and Josephine (Gray) P.; m. Bettimae Scrivener, Aug. 8, 1953; children: James Roderick, Deidre Lynn. BA, Tex. A&M Coll., 1953. Farm dir. KADA Radio, Ada, Okla., 1953-56, KGNO Radio, Dodge City, Kans., 1956-59, KLIK Radio, Jefferson City, Mo., 1959; assoc. farm dir. KWFT Radio, Wichita Falls, Tex., 1959-64; sr. farm broadcaster, former owner Voice of S.W. Agt. Radio Network, San Angelo, Tex., 1964—; mem. adv. bd. Tex. Agrl. Lifetime Leadership Program, College Station, 1987—, West Tex. Boys Ranch, San Angelo, 1966—. Named Man of Yr. in Tex. Agr., Tex. Assn. County Agrl. Agts., 1984, Disting. Alumnus Coll. Agr. and Life Scis., Tex. A&M Univ., 1995; recipient Ann. Comms. award Tex. Profl. Agrl. Workers, 1982, Knapp-Porter award, Tex. Agrl. Extension Svc., 1995. Mem. Nat. Assn. Farm Broadcasters (pres. 1982, Farm Broadcaster of Yr. 1992), San Angelo C. of C. Republican. Methodist. Avocations: flying, music, photography.

PEEPLES, WILLIAM DEWEY, JR., mathematics educator; b. Bessemer, Ala., Apr. 19, 1928; s. William Dewey and Thelma Jeannette (Chastain) P.; m. Katie Ray Blackerby, Aug. 30, 1956; children: Mary Jeannette, William Dewey III, Gerald Lewis, Stephen Ray. B.S., Samford U., 1948; M.S., U. Wis., 1949; Ph.D., U. Ga., 1951. Rsch. mathematician Ballistics Rsch. Lab., Aberdeen, Md., summer 1951; mem. faculty Samford U., Birmingham, Ala., 1951-56, prof. math., 1959-95, head dept., 1967-95; mem. faculty Auburn U., 1956-59; ret., 1995; cons. Hayes Internat. Corp. Co-author: Modern Mathematics for Business Students, 1969, Finite Mathematics, 1974, Modern Mathematics with Applications to Business and the Social Sciences, 4th edit, 1986, Finite Mathematics with Applications to Business and the Social Sciences, 1981, 2d edit., 1987; Contbr. articles to profl. publs. Served to 1st lt. AUS, 1954-56. Mem. Am. Math. Soc., Math. Assn. Am., Nat. Council Tchrs. Math., Ala. Coll. Tchrs. Math. (pres. 1969), Sigma Xi, Pi Mu Epsilon, Phi Kappa Phi (pres. 1977), Lambda Chi Alpha. Baptist (deacon, chmn. 1986). Club: Mason (Shriner). Home: 419 Poinciana Dr Birmingham AL 35209-4129

PEER, GEORGE JOSEPH, metals company executive; b. St. Louis, Aug. 26, 1925; s. George J. and Melba (Rahning) P.; m. Mary Jane Hazlewood, Feb. 14, 1948; children—Linda, Gary, Steven, Scott. B.S., Purdue U., 1945, M.S., 1948; postgrad., Advanced Mgmt. Program, Harvard, 1967. Operating supr. Republic Steel Corp., Canton, Ohio, 1948-54; various sales positions to v.p. sales Basic, Inc., Chgo., Cleve., 1954-63; v.p. marketing Handy & Harman, N.Y.C., 1963-71; dir. Handy & Harman, 1971-75, group v.p. precious metals, 1972-75; chmn., pres., chief exec. officer Multi-Metal Wire Cloth, Inc., 1975-88; pres. Holyoke Wire Cloth Co., 1975-88, Multi-Wedge Corp., 1976-88, United-Holyoke Corp., 1980-86; pres., chief exec. officer Liquid-Solids Separation Corp., 1988-93, dir., 1988-96; retired; bd. dirs. Lewis Corp.; chmn. Phillips Steel Fabricators, Inc., 1989-93. Chmn. bd. Lucas Milhaupt, Inc., Cudahy, Wis., 1967-75. Served with USNR, 1943-46, 51-53. Mem. Am. Mgmt. Assn., Nat. Indsl. Conf. Bd., Am. Inst. Mining and Metall. Engrs., Tau Beta Pi, Kappa Delta Rho. Republican. Conglist. Clubs: Landings Club (Savannah, Ga.), Cornell of N.Y. Home: 9 Springdale Ln Savannah GA 31411

PEER, LARRY HOWARD, literature educator; b. Ogden, Utah, Jan. 2, 1942; s. Howard Harvey and Edna Celina (Baron) P.; m. Janet Priday; 9 children. BA, Brigham Young U., 1963, MA, 1965; PhD, U. Md., 1969. From asst. to assoc. prof. U. Ga., Athens, 1968-75; assoc. prof. Brigham Young U., Provo, Utah, 1975-78, prof., 1978—; acting head dept. comparative lit. U. Ga., Athens, 1973-74, Brigham Young U., Provo, 1978-81; pres. Western Regional Honors Coun., 1978-79; exec. dir. Am. Conf. on Romanticism, 1992—. Author: Beyond Haworth, 1984, The Reasonable Romantic, 1986, The Romantic Manifesto, 1988. Mem. MLA, Am. Comparative Lit. Assn. (exec. officer 1988-94), Am. Soc. for Aesthetics, Rocky Mountain Soc. for Aesthetics (pres. 1986-87), Internat. Byron Soc., Internat. Brontë Soc. Mem. LDS Ch. Avocation: travel. Office: Brigham Young U Comparative Lit Dept Provo UT 84602

PEERCE, LARRY, film director; b. Bronx, N.Y.; s. Jan Peerce. Dir.: One Potato, Two Potato, 1964, The Incident, 1967, Goodbye Columbus, 1969, The Sporting Club, 1971, A Separate Peace, 1972, Ash Wednesday, 1973, The Other Side of the Mountain, 1975, Two Minute Warning, 1976, The Other Side of the Mountain-Part II, 1978, The Bell Jar, 1979, Why Would I Lie?, 1980, Love Child, 1982, Hard to Hold, 1984, Wired, 1989; TV films include A Stranger Who Looks Like Me, 1974, I Take These Men, 1983, Love Lives On, 1985, The Fifth Missile, 1986, Prison for Children, 1987, Elvis and Me, 1988, The Court-Martial of Jackie Robinson, 1990, Murder at the PTA Luncheon, 1990, A Woman Named Jackie, 1991, Child of Rage, 1992, Poisoned by Love: The Kern County Murders, 1993, A Burning Passion: The Margaret Mitchell Story, 1994, An Element of Truth, 1995, The Abduction, 1996, Christmas Everyday, 1996, Love Struck, 1997; miniseries include Queenie, 1987, The Neon Empire, 1989, Heaven and Hell: Part III of the North and the South, 1993. Office: 12700 Ventura Blvd Studio City CA 91604-2469 also: 350 Fifth Ave Ste 3505 New York NY 10118 also: Agy Performing Arts 9000 Sunset Blvd Ste 1200 Los Angeles CA 90012*

PEERMAN, DEAN GORDON, magazine editor; b. Mattoon, Ill., Apr. 25, 1931; s. Staley Jacob and Irene (Monen) P. B.S. with highest distinction, Northwestern U., 1953; postgrad., Cornell U., 1953-54; B.D., Yale, 1959; D.D., Kalamazoo Coll., 1967. With Christian Century Found., 1959—; copy editor Christian Century mag., 1959-61, assoc. editor, 1961-64, mng. editor, 1964-81, exec. editor, 1981-85, sr. editor, 1985—. Author: (with M.E. Marty) Pen-ultimates, 1963, (with Marty, L.M. Delloff, J.M. Wall) A Century of The Century, 1987; editor: Frontline Theology, 1967; co-editor: (with Marty) New Theology 1-10, 1964-73, A Handbook of Christian Theologians, 1965, enlarged edit., 1984, (with Alan Geyer) Theological Crossings, 1971. Contbr.: Chile: Under Military Rule, 1974. Active Chgo. community theater groups. Recipient award for distinction in lay ministry within the church Yale Div. Sch., 1995. Mem. ACLU, Fellowship of Reconciliation, Amnesty Internat., Clergy and Laity Concerned, Phi Beta Kappa. Democrat. Baptist. Office: Christian Century Mag 407 S Dearborn St Chicago IL 60605-1106

PEERS, MICHAEL GEOFFREY, archbishop; b. Vancouver, B.C., Can., July 31, 1934; s. Geoffrey Hugh and Dorothy Enid (Mantle) P.; m. Dorothy Elizabeth Bradley, June 29, 1963; children: Valerie Anne Leslie, Richard Christopher Andre, Geoffrey Stephen Arthur. Zert.dolm., U. Heidelberg, Germany, 1955; BA, U. B.C., Vancouver, 1956; Licentiate in Theology, Trinity Coll., Toronto, Ont., 1959, DD (hon.), 1977; DD (hon.), St. John's Coll., Winnipeg, Man., 1981, Wycliffe Coll., Toronto, 1987, Kent U., Canterbury, Eng., 1988, Montreal Diocesan Coll., Que., Can., 1989, Coll. of Emmanuel and St. Chad, Sask., Can., 1990, Thorneloe U., 1991; DCL (hon.), Bishop's U., Lennoxville, Que., 1993. Ordained to ministry Anglican Ch. as deacon, 1959, as priest, 1960, consecrated bishop, 1977. Asst. curate St. Thomas Ch., Ottawa, 1959-61; chaplain U. Ottawa, 1961-66; rector St. Bede's Ch., Winnipeg, 1966-72, St. Martin's Ch., Winnipeg, 1972-74; dean of Qu'Appelle, Regina, Sask., 1974-77; bishop Qu'Appelle, 1977-82, archbishop, 1982-86; instr. Ottawa Tchrs. Coll., 1962-66, St. Paul's High Sch., Winnipeg, 1967-69; pres. Coun. Coll. Emmanuel, St. Chad, Saskatoon, 1979-83.

PEET, CHARLES D., JR., lawyer; b. N.Y.C., Sept. 3, 1935; s. Charles D. and Margaret Louise (Sherman) P.; children: Alisa, Amanda. B.A., Yale U., 1957; J.D., Harvard U., 1960. Bar: N.Y. 1962. Assoc. Milbank, Tweed, Hadley & McCloy, N.Y.C., 1960-68, ptnr., 1969—. Mem. ABA, N.Y. State Bar Assn., Assn. Bar N.Y.C., Internat. Bar Assn. Office: Milbank Tweed Hadley & McCloy 1 Chase Manhattan Plz New York NY 10005-1401

PEET, HOWARD DAVID, English language and literature educator, writer; b. Fargo, N.D., Oct. 7, 1930; s. Howard Morrison and Beatrice Katherine (Gunness) P.; m. Jacquelyn Marie Hegge, June 20, 1953; children: Terry H., Pamela Peet Astrup. BA, Macalaster Coll., St. Paul, 1956; BS, Moorhead State U., 1965, MS, 1965; postgrad., U. Minn., 1970. Ride trumpet Ray Palmer Orch., Chgo., 1950-52; lead trumpet Kliff Riggs Orch., Omaha, 1954-55; ins. investigator Retail Credit Assn., St. Paul, 1955-60; prof. English N.D. State U., Fargo, 1965-86, prof. emeritus, 1986—, dir. concentrated approach program, 1970-80. Author and co-author 65 books including The English Book: A Complete Course, 1980, Wordskill for The Micro Computer, 1982, MacMillan Spelling, 1983, Vocabulary for College Reading and Writing, 1984, Linguistics For Teachers, 1993, Wordskills, 1993, (audio tapes) Skits to Success, 1997. Pres. Young Reps., Wilkin county, Minn., 1970's, PTA, Barnesville, Minn., 1970's; treas. Presbyn. Ch., Deerhorn, Minn., 1970's. With USN, 1952-54, Korea. Named Red River Valley Educator, Red River Valley Heritage Soc., 1992. Mem. Nat. Coun. Tchrs. English, Writers of the Purple Sage, Am. Legion, La. Soc. Des 40 Hommes Et 8 Chevauk. Avocations: music, reading, traveling, writing poetry. Home: 25 Prairiewood Xing Fargo ND 58103-4667

PEET, PHYLLIS IRENE, women's studies educator; b. Winnipeg, Man., Can., Mar. 3, 1943; came to the U.S., 1948; d. Harold Parsons and Gladys Mae (Riley) Harrison; m. Thomas Peter Richman, June 14, 1963 (div. 1969); m. Charles Francis Peet, Sept. 9, 1972. BA in Art, Calif. State U., Northridge, 1972; MA in Art History, U. Calif., L.A., 1976, PhD in Art History, 1987. Sec. L.A. County Supr. Kenneth Hahn, 1960-68; assoc. in art history L.A. County Mus. Art, 1974-75; asst. dir., curator Grunwald Ctr. for the Graphic Arts, U. Calif., L.A., 1975-78; Am. art scholar High Mus. Art, Atlanta, 1984-90; instr. women's studies Monterey (Calif.) Peninsula Coll., 1986—, dir., instr. women's programs/women's studies, 1989—; dirs.' adv. com. The Art Mus. of Santa Cruz County, 1981-84, 89-94; vis. lectr. Calif. State U., Fresno, fall 1984; program coord. conf. Inst. for Hist. Study, San Francisco, 1987; lectr. bd. studies in art U. Calif. Santa Cruz, 1991-94. Author, co-curator, editor, compiler: (book and exhbn.) The American Personality: The Artist Illustrator of Life in the United States, 1860-1930, 1976; author, curator: (book and exhbn.) American Women of the Etching Revival, 1988; co-author: American Paintings in the High Museum of Art, 1994; contbr. articles to profl. jours. Vol., activist Dem. Party, L.A., 1960-66, Peace and Freedom Party, L.A., 1967-71; vol. Dem. Party Candidates, Santa Cruz, Calif., 1979-96, Santa Cruz Action Network, 1980-85; mem. nominating com. Girl Scouts of Am., Monterey Bay, 1991-93. Rockefeller Found. fellow U. Calif. L.A., 1978-79, 79-80, Dickson grantee U. Calif. L.A., 1981-82; recipient Women Helping Women award Soroptimists, Monterey and Carmel, Calif., 1991, 95, Allen Griffin for Excellence in Edn. award Cmty. Found. of Monterey County, 1993, Quality of Life award Econ. Devel. Corp., Monterey, 1994. Mem. NOW, AAUW, Nat. Women's Studies Assn., Inst. for Hist. Study, Western Assn. Women Historians, Women's Internat. League for Peace and Freedom, Monterey Bay Women's Caucus for Art (founder, bd. dirs. 1988-93). Avocations: print collecting, photography.

Office: Womens Programs Monterey Peninsula Coll 980 Fremont St Monterey CA 93940-4704

PEETE, RUSSELL FITCH, JR., aircraft appraiser; b. Memphis, June 15, 1920; s. Russell Fitch and Louise Gift (Edmondson) P.; m. Esther Eletha Mosley, Feb. 7, 1942 (dec. Jan. 1987); children: Miriam, Russell III, William; m. Margery May George, Sept. 2, 1988. BS in Aerospace Engring., Miss. State U., 1942. Dredge hand U.S. Corp. Engrs., West Memphis, Ark., 1937; rodman U.S. Corp. Engrs., Mobile, Ala., 1939; rsch. engr. Chicago & Southern Airlines, Memphis, 1941-51; tech. sales rep. Lockheed Corp., Burbank, Calif., 1951-82; ops. analyst Flying Tiger Line, L.A., 1982; dir. sales engring. Cammacorp, El Segundo, Calif., 1982-85, Anacorp, Marina Del Rey, Calif., 1987-89; aviation cons. Avcons, Tucson, 1993—; aircraft appraiser Nat. Aircraft Appraiser Assn., Tucson, 1993—; cons. Avcons, Camarillo, Calif., 1985-86. Sec. Conejo Y's Mens Clubs, Thousand Oaks, Calif., 1960-63. With U.S. Army, 1944-46. Mem. Soc. Automotive Engrs., Exptl. Aircraft Assn., Aircraft Owners and Pilots Assn., Confederate Air Force, Internat. Aerobatic Club. Republican. Lutheran. Avocations: flying, photography, golf, travel. Office: 63652 E Squash Blossom Ln Tucson AZ 85739-1263

PEETE, WILLIAM PETTWAY JONES, surgeon; b. Warrenton, N.C., Mar. 29, 1921; s. Charles Henry and Lucy Pettway (Jones) P.; m. Mary Frances Hart, Feb. 7, 1960; 1 child, Marianna Jones. AB, U. N.C., 1942; MD, Harvard U., 1947. Fellow in pathology Peter Bent Brigham Hosp., Boston, 1943-44; house officer Mass. Gen. Hosp., Boston, 1947-54; instr. Harvard U. Med. Sch., 1953-55; asst. to dean Duke U. Med. Sch., Durham, N.C., 1955-63; asst. prof., asso. prof. Duke U. Med. Sch., 1955-64, prof. surgery, 1964-92, prof. emeritus surgery, 1992—; bd. dirs. Nations Bank, Durham; cons. Physicians for Peace, Am. Family Life, Inc., Rsch. Triangle Park, Batelle Corp., Patient Problems. Moseley fellow, 1954-55. Mem. N.C., Surg. Assn., So. Surg. Assn., So. Surg. Club, Soc. for Surgery of Alimentary Tract.

PEFLEY, NORMAN GORDON, financial analyst; b. Eugene, Oreg., Dec. 15, 1955; s. Gordon Vergne Pefley and Jean Pefley (Lee) Hawley; m. Emma Ginete Lacuesta, July 5, 1986. BA, U. Calif., Davis, 1977; MA, Johns Hopkins U., 1979; MBA, U. Chgo., 1981. CFA. Rsch. analyst Chgo. Bd. Options Exch., 1981-83; sr. fin. analyst Bank of Am., San Francisco, 1983-89, v.p., 1989—; referee Jour. Futures Market, N.Y.C., 1984-87. Mem. Am. Fin. Assn., Am. Econ. Assn., Assn. for Investment Mgmt. and Rsch., The Security Analysts of San Francisco, Commonwealth Club of Calif., Toastmasters Internat., Phi Beta Kappa, Delta Phi Alpha, Omicron Delta Epsilon. Avocation: foreign languages.

PEGELS, C. CARL, management science and systems educator; b. Barendrecht, South Holland, Netherlands, Feb. 26, 1933; came to U.S., 1962, naturalized, 1968; s. Bertus and Adriana Maria (Denotter) P.; children—Janice Joy, Kevin Carl. BS in Mech. Engring., Detroit Inst. of Tech., 1961, MS, PhD; Mgmt., Purdue U., 1963, 66. Prodn. engr. Ford Motor, Windsor, Can., 1955-62; instr. Purdue U., W. Lafayette, Ind., 1962-66; prof. SUNY-Buffalo, 1966—; v.p. Ctr. for Mgmt. Systems, Buffalo, 1978-91. Author: Basic for Business, 1973, Health Care & Elderly, 1980, Japan vs The West, 1984, Q.C. in Health Care, 1985, Decision Support Systems for Production and Operations Management, 1986, Management and Industry in China, 1987, Strategic Management for Hospitals and Health Care Corporations, 1987, Health Care and the Older Citizen, 1988, Decision Support Systems for Management Science/Operations Research, 1989, Strategic Information Systems, 1993. Krannert fellow, 1966; Krannert scholar Purdue U., 1963. Mem. Ops. Research Soc. Am., Inst. Mgmt. Sci., Am. Inst. Decision Scis. Avocations: long distance runner. Home: 63 Ruskin Rd Buffalo NY 14226-4255 Office: Sch of Mgmt Suny At Buffalo Buffalo NY 14214-3001

PEGIS, ANTON GEORGE, English educator; b. Milw., Feb. 21, 1920; s. George Anton and Eugenia (Stathas) P.; m. Harriet Louise Stevens, June 1, 1949; children: Stefani Elizabeth, Penelope Eugenia. A.B., Western State Coll. Colo., 1949; M.A., Denver U., 1951, Ph.D., 1956. Jr. engr. N. Shore Gas Co., Waukegan, Ill., 1946-47; instr. Ft. Lewis Coll., 1952-53; process control technician Gates Rubber Co., Denver, 1953-54; prof. English Colo. Sch. Mines, Golden, 1954—; asst. to pres. Colo. Sch. Mines, 1964-68, v.p. for devel., 1968-73, v.p. for external affairs, 1973-74, prof. English, 1975-82, prof. emeritus, 1982—; cons. U.S. Bur. Mines, Office of Mineral Reports, Washington, Regional Tng. Center, Office of Personnel Mgmt., Denver, 1983, CSC, San Francisco, 1974-94. Author: Social Theory in the Novels of Ford Madox Ford, 1956, An Intensive Course in English for Foreign Engineering Students, 1957, Humanism and the Practical Order, 1964, Excellence and the Odyssean Philosophy, 1965, Platonism in the Renaissance Lyric, 1965, Education for Leadership, 1966, Totality in Engineering Education, 1968, Course Recommendations for the Resource Engineer, 1968, Encroachment of Competing Land Uses on Mineral Development, 1976. Chmn. United Way Fund; sec. Colo. Sch. Mines Found.; pres. Roland Valley Civic Assn., 1974-75. Served with AUS, 1940-46; maj. AUS, ret. Appointed hon. disting. sgt. 121st Field Arty. Regiment, 1988. Named Outstanding Prof., Tau Beta Pi, 1963, Hon. Colonel 115th Engring. Rgt., 1988; recipient Outstanding Prof. award Colo. Sch. Mines, 1976; Amoco Found. awards. Mem. Golden C. of C. (pres. 1968), Am. Soc. Engring. Edn. (chmn. Rocky Mountain sect.), Am. Alumni Council (chmn. dist. VII 1971-72), Modern Lang. Assn., Blue Key, Theta Chi, Alpha Psi Omega. Home: 415 Scenic Ct Golden CO 80401-2533

PEHL, GLEN EUGENE, risk and insurance consultant; b. Woodford, Wis., Aug. 10, 1932; s. Henry Earnest and Ella Viola Pehl; m. Mazie Lee McCrackin, July 9, 1960; children: Keith, Tracey. BSBA, Ala. Poly. Inst., 1958. Indsl. account rep. Am. Mut. Liability Ins. Co., Charlotte, N.C., 1958-60, br. sales mgr., 1960-66, dist. sales mgr., 1967-91; chmn., pres., treas. Indsl. Ins. Mgmt. Corp. and Corp. Life Cons., Inc., Charlotte, 1991-92; vice chmn. McNeery Ins. Consulting Inc., Charlotte, 1992-97, pres., CEO, 1992-95, chmn., 1995-97; dir. N.C. Self-Insurers Assn., 1976-80; lectr. Trustee Alexander Children's Home, Charlotte, 1982-87, treas., bd. dirs., 1992-95, chmn. bd. dirs., 1995-97. With USAF, 1951-55. Decorated Nat. Def. medal. Mem. N.C. Citizens Assn., Charlotte City Club, Cedarwood Country Club, Masons. Republican. Presbyterian. Office: McNeery Ins Consulting Inc PO Box 220926 Charlotte NC 28222

PEHLKE, ROBERT DONALD, materials and metallurgical engineering educator; b. Ferndale, Mich., Feb. 11, 1933; s. Robert William and Florence Jenny (McLaren) P.; m. Julie Anne Kehoe, June 2, 1956; children: Robert Donald, Elizabeth Anne, David Richard. B.S. in Engring, U. Mich., 1955; S.M., Mass. Inst. Tech., 1958, Sc.D., 1960; postgrad., Tech. Inst., Aachen, Ger., 1956-57. Registered profl. engr., Mich. Mem. faculty U. Mich., 1960—, prof. materials sci. and engring., 1968—, chmn. dept., 1973-84; cons. to metall. industry; vis. prof. Tohoku U., Sendai, Japan, 1994. Author: Unit Processes of Extractive Metallurgy, 1973; Editor, contbr. numerous articles to profl. jours. Pres. Ann Arbor Amateur Hockey Assn., 1977-79. NSF fellow, 1955-56; Fulbright fellow, 1956-57. Fellow Am. Soc. Metals (mem. tech. divs. bd. 1982-84, sec. metals acad. com. 1977), Minerals, Metals and Materials Soc. of AIME (Gold Medal award extractive metallurgy div. 1976); mem. NSPE, Iron and Steel Soc. of AIME (Disting. life mem., chmn. process tech. div. 1976-77, dir. 1976-79, Howe meml. lectr. 1980), Germany, London, Japan Socs. Iron and Steel, Am. Foundrymen's Soc., Am. Soc. Engring. Edn., N.Y. Acad. Sci., Sigma Xi, Tau Beta Pi, Alpha Sigma Mu (pres. 1977-78). Home: 9 Regent Dr Ann Arbor MI 48104-1738 Office: U Mich Materials Sci & Engring Dow Bldg 2300 Hayward St Rm 2146B Ann Arbor MI 48109-2136

PEI, IEOH MING, architect; b. Canton, China, Apr. 26, 1917; came to U.S., 1935, naturalized, 1954; s. Tsu Yee Pei and Lien Kwun Chwong; m. Eileen Loo, June 20, 1942; children: T'ing Chung, Chien Chung, Li Chung, Liane. BArch, MIT, 1940; MArch, Harvard U., 1946; DFA (hon.), U. Pa., 1970, Rensselaer Poly. Inst., 1978, Carnegie Mellon U., 1980, U. Mass., 1980, Brown U., 1982, NYU, 1983, Dartmouth Coll., 1991, Northeastern U.; LLD, Chinese U., Hong Kong, 1970, Pace U.; LHD, Columbia U., 1980, U. Colo., 1982, U. Rochester, 1982, U. Hong Kong, 1990, Am. U., Paris, 1990. Practice architecture N.Y.C., 1939-42; asst. prof. Harvard Grad. Sch. Design, 1945-48; dir. archtl. div. Webb & Knapp, Inc., 1948-55; with Pei Cobb Freed & Partners (formerly I.M. Pei & Ptnrs., I.M. Pei & Assos.), N.Y.C., 1955-96; now ind. architect N.Y.C., 1996—. Prin. projects include Mile High Ctr., Denver, Nat. Ctr. Atmospheric Rsch., Boulder, Colo., Dallas City Hall, John Fitzgerald Kennedy Libr., Boston, Can. Imperial Bank Commerce Complex, Toronto, Overseas Chinese Banking Corp. Ctr., Singapore, Dreyfus Chemistry Bldg. MIT, East-West Ctr. U. Hawaii, Honolulu, Mellon Art Ctr. and Choate Rosemary Hall Sci. Ctr., Wallingford, Conn., Univ. Plz. NYU, Johnson Mus. Art Cornell U., Ithaca, N.Y., Washington Sq. East, Phila, Everson Mus. Art, Syracuse, N.Y., Nat. Gallery Art, East Bldg., Washington, Wilmington Tower, Raffles City, Singapore, West Wing Mus. Fine Arts, Boston, expansion and modernization of Louvre Mus., Paris, Morton H. Meyerson Symphony Ctr., Dallas, MIT Arts and Media Ctr., Jacob K. Javits Conv. Ctr., N.Y.C., Fragrant Hill Hotel, Beijing, Tex. Commerce Tower, Houston, Bank of China, Hong Kong, Creative Artists Agy., Beverly Hills, Calif., Guggenheim Pavilion, Mount Sinai Med. Ctr., N.Y.C., Rock n' Roll Hall of Fame and Mus., Cleve., Mus. Modern Art, Athens, Greece, Miho Mus. of Art, Shiga, Japan, Bilbao (Spain) Estuary Project, Four Seasons Hotel, N.Y.C., others; planning projects include S.W. Washington Redevelopment Plan, Govt. Ctr. Redevelopment Plan, Boston, Oklahoma City Downtown Redevelopment Plan, Bedford Stuyvesant Super Block, Bklyn., master plan Columbia U. Mem. Nat. Def. Rsch. Com., Princeton, N.J., 1943-45, Nat. Coun. Humanities, 1966-70, Nat. Coun. on Arts, 1981-84. MIT traveling fellow, 1940, Wheelwright fellow Harvard, 1951; Thomas Jefferson Meml. medal for Architecture, 1976, gold medal for architecture Am. Acad. Arts and Letters, 1979, Nat. Arts Club Gold medal of honor, 1981, Mayor's award of Honor for Art and Culture, N.Y.C., 1981, La Grande Medaille D'or L'Académie d'Architecture, 1981, Pritzker Architecture prize, 1983, Medal of Liberty, 1986, Medal of French Legion of Honor, 1988, Nat. Medal of Art, 1988, Praemium Imperiale Japan Art Assn., 1989, UCLA Gold medal, 1990, Colbert Found. first award for Excellence, 1991, Excellence 2000 award, 1991, Freedom medal, 1993. Fellow AIA (Medal of Honor N.Y. chpt. 1963, Gold Medal 1979); hon. fellow ASID; mem. Nat. Inst. Arts and Letters (Arnold Brunner award 1961), Am. Acad. Arts and Scis., Am. Acad. and Inst. Arts and Letters (chancellor 1978-80), Royal Inst. Brit. Architects, NAD, Urban Design Council. Office: care Pei Cobb Freed & Ptnrs 600 Madison Ave New York NY 10022-1615

PEIFFER, RANDEL AARON, agricultural sciences educator, researcher; b. Ligonier, Pa., Aug. 4, 1944; s. Tony and Emma E. (Leighty) P. BS, Delaware Valley Coll., 1968; MS, Pa. State U., 1970, PhD, 1976. Rsch. asst. prof. Del. State U., Dover, 1986; asst. prof. Del. State Coll., Dover, 1986-93, assoc. prof., 1993—; vis. prof. Farmers Home Adminstrn. Advisor carpentry adv. com. Vocat. Tech. Sch., Kent County, Del., 1987—; mem. Del. Agr. Mus., Dover, 1986—; mem. tech. com. NE-SARE, 1994—. Recipient First Pl. Sci. Poster in Plant and Soil Sci., 9th Biennial Rsch. Symposium, Assn. Rsch. Dirs. 1890 Land-Grant Colls. and Univs., Atlanta, 1992—. Mem. Am. Soc. Agronomy, Crop Sci. Soc. Am., Fraternal Order Police, Silver Lake Fishing Club (editor newsletter Dover chpt. 1984—). Achievements include research inforage management and utilization, biological control of gypsy moth in urban forest and crop ecology. Office: Del State U Dept Agr Natural Resources Dover DE 19901

PEIMBERT, MANUEL, astronomer; b. Mexico City, June 9, 1941; s. Gonzalo Peimbert and Catalina Sierra; m. Silvia Torres, Aug. 25, 1962; children: Antonio, Mariana. BS, U. Nacional Autónoma de Mex., 1962; PhD in Astronomy, U. Calif., Berkeley, 1967. Postdoctoral fellow U. Calif., Berkeley, 1967-68; prof. astronomy U. Nacional Autónoma de Mex., Mexico City, 1968—. Author over 100 research articles, 1960—; editor Revista Mexicana de Fisica, 1981-85. Recipient Guillaume Budé medal Coll. de France, Paris, 1974, Nat. Prize of Scis. Govt. of Mex., 1981. Fellow Third World Acad. Scis.; mem. NAS (fgn. assoc.), Am. Astron. Soc. (councilor 1975-78), Internat. Astron. Union (v.p. 1982-88), Royal Astron. Soc. U.K. (fgn. assoc.), Acad. de la Investigacion Cientifica (Scis. prize 1971), Soc. Mexicana de Fisica. Office: Inst de Astronomia, APDO Postal 70-264, 04510 Mexico City Mexico

PEIPERL, ADAM, kinetic sculptor, photographer; b. Sosnowiec, Poland, June 4, 1935; came to U.S., 1953, naturalized, 1958; s. Jacob and Fanny (Alster) P.; m. Martha Rose Dorf, June 15, 1958; children: Maury, Laurence, Linda. Grad., Cours Complémentaire Général, Paris, 1952; B.S. in Chemistry, George Washington U., 1957; postgrad., Pa. State U., 1959. Cons. in Russian sci. lit. Libr. Congress, Washington, 1959-61, 66-67; chemist Nat. Bur. Standards, Washington, 1961-63; sci. translator Am. Inst. Physics, N.Y.C., 1973-94, Plenum Pub., 1993—. One-man shows include Balt. Mus. Art, 1969, Pa. Acad. Fine Arts, 1969, Marlborough Gerson Gallery, N.Y.C., 1969, Smithsonian Mus. History and Tech., 1972, Electric Gallery, Toronto, Ont., Can., 1975, Phila. Art Alliance, 1978; group shows include Washington Gallery Modern Art, 1968, Corcoran Gallery Art, 1968, Kent State U., McKay Art Inst., San Antonio, 1969, NASA Manned Spacecraft, Houston, 1970-71, Nat. Mus. Am. Art, 1972-82, Meml. Art Gallery, U. Rochester, 1978, Foster Harmon Galleries Am. Art, Sarasota, Fla., 1982-83, Artworks Gallery, Santa Barbara, Calif., 1989; represented in permanent collections Pa. Acad. Fine Arts, Mus. Boymans-van Beuningen, Rotterdam, The Netherlands, John F. Kennedy Ctr. for Performing Arts, Hirshhorn Mus. and Sculpture Garden, Kreeger Mus.; made first kinetic polarized-light sculpture in water, 1968; designed polarized-light kaleidoscope interiors, 1989; kaleidoscope photographs pub. on book covers for Prentice-Hall/Simon & Schuster, 1991, 92, 97, Mayfield Pub. Co., 1992, 94, Modern Curriculum Press, 1993; poster for Elektra Entertainment Deee-Lite, 1990 (reproduced in book 1995); art for Andersen Consulting brochure, 1995, Time-Life Book-of-the-Month brochures, 1995—; collaborated with choreographer Maida Rust Withers on UTAH * Spirit Place * Spirit Planet * Tukuhnikivatz, 1996 (multimedia dance theater); photography represented by The Stock Market Photo Agy.; collaborated with Chesnik Kaleidoscopes on "Polaris", 1997. Home: 1135 Loxford Ter Silver Spring MD 20901-1130

PEIPERT, JAMES RAYMOND, journalist; b. Alton, Ill., Nov. 15, 1942; s. Lawrence George and Virginia Pauline (Sieve) P.; m. Mary Ellen Finney, Aug. 1, 1970; children: Benjamin, Matthew, Thomas. BA, So. Ill. U., 1965. Reporter, editor AP, Chgo., 1965-68, N.Y.C., 1968-70; corr. AP, Moscow, 1970-74, London, 1974-80; news editor AP, Johannesburg, South Africa, 1980-81; East Africa bur. chief AP, Nairobi, Kenya, 1981-86; nat./fgn. editor Fort Worth Star-Telegram, 1986—. With U.S. Army, 1965-67. Roman Catholic. Avocations: bicycling, maintaining 1967 Mustang, reading. Office: Fort Worth Star Telegram PO Box 1870 Fort Worth TX 76101-1870

PEIRANO, LAWRENCE EDWARD, civil engineer; b. Stockton, Calif., May 13, 1929; s. Frank Lloyd and Esther Marie (Carigiet) P.; m. Mary Ellen Alabaster, July 26, 1952; children: Thomas Lawrence, Ellen Marie. BSCE, U. Calif., Berkeley, 1951, MSCE, 1952. Registered profl. engr., Calif., Nev.; diplomate Am. Acad. Environ. Engrs. Assoc. civil engr. Calif. Div. Water Resources, 1952-53; with Kennedy Engrs., Inc., San Francisco, 1955-94, project mgr., 1960-79, v.p., chief environ. engr., 1974-79; dir. ops. Kennedy/Jenks Engrs., Inc., San Francisco, 1979-86; sr. v.p., regional mgr. Kennedy/Jenks/Chilton, Inc., San Francisco, 1986-90; exec. v.p., chief tech. officer Kennedy/Jenks Cons., Inc. (formerly Kennedy Engrs., Inc.), San Francisco, 1990-94, also bd. dirs., chmn. bd., 1972-94; ret., 1994; spl. lectr. san. engring. U. Calif., Berkeley, 1976. Served in U.S. Army, 1953-55, Korea, Okinawa. James Monroe McDonald scholar, 1950-51; recipient Trustees' citation U. Calif., Berkeley, 1996. Fellow ASCE (life); mem. Water Environ. Fedn., U. Calif. Alumni Assn., Sierra Club, Tau Beta Pi, Chi Epsilon. Republican. Roman Catholic. Home: 3435 Black Hawk Rd Lafayette CA 94549-2326
Focus on serving clients and rewards will follow.

PEIRCE, BROOKE, English language educator; b. Washington, Jan. 2, 1922; s. Charles Brooke, Jr. and Nancy Ley (Bass) P.; m. Carol Emily Marshall, July 12, 1952. B.A., U.Va., 1943; M.A., Harvard U., 1947, Ph.D., 1954. Teaching fellow Harvard U., 1948-51; instr. English U. Va., 1951-54; mem. faculty Goucher Coll., 1954-85, prof. English, 1966-85, prof. emeritus, 1985—, chmn. dept. English and dramatic arts, 1964-69, 72-75, chmn. faculty humanities, 1964-66, 72-73, 79; vis. prof. English, SUNY Coll.-Oswego, 1985-87; lectr. Villa Julie Coll., 1989—. Author: (with Carol Peirce) Introduction to English Literature, 2 vols., 1954. Treas. Edgar Allan Poe Soc., Balt., 1959-66, mem. bd., 1959—. Served with U.S. Army, 1943-45. Nat. Endowment for Humanities fellow, 1977-78; recipient Disting. Tchr. award, 1979. Mem. Modern Lang. Assn., Raven Soc. of U. Va., Classical Assn., Phi Beta Kappa. Democrat. Home: 705 Warren Rd Cockeysville Hunt Valley MD 21030-2824

PEIRCE, CAROL MARSHALL, English educator; b. Columbia, Mo., Feb. 1, 1922; d. Charles Hamilton and Helen Emily (Davault) Williams; m. Brooke Peirce, July 12, 1952. AB, Fla. State U., 1942; MA, U. Va., 1943; PhD, Harvard U., 1951. Head English dept. Fairfax Hall, Waynesboro, Va., 1943-44; instr. English Cedar Crest Coll., Allentown, Pa., 1944-46, Harvard U., 1952-53; asst. dean instrn. Radcliffe Coll., Cambridge, 1950-53; head English extension home study U. Va., Charlottesville, 1953-54; asst. dir. admissions Goucher Coll., Towson, Md., 1956-62; prof. English and comm. design U. Balt., 1968—, chmn. dept., 1968-94, gen. edn. core coord., 1985-87, Disting. teaching prof. Coll. Liberal Arts, 1981-82, chmn. humanities div., 1972-79; gen. edn. dir., 1995-97; chmn. bd. New Poets Series, 1975—; vis. scholar Lucy Cavendish Coll., U. Cambridge, Eng., 1977-78; co-coord. On Miracle Ground: The Internat. Lawrence Durrell Conf., 1980, 82, 90; co-coord. conf. Evermore! Celebrating the 150th Anniversary of Edgar Allan Poe's "Raven," 1995. Author: (with Brooke Peirce) A Study of Literary Types and an Introduction to English Literature from Chaucer to the Eighteenth Century, 1954, A Study of Literary Types and an Introduction to English Literature from the Eighteenth Century to the Present, 1954; editor: (with Lawrence Markert) On Miracle Ground: Second Lawrence Durrell Conference Proceedings, 1984; guest editor: (with Ian S. MacNiven) Lawrence Durrell Issue, Parts 1 and II, Twentieth Century Literature, Fall, Winter, 1987; contbr. essays to: Poe and Our Times, 1986, Critical Essays on Lawrence Durrell, 1987, Into the Labyrinth: Essays on the Art of Lawrence Durrell, 1989, On Miracle Ground: Essays on the Fiction of Lawrence Durrell, 1990, Dictionary of Literary Biography Yearbook, 1990, St. James Reference Guide to English Literature, 1991, Poe's Pym: Critical Explorations, 1992, Selected Essays on the Humor of Lawrence Durrell, 1993, Lawrence Durrell: Comprehending The Whole, 1994, D.H. Lawrence: The Cosmic Adventure, 1996, Anais Nin: A Book of Mirrors, 1996, others; assoc editor: Deus Loci: The Lawrence Durrell Jour., 1990-92, co-editor, 1993—. McGregor fellow, DuPont fellow U. Va., 1943; Harvard tutor, Anne Radcliffe traveling fellow Harvard U., 1951. Mem. MLA, Edgar Allan Poe Soc. of Balt. (bd. dirs. 1973-89, pres. 1989—), Lawrence Durrell Soc. (nat. pres. 1980-82, internat. pres. 1994—), Md. Assn. Depts. English, Phi Beta Kappa, Chi Delta Phi, Phi Alpha theta, Phi Kappa Phi. Home: 705 Warren Rd Cockeysville Hunt Valley MD 21030-2824 Office: Univ Balt Dept Lang Lit and Comm Dsgn Baltimore MD 21201

PEIRCE, DONALD OLUF, elementary education educator; b. Boulder, Colo., Mar. 5, 1939; s. James Girdwood and Ruth Julia (Wagner) P.; m. Joyce Arleen Kovatch. BS, Temple U., 1971, MEd, 1978. Cert. elem. tchr., reading specialist, Pa. Remedial reading tchr. Bartram High Sch., Phila., 1975-80; piano, reading, English tchr. Locke Elem. Sch., Phila., 1981—. With USMCR, 1963-68. Mem. Del. Valley Reading Assn. Republican. Episcopalian. Avocations: music composition, piano, swimming, cinema, travel. Office: Locke Elementary School 46th & Haverford Ave Philadelphia PA 19139

PEIRCE, GEORGE LEIGHTON, airport administrator; b. Worcester, Mass., Mar. 9, 1933; s. George Leighton and Grace Hislop (McDougall) P.; m. Carolyn Janasy, Oct. 7, 1968; children: Jennifer Lindsey, Amanda Leighton. B.B.A., U. Mass., 1961. Supr. mgmt. engring. services Port Authority of N.Y. and N.J., 1961-69; airport mgr. Stewart Airport, Newburgh, N.Y., 1970; asst. mgr. LaGuardia Airport, Flushing, N.Y., 1970-75; gen. mgr. LaGuardia Airport, 1975-94; bd. dirs. Lighthouse, Inc., N.Y.C., 1989-94, Americas' Sail, Huntington, N.Y. Mem. Queens adv. bd. Salvation Army, 1980-94; chmn. adv. bd. Queens Lighthouse for Blind, 1980-94; bd. dirs., treas., vice chmn. OPSAIL; bd. dirs. Couri Found. Ridgefield, Conn. With USAF, 1954-58, Mass. Air N.G., 1959-61. Recipient Outstanding Community Svc. award Greater N.Y. Coun. Boy Scouts Am., 1978, Outstanding Pub. Svc. award Dept. Transp., 1986, Meritorious Pub. Svc. award USCG, 1986, Pub. Svc. award N.Y. Urban League, 1991, Disting. Svc. award Port Authority N.Y., N.J., 1992, George W. Hixson fellow award Kiwanis Internat., 1996. Mem. Queens C. of C., Coll. Aeronautics, Acad. Aero. (adv. bd.), 1976-94, LaGuardia Kiwanis (bd. dirs., past pres.), North Beach Club (past pres., bd. dirs.). Home: 392 Brett Rd Fairfield CT 06430-1720

PEIRCE, JOHN WENTWORTH, architect; b. Boston, Feb. 9, 1912; s. Thomas W. and Gabrielle (Dexter) P.; m. Grace Minot, June 27, 1934; children—Thomas W., Lucy (Mrs. David Scanlon III), John W. A.B. cum laude, Harvard, 1933; postgrad. Archtl. Sch., 1933-35; M.Arch., MIT, 1947. Individual practice architecture Boston, 1938-42; assoc. Shepley, Bulfinch, Richardson & Abbott, Boston, 1948-60; ptnr. Peirce & Pierce, Boston, 1960-71, Peirce Pierce & Kramer, 1971-75; Mem. Mass. Bd. Registration for Architects, 1954-59, chmn., 1957; mem. Mass. Insp.-Gen. Council, 1981-85. Prin. archtl. works include Shields Warren Radiation Lab, N.E. Deaconess Hosp., Boston, Trinity Episcopal Ch, Topsfield, Mass., Loeb Marine Lab, Woods Hole, Mass., Art/Music Bldg., St. Mark's Sch., Southboro, Mass. Chmn. Topsfield Conservation Commn., 1965-71; commr. Ipswich River Watershed Dist., 1968—, chmn., 1976-80; bd. dirs. Ipswich River Watershed Assn., 1976-87; trustee Essex County Greenbelt Assn., 1961-71, pres., 1966-77, dir., 1977-80, hon. dir., 1980—; trustee Trustees Pub. Reservations, 1966-83; bd. dirs. Plymouth County Wildlands Trust, 1973-79, 81-84, 87-95, trustee, 1984-87. Served to lt. comdr. USNR, 1942-46. Recipient Ann. Conservation award Mass. Trustees of Reservations, 1975, Open Space award Mass. Conservation Council, 1977, Conservation award Ipswich River Watershed Assn., 1984, Conservation award New Eng. Wildflower Soc., 1988. Fellow AIA; mem. Mass. Assn. Architects (pres. 1968), Boston Soc. Architects (v.p. 1968, pres. 1969). Clubs: Bournes Cove Yacht (Wareham, Mass.) (commodore 1966-68); St. Botolph (Boston). Home and Office: Witch Hill 9 Garden St Topsfield MA 01983-2401

PEIRCE, NEAL R., journalist; b. Phila., Jan. 5, 1932; s. J. Trevor and Miriam deS. (Litchfield) P.; m. Barbara von dem Bach-Zelewski, Apr. 18, 1959; children: Celia, Andrea, Trevor. B.A., Princeton U., 1954; postgrad., Harvard U., 1957-58. Legis. asst. Office of U.S. Rep. Silvio Conte of Mass., 1959; polit. editor Congl. Quar., 1960-69; co-founder, contbg. editor Nat. Jour., Washington, 1969—; cons. and commentator elections CBS News, 1962, 67-76, NBC News, 1964-66; lectr. in field; syndicated newspaper columnist Washington Post Writers Group, The Citistates Group; dir. Peirce-Phelps, Inc., Phila.; mem. faculty Salzburg (Austria) Seminar, 1980, 84, 97; 1st Weinberg prof. Princeton U.'s Woodrow Wilson Sch. Pub. and Internat. Affairs, 1992. Author: The People's President, 1968, 2d edit., 1981, The Megastates of America, 1972, The Pacific States of America, 1972, The Mountain States of America, 1972, The Great Plains States America, 1973, The Deep South States of America, 1974, The Border South States, 1975, The New England States, 1976, The Mid-Atlantic States of America, 1977, The Great Lakes States of America, 1980, The Book of America: Inside Fifty States Today, 1983, Citistates: How Urban America Can Prosper in A Competitive World, 1993, Breakthroughs: Recreating The American City, 1993; Corrective Capitalism, 1987; editor Peirce Report series on Citistate futures starting with Phoenix Republic and Gazette, 1987. Founder, chmn. S.W. Neighborhood Assembly and Cmty. Coun., Washington, 1963-65; mem. exec. com. Nat. Civic League, 1990-95; trustee German Marshall Fund of U.S., 1987—; adv. com. Trust for Pub. Land, 1984—, Nat. Acad. Pub. Adminstrn., 1992—, Alliance for Redesign of Govt., 1993—. With CIC, AUS, 1954-57. Fellow Woodrow Wilson Internat. Center Scholars, 1971-74. Mem. Newfound Lake Regional Assn. (v.p. 1989-92), Phi Beta Kappa. Episcopalian. Club: Federal City (Washington). Home and Office: 610 G St SW Washington DC 20024-2440

PEIRSON, GEORGE EWELL, film producer, art director, educator; b. L.A., May 16, 1957; s. Malcolm Alan and Beth (Wanlass) P. BFA, Art Ctr. Coll. of Design, Pasadena, Calif., 1986. Photographer Griffith Park Observatory, L.A., 1981-84; owner, art dir. Peirson to Peirson Studio, West Hills, Calif., 1983—; instr. Art Workshops, L.A., 1988-89, Learning Tree U., Chatsworth, Calif., 1990-93. Art dir., films include Valentine's Day, 1986, Private Demons, 1986, The Courtyard, 1987, Hope of the Future, Escape from Lethargia, 1988, Time Scrambler, 1988, Star Quest, 1988, Star Runner, 1989, The World of Early Bird, 1989, Dominic's Castle, 1991, The Deadly Avenger, 1991, Hell Comes to Frogtown II, 1991, The Minister's Wife, 1991, Eye of the Stranger, 1992, Showtime, 1992, Star Runners, 1992, Monty, 1992, Guyver, Dark Hero, 1993, Tiger Mask, The Star, 1994, Dragon Fury,

1994, Arizona Werewolf, 1994, Drifting School, 1994; prodr., films include Jurassic Women, 1994, Wolves Carnival, 1995, King of Hearts, 1995, Rollergator, 1995, Lord Protector, 1996, Lancelot: Guardian of Time, 1997. Mem. Assn. for Astron. Arts (bd. mem., v.p. 1987-89), Costumers Guild West, Assn. of Sci. Fiction and Fantasy Artists. Republican. Avocations: computers, skiing, running, bicycling, scuba diving. Office: Peirson to Peirson Studio 20022 Strathern St Winnetka CA 91306-2336

PEISER, JOHN GEORGE, accountant, consultant; b. Chgo., June 2, 1944; m. Liora Rappaport, June 29, 1969; children: Daniela Jacqui, Gary Dean. BSc, U. Witwatersrand, South Africa, 1965, BSc (hon.), 1969; M in Bus. Leadership, U. South Africa, Pretoria, 1977. CPA; cert. valuation analyst. Researcher Nat. Inst. for Pers. Rsch., Johannesburg, South Africa, 1966-69; various mgmt. positions Lindsay Saker, Johannesburg, South Africa, 1970-76, bd. dir. pers., 1976 -78; mgr. human resource planning & devel. Fox & Jacobs, Dallas, 1978-83, regional sales dir., 1984-85; pres. Sidran, Inc., Dallas, 1985-90; CPA, ptnr., exec. cons. Peiser & Peiser, CPAs, Dallas, 1990-93; ptnr., exec. cons. bus. valuations Goldin Peiser & Peiser, CPAs, L.L.P., Dallas, 1993—; Bd. dirs. Solomon Schechter Acad. Dallas, chmn., 1984-86. Bd. dirs. Shearith Israel Congregation, Dallas, 1983-86, Zionist Orgn. Am., Dallas; pres. Yavneh Acad. of Dallas, 1993—. Mem. AICPA, Am. Inst. Tng. and Devel., Nat. Assn. Cert. Valuation Analysts, Tex. Soc. CPA, Inst. Personnel Rsch. (branch chair, 1974-75). Avocations: reading, squash, tennis, bridge, travel. Office: Goldin Peiser & Peiser CPAs LLP 470 Signature Pl II 14785 Preston Rd Ste 470 Dallas TX 75240-7882

PEISER, ROBERT ALAN, financial executive; b. N.Y.C., Apr. 17, 1948; s. Donald Edward and Natalie Audrey (Phillips) P.; m. Kathleen Lorraine Reilly, Jan. 11, 1970; children: Karyn, Brian, Craig, Scott. BA, U. Pa., 1969; MBA, Harvard U., 1972. Dir. corp. fin. TWA, N.Y.C., 1972-77, sr. v.p. fin., CFO, 1983-86, exec. v.p. fin , CFO, 1994-96; treas. Hertz Corp., N.Y.C., 1977-80; staff v.p., treas. ops. RCA Corp., N.Y.C., 1980-81; v.p., treas., Trans World Corp., N.Y.C., 1982-83; sr. v.p., CFO ALC Comm. Corp., Birmingham, Mich., 1986-88; sr. v.p. fin., CFO Borman's Inc., Detroit, 1988-89; pres., CEO Orange-Co. Inc., Bartow, Fla., 1989-92; with Bahadur, Balen & Kazerski, Ltd., Southfield, Mich., 1992-94; vice chmn., CEO FoxMeyer Drug Co., Carrollton, Tex., 1996; pres., CEO Western Pacific Airlines, Colorado Springs, Colo., 1996—. Trustee Mich. chpt. Leukemia Soc. Am. Mem. Fin. Execs. Inst., Colo. Springs C. of C. (bd. dirs.), Birmingham Athletic Club, The Wyndgate Country Club. Home: 326 Lakewood Dr Bloomfield Hills MI 48304-3533 Office: 2864 S Circle Dr Ste 1100 Colorado Springs CO 80906-4114

PEIXOTO, JOSE ULYSSES, internist, researcher; b. Crato, Ceará, Brazil, Aug. 29, 1930; s. Adérito de Aquino Silva and Adelite Alencar Peixoto; m. Maria Isolda Teles Cartaxo, May 23, 1958; children: Jose Ulysses Peixoto Filho, Eunice Ulysséia Peixoto Maia, Jorge André Cartaxo Peixoto. 1st degree, State Coll. Goias, Brazil, 1942, postgrad., 1942-49; 2d degree, St. John Coll., Fortaleza, Brazil, 1949; postgrad., Fed. U., Recife, Brazil, 1955; Laurel, Cearense Med. Ctr., 1994. Med. resident St. Michael Hosp., Rio de Janeiro, 1956; intern St. Anthony Hosp., Iguatú, Ceará, 1957; founder Social Providence, Crato, Ceará, 1958-64; attendent St. Frances Hosp., Crato, 1958-69; founder St. Michael Hosp., Crato, 1967-93, pres., dir., 1983-93, internist, researcher, 1993—; founder Faculty of Law, Crato, 1977-78; lectr. faculty of medicine The Fed. U. of Ceará, 1976—. Recipient Good Svc. award Lyons Club, 1992. laurel Cearense Med. Ctr., 1994. Fellow Brazilian Med. Assn. (specialist); mem. AAAS, ACP, Brazilian Soc. Clin. Medicine (specialist), N.Y. Acad. Sci. Roman Catholic. Avocations: reading, walking in woods, cinema, farming.

PEKARSKY, MELVIN HIRSCH, artist; b. Chgo., Sept. 18, 1934; s. Abe and Inda (Levin) P. Student, Sch. of Art Inst., Chgo., 1951-52; B.A., Northwestern U., 1955, M.A., 1956. Faculty Northwestern U., 1955-56; faculty Kendall Coll., 1960-67, chmn. art dept., 1965-67; asst. dean Sch. Visual Arts, N.Y.C., 1967-68; assoc. dean Sch. Visual Arts, 1968-69; grad. faculty NYU, 1970-71; assoc. prof. art SUNY, Stony Brook, 1975-84, prof. art, 1984—; chmn. dept. SUNY, 1977-78, 84-89. One-man shows include Gimpel and Weitzenhoffer, N.Y.C., 1974, Lehigh U., 1975, Ball State U. Gallery, Muncie, Ind., 1975, G.W. Einstein Co., Inc., N.Y.C., 1975, 77, 78, 80, 81, 82, 84, 86, 88, 91, 95, 97, Hull Gallery, Washington, 1978, Centro Colombo-Americano, Bogotá, Colombia, 1980, 112 Greene St. Gallery, N.Y.C., 1980, 82, Marianne Deson Gallery, Chgo., 1987, Butler Inst. Am. Art, Youngstown, Ohio, 1990, The Mus. at Stony Brook, 1993; group shows include Chgo. Art Inst., 1966, Whitney Mus., N.Y.C., 1971, Bklyn. Mus., 1974, Cleve. Mus., 1978, Cooper-Hewitt Mus., 1971, Mus. Modern Art Corp.,Lending and Adv. Svc. Exhbns., Kuznetsky-Most Galleries, Moscow, 1989, NAD, N.Y.C., 1990, public murals commns., Houston and Crosby Sts., N.Y.C., 1972, Lafayette and Bleecker Sts., N.Y.C., 1969; represented in permanent collections Cleve. Mus., Fogg Mus. Art, Harvard U., Indpls. Mus., Westinghouse Corp., Corcoran Gallery Art, Yale U., Notre Dame U., AT&T, Chase Manhattan Bank, other pub. and corp. collections, also pvt. collections. Founding mem., v.p., bd. dirs. City Walls, 1969-77. Served with Combat Engrs. AUS, 1957-59. Recipient grants in public art through City Walls Kaplan Fund, 1969, City Walls Bernhard Found., 1971, City Walls N.Y. State Council on Arts, 1970, City Walls Nat. Endowment for the Arts, 1971. Mem. Coll. Art Assn. Am. Home: PO Box 1575 Stony Brook NY 11790-0875 Office: SUNY Art Dept Stony Brook NY 11794-5400

PEKER, ELYA ABEL, artist; b. Moscow, June 15, 1937; came to U.S. 1972; s. Aba Z. and Frieda I. (Warshavsky) P.; m. Katrina Friedman, May 19, 1977; 1 child, Benjamin E. Diploma of Artist for Theater Decoration, Art Inst., Moscow, 1956. Comml. artist N.Y.C., 1972-88. One-man shows include Nakhamkin Fine Art Gallery, N.Y.C., 1980-85; exhibited in group shows in Basel, Switzerland, Hong Kong, others; represented in permanent collections of Kennedy-Onassis family, Emil Wolf, Frank L'Angella, Campbell family, Benjamin family, others; contemporary flower and still-life poster series published 1991, reproductions published worldwide. Mem. Am. Biog. Inst. (dep. gov., order internat. ambs., Gold Record Achievement 1995, 20th Century Achievement award 1995, Internat. Cultural Diploma Honor 1996), Internat. Platform Assn., Licensing Industry Merchandiser's Assn. Address: 1673 E 16th St Ste 164 Brooklyn NY 11229-2901

PÉLADEAU, MARIUS BEAUDOIN, art consultant, retired museum director; b. Boston, Jan. 27, 1935; s. Marius and Lucienne (Beaudoin) P.; m. Mildred L. Cole, Feb. 26, 1972. B.A. cum laude, St. Michael's Coll., 1956; M.S., Boston U., 1957; M.A., Georgetown U., 1962. Assoc. editor Public Utilities Fortnightly, Washington, 1962-66; adminstrv. asst., press sec. to U.S. Congressman J. P. Vigorito, Washington, 1967-72; dir. Maine League Hist. Socs. and Mus.'s, Monmouth, 1972-76, William A. Farnsworth Library and Art Mus., Rockland, Maine, 1976-87; gen. mgr. The Theater at Monmouth, Maine, 1989; cons. in field, 1990—. Author: The Verse of Royall Tyler, 1968, The Prose of Royall Tyler, 1972, Chansonetta: The Life and Photographs of Chansonetta Stanely Emmons, 1858-1937, 1977. Trustee Jones Mus. Glass and Ceramics; guest curator L.C. Bates Mus., Hinckley, Maine. Fellow Co. Mil. Historians; mem. Vt. Hist. Soc. Democrat. Roman Catholic.

PELADEAU, PIERRE, publishing company executive; b. Montreal, Apr. 11, 1925; s. Henri and Elmire (Fortier) P.; m. Raymonde Chopin, May 26, 1954; children: Eric, Isabelle, Pierre-Karl, Anne-Marie; m. Line Parisien, May 24, 1979; children: Esther, Pierre Jr., Jean. L.Ph., U. Montreal, 1945, M.A., 1947; B.C.L., McGill U., Montreal, 1950; Dr honoris cause, U. Que., U. Sherbrooke. With Quebecor Inc.; pub., printing and forest products holding co. exec. Quebecor Inc., Montreal, 1965—; editor, pres., chief exec. officer Quebecor Inc., 1965—; bd. dirs. Donohue Inc., Sodarcan Inc. 1st chancelor Ste.-Anne U., Novia Scotia, 1988. Mem. Order of Can., Nat. Order Que. Club: Saint-Denis. Office: Quebecor inc, 612 Rue Saint-Jacques ouest, Montreal, PQ Canada H3C 4M8

PELAEZ, ROLANDO FEDERICO, economics educator, consultant; b. Washington, May 5, 1940; s. Rolando Juan and Maria Gertrudis (Bringuier) P. BS, La. State U., 1962, MA, 1964; PhD in Econs., U. Houston, 1973; postgrad., Rice U., 1978-79. Teaching fellow U. Houston-Univ. Park, 1970-71, instr., 1971-73; asst. prof. N.Mex. State U., 1973-74, Southeastern La. U., 1976; asst. prof. U. Houston-Downtown, 1977-80, assoc. prof. fin. Coll. Bus., 1987—; assoc. prof. U. St. Thomas, 1980-87; expert witness forensic economist; vis. asst. prof. U. Houston-Univ. Park, 1974-75; spkr., presenter confs. in field. Contbr. articles to profl. jours. OAS doctoral fellow, 1970. Mem. Am. Econ. Assn., Am. Statis. Assn., So. Finance Assn., Southwestern Econ. Assn., Southwestern Finance Assn., Western Econ. Assn., Nat. Assn. Forensic Economists. Home: 8318 Daycoach Ln Houston TX 77064-8202

PELAN, ALAN D., manufacturing company executive; b. Johnston, R.I., Oct. 18, 1944; s. Howard D. and Marjorie (Stone) P.; m. Mary Jane Nickerson; children: David, Julie. BSBA, Clark U., 1969; MBA, Bryant Coll., 1976. Cost acct. Norton Co., Worcester, Mass., 1965-69; exec. v.p. Acushnet Co., New Bedford, Mass., 1969-83; v.p. contr. Nat. Med. Care, Waltham, Mass., 1983-84, Phalo Corp., Westboro, Mass., 1984-86; pres. Stillman Seal, Carlsbad, Calif., 1986-89; COO Aeroquip, Middleton, Ohio, 1989-90; pres. Fasco Motors, Eldon, Mo., 1990—. Avocations: weightlifting, fishing, reading. Office: Fasco Industries PO Box 309 Eldon MO 65026-0309

PELANDINI, THOMAS FRANCIS, marketing executive; b. Vallejo, Calif., Jan. 6, 1938; s. Francis Lee and Betty (Tucker) P.; m. Sandra Lee Holmes, Sept. 17, 1961; children: Jennifer Lynn, Beth Ann. BA in Comm., U. Wash., Seattle, 1961. Dir. div. public relations Pepsi-Cola Co., N.Y.C. and Chgo., 1966-68; account supr. Patton Agy., Phoenix, 1968-70; v.p. Hill & Knowlton, Inc. (public relations), Los Angeles, 1970-72; corp. dir. communications Avco Corp., Greenwich, Conn., 1972-75; v.p. public affairs Crocker Nat. Bank, San Francisco, 1975-82; sr. v.p. Hoefer-Amidei, Inc., San Francisco, 1982-83; exec. v.p. Manning, Selvage & Lee, Inc., San Jose, Calif., 1983-85; sr. v.p. corp. affairs Austec, Inc., San Jose, 1986-88; pres., chief operating officer Austec, Inc., San Jose, CA, 1988-90; v.p. corp. com. Businessland Inc., San Jose, Calif., 1990-92; v.p. worldwide sales and mktg. Sitka Corp., Alameda, Calif., 1992-93; pres. Channel Focus (Europe) Ltd., Reading, U.K., 1993-95; COO Intermax Solutions, Inc., San Mateo, Calif., 1996—. Bd. dirs. Diablo Community Service Dist. 1st lt. USAF, 1962-65. Mem. Diablo Country Club. Home: Thimble Farm Diablo CA 94528

PELAVIN, MICHAEL ALLEN, lawyer; b. Flint, Mich., Sept. 5, 1936; s. B. Morris and Betty (Weiss) P.; m. Natalie Katz, June 18, 1960; children: Mark, Gordon. Student U. Mich., 1954-55, Wayne State U., 1955-57; JD, Detroit Coll. Law, 1960. Bar: Mich. 1960, U.S. Tax Ct. 1966, U.S. Ct. Appeals (6th cir.) 1969, N.Y. 1989. Assoc. Pelavin & Powers, P.C. (now Pelavin, Powers & Behm P.C.), Flint, Mich., 1960-63, ptnr., 1963-71, pres., 1980—; trustee Mut. of Am. Life Ins. Co., 1981—; chair Nat. Jewish Community Rels. Adv. Coun., 1986-89. Chmn. young leadership cabinet United Jewish Appeal, 1973; pres. Flint Jewish Fedn., 1974-77; chmn. Bishop Internat. Airport Authority, 1990—. Recipient Herbert Lehman Young Leadership award United Jewish Appeal, Sydney B. Melet Humanitarian award Urban Coalition Greater Flint, Donald Riegle Cmty. Svc. award & Pres. award Flint Jewish Fedn., Disting. Svc. award Genesee County Bar Assn. Mem. ABA, N.Y. State Bar Assn., Assn. Trial Lawyers Am., Mich. Bar Assn. Democrat. Home: 6168 Sierra Pass Flint MI 48532-2134 Office: Pelavin Powers & Behm PC 801 S Saginaw St Flint MI 48502-1511

PELAVIN, SOL HERBERT, research company executive; b. Detroit, Dec. 16, 1941; s. Norman J. and Alice A. (Levinson) P.; m. Diane Christine Blakemore, Aug. 14, 1966; children: Shayna Beth, Adam Blake. BA in Math., U. Chgo., 1965, MAT in Math., 1969; MS in Stats., Stanford U., 1974, PhD candidate in mathematical models of edn. research, 1975. Tchr. pub. schs., 1965-70. teaching rsch. asst. Stanford (Calif.) U., 1972-74; cons. Rand Corp., Santa Monica, Calif., 1975; policy analyst SRI Internat., Menlo Park, Calif., 1975-78; exec. officer NTS Research Corp., Durham, N.C., 1978-82; pres. Pelavin Assocs., Inc., Washington, 1982-94; exec. v.p., CFO Am. Inst. Rsch., 1994—; dir. Data Analysis and Tech. Support Ctr., Washington, 1989-93, Policy Analysis Support Ctr., Washington, 1993—; expert witness to U.S. Congress, 1977, 79, Cabinet briefing, 1983; cons. Frank, Bernstein, Conway and Goldman, Balt., 1980-81; dir. Ednl. Analysis Ctr., Washington, 1982-85. Author: (with others) Investigation of the Impact of the Emergency School Assistance Porgrams on Black, Male 10th Grade Student Achievement, 1975, (with P. Barker) A Study of the Generalizability of the Results of Standardized Achievement Tests, 1976, (with J.L. David) Research on the Effectiveness of Compensatory Education Programs: A Reanalysis of Data, 1977, (with others) Federal Expenditures for the Education of Children and Youth With Special Needs, 1981, (with D.C. Pelavin) An Evaluation of the Fund for the Improvement of Postsecondary Education, 1981, 83, (with others) Evaluation of the Commodity Supplemental Food Program, 1982, An Evaluation of the Bilingual Education Evaluation, Dissemination and Assessment Centers, 1984, A Study of a Year-Round School Program, 1978, An Evaluation of the Indian Education Act, Title IV, Part C, Education for Indian Adults, 1984, Teacher Preparation: A Review of State Certification Requirements, 1984, Analysis of the National Availability of Mathematics and Science Teachers, 1983, Minority Participation in Higher Education, 1988, Changing the Odds, 1990, others; contbr. articles to profl. jours. NSF fellow U. Chgo., 1968-69; Cuneo fellow Stanford U., 1973. Mem. AAAS, Am. Ednl. Research Assn., Am. Psychol. Assn. Democrat. Jewish. Office: American Inst Rsch 3333 K St NW Ste 300 Washington DC 20007-3500

PELC, KAROL I., engineering management educator, researcher; b. Czestochowa, Poland, July 29, 1935; came to U.S., 1985; s. Stanislaw Pelc and Kamilla (Hecko) Pelc-Kosna; m. Ryszarda Lidia Ryglewicz, Sept. 24, 1959; 1 child, Dariusz. MScEE, Tech. U. Wroclaw, Poland, 1958, PhD in Econs., 1976; PhD in Electronics, U. Uppsala, Sweden, 1968. Prodn. & engring. mgr. Energopomiar Co., Wroclaw, 1960-65; rsch. asst. dept. electronics U. Uppsala, 1961-62; assoc. dir. divsn. Inst. Electric Power Industry, Wroclaw, 1966-68; founder, dir. Forecasting Rsch. Ctr., Wroclaw, 1971-81; electronic design engr. Rsch. Inst. Tech. U. Wroclaw, $Dland, 1957-60; rsch. dir. Tech. U. Wroclaw, 1968-77, lectr., dir. Jelenia Gora Coll. br., 1982-85; prof. Mich. Technol. U., Houghton, 1985—; vis. prof. Indian Inst. Tech., Bombay, 1981, Stevens Inst. Tech., Hoboken, N.J., 1993; vis. scholar Japan Ctr. for Mich. Univs., Hikone, 1992; mem. innovation task force Internat. Inst. for Applied Systems Analysis, Laxenburg, Austria, 1983-84; chmn. forecasting seminar Polish Acad. Scis., Warsaw, 1974-81; v.p. divsn. Soc. Mgmt. and Orgn., Wroclaw, 1979-80. Author: Planning of Research and Development, 1981; mem. editl. bd. Technol. Forecasting and Social Change, U.S. R&D Mgmt., Eng., Transformations, Poland; contbr. over 90 articles to scholarly jours.; patentee in field. Mem. Internat. Assn. Mgmt. Tech., Internat. Assn. for Rsch. and Devel. Mgmt., Am. Soc. Engring. Mgmt., Engring. Mgmt. Soc. of IEEE, Acad. Mgmt. Roman Catholic. Avocations: classical music, tourism, cross-country skiing, bicycling, swimming. Office: Mich Technol Univ Sch Bus & Econ Houghton MI 49931

PELCZAR, MICHAEL JOSEPH, JR., microbiologist, educator; b. Balt., Jan. 28, 1916; s. Michael Joseph and Josephine (Polek) P.; m. Merna M. Foss, Aug. 28, 1941; children: Ann Foss, Patricia Mary, Michael Rafferty, Rita Margaret, Josephine Merna, Julia Foss. BS, U. Md., 1936, MS, 1938; PhD, U. Iowa, 1941; DSc (hon.), Utah State U., 1986. Diplomate: Am. Bd. Microbiology. Instr. bacteriology U. Iowa, 1940-41; asst. prof., assoc. prof. bacteriology U. Md., College Park, 1946-50; prof. microbiology U. Md., 1950-78; prof. emeritus, 1978—, v.p. grad. studies and research, 1966-78, v.p. emeritus, 1978—; pres. Council Grad. Schs. in U.S., Washington, 1978-84; pres. emeritus Council Grad. Schs. in U.S., 1984—; mem. microbiology adv. panel Office Naval Rsch., 1965-70; spl. cons. Random House Dictionary of English Lang., 1965; councilor Oak Ridge Asso. Univs., Inc., 1959-66; also bd. dirs.; mem. So. Regional Edn. Bd., Coun. Grad. Edn. in Agrl. Scis., 1967; mem. departmental com. on biol. scis. U.S. Dept. Agr. Grad. Sch., 1967-76; chmn. Spl. Meeting on Neisseria WHO, Geneva, Switzerland, 1964, mem. expert adv. panel on bacterial diseases, 1967-77; mem. Gov.'s Sci. Adv. Bd., 1967—, chmn., 1967-72; mem. organizing com. for XVII Gen. Assembly NRC, div. biology and agr. Internat. Union Biol. Scis., 1968; chmn. bd. on human resource data and analysis Commn. on Human Resources, NRC, 1975-79; mem. exec. com. Coun. Grad. Schs., 1976-78; mem. Nat. Sea Grant Rev. Panel, 1979-89; mem. adv. com. Nat. Rsch. Coun., 1987—. Coauthor: Microbiology, 5th edit, 1986, Elements of Microbiology, 1981, Microbiology: Concepts and Applications, 1993; editorial bd.: Jour. of Bacteriology, 1965-69; Contbr. sect. to: Ency. Brit, 1969, 94; articles to profl. jours. Ency. Ednl. Research. Recipient Nat. Sea Grant Assn. award, 1991, ASM Disting. Svc. award, 1995. Fellow AAUP (past br. pres.). Nat. Adminstrn. Acad. Univ. Rsch. (founding mem. 1985); mem. AAAS, Am. Acad. Microbiology, Am. Inst. Biol. Scis. (bd. govs., past vis. lectr.), Am. Soc. Microbiology (bd. govs., past com. chmn., councilor, br. pres., hon. mem. 1986—), Internat. Assn. Microbiology, Washington Acad. Scis., Nat. Assn. State Univs. and Land-Grant Colls. (chmn. coun. for rsch. policy and adminstrn., cons. higher edn. rsch. administrn.), Cosmos Club, Phi Beta Kappa (assoc. 1989), Sigma Xi (ann. award sci. achievement 1968), Phi Kappa Phi, Sigma Alpha Omicron. Research microbial physiology. Home: PO Box 133 300 Avalon Farm Ln Chester MD 21619

PELÉ (EDSON ARANTES DO NASCIMENTO), professional soccer player; b. Três Coracões, Minas Gerais, Brazil, Oct. 23, 1940; came to U.S., 1975; s. João Ramos do Nascimento and Celeste Arantes; m. Rosemeri Cholbi, Feb. 21, 1966 (div.); children: Kely Cristina, Edson, Jennifer; m. Assiria Lemos, April 30, 1994. Grad. in phys. edn., Santos U., 1972. Soccer player with Santos Football Club, Sao Paulo, 1956-74, N.Y. Cosmos, N.Y.C., 1975-77; chmn. Pepsi Internat. Youth Soccer Program, 1972—; pres. Empresas Pelé, Santos; chmn. Pelé Soccer Camps, 1978—; min. sports Govt. of Brazil, 1995—; dir. soccer clinics. Author: Eu Sou Pelé, 1962, Jogando com Pelé, 1974, My Life and the Beautiful Game, 1977, Pelé Soccer Training Program, 1982; appeared in: films Eu sou Pelé, 1964, A Marcha, 1973, Istoé Pelé, 1974, Pelé, The Master and His Method, 1973, Pelé's New World, 1975, Pelé, 1977, Os Trombadinhas, 1979, Victory, 1981, A Minor Miracle, 1983, Hot Shot, 1985; composer: numerous songs in Samba style including Saudacão Criança, 1969, Vexamão, 1970; soundtrack for film Pelé, 1977. Active Spl. Olympics, 1978—. Served with Brazilian Army, 1958. Recipient Internat. Peace award, 1978, WHO medal, 1989; named Athlete of Century, 1980. Player 4 World Cups, 1958, 62, 66, 70, won 3 times, Brazilian Nat. Team, 1957-71; scored 1,282 goals (1,364 games) total; 1088 goals (1114 games) for Santos Football Club, 97 goals (111 games) for Brazilian Nat. Team, 65 goals (108 games) for Cosmos. Address: 75 Rockefeller Plz New York NY 10019-6908*

PELFREY, D. PATTON, lawyer; b. Ky., 1941. BA, Calif. State U., L.A., 1963; JD, U. Louisville, 1968. Bar: Ky. 1968. Trial atty. region 9 NLRB, Cin., 1968-72; mem. Brown, Todd & Heyburn, Louisville; prof. sch. law U. Louisville, 1988-89. Mem. ABA (sect. labor and employment law), Ky. Bar Assn. (labor sect.), Louisville Bar Assn. (mem. labor com. 1983—), Delta Theta Phi. Office: Brown Todd & Heyburn 400 W Market St Ste 3200 Louisville KY 40202-3359

PELHAM, FRAN O'BYRNE, writer, teacher; b. Phila., Oct. 16, 1939; d. Frederick Thomas and Frances Rebecca (Johns) O'Byrne; m. Donald Lacey Pelham, June 15, 1968; children: Mary Frances, Michael. BA, Holy Family Coll., 1967; M in English Edn., Trenton Coll., 1974; EdD, U. Pa., 1993. Cert. secondary tchr. Tchr. Sch. Dist. Bristol (Pa.) Twp., 1967-70; feature writer various publs., Phila. and others, 1980—; prof., dir. Writing Ctr. Holy Family Coll., Phila., 1982-89; asst. prof. lit. and writing LaSalle U., Phila., 1989-93, Beaver Coll., Glenside, Pa., 1994—; dir. tech. communications Internat. Chem. Co., Phila., 1985-90; speaker, workshop leader various orgns. Author: Search for Atocha Treasure, 1989, Downtown America: Philadelphia, 1989; contbr. articles to mags. Participant Home and Sch. Assn., Jenkintown, Pa., 1983, Jenkintown Arts Festival, 1984, Campus Ministry Team Holy Family Coll., Phila., 1986-89, Alliance for a Living Ocean, 1991—, Phila. Children's Reading Roundtable, Authors Guild, Franciscan Adult Sch. Bd., 1995, A Non-denominational Cmty. Harvesting Our Resources, Support Police Immediate Response Intervention Team; bd. dirs. U. Pa. Edn. Alumni Assn. Recipient Citation Mayor's Commn., 1988. Mem. AAUW, Nat. Coun. Tchrs. Eng., Am. Conf. Irish Studies, Nat. League Am. Pen Women (br. pres. 1982-84), Phila. Writers' Conf. (bd. dirs. 1982-86), Pi Lambda Theta, Lambda Iota Tau, Phi Delta Kappa. Democrat. Roman Catholic. Avocations: scuba diving, tennis, boating, travel. Office: Dept of Lit Beaver College Glenside PA 19120

PELHAM, THOMAS GERALD, lawyer; b. Hartford, Ala., Nov. 23, 1943; s. Roy W. and Annie Louise (Blackburn) P.; m. Vivian Holden, Feb. 1, 1969; children: Christopher Holden, Evan Blackburn. BA, Fla. State U., 1965; MA, Duke U., 1967; JD, Fla. State U., 1971; LLM, Harvard U., 1977. Bar: Fla. 1971. Ptnr. Brown, Smith, Young & Pelham, Tallahassee, 1971-76; prof. law So. Meth. U., Dallas, 1977-80; ptnr. Carlton Fields Law Firm, Tallahassee, 1980-82, Akerman, Senterfitt & Edison, Tallahassee, 1982-84, Culpepper, Pelham, Turner & Mannheimer, Tallahassee, 1985-87; sec. Fla. Dept. Community Affairs, Tallahassee, 1987-91; ptnr. Holland & Knight, Tallahassee, 1991-93, Apgar & Pelham, Tallahassee, 1993—; adj. prof. law Fla. State U., Tallahassee, 1992—; chmn. bd. dirs. Legal Environ. Assistance Found., Tallahassee; mem. Gov.'s Environ. Land Mgmt. Study Com., Tallahassee, 1992. Author: State Land Use Planning and Regulation, 1979. Mem. Tallahassee-Leon County Planning Com., 1985-87, Capitol Ctr. Planning Commn., Tallahassee, 1982-85. Recipient Govtl. Conservationist of Yr. award Fla. Audubon Soc., 1990, Spl. Friend of Fla. award 1000 Friends of Fla., 1988, 90, Person of Yr. award Fla. Environ. Mag., 1990. Mem. ABA (state and local law sect.), Fla. Bar (chmn. environ. and lang use law sect. 1990-91), Am. Planning Assn. (Fla. chpt. v.p. chpt. affairs 1992-94, pres.-elect 1994—), Econ. Club Fla. Avocations: reading, travel, jazz, movies, jogging. Office: Apgar & Pelham 909 E Park Ave Tallahassee FL 32301-2646

PELIKAN, JAROSLAV JAN, history educator; b. Akron, Ohio, Dec. 17, 1923; s. Jaroslav Jan and Anna (Buzek) P.; m. Sylvia Burica, June 9, 1946; children: Martin, Michael, Miriam. Grad. summa cum laude, Concordia Jr. Coll., Ft. Wayne, Ind., 1942; BD, Concordia Theol. Sem., St. Louis, 1946; PhD, U. Chgo., 1946; MA (hon.), Yale U., 1961; DD (hon.), Concordia Coll., Moorehead, Minn., 1960, Concordia Sem., 1967, Trinity Coll., Hartford, Conn., 1987, St. Vladimir's Orthodox Theol. Sem., 1988, Victoria U., Toronto, 1989, U. Aberdeen, Scotland, 1995; LittD (hon.), Wittenberg U., 1960, Wheeling Coll., 1966, Gettysburg Coll., 1967, Pacific Luth. U., 1967, Wabash Coll., 1988, Jewish Theol. Sem., 1991; HHD (hon.), Providence Coll., 1966, Moravian Coll., 1986, Jewish Theol. Sem., 1991; LLD (hon.), Keuka Coll., 1967, U. Notre Dame, 1979; LHD (hon.), Valparaiso U., 1966, Rockhurst Coll., 1967, Albertus Magnus Coll., 1973, Coe Coll., 1976, Cath. U. Am., 1977, St. Mary's Coll., 1978, St. Anselm Coll., 1983, U. Nebr.-Omaha, 1984, Tulane U., 1986, Assumption Coll., 1986, LaSalle U., 1987, Carthage Coll., 1991, U. Chgo., 1991, So. Meth. U., 1992, SUNY, Albany, 1993; ThD (hon.), U. Hamburg, 1971, St. Olaf Coll., 1972; STD, Dickinson Coll., 1986; DSc in Hist., Comenius U., Bratislava, 1992; ScD (hon.), Loyola U., Chgo., 1995. Faculty Valparaiso (Ind.) U., 1946-49, Concordia Sem., St. Louis, 1949-53, U. Chgo., 1953-62; Titus Street prof. eccles. history Yale U., 1962-72, Sterling prof. history, 1972-96, William Clyde DeVane lectr., 1984-86, dir. div. humanities, 1974-75, chmn. Medieval studies, 1974-75, 78-80, dean Grad. Sch., 1973-78; Gray lectr. Duke U., 1960, Ingersoll lectr. Harvard U., 1963, Gauss lectr. Princeton U., 1980, Jefferson lectr. NEH, 1983, Richard lectr. U. Va., 1984, Rauschenbusch lectr. Colgate-Rochester Divinity Sch., 1984, Gilson lectr. U. Toronto, 1985, Hale lectr. Seabury-Western Sem., 1986, Mead-Swing lectr. Oberlin Coll., 1986, Gross lectr. Rutgers U., 1989; bd. dirs. Nat. Humanities Ctr., 1984-90, Univ. Support Svcs. Inc., 1992-94; adv. bd. Ctr. Theol. Inquiry, 1984-90; mem. coun. The Smithsonian Instn., 1984-90; U.S. chmn. U.S. Czechoslovak Commn. on Humanities and Social Scis., 1987-92. Author: From Luther to Kierkegaard, 1950, Fools for Christ, 1955, The Riddle of Roman Catholicism, 1959 (Abingdon award 1959), Luther the Expositor, 1959, The Shape of Death, 1961, The Light of the World, 1962, Obedient Rebels, 1964, The Finality of Jesus Christ in an Age of Universal History, 1965, The Christian Intellectual, 1966, Spirit Versus Structure, 1968, Development of Doctrine, 1969, Historical Theology, 1971, The Christian Tradition, 5 vols., 1971-89, Scholarship and Its Survival, 1983, The Vindication of Tradition, 1984, Jesus through the Centuries, 1985, The Mystery of Continuity, 1986, Bach Among the Theologians, 1986, The Excellent Empire, 1987, The Melody of Theology, 1988, Confessor Between East and West, 1990, Imago Dei, 1990, Eternal Feminines, 1990, The Idea of the University: A Reexamination, 1992, Christianity and Classical Culture, 1993, Faust the Theologian, 1995, The Reformation of the Bible/ The Bible of the Reformation, 1996, Mary through the Centuries, 1996, also introductions to works of others; editor, translator: Luther's Works, 22 vols., 1955-71, The Book of Concord, 1959, The Unbounded Community, 1996; editor: Makers of Modern Theology, 5 vols., 1966-68, The Preaching of Chrysostom, 1967, Interpreters of Luther, 1968, Twentieth-Century Theology in the Making, 3 vols., 1969-70, The Preaching of Augustine, 1973, The World Treasury of Modern Religious Thought, 1991, Sacred Writings, 7 vols., 1992; mem. editorial bd. Collected Works of Erasmus, Classics of Western Spirituality, Evangelisches

Kirchenlexikon, Emerson's Nature, 1986, The World Treasury of Modern Religious Thought, 1990; departmental editor Ency. Britannica, 1958-69; adminstrv. bd. Papers of Benjamin Franklin; chmn. publs. com. Yale Univ. Press, 1979-90, 92—, v.p. bd. govs., 1988—; contbr. to many symposia, jours., encys. Pres. 4th Internat. Congress for Luther Research, 1971, New Eng. Congress on Grad. Edn., 1976-77. Recipient Abingdon award, 1959; Pax Christi award St. John's U., Collegeville, Minn., 1966, Colman J. Barry award, 1995; John Gilmary Shea prize Am. Cath. Hist. Assn., 1971, nat. award Slovak World Congress, 1973, religious book award Cath. Press Assn., 1974, Christian Unity award Atonement Friars, 1975, Bicentennial award Czechoslovak Soc. Arts and Scis., 1976, Wilbur Cross medal Yale U. Grad. Sch. Assn., 1979, Profl. Achievement award U. Chgo. Alumni Assn., 1980, Shaw medal Boston Coll., 1984, Comenius medal Moravian Coll., 1986, Alumnus of Yr. award U. Chgo. Div. Sch., 1986, Bicentennial medal Georgetown U., 1989, award for excellence Am. Acad. Religion 1989, Umanità award Newberry Libr., 1990; recipient Festschrift: Schools of Thought in the Christian Tradition, 1984; sr. fellow Carnegie Found. for Advancement Tchg., 1982-83. Fellow Medieval Acad. Am. (councillor, Haskins medal 1985); mem. Am. Hist. Assn., Am. Soc. Ch. History (pres. 1965), Internat. Congress Luther Rsch. (pres. 1971), Am. Acad. Arts and Scis. (v.p. 1976-94, pres. 1994-97), Am. Philos. Soc. (councillor 1984-87), Coun. Scholars of Libr. of Congress (founding chmn. 1980-83), Elizabethan Club, Mory's, Phi Beta Kappa (senator United chpts. 1985-90). Home: 156 Chestnut Ln Hamden CT 06518-1604

PELISEK, FRANK JOHN, lawyer; b. Wauwatosa, Wis., June 8, 1930; s. Frank Pelisek and Virginia Pancost; m. Jane Olga Bauman (div.), Susan M., David P.; m. Jill Ann Grootemaat, Apr. 4, 1975. BS in Econs., U. Wis., 1954, LLB, 1958; D in Comml. Sci. (hon.), U. Wis., Milw., 1990. Sr. ptnr. Michael, Best & Friedrich, Milw., 1958—. 1st lt. U.S. Army, 1954-56. Office: Michael Best & Friedrich 100 E Wisconsin Ave Milwaukee WI 53202-4107

PELL, ARTHUR ROBERT, human resources development consultant, author; b. N.Y.C., Jan. 22, 1920; s. Harry and Rae (Meyers) P.; m. Erica Frost, May 19, 1946; children—Douglas, Hilary. AB, NYU, 1939, MA, 1944; PhD, Calif. Coast U., 1977; profl. diploma, Cornell U., 1943. Personnel dir. Eagle-Electric Mfg. Co., Long Island City, N.Y., 1946-50, North Atlantic Constructors, N.Y.C., 1950-53; v.p. Harper Assos., Inc. (personnel consultants), N.Y.C., 1953-75; cons. Human Resources Mgmt., 1975—; adj. asso. prof. mgmt. Sch. Continuing Edn., NYU, 1962-84; lectr. Baruch Sch. Bus. and Pub. Adminstrn. Coll. City N.Y., 1948-67; adj. asso. prof. mgmt. Coll. Bus. Adminstrn., St. John's U., 1971-76. Author: (with W.B. Patterson) Fire Officer's Guide to Leadership, rev. edit., 1963, Placing Salesmen, 1963, Placing Executives, 1964, Police Leadership, 1967, How to Get the Job You Want After 40, 1967, Recruiting and Selecting Personnel, 1969, (with M. Harper) Starting and Managing an Employment Agency, 1970, Recruiting, Training and Motivating Volunteer Workers, 1972, Be a Better Employment Interviewer, 1972, rev. edits., 1978, 86, 94, The College Graduate Guide to Job Finding, 1973, (with Wilma Rogalin) Women's Guide to Executive Positions, 1975, (with Albert Furbay) College Student's Guide to Career Planning, 1975, (with Dale Carnegie Assocs.) Managing Through People, 1975, rev. edits., 1978, 1987, Choosing a College Major: Business, 1978, Enrich Your Life: The Dale Carnegie Way, 1979, The Part Time Job Book, 1984, Making the Most of Medicare, 1987, rev. edit., 1990, (with George Sadek) Resumes for Engineers, 1982, Resumes for Computer Professionals, 1984, How to Sell Yourself on an Interview, 1982, The Job Finder's Kit, 1989, How to Get the Most from Your People, 1990, Diagnosing Your Doctor, 1991, The Supervisor's Infobank, 1994, The Complete Idiot's Guide to Managing People, 1995; editorial cons. for revision Dale Carnegie's How to Win Friends and Influence People, 1981; author syndicated feature The Human Side; also articles. Served with AUS, 1942-46. Office: 111 Dietz St Hempstead NY 11550-7625

PELL, CLAIBORNE, former senator; b. N.Y.C., Nov. 22, 1918; s. Herbert Claiborne and Matilda (Bigelow) P.; m. Nuala O'Donnell, Dec. 1944; children: Herbert Claiborne III, Christopher T. Hartford, Nuala Dallas Yates, Julia L.W. Student, St. George's Sch., Newport, R.I.; A.B. cum laude, Princeton U., 1940; A.M., Columbia U., 1946; 46 hon. degrees. Enlisted USCGR, 1941; served as seaman, ensign North Atlantic sea duty, Africa, Italy; hospitalized to U.S., 1944; instr. Navy Sch. Mil. Govt., Princeton, 1944-45; capt. USCGR; ret.; on loan to State Dept. at San Francisco Conf., 1945, State Dept., 1945-46, U.S. embassy, Czechoslovakia, 1946-47; established consulate gen. Bratislava, Czechoslovakia, 1947-48; vice consul Genoa, Italy, 1949; assigned State Dept., 1950-52; v.p., dir. Internat. Rescue Com.; senator from R.I., 1961-96; ranking minority mem. Fgn. Rels. Com., Labor and Human Resources Subcom. on Edn., Arts, and Humanities; mem. Rules and Adminstrn. Com., Joint Com. on Libr. and Congl. Intern Program, Senate Dem. Policy Com.; U.S. del. Internat. Maritime Consultative Orgn., London, 1959, 25th Gen. Assembly, 1970. Author: Megalopolis Unbound, 1966, (with Harold L. Goodwin) Challenge of the Seven Seas, 1966, Power and Policy, 1972. Hon. bd. dirs. World Affairs Council R.I.; trustee St. George's Sch.; trustee emeritus Brown U.; Cons. Democratic Nat. Com., 1953-60; exec. asst. to chmn. R.I. State Dem. Com., 1952-54; chmn. R.I. Dem. Fund drive, 1952, Dem. nat. registration, chmn., 1956, co-chmn., 1962; chief delegation tally clk. Dem. Nat. Conv., 1956, 60, 64, 68. Decorated knight Crown of Italy, Grand Cross Order of Merit Italy, Red Cross of Merit Portugal, Legion of Honor France, comdr. Order of Phoenix Greece, Grand Cross Order of Merit Liechtenstein, Grand Cross Order of Christ Portugal, Order of Henry the Navigator, Portugal, Grand Cross Order of N. Star Sweden, Grand Cross of Merit Knights of Malta, Grand Officer of Merit Luxembourg, Grand Comdr. Lebanon; recipient Caritas Elizabeth medal Cardinal Franz Koenig, Grand decoration of honor in silver with sash Austria, Gold medal of St. Barnabas (Cyprus), recipient Pres.'s Fellow award R.I. Sch. Design, medal Nat. Order of Cedar, Hugo Grotius Commemorative medal The Netherlands, recipient Harold W. McGraw, Jr. Prize in Education, McGraw-Hill, 1988. Mem. Soc. Cin. Episcopalian. Clubs: Hope (Providence); Knickerbocker (N.Y.C.), Racquet and Tennis (N.Y.C.), Brook (N.Y.C.); Metropolitan (Washington); Travellers (Paris); Reading Room (Newport); White's (London). Office: 3425 Prospect St NW Washington DC 20007 *I have a seven word definition of my job and of my life: "Translate ideas into events, and help people."*.*

PELL, JANE EILEEN, insurance executive; b. Canton, Ohio, July 23, 1946; d. Edward G. and Alice C. (Snyder) Psolla; m. Richard W. Pell, Feb. 18, 1986. Cert. gen. ins., Ins. Inst. Am., Phila., 1976; Assoc., Am. Ednl. Inst., N.J., 1980. Sec. Glouka Ins. Agy., Cleve., 1964-65; jr. underwriter Employers Group, Cleve., 1965; sec., adjuster Md. Casualty, Phila., 1967-70; claims supr. PMA Ins., Phila., 1970-77; tech. supt. and claims INA, Phila., 1977-86, asst. v.p. major claims, 1986-89, field ops. v.p., 1989-92, regional claims v.p., 1992—. Mem. NAFE. Office: CIGNA One Beaver Valley Rd 4 West Wilmington DE 19850

PELL, JONATHAN LAURENCE, artistic administrator; b. Memphis, Oct. 20, 1949; s. Burton Marshall and Eleanor (Leopold) P. BA, U. So. Calif., 1971. Interior designer Gene Morse Assocs., Wichita, Kans., 1971-77; mgr. Internat. Artists Mgmt., N.Y.C., 1977-79, Robert Lombardo Assocs., N.Y.C., 1979-80; TV producer Sta. WNET, N.Y.C., 1980-83; dir. publicity John Curry Skating Co., N.Y.C., 1983; prodr. Jerome Kern Centennary Gala Town Hall, N.Y.C., 1984; dir. artistic administration The Dallas Opera, 1984—; vocal competition judge Met. Opera Nat. Coun. Auditions, Pavarotti Competition, George London Awards, Ctr. for Contemporary Opera, Marguerite McCammon Competition, San Antonio Opera Guild, Richard Tucker award, others; tchr. master classes for young singers Nat. Opera Assn., Can. Opera Co., S.W. Chpt. NATS; mem. performing arts assistance corp. U. of North Tex. Scenic and Costume designer for plays, musicals and ballets for various cos., 1970-76; host The Dallas Opera Radio Hour, WRR, 1994—. Bd. dirs., chmn. nat. auditions com., mem. award selection com. Richard Tucker Music Found. Mem. Opera Am. Office: Dallas Opera 3102 Oak Lawn Ave Ste 450 Dallas TX 75219-4259

PELL, SIDNEY, epidemiologist; b. N.Y.C., Dec. 13, 1922; m. Lola May, July 2, 1950. MBA, CCNY, 1952; PhD, U. Pitts., 1956. Biostatistician E.I. Du Pont de Nemours and Co., Wilmington, Del., 1955-76, mgr. epidemiology sect., 1976-82, sr. cons., 1982-85; epidemiology cons. Wilmington, 1985—; epidemiology cons. Del. Divsn. Pub. Health, Dover, 1986-95. Contbr. articles to New Eng. Jour. Medicine, Jour. Occupational Medicine, Jour. AMA. With U.S. Army, 1943-45, ETO. Recipient Merit in Authorship Hon. Mention, Inds. Med. Assn., 1959. Fellow Am. Coll. Epidemiology, Am. Heart Assn., Am. Pub. Health Assn. Home: 1416 Emory Rd Wilmington DE 19803-5120

PELL, WILBUR FRANK, JR., federal judge; b. Shelbyville, Ind., Dec. 6, 1915; s. Wilbur Frank and Nelle (Dickerson) P.; m. Mary Lane Chase, Sept. 14, 1940; children: Wilbur Frank III, Charles Chase. A.B., Ind. U., 1937, LL.D. (hon.), 1981; LL.B. cum laude, Harvard U., 1940; LL.D., Yonsei U., Seoul, Korea, 1972, John Marshall Sch. Law, 1973. Bar: Ind. 1940. Pvt. practice Shelbyville, 1940-42, 45-70; spl. agt. FBI, 1942-45; sr. ptnr. Pell & Good, 1949-56, Pell & Matchett, 1956-70; judge U.S. Ct. Appeals (7th cir.), 1970—, now sr. judge; mem. 3 judge spl. divsn. U.S. Ct. Appeals (D.C. cir.), appointing ind. counsel, 1987-92; dep. atty. gen., Ind., 1953-55; dir., chmn. Shelby Nat. Bank, 1947-70. Bd. dirs. Shelbyville Community Chest, 1947-49, Shelby County Fair Assn., 1951-53; dir. Shelby County Tb Assn., 1948-70, pres., 1965-66; dist. chmn. Boy Scouts Am., 1956-57; mem. pres.'s council Nat. Coll. Edn., 1972-87; dir. Westminster Found., Ind. U.; hon. dir. Korean Legal Center. Fellow Am. Coll. Probate Counsel, Am. Bar Found.; mem. ABA (judge Edward R. Finch Law Day USA Speech award 1973), Ind. Bar Assn. (pres. 1962-63, chmn. ho. of dels. 1968-69), Fed. Bar Assn., Ill. Bar Assn., Shelby County Bar Assn. (pres. 1957-58), 7th Fed. Cir. Bar Assn., Am. Judicature Soc., Am. Coun. Assn., Shelby County C. of C., Nat. Conf. Bar Pres.'s, Riley Meml. Assn., Ind. Soc. Chgo. (pres. 1978-79), Harvard Law Soc. Ill. (pres. 1980-81), Rotary (dist. gov. 1952-53, internat. dir 1959-61), Union League, Legal Club (pres. Chgo. 1976-77), Law Club (pres. Chgo. 1984-85), Kappa Sigma, Alpha Phi Omega, Theta Alpha Phi, Tau Kappa Alpha, Phi Alpha Delta (hon.). Republican. Presbyterian (elder, deacon). Office: US Ct Appeals 7th Cir 219 S Dearborn St Ste 2760 Chicago IL 60604-1803 *I have been fortunate - fortunate in having for 55 years a supportive, loving wife, for being selected for the President of the State Bar Association when the nominating committee was split between two others, for being selected as a Federal Judge although never in political office when one was expected to get the position.*

PELLA, MILTON ORVILLE, retired science educator; b. Wilmot, Wis., Feb. 13, 1914; s. Charles August and Ida Marie (Pagel) P.; m. Germaine Marie Reich, Dec. 9, 1944. B.E., Milw. State Tchrs. Coll., 1936; M.S., U. Wis., 1940, Ph.D., 1948. Tchr. sci. and math. Wyler Mil. Acad., 1937-38; tchr. elementary sch. Delavan Pub. Schs., 1938-39; tchr. sci. U. Wis. High Sch., 1939-42; prof. sci. edn. U. Wis., Madison, 1946-80, prof. emeritus, 1980—; With Fgn. Ednl. Service, Turkey, 1959, Iran, Turkey, Jordan, Syria, Lebanon, 1961, 62, Jordan, Lebanon, 1963, 64, 65, 66, 68, Costa Rica, 1967, Saudi Arabia, 1969, Nigeria, 1968, 69, Lebanon and Egypt, 1971-81. Author: Physical Science for Progress, 3d edit, 1970, Science Horizons—The Biological World, (with Branley and Urban), 1965-70. Served with AUS, 1942-46. Fellow A.A.A.S.; mem. Central Assn. Sci. and Math. (pres. 1955), Nat. Assn. for Research in Sci. Teaching (pres. 1966), Nat. Sci. Tchrs. Assn. (dir. 1950, 60). Club: Masons. Home: 5518 Varsity Hl Madison WI 53705-4652

PELLECCHIA, EVE WASSALL, management consultant; b. Columbus, Ohio, Dec. 7, 1956; d. Robert Byron Wassall and Constance Leona (Windey) Moult; m. Dennis John Pellecchia, Oct. 29, 1983; children: Kevin Patrick, Kara René. BS, Lebanon Valley Coll., 1978; MBA, Lehigh U., 1983. CFP. Ops. rsch. analyst Air Products & Chems., Inc., Trexlertown, Pa., 1978-83; ops. rsch. mng. analyst Air Products & Chems., Inc., Trexlertown, 1984-87, ops. rsch. mgr. gas. div., 1987-88; pvt. practice Wyomissing, Pa., 1990—. Mem. Reading Hosp. Aux., Wyomissing, 1987—; fundraiser Am. Heart Assn., 1991—; pres. Cross Keys Wranglers 4-H Club; mem. Wyomissing Hills Shade Tree Commn. Avocations: skiing, tennis, photography, horseback riding. Home: 102 Robert Rd Wyomissing PA 19610-3116

PELLEGRENE, THOMAS JAMES, JR., editor, researcher; b. Wilmington, Del., Dec. 26, 1959; s. Thomas J. and MaryBelle (McGowan) P.; m. Pamela Heinecke, Apr. 5, 1986. BS in Journalism, Northwestern U., 1981, MS in Journalism, 1982. Staff writer Ft. Wayne (Ind.) Journal-Gazette, 1982-87, bus. editor, 1987-95, asst. metro editor, 1995—. Mem. Am. Assn. Pub. Opinion Rsch., Soc. Profl. Journalists. Office: Fort Wayne Journal-Gazette 600 W Main St Fort Wayne IN 46802-1408

PELLEGRINI, ANNA MARIA, soprano; b. Pretoro, Chieti, Italy, July 15, 1944; arrived in Can., 1959, naturalized, 1964; d. Vincenzo and Giuseppina (Pietrantonio) P.; m. Steven Murray Thomas, Aug. 13, 1974; 1 son, Vincent Thomas. Student, U. Toronto, Ont., Can., Faculty of Music, 1962-65. Tchr. voice Italian repertoire. Debut as Gilda in Rigoletto, Can. Opera Co., 1965; leading roles in: Cosi Fan Tutte, La Boheme, Turandot, I Pagliacci, Elektra; title roles in: Madama Butterfly, Manon Lescaut, Can. Broadcasting Corp. TV prodn. Madama Butterfly, 1977; appeared in maj. opera houses throughout the world. Recipient prize Met. Opera Nat. Auditions, 1966, Caravello d'Oro Ufficio Di Turismo, Genova, 1970, medallion honoring her and Puccini Sindico di Teatro Comunale di Treviso, 1974. Mem. Can. Actors Equity, Brit. Equity, Que. (Can.) Union des Artistes, Am. Guild Mus. Artists, Assn. Can. TV and Radio Artists. Office: Sardos Artist Mngmt Corp 180 W End Ave New York NY 10023-4902*

PELLEGRINO, EDMUND DANIEL, physician, educator, former university president; b. Newark, June 22, 1920; s. Michael J. and Marie (Catone) P.; m. Clementine Coakley, Nov. 17, 1944; children: Thomas, Virginia, Michael, Andrea, Alice, Leah. BS, St. John's U., 1941, DSc (hon.), 1971; MD, NYU, 1944; 39 hon. degrees. Diplomate Am. Bd. Internal Medicine. Intern Bellevue Hosp., N.Y.C., 1944-45; asst. resident medicine Bellevue Hosp., 1948-49; resident medicine Goldwater Meml. Hosp., N.Y.C., 1945-46; fellow medicine NYU, 1949-50; supervising Tb physician Homer Folks Hosp., Oneonta, N.Y., 1950-53; dir. internal medicine Hunterdon Med. Center, Flemington, N.J., 1953-59; med. dir. Hunterdon Med. Center, 1955-59; prof., chmn. dept. medicine U. Ky. Med. Center, 1959-66; prof. medicine SUNY, Stony Brook, 1966-72; v.p. for health scis., dir. Health Scis. Center SUNY, 1968-73, dean Sch. Medicine, 1968-72; v.p. health affairs U. Tenn. System; chancellor U. Tenn. Med. Units, Memphis, 1973-75; prof. med. Yale U., New Haven, 1975-78; pres. Yale-New Haven Med. Center, 1975-78, Cath. U. Am., Washington, 1978-82; prof. philosophy and biology Cath. U. Am., 1978-82; John Carroll prof. medicine and med. ethics Georgetown U., Washington, 1982—; dir. Kennedy Inst. Ethics, Washington, 1983-88; dir. Ctr. for Advanced Study Ethics Georgetown U., Washington, 1988-94, dir. Ctr. for Clin. Bioethics, 1991—, acting chief Divsn. Gen. Internal Medicine, 1993-94. Founding editor Jour. Medicine and Philosophy, 1983—. Served with USAAF, 1946-48. Master ACP; fellow N.Y. Acad. Medicine; mem. Inst. Medicine of NAS, AMA, Assn. Am. Physicians, Medieval Acad. Am., Metaphys. Soc. Am., N.Y. Acad. Sci., Am. Clin. and Climatol. Assn. Office: Georgetown U Ctr for Clin Bioethics Washington DC 20007

PELLEGRINO, JAMES WILLIAM, college dean, psychology educator; b. N.Y.C., Dec. 20, 1947; s. Vincent and Emily (Nicosia) P.; m. Barbara Jo Sposato, June 6, 1970 (div. 1975); 1 child, Christopher Michael; m. Susan Rosen Goldman, Dec. 23, 1978; children: Joshua Goldman, Seth Goldman. BS in Psychology, Colgate U., 1969; MS in Experimental, Quantitative Psychology, U. Colo., 1970, PhD in Experimental, Quantitative Psychology, 1973. Asst. prof. U. Pitts., 1973-78, assoc. prof., 1978-79; assoc. prof. U. Calif., Santa Barbara, 1979-83, prof., 1983-89; Frank Mayborn prof. Vanderbilt U., Nashville, Tenn., 1989—, dean Peabody Coll. Edn. and Human Devel., 1991—; co-dir. Learning Tech. Ctr. Vanderbilt U., 1989-91; proposal reviewer NSF, Can. Rsch. Coun., Australian Rsch. Coun.; presenter in field. Author: (with others) Cognitive Psychology and Instruction, 1978, Handbook of Semantic Word Norms, 1978, Memory Organization and Structure, 1979, Aptitude, Learning and Instruction: Cognitive Process Anayses, How Much and How Can Intelligence Be Increased, 1982, Advances in Instructional Psychology, vol. II, 1982, Handbook of Research Methods in Human Memory and Cognition, 1982, Advances in the Psychology of Human Intelligence, 1982, Individual Differences in Cognition, 1983, Human Abilities: An Information Processing Approach, 1984, Test Design: Developments in Psychology and Psychometrics, 1985, International Encyclopedia of Education, 1985, What is Intelligence?, 1986, Arthur Jensen: Consensus and Controversy, 1987, Intelligence and Cognition: Contemporary Frames of Reference, 1987, Metacognition, Motivation and Understanding, 1987, Test Validity, 1988, Learning and Individual Differences: Abilities, Motivation and Methodology, 1989, The Psychology of Learning and Motivation, 1989, The Proceedings of the 22nd Annual Hawaii International Conference on System Sciences, 1989, Vision and Action: The Control of Grasping, 1990, Learning Disabilities: Theoretical and Research Issues, 1990, Intelligence: Reconceptualization and Measurement, 1991, Philosophy of Science, Cognitive Psychology, and Educational Theory and Practice, 1992, New Approaches to Testing: Rethinking Aptitude, Achievement and Assessment, 1992, Cognitive Approaches to Automated Instruction, 1992; co-author: Human Intelligence: Perspectives and Prospects, 1985, Testing: Theoretical and Applied Perspectives, 1989, Instruction: Theoretical and Applied Perspectives, 1991; contbr. numerous articles to profl. jours. NIMH fellow; Colgate U. scholar, N.Y. State Regents scholar, Westchester County Golf Assn. Caddie scholar; recipient Austen Colgate award, Phil R. Miller award, Outstanding Young Men in Am. award. Mem. AAAS, Am. Ednl. Rsch. Assn. (various coms.), Midwestern Psychol. Assn., Rocky Mountain Psychol. Assn., N.Y. Acad. Sci., European Assn. Rsch. on Learning and Instrn., Cognitive Sci. Soc., Soc. Multivariate Experimental Psychology, Computers in Psychology, Soc. Mathematical Psychology, Soc. Rsch. and Child Devel., Psychonomic Soc., Sigma Xi, Phi Beta Kappa, Psi Chi. Avocations: sports, gardening, music. Home: 44 Park Crescent Cir Nashville TN 37215-6115 Office: Vanderbilt U Box 329 Peabody Coll Nashville TN 37203

PELLEGRINO, NANCY DAVIS, middle school educator; b. Newark, Feb. 10, 1944; d. William Francis and Doris (Williams) Davis; m. Donald Nicholas Spano (dec. May 1980); children: Donna, Donald; m. Anthony Joseph Pellegrino Jr., Mar. 17, 1984. BA in Sci., Rutgers U., 1965; MEd, Nat.-Louis U., 1994. Cert. tchr. biology, gen. sci. Biology tchr. Our Lady of Good Coun., Newark, N.J., 1964-67; 4th grade tchr. Most Holy Name of Jesus, Gulfport, Fla., 1974-80; tchr. dropout prevention Pinellas Park (Fla.) Mid. Sch., 1988-93, tchr. sci.-tech. edn. lab., 1993—; chmn. Sch. Adv. Coun., Pinellas Park, 1992-95, pro edn. facilitator, 1993—; presenter Sci.-Tech. Conf., St. Petersburg, Fla., 1993, Edn. at Tech. Conv., Innisbrook, Fla., 1994; curriculum writer Fla. Dept. Edn., Tallahassee, 1994, Improving Edn. in Orlando, 1995; mem. Sch. Adv. Coun.; presenter Quality Expo. Sapp Bookfair scholar Bookfair Assn., 1992; finalist Cigna Tchr. of Yr., 1996. Mem. ASCD, Fla. Assn. Sch. Tchrs., Pinellas Assn. Sci. Tchrs. Avocations: model airplane building, computers. Office: Pinellas Park Mid Sch 6940 70th Ave Pinellas Park FL 33781-3907

PELLEGRINO, PETER, surgeon; b. Camden, N.J., July 7, 1934; s. Peter and Alice (Alchin) P.; m. Barbara Ann Holdon, June 18, 1960; children: Peter Scott, Kathleen Ann, Lisa Marie. AB in Psychology, Franklin-Marshall Coll., 1956; MD, Hahnemann Med. Coll., 1960. Diplomate Am. Bd. Surgery. Intern, Hahnemann Hosp., Phila., 1960-61, surg. resident, 1961-62, surg. resident, 1965-67, 68, attending surgeon, 1969—; chief dept. surgery Kessler Hosp., Hammonton, N.J., 1969—. Served to capt., U.S. Army, 1962-65. Fellow ACS; mem. Am. Acad. Proctology, Soc. Abdominal Surgeons, AMA, N.J. Med. Soc., Hahnemann Alumni Assn. (1st v.p. 1984). Republican. Home: 3 Stafford Ct Berlin NJ 08009-2209 Office: 777 Profl Ctr Hammonton NJ 08037

PELLEGROM, DANIEL EARL, international health and development executive; b. Three Rivers, Mich., May 29, 1944; s. Francis Robert and Regina Elizabeth (Valentine) P.; m. Sally Margaret Stukenbroeker, Nov. 30, 1944; children: Daniel, Jr., Benjamin, Sara. BA, Western Mich. U., 1966; MDiv, Union Theol. Seminary, 1969. Ordained to ministry, Presbyn. Ch., 1970. Dir. coll. programs Planned Parenthood Fedn., N.Y.C., 1969-71; exec. dir. Memphis Planned Parenthood, 1971-75, Md. Planned Parenthood, Balt., 1975-85; pres. Pathfinder Internat., Watertown, Mass., 1985—; bd. dirs. Alan Guttmacher Inst., N.Y.C., InterAction, Washington, Brush Found., Cleve.; bd. dirs. Advocates for Youth, Washington, treas., 1991—; bd. overseers Planned Parenthood League Mass., Cambridge. Mem. Gov.'s conf. on children and youth State of Md., Balt., 1978-80; assoc. sch. hygiene and pub. health Johns Hopkins U., Balt., 1984-85. Recipient Leadership award Greater Balt. Com., 1983-84, UN Population award Pathfinder Internat., 1996, Internat. award Nat. Family Planning and Reproductive Health Assn., 1997. Mem. APHA. Democrat. Avocations: baseball, travel, hiking. Home: 48 Bound Brook Rd Newton MA 02161-2036 Office: Pathfinder Internat 9 Galen St Ste 217 Watertown MA 02172-4521

PELLERZI, LEO MAURICE, lawyer; b. Cumberland, Md., June 14, 1924; s. John and Ida Lezzer (Regis) P.; m. Betty Lou Mearkle, Jan. 17, 1946; children: Jon Lou, Cheryl M., John C., Michele S., Julie A., Laura M., Jeffrey C. LL.B., George Washington U., 1949, LL.M., 1950. Bar: D.C. bar 1949, also U.S. Supreme Ct 1949. Asst. gen. counsel Subversive Activities Control Bd., 1952-56, 1956-59; adminstv. law judge ICC, 1959-65; gen. counsel U.S. Civil Svc. Commn., 1965-68; asst. atty. gen. for adminstrn. Dept. Justice, 1968-73; chmn. bd. Govt. Svcs., Inc., 1971-73; gen. counsel Am. Fedn. Govt. Employees, AFL-CIO, 1973-78; chmn. bd. Flag Filter Corp., 1978-85; pvt. practice law Washington, 1978-90. Gen. counsel Lafayette Fed. Credit Union, 1956-59; pres. Fed. Adminstrv. Law Judges Conf., 1963-65. Served with USAAF, 1943-45; lt. col. Res. Decorated Air medal with 4 oak leaf clusters.; recipient Commrs.'s award U.S. Civil Svc. Commn., 1968, Justice Tom C. Clark award Fed. Bar Assn., 1967. Roman Catholic. Home: 106 Indian Spring Dr Silver Spring MD 20901-3017

PELLETIER, ARTHUR JOSEPH, state legislator, industrial arts and computer programming educator; b. Exeter, N.H., Dec. 13, 1946; s. Joseph Telesphor and Elsie Jane (Dillon) P.; m. Marsha Lynn Mingle, May 19, 1973; 1 child, John. Diploma N.H. Vocat. Tech. Inst., 1966; B.A., Kans. State U., 1970, M.S., 1972. Cert. in secondary edn., guidance. Asst. to dir. Kans. State U. Div. Continuing Edn., Manhattan, 1971-74; tchr. drafting Portsmouth High Sch., N.H., 1974-86; tchr. computer programming McIntosh Coll., Dover, N.H., 1982-84; assoc. prof. N.H. Vocat.-Tech. Coll., Stratham, N.H., 1986-87; kitchen designer Area Kitchen Ctr., Portsmouth, 1987; mem. N.H. Ho. Reps., 1993—; mem. legis. sci., tech. and energy com., 1993-96; mem. legis. edn. com., 1997—; co-founder N.H. Coalition for Edn.; mem. bd. dirs. N.H. Citizen Action, 1991-96; mem. Dover Ready to Learn Task Force, 1995—; mem. Dover Schs. Program Evaluation and Review Com.; mem. Partnership Healthier Cmty., 1995—, Ams. for Non-Smoker's Rights, 1996—; bd. advs. Hub Family Support Ctr., 1996—. Mem. World Future Soc., Seacoast I.B.M. Users Group, Friends of Dover Libr. Avocations: radio-controlled model aircraft; tennis; photography. Home: 94 Back River Rd Dover NH 03820-4411

PELLETIER, LOUIS CONRAD, surgeon, educator; b. Montreal, Que., Can., Mar. 15, 1940; s. Conrad L. and Lucienne (Rochette) P.; m. Louise Montpetit, June 26, 1965; children: Conrad R., Marie-Helene. BA, Brébeuf Coll., Montreal, 1959; MD, U. Montreal, 1964, MBA, 1996. Resident in cardiovascular and thoracic surgery U. Montreal, 1964-70, chmn. dept. surgery, 1986-94; rsch. asst. Mayo Clin. Found., Rochester, Minn., 1970-72; mem. dept. surgery Maisonneuve-Rosemont Hosp., Montreal, 1972-76, Sacré-Coeur Hosp., Montreal, 1972-80; mem. dept. surgery Montreal Heart Inst., 1979—, head dept. surgery, 1979-87. Contbr. articles to profl. jours. Mem. adminstrv. bd. College Stanislas, Montreal, 1979-86, Que. Heart Found., 1980-84, regional healthcare bd., 1991-92, Hotel-Dieu Hosp., 1993-95. Recipient Young Investigator's award Am. Coll. Cardiology, 1972; Med. Rsch. Coun. Can. scholar U. Montreal, 1973-78. Fellow Royal Coll. Physicians and Surgeons Can.; mem. ACS, Association des Medecins de Langue Francaise du Canada, Can. Med. Assn., Royal Coll. Can., Assn. Cardiovascular and Thoracic Surgery Que., Can. Cardiovascular Soc., Montreal Cardiac Soc., Clin. Rsch. Club Que., Soc. Thoracic Surgeons, Can. Assn. Clin. Surgeons, Sociedad de Cardiocirujanos, Coun. on Cardiovasular Surgery, Am. Heart Assn., Internat. Soc. for Heart Transplantation, Can. Soc. Cardiovascular and Thoracic Surgeons, Am. Assn. Thoracic Surgery, Am. Surgical Assn. Roman Catholic. Avocations: skiing, sailing. Office: Montreal Heart Inst, 5000 E Belanger, Montreal, PQ Canada H1T 1C8

PELLETIER, MARSHA LYNN, state legislator, secondary school educator; b. Mt. Pleasant, Mich., July 29, 1950; d. Eugene Russell and Mary Ellen (Edde) Mingle; m. Arthur Joseph Pelletier, May 19, 1973; 1 child, John Frederick. BS in Home Econs. and Edn., Kans. State U., 1971, MS in Edn. Guidance and Counseling, 1972. Lic. rela estate broker, N.H. Conf. coord., guidance counselor Kans. State U., Manhattan, 1971-73; tchr. home econs.

Franklin (Mass.) H.S., 1974, Exeter (N.H.) H.S., 1974-75, Barrington (N.H.) Mid. Sch., 1975-81, Pentucket Regional Jr. H.S., West Newbury, Mass., 1981-82; realtor assoc. Century 21 Ocean and Norword Realty, Portsmouth, N.H., 1983-86; tchr. interior design, cons. U. N.H., Durham, 1986-87; tchr. family and consumer sci. Dover Middle Sch., 1983—; rep. Dist. 12 Dover N.H. Ho. of Reps., Concord, 1992-94, 96—; ind. real estate broker Dover, 1986—;, 1996-98. Bd. dirs. Dover Adult Learning Ctr., 1995—; mem. Health Task Force, Dover and Concord, 1993-94; trustee St. John's Meth. Ch., 1995-97; mem. Dover Friends of the Pub. Libr., 1996—. Mem. NEA (local pres. negotiator, membership chair, leadership exec. com., rep. 1979—), Nat. Coalition for Consumer Edn., Alpha Delta Kappa. (v.p. historian altruistic chmn. 1984-89). Democrat. Avocations: gardening, aerobics, designing, sewing, cooking. Home: 94 Back River Rd Dover NH 03820-4411

PELLETIER, S. WILLIAM, chemistry educator; b. Kankakee, Ill., July 3, 1924; s. Anthony Amos and Estella Edith (Hays) P.; m. Leona Jane Bledsoe, June 18, 1949; children: William Timothy, Jonathan Daniel, Rebecca Jane, Lucy Ruth, David Mark, Sarah Lynn. B.S. with highest honors in Chem. Engring, U. Ill., 1947; Ph.D. in Organic Chemistry, Cornell U., 1950. Instr. chemistry U. Ill., 1950-51; mem. staff Rockefeller Inst., 1951-62, assoc. prof. organic chemistry, 1961-62; prof. chemistry, head dept. U. Ga., 1962-69, Alumni Found. disting. prof., 1969—, provost, 1969-76, Univ. prof., 1976—; dir. Inst. for Natural Products Research, 1976—; Gordon lectr., New Hampton, N.H., 1955, 59, 69; lectr. German Acad. Agrl. Scis., 1959; Am. Swiss Found. lectr., Zurich, Basel, Bern, Geneva, Switzerland, 1960; Commemorative dedication lectr. Shionogi Rsch. Lab., Osaka, Japan, 1961; Victor Coulter lectr. U. Miss., 1965; Nason-Piston lectr. Boston Pub. Libr., 1982; Plenary lectr. 32d Internat. Congress on Medicinal Plant Rsch., Antwerp, Belgium, 1984; lectr. for internat. symposia in Berlin, Melbourne, Hong Kong, Latvia, Prague, Stockholm, London, Riga, Latvia, Varna, Bulgaria, Istanbul, Turkey, also other lectures in Eng., Italy, India, Israel, Taiwan, Japan; mem. health medicinal chemistry study panel NIH, 1968-72. Author: Chemistry of the Alkaloids, 1970, Alkaloids: Chemical and Biological Perspectives, vols. 1-11, 1983-96, 7 monographs on Am. etcher John Taylor Arms, 1975-93, catalog of etchings of Charles Meryon and Jean-Francois Millet, 1994, Adriaen van Ostade, Etchings of Peasant Life in Holland's Golden Age, 1994; editl. bd. Jour. Organic Chemistry, 1966-70, Heterocycles, 1979—, Jour. Natural Products, 1980—, Phytochem. Analysis, 1989—, Trends in Heterocyclic Chemistry, 1994—, Recent Rsch. Devel. in Heterocyclic Chemistry, 1994, Turkish Jour. Chemistry, 1996—, also numerous articles. Pres. bd. Flushing Christian Day Sch., 1956-60; bd. advisers Ga. Mus. Art, 1968—; bd. dirs. Center for Research Libraries, Chgo., 1975-81. Served with USNR, 1944-46. Fellow AAAS, Royal Soc. Arts (London), Royal Soc. Chemistry (London); mem. Am. Chem. Soc. (chmn. N.E. Ga. sect. 1968, Charles Herty medal 1971, So. Chemists award 1972), Am. Soc. Pharmacognosy (hon. life mem., Achievement award 1991), Worldwide Discipleship Assn. (bd. dirs. 1980-88), Sigma Xi, Phi Eta Sigma, Tau Beta Pi, Sigma Tau. Presbyn. (elder). Spl. research structure and stereochemistry diterpenoid alkaloids, applications of carbon-13 nuclear magnetic resonance to structure determination, synthesis of terpenes, X-ray crystallographic structures of natural products. Office: U Ga Dept Chemistry Athens GA 30602-2556 *I have been working in the field of natural products for over forty years now. As we unravel the structures of complex natural products and illuminate their fascinating chemistry. I am impressed over and over with the marvelous design and handiwork of the Creator. In a certain real sense, as I explore and discover new truth about the part of the universe in which I work, I believe that I am thinking God's thoughts after him.*

PELLETREAU, ROBERT HALSEY, diplomat; b. Patchogue, N.Y., July 9, 1935; s. Robert H. and Mary (Pigeon) P.; m. Pamela Day, Dec. 17, 1966; children: Katherine Day, Erica Pigeon, Elizabeth Anne. B.A., Yale U., 1957; LL.B., Harvard U., 1961. Bar: N.Y. 1961. Assoc. firm Chadbourne, Parke, Whiteside & Wolfe, N.Y.C., 1961-62; joined U.S. Fgn. Service, 1962; service in Morocco, Mauritania, Lebanon, Algeria, Jordan and Syria; ambassador to Bahrain, 1979-80, dep. asst. sec. def., 1980-81, 85-87, dep. asst. sec. state, 1983-85, ambassador to Tunisia, 1987-91, ambassador to Egypt, 1991-93; asst. sec. state U.S. Dept. State, Washington, 1994—. Served with USNR, 1957-58. Mem. Am. Fgn. Service Assn., Middle East Inst., Coun. Fgn. Rels. Office: US Dept State Rm 6242 (NEA) Washington DC 20520*

PELLEY, MARVIN HUGH, mining executive; b. St. Anthony, Nfld., Can., Nov. 24, 1947; s. Hugh Albert Pelley and Alma Josie (Harnett) Potter; m. Velma Delilah Gillard, Nov. 5, 1965; 1 child, Rhonda Mary-Jane. Diploma in engring., Meml. U. Nfld., St. John's, 1969, BSc, 1969; B in Engring. with distinction, Tech. U. N.S., Halifax, 1973. Registered profl. engr. Contract miner Whissel Mining Ltd., Nfld., 1969-71; planning engr. Kaiser, N.S., 1972; gen. foreman opers. Iron Ore Co. Can, Nfld., 1973-74, chief engr., 1975-78; exec. v.p./ptnr. Baumgartl & Assoc., Nfld., 1978-81; mgr. tech. svcs. Denison Mines Ltd. Quintette, B.C., 1981-86; v.p. engring./transp. Curragh Resources Inc., Y.T., 1986-87; exec. v.p. mining Curragh Resources Inc., Ont., 1987-91, pres. projects and coal, 1991-92, pres. corp. devel. and projects, 1992-93; pvt. cons., 1993-94; pres. Alagnak Enterprises, Inc., Mississauga, Ont., 1995—; presenter in field. Mem. Am. Inst. Mining Engring., Canadian Inst. Mining and Metallurgy, Assn. Profl. Engrs Nfld., Assn. Profl. Engrs. B.C., Assn. Profl. Engrs. Yukon, B.C. Mining Assn. (bd. dirs. 1989). Avocations: reading, outdoor activities, canoeing, fishing, golf. Office: 1527 Manorbrook Ct, Mississauga, ON Canada L5M 4A9

PELLI, CESAR, architect; b. Tucuman, Argentina, Oct. 12, 1926; came to U.S., 1952, naturalized, 1964; s. Victor V. and Teresa S. (Suppa) P.; m. Diana Balmori, Dec. 15, 1950; children: Denis G., Rafael A. BArch cum laude, U. Tucuman, 1949; MS in Architecture, U. Ill., 1954. Assoc. firm Eero Saarinen & Assocs. (Architects), 1954-64, Daniel, Mann, Johnson & Mendenhall, 1964-68, Gruen Assocs. Inc., L.A., 1968-77, Cesar Pelli & Assocs., New Haven, Conn., 1977—; dean Sch. Architecture, Yale U., New Haven, 1977-84. Works include Pacific Design Ctr. and Expansion, L.A. (Honor award So. Calif. chpt. AIA 1976, Design award from Progressive Architecture 1987), U.S. Embassy, Tokyo, Mus. Modern Art Expansion, N.Y.C., World Fin. Ctr. and Winter Garden, N.Y.C. (Bard award), Cleve. Clinic (Honor award AIA 1986), Herring Hall, Rice U., Houston (Honor award AIA 1986), Carnegie Hall Tower, N.Y.C. (Honor award AIA 1994, Design award AIA/Conn. 1991), Boyer Ctr. Molecular Medicine Yale U. (Design award AIA/Conn.), St. Luke's Med. Tower, Houston (Honor award Modern Healthcare/AIA 1991), NationsBank Corp. Ctr., Charlotte, NTT Corp. Hdqrs., Tokyo, New North Terminal, Washington Nat. Airport, Aronoff Ctr. for the Arts, Cin. (USITT honor award, AIA/Cin. design award), Petronas Twin Towers, Kuala Lumpur, Malaysia, Frances Lehman Loeb Art Ctr. Vassar Coll., Poughkeepsie, N.Y. (AIA/Conn. honor design award); bd. govs. Perspecta mag.; editor Yale Seminars on Architecture, 1981, 82. Fellow AIA (Firm award 1989, named to top ten list of living Am. archs. 1991, Gold medal 1995); mem. NAD (Arnold M. Brunner Meml. prize 1978), Am. Acad. Arts and Letters (academician), Internat. Acad. Architecture (academician). Office: Cesar Pelli & Assocs care Janet Kagan 1056 Chapel St New Haven CT 06510-2402

PELLI, DENIS GUILLERMO, visual perception, psychology educator; b. Champaign, Ill., June 25, 1953; s. Cesar Pelli and Diana Balmori. BA in applied math. magna cum laude, Harvard U., 1975; PhD in physiology, Cambridge U., Eng., 1981. Rsch. fellow Psychology Dept. U. Minn., Mpls., 1979-81; prof. neurosci. Inst. Sensory Rsch. Syracuse (N.Y.) U., 1981-95; prof. psychology and neural sci. NYU, 1995—; dir., founder Computational Neurosci. Program Syracuse U. and SUNY Health Sci. Ctr., 1991-95; adj. prof. dept. psychology Syracuse U., 1991-95; rsch. prof. dept. ophthalmology, SUNY Syracuse Health Ctr., 1991—; freeman Worshipful Co. Spectacle Maker, Brit. Opticians Guild, 1979—; mem. Working Group on Visual Disability Com. on Vision NAS/NRC, Washington, 1993; co-chair low vision panel Nat. Adv. Eye Coun. Vision Rsch. Program Planning Com., 1989-90; mem. reviewers res. NIH, 1993—, visual scis. B study sect., 1989-93, external reviewer, 1989, ad hoc mem., 1986, 87, 88, visual scis. ad hoc study sect., 1986, low vision grants ad hoc study sect., 1985; site visit team mem. Nat. Inst. Aging, 1988; acad. rsch. enhancement awards ad hoc study sect., Nat. Eye Inst., 1985; reviewer NSF, Air Force Office Rsch., Tobacco-Related Disease Rsch. Program of U. Calif. Contbr. articles to profl. jours. Mem. AAAS, APA, Assn. Computing Machinery, Assn Edn. and Rehab. of Blind and Visually Handicapped, Assn. Rsch. Vision and Opthamology, Graphic Arts Tech. Found., IEEE Computer Soc., N.Y. Acad. Scis., Optical Soc. Am., Psychonomics, SIGGRAPH, Soc. Neurosci., Sigma Xi. Achievements include invention of ISR Video Attenuator, 1989, Letters-in-Noise chart, 1987, Pelli-Robson Contrast Sensitivity Chart, 1986, Blurscope and contrast reduction screen for control of resolution and contrast of vision of moving objects, 1986. Home: 110 Bleecker St Apt 15F New York NY 10012-2105 Office: NYU Psychology Dept 6 Washington Pl New York NY 10003-6603

PELLOW, RICHARD MAURICE, state legislator; b. Mpls., 1931; m. Jean Schwaab; 5 children. Grad. h.s. Minn. state rep. Dist. 52B, 1988-92, 95—; former mem. Commerce, Econ. Devel., Edn., Transp. Coms.; currently self-employed. Address: 1471 18th St NW New Brighton MN 55112-5451

PELOFSKY, JOEL, lawyer; b. Kansas City, Mo., June 23, 1937; s. Louis J. and Naomi (Hecht) P.; m. Brenda L. Greenblatt, June 19, 1960; children: Mark, Lisa, Carl. AB, Harvard U., 1959; LLB, 1962. Bar: Mo. 1962, U.S. Dist. Ct. (we. dist.) Mo. 1962, U.S. Ct. Appeals (8th cir.) 1968, U.S. Ct. Appeals (10th cir.) 1970. Law clk. to judge U.S. Dist. Ct. (we. dist.) Mo., 1962-63; mem. Miniace & Pelofsky, Kansas City, Mo., 1965-80; asst. pros. atty. Jackson County (Mo.), 1967-71; mem. Kans. City (Mo.) City Council, 1971-79; judge U.S. Bankruptcy Ct., Western Dist. Mo., Kansas City, 1980-85; ptnr. Shughart, Thomson & Kilroy P.C., Kansas City, 1986-95; apptd. U.S. trustee Ark., Mo., Nebr., 1995—; intermittent lectr. in law U. Mo.; mem. Region I, Law Enforcement Assistance Adminstrn. Bd. dirs. Greater Kansas City Mental Health Found.; mem. adv. bd. Urban League, Kansas City, Mo., chmn. human resource devel. com. Mo. Mcpl. League; bd. dirs., mem. exec. com. Truman Med. Ctr., Kansas City, Mo., pres. bd. 1988-90, chmn. bd., 1990-92; trustee Menorah Med. Ctr., Kansas City, Mo. Served to lt. U.S. Army, 1963-65. Mem. ABA, Mo. Bar, Kansas City Bar Assn., Comml. Law League, Am. Coll. Bankruptcy. Office: US Trustee 818 Grand Blvd Ste 200 Kansas City MO 64106-1910

PELOQUIN, LOUIS OMER, lawyer; b. Tracy, Quebec, Can., June 15, 1957; came to U.S., 1986; s. Gilles and Andree (Gelinas) P.; m. Carole Plante, Aug. 21, 1987; children: Louis-Alexandre, Valerie. BBA, Laval U., Quebec City, Can., 1980; LLB, U. Montreal, Can., 1984; LLM, NYU, 1987. Bar: Que. 1985, N.Y. 1988. Assoc. Martineau Walker, Montreal, Que., Can., 1985-86, Paul, Weiss, Rifkind, Wharton & Garrison, N.Y.C., 1987-89, Shearman & Sterling, N.Y.C., 1989-91, McCarthy Tetrault, Montreal, 1991-93; v.p., gen. counsel, sec. Golden Star Resources Ltd., Denver, 1993—. Contbr. articles to profl. jours. Recipient Richard de Boo prize in Taxation, 1984. Mem. ABA, N.Y. Bar Assn., Quebec Bar Assn., Assn. Am. Corp. Counsel, Rocky Mountain Mineral Law Found. Avocations: golf, skiing, reading, painting. Home: 5300 E Nichols Dr Littleton CO 80122-3892 Office: Golden Star Resources Ltd 1700 Lincoln St Ste 1950 Denver CO 80203-4519

PELOSI, NANCY, congresswoman; b. Balt., Mar. 26, 1941; d. Thomas J. D'Alesandro Jr.; m. Paul Pelosi; children: Nancy Corinne, Christine, Jacqueline, Paul, Alexandra. Grad., Trinity Coll. Former chmn. Calif. State Dem. Com., 1981; committeewoman Dem. Nat. Com., 1976, 80, 84; fin. chmn. Dem. Senatorial Campaign Com., 1987; mem. 99th-102d Congresses from 5th Calif. dist., 1987-1992, 103rd Congress from 8th Calif. dist., 1993—; mem. appropriations com., subcoms. on labor, HHS and edn., fgn. ops., mem. intelligence select com. Office: US House of Rep 2457 Rayburn Bldg Washington DC 20515-0508

PELOSO, JOHN FRANCIS XAVIER, lawyer; b. N.Y., Oct. 7, 1934; s. Rocco C. and Victoria (Musco) P.; m. Elizabeth Byrne Peloso, Oct. 7, 1961; children: Alycia, John, Matthew. BA, Fordham U., 1956, LLB, 1960. Bar: N.Y. 1960, U.S. Dist. Ct. (so. dist.) N.Y. 1962, U.S. Ct. Appeals (2nd cir.) 1967, U.S. Supreme Ct. 1968. Law clk. to judge U.S. Dist. Ct. (so. dist.) N.Y., 1960-61; asst. to U.S. Atty. U.S. Atty.'s Office, N.Y., 1961-65; assoc. Carter Ledyard & Milburn, N.Y., 1965-70; chief trial counsel NYRO-SEC, N.Y., 1970-75; ptnr. Sage Gray Todd & Sims, N.Y., 1975-87, Morgan, Lewis & Bockius, N.Y., 1987—; speaker in field. Contbr. articles to profl. jours. Capt. inf. USAR, 1956-64. Mem. ABA (sect. corp., banking and bus. law, com. fed. regulation securities 1975—, com. bus. and corp. litigation, chair subcom. securities litigation 1993—, litigation co-chmn. com. securities 1983-87, com. on liaison with jud. 1987-88, coun. 1989-91, co-chmn. com. trial evidence 1994-95, co-chmn. task force on the ind. lawyer 1995—), Assn. of Bar of City of N.Y. (arbitration com. 1970-73, fed. legis. com. 1975-78, fed. cts. com. 1982-86), Nat. Assn. Securities Dealers (nat. panel arbitrators 1975—, nat. arbitration com. 1982-85). Office: Morgan Lewis & Bockius 101 Park Ave New York NY 10178

PELOTTE, DONALD EDMOND, bishop; b. Waterville, Maine, Apr. 13, 1945; s. Norris Albert and Margaret Yvonne (LaBrie) P. AA, Eymard Sem. and Jr. Coll., Hyde Park, N.Y., 1965; BA, John Carroll U., 1969; MA, Fordham U., 1971, PhD, 1975. Ordained priest Roman Cath. Ch., 1972. Provincial superior Blessed Sacrament, Cleve., from 1978; ordained coadjutor bishop Diocese of Gallup, N.Mex., 1986-90, bishop, 1990—; nat. bd. dirs. Maj. Superiors of Men, Silver Spring, Md., 1981-86, Tekakwitha Conf., Great Falls, Mont., 1981—. Author: John Courtney Murray: Theologian in Conflict, 1976. 1st native Am. bishop. Mem. Cath. Theol. Soc. Am., Am. Cath. Hist. Soc. *

PELSTER, WILLIAM CHARLES, lawyer; b. St. Louis, May 11, 1942; s. William R. and Marie C. (Graefe) P.; m. Terry C. Cuthbertson, Aug. 9, 1969. BA, Oberlin Coll., 1964; JD, U. Mich., 1967. Bar: Mo. 1967, N.Y. 1968, U.S. Dist. Ct. (so. dist.) N.Y. 1968, U.S. Ct. Appeals (2d cir.) 1968, U.S. Supreme Ct. 1972. Law clk. to presiding justice U.S. Ct. Appeals (2d cir.), N.Y.C., 1967-68; assoc. Donovan, Leisure, Newton & Irvine, N.Y.C., 1968-75; ptnr. Skadden, Arps, Slate, Meagher & Flom, LLP, N.Y.C., 1976—. Trustee Cancer Care Inc., N.Y.C., 1975—. Mem. ABA, Assn. of Bar of City of N.Y. Office: Skadden Arps Slate Meagher & Flom LLP 919 3rd Ave New York NY 10022

PELTASON, JACK WALTER, former university president, educator; b. St. Louis, Aug. 29, 1923; s. Walter B. and Emma (Hartman) P.; m. Suzanne Toll, Dec. 21,1946; children: Nancy Hartman, Timothy Walter H., Jill K. BA, U. Mo., 1943, MA, 1944, LLD (hon.), 1978; AM, Princeton U., 1946, PhD, 1947; LLD (hon.), U. Md., 1979, Ill. Coll., 1979, Gannon U., 1980, U. Maine, 1980, Union Coll., 1981, Moorehead (N.D.) State U., 1980; LHD (hon.), 1980, Ohio State U., 1980, Mont. Coll. Mineral Scis. and Tech., 1982, Buena Vista Coll., 1982, Assumption Coll., 1983, Chapman Coll., 1986, U. Ill., 1989. Asst. prof. Smith Coll., Mass., 1947-51; asst. prof. polit. sci. U. Ill., Urbana, 1951-52, assoc. prof., 1953-59, dean Coll. Liberal Arts and Scis., 1960-64, chancellor, 1967-77; vice chancellor acad. affairs U. Calif., Irvine, 1964-67, chancellor, 1984-92; pres. U. Calif. System, Oakland, 1992-95, Am. Coun. Edn., Washington, 1977-84; prof. emeritus dept. politics and soc. U. Calif., Irvine, 1995—; Cons. Mass. Little Hoover Commn., 1950. Author: The Missouri Plan for the Selection of Judges, 1947, Federal Courts and the Political Process, 1957, Fifty-eight Lonely Men, 1961, Understanding the Constitution, 14th edit., 1997, orig. edition, 1949, (with James M. Burns) Government By the People, 16th edit., 1995, orig. edit., 1952; contbr. articles and revs. to profl. jours. Recipient James Madison medal Princeton U., 1982. Fellow Am. Acad. Arts and Scis.; mem. Am. Polit. Sci. Assn. (council 1952-54), Phi Beta Kappa, Phi Kappa Phi, Omicron Delta Kappa, Alpha Phi Omega, Beta Gamma Sigma. Home: 18 Whistler Ct Irvine CA 92612-4069 Office: U Calif Dept Politics and Society 18 Whistler Ct Irvine CA 92612-4069

PELTIER, EUGENE JOSEPH, civil engineer, former naval officer, business executive; b. Concordia, Kans., Mar. 28, 1910; s. Frederick and Emma Helen (Brasseau) P.; m. Lena Evelyn Gennette, June 28, 1932 (dec.); children: Marion Joyce, Eugene Joseph (dec.), Carole Josephine, Kenneth Noel, Judith Ann. B.S. in Civil Engring., Kans. State U., 1933, LL.D., 1961. Registered profl. engr., Mo., N.Y., Kans., Fla., Va., Calif. Commd. lt. (j.g.) U.S. Navy, 1936, advanced through grades to rear adm., 1957; asst. public works officer Great Lakes, Ill., 1940-42; sr. asst. supt. civil engr. Boston, 1942-44; officer in charge 137th Constrn. Bn. Okinawa, 1945, officer in charge 54th Constrn. Regt., 1945; officer various public works assignments Pensacola, Fla., 1945-46, Memphis, 1946-49, Jacksonville, Fla., 1949-51; dist. public works officer (14th Naval Dist.), 1951-53; asst. chief maintenance and materials Bur. Docks Washington, 1953-56; comdg. officer Pt. Hueneme, 1956-57; chief Bur. Yards and Docks, Navy Dept. Washington, 1957-62; chief of civil engrs., 1957-62, ret., 1962; instrumentman, resident engr. Kans. Hwy. Commn., Norton, Topeka, Chanute, 1934-40; v.p. Sverdrup & Parcel & Assocs., Inc., St. Louis, 1962-64; sr. v.p. Sverdrup & Parcel & Assos., Inc., 1964-66, exec. v.p., 1966-67, pres., dir., 1967-75, chief exec. officer, 1972-75, ptnr., 1966-75, cons., 1975-82; pres., dir. Sverdrup & Parcel & Assos., N.Y., Inc., 1967-75; dir. Sverdrup & Parcel Internat., Inc., 1967-75; v.p., dir. ARO, Inc., Tullahoma, Tenn., 1966-75; cons. EPA, 1976-80; dir. Merc. Trust Co., St. Louis, 1971-81. Mem. emeritus Civic Progress, Inc.; bd. dirs. YMCA, St. Louis, 1972-76. Decorated Legion of Merit; recipient citation Am. Inst. Steel Constrn., 1973. Mem. ASCE (hon.), Am. Public Works Assn. (1 of Top Ten Public Works Men of Year 1960), Soc. Mil. Engrs. (pres. 1960-61), Am. Concrete Inst., Am. Road and Transp. Builders Assn. (pres. 1972-73), Nat. Soc. Profl. Engrs., Mo. Soc. Profl. Engrs., Public Works Hist. Soc. (pres. 1977-78, trustee 1975-79), Nat. Acad. Engring., Cons. Engrs. Council (award of Merit 1962), Sigma Tau, Phi Kappa Phi. Clubs: Army-Navy Country (Washington); Old Warson Country (St. Louis).

PELTIER, JOHN WAYNE (JACK), oil and gas industry executive; b. Merlin, Ont., Can., Dec. 11, 1939; s. Lawrence Joseph and Annabelle (McDonald) P.; m. Irene Lobodowski, Dec. 28, 1965; children: Joy Anne, John Michael. BS, Royal Mil. Coll., 1962; MBA, Queen's U., 1968. Fin. analyst Richardson Secnoitdes, Winnipeg, Can., 1969-77; pres. Unicorp Resources Ltd., Calgary, Can., 1978-84; ptnr. Ipperwash Resources Ltd., Calgary, 1978—; pres. Prodeco Oil & Gas Ltd., Calgary, Can., 1984-85; ptnr. Canson Jennings & Assocs., Calgary, Can., 1985-91, CN Exploration, Inc., Calgary, Can., 1992-97; bd. dirs. Hybridge Exploration, Inc., Calgary, Enermark, Inc., Calgary, Bon Valley Energy Ltd., Belfast Petroleum Ltd., Thunder Energy Ltd.; mem. investment com. Alberta Tchrs. Pension Fund, Edmonton, Can., 1995—. Capt. Can. Infantry, 1958-65. Mem. Calgary Petroleum Club. Avocations: skiing, hiking, mountain biking, mountaineering. Home: 824 Woodpark Way SW, Calgary, AB Canada T2W 2V8

PELTON, CHARLES R., financial institution executive; b. Dayton, Ohio, Mar. 16, 1954; s. Harold N. and Frances (LeFevre) P.; m. Joan E. Madole, Aug. 30, 1975; children: Robert, Nick, Leslie. BBA, U. Cin., 1977. Achievement of Profl. Practice, U. Cin. Asst. v.p. Gem Mortgage Corp. Gem Savs. Assn., Dayton, Ohio, 1974-84; pres. The Kirchman Corp., Altamonte Springs, Fla., 1984-88; sr. v.p. FIS, Inc., Orlando, Fla., 1988—; instr. Inst. Fin. Edn. Sinclair Community Coll., Dayton, Ohio, 1980-82; dir. Bus. Adv. Coun. Valencia Community Coll. Computer Tng. for the Disabled, Olando, Fla., 1991—. Author/editor: Training Guide for IBM Financial Industry, 1983. V.p. Greater Dayton (Ohio) Jr. C. of C., 1976-79, Kettering (Ohio) Optomist Club, 1980-84; allocations chmn. United Way, Warren County, Ohio, 1980-81; dir. Springboro (Ohio) C. of C., 1982-83. Mem. Mortgage Bankers Am., Fla. High Tech. & Industry Coun. Republican. Presbyterian. Avocations: boating, sport fishing, outdoor activities. Home: 199 Sheridan Ave Longwood FL 32750-3967 Office: FIS Inc 401 S Magnolia Ave Orlando FL 32801-3331

PELTON, JAMES RODGER, librarian; b. St. Louis, Mar. 21, 1945; s. Norman C. and Leona V. (Schulte) P.; m. Sandra Lee Birdsell, Mar. 29, 1969; 2 daus., Joni Lee, Vicki Sue. B.A., U. Mo., 1967, M.L.S., 1969. Br. librarian Scenic Regional Library, Union, Mo., 1968-71; adminstr. Daniel Boone Regional Library - Columbia Center, Columbia, Mo., 1971-78; cons. La. State Library, Baton Rouge, 1978-80; dir. Shreve Meml. Library, Shreveport, La., 1980—. Mem. ALA, La. Library Assn. Home: 3201 Old Mooringsport Rd Shreveport LA 71107-3926 Office: 424 Texas St Shreveport LA 71101-3522

PELTON, JOAN ELISABETH MASON, music company owner; b. Bristol, Pa., Feb. 15, 1932; d. William and Mary-Scott (Ryder) Mason; m. Clifford L. Pelton, Feb. 29, 1952 (div. 1977); children: William, Seth, Jesse, Aaron. BA, Pomona Coll., Claremont, Calif., 1953. Owner Silo Inc./Alcazar Inc., Waterbury, Vt., 1977—. Musician recording The Hammered Dulcimer, 1972; producer records Kitchen Junket, 1977, several new releases, particularly children's, 1988-97. Mem. Nat. Assn. Ind. Record Distbrs. (bd. dirs. 1984-91, 91—), Women Bus. Owners Network. Office: Silo Inc/Alcazar Prodns Inc PO Box 686 Waterbury VT 05676-0429

PELTON, JOHN TOM, biochemist; b. Lincoln, Nebr., Oct. 26, 1949; arrived in France, 1987; s. Frederick Lee and Dorothy Avis (Goebel) P.; m. Patricia Diane Lahr, Jan. 3, 1987. BS, U. Nebr., 1971, PhD, 1981. Rsch. assoc. U. Ariz., Tucson, 1981-82, NIH postdoctoral fellow, 1982-84; rsch. scientist Friedrich-Miescher Inst., Basel, Switzerland, 1984-85; sr. rsch. chemist II Merrell Dow Rsch. Inst., Indpls., 1985-87; sr. rsch. biochemist III Merrell Dow Rsch. Inst., Strasbourg, France, 1987-91; rsch. assoc., head peptide and biophys. chemistry Marion Merrell Dow Rsch. Inst., Strasbourg, 1991-94; rsch. scientist, head theoretical and enzyme chemistry Marion Merrell Dow Rsch. Inst., Cin., 1995-97; head phys. methods Hoechst Marion Roussel, Inc., Cin., 1997—. Author, editor books in field; contbr. numerous rsch. articles to profl. publs.; patentee in field. With U.S. Army, 1971-73, Germany. Mem. Am. Chem. Soc., Am. Soc. Biochemistry and Molecular Biology, Am. Peptide Soc., European Peptide Soc., European Fedn. Soc. of Biochemistry, Sigma Xi. Home: 6229 Whileaway Dr Loveland OH 45140-7265 Office: Hoechst Marion Roussel Rsch Inst 2110 Galbraith Rd PO Box 156300 Cincinnati OH 45215-6300

PELTON, RUSSELL GILBERT, lawyer; b. Monticello, N.Y., July 23, 1914; s. William and May (Morgan) P.; m. Marion Gosart, Dec. 14, 1940; children: William, Marjorie, Marilyn Pelton Barringer. BS, Syracuse U., 1935; JD, George Washington U., 1944. Bar: D.C. 1944, N.Y. 1947, U.S. Supreme Ct. 1948, U.S. Dist. Ct. N.Y. 1947; U.S. Dist. Ct. (fed. dist.). Ptnr., Darby & Darby, N.Y.C., 1945-56; sr. v.p. N.Am. Philips Corp., N.Y.C., 1956-75; exec. v.p. U.S. Philips Corp., N.Y.C., 1968-75; of counsel Rogers, Hoge & Hills, N.Y.C., 1976-78; ptnr. Spellman, Joel & Pelton, White Plains, N.Y., 1979-81, Eslinger & Pelton, N.Y.C., 1983-85; officer, dir. Tech. Container Corp., N.Y.C., 1977-95; former dir. Ferroscube Corp., Savgerties, N.Y., Polyseal Corp., N.Y.C.; lectr. Practising Law Inst., 1953-69; arbitrator, mediator Am. Arbitration Assn., 1985—. V.p. Siwanoy coun. Boy Scouts Am., 1948-53; v.p. Rye Neck Bd. Edn., Mamaroneck, N.Y., 1952-62; mem. Zoning Bd. Appeals, 1966-70; town justice, 1970-85; trustee Syracuse U., 1967-73. Patentee in field. Served with Signal Corps, U.S. Army, 1941-45. Mem. ABA, Am. Patent Law Assn. (past chmn. com. antitrust), N.Y. State Bar Assn. (ethics com., Iolta com.), N.Y. Patent Law Assn. (past bd. govs.), State Magistrates Assn., County Magistrates Assn. (treas., v.p., pres.), Westchester County Bar Assn. (dir., chmn. ethics com., alternative dispute resolution com.), Assn. Bar City N.Y. (patent com.), IEEE, Am. Radio Relay League, Aircraft Owners and Pilots Assn., Wings Club, Cloud Club, Winged Foot Golf Club, Waccabuc Country Club, Masons, Elks. Home: 3 Oxford Rd Larchmont NY 10538-1428

PELTON, RUSSELL MEREDITH, JR., lawyer; b. Chgo., May 14, 1938; s. Russell Meredith and Mildred Helen (Baumrucker) P.; m. Patty Jane Rader, Aug. 12, 1961; children: James, Thomas, Michael, Margaret. BA, DePauw U., 1960; JD, U. Chgo., 1963. Bar: Ill. 1963, U.S. Supreme Ct. 1979. Assoc., Peterson, Ross, Schloerb & Seidel, Chgo., 1966-72, ptnr., 1972-90; ptnr. Oppenheimer, Wolff & Donnelly, 1990—, Chgo. mng. ptnr., 1992-95; co-founder, gen. counsel Chgo. Opportunities Industrialization Ctr., 1969-83; gen. counsel Delta Dental Plan Ill., 1979-96; bd. dirs. First United Life Ins. Co., 1979-82. Pres. Wilmette Jaycees, 1970; chmn. Wilmette Sch. Bd. Caucus, 1970-71; Wilmette Dist. 39 Bd. Edn., 1972-80; gen. counsel Am. Assn. Neurol. Surgeons, 1981—; bd. dirs. Wilmette United Way, 1980-86, campaign chmn., 1983-85, pres., 1985-86; Wilmette Zoning Bd. Appeals, 1989—, chmn., 1990—. Served to capt. USAF, 1963-66. Mem. Chgo. Bar Assn., Ill. Bar Assn., ABA, Soc. Trial Lawyers. Office: Oppenheimer Wolff & Donnelly Two Prudential Plz 45th Fl 180 N Stetson Ave Chicago IL 60601-6710

PELTON, SHARON JANICE, emergency physician; b. Cohoes, N.Y., Oct. 21, 1944; d. William Joseph and Lily Marie (Carey) P.; m. John A. Martinec, Sept. 21, 1974 (div. Sept. 1977). BS, Rensselaer Poly. Inst., Troy, N.Y., 1966; MD cum laude, Albany Med. Coll., 1970. Diplomate Am. Bd. Emergency Medicine. Intern and resident Dartmouth Affiliated Hosps.,

Hanover, N.H., 1970-71; emergency physician Ill. Trauma Ctr. Sys., Ill. Emergency Depts., Neenah, Wis., 1971-73; co-initiator emergency physician coverage Theda Clark Hosp., Neenah, Wis., 1973-74; dir. emergency svcs. Oconto Falls (Wis.) Hosp., Naperville, Ill., 1974-76; asst. dir. emergency dept. Edward Hosp., Naperville, Ill., 1976-78; pvt. practice Meml. Hosp., Naperville, Ill., 1978-92; attending physician emergency dept. Meml. Hosp., Carbondale, Ill., 1992—; clin. asst. prof. So. Ill. U., Carbondale, 1994—; lectr. trauma nurse specialist program, Carbondale, 1994—. Advisor N.Am. Riding for Handicapped Assn., Harrisburg, 1995-96. Recipient award for doctor-patient relationship Lamb Found., 1970, Frederich H. Hesser award for excellence in neurology, 1970. Fellow Am. Coll. Emergency Physicians, Am. Acad. Family Physicians; mem. Am. Coll. Sports Medicine, Am. Med. Soc., Ill. State Med. Soc., Alpha Omega Alpha, Pi Delta Epsilon. Avocations: equestrian, animal activist, environmentalist. Office: Meml Hosp Carbondale Carbondale IL 62901

PELTZ, ALAN HOWARD, manufacturing company executive; b. N.Y.C., July 16, 1944; s. Harry and Rachel (Hammer) P.; BBA in Acctg., CCNY, 1966; MBA in Fin., Pace U., 1971; grad. advanced mgmt. program, Harvard U., 1988; m. Frieda Wichter, Nov. 16, 1968; children: Jason, Elissa. Corp. auditor RCA, N.Y.C., 1966-69; sr. fin. analyst Celanese Chem. Co., N.Y.C., 1969-70; asst. treas. Baker Industries, Inc., Parsippany, N.J., 1970-74; v.p. fin., adminstrn., human resources, mgmt. info. systems Burndy Corp., Norwalk, Conn., 1974-93, v.p., CFO, 1993-97, chmn. bd., CEO, 1997—; v.p. fin. Framatome Connectors Internat., Paris, 1993—; mem. faculty Fairfield (Conn.) U., 1979-80; mem. exec. adv. com. Western Conn. State Coll., 1979-80. Bd. dirs. Elderhouse, 1985, Friends of Norwalk Coll., 1986, Hallbrook Hosp. Served as sgt. USMC, 1967-68. Fellow Internat. House Columbia, 1965. Mem. Fin. Execs. Inst., Internat. Treasury Orgn., Norwalk C. of C. (bd. dirs. 1984—), Nat. Assn. Corp. Treas., Mfrs. Alliance Productivity and Innovation Inc. (fin. coun. II), Nat. Elec. Mfrs. Assn. (human resources). Republican. Jewish. Avocations: racquetball, skiing, tennis. Office: Burndy Corp Richards Ave Norwalk CT 06854-2318

PELTZ, PAULETTE BEATRICE, corporate lawyer; b. Bklyn., May 30, 1954; d. Joseph and Margaret P. BA, SUNY, Binghamton, 1976; JD, Am. U., 1979. Bar: D.C. 1980, Va. 1982, Md. 1986. Atty. U.S. EPA, Washington, 1979-83; assoc. Mahn, Franklin & Goldenberg, Washington, 1983-85, Deso, Greenberg & Thomas, P.C., Washington, 1985-87; corp. gen. counsel Western Devel. Corp., Washington, 1987-91; v.p. and corp. gen. counsel Mills Corp., 1992-94; sr. v.p., gen. counsel Charter Oak Ptnrs., 1994—. Home: 11012 Beach Mill Rd Great Falls VA 22066-3026 Office: Charter Oak Ptnrs 8000 Towers Crescent Dr Ste 950 Vienna VA 22182-2700

PELTZER, DOUGLAS LEA, semiconductor device manufacturing company executive; b. Clinton, Ia., July 2, 1938; s. Albert and Mary Ardelle (Messer) P.; m. Nancy Jane Strickler, Dec. 22, 1959; children: Katharine, Eric, Kimberly. BA, Knox Coll., 1960; MS, N.Mex. State U., 1964; MBA, U. Phoenix, 1990. Rsch. engr. Gen. Electric Co., Advanced Computer Lab., Sunnyvale, Calif., 1964-67; large scale integrated circuit engr. Fairchild Camera & Instrument, Rsch. & Devel. Lab., Palo Alto, Calif., 1967-70, bipolar memory divsn., Mountain View, Calif., 1970-83, tech. dir., 1977-83; v.p. tech. ops. Trilogy Systems Corp., Cupertino, Calif., 1983-85; pres. Tactical Fabs, Inc., 1985-89; v.p. process devel. Chips and Techs. Inc., 1989-92; pres, CEO Camlan, Inc., San Jose, Calif., 1992-94; staff Chip Express, Santa Clara, Calif., 1994—; prin. Corp. Tech. Devel., 1994—. NSF fellow, 1962-63; recipient Sherman Fairchild award for tech. excellence, 1980, Semiconductor Equipment and Materials Inst. award, 1988; Inventor of Yr. award Peninsula Patent Law Assn., 1982. Mem. AAAS, IEEE, Sigma Pi Sigma. Inventor in field; patentee in field. Home: 10358 Bonny Dr Cupertino CA 95014-2908

PELTZIE, KENNETH GERALD, hospital administrator, educator; b. Kansas City, Nov. 17, 1933; s. Sam and Leah (Unell) P.; m. Suzan Francis Orringer, July 19, 1964; 1 child, Sharon Lynn. BA, Washington U., 1955; MS, Columbia U., 1958. Adminstrv. officer USAF Hosp., Dyess AFB, Tex., 1958-61; budget examiner Officer Mgmt. & Budget, 1961-66; assoc. adminstr. Sinai Hosp. Detroit, 1966-72; v.p. Chi Systems, Ann Arbor, Mich., 1972-80; sr. v.p. Robert Douglas Assocs., Houston, 1980-82; exec. v.p. Community Hosp. of Indpls., 1982-86; pres. Affiliated Hosps. Ind., Indpls., 1982-86; v.p. corp. strategy Bethesda Healthcare Corp., Boynton Beach, Fla., 1987—; adj. asst. prof. Fla. Atlantic U., Boca Raton, 1991—; mem. adv. bd. Stewart James Rsch. Ctr., Boca Raton, Fla., 1991—. Co-author: Continued Care & Cost Containment, 1974; contbr. articles to profl. jours. Mem. com. United Way of Palm Beach County, West Palm Beach, Fla., 1992-93; active Leadership Palm Beach. Fellow ACHE; mem. Am. Hosp. Assn., Internat. Hosp. Fedn., Soc. Healthcare Plannig & Mktg., Rotary Club Delray Beach. Office: Bethesda Meml Hosp 2815 S Seacrest Blvd Boynton Beach FL 33435-7934

PELTZMAN, SAM, economics educator; b. Bklyn., Jan. 24, 1940; s. Benjamin Raphael and Ceil (Heller) P.; m. Nancy Virginia Bradney, Sept. 7, 1952; children: Shira Malka, Talya Rose. BBA, CCNY, 1960; PhD, U. Chgo., 1965. Prof. econs. UCLA, 1964-73; sr. staff economist Council of Econ. Advisers, Washington, 1970-71; prof. econs. grad. sch. bus. U. Chgo., 1973-87, Sears, Roebuck prof., 1987—; dir. George J. Stigler Ctr. for Study The Economy and the State U. Chgo., U. Chgo., 1992—; vis. fellow Inst. for Advanced Study Hebrew U., Jerusalem, 1978. Co-author: Public Policy Toward Mergers, 1967; editor Jour. Law and Econs.; contbr. articles to profl. jours. Mem. Am. Econ. Assn., Mt. Pelerin Soc. Jewish. Office: U Chgo Grad Sch Bus 1101 E 58th St Chicago IL 60637-1511

PELZ, ROBERT LEON, lawyer; b. N.Y.C., Nov. 18, 1918; s. Leon S. and Fanny M. (Berk) P.; m. Mary Jane Gips, Feb. 11, 1949; children: Kathryn Louise, Robert Leon. AB, Columbia U., 1939, JD, 1942. Bar: N.Y. 1942. Since practiced in N.Y.C.; ptnr. Hess Segall Guterman Pelz Steiner & Barovick, 1953-86, Loeb and Loeb, N.Y.C., 1986—; chmn. bd. dirs. Commentary mag. Life trustee, former v.p. Fedn. Jewish Philanthropies; bd. dirs., chmn. legal com., former chmn. bd. dirs. Fedn. Jewish Philanthropies Svc. Corp.; past trustee Coll. Pharm. Scis. Columbia U.; former chmn. bd. trustees Am. Jewish Com. Capt. AUS, WWII. Office: Loeb and Loeb 345 Park Ave New York NY 10154-0004

PEMBER, JOHN BARTLETT, social worker, educator; b. White Plains, N.Y., June 24, 1951; s. John Raymond and Allyn Marie (Case) P.; m. Deborah Ann Dudley, June 9, 1973; children: John Scott, Matthew Bartlett, Jenna Lynne. BA, Houghton (N.Y.) Coll., 1973; MSW, SUNY, Buffalo, 1978. Cert. social worker, N.Y. Social work asst. Cuba (N.Y.) Meml. Hosp. and Skilled Nursing Facility, 1973-76; staff social worker Wyoming County Mental Health, Warsaw, N.Y., 1978-80, supervising social worker, 1980-85; parole officer N.Y. State Div. Parole, Rochester, 1985-87; team supr., social worker II, Capital Dist. Psychiat. Ctr., Albany, N.Y., 1987—; pvt. practice Capital Area Christian Counseling Svc., Delmar, N.Y., 1988—; social work cons., Warsaw, 1978-87; instr. field work SUNY, Buffalo, 1982-85, SUNY, Albany, 1987—; clin. instr. dept. psychiatry Albany Med. Coll., 1991—. Mem. NASW. Avocations: fishing, hiking, gardening, softball, camping. Office: Capital Area Christian Cons PO Box 313 Delmar NY 12054-0313

PEMBERTON, BOBETTE MARIE (HARMAN), nursing administrator; b. San Mateo, Calif., Oct. 20, 1952; d. William Adolph and Agnes Marie (Costa) Harman; m. William Charles Pemberton (div. Sept. 1993). BSN, U. San Francisco, 1975, PHN. RN, Calif., Hawaii, Fla., Ind.; cert. pub. health nurse, flight nurse, oper. rm. nurse. Recreation supr. Burlingame (Calif.) Recreation Ctr., 1968-74; nursing asst. III Stanford U. Med. Ctr., Palo Alto, Calif., 1974-75, staff nurse, 1976-78; clin. edn. supr., mobile ops. supr. Irwin Meml. Blood Bank, San Francisco Med Soc., 1978-87; OR staff nurse U. Calif., Davis, 1987-88; asst. dir. blood svcs. ARC, Farmington, Conn., 1988-89; coord. blood bank St. Anthony's Med. Ctr., St. Petersburg, Fla., 1989-90; dir. donor svcs. Hunter Blood Ctr., Clearwater, Fla., 1990-93; dir. nursing svcs. Blood Bank of Hawaii, Honolulu, 1993-95; dir. nursing Peninsula Blood Bank, 1995—; chairperson nursing edn. com. Calif. Blood Bank System, No. Calif. region seminar Irwin Meml. Blood Bank; mem. sci. com. Blood Bank Nurses Calif., Calif. Blood Bank System; nursing rep. Local 535; lectr. in field. With USAFR, 1983—. Mem. NAFE, Am. Bus. Women's Assn. (rec. sec., chairperson spring conf. Burlingame charter chpt., del. Kansas City conv.), Am. Assn. Blood Banks, Calif. Blood Bank Soc. (nursing and donor svcs. com., continuing edn. com.), Air Force Assn., Air Force Res. Officers Assn. Republican. Roman Catholic. Avocations: swimming, country dancing, horseback riding, Civil War history. Home: 512 Marin Dr Burlingame CA 94010-2727

PEMBERTON, HARRISON JOSEPH, philosopher, educator; b. Orlando, Fla., Mar. 3, 1925; s. Harrison Joseph and Frances (Chappell) P. A.B., Rollins Coll., 1949; M.A., Yale U., 1951, Ph.D., 1953. Instr. Yale U., 1951-54; asst. prof. U. Va., 1954-62; mem. faculty Washington and Lee U., 1962—, prof. philosophy, chmn. dept., 1967-90; vis. prof. U. Tex., summers 1962, 66, 69, Chung Chi Coll., Chinese U. Hong Kong, 1971. Author: The Parmenides of Plato: The Critical Moment for Socrates. Served with U.S. Army, 1943-46. Fellow Pierson Coll., Yale, 1952-54, NEH fellow U. Tex., 1986. Mem. Phi Beta Kappa. Home: 602 S Main St Lexington VA 24450-2246

PEMBERTON, JOHN DE JARNETTE, JR., lawyer, educator; b. Rochester, Minn., Apr. 21, 1919; s. John de Jarnette and Anna Trego (Hogeland) P.; m. Frances E. Werner, July 23, 1973; children by previous marriage: Ann O., Sarah F., Caro G., Nancy S., James de Jarnette. B.A., Swarthmore (Pa.) Coll., 1940; LL.B., Harvard U., 1947. Bar: N.C. 1949, Minn. 1950, N.Y. 1969, Calif. 1976. Acting asst. prof., then assoc. prof. Duke U. Law Sch., Durham, N.C., 1947-50; ptnr. Pemberton, Michaels, Bishop & Seeger, Rochester, 1950-62; nat. exec. dir. ACLU, 1962-70; prof. U. San Francisco Law Sch., 1973-86; dep. gen. counsel, then acting gen. counsel EEOC, 1971-73; regional atty. dist. office EEOC, San Francisco, 1986-94; adj. lectr. NYU Law Sch., 1968-70, U. San Francisco Law Sch., 1986—; mem. legal com. No. Calif. chpt. ACLU, 1973-86. Assoc. editor and/or editor sects. in law jours. Chmn. Olmsted County (Minn.) Republican Party, 1958-61; commnr. Minn. Fair Employment Practices Com., 1961-62; exec. com Leadership Conf. Civil Rights, 1967-68. Served with Am. Field Service, 1941-45. Mem. ABA, Calif. Bar Assn. Quaker. Home: 11739 Laurel Dell Ave Monte Rio CA 95462-9740

PEÑA, FEDERICO FABIAN, federal official; b. Laredo, Tex., Mar. 15, 1947; s. Gustavo J. and Lucille P.; m. Ellen Hart, May 1988. BA, U. Tex., Austin, 1969, JD, 1972. Bar: Colo. 1973. Ptnr. Pena & Pena, Denver, 1973-83; mayor City and County of Denver, 1983-91; pres. Peña Investment Advisors, Inc., Denver, 1991-93; sec. U.S. Dept. of Energy, Washington, 1993—; assoc. Harvard U. Ctr. for Law and Edn., Cambridge, Mass.; mem. Colo. Bd. Law Examiners. Mem. Colo. Ho. of Reps., 1979-83, Dem. leader, 1981. Named Outstanding House Dem. Legislator, Colo. Gen. Assembly, 1981. Roman Catholic. Home: 3517 Sterling Ave Alexandria VA 22304-1834 Office: Dept of Energy Office Sec 1000 Independence Ave SW Washington DC 20585-0001*

PEÑA, JUAN JOSÉ, interpreter; b. Hagerman, N.Mex., Dec. 13, 1945; s. Rosa Peña; m. Petra Cervantes, Dec. 22, 1974 (div. 1982); children: Federico Ezequiel, Margarita Maria Blea. BA, N.Mex. Highlands U., 1968, MA, 1972, postgrad. With Albert Garcia Gen. Contr., Las Vegas, N.Mex., 1955-67; teaching asst. N.Mex. Highlands U., Las Vegas, 1971-72, prof. Spanish, Chicano studies, 1972--78; teaching asst. U. N.Mex., Albuquerque, 1978-79; attendant N.Mex. State Mental Hosp., Las Vegas, 1982-83; staff and supervisory interpreter U.S. Dist. Ct. N.Mex., Albquerque, 1983—; head Raza Unida del to PLO in Lebanon, 1981, head negotiator with Iranians for release of 2 Chicanos and 1 Indian; supr ct. interpreters and reporters sect. U.S. Dist. Ct. N.Mex.; co-chmn. Cuatro-Centennial Com., Inc.; mem. exec. com. N.Mex. Human Rights Coalition. Author collection of poetry: Angustias y Remembranzas; contbr. articles to profl. jours.; author play: Canto a La Raza, 1978. Pres. Dads Against Discrimination, Albuquerque, 1993—; chmn. bd. trustees No. N.Mex. Legal Svcs., Las Vegas, 1972-81; mem. exec. com. Ind. Socialist Parties of Latin Am.; exec. commn. N.Mex. Human Rights Coalition. Decorated Bronze Star medal. Mem. N.Mex. Translator and Interpreters Assn. (pres. 1984-86), Nat. Assn. Judiciary Interpreters (sec. 1986-88), Nat. Partido Raza Unida (pres. 1976-81), N.Mex. Partido Raza Unida (pres. 1972-75, 77-78), Vietnam Vets. Am. (vice chmn. chpt. 1993—), Vietnam Vets. N.Mex., Am. GI Forum (Albuquerque Chpt. 1 comdr. 1993—), N.Mex. GI Forum (comdr. 1996), Nat. Assn. Chicano Studies (founding mem.), N.Mex. Chicano Studies Assn. (pres. 1972-78), Hispanic Round Table of N.Mex. (chmn. 1995), Barelas Neighborhood Assn. (pres.), Phi Sigma Iota. Democrat. Roman Catholic. Avocations: weight lifting, swimming, ice skating, hiking, camping. Home: 1115 9th St SW Albuquerque NM 87102-4027 Office: US Dist Ct Dist of NM 421 Gold Ave SW Rm 108 Albuquerque NM 87102-3254

PENA, MANUEL, JR., state senator; b. Cashion, Ariz., Nov. 17, 1924; s. Manuel and Elvira (Gomez) P.; student public schs.; m. Aurora Cruz, June 13, 1945; children: Yolanda, Mary, Henry, Steve, Patricia, Geraldine, Manuel III. Owner Pena Realty & Ins. Agy., Phoenix, 1951-90; ret.; pres. emeritus Pena Ins. Agy., 1990; pres. Penasco, Inc.; mem. Ariz. state adv. com. U.S. Commn. Civil Rights, 1974, Ariz. Ho. of Reps., Phoenix, 1967-72, Ariz. Senate, Phoenix, 1973-97. Exec. sec. Ariz. Athletic Commn., 1964-66, 67-71; v.p. bd. dirs. Ariz. Consumers Coun., 1960—; commr. human rels. City of Phoenix, 1967-71. With U.S. Army, 1945-46. Mem. VFW, Am. Legion (comdr.). Democrat. Roman Catholic.

PENA, MARIA GEGES, academic services administrator; b. Torrance, Calif., Nov. 27, 1964; d. Nicholas John and Dina Connie (Vengel) Geges; m. Vicente Gregorio Pena, June 22, 1991. AA, El Camino Coll., 1985; BA, U. Calif., San Diego, 1987; MS, San Diego State U., 1989, postgrad.; postgrad., Claremont Grad. Sch., 1990—, Western State U., 1995—. Peer counselor El Camino Coll., Torrance, Calif., 1982-85; peer advisor U. Calif., San Diego, 1985-87, vice chancellor student affirmative action rsch. intern, 1986-87, outreach asst. disabled student svcs., 1986-89; coord. student svcs. Mira Costa Coll., Oceanside, Calif., 1989—. Contbr. articles to profl. jours. Mem. Calif. Assn. Postsecondary Educators of Disabled. Democrat. Greek Orthodox. Avocations: law, education, CD collecting, collecting Beatles memorabilia. Office: Mira Costa Coll 1 Barnard Dr Oceanside CA 92056-3820

PENA, RAYMUNDO JOSEPH, bishop; b. Corpus Christi, Tex., Feb. 19, 1934; s. Cosme A. and Elisa (Ramon) P. D.D., Assumption Sem., San Antonio, 1957. Ordained priest Roman Catholic Ch., 1957; asst. pastor St. Peter's Ch., Laredo, Tex., 1957-60, St. Joseph's-Our Lady of Fatima, Alamo, Tex., 1960-63, Sacred Heart, Mathis, Tex., 1963-67, Christ the King and Our Lady of Pillar Parishes, Corpus Christi, 1967-69; pastor Our Lady of Guadalupe Parish, Corpus Christi, 1969-76; v.p. Corpus Christi Diocesan Senate of Priests, 1970-76; aux. bishop of San Antonio, 1976-80; bishop El Paso, 1980-95, Brownsville, Tex., 1995—; mem. secretariat to Prep. Synod of Bishops for Am. Mem. Nat. Conf. Cath. Bishops, U.S. Cath. Conf. (chmn. bishops' com. for hispanic affairs 1987-90, bishops' com. for ch. in L.Am. 1994-97). Home: Rt 8 Box 629 7600 Old Military Rd Brownsville TX 78522 Office: PO Box 2279 Brownsville TX 78522-2279

PENACHIO, ANTHONY JOSEPH, JR., psychotherapist, hypnotherapist, behavioral therapist; b. Stamford, Conn., Apr. 3, 1943; 1 child, Ariana. Cert. in psychotherapy, Am. Sch. Hynotherapy, 1978; DD, Aquarian Ch. of Jesus, 1978; PSD, Neotharian Sch. Philosophy, 1980. Cert. clin. registered hypnotherapist, psychotherapist, behavioral therapist. Counseling min., exec. dir. Inst. Clin. Tricotomy, Stamford; lectr., radio and cable TV talk show seminar presenter. Contbr. articles profl. jours. Mem. Am. Coun. Hypnotherapist-Psychotherapist (bd. examiners), N.Y. Acad. Sci. Home and Office: 965 Hope St Stamford CT 06907-2227

PENCE, HOBERT LEE, physician; b. Campton, Ky., July 14, 1941; s. Bruce Elmer and Elva (Banks) P.; m. Marsha Lee Sweet, June 29, 1962; children: Robert, Ryan, Stefanie. BS, Ohio State U., Columbus, 1963, MD, 1968. Residency Walter Reed Gen. Hosp., Washington, 1969-71, fellowship in allergy and clin. immunology, 1971-73; pvt. practice pvt. practice, Louisville, 1975—; asst. clin. prof. medicine U. Louisville, 1976-81, assoc. clin. prof. medicine, 1981—; assoc. clin. prof. Pediat. U. Louisville, 1995—. Contbr. articles to profl. jours. V.p. Jefferson County Med. Soc., Louisville, 1984-86; pres. Greater Louisville Allergy Soc., 1990-92. Major U.S. Army, 1969-75. Mem. Southeastern Allergy Assn. (1st v.p., pres. elect, pres. 1996). Avocations: golf, tennis, reading. Office: Kentuckiana Allergy 9113 Leesgate Rd Louisville KY 40222-5003

PENCE, IRA WILSON, JR., material handling research executive, engineer; b. Pontiac, Mich., June 18, 1939; s. Ira Wilson and Fern Elizabeth (Fraser) P.; m. JoAnna Springer, Sept. 5, 1959; children: Ira W. III, Teresa Ann, Deidre Lynn. BS, U. Mich., 1962, MSEE, 1964, PhD, 1970. Rsch. engr. Willow Run Labs., Ypsilanti, Mich., 1960-67, Dow Lab., Ann Arbor, Mich., 1967-70, GE, Schenectady, N.Y., 1970-80; engring. mgr. GE, Charlottesville, Va., 1980-83; v.p. engring. Unimation, Inc., Danbury, Conn., 1983-87; dir. MHRC Ga. Inst. Tech., Atlanta, 1987-94; cons. Superior Motor, Hartford, 1987-89; bd. dirs. Wesley Foundation; adv. council Westinghouse, Pittsburgh, 1983-87. Editor: Progress in Material Handling and Logistics, 1988; Material Handling for 90's, 1990. Trustee United Meth. Ch., 1988—. Recipient New Product of Yr. award Innovation Today, 1985. Mem. IEEE (sr., sect. chmn. 1978), ASME (Materials Handling Engring. divsn. chair 1994). Republican. Methodist. Avocations: cabinet making, golf. Office: Ga Inst Tech 765 Ferst Dr Atlanta GA 30332-0205

PENCE, MARTIN, federal judge; b. Sterling, Kans., Nov. 18, 1904; m. Eleanor Fisher, Apr. 12, 1975. Bar: Calif. 1928, Hawaii 1933. Practice law Hilo, Hawaii, 1936-45, 50-61; judge 3d Circuit Ct., Hawaii, 1945-50; chief judge U.S. Dist. Ct., Hawaii, 1961-74; sr. judge U.S. Dist. Ct., 1974—. Office: US Dist Ct Rm C-426 PO Box 50128 Honolulu HI 96850*

PENCE, ROBERT DUDLEY, biomedical research administrator, hospital administrator; b. Hillsboro, Ohio, June 16, 1928; s. Glenn Roush and Mildred (Wright) P. BA cum laude, Miami U., Oxford, Ohio, 1950; postgrad., U. Montpellier, France, 1950-51. Mktg. rep. Tex. Petroleum Co., West Africa, 1956-58; mgr. lab. and office svcs. Sloan-Kettering Inst. for Cancer Rsch., N.Y.C., 1958-68; bus. mgr., cancer rsch. inst. New Eng. Deaconess Hosp., Boston, 1968-72, adminstr. Shields Warren Radiation Lab., 1970-78, asst. dir., 1972-86, adminstrv. dir., cancer rsch. inst., 1974-88, adminstrv. dir. Shields Warren Radiation Lab., 1978-88, dir. div. of rsch., 1986-88, cons., 1988—; field liaison fellow ACS, Chgo., 1981-88. Pres. Am. Cancer Soc., Brookline, Mass. Served to lt. (j.g.) USN, 1951-55. Fulbright scholar, Montpellier, 1950. Mem. Assn. Community Cancer Ctrs. (del.), Internat. Union Against Cancer (U.S. standing com.), Assn. Am. Cancer Insts., Soc. Rsch. Adminstrs. (charter), Nat. Coun. Univ. Rsch. Adminstrs., Nat. Tumor Registrars Assn. (advisor 1980—), Tumor Registrars Assn. New Eng. (bd. dirs. 1975—), Phi Beta Kappa. Home: 30 Driftwood Cir Norwood MA 02062-5505

PENCEK, CAROLYN CARLSON, treasurer, educator; b. Appleton, Wis., June 13, 1946; d. Arthur Edward and Mary George (Notaras) Carlson; m. Richard David Pencek, July 10, 1971; children: Richard Carlson, Mallory Barbara Rowlinds. BA in Polit. Sci., Western Coll., 1968; Ma in Polit. Sci., Syracuse U., 1975; postgrad., Temple U., 1991—. Investment analysts asst. Bankers Trust Co., N.Y.C., 1969-71; substitute tchr. Lackawanna Trail Sch. Dist., Factoryville, Pa., 1971-81; instr. polit. sci. Keystone Coll., La Plume, Pa., 1972-73; USGS coding supr. Richard Walsh Assocs., Scranton, Pa., 1975-76; instr. polit. sci. Pa. State U., Dunmore, 1976-77; treas. Creative Planning Ltd., Dunmore, 1988—; bd. trustees Lourdesmont Sch., Clarks Summit, Pa., 1989—. Bd. dirs. Lackawanna County Child and Youth Svcs., Scranton, 1981—, pres., 1988-90; founding mem., sec. Leadership Lackawanna, 1982-84; bd. dirs. N.E. Pa. Regional Tissue and Transplant Bank, Scranton, 1984-88, Vol. Action Ctr., Scranton, 1986-91; founding mem. Women's Resource Ctr. Assn., Scranton, 1986—, pres., 1986-87; v.p. sch. improvement coun. Lackawanna Trail Sch. Dist., 1995-96, sec., 1996-97. Named Vol. of Yr. nominee, Vol. Action Ctr., 1985; Temple U. fellow, Phila., 1991-92. Mem. AAUW (sec. 1973-75, state sel. com. 1979-81), Assn. Jr. Leagues Internat. (area II coun. mem. 1978-79), Jr. League Scranton (v.p. 1980, pres. 1981-83, Margaret L. Richards award 1984), Philharmonic League (v.p. 1976, pres. 1977). Episcopalian. Home: RR 2 Box 2489 Factoryville PA 18419-9649 Office: Creative Planning Ltd 1100 Dunham Dr Dunmore PA 18512-2653

PENDAGAST, EDWARD LESLIE JR., physician; b. Danbury, Conn., Aug. 3, 1932; s. Edward Leslie and Ruth Arlene (Staib) P.; m. Eileen Jean Guerin, Feb. 3, 1968; children: Edward Leslie Pendagast III, Eileen Leslie Pendagast. BS, Yale U., 1954; MD, N.Y. Med. Coll., 1958. Intern St. Vincent's Hosp., Bridgeport, Conn., 1958-59; pvt. practice Bridgeport, 1959-68, pres., St. Vincent's Emergency Physicians, 1969-76; attending emergency physician Norwalk (Conn.) Hosp., 1976-78, courtesy emergency physician, 1979—; dir., emergency dept. New Milford (Conn.) Hosp., 1978—; dir. health Town of Easton (Conn.), 1972—; asst. med. examiner State of Conn., 1980—; med. adv. bd. Bridgeport Visiting Nurse Assn., 1962-65; exec. com. New Milford Hosp., 1978—, Core Content Rev. Family Medicine, Bloomfield, Conn., 1984-87. Co-author: Advanced Skills in Emergency Care, 1982, The First Minutes, 1984, 2d edit., 1988; consulting physician: Emergency Handbook, 1980; editl. bd. Reviewing Basic EMT Skills, 1982. Fire commr. Town of Easton, 1972—; mem. Emergency Med. Svc. Commn., Town of Easton, 1972-75. Mem. Am. Acad. Family Physicians, Conn. Acad. Family Physicians (bd. dirs. 1977-82, 91-93, pres. 1983-84), Am. Coll. Emergency Physicians, Conn. Coll. Emergency Physicians (councillor to nat. 1982), Black Rock Yacht Club, Bridgeport. Republican. Roman Catholic. Avocations: gardening, hunting, sailing, fishing. Home: 94 Burr St Easton CT 06612-1616 Office: New Milford Hospital 21 Elm St New Milford CT 06776-2915

PENDARVIS, DONNA KAYE, elementary and secondary school educator, adminstrator; b. New Orleans, June 19, 1959; d. Ray Haddox and Nita Sims; 1 child, Krista. BS, U. So. Miss., 1979; MEd, William Carey Coll., 1982, EdS, 1984; MEd in Guidance and Counseling, Southeastern La. U., 1992. Cert. elem. tchr., Miss., La.; lic. profl. counselor. Tchr. Sumrall (Miss.) Elem. Sch., 1979-88; tchr. kindergarten Washington Parish Sch. Bd., Franklinton, La., 1988-89; elem. tchr. Columbia (Miss.) Acad., 1989-92; counselor and adminstr. St. Tammany Parish, Covington, La., 1992-94; counselor, adminstr. Varnado (La.) H.S., 1994-96; counselor Sixth Ward Jr. H.S., Pearl River, La., 1996—; mem. La. Disting. Educator Team. Grantee Miss. Power Found. Mem. NEA, ASCD, Am. Assn. Math. Tchrs., Am. Fedn. Tchrs., Miss. Fedn. Tchrs., La. Edn. Assn., Lamar County Classroom Tchrs. Assn., Washington Parish Reading Assn., Miss. Pvt. Sch. Assn., La. Counselors Assn., La. Vocat. Assn., La. Adminstrn. Sch. Employees Assn., Chi Omega Iota. Home: 276 C Lakeview Dr Slidell LA 70458 Office: Sixth Ward Jr High Sch 72360 Highway 41 Pearl River LA 70452-2547

PENDERECKI, KRZYSZTOF, composer, conductor; b. Debica, Poland, Nov. 23, 1933; s. Tadeusz and Zofia P.; m. Elzbieta Solecka; children: Lukasz, Dominique. Grad., State Acad. Music, Krakow, 1958; student, Arthur Malawski and Stanislaw Wiechowicz; Dr. honoris causa, U. Rochester, St. Olaf Coll., Northfield, Minn., Cath U., Leuven, Belgium, U. Bordeaux, France, Georgetown U., Belgrade U., Madrid U., Spain, Adam Mickiewicz U., Warsaw U., Poland, 1993, U. Catolica Argentina, Buenos Aires, 1994, Acad. Music, Cracow, 1994, Acad. Music, Warsaw, 1994, U. Glasgow, 1995. Prof. composition Krakow State Sch. Music, 1959-65, Folkwang Hochschule für Musik, Essen, Fed. Republic Germany, 1966-68; composer-in-residence Sch. Music, Yale U., alternate years; guest condr. London Symphony Orch., Polish Radio Orch., Berlin Philharm. Orch. Composer: Psalms of David for chorus and percussion, 1958, Emanations for 2 string orchs., 1959, Strophes for soprano, narrator and 10 instruments, 1959, Dimensions of time and silence, 1959-61, Anaklasis, 1959-60, Threnody for the Victims of Hiroshima, 1960, Psalmus for tape, 1961, Polymorphia, 1961; Fluorescences, 1961, Stabat Mater, 1962, Canon, 1962, Sonata for cello and orch., 1964, St. Luke Passion, 1965, De Natura Sonoris I, 1966, Dies Irae, 1967, Capriccio for violin and orch., 1967, Capriccio for cello Solo, 1968; opera The Devils of Loudun, 1968-69; Utrenja for double chorus, soloists and orch., 1969-71, Cosmogony, 1970, Utrenja II-Resurrection, 1971, Actions for jazz ensemble, 1971, Partita for harpsichord, 4 solo instruments and orch., 1971-72, Cello Concerto, 1967-72; for double chorus, soloists and orchestra Ecloga VIII for 6 male voices, 1972; Symphony 1, 1972-73, Canticum Canticorum Salomonis for 16 voices and chamber orch., 1970-73, Magnificat, 1973-74, When Jacob Awoke for orch., 1974, Violin Concerto, 1976-77, Paradise Lost (rappresentazione), 1976-78, (Christmas) Symphony No. 2, 1980, Te Deum, 1979-80, Lacrimosa, 1980, Agnus Dei for a cappella chorus, 1981, Cello Concerto No. 2, 1982, Requiem, 1983, Concerto per Viola, 1983, Polish Requiem, 1983-84, The Black Mask, 1986, Der Unterbrochene Gedanke, 1987, Adagio, 1989, Ubu Rex, 1991, Sinfonietta for orchestra, 1990-91, Symphony No. 5 for orchestra, 1991-92, Partita for orchestra, rev. edit., 1991, Flute concerto, 1992-93, Quartet for Clarinet and String Trio, 1993, Divertimento per Cello solo, 1994, Violin Concerto No. 2, 1992-95, Agnus Dei, 1995, Symphony No. 3, also other works; guest condr. NDR Symphony Orch., Hamburg, Federal Republic of Germany. Recipient 1st prize for Strophes Polish Composers Assn., 1959, UNESCO award, Fitelberg prize and Polish Ministry Culture award all for Threnody, 1960, Krakow composition prize for Canon, 1961, grand prize State N. Rhine-Westphalia for St. Luke Passion, 1966, Pax prize Poland, 1966, Jurzykowski prize Polish Inst. Arts and Scis., 1966, Sibelius award, 1967, Prix d'Italia, 1967-68, Polish 1st Class State award, 1968, Gottfried von Herder prize, 1977, prix Arthur Honegger, 1978, Sibelius prize Wihouri Found., 1983, Wolf Found. prize, 1987, 3 Grammy awards, Gamma prize Acad. Rec. Arts and Scis., 1988, Manuel de Falla Gold medal Accademia de Bellas Artes, Granada, 1989, Das Grosse Verdienstkreuz des Verdienstordens der Bundesrepublik Deutschland, 1990, 2 Grammy nominations, 1992, Grawermeyer Music award, 1992, Österreichische Ehrenzeichen für Wissenschaft und Kunst, 1994; grantee several founds., govts., insts. Mem. Royal Acad. Mus. London (hon.), Nat. Acad. of Santa Cecilia (Rome) (hon.), Royal Swedish Acad. Music, Acad. of Kuenste West Berlin (extraord. mem.), Nat. Acad. of Bellas Artes (Buenos Aires) (corr.), Internat. Acad. Philosophy and Art (Berne), Nat. Acad. Scis., Belles-lettres et Arts (Bordeaux), Acad. Scientiarium et Artium Europaea (Salzburg), L'Ordre de Saint Georges de Bourgogne (officer, Brussels). Creator original notational system allowing aleatory freedom for performer within sects. of precise duration. Home: ul Cisowa 22, 30229 Cracow Poland Office: ICM Artists Ltd 8942 Wilshire Blvd Beverly Hills CA 90211-1934 also: Panstwowa Wyzsza Szkola Muzyczna, ul Starowislna, 31-038 Cracow Poland*

PENDERGAST, JOHN JOSEPH, III, lawyer; b. Lewiston, Maine, Jan. 29, 1936; s. John Joseph and Grace (McCarty) P.; m. Joan Shaw Cole, June 14, 1958; children: John Joseph IV, Timothy S., Terrence B., Mary R., Michael C., Joan M. B.A., Yale U., 1957, LL.B., 1960. Bar: R.I. 1961, U.S. dist. Ct. R.I. 1961, U.S. Ct. Appeals (1st cir.) 1963. Assoc. Hinckley, Allen, & Snyder, Providence, 1960-66, ptnr., chmn. labor dept., 1966—; instr. U. R.I., Kingston, 1984-88, adj. prof. Providence Coll., 1984-86. Author: (with others) The Developing Labor Law, 2d edit., 1983, Labor and Employment Arbitration, 1988, NLRA Law & Practice, 1992. Mem. Cath. Charities panel Diocese of Providence, 1976-94; bd. dirs. Smith Hill Center, Providence, 1978-93; v.p. Providence Boys Clubs, 1970-72, bd. dirs., 1990—. Mem. ABA (labor law sect.), The Best Lawyers in Am., Am. Coll. Hosp. Attys., Indsl. Rels. Rsch. Assn., Hosp. Assn. Labor Execs., R.I. Bar Assn., Sakonnet Yacht Club, University Club, Yale Club of R.I. (Providence). Avocations: antiques, fly fishing. Home: 21 Violet St Providence RI 02908-4825 Office: Hinckley Allen & Snyder 1500 Fleet Ctr Providence RI 02903

PENDERGHAST, THOMAS FREDERICK, business educator; b. Cin., Apr. 23, 1936; s. Elmer T. and Dolores C. (Huber) P.; BS, Marquette U., 1958; MBA, Calif. State U., Long Beach, 1967; D in Bus. Adminstrn. Nova U., 1987; m. Marjorie Craig, Aug. 12, 1983; children: Brian, Shawna, Steven, Dean, Maria. Sci. programmer Autonetics, Inc., Anaheim, Calif., 1960-64; bus. programmer Douglas Missile & Space Ctr., Huntington Beach, Calif., 1964-66; computer specialist N.Am. Rockwell Co., 1966-69; asst. prof. Calif. State U., Long Beach, 1969-72; prof. Sch. Bus. and Mgmt., Pepperdine U., Los Angeles, 1972—; spl. adviser Commn. on Engring. Edn., 1968; v.p. Visual Computing Co., 1969-71; founder, pres. Scoreboard Animation Systems, 1971-77; exec. v.p. Microfilm Identification Systems, 1977-79; pres. Data Processing Auditors, Inc., 1981—; data processing cons. designing computer system for fin. health and mfg. orgns., 1972—. Mem. Orange County Blue Ribbon Com. on Data Processing, 1973; mem. Orange County TEC Policy Bd., 1982-87; mgmt. and organization devel. cons. Assn. Psychological Type, 1993—. Served to lt. USNR, 1958-60. Cert. in data processing. Mem. Users of Automatic Info. Display Equipment (pres. 1966). Author: Entrepreneurial Simulation Program, 1988. Home: 17867 Bay St Fountain Valley CA 92708-4443

PENDERGRASS, HENRY PANCOAST, physician, radiology educator; b. Bryn Mawr, Pa., Jan. 29, 1925; s. Eugene Percival and Rebecca (Barker) P.; m. Carol Lowe Dodson, Aug. 27, 1960 (dec. Aug. 1993); children: Sharon (dec. Aug. 1993), Lisa (dec. Aug. 1993), Deborah, Margaret; m. Carol Minster Roberts, Oct. 2, 1994. Student, U.S. Naval Acad., 1944-46; A.B., Princeton U., 1948; M.D., U. Pa., 1952; M.P.H., Harvard U., 1969. Diplomate: Am. Bd. Radiology, Am. Bd. Nuclear Medicine. Intern Pa. Hosp., 1953-54; mem. staff and faculty U. Pa. Med. Sch. and Univ. Hosp., Phila., 1953-58, 60-61; clin. asst. in neuroradiology Inst. Neurology Queen Sq., London, 1959-60; mem. staff and faculty Harvard U. Med. Sch. and Mass. Gen. Hosp., Boston, 1958-59, 61-76; prof. radiology Vanderbilt U. Sch. Medicine, Nashville, 1976-95, prof. emeritus, 1995—, vice chmn., 1976-89; adj. prof. radiology U. Pa. Sch. Medicine, Phila., 1996—. Mem. editorial bd. Am. Family Physician, 1980-94, Jour. Digital Imaging, 1987-96; contbr. chpts. to books, articles to med. jours. Mem. cancer control rev. com. Nat. Cancer Inst., 1975-79; Bd. dirs. state and local div. Am. Cancer Soc., 1976-85; mem. Project Hope Med. Mission, Peru, 1962; trustee Harpeth Hall Sch., Nashville, 1983-88. With U.S. Army, USN, 1943-46. Am. Cancer Soc. grantee, 1956-57; Nat. Cancer Inst. grantee, 1957-58; Nat. Inst. Neurol. Disease and Blindness grantee, 1959-60; Nat. Inst. Gen. Med. Scis. grantee, 1968-69. Fellow Am. Coll. Radiology (life mem., benefactor, counselor, steering com. 1968-73, bd. chancellors 1977-81), AMA (mem. Ho. of Dels. 1986—, sect. coun. on radiology 1978—, sec. 1987—, sect. on med. schs. 1979—, Disting. Svc. Gold medal 1994, grad. med. edn. adv. com. 1994—, chair 1996), Coun. Med. Splty. Socs., Am. Roentgen Ray Soc., Brit. Inst. Radiology, Ea. Radiol. Soc. (pres., trustee 1968-72, sci. program chmn. 1964, 72, 79), Assn. Univ. Radiologists, Mass. Radiol. Soc. (v.p. 1967-68, 75-76), Mass. Med. Soc. (counselor 1968-76), Nashville Acad. Medicine (chmn. com. on ethics 1981-82), Nat. Bd. Med. Examiners, Radiol. Soc. N.Am. (bd. dirs. 1972-77, chmn. 1975-76, pres.-elect and pres. 1977-78, Gold medal 1984, trustee RSNA Rsch. and Edn. Fund 1984-90, fund sec.-treas 1988-90), Am. Soc. Emergency Radiology, Tenn. Med. Assn., Tenn. Radiol. Soc. (pres.-elect, then pres. 1985-86, exec. com. 1984-88), Mid. Tenn. Radiol. Soc. (pres. 1984-85, sec., treas. 1985-94), Soc. Thoracic Imaging, Soc. Magnetic Resonance in Medicine, Sigma Xi, Delta Psi. Clubs: Belle Meade Country, Merion golf, Merion Cricket, Amateur Ski (N.Y.), Cap and Gown (Princeton, N.J.). Office: Vanderbilt U Sch Medicine 1121 21st Ave S Nashville TN 37203

PENDERGRASS, TEDDY (THEODORE D. PENDERGRASS), musician; b. Phila., Mar. 26, 1950; m. Karin Michelle Still, June 20, 1987; children: Tisha, Ladonna, Teddy. Student public schs. Drummer for various groups, 1966-69; Singer, lead singer Harold Melvin & Blue Notes, 1969-75; solo artist, 1975—; pres. Teddy Bear Enterprises, Phila. Squire, Memphis. albums include: Life Is a Song Worth Singing, 1978, Teddy, 1979, T.P., 1980, Live Coast to Coast, 1980, It's Time for Teddy, 1981, Teddy Pendergrass, 1982, This One's For You, 1982, Heaven Only Knows, 1983, Greatest Hits, 1984, Love Language, 1984, Workin' It Back, 1985, Joy, 1988, Truly Blessed, 1991, A Little More Magic, 1993, (with Harold Melvin & The Blue Notes) Teddy Live Coast to Coast, 1994. Recipient civic and pub. service awards., Image award NAACP, 1973, 80, Black Achievement award Ebony Mag., 1979, award outstanding mus. contbn. Afro-Am. Hist. Mus., 1983, award of merit City of Detroit, 12 gold and 7 platinum albums; recipity Keys to Cities, Lakeland (Fla.), Detroit, Savannah (Ga.), Memphis; named New Artist of 1977 for Top Pop Album Billboard Mag. Address: The Right Stuff EMI Music Distbn 21700 Oxnard St # 700 Woodland Hills CA 91367*

PENDERY, EDWARD STUART, deputy county judge; b. Dayton, Ky., June 1, 1931; s. Edward Stuart and Marguerite Garnet (Owens) P.; m. Nancy Jean Burck, Aug. 22, 1958; children: Michael Edward, Darren Frederick, Eric Christopher. Student, U.S. Tech. Sch., 1952. R.R. dep. chief clk. N.Y. Ctrl. R.R., Cin., 1950-51; R.R. comml. agt. C & WC Rlwy., Cin., 1955-58; salesman Pittsburg Paint & Glass, Cin., 1958-63; ops. mgr. Am. Laundry/Econo Sales, Cin., 1963-67; pvt. practice I.P.C.S. Pub., Ft. Thomas, Ky., 1967-68, 74-86; mag. sales and display ads staff Cin. (Ohio) Mag., 1969-74; dep. county judge Campbell County Ky., Newport, Ky., 1986—. Editor, originator: (tabloids) North Ky. Sports Scene, 1976—, Bellevue News, 1980—, Shopping Guides, 1980—. Chmn. site group North Ky. U., Highland Heights, 1968; chmn. study group Ft. Thomas (Ky.) Sch. Sys., 1970; dir. North Ky. U. Norse Club, Highland Heights, 1971-89, Famous Stars H.S. Program, Bellevue, Ky., 1978-94; mem. Bellevue Civic Assn., 1980—, North Ky. Adminstrs. Group, Newport, 1986-94, Libr. Site Com., Cold Spring, Ky., 1993-94, Nat. Alliance Bus., 1993. Staff sgt. USAF, 1951-55. Named Ky. Col., Ky. Gov., 1967; recipient Meritorious Svc. award Cub Scouts, 1968. Mem. Am. Assn. Ret. Persons, Elks, Am. Legion, North Ky. U. Norse Club. Democrat. Avocation: golf. Home: 38 Homestead Pl Fort Thomas KY 41075-1225

PENDLETON, BARBARA JEAN, retired banker; b. Independence, Mo., Aug. 14, 1924; d. Elmer Dean and Martha Lucille (Friess) P. Student, Cen. Mo. State Coll., 1942; D of Bus. Adminstrn. (hon.), Avila Coll., 1986. V.p. Grand Ave. Bank, Kansas City, Mo., 1962-76, exec. v.p., 1976-79; vice chmn. City Bank & Trust Co., Kansas City, 1979-82, chmn., 1982-83; exec. v.p. United Mo. Bank of Kansas City, 1983-93, United Mo. Bancshares, Inc., 1990-93; bd. dirs. Shepherd Ctrs. of Am., Inc., 1992—. Vice chmn., mem. Dept. Def. adv. com. Women in Svc., Washington, 1967-69; chmn. City of Kansas City Employee Retirement Fund, 1985—; mem. bd. dirs. YMCA USA, 1996—. Recipient Matrix award Press Women, 1963, Wohelo award Campfire, Inc., 1979. Mem. Fin. Women Internat. (nat. pres. 1972-73), Am. Humanics, Inc. (chmn. 1987-88). Club: Cen. Exchange (Kansas City) (pres. 1983-84).

PENDLETON, ELMER DEAN, JR., retired military officer, international consultant; b. Kansas City, Mo., June 26, 1927; s. Elmer Dean and Martha Lucille (Friess) P.; m. Anne Bittner, Sept. 10, 1971; children: V. Allison Connor, John K. Lange, Christian D. Pendleton. BS, U.S. Mil. Acad., West Point, 1951; MS, George Washington U., Washington, 1969. Commd. 2d lt. U.S. Army, 1951, advanced through grades to maj. gen., 1977, ret., 1986; platoon leader 11th airborne div., Fort Campbell, Ky., 1951-52; co. commdr. 7th infantry div., Korea, 1952-53, 82d airborne div., Fort Bragg, N.C., 1954-56; instr. Ranger Sch., Eglin AFB, Fla., 1957-58; aide to comdg. gen. Teheran, Iran, 1958; staff officer 3d inf. (Old Guard), Washington, 1958-59, Dept. of Army, Washington, 1960-63; bn. comdr. 24th inf. div., Berlin, Fed. Republic Germany, 1964-65; sector advisor Can Tho, Vietnam, 1965-66; bn. comdr. 1st inf. div., Vietnam, 1966-68; brigade comdr. 1st inf. div. and II field force, G-3, Vietnam, 1969-70; corps G-3 XVIII airborne corps, Fort Bragg, N.C., 1971-74; dep. chief of staff and chief of staff XVIII airborne corps, 1974-75; comdr. 1st corps Support Command, Fort Bragg, N.C., 1975-78, 19th Support Command, Taegu, Korea, 1978-80; logistics officer U.S. Readiness Command, MacDill AFB, Fla., 1980-81; ops. officer U.S. Readiness Command, 1981-82; chief Joint U.S. Mil. Mission for Aid to Turkey, Ankara, 1982-86; cons. Internat. Activities, Washington, 1986—. Decorated D.S.M., Def. D.S.M., Silver Star with 3 oak leaf clusters, Legion of Merit with 2 oak leaf clusters, D.F.C. with 2 oak leaf clusters, Bronze Star with 8 oak leaf clusters and V device, Combat Infantry Badge 2d award, 44 Air medals, Purple Heart, others. Mem. Am. Turkish Coun. (bd. dirs., chmn. def. and security affairs com.), ITEC, Inc. (pres.), Army-Navy Club (Washington). Home and Office: 3028 Knoll Dr Falls Church VA 22042-3111

PENDLETON, EUGENE BARBOUR, JR., business executive; b. nr. Louisa, Va., Apr. 2, 1913; s. Eugene Barbour and Virginia (Goodman) P.; m. Mildred McLean, June 18, 1938; children: Barbara Jane Pendleton Wootton, Sally Anne Pendleton Campbell, Nancy McLean Pendleton Wheeler, Susan Virginia Pendleton Hayden, Martha Christina Pendleton Perry. Student, Va. Mil. Inst., 1930-31, Hampden-Sydney Coll., 1931-34. Organizer, mgr. Gen. Ins. Agy., 1937-42; treas. Louisa County, Va., 1946-58; field rep. Va. Dept. Taxation, 1958-60; treas. State of Va., 1960-64; treas. So. States Coop., 1964-80, v.p. fin., 1977-78; v.p. fin. Truxmore Industries Inc., Richmond, Va., 1978-86, retired, 1986; mem. adv. bd. Jefferson Nat. Bank. Bd. dirs., past pres. Richmond Businessmen's Assn.; v.p., mem. exec. com. Atlantic Rural Expn.; past mem. exec. com. Richmond Home for Boys, Va. Edn. Fund; past bd. dirs. Richmond Symphony.; Mem. bd. suprs., Louisa County, 1937-42; mem. Ho. of Dels., Va. Gen. Assembly, 1966-70; Past pres. Va. Thanksgiving Festival. Served from ensign to lt. USNR, 1942-46, ETO. Mem. Va. Richmond chambers commerce, Bond Club Va., County and City Treas. Assn. Va. (past pres.), Nat. Assn. State Treas., Mil. Order World Wars (past comdr.), Navy League U.S. (pres.), 1st Families Va. (pres., coun.), Soc. of Va. (v.p.), Am. Legion, VFW (past comdr.), Downtown Club (Richmond, past pres.), commonwealth Club, Country Club of Va., Shriners, Masons, Willow Oakes Country Club (past pres.), Sigma Chi. Mem. Christian Ch. (past elder, chmn. bd.). Home: 8007 Dunsmore Rd Richmond VA 23229-7411

PENDLETON, GARY H(ERMAN), life insurance agent; b. Stuart, Va., Mar. 8, 1947; s. Herman P.; m. Laura Jeanes, Feb. 14, 1976; children: Blair J., Gray E. BS, SUNY, Albany. CLU, ChFC. Dir. intergovt. relations N.C. Dept. Transp., Raleigh, 1973-76; pres. Preferred Planning and Ins., Inc., Raleigh, 1976—; mem. N.C. State Banking Commn., 1985-89. Chmn., county commr. Wake County, N.C., 1992-96; mem. N.C. Bd. C.C.'s, 1989-91, N.C. Econ. Devel. Bd., 1991-93; bd. dirs. Wake Med. Ctr., 1994—. Presbyterian. Avocations: snow skiing, boating, fishing, hunting. Home: 2908 Lake Boone Pl Raleigh NC 27608-1151 Office: 2601 Oberlin Rd Ste 201 Raleigh NC 27608-1319

PENDLETON, JOAN MARIE, microprocessor designer; b. Cleve., July 7, 1954; d. Alvin Dial and Alta Beatrice (Brown) P. BS in Physics, Elec. Engring., MIT, 1976; MSEE, Stanford U., 1978; PhDEE, U. Calif., Berkeley, 1985. Sr. design engr. Fairchild Semiconductor, Palo Alto, Calif., 1978-82; staff engr. Sun Microsystems, Mountain View, Calif., 1986-87; dir. engring. Silicon Engring. Inc., Scotts Valley, Calif., 1994-95; cons., designer computer sci. dept. U. Calif., Berkeley, 1988-90. Contbr. articles to profl. jours.; inventor, patentee serpentine charge transfer device. Recipient several 1st, 2d and 3d place awards U.S. Rowing Assn., Fairchild Tech. Achievement award, 1982, 1st place A award Fed. Internat. Soc Aviron, 1991. Mem. IEEE, Assn. for Computing Machinery, Lake Merritt Rowing Club, Stanford Rowing Club, U.S. Rowing Assn. Avocations: rowing, skiing, backpacking.

PENDLETON, MARY CATHERINE, foreign service officer; b. Louisville, Ky., June 15, 1940; d. Joseph S. and Katherine R. (Toebbe) P. BA, Spalding Coll., 1962; MA, Ind. U., 1969; cert., Nat. Def. U., 1990; D (hon.), U. N. Testemitanu, Moldova, 1994. Cert. secondary tchr., Ky. Tchr. Presentation Acad., Louisville, 1962-66; vol. Peace Corps, Tunis, Tunisia, 1966-68; employment counselor Ky. Dept. for Human Resources, Louisville, 1969-75; gen. svcs. Am. Embassy, Khartoum, Sudan, 1975-77; counsular officer Am. Embassy, Manila, Philippines, 1978-79; adminstrv. officer Am. Embassy, Bangui, Cen. African Republic, 1979-82, Lusaka, Zambia, 1982-84; post mgmt. officer Dept. of State Bur. European and Can. Affairs, Washington, 1984-87; adminstrv. counselor Am. Embassy, Bucharest, Romania, 1987-89; dir. adminstrv. tng. divsn. Fgn. Svc. Inst., Arlington, Va., 1990-92; ambassador Am. Embassy, Chisinau, Moldova, 1992-95; adminstrv. counselor Am. Embassy, Brussels, 1995—. Bd. dirs. Am. Sch. of Bucharest, 1987-89. Named to Honorable Order of Ky. Cols., 1988. Democrat. Roman Catholic. Avocations: family history research, outdoor activities. Home and Office: Emb USA, Blvd du Regent 27, B-1000 Brussels Belgium

PENDLETON, MILES STEVENS, JR., diplomat; b. Montclair, N.J., Mar. 22, 1939; s. Miles Stevens and Lucille (Bond) P.; m. Elisabeth Morgan, Aug. 13, 1967; children: Constance Morrow, Nathaniel Palmer. BA, Yale U., 1961; MPA, Harvard U., 1967; diploma, Nat. War Coll., 1980. Tchr. Ghana Secondary Sch., Koforidua, 1962-63, Adisadel Coll., Cape Coast, Ghana, 1963-64; vice consul Am. Embassy, Tel Aviv, Israel, 1968-70; polit. and econ. officer Am. Embassy, Bujumbura, Burundi, 1970-72; watch officer Ops. Ctr. Dept. State, Washington, 1972-73, staff officer Secretariat Staff, 1973-74, spl. asst. to Dep. Sec. of State Office Dep. Sec., 1974-76; polit. officer U.S. Mission to NATO, Brussels, 1976-79; dep. dir. Office of No. European Affairs Dept. State, Washington, 1980-82, dir. Office of Israel and Arab-Israel Affairs, 1982-83, exec. asst. to under sec. of state for polit. affairs, 1983-85; min., counselor for polit. affairs Am. Embassy, London, 1985-89, Paris, 1989-93; prof. strategy Indsl. Coll. Armed Forces Nat. Def. U., Washington, 1993-95; dir. Office of Ecology and Terrestrial Conservation Dept. of State, Washington, 1995—. Avocations: sailing, reading. Home: 3410 Lowell St NW Washington DC 20016

PENDLETON, MOSES ROBERT ANDREW, dancer, choreographer; b. St. Johnsbury, Vt., Mar. 28, 1949; s. Nelson Augustus and Mary Elizabeth (Patchel) P. B.A., Dartmouth Coll., 1971. Co-founder, dir., choreographer, dancer Pilobolus Dance Theater, Washington, Conn., 1971—; founder, artistic dir. Momix Dance Theater, Washington, 1980—. Choreographer, dancer numerous works including Pilobolus, 1971, Anendrom, 1972, Walklyndon, 1972, Ocellus, 1972, Ciona, 1973, Monkshood's Farewell, 1974, Untitled, 1975, Eve of Samhain, 1977, Alraune, 1975, Lost in Fauna, 1976, Shizen, 1977, Bonsai, 1978, Day Two, 1981, Elva, 1987, Debut C, 1988, Accordion, 1989, Fantasy on a Variation on a Theme, 1989; choreographer Am. premiere of Jean Coeteau's Les Marie de la tour Eiffel, 1988; actor, dancer: (film) Pilobolus and Joan, 1974; choreographer: Erik Satie Festival, Paris Opera, 1978; co-choreographer: Molly's Not Dead, 1978; choreographer: (for Pilobolus Dance Theater) Day Two 1981, Stabat Mater, 1985, Carmina Burana Side II, 1985; Joffrey Ballet Relache, 1980, Closing Ceremonies 1980 Winter Olympics, Berlin Opera Tutuguri, 1981, Moses Pendleton Presents Moses Pendelton, 1982, Ballet de Nancy, France, Pulcinella, 1985, (for Momix Dance Theater) Kiss Off Spiderwoman, 1986, Spawning, 1986, Venus Envy, 1986, Medusa, 1986, Preface to Preview, 1986, excerpts from Gifts from the Sea, 1986, (opera for Spoleto Festival) Platee, 1987, Passion, 1991; tchr., artist-in-residence at univs. throughout U.S., 1977; tchr., condr. workshops. Recipient Edinborough Fringe Festival Scotman's award, 1973, Berlin Critic's prize, 1975; Nat. Endowment for Arts grantee, 1975-76; Guggenheim fellow in choreography, 1977. Democrat. Office: Momix PO Box 1035 Washington CT 06793*

PENDLETON, ROBERT GRUBB, pharmacologist; b. Kansas City, Mo., Apr. 24, 1939. AA, Kansas City Jr. Coll., 1959; AB in Chemistry, U. Mo., 1961; PhD in Pharmacology, U. Kans., 1966. Sr. scientist SmithKline and French, Phila., 1966-67, assoc. sr. investigator, 1967-69, sr. investigator, 1969-74, asst. dir., 1974-79, assoc. dir., 1977-80, dir. pharmacology, 1980-81; dir. gastroenterology Merck, West Point, Pa., 1981-86; sr. dir. biology Rper Ctrl. Rsch., King of Prussia, Pa., 1986-90; sr. rsch. scholar Temple U., Phila., 1993—; chief sci. officer Biopharm Cons., 1991—; lectr. pharmacology Thomas Jefferson U., 1991—; lab. sci. cons. Office of the Surgeon Gen., U.S. Army, Washington, 1989—. Col. U.S. Army Res., 1969—. Mem. Am. Soc. Pharmacology Exptl. Therapy, Am. Chem. Soc. (divsn. med. chem.), Soc. of Armed Forces Med. Lab. Scientist. Achievements include 15 patents describing dopamine receptor agonists and PNMT inhibitors; discovery of new drugs to activate dopamine reactors in CNS and kidney, to inhibit epinephrine biosynthesis PNMT in adrenal gland and CNS and to block histamine receptors insurmountably in stomach; discovered that tricyclic antidepressants act in CNS to decrease gastric acid secretion and new approaches to treat ischemia via rightward shifts of hemoglobin/oxygen dissocation curve; research on role of catecholamines in developmental biology and pharmacology of chiral molecules. Home and Office: 1312 Sumneytown Pike Lower Gwynedd PA 19002

PENDLETON, ROBERT LEON, civilian military employee; b. Hackensack, N.J., Jan. 3, 1937; s. Leon Dexter and Pauline Alice (Hopko) P.; m. Elsa Louise Walther, Jan. 25, 1958; children: Bryan Whittier, Phillip Clarke. AB, Oberlin Coll., 1958; PhD, Ind. U., 1964; JD, Loyola U., 1976. Gen. mgr. Penn Battery Mfg. Co., N.Y.C., 1958-60; instr. MIT, Cambridge, Mass., 1964-66; asst. prof. La. State U., Baton Rouge, 1966-70; chmn. math. dept. Whittier (Calif.) Coll., 1970-77; pvt. practice law L.A., 1978-80; software cons. U.S. Coast Guard, Washington, 1980-81; ops. rsch. analyst Naval Air Warfare Ctr. Weapons Divsn., China Lake, Calif., 1981—. NSF fellow, 1963-64. Mem. Res. Officers Assn. U.S. Republican. Unitarian. Avocations: philately, gardening, computers, travel. Home: PO Box 129 Ridgecrest CA 93556 Office: Naval Air Warfare Ctr Weapons Divsn Code 4J1200D 1 Administration Cir China Lake CA 93555

PENDLETON, SUMNER ALDEN, financial consultant; b. Boston, May 2, 1918; s. Sumner Maynard and Ethel Parker (Phinney) P.; m. Nancy Curtiss Welles, June 8, 1941; children: Nancy Alden Pendleton Dyer, John Welles. SB cum laude, Harvard U., 1939, MBA, 1941. With Gen. Electric Co., 1945-50, Ford Motor Co., 1950-53; asst. to corp. contr. to contr. electronics div. Curtiss-Wright Corp., 1953-60; asst. contr. ITT Corp., 1960-63; contr., asst. sec. Joy Mfg. Co., Pitts., 1963-67; v.p. fin. treas. Ryan Homes, Inc., Pitts., 1967-71, v.p. corp. devel., 1971-74; v.p., sec., treas. Ryan Homes Fin. Co., 1970-74; chmn., treas. Unidyne Corp., Pitts., 1975-80, Bergoo (W.Va.) Coal Co., 1975-78; assoc. exec. dir. budget and fin. United Presbyn. Ch. U.S.A., 1976-78; fin. cons., 1978-81; dir., v.p. fin., treas. Hytronics Corp., 1979-81; lic. sales assoc. VR Bus. Brokers, Clearwater, 1990-92, 95—, Metro Bay Assocs., bus. brokers, Clearwater, Fla., 1992-94; mgmt. fin. cons., 1974—; chmn., treas., bd. dirs. Consource Plastic Recycling Corp., Tampa, 1992—; mem. Svc. Corps Ret. Execs., 1981—, v.p., sec., treas. Pinellas chpt., 1983-85, pres., 1985-86, chmn., 1986-87. Gen. campaign chmn. Comty. Chest Ridgewood, Hohokus and Midland Park, N.J., 1959-60, pres., 1960-62; treas. Southminster Presbyn. Ch., Mt. Lebanon, Pa., 1966-76, trustee, 1965-68, elder, 1968-71, past deacon, head usher, Sunday sch. tchr. Lt. comdr. USNR, 1941-45, capt. USNR, ret. Decorated Silver Star; recipient Acctg. Profession Exec. of Yr. award Robert Morris Coll., 1973; Baker scholar Harvard Bus. Sch., 1941. Mem. Fin. Execs. Inst. (dir. Newark 1961-62), Nat. Assn. Accts. (Lybrand cert. 1955, pres. Paterson chpt. 1955-56, nat. dir. 1957-59, v.p. 1965-66, mem. exec. com. 1966-69), Stuart Cameron McLeod Soc. (pres. 1975-76), Harvard Bus. Sch. Assn. Pitts. (v.p. 1968-69, pres. 1969-70, chmn. bd. govs. 1970-71), Harvard Club of Fla. West Coast (v.p. 1982-84, pres. 1984-86, bd. dirs. 1986—), Harvard Bus. Sch. Club Fla. West Coast (bd. dirs. 1986-96). Home: 2163 Waterside Dr Clearwater FL 34624-6658 Office: 4625 E Bay Dr Ste 305 Clearwater FL 33764-5747

PENDLETON, TERRY LEE, baseball player; b. L.A., July 16, 1960; m. Catherine Grindulo Marquey, Oct. 27, 1984. Student, Oxnard Coll., Calif., Fresno State U., Calif. Baseball player St. Louis Cardinals, 1982-90, Atlanta Braves, 1991-94; with Fla. Marlins, 1995-96, Cin. Reds, 1996—. Winner Most Valuable Player award Baseball Writers' Assn. Am., 1991, Gold Glove award, 1987, 89, 92; mem Nat. League All-Star Team, 1992; Nat. League Batting Champion, 1991; named N.L. Comeback Player of the Yr. The Sporting News, 1991, Third Baseman on the Sporting News N.L. All-Star Team, 1991. Office: Cin Reds 100 Cinergy Field Cincinnati OH 45202*

PENDLEY, DONALD LEE, association executive; b. Jersey City, Nov. 5, 1950; s. Donald L. and Loretta M. (Purcell) P.; m. Donna Lynn Meade, Oct. 14, 1984; 1 child, Katelyn. BA, Montclair State Coll., 1972; MA, Syracuse U., 1974. Reporter/rewriter The Herald-News, Passaic, N.J., 1969-72; reporter The Dispatch, Union City, N.J., 1973; writer Keep America Beautiful, Inc., N.Y.C., 1974-75, communications dir., 1976-78, v.p. communications program devel., 1979-84; sr. v.p. communications Greater Newark C. of C., 1985-86; dir. pub. rels. Internat. Coun. Shopping Ctrs., N.Y.C., 1987-92; exec. dir. N.J. Hospice Orgn., Scotch Plains, N.J., 1993—. Creator, dir. theatre composer series William Carlos Williams Ctr., 1987-91; creator, dir. SRO Cabaret Series, 1991—. Pres. State Repertory Opera, South Orange, N.J., 1981-85, 92—, Ars Musica Chorale, Englewood, N.J., 1979-81. Recipient Award of Excellence Am. C. of C. Execs. 1986, Gold Key awards, Pub. Rels. News, 1982, 86. Mem. PRSA (accredited, sec.-treas. assn. sec. 1989-90, vice chmn. assn. sect. 1990-91, chmn. 1991-92), Am. Soc. Assn. Execs. (Gold Circle award 1988, comm. sect. coun. 1994-96), Am. Mensa, Ltd. (nat. devel. officer 1985-89, 96—, regional tng. officer 1989-93), Intertel. Avocations: music, photography. Home: 32 Hamilton Rd Glen Ridge NJ 07028-1109

PENDLEY, WILLIAM TYLER, naval officer, international relations educator; b. Paris, Ky., June 21, 1936; s. Louis Tyler and Virginia Lorene (Poplin) P.; m. Anne Carrol Cooke, Dec. 13, 1958; children: Stephen Tyler, Robert Randolph, Lisa Carrol, Leslie Brooks. BS in Engring., U.S. Naval Acad., 1958; MA, Am. U., Washington, 1965. Commd. ens. USN, 1958, advanced through grades to rear adm., 1983; comdg. officer Patrol Squadron 45, Jacksonville, Fla., 1975-76; ops. officer Patrol Wing 11, U.S. Atlantic Fleet, Jacksonville, 1976-78, commdr., 1979-81; exec. sec. for joint chief of staff matters Chief Naval Ops., Washington, 1978-79, planner for joint chief of staff matters, 1981-82, dir. plans policy and strategy div., 1985-86; exec. asst. to comdr. in chief U.S. Pacific Fleet, Pearl Harbor, Hawaii, 1982-83; commdr. patrol wings U.S. Atlantic Fleet, Brunswick, Maine, 1983-85; commdr. Naval Forces Korea, Seoul, 1986-89; sr. mem. UN Mil. Armistice Commn., 1986-89; dir. strategic plans and policy USCINCPAC, Camp H. M. Smith, Hawaii, 1989-91; dep. asst. sec. def. for East Asia and Pacific affairs Dept. Defense, Washington, 1992-93; prof. internat. rels. Air War Coll., Maxwell AFB, Ala., 1993—; fellow Georgetown U. Leadership

Seminar, Washington, 1985. Co-author: Nuclear Coexistence, 1994; contbr. articles to profl. jours. Decorated Def. D.S.M. with oak leaf cluster, Legion of Merit with 4 gold stars; named hon. Ky. Col., 1975; recipient Def. medal for disting. pub. svc., 1993. Mem. U.S. Naval Inst., Internat. Inst. Strategic Studies, Phi Kappa Phi, Pi Gamma Mu. Methodist. Avocations: flying, golf, tennis, skiing. Home: 6445 Eastwood Glen Dr Montgomery AL 36117-4713 Office: Air War Coll 325 Chennault Cir Maxwell AFB AL 36112-6427

PENFIELD, CAROLE H. (KATE PENFIELD), minister, church official. Grad., Andover Newton Theol. Sch. Co-pastor Ctrl. Bapt. Ch., Providence, 1st Bapt. Ch. Am., Providence; exec. dir. Ministers Coun. of ABC USA; mem. regional and nat. mins. coun. and senate Am. Bapt. Chs., v.p., 1994—; mem. state Senate ethics com. R.I. Legislature; pres. R.I. State Coun. Chs., 1987-89. Editor Ministry, Am. Bapt. Chs. Office: ABC in the USA PO Box 851 Valley Forge PA 19482-0851

PENFIELD, PAUL LIVINGSTONE, JR., electrical engineering educator; b. Detroit, May 28, 1933; s. Paul Livingstone and Charlotte Wentworth (Gilman) P.; m. Martha Elise Dieterle, Aug. 24, 1956 (dec. Apr. 1988); children: David Wesley, Patricia Jane, Michael Baldwin; m. Barbara Jean Buehrig Lory, July 22, 1989. BA, Amherst Coll., 1955; ScD, MIT, 1960. Asst. prof. elec. engring. MIT, Cambridge, 1960-64, assoc. prof., 1964-69, prof., 1969—, head dept. elec. engring. and computer sci., 1989—. Author: Frequency-Power Formulas, 1960, MARTHA User's Manual, 1971; co-author: Varactor Applications, 1962, Electrodynamics of Moving Media, 1967, Tellegen's Theorem and Electrical Networks, 1970. Sr. postdoctoral fellow NSF, 1966-67. Fellow IEEE (chmn. Boston sect. 1971-72, Darlington award 1983, Centennial medal 1984); mem. Nat. Acad. Engring., Am. Phys. Soc., Assn. for Computing Machinery, Audio Engring. Soc., Sigma Xi. Avocation: field identification of ferns and fern hybrids. Office: MIT Dept EECS Cambridge MA 02139

PENG, ZHONG, electrical engineer; b. Tianjin, China, May 20, 1946; came to U.S, 1981; s. Shichang and Rungeng (Bu) P. BSEE, Tianjin U., 1968; MSEE, Purdue U., 1982; MS in Computer Engring., U. So. Calif., 1984. Registered profl. engr., Calif. Elec. engr. Henan Power Adminstrn., Anyang, China, 1968-78; rsch. assoc. Electric Power Rsch. Inst., Beijing, 1980-81; lectr. Calif. State U., L.A., 1985; power system analyst CAE Electronics, Montreal, Que., Can., 1987-89; power system engr. Pacific Gas & Electric, San Francisco, 1985-87, elec. engr., 1989-94; utility engr. Nev. Pub. Svc. Commn., Las Vegas, 1994—. Contbr. articles to profl. jours. Coord. alumni svcs. Grad. Sch. Chinese Acad. Scis., 1991—. Mem. IEEE (sr., prize paper award 1987, 88). Office: State Nev Pub Svc Commn 555 E Washington Ave Ste 4600 Las Vegas NV 89101-1073

PENHOET, EDWARD, biochemicals company executive; b. Oakland, Calif., Dec. 11, 1940. AB, Stanford U., 1963; PhD, U. Wash., 1968. Office: Chiron Corp 4560 Horton St Emeryville CA 94608-2916

PENICK, GEORGE DIAL, pathologistst; b. Columbia, S.C., Sept. 4, 1922; s. Edwin Anderson and Caroline Inglesby (Dial) P.; m. Marguerite Murchison Worth, Feb. 7, 1947; children: George Dial, Hal Worth, David Williams, Anderson Holladay, Marguerite Worth. Student, U. N.C, 1939-42, BS, 1944; MD, Harvard U., 1946. Intern in pathology Presbyn. Hosp. City Hosp., 1946-47; instr. pathology U. N.C., Chapel Hill, 1949-53, asst prof. pathology, 1953-56, assoc. prof. pathology, 1956-63, prof. pathology, 1963-70; prof., head dept. pathology U. Iowa, Iowa City, 1970-81, prof. pathology and dermatology, 1981-93; cons. Watts Hosp., Durham, N.C., 1949-70; attending pathologist N.C. Meml. Hosp., Chapel Hill, 1953-70; bd. dir. Nat. Heart Inst. Program, Project U. N.C.,1962-70; cons., bd. dirs. lab. svc. VA Med. Ctr., Iowa City, 1972-75. Contbr. articles to profl. jours. Capt. U.S. Army, 1947-49. Med. Sci. scholar John and Mary Markle Found., N.Y.C., 1953-58; recipient Disting. Svc. award Sch. of Med. U. N.C., 1979. Fellow Coll. Am Pathologists; mem. AMA, Am. Soc. Clin. Pathologists, Am. Assoc. Pathologists, Internat. Acad. Pathology, Phi Beta Kappa. Democrat. Episcopolian. Avocations; bicycling, tennis. Home: 3712C Reston Ct Wilmington NC 28403-6123

PENICK, GEORGE DIAL, JR., foundation executive; b. San Juan, P.R., Apr. 17, 1948; s. George Dial and Marguerite Murchison (Worth) P.; m. Carol Davis Bonham, Jan. 30, 1971; children: Holladay Bonham, Robert Anderson. BA, Davidson Coll., 1970; EdM, Harvard U., 1976, M in Pub. Adminstrn., 1977, EdD, 1982. Asst. to dir. Learning Inst. N.C., Durham, 1970-71; child devel. adminstr. N.C. Office for Children, Raleigh, 1973-75; sr. research asst. Harvard U.-MIT Joint Ctr. for Urban Studies, Cambridge, 1978-79; assoc. dir. Mary Reynolds Babcock Found., Winston-Salem, N.C., 1979-85; exec. dir. Jessie Ball duPont Fund, Jacksonville, Fla., 1986-90; pres. Found. for the MidSouth, Jackson, Miss., 1990—; bd. dirs. Miss. Chem. Corp.; bd. dirs. Nat. Charities Info. Bus., 1990—, chair, 1996—; bd. dirs. Nat. Cathedral Assn., 1993—, v.p., 1996; bd. dirs. Coun. on Founds., 1994—; bd. dirs. Presiding Bishop's Fund for World Relief, 1994—, chair, 1996—; bd. dirs. Southeastern Coun. Founds., 1983-89. Mem. Leadership Jacksonville, 1987-88, Leadership La., 1994; bd. dirs. Practical and Cultural Edn. Ctr. for Girls, Jacksonville, 1987-90, pres., 1989-90; bd. dirs. Jacksonville Cmty. Coun., Inc., 1987-90, Greater Jackson Found., 1994—. 1st lt. U.S. Army, 1971-73. Democrat. Club: Harvard of N.Y.C. Avocations: jogging, stamp collecting, children. Home: 138 Highland Hills Ln Flora MS 39071-9536 Office: Found for the Mid South 308 E Pearl St Fl 4 Jackson MS 39201-3406

PENIKETT, ANTONY DAVID JOHN, Canadian government official; b. Nov. 14, 1945; s. Erik John Keith and Sarah Ann (Colwell) P.; m. Lula Mary Johns, 1974; children—John Tahmoh, Sarah Lahlil, Stephanie Yahsan. Exec. asst. to nat. leader New Dem. Party, Ottawa, Ont., Canada, 1975-76, nat. pres., 1981-85, fed. councillor, 1973—; leader New Dem. Party, Whitehorse, Y.T., Canada, 1980—; campaign mgr. New Dem. Party, N.W.T., Canada, 1972; city councillor City of Whitehorse, Y.T., Canada, 1977-79; elected mem. Yukon Legis. Assembly, 1978-95; opposition leader Yukon Legis. Assembly, Y.T., Canada, 1982-85, 92-95; elected govt. leader Yukon Terr. Yukon Legis. Assembly, 1985-92; sr. policy advisor, exec. coun. Govt. of Saskatchewan, 1995—. Author (film): The Mad Trapper, 1972; La Patrouille Perdue, 1974. Mem. Christian Socialist Ch. Office: Legislative Bldg Rm 33, Regina, SK Canada S4S 0B3

PENIN, LINDA MARGARET, elementary education educator; b. N.Y.C., May 18, 1946; d. Santos Rodriquez and Dorothea May (Fink) P. BA, Jersey City State Coll., 1969, MA, 1973. Cert. elem. tchr., reading tchr., reading specialist. Tchr. elem. Leonia (N.J.) Bd. Edn., 1969—. Recipient Gov.'s Tchr. Recognition award State of N.J., 1989. Mem. NEA, N.J. Edn. Assn., Bergen County Edn. Assn., Leonia Edn. Assn., Order of Ea. Star N.J. (officer). Republican. Methodist. Avocations: reading, bike riding, relaxing at beach. Home: 24 Kimble Ct Pompton Plains NJ 07444-1656 Office: Leonia Bd Edn 500 Broad Ave Leonia NJ 07605-1537

PENISTEN, GARY DEAN, entrepreneur; b. Lincoln, Nebr., May 14, 1931; s. Martin C. and Jayne (O'Dell) P.; m. Nancy Margaret Golding, June 3, 1951; children: Kris D., Janet L., Carol E., Noel M. B.S. in Bus. Adminstrn., U. Nebr., Omaha, 1953; LLD (hon.), Concordia Coll., 1993. With Gen. Electric Co., 1953-74; mgr. group fin. ops. power generation group Gen. Electric Co., N.Y.C., 1973-74; asst. sec. navy fin. mgmt., 1974-77; sr. v.p. fin., chief fin. officer, dir. Sterling Drug Inc., N.Y.C., 1977-89; sr. v.p. fin., health group Eastman Kodak Co., N.Y.C., 1989-90; bd. dirs. Foster Ptnrs. Inc., Food Ct. Entertainment Network Inc.; chmn. bd. dirs. Acme United Corp. Bd. dirs. Goodwill Industries Internat. Found.; mem. corp. adv. bd. U. Nebr. Coll. Bus., Omaha. Recipient Disting. Public Service award Navy Dept., 1977; Alumni Achievement citation U. Nebr., Omaha, 1975. Mem. Fin. Execs. Inst., Navy League of U.S., Army and Navy Club (Washington), Rotary, Union League, Econs. Club (N.Y.C.), Siwanoy Country Club. (Bronxville, N.Y.), White Eagle Golf Club (Naperville). Republican. Unitarian. Home and Office: 1409 Aberdeen Ct Naperville IL 60564

PENKAVA, ROBERT RAY, radiologist, educator; b. Virginia, Nebr., Jan. 30, 1942; s. Joseph Evert and Velta Mae (Oviatt) P.; m. Kathy Bennett Secrest, Apr. 6, 1973; children: Ashley Secrest, J. Carson Bennett. AB BS, Peru State Coll., Nebr., 1963; MD, U. Nebr., Omaha, 1967. Intern Lincoln Gen. Hosp., Nebr., 1967-68; resident Menorah Med. Cen., Kansas City, 1968-71; chief resident Menorah Med. Ctr., Kansas City, 1970-71; adj. faculty U. Mo., Kansas City, 1970-71; staff radiologist Ireland Army Hosp., Ft. Knox, Ky., 1971-72, chief, dept. radiology & nuclear med., 1972-73; staff radiologist Deaconess Hosp., Evansville, Ind., 1973—, dir. dept. radiology, 1992—; mem. faculty U. So. Ind., Evansville, 1973—; assoc. faculty Ind. U. Coll. Med., Bloomington, 1973—; med. dir. Sch. Radiol. Tech. U. So. Ind., Evansville, 1978—; dep coroner Vanderburgh County, 1991—; chmn. So. Ind. Health Sys., 1980-83; pres. Vanderburgh County Med. Soc. Svc. Bur., 1979—; mem. roentgen soc. liaison com. Ind. Bd. Health, 1968. Author numerous articles on med. ultrasound, nuclear med., angiography, and computed tomography. Chmn. profl. div. United Way of So. Ind., 1983; bd. dirs. S.W. Ind. Pub. Broadcasting, 1978-84, S.W. Ind. PSRO, 1982; v.p. Mesker Zoo Found., bd. dirs., 1991—. Maj. U.S. Army, 1971-73. Named Sci. Tchr. of Year, Lewis & Clark Jr. High Sch., 1963. Mem. AMA, Evansville Med. Radiol. Assn. (treas. 1987—), Tri-State Radiology Assn. (pres.), Vanderburgh County Med. Soc. (pres.), Physicians Svc. Bur. (treas.), Magnetic Resonance Imaging, Inc. (treas.), Am. Coll. Radiology, Radiol. Soc. N.Am., Am. Roentgen Ray Soc., Am. Inst. Ultrasound in Medicine, Soc. Cardiovascular and Interventional Radiology. Avocations: golf, boating, flying. Office: 611 Harriet St Evansville IN 47710-1781

PENLAND, ARNOLD CLIFFORD, JR., college dean, educator; b. Asheville, N.C., Oct. 8, 1933; s. Arnold Clifford and Pearl (Bailey) P.; m. Jean Wall (div. 1967); 1 child, Marcia Jean; m. Joan Eudy; 1 child, Elizabeth Bailey. BS, Western Carolina U., 1956; MA, Vanderbilt U., 1959; MEd, Duke U., 1966; PhD, Fla. State U., 1983. Tchr. of music Reidsville (N.C.) Pub. Schs., 1956-60; supr. of music Raleigh (N.C.) Pub. Schs., 1960-67; supr. of music and rsch. Smoky Mt. Cultural Arts Devel. Assn., Sylva, N.C., 1967, 1968-69; state supr. of music State Dept. of Edn., Columbia, S.C., 1969-70; assoc. prof. of music U. of Fla., Gainesville, 1970-80, prof. of music, 1980—, assoc. dean and prof. Coll. of Fine Arts, 1981—; prog. dir. Raleigh Cultural Ctr., Inc., 1962-67; music dir. various ch. choirs, N.C. and Fla., 1956-80; ednl. cons. Nat. Grass Roots Opera, Co., Raleigh, 1962-67, bd. dirs. Fla. League of the Arts. Contbr. articles to profl. jours. Mem. Gainesville Cultural Commn., 1975-76, v.p. Alachua County Arts Coun., Inc., 1976-77; bd. dirs. Arts Coun. of Raleigh, Inc., 1963-65. Recipient Disting. Service Citation, Federated Music Clubs of N.C., 1966; grantee Office of Edn., 1967-69. Mem. Nat. Assn. Acad. Affairs Adminstrn. (pres. 1990-92, bd. dirs. 1992-96), Reg. Assn. Acad. Affairs Adminstrn. (pres. 1985-86), Music Educators Nat. Conf., Coll. Music Soc. (life), Lions (v.p. Raleigh chpt. 1963-66), Kiwanis (Kiwanian of Yr. 1989-90, bd. dirs. 1992-96), Order of Omega, Phi Delta Kappa (pres. North Ctrl. Fla. chpt. 1985-86), Sigma Phi Epsilon. Democrat. Presbyterian. Avocations: gardening, cooking. Office: U Fla Coll Fine Arts 115800 Gainesville FL 32611-5800 *In life one can do anything one chooses to do if one is genuinely committed.*

PENLAND, JAMES GRANVILLE, psychologist; b. Dallas, Mar. 1, 1951; s. James Marr and Katherine (Lindsley) P.; m. Michelle Elizabeth Stahl, Aug. 13, 1977; children: Abraham Christopher, Simon Peter, Zachary James. BA summa cum laude, Met. State Coll., 1977; MA, U. N.D., 1979, PhD, 1984. Instr. U. N.D., Grand Forks, 1978-83, statistician, 1981-84, psychologist, 1984-85; rsch. psychologist USDA, Agrl. Rsch. Svc., Grand Forks, 1985—; adj. prof. U. N.D., 1984—; cons. in field. Contbr. articles to profl. jours. Met. State Coll. scholar, 1977. Mem. APA, Am. Inst. Nutrition, Midwestern Psychol. Assn., N.D. Acad. Sci., Am. Statis. Assn., Nat. Acad. Sci., Sigma Xi. Home: 1804 S 36th St Grand Forks ND 58201-5740 Office: USDA ARS 2420 2nd Ave N Grand Forks ND 58203-8312

PENLAND, JOHN THOMAS, import and export and development companies executive; b. Guntersville, Ala., Mar. 31, 1930; s. James B. and Kathleen (Bolding) P.; m. Carolyn Joyce White, May 30, 1961; children—Jeffrey K., Mark A., Michael J. B.A., George Washington U., 1957. Vice pres., dir. Rouse, Brewer, Becker & Bryant, Inc., Washington, 1957-63; staff mem. SEC, Washington, 1963-67; pres., dir. INA Trading Corp., Phila., 1968-69; v.p. INA Security Corp., Phila., 1967-69; v.p. Shareholders Mgmt. Co., Los Angeles, 1969, sr. v.p., 1970, exec. v.p., 1970-73, pres., 1973-75, also bd. dirs.; v.p. Shareholders Capital Corp., L.A., 1972-73; v.p., dir. several mut. funds managed by Shareholders Mgmt. Co., 1970-75; pres., chmn., CEO, HMO Internat. and its subs., L.A., 1975; founder, pres., chmn. Pendlar Corp., Atlanta, 1977—; chmn., pres. Bella Vista Developers, Inc., Albuquerque, 1977—; chmn. CompuComp Corp., Atlanta, 1977-81; chmn., pres. Fran Stef Corp., N.Y.C., 1982-89; pres., chmn. Engineered Products Corp., Dandridge, Tenn., 1983-90; founder, chmn., CEO Am. Accessories Inc., Covington, Ga., 1983—; founder, pres., chmn. United Am. Products Corp., Dandridge, 1983-89; founder, chmn. Chamisa Properties, Inc., Albuqueque, 1988-94, Glorieux Ltd., Atlanta, 1988—, Ga. Ptnrs. Ltd., Covington, 1988-94; founder, chmn., dir. Premier Trading Internat., Inc., Atlanta, 1989—; founder, dir. Chamisa Enterprises, Inc., Covington, 1990—; founder, mng. ptnr. Ft. Hill Ptnrs., Knoxville, Tenn., 1990-93; chmn. Einson Freeman & Detroy Corp., Fair Lawn, N.J., 1978-83; founder, dir., pres. West Point Contract Packaging, Inc., Martinsville, Va., 1991—; founder, mng. ptnr. Harbor View, Ltd., Fernandina Beach, Fla., 1992-94; founder, chmn. West Point Tech. Assembly, Inc., Winston-Salem, N.C., 1993—; dir., pres. BKP Industries, Inc., Monroe, Ga., 1995—. Served with AUS, 1948-55. Republican. Episcopalian. Home: PO Box 549 Social Circle GA 30279-0549 Office: 3261 Highway 278 NE Covington GA 30014-2495

PENLIDIS, ALEXANDER, chemical engineering educator; b. Kozani, Greece, Feb. 12, 1957; j. Diploma in engring., U. Thessaloniki, 1980; PhD in Chem. Engring., McMaster U., 1986. Rsch. assoc. Polymer Prodn. Techs., McMaster Inst., Can., 1985-86; from asst. prof. to assoc. prof. chem. engring. U. Waterloo, Ontario, Can., 1986-90; assoc. prof. U. Waterloo, 1990-95, prof., 1995—; assoc. dir. Inst. Polymer Rsch. U. Waterloo, Ont., Can., 1990-95, dir., 1995—; cons. in field, 1985—. Founding co-editor Polymer Reaction Engring. Jour., 1990—. Mem. AIChE, Chem. Inst. Can., Am. Chem. Soc., Can. Soc. Chem. Engring. Office: Univ Waterloo Inst Polymer Rsch, Chem Engring Dept, Waterloo, ON Canada N2L 3G1

PENMAN, PAUL DUANE, nuclear power laboratory executive; b. Williston, N.D., Sept. 25, 1937; s. Robert Roy and Kathryn Erica (Hagstrom) P.; m. Cornelia Dennis, Jan. 9, 1960 (div. June 1986); children: Anne, Robert, Jill; m. Carrie B. Silverblatt, July 14, 1986. BS in Engring. Physics, U. Colo., 1959; MS in Physics, U. Louisville, 1965. Asst. prof. U. Louisville, 1962-65; engr. Bettis Atomic Power Lab., West Mifflin, Pa., 1965-71, mgr., 1971-77, in charge lab. ops., 1977-82, in charge nuclear core mfg., 1982-92; mgr. performance and quality Westinghouse Electro-Mech. Divsn., Cheswick, Pa., 1992-93, mgr. performance quality improvement, 1994—. Leader Boy Scouts Am., Pitts., 1977-80. Lt. USN, 1959-64. Mem. U.S. Naval Inst., Gyro Internat. (bd. dirs., pres. 1988-90), U. Colo. Alumni Assn. (pres. Pitts. 1971-8o). Republican. Home: 105 Urick Ct Monroeville PA 15146-4919 *Make all decisions on first principles - they will carry you through all storms.*

PENN, ARTHUR HILLER, film and theatre producer; b. Phila., Sept. 27, 1922; s. Harvy and Sonia (Greenberg) P.; m. Peggy Maurer, Jan. 27, 1955; children: Matthew, Molly. Student, Joshua Logan's Stage Co., Black Mountain Coll., Asheville, N.C., U. Perugia, Florence, Italy, Actors Studio, Los Angeles; studied with Michael Chekhov. Joined Army Theatre Co. during World War II; worked in TV, 1951-53; producer plays for Broadway theatre including The Miracle Worker (Tony award 1960), All The Way Home, Toys in the Attic, Two for the Seesaw, In the Council House, Wait Until Dark, Sly Fox, Monday After the Miracle; films include The Left-Handed Gun, 1957, The Miracle Worker, 1962, Mickey One, 1964, The Chase, 1965, Bonnie and Clyde, 1967, Alice's Restaurant, 1969, Little Big Man, 1971, Night Moves, 1975, The Missouri Breaks, 1976, Four Friends, 1981, Target, 1985, Dead of Winter, 1987, Penn & Teller Get Killed, 1989, TV films The Portrait, 1993, Lumiere et Compagnie, 1995, Inside, 1996; co-dir. film Visions of Eight, 1973; dir. theatre: Golden Boy, Hunting Cockroaches. Address: Bell and Co Pc 535 Fifth Ave 21st Fl New York NY 10017*

PENN, DAWN TAMARA, entrepreneur; b. Knoxville, Tenn., July 22, 1965; d. Morton Hugh and Virginia Audra (Wilson) P. AS, Bauder Fashion Coll., Atlanta, 1984; postgrad., U. Tenn., 1986; grad., Rasnic Sch. Modeling, Knoxville, 1986. Gen. mgr. Merry-Go-Round, Knoxville, 1984-86; mgr., dancer Lady Adonis Inc. Performing Arts Dance Co., Knoxville, 1987-90; owner, pres. Lady Adonis, Inc. Performing Arts Dance Co., Knoxville, 1990—, also chmn.; owner/pres. Penn Mgmt and Investment Co. Comml. Real Estate, Knoxville, 1989—; deputized bonded rep. Knox County Sheriff's Dept., Knoxville, 1989-90; fgn. dance tours include Aruba, Curacao, Caracas, Barbados, Ont., Que., Montreal, Nfld., Labrador, N.S., New Brunswick; cons. The John Reinhardt Agy., Winston-Salem, N.C., 1987—, Gen. Talent Agy., Monroeville, Pa., 1990—, Xanadu, Inc., Myrtle Beach, S.C., 1991—. Author, editor: Lady Adonis Performing Arts promotional mag., 1988; TV and motion picture credits include: Innocent Blood, 1992, The Phil Donahue Show, N.Y.C., 1989, 91. Coord. bridal fair Big. Bros./Big Sisters Knox County, Knoxville, 1985, 86; judge Southeastern Entertainer of Yr. Pageant, Knoxville, 1992—, Miss Knoxville U.S.A. Pageant, Knoxville, 1990—; active Knoxville Conv. and Visitors Bur., 1993-94. Recipient 1st Pl. award for swimsuit TV comml. and runway modeling Internat. Model's Hall of Fame, 1986, 1st Pl. award for media presentation Modeling Assn. Am. Internat., 1986; nominee The Pres.'s Commn. on White House Fellowships, U.S. Office Pers. Mgmt., 1994-95. Mem. Internat. Platform Assn., Profl. Assn. Diving Instrs. (cert.). Methodist. Avocations: scuba diving, racquetball, horseback riding, piano, theology. Home: 5109 Ridgemont Dr Knoxville TN 37918-4539 Office: Lady Adonis Inc/Penn Mgmt Ste 4 7320 Old Clinton Hwy Knoxville TN 37921-1064

PENN, GERALD MELVILLE, pathologist; b. Toledo, Mar. 24, 1937; s. Melville Delroy and Hildegarde Agnes (Wammus) P.; m. Joyce Earl, June 5, 1965; children: Gerald Bradley, David Joshua. MD, Ohio State U., 1964, PhD, 1975. Cert. Am. Bd. Pathology. Head hematology sect. Bethesda (Md.) Naval Hosp., 1970-72; chief clin. pathology Children's Hosp., Columbus, Ohio, 1972-81; dir. lab. medicine Grant Med. Ctr., Columbus, 1981-96; med. dir. Cytometry Assocs., Columbus, 1996—; assoc. dir. Consolidated Bio-Med. Labs., Dublin, Ohio, 1972-78; chmn. Am. Bd. Med. Lab. Immunology, Washington, 1982-85. Author: Interpretation of Immunoelectrophoretic Patterns, 1978, The Clinical Use and Interpretation of Agarose Gel Electrophoresis Patterns, 1982; editor: Manual of Clinical Laboratory Immunology, 1992. Chmn. med. coun. Health Coalition of Ctrl. Ohio, Columbus, 1991—. Lt. comdr. USN, 1970-72. Recipient Commendation for Meritorious Svc., USN Nat. Naval Med. Ctr., Bethesda, 1972. Fellow Am. Soc. Clin. Pathology (dep. sec. 1973-78, CCE Meritorious Svc.), Coll. Am. Pathologists; mem. Acad. Medicine Columbus (sec.-treas. 1992-96). Republican. Roman Catholic. Office: Cytometry Assocs 181 Granville St Gahanna OH 43230-2967

PENN, HUGH FRANKLIN, small business owner; b. Morgan County, Ala., Aug. 15, 1917; s. Charles Franklin and Bessie Melinda (Praytor) P.; m. Marynelle Walter, Nov. 12, 1939 (dec. Dec. 1993); children: Hugh Franklin, Charles Phillip, Beverly Ann; m. Martha Ann Jordan Phillips, Feb. 11, 1994. Student, U. Ala., 1936-37. Asst. purchasing agt. for contractors constructing Huntsville Arsenal and Redstone Arsenal, Ala., 1941-43; purchasing agt. U.S. Army Air Force, Courtland Army Air Field, Ala., 1943-46; owner, mgr. Hugh Penn Lumber Co., Hartselle, Ala., 1946-60; owner, mgr. C.F. Penn Hamburgers, Hartselle, 1958-81, chmn. bd., 1981—; postmaster City of Hartselle, 1957-81; office mgr., realtor assoc. Charlie Penn Realty, 1981-85; bd. dirs. Terrell Industries, Inc. Moderator Morgan County Baptist Assn., 1955, 56; chmn. Hartselle Bd. Zoning Adjustment, 1956-76; founder, bd. dirs. Hartselle Downtown Action Com., 1971—; bd. dirs. Morgan County Combined Fed. Campaign, 1971-81, Hartselle Clean City Assn. 1990-93; apptd. to aging adv. coun. North Cen. Ala. Regional Coun. Govt., 1991; bd. dirs., trustee North Cen. Ala. Mental Health Found., 1992. Recipient Hartselle Civitan Unselfish Svc. award, 1995. Mem. Nat. Assn. Post Masters U.S., Hartselle C. of C. (pres. 1976-77); appointed mem. City of Hartselle Industrial Devel. Bd., 1995—. Republican. Baptist. Lodge: Kiwanis (life, Legion of Honor award 1977, Perfect Attendance award 1992). Home: 424 Crescent Dr SW Hartselle AL 35640-3825 Office: PO Box 8 Hartselle AL 35640-0008

PENN, HUGH FRANKLIN, JR., psychology educator; b. Hartselle, Ala., Jan. 28, 1941; s. Hugh Franklin and Marynelle (Walter) P.; m. Susan Irwin Adams, June 5, 1976; children: Charles Bracken, Caryn Elizabeth. BS, Florence State Coll., 1964; MA, Florence State Univ., 1967; grad. ednl. specialist, U. Ala., 1972, PhD, 1982. Psychology tchr. Hartselle (Ala.) H.S., 1964-89, sch. counselor, 1989-91, spl. svcs. counselor, 1991—; psychology instr. Calhoun C.C., Decatur, Ala., 1970—; chmn. bd. North Ctrl. Ala. Mental Health Bd., 1984-87, bd. dirs.; pres. of advisors Ala. Assn. Student Couns., 1970; ea. states head advisor So. Assn. Student Couns., 1973-74; mem. adv. bd. Mental Health Assn. Morgan County, 1996—. Named Outstanding Young Educator of Ala., Ala. Jaycees, 1973. Mem. APA, ACA, Coun. for Exceptional Children, Learning Disabilities Assn., Am. Sch. Counselor Assn., Autism Soc. Am., Orton Dyslexia Soc., Hartselle C. of C. (Thomas Guyton Humanitarian award 1994). Methodist. Home: 412 Aquarius Dr SW Hartselle AL 35640-4000 Office: Hartselle City Schs 130 Petain St SW Hartselle AL 35640-3228

PENN, JOHN GARRETT, federal judge; b. Pittsfield, Mass., Mar. 19, 1932; s. John and Eugenie Gwendolyn (Heyliger) P.; m. Ann Elizabeth Rollison, May 7, 1966; cildren: John Garett II, Karen Renee, David Brandon. BA, U. Mass., 1954; LLB, Boston U., 1957; postgrad. pub. and internat. affairs, Princeton U., 1967-68. Bar: Mass 1957, D.C. 1970. Trial atty. U.S. Dept. Justice, Washington, 1961-65, atty. tax divsn., 1961-70; then reviewer, asst. chief gen. litigation sect., assoc. judge Superior Ct. of D.C., Washington, 1970-79; judge U.S. Dist. Ct. D.C., Washington, 1979-92, chief judge, 1992—. Ex-officio dir. day care program D.C. Dept. Recreation, 1978—. With JAG U.S. Army, 1958-61. Nat. Inst. Pub. Affairs fellow, 1967. Mem. Nat. Bar Assn., Mass. Bar Assn., Washington Bar Assn., D.C. Bar Assn., Bar Assn. D.C. (hon.), Am. Judicature Soc., Boston U. Law Sch. Alumni Assn. Episcopalian. Office: US Dist Ct DC US Courthouse 333 Constitution Ave NW Washington DC 20001-2802

PENN, STANLEY WILLIAM, journalist; b. N.Y.C., Jan. 12, 1928; s. Murray and Lillian (Richman) P.; m. Esther Aronson, July 12, 1952; children—Michael, Laurel. Student, Bklyn. Coll., 1945-47; B. Journalism, U. Mo., 1949. With Wall St. Jour., 1952-90; investigative reporter N.Y. bur., 1957-90. (Co-recipient Pulitzer prize for nat. reporting 1967). Home: 380 Riverside Dr New York NY 10025-1858

PENNACCHIO, LINDA MARIE, secondary school educator; b. Boston, Oct. 8, 1947; d. Antonio and Florence (Delano) P. BA in Math., U. Mass., 1969; MEd in Guidance, Boston State Coll., 1974, cert. advanced study in adminstrn., 1976. Cert. math., guidance counselor, prin. Math. tchr. Abraham Lincoln Sch., Revere, Mass., 1969-91; computer tchr. grades K-8 Abraham Lincoln Sch., Revere, 1985-91; math. tchr. Beachmont Middle Sch., Revere, 1991—, equity coord., mentor tchr., 1995; office asst. Mass. Gen. Hosp., Bunker Hill Health Ctr., Charlestown, Mass., 1982—; adviser Nat. Jr. Honor Soc., Revere, 1985-94; mem. math. Curriculum Revision Com., Revere, 1985-86, 94-95, Com. to Establish Gifted and Talented Program, Revere, 1988; participant U.S. Dept. Edn. Tech. Grant, Revere, 1989-92; mem. math. portfolio pilot study Commonwealth of Mass. Dept. Edn., 1992-95; co-adviser Beachmont Sch. Aspirers Club. Mem. ASCD, Nat. Coun. Tchrs. Math., Mass. Tchrs. Assn., Assn. Tchrs. Math. in Mass., Nat. Assn. Student Activity Advisers. Democrat. Roman Catholic. Office: Beachmont Sch 15 Everard Ave Revere MA 02151-5516

PENNANT-REA, RUPERT LASCELLES, banker, economist; b. Harare, Zimbabwe, Jan. 23, 1948; came to Britain, 1966; s. Peter Athelwold and Pauline Elizabeth (Creasy) Pennant-Rea; m. Louise Greer, Oct. 3, 1970 (div. 1976); m. Jane Trevelyan Hamilton, Aug. 18, 1979 (div. 1986); children: Emily Trevelyan, Rory Marcus; m. Helen Jay, June 24, 1986; 1 child, Edward Peter. B.A. with honors, Trinity Coll., Dublin, 1970; M.A., U. Manchester, 1972. Economist, Confedn. Irish Industry, Dublin, 1970-71, Gen. and Mcpl. Workers Union, Eng., 1972-73, Bank of Eng., 1973-77; journalist The Economist, London, 1977-93, editor, 1986-93; dep. gov. Bank of Eng., London, 1993-95; chmn. Caspian, London, 1995—; chmn. The Stationery Office, London, 1996—. Author: Gold Foil, 1979; The Pocket Economist, 1983; The Economist Economics, 1986. Recipient Wincott prize for fin. journalism Wincott Found., London, 1984. Mem. Ch. of Eng. Clubs: Marylebone Cricket, Reform (London), Harare (Zimbabwe). Avocations: music; tennis. Office: Caspian, 199 Bishopsgate, London EC2, England

PENNEL, MARIE LUCILLE HUNZIGER, elementary education educator; b. Oregon, Mo., Jan. 16, 1934; d. William Henry and Milree (Huff) Hunziger; m. Berres H. Pennel, Mar. 6, 1955; children: Patricia Lu Pennel Wolfe, Pamela Cille Pennel Ginther. BS, Northwest Mo. State U., 1954; MS, Kans. U., 1959; postgrad., Kans. State U. Cert. elem. tchr., Kans. 1st grade tchr. Lawrence, Kans.; kindergarten tchr. Atchison, Kans., Unified Sch. Dist. 415, Hiawatha, Kans., 1972-94. Recipient Outstanding Svc. award, Lawrence Jaycees, 1958, 59. Mem. NEA, Kans. Edn. Assn., ASCD, Assn. for Childhood Edn. Internat., Kappa Delta Pi, Delta Kappa Gamma. Home: 403 Woodbury Ln Hiawatha KS 66434-1525

PENNELL, LINDA BENNETT, secondary school educator; b. Macon, Ga., Nov. 30, 1947; d. Frank Autrelle and Blance (Fraser) Bennett; m. John Clarence Pennell, Dec. 28, 1969; children: John Jacob, Frank McClinton. BA, Valdosta State Coll., 1969; MEd, Ga. State U., 1974. Cert. reading specialist, Tex.; mid-mgmt. cert. Tchr. Freehome Elem. Sch., Canton, Ga., 1973-74, Cypress-Fairbanks Ind. Sch. Dist., Houston, 1975—; team leader Cook Jr. High, Houston, 1988-91, dept. chair, 1991-95; asst. prin. Truitt Jr. High, Houston, 1995—; presenter in field. Ruling elder Windwood Presbyn. Ch., Cypress, Tex., 1986-89, 90-91. Recipient Guiding Star award Star Furniture and Houston Chronicle, 1993, Middle Sch. Start Educator Achievement award Jr. Achievement, 1993. Mem. ASCD, Nat. Assn. Secondary Sch. Prins., Assn. Tex. Profl. Educators (membership chair 1985, treas. 1988-89, pres. 1991), Tex. Reading Assn., Internat. Reading Assn. Presbyterian. Avocations: riding horses, reading, traveling, singing, theater. Home: PO Box 610 Cypress TX 77429-0610 Office: Truitt Jr High 6600 Addicks Satsuma Rd Houston TX 77084-1520

PENNELL, WILLIAM BROOKE, lawyer; b. Mineral Ridge, Ohio, Oct. 28, 1935; s. George Albert and Katherine Nancy (McMeen) P. AB, Harvard U., 1957; LLB cum laude, U. Pa., 1961; m. Peggy Polsky, June 17, 1958; children: Katherine, Thomas Brooke. Bar: N.Y. 1963, U.S. Dist. Ct. (so. dist.) N.Y. 1964, U.S. Dist. Ct. (ea. dist.) N.Y. 1964, U.S. Ct. Appeals (2d cir.) 1966, U.S. Ct. Claims 1966, U.S. Tax Ct. 1967, U.S. Supreme Ct. 1967. Clk. U.S. Dist. Ct., (so. dist.) N.Y., N.Y.C., 1961-62; assoc. Shearman & Sterling, N.Y.C., 1962-71, ptnr., 1971-91. Recent case editor U. Pa. Law Rev., 1960-61. Bd. govs. Bklyn. Heights Assn., 1964-74, pres., 1969-71; chmn. bd. Willoughby House Settlement, 1972-95. Served with U.S. Army, 1957. Fellow Salzburg Seminar Am. Studies, 1965. Mem. Rembrandt Club. Office: PO Box 249 Canaan NY 12029-0249

PENNEMAN, ROBERT ALLEN, retired chemist; b. Springfield, Ill., Feb. 5, 1919; s. Allen Frederick and Beryl (McNeeley) P.; m. Mary Ellen Emerick, July 25, 1942; children: Jacqueline, Cindy, Dean. A.B. summa cum laude, Millikin U., Decatur, Ill., 1941, Sc.D. (hon.), 1961; M.S., U. Ill., 1942, Ph.D. in Inorganic Chemistry, 1947. Chemist Ill. Hwy. Lab., Springfield, 1941; chemist metall. lab. U. Chgo., 1942-45; research assoc. Clinton Labs., Oak Ridge, 1945-46; chemist, staff mem., group and assoc. div. leader Los Alamos Nat. Lab., 1947-84, ret., 1984; adj. prof. U. N.Mex., 1950—; cons., lectr. in field. Editl. bd. Inorganic Cheistry, 1962-66 (founding mem.), Inorganic and Nuclear Chemistry Letters, 1968—; contbr. articles to profl. jours. Recipient Disting. Performance award Los Alamos Nat. Lab., 1981, award of excellence Los Alamos Nat. Lab., 1986, Seaborg award Actinide Separations Chemistry, 1995. Mem. Am. Chem. Soc. (chmn. N.Mex. chpt. 1956), Nat. Acad. Scis. (participant workshop 1983, panelist 1996-97), Sigma Xi, Phi Kappa Phi, Alpha Chi Sigma. Home: 12201 LaVista Grande Dr Albuquerque NM 87111-6710 Office: Los Alamos Nat Lab PO Box 1663 Los Alamos NM 87545-0001

PENNER, HANS HENRY, historian; b. Sacramento, Jan. 29, 1934; s. Hans Henry and Frieda Marie (Haehnel) P.; m. Anna M. Tardiff, Sept. 27, 1958. D.B., U. Chgo., 1958, M.A., 1962, Ph.D., 1965. Instr. U. Vt., 1962-65; asst. prof. Dartmouth Coll., 1965-71, Preston Kelsey prof. religion, 1991—, dean faculty, 1980-85; Pres. Am. Acad. Religion New Eng., 1980-81. Author: Impasse and Resolution: A Critique of the Study of Religion, 1989; editl. bd. Am. Acad. Religion; contbr. articles to profl. jours. Danforth fellow, 1968-69; Dartmouth Faculty fellow, 1967; Fulbright research grantee, 1966; Am. Council Learned Socs. grantee, 1979. Mem. Assn. Asian Studie, Am. Soc. St. Religion, Internat. Assn. History of Religion. Home: PO Box 642 Hanover NH 03755-0642 Office: Dartmouth Coll 6306 Thornton Hanover NH 03755

PENNER, KEITH, Canadian government official; b. Sask., Can., May 1, 1933. BA, U. Alberta, Can., 1955; MEd, U. Ottawa, Can., 1971. Secondary sch. tchr. Dryden, Ont., Can., 1961-68; mem. parliament Cochrane-Superior, Ont., 1968-88; mem. Can. Transp. Agy., Ottawa, Ont., 1988—; past parliamentary sec. to Min. of State for Sci. and Tech., past parliamentary sec. to Min. of Indian Affairs and No. Devel., past chmn. Standing Com. on Indian Affairs and No. Devel.; vis. fellow Sch. of Polit. Sci., Queen's U., 1987-88. Office: Can Transp Agy, Ottawa, ON Canada K1A 0N9

PENNER, STANFORD SOLOMON, engineering educator; b. Unna, Germany, July 5, 1921; came to U.S., 1936, naturalized, 1943; s. Heinrich and Regina (Saal) P.; m. Beverly Preston, Dec. 28, 1942; children: Merilynn Jean, Robert Clark. BS, Union Coll., 1942; MS, U. Wis., 1943, PhD, 1946; Dr. rer. nat. (hon.), Technische Hochschule Aachen, Germany, 1981. Research asso. Allegany Ballistics Lab., Cumberland, Md., 1944-45; research scientist Standard Oil Devel. Co., Esso Labs., Linden, N.J., 1946; sr. research engr. Jet Propulsion Lab., Pasadena, Calif., 1947-50; mem. faculty Calif. Inst. Tech., 1950-63, prof. div. engring., jet propulsion, 1957-63; dir. research engring. div. Inst. Def. Analyses, Washington, 1962-64; prof. engring. physics, chmn. dept. aerospace and mech. engring. U. Calif. at San Diego, 1964-68, vice chancellor for acad. affairs, 1968-69, dir. Inst. for Pure and Applied Phys. Scis., 1968-71, dir. Energy Ctr., 1973-91; bd. dirs. Ogden Corp., Optodyne Corp.; U.S. mem. adv. group aero. rsch. and devel. NATO, 1952-68, chmn. combustion and propulsion panel, 1958-60; mem. adv. com. engring. scis. USAF-Office Sci. Rsch., 1961-65; mem. subcom. on combustion NACA, 1954-58; mem. rsch. adv. com. on air-breathing engines NASA, 1962-64; mem. coms. on gas dynamics and edn. Internat. Acad. Astronautics, 1969-80; nat. lectr. Sigma Xi, 1977-79; chmn. fossil energy rsch. working group Dept. Energy, 1978-82, chmn. advanced fuel cell commercialization working group, 1993-95; chmn. assembly engring. NAE, 1978-82; chmn. NAS-NRC U.S. Nat. Com. IIASA, 1978-82; mem. commn. engring. tech. sys. NRC, 1982-84; spl. guest Internat. Coal Sci. Confs., 1983, 85, 87, 89, 91; mentor Def. Sci. Studies Group, 1985-93; chmn. studies mcpl. waste incineration NSF, 1988-89, Calif. Coun. Sci. Tech., 1992; pub. info. adv. com. Nat. Acad. Engring., 1994—, Independent Commn. on Environ. Edn., 1995-97, sci. adv. com., San Diego County, 1997—. Author: Chemical Reactions in Flow Systems, 1955, Chemistry Problems in Jet Propulsion, 1957, Quantitative Molecular Spectroscopy and Gas Emissivities, 1959, Chemical Rocket Propulsion and Combustion Research, 1962, Thermodynamics, 1968, Radiation and Reentry, 1968; sr. author: Energy, Vol. I (Demands, Resources, Impact, Technology and Policy), 1974, 81, Energy, Vol. II (Non-nuclear Energy Technologies), 1975, 77, 84, Energy, Vol. III (Nuclear Energy and Energy Policies), 1976; editor: Chemistry of Propellants, 1960, Advanced Propulsion Techniques, 1961, Detonations and Two-Phase Flow, 1962, Combustion and Propulsion, 1963, Advances in Tactical Rocket Propulsion, 1968, In Situ Shale Oil Recovery, 1975, New Sources of Oil and Gas, 1982, Coal Combustion and Applications, 1984, Advanced Fuel Cells, 1986, Coal Gasification: Direct Applications and Syntheses of Chemicals and Fuels, 1987, CO2 Emissions and Climate Change, 1991, Commercialization of Fuel Cells, 1995; assoc. editor Jour. Chem. Physics, 1953-56; editor Jour. Quantitative Spectroscopy and Radiative Transfer, 1960-92, Jour. Def. Rsch., 1963-67, Energy-The Internat. Jour., 1975—. Recipient spl. award People-to-People program, NATO, pub. svc. award U. Calif., San Diego, N. Manson medal Internat. Colloquia on Gasdynamics of Explosions and Reactive Systems, 1979, internat. Columbus award Internat. Inst. Comm., Genoa, Italy, 1981, disting. assoc. award U.S. Dept. Energy, 1990; Guggenheim fellow, 1971-72. Fellow Am. Phys. Soc., Optical Soc. Am., AAAS, N.Y. Acad. Scis., AIAA (dir. 1964-66, past chmn. com., G. Edward Pendray award 1975, Thermophysics award 1983, Energy Systems award 1983), Am. Acad. Arts and Scis.; mem. Nat. Acad. Engring., Internat. Acad. Astronautics, Am. Chem. Soc., Sigma Xi. Home: 5912 Avenida Chamnez La Jolla CA 92037-7402 Office: U Calif San Diego 9500 Gilman Dr La Jolla CA 92093-5003

PENNER-SEKERA, CYNTHIA DAWN, secondary education educator; b. Stockton, Calif., Mar. 23, 1959; d. Donald Dean and Frances Lee (Cox) Penner; m. Carl Joseph Sekera, June 21, 1981; children: Matthew Carl, Samantha Dawn. BA, Calif. State U., 1981, postgrad., 1983, MA in Edn., 1984, postgrad., 1991. Cert. tchr., Calif. Tchr. KinderCare Schs., Santa Ana, Calif., 1981-84, Long Beach (Calif.) Sch. Dist., 1984-87, Tracy (Calif.) Adult/Elem. Dist., 1987-95; tech. tchr. Tracy High Sch. Dist., 1995-96; math. tchr. San Ramon Valley Sch. Dist., 1996—; mem. Tracy Dist. Tech. Steering Com., 1991-96; tech. mentor tchr. Tracy Elem. Dist., 1992-95; pub. C.U.E. (Computer Using Educators) Newsletter, 1994-95. Contbr. articles to profl. jours. Tchr. McHenry House for the Homeless, Tracy, 1990-93. Mem. AAUW (vol. coord. 1988-90, v.p. 1990-91). Avocations: computers, children, music, laughter. Office: Charlotte Wood Mid Sch 600 El Capitan Dr Danville CA 94526-5000

PENNEY, CHARLES RAND, lawyer, civic worker; b. Buffalo, July 26, 1923; s. Charles Patterson and Gretchen (R) P. BA, Yale U., 1945; JD, U. Va., 1951; DFA (hon.), SUNY, 1995. Bar: Md. 1952, N.Y. 1958, U.S. Supreme Ct. 1958. Law sec. to U.S. Dist. Ct. Judge W.C. Coleman, Balt., 1951-52; dir. devel. office Children's Hosp., Buffalo, 1952-54; sales mgr. Amherst Mfg. Corp., Williamsville, N.Y., 1954-56, also; Delevan Electronics Corp., East Aurora, N.Y.; mem. firm Penney & Penney, Buffalo, 1958-61; pvt. practice, Niagara County, N.Y., 1961—. Numerous contemporary art collection exhbns. include Mus. Modern Art, N.Y.C., 1962, Whitney Mus. Am. Art, N.Y.C., 1963, 79, 80, Burchfield-Penney Art Ctr., 1973, 92-96, Meml. Art Gallery, Rochester, 1976, 78, 83, 88, U. Iowa, 1978, Columbus (Ohio) Gallery Fine Arts, 1979, Whitte Meml. Mus., San Antonio, 1979, U. N.C., 1979, Ga. Mus. Art, 1979, Hunter Mus. Art, Chattanoga, Tenn., 1980, Brooks Meml. Art Gallery, Memphis, 1980, Portland (Maine Mus. Art), 1980, Arts Ctr., South Bend, Ind., 1980, The Bowers Mus., Santa Ana, Calif., 1980, Beaumont (Tex.) Art Mus., 1981, 88, Meadows Mus. Art, Shreveport, La., 1981, 88, Cedar Rapids (Iowa) Mus. Art, 1983, Roland Gibson Art Gallery, Potsdam, N.Y., 1983, 84, Met. Mus. Art, 1984, San Jose Mus. Art, 1985, Tampa Mus., 1986, Boston Athenaeum, Mass., 1986, The New Britain (Conn.) Mus. Art, 1986, Currier Gallery Art, Manchester, N.H., 1987, Miss. Mus. Art, Jackson, 1987, others; selected works from art collections exhibited at Met. Mus. Art, N.Y. Hist. Soc., 1987, San Francisco Mus. Art, 1963, Walker Art Ctr., Mpls., 1963, Pa. Acad. Fine Arts, 1964, and 25 U.S. Embassies, 1965-72, U. Ariz., Tucson, 1965, 66, Albright-Knox Art Gallery, Buffalo, 1967, 87, Cleve. Mus., Art, 1972, Indpls. Mus. Art, 1973, Whitney Mus. Am. Art, N.Y., 1979, 80, Milw. Mus. Art, 1984, Wadsworth Atheneum, Hartford, 1986, Corcoran Gallery Art, Washington, 1987, U. Mich., 1993, Terra Mus. Am. Art, 1993. Bd. dirs. Buffalo State Coll. Found.; hon. life trustee Burchfield-Penney Art Ctr.; mem. Kenan Ctr., Lockport, N.Y., Hallwalls Contemporary Arts Ctr., Buffalo, N.Y. 2d lt. U.S. Army, 1943-46. Recipient Pres.'s Disting. Svc. award Buffalo State Coll., 1991, Disting. Svc. to Culture award Coll. Arts and Scis., SUNY, Potsdam, 1983; named Disting. fellow Cultural Studies of the Burchfield-Penney Art Ctr., 1994, Outstanding Individual Philanthropist, Nat. Soc. Fund Raising Execs. Western N.Y., 1996, Individual Patron of the Arts award Buffalo and Erie County Arts Coun. and Buffalo C. of C., 1997. Fellow The Explorers Club: mem. AARP, Albright-Knox Art Gallery Buffalo (life), Buffalo Mus. Sci. (Life), Buffalo and Erie County Hist. Soc. (life), Niagara County Hist. Soc. (life), Old Ft. Niagara (life), Buffalo Soc. Artists (hon. trustee), Hist. Lockport (life), Landmark Soc. Western N.Y. (life), Nat. Trust Hist. Preservation, Am. Ceramic Cir., Hist. Lewiston (life), Friends of U. Rochester Librs. (life) Meml. Art Gallery U. Rochester (hon. bd. mgrs., hon. life), Winslow Homer Soc. of Dirs. Cir. (hon. life), Smithsonian Instn. (benefactors cir.), Rochester Hist. Soc. (life), Am. Hist. Print Collectors Soc. (life), Burchfield Homestead Soc. (hon. life), Archives Am. Art, Mark Twain Soc. (hon.), Landmark Soc. fo the Niagara Frontier, U. Rochester's Pres.'s Soc. (hon. life), U. Iowa's Pres.'s Club (hon. life), Va. Law Found., Nat. Geog. Soc. (life), World's Fair Collectors Soc., Helsey Collectors Am., Brit. Commemorative Collectors, Hist. Soc. of Tonawandas (life), Pres.'s Cir. Buffalo State Coll. (hon. life), Peanut Pals, Grolier Club, Pan Am. Expo Collectors Soc., Columbus (Ohio) Mus. of Art, Castellani Art Mus./Niagara U., Yale Club of N.Y.C., Roycrofters-at-Large Assn. (life), Arctic Circle Club, Order of the Alaska Walrus, Chi Psi, Phi Alpha Delta. Clubs: Automobile (Lockport); Zwicker Aquatic, Niagara County Antiques (hon.); Rochester Art (hon. life). Office: 538 Bewley Building Lockport NY 14094-2944 *I have tried to strive for excellence in whatever I undertake, be it small or large. What success I may have achieved has required initiative, imagination, and dedication to the task at hand. Satisfaction comes from the hard work that leads to an objective. In all that I do I adhere to the Golden Rule and to fairness, honesty, and understanding in human relationships. I try to maintain a sense of humor at all times. And I enjoy living in a small community because it is from such areas that the strength of America comes.*

PENNEY, LINDA HELEN, music educator; b. Poquonnock, N.J., Mar. 22, 1958; d. John J. and Edith (Cook) P. B in Music cum laude, U. Hartford, 1979; MS in Edn., Fordham U., 1986; MMusic, U Conn., 1996. Cert. tchr., N.Y., Conn.; cert. adminstr., N.Y. Choral dir. Middletown (Conn.) High Sch., 1979-82, Bronxville (N.Y.) Mid. Sch.-High Sch., 1983-87; dir. music Canaan (Vt.) Pub. Sch., 1987-88; dir. chorus, drama Ardsley (N.Y.) Mid. Sch.-High Sch., 1988-92; vocal and choral dir., instr. music theory, theater Port Chester (N.Y.) High Sch., 1992—; dir. performing arts Woodside on the Move-N.Y.C. Cultural Youth Bd., 1983-85; mem. faculty Ossining (N.Y.) Studio Music, 1989-91. Mem. Am. Choral Dirs. Assn., Music Educators Nat. Conf. (nat. registry), Internat. Assn. Jazz Edn., Westchester Coun. for Arts, N.Y. State Schs. Music Assn., Westchester County Schs. Music Assn. (chair area all-state music festival 1985-87). Avocations: concerts, reading, hiking. Home: 39 Main St Bedford Hills NY 10507 Office: Port Chester High Sch Tamarack Rd Port Chester NY 10573

PENNEY, SHERRY HOOD, university president, educator; b. Marlette, Mich., Sept. 4, 1937; d. Terrance and B. Jean (Stoutenburg) Hood; m. Carl Murray Penney, July 8, 1961 (div. 1978); children: Michael Murray, Jeffrey Hood; m. James Duane Livingston, Mar. 30, 1985. BA, Albion Coll., 1959, LLD (hon.), 1989; MA, U. Mich., 1961; PhD, SUNY, Albany, 1972. Vis. asst. prof. Union Coll., Schenectady, N.Y., 1972-73; assoc. higher edn. N.Y. State Edn. Dept., Albany, 1973-76; assoc. provost Yale U., New Haven, Conn., 1976-82; vice chancellor acad. programs, policy and planning SUNY System, Albany, 1982-88; acting pres. SUNY, Plattsburgh, 1986-87; chancellor U. Mass., Boston, 1988-95, pres., 1995, chancellor, 1996—; chmn., bd. dirs. Nat. Higher Edn. Mgmt. Sys., Boulder, Colo., 1985-87; mem. commn. on higher edn. New Eng. Assn. Schs. and Colls., Boston, 1979-82, Mid. States Assn. Schs. and Colls., Phila., 1986-88; mem. commn. on women Am. Coun. Edn., Washington, 1979-81, commn. on govt. rels., 1990-94; bd. dirs. Boston Edison Co., Am. Coun. on Edn., Carnegie Found. for Advancement of Teaching, The Boston Pvt. Industry Coun. Author: Patrician in Politics, 1974; editor: Women in Management in Higher Education, 1975; cons. editor Change mag. and Jour. Higher Edn. Mgmt.; contbr. articles to profl. jours. Mem. Bus.-Higher Edn. Forum, Internat. Trade Task Force, 1994-96; mem. exec. com., Challenge to Leadership, 1988, chair, 1996; mem. Mid-Am. adv. bd. HERS, 1992—; trustee Berkeley Div. Sch., Yale U., 1978-82, John F. Kennedy Libr. Found.; bd. dirs. Albany Symphony Orch., 1982-88, U. Mass. Found., 1988—, Mcpl. Rsch. Bur., Boston, 1990—, New Eng. Coun., New Eng. Aquarium, Boston Plan for Excellence, Boston Pvt. Industry Coun., Greater Boston One to One Leadership Coun., Hers Mid Atlantic Adv. Bd., NASULGC Commn. Urban Affairs, The Ednl. Resource Inst., 1994, The Environ. Bus. Coun., 1991—. Recipient Disting. Alumna award Albion Coll., 1978, Disting. Citizen award for racial harmony Black/White Boston, 1994, Am. Coun. on Edn./Nat. Identification Program Mass. Leadership award, 1995, New Eng. Women's Leadership award, 1996. Mem. Am. Coun. Edn. (bd. dirs.), Am. Assn. Higher Edn., Orgn. Am. Historians, Nat. Assn. State Univs. and Land Grant Colls., Greater Boston C. of C. (bd. dirs.), St. Botolph Club, Comml. Club (Boston). Unitarian. Office: U Mass Boston 100 Morrissey Blvd Boston MA 02125

PENNIMAN, CLARA, political scientist, educator; b. Steger, Ill., Apr. 5, 1914; d. Rae Ernest and Alethea (Bates) P. B.A., U. Wis., 1950, M.A., 1951; Ph.D., U. Minn., 1954. Legal sec., 1934-37; adminstrv. asst. Wis. Employment Service, 1937-47; mem. faculty U. Wis., 1953—, prof. polit. sci., 1961-84, prof. emeritus, 1984—, chmn. dept., 1963-66; dir. Center for Pub. Policy and Administrn., 1968-74, Oscar Rennebohm prof. pub. adminstrn., 1974-84; Asso. Brookings Instn., 1972-76; examiner-cons., mem. higher edn. commn. N. Central Assn. Colls.; vis. lectr. Johns Hopkins, summer 1958. Author: State Income Taxation, 1980; co-author: The Minnesota Department of Taxation, 1955, State Income Tax Administration, 1959, Government in the Fifty States, 1960; Contbr. to: Politics in the American States, 1965, 71, 76. Pres. League Women Voters, Madison, 1956-58; mem. Gov. Wis. Tax Impact Study Commn., 1959, Gov.'s Higher Edn. Merger Com., 1971-73; Mayor Madison Met. Com., 1957-58, Madison Redistricting Com., 1960-63; mem. adv. com. govts. div. Bur. Census, 1962-65, mem. state compensation study com., 1983. Recipient Outstanding Achievement award U. Minn., Disting. Service award U. Wis.-Madison. Mem. Am. Polit. Sci. Assn. (v.p. 1971-72, past mem. nat. coun.), Midwest Polit. Sci. Assn. (pres. 1965), ASPA, AAUP (pres. state conf. 1972-73), Nat. Assn. Schs. Pub. Adminstrn. (coun. 1973-75), Am. Acad. Pub. Adminstrn., Altrusa (pres. Madison chpt. 1968-69), Phi Beta Kappa, Phi Kappa Phi. Home: 6209 Mineral Pt Rd Apt 1402 Madison WI 53705-4558

PENNIMAN, NICHOLAS GRIFFITH, IV, newspaper publisher; b. Balt., Mar. 7, 1938; s. Nicholas Griffith Penniman III and Esther Cox Lony (Wight) Keeney; m. Linda Jane Simmons, Feb. 4, 1967; children: Rebecca Helmle, Nicholas G. V. AB, Princeton U., 1960. Asst. bus. mgr. Ill. State Jour. Register, Springfield, 1964-69, bus. mgr., 1969-75; asst. gen. mgr. St. Louis Post-Dispatch, 1975-84, gen. mgr., 1984-86, pub., 1986—. Chmn. Downtown St. Louis, Inc., 1988-90, Mo. Health and Ednl. Facilities Adminstrn., 1982-85, Ill. State Fair Bd., Springfield, 1973-75, St. Louis Sports Com., 1992-93; trustee St. Louis Country Day Sch., 1983-86; bd. dirsd. St. Louis Area Boy Scouts Am., 1987—; trustee Mercantile Libr., 1995—, Regional Commerce Assn., 1995—, sec.-treas. Gateway Arch Park Expansion; chmn. Forest Park Forever, 1991-93, Caring Found. for Children, 1988-91. With U.S. Army, 1962-67. Clubs: St. Louis Country, Noonday (pres. 1994). Avocation: tennis. Home: 7540 Maryland Ave Saint Louis MO 63105-3802 Office: Pulitzer Pub Co 900 N Tucker Blvd Saint Louis MO 63101-1069

PENNIMAN, RICHARD WAYNE See LITTLE RICHARD

PENNIMAN, W. DAVID, information scientist, educator, consultant; b. St. Louis, Dec. 19, 1937; s. William Leon and Laura Mae (Van Winkle) P.; m. Charlotte Ann Meder, Mar. 17, 1973; children: Kara, Rachel, John; 1 child by previous marriage, Jessica. BS in ME, U. Ill., 1960, MS in Journalism, Communications, 1962; PhD in Communication Theory, Ohio State U., 1975. Registered profl. engr., Ohio. Assoc. dir. engring. publs. U. Ill. Coll. Engring., Urbana, 1965-66; research scientist info. systems Battelle Columbus Labs., Columbus, Ohio, 1966-69, assoc. mgr. info. systems, 1969-77; research scholar Internat. Inst. Applied Systems Analysis, Laxenburg, Austria, 1977; mgr. research Online Computer Library Ctr., Dublin, Ohio, 1978-79, dir. software devel., 1979-82, v.p. planning and research, 1982-84; dir. libraries and info. systems AT&T Bell Labs., Murray Hill, N.J., 1984-90, dir. info. svcs. group, 1990-91; pres. Coun. on Libr. Resources, Inc., Washington, 1991-95; dir. Ctr. for Info. Studies, 1995—; prof. sch. of Info. Scis. Univ. Tenn., 1995—; bd. dirs., chmn. Engring. Info. Inc., N.Y.C., 1983-91; governing com. Forest Press Inc., Albany, N.Y., 1985-88; adv. com. info. sci. Rutgers U., 1982-91. Author numerous book chpts. and articles in profl. jours. Advisor United Way, Columbus, 1981-83. Served with U.S. Army, 1963-65. Named Tech. Person of the Yr. Columbus Tech. Council, 1982, U.S. Del. to Internat. Inst. for Applied Systems Analysis, 1977. Fellow AAAS; mem. IEEE (sr.), ALA, Am. Soc. Info. Sci. (pres. 1988-89), Assn. for Computing Machinery. Avocations: antique automobiles, hiking. Home and Office: 39 Palisades Pkwy Oak Ridge TN 37830 Office: U Tenn 804 Volunteer Blvd Knoxville TN 37916-3106

PENNING, PATRICIA JEAN, elementary education educator; b. Springfield, Ill., Sept. 3, 1952; d. Howard Louis and Jean Lenore (Hartley) P. AA, Lincoln Land C.C., Springfield, 1972; BA, Millikin U., 1975. Cert. tchr. grades K-9. Receptionist Drs. Penning, Marty & Teich, Springfield, 1968-72; child care asst. La Petite Acad., Springfield, 1970-72; tchr. St. Agnes Sch., Springfield, 1975—; mail clk. St. John's Hosp., Springfield, 1977-88; mem. dir. instrnl. tv St. Agnes Sch., Springfield, 1981—, sec. primary level, 1993—, mem. reading com., 1994—, mem. social com., 1994—. Mem. St. Agnes Folk Choir, Springfield, 1976—; cantor, St. Agnes Ch., Springfield, 1976—. Recipient Outstanding Tchr. award Office Cath. Edn., Springfield, 1988, Golden Apple award Ch. 20 and Town and Country Bank, Springfield, 1993; named Apprentice Cathechist, Diocese of Springfield, Ill., 1992. Mem. Internat. Reading Assn., Nat. Coun. Math., Nat. Cath. Edn. Assn. (Grad. award 1991), Ill. State Assn. Curriculum and Devel. Roman Catholic. Avocations: reading, crafts, gardening, classical music. Home: 22 Westminster Rd Chatham IL 62629-1254 Office: St Agnes Sch 251 N Amos Ave Springfield IL 62702-4796

PENNINGER, FRIEDA ELAINE, retired English language educator; b. Marion, N.C., Apr. 11, 1927; d. Fred Hoyle and Lena Frances (Young) P. AB, U. N.C., Greensboro, 1948; MA, Duke U., 1950, PhD, 1961. Copywriter Sta. WSJS, Winston-Salem, N.C., 1948-49; asst. prof. English Flora Macdonald Coll., Red Springs, N.C., 1950-51; tchr. English Barnwell, S.C., 1951-52, Brunswick, Ga., 1952-53; instr. English U. Tenn., Knoxville, 1953-56; instr., asst. prof. Woman's Coll., U. N.C., Greensboro, 1956-58, 60-63; asst. prof., assoc. prof. U. Richmond (Va.), 1963-71; chair., dept. English Westhampton Coll., Richmond, 1971-78; prof. English U. Richmond, 1971-91, Bostwick prof. English, 1987-91; ret., 1991. Author: William Caxton, 1979, Chaucer's "Troilus and Criseyde" and "The Knight's Tale": Fictions Used, 1993, (novel) Look at Them, 1990; compiler, editor: English Drama to 1660, 1976; editor: Festschrift for Prof. Marguerite Roberts, 1976. Fellow Southeastern Inst. of Mediaeval and Renaissance Studies, 1965, 67, 69. Democrat. Presbyterian. Home: 2701 Camden Rd Greensboro NC 27403-1438

PENNINGER, WILLIAM HOLT, JR., lawyer; b. Springfield, Mo., May 4, 1954; s. William Holt Sr. and Marjorie Marie (Emanuel) P.; m. Una Lee McLeer, Aug. 8, 1981; children: Una Lee, William Holt III. BS, MIT, 1976; JD, MBA, Tulane U., 1981; LLM, Tulane, 1983. Bar: La. 1981, N.Y. 1984, Mo. 1987. Customer service rep. CIT Fin. Services, Inc., Springfield, Mo., 1976-77; lexis rep. Mead Data Cen., New Orleans, 1981-83; assoc. Hill, Betts & Nash, N.Y.C., 1983-85, Cole & Deitz, N.Y.C., 1985-86; fin. planner IDS Fin. Services Inc., Springfield, Mo., 1986-87; assoc. Farrington & Curtis, Springfield, 1987-90; legal counsel Med. Def. Assocs., Springfield, 1990—; bd. dirs. Med. Def. Ins. Co., Med. Def. Assoc. Composer, performer: The Accessible Penninger, 1991, Man/Machine/Music, 1991, Fdt=mdv, 1992, The Coyote, The Scorpion & The Goat, 1993, The Ministry for the Absorption of Protohumans, Androids & Cyborgs, 1996. Mem. Greene County Estate Planning Coun., 1987-91; bd. dirs. Springfield Regional Opera, 1989-93. Mem. ABA, Mo. Bar Assn. (ins. law com.), Springfield Met. Bar Assn., Nat. Assn. Securities Dealers (lic. 1986-89). Republican. Presbyterian. Avocations: sailing, skin and scuba diving, theoretical physics, electronic music composition, photography. Home: 2705 S Patterson Ave Springfield MO 65804-3913 Office: Legal Counsel Med Def Assoc 1311 E Woodhurst Dr Springfield MO 65804-4282

PENNINGTON, BEVERLY MELCHER, financial services company executive; b. Vermillion, SD, Feb. 8, 1931; d. Cecil Lloyd and Phyllis Cecelia (Walz) M.; m. Glen D., Sept. 1, 1965 (dec. Aug. 1986); 1 child, Terri Lynn. BS, U. S.D., Vermillion, 1952. Enrolled agt. cert. IRS 1989. Sec. budget dept. Bur. of Indian Affairs, Aberdeen, S.D., 1952-53, pvt. sec., 1953-54; pvt. sec. U.S. P.H.S. Indian Health, Aberdeen, 1954-55; adminstr. asst. U.S. Pub. Health Svc., Anchorage, 1955-58, U.S. Pub. Health, Dental Pub. Health, Washington, 1958-61; grant adminstr. Dental Pub. Health, Washington, 1961-65; co-owner Penn Mel Marina, Platte, S.D, 1965-74; co-owner Pennington Tax Service, Platte, 1974-86, owner, 1986-93; pres., CEO, White Tiger Fin. Svc., Inc., Platte, 1994—. Contbr. articles to profl. jours. Mem. Platte Women's Club, sec., 1965-68, pres., 1968-70, 89-91; mem. Libr. Bd., Sec., 1982-85, treas., 1995—. Fellow Am. Soc. Tax Profls. (sec. 1989-91, 2d v.p. 1995, 1st v.p. 1996, pres. 1997); mem. NAFE, Platte C. of C. (v.p. 1989, pres. 1990), Lyric Theatre Mus. Soc. (pres. 1988-92), U.S. C. of C., Washington Dakota Cen. Com. Republican. Presbyterian. Avocations: collecting jewelry, reading, dress designing, gourmet cooking. Office: White Tiger Fin Svc Inc 420 Main Platte SD 57369

PENNINGTON, DONALD HARRIS, physician; b. Clarksville, Ark., Sept. 13, 1945; s. John Powers and Verna Olive (Harris) P.; m. Susan Myree

Snyder, Aug. 27, 1966 (div. Aug. 1982); children: Thomas Walter, Aimee Myree, John Herrick. BA, U. of the Ozarks, 1968; MD, U. Ark., 1972; wine diploma, Calif. Dept. Agr., 1973. Intern St. Vincent Infirmary, Little Rock, 1973; physician, founding ptnr. Clarksville Med. Group, P.A., 1972-93; physician Mercy Med. Svcs., Inc., Ft. Smith, Ark., 1993—; cons. family planning svcs. Ark. State Bd. of Health, 1973-93; mem. physician adv. bd. Mercy Med. Group, 1996—. Founding mem., musician Ft. Douglas (Ark.) Backporch Bluegrass Symphony, 1976-91; acoustic double bassist River Valley Jazz Union, Russellville, Ark., 1991-97. Bd. dirs. Johnson County Regional Hosp., Clarksville, 1973-82; asst. ch. organist 1st United Meth. Ch., Clarkville, 1968—; full time organist 1st Presbyn. Ch., 1994—; active ACLU, Planned Parenthood Fedn., The League to Make a Difference, Sierra Club Legal Defense Fund, The Nature Conservancy; mem. Nat. Trust for Hist. Preservation, 1982—; mem. governing bd. Oakland Cemetery Assn., 1997—. Mem. AMA, Assn. Am. Physicians for Human Rights, Nat. Trust for Historic Preservation, Ark. Med. Soc. (county del. 1972-96), Ark. Acad. Family Practice, Sierra Club, Legal Def. Fund, Drug Policy Found., Am. Guild Organists. Democrat. Avocations: restoration of historic homes, antiques, family history, music, historical preservation. Home: 317 N Johnson St Clarksville AR 72830-2931 *I make as much music as I can; practice medicine as best as I know how. My goal is to keep breathing in and out and enjoy the happiness of each day as it comes.*

PENNINGTON, MARY ANNE, art museum director, museum management consultant, art educator; b. Franklin, Va., Apr. 12, 1943; d. James Clifton and Martha Julia (Futrell) P.; m. Walter Joseph Shackelford, Nov. 26, 1981. Student East Carolina U., 1962; BFA, Va. Commonwealth U., 1965, MFA, 1966; postgrad. Cameron U., 1970, East Carolina U., 1972, U. N.C., Chapel Hill, 1980. Instr. art Presbyn. Coll., Clinton, S.C., 1966-69; tchr. art in Pitt County, 1970-71, Greenville City (N.C.) Sch. Systems, 1971-73; instr. art Pitt Community Coll., 1972-73; coordinator visual arts and humanities program, Ludwigsberg, Fed. Republic Germany, 1974-76; vis. artist-in-residence Salt Pond Art Ctr., Blacksburg, Va., summer, 1978; asst. prof. art Pembroke State U., N.C., 1976-80; exec. dir. Greenville Mus. Art, 1980-87, The Lauren Rogers Mus. of Art, Laurel, Miss., 1987-93, Huntington (W.Va.) Mus. Art, 1994—; guest curator Slidell (La.) Arts Ctr., 1993, Artemis. Roanoke, Va., 1995; judge art competition, 1980—; speaker N.C. Dept. Corrections, 1980-87; guest lectr. art Converse Coll., Spartanburg, S.C., 1966, U. So. Miss., 1993; coord. cultural arts program Jones County Leadership Inst., 1989-90, participant, 1990-91, chair curriculum com., 1991-92, chair bd. dirs.; field reviewer Inst. Mus. Svcs., 1986-92; mem. project support grants panel Miss. Arts Commn., 1990-93; mem. Jones County Competitive Cmty. Program Team, chair edn. task force, 1991-92; adj. prof. visual art U. So. Miss. and Jones County Jr. Coll., 1993-94; mem. fed. art project rev. panel, 1994-96; co-chmn. Huntington 125th Anniversary Celebration, 1994-96. Author: Application of Industrial Sand Casting to Sculpture, 1966, Handbook to the Collection of the Lauren Rogers Mus. Art, 1989, Museum in The Schools Education Program, 1989, moderator Long Range Plan Panel, 1992, Ms. Conf. on the Arts; art columnist Laurel Leader Call, 1990-93, The Herald Dispatch, 1994—; also articles. Bd. dirs. Pitt-Greenville Arts Coun., InterMus. Lab. Consortium, 1996—, Our Jobs, Our Children; chmn. cmty. enhancement com. Our Future, Inc. 1994—; comm. com. Huntington C. of C., 1995-96; program coordinator Pitt-Greenville Leadership Inst., 1982-87; bd. dirs., v.p. Parents As Resource Tchrs., 1990-91; advisory bd. chmn. Marshall Artists Series Edn. Com., 1994—; bd. dirs. Huntington Chamber Orch., 1994—. Recipient Vol. award N.C. Gov., 1981; 2 N.C. Arts Council scholarship awards, 1980, 87. Mem. Am. Assn. Mus. (accreditation surveyor 1990—, mus. assessment program surveyor 1990—), Southeastern Mus. Conf., Inc. (steering com. 1990-91, program com. 1995-96), N.C. Mus. Council (bd. dirs. 1986-87), Miss. Mus. Assn. (bd. dirs. 1990-94, v.p. 1992-94), Miss. Inst. Arts and Letters (bd. govs. 1990-94, v.p. 1992-93, pres. 1993-94, chair Visual Arts Award, 1991, 92), Jones County C. of C. (adv. bd. dirs. 1990-93).

PENNINGTON, RICHARD J., police chief. Chief of police New Orleans. Office: 715 S Broad St New Orleans LA 70119-7416

PENNINGTON, RICHARD MAIER, lawyer, retired insurance company executive; b. Phila., Aug. 2, 1926; s. Richard and Mildred (Locke) P.; m. Apr. 20, 1963; children—Elizabeth Ann, Catherine Carter. BA, Haverford Coll., 1950; LL.B., Temple U., 1961. Bar: Pa. 1963. Claims work with INA, Phila., 1953-57, 1957-76, Asst. v.p., 1976-77; v.p. Atlantic Mut. Ins. Co., N.Y.C., 1977-78, sr. v.p., 1979-92; mem. exec. com. Ins. Com. for Arson Control, Chgo., 1982-91. Served with U.S. Army, 1945-46. Mem. ABA, Phila. Bar Assn.

PENNINGTON, WILLIAM MARK, sportswriter; b. Hartford, Conn., Dec. 12, 1956; s. Albert William and Lillian Anne (Lewis) P.; m. Joyce Hand, July 14, 1990; children: Anne D'Amour, Elise Holly. BS, Boston U., 1978. Reporter The Bristol Press, Bristol, Conn., 1976-77, The Associated Press, Boston, 1977, The Providence Jour.-Bull., Providence, 1977-79, The Stamford Advocate, Stamford, Conn., 1979-84; reporter The Record, Hackensack, N.J., 1984-89, syndicated columnist, sr. writer, 1989-97; staff writer The New York Times, 1997—. Author: The Winning Spirit, 1991; contbg. author: (book) Best Sports Stories, 1983, 85, 87, 94. Recipient Best Story award Associated Press Sports Editors, 1985, 89, 91, 93, 96, Best Columnist award, 1983, 89, 95, 96. Mem. Baseball Writers Assn. of Am., Boston U. Football Alumni Assn., New England Hist. Genealogical Soc. Roman Catholic. Office: The Record 150 River St Hackensack NJ 07601-7110

PENNISTEN, JOHN WILLIAM, computer scientist, linguist, actuary; b. Buffalo, Jan. 25, 1939; s. George William and Lucy Josephine (Gates) P. AB in Math. and Chemistry with honors, Hamilton Coll., 1960; postgrad., Harvard U., 1960-61, U.S. Army Lang. Sch., 1962-63; MS in Computer Sci. with honors, N.Y. Inst. Tech., 1987; cert. in taxation, NYU, 1982; cert. in profl. banking, Am. Inst. of Banking of Am. Bankers Assn., 1988.; cert. Asian Langs., NYU, 1992. Actuarial asst. New Eng. Mut. Life Ins. Co., Boston, 1965-66; asst. actuary Mass. Gen. Life Ins. Co., Boston, 1966-68; actuarial assoc. John Hancock Mut. Life Ins. Co., Boston, 1968-71; asst. actuary George B. Buck Cons. Actuaries, Inc., N.Y.C., 1971-75, Martin E. Segal Co., N.Y.C., 1975-80; actuary Laiken Siegel & Co., N.Y.C., 1980; cons. Bklyn., 1981—; timesharing and database analyst banklink corp. cash mgmt. div. Chem. Bank N.Y.C., 1983-85; programmer analyst Empire Blue Cross and Blue Shield, N.Y.C., 1986-88, Mt. Sinai Med. Ctr., N.Y.C., 1988-89, French Am. Banking Corp. (subs. Banque National de Paris), N.Y.C., 1989; sr. programmer analyst Dean Witter Reynolds, Inc., N.Y.C., 1989-92; computer specialist for software N.Y.C. Dept. Fin., 1992—; enrolled actuary U.S. Fed. Pension Legis. Bklyn., 1976—. Contbr. articles to profl. jours. With U.S. Army, 1961-64. Mem. AAAS, MLA, Soc. Actuaries (fellow), Practising Law Inst., Assn. Computing Machinery, IEEE Computer Soc., Am. Assn. Artificial Intelligence, Linguistic Soc. Am., Assn. Computational Linguistics, Am. Math. Soc., Math. Assn. Am., Nat. Model R.R. Assn. (life), Nat. Ry. Hist. Soc., Ry. and Locomotive Hist. Soc. (life), Bklyn. Heights Assn., Met. Opera Guild, Am. Friends of Covent Garden, Harvard Gra. Soc., Am. Legion, Phi Beta Kappa, others. Home: 135 Willow St Brooklyn NY 11201-2255

PENNOCK, DONALD WILLIAM, retired mechanical engineer; b. Ludlow, Ky., Aug. 8, 1915; s. Donald and Melvin (Evans) P.; B.S. in M.E., U. Ky., 1940, M.E., 1948; m. Vivian C. Kern, Aug. 11, 1951; 1 son, Douglas. Stationary engring., constrn. and maintenance Schenley Corp., 1935-39; mech. equipment design engr. mech. lab. U. of Ky., 1939; exptl. test engr. Wright Aero. Corp., Paterson, N.J., 1940, 1941, investigative and adv. engr. to personnel div., 1941-43; indsl. engr. Eastern Aircraft, div. Gen. Motors, Linden, N.J., 1943-45; factory engr. Carrier Corp., Syracuse, N.Y., 1945-58, sr. facilities engr., 1958-60, corporate material handling engr., 1960-63, mgr. facilities engring. dept., 1963-66, mgr. archtl. engring., 1966-68, mgr. facilities engring. dept., 1966-78. Staff, Indsl. Mgmt. Center, 1962, midwest work course U. Kan., 1959-67. Mem. munitions bd. SHIAC, 1950-52; trustee Primitive Hall Found., 1985—. Elected to Exec. and Profl. Hall of Fame, 1966. Registered profl. engr., Ky., N.J. Fellow Soc. Advancement Mgmt. (life mem., nat. v.p. material handling div. 1953-54); mem. ASME, NSPE, Am. Material Handling Soc. (dir. 1950-57, chmn. bd., pres. 1950-52), Am. Soc. Mil. Engrs., Am. Mgmt. Assn. (men. packaging council 1950-55, life mem. planning council), Nat. Material Handling Conf. (exec. com. 1951), Found. N.Am. Wild Sheep (life), Internat. Platform Assn., Tau Beta Pi. Protestant. Mng. editor Materials Handling Engring. (mag. sect.), 1949-50; mem. editorial adv. bd. Modern Materials Handling (mag.), 1949-52. Contbr. articles to tech. jours. Contbg., cons. editor: Materials Handling Handbook, 1958. Home: 24 Pebble Hill Rd Syracuse NY 13214

PENNOYER, PAUL GEDDES, JR., lawyer; b. N.Y.C., Feb. 11, 1920; s. Paul G. and Frances (Morgan) P.; m. Cecily Henderson, Feb. 5, 1949; children—Jennifer, Deidre, Paul T., Sheldon K., William M. B.S., Harvard U., 1942, LL.B., 1948. Bar: N.Y. 1949, U.S. Dist. Ct. (so. and ea. dists.) N.Y. 1952, U.S. Supreme Ct. 1972, U.S. Ct. Appeals (2d cir.) 1964, U.S. Ct. Appeals (4th cir.) 1986, U.S. Ct. Appeals (11th cir.) 1987. Assoc. Bingham Englar Jones & Houston, N.Y.C., 1949-55, ptnr., 1955-63; ptnr. Chadbourne & Parke, N.Y.C., 1963-89; of counsel, 1989—. Vice pres., trustee Frick Collection, 1975—; trustee L.I. U., 1975-85. Served to lt. USN, 1942-45. Decorated Navy Cross, Air Medal (2). Mem. ABA, N.Y. State Bar Assn., Assn. Bar City N.Y., N.Y. Bar found., Am. Coll. Trial Lawyers, N.Y. Yacht Club. Republican. Episcopalian. Office: Chadbourne & Parke 30 Rockefeller Plz New York NY 10112

PENNOYER, ROBERT M., lawyer; b. N.Y.C., Apr. 9, 1925. B.A., Harvard U., 1946; LL.B., Columbia U., 1950. Bar: N.Y. 1951, U.S. Supreme Ct. 1971. Partner firm Patterson, Belknap, Webb & Tyler, N.Y.C., 1962—; asst. U.S. atty. criminal div. So. Dist., N.Y., 1953-55; asst. to gen. counsel Office of Sec. of Def., Dept. Def., Washington, 1955-57; spl. asst. to asst. sec. of def. for internat. security affairs Office of Sec. of Def., Dept. Def., 1957-58. Trustee Carnegie Instn., Washington, 1968-79, John Merck Fund, 1982—, Mrs. Giles Whiting Found., 1970—, Met. Mus. Art, 1966—, Pierpont Morgan Libr., 1969—, columbia U., 1982-88, Boyce Thompson Inst. for Plant Rsch., Cornell U., 1974—. Lt. (j.g.) USNR, 1944-46. Mem. ABA, N.Y. State Bar Assn., Assn. Bar City N.Y., Century Assn. Office: Patterson Belknap 1133 Avenue Of The Americas New York NY 10036-6710

PENNY, JOSEPHINE B., retired banker; b. N.Y.C., July 7, 1925; d. Charles and Delia (Fahey) Booy; student Columbia U., Am. Inst. Banking; grad. Sch. Bank Adminstrn. U. Wis., 1975; m. John T. Penny, July 15, 1950 (div.); children—John T., Charleen Penny DeMauro, Patricia Penny Paras. With Prentice-Hall, N.Y.C., 1942-43; with Trade Bank & Trust Co., 1943-52, 61-70; with Nat. Westminster Bank U.S.A., 1970-85, v.p., dep. auditor, 1978-85. Mem. Bank Adminstrn. Inst. (chpt. dir. 1983-85), Inst. Internal Auditing, Nat. Assn. Bank Women (chpt. chmn. 1980-81). Home: 221A Manchester Ln Jamesburg NJ 08831-1711

PENNY, ROGER PRATT, management executive; b. Buffalo, July 13, 1936; s. George Albert and Louise (Mings) P.; m. Judith Stevens, Aug. 25, 1957; children: David, Sarah, Julia. BA in Adminstrv. Engring., Union Coll., 1958. Registered profl. engr., N.Y., Ind., Pa. From supt. to sr. mgr. Bethlehem Steel Corp., Lackawanna, N.Y., 1958-83; gen. mgr. Bethlehem Steel Corp., Burns Harbor, Ind., 1983-87; sr. v.p. Bethlehem (Pa.) Steel Corp., 1987-92, bd. dirs., bd. dirs., pres., chief oper. officer, 1992—. Mem. United Way, Buffalo, 1960-82; chmn. campaign United Way Porter County, Valparaiso, Ind., 1986; mem. Orchard Park Town Coun., 1970-82; mem. adv. bd. Purdue U., West Lafayette, Ind., 1985-86, Bus. Sch., Valparaiso U., 1986; bd. dirs. Minsi Trails coun. Boy Scouts Am., Lehigh Valley, Pa., 1988—, pres., 1996; trustee St. Luke's Hosp. Mem. Am. Iron and Steel Inst., Assn. Iron and Steel Engrs., Valparaiso C. of C. (dir. 1985-86), Orchard Park C. of C., Buffalo C. of C., Sand Creek Club (pres. 1983-86), Buffalo Soccer Club (pres. 1960-75, sec.), Saucon Valley Country Club. Republican. Episcopalian. Office: Martin Tower 1170 8th Ave Bethlehem PA 18016-7600

PENNY, TIMOTHY JOSEPH, congressman; b. Albert Lea, Minn., Nov. 19, 1951; s. Jay C. and Donna (Haukoos) P.; m. Barbara J. Christianson, Oct. 18, 1975; children: Jamison, Joseph, Molly, Marcus. B.A., Winona State U., 1974; postgrad., U. Minn., 1975. Mem. Minn. Senate from Dist. 30, 1977-82, 98th-103d Congresses from 1st Minn. Dist., 1983-94; mem. agr. com., vets affairs com., chmn. fgn. agr. and hunger subcom. Mem. Minn. State Univ. Bd., 1974-77; co-chmn. Dem. budget study group Whip-At-Large. With USNR. Recipient Disting. Service award U. Minn., 1982, Spark Plug award Communicating for Agr., 1980, Nat. Comdr.'s award DAV, 1989. Mem. New Richland (Minn.) Jaycees, Waseca Pals, Inc., Waseca and Freeborn County Assn. for Retarded Citizens. Democrat. Lutheran.

PENROD, JAMES WILFORD, choreographer, dancer; b. Provo, Utah, July 22, 1934; s. Joseph Keller and Virginia Rose (Zobell) P. BA in English, U. So. Calif., 1964; MFA in Dance, U. Calif., Irvine, 1974; CMA, Inst. Movement Studies, 1990. Mem. faculty Am. Sch. Dance, Hollywood, Calif., 1958-68, U. So. Calif., Idyllwild, 1957-59; prof. dance U. Calif., Irvine, 1966—, chmn. dept., 1981-89, 91-94; co-artistic dir. Dancer's Dance Co., Los Angeles, 1968-69, Penrod Plastino Movement Theatre, Irvine, 1968-84, choreographer, 1958—. Profl. dancer on TV, in movies and on stage; choreographer original works.; Author: Movement for the Performing Artist, 1974; co-author: Dancer Prepares, 1970. Grantee U. Calif., 1967—. Mem. SAG, AFTRA, AGVA, Nat Dance Assn., Congress Rsch. in Dance (dir. 1983-85), Orange County Performing Arts Dance Alliance (bd. dirs. 1986-89), Dance Notation Bur. (adv. bd. dirs. 1988-90), Screen Extras Guild, Actors Equity, Am. Guild Mus. Artists. Home: 4645 Green Tree Ln Irvine CA 92612-2250

PENROD, KENNETH EARL, medical education consultant, retired; b. Blanchester, Ohio, Mar. 30, 1916; s. William F. and Josie Alma (Carman) P.; m. Virginia Hogue, June 29, 1942; children: Caroline (dec.), Bruce Hogue. B.S., Miami (Ohio) U., 1938; Ph.D., Iowa State Coll., 1942. Asst. prof. physiology Boston U. Sch. Medicine, 1946-50; asso. prof. physiology Duke U. Sch. Medicine, 1950-57, prof., 1957-59, asst. dean, 1952-59; founding v.p. for med. affairs, prof. physiology W.Va. U., 1959-65; provost for med. ctr., prof. physiology Ind. U., Indpls., 1965-69; vice chancellor for med. and health scis. State U. System Fla., Tallahassee, 1969-74; exec. dir. community hosp. grad. med. edn. program Fla. Bd. Regents, Tallahassee, 1974-85; retired, 1992; spl. cons. AID, Latin Am. Mem. editorial bd. Jour. Med. Edn, 1957-65; contbr. to sci. jours. in physiol. and health edn. Served from 2d lt. to capt. USAAF, 1942-46. Mem. Am. Physiol. Soc., Assn. for Acad. Health Centers (incorporator), Assn. Am. Med. Colls., AAAS, Rotary, Phi Beta Kappa, Sigma Xi, Phi Kappa Phi, Phi Kappa Tau, Alpha Omega Alpha. Presbyterian. Home: 913 Lasswade Dr Tallahassee FL 32312-2831

PENROSE, CHARLES, JR., professional society administrator; b. Phila., Oct. 9, 1921; s. Charles and Beatrice (d,Este) P.; m. Ann Lucille Cantwell, Apr. 17, 1943; children: James, Thomas, John. Grad., Episcopal Acad., Overbrook, Pa., 1940. Exec. sec. Newcomen Soc. N.Am. (N.A.), Phila., 1946-48; dist. sales mgr. Fitchburg Paper Co., Mass., 1948-50, 52-53; from sales mgr. to v.p. sales A.M. Collins Mfg. Co., Phila., 1953-55; sales mgr. A.M. Collins divsn. Internat. Paper Co., N.Y.C., 1955; asst. to sales mgr. fine paper and bleached bd. divsn., 1956-57; sr. v.p., CEO Newcomen Soc. in N.Am., Downingtown, Pa., 1957-61; also bd. dirs. Newcomen Soc. in N.Am.; pres., CEO Newcomen Soc. U.S., 1961-87, chmn., 1987-89, chmn. emeritus, 1989—; sr. v.p. N. Am. Newcomen Soc., London, 1957-89, hon. v.p., 1989—; pres., CEO Newcomen publs. in N. Am., Inc., 1958-61, trustee, 1948-61; pres., dir. Rocaton, Inc., Darien, Conn., 1960-61. Author: They Live on a Rock in the Sea The Isles of Shoals in Colonial Days, 1957. Sec., asst. treas. Chester County Investment Fund Assn., Phila., 1959-64; v.p. Brit. Am. Ednl. Found., Inc., N.Y.C., 1968-70, pres., 1970-75, trustee, 1968-81; trustee The Stanley Mus., Kingfield, Maine, 1995—. Capt. USAAF, 1940-46, S.W. Pacific; capt. AUS, 1950-52, Germany. Mem. Most Venerable Order Hospice of St. John of Jerusalem (London). Mem. Newcomen Soc. U.S., Newcomen Soc. London, Royal Soc. Arts (Benjamin Franklin fellow 1980), Pilgrims of U.S., First Troop Phila. City Calvary (hon.), Nat. Inst. Social Scis., Soc. Am. Historians, Marine Hist. Assn., N.H. Hist. Soc., Mt. Washington Obs., Sandwich (N.H.) Hist. Soc. (trustee 1992-94, v.p. 1994—), Chi Psi Omicron. Republican. Episcopalian. Clubs: Tokeneke (Darien); Tamworth Outing (N.H.); Wonalancet Outdoors (N.H.). Home: Briar Farm 232 Quaker Whiteface Rd North Sandwich NH 03259 Office: 412 Newcomen Rd Exton PA 19341-1934

PENSE, ALAN WIGGINS, metallurgical engineer, academic administrator; b. Sharon, Conn., Feb. 3, 1934; s. Arthur Wilton and May Beatrice (Wiggins) P.; m. Muriel Drews Taylor, June 28, 1958; children—Daniel Alan, Steven Taylor, Christine Muriel. B.Metall. Engring., Cornell U., 1957; M.S., Lehigh U., 1959, Ph.D., 1962. Research asst. Lehigh U., Bethlehem, Pa., 1957-59, instr., 1960-62, asst. prof., 1962-65, asso. prof., 1965-71, prof., 1971-96, chmn. dept. metallurgy and materials engring., 1977-83, assoc. dean Coll. Engring. and Applied Scis., 1984-88, dean, 1988-90, v.p., provost, 1990-96, prof. emeritus, 1997—; assoc. dir. Ctr. Advanced Tech. for Large Structural Systems NSF, 1986-89; cons. adv. com. on reactor safeguards NRC, 1965-86. Author: (with R.M. Brick and R.B. Gordon) Structure and Properties of Engineering Materials, 4th edit, 1978; also articles. Recipient Robinson award Lehigh U., 1965, Stabler award, 1972; Danforth fellow, 1974-86. Fellow Am. Soc. Metals, Am. Welding Soc. (William Spraragan award 1963, Adams Membership award 1966, Jennings award 1970, Adams lectr. 1980, William Hobart medal 1982, Plummer lectr. 1995); mem. ASTM, Am. Soc. Engring. Edn. (Western Elec. award 1986), Internat. Inst. Welding, Nat. Acad. Engring. Republican. Evang. Congregationalist (pres. bd. trustees Evang. Sch. Theology). Home: 2227 West Blvd Bethlehem PA 18017-5025 Office: 117 Atlss St Bethlehem PA 18015-4728 *Achievement of significant goals in our life must be balanced by the quality of that life itself, for what we are is as important as what we do.*

PENSKAR, MARK HOWARD, lawyer; b. Detroit, Mar. 4, 1953; s. Sol Leonard and Frances (Rosenthal) P.; m. Carol Ann Stewart, Aug. 7, 1977; children: David, Rebecca. BA, U. Mich., 1974, M in Pub. Policy, 1975, JD, 1977. Bar: Calif. 1977, U.S. Dist. Ct. (no. dist.) Calif. 1977, (ea. and cen. dists.) Calif. 1983, (so. dist.) 1988, U.S. Ct. Appeals (9th cir.) 1987, U.S. Tax Ct. 1993. Assoc. Pillsbury, Madison and Sutro, San Francisco, 1977-84, ptnr., 1985-96; sr. bus. litigation atty. Pacific Gas and Electric Co., San Francisco, 1996—; mediator Superior Court early settlement program, San Francisco. Mem. Com. for Sch. of Pub. Policy. Mem. ABA, San Francisco Bar Assn., Commonwealth Club, Phi Gamma Delta (past pres. Bay Area grad. chpt.). Avocations: camping, golf, wine collecting. Home: 29 E Altarinda Dr Orinda CA 94563-2415 Office: Pacific Gas and Electric Co Law Dept B30A PO Box 7442 San Francisco CA 94120

PENSKE, ROGER S., manufacturing and transportation executive; b. 1937; married. Grad., Lehigh U., 1958. With Alcoa Aluminum, Pitts., 1958-63, George McKean Chevrolet, Phila., 1963-65; prin. Penske Corp., Red Bank, N.J., pres., chmn. bd.; chmn. bd. dirs., pres., CEO Penske Transp. Inc., Detroit; chmn. bd. dirs., pres. Pa. Internat. Raceway, Nazareth, 1986—; CEO Detroit Diesel Corp., chmn. bd. dirs.; pres. Competition Tire West, inc., Brooklyn, Mich.; chmn. bd. dirs. Penske Truck Leasing Corp., Penske Speedway, Inc., Detroit, Penske Automotive Group, Detroit, Outer Drive Holidays, Inc., Detroit, D Longo, Inc., El Monte, Calif.; sec. Ilmore Engring., Inc., Redford, Mich. *

PENSMITH, SHARYN ELAINE, communications executive; b. Washington, Mar. 22, 1945; d. Alfred Munk and Helen Victoria (Sollers) Lawson; m. Charles Lee Pensmith, Oct. 18, 1986. BA in Psychology, U. Md., 1967. Sales/acct. rep. GE, Bethesda, Md., 1967-75; sr. sales Nat. CSS, Arlington, Va., 1975-79, Itel Corp., McLean, Va., 1978-80; br. mgr. On-Line Systems, McLean, Va., 1980-82; dist. sales support AT&T, Rosslyn, Va., 1982-84; dir. bus. devel. Govt. Systems Inc., Fairfax, Va., 1984-96; v.p. Fed. Sources Inc., 1996—; pres. ARI Consulting Group, Fairfax, 1993—; cons. Mint Corp., Fairfax, 1993—. Founder Migration Methodology strategy. Annual recipient pres.'s award Infonet, 1986-96, Best of the Best Infonet award, 1992, 93, 94, 96. Mem. NAFE, Women in Tech., Inter Agy. Com., Armed Forces Comm. and Electronics Assn. Avocations: cooking, investments. Home: 775 Bon Haven Dr Annapolis MD 21401 Office: Fed Sources Inc 4th Fl 8400 Westpark Dr Ste 4 Mc Lean VA 22102-3522

PENSON, EDWARD MARTIN, management consulting company executive; b. N.Y.C., Aug. 30, 1927; s. Michael and Cecile (Cohan) P.; m. Georgann Ellen McCune, June 25, 1975; children: Jeffery, Albert, Cynthia. B.A. cum laude, U. Fla., 1950, Ph.D., 1955; M.A., Ohio U., 1951. Prof. communication Ohio U., Athens, 1955-75, dean, 1965-68, v.p., 1969-75; pres., prof. Salem State Coll., Mass., 1975-78; prof., chancellor U. Wis.-Oshkosh, 1978-89, chancellor emeritus, 1989—; pres. Penson-Strawbridge, Inc., mgmt. cons., 1989—; cons. Royal McBee, Litton Industries, Ohio Credit Union, Battelle Meml. Inst., 1963-66, U. Nev., 1980-81, Paine Art Ctr., 1985, Acad. Ednl. Devel., King Fiesal U., 1986, OshKosh B'Gosh, Inc., 1987, Akron U., 1988, Baker Paper Co., 1990; bd. dirs. Valley Bank, Wis. Contbr. numerous articles to profl. jours., chpts. to books. Bd. dirs. Assn. Retarded Citizens, Salem, Mass., 1975-78; bd. dirs. Econ. Devel. Council, North Shore, Mass., 1976-78, Ohio student loan commr., Columbus, 1971-75. Mem. Communication Assn. Am., Internat. Communication Assn., Am. Assn. State Colls. and Univs., Nat. Assn. Student Personnel Adminstrs., Sigma Alpha Eta, Phi Kappa Phi, Alpha Lambda Delta, Psi Chi, Rotary (Salem, Mass. and Oshkosh, Wis.). Home and Office: 924 Summerbrooke Dr Tallahassee FL 32312

PENTKOWSKI, RAYMOND J., superintendent. Supt. Battenkill (Vt.) Valley Supervisory Union. Named state finalist Nat. Supt. of Yr. award, 1989. Office: East Arlington Rd Arlington VT 05250

PENTNEY, ROBERTA JEAN, neuroanatomist, educator; b. Van Nuys, Calif., Jan. 11, 1936; d. Bernard Andrew and Helen Amelia (Sahm) Pierson; m. William M. Pentney, July 5, 1975; 1 child, William Robert. BA, Coll. Notre Dame, Belmont, Calif., 1960; PhD, U. Notre Dame, 1965. Asst. then assoc. prof. Coll. Notre Dame, Belmont, 1965-71; spl. fellow Coll. Phys. and Surgeons, Columbia U., N.Y.C., 1971-74; from asst. prof. to prof. Sch. Medicine and Biomed. Sci. SUNY, Buffalo, 1974—; interim chmn. dept. anat. cell biology Sch. Medicine and Biomed. Sci. SUNY, Buffalo, 1992—. Contbr. articles to profl. jours. Mem. Am. Assn. Anatomists, Soc. for Neuroscis., Rsch. Soc. on Alcoholism, Gerontol. Soc., Sigma Xi. Office: SUNY Dept Anatomy Cell Bio 317 Farber Hall Buffalo NY 14214-8001

PENWELL, JONES CLARK, real estate appraiser, consultant; b. Crisp, Tex., Dec. 19, 1921; s. Clark Moses and Sarah Lucille (Jones) P.; BS, Colo. State U., 1949; m. A. Jerry Jones, July 1, 1967; children: Dale Maria, Alan Lee, John Steven, Laurel Anne, Tracy Lynn. Farm mgmt. supr. Farmers Home Adminstrn., Dept. Agr., 1949-58; rancher 1958-61; real estate appraiser/realty officer Dept. Interior, Tex., Calif., Ariz., Colo., Washington, 1961-78, chief appraiser Bur. Reclamation, Lakewood, Colo., 1978-80; ind. fee appraiser, cons., 1980-94; ret., 1995. Served with USN, 1940-46. Accredited rural appraiser; cert. review appraiser, gen. appraiser; recipient Outstanding Performance awards U.S. Bur. Reclamation, 1964, 75, 80. Mem. Am. Soc. Farm Mgrs. and Rural Appraisers, Internat. Right-of-Way Assn., Nat. Assn. Rev. Appraisers (regional v.p. 1978-79), Jefferson County Bd. Realtors. Democrat. Presbyterian. Clubs: Elks, Rotary, Mt. Vernon Country. Author: Reviewing Condemnation Appraisal Reports, 1980; The Valuation of Easements, 1980. Home and office: 10100 W 21st Pl Lakewood CO 80215-1406 *Personal philosophy: Great personal satisfaction and benefit to society follows a person's development, constant improvement and marketing of talents in a line of work which is enjoyable and most comfortable for him to deliver.*

PENZ, ANTON JACOB, retired accounting educator; b. Cleve., Feb. 22, 1906; s. Stephen F. and Elizabeth (Prokosch) P.; (married); children—Alton Jeffry, David Alan. B.S. in Elec. Engring, Cleve. State U., 1933; M.A. in Edn, Western Res. U., 1936; M.B.A., Northwestern U., 1942; Ph.D., Ohio State U., 1947. Prof. Davis and Elkins Coll., 1937-40; lectr. Rennselaer Poly. Inst., 1944; asst. prof. La. State U., 1944-47; prof. accounting, head dept. U. Ala., 1947-71, prof. emeritus, 1971—; Distinguished vis. prof. U. Nev., Reno, spring 1972, U. Colo., Boulder, spring 1973, Va. Commonwealth U., Richmond, spring 1975, U. Md., College Park, spring 1979; cons., lectr. AID, Lima, Peru, 1965-66, Guyana, 1967. Author: Manual De Contabilidad Y Costos, 1966; Editor: Accounting Teachers Guide, 1953, Professional Developments: Accounting Teachers Guide, 1953, Accountancy, A Vocation and Profession, 1958, Guide to Accounting Instruction: Concepts and Practices, 1968, Introducing the Profession: A Guide to Accounting Instruction, 1968. Del. various congresses. Mem. Nat. Assn. Accountants (Lybrand award 1951), Fin. Execs. Inst., Am. Accounting Assn. (v.p. 1962-63), Beta Alpha Psi (pres. 1955-56, editor newsletter 1953-

55). Home: Pine Valley # F-31 800 Rice Valley Rd N Tuscaloosa AL 35406-1671 Office: Box AC Tuscaloosa AL 35486

PENZER, MARK, lawyer, editor, corporate trainer, former publisher; b. Bklyn., Nov. 22, 1932; s. Ed and Fay (Weinberg) P.; m. Eileen Malen, Aug. 12, 1962; children: Matthew, Nicole; m. Nydia A. Rey, Nov. 25, 1984. B.B.A., CCNY; J.D., Fordham U. Bar: N.Y. 1968, D.C. 1973, Fla. 1982, U.S. Dist. Ct. (ea. dist.) N.Y. 1976, U.S. Dist. Ct. (so. dist.) Fla. 1991; cert. instr. DMA, 1986. Free-lance writer, 1950-83; editorial asst. Hearst mags., N.Y.C., 1955; asst. editor Hearst mags., 1956, assoc. editor, 1957-66; columnist N.Y. Jour.-Am., 1960-62; editor in chief Rudder mag., 1967-69, editorial dir., 1970-74; editor in chief True, 1970-73, editor at large, 1973-75; pub., editor in chief Jour. Energy Medicine, 1978-81; Medicare hearing officer Miami, Fla., 1981-82; pres. Success Internat., Inc., Coral Gables, Fla., 1984-85; adj. prof. bus. and tech. writing Fla. Internat. U., small bus. mgmt., U. Miami, 1986-89; pres. Heroica, Inc., Miami Lakes, Fla., 1989-90; pvt. practice Law Offices of Mark Penzer, Hialeah and Miami Lakes, Fla., 1991—; tchr. creative writing Dade County Off Campus Edn. Author: The Motorboatman's Bible, 1965, The Powerboatman's Bible, 1977; asst. editor: The Path of Least Resistance, 1989, Do It!, 1991. Served with AUS, 1953-55. Mem. Hialeah-Miami Lakes Bar Assn. (pres. 1990-92).

PENZIAS, ARNO ALLAN, astrophysicist, research scientist, information systems specialist; b. Munich, Germany, Apr. 26, 1933; came to U.S., 1940, naturalized, 1946; s. Karl and Justine (Eisenreich) P.; m. Sherry Chamovelevit, Aug. 2, 1996; children: David Simon, Mindy Gail, Laurie Shifra. BS in Physics, CCNY, 1954; MA in Physics, Columbia U., 1958, PhD in Physics, 1962; Dr. honoris causa, Observatoire de Paris, 1976; ScD (hon.), Rutgers U., 1979, Wilkes Coll., 1979, CCNY, 1979, Yeshiva U., 1979, Bar Ilan U., 1983, Monmouth Coll., 1984, Technion-Israel Inst. Tech., 1986, U. Pitts., 1986, Ball State U., 1986, Kean Coll., 1986, U. Pa., 1992, Ohio State U., 1988, Iona Coll., 1988; Drew U., 1989; ScD (hon.), Lafayette Coll., 1990, Columbia U., 1990, George Washington U., 1992, Rensselaer Univ., 1992, U. Pa., 1992; Bloomfield Coll., 1994, Rankin Tech. U., 1997, Hebrew Union Coll., 1997. Mem. tech. staff Bell Labs., Holmdel, N.J., 1961-72, head radiophysics rsch. dept., 1972-76; dir. radio research lab. Bell Labs., 1976-79, exec. dir. rsch., communications scis. div., 1979-81, v.p. rsch., 1981-95, v.p., chief scientist, 1995—; bd. dirs. A.D. Little, LCC Internat., Warpspeed Comm., Fibex Techs.; adj. prof. earth and scis. SUNY, Stony Brook, 1974-84, Univ. Disting. lectr., 1990; lectr. dept. astrophys. scis. Princeton U., 1967-72, vis. prof., 1972-85; rsch. assoc. Harvard Coll. Obs., 1968-80; Edison lectr. U.S. Naval Rsch. Lab., 1979; Kompfner lectr. Stanford U., 1979; Gamow lectr. U. Colo., 1980; Jansky lectr. Nat. Radio Astronomy Obs., 1983; Michelson Meml. lectr., 1985; Grace Adams Tanner lectr., 1987; Klopsteg lectr. Northwestern U., 1987; grad. faculties alumni Columbia U., 1987-89; Regents' lectr. U. Calif., Berkeley, 1990; Lee Kuan Yew Disting. vis. Nat. U. Singapore, 1991; mem. astronomy adv. panel NSF, 1978-79, mem. indsl. panel on sci. and tech., 1982—, disting. lectr., 1987, affiliate Max-Planck Inst. for Radioastronomy, 1978-85, chmn. Fachbeirat, 1981-83; rschr. in astrophysics, info. tech., its applications and impacts. Author: Ideas and Information Managing in a High-Tech World, 1989 (pub. in 10 langs.), Harmony-Business, Technology and Life After Paperwork, 1995; mem. editl. bd. Ann. Rev. Astronomy and Astrophysics, 1974-78; mem. editl. bd. AT&T Bell Labs. Tech. Jour., 1978-84, chmn., 1981-84; assoc. editor Astrophys. Jour., 1978-82; contbr. over 100 articles to tech. jours.; several patents in field. Trustee Trenton (N.J.) State Coll., 1977-79; mem. bd. overseers U. Pa. Sch. Engring. and Applied Sci., 1983-86; mem. vis. com. Calif. Inst. Tech., 1977-79; mem. Com. Concerned Scientists, 1975—, vice chmn., 1976—; mem. adv. bd. Union of Couns. for Soviet Jews, 1983—; bd. dirs. IMNET, 1986-91, Duracell, 1995-96, Coun. on Competitiveness, 1989-92. With U.S. Army, 1954-56. Named to NJ Lit, Hall of Fame, 1991; recipient Herschel medal Royal Astron. Soc, 1977, Nobel prize in Physics, 1978, Townsend Harris medal CCNY, 1979, Newman award, 1983, Joseph Handleman prize in the scis., 1983, Grad. Faculties Alumni award Columbia U., 1984, Achievement in Science award Big Brothers Inc., N.Y.C., 1985, Priestly award Dickinson Coll., 1989, Pender award U. Pa., 1992. Mem. NAE, NAS (Henry Draper medal 1977), AAAS, IEEE (hon.), Am. Astron. Soc., Am. Phys. Soc. (Pake prize 1990), Internat. Astron. Union, World Acad. Arts and Sci.

PENZIEN, JOSEPH, structural engineering educator; b. Philip, S.D., Nov. 27, 1924; s. John Chris and Ella (Stebbins) P.; m. Jeanne Ellen Hunson, Apr. 29, 1950 (dec. 1985); children—Robert Joseph, Karen Estelle, Donna Marie, Charlene May; m. Mi-jung Park, June 16, 1988. Student, Coll. Idaho, 1942-43; B.S., U. Wash., 1945; Sc.D., Mass. Inst. Tech., 1950. Mem. staff Sandia Corp., 1950-51; sr. structures engr. Consol. Vultee Aircraft Corp., Fort Worth, 1951-53; asst. prof. U. Calif. at Berkeley, 1953-57, asso. prof., 1957-62, prof. structual engring., 1962-88, prof. emeritus, 1988—; dir. Earthquake Engring. Research Center, 1968-73, 77-80; cons. engring. firms; chief tech. adv. Internat. Inst. of Seismology and Earthquake Engring., Tokyo, Japan, 1964-65; chmn. bd. Ea. Internat. Engrs., Inc., 1980-90, Internat. Civil Engring. Cons., Inc., 1990—. NATO Sr. Sci. fellow., 1969. Fellow Am. Acad. Mechanics; hon. mem. ASCE (Walter Huber Rsch. award, Alfred M. Freudenthal medal, Nathan M. Newmark medal), Earthquake Engring. Rsch. Inst. (hon., Hausner medal), IAEE (hon.), EERI (Alfred E. Alquist award); mem. Am. Concrete Inst., Structural Engrs. Assn. Calif., Seismol. Soc. Am., Nat. Acad. Engring. Home: 800 Solana Dr Lafayette CA 94549-5004 Office: Davis Hall Univ Calif Berkeley CA 94720

PEOPLES, DAVID WEBB, screenwriter; b. Middletown, CT; s. Joe Webb Peoples. B.A. English, UC Berkeley, 1962. Scripts include Blade Runner, 1982, Leviathan, 1989, Dead Fall, 1990, Unforgiven, 1992 (Academy award nomination best original screenplay 1992), Hero, 1992; dir., writer: The Blood of Heroes, 1990. Office: 2899 Buena Vista Way Berkeley CA 94708-2015*

PEOPLES, JOHN ARTHUR, JR., former university president, consultant; b. Starkville, Miss., Aug. 26, 1926; s. John Arthur and Maggie Rose (Peoples) P.; m. Mary E. Galloway, July 13, 1951; children: Kathleen, Mark Adam. B.S., Jackson State U., 1950; M.A., U. Chgo., 1951, Ph.D., 1961. Tchr. math. Froebel Sch., Gary, Ind., 1951-58; asst. prin. Lincoln Sch., Gary, 1958-62; prin. Banneker Sch., Gary, 1962-64; asst. to pres. Jackson (Miss.) State U., 1964-66, v.p., 1966-67, pres., 1967-84; Trustees disting. prof. Univs. Ctr. of Jackson, 1984-85; asst. to pres. SUNY, Binghamton, 1965-66; cons. in higher edn., 1985—; lectr. summers numerous univs. and colls. Contbr. articles to profl. jours. Active Boy Scouts Am.; bd. govs. So. Regional Edn. Bd.; bd. visitors Air U.; adv. com. U.S. Army Command and Gen. Staff Coll.; mem. Commn. Excellence Am. Assn. State Colls. and Univs.; bd. commrs. Jackson Airport Authority. Served with USMCR, 1944-47. Recipient Disting. Am. award Nat. Football Found., Presdl. citation, Lifetime Achievement award Nat. Black Coll. Alumni Found., 1993—; named to Southwestern Athletic Hall of Fame. Mem. Am. Council Edn. (chmn. dir. 1975), Am. Assn. Higher Edn. (dir. 1971-74), NEA, Miss. Tchrs. Assn., Jackson C. of C. (econ. council), Alpha Kappa Mu, Phi Kappa Phi, Phi Delta Kappa, Omega Psi Phi (Man of Year, Sigma Omega chpt. 1966), Sigma Pi Phi. Lodge: Masons (33 deg.).

PEOPLES, THOMAS EDWARD, publisher, executive, writer; b. Cleve., Oct. 26, 1915; s. Robert Stephen and Mary Frances (Box) P.; m. Helen Catherine Mullaney, Jan. 9, 1943; children—Michael Thomas, Mary Dennis, Thomas Edward, James Robert. Student, John Carroll U., 1933-37. Staff photographer Central Press Assn. div. Hearst Corp., 1938-41; staff photographer Internat. News Photos, Cleve., 1946, bur. mgr., 1947-52; picture editor Newspaper Enterprise Assn., Cleve., 1953-58; comics prodn. editor Newspaper Enterprise Assn., 1958-68, dir. comic art, 1968-76, v.p., 1972-76. Author: syndicated comic page Our Boarding House with Maj. Hoople, 1959-69, Major Hoople Football Forecast, 1959-91. Served to 1st lt. U.S. Army, 1941-46, PTO. Mem. Cleve. Newspaper and Newsreel Cameramens Assn. (pres. 1950-51), Newspaper Comics Council (exec. bd. 1968-76, promotion dir. 1972-73), Nat. Cartoonists Soc., Sigma Delta Chi. Democrat. Roman Catholic. Home: 1095 Circle Ter W # B Delray Beach FL 33445-2905 *Every day we should attempt to do some deed for the betterment of society and one's fellowmen. The performance of these deeds may or may not be anonymous but they must never be done with the aim of financial reward or personal or social gain. Our efforts to help our fellowmen may not be crowned with success every time, but it is in the trying we receive our reward.*

PEPE, FRANK A., cell and developmental biology educator; b. Schenectady, May 22, 1931; s. Rocco and Margherita (Ruggiero) P. B.S., Union Coll., 1953; Ph.D., Yale U., 1957. Instr. anatomy U. Pa., Phila., 1957-60, assoc. in anatomy, 1960-63, asst. prof., 1963-65, assoc. prof., 1965-70, prof., 1970-92, chmn. dept. anatomy, 1977-90, prof. cell. and devel. biology, 1992-96, emeritus prof., 1996—. Editor: Motility in Cell Function, 1979. Recipient Rsch. Career Devel. award USPHS, 1968-73, Raymond C. Truex Disting. Lecture award Hahneman U., 1988. Fellow AAAS; mem. Am. Assn. Anatomists, Am. Chem. Soc., Biophys. Soc., Microscopy Soc. Am., Sigma Xi. Home: 4614 Pine St Philadelphia PA 19143-1808 Office: U Pa Sch Medicine Philadelphia PA 19104-6508

PEPE, LOUIS ROBERT, lawyer; b. Derby, Conn., Mar. 7, 1943; s. Louis F. and Mildred R. (Vollaro) P.; m. Carole Anita Roman, June 8, 1969; children: Marissa Lee, Christopher Justin, Alexander Drew. B.Mgmt.Engring., Rensselaer Poly. Inst., 1964, M.S., 1967; J.D. with distinction, Cornell U., 1970. Bar: Conn. 1970, U.S. Dist. Ct. Conn. 1970, U.S. Ct. Appeals (2d cir.) 1971, U.S. Supreme Ct. 1975, U.S. Ct. Claims 1978. Assoc., Alcorn, Bakewell & Smith, Hartford, Conn., 1970-75, ptnr., 1975-82; sr. ptnr. Pepe & Hazard, Hartford, 1983—; dir. BayBank Conn., 1987-93; adj. assoc. prof. Hartford Grad. Ctr., 1972-87. Adv. coun. Cornell Law Sch., 1990—. Mem. New Hartford Planning and Zoning Commn., 1973-84, chmn., 1980-84; mem. New Hartford Inland Wetlands Commn., 1975-78, New Hartford Housing Authority, 1971-72; dir. Capitol Area Found. Equal Justice, 1993—. Served to 1st lt., U.S. Army, 1964-66. Decorated Army Commendation Medal; recipient Frazer prize and Robinson Moot Ct. award Cornell U., 1970. Fellow Am. Bar Found.; mem. ABA, Am. Coll. Trial Lawyers, Am. Bd. Trial Advs., Conn. Bar Assn. (chmn. constrn. law sect. 1989-92), Conn. Trial Lawyers Assn., Hartford County Bar Assn., Phi Kappa Phi. Home: 3 Metacom Dr Simsbury CT 06070-1851 Office: Goodwin Sq Hartford CT 06103-4300

PEPE, MICHAEL, publishing executive; b. Chester, Pa., May 1, 1954; s. John F. and Adele (Davis) P.; m. Laurie Ann Huckins, June 12, 1976; children: Matthew Eliot, Gordon Michael. BA, U. Del., 1976; MBA, Harvard U., 1981. Area mgr. Surgicot, Inc., Hauppauge, N.Y., 1976-78, dir. mktg., 1978-79; assoc. Morgan Stanley & Co., N.Y.C., 1981-82; asst. brand mgr. Procter & Gamble, Cin., 1982-84; v.p. mktg. Patient Tech., Inc., Hauppauge, 1984, pres., chief operating officer, 1984-86; dir. strategic planning People mag. div. Time, Inc., N.Y.C., 1986-87, dir. prod., sr. v.p., 1987—; Group Pub Fortune, N.Y.C. Walter C. Teagle fellow, Harvard U., 1979. Phi Beta Kappa. Club: Harvard. Avocations: fly fishing, running, cooking, wine. Office: Time Inc Time & Life Bldg Rockefeller Ctr New York NY 10020-1302*

PEPE, PAUL ERNEST, emergency physician, educator; b. New Haven, Conn., July 13, 1950; s. Vincent and June Rose (Segnella) P.; m. Linda Lou Miller, Sept. 23, 1990; children: Lauren June, Michael Vincent. BA magna cum laude, Boston U., 1972; MD, U. Calif., 1976; MPH, U. Tex., 1995. Diplomate Am. Bd. Internal Medicine, Am. Bd. Emergency Medicine, Am. Bd. Forensic Medicine, Am. Bd. Pulmonary Medicine. Resident in internal medicine U. Wash. Hosp., Seattle, 1976-79, sr. fellow in critical care and pulmonary medicine, 1979-81, sr. fellow in trauma medicine, 1981-82; dir. emergency med. svcs. City of Houston, 1982-96; prof. medicine Baylor Coll. of Medicine, Houston, 1982-96; dir. and chmn. dept. emergency medicine Allegheny U. of the Health Scis., Pitts., 1996—; dir. emergency svcs. Allegheny Gen. Hosp., Pitts., 1996—. Contbr. nearly 400 sci. manuscripts and abstracts to profl. jours. and sci. confs. Med. dir. Econ. Summit of Nations, Houston, 1990, Rep. Nat. Conv., 1992; mem. emergency med. adv. panel U.S. Secret Svc., Washington, 1993—, emergency med. and trauma adv. com. U.S. Dept. Health and Human Svcs., Washington, 1994-96; trauma and emergency medicine cons. White House Med. Unit, 1996—. Grantee numerous fed. and other grants, 1981—; recipient Alumni Achievement award Boston U., 1986, Health Policy Leadership award Houston Area Health Coalition, 1991, Disting. Pub. Svc. award City of Houston, 1995, '96. Fellow ACP, Am. Coll. Emergency Physicians, Am. Coll. Chest Physicians, Am. Coll. Critical Care Medicine; mem. Am. Heart Assn. (bd. dirs. Gulf coast divsn., nat. subcom. on basic and advanced life support), others. Avocations: travel, piano, photography. skiing, free diving. Office: Allegheny Gen Hosp 320 E North Ave Pittsburgh PA 15212-4756

PEPE, STEPHEN PHILLIP, lawyer; b. Paterson, N.J., Oct. 30, 1943; s. Vincent Attilio and Emma (Opletal) P.; m. Catherine B. Hagen, Dec. 8, 1990. BA, Montclair (N.J.) State Coll., 1965; JD, Duke U., 1968. Bar: Calif. 1969, J.S. Dist. Ct. (no., so., ea. and cen. dists.) Calif. 1975, U.S. Ct. Appeals (9th cir.) 1975, U.S. Sup. Ct. 1978. Assoc. O'Melveny & Myers, L.A., 1968-75, ptnr., 1976—, chmn. lab. and employment law dept., 1989-92. Co-author: Avoiding and Defending Wrongful Discharge Claims, 1987, Privacy in the Work Place, 1993, Corporate Compliance Series: Designing an Effective Fair Fining and Termination Compliance Program, 1993, The Law of Libel & Slander, 1994; co-editor: Guide to Acquiring and Managing a U.S. Business, 1992, Calif. Employment Law Letter, 1990-94. Bd. visitors Duke Law Sch., 1992-96; bd. trustees Montclair State Coll. Found., 1991; pres. Inst. Indsl. Rels. Assn. With USAR, 1969-75. Mem. Am. Hosp. Assn. (labor adv. com. 1975-90), The Employers Group (bd. dirs., chmn. legal com. 1989—), Calif. Club (chmn. employee rels. com. 1980—). Democrat. Roman Catholic. Avocations: wine collecting, wine making, wine judging, vineyard owner. Office: O'Melveny & Myers 610 Newport Center Dr Newport Beach CA 92660

PEPE, STEVEN DOUGLAS, federal magistrate judge; b. Indpls., Jan. 29, 1943; s. Wilfrid Julius and Roselda (Gehring) P. BA cum laude, U. Notre Dame, 1965; JD magna cum laude, U. Mich., 1968; postgrad., London Sch. Econs. and Polit. Sci., 1970-72; LLM, Harvard U., 1974. Bar: Ind. 1968, U.S. Dist. Ct. Ind. 1968, D.C. 1969, U.S. Dist. Ct. D.C. 1969, mass. 1973, Mich. 1974, U.S. Dist. Ct. (ea. dist.) Mich., 1983. Law clk. Hon. Harold Leventhal U.S. Cir. Ct. Appeals, Washington, 1968-69; staff atty. Neighborhood Legal Svcs. Program, 1969-70; cons. Office of Svcs. to Aging, Lansing, Mich., 1976-77, Administrn. Aging, Dept. Health and Human Svcs., 1976-78; U.S. magistrate judge Eastern Dist., Ann Arbor, Mich., 1983—; mem. Biregional Older Am. Advocacy Assistance Resource and Support Ctr., 1979-81; cons., bd. dirs. Ctr. Social Gerontology (1988-93); clin. prof. law, dir. Mich. Clin. Law Program, U. Mich. Law Sch., 1974-83; adj. prof. law Detroit Mercy Sch. Law, 1985; lectr. U. Mich. Law Sch., 1985-96. Editor Mich. Law Rev.; contbr. articles to profl. jours. Recipient Reginald Heber Smith Cmty. Lawyer fellowship, 1969-70; Mich.-Ford Internat. Studies fellow, 1970-72, Harvard Law Sch. Clin. Teaching fellow, 1972-73. Mem. ABA, State Bar Mich., State Bar Ind., D.C. Bar, Fed. Bar Assn., Washtenaw County Bar Assn., Vanzetti M. Hamilton Bar Assn., Am. Inn Court XI, U. Detroit Mercy, Pi Sigma Alpha, Order of Coif. Office: US District Court PO Box 7150 Ann Arbor MI 48107-7150

PEPER, CHRISTIAN BAIRD, lawyer; b. St. Louis, Dec. 5, 1910; s. Clarence F. and Christine (Baird) P.; m. Ethel C. Kingsland, June 5, 1935 (dec. Sept. 1995); children: Catherine K. Peper Larson, Anne Peper Sale, Christian B.; m. Barbara C. Pleiter, Jan. 25, 1996. AB cum laude, Harvard U., 1932; LLB, Washington U., 1935; LLM, Yale U., 1937. Bar: Mo. 1934. Since practiced in St. Louis; of counsel Peper, Martin, Jensen, Maichel & Hetlage.; lectr. various subjects Washington U. Law Sch., St. Louis, 1943-61; ptnr. A.G. Edwards & Sons, 1945-67; pres. St. Charles Gas Corp., 1953-72; bd. dirs. St. Louis Steel Casting Inc., Hydraulic Press Brick Co., El Dorado Paper Bag Mfg. Co., Inc. Editor: An Historian's Conscience: The Correspondence of Arnold J. Toynbee and Columba Cary-Elwes, 1986. Contbr. articles to profl. jours. Mem. vis. com. Harvard Div. Sch., 1964-70; counsel St. Louis Art Mus. Sterling fellow Yale U., 1937. Mem. ABA, Mo. Bar Assn., St. Louis Bar Assn., Noonday Club, Harvard Club, East India Club (London), Order of Coif, Phi Delta Phi. Roman Catholic. Home: 1454 Mason Rd Saint Louis MO 63131-1211 Office: 720 Olive St Saint Louis MO 63101

PEPER, GEORGE FREDERICK, editor; b. Nyack, N.Y., Jan. 25, 1950; s. Gerhard Wilhelm and Doris Elene (Bargfrede) P.; m. Elizabeth Marshall White, May 20, 1978; children: Timothy William, Christopher Scott. BA in English and Comparative Lit., Princeton U., 1972; postgrad., Yale U., 1973. Assoc. editor Winchester Press, N.Y.C., 1973-75; communications dir. Met. Golf Assn., N.Y.C., 1976; assoc. editor, exec. editor Golf mag., N.Y.C., 1976-78; editor Golf mag., 1979-90; editor-in-chief Golf Mag., 1990—; editl. dir. Golf Mag. Properties, N.Y.C., 1992—, sr. v.p., editl. dir., 1994. Author: Scrambling Golf, 1977, Golf's Supershots, 1982, Masters Tournament anns., 1983—, The PGA Championship, 1916-84, 1985, Golf Courses of the PGA Tour, 1986, 94, Grand Slam Golf, 1991, Golfwatching: A Viewer's Guide to World Golf, 1995; (with Greg Norman) Shark Attack: Greg Norman's Guide to Aggressive Golf, 1988, Greg Norman's Instant Lessons, 1993; co-author: Golf Magazine's Complete Book of Golf Instruction, 1997; script-writer: Jack Nicklaus—The Year in Golf, 1994, Official U.S. Open Video, 1994, 95, 96, 97, Official PGA Championship Video, 1994, 95, 96, 97; editor: Golf in America: The First 100 Years, 1988, Shinnecock Hills Golf Club, 1891-91, 1997. Recipient Times Mirror Chmn.'s award, 1997. Mem. Nat. Golf Found. (bd. dirs. 1996—), Golf Writers Assn., Am. Met. Golf Writers Assn., Am. Soc. Mag. Editors, Sleepy Hollow Country Club (Scarborough, N.Y.), Loch Lomond Golf Club (Scotland), Royal and Ancient Golf Club of St. Andrews (Scotland), Turnberry Golf Club (Scotland). Office: Golf Magazine 2 Park Ave New York NY 10016-5675

PEPIN, JOHN NELSON, materials research and design engineer; b. Lowell, Mass., June 5, 1946; s. Nelson Andre and Leanne Florine (Boucher) P. BS in Mech. Engring., Northeastern U., 1968; MS in Aerospace Engring., MIT, 1970. Aero. engr. Bradway STOL Amphibian Ltd., Raymond, Maine, 1979; staff engr. Fiber Materials, Inc., Biddeford, Maine, 1979-84; pres. Pepin Assocs., Inc., Greenville, Maine, 1984—; cons. Foster-Miller Engrs., Waltham, Mass., 1985-95, Johnson & Johnson Orthopedic Divsn., Braintree, Mass., 1984-86, Allied Signal Aerospace, South Bend, Inc., 1985-93, B.F. Goodrich, Akron, Ohio and Marlboro, Mass., 1986-87. Patentee in field. U.S. Dept. Transp. grantee, 1989—, U.S. Dept. of Energy grantee, 1990-93; NIH grantee, 1994—; U.S. Dept. Commerce grantee, 1996—. Mem. Soc. for Advancement of Materials and Process Engring., Seaplane Pilots Assn., MIT Club of Maine (bd. dirs. Portland chpt. 1988). Achievements include research contributions in lightweight structures to contain turbine engine rotor failures, process to recycle plastics into automotive structures, and advanced bone replacement materials. Home: PO Box 143 Greenville ME 04441-0143

PÉPIN, MARCEL, broadcast executive; b. Ste-Cécile-de-Lévrard, Que., Can., 1941. BA, U. Ottawa, Can., 1961, Etudes supérieures en Lettres françaises, 1962-64; B in Pedagogy, U. Montreal, Can., 1962. Lectr. U. Ottawa, 1962-64; corr. Parliament Le Droit, Ottawa, 1964-68; gen. mgr. Conseil économique de l'Outaouais, 1968-69; asst. to mng. editor info. La presse, 1970-73, columnist labor sect., 1973-74; chief parliamentary bur. La presse, Ottawa, 1974-77; chief editor Le Soleil, Que., 1977-82; pres. Commn. d'accès à l'information, 1982-88; chief editor French Radio News CBC, 1988-90, gen. mgr. programs French Radio Info., 1990-91; v.p. French Radio SRC CBC, 1991—; former treas. Conseil de presse du Que.; bd. dirs. Digital Radio Rsch. Inc., com. mem. La Recherche sur la radio numérique Inc.; bd. dirs. Alliance for Canada's Audio-Visuel Heritage, 1996, com. mem. de direction. Mem. conseil d'adm. Musée des religions de Nicolet. Recipient Prix Olivar-Asselin, 1982. Mem. La tribune des journalists (former bd. dirs.), Syndicat des journalistes de La Presse (former pres.), Fédn. professionnelle des journalistes du Que. (former v.p.). Office: PO Box 6000, 1400 René-Lévesque Blvd E, Montreal, PQ Canada H3C 3A8

PEPITONE, BYRON VINCENT, former government official; b. New Brunswick, N.J., June 9, 1918; s. Joseph James and Sarah Frances (Byron) P.; m. Marolynn Mary Mills, June 9, 1940; children: Byron II, James S. Student, U.S. Army Command and Gen. Staff Coll., 1944, Air. U. Air Command and Staff Coll., 1950, NATO Def. Coll., 1955. Commd. 2d lt. USAAF, 1942; advanced through grades to col. USAF, 1953; ret., 1970; dep. dir. SSS, Washington, 1970-72; acting dir. SSS, 1972-73, dir., 1973-77; ret., 1977. Decorated D.S.M., Legion of Merit with 2 oak leaf clusters, USAF Commendation medal, U.S. Army Commendation medal with oak leaf cluster; recipient Distinguished Service medal SSS, 1972. Mem. USAF Assn. Home: 2265 SW Creekside Dr Palm City FL 34990-2528

PEPLAU, HILDEGARD ELIZABETH, nursing educator; b. Reading, Pa., Sept. 1, 1909; d. Gustav and Ottylie (Elgert) P. Diploma, Pottstown Hosp. Sch. Nursing, 1931; BA, Bennington Coll., 1943; MA, Columbia U., 1947, EdD, 1953, DSc (hon.), 1983; cert., William Alanson White Inst., 1953; DSc (hon.), Alfred U., 1970, Duke U., 1974, Rutgers U., 1985, Ind. U., 1994, U. Ulster, No. Ireland, 1994; D of Nursing Sci. (hon.), Boston Coll., 1972; LHD (hon.), U. Indpls., 1987, Ohio State U., 1990. RN, N.J., Calif. Exec. officer Coll. Health Svc., Bennington (Vt.) Coll., 1938-43; dir. grad. program psychiatric nursing Tchrs. Coll., Columbia U., N.Y.C., 1948-53; exec. dir. ANA, Washington, 1969-70; dir. grad. program psychiatric nursing Rutgers U., New Brunswick, N.J., 1955-74, prof. emerita, 1974—. Author: Interpersonal Relations in Nursing, 1952; contbr. numerous articles to profl. publs. and jours., 1942—. 1st lt. Nurse Corps, U.S. Army, 1943-45. Mem. ANA, Am. Acad. Nursing (designated Living Legend 1994), Internat. Coun. Nurses (3d v.p. 1977-81, bd. dirs. 1973-77), Nat. League Nursing. Democrat. Lutheran. Home: 14024 Otsego St Sherman Oaks CA 91423-1225

PEPONIS, HAROLD ARTHUR, insurance agent, broker; b. Chgo., Dec. 12, 1928; s. Arthur Harold and Ethel (Karambis) P.; m. Toula H. Preketes, Mar. 1, 1952 (dec. Dec. 1984); 1 child, Arthur Harold II; m. Aphrodite E. Stavros, May 26, 1990. BS, Loyola U., Chgo., 1950, postgrad., 1991—. Treas. Plaza Cleaners & Dyers, Inc., Chgo., 1950-58; owner Exch. Cleaners, Chgo., 1958-63, Park West Plaza Cleaners, Chgo., 1963-69; ins. agt. Aetna Life & Casualty, Lisle, Ill., 1969—; ptnr. lecture series/pub. co. Images of Orthodoxy; pres. Tesera Assoc., Evanston, Ill., 1973—. Mem. editl. bd. Christianity and Arts mag., 1996—. Pres. parish coun. United Greek Orthodox Chs. of Chgo., 1963-64, Annunciation Cathedral, 1991-92, 94; archon Order of St. Andrew, Greek Orthodox Ch., state comdr., 1994—; mem. diocesan coun. Diocese of Chgo. Greek Orthodox Ch., 1994, mem. archdiocesan coun., 1997-98. Mem. Pan Arcadian Fedn. Am. (nat. pres. Chgo. 1963-64), Du Page Life Underwriters Assn.. Home: 715 Sheridan Rd Wilmette IL 60091-1959 Office: 2956 Central St Evanston IL 60201-1246

PEPPAS, NIKOLAOS ATHANASSIOU, chemical engineering educator, consultant; b. Athens, Greece, Aug. 25, 1948; s. Athanassios Nikolaou Peppas and Alice Petrou Rousopoulou; m. Lisa Brannon, Aug. 10, 1988. Diploma in Engring., Nat. Tech. U., Athens, 1971; ScD, MIT, 1973. Rsch. assoc. MIT, Cambridge, Mass., 1975-76; asst. prof. chem. engring. Purdue U., West Lafayette, Ind., 1976-78, assoc. prof., 1978-81, prof., 1981—, Showalter Disting. prof., 1993—; vis. prof. U. Geneva, 1982-83, Calif. Inst. Tech., Pasadena, 1983, U. Paris, 1986, Hoshi U., Japan, 1994, Hebrew U., Jerusalem, 1994, U. Naples, 1995; adj. prof. U. Parma, Italy, 1987; cons. in field; mem. adv. bd. several cos. Author: Biomaterials, 1982, Hydrogels in Medicine and Pharmacy, 1987, One Hundred Years of Chemical Engineering, 1989, Pulsatile Drug Delivery, 1993, Biopolymers, 1993, Superabsorbent Polymers, 1994, Polymer/Inorganic Interfaces, 1995, Biomaterials for Drug and Cell Delivery, 1994; contbr. over 500 articles and over 300 abstracts to jours. Active Indpls. Symphony Orch., Indpls. Mus. Arts, Holy Trinity Orthodox Ch. Indpls. Recipient APV Silver medal U. Parma. Fellow AICE (chmn. materials divsn. 1988-90, dir. bioengring. divsn. 1994—, Materials Engring. Sci. award 1984, Bioengring award 1994, Best Paper award 1994), Am. Inst. Med. Biol. Engrs., Am. Assn. Pharm. Scientists, Soc. Biomaterials, Helian Soc. Medicine and Scis.; mem. Am. Chem. Soc., Am. Phys. Soc., N.Y. Acad. Sci., Controlled Release Soc. (pres. 1987-88, Founders award 1991), Soc. Biomaterials (Clemson award 1992), Am. Soc. Engring. Edn. (AT&T award 1982, Curtis McGraw award 1988, G. Westinghouse award 1992), Polymer Pioneer, numerous others. Avocations: linguistics (conversant in 8 langs.), opera, rare maps, classical record collecting, wine collecting. Office: Purdue U Sch Chem Engring West Lafayette IN 47907

PEPPER, ALLAN MICHAEL, lawyer; b. Bklyn., July 5, 1943; s. Julius and Jeanette (Lasovsky) P.; m. Barbara Benjamin, Aug. 30, 1964; children—Leslie Anne, Joshua Benjamin, Adam Richard, Robert Benjamin. B.A. summa cum laude, Brandeis U., 1964; LL.B. magna cum laude, Harvard U., 1967. Bar: N.Y. 1968, U.S. Dist. Ct. (so. and ea. dists.)

N.Y. 1968, U.S. Ct. Appeals (2d cir.) 1968, U.S. Supreme Ct. 1988. Law clk. U.S. Ct. Appeals for 2d Circuit, N.Y.C., 1967-68; assoc. Kaye, Scholer, Fierman, Hays & Handler, N.Y.C., 1968-74, ptnr., 1975—; lectr. in field. Mem. exec. com., assoc. nat. chmn. Brandeis U. Alumni Fund, 1979-82, nat. chmn., 1982-85, chmn. 25th Reunion gift com., 1989, devel. com., trustee, 1982-85, pres., councillor, 1980—; trustee Brandeis U., 1985-95, sec., 1992-93, budget and fin. com., 1988-95, chmn. com. strategic plan, 1990-91, acad. affairs com., 1985-92, student life and phys. facilities com., 1985-89, vice chmn. ad hoc by-laws com., 1988-89, long range planning com., 1989-91, chmn. audit com., 1991-95, exec. com., 1990-91; bd. dirs. Styles Brook Homeowners Assn., 1990—, exec. com., 1994—; nominating com. Edgemont Sch. Bd., 1992-93; trustee Edgemont Sch. Found., 1994—. Recipient Henry Jones-Golda Meier Bnai Brith Youth Services award, 1986, L.I. Press Valedictory medal, 1960; Felix Frankfurter scholar Harvard U. Law Sch., 1964-65; Louis D. Brandeis hon. scholar Brandeis U., 1964. Mem. ABA, Assn. of Bar of City of N.Y. (mem. law firm mgmt. com. 1987-91), N.Y. State Bar Assn. (comml. and fed. lit. sect., vice chmn. com. on discovery 1993—), Brandeis U. Alumni Assn. (exec. com. 1982-85, alumni giving strategic planning com., 1992, Alumni Svc. award 1988), Phi Beta Kappa (L.I. Alumni award 1960). Democrat. Jewish. Lodge: B'nai B'rith (pres. Henry Jones Lodge 1982-84, mem. Westchester-Putnam council 1982-85, bd. govs. dist. 1, 1985-86). Office: Kaye Scholer Fierman Hays & Handler LLP 425 Park Ave New York NY 10022-3506

PEPPER, BEVERLY, artist, sculptor; b. Bklyn., Dec. 20, 1924; d. Irwin Edward and Beatrice Evadne Stoll; m. Curtis G. Pepper, Oct. 11, 1949; children: Jorie Graham, John Randolph. Studied with, Fernand Leger, Andre L'Hote; student, Pratt Inst., 1939-41, D.F.A. (hon.), 1982; student, Art Students League, N.Y.C., 1944; D.F.A. (hon.), Md. Inst., 1983. Prof. meritus U. Perugia, Italy, 1987. One-woman shows include Marlborough Gallery, N.Y.C., 1969, Mus. Contemporary Art, Chgo., 1969, Galerie Hella Nebelung, Dusseldorf, Ger., 1971, Piazza Margana, Rome, 1971, Parker St. Gallery, Boston, 1971, Qui Arte Contemporanea, Rome, 1972, Marlborough Galleria d'Arte, Rome, 1972, Tyler Sch. of Art, Temple U. Abroad, Rome, 1973, Hammarskjold Plaza Sculpture Garden, N.Y.C., 1975, Met. Mus. Art, Miami, Fla., 1976, San Francisco Mus. Art, 1976, 86, Seattle Mus. Art, 1977, Princeton U., 1978, Indpls. Mus. Art, 1978, Todi Piazza and Sala delle Pietra, 1979, Gimple-Hanover Gallery, Zurich, 1980, Ronald Greenberg Gallery, St. Louis, 1980, Davenport Art Gallery, 1981, Hansen Fuller Goldeen Gallery, San Francisco, 1981, Laumeier Internat. Sculpture Park, St. Louis, 1982 Galleria Il Ponte, Rome, 1982, John Berggrun Gallery, San Francisco, 1983, 1985, Adams-Middleton Gallery, Dallas, 1985, Andre Emmerich Gallery, N.Y.C., 1975, 77, 79, 80, 82, 84, 86, 87, 89, 90, 91, 93, Columbus (Ohio) Mus. Art, 1986, Bklyn. Mus. Art, 1986, Charles Cowles Gallery, N.Y.C., 1987, 90, 94, Albright-Knox Art Gallery 20 yr. traveling survey exhbn., 1986, Visual Arts Ctr. MIT, Cambridge, Mass., 1989, James Corcoran Gallery, Santa Monica, Calif., 1989, 90, Contemporary Sculpture Ctr., Tokyo, 1991, Met. Mus. Art, N.Y.C., 1991, Narni all Rocca, Narna, Italy, 1991; group shows include XXIII Biennale di Venezia, Venice, Italy, 1972, Mus. Phila. Civic Center, 1974, Finch Coll. Mus. Art, N.Y.C., 1974, Marlborough Gallery, N.Y.C., 1974, Janie C. Lee Gallery, Houston, 1975, New Orleans Mus. Art, 1976, Documenta 6, Kassel, Ger., 1977, Quadriennale di Roma, Rome, 1977, Seattle Mus., 1979, Bklyn. Mus. Art, 1987, Bienale de Sculpture, Monte Carlo, 1991, Galleria Comunale d'Arte Moderna, Spoletto, Italy, 1992, Chelsea Harbour Sculpture '93, London, 1993, Queens Mus. Art, Corona Park, N.Y., 1994; represented in numerous permanent collections including Met. Mus. Art, N.Y.C., Fogg Mus., Cambridge, Mass., Albright-Knox Art Gallery, Buffalo, Jacksonville (Fla.) Mus. Modern Art, Galleria d'Arte Moderna, Florence, Italy, Walker Art Center, Mpls., Instituto Italiano di Cultura, Stockholm, Sweden, Power Inst. Fine Arts, Sydney, Australia, Galleria Civica d'Arte Moderna, Turin, Italy, Albertina Mus., Vienna, Hirshhorn Mus. and Sculpture Garden, Washington, Worcester (Mass.) Art Mus., Parkersburg (W.Va.) Art Mus., Smithsonian Inst., Washington, Dartmouth Coll., Hanover, N.H., Atlantic Richfield Co., L.A., Rutgers U., Wright, Runstad & Co., Seattle, Niagara Frontier Transp. Authority, Buffalo, Johns Hopkins Hosp., John Deere Foundry, East Moline, Ill.; commns. include Amphisculpture, AT&T, Bedminster, N.J., 1974-76, Dartmouth Coll., 1976-77, Sol i Onbra Park, 1986-91, City Barcelona, 1986—, Teatre Celle, Villa Celle, Postoia, Italy, 1989-91, Terana Altar II, Smithsonian Inst., Nat. Mus. Am. Art, Washington, 1990-91, Gotanno Community Park, Adachi-ku Machizukuri Corp., Neo-Hodos, Tokyo, 1992, Split Ritual, U.S. Nat. Arboretum, Washington, 1992, Palingenesis, Credit-Suisse, Zurich, 1992-94, The Garden at 26 Fed/Plz., Gen. Svcs. Adminstrn., N.Y.C., 1992—, Jerusalem Ritual, Jerusalem Found., Israel, 1994. Recipient award Nat. Endowment of Arts, 1976, 79, award GSA, 1975, Honor award Nat. Women's Caucus for Art, 1994. Home: Torre Gentile di Todi (PG) Italy 06059 Office: 84 Thomas St New York NY 10013-3371

PEPPER, DAVID M., physicist, educator, author, inventor; b. L.A., Mar. 9, 1949; s. Harold and Edith (Kleinplatz) P.; m. Denise Danyelle Koster, Mar. 19, 1992. BS in Physics summa cum laude, UCLA, 1971; MS in Applied Physics, Calif. Inst. Tech., 1974, PhD in Applied Physics, 1980. Mem. tech. staff Hughes Rsch. Labs., Malibu, Calif., 1973-87, sr. staff physicist, 1987-91, head nonlinear and electro-optic devices sect., 1989-91, sr. scientist, 1991-94; sr. rsch. scientist Hughes Rsch. Labs., Malibu, 1994—; adj. prof. math. and physics Pepperdine U., Malibu, 1981—; mem. adv. panel NSF, Washington, 1997. co-author: Optical Phase Conjugation, 1983, Laser Handbook, Vol. 4, 1985, Optical Phase Conjugation, 1995, Spatial Light Modulator Technology, 1995, CRC Handbook of Laser Science and Technology, 1995; tech. referee profl. jours.; contbr. articles to tech. jours. including Sci. Am.; holder 18 patents. Mem. Sons and Daughters of 1939 Club, 2d Generation of Martyrs Meml., Mus. Holocaust. Recipient Rudolf Kingslake award Soc. Photo-Optical Instrumentation Engrs., 1982, Publ. of Yr. award Hughes Rsch. Lab., 1986; NSF trainee Calif. Inst. Tech., 1971; Howard Hughes fellow Hughes Aircraft Co., 1973-80. Fellow Optical Soc. Am. (conf. adv. com. 1996; mem. adv. bd. topical conf. on nonlinear optics, Hawaii 1996); mem. AAAS, IEEE (guest editor, assoc. editor; mem. program com. lasers and electro-optics, Balt. 1997), SPIE (guest editor), N.Y. Acad. Scis., Am. Phys. Soc., Laser Inst. Am., Internat. Coun. Sci. Unions (com. on sci. and tech. in developing countries), Sigma Xi (v.p. 1986-87, chpt. pres. 1987-88, 90-91, 91-92), Sigma Pi Sigma. Jewish. Avocations: classical music, travel, sports, astronomy, nature. Office: Hughes Rsch Labs 3011 Malibu Canyon Rd Malibu CA 90265-4737 *Personal philosophy: We all have a profound, meaningful purpose and mission in life—the challenge is to identify, appreciate, realize and embrace our dreams and goals.*

PEPPER, DOROTHY MAE, nurse; b. Merill, Maine, Oct. 16, 1932; d. Walter Edwin and Alva Lois (Leavitt) Stanley; m. Thomas Edward Pepper, July 1, 1960; children: Walter Frank, James Thomas. RN, Maine Med. Ctr. Sch. Nursing, Portland, 1954. RN, Calif. Pvt. duty nurse Lafayette, Calif.; staff nurse Maine Med. Ctr., Portland, 1954-56, Oakland (Calif.) VA Hosp., 1956-58; pvt. duty nurse, dir. RN's Alameda County, Oakland. Mem. Profl. Nurses Bur. Registry, Maine Writers and Pubs. Alliance. Avocation: writing.

PEPPER, IAN L., environmental microbiologist, research scientist, educator; b. Tonypandy, Wales, U.K., Oct. 5, 1946. BSc in Chemistry, U. Birmingham, U.K., 1970; MS in Soil Biochemistry, Ohio State U., 1972, PhD in Soil Microbiology, 1975. Post-doctoral rsch. assoc. Wash. State U., 1975-76; asst. prof., asst. rsch. sci. dept. soil, water & environ. U. Ariz., 1971-81, assoc. prof., assoc. rsch. sci., 1971-88, prof., rsch. sci. dept. soil and water sci. and microbiology, 1988—, chair undergrad. program in environ. sci., 1993—. Contbr. articles to profl. jours. Recipient Ciba-Geigy award, 1983. Fellow Am. Acad. Microbiology, Am. Soc. Agronomy, Soil Sci. Soc. Am. Office: Univ of Arizona 429 Shantz Bldg Tucson AZ 85721

PEPPER, JEFFREY MACKENZIE, publishing executive; b. Dallas, June 11, 1957; s. Doris Jane (Mackenzie) P.; m. Martha Helen Stearns, July 27, 1985; children: Katherine McRaven, Anne Mackenzie. BA, Coll. Wooster, 1979. Sales rep. Acad. Press, N.Y.C., 1979-82; program editor Addison-Wesley Pub. Co., Reading, Mass., 1982-83, acquisitions editor, 1983-86; sr. editor Osborne McGraw-Hill, Berkeley, Calif., 1986-90, editor-in-chief, 1990-95; v.p., editl. dir. Acad. Press Profl., Chestnut Hill, Mass., 1995—. Contbr. articles to profl. jours. Avocations: storytelling, computers, gardening.

PEPPER, JOHN ENNIS, JR., consumer products company executive; b. Pottsville, Pa., Aug. 2, 1938; s. John Ennis Sr. and Irma Elizabeth (O'Connor) P.; m. Frances Graham Garber, Sept. 9, 1967; children: John, David, Douglas, Susan. BA, Yale U., 1960; PhD (hon.), Mt. St. Joseph Coll., St. Petersburg (Russia) U., Xavier U. From staff asst. to advt. mgr. Procter & Gamble Co., Cin., 1963-74, gen. mgr. Italian subs., 1974-77; v.p., gen. mgr. divsn. packaged soap and detergent Proctor & Gamble Co., Cin., 1977-80, group v.p. divsns. packaged soap and bar soap and household cleaning products, 1980-84, group v.p. European ops., 1981, exec. v.p., bd. dirs., 1984-86, pres. U.S. bus., 1986—, pres. internat. bus., 1990-95, chmn. bd., CEO, 1995—; bd. dirs. Xerox Corp., Motorola, Inc. Group chmn. Cin. United Appeal Campaign, 1980; trustee Xavier U., 1985-89, mem. exec. com., 1989; trustee Cin. Coun. World Affairs, Cin. Art Mus., Ctr. Strategic & Internat. Studies, Christ Ch. Endowment Fund, Yale Corp.; gen. chmn. United Way Campaign, 1994; co-chair Gov.'s Edn. Coun., State of Ohio; mem. adv. coun. Yale Sch. Mgmt.; mem. schs. com. Cin. Bus. Com.; co-chmn. Cin. Youth Collaborative; mem. Total Quality Leadership steering com. Served to lt. USN, 1960-63. Mem. Am. Soc. Corp. Execs., Grocery Mfrs. Am., Nat. Alliance Businessmen (chmn. communication com.), Soap and Detergent Assn. (bd. dirs.), The Bus. Coun., Bus. Roundtable, Yale Club, Queen City Club, Commonwealth Club, Comml. Club. Office: Procter & Gamble Co 1 Procter And Gamble Plz Cincinnati OH 45202-3315*

PEPPER, JONATHON L., newspaper columnist; b. Dearborn, Mich., Aug. 23, 1955; s. Joseph Daniel and Norma (McIntyre) P.; m. Diane Sharon Garelis, May 12, 1984; children: Jonathon Jay, Lauren Claire, Scott Joseph. BA, Mich. State U., 1977. Copywriter Detroit Free Press, 1977-84, reporter, 1984-87; nat. corr. Detroit News, 1987-91, bus. columnist, 1991—; host talk show Sta. WXYT, 1995-96; assoc. bus. editor Detroit News, 1997—. Mem. Writers Guild Am. Office: The Detroit News 615 W Lafayette Blvd Detroit MI 48226-3124

PEPPERDENE, MARGARET WILLIAMS, English educator; b. Vicksburg, Miss., Dec. 25, 1919; d. O.L. and Jane (Stocks) Williams. B.S., La. State U., 1941; M.A., Vanderbilt U., 1948, Ph.D., 1953. Div. Instr. English U. Oreg., 1946-47; teaching fellow Vanderbilt U., 1948-50; instr., then asst. prof. Miami U., Oxford, Ohio, 1952-56; mem. faculty Agnes Scott Coll., 1956—, prof. English, chmn. dept., 1967—. Author articles.; Editor: That Subtile Wreath: Lectures Presented at the Quartercentenary Celebratiom of the Birth of John Donne, 1973. Served to lt. USNR, 1943-46. Fulbright fellow, 1950-51; Ford Found. grad. fellow, 1951-52; AAUW fellow, 1954-55; research fellow Dublin Inst. Advanced Studies, 1954-55; Guggenheim fellow, 1956-57; recipient Gov.'s Award in Humanities, Ga., 1987. Home: 418 Glendale Ave Decatur GA 30030-1922

PEPPERS, JERRY P., lawyer; b. Cleve., Mar. 8, 1946; s. Jerry P. and Katherine M. Peppers; m. Sue E. Schafer, June 14, 1969; children: Amy E., Erica K., Christina A., Michele S. BBA, Ohio U., 1968; JD, Duke U., 1971. Bar: N.Y. 1972. Assoc. Winthrop, Stimson, Putnam & Roberts, N.Y.C., 1971-81, ptnr., 1982—; mgmt. com., 1995—; bd. dirs. Firth Rixson, Inc., Rochester, N.Y., Monroe Forgings, Inc., Rochester, Progenitor, Inc., Columbus, Ohio, Viking Metall. Corp., Reno; N. Am. pension oversight com. The Morgan Crucible Co., Windsor, U.K. Editor: (booklet) Outline of Mergers and Acquisitions in the United States, 14th edit., 1995. Trustee Ohio Univ. Found., Athens, 1991—, Fox Meadow Athletic Assn., Scarsdale, Scarsdale Youth Soccer Club, Inc.; dir., treas. Scarsdale Maroon and White Club. Mem. ABA, Internat. Bar Assn., India House, Fox Meadow Tennis Club (Scarsdale, N.Y.). Avocation: coaching soccer (lic. FIFA). Office: Winthrop Stimson Putnam & Roberts 1 Battery Park Plz New York NY 10004-1405

PEPPET, RUSSELL FREDERICK, accountant; b. Chgo., Oct. 3, 1939; s. George Russell and Elizabeth (Foster) P.; m. Rosemary Meyer, June 18, 1960; children—Cynthia, Jeffrey, Scott. B.S. in Math, Mich. State U., 1960; M.B.A., Northwestern U., 1963. C.P.A., Ill., Minn. Cons. Peat, Marwick, Mitchell & Co., Chgo., 1961-68; head mgmt. cons. dept. Peat, Marwick, Mitchell & Co., Mpls., 1968-72; partner Peat, Marwick, Mitchell & Co., 1969-88; sr. cons. partner for Continental Europe, Paris, 1972-78, partner-in-charge mgmt. cons. dept., N.Y. office, 1978-81, vice chmn. mgmt. cons., 1981-86; mng. ptnr. San Jose Bus. Unit, 1986-88; v.p. internat. devel. Towers Perrin, N.Y.C., 1989-90; vice-chmn. Quirk Carson Peppet Inc., N.Y.C., 1990—; bd. dirs. AFS-USA, chmn., 1992-96; bd. dirs. Park Ave. Bank, Zahren Alternative Power Corp. With U.S. Army, 1962-64. Mem. AICPA, Country Club of Darien (Conn.), Sky Club (N.Y.C.). Club: Sky (N.Y.C.). Office: Quirk Carson Peppet Inc 126 E 56th St New York NY 10022

PEPPLER, WILLIAM NORMAN, aviation association executive; b. Hanover, Ont., Can., June 29, 1925. Student public shcs., Hanover. Charter pilot Leavens Bros., Toronto, Ont., 1945-48; chief flying instr. Sky Harbour Air Service, Goderich, Ont., 1949-51; survey pilot Spartan Air Services, Ottawa, Ont., 1951-57; mgr. Can. Owners and Pilots Assn., Ottawa, 1957-96; editor Can. Flight Mag., 1957-94; Can. Gen. Aviation News, 1957-94; Can. rep. Aircraft Owners and Pilots Assn., 1996—.

PEPPLES, ERNEST, tobacco company executive; b. Louisville, Feb. 13, 1935; s. Ernest Clifton and Goldie Mae (Byington) P.; m. Martha Scott Norman; children: J. Craig, Eleanor Evans, Cindy. AB, Yale U., 1957; LLB, U. Va., 1963. Bar: Ky., 1963. Ptnr. Wyatt, Grafton & Sloss (name changed to Wyatt, Tarrant & Combs), Louisville, 1963-75; sr. v.p. Brown & Williamson Tobacco Corp., Louisville, 1975-80, 1980—, also bd. dirs.; chmn. bd. dirs. Tobacco Merchants Assn. U.S.A., Inc., Princeton, N.J.; bd. dirs. Tobacco Inst., Washington, Coun. for Tobacco Rsch., Inc., N.Y., Ky. Tobacco Rsch. Bd., Lexington. Pres. Louisville and Jefferson County Health and Welfare Council, 1972-73, Neighborhood Housing Services Inc., Louisville, 1986-87. Served to 1st lt. U.S. Army, 1957-60. Mem. ABA, Ky. Bar Assn., Tobacco Mchts. Assn. (bd. dirs. 1975—, chmn. 1990—). Democrat. Mem. Christian Ch. Clubs: Louisville Country, Pendennis, Wynn-Stay. Home: 2432 Ransdell Ave Louisville KY 40204-2113 Office: Brown & Williamson Tobacco Corp 200 Brown Williamson Tower Louisville KY 40202-3404

PEPYNE, EDWARD WALTER, lawyer, psychologist, former educator; b. Springfield, Mass., Dec. 27, 1925; s. Walter Henry and Frances A. (Carroll) P.; m. Carol Jean Dutcher, Aug. 2, 1958; children—Deborah, Edward, Jr., Susan, Byron, Shari, Randy, David, Allison, Jennifer. B.A., Am. Internat. Coll., 1948; M.S., U. Mass., 1951, Ed.D., 1968; postgrad., NYU, 1952-55; prof. diploma, U. Conn., 1964; J.D., Western New Eng. Coll., 1978. Bar: Mass. 1978, U.S. Supreme Ct. 1981. Prin., tchr. Gilbertville Grammar Sch., Hardwick, Mass., 1948-49; sch. counselor West Springfield High Sch., Mass., 1949-53; instr. NYU, 1953-54; supt. schs. New Shoreham, R.I., 1954-56; asst. prof. edn. Mich. State U., 1956-58; sch. psychologist, guidance dir. Pub. Sch. System, East Long, Mass., 1958-62; lectr. Westfield State Coll., 1961-65; dir. pupil services Chicopee Pub. Sch., 1965-68; assoc. prof. counselor edn. U. Hartford, West Hartford, Mass., 1968-71, prof., 1971-85, dir. Inst. Coll. Counselors Minority and Low Income Students, 1971-72, dir. Div. Human Services, 1972-77; cons. Aetna Life & Casualty Co., Hartford, 1962-75; hearing officer Conn. State Bd. Edn., 1980—; exec. dir. Sinapi Assocs., 1959-78; pvt. practice, Ashfield, Mass., 1978—. Co-author: Better Driving, 1958; assoc. editor: Highway Safety and Driver Education, 1954; chmn. editorial com.: Man and the Motor Car, 5th edit., 1954; contbr. numerous articles to profl. jours. Chief Welfare Svcs. Civil Def., Levittown, N.Y., 1953-54; chmn. Ashfield Planning Bd., Mass., 1979-83; moderator Town of Ashfield, 1980-81, town counsel, Charlemont, Mass., 1983-84; mem. jud. nominating coun. Western Regional Com., 1993—. Mem. ABA, APA, Mass. Bar Assn., Mass. Acad. Trial Attys., Am. Pers. and Guidance Assn., New Eng. Pers. and Guidance Assn. (bd. dirs.), New Eng. Ednl. Rsch. Orgn. (pres. 1971), Am. Assn. Sch. Adminstrs., Am. Ednl. Rsch. Assn., Mt. Tom Amateur Radio Assn., Franklin County Amateur Radio Club, Elks, Kiwanis (pres. 1988-89, lt. gov. div. 12, 1991-92), Masons (master 1994—), Shriners, Phi Delta Kappa. Home: PO Box 31 134 Ashfield Mountain Rd Ashfield MA 01330-9622 Office: PO Box 345 134 Ashfield Mountain Rd Ashfield MA 01330-9622

PERADOTTO, JOHN JOSEPH, classics educator, editor; b. Ottawa, Ill., May 11, 1933; s. John Joseph and Mary Louise (Giacometti) P.; m. Noreen Doran, Aug. 29, 1959 (div. 1982); m. Marlene Rosen, Aug. 29, 1992; children: Erin, Monica, Noreen, Nicole. B.A., St. Louis U., 1957, M.A., 1958; Ph.D., Northwestern U., 1963. Instr. classics and English Western Wash. U., Bellingham, 1960-61; instr. Georgetown U., 1961-63, asst. prof. classics, 1963-66; asst. prof. classics SUNY, Buffalo, 1966-69, asso. prof., 1969-73; prof., chmn. classics U. Tex., Austin, 1973-74; prof. classics SUNY-Buffalo, 1974—, Andrew V.V. Raymond prof. classics, 1984—, Disting. teaching prof., 1990—, chmn. dept., 1974-77, dean div. undergrad. edn., 1978-82; Martin lectr. Oberlin Coll., 1987; dir. summer seminar for coll. tchrs. NEH, 1976, for secondary sch. tchrs., 1984. Author: Classical Mythology: An Annotated Bibliographical Survey, 1973, Man in the Middle Voice: Name and Narration in the Odyssey, 1990; also articles and revs.; founding assoc. editor: Arethusa, editor-in-chief, 1974-95; mem. bd. editors SUNY Press, 1978-81; editor: SUNY Press Classical Series, 1981—, Classical Literature and Contemporary Literary Analysis, 1977, Women in the Ancient World, 1978, 83; co-editor: Population Policy in Plato and Aristotle, 1975, The New Archilochus, 1976, Augustan Poetry Books, 1980, Indo-European Roots of Classical Culture, 1980, Vergil: 2000 Years, 1981, Texts and Contexts: American Classical Studies in Honor of J.P. Vernant, 1982, Semiotics and Classical Studies, 1983, Audience-oriented Criticism and the Classics, 1986, Herodotus and the Invention of History, 1987, The Challenge of Black Athena, 1989, Pastoral Revisions, 1990, Reconsidering Ovid's Fasti, 1992, Bakhtin and Classical Studies, 1993, Rethinking the Classical Canon, 1994, Horace: 2000 Years, 1995, The New Simonides, 1996, The Iliad and its Contexts, 1997. Fellow Center for Hellenic Studies, 1972-73; recipient Chancellor's award for teaching excellence State U. N.Y., 1975, Disting. Retiring Editor award Coun. of Editors of Learned Jours., 1995. Mem. Am. Philol. Assn. (dir. 1974-77, pres. 1990), Classical Assn. Atlantic States (exec. com. 1976-78). Office: Dept Classics State U NY Buffalo NY 14260

PERAHIA, MURRAY, pianist; b. N.Y.C., Apr. 19, 1947; m. Naomi Shohet, 1980; 2 children. MS, Mannes Coll. Music; student, Jeannette Haien, Artur Balsam, Mieczyslaw Horszowski. Appeared with Berlin Philharm., Chgo. Symphony Orch., English Chamber Orch., Boston Symphony Orch., N.Y. Philharm., Cleve. Orch., Los Angeles Philharm., Phila. Orch., others; performed with Budapest, Guarneri and Galimir string quartets; frequent performer, artistic dir.: Aldeburgh Festival, 1983-89; past participant: Marlboro Music Festival; recital tours in U.S., Can., Europe and Japan; recs. for SONY Classical; 1st Am. to record the Complete Mozart Concertos as condr. with English Chamber Orch., recorded complete Beethoven concertos with Haitink concertgebouw Orch. Recipient Kosciusko Chopin prize, 1965, Avery Fisher prize, 1975, numerous maj. rec. awards including Leeds Competition, 1972. Office: care Edna Landau IMG 22 E 71st St New York NY 10021-4911

PERALTA, ANTONIO MARTINEZ, family physician; b. Legaspi, Luzon, The Philippines, Nov. 20, 1937; came to U.S., 1972; s. Federico Aseneta and Maria Luisa (Martinez) P.; m. Celia Elepano, June 20, 1970; children: Antonio Jr., Alan, Anne Marie, Michael-Andrew. BS, U. of East, Manila, 1960; MD, Far Eastern U., Manila, 1966. Intern Englewood (N.J.) Hosp. Assn., 1977-78; resident in family practice Yonkers (N.Y.) Gen. Hosp., 1978-80; emergency room physician Mattie Wills Hosp., Richland, Va., 1979-82; pvt. practice family medicine Whitewood, Va., 1982-83, Bradshaw, W.Va., 1983-90; assoc. physician Merit Med. Group Managed Care, Richlands, 1990-96; physician Columbia-Clinch Valley Med. Ctr., Richlands, 1996—. Vol. physician Tri-County Med. Clinic, Richlands, 1991—. Capt. M.C. Philippine Army. Fellow Am. Acad. Family Physicians; mem. So. Med. Assn., Tazewell County Med. Soc. (treas. 1995), S.W. Va. Assn. of Philippine Physicians (pres. 1992-94). Republican. Roman Catholic. Avocation: golf. Home: 737 Sandy Ln Richlands VA 24641 Office: Columbia-Clinch Valley Medical Center Ste 1100 Richlands VA 24641

PERALTA, JOSEPH SORIANO, financial planner; b. Davao City, Philippines, Mar. 11, 1962; came to the U.S., 1984; s. Edward Embry and Rosamar Marfori (Soriano) P.; m. Leslie Sison-Aquino. BS in Commerce with honors, De LaSalle U., 1983, BA in Econs., 1983; grad. profl. edn. program, Coll. for Fin. Planning, 1992. CFP; registered prin. series 24, registered rep. series 7. Gen. mgr. RSP Enterprises, Davao City, 1983-84; market rsch. supr. Sheer Communications, Albertson, N.Y., 1985-86; dir. fin. Apex Health Svcs./Kidney Ctr. of Vernon, Tex., 1987-89; CFP FFP Securities, Inc., Orange, Calif., 1990—. Co-author: Econometric Investigation of the Debt Service Capacity of the Philippines, 1982, Role of Government in the Development of Private Investment Houses, 1983. Mem. CFP Bd. of Standards, Orange County Soc. Inst. CPF, Inst. CFPs (registry of CFP lic. practitioners), Internat. Assn. for Fin. Planning (mem. practitioner divsn.), L.A. Athletic Club. Democrat. Roman Catholic. Avocations: reading, travel, performing arts, basketball, swimming. Home: 1300 Doremus Rd Pasadena CA 91105-2741 Office: FFP Securities Inc 333 S Anita Dr Ste 625 Orange CA 92868-3320

PERCAS DE PONSETI, HELENA, foreign language and literature educator; b. Valencia, Spain, Jan. 17, 1921; came to U.S., 1940, naturalized, 1950; m. Ignacio V. Ponseti, 1961. Baccalaureat, Paris, France, 1939; B.A., Barnard Coll., 1942; M.A., Columbia, 1943, Ph.D., 1951. Tchr. lang. and lit. Barnard Coll., 1942-43, Russell Sage Coll., 1943-45, Columbia U., 1945-47, Queens Coll., 1946-48; mem. faculty Grinnell Coll., 1948—, prof. lang. and lit., 1957—, Roberts Honor prof. modern fgn. langs., 1961-62, Richards prof. modern fgn. langs., 1963-82, prof. emerita, 1982—. Author: La Poesia Femenina Argentina, 1810-1950, 1958, Cervantes y su concepto del arte, 1975, Cervantes the Writer and Painter of Don Quijote, 1988. Mem. Cervantes Soc. Am. (founding mem., mem. exec. com. 1979—, assoc. editor jour. Cervantes 1981), Asociacion de Cervantistas Alcala de Henares Spain, 1987 (charter). Home: 110 Oakridge Ave Iowa City IA 52246-2935

PERCIASEPE, ROBERT, federal agency administrator. BS in Environ. Scis., Cornell U.; MS in Planning, Syracuse U. Various positions county and regional planning agys. and SUNY; asst. dir. planning City of Balt.; asst. sec. for planning and capital programs Md. Dept. Environ., Annapolis, dep. sec., sec. of environ., 1991-93; asst. adminstr. for water EPA, Washington, 1993—; lectr. Johns Hopkins U., Morgan Stte U., U. Md.; former chmn. Md. Asbestos Oversight Com., Chesapeake Bay Agreement States' Nutrient Reduction Work Group; former vice chmn. Appalachian Low-Level Radioactive Waste Commn.; former 1st chmn. N.E. Ozone Transport Commn.; former mem. bd. dirs. Chesapeake Bay Trust; former mem. Md. Gov.'s Internat. Cabinet and Md. Gov.'s Commn. on Lead Paint Poisoning. Contbr. articles to profl. jours. Mem. profl. orgns. Avocations: biking, hiking, softball. Office: Water 401 M St SW Washington DC 20460-0001

PERCOCO, THELMA ANN, nurse, educator; b. Newton, Kans., Sept. 11, 1935; d. Menno J. and Lydia A. (Miller) Hirschler; m. Richard A. Percoco, June 5, 1960. Diploma in nursing, Bethel Deaconess Hosp., Newton, 1957; BS in Nursing, Fla. State U., 1960; MS in Nursing, Tex. Women's U., 1977. RN, Tex. Staff nurse, team leader VA Hosp., Albuquerque, 1957-58, 60; staff nurse State Tuberculosis Hosp., Tallahassee, 1960, West Haven (Conn.) VA Hosp., 1960, 61; staff nurse, team leader, than head nurse and surg. supr. Houston VA Hosp., 1961-79; instr. Lee Coll., Baytown, Tex., 1979—, Lead Inst., 1987-93; acting divsn. chair allied health Lee Coll., Baytown, Tex., 1993-94; com. mem. Am. Cancer Soc. Contbr. articles to various publs. Chair Pine Bluff Civic Assn., La Porte, Tex., 1984—. Named Tchr. of Yr., Lee Coll., 1987. Mem. ANA, Nat. League for Nursing, Tex. League for Nursing (pub. rels. com. 1990), Tex. Nurses Assn. (chair legis. com. 1987-91), Sigma Theta Tau (acting chair allied health divsn. 1992-93).d. Avocation: sailboat racing. Home: 1 Pine Bluff St La Porte TX 77571-6677 Office: Lee Coll 511 S Whiting St Baytown TX 77520-4703

PERCUS, JEROME KENNETH, physicist, educator; b. N.Y.C., June 21, 1926; s. Philip M. and Gertrude B. (Schweiger) P.; m. Ora Engelberg, May 20, 1965; children: Orin, Allon. B.S.E.E., Columbia U., 1947, M.A., 1948, Ph.D., 1954. Instr. elec. engring. Columbia U., N.Y.C., 1952-54; asst. prof. Stevens Inst. Tech., Hoboken, N.J., 1955-58; assoc. prof. NYU, N.Y.C., 1958-65; prof. physics NYU, 1965—; dir. Nat. Biomed. Research Found. Author: Many-Body Problem, 1963, Kinetic Theory and Statistical Mechanics, 1969, Combinatorial Methods, 1971, Combinatorial Methods in Developmental Biology, 1977, Mathematical Methods in Developmental Biology, 1978, Mathematical Methods in Enzymology, 1984, Lectures on the Mathematics of Immunology, 1986; editor: Pattern Recognition, Jour. Statis. Physics, Jour. Comp. Molecular Biology. With USN, 1944-46. Recipient

Pregel Chemistry Physics award N.Y. Acad. Scis., 1975, Joel Henry Hildebrand award in the Theoretical and Exptl. Chemistry of Liquids, Am. Chem. Soc., 1993, Pattern Rec. Soc. award, 1992. Fellow AAAS, Am. Phys. Soc.; mem. Am. Math. Soc., Sigma Xi. Office: NYU 251 Mercer St New York NY 10012-1110

PERCY, LEE EDWARD, motion picture film editor; b. Kalamazoo, Feb. 10, 1953; s. Richard Noyes and Helen Louise (Sheffield) P. Student, Goodman Sch., Chgo., 1971, Juilliard Sch., 1972; AB, U. Calif., Santa Cruz, 1977. Radio news reporter McGovern Campaign, Chgo., 1972; cons. Kjos Pub. Co., Chgo., 1973-74; dir. VisArt, Ltd., San Francisco, 1977; ind. film editor L.A., 1978—. Editor: motion pictures: Re-Animator, 1984, Kiss of the Spiderwoman, 1985, Slam Dance, 1987, Checking Out, 1988, Blue Steel, 1989, Reversal of Fortune, 1990, Year of the Gun, 1991, Single White Female, 1992, Against the Wall, 1993 (Eddie award 1995, nominated for Cable ACE award), Corrina, Corrina, 1994, Kiss of Death, 1995, Before and After, 1996, Desperate Measures, 1997. Mem. Am. Cinema Editors, Editors Guild Hollywood, Motion Picture Editors N.Y.

PERDEW, JOHN PAUL, physics educator, condensed matter and density functional theorist; b. Cumberland, Md., Aug. 30, 1943. BS, Gettysburg Coll., 1965; PhD, Cornell U., 1971. Postdoctoral fellow U. Toronto (Ont., Can.), 1971-74, Rutgers U., New Brunswick, N.J., 1974-77; prof. physics Tulane U., New Orleans, 1977—, chair physics dept., 1991-94; vis. scientist Nordita, Copenhagen, Argonne Nat. Lab., ETH Zurich, ITP Santa Barbara, Naval Rsch. Lab., Washington; invited lectr. more than 35 internat. confs. Contbr. more than 125 sci. articles to profl. jours. NSF Rsch. grantee, 1978—; recipient Tulane LAS award for excellence in rsch., 1990. Fellow Am. Phys. Soc.; mem. Am. Chem. Soc., Am. Assn. Physics Tchrs., Phi Beta Kappa. Office: Tulane U Dept Physics New Orleans LA 70118

PERDIGAO, GEORGE MICHAEL, advertising executive; b. Sacramento, Jan. 23, 1965; s. George Vierra and Carolyn Sue (Creager) P. B in Journalism, U. So. Calif., 1987. Dir. advt. Mike Glickman Realty, Inc., Brentwood, Calif., 1987-90; sr. acct. exec. Bozell, Inc., West L.A., 1990-92; v.p. Dailey & Assocs., L.A., 1992—. Recipient Trojan 4th Estate award U. So. Calif., 1987. Home: 7320 Balboa Blvd Apt 123 Van Nuys CA 91406-2761 Office: Dailey & Assocs 3055 Wilshire Blvd Los Angeles CA 90010-1108

PERDREAU, CORNELIA RUTH WHITENER (CONNIE PERDREAU), English as a second language educator, international exchange specialist; b. Beacon, N.Y.; d. Henry Kato Whitener and Mazie Althea (Martin) Whitener-Johnson; m. Michel Serge Yves Perdreau, June 14, 1969; 1 child, Maurice Laurence Henri. BA, SUNY, Potsdam, 1969; MA, Ohio U., 1971, 72. French/Latin tchr. Walt Whitman Jr. High Sch., Yonkers, N.Y., 1969-70; French teaching asst. Ohio U., Athens, 1970-71, ESL tchr., 1976—; English/French tchr. Lycee de Chambery, France, 1972; English tchr. Acad. de Paris, France, 1984; study abroad coord. Ohio U., Athens. Contbr. articles to profl. jours. Chair Tri-County Community Action Agy., Sugarcreek, Ohio, 1982; mem. bd. Dairy Barn Arts Ctr., Athens, 1985-91; trustee Ohioana Bd. Trustees, Columbus, 1987-96. Mem. NAFSA Assn. Internat. Educators (pres.-elect 1995-96, pres. 1996-97), TESOL (chair rules and resolutions com. 1993-95), Internat. Assn. Black Profls. in Internat. Affairs (founder), Adminstrs. and Tchrs. in ESL (chair 1992-93), Internat. Black Profls. in TESOL (founder, chair 1992-95), Ohio TESOL (pres. 1986-87), Assn. Internat. Educators (pres.-elect 1995). Office: Ohio U Study Abroad Office 243 Scott Quadrangle Athens OH 45701

PERDUE, BEVERLY MOORE, state legislator, geriatric consultant; b. Grundy, Va., Jan. 14; d. Alfred P. and Irene E. (Morefield) (dec.) Moore; children: Garrett, Emmett. BA, U. Ky., 1969; MEd, U. Fla., 1974, PhD, 1976. Pvt. lectr., writer, cons., 1980-86; pres. The Perdue Co., New Bern, N.C., 1985—; rep. N.C. State Gen. Assembly, Raleigh, 1986-90; senator N.C. Gen. Assembly, Raleigh, 1990—; bd. dirs. Nations Bank, New Bern. Bd. dirs. N.C. United Way, Greensboro, 1990-92; exec. mem. N.C. Dem. Party, Raleigh, 1989—; mem. N.C. travel bd. Nat. Conf. State Legislators. Named Outstanding Legislator, N.C. Aging Network, 1989, 92, Toll fellow Nat. Conf. State Legislators, Lexington, Ky., 1992. Mem. Nat. Coun. on Aging, Bus. and Profl. Women, Rotary. Episcopalian. Home: 211 Wilson Point Rd New Bern NC 28562-7519 Office: Perdue & Co PO Box 991 507 Pollack St New Bern NC 28563 also: NC Senate Raleigh NC 27601

PERDUE, CHARLES L., JR., anthropology and English educator; b. Panthersville, Ga., Dec. 1, 1930; s. Charles L. Sr. and Eva Mae (Samples) P.; m. Nancy J. Martin; children: Martin Clay, Marc Charles, Kelly Scott, Kevin Barry (dec.). Student, North Ga. Coll., 1948-49, Santa Rosa (Calif.) Jr. Coll., 1953; AB in Geology, U. Calif., Berkeley, 1958, postgrad., 1958-59; MA in Folklore, U. Pa., 1968, PhD in Folklore, 1971. Engring. writer Convair Astronautics, Vandenberg AFB, Calif., 1959-60; geologist, mineral classification branch U.S. Geological Survey, Washington, 1960-67; asst. prof. English dept. U. Va., Charlottesville, 1971-72, asst. prof. English and sociology, anthropology depts., 1972-73, asst. prof. English and anthropology depts., 1973-76, assoc. prof., 1976-92, prof., 1992—; cons. in field. Author: Outwitting the Devil: Jack Tales from Wise County, Virginia, 1987, Pig's Foot Jelly and Persimmon Beer: Foodways from the Virginia Writers' Project, 1992, (with others) Weevils in the Wheat: Interviews with Virginia Ex-Slaves, 1976, (with Nancy J. Martin-Perdue) Talk about Trouble: A New Deal Portrait of Virginians in the Great Depression, 1996; contbr. articles to profl.jours. With U.S. Army, 1951-54. Univ. Predoctoral fellow U. Pa., 1967-71; Wilson Gee Inst. Rsch. grant U. Va., 1974, 75; Rsch. grant NEH, 1980-81, 84; Sesquicentennial Assoc. award Ctr. for Advanced Studies U. Va. 1978-79, 87-88. Mem. Am. Folklore Soc. (exec. bd. 1980-83, book rev. editor jour. 1986-87), Mid. Atlantic Folklore Assn. (founding mem., bd. dirs.), Nat. Coun. for Traditional Arts (bd. dirs. 1971-87, pres. 1973-79), Va. Folklore Soc. (archivist/editor 1974-89, archivist 1990-94, archivist/pres. 1995-96, archivist 1997—). Office: U Va Dept Anthropology 303 Brooks Hall Charlottesville VA 22903

PERDUE, FRANKLIN P., poultry products company executive; m. Mitzi Henderson Ayala, July 1988. Chmn. exec. com. Perdue Farms Inc., Salisbury, Md., Perdue Inc. subs. Perdue Farms Inc., Salisbury; chrm., dir. Perdue Farms, Inc. Office: Perdue Farms Inc PO Box 1537 Salisbury MD 21802-1537*

PERDUE, JAMES, food products executive; b. 1949. BS, Wake Forest U., 1973; MA in Marine Biology, Southeastern Mass. U., 1976; PhD in Fisheries, U. Wash., 1983. With U. Md., Cambridge, 1976-78; chmn. bd. Perdue Transp., Inc., Salisbury, Md., 1983—; chmn. bd. Perdue Farms Inc., 1983—, now CEO. Office: Perdue Farms Inc PO Box 1537 Salisbury MD 21802*

PERDUE, JAMES EVERETT, university vice chancellor emeritus; b. Auburn, Nebr., June 24, 1916; s. James O. and Hazel D. Perdue; m. Raedeen Tibbetts, Apr. 9, 1939; children: Pamela Jane, Darcy Clare; m. 2d, June Harrison Ward, Aug. 14, 1988. Student, Nebr. Wesleyan U., 1933-34; A.B., Nebr. State Tchrs. Coll., 1937; A.M., No. Colo. State U., Greely, 1940; Ph.D., Stanford U., 1952; LL.D., U. Denver, 1965. Coach, tchr. social studies DeWitt High Sch., Nebr., 1937-38; head social sci. dept. Ft. Morgan High Sch., Colo., 1938-41; ednl. rep. Row, Peterson and Co., 1941-43; acting dean Coll. Arts and Scis., U. Denver, 1946-48, assoc. dean, 1948-51; univ. budget officer U. Denver, 1951-52, asst. to chancellor, 1952-53; prof. social sci., dean Coll. Arts and Scis., U. Denver, 1953-65; pres., prof. social sci. SUNY-Oswego, 1965-77; assoc. chancellor SUNY System, 1977-78, vice chancellor for acad. programs, policy and planning, 1978-81; acting v.p. acad. affairs SUNY-Oswego, 1981; founding dean Coll. Arts and Sci. Ark. State U., 1981-82; provost, chief operating officer U. Ark., 1983; cons. to colls. and univs., 1981—; cons. N.J. State System Higher Edn., 1988; interim v.p. Met. State Coll., Denver; trustee Oswego City Savs. Bank; dir. Oswego br. Marine Midland Trust Co. Author: (autobiography) The First 75 Years, 1991. Mem. adv. com. on higher edn. Legis. Council State of Colo.; mem. Colo. Mental Health Planning Com., Colo. Council on Instrn., Hosp. Rev. and Planning Council Central N.Y.; mem. Colo. Com. to Secure the Super Conducting Super Collider, 1988; bd. dirs. Acad. Collective Bargaining Service, 1973—, chmn., 1974—; chmn. Oswego County Heart Fund, 1973; vestry mem. St. Charles Episcopal Ch., 1988; bd. dirs. Heritage Found., 1990—; trustee Morgan C.C. Found., 1990-95, pres. 1992-95. Served as ops. and communications officer USNR, 1943-46. Recipient Disting. Ednl. Service award Peru State, 1966; Outstanding Male Educator award U. N.C., 1975; Meritorious Service award Am. Assn. State Colls. and Univs., 1972; Adminstrv. Leave award Danforth Found., 1972. Mem. Am. Conf. Acad. Deans (vice chmn. 1963-64, exec. bd. 1959-64, nat. chmn. 1965-66), Am. Assn. State Colls. and Univs. (dir. 1967-72, pres.-elect 1976), Ft. Morgan Country Club (trustee 1990-93), Phi Beta Kappa, Pi Gamma Mu, Phi Delta Kappa. Home: 504 E 6th Ave Fort Morgan CO 80701-3217

PERDUNN, RICHARD FRANCIS, management consultant; b. Trenton, N.J., Dec. 12, 1915; s. Francis R. and Edith (Nogle) P.; m. Eugenia E. Morel, June 7, 1941; 1 child, Justine Reneau; m. Doris D. Andrus, Jan. 30, 1993. B.S., Lehigh U., 1939; postgrad. student, U. Pitts., 1939-40, Johns Hopkins, 1941-42. With U.S. Steel Co., also Glenn L. Martin, 1939-43, supt. machine and assembly, 1941-43; partner Nelson & Perdunn (engrs. and cons., also); v.p. Penco Corp., 1947-49; with Merck & Co., 1949-54, mgr. adminstrn., 1951-54; with Stevenson, Jordan & Harrison (mgmt. engrs.), N.Y.C., 1954-68; exec. v.p. Stevenson, Jordan & Harrison (mgmt. engrs.), 1962-64, pres., 1964-68; pres., chief exec. officer Bachman-Jacks, Inc., Reading, Pa., 1968-71; sr. v.p. Golightly Internat., N.Y.C., 1971—; also dir. Golightly Internat.; chmn. Perdunn Assocs., Inc., 1979—, dir. West Point & Annapolis Text Book Pub. Co., 1948—, Indsl. Edn. Films Inc., 1966—, Eldun Corp., 1964—, Security Nat. Bank, Newark, 1964—, Surburban Life Ins. Co., 1966—, Mainstem Inc., 1965—, Greenhouse Decor Inc., 1961—, Neuwirth Mut. Fund Inc., 1975—; Lectr. on finance and mfg. in, U.S., Can., Eng., Sweden. Assoc. editor: Systems and Procedures Quar, 1948-51; Contbr. articles to profl. publs. Bd. dirs. Inst. Better Confs., Internat. Inst. Bus. Devel., Inst. Urban Affairs, People Care, Inc.; dir. finance Assn. Help for Retarded Children. Served with USAAF, 1942-47. Mem. N.Y.C. C. of C., Council Econ. Devel., Am. Mgmt. Assn., AIM (pres.'s council), Newcomen Soc. N.Am., Systems and Procedures Assn. Am., Soc. Advanced Mgmt. Address (winter): 99 Bird Song Way Apt D306 Hilton Head Island SC 29926-1373 also: 600 Square Brielle NJ 08730 Address (summer): 99 Birdsong Way Apt D306 Hilton Head Island SC 29926-1373

PEREIRA, JULIO CESAR, middle school educator; b. Vila Nova Sintra, Cape Verde, Cape Verde, Oct. 12, 1937; came to U.S., 1983; s. Julio Feijoo Pereira and Beatriz Feijoo Pereira. Student, Mil. Sch., Coimbra, Portugal, 1958-61; MAEE, U. Lisbon, Portugal, 1976; cert. in teaching, Afonso Domingues, Lisbon, 1979, Ea. Nazarene Coll., Quincy, Mass., 1988. Registered profl. engr., Portugal. Vocat. sch. tchr. Portuguese Sch., Lisbon, 1969-83, dir. instrn., 1980-81; social studies tchr. Madison Park H.S., Boston, 1984-85; math. tchr. Dearborn Mid. Sch., Boston, 1985—. Inventor slide model for algebraic addition. Lt. Portuguese Army, 1961-65. Recipient Tchr. Appreciation award Algebra Project Boston, 1992, Multicultural Recognition award Mass. Dept. Edn., 1992, Ofcl. citation Mass. Senate, 1993, Presdl. award for Excellence in Math. Teaching, Pres. of U.S., 1994. Mem. Coun. Presdl. Awardees in Math. Avocations: reading, research, computer programming, gardening, travel. Home: 116 Park St Stoughton MA 02072-2925 Office: Dearborn Mid Sch 35 Greenville St Boston MA 02119-2315

PEREL, MICHAEL JOSEPH, dermatologist, inventor; b. Memphis, Oct. 29, 1947; s. Philip Alexander and Dorothy Louise (Dansby) P.; m. Georgia Chris Roberts, Nov. 20, 1973; 1 child, Eric. BS, Tulane U., 1969; MD, U. Tenn., Memphis, 1972. Diplomate Am. Bd. Dermatology. Pvt. practice dermatology Oxnard, Calif., 1977-89; dermatologist Riverside (Calif.) Med. Clinic, 1989—; owner Dreamscape Masonry & Landscaping Co., 1995—. Songwriter for rock group Killing Culture; inventor electronic med. record, 1993, Dr. Perel's hair regrowth formula, 1995. Mem. Inland Counties Dermatologic Soc., Calif. Med. Soc. Libertarian. Avocations: skiing, tennis. Home: 2328 Caserta Ct Henderson NV 89014-5316

PERELLA, MARIE LOUISE, lawyer; b. Akron, Ohio, Feb. 5, 1967; d. Manuel James and Jean Ann (Nalencz) P. BA in Spanish, John Carroll U., 1989; student, Univ. Ibero Americana, Mexico City, 1988; JD, Akron U., 1992. Bar: Ohio 1992, U.S. Dist. Ct. (no. dist.) Ohio 1993, U.S. Supreme Ct. 1996. Law clk. Akron Law Dept., 1990; legal intern Cuyahoga Falls (Ohio) Law Dept., 1990-92; law clk. Ticktin, Baron, Koepper & Co. LPA, Cleve., 1992, assoc. atty., 1992—; commed. to take marriage licence applications at penal instns. Probate Ct. of Cuyahoga County, 1994—. Guest spkr. Cleve. Legal Secs. Assn. meeting, 1995. John Carroll U. scholar, 1988-89, Presdl. Honor scholar, 1985-89, Am. Values scholar, 1985-89, others. Mem. ABA, ATLA, Ohio State Bar Assn., Cuyahoga County Bar Assn. (family law sect.), Cleve. Bar Assn., U.S. Supreme Ct. Hist. Soc., Centro Cultural Hispano, Justinian Forum, Phi Alpha Delta (clk. law sch./grant chpt. 1991-92), Sigma Delta Pi. Avocations: sports, travel, flute. Office: Ticktin Baron Koepper & Co LPA 1621 Euclid Ave Cleveland OH 44115-2107

PERELLA, SUSANNE BRENNAN, librarian; b. Providence, Mar. 19, 1936; d. Laurence J. and Harriet E. (Delaplane) Brennan. B.A., U. Conn., 1960; M.L.S., U. Mich., 1967. Head M.B.A. Library, Univ. Conn., Hartford, 1964-66; asst. librarian Cornell Univ. Grad. Sch. Bus., Ithaca, N.Y., 1967-72; head reader's services FTC Library, Washington, 1972-79; library dir. FTC Library, 1979-92; libr. dir. Libr. and Info. Svcs. U.S. Treasury, Washington, 1992—. Mem. Law Librarians Soc., Spl. Libraries Assn., Am. Assn. Law Libraries, Fed. Library and Info. Ctr. Com. Office: US Dept Treasury Libr 1500 Pennsylvania Ave NW Washington DC 20005-1007

PERELLE, IRA B., psychologist; b. Mt. Vernon, N.Y., Sept. 16, 1925; s. Joseph Yale and Lillian (Schaffer) P.; student U. Tex.; grad. in elec. engring. R.C.A. Inst., 1951; student Iona Coll.; B.S., M.S., Ph.D., Fordham U.; m. Diane A. Granville, 1982; 1 child, Jessica Eve. Prodn. mgr. Arden Jewelry Case Co., 1946-49; became chief engr. Westlab Electronic Service Engrs., 1949; ptnr. Westlab, 1954; pres. Westlab, Inc., 1955-64, chmn. bd., 1956; pres. Westchester Research and Devel. Labs., 1953-65; exec. dir. Interlink, Ltd., 1966—; dir. Atlantic Research Inst., 1975—; cons. higher edn. divsn. U.S. Dept. of Edn., 1994—; cons. ednl. research Fordham U., Catholic U. of P.R., Bayamon (P.R.) Central U., World U., San Juan, P.R., John Jay Coll., N.Y.C., Rockland C.C., N.Y.; rsch. cons. So. Westchester County Bd. Coop. Ednl. Services; stats. cons. City of Mt. Vernon (N.Y.), Reader's Digest, Pleasantville, N.Y., GT&E Inc., CUNY; served as expert witness for N.Y. State Tax Ct.; assoc. Columbia U. Seminars; prof. dept. psychology NYU; prof. dept. bus. and econs., dept. psychology Mercy Coll., Dobbs Ferry, N.Y.; prof. Grad. Sch. Bus., L.I. U.; adj. prof. SUNY-Purchase, Fordham U., N.Y.C.; vis. prof. Fairleigh Dickenson U.; faculty adv. com. Mercer County Coll., 1969-73; conf. leader Nat. Conf. Ednl. Tech., 1971-73. Mem. staff Civil Def., 1954-74; bd. dirs. Mid-Hudson Inst., Dobbs Ferry, N.Y. Served as radio instr. USAAF, 1943-46. Mem. IEEE, AAAS, N.Y. Zool. Soc., Assn. Ednl. Communication and Tech., N.Y. State Ednl. Communication Assn., Audio Engring. Soc., Acoustical Soc. Am., Am. Inst. Physics, Am. Psychol. Assn., Am. Ednl. Rsch. Assn., Am. Statis. Assn., Animal Behavior Soc., Am. Genetic Soc., N.Y. Acad. Scis. Author: A Practical Guide to Educational Media for the Classroom Teacher, 1974; also articles; research on laterality for evolutionary biology. Discoverer Perelle Phenomenon, psychology-attention. Office: Dept of Psychology Mercy Coll Dobbs Ferry NY 10522

PERELMAN, LEON JOSEPH, paper manufacturing executive, university president; b. Phila., Aug. 28, 1911; s. Morris and Jennie (Davis) P.; m. Beverly Waxman, Jan. 27, 1945 (div. Apr. 1960); children: Cynthia, David. B.A., LaSalle Coll., 1933, LL.D., 1978; postgrad., U. Pa. Law Sch., 1933-35; L.H.D. (hon.), Dropsie U., 1976. Ptnr. Am. Paper Products Co. (later Am. Paper Products Inc.), Phila., 1935-42, pres., 1943—; pres. Am. Cone & Tube Co. Inc., Phila., 1953—, United Ammunition Container Inc., Phila., 1961—, Ajax Paper Tube Co., Phila., 1962—; vice chmn. bd. Belmont Industries, Phila., 1963—; pres. Dropsie U., Phila., 1978—. Author: Perelman Antique Toy Mus., 1972. Fin. chmn. Valley Forge council Boy Scouts Am., 1968; founder, bd. dirs. Perelman Antique Toy Mus., Phila., 1969; pres. West Park Hosp., 1975-78, 81—; trustee La Salle U., Balch Inst. Ethnic Studies. Served to 1st lt. USAAF, 1942-45. Recipient citation Jewish Theol. Sem., 1965; Beth Jacob award, 1966; award Pop Warner Little Scholars Inc., 1972; Cyrus Adler award Jewish Theol. Sem., 1976. Mem. AAUP, Jewish Publ. Soc. Am. (treas. 1983, v.p. 1991), Franklin Inst., Am. Assn. Mus. Republican. Jewish. Clubs: Union League (Phila.); Masons, Shriners. *One of the highlights of my life was the establishment of an antique toy museum to keep intact in a permanent place, in order to provide inspiration and pleasure for the general public and stimulate interest in old toys and to give students, antiquarians and collectors an opportunity for study and research in the history and development of one of the world's largest collections of children's toys during the past hundred years.*

PERELMAN, RONALD OWEN, diversified holding company executive; b. Greensboro, N.C., 1943; s. Raymond and Ruth (Caplan) P.; m. Claudia Cohen; 4 children. BA, U. Pa., 1964; MBA, Wharton Sch. Fin., 1966. With Belmont Industries Inc., 1966-78; chmn., chief exec. officer, dir. MacAndrews & Forbes Holdings Inc., Wilmington, Del., 1983—; chmn., chief exec. officer MacAndrews & Forbes Group Inc. (subs.), N.Y.C., 1978—; chmn., chief exec. officer, dir. Revlon Group Inc. (subs. MacAndrews & Forbes Group Inc.), N.Y.C., 1985—, Revlon Inc. (subs.), N.Y.C., 1985—; also chmn. Nat. Health Labs. Inc., La Jolla, Calif., 1985—, Andrews Group Inc., N.Y.C., 1985—. Jewish. Office: Revlon Group Inc 625 Madison Ave New York NY 10022-1801 also: MacAndrews & Forbes Group Inc 35 E 62nd St New York NY 10021-8005*

PERENCHIO, ANDREW JERROLD, film and television executive; b. Fresno, Calif., Dec. 20, 1930; s. Andrew Joseph and Dorothea (Harvey) P.; m. Robin Green, July 16, 1954 (div.); children: Candace L., Catherine M., John Gardner; m. Jacquelyn Claire, Nov. 14, 1969. BS, UCLA, 1954. V.p. Music Corp. Am., 1958-62, Gen. Artists Corp., 1962-64; pres., owner theatrical agy. Chartwell Artists, Ltd., L.A., from 1964; chmn. bd. Tandem Prodns., Inc. and TAT Communications Co., L.A., 1973-83; pres., CEO Embassy Pictures, L.A., from 1983; now pres. Chartwell Partnerships Group, L.A. Promoter Muhammad Ali-Joe Frazier heavyweight fight, 1971, Bobby Riggs-Billie Jean King tennis match, 1973. Served to 1st lt. USAF, 1954-57. Clubs: Bel-Air Country (Los Angeles); Westchester (N.Y.) Country; Friars (N.Y.C.). Office: Chartwell Partnerships Group 1999 Ave Of Stars Ste 3050 Los Angeles CA 90067-6022*

PERERA, GEORGE A., physician; b. N.Y.C., Dec. 29, 1911; s. Lionello and Carolyn (Allen) P.; m. Anna Paxson Rhoads, Dec. 22, 1934; children: Marcia (Mrs. Nicholas B. Van Dyck), David Rhoads. A.B., Princeton U., 1933; M.D., Columbia U., 1937, Sc.D. in Medicine, 1942. Diplomate: Am. Bd. Internal Medicine (dir. 1957-64, vice chmn. 1963-64). Intern Presbyn. Hosp., N.Y.C., 1937-39; resident medicine Presbyn. Hosp., 1941-43; asst. resident Peter Bent Brigham Hosp., Boston, 1939-40; asst. physiology N.Y. U., 1940-41; mem. staff Presbyn. Hosp., 1943-71, attending physician, 1960-71; faculty Columbia U. Coll. Physicians and Surgeons, 1946-71, prof. medicine, 1958-71, asso. dean, 1962-70. Trustee Riverdale Country Sch., N.Y.C., 1949-80, pres., 1977-80; trustee Mary Imogene Bassett Hosp., Cooperstown, N.Y., 1961-80, Columbia U. Press, 1961-64, 66-69, Bridges of Understanding Found., 1973-77; trustee Concern for Dying, 1975-81, v.p., 1978-79, 80-81; alumni trustee Columbia U., 1974-80; mem. corp. Haverford Coll., 1979-87; bd. dirs. Kendal-Crosslands Comty., 1983-94. Fellow ACP, AAAS; mem. N.Y. Acad. Medicine (v.p. 1968-70, trustee 1973-78), Assn. Am. Physicians (emeritus), Alpha Omega Alpha. Home: 159 Kendal Dr Kennett Square PA 19348-2332

PERERA, LAWRENCE THACHER, lawyer; b. Boston, June 23, 1935; s. Guido R. and Faith (Phillips) P.; m. Elizabeth A. Wentworth, July 5, 1961; children: Alice V. Perera Lucey, Caroline F. Perera Barry, Lucy E., Lawrence Thacher. B.A., Harvard U., 1957, LL.B., 1961. Bar: Mass. 1961, U.S. Supreme Ct. 1973. Clk. Judge R. Ammi Cutter, Mass. Supreme Jud. Ct., Boston, 1961-62; assoc. Palmer & Dodge, Boston, 1962-69; ptnr. Palmer & Dodge, 1969-74; judge Middlesex County Probate Ct., East Cambridge, Mass., 1974-79; ptnr. Hemenway & Barnes, Boston, 1979—; mem. faculty and nat. coun. Hon. Nat. Jud. Coll., Reno, prof./pres. Mass. Continuing Legal Edn., Inc., 1988-90. Chmn. Boston Fin. Commn., 1969-71; overseer Brigham and Women's Hosp., Boston, Boston Lyric Opera; chmn. bd. overseers Boston Opera Assn.; chmn. Back Bay Archtl. Commn., 1966-72; trustee emeritus Sta. WGBH Ednl. Found., Boston Athenaeum, Wang Ctr. Performing Arts; trustee Social Law Libr., Boston. Fellow Am. Acad. Matrimonial Lawyers, Am. Coll. Trust and Estate Counsel; mem. ABA, Am. Bar Found., Am. Law Inst., Mass. Bar Assn., Mass. Bar Found., Boston Bar Assn.. Home: 18 Marlborough St Boston MA 02116-2101 Office: 60 State St Boston MA 02109-1800

PERERA, VICUMPRIYA SRIYANTHA, mathematics educator; b. Colombo, Sri Lanka, Feb. 19, 1961; came to U.S., 1986; s. George Paul and Chandrawathi (Perera) P.; m. Lilani Devika Silva, June 21, 1986; children: Vidushani Sriyanka, Vindya Sumedhika, Vihanga Sandunika. BSc in Math. with honors, U. Colombo, 1984; MS in Math., Purdue U., Indpls., 1988; PhD in Pure Math, Purdue U., West Lafayette, 1993. Postdoctoral fellow in math. Purdue U., Indpls., 1986-94; lectr. Ohio State U., Newark, 1994—. Mem. Am. Math. Soc. Roman Catholic. Avocations: chess, computer languages. Home: 22E S Terrace Ave Newark OH 43055 Office: Ohio State U Dept Math 1179 University Dr Newark OH 43055-1766

PERES, JUDITH MAY, journalist; b. Chgo., June 30, 1946; d. Leonard H. and Eleanor (Seltzer) Zurakov; m. Michael Peres, June 27, 1972; children: Dana, Avital. BA, U. Ill., 1967. Acct. exec. Daniel J. Edelman Inc., Chgo., 1967-68; copy editor Jerusalem (Israel) Post, 1968-71, news editor, 1971-75, chief night editor, 1975-80, editor, style book, 1978-80; copy editor Chgo. Tribune, 1980-82, rewriter, 1982-84, assoc. fgn. editor, 1984-90, nat. editor, 1990-95, nat./fgn. editor, 1995—. Office: Chicago Tribune 435 N Michigan Ave Chicago IL 60611*

PERESS, MAURICE, symphony conductor, musicologist; b. N.Y.C., Mar. 18, 1930; s. Haskell Ben Ezra and Elka (Tygier) P. B.A., N.Y.U., 1951; postgrad., Mannes Coll. Music, NYU Grad. Sch. Musicology. Asst. condr. Mannes Coll. Music, 1957-60; music dir. NYU, 1958-61; asst. condr. New York Philharmonic, 1961-62; music dir. Corpus Christi (Tex.) Symphony, 1961-74, Austin Symphony, 1970-72, Kansas City Philharm., 1974-80; dir. Bur. Indian Affairs pilot project Communication through Music, 1968; faculty Queens Coll., 1969-70, 83—; mus. dir. world premiere Bernstein Mass, J.F. Kennedy Center, Washington, 1971. Pub.: musical adaptation and devel. Ellington Opera, Queenie Pie; orchestrations: Ellington, New World 'a Comin', Black Brown and Beige, Bernstein West Side Story Overture; reconstrn. Gershwin's "Strike Up the Band", 1929, Paul Whiteman's Historic Aeolian Hall concert of 1924 (recorded Musical Heritage Soc.), Duke Ellington's First Carnegie Hall concert, 1944; George Antheil's 1927 Carnegie Hall "Ballets Mécanique" concert (recorded Musical Heritage Soc.); James Reese Europes Clef Club concert, 1912, First "All Negro" concert composed and performed by African Ams. in Carnegie Hall; author: Some Music Lessons for American Indian Youngsters, 1968; contbr. articles profl. jours. Served with AUS, 1953-55. Named Millicent James fellow NYU, 1955; Mannes Coll. scholar, 1955-57. Mem. ASCAP, Conductor's Guild, The Friends of Earl Robinson (pres.), Dvorak Am. Soc. (bd. dirs.), Am. Soc. for Jewish Music (bd. dirs.). Jewish. Home: 310 W 72nd St New York NY 10023-2675

PERETTI, MARILYN GAY WOERNER, human services professional; b. Indpls., July 30, 1935; d. Philip E. and Harriet E. (Meyer) Woerner; children: Thomas A., Christopher P. BS, Purdue U., 1957; postgrad., Coll. DuPage, 1980—, U. Wis., 1981—. Nursery sch. lab. asst. Mary Baldwin Coll., Staunton, Va., 1957-58; tchr. 1st grade, nursery sch. No. Ill. area schs., 1958-61; asst. tchr. of blind Glenbard E. H.S., Lombard, Ill., 1978-80; adminstrv. asst. Elmhurst Coll., 1980-81; dir. vol. svcs. DuPage Convalescent Ctr., Wheaton, 1981-95; dir. cmty. outreach Sr. Home Sharing, Inc., Lombard, Ill., 1996—; developer new vol. pos. for vis. the non-verbal handicapped, 1994; prodr. 4 ednl. slide programs on devel. countries, 1988-91; initiator used book collection for library project U. Zululand, S. Africa, 1993-94. Editor, designer newsletter Our Developing World's Voices, 1994—, leaflet newsletter Guide of the Morton Arboretum, 1997—. Bd. dirs. Lombard YMCA, 1977-83, pres., 1980; vol. Chgo. Uptown Ministry, 1979; participant fact finding trips El Salvador, 1988, Honduras, 1989, Nicaragua, 1989, Republic of South Africa, 1991; mem. Nature Artists Guild of Morton Arboretum; vol. PADS, 1994—. Mem. Nature Artists Guild of Morton Arboretum. Avocations: swimming, poetry writing, desktop publishing, Third World concerns, botanical watercolors.

PERETZ, EILEEN, interior designer; b. N.Y.C., Oct. 29, 1934; d. Leo and Mary Miller; m. David Peretz, Aug. 28, 1955; children: Deborah, Adam. BA in Fine Art, CCNY, 1956; Cert. in Interior Design, N.Y. Sch. Interior Design, N.Y.C., 1964. Interior design asst. Narden & Radoszy, N.Y.C., 1956; assoc. interior designer Renee Ross Interiors, N.Y.C., 1964-70; chief interior designer Peretz & Marks Interiors, N.Y.C., 1972-82; sole propr. Eileen Peretz Interiors Inc., N.Y.C., 1970-72, pres., 1982—; cons., mentor, lectr. Marymount Coll., N.Y.C., 1980; lectr. Fashion Inst. Tech.; cons., Paris. Columnist for weekly newspaper Our Town, N.Y.C., 1976-79. Mem. ASID (assoc.), Allied Bd. Trade. Home and Office: 300 Central Park W New York NY 10024-1513 also: 32 Rue de Varenne, Paris 75007, France

PEREYRA-SUAREZ, CHARLES ALBERT, lawyer; b. Paysandu, Uruguay, Sept. 7, 1947; came to U.S., 1954, naturalized, 1962; s. Hector and Esther (Enriquez-Sarano) P.-S.; m. Susan H. Cross, Dec. 30, 1983. BA in History magna cum laude, Pacific Union Coll., 1970; postgrad., UCLA, 1970-71; JD, U. Calif., Berkeley, 1975. Bar: Calif. 1975, D.C. 1980. Staff atty. Western Ctr. Law and Poverty, Inc., Los Angeles, L.A., 1976; trial atty. civil rights div. U.S. Dept. Justice, Washington, 1976-79; asst. U.S. atty., criminal div. U.S. Dept. Justice, Los Angeles, L.A., 1979-82; sr. litigation assoc. Gibson, Dunn & Crutcher, Los Angeles, L.A., 1982-84; sole practice Los Angeles, L.A., 1984-86; ptnr. McKenna & Cuneo, Los Angeles, L.A., 1986-95, Davis Wright Tremaine, L.A., 1995—. Democrat. Avocations: tennis, jogging, travel.

PEREZ, ANDREW, III, architect; m. Cynthia A. Jonston; children: Andrew, Chrstina Alexia, David Alexander. Student, Georgetown U., 1958; BArch, U. Tex., 1961; postgrad., U. Calif., Berkeley, 1965-66. Registered architect, Tex., Calif.; cert. Nat. Coun. Archtl. Registration Bd. Founder, mng. ptnr. O'Neill & Perez, Architects, 1969-84, Andrew Perez Assocs., Architects, 1984—; dir., coord. architecture and interior design programs U. Tex., San Antonio, 1988—; prin.-in-charge master planning and urban design svcs. City of San Antonio, Pan Am. U., Ft. Hood, Tex., various Tex. communities; vis. lectr. Universidad Nacional Autonoma de Mex., Instituto Tecnologico de Nuevo Laredo y la Academia de Arquitectura, Tex. A&M u., U. Houston, 1987; vis. critic U. Tex., San Antonio, San Antonio Coll., Trinity U.; juror various archtl. design competitions. Prin. works include Bank of San Antonio, 1974 (Design Excellence award Bldg./Owners Mgmt. Assn., Pre-cast Concrete Inst. 1976), Gill Cos. Office Bldg., 1975 (Design Excellence award Bldg./Owners Mgmt. Assn. 1977), Mullins Ranch Ho., Muldoon, Tex., (Design Excellence award San Antonio chpt. AIA 1978, Honor award Tex. Soc. Architects 1979), Baird Residence, Marble Falls, Tex. (Honor award Tex. Soc. Architects 1978), Mexican Am. Unity Coun. Ctr., 1978 (Design Excellence award San Antonio chpt. AIA 1978, Adaptive Reuse award San Antonio Conservation Soc. 1979), Bandera br. Gill Savs. (Honor award Tex. Soc. Architects 1981, Design Excelllence award San Antonio chpt. AIA 1984), Victoria Cts. Phases I & II renovation, 1979-86 (Design Excellence award San Antonio chpt. AIA 1982), Child Care Ctr., Brooks AFB, Tex., 1981 (1st Honor award USAF Design Awards 1980, 1st Pl. Design award USAF Design Competition, 1980), St. Paul Sq. Block Improvements, 1982 (Honor award, Design Excellence award San Antonio chpt. AIA 1982), Diagnostic Unit Tex. Dept. Corrections, Huntsville, Tex., 1983, Straus Ranch Ho., Bexar County, Tex. (2 Design Excellence awards San Antonio chpt. AIA 1984, Honor award Tex. Soc. Architects 1984, one of 8 Outstanding Examples of Architecture in Tex. during Past 150 Yrs. Tex. Architect Mag. 1986), Logistical Systems Ops. Ctr., Kelly AFB, 1984, adminstrv. offices Alamo C.C. Dist., 1984, U.S. Border Patrol Sta., Eagle Pass, Tex., 1984 (Design Excellence award San Antonio chpt. AIA 1984), City Pub. Libr. & Lagoon/Pk. Devel., Farmers Branch, Tex., 1985 (Design Excellence, Honor award San Antonio chpt. AIA 1987), McAllister Ranch Ho., Magic Springs, Tex. (Design Excellence award San Antonio chpt. AIA 1985), U.S. Post Office, San Antonio, 1985, Consolidated Support Ctr., Brooks AFB, Tex., 1985, Univ. Ctr. U. Tex., San Antonio, 1986, Health & Phys. Edn. Facility Pan Am. U., 1986, Minten Residence, 1986 (Design Excellence award San Antonio chpt. AIA 1987), The Edn. Ctr., 1986 (John & Joyce Karr award Tex. Hist. Commn. 1987, Design Excellence award San Antonio chpt. AIA 1987), Manske Meml. Libr., Farmers Branch (1st Pl. Design award City of Farmers Branch Design Competition 1981, Design Excellence award San Antonio chpt. AIA 1987), County Line Rad Fire Sta., New Braunfels, Tex., 1987, Tex. Air N.G. Hdqs., 1990, Cahill Residence, San Antonio, 1991, Longoria Residence, Helotes, Tex., 1993-94, others. Pres. parents-tchrs. coun. St. Anthony Sch., 1979, founding treas., bd. dirs., 1985-88, mem. devel. com.; mem. parish bd. Our Lady Grace Ch., 1980-82; chmn. Mayor & City Coun.'s Hist. Sites and Structures Task Force, 1982-87, Task Force Redrafting San Antonio Hist. Preservation Ordinance, 1985-87, Master Plan Task Force for City of San Antonio, 1992, City of San Antonio Hist. Rev. Bd., 1991-92, City of San Antonio Hist. and Design Rev. Commn., 1992—; mem. Task Force Developing hist. Preservation Incentives Program, 1986; founder/v.p. San Antonio Hist. Found., 1988; bd. dirs. Stas. KSTX and KPAC, 1984—, San Antonio Mus. Assn., 1986—, chmn. facilities com., 1987—, sec. bd. dirs., 1991—. With USN, 1963-65, capt. Res. ret. Fellow AIA (past pres., v.p., sec. San Antonio chpt., mem. urban design com. 1984-86, mem. and past chmn. San Antonio chpt. found., co-chmn. graphic and publs. com. nat. conv. 1986); mem. Nat. Trust Hist. Preservation, Tex. Soc. Architects (bd. dirs. 1982-85), Urban Design Inst. Office: Andrew Perez Assocs Architects 100 W Almos Ste 102 San Antonio TX 78212-6547*

PEREZ, CARLOS A., radiation oncologist, educator; b. Colombia, Nov. 10, 1934; came to U.S., 1960, naturalized, 1969; children: Carlos S., Bernardo, Edward P. BS, U. de Antioquia, Medellin, 1952, MD, 1960. Diplomate: Am. Bd. Radiology (trustee 1985-97). Rotating intern Hosp. U. St. Vincente de Paul, Medellin and Caldas, 1958-59; resident Mallinckrodt Inst. Radiology Hosp. U. St. Vincente de Paul, St. Louis, 1960-63, mem. faculty, 1964—; prof. radiology Mallinckrodt Inst. Radiology Washington U., St. Louis, 1972—, dir. radiation oncology ctr., 1976—; fellow radiotherapy M.D. Anderson Hosp. and Tumor Inst., U. Tex., Houston, 1963-64. Coeditor: Principles and Clinical Practice of Radiation Oncology, Principles and Practice of Gynecologic Oncology; mem. editl. bd. Internat. Jour. Radiation and Physics, 1975—, Cancer, 1993—; contbr. articles to med. jours. Fellow Am. Coll. Radiology; mem. AAAS, AMA, Internat. Assn. Study Lung Cancer, Am. Soc. Clin. Oncology, Am. Soc. Therapeutic Radiologists (pres. 1981-82, Gold medal 1992), Am. Radium Soc., Am. Assn. Cancer Rsch., Am. Assn. Cancer Edn., Radiol. Soc. N.Am., Brit. Inst. Radiology, Mo. Radiol. Soc., Mo. Acad. Sci., Mo. Med. Soc., St. Louis Med. Soc., Greater St. Louis Soc. Radiologists, Radiation Rsch. Soc. Home: 78 Lake Frst Saint Louis MO 63117-1359 Office: Washington U Radiation Oncology Ctr 4511 Forest Park Ave Saint Louis MO 63108-2138

PEREZ, CARLOS GROSS, professional baseball player; b. Nigua, Dominican Republic, Apr. 14, 1971. Pitcher Montreal Expos, 1995—. Selected to N.L. All-Star Team, 1995. Office: Montreal Expos, 4540 Pierre-de-Coubertin Av, Montreal, PQ Canada H1V 3N7*

PEREZ, DIANNE M., medical researcher; b. Cleve., Dec. 13, 1959. BA in Chemistry and Biology with honors, Coll. of Wooster, 1982; PhD in Chemistry, Calif. Inst. Tech., 1988. Grad. rsch. asst. dept. chemistry Calif. Inst. Tech., Pasadena, 1982-87, grad. teaching asst. introductory chemistry and biochemistry, 1982-87; sr. rsch. scientist Specialty Labs., Inc., Santa Monica, Calif., 1987-88; fellow dept. eye rsch. Doheny Eye Inst., L.A., 1988-89; fellow dept. heart and hypertension rsch. Cleve. Clinic Found., 1989-91, rsch. assoc. dept. cardiovascular biology, 1992-93, project scientist dept. molecular cardiology, 1993-95, mem. asst. staff dept. molecular cardiology, 1996—; coord. Molecular Cardiology's Protein Group Seminar Series, Cleve. Clinic Found., 1994-95, supr. DNA Synthesis Core Facility Rsch. Inst., fellow's rep. Dept. Heart and Hypertension Rsch. to Divsn. Edn. Com.; adj. asst. prof. dept. pharmacology U. Ky., Lexington, 1994—; manuscript referee Molecular Pharmacology, Circulation Rsch., Cardiovascular Rsch., Jour. Pharmacology and Exptl. Therapeutics, Gene, Biochemistry; lectr. in field. Contbr. articles to profl. jours.; patentee in field. Lubrizol scholar Coll. of Wooster, 1980; recipient Nat. Rsch. Svc. award NIH, 1991; Glaxo grantee, 1994—. Mem. AAAS, Am. Soc. Pharmacology and Exptl. Therapeutics, Am. Heart Assn. (Established Investigator award 1996), Am. Chem. Soc. (cert.), Am. Soc. Biochemistry and Molecular Biology, Phi Beta Kappa, Iota Sigma Pi, Sigma Xi. Office: Cleve Clinic Found Rsch Inst 9500 Euclid Ave Cleveland OH 44195-0001

PEREZ, JEAN-YVES, engineering company executive; b. 1945. Ingenieur Civil Engring., Ecole Centrale des Arts et Manufactures, Paris, 1967; MS, U. Ill., 1970. With Soletanche Enterprise, 1971-72; pres., CEO Woodward-Clyde Group, Inc., Denver, 1967-70, 73—. With French Air Force, 1970-71. Office: Woodward-Clyde Group Inc 4582 S Ulster St Ste 600 Denver CO 80237-2635

PEREZ, JOHN CARLOS, biology educator; b. Park City, Utah, Apr. 29, 1941; s. John Cano and Elma May (Ivie) P.; m. Patsy May Sudden, Oct. 26, 1963; 9 children. B.S. in Molecular and Genetic Biology, U. Utah, 1967; M.A. in Zoology, Mankato State Coll., Minn., 1972; Ph.D. in Bacteriology, Utah State U., 1972. Research assoc. in bacteriology Utah State U., Logan, 1970-72; asst. prof. biology Tex. A&M U., Kingsville, 1972-75, a prof., dir. MBRS-NIH program, 1975-85, prof., 1981—. Contbr. articles to profl. jours. Served with U.S. Army, 1960-63. Named Outstanding Citizen of Kingsville, 1976; recipient Disting. Research award Tex. A&I U., 1979; recipient numerous grants for research and teaching, 1976—. Mem. Am. Soc. Microbiology, Internat. Soc. Toxinology, Tex. Assn. Coll. Tchrs., Sigma Xi. Mormon (stake pres.). Office: Tex A&M U Biology Dept Campus Box 158 A&I Kingsville TX 78363

PEREZ, JOSEPHINE, psychiatrist, educator; b. Tijuana, Mex., Feb. 10, 1941; came to U.S., 1960, naturalized, 1968. BS in Biology, U. Santiago de Compostela, Spain, 1971; MD, 1975. Clerkships in internal medicine, gen. surgery, otorhinolaryngology, dermatology and venereology Gen. Hosp. of Galicia (Spain), 1972-75; resident in gen. psychiatry U. Miami (Fla.), Jackson Meml. Hosp. and VA Hosp., Miami, 1976-78; practice medicine specializing in psychiatry, marital and family therapy, individual psychotherapy, Miami, Fla., 1979—; nuclear medicine technician, EEG technician, supr. Electrographic Labs., Encino, Calif., 1963-71; emergency room physician Miami Dade Hosp., 1975; attending psychiatrist Jackson Meml. Hosp., 1979—, asst. dir. adolescent psychiat. unit, 1979-83; mem. clin. faculty U. Miami Sch. Medicine, 1979—, clin. instr. psychiatry, 1979—. Mem. AMA (Physicians' Recognition award 1980, 83, 86, 89), Am. Assn. for Marital and Family Therapy (cert. clin. mem., treas. 1982-84, pres.-elect 1985-87, pres. 1987-89), Am. Psychiat. Assn., Am. Med. Women's Assn., Assn. Women Psychiatrists, South Fla. Psychiat. Soc., South Dade Women Physicians Assn. Office: 420 S Dixie Hwy Ste 4A Coral Gables FL 33146-2222

PEREZ, LOUIS ANTHONY, radiologist; b. N.Y.C., June 11, 1939; s. Salvatore Lawrence and Valvadina Rose (Ruscillo) P.; divorced, 1988; children: Lisa, Gregg, Nicole; m. Patricia Ann McVey, May 19, 1990; 1 child, Kelsey. BEE, Manhattan Coll., 1962; MD, SUNY, Bklyn., 1966. Diplomate Am. Bd. Radiology, Am. Bd. Nuclear Medicine. Chief nuclear medicine Misericordia Hosp., Bronx, 1973-75; cons. Manhattan Coll., Radiology Inst., Riverdale, N.Y., 1974-81; chief nuclear medicine Norwalk (Conn.) Hosp., 1975-82; dir. radiology Lawrence Hosp., Bronxville, N.Y., 1982—; asst. clin. prof. radiology Columbia U. Coll. Physicians and Surgeons, N.Y.C., 1995—. Contbr. articles to profl. jours., chpts. to books. Lt. comdr. USN, 1963-77. Grantee, Am. Cancer Soc., 1968-70, USPHS, 1974-75. Fellow Am. Coll. Radiology; mem. Soc. Nuclear Medicine (trustee 1985-89, 92—, chmn. sci. subcom. 1988—, chpt. pres. 1982), Am. Coll. Physician Execs., N.Y. State Med. Soc., Explorers Club, Alpine Club. Republican. Roman Catholic. Office: Diagnostic Imaging Svcs of Bronxville 45 Parkview Ave Bronxville NY 10708-2901 also: Lawrence Hosp Dept Radiology 55 Palmer Rd Yonkers NY 10708-5826

PEREZ, LOUIS MICHAEL, newspaper editor; b. Tampa, Fla., May 30, 1946; s. Louis H. and Mary Elizabeth (Mansell) P.; m. Betty Louise Yates, Mar. 22, 1969 (div. May 1980); 1 child, Christian Marcos; m. Donna Marie Pence, Oct. 8, 1982; children: Louis Michael Jr., Ty Pence, Shea Marie. Student, Loyola U., New Orleans, 1964-66; BS in Journalism, U. Fla., 1969. Reporter/corr. Tampa Tribune, Gainesville, Fla., 1966-69; asst. to dean Coll. Edn. U. Fla., Gainesville, 1969-70, adj. prof. Coll. Journalism, 1975-76; reporter Gainesville Sun, 1970-76, editorial writer, 1974-76; editorial page editor The Ledger, Lakeland, Fla., 1976-81, exec. editor, 1981—; vis. prof. Coll. Journalism U. Fla., 1982; judge journalism awards Scripps-Howard Found., 1988; juror Pultizer Prizes com., 1994, 95. Recipient Best Editorial award Fla. Bar Assn., 1977. Mem. Am. Soc. Newspaper Editors, Fla. Soc. Newspaper Editors (pres. 1981-82, bd. dirs. 1980-83, 88-90, 1st pl. Best Feature Article award 1972). Roman Catholic. Home: 5220 Waterwood Run Bartow FL 33830-9768 Office: The Ledger PO Box 408 Lakeland FL 33802-0408

PEREZ, MARY ANGELICA, bilingual specialist, educational administrator; b. San Benito, Tex., Sept. 3; d. Refugio P. and Maria G. (Guerra) P. AA, Tex. Southmonost Coll., Brownsville, Tex., 1955; BS in Elem. Edn., Tex. A&I U. (now Tex. A&M U.), 1959. Cert. elem. tchr., Tex., Calif. Substitute tchr. Bassett Unified Sch. Dist., La Puente, Calif.; tchr. kindergarten West Covina (Calif.) Unified Sch. Dist., ret.; tchr. ESL Tulane U., New Orleans; tchr. bilingual kindergarten San Benito (Tex.) Consolidated Sch. Dist.; tchr. bilingual 4th grade Brownsville (Tex.) Consolidated Sch. Dist.; tchr., head coord. Headstart St. Benedict Ch., San Benito, Tex. Delta Kappa Gamma scholar, 1953; grantee NDEA, 1963, EEOC, 1969, U. Madrid, 1991. Mem. NEA, Nat. Assn. Bilingual Edn., Calif. Tchrs. Assn., Calif. Assn. Bilingual Educators, Tex. Tchrs. Assn. (pres. 1966), Catholic Tchrs. Guild (pres. Brownsville Diocese 1965), Hispanic Women's Coun.. Democrat. Roman Catholic. Avocation: making and selling crafts. Home: 1829 S Lark Ellen Ave West Covina CA 91792-1104

PEREZ, ROSIE, actress; b. Bklyn.; d. Ismael Serrano and Lydia Perez. D-ramatic appearances include: (T.V.) 21 Jump Street, WIOU, (film) Do the Right Thing, 1989, White Men Can't Jump, 1992, Night on Earth, 1992, Untamed Heart, 1993, Fearless, 1993 (Acad. award nom. Best Supporting Actress 1994), It Could Happen To You, 1994, Somebody to Love, 1995, (TV series) House of Buggin, 1995. Office: CAA 9830 Wilshire Blvd Beverly Hills CA 90212-1804

PEREZ-BORJA, CARLOS M., neurologist, hospital executive; b. Quito, Ecuador, Oct. 24, 1927; came to U.S., 1959; s. Manuel V. Perez and Margot Borja; m. Rosa Enriquez, Sept. 6, 1954; children: Carmen, Patricia, Maria, Helena, Carlos. MD, U. Quito, 1952. Diplomate Am. Bd. Psychiatry and Neurology; Am. Bd. Electroencephalography. Asst. prof. neurology Wash. Med. Sch., Seattle, 1965-66; chief of medicine Macomb Hosp. Ctr., Warren, Mich., 1982-84, chief of neurology, 1969-96, vice chief of staff, 1995-96; dir. bd. dirs Detroit Macomb Hosp. Corp., 1985-87, 89-91. Contbr. numerous rsch. papers to profl. jours. Fellow ACP, Am. Acad. Neurology, Am. EEG Soc., Pan Am. Coll. Physicians. Roman Catholic. Avocations: reading, foreign languages. Office: 556 Coventry Ln Grosse Pointe MI 48236-1503

PEREZ-CRUET, JORGE, psychiatrist, psychopharmacologist, psychophysiologist, educator; b. Santurce, P.R., Oct. 15, 1931; s. Jose Maria Perez-Vicente and Emilia Cruet-Burgos; m. Anyes Heimendinger, Oct. 4, 1958; children: Antonio, Mick, Graciela, Isabelle. BS magna cum laude, U. P.R., 1953, MD, 1957; diploma psychiatry McGill U., Montreal, Que., Can., 1976. Diplomate Am. Bd. Psychiatry and Neurology, Nat. Bd. Med. Examiners, Am. Bd. Geriatric Psychiatry; lic. Can. Coun. Med. Examiners; cert. in quality assurance. Rotating intern Michael Reese Hosp., Chgo., 1957-58; fellow in psychiatry Johns Hopkins U. Med. Sch., 1958-60, instr., then asst. prof. psychiatry, 1962-73; lab. neurophysiologist and psychomatic lab. Walter Reed Army Inst. Rsch., Washington, 1960-62, cons., 1963-65; rsch. assoc. lab. chem. pharmacology NIH, Bethesda, Md., also rsch. assoc. adult psychiatry br. and lab. clin. sci. NIMH, Bethesda, 1969-73; psychiatry resident diploma course in psychiatry McGill U. Sch. Medicine, Montreal Gen. Hosp., 1973-76, Montreal Children's Hosp., 1975; prof. psychiatry U. Mo.-Mo. Inst. Psychiatry, St. Louis, 1976-78; chief psychiatry svc. San Juan (P.R.) VA Hosp., pharmacy and therapeutic com. 1978-92; also prof. psychiatry U. P.R. Med. Sch., 1978-92; prof. psychiatry U. Okla. Health Scis. Ctr., Okla. City VA Med. Ctr., 1992—, mem. pharmacy and therapeutic com., 1993—; spl. adviser on mental health P.R. Senate, P.R. sec. health, 1989; spl. cons. NASA, 1965-69; cons. divsn. narcotic addiction and drug abuse NIDA, 1972-73. Capt. M.C., USAR, 1960-62; sr. surgeon USPHS, 1969-71, med. dir., 1971-73. Recipient Coronas award, 1957, Ruiz-Arnau award, 1957, Diaz-Garcia award, 1957, Geigy award, 1975, 76, AMA Recognition award, 1971, 76, 81, Horner's award, 1975, 76, Pavlovian award, 1978, Recognition cert. Senate of P.R., 1986, cert. of merit Gov. of P.R., 1986. Fellow Interam. Coll. Physicians and Surgeons, Royal Coll. Physicians and Surgeons Can. (sr., cert.); mem. Am. Psychiat. Assn., Am. Physiol. Soc., Pavlovian Soc., Am. Fedn. Clin. Rsch., Am. Fedn. Med. Rsch., Am. Assn. Geriatric Psychiatry, Am. Soc. Clin. Pharmacology and Therapeutics, Am. Soc. Pharmacology and Experimental Therapeutics, Soc. Neurosci., Nat. Assn. Healthcare Quality, Internat. Soc. Rsch. Aggression, Okla. Psychiat. Assn., Am. Soc. Clin. Psychopharmacology, Menninger Found., Charles F. Menninger Soc., Okla. Assn. Health Care Quality. Roman Catholic. Home: 3304 Rosewood Ln Oklahoma City OK 73120-5604 Office: Oklahoma City VA Med Ctr 921 NE 13th St Oklahoma City OK 73104-5007

PEREZ-GIMENEZ, JUAN MANUEL, federal judge; b. San Juan, P.R., Mar. 28, 1941; s. Francisco and Elisa (Gimenez) P.; m. Carmen R. Ramirez, July 16, 1964; children: Carmen E., Juan C., Jorge E., Jose A., Magdalena. BBA, U. P.R., 1963, JD, 1968; MBA, George Washington U., 1965. Bar: P.R. 1968. Ptnr. Goldman, Antonetti & Davila, San Juan, 1968-71; asst. U.S. atty. San Juan, 1971-75, U.S. magistrate, 1975-79; judge U.S. Dist. Ct. P.R., San Juan, 1979—. Mem. ABA, Fed. Bar Assn., Colegio de Abogados. Roman Catholic. Office: US Courthouse CH-125 Fed Bldg 150 Carlos Chardon Ave San Juan PR 00918-1765*

PÉREZ-GONZALEZ, ESMERALDA, principal, educator; b. Alice, Tex., Sept. 7, 1963; d. Felipe Perez and Cora Cantu Perez Carrillo. BS, Corpus Christi State U., 1987, MS, 1993; AA, Del Mar Coll., 1987. Tchr. Holy Family Sch., Corpus Christi, Tex.; prin. Archbishop Oscar Romero Middle Sch., Corpus Christi, Tex. Title VII Bilingual Edn. Fellowship grantee, Gov. Fellowship award, 1994. Mem. Tex. Assn. Bilingual Edn., PTA, Nat. Cath. Edn. Assoc., Assoc. Supervision, Curriculum Devel., Nat. Assoc. Secondary Sch. Prin., Year Round Edn., Tex. Middle Sch. Assoc., Nat. Middle Sch. Assoc., Nat. Coun. of tchrs. of Math., tex. Coun. of Tchrs. of Math. Avocations: continuing education, walks on the beach, collecting sanddollars, family. Home: 7130 Everhart Rd #23 Corpus Christi TX 78413

PEREZ-MENDEZ, VICTOR, physics educator; b. Guatemala, Aug. 8, 1923; came to U.S., 1946; m. 1949; 2 children. MS, Hebrew U., Israel, 1947; PhD, Columbia U., 1951. Rsch. assoc. Columbia U., N.Y.C., 1951-53, staff physicist, 1953-61; sr. scientist Lawrence Berkeley Lab., U. Calif., Berkeley, 1960—; vis. lectr. Hebrew U., 1959—; prof. physics dept. radiology U. Calif., San Francisco, 1968—. Fellow IEEE, AAAS, Am. Phys. Soc., N.Y. Acad. Sci.; mem. Soc. Photo Instrumentation Engrs. Office: U Calif Lawrence Berkeley Lab Berkeley CA 94720

PÉREZ-RIVERA, FRANCISCO, writer; b. Vertientes, Cuba, Oct. 3, 1938; came to U.S., 1968, naturalized, 1974; s. Francisco Daniel Pérez and María Eloísa Rivera. BA, Camagüey Coll., Cuba, 1955; MA in Romance Langs., U. Munich, 1967. Newsman, script writer Bavarian Radio, Munich, 1964-68; newsman Associated Press, N.Y.C., 1968-92, arts and entertainment editor, 1992—; dir. Spanish programs for lang. labs., 1987. Author: (poetry) Construcciones, 1979, (novel) Las sabanas y el tiempo, 1986, (short stories) Cuentos cubanos, 1992; co-author: Introducción a la literatura española, 1982; short stories in the anthologies New Cuban Storytellers, 1961, Cuba: Nouvelles et contes d'aujourd'hui, 1985, Narrative and Liberty: Cuban Tales of the Dispersion, 1996, Prosa moderna del mundo hispánico, 1997. Grantee German Academic Exchange Svc., Munich, 1961-67; fellow Cintas Found., N.Y., 1980. Home: 212 E 77th St Apt 1G New York NY 10021-2111 Office: AP 50 Rockefeller Plz New York NY 10020-1605

PEREZ-SILVA, GLAISMA, special education teacher; b. Mayagüez, P.R., Oct. 19, 1957; d. Ismael Pérez and Gladys (Silva) Valentin; 1 child, Andrés Guillermo Figueroa. BA in Spl. Edn., Catholic U., Ponce, P.R., 1980; MS in Spl. Edn. summa cum laude, Interam. U., Rio Piedras, P.R., 1987. Spl. edn. tchr. Manuel G. Tavarez Sch., Ponce, P.R., 1980-81, Amalia Marin Sch., Rio Piedras, P.R., 1981-82, 83-87, Carmen Gomez Tejera Sch., Rio Piedras, 1982-83, Victor Pares Sch., Rio Piedras, 1987-88; bilingual spl. edn. tchr. R. J. Kinsella Cmty. Sch., Hartford, Conn., 1988-96; spl. edn. monitor R. J. Kinsella Cmty. Sch., 1993-95, program coord. enrichment program, 1994-95, coord. cultural and artistic program, 1991-96, mem. governance team, 1994-96; bilingual spl. edn. tchr. T.J. Quirk Middle Sch., 1996—; spl. edn. tchr. Hartford Bd. Edn. Summer Cmp, 1989; site supr. Ctr. City Chs. Summer Camp, Hartford, 1992, 94; tchr. coord. The Village for Families and Children Summer Program, 1995; charter Oak Cultural Ctr. Arts Enrichment Camp, 1996, 97; staff writer El Extra News, Hartford, 1992-95; Spanish music dir. WFCS-FM, New Britain, Conn., 1993—; spl. reporter WFCR-Tertulia, Amherst, Mass., 1994—; lectr. in field. Tchr. Spanish Noah Webster Enrichment Program, Hartford, 1991, bd. dirs. PTA, 1991-92; collaborator D.J. WRTC, Hartford, 1991-93, Guakia, Inc., Hartford, 1991-96, vis. artist, 1996—, ARTS program cons., 1997—; bd. dirs. Kinsella's Union Sch. Com., Hartford, 1991-93, Padres Abriendo Puertas, 1994-97; mem. adv. bd. The Writers Voice, Fairfield, Conn., 1995-96; advisor Kinsella Sch. and Cmty. Partnership, 1992-96; ednl. advisor cultural and cmty. issues Charter Oak Cultural Ctr., Hartford, 1993, bd. dirs., 1995; mem. steering com. P.R. Cultural Day Wadsworth Atheneum, Hartford, 1993-94, 94-96, co-chair, 1994-95, bd. electors, 1995; bd. dirs. Cimarrona: Centro de la Mujer Puertorriquena (Puerto Rican Woman Center), Hartford, 1995, pres., 1996—; advisory bd. mem. Centro de Reafirmaciñn Familiar, Hartford, 1996—; dir. Charter Oak Cultural Ctr. Arts Enrichment Camp.; cons. creative writing Spanish Am. Union, Mass., 1996. Mem. Hartford Fedn. Tchrs. Avocations: reading, drawing, crafts, music, poetry. Office: TJ Quirk Middle Sch 85 Edwards St Hartford CT 06120-2812

PERFETTI, ROBERT NICKOLAS, educational services administrator; b. Staples, Minn., Jan. 8, 1937; s. Nickolas Albert and Lila Bertha (Beurge) P. BS, St. Cloud State U., 1960; postgrad., Bemidji State U., 1961-62, Calif. State U., L.A., 1964-68, Pepperdine U., 1967-68; MA, La Verne U., 1970; postgrad., U. So. Calif., 1972-73, Point Loma U., Pasadena, Calif., 1974-75; EdD, Pacific States U., 1975. Cert. adminstr., counselor, secondary, community coll., jr. high sch., adult, and elem. edn. Calif. Prin. Richmond (Minn.) Pub. Schs., 1960-62; elem. tchr. Sebeka (Minn.) Sch. Dist., 1962-63; team leader lang. arts, social sci. and summer sch. Rowland Unified Sch. Dist., Rowland Heights, Calif., 1965-76, coord. math. lab., 1976-79, secondary counselor, 1979-81, coord. work experience edn., career edn. and career ctr., 1981—, home ind. study coord., ednl. cons., 1992—; coord. Gender Equity, 1980-, Job Tng. Partnership Act, 1980--; advisor Nat. Vocat. Tech. Honor Soc., 1991--; alumni dir. Sacred Heart Sch., Staples. Editor: (profl. newspaper) Reaction. Officer parish coun. Our Lady of the Assumption Ch., Claremont, Calif., chmn. edn. com.; chmn. PTA, Rowland Heights; rep. fed. project, Rowland Heights; scoutmaster, chmn. troop com. Boy Scouts Am. Recipient Svc. Commendation Rowland Unified Sch. Dist., 1978; named. L.A. County Tchr. of Yr. Calif. State Dept. Edn., 1975, Outstanding Secondary Educator of Am., 1974, Giano Tchr. of Yr. Giano Intermediate Sch., 1973, Tchr. of Yr. Rowland Unified Sch. Dist., 1974. Mem. NEA (life), Calif. Tchrs. Assn., Assn. Rowland Educators (v.p.), Calif. Assn. Work Experience Educators (Alpha chpt. v.p.), Alpha Phi Omega (pres.), Pi Delta Epsilon (pres.), KC (3d degree). Roman CAtholic. Avocations: water sports, traveling, research, writing. Home: RR 1 Box 193A Cushing MN 56443-9801 Office: Rowland High Sch 2000 Otterbein Ave Rowland Heights CA 91748-3949

PERHACH, JAMES LAWRENCE, pharmaceutical company executive; b. Pitts., Oct. 26, 1943; s. James Lawrence and Elizabeth Louise (Hoffman) P.; m. Judith Irene Selter, Apr. 15, 1967; children: Laura Anne, Amy Elizabeth. BS, U. Dayton, 1966; MS, U. Pitts., 1969, PhD, 1971. Sr. scientist dept. pharmacology Mead Johnson Rsch. Ctr., 1971-74, sr. investigator dept. biol. rsch., 1974-76, sr. rsch. assoc. dept. biol. rsch., 1976-77, sr. rsch. assoc. dept. pathology and toxicology, 1977-78, prin. rsch. assoc. dept. pathology and toxicology, 1978-80; from dir. pharmacology to dir. clinical investigation Wallace Biol. Rsch., Wallace Labs. div. Carter-Wallace Inc., Cranbury, N.J., 1980-87, v.p. clin. pharmacology and pharmacokinetics, 1987—; vis. asst. prof. dept. pharmacy practice and adminstrn. Coll. Pharmacy Rutgers U., 1993—; adj. prof. toxicology Phila. Coll. Pharmacy and Sci., 1981—; assoc. faculty Evansville Ctr. Med. Edn., Ind. U., 1973-80; lectr. grad. physiology U. Evansville, 1973-79; mem. adv. bd. clin. rsch. ctr. U. Medicine and Dentistry N.J., 1995—; mem. Drug Utilization Rev. Coun., State of N.J., 1983—, med. pharmacologist, 1983, sec., 1984, chmn., 1985-87; mem. substance abuse com. Tri-State Area Health Planning Coun., Evansville, 1972-75; mem. addictions mem. edn. program Evansville Ctr. for Med. Edn., 1972-78. Fellow Am. Coll. Clin. Pharmacology; mem. AAAS, Am. Soc. Clin. Pharmacology and Therapeutics, Am. Soc. Pharmacology and Exptl. Therapeutics, Am. Coll. Toxicology, European Soc. Toxicology, Soc. Exptl. Biology and Medicine, Soc. Neurosci., N.Y. Acad. Sci., Physiol. Soc. Phila., Drug Info. Assn., Sigma Xi. Research in drug discovery, elucidation of mechanism of action and safety evaluation of new therapeutic agents. Home: 6 Highfield Ct Lawrenceville NJ 08648-1077 Office: Wallace Labs PO Box 1001 Half Acre Rd Cranbury NJ 08512

PERHACS, MARYLOUISE HELEN, musician, educator; b. Teaneck, N.J., June 15, 1944; d. John Andrew and Helen Audrey (Hosage) P.; m. Robert Theodore Sirinek, Jan. 27, 1968 (div. Jan. 1975). Student, Ithaca (N.Y.) Coll., 1962-64; BS, Juilliard Sch., 1967, MS, 1968; postgrad., Hunter Coll., 1976, St. Peter's Coll., Jersey City, N.J., 1977. Cert. music tchr., N.Y., N.J. Instr. Carnegie Hall, N.Y.C., 1966-69; program developer, coord., instr. urban edn. program Newburgh (N.Y.) Pub. Sch. System, 1968-69; adj. prof. dept. edn. St. Peter's Coll., Jersey City, 1976-92; tchr. brass instruments Indian Hills High Sch., Oakland, N.J., 1976; tchr. Jersey City Pub. Schs., 1976-77, N.Y.C. Pub. Sch., Bronx, 1980-84; pvt. tchr. Cliffside Park, N.J., 1976—; vocal music tchr. East Rutherford, N.J., 1990; tchr. music Bergen County Spl. Svcs. Sch. Dist., 1990-91; tchr. gen. music Little Ferry (N.J.) Pub. Schs., 1991-92; tchr. mid. sch. instrumental Paramus (N.J.) Pub. Schs., 1993-94; tchr. vocal music West New York (N.J.) Pub Schs., 1995—; Park Ridge N.J. High Sch. Summer Instrumental Music Pgm., 1995, 96; tchr., singer, trumpeter Norwegian Caribbean Lines, 1981-82, Jimmy Dorsey Band, Paris and London, 1974; music and edn. lect. cir., 1992—. Singer with Original PDQ Bach Okay Chorale, 1966, Live from Carnegie Hall Recordings, 1970, St. Louis Mcpl. Opera, 1970, Ed Sullivan Show, 1970; singer, dancer, actress (Broadway shows) Promises, Promises, 1969-71, Sugar, 1971-72, Lysistrata, 1972; trumpeter (Broadway shows) Jesus Christ Superstar, 1973, Debbie!, 1976, Sarava!, 1979, Fiddler on the Roof, Lincoln Ctr., 1981, Sophisticated Ladies, 1982; writer, host series on women in music Columbia Cable/United Artists, 1984; recordings: Carnegie Hall Live, Avery Fisher Hall, Lincoln Ctr. Cons. to cadette troop Girl Scouts U.S., Jersey City, 1967-68, Bergen County N.J. Coun., 1995—; founding mem. Cliffside Park (N.J.) Arts Coun., 1997. Mem. NEA, AFTRA, Actors Equity Assn., Am. Fedn. Musicians (mem. theatre com. local 802 N.Y.C. 1972—, chmn. 1973), AFM Local N.J. 248, Music Educators Nat. Conf., N.J. Music Educators Assn., N.J. Sch. Music Assn., N.J. Edn. Assn., Internat. Women's Brass Conf. (charter mem.), Internat. Trumpet Guild, Women of Accomplishment (charter mem. 1992), Mu Phi Epsilon. Democrat. Episcopalian. Avocations: cats, cake decorating, food sculpting, horticulture, sewing. Home and Office: 23 Crescent Ave Cliffside Park NJ 07010-3003

PERI, WINNIE LEE BRANCH, educational director; b. Dallas; d. Floyd Hamilton and Eula Dee (Richardson) Branch; m. Fred Ronald Peri; children: Kenneth Michael, Michael Anthony, Desiree Denise. BA in Psychology, Calif. State U., Long Beach, 1978, English teaching credential, 1988; social sci. teaching credential, Calif. State U., Northridge, 1979. Republic of South Africa tchr. Internat. Sch. Svcs., Princeton, N.J., 1980-82; tchr. English, St. Jeanne de Lestonnac Sch., Tustin, Calif., 1988-91; dir. edn. Sylvan Learning Ctr., Mission Viejo, Calif., 1993-94; self-employed as tutor, 1994—; facilitator Rainbows for All God's Children, 1989; mem. team experience sch. evaluation com. WASC/WCEA. Mem. adv. bd. Thomas Paine Sch. PTA; dep. sheriff Los Angeles County. Mem. Psi Chi.

PERICH, TERRY MILLER, secondary school educator; b. Greensburg, Pa., Sept. 22, 1948; s. Miller and Eleanor Ann (Schmuck) P.; m. Kathleen Ann Ferrari, July 26, 1975. BA in Elem. Edn., Edinboro U., 1970; elem. cert., Pa. State U., 1973; Masters equivalency degree, U. Pitts., 1994; postgrad., Carlow Coll., 1994. Trained student assistance profl., Pa.; cert. tchr. elem. edn. Tchr. sci. and math. Penn Trafford Schs., Harrison City, Pa., 1970—; mentor, tchr. Tchr. Enhancement Inst. St. Vincent Coll., Latrobe, Pa.; selected tchr. Watershed Restoration St. Vincent Coll., Latrobe. County committeeman Dem. Party, Penn Twp., Pa., 1994—; lion tamer Bushy Run Lions Club, Claridge, Pa., 1993—, 3rd v.p., 1995, 2d v.p., 1996, 1st v.p., 1997—. Recipient Commendation, Pres.-elect Clinton, Student Assistance Program award for working with students at risk St. Vincent Coll. Prevention Projects, 1991. Mem. NEA, ASCD, PACE, Nat. Sci. Tchrs. Assn., Pa. Tchrs. Edn. Assn., Pa. Sci. Tchrs. Assn., Westmoreland County Assn. Student Assistance Profls. (bd. dirs. 1992-94, mem. Westmoreland county student assistance team 1995-96, 96-97), Penn Trafford Edn. Assn. (exec. bd. dirs. 1990-91). Roman Catholic. Avocations: travel, education. Home: 13 Rizzi Dr Irwin PA 15642-8902 Office: Penn Mid Sch PO Box 368 Watt Rd Claridge PA 15623

PERILSTEIN, FRED MICHAEL, electrical engineer, consultant; b. Phila., Oct. 25, 1945; s. Paul Pincus and Adeline Sylvia (Schneyer) P.; m. Abigail Siff, June 13, 1971. BS in Econs., CCNY, 1968; BSEE, Newark Coll. Engring., 1972; MSEE Power, N.J. Inst. Tech., 1977. Registered profl. engr., N.J., Pa., N.Y., Calif. Applications engr. Fed. Pacific Electric Corp., Newark, 1972-78; cons. in field, 1978-82, 97—; pres. Tramlec Corp., Cons. Engrs., Springfield, 1982-97; seminar instr. Multi-Amp Corp., Springfield, 1980; mem. IEEE Cons.' Network, no. N.J., 1992-96; lectr. IEEE Montech 86, Montreal, Can., 1986, ASME/IEEE joint railroad conf., Chgo., 1994, Boston, 1997. Contbr. articles to IEEE Transactions, EC&M Mag. Regents scholar N.Y. Bd. Regents, 1963; recipient 3d prize trophy World Wide Inventor Expo '82, 1982. Mem. IEEE (power engring., vehicular tech., and indsl. application socs., contbr., mem. 4 worldwide transit railcar standards coms., 1996—), NSPE. Achievements include U.S. patent for Polyphase Variable Frequency Inverter. Office: 30 Benjamin Dr Springfield NJ 07081-3019

PERIN, DONALD WISE, JR., former association executive; b. Newton, Mass., Feb. 28, 1915; s. Donald Wise and Beatrice Franklin (Cobb) P.; m. Jean Newcomb Mulcahy, Dec. 5, 1942; children: William Kirk, Betsy Cobb, Donald Wise. Student, Norwich U., 1932-34; B.A., Columbia U., 1936. With Gt. Am. Indemnity Co., N.Y.C., 1936-50; asst. sec. Gt. Am. Indemnity Co., 1946-50; asst. sec.-treas. Nat. Assn. Ins. Agts., N.Y.C., 1950-54; v.p. Alexander & Co., Chgo., 1954-63, Great Am. Ins. Co., N.Y.C., 1964-69; dir. research Ind. Ins. Agts. of Am., N.Y.C., 1970-79; exec. v.p. Ind. Ins. Agts. of Am., 1979-81, exec. v.p. emeritus, 1981. Served with U.S. Army, 1940-46, PTO. Mem. Am. Soc. Assn. Execs., Soc. C.P.C.U.'s, Sigma Alpha Epsilon. Republican. Home: RR 1 Box 3498 Bennington VT 05201

PERITORE, LAURA, law librarian; b. San Francisco, Nov. 28, 1945; d. Attilio and Anita (Firenzi) Marcenaro; children: Victor Anthony, Phillip Michael. BA, U. Calif., Santa Barbara, 1967, MA, 1970; MLS, U. Mo., 1974. Asst. libr. Mo. Hist. Soc., Columbia, 1971-74, 77-79; asst. libr. Hastings Law Libr., San Francisco, 1980-86, assoc. libr., 1986—; part-time tchr. legal rsch. City Coll., San Francisco, 1990-91. Author: Guide to California County Probate and Vital Records, 1994; contbr. articles and monographs to profl. jours. Mem. Am. Assn. Law Librs., No. Calif. Assn. Law Librs. (asst. editor newsletter 1984-86, workshop com. 1988, advt. editor 1990-91, sec. 1993-94, grantee 1984). Avocations: piano, yoga, cooking. Office: Hastings Law Libr 200 Mcallister St San Francisco CA 94102-4707

PERITZ, ABRAHAM DANIEL, business executive; b. Ellenville, N.Y., Aug. 12, 1940; s. Harry and Ida (Koblin) P.; m. Marleen Minkoff, Dec. 12, 1964; children—Alaine, Marc. B.A., Hartwick Coll., Oneonta, N.Y., 1962; postgrad., Baruch Coll., 1967. Asst. restaurant mgr. Concord Hotel, Kiamesha Lake, N.Y., 1962-64; with Ruder Finn, Inc., N.Y.C., 1965—, v.p., controller, 1972-75, chief fin. officer, 1976-82, treas., 1983—. Treas. Kingsley Sq. Townhouse Assn., Freehold, N.J., 1974-75. Served with USAR, 1964. Democrat. Jewish. Home: 127 Kingsley Way Freehold NJ 07728-1667 Office: Ruder Finn Inc 301 E 57th St New York NY 10022-2900

PERKEL, ROBERT SIMON, photojournalist, educator; b. Jersey City, Apr. 23, 1925; s. Louis Leo and Flora Sonia (Levin) P.; BS, NYU, 1948; MS, Barry U., 1964; postgrad. Columbia U. Owner, operator Gulfstream Color Labs., Miami Beach, Fla., 1955-61; graphic instr. Dade County Pub. Schs., 1962-66; freelance photojournalist, 1967—; rep. News Events Photo Svc., Ft. Lauderdale, Fla.; instr. photography Broward Community Coll., 1982-92; rep. Patch Communications, Titusville, Fla., 1985-88; pub. Biograph/Communications, North Miami Beach, Fla., 1987-90; contbr. photo stories, and photographs to numerous mags. and indsl. trade publs. including Women's World, Merck, Sharp & Dohme's Frontline Mag., Gt. Am. Combank News, Nat. Utility Contractor, Mainstream, Nat. Jewish Monthly, Delta Digest, Textile Rental, Sprint Communicator, Rag, the All-Music Mag., DAV Mag., Hallandale Digest, Miami Herald, record jacket C.P. Records, Inc.; exhibited at Met. Mus. and Art Center, Coral Gables, Fla., Mus. of Fine Arts, Boston. Former publicity dir. Coun. for Internat. Visitors of Greater Miami; Served with AUS, 1943-46; ETO. Recipient Community Spirit award Zonta Club Greater Miami, 1980. Fellow Nat. Press Photographers Found.; mem. NYU Alumni Fedn. (Leadership award for 1982-83 fund campaign), Barry U. Alumni Assn., Nat. Press Photographers Assn. (life), Nielsen Media Rsch., DAV (nat. citation for disting. service 1969, trustee Jack Schwartz chpt., past comdr. Miami Beach-Surfside chpt.), Steamship Hist. Soc. Am. (S.E. Fla. chpt.), Am. Legion, Alpha Mu Gamma. Clubs: Mus. of Art (Fort Lauderdale). Home: 617 SE 16th St Apt 3 Fort Lauderdale FL 33316-2629

PERKIEL, MITCHEL H., lawyer; b. N.Y.C., Oct. 26, 1949; s. Frank and Ella Perkiel; m. Lois E. Perkiel, June 24, 1984; children: Joshua L., Alexa Kim, Griffin. BA, SUNY, Stony Brook, 1971; JD, New York Law Sch., 1974. Bar: N.Y. 1975, U.S. Dist. Ct. (so. and ea. dists.) N.Y. 1975, U.S. Ct. Appeals (2d cir.) 1975, Conn. 1988. Law clk. to presiding justice N.Y. County Civil Ct., 1975; assoc. Levin & Weintraub & Crames, N.Y.C., 1975-80, ptnr., 1980-90; with Kaye, Scholer, Fierman, Hayes & Handler, N.Y.C. Notes and comments editor New York Law Rev., 1973-74. Served with USAR, 1969-73. Mem. ABA, Assn. of Bar of City of N.Y., Am. Bankruptcy Inst. Office: Kaye Scholer Fierman Hayes & Handler 425 Park Ave New York NY 10022-3506

PERKIN, GORDON WESLEY, international health agency executive; b. Toronto, Ont., Can., Apr. 25, 1935; came to U.S., 1962; s. Irvine Boyer and Jean (Laing) P.; m. Elizabeth Scott, Dec. 21, 1957; children: Scott, Stuart. MD, U. Toronto, 1959. Asst. dir. clin. research Ortho Research Found., Raritan, N.J., 1962-64; assoc. med. dir. Planned Parenthood Fedn. Am., N.Y.C., 1964-66; program advisor Ford Found., N.Y.C., 1966-67; regional program advisor Ford Found., Bangkok, 1967-69, Rio de Janeiro, 1973-76; program officer Ford Found., Mexico City, 1976-80; project specialist Ministry Fin. and Econ. Planning, Accra, Ghana, 1969-70; cons. World Health Orgn., Geneva, 1971-73; pres. Program for Appropriate Tech. in Health, Seattle, 1980—; affiliate prof. pub. health, U. Wash., Seattle. Contbr. numerous articles to profl. jours. Am. Pub. Health Assn. fellow, 1970. Mem. Planned Parenthood Fedn. Am. (bd. dirs. 1983-89), Planned Parenthood Seattle-King County (bd. dirs. 1982-96, mem. exec. com. 1983-86), Planned Parenthood Western Wash. (bd. dirs. 1996—), Nat. Coun. for Internat. Health (bd. govs. 1984-95), Nat. Acad. Scis. (com. mem. 1987-90), Alan Guttmacher Inst. (bd. dirs. 1985-90), Assn. Reproductive Health Profls., Alpha Omega Alpha. Office: PATH 4 Nickerson St Seattle WA 98109-1651

PERKIN, HAROLD JAMES, retired social historian, educator; b. Stoke-on-Trent, Eng., Nov. 11, 1926; s. Robert James and Hilda May (Dillon) P.; BA 1st class with distinction (major scholar coll., Bell exhibitioner univ.), Cambridge U., 1948, MA, 1952; m. Joan Griffiths, July 3, 1948; children: Deborah Jane, Julian Robert. Asst. lectr., then lectr. social history Manchester U., 1951-65; sr. lectr. Lancaster U., 1965-67, prof. social history, 1967-84, dir. centre social history, 1975-84; Andrew W. Mellon disting. prof. humanities Rice U., Houston, 1984; prof. history Northwestern U., Evanston, Ill., 1985-97, prof. higher edn., 1987-97; vis. fellow Princeton U., 1979-80; fellow Nat. Humanities Center, N.C., 1982-83. Served with RAF, 1948-50. Recipient Gold medal Nat. Inst. Ednl. Research, Tokyo, 1982. Fellow Royal Hist. Soc., 1969—, John Simon Guggenheim fellow, 1989-90; v.p. Social History Soc. U.K. (founding chmn. 1976), Econ. History Soc., Soc. Study Labour History, History of Edn. Soc., Assn. U. Tchrs. (pres. 1970-71). Author: The Origins of Modern English Society, 1780-1880, 1969; Key Profession: The History of the Association of University Teachers, 1969; New Universities in the U.K., 1969; The Age of the Railway, 1970; The Age of the Automobile, 1976; The Structured Crowd, 1980; Professionalism, Property and English Society since 1880, 1981; The Rise of Professional Society: England since 1880, 1989, Higher Education and English Society, Japanese translation, 1993, The Third Revolution: International Professional Elites in the Modern World, 1996. Home: 106 St Mary's Mansions, London W2 1SZ, England

PERKINS, BOB(BY) F(RANK), geologist, dean; b. Greenville, Tex., Dec. 9, 1929; s. William Frank and Vela Beatrice (Richey) P.; m. Patricia Katharine Woodhull, May 25, 1954; children: Katharine Harriet, Marianna Lea, Orrin Woodhull. B.S., So. Methodist U., 1949, M.S., 1950; Ph.D., U. Mich., 1956. Instr. geology and biology So. Meth. U., 1950-51, 53-56; asst. prof. geology U. Houston, 1956-57; rsch. paleontologist Shell Devel. Corp., Houston, 1957-66; prof. geology La. State U., Baton Rouge, 1966-75; chmn., dir. Sch. Geosci. La. State U., 1973-75; prof. geology, dean Grad. Sch. U. Tex., Arlington, 1975-95; also assoc. v.p. research Grad. Sch., U. Tex., Arlington, 1975-93; exec. dir. Gulf Coast sect. Soc. Econ. Paleontologists and Mineralogists Found., 1983—. Editor: 15 vol. series Geoscience and Man, 1970-75; contbr. articles to profl. jours. Fellow Geol. Soc. Am., AAAS, Tex. Acad. Sci.; mem. Paleontol. Soc., Am. Assn. Petroleum Geologists, Paleontol. Soc. Gt. Britain, Soc. Econ. Paleontologists and Mineralogists, Malacological Soc. London. Home: 165 Pinehurst Rd West Hartland CT 06091

PERKINS, BRADFORD, history educator; b. Rochester, N.Y., Mar. 6, 1925; s. Dexter and Wilma (Lord) P.; m. Nancy Nash Tucker, June 18, 1949 (dec.); children: Dexter III, Matthew Edward, Martha Nash. A.B., Harvard U., 1946, Ph.D., 1952. From instr. to asso. prof. history U. Calif. at, Los Angeles, 1952-62; prof. history U. Mich., 1962—, chmn. dept., 1971-72, 80-81; Commonwealth Fund lectr. Univ. Coll., London, Eng., 1964; vis. prof. history Brandeis U., 1970, Ecole des Hautes Etudes en Sciences Sociales, Paris, 1983; Albert Shaw lectr. Johns Hopkins U., 1979; mem. council Inst. Early Am. History and Culture, 1968-71; program dir. Nat. Endowment for Humanities Fellowships in Residence for Coll. Tchrs., 1974-75. Author: The First Rapprochement: England and the United States, 1795-1805, 1955, Youthful America, 1960, Prologue to War: England and the United States, 1805-1812, 1961, Causes of the War of 1812, 1962, Castlereagh and Adams: England and the United States, 1812- 1823, 1964, The Great Rapprochement: England and the United States, 1895-1914, 1968, The Creation of a Republican Empire, 1993. Served with AUS, 1943-45, ETO. Decorated Bronze Star.; Recipient Bancroft prize, 1965, Disting. Faculty award U. Mich., 1986; Warren fellow, 1969-70; Social Sci. Research Council faculty research fellow, 1957-60; Guggenheim fellow, 1962-63. Mem. Am. Hist. Assn., Soc. Am. Historians, Orgn. Am. Historians (coun. 1969-72), Soc. Historians Am. Fgn. Rels. (coun. 1967-72, pres. 1974, Graebner award 1992), Mass. Hist. Soc., Am. Antiquarian Soc. Home: 3401 Berry Rd Ypsilanti MI 48198-9423

PERKINS, CHARLES, III, newspaper editor; b. Brockton, Mass., July 25, 1952; s. Charles II and Barbara Perkins; m. Linda C. Burroughs, Jan. 4, 1985. BA, Dartmouth Coll., 1975. Editor Journal-Opinion, Bradford, Vt., 1977-78; reporter, editor The Union Leader and N.H. Sunday News, Manchester, N.H., 1978-81; Sunday editor N.H. Sunday News, Manchester, 1981-84; mng. editor The Union Leader and N.H. Sunday News, Manchester, 1984-92, exec. editor, 1992—. Office: PO Box 9555 Manchester NH 03108-9555

PERKINS, CHARLES THEODORE, real estate developer, consultant; b. Houston, Aug. 16, 1967; s. Charles Abraham and Mary Margaret Perkins. Attended, St. John's Coll., Santa Fe, 1985-86; AB in Psychology, AB in French, Washington U., St. Louis, 1989; MBA, Institut Superieur Des Affaires/Groupe HEC Paris, 1994; postgrad. The Wharton Sch., U. Pa., 1994-95. Lic. broker, N.Y. Asset mgr. A. David Schwarz, III, Inc., Houston, 1989-93; pres. CTP Interests, Inc., Houston, 1991—; projet mgr. Washington Sq. Ptnrs., N.Y., 1995—, The Arete Group, N.Y., 1995—; broker's lic. Tex. Real Estate Commn., Austin, 1991—. Dir. Washington Crew Classic Regata, St. Louis, 1989; founding coach Rice U. Crew, Houston, 1990; lic. judge referee U.S. Rowing Assn., 1991—, level I coach, 1991—. Recipient Prix De L'excellence BDE, Groupe HEC-ISA, Paris, 1994. Mem. The Penn Club of N.Y., N.Y. Sports Club, Mensa. Episcopalian.

PERKINS, DAVID, English language educator; b. Philadelphia, Pa., Oct. 25, 1928; s. Dwight Goss and Esther M. (Williams) P. A.B., Harvard U., 1951, M.A., 1952, Ph.D., 1955. Mem. faculty Harvard U., 1957—, prof. English, 1964-94, chmn. dept. English, 1976-81, chmn. dept. lit., 1987-89, prof. emeritus, 1994—; vis. prof. Goettingen U., 1968-69. Author: The Quest for Permanence: the Symbolism of Wordsworth, Shelley and Keats, 1959, Wordsworth and the Poetry of Sincerity, 1964, English Romantic Writers, 1967, A History of Modern Poetry: From the 1890's to the High Modernist Mode, 1976, A History of Modern Poetry, Vol. 2, Modernism and After, 1987; (with W. Jackson Bate) British and American Poets: Chaucer to the Present, 1986, Is Literary History Possible, 1991; editor: The Teaching of Literature: What is Needed Now, 1988, Theoretical Issues in Literary History, 1991; mem. editorial adv. bd. Keats-Shelley Jour., 1962-89, The Wordsworth Circle. Served with AUS, 1955-57. Guggenheim fellow, 1962, 73; Fulbright fellow, 1968-69; Am. Council Learned Socs. fellow, 1977. Mem. Am. Acad. Arts and Scis., Cambridge Sci. Club. Home: 984 Memorial Dr Apt 304 Cambridge MA 02138-5741

PERKINS, DAVID LAYNE, SR., architect; b. Picayune, Miss., Mar. 3, 1925; s. Robert E. and Henrietta (Browne) P.; m. Edna Blanche Rice, Jan. 23, 1954; children—David Layne Jr., Richard Scott. B.Arch., Tulane U., 1954. Registered architect, La. Designer, draftsman Curtis & Davis Architects, New Orleans, 1948-53; designer M. Wayne Stoffle, Architect, New Orleans, 1954; asst. prof. of architecture U. Southwestern La., Lafayette, 1954-57, 86-87, 88; prin. David L. Perkins, Architect, Lafayette, 1955-75; pres., sr. ptnr. Perkins-Guidry-Young, Architects, Inc., Lafayette, 1975-88; pres., sr. ptnr., chmn. Perkins-Guidry-Beazley-Osteen, Architects, Inc., Lafayette, 1985-90; pvt. practice cons. architect Lafayette, 1988—; bd. dirs. St. Joseph's Home; past pres., 1st v.p., treas., bd. dirs. Nat. Archtl. Accrediting Bd.; past dir. gulf states region AIA Nat Bd. Dirs.; past pres., v.p., bd. dirs. La. Architects Assn.; mem. dean's council Tulane U. Sch. Arch. Prin. works include office bldgs., Lafayette Pub. Library, neuropsychiat. clinic. Mem. adv. bd. Lafayette Cath. Service Ctr. Inc. Served to capt. USAF, 1943-45, 51-52. Fellow AIA (pres. So. La. chpt. 1963-64, honor award So. La. chpt. 1982, 83, 85, bd. dirs. 1975-78, award of excellence 1982); mem. La. Architects Assn. (honor award 1963, 64, 70, 74, 82, 83). Republican. Presbyterian. Avocation: boating, woodworking. Home: 503 Marjorie Blvd Lafayette LA 70503-3147 Office: PO Box 51762 Lafayette LA 70505-1762

PERKINS, DWIGHT HEALD, economics educator; b. Chgo., Oct. 20, 1934; s. Lawrence Bradford and Margery (Blair) P.; m. Julie Rate, June 15, 1957; children: Lucy Fitch, Dwight Edward, Caleb Blair. B.A., Cornell U., 1956; A.M., Harvard U., 1961, Ph.D., 1964. From instr. to assoc. prof. Harvard U., Cambridge, Mass., 1963-69, prof. econs., 1969-81, assoc. dir. East Asian Research Ctr., 1973-77, chmn. dept. econs., 1977-80, H.H. Burbank prof. polit. economy, 1981—; dir. Harvard Inst. Internat. Devel., Cambridge, 1980-95; dir. Nat. Com. on U.S.-China Rels., 1991—; trustee China Med. Bd., 1995—; cons. permanent subcom. on investigations U.S. Senate, 1974-80; H.M. Jackson vis. prof. Chinese studies U. Wash., 1985, Phi Beta Kappa lectr., 1992-93, Faculty Salzburg seminar, 1996; lectr. Fulbright econ. policy program, Vietnam, 1997; mem. Internat. Adv. Group to Prime Min. of Papua, New Guinea, 1991-92; cons. Korea Devel. Inst., 1972-80. Author: Agricultural Develoopment in China, 1368-1968, 1969, Market Control and Planning in Communist China, 1966, China: Asia's Next Economic Giant?, 1986, (with E.S. Mason and others) The Economic Modernization of Korea, 1980, (with S. Yusuf) Rural Development in China, 1984, (with M. Gillis and others) Economics of Development, 1983, 4th edit., 1996; editor: China's Modern Economy in Historical Perspective, 1975, (with M. Roemer) Reforming Economic Systems in Developing Countries, 1991, (with J. Stern and others) Industrialization and the State: The Korean Heavy and Chemical Industry Drive, 1995. Mem. Vis. Com. Far Ea. Studies, U. Chgo., 1973-77; mem. bd. govs. East-West Ctr., Honolulu, 1979-82; co-moderator Aspen Inst. Seminar on Korea, Colo., 1980-83. Lt. (j.g.) USNR, 1956-58. Fgn. Area Tng. fellow Ford Found., N.Y., 1958-62; NSF Sci. Faculty fellow Tokyo, 1968-69. Mem. Assn. Asian Studies, Assn. Comparative Econ. Systems (past pres.), Am. Econ. Assn., Phi Beta Kappa. Home: 64 Pinehurst Rd Belmont MA 02178-1504 Office: Harvard Inst Internat Devel One Eliot St Cambridge MA 02138-5781

PERKINS, EDWARD J., diplomat; b. Sterlington, La., June 8, 1928; m. Lucy Liu; children: Katherine, Sarah. Student, U. Calif., Lewis and Clark Coll.; BA, U. Md., 1967; MPA, U. So. Calif., 1972, DPA, 1978; studied French, Fgn. Service Inst., 1983; LLD (hon.), U. Md., 1990, St. John's U., 1990, Lewis and Clark Coll., 1988; LHD (hon., Winston-Salem State U., 1990; LHD (hon.), Bowie State Coll., 1993; HHD (hon.), St. Augustine Coll., 1991, Beloit Coll., 1990, U. So. Calif., 1995. Chief of pers. Army and Air Force Exch. Svc., Taipei, Taiwan, 1958-62; dep. chief Army and Air Force Exch. Svc., Okinawa, Japan, 1962-64; chief pers. and adminstrn. Army and Air Force Exchange Service, Okinawa, Japan, 1964-66; asst. gen. svcs. officer Far East bur. AID, 1967-69, mgmt. analyst, 1969-70; asst. dir. for mgmt. U.S. Ops. Mission to Thailand, 1970-72; staff asst. Office of Dir. Gen. Fgn. Svc., 1972, personnel officer, 1972-74; adminstrv. officer Bur. Near Eastern and South Asian Affairs, 1974-75; mgmt. analysis officer Office Mgmt. Ops., Dept. State, 1975-78; counselor for polit. affairs Accra, Ghana, 1978-81; dep. chief of mission Monrovia, Liberia, 1981-83; dir. Office of West African Affairs, Bur. African Affairs, Dept. State, 1983-85; U.S. amb. to Liberia, 1985-86, U.S. amb. to South Africa, 1986-89; dir. gen., dir. pers. Fgn. Svc., Dept. of State, Washington, 1989-92; U.S. rep. to UN N.Y.C., 1992-93; U.S. amb. to Australia Canberra, 1993-96; William J. Crowe chair prof., interim exec. dir. Internat. Programs Ctr. U. Okla., 1996—; William J. Crowe Chair prof. and interim exec. dir. Internat. Programs Ctr., U. Okla., 1996—. Contbr. articles to profl. publs. Bd. trustees Lewis and Clark Coll., 1994—; bd. govs. Joint Ctr. for Polit. and Econ. Studies steering com. Ctr. for Australian and New Zealand Studies, Georgetown U., 1996—; bd. trustees Asia Soc., 1997—; bd. Cranlana Programme; bd. trustees Inst. of Internat. Edn., 1997—. Recipient Presdl. Meritorious Svc. award, 1987, Presdl. Disting. Svc. award, 1989, Meritorious Honor award AID, 1967, Disting. Alumni award U. So. Calif., 1991, Achievement award So. U., 1991, award for outstanding svc. as fgn. svc. officer Una Chapman Cox Found., 1989, Living Legend award The Links, Inc., 1989. Fellow Nat. Acad. Pub. Adminstrn.; mem. VFW, ASPA, Conf. Minority Pub. Adminstrs., Navy League, Am. Polit. Sci. Assn., Fgn. Policy Assn. (ambassadorial fellow), Internat. Studies Assn., Coun. on Fgn. Rels., Am. Consortium Internat. Pub. Adminstrn., Am. Fgn. Svc. Assn., Am. Legion, Ctr. Study of Presidency, Chester A. Arthur Soc., Pub. Svc. Comm., World Affairs Couns. Okla. and Washington, Sigma Pi Phi, Kappa Alpha Psi, Inc. (Laurel Wreath award 1993, C. Rodger Wilson Leadership Conf. award 1990, Disting. Svc. award 1989, Outstanding Achievement award for Fgn. Svc. 1986), Phi Kappa Phi. Office: U Okla Internat Programs Ctr 339 W Boyd St Rm 400 Norman OK 73069-4854

PERKINS, ELIZABETH ANN, actress; b. Queens, N.Y.. Grad., Goodman Theatre, Chgo., 1981. Films include: About Last Night, 1986, From the Hip, 1987, Sweet Hearts Dance, 1988, Big, 1988, Love at Large, 1990, Enid is Sleeping, 1990, Avalon, 1990, He Said/She Said, 1991, The Doctor, 1991, Indian Summer, 1993, The Flintstones, 1994, Miracle on 34th Street, 1994, Moonlight and Valentino, 1995; TV film: For Their Own Good, 1993; theater: Brighton Beach Memoirs, 1984, Playwrights' Horizon, Ensemble Studio Theater, N.Y. Shakespeare Festival, Four Dogs and a Bone, 1995. Office: Creative Artist Agy 9830 Wilshire Blvd # 220 Beverly Hills CA 90212-1804*

PERKINS, ESTHER ROBERTA, literary agent; b. Elkton, Md., May 10, 1927; d. Clarence Roberts and Esther Crouch (Terrell) P.; student West Chester State Tchrs. Coll., 1945-47, U. Del. Acct., E. I. duPont de Nemours & Co., Inc., Wilmington, Del., 1947-65; records specialist U. Del., 1966-78; partner Holly Press, Hockessin, Del., 1977-83; owner Esther R. Perkins Lit. Agy., Childs, Md., 1979—; author's agt. Mem. Cecil County Arts Council. Mem. Authors Guild, Nat. Writer's Club, DAR, Romance Writers Am., Mystery Writers Am. Author: Backroading Through Cecil County Maryland, 1978; Things I Wish I'd Said, 1979; Canal Town, Historic Chesapeake City, Maryland, 1983. Republican. Methodist. Home and Office: PO Box 48 Childs MD 21916-0048

PERKINS, FLOYD JERRY, retired theology educator; b. Bertha, Minn., May 9, 1924; s. Ray Lester and Nancy Emily (Kelley) P.; m. Mary Elizabeth Owen, Sept. 21, 1947 (dec. June 1982); children: Douglas Jerry, David Floyd, Sheryl Pauline; m. Phyllis Genevra Hartley, July 14, 1984. AB, BTh, N.W. Nazarene Coll., 1949; MA, U. Mo., 1952; MDiv, Nazarene Theol. Sem., 1952; ThM, Burton Sem., 1964; PhD, U. Witwatersrand, Johannesburg, South Africa, 1974; ThD, Internat. Sem., 1994. Ordained to Christian ministry, 1951. Pres. South African Nazarene Theol. Sem., Florida Transvaal, Africa, 1955-67; pres. Nazarene Bible Sem., Lourenzo Marques, Mozambique, 1967-73, Campinas, Brazil, 1974-76; prof. missions N.W. Nazarene Coll., Nampa, Idaho, 1976; prof. theology Nazarene Bible Coll., Colorado Springs, Colo., 1976-97; chmn., founder com. higher theol. edn. Ch. of Nazarene in Africa, 1967-74; sec. All African Nazarene Mission Exec., 1967-74; ofcl. Christian Council Mozambique, 1952-74. Author: A History of the Christian Church in Swaziland, 1974. Served with USN, 1944-46. Mem. Soc. Christian Philosophers, Evang. Theol. Soc., Am. Schs. Orientan Rsch., Am. Soc. Missiology, Assn. Evang. Missions Profs. Republican. Avocation: golf. Home: 1529 Lyle Dr Colorado Springs CO 80915-2009 *Personal philosophy: Be cheerful, hopeful, courageous, honest, candid, faithful, committed, loyal, and the whole world will be yours!.*

PERKINS, FRANK OVERTON, marine scientist, educator; b. Fork Union, Va., Feb. 14, 1938; s. Frank Otie and Mary Ella (Hughes) P.; m. Beverly Anne Weeks. BA, U. Va., 1960; MS, Fla. State U., Tallahassee, 1962, PhD, 1966. Marine scientist Va. Inst. Marine Sci., Coll. William and Mary, Gloucester Point, Va., 1966-69; sr. marine scientist Va. Inst. Marine Sci., Coll. William and Mary, Gloucester Point, 1969-77, asst. dir., 1977-81, dir., dean Sch. Marine Sci., 1981-91, prof. marine sci., 1991-97. Baptist. Home: 5313J Creek Ridge Ln Raleigh NC 27607 Office: Dept Zoology Box 7617 NC State U Raleigh NC 27695

PERKINS, FREDERICK MYERS, retired oil company executive; b. Tallahassee, Fla., Oct. 7, 1928; s. Frederick Myers and Nancy Evelyn (Turner) P.; m. Rosemary Ross, Dec. 21, 1950; children: Lucille Lambert Reed, Nancy Evelyn Cavanagh, Matthew Myers. B.Ch.E., U. Fla., 1951, M.S., 1952. Prodn. research engr. Humble Oil & Refining Co., Houston, 1952-62, prodn. staff coordinator, 1963-65; reservoir engr. Humble Oil & Refining Co., New Orleans, 1965-66; prodn. mgr. Humble Oil & Refining Co., Corpus Chrisiti, Tex., 1966-70; petroleum economist Standard Oil Co. N.J., N.Y.C., 1962-63; dep. mng. dir. Esso Australia Ltd., Sydney, 1970-72; gen. mgr. natural gas Exxon Co. U.S.A., Houston, 1972-76, v.p. prodn., 1976-79, dep. mgr. producing Exxon Corp., 1979-80, v.p. gas, 1980-85, v.p. producing, 1985-86; pres. Exxon Prodn. Research Co., Houston, 1986-93; ret., 1993. Patentee in field. Served with U.S. Army, 1946-47, PTO. Mem. Soc. Petroleum Engrs., Galveston Country Club, Petroleum Club.

PERKINS, GEORGE HOLMES, architectural educator, architect; b. Cambridge, Mass., Oct. 10, 1904; s. George Howard and Josephine (Schock) P.; m. Georgia Hencken, June 3, 1933; children—Gray H., Jennifer H. Student, Phillips-Exeter Acad., 1920-22; A.B., Harvard U., 1926, M.Arch., 1929; LL.D., U. Pa., 1972. Instr. architecture U. Mich., 1929-30; instr. architecture Harvard, 1930-36, asst. prof., 1936-39, assoc. prof., 1939-42, Norton prof. regional planning, chmn. dept., 1945-51; dean, chmn. dept. architecture Grad. Sch. Fine Arts, U. Pa., 1951-71, prof. architecture and urbanism, 1971—; practicing architect and city planner, 1933—; asst. regional rep., acting dir. urban devel. div. Nat. Housing Agy., 1942-45; cons. Brit. Ministry of Town and Country Planning, 1946, UN, 1946, 55-56; cons. to Govt. Turkey, 1958-60, Balt. Redevel. Authority, Cambridge Redevel. Authority, Worcester Redevel. Authority.; Mem. Cambridge Planning Bd., 1950-51; dir. Phila. Housing Assn., 1951-56, pres., 1953-56; dir. Citizens Council City Planning, 1951-54; chmn. Phila. Zoning Commn., 1955-58, Phila. City Planning Commn., 1958-68; dir. Phila. Port Corp., Old Phila. Devel. Corp., Phila. Indsl. Devel. Corp. Author: Comparative Outline of Architectural History, 1937; editor: Jour. Am. Inst. Planners, 1950-52; contbr. articles to profl. jours. Mem. Phila. Commn. Higher Edn.; Trustee Fairmount Park Art Assn., 1965—. Fellow A.I.A. (chancellor coll. fellows 1964-66); mem. Am. Inst. Planners, Am. Soc. Planning Ofcls., Nat. Assn. Housing Ofcls., World Soc. Ekistics; hon. corr. mem. Royal Inst. Architects Can. Clubs: The Country (Brookline); Franklin Inn (Phila.), Rittenhouse (Phila.), Philadelphia Cricket (Phila.), Art Alliance (Phila.); Century (N.Y.C.). Home: 82 Bethlehem Pike Philadelphia PA 19118-2821

PERKINS, GEORGE WILLIAM, II, financial services executive, film producer; b. Salem, Mass., Sept. 10, 1926; s. George William and Daisy A. (Chase) P.; m. Mildred Boyle, Oct. 6, 1951; children: George William III, Clifton Alfred Dow, Mark Paige. Student, Northeastern U., 1944-49; B.Sc., Curry Coll., 1952; postgrad., Eastern Sch. Photography, Boston U.; Cert., Coll. Financial Planning, Denver, 1974. Registered investment advisor. Travel lectr., color cinematographer, 1946—; in charge road testing Renault auto, Alcan Hwy., Alaska, 1949; pres. Neily Film Prodns., Inc., 1953-55; Eastern regional v.p. Western Res. Life Assurance Co., Ohio, 1973-75; pres., chmn. bd. Fin. Mktg. Systems, Inc., Nashua, N.H., 1976—; chmn. Holmes Travel Orgn., 1978—; chmn. bd., v.p. Fin. Cons. Group for Women, Inc., 1981—; registered prin. Fin. Cons., Stoneham, Mass., 1975-88, Linsco-Pvt. Ledger, Boston, 1988-96; div. mgr. Calif. Pacific Ins. Services Inc., 1977-80; pres. Fin. Benefits Planning Corp., 1983—; sr. v.p., treas. Penn Distbn. Co, Inc., 1983-87, Penn RE Life Ins. Co., 1984-88; v.p. Polymer Balloon Corp., 1984-88; dir., treas. Linsco Ins. Agy., Inc., 1987-96; registered prin. Linsco-Pvt. Ledger, 1988-96; sr. v.p. corp. rels. Capital Def. Corp., 1990—; dir. Fin. Cons. Mgmt. Corp., Sonolite Corp., Contrex Co., FBP, Inc., FMSINC, Capital Defence Corp., Security Trust Ins. Co.; registered prin. Tri-Merica Securities Corp., 1996—; spkr. on sales and svc. motivation; assoc. prof. bus. adminstrn. Curry Coll., until 1963, also sr. mem. bd. trustees, mem. coll. corp., also chmn. reorgn., 1963; pvt. trustee and executor, 1972—. Chief rsch. team, prodr. first feature length 16 mm Cinemascope motion picture, 1954; narrator, film prodr.: Burton Holmes travelogues, 1950-70; appearances at Carnegie Hall, N.Y. Music Hall, Phila. Symphony Hall, Boston Nat. Geog. Soc., Washington, numerous other cities, U.S., Mexico and Can.; designer world's largest portable cinemascope motion picture screen; contbg. editor: monthly newsletter Fin. Strategies and Money Mgmt. for Women; contbr. articles on ins. and sales to various publ., documentary and world travel motion picture and video prodn. in 36 countries, also photographic and cinematographic publs. Served with USNR, World War II, PTO. Recipient Nat. Quality award Nat. Assn. Life Underwriters. Mem. Merrimack Valley Life Underwriters Assn. (v.p., dir. 1968-69), Boston Life Underwriters Assn., Advt. Club Greater Boston, Internat. Assn. Fin. Planners (charter pres. No. Mass. chpt.), Nat. Assn. Security Dealers (prin.), Northeastern U., Curry Coll. alumni assns., Mass. Brokers Assn., Inst. Cert. Fin. Planners, Ins. Conf. Planners Assn., Am. Soc. Assn. Execs., Masons, Rotary (charter pres. Chelmsford, Mass. 1967-68). Home: 278 Lowell St Lynnfield MA 01940-1115 Office: 33 Main St Nashua NH 03060-2776 *Life tends to be what you encourage it to be as you live it day by day.*

PERKINS, GLADYS PATRICIA, retired aerospace engineer; b. Crenshaw, Miss., Oct. 30, 1921; d. Douglas and Zula Francis (Crenshaw) Franklin; m. Benjamin Franklin Walker, Sept. 26, 1952 (dec.); m. William Silas Perkins, Sept. 16, 1956 (dec.). BS in Math., Le Moyne Coll., 1943; postgrad., U. Mich., 1949, U. Calif., L.A., 1955-62. Mathematician Nat. Adv. Com. for Aeronautics (now NASA), Hampton, Va., 1944-49, Nat. Bur. of Standards, L.A., 1950-53, Aberdeen Bombing Mission, L.A., 1953-55; assoc. engr. Lockheed Missiles Systems Div., Van Nuys, Calif., 1955-57; staff engr. Hughes Aircraft Co., El Segundo, Calif., 1957-80; engring. specialist Rockwell Internat., Downey, Calif., 1980-87, ret., 1987. Contbr. articles to profl. publs. Named Alumnus of Yr. Le Moyne-Owen Coll., 1952; recipient Nat. Assn. for Equal Opportunity in Higher Edn. award Le Moyne-Owen Coll. Mem. Soc. of Women Engrs., Assn. of Computing Machinery, Le Moyne-Owen Alumni Assn. (pres. 1984), U. Mich. Alumni Club, Alpha Kappa Alpha. Democrat. Congregationalist. Home: 4001 W 22nd Pl Los Angeles CA 90018-1029

ERKINS, HERBERT ASA, physician; b. Boston, Oct. 5, 1918; s. Louis d Anna (Robinson) P.; m. Frances Snyder, Sept. 2, 1942; children: Susan, eborah, Dale, Karen, Ronnie. AB cum laude, Harvard U., 1940; MD summa cum laude, Tufts U., 1943. Intern Boston City Hosp., 1944, resident, 1947-48; practice medicine specializing in transfusion medicine, 1953—; clin. instr. Stanford Med. Sch., 1953-57, asst. clin. prof., 1957-58; hematologist Open Heart Surgery Team, Stanford Hosp., San Francisco, 1955-58, Jewish Hosp., St. Louis, 1958-59; dir. rsch. Irwin Meml. Blood Ctrs., San Francisco, 1959-78, med. and sci. dir., 1978-90, exec. dir., 1987-91, pres., 1991-93, sr. med. scientist, 1993—; asst. prof. medicine Washington U., St. Louis, 1958-59, U. Calif., San Francisco, 1959-66, assoc. prof., 1966-71, clin. prof., 1971—; v.p. Blood Rsch. & Devel. Found., 1995—. Co-editor: Hepatitis and Blood Transfusion, 1972; assoc. editor: Transfusion. Maj. M.C., U.S. Army, 1944-47. Mem. AAAS, Am. Assn. Blood Banks (chmn. sci. adv. com. 1972-73, chmn. stds. com. 1968-71, chmn. com. on organ transplantation and tissue typing 1970-80, bd. dirs. 1982-86), Am. Soc. Hematology, Internat. Transfusion Soc., Am. Soc. Histocompatibility and Immunogenetics (pres. 1985-86), Nat. Marrow Donor Program (chair bd. dirs. 1995-96, chmn. com. on stds. 1987-94, chmn. fin. com. 1987-94). Home: 520 Berkeley Ave Menlo Park CA 94025-2323 Office: Irwin Meml Blood Ctrs 270 Masonic Ave San Francisco CA 94118-4417

PERKINS, HOMER GUY, manufacturing company executive; b. New Haven, Oct. 23, 1916; s. Frank W. and Emily (Oesting) P.; m. Dorothy C. Stock, Jan. 24, 1942; children: Maribeth Perkins Grant, Homer Guy Jr., Hazel Mary Perkins Adolphson, Dorothy Catherine, Caroline Ann, Faith Elizabeth Perkins Crotteau, Ruth Emily Perkins Sico. BA in Internat. Rels., Yale U., 1938; LLD (hon.), Westfield (Mass.) State Coll., 1977. With Stanhome, Inc. (formerly Stanley Home Products, Inc.), Westfield, 1939—, v.p., 1965-66, exec. v.p., 1966-70, pres., CEO, 1970-78, chmn., 1978-81, also bd. dirs. Treas. Stanley Park of Westfield, 1949—; pres. Citizens Scholarship Found., Easthampton, Mass., 1966-67, Easthampton Cmty. Chest, 1960-61; chmn. fin. com., bd. dirs. Western Mass. coun. Girl Scouts U.S., 1966-69; mem. devel. com. Clarke Sch. Deaf, Northampton, 1965-68; mem. fin. com. Town of Easthampton, 1962-70, chmn. fin. com., 1967-68; dir. Frank Stanley Beveridge Found., Westfield, 1956-95, pres., 1966-87; trustee Cooley Dickinson Hosp., Northampton, 1963-70, 84-92, chmn. bd. trustees, 1989-91; pres. bd. trustees Northampton Sch. for Girls, 1964-73; bd. dirs. Porter Phelps Huntington Found., Hadley, Mass., 1960-92, Guild of Holy Child, Westfield, 1969-76; mem. bd. overseers Williston Acad., Easthampton, 1961-64, Old Sturbridge (Mass.) Village, 1970-76; v.p. bd. trustees Williston-Northampton Sch., 1970-75, pres., 1975-78. With USAAF, 1942-46. Mem. Direct Selling Assn. (chmn. 1975, bd. dirs., mem. Hall of Fame), Paperweight Collectors Assn. (pres. 1991-95), Lions (past pres. Easthampton club). Home: 8 Carol Ave Easthampton MA 01027-1904

PERKINS, JACK EDWIN, lawyer; b. Portola, Calif., May 25, 1943; s. Charles James and Vira Almena (Wing) P.; m. Barbara Kay Nielson, Jan. 18, 1969; children: Jill Christy, Kelli Anne. BA, San Jose State Coll., 1966; JD, Hastings Coll. Law, 1972. Bar: Calif. 1972, D.C. 1989. Asst. U.S. Atty., Dept. Justice, San Francisco, 1973-74; staff atty. Dept. Justice, Washington, 1972, 74-80, legis. counsel, 1980-86, dep. asst. atty. gen., 1986-90; chief adminstrv. hearing officer Exec. Office for Immigration Rev., Falls Church, Va., 1990—. Served to capt. USMC, 1966-69, Vietnam. Recipient John Marshall award Dept. Justice, 1986. Avocations: tennis, jogging, racquetball. Home: 3310 Fallen Tree Ct Alexandria VA 22310-2262 Office: Exec Office Immigration Rev 5107 Leesburg Pike Ste 2400 Falls Church VA 22041-3234

PERKINS, JAMES FRANCIS, physicist; b. Hillsdale, Tenn., Jan. 3, 1924; s. Jim D. and Laura Pervis (Goad) P.; A.B., Vanderbilt U., 1948, M.A., 1949; Ph.D., 1953; m. Ida Virginia Phillips, Nov. 23, 1949; 1 son, James F. Sr. engr. Convair, Fort Worth, Tex., 1953-54; scientist Lockheed Aircraft, Marietta, Ga., 1954-61; physicist Army Missile Command Redstone Arsenal, Huntsville, Ala., 1961-77; cons. physicist, 1977—. Served with USAAF, 1943-46. AEC fellow, 1951-52. Mem. Am. Phys. Soc., Sigma Xi. Contbr. articles to profl. jours. Home and Office: 102 Mountain Wood Dr SE Huntsville AL 35801-1809

PERKINS, JAMES WINSLOW, international business consultant, builder, contractor; b. Southington, Conn., Sept. 15, 1955; s. Robert Winslow and Florence Corinne (Angelone) P. Student, Tunxis Community Coll., Farmington, Conn., 1973-75. Owner Town & Country Club, Smithfield, R.I., 1975-80, Ad Mark of Mass, Inc., Ludlow, Mass., 1980-84, Car Stereo Distbrs., Inc., West Palm Beach, Fla., 1983-85, Internat. Imports, Lauderdale Lakes, Fla., 1985-88, Modern Sectional Homes, Inc., Southington, Conn., 1989-93. Mem. Nat. Assn. Realtors, Cen. Conn. Bd. Realtors, New Eng. Mfrd. Housing Assn., 100 Club of Conn. Republican. Avocations: sailing, water skiing. Home: 2587 Meriden-Wtby Rd Marion CT 06444 also: Modern Sectional Homes PO Box 153 Marion CT 06444-0153

PERKINS, JAMES WOOD, lawyer; b. New Bedford, Mass., Oct. 14, 1924; s. Ralph Chamberlain and Louise Bartlett (Allen) P.; m. Margaret Neale Heard, Feb. 3, 1951; children: Charles H., James A., George H. AB, Havard U., 1945, JD, 1948; MTS, Harvard Div. Sch., 1996. Bar: Mass. 1948, U.S. Dist. Ct. Mass. 1948. Engr. Sylvania Electric Products, Inc., Salem, Mass., 1944-45; assoc. Palmer & Dodge, Boston, 1948-54, ptnr., 1955-91, mng. ptnr., 1986-89, of counsel, 1992—. Mem. ABA (chmn. sect. local govt. law 1970-71, sect. del. 1974-78), Nat. Assn. Bond Lawyers (pres. 1985-86). Office: Palmer & Dodge 1 Beacon St Boston MA 02108-3107

PERKINS, JOHN ALLEN, lawyer; b. New Bedford, Mass., Sept. 13, 1919; s. Ralph Chamberlain and Louise Bartlett (Allen) P.; m. Lydia Bullard Cobb, Sept. 9, 1944; children: John A., Susan W., Robert C., William B. A.B., Harvard U., 1940, LL.B., 1943. Bar: Mass. Of counsel Palmer & Dodge, Boston; clk. Social Law Library, 1961-83; grad. researcher Univ. Coll., Oxford U., 1978; bd. dirs. Greater Boston Legal Services, Inc., 1972-91. Author: The Prudent Peace—Law as Foreign Policy, 1981; contbr. articles to profl. jours. Mem. Dedham (Mass.) Sch. Com., 1959-65, chmn., 1963-65, town counsel, Dedham, 1971-72. Mem. Am. Law Inst., Am. Coll. Trust and Estate Counsel, Mass. Bar Assn. (dir. 1973-75), Internat. Acad. Estate and Trust Law (exec. coun. 1990-94), Boston Bar Assn. (council 1972-75, v.p. 1981-82, pres. 1982-84). Home: 203 Highland St Dedham MA 02026-5835 Office: Palmer & Dodge 1 Beacon St Boston MA 02108-3107

PERKINS, JOSEPH JOHN, JR., lawyer; b. Pitts., Feb. 22, 1954; s. Joseph John Sr. and Joan Elizabeth (Challingsworth) P.; m. Rebecca Ellen Graham, Apr. 7, 1984; children: Benjamin Joseph, Nathaniel Graham. BS in Geol. Engring. magna cum laude, Princeton U., 1976; JD, U. Denver, 1979. Bar: Alaska 1979, U.S. Dist. Ct. Alaska 1979, U.S. Ct. Appeals (9th cir.) 1983, U.S. Supreme Ct. 1986. Assoc. Guess & Rudd, Anchorage, 1979-84, shareholder, 1984—. Trustee Rocky Mountain Mineral Law Found., Denver, 1988—. Mem. ABA (vice chmn. hard mineral com., sect. on natural resources and environ. law 1992-93), Alaska Bar Assn. (chmn. natural resources law sect. 1984-88), Sigma Xi, Tau Beta Pi. Republican. Episcopalian. Avocations: swimming, biking, gardening, travel. Home: 7202 Hunter Cir Anchorage AK 99502-4185 Office: Guess & Rudd 510 L St Ste 700 Anchorage AK 99501-1959

PERKINS, LAWRENCE BRADFORD, JR., architect; b. Chgo., Jan. 13, 1943; s. Lawrence Bradford and Margery Isabella (Blair) P.; m. Phyllis Barbara Friedman, Sept. 11, 1966; children: Rachael Naomi, Judith Eve, Rebecca Abigail. BA, Cornell U., 1967; MBA, Stanford U., 1969; BArch, CCNY, 1976. Registered architect, N.Y., Ohio, Ill., Conn., Pa., Mass., Ill., N.J., Ga., Fla., Mo., Ariz., Tex. Pres. Perkins Eastman Archs., N.Y.C., 1983—, Omnidata Svcs., N.Y.C., 1971-73; mng. ptnr. Llewelyn-Davies Assocs., N.Y.C., 1973-77, Perkins & Will, N.Y.C., 1977-81; ptnr. Attia & Perkins, N.Y.C., 1981-83. Author chpts. to books; contbr. articles to profl. jours. Bd. dirs. Castle Gallery Coll. New Rochelle, N.Y., 1985—, Settlement Housing Fund, N.Y.C., 1991—, Helen Keller Internat., N.Y.C., 1993—, various other village bds. and coms. Fellow AIA (mem. various coms.), Am. Inst. Cert. Planners, Cornell U. Coun., Epsilon Assn. (pres. 1993-96—). Home: 4 Rectory Ln Scarsdale NY 10583-4314 Office: Perkins Eastman Archs 437 5th Ave New York NY 10016-2205

PERKINS, LEEMAN LLOYD, music educator, musicologist; b. Salina, Utah, Mar. 27, 1932; s. Milton Lloyd and Ida Margaret (Johnson) P.; m. Marianne Suzanne Contesse, Nov. 14, 1956; children: Eric Raymond, Bruce Philippe, Marc Christian (dec.), Patrick Thierry. BFA, U. Utah, 1954; PhD, Yale U., 1965. Instr. Boston U., 1964; instr. Yale U., 1964-67, asst. prof., 1967-71, dir. undergraduate studies in music history, 1969-70; assoc. prof. music history, coord. for musicology U. Tex., Austin, 1971-75, assoc. prof. music history, grad. adv. for musicology, 1976; prof. music Columbia U., N.Y.C., 1976—, chmn. dept music, 1985-90; instr. advanced seminar in Medieval History, Smith Coll., 1968; vis. assoc. prof. music Columbia U., 1975; vis. prof. Boston U., 1978; dir. NEH Summer Seminar, 1977. Editor: Johannes Lheritier Opera Omnia, 1969, (with Howard Garay) The Mellon Chansonnier, 1979; contbr. to profl. jours. Chmn. grad. musicology com., Columbia U., 1980-84. Sgt. U.S. Army, 1957-59. Recipient James Morris Whiton Fund award Yale U., 1965, The Otto Kinkeldey award Am. Musicological Soc., 1980; Trumbull Coll. fellow Yale U., 1966-71, Lewis-Farmington fellow Yale U., 1962-63, Morse fellow Yale U., 1967-68, Am. Coun. Learned Soc. fellow, 1973-74, NEH fellow, 1979, 1984-85, French Archival Scis. fellow Newberry Libr. Center for Renaissance Studies, 1991; Martha Baird Rockefeller grantee, 1963-64, Paul Mellon Found. grantee, 1972, Am. Coun. Learned Soc., 1972, 82, U. Tex. grantee, 1975,. Mem. Am. Musicological Soc. (chmn. program com. 1979, bd. dirs. 1980-81, adv. bd., 1985-86, chmn. ad hoc sub com., 1985-86, exec. com. delegate, 1989-92), Internat. Musicological Soc., The Renaissance Soc. of Am., Amici Thomae Mori, Phi Beta Kappa, Phi Kappa Phi. Mormon. Office: Columbia U Dept of Music Dodge Hall 703 New York NY 10027

PERKINS, LUCIAN, photographer. Grad., U. Texas. Intern The Washington Post, 1979, now staff photographer. Named Newspaper Photographer of Yr., Pictures of Yr. competition, 1993; recipient Pulitzer Prize for explanatory journalism, 1995, Photo of Yr. award World Press, 1996. Office: The Washington Post 1150 15th St NW Washington DC 20071-0001*

PERKINS, MARVIN EARL, psychiatrist, educator; b. Moberly, Mo., June 1, 1920; s. Marvin Earl and Nannie Mae (Walden) P.; A.B., Albion Coll., 1942; M.D., Harvard U., 1946; M.P.H. (USPHS fellow), Johns Hopkins U., 1956; L.H.D., Albion Coll., 1968; grad. U.S. Army Command and Gen. Staff Coll., 1966, U.S. Army War Coll., 1972; m. Mary MacDonald, May 24, 1943 (div.); children: Keith, Sandra, Cynthia, Marvin, Mary, Irene; m. 2d, Sharon Johnstone, May 20, 1978; 1 dau., Sharon. Intern, Henry Ford Hosp., Detroit, 1946-47; post surgeon, hosp. comdg. officer Fort Eustis, Va., 1948; resident physician psychiatry Walter Reed Army Hosp., Washington, 1949-52; chief psychiatry br., psychiatry and neurology cons. div. Office U.S. Army Surgeon Gen., Washington, 1952-53, chief records rev. br., 1953-55; chief psychiat. svcs. div. D.C. Dept. Pub. Health, 1955-58, chief bur. mental health, 1959-60; lectr. Johns Hopkins U., Balt., 1960-65; adj. prof. Columbia U., 1961-67; prof. psychiatry Mt. Sinai Sch. Medicine of CUNY, 1967-72; clin. prof. psychiatry Coll. Physicians and Surgeons, Columbia U., 1972-77; prof. psychiatry N.Y. Coll. Medicine, 1977-78; prof. behavioral medicine and psychiatry U. Va. Sch. Medicine, 1978—; dir. N.Y.C. Community Mental Health Bd., 1960-68, commr. mental health svcs., 1961-68; dir. psychiatry Beth Israel Medical Center, N.Y.C., 1967-72, dir. Morris J. Bernstein Inst., 1968-72; dir. Community Mental Health Svcs. Westchester County, 1972-77; dir. psychiatry Westchester County Med. Center, 1977-78; med. dir. Mental Health Svcs. of Roanoke Valley, 1978-82; med. dir. Roanoke Valley Psychiat. Ctr., 1980-82, pres. med. staff, 1985-86; med. dir., pres. med. staff Catawba Hosp., 1988-91; psychiat., mental hygiene clinic VA Med. Ctr., Salem, Va., 1992-95; cons. psychiatrist Blue Ridge Cmty. Svcs., 1992—; med. dir. partial hospitalization program Alleghany Regional Hosp., Low Moor, Va., 1995-96. With AUS, 1943-46; col. M.C. Res. ret. Diplomate in psychiatry Am. Bd. Psychiatry and Neurology; certified mental hosp. adminstr. Am. Psychiat. Assn. Fellow Am. Psychiat. Assn. (life), N.Y. Acad. Medicine (life); mem. AMA, Group Advancement Psychiatry, Roanoke Acad. Medicine, N.Y. Psychiat. Soc., Neuropsychiat. Soc. Va., Med. Soc. Va., State Hist. Soc. Mo. (life), Res. Officers Assn. (life) Mil. Order of World Wars (perpetual). Home: 3728 Forest Rd SW Roanoke VA 24015-4510 also: PO Box 20437 Roanoke VA 24018 Office: 1604 Boulevard Salem VA 24153-6420 also: 865 Roanoke Rd Daleville VA 24083

PERKINS, MERLE LESTER, French language educator; b. West Lebanon, N.H., Apr. 16, 1919; s. Charles Elisha and Ethel (Armstrong) P.; m. Barbara Marion Cunningham, June 16, 1951; children: Elizabeth Cunningham, Janet Blair. AB, Dartmouth Coll., 1941; AM, Brown U., 1942, PhD in French, 1950. Instr. French Brown U., 1948-50, U. Chgo., 1950-53; mem. faculty U. Calif., Davis, 1953-67; prof. French U. Calif., 1963-67, chmn. dept. fgn. langs., 1962-65, chmn. dept. Italian and French, 1965-67; prof. French U. Wis., 1967—, chmn. grad. studies French, 1967-74, 77-89, Pickard Bascom prof. French, 1983—; dir. univs. Mich. and Wis. Year in France, Aix-en-Provence, 1976-77, chmn. admissions, 1979-89. Author: The Moral and Political Philosophy of the Abbé de Saint-Pierre, 1959, Voltaire's Concept of International Order, 1965, J.-J. Rousseau on History, Liberty, and National Survival, 1968, Jean-Jacques Rousseau on the Individual and Society, 1974, Diderot on the Time-Space Continuum, 1982, Montesquieu on National Power and International Rivalry, 1986, Six French Philosophes on International Rivalry and War, 1989, Marquis de Sade, His Ethics and Rhetoric: Suspense in Sade, 1989, Diderot: A Study Guide, 1990, Enlightenment Writers, Their Contributions to Two Revolutions, 1993, Ordeal of Arms, Air Combat, Europe and the Balkans, 1993, Recollections of Air Combat, World War II, 1996; also anthology, articles, reviews. Served with USAAF, 1942-45. Decorated Air medal with 3 oak leaf clusters.; Parker fellow Dartmouth Coll., 1941-42; Edwards fellow Brown U., 1948-49; Penrose Fund grantee Am. Philos. Soc., 1956-57, 72-73, 74-75; Fulbright research grantee France, 1960-61, 67-68. Mem. Am. Assn. Tchrs. French, Philol. Assn. Pacific Coast, Modern Lang. Assn. (grantee 1956-57), Internat. Assn. for 18th Century Studies, Modern Humanities Research Assn., Phi Beta Kappa. Episcopalian. Office: U Wis Dept French 1220 Linden Dr Madison WI 53706-1525

PERKINS, NANCY LEEDS, lawyer; b. Washington, June 19, 1956; d. Roswell Burchard and Joan (Titcomb) P. AB, Harvard U., 1979, M in Pub. Policy, 1987, JD, 1987. Bar: Pa. 1988, D.C. 1989, U.S. Dist. Ct. D.C. 1990. Jud. clk. U.S. Dist. Ct. (ea. dist.) N.Y., Bklyn., 1987-88; spl. counsel Arnold & Porter, Washington, 1988—. Contbr. articles to profl. jours. Recipient Pro Bono svc. award Internat. Human Rights Law Group, 1990. Democrat. Avocation: tennis. Office: Arnold & Porter 555 12th St NW Washington DC 20004

PERKINS, RALPH LINWOOD, business executive, public health administration specialist; b. Orono, Maine, July 17, 1914; s. Ralph L. and Zilla (Sawyer) P.; m. Hilda Beatrice Morrison, Sept. 1, 1938; children: Sylvia Lucille Perkins Nespoli, Jacquelyn Sue Perkins Lowe-Vosburgh. BSME, U. Maine, 1935; MS in Hosp. Adminstrn., Columbia, 1950. With U.S. Engrs. Dept., Quoddy, Me., 1935-37, NYA in, Me., Ohio and W.Va., 1937-44; with USPHS, W.Va., Miss., La., D.C. and N.Y., 1944-48; asst. adminstrv. officer USPHS Hosp., S.I., 1949-50, adminstrv. officer, 1950-63; asso. dir. Hosp. U. Pa., 1963-64, exec. dir., 1964-74; sr. adviser Chi Systems, Inc., Ann Arbor, Mich., 1974-78; Lectr. Columbia Sch. Pub. Health and Adminstrv. Medicine, 1961-74. Past chmn. Delaware Valley Hosp. Council Forum.; Former bd. dirs. West Phila. Community Mental Health Consortium. Recipient Commendation Medal USPHS, 1963. Fellow Am. Coll. Health Care Execs. (life); mem. Am. Hosp. Assn. (life), Maine Hosp. Assn., Delaware Valley Hosp. Coun. (past dir., past pres. forum, sec.-treas.), Assn. Am. Med. Colls., Hosp. Assn. Pa. (past trustee), Commd. Officers Assn. USPHS (life). Methodist. Home and Office: 517 Fairfax Rd Drexel Hill PA 19026-1210

PERKINS, RICHARD BURLE, II, chemical engineer, international consultant; b. Houston, May 25, 1960; s. Richard Burle I and Mariam (Jamail) P. BSChemE, U. Tex., Austin, 1983; postgrad., Ariz. State U., 1988-90. Engr. Magcobar group DiChem div. Dresser Industies, Houston, 1979-82; engr. Honeywell Satellite Systems Ops., Phoenix, 1984-92; sr. assoc. ICF Kaiser Internat. Inc., Washington, 1992-95; program mgr. Tex. Natural Resource Conservation Commn., Austin, 1995-96; regional sales mgr. Peteroferm Inc., Austin, 1996—; chmn. electrostatic discharge control com. Honeywell, Inc., Satellite Systems Operation, Phoenix, 1985-92; mem. Honeywell Corp. CFC Reduction Task Force, 1990-92, chmn., 1991-92. Presenter papers at profl. confs. Rep. del., Austin, 1980, alt. del., 1982; chmn. City of Glendale Citizens Recycling Task Force, 1990-92; mem. Glendale Strategic Planning Com., 1991-92, Phoenix Hash House Harriers, 1988-93; grad. Glendale Leadership Advancement and Devel., 1990. Recipient Excellence award Honeywell Mfg. Bd., 1991. Mem. Ariz. EOS/ESD Assn. (founding, sec. 1991), Ariz. Tex. Execs. (pres. 1984, 87, com. chmn. 1988-92), Nat. Assn. Environ. Profls., Austin Hash House Harriers.

Avocations: racquetball, beer, southwestern contemporary art, cycling, cats. Home: 1135 Barton Hills Dr # 226 Austin TX 78704

PERKINS, ROGER ALLAN, lawyer; b. Port Chester, N.Y., Mar. 4, 1943; s. Francis Newton and Winifred Marcella (Smith) P.; m. Katherine Louise Howard, Nov. 10, 1984; children: Marshall, Morgan, Matthew, Justin, Ashley. BA, Pa. State U., 1965; postgrad., U. Ill., 1965-66; JD with honors, George Washington U., 1969. Bar: Md. 1969, Mass. 1975. Trial atty. Nationwide Ins. Co., Annapolis, Md., 1969-72; assoc. Arnold, Beauchemin & Huber, P.A., Balt., 1973; assoc., then ptnr. Goodman & Bloom, P.A., Annapolis, 1973-76; ptnr. Luff and Perkins, Annapolis, 1976-78; sole practice Anapolis, 1978—; temp. adminstrv. hearing officer Anne Arundel County, 1984—; asst. city atty., Annapolis, 1980-82; atty. Bd. Appeals of City of Annapolis, 1986—; mem. Appellate Jud. Nominating Commn., 1995—. Editl. adv. bd. Daily Record, 1996-97. Mem. Gov.'s Task Force on Family Law, 1991-94; adv. coun. on family legal need of low income persons MLSC, 1991-96; coach youth sports. Fellow Am. Acad. Matrimonial Lawyers, Am. Bar Found., Md. Bar Found. (bd. dirs. 1992-95); mem. ABA (ho. dels. 1991-93, 94-96, standing com. on solo and small firm practitioners 1993-97, chair 1996-97), Md. State Bar Assn. (pres. 1992-93, treas. 1988-91, bd. govs. 1985-87, chair spl. com. on lawyer profl. responsibility 1994-95, family and juvenile law sect. coun. 1983-89, chair 1987-88), Anne Arundel County Bar Assn. (pres. 1984-85). Republican. Methodist. Home: 503 Bay Hills Dr Arnold MD 21012-2001 Office: The Courtyards 133 Defense Hwy Ste 202 Annapolis MD 21401-8907

PERKINS, RONALD DEE, geologist, educator; b. Covington, Ky., May 18, 1935; s. Stanley E. and Pauline L. (Green) P.; m. Beverly L. Hughes, June 8, 1957; children—Lisa, Debra. B.S., U. Cin., 1957; M.S., U. N.Mex., 1959; Ph.D. in Geology, Ind. U., 1962. Research geologist Shell Devel. Co., Houston, 1962-63; project leader Shell Devel. Co., Coral Gables, Fla., 1963-68; mem. faculty Duke U., Durham, N.C., 1968—; prof. geology Duke U., 1975—, chmn. dept., 1978-90; cons. to industry. Author numerous papers in field. NSF grantee, 1969-80. Mem. Internat. Assn. Sedimentologists, Soc. Econ. Paleontologists and Mineralogists (sec.-treas. 1978-82), Geol. Soc. Am., Am. Assn. Petroleum Geologists, Sigma Xi. Office: Duke U Dept Geology West Campus Old Chemistry Bldg Durham NC 27708

PERKINS, ROSWELL BURCHARD, lawyer; b. Boston, May 21, 1926. A.B. cum laude, Harvard U., 1945, LL.B. cum laude, 1949, LLD (hon.), Bates Coll., 1988. Bar: Mass. 1949, N.Y. 1949. Assoc. Debevoise, Plimpton & McLean, N.Y.C., 1949-53; ptnr. Debevoise & Plimpton, and predecessor firms, N.Y.C., 1957—; asst. sec. U.S. Dept. Health, Edn. amd Welfare, 1954-56; counsel to Gov. Nelson A. Rockefeller, State of N.Y., 1959; asst. counsel spl. subcom. Senate Commerce Com. to investigate organized crime in interstate commerce, 1950; chmn. N.Y.C. Mayor's Task Force on Transp. Reorgn., 1966; mem. Pres.'s Adv. Panel on Personnel Interchange, 1968; chmn. adv. com. Medicare Adminstrn. Contracting Subcontracting HEW, 1973-74; dir. Fiduciary Trust Co. N.Y., 1963—; trustee Bowery Savs. Bank, 1975-82; mem. legal com. to bd. dirs. N.Y. Stock Exch., 1995—. Mem. N.Y. Lawyers Com. Civil Rights, 1970-73; mem. nat. exec. com., 1973—, co-chmn., 1973-75; mem. adv. coun. Woodrow Wilson Sch. Pub. and Internat. Affairs, Princeton U., 1967-69; bd. dirs. The Commonwealth Fund, 1974—; bd. dirs. Sch. Am. Ballet, 1974-85, chmn. bd., 1976-80; dir., sec. N.Y. Urban Coalition, 1967-74; trustee Pomfret Sch., 1961-76; The Brearley Sch., 1969-75; dir. Salzburg Seminar Am. Studies, 1970-80; mem. overseers vis. com. Kennedy Sch. Govt., Harvard U., 1971-77, Harvard and Radcliffe Colls., 1958-64, 1971-77. Recipient Spl. Merit Citation of Am. Judicature Soc., 1989, Harvard Law Sch. Assn. award, 1994. Mem. ABA (commn. on law and economy 1975-79; mem. house of dels. 1980-93), N.Y. State Bar Assn., Assn. Bar City of N.Y. (chmn. spl. com. on fed. conflict of interest laws 1958-60), Assn. Harvard Alumni (pres. 1970-71), Am. Law Inst. (mem. coun. 1969, pres. 1980-93, chmn. coun. 1993—), Am. Arbitration Assn. (bd. dirs. 1966-71). Author: The New Federal Conflict of Interest Law; editor Harvard Law Rev. Home: 1120 5th Ave New York NY 10128-0144 Office: Debevoise & Plimpton 875 3rd Ave New York NY 10022-6225

PERKINS, SAMUEL, lawyer; b. Boston, Dec. 16, 1948; s. Malcolm and Sheila D. (Redmond) P.; m. Nancy Joy Reed, June 21, 1975; children; Molly, Sara, Benjamin, Emily. AB cum laude, Harvard U., 1970; JD, Boston U., 1976. Bar: Vt. 1977, U.S. Dist. Ct. Vt. 1977, Mass. 1984, U.S. Dist. Ct. Mass. 1984, U.S. Ct. Appeals (1st cir.) 1992. Asst. atty. gen. Atty. Gen.'s Office, Montpelier, Vt., 1977-78; assoc. Welch & Graham, White River Junction, Vt., 1978-81; ptnr. Welch, Graham, Perkins & Manby, White River Junction, 1981-83; assoc. Morrison, Mahoney & Miller, Boston, 1983-87, ptnr., 1987-95; ptnr. Brody, Hardoon, Perkins & Kesten, Boston, 1995—. Mem. Mass. Bar Assn., Boston Bar Assn., Def. Rsch. Inst., Mass. Def. Lawyers Assn. Office: Brody Hardoon Perkins & Kesten 200 State St Boston MA 02109-2605

PERKINS, SUE DENE, editor; b. Wichita Falls, Tex., Jan. 12, 1946; d. Darrye Clayton and Josephine Marie (Hall) P. BA, North Tex. State U., 1968; MA, Stephen F. Austin State U., 1980; postgrad., Angelo State U., 1979. Cert. tchr., Tex. Mag. editor Haire Pubs., N.Y.C., 1968-69; women's editor Arlington (Tex.) Daily News, 1970; police reporter editor Arlington (Tex.) Daily News, 1972; mag. editor Tex. Assn. Bus., Houston, 1972-74; editor in ho. pubs. P.R. Am. Assn. Respiratory Therapy, Dallas, 1974-76; asst. employee pub. rels. Gen. Telephone, San Angelo, 1976-79; dir. student publs. Stephen F. Austin State U., Nacogdoches, Tex., 1980-83, founder Women in Comm. chpt., 1982; instr. journalism Tex. A&M Univ., College Station, 1983-84; owner photo supply Photo-Graphics Co., Lufkin, Tex., 1985-88; adv. student pubs. Diboll (Tex.) Ind. Sch. Dist., 1987-97; editor Escapees Mag., Livingston, Tex., 1997—; computer cons. Deep East Tex. Coun. Govt., Lufkin, 1990, Region VII Edn. Svc. Ctr., Kilgore, Tex., 1994. Editor: (mags.) Handbags & Accessories, 1968-69, Tex. Industry, 1972-74, (newspaper) Arlington Daily News, 1970-72, (newsletter) Am. Assn. for Respiratory Therapy Bull., 1974-76. Pres. Wheeler Cemetery Assn., Corrigan, Tex., 1992, v.p., 1993; sec. Youth for Christ, Diboll, Tex., 1993-95. Named Outstanding Ex-Student, Electra (Tex.) Alumni Assn., 1981-82. Mem. Journalism Educators Am., Tex. Journalism Edn. Assn., Tex. Classroom Tchrs. Assn., Order Ea. Star. Baptist. Avocations: outdoor photography, fishing. Home: RR 1 Box 106 Corrigan TX 75939-9739 Office: Escapees Inc 100 Rainbow Dr Livingston TX 77351-9300

PERKINS, THOMAS HAYES, III, furniture company executive; b. Brookhaven, Miss., Nov. 18, 1922; s. Thomas H. Jr. and Clara Louretta (Whittington) P. BS, La. State U. Owner T.H. Perkins Furniture, Inc. Chmn. Miss. Regional Housing Authority, McComb. With U.S. Army, 1943-44. Decorated Purple Heart, Bronze Star. Mem. Internat. Camellia Soc. (pres. 1988-94). Independent. Office: T H Perkins Furniture 520 Brookway Blvd Brookhaven MS 39601-3267

PERKINS, THOMAS JAMES, venture capital company executive; b. Oak Park, Ill., Jan. 7, 1932; s. Harry H. and Elizabeth P.; m. Gerd Thune-Ellefsen, Dec. 9, 1961; children: Tor Kristian, Elizabeth Siri. B.S.E.E., M.I.T., 1953; M.B.A., Harvard U., 1957. Gen. mgr. computer div. Hewlett Packard Co., Cupertino, Calif., 1965-70, dir. corp. devel., 1970-72; gen. partner Kleiner & Perkins, San Francisco, 1972-80; sr. ptnr. Kleiner Perkins Caufield & Byers, San Francisco, from 1980; chmn. bd. Tandem Computers, Inc., Cupertino, Calif.; chmn. bd. Tandem Computers, Genentech; dir. Spectra Physics., Corning Glass Works, Collagen Corp., LSI Logic Corp., Hybritech Inc., Econics Corp., Vitalink Communications Corp. Author: Classic Supercharged Sports Cars, 1984. Trustee San Francisco Ballet, 1980—. Mem. Nat. Venture Capital Assn. (chmn. 1981-82, pres. 1980-81). Clubs: N.Y. Yacht, Links, Am. Bugatti (pres. 1983—). Office: Tandem Computers Inc 10435 Tantau Ave Cupertino CA 95014-3548 also: Genentech Inc 460 Point San Bruno Blvd South San Francisco CA 94080-4918*

PERKINS, THOMAS KEEBLE, oil company researcher; b. Dallas, Jan. 31, 1932; s. James Thomas and Willie Fae (Keeble) P.; m. Anita Aliene Smith, July 20, 1963; children—Julia, Stephen. B.S., Tex. A&M U., 1952, M.S., 1953; Ph.D., U. Tex., 1957. Engr. Dow Chem. Co., Freeport, Tex., 1952; instr., asst. prof. U. Tex., Austin, 1955-57; from research engr. to disting. research adviser ARCO Exploration and Prodn. Tech., Plano, Tex., 1957-94, ret., 1994; trustee S.W. Rsch. Inst., San Antonio, 1994—, Dickinson Pl. Charitable Corp., Dallas, 1995—. Contbr. numerous articles to profl. jours.; patentee in field. Recipient Atlantic Richfield Tech. Achievement award, 1980, 90, 91. Mem. Soc. Petroleum Engrs. (C.K. Ferguson award com. 1973-75, Disting. lectr. 1977-78, Lester C. Uren award 1978, J. F. Carrl award com. 1984-86, tech. editor jour. 1981-84, J.F. Carrl award 1993), Nat. Acad. Engring. Republican. Methodist.

PERKINS, VAN L., university administrator, educator, conservationist; b. Standardville, Utah, May 22, 1930; s. Howard Edward and Maude (Larsen) P.; m. Colleen Campbell, Feb. 14, 1951 (div. Aug. 1984); children: Mark E., Cheryl, Scott C., Brett C., Regan; m. Katherine Marie Bennett, Jan. 17, 1986. BA, U. Utah, 1956; MA, Harvard U., 1958, PhD, 1966. Purchasing agt. Bechtel Corp., San Francisco, 1951-55; instr. to asst. prof. Brigham Young U., Provo, Utah, 1960-64; asst. prof. U. Calif., Riverside, 1964-68; assoc. prof. U. Calif., 1968-73, prof., 1973-91, prof. emeritus, 1991—; assoc. dean Grad. Sch. U. Calif., Riverside, 1971-73; vice chancellor U. Calif., Riverside, 1973-78, exec. vice chancellor, 1987-88; cons. in higher edn. mgmt., 1977—, mus. orgn. and mgmt., 1982. Author: Crisis in Agriculture, 1969; contbr. articles to profl. jours. Mgr. U.S. Senatorial and Ho. Reps. Campaigns, Dem., Utah and Calif., 1962, 64, 80; mem. adv. com. U.S. Commn. on Civil Rights, 1978-84; conservation chair Santa Fe group Sierra Club, 1992-94; polit. chair Rio Grande chpt. Sierra Club, 1993, 94, exec. com. chair, 1996—. With U.S. Army, 1950-52. Recipient George Emory Fellows prize U. Utah, 1956, Edwards Meml. prize Agrl. History Soc., 1965; Danforth fellow, 1956, co, 1962-64. Mem. ACLU, Sierra Club, Southern Utah Wilderness Alliance, Audubon Soc., Wilderness Soc., Phi Beta Kappa, Phi Kappa Phi. Democrat. Home: RR 19 Box 128H Santa Fe NM 87505-9347 Office: 621 Old Santa Fe Trl Santa Fe NM 87501-4588

PERKINS, WHITNEY TROW, political science educator emeritus; b. Boston, Feb. 28, 1921; s. Wesley Trow and Hazel Alice (Mason) P.; m. Kathryn A. Sylvester, June 28, 1947; children—Rebecca, Mason, Wesley, Rachel. A.B., Tufts U., 1942; Ph.D., Fletcher Sch. Law and Diplomacy, 1948. Asst. prof. internat. relations U. Denver, 1948-53; from assoc. prof. to prof. polit. sci. Brown U., Providence, 1953-84; chmn. Internat. Relations Concentration, Brown U., 1955-84; cons. U.S.-P.R. Commn. on Status of Puerto Rico, 1965. Author: Denial of Empire: The United States and its Dependencies, 1962; Constraint of Empire: The United States and Caribbean Interventions, 1981. Served to capt. USAF, 1942-45, PTO. Recipient Fulbright Research award, 1951-52. Mem. Am. Polit. Sci. Assn., Internat. Studies Assn., Phi Beta Kappa. Democrat. Avocations: tennis; squash; hiking. Home: 11 Catalpa Rd Providence RI 02906-2614

PERKINS, WILLIAM CLINTON, company executive; b. Decatur, Ill., Mar. 7, 1920; s. Glen Rupert and Frances Lola (Clinton) P.; m. Eunice Cagle, Sept. 7, 1939 (div. 1954); stepchildren: William Rea Cagle, Howard Christy Cagle; 1 child, Clinton Colcord; m. Lillian Wuollet, Sept. 7, 1955 (div. 1965); m. Shirley Thomas, Oct. 24, 1969. BS Mil. Sci. and Meteorology, U. Md., 1954; MS in Bus. and Pub. Adminstrn., Sussex Coll., Eng., 1975. Commd. USAF, 1943-73, advanced through grades to col.; with Ship Systems div. Litton Ind., Culver City, Calif., 1973-75; dir. material Hughes Aircraft Co., Tehran, Iran, 1974-78; mgr. internat. s/c Northrop Corp., Dahran, Saudi Arabia, 1978-81; dir. materiel CRS, Riyadh, Saudi Arabia, 1981-83; head major subcontracts Lear Ziegler Corp., Santa Monica, Calif., 1984-88; pres., chmn. bd., CEO Snowtech, Inc., L.A., 1984—; bd. dirs. Ice Village Ctrs., Inc., L.A., Forefront Industries, Maywood, Calif. Bd. dirs. World Children's Transplant Fund, L.A., 1987-95; mem. Mayor's Space Adv. Com., L.A., 1970-74; mem. aerospace hist. com. Mus. Sci. and Industry, L.A., 1988—. Mem. AIAA (sec. chmn. 1970), Ret. Officers Assn. (pres. 1992-95), Soc. for Non-destructive Testing (program chmn. 1973), Am. Soc. Quality Control, Am. Meterol. Soc., Sigma Alpha Epsilon (alumni chpt. pres. 1974-76). Avocations: golf, scuba diving, sailing, flying, gardening. Home: 8027 Hollywood Blvd Los Angeles CA 90046-2510

PERKINS, WILLIAM H., JR., finance company executive; b. Rushville, Ill., Aug. 4, 1921; s. William H. and Sarah Elizabeth (Logsdon) P.; m. Eileen Nelson, Jan. 14, 1949; 1 child, Gary Douglas. Ed., Ill. Coll. Pres. Howlett-Perkins Assos., Chgo.; mem. Ill. AEC, 1963-84, sec., 1970-84; mem. adv. bd. Nat. Armed Forces Mus., Smithsonian Instn., 1964-82. Sgt.-at-arms Democratic Nat. Conv., 1952, 56, del.-at-large, 1964, 68, 72; spl. asst. to chmn. Dem. Nat. Com., 1960; mem. Presdl. Inaugural Com., 1961, 65, 69, 73. Served with U.S. Army, 1944-46. Mem. Ill. Ins. Fedn. (pres. 1965-84), Ill. C. of C. (chmn. legis. com. 1971), Chgo. Assn. Commerce and Industry (legis. com., Raoul Wallenberg Humanitarian award 1993), Sangamo Club, Masons, Shriners. Methodist. Home: 52 N Cowley Rd Riverside IL 60546-2042 Office: 19 Riverside Rd Ste 6 Riverside IL 60546-2237

PERKINSON, DIANA AGNES ZOUZELKA, interior design firm import company executive; b. Prostejov, Czechoslovakia, June 27, 1943; came to U.S., 1962; d. John Charles and Agnes Diana (Sincl) Zouzelka; m. David Francis Perkinson, Mar. 6, 1965; children: Dana Leissa, David. BA, U. Lausanne (Switzerland), 1960; MA, U. Madrid, 1961; MBA, Case Western Res. U., 1963; cert. internat. mktg. Oxford (Eng.) U., 1962. Assoc. Allen Hartman & Schreiber, Cleve., 1963-64; interpreter Tower Internat. Inc., Cleve., 1964-66; pres. Oriental Rug Importers Ltd., Cleve., 1979—; pres. Oriental Rug Designers, Inc., Cleve., 1980—; pres. Oriental Rug Cons., Inc., Cleve., 1980—; chmn. Foxworthy's Inc., Ft. Myers, Naples, Sanibel, Fla.; bd. dir. Beckwith & Assocs., Inc., Cleve., Secura Inc., Dallas, Dix-Bur Investments, Ltd., Real Estate By Design. Trustee, Cleve. Ballet, 1979, exec. com., 1981; mem. Cleve. Mayor's Adv. Com.; trustee Diabetes Assn. Greater Cleve.; mem., chmn. grantsmanship Jr. League of Cleve., 1982; mem. mem. Cleve. Found.-Women in Philanthropy, 1982; trustee Ft. Myers Symphony, 1990. Mem. Women Bus. Owners Assn., Oriental Rug Retailers Am. (bd. dir. 1983), Cleve. Racquet Club, Recreation League, The League Club (Naples, Fla.), Hillbrook Club, Univ. Club (Ft. Myers, Fla.), Captiva Yacht Club. Republican. Roman Catholic. Home: Ravencrest PO Box 477 Sanibel FL 33957-0477 Office: Foxworthys Inc 2430 Periwinkle Way Sanibel FL 33957-3207 also: 17001 Captiva Rd Captiva Island FL 33924

PERKINS SENN, KARON ELAINE, lawyer; b. Lexington, Ky., Nov. 9, 1959; d. John Robert and Sharon Lynn (Cook) Perkins; m. F. Anthony Senn. BA, Purdue U., 1980; cert. of proficiency, Pushkin Inst. Russian Lang., Moscow, 1980; JD, Ind. U., 1983. Bar: Ind. 1984, U.S. Dist. Ct. (so. dist.) Ind. 1984, U.S. Dist. Ct. (no. dist.) Ind. 1990. Internt. mktg. specialist Ind. Dept. Commerce, Indpls., 1980-81; law clk. Mendelson, Kennedy, Miller, Muller & Hall, Indpls., 1981-83; assoc. Jewell, Crump & Angermeier, Columbus, Ind., 1983-86; ptnr. Dalmbert, Marshall & Perkins, Columbus, 1986-92; pvt. practice Columbus, Ind., 1992—; asst. city atty. City of Columbus, 1985-95; town atty. Town of Hope (Ind.), 1987-89; course coord. law for non lawyers Ind. U.-Purdue U., Columbus, 1985-95; course coord. inst. law Sr. Citizen Crt., Columbus, 1990; author, speaker continuing legal edn. seminar, 1988, 89, 90, 91, 92, 94, 96; bd. dirs., sec. Bartholomew Area Legal Aid, 1984-96. Mem. Leadership Bartholomew County, Columbus, 1986; bd. dirs. Salvation Army, Columbus, 1986-92, Columbus Dance Workshop; chmn. Bartholomew County Young Reps., 1986-88, 2d dist. Young Reps., 1987-91; treas. Columbus Task Force on Poor Relief, 1985-90. Recipient Outstanding Female Young Rep., Ind. Young Rep. Fedn., 1987, cert. of appreciation Ind. Tsk Force on Poor Relief, 1987; faculty alumni fellow Ind. U., 1983. Mem. ABA (del. young lawyers div. 1986-87), Ind. Bar Assn. (council, bd. dirs. young lawyers sect., sec.-treas., chair), Bartholomew Bar Assn. (sec., sec.-treas. 1984-90), Ind. Assn. Trial Lawyers, Columbus Jayshees (v.p. 1986, Outstanding New Mem. award 1985), Columbus Jaycees (bd. dirs. 1987), Zonta Club (parliamentarian Columbus 1986-88), Kiwanis. Baptist. Avocations: hiking, reading, sports. Home: 15830 E Lakeshore Dr N Ct Hope IN 47246 Office: 404 Washington St Ste 201 Columbus IN 47201-6786

PERKO, WALTER KIM, computer consultant; b. Mpls., Dec. 8, 1950; s. Eero Nestor and Margie (Hanson) P. AS in Computer Sci./Math./Aeronautics, U. Minn., 1975. Contract computer analyst/cons. Dept. Def., Dept. Justice, NASA and pvt. industry; systems operator The Home Multi Media Hobbyst BBS, San Francisco, 1987-95; owner Natural Digital Musical Productions, San Francisco. Author: This Is America, 1991, EarthCom, 10, 000 Sounds & Songs of the Digital Data Archives, 1993, MegaMODMadNess. With USN, 1968-72, Korea and Vietnam. Mem. Soc. Automotive Engring. Lutheran. Avocations: writing music, playing violin, acoustic guitar and keyboard synthesizer, flying antique airplanes and aerobatics.

PERKOFF, GERALD THOMAS, physician, educator; b. St. Louis, Sept. 22, 1926; s. Nat and Ann (Schwartz) P.; m. Marion Helen Maizner, June 7, 1947; children: David Alan, Judith Ilene, Susan Gail. M.D. cum laude, Washington U., 1948. Intern Salt Lake City Gen. Hosp., 1948-49, resident, 1950-52; from instr. to asso. prof. medicine U. Utah, 1954-63; chief med. service Salt Lake VA Hosp., 1961-63; asso. prof., then prof. medicine Washington U. Sch. Medicine, St. Louis, 1963-79; chief Med. Service, St. Louis City Hosp., 1963-68, prof. preventive medicine and pub. health, dir. div. health care research, 1968-79; Curators prof. and assoc. chmn. dept. family and community medicine and prof. medicine U. Mo., Columbia, 1979-91, Curators prof. emeritus, 1991—; co-dir. program health care and human values U. Mo., 1984-85; chmn. nat. adv. com. Robert Wood Johnson Clin. Scholars Program, 1989-96; dep. dir. Robert Wood Johnson Found. Generalist Physician Initiative, 1991—; career rsch. prof. neuromuscular diseases Nat. Found. Neuromuscular Diseases, 1961; founder, dir. Med. Care Group of Washington U., 1968-78. Contbr. articles profl jours. Served as jr. asst. surgeon USPHS, 1953-54. John and Mary R. Markle scholar med. sci., 1955-60; Henry J. Kaiser Sr. fellow Ctr. Advanced Studies in Behavioral Sci., Stanford, 1976-77, 85-86. Mem. Am. Soc. Clin. Investigation, Soc. Tchrs. Family Medicine, Assn. Am. Physicians, Inst. Medicine (Nat. Acad. Scis.). Home: 1300 Torrey Pines Dr Columbia MO 65203-4826 Office: U Mo Sch Medicine Dept Family & Community Medicine M228 Med Scis Columbia MO 65212

PERKOVIC, ROBERT BRANKO, international management consultant; b. Belgrade, Yugoslavia, Aug. 27, 1925; came to U.S., 1958, naturalized, 1961; s. Slavoljub and Ruza (Pantelic) P.; m. Jacquelyn Lee Lipscomb, Dec. 14, 1957; children: Bonnie Kathryn, Jennifer Lee. M.S. in Econs, U. Belgrade, 1954; B.F.T., Am. Grad. Sch. Internat. Mgmt., 1960; grad. Stanford exec. program, Stanford U., 1970. Auditor Gen. Foods Corp., White Plains, N.Y., 1960-62; controller Gen. Foods Corp., Mexico City, 1962-64; dir. planning Monsanto Co., Barcelona, Spain, 1964-67; dir. fin. Monsanto Co., Europe, Brussels, 1967-70; dir. fin. planning-internat. Monsanto Co., St. Louis, 1970-71; asst. treas. Monsanto Co., 1971-72, Brussels, 1972-74; corp. treas. Fiat-Allis Inc. & BV, Deerfield, Ill., 1974-78; v.p., treas. TRW Inc., Cleve., 1978-88; pres. RBP Internat. Cons., Cleve., 1988—; dir. U.S. Bus. Coun. for Southeastern Europe, Inc. Active Cleve. Commn. on Fgn. Relations. Inc. Served with Yugoslavian Army, 1944-47. Mem. Fin. Execs. Inst., Cleve. Treas. Club (bd. dirs., pres.), Latin Am. Bus. Assn. (co-founder), Mayfield Village (Ohio) Racquet Club. Office: RBP Internat Cons 26 Pepper Creek Dr Cleveland OH 44124-5248

PERKOWITZ, SIDNEY, physicist, educator, author; b. Bklyn., May 1, 1939; s. Morris and Sylvia (Gray) P.; m. Sandra Price; 1 child, Michael Abram. BS, N.Y. Poly., N.Y.C., 1960; MS, U. Pa., 1962, PhD, 1967. Rsch. physicist Gen. Telephone & Electronics Labs., Bayside, N.Y., 1966-69; asst. prof. physics Emory U., Atlanta, 1969-74, assoc. prof., 1974-79, prof., 1979-87, Charles Howard Candler prof., 1987—, chmn. dept., 1980-83; vis. prof. U. Calif.-Santa Barbara, 1983-84; cons. Santa Barbara Rsch. Ctr., 1983-87, Nat. Rsch. Coun. Can., Ottawa, 1988-91, NIST, Gaithersburg, Md., 1990-94; vis. scientist Southeastern Univs. Rsch. Assn., Washington, 1990-91; adj. prof. humanities Atlanta Coll. Arts, 1989—; mem. adv. panel Exptl. Gallery, Smithsonian Inst., Washington. Author: Optical Characterization of Semiconductors, 1993, Empire of Light, 1996; editor, contbr. numerous articles and essays to newspapers and mags. Grantee Sloan Found. Rsch. Corp., AEC, NIH, NSF, Office Naval Rsch., U.S. Dept. Energy, U.S. Dept. Def., TRW Corp., Korea Inst. Sci. and Tech., Lockheed Corp., Oak Ridge Nat. Lab. Mem. AAAS, Am. Phys. Soc., Soc. for Lit. and Sci. (v.p.), Phi Beta Kappa. Avocations: movies, crossword puzzles, music, hiking. Office: Emory U Rollins Rsch Ctr Physics Dept Atlanta GA 30322-2430

PERKOWSKI, JAN LOUIS, language and literature educator; b. Perth Amboy, N.J., Dec. 29, 1936; m. Liliana Asenova Daskalova, May 24, 1989. AB, Harvard U., 1959, AM, 1960, PhD, 1965. Asst. prof. U. Calif., Santa Barbara, 1964-65; assoc. prof. U. Tex., Austin, 1965-74; prof. U. Va., Charlottesville, 1974—. Author: A Kashubian Idiolect in U.S., 1969, Vampires, Dwarves & Witches Among the Ontario Kashubs, 1972, Vampires of the Slavs, 1976, Gusle & Ganga Among the Hercegovinians of Toronto, 1978, The Darkling-A Treatise on Slavic Vampirism, 1989; contbr. more than 50 articles to jours. Grantee, fellow Ford Found., Harvard U., Kościuszko Found., U. Tex., Am. Philos. Soc., Nat. Mus. Man, U. Va., NEH, Kennan Inst., I.R.E.X., Fulbright, numerous others. Mem. Am. Assn. for the Advancement of Slavic Studies, Am. Assn. Tchrs. of Slavic and East European Langs., Slavic and East European Folklore Assn. Office: U Va Dept Slavic Langs & Lits 109 Cabell Hall Charlottesville VA 22903

PERKOWSKI, MAREK ANDRZEJ, electrical engineering educator; b. Warsaw, Poland, Oct. 6, 1946; came to U.S., 1981; s. Adam Perkowski and Hanna (Zielinska) Mystkowska; m. Ewa Kaja Wilkowska, Oct. 26, 1974; 1 child, Mateusz Jan. MS in Electronics with distinction, Tech. U. Warsaw, 1970, PhD in Automatics with distinction, 1980. Sr. asst. Inst. Automatics, Tech. U. Warsaw, 1973-80, asst. prof., 1980-81; vis. asst. prof. dept. elec. engring. U. Minn., Mpls., 1981-83; assoc. prof. elec. engring. Portland (Oreg.) State U., 1983-94, prof., 1994—. Co-author: Theory of Automata, 3d edit., 1976, Problems in Theory of Logic Circuits, 4th edit., 1986, Theory of Logic Circuits-Selected Problems, 3d edit., 1984; contbr. 134 articles to profl. jours., 11 chpts. to books. Mem. Solidarity, Warsaw, 1980-81. Recipient Design Automation award SIGDA/ACM/DATC IEEE, 1986-91; Rsch. grantee NSF, 1991, 94, Commn. for Familites Roman Cath. Ch., Vatican, 1981, Air Force Office Sci. Rsch., 1995. Mem. IEEE (Computer Soc.), Polish Nat. Alliance, Assn. for Computing Machinery, Am. Soc. for Engring. Edn. Roman Catholic. Avocations: tourism, philosophy, woodcarving. Home: 15720 NW Perimeter Dr Beaverton OR 97006-5391 Office: Portland State U Dept Elec Engring PO Box 751 Portland OR 97207-0751

PERKOWSKI, PAUL JAMES, accountant; b. Glen Ridge, N.J., Feb. 19, 1956; s. Benjamin and Adele P.; m. Beth Vasselli, Sept. 17, 1978; children: Thomas, Katelyn. BS, Montclair State Coll., 1978. CPA. Auditor, sr. tax mgr. Ernst & Young, Hackensack, N.J.; ptnr. Perkowski & Assocs., CPAs, Spring Lake, N.J.; presenter in field. Mem. AICPA, Inst. Mgmt. Accts., N.J. Soc. CPAs, Internat. Assn. Fin. Planning (bd. dirs. 1988-94), Spring Lake C. of C. Roman Catholic. Office: Perkowski & Assocs CPAs 302 Washington Ave Spring Lake NJ 07762-1432

PERL, ANDRAS, immunologist, educator, scientist; b. Budapest, Hungary, Sept. 20, 1955; came to U.S., 1985; s. Miklos and Ibolya (Molnar) P.; m. Katalin Banki, July 23, 1983; children: Annamaria, Marcel Adam, Daniel Peter. MD, Semmelweis Med. Sch., Budapest, 1979, PhD, 1984. Resident, fellow Semmelweis U. Med. Sch., 1979-84, asst. prof., 1984-85; cancer rsch. fellow U. Rochester, N.Y., 1985-88; sr. instr. dept. medicine U. Rochester, 1988-89; asst. prof. dept. microbiology and immunology SUNY, Buffalo, 1989-92; cancer rsch. scientist Roswell Park Cancer Inst., Buffalo, 1989-92; assoc. prof. medicine, microbiology & immunology SUNY, Syracuse, 1992—; presenter, lectr. in field. Contbr. articles to profl. publs. Grantee Am. Lupus Soc., 1994. Wilmot Cancer Rsch. fellow, 1985-88; recipient Arthritis Investigator award Arthritis Found., 1989—, Am. Lupus Soc. award, 1995, grant NIH, 1996—, grant Pardee Found. Cancer Rsch., 1991—, grant Nat. Multiple Sclerosis Soc., 1995—. Mem. Am. Assn. Immunologists, N.Y. Acad. Scis., Clin. Immunology Soc. Achievements include discovery of new human endogenous retrovial sequence first to encode protein, cloning of human transaldolase gene, appearing to be involved in autoimmunity and tumorigenesis. Office: SUNY Health Sci Ctr Coll of Medicine 750 E Adams St Syracuse NY 13210-2306

PERL, MARTIN LEWIS, physicist, educator; b. N.Y.C., June 24, 1927; children: Jed, Anne, Matthew, Joseph. B.Chem. Engring., Poly. Inst. Bklyn., 1948; Ph.D., Columbia U., 1955; ScD (hon.), U. Chgo., 1990. Chem. engr. Gen. Electric Co., 1948-50; asst. prof. physics U. Mich., 1955-58, asso. prof., 1958-63; prof. Stanford, 1963—. Author: High Energy Hadron Physics, 1975, Reflections on Experimental Science, 1996; contbr. articles on high energy physics and on relation of sci. to soc. to profl. jours. Served with U.S. Mcht. Marine, 1944-45; Served with AUS, 1945-46. Recipient Wolf prize in physics, 1982, Nobel Prize in Physics, 1995. Fellow Am. Phys.

Soc.; mem. Nat. Acad. Scis., Am. Acad. Arts & Scis. Home: 3737 El Centro Ave Palo Alto CA 94306-2642 Office: Stanford U Stanford Linear Accelerator Ctr Stanford CA 94305

PERLBERG, JULES MARTIN, lawyer; b. Chgo., Jan. 28, 1931; s. Maurice and Louise Mae (Schonberger) P.; m. Dora Ann Morris, Dec. 22, 1968; children: Julia, Michael. BBA with high distinction, U. Mich., 1952, JD with high distinction, 1957. Bar: Ill. 1958, D.C. 1964; C.P.A., Ill. Acct. Arthur Andersen & Co., Chgo., 1954-55; faculty U. Mich. Law Sch., Ann Arbor, 1957-58; assoc. Sidley & Austin and predecessor firm, Chgo., 1958-65, ptnr., 1966—. Mem. Glencoe (Ill.) Bd. Edn., 1980-87, pres., 1985-86; bd. dirs. Juvenile Diabetes Found., Chgo., 1981—, v.p. 1983-85, treas., 1988-90; exec. bd. Am. Jewish Com., Chgo., 1978-88, v.p., 1981-83; trustee New Trier Twp. Schs., 1987-91, pres., 1989-91; class co-chairperson parents com. Duke U., 1992-94. 1st lt. U.S. Army, 1952-54. Recipient Gold medal Ill. Soc. C.P.A.s, 1955. Mem. ABA, Chgo. Bar Assn. Clubs: Legal, Law; Mid-Day (Chgo.); Standard. Home: 568 Westley Rd Glencoe IL 60022-1071 Office: Sidley & Austin 1 First Natl Plz Chicago IL 60603-2003

PERLE, EUGENE GABRIEL, lawyer; b. N.Y.C., Dec. 21, 1922; s. Philip and Simme (Meschenberg) P.; m. Ellen Carlotta Kraus, Nov. 26, 1953 (dec. 1964); 1 child, Elizabeth Perle McKenna; m. Ruth Friedberg Lerner, May 23, 1972 (div. 1977); m. Patricia Fitzpatrick Sinnott, Jan. 24, 1981. BA, Queens Coll., 1943; JD, Yale U., 1949. Bar: N.Y. 1950, Conn. 1995. Assoc. Cravath, Swaine & Moore, N.Y.C., 1949-53; asst. counsel N.Y. State Moreland Commn. Investigation Harness Racing, N.Y.C., 1953-54; assoc. Gordon, Brady, Caffrey & Keller, N.Y.C., 1954-56; assoc. gen. atty. Time Inc., N.Y.C., 1956-66; pub. counsel Time Inc., 1966-73, v.p. law, 1973-80, corp. v.p. law, 1980-85; counsel Proskauer Rose Goetz & Mendelsohn, N.Y.C., 1985-92, Chapman & Fennell, 1992-94; mem. Ohlandt, Greeley, Ruggiero & Perle, Stamford, Conn., 1995—. Co-author: The Publishing Law Handbook, 1988-97; mem. editl. bd. Yale Law Jour., 1948-49; mem. adv. bd. Bur. Nat. Affairs Patent, Trademark and Copyright Jour., 1972-86; contbr. to Bull. Copyright Soc. U.S.A. Trustee Baron deHirsch Fund, 1959-87, hon. trustee, 1988—; commr. Nat. Commn. New Technol. Uses Copyrighted Works, 1975-78; bd. dirs. N.Y. Sch. for Circus Arts, Inc., 1979-87, Am. Arbitration Assn., 1979-84; justice of peace City of Norwalk, Conn., 1960-63. Lt. USNR, 1943-46. Mem. ABA (chmn. copyright divsn. 1970-71, 86-87, chmn. com. copyright and new tech. 1971-73, chmn. com. econs. profession 1976, coun. patent, trademark and copyright sect. 1979-83, governing bd. forum com. comms. law 1979-85, chmn. related fields and future devels. divsn. forum com. entertainment and sports industries 1979), Copyright Soc. U.S.A. (trustee 1962-64, 69-70, 71-74, pres. 1976-78, hon. trustee 1978—), U.S. Trademark Assn. (bd. dirs. 1969-72, 74-77, v.p. 1972-73), Assn. of Bar of City of N.Y., Sunningdale Country Club, Century Assn. Club, Adms. Cove Club. Democrat. Office: Ohlandt Greeley One Landmark Sq Stamford CT 06901

PERLE, GEORGE, composer; b. Bayonne, N.J., May 6, 1915; s. Joseph and Mary (Sanders) Perlman; m. Laura Slobe, 1940; m. Barbara Philips, Aug. 11, 1958 (dec.); children: Kathy, Annette; 1 stepchild, Max Massey; m. Shirley Gabis Rhoads, June 6, 1982; stepchildren: Paul Rhoads, Daisy Rhoads. MusB, DePaul U., 1938; MusM, Am. Conservatory of Music, 1942; Ph.D., NYU, 1956. Mem. faculty U. Louisville, 1949-57, U. Calif., Davis, 1957-61, Juilliard Sch. Music, 1963, Yale U., 1965-66, U. So. Calif., summer 1965, Tanglewood, summers 1967, 80, 87; from asst. prof. to assoc. prof. to prof. CUNY, 1961-85, prof. emeritus, 1985—; composer-in-residence San Francisco Symphony, 1989-91; vis. Birge-Cary prof. music SUNY, Buffalo, 1971-72; vis. prof. U. Pa., 1976, 80, Columbia U., 1979, 83; vis. Ernest Bloch prof. music U. Calif., Berkeley, 1989; vis. disting. prof. music NYU, N.Y.C., 1994. Author: Serial Composition and Atonality 1962, 6th edit., 1991, Twelve-Tone Tonality, 1977, 2d edit., 1996, The Operas of Alban Berg, vol. 1, 1980, vol. 2, 1985, The Listening Composer, 1990, The Right Notes, 1995, Style and Idea in the Lyric Suite of Alban Berg, 1995; contbr. articles in Am., fgn. mus. jours.; composer: Pantomime, Interlude and Fugue, 1937, Little Suite for Piano, 1939, Two Rilke Songs, 1941, Sonata for Solo Viola, 1942, Three Sonatas for Clarinet, 1943, Piano Piece, 1945, Hebrew Melodies for Cello, 1945, Lyric Piece for Cello and Piano, 1946, Six Preludes for Piano, 1946, Sonata for Solo Cello, 1947, Solemn Procession for Band, 1947, Sonata for Piano, 1950, Three Inventions for Piano, 1957, Quintet for Strings, 1958, Wind Quintet I, 1959, Sonata I for Solo Violin, 1959, Wind Quintet II, 1960, Fifth String Quartet, 1960-67, Three Movements for Orchestra, 1960, Monody I for flute, 1960, Music for The Birds of Aristophanes, 1961, Monody II for double bass 1962, Serenade I for Viola and Chamber Ensemble, 1962, Three Inventions for Bassoon, 1962, Sonata II for Solo Violin, 1963, Short Sonata for Piano, 1964, Solo Partita for Violin and Viola, 1965, Six Bagatelles for Orch., 1965, Concerto for Cello and Orch., 1966, Wind Quintet III, 1967, Serenade II for Chamber Ensemble, 1968, Toccata for Piano, 1969, Suite in C for Piano, 1970, Fantasy-Variations for Piano, 1971, Sonata Quasi una Fantasia for Clarinet and Piano, 1972, Seventh String Quartet, 1973, Songs of Praise and Lamentation for chorus and orch. 1974, Six Etudes for Piano, 1976, 13 Dickinson Songs, 1978, Concertino for Piano, Winds, and Timpani, 1979, A Short Symphony, 1980; Ballade for Piano, 1981, Sonata a quattro, 1982, Serenade III for Piano and Chamber Ensemble, 1983, Six New Etudes for Piano, 1984, Wind Quintet IV, 1984, Sonata for Cello and Piano, 1985, Sonatina for Piano, 1986, Sonata a cinque, 1986, Dance Fantasy for Orch., 1986, Lyric Intermezzo for chamber orch., 1987, Lyric Intermezzo for fifteen players, 1987, Lyric Intermezzo for piano, 1987, New Fanfares for brass ensemble, 1987, Sinfonietta, 1987, Windows of Order for string quartet, 1988, Sextet for winds and piano, 1988, Concerto for Piano and Orch., 1990, Sinfonietta II, 1990, Concerto No. 2 for Piano and Orch., 1992, Adagio for Orch., 1992, Transcendental Modulations (commd. for 150 anniversary N.Y. Philharmonic), 1993, Phantasyplay for Piano, 1994, Duos for French horn and string quartet, 1995, Six Celebratory Inventions, 1995. Served with AUS, 1943-46, ETO, PTO. Recipient Nat. Inst. Arts and Letters award, 1977, Pulitzer prize, 1986; Guggenheim fellow, 1966-67, 74-75, MacArthur fellow, 1986; grantee Am. Council Learned Socs., 1968-69, Nat. Endowment for the Arts, 1978-79, 85. Fellow Am. Acad. Arts and Scis.; mem. Am. Musicol. Soc., ASCAP (Deems Taylor award 1973, 78, 81), Am. Acad. Arts and Letters.

PERLE, RICHARD NORMAN, government official; b. N.Y.C., Sept. 16, 1941; s. Jack Harold and Martha Gloria (Needell) P.; m. Leslie Joan Barr, July 31, 1977; 1 child, Jonathan Barr. BA, U. So. Calif., 1964; postgrad. in econs., U. London, 1962-63; MA, Princeton U., 1967. Asst. sec. internat. security policy Dept. Def., Washington, 1981-87; prof. staff mem. subcom. nat. security Senate Com. on Govt. Ops., Washington, 1970-72; profl. staff mem. committee on armed services U.S. Senate, Washington, 1969-80; resident fellow Am. Enterprise Inst. for Pub. Policy Rsch., Washington, 1987—. Office: Am Enterprise Inst Pub Policy Rsch 1150 17th St NW Washington DC 20036-4603*

PERLESS, ELLEN, advertising executive; b. N.Y.C., Sept. 9, 1941; d. Joseph B. and Bertha (Messinger) Kaplan; m. Robert L. Perless, July 2, 1965. Student, Smith Coll., 1958-59; BA, Bard Coll., 1962. Copywriter Doyle, Dane Bernbach, N.Y.C., 1964-70, Young & Rubicam, N.Y.C., 1970-74; creative supr. Young & Rubicam, 1974-76, v.p., creative supr., 1977, v.p., assoc. creative dir., 1978, sr. v.p., assoc. creative dir., 1979-84; v.p., assoc. creative dir. Leber Katz Ptnrs., 1984-85, sr. v.p., creative dir., 1986-87; sr. v.p., sr. creative dir. FCB/Leber Katz Ptnrs., N.Y.C., 1987-93, sr. v.p., group creative dir., 1994—. Recipient Clio awards, Andy awards, awards Art Dirs. Club N.Y., N.Y. Festivals, One Club. Home: 37 Langhorne Ln Greenwich CT 06831-2611 Office: FCB/Leber Katz Ptnrs 150 E 42nd St New York NY 10017-5612

PERLESS, ROBERT L., sculptor; b. N.Y.C., Apr. 23, 1938; s. Meyer and Ethel (Glassman) P.; m. Ellen R. Kaplan, July 2, 1965. Student, U. Miami, Fla., 1955-59. One-man exhbns. include Bodley Gallery, N.Y.C., 1968, 70, Galerie Simonne Stern, New Orleans, 1969, Bernard Danenberg Gallery, N.Y.C., 1970-72, Bonino Gallery, N.Y.C., 1976; group exhbns. include Bodley Gallery, 1970, Whitney Mus., 1970, Forum Gallery, N.Y.C., 1975, Bonino Gallery, 1975, Houston Gallery, 1976, Aldrich Mus., Ridgefield, Conn., 1978, Taft Mus., Cin., 1980, Aldrich Mus., 1987, 94, Stamford (Conn.) Mus., 1989, Bruce Mus., Greenwich, Conn., 1989, Andre Emmerich's Top Gallant Farm, 1991, 92, 93, 94, 95, 96; represented in permanent collections at Whitney Mus., Aldrich Mus., Chrysler Mus., Norfolk, Va., Everson Mus., Syracuse, N.Y., Okla. Art Ctr., Oklahoma City, Phoenix Art Mus., Stamford (Conn.) Mus. Address: 37 Langhorne Ln Greenwich CT 06831-2611

PERLICK, LILLIAN, counselor, therapist; b. Bklyn., Mar. 19, 1928; d. Harry and Rose Kravitz; m. Wallace Perlick; children: Wendy, Wynn, David. BS, Bklyn. Coll., 1949; MS, Hunter Coll., 1962. Cert. guidance counselor, N.Y.C., 1963. Tchr. Pub. Sch. #83, Bklyn., 1949-58, acting asst. prin., 1958-59; guidance counselor Elmont (N.Y.) Meml. H.S., 1959-61; therapist, pvt. practice Great Neck, N.Y., 1970-87; career counselor Nassau (N.Y.) Pub. Librs., 1977-79; cons. parent edn. Great Neck Pub. Schs., 1980-81; asst. dir. Womanspace in Great Neck, 1980-84, dir., 1984-86; counselor, therapist Ctr. Group Counseling, Boca Raton, Fla., 1996—; empathic counselor, fed. grant to Hunter Coll., 1961; exec. dir. Discovery Seminars Assn., Syosset, N.Y., 1980-82. Co-author: Grown Up Children, Grown Up Parents, 1994. Bd. dirs. Copay-Cmty. Clinic, Great Neck, 1981-85. Recipient spl. recognition Town of North Hempstead, Nassau County, N.Y., 1994. Mem. NOW, Poverty Law Ctr., Edgar Cayce Inst., Planned Parenthood, Women in the Arts (charter), Sci. of Mind. Avocations: tennis, golf, skiing, bridge, sculpting, dance. Home: 19750 Sawgrass Dr Boca Raton FL 33434

PERLICK, RICHARD ALLAN, steel company executive; b. Chgo., June 23, 1947; s. Allan Arthur and Lorraine Perlick; m. Sharon Behrendt, Mar. 29, 1969; children: Jill Sharon, Timothy Richard, David Matthew. BS in Metall. Engring., Mich. Tech. U., 1969. Corrosion engr. CarTech Specialty Steel Corp., Reading, Pa., 1969-71; nondestructive test engr. CarTech Specialty Steel Corp., Union, N.J., 1971-75; quality control sr. engr. heavy products AlTech Specialty Steel Corp., Watervliet, N.Y., 1975-78; gen. supt. bar finish AlTech Specialty Steel Corp., Dunkirk, N.Y., 1978-79, sr. supr. metallurgist rod mill, 1979-86, mgr. product metallurgy, 1986-87, wire mill supt., 1987-89, sr. product metallurgist, 1989-90; gen. mgr. Techalloy Co.-Union (Ill.) Wire Plant, Ill., 1990-94; dir. corp. metall. svcs. Techalloy Co., Inc., Union, Ill., 1994-96, v.p. metallurgy, 1997—. Patentee in field. Cubmaster, scoutmaster Boy Scouts Am., Fredonia, N.Y., 1982-90; mem. ch. choir St. Paul Luth., Dunkirk, 1980-82. Recipient Pres.'s Scoutmaster's award Boy Scouts Am., 1988. Mem. Am. Soc. for Materials, Wire Assn. Internat., Am. Soc. Surface Finishing, Kiwanis. Republican. Avocations: vegetable gardening, woodworking, fishing, golfing, family camping. Home: 1758 Woodhaven Dr Crystal Lake IL 60014-1940 Office: Techalloy Co Olson And Jefferson St Union IL 60180

PERLIK, WILLIAM R., lawyer; b. Pitts., May 20, 1925; s. Charles A. and Teresa Anna (Kraft) P.; m. Annabel Virginia Shanklin, June 16, 1949; children—Ronald A., Lynn C. B.A., Oberlin Coll., 1948; J.D., Yale U., 1951. Bar: D.C. 1952, Va. 1955, U.S. Supreme Ct. 1974. Law clk. to judge U.S. Ct. Appeals, Washington, 1951-52; assoc., then ptnr. Cox Langford Stoddard & Cutler, Washington, 1952-62; ptnr., of counsel Wilmer Cutler & Pickering, Washington, 1962—; adj. prof. politics and econs. Oberlin Coll., Ohio, 1973—. Trustee, chmn., mem. exec. com. Oberlin Coll., 1980—; pres. Va. Sch. Bd. Assn., 1971-72; mem. and chmn. Fairfax County Sch. Bd., Va., 1964-72; pres. Fairfax County Fedn. Citizens Assns., 1958. Served with U.S. Army, 1943-46; ETO. Recipient Edn. award Fairfax Edn. Assn., 1960; Citizen of Yr. award Washington Evening Star, 1961. Mem. ABA. Avocations: music, gardening. Home: 1249 Daleview Dr Mc Lean VA 22102-1538 Office: Wilmer Cutler & Pickering 2445 M St NW Washington DC 20037-1435

PERLIN, ARTHUR SAUL, chemistry educator; b. Sydney, N.S., Can., July 7, 1923; s. Benjamin and Eva (Gaum) P.; m. Ruth Laurel Freedman, Nov. 18, 1950; children—Anna, Louise, Deborah, Myra, David. B.Sc., McGill U., Can., 1944, M.Sc., 1946, Ph.D., 1949. Research officer Nat. Research Council Can., Ottawa, Ont., Can., 1948-67; E.B. Eddy prof. chemistry McGill U., Montreal, Que., Can., 1967-91, prof. chemistry emeritus, 1991—; research scientist Pulp and Paper Research Inst. Can., Montreal, Que., 1967—. Contbr. articles to profl. jours., chpts. to books; patentee in field. Fellow Royal Soc. Can., Chem. Inst. Can.; mem. Am. Chem. Soc. (C.S. Hudson award 1979). Office: McGill U, Dept Chemistry, Montreal, PQ Canada H3A 2K6

PERLIN, SEYMOUR, psychiatrist, educator; b. Passaic, N.J., Sept. 27, 1925; s. Samuel and Fanny (Horowitz) P.; m. Ruth Joan Rudolph, Aug. 21, 1958; children: Jonathan Brian, Steven Michael, Jeremy Francis. Student, Johns Hopkins U., 1943-44; B.A. summa cum laude, Princeton U., 1946; M.D., Columbia U., 1950; grad., Washington Psychoanalytic Inst. Diplomate Am. Bd. Psychiatry and Neurology. Intern Univ. Hosp., Ann Arbor, Mich., 1951-52; resident N.Y. State Psychiat. Inst., 1950-51, 53-54, Manhattan State Hosp., 1952; practice medicine specializing in psychiatry and psychoanalysis Bethesda, Md., 1954-59, Stanford, Calif., 1959-60, N.Y.C., 1960-63, Balt., 1964-72, Bethesda, 1974—; chief div. psychiatry Montefiore Hosp., 1960-63; dir. clin. care and tng. Henry Phipps Psychiat. Clinic, Johns Hopkins Hosp., 1964-72; sr. research scholar Ctr. for Bioethics, Kennedy Inst., Georgetown U., Washington, 1974-78; clin. prof. psychiatry UCLA Sch. Medicine, 1973-74; clin. prof. psychiatry George Washington U. Sch. Medicine, 1974-76, prof. to prof. emeritus, 1977-97, 97—, also dir. residency tng., 1977-93; lectr. psychiatry Columbia U., 1963-64; assoc. prof. psychiatry Johns Hopkins Sch. Medicine, 1964-65, prof., 1966-72, dep. chmn. dept. psychiatry and behavioral scis., 1969-72; program dir. Fellowship Program in Suicidology, 1967-72; adv. council Univ. health services Princeton, 1970-82; vis. fellow Princeton U., 1973, Oxford U., 1974; Joseph P. Kennedy fellow medicine, law and ethics, 1974-75; chief sect. psychiatry Lab. Clin. Sci., NIMH, 1955-59, mem. clin. program-project com., 1967-70; fellow Ctr. Advanced Study in Behavioral Scis., 1959-60; chmn. mental health study sect. B, div. research grants NIH, 1964-66; cons. Community Mental Health Services, Md. Dept. Mental Hygiene, 1964-72; chmn. bd. dirs. Youth Suicide Nat. Ctr., 1985-87. Cons. editor: Jour. Suicide and Life Threatening Behavior, 1970-89; editorial bd.: Johns Hopkins Med. Jour, 1970-72; editor: Handbook for the Study of Suicide; co-editor: Ethical Issues in Death and Dying; contbr. numerous articles to med. jours. Served with USNR, 1944-46, with USPHS, 1954-58. Recipient Meirhoff award in pathology, 1950, Bicentennial Silver medal for achievement in psychiatry, 1967, both Coll. Phys. and Surg. Columbia. Fellow Am. Psychiat. Assn.; mem. Am. Coll. Psychiatry, Washington Psychoanalytic Soc., Med. Soc. D.C., Washington Psychiat. Soc., Am. Assn. Suicidology (pres. 1969-70, Dublin award 1978, ann. lectureship in suicidology in his name George Washington U. 1995). Home: 5125 Westbard Ave Bethesda MD 20816-1413 Office: Dept Psychiatry George Washington U Sch Medicine 2150 Pennsylvania Ave NW Washington DC 20037

PERLIS, DONALD M., artist; b. N.Y.C., July 29, 1941; s. Herman and Sylvia M. (Marks) P.; m. Theresa Brown, June 9, 1968. Student, Art Students League, 1961, Sch. Visual Arts, N.Y.C., 1965, Skowhegan Sch., 1965. One-man show Sindin Gallery, N.Y.C., 1994, 95, Walter Wickiser Gallery, N.Y.C., 1996-97; exhibited in group shows Whitney Mus., N.Y.C., Graham Gallery, 1971, 75, Sindin Galleries, 1993, 95, Charas-Elbohio, 1993; documentary film on artist produced by Time Capsule Films, 1993; author: (monograph) Allegories of Love, 1995. Mem. NAD. Home: 105 E 9th St New York NY 10003-5401

PERLIS, MICHAEL FREDRICK, lawyer; b. N.Y.C., June 3, 1947; s. Leo and Betty F. (Gantz) P.; children: Amy Hannah, David Matthew; m. Angela M. Rinaldi, Dec. 23, 1988. BS in Frgn. Svc., Georgetown U., 1968, JD, 1971. Bar: D.C. 1971, N.Y. 1993, U.S. Dist. Ct. D.C. 1971, U.S. Ct. Appeals 1971, D.C. Ct. Appeals 1971, Calif. 1980, U.S. Dist. Ct. (no. dist.) Calif. 1980, U.S. Dist. Ct. (cen. dist.) Calif. 1985, U.S. Ct. Appeals (9th cir.) 1980, U.S. Supreme Ct., 1980, N.Y. 1993. Law clerk D.C. Ct. Appeals, Washington, 1971-72; asst. corp. counsel D.C., Washington, 1972-74; counsel U.S. SEC, div. enforcement, Washington, 1974-75, br. chief, 1975-77, asst. dir., 1977-80; ptnr. Pettit & Martin, San Francisco, 1980-89, Stroock & Stroock & Lavan, L.A., 1989—; adj. prof. Cath. U. Am., 1979-80. Mem. ABA (co-chmn. subcom. securities and commodities litigation 1982-83), D.C. Bar Assn., Calif. State Bar Assn. Office: Stroock & Stroock & Lavan 2029 Century Park E Los Angeles CA 90067-2901

PERLIS, MICHAEL STEVEN, magazine publisher; b. Feb. 12, 1953; s. Sanford and Vivian (Lee) P.; m. Marilyn Dunlap, May 5, 1979; children: Morgan, Steve. BA in Psychology, Syracuse U., 1976. Mktg. dir. Bretton Woods (N.H.) Resort, 1976-78; exec. dir. Mt. Washington Valley C. of C., North Conway, N.H., 1978-80; pub. N.H. Profiles mag., N.Eng. Guide Rumford Nat. Graphics, Concord, N.H., 1980-81; v.p., pub. New Eng. Pubs., Camden, Maine, 1981-82, pres., 1982-84; pub. spls. Rodale Press, Inc., Emmaus, Pa., 1984-85, pub. Runners World mag., 1985-86, group pub., 1986-87; pres. Internat. Data Group, Peterborough, N.H., 1987-89; sr. v.p., pub. Playboy Enterprises, Chicago, 1989-90, sr. v.p., pres. - publishing group, 1990-92, exec. v.p., pres. - publishing group, 1992-94; pub. Details mag., 1994—; pres., pub. Cable Guide, N.Y.C. Mem. Mag. Pubs. Am. (exec. com. 1989—), Young Pres. Org., 1990—. *

PERLIS, SHARON A., lawyer; b. New Orleans; d. Rogers I. and Dorothy (Koehl) P. BA in French, Principia Coll., 1967; JD, Tulane U., 1970. Officer, dir. Perlis, Inc., New Orleans, 1973—; pres. SILREP Internat. Co., Metairie, 1984-97; officer, dir. Internat. Adv. Svcs., Inc., New Orleans, 1985-89; prin. Perlis & Hogg, Metairie, 1985-97; legal counsel La. Ins. Rating Commn., 1980-84; adminstrv. law judge State of La., 1980-84, mem. Econ. Devel. Adv. Coun., 1982-84; dir. The Chamber/New Orleans and The River Region, 1990-97, Bd. of Trade, 1990-97, exec. com. small bus. coun., 1987-89, chmn. small bus. coun., 1988, exec. com. East Jefferson coun., 1989-96; dir. World Trade Co., 1985-96, vice-chmn. internat. bus. com.; dir. New Orleans br. Fed. Res. Bank of Atlanta, 1982-88, chmn., 1984, 86, 88; bd. of commr. Port of New Orleans, 1992-97, vice chmn., 1995, chmn., 1996; del. Joint Civilian Orientation Conf., 1997. Mem. human rels commn. City of New Orleans, 1992-93; mem. exec. bd. La. Coun. Econ. Edn., 1986-89, Pvt. Enterprise Edn. Found., 1986-89; state del. White House Conf. on Small Bus., La. rep. internat. trade issues, 1986; dir. Metro YMCA, 1990-97; exec. com. agy. rels. United Way, 1987-90; mem. exec. com. Jr. Achievement Project Bus., 1987; vice chmn. La. Dist. Export Coun. Recipient Achiever's award Woman Bus. owners Assn., 1994, Jefferson Econ. Devel. Commn. award, 1994, Advocacy of Yr. award Small Bus. Adminstrn., 1988. Mem. Phi Alpha Eta. Avocations: reading, sailing, tennis. Office: Perlis & Hogg 3421 N Causeway Blvd Ste 404 Metairie LA 70002-3722

PERLMAN, BARRY STUART, electrical engineering executive, researcher; b. Bklyn., Dec. 5, 1939; s. Harold Wallace and Jane (Cohen) P.; m. Carolyn Amelia Francis; 1 child, David Matthew. BEE, CCNY, 1961; MSEE, Poly. Inst. N.Y., 1964, PhD in Electrophysics, 1973. Mem. tech. staff, comms. lab. RCA Corp., N.Y.C., 1961-68; mem. tech. staff RCA Labs., Princeton, N.J., 1968-81, mgr. microwave rsch. lab., 1981-86, head design automation rsch., 1986-88; chief microwave photonic devices br. Electronics and Power Source Directorate, Army Rsch. Lab., Ft. Monmouth, N.J., 1988-95; dir. electronics divsn. Phys. Scis. Directorate, Army Rsch. Lab., Ft. Monmouth, 1995-96; chief RF and electronics divsn. Sensor and Electron Devices Directorate, Army Rsch. Lab., Ft. Monmouth and Adelphi, Md., 1996-97; RDEC staff CECOM, Ft. Monmouth, 1997—; pres., mem. bd. dirs. INTEREX, Los Altos, Calif., 1981-83; rep. adv. group on electron devices, chmn. subpanel on RF Components, Office of Indersec. of Def.; chmn, Computational Electronics and Nanoelectronics, HPCMO, 1995—; mem. tech. adv. bd. MURI, Ctr., Photonic Band Gap Devices, UCLA, U. R.I., Ctr. High Frequency Microelectronics, U. Mich.; mem. ind. adv. bd. Computer Applications to Electromagnetics Edn., NSF and U. Utah, 1990—, MIMICAD Ctr., U. Colo., 1989—; Ctr. prof. microwave/lighwave engrng. Drexel U., Phila., 1992—. Editor: Advances in Microwaves, 1974; mem. editl. bd. Wiley Jour. MW.MMW CAD, 1992—; contbr. articles to profl. jours.; patentee in field. Bd. dirs. YMCA, Princeton, 1975-78; pres. Home Owners Assn., E. Windsor, N.J., 1976-78; instr. Am. Heart Assn., N.J., 1978-82; chief rescue squad, E. Windsor, 1978-82. Fellow IEEE (awards and advancement com. 1987—); mem. Microwave Theory and Tech. Soc. of IEEE (editl. bd., chmn. CAD com. MTT-1 1985-92, MTT adcom. 1990-94, chmn. Intersoc. Liaison, 1995—, others), Ultrasonics, Ferroelectrics and Frequency Control, Cirs. and Sys., Automated RF Techniques Group (treas. 1984-88, v.p. 1990-91). Avocations: scouting, woodworking, photography, camping, gardening, tennis. Office: Army Rsch Lab AMSRL-PS-E Fort Monmouth NJ 07703-5000

PERLMAN, BURTON, judge; b. New Haven, Dec. 17, 1924; s. Phillip and Minnie Perlman; m. Alice Weihl, May 20, 1956; children: Elizabeth, Sarah, Nancy, Daniel. B.E., Yale U., 1945, M.E., 1947; LL.B., U. Mich., 1952. Bar: Ohio, 1959, N.Y. 1953, Conn. 1952, U.S. Dist. Ct. (so. and ea. dists.) N.Y. 1954, U.S. Ct. Appeals (2d cir.) 1953, U.S. Ct. Appeals (6th cir.) 1959, U.S. Dist. Ct. (so. dist.) Ohio 1959. Assoc. Armand Lackenbach, N.Y.C., 1952-58; pvt. practice, Cin., 1958-61; assoc. Paxton and Seasongood, 1961-67; ptnr. Schmidt, Effton, Josselson and Weber, 1968-71; U.S. magistrate U.S. Dist. Ct. (so. dist.) Ohio, 1971-76; U.S. bankruptcy judge, 1976—; chief bankruptcy judge so. dist. Ohio, 1986-93; adj. prof. U. Cin. Law Sch., 1976—. Served with U.S. Army, 1944-46. Mem. ABA, Fed. Bar Assn., Am. Judicature Soc., Cin. Bar Assn. Office: US Bankruptcy Ct 221 E 4th St Cincinnati OH 45202-4124

PERLMAN, D(AVID), biochemist, educator; b. Madison, Wis., Feb. 6, 1920; s. Selig and Eva (Shaber) P.; m. Kató Lenárd, Aug. 18, 1968. B.A., U. Wis., 1941, M.S., 1943, Ph.D., 1945. Biochemist Hoffmann-LaRoche, Inc., 1945; microbiologist Merck & Co., 1945-47; biochemist Squibb Inst. for Med. Research, 1947-67; prof. Sch. Pharmacy, U. Wis., Madison, 1967—, dean, 1968-75; Chmn. 3d Internat. Congress Genetics of Indsl. Microorganisms, 1968-75, Kremers prof. pharm. biochemistry, 1979—; chmn. Conf. on Antimicrobial Agts. and Chemotherapy, 1966, 67, Gordon Research Conf. on Coenzymes and Metabolic Pathways, 1966. Editor: Advances Applied Microbiology, 1968—, Ann. Reports Fermentation Processes, 1977—; Contbr. articles to profl. jours. Guggenheim fellow, 1966. Fellow Am. Acad. Microbiology, N.Y. Acad. Scis., Acad. Pharm. Scis.; mem. Am. Chem. Soc. (Disting. Service award div. microbiol and biochem. tech. 1977, Marvin J. Johnson award (same div. 1978), Am. Soc. Microbiology (pres. found. 1974-75, Fisher Sci. Co. award 1979, Pasteur award Ill. sect. 1979), Am. Soc. Pharmacognosists, Tissue Culture Assn., Soc. for Gen. Microbiology, Am. Pharm. Assn., Am. Soc. Biol. Chemistry, Biochem. Soc., Soc. for Indsl. Microbiology (Charles Thom award 1979), Sigma Xi. Home: 1 Chippewa Ct Madison WI 53711-2803

PERLMAN, DAVID, science editor, journalist; b. Balt., Dec. 30, 1918; s. Jess and Sara P.; m. Anne Salz, Oct. 15, 1941; children: Katherine, Eric, Thomas. A.B., Columbia U., 1939, M.S., 1940. Reporter Bismarck (N.D.) Capital, 1940; reporter San Francisco Chronicle, 1940-41, reporter, sci. editor, 1952-77, city editor, 1977-79, assoc. editor, sci. editor, 1979—; reporter New York Herald Tribune, Paris, N.Y.C., 1945-49; European corr. Colliers mag. and New York Post, 1949-51; Regents prof. human biology U. Calif., San Francisco 1974; vis. lectr. China Assn. Sci. and Tech., Beijing, Chengdu and Shanghai, 1983; sci. writer-in-residence U. Wis., 1989. Contbr. articles to major mags. Founding dir. Squaw Valley (Calif.) Community of Writers; dir. Alan Guttmacher Inst., 1985—; trustee Scientists Inst. for Pub. Info., 1986-94. Served with inf. USAAF, 1941-45. Recipient Atomic Indls. Forum award, 1975, AAAS Sci. Writing award, 1976, Ralph Coates Roe medal ASME, 1978, Margaret Sanger Cmty. Svc. award, 1981, Fellows' medal Calif. Acad. Scis., 1984, Career Achievement award Soc. Profl. Journalists, 1989, Glenn T. Seaborg award Internat. Platform Assn., 1993; Poynter fellow Yale U., 1984, Carnegie Corp. fellow Stanford U., 1987. Fellow Calif. Acad. Scis.; mem. AAAS (adv. bd. Science-81-86 mag., com. Pub. Understanding of Sci. 1985-90), Coun. for Advancement Sci. Writing (pres. 1976-80), Nat. Assn. Sci. Writers (pres. 1970-71, Disting. Sci. Journalism award 1994), Astron. Soc. Pacific (dir. 1976-78), Sigma Xi. Office: Chronicle Pub Co 901 Mission St San Francisco CA 94103-2905

PERLMAN, ITZHAK, violinist; b. Tel Aviv, Aug. 31, 1945; s. Chaim and Shoshana P.; m. Toby Lynn Friedlander, 1967; 5 children. Student, Tel Aviv Acad. Music, Juilliard Sch., Meadowmount Sch. Music.; hon. degree in music, Tufts U., 1986. Appeared with N.Y. Philharm., Cleve. Orch., Phila. Orch., Nat. Symphony Orch., most orchs. in U.S., with Berlin Philharm., English Chamber Orch., London Symphony, London Philharm., Royal Philharm., BBC Orch., Vienna Philharm, Israel Philharmonic, Concertgebouw; participant numerous music festivals, including Ravinia Festival, Berkshire Music Festival, Aspen Music Festival, Israel Festival, Wolf Trap Summer Festival, recital tours, U.S., Can., S.Am., Europe, Israel, Australia,

Far East; recorded for Angel, London, RCA Victor, DG, CBS records. Recipient Leventritt prize 1964. Recipient Leventritt prize, 1964, Grammy awards, 1977, 78, 80-82, 87, Award - Medal of Liberty, 1986; hon. doctorates from Harvard U., Yale U, Brandeis U., Hebrew U.-Jerusalem, Brown. Address: EMI Classics/Angel Records care CEMA Distrs 21700 Oxnard St Ste 700 Woodland Hills CA 91367-3666 Address: IMG Artists 420 West 45th St New York NY 10036*

PERLMAN, LAWRENCE, business executive; b. St. Paul, Apr. 8, 1938; s. Irving and Ruth (Mirsky) P.; m. Linda Peterson; children: David, Sara. BA, Carleton Coll., 1960; JD, Harvard U., 1963. Bar: Minn. 1963. Law. clk. for fed. judge, 1963; assoc., ptnr. Fredrikson & Byron, Mpls., 1964-75; gen. counsel, exec. v.p. U.S. pacing ops. Medtronic, Inc., Mpls., 1975-78; sr. ptnr. Oppenheimer, Wolff & Donnelly, Mpls., 1978-80; sec., gen. counsel, v.p. corp. svcs. Control Data Corp., Mpls., 1980-82; pres. Comml. Credit Co., 1983-85, Imprimis Technology, 1985-88; pres., chief oper. officer Control Data Corp., Mpls., 1989; pres., chief exec. officer Control Data Corp. (now Ceridian Corp.), 1990-92; chmn., pres., CEO Ceridian Corp., Mpls., 1992—; bd. dirs. Ceridian Corp., Carlson Cos., Inc., Seagate Tech., Inc., The Valspar Corp., Computer Network Tech.; mem. nat. adv. bd. Chem. Banking Corp. Chmn., bd. dirs. Walker Art Ctr.; regent Univ. of Minn., 1993-95. Mem. Bus. Roundtable (mem. policy com.). Office: Ceridian Corp 8100 34th Ave S Minneapolis MN 55425-1672

PERLMAN, MARK, economist, educator; b. Madison, Wis., Dec. 23, 1923; s. Selig and Eva (Shaber) P.; m. Naomi Gertrude Waxman, June 7, 1953; 1 child, Abigail Ruth Williams. B.A., M.A., U. Wis., 1947; Ph.D., Columbia, 1950. Asst. prof. U. Hawaii, 1951-52, Cornell U., 1952-55; asst. prof., then assoc. prof. Johns Hopkins U., 1955-63; prof. econs., history and pub. health U. Pitts., 1963-94, chmn. dept., 1965-70, univ. prof., 1969-94, prof. emeritus, 1994—; co-chmn. Internat. Econ. Assn. Conf. on Econs. of Health in Industrialized Nations, Tokyo, Japan, 1973, Conf. on Orgn. and Retrieval Econs. Data, Kiel, West Germany, 1975; vis. fellow Clare Hall U. Cambridge, 1977; ofcl. visitor faculty econs. and politics, U. Cambridge, 1976-77; co-chmn., co-editor Internat. Congress on Health Econs., Leyden, The Netherlands, 1980; mem. Princeton Inst. Adv. Study, 1981-82; adj. scholar Am. Enterprise Inst., 1981—; Österreichischer Länderbank Joseph Schumpeter prof. Technische Universität, Vienna, 1982; disting. vis. scholar Beijing Chinese Nat. Acad. Social Scis., 1983; Rockefeller Found. resident scholar Villa Serbelloni, Bellagio, Como, Italy, 1983; vis. prof. Inst. für Weltwirtschaft U. Kiel, 1987, U. Augsburg, 1992, U. Chemnitz, 1996; mem. Internat. Com. for Documentation in the Social Scis., UNESCO, 1988-94, exec. com. 1993-94. Author: Judges in Industry: A Study of Labor Arbitration in Australia, 1954, Labor Union Theories in America, 1958, 2d edit., 1976, The Machinists: A New Study in American Trade Unionism, 1962, (with T.D. Baker) Health Manpower in a Developing Economy, 1967; editor: The Economics of Health and Medical Care, 1974, The Organization and Retrieval of Economic Knowledge, 1977, (with G.K. MacLeod) Health Care Capital: Competition and Control, 1978, (with K. Weiermair) Studies in Economic Rationality: X-Efficiency Examined and Extolled, 1990, (with A. Heertje) Evolving Technology and Market Structure: Studies in Schumpeterian Economics, 1990, (with N.H. Ornstein) Political Power and Social Change: The United States Faces a United Europe, 1991; (with C.E. Barfield) Capital Markets and Trade: The United States Faces a United Europe, 1991, Industry, Services, and Agriculture: The U.S. Faces a United Europe, 1991; Political Power and Social Change: The United States Faces a United Europe, 1991; (with F.M. Scherer), Entrepreneurship, Technological Innovation, and Economic Growth: Studies in Schumpeterian Economics, 1992, (with Yuichi Shionoya) Innovations in Technology Industries and Institutions, 1994, Schumpeter in the History of Ideas, 1994, (with Ernst Helmstadter) The Character of Economic Thought, Economic Characters and Economic Institutions, 1996, Behavioral Norms, Technological Progress, and Economic Dynamics, 1996; also articles, essays on health, population change, econ. devel., orgn. econ. knowledge and methodology, econ. productivity, history of econ. discipline; Festschrifts (Sir John Barry, Edgar M. Hoover), 1972; editor: series Cambridge Surveys of Contemporary Economics 1977-94, Cambridge Surveys of Economic Institutions and Policies, 1991-96; cons. editor, later editorial cons. USIA publ., Portfolio on Internat. Econ. Perspectives, 1972-83; mng. co-editor Jour. Evolutionary Econs., 1989-96; corr. Am. editor Revue d'Economie Politique, 1990—; series editor Great Economists of the World, 1990-96. With U.S. Army, 1943-46. Social Sci. Research Council fellow, 1949-50; Ford Found. fellow, 1962-63; Fulbright lectr. Melbourne U., 1968. Mem. Am. Econ. Assn. (founding and mng. editor Jour. Econ. Lit. 1968-81), Royal Econ. Soc., Internat. Union Sci. Study Population, History Econs. Soc. (v.p. 1979-80, pres. elect 1983-84, pres. 1984-85), J.A. Schumpeter Gesselschaft (editor 1986-96), Phi Beta Kappa. Jewish. Club: Athenaeum (London). Home: 5622 Bartlett St Pittsburgh PA 15217-1514

PERLMAN, MATTHEW SAUL, lawyer; b. Washington, Aug. 30, 1936; s. Jacob and Helen (Aronson) P.; m. Julia Gertrude Hawks, June 22, 1966; children—Penelope Leah, Deborah Jane, Sarah Louise, Jacob Henry. A.B., Brown U., 1957; LL.B., Harvard U., 1960. Bar: D.C. 1960, Md. 1960, U.S. Supreme Ct. 1965. Atty. Air Force Gen. Counsel's Office, Washington, 1960-65; mem. Armed Services Bd. of Contract Appeals, Washington, 1965-67; gen. counsel Pres.' Commn. on Postal Orgn., Washington, 1967; asst. gen. counsel Dept. Transp., Washington, 1967-69; ptnr. Arent, Fox, Kintner, Plotkin & Kahn, Washington, 1969—; mem. Pres. Reagan's Transition Team for GSA, Washington, 1980-81; mem. adv. bd. Fed. Contracts Report, Washington, 1969—; overseas corr. Internat. Constn. Law Rev., London, 1983—. Contbr. articles to profl. jours. Pres. Civic Assn. River Falls, Potomac, Md., 1975-77; mem. Montgomery County Md. Citizens Adv. Commn. for Rock Run AWT Plant, 1979-85. Served to capt. USAF, 1960-63. Mem. ABA (pub. contracts sect.), Fed. Bar Assn., Cosmos Club. Republican. Jewish. Home: 10517 Stable Ln Potomac MD 20854-3867 Office: Arent Fox Kintner Plotkin & Kahn 1050 Connecticut Ave NW Washington DC 20036

PERLMAN, RICHARD WILFRED, economist, educator; b. Mt. Vernon, N.Y., Dec. 15, 1923; s. Uriel and Annie (Feitelberg) P.; m. Irma Lowenthal, Sept. 18, 1949; children: Abel, David, Laura, Jennifer. AB, Cornell U., 1947; PhD, Columbia U., 1953. Asst. prof. econs. Adelphi U., Garden City, N.Y., 1953-57; assoc. prof. Adelphi U., 1957-64; prof. econs. U. Wis., Milw., 1964—, chmn. dept., 1965-68, 74-77; NRC prof. Brookings Instn., 1958-59; Fulbright lectr. Inst. Politecnico Nacional, Mexico City, 1964, Autonomous U. Madrid, 1972. Author: Economics of Education, 1973, Labor Theory, 1969, Economics of Poverty, 1976, (with others) An Anthology of Labor Economics, 1972, Economics of Unemployment, 1984, Issues in Labor Economics, 1989, Sex Discrimination in the Labor Market, 1994. Mem. President's Com. on EEO, 1963. Rsch. fellow U. Melbourne, Australia, 1985, hon. rsch. fellow U. Birmingham, 1990-93, sr. fellow, 1993-98; Fulbright rsch. scholar, Australia, 1987. Mem. Am. Econ. Assn., Indsl. Relations Research Assn., Phi Beta Kappa. Home: 3341 N Summit Ave Milwaukee WI 53211-2930

PERLMUTH, WILLIAM ALAN, lawyer; b. N.Y.C., Nov. 21, 1929; s. Charles and Roe (Schneider) P.; m. Loretta Kaufman, Mar. 14, 1951; children: Carolyn, Diane. AB, Wilkes Coll., 1951; LLB, Columbia U., 1953. Bar: N.Y. 1954. Assoc. Cravath, Swaine & Moore, N.Y.C., 1955-61; ptnr. Stroock & Stroock & Lavan, N.Y.C., 1962—; bd. dirs. Sentry Tech. Corp., Hauppauge, N.Y. Editor Columbia U. Law Rev., 1952-53. Trustee Aeroflex Found., N.Y.C., 1965—, City Ctr. 55th St. Theater Found., 1995—, Harkness Founds. for Dance, N.Y.C., 1976—, Wilkes U., Wilkes-Barre, Pa., 1980—, Weininger Found., 1985—, NYU Med. Ctr., 1995—; trustee Hosp. for Joint Diseases Orthopaedic Inst., N.Y.C., 1980—, chmn. bd. trustees, 1994—. Mem. N.Y. State Bar Assn., Assn. of Bar of City of N.Y., Harmonie Club. Jewish. Home: 880 Fifth Ave New York NY 10021-4951 Office: Stroock & Stroock & Lavan 7 Hanover Sq New York NY 10004-2616

PERLMUTTER, ALVIN HOWARD, television and film producer; b. Poughkeepsie, N.Y., Mar. 24, 1928; s. Fred and Jennie (Albert) P.; children: James F., Stephen H., Tom W. Student, Colgate U., 1945-47; B.A., Syracuse U., 1949. Dir. pub. affairs Sta. WNBC, also Sta. WNBC-TV, N.Y.C., 1957-59; program mgr. Sta. WNBC-TV, 1959-61; exec. producer Nat. Edtl. TV, 1961—; v.p. news documentaries NBC, from 1975; pres. Alvin H. Perlmutter Inc., N.Y.C.; instr. TV news and pub. affairs NYU, 1957, Fairleigh Dickinson U., 1962; cons. John and Mary Markle Found., Pub. Agenda Found.; chmn. Dore Schary Awards for film and TV, Anti-Defamation League. Producer: series Assignment America; Great American Machine, Consumer Reports Presents, Money Matters, Cover Story, Black Journal; various spl. programs including: Native Land, The Primal Mind, Adam Smith's Money World series, Family Computing series, Priceless Treasures of Dresden, The Perpetual People Puzzle; exec. producer: Report From Philadelphia, The Secret Government, The Power of Myth. Chair Dore Schary awards, Anti-Defamation League; bd. dirs. N.Y. Open Ctr. 1st lt. AUS, 1950-53. Recipient various citations and awards including 6 Emmy awards, Peabody award, Robert Kennedy award. Mem. Acad. TV Arts and Scis. (gov. N.Y. chpt., nat. trustee, chmn. awards com. 1968), Assn. Pub. TV Producers (chmn. 1969). Clubs: Overseas Press (N.Y.C.), University; Coffee House. Home: 27 W 86th St New York NY 10024-3615 Office: 45 W 45th St New York NY 10036-4602

PERLMUTTER, DAVID H., physician, educator; b. Bklyn., May 11, 1952; s. Herman Arthur and Ruth (Jacobs) P.; m. Barbara Ann Cohlan, Feb. 7, 1981; children: Andrew, Lisa. BA, U. Rochester, 1974; MD, St. Louis U., 1978. Intern then resident in pediatrics U. Pa. Sch. Medicine, Phila., 1978-81; fellow in pediatric gastroenterology Harvard U. Sch. Medicine, Boston, 1981-84, instr. pediatrics, 1983-85, asst. prof. pediatrics, 1985-86; Donald Strominger prof. of pediatrics Washington U. Sch. Medicine, St. Louis, 1986-89, prof. cell biology, physiology, 1989—. Editor: Pediatric Rsch., 1990—; editl. bd. Gastroenterology, 1990—; dir. divsn. gastrology and nutrition and pediatrics; contbr. articles to profl. jours. Recipient Established Investigator award Am. Heart Assn., 1987, Rsch. Scholar award Am. Gastroent. Assn., 1985, RJR Nabisco Co., 1986. Mem. Soc. Pediatric Rsch. (coun. rep. 1990—), Am. Soc. Cell Biology, Am. Soc. Clin. Investigation. Home: 6344 Wydown Blvd Saint Louis MO 63105-2213 Office: Washington U Sch Medicine Dept Pediatrics 400 S Kingshighway Blvd Saint Louis MO 63110-1014*

PERLMUTTER, DIANE F., communications executive; b. N.Y.C., Aug. 31, 1945; d. Bert H. and Frances (Smith) P. Student, NYU Grad. Sch. of Bus., 1969-70; AB in English, Miami U., Oxford, Ohio, 1967. Writer sales promotion Equitable Life Assurance, N.Y.C., 1967-68; BA de Garmo, Inc., N.Y.C., 1968-69, asst. account exec., 1969-70, account exec., 1970-74, v.p., account supr., 1974-76; mgr. corp. advt. Avon Products, Inc., N.Y.C., 1976-79, dir. communications Latin Am., Spain, Can., 1979-80, dir. brochures, 1980-81, dir. category merchandising, 1981-82, group dir. motivational communications, 1982-83, group dir. sales promotion, 1983-84, v.p. sales promotion, 1984, v.p. internat. bus. devel., 1984-85, area v.p. Latin Am., 1985, v.p. advtg. and campaign mktg., 1985-87, v.p. U.S. operational planning, 1987; cons. N.Y.C., 1987-88; sr. v.p. Burson-Marsteller, N.Y.C., 1988-90, exec. v.p., mng. dir. consumer products, 1991-93, bd. dirs., 1992—, co-chief operating officer, 1993-94, chief operating officer, 1994—; chmn. mktg. practice/U.S., 1996—; chairperson ann. meeting Direct Selling Assn., Washington, 1982; v.p. Nat. Home Fashions League, N.Y.C., 1975-76; adj. instr. SUNY/Fashion Inst. Tech., 1992—; bd. dirs. Double L.P. Industries, Inc. Founding bd. mem. Am. Red Magen David for Israel, N.Y.C., 1970-75; mem. adv. coun. Miami Sch. Bus., 1986—, Miami Sch. Applied Scis., 1978-81. Named to YWCA Acad. Women Achievers, 1996. Mem. Pub. Rels. Soc. Am., Advt. Women of N.Y., Women in Communications, Miami U. Alumni Assn. (pres., chair 1986), Publicity Club N.Y. (bd. dirs. 1994-96), YMCA of Greater N.Y. (bd. dirs. 1996), Beta Gamma Sigma. Avocation: interior design. Office: Burson-Marsteller 230 Park Ave S New York NY 10003-1513

PERLMUTTER, DONNA, music and dance critic; b. Phila.; d. Myer and Bessie (Krasno) Stein; m. Jona Perlmutter, Mar. 21, 1964; children: Aaron, Matthew. BA, Pa. State U., 1958; MS, Yeshiva U., 1959. Music and dance critic L.A. Herald Examiner, 1975-84, L.A. Times, 1984-94, N.Y. Times Contbr., 1994—; dance critic Dance Mag., N.Y.C., 1980—; music critic Opera News, N.Y.C., 1981—, Ovation Mag., N.Y.C., 1983-89, N.Y. Mag., 1995—, L.A. Mag., 1996—, Daily News, L.A., 1996—; panelist, speaker various music and dance orgns. Author Shadowplay: The Life of Antony Tudor, 1991. Recipient Deems Taylor award for excellence in writing on music ASCAP, 1991. Mem. Music Critics Assn. Home: 10507 Le Conte Ave Los Angeles CA 90024-3305

PERLMUTTER, JACK, artist, lithographer; b. N.Y.C., Jan. 23, 1920; s. Morris and Rebecca (Schiffman) P.; m. Norma Mazo, Dec. 24, 1942; children: Judith Faye, Ellen. Staff Dickey Gallery, D.C. Tchrs. Coll., 1951-68, dir., 1962-68, prof. art; prof. art, chmn. printmaking dept. Corcoran Gallery Art, Washington, 1960-82; resident artist St. Olaf Coll., Minn., Gibbs Art Gallery, Charleston, S.C., Mus. Sch. Art, Greenville, S.C.; vis. prof. art U. Costa Rica, San Jose, 1983; Fulbright research prof. painting and printmaking Tokyo U. Arts, 1959-60; art cons. Pres.'s Com. to Hire Handicapped; now curator exhibits Cosmos Club, Washington. NASA artist for: 1st Saturn V moon rocket, Apollo 6, Apollo 16, Orbiter Columbia (space shuttle), Voyager II; contbg. editor: Art Voices South, 1979-80, Art Voices, 1980-82; numerous one-man shows, U.S. and Tokyo, including: Balt. Mus. Art, Brandeis U., Corcoran Gallery Art, Dintenfass Gallery, N.Y.C., Makler Gallery, Phila., Smithsonian Inst., Yoseido Gallery, Tokyo, C. Troup Gallery, Dallas, Nat. Acad. Scis., 1981, Arts Club Washington, 1981, Annapolis, Md., 1982, and gllleries in Amsterdam, Rotterdam, The Hague and Costa Rica; exhibited nat. shows, U.S., Switzerland, Yugoslavia, traveling exhibits, Europe, S.Am., Can.;permanent collections include Bklyn. Mus., Cin. Mus. Art, Carnegie Inst. Art, Corcoran Gallery Art, Library Congress, Met. Mus. Art, N.Y.C., Nat. Gallery Art, Washington, Phila. Mus. Art, Walker Gallery, Mpls., Nat. Mus. Modern Art, Tokyo, U.S. Embassies in Bucharest, Budapest, Bonn, Dublin, London, Prague, Tokyo, others. Recipient awards for paintings and prints from Balt. Mus. Art, Libr. Congress, Corcoran Gallery Art, Butler Inst. Arts, Smithsonian Inst., Soc. Am. Graphic Artists, First Internat. Exhbn. Fine Arts in Saigon, Mus. Fine Arts in Saigon, Mus. Fine Art, Boston, others. Fellow Internat. Inst. Arts and Letters; mem. Soc. Am. Graphic Artists. Club: Cosmos (Washington). Prints, drawings and biog. data in Art Archives Am. Studio: 2511 Cliffborne Pl NW Washington DC 20009-1511

PERLMUTTER, JEROME HERBERT, communications specialist; b. N.Y.C., Oct. 17, 1924; s. Morris and Rebecca (Shiffman) P.; m. Evelyn Lea Friedman, Sept. 19, 1948; children: Diane Muriel, Sandra Pauline, Bruce Steven. AB cum laude, George Washington U., 1949; MA, Am. U., 1957. Chief editor svc., prodn. editor NEA, Washington, 1949-50; editor in chief Jour. AAHPER, Washington, 1950-51; editor Rural Elec. News, REA, USDA, Washington, 1951-53; publ. writer Agrl. Rsch. Svc., 1953-56; chief, editor br. Office Info., 1956-60; sec. Outlook and Situation Bd., 1960-62; chief econ. reports Econ. Rsch. Svc., 1960-62; chief div. pub. and reprodn. svcs. U.S. Dept. State, Washington, 1962-79; pres. Perlmutter Assocs., 1979—; writing cons. CSC, 1956, World Bank, 1967—; communication cons. European Investment Bank, Can. Internat. Devel. Agy., Inter-Am. Devel. Bank, Internat. Monetary Fund; faculty agr. grad. sch. U. Md., also Fgn. Svc. Inst.; pub. cons. White House Conf. on Children and Youth, 1971. Author: A Practical Guide to Effective Writing, 1965; Contbr. articles profl. jours. Coord. fed. graphics Nat. Endowment for Arts, 1972-79, graphic designer, conv. of maj. polit. com., 1980. With USNR, 1943-46. Recipient award U.S. Jr. C. of C., 1963. Mem. Am. Assn. Agr. Coll. Editors, Assn. Editl. Bus. (bd. dirs.), Fed. Editors Assn., Am. Farm Econ. Assn., Soc. Tech. Comm. (bd. dirs.), Md. Literacy Coun., Soc. Profl. Journalists, Phi Beta Kappa, Phi Eta Sigma, Artus. Home: 15111 Glade Dr Silver Spring MD 20906

PERLMUTTER, LOUIS, investment banker, lawyer; b. Cambridge, Mass., Oct. 3, 1934; s. Kermit H. and Rachel (Ehrlich) P.; m. Barbara Patricia Sondik, Dec. 11, 1966; children: Kermit, Eric. B.A., Brandeis U., 1956; J.D., U. Mich., 1959; LHD (hon.), Brandeis U., 1995. Bar: Mass. 1959, N.Y. 1961. Law practice N.Y.C., 1960-65; asst. to pres. New Eng. Industries, N.Y.C., 1965-67; pres. Octagon Assocs., N.Y.C., 1967-75; sr. v.p. White Weld, N.Y.C., 1975-78; mgn. dir. Merrill Lynch, White, Weld, N.Y.C., 1978; mng. dir. Lazard Freres & Co. LLC, N.Y.C., 1978—. Contbr. articles to profl. and gen. interest publs. Chmn. bd. trustees Brandeis U., Waltham, Mass., 1988-95, Am. Jewish Congress, N.Y.C., 1988-94; chmn. exec. com., bd. govs. UN Assn. USA; chmn. econ. adv. com. US/ME Project of Coun. Fgn. Rels.; mem. Coun. Fgn. Rels., Overseas Devel. Coun., Washington; mem. com. visitors U. Mich. Law Sch. Recipient Human Rels. award Am. Jewish Com., 1995. Mem. Econ. Club of N.Y. Home: 39 E 79th St New York NY 10021-0216 Office: Lazard Freres & Co LLC 30 Rockefeller Plz New York NY 10112

PERLMUTTER, LYNN SUSAN, neuroscientist; b. N.Y.C., Oct. 12, 1954; d. David Louis and Audrey Marilyn (Cherkoss) P.; m. Howard Jay Deiner, May 30, 1976; 1 child, Jocelyn Rae Perldeiner. BA with highest honors, SUNY, Stony Brook, 1976; MA, Mich. State U., 1980, PhD, 1984. Postdoctoral fellow U. Calif., Irvine, 1984-87; asst. prof. neurology and pathology U. So. Calif., L.A., 1987-94, sec. med. faculty assembly, 1990-92, assoc. prof. neurology and pathology, 1994; sci. coord. U. So. Calif. Bravo Med. Magnet H.S. Partnership, 1993-94; staff scientist pharm. divsn. Inst. Dementia Rsch., Bayer Corp., West Haven, Conn., 1994—; ad hoc reviewer John Douglas French Found., L.A., 1988, 91, Calif. Dept. Alzheimer's Disease Program, Sacramento, 1990, 92; mem. neurology rev. panel NIH, 1993, 94; chmn. blood-brain barrier session Internat. Conf. Alzheimer's Disease, Italy, 1992; organizer internat. symposium at Soc. Neuroscientists Africa, 1995; invited spkr. Internat. Alzheimer's Disease Conf., Israel, 1997. Contbr. articles to sci. jours. Coach Conn. state champions problem I, divsn. I, Odyssey of the Mind program, 1996. Travel fellow Internat. Conf. on Alzheimer's Disease, 1990, 92. Mem. AAAS, Soc. Neurosci., Electron Microscopy Soc. Am., Internat. Platform Assn., N.Y. Acad. Scis., Med. Faculty Women's Assn. (chmn. membership 1989-91), Phi Kappa Phi. Democrat. Jewish. Avocations: folk festivals, early and world music, films. Office: Bayer Corp Pharm Divsn Inst Dementia Rsch 400 Morgan Ln West Haven CT 06516-4140

PERLOE, SIDNEY IRWIN, psychologist, primatologist, educator; b. Bklyn., June 21, 1932; s. Herman and Helen (Cutler) P.; m. Judith Gregory, June 9, 1957 (dec. Feb. 1971); children: Deborah, Jonathan; m. Paulette Jellinek, May 20, 1977; children: Alexandra, Gabriel. AB, NYU, 1953; PhD, U. Mich., 1959. Asst. prof. Yale U., New Haven, Conn., 1958-61; asst. prof. Haverford (Pa.) Coll., 1961-64, assoc. prof., 1964-68, prof., 1968—. Contbr. articles to profl. jours. Mem. Am. Psychol. Soc., Am. Soc. Primatologists, Internat. Primatological Soc., Internat. Soc. Human Ethology. Office: Haverford Coll 370 Lancaster Ave Haverford PA 19041-1336

PERLOFF, JEAN MARCOSSON, lawyer; b. Lakewood, Ohio, June 25, 1942; d. John Solomon and Marcella Catherine (Borngen) Marcosson; m. Lawrence Storch, Sept. 8, 1991. BA magna cum laude, Lake Erie Coll., 1965; MA in Italian, UCLA, 1967; JD magna cum laude, Ventura Coll. Law, 1976. Bar: Calif. 1976, U.S. Dist. Ct. (cen. dist.) Calif. 1978. Assoc. in Italian U. Calif.-Santa Barbara, 1967-70; law clk., paralegal Ventura County Pub. Defender's Office, Ventura, Calif., 1975; sole practice, Ventura, 1976-79; coprin. Clabaugh & Perloff, A Profl. Corp., Ventura, 1979-82; sr. jud. atty. to presiding justice 6th div. 2d Dist. Ct. Appeals, L.A., 1982-97; instr. Ventura Coll. Law, 1976-79. Pres., bd. dirs. Santa Barbara Zool. Gardens, 1987-88; bd. trustees Lake Erie Coll., 1993—. Named Woman of Yr., 18th Senatorial dist. and 35th Assembly dist. Calif. Legislature, 1992; recipient Disting. Alumnae award Lake Erie Coll., 1996. Mem. ABA, Calif. Bar Assn. (mem. appellate ct. com. 1993-95), Kappa Alpha Sigma. Democrat. Club: Fiesta City. Avocations: tennis, jogging, biking, reading, music. Home: 1384 Plaza Pacifica Santa Barbara CA 93108-2877

PERLOFF, JOSEPH KAYLE, cardiologist; b. New Orleans, Dec. 21, 1924; s. Richard and Rose (Cohen) P.; m. Marjorie G. Mintz; children: Nancy L., Carey E. BA, Tulane U., 1945; postgrad., U. Chgo., 1946-47; MD, La. State U., New Orleans, 1951; MA (hon.), U. Pa., 1973. Diplomate Am. Bd. Internal Medicine, Am. Bd. Cardiovascular Disease. Intern Mr. Sinai Hosp., N.Y.C., 1951-52, resident in pathology, 1952-53, resident in medicine, 1953-54; Fulbright fellow Inst. Cardiology, London, 1954-55; resident in medicine Georgetown U. Hosp., Washington, 1955-56, fellow in cardiology, 1956-57; from clin. instr. to prof. Georgetown U. Sch. Medicine, Washington, 1957-72, dir. cardiac diagnostic lab., 1959-68, asst. dir. divsn. cardiology, 1968-72; prof. medicine and pediat. U. Pa. Sch. Medicine, Phila., 1972-77, chief cardiovascular sect., 1972-77; prof. medicine and pediatrics UCLA Sch. Medicine, 1977—, Streisand/AMA chair in cardiology, 1983; cons. Nat. Heart, Blood and Lung Inst.; dir. UCLA Adult Congenital Heart Disease Ctr. Author: The Cardiomyopathies, 1988, Physical Exam Heart and Circulation, 1990, Clinical Recognition of Congenital Heart Disease, 1994, Congenital Heart Disease in Adults, 1997; co-author: Congenital Heart Disease After Surgery, 1983. Ensign USN, 1943-46, PTO. Recipient The Best of UCLA award Chancellor's Selection, 1987; Residency Career Devel. award NIH, 1959-69. Fellow ACP, Am. Coll. Cardiology; mem. Am. Fedn. Clin. Rsch., Assn. Univ. Cardiologists, Alpha Omega Alpha. Office: UCLA Sch Medicine Cardiology 47 123 Chs Los Angeles CA 90024

PERLOFF, MARJORIE GABRIELLE, English and comparative literature educator; b. Vienna, Austria, Sept. 28, 1931; d. Maximilian and Ilse (Schueller) Mintz; m. Joseph K. Perloff, July 31, 1953; children—Nancy Lynn, Carey Elizabeth. A.B., Barnard Coll., 1953; M.A., Cath. U., 1956, Ph.D., 1965. Asst. prof. English and comparative lit. Cath. U., Washington, 1966-68; asso. prof. Cath. U., 1969-71; asso. prof. U. Md., 1971-73, prof., 1973-76; Florence R. Scott prof. English U. So. Calif., Los Angeles, 1976—; prof. English and comparative lit. Stanford U., Calif., 1986—, Sadie Dernham prof. humanities, 1990—. Author: Rhyme and Meaning in the Poetry of Yeats, 1970, The Poetic Art of Robert Lowell, 1973, Frank O'Hara, Poet Among Painters, 1977, The Poetics of Indeterminacy: Rimbaud to Cage, 1981, The Dance of the Intellect: Studies in the Poetry of the Pound Tradition, 1985, 2d edit., 1996, The Futurist Moment: Avant-Garde, Avant-Guerre and the Language of Rupture, 1986, Poetic License: Essays in Modern and Postmodern Lyric, 1990, Radical Artifice: Writing Poetry in the Age of Media, 1991, Wittgenstein's Ladder: Poetic Language and the Strangeness of the Ordinary, 1996; editor: Postmodern Genres, 1990; co-editor: John Cage: Composed in America, 1994; contbg. editor: Columbia Literary History of the U.S., 1987; contbr. preface to Contemporary Poets, 1980, A John Cage Reader, 1983. Guggenheim fellow, 1981-82, NEA fellow, 1985; Phi Beta Kappa scholar, 1994-95. Fellow Am. Acad. Arts and Scis.; mem. MLA (exec. coun. 1977-81, Am. lit. sect. 1993—), Comparative Lit. Assn. (pres. 1993-94), Lit. Studies Acad. Home: 1467 Amalfi Dr Pacific Palisades CA 90272-2752 Office: Stanford U Dept English Stanford CA 94305

PERLOFF, ROBERT, psychologist, educator; b. Phila., Feb. 3, 1921; s. Myer and Elizabeth (Sherman) P.; m. Evelyn Potechin, Sept. 22, 1946; children: Richard Mark, Linda Sue, Judith Kay. AB, Temple U., 1949; MA, Ohio State U., 1949, PhD, 1951; DSc (hon.), Oreg. Grad. Sch. Profl. Psychology, 1984; DLitt (hon.), Calif. Sch. Profl. Psychology, 1985. Diplomate Am. Bd. Profl. Psychology. Instr. edn. Antioch Coll., 1950-51; with pers. rsch. br. Dept. Army, 1951-55, chief statis. rsch. and cons. unit., 1953-55; dir. R & D Sci. Rsch. Assos., Inc., Chgo., 1955-59; vis. lectr. Chgo. Tchrs. Coll., 1955-56; mem. faculty Purdue U., 1959-69, prof. psychology, 1964-69; field assessment officer univ. Peace Corps Chile III project, 1962; Disting. Svc. prof. bus. adminstrn. and psychology U. Pitts. Joseph M. Katz Grad. Sch. Bus., 1969-90, Disting. Svc. prof. emeritus, 1991—; dir. rsch. programs U. Pitts. Grad. Sch. Bus., 1969-77; dir. Consumer Panel, 1980-83; bd. dirs. Book Ctr.; cons. in field, 1959—; adv. com. assessment exptl. manpower R & D labs. Nat. Acad. Scis., 1972-74; mem. rsch. rev. com. NIMH, 1976-80, Stress and Families rsch. project, 1976-79. Contbr. articles to profl. jours.; editor Indsl. Psychologist, 1963-65, Evaluator Intervention: Pros and Cons; book rev. editor Personnel Psychology, 1952-55; co-editor: Values, Ethics and Standards Sourcebook, 1979, Improving Evaluations; bd. cons. editors Jour. Applied Psychology; bd. advs. Archives History Am. Psychology, Psychol. Svc. Pitts., Recorded Psychol. Jours.; guest editor Am. Psychologist, 1972, Edn. and Urban Soc., 1977, Profl. Psychology, 1977; adv. editor Contemporary Psychology, 1994—. Bd. dirs., v.p. Sr. Citizens Svc. Corp., Calif. Sch. Profl. Psychology; bd. dirs. Greater Pitts. chpt. ACLU, sec., 1997—; chmn. nat. adv. com. Inst. Govt. and Pub. Affairs, U. Ill., 1986-89, sec. nat. adv. com., 1997—. Decorated Bronze Star; Robert Perloff Grad. Rsch. Assistantship in Inst. Govt. and Pub. Affairs, U. Ill., named in his honor, 1990; Robert Perloff Career Achievement award Knowledge Utilization Soc., named in his honor, 1991. Fellow AAAS, APA (mem.-at-large exec. com. divsn. consumer psychology 1964-67, 70-71, pres. divsn. 1967-68, mem. coun. reps. 1965-68, 72-74, chmn. sci. affairs com., divsn. consumer psychology 1968-69, edn. and tng. bd. 1969-72, chmn.

finance com., treas. 1975-84, dir. 1974-82, chmn. investment com. 1977-82, pres. 1985, mem. adv. bd., mem. bd. sci. affairs 1994-96, mem task force intellegence and Intelligence Tests, author column Standard Deviations in jour.), Ea. Psychol. Assn. (pres. 1980-81, dir. 1977-80); mem. Am. Psychol. Soc., Internat. Assn. Applied Psychology, Pa. Psychol. Assn. (Disting. Svc. award 1985), Assn. for Consumer Rsch. (chmn. 1970-71), Am. Psychol. Found. (v.p. 1988-89, pres. 1990-92, trustee 1995—), Am. Evaluation Assn. (pres. 1977-78), Soc. Psychologists in Mgmt. (Disting. Contbn. to Psychology Mgmt. award 1989, pres. 1993-94), Knowledge Utilization Soc. (pres. 1993-95), Sigma Xi (pres. U. Pitts. chpt. 1989-91), Beta Gamma Sigma, Psi Chi. Home: 815 Saint James St Pittsburgh PA 15232-2112 *Experiment. Innovate responsibly. Take risks judiciously. Do not shrink from new ventures for fear of failure. No one is immune from adversity. The hallmark of a successful achieving person is his or her ability to snap back after misfortune, and to benefit from and not be immobilized by failure.*

PERLONGO, DANIEL JAMES, composer; b. Gaastra, Mich., Sept. 23, 1942; s. James and Camille (Fittante) P. Mus.B. in Composition, U. Mich., 1964, Mus.M., 1966; Corso di Perfezionamento, Accademia di S. Cecilia, Rome, 1968. Assoc. prof. music Indiana (Pa.) U., 1968—. Composer (for orchestra) Myriad, 1968, Ephemeron, 1972, Concertino, 1980, Lake Breezes, 1990, Concerto for Piano and Orchestra, 1992, Shortcut from Bratislava for Piano and Orch., 1994, Sunburst for Clarinet and Orch., 1995, Two Movements, 1996, (chamber orch.) Variations 1973, Voyage, 1975, (chamber music) Improvision for Four, 1965, Improvisation 2, 1966, Eufonia, poetica e sonora, 1966, (string trio) Intervals, 1967, (ensemble pieces) Movement for 8 Players, 1967, Semblance for string quartet, 1969-70, String Quartet II, 1983, (percussion quartet) For Bichi, 1968, Movement in Brass, 1969, (various works) Process 7, 5, 3 for 6 in 12, for flute, oboe, clarinet, 3 percussions, 1969, Tre Tempi for flute, oboe, clarinet, violin, cello, 1971, Fragments for flute and cello, 1972, Structure, Semblance and Tune for tuba and percussion, 1973, (wind ensemble) Changes, 1970, (violin) Violin Solo, 1971, (double bass) Episodes, 1966, (for oboe, clarinet and bassoon) Ricercar, 1976, (solo piano) Piano Sonata, 1965, Suite for Piano, 1988, Serenade, 1977, First Set, 1990, (saxophone quartet) Aureole, 1978, (brass quintet) Summer Music, 1979, (solo bass clarinet) Soliloquy, 1980, (soprano voice and piano) Six Songs, 1980, (solo organ) Tapestry, 1981, (winds, percussion and piano) Montalvo Overture, 1984, (piano and woodwind quintet) A Day At Xochimilco, 1987, (trombone and organ) Novella, 1988, (mezzo soprano, violin, clarinet and piano) By Verse Distills, 1989, (wind ensemble) Preludes and Variations, 1991, (horn and harp) Arcadian Suite, 1993. Fulbright fellow Italy, 1966; Italian Govt. grantee, 1967; recipient Joseph Bearns prize Columbia U., 1966; Rome prize, 1971, 72; award Nat. Inst. Arts and Letters, 1975, Internat. Double Reed Soc. prize, 1979, New Music for Young Ensembles prize, 1979, Nebr. Sinfonia prize, 1981; Nat. Endowment Arts grantee, 1981, 95; Guggenheim fellow, 1982. Office: Indiana U of Pa Cogswell Hall Indiana PA 15705

PERLOV, DADIE, management consultant; b. N.Y.C., June 8, 1929; d. Aaron and Anna (Leight) Heitman; m. Norman B. Perlov, May 29, 1950; children—Nancy Perlov Rosenbach, Jane, Amy Perlov Schenkein. BA, NYU, 1950; postgrad., Adelphi U., 1963, Vanderbilt U., 1973. Cert. assn. exec., N.Y. Exec. dir. ops. Open City, N.Y.C., 1962-64; field svcs. dir. Nat. Coun. Jewish Women, N.Y.C., 1968-74; exec. dir. N.Y. Libr. Assn., N.Y.C., 1974-81, Nat. Coun. Jewish Women, N.Y.C., 1981-90; founder, prin. Consensus Mgmt. Group, N.Y.C. and Washington, 1989—; cons. HEW 1975-76; pres.-elect Internat. Coun. Libr. Assn. Execs., 1979-80; exec. mem. Conf. of Pres., 1981-90; strategic planner, lectr., merger facilitator, trainer in field. Contbr. articles to profl. jours. Dem. committeewoman, 1966; mem. N.Y. Zool. Soc., 1959—, adv. bd. Nat. Inst. Against Prejudice and Violence, 1985-89, profl. adv. com. for Hornstein program in Jewish communal svc. Brandeis U., 1986-90; bd. visitors Pratt Inst., Bklyn., 1980-84; bd. dirs. Pres. Coun. on Handicapped, 1981—; facilitator Nursing Summit, 1994. Recipient Recognition award N.Y. Libr. Assn., 1978, BUDDY award NOW Legal Def. and Edn. Found., 1989, cert. N.Y. State Legislature, 1978; named N.Y. State Exec. of Yr., 1980, One of Am.'s 100 Most Important Women, Ladies' Home Jour., 1988. Fellow Am. Soc. Assn. Execs. (cert. 1978, evaluator 1980-91, bd. dirs. 1987-90, bd. found. 1990-92, Excellence award 1983); mem. LWV (chpt. pres. 1960-62), N.Y. Soc. Assn. Execs. (pres. 1985, Outstanding Assn. Exec. 1989, Outstanding Svc. award 1991), Global Perspectives in Edn. (bd. dirs.), Nat. Orgn. Continuing Edn. (coun.), Audubon Soc., N.Y. Citizens Coun. on Librs. (bd. dirs. 1981-84), Am. Arbitration Assn. (mem. panel). Avocations: writing, mycology, history, music, art.

PERLOW, GILBERT J(EROME), physicist, editor; b. N.Y.C., Feb. 10, 1916; s. David and Esther (German) P.; m. Mina Rea Jones. AB, Cornell U., 1936, MA, 1937; PhD, U. Chgo., 1940. Instr. physics U. Minn., Mpls., 1940-41; physicist Naval Ordnance Lab., Washington, 1941-42, Naval Rsch. Lab., Washington, 1942-52; rsch. assoc. physics dept. U. Minn., Mpls., 1952-53; assoc. physicist Argonne (Ill.) Nat. Lab., 1953-57, sr. physicist, 1957—; editor Jour. Applied Physics Am. Inst. Physics/Argonne Nat. Lab., 1970-73, editor Applied Physics Letters, 1970-90, consulting editor Applied Physics Letters, 1990—; vis. assoc. prof. physics U. Wash., Seattle, 1957; vis. prof. German univs., Munich, Berlin; exch. physicist AERE Harwell, Berkshire, Eng., 1961. Contbr. over 70 articles to profl. jours., also chpts. to books; author numerous U.S. patents. Recipient Alexander von Humboldt award Alexander von Humboldt Found., Tech. U. Munich, 1972. Fellow Am. Phys. Soc.; mem. Chgo. Corinthian Yacht Club (life mem., commodore 1974). Avocations: sailing, woodworking, painting. Home: 4919 Northcott Ave Downers Grove IL 60515-3434 Office: Argonne Nat Lab Physics Divsn 9700 Cass Ave Argonne IL 60439-4803

PERLSTADT, SIDNEY MORRIS, lawyer; b. Warsaw, Poland, May 9, 1907; came to U.S. 1916, naturalized, 1920; s. Isaac H. and Sarah (Carmel) P.; m. Mildred Penn, Mar. 5, 1935 (dec.); children—Harry, Susan Perlstadt Serota; m. Bessie Lendrum, Jan. 25, 1961 (dec.). Ph.B., U. Chgo., 1928; J.D., DePaul U., 1942. C.P.A., Ill. Bar: Ill. 1943, U.S. Dist. Ct. (no. dist.) Ill. 1944, U.S. Tax Ct. 1944. Revenue agt. IRS, San Francisco and Chgo., 1935-43; ptnr. Sonnenschein, Nath & Rosenthal, Chgo., 1944—. Mem. Ill. Pub. Employees Pension Laws Commn., 1973-84; trustee Indsl. Areas Found. Mem. Chgo. Bar Assn., Ill. Bar Assn., ABA. Club: Cliff Dwellers (Chgo.). Home: 175 E Delaware Pl Chicago IL 60611-1756 Office: Sonnenschein Nath Rosenthal Suite 8000 233 S Wacker Dr Ste 8000 Chicago IL 60606-6342

PERLSTEIN, ABRAHAM PHILLIP, psychiatrist; b. N.Y.C., Apr. 15, 1926; s. Benjamin William and Pauline (Gittler) P.; m. Shirley Anne Rubenstein, July 10, 1949; children: Judith Paula, Susan Carol, Bernard William. BS, U. Oreg., 1949; MD, NYU, 1953. Diplomate Am. Bd. Psychiatry and Neurology with added qualifications in Geriat. Psychiatry. Cons. alcoholism dir. SUNY, Bklyn., 1958—, clin. asst. prof. psychiatry, 1957—; med. dir. Peninsula Counseling Ctr., Woodmere, N.Y., 1973-78, psychiat. cons. geriatrics, 1978-90; pvt. practice Elmont, N.Y., 1957-90; assoc. psychiat. dir. Frankling Gen. Hosp., Valley Stream, N.Y., 1980-82; attending psychiatrist Kings County Hosp. Ctr., Bklyn., 1957-90, SUNY, U. Hosp. Bklyn., 1963-90, Franklin Gen. Hosp., Valley Stream, 1969-90; adj. clin. asst. prof. psychiatry Cornell U. Med. Coll., N.Y.C., 1978-90; assoc. attending psychiatrist North Shore U. Hosp., Manhasset, N.Y., 1978-90. Sgt. U.S. Army, 1944-46. Fellow Am. Psychiat. Assn. (life). Avocations: music, art, literature, sports. Office: Columbia River Mental Health Svcs PO Box 1337 1950 Fort Vancouver Way Ste A Vancouver WA 98666

PERLSTEIN, WILLIAM JAMES, lawyer; b. N.Y.C., Feb. 7, 1950; s. Justin Sol and Jane (Goldberg) P.; m. Teresa Catherine Lotito, Dec. 20, 1970; children—David, Jonathan. B.A. summa cum laude, Union Coll., 1971; student London Sch. Econs., 1969-70; J.D., Yale U., 1974. Bar: Conn. 1974, D.C. 1976, U.S. Dist. Ct. D.C. 1977, U.S. Ct. Appeals D.C. cir. 1978, U.S. Supreme Ct. 1993. Law clk. Judge Marvin Frankel, U.S. Dist. Ct., N.Y.C., 1974-75; assoc. Wilmer, Cutler & Pickering, Washington, 1975-82, ptnr., 1982—, mem. mgmt. com. 1995—. Mng. editor Yale Law Jour., 1973-74; contbg. author The Workout Game, 1987. Mem. ABA (bus. bankruptcy com. 1983—, vice-chmn. executory contracts subcom. of bus. bankruptcy com. 1988-90, bankruptcy cts. subcom. 1990-97, chmn. legislation subcom. 1997—), Am. Bankruptcy Inst. (chmn. legis. com. 1986-89, bd. dirs. 1989-93, 97—), Am. Law Inst., Am. Coll. Bankruptcy, Union Coll. Alumni Coun., Phi Beta Kappa (at-large regent). Jewish.

PERMAN, NORMAN WILFORD, graphic designer; b. Chgo., Feb. 17, 1928; s. Jacob and Ida (Ladenson) P.; m. Lorraine Shaffer, July 22, 1956; children: Jonathan Dean, Margot Bess. Student, Corcoran Sch. Art, Washington, 1946-47, Northwestern U., 1948-50; BFA, Art Inst. Chgo., 1951. Asst. to designer Everett McNear, Chgo., 1951-52; ind. graphic designer specializing booklets, annual reports, exhibits, packaging and books Chgo., 1953—; guest lectr. U. Ill., Chgo.; curator 75th Anniversary Exhbn. Arts Club of Chgo., 1992; lectr. in field; juror various nat. and regional exhbns. Designer: (records and ednl. materials) Invitations to Personal Reading, 165 vols., 1965, Sounds I Can Hear, Talkstarters, 1966, Health and Growth, 1970, Mathematics Around Us, 1974, Good for Life Exhibit, 1978, Invitation to Mathematics, 1984, Health for Life, 1986; editor: Form and Meaning, 1962; exhbns. include Art Inst. Chgo., 1954-62, 68, U. Ill., 1960, 62, 64, U. Wis., 1957, Am. Inst. Graphic Arts, 1958, 60-61, 63-64, 66, 68, 70, 72, 74, 76, 79-81, 83, State Dept. USSR, 1964, Art Dirs. Club, N.Y.C., 1961, 63, 65, 69, HUD Art in Architecture Exhibit, Smithsonian Instn., 1973, 50 Yrs. Graphic Design in Chgo. Exhibit, 1977; represented in numerous design jours., annuals and graphics books. With USN, 1946-48. Recipient award Art Dirs. Club, Chgo., 1960, 62, 65, 68, award Art Dirs. Club, N.Y.C., 1961-82, Gold medal Direct Mail Assn., 1961, 64. Fellow Am. Ctr. for Design (bd. dirs., chmn. Allerton Park Conf. 1962, nat. pres. 1965-66, exhibits 1952-89, award 1952-86); mem. Assn. Corp. Art Curators (v.p. 1982), Am. Inst. Graphic Arts (award 1960-85), 27 Chgo. Designers, Art Inst. Chgo. (chmn. alumni fund), Oriental Inst., Coun. Fgn. Rels., Arts Club of Chgo. (bd. dirs.). Democrat. Avocations: photography, mountain trekking, travel, music.

PERMUTT, SOLBERT, physiologist, physician; b. Birmingham, Ala., Mar. 6, 1925; s. Harry and Rachel (Damsky) P.; m. Loretta Paul, Jan. 17, 1952; children—Nina Rachel, Thomas Joshua, Lisa Ellen. M.D., U. So. Calif., 1949. Intern U. Chgo. Clinics, 1949-50, resident medicine, 1952, research assoc. dept. anatomy, 1950-52; resident medicine Montefiore Hosp., N.Y.C., 1954-56; fellow medicine and environmental medicine Johns Hopkins Med. Sch., 1956-58; chief div. cardiopulmonary physiology Nat. Jewish Hosp., Denver, 1958-61; asst. prof. physiology Sch. Medicine, U. Colo., 1960-61; mem. faculty Sch. Hygiene and Pub. Health, Johns Hopkins, 1961, prof. environ. health sci., 1965—; prof. medicine Johns Hopkins U. Sch. Med., 1972—, dir. respiratory div. dept. medicine, 1972-81, prof. anesthesiology, 1978—; head physiology div., environ. health sci. John Hopkins Sch. Hygiene and Pub. Health, 1976-79; dir. pulmonary div. Francis Scott Key Med. Ctr. (John Hopkins Med. Instn.), 1981-87, dir. pulmonary rsch., div. pulmonary medicine, 1986-87, dir. rsch. div. pulmonary and critical care medicine, 1988—; assoc. dir. Johns Hopkins Asthma and Allergy Ctr., 1990—; Cons. space sci. bd. Nat. Acad. Sci., 1966-67, mem. com. effects atmospheric contaminants human health, 1968-70; mem. project com. Heart and Lung Program, NIH, 1970-74; mem. sci. adv. council Children's Asthma Research Inst. and Hosp., Denver, 1973-75; mem. expert panel Nat. Inst. Allergy and Infectious Diseases, 1972-74; mem. nat. adv. com. for Cal. Primate Research Center, 1972-75; vice chmn. council on cardiopulmonary diseases Am. Heart Assn., 1974-75, chmn., 1976—, mem. research com., 1979-85; nat. adviser Aspen Lung Confs., 1974—; mem. pulmonary disease adv. com. HHS and NIH, 1979-83. Mem. editorial bd. publs. Am. Physiol. Soc. Circulation Research, 1965—, La Revue Française des Maladies Respiratoires, 1975—; contbr. articles to profl. jours. Served with U.S. Army, 1943-46, 53-54. Recipient Gold medal Am. Coll. Chest Physicians, 1977, Louis and Artur Lucian award McGill U., 1980; fellow Nat. Found. Infantile Paralysis, 1956-58. Mem. Am. Lung Assn. (George Wills Comstock award 1988, Edward Livingston Trudeau medal 1992), Cardiovascular System Dynamics Soc., Am. Med. Assn. (reference panel for diagnostic and therapeutic tech. assessment-DATTA), Assn. Am. Physicians, Johns Hopkins Med. and Surg. Assn., Md. Soc. Med. Rsch., Am. Thoracic Soc., Am. Physiol. Soc., AAAS, Am. Heart Assn. (Citation for Disting. Svc. to Rsch. 1979-84, Disting. Achievement award Cardiopulmonary Coun. 1986). Home: 2303 Sulgrave Ave Baltimore MD 21209-4405

PERNEY, LINDA, newspaper editor. Travel editor The Daily News, N.Y.C. Office: The Daily News 450 E 33rd St New York NY 10016

PERO, JOSEPH JOHN, retired insurance company executive; b. N.Y.C., Nov. 5, 1939; s. Joseph John and Grace Margaret (Picchione) P.; m. Margaret Ann Carey, July 11, 1964; children: Ann Marie, Christopher. B.S., Manhattan Coll., 1961; M.B.A., NYU, 1967. With GM, 1963-94; dir. profit and investment analysis Gen. Motors Corp., N.Y.C., 1973-76; asst. treas., sec. to exec. com. Gen. Motors Corp., Detroit, 1976-79, N.Y.C., 1980-81; exec. v.p.-fin. Motors Ins. Corp. (subs. Gen. Motors Corp.), Detroit, 1981-87, pres., 1987-94; ret., 1994. Bd. dirs. Inner City Bus. Improvement Forum, Detroit, 1978-79; trustee Mt. Elliot Cemetery Assn., 1978-79; bd. dirs., treas. Ryan Sr. Residences of Archdiocese of Detroit. With Army N.G., 1963-69. Mem. Forest Lake Country Club. Home: 4097 Waterwheel Ln Bloomfield Hills MI 48302-1871

PERONI, PETER A., II, psychologist, educator; b. Trenton, N.J., Nov. 14, 1942; s. Peter A. and Mary D. (DiLeo) P. BA, LaSalle U., 1964; MA, Trenton State Coll., 1967, MAT, 1969; EdD, Rutgers U., 1977. Cert. secondary sch. social studies, student pers. svcs.; lic. psychologist, Pa. Tchr. St. Anthony High Sch., Trenton, 1964-67, Lawrence Twp. (N.J.) Pub. Schs., 1967-68; counselor Bucks County C.C., Newtown, Pa., 1968-72, prof., 1972-95; cons. psychologist, 1995—; consulting psychologist N.J. Dept. Health, Trenton, 1977-84; dir. clin. svcs. New Horizon Treatment Svcs., Trenton, 1984-88. Author: The Burg: An Italian-American Community at Bay in Trenton, 1979; writer, co-producer (TV): The Burg: A State of Mind, 1980; author: Academic Success Through Self-Conditioning, 1982. N.J. Commn. for Humanities grantee, 1980. Avocation: motorcycle touring. Home: 52 Hollynoll Dr Trenton NJ 08619-2208

PEROTTI, BEATRICE YEE-WA TAM, pharmacokineticist, research scientist; b. Hong Kong, Nov. 16, 1964; came to U.S., 1984; d. Kin-Fan Tam and Kam-Sheung So; m. Ronald Anthony Perotti, Jan. 29, 1988. Internat. baccalaureate, Lester Pearson Coll. Pacific, Victoria, B.C., 1984; BA, Mills Coll., 1988; PhD, U. Calif., San Francisco, 1994. Sr. rsch. scientist Pfizer Ctrl. Rsch., Groton, Conn., 1994—; guest lectr. U. Calif., San Francisco, 1993. Author: Burger's Medicinal Chemistry and Drug Discovery, 1995; producer, performer (soprano recital) 300 Years of Classical Songs, 1986, Love Songs From the East and West, 1987; contbr. articles to profl. jours. Tutor Upward Bound, Oakland, Calif., 1985-87; soloist Brookside Cmty. Ch., Oakland, 1988-94, youth counselor, charity coord., 1989-94; vol. Project Open Hands, Oakland, 1993-94; chair publicity com. Waterford Rep. Town Com. U. Calif. rsch. fellow, 1986, AFPE Assn. fellow, 1992-94; Sir. Jack Cater trust scholar Hong Kong Edn. Dept., 1982-84; recipient Hong Kong Mills Club scholarship, 1984-87, Hellman music award Mills Coll., 1986-87, Gordon Rsch. Conf. Student Travel award, 1993, Greater Victoria Music award, 1983. Mem. AAAS, Internat. Soc. Study Xenobiotics, Am. Assn. Pharm. Scientists (award 1992), Brit. Sub Agua Club. Avocations: Brit. Sub Aqua Club class 3 diver, swimming, target shooting, in-line skating, golfing. Home: 268 Shore Rd Waterford CT 06385-3425 Office: Pfizer Ctrl Rsch Eastern Point Rd Groton CT 06340

PERRAUD, PAMELA BROOKS, human resources professional; b. Mpls., May 27, 1948; d. Wright William and Gladys Brooks; m. Jean-Marc Francois Perraud, Nov. 22, 1975; children: Marc Alexander, Andrea Elizabeth. BA, Conn. Coll., 1970; MA in Urban Studies, Occidental Coll., 1972; MA in Indsl. Rels., U. Minn., 1977. Cert. sr. profl. in human resources, compensation profl., benefits profl. Dir. personnel Mpls. Housing and ReDevel. Authority, Mpls., 1973-75; dir. adminstrn. United Svcs. Orgn., Paris, 1976-78; dir. office svcs. Pechiney Ughine Kuhlmann, Greenwich, Conn., 1979-80; lectr., trainer Monodnock Internat., London, 1981-85; personnel recruiter IBM Europe, Paris, 1989; prof. bus. Am. Bus. Sch., Paris, 1988-92; pres. Women's Inst. for Continuing Edn., Paris, 1992-93; human resource cons. N.Y.C., 1994—; chair Women on the Move, Paris, 1990-93; v.p. Women's Inst. for Continuing Edn., Paris, 1988-93. Co-author: (books) Living in France, 1994. Co-founder Focus Info. and Referral, London, 1982, Women in Mgmt., Mpls., 1973; trustee Conn. Coll., New London, 1970. Fellow in Pub. Affairs, Coro Found., L.A., 1970. Mem. Friends of WICE, Am. Compensation Assn., Soc. for Human Resources Mgmt., Soc. for Intercultural Edn., Tng. and Rsch., bd. mem. Metro Intl., N.Y.C. Avocations: tennis, skiing. Home: Ste 21E 200 E 90th St New York NY 10128

PERREAULT, SISTER JEANNE, college president; b. Providence, Dec. 13, 1929; d. Alphonse and Malvina I. (Chevalier) P. BSEd, Cath. Tchrs. Coll., Providence, 1959; MS, Cath. U., Washington, 1968; EdD (hon.), Salve Regina U., 1990. Tchr. elem. sch. St. Ann Sch., West Warwick, R.I.; tchr. jr. high sch. St. John Jr. High Sch., West Warwick; tchr. high sch. Notre Dame High Sch., Berlin, N.H.; assoc. prof. Rivier Coll., Nashua, N.H., pres., 1980—; mem. Gov.'s Task Force for Edn. Mem. State of N.H. Post-Secondary Edn. Commn., Concord; bd. dirs. Ctr. for Econ. Devel. for Nashua Area, Bishop Guertin H.S., Nashua; commr. New Eng. Assn. Schs. & Colls.; provincial coun. Sisters of Presentation of Mary. Mem. AAUP, Am. Coun. Colls., Assn. Cath. Colls. and Univs., N.H. Coll. and Univ. Coun.

PERREAULT, WILLIAM DANIEL, JR., business administration educator; b. N.Y.C., Apr. 7, 1948; s. William Daniel Sr. and Barbara Louise (Peckham) P.; m. Pamela Pittard, May 27, 1972; children: Suzanne Elizabeth, William Daniel III. BS, U. N.C., 1970, PhD, 1973. Asst. prof. U. Ga., Athens, 1973-76; asst. prof. U. N.C., Chapel Hill, 1976-79, assoc. prof., 1979-81, prof., 1981-83, Hanes prof., 1983-88; vis. prof. Stanford (Calif.) U., 1986-87, assoc. dean, 1988-92. Kenan prof., 1988—; vis. prof. Cambridge (Eng.) U., 1997. Co-author: The Marketing Game, 1994, Essentials Marketing, 1997, Basic Marketing, 1996; editor: Jour. Mktg. Rsch., 1982-85; contbr. articles to profl. jours. Chmn. adv. com. Bur. Census, Washington, 1982-86. Mem. Am. Mktg. Assn. (v.p. 1986, 95, bd. dirs. 1986-89, 949-95), Acad. Mktg. Sci. (Outstanding Edn. award 1995), Decision Scis. Inst. (coun. 1977), Assn. Dir. Consumer Rsch. Conf. (chmn. 1976—), Mktg. Sci. Inst. (trustee 1989-94), Phi Beta Kappa. Republican. Presbyterian. Office: U NC CB 3490 Carroll Hall # 012A Chapel Hill NC 27599-3490

PERRELLA, JAMES ELBERT, manufacturing company executive; b. Gloversville, N.Y., May 30, 1935; s. James E. and A. Irene (Ferguson) P.; m. Diane F. Campesi; 1 child, Joy. B.S.M.E., Purdue U., 1960, M.S.I.M., 1961. Gen. mgr. Centac div. Ingersoll-Rand Co., Mayfield, Ky., 1972-75; gen. mgr. Air Compressor Group Ingersoll-Rand Co., Woodcliff Lake, N.J., 1975-77, corp. v.p., pres. Air Compressor Group, 1977-82, exec. v.p., 1982-92, pres., 1992—, chmn., CEO, 1993—, also dir.; bd. dirs. Becton Dickinson and Co., Cin. Milacron Inc. Named Disting. Alumnus Sch. Mech. Engring., Purdue U., 1982; named Disting. Alumnus Krammert Mgmt. Sch., Purdue U., 1982. Office: Ingersoll-Rand Co 200 Chestnut Ridge Rd Woodcliff Lk NJ 07675-7703

PERRENOD, DOUGLAS ARTHUR, aeronautical engineer; b. Weehawken, N.J., Sept. 13, 1947; s. George Edward and Eunice Lillian (Cohn) P. Student, Fla. Inst. Tech., 1968-72; B.A. in Interdisciplinary Sci. U. South Fla., 1973; postgrad. Calif. State U., 1982—; grad. engr. mgmt. cert. program Calif. Inst. Tech., 1987; bioenvironmental engr. USAF Sch. Aerospace Medicine, 1992. Cert. glider flight instr. FAA. Engr. trainee NASA Kennedy Space Ctr., Fla., 1969-73; quality control engr. Pelletech Corp., Fontana, Calif., 1976-77; electronics specialist Gen. Telephone Co., San Bernardino, Calif., 1977-79; aerospace and project engr. Rockwell Internat., Downey, Calif., 1979-85, Lockheed Corp., Ontario, Calif., 1986-87, Lockheed Engring. Mgmt. Svc. Co., 1987, Eagle Engring., 1988—, Eagle Tech. Svcs., 1989—; aviation cons., owner-founder Flight Unltd., Long Beach, Calif.; mission pilot, project engr. Flight Level 500 High Altitude Soaring Project. Vol. mem. Orange County Human Services Agy., 1981-86; active Big Bros. of Am., 1978. Lt. Col. USAFR, 1973—. Recipient Amelia Earhart award CAP, 1968, Manned Flight Awareness Apollo 11 medallion NASA, 1971, 1st Shuttle Flight award NASA, 1981, Aerospace Maintenance Officer of Yr. award USAFR, 1979; named to Engr. Honor Roll, Rockwell Internat., 1982, 83, 85. Mem. AIAA, Assn. Mil. Surgeons U.S., Res. Officers Assn., Officers Assn., Air Force Assn., Soc. Flight Test Engrs., Assoc. Glider Club of So. Calif., Long Beach Navy Aero. Club. Developed concept for, and co-authored unprecedented Inter-agency agreement between USAF and NASA for exchange of advanced environmental technology, 1994. Designer telescope mount for 1st astronomy obs. Fla. Inst. Tech., 1969.

PERRET, PETER JAMES, symphony conductor; b. Rochester, Minn., Mar. 25, 1941; s. George E. and Margaret (Minge) P.; m. Chao Mei-Wah, Mar. 23, 1966 (div. Apr. 1978); 1 child, Ondine; m. Debra Skeen, May 24, 1986; children: Zachary, Michael. Student, Royal Conservatory, Brussels, 1964, Diplome Superieur, 1966. Chief producer Swiss Broadcasting Corp., Geneva, 1967-72; prin. condr. Capetown (Peoples Republic of Africa) Symphony, 1972-74; Exxon arts endowment condr. Buffalo Philharmonic, 1975-78; music dir. Winston-Salem (N.C.) Symphony, 1978—; vis. prof. U. Capetown, 1973-74; scholar-in-residence Canisius Coll., Buffalo, 1976, 77; prof. conducting N.C. Sch. of the Arts, Winston-Salem, 1980-88. Composer: (classical music) Symphonie Élégiaque, 1989; recordings on Koch Internat., Albany Records, Vienna Modern Masters. Avocations: cooking, tennis, sailing, mycology, reading. Home: 4230 Stoney Brook Rd Clemmons NC 27012 Office: Winston-Salem Symphony 610 Coliseum Dr Winston Salem NC 27106-5325

PERRICONE, CHARLES, state legislator; b. Oct. 10, 1960. Student, Kalamazoo Coll., Western Mich. U. Rep. Mich. State Dist. 61, 1995—; vice chair tax policy com.; mem. corrections com., house oversight and ethics com., legis. coun.; asst. Rep. leader. Address: PO Box 30014 Lansing MI 48909-7514

PERRIN, EDWARD BURTON, health services researcher, biostatistician, public health educator; b. Greensboro, Vt., Sept. 19, 1931; s. J. Newton and Dorothy E. (Willey) P.; m. Carol Anne Hendricks, Aug. 18, 1956; children: Jenifer, Scott. BA, Middlebury Coll., 1953; postgrad. (Fulbright scholar) in stats, Edinburgh (Scotland) U., 1953-54; MA in Math. Stats., Columbia U., 1956; PhD, Stanford U., 1960. Asst. prof. dept. biostats. U. Pitts., 1959-62; asst. prof. dept. preventive medicine U. Wash., Seattle, 1962-65; assoc. prof. U. Wash., 1965-69, prof., 1969-70, prof., chmn. dept. biostats., 1970-72, prof. dept. health svcs., adj. prof. dept. biostats., 1975—, chmn. dept., 1983-94; prof. (hon.) West China U. of Med. Scis., Szechwan, Peoples Republic of China, 1988—; overseas fellow Churchill Coll., Cambridge U., 1991-92; sr. scientist Seattle Vets. Affairs Med. Ctr., 1994—; clin. prof. dept. cmty. medicine and internat. health Sch. Medicine, Georgetown U., Washington, 1972-75; dep. dir. Nat. Ctr. for Health Stats., HEW, 1972-73, dir., 1973-75; rsch. scientist Health Care Study Ctr., Battelle Human Affairs Rsch. Ctrs., Seattle, 1975-76, dir., 1976-78; dir. Health and Population Study Ctr. Battelle Human Affairs Rsch. Ctrs., Seattle, 1978-83; sr. cons. biostats. Wash./Alaska regional med. programs, 1967-72; biometrician VA Co-op Study on Treatment of Esopageal Varices, 1961-73; mem. Epidemiology and Disease Control Study Sect., NIH, 1969-73; chmn. health svcs. rsch. study sect., HEW, 1976-79; chmn. health svcs. R&D field program rev. panel, VA, 1988-91; chmn. health svcs. info. steering com. State of Washington, 1993-94; mem. nat. adv. coun. Agy. for Health Care Policy and Rsch. Dept. Health and Human Svcs., U.S. Govt., 1994—; mem. com. on nat. stats. NRC, NAS, 1994—; chmn. scientific adv. com. Med. Outcomes Trust, 1994—. Contbr. articles on biostats., health services and population studies to profl. pubs.; mem. editorial bd.: Jour. Family Practice, 1978-90, Public Health Nursing, 1992—. Mem. tech. bd. Milbank Meml. Fund, 1974-76. Recipient Outstanding Service citation HEW, 1975. Fellow AAAS, Am. Pub. Health Assn. (Spiegelman Health Stats. award 1970, program devel. bd. 1971, chmn. stats. sect. 1978-80, governing coun. 1983-85, stats. sect. recognition award 1989), Am. Statis. Assn. (mem. adv. com. to divsn. statis. policy 1975-77); mem. Assn. Health Svcs. Rsch. (pres. 1994-95), Inst. Medicine of Nat. Acad. Sci. (chmn. membership com. 1984-86, mem. bd. on health care svcs. 1987-96, forum health stats. 1994-95, chmn. com. on clin. evaluation 1990-93), Biometrics Soc. (pres. Western N.Am. Region 1971), Inst. Math. Stats., Internat. Epidemiologic Assn., Sigma Xi, Phi Beta Kappa. Home: 4900 NE 39th St Seattle WA 98105-5209 Office: U Wash Dept Health Svcs PO Box 357660 Seattle WA 98195-7660

PERRIN, GAIL, editor; b. Boston, Oct. 14, 1938; d. Hugh and Helen (Baxter) P. B.A., Wellesley Coll., 1960. Copy girl Washington Daily News, summers, 1954-57, reporter, 1958, 60-61, acting women's editor, food editor, 1961-62, rewrite reporter, 1963-65; reporter Honolulu Star Bull., 1959; women's editor Boston Globe, 1965-71, asst. met. editor, 1971-74, food editor, 1974-92; food cons., free-lance writer, 1992—. Mem. Assn. Food Journalists, Women's Culinary Guild.

PERRIN, KENNETH LYNN, university chancellor; b. L.A., July 29, 1937; s. Freeman Whitaker and Lois Eileen (Bowen) P.; m. Shirley Anne Cupp, Apr. 2, 1960; children: Steven, Lynne. BA, Occidental Coll., 1959; MA, Calif. State U., Long Beach, 1964; PhD, Stanford U., 1969. Lic. in speech pathology, Calif. Chmn. dept. communicative disorders U. Pacific, Stockton, Calif., 1969-77; dir. edn. and sci. programs Am. Speech-Lang.-Hearing Assn., Rockville, Md., 1977-80; dean Faculty Profl. Studies West Chester U., Pa., 1980-82; acting acad. v.p. West Chester U., 1982, pres., 1983-91; pres. Coun. on Postsecondary Edn., Washington, 1991-93; chancellor, system sr. v.p. U. Hawaii, Hilo and West Oahu, 1993-97; chancellor Ind. U. South Bend, 1997—; cons. in field, 1969-76; pres. north region Calif. Speech Hearing Assn., 1975-76. Co-author: monograph Prevalence of Communicative Disorders, 1981; contbr. articles to profl. jours.; editor: Guide to Graduate Education Speech Pathology and Audiology, 1980. Chmn. Southeastern chpt. Greater Brandywine Br. ARC; trainee Vocat. Rehab. Adminstrn., 1965-69. Named Disting. Alumnus Sch. Humanities Calif. State U., Long Beach, 1988. Fellow Am. Speech-Lang.-Hearing Assn. (vice chmn. edn. tng. bd. 1975-77 cert. clin. competence in speech pathology); mem. West Chester C. of C. (pres. 1988). Home: 543 Kaanini St Hilo HI 96720 Office: Indiana U South Bend 1700 Wishawaka Ave PO Box 7111 South Bend IN 46634*

PERRIN, NOEL, environmental studies educator; b. N.Y.C., Sept. 18, 1927; s. Edwin Oscar and Blanche Browning (Chenery) P.; m. Nancy Hunnicutt, Nov. 26, 1960 (div. 1971); children: Elisabeth, Amy; m. 2d Annemarie Price, June 20, 1975 (div. 1980); m. Anne Spencer Lindbergh, Dec. 26, 1988 (dec. 1993). B.A., Williams Coll., 1949; M.A., Duke U., 1950; M.Litt., Cambridge U., 1958. Copy boy Daily News, N.Y.C., 1950-51; assoc. editor Med. Econs., Oradell, N.J., 1953-56; instr. U. N.C. Woman's Coll., Greensboro, 1956-59; from instr. to prof. English Dartmouth Coll., Hanover, N.H., 1959-90, prof. environ. studies, 1991—. Author: A Passport Secretly Green, 1961, Dr. Bowdler's Legacy, 1969, Giving Up the Gun, 1979, Second Person Rural, 1980, Third Person Rural, 1983, A Reader's Delight, 1988, A Noel Perrin Sampler, 1991, Last Person Rural, 1991, Solo: Life with an Electric Car, 1992; columnist, Washington Post Book World, 1980-86, 89-91. Served to 1st lt. arty. AUS, 1951-52. Decorated Bronze Star; Guggenheim Found. fellow, 1970, 85. Episcopalian. Home: RR 1 Box 8 Thetford Center VT 05075-9701 Office: Dartmouth College Environ Studies Program Hanover NH 03755

PERRIN, ROBERT, federal agency consultant, writer; b. Ann Arbor, Mich., Aug. 21, 1925; s. John Stephenson and Narcissa Elizabeth (Merkel) P.; m. Barbara J. Groom, June 25, 1949; children: Stephen, Jennifer Perrin Hummel. BS, U. Minn., 1945. Reporter United Press Assn., Detroit, 1948-49, Detroit Free Press, 1949-55; adminstrv. asst. U.S. Senate, Washington, 1955-66; asst. dir. U.S. Office Econ. Opportunity, Washington, 1966-68, dep. dir., 1968-70; v.p. Mich. State U., East Lansing, 1970-79; vice chancellor SUNY System, Albany, 1979-85; exec. v.p. Tchrs. Ins. and Annuity Assn.—Coll. Retirement Equities Fund, N.Y.C., 1987-92; cons. Dept. State, 1993-94. Contbr. articles to mags., newspapers. Mem. U.S.-Mex. Commn. on Border Devel., Washington, 1967-68. Lt. USNR, 1943-46, PTO. Fellow Reid Found., 1954. Home: 2435 Emerald Lake Dr East Lansing MI 48823-7256

PERRINE, RICHARD LEROY, environmental engineering educator; b. Mountain View, Calif., May 15, 1924; s. George Alexander and Marie (Axelson) P.; m. Barbara Jean Gale, Apr. 12, 1945; children: Cynthia Gale, Jeffrey Richard. A.B., San Jose State Coll., 1949; M.S., Stanford U., 1950, Ph.D. in Chemistry, 1953. Cert. environ. profl., 1987. Research chemist Calif. Research Corp., La Habra, 1953-59; assoc. prof. UCLA, 1959-63, prof. engring. and applied sci., 1963-92, prof. emeritus, 1992—, chmn. environ. sci. and engring., 1971-82; prin. Aspen Environ. Group, 1990-93; v.p. Sage Resources, 1988-91; cons. environ. sci. and engring., energy resources, flow in porous media; mem. Los Angeles County Energy Commn., 1973-81; mem. adv. council South Coast Air Quality Mgmt. Dist., 1977-82; mem. air conservation com. Los Angeles County Lung Assn., 1970-84; mem. adv. com. energy div. Oak Ridge Nat. Lab., 1987-90; mem. policy bd. Inst. Environ. and Natural Resource Rsch. and Policy U. Wyo., 1994—. Editor in chief The Environ. Profl., 1985-90. Served with AUS, 1943-46. Recipient Outstanding Engr. Merit award in environ. engring. Inst. Advancement Engring., 1975; ACT-SO award in field of chemistry West Coast region NAACP, 1984. Fellow AAAS; mem. Am. Chem. Soc., Soc. Petroleum Engrs., Am. Inst. Chem. Engrs., Can. Inst. Mining and Metallurgy, N.Am. Assn. Environ. Edn., Nat. Assn. Environ. Profls. (cert.), Air and Waste Mgmt. Assn., Assn. Environ. Enging. Profs., Sierra Club, Wilderness Soc., Audubon Soc., Sigma Xi, Tau Beta Pi, Phi Lambda Upsilon. Home: 22611 Kittridge St West Hills CA 91307-3609 Office: Univ Calif Engring Bldg I Rm 2066D Los Angeles CA 90095-1593

PERRIS, TERRENCE GEORGE, lawyer; b. L.A., Oct. 18, 1947; s. Theodore John Grivas and Penny (Sfakianos) Perris. BA magna cum laude, U. Toledo, 1969; JD summa cum laude, U. Mich., 1972. Bar: Ohio 1972, U.S. Tax Ct. 1982, U.S. Ct. Claims 1983, U.S. Supreme Ct. 1983. Law clk. to judge U.S. Ct. Appeals (2d cir.), N.Y.C., 1972-73; law clk. to Justice Potter Stewart U.S. Supreme Ct., Washington, 1973-74; assoc. Squire, Sanders & Dempsey, Cleve., 1974-80, ptnr., 1980—; v.p., trustee SS&D Found., Cleve., 1984—; nat. coord. Taxation Practice Area, 1987—, mem. mgmt. com., 1996—; chmn. Cleve. Tax Inst., 1993; vis. prof. law U. Mich., 1996; lectr. in field. Mem. vis. com. U. Mich. Law Sch., 1986—. Capt. U.S. Army, 1974. Mem. ABA, Ohio Bar Assn., Cleve. Bar Assn. (subchpt. C of internal revenue code task force), Supreme Ct. Hist. Soc., Tax Club Cleve., Order of Coif, Union Club of Cleve., U. Mich. Club of Cleve., The Club of Cleve., Pres.'s Club (Ann Arbor, Mich.), Phi Kappa Phi. Republican. Eastern Orthodox. Avocation: landscape gardening. Office: Squire Sanders & Dempsey LLP 4900 Key Tower 127 Public Sq Cleveland OH 44114-1216

PERRISH, ALBERT, steel company executive; b. Vancouver, B.C., Can., Nov. 18, 1914; came to U.S., 1920; s. Sam and Nettie (Prezant) P.; m. Leora Claire Quiat, Jan. 12, 1962 (dec. 1984); m. Helen Ann Frazin, June 11, 1985; children: Peggy, Kathleen. BSBA, UCLA, 1938. Commr. City of L.A. Harbor Dept., 1961-64, pres., 1964; exec. Ferro Union Inc., Torrance, Calif., 1964—; mem. adv. bd. U.S. Dept. Commerce, Washington, 1946-50, Small Bus. Adminstrn., Washington, 1955-56. Capt. USAAF, 1942-46. Recipient Star of Solidarity, Pres. of Italy, 1954, Order of Leopold, King of Belgium, 1962, Order of Merit, Govt. of France, 1962. Mem. Am. Inst. Internat. Steel (founder, pres. West Coast chpt. 1959—). Office: Ferro Union Inc 1000 Francisco St Torrance CA 90502-1216

PERRITT, HENRY HARDY, JR., law educator; b. Little Rock, Ark., Dec. 30, 1944; s. Henry Hardy and Margaret Frances (Floyd) P. SB in Engring., MIT, 1966, SM in Mgmt., 1970; JD, Georgetown U., 1975. Bar: Va. 1976, Pa. 1977, D.C. 1981, U.S. Supreme Ct. 1981, U.S. Ct. Appeals (3d cir.) 1979, U.S. Ct. Appeals (2d cir.) 1979, U.S. Ct. Appeals (6th cir.) 1983. Sr. sales planner Lockheed Corp., Marietta, Ga., 1968-71; exec. sec. Cost of Living Coun., Washington, 1972-75; legis. analyst U.S. Dept. Commerce, 1971-72; mem. staff White House, Washington, 1975; dep. undersec. U.S. Dept. Labor, Washington, 1975-76; gen. counsel labor Conrail, Phila., 1976-81; prof. law Villanova U., 1981—, dir. Villanova Ctr. for Info. Law and Policy, 1992—, dir. Project Bosnia, 1996—; cons. atty. Morgan, Lewis & Bockius, Washington, 1981-90, Conrail, 1981-90. Author: Employee Dismissal Law and Practice, 1984, 2d edition, 1987, Labor Injunctions, 1986, How to Practice Law With Computers, 1988, Employee Benefits Claims Law and Practice, 1989, Workplace Torts Rights and Liabilities, 1990, Americans With Disabilities Act Handbook, 1990, Trade Secrets: A Practitioner's Guide, 1994, The Information Superhighway, 1996; contbr. articles to profl. jours. Apptd. vice chmn. Coal Commn. U.S. Sec. of Labor, 1990. Mem. ABA (chmn. com. on r.r. and airline labor law 1983-86, chmn. com. on regulatory initiatives and info. tech., adminstrv. law sect., co-vice chmn. dispute resolution com., adminstrv. law sect. 1987-90), Assn. Am. Law Schs. (chmn. sect. on law and computers 1991), Racquet Club. Republican. Unitarian. Home: 38 Rosemont Ave Bryn Mawr PA 19010-2718 Office: Villanova Law Sch Villanova PA 19085

PERRONE, NICHOLAS, mechanical engineer, business executive; b. Apr. 30, 1930. B. Aero. Engring., Poly. Inst. Bklyn., 1951, M.S., 1953, Ph.D., 1958. Research asst., then assoc. applied mechanics Bklyn. Poly. Inst., 1951-58; asst. prof., then assoc. prof. Pratt Inst., 1958-62; sr. scientist Structural Mechanics br. Office Naval Research, Washington, 1962-67; acting head dept. Structural Mechanics br. Office Naval Research, 1967-68, dir. program, 1968-69, 71-82; pres. CASA Gifts Inc., 1983-85; dep. to pres. Advanced Tech. and Research Inc., 1986-87; pres. Perrone Forensic Cons. Inc., 1987—; lectr. civil engring. Cath U. Am., 1962-64, adj. prof., 1965—; spl. research fellow NIH, Georgetown U., 1969-70; participant numerous workshops, confs., symposia; lectr. in field. Contbg. author: Biodynamics, 1980; editor or co-editor numerous monographs; editorial adv. bd.: Advances in Engring. Software, Computers and Structures, Engineering Fracture, Pressure Vessels and Piping; contbr. numerous articles to profl. jours. Fellow AAAS, ASME, Am. Acad. Mechanics; mem. ASCE, AIAA, N.Y. Acad. Sci., Am. Soc. Engring. Edn., Soc. Automotive Engrs., Soc. Mfg. Engrs. Address: 8 Cherry Ln Newtown Square PA 19073

PERRONE, RUTH ELLYN, university administrator; b. Hearne, Tex., July 2, 1951; d. John Paul Perrone and Ellen Gayle (Sullivan) Perrone-Robertson. BS, Stephen F. Austin State U., 1973; MPA, Tex. A&M U., 1986. Social worker Tex. Dept. Pub. Welfare, Nacogdoches, Tex., 1974-76; licensing rep. Tex. Dept. Human Resources, Bryan, 1976-85; spl. asst. to vice chancellor for state affairs Tex. A&M Univ. System, Austin, 1987-90; asst. to pres. Tex. A&M U., College Station, 1990-92, dir. external rels., 1992—; advisor legis. study group Tex. A&M U., 1992—; bd. dirs. Scott & White Hosp. Health Plan, 1995—. Chair governing bd. John Ben Shepperd Pub. Leadership Found., Odessa, Tex., 1993-94; bd. dirs. Tex. Lyceum, Austin, 1992—; assoc. mem. St. Joseph Hosp. Aux., Bryan, 1993—. Mem. Nat. Assn. State Univ. and Land Grant Coll. (coun. on govtl. affairs), Coun. for Advancement and Support of Edn., Bryan/College Station C. of C. (coun. on govtl. affairs). Avocations: ballet, theatre, reading, dinner parties. Office: Texas A&M University Office of President 805 Rudder Tower College Station TX 77843

PERRONI, CAROL, artist, painter; b. Boston, July 28, 1952; d. Michael John and Mary Agnes (Collett) P.; m. John Richard Mugford, May 23, 1987; 1 child, Jonathan Perroni. Student, Boston Mus. Sch., 1970-71; BA in Art, Bennington Coll., 1976; student, Skowhegan Sch. Painting and Sculpture, 1978; MFA in Art, Hunter Coll., 1983. Studio asst. for artist Isaac Witkin, Bennington, Vt., 1973-74; libr. asst. Simmons Coll. Libr., Boston, 1977-78; studio asst. for artist Mel Bochner N.Y.C., 1979; bookkeeper Internat. House, N.Y.C., 1979-80; studio asst. for Lee Krasner East Hampton, N.Y., 1980; rsch. asst. Art News Mag., N.Y.C., 1981; intern Greenespace Gallery, N.Y.C., 1982-83; tech. asst. Avery Architectural and Fine Arts Libr. Columbia U., N.Y.C., 1981-83; libr., rechr. Kennedy Galleries, Inc., N.Y.C., 1984-86; program specialist, art tchr. Swinging Sixties Sr. Citizen Ctr., Bklyn., 1986-87; with Arts in Edn. Program, R.I., 1993-96. One-woman shows include Boston City Hall, 1978, Hunter Coll. Gallery, N.Y.C., 1983, Ten Worlds Gallery, N.Y.C., 1986, Gallery X, New Bedford, Mass., 1993-94, Hera Gallery, Wakefield, R.I., 1995, AS220, Providence, R.I., 1996, C.C. of R.I., Lincoln, 1996; group shows include Salem State Coll., Mass., 1978, Fuller Mus. Art, Brockton, Mass., 1989-90, Danforth Mus. Art, Framingham, Mass., 1989, Attleboro Mus., Mass., 1989, Gallery One, Providence, 1992, Gallery X, New Bedford, Mass., 1992-96, Grove St. Gallery, Worcester, Mass., 1993, Bell St. Chapel, Providence, 1994-95, AS220, Providence, 1994, Hera Gallery, Wakefield, R.I., 1993-96, St. Andrew's Sch., Barrington, R.I., 1994, McKillop Gallery Salve Regina U., Newport, R.I., 1995, North River Arts Soc., Marshfield Hills Village, Mass., 1995, Providence Art Club, 1995, The Sarah Doyle Gallery Brown U., Providence, 1995-96, R.I. Watercolor Soc. Slater Meml. Park, Pawtucket, 1995, Fed. Reserve Bank, Boston, 1996, Art Advisory/Boston, Quincy, Mass., 1996, Rotch-Jones-Duff Mus., New Bedford, Mass., 1997; represented in permanent collection at R.I. Hosp. Art Collection and pvt. collections. Bd. dirs. Hera Ednl. Found., 1994—. Recipient grant Artists Space, 1986, grant Flintridge Found., 1993, fellowship Vt. Studio Ctr., Johnson, 1990. Mem. SOHO 20 Gallery (nat. affiliate mem.). Home: 154 Lancaster St Providence RI 02906-2533

PERROS, THEODORE PETER, chemist, educator; b. Cumberland, Md., Aug. 16, 1921; s. Peter G. and Christina (Sioris) P.; m. Electra Paula Zolotas, July 21, 1973 (div.). BS, George Washington U., 1946, MS, 1947, Ph.D., 1952; postgrad., Technische Hochschule, Munich, Germany. Analyst research div. U.S. Naval Ordnance Lab., 1943-46; faculty George Washington U., Washington, 1946—, prof. chemistry and forensic scis., 1960—, chmn. dept. forensic sci., 1971-73, chmn. dept. chemistry, 1980-88; v.p. Meridian-West Assos., 1978—; rsch. chemist Bur. Ordnance, 1949; rsch. dir. Air Force Office Sci. R&D, 1958-59; cons. U.S. Naval Ordnance Lab., 1953-56; fed. commr., chmn. bd. dirs. Interstate Commn. Potomac River Basin, 1980; sec. Ahepa Ednl. Found., 1969-78; mem. Chesapeake Bay Sci. and Tech. Adv. Com., 1993. Author: (with William F. Sager) Chemical Principles, 1961, (with C.R. Naeser, W. Harkness) Experiments in General Chemistry, 1961, College Chemistry, 1966; Contbr. (with C.R. Naeser, W. Harkness) articles to profl. jours. Pres. So. Intercollegiate Athletic Conf., 1968, Hellenic Rep. Club of Washington, 1968-70, D.C. Heritage Groups Coun., 1980; campaign chmn. Nat. Rep. Heritage Groups Coun., 1977-78, recipient Kurt Voldemars Meml. award for disting. svc., 1985; mem. D.C. Rep. State Com., 1980—; exec. com. Rep. Nat. Com., 1994-95; chmn. Nat. Rep. Heritage Groups Coun., 1994-95; elected Bob Dole del. San Diego Rep. Conv., 1996. Named Disting. Prof. in Edn. George Washington U., 1990, Award of Distinction, CHS Alumni Assn., 1992; NSF fellow, 1959; AEC grantee, 1951-53, Rsch. Corp. grantee, 1953-54. Fellow Am. Inst. Chemists, Am. Acad. Forensic Scis., Washington Acad. Scis.; mem. Am. Chem. Soc., Soc. Applied Spectroscopy, German Lang. Soc., Chem. Soc. London, Gesellschaft Deutscher Chemiker, Philos. Soc. Washington, Am. Hellenic Ednl. Progressive Assn. (pres. Inst. Arts and Scis., pres. Washington chpt. 1976-78, dist. gov. 1982-83, supreme gov. 1985-86, AHEPA Acad. Achievement award 1984), Sigma Xi, Omicron Delta Kappa, Alpha Chi Sigma (pres. 1964, bd. gov.'s 1986-88, Profl. Merit award 1985, Profl. Chemistry award 1985). Research on stabilities of inorganic coordination polymers, preparation and characterization fluorine containing compounds transition metals. Home: 5825 3rd Pl NW Washington DC 20011-2106

PERROT, PAUL NORMAN, museum director; b. Paris, France, July 28, 1926; came to U.S., 1946, naturalized, 1954; s. Paul and K. Norman (Derr) P.; m. Joanne Stovall, Oct. 23, 1954; children—Paul Latham, Chantal Marie Claire, Jeannine, Robert. Student, Ecole du Louvre, 1945-46, N.Y. U. Inst. Fine Arts, 1946-52. Asst. The Cloisters, Met. Mus. Art, 1948-52; asst. to dir. Corning (N.Y.) Mus. Glass, 1952-54, asst. dir. mus., 1954-60, dir., 1960-72; editor Jour. Glass Studies, 1959-72; asst. sec. for mus. programs Smithsonian Instn., Washington, 1972-84; dir. Va. Mus. Fine Arts, 1984-91; dir. Santa Barbara Mus. Art, 1991-94, mus. cons., 1995—; lectr. glass history, aesthetics, museology; past v.p. Internat. Coun. Mus. Found.; past pres. N.E. Conf. Mus.; past pres. Internat. Centre for Study of Preservation and Restoration of Cultural Property, Rome, mem. coun., 1974-88. Author: Three Great Centuries of Venetian Glass, 1958, also numerous articles on various hist. and archael. subjects. Former trustee Winterthur Mus.; former trustee, treas. Mus. Computer NEtwork; mem. Internat. Cons. Com. for the Preservation of Moenjodaro; chmn. adv. com. World Monuments Fund; chmn. vis. com. Getty Conservation Inst. Mem. Am. Assn. Mus. (past v.p., coun. 1967-78), N.Y. State Assn. Mus. (past pres), Internat. Assn. History Glass (past v.p.) Corning Friends of Library (past pres.), So. Tier Library System (past pres.).

PERRUCCI, ROBERT, sociologist, educator; b. N.Y.C., Nov. 11, 1931; s. Dan and Inez (Mucci) P.; m. Carolyn Land Cummings, Aug. 4, 1965; children: Mark Robert, Celeste Ann, Christopher Robert, Alissa Cummings, Martin Cummings. B.S., SUNY, Cortland, 1958; M.S. (Social Sci. Research Council fellow), Purdue U., Ph.D., 1962. Asst. prof. sociology Purdue U., West Lafayette, Ind., 1962-65; assoc. prof. Purdue U., 1965-67, prof., 1967—, head dept., 1978-87; vis. Simon prof. U. Manchester (Eng.), 1968-69; Bd. dirs. Ind. Center on Law and Poverty, 1973-76. Author: Sociology, 1983, Circle of Madness, 1974, Divided Loyalties, 1980, The Triple Revolution, 1971, Profession Without Community, 1968, The Engineers and the Social System, 1968, Mental Patients and Social Networks, 1982, Plant Closings: International Context and Local Consequences, 1988, Networks of Power, 1989, Japanese Auto Transplants in the Heartland: Corporatism and Community, 1994; editor: The American Sociologist, 1982—, Social Problems, 1993-96; contbr. articles to profl. jours. Served with USMC, 1951-53. Recipient grants NSF, 1966-68, 76-78, grants NIMH, 1969-72. Mem. Am. Sociol. Assn., Soc. Study Social Problems (dir. 1980-83, v.p. 1996-97), N. Central Sociol. Assn. (pres. 1973-74). Home: 305 Leslie Ave West Lafayette IN 47906-2411 Office: Dept Sociology Purdue U West Lafayette IN 47907

PERRY, ANTHONY FRANK, entertainment company executive, printing company executive, graphic designer; b. L.A., Oct. 23, 1965; s. Frank Guy and Verna Dean Perry. Artist Thunderbird Printing Co., Inc., Reno, Nev., 1983-87; pres., chief exec. officer T-Bird Entertainment, Inc., Reno, 1987-91; mktg. dir. Thunderbird Printing and Screening Inc., Reno, 1991-92; pres., CEO Perri Entertainment Svcs., Inc., Reno, 1992—; tour pass security designer Rolling Stones World Tour, 1989-90, Billy Joel Storm Front Tour, 1990, New Kids on the Block, 1990-91, Jimmy Buffett Chameleon Caravan, 1994, Billy Joel River of Dreams, 1994, ZZ Top Antenna World Tour, 1994; designer credentials for San Francisco 49ers, 1995 season; founder Knotty Baker Pretzel Co.; promoter Big Bang New Years Party, 1987-91; founder Webcarvers Am. Interactive Devel. Co.; creator StreetMagic web site and products. Author: The Expert from Out of Town; lighting designer Sheep Dip Show, Reno Hilton, 1986, 87, 89; designer tour logo Doobie Brothers and Foreigner Tour 1994; designer Michael Jackson History World Tour, 1996-97, U2 World Tour. Mem. Nev. Repertory Co., 1983-89. Mem. Reno Advt. Club, Rotary Internat. Roman Catholic. Office: Perri Entertainment Svcs Inc PO Box 11852 Reno NV 89510-1852

PERRY, ANTHONY JOHN, retired hospital executive; b. Dighton, Mass., Oct. 19, 1919; s. Antone and Jessie P.; m. Harriet M. McGirr, Nov. 26, 1949; children: Joan Perry, Martha. B.S. in Edn, State Coll. Mass. at Bridgewater, 1942; MHA, Northwestern U., 1952. Flight supt. Trans World Airlines, Lisbon, Portugal, 1946-47; sta. mgr. Peruvian Internat. Airlines, N.Y.C., 1947-49; with adminstrn. Decatur and Macon County Hosp. (now Decatur Meml. Hosp.), Decatur, Ill., 1952-86, adminstr., 1961-69, exec. v.p., 1969-74, pres., CEO, 1974-86; ret., 1996; cons. in field, 1986—; bd. dirs. MMI Cos., 1985-95, chmn., 1985-94; pres. Mental Health Assn. Macon County, 1957; mem. Tech. Coun. Means and Methods of Financing Health Care for Ill. Bd. dirs. Macon County chpt. ARC, 1960-66, South Cen. Ill. Health Planning Council, 1969—, United Way Decatur and Macon County, 1960-66, Voluntary Hosps. Am., 1977-86; mem. adv. bd. Grad. Studies Ctr., Millikin U. Served with USAAF, 1942-46. Fellow Am. Coll. Hosp. Adminstrs.; mem. Am. Hosp. Assn. (trustee, mem. regional adv. bd., chmn. coun. on fin. 1975-79), Ill. Hosp. Assn. (pres. 1972, chmn. rate rev. steering com. 1979—), Decatur Country Club, La Quinta (Calif.) Resort Golf Club. Home: 421 Hackberry Dr Decatur IL 62521-5501

PERRY, ARTHUR WILLIAM, plastic surgeon; b. Cornwall, N.Y., Jan. 2, 1957; s. Michael Martin and Harriet (Estrin) P. AB magna cum laude, Rutgers Coll., 1977; MD with distinction, Albany Med. Coll., 1981. Diplomate Am. Bd. Plastic Surgery. Clin. fellow in surgery Harvard Med. Sch., Boston, 1981-84; fellow in burn surgery Cornell U. Med. Coll., N.Y.c., 1984-85; resident in plastic surgery U. Chgo., 1985-87; clin. asst. prof. surgery UMDNJ-Robert Wood Johnson Med. Sch., New Brunswick, 1987—; clin. assoc. in surgery U. Pa., Phila., 1993—; mem. N.J. Bd. Med. Examiners, Trenton, 1995—; mem. bus. devel. com. Carnegie Bank, Princeton, N.J., 1990—. Co-author: Cosmetic Surgery, 1997; contbr. chpt. to book, articles to profl. jours. Recipient Gingrass award Plastic Surgery Rsch. Coun., 1981, best paper award Midwestern Assn. Plastic Surgeons, 1987. Fellow ACS; mem. Am. Soc. Plastic and Reconstructive Surgeons, Am. Soc. Aesthetic Plastic Surgery, Alpha Omega Alpha. Office: 3055 State Route 27 Franklin Park NJ 08823-1315

PERRY, BILL, photojournalist. Photo editor Gannett News Svc., Arlington, Va. Office: Gannett News Svc 1000 Wilson Blvd Lowr 10 Arlington VA 22209-3901

PERRY, B(ILLY) DWIGHT, lawyer; b. Oklahoma City, Jan. 28, 1933; s. William C. and Julia Walton (Bray) P.; m. Shirley Andersen, June 16, 1959 (div. 1973); m. Suzanne Meyer , Sept. 15, 1973; children: Scott R., Ryan W., Samantha G., Devin D. BA, U. Okla., 1955; JD, Georgetown U., 1963. Bar: D.C. 1964, U.S. Supreme Ct. 1968. Law clk. to Judge E. Barrett Prettyman U.S. Ct. Appeals (D.C. cir.), 1963-64; assoc. McCarty & Wheatley, Washington, 1964-67; assoc., then ptnr. Dow, Lohnes & Albertson, Washington, 1967-91, mng. ptnr., 1991—. Lt. arty. U.S. Army, 1956-60. Mem. ABA, Fed. Communications Bar Assn., D.C. Bar Assn. (Young Lawyer of Yr. 1967-68), Washington Golf and Country Club. Episcopalian. Avocations: fishing, hunting, scuba diving. Office: Dow Lohnes & Albertson Ste 800 1200 New Hampshire Ave NW Washington DC 20036-6802

PERRY, BRADFORD KENT, academic administrator; b. Boston, Oct. 26, 1942; s. Robert Woodward and Louise (Kent) P.; m. Marilyn Ann Scott, June 13, 1964; children: Katherine, Susan. BA, Harvard U., 1964; MBA, Stanford U., 1970. Commd. ensign USN, 1964, advanced through grades to lt., 1967, served in various locations, 1964-71, resigned, 1971; with Stanford (Calif.) U., 1971-88, asoc. contr., 1981-88; vice chancellor Univ. System N.H., Durham, 1988—; exec. dir. Bus. Mgmt. Inst., Stanford, 1981-86; bd. govs. N.H. Pub. TV, Durham, 1988—; pres. adv. bd. The Common Fund, 1996—. Office: Univ System NH Meyers Ctr Durham NH 03824

PERRY, BURTON LARS, pediatrician; b. Midland, Mich., Dec. 8, 1931; s. Willard Russell and Myrl Alice (Jacobsen) P.; m. Nancy Fawn Towsley, Aug. 24, 1956; children: Ellen, Willard. BS, U. Mich., 1953, MD, 1960. Diplomate Am. Bd. Pediats.; sub-bd. pediat. cardiology. Physician U. Mich., Ann Arbor, 1960-78, Childrens Hosp. Mich., Detroit, 1978—. 1st lt. infantry, U.S. Army, 1954-56. Home: 1416 Dicken Dr Ann Arbor MI 48103-4417 Office: Childrens Hosp Mich 3901 Beaubien St Detroit MI 48201-2119

PERRY, CATHERINE D., judge; b. 1952. BA, Univ. of Okla., 1977; JS, Wash. Univ. Sch. of Law, 1980. Sec., law clk. Gillespie, Perry & Gentry, Sentinel, Okla., 1970, 77-78; with Armstrong, Teasdale, Kramer & Vaughn, St. Louis, 1980-90; magistrate judge U.S. Dist. Ct. (Mo. ea. dist.), 8th circuit, St. Louis, 1990-94, district judge, 1994—. Mem. Fed. Magistrate Judges Assn., Nat. Assn. of Women Judges, Am. Bar Assn., Mo. Bar Assn., Bar Assn. of Metropolitan St. Louis, Women Lawyers Assn. of Greater St. Louis. Office: US Courthouse 1114 Market St Rm 319 Saint Louis MO 63101-2038*

PERRY, CHARLES OWEN, sculptor; b. Helena, Mont., Oct. 18, 1929; s. Owen Hindmarch and Margaret Carroll (Bache) P.; m. Sheila Alicia Henry, June 22, 1962; children—Paul, Carlo, Daniela, Patrick, Marco. Student, Columbia U., 1953; M.Arch., Yale U., 1958. Architect Skidmore Owings & Merrill, San Francisco, 1958-64, Prix de Rome Architecture, 1964-66; sculptor-in-residence Dartmouth Coll., 1973. One-man shows include Hansen Gallery, San Francisco, 1964, Waddell Gallery, N.Y.C., 1967, 70, Dartmouth Coll., 1973, Arts Club, Chgo., 1973; exhibited in group shows at Whitney Mus., 1964, 66, Spoleto Festival, 1967, Venice Biennale, 1970, Quadrienalle di Arte de Roma, 1977, Katonah Gallery, N.Y.; represented in permanent collections at Mus. Modern Art, N.Y.C., Art Inst. Chgo., San Francisco Mus. Art, U. Ind. Mus. Art, Dartmouth Coll., U. Mich., Nat. Air and Space Mus., IBM, Charlotte, N.C., Hyatt Regency, San Francisco, Fed. Res. Bank, Mpls., Barnett Plaza, Tampa, Lincoln Ctr., Dallas, Shell Oil Bldg., Melbourne, Australia, GE Hdqrs., Fairfield, Conn., Bushnell Park, Hartford, Conn., Crystal City, Arlington, Va.; patentee in furniture design field. Served with U.S. Army, 1951-53. Decorated Bronze star. Fellow Am. Acad. Rome, Nat. Acad. Design; mem. Sculptors Guild, Silvermine Guild, Century Assn. (N.Y.C.). Roman Catholic. Home: 20 Shorehaven Rd Norwalk CT 06855-2807 Studio: 3 Raymond St Norwalk CT 06854-3107

PERRY, DALE LYNN, chemist; b. Greenville, Tex., May 12, 1947; s. Francis Leon and Violet (Inabinette) P. BS, Midwestern U., 1969; MS, Lamar U., 1972; PhD, U. Houston, 1974. NSF fellow dept. chemistry Rice U., Houston, 1976-77; Miller Research fellow dept. chemistry U. Calif.-Berkeley, 1977-79; prin. investigator solid state chemistry and spectroscopy Lawrence Berkeley Lab. U. Calif., 1979—, sr. scientist, 1987—; lectr. Ana G. Mendez Ednl. Found., 1988; rsch. mem. G.T. Seaborg Inst. for Transactinium Sci. Author, editor: Instrumental Surface Analysis of Geologic Materials, 1990, Applications of Analytical Techniques to the Characterization of Materials, 1992, Applications of Synchrotron Radiation Techniques to Materials Science, 1993, II, 1995, III, 1996; contbr. articles to profl. jours. Fellow Royal Soc. Chemistry (London); mem. Am. Chem. Soc. (chmn. materials chemistry and engring. subdivsn., indsl. and engring. chemistry divsn., 1992-96), Soc. Applied Spectroscopy, Coblentz Soc., Materials Rsch. Soc. (corp. participation com. 1991—), Sigma Xi (nat. rsch. award 1994). Office: U Calif Lawrence Berkeley Lab Mail Stop 70A-1150 Berkeley CA 94720

PERRY, DAVID, priest. Ecumenical officer Nat. Episcopal Ch., N.Y.C. Office: Episcopal Ch Ctr 815 2nd Ave New York NY 10017-4503

PERRY, DONALD A., cable television consultant; b. Newport News, Va., July 18, 1938. With James Broadcasting, 1961; v.p., gen. mgr. Hampton Rds. Music Corp., Hampton Rds. Cablevision Corp., Danville Cablevision Corp., 1971-70; pres., treas. Donald A. Perry & Assocs., Inc., Gloucester, Va., 1970—; prin. Am. Cablevision Corp., 1970—; sec., treas. Communications East Corp.; sec., treas. 1st Commonwealth Communications, Inc., also chmn. bd. dirs.; pres., chief oper. officer 1st Commonwealth Cablevision, Ltd.; sec. Atlantic Metrovision Corp.; owner Gourmet Mkt., Ltd. With USCG, 1956-60. Recipient J.L. Johnson award, 1984; Paul Harris fellow. Mem. Nat. Cable TV Assn., Community Antenna TV Assn. (bd. dirs.), Va. Cable TV Assn. (past pres.), So. Cable TV Assn. (past officer, past dir.), Rotary (Newport News chpt., past pres.), Tower Club. Home: 201 Country Club Rd Newport News VA 23606-3705 Office: Donald A Perry & Assocs Inc PO Box 1275 Newport News VA 23601-0275 also: Summerville Plantation Gloucester VA 23061

PERRY, DONALD LESTER, II, venture capitalist; b. Culver City, Calif., Jan. 21, 1958; s. Donald Lester Sr. and Joyce Estella (Kirklin) P.; m. Michael Albert Behn, July 24, 1982. BA in Econs. and Polit. Sci., Williams Coll., 1979; MBA in Strategic Mgmt., Claremont (Calif.) Grad. Sch., 1990. Fgn. exch. trader Morgan Guaranty Trust Co., N.Y.C., 1979-80; exec. recruiter Benson-McBride & Assoc., Beverly Hills, Calif., 1980-82; asst. v.p. money markets divsn. Nat. Australia Bank, L.A., 1982-86; v.p., eurodollar trader Sanwa Bank of Calif., L.A., 1986-88; v.p. comml. loans Union Bank, L.A., 1989-90; mng. ptnr. Pine Cobble Ptnrs., L.A., 1990—; speaker Pacific Coast Regional SBDC, L.A., 1989—, Nat. Assn. Black MBAs, L.A., 1990—, So. Calif. Edison/Joint Coun., L.A., 1990—. Contbr. articles to mags. Mem. Town Hall of Calif., L.A., 1990. Recipient Outstanding Entrepreneur of Yr., Peter F. Drucker Ctr. at Claremont Grad. Sch., 1995; named Positive Black Role Model, Assn. Black Women Entrepreneurs, 1993. Mem. L.A. Venture Assn., L.A. Urban Bankers, Pacific Coast Regional Small Bus. Devel. Corp. (mem. loan com. 1990-94), L.A. World Affairs Coun. Republican. Avocations: reading, golf, travel. Office: 811 W 7th St Ste 1000 Los Angeles CA 90017-3421

PERRY, DONNY RAY, electrician; b. Amarillo, Tex., Apr. 29, 1959; s. Ernest Elwood and Donnie Mae Perry; m. Tina Marie Conn, Sept. 9, 1988; children: Contessa, Jason, Stephen, Christopher. Cert. in fiber optics, Tex. State Tech. Inst., 1988; student, Amarillo Coll., 1990—. Electrician Mason & Hanger, Amarillo, 1979—; mem. negotiating com. Mason & Hanger, 1989-90, mem. sick leave and team concept coms., 1991, mem. elec. safety com., 1992, mem. job track analysis and procedure adherence coms., 1993. Mem. Internat. Brotherhood Elec. Workers, Metal Trades Coun. (negotiating com. 1989-90, exec. bd. 1989-90, co-chair elec. safety com. 1995—, team leader Hazard Identification Team 1995—, legis. and polit. action com. 1996—, apprenticeship com. 1996—), Phi Theta Kappa, Nat. Dean's List. Avocations: snow skiing, water skiing, running.

PERRY, DOUGLAS, opera singer. B.M., Wittenberg U.; M.A., Ball State U. Made debut as Don Basilio in Marriage of Figaro, with N.Y.C. Opera; appeared as King Kaspar in: Amahl and the Night Visitors; appeared as Timothy in: Help! Help! The Globolinks; appeared as Guillot in: Manon; Dancing Master and Brighella in: Ariadne auf Naxos; Met. Opera debut as scientist/first mate in: The Voyage (Philip Glass); European debut with Netherlands Opera as Mahatma Gandhi in Satyagraha (Philip Glass); appeared as analyst in A Quiet Place (Bernstein), La Scala and Vienna Stadtsoper; featured soloist on tours and recs. with Gregg Smith Singers and Camerata Singers; performed with Sante Fe Opera, also performed with Ft. Worth Opera, Chatauqua Opera, N.Y.C. Opera, Opera Co. of Boston, Houston Grand Opera, Balt. Opera., Miami Opera, Chgo. Lyric Opera, Seattle Opera, San Francisco Opera, Opera Co. Phila.; recs. include Satyagraha, Songs from Liquid Days, A Quiet Place, Mother of Us All. Address: 170 W End Ave New York NY 10023-5401 Office: Trawick Artists Mgmt Inc 1926 Broadway New York NY 10023-6915

PERRY, E. ELIZABETH, social worker, real estate manager; b. Balt., Oct. 2, 1954; d. James Glenn and Pearl Elizabeth (Christopher) P.; 1 child, Linden Andrew. AA, C.C. of Balt., 1973; B in Art, Psychology, Social Work, U. Md., Balt., 1975, MSW, 1978. Asst. grant coord. Md. Conf. Social Concern, Balt., 1975; dir. social svcs. West Balt. Cmty. Health Care Corp., 1978-80; tng. counselor NutriSystem Inc. of Md., Balt., 1983-86; counselor/psychotherapist Switlik Elem. Sch., Marathon, Fla., 1988-89; program dir. emergency shelter Children's Home Soc., Miami, 1990-91; health educator, spokesperson Rape Treatment Ctr., Miami, 1991-94; CEO, pres. bd. Child Assault Prevention Project, Miami, 1993—; self-employed in real estate rehab. and mgmt., 1980—; pub. spkr. on women's and children's issues/sexual assault issues, 1990—. Bd. dirs. Partnership Way, 1993-95, ACHIEVE, 1995—; pub. citizen Dem. Nat. Com. Mem. AAUW, NOW (bd. dirs. Dade County 1994-95), Nat. Abortion Rights Action League, Amnesty Internat., People for the Am. Way, Psi Chi, Phi Theta Kappa. Democrat. Avocations: hiking, skating, dogs, sewing, knitting. Home: 5161 Alton Rd Miami Beach FL 33140 Office: Child Assault Prev Project Omni Mall Ste 1195 1601 Biscayne Blvd Miami FL 33132-1224

PERRY, EDNA BURRELL, retired elementary school principal; b. Washington, July 30, 1934; d. Harold Flowers and Annie Mae (Harrison) Burrell; m. Sidney Lee Perry, Jr., June 5, 1954; children: Angela, Andrea R. BME magna cum laude, Howard U., Washington, 1956; MA in Adminstrn./Supervision, Roosevelt U., Chgo., 1972. Cert. prin., nat. cert. counselor. Tchr. Healy Sch., Chgo., 1959-62; from asst. prin. to prin., counselor C.H. Wacker Sch., Chgo., 1962-94; ret.; team dir. Golden NeoLife Diamite Internat., Milpitas, Calif., 1986—. Vol. Am. Cancer Soc., Chgo., 1960-80; minister of music Ch. of the Good Shepherd, Chgo., 1959—, condr. choir, 1959—. Named Lay Person of the Yr., Ch. of Good Shepherd, 1980, Woman of the Yr., 1992, Music award, 1994. Mem. Nat. Assn. Negro Musicians, Nat. Pharm. Assn. Aux. (nat. pres. 1977-79, 90-93), Delta Sigma Theta. United Ch. of Christ. Avocations: nutritional counseling. Home: 9201 S Cregier Ave Chicago IL 60617-3602

PERRY, EDWIN CHARLES, lawyer; b. Lincoln, Nebr., Sept. 29, 1931; s. Arthur Edwin and Charlotte C. (Peterson) P.; m. Joan Mary Hanson, June 5, 1954; children: Mary Mills, Judy Phipps, James Perry, Greg Perry, Jack Perry, Pricilla Perry. BS, U. Nebr., 1953, JD, 1955. Bar: Nebr. 1955, U.S. Dist. Ct. Nebr., 1955; U.S. Ct. Appeals Nebr., 1968. Prin. Perry, Guthery, Haase & Gessford, P.C., Lincoln, 1957—. Chmn. Lincoln Lancaster County Planning Com., Madonna Rehab. Hosp. Fellow Am. Bar Found., Nebr. Bar Found.; mem. Nebr. State Bar Assn. (chair ho. dels. 1987-88, pres. 1991-92), Nebr. Coun. Sch. Attys. (pres. 1978-79), Lincoln Bar Assn. (pres. 1982-83). Republican. Roman Catholic. Office: Perry Guthery Haase & Gessford PC 1400 Firstier Brk Bldg Lincoln NE 68508

PERRY, ESTON LEE, real estate and equipment leasing company executive; b. Wartburg, Tenn., June 16, 1936; s. Eston Lee and Willimae (Heidle) P.; m. Alice Anne Schmidt, Oct. 21, 1961; children: Julie Anne, Jeffrey John, Jennifer Lee. B.S., Ind. State U., 1961. With Oakley Corp., 1961—, dir., 1965—, v.p., 1981-86, pres., 1986—; corp. officer Ind. State Bank, Terre Haute, 1975-80; pres. One Twenty Four Madison Corp., Terre Haute, 1979—, also bd. dirs., chmn. bd., 1981—. Bd. dirs. Aviation Commn., Terre Haute, pres., 1970; bd. dirs. Salvation Army, Terre Haute, 1975-91, mem. exec. adv. bd., 1979-87; bd. dirs. Vigo County Dept. Pub. Welfare, 1979-82, Jr. Achievement Wabash Valley, 1980-86; bd. dirs. United Way of Wabash Valley, 1984-89, chmn. fund campaign, 1984, bd. dirs. United Way of Ind., 1984-90, v.p., 1986, pres. 1988-89; trustee Oakley Found., 1970—; bd. dirs. Terre Haute Symphony Orch., 1984-87, Ind. State U. Found., 1988—, Goodwill Industries of Terre Haute, 1984-97, Leadership Terre Haute, 1984-88, Cen. Eastside Assocs., 1984-88, pres., 1984-85; mem. exec. com. Ind. State U. Found., 1990-94; bd. dirs. City of Terre Haute Hulman Links Commn., pres., 1986-91; mem. President's Assocs., Ind. State U., adv. bd.; bd. overseers Sheldon Swope Art Gallery of Terre Haute, 1984-87; nat. mem. Council on Founds.; mem. adv. com. comml. air service study Ind. Dept. Commerce; bd. assocs. Rose Hulman Inst. Tech., 1986—; bd. dirs. Citizens Bank of Western Ind., 1996—. Served with U.S. Army, 1955-57. Mem. Jaycees Terre Haute (v.p. 1967-69), C. of C. Terre Haute (bd. dirs. 1984-93, vice chmn. 1986-88, chmn. 1990), Wabash Valley Pilots Assn., Aircraft Owners and Pilots Assn., Air Safety Found., Aviation Trades Assn., Lambda Chi Alpha. Clubs: Country of Terre Haute (bd. dirs.), Aero of Terre Haute; Sycamore Varsity (Ind. State U.). Lodges: Lions (pres. Terre Haute 1983-84), Elks. Home: 25 Bogart Dr Terre Haute IN 47803-2401 Office: 8 S 16th St Terre Haute IN 47807-4102

PERRY, EVELYN REIS, communications company executive; b. N.Y.C., Mar. 9; d. Lou L. and Bertl (Wolf) Reis; m. Charles G. Perry III, Jan. 7, 1968; children: Charles G. IV, David Reis. BA, Univ. Wis., 1963; student Am. Acad. Dramatic Arts, 1958-59, Univ. N.Mex., 1963-64. Lic. real estate broker, N.C. Vol. ETV project Peace Corps, 1963-65; program officer-radio/tv Peace Corps, Washington, 1965-68; dir. Vols. in Svc. to Am. (VISTA), Raleigh, N.C., 1977-80; exec. dir. CETA Program for Displaced Homemakers, Raleigh, 1980-81; cons. exec. dir. to Recycle Raleigh for Food and Fuel, Theater in the Park, 1981-83, Artspace, Inc., Raleigh, 1983-84; pres., chief exec. officer Carolina Sound Comm., MUZAK, Charleston, S.C. and 12 counties in S.C., 1984—; pub. rels. account exec. various cos., Washington, Syracuse, N.Y., 1969-71; cons. pub. rels. and orgn. Olympic Organizing Com., Mexico City, 1968; cons. pub. rels., fundraising, arts mgmt. pub. speaking, Ill., Pa., N.C., 1971-77; orgnl. and pub. speaking cons. Perry & Assocs., Raleigh, 1980—. Mem. adv. bd. Gov.'s Office Citizen Affairs, Raleigh, 1981-85; mem. Involvement Coun. of Wake County, N.C., Raleigh, 1981-84; mem. Adv. Coun. to Vols. in Svc. to Am., Raleigh, 1980-84; mem. Pres.'s adv. bd. Peace Corps, Washington, 1980-82; v.p., bd. dirs. Voluntary Action Ctr., Raleigh, 1980-84, bd. dirs., Charleston, 1988-94; sec. bd. dirs. Temple Kahil Kadosh Beth Elohim, 1987-89, sec. fin., 1989-90, v.p. programming, 1990-93, v.p. adminstrn. 1993-95; bd. dirs. Chopstik Theater, Charleston, 1989-90; del., chmn. S.C. Delegation to White House Conf. Small Bus., 1995. Mem. N.C. Coun. of Women's Orgns. (pres., v.p. 1982-84), Charleston Hotel and Motel Assn., N.C. Assn. Vol. Adminstrs. (bd. dirs. 1980-84), S.C. Restaurant Assn., Nat. Assn. Women Bus. Owners, Internat. Planned Music Assn. (bd. dirs. 1986—, newsletter editor), NAFE, Nat. Fedn. Ind. Businesses (mem. adv. bd. 1987—, chmn. leadership coun. 1994—), Internat. Platform Assn., Theaterworks (bd. dirs. 1994—), Charleston C. of C. Office: Carolina Sound Comm Inc 1941 Savage Rd Ste 200G Charleston SC 29407

PERRY, FREDERICK SAYWARD, JR., electronics company executive; b. Kittery Point, Maine, Aug. 14, 1940; s. Frederick Sayward Sr. and Rita Alice (Contant) P.; m. Judith Ann Golden, June 21, 1963 (div. 1973); 1 child, Elizabeth; m. Sarah Winthrop Smith, Aug. 26, 1979; children: Mariah, Justus. BA in Math., Harvard U., 1963. Applications engr. Block Engring. Inc., Cambridge, Mass., 1963-67, 69-71; sci. officer Arms Control and Disarmament Agy., Washington, 1967-69; sales mgr. Infrared Industries Inc., Waltham, Mass., 1971-75; mktg. rep. Honeywell Radiation Ctr., Lexington, Mass., 1975-77; pres. Boston Electronics Corp., Brookline, Mass., 1977—. Contbr. article to Laser Focus mag. Mem. Alexandria (Va.) Dem. Com., 1969-70, Brookline Town Meeting, 1988, mem. fin. com., 1993-95, conservation commr., 1995-96; bd. dirs. Brookline Green Space Alliance, 1987—, v.p., 1995-96, pres., 1996—. Mem. Optical Soc. Am., Laser Inst. Am., Internat. Soc. Optical Engring. Home: 32 Bowker St Brookline MA 02146-6955 Office: Boston Electronics Corp 72 Kent St Brookline MA 02146-7347

PERRY, GAYLORD JACKSON, former professional baseball player; b. Williamston, N.C., Sept. 15, 1938. Student, Campbell Coll. Began profl. career with St. Cloud team, No. League; pitcher San Francisco Giants, 1962-71, Cleve. Indians, 1972-75, Tex. Rangers, 1975-77, 80, San Diego Padres, 1978-79, N.Y. Yankees, 1980, Atlanta Braves, 1981, Seattle Mariners, 1982-83, Kansas City Royals, 1983. Co-author: Me and the Spitter: An Autobiographical Confession, 1974. Recipient Cy Young Mem. award Am. League, 1972, Cy Young award Nat. League, 1978; mem. Nat. League All-Star team, 1966, 70, 79, Am. League All-Star team, 1972, 74; inducted into Baseball Hall of Fame, Cooperstown, N.Y., 1991. Address: PO Box 1958 Kill Devil Hills NC 27948-1958*

PERRY, GEORGE, neuroscience researcher; b. Lompoc, Calif., Apr. 12, 1953; s. George Richard and Mary Arlene (George) P.; m. Paloma Aguilar, May 21, 1983; children: Anne A., Elizabeth A. BA, U. Calif., Santa Barbara, 1974; PhD, U. Calif., Scripps Inst. of Oceanography, San Diego, 1979. Postdoctoral fellow Baylor Coll. Medicine, Houston, 1979-82; from asst. prof. to prof. pathology, neurosci. Case Western Res. U., Cleve., 1982—, chmn. med. sch. faculty coun., 1994-95, mem. faculty senate, 1996-97; chmn. study sect. NIH, Bethesda, Md., 1988-93. Editor: Alterations in the Neuronal Cytoskeleton in Alzheimer Disease, Clin. Neurosci.; assoc. editor Am. Jour. Pathology, 1994—; mem. editl. bd. Am. Jour. Pathology, 1992—, African Jour. Neurosci., Alzheimer Assoc. Disorder, Alzehimer's Disease Review; contbr. papers to profl. publs. Fellow Muscular Dystrophy Assn., 1980; recipient Career Devel. award NIH, 1988; grantee NIH, 1988—. Mem. AAAS, Microcsopy Soc. N.E. Ohio (treas. 1986-88, trustee 1988-90, pres. 1990-91), Am. Soc. Cell Biology, Soc. Neurosci., Am. Assn. Investigative Pathologists, Am. Assn. Neuropathologists (awards com. 1992-96, coun. 1995—). Democrat. Roman Catholic. Home: 2500 Eaton Rd University Ht OH 44118-4339 Office: Case Western Res U 2085 Adelbert Rd Cleveland OH 44106-2622

PERRY, GEORGE LEWIS, research economist, consultant; b. N.Y.C., Jan. 23, 1934; s. Lewis G. and Helen L. (Couloumbis) P.; m. Jean Marion West, 1956; children: Elizabeth, Lewis G., George A.; m. 2d, Dina Needleman, 1987. BS, MIT, 1954, PhD, 1961. Editor Brookings Papers on Econ. Activity, 1970—; columnist L.A. Times, 1981-93; bd. dirs. State Farm Mut. Automobile Ins. Co., Bloomington, Ill., Dreyfus Mut. Funds, N.Y.C., Fed. Realty, Bethesda, Md.; co-dir. Brookings Panel Econ. Activity. Author: Unemployment, Money Wage Rates and Inflation, 1966; editor: Curing Chronic Inflation, 1978; contbr. articles to profl. jours. Mem. Am. Econs. Assn. Office: Brookings Instn 1775 Massachusetts Ave NW Washington DC 20036-2188

PERRY, GEORGE WILLIAMSON, lawyer; b. Cleve., Dec. 4, 1926; s. George William and Melda Patricia (Arther-Holt) P. B.A. in Econs., Yale U., 1949; J.D., U. Va., 1953. Bar: Ohio 1953, D.C. 1958, U.S. Supreme Ct. 1958, U.S. Ct. Appeals (D.C. cir.) 1959. Atty. U.S. Dept. Justice, Washington, 1954-56; assoc. Roberts and McInnis, Washington, 1957-59; atty. assoc. counsel Com. on Interstate Fgn. Commerce, U.S. Ho. of Reps., Washington, 1960-65; atty., advisor ICC, Washington, 1965-68; asst. dir. devel. Yale U., New Haven, 1968-70; dir. tax research Pan Am. World Airways, N.Y.C., 1973-75; hearing officer Indsl. Commn. Ohio, Cleve., 1978-81; sole practice, Cleve., 1981—. Served with U.S. Army, 1945-46. Mem. Soc. of Cincinnati in State of Conn., Concord Coalition, Ancient & Hon. Artillery Co. (Boston, hereditary mem.), Phi Delta Phi. Episcopalian.

PERRY, GEORGE WILSON, oil and gas company executive; b. Pampa, Tex., July 18, 1929; s. Frank M. and Ruth (Ingersoll) P.; m. Patricia Carberry Bowen; children: Sally, Jett Perry Pemrick, Susan Jeanne Perry Bynder, Virginia Anne Perry Haynie, Tobe Jackson Perry. BS in Petroleum Engring., U. Tulsa, 1952. Registered profl. engr., Tex. Engr. Stanolind Oil & Gas Co., Oklahoma City, 1952-53, Parker Drilling Co., Tulsa, 1953-54; drilling engr. Holm Drilling Co., Tulsa, 1954-55; drilling mgr. Mobil Oil, Victoria, Tex., Lake Charles, La., Paris, France, Anaco, Venezuela, N.Y.C., Tehran, Iran, Stavanger, Norway, New Orleans, La., 1955-79; exec. v.p. Loffland Bros. Co., Tulsa, 1979-89; pres., CEO Gas Well Properties, Inc., Dallas, 1989—; pres. George Perry Farms, Tunica, Miss., 1989—. Mem. Delta Tau Delta. Office: Gas Well Properties Inc PO Box 795302 5995 Summerside Dr Dallas TX 75379-5302

PERRY, HAROLD OTTO, dermatologist; b. Rochester, Minn., Nov. 18, 1921; s. Oliver and Hedwig Clara (Tornow) P.; m. Loraine Thelma Moehnke, Aug. 27, 1944; children—Preston, Oliver, Ann, John. AA, Rochester Jr. Coll., 1942; BS, U. Minn., 1944, MB, 1946, MD, 1947; MS, Mayo Grad. Sch. Medicine, 1953. Diplomate Am. Bd. Dermatology with spl. competence in dermatopathology (mem. 197979-90, v.p. 1989, pres. 1990). Intern Naval Hosp., Oakland, Calif., 1946-47; resident in dermatology Mayo Grad. Sch. Medicine, 1949-52; practice medicine specializing in dermatology Rochester, 1953-86; mem. staff Mayo Clinic, 1953-86, mem. emeritus staff, 1987—; instr., asst. prof., asso. prof. Mayo Med. Sch., 1953-86, prof., 1978-83, Robert H. Kieckhefer prof. dermatology, 1978-83, head dept. dermatology, 1975-83, emeritus prof. dermatology, 1987—; civilian cons. dermatology to surgeon gen. USAF, 1979—. Contbr. articles to med. jours. and, chpts. to books. With USNR, 1943-45, 46-49. Inducted into Rochester (Minn.) C.C. Alumni Hall of Fame, 1993; recipient Disting. Alumnus award May Found., 1995. Mem. AMA, Am. Acad. Dermatology (pres. 1981, Sulzberger internat. lectr. 1986), Am. Dermatol. Assn. (bd. dirs. 1985-89, pres. 1989-90), Noah Worcester Dermatol. Soc. (pres. 1969), Minn. Dermatol. Soc. (pres. 1967), Chgo. Dermatol. Soc., Internat. Soc. Tropical Dermatology, Minn. Med. Assn.; hon. mem. French Dermatol. Soc., Spanish Acad. Dermatology, Brazilian Dermatol. Soc., Ga. Dermatol. Soc., Iowa Dermatol. Soc., Korean Dermatol. Soc., Bolivar Soc. Dermatology, Jacksonville Dermatol. Soc., N.Am. Clin. Dermatol. Soc. Home: 3625 SW Bamber Valley Rd Rochester MN 55902 Office: Mayo Clinic Dermatology Dept Rochester MN 55905

PERRY, HAROLD TYNER, dentist, educator; b. Bismarck, N.D., Jan. 26, 1926; s. Harold Tyner and Isabel (McGillis) P.; m. Mary Lynn Moss, 1952; children: Harold Tyner III, Dana Lynn. Student, Bismarck Jr. Coll., 1946-47, U. N.D., 1948; DDS, Northwestern U., 1952, PhD in Physiology, 1961. USPHS rsch. fellow, 1952-56; practice dentistry Elgin, Ill., 1956—; mem. faculty Dental Sch. Northwestern U., 1954—, prof., chmn. dept. orthodontics, 1961-86; rsch. assoc. Mooseheart (Ill.) Hosp.; guest lectr. U. Nebr.; dental cons. Middle East sect. WHO; bd. dirs. Union Nat. Bank & Trust Co., Elgin; cons. VA; specialist cons. N.E. Regional Dental Bds. (NERB), 1987-90. Editorial chmn. Jour. Craniomandibular Disorders, Facial/Oral Pain, 1986—. Bd. dirs. Fox Valley coun. Boy Scouts Am., Elgin YMCA, Found. Ill. Archeology, 1980-90, Max McGraw Wildlife Found., 1979—, CAA; bd. govs. United Community Fund, Elgin. With inf. AUS, 1944-46, ETO. Decorated Bronze Star medal, Combat Inf. badge, Croix de Guerre; named Young Man of Year Elgin Jr. C. of C., 1961; recipient Award of Merit Northwestern U., 1974. Fellow Internat., Am. Colls. Dentists, Inst. Medicine Chgo.; mem. ADA, Am. Assn. Orthodonists, AAAS, Soc. Paulista de Orthodontia (hon.), South African Soc. Orthodontists (hon.), Sigma Xi, Alpha Tau Omega, Delta Sigma Delta, Omicron Kappa Upsilon. Methodist. Home: 413 N Alfred Ave Elgin IL 60123-3319 Office: 100 E Chicago St Elgin IL 60120-5585

PERRY, I. CHET, petroleum company executive; b. Phila., Jan. 18, 1943; s. Irving Chester Sr. and Erma Jackson (McNeil) P.; 1 child, London Schade. BA in Psychology, Bus., Lake Forest Coll., 1965. Lic. real estate broker, Ill. Sr. mgmt. trainee British Overseas Airways Corp., London, Eng., 1968-69; owner Itec Internat. Ltd., Barrington, Ill., 1970—; owner Itec Refining & Mktg. Co., Ltd., Barrington, 1970—, CEO, mng. dir., 1986—. Lt. U.S. Army, 1965-68, Vietnam. Decorated Bronze Star, Purple Heart. Mem. Am. Petroleum Inst., European Petrochem. Assn., Barrington Bd. Realtors (bd. dirs. 1974-78), Forest Grove Club, Barrington Tennis Club. Republican. Quaker. Avocations: tennis, photography. Home: 444 W Russell St Barrington IL 60010-4123

PERRY, J. WARREN, health sciences educator, administrator; b. Richmond, Ind., Oct. 25, 1921; s. Charles Thomas and Zona M. (Ohler) P. BA, DePauw U., 1944; postgrad., Harvard U., 1948-49; MA, Northwestern U., 1952, PhD, 1955; DSc (hon.), D'Youville Coll., 1990, Med. Coll. of Ohio, 1996. Instr. St. John's Mil. Acad., Delafield, Wis., 1944-47; counselor, asst. prof. psychology U. Ill.-Chgo., 1953-56; dir. prosthetic-orthotic edn., asst. prof. orthopaedic surgery Northwestern U. Med. Sch., 1957-61; lectr. psychology U. Chgo., 1957-61; asst. chief div. tng. Vocat. Rehab. Adminstrn., HEW, 1961-64, dep. asst. commr. research and tng., 1964-66; prof. health scis. adminstrn. SUNY-Buffalo, 1966-85, founding dean Sch. Health Related Professions, 1966-77, dean and prof. emeritus, 1985—; Mary E. Switzer Meml. lectr. Dallas, 1977, Lexington, 1991; mem. task force for Legislation for Allied Health Professions, 1966-67; com. edn. allied health professions and svcs., coun. med. edn. AMA, 1968-73; nat. adv. com. Am. Dietetic Assn., 1970-75, chmn., 1972-75; nat. rev. com., regional med. programs HEW, 1969-72; mem. Inst. Medicine, NAS, 1973—, steering com. on manpower policy for primary care, bd. health promotion and disease prevention, 1981-83, sr. advisor, com. to study the role allied health, com. to study med. manpower in VA, 1988-91; spl. med. adv. com. VA, 1974-77; task force on manpower for prevention Fogarty Internat. Inst., NIH, 1975-76; acad. planning com. Mass. Gen. Hosp. Founding editor: Jour. Allied Health, 1972-78, editor emeritus, 1985—; contbr. articles to profl. jours. Bd. dirs., dir. com. opera edn. Lyric Opera Guild, Chgo., 1957-61; chmn. acad. divsn. dr., coun. trustees Buffalo Philharm. Orch., 1987-93; bd. dirs. Goodwill Industries Buffalo, 1969-76; trustee Cmty. Music Sch. Buffalo, 1977-80; adv. bd., v.p. Sisters of Charity Hosp., Buffalo, 1969-87, pres., 1986-88; bd. visitors U. Pitts., 1977-80; coun. trustees D'Youville Coll., Buffalo, 1978-88, trustee emeritus, 1989-95; bd. dirs. Am. Lung Assn. Western N.Y., 1975-92, pres., 1983; bd. dirs. ARC, Buffalo, Artpark State Performing Arts Ctr., Lewiston, N.Y., 1986—; Am. Lung Assn. N.Y. State, 1981-85, exec. com., 1989-92; chmn. N.Y. State Coalition Smoking or Health, Albany, N.Y., 1987-91; trustee Theodore Roosevelt Inaugural Site Found., 1987, pres., 1991-94; bd. advisors Buffalo Coun. on World Affairs, 1987-88; trustee Buffalo Opera Co., 1989-94, chmn. opera adv. coun., 1995—. Recipient Sustained Superior Svc. award HEW, 1965, Disting. Svc. award Am. Orthotics-Prosthetics Assn., 1966, Buffalo Opera Co., 1995, Chancellors award for adminstrv. svc. SUNY, 1977, 1st Allied Health Leadership award, 1988, Disting. Author award Jour. Allied Health, 1978, Cert. of Merit, AMA, 1979, Pres. Cir. PIN, Buffalo State Coll., 1993, 50th Anniversary Alumni citation De Pauw U., 1994, Outstanding Svc. award Theodore Roosevelt Inaugural Site Found., 1994, Brotherhood/Sisterhood award in health NCCJ Western N.Y., 1995, Christmas Seal Hall of Fame award ALA N.Y. State, 1995, Disting. Citizenship award Mayor of Buffalo, 1995; named Outstanding Individual Philanthropist, Nat. Soc. Fundraising Execs. Western N.Y., 1992, Ky. Col., 1969, Nebr. admn., 1964; J. Warren Perry Disting. Author award named in his honor Jour. Allied Health, 1984—, J. Warren Perry Meml. lectr. named in his honor SUNY, Buffalo, 1990—, J. Warren Perry Outstanding Vol. Leadership award named in his honor Western N.Y. chpt. ALA, 1994—; Perry Scholarships presented in his honor U. Buffalo Found., 1991—. Fellow Assn. Schs. of Allied Health Professions (pres. 1969-70, cert. of merit 1977, Pres.'s award 1978, Honors of Society 1984); mem. APA, Am. Dietetics Assn. (hon.), Am. Personnel and Guidance Assn., Nat. Rehab. Assn., Phi Beta Kappa, Phi Delta Kappa (pres. 1955), Delta Tau Delta. Home: 83 Bryant St Buffalo NY 14209-1836

PERRY, JAMES ALFRED, environmental scientist, consultant, educator, administrator; b. Dallas, Sept. 27, 1945. BA in Fisheries, Colo. State U., 1968; MA, Western State Coll., 1973; PhD, Idaho State U., 1981. Sr. water quality specialist Idaho Div. Environ., Pocatello, 1974-82; area mgr. Centrac Assocs., Salt Lake City, 1982; prof. forest water quality U. Minn., St. Paul, 1982—, dir. natural resources policy and mgmt., 1985—, dir. grad. studies in water resources, 1988-92; dep. dir. AID-funded Environ. Tng. Project for Ctrl. and Ea. Europe, 1992-96; spl. asst. to dean grad. sch. U. Minn., St. Paul, 1996—; vis. scholar Oxford U., Green College, Eng., 1990-91; internat. cons. in water quality. Author: Water Quality Management a Natural Resource, 1996. Charter mem. Leadership Devel. Acad., Lakewood, Minn., 1988. ACOP/ESCOP nat. leadership fellow, 1995-96. Mem. Minn. Acad. Scis. (bd. dirs. 1987-90), Am. Water Resources Assn., Internat. Water Resources Assn., Internat. Soc. Theoretica and Applied Limnology, N.Am. Benthol Soc. (exec. bd. Albuquerque 1990-91), Sigma Xi, Xi Sigma Pi, Gamma Sigma Delta. Office: U Minn Dept Forest Resource 115 Green Hall 1530 Cleveland Ave N Saint Paul MN 55108-1027

PERRY, JAMES FREDERIC, philosophy educator, author; b. Washington, Jan. 21, 1936; s. Albert Walter and Helene Anna Maria (Neumeyer) P.; m. Sandra Jean Huizing, Feb. 18, 1957 (div. May 1972); children: Sandra Elaine, James Frederic Jr., Bartholomew; m. Roberta Schofield, June 6, 1984. Student, Princeton U., 1953-56, Marietta (Ohio) Coll., 1958-60; BA with honors in Philosophy, Ind. U., 1962, PhD in Philosophy of Edn., 1972. NDEA fellow in philosophy U. N.C., 1962-65; instr. N.C. State U., Raleigh, 1965-66; Univ. fellow Ind. U., 1971; adj. lectr. Ind. U., Bloomington, 1972-

75; prof. philosophy Hillsborough Community Coll., Tampa, Fla., 1975—. Author: Random, Routine, Reflective, 1989; contbr. articles to profl. jours. Precinct committeeman Dem. Party, Tampa, 1988—. Nat. Def. Edn. Act fellow U. N.C., 1962-65, Univ. fellow Ind. U., 1970-71. Mem. AAUP (pres. Fla. conf. 1986-89, chair com. "A" on acad. freedom 1989—), C.C. Humanities Assn. (so. divsn. exec. bd. 1981-89), Internat. Soc. Philos. Enquiry, Internat. Congress for Critical Thinking and Moral Critiques (founding mem. S.E. coun. 1991), Princeton Alumni Assn. of Fla. Suncoast (sec. 1983-86, pres. 1986-95), Mensa, Authors Guild, Textbook and Acad. Authors Assn. Avocations: travel, foreign travel, genealogy, commercial piloting, flight instruction. Office: Hillsborough C C PO Box 10561 Tampa FL 33679-0561

PERRY, JEAN LOUISE, dean; b. Richland, Wash., May 13, 1950; d. Russell S. and Sue W. Perry. BS, Miami U., Oxford, Ohio, 1972; MS, U. Ill., Urbana, 1973, PhD, 1976. Cons. ednl. placement office U. Ill., 1973-75; adminstrv. intern Coll. Applied Life Studies, 1975-76, asst. dean, 1976-77, assoc. dean, 1978-81, asst. prof. dept. phys. edn., 1976-81; assoc. prof. phys. edn. San Francisco State U., 1981-84, prof., 1984-90, chair, 1981-90; dean Coll. of Human and Community Scis. U. Nev., Reno, 1990—. Named to excellent tchr. list U. Ill., 1973-79. Mem. AAHPERD (fellow research consortium, pres. 1988-89), Am. Assn. Higher Edn., Am. Ednl. Research Assn., Nat. Assn. Phys. Edn. in Higher Edn., Nat. Assn. Girls and Women in Sports (guide coordinator, pres.), Delta Psi Kappa, Phi Delta Kappa. Home: 3713 Ranchview Ct Reno NV 89509-7437 Office: U Nev Coll Human and Cmty Scis 136 Reno NV 89557

PERRY, JEANNE ELYCE, principal; b. Ft. Collins, Colo., Jan. 23, 1953; d. Franklin Clyde and Ruth Caroline (Skoglund) Stewart; m. William Kay Perry, Dec. 28, 1974; children: Belinda Eve, Angela Marie. BA in Elem. Edn., Western State Coll., 1975; MA in Ednl. Leadership, U. No. Colo., 1992. Tchr. elem. sch. Soroco Sch. Dist., Oak Creek, Colo., 1977-86, L.A. Unified Sch. Dist., 1986-88; coord. elem. computer Weld RE-1 Sch. Dist., Gilcrest, Colo., 1988-93; prin. Delta (Colo.) Coun. Sch. Dist., 1993—. Leader Girl Scouts Am., Yampa, Colo., 1984-86, Platteville, Colo., 1988-89; precinct committeewoman Rep. Party, Platteville, 1991-93. Colo. Gov.'s grantee, 1990, 91. Mem. ASCD, NAESP. Baptist. Avocations: hiking, skiing, gardening, crafts. Office: Hotchkiss Elem Sch PO Box 309 Hotchkiss CO 81419

PERRY, JOE, guitarist; b. Boston, Sept. 10, 1950. With Aerosmith, 1970-80, 84—, The Joe Perry Project, 1980-84. Albums: (with Aerosmith) Aerosmith, 1973, Get Your Wings, 1974, Toys in the Attic, 1975, Rocks, 1976, Pure Gold, 1976, Draw the Line, 1977, Live Bootleg, 1978, A Night in the Ruts, 1979, Greatest Hits, 1980, Rock in a Hard Place, 1982, Done with Mirrors, 1986, Classics Live, 1986, Permanent Vacation, 1987, Gems, 1989, Pump, 1989, Pandora's Box, 1991, Get a Grip, 1993, Big Ones, 1994, Box of Fire, 1994, Nine Lives, 1997; (with Joe Perry Project) I've Got the Rock n' Rolls Again, Let the Music Do the Talking; composer music for films including The Karate Kid III, 1989, Repossessed, 1990, Wayne's World 2, 1993, Hot Shots! Part Deux, 1993, TV movie Ray Alexander: A Taste for Justice, 1994, TV series theme Spider-Man, 1995. Recipient (with Aerosmith) Grammy award Best Rock Group, 1994. Office: c/o Aerosmith Geffen/Columbia Records 9130 W Sunset Blvd Los Angeles CA 90069-3110*

PERRY, JOHN RICHARD, philosophy educator; b. Lincoln, Nebr., Jan. 16, 1943; s. Ralph Robert and Ann (Roscow) P.; m. Louise Elizabeth French, Mar. 31, 1962; children: James Merton, Sarah Louise, Joseph Glenn. BA, Doane Coll., Crete, Nebr., 1964; PhD, Cornell U., Ithaca, N.Y., 1968; DLitt (hon.), Doane Coll., 1982. Asst. prof. philosophy UCLA, 1968-72; vis. asst. prof. U. Mich., Ann Arbor, 1971-72; assoc. prof. UCLA, 1972-74, Stanford (Calif.) U., 1974-77; prof. Stanford U., 1977-85, Henry Waldgrave Stuart prof., 1985—, chmn. dept. philosophy, 1976-82, 90-91, dir. ctr. study lang. and info., 1985-86, 93—, resident fellow Soto House, 1985-91. Author: Dialogue on Identity and Immortality, 1978, (with Jon Barwise) Situations and Attitudes, 1983, The Problem of the Essential Indexical, 1993. Pres. Santa Monica Dem. Club, Calif., 1972-74. Woodrow Wilson fellow, 1964-65, Danforth fellow, 1964-68, Guggenheim fellow, 1975-76, NEH fellow, 1980-81. Mem. Am. Philos. Assn. (v.p. Pacific divsn. 1992-93, pres. 1993-94). Office: Stanford U Ctr Study Language & Information Stanford CA 94305

PERRY, KENNETH WALTER, integrated oil company executive; b. Shamrock, Tex., Feb. 24, 1932; s. Charles Bowman and Sunshine Virginia (Grady) P.; m. Mary Dean Sudderth, Aug. 28, 1953; children: Mary Martha Perry Mitchell, Kathryn Virginia. BSME, U. Okla., 1954. Sales engr. Mid-Continent Oil Well Supply Co., 1954-55; with Cosden Oil & Chem. Co., Big Spring, Tex., from 1957, jr. engr., 1957-59, project engr., 1959-60, chem. salesman, 1960-64, chem. products mgr., 1964-65, mktg. mgr., then v.p. mktg., 1965-69, v.p. chems., 1969-72, sr. v.p., 1972-76, pres., from 1976; group v.p. Am. Petrofina, Inc., Dallas, 1976-85, sr. v.p., 1985-86, pres., CEO, 1986-88, vice chmn., bd. dirs., 1989-92; CEO Nimir Petroleum Co. Ltd., Dallas, 1992—; chmn. bd. dirs. United Commerce Bank, Highland Village, Tex., 1989-92, CEO, 1990-91. Mem. bd. govs. Dallas Symphony Orch., 1987-93; bd. dirs. Dallas Coun. World Affairs, 1980; mem. engring. com. U. Okla. Aerospace, Nuclear, 1982; bd. dirs. Colo. Mcpl. Water Dist., 1972; bd. visitors Coll. Engring., U. Okla., 1990—. 1st lt. USASC, 1955-57. Mem. Am. Petroleum Inst. (bd. dirs. 1986-90), Nat. Petroleum Coun., Nat. Petroleum Refiners Assn. (chmn. petrochem. com. 1984-87), Ctr. Strategic and Internat. Studies, 25-Yr. Clubs, Petroleum Industry Club, Petrochem. Industry Club, Northwood Club, Dallas Petroleum Club.

PERRY, KENNETH WILBUR, accounting educator; b. Lawrenceburg, Ky., May 21, 1919; s. Ollie Townsend and Minnie (Monroe) P.; m. Shirley Jane Kimball, Sept. 5, 1942; 1 dau., Constance June (Mrs. Linden Warfel). B.S., Eastern Ky. U., 1942; M.S., Ohio U., 1949; Ph.D., U. Ill., 1953; LL.D., Eastern Ky. U., 1983. C.P.A., Ill. Instr. Berea Coll., 1949-50, U. Ky., summer 1950; teaching asst. U. Ill. at Champaign, 1950-53, asst. prof. accounting, 1953-55, asso. prof., 1955-58, prof., 1958—, Alexander Grant prof., 1975—; vis. prof. Northeastern U., summer 1966, Parsons Coll., 1966-67, Fla. A. and M. U., fall 1971; Carman G. Blough prof. U. Va., fall 1975; dir. Illini Pub. Co. Author: Accounting: An Introduction, 1971, Passing the C.P.A. Examination, 1964, (with N. Bedford and A. Wyatt) Advanced Accounting, 1960; contbg. author: Complete Guide to a Profitable Accounting Practice, 1965, C.P.A. Review Manual, 1971; Editor: The Ill. C.P.A, 1968-70; contbg. editor: Accountants' Cost Handbook, 1960. Served to maj. AUS, 1942-46; col. Res. ret. Named outstanding alumnus Eastern Ky. U., 1969. Mem. Am. Accounting Assn. (v.p. 1963, Outstanding Educator award 1974), Am. Inst. C.P.A.'s, Am. Statis. Assn., Nat. Assn. Accountants (dir. 1969-71), Ill. Soc. C.P.A.s (chair in accountancy), Beta Alpha Psi, Beta Gamma Sigma (Distinguished scholar 1977-78), Omicron Delta Kappa. Methodist. Home: 2314 Fields South Dr Champaign IL 61821-9302 Office: Commerce W U Ill Champaign IL 61820

PERRY, KENNY, professional golfer; b. Elizabethtown, Ky., Aug. 10, 1960. Grad., Western Ky. U. Profl. golfer, 1982—. Won Meml. Tournament, 1991, New Eng. Classic, 1994, Bob Hope Chrysler Classic, 1995. Office: c/o PGA Box 109601 100 Ave of Champions Palm Beach Gardens FL 33410

PERRY, LANSFORD WILDER, manufacturing executive, consultant; b. Hartford, Conn., Dec. 29, 1955; s. Thomas McFaul and Margaret Houghton (Hepburn) P.; m. Elaine Frances Zils; children: Robert, Lewis, Nelson, Lara. AB in Econs., Dartmouth Coll., 1977; postgrad., Amos Tuck Sch. Bus. Adminstrn., 1984-85. V.p., dir. T.M. Perry Co., Canton Ctr., Conn., 1983-86; supr. mfg. engr. Colt Industries Chandler Evans, West Hartford, Conn., 1981-83; pres. Perry Tech. Corp., New Hartford, Conn., 1986—; mng. ptnr. Perry Bros. Ptnrship., Canton, 1986—; mem., pres. Snowy Night, Firelight, Woodsmoke & Warmth LLC, 1994—; chmn. bd. Collinsville Co., 1989—; bd. dirs., treas. Sun Wind & Woodland Inc., Canton, The Greenwoods Co., New Hartford, Conn.; mem., pres. Bolder Dive, LLC, 1996—. Bd. dirs., sec. Canton Land Conservation Trust, Inc., 1986-91, Canton Concerned Citizens Alliance, 1989-91; constable Town of Canton, 1975-83. Mem. Am. Soc. Quality Control (cert.), Soc. Mfg. Engrs. (cert.), Nat. Assn. Purchasing Mgrs. (cert.), Abrasive Engring. Soc. (cert.), Am. Prodn. and Inventory Control Soc. (cert.), Canton Creamery Assn. (bd. dirs., sec. 1978), Dartmouth Outing Club (life), Amateur Trapshooting Assn. (life), NRA (life). Home: PO Box #1 54 Barbourtown Rd Canton Center CT 06020-0001 Office: Perry Tech Corp PO Box 21 29 Industrial Park Rd New Hartford CT 06057-0021

PERRY, LEE ROWAN, lawyer; b. Chgo., Sept. 23, 1933; s. Watson Bishop and Helen (Rowan) P.; m. Barbara Ashcraft Mitchell, July 2, 1955; children: Christopher, Constance, Geoffrey. B.A., U. Ariz., 1955, LL.B., 1961. Bar: Ariz. 1961. Since practiced in Phoenix; clk. Udall & Udall, Tucson, 1960-61; mem. firm Carson, Messinger, Elliott, Laughlin & Ragan, 1961—. Mem. law rev. staff, U. Ariz., 1959-61. Mem. bd. edn. Paradise Valley Elementary and High Sch. Dists., Phoenix, 1964-68, pres., 1968; treas. troop Boy Scouts Am., 1970-72; mem. Ariz. adv. bd. Girl Scouts U.S.A., 1972-74, mem. nominating bd., 1978-79; bd. dirs. Florence Crittenton Services Ariz., 1967-72, pres., 1970-72; bd. dirs. U. Ariz. Alumni, Phoenix, 1968-72, pres., 1969-70; bd. dirs. Family Service Phoenix, 1974-75; bd. dirs. Travelers Aid Assn. Am., 1985-89; bd. dirs. Vol. Bur. Maricopa County, 1975-81, 83-86, pres., 1984-85; bd. dirs. Ariz. div. Am. Cancer Soc., 1978-80, Florence Crittenton div. Child Welfare League Am., 1976-81; bd. dirs. Crisis Nursery for Prevention of Child Abuse, 1978-81, pres., 1978-80; Ariz. dir. Devereux Found., 1996—, vice chmn. 1996-97. Served to 1st lt. USAF, 1955-58. Mem. State Bar Ariz. (conv. chmn. 1972), Rotary (dir. 1971-77, 95-96, pres. 1975-76, West Leadership award 1989), Ariz. Club (bd. dirs. 1994—), Phoenix Country Club, Phi Delta Phi, Phi Delta Theta (pres. 1954). Republican. Episcopalian. Office: Carson Messinger Elliott Laughlin & Ragan Norwest Bank Tower PO Box 33907 Phoenix AZ 85067-3907

PERRY, LEWIS CHARLES, emergency medicine physician, osteopath; b. La Plata, Mo., Apr. 22, 1931; s. Lewis C. and Emily B. Perry; m. M. Sheryl Gupton, Oct. 30, 1953; children: David, Susan, Stephen, John. BS, U. Mo., 1958; postgrad., Louisville Presbyn. Sem., 1958-60; DO, Kirksville Coll. Osteo. Medicine, 1967. Intern Midcities Meml. Hosp., Arlington, Tex.; parish min. Presbyn. Bd. Nat. Missions, Canada, Ky., 1960-62; intern Mid Cities Meml. Hosp., Arlington; pvt. practice, Ingleside, Tex., 1968-72, Tucson, 1972-81; emergency physician Tucson Gen. Hosp., 1981-88, pres. med. staff, 1978-79, clin. instr., 1981-88; emergency physician Meml. Med. Ctr. East Tex., Lufkin, 1988—; clin. instr. Osteo. Coll. Pacific, Pomona, Calif., 1985-88. Pres. Helping Hands, Ingleside, 1969-72; bd. dirs., pres. Salvation Army, Tucson, 1978-81; commr. Cub Scouts Am., Tucson, 1975-76; bd. dirs. Unity of Tucson, Inc., 1986-88; pres. bd. dirs. Unity of Nacogdoches, 1993-94. 1st lt. USAF, 1952-56. Named Physician of Yr., Tucson Gen. Hosp., 1978; recipient God and Country award Boy Scouts of Am., 1960. Mem. Am. Legion, Rotary (recipient God and Country award), Masons, Scottish Rite, Shrine. Avocations: cooking, gardening. Home: 1 Columbia Ct Lufkin TX 75901-7212

PERRY, LEWIS CURTIS, historian, educator; b. Somerville, Mass., Nov. 21, 1938; s. Albert Quillen and Irene (Lewis) P.; m. Ruth Opler, June 5, 1962 (div. 1970); 1 child, Curtis Allen; m. Elisabeth Israels, Nov. 26, 1970; children: Susanna Irene, David Mordecai. A.B., Oberlin Coll., 1960; M.S., Cornell U., Ithaca, N.Y., 1964; Ph.D., Cornell U., 1967. Asst. prof. history SUNY, Buffalo, 1966-72, assoc. prof., 1972-78; prof. Ind. U. Bloomington, 1978-84; Andrew Jackson prof. history Vanderbilt U., 1984—, dir. Am. Studies, 1992-95; Ampart lectr. U.S. Info. Service, India and Nepal, 1986, France, 1989; vis. prof. U. Leeds, 1988-89; vis. Raoul Wallenberg fellow Rutgers U., 1991-92. Author: Radical Abolitionism, 1973, reissue, 1995, Childhood, Marriage, and Reform, 1980, Intellectual Life in America, 1984, Boats Against the Current, 1993; co-author: Patterns of Anarchy, 1966, Antislavery Reconsidered, 1979; editor: Jour. Am. History, 1978-84, Twayne's American Thought and Culture Series, 1985—. Pres. Unitarian-Universalist Ch., Bloomington, 1983-84. N.Y. State Regents fellow, 1965-66, Am. Coun. Learned Socs. fellow, 1972-73, Nat. Humanities Inst. fellow, 1975-76, John Simon Guggenheim Found. fellow, 1991, NEH fellow, 1987-88. Mem. Orgn. Am. Historians (editor 1978-84, exec. bd. 1996-99), Am. Hist. Assn., Am. Studies Assn., Soc. Historians Early Am. Republic. Home: 1917 Capers Ave Nashville TN 37212-3107 Office: Vanderbilt U PO Box 95B Nashville TN 37235-0095

PERRY, LOUIS BARNES, retired insurance company executive; b. Los Angeles, Mar. 4, 1918; s. Louis Henry and Julia (Stoddard) P.; m. Genevieve Patterson, Feb. 8, 1942; children: Robert Barnes, Barbara Ann, Donna Lou. B.A., UCLA, 1938, M.A., 1940, Ph.D., 1950; fellow in econs., Yale U., 1941; LL.D., Pacific U., 1964; L.H.D., Whitman Coll., 1967, Linfield Coll., 1981; D.C.S., Willamette U., 1977. Teaching asst. UCLA, 1940-41, research teaching asst., 1946-47; faculty Pomona Coll., 1947-59, asst. to pres., 1955-57, prof. econs., 1957-59; pres. Whitman Coll., Walla Walla, Wash., 1959-67; v.p., treas. Standard Ins. Co., Portland, Oreg., 1967-68; exec. v.p. Standard Ins. Co., 1968-71, pres., 1972-83, chmn., 1983-85, also bd. dirs.; investment counselor, broker Wagenseller & Durst, L.A., 1951-59; rsch. coord. So. Calif. Rsch. Coun., 1952-54; cons. Carnegie Survey Bus. Edn., 1957-58. Author: (with others) Our Needy Aged, 1954, A History of the Los Angeles Labor Movement, 1963; Contbr. (with others) articles to profl. jours. Mem. Oreg. Bd. Higher Edn., 1975-87, pres., 1975-80. Served to maj. AUS, World War II; lt. col. Res. Mem. Am. Coll. Life Underwriters (trustee 1972-81), Rotary, Phi Beta Kappa, Beta Gamma Sigma, Phi Delta Kappa, Pi Gamma Mu, Alpha Gamma Omega, Artus. Methodist. Home: 1585 Gray Lynn Dr Walla Walla WA 99362-9282 *In looking back over the years, an unspoken and oftentime subliminal guiding principle has been to reach beyond one's realistic grasp. This concept coupled with an interest in treating others as one would like to be treated has made it possible to react to new challenges. Successfully meeting the latter has provided a varied career in a number of different fields of activity.*

PERRY, LUKE (COY LUTHER PERRY, III), actor; b. Fredericktown, Ohio, Oct. 11, 1966; s. Coy Sr. and Ann Perry; m. Minnie Sharp, Nov. 18, 1993; 1 child, Jack. Appeared in TV series Loving, 1987, Another World, 1989, Beverly Hills, 90210, 1990—, appeared in films Terminal Bliss, 1992, Buffy the Vampire Slayer, 1992, The Webbers, 1993, 8 Seconds, 1994. Office: Nigro Karlin & Segal 10100 Santa Monica Blvd Los Angeles CA 90067-4003

PERRY, MALCOLM BLYTHE, biologist; b. Birkenhead, Cheshire, Eng., Apr. 26, 1930; s. Cyril A. and Hilda (Blythe) P.; m. Eileen M. Perry, Aug. 10, 1956 (dec. 1981); children: Sara Jane, Judith Anne. B.Sc., U. Bristol, Eng., 1953; Ph.D., U. Bristol, 1956, D.Sc., 1969. Banting research fellow Queen's U., Kingston, Ont., Can., 1955; asst. prof. Queen's U., 1956-60, R.S. McLaughlin research prof., 1960-62; sr. research officer Nat. Research Council, Ottawa, Ont., 1962-81; prin. research officer Nat. Research Council, 1981—; scientist U. Cambridge, Eng., 1969, U. Paris, 1979; prof. U. Ottawa, 1982. Contbr. articles to profl. jours. Fellow Royal Soc. Can., Royal Inst. Chemistry; mem. Can. Soc. Microbiology (award 1991), Am. Soc. Microbiology. Home: 769 Hemlock Rd, Ottawa, ON Canada K1K 0K6 Office: NRC, 100 Sussex Dr, Ottawa, ON Canada K1A 0R6

PERRY, MALCOLM OLIVER, vascular surgeon; b. Allen, Tex., Sept. 3, 1929. BA, U. Tex., 1951; MD, U. Tex., Dallas, 1955. Diplomate Am. Bd. Surgery, Am. Bd. Gen. Vascular Surgery. Intern Letterman Army Hosp., San Francisco, 1955-56; resident in surgery Parkland Meml. Hosp., Dallas, 1958-62; fellow in vascular surgery U. Calif., San Francisco, 1962-63; asst. prof. surgery U. Tex., Dallas, 1962-67, assoc. prof. surgery, chief vascular surgery, 1967-71, prof. surgery, chief vascular surgery, 1971-74; prof. surgery U. Wash., Seattle, 1974-77; prof. surgery, chief vascular surgery Cornell U. Med. Coll., N.Y.C., 1978-87, Vanderbilt U. Sch. Medicine, Nashville, 1987-91; chief vascular surgery Tex. Tech U. Health Scis. Ctr., Lubbock, 1991-95; prof. surgery Southwestern Med. Sch., Dallas. Capt. USAF, 1955-58; major Tex. Air N.G., 1960-66. Home: 4442 Westway Ave Dallas TX 75205 Office: U Tex Dept Surgery Southwestern Med Sch 5323 Harry Hines Blvd Dallas TX 75235-7208 also: St Paul Med Ctr Dept Surgery 5909 Harry Hines Blvd Dallas TX 75235

PERRY, MARGARET, librarian, writer; b. Cin., Nov. 15, 1933; d. Rufus Patterson and Elizabeth Munford (Anthony) P. AB, Western Mich. U., 1954; Cert. d'etudes Francaises, U. Paris, 1956; MSLS, Cath. U. Am., 1959. Young adult and reference libr. N.Y. Pub. Libr., N.Y.C., 1954-55, 57-58; libr. U.S. Army, France and Germany, 1959-63, 64-67; chief circulation U.S. Mil. Libr., West Point, N.Y., 1967-70; head edn. libr. U. Rochester, N.Y., 1970-75, asst. prof., 1973-75, assoc. prof., 1975-82, asst. dir. librs. for reader svcs., 1975-82, acting dir. librs., 1976-77, 80; univ. libr. Valparaiso U., Ind., 1982-93; ret., 1993; mem. Task Force on Coop. Edn., Rochester, 1972; freelance writer Mich. Land Use Inst., 1995—. Author: A Bio-bibliography of Countee P. Cullen, 1903-1946, 1971, Silence to the Drums: A Survey of the Literature of the Harlem Renaissance, 1976, The Harlem Renaissance, 1982, The Short Fiction of Rudolph Fisher, 1987; also numerous short stories; contbr. articles to profl. jours. Bd. dirs. Urban League, 1978-80. Recipient 1st prize short story contest Armed Forces Writers League, 1966; 2d prize Frances Steloff Fiction prze, 1968, 1st prize short story Arts Alive, 1990, 2d prize short story Willow Rev., 1990; seminar scholar Schloss Leopoldskron, Salzburg, Austria, 1956, 3d prize short story West Shore C.C., Scottville, Mich., 1995. Mem. ALA. Democrat. Roman Catholic. Avocations: violin, collecting book marks, gardening, reading, travel. Home: 15050 Roaring Brook Rd Thompsonville MI 49683-9216

PERRY, MATTHEW, actor; b. Williamstown, Mass., Aug. 19, 1969. Actor Friends, 1994—. Appeared on TV series including Boys Will Be Boys, Sydney, Growing Pains; TV movies include Deadly Relations, Call Me Anna, Dance 'Til Dawn; films include A Night in the Life of Jimmy Reardon, 1988, She's Out of Control, 1989, Parrallel Lives, 1994, Gettin In, 1994, Fools Rush In, 1997, Edwards and Hunt: The First American Road Trip, 1997. Office: William Morris Agy 151 S El Camino Dr Beverly Hills CA 90212-2704*

PERRY, MATTHEW EDWARD, JR., telecommunications professional; b. Albany, Ga., Aug. 30, 1946; s. Matthew Sr. and Lucy Bell (Haynes) P.; m. Alverta Phelps, July 15, 1967; children: Matthew Edward III, Michael Evane. BS in Indsl. Mgmt., N.J. Inst. Tech., 1976, MS in Indsl. Mgmt., 1978. Mgr. data ctr. AT&T, Piscataway, N.J., 1980-85, mgr. contracts devel. and negotiations, 1985-87; mgr. sys. engring. AT&T, Morristown, N.J., 1986-87; mgr. fin., customer billing AT&T, Morristown, 1987-88; mgr. billing specs AT&T, Somerset, N.J., 1988-90; mgr. sys. devel. AT&T, Somerset, 1990-92; mgr. wireless ops. AT&T, Basking Ridge, N.J., 1992—. Pres. Franklin Twp. POP Warner, 1991—; chair EOP adv. bd. N.J. Inst. Tech., Newark, 1991-94; AT&T campus rep. U. Va., Charlottesville, 1992-94; trustee, dir. Ctrl. Jersey POP Warner, Sayreville, N.J., 1995. Mem. Alliance of Black Telecomm. Employees (founder 1984, treas./CFO 1986-92, v.p. ops. 1993-95, Founders award 1995). Democrat. Baptist. Avocations: youth sports, football, baseball, basketball, card games. Home: 6 Hexham Dr Somerset NJ 08873-4744 Office: AT&T 131 Morristown Rd Basking Ridge NJ 07920-1650

PERRY, MICHAEL CLINTON, physician, medical educator, academic administrator; b. Wyandotte, Mich., Jan. 27, 1945; s. Clarence Clinton and Hilda Grace (Wigginton) P.; m. Nancy Ann Kaluzny, June 22, 1968; children: Rebecca Carolyn, Katherine Grace. BA, Wayne State U., 1966, MD, 1970; MS in Medicine, U. Minn., 1975. Diplomate Am. Bd. Internal Medicine, Am. Bd. Hematology, Am. Bd. Oncology. Intern in internal medicine Mayo Grad. Sch. Medicine, Rochester, Minn., 1970-71, resident, 1971-72, fellow, 1972-75; instr. Mayo Med. Sch., Rochester, 1974-75; asst. prof. U. Mo., Columbia, 1975-80, assoc. prof., 1980-85, prof., 1985—, chmn. dept. medicine, 1983-91, sr. assoc. dean, 1991-94, Nellie A Smith chair oncology, dir. div. hematology/oncology, 1994—; prin. investigator Cancer and Leukemia Group B, Nat. Cancer Inst., Hanover, N.H., 1982—, exec. com., 1982-84, 1987-90. Author, co-author 30 book chpts.; editor: Toxicity of Chemotherapy, 1984, The Chemotherapy Source Book, 1992, 96, Comprehensive Textbook of Thoracic Oncology, 1996; contbr. articles to profl. jours. Recipient Faculty Alumni award U. Mo., Columbia, 1985, Disting. Alumnus award Wayne State U., 1995. Fellow ACP; mem. Am. Soc. Hematology, Am. Soc. Clin. Oncology, Cen. Soc. Clin. Research, Am. Soc. Internal Medicine (Young Internist of Yr. 1981), Sigma Xi, Alpha Omega Alpha. Home: 1112 Pheasant Run Columbia MO 65201-6254 Office: U Mo-Columbia 516 Ellis Fischel Cancer Ctr 115 Business Loop 70 W Columbia MO 65203-3244

PERRY, MICHAEL DEAN, professional football player; b. Aiken, S.C., Aug. 27, 1965. Student, Clemson. Defensive tackle Cleveland Browns, 1988-94, Denver Broncos, 1994—. Voted to Pro Bowl, 1989-91, 93, 94-96; named defensive tackle The Sporting News All-Pro team, 1989-93. Office: Denver Broncos 13655 Broncos Pkwy Englewood CO 80112-4150*

PERRY, NELSON ALLEN, radiation safety engineer, radiological consultant; b. Louisville, Mar. 26, 1937; s. Leslie Irvin and Sue Helen (Harris) P.; m. Sarita Sue Cornn, Apr. 28, 1956; children: Melody S. Doyle, Kimberly D. Horne. AS, Campbellsville (Ky.) Coll., 1954; BS, U. Louisville, 1961; MS, U. Okla., 1966. Cert. hazard control mgr., hazart material mgt.; lic. med. physicist, Tex. Assoc. prof. Ind. Christian U., Indpls., 1974-76; asst. prof. Ind. U., Indpls., 1971-75; instr. Ind. Voc. Tech. Coll., Indpls., 1968-76; health physicist Michael Reese Hosp., Chgo., 1966-68; radiation safety officer St. Francis Hosp., Beech Grove, Ind., 1968-76, Ind. U., Indpls., 1971-74; radiation safety officer U. South Ala., Mobile, 1976—, assoc. prof., 1981—; radiol. cons. Perry Radiol. Cons., Inc., 1974—; radiol. cons., 1974—. Contbr. articles to profl. jours. Named Ky. Col., 1964; USPHS trainee, 1965-66. Mem. Am. Assn. Physicists in Medicine, Health Physics Soc., Ala. Health Physics Soc. (sec. 1977-79, pres. 1980-81). Republican. Baptist. Avocation: collecting miniatures. Office: U South Ala 257 Clay St Mobile AL 36603-5615

PERRY, NORMAN ROBERT, priest, magazine editor; b. Cin., Dec. 17, 1929; s. Joseph Sylvester and May Ann (Hafertepe) P. B.A. cum laude, Duns Scotus Coll., 1954. Joined Franciscan Order, Roman Cath. Ch., 1950, ordained priest, 1958. Assoc. pastor St. Clement Ch., St. Bernard, Ohio, 1959-61, St. Therese Ch., Fort Wayne, Ind., 1961-62; tchr. Bishop Luers High Sch., Fort Wayne, 1961-62; preaching band Franciscan Friars, 1962-66; definitor St. John the Baptist Province, Cin., 1972-75; vicar provincial St. John the Baptist Province, 1975-81; editor St. Anthony Messenger, 1981—; visitator gen. Order of Friars Minor, Commissariat of the Holy Land, Washington, 1980, Acad. Am. Franciscan History, Washington, 1981; mem. office of due process Archdiocesan Adminstrv. Review Bd.; trustee Franciscan Terrace; pro-syndol judge Cin. Archdiocesan Tribunal. Author: Best of the Wiseman, 1981; assoc. editor St. Anthony Messenger, 1966-81. Recipient Cath. Press Assn. St. Francis de Sales award, 1997, numerous awards for reporting, editorials, opinion and review writing. Home: St Francis Friary 1615 Vine St Cincinnati OH 45210-1200 Office: St Anthony Messenger 1615 Republic St Cincinnati OH 45210-1219

PERRY, PAUL ALVERSON, utility executive; b. Farwell, Mich., Apr. 19, 1929; s. LaVerne Seneca and Ruth Valeria (McNeal) P.; m. Mildred Mayhew Small, Apr. 13, 1957; children: Patricia Perry Larson, Ruth Perry Watkins, Robert Paul, Donna Jean. B.S.B.A., Central Mich. U., 1952. With Consumers Power Co., Jackson, Mich., 1954-84; asst. sec. Consumers Power Co., 1960-68, sec., 1968-84; sec., dir. Mich. Gas Storage Co., Jackson, 1969-84; dir. No. Mich. Exploration Co.; sec. Plateau Resources Ltd.; sec., dir. Mich. Utility Collection Service Co., Inc. Served with U.S. Army, 1952-54. Mem. Am. Soc. Corp. Secs. Home: 9110 42nd St Pinellas Park FL 33782

PERRY, RALPH BARTON, III, lawyer; b. N.Y.C., Mar. 17, 1936; s. Ralph Barton and Harriet Armington (Seelye) P.; m. Mary Elizabeth Colburn, Sept. 2, 1961; children: Katherine Suzanne, Daniel Berenson. A.B., Harvard U., 1958; LL.B., Stanford U., 1963. Bar: Calif. 1964. Assoc. and mem. Keatinge & Sterling, Los Angeles, 1963-68; mem. firm Graven Perry Block Brody & Qualls, Los Angeles, 1968—. Bd. dirs. Planning and Conservation League, 1968—; v.p. Coalition for Clean Air, pres. 1972-80, 85-88. Served with U.S. Army, 1956-58. Mem. ABA (ho. of dels. 1975-95), State Bar Calif., L.S. County Bar Assn., Lawyers Club L.A. County (gov. 1968-82), Keep Tahoe Blue, Nat. Wildlife Fedn., Internat. Wildlife Fedn., Sierra Club. Club: Los Angeles Athletic. Home: 296 Redwood Dr Pasadena CA 91105-1339 Office: Graven Perry Block Brody & Qualls 523 W 6th St Ste 1130 Los Angeles CA 90014-1219

PERRY, RAYMOND CARVER, education educator; b. Anaheim, Calif., July 6, 1906; s. Arthur Raymond and Helen (Carver) P.; m. Evelyn Lucile Wright, July 7, 1940; children: Douglas Wright, David Wright. AB, Stanford U., 1926; MA, U. So. Calif., L.A., 1928, EdD, 1933. Cert.

psychologist, Calif. Secondary tchr. Mexia (Tex.) Sch. Dist., 1926-27; elem. tchr. Artesia (Calif.) Sch. Dist., 1927-28; tchr. jr. high L.A. Sch. Dist., 1928-30, tchr. jr. coll., 1930-35; prof. and dean San Diego State Coll., 1935-40; divsn. chief Calif. Dept. Edn., Sacramento, 1940-45; prof. edn. U. So. Calif., L.A., 1945-72, prof. edn. emeritus, 1972—; curriculum cons., psychologist Fontana (Calif.) Sch. Dist., 1947-51; curriculum survey staff Melbo Assocs., L.A., 1948-71; curriculum cons. Sulphur Springs Sch. Dist., L.A. County, 1965-69. Author: Basic Mathematics for College Students, 1957, Group Factor Analysis of Adjustment Questionnaire, 1934, Cross My Heart, 1990; co-author: Review of Educational Research, 1965. Svc. group rep. City Coordination Coun., Long Beach, Calif., 1933-35. Lt. comdr. USNR, 1942-45. Mem. Nat. Coun. Tchrs. Math., Andrus Ctr. Assocs., U. So. Calif. Ret. Faculty, Phi Delta Kappa (San Diego chpt. pres. 1935-40). Republican. Presbyterian. Avocations: photography, travel.

PERRY, RICHARD JAY, physician; b. Ft. Worth, Tex., Jan. 21, 1961; s. Billy Jay and Carol Joann (Evans) R.; m. Norma Jean Silva, June 9, 1990; children: Miles Jordan, Bryce Nicole. BS, Tex. A&M Univ., 1983, MS, 1985; DO, Tex. Coll. Osteopathic Med, 1990. Diplomate Am. Bd. Osteopathic. Internship Mt. Clemens (Mich.) Hosp., 1990-91; solo practice Sanger, Tex., 1991—; medical dir. Valley View (Tex.) Rural Clinic, 1996—, Cottonwood Manor, Denton, Tex., 1996—; utilization review com., Care Inn, Sanger, 1994—; clinical assoc. prof. UNT Health Sci., Ft. Worth, 1995—. Contbr. articles to profl. jours. Mem. Am. Osteopathic Assn., Tex. Osteopathic Medical Assn., Am. Osteopathic Acad. Sports Medicine, Am. Medical Soc. Sports Medicine (charter), Am. Osteopathic Coll. Family Practitioners, Tex. Soc. Osteopathic Family Practitioners, Tex. Medical Assn., Denton County Medical Soc., Sigma Sigma Phi, Lions Club. Office: Richard J. Perry DO P O Box 228 Sanger TX 76266

PERRY, ROBERT MICHAEL, consulting engineering company executive; b. N.Y.C., Dec. 5, 1931; s. Jerome and Rose P.; m. Frances Diane Gross, Feb. 2, 1957; children—Karen, David, Janice. B.S.E., U. Mich., 1953; postgrad., Columbia U., 1955-57. Engr. Dames & Moore (Cons. Engrs.), L.A., 1955-60, assoc., 1960-65, partner, 1965-75, mng. partner, 1975-89, CFO, 1980-96, dir., 1981—, exec. v.p., 1992—; pres., dir. RMP Inc., 1972—. Served with C.E. U.S. Army, 1953-55. Mem. ASCE (dir., treas. N.Y. sect. 1964-68), Profl. Services Mgmt. Assn. Home: 2736 Via Victoria Palos Verdes Peninsula CA 90274-4478 Office: Dames & Moore Inc 911 Wilshire Blvd Ste 700 Los Angeles CA 90017-3436

PERRY, ROBERT PALESE, molecular biologist, educator; b. Chgo., Jan. 10, 1931; s. Robert John and Gertrude Katherine (Hyman) Palese-Perry; m. Zoila Figueroa, Apr. 28, 1957; children—Rocco, Adele, Monique. B.S., Northwestern U., 1951; Ph.D., U. Chgo., 1956; Docteur Honoris Causa, U. Paris, 1983. Research assoc. Inst. for Cancer Research, Fox Chase Cancer Ctr., Phila., 1960-62, asst. mem., 1962-65, assoc. mem., 1965-69, sr. mem., 1969—; Stanley Reimann chair in rsch. Fox Chase Cancer Ctr., Phila., 1994—; assoc. dir. Inst. for Cancer Research, Fox Chase Cancer Ctr., 1971-74; prof. biophysics U. Pa., Phila., 1973-95. Contbr. numerous research articles to profl. jours., 1957—. Guggenheim fellow, 1974; Nat. Acad. scholar USA/USSR Exch. Program, 1987. Mem. Nat. Acad. Scis. (com. on human rights 1979-86), Internat. Cell Rsch. Orgn. (pres. 1983-86), European Molecular Biology Organization. Home: 1808 Bustleton Pike Southampton PA 18966-4608 Office: Inst Cancer Research 7701 Burholme Ave Philadelphia PA 19111-2412

PERRY, ROGER LAWRENCE, printing executive; b. Ironwood, Mich., Apr. 3, 1923; s. Lawrence E. and Bessie (Thompson) P.; m. Ellen Schwandt, June 28, 1947; children: Pamela, Allison. BBA, U. Wis., 1948. V.p. Hamilton Mfg. Co., Two Rivers, Wis., 1949-56; chmn., chief exec. officer Perry Printing Co., Waterloo, Wis., 1956-90, ret. Ensign USN, 1942-45. Named to Printing Hall of Fame, 1990; named Printing Industry Exec. of Yr., 1991. Republican. Methodist. Avocations: golf, fishing, guns. Mailing Address: 2081 W Picamaderos Green Valley AZ 85614

PERRY, SEYMOUR MONROE, physician; b. N.Y.C., May 26, 1921; s. Max and Manya (Rosenthal) P.; m. Judith Kaplan, Mar. 18, 1951; children: Grant Matthew, Anne Lisa, David Bennett. BA with honors, UCLA, 1943; MD with honors, U. So. Calif., 1947. Diplomate: Am. Bd. Internal Medicine. Intern L.A. County Hosp., 1946-48, resident, 1948-51, mem. staff outpatient dept., 1951; examining physician L.A. Pub. Schs., 1951-52; sr. asst. surgeon Phoenix Indian Gen. Hosp., USPHS, 1952; charge internal medicine USPHS Outpatient Clinic, Washington, 1952-54; fellow hematology UCLA, 1954-55, asst. rsch. physician atomic energy project, 1955-57; asst. prof. medicine, head Hematology Tng. Program, Med. Ctr., 1957-60; instr. medicine Coll. Med. Evangelists, 1951-57; attending specialist internal medicine Wadsworth VA Hosp., Los Angeles, 1958-61; sr. investigator, medicine br. Nat. Cancer Inst., 1961-65, chief medicine br., 1965-68, mem. clin. cancer tng. com., 1966-69, chief human tumor cell biology br., 1968-71, assoc. sci. director clin. trials, 1966-71, assoc. sci. dir. program planning, divsn. cancer treatment, 1971-73, dep. dir., 1973-74, acting dir., 1974; spl. asst. to dir. NIH, 1974-78, assoc. dir., 1978-80, acting dep. asst. sec. health (tech.), 1978-79; acting dir. Nat. Ctr. Health Care Tech., OASH, 1978-80, dir., 1980-82; dep. dir. Inst. for Health Policy Analysis Georgetown U. Med. Ctr., Washington, 1983-89, prof. medicine, prof. cmty. and family medicine, 1983-93, adj. prof., 1993—, interim chmn. dept., 1989-90, chmn., 1990-93, dir. Inst. for Health Care Rsch. and Policy; sr. scholar Med. Tech. and Practice Patterns Inst., Washington, 1993—; dir. WHO Collaborating Ctr. on Health Tech., 1995—; mem. adv. com. on rsch. and on the therapy of cancer Am. Cancer Soc., 1966-70, adv. com. chemotherapy and hematology, 1975-77, chmn. epidemiology, diagnosis and therapy com., 1971, grantee, 1959-60; med. dir. USPHS, 1961-80; asst. surg. gen., 1980-82; mem. radiation com. NIH, 1963-70, co-chmn., 1971-73; pres. Nat. Blood Club, 1971; chmn. Interagy. Com. on New Therapies for Pain and Discomfort, 1978-80; mem. adv. panel on med. tech. and costs of medicare program Congress of U.S., 1982-84; chmn. criteria working group (bioseparation) NASA, 1984; cons. Nat. Ctr. Health Svcs. Rsch. and Health Care Tech., DHHS, 1985-90, Nat. Libr. of Medicine, 1985-89, Agy. for Health Care Policy and Rsch, DHHS, 1990—, Hosp. Assn. N.Y. State, 1990-91; mem. procedures rev. com. and profl. adv. panel Blue Cross/Blue Shield Nat. Capitol Area, 1987-93; advisor WHO Programme on Tech. Devel., Assessment and Transfer; mem. sci. com. Catalan office of Tech. Assessment, Barcelona, Spain, 1994-96. Assoc. editor Internat. Jour. Tech. Assessment in Health Care, 1984—; mem. editl. bd. Jour. Health Care Tech., 1984-87, Health Tech.: Critical Issues for Decision Makers, 1987-90, Cts., Health and the Law, 1990-91. Bd. dirs. NIH Alumni Assn. Decorated comendador Order of Merit, Peru; comendador Orden Hipólito Unanue, Peru; Pub. Health Service commendation, 1967; Meritorious Service medal USPHS, 1980. Master ACP (adv. com. to gov. Md. on coll. affairs 1969-76, gov. for USPHS and HHS 1980-82, subcom. on clin. efficacy assessment 1982-85, chmn. health and pub. policy com. D.C. met. area 1987—, mem. gov.'s coun., D.C., 1992—); mem. APHA, Inst. Medicine of NAS (mem. evaluation panel coun. health care tech. 1987-90, com. on evaluation med. techs. in clin. use 1981-84, chmn. rev. com. on Inst. Medicine Report on Hip Fracture 1990, mem. rev. com. on renal disease 1990, rev. com. on artificial heart 1991), Patient Outcome Rsch. Team (chmn. adv. com. analysis of practice, hip fracture repair and hip replacement for osteoarthritis U. Md. 1990-94), Assn. Health Svcs. Rsch. (health svcs. rsch. adv. com. 1990-93), Assn. Acad. Health Ctrs., Internat. Soc. Tech. Assessment in Health Care (pres. 1985-87, bd. dirs. 1989-95, coord. spl. interest group on developing countries 1996—), NIH Alumni Assn. (bd. dirs. 1993—), Cosmos Club. Achievements include elucidation of leukocyte physiology; initiation of the consensus development process and the technology assessment forum method to resolve controversial issues in medical care. Office: Med Tech and Practice 2121 Wisconsin Ave NW Ste 220 Washington DC 20007-2270

PERRY, SPENCE WILLIAM, lawyer; b. Jacksonville, Fla., Mar. 1, 1942; s. Florence McCarthy and Inez (Holtsford) P.; m. Susan Elizabeth Clarke, Aug. 22, 1964 (div.); m. Cinda Brandenburg, Sept. 22, 1990. BA, Harvard U., 1963; JD, Duke U., 1966. Bar: N.H., Mass., D.C. Assoc. Sullivan & Worcester, Boston, 1969-71; planning officer Office of Emergency Preparedness, Washington, 1971-73; gen. counsel SIGMA, Washington, 1973-74; asst. gen. counsel GSA, Washington, 1975-80; dep. dir. regulatory litigation Dept. Energy, Washington, 1980-81; assoc. gen. counsel Fed. Energy Mgmt. Agy., Washington, 1981-85, gen. counsel, 1985-88; sr. policy advisor Fed. Energy Mgmt. Agy., Washington, DC, 1988-93, dep. gen. counsel, 1993-96; exec. adminstr. Fed. Ins. Adminstrn., 1996—; adj. faculty Indsl. Coll. of Armed Forces, 1985-88. contbr. articles to numerous jours. Comdr. USNR, 1966-90. Office: Fed Emergency Mgmt Agy Office of the Dir 500 C St SW Washington DC 20024-2523

PERRY, THOMAS AMHERST, English literature and language educator; b. Beaver City, Nebr., Apr. 26, 1912; s. Thomas Charles and Mable Laura (Avis) P.; m. Lora Margaret Turner, June 20, 1937; children: Laura E. Perry Massie, Robert Thomas, Timothy T., Charles Lee. BA with honors, Park Coll., 1934; MA, U. Iowa, 1936, PhD, 1943; postgrad., Oxford (Eng.) U., 1964. Prin. grade sch., Des Moines, N.Mex., 1934-35; asst. prof. English, Park Coll., Parkville, Mo., 1936-42; instr. U. Iowa, Iowa City, 1943; prof., dept. head Ctrl. Meth. Coll., Fayette, Mo., 1943-63; Fulbright lectr. Am. lang. and lit. U. Bucharest, Romania, 1963-64; Hermann Brown prof. English, Southwestern U., Georgetown, Tex., 1964-65; prof. English, East Tex. State U., Commerce, 1965-80, head dept., 1969-72, prof. emeritus lit. and langs., 1980—; vis. prof. English, U. Mo., Columbia, 1951-52, U. Autonoma Estado Mex., Toluca, 1959, N.E. Mo. State U., Kirksville, summer 1965; mem. com. on doctorate in English, Fedn. North Tex. State Univs., 1972-75; mem. com. on Variorum Glossary, World Shakespeare Congress, Vancouver, B.C., Can., 1970-71; mem. steering com. Romanian Studies Congress, Auckland, New Zealand, summer 1973. Author: A Bibliography of American Literature Translated into Romanian, 1984, From These Roots and Other Poems, 1996; co-author: Romanian Poetry in English Translation: an Annotated Bibliography, 1989, with supplement An Update with Over 60 Newer Poets, 1997; contbr. articles and criticsmm to profl. jours., poems and poem transls. to lit. mags. Past mem. Fayette Libr. Bd.; past mem. local bd. Salvation Army, Commerce; mem. exec. com. Hunt County Rep. Party, Greenville, Tex., 1970-80; past mem. adminstrv. bd. Meth. Ch., Fayette; past mem. adminstrv. bd. 1st Meth. Ch., Commerce. Recipient Disting. Alumnus award Park Coll., 1984; Smith-Mundt grantee, Toluca, Mexico, 1959, Rsch. Assocs. travel grantee U. Bucharest and U. Cluj, 1968, Am. Coun. Learned Socs. rsch. grantee, Romania, 1978. Mem. MLA (sr. bibliographer 1969—), Comparative Lit. Assn. Am., Shakespeare Assn. Am., Am. Lit. Translators Assn., Internat. Comparative Lit. Assn., Internat. Shakespeare Assn., Am. Romanian Acad. Arts and Scis., Romanian Studies Assn. (exec. bd. 1946-48), Soc. Romanian Studies, Tex. Assn. Coll. Tchrs., Tex. Folklore Soc., Omicron Delta Kappa. Avocations: numismatics, photography, travel. Home: 214 Brookhaven Ter Commerce TX 75428 Office: Tex A&M U Dept Lit and Langs Commerce TX 75428

PERRY, TIMOTHY SEWELL, lawyer; b. Hamlet, N.C., Feb. 28, 1947; s. Edwin Fleetwood and June Faye (Sewell) P.; children: Courtney, Kate, Bart, Carrie, Jeff, Kevin. BA, Princeton U., 1969; JD, Yale U., 1972. Bar: Ga. 1972. Assoc. Alston & Bird and predecessor firms, Atlanta, 1972—; ptnr. Alston & Bird and predecessor firms, 1977—. Sec., Urban Study Inst., Atlanta, 1979—; pres. Andover Reg. Attn./Atlanta, 1987-89. Mem. Atlanta Bar Assn., Ga. Bar Assn. (corp. law sect.), Phillips Acad. Alumni Assn. Presbyterian. Avocation: Spanish. Office: Alston & Bird 1 Atlantic Ctr 1201 W Peachtree St NW Atlanta GA 30309-3400

PERRY, TROY D., clergyman, church administrator; divorced; 2 children. Student Midwest Bible Sch.; D in Ministry (hon.), Samaritan Coll., L.A.; D in Human Svcs., Sierra U., Santa Monica, Calif. Former pastor Ch. of God of Prophecy, Santa Ana, Calif.; founder, moderator Universal Fellowship Met. Community Chs., L.A.; rep. Met. Community Chs. and gay and lesbian rights movement numerous TV shows including 60 Minutes, Phil Donahue, The Mike Douglas Show. Author: The Lord is My Shepherd and Knows I'm Gay, Don't Be Afraid Anymore, 1991, (video) God, Gays & The Gospel: This is Our Story; contbg. editor Is Gay Good? Mem. Los Angeles County Commn. Human Rels. Recipient Humanitarian award ACLU Lesbian and Gay Rights chpt., 1978, Humanitarian award Gay Press Assn., Equality award Human Rights Campaign, 1996. Office: Universal Fellowship Met Comm Chs 8704 Santa Monica Blvd Ph 2 West Hollywood CA 90069-4548

PERRY, VINCENT ALOYSIUS, corporate executive; b. Weehawken, N.J.; s. Edwin Robert and Florence Loretta (Gutberlet) P.; m. Doris Lucille Wanckel, Dec. 3, 1944 (dec. July 1988); children: Cynthia Jeanne, Bradford Kimball. A.B., NYU, 1948, M.A., 1949. Asst. prof. fin. Lehigh U., Bethlehem, Pa., 1949-51; mgr. econs. and fin. analysis div. Gen. Foods Corp., White Plains, N.Y., 1951-59; v.p., treas. Universal Match Corp., St. Louis, 1959-61; asst. treas. Internat. Paper Co., N.Y.C., 1961-71; v.p., treas. Bangor Punta Corp., Greenwich, Conn., 1971-75; fin. v.p., treas. Ziff-Davis Pub. Co., N.Y.C., 1975-77; sr. v.p. fin. The Viguerie Co., Inc., Falls Church, Va., 1977-79. Treas. Workshop for Bus. Opportunities, N.Y.C., 1969-88. Served to capt. AUS, 1942-46, ETO. Mem. Lambda Chi Alpha. Home: 110 Southport Wood Dr Southport CT 06490

PERRY, WILLIAM JAMES, educator, former federal official; b. Vandergrift, Pa., Oct. 11, 1927; s. Edward Martin and Mabelle Estelle (Dunlap) P.; m. Leonilla Green, Dec. 29, 1947; children: David, William, Rebecca, Robin, Mark. B.S. in Math, Stanford U., 1949, M.S., 1950; Ph.D., Pa. State U., 1957. Instr. math. Pa. State U., 1951-54; sr. mathematician HRB-Singer Co., State College, Pa., 1952-54; dir. electronic def. labs. GTE Sylvania Co., Mountain View, Calif., 1954-64; pres. ESL, Inc., Sunnyvale, Calif., 1964-77; tech. cons. Dept. Def., Washington, 1967-77, under sec. def. for research and engring., 1977-81; mng. dir. Hambrecht & Quist (investment bankers), San Francisco, 1981-85; chmn. Tech. Strategies & Alliances, Menlo Park, Calif., 1985-93; prof., co-dir. Ctr. for Internat. Security and Arms Control Stanford U., 1989-93; apptd. Dep. Sec. Def. Pentagon, Washington, 1993-94, appt. Sec. Def., 1994-97; prof. Stanford (Calif.) U., 1997—. Served with U.S. Army, 1946-47. Recipient Def. Disting. Svc. medal U.S. Govt., 1980, 81, Achievement medal Am. Elec. Assn., 1980, Forrestal Medal, 1994, Henry Stimson medal, 1994, Arthur Bueche medal NAE, 1996, Eisenhower award, 1996, Presdl. Medal Freedom, 1997, Outstanding Civilian Svc. medals U.S. Army, 1997, USN, 1997, USAF, 1997, USCG, 1997, NASA, 1997, Def. Intelligence Agy., 1997. Office: Stanford U Stanford CA 94305

PERRY, WILLIAM JOSEPH, food processing company executive; b. Sacramento, Calif., Nov. 4, 1930; s. Joseph Nasciemeto and Jennie (Nunez) P.; m. Beverly Ann Styles, Dec. 9, 1956 (div. May 1981); children: Katherine, Bill Jr., Kathleen, Barbara; m. Leslie Z. Blumberg, June 30, 1986. BS, U. Calif., Berkeley, 1953; MBA, U. So. Calif., 1995. Quality control supr. Stokely Van Camp, Oakland, Calif., 1953-54; plant mgr. Safeway Stores, Brookside div., Grandview, Wash., 1954-61, Gallo Winery, Modesto, Calif., 1961-62; gen. mgr. Bocca Bella Olive Assoc., Wallace, Calif., 1962-65; v.p. Early Calif. Ind., L.A., 1965-74, Fairmont Foods, Santa Ana, Calif., 1974-75; pres. Cal Agra Ind., Stockton, Calif., 1975-76; exec. v.p. Food Brokers Internat., L.A., 1976—; pres., co-owner G.F.F., Inc., L.A., 1981—; dir. G.F.F., Inc., L.A., 1981—, Food Brokers, Inc., L.A., 1976—, Cozad & Assoc. Ad Agy., Encino, Calif., 1985-87. Wrestling com., dir. protocol, L.A. Olympic Com., 1981-84. Mem. Nat. Food Brokers Assn., Assn. of Dressings and Sauces, Product Mktg. Assn., Nat. Single Svc. Assn., Am. Chem. Soc., U. Calif. Alumni Assn., U. So. Calif. Alumni Assn., Westlake Tennis and Swim Club. Republican. Roman Catholic. Avocations: tennis, photography, bicycling, amateur sports associations. Home: 3700 Brigantine Cir Westlake Vlg CA 91361-3816 Office: 5422 Jillson St Los Angeles CA 90040-2118

PERRY-WIDNEY, MARILYN (MARILYN PERRY), international finance and real estate executive, television producer; b. N.Y.C., Feb. 11, 1939; d. Henry William Patrick and Edna May (Bown) Perry; m. Charles Leonidas Widney (dec. Sept. 1981). BA, Mexico City Coll., 1957. Pres. Marilyn Perry TV Prodns., Inc., N.Y.C., 1970—, C.L. Widney Internat., Inc., N.Y.C., 1977—; mng. dir. Donerail Corp., N.Y.C., 1980-88, Lancer, N.Y.C., 1980-88, Assawata, N.Y.C., 1980-88. Prodr., host TV program Internat. Byline, series of more than 90 documentaries on the UN; host 54 radio and internel series Internat. Byline-mem. nations UN for Nat. Pub. Radio satellite, PBS, in S.C., N.C., Ga., Tenn., WNYE-FM, N.Y.C., 1996—. Bd. dirs. UN After Sch. Program; ambassadorial candidate Pres. Bush., 1989; mem. Gibbes Mus., S.C. Recipient U.S. Indsl. Film Festival award, CINE Golden Eagle award, Bronze medal Internat. Film & TV Festival of N.., Bronzenen Urkinde, Berlin, award for superior quality Intercom-Chgo. Internat. Film Festival, Knights of Malta Trophy award for superior programming from Min. of Tourism, Internationales Tourismus award Film festival, Vienna, Manhattan Cable Ten Year award for continuous programming, citations from former pres. Ford and Carter, King Hussein Jordan and Pres. Clinton. Mem. Asia Soc., UN Corrs. Assn., UN After Sch. Programs, Rep. Presdl. Task Force (charter mem.), Rep. Nat. Com., Harbour Club (S.C.), Gibbes Mus. (S.C.). Avocations: music, art and antiques collecting, travel. Home: 211 E 70th St New York NY 10021

PERSAUD, TRIVEDI VIDHYA NANDAN, anatomy educator, researcher, consultant; b. Port Mourant, Berbice, Guyana, Feb. 19, 1940; arrived in Canada, 1972; s. Ram Nandan and Deen (Raggy) P.; m. Gisela Gerda Zehden, Jan. 29, 1965; children: Indrani Uta and Sunita Heidi (twins), Rainer Narendra. MD, Rostock U., Germany, 1965, DSc, 1974; PhD in Anatomy, U. West Indies, Kingston, Jamaica, 1970. Intern Potsdam, Germany, 1965-66; govtl. med. officer Guyana, 1966-67; lectr., sr. lectr. anatomy dept. U. West Indies, 1967-72; assoc. prof. anatomy dept. U. Man., Winnipeg, 1972-75, prof., 1975—, prof. ob-gyn., reproductive scis., 1979—, prof. pediatrics and child health, 1989—, prof., chmn./head dept. anatomy, 1977-93, dir. Teratology Rsch. Lab., 1972—; cons. in teratology, Children's Centre, Winnipeg, 1973—; mem. sci. staff Health Scis. Centre, Winnipeg, 1973—. Author, editor 22 med. textbooks, including: Early History of Human Anatomy: From Antiquity to the Beginning of the Modern Era, 1984, (with others) Basic Concepts in Teratology, 1985, Environmental Causes of Human Birth Defects, 1991, (with K.L. Moore) The Developing Human, 5th edit., 1993, Before We Are Born, 4th edit., 1993; contbr. numerous chpts. to books, over 150 articles to profl. jours. Recipient Carveth Jr. Scientist award Can. Assn. Pathologists, 1974, Albert Einstein Centennial medal German Acad. Scis., 1975, Dr. & Mrs. H.H. Saunderson award U. Manitoba, 1985, 12th Raymond Truex Disting. Lectureship award Hahnemann U., 1990. Fellow Royal Coll. Pathologists of London; mem. Can. Assn. Anatomists (pres. 1981-83, J.C.B. Grant award 1991), Am. Assn. Anatomists, Teratology Soc., European Teratology Soc. Office: U Man Dept Anatomy, 730 William Ave, Winnipeg, MB Canada R3E OW3

PERSAVICH, WARREN DALE, diversified manufacturing company executive; b. Cleve., Dec. 15, 1952; s. Nick and Sophie (Makris) P.; m. Anita Geraldine Zeleznik, Oct. 12, 1974; children: Nicholas, Katherine. BBA, Kent State U., 1975. CPA, Ohio. Staff acct. Price Water House, Cleve., 1975-76; asst. contr. Banner Industries Inc., Cleve., 1976-79, contr., 1979-86, treas., 1986-88, v.p., treas., 1988-90; sr. v.p., chief fin. officer Banner Aerospace Inc., 1990—. Mem. AICPA, Ohio Soc. CPAs. Republican. Office: Banner Aerospace Inc Washington Dulles Airport PO Box 20260 / 300 W Service Rd Washington DC 20041

PERSCHETZ, MARTIN L., lawyer; b. Bklyn., Sept. 15, 1952; s. Louis and Edith (Sandhaus) P.; m. Babs D. Hanfling, Mar. 23, 1980; children: Monica, Keith, Evan. BA, U. Md., 1974; JD, SUNY, Buffalo, 1977. Bar: N.Y. 1978, U.S. Dist. Ct. (so. dist.) N.Y. 1978, U.S. Dist. Ct. (ea. dist.) N.Y. 1979, U.S. Ct. Appeals (2d cir.) 1984, U.S. Dist. Ct. (no. dist.) N.Y. 1989. Assoc. Obermaier, Morvillo & Abramowitz, N.Y.C., 1977-80; asst. U.S. atty. So. Dist. N.Y., N.Y.C., 1980-86, chief major crimes unit, 1985-86; chief counsel N.Y.C. Spl. Commn. to Investigate City Contracts, N.Y.C., 1986; dep. commr. N.Y.C. Dept. Investigation, N.Y.C., 1986; spl. counsel Schulte, Roth & Zabel, N.Y.C., 1986-87; ptnr. Schulte, Roth & Zabel, 1988—. Contbr. article to profl. jour. Recipient Joseph Halpern award Buffalo Law Rev., 1977. Mem. ABA, N.Y.C. Bar Assn., N.Y. Coun. Def. Lawyers. Home: 271 Clayton Rd Scarsdale NY 10583-1517 Office: Schulte Roth & Zabel 900 3rd Ave New York NY 10022-4728

PERSCHINO, ARTHUR J., elementary school principal. Prin. Columbus Magnet Sch. Recipient Elem. Sch. Recognition award U.S. Dept. Edn., 1989-90; named Young Astronaut Leader of Yr. by Pres. Bush, 1991. Office: Columbus Magnet Sch 46 Concord St Norwalk CT 06854-2904

PERSE, ARIA LEON, international business advanced technologies executive; b. L.A., Dec. 30, 1962; s. Constante A. and Marianne (Cobetti) P. PhD, UCLA, 1989. Chmn., CEO Advanced Tech. USA, Inc., Wilmington, Del., 1991—. Mem. exec. campaign bd. Republican Party, L.A., 1992. Mem. AAAS, Nat. Aero. Assn., Planetary Soc. (Pasadena, Calif.), L.A. World Affairs Coun. Office: Advanced Tech USA Inc 1201 N Market St Wilmington DE 19801-1147

PERSELL, CAROLINE HODGES, sociologist, educator, author, researcher, consultant; b. Fort Wayne, Ind., Jan. 16, 1941; d. Albert Randolph and Katherine (Rogers) Hodges; m. Charles Bowen Persell, III, June 17, 1967; children: Patricia Emily, Stephen David. BA, Swarthmore Coll., 1962; MA, Columbia U., 1967, PhD, 1971. Sr. assoc., then nat. coordinator Nat. Scholarship Service and Fund for Negro Students, N.Y.C., 1962-66; project dir. Bur. Applied Social Research, N.Y.C., 1968-71; asst. prof. NYU, 1971-76, assoc. prof., 1976-86, prof. 1986—, dir. grad. studies dept. sociology, 1984-87, chair, 1987-93, Robin Williams Disting. Lectr., 1993-94. Author: Education and Inequality, 1977, Understanding Society, 1984, 2d edit., 1987, 3d edit., 1990; co-author: (with Cookson) Preparing for Power, 1985, Making Sense of Society, 1992, (with Maisel) How Sampling Works, 1996; assoc. editor: Teaching Sociology, 1983-85, Sociology of Edn., 1992-95, Gender & Soc., 1992-95; contbr. articles to profl. jours. Recipient Faculty Devel. award NSF, 1978-79, Women Educators' Research award, 1978; grantee Fund for Improvement of Postsecondary Edn., 1989-92, NSF Equipment Fund, 1993-96. Mem. Am. Sociol. Assn. (chair sec. 1983-84, 88-89, chmn. pubs. com. 1987-89), Am. Edn. Rsch. Assn., Author's Guild, Eastern Sociol. Soc. (pres. 1995-96), Internat. Sociol. Assn., Sociologists for Women in Soc. Avocations: violin, gardening, opera, sports. Office: NYU Dept Sociology 269 Mercer St New York NY 10003-6633

PERSELLIN, ROBERT HAROLD, physician; b. Fargo, N.D., July 3, 1930; s. James Harry and Bessie (Hoffman) P.; m. Bonnie Feibleman, June 27, 1957 (dec. 1983); children: Kathleen, Jamie; m. Diane Cummings, June 14, 1986. B.S., Northwestern U., 1952, M.D., 1956, M.S., 1959. Diplomate: Am. Bd. Internal Medicine, Am. Bd. Rheumatology. Intern Charity Hosp., New Orleans, 1956-57; resident in internal medicine Northwestern U. Med. Center, 1957-60; fellow in rheumatology Southwestern Med. Sch., 1962-64; asst. prof. medicine U. Oreg. Med. Sch., 1964-68; prof. medicine, head div. rheumatology U. Tex. Health Sci. Center, San Antonio, 1968-81; prof. family practice U. Tex. Health Sci. Ctr., San Antonio, 1993—; cons. rheumatology VA Hosps., U.S. Army, Coastal Bend Health Plan; vis. prof. rheumatology Kingstown Med. Coll.; vis. scholar Corpus Christi Coll., Cambridge U., 1979-80; vis. scientist Strangeways Rsch. Lab., Cambridge. Contbr chpts. to books, articles to profl. jours. Bd. dirs. San Antonio Chamber Music Soc., 1970-75, 80-96, pres., 1983-85; bd. dirs. Friends of Strings, 1972-75, San Antonio Bot. Soc., 1985-87; Dem. precinct committeeman Washington County, Oreg., 1966-68. Served to capt. M.C. U.S. Army, 1960-62. Fellow ACP, Am. Coll. Rheumatology (exec. com. mem.); mem. Arthritis Found. (chmn. med. and sci. com. South Ctrl. Tex. chpt.), Heberden Soc., Am. Fedn. Clin. Rsch., So. Soc. Clin. Investigation, Tex. Rheumatism Assn. (pres.), Nat. Soc. Clin. Rheumatology, Mex. Rheumatology Soc. (hon.). Office: 635 E Olmos Dr San Antonio TX 78212-2504

PERSHAN, PETER SILAS, physicist, educator; b. Bklyn., Nov. 9, 1934; s. Max J. and Rosa (Bernekow) P.; m. Patricia S. Birke, Aug. 31, 1957; children: Marc, Jill. BS, Poly. Inst. Bklyn., 1956; AM, Harvard U., 1957, PhD, 1960. Rsch. fellow Harvard U., Cambridge, Mass., 1960, asst. prof., 1961-64, assoc. prof., 1964-68, prof., 1968—; mem. lab. tech. Bell Telephone, Murray Hill, N.J., 1963-64; dir. Materials Rsch. Lab., Cambridge, 1974-78; vis. prof. MIT, Cambridge, 1978-79; vis. scientist Brookhaven Nat. Lab., Upton, N.Y., 1985-86, guest scientist, 1986—; cons. Sperry Gyroscope Co., Great Neck, N.Y., 1961-63, RCA Corp., Princeton, N.J., 1966-73, Battelle Meml. Inst. Naval Ordnance Lab., Silver Springs, Md., 1969-71; mem. proposal rev. panel Stanford Synchtotron Radiation Lab., 1989—; mem. adv. bd. Advanced Liquid Crystalline Optical Materials Consortium, 1991-94; guest scientist RISØ Nat. Lab., Denmark, 1993. Author: Structure of Liquid Crystal Phases, 1988; co-editor: Resonances, 1990; contbr. articles to profl. jours. Fellow Am. Phys. Soc. (com. internat. freedom scientists 1984-86). Home: 218 Follen Rd Lexington MA 02173-5825 Office: Harvard U Div Applied Scis 29 Oxford St Cambridge MA 02138-2901

PERSHAN, RICHARD HENRY, lawyer; b. N.Y.C., Jan. 4, 1930; s. Benjamin and Sadie (Aronowsky) P.; m. Kathryn Schaefler, June 11, 1952; children: Lee S., Richard H., Pamela, Julia B. BA, Yale U., 1951, LLB, 1956. Bar: N.Y. 1956, U.S. Supreme Ct.1969. Assoc. Davis, Polk & Wardwell, N.Y.C., 1956-60; ptnr. Finch & Schaefler, N.Y.C., 1960-85; ptnr. LeBoeuf, Lamb, Greene & MacRae, N.Y.C., 1986-94, of counsel, 1995—. Counsel Mcpl. Art Soc., N.Y.C., 1965-70, Fine Arts Fedn., N.Y.C., 1975-80. Served to 1st lt. USAF. Fellow Am. Coll. Trust and Estate Counsel (author, editor, articles and studies 1960—); mem. Assn. of Bar of City of N.Y., Yale Club, N.Y. Croquet Club, Newport Casino Croquet Club. Democrat. Avocations: indoor rowing, croquet. Home: 1435 Lexington Ave New York NY 10128-1625 Office: LeBoeuf Lamb Greene & MacRae 125 W 55th St New York NY 10019-5369

PERSHING, DAVID WALTER, chemical engineering educator, researcher; b. Anderson, Ind., Oct. 2, 1948; s. Walter L. and Treva B. (Crane) P.; m. Lynn Marie Kennard, Apr. 9, 1977; 1 child, Nicole. BSChemE, Purdue U., 1970; PhDChemE, U. Ariz., 1976. Rsch. asst. Exxon Prodn. Rsch., Houston, 1969; project engr. EPA, 1970-73; asst. prof. chem. engring. U. Utah, Salt Lake City, 1977-82, assoc. prof., 1982-85, prof., 1985—, assoc. dean Grad. Sch., 1983-87, dean Coll. Engring., 1987—; asst. to pres. Reaction Engring. Inc., Salt Lake City, 1990—; vis. scientist Internat. Flame Rsch. Found., Ijmuiden, The Netherlands, 1972-73; vis. assoc. prof. chem. engring. U. Ariz., Tuscon, 1976-77; cons. Energy and Environ. Rsch. Ctr., Irvine, Calif., 1974-90, Acurex Corp., Mountain View, Calif., 1974-79, Kennecott Corp., Salt Lake City, 1979-81, Nat. Bur. Standards, Washington, 1976-78, Geneva Steel, 1989—; assoc. dir. Engring. Rsch. Ctr., NSF, 1986—. Contbr. articles to profl. publs.; patentee in field. Maj. USPHS, 1970-73. Recipient Disting. Teaching award U. Utah, 1982, Disting. Rsch. award U. Utah, 1990; grantee NSF, PYI, 1984-90. Mem. Am. Inst. Chem. Engrs., Combustion Inst. Methodist. Office: U Utah Coll Engring 214 KRC Salt Lake City UT 84112

PERSHING, RICHARD WILSON, communications company executive, consultant; b. L.A., June 14, 1927; s. Howard Louis and Myrtle Edith (Wilson) P.; m. Norma Louise Davis, Aug. 19, 1950; children: Tina Ann Baine, Timothy Alan. BA, Pepperdine U., 1950. Various positions Security Pacific Bank, L.A., 1950-62; sr. v.p. Home Savs. & Loan Assn., L.A., 1962-64; exec. v.p. Hale Bros. Assocs., Inc., San Francisco, 1964-68, Internat. Controls Corp., Fairfield, N.J., 1968-69; pres., CEO Hale Tech. Corp., San Francisco, 1970-84; chmn. bd. Datron Sys. Inc., Escondido, Calif., 1984—. Serves with USNR, 1945-46, PTO. Home: Datron Systems Inc 75-572 Debby Ln Indian Wells CA 92210 Office: Datron Sys Inc 304 Enterprise St Escondido CA 92029-1239

PERSHING, ROBERT GEORGE, telecommunications company executive; b. Battle Creek, Mich., Aug. 10, 1941; s. James Arthur and Beulah Francis P.; BS in Elec. Engring., Tri-State Coll., Angola, Inc., 1961; m. Diana Kay Prill, Sept. 16, 1961, (div. Jan. 1989); children: Carolyn, Robert; m. Charlene Jean Reed Wallis, Mar. 18, 1989 (div. Dec. 1995). Comm. engr. Am. Elec. Power, Ind., N.Y. and Ohio, 1961-69; design supr. Wescom, Inc., Ill., 1969-74; dir. engring. Tellabs, Inc., Lisle, Ill., 1974-78; pres., CEO, bd. dirs. Teltrend, Inc., St. Charles, Ill., 1979-89, chmn. bd., 1979-88; CEO DKP Prodns. Inc., St. Charles, Ill., 1986-89; exec. cons. Teltrend, 1979-93, bd. dirs., 1988-93; asst. treas. Magnekopy Inc., Villa Park, Ill, chmn. bd.; bd. dirs. TI Investors, Inc.; advisor entrepreneurial studies U. Ill.; engring. cons. Recipient Chgo. Area Small Bus. award, 1986, INC 500 awards, 1987, 88. Mem. IEEE. Office: 1519 Kirkwood Dr Geneva IL 60134-1659

PERSICO, JOSEPH EDWARD, author; b. Gloversville, N.Y., July 19, 1930; s. Thomas Louis and Blanche (Perrone) P.; m. Sylvia La Vista, May 23, 1959; children: Vanya, Andrea. B.A., SUNY-Albany, 1952, PhD (hon.), 1996; postgrad., Columbia U., 1955. Writer on staff of gov. N.Y. State, Albany, 1955-59; commd. fgn. service officer USIA, 1959; served in USIA, Buenos Aires, Argentina, Rio de Janeiro, Brazil, 1959-62; exec. asst. to commr. N.Y. State Health Dept., Albany, 1963-66; chief speechwriter for gov. N.Y. State, Albany, 1966-74; speechwriter for v.p. U.S., Washington, 1975-77. Author: My Enemy My Brother: Men and Days of Gettysburg, 1977; (novel) The Spiderweb, 1979, Piercing the Reich: The Penetration of Nazi Germany by American Secret Agents during World War II, 1979 (Nat. Intelligence Study Ctr. prize for best book on intelligence 1979), The Imperial Rockefeller: A Biography of Nelson A. Rockefeller, 1982, Murrow: An American Original, 1988, Casey: William J. Casey, From the OSS to the CIA, 1990, Nuremberg: Infamy on Trial, 1994; collaborator: Colin Powell: My American Journey, 1995. Served to lt. (j.g.) USN, 1952-55. Recipient Disting. Alumnus award SUNY-Albany, 1982. Mem. Authors Guild, Inc. Home and Office: 222 Heritage Rd Guilderland NY 12084-9314

PERSINGER, JUDITH EILEEN, management plan clerk; b. Weston, W.Va., Aug. 4, 1944; d. William Edward and Pearl Lenna (Blake) Skinner; m. Claude Calvin Persinger, Sept. 4, 1962; children: Lisa, Shawn. Grad. high sch., Burnsville, W.Va. Telephone operator Chesapeake and Potomac Telephone Co., Morgantown, W.Va., 1965-68, plant clk., 1969-71; RAAS clk. Bell Atlantic Va., Culpeper, 1978-79; assignment clk. Bell Atlantic Va., Fairfax, 1979-86; mgmt. plan clk. Bell Atlantic Va., Falls Church, 1987—. Pres. Home Owners Assn., Slidell, La., 1975, Cmty. Rel. Bell Atlantic, Warrenton, Va., 1982-89; v.p. Literacy Vol., Warrenton, 1994; pres. Bell Atlantic Pioneers, Richmond, 1995—. Recipient Govs. award, State of Va., 1994. Mem. Eta Sigma (pres. 1989-90). Home: 5647 Wilshire Dr Warrenton VA 20187 Office: Bell Atlantic Va 2980 Fairview Park Dr Falls Church VA 22042-4525

PERSON, CURTIS S., JR., state senator, lawyer; b. Nov. 27, 1934; married; 6 children. BS, Memphis State U., 1956; LLB, U. Miss., 1959. Practice law, Memphis; former mem. Tenn. Ho. of Reps.; mem. Tenn. Senate, 1968—; Senate Rep. whip, 1973-76, minority caucus chmn., 1976-82; chmn. Senate Judiciary com. 95th-100th Gen. Assemblies; chief legal officer Juvenile Ct. of Memphis and Shelby County. Pres., Memphis-Shelby County Mental Health Assn., 1969-73, Handicapped Inc., 1972-74; chmn. Memphis Commn. on Drug Abuse, 1970-71; charter pres. Memphis State Tiger Rebounders; past trustee Memphis State U.; exec. committeeman St. Jude's Memphis Open Golf Classic; co-chmn. Shelby County Legis. Del., 1973-74, vice chmn., 1970, 75, 76, 85-88; chmn. Shelby Rep. Del., 1977, 83-84. Named Memphis and Tenn. Outstanding Young Man of Yr., Jaycees, 1969, Outstanding Legislator of Yr., Government Leader Against Drunk Driving, Tenn. MADD, 1988, Legislator of Yr., Tenn. Alcohol and Drug Assn., 1988; recipient Liberty Bell Freedom award Memphis/Shelby County Bar Assn., 1969, Tenn. Adv. of Year for Handicapped children, 1978, Outstanding Svc to Children award Tenn. Coun. Juvenile Ct. Judges, 1981, Pres'. Svc. award Tenn. Juvenile Ct. Svcs. Assn., 1981, Americanism award Memphis Civitan Club, 1986, Disting. Svc. award County Officials Assn. Tenn., 1989, Community Svc. award Tenn. Med. Assn., 1989, Eagle award Eagle Forum, 1994, Bill Bates Legis. award United Tenn. League, 1994, Champion for Children award Tenn. Assn. Child Care, 1995, Outstanding Legislator award County Officials Assn. Tenn., 1996. Mem. Tenn. Bar Assn., Miss. Bar Assn., Memphis/Shelby County Bar Assn., Memphis State U. Nat. Alumni Assn. (pres. 1970, 71), So. Golf Assn. (past dir.), Nat. Rifle Assn. (life), Phi Alpha Delta, Phi Alpha Theta, Kappa Sigma, Omicron Delta Kappa. Presbyterian. Clubs: Masons, Shriners. Office: War Meml Bldg Rm 308 Nashville TN 37243

PERSON, DONALD AMES, SR., pediatrician, rheumatologist; b. Fargo, N.D., July 17, 1938; s. Ingwald Haldor and Elma Wilhelmenia (Karlstrom) P.; m. Blanche Durand, Apr. 28, 1962; children: Donald Ames Jr., David Wesley. Student, Gustavus Adolphus Coll., 1956-58, U. Minn., 1958-59; BS, U. N.D., 1961; MD, U. Minn., 1963. Intern Mpls.-Hennepin County Gen. Hosp., 1963-64; resident neurol. surgery Mayo Clinic and Mayo Grad. Sch. Medicine, Rochester, Minn., 1967, fellow in microbiology, 1968-70; rsch. assoc. Baylor Coll. Medicine, Houston, 1971, Arthritis Found. fellow, 1972-74, mem. faculty, asst. prof. internal medicine, 1971-78, asst. prof. pediatrics, 1980-87, resident in pediatrics, 1978-80; asst. attending pediatrics Harris County Hosp. Dist., 1980-88; rheumatologist Tex. Children's Hosp., 1980-88, attending pediatrician, 1982-88; cons. Kelsey Seybold Clinic, 1980-88, Houston Shriner's Crippled Children's Hosp., 1983-88 , Houston Meth. Hosp., 1983-88, St. Luke's Episcopal Hosp., 1983-88, Honolulu Shriner's Crippled Children's Hosp., 1988—; prof. clin. pediatrics U. Hawaii Sch. Medicine, Honolulu, 1991—; prof. clin. pediatrics Uniformed Svcs. U. Health Scis., Bethesda, Md., 1993—, chief gen. pediatric svc., 1991-94; chief ambulatory pediatrics, Tripler Army Med. Ctr., Tripler AMC, Hawaii, 1988-94, asst. chief dept. pediatrics, 1988-94, chief dept. pediatrics, 1994—; "A" proficiency designator in pediatrics from Surgeon Gen. of the Army, 1990. Contbr. articles to profl. jours. With AUS, 1964-66, col. regular army, 1987—, Arthritis Found. sr. investigator, 1975-77. Fellow Am. Acad. Pediatrics (v.p. chpt. west uniformed svcs. sect. 1994-95, mem. exec. com. uniformed svcs. sect., 1995-96, adv. mem. exec. com. Hawaii chpt. 1994—), Am. Coll. Rheumatology; mem. AAAS, AMA, Am. Fedn. Clin. Rsch., Am. Soc. Microbiology, Soc. Pediat. Rsch., Am. Soc. Tropical Medicine and Hygiene, Am. Pediat. Soc., Arthritis Found. (dir., med. adv. bd.), Assn. Mil. Surgeons U.S. (Philip Hench award 1990), Harris County Med. Soc., Houston Acad. Medicine, Houston Pediatric Soc., Internat. Orgn. Mycoplasmologists, N.Y. Acad. Sci., N.D. Acad. Sci., Soc. Exptl. Biology and Medicine, So. Soc. Pediatric Rsch., S.W. Sci. Forum, Tex. Med. Assn., Tex. Pediatric Soc., Tex. Rheumatism Assn., Tissue Culture Assn., Honolulu Pediatric Soc., U.S. Fedn. Culture Collections. Mem. Evang. Luth. Ch. in Am., deacon, 1991-94. Home: 1321 Parks Rd Honolulu HI 96819-2131 Office: Tripler Army Med Ctr 1 Jarrett White Rd Tripler Army HI 96859-5000

PERSON, EVERT BERTIL, newspaper and radio executive; b. Berkeley, Calif., Apr. 6, 1914; s. Emil P. and Elida (Swanson) P.; m. Ruth Finley, Jan. 26, 1944 (dec. May 1985); m. 2d, Norma Joan Betz, Mar. 12, 1986. Student, U. Calif., Berkeley, 1937; LHD, Calif. State Univs., 1983, Sonoma State U., 1993. Co-publisher, sec.-treas. Press Democrat Pub. Co., Santa Rosa, Calif., 1945-72, editor, 1972-73, pres., pub., editor-in-chief, 1973-85; sec.-treas. Finley Broadcasting Co., Santa Rosa, 1945-72; pres. Finley Broadcasting Co., 1972-89, Kawana Pubs., 1975-85; pub. Healdsburg Tribune, 1975-85; prin. Evert B. Person Investments, Santa Rosa, 1985—; pres. Person Properties Co., Santa Rosa, 1945-70; v.p. Finley Ranch & Land Co., Santa Rosa, 1947-72, pres., 1972-79; pres. Baker Pub. Co., Oreg., 1957-67, Sebastopol (Calif.) Times, 1978-81, Russian River News, Guerneville, Calif., 1978-81; pres. publ. Kawana Pubs., 1978-85; mem. nominating com. AP, 1982-84, mem. auditing com., 1984-85. Bd. dirs. Empire Coll., Santa Rosa, 1972—, Sonoma County Taxpayers Assn., 1966-69, San Francisco Spring Opera Assn., 1974-79; bd. dirs. San Francisco Opera, 1986—, v.p., 1988—; pres. Calif. Newspaperboy Found., 1957-58; chmn. Santa Rosa Civic Arts Commn., 1961-62; pres. Santa Rosa Sonoma County Symphony Assn., 1966-68, Luther Burbank Meml. Found., 1979, Santa Rosa Symphony Found., 1967-77; adv. bd. Santa Rosa Salvation Army, 1959-67; commodore 12th Coast Guard Dist. Aux., 1969-70; trustee Desert Mus., Palm Springs, 1987-92, v.p. Nat. Bd. Canine Companions, Inc., 1989-92. Mem. Calif. Newspaper Pubs. Assn. (pres. 1981-82), Internat. Newspaper Fin. Execs. (pres. 1961-62), Bohemian Club, Sonoma County Press Club, Santa Rosa Golf and Country club, The Springs Club, Santa Rosa Rotary (past pres.), Masons (33 degree, Legion of Merit), Shriners. Roman Catholic. Home: 1020 Mcdonald Ave Santa Rosa CA 95404-3525 Office: The Oaks 1400 N Dutton Ave Ste 12 Santa Rosa CA 95401-4644

PERSON, ROBERT JOHN, financial management consultant; b. Mpls., Mar. 7, 1927; s. Otto Carl and Alice Kathryn (Kasper) P.; m. Jeanette Haines, Mar. 11, 1948; 1 dau., Julie Ann. BBA, U. Minn., 1947; MS, Columbia u., 1953. Financial analyst Equitable Life Assurance Soc. U.S., N.Y.C., 1947-53; asst. v.p. bus. devel. met. banking dept. Bankers Trust Co., N.Y.C., 1953-64; v.p. bus. devel. div. Union Bank, Los Angeles, 1964-67; v.p., dir. mktg. Bank of Calif., San Francisco, 1967-70; sr. v.p. Central Nat. Bank of Chgo., 1970-72, 1st v.p., 1973-76; 1st v.p. Central Nat. Chgo. Corp., 1973-76; v.p., regional mgr. Lester B. Knight & Assos., Inc., San Francisco, 1976-77; dir. bank cons. Coopers & Lybrand, San Francisco, 1977-80; partner-in-charge, nat. dir. bank cons. Coopers & Lybrand, Chgo., 1980-89; exec. v.p. RJP Assocs., Inc., Stockton, Calif., 1989-92; instr. salesmanship sch. pub. relations N.Y. Bankers Assn., 1960-63; instr. mktg. research Stonier Grad. Sch. Banking, Rutgers U., 1964-65, 73, 75-77, Brown U., 1964; instr. Agrl. Lending Sch., Ill. Bankers Assn., 1973-76, Nat. Comml. Lending Sch., Am. Bankers Assn., 1973-76, Sch. Bank Adminstrn., U. Wis., 1982-85, Nat. Grad. Trust Sch., Northwestern U., 1982-84, Southwestern Grad. Sch. Banking, 1983-84; Vice chmn. mgmt. effectiveness com. Community Fund Chgo. Treas. Sch. Bd., Huntington, N.Y., 1957-59; Bd. dirs. Am. Cancer Soc., Chgo.; chief crusader Crusade of Mercy. Served to lt. comdr. USNR, 1944-46, ret. Recipient Florence McNeil Stanley award Columbia, 1953. Mem. Am. Bankers Assn., Bank Mktg. Assn., Am. Mgmt. Assn. (mktg. planning council), Mgmt. Centre-Europe (fin. mgmt. adv. com. 1971—), Sales and Mktg. Execs. Internat., Stockton Symphony Assn. (bd. dirs. 1989-92), Beta Gamma Sigma. Republican. Presbyn. Clubs: Eastward Ho (Cape Cod); Stockton Golf and Country (Calif.). Lodge: Elks. Home: 14406 W Trading Post Dr Sun City West AZ 85375-5791 also: 81 Joshua Jethro Rd Chatham MA 02633-1104

PERSON, RUTH JANSSEN, academic administrator; b. Washington, Aug. 27, 1945; d. Theodore Armin and Ruth Katherine (Mahoney) Janssen. BA, Gettysburg (Pa.) Coll., 1967; AMLS, U. Mich., 1969, PhD, 1980; MS in Adminstrn., George Washington U., 1974. Head of reference/asst. prof. Thomas Nelson C.C., Hampton, Va., 1971-74; lectr. U. Mich., Ann Arbor, 1975-79, coord. of continuing edn., 1977-79; asst. prof. Cath. U., Washington, 1979-85, assoc. prof., 1985-86, assoc. dean Sch. of Libr. and Info. Sci., 1983-86; dean Coll. Libr. Sci. Clarion (Pa.) U., 1986-88; assoc. vice chancellor U. Mo., St. Louis, 1988-93; v.p. for acad. affairs Ashland (Ohio) U., 1993-95; v.p. acad. affairs, prof. bus. adminstrn. Angelo State U., San Angelo, Tex., 1995—; reviewer U.S. Dept. Edn., Washington, 1987-89, 92; trustee Pitts. Regional Libr. Ctr., 1986-88; chair publs. com. Assn. of Coll. and Rsch. Librs., Chgo., 1986-90; cons. United Way, Alexandria, Va., 1985; cons.-evaluator North Ctrl. Assn., 1993-95; nat. vis. com. Southwest Ctr. Advanced Tech. Edn., 1996—. Co-editor: (book) Academic Libraries: Their Role and Rationale in Higher Education, 1995; editor: (book) The Management Process, 1983; editl. bd. Coll. & Rsch. Librs., 1990-96; contr. articles to profl. jours. Mem. Strategic Planning Task Force, Ashland C. of C., 1994; bd. dirs. Alternatives for Living in Violent Environs., Inc., St. Louis, 1992-94; commr. Commn. for Women, Anne Arundel County, Md., 1984-86; mem. Citizens Adv. Bd., Clarion, Pa., 1986-88; mem. Olivette, Mo. Human Rels. Commn., 1992-94, San Angelo Bus. and Profl. Women's Club, 1995—, pres.-elect, 1996-97, pres., 1997—; mem. bldg. design oversight com. San Angelo Mus. Fine Arts, 1995—; mem. com. Cactus Jazz Festival, 1995—; bd. dirs. San Angelo Bus. and Edn. Coalition, 1997—. Fellow Am. Coun. Edn., 1990, Harvard Inst. Ednl. Mgmt., 1989, Rackham fellow U. Mich., 1976; ACE fellow Ariz. Bd. Regents, 1990-91; recipient Washington Woman award Washington Woman mag., 1986. Mem. ALA (com. on accreditation 1993-97), Am. Assn. Univ. Adminstrs. (bd. dirs. 1993—), Coun. for the Preservation of Anthropol. Records (bd. dirs.), Psi Chi, Beta Phi Mu, Pi Lambda Theta, Kappa Delta Pi, Phi Alpha Theta. Lutheran. Avocations: piano, herb gardening, antiques, cooking, sailing. Home: 5218 N Bentwood Dr San Angelo TX 76904 Office: Angelo State U Box 11008 ASU Station San Angelo TX 76909

PERSON, WILLIS BAGLEY, chemistry educator; b. Salem, Oreg., Apr. 23, 1928; s. Carl Waldo and Grace Cassity (Bagley) P.; m. Krystyna Szczepaniak, 1985. BS, Willamette U., 1947; MS, Oreg. State Coll., Corvallis, 1949; PhD, U. Calif., Berkeley, 1953. Rsch. fellow U. Minn., 1952-54; instr. Harvard U., 1954-55; asst. prof. U. Iowa, 1955-61, assoc. prof., 1961-66; NSF sr. postdoctoral fellow, vis. assoc. prof. U. Chgo., 1965-66; prof. chemistry U. Fla., Gainesville, 1966—; vis. staff Los Alamos (N.Mex.) Nat. Lab., 1975-89; UNESCO cons. state U. Campinas, Brazil, 1980; vis. prof. Royal Holloway Coll., U. London, 1978, Inst. Molecular Sci., Okazaki, Japan, 1984, U. Pierre et Marie Curie, Paris, 1985; assoc. mem. commn. molecular spectroscopy IUPAC, 1982-89; mem. spectroscopy com. IUPAC Commn., 1989—; vis. scientist Lab. Chem. Phys. NIDDK/NIH, Bethesda, Md., 1993. Author: (with R.S. Mulliken) Molecular Complexes, 1969; editor: (with G. Zerbi) Vibrational Intensities in Infrared and Raman Spectroscopy, 1982; contbr. numerous articles to profl. jours. Guggenheim fellow U. Chgo., 1960-61, Chem. Soc. Sr. Postdoctoral fellow, 1978. Mem. AAAS, Am. Chem. Soc., Optical Soc. Am., Royal Soc. Chemists (London), Coblentz Soc., Soc. Applied Spectroscopy. Office: U Fla Dept Chemistry PO Box 117200 Gainesville FL 32611-7200

PERSONICK, STEWART DAVID, electrical engineer; b. Bklyn., Feb. 22, 1947; s. Louis and Mamie (Katz) P.; m. Carol Ann Cooke, Apr. 12, 1986. B.E.E., CCNY, 1967; S.M., MIT, 1968, Sc.D., 1970. Engr. Bell Labs., Holmdel, N.J., 1967-75, engring. supr., 1975-78, dept. head, 1983-84; engring. mgr. Vidar div. TRW, Mountain View, Calif., 1978-81; research mgr. Tech. Research Ctr. TRW, El Segundo, Calif., 1981-83; cons. Pacific Palisades, Calif., 1983-84; com. mem. NRC, Washington, 1983—; div. mgr. Bell Communications Research, Red Bank, N.J., 1984-85, asst. v.p., 1985-95, v.p., gen. mgr., 1995—. Author: Optical Fiber Transmission Systems, 1981, Fiber Optics Technology and Applications, 1985; editor spl. issue on fiber optic systems, IEEE Trans., 1978, 83; IEEE misc. jours., 1975—; patentee fiber optics; contbr. chpts. in books. Fellow IEEE, Optical Soc. Am.; mem. NAE, IEEE Communications Soc. Office: Bell Communications Rsch 445 South St Rm 1C-201B Morristown NJ 07960-6454

PERSONS, OSCAR NEWTON, lawyer; b. McCormick, S.C., Jan. 7, 1939; s. Abner Thaddeus and Esther (Dumas) P.; m. Virginia Van Landingham, July 16, 1988; children: Thaddeus William, Anne Laura Lacour. B in Indsl. Engring., Ga. Inst. Tech., 1960; JD, Emory U., 1967. Bar: Ga. Ptnr. Alston & Bird, Atlanta, 1967—. Mem. Ga. Election Bd., 1976-96; gen. counsel Ga. Rep. Com., 1971-93; Ga. chmn. Dole for Pres. campaign, 1987, 95-96; Ga. vice chmn. Bush for Pres. campaign, 1988; gen. co-chmn. Bush-Quayle campaign, 1992; chmn. Coverdell for U.S. Senate campaign, 1992, Senator Coverdell's Citizens' Senate Del., 1993—; chmn. Ga. Electoral Coll., 1996. Presbyterian. Office: Alston & Bird One Atlantic Ctr 1201 W Peachtree St NW Atlanta GA 30309-3400

PERSONS, STOW SPAULDING, historian, educator; b. Mt. Carmel, Conn., June 15, 1913; s. Frederick Torrell and Florence Isabel (Cummings) P.; m. Dorothy Mae Reuss, Sept. 4, 1943; 1 dau., Catherine. BA, Yale U., 1936, PhD, 1940. Instr. history Princeton U., 1940-45, asst. prof., 1945-50; prof. history U. Iowa, 1950—, rsch. prof., 1956-57, Carver Disting. prof., 1978-81, prof. emeritus, 1981—, acting dean Grad. Coll., 1960-61; sr. rsch. fellow NEH, 1967-68; Vis. prof. Salzburg (Austria) Seminar, 1955, 61, Stetson U., 1957, San Francisco Coll., 1959, U. Wyo., 1960, U. Colo., 1964. Author: Free Religion, 1947, American Minds, 1958, The Decline of American Gentility, 1973, Ethnic Studies at Chicago, 1987, The University of Iowa in the 20th Century, 1990; editor: Evolutionary Thought in America, 1950, (with D. Egbert and T.D.S. Bassett) Socialism and American Life, 1952, Social Darwinism: Selected Essays of William Graham Sumner, 1963, The Cooperative Commonwealth (Laurence Gronlund); mem. editorial bd. Am. Quar., 1958-61, Mississippi Valley Hist. Rev., 1954-57. Fellow Fund Advancement Edn., 1954-55. Mem. Am. Hist. Assn., Orgn. Am. Historians (exec. com. 1960-63). Home: 1433 Oaklawn Ave Iowa City IA 52245-5648

PERSSON, ERLAND KARL, electrical engineer, electrical company executive; b. Soderala, Sweden, Oct. 9, 1923; came to U.S., 1949, naturalized, 1953; m. Elaine Darm; children—Ann Monn, Eric. B.S.E.E., U. Minn., 1955. Registered profl. engr., Minn. Prin. engr. Gen. Mills, Mpls., 1956-61; v.p. engring. Electro-Craft Corp., Hopkins, Minn., 1961-72, v.p. research and devel., 1972-83, sr. v.p., chief tech. officer, 1983-86; pres. Erland Persson Co., Mpls., 1987—. Contbr. articles to profl. jours. Contbr. chpts. to books. Patentee in field. Mem. Mech. Engring. Adv. Com. U. Minn.; bd. dirs. Minn. High Tech. Council, 1984-86, mem., 1987. Fellow IEEE (mem. subcom. electric machines com., indsl. drives com.), Audio Engring. Soc. (founder Midwest chpt. 1974); mem. Eta Kappa Nu. Office: Erland Persson Co Interchange Tower 600 Highway 169 S Ste 1275 Minneapolis MN 55426-1215

PERSYN, MARY GERALDINE, law librarian, law educator; b. Elizabeth, N.J., Feb. 25, 1945; d. Henry Anthony and Geraldine (Sumption) P. AB, Creighton U., 1967; MLS, U. Oreg., 1969; JD, Notre Dame U., 1982. Bar: Ind. 1982, U.S. Dist. Ct. (no. and so. dists.) Ind. 1982, U.S. Supreme Ct. 1995. Social scis. libr. Miami U., Oxford, Ohio, 1969-78; staff law libr. Notre Dame (Ind.) Law Sch., 1982-84; dir. law libr. Valparaiso (Ind.) U., 1984-87, law libr., assoc. prof. law, 1987—. Editor Journal of Legislation, 1981-82; mng. editor Third World Legal Studies, 1986—. V.p. Ind. Coop. Libr. Svcs. Auth., 1997-98, pres., 1998—. Mem. ABA, Ind. State Bar Assn., Am. Assn. Law Librs. Ohio Regional Assn. Law Librs. (pres. 1990-91), Ind. State Quilt Guild (pres. 1996-98). Roman Catholic. Home: 1308 Tuckahoe Park Dr Valparaiso IN 46383-4032 Office: Valparaiso U Law Libr Sch Law Valparaiso IN 46383

PERTSCHUK, LOUIS PHILIP, pathologist; b. London, July 4, 1925; s. Isaac M. and Rose P.; m. Andrea Roberts, June 28, 1985; children: Eric, Shawn, Brandy. AB, NYU, 1946; D.O., Phila. Coll. Osteo. Medicine, 1950. Diplomate: Am. Bd. Pathology. Instr. Downstate Med. Ctr., SUNY-Bklyn., 1974-75, asst. prof., 1975-79, assoc. prof., 1979-86, prof., 1986—; cons. Corning (N.Y.) Glass Works, 1982-86, Zeus Sci. Co., 1982—, Abbott Labs., 1982-92, Lifecodes Corp., 1989-93, Oncor, Inc., Gaithersburg, Md., 1994—, Internat. Bioimmune Sys., Great Neck, N.Y., 1996—, BioGenex, San Ramon, Calif., 1996—. Author: Immunocytochemistry for Steroid Receptors, 1990; editor: Localization of Putative Steroid Receptors, 1985. Served with U.S. Army, 1943-46. NCI/NIH grantee, 1979, 82, 85, 92. Fellow Coll. Am. Pathologists, Am. Soc. Clin. Pathologists; mem. Am. Assn. Pathologists, AAAS, Internat. Acad. Pathology, N.Y. Acad. Sci., Histochemical Soc. Current Work: Identification of steroid hormone binding sites in human neoplasms by histochemical and immunohistological techniques. Subspecialty: Pathology (medicine). Office: SUNY Health Sci Ctr at Bklyn 450 Clarkson Ave # 25 Brooklyn NY 11203-2012

PERVIN, WILLIAM JOSEPH, computer science educator; b. Pitts., Oct. 31, 1930; s. Abraham and Stella (Greenberger) P.; m. Susan P. Chizeck, 1981; 1 child, Hannah; children by previous marriage: Edward, James, Rachel. B.S., U. Mich., 1952, M.S., 1952; Ph.D., U. Pitts., 1957. Prof. Pa. State U., 1957-63; vis. prof. Heidelberg (Germany) U., 1963-64; prof., chmn. U. Wis.-Milw., 1964-67; dir. Computer Center, prof. math. Drexel U., Phila., 1967-73; dir. Regional Computer Center U. Tex., Dallas, 1973-78, prof. computer scis., 1973—, chmn. computer scis., 1983-85, master sch. engring. and computer scis., 1987-94. Author: Foundations of General Topology, 1964. Mem. Assn. Computing Machinery, Am. Math. Soc., IEEE Computer Soc., Soc. Indsl. and Applied Math., Math. Assn. Am. Office: U Tex Dallas PO Box 830688 M/S EC 31 Richardson TX 75083-0688

PESCE, GAETANO, architectural, interior, industrial and graphic designer; b. La Spezia, Italy, Nov. 8, 1939; m. Francesca Lucco, 1969; children: Tata, Tato. Studied architecture, U. Venice, 1959-65, Inst. Indsl. Design, Venice, 1961-65. Ind. artist, filmaker, also co-founder Gruppo N, Padua, Italy, 1959-67; freelance designer Padua, 1962-67, Venice, 1968—; prof. archtl. planning Inst. d'Architecture et d'Etudes Urbaines, Strasbourg, France, 1975—; vis. prof., lectr. Ohio State U., Columbus, 1974, Cooper Union, N.Y., 1975, 79, 80, 83, 85, 86, Pratt Inst., N.Y., 1979, 80, 84, Ecole des Beaux-Arts, Nancy, France, 1981, U. Tech., Compiègne, 1981, Yale U., New Haven, 1983, U. Que., 1984, U. Montreal, 1984, Poly. of Hong Kong, 1985, Domus Acad., Milan, 1986, 87, U. São Paulo, 1987, others; conf. guest spkr. and jury mem. numerous venues and countries. Exhbns. include Galleria Bevilacqua La Masa, Venice, 1961, Hochschule für Gestaltung, Ulm, Fed. Republic Germany, 1964, Finnish Design Ctr., Helsinki, 1964, Keski Suomen Mu., Jyvsakyla, 1965, Galleria Il Canale, Venice, 1966, Galleria La Carabaga, Genoa, 1966, Galleria La Chiocciola, Padua, 1966, Linea Sud Gallery, Naples, 1967, Atelier d'Urbanisme at Architecture, Paris, 1969, Galleria Luca Palazzoli, Milan, 1974, Mus. Arts Dècoratifs, Paris, 1975, Archtl. Assn., London, 1978, JDC Gallery, Tokyo, 1978, Mus. Modern Art, N.Y.C., 1979, Carnegie-Mellon U., Pitts., 1980, Centro de Arte y Comunicación, Buenos Aires, 1981, Yale U., 1983, Mus. Arts Dècoratifs, Montreal, 1984, Harvard U., Cambridge, Mass., 1985, U. Architecture, Hong Kong, 1985, Mus. d'Art Moderne, Strabourg, 1986, Galerie Leptien 3, Frankfurt, 1988, Deutsches Architekturmuseum, Frankfurt, 1988, Max Protech Gallery, N.Y.C., 1989, Sapporo Brewery, Tokyo, 1989, U. Que., Montreal, 1989, Tel Aviv Mus., 1991, CIRVA Ctr. Rsch. on Glass, 1992, Pompidov Ctr., Paris, 1996; represented in collections Mus. Modern Art, N.Y.C., Met. Mus., N.Y.C., Centre Georges Pompidou, Paris, Mus. Arts Dècoratifs, Paris, Keski Suomen Mus., Helsinki, Mus. d'Arte Moderna, Turin, Centre Canadien d'Architecture, Montreal, Mus. Arts Dècoratifs, Montreal, others; contbr. articles to profl. jours. Recipient Locarno Film Festival award, 1968, Tokyo Lighting Design Competition award, 1973, Parc de la Villette award, Paris, 1983, Office Furniture Competition award, Paris, 1983, Chryler award 1993; named Best of Category Accessories for Fish Design Collection, 1995. Address: Pesce Ltd/Fish Design 543 Broadway New York NY 10012-3931

PESEC, DAVID JOHN, data systems executive; b. Cleve., Apr. 19, 1956; s. Rudolph J. and Martha C. (Kessler) P. BS, Cleve. State U., 1988. Pvt. practice cons. Cleve., 1976-78; programmer Champion Svc. Corp., Cleve., 1978; sr. systems programmer United Telephone of Ohio, Mansfield, 1978-89; dir. devel. Broderick Data Systems, Mansfield, 1989—; bd. dirs. Park Ave. Pets, Inc. Bd. dirs. ARC, Mansfield, 1989—, Mansfield Emergency Svc., 1986; assoc. pastor Cornerstone Grace Brethren Ch., 1995—; life mem. Rep. Nat. com., 1991—, Rep. Senatorial Inner Circle, 1991—. Recipient Senatorial medal of freedom, 1996. Mem. Am. Mgmt. Assn., Assn. Computing Machinery, Intercity Radio Club (pres. 1987-90), NRA, Gideons (v.p. 1992), Profl. Photographers. Republican. Mem. Grace Brethren Ch. Avocations: flying, auto racing. Home: 1633 Hickory Ln Mansfield OH 44905-2945 Office: Broderick Data Systems 777 Laver Rd Mansfield OH 44905-2307

PESEK, JAMES ROBERT, management consultant; b. Chgo., May 30, 1941; s. James F. and Elizabeth A. (Ord) P.; children: Becky, Shelly. B.S.M.E. with honors, U. Ill., 1964; M.B.A., U. Nebr., 1966. Cert. mgmt. cons. Adminstrv. services mgr. Cummins Engine Co., Columbus, Ind., 1966-68; cons. div. Arthur Andersen & Co., Milw., 1968-72; mgr. distbn. div. ADG, Indpls., 1972-74; mgr. Mgmt. Adv. Services Wolf & Co., Chgo., 1974-79; pres. Ind. Mgmt. Services, Hinsdale, Ill., 1979—; cons.; spkr., tchr. Mem. Am. Prodn. and Inventory Control Soc., Inst. Mgmt. Cons., Am. Arbitration Assn. Home: RR 1 Box 230 Milltown IN 47145-9749

PESERIK, JAMES E., electrical, controls and computer engineer, consultant, forensics and safety engineer, fire cause and origin investigator; b. Beloit, Wis., Sept. 30, 1945; s. Edward J. and G. Lucille Peserik; m. Elaine L. Peserik, May 6, 1972. BSEE, U. Wis., 1968; MS, St. Joseph's U., 1990. Registered profl. engr., registered profl. land surveyor; cert. fire and explosion investigator, cert. fire investigation instr. Development and instrumentation engr. Square D Co., Milw., 1968-71; product engr. I-T-E Imperial Corp., Ardmore, Pa., 1971-72; project engr. Harris-Intertype Corp., Easton, Pa., 1972-74; elec. engr. Day & Zimmerman, Inc., Phila., 1974-76; pvt. practice Coopersburg, Pa., 1976—; sr. elec. engr. S.T. Hudson Engrs., Inc., Phila., 1980-81; mem. adv. coun. Swenson Skills Ctr., Phila., 1990-95. Treas. Salford-Fraconia Joint Parks Commn., Montgomery County, Pa., 1980-83. Mem. IEEE (sec. indsl. applications group Phila. chpt. 1980, chmn. 1981), NSPE, Pa. Soc. Profl. Engrs., Del. Assn. Profl. Engrs. (external affairs com. 1995—), Nat. Fire Protection Assn., Internat. Assn. Arson Investigators, Nat. Assn. Fire Investigators. Office: PO Box 181 Coopersburg PA 18036-0181

PESHKIN, MURRAY, physicist; b. Bklyn., May 17, 1925; s. Jacob and Bella Ruth (Zuckerman) P.; m. Frances Julie Ehrlich, June 12, 1955; children—Michael, Sharon, Joel. B.A., Cornell U., 1947, Ph.D., 1951. Instr., then asst. prof. physics Northwestern U., 1951-59; physicist, then sr. scientist Argonne (Ill.) Nat. Lab., 1959—, assoc. dir. physics div., 1972-83; fellow Weizmann Inst. Sci., Rehovoth, Israel, 1959-60, 68-69; sr. scientist SciTech Mus., Aurora, Ill., 1991—. Served with AUS, 1944-46. Home: 838 Parkside Ave Elmhurst IL 60126-4813 Office: Argonne Nat Lab Argonne IL 60439

PESHKIN, SAMUEL DAVID, lawyer; b. Des Moines, Oct. 6, 1925; s. Louis and Mary (Grund) P.; m. Shirley R. Isenberg, Aug. 17, 1947; children—Lawrence Allen, Linda Ann. BA, State U. Iowa, 1948, JD, 1951. Bar: Iowa 1951. Ptnr. Bridges & Peshkin, Des Moines, 1953-66, Peshkin & Robinson, Des Moines, 1966-82; Mem. Iowa Bd. Law Examiners, 1970—. Bd. dirs. State U. Iowa Found., 1957—, Old Gold Devel. Fund, 1956—, Sch. Religion U. Iowa, 1966—. Fellow Am. Bar Found., Internat. Soc. Barristers; mem. ABA (chmn. standing com. membership 1959—, ho. of dels. 1968—, bd. govs. 1973—), Iowa Bar Assn. (bd. govs. 1958—, pres. jr. bar sect. 1958-59, award of merit 1974), Inter-Am. Bar Assn., Internat. Bar Assn., Am. Judicature Soc., State U. Iowa Alumni Assn. (dir., pres. 1957). Home: Apt 2064 6735 E Greenway Pkwy Scottsdale AZ 85254

PESIN, ELLA MICHELE, journalist, public relations professional; b. North Bergen, N.J., Aug. 29, 1956; d. Edward and Helene Sylvia (Rattner) P. BA, Sarah Lawrence Coll., 1978. Press rep. CBS-TV News and Entertainment, N.Y.C., 1978-80; publicist Newsweek Mag., N.Y.C., 1980-81; prin. Pesin Pub. Rels., N.Y.C., 1980-94; freelance journalist N.Y.C., 1981—; publicist Universal Studios MCA Inc., L.A., 1982-83; with publicity and mktg. NBC-TV News, N.Y.C., 1985-86; media exec. Burson Marsteller Pub. Rels.-Press/Media Execs., N.Y.C., 1986-87. Contbg. editor Cable Age mag., TV Radio Age mag., Advt. Forum, Facts Figures & Film, Advt. Compliance Svc.; syndicated newspaper columnist. Active Israel Bonds/United Jewish Appeal, N.Y.C., Rudolph Giuliani for N.Y.C. Mayor campaign. Mem. Pub. Rels. Soc. Am., Am. Soc. Journalists and Authors, N.Y. Fin. Writers Group, N.Y. Venture Group, Women Comm., Women Bus., Publicity Club N.Y. Avocations: photography, sculpture, modern dance, tennis, skiing. Home and Office: 7000 Boulevard East Guttenberg NJ 07093

PESMEN, SANDRA (MRS. HAROLD WILLIAM PESMEN), editor; b. Chgo., Mar. 26, 1931; s. Benjamin S. and Emma (Lipschultz) P.; m. Harold W. Pesmen, Aug. 16, 1952; children: Bethann, Curtis. B.S., U. Ill., 1952. Reporter Radio and Community News Service, Chgo., 1952-53; wire editor Champaign-Urbana (Ill.) Courier, 1953; reporter, feature writer Lerner Chgo. N. Side Newspapers, 1953-55; stringer corr. Wayne (Mich.) Eagle, 1958-61; reporter, feature writer Chgo. Daily News, 1968-78; features editor Crain's Chgo. Business mag., 1978-89; corp. features editor Crain Communications, Inc., 1989-95; tchr. feature writing Northwestern U. Evening Sch., 1972-81. Author: Writing for the Media, 1983, Dr. Job's Complete Career Guide, 1995; assoc. editor: Career News Service; author syndicated column Dr. Job, 1985—. Recipient Golden Key award Ill. Mental Health Dept., 1966, 71, award Inst. Psychoanalysis, 1971, Penny Mo. award, 1978, Stick o'Type award Chgo. Newspaper Guild, 1978, award AP, 1975, Peter Lisagor award Soc. Profl. Journalists, 1991; inductee Chgo. Journalism Hall of Fame, 1997. Home: 2811 Fern Ave Northbrook IL 60062-5809

PESNER, CAROLE MANISHIN, art gallery owner; b. Boston, Aug. 5, 1937; m. Robert Pesner (dec. 1983); children: Ben, Jonah; m. Martin Cherkasky, 1995. BA, Smith Coll., 1959. Asst. dir. Kraushaar Galleries, Inc., N.Y.C., 1959-86, dir., 1986-90, pres., 1991—. Author, editor publs., catalogues in field. Mem. Art Dealers Assn. Am., Internat. Fine Print Dealers Assn. Office: Kraushaar Galleries Inc 724 5th Ave New York NY 10019-4106

PESNER, SUSAN M., lawyer; b. Suffern, N.Y., July 17, 1951; d. Leon and Doris (Elias) P.; m. Steven M. Elliott, Sept. 22, 1978. BA, Am. U., Washington, 1973, JD, 1976. Bar: Va. 1980, U.S. Ct. Appeals (4th cir.) 1980, U.S. Dist. Ct. (ea. dist.) Va. 1981, U.S. Supreme Ct. 1993. Paralegal Walstad, Wickwire, Peterson, Gavin & Asselin, Vienna, Va., 1978-80; assoc. Walstad, Wickwire, Peterson, Gavin & Asselin, Vienna, 1980, Peterson & Assocs., Vienna, 1980-83; ptnr. Peterson & Pesner, P.C., Vienna, 1983-90, Peterson, Pesner, Cochran & Basha, P.C., Vienna, 1991—, Gordon, Estabrook & Pesner, P.C., McLean, Va., 1992-95, Gordon & Pesner, McLean, 1995—. Mem. ABA, Va. Bar Assn., Va. State Bar (area rep. 1988-91, gov. 1991—, vice chair 1995-96, chmn., 1996—, bd. govs. real estate sect. 1988—), No. Va. Bldg. Industry Assn. (chmn. regional real estate fin. conf. 1985-87), No. Va. Young Lawyers (v.p. 1983-85), Fairfax Bar Assn. Jewish. Avocations: gardening, photography, hiking. Home: 2008 Wolftrap Oaks Ct Vienna VA 22182-5070 Office: Gordon & Pesner LC 7926 Jones Branch Dr Ste 570 Mc Lean VA 22102-3303

PESTANA, CARLOS, physician, educator; b. Tacoronte, Tenerife, Canary Islands, Spain, June 10, 1936; came to U.S., 1968, naturalized, 1973; s. Francisco and Blanca (Suarez) P.; m. Myrna Lorena Serrato, Aug. 25, 1966; children—Becky Elizabeth, George Byron. B.S., Nat. U. Mex., 1952, M.D., 1959; Ph.D. in Surgery, U. Minn., 1965. Intern St. Mary of Nazareth Hosp., Chgo., 1959-60; resident Mayo Clinic, Rochester, Minn., 1961-65; surgeon Hosp. 20 de Noviembre Mexico City; asst. prof. surgery Nat. U. Mex., 1966-67; asst. prof. surgery U. Tex. Med. Sch. at San Antonio, 1968-70, asso. prof., 1970-74, prof., 1974—, asso. dean for acad. devel., 1971-73, asso. dean for student affairs, 1973-86, assoc. dean acad. affairs, 1986—. Recipient Edward John Noble Found. award, 1965, Piper Prof. award Minnie Stevens Piper Founds., 1972. Mem. San Antonio Surg. Soc., Assn. Am. Med. Colls., Sigma Xi, Alpha Omega Alpha. Home: 10123 N Manton Ln San Antonio TX 78213-1932 Office: 7703 Floyd Curl Dr San Antonio TX 78284-6200

PESTER, JACK CLOYD, oil company executive; b. Seymour, Iowa, Mar. 12, 1935; s. Cloyd Russell Pester and Esther O. (Long) Marston; m. Patricia Joanne Shay, July 21, 1956 (div. 1979); m. Barbara Dee Brazil, Aug. 13, 1979. BS in Bus. Adminstrn., Drake U. Dealer Pester Corp., Grinnell, Iowa, pres., Corydon, Iowa, CEO, Des Moines; sr. v.p. Coastal Corp., Houston; bd. dirs., Am. Mutual Life Ins. Co., Des Moines. Bd. dirs. KFx Inc., Denver. Bd. govs. Drake U. Served with U.S. Army, 1957. Reciepient Disting. Alumni award Drake U., 1979, One in a Hundred Alumni award Drake U., 1981. Republican. Roman Catholic. Clubs: Houston City. Home: 3751 Arnold Houston TX 77005-2162

PESTERFIELD, LINDA CAROL, school administrator, educator; b. Pauls Valley, Okla., May 3, 1939; d. D.J. and Geneva Lewis (Sheegog) Butler; m. W.C. Peterfield, Aug. 30, 1958; children: Ginger Carol, Walt James, Jason Kent. Student, E. Cen. State U., Ada, Okla., 1957, 76, 79; BS, Okla. State U., 1961; postgrad., Ottawa U., Ottawa, Kans., 1970, Okla. U., 1979. Tchr. Sumner Elem. Sch., Perry, Okla., 1961-62; tchr. Whitebead D-16, Pauls Valley, Okla., 1964-65, Cen. Heights Unified, Ottawa, Kans., 1969-71; prin., tchr. Whitebead D-16, Pauls Valley, 1975-91; Pauls Valley Sch., P.V., 1991—; mem. profl. standard bd. State Dept. Edn., Okla., 1988—; presenter in field. Bd. dirs. Positively Pauls Valley, 1987-97; county chmn. Nat. and Okla. 4-H Fund Drive, Garvin County, Okla., 1987-88; mem. organizational com. C-CAP-Child Abuse Prevention Orgn., Pauls Valley, 1987—; mem. vision 2000 com. Garvin County Assn. Svcs. Named to Gov.'s Honor Roll Recognition and Appreciation for Community Activities, Pauls Valley, Okla., 1985-86; named Pauls Valley Citizen of Yr., 1996. Mem. Cooperative Coun. Okla. Sch. Adminstrn., NEA, Okla. Ednl. Assn., Whitebead Ednl. Assn., Okla. Orgn. Dependent Sch., Okla. Assn. Elem. Sch. Prins., AAUW, All Sports Club (v.p. 1984-89, pres. 1985, 90), Okla. Heritage Assn., Pauls Valley Hist. Soc., Rotary (bd. dirs. 1993-96, Paul Harris fellow 1997), Pauls Valley C. of C. (pres. 1997), Delta Kappa Gamma (past local auditor, parliamentarian, v.p., pres. 1979-96), Phi Delta Kappa. Democrat. Mem. Ch. of Christ. Home: RR 3 Box 306 Pauls Valley OK 73075-9232 Office: Pauls Valley Sch Superintendents Office 301 N Chickasaw St Pauls Valley OK 73075-3428

PESTLE, JOHN WILLIAM, lawyer; b. Brattleboro, Vt., Feb. 28, 1948; s. Ray Irving and Annette Adelia (Lilley) P.; m. Penelope Mendenhall, Oct. 11, 1969; children: William Joseph, Sarah Lilley. BA magna cum laude, Harvard U., 1970; MA magna cum laude, Yale U., 1972; JD magna cum laude, U. Mich., 1975. Bar: Mich. 1975, U.S. Dist. Ct. (we. dist.) Mich. 1975, U.S. Dist. Ct (ea. dist.) Mich. 1978, U.S. Ct. Appeals (6th and D.C. cirs.) 1979, U.S. Supreme Ct. 1980. Assoc. Varnum, Riddering, Wierengo & Christenson, Grand Rapids, Mich., 1975-80; ptnr. Varnum, Riddering, Schmidt & Howlett, Grand Rapids, 1980—, co-chmn. energy and telecommunications practice group, 1986—. Contb. articles to profl. jours. Pres. Blodgett Neighborhood Assn., Grand Rapids, 1982-88; bd. dirs. Blodgett Meml. Med. Ctr. Community Rels., 1983-88, Mich. Trails coun. Girl Scouts U.S., 1982-87; trustee Harvard Glee Club Found., 1987—; sec. Nuclear Non-Oper. Owners Group, 1988-93. Mem. ABA, Fed. Energy Bar Assn. (cogeneration and small power prodn. commn.), Mich. State Bar Assn. (chmn. mcpl. utilities commn., chmn. pub. corp. law sect.), State Bar Mich. Found., Grand Rapids Bar Assn., Am. Pub. Power Assn. (vice chmn. legal sect. 1985-86, chmn. 1986-87), Harvard Club Western Mich. (sec. 1976-82). Avocations: skiing, skating, photography, gardening. Home: 515 Plymouth Ave SE Grand Rapids MI 49506-2841

PESTUREAU, PIERRE GILBERT, literature educator, literary critic, editor; b. Civray, Vienne, France, Feb. 8, 1933; came to U.S., 1991; s. Pierre and Madeleine (Bernard) P.; divorced; children: Véronique, Christophe, Charlotte; m. Ann Shepstone Wakefield, July 12, 1980. MA in Lit., U. Poitiers, France, 1955; profl. degree, Paris, 1956; PhD, Sorbonne U., Paris, 1975, SD in Lit., 1981. Prof. Nat. Edn., France, 1956-65, Tahiti, 1966-70; prof. The French Embassy, Madagascar, 1971-73, U. Natal, Durban, South Africa, 1974-80, U. Ocean Indien, La Reunion, France, 1981-83, U. Nantes, France, 1986-91, Loyola U., Chgo., 1991—; lectr. Alliance Francaise, South Africa, U.S., 1976-97; vis. prof. San Diego State U., spring 1988, Loyola U. Chgo., spring 1990. Author: Boris Vian, 1978, Dictionnaire Vian, 1985, 93; editor: Boris Vian Oeuvres Choisies, 1991, Romans, 1992, 93, 94, André Brink, 1992, Raymond Queneau, 1993, 96. Rep. Prof.'s Union, France, 1956-70. Sgt. Svc. Corps French Mil., 1960-62. Decorated chevalier Palmes Académiques. Office: Loyola U 6525 N Sheridan Rd Chicago IL 60626-5311

PESUT, TIMOTHY S., investment advisor, professional speaker, consultant; b. Gary, Ind., June 30, 1956; s. Anton and Virginia Udean (Carahoff) P.; m. Michelle Angela Durdov, May 25, 1985; children: Ariel Fay, Caitlin Michelle. AAS in Elec. Engring. Tech., Purdue U., 1978, AAS Supervision, BS Elec. Engring. Tech., 1980. CFP Coll. Fin. Planning; cert. funds specialist, trust and estate planning advisor, investment mgmt. cons.; registered investment advisor. Cardiology clin. rsch. assoc. Cordis Corp., Miami, Fla., 1980-82, neurosurg. specialist, 1982; investment broker A. G. Edwards Sons, Merrillville, Ind., 1982-86, Shearson Lehman, Sarasota, Fla., 1986-88; portfolio mgr. Prudential Securities, Inc., Venice, Fla., 1988-91; registered investment advisor First Southeastern & Co., Sarasota, Fla., 1991—; arbitrator Am. Arbitration Assn., 1992—; founder Inst. of Cert. Estate Planners. Columnist Money Talks, 1988—, Money Mgmt., 1991—. Guardian ad litem 12th Dist. Ct., Sarasota, 1988—; mem. adv. bd. Wilkinson Sch., Sarasota H.S.; bd. dirs. Jr. Achievement of Sarasota County; founding mem. Anthony Robbins Found., 1990. Cpl. USMC, 1974-76. Mem. Profl. Assn. Diving Instrs. (Divemaster), Nat. Speakers Assn., Toastmasters Internat. (gov. divsn. 1, 1994-95, lt. gov. mktg. 1996-97, dist. treas. 1995-96, lt. gov. edn. and tng. 1997—, Area Gov. of Yr. 1994). Republican. Methodist. Avocations: scuba diving, skiing, sailing, woodworking, fine arts. Office: First Southeastern & Co 1819 Main St Ste 218 Sarasota FL 34236-5983

PESZKE, MICHAEL ALFRED, psychiatrist, educator; b. Deblin, Poland, Dec. 19, 1932; s. Alfred Bartlomiej and Eugenia Halina (Grebocka) P.; m. Alice Margaret Sherman, Sept. 20, 1958; children: Michele Halina Olender, Michael Alexander. BA, Trinity Coll., Dublin, Ireland, 1956; MB, BCh, BAO, Dublin U., 1956. Bd. cert. psychiatrist. Staff psychiatrist Yale Student Health Svc., New Haven, 1961-64; asst. prof. sch. medicine U. Chgo., 1964-68; cons. psychiatrist Wesleyan U., Middletown, Conn., 1968-70; asst. prof. Sch. Medicine U. Conn., Farmington, 1970-73, assoc. prof., 1973-80, prof. psychiatry, 1980-90; clin. prof. U. Md. Sch. Medicine, Balt., 1991—; chief psychiatry Perry Point (Md.) VA Med. Ctr., 1991—; dir. psychiat. clin. svcs. John Dempsey Hosp., U. Conn. Health Ctr., Farmington, 1983-87; chief VA Med. Ctr., Newington, Conn., 1987-90. Author: Involuntary Treatment of the Mentally Ill: The Problem of Autonomy, 1975, Battle for Warsaw, 1939-44, 1995; co-author: (edited by L.A. Pervin, L.R. Reik, W. Dalrymple) The College Drop-out and the Utilization of Talent, 1966, (edited by J. Zusman, E. Bertsch) The Future of Psychiatric State Hospitals, 1975; contbr. articles to profl. jours.; book reviewer Univ. Chgo. Law Rev., 1968, Conn. Law Rev., 1976, Am. Jour. Psychiatry, 1976-93. Mem. Conn.'s Jud. Law Revision Com., 1982-86, Whiting Forensic Adv. Bd., 1975-87; co-chair Commr. Mental Health's Com. to Re-write Conn. Civil Commitment Statutes, 1976-77. WHO travel fellow, United Kingdom, Denmark, Poland, 1977; U. Conn. Research grantee, 1972-87. Fellow APA (life); mem. Am. Coll. Psychiatrists, Soc. for Mil. History. Avocations: World War II military and diplomatic history, sailing. Home: PO Box 165 Perry Point MD 21902-0165

PETAK, WILLIAM JOHN, systems management educator; b. Johnstown, Pa., June 23, 1932; s. Val Andrew and Lola Agatha (Boroski) P.; m. Ramona Janet Cayuela, Dec. 28, 1957; children: Elizabeth Ann Petak-Aaron, William Matthew, Michael David. BS in Mech. Engring., U. Pitts., 1956; MBA, U. So. Calif., 1963, DPA, 1969. Engr. Northrop Corp., Hawthorne, Calif., 1956-59; test engr. Wyle Labs., El Segundo, Calif., 1959-63; we. regional mgr. Instrument div. Budd Co., Phoenixville, Pa., 1963-69; v.p., dir. J.H. Wiggins Co., Redondo Beach, Calif., 1969-81; prof. systems mgmt. U. So. Calif., L.A., 1982—, exec. dir. Inst. Safety and Sys. Mgmt., 1987—; chmn. earthquake mitigation com. Nat. Com. on Property Ins., Boston, 1990-92; mem. com. on natural disasters NRC, Washington, 1985-91, mem. U.S. nat. com. for the decade for natural disaster reduction, 1989-92. Co-author: Natural Hazard Risk Assessment and Public Policy, 1982, Politics and Economics of Earthquake Hazard Reduction, 1986, Disabled Persons and Earthquake Hazards, 1988; editor spl. issue Pub. Adminstrn. Rev., 1985. Commr. County of Los Angeles, 1994—; mem. policy bd. So. Calif. Earthquake Prep. Project, L.A., 1986-92; trustee Marymount Coll., Palos Verdes, Calif., 1974—. Sgt. U.S. Army, 1950-52. Mem. Soc. for Risk Analysis, Earthquake Engrng. Rsch. Inst., Am. Soc. for Pub. Adminstrn., Sigma Xi. Republican. Roman Catholic. Avocations: skiing, fishing, hiking. Office: U So Calif MC 0021 Inst Safety and Systems Mgmt Los Angeles CA 90089

PETCHESKY, ROSALIND POLLACK, political science and women's studies educator; b. Bay City, Tex., Aug. 16, 1942. BA, Smith Coll., 1964; MA, Columbia U., 1966, PhD, 1974. Prof. Hunter Coll. CUNY. Author: (books) The Individual's Rights and International Organization, 1966, Abortion and Women's Choice: The State, Sexuality and Reproductive Freedom, 1984, 2d edit. 1990 (Joan Kelly Meml. prize Am. Hist. Assn. 1984). Founder Internat. Reproductive Rights Rsch. Action Group. MacArthur fellow, 1995. Office: CUNY Hunter Coll Dept Polit Sci 695 Park Ave New York NY 10021-5024

PETER See L'HUILLIER, PETER

PETER, ARNOLD PHILIMON, lawyer; b. Karachi, Pakistan, Apr. 3, 1957; came to U.S., 1968; s. Kundan Lal and Irene Primrose (Mall) P. BS, Calif. State U., Long Beach, 1981; JD, Loyola U., L.A., 1984; MS, Calif. State U., Fresno, 1991. Bar: Calif. 1985, U.S. Dist. Ct. (ea., so., no. and cen. dists.) Calif. 1986, U.S. Ct. Appeals (9th cir.) 1989, U.S. Ct. Appeals (11th cir.) 1990. Law clk. appellate dept. Superior Ct., L.A., 1984-85, U.S. Dist. Ct. (ea. dist.) Calif., Fresno, 1986-88; assoc. Pepper, Hamilton & Scheetz, L.A., 1988-89, McDermott, Will & Emery, P.A., L.A., 1989-90, Cadwalader, Wickersham & Taft, L.A., 1990-91; labor and employment counsel City of Fresno, Calif., 1991-94; v.p. labor rels. and litigation Universal Studios, Hollywood, Calif.; adj. prof. law San Joaquin (Calif.) Sch. Law, 1993—, Calif. State U., Fresno, 1993—, acad. inquiry officer, 1993—, Calif. State U., Fresno. Contbr. articles to profl. jours. Mem. ABA, L.A. County Bar Assn. (mem. conf. of dels., com. on fed. cts.), Calif. State Bar Assn. (chmn. com. on fed. cts., chmn. exec. com. labor and employment law sect.), L.A. Athletic Club. Office: Universal Studios 100 Universal City Plz Universal Cty CA 91608-1002

PETER, FRANCES MARCHBANK, author, editor, publisher, research agency administrator; b. Paterson, N.J.; d. Frederick James Marchbank, Jr. and Frances Grace (Witbeck) Marchbank Filter. BA with honors, Syracuse (N.Y.) U., 1959; postgrad. NYU, U. Md., The Wharton Sch. Tech. writer GE Corp., 1959-60; assoc. producer Met. Opera Broadcasts, 1960-62; treas. Souvaine Assocs., Inc., 1960-62; asst. to music critic Edward Downes, 1962-63; staff program mgmt. Gen. Electric Co., Wiesbaden, W.Ger., 1963-65, Fed. Electric Co., Frankfurt, W.Ger., 1965, Page Communications Engrs., Inc., Saigon, Vietnam and Tripoli, Libya, 1966-70; head publs. dept., mng. editor BioSci., jour. Am. Inst. Biol. Scis., Washington, 1972-75; editor Commn. on Life Scis., NRC-NAS, Washington, 1975-88, dep. dir. food and nutrition bd., 1987-90, dir. long-range planning for adminstrn., 1990-92; v.p. Peter, Marchbank and Palmer, Inc., 1980-92; cons. in field, 1992—. Recipient cert. merit Am. Inst. Biol. Scis., 1975. Mem. Soc. Scholarly Pub. (charter, editor SSP Letter 1982-84, asst. sec.-treas. 1982-84, mem. edit. com. 1996—), Washington Ind. Writers, Coun. Biology Editors (publs. com.), Washington Book Pubs., Delta Delta Delta. Editorial bd. Am. Biology Tchr., 1975-76. Home and Office: 2500 Q St NW #212 Washington DC 20007

PETER, LAURA ANNE, lawyer; b. Santa Monica, Calif., June 17, 1964; d. Gabriel George Pitta and Barbara Joyce (Leomazzi) P. BS, Cornell U., 1986; MA, U. Chgo., 1988; JD, Santa Clara U., 1992; LLM, U. London, 1994. Bar: U.S. Patent and Trademark Office, 1989, Calif. 1992, U.S. Dist. Ct. (no. dist.) Calif. 1992, U.S. Ct. Appeals (9th cir.) 1992. Assoc. Law Offices of Rafael Chodos, Santa Monica, 1995-97; mgr. Rancho de Vino, Monterey, Calif., 1991-93; adj. prof. Santa Clara U. Contbr. articles to profl. jours. Fellow The UN Grad. Study Programme, Geneva, Switzerland, 1987; recipient Hague (The Netherlands) Acad. Internat., 1993. Mem. ABA, Internat. Bar Assn., Internat. Lit. and Artistic Assn., Licensing Execs. Soc. Office: Townsend & Townsend & Crew 2 Embarcadero Ctr Lbby 8 San Francisco CA 94111-3823

PETER, PHILLIPS SMITH, lawyer; b. Washington, Jan. 24, 1932; s. Edward Compston and Anita Phillips (Smith) P.; m. Jania Jayne Hutchins, Apr. 8, 1961; children: Phillips Smith Peter Jr., Jania Jayne Hutchins Stone. BA, U. Va., 1954, JD, 1959. Bar: Calif. 1959. Assoc. McCutchen, Doyle, Brown, Enerson, San Francisco, 1959-63; with GE (and subs.), various locations, 1963-94; v.p. corp. bus. devel. GE (and subs.), 1973-76; v.p. GE (and subs.), Washington, 1976-79, v.p. corp. govtl. rels., 1980-94; counsel, head govt. rels. dept. Reed Smith Shaw & McClay, Washington, 1994—; chmn. bd. govs. Bryce Harlow Found., 1990-92, bd. dirs. Mem. editl. bd. Va. Law Rev., 1957-59. Trustee Howard U., 1981-89; bd. dirs., exec. com. Nat. Bank of Washington, 1981-86; v.p. Fed. City Coun., Washington, 1979-85; bd. dirs. Carlton, 1987-90, 95—, pres., 1995-96. With transp. corps U.S. Army, 1954-56. Mem. Calif. Bar Assn., Order of Coif, Wee Burn Club, Ea. Yacht Club, Farmington Country Club, Ponte Vedra Club, Lago Mar Club, Landmark Club, Congl. Country Club, Georgetown Club, Chevy Chase Club, Pisces Club, F Street Club, Fairfax Club, Carlton Club (bd. dirs. 1990—), Coral Beach and Tennis Club, Johns Island Club, The Windsor Club, Omicron Delta Kappa. Episcopalian. Home: 10805 Tara Rd Potomac MD 20854-1341 also: Johns Island 1000 Beach Rd & 690 Ocean Vero Beach FL 32963-3429

PETER, RICHARD ECTOR, zoology educator; b. Medicine Hat, Alta., Can., Mar. 7, 1943; s. Arthur E. and Josephine (Wrobleski) P.; m. Leona L. Booth, Dec. 27, 1965; children: Jason E., Matthew T.B. BSc with honors, U. Atla., 1965; PhD, U. Wash., 1969. Postdoctoral fellow U. Bristol, Eng., 1969-70; asst. prof. U. Alta., Edmonton, 1971-74, assoc. prof., 1974-79, prof., 1979—, chmn. dept. zoology, 1983-89, 90-92, dean of sci., 1992—. Contbr. over 270 papers to sci. publs. Recipient Pickford medal Internat. Com. on Comparative Endocrinology, 1985. Fellow AAAS, Royal Soc. Can.; mem. Can. Soc. Zoology (pres. 1991-92), Endocrine Soc., Soc. for Study of Reproduction, Internat. Soc. Neuroendocrinology, Can. Coun. of Univ. Biology Chmn. (pres. 1986-87), Internat. Fedn. Comparative Endocrinol. Socs. (pres. 1989-93), Canadian Conf. of Deans of Sci., 1995-96 (pres.).

PETER, SEBASTIAN AUGUSTINE, endocrinologist; b. St. Georges, Grenada, Jan. 20, 1944; came to U.S., 1975; s. Sidney Augustine and Cisly (Scoon) P.; m. Angela Missouri Sherman, July 18, 1970; children: Sebastian Augustine Jr., Senaka Akalbi. MBBS, U. W.I., 1969. Intern U. W.I., Nassau, 1970; resident in medicine Dalhousie U., Halifax, N.S., Can., 1971-72; resident in medicine U. Ottawa, Ont., Can., 1972-74, resident in endocrinology, 1974-75; fellow in endocrinology SUNY Health Sci. Ctr., Bklyn., 1975-76, assoc. clin. prof. medicine, 1992—; chief of endocrinology St. Mary's Hosp., Bklyn., 1992—. Contbr. articles to profl. jours. Recipient Community award Grenada Ex-Students Assn., 1991. Democrat. Avocations: music, jazz, playing musical instrument, reading. Home and Office: 1717 Ditmas Ave Brooklyn NY 11226-6603

PETER, VAL JOSEPH, social services administrator, author; b. Omaha, Nov. 20, 1934. PhB, Gregorian U., Rome, 1956, Licentiate in Sacred Theology, 1960; STD, U. St. Thomas, Rome, 1965; JCD, Lateran U., Rome, 1967; PhD (hon.), Creighton U., 1992, Coll. St. Mary, 1993. Ordained priest Roman Cath. Ch., 1960. Defender of bond Archdiocese of Omaha, 1966—; chmn. dept. theology Coll. of St. Mary, Omaha, 1966-70; prof. theology Creighton U., Omaha, 1970-84; pres., exec. dir. Father Flanagan's Boys Home, Boys Town, Nebr., 1984—. Bd. dirs. St. Joseph Ctr. for Mental Health, 1985—, Boy Scouts Am., 1985—, NCCJ, 1985-93; del. Pres. Summit for Ams. Future; dir. nat. programs for abused and neglected youth, advocate for troubled youth and nat. stds. for residential care. Recipient Disting. Faculty award Creighton U., 1983, Presdl. citation, 1984, Archbishop Gerald T. Bergan award, 1986, Svc. to Mankind award Sertoma Internat., 1987, Creighton Prep Alumnus of Yr. award, 1988, Douglas County Bd. Commrs.

award, 1990, Person of Yr. award U. Notre Dame, 1991, River City Roundup Heritage award, 1992, Toastmasters Internat. Comm. and Leadership award, 1992, Pope John XXIII award Roncalli H.S., 1993, AK-SAR-BEN Excellence in Edn. award, 1993, Nat. Direct Mktg. award Direct Mktg. Assn., 1993, Golden Apple award Met. C.C. Found., 1994, Silver Beaver award Boy Scouts Am., 1995; named Outstanding Humanitarian, Order Sons of Italy, 1987, Raoul Wallenberg Humanitarian of Yr., 1991. Mem. Nat. Assn. Homes and Svcs. for Children (bd. dirs. 1986-95), League Civil Rights (bd. dirs. 1986-92), Am. Our Sunday Visitor Inst. (bd. dirs. 1986—), Greater Omaha C. of C. (exec. com. 1991—), Omaha Cmty. Partnership, Canon Law Soc. Am., Cath. Theol. Soc. Am., Omaha 2000, Equestrian Order of Holy Sepulchre, 1989. Roman Catholic. Home and Office: Father Flanagan's Boy's Home 14100 Crawford St Boys Town NE 68010-7520

PETERKIN, ALBERT GORDON, retired education educator; b. Phila., May 25, 1915; s. Albert Gordon and Eleanor Frances (Fricke) P.; m. Helen Webster, June 14, 1947; children: Eleanor Fricke, Scott Boddington, Mark Webster. BA, U. Pa., 1936; MAT, Harvard U., 1946; EdD, Columbia U., 1954. Cert. sch. adminstr., N.J., Conn., Ill. Tchr. Arms Acad., Shelburne Falls, Mass., 1938-39, Park Sch. of Buffalo, Snyder, N.Y., 1939-41; asst. prof. Lehigh U., Bethlehem, Pa., 1948-55; founding supt. Watchung Hills Regional H.S., Warren, N.J., 1955-60; supt. Westport (Conn.) Pub. Schs., 1960-70, Winnetka (Ill.) Sch. Dist. 36, 1971-77; prof. edn. Vanderbilt U., Nashville, 1977-81; ret., 1981; cons. Nat. Assn. Sch. Bus. Officers, Washington, 1968-70, Tenn. State U., Nashville, 1980-81; advisor Coun. Basic Edn., Washington, 1975; trustee Country Sch., Madison, Conn., 1985-91; chmn. master's program Iranian Sch. Devel., 1978-80, assessment instrument student devel., 1974; initiator Cooperative Individualized Reading Project, U.S. Office Edn., 1970-73. Initiator Urban Coalition Sch. Study, Bridgeport, Conn., 1969-70; pres. Friends of Libr., Madison, 1984-85; prodr. cmty. TV, Madison, 1984-90; mem. Madison Inland Wetlands Commn., 1985—, chmn., 1990-92. Lt. comdr. USNR, 1941-45. John Hay fellow Greenwood Found., 1965; Kettering Found. fellow, 1966, 69; Whitehead fellow Harvard Sch. Edn., 1970-71; named to Supt.'s Hall of Fame Sch. Mgmt. Study Group, 1973. Mem. Am. Assn. Sch. Adminstrs., Suburban Sch. Supts., Madison Country Club, Madison Beach Club, Phi Delta Kappa. Mem. Religious Soc. of Friends. Avocations: garden design, travel, home video, golf, music. Home: 210 Neck Rd Madison CT 06443-2720

PETERKIN, GEORGE ALEXANDER, JR., marine transportation company executive; b. Baton Rouge, Apr. 12, 1927; s. George Alexander and Genevieve (Favrot) P.; m. Nancy Girling, Jan. 27, 1965; children—George Alexander III, Julie, John Thomas, Susan, Lynn. B.B.A., U. Tex., 1948. With Dixie Carriers, Inc., Galveston, Tex.; soliciting freight agt. Dixie Carriers, Inc., New Orleans, Houston, 1949-50; asst. to pres. Dixie Carriers, Inc., Houston, 1953, pres., 1953-73, chmn. bd., 1973—; pres. Kirby Industries, Inc., Houston, 1973-76; pres. Kirby Corp., 1976-95, chmn. bd., 1995—. Bd. dirs. Tex. Med. Center, 1965—, Living Bank, 1968-86; trustee Tex. Children's Hosp., 1964—. Served with USN, 1945-46. Mem. World Pres. Orgn., Chief Execs. Orgn., Am. Bur. Shipping, Ramada Club, Houston Country Club, Bayou Club, Univ. Club N.Y. Avocations: swimming, croquet, golf, shooting. Home: 5787 Indian Cir Houston TX 77057-1302 Office: Kirby Corp Ste 200 1775 Saint James Pl Houston TX 77056-3403

PETERLE, TONY JOHN, zoologist, educator; b. Cleve., July 7, 1925; s. Anton and Anna (Katic) P.; m. Thelma Josephine Coleman, July 30, 1949; children—Ann Faulkner, Tony Scott. BS, Utah State U., 1949; MS, U. Mich., 1950, PhD (univ. scholar), 1954; Fulbright scholar, U. Aberdeen, Scotland, 1954-55; postgrad., Oak Ridge Inst. Nuclear Studies, 1961. With Niederhauser Lumber Co., 1947-49, Macfarland Tree Svc., 1949-51; rsch. biologist Mich. Dept. Conservation, 1951-54; asst. dir. Rose Lake Expt. Sta., 1955-59; leader Ohio Coop. Wildlife Rsch. unit U.S. Fish and Wildlife Svc., Dept. Interior, 1959-63; asso. prof., then prof. zoology Ohio State U., Columbus, 1959-89, prof. emeritus, 1989; chmn. faculty population and environmental biology Ohio State U., 1968-69, chmn. dept. zoology, 1969-81, dir. program in environ. biology, 1970-71; liaison officer Internat. Union Game Biologists, 1965-93; co-organizer, chmn. internat. affairs com., mem. com. ecotoxicology XIII Internat. Congress Game Biology, 1979-80; proprietor The Iron Works; pvt. cons., 1989—; mem. com. rev. EPA pesticide decision making Nat. Acad. Scis.-NRC; mem. vis. scientists program Am. Inst. Biol. Scis.-ERDA, 1971-77; mem. com. pesticides Nat. Acad. Scis., com. on emerging trends in agr. and effects on fish and wildlife; mem. ecology com. of sci. adv. council EPA, 1979-87; mem. research units coordinating com. Ohio Coop. Wildlife and Fisheries, 1963-89; vis. scientist EPA, Corvallis, 1987. Author: Wildlife Toxicology, 1991; editor: Jour. of Wildlife Mgmt., 1969-70, 84-85, 2020 Vision Meeting the Fish and Wildlife Conservation Challenges of the 21st Century, 1992. Served with AUS, 1943-46. Fellow AAAS, Am. Inst. Biol. Scis., Ohio Acad. Sci.; mem. Wildlife Disease Assn., Wildlife Soc. (regional rep. 1962-67, v.p. 1968, pres. 1972, Leopold award 1990, hon. mem. 1990, Profl. award of merit North Ctrl. sect. 1993), Nat. Audubon Soc. (bd. dirs. 1985-87), Ecol. Soc., INTECOL-NSF panel U.S.-Japan Program, Xi Sigma Pi, Phi Kappa Phi. Home: 4072 Klondike Rd Delaware OH 43015-9513 Office: Ohio State U Dept Zoology 1735 Neil Ave Columbus OH 43210-1220

PETERMAN, BRUCE EDGAR, aircraft company executive, retired; b. Merrill, Wis., Jan. 27, 1931; s. Neton Elmer and Grace Elisabeth (Schroeder) P.; m. Constance Lenore Callsen, Feb. 9, 1952; children: Michael Lee, Jeffrey Dean, Elizabeth Ann. AA in Aero. Engring., Spartan Coll., 1951; BS in Aero. Engring., Wichita State Univ., 1955, MS in Aero. Engring., 1961. With detail design and drafting dept. Beech Aircraft Corp., Wichita, Kans., 1951-53; with design, flight test and tech. engring. depts. Cessna Aircraft Co., Wichita, 1953-72, chief engr. Wallace div., 1972-81, v.p. product engring., 1981-87, v.p. ops., 1987-89, sr. v.p., 1989-96; trustee U. Kans. Ctr. for Rsch., Lawrence, 1985-88, Cessna Found., 1987-96; mem. industry adv. com. Nat. Inst. Aviation Rsch., Wichita State U., 1985—; mem. aerospace engring. adv. com. U. Kans., Lawrence, 1975-89, engring. dept. adv. com., 1987-91; mem. Kans. Tech. Enterprise Corp. Ctrs. Com., 1992—, bd. dirs., 1994—. Mem. nat. adv. coun. Endowment Assn. Wichita State U., 1993—; co-chair Kans. Math. and Sci. Coalition, 1992-96. Assoc. fellow AIAA; mem. Soc. Automotive Engrs. (aerospace coun. 1976-91, tech. bd. 1987-91). Avocations: instrument rated multi-engine pilot. Home: 15606 Moscelyn Ln Goddard KS 67052-9331

PETERMAN, DONNA COLE, communications executive; b. St. Louis, Nov. 9, 1947; d. William H. Cole and Helen A. Morris; m. John A. Peterman, Feb. 7, 1970. BA in Journalism, U. Mo., 1969; MBA, U. Chgo., 1984. Mgr. employee comm. Sears Merchandise Group, Chgo., 1975-80; dir. corp. comm. Sears, Roebuck and Co., Chgo., 1982-85; affairs and mktg. comm. Seraco Real Estate, Chgo., 1980-82; sr. v.p., dir. corp. comm. Dean Witter Fin. Svcs. Group, N.Y., 1985-88; sr. v.p., mng. dir. Hill and Knowlton, Inc., Chgo., 1988-94; exec. v.p. Hill and Knowlton, Inc., N.Y.C., 1994-96; sr. v.p., dir. corp. comm. Paine Webber Group, Inc., N.Y.C., 1996—; Media chmn. DeKalb County Comm., Ga., 1975; media dir., Mo. Atty. Gen., 1971, Rep. Govs. Conf., 1974; copywriter Govt. fo Mo., 1971. Trustee Met. Planning Coun. Mem. Internat. Assn. Bus. Communicators, Pub. Relations Soc. Am., City Midday Club, Univ. Club, Women Execs. in Pub. Rels. Republican. Catholic. Avocations: sailing, skiing, bridge, piano, reading.

PETERS, ALAN, anatomy educator; b. Nottingham, Eng., Dec. 6, 1929; came to U.S., 1966; s. Robert and Mabel (Woplington) P.; m. Verona Muriel Shipman, Sept. 30, 1955; children: Ann Verona, Sally Elizabeth, Susan Clare. BSc, Bristol (Eng.) U., 1951, PhD, 1954. Lectr. anatomy Edinburgh (Scotland) U., 1958-66; vis. lectr. Harvard, 1963-64; prof., chmn. dept. anatomy and neurobiology Boston U., 1966—; anatomy com. Nat. Bd. Med. Examiners, 1971-75; mem. neurology B study sect. NIH, 1975-79, chmn., 1978-79; affiliate scientist Yerkes Regional Primate Rsch. Ctr., 1984—. Author: (with S.L. Palay and H. deF Webster) The Fine Structure of the Nervous System, 1970, 3rd edit., 1991, Myelination, 1970; contbr. (with A.N. Davison) articles profl. jours.; mem. editorial bd. Anat. Record, 1972-81, Jour. Comparative Neurology, 1981-97, Neurocytology, 1972-89, 93—, Cerebral Cortex, 1990—, Studies of Brain Function, Anat. and Embryology, 1989-92; editor book series: (with E.G. Jones) Cerebral Cortex, 1984—. Served to 2d lt. Royal Army Med. Corps, 1955-57. Recipient Javits neurosci. investigator award NIH, 1986. Mem. Anat. Soc. Gt. Britain and Ireland (Symington prize anatomy 1962, overseas mem. coun. 1969), Assn. Anatomy Chmn. (pres. 1976-77), Am. Anat. Assn. (exec. com. 1986-90, pres. 1992-93), Am. Soc. Cell Biology, Soc. Neuroscis., Internat. Primatological Soc., Cajal Club (Harman lectr. 1990, Cortical Discoverer award 1991). Home: 16 High Rock Cir Waltham MA 02154-2207 Office: Boston U Sch Medicine Dept Anatomy and Neurobiology 80 E Concord St Roxbury MA 02118-2307

PETERS, ALTON EMIL, lawyer; b. Albany, N.Y., Mar. 21, 1935; s. Emil and Winifred (Rosch) P.; m. Elizabeth Irving Berlin, Feb. 27, 1970; children: Rachel Canfield, Emily Anstice Fletcher. A.B. cum laude, Harvard U., 1955, LL.B., 1958. Bar: N.Y. 1958, U.S. Dist. Ct. (so. dist.) N.Y. 1963. Assoc. Bleakley, Platt, Schmidt & Fritz, 1959-65, mem., 1956-81; ptnr. Miller, Montgomery, Sogi & Brady, 1981-83, Kelley Drye & Warren, N.Y.C., 1983—. Bd. dirs. Am. Friends of Covent Garden and the Royal Ballet, N.Y.C., 1971—, v.p., 1971—; mem. coun. Am. Mus. in Britain, Bath, Eng., 1970—, chmn. U.S.A., 1975-92; bd. dirs. Brit. Am. Arts Assn., N.Y.C., 1983—, chmn., 1984—; bd. dirs. N.Y. br. English-Speaking Union U.S., 1963—, chmn., 1972-88; bd. dirs. Goodwill Industries of Greater N.Y., 1965—, pres., 1970-82, chmn., 1982—; mng. dir. Met. Opera Assn., N.Y.C., 1966—, sec., 1974-86, v.p., 1986-93, chmn. Exec. Com., 1993—; bd. dirs. Met. Opera Guild, Inc., N.Y.C., 1965—, chmn. exec. com., 1968-70, 74-79, 1st v.p., 1979-86, pres., 1986—; bd. dirs. Lincoln Ctr. for Performing Arts, N.Y.C., 1986—; trustee Signet Assocs., Cambridge, Mass., 1957-73, treas., 1957-73, hon. trustee, 1973—; Coun. Fellows Pierpont Morgan Libr., 1995—, vice chmn., 1996—, fellow Frick Collection; trustee Acad. Am. Poets, N.Y.C., 1988—, treas., 1993—; trustee Cathedral of St. John the Divine, 1991—. Decorated Knight Order of St. John of Jerusalem, Officer Order of Brit. Empire. Mem. ABA, N.Y. State Bar Assn., Assn. of Bar of City of N.Y., Am. Judicature Soc., Am. Coll. Probate Counsel, Century Assn., Church Club, Grolier Club (coun. 1994—), Harvard Club N.Y.C., Knickerbocker Club (bd. govs. 1986-92, 94—), Pilgrims Club of Odd Volumes. Home: 211 Central Park W New York NY 10024-6020 Office: Kelley Drye and Warren 101 Park Ave New York NY 10178

PETERS, ANDREA JEAN, artist; b. Boston, Dec. 27, 1947; d. Andrew A. and Mary M. (Badessa) De Francesco; m. Mark Douglas Peters, Aug. 9, 1970; children: Melissa J., Christine M. Cert. of completion/diploma, Vesper George Sch. Art, 1966; student, Mass. Coll. Art, 1966-68. drawing and painting tchr. Tewksbury (Mass.) Fine Art Ctr., 1975-76, Wilmington, Mass., 1975-79. Gallery representation Art 3, Inc., Manchester, N.H., 1985—, Diana Levine Fine Art, Boston, 1988—; Gleason Fine Art, Boothbay Harbor, Maine, 1992—; (cover illustrations) Community Connection Phone Book, 1993, 94. Recipient Daniel V. Hoye Meml. award Hoyt Inst. Fine Art, New Castle, Pa., 1986, Jurors award Whistler Mus., Lowell, Mass., 1987. Mem. Pastel Soc. Am. (master pastelist, Pearl Paint award 1987, J.G. Sher award 1988), Copley Soc. Boston (Jurors award 1988), North Shore Arts Assn. (J.S.G. Saunders Meml. award 1984), Am. Artist Profl. League, Allied Artists Am., Maine Coast Artists. Home: Boothbay Shores PO Box 245 East Boothbay ME 04544

PETERS, ANN LOUISE, accounting manager; b. Knoxville, Tenn., Jan. 26, 1954; d. William Brown and Louise (Emerson) Nixon; m. Raymond Peters, July 11, 1975. BBA, Miami U., Oxford, Ohio, 1976; MBA, Xavier U., 1985. Cert. internal auditor. Acctg. officer Soc. Bank (formerly Citizens Bank), Hamilton, Ohio, 1977-85; internal auditor Procter & Gamble Co., Cin., 1985-86, audit sect. mgr., 1986-88, sr. cost analyst, beauty care, 1988-90; plant fin. mgr. Procter & Gamble Mfg. Co., Phoenix, 1990-92; sr. fin. analyst, beauty care Procter & Gamble Co., Cin., 1992-93, group mgr., gen. acctg., 1993-96, group mgr. R&D fin., 1996—. Mem. Inst. Internal Auditors, Inst. Mgmt. Accts. Republican. Congregationalist. Avocations: golf, swimming. Home: 7889 Ironwood Way West Chester OH 45069-1623 Office: Procter & Gamble Co Sharon Woods Tech Ctr Box 221 HB2J14A 11511 Reed Hartman Hwy Cincinnati OH 45241-2421

PETERS, AULANA LOUISE, government agency commissioner, lawyer; b. Shreveport, La., Nov. 30, 1941; d. Clyde A. and Eula Mae (Faulkner) Pharis; m. Bruce F. Peters, Oct. 6, 1967. BA in Philosophy, Coll. New Rochelle, 1963; JD, U. So. Calif., 1973. Bar: Calif., 1974. Sec., English corr. Publimondial, Spa, Milan, Italy, 1963-64, Fibramianto, Spa, Milan, 1964-65, Turkish del. to Office for Econ. Cooperation & Devel., Paris, 1965-66; adminstrv. asst. Office for Econ. Cooperation & Devel., Paris, 1966-67; assoc. Gibson, Dunn & Crutcher, L.A., 1973-80, ptnr., 1980-84, 88—; commr. SEC, Washington, 1984-88. Recipient Disting. Alumnus award Econs. Club So. Calif., 1984, Washington Achiever award Nat. Assn. Bank Women, 1986. Mem. ABA, State Bar of Calif. (civil litigation cons. group 1983-84), Los Angeles County Bar Assn., Black Women Lawyers Assn. L.A., Assn. Bus. Trial Lawyers (panelist L.A. 1982), Women's Forum, Washington. Office: Gibson Dunn & Crutcher 333 S Grand Ave Los Angeles CA 90071-1504

PETERS, CAROL BEATTIE TAYLOR (MRS. FRANK ALBERT PETERS), mathematician; b. Washington, May 10, 1932; d. Edwin Lucius and Lois (Beattie) Taylor; B.S., U. Md., 1954, M.A., 1958; m. Frank Albert Peters, Feb. 26, 1955; children—Thomas, June, Erick, Victor. Group mgr. Tech. Operations, Inc., Arlington, Va., 1957-62, sr. staff scientist, 1964-66; supervisory analyst Datatrol Corp., Silver Spring, Md., 1962; project dir. Computer Concept, Inc., Silver Spring, 1963-64; mem. tech. staff, then mem. sr. staff Informatics Inc., Bethesda, Md., 1966-70, mgr. systems projects, 1970-71, tech. dir., 1971-76; sr. tech. dir. Ocean Data Systems, Inc., Rockville, Md., 1976-83; dir. Informatics Gen. Co., 1983-89; pres. Carol Peters Assocs., 1989—. Mem. Assn. Computing Machinery, IEEE Computer Group. Home and Office: 12311 Glen Mill Rd Potomac MD 20854-1928

PETERS, CHARLES GIVEN, JR., editor; b. Charleston, W.Va., Dec. 22, 1926; s. Charles Given and Esther (Teague) P.; m. Elizabeth Bostwick Hubbell, Aug. 3, 1957; 1 child, Christian Avery. BA in Humanities, Columbia U., 1949, MA in English, 1951; LLB, U. Va., 1957; LLD (hon.), U. Charleston, 1979. Bar: W.Va. 1957, D.C. 1981. Atty. Peters, Merrick, Leslie & Mohler, Charleston, 1957-61; mem. W.Va State Legislature, Charleston, 1960-62; dir. evaluation Peace Corps, Washington, 1962-68; founder, editor in chief The Washington Monthly, 1968—; Delacorte lectr. Columbia U., 1990. Author: How Washington Really Works, 1980, Tilting at Windmills, 1988; editor: (with Taylor Branch) Blowing the Whistle, 1972, (with James Fallows) The System, 1975, (with Michael Nelson) The Culture of Bureaucracy, 1977, (with Jonathan Alter) Inside the System, 5th edit., 1985. Mgr. John F. Kennedy campaign, Kanawha County, W.Va., 1960. Served with inf. U.S. Army, 1944-46. Recipient Columbia Journalism award, 1978, Richard S. Clurman award, 1996; named West Virginian of Yr., Charleston Gazette-Mail, 1980; Poynter fellow Yale U., 1980. Democrat. Presbyterian. Office: The Washington Monthly Co 1611 Connecticut Ave NW Washington DC 20009-1033*

PETERS, CHARLES WILLIAM, research and development company manager; b. Pierceton, Ind., Dec. 9, 1927; s. Charles Frederick and Zelda May (Line) P.; m. Katharine Louise Schuman, May 29, 1953; 1 child, Susan Kay; m. 2d, Patricia Ann Miles, Jan. 2, 1981; children: Bruce Miles Merkle, Leslie Ann Merkle Sanaie, Philip Frank Merkle, William Macneil Merkle. AB, Ind. U., 1950; postgrad. U. Md., 1952-58. Supervisory rsch. physicist Naval Rsch. Lab., Washington, 1950-71; physicist EPA, Washington, 1971-76; mgr. advanced systems EATON-Consol. Controls Corp., Springfield, Va., 1976-89, v.p. Nuclear Diagnostic Systems, Inc., Springfield, Va, 1989-92, cons. Am. Tech. Inst., 1993—. With U.S. Army, 1945-47. Mem. IEEE, AAAS, Am. Phys. Soc. Home and Office: 5235 N Whispering Hills Ln Tucson AZ 85704-2510

PETERS, CHRISTOPHER ALLEN, computer consultant; b. Syracuse, N.Y., Apr. 26, 1967; s. William F. and Mary Jo (N.) P. BA, Syracuse U., 1989, MLS, 1994. Info. analyst Syracuse U., 1990-96, asst. dir. devel. for sys. mgmt., 1996—. Mem. Assn. Profl. Rschrs. for Advancement. Home: 103 Smith Ln Apt 34 Syracuse NY 13210

PETERS, DAVID ALLEN, mechanical engineering educator, consultant; b. East St. Louis, Ill., Jan. 31, 1947; s. Bernell Louis and Marian Louise (Blum) P.; m. Linda J. Conley, Jan. 25, 1969; children: Michael H., Laura A., Nathan C. BS in Applied Mechanics, Washington U., St. Louis, 1969, MS in Applied Mechanics, 1970; PhD in Aeros. and Astronautics, Stanford U., 1974. Assoc. engr. McDonnell Astronautics, 1969-70; rsch. scientist Army Aeronautics Lab., 1970-74; asst. prof. Washington U., 1975-77, assoc. prof., 1977-80, prof. mech. engring., 1980-85, chmn. dept., 1982-85; prof. aerospace engring. Ga. Inst Tech., Atlanta, 1985-91; dir. NASA Space Grant Consortium Ga. Inst. Tech., Atlanta, 1989-91; dir. Ctr. for Computational Mechanics Washington U., 1992—; prof. dept. mech. engring. Washington U., St. Louis, 1991—, chmn. dept. mech. engring., 1997—. Contbr. 50 articles to profl. jours. Recipient sci. contbn. award NASA, 1975, 76. Fellow AIAA, ASME; mem. Am. Helicopter Soc. (jour. editor 1987-90), Am. Soc. for Engring. Edn., Internat. Assn. for Computational Mechanics (charter), Am. Acad. Mechs., Pi Tau Sigma (gold medal 1978). Baptist. Home: 7629 Balson Ave Saint Louis MO 63130-2150 Office: Washington U Dept Mech Engring Campus Box 1185 Saint Louis MO 63130

PETERS, DAVID FRANKMAN, lawyer; b. Hagerstown, Md., Aug. 15, 1941; s. Harold E. and Lois (Frankman) P.; m. Jane Catherine Witherspoon, Aug. 21, 1965; children: Catherine, Elizabeth. BA, Washington and Lee U., 1963; LLB, Duke U., 1966. Bar: Va. 1966, U.S. Dist. Ct. (ea. and we. dists.) Va., U.S. Ct. Appeals (2d, 4th, 6th, 7th and D.C. cirs.). Assoc. Hunton & Williams, Richmond, Va., 1966-73, ptnr., 1973—. Pres. Children's Home Soc. Va., Richmond, 1977-78, bd. dirs., 1970-91; trustee Westminster-Canterbury Corp., 1995—; elder, trustee 1st Presbyn. Ch., Richmond. Mem. ABA, Va. Bar Assn. (chmn. adminstrn. law com. 1985-88), Richmond Bar Assn. Lodge: Kiwanis. Avocations: photography, travel. Home: 3 Windsor Way Richmond VA 23221-3232 Office: Hunton & Williams 951 E Byrd St Richmond VA 23219-4040

PETERS, DENNIS GAIL, chemist; b. L.A., Apr. 17, 1937; s. Samuel and Phyllis Dorothy (Pope) P. BS cum laude, Calif. Inst. Tech., 1958; PhD, Harvard U., 1962. Mem. faculty Ind. U., 1962—, prof. chemistry, 1974—, Herman T. Briscoe prof., 1975—. Co-author textbooks, contbr. articles profl. jours. Woodrow Wilson fellow, 1958-59; NIH predoctoral fellow, 1959-62; vis. fellow Japan Soc. for Promotion Sci., 1980; recipient Ulysses G. Weatherly award disting. teaching Ind. U., 1969, Disting. Teaching award Coll. Arts and Scis. Grad. Alumni Assn. Ind. U., 1984, Nat. Catalyst award for Disting. Teaching Chem. Mfrs. Assn., 1988; grantee NSF. Fellow Ind. Acad. Sci., Am. Inst. Chemists; mem. Am. Chem. Soc. (grantee, Div. of Analytical Chemistry award for excellence in teaching 1990), N.Y. Acad. Scis. Home: 1401 S Nancy St Bloomington IN 47401-6051 Office: Dept Chemistry Ind U Bloomington IN 47405

PETERS, DONALD CAMERON, construction company executive; b. Milw., Mar. 25, 1915; s. Simon C. and May (Gnewuch) P.; m. Twila Bingel, Dec. 7, 1940; children: Susan (Mrs. Douglas Ingram), David C., Bruce C., Douglas C. B.S. in Civil Engring, Marquette U., 1938. Registered profl. engr., Wis., Pa. Engr. Siesel Constrn. Co., Milw., 1938-44; v.p., dir. Crump, Inc., Pitts., 1944-51; pres. Mellon-Stuart Co., Pitts., 1951-73, also bd. dirs., chmn., 1973-81; mem. 5 man gen. com. rewriting Pitts. Bldg. Code, 1947; mem., chmn. Pa. Registration Bd. Profl. Engrs., 1962-82; chmn. bd. standards and appeals Pitts. Bur. Bldg. Inspection, 1960-72; past pres. Pitts. Builders Exch.; adv. bd. Liberty Mut. Ins., 1968—. Chmn. bd. suprs. Pine Twp., Allegheny County, 1953-80; chmn. Constrn. Industry Advancement Program We. Pa., 1975-93; trustee La Roche Coll., Pitts., 1967—, chmn., 1983-84; bd. dirs. North Hills Passavant Hosp., 1963-90, chmn., 1983-84. Fellow ASCE; mem. NSPE (nat. dir. 1954-57, chmn. bd. ethical rev. 1978-79), Pa. Soc. Profl. Engrs. (pres. 1953-54), Assn. Gen. Contractors Am. (nat. dir.), Pitts. C. of C. (chmn., dir. 1973-81), Master Builders Assn. Western Pa. (past pres.), SBA, Triangle, Tau Beta Pi, Alpha Sigma Nu. Club: Duquesne (Pitts.). Home: 2803 SE 18th Ct Cape Coral FL 33904-4077

PETERS, DOUGLAS ALAN, neurology nurse; b. Portsmouth, Va., Oct. 4, 1968; s. Terrance Gene and Pamela (Haffner) P. BA in Philosophy, Va. Poly. Inst. and State U., 1992; BSN summa cum laude, James Madison U., 1995; postgrad., Johns Hopkins U., 1997—. RN, Va. Photojournalist CVNI/The Greene County Record, Stanardsville, Va., 1992; nursing asst. Rockingham Meml. Hosp., Harrisonburg, Va., 1993-95; clin. nurse Bapt. Hosp., Pensacola, Fla., 1995-96; neurology nurse Tallahassee Meml. Regional Med. Hosp., 1996; nurse mgr./quality assurance Escambia County Jail Infirmary, Pensacola, 1996-97, crisis intervention mgr., RN, 1996—; quality control team advisor Bapt. Health Care, Pensacola, 1995. Vol. hospice unit Rockingham Meml. Hosp., 1994-95; vol. tourette Syndrome Assn., 1996—. Mem. Nat. League for Nursing, Alpha Chi Sigma, Phi Sigma Pi. Avocations: writing creative fiction, photography. Office: 6907 Jones View Dr Apt 1A Baltimore MD 21209-5135

PETERS, DOUGLAS DENNISON, Canadian government official, member of Parliament; b. Brandon, Man., Can., Mar. 3, 1930; s. Wilfrid Seymour and Mary Gladys (Dennison) P.; m. Audrey Catherine Clark, June 26, 1954; children: David Wilfrid, Catherine Elaine Peters Gilchrist. B Commerce, Queen's U., Kingston, Ont., Can., 1963; PhD in Fin. and Commerce, U. Pa., 1969. With Bank of Montreal, Winnipeg, Man., 1950-60; chief economist Toronto (Ont., Can.)-Dominion Bank, 1966—, v.p., chief economist, 1971—, sr. v.p., chief economist, 1980-93; M.P. for Scarborough East House of Commons, Ottawa, Ont., 1993—, sec. of state for fin., 1993—. Author: The Monetarist Counterrevolution - A Critique of Canada's Monetary Policy, 1975-1980, 1980; contbr. articles to profl. publs. Scholar Can. Coun., 1963, 64, Ford Found., 1965. Liberal. Avocation: tennis. Home: 66 Collier St Apt 2A, Toronto, ON Canada M4W 1L9 Office: House of Commons, Parliament Bldg Rm 442N, Wellington St, Ottawa, ON Canada K1A 0A6

PETERS, EDWARD MURRAY, history educator; b. New Haven, Conn., May 21, 1936; s. Edward Murray and Marjorie (Corcoran) P.; m. Patricia Ann Knapp, July 8, 1961; children—Nicole, Moira, Edward. B.A., Yale U., 1963, M.A., 1965, Ph.D., 1967. Instr. in English and history Quinnipiac Coll., Hamden, Conn., 1964-67; asst. prof. history U. Calif., San Diego, 1967-68; asst. prof. medieval history U. Pa., Phila., 1968-70, assoc. prof., 1970-81, Henry Charles Lea prof. history, 1981—, curator Henry Charles Lea Library, 1968—; gasthoogleraar KU Leuven, Belgium, 1992. Author: The Shadow King, 1970, (with A.C. Kors) Witchcraft in Europe, 1100-1750, 1972, Europe: The World of the Middle Ages, 1977, The Magician, The Witch and The Law, 1978, Europe and the Middle Ages, 1983, Torture, 1985, expanded edition, 1996, Inquistion, 1988, (TV series) The World of the Middle Ages, 1974, The World Around the Revolution, 1977, also articles, revs. and introductions; editor, translator: (with Jeanne Krochalis) The World of Piers Plowman, 1975; editor: Heresy and Authority in Medieval Europe, 1980. Served with AUS, 1956-59. Woodrow Wilson fellow, 1963-64, dissertation fellow, 1966-67, hon. Sterling fellow, 1966-67, ACLS fellow, 1981-82, Guggenheim fellow, 1988-89. Fellow Medieval Acad. Am., Royal Hist. Soc.; mem. Am. Hist. Assn., Medieval Acad. Am., Am. Soc. Legal History, Maiestas, Iuris Canonici Medii Aevi Consociatio, Soc. Jean Bodin, Dante Soc. Am. Home: 4225 Regent Sq Philadelphia PA 19104-4438 Office: U Pa Dept History Philadelphia PA 19104

PETERS, ELEANOR WHITE, retired mental health nurse; b. Highland Park, Mich., Aug. 11, 1920; d. Alfred Mortimer and Jane Ann (Evans) White; m. William J. Peters, 1947 (div. 1953); children: Susannah J., William J. (dec.). RN, Christ Hosp. Sch. Nursing, Jersey City, 1941; BA, Jersey City State Coll., 1968; postgrad., U. Del., 1969-70; MS, SUNY, New Paltz, 1983. RN, N.J., N.Y. Mem. staff various area hosps. N.J., 1941-58; indsl. nurse Abex, Mahwah, N.J., 1958-68; sch. nurse Liberty (N.Y.) Ctrl. Sch., 1971-76; coord. practical nurse program Hudson County C.C., Jersey City, 1979-80; community mental health nurse Letchworth Village, Thiells, N.Y., 1981-96. Historian, Bishop House Found., Saddle River, N.J. Mem. AAUW (pres. Liberty-Monticello br. 1988-92), Am. Sch. Health Assn., Alpha Delta Kappa (sec. Mu chpt. 1973-75), Sigma Theta Tau (Kappa Eta chpt.). Republican. Lutheran. Avocations: antiques, history, traveling, education of children. Home: PO Box 224 Saddle River NJ 07458-0224

PETERS, ELIZABETH ANN HAMPTON, nursing educator; b. Detroit, Sept. 27, 1934; d. Grinsfield Taylor and Ida Victoria (Jones) Hampton; m. James Marvin Peters, Dec. 1, 1956; children: Douglas Taylor, Sara Elizabeth. Diploma, Berea Coll. Hosp. Sch. Nursing, 1956; BSN, Wright State U., Dayton, Ohio, 1975; MSN, Ohio State U., Columbus, 1978. Therapist-RN Eastway, Inc., Dayton, Ohio, 1979-81; therapist family counseling svc. Good Samaritan-Cmty. Mental Health Ctr., Dayton, Ohio, 1981-83; instr. Wright State U. Sch. Nursing, Dayton, 1983-84; clin. nurse specialist, pain mgmt. program UPSA, Inc., Dayton, 1983-86; staff nurse Hospice of Dayton, Inc., 1985-86, dir. vol. svcs., 1986-89, dir. bereavement svcs., 1986-87; asst. prof. Cmty. Hosp. Sch. Nursing, Springfield, Ohio, 1990-93, prof., 1993—. Author: (with others) Oncologic Pain, 1987. Mem. Clark County Mental Health Bd., Springfield, 1986-95; mem. New Carlisle (Ohio) Bd. Health, 1990—. Mem. ANA, Ohio Nurses Assn., Sigma Theta Tau. Home: 402 Flora Ave New Carlisle OH 45344-1329

PETERS, ELLEN ASH, state supreme court senior justice; b. Berlin, Mar. 21, 1930; came to U.S., 1939, naturalized, 1947; d. Ernest Edward and Hildegard (Simon) Ash; m. Phillip I. Blumberg; children: David Bryan Peters, James Douglas Peters, Julie Peters Haden. BA with honors, Swarthmore Coll., 1951, LLD (hon.), 1983; LLB cum laude, Yale U., 1954, MA (hon.), 1964, LLD (hon.), 1985; LLD (hon.), U. Hartford, 1983; Georgetown U., 1984; LLD (hon.), Yale U., 1985, Conn. Coll., 1985, N.Y. Law Sch., 1985; HLD (hon.), St. Joseph Coll., 1986; LLD (hon.), Colgate U., 1986, Trinity Coll., 1987, Bates Coll., 1987, Wesleyan U., 1987, DePaul U., 1988; HLD (hon.), Albertus Magnus Coll., 1990; LLD (hon.), U. Conn., 1992; LLD, U. Rochester, 1994. Bar: Conn. 1957. Law clk. to judge U.S. Circuit Ct., 1954-55; assoc. in law U. Calif., Berkeley, 1955-56; prof. law Yale U., New Haven, 1956-78, adj. prof. law, 1978-84; assoc. justice Conn. Supreme Ct., Hartford, 1978-84, chief justice, 1984-96, sr. justice, 1996—. Author: Commercial Transactions: Cases, Texts, and Problems, 1971, Negotiable Instruments Primer, 1974; contbr. articles to profl. jours. Bd. mgrs. Swarthmore Coll., 1970-81; trustee Yale-New Haven Hosp., 1981-85, Yale Corp., 1986-92; mem. conf. Chief Justices, 1984—, pres., 1994; hon. chmn. U.S. Constl. Bicentennial Com., 1986-91; mem. Conn. Permanent Commn. on Status of Women, 1973-74, Conn. Bd. Pardons, 1978-80, Conn. Law Revision Commn., 1978-84; bd. dirs. Nat. Ctr. State Cts., 1992-96, chmn., 1994, Hartford Found., 1997—. Recipient Ella Grasso award, 1982, Jud. award Conn. Trial Lawyers Assn., 1982, citation of merit Yale Law Sch., 1983, Pioneer Woman award Hartford Coll. for Women, 1988, Disting. Svc. award U. Conn. Law Sch. Alumni Assn., 1993, Raymond E. Baldwin Pub. Svc. award Quinnipiac Coll. Law Sch., 1995, Disting. Svc. award Conn. Law Tribune, 1996, Nat. Ctr. State Cts., 1996; named Laura A. Johnson Woman of Yr. Hartford Coll., 1996. Mem. ABA, Conn. Bar Assn. (Jud. award 1992, Spl. award 1996), Am. Law Inst. (coun.), Am. Acad. Arts and Scis., Am. Philos. Soc. Office: Conn Supreme Ct Drawer N Sta A 231 Capitol Ave Hartford CT 06106-1548

PETERS, ERNEST, metallurgy educator, consultant; b. Steinbach, Man., Can., Jan. 27, 1926; s. Franz Isaac Peters and Margaretha (Klassen) MacLachlan; m. Gwynneth Salome Walker, Sept. 21, 1949; children: Charlotte Ann Peters Garcia, Gwynneth Elizabeth Peters Becker. BASc, U. B.C., Can., 1949, MASc, 1951, PhD, 1956. Registered profl. engr., B.C. Metallurgist Geneva Steel Co., Provo, Utah, 1949-50; rsch. engr. Cominco, Ltd., Trail, B.C., Can., 1951-53, Union Carbide Metals Co., Niagara Falls, N.Y., 1956-58; instr. U. B.C., Vancouver, 1955-56, asst. prof., 1958-65, assoc. prof., 1966-68, prof., 1968-91, prof. emeritis, 1991—; cons. Cominco, Ltd., Trail, 1958-92, Kennecott Copper Corp., Salt Lake City, 1969-71, E Z Australasia, Melbourne, Australia, 1977-78, Bacon, Donaldson & Assocs., Vancouver, 1981-90, Westmin Resources Ltd., 1991—; mem. selection com. NRC Can., Ottawa, 1967-68; extractive metallurgy lectr. The Metals Soc. of AIME, Las Vegas, Nev., 1976; keynote lectr. Benelux Metallurgie, Brussels, 1977. Contbr. articles to profl. jours.; patentee in Hydromet. Mem. selection com. Killam fellowships Can. Coun., Ottawa, 1988-91. Sgt. RCAF, 1943-45. Recipient C.I.M.. Alcan award, 1983, James Douglas Gold medal AIME, 1986, Mineral Scis. Edn. award AIME, 1993, Can. Materials Sci. Conf. Metal Chemistry award, 1993; named Indsl. Rsch. chair, 11 Can. cos., 1987-92; Killam fellow Can. Coun., 1983-85. Fellow Royal Soc. Can., The Metall. Soc. of AIME, Can. Inst. Mining & Metallurgy; mem. B.C. Assn. Profl. Engrs. Baptist. Avocations: skiing, windsurfing, radio control model planes. Home: 2708 W 33d Ave, Vancouver, BC Canada V6N 2G1 Office: U BC Dept Metals and Materials Enging, 309-6350 Stores Rd, Vancouver, BC Canada V6T 1Z4

PETERS, ESTHER CAROLINE, aquatic toxicologist, pathobiologist, consultant; b. Greenville, S.C., May 9, 1952; d. Otto Emanuel and Winifred Ellen (Bahan) P.; m. Harry Brinton McCarty, Jr., May 27, 1984; children: Rachel Elizabeth, William Brinton. BS, Furman U., 1974; MS, U. South Fla., 1978; PhD, U. R.I., 1984. Rsch. asst. Environ. Rsch. Lab., U.S. EPA, Narragansett, R.I., 1980-81; grad. rsch. asst. U. R.I., Kingston, 1981-84; assoc. biologist JRB Assocs., Narragansett, 1984-85; postdoctoral fellow Dept. of Invertebrate Zoology, Nat. Mus. Natural History, Washington, 1985-86, resident rsch. assoc., 1986-89; rsch. fellow Registry Tumors in Lower Animals, Nat. Mus. of Natural History, Washington, 1987-91; sr. scientist Tetra Tech, Inc., Fairfax, Va., 1991—; sci. adv. panel Project Reefkeeper, Am. Littoral Soc., Miami, Fla., 1988—; courtesy asst. prof. Dept. Marine Sci., U. South Fla., St. Petersburg, 1987—; cons. The Nature Conservancy, Arlington, Va., 1991. Author: (with others) Pathobiology of Marine and Estuarine Organisms, 1993, Disease Processes of Marine Bivalve Molluscs, 1988, Life and Death of Coral Reefs, 1997; contbr. articles to profl. jours. Recipient Nat. Rsch. Svc. postdoctoral tng. fellowship NIH, Bethesda, Md., 1987-91. Fellow AAAS; mem. Am. Fisheries Soc., N.Y. Acad. Scis., Soc. for Environ. Toxicology and Chemistry, Soc. Invertebrate Pathology, Sigma Xi. Office: Tetra Tech Inc 10306 Eaton Pl Ste 340 Fairfax VA 22030-2201

PETERS, FRANK ALBERT, retired chemical engineer; b. Washington, June 3, 1931; s. Charles Albert and Dorothy Lynette (Paine) P.; m. Carol Beattie Taylor, Feb. 25, 1955; children: Thomas, June, Erick, Victor. B-SChemE, U. Md., 1955. Devel. engr. Celanese Corp. Am., Cumberland, Md., 1955-58; chem. Engr. U.S. Bur. Mines, College Park, Md., 1958-66; project leader U.S. Bur. Mines, College Park, 1966-70, rsch. supr., 1970-77; chief process evaluation U.S. Bur. Mines, Washington, 1977-94, ret., 1994. Contbr. over 20 articles to profl. jours. Avocations: photography, model railroading. Home: 12311 Glen Mill Rd Potomac MD 20854-1928

PETERS, FREDERICK WHITTEN, lawyer; b. Omaha, Aug. 20, 1946; s. Jordan Holt and Elizabeth (O'Bryant) P.; m. Mary Gores Peters, Jan. 2, 1969; children: Mary Irvin, Elizabeth Holt, Margaret Etheridge. BA magna cum laude, Harvard U., 1968; MS with distinction, London Sch. Econs., 1973; JD magna cum laude, Harvard U., 1976. Bar: D.C. 1978, U.S. Dist. Ct. D.C. 1978, U.S. Dist. Ct. Md., 1994, U.S. Ct. Appeals (3d and D.C. cirs.) 1979, U.S. Ct. Claims 1981, U.S. Ct. Appeals (11th cir.) 1986, U.S. Ct. Mil. Appeals 1993. Law clk. to presiding judge U.S. Ct. Appeals (D.C. cir.), Washington, 1976-77; law clk. to justice William J. Brennan U.S. Supreme Ct., Washington, 1977-78; assoc. Williams & Connolly, Washington, 1978-84, ptnr., 1984-95; prin. dep. gen. counsel Dept. of Defense, 1995—; mem. legal ethics com. D.C. Bar, 1988-94, chmn. rules rev. com., 1991-96; rules com. U.S. Ct. Mil. Appeals, 1993-95. Pres. Harvard Law Rev., 1975-76. Bd. dirs. Cleveland Park Hist. Soc., Washington, 1986-91, Washington Area Lawyers for the Arts, 1987-93; mem. adv. com. on streamlining procurement laws DOD, 1991-93. Lt. USNR, 1969-72. Fellow Am. Bar Found.; mem. ABA. Democrat. Episcopalian. Avocations: sailing, tennis, computer sci. Home: 3250 Highland Pl NW Washington DC 20008-3231 Office: Dept Def/ Office Gen Counsel Rm 3E980 1600 Defense Pentagon Washington DC 20301-1600

PETERS, GARY CHARLES, state senator, lawyer, educator; b. Pontiac, Mich., Dec. 1, 1958; s. Herbert Garrett and Madeleine (Vignier) P.; m. Colleen Ochoa; children: Gary Jr., Madeleine. BA, Alma Coll., 1980; MBA, U. Detroit, 1984; JD, Wayne State U., 1989. Bar: Mich. 1990. Fin. cons., resident mgr., asst. v.p. Merrill Lynch, Pierce, Fenner & Smith, Inc., Rochester, Mich., 1980-89; br. mgr., v.p. Paine Webber, Inc., Rochester, Mich., 1989—; state senator Mich., Lansing, 1994—; securities arbitrator, Nat. Assn. Securities Dealers, N.Y. Stock Exchange, Am. Arbitration Assn., 1990—; adj. prof. Oakland U., Rochester, 1991—, instr. Wayne State U., 1992-94; vice chair Mich. Senate fin. com.; mem. edn. com., judiciary com., families, mental health and svcs. com., law revision com. Councilman City of Rochester Hills, 1992-94, mem. zoning bd. appeals and Paint Creek Trailways Commn., 1992-94; officer-at-large Mich. Dem. Party, 1996. Officer USNR. Mem. Mich. State Bar Assn., Sierra Club. Avocations: hiking, cycling, world travel, boating. Home: 2645 Bloomfield Xing Bloomfield Hills MI 48304-1710 Office: PaineWebber Inc PO Box 80730 Rochester MI 48308-0730

PETERS, GORDON BENES, musician; b. Oak Park, Ill., Jan. 4, 1931; s. Arthur George and Julia Anne (Benes) P. Student, Northwestern U., 1949-50; Mus.B., Eastman Sch. Music, 1956, Mus.M., 1962. Percussionist Rochester (N.Y.) Philharmonic Orch., 1955-59; prin. percussionist Grant Park Symphony Orch., Chgo., 1955-58; mem. faculty Rochester Bd. Edn., 1956-57, Geneseo State Tchrs. Coll., 1957-58; acting prin. percussionist Rochester, N.Y., 1958-59; prin. percussionist and asst. timpanist Chgo. Symphony Orch., 1959—; condr., adminstr. Civic Orch. Chgo., 1966-87; condr. Elmhurst Symphony Orch., 1968-73; instr. percussion instruments Northwestern U., 1963-68, lectr., 1991; guest conductor Bangor (Maine) Symphony, 1993. Author, pub. The Drummer: Man, 1975; arranger-pub. Marimba Ensemble arrangements; composer-pub.: Swords of Moda-Ling; editor: percussion column Instrumentalist mag, 1963-69; contbr. articles to profl. jours. Bd. dirs. Pierre Monteux Sch., Hancock, Maine, 1965-95. With U.S. Mil. Acad. Band, 1950-53. Recipient Pierre Monteux disciple award conducting, 1962. Mem. Percussion Arts Soc. (pres. 1962-66), Am. Symphony Orch. League, Condrs. Guild (treas., exec. com. 1979-82, 86-90). Home: 824 Hinman Ave # 2N Evanston IL 60202-2302 Office: Chgo Symphony Orch 220 S Michigan Ave Chicago IL 60604-2501

PETERS, HENRY AUGUSTUS, neuropsychiatrist; b. Oconomowoc, Wis., Dec. 21, 1920; s. Henry Augustus and Emma N. P.; m. Jean McWilliams, 1950; children—Henry, Kurt, Eric, Mark. BA, MD, U. Wis. Prof. dept. neurology and rehab. medicine U. Wis. Med. Sch., Madison, emeritus prof., 1996—; mem. med. adv. bd. Muscular Dystrophy Assn. Served to lt. M.C. U.S. Navy. Fellow A.C.P.; mem. Wis. Med. Assn., Am. Acad. Neurology, Am. Psychiatric Assn. Club: Rotary. Office: 600 Highland Ave Madison WI 53792-0001

PETERS, HENRY BUCKLAND, optometrist, educator; b. Oakland, Calif., Nov. 2, 1916; s. Thomas Henry and Eleanor Bernice (Hough) P.; m. Anne Zara Ledin, Feb. 3, 1968; children—Lynn, Thomas Henry, James Clifton, Christopher Patrick, Elizabeth Anne. A.B., U. Calif. at, Berkeley, 1938; M.A., U. Nebr., 1939; D.O.S., So. Coll. Optometry, 1971, New England Coll. Optometry, 1985; D.O.S. (hon.), SUNY, 1990. Pvt. practice optometry Chico, Calif., 1939-40, Oakland, 1946-59; instr., asst. prof. U. Calif., Berkeley, 1947-62; assoc. prof., asst. dean U. Calif. (Sch. Optometry), 1962-69; prof., dean (Sch. Optometry), 1969-86; prof. public health Med. Center, U. Ala., Birmingham, 1969-87; dean and prof. emeritus U. Ala., Birmingham, 1988—; exec. dir. Research Found. U. Ala., Birmingham, 1986-89; dir. Nat. Bd. Examiners in Optometry, 1984-91; pres. Nat. Health Council, 1978-79; cons. So. Regional Edn. Bd., S.C. Commn. Higher Edn., Calif. Dept. Public Health, Lawrence Radiation Lab., Aerojet Gen., Nat. Acad. Sci. Inst. Medicine; v.p. Children's Vision Center, Oakland, 1963-69; dir. Calif. Vision Service, 1953-59; mem. optometric rev. com. Bur. Health, Manpower and Edn., HEW, 1970-73, Rev. and Program Council, Medicaid, Calif., 1966-69; dir. Community Service Council, Birmingham, 1969-76; mem. deans com. VA Hosp., Birmingham; bd. dirs. Birmingham Health Services Agy., 1976-79, chmn. manpower com., 1976-79; chmn. optometry services adv. com. VA, 1977-88, chmn. spl. adv. com. on legally blind, 1977; mem. Nat. Rev. Bd. Health Promotion with Elderly, 1980-82; mem. adv. bd. Health Policy Council N.Y., 1980-88; mem. Adv. Council on Phys. Therapy Edn., 1986-89. Author: (with Blum and Bettman) Vision Screening for Elementary Schools, 1959; History of School of Optometry, University of Alabama at Birmingham, 1994; also articles. Served to lt. USNR, 1942-46. Named Optometrist of Year, Calif. Optometric Assn., 1959; Optometrist of South, So. Council Optometrists, 1982; Thomas P. Carpenter award for disting. service Nat. Health Council, 1983. Fellow Am. Public Health Assn. (Vision Care Disting. Achievement award 1982), Am. Acad. Optometry (life, pres. 1973-74, Carel C. Koch medal 1974, diplomate pub. health sect. 1989); mem. Am. Optometric Assn. (Disting. Service award 1981), Ala. Optometric Assn. (Optometrist of Year 1973), Assn. Schs. and Colls. Optometry (pres. 1967-68, dir.), Phi Beta Kappa, Sigma Xi, Phi Delta Kappa, Beta Sigma Kappa. Home: 712 Vestavia Lake Dr Birmingham AL 35216-2063

PETERS, HOWARD NEVIN, foreign language educator; b. Hazleton, Pa., June 29, 1938; s. Howard Eugene and Verna Catherine (Miller) P.; m. Judith Anne Griessel, Aug. 24, 1963; children: Elisabeth Anne, Nevin Edward. BA, Gettysburg Coll., 1960; PhD, U. Colo., 1965. Asst. prof. fgn. langs. Valparaiso (Ind.) U., 1965-69, assoc. prof., 1969-75, dir. grad. divsn., 1967-70, acting dean Coll. Arts and Scis., 1970-71, assoc. dean Coll. Arts and Scis., 1971-74, dean Coll. Arts and Scis., 1974-81, prof. fgn. langs., 1975—, chair dept. fgn. langs. and lits., 1994-96. NDEA fellow, 1960-63. Mem. Midwest MLA, Phi Beta Kappa, Sigma Delta Pi, Phi Sigma Iota. Lutheran. Home: 860 N Cr 500 E Valparaiso IN 46383 Office: Meier Hall Rm 113 Valparaiso U Valparaiso IN 46383

PETERS, LAURALEE MILBERG, diplomat; b. Monroe, N.C., Jan. 28, 1943; d. Arthur W. and Opal I. (Mueller) Milberg; m. Lee M. Peters, May 30, 1964; children: David, Evelyn, Edward, Matthew. BA with highest honors, U. Kans., 1964, postgrad., 1965-67; student, Fgn Svc. Inst., 1975. Asst. pub. info. officer NAS, Washington, 1967-69; joined Fgn. Svc., Dept. State, 1972, commd. sr. fgn. svc. officer, 1985; chief visa sect. Am. Embassy, Saigon, Vietnam, 1972-74; internat. fin. officer Dept. State, Washington, 1975-79; U.S. rep. to Econ. and Social Commn. for Asia and Pacific, UN, Bangkok, Thailand, 1979-81; devel. fin. officer Dept. State, Washington, 1981-82; econ. officer Israel, West Bank, Gaza, 1982-84; dir. Office Monetary Affairs Dept. State, Washington, 1984-86; econ. counselor Am. Embassy, Islamabad, Pakistan, 1986-88; career devel. officer Dept. State, Washington, 1988-89, dep. asst. sec. for personnel, 1989-91; mem. Sr. Seminar, 1991-92; U.S. Ambassador to Sierra Leone, 1992-95; internat. affairs adviser to pres. Naval War Coll., 1995—. Various leadership positions Boy Scouts Am., 1977-88. Recipient Disting. award of merit Nat. Capitol Area Coun. Boy Scouts Am., 1986. Mem. Am. Fgn. Svc. Protective Assn. (v.p. 1981-84), Consular Officer's Assn. (sec. 1974-75), Phi Beta Kappa. Home: 9 Jackson Rd Newport RI 02840-3711 Office: Naval War Coll Code 002 686 Cushing Rd Newport RI 02841-1201

PETERS, LEO FRANCIS, environmental engineer; b. Melrose, Mass., Aug. 14, 1937; s. Joseph Leander and Mary Gertrude (Phalen) P.; m. Joan Catherine Anderson, May 20, 1961; children: Elizabeth M., Susan J., Carolyn A., Jennifer L. BS in Civil Engring., Northeastern U., Boston, 1960, MS in Civil Engring., 1966; postgrad., Harvard U., 1989. Registered profl. engr., Mass., N.H.; diplomate Am. Acad. Environ. Engrs. Jr. engr. N.Y. Dept. Transp., Albany, 1960-61; chief engr. John M. Cashman, Weymouth, Mass., 1961-62; project engr. Metcalf & Eddy, Inc., Boston, 1962-65; project engr. Weston & Sampson, Boston, 1965-67, assoc., 1967-70, ptnr., 1970-76; exec. v.p. Weston & Sampson Engrs., Inc., Boston, 1976-82; pres. Weston & Sampson Engrs., Inc., Wakefield and Peabody, Mass., 1982—; mem. Northeastern U. Corp., 1992; trust. The Engring. Ctr., 1991-93; pres. The Engring. Ctr. Edn. Trust, 1994-95. Clk., mem. Melrose (Mass.) Planning Bd., 1969-91. Named Young Engr. of Yr. Mass. Soc. Profl. Engrs. Fellow Am. Cons. Engrs. Coun. (v.p. 1995—); mem. Am. Water Works Assn., Am. Pub. Works Assn., Water Environ. Fedn., Am. Cons. Engrs. Coun. New Eng. (pres. 1990-91), New Eng. Water Works Assn. (pres. 1989-90). Roman Catholic. Home: 187 E Emerson St Melrose MA 02176-3534 Office: Weston & Sampson Engrs Inc 5 Centennial Dr Peabody MA 01960-7906*

PETERS, LEON, JR., electrical engineering educator, research administrator; b. Columbus, Ohio, May 28, 1923; s. Leon P. and Ethel (Howland) Pierce; m. Mabel Marie Johnson, June 6, 1953; children: Amy T. Peters Thomas, Melinda A. Peters Todaro, Maria C., Patricia D., Lee A., Roberta J. Peters Cameruca, Karen E. Peters Ellingson. B.S.E.E., Ohio State U., 1950, M.S., 1954, Ph.D., 1959. Asst. prof. elec. engring. Ohio State U., Columbus, 1959-63; assoc. prof. Ohio State U., 1963-67, prof., 1967-93, prof. emeritus, 1993—; assoc. dept. chmn. for rsch. Ohio State U., Columbus, 1990-92, dir. electro sci. lab., 1983-94. Contbr. articles to profl. jours. Served to 2d lt. U.S. Army, 1942-46, ETO. Fellow IEEE. Home: 2087 Ellington Rd Columbus OH 43221-4138 Office: Ohio State U Electrosci Lab 1320 Kinnear Rd Columbus OH 43212-1156

PETERS, MERCEDES, psychoanalyst; b. N.Y.C. Student Columbia U., 1944-45; BS, L.I. U., 1945; MS, U. Conn., 1953; tng. in psychotherapy Am. Inst. Psychotherapy and Psychoanalysis, 1960-70; cert. in Psychoanalysis Postgrad. Ctr. For Mental Health, 1976; PhD in Psychoanalysis, Union Inst., 1989. Cert. psychoanalyst Am. Examining Bd. Psychoanalysis; cert. mental health cons. Sr. psychotherapist Cmty. Guidance Svc., 1960-75; staff affiliate Postgrad. Ctr. for Mental Health, 1974-76; pvt. practice psychoanalysis and psychotherapy, Bklyn., 1961—. Contbr. articles to profl. jours. Bd. dirs. Brookwood Child Care Assn.; mem. vestry Grace Ch., Brooklyn Heights. Fellow Am. Orthopsychiat. Assn.; mem. LWV, NAACP, NASW, Postgrad. Psychoanalytic Soc., Wednesday Club. Office: 142 Joralemon St Brooklyn NY 11201-4709

PETERS, R. JONATHAN, lawyer, chemical company executive; b. Janesville, Wis., Sept. 6, 1927; m. Ingrid H. Varvayn, 1953; 1 dau., Christina. B.S. in Chemistry, U. Ill., 1951; J.D., Northwestern U., 1954. Bar: Ill. 1954. Chief patent counsel Englehard Industries, 1972-82, Kimberly-Clark Corp., Neenah, Wis., 1982-85; gen. counsel Lanxide Corp., Newark, Del., 1985-87; pvt. practice Chgo., 1985—. Served with CIC, U.S. Army, 1955-57. Patentee in field. Mem. ABA, Am. Intellectual Property Law Assn., Lic. Execs. Soc., Assn. Corp. Patent Counsel. Clubs: North Shore Golf (Menasha, Wis.), Masons, Scottish Rite, Shriners.

PETERS, RALPH EDGAR, architectural and engineering executive; b. Harrisburg, Pa., Feb. 20, 1923; s. George Edward and Rebecca Flavia (Michener) P.; m. Roberta Jane Shaffer, June 12, 1948; children: Sheila Jane, Gail Marie, Ralph Jr., Bret Edward. Student, U. Pa., 1942; BA in Bus. Adminstrn., Pa. State U., 1948. From payroll supr. to asst. budget supr. Pa. State U., 1948-52; chief acct., pers. officer Haller, Raymond & Brown, State College, Pa., 1952-54; from contr. to CEO and chmn. bd. Benatec Assocs., Inc. (formerly Berger Assocs., Inc.), Camp Hill, Pa., 1954—; bd. dirs. CCNB Bank, New Cumberland, Pa., 1972-93. Chmn. bd. advisors Pa. State U., Harrisburg, 1979—; chmn. bd. dirs. Holy Spirit Hosp., Camp Hill, 1982—; past pres. Tri-County United Way, Harrisburg, from 1978; chmn. Pvt. Industry Coun., Harrisburg, 1982-87. With U.S. Army, 1943-45, ETO, 1952-53, Korea. Recipient Community Svc. award Salvation Army, 1980, Disting. Alumnus award Pa. State U., 1980, Disting. Pennsylvanian award Greater Phila. C. of C., 1981, Catalyst award Capital Region Economic Devel., 1992; finalist Ctrl. Pa. Entrpreneur of Yr. award, 1996. Mem. Pa. C. of C. (bd. dir., transp. com. chmn. 1972-90), Harrisburg Area C. of C. (pres., chmn. 1979-83), Ams. for Competitive Enterprise System (pres. 1981-83), Cumberland County Transp. Authority, Susquehanna Valley Regional Airport Authority, Lions, Masons, Pa. Jaycees (pres. 1955-56, nat. v.p. 1956-57), Delta Sigma Pi. Lutheran. Office: Benatec Assocs Inc 101 Erford Rd Camp Hill PA 17011-1808

PETERS, RALPH FREW, investment banker; b. Mineola, N.Y., Mar. 21, 1929; s. Ralph and Helen Louise (Frew) P.; m. Diana Joyce Clayton, Dec. 19, 1969; children: Louise Frew, Jean Reid, Ralph Frew, Melvyn T., Richard Clayton. B.A., Princeton U., 1951; postgrad., Stonier Grad. Sch. Banking, Rutgers U., 1962. With Corn Exchange Bank & Trust Co., 1947-52; chmn. bd., dir. Discount Corp. N.Y., N.Y.C., 1955-93; bd. dirs. Van Eck Funds, Sun Life Ins. & Annuity of N.Y., U.S. Life Ins. Fund. Served with USNR, 1948-55. Mem. Pub. Securities Assn. (gov.), Anglers Club, Leash Club, Links Club, North Woods Club. Episcopalian.

PETERS, RALPH MARTIN, education educator; b. Knoxville, Tenn., May 9, 1926; s. Tim C. and Alma (Shannon) P.; m. Lorraine Daniel, 1949; children—Teresa, Marta. B.S., Lincoln Meml. U., 1949; M.S., U. Tenn., 1953, Ed.D., 1960. Tchr. pub. schs. Lincoln Meml. U., 1956-63, prof., dept. chmn., v.p., 1956-63, 92-97; prof. edn., dean students, dean Grad. Sch. Tenn. Tech. U., Cookeville, 1963-89; dean emeritus, 1989. Editor publs. Served with Armed Forces, World War II. Mem. Phi Kappa Phi, Phi Delta Kappa, Omicron Delta Kappa. Baptist. Club: Rotary. Home: 927 Mt Vernon Rd Cookeville TN 38501-1576

PETERS, RAYMOND EUGENE, computer systems company executive; b. New Haven, Aug. 24, 1933; s. Raymond and Doris Winthrop (Smith) P.; m. Millie Mather, July 14, 1978 (div. Nov. 1983). Student, San Diego City Coll., 1956-61; cert., Lumbleau Real Estate Sch., 1973, Southwestern Coll., Chula Vista, Calif., 1980. Cert. quality assurance engr. Founder, pub. Silhouette Pub. Co., San Diego, 1960-75; co-founder, news dir. Sta. XEGM, San Diego, 1964-68; news dir. Sta. XERB, Tijuana, Mex., 1973-74; founder, chief exec. officer New World Airways, Inc., San Diego, 1968-77; co-founder, exec. vice chmn. bd. San Cal Rail, Inc.-San Diego Trolley, San Diego, 1974-77; founder, pres., CEO Ansonia Sta., micro systems, San Diego, 1986—; cons. on multimedia and electronic commerce sys., 1995—; co-founder, dir. S.E. Cmty. Theatre, San Diego, 1960-68; commr. New World Aviation Acad., Otay Mesa, Calif., 1971-77; co-founder New World Internat. Trade and Commerce Comm., Inc., 1991-94. Author: Black Americans in Aviation, 1971, Profiles in Black American History, 1974, Eagles Don't Cry, 1988; founder, pub., editor Oceanside Lighthouse, 1958-60, San Diego Herald Dispatch, 1959-60. Co-founder, bd. dirs. San Diego County Econ. Opportunity Commn., 1964-67; co-founder Edn. Cultural Complex, San Diego, 1966-75; co-founder, exec. dir. S.E. Anti-Poverty Planning Coun., Inc., 1964-67; mem. U.S. Rep. Senatorial Inner Circle Com., Washington, 1990—; mem. bus. adv. bd. Value Add Reseller, 1995. With U.S. Army, 1950-53, Korea. Decorated (2) Bronze stars, UN medal. Mem. Am. Soc. Quality Control, Nat. City C. of C., Afro-Am. Micro Sys. Soc. (exec. dir. 1987—), Negro Airmen Internat. (Calif. pres. 1970-75, nat. v.p. 1975-77), Tuskegee Airmen (charter, bd. dirs. Benjamin O. Davis San Diego chpt. 1995—), Internat. Platform Assn., U.S. C. of C., Greater San Diego Minority C. of C. (bd. dirs. 1974—, past chmn. bd.), Masons (most worshipful grand master, supreme coun.), Shriners (Al Kadosh Disting. Cmty. Svc. award 1975). Republican. Avocations: creative writing, golf, world history. Home: Meadowbrook Estates # 245 8301 Mission Gorge Rd Santee CA 92071-3500

PETERS, RICHARD T., lawyer; b. La Mesa, Calif., Sept. 24, 1946. BA, Santa Clara U., 1968; JD, UCLA, 1971. Bar: Calif. 1972. Ptnr. Sidley & Austin, L.A. Fellow Am. Coll. Bankruptcy; mem. State Bar Calif. (mem. debtor-creditor rels. and bankruptcy subcom. bus. law sect. 1979-81, chmn. 1981-82, mem. exec. com. bus. law sect. 1982-85, vice chmn. 1984-85), Calif. Continuing Edn. Bar (cons. 1984, 95), L.A. Fin. Lawyers Conf. (bd. govs. 1976-80), L.A. County Bar Assn. (comml. law and bankruptcy sect., bankruptcy com. 1996—). Office: Sidley & Austin 555 W 5th St Fl 40 Los Angeles CA 90013-1010

PETERS, ROBERT WAYNE, organization executive, lawyer; b. LaSalle, Ill., Jan. 13, 1949; s. Earl Edward and Lucille Anne (Hinrichsen) P.; m. Josie M. Browne, Mar. 28, 1992. BA, Dartmouth Coll., 1971; JD, NYU, 1975. Bar: N.Y. 1976. Staff atty. Morality in Media, Inc., N.Y.C., 1985-87, asst. dir. Nat. Obscenity Law Ctr., 1987-92, pres., 1992—; guest lectr. cmty. and profl. groups. Recipient Effective Citizenship award Archdiocese of N.Y., 1987. Republican. Evangelical. Achievements include the drafting of many laws and amendments pertaining to obscenity and related matters, frequently quoted by national and local press and frequently a guest on electronic media on subjects of pornography and TV indecency and violence. Avocations: walking and hiking with my wife. Office: Morality in Media Inc 475 Riverside Dr New York NY 10115-0122

PETERS, ROBERT WOOLSEY, architect; b. Mpls., Mar. 24, 1935; s. John Eugene and Adelaide Elizabeth (Woolsey) P. BArch., U. Minn., 1958; MArch., Yale U., 1961. Registered architect, N.Mex., Ariz. Dir. design Schaefer & Assocs., Wichita, Kans., 1975-76; participating assoc. Skidmore Owings & Merrill, Chgo., 1961-74; ptnr. Addy & Peters, Albuquerque, 1979-82; owner Robert W. Peters AIA Architect, Albuquerque, 1982—. Exhibited work Centre Georges Pompidou, Paris, 1980; Univ. Art Mus., Albuquerque, 1982, 92, Albuquerque Mus., 1988. Bd. dirs. Contemporary Art Soc. N.Mex. Contbr. articles to Century Mag., Progressive Architecture, House & Garden, House Beautiful, also others. Recipient honor awards N.Mex. Soc. Architects, 1980-83, 86, 87, 92; honor award HUD, 1980, 5th Nat. Passive Solar Conf., Amherst, Mass., 1981. Fellow AIA. Democrat. Roman Catholic. Club: Yale of N.Mex.

PETERS, ROBERTA, soprano; b. N.Y.C., May 4, 1930; d. Sol and Ruth (Hirsch) P.; m. Bertram Fields, Apr. 10, 1955; children: Paul, Bruce. Ed. privately; Litt.D., Elmira Coll., 1967; Mus. D., Ithaca Coll., 1968, Colby Coll., 1980; L.H.D., Westminster Coll., 1974, Lehigh U., 1977; D.F.A., St. John's U., 1982; LittD, Coll. New Rochelle, 1989; MusD, U. R.I., 1992. Author: Debut at the Met; Met. Opera debut as Zerlina in Don Giovanni,

1950; recorded numerous operas; appeared motion pictures; frequent appearances radio and TV; sang at Royal Opera House, Covent Garden, London, Vienna State Opera, Munich Opera, West Berlin Opera, Salzburg Festival, debuts at festivals in Vienna and Munich; concert tours in U.S., Soviet Union, Scandinavian countries, Israel, China, Japan, Taiwan, South Korea, debut, Kirov Opera, Leningrad, USSR, sang at Bolshoi Opera, Moscow (1st Am. to receive Bolshoi medal). Trustee Carnegie Hall; dir. Met. Opera Guild; chmn. Nat. Inst. Music Theater, 1991—; apptd. by Pres. Bush to Nat. Coun. Arts, 1992. Named Woman of Yr. Fedn. Women's Clubs, 1964; honored spl. ceremony on 35th anniversary with the Met. Opera Co., 1985; was 1st Am. to receive Bolshoi medal, 1972. Office: ICM Artists Ltd 40 W 57th St New York NY 10019-4001 *I believe that life is a series of just one darn thing after another. If we can learn that, we can expect, meet, and solve our problems.*

PETERS, SARAH WHITAKER, art historian, writer, lecturer; b. Kenosha, Wis., Aug. 17, 1924; d. Robert Burbank and Margaret Jebb (Allen) Whitaker; m. Arthur King Peters, Oct. 21, 1943; children: Robert Bruce, Margaret Allen, Michael Whitaker. BA, Sarah Lawrence Coll., 1954; MA, Columbia U., 1966; student, L'Ecole du Louvre, Paris, 1967-68; diplome, Ecole des Trois Gourmandes, Paris, 1968; PhD, CUNY, 1987. Freelance critic Art in Am., N.Y.C.; lectr.-in-residence Garrison Forest Sch., Owings Mills, Md.; adj. asst. prof. art history C.W. Post, U. L.I.; lectr. Bronxville (N.Y.) Adult Sch., Internat. Mus. Photography, 1979, Tufts U., 1979, Madison (Wis.) Art Ctr., 1984, Meml. Art Gallery, Rochester, N.Y., 1988, 91, Caramoor Mus., Katonah, N.Y., 1988, Yale U. Art Gallery, New Haven, Conn., 1989, The Cosmopolitan Club, N.Y.C., 1977, 91, Sarah Lawrence Coll., Bronxville, 1992, The Phillips Collection, Washington, 1993, Mpls. Inst. Arts, 1993, Whitney Mus. Am. Art, Champion, 1994, U. Wis., Parkside, 1994, Nat. Mus. Wildlife Art, Jackson Hole, Wyo., 1995, The Georgia O'Keeffe Mus., Santa Fe, 1997. Author: Becoming O'Keeffe: The Early Years, 1991, The Dictionary of Art, 1996; contbr. articles to profl. jours. Mem. Coll. Art Assn., Bronxville Field Club, The Cosmopolitan Club. Avocations: horsemanship, mountaineering, tennis, cooking. Home: 14 Village Ln Bronxville NY 10708-4806

PETERS, TED HOPKINS, insurance company executive; b. Greenville, Tex., Dec. 30, 1943; s. Joe Becton and Teddy Rose (Hopkins) P.; B.B.A., E. Tex. State U., 1965; postgrad. U. Tex., 1965-66; m. Fonda Lynn Carter, June 3, 1966; children—Amy Teigh, Andrew Lathen. Fire rate actuary State Bd. Ins., Austin, Tex., 1966; agency dir. Union Security Life Ins. Co., Greenville, Tex., 1967-72, exec. v.p., dir., 1972—; sec. Greenville Hosp. Dist., 1975-78. Bd. dirs. East Tex. State U. Found., 1977-78; mem. exec. bd. N. Central Tex. Council Govts., 1978-80; foreman Hunt County Grand Jury, 1974; dir. Salvation Army adv. bd., sec. Greenville Indsl. Devel. Fund, 1966-70, pres., 1970—; mem. Nat. Eagle Scout Assn., Nat. Genealogy Soc.; tchr. Bible study class Aldersgate Ch., 1985—; mem. bd. regents East Tex. State U., 1983, bd. dirs. The Selwyn Sch.; mem. Hunt County Juvenile Bd. Recipient Spl. Service award Greenville United Fund, 1971. Mem. Tex. Assn. Life Ins. Ofcls. (pres. 1970-71), Life Ins. Advertisers Assn., Lambda Chi Alpha. Democrat. Author: Peters Family History, 1977. Home: 5401 Vale St Greenville TX 75402-6437 Office: 2612 Woodrow Blvd Greenville TX 75402-6467

PETERS, THEODORE, JR., research biochemist, consultant; b. Chambersburg, Pa., May 12, 1922; s. Theodore and Miriam (Lenhardt) P.; m. Margaret Campbell, June 9, 1945; children: Theodore D., James C., Melissa Peters Barry, William L. BS in Chem. Engring., Lehigh U., 1943; PhD in Biol. Chemistry, Harvard U., 1950. Diplomate Am. Bd. Clin. Chemistry. Grad. asst. MIT, Cambridge, 1943-44; rsch. fellow Harvard Med. Sch., Boston, 1948-50; instr. U. Pa. Sch. Medicine, Phila., 1950-51; biochemist U.S. VA Hosp., Boston, 1953-55; rsch. biochemist Mary Imogene Bassett Hosp., Cooperstown, N.Y., 1955-88, rsch. scientist emeritus, 1988—; vis. scientist Carlsberg Laboratorium, Copenhagen, Denmark, 1958-59; guest worker NIH, Bethesda, Md., 1971-72; vis. rsch. prof. U. Western Australia, Perth, 1982; chmn. classification panel FDA, Washington, 1976-79; bd. dirs. Nat. Com. for Clin. Lab. Standards, Villanova, Pa., 1986-87. Author: All About Albumin, Biochemistry, Genetics, and Medical Applications, 1996; chmn. bd. editors Clin. Chemistry, 1979-84; contbr. articles to profl. jours. Chmn. Sewer Bd., Cooperstown, 1975—; mem. Water Bd., Cooperstown, 1973—; chmn. lake com. Otsego County Conservation Assn., Cooperstown, 1972-78. Comdr. USNR, 1944-47, 51-53. Recipient Gold medal Biol. div. Electron Microscope Soc. Am., 1966. Fellow Am. Assn. Clin. Chemistry (pres. 1988, awards 1976, 77, 91); mem. Am. Chem. Soc., Am. Soc. Biol. Chem. Molecular Biology (emeritus), Am. Soc. for Cell Biology (emeritus), Protein Soc., Nat. Acad. for Clin. Biochemistry (diplomate), Acad. Clin. Lab. Physicians and Scientists, Phi Beta Kappa. Avocations: tennis, hiking, music. Home: 30 River St Cooperstown NY 13326-1317 Office: Mary Imogene Bassett Hosp Atwell Rd Cooperstown NY 13326

PETERS, THOMAS ROBERT, English language educator, writer; b. Detroit, Nov. 14, 1929; s. Norman Addison and Eleanor H. (Schneider) P.; m. Lillian J. Tremonti, Aug. 21, 1954; children: Jennifer Leigh Hartman, Thomas R. Jr., Sarah Jeanne. BA, Hillsdale Coll., 1954; MA, Wayne State U., 1963. Screen writer Jam Handy Film Prodns., Detroit, 1956-59; secondary tchr. English, Detroit Pub. Schs., 1960-69; edn. coord. Detroit Free Press, 1969-72; mgr. pub. rels. Blue Cross, Blue Shield Mich., Detroit, 1972-86; prof. English Macomb C.C, Warren, Mich., 1986-95; guest speaker Mich. Schs. and Colls., 1970—. Author: (novels) Education of Tom Webber, 1977, Two Weeks in the Forties, 1988 (Opus Magnum award 1996), Selected Works, 1995, (play) Mensa Meeting, 1987; contbr. numerous stories, articles and poems to nat. mags., anthologies; writer several published speeches. Bd. dirs. Friends of Grosse Pointe Librs., 1978-84. With U.S. Army, 1948-49; U.S. Army Res. 1950-55. Recipient Alumni Achievement award in Literature Hillsdale Coll., 1993; grantee: Grosse Pointe Found., 1978, Utica Community Schs., 1989. Mem. Fine Arts Soc. Detroit (pres. 1978-79). Roman Catholic. Avocations: pianist, actor, tennis player. Home: 350 Moselle Pl Grosse Pointe MI 48236-3307

PETERS, VIRGINIA, actress; b. Los Angeles, July 15, 1924; d. Peter and Tessie (Skiller) Stetzenko. Grad., Pasadena (Calif.) Playhouse, 1944; student, L.A. City Coll. Tchr. Burbank (Calif.) Little Theatre, 1978-80, Burbank Acad. Performing Arts, 1979—. TV appearances in Night Strangler, 1972, Dallas, 1980, The Waltons, 1981, House Detective, 1985, Knight Rider, 1985, Murder She Wrote, 1986, Hunter, 1986, Hardcastle and McCormick, 1986, Cavanaughs, 1986, Paper Chase, 1986, also Days of Our Lives, Divorce Court, Grace Under Fire, 1993; film appearances include The Arrangement, 1968, The Cat People, 1981, Fast Times at Ridgemont High, 1982, Rat Boy, 1985, The Deacon Street Deer, 1985, My Demon Lover, Mr. President, The Judge, Stripped to Kill II, 1988, Hero, My Girl II, Yankovic-Disney Spl., Father's Day; appeared in numerous commls. Mem. Masquers Club (past dir.), Pasadena Playhouse Alumni Assos. (past dir.). Democrat. Roman Catholic.

PETERS, WILLIAM, author, producer, director; b. San Francisco, July 30, 1921; s. William Ernest and Dorothy Louise (Wright) P.; m. Mercy Ann Miller, Oct. 12, 1942 (div. 1968); children: Suzanne Peters Payne, Geoffrey Wright, Jennifer Peters Johnson, Gretchen Peters Daniel; m. Helene Louise Yager White, May 31, 1987. BS, Northwestern U., 1947. Account exec. pub. relations J. Walter Thompson Co., Chgo., 1947-51; mem. fiction staff Ladies' Home Jour., 1951-52; article editor Woman's Home Companion, N.Y.C., 1952-53; freelance writer, Pelham, N.Y., 1953-62; producer CBS Reports, CBS News, N.Y.C., 1962-66; freelance writer, film dir. and TV producer/exec. producer N.Y.C., 1966-82; dir. Yale U. Films, New Haven, 1982-89; freelance writer, film dir., TV producer/exec. producer Guilford, Conn., 1990—; cons. race relations, 1959—, hist. TV documentaries, 1976—. Author: American Memorial Hospital--Reims, France: A History, 1955, Passport to Friendship--The Story of the Experiment in International Living, 1957, The Southern Temper, 1959, (with Mrs. Medgar Evers) For Us, The Living, 1967, A Class Divided, 1971; A More Perfect Union, 1987, A Class Divided: Then and Now, 1987; producer, writer, dir. documentaries Storm Over the Supreme Court, Parts II and III, 1963 (George F. Peabody award, Golden Gavel award ABA), (co-producer) After Ten Years: The Court and the Schools, 1964 (Nat. Sch. Bell award NEA), The Eye of the Storm, 1970 (George Foster Peabody award, Christopher award, Cine Golden Eagle award), Suddenly an Eagle, 1976 (George Foster Peabody award, Cine Golden Eagle award), Death of a Family, 1979 (Writers Guild Am. award), A Bond of Iron, 1982, A Class Divided, 1985 (Emmy award, Sidney Hillman award, Cine Golden Eagle award), others; exec. producer dramas Boswell's London Journal, 1986, others. Co-founder North Shore Citizens Com., 1946, bd. dirs., 1946-51; co-founder Pelham Com. Human Relations, 1963, vice chmn., 1963-65, chmn., 1965-66. Served to capt. USAAF, 1942-45, ETO. Decorated Air medal with 2 oak leaf clusters, D.F.C.; recipient Benjamin Franklin mag. award, 1954; Peabody TV award, 1963, 70, 76, Golden Gavel award ABA, 1963, Sch. Bell award NEA, 1964, Emmy award, Sidney Hillman award, 1985. Mem. Dirs. Guild Am., Writers Guild Am. Democrat. Home: 3108 Long Hill Rd Guilford CT 06437-3619

PETERS, WILLIAM P., oncologist, science administrator, educator; b. Buffalo, Aug. 26, 1950; m. Elizabeth Zentai; children: Emily, Abigail, James. BS, BS, BA, Pa. State U., 1972; MPhil, PhD, Columbia U., 1976, MD, 1978; postgrad., Harvard U., 1984; MBA, Duke U., 1990. Diplomate Am. Bd. Internal Medicine, Am. Bd. Med. Oncology. Prof. medicine Duke U. Med. Ctr., Durham, N.C., assoc. dir. for clin. ops. Duke Comprehensive Cancer Ctr., dir. bone marrow transplant program, 1984-95; pres., CEO, Mich. Cancer Found., Detroit, 1995—; pres., dir., CEO Karmanos Cancer Inst., Detroit, 1995—; prof. oncology, medicine, surgery and radiation oncology Wayne State U., Detroit, 1995—, assoc. dean for cancer programs, 1995—; sr. v.p. for cancer svcs. Detroit Med. Ctr.,, 1995—. Office: Karmanos Cancer Ctr President's Office 4100 John R St Detroit MI 48201-2013

PETERSDORF, ROBERT GEORGE, physician, medical educator; b. Berlin, Feb. 14, 1926; s. Hans H. and Sonja P.; m. Patricia Horton Qua, June 2, 1951; children: Stephen Hans, John Eric. BA, Brown U., 1948, DMS (hon.), 1983; MD cum laude, Yale U., 1952; ScD (hon.), Albany Med. Coll., 1979; MA (hon.), Harvard U., 1980; DMS (hon.), Med. Coll. Pa., 1982, Brown U., 1983; DMS, Bowman-Gray Sch. Medicine, 1986; LHD (hon.), N.Y. Med. Coll., 1986; DSc (hon.), SUNY, Bklyn., 1987, Med. Coll. Ohio, 1987, Univ. Health Scis., The Chgo. Med. Sch., 1987, St. Louis U., 1988; LHD (hon.), Ea. Va. Med. Sch., 1988; DSc (hon.), Sch. Medicine, Georgetown U., 1991, Emory U., 1992, Tufts U., 1993, Mt. Sinai Sch. Medicine, 1993, George Washington U., 1994; other hon. degrees. Diplomate Am. Bd. Internal Medicine. Intern, asst. resident Yale U., New Haven, 1952-54; sr. asst. resident Peter Bent Brigham Hosp., Boston, 1954-55; fellow Johns Hopkins Hosp., Balt., 1955-59; chief resident, instr. medicine Yale U., 1957-58; asst. prof. medicine Johns Hopkins U., 1957-60, physician, 1958-60; assoc. prof. medicine U. Wash., Seattle, 1960-62, prof., 1962-79, chmn. dept. medicine, 1964-79; physician-in-chief U. Wash. Hosp., 1964-79; pres. Brigham and Women's Hosp., Boston, 1979-81; prof. medicine Harvard U. Med. Sch., Boston, 1979-81; dean, vice chancellor health scis. U. Calif.-San Diego Sch. Medicine, 1981-86; clin. prof. infectious diseases Sch. Medicine Georgetown U., 1986-94; pres. Assn. Am. Med. Colls., Washington, 1986-94, pres. emeritus, 1994—; prof. medicine U. Wash., 1994—, disting. prof., 1995; disting. physician Vets. Health Adminstrn., Seattle, 1994—; cons. to surgeon gen. USPHS, 1960-79; cons. USPHS Hosp., Seattle, 1962-79; mem. spl. med. adv. group VA, 1987-94. Editor: Harrison's Priciples of Internal Medicine, 1968-90; contbr. numerous articles to profl. jours. Served with USAAF, 1944-46. Recipient Lilly medal Royal Coll. Physicians, London, 1978, Wiggers award Albany Med. Coll., 1979, Robert H. Williams award Assn. Profs. Medicine, 1983, Keen award Brown U., 1980, Disting. Svc. award Baylor Coll. Medicine, 1989, Scroll of Merit Nat. Med. Assn., 1990, 2d Ann. Founder's award Assn. Program Dirs. in Internal Medicine, 1991, Flexner award Assn. Amer. Med. Coll., 1994; named Disting. Internist of 1987. Felow AAAS, ACP (pres. 1975-76, Stengel award 1980, Disting. Tchr. award 1993), Am. Coll. Physician Execs. (hon.); mem. Inst. Medicine of NAS (councillor 1977-80), Assn. Am. Physicians (pres. 1976-77, Kober medal 1996), Cosmos Club, Rainier Club. Home and Office: 1219 Parkside Dr E Seattle WA 98112-3717

PETERSEN, ANN NEVIN, computer systems administrator, consultant; b. Mexico City, Aug. 7, 1937; parents Am. citizens; d. Thomas Marshall and Gerry (Cox) Nevin; m. Norman William Petersen, Aug. 24, 1956; children: Richard, Robert, Thomas, Anita, David. AS in Electronics, Monterey Peninsula Coll., Monterey, Calif., 1962; student, U. N.Mex., 1956, Las Positas Coll., Livermore, Calif., 1992. Cert. computer profl. CAD mgr. Naval Air Rework Facility, Alameda, Calif., 1979-80; computer systems analyst Space and Naval Warfare System Command, Washington, 1980-84, Facilities Computer Systems Office, Port Hueneme, Calif., 1984-86; systems mgr. Lawrence Livermore Nat. Lab., Livermore, 1986-89; data base mgr. Clayton Environ. Cons., Pleasanton, Calif., 1989-90; computer systems mgr. Waltrip & Assocs., Sacramento, 1990-94; dir. computer systems, CFO Innovative Techs. Inc., Pleasanton, 1992—. Author databases. Bd. dirs. Am. Field Svc., Port Hueneme, 1976-78; mem. various adv. bds. U.S. Navy, 1957-86; mem. adv. bd. Calif. Deaf/Blind Regional Ctr., Sacramento, 1976-80; bd. dirs. ARC Alameda County, Hayward, Calif., 1992—. Recipient Superior Performance award U.S. Navy, 1980, Speaker of Month award Toastmsters, 1985. Mem. Data Processing Mgmt. Assn., bd. dirs., sec.), Assn. for Computing Machinery, Tri Valley MacIntosh Users Group, Inst. for Cert. of Computer Profls. Avocations: astronomy, rockhounding, sewing, tennis, painting. Office: Innovative Techs Inc 5238 Riverdale Ct Pleasanton CA 94588-3759

PETERSEN, ARNE JOAQUIN, chemist; b. L.A., Jan. 27, 1932; s. Hans Marie Theodore and Astrid Maria (Pedersen) P.; m. Sandra Joyce Sharp, Aug. 12, 1961; children: Christina Lynn, Kurt Arne. AA, Compton Coll., 1957; BS, Calif. State U., Long Beach, 1959; BA, U. Calif., Irvine, 1975. Comml. pilots lic. Chemist/scientist Beckman Instruments, Inc., Fullerton, Calif., 1959-62, engr., scientist, 1962-65, project, sr. project engr., 1965-74; project/program mgr. Beckman Clin. Ops., Fullerton/Brea, Calif., 1974-80; ops. mgr. Graphic Controls Corp., Irvine, 1980-82; engr./rsch. and devel. mgr. Carle Instruments Chromatography, Anaheim, Calif., 1982-84; ops. mgr. Magnaflux/X-Ray Devel., L.A., 1984-85; rsch. and devel. dir., new products Am. Chem. Systems, Irvine, Calif., 1985-86; rsch. assoc. U. Calif., Irvine, 1987-88; ind. cons., contractor, sales real estate investment, 1989—; career guidance counselor U. Calif., Irvine, 1976. Author scientific papers in field; patentee in field. Vol. F.I.S.H., Costa Mesa and Newport Beach, Calif.; basketball coach Boys-Girls Club, Newport Beach, 1975-78, baseball coach Newport Beach Parks, 1975-78; adv. com. Newport/Costa Mesa Sch. Bd., 1974-75. Sgt. USAF, 1951-55. Mem. Biomed. Engring. Soc., Internat. Exec. Svc. Corps (exec. svc. with Agy Internat. Devel., 1993, 94), U. Calif. Irvine Club (bd. dirs.), Kappa Sigma (founder Calif. State. U., Long Beach). Avocations: flying, photography, swimming, travel, Bridge.

PETERSEN, BENT EDVARD, mathematician, educator; b. Copenhagen, July 31, 1942; came to U.S., 1964; s. Edvard Valdemar and Grethe Julie (Larsen) P.; m. Marguerite Kathleen Anne McCrindle, Aug. 21, 1965; children: Erik, Poul, Kirsten. BS, U. B.C., Vancouver, Can., 1964; PhD, MIT, 1968. Asst. prof. math. Oreg. State U., Corvallis, 1968-74, assoc. prof. math., 1974-80, prof. math., 1980—; vis. mem. Inst. Advanced Study, Princeton, N.J., 1973-74; guest scientist Internat. Atomic Energy Agy., Trieste, Italy, 1975. Author: Introduction to the Fourier Transform and Pseudo-differential Operators, 1983. Mem. Am. Math. Soc., Math. Assn. Am., Oreg. Acad. Sci., Sigma Xi. Office: Oreg State U Dept Math Corvallis OR 97331-4605

PETERSEN, BENTON LAURITZ, paralegal; b. Salt Lake City, Jan. 1, 1942; s. Lauritz George and Arleane (Curtis) P.; m. Sharon Donnette Higgins, Sept. 20, 1974 (div. Aug. 9, 1989); children: Grant Lauritz, Tashya Eileen, Nicholas Robert, Katrina Arleane. AA, Weber State Coll., 1966, BA, 1968; BA, Weber State Coll., 1968; M of Liberal Studies, U. Okla., 1980; diploma, Nat. Radio Inst. Paralegal Sch., 1991. Registered paralegal. Announcer/news dir. KWHO Radio, Salt Lake City, 1968-70, KDXU Radio, St. George, Utah, 1970-73, KSOP Radio, Salt Lake City, 1973-76; case worker/counselor Salvation Army, Midland, Tex., 1976-84; announcer/news dir. KBRS Radio, Springdale, Ark., 1984-86; case worker/counselor Office of Human Concern, Rogers, Ark., 1986-88; announcer KAZM Radio, Sedona, Ariz., 1988-91; paralegal Benton L. Petersen, Manti, Utah, 1991—; cons. Sanpete County Srs., Manti, 1992—. Award judge Manti City Beautification, 1992-96; treas. Manti Destiny Com., 1993—; tourism com. Sanpete County Econ. Devel., Ephraim, Utah, 1993-96. Served with U.S. Army N.G., 1959-66. Mem. Am. Soc. Notaries, Nat. Assn. Federated Tax Preparers, Nat. Paralegal Assn., Am. Legion. Mem. LDS Ch. Avocations: reading, participating in Doctor Who role playing games. Home: 470 E 120 N Manti UT 84642-0011 Office: Benton L Petersen ND Paralegal Svcs 470 E 120 N Manti UT 84642-0011

PETERSEN, CATHERINE HOLLAND, lawyer; b. Norman, Okla., Apr. 24, 1951; d. John Hays and Helen Ann (Turner) Holland; m. James Frederick Petersen, June 26, 1973 (div.); children: T. Kyle, Lindsay Diane. B.A., Hastings Coll., 1973; J.D., Okla. U., 1976. Bar: Okla. 1976, U.S. Dist. Ct. (we. dist.) Okla. 1978. Legal intern, police legal advisor City of Norman, 1974-76; sole practice, Norman, 1976-81; ptnr. Williams Petersen & Denny, Norman, 1981-82; pres. Petersen Assocs., Inc., Norman, 1982—; adj. prof. Okla. City U. Coll. Law, 1982, U. Okla. Law Ctr., 1987; instr. continuing legal edn. U. Okla. Law Ctr., Norman, 1977, 79, 81, 83, 84, 86, 89-95. Bd. dirs. United Way, Norman, 1978-84, pres., 1981; bd. dirs. Women's Resource Ctr., Norman, 1975-77, 82-84; mem. Jr. League, Norman, 1980-83, Norman Hosp. Aux., Norman, 1982-84; trustee 1st Presbyn. Ch., 1986-87. Named to Outstanding Okla. Women of 1980's, Women's Polit. Caucus, 1980, Outstanding Women Am., 1981, 83. Fellow Am. Acad. Matrimonial Lawyers (pres. Okla. chpt. 1990-91, bd. govs. 1991-95); mem. ABA (seminar instr. 1993, 95, 96), Cleve. County Bar Assn., Okla. Bar Assn. (chmn. family law sect. 1987-88, seminar instr. 1986-93, 95), Phi Delta Phi. Republican. Home: 4716 Sundance Ct Norman OK 73072-3900 Office: PO Box 1243 314 E Comanche St Norman OK 73069-6009

PETERSEN, DAVID L., lawyer. AA, Concordia Jr. Coll., Milw., 1963; BA, Concordia Sr. Coll., Ft. Wayne, Ind., 1965; JD, Valparaiso U., Ind., 1968. Bar: Wis. 1968, U.S. Dist. Ct. (ea. dist.) Wis. 1969, U.S. Ct. Appeals (7th cir.) 1972, U.S. Supreme Ct. 1988, Fla. 1989. Ptnr. Quarles & Brady, Milw. and West Palm Beach, Fla., 1968—. Author: Wisconsin Condominium Law, 1988, 94; editor Valparaiso U. Law Rev., 1967-68; contbr. articles to profl. jours. Mem. Greater Milw. Com. Community Devel., 1983; bd. dirs. Goals for Greater Milw. 2000, 1982, Broward Com. of 100. Lt. col., instr. pilot USAF/Wis. Air N.G., 1970-90. Mem. ABA, Wis. Bar Assn., Milw. Bar Assn., Fla. Bar Assn., Broward County Bar Assn., Palm Beach County Bar, Wis. Mortgage Bankers Assn., Am. Coll. Real Estate Lawyers, Milw. Yacht Club, Palm Beach Yacht Club. Office: Quarles & Brady 222 Lakeview Ave Fl 4 West Palm Beach FL 33401-6147 also: Quarles & Brady 411 E Wisconsin Ave Milwaukee WI 53202-4409

PETERSEN, DEAN MITCHELL, computer systems operator; b. Waterloo, Iowa, Nov. 13, 1950; s. Guy Albert and Valeria Catherine (Mitchell) P.; m. Maria Rosario Artuz, Mar. 1972 (div. Feb. 1978); m. Sandra Jean Asselin, Aug. 15, 1980 (div. Nov. 1992); children: Liesa Jan, Michael Charles. Student, Ill. Cen. Coll., 1978-79, Rhodes Coll., 1988; A in Bus. Adminstrn. magna cum laude, Shelby State Community Coll., Memphis, 1988. Enlisted USN, 1969, hull maintenance technician, 1969-77; lab mgr. Peoria Color Lab, Peoria Heights, Ill., 1977-79; owner Mitchell-Petersen Photography, Peoria, Ill., 1978-79; purchasing agt., parts mgr., office mgr. Weissman Industries, Waterloo, 1980-84; fleet maintenance mgr. Ben Mogy & Sons, Memphis, 1985-86; program devel. coord. Nesretep Bus. Svcs., Lewiston, Maine, 1988-93, C.I.C., Lewiston, Maine, 1993—. Author: Vietnam Veteran's Lament, 1986, Lost Valley Scrolls, 1989, Lost Valley Scrolls-With Annotation, 1991, Collection, 1991, Dancing Girl, 1991, Lyrics, 1991, Recycling as a Component of Economic Development, 1992, Divestment, 1992, Love, Loss, and the Foolish Heart, 1992, Maintenance Planning for Sawmills and Forest Products Industries, 1992; composer: Life of Love, 1988; contbr. articles, photographs to profl. publs.; inventor, designer in field. Recipient Presdl. citation Pres. Ferdinand Marcos, Manila, 1973, Achievement cert. Kodak, 1978. Avocations: writing, camping, gardening, woodcrafting, photography. Office: Nesretep Bus Svcs PO Box 1961 Lewiston ME 04241-1961

PETERSEN, DONALD SONDERGAARD, lawyer; b. Pontiac, Ill., May 14, 1929; s. Clarence Marius and Esther (Sondergaard) P.; m. Alice Thorup, June 5, 1954; children: Stephen, Susan Petersen Schuh, Sally Petersen Riordan. Student, Grand View Coll., 1946-48; B.A., Augustana Coll., Rock Island, Ill., 1951; J.D., Northwestern U., 1956. Bar: Ill. 1957. Assoc. Norman & Billick and predecessors, Chgo., 1956-64, ptnr., 1965-78; counsel Sidley & Austin, Chgo., 1978-80, ptnr., 1980-93, ret., 1993; pres. Chgo. Exhibitors Corp., Chgo., 1978-85. Bd. dirs. Mount Olive Cemetery Co. Inc., Chgo., 1972-90; bd. dirs. Augustana Hosp., 1983-87, Danish Old People's Home, 1976—; bd. dirs. Luth. Gen. Hosp., Park Ridge, Ill., 1968—, chmn., 1979-81, 89-91; bd. dirs. Luth. Gen. Health System and predecessors, Park Ridge, 1980-95, chmn., 1980-81, 83-85; bd. dirs., chmn. Parkside Health Mgmt. Corp., Parkside Home Health Svcs., 1985-88. With U.S. Army, 1951-53. Mem. Chgo. Bar Assn., Ill. State Bar Assn. Club: Union League (Chgo.). Home: 241 N Aldine Ave Park Ridge IL 60068-3009 Office: 55 W Monroe St Ste 2000 Chicago IL 60603-5008

PETERSEN, EVELYN ANN, education consultant; b. Gary, Ind., July 2, 1936; d. Eric Maxwell and Julia Ann (Kustron) Ivany; m. Ozzie G. Hebert, Feb. 27, 1957 (div. July 1963); children: Heather Lynn Petersen Hewett, Eric Dean Hebert; m. Jon Edwin Petersen, June 13, 1964; children: Karin Patricia, Kristin Shawn. BS, Purdue U., 1964; MA, Cen. Mich. U., 1977. Cert. tchr. elem. edn. with early childhood and vocat. edn. endorsements, Mich. Elem. tchr. Harford Day Sch., Bel Air, Md., 1958-62, Interlochen (Mich.) Elem. Sch., 1964-67; dir., tchr. Traverse City (Mich.) Coop. Presch., 1969-77; off-campus instr. grad. level Cen. Mich. U., Mt. Pleasant, 1977-92; Child Devel. Assoc. nat. rep. Coun. for Early Childhood Profl. Recognition, Washington, 1981—; instr. N.W. Mich. Coll., Traverse City, 1974-75, 78, U. Wis., Sheboygan, 1981-83; project dir., instr. West Shore C.C., Scotville, Mich., 1984-86, 89; ednl. cons., 1980—; parenting columnist Detroit Free Press, Knight Ridder Tribune Wire, 1984—; bd. mem. Children's Trust Fund, Lansing, Mich., 1983-85; mem. ad hoc adv. com. Bd. Edn. State of Mich., Lansing, 1985-86, child care provider trainer Dept. Social Svcs., 1988; chairperson adv. bd. Traverse Bay Vocat. Edn. Child Care Program, 1976-79; panelist Nat. Parenting Ctr., L.A., 1992—. Author: A Practical Guide to Early Childhood Planning, Methods and Materials: The What, Why and How of Lesson Plans, 1996; author, co-prodr. (audio and video cassette series) Parent Talk, 1990, Effective Home Visits: Video Training, 1994. County coord. Week of the Young Child, Traverse City, 1974-78; vol. probate ct. Traverse City, 1973-83; commr. Traverse City Human Rights Commn., 1981-82. Mem. AAUW (chairperson, coord. Touch & Do Exploratorium 1974-76), Nat. Fedn. Press Women, Nat. Assn. for Edn. of Young Children, Children's Trust Fund for Abuse Prevention, Mich. Assn. for Edn. of Young Children, Mich. Mental Health Assn., Assn. for Childhood Edn. Internat., Author's Guild. Avocations: writing, reading, travel, snorkeling. Home and Office: 843 S Long Lake Rd Traverse City MI 49684

PETERSEN, GARY N., utility company executive; b. Hartley, Iowa, Sept. 3, 1951; s. Alvin Edward and Lorene Katherine (Seegers) P.; m. Barbara Lund, Sept. 29, 1984; 1 child, Nicholas. Degree in computer sci., Iowa State U., 1973. Sr. acct. Arthur Andersen & Co., 1973-77; asst. to contr. Minnegasco, Mpls., 1977-82; dir. fin. planning and analysis Minnegas Co., Mpls., 1982-85, v.p. gas supply and regulatory adminstrn., 1985-87, exec. v.p., COO, 1987-91, pres., COO, 1991—. Bd. dirs. Dunwoody Inst., Mpls., 1988—, Greater Mpls. Met. Housing Corp., 1991—; past chmn. Mpls. Downtown Coun., 1994; chmn. Mpls. Met. YMCA, 1995—. Mem. Am. Gas Assn., Midwest Gas Assn. (chmn. 1996-97). Avocations: golf, gardening, fishing, stained glass. Office: Minnegasco divsn NorAm Energy Corp Fl 11 800 LaSalle Ave Fl 11 Minneapolis MN 55402-2006

PETERSEN, GEORGE JAMES, educational administration educator; b. L.A., Nov. 11, 1957; s. George James Sr. and Mabel Marie (Crabtree) P.; m. Jennifer Lynn Faue, Dec. 22, 1984; children: Elijah F., Jacob Warren. BA in Philosophy, Angelicum U., Rome, 1981; BA in Anthropology, U. Calif., Santa Barbara, 1986, MA in Ednl. Adminstrn., 1991, PhD in Ednl. Adminstrn., 1993. Cert. social studies tchr., Calif. Tchr. social studies Bishop Garcia Diego High Sch., Santa Barbara, 1981-82, Hollister (Calif.) High Sch., 1987-89; lectr. Grad. Sch. Edn., U. Calif., Santa Barbara, 1990—; assoc. prof. ednl. adminstrn. S.W. Mo. State U., Springfield; cons. Bishop Diego High Sch., 1991-92, Calif. Dairy Coun., Santa Barbara, summer 1992. Named Sallie Mae Outstanding Tchr., Sallie Mae Mktg. Assn., 1988; U. Calif. regents fellow, U. Calif. gen. affiliates grad. fellow. Mem. ASCD, Am. Ednl. Rsch. Assn., Mid-Western Ednl. Rsch. Assn., Assn. of Tchr. Educators, Nat. Coun. of States Inservice Educators, Ea. Ednl. Rsch. Assn., Soc. Am. Baseball Rsch., Phi Delta Kappa, Phi Beta Kappa. Avocations: baseball. Office: SW Mo State U Dept Ednl Admin Springfield MO 65804

PETERSEN, JAMES L., lawyer; b. Bloomington, Ill., Feb. 3, 1947; s. Eugene and Cathryn Teresa (Hemmele) P.; m. Helen Louise Moser, Nov. 20, 1971; children: Christine Louise, Margaret Teresa. BA, Ill. State U., 1970; MA, Sangamon State U., 1973; JD magna cum laude, Ind. U., 1976. Bar: Ind. 1976, Fla. 1980, U.S. Dist. Cts. (no. and so. Ind.), U.S. Ct. Appeals (7th cir.), U.S. Supreme Ct. Admissions officer U. Ill., Springfield, 1970-71, asst. to v.p., 1971-72, registrar, 1972-73; assoc. Ice Miller Donadio & Ryan, Indpls., 1976-83, ptnr., 1983—. Pres. United Cerebral Palsy of Ctrl. Ind., 1981-83, pres. Found., 1988-90. Mem. ABA, Fla. Bar Assn., Ind. Bar Assn., Internat. Assn. Def. Counsel, Ill. State U. Alumni Assn. (pres. 1990-92), Ind. U. Law Alumni Assn. (bd. dirs. 1992—). Home: 11827 Sea Star Dr Indianapolis IN 46256-9400 Office: Ice Miller Donadio & Ryan PO Box 82001 One American Sq Indianapolis IN 46282

PETERSEN, JEAN SNYDER, association executive; b. N.Y.C., Oct. 16, 1931; d. Peter Eugene and Helyn Brownell (Parker) Snyder; m. Elton Reed Petersen, Sept. 16, 1954; children—Bruce Brownell, Craig Reed. Student, N.Y. U., 1949-51; degree fgn. banking, Am. Inst. Banking, 1952. Fgn. credit investigator Chase Nat. Bank Hdqrs., N.Y.C., 1952-56; nat. exec. dir. Assn. Children and Adults with Learning Disabilities (name changed to Learning Disabilities Assn. of Am.), Pitts., 1972—. Mem. exec. com., treas. Jr. League, Pitts.; bd. dirs. Found. for Children with Learning Disabilities, N.Y.C., Children's Hosp., Pitts., Music for Mt. Lebanon, Vocat. Rehab. Ctr., Pitts.; bd. dirs., v.p., mem. exec. com. Assn. Retarded Citizens Pa.; ptnr. UN Internat. Yr. of Disabled; ruling elder Presbyn. Ch.Assn. Retarded Citizens Pa.; mem. exec. com. Pat Buckley Moss Nat. Children's Charity Found. Recipient Sustainers award Jr. League, 1977, Recognition award, 1975, Pres.'s award, 1978. Mem. Meeting Planners Internat. (treas.), Am. Soc. Assn. Execs. Republican. Presbyterian. Home: 343 Shadowlawn Ave Pittsburgh PA 15216-1239 Office: 4156 Library Rd Pittsburgh PA 15234-1349

PETERSEN, KENNETH CLARENCE, chemical company executive; b. Chgo., Mar. 17, 1936; s. Clarence and Theresa (Tomazin) P.; m. Gladys Marie Boyte, Jan. 21, 1956; children: Robert, Michael, Karen, William, Eric, John. Student, Crane Jr. Coll., 1956-57, Wright Jr. Coll., 1957-58; BS in Chemistry, Northwestern U., 1960, MS in Organic Chemistry, 1963. Chem. lab. tech. Glidden Paint Co., Chgo., 1956-58; chemist, group leader Acme Resin Co., Forest Pk., Ill., 1958-64; group leader, research coordinator, research mgr. resin div., mgr. chemistry & tech., mgr. chem. div. mfg., v.p. mfg. then exec. v.p. Schenectady (N.Y.) Chems., Inc., 1964-81, pres., 1981-93; pres. Schenectady Internat. Inc. (formerly Schenectady Chems., Inc.), 1993—; bd. dirs. TRUSTCO, Schenectady; mem. The Fifty Group, tri-city area, 1981—. Contbr. articles to profl. jours.; holder 12 patents. bd. dirs. Schenectady Boys and Girls Club, 1980—, Sunnyview Hosp., Schenectady, 1982—, Schenctady Econ. Devel. Council, 1984—, Fund Raising Rev. Bd. Schenectady, 1985—. Mem. Am. Chem. Soc. (chmn. eastern N.Y. sect. 1979). Clubs: Mohawk, Mohawk Golf (Schenectady). Avocations: fishing, golf, bridge, poker. Office: Schenectady Internat Inc Congress And # 10th Sts Schenectady NY 12303

PETERSEN, LADDIAN WALTER, flight operations director; b. Aberdeen, S.D., July 10, 1952; s. Walter Theodore and Frieda Marie (Holscher) P.; m. Jeanette Lynn Hoffman, June 7, 1975 (div. June 1988); m. Linda Sue Hastings, May 27, 1994; 1 child, David Allen. BS, S.D. State U., 1974. Designated pilot examiner, airline transport pilot; cert. flight instr. FAA. Civil engr. FAA, Des Plaines, Ill., 1975-77; air traffic contr. FAA, Moline, Ill., 1977-81; airport mgr. Clinton (Ark.) Mcpl. Airport, 1981-90; dir. flight ops. Acxiom, Inc., Conway, Ark., 1990—. Republican. Baptist. Avocations: golf, gardening, camping, computers. Home: 120 Eve Ln Conway AR 72032 Office: Conway Aviation 425 6th St Conway AR 72032

PETERSEN, MARTIN EUGENE, museum curator; b. Grafton, Iowa, Apr. 21, 1931; s. Martin S. and Martha Dorothea (Paulsen) P. B.A., State U. Iowa, 1951, M.A., 1957; postgrad., The Hague (Netherlands), 1964. Curator San Diego Mus. Art, 1957-96; advisor Olaf Wieghorst Mus., El Cajon, Calif., 1996—; extension instr. U. Calif., 1958, lectr., 1960. Author art catalogues, books, articles in field. Served with AUS, 1952-54. Mem. So. Calif. Art Historians. Home: 4571 Narragansett Ave San Diego CA 92107-2915

PETERSEN, MICHAEL KEVIN, internist, osteopathic physician; b. Petaluma, Calif., Aug. 11, 1959; s. Richard Frederick and Marilyn Floy (Hough) P.; m. Marianne Cook, Apr. 24, 1981; children: Alayna, Natalie, Jessica, Erik. Student, Brigham Young U., 1977-78, Santa Rosa Jr. Coll., 1981-83; BA, Sonoma State U., 1986; DO, U. Osteo. Medicine and Health, 1991. Missionary Canada Toronto Mission, 1979-81; data quality control analyst Union Pacific R.R., San Francisco, 1981-83; rsch. assoc. dept. biochemistry, biophysics U. Calif., San Francisco, 1984-86; scientist molecular genetics group Henkel Rsch. Corp., Santa Rosa, Calif., 1987; intern U. Nev., Reno, 1991, resident, 1992-94, chief resident of internal medicine, 1993-94; med. dir. Rogue Med. Group, Grants Pass, Oreg., 1994—, Rogue River (Oreg.) Rural Health Clinic, 1996—; CEO MutualMed Pharm. Corp., 1996—. Author: (computer software) Heart sounds and phonocardiogram simulator, 1989. V.p. program, bd. dirs., exec. bd. Boy Scouts Am., Crater Lake Coun., 1996—. Capt. USAR, 1989—. Mem. ACP, AMA, Am. Osteo. Assn., Assn. Mil. Surgeons U.S., Sigma Xi. LDS Ch. Avocations: fly fishing, volleyball, guitar playing. Office: Rogue Med Group 1465 NE 7th St Grants Pass OR 97526-1303

PETERSEN, RICHARD HERMAN, government executive, aeronautical engineer; b. Quincy, Ill., Oct. 9, 1934; s. Herman Hiese and Nancy (Getty) P.; m. Joandra Windsor Shenk, Sept. 15, 1959; children: Eric Norman, Kristin. BS in Aero. Engring., Purdue U., 1956, Dr. Engring. (hon.), 1986; MS in Aeronautics, Calif. Inst. Tech., 1957; D in Pub. Service (hon.), George Washington U., 1987; DSc (hon.), Coll. of William and Mary, 1992. Rsch. engr. NASA Ames Rsch. Ctr., Moffett Field, Calif., 1957-63, aerospace engr., 1963-65, 66-70, br. chief, 1970-73, div. chief, 1975-80; aerospace engr. NASA, Washington, 1965-66; exec. Nielsen Engring. & Rsch. Inc., Mountain View, Calif., 1973-75; dep. dir. NASA Langley Research Ctr., Hampton, Va., 1980-85, dir., 1985-91; assoc. adminstr. Aeronautics and Space Tech. NASA Hdqrs., Washington, 1991-93, retired, 1993; aerospace cons., 1993—. 1st lt. USAF, 1957-60. Recipient Disting. Alumnus award Purdue U., 1980, Meritorious Exec. award U.S. Pres., 1982, Disting. Exec. award U.S. Pres., 1989; Sloan exec. fellow Stanford U., 1973. Fellow AIAA (bd. dirs. 1984-90, Sylvanus A. Reed Aeronautics award 1991), Nat. Acad. Engring. Republican. Avocations: golf, skiing. Home and office: 6 Bray Wood Williamsburg VA 23185-5504

PETERSEN, ROBERT ALLEN, pediatric ophthalmologist; b. N.Y.C., Dec. 30, 1933; s. Harold Marinus and Elinor Louise (Buckley) P.; m. Veronica Margiana Stinnes, Dec. 22, 1956; children: Anne, Catherine, John. BS, CUNY, 1955; MD, Columbia U., 1959, DrMedSc, 1964. Diplomate Am. Bd. Ophthalmology. Med. resident Presbyn. Hosp., N.Y.C., 1959-61; USPHS postdoctoral fellow Columbia U. Coll. Physicians and Surgeons, N.Y.C., 1961-62; USPHS preclin. trainee Howe Lab. of Ophthalmology, MEEI, Boston, 1962-63; resident in ophthalmology Mass. Eye and Ear Infirmary, Boston, 1963-66; instr. in ophthalmology to asst. prof. Harvard Med. Sch., Boston, 1970—; assoc. in ophthalmology to sr. assoc. Children's Hosp., Boston, 1966—. Contbr. over 40 articles to profl. jours. Cons., vision task force Mass. Dept. Pub. Health, 1981-85. Major U.S. Army, 1967-69, South Vietnam. Various rsch. grants NIH, 1961-63, 94—. Fellow Am. Acd. Ophthalmology, Am. Acad. Pediatrics; mem. Am. Assn. for Pediatric Ophthalmology and Strabismus (bd. dirs. 1974-76, edn. com. 1987-93, chair Costenbader Lectureship com. 1993-96, chair site selection com. 1995-97), New Eng. Ophthal. Soc. Mem. Soc. of Friends. Achievements include rsch. on the genetics of reinoblastoma; first to describe optic nerve hypoplasia in the children of diabetic mothers, to describe eye findings in a variety of systemic anomalies. Office: Children's Hosp 300 Longwood Ave Boston MA 02115-5724

PETERSEN, ROBERT E., publisher; b. Los Angeles, Sept. 10, 1926; s. Einar and Bertha (Putera) P.; m. Margie McNally, Jan. 26, 1963. Founder, chmn. bd. emeritus Petersen Pub. Co. (pubs. Hot Rod, Motor Trend, Car Craft, Motorcyclist, Photog., Skin Diver, Teen, Hunting, Guns & Ammo, Circle Track, Dirt Rider, Los Angeles, 1948—; owner, chmn. bd. Petersen Properties, L.A., 1996—; owner Petersen Aviation, Van Nuys, Calif., 1996—. Mem. Los Angeles Library Commn., 1963-64; Bd. dirs. Boys Club Am., past pres. Hollywood br.; bd. dirs. Thalians; founder Petersen Automotive Mus., L.A. Served with USAF. Clubs: So. Calif Safari, Balboa Bay, Catalina Island Yacht, Confrerie de la Chaine des Rotisseurs, Chevaliers du Tastevin. Office: Petersen Publishing Co 6420 Wilshire Blvd Los Angeles CA 90048-5502

PETERSEN, ROLAND, artist, printmaker; b. Endelave, Horsens, Denmark, 1926; came to U.S., 1928; m. Sharane Havlina, Aug. 12, 1950; children—Dana Mark, Maura Brooke, Julien Conrad, Karena Caia. B.A., U. Calif.-Berkeley, 1949, M.A., 1950; postgrad., Han Hofmann's Sch. Fine Arts, summers 1950-51, S.W. Hayter's Atelier 17, Paris, 1950, 63, 70, Islington Studio, London, 1976, The Print Workshop, London, 1980. Tchr. State Coll. Wash., Pullman, 1952-56; mem. faculty U. Calif., Davis, 1956-91, prof. art, 1991; ret., 1991. Exhibited one-man shows: Gump's Gallery, San Francisco, 1962, Staempfli Gallery, N.Y.C., 1963, 65, 67, Adele Bednarz Gallery, Los Angeles, 1966, 69, 70, 72, 73, 75, 76, Crocker Art Gallery, Sacramento, 1965, de Young Mus., San Francisco, 1968, La Jolla Mus., 1971, Phoenix Mus., 1972, Santa Barbara Mus., 1973, USIS sponsored touring one-man exhbn., Turkey, U. Reading, Eng., 1977, 80, U. Calif., Davis, 1978, 92, Brubaker Gallery, Sarasota, Fla., 1979, Rorick Gallery, San Francisco, 1981, 82, 83, 84, 85, Himovitz-Salomon Gallery, Sacramento, 1987-88, 91, Vanderwoude Tananbaum Gallery, N.Y.C., 1987-89, Harcourts Gallery, San Francisco, 1989, 91, 93, U. Calif., Davis, 1992, Maxwell Galleries, San Francisco, 1995, Endelave (Denmark) Mus., 1996; group shows include Calif. Palace Legion of Honor, San Francisco Art Inst., 1962, Mus. Art, Carnegie Inst., Pitts., 1964, Obelisk Gallery, Washington, John Herron Art Inst., Indpls., 1964, Pa. Acad. Fine Arts, Phila., Crocker Art Gallery, Sacramento, 1965, 81, Art Inst. Chgo., 1965, Va. Mus. Fine Arts, Richmond, 1966, U. Ariz. Art Gallery, Tucson, 1967, Am. Cultural Center, Paris, 1971, Nat. Gallery, Washington, 1972, Otis Art Inst. Gallery, Los Angeles, 1974, Auerbach Fine Art Gallery, London, 1977, U. Wis., Madison, 1977, Bklyn. Mus., 1978, U. Ill., 1978, U. Nev., Las Vegas, 1980, Brubaker Gallery, Sarasota, Fla., 1983, U.S.A. World Print Council, San Francisco, Nat. Mus., Singapore, Nat. Gallery, Bangkok, Thailand, Amerika Haus, Berlin, Malmo Konsthall, Sweden, Museo Carrillo Gil, Mexico City, all 1984-86, Crocker Art Mus., 1991, Fresno Met. Mus., 1992, Hall of Pictures, Uman, Russia, 1992, Calif. State U., L.A., 1992, San Bernardino, 1993 Pence Gallery, Davis, Calif., 1993, Artists Contemporary Gallery, Sacramento, 1994, Andre Milan Gallery, Sao Paulo, Brazil, 1995; represented in permanent collections: de Young Mus., San Francisco, San Francisco Mus. Modern Art, Va. Mus. Fine Arts, Richmond, Mus. Modern Art, N.Y.C., Phila. Mus. Art, Whitney Mus. Am. Art, Phoenix Mus., Santa Barbara Mus., Musée Municipal, Brest, France, Smithsonian Instn. Nat. Collection Fine Arts & Archives of Am. Art, Hirschorn Coll., Washington, others. Served with USN, 1944-46, PTO. Recipient numerous prizes and awards, 1950—; Guggenheim fellow, 1963; U. Calif. creative arts fellow, 1967, 70, 77; Fulbright grantee, 1970. Mem. AAUP, San Francisco Art Assn., Calif. Soc. Printmakers. Home: 6 Lanai Way PO Box 1 Dillon Beach CA 94929-0001 Office: John Natsoulas Gallery Davis CA 95616

PETERSEN, ULRICH, geology educator; b. Negritos, Peru, Dec. 1, 1927; s. Georg and Harriet (Bluhme) P.; m. Edith Martensen, Apr. 27, 1952 (dec. Aug. 1978); children: Erich, Armin (dec.), Heidi.; m. Eileen Bourque, June 19, 1982. Mining Engr., Escuela Nacional de Ingenieros, Lima, Peru, 1954; M.A., Harvard U., 1955, Ph.D., 1963. Geologist Instituto Geológico del Peru and Instituto Nacional de Investigación y Fomento Mineros, 1946-51; geologist Cerro de Pasco Corp., Peru, 1951-54; asst. chief geologist Cerro de Pasco Corp., 1956-57, chief geologist, 1958-63; lectr. Harvard, 1963-66; assoc. prof. Harvard U., 1966-69, prof. mining geology, 1969-81, Harry C. Dudley prof. econ. geology, 1981-95; cons. geologist, 1963—, prof. emeritus, 1996—. Named comendador de la orden al Merito por Servicios Distinguidos Peru, 1968; recipient A. von Humboldt rsch. award, 1992-93. Mem. Soc. Econ. Geologists (pres. 1988-89), Geol. Soc. Am., Soc. Geologica del Peru (hon.), Am. Inst. Mining and Metall. Engrs. Home: 414 Marsh St Belmont MA 02178-1109 Office: 20 Oxford St Cambridge MA 02138-2902

PETERSEN, WILLIAM OTTO, lawyer; b. Chgo., Nov. 28, 1926; s. William Ferdinand and Alma Schmidt P.; m. Jane Browne, Nov. 25, 1978. AB cum laude, Harvard U., 1949, LLB, 1952. Bar: Ill., 1952. Atty. No. Trust. Co., Chgo., 1952-55; ptnr. Vedder, Price, Kaufman & Kamholz, Chgo., 1955-97. Mem. exec. bd. Ct. Theatre, 1992—; mem. vis. to U. Chgo. Libr., 1992—; bd. dirs. Chgo. Youth Ctrs., 1958—, pres., 1971, 72; bd. dirs., v.p. Luther I. Replogle Found., Chgo. and Washington, 1986—. With USN, 1944-46. Mem. ABA, Ill. State Bar Assn., Chgo. Bar Assn. (chmn. corp. law com. 1976), Racquet Club of Chgo. (pres. 1981, 82), Univ. Club, Lake Geneva (Wis.) Country Club, Lake Geneva Yacht Club, Caxton Club. Lutheran. Home: 1120 N Lake Shore Dr Chicago IL 60611-1042

PETERSEN-FREY, ROLAND, manufacturing executive; b. Hamburg, Fed. Republic Germany, Aug. 17, 1937; came to U.S., 1958; s. Georg and Erna (Coltzau) P.-F.; m. Pamela Susan Mobley, Feb. 2, 1993; children: Martin, Anya, Daniel. BA in Fin., CUNY, 1967, MA in Fin., 1970. Asst. v.p. Mfrs. Hanover, N.Y.C., 1961-70; v.p. gen. mgr. Rusch Inc., N.Y.C., 1970-75; CEO, chmn. bd. dirs. Inmed Corp., Atlanta, 1975-89; chmn. bd. Burrellco, Inc., Atlanta, 1989-90; bd. dirs. Albert Internat., Gainesville, Ga.; chmn. bd. Magnolia Studios, Atlanta, 1991—; mng. ptnr. Bunter Holdings Ltd., Atlanta, chmn. bd. Bd. dirs. Metro. Atlanta chpt. ARC. Served with U.S. Army, 1959-61. Fellow Inst. Dirs. Republican. Club: WCT Peachtree Tennis (Atlanta). Avocations: tennis, hiking, swimming. Office: Magnolia Studios Inc 120 Interstate North Pkwy SE Atlanta GA 30339-2164

PETERSON, ALFRED EDWARD, family physician; b. Bridgeport, Conn., Mar. 23, 1922; s. Carl Emil Rudolf and Elin Maria (Lindholm) P.; m. June Meadows, May 27, 1944; children: Christina, Elin, Martha, Amy. BA, Dartmouth Coll., 1946; MD, U. Vt., 1950. Diplomate Nat. Bd. Med. Examiners. Intern Binghamton (N.Y.) City Hosp., 1950-51; pvt. practice, Binghamton, N.Y., 1952—; a founding mem. Chenango Bridge Med. Group; sch. physician Chenango Forks (N.Y.) Ctrl. Schs., 1953-94. Bd. dirs. Chenango Emergency Squad, Binghamton, 1980-85, Robert W. Smith Found., Rotary Club, 1980—; bd. dirs. med. records Broome C.C., Binghamton, 1988—. Capt. USAAF, 1943-45. Fellow Am. Acad. Family Physicians; mem. AMA, N.Y. State Med. Soc., Broome County Med. Soc., N.Y. State Acad. Family Physicians. Democrat. Avocations: cabinet making, environmental and animal welfare causes, travel, history. Office: Chenango Bridge Med Group 91 Chenango Bridge Rd Binghamton NY 13901-1293

PETERSON, ALLEN JAY, lawyer, educator; b. Los Alamos, N.C., Oct. 26, 1949; s. Lyle Jay and Lois May (Richards) P.; m. Beverly White, May 27, 1989; children: Elizabeth Bishop, Adam Bryant. AA, St. Petersburg Jr. Coll., 1969; BA, Davidson Coll., 1971; postgrad., Harvard U., 1972; JD, U. N.C., 1976. Bar: N.C. 1974, U.S. Dist. Ct. (we. dist.) N.C. 1976. Ptnr. James, McElroy & Diehl, Charlotte, N.C., 1976-84, Howell & Peterson, Burnsville, N.C., 1984-87, Norris & Peterson, Burnsville, N.C., 1987-94; v.p., gen. counsel North State Foods, Inc., 1995—; constnl. law instr. U. N.C., Charlotte, 1977-78. Sunday sch. tchr. Higgins Meml. Meth. Ch., Burnsville, 1991-93, mem. adminstrv. bd., 1990-93. Mem. Am. Assn. Trial Lawyers, N.C. Acad. Trial Lawyers. Avocation: trout fishing. Home: RR 6 Box 944 Burnsville NC 28714-9632

PETERSON, AMY, Olympic athlete; b. Maplewood, Minn., 1971. Bronze medalist, women's 500m short-track speedskating Olympic Games, Lillehammer, Norway, 1994; Bronze medalist, women's 3000m short-track speedskating Olympic Games, 1994. Office: US Olympic Committee 1750 E Boulder St Colorado Springs CO 80909-5724

PETERSON, ANN SULLIVAN, physician, health care consultant; b. Rhinebeck, N.Y., Oct. 11, 1928; A.B., Cornell U., 1950, M.D., 1954; M.S. (Alfred P. Sloan fellow 1979-80), M.I.T., 1980. Diplomate Am. Bd. Internal Medicine. Intern, Cornell Med. Div.-Bellevue Hosp., N.Y.C., 1954-55, resident, 1955-57; fellow in medicine and physiology Meml.-Sloan Kettering Cancer Ctr., Cornell Med. Coll., N.Y.C., 1957-60; instr. medicine Georgetown U. Sch. Medicine, Washington, 1962-65, asst. prof., 1965-69, asst. dir. clin. research unit, 1962-69; assoc. prof. medicine U. Ill., Chgo., 1969-72, asst. dean, 1969-71, assoc. dean, 1971-72; assoc. prof. medicine, assoc. dean Coll. Physicians and Surgeons, Columbia U., N.Y.C., 1972-80; assoc. prof. medicine, assoc. dean Cornell U. Med. Coll., N.Y.C., 1980-83; assoc. dir. div. med. edn. AMA, Chgo., 1983-86, dir. div. grad. med. edn., 1986-89; v.p. Mgmt. Cons. Corp., 1989-93; ind. cons., Chgo., 1993—; mem. bd. regents Uniformed Svcs. U. of Health Scis., 1984-90. John and Mary R. Markle scholar, 1965-70. Fellow ACP; mem. Mortar Board, Alpha Omega Alpha, Alpha Epsilon Delta. Contbr. articles to med. jours.

PETERSON, ARTHUR LAVERNE, former college president; b. Glyndon, Minn., June 27, 1926; s. John M. and Hilda C. (Moline) P.; m. Connie Lucille Harr, June 14, 1952; children: Jon Martin, Rebecca Ruth, Donna Harr, Ingrid Bliss. AB, Yale U., 1947; MSPA, U. So. Calif., 1949; postgrad., U. Chgo., 1949-50; PhD, U. Minn., 1962; LLD, Lebanon Valley Coll., 1988. Mem. Wis. State Legislature, 1951-55; from instr. to asst. prof. polit. sci. U. Wis., Eau Claire, 1954-60; assoc. prof. to prof. polit. sci. Ohio Wesleyan U., Delaware, 1961-65, 70-80; pres. Am. Grad. Sch. Internat. Mgmt., Phoenix, 1966-70; dean spl. programs Eckerd Coll., St. Petersburg, Fla., 1980-84, dir. Acad. Sr. Profls., 1987-94; pres. Lebanon Valley Coll., Annville, Pa., 1984-87; bd. dirs. Arnold Industries; asst. to chmn. Rep. Nat. Com., Washington, 1960-61; founding dir. Ctr. Internat. Bus., L.A., 1969-70; cons. Novin Inst. Polit. Affairs, Tehran, Iran, 1973; exec. dir. Fla. Assn. Colls. and Univs., 1988—. Author: McCarthyism: Ideology and Foundations, 1962; co-author: Electing the President, 1968; contbr. articles to scholarly jours. Chmn. Ohio Civil Rights Commn., 1963-65; dep. chmn. Republican Nat. Com., 1965-66; mem. Ohio Ethics Commn., 1976-80. Served to capt. USMC, 1951-52; Korea. Citizenship Clearing House Nat. Faculty fellow, 1960; recipient citation for excellence Sigma Phi Epsilon, 1977; Marshall award Ohio Wesleyan Students, 1979. Mem. Am. Polit. Sci. Assn., Am. Judicature Soc. (dir. 1975—), Soc. Polit. Enquiries (pres. 1985—), Acad. Polit. Sci., Pi Sigma Alpha (dir. 1972—), Phi Mu Alpha Sinfonia, Omicron Delta Kappa. Republican. Mem. United Ch. of Christ. Lodges: Rotary, Masons. Avocations: sailing; flying; music. Home: 552 Johns Pass Ave Saint Petersburg FL 33708-2366 *Give the most you can give, of what you are and what you believe, both talent and treasure - where you are - now!.*

PETERSON, BARBARA ANN BENNETT, history educator, television personality; b. Portland, Oreg., Sept. 6, 1942; d. George Wright and Hope (Chatfield) Bennett; m. Frank Lynn Peterson, July 1, 1967. BA, BS, Oreg. State U., 1964; MA, Stanford U., 1965; PhD, U. Hawaii, 1978; PhD (hon.), London Inst. Applied Rsch., 1991, Australian Inst. Coordinated R, 1995. Prof. history U. Hawaii, Honolulu, 1967-96; prof. emeritus history, 1996—; chmn. social scis. dept. U. Hawaii, Honolulu, 1971-73, 75-76, asst. dean, 1973-74; prof. Asian history and European colonial history and world problems Chapman Coll. World Campus Afloat, 1974, European overseas exploration, expansion and colonialism U. Colo., Boulder, 1978; assoc. prof. U. Hawaii-Manoa Coll. Continuing Edn., 1981; Fulbright prof. history Wuhan (China) U., 1988-89; Fulbright rsch. prof. Sophia U., Japan, 1978; rsch. assoc. Bishop Mus., 1995—; lectr. Capital Spkrs., Washington, 1987—; tchr. Hawaii State Ednl. Channel, 1993—. Co-author: Women's Place is in the History Books, Her Story, 1962-1980: A Curriculum Guide for American History Teachers, 1980; author: America in British Eyes, 1988; editor: Notable Women of Hawaii, 1984, (with W. Solheim) The Pacific Region, 1990, 91, American History: 17th, 18th and 19th Centuries, 1993, America: 19th and 20th Centuries, 1993, John Bull's Eye on America, 1995; assoc. editor Am. Nat. Biography; contbr. articles to profl. publs. Participant People-to-People Program, Eng., 1964, Expt. in Internat. Living Program, Nigeria, 1966; chmn. 1st Nat. Women's History Week, Hawaii, 1982; pres. Bishop Mus. Coun., 1993-94; active Hawaii Commn. on Status of Women. Fulbright scholar, Japan, 1967, China, 1988-89; NEH-Woodrow Wilson fellow Princeton U., 1980; recipient state proclamations Gov. of Hawaii, 1982, City of Honolulu, 1982, Outstanding Tchr. of Yr. award Wuhan (China), U., 1988, Medallion of Excellence award Am. Biog. Assn., 1989, Woman of Yr. award, 1991; inducted into the Women's Hall of Fame, Seneca Falls, N.Y., 1991; named Hawaii State Mixed Doubles Tennis Champion, 1985. Fellow World Literacy Acad. (Eng.), Internat. Biog. Assn. (Cambridge, Eng. chpt.); mem. AAUW, Am. Hist. Assn. (mem. numerous coms.), Am. Studies Assn. (pres. 1984-85), Fulbright Alumni Assn. (founding pres. Hawaii chpt. 1984-88, mem. nat. steering com. chairwomen Fulbright Assn. ann. conf. 1990), Am. Coun. on Edn., Maison Internat. des Intellectuals, France, Hawaii Found. History and Humanities (mem. editl. bd. 1972-73), Hawaii Found. Women's History, Hawaii Hist. Assn., Nat. League Am. Pen Women (contest chairperson 1986), Women in Acad. Adminstrn., Phi Beta Phi, Phi Kappa Phi. Avocation: tennis.

PETERSON, BARBARA MAE BITTNER OWECKE, artist, nurse, realtor; b. Winona, Minn., Nov. 25, 1932; d. Adelbert Paul and Hermanda Gilda (Pellowski) Bittner; m. Jerome Francis Owecke, Nov. 28, 1953 (div. 1974); children: Paul Richard Owecke, Michael Jerome Owecke, Margaret Francis Owecke (dec.), Stacy Ann Owecke, Wendy Alane Owecke (dec.), James William Owecke, William Harold Owecke; m. Roy Eugene Peterson, May 28, 1983. RN, St. Francis Sch. Nursing, 1953; B Individualized Study, George Mason U., 1994. RN, Va., Wis., Mich., Ill., Ohio. Staff nurse Commonwealth Hosp., Fairfax, Va., 1973-74; realtor Century 21 United, Fairfax, Va., 1974-91; telemetry nurse Fairfax Hosp., 1974-76; med. sales rep. CB Fleet Pharm., Lynchburg, Va., 1976-78; territory mgr. Bristol-Myers Squibb, Northern Va., Washington, 1978-92; ret., 1992; v.p. B&R Farm, Goldvein, Va., 1989—; artist Goldvein, Va., 1993—; bd. dirs. Fauquier Artists' Alliance, Warrenton, Va., pres., 1994-95. Exhibited in group shows at Alexandria Art League, 1994, Ctr. for Creative Art, 1994-95, George Mason U., 1994. RN Fauquier Free Clinic, Warrenton, 1993—; mem. Goldvein Vol. Fire Dept., 1989-94. Mem. Alexandria Art League, Va. Mus. Fine Arts, Nat. Artists' Equity Assn., Va. Thoroughbred Assn., Va. Horseman's Assn. Roman Catholic. Avocations: training, breeding and riding thoroughbred horses, tennis. Home: 13483 Oakview Dr Goldvein VA 22720 Office: BaMaBi PO Box 100 Goldvein VA 22720

PETERSON, BONNIE LU, mathematics educator; b. Escanaba, Mich., Jan. 19, 1946; d. Herbert Erick and Ruth Albertha (Erickson) P. AA, Bay de Noc C.C., 1966; BS, No. Mich. U., 1968, MA in Math., 1969; EdD, Tenn. State U., 1989. Tchr. Lapeer (Mich.) High Sch., 1969-70, Nova High Sch., Ft. Lauderdale, Fla., 1970-79, Hendersonville (Tenn.) High Sch., 1979—; adj. faculty Vol. State C.C., Gallatin, Tenn., 1989—; chair Sumner County Schs. Tchrs. Insvc., Gallatin, 1990-92; mem. math. specialist team State of Tenn., 1991-93; spkr. in field. Mem. edn. com. Vision 2000-City of Hendersonville, 1993-94. Tenn. State Bd. grantee, 1989-92; Woodrow Wilson fellow, 1993; State-Level Presdl. awardee, 1994, 95, 96; Tandy Scholars award, 1995. Mem. ASCD, Nat. Coun. Tchrs. Math. (chair workshop support com. 1990), Tenn. Math. Tchrs. Assn., Mid. Tenn. Math. Tchrs. Assn. (pres.), Phi Delta Kappa (past pres.). Avocations: cooking, counted cross stitch. Home: 1081 Coon Creek Rd Dickson TN 37055-4014

PETERSON, CARL, professional football team executive; b. Long Beach, Calif.; 1 child, Dawn. BS in Kinesiology, UCLA, 1966, M in Kinesiology, 1967, D in Adminstrn. in Higher Edn., 1970. Asst. coach Wilson High Sch., Calif., 1966, Loyola High Sch., 1967-68, Calif. State U., Somona, 1969-70; head coach Calif. State U., 1970-72; receivers coach UCLA, 1972-74, receivers coach, adminstrv. asst., 1974-76; coach recievers and tight ends Phila. Eagles, 1976, dir. player personnel, 1977-82; pres., gen. mgr. Phila. Stars, 1982-88; pres., gen. mgr., COO Kansas City Chiefs, Mo., 1988—; pres., CEO PhillySport Mag., Phila.; mem. nat. bd. Maxwell Football Club and Pop Warner Little Scholar Orgn. Recipient USFL Exec. of Yr. award Sporting News, 1983, 84. Mem. Young Pres. Orgn. (Kansas City chpt.). Office: Kansas City Chiefs 1 Arrowhead Dr Kansas City MO 64129-1651*

PETERSON, CARL ERIC, metals company executive, banker; b. Wareham, Mass., Apr. 8, 1944; s. E. Gunnar and Ruth (Kramer) P.; m. Frances Harkness, Sept. 7, 1966; children—Robin, Alec Harkness. BA, Brown U., 1966; MA, U. Pa., 1971; grad., Sch. for Internat. Banking, 1974, Stonier Grad. Sch. Banking, 1978. With R.I. Hosp. Trust Nat. Bank, Providence, 1971-82; with Engelhard Corp., Iselin, N.J., 1982-85, Dryvit System, Inc., West Warwick, R.I., 1986, Gerald Metals, Inc., Stamford, Conn., 1987—; lectr. World Gold Markets Conf., London, 1981, Am. Mining Congress,

Phoenix, 1984, 12th Internat. Precious Metals Inst. Conf., Boston, 1988. Bd. dirs., mem. adv. coun. Internat. House of R.I., 1974-79; mem. of corp. Woods Hole Oceanographic Instn., 1981-94, audit com., 1988-94; mem. R.I. Pub. Expenditure Coun., 1974-82, Internat. Ctr. New Eng., 1980-81. Mem. Hope Club (Providence), Willow Dell Beach Club (Matunuck, R.I.), N.Y. Yacht Club. Episcopalian. Clubs: Hope (Providence); Willow Dell Beach (Matunuck, R.I.). Office: Gerald Metals Inc High Ridge Park Stamford CT 06905-1328

PETERSON, CHARLES GORDON, retired lawyer; b. Lansing, Mich., May 21, 1926; s. Russell V. and Edna E. (Jones) P.; m. Clara Elizabeth Parmelee, Mar. 8, 1947; children—Wendy, Pamela, Christopher. B.S., Columbia U. Sch. Gen. Studies, 1954; LL.B., Columbia U. Sch. Law, 1956. Bar: N.Y., 1957. Legal assoc. Beekman & Bogue, N.Y.C., 1956-67; mem. Gaston & Snow, N.Y.C., 1967-91; of counsel Reid & Priest, N.Y.C., 1991-93; ret., 1993. Trustee The Riverside Ch., N.Y.C., 1968-80, 82-89, mem. bd. deacons, 1960-68; pres. Lincoln Guild Housing Corp., N.Y.C., 1961-62, 84-87, v.p., 1987-89, 94-96, bd. dirs., 1961-62, 84-89, 94-96. Mem. Phi Beta Kappa. Republican. Mem. United Ch. of Christ. Avocations: piano, reading, travel. Home: 303 W 66th St Apt 20ee New York NY 10023-6347

PETERSON, CHARLES HAYES, lawyer; b. St. Louis, May 8, 1938; s. Edmund Herbert and Dorothy Marie (Brennan) P.; m. Auli Irene Ahonen, Nov. 28, 1981; children: Mika, Charles, Michael, Katja. BS, U.S. Naval Acad., 1960; MBA, Stanford U., 1971, JD, 1974. Commd. ensign USN, 1956, advanced through grades to capt., resigned, 1969; with USNR, 1969-89; counsel Gen. Electric, San Jose, Calif., 1973-79; div. counsel Syracuse, N.Y., 1980-83; v.p. COGEMA, Inc., Washington, 1983-87; pres. NUEXCO Trading Co., Washington, 1987-95; spl. counsel Morgan, Lewis & Bockius, LLP, 1995—. Recipient Meritorious Service medal State of Calif., 1986. Mem. Calif. and Washington Bar Assns. Lutheran. Home: 8407 River Rock Ter Bethesda MD 20817-4300 Office: Morgan Lewis & Bockius 1800 M St NW Ste 500 Sout Washington DC 20036-5802

PETERSON, CHARLES LOREN, agricultural engineer, educator; b. Emmett, Idaho, Dec. 27, 1938; s. Clarence James and Jane (Shelton) P.; m. Julianne Rekow, Sept. 7, 1962; children—Val, Karl, Marianne, Cheryl Ann, Charles Lauritz, Brent. B.S., U. Idaho, 1961, M.S., 1965; Ph.D. in Engring. Sci, Wash. State U., Pullman, 1973. Registered profl. engr., Idaho, Wash. Exptl. engr. Oliver Corp., Charles City, Iowa, 1961; farmer Emmett, 1962-65; instr. math. Emmett High Sch., 1962-63; instr. freshman engring., then extension agrl. engr. U. Idaho, Moscow, 1963-67; prof. agrl. engring. U. Idaho, 1973—; asst. prof. Wash. State U., 1968-73; cons. in field. Contbr. numerous articles profl. jours. Rep. precinct committeeman, 1972-75; sec. 5th legis. dist. Idaho, 1976-79; mem. Latah County Planning and Zoning Commn., 1980-90, 1st counselor Pullman Wash. Stake Presidency, 1989—. Grantee Wash. Potato, 1971-73, U & I, Inc., 1974, Amalgamated Sugar Co., 1974, 1992-95m Nat. Biodiesel Bd. 1994-95, BPA/USDOE 1993-95, Beet Sugar Devel. Found., 1975-85, Phillips Chem. Co., 1976-80, USDA, 1976-95, Idaho Dept. Water Resources, Energy div., 1992-93, Star Found., 1978, U.S. Dept. Energy and Alaska Regional Bioenergy Program, 1994—; Recipient Excellence in Rsch. award U. Idaho, 1992-93, Best in Category award Transp. Tech. U.S. Dept. Energy, 1994, Biomass Energy Program Outstanding Achievement award, 1996, Silver Beaver award Boy Scouts Am., 1996, Regional Bioenergy Program award for excellence in rsch. U.S. Dept. Energy, 1996. Fellow Am. Soc. Agrl. Engrs. (chmn. Inland Empire chpt. 1978-79, chmn. nat. environ. stored products com. 1978-80, chmn. biomass energy com. 1985-86, chmn. Pacific N.W. region 1984-85, chmn. T-11 Energy com. 1989-90, dir. dist. 5, 1989-91, Engr. of Year award Inland Empire chpt., 1978, nat. Blue Ribbon award 1975, Engr. of Yr. award Pacific N.W. sect. 1990, Outstanding Paper award 1990); mem. Nat. Soc. Profl. Engrs., Am. Soc. Engring. Edn., Potato Assn. Am., Am. Soc. Sugarbeet Technologists, Idaho Soc. Profl. Engrs., Nat. Assn. Colls. and Tchrs. of Agriculture (Tchr. award 1990), Soc. Automotive Engrs., Phi Kappa Phi (Disting. Faculty award Idaho chpt. 1997), Sigma Xi, Gamma Sigma Delta (Outstanding Rsch. in Agriculture award 1989). Mem. LDS Ch. Office: U Idaho Agrl Engring JML # 81-b Moscow ID 83844-2040

PETERSON, CHARLES MARQUIS, medical educator; b. N.Y.C., Mar. 8, 1943; s. Charles William and Elisabeth (Marquis) P.; m. Karen Pielop, Dec. 26, 1996; children: Caroline, Elisabeth. BA in cum laude, Carleton Coll., 1965; MD, Columbia Coll., 1969. Intern Harlem Hosp., 1969-70, resident, 1970-73, chief resident, 1972-73; guest investigator, asst. physician The Rockefeller Univ., 1971-73, assoc. physician, 1973-78, asst. prof., 1973-78, assoc. prof., 1978-84; clin. prof. medicine U. So. Calif., 1985—; vis. clin. fellow Columbia Coll. Physicians and Surgeons, 1970-73; asst. vis. physician Harlem Hosp., 1973-84; cons. pediatrics Cornell U. Med. Ctr., 1975-84; assoc. attending medicine Beth Israel Med. Ctr., 1976-84; lectr. Mt. Sinai Sch. Medicine, 1977—; adj. assoc. prof. dept. medicine Cornell U. Med. Ctr., 980-84; assoc. attending physician dept. medicine N.Y. Hosp., 1980-84; attending physician in medicine Cottage Hosp., Santa Barbara, Calif., 1984—; dir. rsch., med. dir. Sansum Med. Rsch. Found., 1984-96, sr. scientist, 1997—; dir. diabetes Endocrine Clinic, Santa Barbara County, 1989—; CEO, Sansum Med. Rsch. Found., 1995-96. Author: Self Monitoring of Blood Glucose: A Physician's Guide, 1981, Take Charge of Your Diabetes, 1982, Diabetes Management in the 80's, 1982; co-author: The Diabetes Self-Care Method, 1990, A Touch of Diabetes, 1991, Vivere con il Diabete, 1992, and many others; mem. editorial bd. Diabetes Care, 1980-84, Diabetes in the News, 1985—, Diabetes News Bureau, 1985—, Diabetes Profl., editor-in-chief, 1988-91, Diabetic Nephropathy/Jour. of Diabetic Complications, 1982-91; contbr. numerous articles to Prensa Medica, Jour. Lab. and Clin. Medicine, New England Jour. Medicine, Annals of Internal Medicine, Archives of Neurology, Blood, Jour. Nat. Med. Assn., Am. Jour. Obstetrics and Gynecology, many others. Mem. med. adv. bd. Cooley's Anemia Vols., 1975-84; bd. mem. Diabetes Control Found., 1980-88; dir. Diabetes Self Care Program, 1978-84, med. dir., 1981-84; bd. mem. Leake and Watts, 1978-84, Gifts for Life, 1986-89; bd. dirs. Sports Tng. Inst., 1984-86, others. Fellow ACP; mem. AAAS, Am. Chem. Soc., Am. Diabetes Assn., Am. Fedn. Clin. Rsch., Am. Med. Writers Assn., Am. Soc. Clin. Investigation, Am. Soc. Hematology, Am. Soc. Pharmacology and Experimental Therapeutics, Coun. Biology Editors, Diabetes and Pregnancy Study Group West (founder), N.Y. Acad. Scis., Rsch. Soc. Alcoholsim, Soc. Experimental Medicine and Biology, Am. Med. Writers Assn., Am. Diabetes Assn. (founding bd. mem. Santa Barbara chpt. 1988—, pres. 1991-92), Sigma Xi. Home: 1075 San Antonio Creek Rd Santa Barbara CA 93111-1309 Office: Sansum Med Rsch Found 2219 Bath St Santa Barbara CA 93105-4321

PETERSON, CHASE N., university president; b. Logan, Utah, Dec. 27, 1929; s. E.G. and Phebe (Nebeker) P.; m. Grethe Ballif, 1956; children: Erika Elizabeth, Stuart Ballif, Edward Chase. A.B., Harvard U., 1952, M.D., 1956. Diplomate: Am. Bd. Internal Medicine. Asst. prof. medicine U. Utah Med. Sch., 1965-67; assoc. Salt Lake Clinic; dean admissions and fin. aids to students Harvard U., 1967-72, v.p. univ., 1972-78; v.p. health scis. U. Utah, Salt Lake City, 1978-83, prof. medicine, 1983—, pres., 1983-91, clin. prof. medicine, 1991—; pres. emeritus U. Utah, Salt Lake City, 1992—; bd. dirs. First Security Corp., Utah Power & Light Co., D.C. Tanner Co., OEC Med. Systems. Mem. Nat. Assn. State Univs. and Land-Grant Colls. (chmn. 1988-89, chair U.S. Ofc. Tech. Assessment adv. bd. 1990-92). Home: 66 Thaynes Canyon Dr Park City UT 84060-6711 Office: U Utah 1C26 Sch Medicine Salt Lake City UT 84112

PETERSON, COLLIN C., congressman; b. Fargo, N.D., June 29, 1944; children: Sean, Jason, Elliott. BA in Bus. Adminstrn. and Acctg., Moorhead State U., 1966. CPA, Minn. Senator State of Minn., 1976-86; mem. 102nd-105th Congresses from 7th Minn. dist., 1991—; mem. agrl. com., subcoms. gen. farm commodities, specialty crops and natural resources, livestock, environ. credit and rural devel., mem. govt. ops. com., chmn. subcom. employment housing and aviation, chmn. subcom. employment, housing and aviation, mem. 104th Cong. resource conservation com., rsch. and forestry subcom., livestock, dairy and poultry subcom., govt. reform and oversight com., nat. econ. growth com., nat. resources and regulatory affairs com.-ranking minority mem. With U.S. Army N.G., 1963-69. Mem. Am. Legion, Ducks Unltd., Elks, Sportsmen's Club, Rural Caucus, Mainstream Forum, Cormorant Lakes Sportsmen Club, Congl. Sportsmen's Caucus, Mainstream Forum, Congl. Rural Caucus. Democrat. Office: US Ho of Reps 2159 Rayburn Washington DC 20515-0107*

PETERSON, COURTLAND HARRY, law educator; b. Denver, June 28, 1930; s. Harry James and Courtney (Caple) P.; m. Susan Schwab, Gisvold, Jan. 28, 1966; children: Brooke, Linda, Patrick. B.A., U. Colo., 1951, LL.B., 1953; M.C.L., U. Chgo., 1959; J.D., U. Freiburg, Ger., 1964. Bar: Colo. 1953. Mem. faculty U. Colo. Law Sch., 1959—, prof., 1963—, dean, 1974-79, Nicholas Rosenbaum prof., 1991-94, Nicholas Doman prof. emeritus, 1995—; vis. prof. U. Calif. Law Sch., Los Angeles, 1965, Max Planck Inst., Hamburg, Ger., 1969-70, U. Tex. Law Sch., Austin, 1973-74, Summer Program Tulane U., Rodos, Greece, 1993; bd. dirs. Continuing Legal Edn. in Colo., 1974-77. Author: Die Anerkennung Auslandischer Urteile, 1964; Translator: (Bauer) An Introduction to German Law, 1965. Served to 1st lt. USAF, 1954-56. Fgn. Law fellow U. Chgo., 1957-59; Ford Found. Law Faculty fellow, 1964; Alexander von Humboldt Stiftun fellow, 1969-70. Mem. ABA, Colo. Bar Assn. (bd. govs. 1974-79), Boulder County Bar Assn., Am. Soc. Comparative Law (dir., bd. editors, treas. 1978-89, hon. pres. 1996—), Internat. Acad. Comparative Law, Am. Law Inst. Home: 205 Camden Pl Boulder CO 80302-8032 Office: U Colo Law Sch Boulder CO 80309

PETERSON, DAVE LEONARD, psychologist; b. Memphis, Nov. 29, 1952; s. Leroy Leonard and Mary Elizabeth (Linker) P.; m. Eleanor M. Hjelvik, Aug. 14, 1980. Student, U. Wis., 1972-74; BA, Sonoma State U., Rohnert Park, Calif., 1976; MA, U.S. Internat. U., San Diego, 1982, PhD, 1990. Psychology intern, 1986; forensic psychologist, forensic psychology coord. Ctrl. State Hosp., Milledgeville, Ga., 1995-97; staff sr. psychologist Winnebago (Wis.) Mental Health Inst., 1992-95. Mem. APA, Am. Psychology and Law Soc., Ga. Psychol. Assn., Mid. Ga. Psychol. Assn., Psi Chi. Avocations: philosophy, hunting, long-range rifle shooting. Home: 253 Ivey Dr SW Milledgeville GA 31061 also: PO Box 2233 Sylacauga AL 35150-5233 Office: Ctrl State Hosp Forensic Svc Divsn Milledgeville GA 31062

PETERSON, DAVID CHARLES, photojournalist; b. Kansas City, Mo., Oct. 22, 1949; s. John Edward and Florence Athene (Hobbs) P.; m. Adele Mae Johnson, Dec. 31, 1952; children: Brian David, Scott Ryun, Anna Victoria. BS in Edn., Kansas State U., 1971; BS in Journalism, U. Kans., 1973, U. Kans., 1974. Staff photographer Topeka Capital-Jour., 1975-77, Des Moines Register, 1977—. Photographer (photo essay) Shattered Dreams-Iowa's Rural Crisis, 1986 (Pulitzer prize 1987); exhibited at Creative Ctr. Photography, Tucson, 1989. Mem. Nat. Press Photographers Assn. (Nikon sabbatical 1986). Democrat. Home: 2024 35th St Des Moines IA 50310-4438 Office: Des Moines Register News Dept 715 Locust St Des Moines IA 50309-3703*

PETERSON, DAVID FREDERICK, government agency executive; b. Washington, Apr. 4, 1937; s. Victor Henry and Alice Augusta (Vogle) P.; m. Laurie A. Cadigan, June 11, 1988. A.B., Harvard U., 1959; LL.B., Cornell U., 1962. Bar: D.C. 1963. With Metromedia Inc., N.Y.C. and Los Angeles, 1963-70; exec. dir. consumer info. ctr. GSA, Washington, 1970-76, dir. consumer affairs, 1976-82, assoc. archivist for mgmt. Nat. Archives and Records Service, 1982-83; asst. archivist for Fed. Records Ctrs. Nat. Archives and Records Adminstrn., Washington, 1983-96; asst. archivist Presdl. Librs., 1996—. Served with U.S. Army, 1963. Home: 2315 N Glebe Rd Arlington VA 22207-3410 Office: Nat Archives & Records Admn 8601 Adelphi Rd College Park MD 20740-6002

PETERSON, DAVID GLENN, retired career officer; b. Seattle, May 4, 1952; s. Wilbur Glenn and Donna Jean (Nielsen) P.; m. Marjorie Ann Erickson, Aug. 6, 1977; 1 stepchild, David Charles Erickson. BA in Social Studies, McKendree Coll., 1978; postgrad., U. Okla., 1981-87. Correctional officer Minn. State Reformatory, St. Cloud, 1973-75; commd. 2d lt. U.S. Army, 1976, advanced through grades to maj., 1987, served in 7th infantry div., 1975-76, adminstrv. officer Armor Sch., 1976-80, served in 1st armored div., 1980-81, 83-84, comdr. 501st adjutant gen. co., 1981-83, deputy adjutant gen. mil. dist. Washington, 1984-87, pers. policy analyst hdqrs. dept. Army, 1987-94; ret., 1994; dir. adminstrn. Nat. Presbyn. Ch., Washington, 1994—. Elder Nat. Presbyn. Ch., Washington, 1990—; bd. dirs. Westhampton Mens Condominium Assn., 1989-93; trustee N.Y. Ave. Presbyn. Ch., Washington, 1985-87. Mem. Retired Officers Assn., Rails to Trails Conservancy, Nat. Assn. of Ch. Bus. Adminstrn. Republican. Avocations: computers, biking. Home: 4918 Albemarle St NW Washington DC 20016

PETERSON, DAVID MAURICE, plant physiologist, research leader; b. Woodward, Okla., July 3, 1940; s. Maurice Llewellyn and Katharine Anne (Jones) P.; m. Margaret Ingegerd Sundberg, June 18, 1965; children: Mark David, Elise Marie. BS, U. Calif., Davis, 1962; MS, U. Ill., 1964; PhD, Harvard U., 1968. Rsch. biologist Allied Chem. Corp., Morristown, N.J., 1970-71; plant physiologist U.S. Dept. Agr.-Agrl. Rsch. Svc., Madison, Wis., 1971—; from asst. to full prof. U. Wis., Madison, 1971—. Capt. U.S. Army, 1968-70. Fellow AAAS; mem. Am. Soc. Plant Physiologists (editorial bd. 1984-86), Am. Assn. Cereal Chemists (assoc. editor 1988-91), Crop Sci. Soc. Am. (assoc. editor 1975-78). Office: USDA Cereal Crops Rsch Unit 501 Walnut St Madison WI 53705-2334

PETERSON, DAVID ROBERT, lawyer, former Canadian government official; b. Toronto, Dec. 28, 1943; s. Clarence and Laura Marie (Scott) P.; m. Shelley Peterson, Jan. 16, 1974; children: Benjamin David, Chloe Matthews, Adam Drake Scott. BA, U. Western Ont., 1964; LLB, U. Toronto, 1967; LLD (hon.), U. Ottawa, Am. U. of Caribbean, U. Tel Aviv, U. Toronto. Bar: Ont. 1969, Queens counsel 1981. Chmn., pres. C.M. Peterson Co. Ltd., 1969-75, Cambridge Acceptance Corp., 1969-75; M.P. Ontario Parliament, Can., 1975—; leader Ont. Liberal Party, 1982; premier Province of Ont., 1985-90; sr. counsel Cassels Brock & Blackwell, Toronto, 1991—; chmn. Toronto Raptors Basketball Club, Inc.; bd. dirs. Rogers Comms., Ltd., Nat. Life Assurance Co., Industrielle-Alliance Life Assurance Co., Nat. Trust, Banque Nationale de Paris (Can.), Cascades Paperboard Internat. Inc., SHL Systemhouse, Inc., Speedy Muffler King Inc., Quorum Growth Inc., Euro-Nev. Mining Corp. Ltd. Leader of the official opposition party, Liberal Party, Ont., 1982-85; dir. Legal Svcs., Yorkville; mem. Kidney Found. Can., Ont., Cystic Fibrosis Found. Fellow McLaughlin Coll., 1985; appointed Knight of Order of Legion of Honor, Govt. France, 1994; recipient Ordre de la Pléiade, Internat. Assembly French-Speaking Parliamentarians, 1995. Mem. Law Soc. U.C., Young Pres. Orgn., London C. of C., London Hunt Country Club, London Racquets Club, Can. Club. Mem. United Ch. Christ. Avocations: theatre, riding, jogging, skiing, tennis, reading. Office: Cassels Brock & Blackwell, 40 King St W Ste 2100, Toronto, ON Canada M5H 3C2

PETERSON, DONALD CURTIS, life care executive, consultant; b. Seattle, Feb. 27, 1931; s. Arthur O. and Agnes V. (Erickson) P.; m. Marilyn Jane, June 21, 1952; children: Bruce D., Mark A., Daryl R., Debra L., Joseph J. AA, North Park Coll., 1950; cert. in mgmt., Am. Mgmt. Assn., 1965. With fgn. ops. staff Internat. Harvester Co., Chgo., 1950-54; mktg. exec. UARCO, Inc., Barrington, Ill., 1954-67; group v.p. Victor Comptometer, Lincoln, Nebr., 1967-68; pres. Nationwide Data, Wheeling, Ill., 1968-71, Nationwide Bus. Forms, Wheeling, 1968-71, Ins. Producers Bulletin, Wheeling, 1968-71, Alpha Internat., Sawyer, Mich., 1971-83; exec. dir. Freedom Sq. U.S.A., Seminole, Fla., 1983-92; adminstr., CEO Mount Miguel Covenant Village, Spring Valley, Calif., 1992—; mktg. cons. Balt. Bus. Forms., Hunt Valley, Md., 1974-76. Supr., chmn. water bd., sanitary bd. Chikaming Twp., Lakeside, Mich., 1972-76. Served with U.S. Army, 1952-57. Republican. Baptist. Home: 10405 Pine Grove St Spring Valley CA 91978-1505

PETERSON, DONALD MATTHEW, insurance company executive; b. Mt. Vernon, N.Y., Dec. 22, 1936; s. Cornelius J. and Catherine M. (Carney) P.; m. Patricia A. Frusciante, Sept. 10, 1960; children: Daniel, Linda, David, Debra, James. BA in Econs., LaSalle U., 1958. CLU; ChFC; FSA, MAAA, EA, RHU. Actuarial analyst Met. Life, N.Y.C., 1958-63; actuarial assoc. N.Am. Co. for Life and Health, Chgo., 1963-66; chmn., CEO Trustmark Ins. Co., Lake Forest, Ill., 1966—; bd. dirs. Trustmark Ins. Co., Trustmark Life Ins. Co., Star Mktg. and Adminstrs. Bd. dirs. Glenview (Ill.) Pub. Schs., 1973-76, Lake County (Ill.) United Way, 1989-96, Glenview Dist. 34 Found., 1990-93, Lake Forest Hosp., 1992—, Ill. Life Ins. Coun., 1990-94, Barat Coll., 1994—, Lake Forest Grad. Sch. Mgmt., 1995—. Mem. NALU, Nat. Assn. Health Underwriters, Am. Acad. Actuaries, Health Ins. Assn. Am. (bd. dirs. 1992—), Am. Coun. Life Ins. (bd. dirs. 1995—), Econ. Club Chgo., North Shore Country Club, Conway Farms Golf Club, Pelican Nest Golf Club. Republican. Roman Catholic. Avocations: golf, curling, swimming, running. Office: Trustmark Ins Co 400 N Field Dr Lake Forest IL 60045-4809

PETERSON, DONALD ROBERT, psychologist, educator, university administrator; b. Pillager, Minn., Sept. 10, 1923; s. Frank Gordon and Ruth (Friedland) P.; m. Jean Hole, Feb. 10, 1952 (div.); children: Wendy, Jeffrey, Roger, Lisa; m. Jane Snyder Salmon, Dec. 21, 1974. BA, U. Minn., 1948, MA, 1950, PhD, 1952. Mem. faculty U. Ill., Urbana, 1952-75, prof. clin. psychology, 1963-75, head div. clin. psychology, 1963-70, dir. Psychol. Clinic, 1961-70, dir. D. Psychology program, 1970-75; dean Grad. Sch. Applied and Profl. Psychology Rutgers U., New Brunswick, 1975-89; pres. Nat. Coun. Schs. of Profl. Psychology, 1981-83. Author: The Clinical Study of Social Behavior, 1968, Educating Professional Psychologists, 1997; co-author: Close Relationships, 1983; also articles; editor Jour. Abnormal Psychology, 1970-72. With AUS, 1943-46. Mem. N.J. Psychol. Assn., Am. Psychol. Assn. (awards for disting. contbns. to practice of psychology 1983, disting. contbns. to edn. and tng. 1989). Office: Rutgers U Grad Sch Applied & Profl Psychology New Brunswick NJ 08903

PETERSON, DONALD ROBERT, magazine editor, vintage automobile consultant; b. Sandstone, Minn., Apr. 1, 1929; s. Martin Theodore and Margaret Mildred (Dezell) P.; m. Lois Taylor, Dec. 31, 1951 (div. 1975); children: Wyatt A., Winston B., Whitney C. (dec.), Westley D., Webster E.; m. Edie Tannenbaum, Aug. 31, 1975; 1 child, Ryan Kerry. Student, U. Minn., 1947-50; B.S., Gustavus Adolphus Coll., 1952. Asst. underwriter Prudential Ins. Co. Am., Mpls., 1953-64; chief health underwriter North Central Life, St. Paul, 1964-66; pres. 1st State Bank Murdock, Minn., 1967-73, EDON, Inc., Roswell, Ga., 1974—; editor Car Collector mag., Roswell, 1977-91, editor emeritus, 1992—; v.p., dir. Classic Pub. Inc., Atlanta, 1979-97. Contbr. chpt. to book. Councilman, City of Murdock, 1968-72, mayor, 1972-74; del. State Republican Conv., 1970-72; treas. Swift County Rep. Com., 1970-73. Served with U.S. Navy, 1946-47. Recipient citation for disting. service Classic Car Club Am., 1965. Mem. Internat. Soc. Philos. Enquiry, Swift County Bankers Assn. (pres. 1970-73), Soc. Automotive Historians, Am. Legion, Mensa (pres. Ga. chpt. 1976-78), Milestone Car Soc., Classic Car Club Am. (chpt. pres. 1959, 60, 63, nat. bd. dirs. 1978-81, 97—), Rolls-Royce Owners Club, Antique Automobile Club, Vet. Motor Car Club Am., Packard Club, Horseless Carriage Club Am. Republican. Avocations: automobile collecting, internat. traveling. Home: 1400 Lake Ridge Ct Roswell GA 30076-2869

PETERSON, DONN NEAL, forensic engineer; b. Northwood, N.D., Jan. 1, 1942; s. Emil H. and Dorothy (Neal) P.; m. Lorna Jean Kappedal, July 8, 1962 (div. July 1966); m. Donna Sue Butts Daiker, Aug. 26, 1967; children: Barbara Daiker, Elizabeth Plamondon, Phoebe, Phaedra, Rosalind Peterson. BSME, U. N.D., 1963; MSME, U. Minn., 1972. Registered profl. engr. Advanced engring. courses student GE, Evendale, Ohio, 1963-66; systems engr. GE Aircraft Engine Group, Evendale, Ohio, 1963-70; prin. Donn N. Peterson & Assocs., Mpls., 1971-74; pres. Donn N. Peterson & Assocs., Inc., Mpls., 1974-85, Peterson Engring., Inc., Mpls., 1985—; instr. GE Edn. Program, 1968-69; seminar presenter State Bd. of Registration, Mpls., 1980; seminar leader Minn. Fedn. Engring. Socs., Mpls., 1990-91; speaker in field; expert witness 100 ct. trials and 100 depositions. Del. Minn. 6th Dist. Rep. Conv., Brooklyn Park, Minn., 1982. Fellow Am. Acad. Forensic Scis. (sect. chmn. 1989-90, Founders award 1991), Nat. Acad. Forensic Engrs. (v.p. 1996, sr. v.p. 1997—); mem. ASME (Young Engr. of Yr. 1976, state chmn. 1979-80), NSPE, Profl. Engrs. in Pvt. Practice (state pres. 1987-88, Svc. award 1988), Soc. of Automotive Engrs., Rotary Club (sec. Brooklyn Park chpt. 1990-93, v.p. 1993-94, pres.-elect 1994-95, pres. 1995-96, Svc. award 1992), Brooklyn Park C. of C. (city hwy. 610 corridor com. 1992-94). Lutheran. Achievements include devel. of successful math. models to simulate jet engine transient performance and wave dynamics in gas flow, computer simulations for vehicle and occupant dynamics during collisions. Home: 15720 15th Pl N Plymouth MN 55447-2405 Office: 4455 Highway 169 N Plymouth MN 55442-2856 Office: 4455 Highway 169 N Plymouth MN 55442-2856

PETERSON, DOROTHY LULU, artist, writer; b. Venice, Calif., Mar. 10, 1932; d. Marvin Henry and Fay (Brown) Case; m. Leon Albert Peterson, June 21, 1955; 1 child, David. AD, Compton (Calif.) Coll., 1950. Artist Moran Printing Co., Lockport, N.Y., 1955-59; caricature artist West Seneca and Kenmore Creative Artist Socs., 1973-86; commd. artist in pvt. practice, 1986—; comml. artist Boulevard Mall, Kenmore (N.Y.) Arts Soc., 1974—. Works include portraits of Pres. and Mrs. Reagan in Presdl. Libr. Collection, also portraits of Geraldine Ferraro, Presidents Clinton, Bush, Nixon, Ford, also Bette Davis, Lucille Ball, Bing Crosby, Elizabeth Taylor, 1971-94; sculpture of Pres. Bush; author articles. Recipient awards West. Seneca Art Soc., 1975, Kenmore Art Soc., 1982, 86. Democrat. Baptist. Home: 247 Pryor Ave Tonawanda NY 14150

PETERSON, DOUGLAS ARTHUR, physician; b. Princeton, N.Y., Sept. 13, 1945; s. Arthur Roy William and Marie Hilma (Anderson) P.; m. Virginia Kay Eng., June 24, 1967; children: Rachel, Daniel, Rebecca. BA, St. Olaf, 1966; PhD, U. Minn., 1971, MD, 1975. Postdoctoral fellow U. Pitts., 1971-72; intern Hennepin County Med. Ctr., Mpls., 1975-76, resident in medicine, 1976-78; physician Bloomington Lake Clinic, Mpls., 1978-82; staff physician Mpls. VA Med. Ctr., Mpls., 1992—, chief compensation and pension, 1992—; asst. prof. U. Minn., 1985—. Bd. dirs. Rolling Acres Home, Victoria, Minn., 1985—. Lt. Col. M.C., USAR. Mem. AAAS. Achievements include introduction of concept of reductive activation of receptors. Home: 5008 Queen Ave S Minneapolis MN 55410-2207 Office: VA Med Ctr One Veterans Dr Minneapolis MN 55417

PETERSON, DOUGLAS PETE (PETE PETERSON), ambassador, former congressman; b. Omaha, Nebr., June 26, 1935; m. Carlotta Ann Neal; children: Michael, Paula, Douglas. Grad., Nat. War Coll., 1975; BA, U. Tampa, 1976; postgrad., U. Ctrl. Mich., 1977. Commd. USAF, 1954, advanced through grades to col., ret., 1980; exec. CRT Computers, 1984-90; adminstr. Dozier Sch. for Boys, 1985-90; mem. 101st-104th Congresses from 2nd Fla. Dist., 1991-96; mem. appropriation com.-energy and water, agrl., amb. to Vietnam, 1996—. Prisoner of war, Vietnam. Mem. DAV, Am. Legion, Elks. Roman Catholic. Office: 7 Lang Ha Rd, Hanoi Ba Denh District, Vietnam

PETERSON, EDWARD ADRIAN, lawyer; b. St. Louis, May 19, 1941; s. Adrian J. and Virginia (Hamlin) P.; m. Catherine Frances Younghouse, Dec. 17, 1960; children: Kristin, Kendra. B.S.B.A., Washington U., St. Louis, 1963; LL.B., So. Methodist U., 1966. Bar: Tex. 1966, U.S. Dist. Ct. (no. and so. dists.) Tex. Instr. bus. law and acctg. Midwestern U., Wichita Falls, Tex., 1966-67; assoc. Schenk & Wesbrooks, Wichita Falls, 1966-67, Newman & Pickering, Dallas, 1967-72; ptnr. Moore & Peterson, Dallas, 1972-89, Winstead Sechrest & Minick P.C., Dallas, 1989—; speaker in field. Contbr. articles to legal jours. Bd. dirs. Leukemia Soc., 1970-71, North Tex. Commn., 1992-96, South Dallas/Fair Park Trust Fund, 1992. Fellow Tex. Bar Found. (life); mem. ABA, Am. Coll. Real Estate Lawyers (chmn. professionalism and practice com.), State Bar Tex., Coll. State Bar Tex., Tex. Coll. Real Estate Attys., Dallas Bar Assn., Phi Alpha Delta, Sigma Alpha Epsilon. Lutheran. Avocation: snow skiing. Home: 9442 Spring Hollow Dr Dallas TX 75243-7533 Office: Winstead Sechrest & Minick PC 5400 Renaissance Tower Dallas TX 75270

PETERSON, EDWIN J., retired supreme court justice, law educator; b. Gilmanton, Wis., Mar. 30, 1930; s. Edwin A. and Leora Grace (Kitelinger) P.; m. Anna Chadwick, Feb. 7, 1971; children: Patricia, Andrew, Sherry. B.S., U. Oreg., 1951, LL.B., 1957. Bar: Oreg. 1957. Assoc. firm Tooze, Kerr, Peterson, Marshall & Shenker, Portland, 1957-61; mem. firm Tooze, Kerr, Peterson, Marshall & Shenker, 1961-79; assoc. justice Supreme Ct. Oreg., Salem, 1979-83, 91-93, chief justice, 1983-91; ret., 1993; disting. jurist-in-residence, adj. instr. Willamette Coll. of Law, Salem, Oreg., 1994—; chmn. Supreme Ct. Task Force on Racial Issues, 1992-94; mem. standing com. on fed. rules of practice and procedure, 1987-93; bd. dirs. Conf. Chief Justices, 1985-87, 88-91. Chmn. Portland Citizens Sch. Com., 1968-70; vice chmn. Young Republican Fedn. Orgn., 1951; bd. visitors U. Oreg. Law Sch., 1978-83, 87-93, chmn. bd. visitors, 1981-83. Served to 1st lt. USAF, 1952-54.

Mem. Oreg. State Bar (bd. examiners 1963-66, gov. 1973-76, vice chmn. profl. liability fund 1977-78), Multnomah County Bar Assn. (pres. 1972-73), Phi Alpha Delta, Lambda Chi Alpha. Episcopalian. Home: 3365 Sunridge Dr S Salem OR 97302-5950 Office: Willamette Univ Coll Law 245 Winter St SE Salem OR 97301-3916

PETERSON, EILEEN M., state agency administrator; b. Trenton, N.J., Sept. 22, 1942; d. Leonard James and Mary (Soganic) Olschewski; m. Lars N. Peterson, Jr., 1970 (div. 1983); children: Leslie, Valerie, Erica. Student, Boise State U. Adminstrv. sec. State Ins. Fund, Boise, 1983-85; legal asst. Bd. Tax Appeals, Boise, 1985-87, exec. asst., 1987-92, dir., 1992—; ind. distbr. for USANA nutritional products; outside referring travel agt. Travelmax Intenrat. Vol. Boise Art Mus., Idaho Refugee Svc. Recipient Gov's. Cert. of Recognition for Outstanding Achievement, 1995. Mem. Mensa, Investment Club (pres.), Mountains West Outdoor Club, Idaho Rivers United. Democrat. Avocations: white water rafting, teaching ESL, non-fiction reading. Home: 3317 Mountain View Dr Boise ID 83704-4638 Office: Idaho State Bd Tax Appeals 1109 Main St Boise ID 83702-5640

PETERSON, ELAINE GRACE, technology director; b. Chgo., Feb. 6, 1943; d. Lincoln and Martha (Guthmiller) Wyman; m. Robert J. Peterson, June 5, 1965; children: Wesley, Christian. Certificate in computer programming, Moraine Valley Coll., Palos Hills, 1975; BA in Edn., Governors State U., 1981, MA in Comm. Sci. and Adminstrn., 1981. Computer coord. Dist. 144, Hazel Crest, Ill., 1984-86; adj. prof. Governors State U., University Park, Ill., 1986-87; program coord. ISBE - Edml. Svc. Ctr., Flossmoor, Ill., 1986-92; rsch. assoc. Argonne Nat. Lab., Argonne, Ill., 1991-93; dist. tech. dir. Lombard Dist. 44, Lombard, Ill., 1991-92; dir. tech./ media svcs. DuPage H.S. Dist. 88, Villa Park, Ill., 1992—; dir. tech./Media Svcs. DuPage H.S. Dist. 88, Addison, Ill., 1992—; grant writer Layne Cons., Addison, Ill., 1993-94; bd. dirs. Audio-Visual Inst. of DuPage, Lombard, 1991—; mem. Bus. Profl. of Am., Flossmoor, 1990-92, Reg. Ofc. Edn./Profl. Dev. Ctr., Lombard, 1993—; tech. mem. Addison 2000 Cmty. Org. of Village and Schs., Addison, 1993—; tech. com. adv. Dist. 45 - Feeder Sch., Villa Park, 1994—; grant reader Ednl. Svc. Ctrl. Ill. Math Sci. Acad., Aurora, Ill., 1992-94, Ill. State Bd. of Edn., Springfield, Ill., 1995—; mem. adv. bd. ISBE Area # 1 tech. hub. 1996. Contbr. articles to profl. jours. Mem. Internat. Soc. for Tchr. Edn., Ill. Computing Educators, Tech 2000, Ill. Sch. Libr. Media Assn., Argonne Cmty. of Tchrs., Ill. Assn. for Sch. Curriculum Devel., Phi Delta Kappa of DuPage County (treas.). Avocations: bowling, investing, computing, boating, shopping. Home: 21424 W Sycamore Ct Plainfield IL 60544 Office: DuPage HS Dist 88 101 W Highridge Rd Villa Park IL 60181-3100

PETERSON, ELMOR LEE, mathematical scientist, educator; b. McKeesport, Pa., Dec. 6, 1938; s. William James and Emma Elizabeth (Scott) P.; m. Sharon Louise Walker, Aug., 1957 (div. Jan. 1961); 1 child, Lisa Ann Peterson Loop; m. Miriam Drake Mears, Dec. 23, 1966; 1 child, David Scott. BS in Physics, Carnegie Mellon U., 1960, MS in Math., 1961, PhD in Math., 1964. Technician U.S. Steel Rsch. Ctr., Monroeville, Pa., summer 1959; engr. Westinghouse Atomic Power, Forest Hills, Pa., summer 1960; rsch. engr. Atomics Internat., Canoga Park, Calif., summer 1961; physicist Lawrence Radiation Labs., Livermore, Calif., summer 1963; sr. math. Westinghouse R & D, Churchill Boro, Pa., 1963-66; asst. prof. math. U. Mich., Ann Arbor, 1967-69; assoc. prof. math. and mgmt. sci. Northwestern U., Evanston, Ill., 1969-73, prof. math. and mgmt. sci., 1973-77, prof. applied math. and mgmt. sci., 1977-79; prof. math. and ops. rsch. N.C. State U., Raleigh, 1979—; vis. asst. prof. W.Va. U., dept. Math., Morgantown, 1966; vis. assoc. prof. U. Wis. Math. Rsch. Ctr., Madison, 1968-69; vis. prof. Stanford U. Ops. Rsch. Dept., 1976-77. Author: (with others) Geometric Programming, 1967, Russian trans., 1971; contbr. articles to profl. jours. Mobil Found. Rsch. grantee, 1967-69, Air Force Office Sci. Rsch. grantee, 1973-75, 76-78, NSF grantee, 1985-86. Mem. Soc. for Indsl. and Applied Math., Ops. Rsch. Soc. Am., Am. Math. Soc., Math. Assn. Am. Avocations: aerobic exercise, antique furniture. Home: 3717 Williamsborough Ct Raleigh NC 27609-6357 Office: NC State U Hillsborough St Raleigh NC 27695

PETERSON, ERLE VIDAILLET, retired metallurgical engineer; b. Idaho Falls, Idaho, Apr. 29, 1915; s. Vier P. and Marie (Vidaillet) P.; m. Rosemary Sherwood, June 3, 1955; children: Kent Sherwood, Pamela Jo. BS in Mining Engring., U. Idaho, 1940; MS in Mining Engring., U. Utah, 1941. Tech. advisor Remington Arms Co., Salt Lake City, 1941-43; constrn. engr. plutonium plant duPont, Hanford, Wash., 1943-44; R & D engr. exptl. sta. duPont, Wilmington, Del., 1944-51; plant metallurgist heavy water plant duPont, Newport, Ind., 1951-57; rsch. metallurgist metals program duPont, Balt., 1957-62, prin. project engr. USAF contracts, 1962-68; devel. engr. duPont, Wilmington, 1969-80; ret., 1980. Patentee in field; contbr. articles to profl. jours. Candidate for State Senate-Am. Party, Wilmington, 1974; com. chmn. Boy Scouts Am., Wilmington, 1975-78; treas. Local Civic Assn., Wilmington, 1977-79. Rsch. fellow U. Utah, 1940. Mem. Am. Soc. Metallurgists Internat., Del. Assn. Profl. Engrs. Republican. Avocations: lapidary, jewelry making, photography, prospecting, gardening. Home: PO Box 74 Rigby ID 83442-0074 *It matters not that you grow up on homestead and graduate from a country high school in a class of five during a great depression. With persistence and dedication toward your objectives, you can achieve goals that appear impossible.*

PETERSON, ESTHER, consumer advocate; b. Provo, Utah, Dec. 9, 1906; d. Lars and Annie (Nielsen) Eggertsen; m. Oliver A. Peterson, May 28, 1932; children: Karen Kristine, Eric N., Iver E., Lars E. A.B., Brigham Young U., 1927; M.A., Columbia Tchrs. Coll., 1930; M.A. hon. degrees, Smith Coll., Bryant Coll., Carnegie Inst. Tech., Montclair Coll., Hood Coll., Maryhurst Coll., Simmons Coll., Northeastern U., U South Utah, Western Coll. Women, Oxford, Ohio, Mich. State U., U. Mich., U. Utah, Williams Coll., Georgetown U., Temple U., Goucher Coll., Tufts U. Tchr. Branch Agr. Coll., Cedar City, Utah, 1927-29, Utah State U., Winsor Sch., Boston, 1930-36, Bryn Mawr Summer Sch. for Women Workers in Industry, 1932-39; asst. dir. edn. Amal. Clothing Workers Am., 1939-44, Washington legis. rep., 1945-48; legis. rep. indsl. union dept. AFL-CIO, 1958-61; dir. Women's Bur., U.S. Dept. Labor, 1961-64, asst. sec. labor for labor standards, 1961-69; exec. vice chmn. Pres.'s Commn. on Status of Women, 1961-63, Interdeptl. Com. Status Women, 1963-65; chmn. Pres.'s Com. Consumer Interests, 1964-67, spl. asst. to President for consumer affairs, 1964-67; legis. rep. Amal. Clothing Workers Am., Washington, 1969-70; consumer adviser Giant Food Corp., 1970-77; spl. asst. to Pres. for consumer affairs, 1977-80; chmn. Consumer Affairs Council, 1979-80. Active Internat. Med. Svcs. for Health, 1987, United Srs. Health Coop., 1987, Ctr. Sci. in Pub. Interest, 1964; mem. Women's Nat. Dem. Club; NGO rep. Internat. Orgn. Consumers Union at Econ. and Social Coun. UN, 1985, appointed pub. mem. U.S. Del. to Gen. Assembly, 1993. Decorated Presdl. medal of Freedom, 1981; recipient Food Industry Consumer award, 1986, Mgmt. award Brigham Young U., 1989. Mem. AAUW, Am. Home Econs. Assn. (hon.), Nat. Consumers League (pres. 1974-76, hon. pres. 1981), Cosmos Club, Phi Chi Theta (hon.), Delta Sigma Theta (hon.). Home: 3032 Stephenson Pl NW Washington DC 20015

PETERSON, FRED MCCRAE, librarian; b. Mpls., Dec. 29, 1936. B.A., U. Minn., 1958, M.S., 1960; Ph.D. in L.S., Ind. U., 1974. Asst. to dir. Iowa State U. Library, 1961-64, head catalog dept., 1964-67, asst. dir. library, 1967-69, assoc. dir. library, 1969-70; with Catholic U. Am., Washington, 1970-82, asst. prof., assoc. chairperson, 1973-77, acting dir. libraries, 1977-78, dir., 1978-82; univ. librarian Ill. State U., Normal, 1982-96. Mem. ALA, Ill. Library Assn. (past pres., Librian of Year 1994). Home: RR 2 Box 160 Bloomington IL 61704-9628

PETERSON, GALE EUGENE, historian; b. Sioux Rapids, Iowa, May 23, 1944; s. George Edmund and Vergene Elizabeth (Wilson) P. B.S., Iowa State U., 1965; M.A., U. Md., 1968, Ph.D., 1973. Instr. dept. history U. Md., College Park, 1971-72, Cath. U. Am., Washington, 1972-73; prin. investigator Gregory Directory project Orgn. Am. Historians, Bloomington, Ind., 1973-75; instr. dept. history Purdue U., West Lafayette, Ind., 1975-76; dir. U.S. Newspaper Project, Orgn. Am. Historians, Bloomington, Ind., 1976-78; exec. dir. Cin. Hist. Soc., 1978-96; exec. dir. emeritus, 1996—. Author: (with John T. Schlebecker) Living Historical Farms Handbook, 1970, Harry S Truman and the Independent Regulatory Commissions 1945-52, 1985. Mem. Cin. Bicentennial Commn., 1983-88. Mem. Orgn. Am. Historians (treas. 1993—), Am. Assn. State and Local History, Am. Hist. Assn., Am. Assn. Mus., Midwestern Mus. Conf. (v.p.-at-large 1993-95, exec. v.p. 1996-96, pres. 1996—), Cincinnatus Assn., Nat. Coun. on Pub. History (bd. dirs. 1992-95). Home: 3767 Middleton Ave Cincinnati OH 45220-1143

PETERSON, GARY ANDREW, agronomics researcher; b. Holdrege, Nebr., Apr. 30, 1940; s. Walter Andrew and Evelyn Christine (Johnson) P.; m. Jacquelyn Charlene Flick, June 18, 1965; children: Kerstin, Ingrid. BS, U. Nebr., 1963, MS, 1965; PhD, Iowa State U., 1967. Research assoc. agronomy Iowa State U., Ames, 1964-67; prof. U. Nebr., Lincoln, 1967-84; prof. soil and crop scis. Colo. State U., Ft. Collins, 1984—. Assoc. editor AGronomy Jour., 1979-81, tech. editor, 1981-83, editor, 1984-89, editor-in-chief, 1991-96; contbr. articles to profl. jours. Fellow Am. Soc. Agronomy (Ciba-Geigy Agr. Achievement award 1974, Agronomic Achievement award-Soils 1990), Soil Sci. Soc. Am. (Applied Rsch. award 1987); mem. Soil Conservation Soc. Am. Republican. Avocations: reading, hiking, skiing. Office: Colo State U Dept Soil Crop Scis Fort Collins CO 80523

PETERSON, GEORGE EMANUEL, JR., lawyer, business executive; b. Mt. Vernon, N.Y., Mar. 8, 1931; s. George E. and Lydia Evelyn (Peterson) P.; m. Barbara Ritter, Aug. 30, 1957; children—Lisa Manvel, George Emanuel III. B.A., Yale, 1953; LL.B., U. Va., 1958. Bar: N.Y. State 1959, Conn. 1974. Assoc. firm Reid & Priest, N.Y.C., 1958-68, ptnr., 1968-70; v.p., gen. counsel Insilco Corp., Meriden, Conn., 1970-72, v.p. fin., 1972-76, v.p., sec., 1976-79, v.p., gen. counsel, 1976-89; pvt. practice North Haven, Conn., 1989—. Served to lt. USNR, 1953-55. Mem. ABA, N.Y. State Bar Assn. Home and Office: 225 Blue Trl Hamden CT 06518-1601

PETERSON, GERALD ALVIN, physics educator; b. Chesterton, Ind., Apr. 12, 1931; s. Gustaf Albert and Esther Josephine (Carlson) P.; m. Doris Lee DeJonge, Dec. 22, 1953; children—Curtis Mark, Thomas Andrew, Anna Beth. BS, Purdue U., 1953, MS, 1955; PhD, Stanford U., 1962. Lectr. Yale U., New Haven, 1962-64; asst. prof., 1964-67; research scientist Inst. voor Kernphysisch Onderzoek, Amsterdam, 1967-68; assoc. prof. physics U. Mass., Amherst, 1968-73, prof., 1973—; vis. prof. U. Mainz, Fed. Republic Germany, 1975, Japan Soc. Promotion Sci., 1972, 89; U.S.-Israel Binat. Sci. Found. vis. prof. Tel Aviv U., 1983; cons. in field. Contbr. articles to profl. jours. Served with U.S. Army, 1955-57. NATO fellow, 1969, U.K. sr. rsch. fellow, 1970. Fellow Am. Phys. Soc. (chmn. New Eng. sect. 1996); mem. Sigma Xi. Congregationalist. Research in electron scattering and nuclear structure. Home: 10 Old Briggs Rd Leverett MA 01054-9759 Office: U Mass Nuclear Physics Grad Rsch Ctr Amherst MA 01003

PETERSON, HARRIES-CLICHY, financial adviser; b. Boston, Sept. 7, 1924; s. Edwin William and Annekathe (Lieske) P. AB, Harvard U., 1946, MBA, 1950; MA in Edn., San Francisco State U., 1993. Sci. officer Ronne Antarctic Expdn., 1947-48; staff asst. Kidder Peabody & Co., N.Y.C., 1952-53, Devel. and Resources Corp., N.Y.C., 1959-61; dir. indsl. devel. W.R. Grace & Co., Lima, Peru, 1953-57; staff asst. Devel. & Resources Corp., N.Y.C., 1959-61; bus. cons. Lima, 1961-65; v.p. internat. div. Foremost Dairies, Inc. (now McKesson Corp.), San Francisco, 1965-67; v.p. H.K. Porter Co., Inc., Pitts., 1967-68; also chmn. and dir. overseas affiliates H.K. Porter Co., Inc., 1967-68; independent fin. adviser San Francisco and Los Angeles, 1968—; cons. investment banking projects for 3d world countries, Brazil, 1981, 82, 84, Nepal, 1987, Ecuador, 1988, Kenya, 1989, Indonesia, 1989, Peru, 1989, 90, 92, 93, 95, 96, Hungary, 1992, Argentina, 1993, Bolivia, 1993; ind. cons. in field. Author: Development of Titanium Metals Industry, 1950, Che Guevara on Guerrilla Warfare, 1961, Petróleo: Hora Céro, 1964, Islamic Banking, 1979; contbr. articles gen. interest, bus., mil. publs. Served to col. USMCR, 1943-45, 51-52, 57-59. Decorated Silver Star. Mem. Colegio de Economistas del Peru (co-founder, past dir.), Am. Mgmt. Assn. (conf. chmn.). Address: PO Box 190002 San Francisco CA 94119-0002 also: Donatello 131, San Borja, Lima 41, Peru *I am grateful to classical education for having shown me truth and beauty. But the challenge to apply ideals and innovation into tradition and hierarchy requires endless self-appraisal and adjustment, sometimes exhilarating, sometimes disheartening, sometimes edifying, sometimes extracting great sacrifices from self and others I might have better served. Yet, the pursuit of uncynical truth and harmonious beauty remains an unshakeable mistress needed to satisfy soul and spirit.*

PETERSON, H(ARRY) WILLIAM, chemicals executive, consultant; b. Yokohama, Honshu Island, Japan, Mar. 9, 1922; came to U.S., 1924; s. Harry William and Alice (Mateer) P.; m. Doris Jane Howe, Apr. 27, 1946; children: Robert, Christine Fitzpatrick, Janet McMillan. BA in Chemistry and Botany, Colgate U., 1946; postgrad., Princeton U., 1949-50, U. Del., 1982-83. Lic. capt. U.S. inland waters U.S. Coast Guard. Researcher, developer ESSO Standard Oil Co., Bayway, N.J., 1946-51; various positions Enjay Chem. Co., N.Y.C., 1951-65; coord. world-wide chem. Gulf Oil Corp., Pitts., 1965-67; gen. mktg. mgr. Gulf Oil-Eastern Hemisphere, London, 1967-71; corp. v.p. chem. mktg., corp. v.p. mktg. Gulf Oil Can. Ltd., Montreal, Que., Can., 1971-77; CEO chems. divsn., corp. v.p. Golfoil Can., Montreal, Quebec, Can., 1971-77; chief operating officer Corpus Christi Chem. Co., Wilmington, Del., 1971—; mng. dir. Food Machinery & Chem. Corp. Internat. Chems., Phila., 1979-80; internat. cons. Bozman, Md., 1980—. Patentee in field. Leader Young Christians Assn., 1st Bapt. Ch., Somerville, N.J., 1948-53; lay speaker, mem. adminstrn. bd. Riverview Charge, United Meth. Ch.; chaplain Mil. Order Purple Heart. With USMC, 1942-46, PTO. Decorated Purple Heart, two battle stars. Fellow Am. Inst. Chemists; mem. Am. Chem. Soc. (emeritus). Avocations: writing, philosophy, religion. Home and Office: Quakerneck Rd Mulberry Pt Bozman MD 21612

PETERSON, HOWARD COOPER, lawyer, accountant; b. Decatur, Ill., Oct. 12, 1939; s. Howard and Lorraine (Cooper) P.; BEE, U. Ill., 1963; MEE, San Diego State Coll., 1967; MBA, Columbia U., 1969; JD, Calif. Western Sch. Law, 1983; LLM in Taxation NYU, 1985. Bar: Calif., cert. fin. planner.; CPA, Tex.; registered profl. Engr., Calif.; cert. neuro-linguistic profl. Elec. engr. Convair divsn. Gen. Dynamics Corp., San Diego, 1963-67, sr. electronics engr., 1967-68; gen. ptnr. Costumes Characters & Classics Co., San Diego, 1979-86; v.p., dir. Equity Programs Corp., San Diego, 1973-83; pres., dir. Coastal Properties Trust, San Diego, 1979-89, Juno Securities, Inc., 1983-96, Juno Real Estate Inc., 1974—, Scripps Mortgage Corp., 1987-90, Juno Transport Inc., 1988—; CFO, dir. Imperial Screens of San Diego, 1977-96, Heritage Transp. Mgmt. Inc., 1989-91, A.S.A.P. Ins. Svcs. Inc., 1983-85. Mem. ABA, Interam. Bar Assn., Nat. Soc. Public Accts., Internat. Assn. Fin. Planning, Assn. Enrolled Agts.

PETERSON, JAMES ALGERT, geologist, educator; b. Baroda, Mich., Apr. 17, 1915; s. Djalma Hardaman and Mary Avis (McAnally) P.; m. Gladys Marie Pearson, Aug. 18, 1944; children—James D., Wendy A., Brian H. Student, Northwestern U., 1941-43, U. Wis., 1943; B.S. magna cum laude, St. Louis U., 1948; M.S. (Shell fellow), U. Minn., 1950, Ph.D., 1951. Mem. staff U.S. Geol. Survey, Spokane, Wash., 1949-51; instr. geology Wash. State U., Pullman, 1951; geologist Shell Oil Co., 1952-65; geologist div. stratigrapher, 1958-63, sr. geologist, 1963-65; instr. geology N. Mex. State U., San Juan, (P.R.), br., 1959-65; prof. geology U. Mont., Missoula, 1965—; cons. U.S. Geol. Survey, 1976-82, rsch. geologist, 1982—. Editor: Geology of East Central Utah, 1956, Geometry of Sandstone Bodies, 1960, Rocky Mountain Sedimentary Basins, 1965, (with others) Pacific Geology, Paleotectonics and Sedimentation, 1986; Contbr. (with others) articles to profl. jours. Served to 1st lt. USAAF, 1943-46. Recipient Alumni Merit award St. Louis U., 1960, Outstanding Achievement award U. Minn., 1995. Fellow AAAS, Geol. Soc. Am.; mem. Am. Assn. Petroleum Geologists (hon., pres. Rocky Mountain sect. 1964, Pres.'s award 1988, Disting. Svc. award 1992), Rocky Mountain Assn. Geologists (Outstanding Scientist award 1987), Four Corners Geol. Soc. (hon., pres. 1962), Am. Inst. Profl. Geologists (pres. Mont. sect. 1971), Soc. Econ. Paleontologists and Mineralogists (hon. 1985, sec.-treas. 1969-71, editor 1976-78, Disting. Pioneer Geologist award 1988), Mont. Geol. Soc. (hon. 1987), Utah Geol. Soc., Explorers Club. Home: 301 Pattee Canyon Dr Missoula MT 59803-1624

PETERSON, JAMES KENNETH, manufacturing company executive; b. Sioux City, Iowa, Oct. 17, 1934; s. David Winfield and Beulah Lillian (Johnson) P.; m. Nanette Kay Olin, Feb. 2, 1957; children: Kimberly, Kristin, David. B.A. in Econs, Mich. State U., 1956. Research/devel. engr. Reynolds Metals Co., Richmond, Va., 1957-59, sales rep., 1959-61, dist. sales mgr., 1961-65, regional sales mgr., 1965-67, asst. to exec. v.p., 1968, mktg. dir., 1969-71; dir. nat. account sales The Continental Group, Stamford, Conn., 1971, gen. mgr. sales, 1972-73, div. gen. mgr., 1974-78, v.p., corp. officer, 1974-80, v.p., gen. mgr. global bus. devel., 1979; pres., chief oper. officer Ludlow Corp., Needham, Mass., 1980-82, also bd. dirs.; pres., CEO, dir. Graphic Packaging Corp., Paoli, Pa., 1982-89; pres., CEO Peterson Group, Easton, Md., 1989—; chmn., CEO The Petters Co., Lititz, Pa.; chmn. bd. dirs. Comml. Printers of Conn.; bd. dirs. Graphic Packaging Corp., South Chester Tube Co.; mem. Precision Strip Inc. Served to 1st lt. U.S. Army, 1957. Mem. Merion Golf Club, Merion Cricket Club, Talbot Country Club. Home: 27779 Waverly Rd Easton MD 21601-8121 Office: Peterson Group PO Box 738 Easton MD 21601-0738 also: The Petters Co 2077 Main St Lititz PA 17543-3029

PETERSON, JAMES LINCOLN, museum executive; b. Kewanee, Ill., Nov. 12, 1942; s. Reinold Gustav and Florence Josephine (Kjellgren) P.; m. M. Susan Pepin, Aug. 15, 1964; children: Hans C., Erika C. BA, Gustavus Adolphus Coll., 1964; PhD, U. Nebr., 1972. Sci. tchr. pub. schs. Ill. and Minn., 1964-68; research asst. U. Nebr., Lincoln, 1968-72; research assoc. U. Wis., Madison, 1972-74; staff ecologist Nat. Commn. Water Quality, Washington, 1974-75; v.p. research Acad. Nat. Scis., Phila., 1976-84, v.p. devel., 1982-84; pres. Sci. Mus. Minn., St. Paul, 1984—. Bd. dirs. Ea. Pa. chpt. Nature Conservancy, Phila., 1982-84, Downtown Coun., St. Paul, 1986-93, Keystone (Colo.) Ctr., 1989-93; mem. St. Paul Riverfront Commn., 1987-91; mem. adv. com. U. Minn. Coll. Biol. Scis., 1989-95. Mem. Assn. Sci. Mus. Dirs., Assn. Sci. and Tech. Ctrs. (pres. 1993-95), Sci. Mus. Exhibit Collaborative (pres. 1986-89), St. Paul C. of C. (bd. dirs. 1985-89), Informal Club. Office: Sci Mus Minn 30 10th St E Saint Paul MN 55101-2205

PETERSON, JAMES ROBERT, retired engineering psychologist; b. St. Paul, Apr. 16, 1932; s. Palmer Elliot and Helen Evelyn (Carlson) P.; BA in Psychology cum laude, U. Minn., 1954; MA in Exptl. Psychology, 1958; PhD in Engring. Psychology, U. Mich., 1965; m. Marianna J. Stockvig, June 26, 1954; 1 child, Anne Christine. Devel. engr. Honeywell Inc., 1961-65, sr. devel. engr., 1965-67, staff engr., 1967-90, sr. project staff engr., 1990-93, ret., 1993; Honeywell sponsor rep. Shuttle Student Involvement Program, 1982, 84. Served with USMC, 1954-57, with Res., 1957-62. Assoc. fellow AIAA; mem. Human Factors and Ergonomics Soc. (life), Air & Space Mus. (charter), Smithsonian Inst. Club: Mason. Contbr. articles to profl. jours. Achievements include invention of Apollo translation hand controller; participation in development work on all U.S. Manned Space Programs (Mercury, Gemini, Apollo, Lunar Excursion Module, Manned Orbiting Laboratory, Space Shuttle and Space Station) as member/manager of associated human factors groups. Home: 3303 San Gabriel St Clearwater FL 34619-3341

PETERSON, JAMES ROBERT, retired writing instrument manufacturing executive; b. Momence, Ill., Oct. 28, 1927; s. Clyde and Pearl (Deliere) P.; m. Betty Windham, May 12, 1949; children: Richard James, Lynn Peterson Anderson, Susan Peterson Hanske, John Windham. Student, St. Thomas Coll., 1945, Iowa State U., 1945-46, U. Colo., 1946, Northwestern U., 1946; BS in Mktg. cum laude, U. Ill., 1952; grad. exec. MBA program, Stanford U., 1967. With Pillsbury Co., Mpls., 1952-76; brand mgr. grocery products Pillsbury Co., 1953-57, brand supr. flour, 1957-61, dir. mktg., 1961-66, v.p. mktg., 1966-68; v.p., gen. mgr. Grocery Products Co., 1968-71, group v.p. consumer cos., 1971-73, pres., dir., 1973-76; exec. v.p., dir. R.J. Reynolds Industries, Inc., Winston-Salem, N.C., 1976-82; pres., chief exec. officer, dir. Parker Pen Co., Janesville, Wis., 1982-85; dir. Dun & Bradstreet Corp., N.Y.C., 1977, Waste Mgmt., Inc., Oak Brook, Ill., 1980, Cogniz Corp., Westport, Conn., 1996. Former mem. bd. dirs. Boy Scouts Am., past pres. Viking coun.; mem. bd. regents St. Olaf Coll., 1974-91. Lt. USN, 1945-50. Recipient Bronze Tablet award U. Ill. Mem. Pilgrims of U.S., Tequesta Country Club, Janesville Country Club, Bodega Harbour Golf, Links Club, Jupiter Hills Club. Methodist. Address: 19750 Beach Rd # 505 Tequesta FL 33469

PETERSON, JANE WHITE, nursing educator, anthropologist; b. San Juan, P.R., Feb. 15, 1941; d. Jerome Sidney and Vera (Joseph) Peterson; 1 child, Claire Marie. BS, Boston U., 1968; M in Nursing, U. Wash., 1969, PhD, 1981. Staff nurse Visiting Nurse Assn., Boston, 1964-66; prof. Seattle U., 1969—, dir. nursing home project, 1990-92, chair pers. com., 1988-90; chair dept. Community Health and Psychiat. Mental Health Nursing, 1987-89; sec. Coun. on Nursing and Anthropology, 1984-86; pres. Wash. League Nursing, Seattle, 1988-90; pres. bd. Vis. Nurses Svcs., Seattle, 1988-90; contbg. cons. CSI Prodn., Okla., 1987; cons. in nursing WHO/U. Indonesia, Jakarta, fall 1989, Myanmar (Burma), Yangon, winter 1995, Beijing, 1995. Contbr. articles to profl. jours., chptrs. to books. Co-owner (with Robert Colley) North End Train Ctr., Seattle; mem. Seattle Art Mus., 1986—. Fellow: Soc. for Applied Anthropology; mem. Am. Anthropological Assn., Soc. for Med. Anthropology, Nat. League for Nursing, Am. Ethological Soc. Office: Seattle U Sch Nursing Broadway and Madison Seattle WA 98122

PETERSON, JOHN DOUGLAS, museum administrator; b. Peshtigo, Wis., July 9, 1939; s. Rubin and Ruth (Erickson) P.; m. Beth L. Lynch, July 22, 1965; children: Marie Storm, Beth Storm. BFA, Layton Sch. Art, 1962, cert. in indsl. design, 1962; MFA, Cranbrook Acad. Art, Bloomfield Hills, Mich., 1966. Asst. dir. Cranbrook Acad. Art Mus., Bloomfield Hills, Mich., 1969-70, assoc. dir., 1970-71, dir., 1971-77; exec. dir. Lakeview Mus. Arts and Scis., Peoria, Ill., 1977-82, The Morris Mus., Inc., Morristown, N.J., 1982-94; v.p. The Morris Mus. Found., Morristown, 1990-94; exec. dir. Scienceport, Rye, N.Y., 1994-95; bd. dirs. Morristown Inf. Ctr., Gill St. Bernard Sch., 1988-94, Mng. Mainstreet, J/B Peterson, Inc.; mem. adv. panel Ill. Arts Coun., Chgo., 1980-82, N.J. State Coun. Arts, Trenton, 1984-85; reviewer Inst. Mus. Svcs., Washington, 1985-87. Bd. dirs. Peoria City Beautiful, 1978-82, Met. Detroit Arts Coun., 1972-77, New Philharmonic Orch., N.J.; chmn. Arts Coun., Triangle, 1972-73; co-chmn. Pub. Arts Com., Peoria, 1977-78. Mem. Am. Assn. Mus., Am. Assn. State and Local History, Advocates for the Arts, Mid-Atlantic Mus. Assn., New England Mus. Assn., N.J. Assn. Mus. (bd. dirs. 1990-94), Somerset Art Assn. (bd. dirs. 1990-94), N.J. Art Pride (bd. dirs. 1990-94), Morris Area Mus. Assn., Park Ave Club, Morristown Club. Home: 215 E Cliff St Somerville NJ 08876-2414

PETERSON, JOHN E., congressman; b. Titusville, Pa., Dec. 25, 1938; s. Axel Benjamin and Mary Elizabeth (Baker) P.; m. Saundra June Watson, 1968; children: Richard D., Florence Waychoff. Student, Pa. State U. Owner retail food market Pleasantville, Pa., 1958-84; mem. Pa. Ho. of Reps., 1977-84, Pa. State Senate, 1984-96, 105th Congress from 5th Pa. dist., 1997—; former mem. nat. adv. coun. U.S. Small Bus. Adminstrn.; mem. Pub. Health and Welfare Com., now chmn.;active PENNVEST Bd., Pa. Hardwoods Devel. Coun.; sec. Ctr. Rural Pa. Former dist. asst. U.S. Congressman Albert Johnson; mem. regional adv. coun. Pitts. Cancer Inst.; former lay leader Pleasantville United Meth. Ch., former chmn. pastoral parish com.; bd. advisors Foxview Manor, Inc.; mem. adv. bd. U. Pitts., Titusville and Bradford campuses; mem. adv. coun. Ind. U. of Pa. Culinary Sch.; active Pa. Trauma Ctr. Found., Venango County Indsl. Bd. Served U.S. Army. Recipient John Heinz Meml. award; Presdl. Distinction medal U. Pitts. at Bradford, Recognition award Pa. Acad. Family Physicians, Appreciation award, Better Life award Pa Health Care Assn., Guardian of Small Bus. award Nat. Fedn. Ind. Bus., Spl. Achievement award Pa. Bar Assn., Elected Officials award Pa. Home Health Assn., 1994; named Senator of Yr., Pa. Jewish Coalition, Legislator of Yr., Pa. Assn. County Human Svc. Adminstrs., 1993, Pa. Home Health Care Assn., 1993. Mem. Titusville Area C. of C. (past pres.), Pleasantville Parent-Tchr. Assn. (past pres.), Lions. Republican. Methodist. Home: PO Box 295 248 N Main St Pleasantville PA 16341 Office: 1020 Longworth Washington DC 20515-3805*

PETERSON, JOHN ERIC, physician, educator; b. Norwalk, Ohio, Oct. 26, 1914; s. Charles Augustus and Fannie Helen (Stanford) P.; m. Lodene C. Pruett, Aug. 18, 1938; children—Carol Peterson Haviland, John Eric. Student, Columbia Jr. Coll., 1932-34; M.D., Coll. Med. Evangelists, 1938. Diplomate: Nat. Bd. Med. Examiners, Am. Bd. Internal Medicine. Intern Henry Ford Hosp., Detroit, 1938-39; resident Henry Ford Hosp., 1939-42; practice medicine specializing in internal medicine Los Angeles, 1942-56, Loma Linda, Calif., 1956—; mem. staff Los Angeles County Hosp., Riverside (Calif.) County Gen. Hosp.; mem. faculty Sch. Medicine, Loma

Linda U., 1942—, prof. medicine, 1967-88, prof. medicine emeritus, 1988—, chmn. dept., 1969-80; asso. dean Sch. Medicine, Loma Linda U. (Sch. Medicine), 1965-75; mem. staff Loma Linda U. Hosp., 1967—, chief medicine service, 1969-80; rsch. assoc. Harvard Med. Sch., 1960-61; cons. to univs. and fgn. govts. Contbr. articles to various publs. Fellow ACP; mem. AMA, Calif. Med. Assn., San Bernardino County Med. Assn., Calif. Soc. Internal Medicine, Inland Soc. Internal. Medicine, Am. Diabetes Assn., Western Soc. Clin. Investigation, Assn. Profs. of Medicine, L.A. Acad. Medicine, Diabetes Assn. So. Calif., Sigma Xi, Alpha Omega Alpha. Office: Loma Linda U Med Ctr Dept Medicine Rm 1576 Loma Linda CA 92350

PETERSON, JOHN LEONARD, lawyer, judge; b. Butte, Mont., Sept. 11, 1933; s. Roy Victor and Lena Pauline (Umhang) P.; m. Jean Marie Hollingsworth, June 10, 1957; children: Michael R., John Robert, Carol Jean. BA in Bus., U. Mont., 1957, JD, 1957. Bar: Mont. 1957, U.S. Supreme Ct. 1964, U.S. Ct. Appeals (9th cir.) 1974, U.S. Tax Ct. 1978. Assoc., McCaffery, Roe, Kiely & Joyce, 1957-63; ptnr. McCaffery & Peterson, 1963-79; sole practice, Butte, Mont., 1979-85; part-time U.S. bankruptcy judge, 1963-85; U.S. bankruptcy judge, Mont., 1985—. Bd. govs. Nat. Conf. Bankruptcy Judges, 1989-92; mem. Mont. Bd. Regents Higher Edn., 1975-82; del. Democratic Nat. Conv., 1968. Mem. Nat. Conf. Bankruptcy Judges, Mont. Bar Assn., Silver Bow County Bar Assn., Butte Country Club. Democrat. Lutheran. Office: US Dist Ct 215 Fed Bldg Butte MT 59701

PETERSON, KAREN IDA, marketing research company executive; b. Rahway, N.J., Dec. 30, 1939; d. Sigurd Thage and Harriet Erma (Pearson) P.; m. Thomas Lea Davidson, Oct. 7, 1978 (dec.). BA, Wellesley Coll., 1961; postgrad., CCNY, 1963-66. Rsch. asst. Opinion Rsch. Corp., Princeton, N.J., 1961-63; rsch. sec. Interpub. Group of Cos., N.Y.C., 1963-65; project dir., account supr., group head, v.p. Oxtoby Smith, Inc., N.Y.C., 1965-74; founder, prin., pres. Davidson-Peterson Assoc., N.Y.C. and York, Maine, 1974—; treas. Coun. Am. Survey Rsch. Orgn., Pt. Jefferson, N.Y., 1978-83, bd. mem., 1979-82, 90-92. Co-author: Rural Tourism Marketing, 1994; mem. editl. rev. bd. Jour. Travel Rsch., 1993—. Dir. Seashore Trolley Mus., Kennebunk, Maine, 1994—. Recipient Noah award Acad. of Travel, 1986. Mem. S.E. Tourism Soc., Women Execs. Internat. Tourism Assn. (bd. dirs., pres. 1984-89), Travel & Tourism Rsch. Assn. Internat. (bd. dirs. 1990-92). Avocations: photography, travel, antiques. Office: Davidson-Peterson Assoc Inc PO Box 350 York ME 03909-0350

PETERSON, KENT WRIGHT, physician; b. Portsmouth, Va., Apr. 16, 1943; s. Gerald Milton and Julia Elizabeth (Hoover) P.; m. Virginia Mae Sonne, Dec. 26, 1979; children: Liesl Lynn, Owen Sonne. B.A., U. N.C., Chapel Hill, 1964; M.D., U. Pa., 1968. Diplomate Am. Bd. Gen. Preventive Medicine and Occupational Medicine; cert. gen. preventive medicine. Intern U. Wis., 1968-69, resident, 1970-71; Robert Wood Johnson clin. scholar George Washington U., 1975-77; family physician E. Madison Clinic, Madison, Wis., 1969; chief med. officer policy devel. U.S. Cost of Living Council, Washington, 1973-74; assoc. dir. Assn. Univ. Programs in Health Adminstrn., Washington, 1974-77; exec. v.p. Am. Coll. Preventive Medicine, Washington, 1977-81; corp. mgr. preventive and environ. medicine IBM Corp., White Plains, N.Y., 1981-84; corp. med. dir. Am. Standard, N.Y.C., 1984-86; pres. Occupational Health Strategies, Charlottesville, Va., 1984—; clin. asst. prof. Georgetown U. Sch. Medicine, 1979-85; clin. assoc. prof. NYU dept. environ. medicine, 1985—; rep. to Coun. Med. Specialty Socs., 1980-86; mem. Accreditation Coun. for Continuing Med. Edn., 1981-86; treas. Med. Rev. Officer Cert. Coun., 1992—; v.p. Am. Bd. of Ind. Med. Examiners, 1995—. Author books including Directory of Occupational Health and Safety Software, 10th edit., 1997, Handbook of Health Risk Appraisals, 3d edit., 1996; contbr. numerous articles to profl. jours. and chpts. to books. Pres. Children of the Americas Found., 1979-84. Served to maj. M.C. U.S. Army, 1971-73. Fellow Am. Coll. Preventive Medicine, Am. Coll. Occupl. and Environ. medicine (chmn. computers in occupl. medicine com. 1986-90, pres. 1996-97); mem. AMA, APHA, Assn. Tchrs. Preventive Medicine, N.Y. Acad. Medicine, Ramazzini Soc., Soc. Prospective Medicine (officer) World Future Soc., Coun. for Liveable World, Va. Occupl. Medicine Assn. (pres. 1988-90). Home: 7767 Faber Rd Faber VA 22938-9715 Office: Occupational Health Strategies Inc 901 Preston Ave Ste 400 Charlottesville VA 22903-4491

PETERSON, KEVIN BRUCE, newspaper editor, publishing executive; b. Kitchener, Ont., Can., Feb. 11, 1948; s. Bruce Russell and Marguerite Elizabeth (Hammond) P.; m. Constance Maureen Bailey, Feb. 11, 1975 (dec. May 1975); m. Sheila Helen O'Brien, Jan. 9, 1981. B.A., U. Calgary, Alta., Can., 1968. Chief bur. Calgary Herald, 1972-75, city editor, 1976-77, news editor, 1977-78, bus. editor, 1978, mng. editor, 1978-86, editor, asst. pub., 1986-87, gen. mgr., 1987-88, pub., 1989-96; pres. Canadian Univ. Press, Ottawa, Ont., Can., 1968-69; dir. New Directions for News. Harry Brittain Meml. fellow Commonwealth Press Union, London, 1979. Mem. Can. Mng. Editors (bd. dirs. 1983-87), Am. Soc. Newspaper Editors, Horsemen's Benevolent and Protective Assn., Alta. Legis. Press Gallery Assn. (v.p. 1971-76), Can. Daily Newspaper Assn. (bd. dirs. 1990-96, vice chmn. , treas 1992, chmn. 1993-96), Calgary Petroleum Club, Ranchmen's Club, 100-t-1 Club, (Arcadia, Calif.). Avocations: thoroughbred horse racing; art collecting.

PETERSON, LAURENCE E., physics educator; b. Grantsburg, Wis., July 26, 1931; m. Joelle Dallancon, 1956; children: Mark L., Daniel F., Lynn M., Julianne. BS, U. Minn., 1954, PhD, 1960. Rsch. assoc. in physics U. Minn., Mpls., 1960-62; from resident physicist to prof. physics U. Calif., San Diego, 1962—; physics subcom. NASA Space Sci. Steering Com., 1964—, assoc. dir. sci. astrophysics divsn., 1986-88; dir. Ctr. Astrophysics & Space Sci., U. Calif., San Diego, 1988—. Fellow NSF, 1958-59, Guggenheim Found., 1973-74. Fellow Am. Phys. Soc.; mem. AIAA (space sci. award 1978), AAAS, Am. Astron. Soc., Internat. Astronomical Union. Office: U Calif-San Diego Ctr. Astrophysics & Space Scis MC 0424 9500 Gilman Dr La Jolla CA 92093*

PETERSON, LESLIE ERNEST, bishop; b. Noranda, Que., Can., Nov. 4, 1928; s. Ernest Victor and Blanch (Marsh) P.; m. Yvonne Hazel Lawton, July 16, 1953; children—Shauna Peterson Van Hoof, Tom, Jennifer Peterson Glage, Kathryn Peterson Scott, Jonathan. B.A., U. Western Ont., London, Ont., Can., 1952; L.T.H., Huron Coll., London, Ont., Can., 1954, D.D. (hon.), 1984; tchr.'s cert., North Bay Tchrs. Coll., Ont., 1970. Ordained to ministry Anglican Ch., 1954. Priest Diocese of Algoma, Coniston, Ont., 1954-58; priest Diocese of Algoma, Elliot Lake, Ont., 1959-63, rural dean, 1961-63; priest Diocese of Algoma, North Bay, 1963-78; priest Diocese of Algoma, Parry Sound, Ont., 1978-83, archdeacon, 1980-83; bishop Diocese of Algoma, Sault Ste. Marie, Ont., 1983-94; tchr. North Bay Elem. Sch., 1970-78; ret., 1994. Avocations: canoeing, woodworking, gardening. Address: 615 Santa Monica Rd, London, ON Canada N6H 3W2

PETERSON, LESLIE RAYMOND, barrister; b. Viking, Alta., Can., Oct. 6, 1923; s. Herman S. and Margaret (Karen) P.; m. Agnes Rose Hine, June 24, 1950; children: Raymond Erik, Karen Isabelle. Student, Camrose Luth. Coll., Alta., McGill. U., Can., London U., Eng.; LLB, U. B.C., Can., 1949; LLD, Simon Fraser U., Can., 1965, U. B.C., 1993; EdD, Notre Dame U., Nelson, Can., 1966; hon. diploma tech., B.C. Inst. Tech., 1994. Bar: B.C. 1949; called to Queens Counsel, 1960. Pvt. practice barrister Vancouver, B.C., 1949-52; with Peterson & Anderson, 1952; then with Boughton & Co. (now Boughton Peterson Yang Anderson).; mem. B.C. Legislature for Vancouver Centre, 1956-63, Vancouver-Little Mountain, 1966; min. of edn., 1956-68, min. of labour, 1960-71, atty. gen., 1968-72; bd. govs. U. B.C., Vancouver, 1979-83, chancellor, 1987-93; bd. dirs. Can. Found. Econ. Edn., Inst. Corp. Dirs. Can., Tordiam Inc., West Vancouver Found., Karay Holdings Ltd., Amaric Prodns. Inc., Rick Hansen Enterprises Inc.; trustee Peter Wall Inst. for Advanced Studies; chmn. U. B.C. Found., 1990-96. Bd. dirs. Portland unit Shriners Hosp. for Crippled Children, 1994-96; past bd. dirs. Western Soc. of Rehab., YMCA, Victoria B.C.; past pres. Twenty Club; hon. mem. Vancouver Jr. C. of C.; former v.p. Normanna Old People's Home; founding mem. Convocation, Simon Fraser U. and U. Victoria, pres., 1964-65; hon. dep. French Nat. Assembly, Paris; hon. commr. labor State of Okla.; gov. Downtown Vancouver Assn. With Can. Army, 1942-46, ETO. Recipient Disting. Alumnus award Camrose Luth. Coll., 1980. Fellow Royal Soc. Arts; mem. Internat. Bar Assn., Vancouver Bar Assn., Law Soc. B.C., Internat. Assn. of Govt. Labour Ofcls. (chmn. standing com., Can. mins. of edn. 1965-66), Terminal City Club (pres. 1991—), Scandinavian Bus. Men's Club (past pres.), Hazelmere Golf and Tennis Club (bd. dirs.), Union Club (Victoria), Wesbrook Soc. of U. B.C. (chmn. 1987), Order of St. Lazarus (knight comdr.), Freemason (potentate Gizeh Temple Shrine 1988). Avocations: skiing, golf, fishing, hunting. Home: 814 Highland, West Vancouver, BC Canada V7S 2G5 Office: Boughton Peterson Yang Anderson, 1055 Dunsmuir St PO Box 49290, Vancouver, BC Canada V7X 1S8

PETERSON, LINDA H., English language and literature educator; b. Saginaw, Mich., Oct. 11, 1948. BA in Lit. summa cum laude, Wheaton Coll., 1969; MA in English, U. R.I., 1973; PhD in English, Brown U., 1978. From lectr. to assoc. prof. Yale U., New Haven, 1977-92, prof., 1992—, dir. undergrad. studies English, 1990-94, chair, 1994—; dir. Bass writing program Yale Coll., 1979-89, 90—; mem. various departmental and univ. coms. Yale U., 1977—; presenter in field. Author: Victorian Autobiography: The Tradition of Self-Interpretation, 1986; co-author: Writing Prose, 1989, A Struggle for Fame: Victorian Women Artists and Authors, 1994; co-editor: Wuthering Heights: A Case Study in Contemporary Criticism, 1992, The Norton Reader, 9th edit., 1996, Instructor's Guide to the Norton Reader, 1996; mem. editl. bd. Writing Program Adminstrn., 1983-85, Coll. Composition and Comm., 1986-88, Auto/Biography Studies, 1990-96; contbr. articles to profl. jours. Resident fellow Branford Coll., 1979-87, Mellon fellow Whitney Humanities Ctr., 1984-85, fellow NEH, 1989-90. Mem. MLA (del. assembly 1984-86, mem. program com. 1986-89, mem. non-fiction divsn. com. 1988-92, mem. nominating com. 1993-94, mem. teaching of writing divsn. 1993—), Nat. Writing Program Adminstrs. (mem. cons.-evaluator program 1982—, mem. exec. bd. 1982-84, 89-90, v.p. 1985-86, pres. 1987-88), Nat. Coun. Tchrs. English (mem. CCCC nominating com. 1985, mem. coll. sect. com. 1987-90). Home: 53 Edgehill Rd New Haven CT 06511-1343 Office: Yale U Dept English PO Box 208302 New Haven CT 06520-8302

PETERSON, LOUIS ROBERT, retired consumer products company executive; b. Racine, Wis., Nov. 11, 1923; s. Edward J. and Effie (Buenning) P.; m. Marian Francis Barber, Nov. 22, 1947; children: Karen Jean, Kathleen Alice, Jill Ann. Student, Utah State Agrl. Coll., U. Wis.-Racine. With Johnson Wax Co., Racine, Wis., 1947—; sales rep. Johnson Wax Co., 1970-72, v.p. household sales, 1972-76, exec. v.p. U.S. consumer products, ptnr. in office of the chmn., 1976-86, exec. v.p. internat. consumer products, 1980—; bd. dirs. Biltmore Investors Bank, Phoenix. Past pres., bd. dirs. Racine Area United Way.; bd. dirs. St. Mary's Med. Ctr. With U.S. Army, 1943-46. Mem. Northwestern U. Assocs., Conf. Bd. (internat. council), Internat. C. of C. (U.S. Council internat. bus.). Republican. Roman Catholic. Clubs: Somerset (Racine, Wis.); Pinnacle Peak Country (Scottsdale, Ariz.) (bd. dirs.). Home: RR 1 Box 1168 Hayward WI 54843-9727 also: 8723 E Clubhouse Way Scottsdale AZ 85255-4231

PETERSON, M. ROGER, international banker, retired manufacturing executive, retired air force officer; b. Chgo., June 6, 1929; s. Milton Albert and LaVergne Geraldine (Andelin) P.; m. Sally Ann Alder, Apr. 25, 1952; children: Bruce Roger, Dale Alder, Drew Alan. B.S. in Acctg., UCLA, 1955; M.S. in Mgmt., U. Colo., 1964; grad., Air Command and Staff Coll. Air U., Ala., 1965; grad. Exec. Program for Internat. and Nat. Security, J.F. Kennedy Sch. Govt., Harvard U., 1983. Joined USAF, 1955, advanced through grades to maj. gen., 1981, pilot, 1956-61, mgr. tactical missile site constrn., 1961; air officer comdg. 11th Cadet Squadron, Air Force Cadet Wing USAF Acad., 1961-64; asst. sec. Joint Chiefs of Staff and NSC matters for Hdqrs. Pentagon, 1965-68; transport pilot USAF, Vietnam, 1968; asst. chmn. U.S.-Japan Joint Com., Adminstrn. of Status of Forces Agreement USAF, 1968-73, chief program cost, dir. budget, 1973-76, chief plans, comptroller of Air Force, 1976-78, dir. mgmt. analysis, 1978-79, dir. programs, asst. chief of staff for research and devel., 1979-81; asst. dir. plans, policies and programs Def. Logistics Agy., Alexandria, Va., 1981-82, dep. dir., 1982-83; asst. dep. chief staff for logistics and engrng. Hdqrs. USAF, Washington, 1983-84; pres., chief exec. officer advanced tech. factory, 1984-85; strategic planner United Techs. Corp., 1985-88; v.p., chief oper. officer Sikorsky Support Svcs. Inc., 1988-90; exec. asst. to mng. ptnr. O'Connor & Assocs., 1990-92; mng. dir. global ops. and svcs. Swiss Bank Corp., Zurich, 1992-96; chief of staff Swiss Bank Corp. N.Am., Chgo., 1996—, N.Am. and S.Am., 1996—; mng. dir. Swiss Bank Corp. N.Am., N.Y., 1996—. Decorated D.S.M., Legion of Merit, Air medal with oak leaf cluster, Joint Service Commendation medal, Air Force Commendation medal with two oak leaf clusters. Mem. Air Force Assn., Beta Gamma Sigma, Sigma Iota Epsilon. Presbyterian. Designed and negotiated consolidation of U.S. Air Force bases in Tokyo, 1970-73; negotiated mil. and civil aviation agreement for return of Okinawa to Japan; created global bus. mgmt. system for Swiss Bank Corp. Home: 175 N Harbor Dr Apt 3902/03 Chicago IL 60601-7344 Office: Swiss Bank Corp 222 Broadway New York NY 10038-2510 also: Swiss Bank Corp c/o Jan Galayda 141 W Jackson Blvd Chicago IL 60604-2901 *Always with honor.*

PETERSON, MARY L., state agency official. BA in English, Carleton Coll., 1972; MA in Tchg. in Edn. and English, Duke U., 1974; postgrad., U. Utah, 1977-80. Tchr. English, New Canaan (Conn.) Sch. Dist., from 1973, Brighton Ctrl. Sch. Dist., Rochester, N.Y., Davis County Sch. Dist., Kaysville, Utah, until 1977; rsch. asst. in cultural founds. and ednl. adminstrn. U. Utah, Salt Lake City, 1977-79; prin. St. Nicholas Elem. Sch., Rupert, Idaho, 1979-81; cons. Nev. Dept. Edn., Carson City, 1981-92, dep. supt. instrnl., rsch. and evaluative svcs., 1992-94, supt. pub. instrn., 1994—; assessor Nev. Assessment Ctr., Nat. Assn. Secondary Sch. Prins.; mem. accreditation team N.W. Assn. Schs. and Colls.; trainer Tchr. Effectiveness for Student Achievement, Correlates Effective Schs.; facilitator Assisting Change in Edn.; mem. state team Nat. Coun. for Accreditation Tchr. Edn. Asst. editor: Work, Family and Careers (C. Brooklyn Derr), 1980; contbr. to profl. publs. Scholar Carleton Coll., Duke U. Mem. Phi Kappa Phi, Delta Kappa Gamma. Office: Nev Dept Edn Capitol Complex 700 E 5th St Carson City NV 89701-5096*

PETERSON, MERRILL DANIEL, history educator; b. Manhattan, Kans., Mar. 31, 1921; s. William Oscar and Alice Dwinell (Merrill) P.; m. Jean Hymphrey, May 24, 1944 (dec. Nov. 1995); children: Jeffrey Ward, Kent Merrill. Student, Kans. State U., 1939-41; AB, U. Kans., 1943; PhD in History of Am. Civilization, Harvard U., 1950. Teaching fellow Harvard U., Cambridge, Mass., 1948-49; instr., then asst. prof. history Brandeis U., Waltham, Mass., 1949-55; asst. prof., bicentennial preceptor Princeton U., N.J., 1955-58; mem. faculty Brandeis U., Waltham, Mass., 1958-62, dean students, 1960-62; Thomas Jefferson Found. prof. U. Va., Charlottesville, 1962-87, Thomas Jefferson Found. prof. emeritus, 1987—, chmn. dept. history, 1966-72, dean of faculty Arts and Scis., 1981-85; Mary Ball Washington prof. Am. History University Coll., Dublin, Ireland, 1988-89; vol. Peace Corps, Armenia, 1997—; scholar in residence Bellagio Study Ctr., 1974; faculty Salzburg Seminar in Am. Studies, 1975; Lamar lectr. Mercer U., 1975; Fleming lectr. La. State U., 1980; lectr. at 15 European univs., 40 Am. colls. and univs. Author: The Jefferson Image in the American Mind, 1960 (Bancroft prize, Gold medal Thomas Jefferson Meml. Found.), Major Crises in American History, 2 vols., 1962, Democracy, Liberty and Property: The State Constitutional Convention Debates of the 1820s, 1966, Thomas Jefferson and the New Nation: A Biography, 1970, James Madison: A Biography in His Own Word, 1974, Adams and Jefferson: A Revolutionary Dialogue, 1976, Olive Branch and Sword: The Compromise of 1933, 1982, The Great Triumvirate: Webster, Clay and Calhoun, 1987; editor: Thomas Jefferson: A Historical Profile, 1966, The Portable Thomas Jefferson, 1975, Thomas Jefferson Writings, 1984, Thomas Jefferson: A Reference Biography, 1986, The Virginia Statute for Religious Freedom: Its Evolution and Consequences in American History, 1988, Visitors to Monticello, 1989, Lincoln in American Memory, 1994 (History finalist, Pulitzer prize, PBK Book award U. Va.). Bd. dirs. Thomas Meml. Found.; chmn. Thomas Jefferson Commemoration Commn., 1993-94. Guggenheim fellow, 1962-63, Ctr. for Advanced Study in Behavioral Scis. fellow, 1968-69, NEH and Nat. Humanities Ctr. fellow, 1980-81; recipient 20th Anniversary award Va. Found. for Humanities, 1994, Nat. First Freedom award First Freedom Coun., 1997. Fellow Am. Acad. Arts and Scis.; mem. Am. Hist. Assn., So. Hist. Assn., Soc. Am. Historians, Am. Antiquarian Soc., Mass. Hist. Soc., Phi Beta Kappa. Home: # 6 250 Pantops Mountain Rd Charlottesville VA 22911

PETERSON, MILDRED OTHMER (MRS. HOWARD R. PETERSON), civic leader, lecturer, writer, librarian; b. Omaha, Oct. 19, 1902; d. Frederick George and Freda Darling (Snyder) Othmer; m. Howard R. Peterson, Aug. 25, 1923 (dec. Feb. 9, 1970). Student, U. Iowa, 1919, U. Nebr., 1921-23, Northwestern U., 1935, U. Chgo., 1943, Am. U. Switzerland, 1985. Asst. purchasing agt. Met. Utilities Dist., 1920-21; asst. U. Nebr. Library, 1921-23; tchr. piano, dir. choir Harlan, Iowa, 1924-26; dir. pub. relations and gen. asst. Des Moines Pub. Library, 1928-35; broadcaster weekly book programs Sta. WHO, Des Moines, and other Iowa radio stas.; columnist, writer Mid-West News Syndicate, Des Moines Register and Tribune; editor Book Marks, 1929-35; writer for Drug Topics, Drug Trade News, others, No. Ill., 1935; writer, spl. asst. ALA, Chgo., 1935-59, Chgo. Tribune, 1941—; travel writer Hyde Park Herald, 1974—; lectr. SS. Rotterdam of Holland Am. Line, 1971; lectr. tours U.S., Can., Mexico, 1970—; internat. lectr. on travel, fgn. jewelry and internat. relations, 1940—; guest lectr. on Golden Odyssey Ship Royal Cruise Line to Orient, world trip with Purdue U. Alumni, Feb.-Mar., 1988; del. 1st Assembly Librarians Ams., Washington, 1947. Contbr. articles to newspapers, periodicals, encys. and yearbooks. Chmn. India Famine Relief, 1943; a founder Pan Am. Coun., 1939, v.p., 1982-86, numerous other coms.; founder, past pres. Pan Am. Bd. Edn., 1955-58, Internat. Visitors Ctr., 1952-56, a founder, 1st pres. and hon. life dir., 1986; rep. Chgo. at State Dept. Conf. on Cmty. Svcs. to Fgn. Visitors; a founder COSERV (Nat. Coun. Cmty. Svcs. to Internat. Visitors), Washington, 1957; mem. exec. bd., awards com. Mayor's Com. on Chgo. Beautiful; mem. Ill. Gov.'s Com. on Ptnrs. of The Ams., São Paulo, Brazil and Ill. sister states; mem. U.S. Dept. State conf. for Ptnrs. of Am., Dominican Republic, 1985, Little Rock, 1986, Jamaica, 1987 (Superior Svc. award 1987), Miami Beach, Fla., 1988; mem. chancellor's com. U. Nebr., conf. com. U. Chgo., 1990; former bd. dirs. coun., troop leader Girl Scouts U.S., Council Bluffs, Iowa, 1926-28; mem. Women's Soc., coun., stewardship and mission bds. Hyde Pk. Union Ch., also 75th, 100th and 110th anniversary coms.; bd. dirs. YWCA, Chgo. Lung Assn.; women's bd. Camp Brueckner-Farr, Grad. Bapt. Student Ctr.; mem. exec. coun. Friends of Sta. WTTW-TV; chairwoman Hyde Pk. Christmas Seals Campaign, 1985-86, 87-88 (Outstanding Svc. award 1987); bd. dirs. Maridian Hospice; mem. centennial com. U. Chgo. Svc. League, 1995; mem. benefit com. Chgo. Svc. League, 1995, mem. music and travel sects.; v.p. U. Chgo. Internat. House Assn.; mem. Vista Homes Garden Assn., Mus. Sci. and Industry, Chgo. Art Inst. Decorated Uruguayan medal, 1952; Internat. Eloy Alfaro medal, 1952; Order of Carlos Manuel de Cespedes Cuba; Order of Vasco Nuñez de Balboa Panama; cited by Chgo. Sun, Ill. Adult Edn. Council, 1953; recipient scholarship in Latin-Am. field U. Chgo. and Coordinator Inter-Am. Affairs, U.S. Govt., 1943, world understanding merit award Chgo. Council on Fgn. Relations, 1955, Disting. Service award Hospitality Center, 1958, Disting. Service medal U. Nebr., Disting. Service medal U. Nebr. Alumni Assn., 1963, Disting. Achievement award, 1975, Ambassador of Friendship award Am. Friendship Club, 1963, merit award YWCA for 10 yrs. as mem. bd., 1964 and Disting. Service award, 1975; Civic salute WMAQ radio, Chgo., 1965; Disting. Service award Pan-Am. Bd. Edn., 1966; also founders award, 1968; Laura Hughes Lunde Meml. award Citizens Greater Chgo., 1968; Friendship award Philippine Girl Scouts, 1971; Disting. Service award OAS, 1971; named Woman of Yr. Friends of Chgo. Sch. and Workshop for Retarded, 1975; Disting. Service trophy Fedn. Latin Am. Orgns., 1976; Merit Award WTTW-TV, Chgo., 1983; named to Sr. Citizens Hall of Fame, 1992, Chgo. Hall of Fame, 1992. Fellow Am. Internat. Acad. (life mem.); mem. Nat. Council Women U.S., Chgo. Council for USA-USSR Friendship (mem. Leaders Tour of China 1990), English Speaking Union, Japan-Am. Com., U.S.-China Friendship Assn. (bd. dirs. 1987—, Vol. award 1990), Internat. House Assn. (v.p.), Pan-Am. Bd. Edn. (founder, pres., Merit award), U.S. Capitol Hist. Soc., Ill. Hist. Soc., Nebr. Hist. Soc., Chgo. Hist. Soc., Hyde Park Hist. Soc. (charter mem. award 1978), Field Mus. Natural History, Mus. Sci. and Industry, Lincoln Park Zool. Soc., Citizenship Council Met. Chgo., Oriental Inst., Am. Heritage Coun., ALA, Ill. Libr. Assn. (local arrangements com. of nat. conf. 1976, 78, 85, 95), Internat. Fedn. Libr. Assns. (local arrangements com. 1985 Chgo.), Soc. Woman Geographers (pres. Chgo. chpt., v.p. internat. coun. 1987—), Coun. Fgn. Rels. (speakers bur.), Nat. Assn. Travel Ofcls. (Chgo. Tribune rep.), Library Internat. Rels. (ball com. 1969—), U. Nebr. Alumni Assn. (past pres. Des Moines, Rockford and Chgo. chpts.), U. Nebr. Found., U. Chgo. Internat. House Assn. (v.p. 1976—), Art Inst. Chgo., U. Chgo. Svc. League (past bd. mem., now bd. dirs. Camp Brueckner-Farr Aux.), Am. Legion Aux. (mem. state bds. Iowa and Ill.), AAUW, LWV, Children's Benefit League, Woman's Bd. United Negro Coll. Fund, Renaissance Soc., Peruvian Arts Soc., Hispanic Soc. Chgo., Chgo. Acad. Scis. (woman's bd.), Chgo. Chamber Orch. Assn., John G. Shedd Soc., Japan Am. Soc., Friends Chgo. Pub. Library, Chgo. Symphony Soc., Citizens Greater Chgo., Found. for Ill. Archaeology, Cook County Hosp. Aux., Lyric Opera Guild, Crossroads Student Center, Internat. Platform Assn., Exec. Service Corps Chgo., Friends of Grant Park Concerts, Chgo. Council for USA-USSR, Friendship U. Ill., Chgo. Internat. Programs, Friends of Parks, Friends of Downtown, Friends of Chgo. River, Met. Planning Coun., Chgo. Architecture Found., Landmarks Presrvation Coun., Open Lands Project, Women in Arts (charter mem. Washington chpt.), Geographic Soc. Chgo., Alpha Delta Pi (past pres. Omaha, Des Moines and Chgo. alumnae chpts., editor Adephean 1938-39, woman of year award U.S. and Can. 1955), Xi Delta. Clubs: Mem. Order Eastern Star, South Shore Country, College, Quadrangle, Ill. Athletic, University of Chicago Dames, Iowa Authors, Lakeside Lawn Bowling, Hyde Park Neighborhood, Travellers Century (World's Most Travelled Person plaque 1993). Travelled to and lecturer on over 250 countries, including China and Albania; extensive foreign Christmas card collection Exhibited at Museum Scienc and Industry, Chicago Public Library, Chicago Sun Times, Des Moines Public Library, others, given to Chicago Pub Library; donor sheet music, musical records, thousands of colored slides taken during her extensive travels to Chicago Public Library, Egyptian jewelry to University of Chicago Oriental Institute, East Indian rose cut diamonds and other jewels to Smart Gallery, University of Chicago, Cruise of the Americas through Panama Canal from East to West. Address: 5834 S Stony Island Ave Chicago IL 60637-2060

PETERSON, MONICA DOROTHY, actress, singer, model, writer, entrepreneur. Drama cert., Neighborhood Playhouse, N.Y.C., 1963, Jeff Corey Sch. Acting, 1967; student Sch. Music and Dance, Covent Garden, London, 1972; AA, Santa Monica Coll., 1983; BA, U. So. Calif., 1986. Editorial sec., writer Look mag., N.Y.C., 1964-66; asst. mgr. Venture Mag. Advt., N.Y.C., 1965-66; actress, singer, performer William Morris Agy., Hollywood, Calif., 1967-70, also London, Spain, Italy; contract player 20th Century Fox, 1967-70; contract singer, dancer, actress L.A. City Hall Theatre of Arts, 1975-80; staff writer USC Trojan Newspaper, L.A., 1981-83; newspaper editor SMC, L.A., 1983-84; writer USC Trojan Newspaper, 1985-86; exec. asst., 1986—; chair, writer Crystal Awards Show, 1992, 1993; with Dem. Leadership for 21st Century L.A. Chpt., 1993, asst. p.r. media Mayoral Roundtable Whittle Communications, 1993; jazz singer and actress, 1987—; active in telecomm., 1987—; comml. agt. Tisherman Agy., L.A.; theatrical agt. Dorothy Day Otis Agy., Beverly Hills, Calif., R.H. Talen Agy. for comml. meredian for print; Paris fashion runway model, 1993; scriptwriter, 1993; asst. pub. rels./media Dem. Leadership 21st Century Mayoral Roundtable for Whittle Comm. Raleigh Studioes, 1993, working with L.A. chpt., 1993; entrepreneur Herbal Essence. Editorial and entertainment editor, prodr., writer, reporter Sta. KCRW Radio Programs, 1995, several musical videos; extensive travel as a performer (including 2-month concert in Japan), theatre, stage, TV, radio; one-woman shows include Toys for Tots Shows, L.A., Biltmore Jazz Club, other jazz, supper clubs with continuous return engagements; contbr. articles to mags.; scriptwriter Crystal awards, 1995, infomercials, 1995, 96. Script analyst, editor, asst. casting dir. Inner City Cultural City, L.A., 1974-76; vol. Easter Seals, also vol. work for diabetics, homeless, needy, elderly and sick; v.p. Internat. Coun.; active Bill Clinton for Pres. Campaign, 1992, Voters Revolt Campaign, 1992; mem. Dem. Com., Washington; elected Community Bd. Dirs. Recipient Hollywood Star of Tomorrow award ABC, 1968, Overseas award USO, 1969, Poetry award N.Am. Poetry Contest, 1996, others. Mem. SAG (v.p. minority com. 1969-71, rep. Image award 1969-72), AFTRA, Women in Film (scriptwriter, prodr. Cannes Film Festival, scriptwriter Crystal awards 1992, chair and writer Crystal awards 1993), Equity, Internat. Platform Assn., Women In Comm. (del. Cannes Film Festival 1993), U. So. Calif. Alumni Assn., Soc. of Singers, Cabaret West. Democrat. Roman Catholic. Avocations: jogging (ran L.A. marathon 94, 95, 96), reading, softball, music.

PETERSON, MYRA M., special education educator; b. Eagle Bend, Minn., July 1, 1937; children: Randy E., Vicky L. Rholl. Assoc. in Edn., St. Cloud State U., 1957, BS in Elem. Edn., 1963; cert. in learning disabilities, Bemidji State U., 1979. Cert. edn. Elem. instr. Wadena (Minn.) Pub. Sch., 1957-60;

supplemental edn. and secondary devel. reading Bertha-Hewitt (Minn.) Sch., 1964-75, learning disabilities instr., 1975—; coord. for local sch. Minn. Basic Skills Program, Bertha-Hewitt (Minn.) Sch., 1980-85; adv. bd. for spl. needs N.W. Tech. Coll., Wadena, 1992—. Mem., edn. com. United Meth. Ch., Wadena; pres. Am. Legion Aux., Wadena, 1990—. Named Tchr. of Yr., Bertha-Hewitt (Minn.) Edn. Assn., 1981. Mem. NEA, Minn. State Edn. Assn., Bertha-Hewitt Edn. Assn., N.W. Reading Coun. (pres. 1987-88), Delta Kappa Gamma Internat. (pres. Alpha Eta chpt. 1993-95, Woman of Achievement 1991). Office: Bertha-Hewitt Sch PO Box 8 Bertha MN 56437

PETERSON, NAD A., lawyer, retired corporate executive; b. Mt. Pleasant, Utah, 1926; m. Martha Peterson, 1948; children: Anne Carroll (Mrs. Stanford P. Darger, Jr.), Christian, Elizabeth (Mrs. Henry G. Ingersoll), Robert and Lane (twins). A.B., George Washington U., 1950, J.D., 1953. Bar: D.C. 1953, Calif. 1960, U.S. Supreme Ct. 1958. Law practice Washington, 1953-60; sec., asst. gen. counsel Dart Industries, Los Angeles, 1960-67; chief counsel, 1967-73; gen. counsel Fluor Corp., 1973-79, v.p. law, 1979-82, sr. v.p. law, 1983-84; sr. v.p., sec. Fluor Corp., Irvine, Calif., 1984-93; sr. v.p., gen. counsel San Diego Gas & Electric Co., 1993-95. Mem. ABA, Calif. Bar Assn., Phi Delta Phi. Home: PO Box 9101 Rancho Santa Fe CA 92067

PETERSON, OSCAR EMMANUEL, pianist; b. Montreal, Que., Can., Aug. 15, 1925; s. Daniel and Olivia (John) P. Studied with Paul deMarky; LLD (hon.), Carleton U., 1973, Queen's U., 1976, Concordia U., 1979, McMaster U., 1981, U. of Victoria, 1981, U. Toronto, 1985, U. B.C., 1994; DMus (hon.), Mount Alison, N.B., 1980, U. Laval, 1985; LittD (hon.), York U., 1982; D.F.A. (hon.), Northwestern U., Evanston, Ill., 1983, Niagara U., 1996; MusD (hon.), U. Laval, 1985. Founder Advanced Sch. Contemporary Music, Toronto; former chancellor York U., 1991-94; chancellor emeritus York U., 1994. Began music career on weekly radio show, then with Johny Holmes Orchestra, Can., 1944-49; recorded with RCA Victor Records; appeared with Jazz at the Philharmonic, Carnegie Hall, 1949; toured the U.S. and Europe, 1950—; leader trio with Ray Brown, Irving Ashby, later Barney Kessel, Herb Ellis, Ed Thigpen, Sam Jones, Louie Hayes, concert appearances with Ella Fitzgerald, Eng., Scotland, 1955; appeared Stratford (Ont.) Shakespeare Festival, Newport Jazz Festival; recorded and performed solo piano works, 1972—; toured USSR, 1974, recordings with Billie Holiday, Fred Astaire, Benny Carter, Count Basie, Roy Eldridge, Lester Young, Ella Fitzgerald, Niels-Henning Orsted Pederson, Dizzy Gillespie, Harry Edison, Clark Terry; composer: Canadiana Suite, Hymn to Freedom, Fields of Endless Day, City Lights, Begone Dull Care, (with Norman McLaren) salute to Johann Sebastian Bach, music for films Big North and Silent Partner; author: Jazz Exercises and Pieces: Oscar Peterson New Piano Solos; numerous TV specials. Decorated officer Order of Canada, 1972, companion, 1984; recipient award for piano Down Beat mag. 13 times, Metronome mag. award, 1953-54, Edison award, 1962, Award of merit City of Toronto, (1st mention) 1973 (2d mention 1983), Diplome d'honneur Can. Conf. of the Arts, 1975, Grammy award 7 times, Olympic Key to Montreal, The Queen's medal, 1977, Genie Film award for film score The Silent Partner, 1978, Grand-Prix du Disques for Night Child album, 1981, Canadian Band Festival Award, 1982, Juno Hall of Fame award, 1982, George Peabody medal Peabody Conservatory of Music, Balt., 1987, Volunteer award Roy Thompson Hall, Toronto, 1987, Can. Club Arts and Letters award, N.Y.C., 1987, Officer in Order of Arts and Letters, France, 1989, Chevalier Order of Que., 1991, Lifetime Achievement Toronto Arts Award, 1991, appointed Order of Ontario, 1992, Lifetime Achievement Gov. Gens. award, 1992, Glenn Gould prize, 1993, Gemini Film award, 1993, Three-Key award Bern Internat. Jazz Festival, 1995, NARAS Grammy award for Lifetime Achievement, 1997, Loyola medal, 1997, Carnegie Hall Anniversary medal, Charlie Parker bronze medal, Ville de Salon de Provence medal, Award of Thanks, Mexico City; 12-time jazz poll winner Playboy mag.; named number one (piano) Jazz and Pop, Readers Poll 1968, 85; named to U. Calif. at Berkeley Hall of Fame, 1983, Contemporary Keyboard Hall of Fame, 1983; Oscar Peterson Day proclaimed by Baltimore, Oreg., 1981, 83; Oscar Peterson Scholarship founded in his honor Berklee Sch. of Music, Boston, 1982. Avocations: fly fishing, photography, astronomy. Office: Regal Recordings Ltd, 2421 Hammond Rd, Mississauga, ON Canada L5K 1T3

PETERSON, PATTI MCGILL, academic administrator; b. Johnstown, Pa., May 20, 1943; d. Earl Frampton and Helen G. McGill; m. Luther D. Peterson, Aug. 31, 1968; 1 son, Lars-Anders. B.A. in Polit. Sci., Pa. State U., 1965; M.A. in Polit. Sci., U. Wis., 1968, Ph.D. in Polit. Sci. and Ednl. Policy, 1974; cert. advance study, Harvard U., 1977; D.Litt (hon.), Le Moyne Coll. Clarkson U., 1983. Asst. prof. polit. sci., dean of freshman women Schiller Coll., Ger., 1968-69; asst. prof. polit. sci. SUNY-Oswego, 1971-72, asst. to pres., adj. prof., 1972-77, v.p. acad. services and planning, assoc. prof., 1978-80; pres. Wells Coll., Aurora, N.Y., 1980-87, St. Lawrence U., Canton, N.Y., 1987-96; pres. emerita St. Lawrence U., 1996—, Wells Coll., 1996—; sr. fellow Inst. for Public Policy, Cornell U., 1996—; bd. dirs. Nia. Mo. Power Corp., John Hancock Mut. Funds. Author numerous articles in field. Trustee Northwood Sch. Sta.; bd. overseers The Nelson A. Rockefeller Inst. Govt., 1988; trustee Assn. Am. Colls., 1987; chmn. Pub. Leadership Edn. Network, 1983-85; mem. Gov.'s Com. on Vol. Enterprise, 1983-85; pres. Assn. Colls. and Univs., N.Y., 1984-86; chair Women's Coll. Coalition, 1983-85, U.S.-Can. Fulbright Com., 1990-93; mem. Com. on Nat. Challenges in Higher Edn., 1986-88. Carnegie fellow Harvard U., 1977. Mem. Am. Coun. Edn. (chmn. com. on leadership devel. and acad. adminstrn. 1982-84), Mid. States Assn. Colls. and Schs. (cons., chmn.). Home: Brown Rd King Ferry NY 13081 Office: Inst for Public Affairs Cornell Univ 473 Hollister Hall Ithaca NY 14853-3501

PETERSON, PAUL QUAYLE, retired university dean, physician; b. Marissa, Ill., June 30, 1912; s. Charles Logan and Phoebe (Lewis) P.; m. Kathryn Lentz, Aug. 1936; children—Philip Lewis, Frances Anne; m. Mildred Cook Allison, Dec. 7, 1957; foster children—Patricia Elaine Allison, Susan Claire Allison. B.S., U. Ill., 1933, M.D., 1937; M.P.H., U. Mich., 1946. Diplomte Am. Bd. Preventive Medicine (service mem., vice chmn. 1976—). Intern Bethesda Hosp., Cin., 1936-37; gen. resident Meml. Hosp., Lima, Ohio, 1937-38; gen. practice medicine McLeansboro, Ill., 1939-40; practice medicine specializing in preventive medicine, 1940-46; health officer Breckenridge, Meade and Hancock counties, Ky., 1940-41, Warren, Simpson and Allen counties, 1942-45; regional cons., div. local health Ky. Health Dept., 1946-47; chief bur. direct services, asst. to dir. Ohio Dept. Health, 1948-51; asst. prof. preventive medicine Ohio State U., 1948-51; chief health div. Mut. Security Mission to China, Taipei, Taiwan, 1952-53; chief health and sanitation div. USOM (asso. states Cambodia, Laos and Vietnam), 1954; chief program services, div. internat. health USPHS, Washington, 1955; chronic disease program USPHS, 1957; asst. dir. Nat. Inst. Allergy and Infectious Diseases, NIH, 1958-61; dep. chief div. pub. health methods Office Surgeon Gen., 1961-62, chief div., 1962-64; asst. surgeon gen. USPHS, 1964, asso. chief bur. state services (community health), 1964-67; dep. dir. Bur. Health Services, 1967-68; asso. adminstr. Health Services and Mental Health Adminstrn., 1968-70; dep. surgeon gen., 1970; dean Grad. Sch. Pub. Health, U. Ill., Chgo., 1971-82, dean emeritus, 1982—; dir. office rsch. Ctr. Study Patient Care, U. Ill. Med. Ctr., 1979-86; dir. Ill. Dept. Pub. Health, 1977-79, Am. Bur. Med. Aid to China; mem. residency rev. com. Liaison Com. Grad. Med. Edn., 1976—; cons. Ctr. for Health Services Research, 1982—. mem. editorial bd. Pub. Health Service World, Mil. Medicine. Commr. USPHS, 1941. Recipient Disting. Service award U. Ill. Alumni Assn., 1984. Fellow Am. Pub. Health Assn. (chmn. program area com. pub. health adminstrn.); mem. Am. Assn. Pub. Health Physicians (pres. 1975-76), AMA (intersplty. adv. bd. 1975-77), Assn. Schs. Pub. Health (exec. com. 1975—), Pub. Health Service Commd. Officers Assn. (sec. D.C. 1959), AAAS, Assn. Mil Surgeons, Am. Coll. Preventive Medicine (regent 1975—), Ill. Hosp. Assn. (exec. bd. 1974-77, cert. correctional health com. of profl. cert. bd. 1990), Nat. Inst. of Health Alumni Assn. bd. dirs., 1993—, Phi Beta Pi (pres. 1935), Delta Omega. Methodist. Home: 1600 N Oak St Arlington VA 22209-2751

PETERSON, PETE, ambassador, former congressman. Mem. from Fla. U.S. Ho. of Reps., Washington; amb. U.S. Dept. State, Hanoi, Vietnam. Office: US Embassy, 7 Lang Ha Rd, Ba Dinh Dist Hanoi Vietnam*

PETERSON, PETER G., investment banker; b. Kearney Nebr., June 5, 1926; s. George and Venetia P.; m. Sally H., May 1953 (div. 1979); children: John, Jim, David, Holly, Michael; m. Joan Ganz Cooney, Apr. 26, 1980. BS, Northwestern U., 1947; MBA, U. Chgo. 1951; PhD (hon.) Colgate U., George Washington U., Northwestern U., Georgetown U., U. Rochester, Southampton Coll. at L.I., Exec. v.p. Market Facts, Chgo., 1948-52; v.p. McCann Erickson, Chgo. 1952-58; pres. Bell and Howell, Chgo., 1958-71, exec. v.p. 1958-61, CEO, 1963-71; asst. to Pres. of U.S. for Internat. Econ. Affairs, Washington, 1961-63; sec. of commerce U.S. Govt., 1972-73; CEO, chmn. bd. Lehman Bros. and Lehman Bros., Kuhn, Loeb, Inc., N.Y.C., 1973-84; chmn. The Blackstone Group, 1985—. Author: Will America Grow Up Before it Grows Old, Facing Up: How to Rescue the Economy from Crushing Debt and Restore the American Dream; editor: Readings in Market Organization and Price Policies; co-author: On Borrowed Time: How The Growth In Entitlement Spending Threatens America's Future. founding mem. Bi-Partisan Budget Appeal; pres. The Concord Coalition; trustee Commn. for Econ. Devel., Mus. Modern Art, N.Y.C. Recipient Outstanding Service award, Phoenix House, N.Y.C., 1976, Stephen Wise award, Am. Jewish Congress, 1981, U. Chgo. Alumni medal, 1983, Man of Vision award, 1994, Nebraskalander award, 1994; named to Pres. Clinton's Bi-Partisan Comm. on Entitlement Refirm, 1994. Mem. Council Fgn. Relations (chmn. bd. 1985—), Inst. Internat. Econs. (chmn. bd.), Nat. Bur. Econ. Research (trustee), Japan Soc. Republican. Clubs: Maidstone (Easthampton, N.Y.); Chgo., River, Links (Chgo.); Augusta Nat.; Burning Tree (Washington), Atlantic. Home: 435 E 52nd St Apt 11G New York NY 10022-6445 Office: The Blackstone Group 345 Park Ave New York NY 10154-0004

PETERSON, PHILIP EVERETT, legal educator; b. Galena, Ill., July 10, 1922; s. Everett Marvin and Marie Isabelle (Gleason) P.; m. Jeanne Rosanna Payette, Nov. 17, 1947; children—Christine Marie, Barbara Ellen, Claudia Ann, Patricia Eileen, Eric Karl, Kurt Kevin. Student, Loras Coll., 1948; B.S., U. Ill., 1950, J.D., 1952; LL.M., Harvard, 1958. Bar: Ill. bar 1951, Idaho bar 1955, U.S. Supreme Ct. bar 1958. Practice in Urbana, Ill., 1951-52; mem. faculty U. Idaho Law Sch., 1952-88, prof. law, 1961-88, dean, 1962-67; legal cons., 1955—. Served with AUS, 1942-48. Mem. ABA, Ill. Bar Assn., Idaho Bar Assn., AAUP. Home: 318 5th St Lewiston ID 83501-2408

PETERSON, RALPH R., engineering executive; b. 1944. BS in Civil Engring., Oreg. State U., 1969; MS in Environ. Engring., Stanford U., 1970; AMP, Harvard Bus. Sch., 1991. Engring. aide Johnson, Underkofler & Briggs, Boise, 1962-63; surveyor Smith, Keyes & Blakely, Caldwell, Idaho, 1963-64; with Chronic & Assocs., Boise, 1964-65; with CH2M Hill Cos., Ltd., 1965—, sr. v.p., dir. tech., 1988, pres., CEO, 1990. Office: CH2M Hill Cos Ltd 6060 S Willow Dr Greenwood Vlg CO 80111-5142

PETERSON, RICHARD ELTON, publisher; b. Spokane, Wash., Apr. 26, 1941; s. Darrel Emil and Katherine (Millar) P.; m. Ruthanne Hawkins, Aug. 12, 1977; children—Scott Edward, Andrew Richard; stepchildren—Troy Donald Slocum, Sean James Slocum. B.S. in Edn., U. Mo., 1963; M.B.A., U. Chgo., 1975; postgrad., Stanford U. Tchr. high sch. math. Brunswick, Mo.; tchr. Park Ridge, Ill., 1963-65; profl. baseball player N.Y. Mets., 1963-65; with Scott, Foresman & Co., 1965-93, sales rep., 1965-70, market rsch. profl., 1970-73; mktg. coord. Scott, Foresman & Co., Calif., 1973-77; regional v.p., mgr. ea. region Scott, Foresman & Co., Oakland, N.J., 1977-78; sr. v.p. mktg. Scott, Foresman & Co., Glenview, Ill., 1978-84, sr. v.p., gen. mgr. sch. div., 1984-88, pres., CEO, 1988-93, also bd. dirs.; group v.p. Harper/Collins Pub., N.Y.C., 1992-93. Bd. dirs. Evanston Hosp. Corp., 1991—; bd. govs. Northwestern U. Libr., Evanston, Ill., 1993—; bd. dirs. The Youth Campass, Park Ridge, Ill., 1995—. Mem. Assn. Am. Pubs. (chmn. Calif. com. 1980-86, exec. com. sch. divsn. 1985-88, 90-93, chmn. exec. com. 1986-88), Western Golf Assn. (bd. dirs. 1987—). Home: 707 Edgemont Ln Park Ridge IL 60068-2652

PETERSON, RICHARD WILLIAM, magistrate judge, lawyer; b. Council Bluffs, Iowa, Sept. 29, 1925; s. Henry K. and Laura May (Robinson) P.; m. Patricia Mae Fox, Aug. 14, 1949; children: Katherine Ilene Peterson Sherbondy, Jon Eric, Timothy Richard. BA, U. Iowa, 1949, JD with distinction, 1951; postgrad., U. Nebr.-Omaha, 1972-80, 86. Bar: Iowa 1951, U.S. Dist. Ct. (so. dist.) Iowa 1951, U.S. Supreme Ct. 1991. Pvt. practice law Council Bluffs, 1951—; U.S. commr. U.S. Dist. Ct. (so. dist.) Iowa, 1958-70; part-time U.S. magistrate judge U.S. Dist. Ct. (so. dist.) Iowa, 1970—; mem. nat. faculty Fed. Jud. Ctr., Washington, 1972-82; emeritus trustee Children's Square, U.S.A.; verifying ofcl. Internat. Prisoner Transfer Treaties, Mexico City, 1977, La Paz, Bolivia, 1980, 81, Lima, Peru, 1981. Contbr. articles to legal publs. Bd. dirs. Pottawattamie County (Iowa) chpt. ARC, state fund chmn., 1957-58; state chmn. Radio Free Europe, 1960-61; dist. chmn. Trailblazer dist. Boy Scouts Am., 1952-55; mem. exec. coun. Mid-Am. Coun., 1976—. With inf. U.S. Army, 1943-46. Decorated Purple Heart, Bronze Star; named Outstanding Young Man Council Bluffs C. of C., 1959. Fellow Am. Bar Found.; mem. ABA, Am. Judicature Soc., Iowa Bar Assn. (chmn. com. fed. practice 1978-80), Pottawattamie County Bar Assn. (pres. 1979-80), Fed. Bar Assn., Inter-Am. Bar Assn., Supreme Ct. Hist. Soc., Fed. Magistrate Judges Assn. (pres. 1978-79), Iowa Conf. Bar Assn. Pres. (pres. 1985-87), Hist. Soc. of U.S. Cts. Eighth Jud. Cir. (pres. 1989—), Kiwanis (pres. Council Bluffs club 1957), Masons, Phi Delta Phi, Delta Sigma Rho, Omicron Delta Kappa. Republican. Lutheran. Home: 1007 Arbor Ridge Cir Council Bluffs IA 51503-5000 Office: PO Box 248 25 Main Pl Ste 200 Council Bluffs IA 51503

PETERSON, ROBERT ALLEN, marketing educator; b. N.Y.C., Mar. 25, 1944; s. Robert A. and Carrol D. (Collins) P.; m. Diane S. Femrite, June 18, 1966; children: Jeffrey, Jennifer, Matthew. B.S., U. Minn., 1966, M.S., 1968, Ph.D., 1970. Asst. prof. mktg. U. Tex., Austin, 1970-73, assoc. prof., 1973-77, prof., 1977—, John T. Stuart chair, 1985—, chmn. dept. mktg. adminstrn., 1983-85; prin. Group Seven Assocs., Austin. Author: Marketing Research, 1982, 2d edit., 1988; co-author: Modern American Capitalism, 1990, Strategic Marketing, 7th edit., 1995; editor: Jour. Mktg. Rsch., 1985-88, Jour. Acad. Mktg. Sci., 1991-96; mem. editorial bd. Jour. Mktg., Bus. Rev., Internat. Mktg. Rev. Recipient rsch. award AMA, 1988, Charles Hurwitz fellow, 1983—. Fellow Southwestern Mktg. Assn. (pres. 1977-78), Am. Mktg. Assn. (v.p. 1980-81), Acad. Mktg. Sci. (bd. govs. 1982-86, chmn. 1994—, Am. Inst. Decision Scis. (dir. 1974-75). Lutheran. Office: Univ Texas Dept Mktg Austin TX 78712

PETERSON, ROBERT AUSTIN, manufacturing company executive retired; b. Sioux City, Iowa, July 5, 1925; s. Austen W. and Marie (Mueller) P.; m. Carol May Hudy, May 17, 1952; children: Roberta, Richard., Bruce. BS, U. Minn., 1946, BBA, 1947. Credit mgr. New Holland Machine div. Sperry Rand Corp., Mpls., 1952-61; from credit mgr. to treas. Toro Co., Mpls., 1961-70; v.p., treas. internat. fin. Toro Co., 1970-83; v.p., fin., pres. Toro Credit Co., 1983-93; bd. dirs. Tesco, South Miami, Fla., Wesco Turf, Sarasota, Fla., Toro Credit Co. Chmn. Prior Lake Spring Lake Watershed Dist., 1970-80; chmn., bd. dirs. Prior Lake Bd. Edn., 1965-71; chmn. Scott County Republican Party, 1969-70; bd. dirs. Scott Carver Mental Health Center, 1969-73, Minn. Watershed Assn., 1972-76. Served to ensign USNR, 1943-46. Mem. Prior Lake Yacht Club (bd. dirs.).

PETERSON, ROBERT B., petroleum company executive; b. Regina, Sask., Can.. BSc in Chem. Engring., Queen's U., Kingston, Ont., Can., 1959, MSc in Chem. Engring., 1961. Various prodn. positions Imperial Oil Ltd. and affiliates, Can. and U.S., 1960-81; pres. and dir. Esso Resources, Calgary, Alta., Can., 1981; dir., pres. & CEO Esso Resources, Toronto, Ont., Can., 1982; exec. v.p., chief operating officer Imperial Oil Ltd., Toronto, 1988-92; chmn. Esso Resources, Toronto, 1988-92; chmn., CEO Imperial Oil Ltd., Toronto, 1994—; bd. dirs. Royal Bank Can., C.D. Howe Inst., Bus. Coun. Nat. Issues. Gov. Jr. Achievement Can.; past chmn. The Conf. Bd. Can. Mem. Assn. Profl. Engrs. Geologists and Geophysicists of Alta. Office: Imperial Oil Ltd, 111 St Clair Ave W, Toronto, ON Canada M5W 1K3

PETERSON, ROBERT L., meat processing executive; b. Nebr., July 14, 1932; married; children: Mark R., Susan P. Student, U. Nebr., 1950. With Wilson & Co., Jim Boyle Order Buying Co.; cattle buyer R&C Packing Co., 1956-61; cattle buyer, plant mgr., v.p. carcass prodn. Iowa Beef Processors, 1961-69; exec. v.p. ops. Spencer Foods, 1969-71; founder, pres., chmn., chief exec. officer Madison (Nebr.) Foods, 1971-76; group v.p. carcass div. Iowa Beef Processors, Inc. (name now IBP, Inc.) div. Occidental Petroleum Corp., Dakota City, Nebr., 1976-77, pres., chief operating officer, 1977-80, chief exec. officer, 1980-81, co-chmn. bd. dirs., 1981-82, chief exec. officer, CFO, 1980—. Served with Q.M.C. U.S. Army, 1952-54. Mem. Sioux City Country Club. Office: IBP Inc IBP Ave PO Box 515 Dakota City NE 68731-0515*

PETERSON, ROBIN TUCKER, marketing educator; b. Casper, Wyo., July 31, 1937; s. Walfred Arthur and Mary Lurene Peterson; m. Marjorie K. Greenwald, June 25, 1963; children: Timothy, Kimberly. BS, U. Wyo., 1959, MS in Bus., 1961; PhD., U. Wash., 1967. Mem. faculty Idaho State U., Pocatello, 1963-73; prof. mktg., head mktg. dept. St. Cloud (Minn.) State U., 1973-76, N.Mex. State U., Las Cruces, 1976—; Fulbright lectr., Yugoslavia, 1973; vis. scholar Ea. Mont. State Coll., 1985; Sunwest Fin. Svcs. Disting. Centennial prof. N.Mex. State U., 1991, 92. Author: Marketing-A Contemporary Introduction, 1976, Forecasting, 1976, edit., 1983, Personal Selling, 1977, Marketing in Action, 1977, Lernbook Marketing, 1984, Marketing: Concepts and Decision Making, 1987, Principles of Marketing, 1989, Argentina, 1990, Managing the Distributor Sales Network, 1990, Business Forecasting, 1992, Getting New Products to Market Rapidly, 1994; exec. editor Bus. Forecaster, 1993-94; editor Jour. Bus. and Entrepreneurship, 1994-97; also contbr. articles to profl. publs. Served with USAR, 1962-63. Mem. Am. Mktg. Assn., Sales and Mktg. Execs. Internat., Acad. Mktg. Sci. (pres. 1977-78, 80-82), Am. Arbitration Assn. (Outstanding Educators Am. award), S.W. Small Bus. Assn. (pres. 1983-84, Outstanding Mktg. Educators award), S.W. Mktg. Assn., Western Mktg. Educators, Las Cruces C. of C., Las Cruces Sales and Mktg. Club, Beta Gamma Sigma, Phi Kappa Psi, Alpha Kappa Psi, Alpha Mu Alpha. Republican. Presbyterian. Home: 4350 Diamondback Las Cruces NM 88011 Office: NMex State U Box 5280 Las Cruces NM 88001

PETERSON, RODERICK WILLIAM, television writer, producer; b. Phoenix, July 7, 1921; s. Paul Culver and Elizabeth (Butler) P.; m. Jewell Nichols, Feb. 28, 1943 (div. 1972); children: Eric, Lisa Peterson Winslow, Sally Peterson Hinson; m. Claire Whitaker, Nov. 18, 1972. Student, Phoenix Community Coll., 1939-41; B.A., U. Ariz., 1949. Program dir., writer Sta. KTAR, Phoenix, 1949-56; program dir. Sta. KGUN-TV, Tucson, 1956-57. Freelance network radio writer NBC, CBS, Mut. Broadcasting Sys.; freelance writer: (TV) Bonanza, Emergency, Black Saddle, Kilpatricks, Combat, The Deputy, Wonderful World of Disney, Laramie, (film) The Chartroose Caboose, 1959, (TV series) Laramie, 1960-64; writer, assoc. prodr. Walt Disney Prodns., 1965-75; writer, prodr.: (TV) The Waltons, 1977-79, exec. prodr., 1980-81; writer, prodr. MTM Studios, 1981-83; exec. supervising prodr., writer: (TV) Falcon Crest, 1984-86; writer: (TV spls.) (with Claire Whitaker) Walton Thanksgiving Reunion, 1993, A Walton Wedding, 1995. Served with USAAF, 1943-46, PTO. Mem. Writers Guild Am., Hollywood TV Acad., Am. Film Inst., ASCAP. Democrat.

PETERSON, RODNEY DELOS, mediator, forensic economist; b. Sioux Falls, S.D., Nov. 10, 1932; s. Severin Ingvald and Vera (Blow) P.; m. Evelyn Koubsky, Dec. 26, 1965; children: Douglas, Russell, Stuart. B.A., Huron (S.D.) Coll., 1958; M.S. in Econs, S.D. State U., 1959; Ph.D. in Econs. and Bus. Orgn, U. Nebr., 1964; J.D., U. Denver, 1982. Instr. U. Nebr., Lincoln, 1959-64; vis. asst. prof. agrl. econs. U. Nebr., summers 1964-66; instr. adult edn. U. Omaha, part-time 1963-64; asst. prof. econs. Cen. Wash. State U., Ellensburg, 1964-65; asst. prof., then assoc. prof. U. Idaho, Moscow, 1965-68; mem. faculty Colo. State U., Ft. Collins, 1968-91; prof. econs. Colo. State U., 1971-91, dir. Ctr. Econ. Edn., 1976-77, mediation officer, 1985-91, prof. emeritus, 1991; economist Fla. Dept. Commerce, 1991-96, Fla. Dept. Labor, 1996—; dir. Ctr. Econ. Edn. Colo. State U., 1976-77; vis. prof. Simon Fraser U., Vancouver, B.C., Can., 1974-75, univ. mediation officer, 1985-91. Author: Student Guide to Accompany Our Changing Economy, 1976, Economic Organization in Medical Equipment and Supply, 1973, Political Economy & American Capitalism, 1991; contbr. numerous articles to profl. jours. NSF fellow, summers 1971, 73, expert witness personal injury and antitrust cases. Mem. Am. Econ. Assn., Midwest Econs. Assn., Sigma Xi, Delta Sigma Pi, Beta Gamma Sigma, Omicron Delta Epsilon (regional dir. 1975-76). Home: 5433 Pinderton Way Tallahassee FL 32311-1412 Office: Fla Dept Labor Ste 200 Hartman Bldg Tallahassee FL 32399

PETERSON, ROGER LYMAN, insurance company executive; b. Cumberland, Wis., Apr. 14, 1938; s. Oscar Adolph and Myrtle (Nelson) P.; children: Jeffrey, Scott, Robert Michael. BS in Econs., Ill. Inst. Tech., 1960. CPCU, CLU; cert. assoc. in risk mgmt.; cert. ins. counselor. Field rep. Sun Atlas, Chgo., 1961-64, Western Casualty & Surety, Champaign, 1964-67, Am. States Ins. Co., Champaign, 1967-73; field rep., v.p. Tyler, Fletcher, Fink, Peterson, Champaign, 1973-83; v.p. Ins. Risk Mgrs., Champaign, 1983-94, sr. v.p., 1994—; chmn. Arm Internat., Austin, Tex., 1980-95. Bd. dirs. YMCA, Champaign, 1979—. With USCG, 1960-68. Mem. CPCU Soc., CLU Soc., Champaign County Ind. Ins. Agts. Assn. (past pres.), Lincolnshire Fields Country Club (past pres.), Cert. Ins. Counselors Soc., Chgo. Dist. Golf Assn. (bd. dirs.). Republican. Lutheran. Avocations: golf, basketball, bridge, reading. Home: 2308 Briar Hill Dr Champaign IL 61821-6141 Office: Ins Risk Mgrs Ltd 2507 S Neil St Champaign IL 61820-7713

PETERSON, RONALD ROGER, lawyer; b. Chgo., July 27, 1948; married; children: Elizabeth G., Ronald W. AB, Ripon, 1970; JD, U. Chgo., 1973. Bar: Ill. 1974, U.S. Dist. Ct. (no. dist.) Ill. 1974, U.S. Ct. Appeals (7th cir.) 1974, U.S. Dist. Ct. (ea. dist.) Wis. 1975, U.S. Dist. Ct. (no. dist.) Ind. 1978, U.S. Dist. Ct. (cen. dist.) Ill. 1980, U.S. Ct. Appeals (8th cir.) 1984, U.S. Ct. Appeals (6th cir.) 1990. Ptnr. Jenner & Block, Chgo., 1974—; commd. 2d lt. U.S. Army, 1968, advanced through grades to 1st lt., 1973, ret., 1978, with mil. intelligence, 1968-78. Mem. ABA, Chgo. Bar Assn., Internat. Soc. Insolvency Practitioners, Comml. Law League, Am. Bankruptcy Inst., Am. Coll. Bankruptcy, Am. Coll. Bankruptcy Lawyers. Avocation: skiing. Office: Jenner & Block 1 E Ibm Plz Chicago IL 60611-3586

PETERSON, ROY JEROME, physics educator; b. Everett, Wash., Oct. 18, 1939; married; four children. BS, U. Wash., 1961, PHD, 1966. Instr. physics Princeton (N.J.) U., 1966-68; rsch. assoc. Yale U., New Haven, 1968-70; from rsch. assoc. to prof. physics U. Colo., Boulder, 1970—, asst. vice chancellor rsch., 1996—; program dir. Intermediate Energy Physics NSF, 1978-79. Fellow Am. Phys. Soc.; mem. Pakistan Acad. Scis. Office: U Colo Box 446 Nuclear Physics Lab Boulder CO 80309

PETERSON, RUDOLPH A., banker; b. Svenljunga, Sweden, Dec. 6, 1904; s. Aaron and Anna (Johannson) P.; m. Barbara Welser Lindsay, Dec. 25, 1962; children: Linnea Peterson Bennett, R. Price; stepchildren: Robert I. Lindsay, Lorna Lindsay, Anne Lindsay, Margaret Lindsay. B.S. in Commerce, U. Calif., 1925, LL.D., 1968; L.H.D., U. Redlands, 1967. With Comml. Credit Co., 1925-36; successively asst. mgr. Comml. Credit Co., San Francisco; v.p., gen. mgr. Comml. Credit Co., Mexico City; div. operations mgr. Comml. Credit Co., Chgo.; dist. mgr. Bank Am. Nat. Trust & Savs. Assn., Fresno, Calif., 1936-41; v.p. Bank Am. Nat. Trust & Savs. Assn., San Francisco, 1941-46; pres., chief exec. officer Allied Bldg. Credits, 1946-52; v.p. Transam. Corp., San Francisco, 1952-55; pres., chief exec. officer Bank of Hawaii, Honolulu, 1956-61; pres., CEO BankAm. Corp., San Francisco, 1961-70, chmn. exec. com., 1970-76, also dir., 1968—; adminstr. UN Devel. Programme, 1971-76; bd. dirs. Alza Corp., Mcpl. Fund for Calif. Investors, Inc., Asia Found.; chmn. Euro Can. Bank, 1982-94; adminstr. UN Devel. Programme, 1972-76. Mem. adv. coun. Calif. Acad. Scis. Decorated Grand Cross of Civil Merit Spain; Order of Merit Italy; named Swedish-Am. of Year Vasa Order, 1965; U. Calif. Alumnus of Year, 1968; recipient Capt. Robert Dollar Meml. award for contbn. to advancement Am. fgn. trade, 1970, Chancellor's award U. Calif., 1992, Great Swedish Heritage award, 1996. Clubs: Bohemian (San Francisco), Pacific-Union (San Francisco). Home: 86 Sea View Ave Piedmont CA 94611-3519 Office: Bank Am Ctr 555 California St Fl 11 San Francisco CA 94104

PETERSON, RUSSELL WILBUR, former association executive, former state governor; b. Portage, Wis., Oct. 3, 1916; s. John Anton and Emma (Anthony) P.; m. E. Lillian Turner, June 30, 1937 (dec. Apr. 28, 1994); children: Russell Glen, Peter Jon, Kristin, Elin; m. June B. Jenkins, Oct. 21, 1995. B.S., U. Wis., 1938, Ph.D., 1942, LL.D. (hon.), 1984; D.Sc. (hon.), Williams Coll., 1975, Butler U., Springfield Coll., Stevens Inst. Tech., 1979, Gettysburg Coll., 1980, Alma Coll., 1981, Ohio State U., SUNY-Syracuse, Northland Coll., Fairleigh Dickinson U., 1981; LL.D. (hon.), Monmouth

Coll., 1982, Salisbury State U., 1988; D of Humane Letters, Meadville-Lombard Theol. Sch., 1992. With E. I. DuPont de Nemours & Co., Inc., 1942-69, research dir. textile fibers dept., 1954-55, 56-59, merchandising mgr. textile fibers, 1955-56, dir. new products div. textile fibers, 1959-62, dir. research and devel. div. devel. dept., 1963-69; bd. dirs. Textile Research Inst., Princeton, N.J., 1956-63, chmn. exec. com., 1959-61, chmn. bd. dirs., 1961-63, fellow, 1969; gov. of Del., 1969-73; chmn. exec. com. Nat. Commn. Critical Choices for Am., 1973; chmn. U.S. Council on Environ. Quality, 1973-76; pres. New Directions, 1976-77, Nat. Audubon Soc., 1979-85; mem. Nat. Commn. Critical Choices for Am., 1973-74; dir. Office Tech. Assessment, U.S. Congress, 1978-79; regional v.p. Nat. Mcpl. League, 1968-78; chmn. Edn. Commn. States, 1970; chmn. com. nuclear energy and space tech. So. Govs. Conf., 1970-71; chmn. Nat. Adv. Commn. on Criminal Justice Standards and Goals, 1971-73; chmn. com. law enforcement, justice and pub. safety Nat. Govs. Conf., 1970-73; v.p. Council State Govts., 1970-71; chmn. adv. bd. Solar Energy Research Inst., 1979-83; vis prof. Dartmouth Coll., 1985, Carleton Coll., 1986, U. Wis.-Madison, 1987; chmn. Centennial Internat. Symposium, Nat. Geog. Soc., 1986-88. Chmn. Del. River Basin Commn., 1971-72; founding chmn. Bio-Energy Coun., 1976-78; bd. dirs. World Wildlife Fund, 1976-82, Population Action Internat., 1973-97 , Alliance to Save Energy, 1979-93; bd. dirs. Global Tomorrow Coalition, 1981-91, chmn., 1981-87; regional councillor Internat. Union Conservation Nature and Natural Resources, 1981-88, v.p., 1984-88; mem. Pres.'s Commn. on Accident at Three Mile Island, 1979; pres. Internat. Coun. Bird Preservation, 1982-90; chmn. Ctr. on Consequences of Nuclear War, 1983-87; vice chmn. Better World Soc., 1985-90, pres., 1985-87; vis. com. John F. Kennedy Sch. Govt., 1979-85; Goodwill amb. UN Environ. Program, 1984—, mem. world environ. prize com., 1989—; mem. Gov. Cuomo's Environ. Adv. Bd., 1985-94; mem. adv. bd. Pace U. Sch. Law, 1988—, Earth Island Inst., 1988—; chmn. bd. Earth Lobby, 1992-96; co-chmn. gov.'s task force on rejuvenating Wilmington waterfront, 1992-95; mem. Del. Riverfront Devel. Corp., 1995—. Decorated Order of Golden Ark (The Netherlands); recipient Ann. award NCCJ, 1966, Gold medal World Wildlife Fund, 1971, Ann. award Comml. Devel. Assn., 1971, Gold Plate award Nat. Acad. Achievement, 1971, Parsons award Am. Chem. Soc., 1974, Audubon award Nat. Audubon Soc., 1977, Proctor prize Sigma Xi, 1978, Frances K. Hutchinson medal Garden Club Am., 1980, Robert Marshall award Wilderness Soc., 1984, Nat. Conservation medal DAR, 1989, Human and Civil Rights award Del. Human Rights Commn., 1989, Environ. Law Inst. award, 1990, Ann. award Am. Civil Liberties Found. Del., 1992, Lawrence Solid Waste award Assn. N.Am., 1993, Kiwanis Cmty. Svc. award, 1993, Lifetime Achievement award Global Tomorrow Coalition, 1994, Lifetime Achievement award League of Conservation Voters, 1995; named Conservationist of Yr., Nat. Wildlife Fedn., 1972, Swedish-Am. of Yr., Vasa Order of Am. In Sweden, 1982,. Hon. fellow Am. Inst. Chemists, AAAS (past bd. dirs.); mem. Am. Ornithologists' Union, Linnaean Soc., Fedn. Am. Scientists, Am. Chem. Soc., Del. Acad. Sci., U.S. Assn. for Club of Rome, Cosmos Club, Phi Beta Kappa, Sigma Xi (Proctor prize 1978), Phi Lambda Upsilon, Phi Kappa Phi. Unitarian. Address: 11 E Mozart Dr Wilmington DE 19807

PETERSON, SKIP (ORLEY R. PETERSON, III), newspaper photographer; b. Dayton, Ohio, July 6, 1951; s. Orley Ray and Helen Louise (Stafford) P.; m. Jennifer Susan Hinders, Sept. 22, 1990; children from previous marriage: Meredith, Sam, Elizabeth; 1 stepchild, Erin. BS in Journalism, Ohio U., 1973. Staff photographer Dayton Daily News, 1973-82, chief photographer, 1982—; part-time faculty mem. U. Dayton. Contbr. photographs to mags., including Life, Time, Newsweek, Sports Illustrated, also book Photojournalism. Judge ann. contests for White House News Photographers, Ind. News Photographers Assn., Mich. Press Photographers Assn., Ky. News Photographers Assn., Soc. Profl. Journalists. Recipient awards Soc. Profl. Journalists, 1st Place Sports Feature award Pictures of Yr. Competition, 1985, Robert Carson award for outstanding contbn. to photojournalism in Ohio, Ohio Understanding award for documentary. Mem. Ohio News Photographers Assn. (chmn. bd. dirs., past pres., awards), Nat. Press Photographers Assn. (past regional dir., exec. com. bd. rep., awards). Methodist. Avocations: restoring British sports cars, golf, auto racing. Home: 440 Wing View Ln Kettering OH 45429 Office: Dayton Daily News 45 S Ludlow St Dayton OH 45402-1810

PETERSON, SOPHIA, international studies educator; b. Astoria, N.Y., Nov. 24, 1929; d. George Loizos and Caroline (Hofstetter) Yimoyines; m. Virgil Allison Peterson, Dec. 28, 1951; children: Mark Jeffrey, Lynn Marie. BA, Wellesley (Mass.) Coll., 1951; MA, UCLA, 1956, PhD, 1969; DHL (hon.), Wheeling Jesuit U., 1997. Instr. Miami U., Oxford, Ohio, 1961-63; with W.Va. U., Morgantown, 1966—, assoc. prof., 1972-79, prof., 1979—, dir., internat. studies maj., 1980-92; dir. W.Va. Consortium for Faculty & Course Devel. in Internat. Studies, Morgantown, 1980—. Author: monograph Monograph Series in World Affairs, 1979. Recipient gold medal semi-finalist CASE Prof. of Yr. award Coun. for Advancement and Support of Edn., 1987, Outstanding Tchr. award W.Va. U., W.Va. U. Coll. Arts and Scis., 1988, finalist Prof. of Yr. award W.Va. Faculty Merit Found., 1991, Heebink award for disting. state svc. W.Va. U., 1984. Mem. Internat. Studies Assn. (v.p. Mid-Atlantic chpt. 1978-86), W.Va. Polit. Sci. Assn. (pres. 1984-85), AAAUP (pres. W.Va. U. chpt. 1976-78). Democrat. Avocation: sailing. Home: 849 Vandalia Dr Morgantown WV 26505-6247 Office: WVa U Dept Polit Sci Morgantown WV 26506

PETERSON, THEODORE BERNARD, retired journalism educator; b. Albert Lea, Minn., June 8, 1918; s. Theodore B. and Emilie (Jensen) P.; m. Helen M. Clegg, Sept. 13, 1946; children: Thane Eric, Kristin, Megan, Daniel Alan. B.A., U. Minn., 1941; M.S., Kans. State Coll., 1948; Ph.D., U. Ill., 1955. Instr., then asst. prof. journalism Kans. State Coll., 1945-48, head coll. news bur., 1945-47; instr. journalism U. Ill., 1948-55, assoc. prof., 1955-57, prof., 1957-87; dean U. Ill. (Coll. Communications), 1957-79; judge Nat. Mag. Awards, 1967-88. Author: Writing Nonfiction for Magazines, 1949, Magazines in the Twentieth Century, 1956, rev., 1964, (with F.S. Siebert, Wilbur Schramm) Four Theories of the Press, 1956, (with J.W. Jensen, Wm. L. Rivers) The Mass Media in Modern Society, 1965, rev., 1971. Recipient award for distinguished research journalism Sigma Delta Chi, Kappa Tau Alpha, 1956, Outstanding Achievement award U. Minn., 1973, Outstanding Undergraduate Teaching award U. Ill., 1987. Mem. Assn. Edn. Journalism (1st v.p. 1962, pres. 1963), Am. Council on Edn. Journalism (accrediting com. 1961-70, 72-81), Am. Assn. Schs. and Depts. Journalism (pres. 1965), Kappa Tau Alpha, Phi Kappa Phi. Home: 103 E George Huff Dr Urbana IL 61801-5807

PETERSON, TRUDY HUSKAMP, archivist; b. Estherville, Iowa, Jan. 25, 1945. BS, Iowa State U., 1967; MA, U. Iowa, 1972, PhD, 1975. Various positions Nat. Archives, Washington, 1968-87, asst. archivist, 1987-93, dep. archivist of U.S., 1993-95, acting archivist, 1993-95; exec. dir. Open Soc. Archives, Budapest, 1995—; Fulbright lectr. in Am. studies, 1983-84; commr. U.S.-Russia Joint Commn. on MIA/POWs, 1992-95; sec. Internat. Conf. on Round Table on Archives, 1992-93, pres., 1993-95; mem. European Bd. on Archives, 1995-96; v.p. program support commn. Internat. Coun. on ARchives, 1996—. Author: Agricultural Exports, Farm Income and the Eisenhower Administration, 1979, Basic Archival Workshop Exercises, 1982, Archives and Manuscripts: Law, 1985; editor: Farmers, Bureaucrats and Middlemen: Historical Perspectives on American Agriculture, 1980; mem. editl. bd. The Am. Archivist, 1978-81; contbr. articles to profl. jours. Pres. Capitol Hill Restoration Soc., 1987-88. Recipient Order of Arts and Letters Republic of France, 1995, Hancher-Finkbine Medallion, Disting. Alumni award U. Iowa, 1995; named Samuel Lazerow Lectr. Simmons Coll., 1995. Fellow Soc. Am. Archivists (mem. coun. 1984-87, pres. 1990-91, held various offices, Gondos Meml. award 1973, Fellows Posner prize 1987); mem. Agrl. History Soc. (mem. exec. com. 1982-85, pres. 1988-89), Soc. History in Fed. Govt. (mem. exec. com. 1987-89). Office: Open Soc Archives, October 6 u 12, H-1051 Budapest Hungary

PETERSON, VICTOR LOWELL, aerospace engineer, management consultant; b. Saskatoon, Sask., Can., June 11, 1934; came to U.S., 1937; s. Edwin Galladet and Ruth Mildred (McKeeby) P.; m. Jacqueline Dianne Hubbard, Dec. 21, 1955; children: Linda Kay Peterson Landrith, Janet Gale, Victor Craig. BS in Aero. Engring., Oreg. State U., 1956; MS in Aerospace Engring., Stanford U., 1964; MS in Mgmt., MIT, 1973. Rsch. scientist NASA-Ames Rsch. Ctr., Moffett Field, Calif., 1956-68, asst. chief hypersonic aerodyns., 1968-71, chief aerodyns. br., 1971-74, chief thermo and gas dynamics div., 1974-84, dir. aerophysics, 1984-90, dep. dir., 1990-94; pvt. mgmt. cons., 1994—; mem. nat. adv. bd. U. Tenn. Space Inst., Tullahoma, 1984-94. Contbr. numerous articles to profl. jours. Treas. Woodland Acres Homeowners Assn., Los Altos, Calif., 1978—. Capt. USAF, 1957-60. Recipient medal for outstanding leadership NASA, 1982; Alfred P. Sloan fellow MIT, 1972-73. Fellow AIAA. Republican. Methodist. Achievements include development of numerical aerodynamic simulation system for aerospace, of method for reconstructing planetary atmosphere structure from accelerations of body entering atmosphere, of theory for motions of tumbling bodies entering planetary atmospheres. Home: 484 Aspen Way Los Altos CA 94024-7126 *Achievements in life are maximized by creating visions of success and focussing relentlessly on successful accomplishment of intermediate objectives.*

PETERSON, WALLACE CARROLL, SR., economics educator; b. Omaha, Mar. 28, 1921; s. Fred Nels and Grace (Brown) P.; m. Eunice V. Peterson, Aug. 16, 1944 (dec. Nov. 1985); children: Wallace Carroll Jr., Shelley Lorraine; m. Bonnie B. Watson, Nov. 11, 1988 (dec. Oct. 1996). Student, U. Omaha, 1939-40, U. Mo., 1940-42; BA in Econs. and European History, U. Nebr., 1947, MA in Econs. and European History, 1948, PhD in Econs. and European History, 1953; postgrad., Handelshochschule, St. Gallen, Switzerland, 1948-49, U. Minn., 1951, London Sch. Econs. and Polit. Sci., 1952. Reporter Lincoln (Nebr.) Jour., 1946; instr. econs. U. Nebr., Lincoln, 1951-54, asst. prof., 1954-57, assoc. prof., 1957-61, prof., 1962—, chmn. dept. econs., 1965-75, George Holmes prof. econs., 1966-92; George Holmes prof. econs. emeritus, 1992—; v.p. faculty senate U. Nebr., Lincoln, 1972-73, pres. faculty senate, 1973-74; S.J. Hall disting. vis. prof. U. Nev., Las Vegas, 1983-84. Author: The Welfare State in France, 1960, Elements of Economics, 1973, Our Overloaded Economy: Inflation, Unemployment and the Crisis in American Capitalism, 1982, Market Power and the Economy, 1988, Transfer Spending, Taxes and the American Welfare State, 1991, Income, Employment and Economic Growth, 8th edit., 1996, Silent Depression: The Fate of the American Dream, 1994; contbr. articles to profl. jours. and columns to newspapers. Mem. Nebr. Dem. Cen. Com., 1968-74, vice-chmn., chmn. Nebr. Polit. Accountability and Disclosure Commn., 1977-80; chmn. Nebr. Coun. Econ. Edn., 1976-77. Capt. USAAF, 1942-46. Recipient Champion Media award for Econ. Understanding, 1981; Fulbright fellow, 1957-58, 64-65; Mid-Am. State Univs. honor scholar, 1982-83. Mem. ACLU, AAUP (pres. Nebr. 1963-64, nat. coun.), Assn. for Evolutionary Econs. (pres. 1976, Veblen-Commons award 1991), Am. Econs. Assn., Midwest Econs. Assn. (pres. 1968-69), Mo. Valley Econ. Assn. (pres. 1989), Assn. Social Econs. (pres. 1992, Thomas F. Devine award 1995), Fedn. Am. Scientists. Home: 4549 South St Lincoln NE 68506-1253 Office: U Nebr Dept Econs CBA Lincoln NE 68588-0489

PETERSON, WALTER FRITIOF, academic administrator; b. Idaho Falls, Idaho, July 15, 1920; s. Walter Fritiof and Florence (Danielson) P.; m. Barbara Mae Kempe, Jan. 13, 1946; children: Walter Fritiof III, Daniel John. BA, State U. Iowa, 1942, MA, 1948, PhD, 1951; HHD (hon.), Loras Coll., 1983; LHD (hon.), Clarke Coll., 1991; DHum (hon.), U. Dubuque, 1997. Asst. prof. history, chmn. dept. history Milw. Downer Coll., 1952-57, assoc. prof. history, chmn. social sci. div., 1957-64; assoc. prof. history Lawrence U., Appleton, Wis., 1964-67; prof. history, Alice G. Chapman libr. Lawrence U., 1967-70; pres. U. Dubuque, 1970-90, chancellor, 1990—; regional tng. officer Peace Corps, 1965-68; cons. history Allis-Chalmers Mfg. Co., 1959-75, Secura Ins. Group, 1968-92, Wm. C. Brown Pub. Co., 1981-92, bd. dirs. Editor: Transactions of Wis. Acad. Scis., Arts and Letters, 1965-72, The Allis-Chalmers Corporation: An Industrial History, 1977, A History of Wm. C. Brown Cos., 1994, A History of Hawkeye Bancorporation, 1996. Advisor Templeton Prize for Progress in Religion, 1986-91; bd. dirs. Finley Hosp., pres., 1983-84; chmn. Finley Health Found., 1986-95; pres. Grand Opera House Found., 1996—; bd. dirs. Dubuque Symphony Orch., Dubuque Art Assn., Jr. Achievement, Nat. River Hall of Fame, 1984; chmn. Iowa Assn. Coll. and Univ. Pres., 1975-76; chmn. Iowa Coll. Found., 1982-83. With USAAF, 1942-45, PTO. Recipient Dubuque Citizen award, 1990, Disting. Civic Svc. award, 1991, Benjamin Franklin award Nat. Soc. Fundraising Execs., 1994, Paul Harris fellowship, Duduque Rotary Club, 1993; named to Dubuque Bus. Hall of Fame, 1990. Mem. Iowa Assn. Ind. Colls. and Univs. (chmn. 1988-89), Dubuque County Hist. Soc. (bd. dirs.), Dubuque Golf and Country Club, Phi Alpha Theta, Kappa Delta Pi, Phi Delta Kappa. Office: U Dubuque Office of Chancellor 2000 University Ave Dubuque IA 52001-5050

PETERSON, WAYNE TURNER, composer, pianist; b. Albert Sea, Minn., Sept. 3, 1927; s. Leslie Jules and Irma Thelma (Turner) P.; m. Harriet Christiansen, 1948 (div. 1978); children: Alan, Craig, Drew, Grant. BA, U. Minn., 1951, MA, 1953; postgrad., Royal Acad. Music, London, 1953-54; PhD, U. Minn. Instr. music U. Minn., 1955-59; asst. prof. music Chico (Calif.) State U., 1959-60; prof. music San Francisco State U., 1960—; vis. prof. composition U. Ind., Bloomington, 1992, Stanford U., 1992-94; artist in residence Briarcombe Found., Bolinas, Calif., 1983; vis. artist Am. Acad. in Rome, 1990. Composer: Allegro for String Quartet, 1952, Introduction and Allegro, 1953, Free Variations for Orch., 1954-58, Can Death Be Sleep, 1955, Earth, Sweet Earth, 1956, (cappella chorus) Cape Ann, 1957, Three Songs for Soprano and Piano, 1957, (cappella chorus) Psalm 56, 1959, Exaltation, Dithyramb and Caprice, full orchestra, 1959-60, (cappella chorus) An e e Cummings Triptych, 1962, Tangents for flute, clarinet, horn and violin, 1963, An e e Cummings Cantata, 1964, Fantasy Concertante for violin and piano, 1965, Reflections, ballet, full orchestra, 1965, Metamorphosis for Wind Quintet, 1967, Phantasmagoria for flute, clarinet, double bass, 1968, Cataclysms, full orchestra, 1968, Clusters and Fragments for string orch., 1969, Ceremony After a Fire Raid, Soprano and piano, 1969, Sinfonia and Canticle for baritone voice and organ, 1969, Capriccio for Flute and Piano, 1973, Transformations for String Quartet, 1974, Trialogue for violin, cello and piano, 1975, Diatribe for violin and piano, 1975, Encounters mixed ensemble of mini instrument, 1976, Rhapsody for Cello and Piano, 1976, An Interrupted Serenade for flute, harp and cello, 1978, Dark Reflections (cycle of four songs for high voice, violin and piano), 1980, Mallets Aforethought (symphony for percussion ensemble), 1981, Sextet for flute, clarinet, percussion, harp, violin and cello, 1982, Doubles for 2 flutes and 2 clarinets, 1982, Debussy Song Cycle transcribe for voice and small orchestra, 1983, String Quartet, 1983-84, Ariadne's Thread for harp, flute, clarinet, horn, percussion and violin, 1985, Transformations for chamber orch., 1986, Duo for viola and cello, 1986-87, Trilogy for Orch., 1987, Labyrinth for flute, clarinet, violin and piano, 1987, The Widening Gyre for full orch., 1991, The Face of the Night, the Heart of the Dark for full orch., 1991 (Pulitzer prize for music 1992), Mallets Aforthought percussion symphony revision, 1991, String Quartet # 2, 1992, Diptych, fl, cl, pec., po, rn,vc, 1992, Janus, mixed ensemble of ten instrument, 1993, Duo for Violin and Piano, 1993, And the Winds Shall Blow, a fantasy for saxophone quartet, symphony winds, brass and percussion, 1994; Theseus for smaller orchestra, Vicissiyude (fl, cl, perc, po, vn, vc, 1995, A Robert Herrick Motley (five a capella Choruses) Windup Saxaphone Quartet, Peregrinations (solo clarinet) 1996; recs. with Mercury Records, Desto Records, Arch Records, Grenadilla Records, Koch Internat. CRI, Innova, Foghorn, Centur, San Francisco Chamber Singers; Recordings commd. Am. Music Ctr., 1959, Virtuosi of San Francisco, 1968, Unitarian Ch., 1969, Paul Mason, Inc., 1974, 87, NEA Consortium Commn., 1982, Charles Wuorinen and San Francisco Symphony, 1985, Am. Composers Symphony, Inc., 1987, San Francisco Symphony, 1991, Gerbode Found., 1990, Koussevitzky Found., 1990, Fromm Music Found., 1992, Philharmonic Orch. of Freiburg in Breisgau, Germany, 1993, U. Minn., 1995, Neel the Composer (Consortium, Comm.) 1996, Allen Blustine, 1996. Recipient 11th Ann. Norman Fromm Composer's award, 1982, Meritorious Svc. award Calif. State U. System, 1984, Top award Am. Harp Soc., 1985, Composer's award Am. Acad. and Inst. Arts and Letters, 1986, Pulitzer Prize for music, 1992; Fulbright scholar, Royal Acad. Music, 1953-54; NEA grantee, 1976; Guggenheim fellow, 1989-90, Djerassi Found. fellow, 1989-91. Home: 140 S Lake Merced Hill San Francisco CA 94132-2935

PETERSON, WILLARD JAMES, Chinese history educator; b. Oak Park, Aug. 1, 1938; s. Otto Stewart and Catherine (Esin) P.; m. Toby Black, Aug 27, 1960. BA, U. Rochester, 1960; MA, U. London, 1964; PhD, Harvard U., 1970. Asst. prof. Dartmouth Coll., Hanover, N.H., 1970-71; prof. East Asian Studies and History Princeton (N.J.) U., 1971—. Author: Bitter Gourd, 1979, Power of Culture, 1994. Office: Dept of East Asian Studies & Hist Princeton U Princeton NJ 08544

PETERSON, WILLIAM FRANK, physician, administrator; b. Newark, Sept. 28, 1922; s. Edgar Charles and Margaret Benedict (Heyn) P.; m. Margaret Henderson Lee, June 28, 1946 (div. 1978); children: Margaret Lee, Edward Charles; m. 2d, Mary Ann Estelle McGrath, Nov. 29, 1980. Student, Cornell U., 1940-43; MD, N.Y. Med. Coll., 1946. Commd. lt. U.S. Air Force, 1946, advanced through grades to col., 1963; med. officer U.S. Air Force, 1946-70; chmn. dept. ob-gyn Washington Hosp. Ctr. 1970-92; dir. Women's Clinic. Washington, 1971-96, Ob-Gyn Ultrasound Lab., Washington, 1974-92; ret. 1996. Contbr. articles to profl. jours. Chmn., Maternal Mortality Com., 1981-96. Decorated Legion of Merit, 1960, 70; Cert. Achievement, Office Surgeon Gen., USAF, 1967. Fellow Am. Coll. Ob-Gyn, ACS, Nat. Bd. Med. Examiners (diplomate), Washington Gynecol. Soc. (exec. council 1980-85). Republican. Episcopalian. Home: 50 Stonegate Dr Colesville MD 20905-5701

PETERSON, WILLIS LESTER, economics educator; b. Mpls., Mar. 3, 1932; s. Lester Wilfred and Valeria Leone (Slatoski) P.; m. Dorothy Feiertag, July 5, 1969. BS, U. Minn., 1960, MS, 1962; PhD, U. Chgo., 1966. Rsch. fellow U. Chgo., 1962-65; mem. faculty U. Minn., St. Paul, 1965—, prof. econs., 1972—. Author: Principles of Economics: Macro, 1971, 10th edit., 1997, Principles of Economics: Micro, 1971, 10th edit., 1997, Introduction to Economics, 1977, rev. edit., 1995. With U.S. Army, 1952-54. Home: 500 Constance Blvd Anoka MN 55304 Office: U Minn 337 Cla Ofc Bldg Saint Paul MN 55108

PETHICK, CHRISTOPHER JOHN, physicist; b. Horsham, Sussex, Eng., Feb. 22, 1942; s. Richard Hope and Norah Betty (Hill) P. BA, Magdalen Coll., Oxford (Eng.) U., 1962, PhD, 1965. Fellow Magdalen Coll., Oxford U., 1965-70; research assoc. U. Ill., Urbana, 1966-68, research asst. prof., 1968-69, assoc. prof. physics, 1970-73, prof. physics, 1973-95; prof. physics Nordita, Copenhagen, 1975—. A.P. Sloan research fellow, 1970-72. Fellow Am. Phys. Soc.; mem. Am. Astron. Soc., European Phys. Soc. Home: Niels W Gades Gade 34, DK-2100 Copenhagen Denmark Office: Nordita, Blegdamsvej 17, DK-2100 Copenhagen Denmark also: Nordita, Blegdamsvej 17, DK-2100 Copenhagen Denmark

PETICOLAS, WARNER LELAND, physical chemistry educator; b. Lubbock, Tex., July 29, 1929; s. Warner Marion and Beulah Francis (Lowe) P.; m. Virginia Marie Wolf, June 30, 1969; children—Laura M., Alicia B.; children by previous marriage—Cynthia M., Nina P., Phillip W. B.S., Tex. Technol. Coll., 1950; Ph.D., Northwestern U., 1954. Research asso. DuPont Co., Wilmington, Del., 1954-60; research div. IBM, San Jose, Calif., 1960-67; cons. IBM, 1967-69, mgr. chem. physics group, 1965-67; prof. phys. chemistry U. Oreg., 1967—; vis. prof. U. Paris-Pierre and Marie Curie, 1980-81; vis. prof. Weizmann Inst. Sci., Rahovat, Israel, 1991, vis. prof. U. Reims, 1996. Committeeman Democratic party, Eugene, Oreg., 1967-70. Served with USPHS, 1955-57. Recipient Alexander von Humboldt award, W. Ger., 1984-85. Guggenheim fellow Max von Laue-Paul Langevin Inst., Grenoble, France, 1973-74. Fellow Am. Phys. Soc.; mem. Am. Chem. Soc., Am. Phys. Soc., Sigma Xi, Alpha Chi Sigma, Tau Beta Pi. Episcopalian. Home: 2829 Arline Way Eugene OR 97403-2527 Office: U Oregon Dept Of Chemistry Eugene OR 97403

PETILLON, LEE RITCHEY, lawyer; b. Gary, Ind., May 6, 1929; s. Charles Ernest and Blanche Lurene (Mackay) P.; m. Mary Anne Keeton, Feb. 20, 1960; children: Andrew G., Joseph R. BBA, U. Minn., 1952; LLB, U. Calif., Berkeley, 1959. Bar: Calif. 1960, U.S. Dist. Ct. (so. dist.) Calif. 1960. V.p. Creative Investment Capital, Inc., L.A., 1969-70; corp. counsel Harvest Industries, L.A., 1970-71; v.p., gen. counsel, dir. Tech. Svcs. Corp., Santa Monica, Calif., 1971-78; ptnr. Petillon & Davidoff, L.A., 1978-92, Gipson Hoffman & Pancione, 1992-93; pvt. practice Torrance, Calif., 1993-94; ptnr. Petillon & Hansen, Torrance, Calif., 1994—. Co-author: R&D Partnerships, 2d edit., 1985, Representing Start-Up Companies, 1992, 3d edit., 1996, California Transaction Forms, 1996. Chmn. Neighborhood Justice Ctr. Com., 1983-85, Middle Income Co., 1983085; active Calif. Senate Commn. on Corp. Governance, State Bar Calif. Task Force on Alternative Dispute Resolution, 1984-85; chmn. South Bay Sci. Found., Inc.; vice-chmn. Calif. Capital Access Forum, Inc. Recipient Cert. of Appreciation L.A. City Demonstration Agy., 1975, United Indian Devel. Assn., 1981, City of L.A. for Outstanding Vol. Svcs., 1984. Mem. ABA, Calif. State Bar Assn. (pres., Pro Bono Svcs. award 1983), L.A. County Bar Found. (bd. dirs. 1986-89), L.A. County Bar Assn. (chmn. law tech. sect., alt. dispute resolution sect. 1992-94, trustee 1984-85, Griffin Bell Vol. Svc. award 1993). Avocations: backpacking, reading, music, painting. Home: 1636 Via Machado Palos Verdes Estates CA 90274-1930 Office: Petillon & Hansen 21515 Hawthorne Blvd Ste 1260 Torrance CA 90503-6503

PETINGA, CHARLES MICHAEL, business executive; b. Atlantic City, July 9, 1946; s. Thomas Joseph and Rose Marie (Merindino) P.; m. Velna Mae McVicker, June 7, 1969; children: Scott, Jeffery. BS in Geology, Geography, U. Wis., Superior, 1969. Ops. supr. Schneider Transport, Inc., Green Bay, Wis., 1973-74, prodn. mgr., 1974-76, safety dir., 1976-79; dir. safety Schneider Nat., Inc., Green Bay, 1979-82, dir. risk mgmt., 1982-87; gen. mgr. Petinga Candy Co., Atlantic City, 1987-89; mgr. bus. devel., sr. v.p. Marsh and McLennan, Appleton, Wis., 1989—; cons. local charitable groups, Green Bay, 1985-88; adviser, cons. Small Bus. Execs., Green Bay, 1989; mem. worker compensation task force Wis. Motor Carriers, Madison, 1991; speaker at vocat. schs. and high schs.; speaker to motor carrier assns. and industry mgmt. goups. Co. liaison Green Bay United Way, 1985, 86. With U.S. Army, 1971-73. Mem. Wis. Coun. Safety Suprs., Nat. Safety Mgmt. Soc., Wis. Motor Carriers Assn., Risk and Ins. Mgmt. Soc., Nat. Safety Coun., Am. Trucking Assn. Avocations: martial arts, physical fitness, weight lifting. Office: Marsh and McLennan Inc 59 Park Pl Appleton WI 54915-8230

PETIT, ELLEN JAYNE, casino supervisor; b. Jersey City, N.J., Nov. 9, 1956; d. William Henry and Margene Emma (Garrison) Scheurle; m. Joseph Edward Scarlatella, June 9, 1979 (div. 1987); children: Amy Jo, Joseph William, David Gene; m. Kim Alan Petit, May 19, 1997. Grad. h.s., Ventura, Calif. Owner, operator Joe's Mountain Copy, Running Springs, Calif., 1983-88; gaming dealer Sam's Town Goldriver, Laughlin, Nev., 1988-90; dual rate floor person Flamingo Hilton, Laughlin, 1990-95; supr. casino pit Avi Hotel & Casino, Laughlin, 1995—; instr. Mohave C.C., Bullhead City, Ariz., 1994-96. Leader Girl Scouts Am., Needles, Calif., 1988; founder Sheriff's Safety Kids, Needles, 1989. Lutheran. Avocations: dancing, reading, bowling, sewing, yard sales. Home: 2047 Carty Way Needles CA 92363-3053 Office: Avi Hotel & Casino 10000 Aha Macav Pkwy Laughlin NV 89028

PETIT, PARKER HOLMES, health care corporation executive; b. Decatur, Ga., Aug. 4, 1939; s. James Percival and Ethel (Holmes) P.; children: William Wright, Patricia Monique, Meredith Katherine. BS in Mech. Engring., Ga. Inst. Tech., 1962, MS in Engring. Mechanics, 1964; MBA, Ga. State U., 1973. Engr. Gen. Dynamics Corp., Fort Worth, Tex., 1966-67; engring. project mgr. Lockheed-Ga. Co., Marietta, 1967-71; pres., founder, chief exec. officer Healthdyne, Inc., Marietta, 1971—; bd. dirs. Atlantic S.E. Airlines, Atlanta, Healthdyne Technologies, Inc., Atlanta, Healthdyne Info. Enterprises, Inc., Marietta, Ga., Matria Healthcare, Inc., Marietta. Author: Primer on Composite Materials, 1968; patentee in field. Chmn. bd. dirs. Sudden Infant Death Syndrome Alliance, Washington, 1986; active nat. adv. coun. Emory U. Med. Sch., Coun. fellows for the Emory, Ga. Tech. Biomed. Tech. Rsch. Ctr.; bd. dirs. Ga. Rsch. Alliance, 1995. 1st lt. U.S. Army, 1964-67. Recipient Humanitarian award La SocieteFrancaise de Bienfaisance, 1981; mem. Tech. Hall of Fame of Ga.; mem. Ga. Tech. Acad. Disting. Alumni, 1994; Internat. Bus. fellow, 1986. Mem. Health Industry Mfrs. Assn., Cobb County C. of C. (bd. dirs. 1980-82), Pi Kappa Phi. Republican. Methodist. Avocations: flying; oil painting; golf; tennis. Office: Healthdyne Inc 1850 Parkway Pl SE Marietta GA 30067-4439

PETITO, MARGARET L., public relations executive, consultant; b. Dallas, Sept. 28, 1950; d. Jacob Charles and Eileen (Shank) Loehr; m. John Haven Petito, 1978 (div. 1984); children: John Christian Robert, David Nelson. BA, So. Meth. U., 1972. Mem. Action/Vista Program U.S. Govt., Middlesex, N.Y., 1972-74; dir., curator Oliver House Mus., Penn Yan, N.Y., 1975-77; staff asst. Williams & Jensen, P.C., Washington, 1986-91; dir. fed. rels. Chambers Devel. Co., Inc., 1989-92; dir. fed. affairs DSSI-U.S. Biotech.,

Washington, 1992-94; cons., dir. pub. affairs Embassy Ecuador, Govt. Ecuador, Washington, 1994—; prin. Petito & Assocs.; dir. external events Internat. Cancer Alliance, Bethesda, Md., 1996-97. Dir. Marshall House Mus., Lambertville, N.J., 1980-82; spl. legis. advisor Drugwatch Internat., Chgo., 1993—; bd. dirs., Nyumbani Orphanage for Kenyan Children with AIDS, Africa, Washington, 1989—; mem. Women's Coun. Energy and Environ., Washington, 1990—; mem. task force Women in Govt. Rels., Washington, 1990—; founder, co-chair Forum for the Environ., Washington, 1989-91. Mem. Tex. State Soc., Tex. Breakfast Club. Roman Catholic. Avocations: squash, needlepoint, fishing. Home: 6008 34th Pl NW Washington DC 20015-1914 Office: Embassy of Ecuador 2533 15th St NW Washington DC 20009-4102

PETITO, VICTOR THOMAS, JR., credit bureau executive; b. Bklyn., Jan. 29, 1936; s. Victor Sr. and Domenica (DeCarlo) P.; m. Geneva Mae Macom, June 5, 1957 (div. Aug. 1980); children: Victor Bret, Rick Thomas, Gina Lynn; m. Jean Austin, Nov. 22, 1988. Student, Tex. Christian U., 1953-55. Credit mgt. Family Loan, Lubbock, Tex., 1959-62, Goodyear Tire & Rubber, Ft. Worth, 1962-63, Montgomery Wards, Ft. Worth, 1963-68; pres., chief exec. officer The Credit Bur. of Oklahoma City, 1969—; pres. Consumer Credit Counseling, Oklahoma City, 1985-86. Bd. dirs. Okla. Spl. Olympics, Oklahoma City, 1984—; coach track and field Jr. Amateur Athletic Union U.S., Oklahoma City, 1980; deacon Village Christian Ch., Disciples of Christ. With USAF, 1955-57. Mem. Assoc. Credit Burs. (bd. dirs. 1987—, Gemini award 1976, award of excellence 1989), Assoc. Credit Burs. Okla. (pres. 1985-86), Internat. Credit Assn. (exec. dist. 1985—, disting. svc. award 1986, merit award 1987, internat. legis. award 1988), Internat. Soc. Cert. Credit Execs. (chmn. 1987—, Fellow Yr. award 1986), Okla. Soc. Cert. Credit Execs. (founder, pres. 1983-84), Retail Credit Mgrs. Assn. (pres. 1984-85), U.S. C. of C., Oklahoma City C. of C., Del City C. of C., Moore (Okla.) C. of C., Norman (Okla.) C. of C., Edmond (Okla.) C. of C., Moose. Republican. Avocations: golf, fishng, photography. Office: The Credit Bur of Oklahoma City 2519 NW 23rd St Oklahoma City OK 73107-2249

PETITTO, BARBARA BUSCHELL, artist; b. Jersey City; d. John Edward and Anna (Barnaba) Buschell; m. Joseph Bruno Petitto, Feb. 1, 1964; children: Vincent John, Christopher Joseph. Student, Fairleigh Dickinson U., 1969-70; studio art cert., N.J. Ctr. Visual Arts, Summit, 1985; student, Art Students League, N.Y.C., 1980, 89-92, Montclair Art Mus., 1991-93. Artist-in-resident art faculty Acad. St. Elizabeth, Convent Stations, N.J., 1989, 90, 91; art faculty Morris County Art Assn., Morristown, N.J., 1989; curator Olcott Studio Gallery Art Show, Bernardsville, N.J., 1985; curator Color/Divine Madness Ward-Nasse Gallery, N.Y.C., 1996; demonstrator Acad. St. Elizabeth Convent Station, 1989, 90, DuCret Sch. of the Arts Student Art Exhbn.; organizer for acad. students, 1989; dir. Student's Art Festival WNET/Thirteen, Acad. St. Elizabeth, 1989. One-woman shows include County Coll. Morris, 1989, Allied Corp., N.J., 1989, Ariel Gallery, N.Y.C., 1987, 88, Corner Gallery, World Trade Ctr., N.Y.C., 1989, 90, Montserrat Gallery, N.Y.C., 1992-97; internat. juried shows include N.J. Ctr. Visual Arts, Summit, 1985, 92, Nat. Assn. Women Artists, Inc., 420 West Broadway Mems. Exhbn., 1995-96, 97, Meadowlands Cultural Ctr. for Arts, Rutherford, N.J., 1995; exhibited in group shows at Ward-Nasse Gallery, 1989-94, 95, 96, 97, Artworks-Trenton, N.J., 1989, 92, N.J. Assn. Ind. Schs., Gill St., Bernard, 1989, Jain Gallery, N.Y.C., 1989, 91, Blackwell St. Gallery, Dover, N.J., 1993, Montclair Art Mus., Bloomfield Coll., 1990, Ben-Shahn Gallery, William Paterson Coll., 1992, 94, Jain-Marunouchi Gallery, N.Y.C., 1992, 93, Cmty. Arts Assn., Ridgewood, N.J., 1995, Nat. Assn. Women Artists, Inc., SoHo, N.Y., 1995, 96, 97, Nat. Soc. Painters in Casein and Acrylic, Salmagundi Gallery, 1996, Hunterdon Art Ctr., 1997; represented in permanent collections Ethicon Corp., divsn. Johnson & Johnson Corp., New Brunswick, N.J., 1996, Allied Corp., N.J., Interior Sensations, Marinac, N.Y., Palisades Amusement Pk. Hist. Soc., Cliffside Park Libr., ACI Art Communication Internat. Juried-Curated Art Collection CD-ROM and Internet, The Best Contemporary Art, Phila., 1996, 97. Named Miss Livingston N.J., Livingston C. of C., 1956; recipient Rudolph A. Voelcker Meml. award Art Ctr. N.J., 1982, Excellence award Hunterdon Art Mus., 1988, award for excellence Artists League Ctrl. N.J., 1989, Cornelius Low House, Middlesex County Mus., Montclair Art Mus., 1990, award for mixed media Millburn-Short Hills Art Assn., 1989, 1st Pl. award N.E. Caldwell Arts Festival, 1989, award Nabisco Brands, Inc., East Hanover, N.J., 1990, Excellence award Ann. Tri-State Artists League Ctrl. N.J., 1991, 92, Winsor & Newton plaque, Visual Arts League, Edison, N.J., 1992, Excellence award Manhattan Arts Internat. Cover Art Competition, 1994, Hunterdon Art Ctr. award for acrylic/mixed media, 1996, award Livingston Art Assn., Newark Acad., 1996. Mem. Nat. Soc. Painters in Casein and Acrylic, Nat. Assn. Women Artists, Inc., Artists Equity, N.J. Ctr. Visual Arts, Nat. Mus. Women in Arts, Jersey City Mus., Catherine Lorillaird Wolfe Art Club, World Wildlife Fedn., Ward-Nasse Gallery, N.Y.C., Livingston Art Assn. (Award for Acrylic 1996), Smithsonian, Newark Acad. Avocations: opera, vocalist, piano, concerts, museums. Office: PO Box 515 Whippany NJ 07981-0515

PETKANICS, BRYAN G., lawyer; b. N.Y.C., Dec. 29, 1955. BA cum laude, Fordham U., 1976; JD, Georgetown U., 1980. Bar: N.J. 1980, N.Y. 1986. Atty. St. John & Wayne, N.Y.C. Mem. N.Y. State Bar Assn. (mem. internat. law and practice sect. and com. on internat. banking, securities and internat. transactions), Assn. Bar City N.Y., Phi Sigma Alpha. Office: St John & Wayne 70 E 55th St New York NY 10022-3222

PETKUS, ALAN FRANCIS, microbiologist; b. Chgo., Feb. 4, 1956; s. Frank Anthony and Valeria (Shimkus) P.; m. Karan Elaine Blakely, Apr. 21, 1990; children: Sabrina Marie, Alexandra Louise, Emerson Alan. BS, Ill. Benedictine Coll., Lisle, 1979; PhD, Chgo. Med. Sch., North Chicago, 1986. Technologist Palos Community Hosp., Palos Heights, Ill., 1973-79, med. technologist, 1979-86; microbiologist South Bend (Ind.) Med. Found., 1986-91; microbiology dir. Met. Hosp., Grand Rapids, Mich., 1991—. Mem. AAAS, Am. Soc. Clin. Pathologists, Am. Soc. Microbiology, N.Y. Acad. Sci., Ill. Soc. Microbiology, South Ctrl. Assn. Microbiology. Roman Catholic. Avocations: designing computer programs, fishing, skiing. Office: Met Hosp 1919 Boston St SE Grand Rapids MI 49506-4160

PETOK, SAMUEL, retired manufacturing company executive; b. Detroit, Aug. 12, 1922; s. Harry and Jennie (Weingarten) P.; m. Fayne Joyce Myers, June 26, 1952; children—Carol, Seth, Michael. B.A. in History, Wayne State U., Detroit, 1945; postgrad., Medill Sch. Journalism, Northwestern U., 1946. Reporter Detroit Free Press, 1946-50; account exec. McCann Erickson, 1950-52; pub. relations exec. Chrysler Corp., 1952-70; Vice pres. public relations and advt. White Motor Corp., Cleve., 1971-76; dir. communications automotive ops. Rockwell Internat. Co., Troy, Mich., 1976-77; corp. staff v.p. public relations Rockwell Internat. Co., Pitts., 1977-78; v.p. communications Rockwell Internat. Co., 1978-82, sr. v.p. communications, mem. mgmt. com., 1982-88; retired. Former trustee Arthur W. Page Soc. Recipient Page One award Newspaper Guild Detroit, 1948. Mem. Pub. Rels. Soc. Am. (Silver Anvil award 1964, award Cleve. chpt. 1975), Internat. Pub. Rels. Assn., Overseas Press Club Am., The Old Guard of Princeton, Green Acres Country Club.

PETOSA, JASON JOSEPH, publisher; b. Des Moines, Iowa, Apr. 26, 1939; s. Joseph John and Mildred Margaret (Cardamon) P.; m. Theodora Anne Doleski, Aug. 12, 1972; 1 son, Justin James. Student, Marquette U., 1957-59, St. Paul Sem., 1959-63, 65-67, Colegio Paolino Internationale, Rome, 1963-65. Asso. editor Cath. Home Mag., Canfield, Ohio, 1965-67; editor Cath. Home Mag., 1968; dir. Alba House Communications, Canfield, 1968-71; with Office of Radio and TV, Diocese of Youngstown, Ohio, 1969-71; dir. pub. relations, instr. Alice Lloyd Coll., Pippa Passes, Ky., 1971-76; writer, cons. Bethesda, Ohio, 1976-79; pres., pub. Nat. Cath. Reporter, Kansas City, Mo., 1979-85; v.p., gen. mgr. Towsend-Kraft Pub. Co., Liberty, Mo., 1985-86; pres., pub. Steadfast Pub. Co., Kansas City, 1986—; owner CF&E Ptnrs. Bd. dirs. David (Ky.) Sch., 1973-79; mem. Mayor's UN Day Com., Kansas City. Mem. Kansas City Direct Mktg. Assn., UN Assn. (bd. dirs. Met. Kansas City chpt.), Sigma Delta Chi. Roman Catholic. Office: 19 W Linwood Blvd PO Box 410265 Kansas City MO 64141

PETOSKEY, THOMAS W., secondary school educator; b. Bay City, Mich., Feb. 17, 1955; s. Walton R. and Henrietta (Wesolowski) P. BS, U. Detroit, 1977; MS, Oklahoma City U., 1982, EdD, 1984. Cert. tchr., Okla., Mich., Calif. Tchr. sci. Oklahoma City Pub. Schs.; now tchr. sci. Archdiocese of L.A. Com. mem. Loyola Marymount U. Named Vol. of Yr., Oklahoma City Pub. Schs., 1982, 83, Tchr. of Yr., 1992. mem. ASCD, Am. Fedn. Tchrs., Calif. Sci. Tchrs. Assn., Nat. Cath. Edn. Assn., Nat. Sci. Tchrs. Assn.

PETRAIT, BROTHER JAMES ANTHONY, secondary education educator, clergy member; b. Phila., May 4, 1937; s. John Joseph and Antonina Frances (Cizek) P. BA, U. Detroit, 1969; MEd, U. Ga., 1971; postgrad. in Scis. and Edn., 8 Univs. and Colls. in U.S., 1971—. Joined Oblates of St Francis de Sales, Roman Cath. Ch., 1957. Sci. tchr. Salesian H.S., Detroit, 1961-70, Judge Meml. H.S., Salt Lake City, 1972-76, Benedictine H.S., Detroit, 1976-82; sci. tchr. St. Joseph H.S., Ogden, Utah, 1983-88, Fredriksted, V.I., 1988—; tchr. resource agt. Am. Astron. Soc., 1995—; pres. Mich. Assn. of Biology Tchrs., 1978-82, Utah Biology Tchrs. Assn., 1985-88; bd. dirs. Utah Sci. Tchrs. Assn., 1985-88; presenter at workshops, speaker in Chgo., New Orleans, Las Vegas, Detroit, Phila., Salt Lake City, Layton, Orlando, Purdue U., Anaheim, Australian Nat. Univ., Canberra; participant in 8 NSF-funded programs: U. Ga., Christian Bros. Colls., Vanderbilt U., St. Lawrence U., Ball State U., W. Va. U., No. Ariz. U. Contbr. article to teacher's mags. and ednl. jours. including The Am. Biology Tchr., The Sci. Tchr., The Cath. Digest., Congrl. Record. Anti nuclear weapons activist, founder and leader Nuclear Free Utah, Ogden, 1986-88; led boycott against Morton Salt Co., maker of nuclear weapons.. Recipient Outstanding Biology Tchr. award Nat. Assn. Biology Tchrs., 1975, Nat. Finalist in Presdl. awards for excellence in sci. and math. tchg. Nat. Sci. Tchrs. Assn./NSF/The White House, 1995; fellow Access Excellence fellow Genentech Inc. program for Outstanding Biology Tchrs., 1996. Mem. Nat. Sci. Tchrs. Assn. (cert. in biology and gen. sci., Star award 1976, Ohaus awards, 1980, 84), Am. Astron. Soc., Soc. of Amateur Radio Astronomers. Avocations: radio amateur, computers, photography, videography. Home and Office: Saint Joseph H S Plot 3 Rte 2 Frederiksted VI 00840

PETRAKIS, HARRY MARK, author; b. St. Louis, June 5, 1923; s. Mark E. and Stella (Christoulakis) P.; m. Diane Perparos, Sept. 30, 1945; children: Mark, John, Dean. Student, U. Ill., 1940-41, L.H.D., 1971; L.H.D., Governor's State U., 1980, Hellenic Coll., 1984, Roosevelt U., 1987. Free-lance writer, tchr., lectr.; tchr. workshop classes in novel, short story; McGuffey vis. lectr. Ohio U., Athens, 1971; writer-in-residence Chgo. Pub. Library, 1976-77, Chgo. Bd. Edn., 1978-79; Kazantzakis Prof. San Francisco State U., 1992. Author: Lion at My Heart, 1959, The Odyssey of Kostas Volakis, 1963, Pericles on 31st Street, 1965 (nominated for Nat. Book award), The Founder's Touch, 1965, A Dream of Kings, 1966 (Nat. Book award nomination), The Waves of Night, 1969, Stelmark: A Family Recollection, 1970, In the Land of Morning, 1973, The Hour of the Bell, 1976, A Petrakis Reader, 28 Stories, 1978, Nick the Greek, 1979, Days of Vengeance, 1983, Reflections on a Writer's Life and Work, 1983, Collected Stories, 1986, Ghost of the Sun, 1990; contbr. short stores to mags. including, Atlantic Monthly, Sat. Eve. Post, Harper's Bazaar, Country Beautiful. (Story included in Prize Stories, also O. Henry Award 1966). Recipient awards Friends of Am. Writers, Friends of Lit., Soc. Midland Authors, Carl Sandburg award, Ellis Island medal of honor, 1995. Mem. Authors Guild, PEN, Writers Guild Am.-West. Address: Dune Acres 80 East Rd Chesterton IN 46304 *"...The older I become, the more clearly I see that there is a stunning purity in the writing of a book that I cannot achieve in my own life with its frailty and desperation. The work takes over with a life of its own. In those moments, I wouldn't trade writing with all its loneliness and sometimes with its pain, for any other profession in the world.*

PETRAKIS, LEONIDAS, research scientist, educator, administrator; b. Sparta, Greece, July 23, 1935; came to U.S., 1951, naturalized, 1956; s. Lina Contos P.; m. Ismene Lempesis, June 21, 1959; children: Ismene L., Alexis L. BS, Northeastern U., 1958; PhD, U. Calif., Berkeley, 1961. Faculty research grantee Nat. Research Council, Can., 1961-62; prof. chemistry U. Md., College Park, 1962-63; researcher DuPont Co., Wilmington, Del., 1963-65; sr. scientist Gulf-Chevron Research Co., Richmond, Calif., 1965-89; sr. scientist Brookhaven Nat. Lab., Upton, N.Y., 1989—, chmn. dept. applied scis., 1989-94; sr. vis. lectr. Carnegie-Mellon U., Pitts., 1972-73; vis. prof. U. Paris, 1985, 91, 95; adj. prof. U. Pitts., 1981-85; mem. Coun. for Chem. Rsch. Author: Free Radicals in Syn Fuels, 1983, NMR for Liquid Fuels, 1986; editor and author four books on chemistry for fossil energy, 1978, 80, 84, 94; contbr. articles to profl. jours. Mem. environ. com. L.I. Assn.; bd. advisors Barnett Inst., Northeastern U.; mem. Organizing Group and Sci. and Bus. Adv. Bd. for L.I. Rsch. Inst. Advanced Study Inst. rsch. grantee Dept. Energy, Nat. Sci. Found, NATO, Washington, 1979-83. Mem. Am. Chem. Soc. (adv. bd. 1979-83, officer 1974-78, Pitts. award 1984), Am. Phys. Soc.(symposium organizer), AAAS, NSF (grantee, Washington 1981-85, also symposium organizer), Sigma Xi. Office: Brookhaven Nat Lab Dept Of Applied Sci Upton NY 11973 *Technological progress has its downside: complexity, obfuscation, lack of depth, alienation; homo sapiens become homo economicus and now auto-sapiens; quantity become quality, although it is clear enough that more, as in cancer, is not always better; and the wrappings are the package. It is time to take time with the poets and listen to the raindrops, time to read again the myth of the Tower of Babel, and to rediscover the lessons of entropy in everyday life.*

PETRAKIS, NICHOLAS LOUIS, physician, medical researcher, educator; b. San Francisco, Feb. 6, 1922; s. Louis Nicholas and Stamatina (Boosalis) P.; m. Patricia Elizabeth Kelly, June 24, 1947; children: Steven John, Susan Lynn, Sandra Kay. BA, Augustana Coll., 1943; BS in Medicine, U. S.D., 1944; MD, Washington U., St. Louis, 1946. Intern Mpls. Gen. Hosp., 1946-47; physician-researcher U.S. Naval Radiol. Def. Lab., San Francisco, 1947-49; resident physician Mpls. Gen. Hosp., 1949-50; sr. asst. surgeon Nat. Cancer Inst., USPHS, San Francisco, 1950-54; asst. research physician Cancer Research Inst., U. Calif., San Francisco, 1954-56; asst. prof. preventive medicine U. Calif. Sch. Medicine, San Francisco, 1956-60, assoc. prof., 1960-66, prof., 1966-91, chmn. dept. epidemiology and internat. health, 1978-88, prof. emeritus, 1991—; prof. epidemiology U. Calif. Sch. Pub. Health, Berkeley, 1981-91; assoc. dir. G.W. Hooper Edn., U. Calif., San Francisco, 1970-74, acting dir., 1974-77, chmn. dept. epidemiology and internat. health, 1979-89; co-dir. Breast Screening Ctr. of No. Calif., Oakland, 1976-81; cons. Breast Cancer Task Force, Nat. Cancer Inst., Bethesda, Md., 1972-76; chmn. Biometry & Epidemiology Contract Rev. Com., Bethesda, 1977-81; mem. bd. sci. counselors, div. cancer etiology Nat. Cancer Inst., Bethesda, 1982-86; mem. scientific adv. com. Calif. State Tobacco-Related Disease Rsch. Program, 1991-93; cons. U. Crete Sch. Medicine, Heraklion, Greece, 1984; bd. dirs. No. Calif. Cancer Ctr., 1991. Contbr. over 200 research papers on breast cancer, med. oncology and hematology. Eleanor Roosevelt Internat. Cancer fellow Am. Cancer Soc., Comitato Reserche Nucleari, Cassacia, Italy, 1962; U.S. Pub. Health Service Spl. fellow Galton Lab., U. London, 1969-70; recipient Alumni Achievement award Augustana Coll., Sioux Falls, S.D., 1979, Axion award Hellenic-Am. Profl. Soc. of Calif., San Francisco, 1984, Lewis C. Robbins award Soc. for Prospective Medicine, Indpls., 1985. Mem. Am. Soc. Preventive Oncology (founding, pres. 1984-85, Disting. Achievement award 1992), Soc. for Prospective Medicine (founding), Am. Assn. Cancer Rsch., Am. Epidemiol. Soc., Am. Soc. Clin. Investigation, Am. Bd. Preventive Medicine (cert.). Home: 335 Juanita Way San Francisco CA 94127-1657 Office: U Calif Sch Medicine Dept Epidemiology and Biostats 1699 HSW San Francisco CA 94143-0560

PETRALIA, RONALD SEBASTIAN, entomologist, neurobiologist; b. Lawrence, Mass., Nov. 7, 1954; s. Samuel and Rosalie (Zanfagna) P.; B.S. summa cum laude in Entomology, U. Mass., 1975; Ph.D. in Entomology and Biology, Tex. A&M U., 1979. Rsch. asst., 1975-79, rsch. assoc. Tex. A&M U., College Station, 1979-80; asst. prof. biology St. Ambrose Coll., Davenport, Iowa, 1980-85; rsch. fellow dept. anatomy George Washington U., Washington, 1985-90; sr. staff fellow Nat. Inst. for Deafness and Other Comm. Disorders., NIH, Bethesda, Md., 1991-97, staff scientist, 1997—; presenter in field. Co-author: (book chpts. with others) Excitatory Amino Acids, 1992, The Mammalian Cochlear Nuclei: Organization and Function, 1993, Excitatory Amino Acids: Their Role in Neuroendocrine Function, 1996, The Ionotropic Glutamate Receptors, 1997; contbr. articles to profl. jours. Mem. AAAS, Chesapeake Soc. for Microscopy (coun. mem., newsletter editor, past pres.), Soc. for Neurosci., Entomol. Soc. Am., Microscopy Soc. Am., Assn. Rsch. in Otolaryngology, Cambridge Entomol. Club, Sigma Xi. Roman Catholic. Home: 78 Boston St Methuen MA 01844-5359 Office: NIDCD NIH 9000 Rockville Pike Rm 5d08 Bethesda MD 20814-1436

PETRASH, JEFFREY MICHAEL, lawyer; b. Cleve., Dec. 14, 1948; s. Robert Anthony and Naomi Marjorie (Close) P.; m. Patricia Ann Early, May 29, 1971 (div. Mar. 1986); 1 child, Michael Stewart. AB, U. Mich., 1969, JD, 1973. Bar: Mich. 1974, D.C. 1975. Assoc. Dickinson, Wright, McKean, Cudlip & Moon, Detroit, 1973-75, Hamel, Park, McCabe & Saunders, Washington, 1975-78; from assoc. to ptnr. Dickinson, Wright, Moon, Van Dusen & Freeman, Washington, 1978—. Served to capt. U.S. Army, 1973-74. Mem. Soc. Barristers. Episcopalian. Avocation: sailing. Home: 6606 Hillandale Rd Bethesda MD 20815-6406 Office: Dickinson Wright Moon Van Dusen & Freeman 1901 L St NW Washington DC 20036-3506

PETREE, WILLIAM HORTON, lawyer; b. Winston-Salem, N.C., Nov. 4, 1920; s. Elbert Heaton and Ethel (Tucker) P.; m. Lena Morris, Dec. 23, 1943; children: William Horton Jr., Mary Jo. BS, U. N.C., 1944, JD, 1948. Bar: N.C. 1948. Ptnr. Petree Stockton and predecessors, 1956—; past chmn. local bd. dirs. First Union Nat. Bank, Winston-Salem. Past bd. dirs., mem. exec. com. Old Salem, Inc.; past mem. campaign coordinating com. Forsyth County, N.C.; past chmn. found. com. Winston-Salem Found.; past pres. Forsyth County Tb and Health Assn.; trustee, elder, past bd. dirs. Moravian Home; past chmn. fin. bd. Moravian Ch. in Am., South; past trustee, exec. com. Salem Coll., bd. visitors, 1995—. 1st lt. USMCR, 1944-46. Mem. Forsyth County Bar Assn. (past pres.), Forsyth Country Club (past dir.), Piedmont Club, Kiwanis (bd. dirs. Winston-Salem club, pres. 1976-77), Alpha Tau Omega, Phi Delta Phi. Democrat. Mem. Moravian Ch. Home: 144 Muirfield Dr Winston Salem NC 27104-3949 Office: Petree Stockton 1001 W 4th St Winston Salem NC 27101-2410 *Enthusiasm, coupled with proper motivation, contributes most to a successful, happy and fulfilling life.*

PETREK, WILLIAM JOSEPH, college president emeritus; b. Arcadia, Wis., Feb. 26, 1928; s. Roman Casper and Agnes (Jankowski) P.; m. Sandra Lucille Nash, Nov. 24, 1961; children: Michele, Søren. B.A. cum laude, St. John's U., Minn., 1948; S.T.L. magna cum laude, Gregorian U., Rome, 1952; Ph.D. with great distinction, Higher Inst. Philosophy, U. Louvain, Belgium, 1956; DHumLitt, Richmond Coll., London. Asst. prof. philosophy, chmn. dept. philosophy Holy Cross Coll., La Crosse, Wis., 1956-60; from asst. prof. to prof. philosophy and religion DePauw U., Greencastle, Ind., 1961-71; dir. internat. edn., asst. dean internat. edn. and off-campus programs DePauw U., 1966-71; v.p. Gt. Lakes Colls. Assn., Ann Arbor, Mich., 1971-72; dean Coll. Liberal Arts, Hofstra U., Hempstead, N.Y., 1972-74; provost, dean faculties Hofstra U., 1974-76; acad. v.p. Southeast Mo. State U., Cape Girardeau, 1976-80; pres. Richmond Coll., London, 1980-92. Translator, author: introduction (Jean Nabert) Elements for an Ethic, 1969. Trustee Nassau Higher Edn. Consortium, 1973-76; exec. com. bd. Council Intercultural Studies and Programs, 1974-88; bd. nat. cons. Nat. Endowment Humanities, 1974—; bd. dirs. World Univ. Service, 1976-80; mem. Ct. Govs. Mill Hill Sch., London, 1989-94. Danforth asso., 1964; recipient Best Prof. award DePauw U., 1965; Ford Found. humanities grantee, 1970; Gt. Lakes Colls. Assn. Non-Western research grantee, 1965; hon. fellow Inst. Am. Univs., Aix-en-Provence, France, 1973. Mem. Soc. Phenomenology and Existential Philosophy, Assn. Internat. Colls. and Univs. (pres. 1984-89). Office: Richmond Coll, Queens Rd Richmond, Surrey TW10 6JP, England

PETREQUIN, HARRY JOSEPH, JR., foreign service officer; b. Ste. Genevieve, Mo., July 1, 1929; s. Harry Joseph and Crescentia Ellen (Bechter) P.; m. Katharine McDonnell Drouin, Oct. 7, 1980; children: John Andrew, Marc Christopher, Paul Nicholas. AB, Westminster Coll., 1950; B of Fgn. Trade, Am. Grad. Sch. Internat. Mgmt., 1954; postgrad., Johns Hopkins U., 1960; MA, Tufts U., 1970. Joined U.S. Fgn. Svc., 1955; assigned AID and predecessor agys., 1955—; dep. dir. S.E. Asia Regional Econ. Devel. Office, Thailand, 1970-74; U.S. coord. Senegal River Basin Authority, Dakar, 1975-76; dir. ASEAN and South Pacific Affairs, 1977-80; dir. program devel. and evaluation staff Bur. Internat. Orgn. Affairs State Dept., 1980-81; dep. dir. AID Mission, Morocco, 1981-85; coord. AID Sr. Mgmt. Course, 1985-86, Indsl. Coll. of the Armed Forces, 1986-87; faculty dept. nat. security policy Nat. War Coll., Washington, 1987-89; internat. devel. cons. Black Mountain, N.C., 1989—; adj. prof. polit. sci. Warren Wilson Coll., Swannanoa, N.C., 1993—. Lt. (j.g.) USCGR, 1951-53, comdr. Res. Recipient Superior Honor award AID, 1979, State Dept. Superior Honor award, 1981, Comdrs. award for Civilian Svc., Dept. of the Army, 1989. Mem. Soc. Internt. Devel., World Federalist Assn. (nat. bd. dirs.), Am. Fgn. Svc. Assn., UN Assn. U.S., Acad. Polit. Sci., Cousteau Soc., Common Cause, Inst. Noetic Scis., World Future Soc., Amnesty Internat., Coast Guard Combat Vets Assn., Greenpeace, Vets. for Peace, The Land Inst., Phi Alpha Theta.

PETRI, THOMAS EVERT, congressman; b. Marinette, Wis., May 28, 1940; s. Robert and Marian (Humleker) P.; m. Anne Neal, Mar. 26, 1983; 1 child, Alexandra. BA in Govt., Harvard U., 1962, JD, 1965. Bar: Wis. 1965. Law clk. to presiding justice U.S. Dist. (we. dist.) Wis., Madison, 1965-66; vol. Peace Corps, Somalia, 1966-67; aide White House, Washington, 1969-70; dir. crime and drug studies Pres.'s Nat. Adv. Coun. on Exec. Orgn., 1969; pvt. practice Fond du Lac, Wis., 1970-79; mem. Wis. State Senate, Madison, 1973-79, 96th-105th Congress from 6th Wis. Dist., Washington, 1979—; mem. edn. and workforce com., trans. and infrastructure com. Editor: National Industrial Policy: Solution or Illusion, 1984. Republican. Lutheran. Avocations: reading, swimming, hiking, biking, skiing. Office: US Ho of Reps 2262 Rayburn Bldg Washington DC 20515-4906

PETRIC, ERNEST, Slovenian ambassador; b. Trzic, Slovenia, 1936; married; 3 children. D of Internat. Law, U. Ljubljana, Slovenia, 1960; student, U. Vienna, 1962-63. Minister of sci. and tech. Republic of Slovenia, 1967-72; prof., dean faculty of sociology, polit. sci. and journalism U. Ljubljana, 1972-83; prof. internat. law U. Addis Ababa, Ethiopia, 1983-86; amb. to India and Nepal from Republic of Yugoslavia, New Delhi, 1989-91; amb. to U.S. and Mex. from Republic of Slovenia, Washington, 1991—; chmn. Yugoslav Assn. for UN, 1987-88. Author: International Protection of Minorities, 1977, Right to Self Determination, 1984, From Emperor to Leader, 1987, others; contbr. numerous articles to internat. law and internat. rels. jours. Mem. Internat. Law Assn. (human rights com.). Home: Na Rebri 4a, Bled Slovenia Office: Embassy of Slovenia 1525 New Hampshire Ave NW Washington DC 20036-1203

PETRICK, ALFRED, JR., mineral economics educator, consultant; b. Mt. Vernon, N.Y., Dec. 30, 1926; s. Alfred and Ruth (Updike) P.; m. Ruth Goodridge, Jan. 2, 1956; children: Elizabeth, Andrew Wayne. B.S., B.A., Columbia U., 1952, M.S., 1962; M.B.A., Denver U., 1966; Ph.D., U. Colo., 1969. Registered profl. engr., Colo. Sales engr. Ingersoll Rand Co., N.Y.C., 1953-54; project engr. U.S. AEC, Grand Junction, Colo., 1954-57; mining engr. Reynolds Metals Co., Bauxite, Ark., 1957-61, Guyana, 1957-61; mineral economist U.S. Bur. Mines, Denver, 1963-70; Coulter prof. Colo. Sch. Mines, Golden, 1970-84, emeritus prof., 1984—; dir. Petrick Assocs., Evergreen, Colo. Author: Economics International Development, 1977, Economics of Minerals, 1980, Preparacion y Evaluacion, 1982. Mem. com. tech. aspects strategic materials Nat. Acad. Sci., Washington, 1973-76, mem. com. surface mining and reclamation, 1979. Served with USAF, 1945-47, PTO. Fulbright research scholar U. Otago, Dunedin, New Zealand, 1986; recipient Edn. award Instituto Para Funcionarios De Las Industrias Minera y Siderurgica, Mexico City, 1981; recipient Service award Office Tech. Assessment, U.S. Congress, 1981. Mem. AIME (chmn. council econs. 1977-78, Henry Krumb lectr. 1986, service award), Profl. Engrs. Colo. Presbyterian. Home: 5544 S Hatch Dr Evergreen CO 80439-7233 Office: Colo Sch Mines Golden CO 80401

PETRICK, ERNEST NICHOLAS, mechanical engineer; b. Pa., Apr. 9, 1922; s. Aurelius and Anna (Kaschak) P.; m. Magdalene Simcoe, June 13, 1946; children: Deborah Petrick Healey, Katherine, Denise, Victoria Petrick Kropp. B.S. in Mech. Engring, Carnegie Inst. Tech., 1943; M.S., Purdue U., 1948, Ph.D., 1955. Registered profl. engr., Mich. Faculty Purdue U., 1946-53; dir. heat transfer research Curtiss-Wright Corp., Woodridge, N.J., 1953-56; chief advanced propulson systems Curtiss-Wright Research divsn., Quehanna, Pa., 1957-60; chief research engr. Kelsey-Hayes Co., Detroit, 1960-65; chief scientist, tech. dir. U.S. Army Tank-Automotive Command, Warren, Mich., 1965-82; chief scientist, dir. engring. labs. Gen. Dynamics, 1982-87; engring. cons., 1987—; panel mem. combat vehicles NATO, 1973-82; mem. adv. bd. on basic combustion research NSF, 1973; chmn. advanced transp. systems com. White House Energy Project, 1973; mem. adv. com.

NSF-RANN research program Drexel U. Coll. Engring., 1976-78; mem. Army Sci. Bd., 1983-89; cons. Air Force Studies Bd. NRC, 1991-93, cons. Def. Sci. Bd., 1994-95; adj. prof. engring. Wayne State U., Detroit, 1972-82, U. Mich., Ann Arbor, 1982-83. Contbr. articles on transp., ground vehicles, flight propulsion and project mgmt. to profl. jours. Mem. adv. bd. Wayne State U. Engring., Detroit. Served to lt. USN, 1942-46; to lt. comdr. USNR, 1946-54. Recipient certificate of achievement U.S. Army, 1967, Outstanding Performance awards, 1970, 71, 76, 82, Outstanding Mech. Engring. award Purdue U., 1991; named Disting. Engring. Alumnus Purdue U., 1966. Mem. Soc. Automotive Engrs. (nat. dir. 1978-80), Am. Def. Preparedness Assn. (chmn. land warfare survivability divsn. 1990-95, Silver medal 1992), Assn. U.S. Army, Sigma Xi, Pi Tau Sigma. Home: 1540 Stonehaven Rd Ann Arbor MI 48104-4150

PETRICOFF, M. HOWARD, lawyer, educator; b. Cin., Dec. 22, 1949; s. Herman and Neoma P.; m. Hanna Sue, Aug. 11, 1974; children: Nicholas, Eve. BS, Am. U., 1967-71; JD, U. Cin., 1971-74; M in Pub. Adminstrn., Harvard U., 1980-81. Bar: Ohio, U.S. Ct. Appeals (D.C. cir.) 1977, U.S. Ct. Appeals (10th cir.) 1985, U.S. Ct. Appeals (6th cir.) 1989, U.S. Supreme Ct. 1989. Asst. city law dir. City of Toledo (Ohio), 1975-77; asst. atty. gen. Ohio Atty. Gen. Office, Columbus, 1977-82; ptnr. Vorys, Sater, Seymour & Pease, Columbus, 1982—; adj. prof. law Capital U. Law Sch., Columbus, 1991—. Contbr. articles to profl. jours. Reginald Heber Smith Found. fellow Washnigton, 1974-75. Mem. Ohio Bar Assn., Columbus Bar Assn., Ohio Oil and Gas Assn. Office: Vorys Sater Seymour & Pease PO Box 1008 52 E Gay St Columbus OH 43215-3161

PETRIDES, GEORGE ATHAN, ecologist, educator; b. N.Y.C., Aug. 1, 1916; s. George Athan and Grace Emeline (Ladd) P.; m. Miriam Clarissa Pasma, Nov. 30, 1940; children: George H., Olivia L., Lisa B. B.S., George Washington U., 1938; M.S., Cornell U., 1940; Ph.D., Ohio State U., 1948; postdoctoral fellow, U. Ga., 1963-64. Naturalist Nat. Park Service, Washington and Yosemite, Calif., 1938-43, Glacier Nat. Park, Mont., 1947, Mt. McKinley Nat. Park, Alaska, 1959; game technician W.Va. Conservation Commn., Charleston, 1941; instr. Am. U., 1942-43, Ohio State U., 1946-48; leader Tex. Coop. Wildlife Unit; assoc. prof. wildlife mgmt. Tex. A. and M. Coll., 1948-50; assoc. prof. wildlife mgmt., zool. and African studies Mich. State U., 1950-58, prof., 1958—; research prof. U. Pretoria, S. Africa, 1965; vis. prof. U. Kiel, Germany, 1967; vis. prof. wildlife mgmt. Kanha Nat. Park, India, 1983; del. sci. confs. Warsaw, 1960, Nairobi and Salisbury, 1963, Sao Paulo, Aberdeen, 1965, Lucerne, 1966, Varanasi, India, Nairobi, 1967, Oxford, Eng., Paris, 1968, Durban, 1971, Mexico City, 1971, 73, Banff, 1972, Nairobi, Moscow, The Hague, 1974, Johannesburg, 1977, Sydney, 1978, Kuala Lumpur, 1979, Cairns, Australia, Mogadishu, Somalia, Peshawar, Pakistan, 1980; participant NSF Expdn., Antarctic, 1972, FAO mission to, Afghanistan, 1972, World Bank mission to, Malaysia, 1975. Author: Field Guide to Trees and Shrubs, 1958, 2d edit., 1972, Field Guide to Eastern Trees, 1988, Field Guide to Western Trees, 1992, First Guide to Trees, 1993, Trees of the California Sierra Nevada, 1996; Editor wildlife mgmt. terrestial sect.: Biol. Abstracts, 1947-72; Contbr. articles to biol. publs. Served to lt. USNR, 1943-46. Fulbright research awards in E. Africa Nat. Parks Kenya, 1953-54; Fulbright research awards in E. Africa Nat. Parks Kenya, Uganda, 1956-57; N.Y. Zool. Soc. grantee Ethiopia, Sudan, 1957; N.Y. Zool. Soc. grantee Thailand, 1977; Mich. State U. grantee Nigeria, 1962; Mich. State U. grantee Zambia, 1966; Mich. State U. grantee Kenya, 1969; Mich. State U. grantee Africa, 1970, 71, 73, 81; Mich. State U. grantee Greece, 1974, 83; Mich. State U. grantee Iran, 1974; Mich. State U. grantee Botswana, 1977; Mich. State U. grantee Papua New Guinea, Thailand, 1979; Iran Dept. Environment grantee, 1977; Smithsonian Instn. grantee India and Nepal, 1967, 68, 75, 77, 83, 85; World Wildlife Fund grantee W. Africa, 1968. Mem. Am. Ornithologists Union, Am. Soc. Mammalogists, Wildlife Soc. (exec. sec. 1953), Wilderness Soc., Am. Comm. Internat. Wildlife Protection, Ecol. Soc., Fauna Preservation Soc., E. African Wildlife Soc., Internat. Union Conservation Nature, Zool. Soc. So. Africa, Sigma Xi. Presbyterian. Home: 4895 Barton Rd Williamston MI 48895-9305 Office: Mich State U Dept Fisheries And Wil East Lansing MI 48824

PETRIE, BRUCE INGLIS, lawyer; b. Washington, Nov. 8, 1926; s. Robert Inglis and Marion (Douglas) P.; m. Beverly Ann Stevens, Nov. 3, 1950 (dec. Oct. 6 1993); children: Laurie Ann Roche, Bruce Inglis, Karen Elizabeth Medsger. BBA, U. Cin., 1948, JD, 1950. Bar: Ohio 1950, U.S. Dist. Ct. (so. dist.) Ohio 1951, U.S. Ct. Appeals (6th cir.) 1960, U.S. Supreme Ct. Assoc. Kunkel & Kunkel, Cin., 1950-51; assoc. Graydon, Head & Ritchey, 1951-57, ptnr., 1957—. Mem. bd. Charter Com. Greater Cin., 1952-76; mem. bd. edn. Indian Hill Exempted Village Sch. Dist., 1965-67, pres., 1967; mem. adv. bd. William A. Mitchell Ctr., 1969-86; mem. Green Areas adv. com. Village of Indian Hill (Ohio), 1969-80, chmn., 1976-80; mem. Ohio Ethics Com., 1974-75; founder Sta. WGUC-FM; mem. WGUC-FM Community Bd., 1974—, chmn., 1974-76; bd. dirs. Murray Seasongood Good Govt. Fund, 1975—, pres., 1989—; life dir. Nat. Civic League; bd. dirs. Cin. Vol. Lawyers for Poor Found.; parents as tchrs. Metro Housing Auth. Commn., 1991—; bd. dirs. Linton Music Series; bd. Amernet Chamber Music Soc.; elder, trustee, deacon Knox Presbyn. Ch. Fellow Am. Bar Found.; mem. ABA, Ohio Bar Assn., Cin. Bar Assn. (pres. 1981), Am. Judicature Soc. (Herbert Lincoln Harley award 1973; dir.), Nat. Civic League (Disting. Citizen award 1985, coun. 1984—), Am. Law Inst., Ohio State Bar Assn. Found. (Outstanding Rsch. in Law and Govt. award 1986, Charles P. Taft Civic Gumption award 1988, Ohio Bar medal 1988), Cincinnatus Assn., Order of Coif, Literary Club, Univ. Club, Cin. Club. Recipient Pres.'s award U. Cin., 1976, Disting. Alumnus award, 1995. Contbr. articles to legal jours. Avocations: tennis, squash, woodworking, writing, horticulture, music. Home: 2787 Walsh Rd Cincinnati OH 45208-3428 Office: Graydon Head & Ritchey 1900 Fifth 3d Ctr 511 Walnut St Cincinnati OH 45202-3115

PETRIE, DANIEL MANNIX, film, theatre and television director; b. Glace Bay, N.S., Can., Nov. 26, 1920; came to U.S., 1945; s. William Mark and Mary (Campbell) P.; m. Dorothea Grundy, Oct. 27, 1946; children: Daniel Mannix, Donald Mark, Mary Susan and June Anne (twins). BA, St. Francis Xavier U., Antigonish, N.S., 1942, LittD (hon.), 1974; MA, Columbia U., 1945; postgrad., Northwestern U., 1947-48; LittD (hon.), St. Francis Xavier U.; LLD (hon.), U. Coll. Cape Breton. chmn. Ctr. for Advanced Film and TV Studies Am. Film Inst. Broadway actor, 1945-46, TV dir., 1950—; TV shows include Eleanor and Franklin, ABC, 1976 (Outstanding Drama award 1976, Emmy award 1976, Critics Circle award 1976, Peabody award 1976), Harry Truman Plain Speaking, Pub. Broadcasting Sta., 1976 (Emmy nomination), Sybil, NBC, 1976 (Emmy award for Outstanding Spl. 1977, Peabody award 1976), Eleanor and Franklin: The White House Years, ABC, 1977 (Emmy award, Dirs. Guild award), Silent Night, Lonely Night, 1969, The Quinns, 1977, The Dollmaker, 1984 (Emmy nomination), The Execution of Raymond Graham, 1985 (Emmy nomination), Half a Lifetime, 1986 (Cable award), film My Name is Bill W. (Emmy and Golden Globe nominations), 1989, (also prodr.) Mark Twain and Me (Emmy award), 1991, A Town Torn Apart (Emmy nomination), 1992; dir. films including. Served as lt. Canadian Army, 1942. Recipient Humanitas award Cannes, DGA award, Christopher award, 1958, 84, 89, 92. Mem. Acad. Motion Picture Arts and Scis., Dir.'s Guild Am. (1st v.p. 1981-95), Am. Film Inst. (chmn.), Acad. TV Arts. *

PETRIE, DONALD JOSEPH, banker; b. N.Y.C., Sept. 2, 1921; s. John and Elizabeth (Thomson) P.; m. Jane Adams, Aug. 27, 1949; children: R. Scott, Anne, Elizabeth, Douglas, Susan. B.B.A., Manhattan Coll., 1950. Personnel mgr. Otis Elevator Co., N.Y.C., 1951-59; personnel dir. Brown Bros. Harriman & Co., N.Y.C., 1959-68; exec. v.p. U.S. Trust Co., N.Y.C., 1968-79; sr. v.p. Marine Midland Bank, N.Y.C., 1979-86, Drake Beam Morin Inc., N.Y.C., 1986-90; chmn., chief exec. officer Webster Corp., N.Y.C., 1990—; lectr. Baruch Sch. Bus., Coll. City N.Y., 1955-58; pres., chmn. exec. and fin. coms., dir. Webster Apts., N.Y.C., 1973—; adj. prof. mgmt. Hofstra U., Hempstead, N.Y., 1986-93. Author: Explaining Pay Policy, 1969, Handling Employee Questions About Pay, 1976. Capt. USAAF, 1942-46. Mem. N.Y. Chamber Commerce and Industry (chmn. mgmt. edn. and adv. com. 1964—). Home: 11 Fairview Ave Great Neck NY 11023-1462 Office: 419 W 34th St New York NY 10001-1596

PETRIE, FERDINAND RALPH, illustrator, artist; b. Hackensack, N.J., Sept. 17, 1925; s. Archibald John and Bessie (Rutherford) P.; m. Phyllis C. Haddow, Oct. 19, 1951; children: Beth, David. Advt. cert., Parson's Sch. Design, N.Y.C., 1949; student, Art Students League, 1947-49, Famous Artists Course in Illustration, 1958-59. Illustrator J. Gans Assos., N.Y.C., 1950-69. Free lance illustrator, artist, 1969—, owner, Petrie Gallery, Rockport, Mass., 1971-95; represented in permanent collections, U.S. Supreme Ct., Smithsonian Instn., Washington, Indpls. Mus. Art; designer U.S. commemorative stamp design, 2 Zaire commemorative stamps, 1980; Author: Drawing Landscapes in Pencil, 1979; illustrator: The Drawing Book, 1980, The Color Book, 1981, The Alkyd Book, 1982, The Watercolorists Guide to Painting Trees, 1983, The Watercolorists Guide to Painting Skies, 1984; The Watercolorists Guide to Painting Water, 1985, Painting Nature in Watercolor, 1990. Served with U.S. Maritime Service, 1943-46. Mem. Artists Fellowship, Rockport Art Assn., Am. Artists Profl. League, N.J. Watercolor Soc. Presbyterian. Address: 51 Vreeland Ave Rutherford NJ 07070-2227

PETRIE, GEOFF, professional basketball team executive. Grad., Princeton U., 1970. Guard Portland Trail Blazers, 1970-76, exec., 1976-93; v.p. basketball ops. Sacramento Kings, 1994—. Named NBA Rookie of the Yr., 1970; selected to NBA All-Star Team, 1971, 74. Avocations: working out, golfing. Office: Sacramento Kings One Sports Parkway Sacramento CA 95834*

PETRIE, GREGORY STEVEN, lawyer; b. Seattle, Feb. 25, 1951; s. George C. and Pauline P.; m. Margaret Fuhrman, Oct. 6, 1979; children: Kathryn Jean, Thomas George. AB in Polit. Sci and Econs., UCLA, 1973; JD, Boston U., 1976. Bar: Wash. 1976, U.S. Dist. Ct. (we. dist.) Wash. 1976. Adminstr. Action/Peace Corps, Washington, 1973, Fed. Power Commn., Washington, 1974; assoc. Oles Morrison et al, Seattle, 1976-80; ptnr. Schwabe Williamson Ferguson & Burdell, Seattle, 1981-94; shareholder Krutch Lindell, PSC, Seattle, 1994—. Mem. ABA, Seattle-King County Bar Assn., Profl. Liability Architects and Engrs., Wash. Athletic Club. Avocations: woodworking, skiing. Office: Krutch Lindell PSC 1201 3rd Ave Ste 3100 Seattle WA 98101-3079

PETRIE, HUGH GILBERT, university dean, philosophy of education educator; b. Lamar, Colo., Sept. 21, 1937; s. Charles Albert and Mary Madeleine (Ocsay) P.; m. Patricia Donahoe Bradasich, June 3, 1959 (div. 1978); children: Trent Anthony, Ragan Andrea, Brock Asher; m. Carol Ann Hodges, Aug. 26, 1978; stepchildren: Lara Wardrop, Amy Wardrop. BS in Bus., BS in Applied Math., U. Colo., 1960; Phd in Philosophy, Stanford U., 1965. Asst. prof. Northwestern U., Evanston, Ill., 1965-71; assoc. prof. U. Ill., Champaign/Urbana, 1971-75, prof., 1975-81, assoc. vice chancellor for academic affairs, 1977-80; dean Grad. Sch. Edn. SUNY, Buffalo, 1981-97, prof., 1981—; coord. N.E. region Holmes Group, 1986-90, bd. dirs.; mem. bd. overseers N.E. Regional Lab., 1986-92, chmn., 1986-87; co-chmn. N.Y. State Task Force on Preparation and Licensure Sch. Adminstrs., 1988-89; mem. N.Y. State Spl. Commn. on Edn., Structure, Policies, and Practices, 1993; bd. dirs. Orgn. Internat. Affiliates, Am. Edn. Rsch. Assn., 1991-93; pres. Tchr. Edn. Conf. Bd., N.Y., 1991-95; mem. N.Y. State Comm. Cert. of Edn. Profl., 1996-97. Author: The Dilemma of Enquiry and Learning, 1981; editor jour. Ednl. Theory, 1980-81; founding mem. bd. editors jour. Ednl. Policy, 1986—; contbr. numerous articles to profl. jours. Mem. commn. on teaching Nat. Assn. State Univs. and Land Grant Colls., 1988-92. Resident assoc. Ctr. for Advanced Study, U. Ill., 1980-81. Fellow Philosophy of Edn. Soc. (pres. 1984-85, mem. exec. com. 1974-76, 82-83); mem. Am. Ednl. Rsch. Assn., Am. Philos. Assn. Office: SUNY 367 Baldy Hall Buffalo NY 14260

PETRIE, WILLIAM, physicist; b. Victoria, B.C., Can., Dec. 30, 1912; s. James and Amelia (Robertson) P.; m. Isabelle Ruth Chodat, May 8, 1944; children: Heather Louise (dec.), Douglas Bruce. B.A., U. B.C., Vancouver, Can., 1938; A.M., Harvard U., 1941, Ph.D., 1944. Assoc. prof. U. Sask., Saskatoon, Can., 1945-51; chief ops. research Def. Research Bd., Ottawa, Ont., Can., 1954-60, dep. chmn., 1966-68; chief Can. def. research staff Def. Research Bd., London, 1968-71; sci. advisor Apollo Energy, Victoria, 1981-83; mem. numerous sci. bds. and coms. Author: The Story of the Aurora Borealis, 1963, Guide to Orchids of North America, 1981; also numerous articles. Recipient Centennial medal Govt. of Can., 1967, numerous research grants and contracts. Fellow Royal Soc. Can. Avocations: gardening; fishing. Home: 52-1255 Wain Rd, Rural Rt 4, Sidney, BC Canada V8L 4R4

PETRILLO, LEONARD PHILIP, corporate securities executive, lawyer; b. Toronto, Ont., Can., June 20, 1941; s. Philip Ralph and Bernice (Kowalski) P.; children: Larissa, Matthew. BSc, U. Toronto, 1964; LLB, Osgoode Hall Law Sch., Toronto, 1967. Bar: Ont. 1969. Ptnr. Robinson & Petrillo, 1969-79; corp. counsel Seel Enterprises Ltd., 1979-81; gen. counsel Toronto Stock Exch., 1981, corp. sec., sec. to bd. govs., 1984-96, v.p., gen. counsel, sec., 1996—; bd. dirs. Can. Dealing Network, Inc. Office: Toronto Stock Exch, 2 First Canadian Pl, Toronto, ON Canada M5X 1J2

PETRIN, HELEN FITE, lawyer, consultant; b. Bklyn., June 22, 1940; d. Clyde David and Connie Marie Keaton; m. Michael Richard Petrin, June 29, 1963; children: Jennifer Lee, Michael James, Daniel John. BS, Rider Coll. (now Rider U.), 1962, MA, 1980; postgrad., Glassboro (N.J.) Coll. (now Rowan Coll.), 1981; JD, Widener U., 1987. Bar: Pa. 1989, N.J. 1990, U.S. Dist. N.J. 1990. Tchr. bus. edn. Pennsville (N.J.) Meml. High Sch., 1962-66; asst. prof. Salem Community Coll., Carney's Point, N.J., 1977-81; asst. prof. Brandywine Coll. Widener U., Wilmington, Del., 1981-87, asst. prof., adminstr., dir. paralegal program, 1987-88; dir. continuing legal edn. Widener U. Sch. Law, Brandywine, 1987-88; pvt. practice computer cons. Phila., N.J. and Del., Del., Pa., N.J., 1988—; pvt. practice law Salem, N.J., 1989—; prosecutor Pilesgrove Township, N.J., 1990-91; dep. surrogate Salem County, N.J., 1991—; word processing cons. New Castle County (Del.) Pers. Dept., 1983; mem. dist. I ethics com. N.J. Supreme Ct., 1993-96; instr. N.J. Inst. for CLE, 1995—; adv. com. on minority concerns Ct. N.J. Vicinage 15, 1995—; judge mock trial N.J. State Bar, 1994—. Pres. bd. Salem County YMCA, 1983, bd. dirs., 1980—; dir. mediator Salem County YMCA Mediation Svcs., 1995—; col. atty. Phila. Vols. for Indigent Program, 1990-95, Camden Legal Svcs., Inc. for Salem County, 1990—; bd. dirs. United Way Salem County, 1991-97, treas., 1994-95; bd. dirs. United Ways of Pa. & N.J., 1994-97; mem. Hope III com. (Home Ownership and Opportunity for People Everywhere), Salem, N.J., 1992—; vol. atty. Salem County N.J. Office Aging Sr. Law Day, 1991—, vol. dir. Guardianship Monitoring Program, 1993—. Mem. ABA (chmn. young lawyers econs. com. 1990-93, vice chmn. mktg. legal svcs. com. gen. practice sect. 1993—), ATLA, N.J. Bar Assn. (exec. com. 1990-93), N.J. State Bar Assn. (mock trial judge 1992—), Pa. Bar Assn., Phila. Bar Assn. (probate adv. panel 1992-94), Salem County Bar Assn. (treas. 1991-92, sec. 1992-93, v.p., pres.-elect 1993-94, pres. 1994-95, dir. of Salem County, N.J. YMCA Family Ct. Mediation program 1995—), Delta Pi Epsilon (sec. bd. dirs. 1980-82). Avocations: swimming, music, walking, reading. Home: 99 Marlton Rd Woodstown NJ 08098-2722 Office: 51 Market St Salem NJ 08079-1909

PETRIN, JOHN DONALD, town administrator; b. Woonsocket, R.I., Feb. 26, 1959; s. Hector Arthur and Claire Jeannette (Dalpe) P.; m. Kimberly Ann Marcotte, May 30, 1986. BA, Stonehill Coll., 1981; MPA, Northeastern U., 1987. Accredited assessor Mass. Assn. Assessing Officers, 1985. Assessor Town of Bellingham, Mass., 1982-85; town adminstr. Town of Pepperell, Mass., 1985-88, Town of Harvard, Mass., 1988—; vice-chmn. Minuteman-Nashoba Health Group, Concord, Mass., 1990-94, chmn., 95-96. Pres. Bellingham (Mass.) Youth Baseball, 1979-82, v.p., 1980-85; elected mem. Bellingham (Mass.) Pk. Commn., 1980-85; elected town com. mem. Dem. Com., Bellingham, 1984-88; corporator Boys & Girls Club Greater Marlboro Inc., 1995, bd. dirs., treas., 1996—. Recipient citation Mass. Ho. of Reps., 1985. Mem. Internat. City/County Mgmt. Assn., Mass. Mcpl. Assn. (bd. dirs.), Mass. Mcpl. Mgmt. Assn. (past pres. 1995). Roman Catholic. Avocations: swimming, racquetball, woodworking, reading, history. Home: 41 Eager Ct Marlborough MA 01752-2360

PETRINA, ANTHONY J., retired mining executive. Former pres., CEO Placer Dome Inc., Vancouver, B.C., Can., 1988-93; ret., 1993; bd. dirs. Miramar Mining Corp., Vancouver, Inmet Mining Corp., Toronto, Pegasus Gold Corp., Vancouver, Wajax Inc., Vancouver. Mem. Mining Assn. B.C., Mining Assn. Can. (past chmn.). Office: Ste 822, 510 W Hastings St, Vancouver, BC Canada V6B 1L8

PETRINOVICH, LEWIS F., psychology educator; b. Wallace, Idaho, June 12, 1930; s. John F. and Ollie (Steward) P. BS, U. Idaho, 1952; PhD, U. Calif., Berkeley, 1962. Asst. prof. San Francisco State Coll., 1957-63; from assoc. to prof. SUNY, Stony Brook, 1963-68; prof. U. Calif., Riverside, 1968-91, chmn. psychology, 1968-71, 86-89, prof. emeritus, 1991—. Author: Understanding Research in Social Sciences, 1975, Introduction to Statistics, 1976, Human Evolution, Reproduction and Mortality, 1995, Living and Dying Well, 1996; editor: Behavioral Development, 1981, Habituation, Sensitization and Behavior, 1984; cons. editor Behavioral and Neural Biology, 1972-90, Jour. Physiol. and Comparative Psychology, 1980-82, Jour. Comparative Psychology, 1983-90. Fellow Am. Psychol. Assn., Am. Psychol. Soc., Calif. Acad. Scis., Human Behavior and Evolution Soc., Western Psychol. Assn.; mem. Am. Ornithological Union (elected), Animal Behavior Soc., Sigma Xi. Home: 415 Boynton Ave Berkeley CA 94707-1701 Office: U Calif Riverside Dept of Psychology Riverside CA 92521

PETRO, JAMES MICHAEL, lawyer, politician; b. Cleve., Oct. 25, 1948; s. William John and Lila Helen (Janca) P.; m. Nancy Ellen Bero, Dec. 16, 1972; children: John Bero, Corbin Marie. BA, Denison U., 1970; JD, Case Western Res., 1973. Bar: Ohio 1973, U.S. Dist. Ct. (no. dist.) Ohio 1974, U.S. Ct. Appeals (6th cir.) 1981. Spl. asst. U.S. senator W.B. Saxbe, Cleve., 1972-73; asst. pros. atty. Franklin County, Ohio, 1973-74; asst. dir. law City of Cleve., 1974; ptnr. Petro & Troia, Cleve., 1974-84; dir. govt. affairs Standard Oil Co., Cleve., 1984-86; ptnr. Petro, Rademaker, Matty & McClelland, Cleve., 1986-93, Buckingham, Doolittle & Burroughs, Cleve., 1993-95. Mem. city coun. Rocky River, Ohio, 1977-79, dir. law, 1980; mem. Ohio Ho. of Reps., Columbus, 1981-84, 86-90; commr. Cuyahoga County, Ohio, 1991-95; Auditor of State of Ohio, 1995—. Mem. ABA, Ohio State Bar Assn., Cleve. Bar Assn. Republican. Methodist. Home: 315 Falmouth Dr Cleveland OH 44116-1326 Office: 88 E Broad St Columbus OH 43215-3506

PETROCELLI, ANTHONY JOSEPH, management executive, consultant; b. Bklyn., Sept. 25, 1937; s. Lucio and Carmela (Carrione) P.; m. Antoinette Cassata, May 25, 1963; 1 child, Serena Ann. BS in Mgmt., Fairleigh Dickinson, Madison, N.J., 1969, MBA, 1972. Pres. Met. Consolidated Inc., N.Y.C., 1978-84; pvt. practice mgmt. cons., 1984-88; ptnr., mng. dir. D. George Harris & Assocs., N.Y.C., 1984—, vice chmn., 1989—; vice chmn. Novacarb, France, 1996—, Salt Union Ltd., U.K., 1992—, Societa Chimica Larderello SpA, Italy, 1993—, Harris Chem. Group, 1993—, Harris Specialty Chemicals, Inc., 1994—, Matthes & Weber GmbH, Germany, 1993, U.S. Silica, 1996—, Penrice Soda Products, Australia, 1996—. Trustee Italian Am. Club, North Brunswick, N.J. With U.S. Army, 1956-58, Germany. Office: D George Harris & Assocs 399 Park Ave New York NY 10022

PETROS, RAYMOND LOUIS, JR., lawyer; b. Pueblo, Colo., Sept. 19, 1950. BS, Colo. Coll., 1972; JD, U. Colo., 1975. Bar: Colo. 1975. Jud. clk. to Justice Paul V. Hodges Colo. Supreme Ct., Denver, 1975-77; assoc. Bermingham, White, Burke & Ipsen, Denver, 1977-78; from assoc. to ptnr. Hall & Evans, Denver, 1978-81; ptnr. Kirkland & Ellis, Denver, 1981-86; mem. Holme, Roberts & Owen, Denver, 1986-96, Petros & White, LLC, 1996—. Contbr. articles to profl. jours. Bd. dirs. Rocky Mountain Poison Control Found., Denver, 1988-94. Office: Petros & White LLC Ste 820 730 Seventeenth St Denver CO 80202-3518

PETROSIAN, VAHÉ, astrophysicist, educator; b. Arak, Iran, Sept. 13, 1938; came to U.S., 1958; s. Armenak and Chnarik (Beglarian) P.; m. Maude Denney Voegeli, Aug. 21, 1965 (div. 1992); children: Gabrielle Elane, Meline Chnar. B.E.E., Cornell U., 1962, M.S., 1963, Ph.D., 1967. Research fellow Calif. Inst. Tech., Pasadena, Calif., 1967-69; vis. scientist Inst. Theoretical Astronomy, Cambridge, Eng., summer 1969; asst.prof. Stanford U., (Calif.), 1969-71; assoc. prof. Stanford U., 1972-79, prof., 1980—, chmn. astronomy program; vis. cons. Kitt Peak Nat. Obs., Tucson. Alfred P. Sloan fellow, 1972-74; NASA grantee, 1970—; NSF grantee, 1980—. Fellow Royal Astron. Soc.; mem. Internat. Astron. Union, Am. Astron. Soc., U.S. Volleyball Assn. Achievements include the co-discovery of giant luminous arcs in clusters of galaxies. Home: 4114 Willmar Dr Palo Alto CA 94306-3835 Office: Stanford U Astronomy Program Varian 302C Stanford CA 94305

PETRU, SUZANNE MITTON, health care finance executive; b. Shawano, Wis., Sept. 26, 1947; d. William Wallace and Gertrude Priscilla Mitton; m. W. James Petru, Jan. 2, 1987. BSBA, Northwestern U., 1970, MBA, 1971. CPA, Ill., Wis. Diplomate Am. Coll. Healthcare Execs. Sr. acct. Arthur Andersen & Co., Chgo., 1971-77; v.p. fin. Thorek Hosp. and Med. Ctr., Chgo., 1977-82; sec./treas. La Grange (Ill.) Meml. Health Sys., 1982-85; v.p. fin. La Grange Meml. Hosp., 1982-85; audit prin. Deloitte & Touche (formerly Touche Ross & Co.), Chgo., 1985-88; sr. v.p. fin., treas. SSM Health Care Sys., St. Louis, 1988-95; pres. healthcare divsn. Am. Home Assurance Co. (subs. Am. Internat. Group, Inc.), 1995-96; v.p., CFO, treas. Group Health Plan (subs. Coventry Corp.), 1996—. Mem. investment com. Sisters of Charity Healthcare Sys., Cin., 1993-96, mem. fin. com., 1994-96; mem. assoc. bd. La Grange Meml. Hosp., 1988-95; advisor Jr. Achievement, 1971-76. Fellow Healthcare Fin. Mgmt. Assn. (bd. dirs. 1989-91), principles and practices bd. 1992-95, nat. matrix 1985-86, 88-89, pres., pres.-elect, sec., bd. First Ill. chpt. 1979-86, Follmer Bronze award 1982, Reeves Silver award 1985, Muncie Gold ward 1988, Alice V. Runyan chpt. 1988); mem. Fin. Execs. Inst., Country Club at Legends (adv. bd. 1991-93), St. Louis Club (house com. 1991-95). Republican. Presbyterian. Avocations: golf, travel. Home: 12033 Tindall Dr Saint Louis MO 63131-3135 Office: Group Health Plan 940 Westport Plz Ste 300 Saint Louis MO 63146-3118

PETRUCELLI, JAMES MICHAEL, lawyer; b. Fresno, Calif., Dec. 28, 1949; s. Gene Vincent and Josephine Marie (Frediani) P.; 1 child, Vincent Michael. BS, Fresno State Coll., 1972; JD, San Joaquin Coll., 1989. Bar: Calif. 1989, U.S. Dist. Ct. (ea. dist.) Calif. 1989, U.S. Dist. Ct. (no. dist.) Calif. 1990, U.S. Ct. Appeals (9th cir.) 1990, U.S. Supreme Ct., 1993. Dep. sheriff Fresno County Sheriff's Dept., 1974-89; pvt. practice Fresno, 1989—; del. State Bar Conf. of Dels., Fresno, 1990—; State Bar Law Practice Mgmt. Sect., 1994—, dir. Commn. For Adv. Calif. Paralegal Specialation Inc., 1995—. Pres. San Joaquin Coll. Law Alumni Assn., Fresno, 1990—; mem. exec. com. San Joaquin Coll. Law, 1990-91, 20th anniversary com., 1990-91; trustee Kerman (Calif.) Unified Sch. Dist., 1982-88; bd. dirs. North Cen. Fire Protection Dist., Kerman, 1990—. Mem. ABA, Am. Trial Lawyers Assn., Consumer Attorney of Calif., Calif. Bar Assn., Fresno County Bar Assn., Inns of Ct. Office: 2350 W Shaw Ave Ste 137 Fresno CA 93711-3412

PETRUS, ROBERT THOMAS, distribution executive, real estate executive; b. Manchester, Conn., 1957; s. John Joseph and Geraldine Petrus; m. Laura Lee Waggoner, Nov. 22, 1986; children: Elizabeth Ashley, Nicholas Kent. BA with honors, Trinity Coll., Hartford, Conn., 1979. Mgmt. intern Aetna Life & Casualty Co., Hartford, 1979-82, sr. adminstr. data processing ops., 1982-85, cons. Tech. Ctr., 1985-90; pres. Omoo Distbn. Corp., Mansfield, Conn., 1990—; v.p. Cogitore, Inc., 1990—. Author: Get Organized!, 1991. Chmn. Conn. Youth for Pres. Ford, 1976; com. mem. Big Bros.-Big Sisters, Hartford, 1982-83; loaned exec. Greater Hartford United Way-Combined Health Appeals Campaign, 1985. Recipient ofcl. citation Conn. Ho. of Reps., 1985. Mem. Phi Beta Kappa, Pi Gamma Mu, Mu Alpha Theta. Republican. Avocations: photography, golf, skiing. Office: Omoo Corp 27 Wormwood Hill Rd Ste 101 Mansfield Center CT 06250-1135

PETRUSKI, JENNIFER ANDREA, speech and language pathologist; b. Kingston, N.Y., Jan. 28, 1968; d. Andrew Francis and Judith (Cruger) P. BS, SUNY, Buffalo, 1990; MSEd, SUNY, 1992. Cert. tchr. speech-hearing handicapped, N.Y.; cert. clin. competence; lic. speech-lang. pathology, N.Y. Speech-lang. pathologist Kingston (N.Y.) City Schs., 1992—; cooperating tchr. SUNY, New Paltz, 1995—, clinic supr., 1996—. Mem. Am. Speech and Hearing Assn., N.Y. State Speech-Lang. and Hearing Assn., Speech and Hearing Assn. Hudson Valley (corr. sec. 1995—, membership com. 1995—, editor newsletter 1995—). Home: 342 Hurley Ave # 10-64 Kingston NY 12401 Office: Kingston City Schs 61 Crown St Kingston NY 12401-3833

PETRUSKY, JOHN W., banker, consultant; b. Johnstown, Pa.; children: John T., Dianna L., James W. B.S. in Acctg., Pa. State U., 1961. With Bank of N.Y., N.Y.C., 1961-64; asst. v.p. Dry Dock Savs. Bank, N.Y.C., 1964-68,

Leasco Systems Internat., N.Y.C., 1968-69; sr. v.p. Phoenix Systems Internat., N.Y.C., 1969-70; (with Dollar Dry Dock Savs. Bank, N.Y.C., 1970-87, pres., 1985-87; founder, pres. The Petrusky Group, Inc., 1987—. Internat. rep. for banking standards The Am. Banker's Assn.; chmn. Am. Nat. Standards Inst., 1979-81; chmn. Internat. Standards Orgn. 68, Geneva, 1979-86; trustee Waldorf Sch., Garden City, N.Y., 1986-96; bd. dirs. Am. Nat. Standards Inst., 1979-81; Served with USAF, 1955-59. Recipient IBM Point of Sale award, 1976; Electronic Funds Transfer award Mutual Inst. Nat. Transfer System, 1980. Copyright computer software for tele-mktg. system, 1989, mortgage systems, 1992. Republican. Home and Office: 22 S Lakeshore Dr Brookfield CT 06804

PETSCHEK, ALBERT GEORGE, physicist, consultant; b. Prague, Bohemia, Czechoslovakia, Jan. 31, 1928; came to U.S., 1938; s. Hans Petschek and Eva (Epler) Petschek-Newman; m. Marilyn Adiene Poth, June 25, 1948; children: Evelyn A., Rolfe G., Elaine L., Mark A. BS, MIT, 1947; MS, U. Mich., 1949; PhD, U. Rochester, 1953. Jr. physicist Carter Oil Co., Tulsa, 1948-49; sr. rsch. scientist Systems, Science and Software, San Diego, Calif., 1968-71; staff mem., group leader, fellow, cons. Los Alamos (N. Mex.) Nat. Lab., 1953—; prof. of physics N. Mex. Inst. Mining and Tech., Socorro, 1966-68, 71—, prof. emeritus, 1994—; vis. asst. prof. Cornell U., Ithaca, N.Y., 1960-61; vis. prof. Tel Aviv U., Israel, 1978; cons. Sandia Corp., Albuquerque, N. Mex., 1966-70. Editor: (book) Supernovae, 1990; contbr. more than 50 articles to profl. jours. Fellow AAAS; mem. AAUP, Am. Phys. Soc., Am. Astron. Soc. Republican. Unitarian. Avocations: bicycling, skiing. Home: 122 Piedra Loop White Rock NM 87544 Office: Los Alamos Nat Lab Box 1663 Los Alamos NM 87545

PETSKO, GREGORY ANTHONY, chemistry and biochemistry educator; b. Washington, Aug. 7, 1948; s. John and Mary (Santoro) P.; m. Carol Bannister Chamberlain, July 3, 1971 (div. 1982). BA, Princeton U., 1970; DPhil, Oxford U., 1973. Instr. Wayne State U. Med. Sch., Detroit, 1973-75, asst. prof., 1975-78; assoc. prof. MIT, 1979-85, prof. chemistry, 1985-90; Lucille P. Markey prof. biochemistry and chemistry Brandeis U., Waltham, Mass., 1990-96; Gyula & Katica Tauber prof. biochemistry & Pharmacodynamics Brandeis U., Waltham, 1997—; dir. Rosenstiel Basic Med. Scis. Rsch. Ctr. Brandeis U., Waltham, Mass., 1994—; founding scientist, cons. Arqule, Inc., Medford, 1993—. Editor. Jour. Protein Engring., 1988—. Recipient Max Planck prize Mack Planck Gesellschaft, 1992; Rhodes scholar Oxford U., 1970, Danforth fellow, 1980; Alfred P. Sloan fellow MIT, 1978; elected to NAS, 1995. Mem. NAS, Am. Crystallographic Assn. (Siddhu award 1981), Am. Chem. Soc. (Pfizer award 1987), Biophys. Soc., Am. Soc. Biochemistry and Molecular Biology, Am. Soc. Microbiology. Avocations: writing poetry and fiction, hiking, basketball, old movies, sports cars. Home: 8 Jason Rd Belmont MA 02178-3129 Office: Brandeis U Rosenstiel Ctr Waltham MA 02254-9110

PETTEE, DANIEL STARR, neurologist; b. N.Y.C., Feb. 15, 1925; s. Allen Danforth and Helen Marien (Starr) P.; m. Dimetra Marie Peters, June 24, 1961; children: William, Margaret, Allen. BA, Yale U., 1951; MD, Columbia U., 1955. Diplomate Am. Bd. Psychiatry and Neurology, 1965, Am. Bd. Clin. Neurophysiology, 1984. Rotating internship Strong Meml. Hosp. U. Rochester, N.Y., 1955-57, residency neurology, 1957-62; neurologist pvt. practice, Rochester, N.Y., 1962-96; clinic dir. Rochester (N.Y.) Area Multiple Sclerosis Chpt., Rochester, N.Y., 1962-76; assoc. prof. neurology U. Rochester (N.Y.) Sch. Medicine, 1978-96, emeritus assoc. prof., 1996—; clin. assoc. dept. neurology Strong Meml. Hosp., Rochester, 1978-96; head neurology div. dept. medicine The Genesee Hosp., Rochester, 1972-96; pres. Genesee Neurol. Assocs., Rochester, 1974-96; mem. bd. dirs. Rochester (N.Y.) Area Multiple Sclerosis Chpt., 1970-76. Contbr. articles to profl. jours. Mem. bd. dirs., singer Rochester (N.Y.) Oratorio Soc., 1960-61, 1955-78. Recipient Purple Heart, Bronze Star U.S. Army, 1944, Bronze Hope Chest for Svc. award Rochester (N.Y.) Area Multiple Sclerosis Chpt., 1976. Mem. N.Y. Acad. Sci., Rochester Acad. Sci. (astronomy sect. 1989—, bd. dirs. astronomy sect. 1993-94). Home: 150 Summit Dr Rochester NY 14620-3130 Office: Genesee Neurol Assocs 222 Alexander St Rochester NY 14607-4005

PETTENGILL, GORDON H(EMENWAY), physicist, educator; b. Providence, Feb. 10, 1926; s. Rodney Gordon and Frances (Hemenway) P.; m. Pamela Anne Wolfenden, Oct. 28, 1967; children—Mark Robert, Rebecca Jane. B.S., MIT, 1948; Ph.D., U. Calif., Berkeley, 1955. Staff mem. Lincoln Lab. MIT, Lexington, 1954-63, 65-68; prof. planetary physics, dept. earth, atmospheric and planetary scis. MIT, Cambridge, 1971—, dir. Ctr. Space Rsch., 1984-90; assoc. dir. Arecibo (P.R.) Obs., 1963-65, dir., 1968-71. Served with inf., Signal Corps AUS, 1944-46. Decorated Combat Inf. badge; recipient Magellanic Premium, Am. Philos. Soc., 1994. Fellow Am. Geophys. Union (Whipple award 1995); mem. AAAS, Am. Phys. Soc., Am. Astron. Soc., Internat. Astron. Union, Internat. Radio Sci. Union, Nat. Acad. Sci., Am. Acad. Arts and Sci. Pioneer several techniques in radar astronomy for describing properties of planets and satellites; discovered 59-day rotational period of planet Mercury. Office: MIT 77 Massachusetts Ave Rm 37-641 Cambridge MA 02139-4301

PETTENGILL, HARRY JUNIOR, federal agency administrator; b. Lock Haven, Pa., Apr. 16, 1946; s. Harry Blair and Bertha Irene (Quigg) P.; m. Sandra Kaye Conway, Sept. 3, 1970; children: Keri-Beth Irene, Justin Matthew, Rebekah Ann Louise. BA, Lock Haven U., 1968; MS, Temple U., 1971; PhD, U. Mich., 1974. Dep. mgr. waste environ. studies project U.S. EPA, Washington, 1975-80; chief uranium mills licensing NRC, Washington, 1980-83; chief uranium recovery licensing NRC, Denver, 1983-88; dir. nuclear safety tech. div. Dept. Energy, Washington, 1988-90, dep. asst. sec. for health, 1990—. U.S. AEC fellow Temple U., 1968, USPHS fellow U. Mich., 1971. Mem. OECD-NEA (com. radiology protection and pub. health), Health Physics Soc. Lt. comdr. USPHS, 1977-79. Office: US Dept Energy 1000 Independence Ave SW Washington DC 20585-0001

PETTERCHAK, JANICE A., researcher, writer; b. Springfield, Ill., Sept. 15, 1942; d. Emil H. and Vera C. (Einhoff) Stukenberg; m. John J. Petterchak, Oct. 5, 1963; children: John A., Julie Gilmour, James. AA, Springfield Coll., 1962; BS, Sangamon State U., 1972, MA, 1982. Supr. hist. markers Ill. State Hist. Soc., Springfield, 1973-74, asst. exec. dir., 1985-87; curator photographs Ill. State Hist. Libr., Springfield, 1974-79, assoc. editor, 1979-83, rep. local history svcs., 1983-85, libr. dir., 1987-95; project dir. NEH/Ill. newspaper cataloging project. Author: Mapping a Life's Journey: The Legacy of Andrew McNally III, 1995, Jack Brickhouse: A Voice for All Seasons, 1996, (booklets) Researching and Writing Local History in Illinois: A Guide to the Sources, 1987; editor: Illinois History: An Annotated Bibliography, 1995; assoc. editor Illinois Historical Jour.; contbr. articles to profl. jours. Grantee NEH, 1987-95. Mem. Ill. State Hist. Soc., Abraham Lincoln Assn. (co-editor Papers Abraham Lincoln Assn. 1981-82), Stephen A. Douglas Assn., Sangamon County Hist. Soc. (bd. dirs. 1991-94, v.p. 1996-97, pres. 1995-96), Soc. of Midland Authors. Home: 11381 Mallard Dr Rochester IL 62563-8011

PETTERS, SAMUEL BRIAN, air force officer; b. Lakeland, Fla., Feb. 7, 1967; s. Clement Edward and Joan Agnes (Barthle) P.; m. Vicki Jean LaBauve, Dec. 17, 1988; children: John Clement, Benjamin Howard, Leo Alfred. BA, La. State U., 1989. Commd. 2d lt. U.S. Air Force, 1990, advanced through grades to capt., 1994; edn. and tng. officer 323 Ops. Support Squadron, Mather AFB, Calif., 1991-93; historical officer Air Force Historical Rsch. Agency, Maxwell AFB, Ala., 1993-96; chief curriculum devel. B-52 divsn USAF Weapons Sch., Barksdale AFB, La., 1996—. Republican. Roman Catholic. Avocations: swimming, bicycling, soccer, fishing. Home: 2136 Rossie Lee Dr Bossier City LA 71112 Office: Det 5.57 wg/WCM 50 Vandenberg Ave Barksdale AFB LA 71110-2079

PETTERSEN, KEVIN WILL, investment company executive; b. Yonkers, N.Y., July 4, 1956; s. Kjell Will and Marilyn Ann (Stevens) P.; m. Mary Elizabeth Murphy, Aug. 30, 1981; children: Kelly, Elizabeth, Erin. Diploma academia, Chaminade, Mineola, N.Y., 1974; BA in Econs., SUNY at Stony Brook, 1978. Buyer JC Penney Co., Inc., N.Y.C., 1979-82; nat. sales mgr. Randa Corp., Inc., N.Y.C., 1982-83; dir. sales Wemco, Inc., N.Y.C., 1983-86; mng. dir., sr. v.p. D.H. Blair & Co., Inc., N.Y.C., 1986-89; exec. v.p. Brean Murray, Foster Securities, Inc., N.Y.C., 1989-90; v.p., br. mgr., corp. officer A.G. Edwards and Sons, Inc., Huntington, N.Y., 1990—; cons. Oncor Inc., Gaithersburg, Md., 1987-93, Wedding Info. Network, Inc., Omaha, 1987-91; fin. adviser European banking, ins. and investment industry, 1987—; mem. Pres. Coun. A.G. Edwards, Million Dollar Club A.G. Edwards; mem. pres.'s adv. coun. The Rochester Funds, exec. coun. The Oppeneheimer Funds Group; mem. All=Am. team The Am. Funds Group, 1990-94, mem. Pres. club, 1997. Bd. dirs. Harbour Green L.I. Assn., 1990-94, pres., 1991; mem. Oyster Bay Supr.'s Adv. Com. on Crime, 1993—; del. Rep. Party Planning Com., 1996. Recipient Outstanding Character award Chaminade, 1974. Mem. ASPCA, U.S. Golf. Assn., Sons of Norway, Chaminade Wall St. Assn., SUNYStony Brook Alumni Assn., Green Harbour Green Beach Club (bd. dirs. 1994—), Swan Lake Country Club, Southward Ho Country Club, Chaminade Torch Club. Republican. Roman Catholic. Avocations: golf. skiing, swimming. Home: 122 Exeter Rd Massapequa NY 11758-8128 Office: AG Edwards and Sons Inc 24 W Carver St Huntington NY 11743-3309

PETTERSEN, KJELL WILL, stockbroker, consultant; b. Oslo, Norway, June 19, 1927; came to U.S., 1946, naturalized, 1957; s. Jens Will and Ragna O. (Wickstrom) P.; m. Marilyn Ann Stevens, Aug. 16, 1952; children: Thomas W., Maureen, Kevin W., Maryann, Kathleen. Student, Zion Theol. Sch., 1945-49, N.Y. Inst. Finance, 1955-56. Mgr. A.M. Kidder & Co., N.Y.C., 1954-64; sr. v.p., sec., dir. Halle & Stieglitz, Fillor Bullard Co., Inc., 1964-73; sr. v.p., dir. mktg. Parrish Securities, Inc., N.Y.C., 1973-74; cons. Loeb, Rhoades & Co., N.Y.C., 1974-79; mng. dir. Prudential Securities, N.Y.C., 1979-89; pres. Arbitration Recovery Cons., Marco, Fla., 1992-93; vice chmn. Noddings Investment Group, Inc., Oakbrook Terrace, Ill., 1993-95, cons., 1996—; dir. Ski for Light Inc., Mpls., Creative Arts Rehab. Ctr. Inc., N.Y.C. Dem. candidate N.Y. State Assembly, Nassau County, 1962; past dir. Guadalupe Ctr., Marco YMCA; pres. Quest for Peace Internat. Mem. Security Industry Assn., Nat. Assn. Security Dealers (bd. arbitrators), N.Y. C. of C. (past dir.), Norwegian-Am. C. of C. (dir. Guadalupe Ctr.), Scandinavian Found., Bankers Club of Am., Norwegian Club (N.Y.C.), Rotary (dir.). Mem. Security Industry Assn., Nat. Assn. Security Dealers (bd. arbitrators), N.Y. C. of C., Norwegian-Am. C. of C. (dir. Guadalope Ctr.), Scandinavian Found., Bankers Club of Am., Norwegian Club (N.Y.C.), Marco Bay Yacht Club, Rotary. Home: 350 Rockhill Ct Marco Island FL 34145-3860

PETTEWAY, SAMUEL BRUCE, college president; b. Fayetteville, N.C., July 18, 1924; s. Walter Bernard and Margaret Maysie (Cole) P.; m. Eleanor Glenn Sugg, Nov. 27, 1948; children—Margaret Petteway Small, Samuel Bruce. B.S., N.C. State U., 1949, M.Ed., 1966, Ed.D., 1968. Gen. mgr. Homeowners Ins. and Realty Co., 1960-63; engring. tech. dept. chmn., dean occupational and transfer programs, dir. evening programs Lenoir County Community Coll., 1963-68; pres. Coll. of the Albemarie, Elizabeth City, N.C., 1968-75, N.C. Wesleyan Coll., Rocky Mount, 1975-86; prof. Va. Poly. Inst. and State U., 1973-75, East Carolina U., 1994—; pres. Philanthropic Cons., Inc., Kinston, N.C., 1986—; sec. Coll. Mgmt. Svcs., Inc., Raleigh, N.C., 1989; lic. amateur radio operator, 1992—. Pres. chpt. Am. Cancer Soc., 1960-61, Boys' Club Lenoir County, 1987-91, Westminter Homeowners Assn., 1997; bd. dirs. Rocky Mount Acad., 1979-80, Triangle East, Inc., 1985-86, Meth. Home for Children, Cypress Glen Retirement Home, chmn. 1996; chmn. deferred giving com. N.C. Meth. Found., 1979-86; chmn. coun. on ministries 1st United Meth. Ch., Rocky Mount, 1980-81, Westminster United Meth. Ch., 1989-90, chmn. bd. trustees, 1994—; chmn. bd. trustees Art Edn. Found., 1980; mem. Nash County Bd. Health, 1985-86; bd. trustees United Meth. Retirement Homes, Inc., 1996—. Named Tar Heel of Week News and Observer, 1975, Today's Outstanding N.C. Citizen WNCT-TV, 1975; NSF fellow U. Ill., 1963. Mem. Nat. Assn. for Hosp. Devel., N.C. Assn. Colls. and Univs., N.C. Conf. United Meth. Ch. (chmn. bd. trustees 1973-79), Nat. Soc. Fund Raising Execs. (cert.), Rocky Mount C. of C. (bd. dirs. 1980-84), Rotary (scholarship com. dist. 7730 1995—), Phi Kappa Phi, Theta Alpha Phi. Democrat. Clubs: Benvenue Country, Galaxy Social; Kinston Country. Lodge: Rotary (pres. 1980-81, bd. dirs. Kinston chpt. 1988-92). Office: 708 Westminster Ln Kinston NC 28501-2770

PETTEY, WALTER GRAVES, III, lawyer; b. Bessemer, Ala., Aug. 24, 1949; s. Walter Graves Jr. and Mildred Louise (Nebrig) P.; m. Virginia McWherter Lott, Feb. 28, 1976; 1 child, Stephen Blacksher. BA, Washington & Lee U., 1971; JD, U. Ala., 1976. Bar: Ala. 1976, Tex. 1977. Law clk. to Hon. Walter P. Gewin U.S. Ct. Appeals (5th cir.), Tuscaloosa, Ala., 1976-77; assoc. Hughes & Hill, Dallas, 1977-82; assoc. Pettit & Martin, Dallas, 1983-84, ptnr., 1985-92; ptnr. Hughes & Luce, L.L.P., Dallas, 1992—. 1st lt. U.S. Army, 1971-73. Office: Hughes & Luce L L P 1717 Main St Ste 2800 Dallas TX 75201-7342

PETTIBONE, PETER JOHN, lawyer; b. Schenectady, N.Y., Dec. 11, 1939; s. George Howard and Caryl Grey (Ketchum) P.; m. Jean Kellogg, Apr. 23, 1966; children: Stephen, Victoria. AB summa cum laude, Princeton U., 1961; JD, Harvard U., 1964; LLM, NYU, 1971. Bar: Pa. 1965, D.C. 1965, N.Y. 1968, U.S. Supreme Ct. 1974, Russia (fgn. legal cons.) 1995. Lectr. Heidelberg (Fed. Republic Germany) U., 1965-67; assoc. Cravath, Swaine & Moore, N.Y.C., 1967-74, Lord Day & Lord, Barrett Smith, N.Y.C., 1974-76; ptnr. Lord Day & Lord, Barrett Smith, N.Y.C. and Washington, 1976-94, Patterson, Belknap, Webb & Tyler LLP, N.Y.C. and Washington, 1994—; pres. 1158 Fifth Ave. Corp., N.Y.C., 1991-94; pres. North Ferry Co., Shelter Island, N.Y., 1987-90; bd. dirs., vice-chmn. N.Y. State Facilities Devel. Corp., N.Y.C., 1983-89. Editor USSR Legal Materials, 1990-92. Trustee, treas. Hosp. Chaplaincy Inc., N.Y.C., 1980-86, Civitas, N.Y.C., 1984-92; mem. Coun. Fgn. Rels., 1993—; trustee Union Chapel, Shelter Island, N.Y., 1990—, CEC Internat. Ptnrs., 1996—; bd. dirs., vice chmn. Geonomics Inst., Middlebury, Vt., 1991—; mem. vestry Ch. of Heavenly Rest, N.Y.C., 1987-93; mem. Nat. Adv. Coun. Harriman Inst. Columbia U., 1996—; mem. Russia com. Episcopal Diocese of N.Y. Capt. U.S. Army, 1965-67, Heidelberg, Germany. Mem. ABA, Assn. Bar City N.Y. (chmn. com. on CIS affairs 1991-94), U.S.-USSR Trade and Econ. Coun. Inc. (U.S. co-chmn. legal com. 1980-92), U.S.-Russia Bus. Coun. (bd. dirs.), Soc. of Cin., Anglers Club N.Y.C., Shelter Island Yacht Club, Amateur Ski Club N.Y. (pres. 1980-82), Canterbury Choral Soc. (pres. 1983-84), Phi Beta Kappa. Episcopalian. Home: 1158 Fifth Ave New York NY 10029-6917 also: 10 Wesley Ave Shelter Island Heights NY 11965 Office: Patterson Belknap Webb & Tyler LLP 1133 Avenue Of The Americas New York NY 10036-6710

PETTIGREW, CLAIRE RUDOLPH, music educator; b. Chambersburg, Pa., Aug. 3, 1961; d. Herman Leon and Helen Frances (Tobey) Rudolph; m. Daniel Pettigrew III, Mar. 10, 1991; stepchildren: Christine, Sara. BS in Edn. in Music, West Chester U., 1983, MEd in Elem. Edn., 1991. Tchr. music West Chester (Pa.) Area Sch. Dist., 1989—; co-dir. summer music program West Chester Cmty. Ctr., 1986. Mem. West Chester Cmty. Band, 1987—, sec., 1993—; charter mem. Gilbert and Sullivan Soc. Chester County. Mem. NEA, Pa. Sch. Edn. Assn., Music Educator Nat. Conf., Am. ORFF-Schulwerk Assn., Phi Delta Kappa, Sigma Alpha Iota (Coll. Honor award 1983). Avocations: counted cross-stitch, playing flute and piccolo. Office: Starkweather Elem Sch 1050 Wilmington Pike West Chester PA 19382-7368

PETTIGREW, EDWARD W., lawyer; b. Aurora, Ill., July 16, 1943. AB, Kenyon Coll., 1965; JD, U. Mich., 1968. Bar: Wash. 1970, Mich. 1971, U.S. Ct. Appeals (9th cir.) 1971, U.S. Dist. Ct. (we. and ea. dists.) Wash. 1971. Mem. Graham & Dunn, Seattle. Mem. Fed. Bar Assn. (pres. western dist. Wash. 1987-88). Office: Graham & Dunn 1420 5th Ave Fl 33 Seattle WA 98101-2333

PETTIGREW, L. EUDORA, academic administrator; b. Hopkinsville, Ky., Mar. 1, 1928; d. Warren Cicero and Corrye Lee (Newell) Williams; children: Peter W. Woodard, Jonathan R. (dec.). MusB, W.Va. State Coll., 1950; MA, So. Ill. U., 1964, PhD, 1966. Music/English instr. Swift Meml. Jr. Coll., Rogersville, Tenn., 1950-51; music instr., librarian Western Ky. Vocat. Sch., Paducah, 1951-52; music/English instr. Voorhees Coll., Denmark, S.C., 1954-55; dir. music and recreation therapy W.Ky. State Psychiatric Hosp., Hopkinsville, 1956-61; research fellow Rehab. Inst., So. Ill. U., Carbondale, 1961-63, instr., resident counselor, 1963-66, coordinator undergrad. ednl. psychology, 1963-66, acting chmn. ednl. psychology, tchr. corps instr., 1966; asst. prof. to assoc. prof. dept. psychology U. Bridgeport, Conn., 1966-70; prof., chmn. dept. urban and met. studies Coll. Urban Devel. Mich. State U., East Lansing, 1974-80; assoc. provost, prof. U. Del., Newark, 1981-86; pres. SUNY Coll. at Old Westbury, 1986—; cons. for rsch. and evaluation Hall Neighborhood House Day Care Tng. Project, Bridgeport, 1966-68, U.S. Ea. Regional Lab., Edn. Devel. Ctr., Newton, Mass., 1967-69; coordinator for edn. devel., 1968-69; cons. Bridgeport Public Schs. lang. devel. project, 1967-68, 70; Lansing Model Cities Agy., Day Care Program, 1971; U. Pitts., 1973, 74, Leadership Program, U. Mich. and Wayne State U., 1975, Wayne County Pub. Health Nurses Assn., 1976, Ill. State Bd. Edn., 1976-77; assoc. prof. U. Bridgeport, 1970, Ctr. for Urban Affairs and Coll. of Edn., Mich. State U., East Lansing, 1970-73; trustee L.I. Community Found.; program devel. specialist Lansing Public Schs. Tchr. Corps program, 1971-73; chair commn. SUNY Higher Edn. in Africa, 1994—; coord. workshop Conflict Resolution the Woman's Role in Our World, 4th Internat. IAUP/UN Conf., Beijing, China, 1995; lectr. in field; condr. workshops in field; mem. adv. com. Economists Allied for Arms Reduction, 1996; chmn. SUNY commn. on higher edn. in Africa; guest spkr. Internat. Conf. on The New Role of Higher Edn. in the Context of an Ind. Palestinian State, An-Najah Nat. U., Nablus, Palestine, 1996. Tv/radio appearances on: Black Women in Edn, Channel 23, WKAR, East Lansing, 1973, Black Women and Equality, Channel 2, Detroit, 1974, Women and Careers, Channel 7, Detroit, 1974, Black Women and Work: Integration in Schools, WITL Radio, Lansing, 1974, others.; Contbr. articles to profl. jours. Recipient Diana award Lansing YWCA, 1977, Outstanding Profl. Achievement award, 1977, award L.I. Ctr. for Bus. and Profl. Women, 1988, Educator of Yr. 100 Black Men of L.I., 1988, Black Women's Agenda award, 1988, Woman of Yr. Nassau/Suffolk Coun. of Adminstrv. Women in Edn., 1989, Disting. Ednl. Leadership award L.I. Women's Coun. for Equal Edn. Tng. and Employment, 1989, L.I. Disting. Leadership award L.I. Bus. News, 1990, Disting. Black Women in Edn. award Nat. Coun. Negro Women, 1991; named Outstanding Black Educator, NAACP, 1968, Oustanding Woman Educator, Mich. Women's Lawyers Assn. and Mich. Trial Lawyers Assn., 1975, Disting. Alumna, Nat. Assn. for Equal Opportunity in Higher Edn., 1990, Woman of Yr., Nassau County League of Women Voters, 1991. Mem. AAAS, Nat. Assn. Acad. Affairs Adminstrs., Internat. Assn. Univ. Pres. (exec. com.), Phi Delta Kappa. Office: SUNY-Old Westbury PO Box 210 Old Westbury NY 11568-0210

PETTIGREW, THOMAS FRASER, social psychologist, educator; b. Richmond, Va., Mar. 14, 1931; s. Joseph Crane and Janet (Gibb) P.; m. Ann Hallman, Feb. 25, 1956; 1 son, Mark Fraser. A.B. in Psychology, U. Va., 1952; M.A. in Social Psychology, Harvard U., 1955, Ph.D., 1956; D.H.L. (hon.), Governor's State U., 1979. Rsch. assoc. Inst. Social Rsch., U. Natal, Republic South Africa, 1956; asst. prof. psychology U. N.C., 1956-57; asst. prof. social psychology Harvard U., Cambridge, Mass., 1957-62, lectr., 1962-64, assoc. prof., 1964-68, prof., 1968-74, prof. social psychology and sociology, 1974-80; prof. social psychology U. Calif., Santa Cruz, 1980-94, rsch. prof. social psychology, 1994—; prof. social psychology U. Amsterdam, 1986-91; mem. com. status black Ams. NRC, 1985-88; adj. fellow Joint Ctr. Polit. and Econ. Studies, Washington, 1982—; mem. adv. bd. women's studies program Princeton (N.J.) U., 1985—. Author: (with E.Q. Campbell) Christians in Racial Crisis: A Study of the Little Rock Ministry, 1959, A Profile of the Negro American, 1964, Racially Separate or Together?, 1971, (with Frederickson, Knobol, Glazer and Veda) Prejudice, 1982, (with Alston) Tom Bradley's Campaigns for Governor: The Dilemma of Race and Political Strategies, 1988, How to Think Like a Social Scientist, 1996; editor: Racial Discrimination in the United States, 1975, The Sociology of Race Relations: Reflection and Reform, 1980, (with C. Stephan & W. Stephan) The Future of Social Psychology: Defining the Relationship Between Sociology and Psychology, 1991; mem. editorial bd. Jour. Social Issues, 1959-64, Social Psychology Quarterly, 1977-80; assoc. editor Am. Sociol. Rev, 1963-65; mem. adv. bd. Integrated Edn, 1963-84, Phylon, 1965-93, Edn. and Urban Society, 1968-90, Race, 1972-74, Ethnic and Racial Studies, 1978-95, Rev. of Personality and Social Psychology, 1980-85, Community and Applied Social Psychology, 1989—, Individual and Politics, 1989-93, New Cmty., 1994—; contbr. articles to profl. publs. Chmn. Episcopal presiding Bishop's Adv. Com. on Race Relations, 1961-63; v.p. Episcopal Soc. Cultural and Racial Unity, 1962-63; mem. Mass. Gov.'s Adv. Com. on Civil Rights, 1962-64; social sci. cons. U.S. Commn. Civil Rights, 1966-71; mem. White House Task Force on Edn., 1967; mem. nat. task force on desegregation policies Edn. Commn. of States, 1977-79; trustee Ella Lyman Cabot Trust, Boston, 1977-79; mem. Emerson Book Award com. United Chpts. Phi Beta Kappa, 1971-73. Guggenheim fellow, 1967-68; NATO sr. scientist fellow, 1974; fellow Center Advanced Study in Behavioral Scis., 1975-76; Sydney Spivack fellow in intergroup relations Am. Sociol. Assn., 1978; Netherlands Inst. Advanced Study fellow, 1984-85; recipient Kurt Lewin Meml. award Soc. for Psychological Study of Social Issues, 1987, (with Martin) Gordon Allport Intergroup Rels. Rsch. prize, 1988, Faculty Rsch. award U. Calif., Santa Cruz, 1988; Bellagio (Italy) Study Ctr. resident fellow, Rockefeller Found., 1991. Fellow Am. Psychol. Assn., Am. Sociol. Assn. (council 1979-82); mem. Soc. Psychol. Study Social Issues (council 1962-66, pres. 1967-68), NRC (com. status black Ams. 1985-88), European Assn. Social Psychology. Home: 524 Van Ness Ave Santa Cruz CA 95060-3556

PETTIJOHN, FRANCIS JOHN, geology educator; b. Waterford, Wis., June 20, 1904; m. Dorothy Bracken, 1930 (dec.); children: Norma Pettijohn Friedemann, Clare Pettijohn Maher, Loren; m. Virginia Romberger, 1990 (dec.). A.B., U. Minn., 1924, A.M., 1925, Ph.D., 1930; D.H.L. (hon.), Johns Hopkins U., 1978; Sc.D. (hon.), U. Minn., 1986. Instr. Macalester Coll., 1924-25, Oberlin Coll., 1925-29, U. Minn., 1928-29; instr. U. Chgo., 1929-31, asst. prof., 1931-39, asso. prof., 1939-46, prof., 1946-52; prof. Johns Hopkins U., Balt., 1952-73; prof. emeritus Johns Hopkins U., 1973—, chmn. dept. geology, 1963-68, acting chmn. dept. earth and planetary scis., 1970; geologist U.S. Geol. Survey, 1943-53; cons. Shell Oil Co., 1953-63; mem. adv. panel for earth scis. NSF, 1959-62; mem. adv. bd. Petroleum Research Fund., 1963-65. Author: numerous books in field including Sedimentary Rocks, 1949, 3d edit., 1973, (with P.E. Potter) Paleocurrents and Basin Analysis, 1963, 2d edit., 1977, (with P.E. Potter, R. Siever) Sand and Sandstone, 1987, 2d edit.; contbr. articles to profl. jours.; editor: Jour. Geology, 1947-52. Recipient Sorby medal Internat. Assn. Sedimentologists, 1982. Fellow AAAS, Geol. Soc. London (Wollaston medal 1974), Geol. Soc. Am. (Penrose medal 1975); mem. Soc. Econ. Paleontologists and Mineralogists (hon., pres. 1955-56, Twenhofel medal 1974), Geol. Soc. India (hon.), Geol. Soc. Finland (corr.), Soc. for Sedimentary Geology (established Francis J. Pettijohn medal 1992), Am. Assn. Petroleum Geologists, Am. Acad. Arts and Scis., Nat. Acad. Scis., Explorers Club (life), Phi Beta Kappa, Sigma Xi. Home: U38 11630 Glen Arm Rd Glen Arm MD 21057-9448 Office: Johns Hopkins U Dept Earth And Scis Baltimore MD 21218

PETTIJOHN, FRED PHILLIPS, retired newspaper executive, consultant; b. Balt., May 11, 1917; s. Fred and Adelaide Josephine (Phillips) P.; m. Elaine Wilson, Dec. 7, 1946; children: Fred Phillips, Mark Clay. B.A.E., U. Fla., 1941. Sports editor Tallahassee Democrat, 1946-53; with Fort Lauderdale (Fla.) News, 1953-82, exec. editor, 1960-68, gen. mgr., 1968-77, editorial dir., from 1977; 1st v.p. Gore Newspapers Co., from 1960; now cons. Bd. dirs. Salvation Army, 1975-79, v.p., 1979; bd. dirs. Fla. Council 100, 1976-78. Served with AUS, 1943-45. Recipient Disting. Service award Fla. Press Assn., 1976, Disting. Alumnus award U. Fla., 1977; inducted into Fla. Newspaper Hall of Fame, 1990. Mem. Fla. Press Assn. (pres. 1963-64, 69-70), AP Mng. Editors (bd. dirs. 1964-66), So. Newspaper Pubs. Assn., Lauderdale Yacht Club, Tower Club, Sigma Delta Chi, Theta Chi. Democrat. Presbyterian. Home: 911 N Rio Vista Blvd Fort Lauderdale FL 33301-3037

PETTINELLA, NICHOLAS ANTHONY, financial executive; b. Little Falls, N.Y., Sept. 9, 1942; s. Nicholas and Rose (Zuccaro) P.; m. Nancy C. Whitehouse, Oct. 28, 1978; children: Albert J., Michael A. BS, Bentley Coll., 1968; MBA, Babson Coll., 1975; postgrad. Harvard U., 1979, Stanford U., 1983. CPA, Mass. Auditor, Coopers & Lybrand, Boston, 1970-76; treas. Courier Corp., Lowell, Mass., 1976-80; controller corp. ops. Digital Equipment Corp., Maynard, Mass., 1980-81; dir. fin. Intermetrics, Inc., Burlington, Mass., 1981-83; v.p. fin., chief fin. officer, treas., 1983—; bd. dirs. The Computer Mus., Boston, 1986—, treas. 1988—. Chmn. fin. com. Town of Ashland, Mass., 1980-82. Served with U.S. Army, 1964-66. Mem. Fin. Execs. Inst., AICPA, Inst. Mgmt. Accts., Mass. Soc. CPAs, Treas. Club Boston, Pacioli Soc. Roman Catholic. Home: 141 South St Ashland MA 01721-2263 Office: Intermetrics Inc 23 4th Ave Burlington MA 01803-3303

PETTINGA, CORNELIUS WESLEY, pharmaceutical company executive; b. Mille Lacs, Minn., Nov. 10, 1921; s. R.C. and Adrianna (Landaal) P.; m. Yvonne Imogene Svoboda, Dec. 22, 1943; children—Julie, Steven, Mark, Tom, Jennifer. A.B., Hope Coll., 1942; postgrad., Syracuse U., 1943; Ph.D. in Chemistry, Iowa State Coll., 1949; DSc with honors, Hope Coll., 1985; DSc (hon.), Ind. U., 1988. With Eli Lilly & Co., Indpls., 1949-86, v.p. research, devel. and control, 1964-70, v.p., asst. to pres., 1970-72, exec. v.p., 1972-86, bd. dirs., 1966-86, cons. bus. & tech., 1987—. Contbr. articles to profl. jours. Bd. overseers Sweet Briar Coll.; trustee, bd. govs., fin. com., exec. com. Indpls. Mus. Art; bd. dirs. Hanover Coll.; trustee Park-Tudor Sch., Coe Coll.; mem. corp. vis. com. dept. nutrition and food sci. M.I.T.; mem. Purdue Rsch. Found. With USNR, 1943-45. Fellow Nat. Cancer Inst., 1949; recipient Charles H. Best award ADA, 1986. Mem. Am. Chem. Soc., AAAS, Ind. Acad. Sci., Bus. Com. for Arts, Indpls. C. of C. (new bus. devel. com.), Sigma Xi. Clubs: Lambs (Indpls.), University (Indpls.), Woodstock (Indpls.), Meridian Hills Country (Indpls.); Piedmont (Lynchburg, Va.); John's Island (Vero Beach, Fla.). Home: 445 Somerset Dr W Indianapolis IN 46260-2919 also: 200 Ocean Rd 3A Johns Island Vero Beach FL 32963 Office: 2B 1020 Bldg Winterton 1040 E 86th St Indianapolis IN 46240-1829

PETTIS-ROBERSON, SHIRLEY MCCUMBER, former congresswoman; b. Mountain View, Calif.; d. Harold Oliver and Dorothy Susan (O'Neil) McCumber; m. John J. McNulty (dec.); m. Jerry L. Pettis (dec. Feb. 1975); m. Ben Roberson, Feb. 6, 1988; children: Peter Dwight Pettis, Deborah Neil Pettis Moyer. Student, Andrews U., U. Calif., Berkeley. Mgr. Audio-Digest Found., L.A., Glendale; sec.-treas. Pettis, Inc., Hollywood, 1958-68; mem. 94th-95th Congresses from 37th Calif. Dist., mem. coms. on interior, internat. rels., edn. and labor; pres. Women's Rsch. and Edn. Inst., 1979-80; bd. dirs. Kemper Nat. Ins. Cos., 1979—, Lumbermines Mut. Ins. Co. Mem. Pres.'s Commn. on Arms Control and Disarmament, 1980-83, Commn. on Presdl. Scholars, 1990-93; trustee U. Redlands, Calif., 1980-83, Loma Linda (Calif.) U. and Med. Ctr., 1990-95; chair Loma Linda U. Children's Hosp. Found.; mem. Former Mems. Congress, 1988—. Mem. Morningside Country Club (Rancho Mirage, Calif.), Capitol Hill Club (Washington).

PETTIT, FREDERICK SIDNEY, metallurgical engineering educator, researcher; b. Wilkes Barre, Pa., Mar. 10, 1930; s. Edwin Humes and Edith Mae (Barnecut) P.; m. Lou-Jean Mary Corso, Aug. 30, 1958; children: Frederick N., Theodore E., John C., Charles A. B in Engring., Yale U., 1952, M in Engring., 1960, D in Engring., 1962. Jr. engr. Westinghouse Electric Corp., Pitts., 1952-54; engr. Avco-Lycoming, Stratford, Conn., 1957-58; postdoctoral student Max Planck Inst. Phys. Chemistry, Gottingen, Fed. Republic Germany, 1962-63; sr. staff scientist Pratt & Whitney Aircraft Co., East Hartford, Conn., 1963-79; prof. metall.-material engring. dept., chmn. U. Pitts., Pa., 1979-88; prof. U. Pitts., 1988—, Harry S. Tack prof. materials engring., 1992—; mem. adv. bd. Jour. Oxidation of Metals, Plenum Press, N.Y., 1975—. 1st lt USMC, 1954-57. NSF fellow, 1962-63. Mem. Metall. Soc. (program dir. 1982-83), Electrochem. Soc. (sec.-treas. high temperature materials div. 1979-83), Am. Soc. Metals, Materials Rsch. Soc. Roman Catholic. Home: 201 Ennerdale Dr Pittsburgh PA 15237-4026 Office: U Pitts 848 Benedum Hall Pittsburgh PA 15261-2208

PETTIT, GEORGE ROBERT, chemistry educator, cancer researcher; b. Long Branch, N.J., June 8, 1929; s. George Robert and Florence Elizabeth (Seymour) P.; m. Margaret Jean Benger, June 20, 1953; children: William Edward, Margaret Sharon, Robin Kathleen, Lynn Benger, George Robert III. B.S., Wash. State U., 1952; M.S. Wayne State U., 1954, Ph.D., 1956. Teaching asst. Wash. State U., 1950-52, lecture demonstrator, 1952; rsch. chemist E.I. duPont de Nemours and Co., 1953; grad. teaching asst. Wayne State U., 1952-53, rsch. fellow, 1954-56; sr. rsch. chemist Norwich Eaton Pharms., Inc., 1956-57; asst. prof. chemistry U. Maine, 1957-61, assoc. prof. chemistry, 1961-65, prof. chemistry, 1965; vis. prof. chemistry Stanford U., 1965; chmn. organic div. Ariz. State U., 1966-68, prof. chemistry, 1965—; vis. prof. So. African, Univs., 1978; dir. Cancer Rsch. Lab., 1974-75, Cancer Rsch. Inst., 1975—; lectr. various colls. and univs.; cons. in field. Contbr. articles to profl. jours. Mem. adv. bd. Wash. State U. Found., 1981-85. Served with USAFR, 1951-54. Recipient Disting. Rsch. Professorship award Ariz. State U., 1978-79, Alumni Achievement award Wash. State U., 1984; recipient Rsch. Achievement award Am. Soc. Pharmacolgnosy, 1995; named Dalton Prof. Medicinal Chemistry and Cancer Rsch., 1986—, Regents Prof. Chemistry, 1990—. Fellow Am. Inst. Chemists (Pioneer award 1989, Ariz. Gov.'s Excellence award 1993); mem. Am. Chem. Soc. (awards com. 1968-71, 78-81), Chem. Soc. (London), Pharmacognosy Soc., Am. Assn. Cancer Rsch., Sigma Xi, Phi Lambda Upsilon. Office: Ariz State U Cancer Rsch Inst Tempe AZ 85287

PETTIT, GHERY DEWITT, retired veterinary medicine educator; b. Oakland, Calif., Sept. 6, 1926; s. Hermon DeWitt Pettit and Marion Esther (St. John) Menzies; m. Frances Marie Seitz, July 5, 1948; children: Ghery St. John, Paul Michael. BS in Animal Sci., U. Calif., Davis, 1948, BS in Vet. Sci., 1951, DVM, 1953. Diplomate Am. Coll. Vet. Surgeons (recorder 1970-77, pres., chmn. bd. dirs. 1978-80). Asst. prof. vet. surgery U. Calif., Davis, 1953-61; prof. vet. surgery Wash. State U., Pullman, 1961-91, prof. emeritus, 1991—; mem. Wash. State Vet. Bd. Govs., 1981-88, chmn., 1987; vis. fellow Sydney (Australia) U., 1977. Author/editor: Intervertebral Disc Protrusion in the Dog, 1966; cons. editoral bd. Jour. Small Animal Practice, Eng., 1970-88; mem. editoral bd. Compendium on C.E., Lawrenceville, N.J., 1983-86, editoral rev. bd. Jour. Vet. Surgery, Phila., 1984-86, editor 1987-92; contbr. articles to profl. jours., chpts. to books. Elder Presbyn. Ch., Pullman, 1967—. Served with USN, 1944-46. Recipient Norden Disting. Tchr. award Wash. State U. Class 1971, Faculty of Yr. award Wash. State U. Student Com., 1985. Mem. AVMA, Am. Legion, Kiwanis Internat., Sigma Xi, Phi Zeta, Phi Kappa Sigma (chpt. advisor 1981-93, 2d v.p. 1993-98). Republican. Avocations: camping, small boat sailing.

PETTIT, GHERY ST. JOHN, electronics engineer; b. Woodland, Calif., Apr. 6, 1952; s. Ghery DeWitt and Frances Marie (Seitz) P.; m. Marilyn Jo Van Hoose, July 28, 1973; children: Ghery Christopher, Heather Kathleen. BS in Electrical Engring., Wash. State U., 1975. Nuclear engr. Mare Island Naval Shipyard, Vallejo, Calif., 1975-76; electronics engr. Naval Electronic Systems Engring. Ctr., Vallejo, 1976-79; sr. engr. Martin Marietta Denver Aerospace, 1979-83; staff engr. Tandem Computers Inc., Santa Clara, Calif., 1983-90; mgr. electromagnetic capability Tandem Computers Inc., Cupertino, Calif., 1990-91, electromagnetic compatibility lead engr., 1991-95; EMC engr. Intel Corp., Hillsboro, Oreg., 1995-96, DuPont, Wash., 1996—. Asst. cubmaster Boy Scouts Am., San Jose, Calif., 1985-86, cubmaster, 1986-88, ast. scoutmaster, 1988-90, scoutmaster, 1990-93. Mem. IEEE (sr.), Electromagnetic Capability Soc. (sec.-treas. Littleton, Colo. chpt. 1983, sec. Santa Clara Valley chpt. 1985-87, vice chmn. 1987-89, chmn. 1989-91, sec. Santa Clara Valley sect. 1991-92, treas. 1992-93, vice chmn. 1993-94, chmn. 1994-95), IEEE EMC Soc. (chmn. Seattle chpt. 1997—). Republican. Presbyterian. Avocations: target shooting, hiking, camping, amateur radio, sailing. Office: Intel Corp 2800 Center St Dupont WA 98327-9728

PETTIT, JOHN W., administrator; b. Detroit, Mar. 6, 1942; s. John W. and Clara (Schartz) P.; m. Kathleen Endres, Aug. 8, 1970; children: Julie, Andrew, Michael. BBA, U. Notre Dame, 1964; MBA, Mich. State U., 1974. CPA, Mich. Acct. Ernst & Ernst, Detroit, 1964-67; chief acct. Detroit Inst. Tech., Detroit, 1967-69; controller, dir. adminstrn. & fin. Mich. Cancer Found., Detroit, 1969-80; chief adminstrv. officer Dana-Farber Cancer Inst., Boston, 1980-94; exec. v.p., chief oper. officer John Wayne Cancer Inst., Santa Monica, Calif., 1995—; grant reviewer Nat. Cancer Inst., Bethesda, Md., 1979—. Pres. advanced mgmt. program Mich. State U., 1978-79. Mem. Am. Inst. CPA's. Avocations: sailing, woodworking, photography, music. Office: John Wayne Cancer Inst 2200 Santa Monica Blvd Santa Monica CA 90404-2302

PETTIT, JOHN WHITNEY, lawyer; b. Washington, Mar. 20, 1935; s. Manson Bowers and Dagny Bernice (Rudback) P.; m. Anne McCullough, Jan. 20, 1939; children: John Whitney, Jennifer Read. BA, Duke U., 1957; JD, Georgetown U., 1960. Bar: D.C. 1960, U.S. Supreme Ct. 1965. Gen. counsel FCC, 1972-74; assoc. Hamel & Park, Washington, 1963-67, ptnr., 1967-72; gen. counsel FCC, Washington, 1972-74; ptnr. Hamel & Park, Washington, 1974-88, mng. ptnr., 1978-80, 86-88; mng. ptnr. Hopkins & Sutter, Washington, 1988-94; ptnr. Drinker Biddle & Reath, Washington, 1994—, ptnr.-in-charge, 1995—, mng. ptnr., 1996—. Fellow Am. Bar Found.; mem. ABA, Fed. Comms. Bar Assn., Vis. Nurse Assn. Washington (chair, bd. dirs. 1990-95), Met. Club, Chevy Chase (Md.) Club, Talbot (Md.) Country Club. Office: Drinker Biddle & Reath 901 15th St NW Washington DC 20005-2327

PETTIT, LAWRENCE KAY, university president; b. Lewistown, Mont., May 2, 1937; s. George Edwin and Dorothy Bertha (Brown) P.; m. Sharon Lee Anderson, June 21, 1961 (div. Oct. 1976); children: Jennifer Anna, Matthew Anderson, Allison Carol, Edward McLean; m. Elizabeth DuBois Medley, July 11, 1980; 3 stepchildren. BA cum laude, U. Mont., 1959; AM, Washington U., St. Louis, 1962; PhD, U. Wis., 1965. Legis. asst. U.S. Senate, 1959-60, 62; asst. & assoc. prof. dept. polit. sci. Pa. State U., 1964-67; assoc. dir. fed. rels. Am. Council Edn., Washington, 1967-69; chmn. dept. polit. sci. Mont. State U., 1969-72; adminstrv. asst. to gov. State of Mont., 1973; chancellor Mont. Univ. System, Helena, 1973-79; pvt. practice ednl. cons. Mont., 1979-81; dep. commr. for acad. affairs Tex. Coordinating Bd. for Higher Edn., 1981-83; chancellor Univ. System of South Tex., 1983-86; chancellor So. Ill. U., Carbondale and Edwardsville, 1986-91, Disting. svc. prof., 1991-92; pres. Indiana U. Pa., 1992—; mem. various nat. and regional bds. and coms. on higher edn. Author: (with H. Albinski) European Political Processes, 2d edit., 1974, (with E. Keynes) Legislative Process in the U.S. Senate, 1969, (with S. Kirkpatrick) Social Psychology of Political Life, 1972, (with J. Goetz and S. Thomas) Legislative Process in Montana, 1975; mem. editorial bd. Ednl. Record, 1985—. Mem. adv. bd. Leadership Ctr. Ams., 1988-90, Ill. Coalition, 1989-92; candidate for 2d dist. U.S. Ho. of Reps., Mont., 1980; mem. Ill. Gov.'s Com. on Sci. and Tech., 1986-90; bd. dirs. Tex. Guaranteed Student Loan Corp., 1985-86; chmn. Ill.-Niigata Commn. on Edn. and Econ. Devel., 1990-92; chair bd. dirs. Nat. Environ. Edn. and Tng. Ctr., 1994—. U. Wis. fellow 1962-63, Vilas fellow U. Wis., 1963-64. Mem. AAUP (pres. Mont. conf. 1971-72), Nat. Assn. Sys. Heads (pres. 1989), Am. Coun. on Edn. (chmn. leadership commn. 1989-90, sr. fellow 1991-92), Am. Assn. Higher Edn., Am. Assn. State Colls. and Univs. (Disting. Svc. award 1991), Newcomen Soc., Duquesne Club Pitts., Allegheny Club Pitts., World Affairs Coun. Pitts., Univ. Club Pitts., Pa. Soc., Ind. Country Club, Rotary, Sigma Chi (Significant Sig award 1988), Phi Kappa Phi. Episcopalian. Office: Indiana U President's Office 201 John Sutton Hall Indiana PA 15705

PETTIT, ROBERT, retired basketball player; b. Baton Rouge, Dec. 12, 1932. Grad., La. State U., 1954. Basketball player Milw. Hawks, 1954-55; basketball player St. Louis Hawks, 1955-65, coach, 1961-62. Named to Basketball Hall of Fame, 1970, NBA All-Star Most Valuable Player, 1956, 58, 62, All-Star Game co-Most Valuable Player, 1959; selected NBA 25th Anniversary All-Time Team, 1970, 35th Anniversary All-Time Team, 1980, All-NBA 1st Team, 1955, 56, 57, 58, 59, 60, 61, 62, 63, 64, All-NBA 2d Team, 1965; recipient Most Valuable Player award NBA, 1956, 59, Rookie of Yr. award, 1955; mem. NBA Championship Team, 1958; record-holder all time leading rebounder Atlanta Hawks, 1954-55, 64-65. Office: c/o Basketball Hall Fame PO Box 179 Springfield MA 01101-0179

PETTITE, WILLIAM CLINTON, public affairs consultant; b. Reno, Nev.; s. Sidney Clinton and Wilma (Stibal) P.; m. Charlotte Denise Fryer; children: Patrick Keane, William Ellis, Joseph Clinton. Owner, Market Lake Citizen & Clark County Enterprise Newspapers, Roberts, Idaho, 1959-70, pub., 1959-61; publicity dir. Golden Days World Boxing Champs, Reno, 1970; pub. Virginia City (Nev.) Legend newspaper, 1970; public affairs cons., Fair Oaks, Calif., 1966—, owner PT Cattle Co., Firth, Idaho; cons. in Ireland, Wales, Korea, Japan, France, Czech Republic, Scotland, Alberta, British Columbia, New Brunswick, Prince Edward Island, Nova Scotia, Can., Channel Islands, Costa Rica, Macau, Hong Kong, 1984—. County probate judge, Idaho, 1959-61; acting County coroner, 1960-61; sec., trustee Fair Oaks Cemetery Dist., 1963-72; bd. dir. Fair Oaks Water Dist., 1964-72, v.p., 1967-68, pres., 1968-70; dir., v.p. San Juan Cmty. Svcs. Dist., 1962-66, 68-72; exec. sec. Calif. Bd. Landscape Archs., 1976-78, Calif. Assn. Collectors, 1966-68. Cons. Senate-Assembly Joint Audit Com. Calif. Legislature, 1971-73; exec. officer Occupational Safety and Health Appeals Bd., 1981-83; mem. regulatory rev. commn. Calif. FabricCare Bd., 1981-82; mem. Sacramento County Grand Jury, 1973-74, 1981-82, cons. bd. supvs. Sacramento County, 1985-87; chmn. bus. adv. bd. East Lawn Corp, 1991—; devel. coord. Sacramento Diocese Cath. Cemeteries, 1996—. Election campaign coord. for E.S. Wright, majority leader Idaho Senate, 1968, Henry Dworshak, U.S. Senator, 1960, Hamer Budge, U.S. Rep., 1960, Charles C. Gossett, former Gov. Idaho, 1959-74; asst. sgt. at arms Rep. Nat. Conv., 1956; chmn. Rep. County Cen. Com., 1959-61; del. Rep. State Conv., 1960. Chmn. Idaho County Centennial Commn., 1959-61. Recipient Idaho Centennial award, 1968, 69. Mem. Assn. Sacramento County Water Dists. (bd. dir. 1967-72, pres. 1970-72), No. Calif. Peace Officers Assn., Nat. Coun. Juvenile Ct. Judges (com. 1959-61). Club. Author: Memories of Market Lake, Vol. I, 1965; A History of Southeastern Idaho, Vol. II, 1977, Vol. III, 1983, Vol. IV, 1990; contbr. articles to newspapers, profl. jours. Home: PO Box 2127 Fair Oaks CA 95628-2127 Office: 2631 K St Sacramento CA 95816-5103 *Personal philosophy: Proverbs 3:3 "Never forget to be truthful and kind. Hold these virtues tightly. Write them deep within your heart."*

PETTITT, JAY S., architect, consultant; b. Redford, Mich., Jan. 6, 1926; s. Jay S. and Florence Marian (Newman) P.; m. Ruth Elizabeth Voigt, June 21, 1947; children—J. Stuart, Laura Ellen, Patricia Lynn, Carol Ann. B.Arch., U. Mich., 1951. Registered architect, Mich. Draftsman Frank J. Stepnoski and Son, Fond du Lac, Wis., 1951; project architect Albert Kahn Assocs., Inc., Detroit, 1951-62; chief archtl. devel. Albert Kahn Assocs., Inc., 1962-67, v.p., 1967-88, dir. architecture, 1975-88; archtl. cons. Beulah, Mich., 1988—. Active Jr. Athletic Assn., Redford, Mich., 1959-63; com. chmn. Boy Scouts Am., 1960-65; supr. Benzonia Twp. Served with U.S. Army, 1943-46, ETO. Fellow AIA; mem. Mich. Soc. Architects (pres. 1967), Am. Arbitration Assn., Am. Assn. Hosp. Planning, Engring. Soc. Detroit, U. Mich. Pres.' Club. Avocations: sailing; skiing.

PETTUS, BARBARA WYPER, bank executive; b. Hartford, Conn., Nov. 9, 1947; d. John Stuurman Wyper and Mary Blair (Goodell) Crolius; m. Charlton Messick Pettus, Apr. 19, 1975 (div., 1985). BA, Smith Coll., 1969; MLS, Simmons Coll., 1972, MBA, 1980. Adminstrv. asst. Perkins & Will Architects, Washington, 1969-71; head reference libr. Memorial Hall Libr., Andover, Mass., 1972-77; asst. dir. Memorial Hall Libr., Andover, 1977-79; asst. treas. Chase Manhattan Bank, N.Y.C., 1981-83, 2nd v.p., 1983-88, v.p. U.S. pvt. banking div., 1988-90; team leader, pvt. banking Mfrs. Hanover Trust Co., 1990-91; team leader, pvt. banking Chem. Bank, N.Y.C., 1991-94, unit mgr. pvt. banking, 1994-96; team leader pvt. banking Chase Manhatten Bank. Editor: (mag.) Bay State Librarian, 1977-79. Bd. dirs. Simmons Coll. Alumni Assn., Boston, 1982-84; mem. N.Y. Jr. League, 1987-90. Mem. Fin. Women's Assn. of N.Y. (bd. dirs. 1997), N.Y. Soc. Inst. Cert. Fin. Planners (bd. dirs. 1995—). Congregationalist. Office: Chase Manhattan Bank 1211 Sixth Ave New York NY 10036

PETTY, CHARLES SUTHERLAND, pathologist; b. Lewistown, Mont., Apr. 16, 1920; s. Charles Frederic and Mae (Reichert) P.; m. Lois Muriel Swenson, Dec. 14, 1957; children—Heather Ann, Charles Sutherland II; children by previous marriage—Daniel S., Carol L. B.S., U. Wash., 1941, M.S., 1946; M.D., Harvard U., 1950. Intern Mary Imogene Bassett Hosp., Coopertown, N.Y., 1950-52; resident in pathology Peter Bent Brigham Hosp., Children's Med. Center, New Eng. Deaconness Hosp., Boston, 1952-55; instr. pathology La. State U. Sch. Medicine, 1955-56, asst. prof., 1956-58; asst. med. examiner State of Md., 1958-67; asst. prof. forensic pathology U. Md. Sch. Medicine, 1958-64, asso. prof., 1964-67; lectr., then asso. Johns Hopkins U. Sch. Hygiene and Public Health, 1959-67; adj. prof. police adminstrn. U. Louisville, 1978—; dir. Balt. Regional ARC Blood Program, 1959-67; prof. forensic pathology Ind. U. Sch. Medicine, Indpls., 1967-69; dir. lab. Ind. Commn. on Forensic Scis., 1967-69; chief med. examiner Dallas County, 1969-91; prof. forensic scis., pathology U. Tex. Southwestern Med. Sch., Dallas, 1969—; dir. Southwestern Inst. Forensic Scis., 1969-91. Served from ensign to lt. comdr. USNR, 1941-45. Fellow Coll. Am. Pathologists, Am. Soc. Clin. Pathologists, A.C.P., Am. Acad. Forensic Scis. (pres. 1967-68); mem. Sigma Xi. Episcopalian. Home: 3964 Goodfellow Dr Dallas TX 75229-2722 Office: 5601 Med Ctr Dr Dallas TX 75235-7200

PETTY, GEORGE OLIVER, lawyer; b. L.A., Mar. 31, 1939; s. Hugh Morton and May (Johnson) P.; m. Sandra Diane Kilpatrick, July 14, 1962; children: Ross Morton, Alison Lee, Christopher Henry. AB, U. Calif., Berkeley, 1961; LLB, U. Calif., 1964. Bar: Calif. 1965, Eng. and Wales 1986, U.S. Supreme Ct. 1976. Atty. Huovinen & White, Oakland, Calif., 1967-69; counsel Bechtel Power Corp., San Francisco, 1969-83; prin. counsel Bechtel Ltd., London, 1983-86; gen. counsel Sun-Diamond Growers of Calif., Pleasanton, Calif., 1987-95; pvt. practice, 1995—. Capt. U.S. Army, 1965-67. Mem. Calif. State Bar Assn., Alameda County Bar Assn., Eng. and Wales Bar Assn., Bar Assn. for Commerce, Fin. & Industry (Eng.), Middle Temple Inn. Office: 843 Arlington Ave Berkeley CA 94707-1926

PETTY, JOHN ROBERT, banker; b. Chgo., Apr. 16, 1930; s. Dewitt Talmage and Beatrice (Worthington) P.; children: L. Talmage, Robert D., George M., Victoria Lee. AB, Brown U., 1951; postgrad., NYU, 1953-54. With Chase Manhattan Bank, N.Y.C. and Paris, 1953-66; v.p. Chase Manhattan Bank, 1964-66; dep. asst. sec. Dept. Treasury, Washington, 1966-68, asst. sec. for internat. affairs, 1968-72; partner Lehman Bros., N.Y.C., 1972-76; pres., dir., chmn. exec. com. Marine Midland Banks, Inc., from 1976, chmn., chief exec. officer, 1976-88; mng. gen. ptnr. Petty-FBW Assocs., Washington, 1989-91; chmn. Fed. Nat. Payables Inc. Washington, 1992—, Fed. Nat. Svcs. Inc., 1992—; chmn. Nippon Credit Trust Co., N.Y.C.; chmn. Hydro-Icona, Inc., Czech & Slovak Am. Enterprise Fund, 1991-95; bd. dirs. Antec Corp., Magnetic Analysis Corp., Anixter Internat. Corp.; trustee Am. Univ. With USNR, 1951-53. Mem. Council Fgn. Relations, Fgn. Bondholders Protective Council (pres.). Office: 7315 Wisconsin Ave Ste 322E Bethesda MD 20814-3208

PETTY, KYLE, professional stock car driver; s. Richard and Lynda P. 5th in NASCAR money leaders, 1992. Winner Champion Spark Plug 500, 1993. Office: c/o NASCAR PO Box 2875 Daytona Beach FL 32120-2875*

PETTY, RICHARD, retired professional race car driver; s. Lee and Elizabeth T. P.; m. Lynda Owens; children: Kyle, Sharon, Lisa, Rebecca. Auto racer, 35 years, ret., 1992; owner Car # 43. Mem. Pres.'s Coun. Fitness and Sport. Recipient Myers Bros. award Nat. Motorsports Press Assn., 1961, 67, 71, Excellence award NASCAR, 1987; named Grand Nat. Rookie of Year, 1959; Most Popular Driver in Grand Nat., 1962, 64, 68, 70, 74, 75, 76, 77, 78; Martini & Rossi Am. Driver of Year, 1971; Driver of Year Nat. Motorsport Press Assn., 1974-75; Driver of Quarter Century, 1991; inducted into N.C. Athletic Hall of Fame, 1973. Mem. Nat. Assn. Stock Car Auto Racing (7 time champion; Winston Cup grand nat. champion 1964, 67, 71, 72, 74, 75, 79). Entered 1015 Grand Nat. Races, winner 200, 1958-86, with 55 Superspeedway wins; winner Daytona 500, 1964, 66, 71, 73, 74, 79, 81; 1000th career Winston Cup start June 15, 1986 at Mich. Internat. Speedway; 500th consecutive start on Aug. 21, 1988 in Champion Spark Plug 500. Address: Petty Interprises Inc 311 Branson Mill Rd Randleman NC 27317-8008*

PETTY, RICHARD EDWARD, psychologist, educator, researcher; b. Garden City, N.Y., May 22, 1951; s. Edmund and Josephine (Serzo) P.; m. Virginia Lynn Oliver, Aug. 29, 1978. BA, U. Va., 1973; PhD, Ohio State U., 1977. Asst. prof. psychology U. Mo., Columbia, 1977-80, assoc. prof. psychology, 1981-83, Middlebush prof. psychology, 1984-85; vis. fellow Yale U., New Haven, Conn., 1986; prof. psychology Ohio State U., Columbus, 1987—; vis. prof. Princeton U., 1995; advisor com. on dietary guidelines implementation NAS, 1989-91; chair NIMH Social and Group Processes Panel. Author: Attitudes and Persuasion, 1981, Communication and Persuasion, 1986, Attitude Strength, 1995; editor Personality and Social Psychology Bull., 1988-92; mem. editl. bd. of 7 jours.; contbr. articles to profl. jours. Grantee NIMH, 1978-79, NSF, 1984-88, 90-94, 95—. Fellow AAAS, APA, Am. Psychol. Soc. Achievements include origination of the elaboration likelihood model of persuasion. Home: 2955 Scioto Pl Columbus OH 43221-4753 Office: Ohio State U 1885 Neil Ave Columbus OH 43210-1222

PETTY, SCOTT, JR., rancher; b. San Antonio, Apr. 10, 1937; s. Olive Scott and Edwina (Harris) P.; m. Marie Louise James, June 10, 1959 (dec. Dec. 1981); children: Joan Louise Oliver, Susan Harris Arnim, Scott James; m. Eleanor Oliver, Apr. 30, 1983; children: Tim A. Weed, Richard Oliver Weed. BS in Petroleum Engring., U. Tex., 1960, MS in Petroleum Engring., 1961. cert. engr. Tex., La. Asst. to pres. Petty Geophys. Engring., 1961-63, v.p., 1963-65; pres., exec. officer Petty Labs., 1965-67; pres., dir. Petty Geophys. Engring., 1967-73; exec. v.p. Petty-Ray Geophys., 1973-74; cons. Geosource Internat., 1974-76; chmn. bd. Pioneer Flour Mills, San Antonio, 1982—, White Lily Foods Co., Knoxville, Tenn. Mem. chancellor's coun. U. Tex., Austin, devel. bd., San Antonio; bd. dirs. U. Tex. Inst. Tex. Cultures, San Antonio, San Antonio Zool. Soc., Tex. and Southwestern Cattle Raisers, Ft. Worth, S.W. Tex. Property Rights Assn., Hondo, N.Am. Deer Farmers Assn. Mem. Am. Assn. Petroleum Geologists, Am. Inst. Mining, Metall. & Petroleum Engrs., Am. Petroleum Inst., Assn. Profl. Engrs., Geologists & Geophysicists of Alberta, Geophys. Soc. Houston, Internat. Assn. Geophys. Contractors, Internat. Oceanographic Found., Soc. Exploration Geophysicists, Soc. Petroleum Engrs., South Tex. Geol. Soc., Tex. Soc. Profl. Engrs. Republican. Episcopalian. Home: 202 La Jara Blvd San Antonio TX 78209-4444 Office: Petty Ranch Co 711 Navarro St Ste 235 San Antonio TX 78205-1710

PETTY, THOMAS LEE, physician, educator; b. Boulder, Colo., Dec. 24, 1932; s. Roy Stone and Eleanor Marie (Kudrna) P.; m. Carol Lee Piepho, Aug. 7, 1954; children: Caryn, Thomas, John. B.A., U. Colo., 1955, M.D., 1958. Intern Phila. Gen. Hosp., 1958-59; resident U. Mich., 1959-60, U. Colo., Denver, 1960-62; pulmonary fellow U. Colo., 1962-63, chief resident medicine, 1963-64, instr. medicine, 1962-64, asst. prof., 1964-68, assoc. prof., 1968-74, prof. medicine, 1974—; pres. Presbyn./St. Luke's Ctr. for Health Scis. Edn., 1989-95; practice medicine, specializing in internal medicine, pulmonary medicine Denver, 1962—; prof. medicine Rush Univ., 1992—; Cons. Fitzsimmons Army Hosp., 1970-96. Author: For Those Who Live and Breathe, 1967, 2d edit., 1972, Intensive and Rehabilitative Respiratory Care, 1971, 3d edit., 1982, Chronic Obstructive Pulmonary Disease, 1978, 2d edit., 1985, Principles and Practice of Pulmonary Rehabilitation, 1993, Enjoying Life With COPD, 1995, 3d edit., others; contbr. articles to profl. jours. NIH and Found. grantee, 1966-88. Master ACP, Am. Coll. Chest Physicians (pres. 1982); mem. Assn. Am. Physicians, Assn. of Pulmonary Program Dirs. (founding pres. 1983-84), Am. Bd. Internal Medicine (bd. govs. 1986-92), Am. Thoracic Soc. (Disting. Achievement award), Phi Beta Kappa, Phi Delta Theta, Alpha Omega Alpha, Phi Rho Sigma (pres. 1976-78). Home: 1940 Grape St Denver CO 80220-1353 Office: Presbyn Hosp Dept Internal Medicine Denver CO 80218

PETTY, TOM, rock guitarist, band leader, composer; b. Gainesville, Fla., Oct. 20, 1950; s. Earl Petty. Rock guitarist, 1969—; leader Tom Petty and the Heartbreakers, 1975—. Played in local bands The Epics, Mudcrutch while in Gainesville; songwriter, musician for Leon Russell, 1974; rec. and touring artist with the Heartbreakers, albums include Tom Petty and the Heartbreakers, 1976, You're Gonna Get It, 1978, Damn the Torpedoes, 1979, Hard Promises, 1981, Long After Dark, 1982, Southern Accents, 1985, Pack Up the Plantation, 1986, Let Me Up (I've Had Enough), 1987, Full Moon Fever, 1989, Into the Great Wide Open, 1991, Tom Petty and the Heartbreakers' Greatest Hits, 1993, Wildflowers, 1994; (with The Traveling Wilburys) Traveling Wilburys Vol. 1, 1989, Traveling Wilburys Vol. 3, 1990; hit singles include Breakdown, 1978, Here Comes My Girl, 1979, Refugee, 1979, The Waiting, 1981, You Got Lucky, 1982, Don't Come Around Here No More, 1985, Jammin' Me, 1987, Free Fallin', 1989 (solo album), Playback, 1994, Wildflowers, 1995; toured the world with Bob Dylan, 1986, toured America with Georgia Satellites and Del Fuegos (Rock 'n' Roll Caravan tour), 1987; film composer She's the One, 1996. Grammy nomination (Best Rock Duo or Group Performance, 1994) for My Back Pages (with Bob Dylan, Roger McGuinn, Neil Young, Eric Clapton, and George Harrison); MTV Best Male Video (with the Heartbreakers) for Mary Jane's Last Dance; recipient MTV Video Vanguard award. Office: Warner Bros Records 3300 Warner Blvd Burbank CA 91505*

PETTYJOHN, SHIRLEY ELLIS, lawyer, real estate executive; b. Liberty, Ky., Aug. 16, 1935; d. Wesley Barker and Ada Lou (Bryant) Ellis; m. Flem D. Pettyjohn, Sept. 24, 1955; children: Deena Renee, Ellisa Denise. BS in

Commerce, U. Louisville, 1974, JD, 1977. Bar: Ky. 1978, Ind. 1988; lic. real estate broker, Ky., Ind.; cert. mediator. Pres. Universal Devel. Corp., Ky. and Fla., 1984—, Pettyjohn Inc., Ky. and Ind., 1967—, Ind. Mediation Svcs., Inc., 1990—, Ky. Mediation Svcs., Inc., 1991—; v.p. Continental Investments Corp., 1986—; sr. ptnr. Pettyjohn & Assocs., Attys., 1987—. Editor Law-Hers Jour. Vice chmn. Louisville and Jefferson County Planning Commn., 1971-75; mem. Gov.'s Conf. on Edn., 1977, jud. nominee, 1981, Met. Louisville Women's Polit. Caucus, Bluegrass State Skills Corp., 1992-96, Ky. Opera Assn. Guild; elected mem. Ky. State Dem. Exec. Com., 1988-92; del. Nat. Dem. Conv. and Dem. Nat. Platform Com., 1988; bd. dirs. Ky. Dem. Hdqs., Inc., 1988-92, Pegasus Rising, Inc.; chmn. Okolona Libr. Task Force; mem. Clinton-Gore Nat. Steering Com., 1995. Recipient Mayor's Cert. Recognition, 1974, Mayor's Fleur de lis award, 1969-73, Excellence in Writing award Arts Club Louisville, 1986, 87, 93. Mem. ABA, NAFE, Nat. Assn. Adminstrv. Law Judges (Casey County Alumni Assn. Hall of Fame 1997), Ky. Bar Assn., Louisville Bar Assn., Women Lawyers Assn. of Jefferson County, Am. Judicature Soc., Clark County Bar Assn., Ind. Bar Assn., Ind. Assn. Mediators, Am. Inst. Planners, Women's C. of C. of Ky. (past bd. dirs., chmn. legis. com.), Am. Legion (aux.), Fraternal Order Police Assn. (award 1982), Louisville Legal Secs. (past pres., editor Law-Hers Jour.), Coun. of Women Pres. (past pres., Woman of Achievement award 1974), Louisville Visual Arts Assn. (former bd. dirs.), Louisville Ballet Guild (chair audience devel. 1989-91), Dem. Leadership Coun. (Friends of Casey County v.p. 1997—), Jefferson County Dem. Women's Club (past v.p.), Nat. Fedn. Dem. Women's Clubs, Spirit of 46th Club, Mose Green Club, North End Club, 12th Ward Club, S. End Club, 3rd Ward Club, Highland Pk. Club, Grass Roots Club, Harry S. Truman Club, Beargrass Club, Arts Club of Louisville (past pres.), Sigma Delta Kappa, Chi Thi Theta, Century 2000 Democrat Club. Home: 6924 Norlynn Dr Louisville KY 40228-1471 Office: 4500 Poplar Level Rd Louisville KY 40213-2124 Office: 4500 Poplar Level Rd Louisville KY 40213-2124

PETZ, EDWIN V., real estate executive, lawyer; b. Beatrice, Nebr., May 14, 1935; s. Virgil Leonard and Ruth Elenor (Thomsen) P.; m. Daphne Cross, May 17, 1958 (div. June 1964); 1 dau., Katherine J.; m. Anne Higgins, Dec. 3, 1964 (div. Sept. 1993); 1 son, W. Christopher; m. Louise Loosli, Jan. 9, 1997. B.A., Principia Coll., Elsah, Ill., 1955; J.D., Harvard U., 1958. Bar: N.Y. 1959, Mass. 1976. Assoc. Chadbourne, Parke, Whiteside & Wolff, N.Y.C., 1958-62; asst. gen. counsel Martin Marietta Corp., Bethesda, Md., 1963-64, 1965-75; gen. atty. sec. Bunker-Ramo Corp., Oakbrook, Ill., 1964-65; asst. gen. counsel United Brands Co., N.Y.C., 1975-82, v.p., gen. counsel, sec., 1982-84; sr. v.p., gen. counsel Milstein Properties Corp., 1985—; sr. v.p., gen counsel The Milstein Group Inc., 1992—. Mem. ABA, Assn. of Bar of City N.Y. Republican. Episcopalian. Club: University (N.Y.C.). Office: Milstein Properties Corp 1271 Avenue Of The Americas New York NY 10020-1300

PETZAL, DAVID ELIAS, editor, writer; b. N.Y.C., Oct. 21, 1941; s. Henry and Aline Born (Bixer) P.; m. Arlene Anne Taylor, May 29, 1974. B.A., Colgate U., 1963. Editor Maco Publs., N.Y.C., 1964-69; mng. editor Davis Publs., N.Y.C., 1969-70; features editor Hearst Publs., N.Y.C., 1970-72; mng. editor CBS Publs., N.Y.C., 1972-79, editor, 1979-83, exec. editor, 1983-87; exec. editor Times-Mirror Mags., N.Y.C., 1987—. Author: The .22 Rifle, 1972; editor: The Experts Book of the Shooting Sports, 1972, The Experts Book of Upland Game and Waterfowl Hunting, 1975, The Experts Book of Big-Game Hunting in North America, 1976, The Ency. of Sporting Firearms, 1991. Home: PO Box 219 Bedford NY 10506-0219 Office: Times Mirror Mags 2 Park Ave New York NY 10016-5675

PETZEL, FLORENCE ELOISE, textiles educator; b. Crosbyton, Tex., Apr. 1, 1911; d. William D. and A. Eloise (Punchard) P. PhB, U. Chgo., 1931, AM, 1934; PhD, U. Minn., 1954. Instr., Judson Coll., 1936-38; asst. prof. textiles Ohio State U., 1938-48; assoc. prof. U. Ala., 1950-54; prof. Oreg. State U., 1954-61, 67-75, 77, prof. emeritus, 1975—, dept. head, 1954-61, 67-75; prof., div. head U. Tex., 1961-63; prof. Tex. Tech U., 1963-67; vis. instr. Tex. State Coll. for Women, 1937; vis. prof. Wash. State U., 1967. Effie I. Raitt fellow, 1949-50. Mem. Met. Opera Guild, High Mus. Art, Sigma Xi, Phi Kappa Phi, Omicron Nu, Iota Sigma Pi, Sigma Delta Epsilon. Author Textiles of Ancient Mesopotamia, Persia and Egypt, 1987; contbr. articles to profl. jours. Home: 150 Downs Blvd Apt D205 Clemson SC 29631-2049

PETZOLD, ANITA MARIE, psychotherapist; b. Princeton, N.J., June 2, 1957; d. Charles Bernard and Kathleen Marie (McDonald) P. AS in Bus., Indian River C.C., Ft. Pierce, Fla., 1986; BS in Liberal Studies, Barry U., 1988; MS in Human Svcs. Adminstrn., Nova U., 1989, postgrad., 1989-91; PhD in Human Svcs. Adminstrn., LaSalle U., 1994. Lic. mental health counselor, Fla.; cert. addictions profl.; internat. cert. alcohol and drug abuse counselor; nat. cert. counselor; cert. employee assistance counselor; nat. cert. clin. mental health counselor; nat. cert. addictions counselor; cert. DUI instr. Admissions coord. The Palm Beach Inst., West Palm Beach, Fla., 1985-86; dir. admissions Heritage Health Corp., Jensen Beach, Fla., 1986-89; drug abuse strategy coord. Martin County Bd. of County Commrs., Stuart, Fla., 1989—; mem. Drug Resource Team for the 12th Congl. Dist., Fla., 1990—, Juvenile Justice Assn. of the 19th Jud. Ct., Fla., 1993—; grant writer in field. Vol. Hist. Soc. Martin County, Stuart, 1986—; mem. United Way Martin County, Stuart, 1993, mem. bd. dirs. Cmty. AIDS Adv. Project, Stuart, 1993; chmn. treatment com. Martin County Task Force on Substance Abused Children, Stuart, 1993—. Recipient Outstanding Cmty. Svc. award United Way Martin County, Stuart, 1993. Mem. NASW, Am. Mental Health Counselors Assn., Nat. Criminal Justice Assn., Nat. Assn. Alcoholism and Drug Abuse Counselors, Nat. Consortium Treatment Alternatives to St. Crime Programs, Am. Coll. Addiction Treatment Adminstrs., Am. Labor-Mgmt. Adminstrs., Fla. Alcohol and Drug Abuse Assn. Republican. Roman Catholic. Avocations: walking, reading. Office: Martin County Bd County Commrs 400 SE Osceola St Stuart FL 34994-2577

PETZOLD, CAROL STOKER, state legislator; b. St. Louis, July 28; d. Harold William and Mabel Lucille (Wilson) Stoker; m. Walter John Petzold, June 27, 1959; children: Ann, Ruth, David. BS, Valparaiso U., 1959. Tchr. John Muir Elem. Sch., Alameda, Calif., 1959-60, Parkwood Elem. Sch., Kensington, Md., 1960-62; legis. aide Md. Gen. Assembly, Annapolis, 1975-79; legis. asst. Montgomery County Bd. Edn., Rockville, Md., 1980; cmty. sch. coord. Parkland Jr. H.S., Rockville, 1981-87; mem. Md. Ho. of Dels., Annapolis, 1987—, mem. consl. and adminstrv. law com., 1987-93, mem. judiciary com., 1994—, vice chair Montgomery County del., 1995—; mem. transp. planning bd. Nat. Capitol Region, 1989—; vice chmn. assembly on fed. issues Nat. Conf. State Legislatures. Editor Child Care Sampler, 1974, Stoker Family Cookbook, 1976. Pres. Montgomery Child Care Assn., 1976-78; mem. Md. State Scholarship Bd., 1978-87, chmn. 1985-87; chmn. Legis. Com. Montgomery County Commn. for Children and Youth, 1979-84; mem., v.p. Luth. Social Services Nat. Capitol Area, Washington, 1980-86; mem. exec. com. coun. Montgomery United Way, 1981—. Recipient Statewide award Gov.'s Adv. Bd. on Homelessness, 1994; recognized for outstanding commitment to children U.S. Dept. HEW, 1980. Mem. AAUW (honoree Kensington br. 1971, honoree Md. div. 1981), Women's Polit. Caucus (chmn. Montgomery County 1981-83), Md. Women Legislators Caucus. Democrat. Lutheran. Home: 14113 Chadwick Ln Rockville MD 20853-2103

PEUGEOT, PATRICK, insurance executive; b. Paris, Aug. 3, 1937; s. Jacques Louis and Edith (Genoyer) P.; m. Catherine Dupont, 1963; children: Hubert, Thomas, Camille. Degree, Ecole Poly., Paris, 1959, Ecole Nat. D'Adminstrn., Paris, 1965. Ins. auditor Ministry of Fin., Paris, 1962-65; auditor Cour des Comptes, Paris, 1965-83; spl. asst. Bur. Planning, Paris, 1966-70; sr. v.p. EMC, Toulouse, France, 1970-72, Hachette Inc., Paris, 1972-74; exec. v.p. ops. AGF Life, Paris, 1974-78; exec. v.p. AGF Reins., Paris, 1979-82; pres. Caisse Cen. de Reassurance, Paris, 1983-85; chmn. Scor S.A., Paris, 1984-94, hon. chmn., 1994, 1994—; dir. SCOR U.S., 1994—; vice chmn., CEO La Mondiale, Paris, chmn., CEO, 1996—. Home: 82 Rue Notre Dame Champs, 75006 Paris France Office: La Mondiale, 22 Blvd Jalesherbes, 75008 Paris France

PEURA, ROBERT ALLAN, electrical and biomedical engineering educator; b. Worcester, Mass., Jan. 26, 1943; married; four children. BS, Worcester Poly. Inst., 1964; MS, Iowa State U., 1967, PhD, 1969. From asst. prof. to assoc. prof. edn./biomed. engring. Worcester (Mass.) Poly. Inst., 1968—; sir. dir. St. Vincent Hosp. Internship Ctr., Worcester, 1972—; lectr. biomed. engring. Med. Sch. U. Mass., 1974—; vis. assoc. prof. health sci. & technol. divsn. Mass. Inst. Tech., Cambridge, 1981-82. Mem. IEEE, Am. Heart Assn., Am. Soc. Engring. Edn., Assn. Advanced Med. Instrumentation. Office: Worcester Polytechnic Inst Applied Bioengineering Ctr 100 Institute Rd Worcester MA 01609-2247*

PEVEC, ANTHONY EDWARD, bishop; b. Cleve., Apr. 16, 1925; s. Anton and Frances (Darovec) P. MA, John Carroll U., Cleve., 1956; PhD, Western Res. U., Cleve., 1964. Ordained priest Roman Catholic Ch., 1950. Assoc. pastor St. Mary Church, Elyria, Ohio, 1950-52, St. Lawrence Ch., Cleve., 1952-53; rector-prin. Borromeo Sem. High Sch., Wickliffe, Ohio, 1953-75; adminstrv. bd. Nat. Cath. Edn. Assn., 1972-75; pastor St. Vitus Ch., Cleve., 1975-79; rector-pres. Borromeo Coll., Wickliffe, 1979-82; aux. bishop Diocese of Cleve., 1982—. Mem. v.p. Slovenian-Am. Heritage Found., Cleve., 1975—. Honoree, Heritage Found., Cleve., 1982; named Man of Yr., Fedn. Slovenian Nat. Homes, Cleve., 1985; inducted into Hall of Fame, St. Vitus Alumni Assn., 1989. Mem. Nat. Conf. Cath. Bishops (com. on vocations 1984-86, com. on pro-life activities, 1990-92, com. on sci. and human values 1993-96, com. on priestly formation 1993—), U.S. Cath. Conf. (nat. adv. coun. 1996—). Democrat. Roman Catholic. Avocations: reading; music. Home and Office: Diocese of Cleve 28700 Euclid Ave Wickliffe OH 44092-2527 *Ultimately I must always remember that the Lord is totally in control of my life, no matter how complicated it may seem to be. I am here to do the Lord's will,, and wherever I go I come to do His will.*

PEW, JOHN GLENN, JR., lawyer; b. Dallas, Apr. 18, 1932; s. John Glenn Sr. and Roberta (Haughton) P. BA, U. Tex., 1954. LLB, 1955. Bar: Tex. 1955, U.S. Dist. Ct. (no. dist.) Tex. 1959, U.S. Supreme Ct. 1959, U.S. Ct. Appeals (5th cir.) 1961, U.S. Ct. Appeals (10th cir.) 1982. Ptnr., Jackson & Walker, L.L.P., Dallas, 1964—. With USNR, 1955-58. Mem. Order of Coif, Phi Beta Kappa. Republican. Presbyterian. Office: Jackson & Walker LLP 901 Main St Ste 6000 Dallas TX 75202-3748

PEW, KEVIN DALE, association executive; b. San Jose, Apr. 4, 1962; s. Dale Duane and Barbara Jean (Cooper) P.; m. Nancy Ann Alderman, Oct. 12, 1996; children: Eric Scott, Janelle Kelly. BA, Kans. State U., 1985. Dir. show prodn. United Sports of Am., Kansas City, Mo., 1985—; tour dir. Monster Truck Challenge 91, Australia, 1991, asst. tour dir. Monster Truck Challenge 89. Prodn. dir. video: Monster Mania, 1986; event dir. video: Monster Truck Bloopers, 1992. Mem. Monster Truck Racing Assn. (tech. dir. 1989—), Nat. Mud Racing Assn. (Most Valuable Person 1989, Thom Bachman Meml. award 1989). Republican. Methodist. Avocations: golf, softball, video photography, world travel. Office: United Sports of Am 2310 W 75th St Prairie Village KS 66208

PEW, ROBERT ANDERSON, retired real estate corporation officer; b. Phila., Aug. 22, 1936; s. Arthur Edmund and Mary Elizabeth (Elliott) P.; children from previous marriage: Robert Anderson (dec.), James Cunningham, Glenn Edgar, Joan Elliott; m. Daria S. Decerio, June 19, 1993; 1 child, Richard Westerman. Student, Princeton U., 1954-56; B.S., Temple U., 1959; M.S. in Mgmt. (Alfred P. Sloan fellow), MIT, 1970; LL.D. (hon.), Widener U., 1982; D.P.S. (hon.), Temple U., 1983; L.H.D. (hon.), Gettysburg Coll., 1984. Ops. asst. prodn. div. Sun Oil Co., Premont, Tex., 1959-60; ops. asst. prodn. div. Sun Oil Co., Morgan City, La.; auditor internal audit dept. Sun Oil Co., Phila., 1960-65, staff asst. treasury dept., 1965-69, asst. to exec. v.p. corp. projects group, 1970-71, sec.-treas., mgr. financial control of products group, 1971-74, corp. sec., 1974-77; pres. Helios Capital Corp., 1977-96; CEO Radnor Corp., 1995-96; bd. dirs. Sun Co., Inc., Phila., Glenmede Corp., Phila., Pew Charitable Trusts, Phila., Glenmede Trust Co., Phila., Alex Brown Capital Adv. & Trust Co., Balt. Trustee Children's Hosp. Phila., vice chmn. 1991—, Bryn Mawr (Pa.) Coll., vice chmn., 1991—, Curtis Inst. Music, 1993—. Served Pa. Air N.G., 1956-59. Recipient R. Kelso Carter award Widener U., 1971. Mem. Aircraft Owners and Pilots Assn. (trustee, chmn. 1974-77, 85—, vice-chmn. 1979-85), Am. Hosp. Assn. (hon.), Union League Club, Seal Harbor Club (pres. 1992-96), Phila. Aviation Country Club, Merion Cricket Club, N.E. Harbor Fleet. Republican. Presbyterian. Home: 916 Muirfield Rd Bryn Mawr PA 19010-1921 Office: Sun Co Ten Penn Ctr 17th Flr 1801 Market St Philadelphia PA 19103-1628

PEW, ROBERT CUNNINGHAM, II, office equipment manufacturing company executive; b. Syracuse, N.Y., June 4, 1923; s. Robert Carroll and Bernice (Evans) P.; m. Mary Bonnell Idema, Aug. 23, 1947; children: Robert Cunningham, John Evans, Kate Bonnell. B.A., Wesleyan U., Middletown Conn.; HHD (hon.), Aquinas Coll., LLD (hon.). Labor relations exec. Doehler-Jarvis Corp., Grand Rapids, Mich., 1948-51; with Steelcase Inc., Grand Rapids, 1952—; exec. v.p. Steelcase Inc., 1964-66, pres., 1966-75, chmn. bd., pres., from 1975, formerly chmn., chief exec. officer, now chmn. bd.; dir. Old Kent Financial Corp., Foremost Corp. Am. Bd. control Grand Valley State Coll.; bd. dirs. Econ. Devel. Corp. Grand Rapids, Mich. Strategic Fund, Nat. Orgn. on Disability; mem. Gov.'s Commn. on Jobs and Econ. Devel. Served to 1st lt. USAAF, 1942-45; to capt. USAF, 1951-52. Decorated Purple Heart, Air medal with 2 oak leaf clusters. Mem. Grand Rapids C. of C. (dir.), Grand Rapids Employers Assn. (dir.), Chi Psi. Episcopalian. Clubs: Lost Tree (North Palm Beach Fla.); Peninsular; University, Kent Country (Grand Rapids). Home: 11307 Old Harbour Rd No Palm Beach FL 33408-3406 Office: PO Box 1967 Grand Rapids MI 49501-1967 Office: 901 44th St SE Grand Rapids MI 49508-7575

PEW, THOMAS W., JR., advertising executive; b. Houston, Sept. 14, 1938; s. Thomas William and Floranz (Leebove) P.; m. Laura Rice Neuhaus, June 10, 1964; children—Katherine, William, David. B.A., Cornell U., 1961. Editor, assoc. pub. Troy Daily News, Ohio, 1965-72; freelance writer, 1972-80; editor, pres. Am. West mag. Am. West Pub. Co., Tucson, 1981-89; pres. Hawkeye West, Tucson, 1986—; advt. dir. Sturm Ruger & Co., 1986—; pres. Merlin Inc., Advt. Agy., Inc., 1991—. Contbr. articles to Smithsonian Mag., Am. Heritage Mag., numerous others. Served with inf. U.S. Army, 1961-63. Avocations: skiing; guitar; backpacking.

PÉWÉ, TROY LEWIS, geologist, educator; b. Rock Island, Ill., June 28, 1918; s. Richard E. and Olga (Pomrank) P.; m. Mary Jean Hill, Dec. 21, 1944; children: David Lee, Richard Hill, Elizabeth Anne. AB in Geology, Augustana Coll., 1940; MS, State U. Iowa, 1942; PhD, Stanford U., 1952; DSc (hon.), U. Alaska, 1991. Head dept. geology Augustana Coll., 1942-46; civilian instr. USAAC, 1943-44; instr. geomorphology Stanford, 1946; geologist Alaskan br. U.S. Geol. Survey, 1946-93; chief glacial geologist U.S. Nat. Com. Internat. Geophys. Year, Antarctica, 1958; prof. geology, head dept. U. Alaska, 1958-65; prof. geology Ariz. State U., 1965-88, prof. emeritus, 1988—, chmn. dept., 1965-76; dir. Mus. Geology, 1976-97, dir. emeritus, 1997—; lectr. in field, 1942—; mem. organizing com. 1st Internat. Permafrost Conf. Nat. Acad. Sci., 1962-63, chmn. U.S. planning com. 2d Internat. Permafrost Conf., 1972-74, chmn. U.S. del. 3d Internat. Permafrost Conf., 1978, chmn. U.S. organizing com. 4th Internat. Permafrost Conf., 1979-83; com. to study Good Friday Alaska Earthquake Nat. Acad. Scis., 1964-70, mem. glaciological com. polar research bd., 1971-73, founding chmn. permafrost com., mem. polar research bd., 1975-81; organizing chmn. Internat. Assn. Quarternary Research Symposium and Internat. Field Trip Alaska, 1965; mem. Internat. Commn. Periglacial Morophology, 1964-71, 80-88 ; mem. polar research bd. NRC, 1975-78, late Cenozoic study group, sci. com. Antarctic research, 1977-80. Contbr. numerous papers to profl. lit. Recipient U.S. Antarctic Svc. medal, 1966, Outstanding Achievement award Augustana Coll., 1969, Disting. Alumnus award U. Iowa, 1994, Internat. Geophysics medal USSR Nat. Acad. Sci., 1985; named 2d hon. internat. fellow Chinese Soc. Glaciology and Geocryology, 1985. Fellow AAAS (pres. Alaska div. 1956, com. on arid lands 1972-79), Geol. Soc. Am. (editorial bd. 1975-82, chmn. cordilleran sect. 1979-80, chmn. geomorphology div. 1981-82), Arctic Inst. N.Am. (bd. govs. 1969-74, exec. bd. 1972-73), Iowa Acad. Sci., Ariz. Acad. Sci. (pres. 1982-83); mem. Assn. Geology Tchrs., Glaciological Soc., N.Z. Antarctic Soc., Am. Soc. Engring. Geologists, Internat. Permafrost Assn. (founding v.p. 1983, pres. 1988-93), Am. Quaternary Assn. (pres. 1984-86), Internat. Geog. Union. Club: Cosmos. Home: 538 E Fairmont Dr Tempe AZ 85282-3723

PEYSER, JOSEPH LEONARD, historical researcher, author, translator; b. N.Y.C., Oct. 19, 1925; s. Samuel and Sadye (Quinto) P.; m. Julia Boxer, May 30, 1948; children: Jay Randall, Jan Ellen. B.A., Duke U., 1947, M.A., 1949; profl. diploma, Columbia U., 1955; postgrad., U. Nancy, France, 1949-50; Ed.D., NYU, 1965. Prof., chmn. fgn. langs., adminstr. Nancy (France) École Normale, 1949-50; Tchr., chmn. fgn. langs. Monroe (N.Y.) Pub. Schs., 1951-54, Uniondale (N.Y.) Pub. Schs., 1954-61; asst. high sch. prin. Plainview, N.Y., 1961-63; mem. faculty Hofstra U., Hempstead, N.Y., 1963-68; assoc. prof. edn. Hofstra U., 1966-68; asst. dean, then asso. dean Hofstra U. (Sch. Edn.), 1964-66; interim dean Sch. Edn. Hofstra U., 1966-68; dean acad. affairs, prof. French and edn. Dowling Coll., Oakdale, N.Y., 1968-70; v.p. acad. affairs, dean faculty Dowling Coll., 1970-73; prof. French and edn. Ind. U., South Bend, 1973-94, prof. emeritus French, 1994—, dean faculties, 1973-75, chmn. fgn. lang. dept., 1987-89; vis. asst. prof. NYU, 1964-66; adj. asst. prof. L.I. U., 1961-63; prin. researcher, translator French Michilimackinac Rsch. Project, Mich., 1991—; rsch. reviewer NEH, 1994—. Author: Letters from New France, 1981, rev. edit. Letters from New France: The Upper Country, 1686-1783, 1992; co-author: The Fox Wars: The Mesquakie Challenge to New France, 1993, Jacques Legardeur de Saint-Pierre: Officer, Gentleman, Entrepreneur, 1996, On the Eve of the Conquest: Chevalier Raymond's Critique of New France in 1754, 1997; translator Fort St. Joseph Manuscripts, 1978, William Henry Harrison's French Correspondence, 1994; contbr. profl. publs. Bd. dirs. South Bend Symphony, 1979-86. Served with USNR, 1943-46. Recipient Founders Day award NYU, 1966, State Hist. Soc. of Wis. Hesseltine award, 1991, French Colonial Hist. Soc. Heggoy Book prize, 1994; tchg. fellow French Ministry Edn., 1949-50, Lilly Endowment faculty fellow, 1985-86, NEH fellow, 1988, 94-95, Lundquist faculty fellow, 1989-90; Newberry Libr. rsch. assoc., 1985-86. Mem. Ind. Hist. Soc. (Thornbrough award 1996), Ind. Assn. Historians, Hist. Soc. Mich., French Colonial Hist. Soc. (v.p. 1988-91, exec. com. 1988-94), Ctr. for French Colonial Studies.

PEYSER, PETER A., former congressman, investment management company executive; b. Cedarhurst, N.Y., Sept. 7, 1921; s. Percy A. and Rubye (Hoeflich) P.; m. Marguerite Richards, Dec. 23, 1949; children: Penny, Carolyn, Peter, James, Tommy. BA, Colgate U., 1943. Mgr. Mut. N.Y. Ins. Co., N.Y.C., 1956-70; mem. 92d Congress from 25th N.Y. dist., mem. Edn. and Labor Com.; mem. 92d-93d-94 Rep. 96th-97th Dem., mem. Edn. and Labor Com., Adminstrn. Com.; mayor City of Irvington, N.Y., 1963-70; nat. dir., v.p. Taft-Hartley Pension Funds. With U.S. Army, 1943-46. Decorated Bronze Star; Belgian Fourragere. Episcopalian. Home: Sunnyside Ln Irvington NY 10533

PEYTON, DONALD LEON, retired standards association executive; b. Portland, Oreg., May 5, 1925; s. Bernard Thomas and Nelle (Moses) P.; m. Jane Frances Kirkman, Aug. 26, 1950; children: Patrick Philip, James Allen. Student, Mont. State U., 1946-47; BA, No. Colo. U., 1950. Civilian edn. specialist USAF, 1951-56; engaged in real estate Cheyenne, Wyo., 1956-57; adminstrv. asst. to congressman, 1957-60; with U.S. C. of C., 1960-66, gen. mgr. govt. relations, 1965-66; pres. Am. Nat. Standards Inst., Inc., 1966-89, ret., 1989, Peyton Assocs., Standards Cons., White Plains, N.Y., 1989—; Lectr. govt. bus. relations Am. U., 1965-66, Amos Tuck Sch., Dartmouth, 1965—. Author: Standards and Trade in the 1990's; author monographs. Pres., Cheyenne Jr. C. of C., 1955-56. Mem. Am. Soc. Assn. Execs., Old Guard of White Plains. Home and Office: 2 Beverly Rd White Plains NY 10605-3306 *My personal philosophy of life parallels that of my philosophy regarding voluntary organizations. In personal and professional life there is no hope for the self-satisfied individual or the self-satisfied organization.*

PEYTON, WILLIAM MAUPIN, financial services executive, educator; b. Richmond, Ky., Jan. 5, 1932; s. Russell Page and Amanda Thomas (Bogie) P.; m. Margaret Christine Dahl, Sept. 8, 1956; children: Michael William, Stephen Todd, John Patrick. B.S. in Bus. Adminstrn., UCLA, 1957; M.B.A. in Fin., U. So. Calif., 1967; postgrad., Harvard U., 1980. Office mgr., cost acct. Ralphs Grocery Co., Los Angeles, 1957-62; cost acctg. supr. Lockheed Air Terminal, Burbank, Calif., 1962-69; chief acct. Lockheed Air Terminal, Burbank, Calif, 1969-72, treas., 1972-80, exec. v.p., 1980-86, also dir.; treas. Lockheed Air Terminal, Panama City, 1976—; pres. Peyco, Inc., Burbank, 1986—; asst. prof. Glendale (Calif.) Coll., 1969—. Served with USAF, 1951-55. Mem. Inst. Mgmt. Accts. (dir. 1963). Republican. Episcopalian. Home: 12525 E Lupine Ave Scottsdale AZ 85259-3447

PEZ, GUIDO PETER, research chemist; b. Fiume, Italy, Feb. 10, 1941; married, 1966; 3 children. BSc, U. NSW, 1962; PhD in Chemistry, Monash U., Australia, 1967. Fellow McMaster U., 1967-69; rsch. chemist Allied Chem. Corp., 1969-74, sr. rsch. chemist, 1974-78, rsch. assoc., 1978-81; sr. rsch. assoc. Air Products & Chems., Inc., 1981-93, chief scientist, 1993—. Recipient award in Inorganic Chem. Am. Chem. Soc., 1995. Mem. Am. Chem. Soc. (Award in Inorganic Chemistry 1995). Achievements include research in synthetic inorganic and organometallic chemistry applied to catalysis, selective gas absorption materials, gas separation membranes, organofluorine chemistry, fluorinating reagents for synthesizing bio-active compounds. Office: Air Products & Chemicals Inc 7201 Hamilton Blvd Allentown PA 18195-1526

PEZACKA, EWA HANNA, biochemist, educator; b. Lodz, Poland, May 22, 1949; came to U.S., 1981; d. Wincenty and Janina (Andrzejewska) Pezacki; m. Jerzy Perkitny, Mar. 14, 1981. BA, Coll. of Helena Modrzejewska, Poznan, 1965; MS with highest honors, U. Adam Mickiewicz, Poznan, 1971; PhD with highest honors, U. Agrl., Poznan, 1976; postgrad., Case Western Res. U., 1981-85. Faculty asst. Biochemistry Inst. U. Agriculture, Poznan, 1971-74, sr. faculty asst., 1974-77, asst. prof., 1977-81; rsch. assoc. Case Western Res. U. Sch. Medicine, Cleve., 1981-85, sr. rsch. assoc., 1985-88; project staff Dept. Lab. Hematology, Cleve. Clinic Found., 1988-91, asst. staff, 1991-92, asst. staff dept. brain and vascular rsch., 1993-95, asst. staff dept. cell biology, 1993-95; assoc. rsch. scientist Allegheny-Singer Rsch. Inst., Pitts., 1995—; assoc. prof. Allegheny U. of the Med. Scis., 1995—; vis. asst. U. Humboldt, Berlin-Buche, Germany, 1973-74; co-investigator Inst. Food Tech., Poznan, 1977-81, MacDonald Hosp. for Women, Cleve., 1985-88; presenter in field. Contbr. more than 60 articles to profl. jours. Fellow Univ. Humboldt, Berlin, 1973-74; grantee Polish Acad. Sci./Polish Soc. Biochemistry, 1976, NIH, 1991—, travel grantee Internat. Union Biochemistry, 1991; recipient Excellence in Biochemistry award Polish Acad. Sci., 1971, Norwegian Rsch. Coun. Internat. award, 1994. Mem. Am. Chem. Soc., Am. Soc. for Biochemistry and Molecular Biology, Internat. Union Biochemistry, N.Y. Acad. Sci., Polish Soc. Biochemistry. Avocations: sailing, horse-back riding, skiing, yard work and travel. Office: ASRI/Dept Human Genetics 11th Floor South Tower 320 E North Ave Pittsburgh PA 15212-4756

PEZESHKI, KAMBIZ A., metallurgical engineer; b. Tabriz, Iran, Sept. 30, 1949; came to U.S., 1970, naturalized; s. Amir Aziz and Azam (Mazi) P.; m. Shiron Cashmir Wisenbaker, Apr. 7, 1976; children: Shahene A., Shahla J. BS in Metall. Engring., U. Utah, 1977; MBA in Mktg. and Human Rels., U. Phoenix, 1983. Cert. tchr., Ariz. Process metallurgist Amax, Inc., Golden, Colo., 1977-79; process, rsch. engr. Cities Svcs. Co./Oxidental, Miami, Ariz., 1979-84; tech. svcs. engr. Am. Cyanamid, Wayne, N.J., 1984-87; mgr. western mining Rhone-Poulenc, Inc., Salt Lake City, 1987-93; nat. sales engr. Hychem, Inc., Salt Lake City, 1993—; polymerization cons. RTZ/Kennecott Copper, Salt Lake City, 1989—. Fund raiser Jake Garn for Senate, Salt Lake City, 1976; fund raiser, motivator Barry Goldwater for Senate re-election, 1980-81; vol. Ted Wilson for Gov., Salt Lake City, 1988. Mem. Am. Mining Engrs. Soc. Republican. Presbyterian. Avocations: wind surfing, running, racquetball, tennis, total fitness.

PEZZELLA, JERRY JAMES, JR., investment and real estate corporation executive; b. Chesapeake, Va., Sept. 30, 1937; s. Jerry James Sr. and Mabel (Aydlett) P.; m. Carolyn Blades; children: James M., Stanley J., Julie Pezzella Scanlon. BS, U. Richmond, 1963; MBA, U. Pa., 1964. Asst. v.p. Va. Nat. Bank (now Nations Bank), Norfolk, 1964-68; chmn. bd., pres. First Am. Investment Corp., First Ga. Investment Corp., Atlanta, 1968-74; v.p. Great Am. Investment Corp., Atlanta, 1974-78; sr. exec. v.p., 1984-85; exec. v.p. Equity Fin. & Mgmt. Co., Chgo., 1978—; pres., chmn. bd. First Capital Fin. Corp., Chgo., 1983-85; pres. GAFGI Holdings Inc., Chgo., 1983—; chmn. bd. 1st Property Mgmt. Corp., 1990-92; bd. dirs. Great Am. Mgmt. and Investment, Inc., Chgo., Nat. Multi Housing Coun., 1992-94, mem. exec. com. Bd. dirs., exec. com. Nat. Multi-Housing Coun., 1991-93. Mem. River Club (Chgo.), Met. Club (Chgo.), Cherokee Golf and Country Club (Murphy, N.C.). Office: 2 N Riverside Plz Ste 700 Chicago IL 60606-2600

PFAELZER, MARIANA R., federal judge; b. L.A., Feb. 4, 1926. AB, U. Calif., 1947; LLB, UCLA, 1957. Bar: Calif. 1958. Assoc. Wyman, Bautzer, Rothman & Kuchel, 1957-69, ptnr., 1969-78; judge U.S. Dist. Ct. (ctrl. dist.) Calif., 1978—; mem. Jud. Conf. Adv. Com. on Fed. Rules of Civil Procedure. pres., v.p., dir. Bd. Police Commrs. City of L.A., 1974-78; bd. vis. Loyola Law Sch. UCLA Alumnus award for Profl. Achievement, 1979, named Alumna of Yr., UCLA Law Sch., 1980, U. Calif. Santa Barbara Disting. Alumnus award, 1983. Mem. ABA, Calif. Bar Assn. (local adminstrv. com., spl. com. study rules procedure 1972, joint subcom. profl. ethics and computers and the law coms. 1972, profl. ethics com. 1972-74, spl. com. juvenile justice, women's rights subcom. human rights sect.), L.A. County Bar Assn. (spl. com. study rules procedure state bar 1974), mem. Judicial Conf. Advisory Comm. on Federal Rules of Civil Procedure. Office: US Dist Ct 312 N Spring St Ste 152 Los Angeles CA 90012-4703*

PFAFF, DONALD W., neurobiology and behavior educator; b. Rochester, N.Y., Dec. 9, 1939; s. Norman J. and Eleanor W. (Blakeslee) P.; married Stephanie Pfaff; children: Robin W., Alexander S., Douglas B. AB magna cum laude, Harvard U., 1961; PhD, MIT, 1965. Rsch. assoc. dept. psychology MIT, Cambridge, 1965-66; trainee Marine Biol. Lab., Woods Hole, Mass., 1966; postdoctoral fellow Rockefeller U., N.Y.C., 1966-68, staff scientist biomed. div. population coun., 1968-69, asst. prof., 1969-71, assoc. prof., 1971-78, prof., 1978—. Author: Estrogens and Brain Function, 1980; editor: The Physiological Mechanisms of Motivation, 1982, Ethical Questions in Brain and Behavior, 1983, Molecular Neurobiology: Endocrine Approaches, 1987, Drives, 1997. Recipient Pres.'s award MIT, 1962-63; Woodrow Wilson fellow, 1961-62, fellow Neuroscis. Rsch. Program, 1969. Fellow Am. Acad. Arts and Scis.; mem. NAS, Am. Physiol. Soc., Soc. for Neurosci., Endocrine Soc., Sigma Xi. Office: Rockefeller U 1230 York Ave New York NY 10021-6307

PFAFF, WILLIAM WALLACE, medical educator; b. Rochester, N.Y., Aug. 14, 1930; s. Norman Joseph and Eleanor Blakesley (Wells) P.; m. Patricia Ann Clark; children: Nancy, Karen, Margaret, Mary Catherine. AB, Harvard U., 1952; MD, SUNY, 1956. Intern U. Chgo., 1956-58; sr. asst. surgeon NIH, Bethesda, Md., 1958-60; resident Stanford U. Med. Ctr., Palo Alto, Calif., 1960-65; asst. prof. U. Fla., Gainesville, 1965-68, assoc. prof., 1968-71, prof. surgery, 1971-95, prof. emeritus, adj. prof., 1995—, dir. organ transplant programs, 1971-95; bd. dirs. United Network for Organ Sharing, Richmond, Va., pres. elect, 1997-98; pres., com. chair Southeastern Organ Procurement Found., Richmond, 1973-95. Fellow Am. Coll. Surgeons; mem. Am. Surg. Assn., Am. Soc. Transplant Surgeons, So. Surg. Assn., Transplantation Soc., Alachua County Med. Soc. (pres. 1977-78). Home: 2445 NW 15 Pl Gainesville FL 32605 Office: U Fla Dept Surgery PO Box 100286 Gainesville FL 32610-0286

PFALMER, CHARLES ELDEN, secondary school educator; b. Trinidad, Colo., Aug. 9, 1937; s. Arthur Joseph and Nettie Mildred (Powell) P.; m. Margaret Christine La Duke, June 25, 1964; children: Betholyn Ann, Garret. AA, Trinidad State Jr. Coll., 1957; BA, Adams State Coll., 1959, MA, 1962. Cert. tchr., Colo. Tchr. Olathe (Colo.) H.S., 1959-60, Yuma (Colo.) H.S., 1960—; instr. Northeastern Jr. Coll., Sterling, Colo., 1980-97. Precinct chmn. Dem. Orgn., Yuma, 1992-96, del. to state conv., 1984-86, 88-90, 92-94, 96; ch. treas. Yuma Episcopal Ch., 1985—; v.p. Citizens Action Com., Yuma, 1994. Recipient Outstanding Educator award West Yuma Sch. Dist., 1987, Colo. State Ho. of Reps., 1987, Local Disting. Svc. award Colo. H.S. Activities Assn., 1991, Outstanding Cmty. Svc. award Colo. Athletic Dirs. Assn., 1990. Mem. NEA, Am. Polit. Collectors, Nat. Coun. for the Social Studies, Colo. Edn. Assn., Phi Delta Kappa. Avocations: collecting political buttons, antiques, sports. Home: 321 E 10th Ave Yuma CO 80759-3001 Office: Yuma HS 1000 S Albany St Yuma CO 80759-3008

PFALTZGRAFF, ROBERT LOUIS, JR., political scientist, educator; b. Phila., June 1, 1934; s. Robert L. and Mary (Warriner) P.; m. Diane A. Kressler, May 20, 1967; children: Suzanne Diane, Robert Louis III. B.A. with honors, Swarthmore Coll., 1956; M.B.A., U. Pa., 1958, Ph.D. in Polit. Sci. (Penfield fellow), 1964; M.A. in Internat. Relations, 1959. Research assoc. Fgn. Policy Research Inst., 1964-71; asst. prof. polit. sci. U. Pa., Phila., 1964-70; dep. dir. Fgn. Policy Research Inst., 1971-73; assoc. prof. internat. politics Fletcher Sch. Law and Diplomacy, Tufts U., Medford, Mass., 1971-78, prof. internat. politics, 1978-83, Shelby Cullom Davis prof. internat. security studies, 1983—; vis. lectr. Fgn. Service Inst. Dept. State, 1970-71; George C. Marshall prof. Coll. of Europe, Bruges, Belgium, 1970-71; pres. Inst. for Fgn. Policy Analysis, Cambridge, Mass., 1976—; short term acad. guest prof. Nat. Defense Coll., Tokyo, Japan, 1981; pres. U.S. Strategic Inst., Washington, 1977-79. Author: Britain Faces Europe, 1957-1967, 1969, Politics and the International System, 1969, The Atlantic Community: A Complex Balance, 1969, The Study of International Relations, 1977, The Cruise Missile: Bargaining Chip or Defense Bargain, 1977, Power Projection and the Long Range Combat Aircraft: Missions, Capabilities and Alternative Designs, 1981, Contending Theories of International Relations: A Comprehensive Survey, 1981; co-editor: Contrasting Approaches to Strategic Arms Control, 1974, SALT: Implications for Arms Control in the 1970s, 1973, The Other Arms Race: New Technologies and Non Nuclear Conflict, 1975, Arms Transfers to the Third World: The Military Build-up in Less Industrial Countries, 1978, Intelligence Policy and National Security, 1981, Projection of Power: Perspectives, Perceptions and Problems, 1982, (with Ra'anan) The U.S. Defense Mobilization Infrastructure: Problems and Priorities, 1983, International Dimensions of Space, 1984, National Security Policy: The Decision-Making Process, 1984, The Peace Movements in Europe and the United States, 1985, co-author: American Foreign Policy: FDR to Reagan, 1986, co-editor: Selling the Rope to Hang Capitalism? The Debate on West-East Trade and Technology Transfer, 1987, Emerging Doctrines and Technologies: Implications for Global and Regional Political-Military Balance, 1987, Protracted Warfare--The Third World Arena: A Dimension of U.S.-Soviet Conflict, 1988, Guerrilla Warfare and Counter-Insurgency: U.S.-Soviet Policy in the third World, 1988, U.S. Defense Policy in an Era of Constrained Resources, 1989; co-author: Contending Theories of International Relations: A Comprehensive Study, 1990; co-editor: National Security Decisions: The Participants Speak, 1990, The United States Army: Challenges and Missions for the 1990s, 1991, The Future of Air Power in the Aftermath of the Gulf War, 1992, Naval Forward Presence and the National Military Strategy, 1993, Ethnic Conflict and Regional Instability: Implications for U.S. Policy and Army Roles and Missions, 1994, Naval Expeditionary Forces and Power Projection: Into the 21st Century, 1994, Long-Range Bombers and the Role of Airpower in the New Century, 1995, Roles and Missions of Special Operations Forces in the Aftermath of the Cold War, 1995, others; contbr. articles to scholarly jours. Guggenheim fellow, 1968-69; Relm Found. grantee, 1969. Mem. Internat. Studies Assn., Coun. Fgn. Rels., Internat. Inst. Strategic Studies, Capitol Hill Club, Army and Navy Club (Washington). Home: 663 Wallace Dr Straford PA 19087 Office: Inst Fgn Policy Analysis 675 Massachusetts Ave Ste 10 Cambridge MA 02139-3309*

PFANSTIEL PARR, DOROTHEA ANN, interior designer; b. San Antonio, Nov. 10, 1931; d. Herbert Andraes and Ethel Missouri (Turner) Pfanstiel; m. Thurmond Charles Parr, Jr., Sept. 15, 1951; children: Thurmond Charles, III, Richard Marshall. AA, Coll. San Antonio, 1951. Asst. dean evening divsn. Alamo C.C., San Antonio, 1951; tchr., cons., dir. Humpty Dumpty Early Childhood Devel. Ctr., San Antonio, 1951-58; exec. sec., cons. Thurmond C. Parr, Jr. & Co., San Antonio, 1960-61; founder, pres. Creative Designs, Ltd., San Antonio, 1962—; liaison, coord. Internat. Students Lang. Sch., Lackland AFB, San Antonio, 1959-65. Adv., cons. Urban Renewal Inner City San Antonio, 1959-61. Named Notable Woman of Tex., Awards and Hons. Soc. Am., 1984-85. Republican. Presbyterian. Avocations: travel, swimming, reading, studying, walking. Office: Creative Designs Ltd PO Box 6822 San Antonio TX 78209

PFAU, GEORGE HAROLD, JR., stockbroker; b. Milw., May 7, 1924; s. George Harold and Elisabeth C. (Hunter) P.; m. Anne Elizabeth Mayhew; 1 child, George Harold III; children by previous marriage: Mary D., Peter W., Elizabeth C. B.S., Yale U., 1948. Tchr., 1948-49; with Fleishhacker Paper Box Co., San Francisco, 1952-54; salesman A.G. Becker & Co., San Francisco, 1954-55; v.p., sec., dir. Carl W. Stern & Co., San Francisco, 1955-57; with White Weld & Co. Inc., San Francisco, 1957-78; 1st v.p. corp. fin. dept. Blyth Eastman Dillon, San Francisco, 1978-79; sr. v.p. Paine Webber, San Francisco, 1979—; bd. dirs. IA Dist. Argl. Assn. Bd. dirs. The Guardsmen, 1966-67, Pathfinder Fund, 1974-82, San Francisco Zool. Soc., 1979-80; trustee Thacher Sch., Ojai, Calif., 1967-76, Town Sch., San Francisco, 1966-70; pres. Planned Parenthood San Francisco-Alameda County, 1968-69, bd. dirs., 1965—; chmn. Lincoln Club of No. Calif, 1993-95, mem., 1982—; chmn. Citizens for Better San Francisco. With C.E. AUS, 1942-44; with Am. Field Svc., 1944-45. Mem. Kappa Beta Phi, San Francisco (Calif.) Bond Club, Bohemian Club (San Francisco), Calif. Tennis Club. Office: Paine Webber 555 California St 32d Fl San Francisco CA 94104-1502

PFAU, RICHARD ANTHONY, college president; b. N.Y.C., Feb. 19, 1942; s. Hugo and Irene Beatrice P.; m. Nancy Ann DiPace, Sept. 12, 1964; children: Bradley Madison, Aleksandra Nicole. AB, Hamilton Coll., 1964; MA, U. Va., 1973, PhD, 1975. Systems analyst Equitable Life Ins. Co., N.Y.C., 1964-66; asst. prof. history Dickinson Coll., Carlisle, Pa., 1975-80; assoc. prof., assoc. dean U. Miami, Coral Gables, Fla., 1980-85; dean of faculty, provost Emory (Va.) and Henry Coll., 1985-93; pres. Ill. Coll., Jacksonville, Ill., 1993—. Author: No Sacrifice Too Great: The Life of Lewis L. Strauss, 1985. Contbr. articles, book revs. to profl. publs. Vestryman St. Thomas Episc. Ch., Abingdon, Va.; chmn., sec.-treas., exec. com., bd. dirs. Va. Found. for Humanities and Pub. Policy, Exec. Com. Fedn. Ind. Ill. Colls. and Univs. Capt. USAF, 1966-71. DuPont fellow, 1974-75; Hoover fellow, 1982. Mem. Omicron Delta Kappa, Alpha Psi Omega, Pi Delta Epsilon, Union League Club (Chgo.). Home: Barnes House 310 Lockwood Pl Jacksonville IL 62650-2225 Office: Ill Coll Pres Office Jacksonville IL 62650

PFAUTCH, ROY, minister, public affairs consultant; b. St. Louis, June 24, 1936; s. Floyd and Bertha Edna (Berghoefer) P. AB, Washington U., St. Louis, 1957; BD, Princeton Theol. Sem., 1961. Ordained to ministry Presbyn. Ch., 1961. Asst. to pres. Princeton Theol. Sem., 1961-63; pres. Civic Service, Inc., St. Louis and Washington, 1963—; mem. adv. com. on voluntary fgn. aid, U.S. Dept. State, 1981-83, Nat. Service Council, 1982-83. Del. Rep. Nat. Conv., Dallas, 1984, Houston, 1992, San Diego, 1996; co-chmn. Nat. Day Prayer, 1985, 89, hon. co-chmn. Presdl. Inaugural, Washington, 1985, 89; chmn. Salute to Pres. Dinner, Washington, 1986; bd. overseers Reagan scholars program Eureka (Ill.) Coll., 1982-89; mem. presbytery Elijah Prish Lovejoy, United Presbyn. Ch., 1961—; bd. dirs. St. Louis Pub. Library System, 1980-86; del. XXIV Olympics, Seoul, 1988; mem. adv. bd. Internat. Ctr. Tropical Ecology, 1991—; bd. dirs. Nat. Found. Improvement of Edn., 1992—. Mem. AMA (hon.), Internat. Assn. Polit. Cons., Am. Assn. Polit. Cons. (v.p., sec., pres. 1980-84) Am. Assn. Pub. Opinion Research, Mktg. Research Assn., Coun. Pub. Polls. Clubs: St. Louis, St. Louis Country, 1929 'F' St. (Washington). Avocations: horse riding, gardening, reading. Home: 52 Portland Pl Saint Louis MO 63108-1242 Office: Civic Srvc Inc 1 Mercantile Ctr Ste 3101 Saint Louis MO 63101-1643 also: Civic Srvc Inc 1050 Connecticut Ave NW Ste 870 Washington DC 20036-5303

PFEFFER, DAVID H., lawyer; b. N.Y.C., Mar. 15, 1935. B. Chem. Engring., CCNY, 1956; J.D., NYU, 1961, LL.M. in Trade Regulation, 1967. Bar: N.Y. 1961. With patent dept. U.S. Rubber Co., Wayne, N.J., 1957-61; assoc. Watson, Leavenworth, Kelton & Taggart, N.Y.C., 1961-63; assoc. Morgan & Finnegan, N.Y.C., 1963-70, ptnr., 1971—; village prosecutor Roslyn Harbor, N.Y., 1976-78, village justice, 1979—; panel of arbitrators Am. Arbitration Assn. Mem. ABA (litigation sect.), N.Y. State Bar Assn., Assn. Bar City N.Y., Nassau County Bar Assn. (coms. on patent and trademarks, fed. practice), Am. Intellectual Property Law Assn. (com. alt. dispute resolution), N.Y. Patent Trademark and Copyright Law Assn., N.Y. State Magistrates Assn., Nassau County Magistrates Assn., Order of Coif. Office: Morgan & Finnegan LLP 345 Park Ave New York NY 10154-0004

PFEFFER, EDWARD ISRAEL, educational administrator; b. Newark, July 1, 1914; s. Jacob and Fannie Bessie (Fisher) P.; m. Anna Chinich, July 14, 1940; children—Cynthia Roberta, Bruce Paul. B.S., N.Y. U., 1937; M.A., N.J. State Tchrs. Coll., Montclair, 1942; Ed.D., Rutgers U., 1954. Tchr. Abington Ave. Sch., Newark, 1937-46; vice prin. Warren St. Sch., 1946-53; prin. Monmouth St. and Coes Pl. schs., 1953-57, Robert Treat Jr. High and Elem. Sch., 1957-64; asst. supt. spl. services Newark Dist. Pub. Schs., 1964-67, dep. supt., 1967-72, 73—, acting supt., 1972-73. Contbr. articles profl. publs. Commr. Newark Sr. Citizens Commn., 1967—; mem. Newark Juvenile Problems Commn., 1958-62; chmn. Children's Resources Commn., Council Social Agys., 1955-60; mem. exec. bd. Family and Children's Div., 1955-62; mem. Newark Commn. for UN Week, 1962—, Newark Disaster Com., 1967—, Bd. Edn., Temple B'nai Abraham, Essex County, N.J., 1964-65; Mem. exec. bd. Newark Central Community Council; mem. adv. bd. Essex County Tech. Sch. Recipient citations Newark Assn. Dirs. and Suprs., 1973, citations Newark Title I Central Parents Council, 1973. Mem. Newark Pub. Sch. Prins. Assn. (pres. 1963-64), N.J. Elementary Sch. Press Assn. (pres.), Congress Parents and Tchrs. (life), NEA (life), Am., N.J. assns. sch. adminstrs., Newark Schoolmens Assn. (bd. govs., named Outstanding Schoolman of Year 1972-73), Columbia Scholastic Press Assn. (v.p., Gold Key 1948), Urban League, NAACP, Phi Delta Kappa. Home: 507 Clinton Pl Newark NJ 07112-1703 Office: 2 Cedar St Newark NJ 07102-3015

PFEFFER, JEFFREY, business educator; b. St. Louis, July 23, 1946; s. Newton Stuart and Shirlee (Krisman) P.; m. Kathleen Frances Fowler, July 23, 1986. BS, MS, Carnegie Mellon U., 1968; PhD, Stanford U., 1972. Mem. tech. staff Research Analysis Corp., McLean, Va., 1968-69; asst. prof. U. Ill., Champaign, 1971-73; from asst. prof. to assoc. prof. U. Calif., Berkeley, 1973-79; prof. Grad. Sch. Bus., Stanford U., Calif., 1979—; vis. prof. Harvard U. Sch. Bus., Boston, 1981-82; dir., mem. compensation com. Portola Packaging, Inc. Author: The External Control of Organizations, 1978, Organizational Design, 1978, Power in Organizations, 1981, Organizations and Organization Theory, 1982 (Terry Book award 1984), Managing with Power, 1992, Competitive Advantage Through People, 1994, New Directions for Organization Theory, 1997. Fellow Acad. Mgmt. (bd. govs. 1984-86, New Concept award 1979, Richard D. Irwin award for scholarly contbns. to mgmt. 1989); mem. Am. Sociol. Assn., Indsl. Rels. Rsch. Assn. Jewish. Avocations: cooking, music. Home: 5 Burnett Ave San Francisco CA 94131-3317 Office: Stanford U Grad Sch of Bus Stanford CA 94305

PFEFFER, PHILIP ELLIOT, biophysicist; b. N.Y.C., Apr. 8, 1941; s. Charles and Della (Smith) P.; m. Judith Stadlen, Dec. 22, 1962; children: Charles, Ari, Shira. AB, Hunter Coll., 1962; MS, Rutgers U., 1964, PhD, 1966. Rsch. asst. dept. chemistry Rutgers U., New Brunswick, N.J., 1964-66; rsch. fellow dept. chemistry U. Chgo., 1966-68; rsch. scientist Ea. Regional Rsch. Ctr. USDA, Phila., 1968-88, rsch. leader Ea. Regional Rsch. Ctr., 1976-88, lead scientist Ea. Regional Rsch. Ctr., 1988—; editor-at-large Marcel Dekker, N.Y.C., 1990—; adj. prof. dept. biosci. and biotech. Drexel U., Phila., 1996—. Editor: Nuclear Magnetic Resonance in Agriculture, 1989, Nuclear Magnetic Resonance in Plant Biology, 1996; mem. editl. bd. Jour. Carbohydrate Chemistry, 1985—, Jour. Magnetic Resonance Analysis; contbr. articles to profl. jours. including Plant Physiology, Carbohydrate Rsch., Biochemica Acta, Biophysica, Jour. Magnetic Resonance. Recipient Bond award Am. Oil Chemists Soc., 1976, Fed. Svcs. award Phila. Fed. Assn., 1979, Science and Edn. award USDA, 1982; fellow Orgn. for Econ. Cooperation and Devel., 1989; Agrl. Rsch. Svc. rsch. fellow, 1989; vis. scientist grantee Centre d'Etudes Nucleaires de Grenoble, 1986, Oxford U., 1989. Mem. AAAS, Internat. Soc. for Magnetic Resonance, Am. Chem. Soc. (Phila. sect. Scientist of Yr. 1982), Soc. for Applied Spectroscopy. Achievements include patents and publs. concerning use of alpha-anions; discovery of deuterium isotope shift NMR method for determining carbohydrate structures; development of P-31 NMR in vivo methodology for studying metal ion transport and C-13 NMR for studying plant/microbe interactions in nitrogen fixing plant nodules and symbiotic mycorrhizae. Office: USDA 600 E Mermaid Ln Wyndmoor PA 19038-8551

PFEFFER, PHILIP MAURICE, book publishing executive; b. St. Louis, Jan. 20, 1945; s. Philip McRae and Jeanne (Kaufman) P.; m. Pamela Jean Korte, Aug. 28, 1965; children: John-Lindell Philip, James Howard, David Maurice. B.A. in Math. and Chemistry, So. Ill. U., 1965, M.A. in Econs., 1966; postgrad., Vanderbilt U., 1966-68; PhD Humane Letters (hon.), So. Ill. U., 1997. Economist Genesco, Inc., Nashville, 1968, mgr. internat. fin., 1969, asst. treas.; pres. Genesco Export Co., Nashville, 1970-75; dir. fin. planning Ingram Distribution Group, Inc., Nashville, 1976-77, v.p. fin. and adminstrn., 1977-78, exec. v.p., 1978, pres. and chief exec. officer, 1978-81, chmn. bd. and chief exec. officer, 1981-96, dir., 1978-96; exec. v.p. Ingram Industries, Inc., Nashville, 1981-96, dir., 1981—; pres., dir. Random House Inc., N.Y.C., 1996—; bd. dirs. Ingram Barge Co., Ingram Micro Inc.; instr. fin. and econs. U. Tenn., Nashville, 1968-77; lectr. corp. fin. Vanderbilt U., 1972-77. Bd. dirs. So. Ill. U. Found., 1982—; mem. exec. bd. mid.-Tenn. coun. Boy Scouts Am., 1982—. Recipient Long Rifle and Silver Beaver award Boy Scouts Am., Nashville, 1981, also Disting. Eagle from Nat. Coun.; Benjamin Gomez award for Disting. Contbns. to the Art of Book Pub. Mem. Fin. Execs. Inst. (pres. 1978-79), Nat. Eagle Scout Assn. (bd. dirs., Silver Wreath award), Nashville Area C. of C. (vice chmn.), Am. Wholesale Booksellers Assn. (past v.p., trustee), So. Ill. U. Alumni Assn. (past bd. dirs.), Young Pres.'s Orgn., World Pres.'s Orgn., Tenn. Assn. Bus., Rotary Internat. Avocations: scouting, sailing, water sports, landscaping. Home: 836 Treemont Ct Nashville TN 37220-1536 Office: Random House Inc 201 E 50th St New York NY 10022-7703

PFEFFER, RICHARD LAWRENCE, geophysics educator; b. Bklyn., Nov. 26, 1930; s. Lester Robert and Anna (Newman) P.; m. Roslyn Ziegler, Aug. 30, 1953; children—Bruce, Lloyd, Scott, Glenn. B.S. cum laude, CCNY, 1952; M.S., Mass. Inst. Tech., 1954, Ph.D., 1957. Research asst. MIT, 1952-55, guest lectr., 1956; atmospheric physicist Air Force Cambridge Research Center, Boston, 1955-59; sr. scientist Columbia U., 1959-61, lectr., 1961-62, asst. prof. geophysics, 1962-64; assoc. prof. meteorology Fla. State U., Tallahassee, 1964-67, prof. meteorology, 1967-96, disting. rsch. prof., 1997—; dir. Geophys. Fluid Dynamics Inst., 1967-93; cons. NASA, 1961-64, N.W. Ayer & Son, Inc., 1962, Ednl. Testing Service, Princeton, N.J., 1963, Voice of Am., 1963, Grolier, Inc., 1963, Naval Research Labs., 1971-76; Mem. Internat. Commn. for Dynamical Meteorology, 1972-76. Editor: Dynamics of Climate, 1960; Contbr. articles to profl. jours. Bd. dirs. B'nai B'rith Anti-Defamation League; chmn. religious concern and social action com. Temple Israel, Tallahassee, 1971-72. Fellow Am. Meterol. Soc. (program chmn. ann. meeting 1963); mem. Am. Geophys. Union, N.Y. Acad. Scis. (chmn. planetary scis. sect. 1961-63), Sigma Xi, Chi Epsilon Pi, Sigma Alpha. Home: 926 Waverly Rd Tallahassee FL 32312-2813

PFEFFER, ROBERT, chemical engineer, academic administrator, educator; b. Vienna, Austria, Nov. 26, 1935; came to U.S., 1938, naturalized, 1944; s. Joseph and Gisela (Aberbach) P.; m. Marcia Borenstein, Dec. 24, 1960; children—Michael, Jacqueline. B.Ch.E., N.Y. U., 1956, M.Ch.E., 1958, D.Eng.Sc., 1962. Mem. faculty CCNY, 1957-92, asst. prof. chem. engring., 1962-66, assoc. prof., 1966-71, prof., 1971-92, chmn. dept. chem. engring., 1973-87, Herbert Kayser prof., 1980-92, dean grad. studies and research, dep. provost, 1987-88, provost, v.p. acad. affairs, 1988-92; v.p. rsch. and grad. studies, prof. chem. engring. N.J. Inst. Tech., Newark, 1992—; vis. prof. Imperial Coll., London, 1969; Fulbright scholar Technion-Israel Inst. Tech., 1976-77; cons. in field. Contbr. articles to tech. publs. Fulbright Hays awardee, 1976-77; DuPont faculty fellow, 1962; NASA faculty fellow, 1964-65. Mem. AIChE (Particle Tech. Forum Nat. award 1995), Am. Soc. Engring. Edn., Sigma Xi, Tau Beta Pi, Phi Lambda Upsilon. Jewish. Office: NJ Inst Tech 323 Dr Martin Luther King Jr Blvd Newark NJ 07102

PFEFFER, RUBIN HARRY, publishing executive; b. Bklyn., Oct. 9, 1951; s. Martie and Idell (Treiber) P.; m. Lurie Horns; children: Stephanie, Ian, Rebecca, Vaughn. BFA in Graphic Design, Carnegie-Mellon U., 1973. Dir. art Harcourt Brace Jovanovich, San Diego, 1979-84; corp. art dir. Harcourt Brace Jovanovich, Orlando, Fla., 1984—; dir. children's books Harcourt Brace Jovanovich, San Diego, 1984-85; pres. Harcourt Brace & Co. Trade Books, San Diego, 1985—. Bd. dirs. Calif. Ballet Co., San Diego, 1986-87, Easter Seal Soc., San Diego, 1988—. Avocation: painting. Office: HB Trade Divsn 525 B St San Diego CA 92101-4403

PFEFFERKORN, MICHAEL GENE, SR., secondary school educator, writer; b. Delano, Calif., July 19, 1939; s. E. Michael and N. Ruth (Ervin) P.; m. Sandra J. Carter, June 15, 1963; children: Michael Jr., Patricia. AB, S.E. Mo. State, 1961, BS in Secondary Edn., 1961; MEd, U. Mo., 1963. Cert. Eng., life Social Studies tchr., Mo. Tchr. De Soto (Mo.) Pub. Schs., 1961-62, Cleveland H.S., St. Louis, 1963-84; tchr. S.W. H.S., St. Louis, 1984-86, tchr., history dept. head, 1987-92; tchr. Gateway Inst. of Tech. H.S., St. Louis, 1992—; cons. Internat. Edn. Consortium, St. Louis, 1989-92. Co-author: Chits, Chiselers, and Funny Money, 1976; editor Mo. Jour. Numismatics; contbr. articles to numis. jours. Pres. Carondelet Hist. Soc., 1977-78, mem., 1970—; mem. Landmarks and Urban Design Com., St. Louis, 1976-80. Mem. ASCD, Am. Fedn. Tchrs., Nat. Coun. Social Studies Tchrs., State Hist. Soc. Mo., Am. Numis. Assn., Mo. Numis Soc. (bd. dirs. 1997—), Numis. Lit. Guild, World Coin Club Mo. Roman Catholic. Avocations: numismatics, writing, genealogy. Home: 6803 Leona St Saint Louis MO 63116-2833 Office: Gateway Inst of Tech 5101 McRee Ave Saint Louis MO 63110-2019

PFEFFERKORN, SANDRA JO, secondary school educator; b. St. Louis, Jan. 14, 1940; d. Albert A. and Alice C. (Lowell) Carter; m. Michael G. Pfefferkorn, June 15, 1963; children: Michael G. Jr., Patricia A. BS in Secondary Edn., S.E. Mo. State Coll., 1961; MEd, U. Mo., 1966. Cert. life English, Spanish, French, and reading tchr., Mo. Tchr. English, head English and fgn. lang. dept. St. Louis Bd. Edn.; English tchr. Cleveland Naval Jr. Res. Officer Tng. Corps H.S., St. Louis. Asst. editor Mo. Jour. Numismatics. Regents scholar, 1957; fellow Mo. Writing Project, 1981. Mem. AAUW, Nat. Coun. Tchrs. English, Internat. Reading Assn., Mo. Assn. Tchrs. English, Delta Kappa Gamma, Phi Delta Kappa. Roman Catholic. Avocations: writing, reading, ceramics. Home: 6803 Leona St Saint Louis MO 63116-2833 Office: Cleve Naval Jr ROTC 4352 Louisiana Ave Saint Louis MO 63111-1046

PFEIFER, HOWARD M(ELFORD), mechanical engineer; b. St. Louis, Aug. 23, 1959; s. Howard William and Ruth Joyce P. BS in Applied Sci. and Tech., Charter Oak State Coll., 1990; BSME, U. Hartford, 1991; MBA, Rensselaer Poly. Inst., 1997. Engr. in tng., Conn. Engr. asst. Pratt & Whitney, East Hartford, Conn., 1984-89; devel. engr. Chromalloy Rsch. and Tech. Divsn., Orangeburg, N.Y., 1991-93; process devel. engr. Howmet Corp., North Haven, Conn., 1993-95; process engr. Windsor Airmotive, The Barnes Group, East Granby, Conn., 1995—; mem. U. Hartford Engring. Alumni Adv. Bd., Bloomfield, Conn., 1992—, chmn., 1996—. Mem. NSPE, Sigma Xi (assoc.). Republican. Achievements include research, design and construction of a human powered helicopter, and research to map acoustical soundboard characteristics in a Steinway Grand Piano. Home: 99 Victoria St Windsor CT 06095 Office: Windsor Airmotive The Barnes Group 7 Connecticut South Dr East Granby CT 06026-9738

PFEIFER, JOANN, hotel executive. V.p. ops. British Columbia and prairies Delta Vancouver Airport Hotel & Marina, Richmond, B.C., Can. Office: Delta Vancouver Airport Hotel & Marina, 3500 Cessna Dr, Richmond, BC Canada V7B 1C7

PFEIFER, LARRY ALAN, public health service coordinator; b. Rock Springs, Wyo., July 20, 1958; s. Jack Albert and Betty Lee (Ethington) P.; m. Sandra Lynn, June 20, 1986. BS cum laude, So. Oreg. State Coll., 1983, MS in Health Edn., 1989; paramedic diploma, Rogue Community Coll., 1984; postgrad., Columbia Pacific U. Cert. paramedic, Oreg. Lt., paramedic Tualatin Valley Fire and Rescue, Portland, Oreg., 1991—; adj. faculty Oreg. Health Scis. U. Sch. of Medicine, Dept. of Emergency Medicine, 1995; lectr. in field. Author (text) Non-Verbal Pre-Hospital Assessment of the Trauma Patient. Mem. Oreg. Paramedic Assn., Phi Kappa Phi, Kappa Delta Pi. Home: 5156 NW 173rd Pl Portland OR 97229-7325

PFEIFER, MICHAEL DAVID, bishop; b. Alamo, Tex., May 18, 1937; s. Frank and Alice (Savage) P. Student, Oblate Sch. Theology. Ordained priest Roman Cath. Ch., 1965, consecrated bishop, 1985; mem. Missionary Oblates of Mary Immaculate. Priest Roman Cath. Ch., Mexico City, 1964-1981; provincial-superior of Oblate So. U.S. Province Roman Cath. Ch., San Antonio, 1981-85; bishop Roman Cath. Ch., San Angelo, Tex., 1985—. Address: PO Box 1829 804 Ford St San Angelo TX 76902

PFEIFER, PAUL E., state supreme court justice; b. Bucyrus, Ohio, Oct. 15, 1942; m. Julia Pfeifer; children: Lisa, Beth, Kurt. BA, Ohio State U., 1963, JD, 1966. Asst. atty. gen. State of Ohio, 1967-70; mem. Ohio Ho. of Reps., 1971-72; asst. prosecuting atty. Crawford County, 1973-76; mem. Ohio Senate, 1976-92, minority floor leader, 1983-84, asst. pres. pro-tempore, 1985-86; ptnr. Cory, Brown & Pfeifer, 1973-92; justice Ohio Supreme Ct., 1992—; chmn. jud. com. Ohio Senate, 10 yrs. Mem. Grace United Meth. Ch., Bucyrus. Mem. Bucyrus Rotary Club. Office: 30 E Broad St Fl 3 Columbus OH 43215-3414

PFEIFER, PETER MARTIN, physics educator; b. Zurich, Switzerland, Apr. 19, 1946; came to U.S., 1986; s. Max and Eva (Korrodi) P.; m. Therese M. Abgottspon, June 13, 1980; children: Anne, Helen. MS in Chemistry, Swiss Fed. Inst. Tech., 1969, PhD in Natural Scis., 1980. Rsch. and tchg. asst. Swiss Fed. Inst. Tech., Zurich, 1970-75, rsch. assoc., instr., 1975-80; rsch. fellow Hebrew U. Jerusalem, 1981-82; asst. prof. chemistry U. Bielefeld, West Germany, 1982-86, habilitation, 1986; assoc. prof. physics U. Mo., Columbia, 1986-95; vis. prof. physics Swiss Fed. Inst. Tech., 1993-94; vis. scientist Ecole Poly., Palaiseau, France, 1994; prof. physics U. Mo., Columbia, 1995—; mem. adv. bd. Symposium on Probability Methods in Physics, Bielefeld, 1984, Symposium on Small Irregular Particles, Cuernavaca, Mex., 1988, Conf. on Fractals in Natural Scis., Budapest, Hungary, 1993, 22d Midwest Solid-State Theory Symposium, Columbia, 1994, 2d Internat. Symposium on Surface Heterogeneity, Zakopane, Poland, 1995, 3d conf. Fractals in Engring., Arcachon, France, 1997; spkr. in field. Mem. editl. bd. Internat. Jour. Fractals, 1992—, Heterogeneous Chemistry Reviews, 1992—; contbr. over 75 articles to profl. jours. Recipient Gränacher Grad. fellowship Found. of Swiss Chem. Industry, 1970-71, fellowship for jr. scientists Swiss Nat. Sci. Found., 1981-82, Outstanding Rsch. prize U.Bielefeld, 1986, Rsch. Coun. fellowship U. Mo., 1986; grantee: Petroleum Rsch. Fund, 1987-98, Rsch. Leave award U. Mo., 1993-94. Mem. Am. Phys. Soc., Materials Rsch. Soc. Achievements include development of fractal analysis in surface science; discovery of first fractal materials and of numerous structure-function relationships (diffusion, scattering, wetting and transport properties); fundamental research in quantum theory: discovery of chiral superselection rule in molecules, unified framework for reduced quantum dynamics, generalized time-energy uncertainty relations, variational bounds for transition probabilities. Office: Univ Mo Dept Physics Columbia MO 65211

PFEIFFER, ECKHARD, computer company executive. BA, Nuremberg Business, 1963; MBA, SMU, 1983. Pres. & CEO Compaq Computer, 1991—. Office: Compaq Computer Corp PO Box 692000 20555 State Hwy Houston TX 77269-2000*

PFEIFFER, ERIC ARMIN, psychiatrist, gerontologist; b. Rauental, Germany, Sept. 15, 1935; came to U.S., 1952; naturalized, 1957; s. Fritz and Emma (Saborowski) P.; m. Natasha Maria Emerson, Mar. 21, 1964; children: Eric Alexander, Michael David, Mark Armin. AB, Washington U., 1956, MD, 1960. Intern Albert Einstein Coll. Medicine, Bronx, N.Y., 1960-61; resident in psychiatry U. Rochester, N.Y., 1961-64; practice medicine specializing in psychiatry Durham, N.C., 1966-76, Denver, 1976-78; asst. prof. Duke U., Durham, 1966-69, assoc. prof., 1969-72, prof., 1973-76, project dir., 1971-76, assoc. dir., 1974-76; dir. Davis Inst. Care and Study Aging, Denver, 1976-77; prof. psychiatry U. Colo., Denver, 1976-78; prof. psychiatry, chief div. geriatric psychiatry U. South Fla. Coll. Medicine, Tampa, 1978—; dir. Suncoast Gerontology Ctr. U. South Fla. Coll. Medicine, 1980—; chief psychiatry svc. Tampa VA Med. Ctr., 1979-80; cons. in field; chmn. bd. Social Systems, Inc., 1975-76; chmn. com. on mental health and mental illness of elderly HEW, 1976-77. Author: Disordered Behavior, 1968, (with E.W. Busse) Behavior and Adaptation in Late Life, 1970, 3d edit., 1977, Successful Aging, 1974, Multidimensional Functional Assessment, 1977, Alzheimer's Disease, 1989. With USPHS, 1964-66. Markle Found. scholar acad. medicine, 1968-73; Eric Pfeiffer Chair in Alzheimer's Disease Rsch. named in his honor, U. S. Fla., 1985. Fellow Gerontol. Soc. (chmn. clin. medicine sect. 1975-76), Am. Psychiat. Assn.; mem. Am. Geriatrics Soc. (Allen Gold medal 1977), So. Psychiat. Soc., Phi Beta Kappa. Home: 5140 W Longfellow Ave Tampa FL 33629-7534 Office: 12901 Bruce B Downs Blvd Tampa FL 33612-4742

PFEIFFER, JANE CAHILL, former broadcasting company executive, consultant; b. Washington, Sept. 29, 1932; d. John Joseph and Helen (Reilly) Cahill; B.A., U. Md., 1954; postgrad., Cath. U. Am., 1956-57; LHD (hon.), Pace Coll., 1978, U. Md., 1979, Manhattanville Coll., 1979, Amherst U., 1980, Babson Coll., 1981, U. Notre Dame, 1991; m. Ralph A. Pfeiffer, Jr., June 3, 1975. With IBM Corp., Armonk, N.Y., 1955-76, sec. mgmt. rev. com., 1970, dir. communications, 1971, v.p. communications and govt. relations, 1972-76, bus. cons., 1976-78; chmn. NBC, Inc., N.Y.C., 1978-80; bus. cons., 1980—; dir. Ashland Oil Co., Mony Fin. Svcs., Internat. Paper Co., J.C. Penney Co.; trustee The Conf. Bd., 1991. Mem. pres.'s adv. com. White House Fellows, 1966, Pres.'s Gen. Adv. Commn. on Arms Control and Disarmament, 1977-80, Pres.'s Commn. Mil. Compensation, trustee Rockefeller Found., U. Md., Carnegie Hall, U. Notre Dame. White House fellow, Washington, 1966; recipient Achievement award Kapppa Kappa Gamma, 1974-80, Eleanor Roosevelt Humanitarian award N.Y. League for Hard of Hearing, 1980, Disting. Alumna award U. Md., 1975, Humanitarian award NOW, 1980, Centennial Alumna Medallion U. Md., 1988. Mem. Council on Fgn. Relations, Overseas Devel. Council. Club: Econ. of N.Y. Office: 90 Field Point Cir Greenwich CT 06830-7011

PFEIFFER, JOHN EDWARD, author; b. N.Y.C., Sept. 27, 1914; s. Edward Heyman and Jeannette (Gross) P.; m. Naomi Ranson, Sept. 9, 1939; 1 son, Anthony John. B.A., Yale U., 1936. Sci. editor Newsweek mag., N.Y.C., 1936-42; sci. dir. CBS, N.Y.C., 1946-48; mem. editorial bd. Sci. Am., N.Y.C., 1948-50; free-lance writer, editor, 1950—; prof. anthropology Livingston Coll., Rutgers U., 1968—; cons. NSF, U. Chgo., Princeton U. Adv. Council for Anthropology, Tulane U., Ednl. Testing Svc. Princeton, N.J., Harvard U. Negotiation Project, Pacific Gas and Electric Co., Berkeley Study of High Risk Orgns., Harper's mag., others; mem. adv. council on anthropology Princeton U. Author: Science in Your Life, 1939, The Human Brain, 1955, The Changing Universe, 1956, From Galaxies to Man, 1959, The Thinking Machine, 1962, The Search For Early Man, 1963, The Cell, 1964, New Look at Education, 1968, The Emergence of Man, 1969, 4th edit., 1985, The Emergence of Society...A Prehistory of the Establishment, 1977, The Creative Explosion....An Inquiry into the Origins of Art and Religion, 1982; reviewer, cons. N.Y. Times Book Rev., 1982—; cons., contbg. editor Smithsonian mag. Trustee Solebury Sch., New Hope, Pa. Recipient CBS TV Writing award, 1959, Wenner-Gren Found. grant, 1961, Carnegie Corp. of N.Y. grants, 1965, 69; John Simon Guggenheim fellow, 1952, 54; Fulbright fellow, 1958; Harry Frank Guggenheim fellow, 1979-80, 80-81. Mem. AAAS, Am. Anthrop. Assn., Acad. Mgmt., Prehistoric Soc. of Eng., Soc. Am. Archeologists, Soc. Am. Anthropology, Antarctic Archaeol. Inst., Nat. Assn. Sci. Writers (past pres.), Prehistoric Soc. London. Home: 331 Lower Dolington Rd Newtown PA 18940-1696

PFEIFFER, LEONARD, IV, executive recruiter, consultant; s. Leonard Jr. and Felicia Pfeiffer; m. Anna Gunnarsson. BA, Harvard U., MBA. Mktg. mgr. Am. Express, N.Y.C., 1970-72; project dir. S.T.I., N.Y.C. and San Francisco, 1972-74; v.p. R. Olivier & Assocs., N.Y.C., 1974-76, A. Kane & Assoc., N.Y.C., 1976-78; v.p., ptnr. Korn/Ferry Internat., Washington and N.Y.C., 1978—. Bd. dirs. Cmty. Found., Washington, 1982-84, Nat. Ctr. for Missing Children, 1989—, Nat. Blood Found., 1995-97; founding mem. jr. bd. dirs. Washington Opera, 1983-93; mem. men's com. Project Hope; devel. com. Nat. Head Injury Found. and Nat. Symphony Orchestra. Lt. U.S. Army, 1968-70. Schepp Found. scholar, 1968-70. Mem. Am. Soc. Assn. Execs., Greater Washington Soc. Assn. Execs., Congl. Country Club, Harvard Club (activities com., admissions com. N.Y.C. chpt. 1975-81, 1st v.p. bd. dirs. Washington chpt. 1985-87). Avocations: water and snow skiing, power and sail boating, tennis. Office: Korn Ferry Internat 900 19th St NW Washington DC 20006-2105

PFEIFFER, MARGARET KOLODNY, lawyer; b. Elkin, N.C., Oct. 7, 1944; d. Isadore Harold and Mary Elizabeth (Brody) K.; m. Carl Frederick Pfeiffer II, Sept. 2, 1968. BA, Duke U., 1967; JD, Rutgers U., 1974. Bar: N.J. 1974, N.Y. 1976, D.C. 1981, U.S. Supreme Ct. 1979. Law clk. to Hon. F.L. Van Dusen U.S. Ct. Appeals 3d cir., Phila., 1974-75; assoc. Sullivan & Cromwell, N.Y.C. and Washington, 1975-82, ptnr., 1982—. Contbr. articles to profl. jours. Mem. ABA, Internat. Bar Assn., D.C. Bar Assn., N.Y. State Bar Assn., Assn. of Bar of City of N.Y. Avocations: hiking, reading, music. Office: Sullivan & Cromwell 1701 Pennsylvania Ave NW Washington DC 20006-5805

PFEIFFER, MICHELLE, actress; b. Santa Ana, Calif., Apr. 29, 1957; d. Dick and Donna P.; m. Peter Horton (div.); 1 adopted child, Claudia Rose; m. David Kelley, Nov. 13, 1993. Student, Golden West Coll., Whitley Coll. Actress: (feature films) Falling in Love Again, 1980, Hollywood Knights, 1980, Charlie Chan and the Curse of the Dragon Queen, 1981, Grease II, 1982, Scarface, 1983, Ladyhawke, 1985, Into the Night, 1985, Sweet Liberty, 1986, Amazon Women on the Moon, 1987, Witches of Eastwick, 1987, Married to the Mob, 1988, Tequila Sunrise, 1988, Dangerous Liaisons, 1988 (Acad. award nominee 1989), The Fabulous Baker Boys, 1989 (Achievement award L.A. Film Critics Assn. 1989, D.W. Griffith award Nat. Bd. Rev. 1989, N.Y. Film Critics award 1989, Nat. Soc. Film Critics award 1990, Golden Globe award 1990, Acad. award nominee 1990), The Russia House, 1990,Frankie & Johnny, 1991, Love Field, 1992 (Acad. award nominee 1993), Batman Returns, 1992, The Age of Innocence, 1993, Wolf, 1994, Dangerous Minds, 1995; (TV movies) The Solitary Man,1979, Callie and Son, 1981, The Children Nobody Wanted, 1981, Splendor in the Grass, 1981, (TV series) Delta House, 1979, B.A.D. Cats, 1980, Up Close and Personel, 1996, To Gillian on her 37th Birthday, 1996, Privacy, 1997. Named Woman of the Yr., Harvard's Hasty Pudding Theater Club, 1995. Office: care ICM 8942 Wilshire Blvd Beverly Hills CA 90211-1934*

PFEIFFER, PHYLLIS KRAMER, publisher; b. N.Y.C., Feb. 11, 1949; d. Jacob N. and Estelle G. Rosenbaum-Pfeiffer. B.S., Cornell U., 1970; postgrad. U. San Diego, 1976-78; m. Stephen M. Pfeiffer, Dec. 21, 1969; children: Andrew Kramer, Elise Kramer. Instr., Miss Porter's Sch., Farmington, Conn., 1970; tchr. N.Y.C. Bd. Edn., Dewey Jr. High Sch., 1970-73; research Hunter Coll., N.Y., 1971-72; account exec. La Jolla (Calif.) Light, 1973-75, advt. dir., 1975-77, gen. mgr., 1977-78, pub., 1978-87 ; exec. v.p. Harte Hanks So. Calif. Newspapers, 1985-87; gen. mgr. San Diego edit. L.A. Times, 1987-93; pres., pub. Marin Ind. Jour., Novato, Calif., 1993—; dir. communications center San Diego State U., 1980-93. Bd. dirs. La Jolla Cancer Research Found., 1979-82; bd. dirs. Alvarado Hosp., 1981-88, chmn. fin. com., 1986, sec. bd., 1986; co-chmn. Operation USS La Jolla, U.S. Navy, 1980—; mem. mktg. com. United Way, 1979-81, chmn., 1983; bd. dirs. YMCA, San Diego Ballet, 1980; trustee La Jollan's Inc., 1975-78; mem. Conv. and Visitors Bur. Blue Ribbon Com. on Future, 1983, resource panel Child Abuse Prevention Found., 1983—; bd. overseers U. Calif., San Diego; mem. violent crimes task force San Diego Police Dept.; bd. dirs. Dominican Coll., San Rafael, Calif., 1994—. N.Y. Bd. Edn. grantee, 1971-72; named publisher of yr. Gannet Co., Inc., 1995. Mem. Newspaper Assn. Am., Calif. Newspaper Pubs. Assn. (bd. dirs., exec. com.), Chancellor's Assn. U. Calif.-San Diego., Tiburon Peninsula Club. Office: Marin Ind Jour 150 Alameda Del Prado Novato CA 94949-6665

PFEIFFER, ROBERT JOHN, business executive; b. Suva, Fiji Islands, Mar. 7, 1920; came to U.S., 1921, naturalized, 1927; s. William Albert and Nina (MacDonald) P.; m. Mary Elizabeth Worts, Nov. 29, 1945; children—Elizabeth Pfeiffer Tumbas, Margaret Pfeiffer Hughes, George, Kathleen. Grad. high sch., Honolulu, 1937; DSc (hon.), Maine Maritime Acad.; HHD (hon.), U. Hawaii; DHL (hon.), Hawaii Loa Coll. With Inter-Island Steam Navigation Co., Ltd., Honolulu, (re-organized to Overseas Terminal Ltd. 1950); with (merged into Oahu Ry. & Land Co. 1954), 1937-55, v.p., gen. mgr., 1950-54, mgr. ship agy. dept., 1954-55; v.p., gen. mgr. Pacific Cut Stone & Granite Co., Inc., Alhambra, Calif., 1955-56, Matcinal Corp., Alameda, Calif., 1956-58; mgr. div. Pacific Far East Line, Inc., San Francisco, 1958-60; with Matson Nav. Co., San Francisco, 1960—, v.p., 1966-70, sr. v.p., 1970-71, exec. v.p., 1971-73, pres., 1973-79, 84-85, 89-90, CEO, 1973-92, chmn. bd., bd.dirs., 1978-95, chmn. emeritus, 1995—; v.p. The Matson Co., San Francisco, 1968-70; pres. The Matson Co., 1970-82; v.p., gen. mgr. Matson Terminals, Inc., San Francisco, 1960-62; pres. Matson Terminals, Inc., 1962-70, chmn. bd., 1970-79; chmn. bd. Matson Svcs. Co., 1973-79, Matson Agys., Inc., 1973-78; sr. v.p. Alexander & Baldwin, Inc., Honolulu, 1973-77; exec. v.p. Alexander & Baldwin, Inc., 1977-79, chmn. bd., 1980-95; chmn. emeritus Alexander & Baldwin, Inc., Honolulu, 1995—; CEO Alexander & Baldwin, Inc., 1980-92, pres., 1979-84, 89-91; chmn. bd., pres., dir. A&B-Hawaii, Inc., 1988-89, chmn. bd., 1989-95; chmn. emeritus A&B-Hawaii, Inc., Honolulu, 1995—; former mem. Gov.'s commn. on exec. salaries State of Hawaii, com. on jud. salaries. Past chmn. maritime transp. rsch. bd. NAS; former mem. select com. for Am. Mcht. Marine Seamanship Trophy Award; mem. commn. sociotech. systems NRC; mem. adv. com. Joint Maritime Congress; Pacific Aerospace Mus., also bd. dirs.; vice-chmn. Hawaii Maritime Ctr.; former chmn. A. Com. on Excellence (ACE), Hawaii; bd. govs. Japanese Cultural Ctr. Hawaii; hon. co-chmn. McKinley H.S. Found. Lt. USNR, WWII; comdr. Res. ret. Mem. VFW (life), Nat. Assn. Stevedores (past pres.), Internat. Cargo Handling Coord. Assn. (past pres. U.S. Com.), Propeller Club U.S. (past pres. Honolulu chpt.), Nat. Def. Transp. Assn., Containerization & Intermodal Inst. (hon. bd. advisors), 200 Club, Aircraft Owners and Pilots Assn., Pacific Club, Outrigger Club, Oahu Country Club, Maui Country Club, Pacific Union Club, Bohemian Club, World Trade Club (San Francisco), Masons, Shriners. Republican. Home: 535 Miner Rd Orinda CA 94563-1429 Office: Alexander & Baldwin Inc 822 Bishop St Honolulu HI 96813-3924

PFEIFFER, SOPHIA DOUGLASS, state legislator, lawyer; b. N.Y.C., Aug. 10, 1918; d. Franklin Chamberlin and Sophie Douglass (White) Wells; m. Timothy Adams Pfeiffer, June 7, 1941; children: Timothy Franklin, Penelope Mersereau Keenan, Sophie Douglass. AB, Vassar Coll., 1939; JD, Northeastern U., 1975. Bar: R.I. 1975, U.S. Ct. Apls. (1st cir.) 1980, U.S. Supreme Ct. 1979. Editl. rschr. Time, Inc., N.Y.C., 1940-41; writer Office War Info., Washington, 1941-43, N.Y.C., 1943-45; editl. staff Nat. Geog. Mag., Washington, 1958-59, 68-70; editor Turkish Jour. Pediatrics, Ankara, 1961-63; staff atty. R.I. Supreme Ct., Providence, 1975-76, chief staff atty., 1976-87; mem. Maine Ho. Reps., 1990-94; lectr. U. So. Maine, 1995; bd. dirs. Death and Dying project. Chair bioethics study League Women Voters. Contbr. in field. Pres., Karachi Am. Sch. (Pakistan), 1955-56; chair, Brunswick Village Review Bd., 1986-89. Home: 15 Franklin St Brunswick ME 04011-2101

PFEIFFER, STEVEN BERNARD, lawyer; b. Orange, N.J., Jan. 19, 1947; s. Bernard Victor and Elizabeth Sophia (Bissell) P.; m. Kristin Reagan, June 27, 1970; children: Victoria Elizabeth, Rachel Catherine, Emily Dorothea, Stephanie Kristin Bissell, Andrew Steven Bernard. BA in Govt., Wesleyan U., 1969; BA in Jurisprudence, Oxford U., 1971, MA, 1983; MA in African Studies, U. London, 1973; JD, Yale U., 1976. Bar: N.J. 1976, D.C. 1978. Assoc. Fulbright & Jaworski, Houston, London, 1976-83; ptnr. Fulbright & Jaworski, London, Washington, 1983—; ptnr.-in-charge Fulbright & Jaworski, London, 1983-86; head internat. dept. Fulbright & Jaworski, Washington, 1989—; bd. dirs. Riggs Nat. Corp., Washington, Riggs Nat. Bank, Washington, Riggs AP Bank, London, U. Cape Town Fund, N.Y.C. Contbr. articles to profl. jours. Alumni-elected trustee Wesleyan U., Middletown, Conn., 1976-79, charter trustee, 1980-92, vice chmn. bd. trustees, 1986-87, chmn. bd. trustees, 1987-92, chmn. emeritus, 1992—. With USN, 1969, 72-74; asst. cinceur plans officer, Office of CNO, Washington, 1972-73; spl. asst. to Sec. of Navy, Washington, 1973-74. Rhodes scholar, 1969-72; Thomas Watson Travel fellow, The Watson Found., 1969. Mem. ABA, N.J. State Bar Assn., Am. Soc. Internat. Law, Internat. Bar Assn. (past chmn. sect. energy and natural resources law 1992-94), Naval Res. Assn., Internat. Inst. Strategic Studies, London Coun. Fgn. Rels. Avocations: tennis, history, fishing, books. Home: 301 N View Ter Alexandria VA 22301-2609 Office: Fulbright & Jaworski LLP 801 Pennsylvania Ave NW Washington DC 20004-2604

PFEIFFER, WERNER BERNHARD, artist, educator; b. Stuttgart, Germany, Oct. 1, 1937; came to U.S., 1961; s. Jakob and Emilie (Nufer) P.; children: Jan-Stephen, Michaela Veronica. Diploma, Grafische Fachschule, Stuttgart, Akademie Fine Arts, Stuttgart. Instr. Pratt Inst., Bklyn., 1961-64, prof., 1968-75, adj. prof., 1976—; asst. prof. N.Y. Inst. Tech., Westbury, 1965-67; dir. Pratt Adlib Press, Bklyn., 1968-75. Exhibited in over 50 one-man shows. Mem. Soc. Am. Graphic Artists. Avocations: skiing, travel, music. Address: Flat Rock Rd Cornwall Bridge CT 06754

PFENDER, EMIL, mechanical engineering educator; b. Stuttgart, Germany, May 25, 1925; came to U.S., 1964, naturalized, 1969; s. Vinzenz and Anna Maria (Dreher) P.; m. Maria Katharina Staiger, Oct. 22, 1954; children: Roland, Norbert, Corinne. Student U. Tuebingen, Germany, 1947-49; Diploma in Physics, U. Stuttgart, 1953, D. Ing. in Elec. Engring., 1959. Assoc. prof. mech. engring. U. Minn., Mpls., 1964-67, prof., 1967—. Contbr. articles to profl. jours. Patentee in field. Fellow ASME, ASM; mem. IEEE (assoc.), NAE, ASM Internat. Home: 1947 Bidwell St Saint Paul MN 55118-4417 Office: U Minn Dept of Mech Engrg 111 Church St SE Minneapolis MN 55455-0150

PFENDT, HENRY GEORGE, retired information systems executive, management consultant; b. Frankfurt, Germany, Sept. 19, 1934; s. Georg and Elisabeth K. (Schuch) P.; m. Jane Ann Gossard, July 15, 1961; children: Katherine Ann, Henry G. Jr., Karen Jane. BS, U. Rochester, N.Y., 1972, postgrad., 1972; postgrad., U. Mich., 1986. Dir. No. info. ctr. Eastman Kodak Internat., Göteborg, Sweden, 1972-73; sr. project mgr. Eastman Kodak Internat., Stuttgart, Fed. Republic of Germany, 1973-75; dir. adminstrv. svcs. Kodak Australasia Party Ltd., Coburg, Australia, 1975-77; dir. customer svcs. div. Kodak Australasia Party Ltd., Coburg, 1977-81; dir. mktg. Kodak Australasia Party Ltd., Australia, 1981-84; dir. architecture devel. Eastman Kodak Info. Systems, Rochester, 1984-86, dir. corp. info. systems, 1986-93; ret., 1993, bus. and info. mgmt. cons., 1993—; bd. dirs. client adv. coun. Compu Ware, Detroit. Creator concepts and mgmt. processes in field. Mem. indsl. devel. agy. adv. bd. Zoning Bd. Appeals Town of Barrington; charter mem. adv. bd. Rochester Inst. Tech. Sch. Computer Sci. and Tech., 1987; bd. dirs. YMCA of Maplewood, Rochester, 1989—; mem. Rep. Nat. Com. With USAF, 1955-59. Recipient Industry Visionary award of 25 Most Influential Communications Execs., 1991. Mem. Soc. for Info. Mgmt., Coun. of Logistics Mgmt., Ctr. for Info. Systems Rsch., Strategic Mgmt. Soc., Internat. Platform Assn., Interact Network (assoc.), C. of C. Lutheran. Avocations: reading, golf, gardening, jogging, travel. Home: 968 E Lake Rd Dundee NY 14837-9749

PFENING, FREDERIC DENVER, III, manufacturing company executive; b. Columbus, Ohio, July 28, 1949; s. Frederic Denver Jr. and Lelia (Bucher) P.; m. Cynthia Gordon, July 1, 1978; children: Lesley, Frederic Denver IV. BA, Ohio Wesleyan U., 1971; MA, Ohio State U., Columbus, 1976. Various positions Fred. D. Pfening Co., Columbus, 1976-88, pres., 1988—. Bd. dirs. Friends of Ohio State U. Librs., 1988-94, Columbus State C.C. Devel. Found., 1991—, Hist. Sites Found., Baraboo, Wis., 1984—, pres., 1987-91. Mem. Am. Soc. Bakery Engrs., Orgn. Am. Historians, Bakery Equipment Mfrs. Assn. (bd. dirs. 1985-91), Young Pres.'s Orgn., Circus Hist. Soc. (pres. 1986-89, mng. editor Bandwagon Jour.), Rotary. Office: 1075 W 5th Ave Columbus OH 43212-2629

PFENNIGER, RICHARD CHARLES, JR., lawyer; b. Akron, Ohio, July 26, 1955; s. Richard Charles Pfenniger and Phyllis Irene (Rutan) Gatto. BBA, Fla. Atlantic U., 1977; JD, U. Fla., 1982. Bar: Fla. 1982; CPA, Fla. Acct. Price Waterhouse & Co., Ft. Lauderdale, Fla., 1977-79; assoc. Stearns, Weaver, Miller, Weisller, Alhadeff & Sitterson, P.A., Miami, Fla., 1982-86; mem. Greer, Homer, Cope & Bonner P.A., Miami, 1986-89; sr. v.p. legal affairs and gen. counsel IVAX Corp., Miami, 1989-94, COO, 1994-97; CEO, vice chmn. Whitman Edn. Group, Inc., Miami, Fla., 1997—; bd. dirs. Pan Am Corp., NaPro Biotherapeutics, Inc., N.Am. Vaccine, Inc. Mem. ABA, AICPA. Office: Whitman Edn Group Inc 4400 Biscayne Blvd Miami FL 33137-3212

PFENNIGSTORF, WERNER, lawyer; b. Hamburg, Germany, Sept. 28, 1934; s. Walter and Ilse (Schroeter) P.; m. Heika Helene Droenner, Apr. 6, 1963. Habilitation, U. Hamburg, Germany, 1974; JD, 1960; MCL, U. Mich. 1961. Bar: Germany 1962. Wissenschaftl asst. U. Hamburg, 1963-66; staff atty. Ins. Laws Rev. Commn., State Wis., Madison, 1967-70; rsch. fellow U. Hamburg, 1970-72; project dir. Am. Bar Found., Chgo., 1973-86; pvt. practice, 1986— . Author: Legal Expense Insurance, 1975, German Insurance Laws, 3rd edit., 1995, A Comparative Study of Liability Law and Compensation Schemes in Ten Countries and the U.S., 1991, Public Law of Insurance, 1996; co-editor: Legal Service Plans, 1977; editor: Personal Injury Compensation, 1993, Pollution Insurance, 1993. Mem. Deutscher Verein für Versicherungswissenschaft, ABA (assoc.), Internat. Assn. Ins. Law. Lutheran. Office: Roethkampstr 3, 21709 Duedenbuettel Germany

PFENNING, ARTHUR GEORGE, social scientist; b. N.Y.C., Feb. 22, 1958; s. Arthur Walter and Helen Susan (Mraz) P. BA, NYU; MS, CUNY; PhD, NYU. Dir. Ruder-Finn, Inc., N.Y.C., 1980-86; rsch. dir. The N.Y. Times Co., N.Y.C., 1986-92; prin. APRR, N.Y.C., 1992—; mng. dir. Nat. Opinion Polling Rsch. Coun., N.Y.C., 1989—. Author: Lathe of Heaven, 1986, Magazine Readers & Social Maneuvers, 1992. Regional dir. NAFARP, N.Y.C.; mem. Dem. Nat. Com. Recipient Johnathon D. Kettler award Nat. Caucus, Chgo., 1993, Mildred F. Feinstein meml. award Dem. Citizens Assn., Seattle, 1993; Wentworth fellow, 1994. Fellow Am. Assn. Pub. Rels. Profls., Trout Unltd. (v.p. N.Y. chpt. 1989—), Am. Assn. Rsch. Profls.; mem. Advt. Rsch. Found. (v.p. 1992), Nat. Assn. Advancement Rsch. Profls. Avocations: fly fishing, home brewing, mountain climbing, rafting. Office: APRR 244 Madison Ave Ste 336 New York NY 10016

PFENNINGER, KARL H., cell biology and neuroscience educator; b. Stafa, Switzerland, Dec. 17, 1944; came to U.S., 1971, naturalized, 1993; s. Hans Rudolf and Delie Maria (Zahn) P.; m. Marie-France Maylié, July 12, 1974; children—Jan Patrick, Alexandra Christina. M.D., U. Zurich, 1971. Research instr. dept. anatomy Washington U., St. Louis, 1971-73; research assoc. sect. cell biology Yale U., New Haven, 1973-76; assoc. prof. dept. anatomy and cell biology Columbia U., N.Y.C., 1976-81, prof., 1981-86; prof., chmn. dept. cellular and structural biology U. Colo. Sch. Medicine, Denver, 1986—; dir. interdeptmental program in cell and molecular biology Columbia U. Coll. Physicians and Surgeons, N.Y.C., 1980-85; chmn. Given Biomed. Inst., Aspen, Colo., 1992-93. Author: Essential Cell Biology, 1990; contbr. articles to profl. jours. Recipient C.J. Herrick award Am. Assn. Anatomists, 1977; I.T. Hirschl Career Scientist award, 1977; Javits neurosci. investigator awards NIH, 1984, 91. Mem. AAAS, Am. Soc. for Cell Biology, Am. Soc. for Biochemistry and Molecular Biology, Toxicology Forum (bd. dirs. 1995—), Harvey Soc., Soc. for Neurosci., Internat. Brain Rsch. Orgn., Internat. Soc. for Neurochemistry. Office: U Colo Health Scis Ctr Dept Cellular and Structural Biology B-111 4200 E 9th Ave Denver CO 80262

PFEUFFER, ROBERT JOHN, musician; b. Cleve., Dec. 25, 1925; s. Henry Vincent and Elmo Alice (Burger) P.; m. Betty June Weller, Sept. 21, 1946; children—Barbara (Mrs. Steven Mosley), Jeanne, Susan, Catherine. B.Mus. in Edn, U. Mich., 1950, M.Mus. in Edn, 1951. Contrabassoonist, bassoonist Detroit Symphony Orch., 1951-61, Phila. Orch., 1962-91; instr. bassoon Wayne State U., 1957-61, New Sch. Music, Phila., 1969—; prin. bassoon Lynchburg Symphony, 1994—. Served with AUS, 1942-44. Mem. U.S. Power Squadron, Kappa Kappa Psi, Pi Mu Alpha. Roman Catholic. Home: 1224 Barnhill Ln Moneta VA 24121

PFISTER, CLOYD HARRY, consultant, former career officer; b. State College, Pa., Dec. 20, 1936; s. Rudolf John Pfister and June Ruth (Braun) Pfister Gray; m. Rita Askerc Kracht, Aug. 17, 1962 (div. Mar. 1982); m. Gail Williams, Apr. 24, 1982; children, Gabriele, Catherine, Michael, Romi, Eric Williams, Lori Williams. BA in Philosophy, Oberlin Coll., 1957; MA in Internat. Rels., Am. U., 1964, postgrad., 1964-67. Enlisted U.S. Army, 1957, advanced through grades to maj. gen., 1989; staff officer Nat. Security Agy., Fort Meade, Md., 1965-68; S3 (Ops.) 303d Radio Rsch. Bn., Plantation, Vietnam, 1968-69; instr. JFK Ctr. and Sch., Fort Bragg, N.C., 1969-72; politico-mil. officer, Office Dep. Chief of Staff for Ops. Hdqrs. Dept. Army, Washington, 1972-75; comdr. 307th U.S. Army Security Agy. Bn., VII U.S. Corps, Ludwigsburg, Fed. Republic Germany, 1975-77; asst. chief of staff intelligence 8th Mech. Inf. Div., Bad Kreuznach, Fed. Republic Germany, 1977-79; Mid. East staff officer Office Sec. Def., The Pentagon, 1979-82; comdr. U.S. Army Field Sta., Berlin, 1982-84; chief of staff U.S. Army Intelligence Ctr. and Sch., Fort Huachuca, Ariz., 1984-85, dep. comdt., 1985-86; dir. intelligence (J2), Hdqrs., U.S. Cen. Command, MacDill AFB, Fla., 1986-88; dep. chief of staff intelligence Hdqrs., U.S. Army Europe and 7th Army, Heidelberg, Fed. Republic Germany, 1988-91; asst. dep. chief of staff Intelligence Hdqrs., Dept. Army, Pentagon, 1991-93; cons. Def. Sci. Bd.,

1994, Def. Airborne Reccon Office, 1994—. Decorated Def. D.S.M., D.S.M. Def. Superior Svc. medal, Legion of Merit with two oak leaf clusters, Nat. Intelligence D.S.M.; Ehrenkreutz der Bundeswehr (gold) (Fed. Republic Germany); other awards. Mem. Internat. Inst. for Strategic Studies, Middle East Inst., Security Affairs Support Assn., Assn. U.S. Army. Avocations: tennis, photography, gardening, computers. Office: Tech Strategies & Alliances 5242 Lyngate Ct Burke VA 22015-1631

PFISTER, KARL ANTON, industrial company executive; b. Ernetschwil St. Gallen, Switzerland, Oct. 17, 1941; came to U.S., 1966; s. Josef Anton and Paula (Hobi) P.; m. Karen Antonie Sievers; children: Kirsten, Marc, Theodore, Alexandra. Student trade sch., Rapperswil, Switzerland, 1957-61; student bus. sch., Zuerich, Switzerland, 1964-65. Tool and die maker H. Schmid, Rapperswil, Switzerland, 1957-61, Neher AG, Ebnat-Kappel, Switzerland, 1962-63; process engr. NCR, Buelach, Switzerland, 1964-66, Gretag, Regensdorf, Switzerland, 1966; tool and die maker Stoffel Fineflow Corp., White Plains, N.Y., 1966-67; mgr. mfg. Finetool Corp., Detroit, 1968; pres. Mich. Precision Ind., Inc., Detroit, 1969—; chmn. bd., pres. Kautex N.Am., Inc., 1994; pres. Kloeckner Automotive, Inc., Rochester Hills, Mich., 1996; dir. Kloeckner Capital Corp., Gordonsville, Va., MPI Internat., Inc., Kautex N.Am., Inc., Kloeckner Automotive, Inc. Consul, consulate Switzerland, Detroit, 1984—. Mem. Plum Hollow Club, Fairlane Club. Republican. Roman Catholic. Office: MPI Internat Inc 2129 Austin Ave Rochester Hills MI 48309

PFISTER, RICHARD CHARLES, physician, radiology educator; b. Ypsilanti, Mich., Nov. 27, 1933; s. Emil Robert and Francis Josephine (LeForge) P.; m. Sally DeAnn Haight, Dec. 31, 1956 (div. 1980); children: Kirk Alan, Gary Raymond, Karen Dawn, James Kevin, William Charles. BS, Ctrl. Mich. U., 1958; MD, Wayne State U., 1962. Assoc. prof. radiology Harvard Med. Sch. and Mass. Gen. Hosp., Boston, 1966-89; med. officer FDA, Washington, 1989-90; prof. radiology U. South Ala., Mobile, 1990-92, La. State U., New Orleans, 1993—. Editor, author: Interventional Radiology, 1982. With U.S. Army Med. Corps, 1953-55. Recipient Investigator award NIH, Washington, 1972. Fellow Am. Coll. Radiology; mem. AMA, Soc. Uroradiology (pres. 1984-85), Radiologic Soc. N.Am., Am. Roentgen Ray Soc., Soc. Cardiovascular Interventional. Avocation: sailing (Trans-Atlantic passages). Office: LSU Med Ctr 1542 Tulane Ave New Orleans LA 70112-2825

PFISTER, ROSWELL ROBERT, ophthalmologist; b. Buffalo, Jan. 19, 1938; s. Milton Albert and Florence P. Student, U. Buffalo, 1955-58; M.D., U. Mich., 1962, M.S., 1969. Diplomate Am. Bd. Ophthalmology. Intern Los Angeles County Hosp., 1962-63; resident in ophthalmology U. Mich., Ann Arbor, 1965-69; research fellow dept. cornea research Retina Found., Boston, 1969-71; clin. fellow cornea service Mass. Eye and Ear Infirmary, 1969-71; assoc. prof. U. Colo. Med. Center, Denver, 1971-75; prof., chmn. dept. ophthalmology Combined Program in Ophthalmology, U. Ala. in Birmingham-The Eye Found. Hosp., 1976-81; head research dept. ophthalmology Ellen Gregg Ingalls Eye Research Instn., 1976-81; dir. eye research labs. Brookwood Med. Ctr. (Birmingham), 1982—. Served with USAF, 1963-65. Mem. Med. Assn. Ala., Jefferson County Med. Soc., Assn. Univ. Profs. in Opthalmology, Research to Prevent Blindness, Am. Acad. Ophthalmology, Assn. Research in Vision and Opthalmology, Ala. Acad. Ophthalmology, AMA, Colo. Ophthalmology Soc., Mich. State Med. Soc., Mass. Eye and Ear Infirmary Alumnus Soc., Corneal Soc., Colo. Soc. Prevention of Blindness (mem. med. adv. bd. 1974-76), Colo. Eye Bank (med. dir. 1974-76), Kerato-Refractive Soc. Office: Brookwood Med Ctr 513 Brookwood Blvd Ste 504 Birmingham AL 35209-6801

PFLANZE, OTTO PAUL, history educator; b. Maryville, Tenn., Apr. 2, 1918; s. Otto Paul and Katrine (Mills) P.; m. Hertha Maria Haberlander, Feb. 20, 1951; children: Stephen, Charles, Katrine. B.A., Maryville Coll., 1940; M.A., Yale U., 1942, Ph.D., 1950. Historian Dept. State, 1948-49; instr. N.Y. U., 1950-51; asst. prof. U. Mass., 1952-58, U. Ill., 1958-61; prof. history U. Minn., 1961-76; prof. history Ind. U., 1977-86, emeritus, 1986; Stevenson Prof. of History Bard Coll., Annandale On Hudson, N.Y., 1987-92, emeritus, 1992; chmn. Conf. Group Central European History, 1978; mem. exam. bd., grad. record exam Ednl. Testing Service, 1972-76; mem. Inst. Advanced Study, 1970-71, mem. Historisches Kolleg, Munich, 1980-81. Author: Bismarck and the Development of Germany: Vol. 1.-The Period of Unification, 1815-1871, 1963 (Biennal Book award Phi Alpha Theta), rev. edit., 1990, Vol. 2-The Period of Consolidation, 1871-1880, 1990, Vol. 3-The Period of Fortification, 1880-1898, 1990 (3 vols. collectively named Most Outstanding Book in History, Govt. & Polit. Sci. by Assn. Am. Pubs., 1991); co-author: A History of the Western World: Modern Times, 3d edit, 1975; editor: Innenpolitische Probleme des Bismarck-Reiches, 1983; co-editor: Documents on German Foreign Policy, 1918-1945, Vols. I-III, 1949-50; editor Am. Hist. Rev., 1976-85; mem. editorial bd. Jour. Modern History, 1971-73, Central European History, 1972-74. Served to 1st lt. U.S. Army, 1942-46. Fulbright research fellow, 1955-57; fellow Am. Council Learned Socs., 1951-52; fellow Guggenheim Found., 1966-67; fellow Nat. Endowment Humanities, 1975-76; fellow Internat. Research and Exchanges Bd., 1976; fellow Thyssen Stiftung, Essen, 1986; recipient Humanities award McKnight Found., 1962. Mem. Am. Hist. Assn., German Studies Assn.

PFLAUM, SUSANNA WHITNEY, college dean; b. Boston, Dec. 7, 1937; d. William T. and Ann. (Van Bibber) Whitney; m. Peter E. Pflaum, Apr. 10, 1963 (div. Mar. 1973); children: Melanie Ann, William E.; m. Joseph C. Grannis, Jan. 30, 1987; stepchild: Eric Grannis. AB cum laude, Radcliffe Coll., 1959; MEd, Harvard U., 1960; PhD, Fla. State U., 1971. Tchr. Newton (Mass.) Pub. Schs., 1960-63, Inter-Am. U., San German and Hato Rey, P.R., 1963-66; instr. Mankato (Minn.) State Coll., 1970-71; from asst. prof. to prof. U. Ill., Chgo., 1971-85, dean Honors Coll., 1982-85; dean Sch. Edn. CUNY Queens Coll., Flushing, N.Y., 1985-90; dean Bank St. Coll., N.Y.C., 1990-95; Fulbright prof. U. Namibia, 1996—. Author: Development of Language and Literacy in Young Children, 3d edit., 1986; editor: Aspects of Reading Education, 1978; co-editor: Celebrating Diverse Voices: Progressive Education and Equity, 1993, Experiencing Diversity: Toward Educational Equity, 1994; contbr. articles to profl. jours., 1973-96. Democrat. Episcopalian.

PFLUEGER, M(ELBA) LEE COUNTS, academic administrator; b. St. Louis, Sept. 2, 1942; d. Pless and Edna Mae (Russell) Counts; m. Raymond Allen Pflueger, Sept. 14, 1963 (div. June 1972); children: Salem Allen, Russell Counts. BS in Home Econs., Univ. Mo., 1969; MEd in Guidance and Counseling, Washington Univ., St. Louis, 1973. Ednl. psychologist Ozark Regional Mental Health Ctr., Harrison, Ark., 1974-75; from account mgr. to mgr. pers. Enterprise Leasing Co., St. Louis, 1977-79; mgr. employee rels. Eaton Corp., Houston, 1979-80; owner Nature's Nuggets Fresh Granola, St. Louis, 1980-83; dir. corp. ednl. svcs. Maryville Coll., St. Louis, 1983-84; adminstr. mgmt. skills devel. McDonnell Douglas, St. Louis, 1984-85, mgr. employee involvement, 1985-86, prin. specialist human resources mgmt., 1988-89; mgr. human resources McDonnell Douglas, Houston, 1986-88; dir. devel. sch. engring. U. Mo., Rolla, 1989-93, dir. devel., corp. and found. rels., 1992-93; regional dir. devel., assoc. dir. maj. gifts and capital projects Washington U., St. Louis, 1994—; part-time leader trainer Maritz Motivation, St. Louis, 1984-89. Chair United Fund Campaign for U. Mo., Rolla, 1991. Mem. PEO. Avocations: reading, theatre, yoga.

PFLUG, DONALD RALPH, electrical engineer; b. Shreveport, La., May 22, 1941; s. Donald Ralph and Yullee Estelle (Yarborough) P.; m. Andrea Garza, Oct. 28, 1967; children; Mark David, Paul Eric. BA in Math., Rice U., 1966; MSEE, Syracuse U., 1985; PhD in Chem. Physics, U. Calif., Santa Barbara, 1975. Sr. engr. Atlantic Rsch. Corp., Rome, N.Y., 1976-84, prin. engr., 1987-92; mem. tech. staff Mitre Corp., Griffiss AFB, N.Y., 1984-85; sr. scientist Kaman Scis. Corp., Utica, N.Y., 1985-87; electronics engr. Rome lab. rome Lab., Griffiss AFB, 1993—; govt. exec. com. Electromagnetic Code Consortium, elected chmn., 1997—. Judge sci. fair, Syracuse, N.Y., 1995. With U.S. Army, 1966-68. Mem. IEEE (sr. mem., reviewer Transactions on Antennas), IEEE Electromagnetic Compatibility Soc. (chpt. chmn. 1994—, reviewer 1994—), Applied Computational Electromagnetics Soc. (com. chmn. 1994—), Am. Phys. Soc., Electromagnetics Soc. Avocations: golf, jogging, weightlifting. Office: Rome Lab ERST 525 Brooks Rd Rome NY 13441-4505

PFLUM, BARBARA ANN, pediatric allergist; b. Cin., Jan. 10, 1943; d. James Frederick and Betty Mae (Doherty) P.; m. Makram I. Gobrail, Oct. 20, 1973; children: Christina, James. BS, Coll. Mt. St. Vincent, 1967; MD, Georgetown U., 1971; MS, Coll. Mt. St. Joseph, 1993. Cons. Children's Med. Ctr., Dayton, Ohio, 1975—, dir. allergy clinic, 1983-89. Fellow Am. Acad. Pediatrics, Am. Acad. Allergy and Immunology, Am. Coll. Allergy and Immunology; mem. Ohio Soc. Allergy and Immunology, Western Ohio Pediatric Soc. (pres. 1985-86). Roman Catholic. Home: 4502 Lytle Rd Waynesville OH 45068-9483 Office: 201 E Stroop Rd Dayton OH 45429-2825

PFLUM, WILLIAM JOHN, physician; b. N.Y.C., July 30, 1924; s. Peter Arthur and Caroline (Schmidt) P.; BS, Georgetown U., 1947; MD, Loyola U., Chgo., 1951; m. Roseann Sarah Stubing, Oct. 13, 1956; children: Carol Jean, Jeannine, Suzanne, Denise, Peter. Intern, St. Vincent's Hosp., N.Y.C., 1951-52, resident in internal medicine, 1954-55; resident in internal medicine NYU div. Goldwater Meml. Hosp., N.Y.C., 1952-53; resident in allergy Inst. Allergy, Roosevelt Hosp., N.Y.C., 1956; attending internal medicine (allergy and immunology) Overlook Hosp., Summit, N.J., 1958—; assoc. attending Inst. Allergy, Immunology and Infectious Diseases, Roosevelt Hosp., N.Y.C., 1957-92; pvt. practice medicine, specializing in allergy and immunology, Summit, 1957-92; ret.; cons. in field. Participant Boston Marathon, 1971-95. Served with USAAF, 1943-45; ETO. Decorated Purple Heart, Air medal with two clusters, POW medal. Diplomate Am. Bd. Allergy and Immunology. Fellow Am. Acad. Allergy, Am. Coll. Allergists, Am. Assn. Clin. Immunology and Allergy; mem. Summit Med. Soc., Am. Assn. Clin. Immunology and Allergy (pres. Mid-Atlantic region 1975-76), Disabled Am. Vets., Mil. Order Purple Heart, Am. Ex-Prisoners of War, 8th Air Force Hist. Soc., World Marathon Runners Assn., Robert A. Cooke Allergy Alumni Assn. Roman Catholic. Home: 16 Packer Ave Rumson NJ 07760-2028

PFNISTER, ALLAN OREL, humanities educator; b. Mason, Ill., July 23, 1925; s. Ardon Orel and Rose Margaret (Sandtner) P.; m. Helen Edith Klobes, Dec. 18, 1948; children: Alicia Ann, Jonathan Karl, Susan Elaine. AB summa cum laude, Augustana Coll., 1945; MDiv summa cum laude, Augustana Theol. Sem., 1949; AM with honors, U. Chgo., 1951, PhD, 1955; LLD (hon.), U. Denver, 1978. Instr. in religion Augustana Coll., 1946-47; instr. in philosophy and German Luther Coll., Wahoo, Nebr., 1949-52; dean Luther Coll., 1953-54; research asst., univ. fellow U. Chgo., 1952-53, instr., 1954-57, asst. prof., 1957-58; dir. research joint bds. parish edn. Lutheran Ch. Am., 1958-59; vis. asso. prof. U. Mich., 1959-62, asso. prof., 1962-63; dean Coll. Liberal Arts, prof. philosophy Wittenberg (Ohio) U., 1963-67, provost, prof., 1967-69, acting pres., 1968-69; prof. higher edn. U. Denver, 1969-77, 78-90, exec. vice chancellor and acting chancellor, 1977-78, vice chancellor acad. affairs, 1984-87, assoc. provost, 1988-89, prof. emeritus, 1990—; dir. study fgn. study programs Fedn. Regional Accrediting Commns. Higher Edn., 1970-72; cons. in field; bd. dirs. Nat. Ctr. for Higher Edn. Mgmt. Systems Mgmt. Svcs.; trustee Capital U., Columbus, Ohio, 1983, vice chmn. bd., 1987-89, 91-94. Author: Teaching Adults, 1967, Trends in Higher Education, 1975, Planning for Higher Education, 1976; contbr. numerous articles on higher edn. to profl. jours. Bd. visitors Air Force Inst. Tech., 1978-83, chmn. bd. visitors, 1981-83. Recipient Outstanding Achievement Alumni award Augustana Coll., 1963, Outstanding Contributions to the Univ. award Univ. Denver, 1995. Mem. Am. Am. Assn. Higher Edn., Assn. for Study Higher Edn., Comparative and Internat. Edn. Soc., Blue Key, Phi Beta Kappa (alumnus mem.). Democrat. Home: 7231 W Linvale Pl Denver CO 80227-3556

PFOUTS, RALPH WILLIAM, economist, consultant; b. Atchison, Kans., Sept. 9, 1920; s. Ralph Ulysses and Alice (Oldham) P.; m. Jane Hoyer, Jan. 31, 1945 (dec. Nov. 1982); children: James William, Susan Jane Pfouts Portman, Thomas Robert (dec.), Elizabeth Ann Pfouts Klenowski; m. Lois Bateson, Dec. 21, 1984 (div.); m. Felicia Sprincenatu, 1993. B.A., U. Kans., 1942, M.A., 1947; Ph.D., U. N.C., 1952. Rsch. asst., instr. econs. U. Kans., Lawrence, 1946-47; instr. U. N.C., Chapel Hill, 1947-50, lectr. econs., 1950-52, assoc. prof. econs., 1952-58, prof. econs., 1958-87, chmn. grad. studies dept. econs. Sch. Bus. Adminstrn., 1957-62, chmn. dept. econs. Sch. Bus. Adminstrn., 1962-68; cons. econs. Chapel Hill, 1987—; vis. prof. U. Leeds, 1983; vis. rsch. scholar Internat. Inst. for Applied Systems Analysis, Laxenberg, Austria, 1983; prof. Cen. European U., Prague, 1991. Author: Elementary Economics-A Mathematical Approach, 1972; editor: So. Econ. Jour, 1955-75; editor, contbr.: Techniques of Urban Economic Analysis, 1960, Essays in Economics and Econometrics, 1960; editorial bd.: Metroeconomica, 1961-80, Atlantic Econ. Jour, 1973—; contbr. articles to profl. jours. Served as deck officer USNR, 1943-46. Social Sci. Research Council fellow U. Cambridge, 1953-54; Ford Found. Faculty Research fellow, 1962-63. Mem. AAAS, Am. Statis. Assn., N.C. Statis. Assn. (past pres.), Am. Econ. Assn., So. Econ. Assn. (past pres.), Atlantic Econ. Soc. (v.p. 1973-76, pres. 1977-78), Population Assn. Am., Econometric Soc., Math. Assn. Am., Phi Beta Kappa, Pi Sigma Alpha, Alpha Kappa Psi, Omicron Delta Epsilon. Home and Office: 127 Summerlin Dr Chapel Hill NC 27514-1925

PFUND, EDWARD THEODORE, JR., electronics company executive; b. Methuen, Mass., Dec. 10, 1923; s. Edward Theodore and Mary Elizabeth (Banning) P.; BS magna cum laude, Tufts Coll., 1950; postgrad U. So. Calif., 1950, Columbia U., 1953, U. Calif., L.A., 1956, 58; m. Marga Emmi Andre, Nov. 10, 1954 (div. 1978); children: Angela M., Gloria I., Edward Theodore III; m. Ann Lorenne Dille, Jan. 10, 1988 (div. 1990). Radio engr., WLAW, Lawrence-Boston, 1942-50; fgn. svc. staff officer Voice of Am., Tangier, Munich, 1950-54; project. engr. Crusade for Freedom, Munich, Ger., 1955; project mgr., materials specialist United Electrodynamics Inc., Pasadena, Calif., 1956-59; cons. H.I. Thompson Fiber Glass Co., L.A., Andrew Corp., Chgo., 1959, Satellite Broadcast Assocs., Encino, Calif., 1982; teaching staff Pasadena City Coll. (Calif.), 1959; dir. engring., chief engr. Electronics Specialty Co., L.A. and Thomaston, Conn., 1959-61; with Hughes Aircraft Co., various locations, 1955, 61-89, mgr. Middle East programs, also Far East, Latin Am. and African market devel., L.A., 1971-89, dir. internat. programs devel., Hughes Comm. Internat., 1985-89; mng. dir. E.T. Satellite Assocs. Internat., Rolling Hills Estates, Calif., 1989—; dir. programs devel. Asia-Pacific TRW Space and Tech. Group, Redondo Beach, Calif., 1990-93, Pacific Telecom. Coun., Honolulu, 1993—. With AUS, 1942-46. Mem. AIAA, Phi Beta Kappa, Sigma Pi Sigma. Contbr. articles to profl. jours. Home: 25 Silver Saddle Ln Palos Verdes Peninsula CA 90274-2437 *Edward Pfund served as chairman of the Sub-committee on Communications, Space Flight Operations group, and chief of Johannesburg Operations, 1961-63. He was director of Spacecraft Performance Analysis and Command, 1964-68, for which he directed the real-time commanding, control, and performance of all United States unmanned soft lunar landings and the world's first lunar liftoff and translation, 1966-68. He was also program manager for the Lunar Rover Ground Data System Design, 1969-70; chairman of the Technical Committee for International Consortium (Japan, France, United States, Jordan), 1974-78. He received an Award of Merit and a Congressional Commendation for materials in design engineering for design development of two unique kinds of coaxial cable having low losses over one thousand degrees Fahrenheit for Mach 3 aerospace vehicles.*

PFUNDER, MALCOLM R., lawyer; b. Mpls., Apr. 29, 1944. AB magna cum laude, Harvard U., 1965; JD, Yale U., 1971. Bar: D.C. 1971. Assoc. dir. Bur. Competition FTC, Washington, 1977-78, asst. dir., 1978-81; ptnr. Hopkins & Sutter, Washington, 1981-93; of counsel Gibson, Dunn & Crutcher, Washington, 1993—. Mem. ABA, D.C. Bar. Office: Gibson Dunn & Crutcher 1050 Connecticut Ave NW Washington DC 20036

PHAIR, JOSEPH BASCHON, lawyer; b. N.Y.C., Apr. 29, 1947; s. James Francis and Mary Elizabeth (Baschon) P.; m. Bonnie Jean Hobbs, Sept. 04, 1971; children: Kelly I., Joseph B., Sean P. BA, U. San Francisco, 1970, JD, 1973. Bar: Calif., U.S. Dist. Ct. (no. dist.) Calif., U.S. Ct. Appeals (9th cir.). Assoc. Berry, Davis & McInerney, Oakland, Calif., 1974-76, Bronson, Bronson & McKinnon, San Francisco, 1976-79; staff atty. Varian Assocs., Inc., Palo Alto, Calif., 1979-83, corp. counsel, 1983-86, sr. corp. counsel, 1986-87, assoc. gen. counsel, 1987-90, v.p., gen. counsel, 1990-91, v.p., gen. counsel, sec., 1991—. Mem. devel. bd. St. Vincent de Paul Devel. Coun., San Francisco, 1992—. Mem. Bay Area Gen. Counsel, Peninsula Assn. Gen. Counsel, The Olympic Culb. Roman Catholic. Office: Varian Assoc Inc M/S V-250 3050 Hansen Way Palo Alto CA 94304-1000

PHALEN, ROBERT FRANKLYNN, environmental scientist; b. Fairview, Okla., Oct. 18, 1940; married, 1966; 2 children. B in Physics, San Diego State U., 1964, M in Physics, 1966; PhD in Biophysics, U. Rochester, 1971. Engring. aide advanced space systems dept. Gen. Dynamics/Astronautics, San Diego, 1962-63; asst. to radiation safety officer, lab. teaching asst. San Diego State U., 1964-66, instr. physics dept., 1966; mem. summer faculty biology dept. Rochester (N.Y.) Inst. Tech., 1970-72; rsch. assoc. aerosol physics dept. Lovelace Found. for Med. Edn. and Rsch., Albuquerque, 1972-74; from adj. asst. prof. to assoc. prof. in residence dept. community and environ. medicine U. Calif., Irvine, 1974-84, prof. in residence, dir. Air Pollution Health Effects Lab., 1985—, faculty Ctr. for Occupl. Environ. Health, 1985—; reviewer Am. Rev. Respiratory Disease, Applied Indsl. Hygiene, Bull. Math. Biology, Exptl. Lung Rsch., Jour. Toxicology and Environ. Health, Jour. Toxicology and Applied Pharmacology, Jour. Aerosol Sci., Sci.; reviewer, mem. editl. bd. Fundamental and Applied Toxicology, 1986-92, Inhalation Toxicology, Jour. Aerosol Medicine; mem. safety and occupl. health study sect. NIH, 1988-90, mem. spl. study sects., 1980, 81, chmn. spl. study sects., 1982, 83, 84, 87, 88, 92, mem. site visit teams, 1980, 81, 82, 83, 84, 88; mem. expert panel on sulfur oxides EPA, mem. inhalation toxicology divsn. peer rev. panel, 1982, session chmn., 1983, participant workshop on non-oncogenic lung disease, 1984, mem. grants rsch. sci. rev. panel on health rsch., 1985-88; mem. task group on respiratory tract kinetic model Nat. Coun. Radiation Protection, 1978-97; mem. adv. panel on asbestos APHA, 1978; chmn. atmospheric sampling com. Am. Coun. Govtl. Indsl. Hygienists, 1982-92; chmn. NIOSH spl. study sect., 1983; panelist workshop Nat. Heart, Lung and Blood Inst., 1982; sci. advisor Prentice Day Sch., 1986—. Author: Inhalation Studies: Foundations and Techniques, 1984, (with others) Advances in Air Sampling, 1997, Concepts in Inhalation Toxicology, 1989, Deposition, Retention and Dosimetry of Inhaled Radioactive Substances, 1997; editor: Methods in Inhalation Toxicology, 1997; contbr. numerous articles to profl. jours. Am. Legion scholar. Mem. AAAS, Am. Assn. Aerosol Rsch. (charter, chmn. ann. meeting 1985), Am. Conf. Govtl. Indsl. Hygienists, Am. Indsl. Hygiene Assn. (jour. reviewer, chmn. ann. conf. 1981, 85, 86), Brit. Occupational Hygiene Soc., Fine Particle Soc., Soc. for Aerosol Rsch., Health Physics Soc., Soc. Toxicology (chmn. 20th ann. meeting 1981, dir. 2 internat. confs. on health effects of particulate air pollution). Achievements include research in nasal, tracheobronchial and pulmonary transport of inhaled deposited particles and effects of pollutant exposure on transport kinetcs, laboratory simulation and characterization of airborne environmental pollutants, respiratory tract deposition and clearance models for inhaled particles, including species comparisons and body size effects, behavior of highly-concentrated aerosols with respect to deposition in the respiratory tract. Office: University of California Air Pollution Health Effects Lab Dept of Community & Environ Irvine CA 92697-1825

PHAM, SI MAI, cadiothoracic surgeon, medical educator; b. Ninh Hoa, Khanh Hoa, Vietnam, Oct. 6, 1955; came to U.S. 1975; s. Tro Pham and Nhung Thi Mai; m. Marie Christine Pham, Sept. 9, 1987; children: Benjamin Bartley, Anthony Ninh. Student, U. Saigon, Sch. Pharmacy, Vietnam, 1973-75; BS in Chem. magna cum laude, Lebanon Valley Coll., Annville, Pa., 1979; MD, U. Pitts., 1983. Diplomate Am. Bd. Surgery, Am. Bd. Thoracic Surgery. Intern, resident gen. surgery U. Pitts., Pitts., Pa., 1983-86, rsch. fellow, cardiothoracic surgery, 1986-87, sr. and chief resident, gen. surgery, 1987-89, resident cardiothoracic surgery, 1989-92, asst. prof. surgery, Sch. of Medicine, 1992—, dir. adult cardiac transplant program, Sch. of Medicine, 1993—; dir. extracorporeal membrane oxygenation svc. Presbyterian U. Hosp., Pitts., Pa., 1993—. Contbr. chpts. to books, articles to profl. jours. Recipient Am. Chem. award, 1979, Radiology award U. Pitts., 1983, Dalsemer rsch. scholar award Am. Lung Assn., 1997—; ACS Faculty fellowship award, 1994—; grantee Children's Hosp. Pitts., 1987, Am. Heart Assn., 1987-89, 94-96, 96—, Thoracic Surgery Found., 1996-97, 97-98, Presbyn. U. Hosp., 1987-89. Fellow Am. Coll. Surgeons; mem. Am. Soc. Artificial Internal Organs, Internat. Soc. Heart and Lung Transplantation, Soc. Critical Care Medicine, Am. Assn. Advancement of Sci., Am. Soc. Transplant Surgeons, Soc. Thoracic Surgeons, Extracorporeal Life Support Organization, Assn. for Acad. Surgery, Phi Alpha Epsilon. Home: 305 Marberry Dr Pittsburgh PA 15215-1437 Office: U Pitts Med Ctr Divsn CTS 200 Lothrop St Rm C-700 Pittsburgh PA 15213-2546

PHAN, TÂM THANH, medical educator, psychotherapist, consultant, researcher; b. Hue, Vietnam, June 10, 1949; d. Quê'Dinh and Chánh Thi (Tô) P. BA, Adams State Coll., 1979; MA, Western State Coll., 1980; PhD in Nutrition, Am. Coll. Nutrition, 1983; D of Nutrimedicine, John Kennedy Nutrisci., Gary, Ind., 1986; PhD in Counseling, Columbus Pacific U., 1988; DSc, Lafayette U., 1989. Lic. profl. counselor, marriage and family therapist; cert. nutrimedicine specialist. Counselor Lamar U., Beaumont, Tex., 1980-82; cons. Vietnamese Cmty., Golden Triangle, Tex., 1980—, The Wholistic Clinic, Beaumont, 1980—; mem. adv. bd. Internat. Homeopathic Clearance, Mo., 1993—. Author: How Western Culture..., 1988, Natural Preventive Medicine, The Wholitic Approach, 1992, How to Prevent Mental Illness, 1995, How to Prevent Diabetes, 1996. Fellow Internat. Nutrimedicine Assn., Am. Nutrimedicine Assn.; mem. Internat. Alliance of Nutrimedical Therapists, Internat. Holistic Med. Soc. (bd. dirs. 1996, Cert. of Merit 1996). Avocations: writing, reading, swimming, cooking, knitting. Office: The Wholistic Clinic 1995 Broadway St Beaumont TX 77701-1941

PHARES, ALAIN JOSEPH, physicist, educator; b. Beirut, Apr. 20, 1942; came to U.S., 1975, naturalized, 1982; s. Joseph Michel and Renee Cecile (Dommar) P.; m. Claude Tawa, July 27, 1968; children—Caroline, Denis, Pascal. B.S. in Engring., St. Joseph U., 1964; Docteur-es-Sciences, U. Paris, 1971; Ph.D., Harvard U., 1973. Research fellow Nat. Council Sci. Research, Lebanon, 1973-75; assoc. prof. Lebanese U., 1973-75; research fellow Internat. Centre Theoretical Physics, Trieste, Italy, 1974, Harvard U., 1975-76; vis. asst. prof. U. Mont., 1976-77; asst. prof. physics Villanova U., Pa., 1977-79, assoc. prof., 1979-82, prof., 1982—, chmn. dept., 1981-91, dir. secondary sch. sci., 1981-94. Contbr. articles to profl. jours. French Govt. fellwo, 1964-66, IAEA fellow, 1974; grantee Villanova Rsch., 1978, NSF, 1991—; recipient Outstanding Faculty Rsch. award Villanova U., 1986;. Mem. Am. Phys. Soc., Internat. Assn. Math. and Computers in Simulation, Sigma Xi. Office: Villanova U Dept Physics Villanova PA 19085

PHARES, E. JERRY, psychology educator; b. Glendale, Ohio, July 21, 1928; s. Bruce and Gladys (West) P.; m. Betty L. Knost, Aug. 6, 1955; 1 dau., Lisa M. B.A., U. Cin., 1951; M.A., Ohio State U., 1953, Ph.D., 1955. Faculty Kans. State U., Manhattan, 1955—, prof. psychology, 1964-91, prof. emeritus, 1991—, head dept., 1967-89; Vis. asso. prof. Ohio State U., Columbus, Ohio Wesleyan U., 1961-62. Author, co-author books.; Contbr. articles to profl. jours. Research grantee NIMH, 1960, 80; Research grantee NSF, 1964-76; Research grantee Population Council, 1971. Fellow Am. Psychol. Assn., Am. Psychol. Soc. Office: Psychology Dept Kan State U Manhattan KS 66506

PHARES, LYNN LEVISAY, public relations communications executive; b. Brownwood, Tex., Aug. 6, 1947; m. C. Kirk Phares, Aug. 22, 1971; children: Laura, Margaret, Adele, Jessica. BA, La. State U., 1970; MA, U. Nebr., 1987. Asst. to advt. mgr. La. Nat. Bank, 1970-71; writer, producer, asst. v.p., account exec. Smith, Kaplan, Allen & Reynolds, Inc., Omaha, 1971-80; assoc. dir. pub. affairs U. Nebr. Med. Ctr., 1980-83; dir. pub. rels. ConAgra, Inc., Omaha, 1985-87, v.p. pub. rels., 1987-90, v.p. pub. rels. and cmty. affairs, 1990-96; v.p., corp. rels. ConAgra, Inc., 1996—; pres. ConAgra Found. Office: ConAgra Inc 1 Conagra Dr Omaha NE 68102-5094

PHARIS, RUTH MCCALISTER, retired banker; b. San Diego, Feb. 13, 1934; d. William L. and Mary E. (Beuk) McC.; grad. Del Mar Coll., Corpus Christi, Tex., 1975-79; m. E. Edwin Pharis, Mar. 14, 1953; children—Beth, Tracey, Todd. Asst. cashier Parkdale State Bank, Corpus Christi, 1970-72, asst. v.p., 1972-76, v.p., 1976-79: v.p. Cullen Center Bank & Trust, Houston, 1979-81, sr. v.p., 1982-93; instr. Am. Inst. Banking, 1977-79. Mem. adv. council Houston Community Colls. Mem. Human Resource Mgmt. Assn., Bank Adminstrn. Inst. (v.p. Coastal Bend chpt. 1979), Nat. Assn. Bank Women (ednl. chmn. Coastal Bend group), Am. Inst. Banking (rep.), Tex. Bankers Assn. (council 1983-84, instr.), Coastal Bend Personnel Soc. (v.p.), Houston Personnel Assn., Corpus Christi C. of C. (mem. women's com. 1976-79). Republican. Baptist. Club: Order Eastern Star. Home: 2750 Laurel Cliff Dr New Braunfels TX 78132-3256

PHELAN, ARTHUR JOSEPH, financial executive; b. N.Y.C., Oct. 26, 1915; s. Arthur Joseph and Josephine Adelaide (Barrett) P.; m. Mary Frances Ryan, Feb. 11, 1939; children—Jane Carolee, Leslie Diane, Sandra Christine. Student, Am. Inst. Banking, 1934-35, NYU, 1935-36. With Guaranty Trust Co. of N.Y., 1933-37; accountant N.Y. Post, 1937-38; accountant Webb & Knapp, Inc., N.Y.C., 1938-41, asst. sec., 1941, comptroller, 1942-44, treas., 1944-53, v.p., treas., 1953-55, sr. v.p., dir., 1955-65; also trustee employees profit sharing plan, exec. v.p. David Greenewald Assocs., Inc., 1965-66; sr. v.p. Lefrak Orgn., Inc.,, Forest Hills, N.Y., 1966-92; exec. v.p., dir. LOGO Inc., Tulsa, Okla., 1976-92. Roman Catholic. Club: North Hempstead Country. Home: 88 Summit Rd Port Washington NY 11050-3341

PHELAN, CHARLOTTE ROBERTSON, journalist, book critic; b. Vernon, Tex., May 12, 1917; d. Macum and Bonita (Robertson) P. BA, Tex. Wesleyan U., 1940. City editor Daily News, Lufkin, Tex., 1941-43; an editor Tex. bur. AP, Dallas, 1943-45; publicity dir., program editor, annotator San Antonio Symphony and Grand Opera, 1945-55; staff writer Houston Post, 1955-70, film and drama critic, 1970-73, book editor, 1973-82; leader workshops, panelist in field. Dir. Guadalupe Valley Telephone Cooperative, Inc.; bd. durs. G.V. Communication Systems, Inc.; past mem. Bishop's com. St. Francis by the Lake Episcopal Ch. Recipient 1st pl. feature writing Headliners Club, Austin, Tex., 1964, 1st pl. women's page series, 1968. Mem. Nat. Book Critics Cir., Pilot Internat., Canyon Lake Golf and Country Club. Democrat. Episcopalian. Home: 679 Irene Dr Canyon Lake TX 78133-5293

PHELAN, ELLEN, artist; b. Detroit, Nov. 3, 1943; d. Thomas Edward and Katherine Louise (Gojlewicz) P; m. Joel Elias Shapiro, Nov. 22, 1978. BFA, Wayne State U., 1969, MFA, 1971. Instr. Wayne State U., Detroit, 1969-72, Fairleigh Dickinson U., 1974, Mich. State U., East Lansing, 1974-75, Calif. Inst. Arts, 1978-79, Bard Coll., 1980, NYU, 1981, Sch. of Visual Arts, 1981-83, Calif. Inst. Arts, 1983; prof. of practice of studio art Harvard U., Cambridge, Mass., 1995—; Milton Avery vis. lectr. Bard Coll., 1994. One-woman exhbns. include Willis Gallery, Detroit, 1972, 74, Artist's Space, N.Y.C., 1975, Susanne Hilberry Gallery, Birmingham, Mich., 1977, 79, 81, 82, 84, 86, 88, 90, 92, 94, Wadsworth Athenaeum, Hartford, Conn., 1979, Ruth Schaffner Gallery, L.A., 1979, The Clocktower, N.Y.C., 1980, Hansen-Fuller-Goldeen Gallery, San Francisco, 1980, 82, Dart Gallery, Chgo., 1981, Barbara Toll Fine Arts, N.Y.C., 1982, 85, 86, 87-88, 89, 90, 92, 93, Asher/Faure, L.A., 1989, 92, 94, Balt. Mus. Art, 1989, Albright-Knox Art Gallery, Buffalo, 1991, U. Mass. Amherst Fine Arts Ctr., 1992, Saidye Bronfman Ctr., Montreal, Que., 1993, Contemporary Mus., Honolulu, 1993, John Stoller, Inc., Mpls., 1993, Cin. Art Mus., 1994; exhibited in group shows at Detroit Inst. Arts, 1970, 80, Willis Gallery, Detroit, 1971, 79, J.L. Hudson Gallery, Detroit, 1972, Cranbrook Acad. Art, Bloomfield Hills, Mich., 1972, 79, 84, Grand Rapids (Mich.) Art Mus., 1974, Paula Cooper Gallery, N.Y.C., 1975, 76, 77, 78, 79, 90, Fine Arts Bldg., N.Y.C., 1976, Acad. der Kunste, Berlin, 1976, Susanne Hilberry Gallery, Birmingham, 1976-77, 83, 85, 91, Willard Gallery, N.Y.C., 1977, Kansas City (Mo.) Art Inst., 1977, N.A.M.E. Gallery, Chgo., 1977, Hallwalls, Buffalo, 1977, Mus. Modern Art, N.Y.C., 1978, 89, 92, Weatherspoon Art Gallery U. N.C., Greensboro, 1979, 92, Albright-Knox Gallery, Buffalo, 1979, Brown U., Providence, 1980, XIII Olympic Winter Games, Lake Placid, N.Y., 1980, Jeffrey Fuller Fine Art, Phila., 1980, Portland (Oreg.) Ctr. for Visual Arts, 1980, The Drawing Ctr., N.Y.C., 1980, 82, Brooke Alexander Gallery, N.Y.C., 1980, Mus. Contemporary Art, Chgo., 1980, 81, P.S. 1 Mus., N.Y.C., 1981, 92, Art Latitude Gallery, N.Y.C., 1981, Leo Castelli Gallery, N.Y.C., 1981, Sutton Place, Guildford, Eng., 1982, Gallerie d'Arte Moderna di Ca'Pesaro, Venice, Italy, 1982, Inst. Contemporary Art of Virgini Mus., Richmond, Va., 1982, Galerie Biedermann, Munich, 1982, Thomas Segal Gallery, Boston, 1983, Fuller-Goldeen Gallery, San Francisco, 1983, 86, William Paterson Coll., Wayne, N.J., 1983, 89, Artist's Space, N.Y.C., 1983, 84, Harborside Indsl. Ctr., Bklyn., 1983, Orgn. Ind. Artists, N.Y.C., 1984, Bernice Steinbaum Gallery, N.Y.C., 1984, Brentwood Gallery, St. Louis, 1984, U. Calif., Irvine, 1984, U. No. Iowa Gallery Art, Cedar Falls, 1984, Hudson River Mus., N.Y.C., 1984, Barbara Toll Fine Arts, N.Y.C., 1984, 85, 86, 87, Detroit Focus Gallery, 1984, Cable Gallery, N.Y.C., 1984, Wayne State U., Detroit, 1984, Matthews Hamilton Gallery, Phila., 1984, Barbara Krakow Gallery, Boston, 1984, BlumHelman Warehouse, N.Y.C., 1984, Pam Adler Gallery, N.Y.C., 1985, Daniel Weinberg Gallery, L.A., 1985, 89, Knight Gallery, Charlotte, N.C., 1985, Bank of Boston, 1986, Whitney Mus. Am. Art, Stamford, Conn., 1987, 89, Scott Hansen Gallery, N.Y.C., 1987, Saxon-Lee Gallery, L.A., 1987, Parrish Art Mus., East Hampton, N.Y., 1987, Curt Marcus Gallery, N.Y., 1988, Loughelton Gallery, N.Y.C., 1988, 90, Whitney Mus. Am. Art, N.Y.C., 1988, 91, Hillwood Art Gallery C.W. Post Campus, Brookville, N.Y., 1989, USIA traveling exbhn., 1989, Edward Thorp Gallery, N.Y.C., 1989, Pine Street Lobby Gallery, San Francisco, 1989, Fuller Gross Gallery, San Francisco, 1989, Solo Press/Soho Gallery, N.Y.C., 1989, Maxwell Davidson Gallery, N.Y.C., 1989, Blum Helman Gallery, N.Y.C., 1989, R.I.S.D., Providence, 1989, Graham Modern, N.Y.C., 1990, Hood Mus. Art Dartmouth Coll., Hanover, N.H., 1990, 92, New Britain Mus. Am. Art, Hartford, Conn., 1991, Asher-Faure, L.A., 1991, Annina Nosei Gallery, N.Y.C., 1991, Lintas Worldwide, N.Y.C., 1991, Nina Fredenheim Gallery, Buffalo, 1991, Molica Guidarte Gallery, N.Y.C., 1991, Squibb Gallery, Princeton, N.J., 1991, Cleve. State U. Gallery, 1992, Ind. Curators Inc., N.Y.C., 1992, Wexner Ctr. for the Arts, Columbus, Ohio, 1992, Transamerica Corp., San Francisco, 1992, The Gallery Three Zero, N.Y.C., 1992, Haggerty Mus. Art, Milw., Barbara Methes Gallery, N.Y.C., Asher Fauve Gallery, L.A., Hillwood Art Mus., Brookville, N.Y., Pamela Auchincloss Gallery, N.Y.C., Leo Castelli Gallery, N.Y.C.; represented in permanent collections Mus. Modern Art, N.Y.C., Whitney Mus. Am. Art, N.Y.C., Bklyn. Mus., Walker Art Ctr., Mpls., Balt. Mus., Toledo Mus. Art, Hood Mus. Dartmouth Coll., High Mus. Art, Albright-Knox Art Gallery, Moderna Museet, Stockholm, Mus. Contemporary Art, Mexico City, Detroit Inst. Arts, MIT, Whitehead Inst., Philip Morris, Inc., Volvo Corp., Chase Manhattan Bank, Chem. Bank, BankAm., Bank of Am., Prudential Ins. Co., U.S. Trust & Co., Inter Metro Industries, Lannan Found., numerous pvt. collections. Nat. Endowment for Arts grantee, 1978-79; recipient Am. Acad. Arts and Letters award, 1995, Arts Achievement award Wayne State U., 1989.

PHELAN, JOHN DENSMORE, insurance executive, consultant; b. Kalamazoo, Aug. 31, 1914; s. John and Ida (Densmore) P.; m. Isabel McLaughlin, July 31, 1937; children: John Walter, William Paul, Daniel Joseph. BA magna cum laude, Carleton Coll., 1935. Reporter New Bedford (Mass.) Standard-Times, 1935-36; with Hardware Mut. Ins. Co. (name now Sentry Ins. Co.), Stevens Point, Wis., 1936-45; with Am. States Ins. Co., Indpls., 1945-90, pres., 1963-76, chmn., 1976-79, also dir. numerous subs.; bd. govs. Internat. Ins. Soc. Author: Business Interruption Primer, 1949, also later edits.; contbr. articles to profl. jours. Past pres. Marion County Assn. Mental Health; chmn. emeritus. CPCU-Harry J. Loman Found. Named to Honorable Order of Ky. Colonels, Sagamore of the Wabash. Mem. CPCU Soc. (past nat pres.), CLU Soc., Woodland Country Club (Indpls.), El Conquistador Country Club (Bradenton, Fla.), Phi Beta Kappa. Presbyterian. Home: 6501 17th Ave W # 206 Bradenton FL 34209

PHELAN, MARTIN DUPONT, retired film company executive; b. Chgo., Dec. 25, 1913; s. Martin Anthony and Margaret Crespo (DuPont) P.; m. Mary Katharine Harris, Aug. 14, 1937; children—Richard H., Jeremy D. A.B., DePauw U., 1934. Mdse. exec. Montgomery Ward, Chgo., 1934-42, Butler Bros., Chgo., 1946-47; corporate officer Eastin-Phelan Corp., Davenport, Iowa, 1947-77. Served to col. U.S. Army, 1942-46. Mem. Iowa Libr. Trustee Assn. (pres. 1980), Ponte Vedra Club, Rotary. Republican. Episcopalian. Home: Guildford 207 Vicar's Landing Ponte Vedra Beach FL 32082

PHELAN, RICHARD MAGRUDER, mechanical engineer; b. Moberly, Mo., Sept. 20, 1921; s. Frederick William and Ethel Ray (Magruder) P.; m. Olive Bernice McIntosh, May 25, 1951; children—William James, Susan Ray. Student, Moberly Jr. Coll., 1939-41; B.S. in Mech. Engring, U. Mo.-Columbia, 1943; M.M.E., Cornell U., 1950; postgrad., U. Mich., 1956-57. Instr. Cornell U., 1947-50, asst. prof. mech. engring., 1950-56, assoc. prof., 1956-62, prof., 1962-87, prof. emeritus, 1988—. Author: Fundamentals of Mechanical Design, 1957, 3d rev. edit., 1970, Dynamics of Machinery, 1967, Automatic Control Systems, 1977. Served with USNR, 1943-46. Mem. ASME, Am. Soc. Engring. Edn., Soc. Exptl. Stress Analysis, Am. Gear Mfrs. Assn., AAUP, AAAS, N.Y. Acad. Scis., Soc. Exptl. Mechanics, Sigma Xi, Phi Kappa Phi, Pi Tau Sigma, Tau Beta Pi. Home: 4 Cornell Walk Ithaca NY 14850-6145 Office: Cornell U Upson Hall Ithaca NY 14853

PHELAN, RICHARD PAUL, bank executive; b. N.Y.C., Oct. 26, 1939; s. Peter James and Florence (Leary) P.; m. Bridget Burke, Sept. 17, 1966; children: Richard Matthew, Peter Michael, Robert William. Student, CCNY, 1957-58; Diploma, Am. Inst. Banking, N.Y.C., 1962; BS, NYU, 1967, MBA, 1969; MA, Columbia U., 1992. Sr. v.p. Chase Manhattan, N.Y.C., 1957—. Mem. Union League Club. Republican. Roman Catholic. Home: 564 Dutch Neck Rd East Windsor NJ 08520-1124

PHELAN, ROBIN ERIC, lawyer; b. Steubenville, Ohio, Dec. 28, 1945; s. Edward John and Dorothy (Borkowski) P.; m. Melinda Jo Ricketts, May 27, 1995; children: Travis McCoy, Tiffany Marie, Trevor Monroe. BSBA, Ohio State U., 1967, JD, 1970. Bar: Tex. 1971, U.S. Ct. Appeals (5th cir.) 1981, U.S. Ct. Appeals (11th cir.) 1981, U.S. Ct. Appeals (6th cir.) 1986, U.S. Ct. Appeals (10th cir.) 1988, U.S. Supreme Ct. Ptnr. Haynes and Boone, Dallas, 1970—; bd. dirs. Am. Bankruptcy Inst., Washington, pres., 1994-96; regent Am. Coll. Bankruptcy. Co-author: Bankruptcy Practice and Strategy, 1987, Cowans Bankruptcy Law and Practice, 1987, Annual Survey of Bankruptcy Law, 1988, Bankruptcy Litigation Manual; contbr. articles to profl. jours. Mem. ABA (chmn. bankruptcy litigation subcom. 1990-95), State Bar Tex. (chmn. bankruptcy law com. sect. bus. law 1989-91), Dallas Bar Assn. Roman Catholic. Avocation: athletics. Home: 4214 Woodfin Dr Dallas TX 75220-6416

PHELAN, THOMAS, clergyman, academic administrator, educator; b. Albany, N.Y., Apr. 11, 1925; s. Thomas William and Helen (Rausch) P. A.B. (N.Y. State Regents scholar 1942, President's medal 1945), Coll. Holy Cross, Worcester, Mass., 1945; S.T.L., Catholic U. Am., 1951; postgrad., Oxford (Eng.) U., 1958-59, 69-70. Ordained priest Roman Cath. Ch., 1951; pastor, tchr., adminstr. Diocese of Albany, 1951-58; resident Cath. chaplain Rensselaer Poly. Inst., Troy, N.Y., 1959-72, prof. history, 1972—, dean Sch. Humanities and Social Scis., 1972-95, inst. historian, inst. dean, sr. adviser to pres., 1995—; chmn. architecture and bldg. commn. Diocese Albany, 1968—; cons. in field. Author: Hudson Mohawk Gateway, 1985, Achieving the Impossible, 1995; author monographs, articles, revs. in field. Treas. The Rensselaer Newman Found., 1962—; pres. Hudson-Mohawk Indsl. Gateway, 1971-84, bd. dirs. exec. com. 1984—; mem. WMHT Ednl. Telecomm. Bd., 1966-77, 84-90, chmn. 1973-77; chmn. Troy Hist. Dist. and Landmarks Rev. Commn., 1975-86, chmn. hist. adv. com., 1987—; v.p. Preservation League N.Y. State, 1979-82, mem. trustees coun., 1982-87, 89—, pres. 1987-89; sec. and bd. dirs. Ptnrs. for Sacred Places, 1989—; bd. dirs. Hall of History Found., 1983-87; trustee Troy Pub. Libr., 1992—, bd. dirs.; mem. Pres.' Coun. Sage Colls. With USN, 1943-46. Recipient Paul J. Hallinan award Nat. Newman Chaplains Assn., 1967, Ann. award Albany Arts League, 1977, Disting. Cmty. Svc. award Rensselaer Poly. Inst., 1979, Edward Fox Demers medal Alumni Assn. Rensselaer Poly. Inst., 1986, Disting. Svc. award Hudson-Mohawk Consortium of Colls. and Univs., 1988; named Acad. Laureate of the SUNY Found. at Albany, 1988; Danforth Found. fellow, 1969-70; grantee Homeland Found., 1958-59, Dorothy Thomas Found., 1969-70. Fellow Soc. Arts, Religion and Contemporary Culture; mem. Ch. Soc. Coll. Work (dir., exec. com. 1970—), Am. Conf. Acad. Deans, Liturgical Conf., Soc. Indsl. Archaeology, Assn. Internat. pour l'Etudes des Religions Prehistoriques et Ethnologiques, Cath. Campus Ministry Assn., Cath. Art Assn., Assn. for Religion and the Intellectual Life (bd. dirs. 1987—), Soc. History of Tech. Clubs: Ft. Orange, Troy Country; Squadron A (N.Y.C.). Home: 5 Whitman Ct Troy NY 12180-4732 Office: Rensselaer Poly Inst Troy NY 12180 *Service and community building have motivated most of my business and personal actions. I received these values from my parents and from the church. I work to make positive contributions towards a world in which there is more justice and consequent hope of peace.*

PHELPS, ARTHUR VAN RENSSELAER, physicist, consultant; b. Dover, N.H., July 20, 1923; s. George Osborne and Helen (Ketchum) P.; m. Gertrude Kanzius, July 21, 1956; children: Wayne Edward, Joan Susan. ScD in Physics, MIT, 1951. Cons. physicist rsch. labs. Westinghouse Elec. Corp., Pitts., 1951-70; sr. rsch. scientist Nat. Bur. Standards, Boulder, Colo., 1970-88; fellow Joint Inst. Lab. Astrophysics U. Colo., Boulder, 1970-88, adjoint fellow, 1988—, chmn., 1979-81; chmn. Gordon Rsch. Conf., Plasma Chemistry, 1990. Recipient Silver Medal award Dept. Commerce, 1978. Fellow Am. Phys. Soc. (Will Allis prize 1990). Achievements include patent for Schulz-Phelps ionization gauge; research on electron and atomic collision processes involving low energy electrons, molecules, ions, metastable atoms and resonance radiation; on laser processes and modeling; on gaseous electronics. Home: 3405 Endicott Dr Boulder CO 80303-6908 Office: U Colo Joint Inst Lab Astrophysics Campus Box 440 Boulder CO 80309-0440

PHELPS, ASHTON, JR., newspaper publisher; b. New Orleans, Nov. 4, 1945; s. Ashton Sr. and Jane Cary (George) P.; m. Mary Ella Sanders, Apr. 10, 1976; children—Cary Clifton, Mary Louise, Sanders. BA, Yale U., 1967; JD, Tulane U., 1970. Trainee Times-Picayune Pub. Corp., New Orleans, 1970-71; asst. to pub. Times-Picayune Pub. Corp., 1971-79, pres., pub., 1979-97, pub., 1997—. Bd. dirs. Bur. Govtl. Rsch., New Orleans, 1973-89, Xavier U. of La., New Orleans, 1974-82, Coun. for Better La., 1982-85, Met. Area Com., New Orleans, Ochsner Found. Hosp., New Orleans, 1982—, Internat. House, New Orleans, 1981-83, Pub. Affairs Rsch., New Orleans, 1982-85, La. Children's Mus., New Orleans, 1983-90, Yale Alumni Assn. of La., 1985, Newspaper Advt. Bur. Future of Advt. Com., 1986-89; chmn. Audit Com. of Associated Press, 1986-90. Mem. So. Newspaper Pubs. Assn. (bd. dirs. 1982-85, found. bd. dirs. 1982-83, pres. 1990-91), La. Press Assn. (bd. dirs. 1984-93, v.p. 1989-90, pres. 1991-92). Avocation: tennis. Office: The Times-Picayune 3800 Howard Ave New Orleans LA 70140-1002*

PHELPS, BARTON CHASE, architect, educator; b. Bklyn., June 27, 1946; s. Julian Orville and Elizabeth Willis (Faulk) P.; m. Karen Joy Simonson; 1 child, Charlotte Simonson Phelps. BA in Art with honors, Williams Coll., 1968; MArch, Yale U., 1973. Registered architect, Calif. With Colin St. John Wilson & Ptnrs., London, 1972-73, Frank O. Gehry and Assocs., Inc., Santa Monica, Calif., 1973-76, Charles Moore/Urban Innovations Group, L.A., 1976-78; dir. architecture Urban Innovations Group, L.A., 1980-84; prin. Barton Phelps & Assocs., L.A., 1984—; asst. prof. architecture Rice U. Sch. of Architecture, Houston, 1977-79; asst. dean Grad. Sch. Architecture and Urban Planning, UCLA, 1980-83; prof. architecture Sch. Arts and Architecture UCLA; faculty mem. Nat. Endowment Arts, Mayors Inst. for City Design, 1990, 92. Author, editor: Architecture California, 1988-92. Fellow Graham Found. for advanced Studies in Fine Art, 1989, Nat. Endowment for the Arts, 1988. Mem. AIA (Coll. of Fellows, chair nat. com. on design, recipient design awards for Arroyo House, Kranz House, North Range Clark Libr. UCLA, L.A. Dept. Water and Power Ctrl. Dist. Hdqrs., No. Hollywood Pump Sta., East Bldg. Seeds U. Elem. Sch., UCLA, Inst. Honor for Collaborative Design, Games XXIII Olympiad L.A. 1984). Democrat. Home: 10256 Lelia Ln Los Angeles CA 90077-3144 Office: Barton Phelps & Assocs 5514 Wilshire Blvd Los Angeles CA 90036-3829

PHELPS, CAROL JO, neuroendocrinologist; b. Sendai, Japan, Apr. 20, 1948; d. Harry J. and Helen I. (Davies) P.; m. James B. Turpen, June 13, 1969 (div. Apr. 1982); children: J. Matthew Turpen, John A. Turpen; m. David L. Hurley, Oct. 12, 1985. BS in Zoology, U. Denver, 1969; PhD in Anatomy, La. State U. Med. Ctr., 1974. Postdoctoral fellow NIH, U. Rochester, N.Y., 1974-76; rsch. assoc. Pa. State U., Univ. Park, 1976-77; instr. Pa. State U., 1977-80, postdoctoral scholar, 1980-82; asst. prof. neurobiology U. Rochester, 1982-90; assoc. prof. anatomy Tulane U. Sch. Medicine, New Orleans, 1990-94; prof., 1994—; nat. scientific adv. coun. Am. Fedn. Aging Rsch., N.Y.C., 1988—; rev. coms. Nat. Inst. on Aging, Bethesda, Md., 1993—; editl. bd. Neuroendocrinology, Paris, 1994—, Endocrinology, 1996—, Jour. of Andrology, 1996—. Com. sec., chair Oteitiana Coun. Pack 10 Boy Scouts Am., Honeoye Falls, N.Y., 1987-89. NIH fellow, 1974-76; grantee NIH, 1983—. Mem. Am. Assn. Anatomists, Soc. Exptl. Biology and Medicine, Endocrine Soc., Soc. Neurosci. (chpt. pres. 1995-96). Avocations: antique restoration, photography. Office: Tulane U Sch Medicine Dept Anatomy 1430 Tulane Ave New Orleans LA 70112-2699

PHELPS, CHARLES ELLIOTT, economics educator; b. N.Y.C., Apr. 20, 1943; s. McKinnie L. and Carolyn (McCleery) P.; m. Dale L. King, Sept. 2, 1967; children: Darin, Teresa. BA in Math., Pomona Coll., 1965; MBA, U. Chgo., 1968, PhD, 1973. Economist RAND Corp., Santa Monica, Calif., 1973-84; prof. econs. U. Rochester, N.Y., 1984—; provost U. Rochester, 1994—; cons. JUREcon, Inc., L.A., 1977-86; pvt. cons., Rochester, N.Y., 1986—. Author: Health Economics, 1996; also over 70 articles. Fellow Nat. Bur. for Econ. Rsch.; mem. Inst. Medicine, Am. Econ. Assn., Soc. for Med. Decision Making (trustee 1991-93), Assn. for Pub. Policy Analysis (sec. 1982-91). Avocations: cycling, photography, archery. Office: Office of the Provost U Rochester 200 Administration Bldg. Rochester NY 14627-0001

PHELPS, DEANNE ELAYNE, educational counselor, consultant; b. Cin., Sept. 4, 1949; d. Carlie Earthel and Marcella (Johnson) Smith; m. Jack L. Phelps, Aug. 9, 1969; children: Lisa Michele Phelps Turner, Amy Kristen Phelps Grantland. BA, Eastern Ky. U., 1971; MS in Counseling Edn., Jacksonville (Ala.) State U., 1990. Cert. secondary and English edn. tchr., Ala. Tchr. English Trinity Christian Acad., Oxford, Ala., 1976-79; dir., tchr. Bynum (Ala.) Bapt. Kindergarten, 1979-80; instr. in English Cen. Tex. Coll., Ft. McClellan, Ala., 1983-84, Jacksonville State U., 1985-88; tchr. English Wellborn High Sch., Anniston, Ala., 1989-90; owner, cons. The Communication Factor, Anniston, 1990-93; pers. counselor Temporary Resources, Inc., Anniston, Ala., 1991-92; resource cons., career/transition counselor Orkand Corp., Ft. McClellan, 1992-93; mgr., sr. counselor Resource Cons., Inc., Ft. McClellan, 1993—. Mem. ACA, NAFE, Ala. Counseling Assn., Nat. Employment Counselors Assn., Nat. Career Devel. Assn., Calhoun County C. of C., Leadership Calhoun County (vice chmn. bd. dirs.), Chi Sigma Iota.

PHELPS, EDMUND STROTHER, economics educator; b. Evanston, Ill., July 26, 1933; s. Edmund Strother and Florence Esther (Stone) P.; m. Viviana Regina Montdor, Oct. 1, 1974. BA, Amherst Coll., 1955, DLitt (hon.), 1985; MA, Yale U., 1956, PhD, 1959. Economist Rand Corp., Santa Monica, Calif., 1959-60; asst. prof. Yale U., Cowles Found., 1960-62, assoc. prof., 1963-66; vis. assoc. prof. M.I.T., 1962-63; prof. econs. U. Pa., Phila., 1966-71; prof. econs. Columbia U., 1971-78, 79-82, McVickar prof. polit. economy, 1982—; scholar Russell Sage Found., 1993-94; prof. NYU, 1978-79; fellow Ctr. for Advanced Study in Behavioiral Scis., 1969-70; sr. advisor Brookings Inst., 1976—; econ. advisor European Bank for Reconstrn. and Devel., 1991-94; mem. econ. policy panel Observatoire Francais des Conjonctures Economiques, 1991—. Author: numerous books including Golden Rules of Economic Growth, 1966, Microeconomic Foundations of Employment and Inflation Theory, 1970, Economic Justice, 1973, Studies in Macroeconomic Theory, Vol. I, 1979, Vol. II, 1980, Political Economy, 1985, The Slump in Europe, 1988, Structural Slumps, 1994, Rewarding Work, 1997. Guggenheim fellow, 1978; Social Sci. Research Council fellow, 1966. Mem., NAS, Fellow Econometric Soc.; Fellow Am. Acad. Arts and Scis.; mem. Am. Econ. Assn. (mem. exec. com. 1976-78, v.p. 1983, Kenan Enterprise award 1996), Phi Beta Kappa. Home: 45 E 89th St New York NY 10128-1251 Office: Columbia Univ Dept Economics New York NY 10027

PHELPS, ESMOND, II, lawyer; b. New Orleans, Sept. 16, 1945. BA, Davidson Coll., 1967; JD, Tulane U., 1970. Bar: La. 1970. Ptnr. Correro, Fishman, Haygood, Phelps, Weiss, Walmsley & Casteix LLP, New Orleans. Mem. ABA, La. State Bar Assn., New Orleans Bar Assn., La. Assn. Def. Counsel, Nat. Assn. Railroad Trial Counsel, Internat. Assn. Def. Counsel. Office: Correro Fishman Haygood Phelps Weiss Walmsley & Casteix LLP 201 St Charles Ave New Orleans LA 70170-4700

PHELPS, FLORA L(OUISE) LEWIS, editor, anthropologist, photographer; b. San Francisco, July 28, 1917; d. George Chase and Louise (Manning) Lewis; m. C(lement) Russell Phelps, Jan. 15, 1944; children: Andrew Russell, Carol Lewis, Gail Bransford. Student, U. Mich.; AB cum laude, Bryn Mawr Coll., 1938; AM, Columbia U., 1954. Acting dean Cape Cod Inst. Music, East Brewster, Mass., summer 1940; assoc. social sci. analyst U.S. Govt., 1942-44; co-adj. staff instr. anthropology Univ. Coll., Rutgers U., 1954-55; mem. editorial bd. Américas mag. OAS, Washington, 1960-82; mng. editor, 1974-82, contbg. editor, 1982-89; N.J. vice chmn. Ams. Dem. Action, 1950; mem. Dem. County Com. N.J., 1948-49. Author articles in fields of anthropology, art, architecture, edn., travel; contbr. Latin Am. newspapers. Mem. AAAS, Am. Anthrop. Assn., Archaeological Inst. Am., Latin Am. Studies Assn., Soc. for Am. Archaeology, Soc. Woman Geographers. Home: Collington # 2212 10450 Lottsford Rd Mitchellville MD 20721-2748

PHELPS, GERRY CHARLOTTE, economist, minister; b. Norman, Okla., Oct. 15, 1931; d. George and Charlotte LeNoir (Yowell) P.; 1 child, Scott. BA, U. Tex., 1963, MA, 1984; MDiv, San Francisco Theol. Seminary, 1981. Cert. tchr., Calif. Lectr. in econs. U. Houston, 1966-69; pastor United Meth. Ch., Kelseyville, Calif., 1980-82; sr. pastor Bethany United Methodist Ch., Bakersfield, Calif., 1982-84; exec. dir. Bethany Svc. Ctr., Bakersfield, 1982-84; pres., exec. dir. Concern for the Poor, Inc., San Jose, Calif., 1985-92; pastor United Meth. Ch., Flatonia, Tex., 1993—; exec. dir. Coun. Econ. Strategies, Austin, 1992—, CRISES, Austin, 1994—. Mem. Task Force on the Homeless, San Jose, 1987, Santa Clara County, 1991. Recipient commendation Mayor of Bakersfield, 1984, Santa Clara County Bd. Suprs., 1992. Avocations: Latin American studies, refugee assistance, homeless assistance, study of connections between economic and social problems. Office: CRISES PO Box 4676 Austin TX 78765-4676

PHELPS, JUDSON HEWETT, therapist, counselor, former marketing sales executive; b. Evanston, Ill., Oct. 18, 1942; s. Sidney Norman and Mary Schyler (Coons) P.; m. Barbara Ann Ray, Dec. 21, 1963; children: Wyeth Hewett, Christopher Ashley, Whitney Magee. BA, Williams Coll., 1964; MS, Springfield Coll., 1993. Cert. addictions counselor. Asst. brand mgr. Procter & Gamble Co., Cin., 1968-70; brand mgr. Memorex, Santa Clara, Calif., 1970-72; product mgr. Chesebrough Ponds Inc., Greenwich, Conn., 1972-76; v.p. mktg. L'Oreal subs. Cosmair, Inc., N.Y.C., 1976-77; v.p. sales Bio Products, Inc., Norwalk, Conn., 1978, exec. v.p., 1979, pres., 1980-86, corp. v.p. Ketchum & Co. parent co. Bio Products, Norwalk, 1982-86; mng. dir. Dameon Ptnrs. Inc., Wilton, Conn., 1987-88, pres. Theracom Corp., Rye, N.Y., 1988-89; v.p. Promotion Info. Bur., Norwalk, 1990; prin. Daniel Adams Co., Danbury, Conn., 1991-92; clin. coord., addictions therapist, counselor The Ctr., Bridgeport, Conn., 1993—; adj. faculty Housatonic Cmty. Tech. Coll., Bridgeport, Conn., 1995—. Pres. Camp Dudley (YMCA) Alumni Assn., Westport, N.Y., 1974-79; family counselor Caregivers, Assn. Religious Communities, Danbury, 1975-79; leader, treas. Ridgefield Emmaus Teenage Christian Retreats, Ridgefield, Conn., 1983-92; chmn. Ridgefield Alcohol and Drug Use Commn., 1992—. Lt. USNR, 1964-68. Home: 5 Wooster Heights Dr Ridgefield CT 06877-3109

PHELPS, KATHRYN ANNETTE, mental health counseling executive, consultant; b. Creswell, Oreg., Aug. 1, 1940; d. Henry Wilbur and Lake Ilene (Wall) M.; children: David Bryan (dec.), Derek Alan, Darla Ailene. BS in edn., Western Oreg. State Coll., 1962; MSW, Columbia State U., 1992, PhD, 1993. Tchr. Germany, Thailand, U.S., 1962-88; acct. exec. ins. industry; weight-loss counselor, alchohol/drug abuse prevention/intervention counselor teens, 1990-93; counselor Eugene, 1989-94; sr. exec. v.p., edn. dir. Light Streams, Inc., Eugene, 1993—; sr. exec. v.p., therapist Comprehensive Assessment Svcs./The Focus Inst., Inc., Eugene, 1994—; mental health counselor in pvt. practice; ednl. cons. specializing in learning disability testing Comprehensive Assessment Svcs., Eugene, 1995—; CEO Comprehensive Assessment Svcs., LLC, 1995—; cons. consumer edn.; mem. Am. Bd. Disability Analysts. Author: Easy Does It, books 1 & 2; hosted weekly TV cooking segment, Portland and U.S. Guardian Jobs Daughters, 1980-82; bd. dirs., den mother Cub Scouts, Boy Scouts, Kansas, Oreg., 1974-82; coach girls volleyball, 1974-80; vol. in orphanages, elderly nursing homes, Thailand, Germany, U.S., 1954-95; sunday sch. tchr., 1956-90; sponsored exchange student, 1984-88. Mem. Am. Bd. Disability Analysts, Eastern Star, Nat. Assn. Social Workers, Am. Counseling Assn., Columbia State U. Alumni Assn., Women's Internat. Bowling Conf. Avocations: cooking, gardening, reading, walking, car races, bowling. Home: 3838 Kendra St Eugene OR 97404

PHELPS, ORME WHEELOCK, economics educator emeritus; b. Hobart, Okla., July 5, 1906; s. William Andrews and Kate Mae (Forman) P.; m. Jean

Wright, Aug. 18, 1940; children—John Jackson, Sarah Hamilton; m. Barbara C. Green, July 25, 1981. A.B., U. Chgo., 1937, M.B.A., 1939, Ph.D., 1945. Asst. prof. bus. adminstrn. U. Chgo., 1942-47; prof. econs. Claremont (Calif.) Men's Coll. and Grad. Sch., 1947-63, sr. prof., 1963-76, emeritus, 1976—, dean faculty, 1970-74; vis. prof. UCLA, 1950, State U. N.Y. at Brockport, 1968-69; Fulbright research prof. Univ. Coll. of W.I., Kingston, Jamaica, 1957-58; Brookings research prof., Washington, 1962-63. Author: Introduction to Labor Economics, 4th edit, 1967, Discipline and Discharge in the Unionized Firm, 1959, Union Security, 1954, Legislative Background of the Fair Labor Standards Act, 1939; Contbr. articles, book revs. to profl. jours. Pub. mem., regional vice-chmn. Wage Stblzn. Bd., 1951-53; labor arbitrator, mem. various govt. bds. Ford found. fellow, 1953-54. Mem. Indsl. Relations Research Assn., Am., Western econ. assns., Am. Assn. U. Profs. Democrat. Episcopalian. Home: 1421 Rust Ct Claremont CA 91711-2732

PHELPS, RICHARD FREDERICK, basketball coach; b. Beacon, N.Y., July 4, 1941; s. Richard Bruce and Margaret Adelle (Sullivan) P.; m. Teresa K. Godwin, June 25, 1965; children: Karen, Richard, Jennifer. B.S. in Commerce, Rider Coll., 1963; M.A. in Bus. Edn, 1964. Head basketball coach St. Gabriel's High Sch., Hazleton, Pa., 1965-66; asst. basketball coach U. Pa., 1966-70; head basketball coach Fordham U., N.Y.C., 1970-71, U. Notre Dame, 1971—. Named Coach of Yr. N.Y. Coll. Basketball Writers Assn., 1971, Coach of Yr. Phila. Coll. Basketball Writers Assn., 1971, Coach of Yr. by UPI, The Sporting News, Basketball Weekly, Metropolitan Basketball Writers Assn., 1974, Coach of Yr. Basketball Weekly, 1987. Office: care ESPN ESPN Plaza Bristol CT 06010*

PHELPS, TIMOTHY MILLER, reporter; b. Newport, R.I., May 18, 1947; s. Walter Kane and Constance (Miller) P.; m. Helen Watson Winternitz; children: Constance, Paul. BA, U. Pa., Phila., 1969. Reporter Providence Jour., 1968-69, St. Petersburg (Fla.) Times, 1972-76, N.Y. Times, N.Y.C., 1980-81; freelance reporter Cairo, 1976-77; reporter Balt. Sun, 1977-80, state editor, 1981-85; Mid. East bur. chief Newsday, Cairo, 1985-91; Washington corr. Newsday, 1991-95, fgn. editor, 1996—. Co-author: Capitol Games: The Inside Story of Clarence Thomas, Anita Hill and a Supreme Court Nomination, 1992. With U.S. Army, 1969-72. Recipient Barnet Novelz award White House Correspondents Assn., 1992. Office: Newsday Fgn Desk 235 Pinelawn Rd Melville NY 11747-4226

PHEMISTER, ROBERT DAVID, veterinary medical educator; b. Framingham, Mass., July 15, 1936; s. Robert Irving and Georgia Nora (Savignac) P.; m. Ann Christine Lyon, June 14, 1960; children: Katherine, David, Susan. D.V.M., Cornell U., 1960; Ph.D., Colo. State U., Ft. Collins, 1967. Diplomate: Am. Coll. Vet. Pathologists. Research assoc. U. Calif., Davis, 1960-61, vis. rsch. pathologist, 1974-75; staff scientist Armed Forces Inst. Pathology, Washington, 1962-64; sect. leader to dir. collaborative radiol. health lab. Colo. State U., 1964-77; mem. faculty Coll. Vet. Medicine and Biomed. Scis., 1968-85, prof. vet. pathology, 1973-85, assoc. dean, 1976-77, assoc. dir. expt. sta., 1977-85, dean, 1977-85, interim acad. v.p. Univ., 1982, interim pres. Univ., 1983-84, spl. counselor to pres., 1984-85; vis. prof. Colo. State U., 1995-96; prof. vet. pathology Cornell U., 1985—, dean Coll. Vet. Medicine, 1985-95; cons. Miss. State U., 1977-81; commr. Colo. Advanced Tech. Inst., 1983-84; mem. governing bd. N.Y. Sea Grant Inst., 1985-95, vice chmn., 1990-92; mem. vet. medicine adv. com. FDA, 1984-88; mem. joint coun. on food and agrl. scis. USDA, 1988-92, mem. exec. com., 1989-92; chmn. Zweig Meml. Fund for Equine Rsch., 1985-95; mem. adv. panel for vet. medicine Pew Health Professions Commn., 1991-93. Author papers in field. Served to comdr. USPHS, 1960-68. Recipient Charles A. Lory award and Disting. Univ. Leadership award Colo. State U., 1984, Disting. Practitioner award Nat. Acad. Practice, 1985, Regional Health Adminstr.'s award, 1985; named Honor Alumnus, Colo. State U., 1989. Mem. AVMA (coun. on edn. 1985-91), Assn. Am. Vet. Med. Colls. (pres. 1982-83), Colo. Vet. Med. Assn. (Disting. Svc. award 1985), N.Y. State Vet. Med. Soc. (Centennial award 1990), Sigma Xi, Phi Zeta, Phi Kappa Phi, Gamma Sigma Delta. Home: 5110 Hogan Ct Fort Collins CO 80525 Office: Coll Vet Medicine Cornell U Ithaca NY 14853

PHEMISTER, THOMAS ALEXANDER, lawyer; b. Framingham, Mass., June 2, 1940; s. Robert Irving and Georgia Nora (Savignac) P.; m. Lois Ann Devol, Dec. 28, 1963; children: Michael Anderson, Elizabeth Lynn, Mary Nicole, Virginia Noel. B.A., Carleton Coll., 1962; J.D., U. Chgo., 1965. Bar: Ill., Colo. 1965. Pvt. practice law Chgo., 1965-69; gen. atty. Western R.R. Assn., Chgo., 1969-71; in law practice with Richard J. Hardy, Washington, 1972-73; gen. atty. Assn. Am. R.R.s, Washington, 1973-79; dir. Bur. Explosives Assn. Am. Railroads, 1979-85; sole practice Washington, 1985-87; lead hazardous materials atty. Office Chief Counsel Fed. R.R. Adminstrn., Washington, 1987—; mem. dept. of transp. intermodal hazardous materials attys. group, 1989—; mem. com. on transp. of hazardous materials Transp. Rsch. Bd., 1980-86; mem. nat. motor carrier adv. com. Fed. Hwy. Adminstrn., 1982-86; mem. Can. Nat. Rail Task Force for Movements of Dangerous Commodities, 1985; mem. hazardous materials control course oversight com. Tex. A&M U., 1981-87; mem. bd. correction mil. records USCG, 1992—. Pub.: Emergency Handling of Hazardous Materials in Surface Transportation, 1981, Hazardous Materials Regulations Excerpted for Railroad Employees, 1981, Emergency Action Guides, 1983; author: A Report on Tank Cars: Federal Oversight of Design Construction and Repair, 1990, Forward through the 90s: A Report on Selected Issues in the Transportation by Rail of Hazardous Materials, 1994. Treas. Ill. Lawyers for McCarthy, 1968; trustee First Congregational Ch., Western Springs, Ill., 1970-71; mem. program ministries council United Christian Parish of Reston, Va., 1980-82, mem. South Lakes vestry, 1984-87, mem. parish bd., 1, deacon, ministries com., 1987-93; bd. dirs. Upper Room Emmaus of nat. capital area, 1989-90, lay leader, 1990; mem. Fairfax County Drug Task Force chpt. Parents Alliance to Neutralize Drug and Alcohol Abuse (PANDAA), 1987-89; adult advisor Fairfax County 4-H Horse Forum, 1988—; adult overall advisor Fairfax County 4H Fair Horse Show. Mem. Hunters Valley Riding Club (bd. dirs., v.p. 1993-94), Short Circuit Horse Show Assn. Home: 10802 Dayflower Ct Reston VA 22091-5110 Office: 400 7th St SW Washington DC 20590-0001 *Integrity is an absolute essential - both preserving my own and dealing with other people so that they, too, do not have to compromise on matters of principle.*

PHENIS, NANCY SUE, educational administrator; b. Anderson, Ind., Oct. 29, 1943; d. Wilma (Anderson) Baker; m. Richard W. Phenis, June 11, 1966; 1 child, Heidi L. BA, Ind. State U., 1965; MA, Ball State U., 1974, postgrad., 1985. Elem. tchr. Highland Park (N.J.) Schs., 1966-68, Anderson City Schs., 1969-71; elem. tchr., tchr. gifted and talented South Madison Schs., Pendleton, Ind., 1974-85, elem. prin., 1985—; K-12 curriculum dir. South Madison Schs., 1984. Bd. dirs. South Madison Community Found., Pendleton, 1991, First Am. Bank FirstGrant; devel. bd. St. John's Health Care Systems. Recipient Outstanding Contbn. award Internat. Reading Assn., 1991; grantee Eli Lilly Found., 1993. Mem. NAEPS, AAUW (pres. 1985-87), Ind. Assn. Sch. Prins. (bd. dirs. 1994—), First Am. (bd. dirs. 1992-95), Phi Delta Kappa (historian 1987, Leadership award 1994), Delta Kappa Gamma (sec. 1990-92, pres. 1992-94, Leadership/Adminstr. award 1993). Office: East Elem Sch 893 E Us Highway 36 Pendleton IN 46064-9580

PHENIX, GLORIA GAYLE, educational association administrator; b. Dallas, Mar. 4, 1956; m. Douglas William Phenix, Aug. 8, 1987; children: David William, Duncan Kenneth. BA, U. North Tex., 1979, postgrad., 1979-81; PhD, ABD, U. Minn., 1981-89. Dean Jordan Coll., Benton Harbor, Mich., 1990; pres. Phenix & Assocs. Tng. Cons., St. Joseph, Mich., 1991—, Topeka, Kans., 1993—; bd. dirs. Cornerstone, Inc. Mem. allocation com. United Way, 1990-92, Literacy Coun., 1991-93; mem. Topeka Race Rels. Task Force, 1994; Mayor's Commn. Status Women, 1996—. Fulbright-Hayes fellow Africa, 1990; Hewlett Mellon Found. grantee, 1987, Benton Found. grantee, 1988. Mem. Am. Polit. Sci. Assn., Minn. Polit. Sci. Assn. (bd. dirs. 1989-90), Midwest Polit. Sci. Assn., Am. Assn. Trainers and Developers, Am. Soc. for Quality Control. Presbyterian. Office: Phenix & Assocs 505 Pleasant St Ste 200 Saint Joseph MI 49085-1269 also: Phenix Assocs 530 S Kansas Ave Topeka KS 66603-3403

PHIBBS, CLIFFORD MATTHEW, surgeon, educator; b. Bemidji, Minn., Feb. 20, 1930; s. Clifford Matthew and Dorothy Jean (Wright) P.; m. Patricia Jean Palmer, June 27, 1953; children—Wayne Robert, Marc Stuart, Nancy Louise. B.S., Wash. State U., 1952; M.D., U. Wash., 1955; M.S., U. Minn., 1960. Diplomate Am. Bd. Surgery. Intern Ancker Hosp., St. Paul, 1955-56; resident in surgery U. Minn. Hosps., 1956-60; practice medicine specializing in surgery Oxboro Clinic, Mpls., 1962—, pres., 1985—; cons. to health risk mgmt. corps., 1994—; mem. Children's Hosp. Ctr., Northwestern-Abbott Hosp., Fairview-Southdale Hosp., Fairview Ridges Hosp.; clin. asst. prof. U. Minn., Mpls., 1975-78, clin. assoc. prof. surgery, 1978—; med. dir. Minn. Protective Life Ins. Co. Contbr. articles to med. jours. Bd. dirs. Bloomington Bd. Edn., Minn., 1974—, treas., 1976, sec., 1977-78, chmn., 1981-83; mem. adv. com. jr. coll. study City of Bloomington, 1964-66, mem. community facilities com., 1966-67, advisor youth study commn., 1966-68; vice chmn. bd. Hillcrest Meth. Ch., 1970-71; mem. Bloomington Adv. and Rsch. Coun., 1969-71; bd. dirs. Bloomington Symphony Orch., 1976—, Wash. State U. Found., trustee, 1990—; dir. bd. mgmt. Minnesota Valley YMCA, 1970-75; bd. govs. Mpls. Met. YMCA, 1970—; bd. dirs. Bloomington Heart-Health Found., 1989—, Martin Luther Manor, 1989; pres. Oxboro Clinics, 1985—; bd. dirs. Bloomington History Clock Tower Assn., 1990—; bd. dirs. Fairview Hosp. Clinic, 1994—. Capt. M.C., U.S. Army, 1960-62. Mem. ACS, AMA (Physician Recognition awards 1969, 73, 76, 79, 82, 85, 88, 91, 94), Assn. Surg. Edn., Royal Soc. Medicine, Am. Coll. Sports Medicine, Minn. Med. Assn. (del. 1991-94), Minn. Surg. Soc., Mpls. Surg. Soc., Hennepin County Med. Soc., Pan-Pacific Surg. Assn., Jaycees, Bloomington C. of C. (chmn. bd. 1984, chmn. 1985-86). Home: 9613 Upton Rd Minneapolis MN 55431-2454 Office: 600 W 98th St Minneapolis MN 55420-4773

PHIBBS, GARNETT ERSIEL, engineer, educator, minister, religious organization administrator; b. Clinchfield, Va., Oct. 12, 1922; s. Willie McDonald and Alma Irene (Horton) P.; m. Aug. 18, 1945 (div. 1972); children: Gerald Edwin, David Miller, Robert Lee. BA, Bridgewater (Va.) Coll., 1943; MRE, Bethany Theol. Sem., 1945; MDiv, Yale U., 1952, STM, 1954; postgrad., Boston U., Princeton U., St. Louis U. Cert. tchr., Calif.; ordained min. Ch. of the Brethren, 1945. Pastor Ch. of the Brethren, Bassett, Va., 1945-50, Champaign, Ill., 1955-56, Wilmington, Del., 1956-57, Glendale, Calif., 1969-70; pastor Niantic (Conn.) Bapt. Ch., 1950-51, Congl. Ch. (now United Ch. of Christ), Killingworth, Conn., 1951-55; exec. dir. Coun. of Chs., Trenton, N.J., 1957-62, Toledo, 1962-69; exec. dir. Citizens Aiding Pub. Offenders, Toledo, 1974-76; engr. Beverly Hills (Calif.) Hotel, 1981-91; mem., cons., leader Parents Without Ptnrs., 1972-90, ; mem. Habitat for Humanity, 1989-91; cons. North Toledo Community Orgn., 1977; co-founder Rescue Crisis Svc.; founder Interfaith Housing Corp., Toledo. Author: Bethel Memory Makers, 1977; contbr. articles to profl. jours. Mem. Toledo Bd. of Cmty. Rels., 1962-69, Ohio State Civil Rights Commn. of N.W. Ohio, Toledo, 1966-68, U.S. Civil Rights Commn., Toledo, 1965-69, Planned Parenthood Bd., Sister City Com. Toledo, Spain; mem., past pres. Kiwanis Internat., 1945-69; founding bd. dirs. West Hollywood Homeless Orgn. founder Charlotte Interfaith Network for Gay and Lesbian Equality; charter mem. Common Cause, Ams. United for Separation Ch. and State. Recipient Community Svc. award NAACP, 1960, So. Calif. Regional award Parents Without Parents, 1980; named Man of the Yr., ACLU, 1969. Mem. Internat. Union Oper. Engrs., Am. Correctional Assn., Am. Assn. for Pub. Adminstrs., Calif. Assn. Marriage and Family Counselors, Halfway House Assn, Parents and Friends of Gays and Lesbians (bd. sec. Time-Out Youth). Democrat. United Church of Christ. Avocations: gardening, theater, camping. Home: 5945 Reddman Rd Box 205 Charlotte NC 28212

PHIBBS, HARRY ALBERT, interior designer, professional speaker, lecturer; b. Denver, Jan. 9, 1933; s. Harry Andrew and Mary May (Perriam) P.; m. Alice Conners Glynn, Oct. 23, 1957 (div. Jan. 1988); children: Kathleen Ann Phibbs Pierz, Paul Robert, Mary Alice Phibbs Hettle, Michael John, Peter James, Daniel Edward; m. Nevelle Haley Jones, Feb. 1988. B.A., U. Colo., 1954, B.F.A., 1957. Interior designer Howard Lorton, Inc., Denver, 1957-68; interior designer, v.p. Ronald Ansay Inc., Wheatridge, Colo., 1969-71; interior designer, pres. Phibbs Design Assos., Inc., Denver, 1972-78; interior designer, mgr. Howard Lorton, Inc., Colorado Springs, Colo., 1979-93; prin. Phibbs Design, Colorado Springs, 1993—; pres. Interior Designers Housing Devel. Corp., 1969-72. V.p. Arvada (Colo.) Hist. Soc., 1973; bd. dirs. Colo. Opera Festival, also pres., 1986; bd. dirs. Downtown Colorado Springs, Inc., also pres., 1984; chmn. bd. trustees Interior Design Inst. Denver, 1991-94. With U.S. Army, 1954-56. Fellow Am. Soc. Interior Designers (nat. pres. 1977); mem. Am. Arbitration Assn., Theta Xi (pres. Denver Area alumni club 1958-64). Democrat. Roman Catholic. Home: 91 W Boulder St Colorado Springs CO 80903-3371 Office: 10 Boulder Crescent St Colorado Springs CO 80903-3344 *Each of God's infinite creations was carefully placed on earth with the same responsibility....to grow. Man has the unique role in that plan in that he can help other things and the people around him to grow. This process is contingent upon "loving your neighbor as yourself." Transposing the equation therefore requires that you love yourself. I wish I had learned at an earlier age to take what you do seriously, but not to take yourself too seriously.*

PHIFER, J. REESE, manufacturing executive; b. Feb. 19, 1916; s. William and Olga (Gough) P.; m. Sue Clarkson; children: Beverly Clarkson, Karen Phifer Brooks, Susan Phifer Cork. BS in Commerce, U. Ala., 1938, JD, 1940, HHD (hon.), 1984. Asst. city solicitor City of Tuscaloosa, Ala.; founder, chmn., CEO Phifer Wire Products (formerly Phifer Aluminum Screening Co.), Tuscaloosa, 1952—. Pilot USAAF, 1941-45. Recipient Human Rights award NAACP, 1981, "E" award Pres. Ronald Reagan, 1984, Presdl. "C" award, 1988; inducted to the U. Ala. Bus. Hall of Fame, 1991; Reese Phifer Hall, U. Ala. named in his honor. Office: Phifer Wire Products PO Box 1700 Tuscaloosa AL 35403-1700

PHILBERT, ROBERT EARL, secondary school educator; b. Anderson, Ind., Nov. 17, 1946; s. James William and Lois Louise (Hartman) P.; m. Cheryl Toney, July 24, 1976. BS, Ball State U., Muncie, Ind., 1969, MA, 1974, EdD, 1987. Cert. social sci. tchr., Ind. Tchr. social sci. Marion (Ind.) Community Schs., 1969—; instr. social sci. methods Ball State U., 1983; cons. St. Paul-Bennett Schs., St. Paul's Sch. Bd., Marion, 1990-93, I.S.T.E.P. validation com., Indpls., 1992; mem. Ind. State Textbook Adv. Bd., Indpls., 1992; participant NASA Tchr. in Space program; Marion Police Dept. candidate interview com., 1997. Mem. Citizen's Amb. Program, Social Studies Delegation to the Republic of Vietnam. Sgt. U.S. Army, 1970-72. Named Outstanding Educator, Marion High Sch., 1977-80. Mem. NEA, VFW, Nat. Coun. Social Studies, Ind. Coun. for the Social Studies, Ind. Tchrs. Assn., Marion Tchrs. Assn., Vietnam Vets Am., Am. Legion, Elks, Phi Alpha Theta, Pi Gamma Mu, Kappa Delta Pi, Phi Delta Kappa, Delta Tau Delta. Democrat. Catholic. Avocations: white water rafting, traveling, dog training, photography. Home: 1703 W 32nd St Marion IN 46953-3435 Office: 750 W 26th St Marion IN 46953-2929

PHILBIN, REGIS, television personality; b. N.Y.C.; s. Frank and Florence P.; m. Kay Faylan, 1957 (div.); children: Amy, Danny; m. Joy Senese, Mar. 1, 1970; children: Joanna, Jennifer. Student, U. Notre Dame. Hollywood stagehand, NBC page The Tonight Show; truck driver, newswriter, sportscaster. Co-host The Joey Bishop Show, 1967-69, host Sta. KABC Am. L.A., Sta. WABC TV Morning Show, 1983-88 (with Kathy Lee Gifford in 1985); co-host (syndicated show) Live! With Regis and Kathie Lee, 1988—, Miss Am. Pageant, 1991, 92, 95; co-author: Cooking with Regis and Kathie Lee, 1993, Entertaining with Regis and Kathie Lee, 1994; author: I'm Only One Man, 1995. Office: Regis & Kathie Lee ABC-TV 7 Lincoln Sq New York NY 10023*

PHILBRICK, DONALD LOCKEY, lawyer; b. Portland, Maine, May 3, 1923; s. Donald Ward and Ruth (Lockey) P.; children: Deborah Palmer, Sarah Peyton; adopted children: Paul Sloat, Mark Whitfield, Andrew Hunter; m. Janet Mitchell Poole, Aug. 7, 1982. A.B., Bowdoin Coll., 1944; J.D., Harvard U., 1948. Bar: Maine 1948. Pvt. practice Portland; ptnr. Verrill & Dana, 1951-82. Selectman, Cape Elizabeth, Maine, 1957-63. Served with AUS, 1943-45; with USAF, 1951-53. Mem. Maine Hist. Soc. (past pres.), N.E. Hist. Gen. Soc., Delta Kappa Epsilon. Republican. Congregationalist. Club: Portland Country. Home: 39 Wildwood Dr Cape Eliz ME 04107-1160 Office: 80 Exchange St Portland ME 04101-5035

PHILBRICK, MARGARET ELDER, artist; b. Northampton, Mass., July 4, 1914; d. David and Mildred (Pattison) Elder; m. Otis Philbrick, May 23, 1941 (dec. Apr. 1973); 1 child, Otis. Grad., Mass. Sch. Art, Boston, 1937; student, De Cordova Mus., Lincoln, Mass., 1966-67. Juror art shows; exhibited one woman show, Bare Cove Gallery, Hingham, Mass., 1979, Greenwich Garden Ctr., Cos Cob, Conn., 1981; retrospective exhbn. graphics, Ainsworth Gallery, Boston, 1972; exhibited 40 yr. retrospective, Westenhook Gallery, Sheffield, Mass., 1977, 50 yr. retrospective, 1985; group shows, Boston Printmakers, 1948—, USIA tour to Far East, 1958-59, Boston Watercolor Soc., 1956—, Pratt Graphic Art Ctr., N.Y.C., 1966, New Eng. Watercolor Soc., 1982—; represented in permanent collections Nat. Mus. Fine Arts, Hanoi, Library of Congress, Washington, Boston Pub. Library, Nat. Bezalel Mus., Jerusalem, Royal Miniature Soc. 100th Ann. Exhbn., London, 1995; artist, designer: Wedgwood Commemorative Plates, Stoke-on-Trent, Eng., 1944-55, Nat. Mus. of Women in the Arts, Washington, Wiggin Collection Boston Pub. Library, The Margaret Philbrick Collection Westwood (Mass.) Pub. Libr.; illustrator books; exhibited "The Book as Art" Nat. Mus. of Women in the Arts, 1987, "The Book as Art II", 1989. Recipient purchase Libr. of Congress, 1948; recipient 1st graphics Acad. Artist, Springfield, Mass., 1957, Multum in Parvo Pratt-2d Internat. Miniature Print Exhbn., 1966, 1st prize in floral Miniature Art Soc. Fla., 1986, Ralph Fabri award. Mem. NAD (Ralph Fabri 1977), Boston Printmakers Presentation Print (exec. bd. 1951—), Acad. Artists, New Eng. Watercolor Soc., Miniature Painters, Washington Sculptors and Gravers Soc. (Founders award), Miniature Art Soc. N.J., World Fedn. Miniature Artists, Miniature Art Soc. Home and Office: 47 Westwood Glen Rd Westwood MA 02090-1614

PHILBRICK, RALPH, botanist; b. San Francisco, Jan. 1, 1934; s. Howard R. and Elizabeth (Jauckens) P.; children—Lauren P. Lester, Winston H., Edward W. B.A., Pomona Coll., 1956; M.A., UCLA, 1958; Ph.D., Cornell U., 1963. Research assoc. Cornell U., 1957-63; assoc. in botany U. Calif., Santa Barbara, 1963-64; biosystematist Santa Barbara Botanic Garden, 1964-73, dir., 1974-87, biol. cons., 1987—; research assoc. U. Calif., Santa Barbara, 1964-82. Mem. Santa Barbara County Planning Commn., 1981-85. Mem. Sigma Xi, Phi Kappa Phi. Office: 29 San Marcos Trout Clb Santa Barbara CA 93105-9726

PHILIP, A. G. DAVIS, astronomer, editor, educator; b. N.Y.C., Jan. 9, 1929; s. Van Ness and Lillian (Davis) P.; m. Kristina Drobavicius, Apr. 25, 1964; 1 dau., Kristina Elizabeth Elanor. B.S., Union Coll., 1951; M.S., N.Mex. State U., 1959; Ph.D., Case Inst. Tech., 1964. Tchr. physics, math. and chemistry Brooks Sch., 1954-59; instr. Case Inst. Tech., 1962-64; asst. prof. astronomy U. N.Mex., 1964-66; asst. prof. astronomy SUNY-Albany, 1966-67, assoc. prof., 1967-76, mem. exec. com. Arts and Scis. Coun., 1975-76; prof. astronomy Union Coll., Schenectady, 1976—, astronomer Dudley Obs., 1967-81, Frank L. Fullam chair astronomy, 1980-81, editor Dudley Obs. Reports, 1977-81; astronomer Van Vleck Obs. Wesleyan U., 1982-94; editor contbns. VVObs., 1982-94; pres. Inst. for Space Observation, 1986—; vis. prof. Yale U., 1972, 73, La. State U., 1974, 76, 86, Acad. Scis. Lithuania, USSR, 1973, 76, 79, 86, Stellar Data Ctr., Strasbourg, France, 1978, 79, 80, 82, 85, 86; vis. astronomer Moletai Obs., 1988, 94; bd. dirs., sec.-treas. N.Y. Astron. Corp.; pres., treas. L. Davis Press, Inc., 1982—; trustee, mem. Grants award com. Fund Astrophys. Rsch., 1985—; dir. Shapley Vis. Lectureship Program, 1994—. Exhibited: 2d Ann. Photography Regional, Albany, 1980; author: (with M. Cullen and R.E. White) UBV Color - Magnitude Diagrams of Galactic Globular Clusters, 1976; (with A. Robucci, M. Frame, K.W. Philip) Mm, Fractal Series, Vol. 1, Midgets on the Spike, 1991; editor: The Evolution of Population II Stars, 1972, (with D.S. Hayes) Multicolor Photometry and the Theoretical HR Diagram, 1975, (with M.F. Mc Carthy) Galactic Structure in the Direction of the Galactic Polar Caps, 1977, (with D. H. DeVorkin In Memory of Henry Norris Russell, 1977, (with Hayes) The HR Diagram, 1978, Problems in Calibration of Multicolor Systems, 1979, (with M.F. McCarthy and G.V. Coyne) Spectral Classification of the Future, 1979, X-Ray Symposium, 1981, (with Hayes) Astrophysical Parameters for Globular Clusters, 1981, (with A.R. Upgren) The Nearby Stars and the Stellar Luminosity Function, 1983, (with Hayes and L. Pasinetti) Calibration of Fundamental Stellar Quantities, 1985, (with D.W. Latham) Stellar Radial Velocities, Horizontal-Branch and UV-Bright Stars, 1985, Spectroscopic and Photometric Classification of Population II Stars, 1986, (with J. Grindley) IAU Symposium No. 126, Globular Cluster Systems in Galaxies, 1987, (with Hayes and Liebert) IAU Colloquium No. 95, The Second Conference on Faint Blue Stars, (with Hayes and Adelman) New Directions in Spectrophotometry, 1988, Calibration of Stellar Ages, 1988, (with A.R. Upgren) Star Catalogues; A Centennial Tribute to A.N. Vyssotsky, 1989, (with P. Lu) The Gravitational Force Perpendicular to the Galactic Plane, 1989, (with D.S. Hayes and S.J. Adelman) CCDs in Astronomy. II. Precision Photometry: Astrophysics of the Galaxy, 1991, (with Robucci, Frame and Philip K.) Midgets on the Spike, vol. I, 1991, (with A.R. Upgren) Objective-Prism and Other Surveys, 1991, N.Y. State Astronomy, 1992, (with B. Hauck and A.R. Upgren) Workshop on Databases for Galactic Structure, 1993, (with K.A. Janes and A.R. Upgren) IAU Symposium No. 167, New Developments in Array Technology and Applications, 1995, (with V. Straizys) Photometric Systems and Standard Stars, 1996, 30 Years of Astronomy at Van Vleck Observatory, 1997, (with J. Liebert and R. Saffer) The Third Conference on Faint Blue Stars, 1997; lectr. tours (with K.W. Philip) An Introduction to the Mandelbrot Set, 1988-91; contbr. chpts. to books, articles to profl. jours. Served with AUS, 1951-53. Yale U. vis. fellow, 1976; rsch. grantee Rsch. Corp., NSF, NASA, Nat. Rsch. Lab., NAS, Am. Astron. Soc. Fellow AAAS, Royal Astron. Soc., Am. Phys. Soc.; mem. Am. Astron. Soc. (Harlow Shapley lectr. 1973—, auditor 1977, 79-85), Am. Math. Soc., Can. Astron. Soc., Internat. Astron. Union (chmn., sec. various coms. and commns., pres. commn. 30 1982-85, chmn. working group on spectroscopic and photometric data 1985-94, chmn. sci. organizing com. symposium # 167), N.Y. Acad. Scis., Astron. Soc. Pacific, Astron. Soc. N.Y. (sec.-treas. 1969—, editor newsletter 1974—), Capital Computer Club (bd. dirs. 1990—, v.p. 1993—), Sigma Xi. Achievements include being 1st U.S. observer Soviet 6M telescope, 1980. Home: 1125 Oxford Pl Schenectady NY 12308-2913 Office: Union Coll Physics Dept Schenectady NY 12308

PHILIP, JAMES (PATE PHILIP), state senator; b. May 26, 1930; married; 4 children. Student, Kansas City Jr. Coll., Kans. State Coll. Ret. dist. sales mgr. Pepperidge Farm, Inc.; rep. State of Ill., 1967-74, senator, 1975—; asst. senate minority leader, 1979, senate minority leader, 1981-93, senate pres., 1993—; chmn. DuPage County Rep. Ctrl. Com.; committeeman Addison Twp. Precinct 52; past Jr. Nat. Rep. Committeeman. Past dir. Nat. Found. March of Dimes; past gen. chmn. Elmhurst March of Dimes; spl. events chmn. DuPage Heart Assn.; mem. DuPage Meml. Hosp. Century Club; dir. Ray Graham Assn. Handicapped Children; mem. bd. sponsors Easter Seal Treatment Ctr.; active Lombard YMCA; bd. dirs. Danada Sculpture Garden. With USMC, 1950-53. Recipient Ill. Coun. on Aging award, 1989, Leaders of 90's award Downers Grove Twp., 1989, Man of Yr. award United Hellenic Voters Am., 1989, Legis. of Yr. award Ill. County Treas.'s Assn., 1990, TaxSavers award Ill. Assn. County Auditors, 1990, Statesman of Yr. award Internat. Union of Operating Engrs. Local 150, 1991, Friend of Youth award Assn. Ill. Twp. Com. on Youth, 1991, Spl. Svc. award Serenity House, 1991, Recognition award DuPage Ctr. Independent Living, 1991. Mem. Am. Legion, Ill. Young Reps. (past pres.), DuPage County Young Rep. Fedn. (past chmn.), DuPage County Marine Corps League (life), DuPage Indsl. and Mfg. Assn. (past dir.), Suburban Bus. Mgmt. Coun. (past v.p.), Mil. Order Devil Dogs, Gocery Mgmt. and Sales Exec. Club Chgo., Exec. Club DuPage County, Shriners, Elks, Masons, Order of DeMolay (life), Moose. Office: Ill State Senate 327 State Capitol Bldg Springfield IL 62706

PHILIP, PETER VAN NESS, former trust company executive; b. N.Y.C., Feb. 23, 1925; s. Van Ness and Lilian (Davis) P.; m. Sabina FitzGibbon, May 3, 1952; children: William Van Ness, Thomas Winslow, Peter Sandys. AB, Yale U., 1945W; MBA, NYU, 1950. With Price, Waterhouse & Co., N.Y.C., 1947-52; W.H. Morton & Co., Inc., N.Y.C., 1952-73; pres., CEO Equitable Securities, Morton & Co., Inc., 1970-73; sr. v.p., dir. White Weld & Co., Inc., N.Y.C., 1974-76; v.p. Morgan Guaranty Trust Co., N.Y.C., 1977-88, ret. With 86th inf. div. AUS, 1943-45. Decorated Purple Heart, Bronze Star. Clubs: Racquet and Tennis (N.Y.C.); Links; Yale (N.Y.C.), Downtown Assn. (N.Y.C.), Bond (N.Y.C.); Bedford ((N.Y.); Golf and Tennis; Ekwanok (Manchester, Vt.). Home: Guard Hill Rd Bedford NY 10506

PHILIP, SUNNY KOIPURATHU, municipal official; b. Ranny, Kerala, India, Sept. 3, 1957; came to U.S., 1983; s. Mathai Koipurathu and Sosamma (Ninan) P.; m. Achamma John; children: Sunny K. Jr., Christine. B in Commerce, U. Kerala, India, 1978; M in Commerce, U. Kerala, 1982. Controller St. Thomas Evang. Ch. Hdqtrs., Kerala, India, 1978-81; instr. Minerva Coll., Kerala, 1981-83; fin. dir. City of La Feria, Tex., 1983-91; exec. dir. La Feria Indsl. Devel. Corp., Tex., 1991-93; city mgr. City of La Feria, Tex., 1993—; controller La Feria Indsl. Found. Corp., 1986—. Chmn. Cub Scouts Pack 47. Mem. Tex. City Mgrs. Assn., Tex. Indsl. Devel. Coun., Tex. Assn. Assessing Officers, Govt. Fin. Officers Assn. Tex. Methodist. Lodge: Lions (treas. La Feria club 1983—). Avocations: fishing, travel, reading. Home: PO Box 671 La Feria TX 78559-0671 Office: City of La Feria 115 E Commercial Ave La Feria TX 78559-5002

PHILIPP, ALICIA, community foundation executive. BA, Emory U.; MBA, Ga. State U. Exec. dir. Met. Atlanta Cmty. Found. Inc., Atlanta, 1977; bd. dirs. Ctrl. Atlanta Progress, Ind. Sector, Funders Concerned About Aids, Investment Fund for Founds, Policy Bd. of Atlanta Project. Mem. Jr. League, Internat. Women's Forum, Acad. of Women. Recipient Roz Cohen Cmty. Action award YWCA; named as One of Top Women Mgrs. in U.S. Working Woman mag. Office: Met Atlanta Cmty Found The Hurt Bldg Ste 449 Atlanta GA 30303

PHILIPP, ELIZABETH R., manufacturing company executive, lawyer. Grad., Harvard U., 1978, Harvard U., 1982. Exec. v.p., gen. counsel, sec. Collins & Aikman Corp., N.Y.C. Office: Collins & Aikman Corp. 210 Madison Ave New York NY 10016-3802

PHILIPP, WALTER VIKTOR, mathematician, educator; b. Vienna, Dec. 14, 1936; came to U.S., 1963, naturalized, 1974; s. Oskar and Anna Julie (Krasucky) P.; m. Ariane Randell, Dec. 10, 1984; children: Petra, Robert, Anthony, Andre. MS in Math. and Physics, PhD in Math., U. Vienna, 1960. Asst. U. Vienna, 1960-63, 65-67, dozent, 1967; asst. prof. U. Mont., 1963-64; vis. asst. prof. U. Ill., Urbana, 1964-65; mem. faculty U. Ill., 1967—, prof. math., 1973—, prof. stats., 1988—, chmn. dept. stats., 1990-95; vis. prof. U. N.C., Chapel Hill, 1972, 88, MIT, 1980, Tufts U., 1981, U. Göttingen, 1982, 85, Imperial Coll., London, 1985; adv. bd. Monatshefte für Mathmatik, 1994—. Assoc. editor Annals of Probability, 1976-81. Fellow Inst. Math. Stats.; mem. Am. Math. Soc., Austrian Math. Soc., Internat. Statis. Inst., Am. Statis. Assn., Austrian Acad. Scis. (corr. mem.). Avocations: mountaineering. Home: 1922 Maynard Dr Champaign IL 61821-5265 Office: U Ill Dept Math Champaign IL 61821

PHILIPPI, DIETER RUDOLPH, academic administrator; b. Frankfurt, Germany, July 26, 1929; came to U.S., 1956, naturalized, 1961; s. Alfred and Ellen Marguerite (Glatzel) P.; BBA, Johann Wolfgang Goethe U., 1952; postgrad. Sorbonne, summers 1951, 52, U. Omaha, U. Tex.; MBA, Canadian Inst. Banking, 1953-55; children: Bianca Maria, Christopher Thomas; m. 2d, Helga Philippi, May 29, 1982; children: Stephan Andreas, Michael Joachim. With Toronto-Dominion Bank, Calgary, Edmonton, Alta., Can., 1953-56; chief acct. Baylor U. Coll. Medicine, Houston, 1956-63; contr. Wittenberg U., Springfield, Ohio, 1963-68; bus. mgr. Park Coll., Kansas City, Mo., 1968-70; bus. mgr., treas. Lone Mountain Coll., San Francisco, 1970-75; v.p. bus. affairs Findlay (Ohio) Coll., 1975-76; bus. mgr. Bologna (Italy) Ctr., The Johns Hopkins U., Balt., 1976-78; dir. bus. and fin. Mt. St. Mary's Coll., Los Angeles, 1978-81; asst. to v.p. overseas programs Boston U., Mannheim, Germany, 1981-85, dir. adminstrn. and finance, 1985-93; bus. mgr., controller Schiller Internat. U., Ingersheim, Germany, 1993—. lectr., Laurence U., Santa Barbara, Calif., 1973-75; fin. cons. various charitable orgns. Pres., German Sch. of East Bay, 1970-75; campaign coord. United Appeals Fund, 1968, recipient Disting. Svc. award, 1970; active Boy Scouts, Germany, 1948-52, Can., 1952-56, U.S., 1956-86, exec. bd. Tecumseh council, 1967-68, recipient Silver Beaver award, Wood badge, 1968. Bd. dirs. Bellaire Gen. Hosp., Greenland Hills Sch., Chaminade Coll. Prep. Sch. Mem. Am. Acctg. Assn., Am., Eastern Fin. Assns., Am. Mgmt. Assn., Am. Assn. Univ. Adminstrs., Nat. Coll. and Univ. Bus. Officers Assn., Western Coll. and Univ. Bus. Officers Assn., Nat. Assn. Accts., Am. Assn. Higher Edn., Coll. and Univ. Personnel Assn., San Francisco Consortium, Alpha Phi Omega. Clubs: Commonwealth of Calif. (San Francisco); Univ. (Kansas City). Office: Schiller Internat Univ, Im Schloss, D-74379 Ingersheim Germany

PHILIPPI, ERVIN WILLIAM, mortician; b. Lodi, Calif., June 4, 1922; s. William and Rebecca (Steinert) P.; m. Emma Grace Mosely, May 8, 1958 (div. Mar. 1979); m. Helen Jo Hunt, June 3, 1979. Grad., Calif. Coll. Motuary Sci., 1948. Embalmer, mortician, mgr. Salas Bros. Chapel, Modesto, Calif., 1946-92; dep. coroner Stanislaus County, Calif., 1955-75. With U.S. Army, 1942-46. Avocations: old car restoration, travel.

PHILIPPS, EDWARD WILLIAM, banker, real estate appraiser; b. N.Y.C., Dec. 19, 1938; s. Edward Charles and Eleanor Elizabeth (Eisenger) P.; m. Diane Rose DiCuffa, June 12, 1960; children: James Michael, Robert Christopher. Appraiser Dry Dock Savs., N.Y.C., 1956-70, Nat. Bank of West, White Plains, N.Y., 1970-72, Aires Real Estate, Yonkers, N.Y., 1972-74; sr. v.p. Am. Savs. Bank (merger Empire Savs. Bank), N.Y.C., 1974-92; self employed real estate appraiser Yonkers, 1992-93; sr. v.p., chief lending officer Stamford (Conn.) Fed. Savs., 1993—; mem. mortgage com. Cmty. Preservation Corp., N.Y.C., 1990-92. Mem. Am. Inst. Real Estate Appraisers, Homebuilders Assn. Fairfield County (bd. dirs.). Avocations: wood working, fishing. Home: 261 Kimball Ave Yonkers NY 10704-3030 Office: 999 Bedford St Stamford CT 06905-5609

PHILIPPS, LOUIS EDWARD, data systems manufacturing company executive; b. Duluth, Minn., Feb. 7, 1906; s. Carl Frederick Ferdin and Sarah Marguerithe (Mortenson) P.; m. Gladys Victoria Monsen, Nov. 13, 1930. Student pub. schs., Duluth. Engr. Cleve. Radioelectric Co., 1946-48; v.p., gen. mgr. Radio Systems, Inc., Cleve., 1948-50, Royal Communications, Inc., Cleve., 1950-56; dir. engring. Auth Electric Co., N.Y.C., 1956-59; chief engr. hosp. products div. Motorola-Dahlberg Co., Mpls., 1959-63; founder, pres., chmn. bd. Medelco Inc., Schiller Park, Ill., 1964-74; founder, 1975; since chmn. bd., dir. Datx Corp., Chgo.; dir. sales, chmn. bd. Smart Controllers, Inc., Skokie, Ill., 1985—; cons. to health care industry. Contbr. to profl. jours. Named Father of Hosp. Systems Industry Am. Hosp. Assn., 1974. Sr. mem. IEEE. Republican. Presbyterian. Clubs: Order Eastern Star (Robbinsdale, Minn.), Masons (Robbinsdale, Minn.); Masons (Chgo.), Shriners (Chgo.). Patentee pulsed audio signaling, radio nurse system, data handling system. Home: 31 W Diversey Ave Addison IL 60101-3527 *My wife's faith and encouragement to use defeat as a stepping stone to success made it possible for me to reach my goals. Encouraging and teaching employees also played an important part.*

PHILIPPUS, AL A., protective services official; b. San Antonio, Mar. 18, 1951; m. Jeanne Theresa Philippus; children: Dawn Michelle, Jason Allen, Mary Lamm. A. in Law Enforcement, San Antonio Coll., 1977; BS in Criminal Justice magna cum laude, S.W. Tex. State U., 1979; MS in Criminal Justice Mgmt./Adminstrn., Sam Houston State U., 1992, PhD in Criminal Justice Mgmt./Adminstrn., 1994adr. Patrol officer City of San Antonio Police Dept., 1975-81, detective homicide unit, 1981-84, sgt. patrol divsn., 1984-86, sgt. internal affairs, 1986-88, lt., dir. rsch. and planning, 1988-89, capt., comdr. fiscal mgmt. and rsch. divs., 1989-94, dep. police chief, comdr. uniform divsn., 1994-95, chief of police, 1995—; adj. prof. St. Mary's U., San Antonio, 1993—. Adv. bd. Police Found. Law Enforcement; law enforcement adv. bd. Alamo Area Coun. Govts.; mem. law enforcement coord. com. U.S. Western Dist. Tex.; bd. dirs. Tex. Ctr. for Legal Ethics and Professionalism. Sgt. USAF, 1969-73. Named Officer of the Yr., Greater San Antonio Builder's Assn., 1979, Optimist Club, 1993. Mem. Internat. City Mgmt. Assn., Nat. Assn. Rschrs. and Planners, Internat. Assn. Law Enforcement Planners, Internat. Assn. Chiefs of Police, Police Exec. Rsch. Found., Am. Pub. Welfare Assn., Assn. of Police Planning and Rsch. Officers, Combined Law Enforcement Assn. of Tex., San Antonio Police Officers Assn. Office: PO Box 839948 214 W Nueva St San Antonio TX 78283*

PHILIPS, DAVID EVAN, English language educator; b. Wilkes-Barre, Pa., Aug. 30, 1926; s. Jesse Evan and Edith Kathleen (Stone) P.; m. Janet Briggs Walker, Aug. 19, 1950; children: Evan Walker, Donald David, Kimberly Anne. B.A., Haverford Coll, 1950; M.A., Johns Hopkins U., 1952; postgrad., U. Pa., 1953-56. Instr. English Tufts U., 1956-62; asst. prof. English Ea. Conn. State U., Willimantic, 1962-68, assoc. prof., 1968-80, prof., 1980-90, prof. emeritus, 1990—, head dept., 1966-68, 81-83, dir. Office Pub. Affairs, 1965-67, dir. freshman writing program, 1978-79; profl. storyteller, 1984—. Co-author: A Guide to College Writing Skills, 1979; author: Legendary Connecticut: Traditional Tales from the Nutmeg State, 1984, paperback reprint, 1992; book and author citation Conn. Gen. Assembly, 1994; book rev. columnist: Down East, 1956-87, contbg. editor, 1979-87; assoc. editor: Conn. History, 1972-75, 82-85, editor, 1986-87. Chmn. Windham (Conn.) Devel. and Indsl. Commn., 1965-68; bd. dirs. Conn. Assn. Mcpl. Devel. Commns., 1965-68, Vis. Nurse Assn., Windham, 1968-72; mem. Windham Dem. Town Com., 1968-85, 90—, rec. sec., 1972-74, 82-84, sec. 1978-82; mem. Windham Charter Commn., 1969-71, vice chmn., 1970-71; bd. dirs. Windham Sch. Dist., 1971-79, vice chmn., 1975-79; mem. Windham Zoning Commn., 1982-83; mem. Windham Planning Commn., 1983—, chmn., 1988—; mem. Windham Hist. Soc., 1985—, bd. dirs., 1991-94. With U.S. Merchant Marine, 1944-51, lic. Third Mate, 1946-51; lt. USNR, 1951-53. Danforth Found. Tchr. Study grantee, 1960-61, summer 1963. Mem. AAUP (sec.-treas. Conn. State conf. 1963-65, sec. 1966-68, Emeritus Assembly 1990—, treas. 1991-95), Conn. State Employees Assn. (sr. v.p. 1971-73), Conn. Hist. Soc. Democrat. Unitarian. Home: 7 Antrim Rd Willimantic CT 06226-3705

PHILIPSON, HERMAN LOUIS, JR., investment banker; b. Dallas, May 14, 1924; s. Herman Louis and Lillian (Adler) P.; m. Sonia Topletz, July 20, 1955; children: Cynthia Ann, Leslie, Nancy, Julie. B.S., Tex. A&M U., 1946; postgrad., Harvard Sch. Bus. Adminstrn., 1947-48. Pres. Philipson's, Inc., 1946-56; pres. Nat. Data Processing Corp., 1957-60, chmn. bd., 1960-61; chmn. bd. Techno-Growth Capital Corp., 1962-72; pres. Recognition Internat. Inc., Dallas, 1961-73; chmn. exec. com. Recognition Internat. Inc., 1973-76; vice chmn. Recognition Equipment Inc., 1976-83; pres. Internat. Bus. Devel. Ltd., Dallas, 1973—, IBDL, Inc., Dallas, 1979—. Mem. Dallas Citizens Coun., also v.p., mem. exec. com.; bd. dirs. Dallas County Camp Fire Girls; trustee So. Meth. U. Found. for Sci. and Engring.; mem. engring. adv. and devel. coun. Tex. A&M U. 1st Lt. AUS, 1943-46. Decorated Bronze Star, Purple Heart with cluster; recipient Dallas Exporter of Yr. award, 1970, Ernest Thompson Seton award, 1975; named to Tex. A&M U. Acad. Disting. Mech. Engring. Grads. Mem. Dallas C. of C. (world trade com.), Japan-Tex. Assn. Lodges: Masons, Shriners. Patentee in field. Home: 9100 Rockbrook Dr Dallas TX 75220-3907 Office: Internat Bus Devel Ltd 1545 W Mockingbird Ln Dallas TX 75235-5014

PHILIPSON, MORRIS, university press director; b. New Haven, June 23, 1926; s. Samuel and Edith (Alderman) P.; m. Susan Antonia Sacher, Apr. 26, 1961; children: Nicholas, Jenny, Alex. Diploma, U. Paris, 1947; B.A., U. Chgo., 1949, M.A., 1952; Ph.D. in Philosophy, Columbia U., 1959; L.H.D. (hon.), Coe Coll., 1985. Instr. English lit. Hofstra Coll., 1954-55; instr. philosophy Juilliard Sch. Music, 1955-56, 57-58; lectr. Hunter Coll., 1957-60; editor Vintage Books, Alfred A. Knopf, Inc., N.Y.C., 1959-61, Modern Library, also trade books Random House, Inc., Pantheon Books, 1961-65; sr. editor Basic Books, N.Y.C., 1965-66; exec. editor U. Chgo. Press, 1966-67, dir., 1967—. Author: Outline of Jungian Aesthetics, 1963, Bourgeois Anonymous, 1964, The Count Who Wished He Were a Peasant: A Life of Leo Tolstoy, 1967, Paradoxes, 1969, Everything Changes, 1972, The Wallpaper Fox, 1976, A Man in Charge, 1979, Secret Understandings, 1983, Somebody Else's Life, 1987; also short stories, articles; editor: Aldous Huxley on Arts and Artists, 1960, Aesthetics Today, 1961, Automation: Implications for the Future, 1962, (with Clapp, Rosenthal) Foundations of Western Thought, 1962. Served with AUS, 1944-46. Decorated comdr. Order Arts and Letters (France). Clubs: Arts (Chgo.), Caxton (Chgo.), Tavern (Chgo.), Quadrangle (Chgo.). Office: U Chgo Press 5801 S Ellis Ave Chicago IL 60637-1476*

PHILLABAUM, LESLIE ERVIN, publisher; b. Cortland, N.Y., June 1, 1936; s. Vern Arthur and Beatrice Elizabeth (Butterfield) P.; m. Roberta Kimbrough Swarr, Mar. 17, 1962; children—Diane Melissa, Scott Christopher. B.S., Pa. State U., 1958, M.A., 1963. Editor Pa. State U. Press, 1961-63; editor-in-chief U. N.C. Press, 1963-70; assoc. dir., editor La. State U. Press, Baton Rouge, 1970-75; dir. La. State U. Press, 1975—. Served to 1st lt. AUS, 1959-61. Mem. Assn. Am. Univ. Presses (dir. 1978-80, 83-86, pres. 1984-85), So. Hist. Assn., Acacia, Omicron Delta Kappa, Alpha Kappa Psi. Democrat. Home: 769 Castle Kirk Dr Baton Rouge LA 70808 Office: La State U Press PO Box 25053 Baton Rouge LA 70894

PHILLIPPI, ELMER JOSEPH, JR., data communications analyst; b. Canton, Ohio, May 31, 1944; s. Elmer Joseph and Rita M. (Tillitski) P.; m. Susan Mary Schrader, July 10, 1971; 1 child, Nathan Audie. AB, Cornell U., 1966; MA, Rice U., 1970. Cert. energy auditor. Tchr. Brackenridge High Sch., San Antonio, 1970-71; asst. prof. engring. tech. Muskingum Tech. Coll., Zanesville, Ohio, 1971-80, sec., treas. AAUP chpt; data communications analyst Chem. Abstracts Services, Columbus, Ohio, 1980-87; sr. software engr. Control Data Corp., Dayton, Ohio, 1987-89, analyst computing Boeing Computer Svcs., Huntsville, Ala., 1989; software engr. specialist Ford Aerospace, Houston, 1989-92; computer systems analyst, Lockheed Engring. and Sciences Co., Houston, 1992-93; computer cons., CIBER, Houston, 1993-94; comm. cons. Genesis Data Systems, Houston, 1994; cons., lead cons. Deloitte & Touche Cons., 1994—; communications cons. Ala. Supercomputer Network; designer, devel. Tech. Order Tracking System USAF, 1988; part-time instr. physics Ohio U. Editorial referee Am. Jour. Physics, 1975-85; network design cons. Aeronautical Systems div. USAF; subsystem mgr. for mission control ctr. upgrade, Johnson Space Ctr.; adjunct instr. physics San Jacinto Coll., 1992—. Recipient Group Achievement award AIS Security Team Johnson Space Ctr., 1992; NSF grantee, 1979. Mem. Assn. Computing Machinery (treas. Central Ohio chpt., mem. symposium com.), N.Y. Acad. Scis., Data Processing Mgmt. Assn., Cornell Club of Houston, Rice Bus. Network, Sigma Xi. Avocations: ham radio, music, bicycling, swimming, volunteer church work. Home: 18618 Prince William Ln Houston TX 77058-4225 Office: 1225 North Loop W Ste 825 Houston TX 77008-1761

PHILLIPPI, WENDELL CRANE, editor; b. Zionsville, Ind., July 4, 1918; s. Jesse F. and Bernice (Brock) P.; m. Georgiana Pittman, Jan. 10, 1942 (dec. July 10, 1978); children—Frank, Ann; m. Barbara Jean Caniff Howden, Oct. 30, 1980. A.B., Ind. U., 1940. Copy editor Indpls. News, 1940-46, state editor, 1946-47, city editor, 1947-52, asst. mng. editor, 1952-62, mng. editor, 1962-84; Pres. Ind. A.P., 1957; dir. Mid-Am. Press Inst., 1969-84; bd. dirs. A.P. Mng. Editors Assn., 1963-66, 69-72, v.p., 1971, pres., 1972; mem. Pulitzer Prize in Journalism Jury, 1971, 75, 76. Author: Dear Ike, 1991. Pres. Ind. Armory Bd., 1968-73; bd. dirs. 500 Festival, v.p. 1963-65; mem. Ind. U. Daily Student Bd., 1968-77; sr. warden Episcopal Ch., 1966, 69, 71. Maj. AUS, 1941-45; commanding gen., 38th divsn., 1959-63; maj. gen. Res. Decorated Silver Star, Bronze Star with cluster, Purple Heart. Mem. VFW, NG Assn., U.S. and Ind. (pres. 1953-55), Army Assn. Ind. (pres. 1957-58), Assn. U.S. Army, Indpls. C. of C. Am. Soc. Newspaper Editors, Am. Legion, Ind. U. Alumni Assn. (mag. bd. 1967-81), Econ. Club of Indpls., Indpls. Columbia Club, Blue Key, Sigma Nu, Sigma Delta Chi. Episcopalian. Home: 2244 Rome Dr Indianapolis IN 46228-3240

PHILLIPS, ADRAN ABNER (ABE PHILLIPS), geologist, oil and gas exploration consultant; b. Sugden, Okla., Feb. 6, 1924; s. James M. and Jennie Elizabeth (Norman) P.; m. Carmel Darlene Pesterfield, Aug. 20, 1949 (div.); 1 son, John David. B.S. in Geology, U. Okla., 1949. With Exxon Corp. and affiliates, 1949-79, dist. geologist, Chico, Calif., 1959-64, ops. geologist, Sydney, Australia, 1964-67, exploration coordinator North Slope Alaska, Houston, 1968-70, div. geologist, Denver, 1970-71, exploration mgr. P.T. Inc., Stanvac, Jakarta, Indonesia, 1971-73, exploration mgr. ESSO exploration, Singapore, 1973-76; div. mgr. Exxon U.S.A., Denver, 1976-79; v.p. Coors Energy div., Golden, Colo., 1979-80, pres., 1980-92; oil and gas exploration cons., 1992—. Bd. dirs. Mountain States Legal Found., 1991—. Mem. Am. Assn. Petroleum Geologists, Ind. Petroleum Assn. Mountain States (past pres.), Ind. Petroleum Assn. Am. (dir.). Home and Office: 2194 S Augusta Dr Evergreen CO 80439-8923

PHILLIPS, ALMARIN, economics educator, consultant; b. Port Jervis, N.Y., Mar. 13, 1925; s. Wendell Edgar and Hazel (Billett) P.; m. Dorothy Kathryn Burns, June 14, 1947 (div. 1976); children: Almarin Paul, Frederick Peter, Thomas Rock, David John, Elizabeth Linett, Charles Sumner; m. Carole Cherry Greenberg, Dec. 19, 1976. B.S., U. Pa., 1948, M.A., 1949; Ph.D., Harvard, 1953. Instr. econs. U. Pa., 1948-50, 51-53, asst. prof. econs., 1953-56, prof. econs. and law, 1963-91; Hower prof. pub. policy U. Pa, 1983-91; chmn. dept. econs. U. Pa., 1968-71, 72-73, assoc. dean Wharton Sch., 1973-74, dean Sch. Pub. and Urban Policy, 1974-77, chair faculty senate, 1990-91; teaching fellow Harvard, 1950-51; assoc. prof. U. Va, 1956-61, prof., 1961-63; vis. prof. U. Hawaii, summer 1968, U. Warwick, London Grad. Sch. Bus. Studies, 1972, Ohio State U., McGill U., 1978, Calif. Inst. Tech, Northwestern U., 1980, Ariz. Coll. Law, 1987, Inst. Europeén d'Adminstrn. des Affairs (INSEAD), France, spring 1990; co-dir. Pres.'s Commn. Fin. Structure and Regulation, 1970-71; mem. Nat. Commn. Electronic Fund Transfers, 1976-77; chmn. bd. Econsult Corp., 1990-96. Author: (with R.W. Cabell) Problems in Basic Operations Research Methods for Management, 1961, Market Structure, Organization and Performance, 1962, Technology and Market Structure: A Study of the Aircraft Industry, 1971, (with P. Phillips and T.R. Phillips) Biz Jets: Technology and Market Structure in the Corporate Jet Aircraft Industry, 1994; Editor: Perspectives on Antitrust Policy, 1965, (with O.E. Williamson) Prices: Issues in Theory, Practice and Policy, 1968, Promoting Competition in Regulated Markets, 1975 ; editor Jour. Indsl. Econs., 1974-90; Contbr. articles to tech. lit. Served with AUS, 1943-45. Decorated Purple Heart, Bronze Star. Fellow Am. Statis. Assn., AAAS; mem. Am. Econ. Assn., Econometic Soc., European Econ. Assn., Internat. Telecommunications Soc. (bd. dirs. 1990—). Home: 1115 Remington Rd Wynnewood PA 19096-4021

PHILLIPS, ANTHONY FRANCIS, lawyer; b. Hartford, Conn., May 18, 1937; s. Frank and Lena Phillips; m. Rosemary Karran McGowan, Jan. 28, 1967; children: Karran, Antonia, Justin. BA, U. Conn., 1959; JD, Cornell U., 1962. Bar: N.Y. 1964, U.S. Dist. Ct. (so. dist., ea. dist.) N.Y. 1965, (ctrl. dist.) Calif. 1980, U.S. Tax Ct. 1981, U.S. Ct. Appeals (2nd cir.) 1967, (3d cir.) 1985, (4th cir.) 1983, (5th cir.) 1972, (7th cir.) 1987, (9th cir.) 1983, (10th cir.) 1983, U.S. Supreme Ct. 1971. Assoc. Willkie, Farr & Gallagher, N.Y.C., 1963-69, ptnr., 1969—. Mem. adv. com. Cornell U. Law Sch., 1994—. Fellow Am. Bar Found.; mem. ABA, N.Y. State Bar Assn., N.Y. County Bar Assn. (bd. dirs. 1989-95), Assn. of Bar of City of N.Y. Home: 3 Elm Rock Rd Bronxville NY 10708-4202 Office: Willkie Farr & Gallagher 1 Citicorp Ctr 153 E 53rd St New York NY 10022-4611

PHILLIPS, ANTHONY GEORGE, neurobiology educator; b. Barrow, Cumbria, Eng., Jan. 30, 1943; came to Can., 1953; s. George William and Mabel Lilian (Wood) P. BA (hon.), U. Western Ont., London, Can., 1966, MA, 1967, PhD, 1970. Asst. prof. psychobiology U. British Columbia, Vancouver, Can., 1970-75, assoc. prof., 1975-80, prof., 1980—; head dept. psychology, 1994—; founder Quadra Logic Tech., Inc., Vancouver. Contbr. numerous papers to sci. jours. Chmn. Can.-India Village Aid, Vancouver, 1981-86, bd. dirs. 1987—; bd. dirs. Tibetian Refuge Aid Soc., Vancouver, 1980—. Recipient Killam rsch. prize Can. Coun., 1977, Killam Rsch. prize U. B.C., 1986, D.O. Hebb award Can. Psychol. Assn.; Steacie fellow Nat. Scis. and Engring. Rsch. Coun. (Can.), 1980. Fellow Royal Soc. Can.; mem. Soc. Neurosci., Can. Soc. for Neurosci., Can. Coll. Neuropsychopharmacology. Office: U BC Dept Psychology, 2136 W Mall, Vancouver, BC Canada V6T 1Z4

PHILLIPS, ARTHUR WILLIAM, JR., biology educator; b. Claremont, N.H., Sept. 25, 1915; s. Arthur William and Jane Helen (Daley) P.; m. Mary Catherine Mich, Oct. 21, 1950; children: Marilynn, William (dec.). BS, U. Notre Dame, 1939, MS, 1941; DSc, MIT, 1947. Rsch. asst. Lobund lab. U. Notre Dame, Ind., 1937-41, rsch. scientist, 1943-45; rsch. assoc. MIT, 1947-49; rsch. assoc. prof., head div. bioengring. Lobund lab. U. Notre Dame, Ind., 1949-54; rsch. scientist dept. biology and bioengring. MIT, Cambridge, 1942-43, rsch. fellow dept. food tech., 1945-47, rsch. assoc. dept. food tech., 1947-49; rsch. assoc. prof. dept. bacteriology Syracuse (N.Y.) U., 1954-58, prof. microbiology, 1959-86, prof. emeritus, 1986—, founder, dir. biol. rsch. labs., 1955-65, head radiation and isotope lab., 1956-63, dir. germ-free life rsch. lab., 1956-84; mem. Internat. Congress on Nutrition, Washington, 1960, Internat. Congress for Microbiology, Montreal, Can., 1962, Moscow, 1966, Internat. Congress for Germ-Free Life Rsch., Nagoya, Japan, 1967; mem. com. on nutrition NAS-NRC, Washington, 1964-66; mem. Conf. on Germ-Free Life and Gnobiotics, Madison, Wis., 1986, Internat. Conf. on Gnotobiology, Versailles, France, 1987; cons. NSF, Washington, Cradle Soc. Inc., Evanston, Ill., GE, Syracuse, Am. Cyanamid, Pearl River, N.Y., Carnation Co., L.A., C.V. Mosby, St. Louis, Can. Dry Corp., Greenwich, Conn., Chocolate Mfrs. Assn., Washington, Continental Can Co., Syracuse. Contbr. articles to profl. jours., chpts. to books. Refrigeration Rsch. Found. fellow, 1945-47; NIH grantee, 1956-80. Mem. Am. Soc. for Microbiology (placement com. 1966-78), Gnotobiotics Assn., Soc. for Gen. Microbiology. Avocations: history, genealogy, hiking. Home: Clark Hollow Rd East Poultney VT 05741-0604 Office: Syracuse U Dept Biology 108 College Pl Syracuse NY 13210-2819

PHILLIPS, BARNET, IV, lawyer; b. New York, N.Y., July 5, 1948; s. Barnet III and Isabelle (Auriema) P.; m. Sharon Walsted Packey, Jan. 2, 1981; children: Victoria Ilonka, Caroline Walsted. BA, Yale U., 1970; JD, Fordham U., 1973; LLM, NYU, 1977. Bar: N.Y. 1974. Assoc. Hughes Hubbard & Reed, N.Y.C., 1973-76; assoc. Skadden, Arps, Slate, Meagher & Flom, N.Y.C., 1977-81, ptnr., 1981—; adj. assoc. prof. Forham U., N.Y.C., 1987-88; articles editor The Tax Lawyer, 1989-91. Co-author: Structuring Corporate Acquisition - Tax Aspects. Bd. dirs Student/Sponsor Partnership, N.Y.C., 1990-95; bd. cons. Portsmouth (R.I.) Abbey Sch., 1991-96. Republican. Avocations: skiing, opera, triathlons. Home: 6 Hycliff Rd Greenwich CT 06831-3223 Office: Skadden Arps Slate Meagher & Flom 919 3rd Ave New York NY 10022

PHILLIPS, BARRY, lawyer; b. Valdosta, Ga., Feb. 16, 1929; s. W. Otis and Gypsy (Mercer) P.; m. Grace Greer, Aug. 3, 1957; children: Mary Grace, Barry Jr., Greer, Quinton. AB, U. Ga., 1949, LLB, 1954. Bar: Ga. 1951, D.C. 1977. Assoc. Kilpatrick Stockton, Atlanta, 1954-60, ptnr., 1960-97, of counsel, 1997—; bd. dirs., mem. exec. com., credit com. Bank South Corp., 1978-96. Mem. bd. regents Univ. Sys. Ga., 1988-94, vice chmn., 1991-93, chmn., 1993-94; trustee U. Ga. Found., Atlanta, 1983-87, treas., 1985-87; mem. bd. visitors U. Ga. Law Sch., 1983-87, chmn., 1995; dir. Ctrl. Atlanta Progress, 1985-86; dir. USA-ROC Econ. Coun., 1985-91; bd. dirs. Ga. Coun. Internat. Visitors, Atlanta, 1986-93, sec., 1986-87, pres., 1987-88; bd. dirs. Atlanta Conv. and Visitor's Bur., 1986-91, sec., 1986-87, v.p., 1987-88; bd. dirs. Ga. Region NCCJ, 1980—, co-chair, 1982-83; chmn. Met. Atlanta Olympic Games Authority, 1990-91; bd. dirs. Nat. H.S. Football Hall of Fame, 1994—, Ga. Sports Hall of Fame, 1990, vice chmn., 1993-95, chmn., 1995-96; attache Can. Olympic Team for 1996 Olympics, 1995-96. 1st lt. U.S. Army, 1951-53, Korea. Decorated Air medal; recipient Brotherhood-Sisterhood award Ga. Regional NCCJ, 1993. Fellow Am. Coll. Investment Counsel (bd. dirs. 1986-88), ABA, Ga. Bar Found., Soc. Internat. Bus. Fellows; mem. Ga. Bar Assn. (chmn. corp. and banking law sect. 1977-78), Atlanta Bar Assn., D.C. Bar Assn., Lawyers Club Atlanta, U. Ga. Law Sch. Alumni Assn. (trustee 1979-84, pres. 1982-83), Can. Am. Soc. (bd. dirs. 1981-90, pres. 1981-83), Brit. Am. Bus. Group (bd. dirs. 1985-95), Sphinx, Gridiron, Phi Beta Kappa, Phi Kappa Phi, Omicron Delta Kappa. Democrat. Methodist. Avocations: reading, travel. Home: 4850 Tanglewood Ct NW Atlanta GA 30327-4558 Office: Kilpatrick Stockton 1100 Peachtree St NE Ste 2800 Atlanta GA 30309-4528

PHILLIPS, BERNICE CECILE GOLDEN, retired vocational education educator; b. Galveston, Tex., June 30, 1920; d. Walter Lee and Minnie (Rothspack) Golden; m. O. Phillips, Mar. 1950 (dec.); children: Dorian Lee, Loren Francis. BBA cum laude, U. Tex., 1945; MEd, U. Houston, 1968. cert. tchr., tchr. coord., vocat. tchr., Tex. Dir. Delphian Soc., Houston, 1955-60; bus. tchr. various private schs., Houston area, 1960-65; vocat. tchr. coord. office edn. program Pasadena (Tex.) Ind. Sch. Dist., 1965-68, Houston Ind. Sch. Dist., John H. Reagan High Sch., 1968-85. Bd. dirs. Regency House Condominium Assn., 1991-93. Recipient numerous awards and recognitions for vocat. bus. work at local and state levels. Mem. AAUW (life, Houston Br. v.p. ednl. found. 1987-90, pres. 1992-94, bd. dirs. 1987-96), NEA, Nat. Bus. Edn. Assn. Am. Vocat. Assn. (life), Tex. State Tchrs. Assn. (life), Tex. Classroom Tchrs. Assn. (life), Tex. Bus. Edn. Assn. (emeritus), Vocat. Office Edn. Tchrs. Assn. Tex. (past bd. dirs.), Greater Houston Bus. Edn. Assn. (reporter), Houston Assn. Ret. Tchrs., Tex. Assn. Ret. Tchrs., Delta Pi Epsilon (emeritus), Beta Gamma Sigma. Avocations:

bridge, reading, arts, crafts, travel, theater. Home: 1123D Royston Pl Bel Air MD 21015

PHILLIPS, BETTIE MAE, elementary school educator; b. Ft. Worth, May 2, 1941; d. Robert Sr. and Charittie Barnes; m. George Vernon Phillips Sr., Aug. 29, 1960 (div. Aug. 1985); 1 child, George Vernon Jr. BS in Elem. Edn., Bishop Coll., 1967; MEd in Early Childhood Edn., East Tex. State U., 1976. Tchr. Dallas Ind. Sch. Dist., 1968—. Author: The Whole Armor, 1979, Petals, 1988, Lights in the Shadows, 1993; composer children's songs Bettie's Songs, Vol. 1, 1987, God's Cloud and There's Love Everywhere, 1994 (recorded by Hilltop Records, included in album America), You and I Free Your Score (recorded by Hilltop Records, included in album Hilltop Country), 1995. Mem. Classroom Tchrs. Dallas. Baptist. Avocations: singing in concerts for children and in church choir. Home: 1312 Mill Stream Dr Dallas TX 75232-4604 Office: Bayles Elem Sch 2444 Telegraph Ave Dallas TX 75228-5819

PHILLIPS, BETTY LOU (ELIZABETH LOUISE PHILLIPS), author, interior designer; b. Cleve.; d. Michael N. and Elizabeth D. (Materna) Suvak; m. John S. Phillips, Jan. 27, 1963 (div. Jan. 1981); children: Bruce, Bryce, Brian; m. John D.C. Roach, Aug. 28, 1982. BS, Syracuse U., 1960; postgrad. in English, Case Western Res. U., 1963-64. Cert. elem. and spl. edn. tchr., N.Y. Tchr. pub. schs. Shaker Heights, Ohio, 1960-66; sportswriter Cleve. Press, 1976-77; spl. features editor Pro Quarterback Mag., N.Y.C., 1976-79; freelance writer specializing in books for young people, 1976—; interior designer residential and comml.; bd. dirs. Cast Specialties Inc., Cleve. Author: Chris Evert: First Lady of Tennis, 1977; Picture Story of Dorothy Hamill (ALA Booklist selection), 1978; American Quarter Horse, 1979; Earl Campbell: Houston Oiler Superstar, 1979; Picture Story of Nancy Lopez, (ALA Notable book), 1980; Go! Fight! Win! The NCA Guide for Cheerleaders (ALA Booklist), 1981; Something for Nothing, 1981; Brush Up on Your Hair (ALA Booklist), 1981; Texas ... The Lone Star State, 1989, Who Needs Friends? We All Do!, 1989; also contbr. articles to young adult and sports mags. Bd. dirs. The Children's Mus., Denver; mem. Friends of Fine Arts Found., Denver Art Mus., Cen. City Opera Guild, Alameda County Cancer League. Mem. Soc. Children's Book Writers, Internat. Interior Design Assn. (profl. mem.), Am. Soc. Interior Designers (profl. mem., cert.), Delta Delta Delta. Republican. Roman Catholic. Home: 4278 Bordeaux Ave Dallas TX 75205

PHILLIPS, BILLY SAXTON, artist, designer, painter; b. Louisville, Nebr., June 20, 1915; d. Charles William and Georgia Hazel (de le Zene) Tremblay; m. John Henry Phillips, Sept. 3, 1937; 1 dau., Terry. Grad., Art Ctr. Coll. of Design, 1950. Free-lance artist L.A., 1951—; package designer Wilson Paper-Disneyland, Anaheim, Calif., 1952-56; inventor Vernon (Calif.) Container Corp., 1952-56; instr. Clatsop C.C., Astoria, Oreg., 1990-92; painter Reva-Reva Gallery, Papeete, French Polynesia, 1972-92, Royal Gallery, Lahaina, Maui, Hawaii, 1993-94; artist P.M. Prodns., L.A., 1951-90; instr., motivator Maoridom, New Zealand, 1980—; instr. Art Ctr. Coll. Design, 1952-53. Designer, patentee Ukili, 1967, packages, 1960 (Zipper openings on cardboard containers); designer Disneyland's Tinkerbell; group shows include Royal Art Gallery, Met. Gallery, Lahanina, Maui, Hawaii, 1994, Kona, Hawaii, 1995. Developer Cultural Exchange Program First Ams.-Maori, S.W. Am. Indians and New Zealand Maoris, 1986. Mem. Art Ctr. Alumni (charter, life), Trail's End Art Assn., Lady Elk, Inventors and Scientists Am. Avocations: travel, graphoanalysis, theatre.

PHILLIPS, CARLA, county official; b. Balt., Nov. 14, 1963; d. Paulo Pereira de Mendonca and June Ann (Lewis) Cortese; m. Wayne Shriver Phillips, Mar. 24, 1990. BS, East Carolina U., 1985; MPA, U. Balt., 1993. Program dir. YMCA of Met. Washington, Alexandria, Va., 1985-86; ctr. supr. Balt. County Govt., Towson, Md., 1986-90, community supr., 1990-92, sr. community supr., 1992-94, asst. therapeutic recreation coord., 1994—. Water safety instr. YMCA of Ctrl. Md., 1986—, Rosedale Recreation Coun., Balt., 1991, 93; track and field coach Md. Spl. Olympics, Balt. County; asst. basketball coach Md. Spl. Olympics, Towson, 1994—, soccer coach, cycling coach, dir. track and field; mem. 6th Dist. Substance Abuse Adv. Coun., Towson, 1990-92, Villa Cresta PTA, Parkville, Md., 1988-92; ski instr. Ski Roundtop, Lewisberry, Pa., 1996—. Mem. Nat. Recreation and Park Assn. (cert. leisure profl.), Md. Recreation and Parks Assn., Profl. Ski Instrs. of Am. (eastern divsn.), York Ski Club, Kappa Delta Pi, Phi Sigma Pi, Pi Alpha Alpha. Avocations: Alpine skiing, bicycling. Home: 1000 Harris Mill Rd PO Box 306 Parkton MD 21120-0306 Office: Balt County Govt Recreation and Parks 301 Washington Ave Baltimore MD 21204-4709

PHILLIPS, CARTER GLASGOW, lawyer; b. Canton, Ohio, Sept. 11, 1952; s. Max Dean and Virginia Scott (Carter) P.; m. Sue Jane Henry, June 5, 1976; children: Jessica, Ryan. BA, Ohio State U., 1973; MA, Northwestern U., 1975, JD, 1977. Bar: Ill. 1977, D.C. 1979, U.S. Dist. Ct. (no. dist.) Ill., U.S. Dist. Ct. (D.C. dist.), U.S. Ct. Appeals (2d, 3d, 4th, 5th, 6th, 7th, 8th, 9th, 10th, 11th, D.C. and fed. cirs.). Law clk. U.S. Ct. Appeals (7th cir.), Chgo., 1977-78; law clk. to chief Justice Warren E. Burger U.S. Supreme Ct., Washington, 1978-79; asst. prof. law U. Ill., Champaign, 1979-81; asst. solicitor gen. U.S. Dept. Justice, Washington, 1981-84; ptnr. Sidley & Austin, Washington, 1984—, mng. ptnr., 1995—. Contbr. articles to profl. jours. Chief counsel Spina Bifida Assn. Am., Rockville, Md., 1987—; mem. bd. advisors state and local legal ctrs., Washington, 1985-91. Mem. Am. Law Inst., Acad. Appellate Lawyers. Republican. Episcopalian. Office: Sidley & Austin 1722 I St NW Washington DC 20006-3705

PHILLIPS, CHARLES ALAN, accounting firm executive; b. Cin., Aug. 12, 1939; s. Charles Stanley and Mary Lucile (Kirkpatrick) P. BS in Bus. Adminstrn., Northwestern U., 1960, MBA, 1961. Cert. systems profl. Investment adviser Continental Ill. Bank, Chgo., 1960-65; asst. to pres. A.S. Hansen, Chgo., 1965-67; investment adviser Francis I. du Pont, N.Y.C., 1967-70; prof. North Central Coll., Mansfield, Ohio, 1970-73; prin. Peat, Marwick, Mitchell (now KPMG Peat Marwick), Cleve., Tulsa, Houston, 1973-88. Presbyterian. Avocations: classical music; natural history; gardening.

PHILLIPS, CHARLES FRANKLIN, economic consultant; b. Nelson, Pa., May 25, 1910; s. Frank G. and Emily Catherine (Stevens) P.; m. Evelyn Minard, June 22, 1932; children—Charles Franklin Jr., Carol Ann. A.B., Colgate U., 1931, LL.D., 1945; Ph.D., Harvard U., 1934; LL.D., Colby Coll., 1949, Bowdoin Coll., 1952, Northeastern U., 1953, Shaw U., 1966, Bates Coll., 1967; L.H.D., U. Maine, 1954; Litt.D., Western New Eng. Coll., 1959, Nasson Coll., 1959, Morehouse Coll., Atlanta, 1963. Asst. econs. Hobart Coll., Geneva, N.Y., 1933-34; instr. econs. Colgate U., 1934-36, asst. prof., 1936-39, prof., 1939-44; on leave of absence, 1941-44; to serve as cons. counsumers div. Nat. Def. Adv. Com., 1941; asst. price exec. OPA, 1941-42, chief tire rationing div., 1942-43, dir. automotive supply rationing div., 1943-44, dep. adminstr. charge rationing dept., 1944; pres. Bates Coll., 1944-67, pres. emeritus, 1967—; former pub. gov. Am. Stock Exch.; ret. dir. several corps. Author: Marketing, 1938, (with Jasper V. Garland) Government Spending and Economic Recovery, 1938, Discussion Methods, 1938, The American Neutrality Problem, 1939, (with Delbert J. Duncan and Stanley C. Hollander) Modern Retailing Management, rev. edit, 1972, (with others) Marketing Principles and Methods, rev. edit, 1973, Marketing by Manufacturers, rev. edit, 1951, A Tax Program to Encourage the Economic Growth of Puerto Rico, 1958; contbr. articles to acad., trade jours. Pres. New Eng. Colls. Fund, 1954. Mem. Phi Beta Kappa, Phi Delta Theta. Address: 117 Maple Hill Rd Auburn ME 04210-8728

PHILLIPS, CHARLES FRANKLIN, JR., economist, educator; b. Geneva, N.Y., Nov. 5, 1934; s. Charles Franklin and Evelyn (Minard) P.; m. Marjorie Hancock, June 22, 1957; children: Charles Franklin, Susan Hancock, Anne Davis. B.A., U. N.H., 1956; Ph.D., Harvard U., 1960. Asst. prof. econs. Washington and Lee U., Lexington, Va., 1959-63; asso. prof. Washington and Lee U., 1963-66, prof., 1966—; mem. adv. bd. Shenandoah Valley area, First Union, 1971—; econ. cons. pub. utilities. Author: Competition in the Synthetic Rubber Industry, 1963, The Economics of Regulation, 1965, rev. edit., 1969, The Regulation of Public Utilities, 1984, 3d edit., 1993; editor: Competition and Monopoly in the Domestic Telecommunications Industry, 1974, Competition and Regulation-Some Economic Concepts, 1976, Expanding Economic Concepts of Regulation in Health, Postal and Telecommunications Services, 1977, Regulation, Competition and Deregulation-An Economic Grab Bag, 1978, Regulation and the Future Economic Environment-Air to Ground, 1980. Mem. city coun. Lexington, 1969-71, mayor, 1971-88; trustee Hebron Acad., Maine, 1971-82, Presbyn. Ch., 1991—, elder, 1993—; mem. Commn. on Rev. of Nat. Policy Toward Gambling, 1972-76; chmn. Valley Program for Aging Svcs., 1993-95, treas., 1996—; bd. dirs. Rockbridge Area Presbyn. Home, 1973—, Nat. Regulatory Rsch. Inst., 1992-95; pres. United Way of Lexington-Rockbridge County, 1996—, Hist. Lexington Found., 1997—. Recipient McKinsey Found. award, 1962; Outstanding Regional Dir. award Omicron Delta Epsilon, 1971. Mem. Am. Econ. Assn., So. Econ. Assn., Am. Mktg. Assn., Phi Beta Kappa, Omicron Delta Epsilon (pres. 1976-77, 78-79, 96—). Republican (mem. Va. central com. 1974-76, 77-96). Home: 414 Morningside Dr Lexington VA 24450-2739 Office: Washington and Lee U Dept Economics Lexington VA 24450

PHILLIPS, CHARLES GORHAM, lawyer; b. Glen Ridge, N.J., Apr. 27, 1921; s. Charles Swayne and Margaret Cook (Atwell) P.; m. Martha Hall Belden, Dec. 19, 1942; children: Webster B., Charles G. Jr., Tacey P. Carroll, Tyler A. AB magna cum laude, Williams Coll., 1943; JD cum laude, Harvard U., 1948. Bar: N.Y. 1949. Assoc. Cadwalader, Wickersham & Taft, N.Y.C., 1948-51; assoc. Dewey Ballantine and predecessor firm, N.Y.C., 1951-57, ptnr., 1958—, chmn. mgmt. com., 1984-88. Assoc. trustee Montclair (N.J.) Art Mus., 1988—. Cpl. USAAF, 1943-46. Mem. ABA, Montclair Golf Club, Riomar Bay Yacht Club, Riomar Country Club (Vero Beach, Fla.). Republican. Congregationalist. Avocations: golfing, bridge, needlepoint. Home: 746 Riomar Dr Vero Beach FL 32963-2013 also: 10 Crestmont Rd Montclair NJ 07042-1930 Office: Dewey Ballantine 1301 Avenue Of The Americas New York NY 10019-6022

PHILLIPS, CHRISTOPHER HALLOWELL, diplomat; b. The Hague, The Netherlands, Dec. 6, 1920; s. William and Caroline A. (Drayton) P.; m. Mabel B. Olsen, May 11, 1943 (dec. May 1995); children: Victoria A. Phillips Corbett, Miriam O. Phillips Eley, David W. A.B., Harvard U., 1943. Reporter, Beverly (Mass.) Evening Times, 1947-48; mem. Mass. Senate, 1948-53; spl. asst. to asst. sec. UN affairs Dept. State, 1953; later dep. asst. sec. of state for internat. orgn. affairs; apptd. U.S. Civil Service commr.; vice chmn. U.S. Civil Service Commn., 1957; U.S. rep. on UN Econ. and Social Council, 1958-61; Chase Manhattan Bank rep. for UN affairs, 2d v.p., mgr. Canadian div., 1961-65; pres. U.S. council Internat. C. of C., 1965-69; ambassador, dep. U.S. rep. UN Security Council, 1969-70; ambassador, dep. permanent U.S. rep. to UN, 1970-73; pres. Nat. Council for U.S.-China Trade, Washington, 1973-86, now hon. mem. bd. dirs.; U.S. ambassador to Brunei Darussalam, 1989-91; presdl. appointee to bd. U.S. Inst. Peace, 1992—; trustee Am. Inst. in Taiwan, 1995—; mem. adv. coun. Sch. Advanced Internat. Studies, Johns Hopkins U. Mass. dist. del. Rep. Nat. Conv., 1952, 60. Served to capt. USAAF, 1942-46. Fellow Am. Acad. Arts and Scis.; mem. UN Assn. U.S.A., Coun. Fgn. Rels., Asia Soc., Coun. Am. Ambassadors (bd. dirs.), Met. Club Washington. Episcopalian. Home: 2801 New Mexico Ave NW Washington DC 20007-3921

PHILLIPS, CLIFTON J., history educator; b. Olean, N.Y., Apr. 11, 1919; s. Charles Clifton and Edith (Grey) P.; m. Rachel Jacqueline Martin, July 19, 1952; children: Peter Martin, Elaine Abigail, Alexis Anne, Patience Cecily. B.A., Hiram Coll., 1941; Th.B., Starr King Sch. Religious Leadership, 1944; M.A., Harvard U., 1950, Ph.D., 1954. Civil edn. officer Dept. Def., Kobe, Japan, 1946-49; faculty history De Pauw U., 1954—, prof., 1965-85, sr. prof., 1985—, chmn. dept. history, 1969-72, 78—; lectr. Am. Studies, Korea, 1968-69. Author: Indiana in Transition: The Emergence of an Industrial Commonwealth, 1880-1920, 1968, Protestant America and the Pagan World: The First Half Century of the American Board of Commissioners for Foreign Missions, 1810-1860, 1969, (with others) The Missionary Enterprise in China and America, 1974, Missionary Ideologies in the Imperialist Era, 1880-1920, 1982; DePauw: A Pictorial History, 1987, From Frontier Circuit to Urban Church: The History of Greencastle Methodism, 1989. Served with inf. AUS, 1944-46, PTO. Fulbright-Hays fellow Chinese civilization Taiwan, summer 1962. Mem. Am. Hist. Assn., Assn. Asian Studies, Orgn. Am. Historians, Ind. Hist. Soc., Ind. Assn. Historians (past pres.). Home: 111 S Spring St Greencastle IN 46135-1712

PHILLIPS, DANA WAYNE, lawyer; b. Corpus Christi, Tex., Oct. 5, 1951; s. David Wayne and Mildred (Elliott) P.; m. Dene' Elaine Batelaan, July 21, 1973 (div. 1981); m. Susan Jeanne Predmore, Mar. 23, 1985; 1 child Tristan Reid Phillips, step daughter: Lindsey Ann Midgley. Student, So. Meth. U., Dallas, 1969-70; BA, U. Calif., Santa Barbara, 1973; JD, U. San Diego, 1976. Bar: Calif. 1976, U.S. Dist. Ct. (ctrl. dist.) Calif. 1977. Atty. Pell & Phillips, Ventura, Calif., 1976-80, Drucker & Steinschriber, Sherman Oaks, Calif., 1980-82; gen. counsel Pension Vest, Inc., Montrose, Calif., 1982-85; atty. Drucker & Steinschriber, Sherman Oaks, Calif., 1985-86; gen. counsel Sacramento Housing & Redevelopment Agy., Sacramento, 1986—; bd. mem. Nat. Assn. Pvt. Placement Syndicators, L.A., 1984-85; v.p., bd. dirs. Calif. Housing Authority Risk Mgmt. Agy., Oakland. Mem. ABA, Sacramento County Bar Assn., Sacramento Mother Lode Govt. Atty. Assn. Office: Sacramento Housing & Redevelopment Agy 630 I St Sacramento CA 95814-2404

PHILLIPS, DANIEL ANTHONY, trust company executive; b. Boston, Feb. 24, 1938; s. Lyman Waldo and Harriet Anthony (Carlow) P.; m. Diana Walcott, Aug. 18, 1962; children: Lisa Walcott Phillips, Bradford Lyman, Phillips. AB cum laude, Harvard U., 1960, MBA, 1963. From v.p. to dir. to mem. exec. com. Fiduciary Trust Co., Boston, 1963-92, exec. v.p., dir., trust com. sec., trust officer, 1992—, exec. v.p., dir., trust com., trust officer, 1993-94, pres., CEO, 1993—. Bd. dirs. Family Svc. Am., chair fin. comn., 1993-95, treas., chair bd. dirs., 1995-97; pres., bd. dirs. Am. Meml. Hosp., Reims, France; bd. dirs. Family Found., N.Am., 1993-97, Grimes-King Found. for the Elderly, Inc.; v.p., treas. Frederick E. Weber Charities Corp.; chair bd. dirs. Families Internat., Inc., 1997—. Mem. Boston Soc. Security Analysts, Harvard U. Alumni Assn. (1st v.p. 1996-97, pres. 1997—, Harvard Alumni Assn. award 1995), Boston Econ. Club, Comml. Club. Home: 975 Memorial Dr Cambridge MA 02138-5753 Office: Fiduciary Trust Co 175 Federal St Boston MA 02110-2210

PHILLIPS, DANIEL MILLER, lawyer; b. Cleve., Mar. 21, 1933; s. Clovis H. and Lillian (Miller) P.; m. Joyce C. Hamilton, July 26, 1958; children: Meegan M., Sarah H., Anthony J. Student, Wesleyan U., Middletown, Conn., 1951-53; B.S., Ohio State U., 1958, J.D., 1961. Bar: Ohio 1961. Since practiced in Toledo; mem. firm Robison, Curphey & O'Connell, 1961-77, ptnr., 1967-77; dir. litigation Owens-Corning Fiberglas Corp., Toledo, 1977-86; spl. cons. Asbestos Claim Facility, Princeton, N.J., 1986-87, dir. adminstrn. and human resources, 1987-89, pres., 1990-92, trustee, 1985-86; cons. UNR Asbestos-Disease Claims Trust, 1991—; lectr. Ohio Legal Ctr. Inst., 1969-70, 73; pres. Found. for Practice Law in Pub. Interest, Toledo, 1976; legal rep. for unknown and future asbestos bodily injury persons Chpt. II Procs. Nat. Gypsum Co., 1992—; trustee Eagle-Pitcher Industries Chpt. II Procs., 1996—. Pres. Toledo Florence Crittenton Services, 1971-72; mem. Lucas County Mental Health and Retardation Bd., 1975-76; trustee Toledo Legal Aid Soc., 1977-82, Community Planning Council of Northwestern Ohio, 1978-82; mem. working group on asbestos litigation Nat. Ctr. for State Cts. Jud. Adminstrn., 1982-83. Served with AUS, 1953-55. Mem. ABA, Ohio Bar Assn. (chmn. negligence law com. 1971-73, mem. ins. law com. 1974-79), Toledo Bar Assn. (exec. com. 1971-80, sec. 1974, pres. 1978-79), Toledo Jr. Bar Assn. (pres. 1970-71), Fedn. Ins. Counsel, Def. Rsch. Inst., Ohio Assn. Civil Trial Lawyers (pres. 1971-72), U.S. Jud. Conf. 6th Cir. (life). Home and Office: 2049 Delaware Dr Ann Arbor MI 48103-6014

PHILLIPS, DENISE, critical care nurse; b. Orange, N.J., July 11, 1960; d. James Henry Phillips and Gracie Estelle (Reed) Brown. Diploma in nursing, Riverside Hosp. Sch. Nursing, Newport News, Va., 1985; cert. in paralegal studies, Hampton U., 1990. RN, Va., Fla., Md., N.Y.; cert. BLS instr., ACLS; instr. cert. nurse asst. and LPN programs. Nurse asst. Riverside Hosp., Newport News, 1981-86; Riverside Hosp. Riverside Regional Med. Ctr., Newport News, 1986-91; staff nurse Traveling Nurse Corp., Malden, Mass., 1991-93; dir. staff devel. Va. Health Svcs., Inc., Newport News, 1993-95; asst. dir. nursing svcs. James Pointe Care Ctr., Newport News, Va., 1995—; per diem nurse adminstr. Sentara Hampton (Va.) Gen. Hosp., 1994—; asst. dir. of nursing svcs. James Point Care Ctr., Newport News, Va., 1995—; LPN, cert. nurse asst. instr. Career Devel. Ctr., Newport News, 1989-91; lectr. on decreasing profl. liability for healthcare workers, 1990—. Contbr. article to Health Care Digest, 1995. Vol. Williamsburg (Va.) area Girl Scouts U.S., 1990-92. Mem. ACCN, Nat. League of Nursing. Avocations: reading, bicycling, volleybal, painting, travel. Home: 93 Post St Newport News VA 23601 Office: 5015 Huntington Ave Newport News VA 23607-2013

PHILLIPS, DOROTHY KAY, lawyer; b. Camden, N.J., Nov. 2, 1945; d. Benjamin L. and Sadye (Levinsky) Phillips; children: Bethann P., David M. Schaffzin. BS in English Lit. magna cum laude, U. Pa., 1964; MA in Family Life and Marriage Counseling and Edn., NYU, 1975; JD, Villanova U., 1978. Bar: Pa. 1978, N.J. 1978, U.S. Dist. Ct. (ea. dist.) Pa. 1978, U.S. Dist. Ct. N.J., 1978, U.S. Ct. Appeals (3d cir.), 1984, U.S. Supreme Ct. 1984. Tchr., Haddon Twp. High Sch. (N.J.), and Haddon Heights High Sch. (N.J.), 1964-70; lectr., counselor Marriage Council of Phila.; lectr. U. Pa. and Hahnemann Med. Schs., Phila., 1970-75; atty. Adler, Barish, Daniels, Levin & Creskoff, Phila., 1978-79, Astor, Weiss & Newman, Phila., 1979-80; ptnr. Romisher & Phillips, P.C., Phila., 1981-86; prin. Law Office of Dorothy K. Phillips, 1986—; faculty Sch. of Law Temple U. Guest speaker on domestic rels. issues on radio and TV shows; featured in newspaper and mag. articles; contbr. articles to profl. jours. Rosenbach Found., Philadanco, Fedn. Allied Jewish Appeal (lawyers. div.), World Affairs Coun.; bd. mem. Anti-Defamation League of B'nai B'rith, Nat. Mus. Jewish History, mem. friends' circle, Athenaeum, Phila., shareholder. Mem. ABA, ATLA (membership com. 1990-91, co-chair 1989-90), Pa. Trial Lawyers Assn. (chair membership com. family sect. 1989-90, presenter ann. update civil litigators-family law, author procedures practice of family law Phila. County Family Law Litigation Sect. County practiced database 1991), Pa. Bar Assn. (continuing legal edn. com. 1990-92, faculty, lectr. Pa. Bar Inst. Continuing Legal Edn. 1990, panel mem. summer meeting 1991), N.J. Bar Assn., Phila. Bar Assn. (chmn. early settlement program 1983-84, mem. custody rules drafting com. for Supreme Ct. Pa., spl. events speaker on pensions, counsel fees, written fee agreements 1989-91, co-chair and moderator of panel mandatory continuing legal edn. 1994), Phila. Trial Lawyers Assn., Montgomery County Bar Assn., Lawyers Club. Office: 1818 Market St Ste 35 Philadelphia PA 19103-3602

PHILLIPS, DOROTHY ORMES, elementary education educator; b. Denver, July 26, 1922; d. Jesse Edward and Belle (Noisette) Ormes; m. James Kermit Phillips, Apr. 28, 1945; children: William K., Dorothy E., Valerie A. BBA, Case Western Res. U., 1946, MA, 1959; PhD, U. Akron, 1989. Cert. tchr., adminstr., Ohio. Tchr. Cleve. Pub. Schs., 1955-68, math. cons., 1968-83, adminstrv. intern, 1970-73; grad. asst. U. Akron, Ohio, 1983-85, lectr. elem. edn., supr. student tchrs., 1985—; math. workshop presenter Norton (Ohio) Pub. Schs., 1986, presenter career day, 1997. Chmn. bd. Centerville Mills YMCA Camp, Chagrin Falls, Ohio, 1996—. Grantee NDEA, 1960, NSF, 1966. Mem. ASCD, Nat. Coun. Tchrs. Math., Ednl. Computer Consortium Ohio, Cleve. Pub. Schs. Math. Cons. (assoc.), Alpha Kappa Alpha, Pi Lambda Theta. Avocations: swimming, camping, reading. Home: 8746 Crackel Rd Chagrin Falls OH 44023-1807 Office: U Akron Ednl Field Experiences Zook Hall # 228 Akron OH 44325

PHILLIPS, EARL NORFLEET, JR., financial services executive; b. High Point, N.C., May 5, 1940; s. Earl Norfleet Phillips and Lillian Jordan; m. Sarah Boyle, Oct. 19, 1971; children: Courtney Dorsett, Jordan Norfleet. BSBA, U. N.C., 1962; MBA, Harvard U., 1965. Security analyst Wertheim & Co., N.Y.C., 1965-67; exec. v.p. Factors Inc., High Point, N.C., 1967-71, exec. v.p. First Factors Corp., High Point, 1972-81, pres., 1982—; bd. dirs. Oakdale Cotton Mills, First Union Nat. Bank N.C., N.C. Enterprise Corp. Bd. dirs. Culp, Inc. Trustee U. N.C., Chapel Hill, 1983-91, chmn. bd., 1989-91, mem. endowment bd. U. N.C., 1987—, U. N.C. Found., 1987-91, bd. govs. U. N.C. System, 1995—; bd. dirs. N.C. Bus. Found., N.C. Citizens for Bus. and Industry; mem. N.C. Econ. Devel. Bd., Raleigh, N.C., 1984-91; mem. nat. adv. coun. SBA, 1988-91; trustee High Point Regional Hosp., Asian Inst. Tech., Bangkok, Thailand, 1993—; mem. Piedmont Triad Airport Authority. Named Young Man of Yr., High Point Jaycees, 1971; named One of Five Outstanding Young Men, N.C. Jaycees, 1971. Mem. Nat. Comml. Fin. Assn. (bd. dirs.). Clubs: The Brook (N.Y.C.), Country of N.C. (Pinehurst), High Point C.C., String and Splinter (High Point), Linville (N.C.) Golf. Lodge: Gorgons Head. Office: First Factors Corp PO Box 2730 101 S Main St High Point NC 27261-2730

PHILLIPS, EDUARDO, surgeon, educator; b. Guadalajara, Mex., Oct. 25, 1943; m. Marion Paulette Khan; children: Mark, Anthony, Cynthia. MD with honors, Nat. U. Mexico City, 1967. Diplomate Am. Bd. Surgery. Rotating intern Hosp. Frances, Mexico City, 1966, resident in gen. surgery, 1967-69; rotating intern Sinai Hosp., Detroit, 1969, resident in gen. surgery, 1970-73, coord. surg. edn., 1974-76, chief surg. endoscopy, 1984—, acting chmn. dept. surgery, 1991, chmn. dept. surgery, 1992—; clin. asst. prof. Wayne State U., Detroit, 1992—. Contbr. articles to profl. jours. Fellow Internat. Coll. Surgeons (pres. Mich. divsn. 1995—, vice regent Mich 1993-95, regent Mich. 1995—, Vice Regent of Yr. 1993), Am. Coll. Surgeons; mem. AMA, Am. Soc. for Laser Medicine and Surgery, Am. Soc. Abdominal Surgeons, Am. Soc. Gastrointestinal Endoscopy, Am. Soc. Bariatric Surgery, Acad. Surgery Detroit (coun mem., chair membership com., chmn. membership com. 1995—), Detroit Gastroent. Soc. (pres. 1985-86), Detroit Surg. Assn., Mich. State Med. Soc., Crohn's and Colitis Found. Am., Inc., Soc. Laparoendoscopic Surgeons, Mich. Soc. Gen. Surgeons, Wayne County Med. Soc., Mich. Soc. Gastrointestinal Endoscopy, Frederick A. Coller Surg. Soc., Southeastern Mich. Surg. Soc. Jewish. Avocations: outdoor activities, classical music, reading classics. Office: Sinai Hosp 6767 W Outer Dr Detroit MI 48235-2893

PHILLIPS, EDWARD JOHN, consulting firm executive; b. Phila., Sept. 8, 1940; s. Harold E. and Mary C. P.; m. Kathleen A. Everett, July 23, 1960; children: Elizabeth J., Edward J. B of Mech. Engring., Villanova U., 1973; MBA, Widener U., 1975. Registered profl. engr., Ill., Kans., Mo., Pa., Ohio; chartered engr., U.K. Tech. ops. mgr. Motorola, Inc., Franklin Park, Ill., 1976-81; v.p. engring. Rival Mfg. Co., Kansas City, Mo., 1981-82; prin., sr. cons. Richard Muther & Assocs., Kansas City, 1982-85; chmn. KANDE, Inc., Overland Park, Kans., 1983-86; pres., CEO Sims Cons. Group Inc., Lancaster, Ohio, 1986—; chmn. bd. dirs. Sims Consulting Group, Lancaster, Ohio; bd. dirs. KANDE, Inc., Wilmington, Del. Author: Manufacturing Plant Layout; contbr. articles to profl. jours. Mem. NSPE, ASME (chmn. material handling divsn. 1989-91, mem. internat. mgmt. com. 1977), MIMechE, Tau Beta Pi, Pi Tau Sigma. Office: Sims Cons Group Inc PO Box 968 111 N Broad St Lancaster OH 43130-0968

PHILLIPS, EDWARD JOHN, computer scientist, writer; b. Bristol, Pa., July 17, 1937; s. Frank Heitman and Margaret Marie (Koch) P. BA Math., Temple U., 1963. Lic. stockbroker, Tex. Planetary rsch. programmer Jet Propulsion Lab./NASA, Pasadena, Calif., 1969-78; brain rsch. programmer U. Calif. Med. Sch., L.A., 1979-80; scientific systems engr. Electronic Data Systems, Riverside, Calif./Dallas, 1980-85; naval weapons systems analyst USN, Corona, Calif., 1986-89; computer scientist Riverside, 1989-92, Dallas, 1992-93, Levittown, Pa., 1993—. Author: (book/invention) The Computer and Statistics: The Prediction of Failure in Automobile Components and Systems, 1993, (song) The Song Beyond Memory, 1995, Timeless Mystery, 1995. Mem. Broadcast Music, Inc. Avocations: writing, med. rsch. Home and Office: 80 Indian Red Rd Levittown PA 19057

PHILLIPS, EDWIN CHARLES, gas transmission company executive; b. Saskatoon, Sask., Can., Oct. 19, 1917; s. Charles Henry and Beatrice Grace (Johnson) P.; m. Elizabeth Winnifred Johnston, June 27, 1942; children: Diane, Carol, Glen, Earl, Jane, Sue. Student, Lethbridge Collegiate Inst., 1931-35. Asst. buyer Loblaw Groceries Co. Ltd., Toronto, 1938-42; advt. mgr. Can. and Dominion Sugar Co., Chatham, Ont., 1945-47; asst. to gen. mgr. Consumers Gas Co., Toronto, 1947-52; with Trane Co. Can., Ltd., 1952-68, exec. v.p., gen. mgr., 1964-65, pres., 1966-68; group v.p. Westcoast Energy Inc., Vancouver, 1968-70, exec. v.p., 1971-72, pres., 1972-82, chief exec. officer, 1976-83, chmn. bd., 1980-83, also dir.; dir. emeritus, 1989; bd. dirs. Balaclava Enterprises Ltd., Cheni Resources, Inc., Cambridge Resources Ltd., Future Shop Ltd., Pe Ben Oilfield Svcs. Ltd., Weiser Inc. Served with RCAF, World War II. Home: 4458 W 2nd Ave, Vancouver, BC Canada V6R 1K5 also: 5125 C Renaissance Ave San Diego CA 92122-5575

PHILLIPS, ELIZABETH JOAN, marketing executive; b. Cleve., July 8, 1938; d. Joseph Tinl and Helen Walter; m. Erwin Phillips, June 1956 (div.

1960); 1 child, Michael A. B.A., Fordham U., 1980. Account exec. David Cogan Mgmt., N.Y.C., 1969-77; account exec. N.F.L. Films, N.Y.C., 1977-78; mgr. sports programs Avon Products, N.Y.C., 1978-83; v.p. Needham, Harper & Steers (now D.D.B. Needham), N.Y.C., 1983-86; v.p. Ted Bates Event Mktg., N.Y.C., 1986-87; pres. Custom Event Mktg. 1987—. adj. prof. NYU, N.Y.C., 1987—. Mem. exec. com. Vanderbilt YMCA, N.Y.C., 1976-84; ofcl. 1984 Olympic Games, L.A.; referee Women's Olympic Marathon, L.A., 1984; pres. Met. Athletics Congress, N.Y.C., 1980-83. Mem. Women's Sports Found. (bd. advisors 1983—), N.Y. Road Runners Club (v.p., mem. exec. com. 1976—, pres. 1970—, bd. dirs. 1992—), Road Runners Club of Am. (bd. dirs. 1992—). Office: Custom Event Mktg Inc 19 W 44th St Ste 1506 New York NY 10036-6101

PHILLIPS, ELIZABETH VELLOM, social worker, educator; b. Visalia, Calif., Nov. 7, 1922; d. Ralph Cauble and Mary Amelia (Cole) Vellom; m. William Clayton Phillips, Sept. 10, 1950 (div. 1976); children: Peter Clayton, David Cole, Ann Harper. BA, UCLA, 1943; MSW, Columbia U., 1950; MPH, Yale U., 1970; PhD, Union Grad. Sch., 1980. Lic. clin. social worker; diplomate Am. Bd. Examiners Clin. Social Work. Psychiat. social worker Jewish Bd. Guardians, N.Y.C., 1950-51, Cmty. Svc. Soc. Family Camp, N.Y.C., 1955-57, Jewish Family Svc., New Haven, 1962-64, New Haven Family Counseling, 1964-68; ass. clin. prof. psychiatry Sch. Medicine Yale U., New Haven, 1973—; pvt. practice New Haven, 1981—; sr. social work supr. mental health dept. Hill Health Ctr., New Haven, 1973-81; prof. Sch. Social Work Smith Coll., Northampton, 1981-84; initiator teen pregnancy program Hill Health Ctr., 1977-81, cons., 1975-79. Found. Women's Health Svcs., New Haven, 1985, Inner City Co-op Farm, New Haven, 1978; organizer Big Brother/Big Sister program Yale U., 1976. Named Disting. Practitioner Nat. Acads. Practice, 1996. Mem. NASW, Am. Group Psychotherapy Assn., Nat. Fedn. Socs. Clin. Social Work (sec. 1988, v.p. 1993, pres.-elect 1994-96, pres. 1996-98), Conn. Soc. Clin. Social Work (pres. 1987-88). Democrat. Jewish. Avocations: playing musical instruments, writing poetry, hiking, bridge, travel. Home: 13 Cooper Rd North Haven CT 06473-3001

PHILLIPS, ELLIOTT HUNTER, lawyer; b. Birmingham, Mich., Feb. 14, 1919; s. Frank Elliott and Gertrude (Zacharias) P.; m. Gail Carolyn Isbey, Apr. 22, 1950; children—Elliott Hunter, Alexandra. A.B. cum laude, Harvard U., 1940, J.D., 1947. Bar: Mich. 1948. Since practiced in Detroit; ptnr. Hill Lewis (formerly Hill, Lewis, Adams, Goodrich & Tait), 1953-89, of counsel, 1989-96; of counsel Clark Hill, 1996—; chmn. bd. dirs. Detroit & Can. Tunnel Corp.; pres., dir. Detroit and Windsor Subway Co.; mem. Mich. Bd. Accountancy, 1965-73. Contbr. to legal and accounting jours. Chmn. bd. dirs. Southeastern Mich. chpt. ARC; pres., trustee McGregor Fund; trustee Boys Republic, Detroit Inst. for Children, United Way Southeastern Mich., Univ. Liggett Sch.; mem. nat. maj. gifts com. Harvard U., Harvard Pres.'s Assocs., 1974—; Pres.'s Coun., 1990, mem. overseers com. to visit Law Sch., overseers com. univ. resouces, Mich. chmn. Harvard Coll. Fund; trustee, pres. Ch. Youth Svc.; mem. Detroit Area coun. Boy Scouts Am. Lt. comdr. USNR, 1946. Recipient Spitzley award Detroit Inst. for Children, 1986, Harvard Alumni Assn. Disting. Svc. award, 1991. Fellow Mich. State Bar Found. (life), Am. Bar Found. (life); mem. ABA, State Bar Mich., Detroit Bar Assn., Lincoln's Inn Soc., Soc. Colonial Wars in Mich. and Fla., Country Club Detroit, Detroit Club (pres. 1988-89), Yondotega Club, Leland Country Club, Grosse Pointe Club, Harvard Ea. Mich. Club (pres. 1955-56, Disting. Alumnus award 1992), Harvard Club N.Y.C., John's Island Club. Episcopalian (vestryman, sr. warden). Home: 193 Ridge Rd Grosse Pointe MI 48236-3554 Office: 333 W Fort St Detroit MI 48226-3134

PHILLIPS, ELVIN WILLIS, lawyer; b. Tampa, Fla., Feb. 27, 1949; s. Claude Everett and Elizabeth (Willis) P.; m. Sharon Gayle Alexander, June 20, 1970; children: Natasha Hope, Tanya Joy, Trey Alexander. BA, U. Fla., 1971; MA, Western Carolina U., 1974, EdS, 1975; JD, Stetson U., 1980. Bar: Fla. 1980, U.S. Dist. Ct. (mid. dist.) Fla. 1981, U.S. Dist. Ct. (so. dist.) Fla. 1982, U.S. Ct. Appeals (11th cir.) 1988. Tchr. Monroe County Schs., Key West, Fla., 1970-73; asst. prin. Habersham County Schs., Clarksville, Ga., 1973-77; assoc. Dixon, Lawson & Brown, Tampa, Fla., 1980-81, Yado, Keel, Nelson et al, Tampa, Fla., 1981; ptnr. Lawson, McWhirter, Grandoff & Reeves, Tampa, Fla., 1981-88, Williams, Parker, Harrison, Dietz & Getzen, Sarasota, Fla., 1988—. Leadership Devel. Program fellow Southern Regional Coun., Atlanta, 1975. Mem. ABA (forum com. constrn. industry 1989-96), Fla. Bar (chmn. 1991-92, vice chmn. 1990-91, mem. benefits com.), Sarasota County Bar Assn., Phi Kappa Phi, Phi Alpha Delta, Phi Delta Kappa. Democrat. Baptist. Home: 3310 Del Prado Ct Tampa FL 33614-2721 Office: Williams Parker Harrison Dietz & Getzen 200 S Orange Ave Sarasota FL 34236-6802

PHILLIPS, ETHEL C. (MRS. LLOYD J. PHILLIPS), writer; b. N.Y.C.; d. Henry and Minnie (Hirshfeld) Cohen; m. Lloyd Jay Phillips, 1930; children: Lloyd James, Anne. B.A., Vassar Coll.; M.A. in Pub. Law, Columbia U. Publs. dir. Am. Jewish Com., Inst. Human Relations, N.Y.C., 1939-65; bd. dirs., mem. exec. com. Nat. Charities Info. Bur., N.Y.C., 1966-90, vice-chmn., 1982-90. Author: Mind Your World, 1964, Record and the Vision, 1965, You in Human Rights, 1968; also pamphlets and media features on civil rights, internat. cooperation, human rights, volunteerism. Mem. N.Y. Soc. for Ethical Culture (trustee 1977-83), Nat. Coun. Women U.S. (pres. 1972-74, hon. pres. 1974-76, UN rep. 1976—), Vassar Club (N.Y.C.), Harvard Club (N.Y.C.), Harvard Club of N.Y. Clubs: Vassar (N.Y.C.), Women's City (N.Y.C.). Home: 201 E 69th St Apt 15G New York NY 10021-5465

PHILLIPS, EUAN HYWEL, publishing executive; b. Chipstead, Surrey, Eng., Mar. 31, 1928; s. Edgar Aneurin and Elsie Llewella (Davies) P.; m. Margaret June Savage, June 12, 1954; children: David John, Janet Margaret. B.A., Emmanuel Coll., Cambridge, Eng., 1949, M.A., 1965. Cost acct. J. Lyons & Co. Ltd., London, 1950-53; dispatch mgr. Pickerings Produce Canners Ltd., Manchester, Eng., 1953-56; mgmt. cons. P.A. Mgmt. Cons. Ltd., London, 1956-65; mng. dir. Unwin Bros. Ltd., Old Woking, Eng., 1965-73; univ. printer designate Cambridge (Eng.) U. Press, 1973-74, univ. printer, 1974-76; dir. Cambridge (Eng.) U. Press (Am. br.), N.Y.C., 1977-82; owner New Canaan Bibles and Manx Knitwear, Stamford, Conn., 1982-87; exec. dir. Assn. Am. Univ. Presses, 1987-90; gov. Guildford Sch. Art, 1966-69, Cambridge Coll. Arts and Tech., 1974-76; dir. East Asian History of Sci., Inc., 1978-81. Contbr. to scholarly pub. With Royal Navy, 1946-48. Mem. Brit. Printing Industries Fedn. (coun. 1966-73, pres. Home Counties Alliance 1970-71), Troupers Light Opera Co., Connestee Falls Golf Assn. (pres. 1996-97). Home: 289 Connestee Trl Brevard NC 28712-9009

PHILLIPS, FRANCES MARIE, history educator; b. Hale Center, Tex., Nov. 8, 1918; d. Clyde C. and Ada (Stutzman) P. B.A., West Tex. State Coll., 1940, M.A., 1946; Ph.D. (Univ. fellow), U. N.Mex., 1956; postgrad. (Fulbright scholar), U. London, 1954-55. Tchr. public schs. Channing, Tex., Miami, Tex., Palisade, Colo., Tucumcari, N.Mex., 1940-46; supr. State Tchrs. Coll. Campus High Sch., Wayne, Nebr., 1947-51; instr. U. Md. Overseas Program, Eng., 1955; grad. asst. U. N.Mex., 1955-56; asst., assoc. prof. history Sul Ross State Coll., Alpine, Tex., 1956-60; prof. history, dean grad. div. Sul Ross State Coll., 1962-71; program dir. sr. colls. Coordinating Bd. Tex. Coll. and Univ. System, Austin, 1971-85; asst. prof. Mankato (Minn.) State Coll., 1960-62; lectr. Lifetime Learning Ins. of Austin, 1994—. Editor: Dear Mother and Folks at Home: Iowa Farm to Clermont-Ferrand, 1917-1918, 1988. Chmn. bd. Carlsbad dist. Wesley Found., 1962-66; mem. Adv. Council for Ednl. Personnel Devel., 1972—, State Bd. Examiners for Tchr. Edn., 1972-79, Tex. Com. on Early Childhood Devel. Careers, 1976—. Mem. AAUW, N.Mex. Hist. Soc., Am. Assn. Higher Edn., Assn. Tex. Grad. Schs. (v.p. 1967-69, pres. 1969-70), Alpha Chi, Phi Kappa Phi, Phi Alpha Theta, Delta Kappa Gamma. Democrat. Methodist (past mem. N.Mex. Conf. Bd. Edn., mem. ofcl. bd.). Research in Anglo-Am. relations, 1954-56, 1962. Home: 8700 Millway Dr Austin TX 78757-6832

PHILLIPS, FREDERICK FALLEY, architect; b. Evanston, Ill., June 18, 1946; s. David Cook and Katharine Edith (Falley) P.; m. Gay Fraker, Feb. 26, 1983 (div. Dec. 1993). BA, Lake Forest Coll., 1969; MArch, U. Pa., 1973. Registered architect, Ill., Wis. Draftsman, Harry Weese & Assocs., 1974, 75; pvt. practice architecture Frederick F. Phillips, Architect, Chgo., 1976-81; pres. Frederick Phillips and Assocs., Chgo., 1981—. Bd. dirs. Landmarks Preservation Coun., 1981-85, Chgo. Acad. Sci., 1988—, Friends of Ceuros de Escazu, Costa Rica, 1992—; mem. aux. bd. Chgo. Architecture Found., 1975-89; chmn. Task Group on Manufactured Housing, AIA Nat. Com. on Design, 1994—. Recipient award Townhouse for Logan Square Competition, AIA and Econ. Redevel. Corp. Logan Square, 1980, Gold medal award Willow St. Houses, Ill. Ind. Masonry Coun., 1981, Silver award for pvt. residence, 1989, Gold medal award for private residence, 1994, Three Record Houses awards Archtl. Record, 1990, 95, award 2d Compact House Design Competition, 1990, award of exellence for pvt. residence AIA/Nat. Concrete Masonry Assn., 1992, award for pvt. residence Am. Wood Coun., 1993, Honorable mention-Best in Am. Living award Profl. Builders Mag., 1995, Builder's Choice award pvt. residence, Builder Mag., 1996, Jury's Choice award for pvt. residence Chgo. Athenaeum, 1996 . Fellow AIA (Disting. Bldg. award for Willow St. Houses, Chgo. chpt. 1982, for Pinewood Farm 1983, for Pvt. Residences 1990, 92); mem. Chgo. Archtl. Club, Racquet Club (bd. govs. 1983-89), Arts Club, Cliff Dwellers Club (bd. govs. 1985-88). Office: Frederick F Phillips & Assocs 53 W Jackson Blvd Ste 1752 Chicago IL 60604-3705

PHILLIPS, GABRIEL, travel marketing executive; b. North Vandergrift, Pa., Aug. 3, 1933; s. Samuel and Margaret (Solomon) P.; m. Margaret Mednis, Sept. 5, 1965 (div. 1970). BS, U. Md., 1956; JD, George Washington U., 1962. Various positions CAB, Washington, 1956-66; dir. internat. programs Air Transport Assn., Washington, 1966-69, exec. sec. fin. and acctg., 1970, v.p. internat. programs, 1970-76, v.p. traffic svcs., 1976-79, sr. v.p. industry svcs., 1979-86, exec. v.p., 1986-91, acting pres., 1988-89, ret., 1991; chmn. Holiday Mktg. Inc., Herndon, Va., 1991—; bd. dirs. Phillips Corp., Columbia, Md. Contbr. articles to profl. jours. Bd. dirs. Nat. Alliance of Sr. Citizens. With U.S. Army, 1956-58. Mem. Travel Industry Assn. Am. (bd. dirs., nat. chmn. 1985-86), Nat. Assn. Arab Ams. (bd. dirs., treas. 1985—, pres. 1990-92). Republican. Roman Catholic.

PHILLIPS, GENEVA FICKER, editor; b. Staunton, Ill., Aug. 1, 1920; d. Arthur Edwin and Lillian Agnes (Woods) Ficker; m. James Emerson Phillips, Jr., June 6, 1955 (dec. 1979). BS in Journalism, U. Ill., 1942; MA in English Lit., UCLA, 1953. Copy desk Chgo. Jour. Commerce, 1942-43; editl. asst. patents Radio Rsch. Lab., Harvard U., Cambridge, Mass., 1943-45; asst. editor adminstrv. publs. U. Ill., Urbana, 1946-47; editorial asst. Quar. of Film, Radio and TV, UCLA, 1952-53; mng. editor The Works of John Dryden, Dept. English, UCLA, 1964—. Bd. dirs. Univ. Religious Conf., L.A., 1979—. UCLA teaching fellow, 1950-53, grad. fellow 1954-55. Mem. Assn. Acad. Women UCLA, Dean's Coun., Coll. Letters and Scis. UCLA, Friends of Huntington Libr., Friends of UCLA Libr., Friends of Ctr. for Medieval and Renaissance Studies, Samuel Johnson Soc. of So. Calif., Assocs. of U. Calif. Press., Conf. Christianity and Lit., Soc. Mayflower Descs. Lutheran. Home: 213 1st Anita Dr Los Angeles CA 90049-3815 Office: UCLA Dept English 2225 Rolfe Hall Los Angeles CA 90024

PHILLIPS, GEORGE LANDON, prosecutor; b. Fulton, Miss., May 24, 1949; s. Gilbert L. and Grace (Staker) P. BS, U. So. Miss., 1971; JD, U. Miss., 1973. Bar: Miss. 1973. Assoc. Johnson, Pittman & Pittman, Hattiesburg, Miss., 1980-94; ptnr. Norris & Phillips, 1975-76; county pros. atty. Forrest County, Miss., 1976-80; U.S. atty. So. Dist. Miss., Jackson, Miss., 1980-94; chmn. investigative agys. subcom. U.S. Atty. Gen.'s Adv. Com., 1983-86, mem. law enforcement coordination subcom. and budget subcom., 1986-88; spl. coun. U.S. Senator T. Cochran, 1995—; chmn. AGAC subcom. law enforcement cooperation and victim/witness assistance, 1989-94; instr. Hattiesburg Police Acad., 1977. Bd. dirs. Forrest County Youth Ct.; pres. South Ctrl. chpt. ARC, 1980-81; bd. dirs. Pine Burr Area coun. Boy Scouts Am.; mem. Atty. Gen.'s Adv. Com., 1981-82, 89-91; bd. dirs. Jackson Zoo, 1989-91. Mem. Miss. Prosecutors Assn. (pres.), Fed. Bar Assn., Miss. Bar Assn. (v.p. southern region), Am. Criminal Justice Assn., Nat. Dist. Attys. Assn., Miss. Trial Lawyers, Miss. Quarter Horse Assn. (pres.), Kiwanis. Baptist. Office: Spl Counsel Office of US Sen T Cochran 188 E Capital Ste 614 Jackson MS 39201-2125

PHILLIPS, GEORGE MICHAEL, food manufacturing company executive; b. New Kensington, Pa., Nov. 6, 1947; s. Samuel and Margaret (Solomon) P.; m. Juliana Marie Orkwis, Nov. 8, 1969; children: Christopher Michael, Kimberly Ann, Jill Michelle. BS in Acctg., U. Md., 1969; MBA, Suffolk U., 1973. Cert. investment adviser. Cost analyst Polaroid Corp., Cambridge, Mass., 1969-73; mgr. fin. analysis Clorox Co., Oakland, Calif., 1973-75; pres., chief operating officer, dir. Acton (Mass.) Corp., 1975-85; chmn., chief exec. officer W.P. Ihrie and Sons, Inc., 1983-92, Chimill Corp., 1983—, Condor Corp., 1985—, Vesper Corp., 1988—. Bd. vis. U. Md. Served with U.S. Army, 1969-70. Republican. Roman Catholic. Club: Pres.'s U. Md.

PHILLIPS, GERALD BAER, internal medicine educator, scientist; b. Bethlehem, Pa., Mar. 20, 1925; s. Abel H. and Cecilia (Blum) P.; m. Maria Bonzi Lewis, July 15, 1970; children: Abigail, Elizabeth. AB, Princeton U., 1948; MD, Harvard U., 1948. Diplomate Am. Bd. Internal Medicine. Intern Presbyn. Hosp., N.Y.C., 1948-50; rsch. fellow Thorndike Meml. Lab., Med. Sch. Harvard U., Boston, 1950-53; vis. fellow biochemistry Columbia U. Coll. Physicians and Surgeons, N.Y.C., 1954-56, from assoc. in medicine to assoc. prof., 1956-73, prof., 1973—; sr. attending physician Roosevelt Hosp.; attending physician Presbyn. Hosp. Sr. asst. surgeon USPHS, 1952-54. Mem. Am. Fedn. for Clin. Rsch., Am. Soc. for Clin. Investigation, Am. Soc. for Biochemistry and Molecular Biology, Alpha Omega Alpha. Home: 196 E 75th St New York NY 10021-3257 Office: 1000 10th Ave New York NY 10019-1147 *I attribute any success I may have had to heredity and luck.*

PHILLIPS, GLYNDA ANN, editor; b. Riverside, Calif.; d. Henry Grady and Patricia (Loflin) P. BA in English, Millsaps Coll., 1977; MS in Comms., Miss. Coll., 1996. News editor The Magee (Miss.) Courier, 1981-84; editor Miss. Farm Bur. Country and Miss. Farm Bur. Producer, Jackson, 1984—. Contbr. articles to profl. jours. Recipient first place personal column Nat. Fedn. Press Women, 1984, first place personal column Miss. Press Women's Assn., 1984, first place feature articles Miss. Press Women's Assn., 1984, Best Media Campaign award AFBF Info. Contest, 1996. Mem. Soc. Profl. Journalists. Avocation: church organist.

PHILLIPS, GRETCHEN, clinical social worker; b. Erie, Pa., July 14, 1941; life ptnr. Beverly Campbell, June 10, 1989. BA, Mercyhurst Coll., 1966; MSW, Yeshiva U., 1972; postgrad., Advanced Ctr. Psychotherapy, 1972-73, Washington Sq. Inst., 1973-77. Bd. cert. diplomate clin. social work; cert. social worker, N.Y. Psychiat. social worker, forensic social worker Creedmoor Psychiat. Ctr., Queens Village, N.Y., 1972-80; Med. social worker Bellevue Hosp. Ctr., N.Y.C., 1980-83; intake probation officer N.Y.C. Probation, Family Court, Bklyn., 1983—. Mem. NASW, Am. Group Psychotherapy Assn., Internat. Soc. for Traumatic Stress Studies (N.Y. chpt.). Home: 125 Radford St # 3C Yonkers NY 10705-3049 Office: Probation Intake Kings Family Ct 283 Adams St Brooklyn NY 11201-2804

PHILLIPS, HARVEY, musician, soloist, music educator, arts consultant; b. Aurora, Mo., Dec. 2, 1929; s. Jesse E. and Lottie A. (Chapman) P.; m. Carol A. Dorvel, Feb. 22, 1954; children: Jesse E., Harvey G., Thomas A. Student, U. Mo., 1947-48, Juilliard Sch. Music, 1950-54, Manhattan Sch. Music, 1956-58; Mus.D. (hon.), New Eng. Conservatory of Music, 1971; HHD (hon.), U. Mo., Columbia, 1987. Founder, v.p. Mentor Music, Inc., N.Y.C., 1958-79; v.p. Wilder Music, Inc., N.Y.C., 1964-77, Magellan Music, Inc., N.Y.C., 1971—, Peaslee Music Inc., 1971—; mem. faculty Aspen Sch. Music, summer 1962, U. Wis., summer 1963, Hartt Sch. Music, Hartford, Conn., 1962-64, Mannes Sch. Music, N.Y.C., 1964-65; exec. v.p. Orchestra USA, N.Y.C., 1962-65; exec. v.p., personnel mgr., tubist Symphony of the Air N.Y.C., 1957-66; v.p. Brass Artists, Inc., N.Y.C., 1964—; adminstrv. asst. to Julius Bloom, Rutgers U., New Brunswick, N.J., 1966-67; v.p. fin. affairs New Eng. Conservatory of Music, Boston, 1967-71; mem. faculty Sch. Music, Ind. U., Bloomington, 1971-94; disting. prof. music, trustee, 1979; disting. prof. emeritus Ind. U., Bloomington, 1994; adv. bd. Am. Brass Chamber Music, Inc., 1971—; chmn. bd. Summit Brass/Keystone Brass Inst., 1986-92, Rafael Mendez Brass Inst., 1993—; cons. Margun Music, Inc., 1977—. Brass coach Festival at Sandpoint, Idaho, 1986-94; mem. faculty Joven Orch., Spain, 1987-94, Festival Casal Orch., San Juan, P.R., 1964-76; dir. 1st Internat. Tuba Symposium Workshop, 1973, Brass-Wind Music Studios, Carnegie Hall, N.Y.C., 1961-67; tubist, King Bros. Circus Band, 1947, Ringling Bros. & Barnum & Bailey Circus Band, 1948-50, N.Y.C. Ballet Orch., 1951-71, N.Y.C. Opera Orch., 1951-62, Voice of Firestone Orch., 1951-53, Sauter-Finegan Orch., 1952-53, Band of Am., 1952-54, NBC Opera Orch., 1956-65, Bell Tel. Hour Orch., 1956-66, Goldman Band, 1957-62; founding mem., tubist N.Y. Brass Quintet, 1954-67; condr., co-prodr. Burke-Phillips All Star Concert Band, 1960-62; co-founder, tubist Matteson-Phillips Tubajazz Consort, 1976—; founding mem. TubaShop Quartet, 1996—; rec. artist Crest Records, 1958-78—; originator Octubafest, TubaChristmas, Tubasantas, Tuba Jazz,Tubaeaster; exec. editor Instrumentalist mag., 1986-96, bd. advisors, 1996—. Founder, pres. Harvey Phillips Found., Inc., N.Y.C., 1977—; bd. dirs. Mid-Am. Festival of the Arts, 1982-90, Bloomington Area Arts Coun., 1983-90; judge 1st Internt. tuba competition of CIEM Internat. Competition for Musical Performers, Geneva, 1991. Served with U.S. Army Field Band, 1955-56. Recipient Disting. Svc. to Music award Kappa Kappa Psi, 1978, Cmty. Svc. award City of Bloomington, 1978, Nat. Assn. Jazz Educators award, 1977, 78, Nat. Music Conf. award, 1977, T.U.B.A. award, 1978, MI Hummel The Tuba Player award, 1990, Disting. Achievement award Ednl. Press Assn. Am., 1991, Mentor Ideal award Assn. Concert Bands, 1994, Lifetime Achievement award United Music Instruments, 1995, Sudler award medal of the Order of Merit Sousa Found., 1995, Summit Brass Outstanding Svc. and Support Internat. Brassfest, 1995, Orpheus award Phi Mu Alpha Sinfonia, 1997; elected to Acad. Wind and Percussion Arts Nat. Band Assn., 1995, Edwin Franko Goldman citation Am. Bandmasters Assn., 1996: Harvey Phillips Day proclaimed New Eng. Conservatory Music, 1971, Harvey Phillips Day proclaimed Marionville, Mo. Bicentennial, 1976, Harvey Phillips Weekend Gov. of Mo., 1982; named hon. mem. U.S. Army Band, 1984. Mem. Am. Fedn. Musicians, Tubists Universal Brotherhood Assn. (bd. advs. 1973—, pres. 1984-87, hon.), Hoagy Carmichael Jazz Soc. (founder, acting pres. 1983—), Tau Beta Sigma, Phi Mu Alpha Sinfonia (Orpheus award 1997), Kappa Gamma Psi. Home and Office: Tubaranch 4769 S Harrell Rd Bloomington IN 47401-9028 Office: Sch of Music Ind U Bloomington IN 47405 *The role of a performer and teacher is to give, to share skills and knowledge. My primary goal in life is to create new opportunities in the music profession, to develop, expand, and preserve the music arts.*

PHILLIPS, HOWARD WILLIAM, investment banker; b. N.Y.C., May 16, 1930; s. Louis and Helen (Klein) P.; children: Jan Davis, Richard Louis; m. Carol Napack, June 9, 1985. B.A., Dartmouth Coll., 1951, M.B.A., 1952; J.D., Harvard U., 1957. Bar: N.Y. 1957. Asso. Cahill, Gordon, Reindel & Ohl, N.Y.C., 1957-64; v.p., gen. counsel McCall Corp., N.Y.C., 1964-68; sr. v.p. McCall Corp., 1968-69; partner Oppenheimer & Co., N.Y.C., 1969-81; chmn. Holmes, Phillips & Co., N.Y.C., 1981-83; dir. corp. fin. D.H. Blair & Co., Inc., 1983—; bd. dirs. Food Ct. Entertainment Network, Inc., N.Y.C., Pioneer Health Care, Boston. Served to lt. (j.g.) USNR, 1952-54. Mem. Easthampton (N.Y.) Tennis Club, Longboat Key Club (Sarasota, Fla.). Home: 885 Park Ave New York NY 10021-0325 Office: 435 L'Ambiance Dr Longboat Key FL 34228

PHILLIPS, JAMES CHARLES, physicist, educator; b. New Orleans, Mar. 9, 1933; s. William D. and Juanita (Hahn) P.; m. Joanna Vandenberg, July 4, 1993. B.A., U. Chgo., 1952, B.S., 1953, M.S., 1955, Ph.D., 1956. Mem. tech. staff Bell Labs., 1956-58; NSF fellow U. Calif. at Berkeley, 1958-59, Cambridge (Eng.) U., 1959-60; faculty U. Chgo., 1960-68, prof. physics, 1965-68; mem. tech. staff Bell Labs., 1968—. Sloan fellow, 1962-66; Guggenheim fellow, 1967. Fellow Am. Phys. Soc. (Buckley prize 1972), Minerals, Metals and Materials Soc. (William Hume-Rothery award 1992); mem. NAS. Home: 204 Springfield Ave Summit NJ 07901-3909

PHILLIPS, JAMES D., retired diplomat; b. Peoria, Ill., Feb. 23, 1933; s. James D. and Ehila (Hardy) P.; m. Rosemary Leeds, Mar. 30, 1957 (div. Dec. 1981); children: Michael, Madolyn, Catherine; m. Lucie Gallistel, Jan. 7, 1984; stepchildren: Charles, David. B.A., Wichita State U., 1956, M.A., 1957; cert., U. Vienna, Austria, 1956; postgrad., Cornell U., 1958-61. Joined fgn. svc. Dept. State, 1961; served at Am. embassy Paris, before 1975; Am. Consulate Zaire, before 1975; Dept. State Washington, before 1975; dep. chief of mission Am. Embassy, Luxembourg, 1975-78; charge d'affaires Am. Embassy, Banjul, The Gambia, 1978-80; student Nat. War Coll., Washington, 1980-81; office dir. Dept. State, Washington, 1981-84; consul gen. Am. Consulate, Casablanca, Morocco, 1984-86; U.S. amb. to Burundi, 1986-90; U.S. amb. Republic of the Congo, 1990-93; diplomat in residence The Carter Ctr., Atlanta, 1993-94; ret., 1994; pres. Dan Phillips & Assocs., Arlington, Va., 1994—; bd. dirs. Gulf Resources, H.M. Salaam Found.; pres. Ctrl. Africa Found. Contbr. articles to Fgn. Svc. Jour. Bd. dirs. Jane Goodall Inst., 1994—. Avocations: golf; tennis; skiing. Home: 3607 Military Rd Arlington VA 22207-4829 Office: 1101 30th St NW Ste 200 Washington DC 20007-3769

PHILLIPS, JAMES DICKSON, JR., federal judge; b. Scotland County, N.C., Sept. 23, 1922; s. James Dickson and Helen (Shepherd) P.; m. Jean Duff Nunalee, July 16, 1960; children: Evelyn, James Dickson, III, Elizabeth Duff, Ida Wills. BS cum laude, Davidson Coll., 1943; JD, U. N.C., 1948. Bar: N.C. 1948. Asst. dir. Inst. Govt., Chapel Hill, N.C., 1948-49; ptnr. firm Phillips & McCoy, Laurinburg, N.C., 1949-55, Sanford, Phillips, McCoy & Weaver, Fayetteville, N.C., 1955-60; from asst. prof. to prof. law U. N.C., 1960-78, dean Sch. Law, 1964-74; circuit judge U.S. Ct. Appeals (4th cir.), 1978—; Mem. N.C. Wildlife Resources Commn., 1961-63; mem. N.C. Cts. Commn., 1963-75; also vice chmn.; chmn. N.C. Bd. Ethics, 1977-78. Served with parachute inf. U.S. Army, 1943-46. Decorated Bronze Arrowhead, Bronze Star, Purple Heart; recipient John J. Parker Meml. award, Thomas Jefferson award, Disting. Alumnus award U. N.C., 1993. Mem. Am. Law Inst. Democrat. Presbyterian.

PHILLIPS, JAMES EDGAR, lawyer; b. N.Y.C., Aug. 30, 1947; s. Jack Louis Phillips and Jacqueline (Kasper) Ehrman; children: Zachary J., Mark H. BA, Boston U., 1971; JD, Case Western Reserve U., 1975. Bar: Ohio 1975, U.S. Supreme Ct. 1977, U.S. Dist. Ct. (so. dist.) 1978, U.S. Ct. Appeals (6th cir.) 1981, U.S. Dist. Ct. (no. dist.) 1982. Asst. prosecutor Franklin County Prosecutor Office, Columbus, Ohio, 1975-77; sr. asst. prosecutor Franklin County Prosecutor Office, Columbus, 1977-79; assoc. Vorys, Sater, Seymour & Pease, Columbus, 1979-84, ptnr., 1984—; spl. prosecutor State of Ohio, 1993—; gen. counsel Nat. Fraternal Order of Police, Washington, 1987—, Conrail Police #1, U.S. Postal Police #2; mem. Bd. Profl. Law Enforcement Certification; pres. Ohio Ctr. for Law-Related Edn., 1985-95. Author: Civil Recovery in Ohio, 1986, Collective Bargaining in the Pub. Sector, 1988; editor Bar Briefs; contbr. articles Jours., 1987-89. Fellow Ohio Bar Found., Columbus Bar Found., Ohio Bar Assn. (chmn. com. law-related edn. 1982-86), Columbus Bar Assn., Am. Judicature Soc., Sixth Cir. Jud. Conf. (life). Office: Vorys Sater Seymour & Pease PO Box 1008 52 E Gay St Columbus OH 43215-3161

PHILLIPS, JAMES MACILDUFF, material handling company executive, engineering and manufacturing executive; b. Carrick, Pa., June 13, 1916; s. John MacFarlane and Harriet (Duff) P.; m., Majorie Watson, June 1940 (div. 1964); children: James M. Jr., William W.; m. Regina Leininger, Apr. 1964 (dec.); children: Jeffrey M., Molly M., Becky J., Thomas S. BSME, Carnegie Inst. of Tech., 1938; grad., Pitts. Inst. Aeronautics, 1939; ME refresher, Pa. State U. State Coll., 1960; grad., Internat. Correspondence Sch., Scranton, Pa., 1988. Profl. engr. Pa. Draftsmen, engr. Phillips Mine & Mill Supply Co., Pitts., 1933-40, v.p., 1941-77; v.p. engring. Salem Brosius, Inc., Carnegie, Pa., 1956-64; pres. Phillips Corp., Bridgeville, Pa., 1977-83, Phillips Jet Flight, Bridgeville, Pa., 1977-83, Phillips Mine & Mill Inc., Pitts., 1964—; also chmn. bd. Phillips Mine & Mill Inc. Inventor in field; contbr. articles to profl. mags. Bd. dirs. Brashear Assn., Pitts. Mem. Air Force Assn., Aero Club of Pitts., Pa. Pilots Coun. (pres.), Quiet Birdmen (pres.), Early Bird Pilots (bd. dirs.), Exptl. Aircraft Assn. Aircraft Owners and Pilots Assn. (founding), OX-5 Pioneer Airmen (pres. 1987, nat. bd. dirs. 1995), St. Clair County Club; Early Birds of Aviation, Inc. Methodist. Avocations: airline transport pilot, flight instructor, golf, tennis. Office: Phillips Mine & Mill Inc 1738 N Highland Rd Pittsburgh PA 15241-1200

PHILLIPS, JAMES OSCAR, minister; b. Greenville, S.C., Sept. 9, 1920; s. James Henry and Ida Louise (Fortner) P.; m. Marie Burns, Jan. 31, 1943; children: Martha Phillips Henderson, Gwendolyn Phillips Mullinax, Linda Phillips Richey. Grad. bible langs., Missionary Bapt. Sem., 1948, M in bible langs., 1949, D in bible langs., 1961; DDiv (hon.), Carolina Missionary Bapt. Theol. Sem., 1959. Pastor Vilonia (Ark.) Bapt. Ch., 1946-48, Harmony Missionary Bapt. Ch., Stephens, Ark., 1948-50, Corinth Missionary Bapt.

Ch., Stephens, Ark., 1948-50, East Union Missionary Bapt. Ch., Hensley, Ark., 1950-52, Glendale Bapt. Ch., Mauldin, S.C., 1952—; pres. Landmark Missionary Inst., Mauldin, 1954—. Sgt. USMC, 1942-45. Mem. Am. Bapt. Assn. (pres. 1992-94, v.p. 1990-91, mem. Bapt. Suncay Sch. com. 1955—). Office: Glendale Bapt Ch 212 E Butler Ave Mauldin SC 29662-2129*

PHILLIPS, JANET COLLEEN, educational association executive, editor; b. Pittsfield, Ill., Apr. 29, 1933; d. Roy Lynn and Catherine Amelia (Wills) Barker; m. David Lee Phillips, Feb 7, 1954; children—Clay Cullen, Sean Vincent. B.S., U. Ill, 1954. Reporter Quincy (Ill.) Herald Whig, 1951, 52, soc. editor, 1953; editorial asst. Pub. Info. Office U. Ill.-Urbana, 1953-54, asst. editor libr., 1954-61; asst. editor Assn. for Libr. and Info. Sci. Edn., State College, Pa., 1960-61, mng. editor, 1961-89, exec. sec., 1970-89; adminstrv. dir. Interlibr. Delivery Svc. of Pa., 1990—. Mem. AAUW, Assn. for Libr. and Info. Sci. Edn., Embroiderer's Guild Am., Pa. State Blue Course Club, Pa. State U. Women's Club, Theta Sigma Phi, Delta Zeta. Presbyterian. Avocations: travel; golf; sewing; needlecraft. Address: 471 Park Ln State College PA 16803-3208

PHILLIPS, JERRY JUAN, law educator; b. Charlotte, N.C., June 16, 1935; s. Vergil Ernest and Mary Blanche (Wade) P.; m. Anne Butler Colville, June 6, 1959; children: Sherman Wade, Dorothy Colville. B.A., Yale U., 1956, J.D., 1961; B.A., Cambridge (Eng.) U., 1958, M.A. (hon.), 1964. Bar: Tenn. bar 1961. Assoc. firm Miller, Martin, Hitching, Tipton & Lenihan, Chattanooga, 1961-67; asst. prof. law U. Tenn., 1967-72, assoc. prof., 1972-73, prof., 1973—, W.P. Toms prof., 1980—; advisor Tenn. Law Revision Commn., 1968-70; mem. Tenn. Jud. Council, 1970-74; adv. Fed. Interagy. Task Force on Products Liability, 1976-77; lectr. in field. Author: Products Liability in a Nutshell, 4th edit., 1993, Products Liability Cases and Materials on Torts and Related Law, 1980, Products Liability Treatise, 3 vols., 1986, Cases and Materials on Tort Law, 1992, Products Liability-Cases, Materials, Problems, 1994; advisor Tenn. U. Law Rev., 1977—. U. Tenn. grantee, 1978. Mem. ABA, Am. Law Inst., Knoxville Bar Assn., Am. Assn. Law Schs., Order of Coif, Phi Beta Kappa. Democrat. Episcopalian. Club: Knoxville Racquet. Office: 1505 Cumberland Ave Knoxville TN 37916-3199

PHILLIPS, JILL META, novelist, critic, astrologer; b. Detroit, Oct. 22, 1952; d. Leyson Kirk and Leona Anna (Rasmussen) P. Student pub. schs., Calif. Lit. counselor Book Builders, Charter Oak, Calif., 1966-77; pres. Moon Dance Astro Graphics, Covina, Calif., 1994—. Author: (with Leona Phillips) A Directory of American Film Scholars, 1975, The Good Morning Cookbook, 1976, G.B. Shaw: A Review of the Literature, 1976, T.E. Lawrence: Portrait of the Artist as Hero, 1977, The Archaeology of the Collective East, 1977, The Occult, 1977, D.H. Lawrence: A Review of the Literature and Biographies, 1978, Film Appreciation: A College Guide Book, 1979, Annus Mirabilis: Europe in the Dark and Middle Centuries, 1979, (with Leona Rasmussen Phillips) The Dark Frame: Occult Cinema, 1979, Misfit: The Films of Montgomery Clift, 1979, Butterflies in the Mind: A Précis of Dreams and Dreamers, 1980; The Rain Maiden: A Novel of History, 1987, Walford's Oak: A Novel, 1990, The Fate Weaver: A Novel in Two Centuries, 1991, Saturn Falls: A Novel of the Apocalypse, 1993; columnist Horoscope Guide Monthly; contbr. book revs. to New Guard mag., 1974-76; contbr. numerous articles to profl. jours. including Dell Horoscope, Midnight Horoscope, Astrology-Your Daily Horoscope, Am. Astrology. Mem. Young Ams. for Freedom, Am. Conservative Union, Elmer Bernstein's Film Music Collection, Ghost Club London, Count Dracula Soc., Dracula Soc. London, Richard III Soc. Republican. Home: 515 E Claraday St Apt 8 Glendora CA 91740 Office: Moon Dancer Astro Graphics 1037 N Grand Ave Ste 202 Covina CA 91724-2048

PHILLIPS, JOHN A(TLAS), III, geneticist, educator; b. Sanford, N.C., Jan. 24, 1944; s. John A. and Rachael (Sloan) P.; m. Gretchen Lynch, Aug. 1, 1965; children: Jennifer Allene, John Atlas IV, Charles Andrew, James William. Student, U. N.C., 1962-65; MD, Wake Forest U., 1969. Diplomate Am. Bd. Pediatrics, Am. Bd. Med. Genetics. Intern Children's Hosp. Med. Ctr., Boston, 1969-70, jr. resident, 1970-71, sr. resident, 1973-74, chief resident, 1974-75; asst. prof. Johns Hopkins U., Balt., 1978-82, assoc. prof., 1982-84; prof. pediatrics Vanderbilt U., Nashville, 1984—, prof. biochemistry, 1986—, David T. Karzon chair genetics, 1992—; bd. sci. counselors Nat. Inst. Child Health, Washington, 1984-88; counsilor Ctr. Study Polymorphisme Humain, Paris, 1988—; mem. adv. com. Ctr. Reproductive Biology, Nashville, 1990-94; bd. dirs. March of Dimes Birth Defects Found., Nashville, 1986—; mem. adv. bd. Nat. Neurofibromatosis Found., Tenn., 1990—; mem. Tenn. Genetics Adv. Com., Nashville, 1984—. Contbr. to profl. publs. Lt. comdr. USNR, 1971-73. Recipient Sidney Farber award Children's Hosp., Boston, 1975, E Mead Johnson award Mead Johnson Co., 1984; Pediatric Postdoctoral fellow Johns Hopkins U. Sch. Medicine, 1975-77. Mem. Am. Soc. Clin. Investigation, Soc. Pediatric Rsch., Am. Coll. Med. Genetics (founding, bd. dirs. 1995—), Phi Beta Kappa, Alpha Omega Alpha. Achievements include discovery of cause of hemoglobin H disease in Black Americans, chromosomal location of multiple genes in humans, improved diagnoses of cystic fibrosis, hemophilia, inborn metabolic errors, familial neurodegenerative diseases. Office: Vanderbilt U Dept Genetics DD 2205 Med Ctr N Nashville TN 37232

PHILLIPS, JOHN D., media company executive. CEO Metromedia Internat. Group Inc., Atlanta. Office: Metromedia Internat Group Inc 945 E Paces Ferry Rd NE Atlanta GA 30326-1125

PHILLIPS, JOHN DAVID, management consultant; b. Exeland, Wis., June 29, 1920; s. Mathew Frank and Iva (Bryant) P.; m. Estelle Margaret Pautsch, July 19, 1941; 1 son, John David. B.S., U. Wis., 1937. Partner Miss Wis. Cheese, 1946-56; dir. marketing Armour & Co., 1956-60; v.p. Am. Home Corp., 1960-66; founder, pres. R.J. Reynolds Foods, Inc., 1966-72; pres., dir. CBS/Columbia Group, N.Y.C., 1973-81; vice chmn. Nat. Exec. Service Corp., N.Y.C., 1981-94, dir., 1981—; ptnr. Edjon Ltd., Ft. Washington, Pa., 1990—; pres. Intercity Oil & Gas Corp., 1980—; bd. dirs. Glenmore Distillers Co., Airwick Industries, Inc., subs. of Ciba-Geigy Corp., Tex. Internat. Co.; founder, chmn. Sr. Careers Planning and Placement Svc., 1987-94. Past trustee N.Y.C. Pub. Libr., Juniata Coll., Mt. Senario Coll., Greenwich Coun. Boy Scouts Am.; adv. bd. Howard U.; trustee Safe Streets, Washington, 1992—. With USAAF, 1944-46; adminstr. Am. Armenian Diocese, 1994—. Mem. Assn. Corp. Growth (past pres. N.Y.C.), Hamilton Coll. Parents Assn. Conglist. (past pres., trustee). Clubs: Greenwich Country, Riverside Yacht, N.Y. Yacht; Links (N.Y.C.); Petroleum (Corpus Christi, Tex.). Home: Pilot Rock Riverside CT 06878 Office: 630 2nd Ave New York NY 10016-4806

PHILLIPS, JOHN DAVID, communications executive; b. Charlotte, N.C., Nov. 27, 1942; s. Louis and A. Viola (Pack) P.; m. Cheryl Helen Rudd; children: Hunter, Scott, Andrew, Lauren. Student, U. Va., 1962-63. Pres. RMS Distbg., Frankfurt, West Germany, 1965-66, NGK Spark Plugs, Atlanta, 1967-82; pres., chief exec. officer Advanced Telecommunication, Atlanta, 1982-88, also bd. dirs., 1982-88; owner Specialized Hauling Trucking Co., 1987-89; pres., CEO Resurgens Comm. Group, Inc., Atlanta, 1989-93; pres., CEO, bd. dirs. Actava Group, Inc., Atlanta, 1994-95; pres., CEO Metromedia Group Internat. Inc., 1995—, also bd. dirs. Served to capt. USMC, 1963-64. Republican. Methodist. Avocations: fishing, automobiles, flying, boating.

PHILLIPS, JOHN DAVISSON, retired lawyer; b. Clarksburg, W.Va., Aug. 21, 1906; s. Robert Bruce and Lela (Davisson) P.; m. Virginia Maxwell, Nov. 12, 1932; children: John Davisson, Julia Anne. Student, Washington and Lee U., 1924-25; A.B., W.Va. U., 1928, LL.B., 1930; postgrad., Oxford U., 1930-32. Bar: W.Va. 1932. Gen. practice law Wheeling, W.Va., 1932-91; of counsel Phillips, Gardill, Kaiser & Altmeyer; ret., 1991; asst. pros. atty. Ohio County, 1937-40; city solicitor City of Wheeling, 1942-47. Past mem. W.Va. State Bd. Law Examiners. Served as capt. USMCR, World War II. Fellow Am. Bar Founds.; mem. ABA, W.Va. Bar Assn. (pres. 1955-56), Am. Judicature Soc., Phi Kappa Psi, Phi Delta Phi, Fort Henry Club. Episcopalian. Home: 4 Arlington Dr Howard Pl Wheeling WV 26003 Office: 61 14th St Wheeling WV 26003-3426

PHILLIPS, JOHN EDWARD, zoologist, educator; b. Montréal, Que., Can., Dec. 20, 1934; s. William Charles and Violet Mildred (Lewis) P.; m. Eleanor Mae Richardson, Sept. 8, 1956; children: Heather Anne, Jayne Elizabeth, Jonathan David, Catherine Melinda, Wendy Susannah. BSc with honors, Dalhousie U., Halifax, N.S., 1956, MSc, 1957; PhD, Cambridge U., Eng., 1961. Asst. prof. Dalhousie U., Halifax, N.S., 1960-64; assoc. prof. U. B.C., Vancouver, Can., 1964-71, prof., 1971—, head dept. zoology, 1991-96; vis. rschr. Cambridge (Eng.) U., 1972, 76, 81; chair grant selection com. Nat. Rsch. Coun. Can., Ottawa, Ont., 1969-71; mem. coun. Nat. Sci. and Engring. Rsch. Coun., Ottawa, 1983-87. Mem. editorial bd.: Can. Jour. Zoology, 1971-75, Am. Jour. Physiology, 1978-93, Jour. Experimental Biology, 1981-85, Am. Zool., 1996—; contbr. articles to profl. jours. Mem. grant selection com. Can. Cystic Fibrosis Found., Toronto, 1989-91; active Vancouver Bach Choir. Named to James chair St. Francis Xavier U., Antigonish, N.S., 1993. Fellow Royal Soc. Can.; mem. Can. Soc. Zoologists (sec. 1972-76, v.p. 1976-78, pres. 1979), Am. Soc. Zoologists (exec. 1983-85, chair divsn. comp. physiol. biochemistry 1983-85). Avocations: music, choir. Home: 12908-22 B Ave, White Rock, BC Canada V4A 6Z3 Office: U BC, Dept Zoology, Vancouver, BC Canada V6T 1Z4

PHILLIPS, JOHN P(AUL), retired neurosurgeon; b. Danville, Ark., Oct. 14, 1932; s. Brewer William Ashley and Wave Audrey (Page) P.; AB cum laude, Hendrix Coll., 1953; MD, U. Tenn., 1956; m. June Helen Dunbar, Dec. 14, 1963; children: Todd Eustace, Timothy John Colin, Tyler William Ashley. Intern, Charity Hosp. La., New Orleans, 1957; resident in surgery U. Tenn. Hosps., 1958; resident in neurol. surgery U. Tenn. Med. Units, 1958-62; practice medicine, specializing in neurol. surgery, Salinas, Calif., 1962-93; retired 1993; chief of staff, chief of surgery Salinas Valley Meml. Hosp.; mem. staffs Community Hosp. Monterey Peninsula, U. Calif. Hosp., San Francisco; asst. clin. prof. U. Calif., 1962—. Commd. Ky. col. Diplomate Am. Bd. Neurol. Surgeons. Mem. ACS, Internat. Coll. Surgery, Harvey Cushing Soc., Congress Neurol. Surgery, Western Neurosurg. Assn., AMA, San Francisco Neurol. Soc., Pan Pacific Surg. Assn., Alpha Omega Alpha, Phi Chi, Alpha Chi. Home: 6 Mesa Del Sol Salinas CA 93908-9324

PHILLIPS, JOHN RICHARD, engineering educator; b. Albany, Calif., Jan. 30, 1934; s. Eric Lester and Adele Catherine (Rengel) P.; m. Joan Elizabeth Soyster, Mar. 23, 1957; children: Elizabeth Huntley, Sarah Rengel, Catherine Hale. BS, U. Calif., Berkeley, 1956; M in Engring., Yale U., 1958, PhD in Engring., 1960. Registered profl. engr., Calif. Chem. engr. Stanford Rsch. Inst., Menlo Park, Calif., 1960; rsch. engr. Chevron Rsch. Co., Richmond, Calif., 1962-66; mem. faculty Harvey Mudd Coll., Claremont, Calif., 1966—, prof. engring., 1974—, James Howard Kindleberger prof. engring., 1991—, dir. engring. clinic, 1977-93, chmn. engring. dept., 1993—; vis. prof. U. Edinburgh, Scotland, 1975, Cambridge (Eng.) U., 1981, ESIEE, France, 1981, Naval Postgrad. Sch., 1984-85, Calif. Poly. U., San Luis Obispo, 1992; vis. scientist So. Calif. Edison Co., 1980; founder Claremont Engring., 1973; cons. in field. Contbr. articles to profl. jours. 1st lt. AUS, 1960-62. Mem. Am. Inst. Chem. Engrs., Sigma Xi, Alpha Delta Phi, Tau Beta Pi. Home: 911 W Maryhurst Dr Claremont CA 91711-3320

PHILLIPS, JOHN ROBERT, college administrator, political scientist; b. Henderson, Ky., Dec. 16, 1942; s. Leander Armstead and Ann Reid (Brown) P. Diploma, Lang. Inst., Chateauroux, France, 1966; BA, Centre Coll., Danville, Ky., 1969; MA, Western Ky. U., Bowling Green, 1973. Instr. Drury Coll., Springfield, Mo., 1971-73, Western Ky. U., Bowling Green, 1975-79; asst. prof. Thiel Coll., Greenville, Pa., 1979-83, scholar-in-residence, 1983-85; pvt. cons. Henderson, Ky., 1985-87; adj. prof. Lockyear Coll., Evansville, Ind., 1987-88, acad. dean, 1988-90, v.p. acad. affairs, dean coll., 1990-91; exec. dir. human rels. commn. Henderson (Ky.) Mcpl. Ctr., 1991-93; dean acad. affairs, prof. political studies/govt. Springfield (Ill.) Coll., 1993—, acting pres., 1996-97; adj. prof. pub. adminstrn. Ind. State U., Terre Haute, 1991-92; field investigator on religion and culture in ancient city of Taxila, 1968, on indsl. pollution of hist. bldgs. and monuments, France, Italy, Austria, 1969; rschr. on nationalism, Scotland, 1972, on local govt. and urban deves., 1993; participant in internat. confs. on The Future of a United Germany, 1991; mem. adv. coun. St. John's Hosp. Sch. respiratory Therapy, 1993, Ursuline Acad Sch. Bd., v.p., 1995-97, fin. com., 1993-97, Cen. Ill. Fgn. Lang. and Internat. Studies Consortium, 1993—, chmn., 1994-96. Mem. editorial bd. Jour. Urban Affairs, 1985-89; manuscript referee Pub. Adminstrn. Rev., 1985-87; contbr. chpts. to multi-vol. reference series The Small City and Regional Cmty. 1981, 85, 87, 95; contbr. articles on urban affairs, policy planning, and federalism/intergovtl. rels. to profl. jours. Policy advisor Lt. Gov.'s Office, Frankfort, Ky., 1985-86; cons. Commn. on Ky.'s Future, Frankfort, 1985-87; mem. Bd. Cath. Edn., Diocese of Springfield, 1994—. With USAF, 1963-68. Mem. Am. Polit. Sci. Assn. (Leon Weaver Disting. Rsch. Award com. 1990-93), Am. Soc. Pub. Adminstrn. (publs. com. 1984-88, 92-95), Urban Affairs Assn. (publs. com. 1985-89, nominating com. 1984-85, 88-89), Am. Philatelic Soc., Am. Guild Organists, Pi Sigma Alpha, Alpha Sigma Lambda. Democrat. Episcopalian. Avocations: reading, classical music, philately. Home: 2605 Delaware Dr Springfield IL 62702-1213

PHILLIPS, J(OHN) TAYLOR, judge; b. Greenville, S.C., Aug. 20, 1923; s. Walter Dixon and Mattie Sue (Taylor) P.; m. Mary Elizabeth Parrish, Dec. 18, 1954; children: John Allen, Susan, Linda-Lea, Julia. AA, Glenville State Coll., 1952; JD, Mercer U., 1955; LLD, Asbury Coll., 1992. Bar: Ga. 1954, U.S. Supreme Ct. 1969. Mem. Ho. of Reps. State of Ga., Atlanta, 1959-62, Senate, 1962-64. With USMC, 1942-51. Methodist. Home: 1735 Winston Dr Macon GA 31206 Office: State Ct Bibb County PO Box 5086 Macon GA 31213

PHILLIPS, JOSEF CLAYTON, insurance and investment company executive; b. Seattle, June 27, 1908; s. Joseph Clinton and Margaret Janet (Branlund) P.; m. Ada May Gummer, Sept. 24, 1931; 1 dau., Barbara Lee (Mrs. Richard Angus). Student, U. Wash., 1925-28, U. Paris, France, 1928-29. With Merrill, Lynch, Pierce, Fenner & Bean, Seattle, 1930-35; with United Pacific Corp., 1936—, pres., 1960-63, chmn. bd., 1963-67; dir., chmn. exec. com. United Pacific Ins. Co., 1957-72, N.W. Bldg. Co., M.G. Norton Corp., Pelican Seafoods. Clubs: Seattle Golf (Seattle); Wailea Golf (Maui, Hawaii). Home: Apt 209 12503 Greenwood Ave N Seattle WA 98133

PHILLIPS, JOSEPH ROBERT, museum director; b. Utica, N.Y., Mar. 14, 1950; m. Dixie Anne Stedman, 1988. BS in Marine Transp., SUNY, 1972; MA in History Mus. Studies, SUNY, Cooperstown, 1981; MBA, New Hampshire Coll., 1990. Capt., exec. dir. Hudson River Sloop Clearwater, Poughkeepsie, N.Y., 1972-75; capt., assoc. project dir. N.Y. Bicentennial Barge, Albany, 1975-76; mgr. hist. shipyard Maine Maritime Mus., Bath, 1978-81; various program mgmt. and mktg. positions Bath Iron Works Corp., Shipbuilders, 1982-92; mus. dir. Maine State Mus., Augusta, 1992—. Bd. dirs. Maine Cmty. Cultural Alliance, Friends of Maine State Mus.; mem. Maine Cultural Affairs Coun., 1992—, State House and Capital Park Commn., 1992—, Blaine House Commn., 1994—; bd. dirs. Maine Assn. Mus., 1996—; mem. bd. advisors Damariscotta River Assn., 1996—. Office: Maine State Mus 83 State House Sta Augusta ME 04333-0083

PHILLIPS, JOYCE MARTHA, human resources executive; b. Bridgeport, Conn., Dec. 18, 1952; d. Stephen and Shirley B. (Howard) Tabory; m. Glenn L. Phillips, July 14, 1974. BA in English, Fairfield (Conn.) U., 1974; MS in Indsl. Rels., U. New Haven, 1982. Tchr. English and Reading Fairfield Woods Jr. High Sch., 1975; asst. to v.p. mktg. Bunker Ramo Corp., Trumbull, Conn., 1975-76; rep. in investor rels. Gen. Electric Co., Fairfield, 1976-77, specialist in manpower rels., 1977-79; specialist in employee benefits Gen. Electric Co., Bridgeport, Conn., 1979-80, specialist in employee rels., orgn. and staffing, 1980-84; mgr. hdqrs. personnel and office svcs. Armtek Corp., New Haven, 1984-87, dir. compensation and benefits, 1987-89; v.p. human resources (div. sr. human resources officer) Citibank, N.Y.C., 1989-91, v.p. compensation global fin., 1991-95; sr. v.p. human resources Barclays Bank/BZW, N.Y.C., 1995-96; mng. dir., global head of human resources CIBC Wood Gundy, N.Y.C., 1996—. Counsel Fairfield U. Alumni Adv. Coun. Avocations: tennis, piano, dance, boating. Office: CIBC Wood Gundy 425 Lexington Ave New York NY 10017-3903

PHILLIPS, JULIA MILLER, film producer; b. N.Y.C., Apr. 7, 1944; d. Adolph and Tanya Miller; m. Michael Phillips (div.); 1 dau., Kate Elizabeth. B.A., Mt. Holyoke Coll., 1965. Former prodn. asst. McCall's Mag.; later advt. copywriter Macmillan Publs.; editorial asst. Ladies Home Journal, 1966-67; later assoc. editor; East Coast story editor Paramount Pictures, N.Y.C., 1969; head Mirisch Prodns., N.Y., 1970; creative exec. First Artists Prodns., N.Y.C., 1971; founded (with Tony Bill and Michael Phillips) Bill/Phillips Prodns., 1971; founder, producer Ruthless Prodns., Los Angeles, 1971—. Author: You'll Never Eat Lunch in This Town Again, 1991, Driving Under the Affluence, 1995; films include Steelyard Blues, 1972, The Sting, 1973 (Acad. award for Best Picture of Yr.), Taxi Driver, 1976 (Palme d'or for best picture), The Big Bus, 1976, Close Encounters of the Third Kind, 1977, The Beat, 1988; dir. The Estate of Billy Buckner, for Women Dirs. Workshop, Am. Film Inst., 1974. Recipient Katherine McFarland Short Story award, 1963, Short Story award Phi Beta Kappa, 1964. Mem. Acad. Motion Picture Arts and Scis., Writers Guild. Office: 1100 Alta Loma Rd Apt 1207 Los Angeles CA 90069-2442

PHILLIPS, KAREN BORLAUG, economist, association executive; b. Long Beach, Calif., Oct. 1, 1956; d. Paul Vincent and Wilma (Tish) Borlaug. Student Cath. U. P.R., 1973-74; B.A., U. N.D., 1977, B.S., 1977; postgrad. George Washington U., 1978-80. Research asst. research and spl. programs adminstrn. U.S. Dept. Transp., Washington, 1977-78, economist, office of sec., Washington, 1978-82; profl. staff mem. (majority) Com. Commerce, Sci., Transp., U.S. Senate, Washington, 1982-85, tax economist (majority) com. on fin., 1985-87, chief economist (minority) senate com. on fin., 1987-88; commr. Interstate Commerce Commn., 1988-94; v.p. legislation Assn. Am. Railroads, Washington, 1994-95, sr. v.p. policy, legis. & econ., 1995—. Contbg. author studies, publs. in field. Recipient award for Meritorious Achievement, Sec. Transp., 1980, Spl. Achievement awards, 1978, 80, Outstanding Performance awards, 1978, 80, 81. Mem. Am. Econ. Assn., Women's Transp. Seminar (Woman of Yr. award 1994), Transp. Research Forum, Assn. Transp. Law, Logistics & Policy, Tax Coalition, Blue Key, Phi Beta Kappa, Omicron Delta Epsilon. Republican. Lutheran. Office: Assn Am Railroads 50 F St NW Washington DC 20001-1530

PHILLIPS, KEITH WENDALL, minister; b. Portland, Oreg., Oct. 21, 1946; s. Frank Clark and Velma Georgina (Black) P.; m. Mary Katherine Garland, July 16, 1973; children: Joshua, Paul, David. BA, UCLA, 1968; MDiv, Fuller Theology Sem., 1971, D. of Ministries, 1972; LHD (hon.), John Brown U., 1990. Dir. Youth For Christ Clubs, L.A., 1965-71; pres. World Impact, L.A., 1971—; commencement speaker Tabor Coll., 1969, 91, John Brown U., 1990. Author: Everybody's Afraid in the Ghetto, 1973, They Dare to Love the Ghetto, 1975, The Making of a Disciple, 1981, No Quick Fix, 1985, Out of Ashes, 1996. Chmn. L.A. Mayor's Prayer Breakfast Com., 1985—; bd. dirs. Christian Cmty. Devel. Assn., 1992—; spkr. Promise Keeper. Named Disting. Staley lectr., 1969. Mem. Evangelistic Com. of Newark (pres. 1976—), World Impact of Can. (pres. 1978—), The Oaks (pres. 1985—), Faith Works (pres. 1987—). Baptist. Office: World Impact 2001 S Vermont Ave Los Angeles CA 90007-1256 *Our knowledge of God's Word outruns our obedience. The challenge for Christians is to live what we know.*

PHILLIPS, KEVIN PRICE, columnist, author; b. N.Y.C., Nov. 30, 1940; s. William Edward and Dorothy Virginia (Price) P.; m. Martha Eleanor Henderson, Sept. 28, 1968; children: Andrew, Alexander. A.B., Colgate U., 1961; postgrad., U. Edinburgh, Scotland, 1959-60; LL.B., Harvard U., 1964. Bar: N.Y. 1965, D.C. 1965. Adminstrv. asst. to Congressman Paul Fino, 1964-68; spl. asst. atty. gen. U.S., 1969-70; newspaper columnist syndicated King Features, 1970-83; pres. Am. Polit. Rsch. Corp., 1971; commentator Nat. Pub. Radio, 1984—; spl. asst. to campaign mgr. Nixon for Pres. Com., 1968. Author: The Emerging Republican Majority, 1969, Electoral Reform and Voter Participation, 1975, Mediacracy, 1975, Post-Conservative America, 1982, The Business Case for a National Industrial Strategy, 1984, The Politics of Rich and Poor, 1990, Boiling Point: Democrats, Republicans and the Decline of Middle-Class Prosperity, 1993, Arrogant Capital: Washington, Wall Street and The Frustration of American Politics, 1994; editor, pub.: The American Political Report, 1971—; contbg. columnist L.A. Tim. Mem. N.Y., D.C. bars, Phi Beta Kappa. Home: PO Box 1542 Litchfield CT 06759-1542

PHILLIPS, KIMBERLY KAY, educator; b. Atlanta, Jan. 27, 1966; d. James H. and Brenda K. (White) Reynolds; m. Roy A. Phillips Jr. BS in Middle Grades Edn., Mercer U., 1988; MEd in Middle Grades Edn., West Ga. Coll., 1994. Tchr. mid. grade math. and reading Haralson County Sch. Sys., Buchanan, Ga., 1988-94; head tchr. before and after program Loveland Sch., Omaha, 1994-95, staff mem., 1996—; instr. study skills and test taking skills course Offutt AFB, 1996—; adult basic edn./gen. edn. diploma program instr. Met. C.C., Omaha, 1995, part-time faculty mem., 1995—. Mem. Kappa Delta Epsilon. Address: 9205 Park View Blvd La Vista NE 68128-2318

PHILLIPS, LARRY EDWARD, lawyer; b. Pitts., July 5, 1942; s. Jack F. and Jean H. (Houghtelin) P.; m. Karla Ann Hennings, June 5, 1976; 1 son, Andrew H.; 1 stepson, John W. Dean IV. BA, Hamilton Coll., 1964; JD, U. Mich., 1967. Bars: Pa. 1967, U.S. Dist. Ct. (we. dist.) Pa. 1967, U.S. Tax Ct. 1969. Assoc. Buchanan, Ingersoll, Rodewald, Kyle & Buerger, P.C. (now Buchanan Ingersoll P.C.), Pitts., 1967-73, mem., 1973—. Mem. Am. Coll. Tax Counsel, Tax Mgmt. Inc. (adv. bd.), Pitts. Tax Club, ABA (sect. taxation, com. on corp. tax and sect. real property, probate and trust law), Allegheny County Bar Assn., Pa. Bar Assn., Duquesne Club. Republican. Presbyterian. Office: Buchanan Ingersoll PC One Oxford Ctr 301 Grant St Ste 20 Pittsburgh PA 15219-1408

PHILLIPS, LAUGHLIN, museum president, former magazine editor; b. Washington, Oct. 20, 1924; s. Duncan and Marjorie Grant (Acker) P.; m. Elizabeth Hood, 1956 (div. 1975); children: Duncan Vance, Elizabeth Laughlin; m. Jennifer Stats Cafritz, 1975. Student, Yale U., 1942-43; M.A., U. Chgo., 1949. Fgn. service officer, 1949-64, Hanoi, Vietnam, 1950-53, Tehran, Iran, 1957-59; co-founder Washingtonian mag., 1965, editor, 1965-74, editor-in-chief, 1974-79; pres. Washington Mag., Inc., 1965-79; dir. Phillips Collection, 1972-92, pres., chmn. of bd., 1967—; bd. dirs. Nat. Capital Area divsn. UN Assn. Am. Trustee MacDowell Colony, 1977-79, Nat. Com. for an Effective Congress, 1966—. With AUS, 1943-46, PTO. Decorated Bronze Star; comendador Orden de Mayo al Mérito (Argentina); chevalier de l'Ordre de la Couronne (Belgium), knight's cross 1st class Order of Danebrog (Denmark); officier Arts et Lettres (France). Mem. UN Assn. Am. (nat. bd. dirs., bd. dirs. Nat. Capital Area divsn.). Clubs: Cosmos (Washington), Metropolitan (Washington), Rolling Rock (Ligonier, Pa.). Home: 3044 O St NW Washington DC 20007-3107

PHILLIPS, LAWRENCE H., II, neurologist, educator; b. Clarksburg, W.Va., Dec. 30, 1947; m. Elayne K. Phillips, 1985; children: Joshua, Melanie. AB, Princeton U., 1970; MD, U. W.Va., 1974. Diplomate Am. Bd. Psychiatry and Neurology. Intern U. Wis. Hosps., Madison, 1974-75; resident in neurology Mayo Clinic, Rochester, Minn., 1975-78, rsch. fellow neurophysiology, 1978-79; instr. neurology Mayo Med. Sch./U. Minn., 1979-80; asst. prof. U. Va. Med. Ctr., Charlottesville, 1981-87, dir. electromyography lab., 1981—, assoc. prof., 1987—; dir. neuromuscular ctr. Muscular Dystrophy Assn. Clinic, Charlottesville, 1983—; prof. U. Va. Med. Ctr., Charlottesville, 1995—; mem. med. adv. com. Diabetes Rsch. and Tng. Ctr., U. Va., 1981-88; cons. neurologist Mayo Clinic, 1979-80, VA Hosp., Salem, 1983—; cons. panel AMA Diagnostic and Therapeutic Tech. Assessment, 1989—, arbitrator panel, 1990—; expert panel mem. NIH, 1991. Recipient Young Investigator Travel award Internat. Congress Electromyography, 1979. Mem. Am. Neurol. Assn., Am. Acad. Neurology, Am. Assn. Electrodiagnostic Medicine, Assn. Univ. Profs. Neurology, Sigma Xi. Office: Univ VA Neuromuscular Ctr UVA Medical Ctr Dept Neurology Box 394 Charlottesville VA 22908

PHILLIPS, LAYN R., lawyer; b. Oklahoma City, Jan. 2, 1952; s. James Arthur Cole and Eloise (Gulick) P.; m. Kathryn Hale, Aug. 17, 1986; children: Amanda, Parker, Graham. BS, U. Tulsa, 1974, JD, 1977; postgrad., Georgetown U., 1978-79. Bar: Okla. 1977, D.C. 1978, Calif. 1981, Tex. 1991. Asst. U.S. atty. Miami, 1980-81, L.A., 1980-83; trial atty. Bur. of Competition, Washington, 1977-80; U.S. atty. U.S. Dist. Ct. (no. dist.) Okla., Tulsa, 1983-87; judge U.S. Dist. Ct. (we. dist.) Okla., Oklahoma City, 1987-91; litigation ptnr. Irell & Manella, Newport Beach, Calif., 1991—; tchr. trial practice U. Tulsa Coll. Law, Okla. City U. Law Sch.; lectr. Attys. Gen's. Adv. Inst., Washington. Pres. Am. Inn of Ct. XXIII, Sch. Law, Okla. U., 1989-90; pres. Am. Inn. of Ct. CVIII, Sch. Law., Okla. City U. 1990-91.

Named one of Outstanding Young Ams., U.S. Jaycees, 1989. Office: Irell & Manella 840 Newport Center Dr Newport Beach CA 92660-6310

PHILLIPS, LEO HAROLD, JR., lawyer; b. Detroit, Jan. 10, 1945; s. Leo Harold and Martha C. (Oberg) P.; m. Patricia Margaret Halcomb, Sept. 3, 1983. BA summa cum laude, Hillsdale Coll., 1967; MA, U. Mich., 1968; JD cum laude, 1973; LLM magna cum laude, Free Univ. of Brussels, 1974. Bar: Mich. 1974, N.Y. 1975, U.S. Supreme Ct. 1977, D.C. 1979. Fgn. lectr. Pusan Nat. U. (Korea), 1969-70; assoc. Alexander & Green, N.Y.C., 1974-77; counsel Overseas Pvt. Investment Corp., Washington, 1977-80, sr. counsel, 1980-82, asst. gen. counsel, 1982-85; asst. gen. counsel Manor Care, Inc., Silver Spring, Md., 1985-91 asst. sec. 1988—, assoc. gen. counsel, 1991—, v.p., 1996—; vol. Peace Corps, Pusan, 1968-71; mem. program for sr. mgrs. in govt. Harvard U., Cambridge, Mass., 1982. Contbr. articles to legal jours. Chmn. legal affairs com. Essex Condominium Assn., Washington, 1979-81; deacon Chevy Chase Presbyn. Ch., Washington, 1984-87, moderator, 1985-87, supt. ch. sch., elder, trustee, 1987-90, pres., 1988-90, mem. nominating com., 1995-96. Recipient Alumni Achievement award Hillsdale Coll., 1980; Meritorious Honor award Overseas Pvt. Investment Corp., 1981, Superior Achievement award, 1984. Mem. ABA (internat. fin. transactions com., vice chmn. com. internat. ins. law), Am. Soc. Internat. Law (Jessup Internat. Law moot ct. judge semi-final rounds 1978-83, chair corp. counsel com. 1993—), Internat. Law Assn. (Am. br.; com. sec. 1982), D.C. Bar, N.Y. State Bar Assn., Royal Asiatic Soc. (Korea br.), State Bar Mich., Washington Fgn. Law Soc. (sec.-treas. 1980-81, bd. dirs., program coordinator 1981-82, v.p. 1982-83, pres.-elect 1983-84, pres. 1984-85, chmn. nominating com. 1986, 88), Washington Internat. Trade Assn. (bd. dirs. 1984-87), Assn. Bar City N.Y., Hillsdale Coll. Alumni Assn. (co-chmn. Washington area 1977-90), Univ. Club (N.Y.C.). Home: 4740 Connecticut Ave NW Apt 702 Washington DC 20008-5632 Office: Manor Care Inc 11555 Darnestown Rd Gaithersburg MD 20878-3290

PHILLIPS, LINDA GOLUCH, plastic surgeon, educator, researcher; b. Chgo., Nov. 11, 1951; d. Edward Walter and Rosemarie (Tomasek) Goluch; m. William Anthony Phillips, July 12, 1975; children: Cooper William, Nolan Edward, Spencer Geoffrey, Corinna Lee. BA, U. Chgo., 1974, MD, 1978. Diplomate Am. Bd. Surgery, Am. Bd. Plastic Surgery (mem. qualifying examination team 1993). Resident U. Chgo., 1978-80; intern in gen. surgery Northwestern U., Chgo., 1980-81, instr., surgeon, 1982-83; asst. prof. Wayne State U., Detroit, 1985-88; asst. prof. plastic surgery U. Tex. Med. Br., Galveston, 1988-91, assoc. prof. plastic surgery, 1991-95; prof. plastic surgery, 1995—; Truman G. Blocker Jr., MD, Disting. chairperson U. Tex. Med. Br., Galveston, chief divsn. plastic surgery, 1994—; mem. consulting med. staff Shriners Burns Inst., Galveston, Tex., 1988—; chmn. basic rsch. grants com. Plastic Surgery Edn. Found., Chgo., 1992—, mem. ednl. assessment com., mem. scholarship com., 1987-92, mem. plastic surgery-in-svc. exam. com., 1987-88, 89-93, mem. instrnl. course com., 1991-92, mem. rsch. fellowship com., mem. rsch. fund proposals com., 1993, 94; parliamentarian Plastic Surgery Rsch. Coun., 1991-93; Morestin lectr. Nat. Med. Assn., 1991; guest speaker Royal Coll. Surgeons, Eng., 1993; speaker in field. Co-author book chpts.; contbr. articles, abstracts to profl. jours. Pres. Blue Marlin Swim Team, Houston, 1993; active Clear Creek Ind. Sch. Dist., Houston, 1992. Grantee in field. Fellow Am. Coll. Surgeons; mem. AMA, Am. Assn. Plastic Surgeons, Am. Burn Assn. (orgn. and delivery of burn care com. 1988-91, ednl. com., 1991-94), Am. Soc. Plastic and Reconstructive Surgeons (program com. 1991-92, exhibits com. 1992, 93, chair, 1993-94, sci. program com. 1994), Am. Soc. Maxillofacial Surgeons (news com. 1992, membership com. 1992-93), Am. Assn. Surgery of Trauma (search com. editor of Jour. Trauma 1992), Am. Soc. Aesthetic Plastic Surgery, Am. Assn. Hand Surgery, Am. Geriatric Soc., Am. Diabetes Assn., Plastic Surgery Rsch. Coun., Surgical Infection Soc., Assn. Women Surgeons (pres. 1992-94, v.p./pres.-elect 1990-92, chair program com. 1990-92, chair membership com. 1988-89, nominating com. 1989-92), Blocker-Lewis Surgery Soc. (exec. sec. 1988-92), Assn. Acad. Chairmen of Plastic Surgery (prerequisite com. 1990, 91), The Wound Healing Soc. (honors and awards com. 1993), Singleton Surg. Soc. (chmn. 1997), Soc. Head and Neck Surgeons, Tex. Soc. Plastic Surgeons, Assn. Acad. Surgery, N.Y. Acad. Sci., Tex. Med. Assn., Galveston Med. Soc., Sigma Xi. Roman Catholic. Avocations: salt water tropical fish, gardening, gourmet cooking. Home: 15823 Sylvan Lake Dr Houston TX 77062-4795 Office: U Tex Med Br 6.124 McCullough Bldg Galveston TX 77555-0724

PHILLIPS, LINDA LOU, pharmacist; b. Mason City, Iowa, Sept. 3, 1952; d. Reece Webster and Bettye Frances (Martin) Phillips. BS in Polit. Sci., So. Meth. U., 1974; BS in Pharmacy, U. Ark., 1976; MS in Pharmacy, U. Houston, 1980. Registered pharmacist, Tex. Pharmacy intern Palace Drug Store, Forrest City, Ark., 1976-77; pharmacy resident Hermann Hosp., Houston, 1978-79; dir. pharmacy Alvin Cmty. Hosp., (Tex.), 1979-80; relief pharmacist Twelve Oaks Hosp., Houston, 1980; cons. pharmacist Health Facilities, Inc., Houston, 1980-81; pharmacy supr. Meth. Hosp., Houston, 1981—; sec. spl. interest group, IBAX Pharmacy, 1990-93; chmn. HBO and Co., Series 4000, materials mgmt. spl. interest group, 1994—. Mem. Am. Soc. Hosp. Pharmacists, So. Meth. U. Alumni Assn., Ark. Alumni Assn., Rho Chi, Pi Sigma Alpha. Republican. Methodist. Club: Girls' Cotillion (bd. dirs. 1983-85). Home: 7400 Bellerive Dr Apt 403 Houston TX 77036-3045 Office: Meth Hosp Pharmacy 6565 Fannin St Houston TX 77030-2704

PHILLIPS, MARGARET A., pharmacology educator. BS in Biochemistry, U. Calif., Davis, 1981; PhD in Pharm. Chemistry, U. Calif., San Francisco, 1988. Asst. prof. dept. pharmacology U. Tex. Southwestern Med. Ctr., Dallas, 1992—. Contbr. articles to profl. jours. Postdoctoral fellow U. Calif., 1988-92; recipient Lyndon Baines Johnson award Am. Heart Assn., 1993, Established Investigator award, 1996, Young Investigator award Burroughs Wellcome, 1995. Mem. AAAS, Am. Chem. Soc., Am. Soc. Biochemistry and Molecular Biology, Protein Soc. Office: U Tex Southwestern Med Ctr Dept Pharmacology 5323 Harry Hines Blvd Dallas TX 75235-7208

PHILLIPS, MICHAEL GRAY, physician assistant, medical association administrator; b. Elnora, Ind., Dec. 30, 1945; s. Grover Gerald and Dora Leona (Gray) P.; m. Channing Lee Schular, June 17, 1987; children Michael Thad, Laurie Lynn, Justin Michael. B in Health Sci., Duke U., 1973, cert. physician assoc., 1988. Cert. Am. Bd. Transplant Coord., Nat. Commn. on Cert. of Physician Assts., Am. Registry Radiol. Technologists. Pvt. practice Boca Raton, Fla., 1973-74, Crescent City, Fla., 1974-75; chief of organ and tissue donation Duke U., Durham, N.C., 1975-81, U. N.C., Durham, N.C., 1975-81; dir. Alabama Organ Ctr., Birmingham, 1981—; instr. surgery Sch. Med. U. Ala., Birmingham, 1988—; adj. prof. Sch. Health Related Professions U. Ala., Birmingham, 1992-95, instr. Sch. Health Related Professions, 1995—. Author, editor (handbook): Organ Procurement Coordinator's Handbook, 1986 (citation 1986), 1987 (merit award 1987), author 3d. rev. edit., 1995; editor: Organ Procurement, Preservation and Distribution in Transplantation, 2nd edit., 1996. Co-chmn. organ procurement and distbn. com. United Network for Organ Sharing, Richmond, Va., 1990-92, mem. liver and intestine com., 1994—; mem. preservation com. Upjohn/Southeastern Organ Procurement Found., Richmond, 1987-88. Fellow Am. Acad. Physician Assts; mem. Internat. Soc. for Heart Transplantation, North Am. Transplant Coord. Orgn.(mem. faculty selection com. 1987-88), Duke U. Physician Assts. Alumni Assn. (pres., merit award 1983). Avocations: gardening, walking, restoring antiques, traveling, basketball. Office: Alabama Organ Center 201 20th St S Ste 1001 Birmingham AL 35210-1635

PHILLIPS, OLIVER, tropical biodiversity scientist. Rsch. fellow U. Leeds, Eng., 1996—; rsch. assoc. Mo. Bot. Garden, 1997—. Recipient Edmund H. Fulling award Soc. Econ. Botany, 1992. Mem. Soc. for Econ. Botany (mem. coun. 1996—). Office: Geography Sch, U Leeds, Leeds LS2 9JT, England

PHILLIPS, OLIVERIO MICHELSEN, chemical engineer; b. Fusagasuga, Colombia, June 6, 1928; s. Oliverio M. and Yolanda V. (Villaveces) P.; m. Yolanda M. Villaveces, Mar. 25, 1950; children: Jorge, Gustavo, Yolanda, Roberto, Francis, Alberto, Jose, Carolina. BS, MIT, 1948, MS, 1950, DSc, 1957. Indsl. cons. Bogota, 1968-95; cons. UN OAS, N.Y.C., Washington, 1972-76; pres. Corp. Nal. Investigacion Forestal, Bogota, 1978-81; project mgr. Arinco S.A., Bogota, 1982-87, gen. mgr., 1987-92. Bd. dirs. Corporacion Financ. Popular, Bogota, 1968-71, Colciencias, Bogota, 1969-77, Ingeominas, Bogota, 1976-82. Mem. Inst. Colombiano de Normas Tecnicas, Inst. Investigaciones Tecnologicas (bd. dirs. 1983-87), Fedesarrollo (bd. dirs. 1969-95), Cooperacion Tecnica Internacional (bd. dirs. 1992-95), MIT Club (pres. 1966-68), Soc. Colombiana de Ciencias Quimicas (pres. 1962), N.Y. Acad. Scis. Roman Catholic. Avocations: music, reading, walking. Home: 6804 Chesterbrook Apt 304 Raleigh NC 27615

PHILLIPS, OWEN MARTIN, oceanographer, geophysicist, educator; b. Parramatta, Australia, Dec. 30, 1930; s. Richard Keith and Madeline (Lofts) P.; m. Merle Winifred Simons, Aug. 8, 1953; children: Lynette Michelle, Christopher Ian, Bronwyn Ann, Michael Stuart. B.Sc., Sydney (Australia) U., 1952; Ph.D., U. Cambridge (Eng.), 1955. Rsch. fellow Imperial Chem. Industries, U. Cambridge, 1955-57; asst. prof., then assoc. prof. Johns Hopkins, 1957-61; asst. dir. rsch. U. Cambridge, 1961-64; prof. geophys. mechanics Johns Hopkins, 1964—, chmn. dept. earth and planetary scis., 1971-77, 88-89, Decker prof. sci. and engring., 1975—; Cons. to industry, 1960—; Mem. council mems. Nat. Center Atmospheric Research, 1964-67, chmn. rev. and goals, 1965-67; mem. com. global atmospheric research project Nat. Acad. Sci., 1967-69; mem. Waterman award com. NSF, 1975-77. Author: The Dynamics of the Upper Ocean, 1966, 2d edit., 1968, 3d edit., 1977, Russian edit., 1969, 2d Russian edit., 1980, Chinese edit., 1986, The Heart of the Earth, 1968, Italian edit., 1970, 74, 77, The Last Chance Energy Book, 1979, 2d edit., 1980, Japanese edit., 1986; editor: Wave Dynamics and Radio Probing of the Ocean Surface, 1986, Flow and Reactions in Permeable Rocks, 1991; assoc. editor Jour. Fluid Mechanics, 1964-95; regional editor Proc. Royal Soc., 1990-96; mem. editl. adv. com. Ann. Rev. Fluid Mechanics, 1994—; contbr. numerous articles to profl. jours. Trustee Roland Park Country Sch., 1974-81; trustee Chesapeake Research Consortium, 1972-76, sec., 1972. Recipient Adams prize U. Cambridge, 1965, Sverdrup Gold medal Am. Meteorol. Soc., 1974. Fellow Royal Soc. (London), Am. Meteorol. Soc. (publs. commn. 1971-77, planning com. 1983-84); mem. Nat. Acad. Engring., Am. Geophys. Union, Md. Acad. Sci. (sci. coun. 1974-85, pres. 1979-85, trustee 1985-87), Phi Beta Kappa, Sigma Xi, Pi Tau Sigma. Home: 23 Merrymount Rd Baltimore MD 21210-1908

PHILLIPS, PAMELA KIM, lawyer; b. San Diego, Feb. 23, 1958; d. John Gerald and Nancy Kimiko (Tabuchi) Phillips; m. R. Richard Zanghetti, Sept. 16, 1989. BA cum laude, The Am. U., 1978; JD, Georgetown U., 1982. Bar: N.Y. 1983, U.S. Dist. Ct. (so. dist.) N.Y. 1983, Fla. 1994, U.S. Dist. Ct. (mid. dist.) Fla. 1994. Assoc. Curtis, Mallet-Prevost, Colt & Mosle, N.Y.C., 1982-84; assoc. LeBoeuf, Lamb, Greene & MacRae, N.Y.C., 1984-90, ptnr., 1991—. Mng. editor The Tax Lawyer, Georgetown U. Law Sch., Washington, 1980-81. Mem. coun. The Fresh Air Fund, 1991-94; bd. dirs. Jacksonville Zool. Soc., Inc., 1996—; pres. First Coast Venture Capital Group, Inc., 1996—. Am. Univ. scholar, Washington, 1976-78. Mem. ABA, Bar Assn. City N.Y. (sec. young lawyers com. 1987-89, chmn. 1989-91, second century com. 1990-93, banking law com. 1991-94), Jacksonville Bar Assn., N.Y. Athletic Club, River Club. Democrat. Roman Catholic. Avocations: tennis, travel. Home: 108 Putters Way Ponte Vedra Beach FL 32082-2580 Office: LeBoeuf Lamb Greene & MacRae 125 W 55th St New York NY 10019-5369 also: 50 N Laura St Ste 2800 Jacksonville FL 32202-3656

PHILLIPS, PATRICIA JEANNE, retired school administrator, consultant; b. Amarillo, Miss., Jan. 13, 1935; d. William Macon and Mary Ann (Cawthon) Patrick; m. William Henry Phillips, June 22, 1962; 1 child, Mary Jeanne. BA, Millsaps Coll., 1954; MA, Vanderbilt/Peabody U., 1957; EdD, U. So. Miss., 1978. Tchr. Jackson (Miss.) Pub. Schs., 1954-73, prin., 1973-75, asst. prin., 1975-77; dir. ednl. program Eden Prairie (Minn.) # 272, 1977-80; dir. elem. edn. Meridian (Miss.) Pub. Schs., 1980-91, asst. supt. curriculum, 1991, ret., 1991; prof. Miss. Coll., Clinton, part-time 1977, Miss. State U., Meridian, 1981-95; ednl. cons. in field. Co-author: (testing practice) Test Taking Tactics, 1987; contbr. articles to profl. jours. pres. Meridian Symphony Orch., 1987; v.p. Meridian Coun. Arts, 1986; bd. dirs. Meridian Art Mus. Named Boss of Yr., Meridian Secretarial Assn., 1985, Arts Education of Yr., Meridian Coun. Arts, 1991; recipient Excellence award Pub. Edn. Forum, 1993. Mem. ASCD, Miss. ASCD, Miss. Assn. Women (pres.), Rotary, Phi Kappa Alpha, Phi Delta Kappa (pres. 1986-87), Alpha Delta Kappa Gamma (pres. 1962). Republican. Methodist. Avocations: grant writing, computers, sewing. Home: 322 51st St Meridian MS 39305-2013 Office: Miss State Univ Meridian Campus 1000 Highway 19 S Meridian MS 39301-8205

PHILLIPS, PETER CHARLES BONEST, economist, educator, researcher; b. Weymouth, Dorset, Eng., Mar. 23, 1948; came to U.S., 1980; s. Charles Bonest and Gladys Eileen (Lade) P.; m. Emily Dowdell Birdling, Feb. 10, 1971 (div. 1980); 1 child, Daniel Lade; m. Deborah Jane Blood, June 13, 1981; children: Justin Bonest, Lara Kimberley. BA, Auckland (New Zealand) U., 1969, MA, 1971; PhD, London U., 1974; MA (hon.), Yale U., 1979. Teaching fellow U. Auckland, 1969-70, jr. lectr., 1970-71; lectr. in econs. U. Essex, Colchester, Eng., 1972-76; prof. econs. U. Birmingham,, Eng., 1976-79; prof. econs. Yale U., New Haven, Conn., 1979-85, Stanley Resor prof. econs., 1985-89, Sterling prof. econs., 1989—; Alumni disting. prof. econs. U. Auckland, 1991—; pres. Predicta Software Inc., Madison, Conn., 1994—; vis. scholar Ecole Polytechnique, Paris, 1977; univ. vis. prof. Monash U., Melbourne, Australia, 1986; vis. prof. Inst. Advanced Studes, Vienna, Austria, 1989; disting. visitor London Sch. Econs., 1989. Editor Econometric Theory jour., 1985; joint editor Asia Pacific Economic Review, 1995—; contbr. over 180 articles, book revs., notes to profl. jours. Recipient award for promotion of sci. Japan Soc., 1983; Commonwealth Grants Com. scholar, Eng., 1971, Guggenheim fellow, N.Y., 1984-85. Fellow Am. Acad. Arts & Scis., Royal Soc. New Zealand (hon.), Econometric Soc., Jour. Econometrics, Am. Statis. Soc.; mem. Inst. Math. Stats. Avocations: building, poetry, reading, tennis. Home: 133 Concord Dr Madison CT 06443-1814 Office: Cowles Found PO Box 208281 New Haven CT 06520-8281

PHILLIPS, RALPH SAUL, mathematics educator; b. Oakland, Calif., June 23, 1913; s. Isadore and Mary (Shaw) P.; m. Jean Adair, Oct. 11, 1942; 1 child, Xanthippe. A.B., UCLA, 1935; Ph.D., U. Mich., 1939. Instr. U. Wash., 1940-41, Harvard U., 1941-42; group leader Radiation Lab., Mass. Inst. Tech., 1942-46; asst. prof. math. NYU, 1946-47; assoc. prof. U. So. Calif., 1947-53, prof., 1953-58; prof. UCLA, 1958-60, Stanford U., 1960—; Rackham fellow Inst. Advanced Study, 1939-40, mem., 1950-51; research assoc. Yale U., 1953-54; Guggenheim fellow, 1954, 74; research asso. N.Y. U., 1958; vis. prof. U. Aarhus, 1968; mem. interacad. exchange program mission to USSR, 1975. Co-author: Theory of Servomechanisms, 1947, Functional Analysis and Semigroups, 1957, Scattering Theory, 1967, Scattering Theory for Automorphic Functions, 1976; co-editor Jour. Functional Analysis. Mem. Am. Acad. Arts and Scis., Am. Math. Soc. (Steele prize Lifetime Achievement 1997). Home: 1076 Cathcart Way Palo Alto CA 94305-1047 Office: Stanford U Dept Math Stanford CA 94305

PHILLIPS, RENEÉ, magazine editor, writer, public speaker; b. Freeport, N.Y.. Student, Art Students League, 1979, Am. Art Sch., 1979, Fashion Inst. Tech., 1980, New Sch. for Social Rsch., 1980. Dir., founder Artopia, not-for-profit art orgn., N.Y.C., 1980-84; pub., editor-in-chief Manhattan Arts Internat., N.Y.C., 1983—; lectr. mus. and galleries, including Katonah Art Mus., N.Y. Artists Equity, Salmagundi Club, Learning Annex, Marymount Manhattan Coll., N.Y.C.; juror Excellence in Arts Awards, 1988, N.Y. Lung Assn. Ann. Exhbn., 1990, Manhattan Arts Internat. Ann. Internat. Cover Art Competition, 1992-95; juror, co-curator Redefining Visionary ARt, Doma Gallery, N.Y.C., 1989; curator Synthesis of Painting and Sculpture exhbn., 1st Women's Bank, N.Y.C., 1984, Salute to Liberty internat. art exhbn., N.Y.C., 1986; organizer over 40 art and cultural events. Author: New York Contemporary Art Galleries Annual Guide, 1995-96, 97-98; editor-in-chief Success Now!, 1991—. Recipient award of merit Muscular Dystrophy Assn., 1986, award for outstanding contbns. to arts Mayor of N.Y.C., 1987. Mem. Internat. Assn. Art Critics, N.Y. Artists Equity (former bd. dirs.). Office: Manhattan Arts Internat 200 E 72nd St New York NY 10021

PHILLIPS, RICHARD HART, psychiatrist; b. Atlanta, June 23, 1922; s. Wendell Brooks and Margaret (Hart) P.; married Mar. 10, 1945; children: Valerie, Richard Jr., Hugh, Nancy, Mark. BS, U. N.C., 1943; MD, NYU, 1945. Intern U.S. Naval Hosp., Camp Lejeune, N.C., 1945-46; resident med.-surg. Harrisburg Hosp., Harrisburg, Pa., 1948; resident, chief resident psychiatry Duke U. Hosp., Durham, N.C., 1949-51; instr. psychiatry U. Pa., Phila., 1952-53; sr. psychiat. cons. Consolidated Industries Greater Syracuse, Syracuse, N.Y., 1976-89; from asst. prof. to prof. health sci. ctr. SUNY, Syracuse, 1953-92, prof. emeritus, 1992—; dir. adult psychiat. clinic health sci. ctr. SUNY, 1981-92. Author: (poetry) Bindweed, 1988; contbr. sci. and popular articles on psychology to jours. Pres. bd. dirs. Marcellus (N.Y.) Free Libr., 1968-75. Lt. (j.g.) USNR, 1943-48. Fellow Am. Psychiat. Assn. (life); mem. Soc. Children's Book Writers, Thursday Night Club. Republican. Avocations: poetry writing, sculpture, nature photography, bees, goats. Home: 4149 Bishop Hill Rd Marcellus NY 13108-9613 Office: SUNY Health Sci Ctr 750 E Adams St Syracuse NY 13210-2306

PHILLIPS, RICHARD L(OVERIDGE), marine corps officer; b. Sacramento, Nov. 27, 1939; s. Will D. and Lorraine (Richardson) P.; m. Linda Shughart; children: Rebecca, Richard. BS in Engring., Calif. Poly. Coll., 1961; MS in Computer Sci., Naval Postgrad. Sch., Monterey, Calif., 1973. Commd. 2d lt. USMC, 1961, advanced through grades to maj. gen., 1991; served in combat as squadron pilot and ground co. comdr. Vietnam, 1966-67, 70-71; project team leader Marine Corps Tactical Systems Support Activity, 1973-76; comdg. officer Marine Aircraft Group 39 and Marine Amphibious Units 11 and 17, Camp Pendleton and San Diego; dep. comdr. Naval Space Command, 1985-87; dep. asst. chief of staff, command, control, communications and computer, intelligence and interoperability Hdqrs. Marine Corps, Washington, 1987-89; dep. comdr. Fleet Marine Force, Pacific, Marine Corps Bases, Pacific, 1990-91; comdg. gen. 1st Marine Expeditionary Brig., Kaneohe Bay, Hawaii, 1989-91; comdr. U.S. Joint Task Force Cobra Gold, Thailand, 1990; dep. asst. sec. Navy Expeditionary Force Programs, Washington, 1992-93; insp. gen. USMC, Washington, 1993-95; ret., 1995; v.p. Wheat Internat. Comm. Corp., Vienna, Va., 1995—. Decorated D.S.M., Legion of Merit, Meritorious Svc. medal, Air medal (26), numerous others. Republican. Presbyterian. Office: Wheat Internat Comm Corp 8229 Boone Blvd Vienna VA 22182-2623

PHILLIPS, RICHARD WENDELL, JR., air force officer; b. Harrisburg, Pa., Nov. 6, 1929; s. Richard Wendell Sr. and Mary Viola (Myers) P.; m. Betty Jo Teel, Mar. 7, 1954; children—David Wendell, Karen Marie, Terry Lee Phillips Woods. B.S. in Engring., U.S. Mil. Acad., 1953; grad., U.S. Air Force Exptl. Test Pilot Sch., Edwards AFB, Calif., 1960, Air Command and Staff Coll., Maxwell AFB, Ala., 1967, Air War Coll., Maxwell AFB, Ala., 1972; M.S. in Pub. Adminstrn., George Washington U., 1967. Commd. 2d lt. U.S. Air Force, 1953, advanced through grades to maj. gen., 1983; fighter pilot 51st Fighter Interceptor Wing, Naha Air Base,Okinawa, Japan, 1954-57; instr. pilot Laredo AFB, Tex., 1958-60; test pilot Eglm AFB, Fla., 1960-64; exchange officer to U.S. Navy Air Devel. Squadron Four/Point Mugu Naval Air Sta., Calif., 1964-66; chief of tactics 366th Tactical Fighter Wing, Da Nang AB, Vietnam, 1967-68; chief of fighter test 4950th Test Wing, Wright-Patterson AFB, Ohio, 1968-71; chief of operational test and eval. div. Hdqrs. U.S. Air Force, Washington, 1972-75; vice comdr. 51st Composite Wing (tactical), Osan AB, Korea, 1975-76; chief aero. systems div. Hdqrs. U.S. Air Force, Washington, 1977-78, dep. dir. requirements - gen. purpose forces, 1978-80; dir. electronic warfare during close air support joint test force Nellis AFB, Nev., 1980-82; comdr. Air Force Operational Test and Evaluation Ctr., Kirtland AFB, N.Mex., 1982-85; comdr. Sheppard Tech. Tng. Ctr., Sheppard AFB, Tex., 1985-87, ret., 1987. Mem. Soc. Exptl. Test Pilots. Avocations: sailing; golf; skiing. Home: 816 Weeden Island Dr Niceville FL 32578-3708

PHILLIPS, ROBERT JAMES, JR., corporate executive; b. Houston, Aug. 4, 1955; s. Robert James and Mary Josephine (Bass) P.; m. Nancy Norris, Apr. 24, 1982; 1 child, Mary Ashton. BBA, So. Meth. U., 1976, JD, 1980. Bar: Tex. 1980. Vp., gen. counsel Aegis Shipping Ltd., London, 1980-81; assoc. Bishop, Larrimore, Lamsens & Brown, 1981-82; pres. Phillips Devel. Corp., Ft. Worth, Tex., 1982—; pvt. practice Ft. Worth, 1982-87, 89—; assoc. Haynes and Boone, Ft. Worth, 1988-89; sr. v.p. Am. Real Estate Group, 1989-93, Am. Savs. Bank, N.A., New West Fed. Savs. and Loan Assn., 1989-93, Am. Savs. Bank, Ft. Worth, 1991-92; chmn., CEO creative risk control Environ. Risk Mgmt. Inc., Ft. Worth, 1992-94; pres., CEO Pangburn Candy Co., 1996—; bd. dirs. Tex. Heritage, Inc. Bd. dirs., exec. com. Ft. Worth Ballet Assn., 1984-85, Van Cliburn Found.; v.p. planning, bd. dirs., exec. com. Ft. Worth Symphony Orch., 1984-85; bd. dirs. Mus. Modern Art, 1986—; bd. dirs., exec. com., chmn. investment com. Tex. Boys Choir, 1983-85. Mem. ABA, Tex. Bar Assn., Ft. Worth Bd. Realtors, Crescent Club, Phi Delta Phi, Kappa Sigma, Beta Gamma Sigma. Clubs: River Crest Country, Ft. Worth. Avocations: hunting, fishing, photography. Home and Office: PO Box 470099 Fort Worth TX 76147-0099

PHILLIPS, ROGER, steel company executive; b. Ottawa, Ont., Can., Dec. 17, 1939; s. Norman William Frederick and Elizabeth (Marshall) P.; m. Katherine Ann Wilson, June 9, 1962; 1 child, Andrée Claire. B.Sc., McGill U., Montreal, 1960. Vice pres. mill products Alcan Can. Products Ltd., Toronto, Ont., Can., 1969-70, exec. v.p., 1971-75; pres. Alcan Smelters and Chems. Ltd., Montreal, Que., Can., 1976-79; v.p. tech. Alcan Aluminium Ltd., Montreal, Que., Can., 1980-81; pres. Alcan Internat. Ltd., Montreal, Que., Can., 1980-81; pres., chief exec. officer IPSCO Inc., Regina, Sask., Can., 1982—; sr. mem. Conf. Bd. Inc., N.Y., 1987—; bd. dirs. Toronto Dominion Bank. Bd. govs. Coun. for Can. Unity, Montreal, 1987—; bd. dirs. Conf. Bd. of Can., 1984-87, Inst. for Polit. Involvement, Toronto, 1982-88. Mem. Can. Assn. Physicists, Bus. Coun. on Nat. Issues, Am. Iron and Steel Inst. (bd. dirs. 1984—), Inst. of Physics U.K. (chartered physicist), Sask. C. of C. (bd. dirs. 1984—), Que. C. of C. (pres. 1981), Pub. Policy Forum (bd. dirs.), Collegium of Work and Learning, Assiniboia Club (Regina), St. Denis Club, Univ. Club (Montreal). Home: 3220 Albert St, Regina, SK Canada S4S 3N9 Office: IPSCO Inc, Armour Rd, Regina, SK Canada S4P 3C7

PHILLIPS, RONALD FRANK, legal educator, academic administrator, dean; b. Houston, Nov. 25, 1934; s. Franklin Jackson and Maudie Ethel (Merrill) P.; m. Jamie Jo Bottoms, Apr. 5, 1957 (dec. Sept. 1996); children: Barbara Celeste Phillips Oliveira, Joel Jackson, Phil Edward. B.S., Abilene Christian U., 1955; J.D., U. Tex., 1965. Bar: Tex. 1965, Calif. 1972. Bldg. contractor Phillips Homes, Abilene, Tex., 1955-56; br. mgr. Phillips Weatherstripping Co., Midland and Austin, Tex., 1957-65; corp. staff atty. McWood Corp., Abilene, 1965-67; sole practice law Abilene, 1967-70; mem. adj. faculty Abilene Christian U., 1967-70; prof. law Pepperdine U., Malibu, Calif., 1970—, dean Sch. Law, 1970-97, dean emeritus, 1997—, vice chancellor, 1995—. Deacon North A and Tenn. Ch. of Christ, Midland, 1959-62; deacon Highland Ch. of Christ, Abilene, 1965-70; elder Malibu Ch. of Christ, 1978-95; mgr., coach Little League Baseball, Abilene, Huntington Beach and Malibu, 1968-78, 90-95; coach Youth Soccer, Huntington Beach, Westlake Village and Malibu, 1972-80, 85-86, 91. Recipient Alumni citation Abilene Christian U., 1974. Fellow Am. Bar Found. (life); mem. ABA, State Bar Tex., State Bar Calif., Christian Legal Soc., L.A. Bar Assn., Assn. Am. Law Schs. (chmn. sect. on adminstrn. law schs. 1982, com. on cts. 1985-87), Am. Law Inst., Nat. Conf. Commrs. on Uniform State Laws. Republican. Office: Pepperdine U Sch Law 24255 Pacific Coast Hwy Malibu CA 90263-0001

PHILLIPS, RONALD LEWIS, plant geneticist, educator; b. Huntington County, Ind., Jan. 1, 1940; s. Philemon Lewis and Louise Alpha (Walker) P.; m. Judith Lee Lind, Aug. 19, 1962; children: Brett, Angela. B.S. in Crop Sci., Purdue U., 1961, M.S. in Plant Breeding and Genetics, 1963; Ph.D. in Genetics, U. Minn., 1966; postgrad., Cornell U., 1966-67. Research and teaching asst. Purdue U., 1961-62; research and teaching asst. U. Minn., St. Paul, 1962-66; research assoc. U. Minn., 1967-68, asst. prof., 1968-72, assoc. prof., 1972-76, prof. genetics and plant breeding, 1976-93, Regents prof., 1993—; program dir. Competitive Rsch. Grants Office, USDA, Washington, 1979; mem. adv. grant panels NSF, USDA, AID; chmn. Gordon Conf. on Plant Cell and Tissue Culture, 1985; mem. sci. adv. coun. U. Calif. Plant Gene Expression Ctr., Berkeley, 1986-93; vis. prof., Italy, 1981, Can., 1983, China, 1986, Japan, 1990, Morocco, 1996; dir. Plant Molecular Genetics Inst., 1991-94; chief scientist USDA, 1996—; trustee Biol. Stain Commn.; mem. Nat. Plant Genetic Resources Bd.; mem. editl. bd. Procs. Nat. Acad. Sci., 1996—. Co-editor: Cytogenetics, 1977, Molecular Genetic Modification of Eucaryotes, 1977, Molecular Biology of Plants, 1979, The Plant Seed: Development, Preservation and Germination, 1979, Genetic Improvement of Crops: Emergent Techniques, 1980, DNA-Based Markers in Plants, 1994;

assoc. editor: Genetics, 1978-81, Can. Jour. Genetics and Cytology and Genome, 1985-90; mem. editl. bd. Maydica, 1978—, In Vitro Cellular and Devel. Biology, 1988-92, Cell Culture and Somatic Cell Genetics of Plants, 1983-91, Elaeis, 1994—, Proc. NAS; contbr. chpts. to Maize Breeding and Genetics, 1978, Staining Procedures, 1981, Cell Culture and Somatic Cell Genetics of Plants, 1984, Chromosome Structure and Function, 1987, Corn and Corn Improvement, 1988, Plant Transposable Elements, 1988, Chromosome Engrng. in Plants, 1991, Maize Handbook, 1994; contbr. sci. articles to profl. jours. Mem. chmn. coun. on ministries, lay leader United Meth. Ch., 1968, dir. Project AgGrad, 1983—; Cub Scout Pack co-chmn. Boy Scouts Am., 1976-77; judge Minn. Regional and State Sci. Fair, 1970-80. Recipient Purdue Agrl. Alumni Achievement award, 1961, Purdue Disting. Agrl. Alumni award, 1993; NSF fellow, 1961; NIH fellow, 1966-67, Northrup King Outstanding Faculty Performance award, 1985, Crop Sci. Rsch. award, 1988. Fellow AAAS, Am. Soc. Agronomy, Crop Sci. Soc. Am. (awards com., div. chmn., bd. rep. 1988-91, rsch. award 1988); mem. NAS, Genetics Soc. Am., Am. Soc. Agronomy (award student sect., Caleb-Dorr award), Sigma Xi, Gamma Alpha (nat. treas.), Gamma Sigma Delta (award of merit 1994), Alpha Zeta. Office: U Minn Dpt Agronomy-Plant Genetics Saint Paul MN 55108

PHILLIPS, RUSSELL ALEXANDER, JR., foundation executive; b. Charlotte, N.C., Sept. 19, 1937; s. Russell Alexander and Robmae (Black) P. A.B., Duke U., 1959; LL.B. (Edward John Noble fellow), Yale U., 1962. Bar: N.C. 1962, D.C. 1966. Clk. to Sr. Judge, U.S. Ct. Appeals, 4th Circuit, 1962-63; legal adv. Ministry of Fin., Govt. No. Nigeria, 1963-65; asst. commr. income tax (legal) East African Common Services Orgn., Nairobi, Kenya, 1965-66; assoc. firm Wilmer, Cutler & Pickering, Washington, 1966-68; program officer Rockefeller Bros. Fund, N.Y.C., 1968-73, corp. sec., 1973-81; v.p. Rockefeller Bros. Fund, 1979-81, exec. v.p., 1982—, acting pres., 1987-88. Trustee Lingnan Found.; trustee, v.p., sec. Asian Cultural Coun. Mem. N.C. Bar Assn., D.C. Bar, Council Fgn. Relations, Phi Beta Kappa. Democrat. Presbyterian. Club: University (N.Y.C.), Century Assn. (N.Y.C.). Home: 40 E 88th St Apt 5D New York NY 10128-1176 Office: Rm 3450 Ste 3450 1290 Avenue Of The Americas New York NY 10104-3499

PHILLIPS, SANDRA ALLEN, primary school educator; b. Newport News, Va., Mar. 10, 1943; d. Cecil Lamar and Mary (Schenk) Allen. BS, Appalachian State U., Boone, N.C., 1965; MEd, U. N.C., Charlotte, 1990. Tchr. Rockwell (N.C.) Elem. Sch., 1964-65, Granite Quarry (N.C.) Elem. Sch., 1965-68, Lillian Black Elem. Sch., Spring Lake, N.C., 1970, Berryhill Elem. Sch., Charlotte, N.C., 1970-71, 77—, J.C. Roe Sch., Wilmington, N.C., 1974-76; elected to tchr.'s adv. coun. Charlotte-Mecklenburg Schs., 1995-96, 96-97. Named Tchr. of Yr., Berryhill Elem. Sch., 1989. Mem. Profl. Educators N.C., Classroom Tchrs. Assn. Office: Berryhill Elem Sch 10501 Walkers Ferry Rd Charlotte NC 28208-9721

PHILLIPS, SIDNEY FREDERICK, gastroenterologist; b. Melbourne, Australia, Sept. 4, 1933; s. Clifford and Eileen Frances (Fitch) P.; m. Decima Honora Jones, Mar. 29, 1957; children: Penelope Jane, Nichola Margaret, David Sidney. M.B.B.S., U. Melbourne, 1956, M.D., 1961. Resident med. officer Royal Melbourne Hosp., 1957-61, asst. sub-dean clin. sch., 1961-62; research asso. Central Middlesex Hosp., London, 1962-63, Mayo Clinic, Rochester, Minn., 1963-66; cons. in gastroenterology Mayo Clinic, 1966—; prof. medicine Mayo Med. Sch., 1976—, dir. gastroenterology research unit, 1977-94; program dir. Mayo Gen. Clin. Research Ctr., 1974-87; dir. Mayo Digestive Diseases Core Ctr., 1984-90; Karl F. and Marjory Hasselman prof. rsch., 1994—. Editor: Digestive Diseases and Sciences, 1977-82, Gastroenterology International, 1990-95; sr. assoc. editor: Gastroenterology, 1991-96; contbr. chpts. to books, articles to profl. jours. Fellow ACP, Royal Coll. Physicians, Royal Australian Coll. Physicians; mem. Am. Motility Soc. (pres. 1994-96), Am. Soc. Clin. Investigation (emeritus), Gastroenterology Soc. Australia, Am. Gastroenterology Assn. Assn. Am. Physicians, Brit. Soc. Gastroenterology (hon.). Home: 524 14th Ave SW Rochester MN 55902-1956 Office: St Mary's Hosp Gastroenterology Unit 200 1st St SW Rochester MN 55902-3008

PHILLIPS, STEPHEN S., lawyer; b. Phila., 1946. BA, Wesleyan U., 1968; JD, Dickinson U., 1971. Bar: Pa. 1971, U.S. Ct. Appeals (3d cir.) 1971, U.S. Supreme Ct. 1980. Sr. ptnr. Pepper, Hamilton & Scheetz, Phila.; bd. dirs. Schindler Enterprises, Inc., Franke Holding USA, Inc., Pepper Internat. Assocs., Inc. Mem. ABA, Internat. Bar Assn., Pa. Bar Assn., Order of Barristers (pres. 1971-72), Phila. Country Club. Office: Pepper Hamilton & Scheetz 3000 Two Logan Sq 18th Arch St Philadelphia PA 19103

PHILLIPS, SUSAN DIANE, secondary school educator; b. Shelbyville, Ky., Aug. 28, 1955; d. James William and Catherine Elizabeth (Jones) P. B of Music Edn., Eastern Ky. U., 1977; postgrad., U. Ky., 1987. Tchr. music Breckinridge County Schs., Hardinsburg, Ky., 1978, Perry County Schs., Hazard, Ky., 1980-83, Music on the Move, Louisville, 1985-86, Cooter (Mo.) R-4 Sch., 1987-90, Lewis County High Sch., Vanceburg, Ky., 1990—; staff-cavalcade of bands Ky. Derby Festival, Louisville, 1984-86. Dir. Simpsonville (Ky.) United Meth. Ch. Handbell Choirs, 1985-86. Named Ky. Colonel Gov. Commonwealth of Ky., 1979. Mem. Nat. Band Assn., Am. Choral Dirs. Assn., Ky. Educators Assn., Ky. Music Educators Assn., Music Educators Nat. Conf. Office: Lewis County High Sch Lions Ln Vanceburg KY 41179

PHILLIPS, SUSAN MEREDITH, financial economist, former university administrator; b. Richmond, Va., Dec. 23, 1944; d. William G. and Nancy (Meredith) P. BA in Math., Agnes Scott Coll., 1967; MS in Fin. and Ins., La. State U., 1971, PhD in Fin. and Economics, 1973. Asst. prof. La. State U., 1973-74, U. Iowa, 1974-78; Brookings Econ. Policy fellow, 1976-77; econ. fellow Directorate of Econ. and Policy Rsch., SEC, 1977-78; assoc. prof. fin. dept. U. Iowa, 1978-83, assoc. v.p. fin. and univ. svcs., 1979-81; commr. Commodity Futures Trading Commn., 1981-83, chmn., 1983-87; prof. fin. dept., v.p. fin. and univ. svcs. U. Iowa, Iowa City, 1987-91; bd. govs. Fed. Res. Bd., Washington, 1991—. Author (with J. Richard Zecher): The SEC and the Public Interest; contbr. articles in field to profl. jours. Office: Fed Res System 20th Constitution St NW Washington DC 20551

PHILLIPS, T. STEPHEN, lawyer; b. Tennyson, Ind., Oct. 1, 1941. AB, DePauw U., 1963; LLB, Duke U., 1966. Bar: Ohio 1966, Ind. 1967. Assoc. Frost & Jacobs, Cin., 1966-72, ptnr., 1972—; adj. prof. North Ky. U. Chase Coll. Law, Highland Hights, 1983—. Contbg. editor: Ohio Probate Practice (Addams and Hosford), Page on Wills. Trustee Spring Grove Cemetery, Cin. Methodist. Office: Frost & Jacobs 2500 PNC Ct 201 E 5th St Cincinnati OH 45202-4117

PHILLIPS, TED RAY, advertising agency executive; b. American Falls, Idaho, Oct. 27, 1948; s. Virn E. and Jessie N. (Aldous) P.; m. Dianne Jacqulynne Walker, May 28, 1971; children: Scott, Russell, Stephen, Michael. BA, Brigham Young U., 1972, MA, 1975. Account exec. David W. Evans, Inc., Salt Lake City, 1972-75; dir. advt. Div. Continuing Edn., U. Utah, Salt Lake City, 1975-78; sr. v.p. Evans/Lowe & Stevens, Inc., Atlanta, 1978, exec. v.p., 1979; pres., CEO David W. Evans/Atlanta, Inc., 1979-80; dir. advt. O.C. Tanner Co., Salt Lake City, 1980-82; pres. Thomas/Phillips/Clawson Advt., Inc., Salt Lake City, 1982-86; pres. Hurst & Phillips, Salt Lake City, 1986-94; CEO, chmn. The Phillips Agy., Salt Lake City, 1994—; advt. instr. div. continuing edn. Brigham Young U., 1983-85. Dir. publicity, promotion Western States Republican Con., 1976. Recipient Silver Beaver award Boy Scouts Am., 1994, Spurgeon award, 1995. Mem. Am. Advt. Fedn. (8 Best-in-West awards, 2 nat. Addy awards, Clio finalist 1984, Telly award 1991, 92), Utah Advt. Fedn. (bd. dirs. 1976-78, 80-87, pres. 1984-85). Mormon. Home: 1792 Cornwall Ct Sandy UT 84092-5436 Office: The Phillips Agy 428 E 6400 S Salt Lake City UT 84107-7500

PHILLIPS, THEODORE LOCKE, radiation oncologist, educator; b. Phila., June 4, 1933; s. Harry Webster and Margaret Amy (Locke) P.; m. Joan Cappello, June 23, 1956; children: Margaret, John, Sally. BSc, Dickinson Coll., 1955; MD, U. Pa., 1959. Intern Western Res. U., Cleve., 1960; resident in therapeutic radiology U. Calif., San Francisco, 1963, clin. instr., 1963-65, asst. prof. radiation oncology, 1965-68, assoc. prof., 1968-70, prof., 1970—, chmn. dept. radiation oncology, 1973—; rsch. radiobiologist U.S. Naval Radiologic Def. Lab., San Francisco, 1963-65; rsch. physician Lawrence Berkeley Lab. Contbr. numerous articles to profl. publs. With USNR, 1963-65. Nat. Cancer Inst. grantee, 1970-97. Mem. Am. Soc. Therapeutic Radiologists (pres. 1984), Am. Soc. Clin. Oncology, Radiol. Soc. N.Am., N.Am. Hyperthermia Soc. (pres. 1994), Am. Assn. Cancer Rsch., Calif. Med. Assn., Am. Coll. Radiology, Radium Soc., No. Calif. Radiation Oncology Assn., Inst. Medicine, Phi Beta Kappa, Alpha Omega Alpha. Democrat. Office: U Calif San Francisco Dept Radiation Oncology L-75 Box 0226 San Francisco CA 94143

PHILLIPS, THOMAS EDWORTH, JR., investment executive, senior consultant; b. Danville, Va., July 7, 1944; s. Thomas Edworth Sr. and Jean (Worley) P.; m. Claudia Mitchell, July 23, 1966; children: Kelly Marie, Melissa Joyce. BS in Econs., Va. Tech., 1966; cert. in investments, N.Y. Inst. Fin., 1969; MS in Bus., Va. Commonwealth U., 1973; postgrad., U. Pa., 1989. Cert. investment mgmt. analyst; registered investment adviser. Edn. coord. Prince William County Schs., Manassas, Va., 1966-67; investment broker Conrad and Co., Richmond, Va., 1967-68; investment exec. Paine Webber, Inc., Richmond, 1968—, divisional v.p., 1980—; registered prin. NYSE, NASD, 1987—; mem. access program nat. com. PaineWebber, N.Y.C., 1989-90, mem. dir.'s coun., 1987-88, mem. managed accounts nat. adv. bd., 1991-93; mem. mut. fund Nat. Adv. Coun., 1996—; bd. dirs. Madison Group, Inc., Richmond, Meadowbrook Assocs., Inc., Richmond; speaker in field. Bd. dirs. Va. Non-Profit Housing Coalition, pres., 1992—; chmn. bd. deacons. Mt. Olivet Ch., Hanover, Va., 1984-85; trustee Hanover Acad., Ashland, Va., 1980-84. Rotary Found. fellow, 1989. Mem. Investment Mgmt. Cons. Assn., Capital Soc., Melody Hills Property Owners Assn. (bd. dirs. 1980—), Va. Tech. Alumni Assn., Rotary, Bull and Bear Club, Omicron Delta Epsilon. Baptist. Avocations: horses, tennis, golf. Home: 15058 Melody Hills Dr Doswell VA 23047-2075 Office: PaineWebber Inc 1021 E Cary St Ste 1800 Richmond VA 23219-4000

PHILLIPS, THOMAS H., writer, journalism educator, editor; b. Montclair, N.J., Jan. 18, 1942; s. William Louis and Josephine (Hoornbeek) P.; m. Mary Jo Dolembo, June 15, 1963 (div. 1975); children: Jennifer, Luke, Django; m. Debra Given, July 7, 1979; children: Talitha, Cassia, Zoey. BA, Grinnell (Iowa) Coll., 1964; MA, New Sch., 1981. Writer N.Y. Times, N.Y.C., 1965-69; writer, producer Sta. WPIX-TV News, N.Y.C., 1969-73; editor CBS Evening News, N.Y.C., 1974-77, 96—, writer, 1986-96; asst. prof. Columbia U., N.Y.C., 1979-87. Contbr. numerous articles and revs. to N.Y. Times, Rolling Stone mag., Village Voice, others. Mem. Writers Guild Am. (Outstanding Achievement award 1987-90). Presbyterian. Avocation: fiddle. Office: CBS News 524 W 57th St New York NY 10019-2902

PHILLIPS, THOMAS JOHN, lawyer; b. Mpls., Nov. 24, 1948. BA, U. Minn., 1970; JD, U. Utah, 1973; LLM in Taxation, NYU, 1974. Bar: Wis. 1974. Assoc. Whyte & Hirschboeck, S.C., Milw., 1974-78, Minahan & Peterson, S.C., Milw., 1978-91, Quarles & Brady, Milw., 1991—; law clk. Utah Supreme Ct., Salt Lake City, 1972-73. Mem. ABA, Wis. Bar Assn., Profl. Inst. Taxation, North Shore Country Club, Order of Coif. Avocations: gardening, golf, hockey, jogging, racquetball. Office: Quarles & Brady 411 E Wisconsin Ave Milwaukee WI 53202-4409

PHILLIPS, THOMAS ROYAL, judge; b. Dallas, Oct. 23, 1949; s. George S. and Marguerite (Andrews) P.; m. Lyn Bracewell, June 26, 1982; 1 son, Daniel Austin Phillips; 1 stepson, Thomas R. Kirkham. BA, Baylor U., 1971; JD, Harvard U., 1974. Bar: Tex. 1974; cert. in civil trial law Tex. Bd. Legal Specialization. Briefing atty. Supreme Ct. Tex., Austin, 1974-75; assoc. Baker & Botts, Houston, 1975-81; judge 280th Dist. Ct., Houston, 1981-88; chief justice Supreme Ct. Tex., Austin, 1988—; mem. com. on fed.-state rels. Jud. Conf. U.S., 1990-96; chair Tex. Jud. Dists. Bd., 1988—; mem. State Judges Mass Tort Litig. Com., 1991-96; bd. dirs. Elmo B. Hunter Citizens Ctr. for Jud. Selection, 1992-94, Southwestern Legal Found.; mem. Nat. Conf. Chief Justices, 1989—, chairperson elect, 1996; adv. dir. Rev. of Litigation, U. Tex. Law Sch., 1990—; chair Nat. Mass Tort Conf. Planning Com., 1993-94. Bd. advisors Ctr. for Pub. Policy Dispute Resolution, U. Tex. Law Sch., 1993—; mem. planning com. South Tex. Coll. of Law Ctr. for Creative Legal Solutions, 1993—. Recipient Outstanding Young Lawyer award Houston Young Lawyers Assn., 1986, award of excellence in govt. Tex. C. of C., 1992; named Appellate Judge of Yr., Tex. Assn. Civil Trial and Appellate Specialists, 1992-93. Mem. ABA, Am. Law Inst., Nat. Ctr. for State Ctrs. (vice chair, bd. dirs. 1996—), State Bar Tex. (chmn. pattern jury charges IV com. 1985-87, vice chmn. adminstrn. justice com. 1986-87, advisor fed. code revision project 1996—), Am. Judicature Soc. (bd. dirs. 1989-95, exec. bd. 1995-96), Conf. Chief Justices (bd. dirs. 1993-95, 1st v.p. 1995-96, pres. elect 1996—), Tex. Philol. Soc., Houston Philol. Soc., Houston Bar Assn., Travis County Bar Assn. Republican. Methodist. Office: Tex Supreme Ct PO Box 12248 Austin TX 78711-2248

PHILLIPS, THOMAS WADE, judge, lawyer; b. Oneida, Tenn., July 6, 1943; s. W.T. and Lucille (Lewallen) P.; m. Dorothy Mills, Jan. 2, 1971; children: Lori Ann, Wade Thomas. BA, Berea (Ky.) Coll., 1965; JD, Vanderbilt U., 1969; LLM in Labor Law, George Washington U., 1973. Bar: Tenn. 1969, U.S. Supreme Ct. 1972, U.S. Ct. Appeals (6th cir.) 1980. Assoc., ptnr. Baker, Worthington, Crosley, Stansberry & Wolfe, Huntsville, Tenn., 1973-77; ptnr. Phillips & Williams, P.C., Oneida, Tenn., 1977-91; U.S. magistrate judge ea. dist., Tenn., 1991—; county atty. Scott County, Huntsville, 1976-91; city atty. Town of Oneida, 1978-91. Capt. JAGC, U.S. Army, 1969-73. Mem. ABA, Tenn. Bar Assn. (ho. of dels. 1989-91), Scott County Bar Assn. Office: US District Court Howard H Baker Jr Courtho 800 Market St Knoxville TN 37902-2312

PHILLIPS, WALTER RAY, lawyer, educator; b. Democrat, N.C., Mar. 19, 1932; s. Walter Yancey and Bonnie (Wilson) P.; m. Patricia Ann Jones, Aug. 28, 1954; children: Bonnie Ann, Rebecca Lee. A.B., U. N.C., 1954; LL.B., Emory U., 1957, LL.M., 1962, J.D., 1970; postgrad., Yale U., 1965-66. Bar: Ga. 1957, Fla. 1958, U.S. Supreme Ct. 1962, Tex. 1969. With firm Jones, Adams, Paine & Foster, West Palm Beach, Fla., 1957-58; law clk. to chief judge U.S. Dist. Ct., Atlanta, 1958-59; with firm Powell, Goldstein, Frazer & Murphy, Atlanta, 1959-60; bankruptcy judge U.S. Cts., Atlanta, 1960-64; prof. law U. N.D., 1964-65; teaching fellow Yale U., 1965-66; prof. law Fla. State U., 1966-68, Tex. Tech. U., Lubbock, 1968-71; Disting. vis. prof. law Baylor U., 1971; atty. Commn. on Bankruptcy Laws of U.S., Washington, 1971-72; dep. dir., adminstrv. officer, 1972-73; prof. Sch. Law, U. Ga., 1973—, assoc. dean, 1975-83, acting dean, 1976, Joseph Henry Lumpkin prof., 1977-94, also dir. univ's self. study, 1978, Herman E. Talmadge prof., 1994—; Chapman disting. vis. prof. law U. Okla., 1985-86; vis. prof. law U. Okla., 1990, U. Mo., Columbia, 1993, 94; reporter Gov.'s Legislation for Ga., 1973; v.p., dir. Killearn Estates, Inc.; mem. Conf. on Consumer Fin. Law. Author: Florida Law and Practice, 1960, Encyclopedia of Georgia Law, 1962, Seminar for Newly Appointed Referees in Bankruptcy, 1964, Damages: Cases and Materials, 1967, (with James William Moore) Debtors' and Creditors' Rights, Cases and Material, 1966, 5th edit., 1979, The Law of Debtor Relief, 1969, 2d edit., 1972, supplement, 1975, (with James William Moore) Rule 6, Moore's Federal Practice, 1969, Adjustment of Debts for Individuals, 1979, 2d edit., 1981, supplement, 1982, 84, 85, Liquidation Under the Bankruptcy Code, 3d edit., 1988, supplement, 1989, 90, 91, 92, 93, 94, Cases and Materials on Corporate Reorganization, 1983, 3d edit., 1986, 4th edit., 1988, 5th edit., 1990, 7th edit., 1996, Family Farmer and Adjustment of Individual Debts, 1987, supplement, 1988, 89, 90, 91, 92, 93, 94, A Primer of Chapters 12 and 13 of the Bankruptcy Code, 1995. Bd. dirs. Lubbock Day Nurseries, 1969, pres., 1970-71. Served with USAF, 1950. Mem. ABA (consumer bankruptcy com. 1973—, chmn. 1986-90), Fed. Bar Assn., Fla. Bar Assn., Tex. Bar Assn., Western Circuit Bar Assn., Ga. Bar Assn. (vice chmn. publs. com. 1977-89, com. on profl. responsibility 1983—), Am. Judicature Soc., Am. Trial Lawyers Assn., Phi Alpha Delta (chief tribune). Baptist. Home: 310 Red Fox Run Athens GA 30605-4409

PHILLIPS, WARREN HENRY, publisher; b. June 28, 1926; s. Abraham and Juliette (Rosenberg) P.; m. Barbara Anne Thomas, June 16, 1951; children: Lisa, Leslie, Nina. AB, Queens Coll., 1947, LHD (hon.), 1987; JD (hon.), U. Portland, 1973; LHD (hon.), Pace U., 1982, L.I. U., 1987. Copyreader Wall St. Jour., 1947-48; fgn. corr. Wall St. Jour., Germany, 1949-50; chief London bur. Wall St. Jour., 1950-51, fgn. editor, 1951-53, news editor, 1953-54, mng. editor Midwest edit., 1954-57, mng. editor, 1957-65, pub., 1975-88; exec. editor Dow Jones & Co., 1965-70, v.p., gen. mgr., 1970-71, exec. v.p., 1972, editl. dir., 1971-88, pres., 1972-79, CEO, 1975-90, also bd. dirs., past chmn., 1972-97; co-pub. Bridge Works Pub. Co., 1992—; bd. dirs. PBS; copyreader European edit. Stars and Stripes, 1949; pres. Am. Coun. Edn. for Journalism, 1971-73; mem. Pulitzer Prize Bd., 1977-87; adj. faculty Grad. Sch. Journalism, Columbia U., 1992, John F. Kennedy Sch. Govt., Harvard Univ., 1992. Author: (with Robert Keatley) China: Behind the Mask, 1973. Trustee Columbia U., 1980-93, trustee emeritus, 1993—; mem. vis. com. John F. Kennedy Sch. Govt., Harvard U., 1984-90, 92-97; corp. adv. bd. Queens Coll., 1986-90, found. bd. trustees, 1990-97. Named one of 10 Outstanding Young Men in U.S., U.S. Jaycees, 1958; inductee Info. Industry Assn.'s Hall of Fame, 1984. Mem. Am. Newspaper Pubs. Assn. (bd. dirs. 1976-84), Am. Soc. Newspaper Editors (pres. 1975-76), Bridgehampton Club, River Club. Office: Bridge Works Publ PO Box 1798 Bridgehampton NY 11932-1798

PHILLIPS, WILLIAM, English language educator, editor, author; b. N.Y.C.; s. Edward and Marie (Berman) P.; m. Edna M. Greenblatt (dec.). BS, CCNY; MA, NYU; postgrad., Columbia U.; DHL, Adelphi U., 1991. Instr. Columbia U., N.Y.C., 1945; lectr. New Sch. Social Rsch., N.Y.C.; vis. lectr. Sarah Lawrence Coll., N.Y., 1951-54, 56-57, U. Minn., 1953; assoc. prof. NYU, 1960, 61-63; prof. English Rutgers U., New Jersey, 1963-78; prof. Boston U., 1978—. Author: A Sense of the Present, 1967, A Partisan View: Five Decades of the Literary Life, 1983; editor-in-chief Partisan Review, 1934—; editor Short Stories of Dostoyevsky; co-editor The Partisan Review Anthology, Literature and Psychoanalysis, 1983, Writers and Politics, 1983; former cons. editor Dial Press, Criterion Books, Random House, Chilmark Press; editor: Our Country, Our Culture: The Politics of Political Correctness, 1994, Sixty Years of Great Fiction from Partisan Review, 1997. Mem. Gov. N.J. Com. Arts, 1964-66, Pres. Carter Task Force Arts and Humanities, arts adv. group Bus. Com. Arts. Rockefeller Found. grantee, 1977-78; NEH fellow, 1978-79, Guggenheim Found. fellow, 1977. Mem. PEN, Assn. Lit. Mags. Am., Author's League, Coord. Coun. Lit. Mags. Am. (chmn. 1967-75, hon. pres., chmn. 1975). Office: Partisan Review 236 Bay State Rd Boston MA 02215-1403

PHILLIPS, WILLIAM A., research animal scientist; m. Barbara Moore, 1969; children: Jeffrey, Bradley, Jennifer. BS in Agr., Mid. Tenn. State U., 1971; MS in Animal Nutrition, Va. Poly. Inst. and State U., 1974, PhD in Animal Nutrition, 1976. Rsch. animal scientist Grazinglands Rsch. Lab., Agrl. Rsch. Svc., USDA, El Reno, Okla., 1976-85, rsch. leader, animal scientist, 1985-93, rsch. scientist, 1993—; mem. adv. com. for agr. Redlands C.C. Mem. Maple Sch. Bd.; baseball coach YMCA; lay leader, pres. Men's Fellowship, Sunday sch. tchr., mem. fin., missions, long range planning, bldg. and pers. coms. Wesley United Meth. Ch. 2d lt. USAR, 1971-77. Mem. Am. Soc. Animala Sci. (program com., editl. bd.), Coun. for Agrl. Sci. and Tech., Okla. Grain and Stocker Prodrs., Am. Registry Profl. Animal Scientists, El Reno C. of C. (bd. dirs., exec. bd., v.p. for orgn.). Office: USDA Agrl Rsch Svc Grazinglands Rsch Lab El Reno OK 73036

PHILLIPS, WILLIAM DANIEL, physicist; b. Wilkes-Barre, Pa., Nov. 5, 1948; s. William Cornelius and Mary Catherine (Savine) P.; m. Jane Van Wynen, June 20, 1970; children: Catherine, Christine. BS, Juniata Coll., Huntingdon, Pa., 1970; PhD, MIT, 1976. Rsch. asst. MIT, Cambridge, 1970-76, Chaim Weizmann fellow, 1976-78; physicist Nat. Inst. Stds. and Tech., Gaithersburg, Md., 1978-90, group leader, 1990-95, fellow, 1995—; vis. prof. Ecole Normale Supérieure, Paris, 1989-90; adj. prof. physics U. Md., College Park, 1991—. Editor/author: Laser Manipulation of Atoms and Ions, 1992; contbr. articles to profl. jours. Named Outstanding Young Scientist Md. Acad. Sci., 1982; recipient Gold Medal U.S. Dept. Commerce, 1993, Albert A. Michelson medal Franklin Institute, 1995. Fellow Am. Phys. Soc., Optical Soc. Am., Am. Acad. Arts & Scis.; mem. NAS. Achievements include demonstrated laser cooling of atomic beams; electromagnetic trapping of neutral atoms; discovered sub-doppler laser cooling; produced sub-microkelvin 3D kinetic temperatures. Office: Nat Inst Stds and Tech PHY A167 Gaithersburg MD 20899

PHILLIPS, WILLIAM E., advertising agency executive; b. Chgo., Jan. 7, 1930; s. William E. and Alice P.; children: Michael, Tom, Sarah. B.S., Cornell U., 1951; M.B.A., Northwestern U., 1955. Brand mgr. Procter & Gamble, Cin., 1955-59; with Ogilvy & Mather, N.Y.C., 1959-90; chief exec. officer Ogilvy Group, 1981-88; exec. in residence, prof. Johnson Grad. Sch. Mgmt. Cornell U., 1989-90; bd. dirs. Lillian Vernon, Inc., Sun Glass Hut, Inc., D.S.M. Internat. Exec. Office Group. chmn. internat. adv. bd. Outward Bound; trustee Cornell U., Achilles Track Club, N.Y.C., Florence Griswold Mus., Old Lyme, Conn.; bd. dirs. Internat. Tennis Hall of Fame, Newport, R.I. Lt. (j.g.) USN, 1951-54. Mem. Old Lyme Country Cub, Am. Alpine Club, Explorers Club, Cornell Club, Naval Mil. Club. Home: 200 N Cove Rd Old Saybrook CT 06475-2537

PHILLIPS, WILLIAM ROBERT, physician; b. Wash., Apr. 26, 1950. BA, U. Wash., 1971, MD, 1975, MPH, 1975. Diplomate Nat. Bd. Med. Examiners, Am. Bd. Family Practice, Am. Bd. Preventive Medicine; lic. physician and surgeon, Wash. Resident family practice Providence Med. Ctr., Seattle, 1975-78; resident preventive medicine U. Wash. Sch. Pub. Health & Cmty. Medicine, Seattle, 1976-79; vis. prof. U. Auckland, New Zealand, 1979, U. Tasmania, Hobart, Australia, 1979, U. Zimbabwe, Harare, 1993; clin. prof. family medicine U. Wash., Seattle, 1994—; chief staff Ballard Cmty. Hosp., Seattle, 1985, chief family practice, 1984. Contbr. articles to profl. jours. Bd. trustees Ballard Cmty. Hosp., Seattle, 1985. Recipient USPHS primary care policy fellowship, 1995. Fellow Am. Acad. Family Physicians (Mead Johnson award 1976, Warner-Chilcott award 1979), Am. Coll. Preventive Medicine; mem. N.Am. Primary Care Rsch. Group (pres., rsch. awards), Soc. Tchrs. of Family Medicine. Office: 1801 NW Market St Seattle WA 98107-3909

PHILLIPS, WILLIAM RUSSELL, SR., lawyer; b. N.Y.C., June 4, 1948; s. Samuel Russell and Annie Laura (Galloway) P.; m. Dorothy Elizabeth Lowery, Apr. 10, 1976; 1 child, William Russell Jr. BS, Washington & Lee U., 1970; JD, Georgetown U., 1974. Bar: Va. 1975, Ga. 1977, U.S. Dist. Ct. (no. dist.) Ga. 1977, U.S. Ct. Appeals (11th cir.) 1979. Law clk., atty. advisor EPA, Washington, 1973-75; asst. regional counsel region IV EPA, Atlanta, 1976-85, assoc. regional counsel region IV, 1986-90; sr. assoc. Thompson, Mann & Hutson, Atlanta, 1990-91; of counsel Peterson, Dillard, Young, Asselin & Powell, Atlanta, 1992—. Editor: Environmental Desk Manual, 1992, 94. Apptd. by gov. to Legis. Wetlands Study Com., 1992; cubmaster Cub Scouts Am., Lilburn, Ga., 1989-92; pres. Wyndemere Neighborhood Assn., Stone Mountain, Ga., 1990-94; v.p. Meth. Men's Fellowship, Glenn Meml. United Meth. Ch., 1989, pres., 1990. 1st lt. U.S. Army, 1972. Mem. Ga. Bar Assn. (sec. environ. law sect. 1985, vice chmn. 1986, chmn. 1987), Va. Bar Assn., Lawyers Club Atlanta. Avocations: golf, tennis, church service. Office: Peterson Dillard Young Asselin Powell & Wilson 230 Peachtree St NW Atlanta GA 30303-1505

PHILLIPS, WINFRED MARSHALL, dean, mechanical engineer; b. Richmond, Va., Oct. 7, 1940; s. Claude Marshall and Gladys Marian (Barden) P.; children—Stephen, Sean. B.S.M.E., Va. Poly. Inst., 1963; M.A.E., U. Va., 1966, D.Sc., 1968. Mech. engr. U.S. Naval Weapons Lab., Dahlgren, Va., 1963; NSF trainee, teaching, research asst. dept. aerospace engrng. U. Va., Charlottesville, 1963-67; research scientist, 1966-67; asst. prof. dept. aerospace engrng. Pa. State U., University Park, 1968-74, from assoc. prof. to prof., 1974-80, assoc. dean research Coll. Engrng., 1979-80; head Sch. Mech. Engrng. Purdue U., West Lafayette, Ind., 1980-88; dean Coll. Engrng. U. Fla., Gainesville, 1988—, dean engrng. and assoc. v.p. engr. rsch., 1989—; chmn. bd. dirs. North Fla. Tech. Innovation Corp., 1995—; vis. prof. U. Paris, 1976-77; bd. dirs. Tokheim Corp., Fla., Tech. Devel. Bd., Southeastern Coalition for Minorities in Engrng., vice chair, 1995—; adv. com. Nimbus Corp., 1985-90, Hong Kong U. Sci. and Tech., 1990-93, Fla. Bd. Profl. Regulation, 1992—; co-founder, v.p., CEO Inc., 1990—; mem. acad. adv. coun. Indsl. Rsch. Inst., 1990-93; mem. sci. adv. com. electric Power Rsch. Inst., 1994—; bd. dirs. Southeastern Coalition for Minorities in Engrng., vice chmn., 1995—. Sect. editor Am. Soc. Artificial Internal Organs Jour.; contbr. more than 140 articles to profl. jours., chpts. to books. Bd. dirs. Ctrl. Pa. Heart Assn., 1974-80, U. Fla. Found., 1989-91, 95—; mem. Ind. Boiler and Pressure Vessel Code Bd., 1981-88. Named Disting. Hoosier Engr., 1987, Sagamore of the Wabash, 1988; recipient Career Rsch. award NIH, 1974-78, Surgery and Bioengrng. Study sect., 1988-91, Fla. High Tech. and Industry Coun., 1990-94, So. Tech. Coun.,

1991—. Fellow AAAS, AIAA (assoc.), ASME (sr. v.p. edn. 1986-88, bd. dirs. 1995—), N.Y. Acad. Scis., Am. Astron. Soc., Am. Inst. Med. and Biol. Engring. (founding fellow, chair coll. fellows 1994-95, pres. 1996-97), Am. Soc. Engring. Edn. (past chmn. long range planning soc. awards 1990—, vice chmn. engring. deans coun. 1991-93, chair 1993—, bd. dirs. 1994—, 1st v.p. 1994-95, pres. 1996-97), Royal Soc. Arts; mem. Am. Soc. Artificial Internal Organs (trustee 1982-90, sec.-treas. 1986-87, pres. 1988-89), Nat. Assn. State Univs. and Land-Grant Colls. (com. quality of engring. edn.), Accreditation Bd. on Engring. and Tech. (bd. dirs. 1989—, exec. com. 1991—, mem. internat. revs. for univs. in Saudi Arabia, USSR, The Netherlands, Kuwait, pres. 1995-96), Univ. Programs in Computer-Aided Engring., Design and Mfg. (bd. dirs. 1985-91), Am. Phys. Soc., Biomed. Engring. Soc., Internat. Soc. Biorheology, Fla. Engring. Soc., Cosmos Club, Fla. Blue Key, Rotary (pres. Lafayette chpt. 1987-88), Sigma Xi, Phi Kappa Phi, Phi Tau Sigma, Sigma Gamma Tau, Tau Beta Pi (eminent engr.). Achievements include development of artificial heart pumps; research on reentry aerodynamics, on blood rheology, on modelling blood flow, on fluid dynamics of artificial hearts, on the use of smooth blood contacting surfaces, on prosthetic valve fluid dynamics and on laser Doppler studies of biofluid dynamics. Home: 4140 NW 44th Ave Gainesville FL 32606-4518 Office: U Fla Coll Engineering 300 Weil Hall Gainesville FL 32611-2083

PHILLIPS, ZAIGA ALKSNIS, pediatrician; b. Riga, Latvia, Sept. 13, 1934; came to U.S., 1949; d. Adolfs and Alma (Ozols) Alksnis; (div. 1972); children: Albert L., Lisa K., Sintija. BS, U. Wash., 1956, MD, 1959. Fellow Colo. Med. Ctr., Denver, 1961-62; sch. physician Bellevue and Issaquah (Wash.) Sch. Dists., 1970-77; pvt. practice Bellevue, 1977—; staff pediatrician Overlake Ctr., 1977—, Childrens Hosp. and Med. Ctr., Seattle, 1977—, Evergreen Med. Ctr., 1977—; cons. physician Allergy Clinic, Childrens Hosp., Seattle, 1988—; cons. and contact to pediatricians in Latvia, 1988—; team mem. to Latvia, Healing the Children Contact with Latvia, 1993-95; bd. mem. Bellevue's Stay in Sch. Program, 1994—. Mem. Am. Latvian Assn., 1972—, Wash. Latvian Assn., Seattle, 1972—; pres. Latvian Sorority Gundega, Seattle, 1990-93; bd. dirs. Sister Cities Assn., Bellevue, 1992—, Wash. Asthma Allergy Found. Am., 1992. Fellow Am. Acad. Pediatricians; mem. Am. Latvian Physicians Assn., Wash. State and Puget Sound Pediatric Assn. Office: Pediatric Assn 2700 Northup Way Bellevue WA 98004-1461

PHILLIS, JOHN WHITFIELD, physiologist, educator; b. Port of Spain, Trinidad, Apr. 1, 1936; came to U.S., 1981; s. Ernest and Sarah Anne (Glover) P.; m. Pamela Julie Popple, 1958 (div. 1968); children: David, Simon, Susan; m. Shane Beverly Wright, Jan. 24, 1969. B in Vet. Sci., Sydney (Australia) U., 1958, D in Vet. Sci., 1976; PhD, Australian Nat. U., Canberra, 1961; DSc, Monash U., Melbourne, Australia, 1970. Lectr./sr. Monash U., 1963-69; vis. prof. Ind. U., Indpls., 1969; prof. physiology, assoc. dean rsch. U. Man., Winnipeg, Can., 1970-73; prof., chmn. dept. physiology U. Sask., Saskatoon, Can., 1973-81, asst. dean rsch., 1973-75; prof. physiology, chmn. dept. physiology Wayne State U., Detroit, 1981—; Wellcome vis. prof. Tulane U., 1986; mem. scholarship and grants com. Can. Med. Rsch. Coun., Ottawa, Ont., 1973-79; mem. sci. adv. bd. Dystonia Med. Rsch. Found., Beverly Hills, Calif., 1980-85; mem. sci. adv. panel World Soc. for Protection of Animals, 1982—. Author: Pharmacology of Synapses, 1970; editor: Veterinary Physiology, 1976, Physiology and Pharmacology of Adenosine Derivatives, 1983, Adenosine and Adenine Nucleotides as Regulators of Cellular Function, 1991, The Regulation of Cerebral Blood Flow, 1993, Novel Therapies for CNS Injuries: Rationales and Results, 1996; editor Can. Jour. Physiology and Pharmacology, 1978-81, Progress in Neurobiology, 1973—. Mem. grants com. Am. Heart Assn. of Mich., 1985-90, mem. rsch. coun., 1991-92, mem. rsch. forum com., 1991-96, chair, 1992-93. Wellcome fellow London, 1961-62; Can. Med. Rsch. Found. grantee, 1970-81, rsch. prof., 1980; NIH grantee, 1983—. Mem. Brit. Pharmacol. Soc., Physiol. Soc., Am. Physiol. Soc., Soc. Neurosci., Internat. Brain Rsch. Orgn. Office: Wayne State U Dept Physiology 540 E Canfield St Detroit MI 48201-1928

PHILLIS, MARILYN HUGHEY, artist; b. Kent, Ohio, Feb. 1, 1927; d. Paul Jones and Helen Margaret (Miller) Hughey; m. Richard Waring Phillis, Mar. 19, 1949; children: Diane E., Hugh R., Randall W. Student, Kent State U., 1945; BS, Ohio State U., 1949. Chemist Battelle Meml. Inst., Columbus, Ohio, 1949-53; sec. Lakewood Park Cemetery, Rocky River, Ohio, 1972-75; illustrator periodical Western Res. Hist. Mag., Garrettsville, Ohio, 1974-78; illustrator book AAUW, Piqua, Ohio, 1976; art instr. Edison State C.C., Piqua, 1976; watermedia instr. Springfield (Ohio) Mus. Art, 1976-84; juror art exhbns. state and nat. art group, 1980—; painting instr. state and nat. orgns., 1980—; dir. Nat. Creativity Seminars, Ohio Watercolor Soc., Fairborn, 1993-95, 97; lectr. art healing Wheeling (W.Va.) Jesuit Coll., 1994-96. Author: Watermedia Techniques for Releasing the Creative Spirit, 1992; contbr. articles and illustrations to profl. jours.; one-woman shows include Stifel Fine Art Ctr., Wheeling, W.Va., Springfield (Ohio) Art Mus., Zanesville (Ohio) Art Ctr., Cleve. Inst. Music, Columbus Mus. Art, Cheekwood Mus. of Art, Bot. Hall, Nashville; exhibited in group shows at No. Ariz. U. Art Mus., Flagstaff, 1993, Taiwan Art Edn. Inst., Taipei, 1994; represented in permanent collections at Springfield Mus. Art, Ohio Watercolor Soc., also corp. collections. Gallery dir. Green St. United Meth. Ch., Piqua, 1972-75; pres. Rocky River (Ohio) H.S. PTA, 1971; chmn. Cmty. Health and Humor Program, Wheeling, 1992. Recipient First awards Watercolor West, Riverside, Calif., 1990, Hudson Soc. award Nat. Collage Soc., 1995, Art Masters award Am. Artist Mag., 1996. Mem. Internat. Soc. Study of Subtle Energies and Energy Medicine (art cons. sci. jour. 1992-96, art and healing workshop 1995), Am. Watercolor Soc. (dir. 1991-93, newsletter editor 1992—, Osborne award 1975), Soc. Layerists in Multi-Media (nat. v.p. 1988-93), Ohio Watercolor Soc. (sec. 1979-82, v.p. 1982-89, pres. 1990-96, Gold medal, Best of Show 1993), Nat. Watercolor Soc., Int. Noetic Sci., West Ohio Watercolor Soc. (pres. 1979-80, 2nd award 1982), Allied Artists N.Y., W.Va. Watercolor Soc. (1st award 1993), Ky. Watercolor Soc., Ga. Watercolor Soc., So. Watercolor Soc. (pres. 1997-98). Avocations: hiking, reading, genealogy, music, travel. Home and Office: Phillis Studio 72 Stamm Cir Wheeling WV 26003-5549

PHILLS, BOBBY RAY, dean, agricultural research director. BS in Horticulture, So. U. and A&M Coll., 1968; MS in Horticulture/Vegetable Crops, La. State U., 1972, PhD in Horticulture/Plant Breeding, 1975. Postdoctoral fellow Cornell U., 1975-76; from asst. prof. plant and soil scis. to prof. plant and soil scis. Tuskegee (Ala.) U., 1976-82, assoc. dir. Carver Rsch. Found., 1982-85, dir. George Washington Carver Agrl. Expt. Sta., 1982-85; dean, rsch. dir. Coll. Agriculture So. U. and A&M Coll., Baton Rouge, 1985-86, prof. plant and soil scis., 1985—, interim dir. Small Farm and Family Resource Devel. Ctr., 1989—, dean, rsch. dir. Coll. Agricultural Family and Human Svcs., 1986—; bd. dirs. Baton Rouge Green, Allegation Bd.; mem. U.S. Dept. Agriculture/1890 Task Force; chmn. 1890 Land-grant Legis. Com. U.S. Dept. Agriculture-CSRS grantee. Mem. Am. Soc. Horticultural Sci., Assn. 1890 Agrl. Adminstrs., Assn. Rsch. Dirs. Nat. Assn. State Land-grant Colls. and Univs. (bd. dirs. divsn. agr. 1985—), Sigma Xi, Alpha Phi Alpha, Beta Kappa Chi. Office: Southern Univ-Agr & Mech College Coop St Research Service Program Southern Branch PO Baton Rouge LA 70813

PHILOGENE, BERNARD J. R., academic administrator, science educator; b. Beau-Bassin, Mauritius, May 4, 1940; came to Can., 1961; s. Raymond Pierre and Simone Marie (Ruffier) P.; m. Hélène Marie Lebreux, July 7, 1964; children: Simone, Catherine. BS, U. Montreal, 1964; MS, McGill U., 1966; PhD, U. Wis., 1970; DSc (hon.), Compiègne, 1995. Research officer Can. Forestry Service, Que., 1966-70, research scientist, 1970-71; asst. prof. U. B.C., Vancouver, 1971-74; asst. prof., assoc. prof., then prof. entomology U. Ottawa, Can., 1974—, vice dean sci. and engring., 1982-85, acting dean, 1985-86, dean faculty of sci., 1986-90, acad. vice rector, 1990-97; pres. Can. Consortium of Sci. Socs., 1992-94; cons. OAS, Washington, 1979-80, Agence de Coop. Culture & Tech., Paris, 1982-83, Can. Internat. Devel. Agy., Ottawa, 1983-85, UN Environ. Program, Geneva, Switzerland, 1985-86, Internat. Devel. Research Ctr., Ottawa, 1985—. Mem. Ont. Pesticide Adv. Com., 1987-91. Decorated officier de l'Ordre des Palmes Académiques (France); knight of merit Order of St. John of Jerusalem. Fellow Entomol. Soc. Can. (bd. dirs. 1977-80); mem. Am. Inst. Biol. Scis., Entomol. Soc. Am., Can. Pest Mgmt. Soc., Assn. Can.-Française Advancement Sci. (bd. dirs. 1984-86). Office: U Ottawa, PO Box 450, 30 Marie Curie St, Ottawa, ON Canada K1N 6N5

PHILPOTT, HARRY MELVIN, former university president; b. Bassett, Va., May 6, 1917; s. Benjamin Cabell and Daisy (Hundley) P.; m. Pauline Breck Moran, Sept. 15, 1943; children: Harry Melvin, Jean Todd, Benjamin Cabell II, Virginia Lee. A.B., Washington and Lee U., 1938, LL.D., 1966; Ph.D., Yale U., 1947; D.D., Stetson U., 1960; LL.D., U. Fla., 1969, U. Ala., 1970; H.H.D., Samford U., 1978, Montevallo U., 1980, Auburn U., 1981. Ordained to ministry Bapt. Ch., 1942; dir. religious activities Washington and Lee U., 1938-40; prof. religion U. Fla., 1947-52, v.p., 1957-65; dean, head dept. religion and philosophy Stephens Coll., 1952-57; pres. Auburn U., 1965-80. Mem. Regional Edn. Bd., 1966-82, vice chmn., 1973-75; chmn. Ala. Edn. Study Commn., 1967-69; pres. Southeastern Conf., 1972-74. Served to 1st lt. Chaplains Corps., USNR, 1943-46. Mem. Nat. Assn. State Univs. and Land-Grant Colls. (chmn. council presidents 1972-73, exec. com. 1973-78, pres. 1976-77), Fla. Blue Key, Kappa Alpha, Omicron Delta Kappa, Kappa Delta Pi, Phi Kappa Phi. Home: PO Box 3037 Auburn AL 36831-3037

PHILPOTT, JAMES ALVIN, JR., lawyer; b. Lexington, Va., Apr. 26, 1947; s. James Alvin and Helen (Gibbs) P.; m. Judy Mauze, June 10, 1968; children: John Harman, Jean Cameron, James Hundley. BS in Commerce, Washington & Lee U., 1969, JD summa cum laude, 1972. Bar: N.Y. 1974, KY. 1980, U.S. Dist. Ct. (so. dist.) N.Y. 1975, U.S. Dist. Ct. (ea. dist.) Ky. 1991, U.S. Ct. Appeals (4th cir.) 1973, (U.S. Ct. Appeals (6th cir.) 1993. Law clk. to justice U.S. Ct. Appeals (4th cir.), Asheville, N.C., 1972-73; assoc. Cravath, Swaine & Moore, N.Y.C., 1974-79; exec. v.p., gen. counsel Gainesway Farm, Lexington, Ky., 1980-85; dir., mem. exec. com., sec. Breeders' Cup Ltd., 1983—. Editor-in chief Washington & Lee U. Law Rev., 1972. Trustee The Lexington Sch., 1984-91. Served to capt. U.S. Army, 1972-73. Mem. ABA (corp., banking and bus. law sect.), Ky. Bar Assn., Ky. Thoroughbred Assn., Washington & Lee U. Law Sch. Assn. (mem. coun. 1986-91), Idle Hour Country Club, The Lexington Club, Omicron Delta Kappa. Presbyterian. Office: PO Box 54350 Lexington KY 40555-4350

PHILPOTT, LARRY LA FAYETTE, horn player; b. Alma, Ark., Apr. 5, 1937; s. Lester and Rena (Owens) P.; m. Elise Robichaud, Nov. 24, 1962 (div. June 1975); children: Daniel, Stacy; m. Anne Sokol, Feb. 14, 1984. B.S., Ga. So. Coll., 1962; Mus.M., Butler U., 1972. Instr. in horn Butler U., De Pauw U.; dir. music Cedarcrest Sch., Marysville, Wash., 1991—; instr. horn Western Wash. U., Dept Music, Bellingham, 1995—. Mem., N.C. Symphony, 1960, Savannah (Ga.) Symphony, L'Orchestre Symphonique de Quebec, Que., Can., 1962-64, prin. horn player, Indpls. Symphony Orch., 1964-89, Flagstaff Summer Festival, 1968—; artist in-residence Ind.-Purdue Indpls.; appeared with, Am. Shakespeare Theatre, summer 1965, Charlottetown Festival, summers 1967-68, Flagstaff Summer Festival, 1968-85, Marrowstone Music Festival, 1985—. Served with USN, 1956-60. Mem. Music Educators Nat. Conf., Am. Fedn. Musicians, Internat. Conf. Symphony and Opera Musicians, Internat. Horn Soc., Coll. Music Soc., Phi Mu Alpha Sinfonia. Home: 14925 63rd Ave SE Snohomish WA 98296-5277 Office: Cedarcrest Sch 6400 88th St NE Marysville WA 98270-2800 also: Western Wash U Dept Music Bellingham WA 98225-9107

PHILPOTT, LINDSEY, civil engineer, researcher, educator; b. Bridestowe, Devonshire, Eng., Aug. 2, 1948; came to U.S., 1983; s. George Anthony and Joyce Thirza (Teeling) P.; m. Christine May Pembury, Aug. 20, 1974 (div.); children: David, Elizabeth; m. Kathleen Linda Matson, Feb. 17, 1982 (div.); children: Nicholas, Benjamin; m. Kim Elaine Moore, Nov. 24, 1991. Higher Nat. Cert. in Civil Engring., Bristol (Eng.) Poly., 1973; BSCE, U. Ariz., 1986, MSCE, 1987. Registered profl. engr., Calif. Area structural engr. Dept. Environment (Property Svcs. Agy.), Bristol, 1971-73; civil engr. Webco Civil Engring., Exeter, Eng., 1973-75; tech. mgr. Devon & Cornwall Housing Assn., Plymouth, Eng., 1975-79; prin., architect S.W. Design, Plymouth, 1979-81; archtl. engr. United Bldg. Factories, Bahrain, 1981-83; jr. engr. Cheyne Owen, Tucson, 1983-87; civil engr. Engring. Sci. Inc., Pasadena, Calif., 1987-89; project engr. Black & Veatch, Santa Ana, Calif., 1989-90; sr. engr. Brown & Caldwell, Irvine, Calif., 1990-91; environ. engr. Met. Water Dist. So. Calif., San Dimas, 1991—; adj. prof. hydraulics and instrumentation, San Antonio Coll., Walnut, Calif., 1995—. Foster parent Foster Parents Plan, Tucson, 1985-87; vol. reader tech. books Recording for the Blind, Hollywood, Calif., 1988-89, South Bay, Calif., 1990-91, Pomona, Calif., 1991—; vol. sailor/tchr. L.A. Maritime Inst. Topsail Youth Program, 1994—. Mem. ASCE, Am. Water Works Assn., Am. Water Resources Assn. (water quality com. 1990—), Water Environment Fedn., Engrs. Soc. (pres. 1985-96), Mensa, South Bay Yacht Racing Club (Marina del Rey, Calif., vice commodore 1995, commodore 1996), Marina Venice Yacht Club (Marina del Rey, fleet capt. 1997). Avocations: hiking, cycling, sailing, crosswords. Office: Met Water Dist Environ Compliance Divsn PO Box 54153 Los Angeles CA 90054-0153

PHINAZEE, HENRY CHARLES, systems analyst, educator; b. Birdnest, Va., Oct. 26, 1956; s. Charlie Phinazee and Johnnie Belle (Harris) Brice. BEd, Fort Hays State U., 1978, B of Psychology, 1979, M of Psychology, 1980; MEd, Wichita State U., 1985. Cert. tchr., Kans., Tex. Minority advisor Fort Hays State U., 1978-80; tchr. Wichita Pub. Schs., 1980—; tchr. Wichita State U., 1988-92, dorm coord. coll. of health professions, 1986-92, work coord. coll. of health profession, 1988-91; computer analyst Beech Aircraft Corp., Wichita, 1992—. Author: (software) Dayreq, 1989. Mentor Grow Your Own Tchrs., Wichita Pub. Schs., 1990; liaison Com. on Polit. Edn., Wichita, 1988—. Recipient Svc. award Big Bros./Big Sisters, 1987. Mem. Am. Amature Racquetball, Wichita Assn. of Black Educators (treas. 1991-92), Wichita Fedn. of Tchrs. (2d v.p. 1988-92, Svc. award 1991), Kans. Assn. of Black Educators (com. head 1991-92), Phi Delta Kappa, Kappa Alpha Psi (polemark 1988-92, Svc. award). Democrat. Baptist. Avocations: racquetball, running, bicycling, reading, church. Home: 4400 Horizon Hill # 4807 San Antonio TX 78229 Office: Brackenridge HS 400 Eagleland Dr San Antonio TX 78210-1230

PHINIZY, ROBERT BURCHALL, electronics company executive; b. Ben Hill, Ga., June 30, 1926; BS, U. Ariz., 1951; postgrad. U. So. Calif., 1952-55, UCLA, 1956-62; children: Robert B., William, David. Pres., LB Products, Santa Monica, Calif., 1954-68, IMC Magnetics Western, South Gate, Calif., 1968-69, Am. Electronics, Fullerton, Calif., 1969-71; gen. mgr. electronics div. Eaton Co., Anaheim, Calif., 1971-82; pres., CEO Genisco Tech. Corp., Compton, Calif., 1972-83; chmn. bd., CEO Genisco Computers Corp., Costa Mesa, Calif., 1983—, Trans Tech. Alliances, Calif., 1986—; bd. dirs. Microsemi Corp., Santa Ana, Calif., 1992—, Biosonics Inc., Seattle, 1989—, Genisco Tech., 1996—, chmn. fin. com. of creditor com.; bd. dirs. Genisco Technology Corp., 1996—. Contbr. articles to tech. jours.; patentee in field. Bd. dirs. U. Calif., Dominguez Hills, 1975-89; mem. L.A. Town Hall; chmn. bd. dirs. Calif. State U. Found., 1986. Served to capt. USN, 1943-47, USNR, 1947-80. Fellow Coll. Engrs. L.A.; mem. IEEE, Communication and Computers Indsl. Assn., Electronics Assn. Calif. (treas. 1986), Am. Electronics Assn. (chmn. small bus. com. Orange County, Calif. 1989-90), Port Ludlow Yacht Club (vice commodore 1997). Democrat.

PHINNEY, JEAN SWIFT, psychology educator; b. Princeton, N.J., Mar. 12, 1933; d. Emerson H. and Anne (Davis) Swift; m. Bernard O. Phinney, Dec. 11, 1965; children: Peter, David. BA, Mass. Wellesley Coll., 1955; MA, UCLA, 1969, PhD, 1973. Asst. prof. psychology Calif. State U., L.A., 1977-81, assoc. prof. psychology, 1981-86, prof. psychology, 1986—. Editor: Children's Ethnic Socialization, 1987; asst. editor Jour. Adolescence; contbr. articles to profl. jours. NIH grantee. Mem. APA, Soc. for Rsch. in Child Devel., Soc. for Rsch. in Adolescence, Internat. Soc. for Study of Behavior Devel. Avocations: skiing, hiking, travel, chamber music. Office: Calif State U Dept Psychology 5151 State University Dr Los Angeles CA 90032-4226

PHINNEY, WILLIAM CHARLES, retired geologist; b. South Portland, Maine, Nov. 16, 1930; s. Clement Woodbridge and Margaret Florence (Foster) P.; m. Colleen Dorothy Murphy, May 31, 1953; children—Glenn, Duane, John, Marla. B.S., MIT, 1953, M.S., 1956, Ph.D., 1959. Faculty geology U. Minn., 1959-70; chief geology br. NASA Lyndon B. Johnson Space Center, Houston, 1970-82; chief planetology br. NASA Lyndon B. Johnson Space Center, 1982-89, ret., 1994; NASA prin. investigator lunar samples. Contbr. articles to profl. jours. Served with C.E. AUS, 1953-55. Recipient NASA Exceptional Sci. Achievement medal, 1972, NASA Cert. of Commendation, 1987; NASA rsch. grantee, 1972-94, NSF rsch. grantee, 1960-70. Mem. Am. Geophys. Union, AAAS, Mineral. Soc. Am., Geol. Soc. Am., Minn. Acad. Sci. (dir.), Sigma Xi. Home: 18063 Judicial Way S Lakeville MN 55044-8839

PHIPPEN, SANFORD EDWIN, secondary school educator, writer; b. White Plains, N.Y., June 19, 1942; s. Francis Eugene and Elizabeth Marie (Clarke) P. BA, U. Maine, 1964; MA, Syracuse U., 1971. Cert. tchr., Maine. English tchr. New Hartford (N.Y.) H.S., 1964-67, Corcoran H.S., Syracuse, N.Y., 1967-79, Orono (Maine) H.S., 1979-96; asst. prof. English U. Maine, Orono, 1987-88. Author: (fiction) The Police Know Everything, 1982, People Trying to Be Good, 1988, Kitchen Boy, 1996; (essays) Cheap Gossip, 1989; editor The Best Maine Stories, 1986, High Clouds Soaring, Storms Driving Low: The Letters of Ruth Moore, 1993, Maine Life Mag., 1976-86; columnist Maine Times, 1993-97; prodr. (video) A Century of Summers, 1987. Mem. Maine Humanities Coun., Portland, 1984-90, vice chmn., 1989-90; mem. lit. panel Maine Arts Commn., Augusta, 1990-94; pres. Hancock (Maine) Hist. Soc., 1979-96. Named Outstanding Maine Author Portland Pub. Libr., 1990. Mem. Nat. Coun. Tchrs. English, Orono Tchrs. Assn. Democrat. Home: HC 77 Box 212 Hancock ME 04640-9709 Office: Orono HS 18 Goodridge Rd Orono ME 04473-1453

PHIPPS, ALLEN MAYHEW, management consultant; b. Seattle, Oct. 3, 1938; s. Donald Mayhew and Virginia (McGinn) P.; B.A. in Econs., U. Calif., Berkeley, 1961; M.B.A. with honors, Stanford U., 1969; m. Joyce Elisabeth Alberti, Aug. 21, 1971; children—Ramsey Mayhew, Justin Beckwith. Security analyst Morgan Guaranty Trust Co., 1968; with Boston Cons. Group, Inc., 1969—, mgr. 1971-74, mem. sr. team, Calif., 1974-77, corp. v.p., dir., 1975—; mgr. Boston Cons. Group, G.mb.H, Munich. W. Ger., 1978-82, partner-in-charge West Coast client devel., Menlo Park, Calif., 1982-84; pres. Techno Digital Systems, Inc., 1984-86; pres., chief exec. officer, Techno Digital System (Sellectek, Inc.), 1984-85; exec. v.p., Regis McKenna Inc., Palo Alto, Calif., 1985-87; pvt. practice mgmt. cons., Menlo Pk., 1987-95; chief exec. officer Bio Electro Systems, Palo Alto, 1989-92; mng. dir., Bus. Engring. Inc., Menlo Park, Calif., 1992-95; sr. v.p. bus. and policy group SRI Internat., Menlo Park, Calif., 1995-96; pres., CEO SRI Consulting, Menlo Park, 1996—. Served to capt. U.S. Army, 1961-67. Decorated Bronze Star, Army Commendation medal with 2 oak leaf clusters. Mem. Alpha Delta Phi. Republican. Presbyterian. Clubs: Bohemian (San Francisco); Sharon Heights Golf and Country (Menlo Park). Home: 33 Prado Secoya St Atherton CA 94027-4126 Office: SRI Consulting 333 Ravenswood Ave Menlo Park CA 94025

PHIPPS, CLAUDE RAYMOND, research scientist; b. Ponca City, Okla., Mar. 15, 1940; s. Claude Raymond Louis and Deva Pauline (DeWitt) P.; m. Lynn Malarney, Dec. 1, 1962 (div. Feb. 1989); 1 child, David Andrew; life ptnr. Shanti E. Bannwart. BS, MIT, 1961, MS, 1963; PhD, Stanford U., 1972. Rsch. staff Lawrence Livermore (Calif.) Nat. Lab., 1972-74; rsch. staff Los Alamos (N.Mex.) Nat. Lab., 1974-95, project leader engine support sys. tech. program, 1993; assoc. dir. Alliance for Photonic Tech., Albuquerque, 1992-95; pres. Photonic Assocs., Santa Fe, 1995—; co-instr. (with Shanti E. Bannwart) "Pairs" Relationship Tng., Santa Fe, N.Mex., 1990—; dir. Santa Fe Investment Conf., 1987; mem. program com. MIT Workshop on High Temperature Superconductors, Cambridge, 1988; mem. Instl. R & D Com., Los Alamos Nat. Lab., 1990-92, project leader laser effects, 1982-87, mem. internat. rsch. tour, Australia, Japan, Scotland, 1988-89; invited discussion leader Gordon Conf. on Laser Particle Interactions, N.H., 1992; invited plenary spkr. Physics of Quantum Electronics meeting, Snowbird, Utah, 1997. Co-author: Laser Ionization Mass Analysis, 1993; author internat. lecture series on laser surface interactions, Berlin, Antwerp, Marseilles, Xiamen, Cape Town, Durban, 1987—; contbr. articles to profl. jours. Lt. USN, 1963-65. Grad. fellow W. Alton Jones Found., N.Y.C., 1962-63. Avocations: writing poetry, reading, travel, photography. Home and Office: Photonic Assocs 1621 Calle Torreon Santa Fe NM 87501

PHIPPS, JOHN RANDOLPH, retired army officer; b. Kansas, Ill, May 16, 1919; s. Charles Winslow and Kelsey Ethel (Torrence) P.; m. Pauline M. Prunty, Feb. 8, 1946; children: Charles W., Kelsey J. Phipps-Selander. B.S. in Econs. with honors, U. Ill., 1941; M.P.A., Sangamon State U., 1976; assoc. course, Command and Gen. Staff Coll., 1959, nuclear weapons employment course, 1962; course, U.S. Army War Coll., 1973, U.S. Nat. Def. U., 1978. Owner, operator chain shoe stores in Eastern Ill., 1946-70; commd. 2d lt. F.A. U.S. Army, 1941, advanced through grades to capt., 1943; service in Philippines and Japan; discharged as maj., 1946; organizer, comdr. Co. E, 130th Inf., Ill.; N.G., Mattoon, 1947; comdg. officer 2d Bn., 130th Inf. N.G., 1951, lt. col. 2d Bn., 130th Inf., 1951; called to fed. service, 1952; adv. (29th Regt., 9th Republic of Korea Div.), 1952-53; comdr. officer 1st Bn., 130th Inf., Ill. N.G., 1954, col., 1959; comdg. officer 2d Brigade, 33d Div., 1963-67; asst. div. comdr. 33d Inf. Div., 1967, brig. gen., 1967; comdr. 33d Inf. Brigade, Chgo., 1967-70; comdr. Ill. Emergency Ops. Hdqrs., 1970, asst. adj. gen. Ill., 1970-77, acting adj. gen., 1977-78, adj. gen., 1978, promoted to maj. gen., 1978, now maj. gen. ret. Decorated Silver Star, Bronze Star, Disting. Service medal, Combat Infantry Badge, Army Disting. Service medal Ill., various Philippine and Korean decorations; State of Ill. Long and Honorable Service medal. Mem. VFW, Adj. Gens. Assn. U.S., N.G. Assn. U.S., N.G. Assn. Ill., Am. Legion, Amvets. Home: 100 Wabash Ave Mattoon IL 61938-4524 Office: Phipps 100 Wabash Ave Mattoon IL 61938-4524

PHIPPS, LYNNE BRYAN, interior architect, clergywoman, parent educator; b. Chapel Hill, N.C., Sept. 23, 1964; d. Floyd Talmadge and Sandra Patricia (McLester) Bryan. BFA, RISD, 1986, B Interior Architecture, 1987; cert. in parent edn., Wheelock Coll., Boston, 1989; MDiv, Andover Newton Theol. Sem., 1997. Nat. cert. interior arch. Apprentice Thompson Ventulett Stainback, Atlanta, 1983-85; jr. designer Flansberg & Assocs., Boston, 1986-87; sr. designer Andrew Samataro & Assocs., Boston, 1986-87; prin. Innovative Designs, Duxbury, Mass., 1987—; ptnr. Synergy Unlimited, 1997—; parent educator Families First, Cambridge, Mass.; youth min. St. Andrew's Episcopal Ch., Hanover, Mass., 1992-95; youth and family min. St. Stephen's Episcopal Ch., Cohasset, Mass., 1993-96; co-founder Synergy Inc., 1997—; guest lectr., jurist Auburn (Ala.) U., 1988, RISD, Providence, 1990; assoc. prof. Mass. Bay C.C., Wellesley, 1987-88; guest jurist Wentworth U., Boston, 1988-89; guest lectr. Architectural and Family Issues; guest jurist U. Memphis, 1995. Designer furniture. Mem. Internat. Interior Design Assn., Internat. Platform Assn., Jr. League Boston. Avocations: sailing, tennis, antique boats. Office: Innovative Designs Synergy Inc The Parenting Puzzle 18 Bayview Rd Duxbury MA 02332-5009

PHISTER, MONTGOMERY, JR., computer engineering consultant, writer; b. San Pedro, Calif., Feb. 26, 1926; s. Montgomery and Helga Laurena (Winther) P.; m. Melinda Miles, Mar. 29, 1974; children—Montgomery, Julia Elizabeth, Roger Benjamin. Student, Stanford U., 1943-44, B.S., 1949, M.S., 1950; Ph.D., Cambridge (Eng.) U., 1953. Mem. tech. staff Hughes Aircraft Co., Culver City, Calif., 1953-55; dir. engring. TRW Products Co., Los Angeles, 1955-60; v.p. engring. Scantlin Electronics Inc. (later Quotron Systems), Los Angeles, 1960-66; v.p. devel. Xerox Data Systems, Los Angeles, 1966-72; pvt. practice cons., writer Santa Fe, 1972—; instr. UCLA, 1954-64, Harvard U., 1974, U. Sydney, Australia, 1975. Author: Logical Design of Digital Computers, 1958, Data Processing Technology and Economics, 1976. Served with USMCR, 1944-46. Fellow IEEE; mem. Assn. for Computing Machinery. Republican. Patentee. Home and Office: 414 Camino De Las Animas Santa Fe NM 87501-4535

PHLEGAR, BENJAMIN FOCHT, retired magazine editor; b. Salina, Kans., Nov. 21, 1921; s. Benjamin Gray and Frances Lucile (Focht) P.; m. Jane Fulton, Sept. 19, 1945 (dec. Sept. 1983); children: Janet Margaret, Benjamin Fulton. B.J., U. Mo., 1943. Reporter St. Louis Star-Times, 1943-44; with AP, 1944-63; newsman, then automotive editor AP, Detroit, 1955-63; Detroit bur. chief, asso. editor, then asst. mng. editor U.S. News & World Report, Washington, 1963-78; exec. editor U.S. News & World Report, 1979-85. Mem. Am. Soc. Mag. Editors. Home: 4740 Connecticut Ave NW Washington DC 20008-5632

PHOCAS, GEORGE JOHN, international lawyer, business executive; b. N.Y.C., Dec. 1, 1927; m. Katrin Gorny, Feb. 26, 1966; 1 child, George Alexander. A.B., U. Chgo., 1950, J.D., 1953. Bar: N.Y. 1955, U.S. Supreme Ct. 1962. Assoc. Sullivan & Cromwell, N.Y.C., 1953-56; counsel Creole

Petroleum Corp., Caracas, Venezuela, 1956-60; internat. negotiator Standard Oil Co. N.J. (Exxon), 1960-63; sr. ptnr. Casey, Lane & Mittendorf, London, 1963-72, counsel, 1972-76; exec. v.p. Occidental Petroleumm Corp., Los Angeles, 1972-74; adv., U.S. del. UN, ECAFE, Teheran, 1963. Trustee Assn. Naval Aviation, Washington, Owl's Head Aviation Mus., Maine; mem. vis. bd. U. Chgo. Law Sch.; bd. visitors U. Chgo. Law Sch. Capt. U.S. Army. Mem. ABA, Law Soc. London, Brit. Inst. Comparative Law, Am. Soc. Internat. Law, Assn. Bar City N.Y.; Clubs: Boodles (London), Met. (N.Y.C.). Home: 28 Aubrey Walk, London W87JG, England also: 1605 Middle Gulf Dr Unit 102 Sanibel FL 33957-7601

PHULL, B. S., scientist. Prin. scientist Laque Ctr. for Corrosion Tech., Wrightsville Beach, N.C. Office: Auditorium Cir Hwy 76 Wrightsville Beach NC

PHUNG, NGUYEN DINH, medical educator; b. Ninh Binh, Vietnam, Sept. 25, 1950; came to U.S., 1975; s. Thu Dinh Nguyen and Minh Tuyet Le; m. Thuy Thanh Tran, Sept. 25, 1974; children: The-Ngoc, Khoi-Nguyen, Thien Huong. MD, Saigon Med. Sch., 1973. Diplomate Am. Bd. Internal Medicine, Am. Bd. Allergy and Immunology. Clin. instr. medicine, staff physician U. Okla. Health Scis. Ctr. & Vets. Hosp., Oklahoma City, 1982-84; clin. asst. prof. medicine U. Tex. Med. Sch., Houston, 1989—. Co-author: Practical Allergy & Immunology, 1983; contbr. articles to profl. jours. Mem. ACP, Am. Acad. Allergy and Immunology. Avocations: writing, music. Office: Allergy and Asthma Clinic 2905 Milam St Houston TX 77006-3609

PIACITELLI, JOHN JOSEPH, county official, educator, pediatrician; b. Providence, Sept. 1, 1936; s. Joseph A. and Elsie (Mignacca) P.; m. Carol Ann Keirn, Aug. 19, 1961; 1 child, James. BS, U. R.I., 1958; MA, SUNY, Buffalo, 1963; MD, Creighton U., 1964. Diplomate Am. Bd. Pediatrics. Intern Buffalo Gen. Hosp., 1964-65; pediatric resident Children's Hosp. of Buffalo, 1965-67; pediatrician U.S. Army Hosp., Ft. Polk, La., 1967-69, East Nassau Med. Group, North Babylon, N.Y., 1969-79; dir. Charlotte County Pub. Health Unit, Punta Gorda, Fla., 1980—; asst. clin. instr. SUNY, Buffalo, 1965-67, instr. in clin. pediatrics, L.I., 1972-79, asst. prof. pediatrics, 1979. Contbr. articles to profl. jours. Mem. health adv. com. Charlotte County Sch., 1981—; mem. local planning orgn. adv. com., Charlotte County, Fla., 1986-87; mem. Indigent Health Care Adv. Bd., Charlotte County, 1988—; chmn. Charlotte County AIDS Task Force, 1988-91; chmn. adv. com. Head Start Health Svcs., 1991-94. Maj. U.S. Army, 1967-69. Fellow Am. Acad Pediatrics (cert.), Internat. Coll. Pediatrics; mem. Am. Coll. Physician Execs., Nat. Assn. County and City Health Officials, Fla. Pub. Health Assn., Fla. Assn. County Health Officers, Fla. Med. Assn., Fla. Pediatric Soc., Charlotte County Med. Soc. Office: Charlotte County Pub 514 E Grace St Punta Gorda FL 33950-6121

PIAKER, PHILIP MARTIN, accountant, educator; b. N.Y.C., Oct. 26, 1921; s. Jacob and Sarah (Schloss) P.; m. Pauline Strum, Sept. 22, 1946; children: Susan, Alan, Matthew. BA, CCNY, 1943, MBA, 1949. Lectr. CCNY, 1949-52; asst. prof. acctg. SUNY, Binghamton, 1952-57, assoc. prof., 1957-62, prof., 1962—, Disting. Svc. prof. acctg., 1980—, chmn. dept. acctg., 1970-76, 77-89; chmn. bd. Endicott Rsch. Group, Inc., Johnson City, N.Y., 1983—; adv. dir. Endicott Bank N.Y.; mem. N.Y. State Bd. for Pub. Accountancy, 1973-83, chmn., 1982-83; v.p. Piaker, Lyons, P.C., CPA's; mem. Nat. Bd. to Evaluate CPA Exams., 1979-83; Danforth Seminar on Bus. Morality fellow Harvard U., 1959; Summer Study on Ethics in Bus. fellow U. So. Calif., 1982. Mem. editorial bd. Binghamton Reporter, 1975—. Bd. dirs. Broome chpt. Am. Cancer Soc., 1974-79, Tri-Cities Opera; trustee Temple Israel Binghamton, 1978—. With U.S. Army, 1943-46. SUNY SWANA fellow Jerusalem, 1966, Am. Profs. for Peace in Middle East fellow Jerusalem, 1974; recipient Chancellors award for teaching excellence, 1975, David Ben Gurion award State of Israel, 1979, Outstanding Contbn. to Acctg. award Found. for Acctg., 1979, Outstanding Educator award Found. for Acctg. Rsch., 1986 . Mem. AICPA, N.Y. State Soc. CPA's (pres. Binghamton chpt. 1963-65), Am. Acctg. Assn., Acctg. Rsch. Assn., Nat. Assn. Accts., Bus. Ethics Soc., SUNY Alumni Assn. (Disting. Svc. award 1989), CHABAD (pres. 1989-92). Home: 301 Manchester Rd Vestal NY 13850-3604 also: 7421 Hearth Stone Ave Boynton Beach FL 33437

PIAN, RULAN CHAO, musicologist, scholar; b. Cambridge, Mass., Apr. 20, 1922; d. Yuen Ren and Buwei (Yang) Chao; m. Theodore Hsueh-huang Pian, Oct. 3, 1945; 1 child, Canta Chao-po. BA, Radcliffe Coll., 1944, MA, 1946, PhD, 1960. Teaching asst., instr. in modern Chinese Harvard U., 1947-60, lectr. Chinese and Chinese music, 1961-74, prof. Ea. Asian langs. and civilizations, prof. music, 1974-92; prof. emerita, 1992—; coordinator modern Chinese lang. instrn. Harvard U., 1962-68, mem. council E. Asian studies, 1975-92, faculty mem. Com. on Degrees in Folklore and Mythology, 1976-92, master of South House, 1975-78; vis. prof. dept. music The Chinese U. Hong Kong, 1975, 78-79, 82, 94, inst. humanities Nat. Tsing Hua U., Taiwan, 1990, Sch. Humanities, Nat. Cen. U., Taiwan, 1992; hon. prof. Cen. China U. of Sci. and Tech., Wuhan, 1990, Chengdu, China, 1994; hon. rsch. fellow Shanghai Conservatory Music, China, 1991, Inst. Music Rsch., China Acad. of Arts, Beijing, 1997; academician Academia Sinica, Taiwan, 1990. Author: A Syllabus for the Mandarin Primer, 1961, Sonq Dynasty Musical Sources and Their Interpretation, 1967; compiler: Complete Musical Works of Yuen Ren Chao, 1987; contbr. articles to scholarly jours. Recipient Caroline Wilby dissertation prize Radcliffe Coll., 1960, Radcliffe Grad. Soc. medal, 1980; NDEA Fulbright-Hayes research grantee Chinese Music Taiwan, 1964; NEH grantee Hong Kong, 1978-79. Mem. Am. Musicological Soc. (coun. 1993—, Otto Kinkeldey book award 1968), Internat. Musicological Soc., Soc. Ethnomusicology (coun. 1968-75, 87-90), Conf. Chinese Oral and Performing Lit. (co-founder, pres. 1983-90, permanent hon. pres. 1995—), Assn. for Chinese Mus. Rsch. (co-founder). Home: 14 Brattle Cir Cambridge MA 02138-4625 Office: 2 Divinity Ave Cambridge MA 02138-2020

PIAN, THEODORE HSUEH-HUANG, engineering educator, consultant; b. Shanghai, China, Jan. 18, 1919; came to U.S., 1943; s. Chao-Hsin Shu-Cheng and Chih-Chuan (Yen) P.; m. Rulan Chao, Oct. 3, 1945; 1 child, Canta Chao-Po. B in Engring., Tsing Hua U., Kunming, China, 1940; MS, MIT, 1944, DSc, 1948; DSc (hon.), Beijing U. Aeros. and Astronautics, 1990; PhD (hon.), Shanghai U., 1991. Engr. Cen. Aircraft Mfg. Co., Loiwing, China, 1940-42, Chengtu Glider Mfg. Factory, 1942-43; tchg. asst. MIT, Cambridge, 1946-47, rsch. assoc., 1947-52, asst. prof., 1952-59, assoc. prof., 1959-66, prof., 1966-89, prof. emeritus, 1989—; vis. assoc. Calif. Inst. Tech., Pasadena, 1965-66; vis. prof. U. Tokyo, 1974, Tech. U., Berlin, 1975; vis. chair prof. Nat. Tsing Hua U., Hsin Chu, Taiwan, 1990, Nat. Ctrl. U., ChungLi, Taiwan, 1992; hon. prof. Beijing U. Aero. and Astronautics, Beijing Inst. Tech., Southwestern Jaiotong U., Dalian U. Tech., Huazhong U. Sci. and Tech., Changsha Rwy. U., Ctrl.-South U. Tech., Hohai U., Nanjing U. of Aero. and Astronautics, Dalian Rwy. U., Shashi U. Recipient von Karman Meml. prize TRE Corp., Beverly Hills, Calif., 1974. Fellow AAAS, AIAA (assoc. editor jour. 1973-75, Structures, Structural Dynamics and Materials award 1975), U.S. Assn. Computational Mechanics (founding mem.); mem. ASME (hon.), Nat. Acad. Engring., Am. Soc. Engring. Edn., Internat. Assn. for Computational Mechanics (hon. mem. gen. coun.). Home: 14 Brattle Cir Cambridge MA 02138-4625 Office: MIT Dept Aeronautics and Astronautics 77 Massachusetts Ave Cambridge MA 02139-4301

PIANKO, THEODORE A., lawyer; b. Dennville, N.J., Sept. 5, 1955; s. Theodore and Pasqualina (Liguori) P.; m. Beatriz Maria Olivera (div. Dec. 1985); m. Kathryn Anne Lindley, Feb. 18, 1990; children: Matthew James, Samuel Wahoo, Zoe Wahoo. BA, SUNY, 1975; JD, U. Mich., 1978. Bar: Mich. 1978, Ill. 1979, Calif. 1980. Atty. Ford Motor Co., Dearborn, Mich., 1978-80; assoc. Lillick McHose & Charles, L.A., 1980-83; ptnr. Sidley & Austin, L.A., 1983-94, Christie, Parker & Hale, Pasadena, Calif., 1994—. Office: Christie Parker & Hale 350 Colorado Blvd Fl 5 Pasadena CA 91109-7068

PIANTINI, CARLOS, conductor; b. Santo Domingo, Dominican Republic, May 9, 1927; s. Alberto and Marina (Espinal) P.; m. Marianne Piantini (div. 1977); children: Susan, Vivian, Albert, Frank; m. Yolanda Trujillo, Dec. 5, 1982. MusB, NYU, 1968. Violinist 1st Recital, Santo Domingo, 1937-44, Mex. Symphony, 1944-47, Juilliard Sch., N.Y.C., 1947-50, N.Y. Philharm. Orch., N.Y.C., 1956-71; condr. Vienna (Austria) Acad. Music, 1971-73; artistic dir. Nat. Theatre, Santo Domingo, 1973-78; condr. Caracas (Venezuela) Philharm., 1979-83, Nat. Symphonic Orch., Santo Domingo, 1983—; Domican amb. to UN; head cultural affairs Dominican Rep. Govt., 1950-56. Contbr. articles to profl. jours. Cons. V Centennial Commemorative, Santo Domingo, 1988. Avocation: stamp collecting. Office: Nat Symphonic Orch, Palacio de Bellas Artes, Santo Domingo Dominican Republic Address: c/o Warden asso Inc 5626 Deer Run Rd Doylestown PA 18901

PIASECKA JOHNSON, BARBARA, philanthropist, art historian and collector, business investor; b. Staniewicze, Poland; d. Pelagia and Wojciech Piasecki; m. J. Seward Johnson (dec.). Chair., dir. trustee Barbara Piasecka Johnson Found., 1974—; owner extensive art collection, Barbara Piasecka Johnson Collection; mem. bd. mgrs. Wistar Inst., Phila., 1989-91; mem. chmn.'s coun. Met. Mus. Art, N.Y.C., 1986; mem. adv. com. Nat. Gallery Art, Washington, 1980-91; bd. dirs. Inst. for Polish-Jewish Studies, Oxford, Eng.; mem. fine arts com. U.S. Dept. State, 1978-85; mem. strategic adv. com. dept. molecular genetics and microbiology Robert Wood Johnson Med. Sch., U. Medicine and Dentistry N.J. Trustee, bd. dirs. Atlantic Found., 1972-85, Harbor Br. Found., 1972-85; trustee, chair Paderewski Ctr.; mem. coun. Found. for U. Wroclaw, 1991-92. Recipient Heritage award Polish Am. Congress, 1989, Nat. Citizen of Yr. award Am-Pol Eagle, 1989, Disting. Svc. award Am. Coun. for Polish Culture, 1990, Award St. Brother Albert Chmielowski, 1990, Hon. Citizen award State of Calif., 1990, Appreciation diploma Min. Fgn. Affairs Republic Poland, 1991, Gold medal U. Wroclaw, 1991, Sci. Devel. award Acad. Agriculture Wroclaw, 1991, Crystal Heart award Found. for Devel. Cardiac Surgery Zabrze, 1992, Merit cert. Pres. Coun. N.Y.C., 1993, Champion of Democracy award Coll. Democracy Washington, 1993, Waclaw Nizynski medal Polish Artists Agy, 1994, Living Legacy award Women's Internat. Ctr., 1994, The Order of Saint Charles Officer decoration conferred by H.S.H. Prince Rainier III in recognition of svcs. rendered to the Principality of Monaco, 1995. Mem. Am. Assn. for Polish-Jewish Studies (hon. chmn.), Rotary Internat. (Paul Harris fellow 1988).

PIASSICK, JOEL BERNARD, lawyer; b. Atlanta, June 2, 1940; s. Louis S. and Sarah (Freeman) P.; m. Karen Pevow, Aug. 11, 1963; children: Joan, Louis. BA in Polit. Sci., Tulane U., 1962; LLB, U. Va., 1965. Bar: Va. 1965, Ga. 1966. Ptnr. Smith, Gambrell & Russell, Atlanta, 1967-90, Kilpatrick Stockton LLP, Atlanta, 1990—; bd. dirs. Southeastern Bankruptcy Law Inst., Inc. Fellow Am. Coll. Bankruptcy. Office: Kilpatrick Stockton LLP 1100 Peachtree St NE Ste 2800 Atlanta GA 30309-4528

PIATIGORSKY, JORAM PAUL, research scientist, molecular biologist; b. Elizabethtown, N.Y., Feb. 4, 1940; s. Gregor and Jacqueline (de Rothschild) P.; m. Lona Anne Shepley, Aug. 24, 1969; children: Auran Paul, Anton Jacob. AB cum laude, Harvard U., 1962; PhD, Calif. Inst. Tech., 1967. Commd. officer USPHS, 1967; postdoctoral fellow Nat. Inst. Neurol. Diseases and Stroke, NIH, Bethesda, Md., 1967-69; sr. staff fellow devel. biology br. Nat. Inst. Child Health and Human Devel., NIH, Bethesda, 1969-72, sr. staff fellow Lab. Molecular Genetics, 1972-74, biologist Lab. Molecular Genetics, 1974-76, head sect. cellular differentiation Lab. Molecular Genetics, 1976-81; chief Lab. Molecular and Devel. Biology Nat. Eye Inst., NIH, Bethesda, 1981—; ad hoc mem. cell biology study sect. NIH, 1973, ad hoc mem. visual scis. A study sect., 1977, mem. com. on convent utilization, 1983, mem. panel for rsch. strategies for primary openangle glaucoma, 1988, mem. panel for rsch. strategies for cornea, 1988; chmn. dept. biology and genetics Found. Advanced Edn. In Scis., Inc., Bethesda, 1974-87, bd. dirs., 1977-80; mem. panel nat. five yr. plan for cataract rsch. Nat. Eye Inst., NIH, Bethesda, 1980-81, mem. evaluation and update com., 1985; mem. adv. panel Fogarty Scholars-in-Residence, 1983-87; mem. sci. adv. bd. Nat. Retinitis Pigmentosa Found., 1985-88; Futterman Meml. lectr. U. Wash., 1986; vis. prof. Peking Union Med. Coll. Hosp., Chinese Acad. Med. Scis., Beijing, 1987; mem. sci. adv. com. for ophthalmology Mass. Eye and Ear Infirmary, Harvard U. Med. Sch., Boston, 1987, mem. rsch. vis. com., 1994-95; Tenth Ann. Basic Neurochemistry lectr. Am. Soc. Neurochemistry, 1988; mem. sci. adv. bd. Whitney Marine Biology Lab., U. Fla., 1988-92, trustee, 1993—; mem. search com. for lab. chief Nat. Dental Inst., 1989; mem. search com. for lab. chief Nat. Inst. Aging/NIH, 1989; Donald P. Abbott Meml. seminar Hopkins Marine Sta., Stanford (Calif.) U., 1992; Welcome lectr. and vis. prof. U. Louisville, 1992; Seventh Robert R. Kohn Meml. lectr. Case Western Res. U., 1993; 12th Frederick H. Verhoeff lectr. Am. Ophthal. Soc., 1993; mem. search com. for dir. Nat. Inst. Neurol. Diseases and Stroke/NIH, Bethesda, 1993-94; mem. awards com. Alcon Rsch. Inst., Ft. Worth, 1993—; co-leader Devel. Biology Interest Group/NIH, 1994—; mem. basic scis. rev. panel March of Dimes, 1994—; chairperson tenure track com. Nat. Inst. Child Health Devel., 1995; mem. sci. adv. bd. Schepens Eye Rsch. Inst., Boston, 1995—; Fifth V. Everett Kinsey lectr. Ophthalmic Biochemistry Conf., Oakland U., 1995; organizer, co-organizer symposia in field; invited spkr. numerous lectures in field. Editor: Molecular Biology of the Eye: Genes, Vision and Ocular Disease, 1988; exec. editor Experimental Eye Rsch., 1976-92; editor Lens Rsch., 1982-88, Molecular Biology Reports, 1985-91, GENE, 1988-93, Investigative Ophthalmology and Visual Sci., 1992-94, Jour. Biol. Chemistry, 1997—; contbr. numerous abstracts and articles to profl. jours. Recipient Alcon Rsch. Inst. award, 1985, 91, First Hans Bloemendal Lecture award Nijmegen, The Netherlands, 1988. Fellow AAAS; mem. Am. Soc. Cell Biology, Am. Soc. Zoologists, Internat. Soc. Devel. Biology, Internat. Soc. Eye Rsch., Assn. Rsch. in Vision and Ophthalmology (mem. program com. biochemistry sect. 1979-81, chmn. 1981, trustee 1986-90, v.p. 1990-91, mem. awards com. 1987-90, Friedenwald award 1986, Spl. Recognition award 1992), N.Y. Acad. Scis., Sigma Xi. Office: Nat Eye Inst/NIH Lab Molecular & Devel Biology 6 Center Dr, Bldg 6 Rm 201 Bethesda MD 20892

PIATT, JACK BOYD, manufacturing executive; b. Washington, Pa., Jan. 8, 1928; s. Harold Boyd and Violet Marie (Amos) P.; m. Thelma Jean Ritchie, Mar. 15, 1948 (div. 1974); children: Jack Boyd, Rod L., Rebecca, Regina; m. Kathleen Mary Shattuck, May 4, 1975. Student schs. Washington, Pa. Chmn. Millcraft Industries, Washington, Pa., 1957—; bd. dirs. Pitts. br. Fed. Res. Bank Cleve. Pres., bd. dirs. Meadowcroft Found., Avella, Pa.; bd. dirs. Southeastern Found., Miami, Fla., 1983-84. Recipient Disting. Svc. award Greater Washington Area Jaycees, 1980; named Tri-State Entrepreneur of Yr. Arthur Young and INC. mag., 1989. Mem. Am. Iron and Steel Inst., Eastern States Blast Furnace Assn., Assn. Iron and Steel Engrs., Duquesne Club (Pitts.) Republican. Home: PO Box 396 Meadow Lands PA 15347-0396 Office: Millcraft Industries 90 W Chestnut St Washington PA 15301-4524

PIATT, MALCOLM KEITH, JR., medical center administrator; b. Santa Fe, N.Mex., Nov. 12, 1955; s. Malcolm Keith Sr. and Delia Catherine (Ferran) P.; m. Janice Phillips, Dec. 27, 1981; children: Michael, JEnnifer Lauren, Kara Lynn. BS, U. N.Mex, 1978, MD, 1985. Diplomate Am. Bd. Internal Medicine. Resident physician Good Samaritan Med. Ctr., Phoenix, 1985-88, chief medicine resident, 1988-89; staff physician VA Med. Ctr., Phoenix, 1989-95, assoc. chief staff ambulatory care svcs., 1995—; dir. Immunodeficiency Clinic, VA Med. Ctr., Phoenix, 1990—. Fellow ACP. Avocations: photography, hiking. Office: VA Med Ctr 650 E Indian School Rd Phoenix AZ 85012-1839

PIAZZA, MARGUERITE, opera singer, actress, entertainer; b. New Orleans, May 6, 1926; d. Albert William and Michaela (Piazza) Luft; m. William J. Condon, July 15, 1953 (dec. Mar. 1968); children: Gregory, James (dec.), Shirley, William J., Marguerite P., Anna Becky; m. Francis Harrison Bergtholdt, Nov. 8, 1970. MusB, Loyola U., New Orleans; MusM, La. State U.; MusD (hon.), Christian Bros. Coll., 1973; LHD honoris causa, Loyola U., Chgo., 1975. Singer N.Y.C. Ctr. Opera, 1948, Met. Opera Co., 1950; TV artist, regular singing star Your Show of Shows NBC, 1950-54; entertainer various supper clubs Cotillion Room, Hotel Pierre, N.Y.C., 1954, Las Vegas, Los Angeles, New Orleans, San Francisco, 1956—; ptnr. Sound Express Music Pub. Co., Memphis, 1987—; bd. dirs. Cemrel, Inc. Appeared as guest performer on numerous mus. TV shows. Nat. crusade chmn. Am. Cancer Soc., 1971; founder, bd. dirs. Marguerite Piazza Gala for the Benefit of St. Jude's Hosp., 1976; bd. dirs. Memphis Opera Co., World Literacy Found., NCCJ; v.p., life bd. dirs. Memphis Symphony Orch.; nat. chmn. Soc. for Cure Epilepsy. Decorated Mil. and Hospittaler Order of St. Lazarus of Jerusalem; recipient svc. award Chgo. Heart Assn., 1956, svc. award Fedn. Jewish Philanthropies of N.Y., 1956, Sesquicentennial medal Carnegie Hall, St. Martin De Porres award So. Dominicans, 1994; named Queen of Memphis, Memphis Cotton Carnival, 1973, Person of Yr., La. Coun. for Performing Arts, 1975, Woman of Yr., Nat. Am. Legion, Woman of Yr., Italian-Am. Soc. Mem. Nat. Speakers Assn., Woman's Exchange, Memphis Country Club, Memphis Hunt and Polo Club, New Orleans Country Club, Summit Club, Beta Sigma Omicron, Phi Beta. Roman Catholic. Home: #301 Park Pl 5400 Park Ave Apt 301 Memphis TN 38119-3639

PIAZZA, MICHAEL JOSEPH, professional baseball player; b. Norristown, Pa., Sept. 4, 1968. Student, Miami (Fla.)-Dade C.C. Player L.A. Dodgers, 1988—; mem. Nat. League All-Star Team, 1993-96. Named Nat. League Rookie Player of Yr., Sporting News, 1993, Catcher on the Sporting News N.L. All-Star Team, 1993-96, N.L. Silver Slugger Team, 1993-94, named to Nat. League Slugger Team, 1993; named Nat. League Rookie of Yr., Baseball Writers Assn., 1993. Office: LA Dodgers Dodger Stadium 100 Elysian Park Ave Los Angeles CA 90012*

PICARD, DENNIS J., electronics company executive; b. 1932. BBA, Northeastern Univ., 1962. With RCA, 1954-55; elec. engr. Raytheon Co., 1955-59, design engr., 1959-61, sect. mgr., 1961-69, dir. equipment div., data acquisition systems directorate, 1969-76, asst. gen. mgr. ops., equipment div., 1976-77, asst. gen. mgr. ops., equipment div., also corp. v.p., 1977-81, v.p. equipment div., 1981-1985, sr. v.p., gen. mgr. missile systems div., 1985-89, pres., 1989-90, chmn. bd., CEO, 1990—, also bd. dirs. Served USAF 1951-53. Mem. NAE. Office: Raytheon Co 141 Spring St Lexington MA 02173-7860*

PICARD, LAURENT A(UGUSTIN), management educator, administrator, consultant; b. Quebec, Que., Can., Oct. 27, 1927; s. Edouard and Alice (Gingras) P.; m. Therese Picard; children: Andre, Marc, Robert (dec.), Denys, Jean-Louis, François (dec.). BA, Laval U., Quebec, 1947, BS, 1954; DBA, Harvard U., 1964. Prof. U. Montreal, Que., Can., 1962-68, dir. bus. adminstrn. dept., 1964-68; exec. v.p. Can. Broadcasting Corp., Ottawa, Ont., 1968-72, pres., chief exec. officer, 1972-75; joint prof. McGill U. and U. Montreal, 1977-78; dean faculty mgmt. McGill U., Montreal, 1978-86, prof., 1986—; mem. Royal Commn. on Newspapers, Royal Commn. on Econ. Union and Devel. Prospects for Can.; conciliation commr. Maritime Employers Assn., Prot of Montreal; bd. dirs. Lombard-Odier Trust Co., Jean Coutu Group, Dorel Ind. Inc.; cons. to industry; guest speaker at internat. meetings. Contbr. articles to profl. jours. Chmn. Nat. Book Festival, 1978-79; chmn. jury Prix Gerin Lajoie, Ministry Cultural Affairs, 1982. Recipient 125th Anniversary medal Can., 1992; decorated companion Order of Can., 1977. Mem. Commonwealth Broadcasting Assn. (1st pres.). Home: 5602 Wilderton Ave, Montreal, PQ Canada H3T 1R9 Office: McGill U Faculty Mgmt, 1001 Sherbrooke St W, Montreal, PQ Canada H3A 1G5

PICCILLO, JOSEPH, artist; b. Buffalo, Jan. 9, 1941. B.S., Buffalo State U., 1961, M.S., 1964. Faculty Buffalo State U. Coll., 1967—, prof. art edn., 1980—. One-man shows include Banfer Gallery, N.Y.C., 1966, 68, 70, Krasner Gallery, N.Y.C., 1971-79, Housitanic (Conn.) Mus., 1977, Galerie Loyse Oppenheim, Geneva, 1978, 79, Monique Knowlton Gallery, N.Y.C., 1980, 81, 83, 84, Betsy Rosenfeld Gallery, Chgo., 1980, 83, 85, 87, 89, 91, 94, Albright-Knox Art Gallery, Buffalo, 1981, Galleria Forni, Bologna, Italy, 1983, Barbara Fendrick Gallery, N.Y.C., 1988, Brendan Walter Gallery, Santa Monica, Calif., 1990, 92, Fay Gold Gallery, Atlanta, 1994, Monique Knowlton Gallery, N.Y.C., 1995; group shows include Fischer Fine Arts Ltd., London, 1977, 78, Galierie Isy Brachot, Brussels, 1977, Art 9'78, Basle, Switzerland, 1978, 79; represented in permanent collections, Mus. Modern Art, N.Y.C., Chgo. Art Inst., Albright-Knox Gallery, Bklyn. Mus., Rochester (N.Y.) Meml. Art Center, Minn. Mus. Art, Mpls., Little Rock Mus., Met. Mus. Art, N.Y.C., Butler Mus. Art, Youngstown, Ohio, San Francisco Mus. Modern Art, Ball State U., Muncie, Ind., So. Ill. U., Carbondale, SUNY, Buffalo, Fredonia, Alfred (N.Y.) U., St. Lawrence U., Canton, N.Y., Kutztown (Pa.) State Coll., Hamline U., St. Paul, 1st Nat. Bank Chgo., others; panelist, Visual Arts Panel, N.Y. State Council on Arts, 1976-78. SUNY fellow, 1968, 69, 72, 76, 79, 80; Creative Artists Pub. Service Program grantee, 1972, grantee Nat. Endowment Arts fellow, 1979. Home: 461 West Ave Buffalo NY 14213-2501

PICCININI, ROBERT M., grocery store chain executive. CEO, chmn. Save Mart Supermarkets, Modesto, Calif. Office: Save Mart Supermarkets 1800 Standiford Ave Modesto CA 95350-0180*

PICCININO, ROCCO MICHAEL, librarian; b. Phila., Aug. 21, 1949; s. Rocco Anthony and Ida Marie (Minicozzi) P. BA in History magna cum laude, LaSalle Coll., 1971; postgrad., U. N.C., 1971-73; MSLS, Drexel U., 1981. Ednl. resources specialist C.C. of Phila., 1973-74; asst./assoc. libr. United Engrs. & Constructors Inc. (A Raytheon Co.) Libr., Phila., 1974-81; head libr. United Engrs. & Constructors Inc. (A Raytheon Co.) Libr., Boston, 1981-84; asst/assoc. dir. Wentworth Inst. of Tech. Libr., Boston, 1984-89; sci. libr. Smith Coll. Librs., Northampton, Mass., 1989-91, coord. br. and media svcs., sci. libr., 1991—. Mem. ALA (Assn. Coll. Rsch. Librs. divsn., Libr. Adminstrn. and Mgmt. Assn. divsn., Libr. and Info. Tech. Assn. divsn), Spl. Librs. Assn. (sci.-tech. divsn. Boston chpt., chair Western Outreach), Beta Phi Mu. Democrat. Roman Catholic. Avocations: travel, biking, reading, films. Home: 104 Woods Rd Northampton MA 01060-3507 Office: Smith Coll Young Sci Libr Northampton MA 01063

PICCOLO, JOSEPH ANTHONY, hospital administrator; b. Phila., Aug. 1, 1953; s. Rudolph and Mary C. (Mellela) P.; m. Elizabeth J. Mullarkey, Mar. 24, 1984; children: Mary E., Sarah C., Theresa N. BA, U. Pa., 1975; MBA, LaSalle U., 1992. Mgr. health sci. store U. Pa., Phila., 1973-76; mgr. univ. store Hahnemann U., Phila., 1976-86, adminstr., clin. sr. instr. dept. pathology/lab. medicine, 1986-94; assoc. adminstr. Fox Chase Cancer Ctr., Phila., 1994—; v.p. Hahnemann Found. Pathology, Phila., 1986-94. Author: (with others): Health Science Store Manual, 1985. Bd. dirs. Big Sisters of Phila., 1996—. Mem. Med. Group Mgmt. Assn., Am. Mgmt. Assn., Healthcare Fin. Mgmt. Assn., Hahnemann Pathology Assocs., Inc. (v.p., treas. 1986-94), Big Sisters of Phila. Inc. (bd. dirs., 1996—). Avocations: golf, music, reading, boating. Office: Fox Chase Cancer Ctr 7701 Burholme Ave Philadelphia PA 19111-2412

PICCOLO, RICHARD ANDREW, artist, educator; b. Hartford, Conn., Sept. 17, 1943; S. John D. and Lenore (Pasqual) P. BID, Pratt Inst., 1966; MFA, Bklyn. Coll., 1968. Instr. Pratt Inst., Bklyn., 1966-68, Rome, 1969—; dir. Pratt Inst., 1980—; instr. U. Notre Dame Rome Program, 1984—. Artist: solo exhibitions include: Robert Schoelkopf Gallery, N.Y.C., 1975, 79, 83, 89, Suffolk C.C., Long Island, N.Y., 1976, Am. Acad. in Rome, 1977, Galleria Temple, Rome 1979, Galleria Il Gabbiano, Rome. 1985, Contemporary Realist Gallery, San Francisco, 1989, 95; exhibited in group shows Six Americans in Italy, 1973, Metaphor in Painting, Fed. Hall Meml., N.Y., 1978, Realism and Metaphor, U. S. Fla. (traveling), 1980, Contemporary Figure Drawings, Robert Schoelkopf Gallery, 1981, Contemporary Arcadian Painting, 1982, Moravian Coll. Invitational, Bethlehem, Pa., 1981, Art on Paper , Weatherspoon Gallery of Art, N.C., 1981, Out of N.Y., Hamilton Coll., Clinton, N.Y., 1981, Galleria Gabbiano, Rome, FIAC, Paris, 1982, Contemporary Arts Mus., Houston, 1984, Umbria: Americans Painting in Italy, Gallery North, Setauket, N.Y., 1985, Storytellers, Contemporary Realist Gallery, San Francisco, Painted from Life, Bayly Mus., Charlottesville, Va., 1987; work in permanent collections Crown Am. Corp., Johnstown, Pa., Grosvenor Internat., Sacramento, Calif., Mrs. Lillian Cole, Sherman Oaks, Calif., Mr and Mrs. Robert Emery, San Francisco, Mr. Graham Gund, Boston, Dr. Robert Gutterman, San Francisco, Mr and Mrs. Joseph Jennings, San Francisco, Dr. and Mrs. Donald Innes, Jr., Charlottesville, Va., Mr. and Mrs. Alan Ovson, San Francisco, Mr. Frank Pasquerilla, Johnstown, Pa., Mr. Jon Roberts and Mr. John Boccardo, L.A. Recipient E. A. Abbey Meml. scholarship for mural painting, 1973-75; grantee NEA, 1989; mural commn. Simplicity Inspiring Invention: An Allegory of the Arts, Crown Am. Corp., Johnstown, Pa., 1989, Aer, Ignis, Terra, Aqua, U.S. Bank Plaz., Sacramento, Calif., 1991-94. Home: Piazza S Apollonia 3, Rome 00153, Italy Office: Hacket-Freedman Gallery 250 Sutter St Fl 4 San Francisco CA 94108-4451

PICHAL, HENRI THOMAS, electronics engineer, physicist, consultant; b. London, Feb. 14, 1923; came to the U.S., 1957; s. Henri and Mary (Conway) P.; m. Vida Eloise Collum Jones, Mar. 7, 1966; children: Chris C., Henri T. III, Thomas William Billingsley. MSc in Engring., U. London, 1953, PhD in Physics, 1955. Registered profl. engr., Wash., Fla. Product engr. John Fluke Mfg. Corp., Everett, Wash., 1970-73; engring. specialist Harris Corp., Melbourne, Fla., 1973-75; pres., prin. Profl. Engring. Co., Inc., Kissimmee, Fla., 1975-91. Contbr. articles to Electronics, Microwaves, and others. Named one of Two Thousand Men Achievement, 1972. Mem. Inst. Physics, Am. Phys. Soc., Fla. Engring. Soc. (sr.), Inst. Environ. Scis. (sr.), IEEE (past chmn. microwave theory and techniques communications systems), Aerospace/Navigational Electronics, Space Electronics and Telemetry, Mil. Electronics. Republican. Achievements include 69 patents in microwave RF, high frequency and high speed analog ultra linear technology, large dynamic range performance and intermodulation phenomena, noise, and congested area systems problems. Home: PO Box 969 Kingston WA 98346-0969

PICHETTE, CLAUDE, former banking executive, university rector, research executive; b. Sherbrooke, Que., Can., June 13, 1936; s. Donat and Juliette (Morin) P.; m. Renée Provencher, Sept. 5, 1959 (dec. 1994); children: Anne-Marie, Martin, Philippe. B.A., U. Sherbrooke, 1956; M.Sc.Soc. (Econ.), U. Laval, 1960; Doct. d'Etat es Sc. Econ, U. D'Aix-Marseille, France, 1970. Prof. U. Sherbrooke, 1960-70; civil servant Govt. Que., 1970-75; vice rector adminstrn. and fins. U. Que., Montreal, 1975-77; rector U. Que., 1977-86; pres., chief exec. officer La Financière prêts-épargne, 1986-90, La Financière Entraide-Cooperants (holding co.), 1987-90; pres. Que. Found. Econ. Edn., 1979-81; CEO Institut Armand-Frappier Rsch. Inst.; chmn. bd. La Financière Entraide-Cooperants (holding co.), 1987-90; pres. Que. Found. Econ. Edn., 1979-81; CEO Institut Armand-Frappier Rsch. Inst.; chmn. bd. La Financière Credit-Bail, 1989-90; bd. dirs. Shermag, Rona-Dismat, Montreal Stock Exch. Author: Analyse micro-economique et cooperative, 1972. Can. Council grantee, 1958; Federation nationale des cooperatives de consommation de France grantee, 1973. Mem. Que. Assn. Econs. (pres. 1977-78). Club: St.-Denis (Montreal). Home: 745 Hartland, Outremont, PQ Canada H2V 2X5 Office: Armand-Frappier Institute, 531 Blvd des Prairies, Laval, PQ Canada H7N 4Z3

PICHLER, JOSEPH ANTON, food products executive; b. St. Louis, Oct. 3, 1939; s. Anton Dominick and Anita Marie (Hughes) P.; m. Susan Ellen Eyerly, Dec. 27, 1962; children: Gretchen, Christopher, Rebecca, Josh. BBA, U. Notre Dame, 1961; MBA, U. Chgo., 1963, PhD, 1966. Asst. prof. bus. U. Kans., 1964-68, assoc. prof., 1968-73, prof., 1973-80; dean U. Kans. (Sch. Bus.), 1974-80; exec. v.p. Dillon Cos. Inc., 1980-82, pres., 1982-86; exec. v.p. Kroger Co., 1985-86, pres., COO, 1986—, also bd. dirs., 1986-90, pres., CEO, 1990, chmn., CEO, 1990—, also dir.; spl. asst. to asst. sec. for manpower U.S. Dept. Labor, 1968-70; chmn. Kans. Manpower Svcs. Coun., 1974-78; bd. dirs. B.F. Goodrich Co., Cin. Milacron Inc.; indsl. cons. Author: (with Joseph McGuire) Inequality: The Poor and the Rich in America, 1969; contbg. author: Creativity and Innovation in Manpower Research and Action Programs, 1970, Contemporary Management: Issues and Viewpoints, 1973, Institutional Issues in Public Accounting, 1974, Co-Creation and Capitalism: John Paul II's Laborem Exercens, 1983; Co-editor, contbg. author: Ethics, Free Enterprise, and Public Policy, 1978; Contbr. articles to profl. jours. Bd. dirs. Kans. Charities, 1973-75, Benedictine Coll., Atchison, Kans., 1979-83, Cin. Opera; nat. bd. dirs. Boys Hope, 1983—, Tougaloo Coll., 1986—; chmn. nat. bd. Nat. Alliance of Bus. Recipient Performance award U.S. Dept. Labor Manpower Adminstrn., 1969, Disting. Svc. citation U. Kans., 1992; Woodrow Wilson fellow, Ford Found. fellow, Standard Oil Indsl. Rels. fellow, 1966, Woodrow Wilson fellow adv. com., 1990-93; named Disting. Alumnus U. Chgo., 1994. Mem. Bus. Roundtable, Queen City Club, Comml. Club of Cin. Office: Kroger Co 1014 Vine St Cincinnati OH 45202-1141

PICHOIS, CLAUDE P., classical studies educator; b. Paris, July 21, 1925; s. Léon and Renée (Bardou) P.; m. Vincenette Rey, Oct. 26, 1961. D ès L, U. Paris, 1963; D (hon.), U. Neuchâtel, Switzerland, 1983, Trinity Coll., Dublin, Ireland, 1984. Asst. prof. U. Aix-en-Provence, France, 1958-61; prof. U., Basel, Switzerland, 1961-70; vis. rsch. prof. U. Wis., Madison, 1968; prof. Vanderbilt U., Nashville, 1970-73, disting. prof., 1973—; prof. Sorbonne Nouvelle, Paris, 1979-84; bd. dirs. W.T. Bandy Ctr. for Baudelaire Studies, Vanderbilt U., Nashville, Centre de recherches Nerval/Baudelaire, Namur, Belgium, Paris. Author: L'Image de Jean-Paul Richter dans les Lettres Francaise, 1963, Ph. Chasles et la vie littéraire au temps du Romantisme, 1965, Baudelaire, 1987, 96, Gérard de Nerval, 1995, Auguste Poulet-Malassis, 1996; editor: Baudelaire, Complete Works, 1975-76, Baudelaire, Correspondence, 1973, 93, Nerval, Complete Works, 1984, 89, 93, Colette, Works, 1984, 86, 91, Litérature Francaise (16 vols.), 1968-79. Recipient Prix de la critique Académie Française; Guggenheim fellow, 1978. Mem. MLA (hon.), Société Hist. litt. de la France (v.p.), Société Etudes Romantiques, Nineteenth-Century French Studies (bd. dirs.), Lettres Romanes, Bull. Baudelairien, Année Baudelaire. Avocation: bibliophilia. Office: Vanderbilt U Station B Nashville TN 37235

PICIRILLI, ROBERT EUGENE, clergyman, college dean, writer; b. High Point, N.C., Oct. 6, 1932; s. Eugene and Lena (Harrell) P.; m. Clara Mae Lee, June 14, 1953; children: Annina Jean, Myra Jane, Mary June, Celina Joy, Roberta Jill. B.A., Free Will Bapt. Bible Coll., Nashville, 1953; M.A., Bob Jones U., 1955, Ph.D., 1963, D.D., 1967. Ordained to ministry Free Will Bapt. Ch., 1952; grad. asst. Bob Jones U., 1954-55; prof. N.T., Free Will Bapt. Bible Coll., 1955—, registrar, 1960-79, dean, 1979—, dean grad. sch., 1982-86; clk. Nat. Assn. Free Will Baptists, 1961-65, moderator, 1966-71, treas. hist. commn., 1974—, mem. bd. of retirement and ins., 1978-89, sec., 1979-89; mem. testing com. Am. Assn. Bible Colls., 1959-72, research commn., 1982-91, chmn., 1989-91; sec.-treas. So. region Evang. Theol. Soc., 1964-68, vice chmn., 1972-73, 84-85 chmn., 1973-74, 85-86. Author: Paul, the Apostle, 1986, 1, 2 Corinthians, 1987, Ephesians & Philippians, 1988, 1, 2 Thessalonians, 1990, 1, 2 Peter, 1992; co-author: The NKJV Greek English Interlinear New Testament, 1993. Pres. Ransom Elementary Sch. P.T.A., 1965-67. Fellow Inst. for Bibl. Rsch.; mem. AAHE, Am. Assn. Bible Colls. (v.p. 1992-94, pres. 1994-96), Nashville Philatelic Soc. (treas. 1980-81, 92—, pres. 1981-82, 1st v.p. 1982-88), Delta Epsilon Chi. Home: 301 Greenway Ave Nashville TN 37205-2307

PICK, ARTHUR JOSEPH, JR., chamber of commerce executive; b. Louisville, Mar. 22, 1931. BS, U. Calif., Riverside, 1959; grad., Coro Found., L.A., 1960; MA in Urban Studies, Occidental Coll., 1969. Pres. Greater Riverside C. of C., 1972—. Mem. Riverside Monday Morning Group, 1978—, pres., 1993-95; pres. Riverside Symphony Orch. Soc., 1966-69; elected Riverside City Coun., 1967, 71; founder Friends of Calif. Bapt. Coll., 1978; trustee La Sierra U., 1992—, Riverside C.C., 1997—; mem. Calif.-Nev. Super Speed Train Commn., 1992-97; treas. Calif. State Citrus Heritage Park Bd.; co-chair Mayor's Vision Com.; chair City/Univ. Task Force Com.; founding chair adv. bd. U. Calif.-Riverside Ext.; founding chair Riverside Festival of Lights. With U.S. Army, 1953-55. Recipient Disting. Svc. award Riverside Jaycees, 1966, Patron of Arts award Cultural Arts Coun., 1977, Vernon Jordan Humanitarian award Riverside Area Urban League, 1989, Citizen of Yr. award Riverside Police Officers Assn., 1990, Atlas award Riverside YWCA, 1990, Community Svc. award, 1990; named Young Man of Yr. Riverside Jaycees, 1966, Citizen of Yr. Internat. Rels. Coun., 1992. Mem. Inland Area Urban League (founder, bd. dirs., Pacesetter award 1982), U. Calif. Riverside Alumni Assn. (bd. dirs. 1981-87), Riverside Jaycees (life), Riverside Raincross Club. Office: Greater Riverside C of C 3685 Main St Ste 350 Riverside CA 92501-2804

PICK, JAMES BLOCK, management and sociology educator; b. Chgo., July 29, 1943; s. Grant Julius and Helen (Block) P. BA, Northwestern U., 1966; MS in Edn., No. Ill. U., 1969; PhD, U. Calif., Irvine, 1974. Cert. computer profl. Asst. rsch. statistician, lectr. Grad. Sch. Mgmt. U. Calif., Riverside, 1975-91, dir. computing, 1984-91; co-dir. U.S.-Mex. Database Project, 1988-91; assoc. prof. mgmt. and bus., dir. info. mgmt. program U. Redlands, Calif., 1991-95, prof. mgmt. and bus., chair dept. mgmt. and bus., 1995-97; cons. U.S. Census Bur. Internat. Div., 1978; mem. Univ. Commons Bd., 1982-86; mem. bd. govs. PCCLAS, Assn. Borderlands Studies, 1989-92. Trustee Newport Harbor Art Mus., 1981-87, 88-96, chmn. permanent collection com., 1987-91, v.p., 1991-96; trustee Orange County Mus. Art, 1996—, chmn. collection com., 1996—. Recipient Thunderbird award Bus. Assn. Latin Am. Studies, 1993. Mem. AAAS, Assn. Computing Machinery, Assn. Systems Mgmt. (pres. Orange County chpt. 1978-79), Am. Statis. Assn., Population Assn. Am., Internat. Union for Sci. Study of Population, Soc. Info. Mgmt. Club, Standard (Chgo.). Author: Geothermal Energy Development, 1982, Computer Systems in Business, 1986, Atlas of Mexico, 1989, The Mexico Handbook, 1994, Mexico Megacity, 1997; condr. research in info. systems, population, environ. studies; contbr. sci. articles to publs. in fields.

PICK, MICHAEL CLAUDE, international exploration consultant; b. Stuttgart, Fed. Republic Germany, Sept. 17, 1931; came to Can., 1963; s. Manfred and Berti (Baer) P.; m. Jeanette Patrucia Zaharko, Mar. 13, 1965; children—David, Christopher. B.A., U. New Zealand, Wellington, 1952, M.A. with honors, 1954; Ph.D., U. Bristol, Eng., 1963. Sr. geologist Todd Bros. Ltd., Wellington, 1954-58; research assoc. Stanford U., Calif., 1958-60; geologist Chevron Standard Ltd., Calgary, Alta., Can., 1963-68; regional geologist BP Oil & Gas Ltd., Calgary, 1968-71; chief geologist, acting exploration mgr. Columbia Gas, Calgary, 1971-80; sr. v.p. Asamera, Inc., Calgary, 1980-87; pres. Torwood Assocs. Ltd., 1988-95, Terrenex Ventures Inc., Calgary, 1996—. Contbr. articles to profl. jours. Mem. Am. Assn. Petroleum Geologists, Can. Soc. Petroleum Geologists. Avocations: music; reading; model railroading. Home and Office: 3359 Varna Crescent NW, Calgary, AB Canada T3A 0E4

PICK, ROBERT YEHUDA, orthopedic surgeon, consultant; b. Haifa, Israel, 1945; came to U.S., 1957; s. Andre B. and Hanna (Gross) P.; m. Roni L. Kestenbaum, Sept. 25, 1977; children: Benjamin A., Joseph E., Jennifer L., Abigail I. BA, B in Hebrew Lit., Yeshiva U., 1967; MD, Albert Einstein Coll. Med., 1971; MPH, Harvard U., 1979. Diplomate Nat. Bd. Med. Examiners, Am. Bd. Orthopaedic Surgery. Intern Brookdale Hosp., Bklyn., 1971-72; resident in orthopedic surgery Albert Einstein-Bronx (N.Y.) Mcpl. Hosp. Ctr., 1972-74; resident in orthopedic surgery USPHS Hosp., Staten Island, N.Y., 1974-75, asst. chief orthopedic surgery, 1975-77; asst. chief orthopedic surgery USPHS Hosp., Boston, 1977-78; fellow orthopedic trauma Boston City Hosp., 1979-80, assoc. dir. orthopedic surgery, 1980-84, dir. pediatric orthopedics, 1981-83; practice medicine specializing in orthopedic surgery Newton Ctr., Mass., 1984—; instr. orthopedic surgery Boston U., 1980-82, asst. prof., 1982—; adj. asst. prof. health scis. and orthopedics Touro Coll., N.Y.C., 1976-78; dir. spinal screening program Dept. Health and Hosps., Boston, 1979-82; dist. med. advisor U.S. Dept. Labor, Boston, 1984—; cons. Boston Retirement Bd., 1983-84, New Eng. Telephone, Boston, 1985—, Commonwealth of Mass. Pub. Employee Retirement Adminstrn., Boston, 1985-90. Contbr. articles on med. issues to profl. jours. Trustee Young Israel Jackson Heights, Queens, N.Y., 1969-76, pres., 1976-77; sec. Young Israel Brookline, Mass., 1978-79; trustee Maimonides Sch., Brookline, 1990—. Served to lt. comdr. USPHS, 1975-78. Fellow Am. Acad. Orthopedic Surgeons; mem. Am. Physicians Fellowship for Medicine in Israel (trustee 1975—, exec. com. 1976—, asst. treas. 1987-90, treas. 1990-96, Man of Yr. award 1977), Nat. Inst. Occupational Safety and Health (traineeship 1978-79), Mensa.

PICK, RUTH, research scientist, physician, educator; b. Carlsbad, Bohemia, Czechoslovakia, Nov. 13, 1913; came to U.S., 1949; d. Arthur and Paula (Lenk) Holub; m. Alfred Pick, May 28, 1938 (dec. Jan. 1982). M.D., German U., 1938. Resident in medicine Priessnitz Hosp., Graefenberg, Czechoslovakia, 1938; resident in psychiatry Hosp. Veleslavin, Prague, Czechoslovakia, 1945-47; extern in pathology State Hosp. Motol, Prague, 1948; research fellow cardiovascular dept. Michael Reese Hosp. & Med. Ctr., Chgo., 1949-50, research assoc., 1950-58, asst. dir., 1958-66, sr. investigator, 1966-71, chief exptl. atherosclerosis lab., 1971-83, attending physician div. cardiovascular diseases dept. medicine, 1964—; chief cardiac morphology lab. Cardiovascular Inst. Michael Reese Hosp. & Med. Ctr., 1983-95; prof. emeritus medicine and pathology U. Chgo., 1973—; part time rsch. assoc. Cardiovascular Inst., 1995—; mem. research council Chgo. Heart Assn., 1979-84, bd. govs., 1983, pres., 1985-86. Fellow Am. Heart Assn. (coun. on arteriosclerosis, coun. on circulation, established investigator), AAAS; mem. Am. Assn. Pathologists and Bacteriologists, Chgo. Heart Assn. (past pres. 1985-86), Am. Fedn. Clin. rsch., Am. Physiol. Soc., Ctrl. Soc. Clin. Rsch. Home: 400 E Randolph St Chicago IL 60601-7329 Office: Michael Reese Hosp and Med Ctr 2929 S Ellis Ave Chicago IL 60616-3302

PICKARD, CAROLYN ROGERS, secondary school educator; b. Steubenville, Ohio, Dec. 13, 1945; d. Thomas Orlando and Alice Marie (Romick) Rogers; 1 child, Carri Alyce. BA, Fla. State U., 1967; AA, Stephens Coll., Columbia, Mo., 1965. Cert. English tchr., Fla. Tchr. English, chair dept. New World Sch. Arts, Dade County Pub. Schs., Miami, Fla., 1969—; sponsor jr. class; advisor yearbook; liason New World Sch. Arts. Vol. Shores Performing Arts Theater Soc. Recipient Tchr. of Yr. award North Miami Beach High Sch., 1982, Presdl. Scholars Tchr. of Excellence award, 1984. Mem. Nat. Coun. Tchrs. English, United Tchrs. Dade County, Delta Kappa Gamma. Home: 11930 N Bayshore Dr #707 Miami FL 33181

PICKARD, DEAN, philosophy and humanities educator; b. Geneva, N.Y., Mar. 12, 1947; s. William Otis and Frances (Dean) P.; children: Justin Matthew, Christopher Dean. BA cum laude, U. Calif., Riverside, 1973; MA, Calif. State U., Long Beach, 1976-77; PhD, Claremont (Calif.) Grad. Sch., 1992. Instr. phys. edn. Pomona Coll., Claremont, 1975-82; instr. philosophy, humanities, and phys. edn. Moorpark (Calif.) Coll., 1978-82; assoc. prof. philosophy, humanities, and phys. edn. Mission Coll., Sylmar, Calif., 1979-83; instr. philosophy Calif. State U., Northridge, 1988-94; prof. philosophy and humanities Pierce Coll., Woodland Hills, Calif., 1983—. Author: Nietzsche, Transformation and Postmodernism; contbr. articles to profl. jours. Marious De Brabent & Henry Carter scholar, 1973; fellow Claremont Grad. Sch., 1988-89; grantee NEH, 1995. Mem. Am. Philos. Assn., Am. Fedn. Tchrs., N.Am. Nietzsche Soc., L.A. Area Nietzsche Soc. (bd. dirs. 1994-97), Phi Beta Kappa. Avocations: guitar, snow skiing, wind surfing, golfing, martial arts (5th degree black belt). Office: Pierce Coll 6201 Winnetka Ave Woodland Hills CA 91371-0001

PICKARD, GEORGE LAWSON, physics educator; b. Cardiff, Wales, July 5, 1913; came to Can., 1947; s. Harry Lawson and Phoebe P.; m. Lilian May Perry; children—Rosemary Ann, Andrew Lawson. B.A., Oxford U., 1935, M.A., 1947, D.Phil., 1937; D.M.S. (hon.), Royal Roads Mil. Coll., Victoria, B.C., Can., 1980. Sci. officer Royal Aircraft Establishment, Farnborough, Eng., 1937-42; sr. sci. officer ops. research sect. Coastal Command, RAF, 1942-46, prin. sci. officer ops. research sect., 1947; assoc. prof. dept. physics U. B.C., Vancouver, Can., 1947-54, prof. dept. physics, 1954-79, prof. emeritus, 1979—, dir. Inst. Oceanography, 1958-79; cons. Seaconsult Marine Research, Vancouver, Can., 1979—. Author: Descriptive Physical Oceanography, 1964, 5th edit., 1990; (with S. Pond) Introductory Dynamical Oceanography, 1978, 2d edit., 1983. Served with RAF, 1942-47. Decorated mem. Order Brit. Empire; recipient J.P. Tully medal Can. Meteorol. and Oceanographic Soc., 1987. Fellow AAAS, Royal Soc. Can. Avocations: aviation; diving; coral reef oceanography. Home: 4546 W 5th Ave, Vancouver, BC Canada V6R 1S7

PICKARD, MYRNA RAE, dean; b. Sulphur Springs, Tex., Oct. 10, 1935; d. George Wallace and Ellie (Williams) Swindell; m. Bobby Ray Pickard, May 17, 1957; 1 child, Bobby Dale. BS summa cum laude, Tex. Wesleyan Coll., 1957, MEd, 1964; MS, Tex. Women's U., 1974; EdD, Nova U., 1976. Instr. John Peter Smith Hosp., Fort Worth, 1956-58; pub. health nurse Forest County Health Dept., Hattiesburg, Miss., 1958-60; asst. nurse adminstrn. John Peter Smith Hosp. Sch. Nursing, Fort Worth, 1960-70, nurse adminstr., 1970-73; assoc. dean, dean U. Tex. System Sch. Nursing, Fort Worth, 1971-76; dean U. Tex. Sch. Nursing, Arlington, 1976-95; prof. nursing, 1976—; cons. in field; adv. com. Rural Health Rsch. Ctr., U. N.D., 1990. Mem. editorial bd. Jour. Rural Health, 1985-92, 94; contbr. articles to profl. jours., chpt. in book. Pres. Tex. League for Nursing, 1986-89; bd. mgrs. Tarrant County Hosp. Dist., 1995—; trustee Columbia Pla. Med. Bd., 1992—. Fellow Am. Acad. Nursing; mem. ANA, Nat. League Nursing, Nat. Rural Health Assn. (bd. dirs., treas. 1990-92), Sigma Theta Tau. Methodist. Avocations: jogging; gardening. Home: 8301 Anglin Dr Fort Worth TX 76140-4213 Office: U Tex Box 19407 Arlington TX 76019

PICKEN, EDITH DARYL, school principal; b. Washington, Jan. 19, 1955; d. Edward George and Edith Kellog (Jones) P. BS, Towson State U., 1978; MS, CAS, Johns Hopkins U., 1985. Cert. English tchr., guidance counselor, prin. and supervision, advanced profl. I, Md. English tchr. Balt. City Pub. Schs., 1979-83; guidance counselor Anne Arundel County Pub. Schs., Md., 1985-94, adminstr., 1994-97, asst. prin., 1997—; counselor Loyola Edn. Counseling Ctr., Balt.; guest speaker and presenter in field. Named Md. Sch. Counselor of Yr., 1989. Mem. NEA, ASCD, ACA, Md. Assn. Counseling and Devel., AAUW, Md. ASCD, Am. Sch. Counselors Assn., Md. Sch. Counselors Assn., Assn. Ednl. Leaders, Chi Sigma Iota, Pi Lambda Theta. Office: North County High Sch 10 1st Ave E Glen Burnie MD 21061-2073

PICKEN, HARRY BELFRAGE, aerospace engineer; b. Grimsby, Ont., Can., Jan. 8, 1916; s. John Belfrage and Leila Lucinda (Jarvis) P.; m. Florence Elizabeth Runciman, July 7, 1945; children: Roger Belfrage, Donald William, Wendy Elizabeth. BSc in Aero. Engring., U. Mich., 1940. Registered profl. engr., Ont., Can. Chief engr. White Can. Aircraft Ltd., Hamilton, Ont., 1940-45, Weston Aircraft Ltd., Oshawa, Ont., 1946-47, Field Aviation Ltd., Oshawa, 1947-51; pres., chief engr. Genaire Ltd. (Aerospace), St. Catharines, 1951-81; v.p., tech. dir. Ardrox Ltd. (Chems.), Niagara on the Lake, 1968-75, Avionics Ltd. (Electronics), Niagara on the Lake, 1953-67; v.p. Rotaire Ltd. (Helicopters), St. Catharines, Ont., 1958-63; design approval rep. acting on behalf of Dept. of Transport Can., Ottawa, 1948-78; mem. bd. govs. Niagara Coll., Welland, Ont., 1974-80. Editor, pub.: Early Architecture Town and Township of Niagara, 1968, architecture student edit., 1991, Map of the Colonial Town of Niagara-on-the-Lake, 1981; composer (music book) Calgary Song Suite, 1983, Chacun a son Goût, 1991;. Chmn. Planning Bd. of Niagara-on-the Lake, 1963-65; pres. Niagara-on-the-Lake C. of C., 1961-62; bd. dirs., v.p. Niagara Found., Niagara-on-the-Lake, 1963-80; mem. tech. adv. bd. Niagara Coll., 1966-74; vice chmn. bd. govs. Niagara Coll. Applied Arts and Tech., 1979-81; mem. ont. Coun. of Regents, 1987-93. Named Citizen of Yr. Niagara-on-the-Lake C. of C., 1968; recipient Award of Merit, Mohawk Community Coll., Hamilton, Ont., 1990, Medal-Community Svc., Profl. Engrs. Ont., 1981, Citation for Outstanding and Meritorious Work, Transport Can. Civil Aviation Ont. Region, 1978, Caring and Sharing award Niagara Regional Govt., 1992, Citation from Premier Ont., 1993. Fellow Can. Aero. and Space Inst. (assoc.); mem. AIAA, Am. Helicopter Soc., Assn. Profl. Engrs. Ont. (lic. profl. engr.), Composers, Authors and Music Pubs. of Can. (assoc.), Am. Fedn. Musicians (bd. dirs. local 298 Niagara Falls, Ont.). Achievements include patent for developing an entirely new type of honeycomb primary structure and beams fabricated using staples and acrylic adhesives; research in thermal electric modules independently used in cooling and refrigeration techniques; also applied rsch. leading to the development of cold vulcanization techniques relative to rubber. Home: 494 Glenwood Dr, Ridgeway, ON Canada L0S 1N0 Office: Genaire Ltd, Niagara Dist Airport Box 84, Saint Catharines, ON Canada L2R 6R4

PICKENPAUGH, THOMAS EDWARD, archaeologist; b. St. Clairsville, Ohio, Feb. 8, 1945; s. Douglas Giffin and Betty June (Brown) P. BA, Kent State U., 1970, MA, 1971; ABD, Cath. U., 1980. Anthropologist, instr. sociology and anthropology Wheeling (W.Va.) Coll., 1972-73; anthropologist, instr., asst. prof. anthropology Ohio U.-Eastern, 1972-74, 78; archaeologist, asst. prof. anthropology Ohio U.-Eastern, St. Clairsville, 1986-95; mus. technician U.S. Dept. Interior, Nat. Pk. Svc., Washington, 1983; mus. technican Nat. Mus. Natural History, Smithsonian Instn., Washington, 1984-87; mus. specialist, loan officer USN, Naval Hist. Ctr., Washington, 1987—; dir. archaeol. excavations Brokaw Village Site, St. Clairsville, Ohio, 1972-74, 76-78, 82, 86-96; mem. archaeol. staff Thunderbird Site, Front Royal, Va., Savannah River, Ga., S.C., Richard B. Russell Dam Project, 1980, El Mirador Site, Guatemala, 1980, Louis Berger Internat. Project, Trenton, N.J., 1983-84, Sully Plantation, Loudon County, Va., 1984, Fells Point Project, Balt., 1984; others. Contbr. articles to profl. publs. Rsch. grantee U.S. Dept. Interior, Nat. Pk. Svc., 1978-79, Nat. Geog. Soc., 1992-93. Mem. Washington Assn. Profl. Anthropologists, Anthropol. Soc. Washington, Am. Assn. Museums, Internat. Platform Assn. Home: # 201 12512 Village Sq Ter Rockville MD 20852 Home: 12512 Village Square Ter Rockville MD 20852 Office: Naval Hist Ctr Washington Navy Yard 9th And M St SE Washington DC 20374

PICKENS, ALEXANDER LEGRAND, education educator; b. Waco, Tex., Aug. 31, 1921; s. Alex LeGrand and Elma L. (Johnson) P.; m. Frances M. Jenkins, Aug. 20, 1955. B.A., So. Methodist U., 1950; M.A., North Tex. State U., Denton, 1952; Ed.D., Columbia U., 1959. Tchr. art public schs. Dallas, 1950-53, Elizabeth, N.J., 1953-54; instr. Coll. Architecture and Design U. Mich., 1954-59; assoc. prof. dept. art U. Ga., Athens, 1959-62; assoc. prof. Coll. Edn. U. Hawaii, Honolulu, 1962-68, prof. edn., 1968—; U. Hawaii; chmn. doctoral studies curriculum instrn. Coll. Edn. U. Hawaii, Honolulu, 1984-89, asst. to dean for coll. devel., 1989—; dir. children's classes Ft. Worth Children's Mus., 1951-53; head art Nat. Music Camp, Interlochen, Mich., summers, 1957-58, U. Oreg., Portland, summers 1959-60, 62; cons. youth art activities Foremost Dairies, 1964-74; cons. art films United World Films, 1970-75; art edn. cons. Honolulu Paper Co., 1970-76, Kamehameha Sch., Bishop Estate, 1978-95. Exhibited ceramics, Wichita Internat. Exhbn., Syracuse (N.Y.) Nat. Exhbn., St. Louis Mus., Dallas Mus., San Antonio Mus., Detroit Art Inst., Hawaii Craftsmen, also others; editorial bd.: Arts and Activities mag, 1955-82; editor: U. Hawaii Ednl. Perspectives, 1964—; contbr. articles to profl. jours. Memm. adult com. Dallas County chpt. Jr. ARC, 1951-53; exec. com. Dallas Crafts Guild, 1950-53; v.p., publicity chmn. U. Ga. Community Concert Assn., 1960-62, mem., program chmn. Gov.'s Commn. Observing 150 Yrs. Pub. Edn. in Hawaii, 1990-91. Served with USAAF. Recipient award merit, Tex. State Fair, 1957, All-Am. award, Ednl. Press Assn. Am., 1968, 70, 72, 75, 79, Regents' medal for excellence in teaching, U. Hawaii, 1989, Gov.'s Commn. Observance of 150 Yrs. Pub. Edn., 1990-91. Mem. AAUP, NEA, Internat. Soc. Edn., Nat. Art Edn. Assn., Coun. for Advancement and Support of Edn., Nat. Soc. Fundraising Execs., Hawaii Planned Giving Coun., Phi Delta Kappa, Kappa Delta Pi. Address: 1471 Kalaepohaku St Honolulu HI 96816-1804

PICKENS, FRANKLIN ACE, lawyer; b. Borger, Texas, Aug. 19, 1936; s. A.O. and Rhoda (Shaw) P.; m. Dianna Barnard, Dec. 17, 1966. BBA, U. Tex., 1958, JD, 1962. Bar: Tex. 1962, U.S. Dist. Ct. (we. dist.) Tex. 1964, U.S. Dist. Ct. (ea. dist.) Tex. 1983, U.S. Dist. Ct. (so. dist.) Tex. 1989; cert. adminstrv. law Tex. Bd. Legal Specialization. Pvt. practice Odessa, Tex., 1962-63; ptnr. McDonald and Pickens, Odessa, Tex., 1963-69; atty. Shafer, Gilliland, Davis, Bunton & McCollum, Odessa, Tex., 1969-71; rep. State of Texas, Odessa, 1964-73; pvt. practice Austin, Texas, 1973-76; ptnr. Brown McCarroll & Oaks Hartline, Austin, Texas, 1976—; state bd. Ins. Adv. Com. HMOs; former gen. counsel Tex. State Bd. Nurse Examiners; former Washington counsel Tex. R.R.; mem. state bar com. Liason with Med. Profession, 1975-82; spkr. in field. Listed Naifeh and Smith, 1993-94; contbr. articles to profl. jours. Chmn. bd. trustees Shoal Creek Hosp., Austin, 1981-96; former mem. strategic planning task force Brackenridge Hosp., Austin; former mem. coun. advisors Austin Children's Cancer Ctr. Lt. comdr. USNR, 1958-60. Mem. ABA, Nat. Health Lawyers Assn., Am. Soc. Law and Medicine, State Bar Tex. (coll., coun., health law sect. 1980-82, legis. com. 1989), Travis County Bar Assn. (adminstrv. law sect., health law sect.). Episcopalian. Home: 713 Windsong Trl Austin TX 78746-3539 Office: Brown McCarroll & Oaks Hartline 1400 Franklin Plz 111 Congress Ave Austin TX 78701-4043

PICKENS, ROBERT BRUCE, accountant; b. Uniontown, Pa., May 20, 1926; s. Joseph Abraham and Margaret Gertrude (Brown) P.; m. Mary Ellen Evans, Sept. 9, 1950; children: Laura Gail Martin, Rachel Diane Rosen, David Bruce. B.S. in Bus. Adminstrn, Waynesburg Coll., 1950. C.P.A., Pa., Ill., Ind. Vice pres. Home Bottle Gas Corp., Uniontown, 1950-51; jr. accountant to sr. accountant Tenney & Co., Uniontown, 1951-56; mgr. Hosp. Service Assn. Western Pa., Pitts., 1956-57; auditor U. Pitts., 1957-58; sr. accountant Eugene A. Conniff Co., Pitts., 1958-59; mgr. Sheppard & Co., Pitts., 1959-63; supr. Alexander Grant & Co., Chgo., 1963-65; asst. to treas. CTS Corp., Elkhart, Ind., 1965, gen. auditor, controller, 1966-81; self-employed as acct., 1981-86; sec., controller, chief acctg. officer SEA Group, Inc. and SEA-ILAN, Inc., 1987-88; pvt. cons., 1989—. Mem. Bower Hill Civic League, 1956-62; active Boy Scouts Am., 1938-62. Served to cpl. USAAC, 1944-45; USAF Res., 1947-50. Mem. AICPA, Pa. Inst. CPAs, Ill. CPA Soc., Ind. CPA Soc. Republican. Presbyn. (elder, trustee 1959-61, treas. 1960-61). Home and Office: 73 Rogers Rd Carmel IN 46032-1467

PICKERELL, JAMES HOWARD, photojournalist; b. Dayton, Ohio, June 9, 1936; s. Howard and Frances (Harrison) P.; m. Mary Louise Fisher, June 26, 1965; children: Cheryl Elizabeth, Stacy Rae. Student, Ohio U., 1954-56; BA, UCLA, 1963. Comml. photographer, 1963—; ind. photographer Vietnam, 1963-67. Author: Vietnam in the Mud, 1966, Marketing Photography in the Digital Evnironment, 1994, Negotiating Stock Photo Prices, 4th edit., 1997; writer, pub. newsletter Taking Stock. With USN, 1956-60. Mem. Nat. Press Photographers Assn. (1st Pl. Spot News award 1965), Am. Soc. Mag. Photographers (nat. bd. 1987-89), Profl. Photographers Am., Beta Theta Pi. Address: 8104 Cindy Ln Bethesda MD 20817-6915

PICKERING, BECKY RUTH THOMPSON, special education educator; b. Springfield, Mo., Nov. 20, 1949; d. Ray Herman Thompson and Virginia Ruth (Baily) Peterson; m. Gary Joe Pickering, Oct. 22, 1967; children: Summer Pickering Austin, Shane Gary, Slade Thompson. BS in Edn. cum laude, S.W. Mo. State U., 1983. Cert. spl. edn. tchr., Mo. Spl. edn. tchr. Fair Grove (Mo.) Schs. RX, 1983—; mem. Profl. Devel. Com., 1989—. Mem. Cmty. Tchr.'s Orgn. (v.p. local 1990), Mo. State Tchrs. Assn. Democrat. Avocations: reading, walking, farming, writing. Home: 9254 E Farm Rd 2 Fair Grove MO 65648-9724 Office: Fair Grove Schs 132 N Main St Fair Grove MO 65648-8436

PICKERING, CHARLES W., federal judge; b. 1937. BA, U. Miss., 1959, JD, 1968; Hon. Doctorate, William Carey Coll. Ptnr. Gartin, Hester and Pickering, Laurel, Miss., 1961-71; judge Laurel Mcpl. Ct., 1969; pvt. practice Laurel, 1971-72, 80; ptnr. Pickering and McKenzie, Laurel, 1973-80, Pickering and Williamson, Laurel, 1981-90; judge U.S. Dist. Ct. (so. dist.) Miss., Hattiesburg, 1990—. Contbr. articles to Mississippi Law Journal. Mem. ABA, Miss. Bar Assn., Jones County Bar. Assn., State 4-H Adv. Coun., Assn. Trial Lawyers in Am., Miss. Trial Lawyers Assn., U. Miss. Alumni Assn., Jones County Jr. Coll., Jones County Farm Bur., Kiwanis Club. Office: US Courthouse 701 N Main St Ste 228 Hattiesburg MS 39401-3471*

PICKERING, CHARLES W., JR., congressman; m. Leisha Jane Prather; children: Will, Ross, Jackson, Asher. BA in Bus. Adminstrn., U. Miss., 1986; MBA, Baylor U. Legis. asst. to U.S. Senator Trent Lott, apptd. to USDA; mem. U.S. House of Reps., 1996—; mem. agriculture com. U.S. House of Reps., livestock, dairy and poultry subcom., forestry, resource conservation, rsch. subcom., Transp. and Infrastructure com., vice chair surface transp. subcom., aviation subcom., Sci. com., vice chair basic rsch. subcom., space subcom.; asst. minority whip; mem. House Rep. Policy com.; mem. exec. com. Nat. Rep. Congrl. com. Office: 427 Cannon Washington DC 20515-2403*

PICKERING, HOWARD WILLIAM, metallurgy engineer, educator; b. Cleve., Dec. 15, 1935; s. Howard William and Marian (Vittes) P.; m. Judith Anne Burch, Apr. 20, 1963; children: John, Kim, Scott, Carolyn. BS in Metall. Engring., U. Cin., 1958; MS, Ohio State U., 1959, PhD, 1961. Scientist U.S. Steel Corp., Monroeville, Pa., 1962-69, sr. scientist, 1969-72; postdoctoral U.S. Steel fellow Max-Planck Inst., Gottingen, Fed. Republic Germany, 1964-65; assoc. prof. metall. engring. Pa. State U., University Park, 1972-76, chmn., 1975-80, prof., 1976-90, disting. prof., 1990—; cons. Ga. Pacific Corp., Newark, 1983-88, Argonne Nat. Lab., 1986-88, Allegheny Ludlum Corp., 1992—; mem. external adv. panel Corrosion Research Ctr., U. Minn., 1980-86. Co-author: Atom Probe Field Ion Microscopy and Its Applications, 1988; editor Corrosion Sci. Jour., 1975-95; contbr. numerous articles to profl. jours. Recipient Disting. Alumnus award Coll. Engring. U. Cin., 1988, Coll. Rsch. award Pa. State U., 1989, Disting. Alumnus award Coll. Engring. Ohio State U., 1990; numerous rsch. grants. Fellow Nat. Assn. Corrosion Engrs. (rsch. com. 1980-89, A.B. Campbell award 1964, Willis Rodney Whitney award 1985), Electrochem. Soc. (chmn. edn. com. 1979, Young Author award 1967, H.H. Uhlig award 1987); mem. AAAS, Metall. Soc. (edn. and profl. affairs com. 1979-83, corrosion resistant metals com. 1974—), Tau Beta Pi, Phi Lambda Upsilon.

PICKERING, JAMES HENRY, III, academic administrator; b. N.Y.C., July 11, 1937; s. James H. and Anita (Felber) P.; m. Patricia Paterson, Aug. 18, 1962; children: David Scott, Susan Elizabeth. BA, Williams Coll., 1959; MA, Northwestern U., 1960, PhD, 1964. Instr. English Northwestern U., 1963-65; mem. faculty Mich. State U., East Lansing, 1965-81; prof. English Mich. State U., 1972-81, grad. and asso. chmn. dept., 1968-75, dir. Honors Coll., 1975-81; dean Coll. Humanities and Fine Arts U. Houston, 1981-90, sr. v.p., provost, 1990-92, pres., 1992-95. Author: Fiction 100, 1974, 78, 82, 85, 88, 92, 95, 97, The World Turned Upside Down: Prose and Poetry of the American Revolution, 1975, The Spy Unmasked, 1975, The City in American Literature, 1977, Concise Companion to Literature, 1981, Literature, 1982, 86, 90, 94, 97, Mountaineering in Colorado, 1987, Wild Life on the Rockies, 1988, A Mountain Boyhood, 1988, The Spell of the Rockies, 1989, Purpose and Process, 1989, Poetry, 1990, In Beaver World, 1990, Rocky Mountain Wonderland, 1991, A Summer Vacation in the Parks and Mountains of Colorado, 1992, Fiction 50, 1993, Knocking Round the Rockies, 1994, Drama, 1994, Fredrick Chapin's Colorado, 1995. Mem. Coll. English Assn. (pres. 1980-81), Phi Beta Kappa, Phi Kappa Phi, Omicron Delta Kappa. Office: U Houston Dept English Houston TX 77204

PICKERING, JOHN HAROLD, lawyer; b. Harrisburg, Ill., Feb. 27, 1916; s. John Leslie and Virginia Lee (Morris) P.; m. Elsa Victoria Mueller, Aug. 23, 1941 (dec. Nov., 1988); children: Leslie Ann, Victoria Lee; m. Helen Patton Wright, Feb. 3, 1990. AB, U. Mich., 1938, JD, 1940, LLD, 1996; LLD, D.C. Sch. Law, 1995. Bar: N.Y. 1941, D.C. 1947. Practiced in N.Y.C., 1941, practiced in Washington, 1946—; assoc. Cravath, de Gersdorff, Swaine & Wood, 1941; law clk. to Justice Murphy, Supreme Ct. U.S., 1941-43; assoc. Wilmer & Broun, 1946-48, ptnr., 1949-62; ptnr. Wilmer, Cutler & Pickering, 1962-79, Wilmer & Pickering, 1979-81; ptnr. Wilmer, Cutler & Pickering, 1981-88, sr. counsel, 1989—; vis. lectr. U. Va. Law Sch., 1958; mem. com. visitors U. Mich. Law Sch., 1962-68, chmn. devel. com., 1973-81; mem. com. on adminstrn. of justice U.S. Ct. Appeals (D.C. cir.), 1966-72, chmn. adv. com. on procedures, 1976-82, chmn. mediation project, 1988—; bd. govs. D.C. Bar, 1975-78, pres., 1979-80; dir. Nat. Ctr. for State Cts., 1987-93. Lt. comdr. USNR, 1943-46. Recipient Outstanding Achievement award U. Mich., 1978, Disting. Svc. award Nat. Ctr. for State Cts., 1985, 50 Yr. award from Fellows Am. Bar Found., 1993, Paul C. Reardon award Nat. Ctr. for State Cts., 1994, Pro Bono award NAACP Legal Def. Fund, 1990, numerous other awards. Mem. ABA (state del. 1984-93, chmn. commn. on legal problems of elderly 1985-93, sr. advisor 1993-95, chmn. 1995-96, commr. emeritus 1996—, chmn. sr. lawyers divsn. 1996-97), D.C. Bar Assn. (Lawyer of the Yr. 1996), Am. Law Inst., Barristers Washington, Lawyers Club, Met. Club, Chevy Chase Club, Wianno Club, Order of Coif, Phi Beta Kappa, Phi Kappa Phi. Democrat. Mem. United Ch. Christ. Home: 5317 Blackistone Rd Bethesda MD 20816-1822 Office: 2445 M St NW Ste 8 Washington DC 20037-1435

PICKERING, THOMAS REEVE, diplomat; b. Orange, N.J., Nov. 5, 1931; s. Hamilton R. and Sarah C. (Chasteney) P.; m. Alice J. Stover, Nov. 24, 1955; children: Timothy R., Margaret S. A.B., Bowdoin Coll., 1953; M.A., Fletcher Sch. Law and Diplomacy, 1954, U. Melbourne, Australia, 1956. Joined U.S. Fgn. Svc., 1959; fgn. affairs officer ACDA, 1961; polit. adviser U.S. del. 18 Nation Disarmament Conf., Geneva, 1962-64; consul Zanzibar, 1965-67; counselor of embassy, dep. chief mission Am. embassy, Dar es Salaam, Tanzania, 1967-69; dep. dir. Bur. Politico-Mil. Affairs, State Dept., 1969-73; spl. asst. to Sec. of State; exec. sec. Dept. State, 1973-74; U.S. amb. to Jordan, 1974-78; asst. sec. for Bur. Oceans, Internat. Environ. and Sci. Affairs, Washington, 1978-81; U.S. amb. to Nigeria, 1981-83, U.S. amb. to El Salvador, 1983-85, U.S. amb. to Israel, 1985-88, U.S. permanent rep. to UN, 1989-92, U.S. amb. to India, 1992-93, U.S. amb. to Russia, 1993-96; pres. Eurasia Found., 1996-97; undersec. of state for polit. affairs Dept. of State, Washington, 1997—. Served to lt. comdr. USNR, 1956-59. Mem. Council Fgn. Relations, Internat. Inst. Strategic Studies, Phi Beta Kappa. Office: 1527 New Hampshire Ave NW Washington DC 20036-1206 Office: Dept of State 2200 C St Washington DC 20520

PICKERING, WILLIAM HAYWARD, physics educator, scientist; b. Wellington, N.Z., Dec. 24, 1910; s. Albert William and Elizabeth (Hayward) P.; m. Muriel Bowler, Dec. 30, 1932 (dec. Mar. 1992); children: William B., Anne E.; m. Inez Chapman, July 28, 1994. B.S., Calif. Inst. Tech., 1932, M.S., 1933, Ph.D. in Physics, 1936; hon. degrees, Clark U., 1966, Occidental Coll., 1966, U. Bologna, 1974. Mem. Cosmic Ray Expdn. to, India, 1939, Mexico, 1941; faculty Calif. Inst. Tech., 1940—, prof. elec. engring., 1946-80, prof. emeritus, 1980—, dir. jet propulsion lab., 1954-76; Mem. sci. adv. bd. USAF, 1945-48; chmn. panel on test range instrumentation (Research and Devel. Bd.), 1948-49; mem. U.S. nat. com. tech. panel Earth Satellite Program, 1955-60; mem. Army Sci. Adv. Panel, 1960-64; dir. rsch. inst. U. Petroleum and Minerals, Dharan, Saudi Arabia, 1977-79; pres. Pickering Rsch. Corp., 1980-91, Lignetics, Inc., 1983—. Decorated Order of Merit Italy, 1966, knight comdr. Order Brit. Empire, 1975; recipient James Wyld Meml. award Am. Rocket Soc., 1957, Columbus medal Genoa, 1964, Prix Galabert for Astronautics; Goddary trophy Nat. Space Club, 1965, NASA Disting. Svc. medal, 1965, Army Disting. Civilian Svc. award, 1959, Spirit of St. Louis medal, 1965, Crozier medal Am. Ordnance Assn., 1965, Man of Yr. award Indsl. Rsch. Inst., 1968, Interprofl. Coop. award Soc. Mfg. Engrs., 1970, Marconi medal Marconi Found., 1974, Nat. Medal of Sci., 1976, Fahrney medal Franklin Inst., 1976, award of merit Am. Cons. Engrs. Coun., 1976, Francoix-Xavier Bagnoud Internat. award, 1994, Japan prize Sci. and Tech. Found. of Japan, 1994. Fellow AIAA (pres. 1963, Louis W. Hill Transp. award 1968, Aerospace Pioneer award 1986), AAAS, IEEE (Edison medal 1972); mem. NAS, Am. Geophys. Union, Internat. Astronautical Fedn. (pres. 1965-66). Home: 294 Saint Katherine Dr Flintridge CA 91011-4109 Office: Lignetics Inc 1150 Foothill Blvd Ste E La Canada Flintridge CA 91011-3248

PICKERING, WILLIAM TODD, minister; b. Pitts., May 24, 1946; s. Thomas Edwin and Lucile Hutchinson (Todd) P.; m. Lee Ann Bunnell, Sept. 5, 1970; children: Matthew Todd, David Merrill, Amy Noreen. BA, Randolph/Macon Coll., 1968; MDiv, Gen. Theol. Sem., 1971. Ordained to ministry Episcopal Ch. as deacon, 1971, as priest 1971. Vicar St. Alban's Episcopal Ch., Murrysville, Pa., 1971-76; rector Christ Episcopal Ch., Greensburg, Pa., 1976-83, St. Paul's Episcopal Ch., Mt. Lebanon, Pa., 1983-97, St. Mark's Parish, New Canaan, Conn., 1997—. Bd. dirs. Sheldon Calvary Camp, Conneaut, Ohio, 1985-91, Commn. on Ministry, Pitts., 1985-96, Parent & Child Guidance Ctr., Pitts., 1987-93, Outreach South Hills, Inc., Mt. Lebanon, 1986-93, Family Hospice, 1993-96; bd. chmn. St. Paul's Episcopal Nursery Sch., Mt. Lebanon, 1986-96; chmn. workship dept. Diocese of Pitts., 1988-95; pres. bd. dirs. Interfaith Re-employment Group, Pitts., 1990-96. Mem. Pitts. Athletic Assn. Republican. Home: 156 Colonial Rd New Canaan CT 06840 Office: St Mark's Parish 111 Oenoke Rdg New Canaan CT 06840-4105 *The rediscovery of being a community of God's people who are mutually responsible and interdependent is the greatest challenge to the Church and culture as we move into the 21st Century.*

PICKETT, ARTHUR WILLIAM, JR., minister; b. Detroit, Aug. 30, 1925; s. Arthur William Sr. and Florence Caroline (Erickson) P.; m. Donna Fredia Prince, Jan. 4, 1964; children: Thomas, Gerald, Susan, Winston. BS in Chemistry, Wayne State U., 1949; BTh, Concordia Sem., Ft. Wayne, Ind., 1962. Ordained min. Luth. Ch., 1962. Writer Brooke, Smith, French & Dorance, Detroit, 1950-53; TV writer D.P. Brother Inc., Detroit, 1954-57; vicar St. Paul's of Tremont, Bronx, N.Y., 1961-62; pastor Our Saviour Luth. Ch., Topsfield, Mass., 1962-63, Outer Drive Faith Luth. Ch., Detroit, 1963-66, Valley Luth. Ch., Chagrin Falls, Ohio, 1966-92; ret., 1993. Author: The Christian Seeker and the Contrary Church, 1994. Avocations: stock speculator, theatre, speaker, golf, writer. Home: 3841 Wiltshire Rd Chagrin Falls OH 44022-1151

PICKETT, BETTY HORENSTEIN, psychologist; b. Providence, R.I., Feb. 15, 1926; d. Isadore Samuel and Etta Lillian (Morrison) Horenstein; m. James McPherson Pickett, Mar. 10, 1952. A.B. magna cum laude, Brown U., 1945, Sc.M., 1947, Ph.D., 1949. Asst. prof. psychology U. Minn., Duluth, 1949-51; asst. prof. U. Nebr., 1951; lectr. U. Conn., 1952; profl. assoc. psychol. scis. Bio-Scis. Info. Exchange, Smithsonian Instn., Washington, 1953-58; exec. sec. behavioral scis. study sect. exptl. psychology study sect. div. research grants NIH, Washington, 1958-61; research cons. to mental health unit HEW, Boston, 1962-63; exec. sec. research career program NIMH, 1963-66, chief cognition and learning sect. div. extramural research program, 1966-68, dep. dir., 1968-74, dir. div. spl. mental health programs, 1974-75, acting dir. div. extramural research program, 1975-77; assoc. dir. for extramural and collaborative research program Nat. Inst. Aging, 1977-79; dep. dir. Nat. Inst. Child Health and Human Devel., Bethesda, Md., 1979-81; acting dir. Nat. Inst. Child Health and Human Devel., 1981-82, dir. Div. Rsch. Resources, 1982-88; mem. health scientist adminstr. panel CSC Bd. Examiners, 1970-76, 81-88; mem. coun. on grad. edn. Brown U. Grad. Sch., 1989-91. Contbr. articles to profl. jours. Mem. APA, Am. Psychol Soc., Psychonomic Soc., Assn. Women in Sci., AAAS, Phi Beta Kappa, Sigma Xi. Home: Morgan Bay Rd PO Box 198 Surry ME 04684-0198

PICKETT, CALDER MARCUS, retired journalism educator; b. Providence, Utah, July 26, 1921; s. Leland M. and Julia (Gessel) P.; m. Nola Agricola, Mar. 20, 1947; children: Carolyn Zeligman, Kathleen Jenson. BS, Utah State U., 1944; MS in Journalism, Northwestern U., 1948; PhD, U. Minn., 1959. Copy editor Salt Lake (City) Tribune, 1946, Deseret News, Salt Lake City, 1948-49; instr. Utah State U., Logan, 1946-48, U. Denver, 1949-51; prof. U. Kans., Lawrence, 1951—, Oscar Stauffer prof. Journalism, 1973-77, Clyde M. Reed prof. Journalism, 1985-88, ret., 1988. Author: Ed Howe: Country Town Philosopher, 1968; author, editor: Voices of the Past, 1977; columnist Lawrence Jour.-World; writer, producer, narrator radio program The Am. Past; contbr. articles to profl. jours. Recipient Disting. Teaching award Standard Oil Found., 1967, Frank Luther Mott award, 1969, George Foster Peabody award, 1974, HOPE award U. Kans., 1975, Mortar Bd. award U. Kans., 1983, Armstrong Broadcasting award, 1983, Chancellor's Club Career Teaching award, 1987. Avocations: history, music. Home: 712 Lawrence Ave Lawrence KS 66049-4521

PICKETT, DOYLE CLAY, employment and training counselor, consultant; b. Greencastle, Ind., July 15, 1930; s. Joseph Virgil and Lora Clay (Phillips) P.; m. Judith Ann Marshall, 1956 (div. 1961); children: Brian Doyle, Marsha Ann; m. Dorothy Newgent McGinnis, 1964. AB, Wabash Coll., 1952; MBA, Ind. U., 1953. Exec. trainee, various staff and line exec. positions, asst. store mgr. L.S. Ayres & Co., Lafayette and Indpls., Ind., 1953-64; mgmt. analyst Cummins Engine Co., Columbus, Ind., 1964-67; adminstrv. asst. to pres., other exec. positions Baker & Taylor Co., 1967-80; v.p. mktg. Baker & Taylor Co. subs. W.R. Grace Co., N.Y.C., Somerville, N.J., 1980-82; pres. UNIPUB subs. Xerox Co., N.Y.C., 1982-86; mem. exec. com. R.R. Bowker Co., N.Y.C., 1982-86; pres. D.C. Pickett Assocs., 1986-93; counselor Work Force Devel. Program N.J. Dept. Labor, Somerville, Perth Amboy, 1993-94; counselor Project Reemployment Opportunities Sys. N.J. Dept. Labor, Somerville, 1994-96; counselor, facilitator Career Transition Ctr., Somerville, 1996—. Co-author: Approval Plans and Academic Libraries, 1977; mem. editorial adv. bd. Technicalities, 1980-81; contbr. articles to profl. jours. Mem. Dean's Assocs., Ind. U. Sch. of Bus., Bloomington, 1983-90. Mem. Assn. Coll. and Rsch. Librs. (publs. com. 1983-87), Soc. Logistics Engrs. (adv. bd. 1981-91), Nat. Assn. Wabash Men (bd. dirs. 1983-90), Logistics Edn. Found., Caleb Mills Soc., Kiwanis (charter pres. N.W. Indpls. club 1958-59), Masons, Blue Key, Alpha Phi Omega, Delta Tau Delta (ednl. found.). Mem. Christian Ch. Home: 240 Great Hills Rd Bridgewater NJ 08807-1516

PICKETT, EDWIN GERALD, financial executive; b. Washington, Aug. 12, 1946; s. Clarence Edwin and Katherine (Molesworth) P.; m. Nancy Johnson, May 30, 1970; children: Karen, Andrew, Allison. BBA, W.Va. U., 1969; MBA, Loyola Coll. Balt., 1981. CPA, Md. Staff acct. Haskins and Sells CPA's, Balt., 1969-73; dir. internal audit Sun Life Ins. of Am., Balt., 1973-77; v.p., treas. Sun Life Group, Atlanta, 1977-80; v.p., treas. Md. Casualty Co., Balt., 1980-82, sr. v.p. fin., 1982-84; sr. v.p., exec. v.p. Am. Gen. Corp., Houston, 1984-86, CFO, 1986-89; exec. v.p., CFO USF&G Corp., Balt., 1990-93, TIG Holdings, Inc., Irving, Tex., 1993—. Treas. Poplar Springs (Md.) Meth. Ch., 1978-84; trustee Poplar Springs Meth. Ch., 1989-93, Hood Coll., 1990-95, Glenelg Country Sch., 1991-93. Mem. Am. Inst. CPA's, Fin. Execs. Inst., Caves Valley Golf Club (bd. dirs. 1991-93). Republican. Methodist. Avocations: golf, outdoor activities. Office: TIG Holdings Inc Ste N1624 5205 N O Connor Blvd Irving TX 75039-3712

PICKETT, GEORGE BIBB, JR., retired military officer; b. Montgomery, Ala., Mar. 20, 1918; s. George B. and Marie (Dow) P.; BS, U.S. Mil. Acad., 1941; student Nat. War Coll., 1959-60; m. Beryl Arlene Robinson, Dec. 27, 1941; children: Barbara Pickett Harrell, James, Kathleen, Thomas; m. 2d, Rachel Copeland Peeples, July 1981. Commd. 2d lt. U.S. Army, 1941, advanced through grades to maj. gen., 1966; instr. Inf. Sch., Fort Benning, Ga., 1947-50, instr. Armed Forces Staff Coll., Norfolk, Va., 1956-59; comdg. officer 2d Armored Cav. Regt., 1961-63; chief of staff Combat Devel. Command, 1963-66; comdg. gen. 2d inf. div., Korea, 1966-67; ret., 1973; field rep. Nat. Rifle Assn., 1973-85. Decorated Purple Heart with oak leaf cluster, D.S.M. with two oak leaf clusters, Bronze Star with two oak leaf clusters and V device, Silver Star, Legion of Merit with two oak leaf clusters, Commendation medal with two oak leaf clusters. Mem. SAR (pres. Ala. Soc. 1984), Old South Hist. Assn. Episcopalian. Club: Kiwanis. Author: (with others) Joint and Combined Staff Officers Manual, 1959; contbr. articles on mil. affairs to profl. jours. Home: 3525 Flowers Dr Montgomery AL 36109-4719 Office: PO Box 4 Montgomery AL 36101-0004

PICKETT, LAWRENCE KIMBALL, physician, educator; b. Balt., Nov. 10, 1919; s. Herbert E. and Emily (Ames) P.; m. Pauline Ferguson, Dec. 17, 1943; children: Lawrence Kimball, Nancy Lee, Paul F., Stephen B. B.A., Yale U., 1941, M.D., 1944. Intern Peter Bent Brigham Hosp., Boston, 1945-46; resident surgery Boston Childrens Hosp., 1946-50; practice medicine specializing in pediatrics and surgery Syracuse, N.Y., 1950-64, New Haven, 1964-84; clin. assoc. prof. surgery Upstate Med. Center, 1953-64; prof. surgery and pediatrics Yale U. Sch. Medicine, 1964-84, prof. emeritus, 1984—, asso. dean, 1973-84; chief of staff Yale-New Haven Hosp., 1973-83; med. dir. Welch Allen Co., Inc., Skaneateles, N.Y., 1983-95. Served to capt. M.C. AUS, 1951-53. Fellow ACS, Am. Acad. Pediatrics (past sect. chmn.); mem. Am. Surg. Assn. Home and Office: 386 Savage Farm Dr Ithaca NY 14850-6505

PICKETT, OWEN B., congressman; b. Richmond, Va., Aug. 31, 1930. BS, Va. Poly. Inst., 1952; LLB, U. Richmond, 1955. Bar: Va. 1955; CPA. Lawyer, acct. Virginia Beach, Va., 1955-72; mem. Va. Ho. of Dels., Richmond, 1972-86, 100th-105th Congresses from 2d Va. dist., Washington, D.C., 1987—; chmn. Va. Dem. State Cen. Com., 1980-82; ranking minority mem. Nat. Security Subcom. on mil. personnel. Mem. Va. Bar Assn., Virginia Beach Bar Assn. Office: US Ho of Reps 2430 Rayburn Bldg Washington DC 20515-4602*

PICKETT, STEPHEN ALAN, hospital executive; b. Ft. Payne, Ala., Dec. 22, 1953; s. James Benjamin Pickett and Dorothy Jane (Howell) Pickett Fancher; m. Nell Annette Horsley, Mar. 5, 1977; children: Stefanie Leigh, Allison Marie. BBA, U. Montevallo, 1976; MPH, Tulane U., 1995. CPA, Ala. Sr. acct. Ernst & Whinney, Birmingham, Ala., 1976-78; contr. East End Meml. Hosp., Birmingham, 1978, v.p. fin., 1979-84; v.p. fin. W.Va. U. Hosps., Morgantown, 1985-87, exec. v.p., adminstr., 1987-91; adminstr., COO Tulane U. Hosp. and Clinic, New Orleans, 1991-95, CEO, 1995—; bd. dirs. Met. Hosp. Coun., 1991—, Associated Hosp. Svcs., 1991—. Active sustaining mem. campaign Birmingham coun. Boy Scouts Am., 1978; mem. Jefferson County Republican Exec. Com., Birmingham, 1982, First Baptist Ch. New Orleans (fin. com. 1993—). Fellow Healthcare Fin. Mgmt. Assn.; mem. Am. Inst. C.P.A.s, Ala. Soc. C.P.A.s, U. Montevallo Alumni Assn. (life), Alpha Tau Omega Alumni Assn. Baptist. Lodge: Rotary. Home: 185 Lakewood Estates Dr New Orleans LA 70131-8364 Office: Tulane U Hosp & Clinic 1415 Tulane Ave New Orleans LA 70112-2605

PICKETT, STEPHEN WESLEY, university official, lecturer and consultant; b. Billings, Mont., May 27, 1956; s. Wesley William and Carol Ann (Bollum) P. BA, Houston Bapt. U., 1980; MS, U. North Tex., 1988. Cert. elem. tchr., rehab. counselor, Tex. Hosp. tchr. Houston Ind. Sch. Dist., 1981-85; asst. to assoc. dean of students U. North Tex., Denton, 1988-90, asst. coord. disabled student svcs. Office V.P. student affairs, 1990-91, dir. Office Disability Accommodation, 1991—, univ. mentor/advisor, 1992—. Co-author: curriculum guide The Newspaper as a Student Communicator, 1982 (winner Exxon Found.'s Impact Two award for creative teaching). Chair Mayor's Com. on Employment of Persons with Disabilities, Denton, 1990; mem. coun.-at-large Sam Houston Area Coun. Boy Scouts Am., Houston, 1975—; grad. Denton C. of C. Leadership Program, 1992; pub. rels. chair leadership Denton Steering Com., 1993-94. Recipient Cmty. Svc. award U. North Tex., 1992, award for svcs. to persons with disabilities North Tex. Rehab. Assn., 1993, Disting. Alumnus award Houston Bapt. U., 1994, Outstanding Alumnus award Ctr. for Rehab. Studies, U. North Tex., 1995. Mem. Assn. Higher Edn. and Disability, Coun. Exceptional Children, Tex. Assn. Coll. and Univ. Student Pers. Adminstrs. (chair multicultural com. 1994-95, v.p. 1995-96, co-chair endowment found. com. 1996-97). Presbyterian. Avocations: reading, travel, stamp collecting. Office: U North Tex Office Disabili 318A Union Bldg 400 Avenue A Denton TX 76201-5874

PICKHARDT, CARL EMILE, JR., artist; b. Westwood, Mass., May 28, 1908; s. Carl Emile and Louise (Fowler) P.; m. Marjorie Sachs, June 15, 1935 (div. 1952); children: Nancy Louise Arnold, Carl Emile III, Sally Anne Duncan; m. Rosamond Forbes Wyman, Mar. 28, 1953. BA, Harvard U., 1931; studied with Harold Zimmerman, 1931-37. Tchr. Fitchburg Art Mus., 1951-62, Worcester Mus. Sch., 1949-50, Sturbridge Art Sch., 1952-60. Author: Portfolio of Etchings, 1942; one-man shows, Berkshire Art Mus., 1941, Doris Meltzer Gallery, N.Y.C., 1961, 68, 70, 71, 72, Jacques Seligmann Gallery, N.Y.C., 1935, 51, 52, 54, Stuart Gallery, Boston, 1946, Margaret Brown Gallery, Boston, 1951, Fitchburg Art Mus., 1951, 91, Lawrence Gallery, Kansas City, Mo., 1955, Artek Gallery, Helsinki, Finland, 1959, Laguna Gloria Art Mus., Austin, Tex., 1966, Radcliffe Coll., 1983, Providence Art Club, 1986, Fitchburg Art Mus., 1991; exhibited in group shows at Carnegie Internat., 1951, Mus. Modern Art, N.Y.C., 1940, 63, 64, Whitney Mus., 1936, Nat. Acad., 1942, 49, Boston Inst. Contemporary Art, 1941, Internat. Exhbn., Japan., 1952, Exhbn. Am. Drawings, France, 1955, Art Inst. Chgo., Calif. Palace of Legion of Honor, 1953, Boston Arts Festival, 1950, Am. Drawing Biennial, Norfolk, 1964, Pa. Acad. Fine Arts, 1968, Laguna Gloria Art Mus., 1973, Fitchburg Art Mus., 1974, 91; represented in permanent collections, Mus. Modern Art, N.Y.C., Boston Mus. Fine Arts, Bklyn. Art Mus., Worcester Art Mus., Library of Congress, N.Y. Pub. Library, Newark Art Mus., Fogg Art Mus., Addison Gallery, Finch Coll. Art Mus., Pa. Acad. Fine Arts, Boston Pub. Library, Fitchburg Art Mus., Wadsworth Athenaeum, De Cordova Mus. Served with USNR, 1942-45. Ford Found. and Am. Fedn. Arts artist-in-residence Laguna Gloria Art Mus. 1966; recipient Shope prize Nat. Acad. 1942. Address: 66 Forest St Sherborn MA 01770-1618 *My life-long purpose has been to create in visual images a new language and to express order in asymetrical terms.*

PICKHOLTZ, RAYMOND LEE, electrical engineering educator, consultant; b. N.Y.C., Apr. 12, 1932; s. Isidore and Rose (Turkish) P.; m. Eda Rebecca Mittler, June 30, 1957. BEE, CUNY, 1954, MEE, 1958; Ph.D., Poly. Inst. N.Y., 1966. Research engr. RCA Labs., Princeton, N.J., 1954-57, ITT Labs., Nutley, N.J., 1957-61; assoc. prof. Poly. Inst. Bklyn., 1962-71; prof. elec. engring., chmn. dept. George Washington U., Washington, 1977-80, prof., 1971—; pres. Telecommunication Assocs., Fairfax, Va., 1963—; cons. Inst. Def. Analyses, 1971-90, IBM Research, Yorktown Heights, N.Y., 1968-72; del. Union Radio Scientifique, Geneva, 1979—, vice chmn., 1987; del. NRC, Washington, 1980-83; vis. prof. U. Que., 1977; vis. scholar U. Calif., 1983; chmn. U.S. Nat. Commn. C, Union Radio Sci. Internat., 1990-92; mem. sci. and indsl. adv. bd. Telecom. Inst. Ont., Can. and Inst. Nacionale de la Recherches Scientique. Editor: book series Computer Science Press, 1979—; IEEE Trans., 1975-80; author: Local Area and Multiple Access Networks, 1986; contbr. articles to profl. jours.; patentee in field. Recipient rsch. award RCA Labs., 1955; rsch. grantee Office of Naval Research, Washington, 1982, E-Systems, Falls Church, Va., 1983, MCI, Falls Church, Va., Instelsat, Washington. Fellow IEEE (bd. govs. 1979-82, digital comm. com., Centennial medal 1984), AAAS, Washington Acad. Scis.; mem. IEEE Comm. Soc. (v.p. 1986-88, pres. 1990-92, Donald W. McLellan award, 1994, Erskine fellow New Zealand 1997), Math. Assn. Am., Cosmos Club, Sigma Xi, Eta Kappa Nu. Home: 3613 Glenbrook Rd Fairfax VA 22031-3210 Office: George Washington U Dept Elec Engring Washington DC 20052

PICKHOLZ, JEROME WALTER, advertising agency executive; b. N.Y.C., Sept. 11, 1932; s. Solomon and Miriam (Schussler) P.; m. Phyllis Rachelle

Plump, July 11, 1954; children: Keith, Michelle. BBA, CCNY, 1953. CPA, N.Y. Sr. acct. Eisner & Lubin (CPAs), 1957-60; contr. Hodes-Daniel Co., Elmsford, N.Y., 1960-65; v.p. Hodes-Daniel Co., 1965-70; pres., mgr. direct mail ops. Cordura Corp. div. Hodes Daniel Co., Elmsford, 1970-74; exec. v.p. Ogilvy & Mather Direct Response, Inc., N.Y.C., 1974-79, pres., 1979-86, chmn., chief exec. officer, 1986-95, chmn. emeritus, 1995—; vice chmn. Ogilvy & Mather Worldwide, N.Y.C., 1991-95; founding prin. Pickholz, Tweedy, Cowan, N.Y.C., 1996—; bd. dirs. Mail-Well, Inc. Bd. dirs. ARC Greater N.Y., 1987—. Lt. (j.g.) USN, 1954-56. Recipient Eddy award Mail Advt. Svcs. Assn., 1988, Silver Apple award Direct Mktg. Club N.Y., 1989, Direct Marketer of Yr., 1992, Malcolm F. Dunn Leadership award, 1994. Mem. Direct Mktg. Assn. (bd. dirs. 1985—, mem. exec. com. 1986-88, chmn. 1991—). Office: Pickholz, Tweedy, Cowan 520 Madison Ave New York NY 10022-4213

PICKLE, JAMES C., hospital administrator; b. Memphis, June 8, 1943; s. John Lott and Sarah Elizabeth (Adams) P.; m. Peggy Jean Massey, Dec. 18, 1965; children: Jeff, Matt. BS in Liberal Arts, Memphis State U., 1967, MPA, 1977. Asst. to pres. Store Devel. Corp., Memphis, 1967-69; investment analyst First Tenn. Adv. Corp., Memphis, 1972-73; v.p., dir. Care Inns Inc., Memphis, 1973-76; dir. shared svcs. Meth. Hosps., Memphis, 1978, v.p. adminstrn., 1978-83, sr. v.p., 1983-84, exec. v.p., 1985-87. Mem. health and welfare ministry bd. Memphis Conf., United Meth. Ch., 1983-87; COO Meth. Hosps., Memphis, 1983-87; pres., CEO Erlanger Med. Ctr., Chattanooga, Tenn., 1987-94; pres. Ky. divsn. Columbia/HCA Healthcare Corp., 1994-96, London Region, 1996—; mem. health adv. bd. Memphis State U., 1984-87; chmn. bd. dirs. Dogwood Village of Memphis and Shelby County Inc., 1984-87. Recipient Humanitarian award Am. Lung Assn., 1991, Mgr. of the Yr award Chattanooga Area Mgr. Assn., 1993. Mem. Am. Coll. Hosp. Adminstrs., Nat. Assn. Pub. Hosps. (bd. dirs., mem. exec. com. 1991-94), Tenn. Hosp. Assn. (bd. dirs., mem. numerous coms.), Memphis Hosp. Coun. (sec.-treas. 1985, pres. 1987), Tenn. Pub. and Tchg. Hosp. Assn. (chmn. 1989-94). Republican. Methodist. Avocations: snow skiing; sailing. Home: 28 St Edmunds Terr, St Johns Wood, London NW8 7QB, England Office: The Wellington Hosp, Wellington Pl, London NW8 9LE, England

PICKLE, JERRY RICHARD, lawyer; b. Paris, Tex., Feb. 2, 1947; s. Joseph Rambert and Martha Marie (Biggers) P.; m. Helen Leigh Russell, May 3, 1975; children: Jonathan Russell, Sarah Elizabeth. BA in History, U. Houston, 1969, JD, 1971. Bar: Tex. 1972, U.S. Dist. Ct. (no. dist.) Tex. 1974, U.S. Dist. Ct. (we. dist.) Tex. 1989. Mem. Luna, Ballard & Pickle, Garland, Tex., 1972-74; assoc. Hightower & Alexander, Dallas, 1974-76, Cuba & Johnson, Temple, Tex., 1976-77; assoc. gen. counsel Scott & White Clinic, Temple, 1977—; assoc. prof. Tex. A&M U. Coll. of Medicine, Temple, 1986—. Contbr. articles to profl. jours. V.p. The Caring House, Temple, 1989, Tex. divsn. Am. Cancer Soc., Temple, 1976-77; adv. bd. R.R. & Pioneer Mus., Temple, 1982-84; hist. preservation bd. City of Temple, 1979-90; chmn. Bell County Hist. Commn., 1980-82; bd. dirs. Bell County Mus., 1992—, Temple Coord. Child Care Coun., 1991-93, Sr. Citizens Activities Ctr., Temple, 1993-94, pres., 1994-95; bd. dirs. Temple Cultural Activities Ctr., 1992—, pres., 1994-95; chair Heart o'Tex. Coun., Chisholm Trail Dist., Boy Scouts Am., 1987-88. Mem. ABA, Am. Acad. Hosp. Attys., State Bar Tex. (health law sect. councilman 1980-84, 85-87, chmn. 1983-84), Tex. Young Lawyers Assn., State Bar Coll., Bell-Lampasas-Mills Counties Bar Assn. (bd. dirs. 1985-90, pres. 1988-89), Bell-Lampasas-Mills Counties Young Lawyers Assn. (pres. 1980-81), Nat. Health Lawyers Assn., Am. Acad. Healthcare Attys., Temple C. of C. (bd. dirs. 1983-85, 88-90), Rotary (chpt. dir. 1981-85, 86-87), Jaycees (chpt. dir. 1977-78). Democrat. Episcopalian. Avocations: reading, golf, music. Office: Scott & White Clinic 2401 S 31st St Temple TX 76508-0001

PICKLE, JOSEPH WESLEY, JR., religion educator; b. Denver, Apr. 8, 1935; s. Joseph Wesley and Wilhelmina (Blacketor) P.; m. Judith Ann Siebert, June 28, 1958; children: David E., Kathryn E., Steven J. BA, Carleton Coll., 1957; B.D., Chgo. Theol. Sem., 1961; MA, U. Chgo., 1962, PhD, 1969. Ordained to ministry Am. Bapt. Conv., 1962. Asst. pastor Judson Meml. Ch., N.Y.C., 1959-60; acting dean summer session Colo. Coll., Colorado Springs, 1969-70, from asst. prof. to prof. religion, 1964—, faculty dir. internat. studies, 1994—; vis. prof. theology Iliff Sch. Theology, Denver, 1984; vis. prof. religious studies U. Zimbabwe, Harare, 1989; cons. Colo. Humanities Program, Denver, 1975-89; coord. Sheffer Meml. Fund, Colo. Coll., Colorado Springs, 1983—. Co-editor Papers of the 19th Century Theology Group, 1978, 88, 93. Pres. bd. dirs. Pikes Peak Mental Health Ctr., Colorado Springs, 1975; chmn. Colo. Health Facilities Rev. Coun., Denver, 1979-84; mem. Colo. Health Facilities Rev. Coun., Denver, 1976-84, Colo. Bd. Health, Denver, 1986-91; bd. dirs. Marson Found., Colorado Springs, 1994—. Am. Bapt. Conv. scholar, 1953-59; Fulbright Hays Grad. fellow U. Tübingen, Fed. Republic Germany, 1963-64, Danforth fellow, 1957-63, Joseph Malone fellow, 1987. Fellow Soc. for Values in Higher Edn.; mem. Am. Theol. Soc. (pres. 1996-97), Am. Acad. Religion (regional pres. 1983-84, 92-93), Cath. Theol. Soc. Am., Fulbright Assn., Phi Beta Kappa. Democrat. Home: 20 W Caramillo St Colorado Springs CO 80907-7314 Office: Colo Coll 14 E Cache La Poudre St Colorado Springs CO 80903-3243

PICKLE, LINDA WILLIAMS, biostatistician; b. Hampton, Va., July 19, 1948; d. Howard Taft and Kathryn Lee (Riggin) Williams; 1 child from previous marriage, Diane Marie; m. James B. Pearson, Jr., Oct. 14, 1984. BA, Johns Hopkins U., 1974, PhD in Biostats., 1977; postgrad., George Washington U., 1986-87. Computer programmer Comml. Credit Computer Corp., Balt., 1966-69; systems analyst, computer programmer Greater Balt. Med. Ctr., Balt., 1969-72; grad. teaching asst. biostats. Johns Hopkins U., Balt., 1974-77; adj. asst. prof. div. biostats. and epidemiology Georgetown U. Med. Sch., Washington, 1983-88, assoc. prof. div. biostats and epidemiology, 1988-91, dir. biostats. unit, V.T. Lombardi Cancer Rsch. Ctr., 1988-91; biostatistician Nat. Cancer Inst. NIH, Bethesda, Md., 1977-88; math. statistician office rsch. methodology Nat. Ctr. for Health Stats., Hyattsville, Md., 1991—. Author: Atlas of U.S. Cancer Mortality Among Whites: 1950-80, 1987, Atlas of U.S. Cancer Mortality Among Nonwhites: 1950-1980, 1990, Atlas of United States Mortality, 1996; contbr. articles to med. and statis. jours. Sr. troop leader Girl Scouts U.S., 1981-83; sci. fair judge, 1983—. Mem. The Biometric Soc., Am. Statis. Assn., Soc. Epidemiologic Research, Soc. Indsl. and Applied Math., Sigma Delta Epsilon (pres. Omicron chpt. 1984), Phi Beta Kappa. Achievements include research in statistical methods in epidemiology, mapping health statistics.

PICKLE, ROBERT DOUGLAS, lawyer, footwear industry executive; b. Knoxville, Tenn., May 22, 1937; s. Robert Lee and Beatrice Jewel (Douglas) P.; m. Rosemary Elaine Noser, May 9, 1964. AA summa cum laude, Schreiner Mil. Coll., Kerrville, Tex., 1957; BSBA magna cum laude, U. Tenn., 1959, JD, 1961; honor grad. seminar, Nat. Def. U., 1979. Bar: Tenn. 1961, Mo. 1964, U.S. Ct. Mil. Appeals 1962, U.S. Supreme Ct. 1970. Atty. Brown Shoe Co., Inc., St. Louis, 1963-69, asst. sec., atty., 1969-74; sec., gen. counsel Brown Group, Inc., St. Louis, 1974-85, v.p., gen. counsel, corp. sec., 1985—; indiv. mobilization augmentee, asst. army judge adv. gen. civil law The Pentagon, Washington, 1984-89. Provisional judge Municipal Ct., Clayton, Mo., summer 1972; chmn. Clayton Region attys. sect., profl. div. United Fund Greater St. Louis Campaign, 1972-73, team capt., 1974-78; chmn. City of Clayton Parks and Recreation Commn., 1985-87; liaison admissions officer, regional and state coordinator U.S. Mil. Acad., 1980—. Col. JAGC, U.S. Army, 1961-63. Decorated Meritorious Svc. medal. Fellow Harry S. Truman Meml. Library; mem. ABA, Tenn. Bar Assn., Mo. Bar Assn., St. Louis County Bar Assn., Bar Assn. Met. St. Louis, St. Louis Bar Found. (bd. dirs. 1979-81), Am. Corp. Counsel Assn., Am. Soc. Corp. Secs. (treas. St. Louis regional group 1976-77, sec. 1977-78, v.p. 1978-79, pres. Quarter-Century Club 1979-80), U. Tenn. Gen. Alumni Assn. (pres., bd. dirs. St. Louis chpt. 1974-76, 80-84, bd. govs. 1982-89), U.S. Trademark Assn. (bd. dirs. 1978-82), Tenn. Soc. St. Louis (bd. dirs. 1980-88, treas., sec., v.p. 1984-87, pres. 1987-88), Smithsonian Nat. Assocs., World Affairs Coun. St. Louis, Inc., Am. Legion, University Club (v.p., sec. St. Louis chpt. 1976-81, bd. dirs. 1976-81), Stadium Club, West Point Soc. St. Louis (hon. mem., bd. dirs. 1992—), Conf. Bd. (coun. chief legal officers), Fontbonne Coll. Pres.'s Assocs., St. Louis U. Billiken Club, St. Louis U. DuBourg Soc. (hon. dean), Scabbard and Blade, Kappa Sigma, Phi Delta Phi, Phi Theta Kappa, Beta Gamma Sigma, Phi Kappa Phi. Republican. Presbyterian. Avocations: reading, spectator sports. Home: 214 Topton Way Saint Louis MO 63105-3638 Office: Brown Group Inc 8300 Maryland Ave Saint Louis MO 63105-3645

PICKLEMANN, JACK R., surgeon. MD, McGill U., Montreal, Que., Can., 1964. Intern Royal Victoria Hosp., Montreal, Que., Can., 1964-65; resident in surgery U. Chgo. Med. Ctr., 1967-73; prof. surgery Loyola U., Chgo.; attending physician Loyola Med. Ctr., Maywood, Ill. Mem. ACS. Office: Loyola U Med Ctr 2160 S 1st Ave Maywood IL 60153-3304

PICKOVER, BETTY ABRAVANEL, retired executive legal secretary, civic volunteer; b. N.Y.C., Apr. 20, 1920; d. Albert and Sultana (Rousso) Abravanel; m. Bernard Builder, Apr. 6, 1941 (div. 1962); children: Ronald, Stuart; m. William Pickover, Aug. 23, 1970 (dec. Nov. 1983). Student, Taft Evening Ctr., 1961-70. Sec. U.S. Treasury Dept., Washington, 1942-43; exec. legal sec. various attys., Bronx, N.Y., 1956-70; exec. legal sec. various attys., Yonkers, N.Y., 1971-83, ret., 1983. Chair Uniongram Sisterhood of Temple Emanu-El, Yonkers, N.Y., 1975—, Honor Roll, 1975—, v.p. 1995-97; sr. citizen cmty. leader Yonkers Officer for Aging, 1984—, Westchester County Sr. Adv. Bd., White Plains, N.Y., 1989-96; v.p. Mayor's Cmty. Rels. Com. of Yonkers, 1985—, historian, photographer, 1988—; v.p. Mayor's cmty. Rels. com. Yonkers, 1995; mem. adv. coun. Westchester County Office Aging Sr., 1993—; bd. legislators task force sr. citizens Westchester County, 1995-97; Mayor Silver City Coun. Yonkers, 1989; mem. Mayor's adv. coun. sr. citizens, 1990. Recipient Appreciation cert. Westchester County, 1992, Pres. Coun., City of Yonkers, 1992, Merit cert., 1993, Cmty. Svc. award Mayor, City of Yonkers, 1995, 96, John E. Andrus Meml. Vol. award, 1995, Appreciation cert. Westchester County Exec., 1993, 94, Merit cert. N.Y. State Senator, 1995, Merit cert. N.Y. State Senator, 1994, Proclamation Mayor of Yonkers, 1985, 89, 92, (2) Awards U.S. Ho. of Reps., 1992, Woman of Excellence award Yonkers C. of C., 1993, Awards Mayors of Yonkers, 1985-96, awards N.Y. State Senator and Assemblyman 1987-96, Resolution City of Yonkers, 1993, Cert. of Appreciation Westchester County Bd. of Legislators, 1996; nominee U.S. Pres.'s Svc. award, 1995; named to Sr. Citizen Hall of Fame, 1992. Democrat. Jewish. Avocations: writing, photography, entertaining at all nursing homes in Yonkers, history, public relations. Home: 200 Valentine Ln Yonkers NY 10705-3608

PICKREL, PAUL, English educator; b. Gilson, Ill., Feb. 2, 1917; s. Clayton and Inez (Murphy) P. A.B., Knox Coll., 1938; M.A., Yale U., 1942, Ph.D., 1944. Instr. English Lafayette Coll., 1941-42; instr. Yale U., 1943-45, asst. prof., 1945-50, lectr. English, 1954-66, chmn. Scholar of House Program, 1959-60, 61-66; fellow Morse Coll., 1962-66; adviser John Hay fellows, 1959-66; vis. prof. English Smith Coll., Northampton, Mass., 1966-67, prof., 1967-87, prof. emeritus, 1987—, chmn. dept., 1972-75, 81-82. Author: (novel) The Moving Stairs, 1948; also essays on fiction, numerous book revs.; mng. editor: Yale Rev., 1949-66; chief book critic: Harper's mag., 1954-65. Mem. Aurelian Honor Soc., Phi Beta Kappa. Clubs: Elizabethan (New Haven), Faculty (Northampton); Yale (N.Y.C.). Office: Smith Coll Wright Hall Northampton MA 01063

PICKRELL, THOMAS RICHARD, retired oil company executive; b. Jermyn, Tex., Dec. 30, 1926; s. Mont Bolt and Martha Alice (Dodson) P.; m. M. Earline Bowen, Sept. 9, 1950; children—Thomas Wayne, Michael Bowen, Kent Richard, Paul Keith. B.S., North Tex. State U., 1951, M.B.A., 1952; postgrad., Ohio State U., 1954-55; advanced mgmt. program, Harvard U., 1979. CPA, Tex. Auditor, acct. Conoco, Inc., Ponca City, Okla., 1955-62; mgr. acctg. Conoco, Inc., Houston, 1965-67; asst. controller Conoco, Inc., Ponca City, 1967-81; v.p., controller Conoco, Inc., Stamford, Conn., 1982-83, Wilmington, Del., 1983-85; asst. prof. Okla. State U., Stillwater, Okla., 1962-63; controller Douglas Oil Co., Los Angeles, 1963-65; mem. adv. bd. dept. acctg. North Tex. State U., Denton, 1978-85; mem. adv. bd. Coll. Bus., Kansas State U., Manhattan, 1979-81. Bd. dirs. YMCA, Ponca City, 1976-78, Kay Guidance Clinic, Ponca City, 1971-74, United Way, Ponca City, 1979-81; chmn. Charter Rev. Com., Ponca City, 1971-72. Served to sgt. U.S. Army, 1944-46; ETO. Mem. AICPA, Fin. Execs. Inst. (pres. Okla. chpt. 1972), Am. Petroleum Inst. (acctg. com., gen. com.), Ponca City Country Club (pres. 1980-81), Rotary (pres. Ponca City club 1973-74), Beta Gamma Sigma, Beta Alpha Psi. Republican. Presbyterian. Home: 10 San Juan Ranch Rd Santa Fe NM 87501-9804

PICOTTE, LEONARD FRANCIS, naval officer; b. Calumet, Mich., Dec. 8, 1939; s. Irving René and Maria (Tamborino) P.; m. Sandra Lees Whiteley, July 14, 1984; children from previous marriage: Mary Elizabeth, Lance, Michael. BS in Econs. cum laude, U. No. Mich., 1963; MA in Polit. Sci., San Diego State U., 1975; grad. with distinction, Armed Forces Staff Coll., Norfolk, Va., 1976; M in Strategic Studies, Naval War Coll., Newport, R.I., 1985. Commd. ensign USN, 1963, advanced through grades to rear adm., 1991; comdg. officer USS Marathon, Vietnam, 1971-73; exec. officer USS Point Defiance, San Diego, 1976-78; exec. officer, officer in charge Surface Warfare Officers' Sch., Coronado, Calif., 1978-80; exec. officer Naval Sta., San Diego, 1980; comdg. officer USS Alamo, San Diego, 1980-82; surface warfare detailer Bur. Naval Pers., Washington, 1982-84; comdg. officer USS Duluth, San Diego, 1986-88; 1st comdg. officer USS Wasp, 1988-90; insp. gen. Comdr. in Chief, U.S. Atlantic Command, Comdr. in Chief, U.S. Atlantic Fleet, Norfolk, 1990-92; comdr. Amphibious Group Two, Norfolk, 1992-95; ret., 1995; lead analyst expeditionary warfare Am. Systems Corp., Chesapeake, Va., 1995—. Decorated Legion of Merit (2); recipient Disting. Svc. medal. Mem. Surface Navy Assn., USS Wasp Assn. (hon.), Army and Navy Club, Town Point Club, Hampton Roads Coun. Navy League (bd. dirs.), Nat. Security Indsl. Assn. (exec. com. Naval Expeditionary Warfare). Republican. Roman Catholic. Avocations: jogging, hunting, reading, gardening, chess. Home: 119 Northgate Ln Suffolk VA 23434 Office: Am Systems Corp Greenbriar Cir Chesapeake VA 23320

PICOWER, WARREN MICHAEL, editor; b. N.Y.C., Aug. 21, 1934; s. Abraham and Nell (Bloom) P.; divorced; children: Jenny Emelia, Eve Julie. BA, Queens Coll., 1956; MA, New Sch. for Social Rsch., 1978; PsyD in Psychology, Heed U., L.A., 1982. Editorial asst. Newsweek mag., N.Y.C., 1956-59; assoc. editor SM Pub. Co., N.Y.C., 1961-63; assoc., mng. editor Fawcett Pubs., N.Y.C., 1963, 64-65; mng. editor Tuesday Publs., N.Y.C., 1965-67, exec. editor, v.p., 1967-73; sr. editor King Features Syndicate, N.Y.C., 1974-78; mng. editor Food & Wine Mag., N.Y.C., 1978-93; consulting editor Travel Holiday Mag., N.Y., 1993-94; mng. editor Zagat Survey restaurant and hotel guides, N.Y.C., 1994-97; sr. project editor Money Mag., N.Y.C., 1997—; cons. in field. Contbr. articles to profl. jours. Mem. Am. Soc. Mag. Editors, Assn. of Food Journalists. Office: Money Magazine Time & Life Bldg New York NY 10020

PICOZZI, ANTHONY, dentistry educator, educational administrator; b. Bklyn., Dec. 24, 1917; s. Louis and Ida (DeRosa) P.; m. Gloria Margaret Patinella, Feb. 9, 1952; children—Kathryn, Lori. B.S., Columbia U., 1939; D.D.S., NYU, 1944. Section chief Lever Bros. Research, Edgewater, N.J., 1955-68; prof. dentistry NYU, N.Y.C., 1968-74; adminstr., researcher Fairleigh Dickinson U., Hackensack, N.J., 1974-89; rsch. cons. Warner Lambert Co., Morris Plains, N.J., 1989—; cons. Lever Research, Edgewater, 1968-74, W.R. Grace, Balt., 1979-81. Contbr. articles to profl. jours. Served to lt. col. USAR. Mem. ADA (mem. coun. on dental rsch. 1987-91), Am. Assn. Dental Research (councillor 1981, bd. dirs. 1988-90), Am. Assn. Dental Schs. (sect. chmn. 1980-81). Home: 21 Ridge Rd Ridgewood NJ 07450-3159 Office: Warner Lambert Co 170 Tabor Rd Morris Plains NJ 07950-2536

PICRAUX, SAMUEL THOMAS, applied science and physics researcher; b. St. Charles, Mo., Mar. 3, 1943; s. Samuel F. and Jeannette D.; m. Danice R. Kent, July 12, 1970; children: Jeanine, Laura, Daryl. BS in Elec. Engring., U. Mo., 1965; postgrad. Cambridge U., Eng., 1965-66; MS in Engring. Sci., Calif. Inst. Tech., 1967, PhD in Engring. Sci. and Physics, 1969. Mem. tech. staff Sandia Nat. Labs., Albuquerque, 1969-72, div. supr., 1972-86, dept. mgr., 1986-96, dir., 1996—; mem. solid state scis. com. NRC; vis. scientist dept. physics Aarhus U., Denmark, 1975; NATO lectr., 1979, 81, 83, 86.; NSF lectr. 1976, 81. Author: Materials Analysis by Ion Channeling, 1982; editor: Applications of Ion Beams to Metals, 1974, Metastable Materials Formation by Ion Implantation, 1982, Nuclear Instruments and Methods International jour., 1983-91, Surface Alloying by Ion Electon and Laser Beams, 1986, Beam-Solid Interactions and Transient Processes, 1987; contbr. numerous articles to profl. jours. Fulbright fellow, 1965-66. Recipient Ernest Orlando Lawrence Meml. award, U.S. Dept. Energy, 1990, 3 Basic Energy Scis. Outstanding Rsch. awards, U.S. Dept. Energy, 1985, 92, 94. Fellow Am. Phys. Soc. (chmn. materials physics divsn., 1990); mem. IEEE, Am. Vacuum Soc., Materials Rsch. Soc. (pres. 1993). Office: Sandia Nat Labs POB 5800 Albuquerque NM 87185-1427

PIDERIT, JOHN J., university educator; b. N.Y.C., Feb. 26, 1944. BA in Math. and Philosophy magna cum laude, Fordham U., 1967; Lic. in Sacred Theology cum laude, Philosophische und Theologische Hochschule Sankt Georgen, Frankfurt, West Germany, 1971; MPhil, Oxford U., 1974; MA, PhD in Econ., Princeton U., 1979. Ordained Jesuit priest Roman Cath. Ch., 1971. Tchr. math. Regis H.S., N.Y.C., 1967-68; asst. campus minister Fordham U., 1971-72; asst. campus minister Princeton U., 1975-78, preceptor, 1976-77; asst. chairperson grad. studies Fordham U., 1984-88, dir. program internat. polit. econ. and devel., 1981-83, 87-88, asst. chairperson dept. econs., 1979-82, 88-89, asst. prof. econs., 1978-89, assoc. prof. econs., 1989-90; corp. v.p. Marquette U., 1990-93; pres. Loyola U. Chgo., 1993—; vis. fellow Woodstock Theol. Ctr., Washington, summer 1982; sabbatical Santa Clara U., 1989-90; master Queen's Ct. Residential Coll., 1987-90; chmn. responsible investment com. N.Y. province SJ, 1986-88, mem. fin. com., 1986-88; mem. joint commn. govtl. rels. of Am. Coun. Edn., 1994—; mem. exec. com. Nat. Planning Com. Jesuit Assembly '89, 1988-90. Contbr. articles to profl. jours. Founder, moderator Friends of Loyola, 1987-90; pres. Univ. Neighborhood Housing Corp., 1986-90, Maroon Enterprises, Inc., 1986-90; trustee Canisius Coll., Buffalo, 1983-88, 89-94, Loyola Marymount U., L.A., 1996—, John Carroll U., University Heights, Ohio, 1996—; bd. dirs. Corp. Cmty. Schs. of Am., 1993—; promoter PIVOT H.S. and Middle Sch. with Milw. Pub. Schs., 1990-93; mem. Greater Milw. Edn. Trust, 1990-93; mem. steering com., chair edn. task force Milw. Cmty. Traffic Safety Com., 1991-93; mem. steering com. Libr. Literacy Soc. Milw., 1991-93; mem. scholarship com. Knitworkers Union Local 155, N.Y.C., 1982-90; mem. Princeton Schs. Com. N.Y. Region, 1985-88. Mellon grantee Fordham U., summer 1983, summer grantee Fordham U., 1979, Princeton U. fellow, 1974-78. Office: Loyola U Chgo 820 N Michigan Ave Chicago IL 60611-2103

PIDGEON, JOHN ANDERSON, headmaster; b. Lawrence, Mass., Dec. 20, 1924; s. Alfred H. and Nora (Regan) P.; children: John Anderson, Regan S., Kelly; m. Barbara Hafer, May 1986. Grad., Phillips Acad., 1943; B.A., Bowdoin Coll., 1949; Ed.D., Bethany Coll., 1973; D.Litt., Washington and Jefferson Coll., 1979. Instr. Latin, adminstrv. asst. to headmaster Deerfield Acad., 1949-57; headmaster Kiskiminetas Springs Sch., Saltsburg, Pa., 1957—; dir. Saltburg Savs. & Trust. Served as ensign USNR, 1943-46. Mem. New Eng. Swimming Coaches Assn. (pres. 1956-57), Cum Laude Soc., Delta Upsilon. Home and Office: Kiski Sch 1888 Brett Ln Saltsburg PA 15681-8951

PIDOT, WHITNEY DEAN, lawyer; b. N.Y.C., Mar. 2, 1944; s. George B. and Virginia (Ulrich) P.; m. Jeanne Stoddard, April 23, 1973; children: Whitney Dean Jr., Philip Martin, Seth Thayer. AB, Harvard U., 1966; JD, Columbia U., 1970, MBA, 1970. Bar: N.Y. 1971. Ptnr. Shearman & Sterling, N.Y.C., 1970—; adv. bd. Barclays Bank N.Y., 1989-92, Molecular Tool, Inc. (biotech.) Balt., 1991-96, Equine Genetic Rsch. Ptnrs., Balt., 1991-95; trustee, vice chair Winthrop Univ. Hosp., Mineola, N.Y.; bd. dirs. Oneida Ltd., R.I. Corp., North Ctrl. Oil Corp., Houston, Cold Spring Harbor Labs., N.Y. Mayor, Village of Matinecock, Locust Valley, N.Y., 1977-92; vice chmn. North Shore Mayors Com., Long Island, N.Y., 1980-92; bd. dirs. Nassau County (N.Y.) Village Officials Assn., 1978-80; commr. Locust Valley Fire Dist., 1979-93. Mem. Piping Rock Club (pres. 1988-94), Links Club N.Y.C. (v.p., sec.). Republican. Home: Piping Rock Rd Locust Valley NY 11560 Office: 599 Lexington Ave Ste C-2 New York NY 10022-6030

PIDTO, BILL, sports network anchorman; b. Apr. 20, 1965. BA in Psychology, Cornell U., 1987. Sports dir. WBNG-TV, Binghampton, N.Y., 1987-89; weekend sports anchor WSTM-TV, Syracuse, N.Y., 1989; anchor Sports News Network, 1990; field prodr. Scholastic Sports Am. ESPN, 1991-92; sports anchor New Eng. Cable News, 1992; anchor SportsSmash ESPN, 1993—; host NHL 2Night ESPN, 1995—, commentator NFL PrimeTime, 1995—. Office: c/o ESPN ESPN Plaza Bristol CT 06010

PIECEWICZ, WALTER MICHAEL, lawyer; b. Concord, Mass., Jan. 27, 1948; s. Benjamin Michael and Cecelia (Makuc) P.; A.B. magna cum laude, Colgate U., 1970; J.D., Columbia U., 1973; m. Anne T. Mikolajczyk, Oct. 28, 1978; children—Tiffany Anne, Stephanie Marie. Admitted to Ill. bar, 1973; mem. firm Peterson & Ross, Chgo., 1987—; bd. dirs. No. Data Systems, Inc., Steiner Co., Inc., Arrow Pattern & Foundry Co., Inc., Steiner Trust Co. Mem. ABA, Ill. Bar Assn., Chgo. Bar Assn., Chgo. Estate Planning Coun., Internat. Bus. Coun. Midwest, Phi Beta Kappa. Roman Catholic. Office: Peterson & Ross 200 E Randolph St Ste 7300 Chicago IL 60601-7012

PIECH, MARGARET ANN, mathematics educator; b. Bridgewater, N.S., Can., Apr. 6, 1942; d. Frederick Cecil and Margaret Florence (Laschinger) Garrett; m. Kenneth Robert Piech, June 19, 1965; children: Garrett Andrew, Marjorie Ann. BA, Mt. Allison U., Sackville, N.B., Can., 1962; PhD, Cornell U., 1967. Asst. prof. SUNY, Buffalo, 1967-72, assoc. prof., 1972-78, prof. math., 1978—; cons. NSF, Washington, 1980-81, Aspen Analytics, Buffalo, 1986—; v.p. Seventy Niagara Svcs., 1990—. Contbr. articles to profl. jours. Woodrow Wilson fellow, 1962-63; grantee NSF, 1976-85, U.S. Army Rsch. Office, 1985-89. Mem. IEEE, Am. Math. Soc., Assn. Computing Machinery, Greater Yellowstone Coalition, Henry's Fork Found. Avocation: fly fishing. Office: SUNY Diefendorf Hall Buffalo NY 14214

PIECUCH, PAMELA GAYLE, systems operator/coordinator; b. Chgo., Aug. 1, 1954; d. Leon Benjamin and Loretta Mae (Skronz) P. BA magna cum laude, Northeastern U., Chgo., 1987. From pension benefit processor to adminstrv. asst. Structural Ironworkers Pension Fund, Chgo., 1976-89; computer systems operator, coord. SIW, Chgo., 1989—. Bd. dirs. Huntington Commons Assn., Mt. Prospect, Ill., 1989; outreach com. St. Michaels Orthodox Ch., Niles, Ill., 1993-96, trustee, 1997—. Mem. Phi Alpha Theta (historian 1987-89), Pi Gamma Mu, Alpha Chi. Orthodox Christian. Avocations: skating, horseback riding, computers, hiking, historical research. Home: 50 Regent Cir Schaumburg IL 60193-1869

PIEHL, DONALD HERBERT, chemist, consultant; b. Chgo., Jan. 18, 1939; s. Herbert Herman and Faye L. (Pentti) P.; m. Ann Elizabeth Guildner; children: Mark Donald, Jennifer Ann. BA in Chemistry, Carthage Coll., 1961; MS in Chemistry, U. Iowa, 1964, PhD in Chemistry, 1966; postgrad. Young Exec. Inst., U. N.C., 1974. Quality control chemist Bowey's, Inc., Chgo., 1961; polymer chemist Borg-Warner Corp., Des Plaines, Ill., 1962; sr. rsch. chemist R.J. Reynolds Tobacco Co., Winston-Salem, N.C., 1965-70, group leader, 1969-70; section head R.J. Reynolds Industries, Winston-Salem, 1970-76, rsch. mgr., 1976-80, dir. applied R & D, 1980-83; dir. tech. svcs. RJR Nabisco, Winston-Salem, 1983-85; v.p. R & D Heublein Inc., Hartford, Conn., 1985-89, v.p. tech. and brand devel., 1989-94; tchr. mgmt. of tech. and total quality mgmt., quality cons., 1994—; head rsch. and devel. PTHM, Sampoerna, Indonesia, 1995—; instr. Am. Mgmt. Assn., organizer, chmn. Pub. Symposium on Energy and Environ, Greensboro, N.C., 1974; mem. adv. com. mgmt. of tech. program U. N.C., Chapel Hill, 1982-84; tchr. bus. inst. Mgmt. Devel., Inc., Chapel Hill, 1975-85. Contbr. articles to profl. jours. Bd. dirs. Sci. and Tech. Inst. of New Eng., Storrs, Conn., 1988—, Sci. Mus. Conn., Hartford, 1989—, Indsl. Rsch. Inst., 1983—, chmn. precoll. edn. com., 1993-94; pres. Optimist CLub, Winston-Salem, 1971. Recipient Outstanding Young Man of Am. award, 1970, Optimist of Yr. award Optimist Club, 1971, Spl. Teaching award U. N.C. Sch. Bus., 1984; fellow Ethyl Corp., 1964-65. Fellow Conn. Acad. Edn.; mem. World Assn. of Alcohol Beverage Industry (v.p. and com. chair Conn. chpt. 1992-94), Am. Chem. Soc. (chmn. local sect. 1962—, Outstanding Svc. award 1974), Inst. Food Technologists, Conn. Quality Coun. (co-founder 1989—), N.C. Acad. Scis., Hartford C. of C. (chmn. bd. tech. coun. 1986-89), Sigma Xi, Alpha Chi Sigma. Republican. Avocations: tennis, golf, skiing, photography.

PIEKARSKI, VICTOR J., lawyer; b. Lawrence, Mass., Feb. 20, 1950. BA cum laude, Boston Coll., 1971; MBA, U. Chgo., 1978; JD cum laude,

Northwestern U., 1974. Bar: Ill. 1974, U.S. Ct. Appeals (7th cir.) 1977, U.S. Supreme Ct. 1978. Ptnr. Querrey & Harrow Ltd., Chgo. Mem. ABA, Ill. State Bar Assn., Chgo. Bar Assn., Ill. Assn. Def. Trial Counsel, Trial Lawyers Club Chgo., Def. Rsch. Inst. Office: Querrey & Harrow Ltd 180 N Stetson Ave Chicago IL 60601-6710

PIEL, CAROLYN FORMAN, pediatrician, educator; b. Birmingham, Ala., Oct. 18, 1918; d. James R. and Mary Elizabeth (Dortch) Forman; m. John Joseph Piel, Aug. 3, 1951; children: John Joseph, Mary Dortch, Elzabeth Forman, William Scott. BA, Agnes Scott Coll., 1940; MS, Emory U., 1943; MD, Washington U., St. Louis, 1946. Diplomate Am. Bd. Pediatrics (examiner 1973-88, pres. 1986-87); diplomate Am. Bd. Pediatric Nephrology. Intern Phila. Gen. Hosp., 1946-47; resident Phila. Children's Hosp., 1947-49; fellow Cornell U. Med. Sch., N.Y.C., 1949-51; from instr. to assoc. clin. prof. Stanford U. Sch. Medicine, San Francisco, 1951-59; from asst. prof. to prof. Sch. Medicine, U. Calif., San Francisco, 1959-89, emeritus prof., 1989—. Author, co-author research articles in field. Bd. mem. San Francisco Home Health Service, 1977-83. Emeritus mem. Soc. for Pediatric Research, Am. Pediatric Soc., Am. Soc. for Pediatric Nephrology, Am. Soc. Nephrology, Western Soc. for Pediatric Nephrology (pres. 1960). Democrat. Presbyterian. Home: 2164 Hyde St San Francisco CA 94109-1701 Office: U Calif PO Box 748 San Francisco CA 94143

PIEL, GERARD, science editor, publisher; b. Woodmere, L.I., N.Y., Mar. 1, 1915; s. William F.J. and Loretto (Scott) P.; m. Mary Tapp Bird, Feb. 4, 1938; children: Jonathan Bird, Samuel Bird (dec.); m. Eleanor Virden Jackson, June 24, 1955; child, Eleanor Jackson. A.B. magna cum laude, Harvard U., 1937; D.Sc., Lawrence Coll., 1956, Colby Coll., 1960; U. B.C., Brandeis U., 1965, Lebanon Valley Coll., 1977, L.I. U., 1978, Bard Coll., 1979, CUNY, 1979, U. Mo., 1985, Blackburn Coll., 1985; Litt.D., Rutgers U., 1961, Bates Coll., 1974; L.H.D., Columbia, 1962, Williams Coll., 1966, Rush U., 1979, Hahnemann Med. Coll., 1981, Mt. Sinai Med. Sch., 1985; LL.D., Tuskegee Inst., 1963, U. Bridgeport, 1964, Bklyn. Poly. Inst., 1965, Carnegie-Mellon U., 1968, Lowell U., 1986; Dr. (honoris causa), Moscow State (Lomonosov) U., 1985. Sci. editor Life mag., 1938-44; asst. to pres. Henry J. Kaiser Co. (and assoc. cos.), 1945-46; organizer (with Dennis Flanagan, Donald H. Miller, Jr.), pres.and pub. Sci. Am., Inc., 1946-84, chmn., 1984-87, chmn. emeritus, 1987-94. Translated edits.: Le Scienze, 1968, Saiensu, 1971, Investigacion y Ciencia, 1976, Pour la Science, 1977, Spektrum der Wissenschaft, 1978, KeXue, 1979, V Mire Nauki, 1983, Tudomany, 1985, Majallat Al Oloom, 1986; author: Science in the Cause of Man, 1961, The Acceleration of History, 1972, Only One World, 1992, Erde im Gleichgewicht, 1994. Chmn. Commn. Delivery Personal Health Services City N.Y., 1967-68; trustee N.Y. Bot. Garden, René Dubos Ctr.; trustee emeritus Am. Mus. Nat. History, Radcliffe Coll., Phillips Acad., Mayo Clinic, Henry J. Kaiser Family Found., Found. for Child Devel.; pub. mem. Am. Bd. Med. Specialities; bd. overseers Harvard U., 1966-68, 73-79. Recipient George Polk award, 1961, Kalinga prize, 1962, Bradford Washburn award, 1966, Arches of Sci. award, 1969; Rosenberger medal U. Chgo., 1973, In Praise of Reason award Com. Scientists for Investigation of Claims of Paranormal, 1987, A.I. Djavakhishvili medal U. Tbilisi, 1985; named Pub. of Yr. Mag. Pubs. Assn., 1980. Fellow Am. Acad. Arts and Scis., AAAS (pres. 1985, chmn. 1986); mem. Coun. Fgn. Rels., Am. Philos. Soc., Nat. Acad. Sci. Inst. Medicine, Harvard Club, Century Club, Met. Opera Club, Cosmos Club, Somerset Club, Phi Beta Kappa, Sigma Xi. Home: 1115 5th Ave New York NY 10128-0100

PIEL, WILLIAM, JR., lawyer, arbitrator; b. N.Y.C., Nov. 28, 1909; s. William and Loretto (Scott) P.; m. Eleanor Green, Dec. 1, 1951; children by former marriage: Michael, Anthony, Thomas. AB, Princeton U., 1932; LLB, Harvard U., 1935. Bar: N.Y. 1935. Practiced in N.Y.C.; partner Sullivan & Cromwell, 1945-80, sr. counsel, 1980—; expert cons. mil. intelligence service War Dept. Gen. Staff, 1944-45; dir. emeritus Campbell Soup Co., Phillips Petroleum Co. Hon. dir. Greater N.Y.. coun. Girl Scouts Am.; hon. trustee Cancer Rsch. Inst.; trustee Internat. Crane Found., Baraboo, Wis. Fellow Am. Coll. Trial Lawyers, N.Y. State Bar Found.; mem. ABA, Assn. Bar City N.Y., Am. Judicature Soc., Fed. Bar Coun., Squadron A Assn., Century Assn., Princeton Club (N.Y.C.). Home: Tree House 44 Briggs Hill Rd Sherman CT 06784-1535

PIELE, PHILIP KERN, education infosystems educator; b. Portland, Oreg., May 14, 1935; s. Theodore R. and Helen D. (Hanson) P.; m. Sandra Jean Wright, Aug. 10, 1963; children: Melissa, Kathryn. BA, Wash. State U., 1957; student, U. Wash., 1960, San Jose State U., 1964; MS, U. Oreg., 1963, PhD, 1968. Prof. dept. ednl. policy and mgmt. U. Oreg., Eugene, 1979—, mem. faculty applied info. mgmt. program, 1989—, dir. numerous ednl. orgns. and coms. Coll. Edn., 1968—, dir. Edn. Resources Info. Ctr. (ERIC) clearinghouse on ednl. mgmt., 1969—, assoc. dir. Ctr. for Ednl. Policy and Mgmt., 1973-76, heqad dept. ednl. leadership, tech. and adminstrn., 1997—; vis. lectr. U. Western Australia, Monashe U., U. New S. Wales, and several other Australian Univs., 1973; vis. prof. Ontario Inst. for Studies in Edn., U. Toronto, 1974; vis. scholar Stanford U., 1984; exec. sec. Oreg. Sch. Study Coun., 1980—; dir. Networks and Comms. Ctr. for Advanced Tech. in Edn., 1984-92. Author numerous books, chpts., monographs; editor numerous books; contbr. articles to profl. jours. Bd. dirs. Oreg. Bach Festival, Eugene, 1980-83, Oreg. Mozart Players, Eugene, 1995-97. Mem. Nat. Orgn. in Legal Problems in Edn. (pres. 1977-78), Nat. Sch. Devel. Coun. (pres. 1985-86), Am. Ednl. Rsch. Assn. (sec. adminstrn. divsn. 1991-93). Home: 2026 Morning View Dr Eugene OR 97405-1632 Office: U Oreg ERIC Clearinghouse on Ednl Mgmt 1787 Agate St Eugene OR 97403-1923

PIELOU, EVELYN C., biologist; m. Patrick Pielou, June 22, 1944; 3 children. B.Sc., U. London, 1950, Ph.D., 1962, DSc, 1975; LLD (hon.), Dalhousie U., 1993. Research scientist Can. Govt., 1963-67; vis. prof. N.C. State U., 1968, Yale, New Haven, 1969; prof. biology Queen's U., Kingston, Ont., 1969-71, Dalhousie U., Halifax, N.S., 1971-84; vis. prof. U. Sydney, Australia, 1975; oil sands environ. vis. research prof. U. Lethbridge, Alta., 1981-86. Author: Introduction to Mathematical Ecology, 1969, Population and Community Ecology, 1974, Ecological Diversity, 1975, Mathematical Ecology, 1977, Biogeography, 1979, Interpretation of Ecological Data, 1984, World of Northern Evergreens, 1988, After the Ice Age, 1991, Naturalist's Guide to the Arctic, 1994; contbr. articles to profl. jours. Recipient Lawson medal Can. Bot. Assn., 1984, Eminent Ecologist award Ecol. Soc. Am., 1986, Disting. Statis. Ecologist award Internat. Congress Ecology, Commemorative medal for 125th Anniversary of Confedn. of Can., 1992. Mem. Brit. Ecol. Soc. (hon. life), Am. Acad. Arts and Scis. (fgn. hon. mem.).

PIEMME, THOMAS E., medical educator. BS with high honors, U. Pitts., 1954, MD, 1958; postgrad., Ohio State U., 1964-65. Diplomate Nat. Bd. Med. Examiners; cert. Am. Bd. Family Practice. Intern Health Ctr. Hosps., Pitts., 1958-59, asst. resident in medicine, 1959-60; jr. asst. resident in medicine Peter Bent Brigham Hosp., Boston, 1960-61, fellow/AHA, asst. in medicine, 1961-63; rsch. cardiologist, chief bioanalysis br. Envrion. Med. Div. USAF, Wright-Patterson AFB, Ohio, 1964-66; asst. prof. medicine U. Pitts. Sch. of Medicine, 1966-69; asst. chief of medicine Presbyn. U. Hosp., Pitts., 1966-69; prof. medicine, dir. Divsn. Gen. Medicine George Washington U. Sch. of Medicine, 1969-74; various to prof. health care scis. and medicine, assoc. dean George Washington U. Sch. Medicine, 1977—, 1987—. Contbr. articles to profl. jours. and publs. Maj. USAF. Scholar of John and Mary Markle Found., 1966-71; recipient Disting. Svc. award Nat. Bd. Med. Examiners, 1984, others. Mem. AAAS, AMA, AAUP, Am. Fedn. Clin. Rsch., Aerospace Med. Assn., Assn. Am. Med. Colls., Am. Soc. Internal Medicine, Am. Heart Assn., Soc. Tchrs. of Family Medicine, Assn. Phys. Asst. Programs, Am. Acad. Family Physicians, Alliance for Continuing Med. Edn., Soc. for Med. Decision Making (adminstrv. dir.), Phi Beta Kappa, Alpha Omega Alpha, others. Office: George Washington U Office Continuing Med Edn 2300 K St NW Washington DC 20037-1700

PIEMONTE, ROBERT VICTOR, association executive; b. N.Y.C., July 28, 1934; s. Rosario and Carmela (Santoro) P. BS, L.I. U., 1967; MA, Columbia U., 1968, MEd, 1970, EdD, 1976; DSc (hon.), L.I. U., Bklyn., 1993. Asst. dir. nursing svc. ANA, N.Y.C., 1968-69, dir. nursing svc., 1971-72, divsn. dir., 1983-85; asst. dir. nursing Univ. Hosp.-NYU, N.Y.C., 1970-71; assoc. dir. ops. N.Y.C. Health and Hosps. Corp., N.Y.C., 1972-76; assoc. prof. Tchr.'s Coll. Columbia U., N.Y.C., 1976-78; exec. dir. N.J. State Nurses Assn., Montclair, 1978-80; dep. exec. dir. Nat. Student Nurses Assn., N.Y.C., 1980-83, exec. dir., 1985-96, cons., 1996—; adj. prof. nursing Tchr.'s Coll. Columbia U., 1990—; cons. Consensus Mgmt., N.Y.C., 1992—. Contbr. articles to profl. publs.; mem. editl. adv. bd. Nursing and Health Care, 1985-95. Areawide chair nursing Greater N.Y. chpt. ARC, N.Y.C., 1990-93. Col. U.S. Army, 1987-94, ret. Recipient Disting. Alumni award L.I. U., 1984, Hon. Recognition award N.Y. State Nurses Assn., 1992. Fellow Am. Acad. Nursing (treas. 1993—); mem. Am. Soc. Assn. Execs. (cert., bd. dirs. 1993-96), Am. Nurses Found. (trustee 1994—), Nursing House, Inc. (pres. 1993—), Nat. Adv. Coun. on Nurse Edn. and Practice, N.Y. Soc. Assn. Execs. (Outstanding Assn. Exec. 1991, pres. 1989-90). Democrat. Roman Catholic. Avocations: theatre, reading, travel. Home: 76 W 86th St New York NY 10024-3607

PIEMONTESE, DAVID STEFANO, pharmaceutical scientist; b. Paterson, N.J., July 9, 1965; s. Gennarino and Alba (Reis) P. BS in Biology, William Paterson Coll., 1988; MS in Pharm. Sci., St. John's U., Jamaica, N.Y., 1995. Asst. scientist Hoffmann-LaRoche, Inc., Nutley, N.J., 1988-95; presenter in field. Contbr. chpts. to books and articles to profl. jours. Mem. Am. Assn. Pharm. Scientists. Avocations: travel, bicycling, music, reading. Home: 152-18 Union Trnpk Bldg 2 Apt 4F Flushing NY 11367

PIEN, FRANCIS D., internist, microbiologist; b. Detroit, Apr. 7, 1945; s. Chung Ling and Nung Chung (Lee) P.; m. Harriet Ho, Dec. 27, 1967; children: Brian, Ethan, Kevin. BA, Johns Hopkins U., Balt., 1965, MPH, 1971; MD, U. Chgo., 1969; MS in Microbiology, U. Minn., 1973. Diplomate Nat. Bd. Med. Examiners, Am. Bd. Internal Medicine, subspecialty in infectious disease, Am. Bd. Med. Microbiology. Intern U. Ill., 1969-70; fellow in microbiology, resident in internal medicine Mayo Grad. Sch. Medicine, Rochester, Minn., 1970-73; fellow in infectious disease Stanford (Calif.) U., 1973-74; assoc. program dir. integrated med. residency program U. Hawaii, Honolulu, 1977-90, assoc. prof. medicine, 1977-88, prof. medicine, 1988-93, chief infectious diseases, 1987-93, clin. prof. tropical medicine and med. microbiology, 1983—; infectious disease cons. Straub Clinic, Honolulu, 1974—; exchange prof. U. Osaka (Japan) Sch. Medicine, 1990; cons. in infeciton control Leahi Hosp., 1993—; bd. dirs. Rehab. Hosp. of Pacific, Honolulu, 1989-93, Interfaith Hosp. Chaplaincy Ministry, 1990-94, Samaritan Counseling Ctr., 1992-95, Straub Clinic and Hosp., 1990-93. Reviewer Hawaii Med. Jour., Reviews of Infectious Diseases, Western Jour. Medicine, Straub Clinic Proceedings; contbr. over 150 articles to profl. jours. Fellow ACP, Am. Acad. Microbiology, Infectious Disease Soc. Am., Royal Soc. Tropical Medicine and Hygiene; mem. AMA, Hawaii Med. Soc. (chmn. communicable disease com. 1979-83), Am. Soc. Tropical Medicine and Hygiene (mem. delegation to Mainland China 1978), Am. Soc. Microbiology (Hawaii br. pres. 1982-83), Christian Med. Soc., Assn. for Practitioners for Infection Control, Internat. Soc. Travel Medicine, Am. Soc. Sexually Transmitted Diseases, Soc. of Hosp. Epidemiologists of Am., European Soc. Clin. Microbiology. Republican. Presbyterian. Avocations: medical missions, research, travel. Office: Straub Clinic 888 S King St Honolulu HI 96813-3009

PIEN, SHYH-JYE JOHN, mechanical engineer; b. Kaohsiung, Taiwan, Republic of China, July 14, 1956; came to U.S., 1980; s. Ke-Lee and Sue-Jean (Shen) P.; m. Fong-Ling Yang, July 15, 1982; children: Irene J., Jennifer M. BSME, Nat. Taiwan U., 1978; MSME, U. Ill., 1982, PhD, 1985. Asst. prof. U. Notre Dame, South Bend, Ind., 1985-89; sr. engr. Alcoa Tech. Ctr., Alcoa Ctr., Pa., 1989-91, staff engr., 1991-95, tech. specialist, 1995—; sr. advisor UN Devel. Program for China, 1995; panelist on heat transfer in mfg. at profl. confs.; panel chmn. and panelist on spray forming tech. at profl. confs. Editor symposium procs.; contbr. articles to profl. publs. Co-chmn. Nat. Youth Day Assembly, Taiwan, 1977; pres. Chinese Inst. Engrs. in USA, U. Ill., Urbana, 1984; v.p. Orgn. Chinese Ams., Pitts., 1993—. Recipient Excellent Youth award Kashiung City Province, Taiwan, Nat. Coll. Excellent Youth award Govt. Taiwan, Rsch. Initiation award NSF, 1988, Alcoa Merit award, 1995, Alcoa Comty. Leadership award, 1996. Mem. ASME (materials processing and mfg. com. heat transfer divsn. 1990—, planning and devel. com. 1993—, chmn. indsl. liaison com. 1996). Roman Catholic. Achievements include 4 patents on continuous casting machine design, patents pending on spray casting device and twin-belt casting device; research on nuclear safety analysis, hysteresis effect in natural convection, thermal/fluid phenomena in continuous casting, electronic packaging, welding process control, extrusion flow modeling, die casting, spray forming. Office: Aluminum Co Am Alcoa Tech Ctr New Kensington PA 15069

PIENE, OTTO, artist, educator; b. Laasphe, Westphalia, Germany, Apr. 18, 1928; s. Otto and Anne (Niemeyer) P.; children—Annette, Herbert, Claudia, Chloe. Student, Acad. Fine Arts, Munich, Germany, 1949-50, Acad. Fine Arts, Dusseldorf, Germany, 1950-52; Staatsexamen in Philosophy, U. Cologne, Germany, 1957; DFA, U. Md., Balt., 1995. Co-founder Group Zero, Dusseldorf, Germany, 1957; vis. prof. Grad. Sch. Art, U. Pa., Phila., 1964; prof. environ. art Sch. Architecture and Planning, MIT, Cambridge, Mass., 1972-93, dir. Ctr. for Advanced Visual Studies, MIT, 1974-94; dir. emeritus Ctr. for Advanced Visual Studies MIT, 1994—; dir. Sky Art Conf. MIT, 1981, 82, 83, 86; vis. artist, guest prof. numerous univs.; prin. artist, designer numerous archtl. and environ. art commns. and pub. celebrations. Author: (with Heinz Mack) Zero 1, 2, 3, 1958, 61, More Sky, 1973, Sky Art Conf. Proc., 1981, 82, 83, Feuerbilder und Texte, 1988; one man exhbns. include Howard Wise Gallery, N.Y.C., 1965, 69, 70, Galerie Heseler, Munich, 1971, 72, 75, 77, 78, 79, 83, 86, MIT, 1975, 93, Galerie Schoeller, Düsseldorf, Fed. Republic Germany, 1977, 79, 83, 87, 91, 95, Fitchburg (Mass.) Art Mus., 1977, Galerie Watari, Tokyo, 1983, Pat Hearn Gallery, N.Y.C., 1985, Gallery 360, Tokyo, 1991, 92, Galèrie d'Art International, Paris, 1993, Städt Kunstmuseum, Düsseldorf, 1996; numerous group exhbns. U.S. and abroad including, Guggenheim Mus., N.Y.C., 1964, 66, 84, Albright-Knox Gallery Buffalo, 1968, Nat. Mus. Modern Art, Tokyo, 1969, Tate Gallery, London, 1974, Smithsonian Instn., Washington, 1978, Royal Acad. Art, London, 1985, National Gallery, Berlin, 1986, Statsgalerie, Stuttgart, 1986, Berlinische Galerie, Berlin, 1988-89, 91-92, MIT, 1994, Haus der Kunst, Munich, 1995, Bundeskunsthalle, Bonn, 1995, others; also represented in numerous permanent collections (recipient award Internat. Exhibition Graphic Art, Ljubljana, Yugoslavia 1967, 69, prize 8th Internat. Biennial Prints Nat. Mus. Modern Art, Tokyo, Japan 1972, Kohler-Maxwell prize 1987). Recipient Sculpture prize Am. Acad. Arts and Letters, N.Y.C., 1996. Mem. Deutscher Kunstlerbund. Office: MIT Ctr Advanced Visual Studies 265 Massachusetts Ave Cambridge MA 02139-4109

PIEPER, DAROLD D., lawyer; b. Vallejo, Calif., Dec. 30, 1944; s. Walter A. H. and Vera Mae (Ellis) P.; m. Barbara Gillis, Dec. 20, 1969; 1 child, Christopher Radcliffe. AB, UCLA, 1967; JD, USC, 1970. Bar: Calif. 1971. Ops. rsch. analyst Naval Weapons Ctr., China Lake, Calif., 1966-69; assoc. Richards, Watson & Gershon, L.A., 1970-76, ptnr., 1976—; spl. counsel L.A. County Transp. Commn., 1984-93, L.A. County Met. Transp. Authority, 1993-94; commr. L.A. County Delinquency and Crime Commn., 1983-94, pres., 1987-94; chmn. L.A. County Delinquency Prevention Planning Coun., 1987-90. Contbr. articles to profl. jours. Peace officer Pasadena (Calif.) Police Res. Unit, 1972-87, dep. comdr., 1979-81, comdr., 1982-84; chmn. pub. safety commn. City of La Canada Flintridge, Calif., 1977-82, commr. 1977-88; bd. dirs. La Canada Flintridge Coordinating Council, 1975-82, pres. 1977-78; exec. dir. Cityhood Action Com., 1975-76; active Calif. Rep. Party, Appellate Circle of Legion Lex U. So. Calif.; chmn. Youth Opportunities United, Inc., 1990-96, vice-chmn. 1988-89, bd. dirs. 1988-96; mem. L.A. County Justice Systems Adv. Group, 1987-92; trustee Lanterman Hist. Mus. Found., 1989-94, Calif. City Mgmt. Found., 1992—. Recipient commendation for Community Service, L.A. County Bd. Suprs., 1978, Commendation for Svc. to Youth, 1996. Mem. La Canada Flintridge C. of C. and Cmty. Assn. (pres. 1981, bd. dirs. 1976-83), Navy League U.S., Pacific Legal Found., Peace Officers Assn., L.A. County, UCLA Alumni Assn. (life), U. So. Calif. Alumni Assn. (life), L.A. County Bar Assn., Calif. Bar Assn., ABA, U. So. Calif. Law Alumni Assn. Office: Richards Watson & Gershon 333 S Hope St Fl 38 Los Angeles CA 90071-1406

PIEPER, HEINZ PAUL, physiology educator; b. Wuppertal, Germany, Mar. 24, 1920; came to U.S., 1957, naturalized, 1963; s. Heinrich Ludwig and Agnes Marie (Koehler) P.; m. Rose Irmgard Hackl, Apr. 23, 1945. M.D., U. Munich, Germany, 1948. Resident 2d Med. Clinic, U. Munich, 1948-50, asst. prof. dept. physiology, 1950-57; asst. prof. dept. physiology Coll. Medicine, Ohio State U., Columbus, 1957-60; assoc. prof. Coll. Medicine, Ohio State U., 1960-68, prof., 1968—, chmn. dept. physiology, 1974-85, prof. emeritus, 1985—; established investigator Am. Heart Assn., 1962-67. Mem. editorial bd.: Am. Jour. Physiology, 1973-82; contbr. articles on cardiovascular physiology to profl. jours. Mem. Am. Physiol. Soc., Ohio Acad. Scis., Sigma Xi. Home: 2206 SE 36th St Cape Coral FL 33904-4434 Office: Ohio State U Coll Medicine 333 W 10th Ave Columbus OH 43210-1239

PIEPER, PATRICIA RITA, artist, photographer; b. Paterson, N.J., Jan. 28, 1923; d. Francis William and Barbara Margareth (Ludwig) Farabaugh. Student, Baron von Palm, 1937-39, Deal (N.J.) Conservatory, 1939, 40, Utah State U., 1950-52; m. George F. Pieper, July 1, 1941 (dec. May 3, 1981); 1 child, Patricia Lynn; m. Russell W. Watson, Dec., 9, 1989. One-woman shows include Charles Russell Mus., Great Falls, Mont., 1955, Fisher Gallery, Washington, 1966, Tampa City Libr., 1977-81, 83, 84, Ctr. Pl. Art Ctr., Brandon, Fla., 1985; exhibited in group shows Davidson Art Gallery, Middletown, Conn., 1968, Helena (Mont.) Hist. Mus., 1955, Dept. Commerce Alaska Statehood Show, 1959, Joslyn Mus., Omaha, 1961, Denver Mus. Natural History, 1955, St. Joseph's Hosp. Gallery, 1980, 82, 84-86; represented in pvt. collections. Pres. Bell Lake Assn., 1976-78, 79. Winner photog. competition Gen. Tel. Co. of Fla., 1979; recipient Outstanding Svc. award Bell Lake Assn., 1987, Meml. award Land O' Lake Bd. of Realtors, 1989, Appreciation award Southwest Fla. Water Mgmt. Dist., 1993; photography winner in top 100 out of 8,000 Nat. Wildlife Fedn. competition, 1986; 1st place photography MacDill AFB, 1991. Mem. Pasco County (Fla.) Water Adv. Coun., 1978—, chmn., 1979-82, 83-84, 86-88, 92—; gov.'s appointee to S.W. Fla. Water Mgmt. Dist., Hillsborough River Basin Bd., 1981-82, 84-87, sec., 1988-91, vice chmn. 1992; active Save Our Rivers program, 1982-84, 85-86, 92—; ad hoc chmn., 1991-92; mem. adv. bd. Fla. Suncoast Expwy., 1988-90; pres. Bell Lake Assn., 1986, 87; mem. adv. bd. Tampa YMCA, 1979-80. Mem. VFW (life), Nat. League Am. Pen Women (v.p. Tampa 1976-78, Woman of Yr. award 1977-78), Tampa Art Mus., Ret. Officer's Wives Assn., Land O' Lakes C. of C. (bd. dir. 1981-82, Outstanding Svc. award 1980), Fla. Geneal. Soc., West State Archaeol. Soc. (distaff mem.), Ret. Officer's Assn., MacDill AFB, 1982—, Lutz Club, Land O' Lakes Women's Club, Moose. Home and Studio: 3304 E Derry Dr Sebastian FL 32958-8577 *I believe that those of us born with the gift of creativity are truly blessed. It is our duty to make the most of, and be worthy of that gift. And if we work hard and sincerely apply ourselves a chosen few will become immortal through the beauty we leave behind for others to enjoy. As an artist and photographer I am truly blessed.*

PIEPHO, ROBERT WALTER, pharmacy educator, researcher; b. Chgo., July 31, 1942; s. Walter August and Irene Elizabeth (Huybrecht) Apfel; m. Mary Lee Wilson, Dec. 10, 1981. BS in Pharmacy, U. Ill.-Chgo., 1965; PhD in Pharmacology, Loyola U., Maywood, Ill., 1972. Registered pharmacist, Ill., Colo. Assoc. prof. U. Nebr. Med. Ctr., Omaha, 1970-78; prof. pharmacy, assoc. dean Sch. Pharmacy U. Colo., Denver, 1978-86; prof. pharmacol., dean U. Mo. Sch. Pharmacy, Kansas City, 1987—. Contbr. articles to profl. jours., chpts. to books. Pres. Club Monaco Homeowners Assn., Denver, 1980-82. Named Outstanding Tchr. U. Nebr. Coll. Pharmacy, 1975; recipient Arthur Hassan Colo. Pharmacal Assn., 1983, Excellence in Teaching U. Colo. Med. Sch., 1983. Fellow Am. Coll. Clin. Pharmacology (regent 1983-88, 91-96, pres.-elect 1997-98), Am. Coll. Apothecaries; mem. Am. Soc. Hosp. Pharmacists, Am. Soc. Pharmacology and Exptl. Therapeutics, Rho Chi. Roman Catholic. Office: U Mo Sch Pharmacy 5005 Rockhill Rd Kansas City MO 64110-2239

PIEPKORN, EVONNE ARLYS, farmer, scriptwriter, producer, director; b. Stanley, N.D., July 4, 1939; d. Bennie C. and Bertina (Gilbertson) Thorvig; m. LeRoy Piepkorn, June 29, 1958; children: Craig, Lorie, Clark. BA in Psychology, U. N.D., 1994. Sec. to ext. agt. Mountrail County, Stanley, 1957-59; adminstrv. clk. Mountrail County Agrl. Stblzn. and Conservation Office, Stanley, 1960-62; clk. Mountrail and Divide Counties, SSS, Stanley, 1971-73; income tax cons., sec. Mell & Jones Acctg., Stanley, 1979-88; ptnr. farm, Stanley, 1958—; bd. dirs. Piepkorn's, Inc., Grand Forks, N.D. Prodr., dir., scriptwriter film Hidden Foundations of Prairie Women, 1994. Mem. Conflict Resolution Ctr. Grand Forks, Phi Beta Kappa, Psi Chi. Lutheran. Avocations: travel, nature excursions, genealogy, spirituality. Home: RR 1 Box 84 Stanley ND 58784-9768

PIERCE, ALLAN DALE, engineering educator, researcher; b. Clarinda, Iowa, Dec. 18, 1936; s. Franklin Dale and Ruth Pauline (Wright) P.; m. Penelope Claffey, Oct. 27, 1961; children: Jennifer Irene, Bradford Loren. BS, N.Mex. Coll. Agrl. and Mechanic Arts, 1957; PhD, MIT, 1962. Registered profl. engr., Mass. Staff researcher Rand Corp., Santa Monica, Calif., 1961-63; sr. staff scientist Avco Corp., Wilmington, Mass., 1963-66; asst. prof. MIT, Cambridge, 1966-68, assoc. prof., 1968-73; prof. mech. engring. Ga. Inst. Tech., Atlanta, 1973-76, Regent's prof., 1976-88; Leonhard chair in engring. Pa. State U., University Park, 1988-93; chmn. dept aerospace and mech. engring. Boston U., 1993—; vis. prof. Max Planck Inst., Goettingen, Fed. Republic Germany, 1976-77; cons. in field. Author: Acoustics: An Introduction to Its Physical Principles and Applications, 1981; editor phys. acoustics monograph series, 1988—; editor Jour. Computation Acoustics, 1992—; contbr. articles on acoustics, wave propagation, vibrations, solid and fluid mechanics to profl. jours. Recipient Sr. U.S. Scientist award Alexander von Humboldt Found., 1976, Cert. of Recognition Nat. Aeronautics and Space Adminstrn., 1984, Per Bruel Gold medal for noise control and acoustics ASME, 1995; NSF fellow, 1957-60, Shell Oil fellow, 1960-61, U.S. Dept. Transp. faculty fellow, 1979-80. Fellow Acoustical Soc. Am. (silver medal 1991), ASME (Rayleigh lectr. 1992, Per Bruel gold medal 1995); mem. IEEE, AIAA. Home: PO Box 339 East Sandwich MA 02537-0339 Office: Boston U Dept Aerospace & Mech Engring 110 Cummington St Boston MA 02215-2407

PIERCE, ANNE-MARIE BERNHEIM, private school administrator; b. Grenoble, Isere, France, Sept. 9, 1943; came to U.S., 1961; d. Joseph and Andreé Georgette (Haguenauer) Bernheim; m. Robert L. Pierce, Mar. 21, 1964; 1 child, Eric. BA, U. Calif., Berkeley, 1965; MA, Hayward State U., 1973. Head fgn. lang. dept. Head-Royce Sch., Oakland, Calif., 1965-75; head fgn. lang. dept. San Francisco U. High Sch., 1975-80, dir. pub. events, 1979-80; headmistress Ecole Bilingue, Berkeley, 1980-89; cons. A.M.P. and Assocs., San Francisco, 1989-91; head Washington Internat. Sch., 1991—. Co-author radio instrn. A Touch of France, 1980—. Bd. dirs. Mid-Atlantic Multi-Cultural Alliance. Named to Cum Laude Soc. Head-Royce Schs., 1982. Mem. Assn. French Schs. in Am. (founder, pres. 1985-86, 87-88), Calif. Assn. Ind. Schs. (exec. bd. dirs. 1985-88, v.p. 1987-88), Internat. Sch. Assn. (exec. bd. dirs.), Assn. Ind. Schs. Greater Washington (exec. bd. dirs.). Democrat. Avocation: skiing.

PIERCE, CHARLES EARL, software engineer; b. Edenton, N.C., July 13, 1955; s. Charles William and Carrie (Rankins) P.; m. Jan Saunders, Nov. 16, 1991. BS in Math., L.I. U., 1977. Rsch. analyst Equitable Life, N.Y.C., 1977-80; systems analyst CTEK Software, N.Y.C., 1980-83; asst. v.p. Bank N.Y., N.Y.C., 1987—; cons. Nibor Assocs., N.Y.C., 1983-85, Vital Cons., N.Y.C., 1985-87. Mem. IEEE, N.Y. Acad. Scis., Data Processing Mgmt. Assn., Assn. for Computing Machinery, Math. Assn. Am. Mem. Pentecostal Ch. Mem. Pentecostal Ch. Achievements include development of English test interpreter/command processing for mainframe at CTEK Software; automated phased conversion of DMS system.

PIERCE, CHARLES ELIOT, JR., library director, educator; b. Springfield, Mass., Dec. 25, 1941; s. C. Eliot and Dora Mason (Redway) P.; m. Barbara G. Hanson, Oct. 18, 1969; children: Sheila H., Charles Eliot III. B.A., Harvard U., 1964, M.A.T., 1966, Ph.D., 1970. Prof. English Vassar Coll., Poughkeepsie, N.Y., 1970-87; dir. Pierpont Morgan Library, N.Y.C., 1987—. Author: (literary criticism) The Religious Life of Samuel Johnson, 1983. Mem. vis. com. Harvard U. Libr. Mem. Johnsonians, Century Assn., Grolier Club, Walpole Soc., Knickerbocker Club. Episcopalian. Home: Clinton Corners Rd Salt Point NY 12578 Office: Pierpont Morgan Libr 29 E 36th St New York NY 10016-3403

PIERCE, CHARLES R., electric company consultant; b. Bar Harbor, Maine, 1922. AB, Hofstra Coll., 1947; LLB, Columbia U., 1949. Bar: N.Y.

1950, U.S. Ct. Appeals (2nd cir.) 1951. Ret. chmn., chief exec. officer L.I. Lighting Co. Mem. Suffolk County Bar Assn., Nat. Assn. Securities Dealers, N.Y. Stock Exch., Am. Arbitration Assn. (bd. arbitration). Office: 33 Walt Whitman Rd Huntington Station NY 11746-3627

PIERCE, CHESTER MIDDLEBROOK, psychiatrist, educator; b. Glen Cove, N.Y., Mar. 4, 1927; s. Samuel Riley and Hettie Elenor (Armstrong) P.; m. Jocelyn Patricia Blanchet, June 15, 1949; children: Diane Blanchet, Deirdre Anona. AB, Harvard U., 1948, MD, 1952; ScD (hon.), Westfield Coll., 1977, Tufts U., 1984. Instr. psychiatry U. Cin., 1957-60; asst. prof. psychiatry U. Okla., 1960-62, prof., 1965-69; prof. edn. and psychiatry Harvard U., 1969—; pres. Am. Bd. Psychiatry and Neurology, 1977-78; mem. Polar Research Bd.; cons. USAF. Author publs. on sleep disturbances, media, polar medicine, sports medicine, racism; mem. editorial bds. Advisor Children's TV Workshop; chmn. Child Devel. Assn. Consortium; bd. dirs. Action Children's TV. With M.C. USNR, 1953-55. Fellow Royal Australian and N.Z. Coll. Psychiatrists (hon.), Gt. Britain Royal Coll. Psychiatrists (hon.); mem. NAS, Inst. Medicine, Black Psychiatrists Am. (chmn.), Am. Orthopsychiat. Assn. (pres. 1983-84), Am. Acad. Arts and Scis., Inst. Medicine. Democrat. Home: 17 Prince St Jamaica Plain MA 02130-2725

PIERCE, DANIEL THORNTON, physicist; b. L.A., July 16, 1940; s. Daniel Gordon Pierce and Celia Francis Thornton Thayer; m. Barbara Harrison, Nov. 19, 1988; children: Jed, Maia, Stephen. BS, Stanford U., 1962, PhD in Applied Physics, 1970; MA, Wesleyan U., Middletown, Conn., 1966. NSF rsch. asst. materials sci. dept. Stanford U., 1961; lectr in physics U.S. Peace Corps, Kathmandu, Nepal, 1962-64; rsch. asst. Wesleyan U., 1964-66; rsch. asst. Stanford Electronics Lab., 1966-70, rsch. assoc., 1970-71; rsch. staff Solid State Physics Lab., Swiss Fed. Inst. Tech., 1971-75; physicist Nat. Inst. Standards and Tech. (formerly Nat. Bur Standards), Gaithersburg, Md., 1975—. Contbr. chpts. to books, more than 150 articles to profl. jours. Trustee Unitarian Ch. of Rockville, Md., 1994-96. Recipient IR-100 award R&D Mag., 1980, 85, Gold medal Dept. Commerce, 1987, William P. Schlichter award Nat. Inst. Standards and Tech., 1992. Gaede-Langmuir Award, 1994, American Vacuum Society. Fellow Am. Phys. Soc., Am. Vacuum Soc. (surface sci. exec. com. 1984-88, Gaede-Langmuir prize 1994). Achievements include patents for source of spin polarized electrons, absorbed current and low energy spin polarization detectors; development of scanning electron microscopy with polarization analysis. Office: Nat Inst Standards and Tech Bldg 220 Rm B206 Gaithersburg MD 20899

PIERCE, DANNY PARCEL, artist, educator; b. Woodlake, Calif., Sept. 10, 1920; s. Frank Lester and Letitia Frances (Parcel) P.; m. Julia Ann Rasmussen, July 19, 1943; children: Julia Ann, Mary L., Danny L., Duane Nels. Student, Art Ctr. Sch., L.A., 1939, Chouinards Art Inst., L.A., 1940-41, 46-47, Am. Art Sch., N.Y.C., 1947-48, Bklyn. Mus. Art Sch., 1950-53; BFA, U. Alaska, 1963. Instr. Hunter Coll., N.Y.C., 1952-53, Burnley Sch. Art, Seattle, 1954-58, Seattle U., 1956-59; publ. Red Door Studio Press, Kent, Wash., 1959—; artist-in-res. U. Alaska, College, 1959-63; asst. prof. U. Wisc., Milw., 1964; head art dept. Cornish Sch. Allied Arts, Seattle, 1964-65; prof. art U. Wisc., Milw., 1965-84, prof. emeritus, 1984—. One person exhibition shows include Contemporaries Gallery, N.Y.C., 1953, Handforth Gallery, Tacoma, Washington, 1958, U. Alaska, College, 1959, 63, 73, 74, Gonzaga U., Bradley Galleries, Milw., 1966, 68, 70, 72, 74, 76, 78-80, 82, Martin-Zambito Gallery, Seattle, 1997; represented in permanent collections Bibliothèque Nationale, Paris, Mus. Modern Art, N.Y.C., Libr. Congress, Washington, Smithsonian Instn., Washington, Seattle Art Mus., U. Washington Henry Art Gallery, Bklyn. Mus., Princeton U., U. Alaska, U. So. Calif., William and Mary Coll., Oostduinkerke (Belgium) Nat. Fishing Mus., Nat. Mus. Sweden, Stockholm, Johnson Wax Found., Racine, Wisc., Gen. Mills Collection Art, Mpls., Huntington Libr., San Marino, Calif., various pvt. collections. Recipient Best Oil Landscape award Conn. Acad. Fine Arts, Hartford, 1st Prize oil Kohler Gallery, Seattle, 1974, others; chosen one of twelve artists to represent State Wash. Expo 70, Osaka, Japan, rep. U.S. Internat. São Paulo Biannual Art Exhbn.; established archives at Golda Meier Libr., U. Wis.-Mils. Mem. Artist Equity Assn. (charter, pres. Seattle chpt. 1958), Am. Colorprint Soc., Internat. Arts and Letters (life). Office: Red Door Studio 330 Summit Ave N Kent WA 98031-4714

PIERCE, DONNA L., lawyer; b. Bermuda, Dec. 25, 1952; came to U.S., 1953; d. William R. and Joyce (Brewer) P.; 1 child, Dylan Pierce Austin. AS, Greenville (S.C.) Coll., 1976; BS, U. S.C., 1978, JD, 1980. Bar: S.C. 1981, U.S. Dist. Ct. (ea. dist.) Tenn. 1981, U.S. Ct. Appeals (4th, 5th, 6th, 11th cirs.) 1981, Tenn. 1982. Trial atty. Tenn. Valley Authority, Knoxville, Tenn., 1981-84; litigation ptnr. Chambliss & Bahner, Chattanooga, 1985-93, Chattanooga Human Rights and Rels. Comsn., 1993; gen. counsel U. of the South, Sewanee, Tenn., 1994; dir. S.E. Tenn. Legal Svcs., Chattanooga, 1988-92; advisor Cleve. State Coll., 1988-92. Mem. Tenn. Supreme Ct. Commn. on CLES and Specialization, 1993—, Tenn. Supreme Ct. Commn. on Gender Fairness, 1994-96. Mem. ABA, Fed. Bar Assn., S.C. Bar Assn., S.E. Tenn. Lawyers Assn. for Women (pres. 1990), Tenn. Lawyers Assn. for Women (bd. dirs. 1988-90), Tenn. Bar Assn., Chattanooga Bar Assn. (bd. govs. 1988-93, pres. 1992-93), Order of Coif. Office: U of the South 735 University Ave Sewanee TN 37383-0001

PIERCE, EDWARD FRANKLIN, retired academic administrator; b. Cambridge, Mass., July 15, 1927; s. John and Kathleen (McCue) P.; m. Sandra Lea, June 8, 1958; children—Valerie, Marc, Adrienne. B.S., Boston Coll., 1949, M.A., 1950; Ph.D., Columbia U., 1959, Ed.D., 1959. Research chemist AEC, 1950-51; mem. faculty Skagit Valley Coll., Mt. Vernon, Wash., 1954; instr. chemistry SUNY, Geneseo, 1959-66; chmn. dept. SUNY, 1962, dean, 1964; dean U. N.H. System, Keene, 1966-72; pres. Quincy (Mass.) Sr. Coll., 1972-82, Mt. Aloysius Coll., 1982-97; mem. New Eng. Dist. Scholarship Com.; cons. in field, seminar lectr. Author: Selected Quantitative Studies in Physical Science, 1962, Modern Chemistry, 1960, Historical Perspectives in the Physical Sciences, 1964, also articles. Chmn. United Fund, 1968; dist. com. Boy Scouts Am., 1951-54, Council for Children, Quincy, 1972-82; pres., treas. South Shore Day Care Services, 1972-76. Served to ensign USNR, 1944-46. Fellow Am. Inst. Chemists; mem. AAAS, N.Y. Acad. Sci. Club: Quincy Kiwanis (past pres.). Lodge: Rotary (Altoona, Pa.). Home: PO Box 67 Wolfebord MA 03894

PIERCE, FRANCIS CASIMIR, civil engineer; b. Warren, R.I., May 19, 1924; s. Frank J. and Eva (Soltys) Pierce; student U. Conn., 1943-44; B.S., U. R.I., 1948; M.S., Harvard U., 1950; postgrad. Northeastern U., 1951-52; Reg. profl. engr. Conn., N.H., Mass., R.I., Vt.; reg. profl. land surveyor R.I.; m. Helen Lynette Steinouer, Apr. 24, 1954; children—Paul F., Kenneth J., Nancy L., Karen H., Charles E. Instr. civil engring. U. R.I., Kingston, 1948-49, U. Conn., Storrs, 1950-51; design engr. Praeger-Maguire & Ole Singstad, Boston, 1951-52; chief found. engr. C.A. Maguire & Assocs., Providence, 1952-59, assoc., 1959-69, v.p., 1969-72; sr. v.p. C.E. Maguire, Inc., 1972-76, officer-in-charge Honolulu office, 1976-78, exec. v.p., corp. dir. ops., 1975-87; dir. The Maguire Group, Inc., 1979—, gen. mgr. East Atlantic Casualty Co., Ltd., 1987-88; also dir.; pres. Magma, Inc., tech. ops. service co., 1986-88; lectr. found. engring. U. R.I., 1968-69, trustee, 1987—; mem. Coll. Engring. adv. council, 1986—, U.S. com. Internat. Commn. on Large Dams; mem. register of expert witnesses in the construction industry ABA. Vice chmn. Planning Bd. East Providence, R.I., 1960-73; bd. dirs. R.I. Civic Chorale and Orch., 1986-90. Served with AUS, 1942-46. Fellow Soc. Am. Mil. Engrs., ASCE (chpt. past pres., dir.); mem. Am. Arbitration Assn., R.I. Soc. Profl. Engrs. (nat. dir., engr. of year award 1973), Am. Soc. Engring. Edn., ASTM, Soc. Marine Engrs. and Naval Architects, Am. Soc. Planning Ofcls., Harvard Soc. Engrs., Scientists, Providence Engrs. Soc., R.I. Soc. Planning Agys. (past pres.). Contbr. articles to profl. jours. Recipient Commendation Min. of Pub. Works Rep. Venezuela, 1970, Geotechnical award ASCE sect. Boston Soc. Civil Engrs., 1979, USCG Meritorious Pub. Service award, 1987, Chester H. Kirk Disting. Engr. award U. R.I. Coll. Engring., 1987. Acad. of fellows, Am. Mil. Engr., 1996. Home: 3830 St Girons Dr Punta Gorda FL 33950-7870 Office: 225 Foxborough Blvd Foxboro MA 02035-2854

PIERCE, GEORGE ADAMS, university administrator, educator; b. Carlsbad, N.Mex., May 21, 1943; s. Jack Colwell and Shirley (Adams) P.; m. Margaret Mary Brakel, Feb. 10, 1980; children: Christopher, Catherine Rose. BA in Polit. Sci., Fairleigh Dickinson U., 1969; MA in Polit. Sci., New Sch. Social Rsch., 1971; PhD in Higher Edn., Claremont Grad. Sch., 1976. Asst. dir. promotion Afco, N.Y.C., 1969-71; dir. spl. programs U. Calif., Riverside, 1971-73; asst. to pres. Claremont (Calif.) Grad. Sch., 1973-75; asst. to pres. Seattle U., 1975-78, dir. planning, 1978-83, v.p. adminstrn., 1983-87, v.p. planning, 1987-89; v.p. bus. and fin. affairs Western Wash. U., Bellingham, 1989—; chmn. regional rev. panel Truman Scholarship Found., 1977-90. Chmn. Seattle Ctr. Adv. Commn., 1977-83; bd. dirs. N.W. Kidney Found., Seattle, 1986—, YMCA, Bellingham, 1990—; chmn. pack 41 Boy Scouts Am., Bellingham, 1992-94, chmn. troop 7, 1995—. With USAF, 1963-65. Recipient Cert. Merit Riverside County Comprehensive Health Planning, 1972, Cert. Appreciation Office Mayor City of Seattle, 1983, Nat. Truman Scholarship Found., 1986. Mem. Am. Assn. Higher Edn., Assn. Instnl. Rsch. (regional pres. 1977), Nat. Assn. Coll. and Univ. Bus. Officers (chmn. pers. and benefits com. 1992-94), Rotary. Democrat. Roman Catholic. Avocations: backpacking, canoeing, swimming, tennis. Home: 421 Morey Ave Bellingham WA 98225-6344 Office: Western Wash U Old Main 300 Bellingham WA 98225

PIERCE, GEORGE FOSTER, JR., architect; b. Dallas, June 22, 1919; s. George Foster and Hallie Louise (Crutchfield) P.; m. Betty Jean Reistle, Oct. 17, 1942; children: Ann Louise Pierce Arnett, George Foster III, Nancy Reistle Pierce Brumback. Student, So. Meth. U., 1937-39; BA, Rice U., 1942, BS in Architecture, 1943; diplome d'architecture, Ecole des Beaux-Arts, Fontainebleau, 1958. Pvt. practice architecture, 1946—; founding ptnr. Pierce, Goodwin, Alexander & Linville (architects, engrs. and planners), 1946-97, of counsel, 1987—; design cons. Dept. Army, 1966-70; instr. archtl. design Rice U., 1945, preceptor dept. architecture, 1962-67; past trustee, mem. exec. com. Rice Ctr. for Community Design and Rsch.; bd. dirs. Billboards Ltd. Prin. works include projects 8 bldgs., Rice U. Campus, Exxon Brook Hollow Bldg. Complex, Houston Mus. Natural Sci. and Planetarium, Michael Debakey Center Biomed. Edn. and Research, Baylor Coll. Medicine; 4 terminal bldgs. and parking garages, master plan Houston Intercontinental Airport; S.W. Bell Telephone Co. office bldg.; U. Tex. Med. Sch. Hosp., Galveston, U. Houston Conrad Hilton Sch. Hotel & Club Mgmt., U. Houston Univ. Center; 40 story office bldg. for Tex. Eastern Transmission Corp.; outpatient facility U. Tex. M.D. Anderson Cancer Hosp.; 44 story Marathon Oil Tower, others; contbr. articles to profl. jours. Mem. exec. adv. bd. Sam Houston Area Coun. Boy Scouts Am.; past mem. grad. coun. Rice U.; adv. coun. Rice Sch. Architecture, chmn. Houston Mcpl. Sign Control Bd.; past chmn. bd. trustee Contemporary Arts Mus., Houston; past trustee Houston Mus. Natural Sci.; trustee emeritus, past pres. Tex. Archtl. Found. With USNR, WWII. Recipient numerous nat., state, local archtl. awards for design, Silver Beaver award Boy Scouts Am.; named one of five Outstanding Young Texans Tex. Jr. C. of C., 1954; named Disting. R Man Rice U., 1992. Fellow AIA (past nat. chmn. com. on aesthetics, student affairs and chpt. affairs, Golden award Houston chpt., 1990), La Soc. Arquitectos Mexicanos (hon.); mem. Tex. Soc. Archs. (bd. dirs. 1982-84, past pres., L.W. Pitts award 1985), Houston C. of C. (past chmn. future studies), Rice U. Pres.'s Club (founding chmn. 1970-72), Rice U. Assocs., SAR, Tex. Golf Assn. (bd. dirs.), Kappa Alpha. Methodist. Home: 5555 Del Monte Dr Apt 1103 Houston TX 77056-4118 Office: 5555 San Felipe St Ste 1000 Houston TX 77056-2737 *I am pleased to have chosen architecture as my profession, whereby I have been able to influence the quality of life of my community and my country, not only in its physical form through building design and planning, but also toward its cultural, educational and political well being.*

PIERCE, HILDA (HILDA HERTA HARMEL), painter; b. Vienna, Austria; came to U.S., 1940; 1 child, Diana Rubin Daly. Student, Art Inst. of Chgo.; studied with Oskar Kokoschka, Salzburg, Austria. Art tchr. Highland Park (Ill.) Art Ctr., Sandburg Village Art Workshop, Chgo., Old Town Art Center, Chgo.; owner, operator Hilda Pierce Art Gallery, Laguna Beach, Calif., 1981-85; guest lectr. major art mus. and Art Tours in France, Switzerland, Austria, Italy; guest lectr. Russian river cruise and major art mus. St. Petersburg and Moscow, 1994. One-woman shows include Fairweather Hardin Gallery, Chgo., Sherman Art Gallery, Chgo., Marshall Field Gallery, Chgo.; exhibited in group shows at Old Orchard Art Festival, Skokie, Ill., Union League Club (awards), North Shore Art League (awards), ARS Gallery of Art Inst. of Chgo.; represented in numerous private and corporate collections; commissioned for all art work including monoprints, oils, and murals for Carnival Cruise Lines megaliner M.S. Fantasy, 1990, 17 murals for megaliner M.S. Imagination, 1995, 49 paintings for megaliner M.S. Imagination, 1995; contbr. articles to Chgo. Tribune Mag., American Artist Mag., Southwest Art Mag., SRA publs., others; featured in video Survivors of the Shoah (Holocaust) visual History Foundation, 1996. Recipient Outstanding Achievement award in Field of Art for Citizen Foreign Birth Chgo. Immigrant's Svc. League. Mem. Arts Club of Chgo. Studio: PO Box 7390 Laguna Niguel CA 92607-7390 *An artist's most precious quality is curiosity. It has kept me young for many years, kept me searching, experimenting and never being complacent, in my life and my work.*

PIERCE, ILONA LAMBSON, educational administrator; b. Blackfoot, Idaho, Dec. 3, 1941; d. Merlin A. Wright and Loa (Adams) Lambson; m. Sherman D. Pierce, Mar. 19, 1960. IBM cert., LDS Bus. Coll., Salt Lake City, 1960; BS, U. Utah, 1969, MEd, 1974, EdD, 1978. Cert. elem. tchr., adminstrv. endorsement, Utah; cert. tchr. ESL, Utah; lic. real estate agt., Utah. Key punch operator Mountain Bell Telephone Co., Salt Lake City, 1960-61; key punch supr. Hercules Powder Co., Bacchus, Utah, 1961-66; tchr. Cottonwood Heights Elem. Sch., Jordan Sch. Dist., Sandy, Utah, 1969-74; tchr. Willow Canyon Elem. Sch., Jordan Sch. Dist., Sandy, Utah, 1974-76; postdoctoral fellow, grad. rsch. asst. U. Utah, Salt Lake City, 1976-78; tchr. Silver Mesa Elem. Sch. Jordan Sch. Dist., Sandy, Utah, 1978-79, tchr. specialist, 1979-80, asst. prin. Mt. Jordan Mid. Sch., 1980-84, prin. Union Mid. Sch., 1984-86, dir. instrnl. media and bilingual edn., 1986-97; retired; Mem. Utah Network Ednl. TV, 1986—; chmn. tech. adv. bd., chmn. bd. dirs. Math. Engring. Sci. Achievement, 1989, bd. dirs., 1987—; treas. State Film Depository Consortium, 1986—; mem. Utah Info. Tech. Consortium, 1987—; mem. prin. mentor program Brigham Young U., 1986. Sch. dist. co-chmn. United Way, 1986—. Recipient recognition award Math Engring. Sci. Achievement, 1991, Valuable Svc. award Emergency Preparedness Action Com., 1988, Disting. Svc. award Utah Ednl. Libr. Media Assn., 1988. Mem. ASCD, Utah ASCD (bd. dirs., editor 1986-89), NEA (life), Utah Edn. Assn., Jžrdan Edn. Assn., Alpha Delta Kappa (state treas. 1980-84, state pres. 1984-86), Delta Kappa Gamma. Avocations: fossil hunting, travel, reading. Home: 8895 S 540 E Sandy UT 84070-1728

PIERCE, JACK, Olympic athlete, track and field. Olympic track and field participant Barcelona, Spain, 1992. Recipient 110m Hurdles Bronze medal Olympics, Barcelona, 1992. Office: US Olympic Com 1750 E Boulder St Colorado Springs CO 80909-5724*

PIERCE, JAMES CLARENCE, surgeon; b. Huron, S.D., Aug. 5, 1929; s. Henry Montraville and Carrie Bernice (Matson) P.; m. Carol Sue Wilson, 1967; children: Henry MacDonald, Richard Matson, Elizabeth Gail. B.A., Carleton Coll., 1951; M.D., Harvard U., 1955; M.S., U. Minn., 1963, Ph.D. in Surgery, 1966. Diplomate: Am. Bd. Surgery. Surg. intern Peter Bent Brigham Hosp., Boston, 1955-56; surg. fellow U. Minn., 1959-66; instr. surgery Med. Coll. Va., Richmond, 1966; prof. surgery and microbiology Med. Coll. Va., 1972-75; dir. Tissue Typing Lab., 1969-75; attending surgeon, dir. surg. research, dir. transplantation service St. Luke's Hosp. Center, N.Y.C., 1975-78; prof. surgery Columbia U., 1976, Ailsa Mellon Bruce prof. surgery, 1977-78; clin. prof. surgery Pa. State U. and, 1979-88; chmn. dept. surgery Geisinger Med. Center, Danville, Pa., 1979-90, chmn. emeritus, 1990—; clin. prof. surgery Jefferson U., 1990—. Contbr. articles to profl. jours. Elder Presbyn. Ch. With M.C., USAF, 1957-59. NIH fellow, 1963-65; Royal Soc. Medicine Found. travelling fellow, 1971; James IV Assn. Surg. traveller, 1978. Mem. ACS (pres. Ctrl. Pa. chpt. 1981-82), Am. Assn. Pathologists, Transplant Soc., Am. Soc. Transplant Surgeons, Ea. Surg. Assn., N.Y. Clin. Soc., Soc. Univ. Surgeons, Sigma Xi. Republican. Home: 1906 Red Ln Danville PA 17821-8415

PIERCE, JAMES ROBERT, magazine executive; b. Stockton, Ill., Apr. 15, 1933; s. Ellsworth B. and Mayme (Smythe) P.; m. Patricia Curran, May 14, 1960; children: Stacy, John Kelly, Shannon. B.A., U. Ill., 1955. Dist. mgr. McGraw Hill Publs., N.Y.C., 1960-75; computer category mgr. Bus. Week mag., N.Y.C., 1976-79; pub. Aviation Week & Space Tech. mag., N.Y.C., 1979-82; v.p., pub. Bus. Week, 1982, sr. v.p., pub., 1983-84, exec. v.p., pub., 1984; pres., chief exec. officer James R. Pierce, Inc., 1985—; chief oper. officer Lotus Pub. Corp, 1986-88; pub. Investment Vision Mag. Fidelity Pub. Corp., 1988-91; pres., chief oper. officer Hunter Pub., Elk Grove Village, Ill., 1991-94; vice chmn. Adams Trade Press, Inc., 1995—; bd. dirs. Adams Trader Press. 1st lt. SAC USAF, 1956-59. Mem. Bus. and Profl. Advt. Assn., LBS Golf Club. Roman Catholic.

PIERCE, JERRY EARL, business executive; b. Hinsdale, Ill., Aug. 3, 1941; s. Earl and Adeline A. (Zaranski) P.; m. Carol Louise Martin, Aug. 15, 1964; children: Patricia, Barbara, Linda, Bradley. BS, U. Ill., 1964. With R.R. Donnelley & Sons, Chgo., 1964-70; with Western Pub. Co., Racine, Wis., from 1970, nat. pubs. sales mgr., from 1975; pres. Pierce Sale Co., Inc., Restaurant Equipment World, Inc., Heat Transfer Engring. Inc.; chmn. bd. Tech Industries & Nillwork, Inc., 1989-93; pres. B.J. Installation Co., Inc., 1989-91, ROI World Equipment, 1993—; v.p., sec. Savers Clubs Am., Inc. 1st lt. U.S. Army, 1968-70. Mem. Printing Industry Am., Sales and Mktg. Execs., Fla. Restaurant Assn., Food Svc. Cons. Soc., Food Equipment Distbrs. Assn. (bd. dirs. 1994—). Republican. Episcopalian. Clubs: Interlochen Country (Winter Park, Fla.), Cleve. Advt. Patentee refrigeration-to-water utility cost control system. Home: 1208 Sharon Rd Winter Park FL 32789-1210 Office: 2413 N Forsyth Rd Orlando FL 32807-6455

PIERCE, JOHN ROBINSON, electrical engineer, educator; b. Des Moines, Mar. 27, 1910; s. John Starr and Harriet Anne (Robinson) P.; m. Martha Peacock, Nov. 5, 1938 (div. Mar. 1964); children: John Jeremy, Elizabeth Anne; m. Ellen R. McKown, Apr. 1, 1964 (dec. Sept. 1986); m. Brenda K. Woodard, Oct. 17, 1987. BS, Calif. Inst. Tech., 1933, MS, 1934, PhD, 1936; D Engring., Newark Coll. Engring., 1961; DSc, Northwestern U., 1961, Poly. Inst. Bklyn, 1963, Yale U., 1963, Columbia U., 1965, U. Nev., 1970, UCLA, 1977; D. Engring., Carnegie Inst. Tech., 1964; D. Elec. Engring., U. Bologna, Italy, 1974; LLD, U. Pa., 1974; DSc, U. So. Calif., 1978. With Bell Telephone Labs., Inc., Murray Hill, N.J., 1936-71; mem. tech. staff, dir. electronics research, 1952-55, dir. research, communication principles, 1958-62, exec. dir. research, communications principles and systems div., 1963-65, exec. dir. research, communications scis. div., 1965-71; prof. engring. Calif. Inst. Tech., Pasadena, 1971-80; chief technologist Jet Propulsion Lab., 1979-82; vis. prof. music emeritus Stanford U., Calif., 1983—; past mem. Pres.'s Sci. Adv. Com., Pres.'s Com. of Nat. Medal of Sci. Author: Theory and Design of Electron Beams, rev. edit., 1954, Traveling Wave Tubes, 1950, Electrons, Waves and Messages, 1956, Man's World of Sound, 1958, Symbols, Signals and Noise, 1961, (with A.G. Tressler) The Research State: A History of Science in New Jersey, 1964, The Beginnings of Satellite Communications, 1968, Science, Art and Communication, 1968, Almost All About Waves, 1973; (with E.C. Posner) Introduction to Communication Science and Systems, 1980, Signals: The Telephone and Beyond, 1981, The Science of Musical Sound, 1983, rev. edit., 1992, (with Hiroshi Inose) Information Technology and Civilization, 1984, (with A. Michael Noll) Signals, The Science of Telecommunications, 1990; editor: (with M.V. Mathews) Current Directions in Computer Music Research, 1989; articles on popular sci.; short stories. Recipient Morris Liebmann meml. prize Inst. Radio Engrs., 1947; Stuart Ballantine medal 1960, Man of Yr., Air Force Assn., 1962; Golden Plate award Acad. Achievement, 1962; General Hoyt S. Vandenberg trophy Arnold Air Soc., 1963; Nat. Medal of Sci., 1963; Edison medal AIEE, 1963; Valdemar Poulsen Gold medal, 1963; H.T. Cedergren medal, 1964; Marconi award, 1974; John C. Scott award, 1975; Japan Prize, 1985; Arthur C. Clarke award, 1987; Pioneer award Internat. Telemetering Conf., 1990, Charles Stark Draper prize Nat. Acad. of Engring., 1995; Marconi Internat. fellow, 1979. Fellow IEEE (medal of honor 1976), Acoustical Soc. Am., Am. Phys. Soc.; mem. NAS, NAE (Founders award 1977, Charles Stark Draper Prize, 1995), Am. Acad. Arts and Scis., Royal Acad. Sci. (Sweden), Inst. Electronics, Info. and Communication Engrs. of Japan (hon.), Inst. TV Engrs. Japan (hon.), Acad. Engring. of Japan (fgn. assoc.), Am. Philos. Soc. Home: 4008 El Cerrito Rd Palo Alto CA 94306-3114 Office: Stanford U Ctr for Computer Rsch in Music and Accoustics Stanford CA 94305

PIERCE, JOHN THOMAS, industrial hygienist, toxicologist; b. Coffeyville, Kans., Mar. 15, 1949; s. John Gordon and Mary Ellen (McGrath) P.; m. Janet D. Brousseau, Aug. 7, 1981. MPH, U. Okla., 1977, PhD, 1978. Assoc. prof., dir. environ. and occupational health U. North Ala., Florence, 1981-88, Va. Commonwealth U., Richmond, 1988-90; prof., chair dept. industrl. hygiene Cen. Mo. State U., Warrensburg, 1990-92; head, Field Svcs. divsn. U. Kans. Med. Ctr., Kansas City, 1992—. Author: Study Guide: Fundamentals of Industrial Hygiene, 1990; asst. editor Applied Occupational and Environ. Hygiene. Capt. USNR, 1968—. Mem. Am. Acad. Insl. Hygiene (local treas. 1993), Am. Acad. Clin. Toxicology, Am. Chem. Soc. (local treas. 1984-87), Am. Bd. Toxicology, Am. Coll. Toxicology, Rotary Club, Am. Legion, Cath. War Vets., Sigma Xi, Phi Kappa Phi. Democrat. Roman Catholic.

PIERCE, JONATHAN LESLIE, planning commission executive; b. Brantford, Ont., Can., Jan. 1, 1949; s. Nathan Leonard and Gertrude (Westman) P.; m. Mary M. McGuire, Sept. 7, 1980; 1 child, Sean. MA, Carleton U., Ottawa, Ont., 1986. Exec. asst. Coun. for Yukon Indians, Whitehorse, Y.T., Can., 1983-85; policy advisor Tungavik Fedn. of Nunavut, Ottawa, 1987-89; exec. dir. Nunavut Planning Commn., Ottawa, 1989—; land mgmt. advisor Nunavut Tunngavik Inc., Ottawa, 1992-94; sr. policy analyst Royal Commn. Aboriginal People, Ottawa, 1993-94; with Xerox Can. Inc., Whitehorse, 1978-83. Alderman Whitehorse City Coun., 1979-84. Anglican. Avocations: music, canoeing, outdoors, photography. Home: 68 Kenilworth St, Ottawa, ON Canada K1Y 3Y4 Office: Nunavut Planning Commn, 1902-130 Albert St, Ottawa, ON Canada K1P 5G4

PIERCE, KENNETH RAY, veterinary medicine educator; b. Snyder, Tex., May 21, 1934; s. Clois Vernon and Ellen (Goolsby) P.; m. Anne Stasney, Aug. 31, 1956; children: Cynthia Cae, Mindy Rae. D.V.M., Tex. A&M U., 1957, M.S., 1962, Ph.D. (NSF fellow), 1965. Diplomate Am. Coll. Vet. Pathologists (pres. 1984). Instr. vet. anatomy Tex. A. and M. U., College Station, 1957-59; asst. prof. vet. pathology Tex. A. and M. U., 1961-65, assoc. prof., 1965-69, prof., 1969—, head dept., 1978-89, chief sect. vet. clin. pathology, 1967-75, 94—; comparative pathologist Inst. Comparative Medicine, Tex. A. and M. U.-Baylor Coll. Medicine, Houston, 1976-79; pvt. vet. practice San Angelo (Tex.) Vet. Hosp., 1959-61; adj. prof. dept. vet. medicine and surgery M.D. Anderson Tumor Inst. and Hosp., Houston, 1971-92; program dir continuing edn. C.L. Davis, D.V.M. Found., 1981-88; vis. scientist Nat. Inst. Environ. Health Scis., 1985. Co-editor: Vet. Pathology Jour, 1971-81; contbr. articles to profl. jours. Mem. AVMA, AAAS, Am. Soc. Vet. Clin. Pathologists, Am. Assn. of Avian Patholgists, U.S.-Can. Acad. Pathology, Tex. Vet. Med. Assn., Am. Assn. Vet. Med. Colls., N.Y. Acad. Scis., Sigma Xi, Phi Kappa Phi, Phi Zeta, Gamma Sigma Delta. Presbyterian (deacon, elder). Home: 12777 Hopes Creek Rd College Station TX 77845-9297 Office: Dept Vet Pathobiology Tex A&M U College Station TX 77843

PIERCE, LAWRENCE WARREN, retired federal judge; b. Phila., Dec. 31, 1924; s. Harold Ernest and Leora (Bellinger) P.; m. Wilma Taylor (dec.); m. Cynthia Straker, July 8, 1979; children: Warren Wood, Michael Lawrence, Mark Taylor. BS, St. Joseph's U., Phila., 1948, DHL, 1967; JD, Fordham U., 1951, LLD, 1982; LLD, Fairfield U., 1972, Hamilton Coll., 1987, St. John's U., 1990. Bar: N.Y. State 1951, U.S. Supreme Ct. 1968. Civil law practice N.Y.C., 1951-61; asst. dist. atty. Kings County, N.Y., 1954-61; dep. police commr. N.Y.C., 1961-63; dir. N.Y. State Div. for Youth, Albany, 1963-66; chmn. N.Y. State Narcotic Addiction Control Commn., 1966-70; vis. prof. criminal justice SUNY, Albany, 1970-71; U.S. dist. judge So. dist. N.Y., 1971-81; judge U.S. Fgn. Intelligence Surveillance Ct., 1979-81; apptd. U.S. cir. judge for 2d Cir., 1981-89, sr. U.S. cir. judge for 2d Cir., 1990-95, ret., 1995. Home: PO Box 2234 Sag Harbor NY 11963

PIERCE, LESTER LAURIN, aviation consultant; b. Merlin, Oreg., Sept. 26, 1907; s. Frank Arthur and Charlotte (Allen) P.; m. Helen Ramona Thomas, Mar. 22, 1937; children: Adrienne C. Freeman, Nancy E. Johnson. Grad. high sch., 1925. Theatre mgr. Redwood Theatres, Inc., Fortuna and Eureka, Calif., 1927-28; salesman, bookkeeper Thomas Furniture House, Eureka, 1930-39; pilot, mgr. Pierce Bros. Flying Svc., Eureka, 1930-41; aerial photographer Pierce Flying Svc., Eureka, 1934-75; chief flight instr. Govt.

Approved Flight Sch., Eureka, 1947-60; aerial seeder, mgr., pres., salesman Pierce Flying Svc., Inc., Eureka, 1946-68; flight examiner FAA, Eureka, 1948-68, aircraft maintenance insp., 1950-68; mapping pilot Stand Aerial Surveys, Newark, 1938. Lt., flight tng., safety officer USNR, 1942, comdr., 1950. Mem. Soc. Aircraft Safety Investigators Aviation Cons., Elks. Home and Office: 3428 Jacoby Creek Rd Bayside CA 95524-9304

PIERCE, MARGARET HUNTER, government official; b. Weedsport, N.Y., June 30, 1910; d. Thomas Murray and Ruby (Sanders) Hunter; m. John R. Pierce, Nov. 4, 1950 (div. May 1959); 1 dau., Barbara Hunter. B.A., Mt. Holyoke Coll., 1932; J.D., N.Y. U., 1939. Bar: N.Y. bar 1941, D.C. bar 1958. Atty. Office Alien Property Custodian, Washington, 1942-43, 45, Office Solicitor, Dept. Labor, 1943-45, NLRB, 1946, 47-48; atty.-adviser U.S. Ct. Claims, 1947-48, 48-59, reporter decisions, 1959-68; commr. U.S. Indian Claims Commn., 1968-78; pvt. practice Washington, 1978—. Pres. Monday Night Musicales, Inc., 1995—. Mem. D.C. Bar Assn. (ct. claims com. 1958—, mil. law com. 1967), Fed. Bar Assn. (Indian law com. 1955—), ABA (sec. adminstrv. law-vets. com., mil. law com., immigration and nationality com.), Women's Bar Assn., Nat. Assn. Women Lawyers, Exec. Women in Govt., Bus. and Profl. Women (Cosmopolitan br.), Am. Women Composers, Zonta (Washington pres. 1977-78), Harvard Club (D.C.). Home: 3829 Garfield St NW Washington DC 20007-1319

PIERCE, MARIANNE LOUISE, pharmaceutical and healthcare companies executive, consultant; b. Atchison, Kans., Apr. 22, 1949; d. James Arthur and Marian Louise (Patton) P.; m. Woodrow Theodore Lewis Jr., June 23, 1973 (div. June 1981). Student, Barnard Coll.; AB, Columbia U., 1970, MBA, 1975. Dep. dir. N.Y. Model Cities, N.Y.C., 1971-73; assoc. corp. fin. Citibank Mcht. Banking, N.Y.C., 1975-77; sr. assoc. N.Y.C., San Francisco, N.Y.C., 1977-82; dep. biotech. dir. Ciba Geigy A.G., Basel, Switzerland, 1982-86; pres., chmn. bd. dirs. Life Scis. Assocs., Ltd., N.Y.C., 1986—; mng. ptnr. Patton, Pierce, Brandon & Co., 1986—; pres., CEO, chmn. XXygen, Inc., New Haven, 1991—. Author: Developing Biotechnology Strategies for Multinational Corporations, 1985, Managing Successful Strategic Alliances, 1990, New Realities in Drug Discovery, 1995, Drug Discovery Economics, 1996, Reflections on the Pharmaceutical Industry: Past and Future, 1996, Economics of Pharmaceutical Industry Mega Mergers, 1997. Mem. Internat. Soc. Pharm. Engring., Brit. Biotech. Assn., Comml. Devel. Assn., Practicing Law Inst., Univ. Club (N.Y.C.), N.Y. Acad. Scis., Japan Soc. Office: Life Scis Assn Ltd 575 Madison Ave Fl 10 New York NY 10022-2511

PIERCE, MARTIN E., JR., fire commissioner; b. Boston, Nov. 13, 1940. Student, Boston Coll., 1958-60; cert. fire sci. program, Mass. Bay C.C., 1974. Fire fighter Boston Fire Dept., 1969-73, fire lt., 1973-76, fire capt., 1976-82, dist. fire chief, 1982-86, dep. fire chief, 1986-91, fire commr., chief dept., 1991—. Mem. Hyde Park Adv. Com.; coach varsity hockey Matignon High Sch., Cambridge, Mass., 1964—. With U.S. Army, 1962, with Res. 1962-68. Mem. Internat. Assn. of Fire Chiefs, Internat. Soc. for Respiratory Protection, Nat. Fire Protection Assn., Met. Fire Chiefs Assn., Urban Fire Forum, Fire Chiefs Assn. of Mass., Inc., Hundred Club of Mass., Inc. Avocation: golf. Office: Fire Dept 115 Southampton St Boston MA 02118-2713

PIERCE, MARY, professional tennis player; b. Montreal, Que., Can., Jan. 15, 1975; d. Jim and Yannick P. 8th ranked woman USTA. Winner, Australian Open, 1995. Office: WTA 133 First St NE Saint Petersburg FL 33701*

PIERCE, MORTON ALLEN, lawyer; b. Liberec, Czechoslovakia, June 25, 1948; m. Nancy Washor, Dec. 14, 1975; children: Matthew J., Nicholas L. BA, Yale Coll., 1970; JD, U. Pa., 1974; postgrad. Oxford U., 1974-75. Bar: N.Y. 1975. Assoc. Reid & Priest, N.Y.C., 1975-83, ptnr., 1983-86; ptnr. Dewey Ballantine, N.Y.C., 1986—. Contbr. articles to profl. jours. Mem. Internat. Bar Assn., ABA (chairman subcom. internat. securities matters 1986-91), Assn. Bar City of N.Y. Home: 161 E 79th St New York NY 10021-0421 Office: Dewey Ballantine 1301 Ave Of The Americas New York NY 10019-6022

PIERCE, NAOMI ELLEN, biology educator, researcher; b. Denver, Oct. 19, 1954; d. Arthur Preble and Ruiko (Ishizaka) P; m. Andrew James Berry, Mar. 9, 1996. BS, Yale U., 1976; PhD, Harvard U., k1983. Fulbright postdoctoral fellow Griffith U., Brisbane, Australia, 1983-84; rsch. lectr. Christ Ch., U. Oxford, Eng., 1984-86; asst. prof. Princeton U., N.J., 1986-91; Sydney A. and John H. Hessel prof. biology, curator lepidoptera Harvard U. and Harvard Mus. Comparative Zoology, Cambridge, Mass., 1991—. Contbr. articles to profl. jours. MacArthur Found. fellow, Chgo., 1988-93. Fellow Harvard Soc. of Fellows (sr.). Office: Harvard U Museum Comparative Zoology Cambridge MA 02138

PIERCE, PONCHITTA ANN, television host, producer, journalist; b. Chgo., Aug. 5, 1942; d. Alfred Leonard and Nora (Vincent) P. Student, Cambridge (Eng.) U., summer 1962; BA cum laude, U. So. Calif., 1964. Asst. editor Ebony mag., 1964-65, assoc. editor, 1965-67; editor Ebony mag. (N.Y.C. office), 1967-68; chief N.Y.C. editl. bur. Johnson Pub. Co., 1967-68; corr. news divsn. CBS, N.Y.C., 1968-71; contbg. editor McCall's mag., 1971-77; editl. cons. Philps Stokes Fund, 1971-78; staff writer Reader's Digest, 1976-77, roving editor, 1977-80; co-prodr., host Today in New York, Sta. WNBC-TV, N.Y.C., 1982-87; freelance writer, TV broadcaster; bd. govs. Overseas Press Club. WNBC-TV co-host: Sunday, 1973-77, The Prime of Your Life, 1976-80; author: Status of American Women Journalists on Magazines, 1968, History of the Phelps Stokes Fund 1911-1972; contbg. editor: Parade mag., 1993. Del. to WHO Conf., Geneva, 1973; bd. dirs. Morris-Jumel Mansion, Hirshhorn Mus. and Sculpture Garden, Housing Enterprise for the Less Privileged, Third St. Music Sch. Settlement, Big Sisters, Inc., Unward, Inc., Inner-City Scholarship Fund, Sta. WNET-TV; mem. women's bd. Madison Sq. Boys and Girls Club; mem. Columbia Presbyn. Health Scis. Adv. Coun. Recipient Penney-Mo. mag. award excellence women's journalism, 1967; John Russwurm award N.Y.C. Urban League, 1968; AMITA Nat. Achievement award in communications, 1974. Mem. NATAS, Women in Comm. (Woman Behind the News award 1969, Nat. Headliner award 1970), Fgn. Policy Assn. (mem. bd. govs., bd. dirs.), Coun. on Fgn. Rels., Calif. Scholarship Fedn. (life), Econs. Club N.Y., Lotos Club, Nat. Honor Soc., Mortar Bd.

PIERCE, RICHARD HARRY, research director for laboratory. Rsch. dir. Mote Marine Lab., Sarasota, Fla. Office: Mote Marine Lab 1600 Ken Thompson Pkwy Sarasota FL 34236-1004

PIERCE, RICHARD HILTON, lawyer; b. Westerly, R.I., May 2, 1935; s. Ralph Wilson and Mildred (Clark) P.; m. Cynthia Nanian, Sept. 8, 1962; children: Stacey, Andrew, Hilary. AB cum laude, Bates Coll., 1957; JD, NYU, 1960. Bar: R.I. 1961, U.S. Dist. Ct. R.I. 1961, Mass. 1985. Assoc. Hinckley, Allen, Salisbury & Parsons, Providence, 1960-66; ptnr. Hinckley, Allen, & Snyder, Providence, 1966—. Councilman City of Cranston, R.I., 1967-68; libr. trustee Cranston Pub. Libr., 1969-85; mem. sch. com., Cranston, 1985-86; pres. St. Andrews Sch. Fellow Am. Coll. Trust and Estate coun.; mem. ABA, Mass. Bar Assn., R.I. Bar Assn. Office: Hinckley Allen Snyder 1500 Fleet Ctr Providence RI 02903

PIERCE, RICKY CHARLES, professional basketball player; b. Dallas, Aug. 19, 1959; m. Joyce Wright. Student, Walla Walla (Wash.) Community Coll., 1978-79, Rice U., 1979-82. Player Detroit Pistons, 1982-83, San Diego (now L.A.) Clippers, 1983-84, Milw. Bucks, 1984-91, Seattle Super Sonics, 1991-94, Golden State Warriors, 1994-95, Ind. Pacers, 1995—; player NBA All-Star Game, 1991. Recipient Sixth Man award NBA, 1987, 90. Office: Ind Pacers 300 E Market St Indianapolis IN 46204*

PIERCE, ROBERT LORNE, petrochemical, oil and gas company executive. Chmn. and chief exec. officer Foothills Pipe Lines Ltd., Calgary, Alta., Can.; bd. dirs. NOVA Corp. of Alta., Bank of N.S. Mem. Interstate Natural Gas Assn. Am. (bd. dirs.). Office: Foothills Pipe Lines Ltd, 3100 707 8th Ave SW, Calgary, AB Canada T2P 3W8

PIERCE, ROBERT NASH, writer; b. Greenville, Miss., Dec. 5, 1931. Student, U. Mo., 1950; BA, Ark. State U., 1951; MJ, U. Tex., Austin, 1955; PhD, U. Minn., 1968. Reporter, asst. state editor, acting state editor Ark. Democrat, Little Rock, 1953-55; reporter, real estate editor San Angelo (Tex.) Standard-Times, 1955-56; news editor, assoc. editor Sarasota (Fla.) News, 1956-60; dir. public relations Eckerd Coll., St. Petersburg, 1960-62; asst. city editor St. Petersburg Evening Independent, 1962-63; asst. prof. La. State U., 1965-70; assoc. prof. U. Fla., Gainesville, 1970-76; legis. corr. La. Legislature Shreveport Jour., summer 1970; copy editor Miami Herald, 1972; prof. U. Fla., 1976-85, prof. emeritus, 1985—, dir. journalism grad. studies, 1978-83; Fulbright-Hays lectr. journalism U. Argentina de la Empresa, 1973; vis. lectr. Cath. U. Minas Gerais, Belo Horizonte, Brazil, 1973; vis. prof. Autonomous U., Barcelona, Spain, 1982-83, U. Yaounde, Cameroon, 1988. Author: Keeping the Flame: Media and Government in Latin America, 1979, A Sacred Trust: Nelson Poynter and the St. Petersburg Times, 1993; contbr. chpts. to Internat. Communication as a Field of Study, 1970, Mass Communication in Mexico, 1975, World Press Ency., 1981, Handbook of Latin Am. Popular Culture, 1985; contbr. monograph, articles to profl. publs. Research grantee Fulbright-Hays Faculty Research Abroad Program.

PIERCE, ROBERT RAYMOND, materials engineer, consultant; b. Helena, Mont., Feb. 17, 1914; s. Raymond Everett and Daisy Mae (Brown) P.; m. Stella Florence Kankos, June 12, 1938; children: Keith R., Patricia L., Diana L. BS in Chem. Engring., Oreg. State U., 1937. Process supr. Pennwalt Corp., Portland, Oreg., 1941-45, asst. tech. svc. mgr., Tacoma, 1945-47, gen. mgr., Phila., 1947-58, Natrona, Pa., 1958-65, tech. mgr., Phila., 1965-78, sr. tech. cons., Phila., 1978-80; self-employed cons., also Ohio State U., 1980-95; former pres. Pierce CorMat Svcs., Inc. Contbr. articles to prof. jours. Patentee in field. Vice chmn. Phila. Air Pollution Control Bd., Phila., 1969-79, chmn. Ad Hoc # 1, 1974-79; Ky. Colonel, Louisville 1975-96; mem. People to People del. on corrosion, People's Republic China, 1986. Recipient Phila. award City of Phila., 1973, Resolution award, City of Phila., 1979, World Decoration of Excellence for Exceptional Contributions to World Communities award, 1980-90. Mem. AIChE (Spl. Half-Century Membership and Contbrns. to the Advancement of Chem. Engring. award 1992), Nat. Assn. of Corrosion Engr. (bd. dirs.), Inter Soc. Corrosion Com. (world chmn. 1960-61), Internat. Com. for Industrial Chimneys (recipient best paper award Dusseldorf, Germany 1970), Rotary (Paul Harris fellow 1988). Lutheran.

PIERCE, ROY, political science educator; b. N.Y.C., June 24, 1923; s. Roy Alexander and Elizabeth (Scott) P.; m. Winnifred Poland, July 19, 1947. Ph.D., Cornell U., 1950. Instr. govt. Smith Coll., Northampton, Mass., 1950-51, asst. prof., 1951-56; asst. prof. polit. sci. U. Mich., Ann Arbor, 1956-59, assoc. prof., 1959-64, prof., 1964-94, prof. emeritus, 1993—; vis. prof. Columbia U., 1959, Stanford U., 1966, U. Oslo, 1976, Ecole des Hautes Etudes en Sciences Sociales, Paris, 1978. Author: Contemporary French Political Thought, 1966, French Politics and Political Institutions, 1968, 2d edit., 1973, (with Philip E. Converse) Political Representation in France, 1986, Choosing the Chief: Presidential Elections in France and the United States, 1995. Served with USAF, 1943-46. Mem. Am. Polit. Sci. Assn. (co-winner Woodrow Wilson Found. award 1987, George H. Hallett Book award 1996). Office: Inst for Social Rsch U Mich Ann Arbor MI 48109

PIERCE, SAMUEL RILEY, JR., government official, lawyer; b. Glen Cove, L.I., N.Y., Sept. 8, 1922; s. Samuel R. and Hettie E. (Armstrong) P.; m. Barbara Penn Wright, Apr. 1, 1948; 1 child, Victoria Wright. AB with honors, Cornell U., 1947, JD, 1949; postgrad. (Ford Found. fellow), Yale U., 1957-58; LLM in Taxation, NYU, 1952, LLD, 1972; various other hon. degrees including LL.D., L.H.D., D.C.L., Litt.D. Bar: N.Y. 1949, Supreme Ct. 1956. Asst. dist. atty. County N.Y., 1949-53; asst. U.S. atty. So. Dist. N.Y., 1953-55; asst. to under sec. Dept. Labor, Washington, 1955-56; assoc. counsel, counsel Jud. Subcom. on Antitrust U.S. Ho. Reps., 1956-57; pvt. practice law, 1957-59, 61-70, 73-81, 89—; sec. HUD, 1981-89; faculty N.Y. U. Sch. Law, 1958-70; guest speaker colls., univs.; judge N.Y. Ct. Gen. Sessions, 1959-61; gen. counsel, head legal div. U.S. Treasury, Washington, 1970-73; cons. Fund Internat. Social and Econ. Edn., 1961-67; chmn. impartial disciplinary rev. bd. N.Y.C. Transit System, 1968-81; chmn. N.Y. State Minimum Wage Bd. Hotel Industry, 1961; mem. N.Y. State Banking Bd., 1961-70, N.Y.C. Bd. Edn., 1961, Adminstrv. Conf. U.S., 1968-70, Battery Park City Authority, 1968-70, N.Y.C. Spl. Commn. Inquiry into Energy Failures, 1977; mem. nat. adv. com. Comptroller of Currency, 1975-80; adv. group commr. IRS, 1974-76; mem. Nat. Wiretapping Commn., 1973-76; dir. N.Y. 1964-65 World's Fair Corp. Contbr. articles to profl. jours. Trustee Inst. Civil Justice, Mt. Holyoke Coll., 1965-75, Hampton Inst., Inst. Internat. Edn., Cornell U., Howard U., 1976-81; bd. dirs. Tax Found. U.S. del. Conf. on Coops., Georgetown, Brit. Guiana, 1956; mem. panel symposium Mil.-Indsl. Conf. on Atomic Energy, Chgo., 1956; fraternal del. All-African People's Conf., Accra, Ghana, 1958; mem. Nat. Def. Exec. Res., 1957-70; mem. nat. exec. bd. Boy Scouts Am., 1969-75; mem. N.Y.C. U.S.O. Com., 1959-61; mem. panel arbitrators Am. Arbitration Assn. and Fed. Mediation and Conciliation Service, 1957—; Bd. dirs. Louis T. Wright Meml. Fund, Inc., Nat. Parkinson Found., Inc., 1959-61; sec., dir. YMCA Greater N.Y., 1960-70; Mem. N.Y. State Republican Campaign Hdqrs. Staff, 1952, 58; gov. N.Y. Young Rep. Club, 1951-53. With AUS, 1943-46; as 1st lt. J.A.G.C. Res., 1950-52. Recipient N.Y.C. Jr. C. of C. Ann. Disting. Svc. award, 1958, Alexander Hamilton award Treasury Dept., 1973, Disting. Alumnus award Cornell Law Sch., 1988, Disting. Svc. Medallion Nassau County Bar Assn., 1988, Reagan Revolution Medal of Honor, 1989, Presdl. Citizens medal, 1989, Salute to Greatness award Martin Luther King Jr. Ctr., 1989; selected mem. of L.I. Sports Hall of Fame, 1988. Fellow Am. Coll. Trial Lawyers; mem. ABA, Assn. of Bar of City of N.Y., Cornell Assn. Class Secs., Telluride Assn. Alumni, Cornell U. Alumni Assn. N.Y.C. (gov.), C.I.D. Agts. Assn. (gov.), N.Y. County Lawyers Assn., Inst. Jud. Adminstrn., Phi Beta Kappa, Phi Kappa Phi, Alpha Phi Alpha, Alpha Phi Omega. Methodist (former mem. commn. on interjurisdictional relations United Meth. Ch.).

PIERCE, SUSAN RESNECK, academic administrator, English educator; b. Janesville, Wis., Feb. 6, 1943; d. Elliott Jack and Dory (Block) Resneck; m. Kenneth H. Pierce; 1 child, Alexandra Parr. AB, Wellesley Coll., 1965; MA, U. Chgo., 1966; PhD, U. Wis., 1972. Lectr. U. Wis., Rock County, 1970-71; from asst. prof. to prof. English Ithaca (N.Y.) Coll., 1973-83, chmn. dept., 1976-79, 81-82; dean Henry Kendall Coll. Arts and Scis., prof. English U. Tulsa, 1984-90; v.p. acad. affairs, prof. English Lewis and Clark Coll., Portland, Oreg., 1990-92; pres. U. of Puget Sound, Tacoma, 1992—; vis. assoc. prof. Princeton (N.J.) U., 1979; program officer div. ednl. programs NEH, 1982-83, asst. dir., 1983-84; bd. dirs. Janet Elson Scholarship Fund, 1984-1990, Tulsa Edn. Fund, Phillips Petroleum Scholarship Fund, 1985-90, Okla. Math. & Sci. High Sch., 1984-90, Hillcrest Med. Ctr., 1988-90, Portland Opera, 1990-92, St. Joseph's Hosp., 1992—, Seattle Symphony, 1993—; cons. U. Oreg., 1985, Drury Coll., Springfield, Mo., 1986; mem. Middle States and N. Cen. Accreditation Bds.; mem. adv. com. Fed. Women's Program, NEH, 1982-83; participant Summit Meeting on Higher Edn., Dept. Edn., Washington, 1985; speaker, participant numerous ednl. meetings, sems., commencements; chair Frederick Ness Book Award Com. Assn. Am. Colls., 1986; mem. award selection com. Dana Found., 1986, 87; mem. Acad. Affairs Council, Univ. Senate, dir. tchr. edn., chmn. adv. group for tchr. preparation, ex-officio mem. all Coll. Arts and Scis. coms. and Faculty Council on Internat. Studies, all U. Tulsa; bd. dirs. Am. Conf. Acad. Deans; bd. trustees Hillcrest Med. Ctr. Author: The Moral of the Story, 1982, also numerous essays, jour. articles, book sects., book revs.; co-editor: Approaches to Teaching "Invisible Man"; reader profl. jours. Bd. dirs. Arts and Humanities Coun., Tulsa, 1984-90; trustee Hillcrest Hosp., Tulsa, 1986-90; mem. cultural series com., community rels. com. Jewish Fedn., Tulsa, 1986-90; bd. dirs. Tulsa chpt. NCCJ, 1986-90. Recipient Best Essay award Arix. Quar., 1979, Excellence in Teaching award N.Y. State Edn. Council, 1982, Superior Group Service award NEH, 1984, other teaching awards; Dana scholar, Ithaca Coll., 1980-81; Dana Research fellow, Ithaca Coll., 82-83; grantee Inst. for Ednl. Affairs, 1980, Ford Found., 1987, NEH, 1989. Mem. MLA (adv. com. on job market 1973-74), South Ctrl. MLA, Soc. for Values in Higher Edn., Assn. Am. Colls. (bd. dirs.), Am. Conf. Acad. Deans (bd. dirs. 1988-91), Coun. of Presidents, Assn. Governing Bds., Phi Beta Kappa, Phi Kappa Phi, Phi Gamma Kappa. Office: U of Puget Sound 1500 N Warner St Tacoma WA 98416-0001

PIERCE, WILLIAM JAMES, law educator; b. Flint, Mich., Dec. 4, 1921; s. Francis Scott and Ellen (Pelton) P.; m. Betty Kathren Wise, Nov. 20, 1954; children—Darrell William, Margery Marie, Constance Ellen, Kathren Elizabeth. A.B. in Econs, U. Mich., 1947, J.D., 1949. Faculty U. Mich., 1953-89; emeritus prof. U. MIch., 1989—; prof. law, dir. Legis. Rsch. Ctr. U. Mich., 1958-89, asso. dean, 1971-79; exec. sec. Mich. Law Revision Commn., 1966-69; chmn. Citizens Adv. Com. Juvenile Ct., 1964-66; pres. Nat. Conf. Commrs. Uniform State Laws, 1969-72, exec. dir., 1969-92, emeritus exec. dir., 1992—. Author: (with Estep, Stason) Atomic Energy and the Law, 1957, (with Lamb, White) Apportionment and Representative Institutions, 1963, (with Read, MacDonald, Fordham) Materials on Legislation, 1973. Mem. Pres.'s Consumer Adv. Coun., 1967-69, Mich. Gov.'s Commn. on Mental Health Laws, 1969-72; mem. exec. com. Inst. Continuing Legal Edn., 1964-89. With AUS, 1943-45. Decorated Bronze Star medal. Mem. Am. Law Inst., Am. Bar Assn. (ho. of dels. 1966-69), State Bar Mich. Home: 1505 Roxbury Rd Ann Arbor MI 48104-4047 Office: U Mich Law Sch Ann Arbor MI 48109-1215

PIERCE, WILLIAM LUTHER, association executive, writer; b. Atlanta, Sept. 11, 1933; s. William Luther and Marguerite (Ferrell) P.; m. Susan Sarka, May 8, 1991. BS, Rice U., 1955; MA, U. Colo., 1958, PhD, 1962. Asst. prof. physics Oreg. State U., Corvallis, 1962-65; chmn. Nat. Youth Alliance, Arlington, Va., 1970-74, Nat. Alliance, Arlington, 1974—, Nat. Vanguard Books, Hillsboro, W.Va., 1988—. Author: The Turner Diaries, 1978, Hunter, 1989, Gun Control in Germany, 1928-1945, 1994; editor Nat. Vanguard mag., 1978—; writer, announcer: (weekly radio program) American Dissident Voices. Home and Office: Nat Vanguard Books PO Box 330 Hillsboro WV 24946-0330

PIERCE, WILLIAM SCHULER, cardiac surgeon, educator; b. Wilkes-Barre, Pa., Jan. 12, 1937; s. William Harold and Doris Louis (Schuler) P.; m. Peggy Jayne Stone, June 12, 1965; children: William Stone, Jonathan Drew. B.S., Lehigh U., 1958; M.D., U. Pa., 1962. Intern U. Pa., 1962-63; resident in surgery Hosp. U. Pa., 1963-70; asst. prof. M.S. Hershey Med. Ctr., Pa. State U. Coll. Medicine, Hershey, 1970-73, assoc. prof., 1973-77, prof. surgery, 1977—, chief divsn. cardiothoracic surgery, 1991-95; assoc. chmn. dept. surgery, dir. rsch., dept. surgery, 1995-97. Contbr. over 300 articles to profl. jours.; inventor cardiac valve, blood pump. Served with USPHS, 1965-67. Fellow ACS; mem. AMA, AAAS, Internat. Cardiovascular Soc., Am. Soc. Artificial Internal Organs, Soc. Vascular Surgery, Am. Heart Assn., Assn. Acad. Surgery, Inst. Medicine, So. Pa. Assn. Thoracic Surgery, Soc. Univ. Surgeons, Am. Surg. Assn., Soc. Clin. Surgery. Office: Milton S Hershey Med Ctr PO Box 850 Hershey PA 17033-0850

PIERCE-ROBERTS, TONY, cinematographer. Cinematographer: (TV movies) Tinker, Tailor, Soldier, Spy, 1979 (Brit. Acad. award), Caught on a Train, 1980 (Brit. Acad. award), A Voyage Round My Father, 1983, The Good Soldier, 1983, The Cold Room, 1984, (films) Moonlighting, 1982, Kipperbang, 1984, A Private Function, 1985, A Room with a View, 1986 (Academy award nomination best cinematography 1986), A Tiger's Tale, 1988, Slaves of New York, 1989, Out Cold, 1989, Mr. & Mrs. Bridge, 1990, White Fang, 1991, The Dark Half, 1993, Howards End (Academy award nomination best cinematography 1992), The Remains of the Day, 1993, The Client, 1994, Disclosure, 1995, Haunted, 1995, Surviving Picasso, 1995, Jungle 2 Jungle, 1996. Office: Treetops 11 Croft Rd, Chalfront St Peter Gerrards Crossing, Buckinghamshire England

PIERCY, GORDON CLAYTON, bank executive; b. Takoma Park, Md., Nov. 23, 1944; s. Gordon Clayton and Dorothy Florence (Brummer) P.; m. Roberta Margaret Walton, 1985; children: Elizabeth Anne, Kenneth Charles, Virginia Walton, Zachary Taylor Walton. BS, Syracuse U., 1966; MBA, Pace U., 1973. Mgmt. trainee Suburban Bank, Bethesda, Md., 1962-66; mktg. planning assoc. Chem. Bank, N.Y.C., 1966-70; sr. market devel. officer Seattle-First Nat. Bank, 1970-74; product expansion adminstr., mktg. planning mgr. VISA, Inc., San Francisco, 1974-76; v.p., dir. mktg. Wash. Mut. Savs. Bank, Seattle, 1976-82; v.p., mktg. dir. First Interstate Bank of Wash. N.A., 1983-86; sr. v.p. mktg., dir. Puget Sound Nat. Bank, Tacoma, 1986-92; sr. v.p., dir. mktg. and sales Key Bank, 1993-94, dir. corp. sales Kiro Inc., 1994; dir. mktg. and sales InterWest Bancorp, Oak Harbor, Wash., 1994—. Mem. Am. Mktg. Assn., Bank Mktg. Assn., Mktg. Communications Execs. Internat., Seattle Advt. Fedn., Ctrl. Whidbey Lions (bd. dirs.), Island County United Way (allocations com.), Northwest Railcar (bd. dirs.), Sigma Nu, Alpha Kappa Psi, Delta Mu Delta. Episcopalian. Home: 750 Snowberry Ln Coupeville WA 98239 Office: InterWest Bancorp PO Box 1649 Oak Harbor WA 98277

PIERCY, MARGE, poet, novelist, essayist; b. Detroit, Mar. 31, 1936; d. Robert Douglas and Bert Bernice (Bunnin) P.; m. Ira Wood, 1982. AB, U. Mich., 1957; MA, Northwestern U., 1958. Instr. Gary extension Ind. U., 1960-62; poet-in-residence U. Kans., 1971; disting. vis. lectr. Thomas Jefferson Coll., Grand Valley State Colls., fall 1975, 76, 78, 80; vis. faculty Women's Writers Conf., Cazenovia (N.Y.) Coll.; Elliston poetry fellow U. Cin., 1986; DeRoy Disting. vis. prof. U. Mich., 1992. Author: Breaking Camp, 1968, Hard Loving, 1969, Going Down Fast, 1969, Dance the Eagle to Sleep, 1970, Small Changes, 1973, To Be of Use, 1973, Living in the Open, 1976, Woman on the Edge of Time, 1976, The High Cost of Living, 1978, Vida, 1980, The Moon is Always Female, 1980, Braided Lives, 1982, Circles on the Water, 1982, Stone, Paper, Knife, 1983, My Mother's Body, 1985, Gone to Soldiers, 1988, Available Light, 1988 (May Sarton award 1991), Summer People, 1989, He, She and It, 1991, Body of Glass, 1991 (Arthur C. Clarke award 1993), Mars and Her Children, 1992, The Longings of Women, 1994, Eight Chambers of the Heart, 1995, City of Darkness, City of Light, 1996, What Are Big Girls Made Of?, 1997. Cons. N.Y. State Coun. on Arts, 1971, Mass. Found. for Humanities and Coun. on Arts, 1974; mem. Writer Bd., 1985-86; bd. dirs. Transition House, Mass. Found. Humanities and Pub. Policy, 1978-85, Am. ha-Yam, 1988—, v.p., 1995-96; gov.'s appointee to Mass. Cultural Coun., 1990-91, Mass. Coun. on Arts and Humanities, 1986-89; artistic adv. bd. ALEPH Alliance for Jewish Renewal, Am. Poetry Ctr., 1988—; lit. adv. panel poetry NEA, 1989. Recipient Borenstone Mountain Poetry award, 1968, 74, Lit. award Gov. Mass. Commn. on Status of Women, 1974, Nat. Endowment of Arts award, 1978, Carolyn Kizer Poetry prize, 1986, 90, Shaeffer-Eaton-PEN New Eng. award, 1989, Golden Rose Poetry prize, 1990, Brit ha-Dorot award The Shalom Ctr., 1992. Mem. PEN, NOW, Authors Guild, Authors League, Writers Union, Am. Poetry Soc., Nat. Audubon Soc., Mass. Audubon Soc., New Eng. Poetry Club. Address: PO Box 1473 Wellfleet MA 02667-1473

PIERLUISI, PEDRO R., lawyer; b. San Juan, P.R., Apr. 26, 1959; s. Jorge A. and Doris (Urrutia) P.; m. Maria E. Rojo, June 20, 1981; children: Anthony, Michael, Jacqueline, Rafael. BA, Tulane U., 1981; JD, George Washington U., 1984. Bar: D.C. 1984, U.S. Dist. Ct. D.C. 1985, U.S. Ct. Appeals (D.C. cir.) 1985, P.R. 1990, U.S. Supreme Ct. 1990, U.S. Dist. Ct. P.R., 1990, U.S. Ct. Appeals (1st cir.), 1993. Assoc. Verner, Liipfert, Bernhard, McPherson & Hand, Washington, 1984-85, Cole, Corette & Abrutyn, Washington, 1985-90; ptnr. Pierluisi Pierluisi & Mayol-Bianchi, San Juan, 1990-93; atty. gen. Govt. of P.R., 1993-96; ptnr. O'Neill & Borges, San Juan, 1997—. Mem. ABA (ho. of dels. 1995-96, standing com. on substance abuse 1995—), Nat. Assn. Attys. Gen. (chair eastern region 1996), Fed. Bar Assn., George Washington U. Internat. Law Soc. (pres. 1982-83), Rotary, Phi Alpha Delta (hon., Munoz chpt.). Avocations: tennis, jogging. Office: O'Neill & Borges 250 Munoz Rivera Ave Am Internat Plz San Juan PR 00918-1808

PIERONI, ROBERT EDWARD, internist, educator; b. Portland, Maine, June 20, 1937; s. Ansel Kirby and Agnes Mary (Dumais) P.; m. Dorothy Louise McDonnell, Oct. 3, 1970; children: Michelle Kirby, Robert Francis. BS, Boston Coll., 1959; MD, Pa. State U., 1971. Chemist Mass. Dept. Pub. Health, Boston, 1962-71; sr. bacteriologist Mass. Dept. Pub. Health, 1971-74; asst. prof. internal medicine U. Ala., Tuscaloosa, 1974-76, assoc. prof. dept. internal medicine and family practice, 1976-81, prof. internal medicine and family practice, 1981—; cons. VA Hosp., Bryce Hosp. and Partlow State Hosp., Tuscaloosa, 1974—. Contbr. more than 250 textbooks, articles and chpts.; mem. editorial bd. various jours. Col. U.S. Army, 1961—. Decorated Bronze Star, 1991, Commendation for Valor; recipient Golden Stethoscope award, 1982, Faculty Recognition award, 1986, Ala. Golden Eagle Humanitarian award Ala. Sr. Citizens Hall of Fame, 1988, Wright A. Garner award Ala. Acad. Sci., 1997. Fellow Am. Bd. Internal Medicine (diplomate), Am. Bd. Family Practice (diplomate), Am. Bd. Allergy and Immunology (diplomate), Am. Bd. Geriatric Medicine (diplomate), Am. Bd. Quality Assurance (diplomate); mem. AMA, ACP, Am. Coll. Allergy and Immunology, Am. Gerontol. Soc., Am. Acad. Family Physicians, Physicians for Human Rights, Undersea and Hyperbaric Med. Soc., C. of C., VFW, Am. Legion. Democrat. Roman Catholic. Avocations: mountain trekking, scuba diving. Home: 398 Riverdale Dr Tuscaloosa AL 35406-1814 Office: U Ala Dept Internal Medicine PO Box 870326 Tuscaloosa AL 35487-0326

PIERPOINT, POWELL, lawyer; b. Phila., Apr. 30, 1922; s. James Reynolds and Ruth (Powell) P.; m. Margaret Shaw Sagar, Mar. 24, 1950; 1 child, Harriet Pierpoint Bos. B.A., Yale, 1944, LL.B., 1948. Bar: N.Y. bar 1949. Assoc. Hughes, Hubbard & Reed (and predecessors), N.Y.C., 1948-53; ptnr. Hughes, Hubbard & Reed (and predecessors), 1955-61, 63-93, of counsel, 1993—; asst. U.S. atty. So. Dist. N.Y., 1953-55; gen. counsel Dept. Army, 1961-63; dir. Legal Aid Soc., 1968-90, pres., 1979-81; mem. N.Y.C. Bd. Ethics, 1972-89, chmn. 1983-89; spl. master appellate divsn. 1st Dept., 1992—. Served with USNR, 1943-46. Fellow Am. Coll. Trial Lawyers; mem. ABA, N.Y. State Bar Assn., Assn. Bar City of N.Y. Home: 155 E 72nd St New York NY 10021-4371 Office: Hughes Hubbard & Reed 1 Battery Park Plz New York NY 10004-1405

PIERPONT, ROBERT, fund raising executive, consultant; b. Somers Point, N.J., Jan. 27, 1932; s. Robert E. and Elise D. (White) P.; m. Marion J. Welde, Oct. 11, 1958; children: Linda J. Staropoli, Nancy P. Oler, Robert W., Richard F. B.S. in Bus. Adminstrn, Pa. Mil. Coll., 1954; postgrad. Inst. Edn. Mgmt, Harvard Grad. Sch. Bus. Adminstrn., 1970. Comml. sales rep. Atlantic City (N.J.) Electric Co., 1956-58; asst. dir. devel. Widener U. (formerly Pa. Mil. Coll.), Chester, 1958-61, asst. to pres., 1961-62, dir. devel., 1962-68, v.p. for devel., 1968-70; sr. cons. v.p. and dir. Brakeley, John Price Jones, Inc., N.Y.C., 1970-79; v.p. devel. Mt. Sinai Med. Center, N.Y.C., 1979-85; ptnr. Pierpont & Wilkerson, 1986—; guest faculty mem. Big 10 Fund Raisers Inst., Mackinac Island, Mich., 1971; mem. adv. com. on application of standards Philanthropic Adv. Service, Council of Better Bus. Burs., Washington, 1978-81; faculty The Fund Raising Sch., Ctr. on Philanthropy, Ind. U., 1989—. Mem. bishops adv. com. on stewardship Diocese of Pa., 1968-69; vestryman Trinity Episcopal Ch., Swarthmore, 1970-72; trustee Putnam Valley Free Libr., 1986-92; pres. Roaring Brook Lake Property Owners Assn., 1995—. Recipient Alumni Svc. award Widener U., 1989; named Disting. Alumnus in Econs., Widener U., 1986. Mem. Nat. Soc. Fund Raising Execs. (dir.-at-large 1970-78, pres. found. 1977-79, chmn. bd. 1979-82, chmn. cert. bd. 1982-87, presdl. search com. 1989, mem. ethics com. 1993—, chmn. 1993-95). Office: The Stone House PO Box 179 Rt 9 Garrison NY 10524

PIERPONT, WILBUR K., retired administrator, accounting educator; b. Winn, Mich., Mar. 15, 1914; s. Clarence N. and Ethel (Kent) P.; m. Maxine Sponseller, Feb. 7, 1941; children: Ann Pierpont Mack, James. AB, Central Mich. U., 1934; MBA (Univ. scholar), U. Mich., 1938, PhD, 1942; LLD, Central Mich. U., 1958, Hope Coll., 1977. Brookings Instn. fellow, 1941; price analyst Ordnance Dept., Washington, 1942-44; teaching fellow U. Mich., 1938-40, instr. Sch. Bus. Adminstrn., 1941-42, asst. prof., 1946-51, controller, 1947-51, v.p., chief fin. officer, prof., 1951-76, prof. acctg., 1977-81; bd. dirs. R and B Machine Tool Co., Chelsea Milling Co. Conbr. articles to numerous jours. Trustee Buhr Found., Redies Found. Served as lt. Bur. Ordnance, USNR, 1944-46. Recipient Outstanding Achievement award U. Mich., Alumni award U. Mich., Alumni award Cen. Mich. U. Mem. Golf and Outing Club, Rotary, Delta Sigma Pi, Beta Gamma Sigma, Phi Kappa Phi. Methodist. Home: 2125 Nature Cove Ct Ann Arbor MI 48104-8325

PIERRE, CHARLES BERNARD, mathematician, statistician, educator; b. Houston, Dec. 2, 1946; s. Rufus and Charles (Ellis) P.; m. Patsy Randle, Aug. 28, 1970 (div. 1971); m. Cynthia Gilliam, June 28, 1980 (div. 1994); 1 child, Kimberly Keri. BS, Tex. So. U., 1970, MS in Edn., 1974; PhD in Math./Math. Edn., Am. U., 1992. Cert. tchr., Tex., D.C. Comml. photographer Photographics Labs., Houston, 1968-69; elec. engr., mathematician Sta. KPRC-TV, Houston, 1970-71; instr. math. Houston Ind. Sch. Dist., 1971-72, Meth. Secondary Sch., Kailahun, Sierra Leone, West Africa, 1972-73; math. researcher West African Regional Math Program, Freetown, Sierra Leona, West Africa, 1973-77; instr. math. Houston Ind. Sch. Dist., 1977-80, 81-87, Episcopal Acad., Merion, Pa., 1980-81, D.C. Pub. Schs., Washington, 1987-91; instr. math. Houston C.C., 1985-87; asst. prof. math. and computer sci. San Jose State U., 1992-94; assoc. prof. math. scis. Clark Atlanta U., 1994—; African cons. Peace Corps, Phila., 1977, Sierra Leone, West Africa; lectr. math. Tex. So. U., U. Sierra Leone, U. Liberia, Bunambu Tchrs. Coll., Port Loko Tchrs. Coll., Inst. Edn., West Africa; assessment coord. Calif. State U. Alliance for Minority Participation, San Jose, 1994; advisor design team SKYMATH Project, Boulder, Colo., 1994-96; assoc. dir. Park City/IAS Math. Inst. Clark Atlanta U., 1994—; participant Inst. History Math., 1994-96; cons. in field. Author: Introduction to Coordinate Analytic Geometry, 1974, Mathematics for Elementary School Teachers, 1976; co-author: The Modern Approach to Trigonometry, 1975, A Resource Book for Teachers, 1975, Picture Book for the West African Regional Math. Program, 1975, textbook 6th grade STEM project U. Mont., 1996. Vol. Peace Corps., Sierra Leone. NSF fellow. Mem. ASCD, NAM, Am. Math. Soc., Math. Assn. Am., Pi Mu Epsilon. Democrat. Baptist. Avocations: writing, tennis, French horn, photography, travel. Home: 3360 Penny Ln Apt C East Point GA 30344-5557

PIERRE, JOSEPH HORACE, JR., commercial artist; b. Salem, Oreg., Oct. 3, 1929; s. Joseph Horace and Miriam Elisabeth (Holder) P.; m. June Anne Rice, Dec. 20, 1952; children: Joseph Horace III, Thomas E., Laurie E., Mark R., Ruth A. Grad., Advt. Art Sch., Portland, Oreg., 1954, Inst. Comml. Art, 1951-52. Lithographic printer Your Town Press, Inc., Salem, Oreg., 1955-58; correctional officer Oreg. State Correctional Instn., 1958-60; owner Illustrators Workshop, Inc., Salem, 1960-61; advt. mgr. North Pacific Lumber Co., Portland, 1961-63; vocat. instr. graphic arts Oreg. Correctional Instn., 1963-70; lithographic printer Lloyd's Printing, Monterey, Calif., 1971-72; illustrator McGraw Hill, 1972-73; owner Publishers Art Svc., Monterey, 1972-81; correctional officer Oreg. State Penitentiary, 1982-90; ret.; owner Northwest Syndicate, 1993—. Editor/publisher: The Pro Cartoonist & Gagwriter; author: The Road to Damascus, 1981, The Descendants of Thomas Pier, 1992, The Origin and History of the Callaway and Holder Families, 1992; author numerous OpEd cols. in Salem, Oreg. Statesman Jour., others; pub. cartoons nat. mags.; mural Mardi Gras Restaurant, Salem; cartoon strip Fabu, Oreg. Agr. mo. Mem. Rep. Nat. Com., Citizens Com. for Right to Keep and Bear Arms. Served with USN, 1946-51. Decorated victory medal WWII, China svc. medal, Korea medal, Navy occupation medal. Mem. U.S. Power Squadron, Nat. Rifle Assn., Acad. of Model Aeronautics, Oreg. Correctional Officers Assn. (co-founder, hon. mem.), Four Corners Rod and Gun Club. Republican. Avocations: sailing, flying, scuba, model aircraft building and flying. Home: 4822 Oak Park Dr NE Salem OR 97305-2931

PIERRE, PERCY ANTHONY, university president; b. nr. Donaldsville, La., Jan. 3, 1939; s. Percy John and Rosa (Villavaso) P.; m. Olga A. Markham, Aug. 8, 1965; children: Kristin Clare, Allison Celeste. BSEE, U. Notre Dame, 1961, MSEE, 1963, D of Engring. (hon.), 1977; PhD in Elec. Engring, Johns Hopkins U., 1967; postgrad., U. Mich., 1968; DSc (hon.), Rensselear Poly. Inst. Asst. prof. elec. engring. So. U., 1963; instr. Johns Hopkins U., Balt., 1963-64; instr. physics Morgan State Coll., 1964-66; instr. info. and control engring. U. Mich., Ann Arbor, 1967-68; instr. systems engring. UCLA, 1968-69; research engr. in communications RAND Corp., 1968-71; White House fellow, spl. asst. Office of Pres., 1969-70; dean Sch. Engring., Howard U., Washington, 1971-77; program officer for engring. edn. Alfred P. Sloan Found., 1973-75; asst. sec. for research, devel. and acquisition U.S. Dept. Army, 1977-81; engring. mgmt. cons., 1981-83; pres. Prairie View (Tex.) Agrl. and Mech. U. System, 1983-89, Honeywell prof. elec. engring., 1989-90; v.p. rsch. and grad. studies Mich. State U., East Lansing, 1990-95, prof. elec. engring., 1995—; chair. engring. coll. council Am. Soc. for Engring. Edn., 1973-75; mem. sci. adv. group Def. Communications Agy., 1974-75; mem. adv. panel Office Exptl. Research and Devel. Incentives, NSF, 1973-74; mem. Commn. Scholars To Rev. Grad. Programs, Ill. Bd. Higher Edn., 1972-74; mem. panel on role U.S. engring. sch. in fgn. tech. assistance, 1972, co-chmn. symposium on minorities in engring., 1973; mem. rev. panel for Inst. for Applied Tech., Nat. Bur. Standards, 1973-77; chmn. com. on minorities Nat. Acad. Engring., 1976-77; cons. to dir. Energy Rsch. and Devel. Adminstrn., 1976-77; mem. Army Sci. Bd., 1984; mem. adv. bd. Sch. Engring., Johns Hopkins U., 1981-84; cons. Office Sec. Def., 1981-84; mem. adv. bd. Lincoln Labs., MIT. Contbr. articles on communications theory to profl. publs. Trustee U. Notre Dame, 1974-77, 81—; trustee, mem. exec. com. Nat. Fund for Minority Engring. Students, 1976-77; bd. dirs. The Hitachi Found., 1987, Ctr. for Naval Analysis, 1986, Assn. Tex. Colls. and Univs.; pres. Southwest Athletic Conf., 1985-87, bd. dirs. CMS Corp., 1990—, Defense Sci., 1992-94, Old Kent Fin. Corp., 1993—, bd. trustee Aerospace Corp., 1991—. Recipient Disting. Civilian Service award Dept. Army, 1981; award of merit from Senator Proxmire, 1979. Mem. IEEE (sr. mem.; Edison award com. 1978-80), Sigma Xi, Tau Beta Pi. Home: 2445 Emerald Lake Dr East Lansing MI 48823-7256 Office: Mich State U 357 Engineering East Lansing MI 48824-1226

PIERRI, MARY KATHRYN MADELINE, cardiologist, critical care physician, educator; b. N.Y.C., Aug. 12, 1948; d. Charles Daniel and Margaret Loyola (Pesce) P. BA, Manhattanville Coll., 1969; MD, Med. Coll. Pa., 1974. Med. resident Med. Coll. Pa., Phila., 1974-77; fellow in cardiology N.Y. Hosp., N.Y.C., 1977-79; asst. physician Meml. Hosp., N.Y.C., 1980-89, assoc. physician, 1989—, chief cardiology svc., 1991—; assoc. prof. medicine Cornell Med. Coll., N.Y.C., 1989—. Fellow Am. Coll. Cardiology, N.Y. Cardiological Soc.; mem. ACP, Soc. Critical Care Medicine, Alpha Omega Alpha. Office: Meml Hosp Sloan Kettering Cancer Ctr 1275 York Ave New York NY 10021-6007

PIERSKALLA, WILLIAM PETER, university dean, management-engineering educator; b. St. Cloud, Minn., Oct. 22, 1934; s. Aloys R. and Hilda A. P.; m. Carol Spargo, Children: Nicholas, William, Michael. AB in Econs., Harvard U., 1956, MBA, 1958; MS in Math., U. Pitts., 1962; PhD in Ops. Rsch., Stanford U., 1965; MA, U. Pa., 1978. Assoc. prof. Case Western Res. U., Cleve., 1965-68, So. Meth. U., Dallas, 1968-70; prof. dept. indsl. engring. and mgmt. scis. Northwestern U., Evanston, Ill., 1970-78; exec. dir. Leonard Davis Inst., U. Pa., Phila., 1978-83; prof., chmn. health care sys. dept. U. Pa., Phila., 1982-90, prof. decision sci. and systems engring., dep. dean acad. affairs Wharton Sch., 1983-89, Ronald A. Rosenfield prof., 1986-93; dir. Huntsman Ctr. Global Competition and Leadership Wharton Sch., U. Pa., 1989-91; John E. Anderson prof. UCLA, 1993—, dean of John E. Anderson Grad Sch. of Mgmt., 1993—; cons. HHS, Bethesda, Md., 1974-87, MDAX, Chgo., 1985-91, MEDICUS, Evanston, 1970-75, Sisters of Charity, Dayton, Ohio, 1982-83, Project Hope, 1990—; bd. dirs. Huntsman Ctr. for Global Competition and Leadership, 1989-93, No. Wilderness Adventures, Griffin Funds, Inc., 1993-95, No. Trust Corp. Calif., The Bush Found., The Gerald Loeb Found., Grad. Mgmt. Edn. Coun. Contbr. articles to various publs. Mem. adv. bd. Lehigh U., 1986-93, U. So. Calif. Bus. Sch., 1987-93. Recipient Harold Larnder Meml. prize Can. Oper. Rsch. Soc., 1993; grantee NSF, 1970-83, HHS, Washington, 1973-82, Office Naval Rsch., Arlington, Va., 1974-77. Mem. Ops. Rsch. Soc. Am. (pres. 1982-83, editor 1979-82, Kimball Disting. Svc. medal 1989), Inst. Mgmt. Scis. (assoc. editor 1970-77), Internat. Fedn. Operational Rsch. Socs. (pres. 1989-91), Omega Rho (hon.). Office: UCLA Anderson Grad Sch Mgmt 110 Westwood Plz Box 951481 Los Angeles CA 90095-1481

PIERSOL, LAWRENCE L., federal judge; b. Vermillion, S.D., Oct. 21, 1940; s. Ralph Nelson and Mildred Alice (Millette) P.; m. Catherine Anne Vogt, June 30, 1962; children: Leah C., William M., Elizabeth J. BA, U. S.D., 1962, JD summa cum laude, 1965. Bar: S.D. 1965, U.S. Ct. Mil. Appeals, 1965, U.S. Dist. Ct. S.D. 1968, U.S. Supreme Ct. 1972, U.S. Dist. Ct. Wyo. 1980, U.S. Dist. Ct. Nebr. 1986, U.S. Dist. Ct. Mont. 1988. Ptnr. Davenport, Evans, Hurwitz & Smith, Sioux Falls, S.D., 1968-93; judge U.S. Dist. Ct., Sioux Falls, 1993—. Majority leader S.D. Ho. of Reps., Pierre, 1973-74, minority whip, 1971-72; del. Dem. Nat. Conv., 1972, 76, 80; S.D. mem. del. select commn. Dem. Nat. Com., 1971-75; mem. 8th Cir. Judicial Coun. Capt. U.S. Army, 1965-68. Mem. ABA, State Bar S.D., Fed. Judges Assn. (bd. dirs.). Roman Catholic. Avocations: reading, running, sailing, mountaineering. Office: US Dist Ct 400 S Phillips Ave Sioux Falls SD 57104-6824

PIERSON, ALBERT CHADWICK, business management educator; b. Pierson, Ill., Jan. 3, 1914; s. Charles Clevel and Gertrude Fannie (Gale) P.; m. Evelyn Matilda Swanson, Sept. 13, 1952; 1 stepson, Jay F. Lynch. B.A. in Liberal Arts and Scis, U. Ill., 1935; M.B.A. with distinction, Harvard U., 1947; Ph.D., Columbia U., 1963. Merchandiser Montgomery Ward & Co., Chgo., 1935-41; mgmt. cons. N.Y.C., 1947-53; prof. mgmt. San Diego State U., 1954—; cons. in field; pub. accountant, Calif.; research editor Jour. Travel Research, 1967—. Author: Trends in Lodging Enterprises, 1939-1963, 1963. Chmn. bd. Nat. Arts Found., N.Y.C.; mem. accreditation vis. teams Am. Assembly Collegiate Schs. Bus., 1977—. Served to col. AUS, 1941-46. Decorated Bronze Star. Fellow Soc. Applied Anthropology; mem. Acad. Mgmt. (pres. Western div. 1974-75), Western Council Travel Research (dir. 1965-67), Acad. Internat. Mgmt., Mil. Logistics Soc., James Joyce Soc., Beta Gamma Sigma, Sigma Iota Epsilon, Tau Sigma. Democrat. Methodist. Clubs: Harvard (Chgo.); Columbia (N.Y.C.); Marine Corps Officers (San Diego). Home: 1245 Park Row La Jolla CA 92037-3706 Office: Coll Bus San Diego State U San Diego CA 92182-0096

PIERSON, DON, sports columnist. Tribune Pro Football columnist Chicago Tribune. Recipient Dick McCann Mem. Award, 1994. Office: Chicago Tribune Sports Dept 435 N Michigan Ave Chicago IL 60611*

PIERSON, EDWARD SAMUEL, engineering educator, consultant; b. Syracuse, N.Y., June 27, 1937; s. Theodore and Marjorie O. (Bronner) P.; m. Elaine M. Grauer, June 6, 1971; 1 child, Alan. BS in Elec. Engring., Syracuse U., 1958; SM, MIT, 1960, ScD, 1964. Asst. prof., fellow MIT, 1965-66; assoc. prof., assoc. dept. head U. Ill., Chgo., 1966-75; program mgr. Argonne Nat. Labs., Ill., 1975-82; head dept. engring. Purdue U. Calumet, Hammond, Ind., 1982-95, spl. asst to chancellor for environ. programs, 1995—; cons. Argonne Nat. Lab., 1972-75, 82—, Solmecs Corp., 1982-88, HMJ Corp., Washington, 1983-88, LM Mfg., 1994—. Contbr. numerous articles to profl. jours. NSF fellow, 1958-60. Mem. IEEE, Am. Soc. Engring. Edn., Am. Soc. Mech. Engrs. Office: Purdue U Calumet Hammond IN 46323

PIERSON, FRANK ROMER, screenwriter, director; b. Chappaqua, N.Y., May 12, 1925; s. Harold C. and Louise (Randall) P.; m. Polly Stokes, 1948 (div.); m. Dori Derfner, 1978 (div.); m. Helene Szamet, June 24, 1990; children: Michael, Eve. BS, Harvard U., 1946. Writer, corr. Time/Life mags., 1950-58; bd. trustees Los Angeles Theatre Ctr., 1984—. Screenwriter: (television) Naked City, 1962, Route 66, 1963, Nichols, 1971, Haywire, 1979, (feature films) Cat Ballou, 1965 (Academy award nomination best adapted screenplay 1965), The Happening, 1967, Cool Hand Luke, 1967 (Academy award nomination best adapted screenplay 1967), The Anderson Tapes, 1970, Dog Day Afternoon, 1975 (Academy award best original screenplay 1975), In Country, 1989, Presumed Innocent, 1990; screenwriter, dir.: The Looking Glass Wars, 1970, A Star is Born, 1976, King ofthe Gypsies, 1978; dir.: (television) The Neon Ceiling, 1972 (San Francisco Film Festival award 1972), Alfred Hitchcock Presents, 1985, Somebody Has to Shoot the Picture, HBO, 1990 (Cable ACE award for best direction 1990), Citizen Cohn, HBO, 1992 (Cable ACE award for best direction 1992, Emmy award nomination for direction 1993); dir., prodr.: (television series) Have Gun Will Travel, 1960-62. Served with U.S. Army, 1943-46. Mem. Writers Guild Am. West (v.p. 1980-81, pres. 1981-83), Humanities Found. (pres. 1994). *

PIERSON, JOHN HERMAN GROESBECK, economist, writer; b. N.Y.C., Mar. 28, 1906; s. Charles Wheeler and Elizabeth Granville (Groesbeck) P.; m. Gertrude Trumbull Robinson, 1930 (div. 1942); children: Elizabeth P. Friend, John Trumbull Robinson Pierson; m. Sherleigh Elizabeth Glad, June 16, 1948 (dec. 1991); m. Harriet-Anne Duell, Feb. 22, 1992. BA, Yale Coll., 1927, PhD in Econ., 1938. Tchr. St. Bernard's Sch., N.Y.C., 1928-29; spl. asst. to v.p. Consol. Gas Co. of N.Y., N.Y.C., 1929-33; instr. econ. Yale Coll., New Haven, 1933-38, Sterling rsch. fellow, 1938-39; assoc. dir. Inst. for Applied Social Analysis, N.Y.C., 1939-41; asst. chief, then chief of Postwar Labor Problems div. Bur. Labor Statistics, Washington, 1941-45, adviser to acting commr., 1945-46; econ. adviser, spl. asst. to asst. and Under Sec. of Labor Washington, 1946-48; econ. adviser to asst. to adminstr. Econ. Cooperation Adminstrn., Washington, 1949-50; econ. adviser, policy adviser Asia/Far East Aid in Econ. Cooperation Adminstrn. and Mutual Security Agy., 1950-53; founder, pres. Voices to Am., Inc., N.Y.C., 1953-54; dir. rsch., planning div. U.N. Econ. Commn. for Asia and the Far East, Bangkok, 1955-59; spl. cons. Bur. Social Affairs U.N., N.Y.C., 1959-61, spl. adviser to Under-Sec. for Econ. and Social Affairs, 1961-66, sec. adv. com. on application of sci. & tech. to devel., 1964-66; free-lance writer, 1966—; chmn. U.S. Govt. interdepartmental com. on full employment and econ. fgn. policy, 1944-46; U.S. del. 3 internat. confs. to draft "Havana Charter", 1946-48; adviser various other internat. meetings; active Nat. Environ. Leadership Coun., 1990-91. Author: (poems) The Circling Beast, 1941, (books) Full Employment, 1941, Full Employment and Free Enterprise, 1947, Insuring Full Employment: A United States Policy for Domestic Prosperity and World Development, 1964, Essays on Full Employment, 1942-72, Island in Greece, 1973, Hubert Benoit's Reasoned Formulation of Zen, 1975, Full Employment Without Inflation: Papers on the Economic Performance Insurance Proposal, 1980, Full Employment: Why We Need It; How to Guarantee It; One Man's Journey, 1996; co-author: Guaranteed Full Employment: A Proposal for Achieving Continuous Work Opportunity for All, Without Inflation, through "Economic Performance Insurance", 1985; contbr. numerous articles to profl. jours. Mem. Am. Econ. Assn., Athens Soc. of the Friends of the Trees, Century Assn., Phi Beta Kappa. Home: 235 Walker St Lenox MA 01240-2762

PIERSON, JOHN THEODORE, JR., manufacturer; b. Kansas City, Mo., Oct. 13, 1931; s. John Theodore and Helen Marguerite (Sherman) P.; m. Susan K. Chadwick, Apr. 16, 1977; children by previous marriage—Merrill Sherman, Karen Louise, Kimberly Ann. B.S.E., Princeton U., 1953; M.B.A., Harvard U., 1958. With Vendo Co., Kansas City, Mo., 1960—, gen. automatic products salesman, 1960-61, mgr. new products, 1961-63; v.p. sales equipment for Coca-Cola, 1963-66; pres. Vendo Internat., 1966-69, exec. v.p., chief operating officer, 1969-71, pres., chief exec. officer, 1971-74; pres. Preco Industries, Inc., 1976-97, chmn., 1997—; chmn. Internat. Trade and Exhbn. Ctr. Co-author: Linear Polyethylene and Polypropylene: Problems and Opportunities, 1958. Trustee Midwest Rsch. Inst.; bd. dirs. and chmn. MidAm. Mfg. Tech. Ctr.; bd. dirs. Johnson County Bus. Tech. Ctr., Youth Symphony Kansas City, 1965-69; past trustee Pembroke-Country Day Sch., Barstow Sch.; past mem. adv. coun. U.S.-Japan Econ. Rels. Coun.; mem. coun. chmn. for exploring Boy Scouts Am., mem. Nat. coun. Lt. M.I. USNR, 1953-56. Mem. Kansas City C. of C. (v.p. interna.), U.S. C. of C. (dir. 1970-74), River Club (pres. 1994-96), Kansas City Country Club. Home: 2801 W 63rd St Shawnee Mission KS 66208-1866 Office: 9705 Commerce Pkwy Lenexa KS 66219-2403

PIERSON, MARILYN EHLE, financial planner; b. Cleve., Feb. 27, 1931; d. Ernest John and Helen Irene (Steudel) Ehle; m. Edward G. Pierson, July 17, 1954; children: Melanie K., Edward G. III. BSBA, Miami U., 1953. Paralegal Kyte, Conlan, Wulsin & Vogeler, Cin., 1974-79; adminstr. United Way Svcs., Cleve., 1982-87; CFP, sr. fin. advisor Advanced Planner Group Pres.'s Adv. Coun. Master Planner Am. Express Fin. Advisors, Cleve., 1987—; corp. presenter, fin. educator East Ohio Gas, AT&T, Cleve., Master Builders, Cleve., Preformed Line Products, Cleve., others; guest lectr. Chagrin Valley C. of C., Chagrin Falls, Ohio; lectr. adult edn. Shaker Heights (Ohio) H.S., 1993-96. Fin. columnist Bainbridge Banter newspaper. Chair stewardship and resources Valley Presbyn. Ch., Bainbridge, Ohio, elder, 1991-93, planned giving chmn., 1991-95; chmn., developer Meals on Wheels, Oil City, Pa., 1971-73. Mem. Internat. Assn. Fin. Planning (treas. exec. com. NE Ohio chpt. 1994—), Exec. Women Internat. (advisor, bd. dirs. 1997), Estate Planning Coun. Cleve. Avocation: travel. Home: 8178 Chagrin Mills Rd Chagrin Falls OH 44022-3807 Office: Am Express Fin Advisors 28601 Chagrin Blvd Ste 200 Cleveland OH 44122-4500

PIERSON, RICHARD ALLEN, hospital administrator; b. Emporia, Kans., Dec. 17, 1944; s. Lea Ross and Irene (Loren) P.; m. LuJean Hiatt, June 24, 1967; children: Lindsey, Alyssa, Jedd, Amanda, Adam, Aaron, Spencer. BS, Kans. State Tchrs. Coll., 1966; MBA, U. Utah, 1971; MHA, U. Minn., 1974. Adminstrv. resident U. Minn. Hosp., Mpls., 1973-74, asst. dir., 1974-77, assoc. dir., 1977-81; hosp. dir. Univ. Hosp. Ark., Little Rock, 1981-86, exec. dir., 1986—; bd. dirs. Univ. Hosp. Consortium, Chgo. Vice chmn., mem. Ark. Kidney Disease Commn., Little Rock, 1982-92, chmn., 1992-95. Capt. USAF, 1966-70. Mem. Am. Hosp. Assn. (governing coun. met. hosps. sect. 1988-90), Am. Coll. Healthcare Execs. (nominee). Mem. LDS Ch. Office: U Hosp Ark 4301 W Markham St Little Rock AR 72205-7101

PIERSON, ROBERT DAVID, banker; b. Orange, N.J., Mar. 5, 1935; s. Carleton Wellington and Muriel Browning (Potter) P.; BA, Lehigh U., 1957; m. Virginia Duncan Knight, Apr. 30, 1960; children: Lisa Boles, Alexandra Mead, Robert Wellington. Exec. asst. 1st Nat. City Bank N.Y., N.Y.C., 1958-61; asst. to pres. Cooper Labs. Inc., N.Y.C., 1961-65; dir. mktg. svcs. Arbrook div. Johnson & Johnson, Somerville, N.J., 1965-69; v.p. Klemtner Advt. Inc., N.Y.C., 1969-71; sr. v.p. Bowery Savs. Bank, N.Y.C., 1972-80; vice chmn., dir. Carteret Bancorp, Inc. Wilmington, Del., 1980-90 , Carteret Savs. Bank, F.A., Morristown, N.J., 1980-90; pres. Collective Fin. Svcs., Inc., Harbor Mortgage Co., (divsns. of Collective Bank, Montclair, N.J.), 1990—. Mayor Township of Mendham, N.J., 1995—. With USCG, 1958-59. Republican. Presbyterian. Clubs: Morris County Golf, Morristown. Home: Green Hills Rd Mendham NJ 07945-3305 Office: Collective Bank 560 Valley Rd Montclair NJ 07043-1805

PIERSON, WAYNE GEORGE, trust company executive; b. L.A., Nov. 5, 1950; s. Norman Einar and Annabelle Florence (McLay) P.; m. Margaret Aileen Boyle, Mar. 18, 1972; children: Heather, Dawn, Mark, Michael. BS in Bus. Adminstrn. with honors, Calif. State U., Northridge, 1973. CPA, Oreg., Calif. Audit supr. Ernst & Whinney (now Ernst & Young), L.A. and Portland, Oreg., 1973-80; treas. Gregory Affiliates, Beaverton, Oreg., 1980-82, Meyer Meml. Trust, Portland, 1982—; mem. adv. com. New Enterprise Assocs., Roanoke Venture, Veta Ptnrs. Investment com. Columbia Cascade Scout Coun. Mem. AICPA, Inst. Chartered Fin. Analysts Fedn., Assn. for Investment Mgmt. and Rsch., Oreg. Soc. CPAs, Portland Soc. Fin. Analysts, Found. Fin. Officers Group (steering com.). Avocations: tennis, scouting, travel. Office: Meyer Meml Trust 1515 SW 5th Ave Ste 500 Portland OR 97201-5450

PIERSON, WILLIAM ROY, chemist; b. Charleston, W.Va., Oct. 21, 1930; s. Roy H. Pierson and Gay Harris; m. Juliet T. Strong, May 20, 1961; children: Elizabeth T., Anne H. Veis. BSE, Princeton U., 1952; PhD, MIT, 1959. Rsch. assoc. Enrico Fermi Inst. for Nuclear Studies U. Chgo., 1959-62; rsch. scientist Ford Motor Co., Dearborn, Mich., 1962-87; exec dir. Energy and Environ. Engring. Ctr. Desert Rsch. Inst., Reno, 1987-95, rsch. prof., 1996—. Contbr. over 100 articles to profl. jours. Bd. dirs Reno Chamber Orch., 1992-96. Lt. USN, 1952-55. Fellow Air and Waste Mgmt. Assn. (Chambers award 1995); mem. AAAS, Am. Phys. Soc., Am. Chem. Soc., Am. Assn. for Aerosol Rsch. (bd. dirs. 1982-85). Office: Desert Rsch Inst 5625 Fox Ave PO Box 60220 Reno NV 89506

PIESTER, DAVID L(EE), magistrate judge; b. Lincoln, Nebr., Nov. 18, 1947; s. George P.; married; children. B.S., U. Nebr., 1969, J.D., 1972. Bar: Nebr. 1972, U.S. Dist. Ct. Nebr. 1972, U.S. Ct. Appeals (8th cir.) 1976, U.S. Supreme Ct. 1979. Staff atty. Legal Services S.E. Nebr., Lincoln, 1972-73, exec. dir., 1973-79; asst. U.S. atty. Dept. Justice, Lincoln, 1979-81; magistrate U.S. Dist. Ct. Nebr., Lincoln, 1981—; cons. Legal Services Corp., Nat. Legal Aid and Defender Assn., 1974-77. Mem. Lincoln Human Rights Commn., 1978-79. Mem. Nebr. State Bar Assn. (dispute resolution com.), ABA (Jud. adminstrn. divsn., Nat. Conf. Fed. Trial Judges), Fed. Magistrate Judges Assn., Lincoln Bar Assn., Eighth cir. Jud. Coun., 1993-96; eighth cir. edn. com., 1990-96. Office: 566 Fed Bldg Lincoln NE 68508

PIETERS, C.M., geology educator, planetary scientist, researcher; b. Ft. Sill, Okla., Nov. 11, 1943; widow. BA, Antioch Coll., 1966; BS, MIT, 1971, MS, 1972, PhD, 1977. Tchr. math. Somerville (Mass.) H.S., 1966-67; tchr. sci. Peace Corps, Sarawak, Malaysia, 1967-69; staff scientist rschr. Planetary Astron. Lab. MIT, 1972-75; space scientist Johnson Space Ctr. NASA, 1977-80; asst. prof. Brown U., Providence, R.I., 1980-83, assoc. prof. geology, 1983-94; prof. geoscis. Brown U., Providence, 1994—. Asteroid named in honor, Pieters. Mem. AAAS, Am. Geophys. Union, Am. Astron. Soc., Meteoritical Soc. Office: Dept Geol Sci Brown University Providence RI 02912

PIETRA, GIUSEPPE GIOVANNI, pathology educator; b. Piacenza, Italy, Dec. 30, 1930; came to U.S., 1957; s. Angelo and Emilia (Veratti) P.; m. Kathy Leuzinger, Nov. 23, 1957; children: Peter A., Philipp J. MD, U. Milan, 1955; BA (hon.), U. Pa., 1976. Diplomate Am. Bd. Pathology. Oncology fellow Chgo. Med. Sch., 1957-60; resident pathology Mass. Gen. Hosp., Boston, 1962-63; prosector pathology U. Zurich, Switzerlaand, 1963-64; asst. prof. pathology Chgo. Med. Sch., 1965-66, U. Ill., Chgo., 1966-69; asst. prof. pathology U. Pa., Phila., 1969-72, assoc. prof., 1972-76, prof., 1976-96, prof. emeritus, 1996—; staff pathologist U. Pa. Hosp., 1969-76, dir. med. pathology, 1976-82, dir. anatomic pathology, 1982-94; vis. prof. Univ. Milano Medical Sch., Italy. Lt. M.C., Italian Army, 1955-57. Fellow ACP; mem. Internat. Acad. Pathology, Microscopy Soc. Am. Office: U Pa Sch Medicine HUP 34th and Spruce Sts Philadelphia PA 19104-1999

PIETRINI, ANDREW GABRIEL, automotive aftermarket executive; b. Bryn Mawr, Pa., Feb. 27, 1937; s. Bernard and Irene (Norcini) P.; m. Pam Mari, Sept. 29, 1962; children: Darrin, Wayne. B.S., Villanova U., 1958. C.P.A., Pa. Jr. acct. Fernald & Co., Phila., 1958-60; sr. acct. O & W Audit Co., Narberth, Pa., 1960-62; asst. sec. James Talcott, Inc., N.Y.C., 1962-68; pres. UIS, Inc., N.Y.C., 1968—, dir., 1972—, now dir., chief oper. officer, chmn bd. dirs. Bd. dirs. Lebensfeld Found., N.Y.C., 1979—. Mem. Am. Inst. C.P.A.s, Fin. Execs. Inst. Republican. Roman Catholic. Avocations: sailing; golf. Office: UIS Inc 15 Exchange Pl Ste 1120 Jersey City NJ 07302*

PIETRUSKA, STANLEY ROBERT, lawyer, jury consultant; b. Bayonne, N.J., Dec. 11, 1963; s. Stanley Thomas and Maureen Margaret (Warren) P. BA, Jersey City State Coll., 1985; JD, Okla. City U., 1993. Bar: N.J. 1994, U.S. Dist. Ct. N.J. 1994, U.S. Ct. Appeals (3d cir.) 1994. Law clk. Legal Aid We. Okla., Oklahoma City, 1992-93, Okla. Indian Legal Svcs., Oklahoma City, 1993-94; sole practice law Jersey City, 1994—; pvt. practice Law Office of Stanley R. Pietruska, 1994—; price guide analyst Sports Collectors Digest, Iola, Wis., 1990—. Author: ESOPS: Corporate Advantages Put Taxpayers at a Disadvantage, Western State U. Law Review, 1996, co-author: Legal Aid of Western Oklahoma Guide to Garnishments, 1993; columnist Collectors Sportslook, 1993-94, Baseball Card News, 1991-92, Sports Card Price Guide, 1992-93; contbr. articles to profl. jours. Fundraiser, organizer Okla. Children's Hosp., Oklahoma City, 1992, 93. Recognized as one of Top 50 Most Influential People in Sports Memorabilia, Autograph News, 1992. Mem. ABA, ATLA, Phi Alpha Delta. Avocations: ice hockey, travel, golf, sports memorabilia, writing. Office: 580 Newark Ave Jersey City NJ 07306-2314 Address: 375 Avenue E Bayonne NJ 07002

PIETRUSKI, JOHN MICHAEL, JR., biotechnology company executive, pharmaceuticals executive; b. Sayreville, N.J., Mar. 12, 1933; m. Roberta Jeanne Talbot, July 3, 1954; children: Glenn David, Clifford John, Susan Jane. BS with honors, Rutgers U., 1954; LLD (hon.), Concordia Coll., 1993. With Proctor and Gamble Co., 1954-63; pres. med. products div. C.R. Bard, Inc., 1963-77; with Sterling Drug, Inc., N.Y.C., 1977-88; pres. Pharm. Group, 1977-81, corp. exec. v.p., 1981-83, pres., chief operating officer, 1983-85, chmn., chief exec. officer, 1985-88, ret., 1988; pres. Dansara Cons., 1988—; chmn. Tex. Biotech. Corp., 1990—; bd. dirs. Hershey Foods Corp., Gen. Pub. Utilities Corp., Lincoln Nat. Corp., McKesson Corp. Regent Concordia Coll. 1st lt. U.S. Army, 1955-57. Mem. Phi Beta Kappa. Club: Union League (N.Y.C.). Home: 27 Paddock Ln Colts Neck NJ 07722-1266 Office: One Penn Plaza Ste 3408 New York NY 10119

PIETRZAK, ALFRED ROBERT, lawyer; b. Glen Cove, N.Y., June 26, 1949; s. Alfred S. and Wanda M. (Wapniarski) P.; m. Sharon Esther Chizek, July 9, 1978; children: Eric A., Daniel J. BA, Fordham U., 1971; JD, Columbia U., 1974. Bar: N.Y. 1975, U.S. Dist. Ct. (so., ea., we. and no. dists.) N.Y. 1975, U.S. Dist. Ct. (no. dist.) Calif. 1983, U.S. Ct. Appeals (2d cir.) 1975, U.S. Ct. Appeals (9th cir.) 1983, U.S. Ct. Appeals (11th cir.) 1985, U.S. Supreme Ct. 1985. Assoc. Brown & Wood (formerly Brown, Wood, Ivey, Mitchell & Petty), N.Y.C., 1974-82, ptnr., 1983—, also head litigation practice group; mem. fin. products adv. com. Commodity Futures Trading Commn.; mem. CLE faculty Fordham U. Sch. Law.; bd. advisors Rev. of Securities & Commodities Regulation; bd. editors Futures Internat. Law Letter; adv. bd. Fordham Internat. Law Jour.; contbr. articles to legal jours. Mem. ABA (litigation, bus law sect.), Assn. of Bar of City of N.Y. (securities regulation com., chair futures regulation com.), Am. Law Inst. (lectr.), Securities Industry Assn., Futures Industry Assn., Univ. Glee Club. Democrat. Roman Catholic. Home: 525 Monterey Ave Pelham NY 10803 Office: Brown & Wood 1 World Trade Ctr Fl 58 New York NY 10048-5899

PIETRZAK, TED S., art gallery director; b. Kitchener, Ont., Can., Sept. 18, 1952; m. Marlene C. Longdon, Aug. 25, 1990; 1 child, Christina. BA in Arts Mgmt., U. Guelph, Banff, Alta., Can.; attended, Mus. Mgmt. Inst., Berkeley, Calif. Asst. to dir. Art Gallery Hamilton, Ont., 1976-80; dir. Burlington Cultural Ctr., 1980-91, Art Gallery Hamilton, 1992—. Mem. Ont. Assn. Art Galleries (pres. 1983-84), Can. Art Mus. Dirs. Orgn. (chair govt. and arts com., treas. 1991-95). Office: Art Gallery of Hamilton, 123 King St W, Hamilton, ON Canada L8P 4S8

PIFER, ALAN (JAY PARRISH), former foundation executive; b. Boston, May 4, 1921; s. Claude Albert and Elizabeth (Parrish) P.; m. Erica Pringle, June 20, 1953 (div. 1994); children: Matthew, Nicholas, Daniel. AB, Harvard U., 1947; Lionel de Jersey Harvard student Emmanuel Coll., Cambridge (Eng.) U., 1947-48; LLD (hon.), Mich. State U., 1971, Hofstra U., 1974, Notre Dame U., 1975; DHL (hon.), Marymount Coll., 1983, Millsaps Coll., 1986; D of Univ. (hon.), Open U., Eng., 1974; JD (hon.), Atlanta U., 1980; DEd (hon.), U. Cape Town, South Africa, 1984. Exec. sec. U.S. Ednl. Commn. in U.K., London, 1948-53; program officer Carnegie Corp. N.Y., 1953-63, v.p., 1963-65, acting pres., 1965-67, pres., 1967-82, pres. emeritus, sr. cons., 1982-87; chmn., pres. Southport Inst. for Policy Analysis, 1987-91, chmn., 1991-94; v.p. Carnegie Found. for Advancement of Teaching, 1963-65, acting pres., 1965-67, pres., 1967-79, trustee, 1979-87; bd. dirs. Technoserve, Inc. Author: (with others) Our Aging Society, 1986, (with others) Women on the Front Lines: Meeting the Challenge of an Aging America, 1993; Government for the People, 1987. Mem. mgmt. com. U.S.-South Africa Leader Exch. Program, 1957—, pub. policy com. Advt. Coun., 1987-91, adv. coun. Columbia U. Sch. Social Work, 1963-69, R & D ctr. panel U.S. Office Edn., 1963-65, adv. com. higher edn. U.S. Dept. Health Edn. and Welfare, 1967-68, bd. of overseers Harvard U., 1969-75, Charles Stark Draper Lab. bd. MIT, 1970-76, Commn. Pvt. Philanthropy and Pub. Needs, 1973-75; chmn. Consortium Advancement Pvt. Higher Edn., 1983-92, mayor's adv. com. Bd. Higher Edn. N.Y.C., 1966-69, Pres.'s Task Force on Edn., 1968, Aging Soc. Project, 1982-87, Nat. Conf. on Social Welfare Project, 1983-87; co-chmn. N.Y. State Nutrition Watch com., 1982; trustee U. Bridgeport, Conn., 1973—, Assn. Governing Bds. Colls. and Univs., 1985-91, African Am. Inst., 1957-71, Found. Libr. Ctr., 1967-71, Am. Ditchley Found., 1973-81; bd. dirs. Bus. Coun. Effective Literacy Inc., 1984-93, N.Y. Urban Coalition, 1967-71, Nat. Assembly for Social Policy and Devel., 1967-71, Coun. on Founds., Inc., 1970-76, Fed. Reserve Bank N.Y., 1970-76, Harry Frank Guggenheim Found., 1989—. Capt. U.S. Army, 1942-46, ETO. Recipient Barnard Coll. medal of distinction, 1980, Cleveland E. Dodge medal of distinction Tchrs. Coll., Columbia U., 1982. Fellow Am. Acad. of Arts and Scis., African Studies Assn. (founding), Royal Soc. Arts (London); mem. Am. Assn. for Higher Edn. (bd. dirs. 1982-90), Century Assn. Democrat. Clubs: Harvard (N.Y.C.). Avocation: gardening.

PIGA, STEPHEN MULRY, lawyer; b. Bklyn., Apr. 9, 1929; s. Stephen Paul and Ella (Mulry) P.; married, Feb. 23, 1952 (div.); children: Maureen, Stephen, Susan, Elizabeth; m. Emilie Halliday, Aug. 1, 1975; 1 dau., Margaret. A.B., Princeton U., 1950; LL.B., Columbia u., 1955. Bar: N.J. 1955, N.Y. 1956. Assoc. White & Case, N.Y.C., 1955-63, ptnr., 1964-92; ret., 1992; lectr. Practicing Law Inst. N.Y. and various insts., bar assns. Served to capt. USMCR, 1951-53. Mem. ABA, N.Y. State Bar Assn. (exec. com. tax sect. 1981-89, chmn. employee benefits com.), Assn. of Bar of City N.Y., N.J. Bar Assn., Am. Contract Bridge League (life master), Profl. Bowlers' Assn. Am. Republican. Clubs: High Mt. Golf (Franklin Lakes, N.J.), Princeton (N.Y.C.). Avocations: fishing, golf, bowling.

PIGNATARO, LOUIS JAMES, engineering educator; b. Bklyn., Nov. 30, 1923; s. Joseph and Rose (Capi) P.; m. Edith Hoffmann, Sept. 12, 1954; 1 child, Thea. B.C.E., Poly. Inst. Bklyn., 1951; M.S., Columbia U., 1954; Dr. Tech. Sci., Tech. U. Graz, Austria, 1961. Registered profl. engr., N.Y., Calif., Fla. Faculty Poly. Inst. N.Y., 1951-85, prof. civil engring., 1965—, dir. div. transp. planning, 1967—, head dept. transp. planning and engring., 1970, dir. Transp. Tng. and Research Center, 1975; Kayser prof. transp. engring. CCNY, N.Y.C., 1985-88; assoc. dir. Inst. for Transp. CCNY, 1985-88; mem. faculty N.J. Inst. Tech., 1988—, disting. prof. transp. engring., 1988—, dir. ctr. transp. studies and research, 1988-93; exec. dir. Inst. for Transp., 1994—; cons. govtl. agys., pvt. firms. Mem. Gov.'s Task Force Advisers on Transp. Problems, Gov.'s Task Force on Alcohol and Hwy. Safety; commr.'s council advisers N.Y. State Dept. Transp.; mem. adv. bd. freight services improvement conf. Port Authority N.Y. and N.J.; mem. adv. com. N.Y.C. Dept. Transp.; mem. rev. com. N.Y.C. Dept. City Planning; mem. Mayor's Transp. Commn., City of Newark. Sr. author: Traffic Engineering-Theory and Practice, 1973; contbr. over 80 papers to profl. jours. Served with AUS, 1943-46. Recipient Distinguished Tchr. citation Poly. Inst. Bklyn., 1965, Dedicated Alumnus award, 1971, Distinguished Alumnus award, 1972; citation for distinguished research Poly. chpt. Sigma Xi, 1975; named Engr. of Year N.Y. State Soc. Profl. Engrs., 1974. Fellow ASCE (dir.), Inst. Transp. Engrs. (Transp. Engr. of Yr. Met. sect. N.Y. and N.J. 1982); mem. Am. Rd. and Transp. Builders Assn. (div. dir.), Transp. Research Bd. (univ. liaison rep., Outstanding Paper award 1980 ann. meeting), Transp. Research Forum, Nat. Soc. Profl. Engrs., Sigma Xi, Chi Epsilon, Tau Beta Pi. Home: 230 Jay St Brooklyn NY 11201-1948 Office: NJ Inst Tech Inst for Transp 323 Martin Luther King Jr Blvd Newark NJ 07102-1824

PIGNATELLI, DEBORA BECKER, state legislator; b. Weehawken, N.J., Oct. 25, 1947; d. Edward and Frances (Fishman) Becker; m. Michael Albert Pignatelli, Aug. 22, 1971; children: Adam Becker, Benjamin Becker. AA, Vt. Coll., 1967; BA, U. Denver, 1969. Exec. dir. Girl's Club Greater Nashua, N.H., 1975-77; dir. tenant svcs. Nashua Housing Authority, 1979-80; vocat. counselor Comprehensive Rehab. Assocs., Bedford, N.H., 1982-85; specialist job placement Crawford & Co., Bedford, 1985-87; mem. appropriations com. N.H. Ho. of Reps., Concord, 1986-91, asst. minority leader, 1989-92; mem. N.H. State Senate, 1992—; Senate Dem. Whip; chairperson transp. com.; mem. environ., econ. devel., judiciary coms., ways and means com., internal affairs com.; del. Am. Coun. Young Polit. Leaders, Germany, 1987. Mem. Nashua Peace Ctr., 1980—; asst. coach Little League Baseball, Nashua, 1987-90; mem. steering com. Gephardt for Pres. Campaign, N.H., 1987-88; del. Dem. Nat. Conv., 1988; mem. Gov.'s Commn. on Domestic Violence. Named One of 10 Most Powerful Women in N.H., N.H. Editions mag., 1995. Mem. N.H. Children's Lobby, Women's Lobby. Jewish. Avocations: skiing, children, swimming, boating. Home: 22 Appletree Grn Nashua NH 03062-2252 Office: NH State Senate State House Rm 115 Concord NH 03301

PIGNO, MARK ANTHONY, prosthodontist, educator, researcher; b. Lake Charles, La., May 17, 1960; s. Frank Anthony and Geraldine (Carnahan) P.; m. Eileen Marie Failla, May 18, 1991; children: Alexandra Constance, Nathaniel Anthony. BS, McNeese State U., 1983; DDS, La. State U., 1989, cert. in prosthodontics, 1991; cert. in maxillofacial prosthetics, MD Anderson Cancer Ctr., Houston, 1992. Asst. prof. U. Mo., Kansas City, 1992-93; asst. prof. U. Tex. Health Sci. Ctr., San Antonio, 1993—, dir. Maxillofacial Prosthetics Tertiary Care Ctr., 1997—; mem. Craniofacial Anomalies Bd. U. Tex. Health Sci. Ctr., San Antonio, 1995—, Head and Neck Tumor Bd., 1997—. Contbr. articles to dental jours. Grantee U. Tex. Health Sci. Ctr., 1995. Fellow (assoc.) Am. Acad. Maxillofacial Prosthetics (Ann. Rsch. award 1992); mem. Am. Dental Assn., Am. Coll. Prosthodontists (com. mem. 1991—), Am. Assn. Dental Schs., Am. Assn. Dental Rsch. Roman Catholic. Avocations: fishing, gardening. Office: U Tex Health Sci Ctr 7703 Floyd Curl Dr San Antonio TX 78284-6200

PIGOTT, CHARLES MCGEE, transportation equipment manufacturing executive; b. Seattle, Apr. 21, 1929; s. Paul and Theiline (McGee) P.; m. Yvonne Flood, Apr. 18, 1953. B.S., Stanford U., 1951. With PACCAR Inc, Seattle, 1959—, exec. v.p., 1962-65, pres., 1965-86, chmn., pres., 1986-87, chmn., chief exec. officer, 1987-97, also bd. dirs., chmn. emeritus, 1997—; dir. The Seattle Times, Chevron Corp., The Boeing Co. Pres. Nat. Boy Scouts Am., 1986-88, mem. exec. bd. Mem. Bus. Council. Office: Paccar Inc 777 106th Ave NE Bellevue WA 98004-5001

PIGOTT, GEORGE MORRIS, food engineering educator, consulting engineer; b. Vancouver, Wash., Oct. 25, 1928; s. Alexander William and Moreita (Howard) P.; m. Joyce Burroughs (div. 1980); children: George Jr., Roy K., Randall E., Julie M., Becky P; m. Barbee W. Tucker. BS in Chem. Engring., U. Wash., 1950, MS in Chem. Engring., 1955, PhD in Food Sci. and Chemistry, 1962. Field engr. Continental Can Co., Seattle, 1951-53; rsch. engr. Fish and Wildlife Svc., Seattle, 1947-51, Nat. Canners Assn., Seattle, 1953-55, Boeing Corp., Seattle, 1957-60; cons. engr., 1960—; prof. food engring. Inst. Food Sci. and Tech. U. Wash., Seattle, 1962—, dir. Inst. Food Sci. and Tech., 1990—; pres. Sea Resources Engring. Inc., Bellevue, Wash., 1965—; bd. dirs. various cos. Author: Pathway to a Healthy Heart, 1983, Fish and Shellfish in Human Nutrition, 1988, Seafood: The Effect of Technology on Nutrition, 1990; contbr. more than 200 tech. papers; patentee in field. Served to lt. U.S. Army, 1951-53. Mem. NSPE, Am. Inst. Chem. Engrs., Am. Inst. Nutrition, Am. Chem. Soc., Inst. Food Technologists, Am. Inst. Chemistry, Am. Dietetic Assn., Am. Soc. Agrl. Engrs. Avocations: skiing, fishing, boating, scuba diving. Office: U Wash Inst for Food Sci and Tech 3707 Brooklyn Ave NE Seattle WA 98105-6715 Address: 4525-105 NE Kirkland WA 98033

PIGOTT, IRINA VSEVOLODOVNA, educational administrator; b. Blagoveschensk, Russia, Dec. 4, 1917; came to U.S., 1939, naturalized, 1947; d. Vsevolod V. and Sophia (Reprev) Obolianinoff; m. Nicholas Prischepenko, Feb. 1945 (dec. Nov. 1964); children: George, Helen. Grad. YMCA Jr. Coll., Manchuria, 1937; BA, Mills Coll., 1942; cert. social work U. Calif.-Berkeley, 1944; MA in Early Childhood Edn., NYU, 1951. Dir.-owner Parsons Nursery Sch., Flushing, N.Y., 1951-59; dir. Montessori Sch., N.Y.C., 1966-67; dir., tchr. Day Care Ctr., Harlem, 1967-68; founder, dir. East Manhattan Sch. for Bright and Gifted, N.Y.C., 1968—; dir.-owner The House for Bright and Gifted Children, Flushing, N.Y., 1988-93; organizer, pres., exec. dir. Non-Profl. Children's Performing Arts Guild, Inc., N.Y.C., 1961-65, 87—. Organizer Back Yard Theatre, Bayside, N.Y., 1959-61. Democrat. Greek Orthodox. Avocations: music, dance, theatre, art, sports. Home and Office: East Manhattan Sch 208 E 18th St New York NY 10003-3605

PIGOTT, JOHN DOWLING, geologist, geophysicist, geochemist, educator, consultant; b. Gorman, Tex., Feb. 2, 1951; s. Edwin Albert and Emma Jane (Poe) P.; m. Kulwadee Lawwongngam, May 28, 1994. BA in Zoology, U. Tex., 1974, BS in Geology, 1974, MA in Geology, 1977; PhD in Geology, Northwestern U., 1981. Geologist Amoco Internat., Chgo., 1978-80; sr. petroleum geologist Amoco Internat., Houston, 1980-81; asst., then assoc. prof. U. Okla., Norman, 1981—; vis. prof. Mus. Natural History, Paris, 1988, Sun Yat Sen U., Kaohsiung, Taiwan, 1991; rsch. dir. 5 nation Red Sea-Gulf of Aden seismic stratigraphy and basis analysis industry consortium, 1992—; internat. energy cons., 1981—; instr. I.H.R.D.C., Boston, 1987-91, O.G.C.I., Tulsa, 1991—. Mem. editl. bd. Geotectonica et Metallogenin Jour., 1992—. Mem. Am. Assn. Petroleum Geologists, Soc. Exploration Geophysicists, Soc. Petroleum Engrs., Geol. Soc. Am., Indonesian Petroleum Assn., Sigma Xi. Roman Catholic; Buddhist. Achievements include discovering relationship between global CO2 and natural tectonic cycles on the scale of millions of years showing previous greenhouse times during the Phanerozoic, processing first three-dimensional amplitude variation with offset seismic survey to quantify rocks, fluids, and pressures in rocks, processing and displaying first ground penetrating radar survey as a seismic section for ultrahigh resolution sequence stratigraphy, developing tectonic subsidence analysis as a practical tool for investigating the comparative anatomy of a sedimentary basins, their tectonic history, and evolving hydrocarbon potential, and constructing first paleo-heatflow maps of the Red Sea for the past 25 ma. Office: U Okla Sch Geology & Geophysics 100 E Boyd St Norman OK 73019-1000

PIGOTT, KAREN GRAY, community health nurse, geriatrics nurse; b. Utica, N.Y., May 15, 1956; d. Charles Philip and Pauline (Nelson) Gray; m. James H. Pigott, Apr. 30, 1977; children: William Charles, Christopher McCabe. Diploma, Albany Med. Ctr. Sch. Nursing, 1978; diploma nurse practitioner, SUNY, Syracuse, 1982. Cert. adult nurse practitioner. Staff nurse Albany (N.Y.) Med. Ctr., 1978-79, St. Elizabeth's Hosp., Utica, 1979-80; staff nurse RN Community Meml. Hosp., Hamilton, N.Y., 1980-81; nurse practitioner pvt. office, Waterville, N.Y., 1982-87, VA Med. Ctr., Gainesville, Fla., 1987-90; nurse practitioner pvt. office Balt., 1990—; cons. in field; preceptor for grad. students U. Fla., 1988-90, U. South Fla., 1989-90, U. Md., faculty assoc. Johns Hopkins U. Vol. health care provider Salvation Army Homeless Clinic, Gainesville, 1989-90, Spl. Olympics Events, Gainesville, 1990. Mem. ANA, Fla. Nurses Assn. (Expert in Clin. Practice award 1990). Presbyterian. Home: 115 Wakely Ter Bel Air MD 21014-5439 Office: 301 St Paul Pl Baltimore MD 21202-2102

PIGOTT, RICHARD J., food company executive; b. Chgo., May 26, 1940; s. Charles Francis and Mary Barbara (Amberg) P.; m. Karen Victoria Nahigian, Aug. 22, 1964; children: Alicia, Christopher. B.B.A., U. Notre Dame, 1961; J.D., U. Wis., 1966. Law ptnr. Winston & Strawn, 1966-77; with Beatrice Foods Co., Chgo., 1977-88, sr. v.p., gen. counsel, 1977-80, exec. v.p., chief adminstrv. officer, 1981-88; merger and acquisition advisor, investor, atty., 1988—; bd. dirs. Rodman & Renshaw Capital Group, Inc., Chgo., Ameriwood Industries, Grand Rapids, Mich. Trustee Chgo. Symphony Orch., 1983—; mem. bus. adv. coun. U. Ill., Chgo., 1983—. 1st lt., U.S. Army, 1961-63. Home: 1038 Longvalley Rd Glenview IL 60025-3414 Office: Three First Nat Plz 70 N Dearborn St Ste 3100 Chicago IL 60602-3001

PIGOZZI, RAYMOND ANTHONY, architect; b. Chgo., Feb. 29, 1928; s. Mario and Milena (Kervin) P.; m. Judith M. Hays, Feb. 12, 1955; children: Raymond J., Thomas M., Robert J., Ellen A., Andrew H. BS in Architecture, U. Ill., 1951. Registered architect, Ill., Iowa, Wis., Mich., Ind., N.C. Designer Ganster & Henninghausen, Waukegan, Ill., 1954-58; prin. designer O'Donnell Wicklund Pigozzi & Peterson Architects, Inc., Deerfield, Ill., 1958—; juror Coun. Ednl. Facility Planners Internat., Chgo., 1977-78, Am. Assn. Sch. Adminstrs., Washington, 1982-83, honor awards program Masonry Inst. Mich., 1987, Am. Sch. and Univ. Award Winning Ednl. Bldg., 1989, Metal Constrn. Assn. Merit awards, 1993; cons. Ednl. Facilities Lab., N.Y.C., 1972-75; Ednl. Environ. Exhbn. Jury, Ill. Assn. Sch. Bds., 1993. Prin. works include Fairview South Elem. Sch. Auditorium and Learning Ctr., Skokie, Ill. (Chgo. Chpt. AIA Disting. Bldg. award 1968), Onwentsia Country Club Tennis and Squash Facility, Lake Forest, Ill. (Chgo. Chpt. AIA Disting. bldg. award 1971), Berkeley Elem. Sch., Arlington Heights, Ill. (Am. Assn. Sch. Adminstrs. citation 1971), Field Elem. Sch. Remodeling, Chgo. (Coun. Ednl. Facility Planners Modernization award 1973), Von Humboldt Child-Parent Ctr. (Assn. Sch. Bus. Ofcls. award of Merit 1981, Met. Chgo. Masonry Coun. Honor award for excellence in masonry 1981), Robert Crown Community Ctr., Evanston, Ill., Loyola U. Humanities Bldg., 1983, Crystal Lake Village Hall, 1987, Frank C. Whiteley Sch. Hoffman Estates, Ill., 1989, Arthur Anderson & Co. Campus Ctr. Expansion, St. Charles, Ill., 1990 (Gold medal Excellence in Masonry Awards), Science Wing Niles H.S., Skokie, Il., 1993 (Disting. Bldg. award, Silver medal Execllence in Masonry AIA, 1994), Niles West H.S. Field House, 1996 (Best Structure award Structural Engrs. Assn. Ill. 1996). mem. ednl. adv. com. Evanston Twp. High Sch., 1979-83; chmn. profl. svc. Evanston United Way, 1982; mem. state's fine arts rev. com. Northeastern Ill. U., 1987. Recipient Metal Construction Assn. Merit award, 1993, Ill. Assn. Sch. Bd. Award of Distinction, Homewood Floosmoor High Sch., 1993. Fellow AIA (mem. nat. com. on architecture for edn. 1980—, juror N.E. chpt. bldg. honor awards program 1989, Disting. Svc. award 1990, Disting. Svc. award Chgo. chpt. 1990); mem. Ill. Sch. Bus. Ofcls., Ill. Libr. Assn., Ill. Assn. Sch. Bus. Ednl. Environments (juror 1992), Coun. Ednl. Facility Planners (pres. Great Lakes region 1988-90), Landmarks Preservation Coun. Ill. Democrat. Roman Catholic. Home: 200 Lee St Evanston IL 60202-1450 Office: O'Donnell Wicklund Pigozzi and Peterson Architecs Inc 570 Lake Cook Rd Deerfield IL 60015-5612 also: 1 N Franklin St Chicago IL 60606-3421

PIHL, JAMES MELVIN, electrical engineer; b. Seattle, May 29, 1943; s. Melvin Charles and Carrie Josephine (Cummings) P.; married; 1 child, Christopher James. AASEE, Seattle, 1971; BSA, City Univ., Bellevue, Wash., 1996. 1st class operators lic., FCC; lic. in real estate sales. Journeyman machinist Svc. Exch. Corp., Seattle, 1964-67; design engr. P.M. Electronics, Seattle, 1970-73, Physio Control Corp., Redmond, Wash., 1973-79; project engr. SeaMed Corp., Redmond, 1979-83; sr. design engr. Internat. Submarine Tech., Redmond, 1983-85; engring. mgr. First Med. Devices, Bellevue, Wash., 1985-89; rsch. engr. Pentco Products, Bothell, Wash., 1989—. Inventor, patentee protection system for preventing defibrillation with incorrect or improperly connected electrodes, impedance measurement circuit. With U.S. Army,, 1961-64. Mem. N.Y. Acad. Scis. Avocations: boating, target shooting, violin. Home: 13623-184th Ave NE Woodinville WA 98072 Office: Traffic Court Consultants 13623-184th Ave NE Woodinville WA 98072

PIHLAJA, MAXINE MURIEL MEAD, orchestra executive; b. Windom, Minn., July 19, 1935; d. Julian Wright and Mildred Eleanor (Ray) Mead; m. Donald Francis Pihlaja, Jan. 4, 1963; children: Geoffrey Blake, Kirsten Louise, Jocelyn Erika. BA, Hamline U., 1957; postgrad., Columbia U., 1957-58. Group worker Fedn. of Chs., L.A., 1956; case worker St. John's Guild Floating Hosp. Ship, N.Y.C., 1957-59; Y-Teen program dir. YWCA, Elizabeth, N.J., 1957-60, Boulder, Colo., 1964-65; spl. svcs. program and club dir. U.S. Army, Ingrandes and Nancy, France, 1960-62; music buyer, salesperson Guinn's Music, Billings, Mont., 1977-78, N.W. Music, Billings 1978-79; office adminstr. Am. Luth. Ch., Billings, 1979-84; gen. mgr. Billings Symphony Orchestra, 1984—; substitute tchr. Community Day Care and Enrichment Ctr., Billings, 1971-76. Dir. Handbell choir 1st Presybn. Ch., Billings, 1973—, Am. Luth. Ch., 1981-84, 1st English Luth. Ch., 1982—; mem. Billings Symphony Chorale, 1965-91, Bellissimo!, 1983-93, Cmty. Concerts Bd., 1967-96. Mem. Mont. Assn. Female Execs. (mem. membership com. 1994-96, retreat com. 1996—, bd. dirs. 1996—), Am. Guild English Handbell Ringers (state chmn. 1988-89, treas. Area X bd. dirs. 1990-94, Mont. membership chmn. 1994-96), Assn. Symphony Orchs. (treas. 1987-92, sec. 1995-96). Lutheran. Office: Billings Symphony Orch Box 7055 401 N 31st St Ste 530 Billings MT 59103

PIIPPO, STEVE, educator. Dir. math. sci. tech. program Richland (Wash.) High Sch. Creator, author Materials Sci.Tech. Recipient A Sites Recognition award U.S. Dept. Edn. Office: Richland High Sch Math Sci Tech Program 930 Long Ave Richland WA 99352-3311*

PIIRMA, IRJA, chemist, educator; b. Tallinn, Estonia, Feb. 4, 1920; came to U.S., 1949; d. Voldemar Juri and Meta Wilhelmine (Lister) Tiits; m. Aleksander Piirma, Mar. 10, 1943; children: Margit Ene, Silvia Ann. Diploma in chemistry, Tech. U., Darmstadt, Fed. Republic of Germany, 1949; MS, U. Akron, 1957, PhD, 1960. Rsch. chemist U. Akron, Ohio, 1952-67, asst. prof., 1967-76, assoc. prof., 1976-81, prof., 1981-90; prof. emerita U. Akron, Ohio, 1990—; dept. head U. Akron, Ohio, 1982-85. Author: Polymeric Surfactants, 1992; editor: Emulsion Polymerization, 1982; contbr. articles to profl. jours. Recipient Extra Mural Rsch. award BP Am., Inc., 1989. Mem. Am. Chem. Soc. Avocations: swimming, skiing. Home: 3528 Adaline Dr Cuyahoga Falls OH 44224-3929 Office: U Akron Akron OH 44325-3909

PIIRTO, DOUGLAS DONALD, 26458810, educator; b. Reno, Nev., Sept. 25, 1948; s. Rueben Arvid and Martha Hilma (Giebel) P.; BS, U. Nev., 1970; MS, Colo. State U., 1971; PhD, U. Calif., Berkeley, 1977; m. Mary Louise Cruz, Oct. 28, 1978. Rsch. asst. Colo. State U., 1970-71, U. Calif., Berkeley, 1972-77; forester, silviculturist U.S. Dept. Agr., Forest Svc., Sierra Nat. Forest, Trimmer and Shaver Lake, Calif., 1977-85; assoc. prof. natural resources mgmt. dept. Calif. Poly. State U., San Luis Obispo, 1985-90, prof. 1990—; researcher in field; instr. part-time Kings River Community Coll., Reedley, Calif.; forestry cons., expert witness. Registered profl. forester, Calif.; cert. silviculturist USDA Forest Svc. Recipient Meritorious Performance and Profl. Promise award CalPoly, 1989, 96, 97, CalPoly Coll. Agr. Outstanding Tchg. award Dole Food Co., 1995. Mem. Soc. Am. Foresters, Am. Forestry Assn., Forest Products Rsch. Soc., Soc. Wood Sci. and Tech., Alpha Zeta, Xi Sigma Pi, Sigma Xi, Beta Beta Beta, Phi Sigma Kappa. Lutheran. Contbr. articles to sci. and forestry jours. Home: 7605 El Retiro Ave Atascadero CA 93422-3722 Office: Calif Poly State U Dept Natural Resources Mgmt San Luis Obispo CA 93407

PIKE, CHARLES JAMES, employee benefits consultant, financial planner; b. Montreal, Apr. 9, 1914; s. Andrew and Frances Alicia (Webster) P.; m. Lois R. Bennet, Dec. 26, 1953 (dec. Aug. 1963); m. Marjorie H. Murdoch, Nov. 25, 1977. Grad. high sch., Montreal. CLU, chartered ins. broker, CFP, registered fin. planner, chartered adminstr. Subscription sales mgr. Hearst Orgn., then Maclean Hunter, Can., 1932-39; sales mgr. Hires Root Beer, Que., 1939-41; from group rep. to group mgr. Sun Life Can., 1941-48; asst. br. mgr. Sun Life Can., Edmonton, Montreal, 1948-54; pvt. group welfare cons. Montreal, 1955—; pres. Fin. and Estate Planning Coun., Montreal, 1954, Life Underwriters Assn. Montreal, 1955; founding pres. Que. chpt. Can. Assn. Fin. Planners, 1982. Ins. editor, weekly columnist Fin. Times Can., 1950-56. Co-founder mktg. execs. course U. Western Ont., London, 1952; pres. Montreal (Que.) Boys' and Girls' Assn., 1960-63; coun. mem. The Montreal (Que.) Bd. Trade, 1970-72. Mem. Life Underwriters Assn. Can. (life), Million Dollar Round Table (life), Montreal Bd. Trade (life), Que. Assn. Fin. Planners (planner emeritus), Can. Alpine Masters Racing Group (life), JB Ski Club Inc. (past pres.), Beaconsfield Golf Club (life), Montreal Hunt Club (past pres.), Montreal Amateur Athletic Assn. (past coun. mem.). Avocations: skiing, horseback fox hunting, roller blading, golfing. Office: Pike Vezina Assurance, 800 Blvd Rene-Levesque O, Montreal, PQ Canada H3B 1X9

PIKE, DOUGLAS EUGENE, educator; b. Cass Lake, Minn., July 27, 1924; s. Clarence Eugene and Esther (Jensen) P.; m. Myrna Louise Johnson, Sept. 15, 1956; children: Andrew Jefferson, Victoria Louise, Ethan Edward. BA, U. Calif., 1953; MA, Am. U., 1961; postgrad., MIT, 1963-64. Writer UN, Korea, 1950-52; fgn. service officer U.S. Govt. State Dept., Washington, Saigon, Hong Kong, Tokyo, and Taipei, Taiwan., 1958-82; dir. Indochina Studies Program U. Calif., Berkeley, 1982-96; prof. Tex. Tech. U., Lubbock, 1997—. Author: Viet Cong: The Organizational Techniques of the National Liberation Front of South Vietnam, 1965, War, Peace and the Viet Cong, 1969, History of Vietnamese Communism, 1978, PAVN: People's Army of Vietnam, 1986, Vietnam and the USSR: Anatomy of an Alliance, 1987, The Bunker Papers: Reports to the President from Vietnam, 1991; editor: Indochina Chronology, 1983—; contbr. numerous articles to profl. jours. Served to master sgt. Signal Corps, U.S. Army, 1943-46, PTO. Recipient Superior Honor award U.S. Info. Agy., 1976, Sec. Def. medal, U.S. Dept. Def., 1981. Mem. Author's Guild, Army-Navy Club (Washington), Fgn. Svc. Club, Faculty Club U. Calif. Methodist. Avocation: philately. Office: Vietnam War Archive Texas Tech Univ Lubbock TX 79409-1013

PIKE, GEORGE HAROLD, JR., religious organization executive, clergyman; b. Summit, N.J., Jan. 14, 1933; s. George Harold and Ann Aurelia (Brewer) P.; m. Pauline Elizabeth Blair, Aug. 27, 1955; children: Elizabeth, George 3d, James. BA, Trinity Coll., Hartford, Conn., 1954; MDiv, Dubuque (Iowa) Theolog. Sch., 1957. Ordained to ministry Presbyn. Ch. USA., 1957. Pastor 1st PResbyn. Ch., Kasson, Minn., 1956-59, 3d Presbyn. Ch., Dubuque, 1959-64; sr. pastor Presbyn. Ch., Bettendorf, Iowa, 1964-68; sr. pastor 1st Presbyn. Ch., Vancouver, Wash., 1968-78, Cranford, N.J., 1978-88; exec. chair Presbyn. Ch. USA, Louisville, 1988-93; interim pastor 2d Presbyn. Ch., Kansas City, Mo., 1993-95; dir. sem. devel. U. Dubuque, Iowa, 1995—; mem. exec. com. Consultation on Ch. Union, Princeton, 1980-89, pres., 1984-88. Dir. Bettendorf Bd. Edn., 1964-68, pres. 1967-68; bd. dirs. Southwest Wash. Hosps., Vancouver, 1969-78. Named Citizen of Yr., Jaycees, Bettendorf, 1967, Citizen of Yr., B'nai B'rith, Cranford, 1988; named to Honorable Order of Ky. Cols., 1989. Avocations: golf, photography. Home: 3650 Keystone Dr Dubuque IA 52002-3757 Office: U Dubuque 2000 University Ave Dubuque IA 52001-5050

PIKE, JOHN NAZARIAN, optical engineering consultant; b. Boston, Feb. 13, 1929; s. Arthur Thorndike and Sarah Lucy (Nazarian) P.; m. Margaretta May Horner, Dec. 28, 1957; children: Sally Katharine, Susan Horner. AB, Princeton U., 1951; PhD in Physics and Optics, U. Rochester, 1958. Staff scientist Parma (Ohio) Rsch. Ctr., Union Carbide Corp., 1956-63; mem. physics faculty Baldwin-Wallace Coll., Berea, Ohio, 1961-63; sr. scientist Tarrytown (N.Y.) Tech. Ctr., Union Carbide Corp., 1963-85; pres. J.J. Pike & Co., Inc., Pleasantville, N.Y., 1986—. Patentee in applied indsl. optics; contbr. numerous articles to profl. jours. Bd. dirs. United Way of Westchester and Putnam, N.Y., 1979-85, 95—, chmn., 1996—; mem. nat. com. for planned giving United Way of Am., 1997—. Recipient Harold J. Marshall Citation for Cmty. Svc., United Way No. Westchester, 1976, Cmty. Svc. award Union Carbide Corp., 1982. Mem. Optical Soc. Am., Soc. Photo-Optical Instrument Engrs., Internat. Soc. for Optical Engring., Phi Beta Kappa, Sigma Xi. Home: 71 Cedar Ave Pleasantville NY 10570-1932 Office: JJ Pike & Co Inc PO Box 186 Pleasantville NY 10570-0186

PIKE, KENNETH LEE, linguist, educator; b. Conn., June 9, 1912; s. Ernest R. and Hattie (Granniss) P.; m. Evelyn Griset, Oct. 20, 1938; children: Judith, Barbara, Stephen. BTh, Gordon Coll., 1933, LHD (hon.), 1982; PhD, U. Mich., 1942; PhD (hon.), Huntington Coll., 1967, Wheaton Coll., Irian Jaya, 1975, René Descartes U., Sorbonne, 1978, Monterrey, Mex.; LHD (hon.), U. Chgo., 1974, Georgetown U., 1984. Assoc. prof. U. Mich., Ann Arbor, 1948-55, prof., 1955-79; adj. prof. U. Tex., Arlington, 1979—; researcher, cons. Summer Inst. Linguistics, Dallas; researcher, lectr. in Mex., Ecuador, Peru, Guatemala, Papua New Guinea, Ghana, Nigeria, Philippines, Irian Jaya, Nepal, Thailand, Chile, Brazil, Singapore, others. Author: Phonetics, 1943, Intonation of American English, 1945, Phonemics, 1947, Tone Languages, 1948, Language in Relation to a Unified Theory of the Structure of Human Behavior, 1954, 2d edit., 1967, (with R. Young and A. Becker) Rhetoric, Discovery and Change, 1971, (with Evelyn G. Pike) Grammatical Analysis, 1977, 2d edit., 1982, Linguistics Concepts--An Introduction to Tagmemics, 1982, (with Evelyn G. Pike) Text and Tagmeme, 1983, (with D. Stark and Angel Merecias) Translator: New Testament Mixtec, With Heart and Mind, 1962, 2d edit., 1996, Stir, Change, Create: Poems and Essays, 1961, On Pain, 1997, On Philosophy of Life, 1997, On the Shepherd, 1997, On Scholarship and Work, 1997, On Love, Laughter, and Life, 1997; editor: (with Thomas N. Headland, Marvin Harris) Emics and Etics—The Insider/Outsider Debate, 1990, Talk, Thought and Thing—The Emic Road Toward Conscious Knowledge, 1993. Bd. dirs. Wycliffe Bible Translators, Huntington Beach, Calif., 1942-79. Recipient Presdl. Medal Merit, Govt. of Philippines, 1974; named Hon. Prof., U. Trujillo, 1987. Mem. Summer Inst. Linguistics (pres. 1979), Linguistic Soc. Am. (pres. 1961), Linguistic Assn. Can. and U.S. (pres. 1978), Am. Anthrop. Assn., Internat. Phonetic Soc., Am. Acad. Arts and Sci., Nat. Acad. Sci. Republican. Presbyterian. Avocation: water polo. Home and Office: Summer Inst Linguistics 7500 W Camp Wisdom Rd Dallas TX 75236-5628

PIKE, KERMIT JEROME, library director; b. East Cleveland, June 19, 1941; s. Frank James and Pauline Frances (Prijatel) P.; m. Joyce Rita Massillo, June 27, 1964; children: Christopher James, Laura Elizabeth. BA, Case Western Res. U., 1963, MA, 1965. Rsch. asst. Western Res. Hist. Soc., Cleve., 1965-66, curator manuscripts, 1966-72, chief libr., 1969-75, dir. libr., 1976—; adj. prof. history, libr. sci. Case Western Res. U., 1975-84. Author: Guide to the Manuscripts and Archives, 1972, Guide to Shaker Manuscripts, 1974; editor: Guide to Jewish History Sources, 1983; Compiler: Guide to Major Manuscript Collections, 1987. Mem. Super Sesquicentennial Com., Cleve., 1971, Cleve. Bicentennial History Com., 1992-96; chmn. Family Heritage adv. bd., Numa Corp., 1995—; trustee Nationalities Svc. Ctr., Cleve., 1979-86; chmn. vis. com. on humanities and arts, Cleve. State U., 1980-82. Recipient Achievement award No. Ohio Live, Cleve., 1987; Spl. Recognition award Gov. Richard F. Celeste of Ohio, 1990. Mem. Soc. Ohio Archivists (co-founder 1968, pres. 1971-72), Black History Archives (founder 1970), Orgn. Am. Historians, Soc. Am. Archivists, Manuscripts Soc., Midwest Archives Conf., Ohio Geneal. Soc., Early Settlers Assn. of the Western Res., Rowfant Club, Lake County Farmers' Conservation Club, Lambda Chi Alpha. Roman Catholic. Home: 3985 Orchard Rd Cleveland OH 44121-2411 Office: Western Res Hist Soc 10825 East Blvd Cleveland OH 44106-1703

PIKE, (JOHN) KEVIN, special effects expert; b. Hartford, Conn., May 9, 1951. Spl. effects expert (films) Heartbeeps, 1981, The Return of the Jedi, 1983, Twilight Zone: The Movie, 1983, Indiana Jones and the Temple of Doom, 1984, The Last Starfighter, 1984, Mrs. Soffel, 1984, Back to the Future, 1985, City Limits, 1985, Warning Sign, 1985, La Bamba, 1987, Everybody's All-American, 1988, Little Monsters, 1989, Ed Wood, 1994, An Eye for an Eye, 1995, Reach the Rock, 1996, (TV) Earth 2 (Emmy award for Outstanding Ind. Achievement in Spl. Visual Effects 1995); dir. (2d unit) Earth 2, Masters of the Universe, Lamborghini Crush and various commls., (sci. fiction video) for L. Ron Hubbard Exhibit, Syntex Pharms.; co-dir. (documentary) Deming Duck Race. Mem. NATAS, IATSE, Acad. Motion Picture Arts and Scis., Dirs. Guild Am. Office: Filmtrix Inc PO Box 715 North Hollywood CA 91603

PIKE, LARRY SAMUEL, lawyer; b. Savannah, Ga., Feb. 23, 1939; s. Abram and Ida (Feinberg) P.; m. Bonnie Jo Haykin, June 21, 1959; children: Douglas, Stacey, Scott. BA, Emory U., 1960, LLB, 1963; postgrad., Leeds (Eng.) U., 1960-61. Assoc. L. Jack Swertfeger Jr. Atty., Decatur, Ga., 1963-65; ptnr. Swertfeger, Scott, Pike & Simmons, Decatur, 1966-75, Simmons, Pike & Warren, Decatur, 1975-76, Lefkoff, Pike & Sims, Atlanta, 1976-85, Branch, Pike & Ganz, Atlanta, 1985-95, Holland & Knight, Atlanta, 1995—; Pres. Ansley Park Civic Assn., Atlanta, 1977-79, Northshore Homeowners Assn., Tybee Island, Ga., 1992-95, The Temple, Atlanta, 1979-81, trustee, 1977—, Am. Cancer Soc., DeKalb County, Ga. unit, 1970-71, crusade chmn., 1969-70; trustee Ansley Park Beautification Found., Inc., Atlanta, 1984—, The Temple Endowment Fund, Atlanta, 1979-87, Atlanta Jewish Cmty. Ctr., 1973-76; bd. overseers Hebrew Union Coll., Cin., 1987-93; alumni coun. Emory U., Atlanta, 1966-72; bd. trustees Union of Am. Hebrew Congregations, 1991—; mem. Rabbinical Placement Commn., 1994—. Editor-in-chief law jour. and newspaper; contbr. numerous articles to profl. jours. Fulbright fellow, 1960-61; named Outstanding Young Man of Yr. North DeKalb Jaycees, 1968. Mem. ABA, State Bar Ga. (exec. coun. Young Lawyers sect. 1968-72), Atlanta Bar Assn., Decatur-DeKalb Bar Assn. (sec. 1965-66), Atlanta Legal Aid Soc. (pres. 1974-75, past bd. dirs.), Atlanta Tax Forum, Lawyers Club Atlanta, B'nai B'rith (pres. Atlanta lodge 1970-71, Ga. pres. 1974-75, dist. 5 bd. govs. 1973-76, chair Youth Orgn. Bd. 1971-73), Phi Beta Kappa, Omicron Delta Kappa. Office: Holland & Knight 2000 One Atlantic Ctr Atlanta GA 30309

PIKE, LAURENCE BRUCE, retired lawyer; b. Brattleboro, Vt., Sept. 11, 1927; s. Lee Ernest and Alice Louise (Temple) P.; m. Norma I. Ecklund, Sept. 2, 1950; children: Barbara L., William T., Jeffrey O., Alan B. B.A., U. Iowa, 1951; J.D., Columbia U., 1954. Bar: N.Y. 1955. Assoc. firm Simpson Thacher & Bartlett, N.Y.C., 1954-64, ptnr., 1964-87. Mem. Scarsdale Town Club, N.Y., 1964-68; mem. capt. Scarsdale Aux. Police, 1960-72. Served with USN, 1945-48. Mem. ABA, Bar Assn. City N.Y., N.Y. State Bar Assn., Ardsley Curling Club (N.Y., dir., sec. 1974-77), Phi Beta Kappa. Congregationalist. Home: 7 Guilford St Brattleboro VT 05301-2607 Office: Simpson Thacher & Bartlett 425 Lexington Ave New York NY 10017-3903

PIKE, PATRICIA LOUISE, psychology educator; b. Mexico City, May 8, 1951; d. Howard Paul and Barbara Jean (Budroe) McKaughan; m. Stephen Bernard Pike, May 23, 1980; 1 child, Andrew Stephen Lee. BA, U. Hawaii, Honolulu, 1973, MA, 1975, PhD, 1979; postgrad., Calif. Sch. Profl. Psychology, L.A., 1986. Lic. psychologist, Calif. Lectr. U. Hawaii, 1978-79; mem. faculty Internat. Linguistics Ctr., Dallas, 1980-83; instr. Mountain View Coll., Dallas, 1981-83; asst. prof. Rosemead Sch. of Psychology Biola U., La Mirada, Calif., 1983-92; assoc. prof., 1992—; dean Biola U., La Mirada, Calif., 1994—; psychologist Child Guidance Ctrs., Inc., Santa Ana, Calif., 1985-86; staff psychologist Biola Counseling Ctr., La Mirada, 1986—; statis. cons. Wycliffe Bible Translators, Dallas, 1982; seminar speaker on parenting. Contbg. editor Jour. Psychology and Theology, 1987-90, editor elect, 1991-92, editor, 1992—; contbr. articles to profl. jours. Member Whittier (Calif.) Area Bapt. Fellowship, 1985. Mem. APA, Soc. for Rsch. in Child Devel., Phi Kappa Phi, Phi Beta Kappa. Office: Biola U Rosemead Sch Psychology 13800 Biola Ave La Mirada CA 90639-0002

PIKE, RALPH WEBSTER, chemical engineer, educator, university administrator; b. Tampa, Fla., Nov. 10, 1935; s. Ralph Webster and Macey (Adams) P.; m. Patricia Jennings, Aug. 23, 1958. B Chem. Engring., Ga. Inst. Tech., 1957, PhD, 1962. Rsch. chem. engr. Exxon R & D Co., Baytown, Tex., 1962-64; Paul M. Horton prof. chem. engring. and sys. sci. La. State U., Baton Rouge, 1964—, assoc. vice chancellor for rsch., 1975—, dir. La. Mineral Inst., 1979—; cons. to chem. and petroleum refining industry, fed. govt. and State of La., 1964—. Author: Formulation and Optimization of Mathematical Models, 1970, Optimization for Engineering Systems, 1986, Optimizacion en Ingenieria, 1989. Active various civic, ch. and community orgns., Baton Rouge, 1964—. 2d lt. U.S. Army, 1958-60. Recipient over 60 rsch. grants, including NASA, NSF, Dept. Interior, EPA, NOAA, state agys. and pvt. industry, 1964—. Fellow Am. Inst. Chem. Engrs. (chmn. nat. program com. 1984, local sect. 1985); mem. Am. Chem. Soc. (Charles E. Coates Mem. Award, 1994, univ. and profl.), Sigma Xi. Democrat. Methodist. Avocation: skiing. Home: 6063 Hibiscus Dr Baton Rouge LA 70808-8844 Office: La State U 210 Ctr Energy Studies Baton Rouge LA 70803

PIKE, ROBERT WILLIAM, insurance company executive, lawyer; b. Lorain, Ohio, July 25, 1941; s. Edward and Catherine (Stack) P.; m. Linda L. Feitz, Dec. 26, 1964; children: Catherine, Robert, Richard. BA, Bowling Green State U., 1963; JD, U. Toledo, 1966. Bar: Ohio 1966, Ill. 1973. Ptnr. Cubbon & Rice Law Firm, Toledo, 1968-72; asst. counsel Allstate Ins. Co., Northbrook, Ill., 1972-74, assoc. counsel, 1974-76, asst. sec., asst. gen. counsel, 1976-77, asst. v.p., asst. gen. counsel, 1977-78, v.p., asst. gen. counsel, 1978-86, sr. v.p., sec., gen. counsel, 1987—, also bd. dirs.; bd. dirs. Allstate subs., including the Northbrook Group of Cos. Bd. dirs., exec. com. Assn. Calif. Ins. Cos., Nat. Assn. Ind. Insurers. Served to capt. inf. U.S. Army, 1966-68. Mem. ABA, Ill. Bar Assn., Ohio Bar Assn., Ivanhoe (Ill.) Club. Roman Catholic. Home: 811 Hawthorne Pl Lake Forest IL 60045-2210 Office: Allstate Ins Co 2775 Sanders Rd Ste F8 Northbrook IL 60062-6110

PIKE, THOMAS HARRISON, plant chemist; b. West Palm Beach, Fla., Oct. 9, 1950; s. Rufus Draper and Dora Marie (Thomason) P.; m. Julie Lynn Simpson, Aug. 19, 1972; 1 child, Thomas Simpson. BS, Baylor U., 1972. Sci. instr. Valliant (Okla.) Pub. Sch., 1975-76; sch. adminstr. Swink (Okla.) Pub. Sch., 1976-81; plant chemist Western Farmers Electric Coop., Ft. Towson, Okla., 1981—; instr. dept. sci. and engring., Eastern Okla. State Coll., 1997—; mem. adv. bd. Kiamichi Vo-Tech Sch., Idabel, Okla., 1985-87. Charter mem. Valliant Youth Assn., 1987-91. Mem. ASME (co-chmn. task force 1988-90), ASTM, Nat. Assn. Corrosion Engrs. Achievements include research in corrosion control of condensers, case history of turbine problems, improving boiler efficiency, preservation of turbines during extended outages, and water clarification. Home: RR 1 Box 299 Garvin OK 74736-9755 Office: Western Farmers Electric Coop PO Box 219 Fort Towson OK 74735-0219

PIKE, WILLIAM EDWARD, business executive; b. Ft. Collins, Colo., Jan. 25, 1929; s. Harry H. and Alice Francis (Swinscoe) P.; m. Catherine Broward Crawford, June 26, 1965; children: Elizabeth Catherine, Robert Crawford, Daniel William. Student, U. Colo., 1947-48; B.S., U.S. Naval Acad., 1952; M.B.A., Harvard, 1960. Commd. ensign USN, 1952, advanced through grades to lt., 1958; ret., 1958; asst. treas. Morgan Guaranty Trust Co., N.Y.C., 1962-64; asst. v.p. Morgan Guaranty Trust Co., 1964-66, v.p., 1966-71, sr. v.p., 1971-74, chmn. credit policy com., 1974-86; exec. v.p. J.P. Morgan & Co. Inc., 1986-89; bd. dirs. VF Corp., Somat Corp., Am. State Fin. Corp.; corp. dir., trustee, pvt. investor. Episcopalian. Club: Country (New Canaan, Conn.). Home: Indian Waters Dr New Canaan CT 06840 Office: 36 Grove St New Canaan CT 06840-5329

PIKLER, CHARLES, musician. Student violin, Norwich, Conn.; student, U. Conn., violin studies with Bronislaw Gimpel; BA in math., U. Minn. Violin soloist Chgo. Symphony Orch., 1987—. Appeared in summer festivals including Tanglewood Young Artist Program, Berkshire Music Ctr., 1965-71; prin. appearances include Hartford Symphony Orch., Ea. Conn. Symphony Orch. and Manchester Civic Orch.; substitute in Chgo. Symphony Orch. viola sect., violin soloist, solo performer on violin and viola; concertmaster of Chgo. Chamber Orch. Office: care Chgo Symphony Orch Orch Hall 220 S Michigan Ave Chicago IL 60604-2501*

PILAND, DONALD SPENCER, internist; b. Austin, Tex., Aug. 19, 1954; s. Dudley Craton and Mary Frances (Spencer) P.; m. April Ann Dean, July 2, 1983; children: Spencer, Rachel, Rebecca. BA in Biology, U. Tex., 1976; MD, U. Tex. Med. Br., Galveston, 1980. Intern in anesthesiology U. Kans., Kansas City, 1980-81, intern in internal medicine, 1981-82, resident, 1982-84; staff physician Lucy Lee Hosp., Poplar Bluff, Mo., 1984—; chief med. staff Lucy Lee Hosp., 1989-90, chief med. svc., 1986-91, exec. com., 1986—, bd. dirs., 1987-91; exec. bd. dirs. N.W. Med. Ctr., 1992—; med. dir. Home Advantage Home Health Ctr., 1995—. Mem. Rep. Senatorial Policy Com., 1994-95; mem. adv. bd. 1st United Meth. Ch., 1990—; mem. exec. bd. dirs. N.W. Med. Ctr., 1992—, Health First Network, 1995—. Recipient Spl. Recognition award Am. Cancer Soc., 1991. Avocations: flyfishing, hunting. Office: NW Med Ctr 2210 Barron Rd Poplar Bluff MO 63901-1908

PILARCZYK, DANIEL EDWARD, archbishop; b. Dayton, Ohio, Aug. 12, 1934; s. Daniel Joseph and Frieda S. (Hilgefort) P. Student, St. Gregory Sem., Cin., 1948-53; PhB, Pontifical Urban U., Rome, 1955, PhL, 1956, STB, 1958, STL, 1960, STD, 1961; MA, Xavier U., 1965; PhD, U. Cin., 1969; LLD (hon.), Xavier U., 1975, Calumet Coll., 1982, U. Dayton, 1990, Marquette U., 1990, Thomas More Coll., 1991. Ordained priest Roman Catholic Ch., 1959; asst. chancellor Archdiocese of Cin., 1961-63; synodal judge Archdiocesan Tribunal, 1971-82; mem. faculty Athenaeum of Ohio, St. Gregory Sem., 1963-74; v.p. Athenaeum of Ohio, 1968-74, trustee, 1974—; also rector St. Gregory Sem., 1968-74; archdiocesan dir. ednl. services, 1974-82, aux. bishop of Cin., 1974-82, vicar gen., 1974-82, archbishop of Cin., 1982—; bd. dirs. Pope John Ctr., 1978-85; trustee Cath. Health Assn., 1982-85, Cath. U. Am., 1997—, Pontifical Coll. Josephinum, 1983-92; v.p. Nat. Conf. Cath. Bishops, 1986-89, pres., 1989-92, chmn. Com. on Doctrine, 1996—; U.S. rep. Episc. Bd. Internat. Commn. on English in Liturgy 1987-97; chmn., 1991-97. Author: Praepositini Cancellarii de Sacramentis et de Novissimis, 1964-65, Twelve Tough Issues, 1988, We Believe, 1989, Living in the Lord, 1990, The Parish: Where God's People Live, 1991, Forgiveness, 1992, What Must I Do?, 1993, Our Priests: Who They Are and What They Do, 1994, Sacraments, 1994, Lenten Lunches, 1995, Bringing Forth Justice, 1996. Ohio Classical Conf. scholar to Athens, 1966. Mem. Am. Philol. Assn. Home and Office: 100 E 8th St Cincinnati OH 45202-2129

PILBOROUGH, BARBARA JEAN, healthcare consultant; b. Phila., Nov. 2, 1944; d. Stanley Anthony Brokowski and Jean (Tomczyk) O'Brien; m. Christopher Pilborough, Dec. 28, 1974; children: Joy, Lotus. BA in Polit. Econs., Holy Family Coll., Phila., 1965; tchg. cert. (master's program), U. San Francisco, 1971. Adminstr. G.I. Assocs. of Grad. Hosp., Phila., 1983-87, Ctr. for Urol. Care, Haddon Heights, N.J., 1987-94; healthcare cons. Button Assocs., Moorestown, N.J., 1994-95, Parente Consulting, Phila., 1995-96; project mgr. profl. fee dept. Allegheny U. Hosp. Sys., Phila., 1997—. Pres. Pennsauken (N.J.) H.S. PTA, 1994. Mem. NOW (pres. Alice Paul chpt. 1991-92, State of N.J. legis. coord. 1992-94), AAUW, ACLU, Med. Group Mgmt. Assn., Amnesty Internat. Democrat. Avocations: biking, tai chi chuan, literacy volunteer. Home: 3238 N 49th St Pennsauken NJ 08109-2120 Office: Ctr Square West Tower 33rd Fl 1500 Market St Fl 33 Philadelphia PA 19102

PILCHEN, IRA A., journal editor; b. Chgo., Jan. 17, 1964; s. Bernard J. and Erna (Lee) P. BA in History, U. Ill., 1986. Assoc. editor Judicature jour., Chgo., 1991—; staff assoc. Am. Judicature Soc., Chgo., 1991—; mem. ad hoc com. for creation of a State Justice Commn., Ill., 1994; mem. adv. coun. Ill. State Jusice Commn., 1995. Vol. interpretive guide Friends of the Chicago River, 1991—. Named Vol. of Yr., Friends of Chicago River, 1993. Avocations: swimming, bicycling, Chgo. history. Office: Am Judicature Soc 180 N Michigan Ave Ste 600 Chicago IL 60601-7401

PILCHIK, ELY EMANUEL, rabbi, writer; b. Russia, June 12, 1913; came to U.S., 1920, naturalized, 1920; s. Abraham and Rebecca (Lipovitch) P.; m. Ruth Schuchat, Nov. 20, 1941 (dec. 1977); children: Susan Pilchik Rosenbaum, Judith Pilchik Zucker; m. Harriet Krichman Perlmutter, June, 1981. A.B., U. Cin., 1935; M.Hebrew Lit., Hebrew Union Coll., 1936, D.D., 1964. Ordained rabbi, 1939; founder, dir. Hillel Found. at U. Md., 1939-40; asst. rabbi Har Sinai Temple, Balt., 1940-41; rabbi Temple Israel, Tulsa, 1942-47, Temple B'nai Jeshurun, Short Hills, N.J., 1947-81; prof. Jewish Thought Upsala Coll., 1969—; pres. Jewish Book Council Am., 1957-58. Author: books, including Hillel, 1951, From the Beginning, 1956, Judaism Outside the Holy Land, 1964, Jeshurun Essays, 1967, A Psalm of David, 1967, Talmud Thought, 1983, Midrash Memoir, 1984, Touches of Einstein, 1987, Luzzatto on Loving Kindness, 1987, Prayer in History, 1989; author: play Toby, 1968; lyricist 6 cantatas; contbr. articles to profl. and gen. jours. Bd. dirs. Newark Mus.; mem. ethics com. N.J. Bar Assn. Served as chaplain USNR, 1944-46. Mem. N.J. Bd. Rabbis (pres. 1955-57), Central Conf. Am. Rabbis (pres. 1977-79). Office: 1025 S Orange Ave Short Hills NJ 07078-3135 *I have been influenced by the teaching of the 1st Century sage Hillel who said: "If I am not for myself, who will be for me? And if I am for myself only, what am I? And if not now, when?".*

PILCZ, MALETA, psychotherapist; b. Poland, June 5, 1945; came to U.S., 1949; s. Victor and Hana (Oks) P. BA in Psychology, Bklyn. Coll., 1967; MA in Social Work, U. Chgo., 1969. Diplomate Am. Bd. Examiners'Clin. Social Work; cert. social worker, N.Y. Psychotherapist Scholarship and Guidance Assn., Chgo., 1969-71; family therapist, supr. Northwestern Meml. Hosp., Chgo., 1972-75; pvt. practice, psychotherapist, cons. Chgo., 1974-80, N.Y.C., 1980—; field work instr. U. Chgo. Sch. of Social Svcs., 1974-75; instr. dept. psychiatry Northwestern U. Med. Sch., 1973-75; cons. faculty Ctr. for Family Studies, Family Inst. Chgo., 1978-80; assoc. staff Ackerman Inst. Family Therapy, N.Y.C., 1983-88; part-time instr. Hunter Coll. Sch. of Social Work, N.Y.C., 1985-88; cons. N.Y.C. Bd. Edn., 1988—. Author: Understanding the Survivor Family; thematic cons. documentary film The Legacy, 1979 (Cigne Gold Eagle, Red Ribbon Am. Film Festival, 1980). Fellow Am. Orthopsychiat. Assn.; mem. NASW (diplomate clin. social work), Am. Group Psychotherapy Assn., Acad. Cert. Social Workers. Avocations: world travel, hiking, theater, the arts. Office: 330 E 46th St Apt 12D New York NY 10017-3076

PILE, ROBERT BENNETT, advertising executive, writer, consultant; b. Pierre, S.D., May 27, 1918; s. Homer Bennett and Ruth (Gleckler) P.; m. Cynthia Way, Feb. 28, 1953; children: Timothy, Benjamin, Robert, Michael, Cynthia, Anthony. BA, U. Minn., 1941. Asst. advt. mgr. Red Owl Stores, Mpls., 1946-47; advt. mgr. Lactona, St. Paul, 1947-48; acct., ptnr. Olmsted & Foley Advt. Agy., Mpls., 1948-55; account exec. Campbell-Mithun, Inc., Mpls., 1955-59; v.p., group head Campbell-Mithun, Inc., 1960-69, sr. v.p., mgmt. rep., 1969-80; founder, pres., dir., mem. exec. com., chief exec. officer Bob's Wide World of Golf, 1980—; bd. dirs. Roberts-Hamilton Co., 1992; cons. in field; instr. St. Thomas Coll., St. Paul, 1980-86; mgr. 4-A Inst. Advt. Studies, 1981-87. Author: Letters from French Windmill, 1986, Panic in the Morning Mail, 1986, Crisis Every Fifteen Minutes, 1988, Top Entrepreneurs and Their Business, 1993, Women Business Leaders, 1995, For the Love of Rose, 1995; contbg. editor Active Lifestyles Mag.; writer Mpls. Tribune, T.C. Mag.; columnist Format mag., Skyway News. Bd. dirs. Big Bros. Mpls., Minn. Heart Assn., St. Mary's Hosp.; bd. dirs., chmn. 4-A's of Twin Cities, bd. govs. Ctrl. Region. Capt. USAAF, 1941-46. Recipient spl. award Mpls. Spruce Up Drive, 1965; named Alumnus of Notable Achievement, U. Minn., 1994. Mem. Northwest Advt. Golf Assn. (pres. 1977-78, gov.), Am. Assn. ADvt. Agys. (chmn. Twin City coun.), Interlachen Country Club (bd. govs., chmn. house com. & food and beverage com., editor monthly newsletter Intercourse), Ham and Eggs Breakfast Club, Mpls. Club, Yo Yo's Club, Phi Kappa Psi. Home: 4315 E Lake Harriet Blvd Minneapolis MN 55409-1725

PILECKI, PAUL STEVEN, lawyer; b. Norristown, Pa., Sept. 12, 1950; m. Barbara Derrickson; children: Derek Steven, Christopher Drew. AB, St. Joseph's Coll., Phila., 1972; JD, Temple U., 1978. Bar: Pa. 1978, D.C. 1985. Sr. counsel Fed. Res. Bd., Washington, 1978-84; ptnr. Shaw, Pittman, Potts & Trowbridge, Washington, 1984—. Mem. ABA (banking law com.). Home: 11108 Deville Estates Dr Oakton VA 22124-1002 Office: Shaw Pittman Potts et al 2300 N St NW Washington DC 20037-1122

PILETTE, PATRICIA CHEHY, health care organizational/management consultant; b. Rutland, Vt., June 28, 1945; d. John Edward and Mary T. (McNamara) Chehy; m. Wilfrid Pilette, July 22, 1972; 1 child, Patrick John. Diploma, Jeanne Mance Sch. Nursing, 1966; BSN magna cum laude, St. Anselm Coll., 1971; MS summa cum laude, Boston U., 1974, EdD in Counseling and Human Svcs. Adminstrn. summa cum laude, 1984. RN, Mass. Clin. specialist adult psychiatry mgmt. and counseling practice

Framingham, Mass.; employee assistance counselor St. Elizabeth's Med. Ctr., 1984—. Contbr. articles to profl. publs., chpts. to books. Mem. Mass. Soc. Nurse Execs., N.E. Assn. for Specialists in Group Work, N.E. Soc. Group Psychotherapists, Mass. Assn., Women Deans, Adminstrs. and Counselors, Assn. for Humanistic Psychologists, N.Am. Soc. Employee Assistance, Am. Mental Health Counselors Assn., Pi Lambda Theta, Sigma Theta Tau.

PILGERAM, LAURENCE OSCAR, biochemist; b. Great Falls, Mont., June 23, 1924; s. John Rudolph and Bertha Roslyn (Phillips) P.; m. Cynthia Ann Moore, Apr. 16, 1971; children: Karl Erich, Kurt John. AA, U. Calif., Berkeley, 1948, BA, 1949, PhD, 1953. Instr. dept. physiology U. Ill. Profl. Coll., Chgo., 1954-55; asst. prof. dept. biochemistry Stanford (Calif.) U. Sch. Medicine, 1955-57; dir. arteriosclerosis research lab. U. Minn. Sch. Medicine, Mpls., 1957-65, Santa Barbara, Calif., 1965-71; dir. coagulation lab., assoc. dir. Cerebrovascular Research Ctr., Baylor Coll. Medicine, Tex. Med. Ctr., Houston, 1971-75; dir. Thrombosis Control Labs., Palo Alto, Calif., 1975-79, Santa Barbara, 1979—; cons. NIH, Bio-Sci. Labs., FDA; del. Council on Thrombosis and Council on Strokes, Am. Heart Assn. Assembly. Co-editor: Nutrition and Thrombosis for the Nat. Dairy Council, 1973; contbr. sci. articles to profl. jours. Recipient CIBA award, London, 1958, Karl Thomae award, Germany, 1973; NIH grantee, 1954-75; LIfe Ins. Med. Research Fund fellow, 1952-54. Mem. Am. Soc. for Biochemistry and Molecular Biology. Office: PO Box 1583 Goleta PO Santa Barbara CA 93116

PILGRIM, DIANNE HAUSERMAN, art museum director; b. Cleve., July 8, 1941; d. John Martin and Norma Hauserman; divorced. BA, Pa. State U., 1963; MA, Inst. Fine Arts, NYU, 1965; postgrad., CUNY, 1971-74; LHD (hon.), Amherst Coll., 1991, Pratt Inst., 1994. Chester Dale fellow Am. wing. Met. Mus. Art, N.Y.C., 1966-68, rsch. cons. Am. paintings and sculpture, 1971-73; asst. to dirs. Pyramid Galleries, Ltd., Washington, 1969-71, Finch Coll. Mus. Art, Washington, 1971; curator dept. decorative arts Bklyn. Mus., 1973-88, chmn. dept., 1988; dir. Cooper-Hewitt Nat. Design Mus., N.Y.C., 1988—; mem. adv. com. Gracie Mansion, N.Y.C., 1980; mem. design adv. com. Art Inst. Chgo., 1988; mem. Hist. House Trust N.Y.C., Mayor's Office, 1989-94. Co-author, curator: (book and exhbn. catalogue) Mr. and Mrs. Raymond Horowitz Collection of American Impressionist and Realist Paintings, 1973, The American Renaissance 1876-1917, 1979; (book) The Machine Age in America 1918-1941, 1986 (Charles F. Montgomery prize Decorative Arts Soc.). Bd. dirs. Nat. Multiple Sclerosis Soc., 1989. Recipient Disting. Alumni award Pa. State U., 1991. Mem. Decorative Arts Soc. (pres. 1977-79), Art Deco Soc., Victorian Soc., Art Table. Office: Smithsonian Instn Cooper-Hewitt Nat Design Mus 2 E 91st St New York NY 10128-0606

PILIAVIN, JANE ALLYN, social psychologist; b. Montclair, N.J., Feb. 21, 1937; d. Horace Warren and Mary Elizabeth (Young) Allyn; m. Curtis Dale Hardyck, Jan. 20, 1962 (div.); 1 child, Allyn Henry Hardyck; m. Irving Morris Piliavin, Dec. 27, 1968; 1 child, Elizabeth Elaine Piliavin. BA in Psychology with high honors, U. Rochester, 1958; PhD in Social Psychology, Stanford U., 1962. Acting instr. Stanford U., 1960-62; rsch. psychologist Survey Rsch. Ctr. U. Calif., Berkeley, 1962-66, lectr. in psychology, 1964-66; asst. prof. psychology U. Pa., 1967-70; assoc. prof. Sch. Family Resources and Consumer Scis. U. Wis., Madison, 1970-73, prof. Sch. Family Resources and Consumer Scis., 1973-76, prof. dept. sociology, 1976—; vis. asst. prof. psychology Mills Coll., 1966-67; reviewer Am. Found. for AIDS Rsch., 19 87—; mem. blood products adv. com. FDA, 1993—. Author: (with others) Adolescent Prejudice, 1975, Emergency Intervention, 1981, Giving Blood: The Development of an Altruistic Identity, 1991, The Psychology of Helping and Altruism: Problems and Puzzles, 1995; assoc. editor Personality and Social Psychology Bull., 1975-77; cons. editor Jour. Personality and Social Psychology, 1974-77, 84-86, European Jour. Social Psychology, 1982—, Jour. Applied Social Psychology, 1982—, Social Psychology Quar., 1988-90, 94—; hon. mem. editorial bd. Polish Psychol. Bull., 1989—; contbr. chpts. to books, articles to profl. jours. Fellow Am. Psychol. Soc.; mem. AAAS, Soc. Exptl. Social Psychology, European Assn. Exptl. Social Psychology, Am. Sociol. Assn. (coun. sect. on social psychology 1983-86, chair 1990-91, mem. profl. affairs com. 1993—), Phi Beta Kappa, Sigma Xi. Democrat. Office: U Wis 8128 Social Sci Bldg Madison WI 53706

PILISUK, MARC, community psychology educator; b. N.Y.C., Jan. 19, 1934; s. Louis and Charlotte (Feferholtz) P.; m. Phyllis E. Kamen, June 16, 1956; children: Tammy, Jeff. BA, Queens Coll., 1955; MA, U. Mich., 1956, PhD, 1961. Asst. prof., assoc. rsch. psychologist U. Mich., Ann Arbor, 1961-65, founder teach-in, 1965; assoc. prof. Purdue U., West Lafayette, Ind., 1965-67; prof.-in-residence U. Calif., Berkeley, 1967-77; prof. community psychology U. Calif., Davis, 1977—; vis. prof. U. Calif., Wright Inst., 1991—; cons. Ctr. for Self Help Rsch., Berkeley, Calif., 1991-93; prof. psychology Saybrook Inst. and Grad. Ctr., San Francisco, 1993—. Author: International Conflict and Social Policy, 1972, The Healing Web: Social Networks and Human Survival, 1986; editor: The Triple Revolution, 1969; Poor Americans, 1970; Triple Revolution Emerging, 1972; How We Lost the War on Poverty, 1973. NIMH fellow, 1959-60; NSF grantee, 1962-66; Nat. Inst. Alcoholism and Drug Abuse tng. grantee, 1973-77. Fellow Soc. for Cmty. Rsch. and Action, Soc. for Psychol. Study Social Issues (coun.), APA (pres.-elect divsn. peace psychology 1996-97), Am. Orthopsychiat. Assn.; mem. APHA, ACLU, Am. Soc. on Aging, Psychologists for Social Responsibility, Faculty for Human Rights in C.Am.

PILKINGTON, MARY ELLEN, stockbroker, trader; b. N.Y.C., Feb. 16, 1955; d. Charles Arthur Bertrand and Mary (Lynch) Perez; m. Scott Douglas Ballin (div. 1986); m. John J. Pilkington, Aug. 19, 1994. BA in Polit. Sci., Mt. Vernon Coll., Washington, 1976. Dir. materials ctr. Gen. Fedn. of Women's Clubs, Washington, 1978-80; broker, asst. to the chmn. Folger Nolan Fleming Douglas, Washington, 1980-85; broker, account exec. Rose & Co., N.Y.C., 1985-86; trader Bear Stearns, N.Y.C., 1986-88; trader, broker Robyns Capital, N.Y.C., 1988-89; trader, v.p. trading Jessop Capital Corp., N.Y.C., 1989-91, Kidder Peabody, 1992-94, Dean Witter, 1994-95, Gabelli & Co., 1996—. Roman Catholic. Avocations: golf, skiing, tennis, squash, photography.

PILLA, ANTHONY MICHAEL, bishop; b. Cleve., Nov. 12, 1932; s. George and Libera (Nista) P. Student, St. Gregory Coll. Sem., 1952-53, Borromeo Coll. Sem., 1955, St. Mary Sem., 1954, 56-59; B.A. in Philosophy, John Carroll U., Cleve., 1961, M.A. in History, 1967. Ordained priest Roman Cath. Ch., 1959. Assoc. St. Bartholomew Parish, Middleburg Hts., Ohio, 1959-60; prof. Borromeo Sem., Wickliffe, Ohio, 1960-72; rector-pres. Borromeo Sem., 1972-75; mem. Diocese Cleve. Liturgical Commn., 1964-69, asst. dir., 1969-72; sec. for services to clergy and religious personnel Diocese Cleve., 1975-79; titular bishop Scardona; and aux. bishop of Cleve. and vicar Eastern region Diocese of Cleve., 1979-80, apostolic adminstr., from 1980; bishop of Cleve., from 1981; trustee Borromeo Sem., 1975-79, Cath. U., 1981-84; trustee, mem. bd. overseers St. Mary Sem., 1975-79; mem. adv. bd. permanent diaconate program Diocese of Cleve., 1975-79, hospitalization and ins. bd., 1979; bd dirs. Cath. Communications Found., 1981—. Bd. dirs. NCCJ, 1986—. Mem. Nat. Cath. Edn. Assn. (dir. 1972-75), U.S. Cath. Conf., Nat. Conf. Cath. Bishops, Cath. Conf. Ohio., Greater Cleve. Roundtable (trustee from 1981). Home and Office: Chancery Office 350 Chancery Bldg 1031 Superior Ave Cleveland OH 44114-2503*

PILLA, FELIX MARIO, hospital administrator; b. Phila., Sept. 22, 1932; s. Domenick and Carmela (DiPalma) P.; m. Sally Irene Bixler, Oct. 2, 1953; children: Mark, Beth Ann, Michael, Matthew. Diploma profl. nursing, Pa. Hosp. Sch. Nursing, 1956; B.S. in Bus. Adminstrn, LaSalle Coll., Phila., 1959; M.S. in Hosp. Adminstrn, Columbia U., 1961. Various progressively responsible positions in health care field, 1957-70; exec. dir. Monmouth Med. Center, 1970-80; adminstrv. dir. U. Ariz. Health Scis. Center, Tucson, 1980-82; pres. Newton-Wellesley Hosp., Newton, Mass., 1982-85, Abington Meml. Hosp., Pa., 1985—; chmn. N.J. State Health Planning Council, 1976-77. USPHS tng. grantee, 1961. Fellow Am. Coll. Hosp. Adminstrs., Am. Pub. Health Assn.; mem. Am. Hosp. Assn. (life, mem. Ho. of Dels., governing coun. met. hosps. 1991-94), N.J. Hosp. Assn. (chmn. 1979-80), Hosp. Assn. of Pa. (trustee 1988-94), Del. Valley Hosp. Coun. (bd. dirs. 1986-94, chmn. bd. 1990-92). Office: Abington Meml Hosp 1200 Old York Rd Abington PA 19001-3720

PILLAI, RAVIRAJ SUKUMAR, chemical engineer, researcher; b. Bombay, July 29, 1961; came to U.S., 1986; s. Sukumar and Ratnavalli Pillai; m. Bina Menon, Jan. 4, 1995; 1 child, Amit. BS, U. Mysore, India, 1984; MS, U. Ill., Chgo., 1991, PhD, 1993. Rsch. asst. U. Ill., Chgo., 1989-93; postdoctoral scientist Eli Lilly and Co., Indpls., 1993-94; rsch. chem. engr. SRI Internat., Menlo Park, Calif., 1995; sr. scientist GeneMedicine, Inc., The Woodlands, Tex., 1995-96; sr. rsch. scientist McNeil Consumer Pharms., Ft. Washington, Pa., 1996—. Sci. reviewer Aerosol Sci. and Tech., 1994, Jour. Pharm. Scis.; contbr. articles to profl. jours. Mem. Am. Assn. for Aerosol Rsch., Am. Assn. Pharm. Scientists, Internat. Soc. for Aerosols in Medicine, Sigma Xi. Hindu. Achievements include development of novel approaches for delivery of aerosolized drugs to the lungs for local and systemic effect. Office: McNeil Consumer Pharms 7050 Camp Hill Rd Fort Washington PA 19034-2210

PILLANS, CHARLES PALMER, III, lawyer; b. Orlando, Fla., Feb. 22, 1940; s. Charles Palmer Jr. and Helen (Scarborough) P.; m. Judith Hart, July 6, 1963; children: Charles Palmer IV, Helen Hart. BA, U. Fla., 1962, JD, 1966. Bar: Fla. 1967, U.S. Dist. Ct. (mid. dist.) Fla. 1967, U.S. Ct. Appeals (2d cir.) 1968, U.S. Supreme Ct. 1971, U.S. Ct. Appeals (3d cir.) 1976, U.S. Ct. Appeals (5th and 11th cirs.) 1981. Assoc. Bedell, Bedell, Dittmar, Smith & Zehmer, Jacksonville, Fla., 1966-70; asst. state atty. 4th jud. cir. Jacksonville, 1970-72; asst. gen. counsel City of Jacksonville, 1972; ptnr. Bedell, Dittmar, DeVault Pillans & Coxe, P.A., Jacksonville, 1972—; mem. Fla. Bd. Bar Examiners, Tallahassee, 1979-84, chmn., 1983-84; mem. Jud. Nominating Commn., 1988-92, chmn., 1990-91, 1st Dist. Ct. Appeal, Tallahassee, 1988-92, chmn., 1990-91. Master Chester Bedell Inn of Ct.; fellow Am. Coll. Trial Lawyers, ABA; mem. Am. Bar Found., Fla. Bar Assn. (mem. profl. ethics com.). Methodist. Home: Villa 110 6740 Epping Forest Way N Jacksonville FL 32217-2687 Office: Bedell Dittmar DeVault Pillans & Coxe PA Bedell Bldg 101 E Adams St Jacksonville FL 32202-3303

PILLARELLA, DEBORAH ANN, elementary education educator, consultant; b. Chgo., Oct. 2, 1960; d. Richard J. and Josephine A. (Miceli) Ban; m. James J. Pillarella, Sept. 1, 1989. BA in Edn., U. Ill., 1983, MEd in Ednl. Leadership, 1992. Tchr. elem. sch. Chgo. Bd. Edn., 1983—; youth and adult cons. Bodyworks, Chgo., 1982—; sec. Profl. PPAC, Chgo., 1990-94; cons. IDEA, San Diego, 1989—; mem. adv. bd. Spl. Devel. Com., Whiting, Ind., 1993—, Am. Coun. on Exercise, 1995. Author: Healthy Choices for Kids, 1993, Step Fitness, 1995, Adventures in Fitness, 1995. Vol. activist City of Hope, Chgo., 1990—; side coord. Cystic Fiborsis Found., Chgo., 1988; vol. Chgo. Heart Assn., 1989. Mem. AAHPERD, Am. Coll. Sports Medicine, Chgo. Tchrs. Union, Internat. Assn. Fitness Profls., Internat. Fitness Assn. Am., Phi Kappa Phi. Avocations: biking, hiking, swimming, walking, reading, piano, sewing. Home: 12916 S Commercial Ave Chicago IL 60633-1209 Office: Chgo Bd Edn Taylor Sch 9912 S Avenue H Chicago IL 60617-5548

PILLIAR, ROBERT MATHEWS, metallurgy educator, materials scientist; b. Beamsville, Ont., Can., Dec. 13, 1939; married; two children. BS, U. Toronto, 1961; PhD in Metall. Engring., U. Leeds, 1965. Univ. grant metall. McMaster U., Can., 1965-67; rsch. engr. Internat. Nickel, Inc., 1967-68; rsch. scientist Ont. Rsch. Found., 1968-78; adj. prof. metall. and material sci., U. Toronto, 1977-78; adj. prof. mech. engring. dept. U. Waterloo, 1976-77; vis. fellow Dental Biomats., Liverpool U., 1984-85. Mem. ASTM, Can. Soc. Biomats (sec./treas. 1977-78, 80-82, pres. 1982-84), Soc. Biomats, Inst. Assn. Dental Rsch. Orthopedic Rsch. Soc. Office: Univ Toronto/Ctr Biomaterials, Mining Bldg/170 College St, Toronto, ON Canada M5S 3E3*

PILLOT, GENE MERRILL, retired school system administrator; b. Canton, Ohio, Apr. 13, 1930; s. John D. Pillot and Vera R. Granstaff; m. Beverly Ann Shaw, June 4, 1982; children: Vera Kathleen Martin, Michael Gene, Patrick Merrill. BS in Math., Ohio State U., 1952; MEd in Adminstrn. and Supvervision, Kent State U., 1957; EdD in Adminstrn. and Supervision, U. Fla., 1970. Asst. prin. North Royalton (Ohio) High Sch., 1959-61, prin., 1961-63; asst. prin. Sarasota (Fla.) Sr. High Sch., 1963-64, prin., 1964-68; dir. staff development Sarasota Dist. Schs., 1968-70, asst. supt., 1970-71, supt., 1971-80; dir. human resources Sarasota Meml Hosp., 1980-83; owner, broker Pillot Realty, Sarasota, 1986-90; commr. Sarasota City, 1989—, vice mayor, 1992-93, 96-97, mayor, 1993-94; mayor, 1997-98; prof. Am. Assn. Sch. Adminstrn., Nat. Acad. Sch. Execs., 1969-73; adj. prof. U. South Fla., Tampa, 1978-81; pvt. cons. edn. orgns., 1969-76. Author (chpt.) Differentiated Staffing, Strategies for D.S., 1971; contbr. articles to profl. jours. Trustee Fla. Sch. Deaf/Blind, St. Augustine, 1989-90, chmn. bd. dirs., 1986-89; bd. dirs. Riverview Found., 1985-94, Girls Club, Sarasota, 1985-89, Hospice Found., Sarasota Opera Assn., Hispanic Am. Alliance; mem. Civil Svc. Bd. Sarasota, 1984-89; mem. adv. bd. Cath. Social Svcs., 1987-89. Mem. Sara Bay Country Club (Sarasota), Phi Delta Kappa (Educator of Yr. 1980). Republican. Roman Catholic. Avocations: writing, Spanish language, ballroom dancing. Home: 1212 Hillview Dr Sarasota FL 34239-2020

PILLSBURY, EDMUND PENNINGTON, museum director; b. San Francisco, Apr. 28, 1943; s. Edmund Pennington and Priscilla Keator (Giesen) P.; m. Mireille Marie-Christine Bernard, Aug. 30, 1969; children: Christine Bullitt, Edmund Pennington III. BA, Yale U., 1965; MA, U. London, 1967, PhD, 1973; DFA, U. North Tex., 1996. Curator European art Yale U. Art Gallery, New Haven, 1972-76; asst. dir. Yale U. Gallery, New Haven, 1975-76; dir. Yale Ctr. Brit. Art, New Haven, 1976-80; chief exec. officer Paul Mellon Ctr. Studies in Brit. Art, London, 1976-80; dir. Kimbell Art Mus., Ft. Worth, 1980—; founding chmn. Villa I Tatti Coun., Harvard U., 1979-84; adj. prof. Yale U., 1976-80, lectr., 1972-76; internat. adv. bd. State Hermitage Mus., 1995—. Author: Florence and the Arts, 1971, Sixteenth-Century Italian Drawings: Form and Function, 1974, David Hockney: Travels with Pen, Pencil and Ink, 1978, The Graphic Art of Federico Barocci, 1978. Trustee Ft. Worth Country Day Sch., 1982-87, 88-94, St. Paul's Sch., Concord, N.H., 1985—, Burlington Mag. Found., London, 1987—; bd. govs. Yale U. Art Gallery, 1990—; chmn. art adv. panel indemnity program Nat. Endowment Arts, 1984-87; mem. vis. com. Sherman Fairchild Paintings Conservation Ctr., Met. Mus. Art, N.Y.C., 1982—; mem. bd. advisors art dept. U. North Tex., Denton, 1990—; mem. art adv. panel IRS, 1982-84. Decorated chevalier Ordre des Arts et des Lettres, 1985; David E. Finley fellow Nat. Gallery Art, Washington, 1970, Ford Found. fellow Cleve. Mus. Art, 1970-71, Nat. Endowment Arts rsch. fellow, 1974, Morse fellow Yale U., 1975. Mem. Assn. Art Mus. Dirs. (trustee 1989-90), Master Drawings Assn. (bd. dirs. 1987—), Coll. Art Assn., Century Club, Ft. Worth Club, Rivercrest Club, City Club. Episcopalian. Home: 1110 Broad Ave Fort Worth TX 76107-1529 Office: Kimbell Art Mus 3333 Camp Bowie Blvd Fort Worth TX 76107-2744

PILLSBURY, GEORGE STURGIS, investment adviser; b. Crystal Bay, Minn., July 17, 1921; s. John S. and Eleanor (Lawler) P.; m. Sally Whitney, Jan. 4, 1947; children: Charles Alfred, George Sturgis, Sarah Kimball, Katharine Whitney. BA, Yale U., 1943. Chmn. Sargent Mgmt. Co. Mem. Seminole Golf Club (Juno Beach, Fla.), Woodhill Club, Minnetonka Yacht Club, Mpls. Athletic Club, Mpls. Club, River Club (N.Y.C.), Everglades Club (Palm Beach, Fla.). Home: 1300 Bracketts Point Rd Wayzata MN 55391-9393 Office: 4800 First Bank Pl Minneapolis MN 55402

PILLSBURY, HAROLD CROCKETT, otolaryngologist; b. Balt., Dec. 5, 1947; m. Sally Adrienne Pillsbury; children: Matthew C., Benjamin C., Thomas C. BA, George Washington U., 1970, MD, 1972. Intern U. N.C., Chapel Hill, 1972-73, resident in surgery, 1973; resident in otolaryngology N.C. Meml. Hosp., Chapel Hill, 1973-76; fellow Kantonsspital, Zurich, 1977; from asst. prof. to assoc. prof. Yale U. Sch. Medicine, New Haven, 1977-82; from assoc. prof. to prof. surgery/otolaryngology U. N.C. Sch. Medicine, Chapel Hill, 1982—. Mem. ACS, AMA, AAFPRS, AAO-NHS, Alpha Omega Alpha. Office: U NC Womack Bldg CB7070 610 Burnett Chapel Hill NC 27599

PILOUS, BETTY SCHEIBEL, nurse; b. Cleve., July 30, 1948; d. Raymond W. and Dorothy E. (Groth) S.; m. Lee Alan Pilous, Sept. 11, 1970; 1 child. Diploma in nursing, Huron Rd. Hosp., Cleve., 1970; BSBA, St. Joseph's Coll., 1989, MHSA, 1996. RN, Ohio; cert. med.-surg. nurse, nursing adminstr. Nurse Huron Rd. Hosp., Cleve., 1970-71, Hillcrest Hosp., Cleve., 1974-77; head nurse, relief supr. Oak Park Hosp., Oakwood, Ohio, 1977-81; head nurse med.-surg. Bedford Hosp., Ohio, 1981-87; dir. inpatient svcs. Meridia Euclid Hosp., Euclid, Ohio, 1987-93, coord. hosp. info. system for nursing, chair nurse practice com., los com. nursing liason; DON, Manor Care, Willoughby, Ohio; team leader referral/assessment Hospice Western Res. Former instr. ARC; chair nurse practice com. Am. Heart Assn.; mem. nursing standards com. Cmty. Hosp. of Bedford; mem. health and safety com. Twinsburg Schs., Ohio, 1984, mem. curriculum com., 1981-83; chairperson standards com. Cmty. Hosp. of Bedford; former counselor jr. high youth 1st Congl. Ch., Twinsburg; past chair adv. bd. chairperson Brecksville Rainbow Assembly for Girls, 1992; mem. Twinsburg Libr. Levy Com., 1991. Recipient Paradiam award, 1991. Mem. Ohio Citizen League Nursing Nurse Execs. Network (former sec.), Ohio Hosp. Assn., Ohio Orgn. Nurse Execs., Ohio Directors of Nursing Assocs. Long Term Care, Nat. League Nursing, Southeast Cleve. Mid Mgrs. Ohio Orgn. Nurse Exec., Acad. Med.-Surg. Nursing (charter mem.), Networking Group Nurse Mgrs. (initiated), Order Eastern Star, Sigma Theta Tau, Iota Psi. Avocation: hiking.

PILSON, MICHAEL EDWARD QUINTON, oceanography educator; b. Ottawa, Ont., Can., Oct. 25, 1933; came to U.S., 1958; s. Edward Charles and Frances Amelia (Ferguson) P.; m. Joan Elaine Johnstone, July 6, 1957; children: Diana Jane, John Edward Quinton. BSc, Bishops U., Lennoxville, Que., Can.; MSc, McGill U., Montreal, Que., Can., 1958; PhD, U. Calif., San Diego, 1964. Chemist Windsor Mills (Can.) Paper Co., 1954-55; asst. chemist Macdonald Coll. of McGill U., 1955-58; biologist Zool. Soc. San Diego, 1963-66; asst. prof. U. R.I., Narragansett, 1966-71, assoc. prof., 1971-78, prof., 1978—; dir. Marine Ecosystems Rsch. Lab., Narragansett, 1976-97. Contbr. articles to profl. and popular jours.; author chpts. for 5 books. Grantee NSF, NOAA, EPA, NIH. Mem. AAAS, AGU, ASLO, Oceanography Soc., Am. Soc. Mammalogists, Saunderstown Yacht Club (bd. govs. 1974-87, commodore 1985-87). Home: PO Box 27 Saunderstown RI 02874-0027 Office: U RI Grad Sch Oceanography Narragansett RI 02882

PILZ, ALFRED NORMAN, manufacturing company executive; b. Evergreen Park, Ill., Oct. 12, 1931; s. Alfred and Erma Louise (Deane) P.; m. Constance Ney, Nov. 1957; children: Kerry, Kurt, Stephen, Matthew. B.S., Ill. Inst. Tech., 1953; M.B.A., Harvard U., 1960. Registered profl. engr., Mass. Indsl. engr. Harnischfeger Corp., Milw., 1956-58; cons. Arthur D. Little Co., Cambridge, Mass., 1959-60; asst. to exec. v.p., mgr. prodn. engring. Nat. Forge Co., Irvine, Pa., 1960-62; mgmt. cons. McKinsey & Co., N.Y.C. and Cleve., 1962-67; pres., gen. mgr. Ajax Iron Works div. Cooper Industries, Corry, Pa., 1967-72; pres., chief exec. officer WDP, Inc., 1972-79, Swank Refractories Co., Johnstown, Pa., 1972-77, Hyde Park (Pa.) Foundry & Machine Co., 1974-79, Shepard-Niles Corp., Montour Falls, N.Y., 1979-82, Acco Babcock Materials Handling, Frederick, Md., 1982-85; ptnr. Fagan and Co., Ligonier, Pa.; bd. dirs. Acco Babcock, Inc., Babcock Internat., Chemung Foundry, Parnell Precision Products Co., Carre-Orban and Partners, Liberty Mut. Ins. Co., Ind. Steel and Engring. Corp., Bedford Crane Co., Shepard Niles Corp., Marine Bank, WDP, Inc.; chmn. Parnell Precision Products, 1980-82, Ind. Steeland Engring., Bedford Crane Co., 1981-82, pres., chmn., chief exec. officer, Greenway Products. Served with USN, 1953-56, Korea. Mem. Crane Mfrs. Assn., Hoist Mfrs. Assn., Conveyor Equipment Mfg. Assn., Nat. Trust Soc. Clubs: HYP (Pitts.). Auburn-Cord-Duesenberg. Home: 139 Ramsey Rd Ligonier PA 15658-0244 Office: 223 E Main St Ligonier PA 15658-1347

PIMENTAL, LAURA, emergency physician; b. Prestwick, Scotland, Jan. 27, 1958; came to U.S., 1958; BS, Georgetown U., 1979, MD, 1983. Diplomate Am. Bd. Emergency Medicine, Nat. Bd. Med. Examiners. Intern Walter Reed Army Med. Ctr., Washington, 1983-84; resident in emergency medicine Madigan Army Med. Ctr., Tacoma, Wash., 1984-86; chief resident dept. emergency medicine Madigan Army Med. Ctr., Tacoma, 1986; staff physician Tripler Army Med. Ctr., Honolulu, 1986-87, asst. chief emergency med. scvs., 1987-88; attending emergency physician Brooke Army Med. Ctr., San Antonio, Tex., 1989-90; dir. edn. dept. emergency medicine Mercy Med. Ctr., Balt., 1992-93; dir. emergency svcs. Bon Secours Hosp., Balt., 1993-94; attending physician dept. emergency medicine Univ. Hosp., Balt., 1990—; attending physician dept. emergency medicine Mercy Med. Ctr., Balt., 1990—, chmn. dept. emergency medicine, 1996—; mem. affiliate faculty ACLS, Mil. Tng. Network, San Antonio, Tex., 1988, emergency medicine tchg. faculty Brooke Army Med. Ctr., San Antonio, 1989-90; asst. prof. dept. surgery U. Md. Sch. of Medicine, Balt., 1990—. Contbr. articles to profl. jours.; presenter, lectr. at nat. and internat. sci. confs. Named Best Resident and Best Overall Presenter, So. Med. Assn.-Am. Coll. Emergency Physicians Case Presentation Competition, New Orleans, 1984. Mem. Am. Coll. Emergency Physicians, Am. Acad. Emergency Medicine, Christian Med. and Dental Soc. Home: 14 Old Dominion Ct Catonsville MD 21228

PIMENTAL, PATRICIA ANN, neuropsychologist, consulting company executive, author; b. Warwick, R.I., Feb. 2, 1956; d. Thomas Robert and Veronica Madeleine (Costa) P.; m. John V. O'Hara, Dec. 16, 1989; children: John Bernard, Padraic James. BS in Pre-Med, Speech Pathology, Northwestern U., 1978, MA in Speech Pathology with honors, 1980; PsyD in Clin. Psychology with honors, Chgo. Sch. Profl. Psychology, 1987. Lic. psychologist, speech pathologist, Ill.; diplomate Am. Bd. Vocat. Neuropsychology, Am. Acad. Pain Mgmt., Am. Bd. Prof. Disability Cons., Am. Bd. Profl. Neuropsychology. Clin. psychology extern child psychology clinic U. Ill., Chgo., 1984-85, dir. psychol. svcs. dept. phys. medicine and rehab., 1987-91, asst. prof. dept. phys. medicine and rehab., 1987-91; clin. psychology extern Filmore Mental Health Ctr., Berwyn-Cicero (Ill.) Sr. Svcs., 1985-86; clin. psychology intern St. Elizabeth's Hosp., Chgo., 1986-87; mem. faculty Chgo. Sch. Profl. Psychology, 1991—; pres. Neurobehavioral Medicine Cons., Ltd., Oak Brook, Ill., 1991—. Sr. author: Neuropsychological Aspects of Right Brain Injury, 1989, The Mini Inventory of Right Brain Injury, 1989; contbr. articles and revs. to profl. jours., chpts. to books; manuscript reviewer Archives Phys. Medicine and Rehab., 1990; book reviewer Contemporary Psychology, 1991. Vol. trainer ARC Disaster Stress Relief Program, 1991—; leader U. Ill. Stroke Club, 1988-91; bd. dirs. Older Adult Rehab. Svcs., Cicero, 1987-90; active Chgo. Anti-Cruelty Soc., Lincoln Park Zool. Soc. Named one of Outstanding Young Women Am., 1984, 92; Am. Cancer Soc. scholar, 1979; recipient Outstanding Manuscript of Yr. award Am. Jour. of Pain Mgmt., 1993. Fellow Am. Coll. Profl. Neuropsychology; mem. APA, Am. Pain Soc., Ill. Psychol. Assn. (adv. bd. 1989-93, chair-elect, chair health and rehab. sect. 1991-92, 92-93, chair prescription privilege task force 1992-95, continuing edn. chair/clin. practice sect. 1993-95, pres.-elect 1995-96, pres. 1996—), Nat. Brain Injury Rsch. Found. (med. adv. coun. 1992—), Internat. Neuropsychol. Soc., Nat. Acad. Neuropsychology, Am. Congress Rehab. Medicine, Soc. Clin. and Exptl. Hypnosis, Midwest Neuropsychology Group, Am. Speech and Hearing Assn. Avocations: gourmet cooking, piano, voice, aerobic exercise, martial arts. Office: Glen Oaks Hosp Med Ctr Neurobehavioral Medicine 701 Winthrop Ave Glendale Heights IL 60139-1405

PIMENTEL, DAVID, entomologist, educator; b. Fresno, Calif., May 24, 1925; s. Frank and Marion V. (Sylva) P.; m. Marcia R. Hutchins, July, 16, 1949; children: Christina, Susan, Mark David. Student, St. John's U., Collegeville, Minn., 1943, Clark U., summer 1946; BS, U. Mass., 1948; PhD, Cornell U., 1951. Chief tropical rsch. lab. USPHS, San Juan; chief tropical research lab. USPHS, P.R., 1951-54; project leader tech. devel. lab USPHS, Savannah, Ga., 1954-55; postdoctoral investigator U. Chgo., winters 1954-55; postdoctoral investigator, OEEC rsch. fellow Oxford (Eng.) U., 1961; postdoctoral investigator, NSF computer scholar MIT, Cambridge, summer 1961; mem. faculty Cornell U., 1955—, prof. insect ecology, 1963—, head dept. entomology and limnology, 1963-69, prof. entomology, ecology and systematics, 1969-76, prof. insect ecology and agrl. scis., 1976—; prof., core faculty Center Environ. Quality Mgmt., 1973-74; cons. Office Sci. and Tech., Exec. Office Pres., 1964-67, 69-70, EPA, 1971; co-chmn. Commn. on Mosquito Control for Developing Countries, Nat. Acad. Scis., 1972-73; mem. commn. on pesticides and pest mgmt. in Inter-Am., 1973-77; mem. Nat. Adv. Coun. on Environ. Edn., 1973-74; chmn. panel on environ. impact of herbicides EPA, 1972-74, pesticide adv. coun., 1975-78; nat. adv. coun. environ. edn. Office Edn., HEW, 1975-78, chmn., 1975; chmn. study team on interdependence of food, population, health, energy, and environment World Food and Nutrition Study, Nat. Acad. Scis., 1976-77, chmn. environ. studies bd., 1980-83; mem. energy rsch. adv. bd. Dept. Energy, 1979-85; mem. rsch. adv. com. USAID, 1979-82, chmn. panel on land productivity; mem. Office of Tech. Assessment, U.S. Congress, 1979-80; hon. prof. Inst. Applied Ecology, Shengang, China, 1995—. Assoc. editor: Am. Midland Naturalist;

contbr. articles to profl. jours. Trustee Village of Cayuga Heights, 1974—. Served to 2d lt., pilot USAAF, 1943-45. Recipient Disting. Svc. award Rural Sociol. Coun., 1992. Mem. AAAS (climate com. 1979-82, population, resource and environ. com. 1985-91, chmn. subcom. on food, population, and resources 1986-87), NAS (chmn. panel on biology and renewable resources, exec. bd. com. on life scis. 1966-68, com. on world food, health and population 1974-75, chmn. panel on econ. and environ. aspects of pest mgmt. in Ctrl. Am. 1974-76, chmn. bd. on sci. and tech. for internat. devel. 1975-79, com. on food and food prodn. 1974-76, alt. agr. com. 1985-89, com. on role of alt. farming methods in modern productive agr. 1985-89), Entomol. Soc. Am. (gov. bd., chmn. editl. bd., pres. Eastern br. 1974-75), Ecol. Soc. Am., Am. Soc. Naturalists, Soc. Study of Evolution, Entomol. Soc. Can., Am. Soc. Zoologists, Nat. Geog. Soc. (com. on rsch. and explorations 1993—), Internat. Union for Conservation of Nature and Natural Resources (commn. on ecology 1981-90), Royal Swedish Acad. Scis. (bd. dirs. Beijer Inst. 1994—), Chinese Acad. Scis. (hon. prof., acad. com. Inst. Applied Ecology 1994—), Sigma Xi, Phi Kappa Phi, Gamma Alpha (nat. recorder 1960-62). Office: Cornell U Dept Entomology Comstock Hall Ithaca NY 14853

PIMLEY, KIM JENSEN, financial training consultant; b. Abington, Pa., Apr. 29, 1960; d. Alvin Christian Jensen and Helen Marie (Kairis) Meinken; m. Michael St. John Pimley, Nov. 10, 1988; 1 child, Oliver Jensen Pimley. BA, Emory U., 1982, MA magna cum laude, 1982; postgrad., U. Chgo., 1985—. Mgr. tng. ops. Continental Bank, Chgo., 1986-88, mgr. coll. rels., 1988-90; mgr. client svcs. The Globecon Group, N.Y.C., 1990-92; prin. Pimley & Pimley, Inc., Princeton, N.J., 1992-93; pres. P&P Tng. Resources, Inc., Princeton, 1993—; owner Jr. League Designer Showhouse, 1997. Contbr. poetry to various jours. Mem. Chgo. Coun. on Fgn. Affairs, 1990—. Scholarship U. Chgo., 1984. Mem. ACLU, NOW, Oxford and Cambridge Club, Poetry Soc. Am. Office: P&P Tng Resources Inc 117 Library Pl Princeton NJ 08540-3019

PINAC, ANDRÉ LOUIS, III, obstetrician, gynecologist; b. New Orleans, Dec. 8, 1955; s. André Louis Jr. and Patricia Elaine (Ledet) P.; m. Deborah Bordelon LaFleur, Nov. 4, 1989; 1 child, Amy Elizabeth; 1 stepchild, Robby Nicholas LaFleur. BS, U. Southwestern La., 1977; MD, La. State U., New Orleans, 1981. Diplomate Am. Bd. Ob-Gyn. Resident ob-gyn La. State U. Affiliated Hosps., New Orleans, Lafayette, Lake Charles and Baton Rouge, 1981-85; practice medicine specializing in ob-gyn Opelousas, La., 1985—; chief of staff Doctor's Hosp. Opelousas, 1993-94; participant Cmty. Health Fair, Opelousas, 1987—; bd. dirs. Drs. Hosp. of Opelousas. Safety officer St. Landry Parish; bd. dirs. Little League, 1992-94. Named Duke at Mardi Gras Festival, Opelousas Garden Club, 1994. Fellow Am. Coll. Ob-Gyn; mem. AMA, So. Med. Assn., La. State Med. Soc., St. Landry Parish Med. Soc., Opelousas Cath. Soccer Assn. (pres. 1991-93), Alpha Phi Alpha (life), Sigma Alpha Epsilon. Roman Catholic. Avocations: golf, jogging, swimming, trivia, basketball. Office: 839 Cresswell Ln Ste A Opelousas LA 70570-5881

PINARD, RAYMOND R., pulp and paper consultant; b. Trois-Rivieres, Que., Can., May 13, 1930; s. Albert and Mariette (Dufresne) P.; m. Estelle Frechette, Nov. 5, 1965; children: Robert, Andree. B.A., U. Laval, (Que., Can.), 1951; B.Eng., McGill U., Montreal, 1955. Registered profl. engr., Que. Process engring. plant mgr. Domtar Inc., East Augus, Que., 1955-68; gen. mgr. Domtar Kraft & Bd. Domtar Inc., Montreal, 1968-73, v.p., gen. mgr. Domtar Newspring & Pulp, 1974-79, pres. Domtar Pulp & Paper, 1979-81, exec. v.p., chief operating officer, 1981-90, also dir.; bd. dirs. South Shore Industries, United Auto Parts, Gen. Accident; bd. dirs., chmn. Centre Canadien de Fusion Magnetique; chmn. St. Laurent Paperboard Inc.; mem. Montreal adv. bd. Nat. Trust. Bd. dirs., past chmn. PPRIC; bd. dirs. Fondation de l'Universite' du Que., Montreal, 1979-92. Mem. TAPPI, Can. Pulp and Paper Assn. (chmn. 1982, bd. dirs.), Corp. Profl. Engrs. Que., Can. Mfrs. Assn. (chmn. 1988-89), Can. Pulp and Paper Tech. Assn. Office: R Pinard Cons Inc Ste 3000, 630 René-Lévesque Blvd W, Montreal, PQ Canada H3B 5C7

PINCKNEY, C. COTESWORTH, lawyer; b. Richmond, Va., Oct. 23, 1939; s. Thomas and Charlotte (Kent) P.; m. Helen Raney, Aug. 13, 1966; children: Sarah Whitley, Thomas. BA, Yale U., 1961; LLB, U. Va., 1967. Bar: Va. 1967. Assoc. Mays, Valentine, Davenport & Moore, Richmond, 1967-72; ptnr. Mays & Valentine, LLP, Richmond, 1972—. Bd. dirs. Sweet Briar Coll., 1996—; pres. Sheltering Arms Hosp., Richmond, 1986-87, bd. dirs., 1972—; trustee William H.-John G.-Emma Scott Found., 1974—, sec., 1994—; campaign vice chmn. United Way Svcs., 1997. Mem. ABA, Va. Bar Assn., Richmond Bar Assn., Phila. Quarry Club (pres. 1985-91), Country Club of Va., Commonwealth Club (bd. govs. 1986-92, pres. 1991-92), Soc. of Cin. Republican. Episcopalian. Home: 2 Roslyn Rd Richmond VA 23226-1610 Office: Mays & Valentine 1111 E Main St PO Box 1122 Richmond VA 23218-1122

PINCKNEY, NEAL THEODORE, psychologist, educator; b. N.Y.C., July 26, 1935; s. Leo Allen and Jean (Wiener) P.; children: Andrew Allen, Jennifer Elizabeth, Matthew Ian. Cert. polit. social and hist. issues, King's Coll., U. Durham, Eng., 1957; A.B., U. So. Calif., 1958, postgrad., 1958-61; Ph.D., Oxford U., 1966; postgrad., U. Vienna, U. Hiroshima, Stanford U. Mem. Pub. Welfare Commn., Los Angeles County, 1958-60; tchr. pub. schs., Los Angeles, 1960-61; tchr., counselor Las Vegas, 1961-62, adminstr. therapist psychiat. clinic, 1962-63; educator, dir. guidance service Dept. Def. Overseas Dependent Schs., England and Japan, 1963-67; pvt. practice clin. psychology, 1967-87; lectr. Calif. State U., Sacramento, 1967-68, asst. prof., 1968-71, assoc. prof., 1971-77, prof. psychology and edn., 1977-87, prof. emeritus, 1987—, chmn. dept. behavioral scis., 1980-82, prof. counseling psychology, coordinator grad. studies, dept. adminstrn., counseling and policy studies, 1982—; founder, clin. dir. A Healing Heart, 1993—; vis. prof. U. Calif.-Davis, 1979—; psychologist, instr. enforcement psychology and human rels. Calif. Hwy. Patrol, 1967-80; dir. Univ. Software Evaluation Project, 1987; tech. cons., adv. Ministry Edn. and Culture, Goft. Brazil, Brasilia, 1974-76; cons. psychologist Calif. Med. Facility, Vacaville, various law enforcement agys.; prof. U. Hawaii, lectr. U. Hawaii Leeward C.C., 1992-93; founder, clin. dir. Healing Heart Found., 1993—; mem. profl. treatment team Preventive Medicine Rsch. Inst.-Ornish Residential Retreat for Revevsing Heart Disease, 1996. Author: Healthy Heart Handbook, 1994, Law and Ethics in Counseling and Psychotherapy, A Casebook, 1961, 86; pub. USER, a Software Report Card, 1987; editor: Incite Newsletter of Hawii Portable Computer Users Assn., 1987-88; editor: Ency. of Psychology, 2d edit. Served with 3d Armored Div. U.S. Army, 1954-55. Queen's scholar Eng., 1956-57; scholar Dept. State Fgn. Service Inst., 1964; fellow Ford Found., 1960-61. Mem. Am. Psychol. Assn., Brit. Psychol. Assn., Japanese Psychol. Assn., Brazilian Psychol. Assn., Am. Ednl. Research Assn., Am. Assn. Counseling and Devel., Am. Radio Relay League (life), Hawaii Portable Computer Users Assn., Hawaii Personal Computer Users Group (pres. 1989-91, system operator Electronic Bulletin Bd. Svc.), Quarter Century Wireless Assn. (life), Vegetarian Assn. of Hawaii (bd. dirs.), No. Calif. DX Club, Hawaii DX Assn., Phi Delta Kappa, Delta Phi Epsilon. Clubs: Commonwealth (San Francisco); Oxonian (Tokyo); Toastmasters (area gov. 1962-63). Lodge: Masons. Home: 84-683 Upena St Waianae HI 96792-1935 *Those who rush through life are merely hurrying toward their death. When one pauses to savor its many subtle varieties one begins to gain some insight and to be in awe of the wonder of it all. Then we begin to place ourselves in perspective and everything has meaning.*

PINCOCK, DOUGLAS GEORGE, electronics company executive; b. Vancouver, B.C., Can., Sept. 29, 1940; s. George Leyland and Sadie McElvenna (Boyle) P.; m. Gloria Dawn Werth, Sept. 5, 1964 (div. 1985); children: Barry, James, David, Lisa; m. Marilyn Marie Spearns, Oct. 28, 1990. BSEE, Man. (Winnipeg, Can.) U., 1963, MSEE, 1967; PhD, New Brunswick U., Fredericton, 1971. Registered profl. engr., N.S. Asst. prof. St. Francis Xavier U., Antigonish, N.S., 1969-70; from lectr. to asst. prof. to assoc. prof. U. N.B., 1970-75, 76-79; maitre de conf. U. Paris, 1975-76; prof. Tech. U. N.S., Halifax, 1979-82; pres., founder Applied Microelectronics Inc., Halifax, 1982—; bd. dirs. Can. Microelectronics Corp., Kingston, Ont., VEMCO, Shad Bay, N.S.; pres., bd. dirs. AMI Techs., Halifax, 1992—; mem. adv. bd. Can. Intellectual Property Orgn. Contbr. 25 papers to profl. jours. Head coach basketball Tech. U. N.S., 1986-95. With Can. Air Force, 1963-66. Achievements include co-invention weatherstar 4000, electronic parking meter, other inventions in underwater telemetry products. Office: Applied Microelectronics Inc, 1046 Barrington St, Halifax, NS Canada B3H 2R1

PINCOCK, GARRY LAMAR, association administrator; b. Phila., June 11, 1949; s. Lamar R. and Barbara (Henry) P.; children: Jacqueline Meredith, Amy Lauren. BS, West Chester (Pa.) U., 1975; postgrad., Ind. U., 1982. Tchr. Penn Delco Sch. Dist., Aston, Pa., 1975-77; v.p. Atlas Maintenance, Inc., Brookhaven, Pa., 1972-83; exec. dir. Pa. div. Am. Cancer Soc., Media, 1979-83; asst. v.p. field svcs. Ga. div. Am. Cancer Soc., Macon, 1983-86; v.p. field svcs. Ga. div. Am. Cancer Soc., Atlanta, 1986-89, sr. v.p. div. ops., 1989-91; exec. v.p., CEO Pa. divsn. Am. Cancer Soc., 1991—, CEO commonwealth divsn., 1996—, vice chair cmty. health campaign, 1996—; instr., cons. S.E. Pa. Cmty. Health Assn., Bethlehem, 1980-81; founding mem. Cmty. Health Campaign, 1993, bd. dirs., 1996—. Mem. bldg. campaign com. Piedmont Baptist Ch., Marietta, Ga., 1987; mem. city com. Young Life, Media, 1982; v.p. Garage Youth Ctr., Brookhaven, Pa., 1970-74. Republican. Avocations: golf, tennis, jogging. Office: Am Cancer Soc Pa Divsn Rt 422 & Sipe Ave Hershey PA 17033

PINCOCK, RICHARD EARL, chemistry educator; b. Ogden, Utah, Sept. 14, 1935; s. Earl Samuel and Virginia (Christenson) P.; m. Elke Gertrud Hermann, Aug. 20, 1960; children—Christina, Gordon, Jennifer. B.S., U. Utah, 1956; A.M., Harvard U., 1957, Ph.D., 1960. Postdoctoral research fellow Calif. Inst. Tech., 1959-60; faculty U. B.C., Vancouver, Can., 1960—; prof. U. B.C., 1969—. Mem. Phi Beta Kappa, Sigma Pi. Office: U BC, Chemistry Dept, Vancouver, BC Canada V6T 1Y6

PINCUS, ANN TERRY, federal agency administrator; b. Little Rock, Sept. 12, 1937; d. Fred William and Cornelia (Witsell) Terry; m. Walter Haskell Pincus, May 1, 1965; children: Ward, Adam, Cornelia Battle. BA, Vassar Coll., 1959. Editorial asst., writer Glamour Mag., 1963; reporter Ridder Pubs., Washington, 1963-66; freelance writer Washington, 1966-76; dir. info. select com. on U.S. population U.S. Ho. Reps., Washington, 1977-79; nat. publicist Nat. Pub. Radio, Washington, 1979-83; press sec. U.S. Sen. Charles Mathias, Washington, 1983-87; profl. staff mem. Senate Com. on Rules, Washington, 1983-87; v.p. communications Stas. WETA-TV/Radio, Washington, 1987-93; dir. Office of Rsch., U.S. Info. Agy., Washington, 1993—; bd. dirs. Fgn. Student Svcs. Coun., Washington, Woodley House. Editor: Kennedy Center Cookbook, 1977; contbr. articles to profl. jours. Avocations: politics, reading, walking, tennis. Home: 3202 Klingle Rd NW Washington DC 20008-3403 Office: Office of Rsch US Info Agy 301 4th St SW Rm 352 Washington DC 20547-0009

PINCUS, HOWARD JONAH, geologist, engineer, educator; b. N.Y.C., June 24, 1922; s. Otto Max and Gertrude (Jankowsky) P.; m. Maud Lydia Roback, Sept. 6, 1953; children: Glenn David, Philip E. BS, CCNY, 1942; PhD, Columbia U., 1949. Mem. faculty Ohio State U., 1949-67, successively instr., asst. prof., assoc. prof., 1949-59, prof., 1959-67, chmn. dept. geology, 1960-65; rsch. geologist U. S. Bur. Mines, summers 1963-67; geologist, rsch. supr. U.S. Bur. Mines, 1967-68; prof. geol. sci. and civil engring. U. Wis., Milw., 1968-87, prof. emeritus, 1987—, dean Coll. Letters and Sci., 1969-72; rsch. assoc. Lamont Geol. Obs., Columbia, 1949, 50, 51; geologist Ohio Dept. Natural Resources, summers 1950-61; cons. geology and rock mechanics, 1954-67, 68—; mem. U.S. nat. com. on tunnelling tech. NAE, 1972-74, mem. U.S. nat. com. on rock mechanics NAS/NAE, 1975-78, 80-89, chmn., 1985-87; mem. U.S. com. Internat. Assn. Engring. Geology/NAS, chmn., 1987-90; sr. postdoctoral fellow NSF, 1962. Tech. editor: Geotech. Testing Jour., 1992-95; editl. bd. Geotech Testing Jour., 1996—. Served to 1st lt. C.E. AUS, 1942-46. Recipient award for teaching excellence U. Wis.-Milw. Alumni Assn., 1978. Fellow ASTM (Reinhart award 1987, Award of Merit 1989), AAAS, Geol. Soc. Am.; mem. NSPE, AAUP (pres. Ohio State U. chpt. 1955-56, mem. coun. 1965-67, pres. U. Wis.-Milw. chpt. 1976-77), Am. Geophys. Union, Geol. Soc. Am. (chmn. engring. geology divsn. 1973-74), Soc. Mining Engrs., Internat. Assn. Engring. Geology, Internat. Soc. Rock Mechanics, Assn. Engring. Geologists, Am. Inst. Profl. Geologists (pres. Ohio sect. 1965-66), Phi Beta Kappa (pres. Ohio State U. chpt. 1959-60, pres. U. Wis.-Milw. chpt. 1976-77), Sigma Xi. Home: 17523 Plaza Marlena San Diego CA 92128-1807 Office: PO Box 27598 San Diego CA 92198-1598

PINCUS, JONATHAN HENRY, neurologist, educator; b. Bklyn., May 4, 1935; s. Joseph Bernhard and Hannah Martha (Palestine) P.; m. Cynthia Sterling Deery, Jan., 1961 (div. 1983); children: Daniel, Jeremy, Adam; m. Fortuna Mizrahi Fries, Nov. 1983 (div. 1995). AB, Amherst Coll., Mass., 1956; MD, Columbia U., 1960; MA, Yale U., 1973. Asst. prof. neurology Yale U., New Haven, 1965-69, assoc. prof. neurology, 1969-73, prof. neurology, 1973-86; prof., chmn. neurology Sch. Medicine Georgetown U., Washington, 1987-95, prof. neurology, 1987—. Author: Behavioral Neurology, 1974, 3d edit., 1986. Fellow Am. Acad. Neurology (v.p. 1991-93); mem. Am. Neurol. Asns. (counselor 1984-86). Achievements include linkage of anticonvulsant properties of phenytoin to reduction of Ca influx; introduction of protein redistribution diet to restore l-dopa responsiveness in end stage Parkinsonism; correlation of neurologic deficits, the experience of abuse and paranoia with episodic violence in delinquents and criminals; proposition of defect in thiamine triphosphate as cause of Leigh's encephalomyelopathy. Office: Georgetown Univ Hosp Dept Neurology 1st Fl Bles Bldg 3800 Reservoir Rd NW Washington DC 20007-2113

PINCUS, JOSEPH, economist, educator; b. N.Y.C., Apr. 17, 1919; s. Samuel and Lillian (Sirotkin) P.; m. Ethel Frances London, July 6, 1952; children: Terri Ellen Pincus Forman, Sally Neila, Robert Alan. BSS, CCNY, 1941; MA, Am. U., 1947, PhD, 1953. Internat. economist Latin Am. studies project U.S. Tariff Commn., Washington, 1946-47, 61-62; economist, fgn. affairs analyst Div. Research Am. Republics, Dept. State, Washington, 1949-58; tariff adviser ICA, USOM, Honduras, 1958-60; rep. with Continental Allied Co. to study indsl. devel., 1961; program officer, econ. adviser AID, Costa Rica, 1962-64; acting dir. mission AID, 1964; econ. adviser, pvt. enterprise adviser Am. Embassy, Asuncion, Paraguay, 1964-66, acting embassy econ. officer, 1967; pvt. enterprise devel. officer Am. Embassy, San Salvador, El Salvador, 1967-69, acting program officer, 1968, loan economist, 1968-69; dir. research Brokers Internat. Ltd., Miami, Fla., 1972-73; adj. prof. econs. Fla. Internat. U., also Embry-Riddle Aero. U., 1974-75; vis. prof. econs. U. Miami, 1974, 79, Fla. Meml. Coll., 1975; pres. Common Market Devel. Corp., Miami, 1975-86; ptnr., chief economist Brown and Pincus Assocs.; hon. fellow U. Asuncion Sch. Advanced Econ. Studies, 1966-67; dir. enterprise devel. program Ctr. for Advanced Internat. Studies, U. Miami; mem. Fla.-Colombia Ptnrs. Program. Mem. indsl. devel., promotion and retention task force Dade County Overall Econ. Devel. Program Com., 1983-85; senator Fla. Silver-Haired Legislature; mem. internat. bus. and commerce task force Beacon Council; founder South Dade-Kendall Rep. Club, Dade County, Fla. Mem. Am. Fgn. Svc. Assn., Nat. Assn. Ret. Fed. Employees, Latin Am. Studies Assn., Soc. Internat. Devel., Acad. for Internat. Bus., Caribbean Studies Assn., U. Miami Consortium on Hunger and Poverty, Omicron Delta Epsilon, Beta Gamma Sigma. Avocations: amateur radio at Sta. KD6TCE. Home and Office: 50 Chumasero Dr San Francisco CA 94132-2338 *To those involved in corporate or governmental bureaucracies, my advice is to exercise initiative, go as far as you can on your own, and then seek advice. If you're wrong, someone in authority will stop you eventually. But you could be RIGHT.*

PINCUS, LIONEL I., venture banker; b. Phila., Mar. 2, 1931; s. Henry and Theresa Celia (Levit) P.; m. Suzanne Storrs Poulton (dec.). BA, U. Pa., 1953; MBA, Columbia U., 1956. Assoc. gen. ptnr. Ladenburg, Thalmann & Co., N.Y.C., 1955-63; pres. Lionel I. Pincus & Co., Inc., N.Y.C., 1964-66; pres., CEO E.M. Warburg & Co., Inc., N.Y.C., 1966-70; chmn., CEO E.M. Warburg, Pincus & Co., Inc., N.Y.C., 1970—. Bd. trustees Montefiore Hosp., N.Y.C.; trustee Ittleson Found., Inc., Columbia U., chmn.; trustee Sch. Am. Ballet, Citizens Budget Commn., German Marshall Fund USA, 1982-88; mem. bd. overseers Columbia Grad. Sch. Bus.; bd. dirs. Nat. Park Found. Mem. Council Fgn. Rels., N.Y.C. Partnership, Nat. Golf Links Am. Club, Meadow Club. Office: EM Warburg Pincus Co Inc 466 Lexington Ave New York NY 10017-3140

PINCUS, ROBERT LAWRENCE, art critic, cultural historian; b. Bridgeport, Conn., June 5, 1953; s. Jules Robert and Carol Sylvia (Rosen) P.; m. Georgianna Manly, June 20, 1981; 1 child, Matthew Manly. BA, U. Calif., Irvine, 1976; MA, U. So. Calif., 1980, PhD, 1987. Instr. U. So. Calif., L.A., 1978-83; art critic L.A. Times, 1981-85, San Diego Union, 1985-92, San Diego Union-Tribune, 1992—; vis. prof. San Diego State U., 1985-86, 92. Author: On A Scale That Competes with the World: The Art of Edward and Nancy Reddin Kienholz, 1990, (with others) West Coast Duchamp, 1991, But Is It Art: The Spirit of Art as Activism, 1994, Paradise, 1994; author introduction to W.D.'s Midnight Carnival, 1988, Manuel Neri Early Work, 1953-78, 97. Recipient Chem. Bank award, 1994, Best Critical Writing award San Diego Press Club, 1994. Mem. Internat. Assn. Art Critics, Coll. Art Assn. Democrat. Office: San Diego Union-Tribune PO Box 191 350 Camino De La Reina San Diego CA 92115

PINCUS, STEPHANIE HOYER, dermatologist, educator; b. Lakehurst, N.J., Feb. 28, 1944; d. Ernest Carl and Aviva (Silbert) Hoyer; m. David Frank Pincus, Aug. 22, 1965 (div. Dec. 1984); children: Matthew Jonah, Tamara Hope; m. Allan Roy Oseroff, Mar. 24, 1985; 1 child, Benjamin Henry Oseroff. BA, Reed Coll., 1964; MD cum laude, Harvard U., 1968. Diplomate Am. Bd. Dermatology, Am. Bd. Internal Medicine. Intern Boston City Hosp., 1968-69; rsch. fellow U. Wash., Seattle, 1969-71, resident internal medicine, 1971-72; resident-fellow dermatology U. Washington, Seattle, 1972-74; fellow instr. dept. dermatology Harvard Med. Sch., Boston, 1974-75; asst. prof. medicine U. Wash., Seattle, 1975-77; lectr. Sch. Medicine Boston U., 1977-89; asst. prof. medicine Sch. Medicine Tufts U., Boston, 1977-82, mem. dept. immunology, 1977-89, asst. prof. dermatology, 1979-82, assoc. prof. dermatology and medicine, vice chairperson dermatology, 1982-89; prof. medicine and dermatology, chairperson dermatology SUNY, Buffalo, 1989—. Dermatology Found. fellow, Evanston, Ill., 1974-75, 77-78; Vets. Adminstrn. rsch. assoc., 1975-77; recipient Clin. Investigator award NIH, Bethesda, Md., 1979-81. Mem. Am. Contact Dermatitis Soc. (mem. liaison com. 1993—), Women's Dermatologic Soc. (bd. dirs. 1992—), Soc. Investigative Dermatology (chmn. com. on govt. and pub. rels. 1992-96), Profs. of Dermatology (mem. program com. 1993—), Internat. Soc. for Study of Vulvar Diseas (mem. exec. com. 1993-95), Harvard Med. Alumni (pres. 1995-96), Phi Beta Kappa, Alpha Omega Alpha. Office: SUNY 100 High St Ste C319 Buffalo NY 14203-1126

PINCUS, THEODORE HENRY, public relations executive; b. Chgo., Sept. 15, 1933; s. Jacob T. and J. (Engel) P.; m. Sharon Barr, Jan. 16, 1988; children: Laura, Mark, Susan, Anne, Jennifer. BS in Journalism, Ind. U., 1955. Free-lance bus. writer, 1955-58; sr. exec. Harshe Rotman & Druck, Chgo., 1958-62; dir. comm. Maremont Corp., Chgo., 1962-64; chmn., CEO, majority owner The Fin. Rels. Bd. Inc., N.Y.C., Chgo., L.A., San Francisco, Boston, Washington, 1964—; pub. affairs advisor to Nelson Rockefeller, N.Y.C., 1960, 68; advisor U.S. Info. Agy., 1993—. Author: Giveaway Day, 1977; contbr. articles to profl. jours. Active presdl. nomination campaigns; vice-chmn. Midwest region Am. Jewish Com.; mem. adv. bd. Ind. U. Bus. Sch. With USAF, 1955-57. Recipient numerous nat. awards for profl. excellence in investor rels. and corp.pub. rels. including Silver Anvil award Pub. Rels. Soc. Am., 1966, Civic Achievement award Am. Jewish Com., 1993. Mem. Young Pres.'s Orgn., Nat. Investor Relations Inst. (founding). Club: Union League. Office: The Financial Relations John Hancock Ctr 875 N Michigan Ave Chicago IL 60611-1803

PINCUS, WALTER HASKELL, editor; b. Bklyn., Dec. 24, 1932; s. Jonas and Clare (Glassman) P.; m. Betty Meskin, Sept. 12, 1954; 1 son, Andrew John; m. Ann Witsell Terry, May 1, 1965; children: Ward Haskell, Adam Witsell, Cornelia Battle Terry. B.A., Yale, 1954; postgrad., Georgetown U., 1995—. Cons. Senate Fgn. Relations Com., 1962-63; spl. writer Washington Evening Star, 1963-66; editor, reporter Washington Post, 1966-69; chief cons. Symington subcom. Senate Fgn. Relations Com., 1969-70; asso. editor New Republic, 1972-74, exec. editor, 1974-75; spl. writer Washington Post, 1975—; Cons. NBC News, 1971-79, CBS News, 1979-86, NBC News, 1987-88, Washington Post Co., 1989—; vis. lectr. Yale U., Fall 1988; dir. N.Y. Rev. Corp., 1979-85. Trustee Shakespeare Theater at the Folger, 1988—, co-chmn. edn. com., 1989-91, chmn. nominating com., 1992-96. Served with AUS, 1955-57. Recipient Page One award, 1960, George Orwell award, 1977, George Polk award, 1978, Emmy award, 1981. Mem. Council Fgn. Relations. Clubs: Federal City (Washington), Yale (Washington). Home: 3202 Klingle Rd NW Washington DC 20008-3403 Office: Washington Post 1150 15th St NW Washington DC 20071-0001

PINCZOWER, KENNETH EPHRAIM, lawyer; b. N.Y.C., Aug. 24, 1964; s. Joachim and Dinah (Cohen) P. BA, Queens Coll., 1985; postgrad., Rabbinical Sem. of Am., N.Y.C., 1983-86; JD, Benjamin N. Cardozo Sch. Law, 1989. Bar: N.Y. 1990, N.J. 1990, D.C. 1991, U.S. Dist. Ct. (so. and ea. dist.) N.Y. 1990, U.S. Dist. Ct. N.J. 1990, Fla. 1993. Auditor Seidman & Seidman/B.D.O., N.Y.C., 1986-87; summer assoc. U.S. Attys. Office, So. Dist. N.Y., N.Y.C., 1988; Alexander jud. fellow U.S. Dist. Judge, So. Dist. N.Y., N.Y.C., 1987-88; asst. corp. counsel N.Y.C. Law Dept., 1989-95; atty. Barron, McDonald, Carroll & Cohen, Bklyn., 1995—. Editor Cardozo Arts & Entertainment Law Jour., 1988-89. Vol. instr. Jewish Edn. Program, N.Y.C., 1983-86; instr. Aish Ha Torah, 1994—; chmn. Torah Chesed Fund, Yeshiva U., 1995—; Talmud assoc. Artscroll Mesorah Heritage Found., 1993—; com. mem. Nat. Conf. Synagogue Youth, 1991—. Avocations: Talmudic law, tennis, basketball. Home: 94-11 69th Ave Forest Hills NY 11375 Office: Barron McDonald et al 195 Montague St Brooklyn NY 11201-3631

PINCZUK, ARON, physicist; b. San Martin, Argentina, Feb. 15, 1939; s. Faiwel and Ester (Wejeman) P.; m. Gladys Norma Teitelman, June 14, 1962; children: Ana Gabriela, Guillermo Fabian. Licenciado, U. Buenos Aires, Argentina, 1962; PhD, U. Pa., 1969; D (hon.), U Autonoma, Madrid, 1997. Staff mem. Nat. Rsch. Coun., Argentina, 1971-76; head physics dept. Faculty of Scis., U. Buenos Aires, Argentina, 1974; vis. scientist Max Planck Inst., Stuttgart, Germany, 1976, IBM Rsch., Yorktown Heights, N.Y., 1976-77; staff mem. AT&T Bell Labs., Murray Hill, N.J., 1978—; sec. Argentina Phys. Soc., Buenos Aires, 1972-75; editor Solid State Communications, 1989-92, assoc. editor in chief, 1992—. Contbr. over 200 articles to profl. jours. and numerous chpts. to books. Recipient Oliver E. Buckley Condensed-Matter Physics prize Am. Physical Soc., 1994. Fellow Am. Phys. Soc. (Oliver E. Buckley prize 1994); mem. AAAS. Achievements include use and devel. novel optical methods in studies of structural phase transitions, semiconductor interfaces and interactions of free electrons in semiconductors; discovered novel phenomena in studies of quantum electron fluids. Office: Bell Labs Lucent Techs 600 Mountain Ave Rm 1d-433 New Providence NJ 07974-2008

PINDELL, HOWARDENA DOREEN, artist; b. Phila., Apr. 14, 1943; s. Howard Douglas and Mildred Edith (Lewis) P. B.F.A., Boston U., 1965; M.F.A., Yale U., 1967. Curatorial asst. Mus. Modern Art, N.Y.C., 1969-71; asst. curator Mus. Modern Art, 1971-77, assoc. curator dept. prints and illus. books, 1977-79; asso. prof. art SUNY, Stony Brook, 1979-84, prof. art, 1984—. Contbr. articles to profl. jours.; exhbns. include, Mus. Modern Art, Stockholm and 5 European mus., 1973, Fogg Art Mus., Cambridge, Mass., 1973, Indpls. Mus., Taft Mus., Cin., 1974, Gerald Piltzer Gallery, Paris, 1975, 9th Paris Biennale, Mus. Modern Art, Paris, 1975, Vassar Coll. Art Gallery, 1977; represented in permanent collections, Mus. Modern Art, N.Y.C., Fogg Art Mus., Met. Mus., N.Y.C., Whitney Mus. Am. Art; represented in travelling exhbns. Brandeis U., U. Calif. at Riverside, Cleve. Inst. Arts, SUNY, Potsdam, New Paltz, Wesleyan U., Davison Art Ctr., others. Recipient Artist award Studio Mus. of Harlem, 1994, Joan Mitchell Painting award Joan Mitchell Found., 1994/95; N.Y.C. Nat. Endowment Arts grantee, 1972-73, 83-84, Women's Caucus for Art award for Disting. Contbns. and Achievement in Arts, 1996; Japan/U.S. Friendship fellow, 1981-82; recipient Boston U. Alumni award, 1983, Ariana Found. grant, 1984-85, Guggenheim fellowship, 1987-88. Mem. ACASA, Coll. Art Assn. (Best Exhbn./Performance award 1990), Internat. Assn. Art Critics, Internat. Hous of Japan (acad.). Office: SUNY Art Dept Stony Brook NY 11794

PINDER, GEORGE FRANCIS, engineering educator, scientist; b. Windsor, Ont., Can., Feb. 6, 1942; s. Percy Samuel and Stella Marie P.; m. Phyllis Marie Charlton, Sept. 14, 1963; children—Wendy Marie, Justin George. B.Sc., U. Western Ont., 1965; Ph.D., U. Ill., 1968. Research hydrologist U.S. Geol. Survey, 1968-72; mem. faculty dept. civil engring. Princeton U., 1972-89, prof., 1972-89, chmn. dept., from 1980, dir. water resources program, 1972-80; dean Coll. Engring. and Math. U. Vt., Burlington, 1989-96, dir. Rsch. Ctr. for Groundwater Remediation Design, 1993—. Recipient O.E. Meinzer award Geol. Soc. Am., 1975, WUC medal, 1992; U. Vt. Univ. scholar, 1993. Fellow Am. Geophys. Union (Robert E. Horton award 1969); mem. ASCE, Soc. Petroleum Engrs. Home: 7 Bishop Rd Shelburne VT 05482-7351 Office: U Vt Coll Engring and Math Burlington VT 05405

PINDERA, JERZY TADEUSZ, mechanical and aeronautical engineer; b. Czchow, Poland, Dec. 4, 1914; immigrated to Can., 1965, naturalized, 1975; s. Jan Stanislaw and Natalia Lucia (Knapik) P.; m. Aleksandra-Anna Szal, Oct. 29, 1949; children: Marek Jerzy, Maciej Zenon. BS in Mech. Engring, Tech. U., Warsaw, 1936; MS in Aero. Engring, Tech. U., Warsaw and Lodz, 1947; D in Applied Scis., Polish Acad. Scis., 1959; DS in Applied Mechanics, Tech. U., Cracow, 1962. Registered profl. engr., Ont. Asst. Lot Polish Airlines, Warsaw, 1947; head lab. Aero. Inst., Warsaw, 1947-52, Inst. Metallography, Warsaw, 1952-54; dep. prof., head lab. Polish Acad. Scis., 1954-59; head lab. Bldg. Research Inst., Warsaw, 1959-62; vis. prof. mechanics Mich. State U., East Lansing, 1963-65; prof. mechanics U. Waterloo (Ont. Can.), 1965-83, adj. prof., 1983-86, Disting. prof. emeritus, 1987—; chmn. Internat. Symposium Exptl. Mechanics, U. Waterloo, 1972, dir. Inst. for Exptl. Mechanics, 1983-86; chmn. 10th Can. Fracture Conf., 1983; hon. adv. prof. Chongqing (Sichuan, China) U., 1988—; hon. prof. Shanghai (China) Coll. Archtl. and Mcpl. Engring., 1988—; hon. chmn. Internat. Conf. on Advanced Exptl. Mechanics, U. Tianjin, People's Republic of China, 1988; co-chmn. Second Internat. Conf. on Composites Engring., New Orleans, 1995; vis. prof. in France, Fed. Republic Germany, Slovenia, U.S.A., China; cons. in field. Bd. editors Mechanics Rsch. Comm., 1974—, Theoretical and Applied Fracture Mechanics, 1984—; mem. editl. adv. bd. Acta Mechanica Sinica, 1990—; guest editor spl. issue Birefringence Methods, Jour. Optics and Lasers in Engring., 1995; patentee in field; contbr. tech. books, articles, and chpts. in books. Served with Polish Army, 1939. Decorated Def. War 1939 medal (Poland), Cross of Oswiecim (Poland),; Comdr.'s Cross of Order of Merit (Fed. Republic Germany). Fellow Soc. Exptl. Mechanics (M.M. Frocht award 1978), Can. Soc. for Mech. Engring. (H.G. Duggan medal 1986); mem. Gesellschaft Angewandte Mathematik und Mechanik, N.Y. Acad. Scis., Soc. Engring. Sci., ASME, Assn. Profl. Engrs. Ont. Home: 310 Grant Crescent, Waterloo, ON Canada N2K 2A2 Office: U Waterloo Dept Civil Engring, 200 University Ave, Waterloo, ON Canada N2L 3G1 *It is true that "Nothing is more practical than a theory," provided however, that the assumptions on which the theory is founded are well understood. But, indeed, nothing can be more disastrous than a theory when applied to a real problem outside of the practical limits of the assumptions made, simply because of an homonymous identity with the problem under consideration!.*

PINDLE, ARTHUR JACKSON, JR., philosopher, researcher; b. Macon, Ga., May 26, 1942; s. Arthur Jackson Sr. and Beatrice Rosetta (Williams) P.; 1 child, Zhinga D. BS in Physics, Morehouse Coll., 1964; MA in Philosophy, Yale U., 1973, MPhil, 1974, PhD in Philosophy, 1978. Physicist IBM, Inc., Poughkeepsie, N.Y., 1964, Naval Ordinance Station, Indian Head, Md., 1966-69, Satellite Experiment Lab, Suitland, Md., 1970-71; philosophy prof. Fayetteville (N.C.) State U., 1976-83; pres. HRG, Inc., New Orleans, 1983—; dir. rsch. NITRT, Inc., New Orleans, 1993—; mem. bd. advs. Inst. Philosoph. Rsch., Boulder, Colo., 1980-83. Contbr. articles to profl. jours. Mem. Dem. Nat. Com., 1993-96. Avocations: yoga, chess. Home: 5000 Good Dr New Orleans LA 70127 Office: NITRT Inc 5000 Good Dr New Orleans LA 70127-3814

PINDYCK, BRUCE EBEN, lawyer, corporate executive; b. N.Y.C., Sept. 21, 1945; s. Sylvester and Lillian (Breslow) P.; m. Mary Ellen Schwartz, Aug. 18, 1968; children: Ashley Beth, Eben Spencer, Blake Michael Lawrence. AB, Columbia U., 1967, JD, 1970, MBA, 1971. Bar: N.Y. 1971, Wis. 1987. Assoc. Olwine, Connelly, Chase, O'Donnell & Weyher, N.Y.C., 1971-80; asst. gen. counsel Peat, Marwick, Mitchell & Co., N.Y.C., 1980-82; ptnr. Hollyer, Jones, Pindyck, Brady & Chira, N.Y.C., 1983-87; pres., CEO Meridian Industries, Inc., Milw., 1985—; also chmn. bd. dirs. Meridian Industries, Inc.; CEO Majilite Corp., Dracut, Mass., 1987—; also chmn. bd. dirs. Majilite Corp.; mem. capital campaign com. Columbia U., 1984-87. Bd. dirs. Harambee Community Sch., 1991-96, Milw. Ballet Co., 1993—, Milw. Pub. Mus., 1994—. Mem. Columbia Coll. Alumni Assn. (regional dir. 1988-94, v.p. 1994—, exec. com.), World Pres.'s Orgn. Office: 100 E Wisconsin Ave Milwaukee WI 53202-4107

PINE, CHARLES JOSEPH, clinical psychologist; b. Excelsior Springs, Mo., July 13, 1951; s. Charles E. and LaVern (Upton) P.; m. Mary Day, Dec. 30, 1979 (div. 1996); children: Charles Andrew, Joseph Scott, Carolyn Marie. BA in Psychology, U. Redlands, 1973; MA, Calif. State U.-L.A., 1975; PhD, U. Wash., 1979; postdoctoral UCLA, 1980-81. Diplomate in Clinical Psych. Am. Bd. Profl. Psych. Lic. psychologist, Calif., Fla. Psychology technician Seattle Indian Health Bd., USPHS Hosp., 1977-78; psychology intern VA Outpatient Clinic, L.A., 1978-79; instr. psychology Okla. State U., 1979-80, asst. prof., 1980; asst. prof. psychology and native Am. studies program Wash. State U., 1981-82; dir. behavioral health services Riverside-San Bernardino County Indian Health Inc., Banning, Calif., 1982-84; clin. psychologist, clin. co-dir. Inland Empire Behavioral Assocs., Colton, Calif., 1982-84; clin. psychologist VA Med. Ctr., Long Beach, Calif., 1984-85; clin. psychologist, psychology coordinator Psychiatry div. VA Med. Ctr., Sepulveda, Calif., 1985-93; clin. dir. Traumatic Stress Treatment Ctr., Thousand Oaks, Calif., 1985-93; assoc. clin. prof. UCLA Sch. Medicine, 1985—, Fuller Grad. Sch. Psychology, Pasadena, Calif., 1985-93, indep. practitioner Orlando, 1993-94; adj. assoc. prof. Calif. Sch. Profl. Psychology, L.A., 1989-95; mem. adj. faculty, psychologist, adminstv. coord. alcohol and drug abuse U. Ctrl. Fla., mem. faculty 1993-94; rsch. assoc. Nat. Ctr. for Am. Indian and Alaska Native Mental Health Rsch., U. Col. Health Sci. Ctr., Denver, 1989—; psychologist and adminstrv. coord. alcohol and drug abuse treatment program, Orlando VA Outpatient divsn. Tampa VA Med. Ctr., 1993—; cons. NIH, 1993—; psychologist stress treatment programs Bay Pines (Fla.) VA Med. Ctr., 1994-96; psychologist, team leader Vets. Counseling Ctr., Upland, Calif., 1997—; mem. L.A. County Am. Indian Mental Health task force, 1987-92. Editorial cons. White Cloud Jour., 1982-85; cons. Dept. Health and Human Services, USPHS, NIMH, 1980. Vol. worker Variety Boys Clubs Am., 1973-75; coach Rialto Jr. All-Am. Football League, 1974, Conejo Youth Flag Football Assn., pres., 1990, coach, bd. dirs. Westlake Youth Football, 1991-92; coach. Conejo Valley Little League, Dr. Phillips Little League, 1993—; co-commr., coach Dr. Phillips Pop Warner Football, 1993—. U. Wash. Inst. Indian Studies grantee, 1975-76, UCLA Inst. Am. Cultures grantee, 1981-82. Fellow Am. Psychol. Assn. (chair task force on service delivery to ethnic minority populations bd. ethnic minority affairs 1988, bd. ethnic minority affairs 1985-87); mem. Soc. Indian Psychologists (pres. 1981-83), Nat. Register Health Svc. Providers in Psychology, Calif. Psychol. Assn. Found. (bd. dirs. 1990-92), Soc. for Psychol. Study Ethnic Minority Issues (exec. com. 1987-88, pres. 1995-96), Sigma Alpha Epsilon. Republican. Roman Catholic. Contbr. psychol. articles to profl. lit.

PINE, JEFFREY BARRY, state attorney general; b. N.Y.C., Jan. 10, 1955; s. Henry F. Pine and Irma (Goldberg) Nass; m. Faith Marcia Scavitti, May 20, 1984; children: Bethany Arielle, Jonathan Ian Lee. BA in Polit. Sci., Haverford Coll., 1976; JD, George Washington U., 1979. Bar: R.I. 1979, Mass. 1979, U.S. Dist. Ct. R.I. 1979. Asst. atty. gen., dep. chief criminal prosecution R.I. Dept. Atty. Gen., Providence, 1979-89; assoc. atty. Decof & Grimm, Providence, 1990-93; atty. gen. State of R.I., 1993—. Bd. dirs. Camp Jori, Providence, 1989—, Jewish Family Svcs., Providence, 1989-92; trustee Temple Beth El, Providence, 1990-92; mem. R.I. Criminal Bench Bar Com., 1979-90, MADD, 1987—, Bd. Bar Overseers Mass. Recipient Beta Rho Sigma award; named top prosecutor by R.I. Monthly. Mem. ABA, R.I. Bar Assn., Assn. Am. Trial Lawyers, R.I. Trial Lawyers Assn., Ledgemont Country Club. Home: 15 Westford Rd Providence RI 02906-4943 Office: Office of Attorney General 72 Pine St Providence RI 02903-2836*

PINEDA, MAURICIO HERNAN, reproductive physiologist, educator; b. Santiago, Chile, Oct. 17, 1930; came to U.S., 1970, naturalized, 1982; s. Teofilo Pineda-Garcia and Bertila Pinto-Bouvret; m. Rosa A. Gomez, July 26, 1956; children—Anamaria, George H., Monserrat. D.V.M., U. Chile, 1955; M.S., Colo. State U., 1965, Ph.D., 1968. Prof. Coll. Vet. Medicine, Austral U. Chile, Valdivia, 1958-63, prof., head animal reprodn. lab., 1968-70; postdoctoral trainee U. Wis., Madison, 1970-72; postdoctoral fellow Colo. State U., Ft. Collins, 1972-74, research assoc., 1972-78; assoc. prof. physiology, dept. physiology and pharmacology Coll. Vet. Medicine, Iowa State U., Ames, 1979-84, prof., 1984—. Assoc. editor: Veterinary Endocrinology and Reproduction, 4th edit., 1989; contbr. chpts. to books, articles to profl. jours.; mem. editl. bds. sci. jours. Recipient Best Student award U. Chile Coll. Vet. Medicine, 1954; Rockefeller Found. scholar, 1963; Morris Animal Found. fellow, 1974. Mem. Chilean Vet. Med. Assn. (Disting. Services award 1987), Soc. for Study of Fertility (Eng.), N.Y. Acad. Scis., Sigma Xi, Beta Beta Beta, Phi Kappa Phi, Gamma Sigma Delta. Office: Iowa State U Dept Physiology and Pharmacology Vet Med Ames IA 50011

PINELESS, HAL STEVEN, neurologist; b. Chgo., Oct. 19, 1954; s. William and Sophie (Lubnicka) P.; m. Edy Dianne Rudnick, Mar. 10, 1985; children: Adam, Emily. BS in Zoology, U. Ill., 1976; DO, Chgo. Coll. Osteo. Medicine, 1981. Diplomate Am. Osteo. Bd. Neurology and Psychiatry. Intern Chgo. Osteo. Hosp., 1981-82; resident Loyola U. Med. Ctr./Hines (Ill.) VA Ctr., 1982-85; asst. prof. neurology Chgo. Coll. Osteo. Medicine, 1985-86; pvt. practice Winter Park, Fla., 1986—; pres. med. staff Fla. Hosp. East Orlando, 1990-93, bd. trustees, 1990-94. Contbr. articles to profl. jours and newspapers. Mem. AMA, Am. Osteo. Assn., Am. Acad. Neurology, Am. Coll. Neuropsychiatrists, Nat. Headache Found. Avocations: golf, racquetball, swimming, computers, photography. Office: 1890 Semoran Blvd Ste 255 Winter Park FL 32792-2285

PINES, ALEXANDER, chemistry educator, researcher, consultant; b. Tel Aviv, June 22, 1945; came to U.S., 1968.; s. Michael and Neima (Ratner) P.; m. Ayala Malach, Aug. 31, 1967 (div. 1983); children: Itai, Shani; m. Ditsa Kafry, May 5, 1983; children: Noami, Jonathan, Talia. BS, Hebrew U., Jerusalem, 1967; PhD, MIT, 1972; D (hon.), U. Paris, 1996. Asst. prof. chemistry U. Calif., Berkeley, 1972-75, assoc. prof., 1975-80, prof., 1980—, Pres.'s chair, 1993-97; faculty sr. scientist materials scis. div. Lawrence Berkeley Lab., 1975—; cons. Mobil Oil Co., Princeton, N.J., 1980-84, Shell Oil Co., Houston, 1981—; chmn. Bytel Corp., Berkeley, Calif., 1981-85; vis. prof. Weizmann Inst. Sci., 1982; adv. prof. East China Normal U., Shanghai, People's Rep. of China, 1985; sci. dir. Naloraç, Martinez, Calif., 1986—; Joliot-Curie prof. Ecole Superieure de Physique et Chemie, Paris, 1987; Walter J. Chute Disting. lectr. Dalhousie U., 1989, Charles A. McDowell lectr. U. B.C., 1989, E. Leon Watkins lectr. Wichita State U., 1990; Hinshelwood lectr., U. Oxford, 1990, A.R. Gordon Disting. lectr. U. Toronto, 1990, Venable lectr. U. N.C., 1990, Max Born lectr. Hebrew U. of Jerusalem, 1990; William Draper Harkins lectr. U. Chgo., 1991, Kolthoff lectr. U. Minn., 1991; Md.-Grace lectr. U. Md., 1992; mem. adv bd. Nat. High Magnetic Field Lab., Inst. Theoretical Physics, U. Calif. Santa Barbara; mem. adv. panel chem. Nat. Sci. Found.; Randolph T. Major Disting. Lectr. U. Conn., 1992; Peter Smith lectr. Duke U., 1993, Arthur William Davidson lect. U. Kansas, 1992, Arthur Birch lect. Australian Nat. U., 1993, Richard C. Lord Meml. lectr. MIT, 1993, Steacie lectr. Nat. Rsch. Coun. Can., 1993, Centenary lectr. Royal Soc. Chemistry, 1994, Morris Loeb lectr. Harvard U., 1994, Jesse Boot Found. lectr., U. Nottingham, 1994, Frontiers in Chemistry lectr. Tex. A&M U., 1995, Bergman lectr. Weizmann Inst. Sci., 1995, faculty rsch. lectr. U. Calif., Berkeley, 1996, Raymond & Beverly Sackler lectr. Tel Aviv U., 1996; Proestley lectr. Pa. State U., 1997. Editor Molecular Physics, 1987-91; mem. bd. editors Chem. Physics, Chem. Physics Letters, Nmr: Basic Principles and Progress, Advances in Magnetic Resonance, Accounts Chemistry Research, Concepts in Magnetic Reson; adv. editor Oxford U. Press; contbr. articles to profl. jours.; patentee in field. Recipient Strait award North Calif. Spectroscopy Soc., Outstanding Achievement award U.S. Dept. of Energy, 1983, 87, 89, R & D 100 awards, 1987, 89, Disting. Teaching award U. Calif., E.O. Lawrence award, 1988, Pitts. Spectroscopy award, 1989, Wolf Prize for chemistry, 1991, Donald Noyce Undergrad. Teaching award U. Calif., 1992, Robert Foster Cherry award for Great Tchrs. Baylor U., Pres.'s Chair for undergrad. edn. U. Calif., 1993; Guggenheim fellow, 1988, Christensen fellow St. Catherine's Coll., Oxford, 1990. Fellow Am. Phys. Soc. (chmn. divsn. chem. physics), Inst. Physics; mem. NAS, Am. Chem. soc. (mem. exec. com. divsn. phys. chemistry, Signature award, Baekeland medal, Harrison Howe award 1991), Royal soc. Chemistry (Bourke lectr.), Internat. Soc. Magnetic Resonance (v.p., pres. 1993-96). Office: U Calif Chemistry Dept D 64 Hildebrand Hall Berkeley CA 94720

PINES, BURTON YALE, broadcasting executive; b. Chgo., Apr. 6, 1940; s. Hyman and Mary Pines; m. Helene Brenner, May 21, 1972. B.A., U. Wis., 1961, M.A., 1963. Instr. U. Wis., Madison, 1962-65; corr. Time mag., Bonn, Saigon and Vienna, 1966-73, editor, N.Y.C., 1973-81; sr. v.p. Heritage Found., Washington, 1981-92; chmn. Nat. Ctr. for Pub. Policy Rsch., Washington, 1982-94; co-founder, exec. v.p., COO NET Polit. Newstalk Network, Washington, 1992-95; pres., CEO BookNet Cable TV Network, N.Y.C., 1995—. Author: Back to Basics, 1982, Out of Focus, 1994; editor: Mandate for Leadership II, 1984, Mandate for Leadership III, 1988. Recipient Page One award N.Y. Newspaper Guild, 1976, 77, 78, Freedom's Found. award, 1983. Jewish. Office: BookNet 45 Rockefeller Plz Fl 20 New York NY 10111-0100

PINES, WAYNE LLOYD, public relations counselor; b. Washington, Dec. 31, 1943; s. Jerome Martin and Ethel (Schnall) P.; B.A., Rutgers U., 1965; postgrad. George Washington U., 1969-71; m. Nancy Freitag, Apr. 16, 1966; children—Noah Morris, Jesse Mireth. Reporter, city editor Middletown (N.Y.) Times Herald-Record, 1965-68; copy editor Reuters News, 1968-69; assoc. editor FDC Reports, Washington, 1969-72; chief Consumer Edn. and Info., FDA, also editor FDA Consumer, 1972-74; exec. editor Product Safety Letter and Devices and Diagnostics Letter, Washington, 1974-75; dep. asst. commr. for pub. affairs, chief press relations FDA, Rockville, Md., 1975-78, assoc. commr. public affairs, 1978-82; adj. prof. Washington Public Affairs Center, U. So. Calif., 1980-81; instr. N.Y.U. Sch. Continuing Edn., 1982-84; instr. Profl. Devel. Inst., 1983-85; spl. asst. to dir. NIMH, 1982-83; sr. v.p., sr. counselor Burson-Marsteller, 1983-87; exec. v.p., dir. med. issues, 1987-93; pres. healthcare practice APCO Assocs., Washington, 1993—, dir. crisis com.; sr. counselor Gross, Townsend, Frank, Hoffman, 1993—; bd. dirs. Transcell Techs., Inc.; columnist Med. Advt. News., 1985-90; mem. adv. bd. Nat. Orgn. Rare Disorders, Orphan Med.; mem. corp. adv. bd. ANA. Author: The Sermons of Jerome Martin Pines, FDA Advertising and Promotional Manual, When Lightning Strikes: A How-to Crisis Manual; contbr. numerous articles in field to profl. jours. Home: 5821 Nevada Ave NW Washington DC 20015-2547 Office: APCO Assocs 1615 L St NW Washington DC 20036-5610

PINET, FRANK SAMUEL, former university dean; b. Topeka, Nov. 8, 1920; s. Frank Leo and Hattie Blanche (McClure) P.; m. Winifred Sarann Meyer, Jan. 27, 1956 (dec. Jan. 1995); children: Christopher Paul, Nancy Ann, Rosemary, Winifred Suzanne, Caroline Michele. BS, U. Kans., 1942, MBA, 1947, PhD, 1955. Mem. faculty U. Kans., Lawrence, 1946—; prof. bus. adminstrn. U. Kans., 1970-80, Telecommunications Industry disting. teaching prof., 1980-85, prof. emeritus, 1986—; asso. dean U. Kans. (Sch. Bus.), 1969-80; vis. prof. OEC, Italy, 1959-60; dir. Dold Foods, Inc.; cons. to industry, 1955—. Author: Probated Estates in Kansas, 3d edit, 1956. Bd. dirs. Spencer Mus. Art, U. Kans., 1997—. Served to lt. comdr. USNR, 1942-46, 50-52. Recipient Standard Oil Co. (Ind.) Outstanding Teaching award, 1973, Henry A. Bubb Outstanding Teaching award, 1972, 84, Pacesetter award U.S. Ind. Telephone Assn., 1982; named Outstanding Educator Mortar Board, 1980; Ford Found. fellow, 1961-62. Mem. Am. Econ. Assn., Indsl. Relations Research Assn. Home: 704 W 12th St Lawrence KS 66044-3212 Office: Univ Kans 202 Summerfield Hall Lawrence KS 66044-7522

PING, CHARLES JACKSON, philosophy educator, retired university president; b. Phila., June 15, 1930; s. Cloudy J. and Mary M. (Marion) P.; m. Claire Oates, June 5, 1951; children: Andrew, Ann Shelton. B.A., Rhodes Coll., 1951; B.D., Louisville Presbyn. Theol. Sem., 1954; Ph.D., Duke, 1961. Assoc. prof. philosophy Alma Coll., 1962-66; prof. philosophy Tusculum Coll., 1966-69, v.p., dean faculty, 1967-68, acting pres., 1968-69; provost Central Mich. U., Mt. Pleasant, 1969-75; pres. Ohio U., Athens, 1975-94, pres. emeritus, Trustee prof. philosophy and edn., 1994—, dir. Planning Inst. for Tchg. Humanities; bd. dirs. Nationwide Corp.; bd. dirs. Wing Lung Bank Internat. Inst. for Bus. Devel., Hong Kong; trustee Louisville Presbyn. Theol. Sem.; mem. adv. bd. Ind. Coll. Program N.W. Area Found., Inst. Ednl. Mgmt. of Harvard U.; chair Commn. Planning for Future of Higher Edn., Kingdom of Swaziland, Internat. Edn. Exch.; mem. Commn. on Higher Edn. Republic of Namibia; exec. dir. Manasseh Cutler Scholars Program. Author: Ohio University in Perspective, 1985, Meaningful Nonsense, 1966, also articles. Fulbright Sr. Rsch. scholar for So. Africa, 1995. Mem. Am. Assn. Higher Edn., Nat. Assn. State Univs. and Land-Grant Colls., Coun. on Internat. Ednl. Exch. (chair bd.), David C. Lam Inst. for East-West Studies (bd. dirs.), Coun. Internat. Exch. Scholars (bd. dirs., chair Africa com.). Office: Ohio U Office of Pres Emeritus Athens OH 45701

PINGATORE, SAM ROBERT, systems analyst, consultant, business executive; b. Chgo., Sept. 14, 1948; s. Samuel and Theresa (Kirchue) P.; m. Alicia Mae Morales, Aug. 16, 1969; 1 child, Joshua S.E. BA in Polit. Sci., Miami U., Oxford, Ohio, 1970; student, Baldwin Wallace Coll., Berea, Ohio, 1980, Ohio State U., 1985, Kent State U., 1973. Buyer, materials analyst FECO-Bangor Punta, Cleve., 1974-76; inventory analyst Van Dorn Co., Strongsville, Ohio, 1976-78; systems analyst Def. Logistics Agy., Dept. Def., Cleve., 1978-85, tng. officer, 1985-86, systems analyst-contracts, 1986-87, program analyst-budget, 1987-90; bus. mgr. ARVIN/CALSPAN NASA Lewis Operation, Cleve., 1990-95; v.p. ops. Morales Svcs., Columbia Station, Ohio, 1995—; bus. mgr., dir. H.R. Medina Co. Bd. MR/DD, Medina, Ohio, 1996-97, NASA Contract Proposal Team, CMT, Inc., 1996—; data processing instr. Bryant and Stratton Coll., Parma, Ohio, 1997—; mem. total quality mgmt. steering com. ARVIN/CALSPAN Corp., Cleve., 1991-95; mem. curriculum com. Polaris Vocat. Sch., Middleburg Heights, Ohio, 1991-95; mem. tng. and devel. com. Greater Cleve. Urban League; cons. Calspan Corp. Space Inds. Internat., North Olmsted, 1995—, CMT, Inc.; instr. data processing Bryant and Stratton Coll., Parma, Ohio, 1997—. Writer speeches, curriculum, position papers. Advisor St. Brendan Youth Group, North Olmsted, 1986; co-chair Pre-Cana, Marriage Preparation com., North Olmsted, 1981-96; co-chair Adult Edn. Commn., North Olmsted, 1979; mem. Human Rels. Coun., Darmstadt, Germany, 1972. With U.S. Army, 1970-73. Decorated Army Commendation medal (2), Army Achievement medal. Mem. Better Bus. Bur., Nat. Contract Mgmt. Assn., Rampant Lion Found., Delta Kappa Epsilon. Republican. Roman Catholic. Avocations: chess, tennis. Home and Office: 24647 Squire Rd Columbia Station OH 44028-9672

PINGEL, JOHN SPENCER, advertising executive; b. Mt. Clemens, Mich., Nov. 6, 1916; s. George F. and Margaret (Dalby) P.; m. Isabel Hardy, Dec. 12, 1939; children—John S. (dec.), Roy Hardy. Student, U.S. Mil. Acad., 1936; B.A., Mich. State U., 1939. Asst. dir. truck merchandising Dodge div. Chrysler Corp., 1940-41, fleet sales rep., 1949; adminstrv. asst. Mich. State U., 1945-46; dir. advt. Reo Motors, Inc., 1947-48; with mdsg. dept. Brooke, Smith, French & Dorrance, Inc., 1949-55, v.p., account supr., 1955-57, v.p., asst. to pres., 1957-60, exec. v.p., 1960; exec. v.p. Ross Roy-BSF & D, Inc., Detroit, 1960-62; exec. v.p. Ross Roy, Inc., 1962-64, pres., 1964—, vice-chmn., 1979—. Exec. bd., pres., chmn. orgn. and extension com. Detroit area council Boy Scouts Am; pres. Inst. for Econ. Edn., 1971; mem. adv. bd. United Found., 1970-71; mem. Pres.'s Council on Phys. Fitness and Sports, 1975—; Trustee Alma Coll., New Detroit, Inc., Harper Grace Hosp., Oakland U. Found.; mem. exec. com. Grosse Pointe U. Sch., 1957-58, trustee, 1959—; bd. dirs. Boys Republic, Inc., Greater Met. Detroit Project Hope, Greater Mich. Found.; trustee emeritus Mich. State U. Served from 2d lt. to lt. col. 95th Inf. Div. AUS, 1941-45. Decorated Bronze Star, Purple Heart; named to Nat. Football Hall of Fame, 1968, to Mich. Sports Hall of Fame, 1973, Mich. State U. Sports Hall of Fame, 1993. Mem. Detroit Sales Execs. Club (v.p. 1951), Am. Assn. Advt. Agys. (chmn. Mich. 1960, nat. chmn. 1978-79), Mich. C. of C. (dir.), Greater Detroit C. of C. (dir. 1970-71, chmn. 1977-78). Presbyterian (elder). Clubs: Detroit Athletic, Country of Detroit, Adcraft (pres. 1960-61), Detroit, Economic, Yondotega (Detroit); Seminole Golf, Everglades (Palm Beach, Fla.); Jupiter Hills. Home: 582 Peachtree Ln Grosse Pointe MI 48236-2717 also: 80 Celestial Way Juno Beach FL 33408-2371 Office: Ross Roy Inc 100 Bloomfield Hills Pky Bloomfield Hills MI 48304-2949

PINGREE, BRUCE DOUGLAS, lawyer; b. Salt Lake City, June 6, 1947; s. Howard W. and Lois (Ivie) P.; m. Lorraine Bertelli, Oct. 11, 1981; children: Christian James, Matthew David, Alexandra Elizabeth, Meredith Gillian, Lauren Ashley, Geoffrey Nicholas. BA in Philosophy, U. Utah, 1970, JD, 1973. Bar: Ariz. 1973, Tex. 1990. Ptnr. Snell & Wilmer, Phoenix, 1973-89; shareholder Johnson & Gibbs, Dallas, 1989-93; ptnr. Gardere & Wynne, Dallas, 1993-95; ptnr. Baker & Botts, L.L.P., Dallas, 1995—; lectr. in field of taxation. Contbr. articles to profl. jours. Served to capt. USAR. Mem. ABA (tax sect., past chair employee benefits com., past vice chair, past chmn. various sub-coms., 1993-94, chair joint com. on employee benefits 1994-95), Western Pension Conf., Southwest Benefits Conf., Order of Coif. Episcopalian. Home: 4065 Bryn Mawr Dr Dallas TX 75225-7032 Office: Baker & Botts LLP 2001 Ross Ave Dallas TX 75201-8001

PINGREE, DIANNE, sociologist, educator, mediator; b. Dallas; m. Harlan Pingree. BFA magna cum laude, So. Methodist U., 1976, MA, 1989; PhD in Sociology, Tex. Women's U., 1994. Cert. Family Life Educator, Mediator, Nat. Coun. Family Relations. Found., editor, pub. Tex. Woman Mag., 1977-80; pres. Tex. Woman Inc., 1980-85; owner, pres. Dianne Pingree & Assoc., 1985-88; pub. cons. Tex. Elite Publications, Dallas, 1988-89; mediator Ctr. for Dispute Resolution Denton County, 1991; tchng. assoc. Tex. Woman's U., 1990-92; postgrad. clin. intern SW Family Inst., Dallas, 1993-94; therapist J&L Human Sys. Devel., Dallas, 1994-95; pschotherapist Child and Family Svc. Inc., Austin, 1995-96; cons. Austin, 1996—; Speaker in field. Recipient Matrix award for outstanding achievement, Women in Comms., Women Helping Women award, Women's Ctr. Dallas, Dallas Press Club award. Am. Sociol. Assn., Sociol. Practice Assn., Assn. Family and Conciliation Courts, Nat. Coun. Family Rels., Acad. Family Mediators, Alpha Kappa Delta, Internat. Sociol. Honor Soc. (pres. Tex. Women's U. chpt. 1992). Home and Office: 1004 Porpoise Dr Austin TX 78734

PINGS, ANTHONY CLAUDE, architect; b. Fresno, Calif., Dec. 16, 1951; s. Clarence Hubert and Mary (Murray) P.; m. Carole Clements, June 25, 1983; children, Adam Reed, Rebecca Mary. AA, Fresno City Coll., 1972; BArch, Calif. Poly. State U., San Luis Obispo, 1976. Lic. architect, Calif.; cert. Nat. Council Archtl. Registration Bds. Architect Aubrey Moore Jr., Fresno, 1976-81; architect, prin. Pings & Assocs., Fresno, 1981-83, 86—, Pings-Taylor Assocs., Fresno, 1983-85. Prin. works include Gollaher Profl. Office (Masonry Merit award 1985, Best Office Bldg. award 1986), Fresno Imaging Ctr. (Best Instnl. Project award 1986, Nat. Healthcare award Modern Health Care mag. 1986), Orthopedic Facility (award of honor Masonry Inst. 1987, award of merit San Joaquin chpt. AIA 1987), Modesto Imaging Ctr. (award of merit San Joaquin chpt. AIA 1991), Peachwood Med. Ctr. (award of merit San Joaquin chpt. AIA). Mem. Calif. Indsl. Tech. Edn. Consortium Calif. State Dept. Edn., 1983, 84. Mem. AIA (bd. dirs. Calif. chpt. 1983-84, v.p. San Joaquin chpt. 1982, pres. 1983, Calif. Coun. evaluation team 1983, team leader Coalinga Emergency Design Assistance team), Fresno Arts (bd. dirs., counsel 1989—, pres. 1990-93), Fig Gardens Home Owners Assn. (bd. dir. 1991—, pres. 1994—). Republican. Home: 4350 N Safford Ave Fresno CA 93704-3509 Office: 1640 W Shaw Ave Ste 107 Fresno CA 93711-3506

PINGS, CORNELIUS JOHN, educational association administrator; b. Conrad, Mont., Mar. 15, 1929; s. Cornelius John and Marjorie (O'Loughlin) P.; m. Marjorie Anna Cheney, June 25, 1960; children: John, Anne, Mary. B.S., Calif. Inst. Tech., 1951, M.S., 1952, Ph.D., 1955. Inst. chem. engring. Stanford U., 1955-56, asst. prof., 1956-59; assoc. prof. chem. engring. Calif. Inst. Tech., 1959-64, prof., 1964-81, exec. officer chem. engring., 1969-73, vice-provost, dean grad. studies, 1970-81; provost, sr. v.p. acad. affairs U. So. Calif., 1981-93; pres. Assn. Am. Univs., Washington, 1993—; mem., dir. Nat. Commn. on Rsch., 1978-80; mem. bd. mgmt. Coun. on Govtl. Rels., 1980-83; bd. dirs. and chmn. Pacific Horizon Funds; mem. bd. dirs. Farmers Group, Inc., L.A.; pres. Assn. Grad. Schs., 1977-78; pres. Western Coll. Assn., 1988-90; mem. sci. engring. and pub. policy com. NAS, 1987-92, chmn., 1988-92. Contbr. articles to tech. jours. Mem., chmn. bd. trustees Mayfield Sr. Sch. Bd., 1979-85; mem. Pasadena Redevel. Agy., 1968-81, chmn., 1974-81; bd. dirs. Huntington Meml. Hosp., Pasadena; chmn. L.A. Ctrl. City Assn. Recipient Arthur Nobel medal, City of Pasadena, 1981, Disting. Alumni award Calif. Inst. Tech., 1989, Presdl. medallion U. So. Calif., 1993. Fellow AIChE, Am. Acad. Arts and Scis.; mem. NAE,

Calif. Club, Twilight Club, Bohemian Club, Cosmos Club, Valley Hunt Club. Roman Catholic. Home: 2330 Massachusetts Ave NW Washington DC 20008-2801 Office: Assn of Am Univs 1200 New York Ave NW Ste 550 Washington DC 20005-3929

PINHEY, FRANCES LOUISE, physical education educator; b. Canton, Ohio, Apr. 18, 1927; d. Frederick Otto and Rose June (Wolf) Sengleitner; m. Donald Charles Pinhey, June 13, 1952; children: Val Don, Shauna Rae, Kaye Dorrell, Lon Pernell. BA, Muskingum Coll., 1949; MS, U. R.I., 1977; postgrad., Ind. U., 1958. Cert. tchr., Ohio. Tchr. Canton Pub. Schs., 1949-50; instr. Muskingum Coll., New Concord, Ohio, 1950-52; tchr. New Concord Pub. Schs., 1950-52, Barberton (Ohio) High Sch., 1952-53, Ottawa (Ont., Can.) Pub. Schs., 1954-57, Ottawa YMCA, 1954-57; instr. Dakota Wesleyan U., Mitchell, S.D., 1959-63, Wilmington (Ohio) Coll., 1963-67; tchr. New London (Conn.) Pub. Schs., 1967-68; asst. prof. phys. edn., coach Mitchell Coll., New London, 1968—; chair, mem. Conn. Sports Officiating Rating Bd., 1968-78. Nat. ofcl. women's volleyball & basketball, 1958-80; pres. PTA, Wilmington, 1967, PTA mem., New London, Conn., 1968-77; vol. New London Recreation Dept., 1986, Little League, 1970-75; vol. condr. CBA Badminton Tournaments. Inducted into Mitchell Coll. Hall of Fame, 1993. Mem. AAHPERD, Nat. Jr. Coll. Field Hockey Coaches Assn. (pres. 1991—), Nat. Jr. Coll. Men's Tennis Assn., U.S. Badminton Assn., Nat. Assn. Sport and Phys. Edn., Nat. Dance Assn., Nat. Dance-Exercise Instrs. Tng. Assn., Nat. Jr. Coll. Athletic Assn. (chmn. New Eng. region XXI field hockey com. 1975-89, women's field hockey Coach of Yr. region XXI 1975, 78, 79, 80, 81, 83, 84, 90, nat. championships and Nat. Coach of Yr. 1979, 81, 83, 84, 90, Men's Tennis Coach of Yr. Region XXI 1983, 87, 89, 90). Avocations: badminton (ranked player, singles and doubles Conn. Badminton Assn. Top 10, 1981, 83, 84, 85, 86 and 87), tennis, gardening. Home: 43 Bellevue Pl New London CT 06320-4701 Office: Mitchell Coll 437 Pequot Ave New London CT 06320-4452

PINIELLA, LOUIS VICTOR, professional baseball team manager; b. Tampa, Fla., Aug. 28, 1943; m. Anita Garcia, Apr. 12, 1967; children: Lou, Kristi, Derrick. Student, U. Tampa. Baseball player various minor-league teams, 1962-68, Cleve. Indians, 1968, Kansas City Royals, 1969-73; baseball player N.Y. Yankees, 1974-84, coach, 1984-85, mgr., 1985-87, 1988, gen. mgr., 1987-88, spl. advisor, TV announcer, 1989; mgr. Cin. Reds, 1990-92, Seattle Mariners, 1992—. Named to Am. League All-Star Team, 1972; recipient Ellis Island Medal of Honor, 1990; Named A.L. Rookie of the Yr Baseball Writers Assoc of Amer, 1969, Named A.L. Manager of the Yr, 1995. Office: Seattle Mariners PO Box 4100 83 S King St Seattle WA 98104-2875

PINILLA, ANA RITA, neuropsychologist, researcher; b. N.Y.C., May 20, 1957; d. Louis and Luz Maria (Diaz) P.; m. Jorge Rosado Rosado, Dec. 01, 1979; children: Jorge Javier, Juan Carlos, Ana Mari. BS magna cum laude, U. P.R., Rio Piedras, 1978; MS, Caribbean Ctr., San Juan, P.R., 1980, PhD, 1988. Lic. psychologist, P.R. Prof. psychology Inter-Am. U., San Juan, 1980-91; neuropsychologist Neuropsychol. Svcs. to Developmental Deficiencies Children, Bayamon, P.R., 1987-88; asst. dir. Gov.'s Prevention Program, San Juan, 1988-90; exec. dir. Learning Disability Ctr., San Juan, 1990-94; external evaluator prevention program Roberto Clemente Sports City, Carolina, P.R., 1990-95; cons. in edn1. programs Gov.'s Office; adviser, evaluator drug prevention programs, 1994-96; clin. dir. Options, P.R.; cons. in field. Author: Analysis of Wisc-R, 1988; contbr. articles to profl. publs. Mem. Internat. Neuropsychol. Soc., Nat. Acad. Neuropsychology. Achievements include development of program of services to learning disabled children using neuropsychological approach, development of tests for measurement character traits.

PINKEL, DONALD PAUL, pediatrician; b. Buffalo, Sept. 7, 1926; s. Lawrence William and Ann (Richardson) P.; m. Marita Donovan, Dec. 26, 1949 (div. 1981); children: Rebecca, Nancy, Christopher, Mary, Thomas, Anne, Sara, John, Ruth; m. Cathryn Barbara Howarth, May 16, 1981; 1 child, Michael. BS, Canisius Coll., 1947; MD, U. Buffalo, 1951. Diplomate Am. Bd. Pediatrics, Pediatric Hematology and Oncology, Nat. Bd. Med. Examiners. From intern to resident to chief resident Children's Hosp., Buffalo, 1951-54; research fellow Children's Hosp. Med. Ctr., Boston, 1955-56; chief. of pediatrics Roswell Park Meml. Inst., Buffalo, 1956-61; med. dir. St. Jude Children's Research Hosp., Memphis, 1961-73; chmn. pediatrics Med. Coll. Wis., Milw., 1974-78; pediatrician-in-chief Milw. Children's Hosp., 1974-78; chief. of pediatrics City of Hope Med. Ctr., Duarte, Calif., 1978-82; chmn. pediatrics Temple U. Sch. Medicine, Phila., 1982-85; prof., Kana Research chmn., dir. pediatric leukemia program U. Tex. System Cancer Ctr., M.D. Anderson Hosp. and Tumor Inst., Houston, 1985-93; prof. emeritus U. Tex.-M.D. Anderson Cancer Ctr., Houston, 1994—. Contbr. numerous articles to profl. jours. Bd. dirs. Lee County Coop. Clinic, Mariana, Ark., 1972-74. Served with USN, 1944-45, served to 1st lt. U.S. Army, 1954-55. Recipient Albert Lasker award for Med. Research Lasker Found., 1972, Windermere Lectureship Brit. Pediatric Assn., 1974, David Karnofsky award Am. Soc. Clin. Oncology, 1978, Zimmerman prize for Cancer Research Zimmerman Found., 1979, Charles Kettering prize Gen. Motors Cancer Research, 1986, Clin. Rsch. award Am. Cancer Soc., 1988, Return of the Child award Leukemia Soc. Am., 1992. Mem. Am. Pediat. Soc., Am. Assn. Cancer Rsch., Soc. Exptl. Biology and Medicine, Am. Soc. Hematology. Democrat. Roman Catholic. Avocations: swimming, sailing. Home: 2501 Addison Rd Houston TX 77030-1811 Office: Driscoll Children's Hosp 3533 S Alameda St Corpus Christi TX 78411-1721

PINKER, STEVEN A., cognitive science educator; b. Montreal, Que., Can., Sept. 18, 1954; came to U.S., 1976; s. Harry and Roslyn (Wiesenfeld) P. BA, McGill U., Montreal, 1976; PhD, Harvard U., 1979. Asst. prof. Harvard U., Cambridge, Mass., 1980-81, Stanford U., Palo Alto, Calif., 1981-82; prof. cognitive sci. MIT, Cambridge, 1982—. Author: Language Learnability and Language Development, 1984, Learnability and Cognition, 1989, The Language Instinct, 1994, How the Mind Works, 1997; assoc. editor Cognition, 1984—. Recipient grad. teaching award MIT, 1986, Troland Rsch. award NAS, 1993. Fellow AAAS, APA (Disting. Early Career award 1984, Boyd McCandless award 1986, William James Book prize 1995), Linguistics Soc. Am. (Linguistics, Lang. and Pub. Svcs. award 1997), Am. Psychol. Soc. Office: MIT Dept Brain-Cognitive Scis E10-016 Cambridge MA 02139

PINKERTON, HELEN JEANETTE, health care executive; b. Chattanooga, Mar. 17, 1956; d. Jesse Robert and Irene Louise (Boyd) Pinkerton. BS, U. Tenn.-Knoxville, 1979, MPH, 1980. Dir. Hypertension/Diabetes Program Alton Park Health Ctr., Chattanooga, 1981—; bd. dirs. Bethlehem Cmty. Ctr., Hospice of Chattanooga; Contbr. to Tenn. Hypertension Control Manual, 1984, 2nd Edit., 1995. Dir. Choirs, fin. officer First Baptist Ch., Hixson; Community Services Club, 1986— (sec.); mem. Chattanooga Jaycees, Chattanooga Hunger Coalition. Doak scholar, 1977. Mem. NAFE, So. Health Assn., Tenn. Pub. Health Assn., Am. Diabetes Assn. (bd. dirs.), Hypertension Coalition (chmn. 1984—), Am. Cancer Soc. (bd. dirs.), Neighbors for Life (chairperson, Am. Cancer Soc.), Alton Park C. of C. (council mem. 1982-86), Alpha Kappa Alpha. Democrat. Avocations: walking, reading, singing, jogging. Home: 5419 Moody Sawyer Rd Hixson TN 37343-3646 Office: Alton Park Health Ctr 100 E 37th St Chattanooga TN 37410-1401

PINKERTON, LINDA F., lawyer; b. Phila., Dec. 4, 1949; d. Vicotr M. and Callie (Noland) Ferreri; m. Michael S. Foster, June 5, 1984. BA, Duke U., 1971; MA, NYU, 1973; JD, U. Tulsa, 1980. Bar: Calif. 1981, N.C. 1991, N.Y. 1996, U.S. Dist. Ct. (all dists.) Calif., U.S. Ct. Appeals (9th and 10th cirs., U.S. Supreme Ct. Atty. Exxon, Los Angeles, 1980-85; assoc. Pillsbury, Madison & Sutro, San Francisco, Calif., 1985-88; sec., gen. counsel J. Paul Getty Trust, L.A., 1988-94; v.p. and gen. counsel Christie's Inc., N.Y.C., 1995-96. Mem. Internat. Bar Assn. Office: 11 N Market St Asheville NC 28801-2907

PINKERTON, RICHARD LADOYT, management educator; b. Huron, S.D., Mar. 5, 1933; s. Abner Pyle and Orral Claudine (Arneson) P.; m. Sandra Louise Lee, Aug. 28, 1965 (div. 1992); children—Elizabeth, Patricia. B.A. (La Verne Noyes scholar 1952-55), U. Mich., 1955; M.B.A., Case Western Res. U., 1962; Ph.D. (Nat. Assn. Purchasing Mgmt. fellow 1967-68), U. Wis., 1969. Sr. market research analyst Harris-Intertype Corp., Cleve., 1957-61; mgr. sales devel. Triax Corp., Cleve., 1962-64; coordinator mktg. program Mgmt. Inst., U. Wis., 1964-67; dir. exec. programs Mgmt. Inst., U. Wis. (Grad. Sch. Bus.), also asst. prof. mktg., 1969-74; prof. mgmt., dean Grad. Sch. Adminstrn., Capital U., Columbus, Ohio, 1974-86; prof. mgmt., dir. Univ. Bus. Ctr., Craig Sch. of Bus. Calif. State U., Fresno, 1986-89, prof. mktg., 1989—, chair mktg. and logistics dept., 1996—; trustee Ohio Coun. Econ. Edn., 1976-87; bd. dirs. Univ. Bus. Ctr.; cons. to govt. and industry, 1960—. Co-author: The Purchasing Manager's Guide to Strategic Proactive Procurement, 1996; contbr. articles to profl. jours. Bd. dirs. The Fresno Townhouse Assn.; bd. govs. Hannah Neil Home for Children, Columbus, 1975-78. Served as officer USAF, 1955-57, lt. col. USAFR, 1957-78. Mem. Nat. Assn. Contract Mgmt. (chmn. validation cert. com. 1990), Nat. Assn. Purchasing Mgmt. (chmn. acad. planning 1979-84, rsch. symposium 1992), Am. Mktg. Assn. (chpt. pres. 1972-73), Res. Officers Assn., Air Forces Assn., Ft. Washington Golf and Country Club, Beta Gamma Sigma, Alpha Kappa Psi, Phi Gamma Delta, Rotary (Paul Harris fellow). Home: 4721 N Cedar Ave Apt 111 Fresno CA 93726-1007 Office: Calif State U Dept of Mktg Fresno CA 93740-0007

PINKERTON, ROBERT BRUCE, mechanical engineer; b. Detroit, Feb. 10, 1941; s. George Fulwell and Janet Lois (Hedke) P.; m. Barbara Ann Bandfield, Aug. 13, 1966; 1 child, Robert Brent. BSME, Detroit Inst. Tech., 1965; MA in Engring., Chrysler Inst. Engring., 1967; JD, Wayne State U., 1976. From mech. engr. to emissions and fuel economy planning specialist Chrysler Engring. Office Chrysler Corp., Highland Park, Mich., 1967-80; dir. engring. Replacement div. TRW, Inc., Cleve., 1980-83; v.p. engring. TRW Automotive Aftermarket Group, 1983-86; v.p. engring. and rsch. Blackstone Corp., Jamestown, N.Y., 1986-89; pres., CEO Blackstone Corp., Jamestown, 1989-90, Athena Corp., Beaufort, S.C., 1990—, Cedar Crest Corp., Beaufort, S.C., 1990—. Active oper. audit com. Beaufort County; bd. dirs. Village Renaissance, Inc., 1994—; exec. com. Beaufort Schs. Oversight Com., 1995—, Pvt. Industry Coun., 1996—; bd. dirs. Greater Beaufort C. of C., 1997—. Mem. Rotary (Asst. dist. gov. 1997—). Presbyterian. Home: PO Box 2417 Beaufort SC 29901-2417 Office: PO Box 2115 128 Castle Rock Rd Beaufort SC 29401-2115

PINKETT, HAROLD THOMAS, archivist, historian; b. Salisbury, Md., Apr. 7, 1914; s. Levin Wilson and Catherine Pinkett; A.B., Morgan Coll., Balt., 1935; A.M., U. Pa., 1938; Ph.D., Am. U., 1953; m. Lucille Cannady, Apr. 24, 1943. Tchr., Douglass High Sch., Balt., 1936-38; mem. faculty Livingstone Coll., Salisbury, N.C., 1938-39, 41-42; staff and supervising archivist Nat. Archives, Washington, 1942-79; archival cons. Howard u., 1980, cons. Nat. Bus. League, 1981-83, cons., United Negro Coll. Fund, 1984, cons. Nat. Urban League, 1984, cons. Cheyney U., 1984-85, cons. Nat. Assn. for Advancement of colored people, 1986-87, cons. Atlanta U., 1992, cons. Eugene and Agnes Meyer Found., 1993-94; adj. prof. history and archival adminstrn. Howard U., 1970-76, Am. U., 1976-77, lectr. in history, Mary Baldwin Coll. 1986; mem. adv. bd. D.C. Hist. Records, 1978—. Served with AUS, 1943-46. Fellow Council Library Resources, 1972; recipient Exceptional Service award Nat. Archives, 1979. Fellow Soc. Am. Archivists, Forest History Soc. (pres. 1976-78, dir. emeritus 1985—); mem. Agrl. History Soc. (pres. 1982-83, Book award 1968), Am. Hist. Assn., Orgn. Am. Historians, Assn. Study Afro-Am. Life and History, So. History Assn., Am. Forestry Assn., U.S. Capitol Hist. Soc., Nat. Coun. Pub. History, Omega Psi Phi, Sigma Pi Phi. Methodist. Club: Cosmos (Washington). Author: Gifford Pinchot, Private and Public Forester, 1970, National Church of Zion Methodism: A History of John Wesley A.M.E. Zion Church, 1989; editor: Research in the Administration of Public Policy, 1975, The Am. Archivist, 1968-71. Address: 5741 27th St NW Washington DC 20015-1101

PINKETT, JADA, actress. Appeared in films Jason's Lyric, 1994, A Low Down Dirty Shame, 1994, Tales From The Crypt Presents Demon Knight, 1995, The Nutty Professor, 1996, Set It Off, 1996. Office: United Talent Agy 9560 Wilshire Blvd 5th Fl Beverly Hills CA 90212*

PINKHAM, DANIEL, composer; b. Lynn, Mass., June 5, 1923; s. Daniel R. and Olive C. (White) P. A.B., M.A., Harvard, 1944; Litt.D. (hon.), Nebr. Wesleyan U., 1976; Mus.D. (hon.), Adrian Coll., 1977, Westminster Choir Coll., 1979, New Eng. Conservatory, 1993, Ithaca Coll., 1994. Mem. faculty New Eng. Conservatory Music, 1959—; music dir. King's Chapel, Boston, 1958—; co-founder Cambridge Festival Orch., 1948. Composer: Sonatas for Organ and Strings, 1943, 54, 86, Piano Concertino, 1950, Concerto for Celesta and Harpsichord, 1954, Wedding Cantata, 1956, Christmas Cantata, 1958, Easter Cantata, 1961, Symphonies, 1961, 64, 85, Signs of the Zodiac, 1964, St. Mark Passion, 1965, Jonah, 1966, In the Beginning of Creation, 1970, Ascension Cantata, 1970, Organ Concerto, 1970, When the Morning Stars Sang Together, 1971, the Other Voices of the Trumpet, 1971, Safe in Their Alabaster Chambers, 1972, To Troubled Friends, 1972, Daniel in the Lions' Den, 1973, The Seven Deadly Sins, 1974, Four Elegies, 1974, The Passion of Judas, 1975, Garden Party, 1976, Blessings, 1977, Company at the Creche, 1977, Miracles, 1978, Epiphanies, 1978, Serenades, 1979, Proverbs, 1979, Diversions for Organ and Harp, 1980, Descent Into Hell, 1980, Before the Dust Returns, 1981, The Death of the Witch of Endor, 1981, Prelude and Scherzo for Wind Quintet, 1981, The Dreadful Dining Car, 1982, Brass Quintet, 1983, In Heaven Soaring Up, 1985, The Left-Behind Beasts, 1985, A Biblical Book of Beasts, 1985, Versets, 1985, A Mast for the Unicorn, 1986, A Crimson Flourish, 1986, Winter Nights, 1986, De Profundis, 1986, In the Isles of the Sea, 1986, Antiphons, 1987, Getting To Heaven, 1987, Angels Are Everywhere, 1987, Heav'n Must Go Home, 1988, Four Marian Antiphons, 1988, Alleluias, 1988, Sonata da Chiesa, 1988, Sonata da Camera, 1988, Petitions, 1988, Pedals, 1988, The Seasons Pass, 1988, Reeds, 1988, Concerto Piccolo, 1989, The Small Passion, 1989, Requiem Collects, 1989, The Saints Preserve Us!, 1989, String Quartet, 1989, Stabat Mater, 1990, Symphony Number 4, 1990, The Book of Hours, 1990, Carols and Cries, 1990, The Dryden Te Deum, 1990, Pentecost Cantata, 1991, Three Canticles from Luke, 1991, For Solace in Solitude, 1991, Advent Cantata, 1991, Smart Set, 1991, First Organbook, 1991, The Small Requiem, 1991, Second Organbook, 1992, Christmas Symphonies, 1992, Overture Concertante, 1992, Nocturnes for Flute and Guitar, 1992, Vowels, 1993, Adagietto for Organ and Strings, 1993, Wondrous Love, 1993, When Love Was Gone, 1993, Missa Domestica, 1993, Miserere mei Deus, 1993, The Guiding Star, 1994, The Creation of the World, 1994, Reed Trio, 1994, Morning Music, 1994, Organ Concerto Number Two, 1995, Preludes for Piano, 1995, Passion Music, 1995, The Tenth Muse, 1995, The Inner Room of the Soul, 1995, Festive Processional, 1995, The White Raven, 1996, O Come, Emanuel, 1996, Called Home, 1996, Organ Concerto Number Three, 1996, Tidings, 1996, Divertimento, 1997, Sagas, 1997. Fellow Am. Acad. Arts and Scis.; mem. Am. Guild Organists (past dean Boston chpt.). Home: 150 Chilton St Cambridge MA 02138-1227

PINKHAM, ELEANOR HUMPHREY, retired university librarian; b. Chgo., May 7, 1926; d. Edward Lemuel and Grace Eleanor (Cushing) Humphrey; m. James Hansen Pinkham, July 10, 1948; children: Laurie Sue, Carol Lynn. AB, Kalamazoo Coll., 1948; MS in Library Sci. (Alice Louise LeFevre scholar), Western Mich. U., 1967. Pub. svcs. libr. Kalamazoo Coll., 1967-68, asst. libr., 1969-70, libr. dir., 1971-93, ret. 1993; vis. lectr. Western Mich. U. Sch. Librarianship, 1970-84; mem. adv. bd., 1977-81, also adv. bd. Inst. Cistercian Studies Libr., 1975-80. Mem. ALA, AAUP, ACRL (chmn. coll. libr. sect. 1988-89), Mich. Libr. Assn. (pres. 1983-84, chmn. acad. div. 1977-78), Mich. Libr. Consortium (exec. coun. 1974-82, chmn. 1977-78, Mich. Libr. of Yr 1986), OCLC Users Coun., Beta Phi Mu. Home: 2519 Glenwood Dr Kalamazoo MI 49008-2405

PINKHAM, FREDERICK OLIVER, foundation executive, consultant; b. Ann Arbor, Mich., June 16, 1920; s. Frederick Oliver and Leah Winifred (Hallett) P.; m. Helen Kostia, June 20, 1943; children: Peter James, Gail Louise, Steven Howard. AB, Kalamazoo Coll., 1942, LLD (hon.), 1958; MA, Stanford U., 1947, EdD, 1950; LLD (hon.), Lawrence Coll., 1957; DSc (hon.), Ripon Coll., 1990. Tchr., counselor Sequoia Union High Sch., Redwood City, Calif., 1947-49; researcher Stanford (Calif.) Consultation Service, 1949-50; asst. to pres. George Washington U., 1950-51; exec. sec. Nat. Commn. on Accrediting, 1951-55; pres. Ripon (Wis.) Coll., 1955-66; dir. The Yardstick Project, Cleve., 1966-67; v.p., dir. Western Pub. Co., 1967-70; founder, pres. Edn. Mgmt. Services, Inc., 1970-76; asst. adminstr. for population and humanitarian affairs AID, Dept. State, 1976-77; chmn., pres. Population Crisis Com., 1977-87; assoc. dir. Inst. for Population and Resource Studies, Stanford U., 1987-90; program officer David and Lucile Packard Found., 1988-92; cons. for population David and Lucille Packard Found., Los Altos, Calif., 1993—; cons. True North Found., Portland, Oreg., 1993—, Compton Found., Menlo Park, Calif., 1996—, Mgmt. Scis. for Health, 1994—, Poptech, Washington, 1995, Neogen Investors LP, San Diego, 1997—; v.p., dir. rsch. Ednl. Recs. Bur., Darien, Conn., 1970-72; founder, pres. Edn. Mgmt. Svcs., Inc., 1970-76; v.p., co-founder World Bus. Coun., 1970-77; pres. Capital Higher Edn. Svc., 1975-76; pres., dir. The Omni Group, 1977-83; treas., co-founder Monterey Peninsula Coll. Found., 1994—; bd. dirs. N.D. Mgmt., Inc. of Neogen Investors L.P., San Diego. Chmn. Wisconsin adv. com. Nat. Commn. on Civil Rights.; bd. visitors Air U.; pres. Wis. Found of Ind. Colls.; chmn. Assn. Colls. Midwest, Midwest Coll. Council; sec., trustee, mem. exec. com. Young Pres.'s Found.; chmn. task force on fgn. assistance Pres.'s Pvt. Sector Survey on Cost Control (Grace Commn.); chmn. bd. Global Tomorrow Coalition, 1985-89; bd. dirs. Internat. Human Assistance Programs, N.Y.C., 1984-87, Mineral Fibre Internat. and Kings Mills Internat., 1986-90, Mgmt. Scis. for Health, 1997—, Neogen Investors, San Diego, 1997—; v.p. Big Sur Land Trust, 1990—; trustee, co-founder Monterey Peninsula Found., Monterey, 1995— . Served with AUS, 1942-45, ETO. Decorated Bronze Star, Purple Heart. Mem. Young Pres. Orgn. (nat. sec., dir., exec. com.), Soc. Internat. Devel., Nat. Heritage Soc. (watchkeeper, bd. dirs.), Old Capital Club Monterey, Calif. (gov.). Home and Office: 25715 Rio Vista Dr Carmel CA 93923-8811

PINKNEY, D. TIMOTHY, investment company executive; b. Long Beach, Calif., June 6, 1948; s. Robert Patten and Mary (Chernus) P.; m. Nancy Dianne Fisher, Aug. 21, 1971; 1 child, Heather Anne. BA, Calif. Luth. U., 1970; MA, Pepperdine U., 1976. CFP. Membership mgr. Seattle C. of C., 1977-79; v.p. mktg. John L. Scott Investment, Bellevue, Wash., 1980-81, SRH Fin., Bellevue, 1981-82, Foster Investment Co., Bellevue, 1982-83; pres., CEO Footprint Fin. Planning, Bellevue, 1983-88, Sheppard & Assocs. Personal Fin. Advs., Bellevue, 1988-91; mgr. and v.p. asset mgmt. div. U.S. Bank, Tacoma, Wash., 1991-92; v.p., Calif. mgr. trust and investment mgmt. U.S. Bank of Calif., Sacramento, 1992-96; prin. Savant/Russell, Inc., Citrus Heights, Calif., 1996—; founder, chief exec. officer Wealth Link Enterprises. Author: book, video and cassete series Pathways to Wealth, Yes IRA's Still Make Cent$?, 1988. Co-chmn. Fin. Independence Week, Western Wash., 1987; bd. dirs. Traveler's Aid Soc., A United Way Agy., Seattle, 1988, pacesetter United Way, 1988-91; alumni class steward Calif. Luth. U., 1992, 93; chmn., bd. dirs. Friends Scouting, Golden Empire coun. Boy Scouts Am., v.p. fin., 1997. Lt. USN, 1970-77, comdr. USNR, ret., 1992. Selected as Jr. Officer of Yr., USNR, 1984, 85. Mem. Nat. Spkrs. Assn. (bd. dirs. N.W. chpt. 1992), Internat. Assn. Fin. Planning (chmn. West Region 1987-90, pres. Western Wash. chpt. 1986-87), Seattle Soc. (CPFs (bd. dirs. 1985-86), Inst. CFPs, Real Estate Securities and Syndication Inst. (v.p. 1980-83), East King County and Pierce County Estate Planning Coun., Seattle Res. Officer Assn. (pres., v.p. 1983-85), Puget Sound Naval Res. Assn. (v.p. 1985-90), Sacramento Rotary (chmn. edn. com. 1994), Sacramento Rotary Found. (bd. dirs. 1996), Seattle Rotary (bd. dirs., chmn. membership devel. com.). Avocations: flying gliders, giant pumpkin growing and sculpting, photography.

PINN, VIVIAN W., pathologist, federal agency administrator; b. Halifax, Va., 1941. BA, Wellesley Coll., 1963; MD, U. Va., 1967. Intern in pathology Mass. Gen. Hosp., Boston, 1967-68, rschr. in pathology, 1968-70; asst. pathologist Tufts U. New England Med. Ctr. Hosp., 1970-77, pathologist, 1977-82; from asst. to assoc. prof. pathology Tufts U., 1971-82, asst. dean student affairs, 1974-82; prof., dept. chair pathology Howard U., 1982-91; first dir. Office Rsch. on Women's Health, NIH, Bethesda, Md., 1991-94, assoc. dir. women's health rsch., 1994—. Office: NIH Office Rsch on Women's Health 9000 Rockville Pike Rm 201 Bethesda MD 20814-1436

PINNELL, SHELDON RICHARD, physician, medical educator; b. Dayton, Ohio, Feb. 3, 1937; s. Jacob and Nevella P.; m. Doren Madey, 1983; children: Kevin, Alden, Tyson. AB, Duke U., 1959; MD, Yale U., 1963. Intern in medicine U. Minn. Hosp., Mpls., 1963-65; resident in dermatology Harvard U., Boston, 1968-71; prof. medicine Duke U. Med. Ctr., Durham, N.C., 1978—, chief div. dermatology, 1982—; asst. prof. of biochemistry, 1988—, J. Lamar Callaway prof. dermatology, 1989—; med. dir. Fibrogen, 1994—. Contbr. over 100 articles to profl. jours.; four patents in field. Office: Duke U Med Ctr PO Box 3135 Durham NC 27715-3135

PINNEY, SIDNEY DILLINGHAM, JR., lawyer; b. Hartford, Conn., Nov. 17, 1924; s. Sydney Dillingham and Louisa (Griswold) Wells P.; m. Judith Munch, Sept. 30, 1990; children from previous marriage: William Griswold, David Rees. Student, Amherst Coll., 1941-43, Brown U., 1943; also, M.I.T., 1943-44; BA cum laude, Amherst Coll., 1947; LLB, Harvard U., 1950. Bar: Conn. 1950. Pvt. practice Hartford, 1950; assoc. Shepherd, Murtha and Merritt, Hartford, 1950-53; ptnr. Shepherd, Murtha and Merritt (name changed to Murtha, Cullina, Richter and Pinney 1967), 1953-92, of counsel, 1993—; lectr. on estate planning. Contbr. to: Estate Planning mag. Bd. dirs. Greater Hartford Area TB and Respiratory Diseases Health Soc., 1956-69, pres., 1966-67; mem. Wethersfield (Conn.) Town Coun., 1958-62; trustee Hartford Conservatory Music, 1967-71, 75-81; trustee, pres. Historic Wethersfield Found., 1961-81; bd. dirs. Hartford Hosp., 1971-80, adv. bd., 1980—; mem. adv. coun. Jefferson House, 1978-82; mem. Mortensen Libr. Bd. of Visitors U. Hartford, 1984—; corporator Hartford Pub. Libr., 1969—, Renbrook Sch., West Hartford, Conn., 1970-75. 1st lt. USAF, 1943-46. Fellow Am. Coll. Trust and Estate Counsel; mem. ABA, Nat. Acad. Elder Law Attys., Conn. Bar Assn. (exec. com. elder law sect.), Hartford County Bar Assn. Republican. Congregationalist. Office: City Place 185 Asylum St Hartford CT 06103-3402

PINNEY, THOMAS CLIVE, English language educator; b. Ottawa, Kans., Apr. 23, 1932; s. John James and Lorene Maude (Owen) P.; m. Sherrill Marie Ohman, Sept. 1, 1956; children—Anne, Jane, Sarah. B.A., Beloit Coll., Wis., 1954; Ph.D., Yale U., New Haven, 1960. Instr. Hamilton Coll., Clinton, N.Y., 1957-61; instr. English Yale U., New Haven, 1961-62; asst. prof. to prof., chmn. dept. English Pomona Coll., Claremont, Calif., 1962—. Editor: Essays of George Eliot, 1963, Selected Writings of Thomas Babington Macaulay, 1972, Letters of Macaulay, 1974-81, Kipling's India, 1986, A History of Wine in America, 1989, Kipling's Something of Myself, 1990, Letters of Rudyard Kipling, 1990, The Vineyards and Wine Cellars of California, 1994, The Wine of Santa Cruz Island, 1994. Guggenheim fellow, 1966, 84,Recipient Disting. Svc. citation Beloit Coll., 1984; fellow NEH, 1980; grantee Am. Coun. Learned Socs., 1974, 84, Am. Philos. Soc., 1968, 82, 94. Mem. MLA, Elizabethan Club (New Haven), Zamorano Club (L.A.), Phi Beta Kappa. Home: 228 W Harrison Ave Claremont CA 91711-4323 Office: Pomona Coll Dept English Claremont CA 91711

PINO, H. EDUARDO, clinical psychologist; b. Santiago, Chile, Sept. 25, 1949; came to U.S., 1968; s. Orozimbo and Sylvia (Garrido) P. BS, St. Joseph's U., Phila., 1973; MS, Hahnemann Med. Coll., 1977; D in Psychology, Hahnemann U. and Hosp. (now called Allegheny U. Health Scis.), 1985; cert. in mediation, Phila. Child Custody Mediation project and Temple U. Law Sch., 1990. Bd. cert. forensic examiner Am. Bd. Forensic Examiners; diplomate Am. Coll. Forensic Examiners. Psychiat. asst. part-time Hahnemann Hosp. Emergency Rm., Phila., 1975-76; psychol. examiner Hahnemann Cmty. Mental Health Ctr., Phila., 1975-78; sr. clin. psychol. intern Montgomery County Emergency Svcs., Norristown, Pa., 1982-84, staff psychologist part-time, 1983-84; staff psychotherapist CAMCARE Health Corp., Camden and Pennsauken, N.J., 1984-85; forensic psychologist Lenape Valley Found., Bucks County, Pa., 1985-86; staff psychologist Eagleville (Pa) Hosp., 1985; cons. clin. psychologist Eugenia Hosp., Flourtown, Pa., 1984-86; ct. clin. psychologist Ct. of Common Pleas, Phila., 1986-91; pvt. practice Phila., 1991—; cons. in group treatment for sexual offenders and individual victims of sexual abuse Joseph J. Peters Inst., Phila., 1991—. Contbr. articles to profl. jours. Recipient award for Outstanding Achievement and Accomplishment in Scholarship Rotary Internat. Fellow Pa. Psychol. Assn. (mem. editl. com. 1989—, cons. editor 1989-90, 91-92, 92-93, 94—); mem. APA (internat. affairs com. chairperson psychology law divsn. 1990-91, 91-92, psychol. hypnosis divsn. 1993—), APHA, Am. Orthopsychiat. Assn., Am. Profl. Soc. on Abuse of Children, Internat. Soc. Family Law, Internat. Soc. Study Dissociation (Phila. study group for MPD and Dissociative States 1992—). Avocations: nature, arts and music, international and multicultural issues on mental health and professional ethics. Office: PO Box 2130 Philadelphia PA 19103-0130

PINO, ROBERT SALVATORE, radiologist; b. Bklyn., May 20, 1939; s. Carmine M. and Olga (Aversa) P. BA, NYU, 1960; MD, SUNY, 1960. Diplomate Am. Bd. Pediatrics, Am. Bd. Radiology. Intern N.Y. Hosp., N.Y.C., 1964-65, resident pediatrics, 1965-67; pvt. practice pediatrics Ft. Lee, N.J., 1969-74; resident radiology N.Y. Hosp., N.Y.C., 1974-76, chief resident radiology, 1976-77; radiologist St. Mary's Hosp., Passaic, N.J., 1977—, dir. radiology, 1986—. Maj. U.S. Army, 1967-69. Home: 2055 Center Ave Fort Lee NJ 07024-4948 Office: St Marys Hosp 211 Pennington Ave Passaic NJ 07055-4617

PINSKER, WALTER, allergist, immunologist; b. Bay Shore, N.Y., Mar. 27, 1933; s. Albert and Irene (Kuchlick) P.; m. Tillene Giller, June 15, 1958; children: Neil, Andrew, Susann. BA, U. Rochester, 1954; MD, Chgo. Med. Sch. U. Health Sci., 1958. Diplomate Am. Bd. Allergy and Immunology. Intern L.I. Jewish Hosp., New Hyde Park, N.Y., 1958-59; resident internal medicine Bklyn. VA Hosp., 1959-60; resident internal medicine Long Beach (Calif.) VA Hosp., 1960-61, resident allergy and immunology, 1961-62; chief of allergy Letterman Army Hosp., San Francisco, 1962-64; pres. Bay Shore Allergy Group, 1964-94; attending physician Mather Hosp., Port Jefferson, N.Y., St. Charles Hosp., Port Jefferson, 1981, Southside Hosp., Bay Shore, 1964—, Good Samaritan Hosp., West Islip, N.Y., 1964—, asst. clin. prof. medicine SUNY, Stony Brook, 1968—; mem. physicians adv. com. Group Health, 1997—. Contbr. articles to profl. jours. Bd. visitors Pilgrim State Hosp., Brentwood, N.Y., 1974-77; pres. Suffolk Assn. Children with Learning Difficulties, N.Y., 1972-74; trustee Leeway Sch., Stony Brook, 1974-75, Bay Shore Jewish Ctr., 1974-84; com. for handicapped West Islip Schs., 1971—. Capt. U.S. Army, 1962-64. Named Co-Humanitarian of Yr. L.I. Adults and Children with Learning and Developmental Disabilities, 1994; recipient Physician's Recognition award AMA, 1969—. Fellow Am. Acad. Allergy and Immunology, Am. Coll. Allergy and Immunology, Am. Assn. Certified Allergists, Am. Coll. Chest Physicians, Am. Assn.- Study of Headaches, N.Y. Acad. Scis., Suffolk Acad. Medicine, Nassau-Suffolk Allergy Soc. (officer, bd. dirs. 1970—, pres. 1980-82). Avocations: golf, boating, photography. Office: Bay Shore Allergy Group P C 649 W Montauk Hwy Bay Shore NY 11706-8222

PINSKY, MICHAEL S., lawyer; b. Chgo., July 25, 1945; s. Joseph and Irene (Sodakoff) P.; m. Judy R. Rabin, Sept. 29, 1974; children: David, Susie, Jodie. BS, U. Ill., 1967; JD, DePaul U., 1971. Bar: Ill. 1971. Conferee, revenue agt. IRS, Chgo., 1967-72; ptnr. Levenfeld & Kanter, Chgo., 1972-80, Levenfeld, Eisenberg Janger, Chgo., 1980-84, Vedder Price, Kaufman & Kammholz, Chgo., 1984-88, Gottlieb & Schwartz, Chgo., 1989-92; with Levin & Schreder, Chgo., 1993—. Bd. dirs. Better Boys Found., Chgo., 1989-96. Mem. Am. Bar Assn., Assn. of Bar of State of Ill., Assn. of Bar of City of Chgo. (com. chmn. 1984-86). Office: 30 N La Salle St Ste 3526 Chicago IL 60602-2507

PINSKY, ROBERT NEAL, poet, educator; b. Long Branch, N.J., Oct. 20, 1940; s. Milford Simon and Sylvia (Eisenberg) P.; m. EllenJane Bailey, Dec. 30, 1961; children: Nicole, Caroline, Elizabeth. B.A., Rutgers U., 1962; Ph.D., Stanford U., 1966. Mem. English faculty U. Chgo., 1967-68, Wellesley Coll., 1968-80; prof. English U. Calif., Berkeley, 1980-89; prof. Boston U., 1980-89, prof. creative writing, 1989—; poetry editor New Republic mag., 1978; vis. lectr. Harvard U.; Hurst prof. Washington U., St. Louis. Author: Landor's Poetry, 1968, Sadness and Happiness, 1975, The Situation of Poetry, 1977, An Explanation of America, 1980, History of My Heart, 1984, Poetry and the World, 1988, The Want Bone, 1990, The Inferno of Dante, 1994, The Figured Wheel: New and Collected Poems 1966-1996, 1996. Recipient Artists award Am. Acad. Arts and Letters, 1979; Saxifrage prize, 1980; William Carlos Williams prize, 1984; Shelley Meml. award, 1996; Guggenheim fellow, 1980; appointed U.S. poet laureate, 1997. Mem. AAAS, PEN. Office: Boston U English Dept 236 Bay State Rd Boston MA 02215-1403

PINSKY, STEVEN MICHAEL, radiologist, educator; b. Milw., Feb. 2, 1942; s. Leo Donald and Louise Miriam (Faldberg) P.; m. Sue Brona Rosenzweig, June 12, 1966; children—Mark Burton, Lisa Rachel. BS, U. Wis., 1964; MD, Loyola U., Chgo., 1967. Resident in radiology and nuclear medicine U. Chgo., 1968-70, chief resident in diagnostic radiology, 1970-71, asst. prof., 1973-77, then assoc. prof. radiology and medicine, 1977-84, prof., 1984-89; prof., chmn. dept. radiology U. Ill., 1989— ; dir. nuclear medicine Michael Reese Med. Ctr., Chgo., 1973-87, vice-chmn. radiology, 1984-87, chmn. radiology, 1987-93, v.p. med. staff, 1986-87, pres., 1988-89, trustee, 1984-86, 90-93; dir. nuclear medicine tech. program Triton Coll., River Grove, Ill., 1974-87. Contbr. chpts. to books, articles to med. jours. Rsch. fellow Am. Cancer Soc., 1969-70. Maj., M.C., U.S. Army, 1971-73. Fellow Am. Coll. Nuclear Physicians (Ill. del., treas. 1982-84), Am. Coll. Radiology (alt. councilor 1986-92, councilor 1993—); mem. Soc. Nuclear Medicine (trustee 1979-87, pres. central chpt. 1980-81), Radiologic Soc. N.Am. (councilor 1994—, chmn. tech. exhibits com. 1994-96, edn. coun. 1994-96), Ill. Radiologic Soc. (sec./treas. 1992-94, pres.-elect 1994-95, pres. 1995-96). Office: U Ill Hosp 1740 W Taylor St Chicago IL 60612-7232

PINSOF, NATHAN, retired advertising executive; b. Havana, Cuba, July 16, 1926; came to U.S., 1928, naturalized, 1952; s. Oscar and Rose (Newman) P.; m. Barbara Cohn, Oct. 28, 1956; children—Ellen, Diane. Student, City Jr. Coll., Chgo., 1944-46; M.B.A., U. Chgo., 1949. Asst. controller Stineway Drugs, 1949-51; mgr. media dept. Weiss & Geller, 1953-60; sr. v.p., media dir. Edward H. Weiss & Co., 1960-67; v.p., mgr. media dept. J. Walter Thompson, 1967-69; sr. v.p., dir. media and fin. Grey-Chgo., Inc., Chgo., 1969-75; exec. v.p. Grey-Chgo., Inc., 1975-88, Lois/USA, Chgo., 1989-92; ret., 1992. Bd. dirs. Off The Street Club; trustee North Shore Cong. Israel.; Bd. dirs. Jewish Children's Bur.; chmn. communications div. Jewish United Fund, 1978-79. Served with U.S. Army, 1951-53. Clubs: B'nai B'rith, The Arts of Chicago. Home: 3900 Mission Hills Rd Apt 101 Northbrook IL 60062-5721

PINSON, ARTIE FRANCES, elementary school educator; b. Rusk, Tex., June 20, 1933; d. Tom and Minerva (McDuff) Neeley; m. Robert H. Pinson, Dec. 14, 1963 (div. Nov. 1967); 1 child, Deidre R. BA magna cum laude, Tex. Coll., 1953; postgrad., U. Tex., 1956, North Tex. U., 1958, 63, New Eng. Conservatory, 1955, 57, 59, 62, Tex. So. U., 1971-72; MEd, U. Houston, 1970. Music tchr. Bullock High Sch., LaRue, Tex., 1953-59; music tchr., 9th grade English tchr. Story High Sch., Palestine, Tex., 1959-64; 3d to 6th grade gifted and talented math. tchr. Turner Elem. Sch., Houston, 1964-66; 3d, 5th and 6th grade tchr. Kay Elem. Sch., Houston, 1966-70; 6th grade tchr. Pilgrim Elem. Sch., Houston, 1970-75; 3d to 6th grade math. tchr. Pleasantville Elem. Sch., Houston, 1975-79; kindergarten to 5th grade computer/math. tchr. Betsy Ross Elem. Sch., Houston, 1979—, instrnl. coord., tchr. technologist; instrnl. coord.; lead tchr. math./sci. program Shell/Houston Ind. Sch. Dist., 1986-87, Say "Yes" program, 1988-89; math. tchr. summer potpourri St. Francis Xavier Cath. Ch., 1991; math. tchr. sci. and engring. awareness and coll. prep. program Tex. So. U., 1993, 94, 95, 96; presenter confs. in field; condr. tchr. tng. workshops. Author computer software in field; contbr. articles to mags. Musician New Hope Bapt. Ch., Houston, 1991—, Sunday sch. tchr.; pianist Buckner Bapt. Haven Nursing Home, Houston, 1990-91; mem. N.E. Concerned Citizens Civic League. Recipient Excellence in Math. Teaching award Exxon Corp., 1990. Mem. Assn. African Am. Math. Educators (Salute to Math. Tchrs. award 1991, treas. 1991-93, sec. 1993—), Nat. Coun. Tchrs. Math., Tex. Coun. Tchrs. Math. (Excellence in Math. Tchg. award 1988), Houston Coun. Tchrs. of Math. (Excellence in Math. Tchg. award 1993), Heoines of Jericho, Palestine Negro Bus. and Profl. Women (charter mem.). Avocations: needlework, number puzzles, piano, photography, gardening. Hom: 5524 Makeig St Houston TX 77026-4021 Office: Betsy Ross Elem Sch 2819 Bay St Houston TX 77026-3203

PINSON, CHARLES WRIGHT, transplant surgeon, educator; b. Albuquerque, May 29, 1952; s. Ernest Alexander and Jean Elizabeth (Farnsworth) P. Student, Miami U., Oxford, Ohio, 1970-72; BA, U. Colo., Boulder, 1972, MBA, 1976; MD, Vanderbilt U., 1980. Diplomate Am. Bd. Surgery, Nat. Bd. Med. Examiners, Tenn., Mass., Oreg. Resident gen. surgery Oreg. Health Scis. U., Portland, 1980-86; fellow gastrointestinal surgery Lahey Clinic, Burlington, Mass., 1986-87; fellow transplant surgery Harvard U., Boston, 1987-88; dir. liver transplant program Vets. Affairs Western region, Portland, 1989-90, Oreg. Health Scis. U., Portland, 1988-90; interim chmn. dept. surgery Vanderbilt U., Nashville, 1993-95, chief divsn. hepatobiliary surgery and liver transplantation, 1990—, vice chmn. dept. surgery, 1995—; dir. Vanderbilt Transplant Ctr., Nashville, 1993—; chmn. med. bd. Vanderbilt U. Med. Ctr., Nashville, 1997—; mem. adv. bd. Pacific N.W. Transplant Bank, Portland, 1989-90, Tenn. Donor Svcs., Nashville, 1991—. Contbr. articles to profl. jours., chpts. to books. Bd. dirs. ARC, Nashville, 1992-94, Am. Liver Found., 1992—. Postdoctoral fellow Am. Heart Assn., Oreg., 1983-84. Mem. Soc. Univ. Surgeons, Soc. Surg. Oncology, Am. Soc. Transplant Surgeons, Am. Soc. Study of Liver Diseases, Am. Gastroenterological Assn., Am. Hepatopancreatobiliary Assn. (exec. com. 1997—), Am. Physiologic Soc., So. Med. Assn. (chmn. sect. surgery 1997—), So. Surg. Assn., Western Surg. Assn., North Pacific Surg. Assn. (sci. program 1990-92), Assn. Acad. Surgery, Soc. Surgery of Alimentary Tract, Internat. Liver Transplantation Soc., Sigma Xi, Phi Beta Kappa, Alpha Omega Alpha. Office: Vanderbilt Transplant Ctr 801 Oxford House Nashville TN 37232

PINSON, ELLIS REX, JR., chemist, consultant; b. Wichita, Kans., Oct. 23, 1925; s. Ellis Rex and Vivian (Neal) P.; m. Betty Ann Hogarth, Dec. 4, 1954; children: Matthew, Martha Pinson Salander, Thomas. B.Sc., U. of South, 1948; Ph.D., U. Rochester, 1951. Research chemist Pfizer Inc., Groton, Conn., 1951-59; project leader Pfizer Inc., 1959-61, sect. mgr., 1961-65, asst. dir. pharmacology research, 1965-67, dir. pharmacology research, 1967-71, dir. research, 1971-72, v.p. medicinal products research and devel., 1972-81; exec. v.p. Pfizer Cen. Research, 1981-86; cons., 1986—. Contbr. articles to profl. jours. Trustee Waterford Pub. Libr., 1980—, pres., 1988-93; bd. dirs., exec. com. Am. Indsl. Health Coun., 1980-86; bd. dirs. S.E. Area Tech. Devel. Ctr., 1992—. With USNR, 1943-46. Fellow N.Y. Acad. Scis.; mem. Am. Chem. Soc., AAAS, Am. Soc. Pharmacology and Exptl. Therapeutics, Phi Beta Kappa, Sigma Xi. Club: Baker Street Irregulars. Patentee in field. Office: Pfizer Inc Eastern Point Rd Groton CT 06340

PINSON, JERRY D., lawyer; b. Harrison, Ark., Sept. 7, 1942; s. Robert L. and Cleta (Keeter) P.; m. Jane Ellis, Sept. 11, 1964; 1 child, Christopher Clifton. BA, U. Ark., 1964, JD, 1967. Bar: Ark. 1967, U.S. Ct. Appeals (8th cir.) 1967, U.S. Supreme Ct. 1967, U.S. Dist. Ct. (ea. and we. dists.) Ark. 1968. Dep. atty. gen. State of Ark., Little Rock, 1967-70; ptnr. Pinson & Reeves, Harrison, 1970-88; sole practice Harrison, 1988—; spl. justice Ark. Supreme Ct., 1991, 94. Pres. United Way Boone County, Harrison, 1974. Mem. ABA, Am. Judicature Soc., Assn. Trial Lawyers Am., Ark. Bar Assn., Boone County Bar Assn., Harrison C. of C. (sec. bd. dirs. 1977). Lodge: Rotary (bd. dirs. 1975, v.p. 1976, pres. 1977). Office: Atty at Law PO Box 1111 Harrison AR 72601

PINSON, LARRY LEE, pharmacist; b. Van Nuys, Calif., Dec. 5, 1947; s. Leland J. and Audrey M. (Frett) P.; m. Margaret K. Pinson, Mar. 18, 1972; children: Scott C., Kelly E. Student, U. Calif., Davis, 1967-69; AA, Am. River Coll., Sacramento, 1969; PharmD, U. Calif., San Francisco, 1973. Staff pharmacist/asst. dir. pharm. svcs. St. Mary's Hosp., Reno, 1973-77; chief pharmacist May Ang Base USAF, 1973-77; owner/chief pharmacist Silverada Pharmacy, Reno, 1979—; adj. prof. Idaho State U., Pocatello, 1989—; cons. pharmacist Physicians Hosp., 1974-93, Reno Med. Plaza, 1973—; pharmacist coordinator Intensive Pharm. Svcs., 1986-87; cons. Calif. Dept. Health & Corrections, Susanville, 1975-76, Nev. Med. Care Adv. Bd., Carson City, 1984-87; provider and reviewer Nev. State Bd. Pharmacy, Reno, 1975-84; instr. we. Nev. Cmty. Coll., 1974-76; cons. Rural Calif. Hosp. Assn., 1973-74. Co-author: Care of Hickman Catheter, 1984. Apptd. by Gov. Bob Miller, Nev. State Bd. Pharmacy, 1995—, pres., 1996—; mem. Nev. Arthritis Found.; bd. dirs. Am. Cancer Soc., 1986—; softball coach Reno/Sparks Recreation Dept., 1973—; cubmaster Pack 153, Verdi, nev.; scoutmaster com. chmn. Reno troop 1, Boy Scouts Am., 1988-92. Recipient Bow of Hygeia award (Pharmacist of the Year), Nev. Pharmacists Assn. and A.H. Robbins Co., 1984. Mem. Nat. Assn. Bds. of Pharmacy, Am. Pharm. Assn., Nev. Pharmacists Assn. (pres. 1981-82), Nev. Profl. Stds. Rev. Orgn., Greater Nev. Health Sys. Agy., Kappa Psi. Avocations: skiing, fishing, backpacking, softball, golf. Home: PO Box 478 Verdi NV 89439-0478 Office: Silverada Pharmacy 2005 Silverada Blvd Ste 160 Reno NV 89512-2057

PINSON, WILLIAM MEREDITH, JR., pastor, writer; b. Ft. Worth, Aug. 3, 1934; s. William Meredith and Ila Lee (Jones) P.; m. Bobbie Ruth Judd, June 4, 1955; children: Meredith Pinson Creasey, Allison Pinson Hopgood. BA, U. N. Tex., 1955; BD, Southwestern Bapt. Theol. Sem., Ft. Worth, 1959, ThD, 1963, MDiv, 1973; LittD (hon.), Calif. Bapt. Coll., Riverside, 1978; DD (hon.), U. Mary Hardin-Baylor, Belton, Tex., 1984; LHD (hon.), Howard Payne U., Brownwood, Tex., 1986; LittD (hon.), Dallas Bapt. U., 1990. Ordained to ministry Bapt. Ch., 1955. Assoc. sec. Christian Life Commn., Dallas, 1957-63; prof. Christian ethics Southwestern Bapt. Theol. Sem., Ft. Worth, 1963-75; pastor First Bapt. Ch., Wichita Falls, Tex., 1975-77; pres. Golden Gate Bapt. Theol. Sem., Mill Valley, Calif., 1977-82; exec. dir. Bapt. Gen. Conv. Tex., 1982—; chmn. program com. Christian Life Commn., So. Bapt. Conv., spl. rschr. for home mission bd., mem. nat. task force planned growth in giving, 1984—, mem. stewardship commn., 1986-96; bd. dirs. T.B. Maston Found., 1991—, Assn. So. Bapt. Schs., 1996—; adj. prof. Southwestern Bapt. Theol. Sem., 1976-77; chmn. study commn. freedom, justice and peace Bapt. World Alliance, 1975-80, mem. study commn. on ethics, 1990—, mem. commmn. on racism, 1992—; v.p. Bapt. Gen. Conv. Tex., 1972-73, mem. state missions commn., 1976-77, vice chmn. urban strategy com., chmn. order of bus. com., 1976, chmn. steering com. Good News Tex., 1976-77, chnmn. resolutions com., exec. dir., 1982—; author, spkr. in field. Contbr. articles to numerous theological publs. Named Lilly Found. scholar Southwestern Bapt. Theol. Sem., 1960-62; Recipient Disting. Alumni award Southwestern Bapt. Theol. Sem., 1979, U. North Tex., 1980, Mosaic Missions award Home Mission Bd., 1984. Avocations: travel, reading. Office: Bapt Gen Conv Tex 333 N Washington Ave Dallas TX 75246-1754

PINSTRUP-ANDERSEN, PER, educational administrator; b. Bislev, Denmark, Apr. 7, 1939; came to U.S., 1965; s. Marinus and Alma (Pinstrup) Andersen; m. Birgit Lund, June 19, 1965; children: Charlotte, Tina. BS, Royal Vet. & Agrl. U., Copenhagen, 1965; MS, Okla. State U., 1967, PhD, 1969; Dr. Tech. Scis. (hon.), Swiss Fed. Inst. Tech., 1996. Agrl. economist Centro Internacional de Agricultura Tropical, Cali, Colombia, 1969-72, head econ. unit, 1972-76; dir. agro.-econ. div. Internat. Fertilizer Devel. Ctr., Florence, Ala., 1976-77; sr. rsch. fellow, assoc. prof. Econ. Inst. Royal Vet. & Agr. U., 1977-80; rsch. fellow Internat. Food Policy Rsch. Inst., Washington, 1980, dir. food consumption and nutrition divsn., 1980-87, dir. gen., 1992—; dir. food and nutrition policy program, prof. food econs. Cornell U., Ithaca, N.Y., 1987-92; cons. The World Bank, Washington, 1978-92, Can. Internat. Devel. Agy., 1982-83, 86, UNICEF, N.Y.C.; cons. subcom. on nutrition UN, Rome, 1980-87. Author: The World Food and Agricultural Situation, 1978, Agricultural Research and Economic Development, 1979, The Role of Fertilizer in World Food Supply, 1980, Agricultural Research and Technology in Economic Development, 1982; editor: (with Magaret Biswas) Nutrition and Development, 1985, Food Subsidies in Developing Countries: Costs, Benefits, and Policy Options, 1988, Macroeconomic Policy Reforms, Poverty, and Nutrition: Analytical Methodologies, 1990, The Political Economy of Food and Nutrition Policies, 1993, (with David Pelletier and Harold Alderman) Child Growth and Nutrition in Developing Countries: Priorities for Action, 1995. With Danish Army, 1958-59. Recipient Ford Internat. fellowship, 1965-66, People to People Cert. of Appreciation, 1967, Kellogg Travel fellowship, 1979, Competition prize Nordic Soc. Agrl. Rschrs. and Norsk Hydro, 1979, Cert. Merit, Gamma Sigma Delta, 1991, Disting. Alumnus award U. Colo., 1993. Mem. Am. Assn. Agrl. Econs. (PhD Thesis award 1970, Outstanding Jour. Article award 1977, bd. dirs. 1996—), Internat. Assn. Agrl. Econs., Columbian Nat. Orgn. Profls. in Agr. (hon.). Home: 1451 Highwood Dr Mc Lean VA 22101-2516 Office: Internat Food Policy Rsch Inst 1200 17th St NW Washington DC 20036-3006

PINTER, GABRIEL GEORGE, physiology educator; b. Bekes, Hungary, June 23, 1925; came to U.S., 1958; s. Lajos and Regina (Szilagyi-Farkas) P.; m. Berit Helgesen, Dec. 19, 1958 (dec. May 1980); children: Renee Astrid, Eva Ingelill; m. Vera Lederer Dallos, May 23, 1984. M.D., U. Sch. of Medicine, Budapest, Hungary, 1951. Asst. prof. U. Sch. Medicine, Budapest, 1951-56; rsch. assoc. U. Inst. Med. Rsch., Oslo, Norway, 1957-58; asst. prof. U. Tenn., Memphis, 1958-61; from asst. prof. to prof. U. Md., Balt., 1961-92, ret.; vis. prof. King's Coll., London, 1990-94. Contbr. articles to profl. jours. Recipient A.V. Humbolt prize Fed. Republic of Germany, 1980; Swedish Royal Med. Soc. fellow, Uppsala, Sweden, 1972. Mem. Am. Physiol. Soc., Physiol. Soc. Great Britain, Scandinavian Physiol. Soc., European Soc. Microcirculation.

PINTER, HAROLD, playwright; b. London, Oct. 10, 1930; s. Hyman and Frances (Mann) P.; m. Vivien Merchant, Sept. 14, 1956 (div. 1980); 1 son, Daniel; m. Antonia Fraser, Nov. 1980. Student, Brit. schs.; D.Litt. (hon.), U. Reading, 1970, U. Birmingham, 1971, U. Glasgow, 1974, U. East Anglia, 1974, U. Stirling, 1979, Brown U., 1982, U. Hull, 1986, U. Sussex, 1990, U. East London, London, 1994, U. Sofia, Bulgaria, 1995; hon. fellow, Queen Mary Coll., London, 1987. Actor in repertory theatres, 1949-57; dir. plays and films, 1970—; assoc. dir. Nat. Theatre, 1973-83; author (plays) The Dumb Waiter, 1957, A Slight Ache, 1958, The Hothouse, 1958, A Night Out, 1959, The Caretaker, 1959, Night School, 1960, The Dwarfs, 1960 (pub. 1990), The Collection, 1961, The Lover, 1962 (Italia prize 1963), Tea Party, 1964, The Homecoming, 1964, The Basement, 1966, Landscape, 1967, Silence, 1968, Night, 1969, Old Times, 1970, Monologue, 1972, No Man's Land, 1974, Betrayal, 1978 (screenplay 1981), Family Voices, 1980, A Kind of Alaska, 1982, Victoria Station, 1982, One for the Road, 1984, Mountain Language, 1988, The New World Order, 1991, Party Time, 1991, Moonlight, 1993, others; (screenplays) The Caretaker, 1962, The Servant, 1962, The Pumpkin Eater, 1963, The Quiller Memorandum, 1965, Accident, 1966, The Birthday Party, 1967, The Go-Between, 1969, The Homecoming, 1969, Langrishe Go Down, 1970, A la Recherche du Temps Perdu, 1972, The Last Tycoon, 1974, The French Lieutenant's Woman, 1980, Betrayal, 1981, Victory, 1982, Turtle Diary, 1984, The Handmaid's Tale, 1987, Reunion, 1988, The Heat of the Day, 1988, The Comfort of Strangers, 1989, The Trial, 1989; (pub.); (novel) Collected Poems and Prose, 1990. Decorated Comdr. Order Brit. Empire; recipient Shakespeare prize Hamburg, Germany, 1970, Austrian prize lit., 1973, Pirandello prize, 1980, Commonwealth award, 1981, Donatello prize, 1982, Elmer H. Bobst award, 1984, David Cohen Brit. Lit. prize, 1995. Office: care Judy Daish Assocs Ltd, 2 St Charles Pl, London W10 6EG, England*

PINTO, ROSALIND, retired educator, civic volunteer; b. N.Y.C.; d. Barney and Jenny Abrams; m. Jesse E. Pinto (dec.); children: Francine, Jerry, Evelyn. BA in Polit. Sci. cum laude, Hunter Coll.; MA in Polit. Sci., History, Columbia U.; postgrad., Queens Coll., LaGuardia Community Coll. Lic. social studies tchr. jr. high sch., N.Y., per diem lifetime substitute; cert. N.Y. State secondary sch. social studies grades 7-12. Substitute tchr., 1966-69, 90, 91—; tchr. social studies I.S. 126Q, L.I. City, N.Y., 1969-88, Jr. High Sch. 217 Briarwood, N.Y.C., 1988-89; ret., 1989; part-time cluster tchr. social studies and communication arts Pub. Sch. 140, Bronx, N.Y., 1990-91, 92; substitute tchr. I.S. 227Q, 1992-93; participant numerous personal and profl. devel. seminars and workshops. Author curriculum materials; contbr. study guide for regent's competency test, 1990; contbr. poems to anthologies, Nat. Libr. Poetry including Tears of Fire, 1994, Dance on the Horizon, 1994, Outstanding Poets of 1994, Best Poems of 1995, Seasons to Come, 1995, The Voice Within, 1996, Best Poems of 1996, Best Poems of 1997; recorded poem for The Sound of Poetry, Nat. Libr. Poetry, 1992 (Editor's Choice award 1993, 94, 96). Enrollment asst. Insight Heart Team, 1989; vol. receptionist Whitney Mus., N.Y.C.; mem. com. on pub. transp. Cmty. Bd. 6, Queens, 1990-96, mem. com. on history, 1990—, chmn. beautification com., 1992—, mem. com. on planning and zoning, 1996—; active Great Smokies Song Chase Warren-Wilson Coll., N.C., 1992; vol. local polit. campaigns; mem. Queens Hist. Soc., Forest Hills Van Ct. Homeowners Assn., Ctrl. Queens Hist. Soc., bd. dirs.; mem. Rego Park Coalition Against Violence, Forest Hills Civic Assn., 1996-97, Neighbors Against Graffiti. Recipient cert. of appreciation for participation in worksite sponsor program Dept. Probate Cmty. Svc. Project, 1993, for participation in Make a Difference Day, 1994, 95, Beautification Com., 1995. Fellow Mcpl. Art Soc. (hon. mention design 2000 award); mem. NAFE, Internat. Soc. Poets (life mem. adv. panel, Internat. Poet of Merit award 1993), N.Y. Insight Alumni Assn., Columbia U. Grad. Sch. Arts and Scis. Alumni Assn., Hunter Coll. Alumni Assn., Robert F. Kennedy Dem. Assn. (bd. dirs.), Ctr. for Sci. in the Pub. Interest. Avocations: poetry and poetry contests, reading, long distance walking, art shows, plays. Home: 97-04 70th Ave Forest Hills NY 11375-5808 *Loving people and having faith in them and the possibility of happy outcomes is the greatest motivation toward achievement of goals.*

PIOMBINO, NICHOLAS, psychotherapist; b. N.Y.C., Oct. 5, 1942; s. Nicholas Bruce and Ruth Mary (Rothbart) P. BA with honors, CCNY, 1964; MSW, Fordham U., 1971; cert. in adult psychoanalysis and psychotherapy, Postgrad. Ctr. Mental Health, N.Y.C., 1982. Diplomate in clin. social work; cert. psychotherapist, social worker, N.Y. Social worker Manhattan State Hosp., N.Y.C., 1971-73; pvt. practice psychotherapy N.Y.C., 1976—; sch. social worker N.Y.C. Bd. Edn., 1974—; staff psychotherapist Postgrad. Ctr. Mental Health, 1978-86; supr., mem. faculty Psychoanalytic Inst. N.Y. Counseling and Guidance Svc., N.Y.C., 1987—. Author: Poems, 1988, Light Street, 1996, (essays) The Boundary of Blur, 1993; contbr. articles and poems to numerous publs. Mem. Postgrad. Psychoanalytic Soc., Soc. Clin. Social Work Psychotherapists. Home: 119 W 95th St New York NY 10025-6636 Office: 680 W End Ave New York NY 10025-6815

PIONKE, HARRY BERNHARD, research leader and soil scientist; b. Bklyn.. BS, U. Wis., 1963, MS, 1966, PhD in Soils, 1967. Asst. prof. soils U. Wis., Madison, 1967-68. Mem. Soil Sci. Soc. Am., Am. Geophys. Union, Am. Soc. Agron., Nat. Water Well Assn.

PIORE, EMANUEL RUBEN, physicist; b. Wilno, Russia, July 19, 1908; came to U.S., 1917; s. Ruben and Olga (Gegusin) P.; m. E. Nora Kahn, Aug. 26, 1931; children—Michael Joseph, Margot Deborah, Jane Ann. A.B., U. Wis., 1930, Ph.D., 1935, D.Sc. (hon.), 1966; D.Sc. (hon.), Union U., 1962. Asst. instr. U. Wis., 1930-35; research physicist RCA, 1935-38; engr.-in-charge TV lab. CBS, 1938-42; head spl. weapons group, bur. ships U.S. Navy, 1942-44; head electronics br. Office Naval Research, 1946-47, dir. phys. sci., 1947-48, dep. for natural sci., 1949-51, chief scientist, dep. dir., 1951-55; v.p., dir. Avco Mfg. Corp., 1955-56; dir. research IBM Corp., 1956-61, v.p. research and engring., 1961-63, v.p., group exec., 1963-65, v.p., chief scientist, 1965-75; also dir.; physicist research lab. electronics MIT, 1948-49; dir. Sci. Research Assocs., Inc., Health Advancement, Inc., Paul Revere Investors, Guardian Mut. Fund.; adj. prof. Rockefeller U., 1974-80. Mem. Pres.'s Sci. Adv. Com., 1959-62; mem. Nat. Sci. Bd., 1961—; bd. dirs. N.Y. State Found. for Sci.; past bd. dirs. NSF; chmn. vis. com. Nat. Bur. Standards; chmn. bd. Hall of Science, N.Y.C.; mem. corp. Woods Hole Oceanographic Instn.; mem. exec. com. Resources for Future; bd. dirs. Stark Draper Lab., Nat. Info. Bur., Meml. Cancer Hosp.; mem. vis. com. to elec. engring. dept. Mass. Inst. Tech., 1956-57; vis. com. Harvard Coll., 1958-70; trustee Sloan-Kettering Inst. Cancer Research; mem. N.Y.C. Bd. Higher Edn., 1976—. Served to lt. comdr. USNR, 1944-46. Recipient Indsl. Research Inst. award, 1967; Disting. Civilian medal Dept. Navy; Kaplun award Hebrew U., 1975, Piore medal-award for young rschrs. IEEE, 1974. Fellow AAAS, Royal Soc. Arts (London, Eng.), Am. Phys. Soc., IEEE, Am. Acad. Arts Scis.; mem. Sci. Research Soc. Am., Sci. Research Assn. (dir.), Nat. Acad. Sci., Nat. Acad. Engring., Am. Inst. Physics (dir.), Am. Philos. Soc. (sec. 1985—), Sigma Xi. Clubs: University (N.Y.C.), Cosmos (Washington), Century (N.Y.C.). Home: 2 Fifth Ave New York NY 10011

PIORE, MICHAEL JOSEPH, educator; b. N.Y.C., Aug. 14, 1940. BA magna cum laude, Harvard U., 1962, PhD in Econs., 1966. Asst. prof. labor econs. MIT, 1966-70, assoc. prof., 1970-75, prof. econs., 1975—, Mitsui prof. of Contemporary Tech., 1981-86; David W. Skinner prof. polit. economy, 1991—; cons. NAACP Legal Def. and Edn. Fund, Inc., 1966-68, Boston Model Cities Adminstrn., 1960, Dept. Labor, 1968-70, Labor, Manpower and Income Maintenance, Commonwealth of P.R., 1970-72, rsch. coord., acting exec. dir., 1970-71, cons., 1977-86; mem. Nat. Manpower Policy Task Force Assocs., 1968-70; mem. Nat. Coun. on Employment Policy, 1977-79; cons. v.p. task force on youth employment; mem. gov. bd. Inst. for Labour Studies, Internat. Labour Orgn., 1990—. Author: Birds of Passage, Migrant Labor and Industrial Societies, 1979, Beyond Individualism, 1995, (with B. Doeringer) Internal Labor Markets and Manpower Adjustment, 1981, (with Charles Sabel) The Second Industrial Divide, 1984; editor: Unemployment and Inflation: Institutionalist and Structuralist Views, 1979, (with Thomas Kochen and Richard Locke) Employment Relations in a Changing World Economy; contbr. articles to profl. jours. and publs. Recipient Harvard Coll. scholarship, 1959-60, Detur Prize, 1960, John Harvard scholarship, 1960-61; Honorary Woodrow Wilson fellowship, 1962-63, MacArthur Found. fellow, 1984-89. Mem. Am. Econ. Assn. (exec. com. 1991-94), Indsl. Rels. Rsch. Assn. Union of Radical Polit. Economists. Home: 295 Beacon St Apt 62 Boston MA 02116-1238 Office: MIT Dept Ecos Rm E52-271C Cambridge MA 02139

PIORE, NORA KAHN, economist, health policy analyst; b. N.Y.C., N.Y., Nov. 28, 1912; d. Alexander and Sara (Rosenbaum) Kahn; m. Emanuel R. Piore, Aug. 26, 1931; children: Michael Joseph, Margot Deborah, Jane Anne. B.A., U. Wis., 1933, MA, 1934. Research economist health legislation subcom. U.S. Senate, Washington, 1950-53; spl. asst. to commr. N.Y.C. Dept. Health, 1957-68; adj. prof. urban affairs Hunter Coll., N.Y.C., 1962-72; dir. N.Y.C. Urban Med. Econs. Research Ctr., 1960-68; vis. scientist Assn. Aid of Crippled Children, N.Y.C., 1968-72, study dir. hosp. ambulatory care svcs. in U.S., 1968-72; prof. pub. health econs. Columbia U. Sch. Pub. Health, N.Y.C., 1972-82; assoc. dir. Columbia U. Ctr. Community Health Systems, N.Y.C., 1971-82, cons. Health Services Research, 1982—; sr. program cons. Commonwealth Fund, N.Y.C., 1982-88; sr. fellow United Hosp. Fund, N.Y.C., 1982-90; dir. Health Svcs. Improvement Fund (Blue Cross-Blue Shield), 1984—, Sun Valley Health Forum, Boise, Idaho, 1978-88; active numerous coms., founds., task forces, funds in field; cons. Carnegie Corp. N.Y., R.I. Health Svcs. Rsch. Corp., Robert Wood Johnson Found., Pew Meml. Trust; mem. N.Y. State Hosp. Rev. and Planning Coun., 1976-84. Contbr. chpts. to books, articles to profl. jours. Recipient Merit award N.Y. Pub. Health Assn., 1977 Career Scientist award N.Y. Health Rsch. Coun., 1961-65, 66-71; Belding scholar Assn. Aid Crippled Children, 1968; grantee USPHS, 1980. Fellow Am. Pub. Health Assn., N.Y. Acad. Medicine; mem. Am. Econs. Assn., AAAS, Health Services Research Assn., Assn. Social Scientists in Health, Inst. Medicine, Nat. Acad. Sci., Phi Beta Kappa. Clubs: Cosmopolitan, Women's City (N.Y.C.).

PIOT, PETER, medical microbiologist, public health officer; b. Leuven, Belgium, Feb. 17, 1949; m. Greet Kimzeke; children: Bram, Sara. MD, U. Ghent, Belgium, 1974; PhD in Microbiology, U. Antwerp, Belgium, 1981; PhD (hon.), Free U., Brussels, 1995, U. Antwerp, 1997. Sr. fellow infectious diseases U. Wash., Seattle, 1978-79; asst. Inst. Tropical Medicine, Antwerp, 1974-78; prof., head dept. microbiology Inst. Tropical Medicine, 1981-92; prof. pub. health Free U., Brussels, 1989-94; assoc. dir. Global Program AIDS/WHO, Geneva, 1995—; exec. dir. Joint UN Program on HIV/AIDS, Geneva, 1995; dir. WHO Collaborating Ctr. on AIDS, Antwerp; bd. dirs. Project SIDA, Kinshasa, Zaire, STD/AIDS Project, Nairobi, Kenya; chair WHO Steering Com. on the Epidemiology of AIDS, 1989-92; prof. med. microbiology U. Nairobi, Kenya, 1986-87. Editor: (with others) Chlamydial Infection, 1982, (with J. Mann) AIDS and HIV Infection in the Tropics, 1988, (with P. Lamptey) The Handbook on AIDS Prevention in Africa, 1990, AIDS in Africa, 1991, (with F. Andre) Hepatitis B, and STD in Heterosexuals, 1991, (with others) Basic Laboratory Procedures in Clinical Bacteriology, 1991, (with others) Reproductive Tract Infections in Women, 1992, (with others) AIDS in Africa: A Handbook for Physicians, 1992; mem. editorial bd. sci. publs. Mem. expert coms. Knighted baron King Albert II, 1995; decorated officier l'Ordre Nat. du Léopard (Zaïre), officier l'Ordre du Lion (Sénégal); NATO fellow, 1978; recipient Health Rsch. award Brussels, 1989, AMICOM award for med. rsch., 1991, Pub. Health award Flemish Community, 1990, H. Breurs prize, 1992, A. Jauniaux prize, 1992, van Thiel award Leiden, 1993, Glaxo award Soc. Infectious Diseases of The Netherlands, 1995, East Flanders Cultural Achievement prize, 1995. Mem. Royal Acad. Medicine (Belgium), Internat. AIDS Soc. (pres.), and other profl. socs. in Europe, U.S.A. and Africa. Home: K Mercierlei 60, 1031 Rte de Tutegny, 2600 Gex France Office: UN AIDS, CH-1211 Geneva Switzerland

PIOTROW, PHYLLIS TILSON, public health educator, international development specialist; b. N.Y.C., Mar. 16, 1933; d. Paul and Phyllis Tilson; children: Diana, Stephen. BA in History summa cum laude, Bryn Mawr Coll., 1954; BA in Modern History first class, Oxford U., England, 1956, MA, 1959; PhD in Pol. Sci. and Population Dynamics, Johns Hopkins U., 1971. Social sci. analyst history and govt. dvsn., legis. reference svc. Libr. Congress, 1956-57; writer Editorial Rsch. Reports (Congresl. quarterly), Washington, 1957-58; instr. St. Anne's Coll. Oxford (England) U., 1958-59; legis. asst. Senator Kenneth B. Keating of N.Y., Washington, 1960-64, Senator G. McGovern of S.D., Washington, 1965; first exec. dir. Population Crisis Com. Population Action Internat., Washington, 1965-69, 71-72, 75-78; adminstr. population info. program Dept. Med. and Pub. Affairs, George Washington U. Med. Ctr., Washington, 1972-75; prin. investigator Population Communication Svcs., Johns Hopkins U., Washington, 1982—; dir. Population Info. Program, Balt., 1978—, Ctr. Communication Programs, Johns Hopkins U., Balt., 1988—; bd. dirs., sec. Population Action Internat., 1969—, mem. exec. com., 1978—; bd. dirs. Ctr. Devel. and Population Activities, Washington, 1975-92, exec. com., 1978-92, sec., 1979-84, chmn., 1984-86; internat. cons. and presenter in field. Author: World Population Crisis: The United States Response, 1972, World Population: The Present and Future Crisis, 1980; (with G. Tapinos) Six Billion People: Demographic Dilemmas and World Politics, 1978; co-author: Family Planning Communication: Lessons for Public Health, 1997; contbr. numerous articles to profl. jours. Advisor U.S. Del. to UN Population Comsn., 1969, 71, 73, 77, U.S. Del. to World Population Conf., Bucharest, 1974; mem. Internat. Adv. Coun. Bryn Mawr Coll., 1972-76, nat. adv. coun. Marshall Scholarship Comsn., 1972-80, Brit. Adv. Coun., 1973-84; mem. adv. com. UN POPIN database, 1982-94; bd. dirs. New Directions, 1977-79; chmn. Informed Choice Task Force, 1988-91. European fellow Bryn Mawr Coll., 1954; Marshall scholar Oxford U., 1954-56; Ford mid-career fellow, 1969-71; recipient Charles A. Dana Found. award, 1991; U.S. AID grantee, 1978-84, 82-87, 84-87, 85-89, 86-91, 87-92, 88-92, 90—; POPLINE database grantee UN Population Fund, 1988. Mem. APHA (chair population and family planning sect. 1979-80, Carl Shultz award 1989), Population Assn. Am., Cosmos Club. Avocations: tennis, gardening, hiking. Office: Johns Hopkins Univ Ctr for Comm Programs 111 Market Pl Ste 310 Baltimore MD 21202-7112

PIOTROWSKI, RICHARD FRANCIS, state agency administrator, council chairman; b. Manchester, N.H., Mar. 13, 1945; s. Stanley J. and Marion G. (Rubino) P.; m. Claudia H. Rund, Aug. 28, 1971; children: Richard Jr., Courtney. AAS in Civil Tech., Hartford (Conn.) State Tech. Coll., 1965; student, U. Conn., 1965-69. Registered profl. engr., Conn. Sr. engr. Henry N. Loomis and Assoc., New Hartford, Conn., 1970-77; quality control engr. Atlantic Pipe Corp., Plainville, Conn., 1977; sr. civil engr. C.E. Maguire, New Britain, Conn., 1977-80; chief civil engr. Anderson-Nichols and Co., Newington, Conn., 1980-83; project engr. Cahn Co., Wallingford, Conn., 1983-84; asst. chief engr. State of Conn. Dept. Pub. Works, Hartford, 1984-85, asst. dir. facilities, design and constrn., 1985-87; dep. commr. dept. pub. works State of Conn., Hartford, 1987—. Councilor Plainville Town Council, 1975-81, 85-87, council chmn./mayor, 1979-81, 1985-87; mem. adv. bd. Colonial Bank, Plainville, 1980-86; pres. Plainville Pre-Sch. Assn., 1984-85; corporator New Britain Gen. Hosp. Recipient Disting. Svc. award Plainville Jaycees, 1980, Conn. Engr. Recognition award, 1991, Dist. Mgr. Svc. award State of Conn., 1994. Mem. Nat. League of Cities (transp. and communications policy com. 1981, 87), Conn. Conf. Municipalities, Conn. Assn. Street and Hwy. Ofcls. Democrat. Roman Catholic. Home: 14 Peace Ct Plainville CT 06062-2836 Office: State of Conn Dept Pub Works 165 Capitol Ave Hartford CT 06106-1659

PIOVANETTI, SIMON, pediatrician; b. Sabana Grande, P.R., Mar. 27, 1920; s. Antonio and Juanita (Bonelli) Prowik; m. Priv K.; 1 child, Yvette. MD, Jefferson Med. Coll., 1951. Dir. dept. pediatrics Ashfor & Presbyn. Cmty. Hosp., Hatorey, P.R., 1985—. 1st lt. U.S. Infantry, 1941-46. Mem. Am. Acad. Pediatrics. Home: 609 Cuevillas Apt 7B San Juan PR 00907 Office: 400 Domenech San Juan PR 00918

PIPER, ADDISON LEWIS, securities executive; b. Mpls., Oct. 10, 1946; s. Harry Cushing and Virginia (Lewis) P.; m. Louise Wakefield (div.); children: Gretchen, Tad, William; m. Cynthia Schuneman, Nov. 14, 1979; children: Elisabeth LaBelle, Richard LaBelle. BA in Econs., Williams Coll., 1968; MBA, Stanford U., 1972. Mktg. cons. Earl Savage and Co., Mpls., 1968-69; mem. capital market dept. Piper and Jaffray, Mpls., 1969-70; asst. syndicate mgr. Piper, Jaffray and Hopwood, Mpls., 1972-73, v.p., 1973-79, dir. trading, 1973-77, dir. sales, 1977-79, exec. v.p., dir. mktg., 1979-83, chief exec. officer, chmn. mgmt. com., 1983—, chmn. bd. dirs., 1988—; adv. com. N.Y. Stock Exch., 1966-90; bd. dirs. Allina Health Systems, Greenspring Corp., Mpls., Minn. Bus. Partnership, Mpls.; vice chair Abbott Northwestern Hosp., Mpls.; trustee CARE Found., Mpls. Fin. chmn. Senator Durenberger Fin. Com., Mpls., 1980-88; chmn. Minn. Pub. Radio, 1985-95. Mem. Securities Industry Assn. (bd. govs. 1986-90, tax policy com.), Country Club of the Rockies (Colo.), Mpls. Club. Republican. Episcopalian. Clubs: Woodhill Country (Wayzata); Minneapolis. Avocations: skiing, golfing, hunting, tennis, horses. Office: Piper Jaffray Cos. PO Box 28 222 S 9th St Minneapolis MN 55440

PIPER, ADRIAN MARGARET SMITH, philosopher, artist, educator; b. N.Y.C., Sept. 20, 1948; d. Daniel Robert and Olive Xavier (Smith) P.; m. Jeffrey Ernest Evans, June 27, 1982 (div. 1987). AA, Sch. Visual Arts, 1969; BA in Philosophy, CCNY, 1974; MA, Harvard U., 1977, PhD, 1981; student, U. Heidelberg, Germany, 1977-78; LHD (hon.), Calif. Inst. Arts, 1992, Mass. Coll. Art, 1994. Asst. prof. U. Mich., Ann Arbor, 1979-86; Mellon rsch. fellow Stanford (Calif.) U., 1982-84; assoc. prof. Georgetown U., Washington, 1986-88, U. Calif., San Diego, 1988; prof. philosophy Wellesley (Mass.) Coll., 1990—; Disting. scholar Getty Rsch. Inst., 1998—; speaker, lectr. on both philosophy and art. Artist: one-woman exhbns. include N.Y. Cultural Ctr., N.Y.C., 1971, Montclair (N.J.) State Coll., 1976, Wadsworth Atheneum, Hartford, Conn., 1980, Nexus COntemporary Art Ctr., Atlanta, 1987, The Alternative Mus., N.Y.C., 1987, Goldie Paley Gallery, Phila., 1989, Power Plant Gallery, Toronto, 1990, Lowe Art Mus., Coral Gables, Fla., 1990-91, Santa Monica (Calif.) Mus. Contemporary Art, 1991, John Weber Gallery, N.Y.C., 1989, 90, 91, 92, Whitney Mus. Am. Art, N.Y.C., 1990, Hirschorn Mus., Washington, 1991, Ikon Gallery, Birmingham, Eng., 1991, Cornerhouse, Manchester, Eng., 1992, Cartwright Hall, Bradford, Eng., 1992, Kunstverein, Munich, Germany, 1992, Indpls. Ctr. Contemporary Art, 1992, Manasterio de Santa Clara, Moguer, Spain, 1992, Grey Art Gallery, N.Y.C., 1992, Paula Cooper Art Galler, 1992, 94; group exhbns. include Paula Cooper Gallery, 1969, Dwan Gallery, N.Y.C., 1969, 70, Seattle Art Mus., 1969, Stadtisches Mus., Leverkusen, Germany, 1969, Kunsthalle Berne, Berne, Switzerland, 1969, N.Y. Cultural Ctr., 1970, Allen Mus., Oberlin, Ohio, 1970, Mus. Modern Art, N.Y.C., 1970, 88, 91, Musee d'Art Moderne, Paris, 1971, 77, 89, Inhibodress Gallery, New South Wales, Australia, 1972, Calif. Inst. Arts, Valencia, 1973, Samuel S. Fleischer Art Meml., Phila., 1974, Mus. Contemporary Art, Chgo., 1975, Newberger Mus., Purchase, N.Y., 1978, Mass. Coll. Art, Boston, 1979, Artemesia Gallery, Chgo., 1979, A.I.R. Gallery, N.Y.C., 1980, Inst. Contemporary Arts, London, 1980, The New Mus., N.Y.C., 1981, 83, 85, Kenkeleba Gallery, N.Y.C., 1983, The Studio Mus. Harlem, N.Y.C., 1985, 89, Mus. Moderner Kunst, Vienna, Austria, 1985, Intar Gallery, N.Y.C., 1988, Whitney Mus. Downtown, N.Y.C., 1988, Art Gallery Ont., Toronto, 1988, Long Beach (Calif.) Art Mus., 1989, Simon Watson Gallery, N.Y.C., 1990, Feigen Gallery, Chgo., 1990, Barbara Krakow Gallery, Boston, 1990, Milw. Art Mus., 1990, Contemporary Arts Ctr., Houston, 1991, John Weber Gallery, 1991, Anne Plumb Gallery, N.Y.C., 1991, Hirschorn Mus., 1991, The Albuquerque Mus. Art, 1991, The Toledo Mus. Art, 1991, Denver Art Mus., Fukui Fine Arts Mus., Fukyui-ken, Japan, 1992-93, N.J. State Mus., Trenton, 1992-93, Philippe Staib Gallery, N.Y.C., 1992, New Loom House, London, 1992, Espace-Lyonnais D'Art Contemporain, Lyon, France, 1993, Am. Acad. Inst. Arts and Letters, N.Y.C., 1993; permanent collections include The Bklyn. Mus., Denver Art Mus., Kunstmuseum Berne, Musee d'Art Moderne, The Mus. Contemporary Art, Chgo., The Wadsworth Atheneum, Met. Mus. Art; art performances include RISD, 1973, The Whitney Mus. Am. Art, 1975, Kurfurstendamm, Berlin, 1977, Hauptstrasse, Heidelberg, Germany, 1978, Allen Meml. Mus., Oberlin, Ohio, 1980, Contemporary Art Inst. Detroit, 1980, San Francisco Art Inst., 1985, Calif. Inst. Art, 1984, The Studio Mus. Harlem, 1988; performances on video, 1987—; contbr. articles to profl. jours. Recipient N.Y. State Coun. on Arts award, 1989, Visual Arts award, 1990, Skowhegan medal for sculptural installation, 1995; NEH Travel fellow, 1979; NEA Visual Artists' fellow, 1979, 82, Andrew Mellon Postdoctoral fellow, 1982-84, Woodrow Wilson Internat. Scholars fellow, 1988-89, Guggenheim Meml. fellow, 1989, non-resident fellow N.Y. Inst. for Humanities, NYU, 1996—; NEA Artists Forums grantee, 1987. Mem. AAUP, Am. Philos. Assn. (mem. ea. divsn.), Am. Soc. Polit. and Legal Philosophy, N.Am. Kant. Soc. Avocations: medieval and renaissance music, fiction, poetry, yoga, German. Office: Wellesley Coll 106 Central St Wellesley MA 02181-8203

PIPER, CLAUDIA ROSEMARY, academic administrator; b. Washington, Nov. 17, 1958; d. Thomas Irving Sr. and Mildred (McCoy) P. BA in Spl. Edn., Math. Edn., Providence Coll., 1981; postgrad., James Madison U., 1982-83; MEd, U. New. Orleans, 1993. Tchr. spl. edn. Grafton Sch., Berryville, Va., 1981-83, PARC Spl. Sch., Kenner, La., 1983-86; Tchr. spl. edn. Waggaman (La.) Spl. Sch., 1989-93, disciplinarian, 1989-93; dean spl. svcs. John H. Martyn H.S., Jefferson, La., 1993—; spl. edn. chmn. Waggaman Spl. Sch., 1986—, substance abuse prevention bd. chmn., 1988—. Mem. chapel choir Mission Circle, editor monthly newsletter. Mem. Assn. Black Psychologists (historian 1991—, program dir. Teen Pregnancy Prevention Program 1991—), Assn. Supervision and Curriculum Devel. Democrat. Baptist. Home: 10950 Jefferson Hwy Apt G23 River Ridge LA 70123 Office: Haynes Mid Sch 1416 Metairie Rd Metairie LA 70005-3921

PIPER, DON COURTNEY, political science educator; b. Washington, July 29, 1932; s. Don Carlos and Alice (Courtney) P.; m. Rowena Inez Wise, July 6, 1956; children: Sharon, Valarie. B.A., U. Md., 1954, M.A., 1958; Ph.D. (James B. Duke fellow), Duke U., 1961. Research assoc. Duke U., 1961-62; exec. sec. Commonwealth-Studies Center, 1962-64; asst. prof. dept. govt. and politics U. Md., College Park, 1964-67; assoc. prof. U. Md., 1967-69, prof., 1969—, head dept. govt. and politics, 1968-74, dir. grad. studies dept., 1982-95, mem. coun. of system faculty, 1989-90; chmn. faculty council College Park Faculty Assembly, 1974-75, chmn. campus senate, 1975-77, 89-90, univ. marshal, 1981-97, mem. Athletic Council, 1986-93, mem. senate ad hoc com. on undergrad. edn., 1986-88, chmn. chancellor's ad hoc com. on campus ceremonies, 1986-87, chmn. acad. com. of Athletic Council, 1986-89; chmn. campaign for College Park, 1988-89; chmn. retention review com. U. Md., 1990-91, chmn. budget and facilities com. athletic coun., 1991-93, chmn. senate com. on programs courses and curriculi, 1991-93, co-chair Mid. States self-study exec. com., 1995-97; teaching fellow Lilly Ctr. for Teaching Excellence, 1994-95; rsch. asst. Am. Coun. on Edn., 1966-68; faculty adv. com., planning adv. com. Md. State Bd. Higher Edn., 1977-82; chmn. com. on dept. chairmen Am. Polit. Sci. Assn., 1973-75; mem. coun. So. Polit. Sci. Assn., 1970-72, chmn. Chastain award com., 1973-75. Author: International Law of Great Lakes, 1967; contbg. author: International Law Standard and Commonwealth Developments, 1966, De Lege Pactorum, 1970, Foreign Policy Analysis, 1975; editor: (with R. Taylor Cole) Post-primary Education and Political and Economic Development, 1964; co-editor, contbg. author: (with Ronald Terchek) Interaction: Foreign Policy and Public Policy, 1983; bd. editors: World Affairs, 1971-94; editl. adv. com.: Internat. Legal Materials, 1977-78. Served to 1st lt. USAF, 1955-58. Recipient U. Md. Regents award for excellence in teaching, 1966, Teaching Excellence award Div. Behavioral and Social Scis., 1982-83, Outstanding Tchr. award Greek System, U. Md., 1982, Pres.'s medal, U. Md., 1992. Mem. Am. Soc. Internat. Law, Internat. Law Assn., Internat. Studies Assn. (chmn. internat. law sect. 1981-83), Am. Peace Soc. (bd. dirs. 1972-94), UN Assn./USA, Phi Beta Kappa (pres. Gamma chpt. 1978-79), Phi Kappa Phi (chpt. pres. 1982-83), Omicron Delta Kappa (faculty adviser 1990-97), Pi Sigma Alpha. Methodist. Home: 4323 Woodberry St Hyattsville MD 20782-1174 Office: U Md Dept Govt & Politics College Park MD 20742

PIPER, MARGARITA SHERERTZ, retired school administrator; b. Petersburg, Va., Dec. 20, 1926; d. Guy Lucas and Olga Doan (Akers) Sherertz; m. Glenn Clair Piper, Feb. 3, 1950; children: Mark Stephen, Susan Leslie Piper Weathersbee. BA in Edn., Mary Washington Coll. of Fredericksburg, 1948; MEd, U. Va., 1973, EdS, 1976. Svc. rep. C&P Telephone, Washington, 1948-55, adminstrv. asst., 1955-56, svc. supr., 1956-62; tchr. Culpeper (Va.) County Pub. Schs., 1970-75, reading lab dir., 1975-80; asst. prin. Rappahannock (Va.) County Pub. Schs., 1980-81, prin., 1981-88, dir. pupil pers., spl. programs, 1988-95; ret., 1995; chair PD 9 regional transition adv. bd. Culpeper, Fauquier, Madison, Orange and Rappahannock Counties, Va., 1991-94; vice chair Family Assessment and Planning Team, Washington, 1992-95. Recipient Va. Gov. Schs. Commendation cert. Commonwealth of Va., 1989-93. Mem. NEA, Va. Edn. Assn., Va. Coun. Adminstrs. Spl. Edn., Va. Assn. Edn. for Gifted, Rappahannock Edn. Assn. Democrat. Episcopalian. Avocations: creative writing, music, walking, crosstitch, knitting.

PIPER, MARK HARRY, retired banker; b. Flint, Mich., Apr. 17, 1931; s. James U. and Dorothy (Weed) P.; m. Wanda L. Hubbard, June 20, 1953; children: Mark T., Kathryn L. BS, St. John's Mil. Acad., 1949; AB with distinction and honors in Econs, U. Mich., 1953, JD cum laude, 1956. Bar: Mich. 1956. With Clark, Klein, Winter, Parsons & Prewitt, Detroit, 1956-57; with Genesee Mchts. Bank & Trust Co., Flint, 1957-88, v.p., sr. trust officer, 1966-72, sr. v.p., 1972-88; sr. v.p. NBD Genesee Bank (formerly United Mich. Corp.), 1985-88, cashier, sec. bd. dirs., 1985-88; adj. instr. bus. adminstrn. U. Mich., Flint, 1976-80; pres. Flint Estate Planning Coun., 1969-70; mem. Flint citizens adv. coun. U. Mich., 1974-82; vice chmn., 1975-82. Bd. dir. Retirement Homes of Detroit Ann. Conf. Meth. Ch., 1964-76, vice chmn. profl. ministry and support, 1975, mem. bd. support systems, 1975, coun. fin. and adminstrn., 1976-84, chmn. coun. fin. and adminstrn., 1980-84; bd. dirs. United Meth. Devel. Fund, 1986-90; gen. bd. pensions United Meth. Ch., 1988-96, mem. investment com., gen. bd. pensions, 1988—; mem. investment com. United Meth. Found. of Detroit. Conf. of United Meth. Ch., 1993—; trustee Flint YMCA Boysfarm Found., 1964-78, chmn., 1976-78; bd. mgmt. Flint YMCA Boysfarm, 1968-74; mem. Detroit Conf. Bd. P. United Meth. Ch., 1968-76, chmn., 1972-75, 88—, mem., 1986—; bd. dirs. U. Mich. Devel. Coun., 1980-82; bd. dirs., asst. treas., sec.-treas. Flint Area Young Life Found., 1979—, Mich. Area Young Life Com., 1980-88; bd. dirs., vice chmn. The Crim Road Race Inc., 1985-87. Mem. Mich. Bar Assn., Genesee County Bar Assn., Inst. Continuing Legal Edn., U. Mich.-Flint Club (bd. dirs., pres. 1973-74), Rotary Club. Home: 1378 Ox Yoke Dr Flint MI 48532-2352 also: PO Box 3121 Estes Park CO 80517

PIPER, ROBERT JOHNSTON, architect, urban planner; b. Byron, Ill., Feb. 2, 1926; s. Leo Edward and Helen Anna (Johnston) P.; m. Carol Jane White, June 23, 1951; children—Christopher White, Brian Douglas, Eric Johnston. B.S. in Archtl. Engring, U. Ill., 1951; M. City and Regional Planning, Cornell U., 1953. Architect, planner Orput & Assos., Rockford, Ill., 1953-61; dir. profl. services AIA, Washington, 1961-67; partner, v.p. Perkins & Will, Chgo., 1967-74; dep. dir. Northeastern Ill. Planning Commn., Chgo., 1974-76; assoc. Metz, Train, Olson & Youngren, Inc., Chgo., 1976-79; dir. community devel. City of Highland Park, Ill., 1980-91; ret. City of Highland Park, 1991; coord. various programs Chgo. Cultural Ctr., 1992—; pres. Landmarks Preservation Council Ill., Chgo., 1976-80. Author: Careers in Architecture, vocat. guidance manuals, 1967, 71, 75, 80, 85, 93; author, editor: Architect's Handbook of Professional Practice, 7th edit., 1963; prin. works include Regional Open Space Plan, Northeastern Ill., Spring Valley Operations Breakthrough Housing Complex, Kalamazoo, CBD Streetscape and Skokie Corridor Master Plan, Highland Park. Trustee Village of Winnetka, Ill., 1978-83; mem. Potomac Planning Task Force Dept. Interior, 1967-68, Commn. on Fed. Procurement, Washington, 1970-71; mem. nat. advisory bd. community characteristics HEW, 1970-78. Served with USNR, 1944-46, PTO. Fellow AIA (mem. Task Force Future of Inst. 1974-75, various coms., pres. AIA Ill. coun. 1986, Disting. Achievement awards AIA Ill., AIA Chgo. 1993); mem. Am. Inst. Cert. Planners (metro chpt. pres. 1971-72), Lambda Alpha. Episcopalian. Home: 1132 Oak St Winnetka IL 60093-2132

PIPER, THOMAS LAURENCE, III, investment banker; b. Washington, June 20, 1941; s. Thomas Laurence and Edna (Milewski) P.; m. Ann Runnette, Apr. 8, 1967; children: Thomas Laurence IV, Andrew Kerr. Student, U. Va., 1959-61. Asso. Hodgdon & Co., Inc., Washington, 1962-65; sr. v.p., dir. Hayden Stone Inc., N.Y.C., 1966-73; mng. dir. New Court Securities Corp., N.Y.C., 1974-81, Dillon, Read & Co., Inc., N.Y.C., 1981—. Chmn. fund dir. New Canaan chpg. ARC, 1978; bd. dirs. Manhattan coun. Boy Scouts Am., Waveny Care Ctr., New Canaan, Our Lady Queen of Angels, Manhattan. Mem. Investment Assn. N.Y. (pres. 1974), Bond Club N.Y. Clubs: Racquet and Tennis, Brook (N.Y.C.); Country of New Canaan. Home: Windrow Ln New Canaan CT 06840 Office: Dillon Read & Co Inc 535 Madison Ave New York NY 10022-4212

PIPER, WILLIAM HOWARD, banker; b. Flint, Mich., Oct. 15, 1933; s. James Underhill P. and Dorothy K. (Weed) Cooper; m. Joyce Rae Foster, June 6, 1959; children: Karen Elizabeth, William Howard, James Raymond. B.A., Yale U., 1955. With NBD Genesee Bank, Flint, 1955—; pres., chief exec. officer, dir. NBD Genesee Bank, 1985-90; sr. v.p. NBD Bancorp, 1990—; head of E. Mich. Banks, 1990—; bd. dirs. U.S. Sugar Corp. Vice chmn., trustee emeritus McLaren Gen. Hosp., Flint, 1974—; trustee, vice chmn. Mott Found., 1985—; mem. adv. bd. Profl., Corp. Flint campus U. Mich., 1982—; dir. YWCA Found.; mem. Greater Flint Community Found.; mem. exec. com. Gen. Motors Inst. Bus. and Industry Ctr.; bd. dirs. Flint Inst. Music, 1983—, Flint Exec. Svc. Corp., 1985-87, Flint Coll. and Cultural Devel. Ctr.; sec., treas. Genesee Area Focus Coun. Mem. Flint C. of C. (bd. dirs. 1983-87). Republican. Methodist. Clubs: Flint Golf, Univ. Home: 63 Chateau Du Lac Dr Linden MI 48451-9022 Office: NBD Bank PO Box 331041 Detroit MI 48232-7041

PIPES, DANIEL, writer, editor; b. Boston, Sept. 9, 1949; s. Richard and Irene (Roth) P.; children: Sarah, Anna. Student, U. Tunis, Institut Bourguiba des Langues Vivantes, 1970; BA in History Sci., Harvard U., 1971; student, U. Cairo, 1971-72, Al-Azhâr U., Cairo, 1971-72, U. Calif. (Berkeley) Ctr. for Arabic Studies Abroad, Cairo, 1971, 1972-73; reader, Orientalisches Sem., Freiburg U., 1976; PhD in Mid. Ea. Studies, Harvard U., 1978; hon. degree, Am. Coll. of Switzerland, 1988. Vis. fellow Princeton U., 1977-78; Harper instr., rsch. assoc. U. Chgo., 1978-82; mem. policy planning staff, spl. advisor U.S. Dept. State, 1982-83; lectr. history Harvard U., 1983-84; prof. U.S. Naval War Coll., 1984-86; dir. Fgn. Policy Rsch. Inst., Phila., 1986-93, Mid. East Forum, 1994—. Author: Slave Soldiers and Islam, 1981, In the Path of God, 1983, An Arabist's Guide to Egyptian Colloquial, 1983, The Long Shadow, 1988, Greater Syria, 1990, The Rushdie Affair, 1990; co-editor: Damascus Courts the West, 1991, Syria Beyond the Peace Process, 1996, The Hidden Hand, 1996, Conspiracy, 1997; Friendly Tyrants, 1991; editor: Sandstorm, 1993, Orbis: Jour. World Affairs, 1986-90, Mid. East Quar., 1994—. Vice chmn. J. William Fulbright Scholarship Bd., 1992-95; mem. adv. com. Internat. Rep. Inst., 1993. Woodrow Wilson nat. fellow, 1971-72, fellow NDEA Title VI, 1974-76, Am. Rsch. Ctr. in Egypt, 1979, vis. fellow Heritage Found., 1984, Japan Soc., Nat. Inst. for Rsch. Advancement, Tokyo, 1985, Washington Inst. for Near East Policy, 1986, 91, 94-95; rsch. grantee Israel Inter-Univ., 1979, Smith Richardson Found., 1980-82, 95-96, Schumann Found., 1990-91, U.S. Inst. Peace, 1990-91, Ford Found., 1992-93, Scaife Found., 1995-96, Bradley Found., 1996—. Mem. Coun. on Fgn. Rels. (internat. affairs fellow 1982-83), Internat. Ho. of Japan. Office: Mid East Quar 1920 Chestnut St Ste 600 Philadelphia PA 19103-4634

PIPES, PAUL RAY, county commissioner; b. Truscott, Tex., Oct. 1, 1928; s. David and Maggie (Brown) Pipes; m. Linda Mullins, Dec. 17, 1961; children: Dana, Tricia. BBA, Sam Houston U., 1956, MEd, 1971. Acct. Pan Am. Petroleum Corp., Thibodaux, La., 1956-61; bus. tchr. Brenham (Tex.) H.S., 1962-90; county commr. Washington County, Brenham, 1991—. With U.S. Army, 1951-53, Korea. Decorated Def. Disting. Svc. medal. Republican. Methodist. Avocations: gardening, nature study. Home: 2106 Jane Ln Brenham TX 77833 Office: Washington County Horton Loop Brenham TX 77833

PIPES, RICHARD, historian, educator; b. Cieszyn, Poland, July 11, 1923; came to U.S., 1940, naturalized, 1943; s. Mark and Sophia (Haskelberg) P.; m. Irene Eugenia Roth, Sept. 1, 1946; children—Daniel, Steven. Student, Muskingum (Ohio) Coll., 1940-43; AB, Cornell U., 1945; PhD, Harvard U., 1950; LLD (hon.), Muskingum Coll., 1988; LHD (hon.), Adelphi U., 1991; Doctor honoris causa, U. Silesia, Poland, 1994. Mem. faculty Harvard U., 1950—, prof. history, 1958-75, Frank B. Baird Jr. prof. history, 1975-96, Baird prof. emeritus, 1996—; assoc. dir. Russian Rsch. Ctr., 1962-64, dir., 1968-73; sr. cons. Stanford Research Inst., 1973-78; dir. East European and Soviet affairs NSC, 1981-82; cons. Ency. Britannica;. Author: Formation of the Soviet Union, rev. edit., 1964, Karamzin's Memoir on Ancient and Modern Russia, 1959, Social Democracy and the St. Petersburg Labor

Movement, 1963, Europe Since 1815, 1970, Struve: Liberal on the Left, 1870-1905, 1970, Russia Under the Old Regime, 1974, Struve: Liberal on the Right, 1905-1944, 1980, U.S.-Soviet Relations in the Era of Detente, 1981, Survival Is Not Enough, 1984, Russia Observed, 1989, The Russian Revolution, 1990, Communism: The Vanished Specter, 1993, Russia Under the Bolshevik Regime, 1994, A Concise History of the Russian Revolution, 1995, Three "Whys" of the Russian Revolution, 1996; editor: Russian Intelligentsia, 1961; (with John Fine) Of the Russe Commonwealth (Giles Fletcher), 1966, Revolutionary Russia, 1968, Collected Works in Fifteen Volumes (P.B. Struve), 1970, Soviet Strategy in Europe, 1976, The Unknown Lenin, 1996; mem. editl. bd. Strategic Rev., Orbis, Comparative Strategy, Jour. Strategic Studies, Internat. Jour. Intelligence and Counterintelligence, Continuity, Arkana. Mem. exec. com. Com. on Present Danger, 1977-92; chmn. Govt. Team B to Rev. Intelligence Estimates, 1976; mem. Reagan transition team Dept. State, 1980. Served with USAAF, 1943-46. Guggenheim fellow, 1956, 65; fellow Am. Coun. Learned Socs., 1965; fellow Ctr. for Advanced Study in Behavioral Scis., Stanford, Calif., 1969-70; lectr. Spring lecture Nobel Norwegian Inst., Oslo, 1993; recipient Comdr.'s Cross of Merit, Republic of Poland, 1996. Fellow Am. Acad. Arts and Scis.; mem. Coun. Fgn. Rels., Polish Acad. (fgn. mem.). Home: 17 Berkeley St Cambridge MA 02138-3409

PIPES, WESLEY O'FERAL, civil engineering educator; b. Dallas, Jan. 28, 1932; s. Wesley O'Feral and Lunnette (Waller) P.; children—Phylis, Victoria (dec.), Wesley, Susan, Gordon. B.S., N. Tex. State U., 1953, M.S., 1955; Ph.D., Northwestern U., 1959. Research engr. U. Calif.-Berkeley, 1955-57; asst. prof. Northwestern U., 1959-62, assoc. prof., 1962-67, prof. civil engring., 1967-74, prof. biol. scis., 1969-74; L. Drew Betz prof. ecology Drexel U., 1975-83, prof. civil engring., 1983—, head civil engring. dept., 1983-87; cons. water pollution and wastewater treatment Office of Drinking Water, EPA, 1986-91, P.R. Aquaduct and Sewer Authority, 1991, Malcolm Pirnie, Inc., 1991-92, Delaware County (Pa.) Regional Authority, 1992, environ. enforcement divsn. U.S. Dept. Justice, 1993-96, Ductile Iron Pipe Rsch. Assn., 1994, Smith & Loveless, Inc., 1994-95. Mem. tech. adv. com. on water resources Northeastern Ill. Planning Commn., 1968-74. Named one of 10 Outstanding Young Men of Chgo. Chgo. Jr. Assn. Commerce and Industry, 1963; recipient Rsch. award Pa. Water Pollution Control Assn., 1989. Mem. ASCE, Assn. Environ. Engring. Profs. (dir. 1970-76, v.p. 1974, pres. 1975), Am. Water Works Assn., Water Pollution Control Fedn., Am. Soc. Microbiology, The Internat. Environmetrics Soc. (dir. 1994—), Sigma Xi, Tau Beta Pi. Research and publs. on microbiology of water and wastewater. Office: Drexel U Dept Civil Engring Philadelphia PA 19104

PIPIA, ROSARIA ANNA, publishing executive, consultant; b. Trapani, Sicily, Italy, Mar. 17, 1962; came to U.S., 1978; d. Gaspare and Gaetana (Nicolosi) P. AA, CUNY, 1985, MA in Italian Lit., 1990; BA in Italian Lang. and Lit., St. John's U., 1987; PhD, NYU. Mgr. book dept. Speedimpex U.S.A., Inc., N.Y.C., 1988-94; pres. Transglobal Books, Inc., 1995—; prof. Italian St. John's U., 1995—; adj. lectr. Italian CUNY, 1989-95; prof. Italian St. John's U., 1995—; Italian tchr. Holy Cross High Sch., 1987-88; Italian tutor Queensborough C.C., 1982-83; book reviewer. Contbr. articles to profl. jours. Mem. MLA, NAFE, Gamma Kappa Alpha. Roman Catholic. Avocation: oil painting. Home: 73-22 72nd St Glendale NY 11385-7352 Office: Transglobal Books Inc 73-22 72d St Glendale NY 11385

PIPKIN, JAMES HAROLD, JR., lawyer; b. Houston, Jan. 3, 1939; s. James Harold and Zenda Marie (Lewis) P. BA, Princeton U., 1960; JD, Harvard U., 1963; Diploma in Law, Oxford (Eng.) U., 1965. Bar: D.C. 1964, U.S. Supreme Ct. 1969, D.C. Ct. Appeals, 1972. Law ck. to assoc. justice U.S. Supreme Ct., Washington, 1963-64; assoc. Steptoe and Johnson, Washington, 1965-70, ptnr., 1971-93; counselor to The Sec. of the Interior U.S. Dept. of the Interior, 1993—; U.S. spl. negotiator for Pacific Salmon, Dept. of State, 1994—; rank of amb. Dept. of State, 1995-96; counsel Friends of Music, Smithsonian Inst., Washington, 1984-88; mem. Nat. Arbitration Panel, 1983-94. Author or co-author: The English Country House: A Grand Tour, 1985, The Country House Garden: A Grand Tour, 1987, Places of Tranquility, 1990; contbr. photographs and articles to mags. including House & Garden, Smithsonian mag., The Mag. Antiques, Archtl. Digest. Grand officier Confrérie des Chevaliers du Tastevin, 1989. Mem. ABA, D.C. Bar Assn., Met. Club. Home: 6109 Davenport Ter Bethesda MD 20817-5827 Office: Office of The Secretary 1849 C St NW Washington DC 20240-0001

PIPPEN, HARVEY G., government official; b. Atlanta, Tex., July 24, 1937; s. Harvey George and Esther P.; m. Sandra Leazar, Aug. 2, 1958; children—Kelly Ann, Robert Christopher. A.S., Arlington State Coll., Tex., 1957; B.A., L.L.B., U. Texas, 1961. Sr. staff assoc. pres. Advisory Council on Exec. Orgn., 1970-71; br. chief grants policy and procedures, EPA, 1971—, dept. dir. grants adminstrn. div., 8 yrs., dir. grants adminstrn. div., 1980-92, dir. office of grants and debarment, 1992—. Contbg. author book on ind. regulatory agys. Pres., Arlington All Stars, 1983-84. Recipient Presdl. Rank award. Mem. Tex. Bar Assn., Nat. Assistance Mgmt. Assn. (dir.). Mem. Disciples of Christ. Home: 2640 N Richmond St Arlington VA 22207-5122*

PIPPEN, SCOTTIE, professional basketball player; b. Hamburg, Ark., Sept. 25, 1965. Student, U. Cen. Ark., 1983-87. With Seattle Super Sonics, 1987; guard/forward Chgo. Bulls, 1987—; player NBA Championship Team, 1991, 92, 93, U.S. Olympic Basketball Team, 1992. Named to All-Star team, 1990, 92-93, NBA All-Defensive First team, 1992, 93, 94, All-Defensive second team, 1991, NBA All-Star Team, 1992-94, NBA All-Star MVP, 1994, All-NBA First Team, 1994; mem. NBA championship team, 1991-93, 96. Office: Chgo Bulls United Ctr 1901 W Madison St Chicago IL 60612-2459*

PIPPIN, JAMES ADRIAN, JR., middle school educator; b. Rockingham, N.C., Aug. 6, 1954; s. James A, Sr. and Essie Juanita (Rorie) P. BS, Appalachian State U., 1976; MEd, Columbus Coll., 1982. Tchr. Eddy Jr. High Sch., Columbus, Ga., 1976-89; dir. N.C. Agrl. Extension Svc., Penn 4-H Ctr., Reidsville, 1980-89, Millstone 4-H Camp, Ellerbe, N.C., 1993; tchr. Arnold Middle Sch., Columbus, Ga., 1989—; mem. multicultural curriculum com., sick leave bank com., textbook adoption com. and tech. com. MCSD; tchg. program participant Found. Internat. Edn., Inverness, Scotland, 1986, Dunedin, New Zealand, 1989; curriculum devel. program participant Ga. Dept. Edn., Germany, 1989, 91; adv. com. Deutsche Welle Video, 1992, 95; internat. edn. adv. com. Ga. Dept. Edn., 1993—. Author: The Physiological and Psychological Effects of Space Flight Environments on Blood Glucose and Circadian Rhythms of the Human Body; contb. author: (curricuums) World Studies, Germany and Georgia: The Search for Unity, Education in Thailand, Germany Unity and Disunity: Ubersichten; Overview of the Federal Republic of Germany, Images of Germany: Past and Present, The Olympic Spirit; A Worldwide Connection, Vol. III. Mem. discovery gallery com. Columbus Mus. Arts & Scis., curriculum devel. com. Atlanta Com. for Olympic Games. Named Ga. Tchr. Yr., 1986, Ga. State Semi-Finalist NASA Tchr. Space Program, 1985; recipient Project award TV Worth Teaching, CBS, 1987; Fulbright Study-Tour scholar, Taiwan and Thailand, 1992. Mem. ASCD, NEA (congl. contact team), Columbus Social Sci. Alliance (bd. dirs.), Ga. Assn. Educators, Nat. Coun. Social Scis., Ga. Coun. Social Scis. (bd. dirs.), Musogee Assn. Edn. (v.p., 2d v.p., chmn. policies and grievences com., legis. com., chmn. officer nominating com.), Columbus Hist. Soc., Columbus Hist. Dist. Preservation Soc. (bd. dirs.), Chattahoochee Valley Archaeol. Soc., Phi Alpha Theta, Phi Delta Kappa.

PIPPIN, JAMES REX, health care company executive, educator; b. Clovis, N.Mex., Apr. 3, 1949; s. C.A. and J. (Davis) P.; m. Annette Jacqueline Charsha, Feb. 6, 1971; children: Ken, Matthew, Sabrina. BS, Ea. N.Mex. U., 1971; MPA, U. Ariz., 1973. Cert. health care adminstr., Ill. Adminstr. The Mayflower, Grinnell, Iowa, 1973-78; exec. dir. Mayflower Homes, Inc., Grinnell, 1978-80; pres., CEO, Lifelink Corp., Bensenville, Ill., 1980—; preceptor, adj. prof. George Washington U., Washington, 1985—. Contbr. articles to profl. jours. Mem. Am. Coll. Health Care Adminstrs., Am. Assn. Homes for Aging (treas. 1988-90, Profl. of Yr. award 1979), Coun. for Health and Human Svcs. (pres. 1990-92, Exec. of Yr. award 1985), Ill. Assn. Homes for Aging (pres. 1986-88), Ill. Child Care Assn. (bd. dirs.), Internat. Assn. Svcs. for the Aging (bd. dirs. 1995—). Republican. Mem. United Ch. of Christ. Avocation: travel. Office: Lifelink Corp 331 S York Rd Bensenville IL 60106-2673

PIPPIN, JOHN JOSEPH, cardiologist; b. Brookline, Mass., Jan. 7, 1950; s. Shirley Ann (Marson) P. AB in History, Harvard U., 1971; MD, U. Mass., 1980. Diplomate Am. Bd. Internal Medicine. Police officer Harvard U., Cambridge, Mass., 1971-76, City of Cambridge, 1976; resident in medicine New Eng. Deaconess Hosp., Boston, 1980-83, chief resident, 1983-84, fellow in cardiology, 1984-86; fellow in nuclear cardiology U. Tex. Southwestern Med. Sch., Dallas, 1986-87; asst. prof. medicine Med. Coll. Va., Richmond, 1987-91; pvt. practice cardiology Okla. Heart Inst., Tulsa, 1991—; assoc. prof. medicine U. Okla. Health Sci. Ctr., Tulsa, 1992—; didr. nuc. cardiology Hillcrest Med. Ctr., Tulsa, 1991—, Cardiovasc. Assessment Ctr., 1991—, dir. James D. Harvey Rsch. Ctr., 1995—; chmn. Instl. Rev. Bd. Author 3 monographs; contbr. more than 50 abstracts, 15 articles to profl. jours. Recipient Clinician-Scientist award Am. Heart Assn., 1986-91. Fellow Am. Coll. Cardiology, Am. Soc. Nuclear Cardiology, Soc. Nuclear Medicine. Avocations: running, weightlifting, music, dogs. Office: Okla Heart Inst 1265 S Utica Ave Tulsa OK 74104-4243

PIPPIN, KATHRYN ANN, state agency administrator; b. Wilmington, Del., July 12, 1947; d. Allen Davis and Mary T. (Thawley) P. BA, U. Del., 1968, MA, 1969; MA, U. N.C., 1972, PhD, 1977. Cert. tchr., Del. Instr. U. Del., Newark, 1969; teaching asst. U. N.C., Chapel Hill, 1972-73; dir. rsch. and info. devel. SOICC-Dept. Labor, Wilmington, 1979-81; adminstrv. asst. to commr. Del. Dept. Correction, Wilmington, 1982-83, rsch. analyst, 1983—; chairperson Deljis Bd. Mgrs., Dover, Del., 1983-84; mem. adj. faculty Wesley Coll., Dover, 1985-86, Wilmington Coll., 1987—; exec. dir. Mother and Child Reading Program, New Castle, Del., 1993—. Author: Chesapeake Lore, 1980, Teachers: Guardians of our Hopes and Dreams, 1992, (play) Chains of Glory, 1983, The Devil's Crossroads, 1996; prodr.: (documentary film) A Secret Road North: Harriet Tubman & The Underground Railroad, 1993, Families in Transition: A Smyrna History, 1995, Living in Harmony with Nature, 1995. Del. Rep. State Conv., Lewes, Del., 1982; active Open Spaces Com., New Castle, 1982-83, Pacem in Terris, Wilmington, 1991—; bd. dirs. St. Patrick's Sr. Ctr., Wilmington, 1982-83. Mem. Am. Correctional Assn. (sec. 1988-90, pres. 1990-92, historian 1993-95), Fort Del. Soc. (historian 1983—), Ea. Evaluation Rsch. Soc., Duck Creek Hist. Soc., Leadership Del., Rotary Internat., Phi Beta Kappa. Roman Catholic. Avocations: reading, writing, travel, hiking, photography. Home: 10 N Delaware St Smyrna DE 19977-1102 Office: Del Dept Correction 80 Monrovia Ave Smyrna DE 19977-1530

PIRANI, CONRAD LEVI, pathologist, educator; b. Pisa, Italy, July 29, 1914; came to U.S., 1939, naturalized, 1945; s. Mario Giacomo Levi and Adriana P.; m. Luciana Nahmias, Mar. 12, 1955; children: Barbara, Sylvia, Robert. Diploma, Ginnasio-Liceo Beccaria, 1932; M.D., U. Milano, Italy, 1938. Intern Columbus Meml. Hosp., Chgo., 1940-42; resident Michael Reese Hosp., Chgo., 1942-45; instr. pathology U. Ill., Chgo., 1945-48; asst. prof. U. Ill., 1948-52, asso. prof., 1952-55, prof., 1955-70; chmn. dept. pathology Michael Reese Hosp., Chgo., 1965-72; prof. pathology Coll. Physicians and Surgeons, Columbia U., N.Y.C., 1972-85; prof. emeritus Coll. Physicians and Surgeons, Columbia U., 1985—; dir. Renal Pathology Lab., 1972-84; cons. Armed Forces Inst. Pathology; mem. sci. com. Kidney Found., N.Y., 1973-80. Contbg. author various books.; assoc. editor Lab. Investigation, 1972-82, Nephron, 1975-92, Clin. Nephrology, 1989-92; contbr. numerous articles to profl. jours. USPHS, NIH grantee. Mem. Am. Assn. Pathologists, AAAS, Internat. Acad. Pathology (counselor 1966-69), Am. Soc. Nephrology (John P. Peters award 1987), Internat. Soc. Nephrology. Home: 28 Bradford St Glen Rock NJ 07452-2102 Office: 630 W 168th St New York NY 10032-3702

PIRCHER, LEO JOSEPH, lawyer; b. Berkeley, Calif., Jan. 4, 1933; s. Leo Charles and Christine (Moore) P.; m. Phyllis McConnell, Aug. 4, 1956 (div. April 1981); children: Christopher, David, Eric; m. Nina Silverman, June 14, 1987; B.S., U. Calif.-Berkeley, 1954, J.D., 1957. Bar: Calif. 1958, N.Y. 1985; cert. specialist taxation law Calif. Bd. Legal Specialization. Assoc. Lawler, Felix & Hall, L.A., 1957-62, ptnr., 1962-65, sr. ptnr., 1965-83; sr. ptnr. Pircher, Nichols & Meeks, L.A., 1983—; adj. prof. Loyola U. Law Sch., L.A., 1959-61; corp. sec. Am. Metal Bearing Co., Gardena, Calif., 1975—, dir. Varco Internat. Inc., Orange, Calif.; speaker various law schs. and bar assns. edn. programs. Author: (with others) Definition and Utility of Leases, 1968. Chmn. pub. fin. and taxation sect. Calif. Town Hall, Los Angeles, 1970-71. Mem. Calif. State Bar, N.Y. State Bar, Los Angeles County Bar Assn. (exec. com. comml. law secton), ABA, Nat. Assn. Real Estate Investment Trusts Inc. (cert. specialist taxation law). Republican. Club: Regency (L.A.). Office: Pircher Nichols & Meeks 1999 Avenue Of The Stars Los Angeles CA 90067-6022

PIRET, MARGUERITE ALICE, investment banker; b. St. Paul, May 10, 1948; d. E.L. and Alice P.; children: Andrew, Anne. AB, Radcliffe Coll., 1969; MBA, Harvard U., 1974. Comml. loan officer Bank of New Eng. (now Fleet Bank), Boston, 1974-79; mng. dir. Kridel Securities, N.Y.C., 1979-81; pres., founder, dir. Newbury, Piret & Co., Inc., Boston, 1981—; trustee, chmn. audit com. Pioneer Mutual Funds, Boston; gov. Investment Co. Inst., 1996—; bd. dirs. Organogenesis, Inc., 1995—. Vis. com. mem. Am. decorative arts and sculpture Mus. Fine Arts, Boston, 1982—; mem. nominating com. for candidates for overseer of Harvard U. and for candidates for dir. of Harvard Alumni Assn.; adv. com. on shareholder responsibility Harvard U., 1986-87; trustee Boston Med. Ctr. and predecessor, 1979—, Mass. Hosp. Assn., 1983-86, Boston Ballet Ctr. for Dance Edn., 1989-93. Mem. Harvard Club. Office: Newbury Piret & Co Inc One Boston Pl Boston MA 02108

PIRIE, ROBERT BURNS, JR., defense analyst; b. San Diego, Sept. 10, 1933; s. Robert Burns and Gertrude May (Freeman) P.; m. Joan Adams, Dec. 23, 1960; children: John Winthrop, Carl Joseph Emil, Susan Gilman. Student, Princeton U., 1950-51; B.S., U.S. Naval Acad., 1955; B.A., Magdalen Coll., Oxford U., 1959, M.A., 1963. Commd. ensign U.S. Navy, 1955, advanced through grades to comdr., 1969; comdg. officer (U.S.S. Skipjack), 1969-72; dep. asst. dir. Congl. Budget Office, 1975-77; prin. dep. asst. sec. for manpower, res. affairs and logistics Dept. Def., Washington, 1977-79; asst. sec. Dept. Def., 1979-81; mgmt. cons., 1981—; def. analyst Ctr. for Naval Analyses, Alexandria, Va., 1981-83; asst. v.p. Inst. for Def. Analyses, Alexandria, Va., 1983-86, v.p., 1986-87; exec. v.p. Essex Corp., Alexandria, Va., 1987, pres., 1987-88; sr. economist Rand Corp., Washington, 1989; dir. strategic studies group U.S. Naval War Coll., 1989-92; v.p. Ctr. Naval Analyses, Alexandria, Va., 1992-94; asst. sec. of Navy for Installations and Environ. USN, Washington, 1994—. Vestryman St. John's Episcopal Ch., Chevy Chase, Md., 1973-76, 81, jr. warden, 1982-84, sr. warden, 1984-87; trustee U.S. Naval Acad. Found., 1980-94. Rhodes scholar, 1956. Mem. U.S. Naval Inst., Internat. Inst. Strategic Studies, U.S. Naval Acad. Alumni Assn. (trustee 1967-70). Club: Vincent's. Office: 1000 Navy Pentagon Washington DC 20350-1000

PIRKL, JAMES JOSEPH, industrial designer, educator, writer; b. Nyack, N.Y., Dec. 27, 1930; s. James and Ida Bertha (Gigrich) P.; m. Sarah B. W. Woolsey, June 8, 1974; children: Theo, James, Philip. Cert. Advt. Design, Pratt Inst., 1951, B of Indsl. Design cum laude, 1958. With design staff Gen. Motors Corp., Warren, Mich., 1958-65; sr. designer Gen. Motors Corp., 1961-64, asst. chief designer, 1964-65; instr. indsl. design Center for Creative Studies, Detroit, 1963-65; faculty dept. design Syracuse (N.Y.) U., 1965-92, assoc. prof., 1969-73, prof. indsl. design, 1974-92, prof. emeritus, 1992—, coord. indsl. design program, 1979-84, chmn. dept. design, 1985-91; exec. council chmn. Sch. Art, 1976-78, 80-81; sr. rsch. fellow All-U. Gerontology Ctr., 1990-92; prin. James J. Pirkl/Design, 1965—; cons. Brownlie Design, Inc., 1972—, Rolland Co., 1993, Am. Soc. on Aging, 1995, Arthritis Found., 1993-96, GE Appliances, 1994, ProMatura Group, 1994-95, Prince Corp., 1991, Ford Motor Design Ctr., 1992, Loretto Geriatric Ctr., Sage Marcom Inc., 1988-90, Hazard Mgmt. Co., 1985, Marcom Switches Inc., 1977-82, Cazenovia Abroad Ltd., 1973-81, Holistic Mgmt. Group, Inc., 1981, Pulos Design Assocs., 1972-80, Beck Assocs., 1976, Fed. Prison Industries, 1974, Gen. Electric Co., 1967-70, Genesee Labs., Inc., 1968, N.Y. State Council on Arts, 1968-69, Stettner-Trush, Inc., 1972-78, Strathmore Chem. Coatings, Inc., 1969, 72, Village of Cazenovia, 1979-93, Xerox Corp., 1975, Age Wave, Inc., 1993—; chmn. accreditation council Design Found., 1982-84; interviewed on Nat. Pub. Radio; invited lectr. Royal Coll. Art, London, 1993, 95, Netherlands Design Inst., Amsterdam, 1993, 95, Inst. for Gerontech., Eindhoven, 1995, Nat. Coll. Art and Design, Dublin, Ireland, 1995, U. Art and Design, Helsinki, 1995, China Instnl. Design Assn., Taiwan, 1990, Korea Indsl. Design Soc., Taijon, 1992. Author: Transgenerational Design: Products for an Aging Population, 1994; co-author: Guidelines and Strategies for Designing Transgenerational Products, 1988; co-editor: State of Art and Science of Design, 1971; co-designer: Gen. Motors Futurama Exhbn., N.Y. World's Fair, 1964-65; contbr. articles to profl. jours. including Jour. Am. Soc. Aging, Design Mgmt. Jour., Jour. Indsl. Designers Soc. Am., Bus. Adminstrn. Jour., Design News, Design Perspectives, Indsl. Design. Mem. Everson Mus. Art, 1977-85; chmn. planning commn. Town of Cazenovia, N.Y., 1988-93; mem. senate Syracuse U., 1973-80; mem. adv. bd. SEARS Project, 1989-91; chmn. chancellor's citation com., 1988-92; mem. exhbns. com. Syracuse Cultural Resources Coun., 1992-93; coord. Tylenol/Arthritis Found. Student Design Awards Program, 1993—. With SeaBees USN, 1951-55. Recipient Gold Indsl. Design Excellence award Indsl. Designers Soc. Am. and Bus. Week Mag., 1994. Fellow Indsl. Designers Soc. Am. (chmn. universal design com. 1991-94, chmn. NASAD liaison com. 1984-88, mem. archives com. 1988-92, nat. bd. dirs. 1977-81, chmn. Cen. N.Y. chpt. 1977-78, v.p. Mid-East region 1978-80, dir., chmn. edn. com. 1980-81, U.S. rep., del. Internat. Congress Socs. Indsl. Design 1989, mem. edn. com. 1989); mem. The Design Found. (chmn. accreditation coun. 1982), Nat. Assn. Schs. Art and Design (accreditation evaluator 1985-95), Nat. Ctr. for a Barrier Free Environment (adv. task force 1981), Human Factors Soc. (life mem.), Am. Soc. Aging (contbr. articles to jour.), Author's Guild. Achievements include patent for 4-way handle. Home: 66 Camino Barranca Placitas NM 87043-9314

PIRKLE, EARL CHARNELL, geologist, educator; b. nr. Buckhead, Ga., Jan. 8, 1922; s. Early Charnell and Eva Lee (Collins) P.; m. Valda Nell Armistead, July 9, 1942; children: Betty Jean, William A., Fredric L. AB, Emory U., 1943; MS, 1947; postgrad., U. Tenn., 1947-50; PhD, U. Cin., 1956. Certified profl. geologist. Prodn. coordinator, research crystallographer Pan-Electronics Labs., Inc., Atlanta, 1942-45; instr. geology U. Tenn., 1947-50; mem. faculty dept. phys. scis. and geology U. Fla., Gainesville, 1950-93, prof. emeritus, 1993—; prof. U. Fla., 1963—, chmn. dept. phys. scis., 1972-79; dir. Phys. Scis., 1979-82; cons. in field; vis. prof. geology Emory U., summers 1959-65; rsch. cons. Fla. Dept. Nat. Resources Bur. Geology, 1950-70. Author: Natural Regions of the United States, 1977, 4th edit., 1985; Editor: Physical Science- Our Environment, 1968, Our Physical Environment, 1980; Contbr. articles to profl. jours. Served with AUS, 1945-46. Fellow Geol. Soc. Am., Soc. Econ. Geologists; mem. Am. Assn. Petroleum Geologists, Am. Soc. Mining, Metall. and Petroleum Engrs., Fla. Acad. Scis., Southeastern Geol. Soc., Phi Beta Kappa, Sigma Gamma Epsilon, Gamma Theta Epsilon, Sigma Chi. Democrat. Methodist.

PIRKLE, ESTUS WASHINGTON, minister; b. Vienna, Ga., Mar. 12, 1930; s. Grover Washington and Bessie Nora (Jones) P.; m. Annie Catherine Gregory, Aug. 18, 1955; children: Letha Dianne, Gregory Don. BA cum laude, Mercer U., 1951; BD, MRE, Southwestern Bapt. Sem., 1956, ThM, 1958; DD, Covington Theol. Sem., 1982. Ordained to ministry So. Bapt. Conv., 1949. Pastor Locust Grove Bapt. Ch., New Albany, Miss.; spkr. Camp Zion, Myrtle, Miss. Author: Wintertime, 1968, Preachers in Space, 1969, Sermon Outlines Book, 1969, Are Horoscopes All Right?, 1971, I Believe God, 1973, Who Will Build Your House?,1978, The 1611 King James Bible: A Study by Dr. Estus Pirkle, 1994; prodr. religious films: If Footmen Tire You, What Will Horses Do?, 1973, The Burning Hell, 1975, Believer's Heaven, 1977. Home and Office: PO Box 80 Myrtle MS 38650-0080

PIRKLE, GEORGE EMORY, television and film actor, director; b. Atlanta, Sept. 3, 1947; s. George Washington and Glanna Adeline (Palmer) P.; m. Karen Leigh Horn, Oct. 20, 1973; 1 child, Charity Caroline. Student North Ga. Coll., 1965-66; BA in Journalism, U. Ga., 1969, MA, 1971. Radio announcer, sportscaster for various radio stas., North Ga. area, 1968-70; TV producer, dir. Instructional Resources Ctr., Athens, Ga., 1969-70; info. officer, Southeastern Signal Sch., U.S. Army, 1971; producer, dir. DA MoPic Svc., Continental Army Command Network and Signal Corps TV Div., 1972-73; pub. info. officer Ga. Dept. Revenue, Atlanta, 1973-78; coord. TV prodn. svcs. So. Co. Svcs., Inc., Birmingham, Ala., 1978-88; exec. v.p. Mgmt. and Human Devel. Assocs., Inc., Birmingham, 1984-86; producer Prodn. Works, Birmingham, 1984-88; actor for various radio and TV commercials, corp. TV programs, radio dramas, stage plays, 1968—; owner Talking Rock Prodns., Cumming, Ga., 1989—. Editor monthly newsletter Ga. Revenews, 1973-78; editor, dir. Bankers TV Network, 1990-92; writer, producer, dir., exec. producer more than 500 corp. and pub. svc. TV and film programs. Recipient So. Superlative outstanding employee award, So. Co. Svcs., 1986. Mem. communications com. Birmingham Area Coun. Boy Scouts Am., 1983-85; Master of ceremonies gov.'s vet. awards presentation World Peace Luncheon, Birmingham, 1981, 82, 84; dir. campaign film Pensacola United Way, 1989; exec. producer videotape for Birmingham Film Coun., 1985; producer, dir. Highway in Crisis, 1986; writer, producer, dir. campaign film Birmingham Area United Way. 1981, 86, 87; writer, producer, narrator, 1987 campaign film; bd. dirs. Birmingham Internat. Ednl. Film Festival, 1987-91; chmn. Sadie award com., student video competition dir.; comml. acting instr. elan/Casablancas Modeling/Career Ctr., 1988-92; instr. Cliff Osmond Acting Program, 1989-92; anchor This Week in Banking, 1990-92; mem. tech. steering com. Forsyth Bd. Edn., 1995—; dir. City Pks. & Recreation Bd., 1996—. 1st lt. U.S. Army, 1971-73. Recipient Battles award, 1988, various others. Mem. Internat. TV Assn. (charter pres. Birmingham chpt. 1984-85, pres. pro tem 1984, editor newsletter Freeze Frame), So. Electric System Visual Communications Subcom. (founding), Ga. Hist. Soc., United Way of Forsyth County (bd. dirs., 1995—), Hist. Soc. Forsyth County (pres. 1996). Avocations: photography, music, genealogy, hist. rsch., archaeology. Office: 105 Brooks Farm Dr Cumming GA 30040-2423

PIRO, ANTHONY JOHN, radiologist; b. Boston, May 28, 1930; s. John Anthony and Josephine (Pepe) P.; m. Marian Giallombardo, Sept. 5, 1955; children—Anthony John, Janet, Jacquelyn. A.B., Boston U., 1952, M.D., 1956. Diplomate: Am. Bd. Internal Medicine, Am. Bd. Radiology. Intern Mass. Meml. Hosp., Boston, 1956-57; resident Boston VA Hosp., 1959-62; practice medicine specializing in internal medicine Framingham, Mass., 1962-63; staff physician Boston VA Hosp., 1963-66; sr. asso. Children's Cancer Research Found., 1966-70; radiotherapist Harvard Joint Center for Radiation Therapy, 1970-77; prof. therapeutic radiology, chmn. dept. therapeutic radiology Tufts-New Eng. Med. Center Hosp., 1977-79; radiation oncologist Salem (Mass.) Hosp., 1979—. Contbr. articles to profl. jours. Served with USAF, 1957-59. Nat. Cancer Inst. grantee, 1977-79. Fellow ACP, Am. Coll. Radiology; mem. Am. Soc. Clin. Oncologists, Am. Soc. Therapeutic Radiologists, Am. Assn. Cancer Rsch., Phi Beta Kappa, Alpha Omega Alpha. Unitarian. Home: 6 Cider Mill Rd Lynnfield MA 01940-1132 Office: 81 Highland Ave Salem MA 01970-2714 also: North Shore Cancer Ctr 17 Centennial Dr Peabody MA 01960

PIRODSKY, DONALD MAX, psychiatrist, educator; b. Freeport, N.Y., Feb. 2, 1945; s. Max and Doris Geilhard (Biedermann) P.; m. Gail Giufre Pallotta, Jan. 4, 1997; children: Laura Anne, Jason Donald. BA, Hofstra U., 1966; MD, SUNY, Syracuse, 1970. Diplomate Am. Bd. Psychiatry and Neurology, Nat. Bd. Med. Examiners. Med. intern Northwestern U. Med. Ctr., Chgo., 1970-71; resident in psychiatry Strong Meml. Hosp., Rochester, N.Y., 1973-74, U. Ariz. Med. Ctr., Tucson, 1974-76; instr. psychiatry SUNY Health Sci. Ctr., Syracuse, 1976-78, attending psychiatrist, 1976—, asst. prof. psychiatry, 1978-85, mem. exec. com. of med. coll. assembly, 1979-82, clin. assoc. prof., 1985—; pvt. practice Syracuse and Fayetteville, N.Y., 1976—; staff psychiatrist, dir. consultation/liaison svc. Syracuse VA Med. Ctr., 1976-87, chmn. pharmacy rev. and therapeutic agts. com., 1980-86; psychiat. cons. Ariz. Sch. for Deaf and Blind, Tucson, 1975-76, Syracuse Devel. Ctr., 1977—, Rochester Sch. for Deaf, 1978-81; ex-officio mem. Family Counseling Agy., Tucson, 1975-76. Author: Primer of Clinical Psychopharmacology: A Practical Guide, 1981, (with Jerry S. Cohn) Clinical Primer of Psychopharmacology: A Practical Guide, 2d edit., 1992; contbr. articles to profl. jours., chpts. to med. books. Lt. comdr. USPHS, 1971-73. Fellow Am. Psychiat. Assn.; mem. AMA, Am. Psychosomatic Soc., Am. Assn. Mental Retardation, Med. Soc. State of N.Y., Onondaga County Med. Soc. Episcopalian. Avocations: sports, collecting baseball cards and other sports memorabilia. Office: 7000 E Genesee St Fayetteville NY 13066-1131

PIRONE, THOMAS PASCAL, plant pathology educator; b. Ithaca, N.Y., Jan. 3, 1936; s. Pascal Pompey and Loretta Muriel (Kelly) P.; m. Sherrill Sevier, Aug. 1, 1961; children—John Sevier, Catherine Sherrill. B.S., Cornell U., 1957; Ph.D., U. Wis., 1960. Asst. prof. La. State U., Baton Rouge, 1960-63; asso. prof. La. State U., 1963-67, U. Ky., Lexington, 1967-71; prof. U. Ky., 1971—, chmn. plant pathology, 1978-86; mem. recombinant DNA adv. com. NIH, 1984-87. Contbr. articles on plant virology to profl. jours.; mem. editorial bd.: Virology, 1974-76, Phytopathology, 1971-73, sr. editor, 1977-78, Ann. Rev. Phytopathology, 1985-90. Sr. Fulbright research fellow U.K., 1974-75. Fellow Am. Phytopathol. Soc. (Ruth Allen award 1989); mem. AAAS, Internat. Soc. Plant Pathology, Am. Soc. Virology. Office: U Ky Dept Plant Pathology Lexington KY 40546

PIRONTI, LAVONNE DE LAERE, developer, fundraiser; b. L.A., Jan. 11, 1946; d. Emil Joseph and Pearl Mary (Vilmur) De Laere; m. Aldo Pironti, May 21, 1977. BA in Internat. Rels., U. So. Calif., L.A., 1967. Commd. ensign USN, 1968-91, advanced through grades to comdr., 1979; pers. officer Lemoore (Calif.) Naval Air Sta., 1972-74; human rels. mgmt. specialist Human Resource Mgmt. Detachment, Naples, Italy, 1975-78; comms. staff officer Supreme Hdqrs. Allied Powers Europe, Shape, Belgium, 1979-83; dir. Navy Family Svc. Ctr. Sigonella Naval Air Sta., Sicily, 1983-85; exec. officer Naval Sta. Guam, Apra Harbor, 1985-87; comms. staff officer NATO Comm. and Info. Sys. Agy., Brussels, Belgium, 1987-89; polit. officer for Guam, trust Territories Pacific Islands Comdr. Naval Forces Marianas, Agana, Guam, 1989-91; store mgr. Sandal Tree, Lihue, Hawaii, 1991-92; CEO, exec. dir. YWCA of Kauai, Lihue, 1992—. Mem. Kauai Children's Justice com., Lihue, 1993—; co-chair Kauai Human Svcs. Coun., Lihue; bd. dirs. Hawaii Health and Human Svcs. Alliance, Lihue, 1993—; chair Kauai County Family Self Sufficiency Program Adv. Bd., Lihue, 1993—. Decorated Navy Commendation medal, Meritorious Svc. Medal with 1 star, Def. Meritorious Svc. Medal with 2 stars, others; named Fed. Woman of the Yr. Comdr. Naval Forces Marianas, 1986-87. Roman Catholic. Avocations: racquetball, reading, aquacise. Office: YWCA of Kauai 3094 Elua St Lihue HI 96766-1209

PIRRO, ALFRED ANTHONY, JR., physician; b. Stamford, Conn., May 17, 1961; s. Alfred Anthony Sr. and Frances (Battaglia) P. BA in Natural Scis., The Johns Hopkins U., 1983; MD, U. Conn., 1987. Surg. resident The Hosp. of St. Raphael, New Haven, Conn., 1987-90; neurosurg. fellow Hartford (Conn.) Hosp., 1991-92, resident in anesthesiology, 1992-95, critical care fellow, 1995-97; emergency medicine physician Windham Hosp., Willamantic, Conn., 1991—; assoc. prof. anesthesiology John Dempsey Hosp. - U. Conn. Sch. Medicine, 1997—; assoc. prof. anesthesiology U. Conn. Sch. Medicine, John Dempsey Hosp., Farmington, Conn. Advisor Lally for Congress campaign, Mineola, N.Y., 1994. Beneficial-Hodson scholarship Johns Hopkins U., 1979, Pitney Bowes scholarship, 1979. Mem. AMA, Internat. Anesthesia Rsch. Soc., NRA (mem. Inst. for Legis. Action 1993—). Republican. Office: Dept Critical Care Hartford Hosp 80 Seymour St Hartford CT 06106-3465

PIRRUNG, MICHAEL CRAIG, chemistry educator, consultant; b. Cin., July 31, 1955; s. Joey Matthew and Grace (Fielman) P. BA, U. Tex., 1975; PhD, U. Calif., Berkeley, 1980. NSF postdoctoral fellow Columbia U., N.Y.C., 1980-81; asst. prof. Stanford (Calif.) U., 1981-89; sr. scientist Affymax Rsch. Inst., Palo Alto, Calif., 1989; assoc. prof. Duke U., Durham, N.C., 1989-94, prof., 1994—; dir. Duke U. program in biol. chemistry, 1994—, dir. biotechnology for bus., 1993—; cons. Am. Cyanamid, 1992—, Wyeth-Ayerst, 1995—, Chroma Xome 1995—; sci. advisor Affymax Rsch. Inst., 1991—. Recipient Newcomb Cleveland prize AAAS, 1991, Intellectual Property Owners Disting. Inventor award, 1993, Outstanding Young Tex. Ex., U. Tex. Ex-Students Assn., 1995. Fellow AAAS, John Simon Guggenheim Mem. Found.; mem. Am. Chem. Soc., Am. Soc. Plant Physiologists. Achievements include invention of spatially directed light addressable parallel chemical synthesis; research on mechanism of ethylene biosynthesis. Office: Duke U Dept Chemistry PM Gross Lab PO Box 90346 Durham NC 27708-0346

PIRSCH, CAROL MCBRIDE, former state senator, community relations administrator; b. Omaha, Dec. 27, 1936; d. Lyle Erwin and Hilfrie Louise (Lebeck) McBride; student U. Miami, Oxford, Ohio, U. Nebr., Omaha; m. Allen I. Pirsch, Mar. 28, 1954; children: Pennie Elizabeth, Pamela Elaine, Patrice Eileen, Phyllis Erika, Peter Allen, Perry Andrew. Former mem. data processing staff Omaha Public Schs.; former mem. wage practices dept. Western Electric Co., Omaha; former legal sec., Omaha; former office mgr. Pirsch Food Brokerage Co., Inc., Omaha; former employment supr. U.S. West Communications, Omaha, mgr. pub. policy; mem. Nebr. Senate, 1979-97. mem. Omaha Pers. Bd.; founder, past pres., bd. dirs. Nebr. Coalition for Victims of Crime. Recipient Golden Elephant award, Kuhle award N.E. Coalition for Victims of Crime, Cert. of Appreciation, Outstanding Legis. Efforts award YWCA, Breaking the Rule of Thumb award Nebr. Domestic Violence Sexual Assault Coalition, Cert. of Appreciation award U.S. Dept. Justice, Kuhle award Nebr. Coalition for Victims of Crime, 1986, Partnership award NE Credit Union League, 1995, Wings award League of Women Voters of Greater Omaha, 1995, NE VFW Spl. Recognition award for Exceptional Svc., 1995, Cert. Appreciation Nebr. Atty. Gen. Mem. VASA, Nat. Orgn. Victim Assistance (Outstanding Legis. Leadership award), Frechom Found., Tangier Women's Aux., Footprinters Internat., Nebr. Hist. Soc., Nebr. Taxpayers Assn., Keystone Citizen Patrol (Keystoner of the Month award), Audubon Soc., Rotary Internat., N.W. Community Club, Benson Rep. Women's Club, Bus. and Profl. Rep. Women Club. Office: State Capitol Lincoln NE 68509

PIRSIG, ROBERT MAYNARD, author; b. Mpls., Sept. 6, 1928; s. Maynard Ernest and Harriet Marie (Sjobeck) P.; m. Nancy Ann James, May 10, 1954 (div. Aug. 1978); children—Christopher (dec. Nov. 17, 1979), Theodore; m. Wendy L. Kimball, Dec. 28, 1978; 1 dau., Nell. B.A., U. Minn., 1950, M.A., 1958. Author: Zen And The Art of Motorcycle Maintenance, 1974, Lila, 1991. Served with AUS, 1946-48. Recipient award AAAL, 1979; Guggenheim fellow, 1974—. Mem. Soc. Tech. Communicators (sec. Minn. chpt. 1970-71, treas. 1971-72). Office: care Bantam Books 1540 Broadway New York NY 10036-4039

PIRTLE, H(AROLD) EDWARD, lawyer; b. Detroit, Apr. 6, 1948; s. Edward Bensen Pirtle and Lorraine Virginia (La Pointe) Schwartz; m. Maxine Mary Stencel, June 10, 1971 (div. May 1981); children: Kimberly, Jeffrey, Michelle; m. Betsy Yvonne Mark, Sept. 1, 1984. AS, Macomb County Cmty. Coll., Warren, Mich., 1977; B in applied sci., Siena Heights Coll., 1983; JD, U. Toldeo, 1990. Bar: Mich. 1990, U.S. Dist. Ct. (ea. dist.) Mich. 1990. Assoc. Beaman & Beaman, Jackson, Mich., 1990-91; solo practitioner H. Edward Pirtle, Atty. at Law, Detroit, 1991-96, Calligaro & Meyering, PC, Taylor, Mich., 1996—. With U.S. Navy, 1967-72. Mem. ABA, Criminal Def. Attys. of Mich., Washtenaw County Bar Assn., Met. Detroit Bar Assn., Am. Mensa (gen. rep. 1984-85, legal counsel Mensa Edn. and Rsch. Found., trustee). Avocations: camping, hunting, fishing. Office: Calligaro & Meyering PC 20600 Eureka Rd Ste 900 Taylor MI 48180-5380

PISANI, JOSEPH MICHAEL, physician; b. N.Y.C., Mar. 22, 1919; s. Antonio David and Josephine Catherine (Walsh) P.; m. Agatha Rita Evaskitis, Nov. 11, 1942; children: Michael, Robert, Richard. AB, Fordham Coll., 1938; MD, NYU, 1942; grad., Army Sch. Tropical Medicine, 1943. Intern Bellevue Hosp., 1942-43; resident medicine Bronx (N.Y.) VA Hosp., 1946-48, asst. chief chest service, 1948-49; dep. exec. dir. Com. on Med. Scis., Research and Devel. Bd., Washington, 1949-50; exec. dir. Com. on Med. Scis., Research and Devel. Bd., 1950-51; asst. dean and instr. medicine State U. Coll. of Medicine at N.Y., Bklyn., 1951-54; asst. dean, asst. prof. medicine State U. Coll. of Medicine at N.Y., 1954-57; asst. vis. physician Kings County Hosp., 1951-57; med. dir. Bankers Trust Co., N.Y.C., 1957-60, Union Family Med. Fund of Hotel Industry of N.Y.C., 1960-64; dep. med. dir. FDA, Dept. Health, Edn. and Welfare, Washington, 1964-66; industry liaison rep. FDA-OTC rev. panels, 1972-76; v.p. for med.-sci. affairs and med. dir. Proprietary Assn., Washington, 1966-84; clin. instr. medicine George Washington U. Sch. Medicine; asso. in medicine George Washington U. Hosp., 1949-51; adj. asso. prof. adminstrv. medicine Columbia U., N.Y.C., 1960-64; asso. clin. prof. adminstrv. medicine George Washington U., 1964-67, asso. clin. prof. medicine, 1968-84, assoc. professorial lectr. medicine, 1984-92, assoc. prof. emeritus clin. medicine, 1992—; domestic and internat. cons. on health affairs, 1984—; exec. sec. Spl. Com. on Med. Rsch., NSF, 1955, cons. on med. rsch., 1956; Del. U.S. Pharmacopeial Convs., 1970, 75, 80; mem. adv. bd. Physicians Desk Reference for Non-Prescription Drugs, 1979-88; mem. instl. rev. bd. Hill Top Rsch., Inc., West Palm Beach, Fla., 1989—. Contbr. articles on adminstrv. aspects med. care, med. edn. and med. research, drug evaluation. Served as capt. M.C. U.S. Army, 1943-46; NATOUSA and MTO with 5th Army, Field and Hosp. Med. Service. Recipient Alumni Achievement award in medicine Fordham U., 1959. Fellow Am. Pub. Health Assn., Indsl. Med. Assn.; mem. A.M.A., Am. Soc. Clin Pharmacology and Therapeutics, D.C. Med. Soc., N.Y. Acad. Scis., Soc. Alumni of Bellevue Hosp., Alumni Assn. N.Y. Univ. Coll Medicine, Celtic Med. Soc., Soc. Med. Cons. to Armed Forces., Am. Med. Tennis Assn. (bd. dirs. 1986-89). Roman Catholic. Home: 484 NE Plantation Rd Apt 4108 Stuart FL 34996-1751 *Whatever small success I may have thus far achieved can be completely attributed to my good fortune in being blessed by a fine heritage, both past and present. The principles of conduct, discipline, ideals and goals in life to which my dear wife and I were exposed in our respective families, have guided us in our own family. No matter how trite it may seem to some, our basic philosophy of life is centered on the golden rule. This involves a fundamental interest in people and trust in them despite disappointments in this regard from time to time.*

PISANKO, HENRY JONATHAN, command and control communications company executive; b. Trenton, N.J., Mar. 14, 1925; s. Isadore Stephen and Victoria (Gula) P.; m. Sophia Emily Zudnak, May 29, 1949; children: Barbara, Henry Jonathan, Jr., Michael. B in Naval Sci., U. Notre Dame, 1945, BA, 1947; cert. in Japanese, U. Colo. and Okla. State U., 1945; postgrad. Woodrow Wilson Sch., Columbia U., 1948-50. Constrn. reporter ea. div. F.W. Dodge div. McGraw-Hill, N.Y.C. and Phila., 1950-52; internat. affairs analyst Dept. Def., Washington, 1953-59; ops. officer Dept. Def., Pacific Rim, Japan and Hong Kong, 1960-63; sr. intelligence officer Internat. Security Affairs, Dept. Def., Washington, 1964-70; overseas adminstr. diplomatic telecommunications Dept. State, Asia, Africa, 1971-73; spl. advisor Def. Intelligence Coll., Washington, 1974-75; ctr. dep. chief, adminstrn. dir. Intelligence Community, Washington, 1976-82; exec. officer USA-EIGO Svcs. Co., Rockville, Md., 1983-87; exec. officer USA-EIGO Svcs. Co., Princeton, N.J., 1983-87, now bd. dirs.; pres. P.K. Co. Ltd., Bethesda, 1987—; chmn. bd. dirs. emeritus P.K. Co. Ltd., Hong Kong; assoc. Dawson Sci. Corp., Hong Kong, 1996—; bd. dirs. Asia Mgmt. Internat., Princeton; assoc. Bi-Lingual U.S.A. Corp., Bethesda, Md., 1984, Mgmt. Logistics Internat., Arlington, Va., 1983-86; hon. dir. Pacific Rim Enterprises, Hong Kong, 1996. Editor, translator: Yoshio Kodama, 1952; author: (monographs) Items of Inquiry Far East, 1983, Japanese Technology-Ancient Culture, 1985, Augur, 1994 (pamphlet) Fiber Optics Across the Pacific, 1989; editor (handbook) Japanese-English Proprietary Business Lexicon for Command Control Communications Intelligence, 1990-93; author, producer handbook: Telecommunications Operations for Pacific Rim Enterprises, 1996. Sponsor, contbr. Pisanko-Kikan, 1982, Hotel Okura, Japan, 1983, Bungei Shunju, Japan, 1988. Lt. J.G., USN, 1942-46. Trenton Times scholar, 1942; recipient Moe Berg award Pub. Security Investigation Agy.-Japan, Tokyo, 1961, Telecommunications award Thai Gen. Staff, Bangkok, 1972, Shimoda Diplomatic award, Japan. Mem. Asian Rsch. Svc., Bus. Devel. Africa, Internat. Inst. Japan, Bus. Execs. for Internat. Security, Internat. Platform Assn., Info. Processing Soc. Japan, Naval Res. Officers Tng. Corps, Unit Alumni Club, Boulder Boys-Japanese Club, Shek-O Club. Avocations: rare book collecting, cryptology, desert safaris. Office: PK Co Ltd Far East Hdqs, Peninsula New Business Ctr, Hong Kong Hong Kong *"I seek no other man's shoes. If I've misdirected my priorities, and I'm confident this is not so, I've had a fair time in lost country. There are no regrets."Moe Berg Pr #23.*

PISANO, A. ROBERT, entertainment company executive, lawyer; b. San Jose, Calif., Mar. 3, 1943; s. Anthony Edward and Carmen Jeanne (Morisoli) P.; m. Carolyn Joan Pollock, May 5, 1979; children: Catherine J., Anthony Daniel, Elizabeth A., Alexandra N. B.A. in Pub. Adminstrn., San Jose State U., 1965; J.D., U. Calif.-Berkeley, 1968. Bar: Calif. Assoc. O'Melveny & Myers, Los Angeles, 1968-75, ptnr., 1976-85, 92-93; exec. v.p. office of chmn., gen. counsel Paramount Pictures, Los Angeles, 1985-91; exec. v.p. Metro-Goldwyn-Mayer Inc., Santa Monica, Calif., 1993-96; vice chmn. Metro-Goldwyn-Mayer, Inc., Santa Monica, Calif., 1997—; bd. dirs. Coppola Group. Bd. dirs. Info. for Pub. Affairs, Sacramento, 1983—. Mem. Motion Picture Assn. Am. (bd. dirs. 1989-91, 93—), Acad. Motion Picture Arts and Scis. Office: Metro-Goldwyn-Mayer Inc 2500 Broadway Santa Monica CA 90404-3065

PISANO, JOEL A., federal judge; b. Orange, N.J., Mar. 3, 1949; s. Salvatore and Rita P.; m. Elizabeth Nee Breckenridge, June 20, 1971. BA, Lafayette Coll., 1971; JD, Seton Hall U., 1974. Asst. dep. Pub. Defender Office Pub. Defender, Newark, 1974-77; ptnr. Schwartz, Pisano, Simon, & Edelstein, Belleville, Livingston, N.J., 1977-91; U.S. Magistrate judge U.S. Dist. Ct. Dist. N.J., Newark, 1991—. Mem. ABA, Essex County Bar Assn., Seton Hall Univ. Inn of Ct. Office: US District Court Us Courthouse PO Ofc Newark NJ 07101

PISANO, RONALD GEORGE, art consultant; b. N.Y.C., Dec. 19, 1948; s. Robert Louis and Mildred Jane Pisano. BA, Adelphi U., 1971; postgrad., U. Del., 1971-73. Dir. exhbns. Baruch Coll. City U., N.Y., 1974-76; assoc. curator William Merritt Chase collection and archives Parrish Art Mus., Southampton, N.Y., 1976; curator mus. William Merritt Chase collection and archives Parrish Art Mus., 1977-78, dir., 1978-82; art cons., 1981—; guest curator Mus. at Stony Brook, N.Y., 1977-79, 85, 90, Henry Art Gallery U. Wash., 1982-83; cons. curator Am. art Heckscher Mus., Huntington, N.Y., 1977-77, guest curator, 1985, 90.. Author: William Merritt Chase, 1979, The Heckscher Mus. Catalogue of the Am. Collection, 1979, An Am. Pl. Exhbn. Catalogue, 1981, A Leading Spirit in American Art: William Merritt Chase, 1849-1916, 1983, The Long Island Landscape, 1820-1920, 1985, The Art Students League; Selections from the Permanent Collection, 1987, A Centennial Celebration of the National Association of Women Artists, 1988, Idle Hours: Americans at Leisure, 1865-1914, 1989, Long Island Landscape Painting in the 20th Century, 1990, Summer Afternoons: Landscape Paintings by William Merritt Chase, 1993, The League at the Cape, 1993, Parodying the American Masters: The Society of Fakirs, 1993, Gifford Beal; Picture Maker, 1993, Photographs from the William Merritt Chase Archives, 1993, William M. Chase and Irving R. Wiles: The Artist as Teacher, 1994, Henry and Edith Prellwitz and the Peconic Art Colony, 1995. Recipient A. Conger Goodyear award, 1971; Disting. Art Historian award Grand Central Art Galleries, 1979; Stebbins Family grantee, 1972-73. Mem. Coll. Art Assn., Am. Assn. Museums. Home: Box 198 Salisbury Mills NY 12577-5408 Office: Ronald G Pisano Inc 375 Riverside Dr Apt 13-b New York NY 10025

PISCHL, ADOLPH JOHN, school administrator; b. East Orange, N.J., Mar. 28, 1920; s. Adolph and Anna (Ellerman) P.; m. Tennessee Wild, Sept. 9, 1947; 1 child, Sallyann. Certificate, Drake Coll., 1940. With Juilliard Sch. of Music, N.Y.C., 1962-86, asst. to concert mgr., 1962-66, dir. pub. relations, 1966-68, concert mgr., 1966-86; adminstr. The Sch. for Strings, N.Y.C., 1987-88; with The Dance Mart, N.Y.C., 1950—, pub. dir. Am. Dance Festival, Conn. Coll., 1964-68; mgr. Betty Jones Dances I Dance, 1966-68, Ruth Currier Dance Co., 1966-68, Anna Sokolow Dance Co., 1966-68, Julliard Sch. Bookstore, 1971-86. Founder, editor: Dance Perspectives, 1958-64, Dance Data, 1977; editor: Juilliard News Bull. and Rev. Ann, 1964-85; pub.: Dance Horizons, 1965-86; Contbr. articles to dance mags. Bd. dirs. Dance Notation Bur.; sec. bd. dirs. Walter W. Naumburg Found., Inc. Served with AUS, 1940-46. Home: 878 Warren Pky Teaneck NJ 07666-5640

PISCIOTTA, ANTHONY VITO, physician, educator; b. N.Y.C., Mar. 3, 1921; s. Andrew and Mary (Zinnanti) P.; m. Lorraine Gault, June 15, 1951; children: Robert Andrew, Nancy Marie, Anthony Vito. B.S., Fordham U., 1941; M.D., Marquette U., 1944, M.S., 1952. Diplomate: Am. Bd. Internal Medicine. Intern Jersey City Med. Center, 1944-45; resident pathology Fordham Hosp., N.Y.C., 1947-48; resident medicine Milwaukee County Gen. Hosp., 1948-51; rsch. fellow hematology New Eng. Center Hosp., 1951-52; instr. medicine Tufts U., 1951-52; mem. faculty Marquette U., 1952-81, prof., 1966-81; vice chmn. Radiation Effects Rsch. Found., Hiroshima, Japan, 1981-83; prof. medicine Med. Coll. Wis., Milw., 1983-97, Robert A. Uihlein, Jr. prof. Hematologic Rsch., 1983-97, prof. emeritus, 1997—; dir. blood rsch. lab., staff hematologist John L. Doyne Hosp. (now Froedtert Meml. Hosp.), 1952-95. Mem. adv. editl. bd. of: Transfusion, 1960-67; mem. editl. bd. of: Jour. Lab. and Clin. Medicine, 1967-70. Served to capt. M.C. AUS, 1945-47. Named Alumnus of Yr. Med. Coll. Wis. Alumni Assn., 1977. Fellow A.C.P.; mem. AMA, Wis., Milw. County med. socs., Assn. Am. Physicians, AAAS, Am. Assn. Immunologists, Am. Soc. for Exptl. Pathology, Am. Soc. Hematology, Central Soc. Clin. Research, Internat. Soc. Hematology, Milw. Acad. Medicine (Achievement award 1987)), Milw. Soc. Internal Medicine, N.Y. Acad. Sci., Soc. Exptl. Biology and Medicine, Nat. Blood Club (sec. 1970-71), Alpha Omega Alpha. Home: 12550 W Grove Ter Elm Grove WI 53122-1973 Office: Med Coll Wis 9200 W Wisconsin Ave Milwaukee WI 53226-3522

PISCIOTTA, VIVIAN VIRGINIA, psychotherapist; b. Chgo., Dec. 7; d. Vito and Mary Lamia; m. Vincent Diago Pisciotta, Apr. 1, 1951; children: E. Christopher, Vittorio, V. Charles, Mary A. Pisciotta Higley, Thomas Sansone. BA in Clin. Psychology, Antioch U., 1974; MSW, George Williams Coll., 1984; postgrad., Erickson Inst. of No. Ill., 1990. Lic. clin. social worker; diplomate in clin. social work. Short-term therapist Woman Line, Dayton, Ohio, 1976-79; psychotherapist Cicero (Ill.) Family Svcs., 1982-83, Maywood (Ill.) - Proviso Family Svcs., 1983-84, Maple Ave. Med. Ctr., Brookfield, Ill., 1985-88, Met. Med. Clinic, Naperville, Ill., 1986-88; allied staff Riveredge Psychiat. Hosp., Forest Park, Ill., 1986-97; psychotherapist, pvt. practice Oakbrook, Ill., 1988-96; psychotherapist, co-founder Archer Austin Counseling Ctr., Chgo., 1988-89; psychotherapist, founder Columbia Hospitals' Columbia Riveredge Hosp., Forest Park, Ill., 1989—; allied staff Linden Oaks Psychiat. Hosp., Naperville, 1990-97; substitute tchr. Chgo. Pub. High Sch., 1981. Author treatment prog., workshops in field. Co-founder Co-op Nursery Sch., Rockford, Ill., 1956; leader Great Books of the Western World series, Piqua, Ohio, 1977, Rockford, 1960-65; leader Girl Scouts U.S., St. Bridget Sch., Rockford, 1968-71. Mem. Assn. Labor-Mgmt. and Cons. on Alcoholism, Soc. Clin. Exptl. Hypnosis, Nat. Assn. Social Workers, Acad. Cert. Social Workers, Nat. Social Work Register (cert.), Antioch Univ. Alumnus Assn. Rockford Coll. Alumnae Orgn. (newsletter contbr. 1972-73), Soc. for Clin. and Exptl. Hypnosis (assoc. mem.), Internat. Soc. for Clin. and Exptl. Hypnosis (assoc. mem.). Republican. Roman Catholic. Avocations: reading, travel, study/rsch., music, religion. Office: Columbia Riveredge Hosp 7002 W Archer Ave Ste 2B Chicago IL 60638-2202

PISHKIN, VLADIMIR, psychologist, educator; b. Belgrade, Yugoslavia, Mar. 12, 1931; came to U.S., 1946, naturalized, 1951; s. Vasili and Olga (Bartosh) P.; m. Dorothy Louise Martin, Sept. 12, 1953; children—Gayle Ann, Mark Vladimir. B.A., Mont. State U., 1951, M.A., 1955; Ph.D., U. Utah, 1958. Dir. neuropsychiat. research labs. VA Hosp., Tomah, Wis., 1959-62; chief research psychologist Behavioral Sci. Labs.,, Oklahoma City, 1962-75; prof. psychiatry Coll. Medicine, U. Okla. Health Scis. Ctr., Oklahoma City, 1973-93, prof. emeritus, 1994; chmn. rsch. coun. dept. psychiatry and behavioral scis., 1972-75; bd. dirs. VA Med Ctr., Oklahoma City; dir. clin rsch. Willow View Hosp., Oklahoma City, 1987—. Author: (with Mathis and Pierce) Basic Psychiatry, rev. 3d edit, 1977; editor in chief: Jour. Clin. Psychology, 1974—; contbr. numerous articles to profl. jours. Served with USAF, 1952-54. Recipient Disting. Service award Jr. C. of C. Fellow Am. Psychol. Assn., Am. Psychol. Soc.; mem. Southwestern Psychol. Assn. (pres. 1973-74), Okla. Psychol. Assn.(Disting. Psychologist award 1986), Midwestern Psychol. Assn., AAAS, Psychonomics Soc. Clubs: Masons, Shriners. Home: 3113 NW 62nd St Oklahoma City OK 73112-4224 Office: 2601 Spencer Rd PO Box 11137 Oklahoma City OK 73136-0137

PISNEY, RAYMOND FRANK, international consulting services executive; b. Lime Springs, Iowa, June 2, 1940; s. Frank A. and Cora H. P. BA, Loras Coll., 1963; postgrad., Cath. U. Am., 1963; MA, U. Del., 1965. Asst. adminstrn. and rsch. Mt. Vernon, Va., 1965-69; historic sites adminstr. N.C. Archives and Hist. Dept., Raleigh, 1969; asst. adminstr. div. historic sites and museums N.C. Dept. Art, Culture and History, Raleigh, 1969-72; cons. Cannon Mills Co., Kannapolis, N.C., 1972-73; exec. dir. Woodrow Wilson Birthplace Found., Staunton, Va., 1973-78, Mo. Hist. Soc., St. Louis, 1978-87; sr. v.p., cons. svcs. ETI Internat., Washington, 1987—; pres., CEO Aurora Internat. Inc., Arlington, Va., 1996—; pres. Va. History and Museums Fedn., 1977-78; pres. Mo. Museums Assoc., 1982-84; cons. assoc. Battelle, Washington, 1994. Author: Historical Markers: A Bibliography, 1977, Historic Markers: Planning Local Programs, 1978, A Preview to Historical Marking, 1976, Old Buildings: New Resources for Work and Play, 1976; editor: Virginians Remember Woodrow Wilson, 1978, Woodrow Wilson in Retrospect, 1978, Woodrow Wilson: Idealism and Realty, 1977, Historic Preservation and Public Policy in Virginia, 1978. Bd. trustees James Clerk Maxwell Mus. and Found., Edinburgh, Scotland, 1993—, Internat. Human Rights Monument and Mus., Moscow, 1991—; sec., trustee Scotland WorldWide Heritage, Glasgow, 1993—; mem. internat. com. Charles A. Lindbergh Anniversary, Paris, 1987; sec. Internat. Assn. Consulting Firms, 1994-96. Recipient Bertha Black Rhoda award NAACP, 1985; Hagley fellow U. Del., 1963-65; Seminar for Hist. Adminstrs. fellow, 1965. Mem. Internat. Assn. Consulting Firms (sec. 1994-96), Washington Ind. Writers, Am. Assn. Museums, Nat. Trust Hist. Preservation U.S., Am. Assn. State and Local History, Can. Museums Assn., Brit. Museums Assn., Internat. Coun. Monuments and Sites, Internat. Coun. Museums, Lindbergh Anniversary Assn. (internat. com. 1987), Phi Alpha Theta. Roman Catholic. *Words that have guided my career were written more than two millennia ago by Marcus Tullius Cicero (106-43 B.C.); the highest level of work is to 'criticize by creating, rather than by finding fault.'*

PISTOLE, THOMAS GORDON, microbiology educator, researcher; b. Detroit, Sept. 17, 1942; s. Leotis Merton Pistole and Lillian Nell (Bosley) Besser; m. Donna Dulcie Straw, Sept. 11, 1965; children: James Alexander, Jennifer Katharine. PhB, Wayne State U., 1964, MS, 1966; PhD, U. Utah, 1969. Postdoctoral fellow U.S. Army, Frederick, Md., 1969-70; research assoc. U. Minn., Mpls., 1970-71; asst. prof. U. N.H., Durham, 1971-77, assoc. prof., 1977-83, prof., 1983—, chmn., 1983-92; vis. scientist Weizmann Inst., Rehovot, Israel, 1979; vis. prof. U. Edinburgh, Scotland, 1986; faculty fellow Office of V.P. for Acad. Affairs U. N.H., 1996—. Co-editor: Biomedical Application of the Horseshoe Crab, 1979; mem. editorial bd. Jour. Invertebrate Pathology, 1988-90. NRC fellow, 1969-70, NIH sr. internat. fellow, 1986; grantee NIH, 1975-77, 89-93, 96—, NSF, 1981-84. Mem. Am. Soc. for Microbiology, Am. Assn. Immunologists, Internat. Soc. Devel. and Comparative Immunology, Soc. for Leukocyte Biology. Avocations: singing, collecting old sheet music, walking, cooking. Office: U NH Rudman Hall Dept Microbiology Durham NH 03824-2617

PISTOR, CHARLES HERMAN, JR., former banker, academic administrator; b. St. Louis, Aug. 26, 1930; s. Charles Herman and Virginia (Brown) P.; m. Regina Prikryl, Sept. 20, 1952; children: Lori Ellen, Charles Herman III, Jeffrey Glenn. BBA, U. Tex., 1952; MBA, Harvard U., 1956, So. Meth. U., 1961. Chmn., chief exec. officer First RepublicBank Dallas, 1980-88, also bd. dirs.; chief exec. officer, chmn. bd. dirs. Northpark Nat. Bank, Dallas, 1988-90; vice chair So. Meth. U., Dallas, 1990-95; bd. dirs. Am. Brands, AMR, Centex Corp., Oryx Corp. Trustee So. Meth. U., Dallas; elder Presbyn. Ch. Served to lt. USNR, 1952-54. Mem. Am. Bankers Assn. (past pres., bd. dirs.). Club: Dallas Country. Home: 4200 Belclaire Ave Dallas TX 75205-3033

PISTORIUS, GEORGE, language educator; b. Prague, Czechoslovakia, Mar. 19, 1922; came to U.S., 1958, naturalized, 1964; s. Theodor and Blazena (Jiranek) P.; m. Marie Skokan, June 30, 1945; 1 dau., Erika. Student, Charles U., Prague, 1945-48; postgrad., Université de Paris, 1948-50; certificats d'etudes superieures, Université de Strasbourg, France, 1950, 1951; Ph.D., U. Pa., 1963. Asst. dept. comparative lit. Charles U., 1946-48; instr. Lafayette Coll., Easton, Pa., 1958-61; asst. prof. French Lafayette Coll., 1961-63; asso. prof. Williams Coll., 1963-68, prof. Romanic langs., 1968-92, chmn. dept., 1971-82, prof. emeritus, 1992—; instr. French, Colby Coll. Summer Sch. Lang., 1959-65. Author: Bibliography of the works of F.X. Salda, 1948, Destin de la culture francaise dans une democratie populaire, 1957, L'Image de l'Allemagne dans le roman francais entre les deux guerres (1919-1939), 1964, Marcel Proust und Deutschland, Eine Bibliographie, 1981, André Gide und Deutschland: Eine internationale Bibliographie, 1990. Mem. MLA, Am. Assn. Tchrs. of French, Assn. Internationale des Etudes Francaises. Home: 54 Cluett Dr Williamstown MA 01267-2805

PI-SUNYER, F. XAVIER, medical educator, medical investigator; b. Barcelona, Catalonia, Spain, Dec. 3, 1933; came to U.S., 1942; s. James and Mercedes (Diaz) Pi-S.; m. Penelope Wheeler; children: Andrea, Olivia, Joanna. BA, Oberlin (Ohio) Coll., 1955; MD, Columbia U., 1959; MPH, Harvard U., 1963. From instr. to asst. prof. Coll. of Physicians & Surgeons, Columbia U., N.Y.C., 1965-76, assoc. prof., 1976-85, prof. clin. medicine, 1985-91; prof. St. Luke's-Roosevelt Hosp. Ctr., N.Y.C., 1991—; from asst. to assoc. attending physician St. Luke's Hosp., N.Y.C., 1965-75; attending physician St. Luke's-Roosevelt Hosp. Ctr., N.Y.C., 1975—, chief div. endocrinology, diabetes and nutrition, 1988—, dir. Obesity Rsch. Ctr., 1988—; dir. Joslin Diabetes Ctr. at St. Luke's Hosp., 1994—, Van Itallie Ctr. for Nutrition and Weight Mgmt., 1994—; mem. adj. faculty Rockefeller U., 1984—; vis. physician Rockefeller U. Hosp., 1984—; attending physician Presbyn. Hosp., 1985—; sr. investigator N.Y. Heart Assn., 1968-73; Hsien Wu investigator St. Luke's-Roosevelt Hosp., 1982-90; Sigma Xi lectr. Pa. State U., 1989; Howard Heinz vis. prof. Med. Coll. Pa., 1987; Pfizer vis. prof. in diabetes Boston U./Tufts U./Harvard U., 1995; mem. C study sect. NIDDKD, 1988-92, mem. task force on obesity, 1990—, mem. nutrition study sect., 1983-87; v.p. Am. Bd. Nutrition, 1987-88; chmn. task force obesity treatment and prevention Nat. Heart and Lung Inst., 1995—. Contbr. numerous articles to profl. jours. Fogarty Internat. fellow NIH, 1979-80. Mem. Am. Soc. for Clin. Nutrition (coun. 1987-90, pres. 1989-90), Am. Diabetes Assn. (exec. com. 1990-93, pres. 1992-93), N.Am. Assn. Study Obesity (v.p. 1992-93, pres. 1994-95), N.Y. State Health Rsch. Coun., N.Y. Acad. Medicine (com. on pub. health 1983-96). Avocations: tennis, skiing, hiking, theater. Home: 305 Riverside Dr New York NY 10025-5286 Office: St Luke's-Roosevelt Hosp Ctr Dept Medicine 1111 Amsterdam Ave New York NY 10025-1716

PITCHELL, ROBERT J., business executive; b. N.Y.C.; m. Louise Clark, Oct. 26, 1974; 1 dau. A.B., Fordham U., 1939; Ph.D., U. Calif., 1955. Mem. faculty Purdue U.; lectr. polit. sci. Butler U.; prof. Ind. U., to 1963; pres. Roosevelt U., 1963-65; formerly dep. adminstr. Fed. Extension Service, Dept. Agr.; later exec. dir. Nat. U. Extension Assn., Washington; pres. Hamden Enterprises Inc., Fairfax, Va.; cons., past dir. Ind. Tax Study Commn. Author books on taxation and continuing edn. Assisted senatorial campaign Birch Bayh, 1962. Home and Office: 3134 Prosperity Ave Fairfax VA 22031-2820

PITCHER, GRIFFITH FONTAINE, lawyer; b. Balt., Nov. 1, 1937; s. William Henry and Virginia Griffith (Stein) P.; m. Sandra E. Barnett, Dec. 16, 1994; children: Virginia T. Pitcher Ballinger, L. Brooke Pitcher Fick, William T. B., Margaret W. Pitcher Lombino. B.A., Johns Hopkins U., 1960; J.D., U. Va., 1963. Bar: Ala. 1963, Fla. 1971. Assoc. Bradley, Arant, Rose & White, Birmingham, Ala., 1963-71; mem. Van den Berg, Gay & Burke, P.A., Orlando, Fla., 1971-76, Mahoney, Hadlow & Adams, P.A., Jacksonville, Fla., 1976-82; ptnr. Squire, Sanders & Dempsey, Miami, Fla., 1982-93, Mershon, Sawyer, Johnston, Dunwoody & Cole, Miami, 1994-95; ptnr. Chamberlain, Hrdlicka, White, Williams & Martin, Atlanta, 1996—. Vice-chmn. Winter Park (Fla.) Planning and Zoning Bd., 1974-75. Served with Army N.G., 1961-64. Fellow Am. Coll. Bond Counsel (dir.); mem. ABA, Nat. Assn. Bond Lawyers, The Fla. Bar, Fla. Econ. Devel. Coun., Fla. Mcpl. Attys. Assn., Fla. Acad. Hosp. Attys., Ala. State Bar Assn., Order of Coif, Delta Phi. Republican. Contbr. articles on law to profl. jours.

PITCHUMONI, CAPECOMORIN SANKAR, gastroenterologist, educator; b. Madura, India, Jan. 20, 1938; came to U.S., 1967; s. Sankara and Jaya (Lekshmi) Iyer; m. Prema Iyer, Nov. 11, 1964; children: Sheila, Shoba, Suresh. Student, St. Xavier Coll., India, 1953-55; MB BS, Trivandrum Med. Coll., India, 1959, MD, 1965. Intern Med. Coll., Trivandurm, India, 1961-63; resident in gastroenterology Yale U., 1967-69; N.Y. Med. Coll., 1969-72; practice medicine specializing in gastroenterology N.Y.C., 1972—; asst. prof. medicine Kottayam Med. Coll., India, 1967; asst. prof. medicine N.Y. Med. Coll., 1972-75, assoc. prof., 1975-80, prof. clin. medicine, 1980-85, prof. medicine, 1985—, assoc. prof. preventive and social medicine, 1975-86, prof. community and preventive medicine, 1986—; chief sect. gastroenterology Our Lady of Mercy Med. Ctr., N.Y., 1980—; assoc. dir. medicine Our Lady of Mercy Med. Ctr., N.Y.C., 1985—, program dir. internal medicine, 1987—; dir. medicine, 1992. Contbg. author med. textbooks; contbr. articles to profl. jours. Recipient Om Prakash award Indian Soc. Gastroenterology, 1976, Outstanding Scientist of Yr. award MV Spltys., Madras, 1994, Oration award Thangavelu Endowment, 1994. Fellow Royal Coll. Physicians and Surgeons Can., ACP, Am. Coll. Gastroenterology (gov. 1996—), Am. Coll. Nutrition; mem. Am. Soc. for Gastrointestinal Endoscopy, Assn. Physicians India, Am. Coll. Nuitrition, Am. Gastroent. Assn., India Soc. Gastroenterology (life), Am. Inst. Nutrition, N.Y. Gastroent. Assn., N.Y. Acad. Scis., N.Y. Soc. Gastrointestinal Endoscopy, Am. Soc. for Clin. Nutrition. Hindu. Home: 178 Fairmount Ave Glen Rock NJ 07452-3014 Office: 600 E 233rd St Bronx NY 10466-2604

PITCOCK, JAMES KENT, head and neck surgical oncologist; b. Tachikawa AFB, Japan, Nov. 18, 1951; s. James Kenneth and Helen (Robertson) P.; m. Cynthia H. Zipperly. Student, U. Houston, 1974; MD, Baylor U., 1979. Diplomate Am. Bd. Otolaryngology. Resident in gen. surgery Baylor Coll. Medicine, Houston, 1979-81, resident in otolaryngology, head and neck surgery, 1981-84; clinician Kelsey-Seybold Clinic, P.A., Houston, 1984-85; lectr. head and neck surgery Inst. Laryngology and Otology, U. London, 1985-86; instr., fellow head and neck surgery U. Chgo., 1986-88; asst. prof. dept. otolaryngology, head and neck surgery, chief div. head and neck surgical oncology U. Calif.-Irvine Med. Ctr., Orange, 1988-92; dir. head and neck oncology clin. & rsch. program Clin. Cancer Ctr. U. Calif., Irvine. Author: Oral and Maxillofacial Trauma, 1989, Musculocutaneous Flap Reconstruction of the Head and Neck, 1989, Surgery of the Skull Base, 1989. Fellow Am. Acad. Otolaryngology, Head and Neck Surgery; mem. ACS. Office: Dauphin W EENT Specialists 3701 Dauphin St Mobile AL 36608-1756

PITEGOFF, PETER ROBERT, lawyer, educator; b. N.Y.C., Mar. 6, 1953; s. Joseph and Libbie (Shapiro) P.; m. Ann Casady, Mar. 22, 1986; children: Maxwell Jacob, Elias Samuel. AB, Brown U., 1975; JD, NYU, 1981. Bar: Mass 1981, N.Y. 1988; cert. tchr., R.I. Tchr. Hope High Sch., Providence, 1974-75; community organizer Nat. Assn. for So. Poor, Petersburg, Va., 1975-76, Citizens Action League, Oakland, Calif., 1976-78; gen. counsel ICA Group, Boston, 1981-88; ptnr. Arrington & Pitegoff, Somerville, Mass., 1986-88; prof. law SUNY, Buffalo, 1988—; adj. asst. prof. law NYU, 1986-88; instr. Harvard Law Sch., 1985; cons. in field, 1978—; legal counsel cmty. devel. worker purchases of bus. corp. fin. dem. corp. structures child care policy and welfare reform. Contbr. to profl. publs. Root-Tilden scholarship NYU, 1978; grantee Pub. Interest Law Found., N.Y.C., 1981. Democrat. Jewish. Avocations: athletics, travel, music. Office: SUNY Sch of Law 507 O'Brian Hall Buffalo NY 14260

PITELKA, FRANK ALOIS, zoologist, educator; b. Chgo., Mar. 27, 1916; s. Frank Joseph and Frances (Laga) P.; m. Dorothy Getchell Riggs, Feb. 5, 1943; children: Louis Frank, Wenzel Karl, Vlasta Kazi Helen. B.S. with highest honors, U. Ill., 1939; summer student, U. Mich., 1938, U. Wash., 1940; Ph.D., U. Calif. at Berkeley, 1946. Mem. faculty U. Calif. at Berkeley, 1944—, prof. zoology, 1958—, chmn. dept., 1963-66, 69-71, Miller research prof., 1965-66; curator birds Mus. Vertebrate Zoology, 1945-63, assoc. dir., 1982—; exec. com. Miller Inst. Basic Rsch. in Sci., 1967-71, chmn., 1967-70; Panel environ. biology NSF, 1959-62, panel polar programs, 1978-80; mem. panel biol. and med. scis., com. polar research Nat. Acad. Scis., 1960-65; research assoc. Naval Arctic Research Lab., Barrow, Alaska, 1951-80; ecol. adv. com. AEC, 1956-1958; adv. coms. U.S. Internat. Biol. Program, 1965-69; mem. adv. com. U. Colo. Inst. Arctic and Alpine Research, 1968-73; mem. U.S. Tundra Biome Program, 1968-73, dir., 1968-69; vis. prof. U. Wash. Friday Harbor Labs, summer 1968; mem. U.S. Commn. for UNESCO, 1970-72. Contbr. research papers in field.; Editorial bd.: Ecology, 1949-51, 60-62, editor, 1962-64; mem. editorial bd. U. Calif. Press, 1953-62, chmn., 1959-62; mem. editorial bd. Pacific Coast Avifauna, 1947-60, Ecol. Monographs, 1957-60, Systematic Zoology, 1961-64, The Veliger, 1961-85, Studies in Ecology, 1972-84, Current Ornithology, 1980-85; asst. editor Condor, 1943-45, assoc. editor, 1945-62; mem. editorial bd. Studies in Avian Biology, 1979-84, editor, 1984-87. Guggenheim fellow, 1949-50; NSF sr. postdoctoral fellow Oxford (Eng.) U., 1957-58; Research fellow Ctr. for Advanced Study in Behavioral Scis., Stanford, 1971; recipient Disting. Teaching award U. Calif.-Berkeley, 1984; The Berkeley citation, 1985, Alumnus Achievement award, U. Ill., 1993. Fellow Arctic Inst. N.Am., Am. Ornithologists Union (Brewster award 1980), Calif. Acad. Scis., AAAS, Animal Behavior Soc.; mem. Ecol. Soc. Am. (Mercer award 1953, Eminent Ecologist award 1992), Soc. Study Evolution, Cooper Ornithol. Soc. (hon. mem.; pres. 1948-50), Brit. Ecol. Soc., Am. Soc. Mammalogists, Am. Soc. Naturalists, Am. Inst. Biol. Scis., Western Soc. Naturalists (pres. 1963-64), Nat. Audubon Soc., Sierra Club, Phi Beta Kappa, Sigma Xi. Home: PO Box 9278 Berkeley CA 94709-0278 *My ideas and goals reflect three important sources of influence: strong university teachers; the excellence of colleagues and the setting of my university base; and, most importantly, the unremitting stimulus and challenge of my graduate students to grow with them over years of dramatic changes in biology.*

PITERNICK, ANNE BREARLEY, librarian, educator; b. Blackburn, Eng., Oct. 13, 1926; emigrated to Can., 1956, naturalized, 1965; d. Walter and Ellen (Harris) Clayton; m. Neil Brearley, 1956 (div. 1971); m. George Piternick, May 6, 1971. B.A., U. Manchester (Eng.), 1948, F.L.A., 1983. Mem. library staff U. B.C., Vancouver, Can., 1956-66; head sci. div. U. B.C., 1960-61, head social scis. div., 1965-66, prof. Sch. Library, Archival and Info. Studies, 1966-91, prof. emerita, 1991—, assoc. dean Faculty of Arts, 1985-90; mem. Nat. Com. Bibliog. Svcs. Can., 1975-80, chmn. com. on bibliography and info. services for social scis. and humanities, 1981-84; mem. adv. acad. panel Social Scis. and Humanities Research Council, 1981-84; mem. adv. bd. Nat. Libr. Can., 1978-84; mem. Nat. Adv. Com. Culture Stats., 1985-90; organizer Confs. on Can. Bibliography, 1974, 81; pres. Can. Assn. Spl. Librs. Info. Svcs., 1969-70, Can. Libr. Assn., 1976-77. Author articles on electronic info. svcs. and scholarly communication. Recipient Queen's Silver Jubilee medal, 1977, award for Spl. Librarianship Can. Assn. Spl. Librs. and Info. Svcs., 1987, 75th Anniversary medal U.B.C., 1990, Can. 125 medal, 1993. Fellow Council on Library Resources (1980). Home: 1849 W 63rd Ave, Vancouver, BC Canada V6P 2H9

PITINO, RICHARD, college basketball coach; b. N.Y.C., Sept. 18, 1952. Student, U. Mass. Asst. coach U. Hawaii, 1975-76, Syracuse U., 1976-78; coach Boston U., 1978-83; asst. coach N.Y. Knicks, 1983-85, coach, 1987-89; coach Providence U., 1986-87; basketball coach U. Ky., Lexington, 1989-97; head coach Boston Celtics, 1997—. Author: (with Dick Weiss) Full Court Pressure: A Year in Kentucky Basketball, 1992. Named Coll. Coach of Yr., Sporting News, 1987. Office: Boston Celtics 151 Merrimae St Boston MA 02114*

PITKIN, EDWARD THADDEUS, aerospace engineer, consultant; b. Putnam, Conn., Dec. 14, 1930; s. Thaddeus Eugene and Florence Mabel (Brown) P.; m. Clara Lucy Modliszewski, June 13, 1953; children—Gayle Linda, Dale Edward. B.S., U. Conn., 1952; M.S. (Guggenheim fellow), Princeton, 1953; Ph.D. (NASA fellow), UCLA, 1964. Project engr. Astro Div. Marquardt Co., Los Angeles, 1956-59; mgr. space propulsion Astro Div. Marquardt Co., 1959-61; engring. cons. Los Angeles, 1961-64; asso. prof. aerospace engring. U. Conn., Storrs, 1964-70, prof. mech. and aerospace engring., 1970-90, prof. emeritus, 1990—; cons. engr., 1990—; asst. dean U. Conn., Storrs, 1977-87. Contbr. articles to tech. publs. Served as lt. USAF, 1953-55. Asso. fellow AIAA. Mem. Solar Energy Soc. Home: 115 Brookside Ln Mansfield Center CT 06250-1001 Office: U Conn Dep Mech Engring U-139 191 Auditorium Rd Storrs CT 06269

PITKIN, ROY MACBETH, retired medical educator; b. Anthon, Iowa, May 24, 1934; s. Roy and Pauline Allie (McBeath) P.; m. Marcia Alice Jenkins, Aug. 17, 1957; children: Barbara, Robert Macbeth, Kathryn, William Charles. B.A. with highest distinction, U. Iowa, 1956, M.D., 1959. Diplomate Am. Bd. Obstetrics & Gynecology, 1967. Intern King County Hosp., Seattle, 1959-60; resident in ob-gyn U. Iowa Hosps. and Clinics, Iowa City, 1960-63; asst. prof. ob-gyn U. Ill., 1965-68; assoc. prof. ob-gyn U. Iowa, Iowa City, 1968-72; prof. U. Iowa, 1972-87, head dept. ob-gyn, 1977-87; prof. UCLA, 1987-97, head dept. ob-gyn., 1987-95, prof. emeritus, 1997—; mem. residency rev. com. ob-gyn, 1981-87, chmn. 1985-87. Editor-in-chief: Year Book of Obstetrics and Gynecology, 1975-86; editor-in-chief: Clinical Obstetrics and Gynecology, 1979; editor: Obstetrics and Gynecology, 1985. Contbr. articles to med. jours. Served to lt. comdr. M.C. USNR, 1963-65. NIH career awardee, 1972-77. Fellow Royal Obstetricians and Gynecologists (ad eundem); mem. AMA (Goldberger award in clin. nutrition 1982), Am. Coll. Obstetricians and Gynecologists, Am. Gynecol. and Obstet. Soc. (pres. 1994-95), German Soc. Gynecology and Obstetrics (hon. 1992), Ctrl. Assn. Obstetricians and Gynecologists, Soc. Gynecologic Investigation (pres. 1985-86), Soc. Perinatal Obstetricians (pres. 1978-79), NAS, Inst. of Medicine. Presbyterian. Office: UCLA Sch Med 1100 Glendon Ave Ste 1655 Los Angeles CA 90024-3520

PITMAN, GROVER ALLEN, music educator; b. Corpus Christi, Tex., Nov. 16, 1943; s. John William and Mae Belle (Reese) P.; m. Jacqueline Kay Dunn, Aug. 29, 1966; children: William Dunn, Karen Joanne. BMus, U. Tex., 1965, MMus, 1967; PhD, Cath. U. Am., 1973. Tchr. Fredericksburg (Tex.) Pub. Schs., 1966-67; instr. Muskingum Coll., New Concord, Ohio, 1967-68; solo hornist U.S. Naval Acad. Band, Annapolis, Md., 1968-72; asst. prof. Winthrop Coll., Rock Hill, S.C., 1972-78; prof. Westminster Coll., New Wilmington, Pa., 1978—; prin. hornist Austin (Tex.) Symphony Orch., 1961-67, Annapolis (Md.) Symphony Orch., 1968-72; hornist Annapolis Brass Quintet, 1968-72, Youngstown (Ohio) Symphony Orch., 1985—. Grantee Winthrop Found., Rock Hill, 1977. Mem. Pa. Collegiate Bandmasters Assn. (pres. 1983-84), Pa. Music Educators Assn. (pres. dist. 5 1984-85), Rotary (pres. New Wilmington chpt. 1986). Episcopalian. Office: Westminster College New Wilmington PA 16172

PITOFSKY, ROBERT, federal agency administrator, law educator; b. Paterson, N.J., Dec. 27, 1929; s. Morris and Sadye (Katz) P.; m. Sally Levy, June 4, 1961; children: Alexander, David, Elizabeth. BA, NYU, 1951; LLB, Columbia U., 1954; LLD (hon.), Georgetown U., 1989. Bar: N.Y. 1956, D.C. 1973, U.S. Supreme Ct. 1972. Atty. Dept. Justice, Washington, 1956-57; assoc. Dewey, Ballantine, Bushby, Palmer & Wood, N.Y.C., 1957-63; prof. law NYU, 1963-70; dir. Bur. Consumer Protection, FTC, 1970-73; prof. law Georgetown U. Law Ctr., Washington, 1973-83, 89—, dean, exec. v.p. law ctr. affairs, 1983-89; commr. FTC, Washington, 1978-81, chmn., 1995—; of counsel Arnold & Porter, Washington, 1973-78, 81-95; guest scholar Brookings Instn., Washington, 1989-90; vis. prof. law Harvard Law Sch., 1975-76; faculty mem. Salzburg (Austria) Seminar in Am. Studies, 1975; chmn. Def. Sci. Bd. task force on antitrust aspects of def. industry downsizing, 1994. Co-author: Cases on Antitrust Law, 1967, Cases on Trade Regulation, 4th edit. 1997; co-editor: Revitalizing Antitrust in Its Second Century, 1991; contbr. articles on consumer protection and antitrust to profl. publs. Served with U.S. Army, 1954-56. Recipient Disting. Service award FTC, 1972; named One of Ten Outstanding Mid-Career Law Profs. Time Mag., 1977. Mem. ABA (coun. antitrust sect. 1986-89), Am. Law Inst., Assn. Am. Law Schs., Columbia U. Ctr. for Law Econ. Studies (adv. bd. 1975-95). Democrat. Jewish. Home: 3809 Blackthorn St Bethesda MD 20815-4905

PITONIAK, GREGORY EDWARD, mayor; b. Detroit, Mich., Aug. 12, 1954; s. Anthony Edward and Constance Elizabeth (Matuszak) P.; m. Denise Ruth Kadi, Apr. 21, 1979; children: Gregory, Mallory. BA, U. Mich., 1976; Masters, U. N.C., 1980. Adminstrv. asst. Taylor (Mich.) Neighborhood Devel. Com., 1977-78; pers. analyst Downriver Community Conf., Southgate, Mich., 1978-79; dir. client svcs. Econ. Devel. Corp. Wayne County, Dearborn, Mich., 1979-84; exec. dir. Econ. Devel. Corp. Wayne County, Livonia, Mich., 1984-88; dir. econ. dev. Downriver Community Conf., Southgate, Mich., 1988; state rep. Mich. Ho. Reps., Lansing, 1989-97; mayor City of Taylor, 1997—. Councilman Taylor City Coun., 1981-88, chmn., 1983-85, 87-88; pres. Mich. Young Dems., 1982-84; treas. 15th Congl. Dist. Dem. Orgn., Taylor, 1988-90. Named Outstanding Young Person, Taylor Jaycees, 1987, State Legislator of Yr., Mich. Credit Union League, 1993. Mem. Am. Econ. Devel. Coun. (cert. econ. developer 1984), Am. Soc. Pub. Adminstrn., Polish Am. Congress, Dem. Club Taylor, KC. Roman Catholic. Home: 9686 Rose St Taylor MI 48180-3046 Office: City of Taylor 23555 Goddard Rd Taylor MI 48180-4116

PITOT, HENRY CLEMENT, III, physician, educator; b. N.Y.C., May 12, 1930; s. Henry Clement and Bertha (Lowe) P.; m. Julie S. Schutten, July 29, 1954; children: Bertha, Anita, Jeanne, Catherine, Henry, Michelle, Lisa, Patrice. BS in Chemistry, Va. Mil. Inst., 1951; MD, Tulane U., 1955, PhD in Biochemistry, 1959, DSc (hon.), 1995. Instr. pathology Med. Sch. Tulane U., New Orleans, 1955-59; postdoctoral fellow McArdle Lab. U. Wis., Madison, 1959-60, mem. faculty Med. Sch., 1960—, prof. pathology and oncology, 1966—, chmn. dept. pathology, 1968-71, acting dean Med. Sch., 1971-73, dir. McArdle Lab., 1973-91. Recipient Borden undergrad. rsch. award, 1955, Lederle Faculty award, 1962, Career Devel. award Nat. Cancer Inst., NIH, 1965, Parke-Davis award in exptl. pathology, 1968, Noble Found. Rsch. award, 1984, Esther Langer award U. Chgo., 1984, Disting. Svc. award Am. Cancer Soc., 1989, Hilldale award U. Wis., 1991, Founders award Chem. Industry Inst. Toxicology, 1993, Midwest Regional chpt. Soc. Toxicology award in toxicology, 1996. Fellow AAAS, N.Y. Acad. Scis.; mem. Am. Soc. Cell Biology, Am. Assn. Cancer Rsch., Am. Soc. Biochemistry and Molecular Biology, Am. Chem. Soc., Am. Soc. Investigative Pathology (pres. 1976-77), Soc. Exptl. Biology and Medicine (pres. 1991-93), Soc. Surg. Oncology (Lucy J. Wortham award 1981), Am. Soc. Preventive Oncology, Soc. Toxicology, Soc. Toxicologic Pathologists, Japanese Cancer Soc. (hon.). Roman Catholic. Home: 314 Robin Pky Madison WI 53705-4931 Office: U Wis McArdle Lab Cancer Rsch 1400 University Ave Madison WI 53706-1526 *Where and who we are today is the result of those whom we have met and known and loved until now.*

PITRELLA, FRANCIS DONALD, human factors professional; b. Seneca Falls, N.Y., Jan. 23, 1934; s. Frank and Minnie Lee (Buchanan) P.; m. Narcissa Voluntad, July 1, 1956 (div. Apr. 1964); children: Paolo, Jason; m. Anke Elly Hofmeyer, Feb. 13, 1970. BA, Bklyn. Coll., 1960; Drs., Tilburg (Netherlands) U., 1981. Cert. human factors profl.; cert. European ergonomist. Human factors analyst ITT Fed. Labs., Nutley, N.J., 1961-64; systems analysis engr. Grumman Aircraft engring. Corp., Bethpage, N.Y., 1964-65; human factors engr. Loral Electronics, Inc., Bronx, 1965; rsch. scientist Matrix Corp., Alexandria, Va., 1966; sr. scientist Dunlap and Assocs., Inc., Santa Monica, Calif., 1967-71; rsch. assoc. traffic safety rsch. group Psychology Dept., Uppsala (Sweden) Univ., 1972; human factors engr. Royal Inst. of Tech., Stockholm, Sweden, 1972; rsch. scientist Rsch. Inst. Human Engring. Forschungs Inst. Anthropotechnik, Wachtberg, Germany, 1972-96; rsch. scientist divsn. ergonomics and info. sys. FFM/FGAN, Wachtberg, 1997—. Contbr. articles to profl. jours. and books. With USN, 1951-55. Mem. Human Factors and Ergonomics Soc. (Europe chpt., founding mem., pres. 1991-93, pres. 1994-96, dir. 1997—). Democrat. Achievements include contributions to the ergonomic design of current military systems, design of a performance test to form matched experimental groups, design of the two-level, sequential judgment rating scale, and design of a cognitive rating model. Office: FGAN/FFM/EFS, Neuenahrer Strasse 20, 53343 Wachtberg Germany

PITRELLI, ELLEN JANE, secondary school educator; b. Bklyn., July 18, 1950; d. Robert Martin and Margaret (Carlo) Timm; m. Fred Pitrelli, Aug. 29, 1971; children: Timothy Robert, Kimberly Marie. BS, St. John's U., 1971; MA, Hofstra U., 1975. Cert. secondary tchr., N.Y., bus. and math tchr. Bus. tchr. Bellport (N.Y.) Sr. High Sch., 1971-72, Longwood Sr. High Sch., Mid. Island, N.Y., 1972—. Mem. Suffolk County Tchrs. Assn., Bus. tchrs. assn., Assn. of Supr. and Curriculm Devel., Phi Delta Kappa. Avocation: reading.

PITT, BERTRAM, cardiologist, educator, consultant; b. Kew Gardens, N.Y., Apr. 27, 1932; s. David and Shirley (Blum) P., m. Elaine Liberstein, Aug. 10, 1962; children—Geoffrey, Jessica, Jillian. BA, Cornell U., 1953; MD, U. Basel, Switzerland, 1959. Diplomate Am. Bd. Internal Medicine, Am. Bd. Cardiology. Intern Beth Israel Hosp., N.Y.C., 1959-60; resident Beth Israel Hosp., Boston, 1960-63; fellow in cardiology Johns Hopkins U., Balt., 1966-67; from instr. to assoc. prof. Johns Hopkins U., 1967-77; prof. medicine, dir. div. cardiology U. Mich., Ann Arbor, 1977-91, assoc. chmn. dept. medicine, 1991—. Author: Atlas of Cardiovascular Nuclear Medicine, 1977; editor: Cardiovascular Nuclear Medicine, 1974. Served to capt. U.S. Army, 1963-65. Mem. ACP, Am. Coll. Cardiology, Am. Soc. Clin. Investigation, Assn. Am. Physicians, Am. Physiol. Soc., Am. Heart Assn., Assn. Univ. Cardiologists, Am. Coll. Chest Physicians, Royal Soc. Mich. Home: 24 Ridgeway St Ann Arbor MI 48104-1739 Office: U Mich Divsn Cardiology 1500 E Medical Center Dr Ann Arbor MI 48109-0005

PITT, BRAD, actor; b. Okla., Dec. 18, 1963; s. Bill and Jane P. Appearences include: (TV series) Dallas, Another World, Growing Pains, The Image(HBO), Glory Days, Two-Fisted Tales; (TV movie) Too Young To Die?, 1989; (films)Cutting Glass, Happy Together, 1989, Across the Tracks, 1990, Contact, Thelma and Louise, 1991, The Favor, 1992, Johnny Suede, 1992, Cool World, 1992, A River Runs Through It, 1992, Kalifornia, 1993, True Romance, 1993, Interview with the Vampire, 1994, Legends of the Fall, 1994, 12 Monkeys, 1995 (Golden Globe award for best supporting actor in film 1996, Acad. award nominee for best supporting actor 1996), Sleepers, 1996, Seven Years in Tibet, 1997. Office: Creative Artists Agy 9830 Wilshire Blvd Beverly Hills CA 90212-1804*

PITT, GEORGE, lawyer; b. Chgo., July 21, 1938; s. Cornelius George and Anastasia (Geocaris) P.; m. Barbara Lynn Goodrich, Dec. 21, 1963 (div. Apr. 1990); children: Elizabeth Nanette, Margaret Leigh; m. Pamela Ann Pittsford, May 19,1990. BA, Northwestern U., 1960, JD, 1963. Bar: Ill. 1963. Assoc. Chapman and Cutler, Chgo., 1963-67; ptnr. Borge and Pitt, and predecessor, 1968-87; ptnr. Katten Muchin & Zavis, Chgo., 1987—. conf. chmn. Bond Buyer's 3rd Ann. Midwest Pub. Fin. Conf., 1994. Notes and Comments editor Northwestern U. Law Rev., 1962-63. Served to 1st lt. AUS, 1964. Fellow Am. Coll. of Bond Counsel; mem. Ill. State Bar Assn., The Monroe Club, Univ. Club Chgo., Michigan City Yacht Club, Ind. Soc. of Chgo., Eta Sigma Phi, Phi Delta Phi, Phi Gamma Delta. Home: 600 N McClurg Ct Chicago IL 60611-3021 Office: Katten Muchin & Zavis 525 W Monroe St Ste 1600 Chicago IL 60661-3629

PITT, HARVEY LLOYD, lawyer; b. Bklyn., Feb. 28, 1945; s. Morris Jacob and Sara (Sapir) P.; m. Saree Ruffin, Jan. 7, 1984; children: Robert Garrett, Sara Dillard; children from previous marriage: Emily Laura, Jonathan Bradley. BA, CUNY, 1965; JD with honors (Univ. scholar), St. John's U., N.Y.C., 1968. Bar: N.Y. 1969, U.S. Supreme Ct. 1972, D.C. 1979. With SEC, Washington, 1968-78; legal asst. to commr. SEC, 1969; editor Instl. Investor Study, 1970-71; spl. counsel Office Gen. Counsel, 1971-72, chief counsel div. market regulation, 1972-73, exec. asst. to chmn., 1973-75, gen. counsel, 1975-78; mng. ptnr. Fried, Frank, Harris, Shriver & Jacobson, Washington, 1978—; adj. prof. law George Washington U. Nat. Law Ctr., 1974-82, U. Pa. Law Sch., 1983-84, vis. practitioner, 1984, Georgetown U. Law Ctr., 1976-84; comml. arbitrator Am. Arbitration Assn. Contbr. articles to profl. jours. V.p. Glen Haven Civic Assn., Silver Spring, Md., 1972-73, pres., 1974. Recipient Learned Hand award Inst. for Human Rels., 1988. Mem. ABA (past chmn. subcom. SEC practice and enforcement, past co-chmn. subcom. state takeover laws), Fed. Bar Assn. (Outstanding Young Lawyer award 1975), Adminstrv. Conf. U.S., Am. Law Inst. (project advisor on restatement law on corp. governance 1981—), Eldwick Homes Assn. (sec. bd. dirs.), Delta Sigma Rho, Tau Kappa Alpha, Phi Delta Phi. Home: 2404 Wyoming Ave NW Washington DC 20008-1643 Office: Fried Frank Harris Shriver & Jacobson 1001 Pennsylvania Ave NW Washington DC 20004-2505 also: Fried Frank Harris Shriver 1 New York Plz New York NY 10004

PITT, JANE, medical educator; b. Frankfurt, Fed. Republic Germany, Aug. 25, 1938; came to U.S., 1939.; d. Ludwig Friederich and Vera (Aberle) Ries; m. Martin Irwin Pitt, Aug. 12, 1962 (dec. 1980); children: Jennifer, Eric Jonathan; m. Robert Harry Socolow, May 25, 1986; stepchildren: David, Seth. BA, Radcliffe Coll., 1960; MD, Harvard U., 1964. Diplomate Am. Bd. Pediatrics. Resident Children's Hosp. Med. Ctr., Boston, 1964-66; fellow Tufts U. Med. Sch., Boston, 1966-67, Harvard U. Med. Sch., Boston, 1967-69; asst. prof. SUNY Downstate Sch. Medicine, N.Y.C., 1970-71; asst. prof. Coll. Physicians and Surgeons Columbia U., N.Y.C., 1971-75, assoc. prof. Coll. Physicians and Surgeons, 1975—; mem. instl. rev. bd. Columbia Health Scis. Campus, N.Y.C., 1982—. Reviewer Jour. of Infectious Diseases, New Eng. Jour. Medicine, 1976—; contbr. articles to profl. jours. NIH grantee, 1974—. Fellow Infectious Disease Soc.; mem. NIH (study sect.), Pediat. Infectious Disease Soc., Soc. Pediat. Rsch. Democrat. Jewish.

Home: 34 Westcott Rd Princeton NJ 08540-3060 Office: Columbia U Coll Physicians Surgeons 630 W 168th St New York NY 10032-3702

PITT, JOSEPH CHARLES, philosophy educator; b. Hempstead, N.Y., Sept. 12, 1944; s. Louis Antony and Miriam (Baumstein) P.; m. Donna Hanlon Smith, Feb. 25, 1946. AB in Philosophy, Coll. William and Mary, 1966; MA in Philosophy, U. We. Ont., London, Ont., Can., 1970; PhD, U. We. Ont., 1972. Instr. Va. Poly. Inst. and State U., Blacksburg, 1971-72; asst. prof. Va. Poly. Inst. and State U., 1972-78; vis. asst. prof. U. Pitts., 1974; assoc. prof. Va. Poly. Inst. and State U., 1978-83, prof. philosophy, 1983—; founding dir. Ctr. for Study of Sci. in Soc., Va. Poly. Inst. and State U., 1980-81, founder, dir. humanities, sci. and tech. program, 1979-89, head dept. philosophy, 1992—. Author: Pictures, Images and Conceptual Change, 1981, Galileo, Human Knowledge and the Book of Nature, 1992, New Directions in the Philosophy of Technology, 1995; editor: New Perspectives on Galileo, 1978, Theories of Explanation, 1988; sr. editor Perspectives on Sci.; mem. bd. editors Philosophy and Tech., 1985-94, Behaviorism, 1985-96, History of Philosophy Quar., 1990—, Sci. and Edn., 1992—; contbr. articles to profl. jours. U. Pitts. Ctr. for Philosophy of Sci. vis. sr. fellow, 1984. Mem. Philosophy of Sci. Assn., Soc. for Philosophy and Tech. (v.p., pres.-elect 1989-91, pres. 1991-93), History of Sci. Soc., Soc. for History of Tech., Am. Philos. Assn., Irish Wolfhound Club Am. (bd. dirs. 1987-95), Sigma Xi. Home: Gavagai Hollow Farm Newport VA 24128 Office: Va Poly Inst and State U Dept Philosophy Blacksburg VA 24061

PITT, JUDSON HAMILTON, publisher, author; b. Glen Cove, N.Y., June 7, 1953; s. Gavin Alexander and Eleanore Gaehler (Whiting) P.; m. Elena U. Tokaeva, Dec. 16, 1995. BS in Communications, Ariz. State U., 1977. Resident advisor fraternity Ohio State U., Columbus, 1977-79; supr. student svcs. Loyola U., Chgo., 1979-81; asst. to CEO Flair Communications Agy., Inc., Chgo., 1981—; v.p. Gavin Pitt Assocs., Inc., Chgo., 1986—; pub. Water Tower Pub. House, Chgo., 1989—; dir. ops. Chgo. Marathon, 1984-93. Author: The Official Hard Rock Cafe Pin Collector's Guide, 1997. Mem. Am. Mktg. Assn., Newcomen Soc. U.S., Chgo. Soc. Assn. Execs., Saddle & Cycle Club, Pi Kappa Alpha. Republican. Presbyterian. Home: 5510 N Sheridan Rd Chicago IL 60640-1633 Office: 214 W Erie St Chicago IL 60610-3611

PITT, REDDING, lawyer; b. Decatur, Ala., Mar. 29, 1944; s. Charles Kermit and Dorothea Rowena (Slaughter) P.; m. Jane Hanify, Sept. 20, 1969 (div. Dec. 1980); 1 child, William Rivers; m. Abigail P. van Alstyne, Aug. 24, 1985. Student, U. Ams., Mexico City, 1963; BA, U. Ala., 1967; JD, Boston Coll., 1977. Staff asst. to chmn. FDIC, Washington, 1977-79; staff asst. to comptr. of currency U.S. Treasury Dept., Washington, 1979-80; asst. atty. gen. State of Ala., Montgomery, 1981-94, counsel to sec. of state, 1981-84, asst. legal adviser to dir. fin., 1984-86, chief dep. atty. gen., 1987-91, counsel to atty. gen., 1991-94; U.S. atty. U.S. Dist Ct. (Mid. Dist.) Ala., Montgomery, 1994—; mem. Ala. Juvenile Justice Coordinating Coun. Supreme Ct. Ala., Montgomery, 1992-94. Editor: Powers and Duties of State Attorneys General, 1988. Mem. Ala. Gov. Drug Adv. Bd., Montgomery, 1994—; mem. adv. bd. Blackburn Inst. U. Ala., 1996—. Capt. U.S. Army, 1969-72. Recipient Pres. award Nat. Assn. Attys. Gen., 1988. Mem. ABA, ATLA, Fed. Bar Assn. (pres. 1995—), Ala. Law Inst. (mem. reform adv. com. 1982-93), Ala. Bar Assn. (mem. com. bench & bar rels. 1994-95). Democrat. Episcopalian. Avocations: history, golf. Office: US Atty Mid Dist Ala 1 Court Sq Ste 201 Montgomery AL 36104-3538

PITT, ROBERT ERVIN, environmental engineer, educator; b. San Francisco, Apr. 25, 1948; s. Wallace and Marjorie (Peterson) P.; m. Kathryn Jay, Mar. 18, 1967; children: Gwendolyn, Brady. BS in Engring. Sci., Humboldt State U., 1970; MSCE, San Jose State U., 1971; PhD in Civil and Environ. Engring., U. Wis., 1987. Registered profl. engr., Wis.; diplomate Am. Acad. Environ. Engrs. Environ. engr. URS Rsch. Co., San Mateo, Calif., 1971-74; sr. engr. Woodward-Clyde Cons., San Francisco, 1974-79; cons. environ. engr. Blue Mounds, Wis., 1979-84; environ. engr. Wis. Dept. Natural Resources, Madison, 1984-87; assoc. prof. depts. civil and environ. engring. and environ. health scis. U. Ala., Birmingham, 1987—; mem. Resource Conservation and Devel. Coun., Jefferson County, Ala., 1992-94; mem. com. on augmenting natural recharge of groundwater with reclaimed wastewater NRC, 1991-94; Ala. state dir. for energy and environment U.S. DOE EPSCOR, 1992-94; guest lectr. U. Gesamthochschule, Essen, Germany, 1994; mem. steering group. U.K. Hwys. Agy., U.K. Environ. Agy., London, 1997—; mem. value engring. com. CSO, Cleve., 1993, mem. tech. adv. com., N.Y.C., 1997—; mem. steering group U.K. Huys Agy., London, 1997—. Author: Small Storm Urban Flow and Particulate Washoff Contributions to Outfall Discharges, 1987, Investigation of Inappropriate Pollutant Entries into Storm Drainage Systems, 1994, Potential Groundwater Contamination from Intentional and Non-Intentional Stormwater Infiltration, 1994, Stormwater Quality Management, 1997, Groundwater Contamination from Stormwater Infiltration, 1996; co-author: Manual for Evaluating Stormwater Runoff Effects in Receiving Waters, 1997; author software in field; mem. editl. bd. Ctr. Watershed Protection, 1994—. Asst. scoutmaster Boy Scouts Am., Birmingham, 1988-94. Recipient 1st Pl. Nat. award U.S. Soil Conservation Svc. Earth Team, 1989, 94, award of recognition USDA, 1990, 1st Pl. Vol. award Take Pride in Am., 1991; Fed. Water Pollution Control Adminstrn. fellow, 1970-71, GE Engring. Edn. fellow, 1984-86. Mem. ASCE, Soc. for Environ. Toxicology and Chemistry, N.Am. Lake Mgmt. Soc. (Profl. Speakers award 1992), Water Environ. Fedn. (1st Pl. Nat. award 1992), Am. Water Resources Assn., Ala. Acad. Sci., Internat. Assn. Water Quality (mem. com. on solids in sewers 1996-96), Sigma Xi. Achievements include development of small storm urban hydrology prediction methods, toxicant control devices for stormwater source flows, methods to identify and correct inappropriate discharges to storm drain systems. Office: U Ala Birmingham Dept Civil/Environ Engring 1150 10th Ave S Birmingham AL 35294-4461

PITT, WOODROW WILSON, JR., engineering educator; b. Rocky Mount, N.C., Aug. 14, 1935; s. Woodrow Wilson Pitt and Stella Marie (Whitley) Wiggins; m. Katherine Ann Morton, Jan. 1, 1958; children: Deborah Ann, Abigail Marie, Katherine Elizabeth. BSChemE, U. S.C., 1957; MS, U. Tenn., 1966, PhD, 1969. Registered profl. engr., Tenn., Tex. Devel. engr. Oak Ridge (Tenn.) Nat. Lab., 1960-72, sr. devel. engr., 1972-81, sect. head, 1981-89; vis. prof. Tex. A&M U., College Station, 1989-90, prof. dept. nuclear engring., asst. dept. head, 1991—. Inventor multi-sample rotor assembly for blood function preparation, differential chromatography; contbr. articles to profl. jours. Councilman Oak Ridge City Coun., 1983-89. Lt. (j.g.) USN, 1957-60; CDR USNR, Ret. Spl. fellow U.S. AEC, 1966-67; recipient IR-100 awards, 1971, 80. Fellow AIChE; mem. ASTM, NSPE, Am. Nuclear Soc., N.Y. Acad. Scis., Sigma Xi, Tau Beta Pi. Methodist. Avocations: golf, tennis. Home: 702 Summerglen Dr College Station TX 77840-2333 Office: Tex A&M U Dept Nuclear Engring 129 Zachry College Station TX 77843

PITTARD, WILLIAM BLACKBURN (BILLY PITTARD), television graphic designer; b. Murfreesboro, Tenn., May 8, 1954; s. Samuel G. and Annette (Batey) P.; m. Linda C. Rheinstein; 1 child, Colby. BS, Middle Tenn. State U., 1978. Art dir. Sta. WKRN-TV, Nashville, 1978-84; design mgr. Sta. KCBS-TV, Los Angeles, 1984-86; pres. Pittard and Sillervin, Calver City, Calif., 1986—. Mem. Broadcast Designer's Assn. (bd. dirs. 1984—, Outstanding Service award, 1986), Nat. Acad. TV Arts and Scis. Office: Pittard and Sillervin 3535 Hayden Ave Culver City CA 90232-2412*

PITTAWAY, DAVID BRUCE, investment banker, lawyer; b. Kansas City, Mo., Oct. 4, 1951; s. Alan Ralph and Joanne (Kenney) P. BA with highest distinction, U. Kans., 1972; JD, Harvard U., 1975, MBA with high distinction, 1982. Bar: Md., D.C., Pa. Assoc. Morgan, Lewis and Bockius, Washington, 1975-80; cons. Bain and Co., Boston, 1982-85; v.p. strategic planning, asst. to pres. Donaldson, Lufkin and Jenrette, N.Y.C., 1985-86; mng. dir. Castle Harlan, Inc., N.Y.C., 1986—; adj. prof. Columbia U., N.Y.C., 1986—; CFO Branford Chain, Inc., N.Y.C., 1987—, bd. dirs., Morton's Restaurant Group, Inc., New Hyde Park, N.Y., McCormick & Schmick Holdings, Inc., Portland, Oreg., Statia Terminals Group, N.V., St. Eustatius, Netherlands Antilles, Commemorative Brands, Inc., Austin, Tex. Bd. dirs. Dystrophic Epidermolysis Bullosa Rsch. Assn. Am., Inc., N.Y.C. Summerfield scholar, 1972, Baker scholar, 1982. Mem. Harvard Club N.Y., Harvard Club Boston, Phi Beta Kappa. Office: Castle Harlan Inc 150 E 58th St New York NY 10155-0099

PITTELKO, ROGER DEAN, clergyman; b. Elk Reno, Okla., Aug. 18, 1932; s. Elmer Henry and Lydia Caroline (Nieman) P.; A.A., Concordia Coll., 1952; B.A., Concordia Sem., St. Louis, 1954, M.Div., 1957, S.T.M., 1958; postgrad. Chgo. Luth. Theol. Sem., 1959-61; Th.D., Am. Div. Sch., Pineland, Fla., 1968; D.Min., Faith Evang. Luth. Sem., Tacoma, 1983; m. Beverly A. Moellendorf, July 6, 1957; children—Dean, Susan. Ordained to ministry, Lutheran Ch.-Mo. Synod, 1958; vicar St. John Luth. Ch., S.I., N.Y., 1955-56; asst. pastor St. John Luth. Ch., New Orleans, 1958-59; pastor Concordia Luth. Ch., Berwyn, Ill., 1959-63; pastor Luth. Ch. of the Holy Spirit, Elk Grove Village, Ill., 1963-87; chmn. Commn. on Worship, Luth. Ch.-Mo. Synod; asst. bishop Midwest region English dist., 1983; pres. and bishop English dist., 1987—. Mem. Luth. Acad. for Scholarship, Concordia Hist. Inst. Republican. Clubs: Maywood (Ill.) Sportsman; Itasca (Ill.) Country. Author: Guide to Introducing Lutheran Worship. Contbr. articles to jours. Home: 19405 Stamford Dr Livonia MI 48152-1240 Office: 33100 Freedom Rd Farmington MI 48336-4030

PITTELKOW, MARK ROBERT, physician, dermatology educator, researcher; b. Milw., Dec. 16, 1952; s. Robert Bernard and Barbara Jean (Thomas) P.; m. Gail L. Gamble, Nov. 26, 1977; children: Thomas, Cameron, Robert. BA, Northwestern U., 1975; MD, Mayo Med. Sch., 1979. Intern then resident Mayo Grad. Sch., 1979-84, post-doctoral exptl. pathology, 1981-83; from asst. to assoc. prof. dermatology Mayo Med. Sch., Rochester, Minn., 1984-95, prof. dermatology, 1995—, assoc. prof. biochemistry and molecular biology, 1992—; cons. Mayo Clinic/Found., Rochester, 1984—. Fellow Am. Acad. Dermatology; mem. AAAS, Am. Dermatol. Assn., Soc. Investigative Dermatology, Am. Burn Assn., Am. Soc. Cell Biology, N.Y. Acad. Scis., Chi Psi. Home: 721 12th Ave SW Rochester MN 55902-2027 Office: Mayo Clinic 200 1st St SW Rochester MN 55902-3008

PITTMAN, CONSTANCE SHEN, physician, educator; b. Nanking, China, Jan. 2, 1929; came to U.S., 1946; d. Leo F.-Z. and Pao Kong (Yang) Shen; m. James Allen Pittman, Jr., Feb. 19, 1955; children: James Clinton, John Merrill. AB in Chemistry, Wellesley Coll., 1951; MD, Harvard U., 1955. Diplomate Am. Bd. Internal Medicine, sub-bd. Endocrinology. Intern Baltimore City Hosp., 1955-56; resident U. Ala., Birmingham, 1956-57; instr. in medicine U. Ala. Med. Ctr., Birmingham, 1956-59, fellow dept. pharmacology, 1957-59, from asst. prof. to assoc. prof., 1959-70, prof., 1970—, Constance & James Pittman lectr., 1993—; prof. medicine Georgetown U., Washington, 1972-73; mem. diabetes and metabolism tng. com. NIH, Bethesda, Md., 1972-76, mem. nat. arthritis, metabolism and digestive disease coun., 1975-78, mem. gen. clin. rsch. ctrs. com., 1979-83, 87-90; dir. Internat. Coun. for the Control of Iodine Deficiency Diseases, 1994—. Master ACP; mem. Assn. Am. Physicians, Am. Soc. for Clin. Investigation, Endocrine Soc. (coun., 1978-79, pres. women's caucus 1978-79), Am. Thyroid Assn. (pres. 1990-91). Achievements include research in activation and metabolism of thyroid hormone; kinetics of thyroxine conversion to triiodothyrine in health and disease states; control of iodine deficiency disorders. Office: U Ala Div Endocrinology/Metab UAB Med Ctr Birmingham AL 35294-0012

PITTMAN, DAVID JOSHUA, sociologist, educator, researcher, consultant; b. Rocky Mount, N.C., Sept. 18, 1927; s. Jay Washington and Laura Frances (Edwards) P. BA, U. N.C., 1949, MA, 1950; postgrad., Columbia U., 1953; PhD, U. Chgo., 1956. Asst. prof. sociology Washington U., St. Louis, 1958-60, assoc. prof., 1960-64, prof., 1964-91, prof. sociology in psychology, 1991-92, prof. psychology, 1992-93, prof. emeritus, 1993—, chmn. dept. sociology, 1976-86, dir. Social Sci. Inst., 1963-76; cons. Jellinek Clinic, Amsterdam, The Netherlands, 1965-68, HEW, Washington, 1977-85, cons. Wine Inst., 1985-94; mem. sci. adv. com. Distilled Spirits Coun., Washington, 1976-86; field editor social scis. Jour. Study Alcoholism, 1985-92, mem. editorial bd., 1992—; Dent Meml. lectr. U. London, 1989. Author: Revolving Door: A Study of Chronic Police Case Inebriates, 1958, The Drug Scene in Great Britain, 1967, Primary Prevention of Alcoholism, 1980; editor: Society, Culture and Drinking Patterns, 1962, Alcoholism, 1967, Society, Culture and Drinking Patterns Reexamined, 1991; mem. editl. bd. Internat. Jour. Advt., 1990—. Bd. dirs. Nat. Gay and Lesbian Task Force, 1993-97—; pres. N.Am. Assn. Alcoholism Programs, 1965-67; chmn. 28th Internat. Congress on Alcohol and Alcoholism, Washington, 1968, Mo. Adv. Coun. on Alcoholism and Drug Abuse, Jefferson City, 1972-75, 87-91; mem. Mo. Mental Health Commn., Jefferson City, 1975-78. Recipient Page One Civic award St. Louis Newspaper Guild, 1967, Bronze Key St. Louis Coun. on Alcoholism, 1976, Silver Key Nat. Coun. on Alcoholism, N.Y.C., 1978, Biennal Rsch. award Soc. of the Med. Friends of Wine, 1992; spl. fellow NIMH, 1966. Fellow Am. Sociol. Soc.; mem. Soc. Study Social Problems (chmn. alcoholism com. 1957-59, Disting. Sr. Scholar award 1993), Internat. Coun. on Alcohol and Addictions (exec. com. 1968-84), Am. Sociol. Assn. (chmn. alcohol and drugs sect. 1992), Phi Beta Kappa, Sigma Xi, Omicron Delta Kappa, mem. Lincoln Club Log Cabin. Republican. Episcopalian. Avocations: collecting elephant replicas, collecting political memorabilia. Office: Washington U Psychol Dept Box 1125 One Brookings Dr Saint Louis MO 63130

PITTMAN, JAMES ALLEN, JR., physician, educator; b. Orlando, Fla., Apr. 12, 1927; s. James Allen and Jean C. (Garretson) P.; m. Constance Ming-Chung Shen, Feb. 19, 1955; children—James Clinton, John Merrill. BS, Davidson Coll., 1948; MD, Harvard, 1952; DSc (hon.), Davidson Coll., 1980, U. Ala., Birmingham, 1984. Intern, asst. resident medicine Mass. Gen. Hosp., Boston, 1952-54; tchg. fellow medicine Harvard U., 1953-54; clin. assoc. NIH, Bethesda, Md., 1954-56; instr. medicine George Washington U., 1955-56; chief resident U. Ala. Med. Ctr., Birmingham, 1956-58, instr. medicine, 1956-59, asst. prof., 1959-62, assoc. prof., 1962-64, prof. medicine, 1964—, dir. endocrinology and metabolism div., 1962-71, co-chmn. dept. medicine, 1969-71, also prof., physiology and biophysics, 1967-92; dean U. Ala. Med. Ctr. (Sch. Medicine), 1973-92; asst. chief med. dir. rsch. and edn. in medicine U.S. VA, 1971-73; prof. medicine Georgetown U. Med. Sch., Washington, 1971-73; mem. endocrinology study sect. NIH, 1963-67; mem. pharmacology and endocrinology fellowships rev. coms., 1967-68; mem. grad. med. edn. nat. adv. com. HEW; mem. HHS coun. on Grad. Med. Edn., 1986-90; mem. nat. adv. rsch. resources coun. NIH, 1991-95; hon. prof. Chung Shan Med. and Dental Coll., Taiwan, 1995; sr. advisor Internat. Coun. on Control of Iodine Deficiency Diseases, 1994-95. Author: Diagnosis and Treatment of Thyroid Diseases, 1963; Contbr. articles in field to profl. jours. Master ACP; fellow Am. Coll. Endocrinology; mem. Assn. Am. Physicians, Endocrine Soc., Am. Assn. Clin. Endocrinologists, Am. Thyroid Assn., N.Y. Acad. Scis. (life), Soc. Nuclear Medicine, Am. Diabetes Assn., Am. Chem. Soc., Wilson Ornithol. Club (life), Am. Ornithologists Union (life), Am. Fedn. Clin. Rsch. (pres. So. sect., nat. coun. 1952-66), So. Soc. Clin. Investigation (Founder's medal 1993), Harvard U. Med. Alumni Assn. (pres. 1986-88), Phi Beta Kappa, Alpha Omega Alpha, Omicron Delta Kappa. Office: U Ala Sch of Med CAMS 1924 7th Ave S Birmingham AL 35294-0007 *I hope that each person I meet leaves the encounter better for it.**

PITTMAN, KATHERINE ANNE ATHERTON, elementary education educator; b. Baytown, Tex., Aug. 20, 1956; d. William Clifford Sr. and Pauline (High) Atherton; children: Richard Neil, Angela Christine, William Charles. Student, Lee Coll., 1973-75, 76, 87; BA in Liberal Arts and History, Tex. A&M U., 1977; cert. in secondary edn., Stephen F. Austin State U., 1978; cert. elem. and secondary edn., U. Houston, 1989, MS in Elem. Edn., 1991. Cert. elem. and high sch. tchr., Tex. Catalog clk. J.C. Penney Co., Baytown, Tex., 1974-75; substitute tchr. San Augustine (Tex.) Ind. Sch. Dist., 1978; math. tchr. Brookeland (Tex.) Ind. Sch. Dist., 1980-81; substitute tchr. Deer Park (Tex.) Ind. Sch. Dist., 1988-89; tchr. 6th grade Channelview (Tex.) Ind. Sch. Dist., 1989-94; tchr. 7th grade English and ESL Houston Ind. Sch. Dist., 1994-95; substitute tchr. Goose Creek Consol. Ind. Sch. Dist., Baytown, 1987-89; tchr. ESL, Harris County Dept. of Edn./Lee Coll., Baytown, 1989-90, substitute ESL tchr., 1990-91; customer svc. assoc. Montgomery Ward Co., Baytown, 1988-89. Mem. Assn. Tex. Profl. Educators, Tex. Computer Edn. Assn., Houston Fedn. Tchrs. Avocations: knitting, crocheting, computers, guitar, reading. Office: Jackson Middle Sch 5100 Polk St Houston TX 77023-1420

PITTMAN, LISA, lawyer; b. Limestone, Maine, Jan. 4, 1959; d. William Franklin and Rowena Paradis (Umphrey) P.; m. Edward Leon Pittman, May 26, 1984; 1 child, Graham Edward Paradis. BA, U. Fla., 1980, MA, 1981, JD, 1984; LLM, George Washington U., 1988. Bar: Fla. 1984, D.C. 1993, U.S Supreme Ct. 1993. Spl. asst. to gen. counsel Nat. Oceanic and Atmospheric Adminstrn., Washington, 1984-85, atty., advisor, 1985-87; minority counsel Com. on Mcht. Marine & Fisheries, Ho. of Reps., Washington, 1987-95; dep. chief counsel Com. on Resources U.S. Ho. of Reps., Washington, 1995—. Home: 6123 Ramshorn Dr Mc Lean VA 22101-2333 Office: US House of Reps 1324 Longworth HOB Washington DC 20515

PITTMAN, PRESTON LAWRENCE, executive assistant; b. Wilson, N.C., May 1, 1951; s. Elmer Lee and Nina Cornelia (Hocutt) P. BA, New Sch. for Social Rsch., 1994. Asst. to the producer Miami Star Theatre, 1974-75; dir. pub. rels. Ex-Cathedra Prodns., N.Y.C., 1976-80; libr. adminstr. Mobil Corp., N.Y.C., 1980-90; records mgmt. coord. Morgan Stanley, N.Y.C., 1991-95; exec. asst. Assn. for the Help of Retarded Children, N.Y.C., 1995—; exec. producer TV show The Gay Cath. Hour, 1996—. Steering com. Dignity N.Y., 1996—. Recipient Calloway leadership award, 1968. Mem. Spl. Librs. Assn., N.Y. Libr. Club, Mid. East Librs. Assn. Democrat. Avocations: fluent Spanish, French, Arabic, Latin. Home: 76 W 86th St New York NY 10024-3607

PITTMAN, ROBERT TURNER, retired newspaper editor; b. Gates, N.C., Sept. 24, 1929; s. Thomas Everett and Lillian (Turner) P.; m. Ruth Fike, Aug. 25, 1956; children—Laura Emily, Mary Ann, Lillian Elizabeth. B.A., Washington and Lee U., 1951; M.A., U. N.C., 1957. Reporter Times Dispatch, Richmond, Va., 1951; editor, pub. Daily Ranger, Glendive, Mont., 1957-58; writer editorials Times Union, Jacksonville, Fla., 1958-63; editorial editor Times, St. Petersburg, Fla., 1963-92; dir. Times Pub. Co., 1968-92; trustee Poynter Inst. Media Studies, St. Petersburg, 1978-92. Editor: (jour.) Masthead, 1980, 81. Active St. Petersburg Charter Revision Com., 1992-93; dir. Fla. Bar Found., 1994-96; mem. Mayor's Cmty. Action com., 1996-97. Lt. (j.g.) USNR, 1951-55. Recipient Pinellas Civil Liberties award, 1993; U. N.C.-Chapel Hill scholarship established in honor, 1994. Mem. Am. Soc. Newspaper Editors, Nat. Conf. Editorial Writers (pres. 1978, life), Nat. Conf. Editorial Writers Found. Inc. (pres. 1984). Methodist. Home: 736 18th Ave NE Saint Petersburg FL 33704-4608

PITTMAN, ROBERT WARREN, entertainment executive; b. Jackson, Miss., Dec. 28, 1953; s. Warren E. and Lanita (Hurdle) P.; m. Sandra Hill, July 27, 1979; 1 son, Robert Thomas. Student, Millsaps Coll., 1971-72, Oakland U., 1972-73, U. Pitts., 1973-74; AMP, Harvard U., 1984-85. Disc. jockey Sta. WJDX-FM, Jackson, Miss., 1970-72, Sta. WRIT, Milw., 1972; research dir. Sta. WDRQ, Detroit, 1972-73; program dir. Sta. WPEZ, Pitts., 1973-74, Stas. WMAQ-WKQZ, NBC Radio, Chgo., 1974-77, Sta. WNBC, N.Y.C., 1977-79; exec. producer Album Tracks, NBC TV, N.Y.C., 1977-78; dir., v.p., then sr. v.p. Warner Amex Satellite Entertainment Co. (now MTV Networks, Inc.), N.Y.C., 1979-82; exec. v.p., chief oper. officer MTV Networks, N.Y.C., 1983-85; pres., chief exec. officer Warner Amex Satellite Entertainment Co., N.Y.C., 1985-86, Quantum Media, Inc., N.Y.C., 1987-89; exec. advisor Warner Communications, Inc., N.Y.C., 1989-90; pres., chief exec. officer Time Warner Enterprises, N.Y.C., 1990-95; CEO Six Flags Entertainment, 1991-95; mng. ptnr., CEO Century 21 Real Estate, 1995-96; pres., CEO Am. On-Line Networks, 1996—; bd. dirs. HFS Inc., Am. Online Internat. Bd. dirs. One to One Found., N.J. Performing Arts Ctr., N.Y.C. Ballet, N.Y. Shakespeare Festival, chmn., 1987-94. Recipient Program Mgr. of Yr. Billboard, 1977, Program Dir. of Yr. Hall Radio Report, 1978, Entrepreneur award White House SB Conf., 1986, Golden Plate award Am. Acad. Achievement, 1990, medal of Excellence Miss. U. Women, 1992, Vision award Retinitis Pigmentosa International, 1992, Lifetime Achievement Internat. Monitor award Internat. Teleproduction Soc., 1993; named Innovator of Yr. Performance Mag., 1981, Humanitarian of Yr., AMC, 1984, Time Mag. Man of Yr. runner-up, 1984, Esquire Mag. Under 40 Leadership, 1985; named one of Pioneers of New Am. Start-Up, Success mag., one of five Original Thinkers of 80s, Life mag, 1990, 8 of 50 Most Influential Baby Boomers, Life mag., 1996. Methodist. Office: Am Online 2200 AOL Way Dulles VA 20166

PITTMAN, STEUART LANSING, lawyer; b. Albany, N.Y., June 6, 1919; s. Ernest Wetmore and Estelle Young (Romeyn) P.; children by previous marriage—Andrew Pinchot, Nancy Steuart, Rosamond Pinchot, Tamara Pickering; m. Barbara Milburn White, Mar. 29, 1958; children—Patricia Milburn, Steuart Lansing, Anne Romeyn. Grad., St. Paul's Sch., Concord, N.H., 1937; B.A., Yale U., 1941, LL.B., 1948. Bar: N.Y. 1948, D.C. 1954. With Pan Am. Airways Africa Ltd., Cairo, 1941-42, China Nat. Aviation Co., Calcutta, India, 1942; with firm Cravath, Swaine & Moore, N.Y.C., 1948-50; with govt. agys. ECA, Mut. Security Agy. and FOA, 1950-54; founder Shaw, Pittman, Potts & Trowbridge (and predecessors), Washington, 1954-61, 64—; asst. sec. of def., 1961-64; cons. 2d Hoover Commn., 1954-55, Dept. State, 1955, Devel. Loan Fund, 1958-59; sr. fellow Inst. Def. Analysis. Bd. dirs. Hudson Inst., Chesapeake Environ. Protection Assn.; mem. Atlantic Coun. 1st lt. USMCR, WWII, CBI. Decorated Silver Star. Mem. Met. Club (Washington). Office: Shaw Pittman Potts & Trowbridge 2300 N St NW Washington DC 20037-1122

PITTMAN, VIRGIL, federal judge; b. Enterprise, Ala., Mar. 28, 1916; s. Walter Oscar and Annie Lee (Logan) P.; m. Floy Lasseter, 1944; children—Karen Pittman Gordy, Walter Lee. B.S., U. Ala., 1939, LL.B., 1940. Bar: Ala. bar 1940. Spl. agt. FBI, 1940-44; practice law Gadsden, Ala., 1946-51; judge Ala. Circuit Ct., Circuit 16, 1951-66; U.S. dist. judge Middle and So. Dist. Ala., 1966-71; chief judge U.S. Dist. Ct. for Ala. So. Dist., 1971-81, sr. judge, 1981—; periodically sits as judge U.S. Ct. Appeals 11th Cir., 1981—; lectr. bus. law, econs. and polit. sci. U. Ala. Center, Gadsden, 1948-66. Author: Circuit Court Proceedings in Acquisition of a Tract of Right of Way, 1959, A Judge Looks at Right of Way Condemnation Proceedings, 1960, Technical Pitfalls in Right of Way Proceedings, 1961. Mem. Ala. Bd. Edn., 1951; trustee Samford U., 1974-90, 92—. Lt. (j.g.) USN, 1944-46. Mem. Ala. State Bar, Etowah County Bar Assn. (pres. 1949), Omicron Delta Kappa. Democrat. Baptist. Office: US Dist Ct PO Box 465 Mobile AL 36601-0465

PITTMAN, WILLIAM CLAUDE, electrical engineer; b. Pontotoc, Miss., Apr. 22, 1921; s. William Claude and Maude Ella (Bennett) P.; m. Eloise Savage, Apr. 20, 1952; children: Patricia A. Pittman Ready, William Claude III, Thomas Allen. BSEE, Miss. State Coll., 1951, MSEE, 1957. From electronic engr. to supr. elec. engring. dept. U.S. Army Labs., Redstone Arsenal, Ala., 1951-59; supr. electronic engr. to aero. engring. supr. NASA/Marshall Space Flight Ctr., 1960; electronic engr. Army Missile Labs., 1962-82; program mgr. Army Labs. and R&D Ctr., Redstone Arsenal, 1982—; organizer numerous sci. and tech. confs. Author patents, reports, papers. Sgt. USMC, 1940-46, PTO. Recipient Medal of Honor, DAR, Meritorious Civilian Svc. award Dept. Army, 1993. Fellow AIAA (assoc.; chmn. Miss.-Ala. chpt. 1981-82, Martin Schilling award 1980); mem. IEEE (sr. life), NSPE, First Marine Div. Assn., DAV, IRE (chmn. Huntsville sect. 1957-58), Madison Hist. Soc., SAR (pres. Tenn. Valley chpt. 1984-85, Ala. Soc. 1990-91, Cert. 1991, Patriot medal), Tau Beta Pi, Phi Kappa Phi, Kappa Mu Epsilon. Avocations: history, genealogy. Home: 704 Desoto Rd SE Huntsville AL 35801-2032 Office: US Army Missile Command Huntsville AL 35809

PITTS, BARBARA TOWLE, accountant, painter; b. St. Paul, Minn., Nov. 8, 1944; d. James Francis and Helen (Gorman) Towle; m. E.R. Pitts, Oct. 19, 1965; 1 child, Paris Tucker Pitts. BSBA, U. Ala., 1980. CPA, Wash., Tenn. Prin. Barbara M. Pitts Assocs., Fayetteville, Tenn., 1982-90, Barbara M. Pitts CPA, Seattle, 1990—. Exhibited in group shows Midwest Watercolor Soc. 20th Ann. Nat. Open Show, 1996, Red River Watercolor Soc. 3d Ann. Nat. Juried Art Exhbn., 1996, Ea. Wash. Watercolor Soc. Ann. Nat. Competition, 1996 (Allied Arts award), Niagara Frontier Watercolor Soc. Nat. Exhbn., 1996 (Winsor and Newton award), City of Brea (Calif.) Gallery, 1996, Ariz. Aqueous '97 Nat. Competition, Tubac (Ariz.) Ctr. of Arts, 1997, Tex. Watercolor Soc. 48th Ann. Mus. of S.W., 1997. Bd. dirs. United Way Lincoln County, Fayetteville, 1989, Lincoln County Bd. Edn., Fayetteville, 1988-90; mem. planning com. Tenn. Hist. Soc., Nashville, 1989. Recipient Cert. of Recognition Tenn. Main St. Program, 1989, Best of Show award Juried Arts Ocean Shores, Wash., 1996, Best of Show awards Tex.

Watercolor Soc. 48th Ann., Traveling Show Tex. Watercolor Soc. 48th Ann., 1996; named Woman of Yr., Fayetteville Bus. and Profl. Women, 1988. Mem. AICPA, Nat. Watercolor Soc., Midwest Watercolor Soc., Am. Watercolor Soc., Wash. Soc. CPA, N.W. Watercolor Soc. (treas.), Red River Watercolor Soc., Tex. Watercolor Soc., Group Health Coop. Puget Sound (cen. regional coun.), Women Painters Wash. Home: 3515 E Marion St Seattle WA 98122-5258

PITTS, GARY BENJAMIN, lawyer; b. Tupelo, Miss., Aug. 23, 1952; s. Dextar Derward Pitts and Eva Margaret (Holcomb) Bush; m. Nicole Palmer; children: Andrew Ross, Caitlan Taylor. Student, U. Miss., Oxford, 1970-71, Coll. Charleston (S.C.), 1971-73; BA, McGill U., Montreal, Que., Can., 1973-74; JD, Tulane U., New Orleans, 1979. Bar: Tex. 1979, U.S. Ct. Appeals (5th cir.) 1980, U.S. Supreme Ct. 1983. Assoc. Julian & Seele, Houston, 1979-84, Ogletree, Pitts & Collard, Houston, 1984-85; ptnr. Pitts & Collard LLP, Houston and Dallas, 1985-96; owner Pitts & Assocs., Houston, 1996—. Organizer, legal counsel for Neighborhood Watch Coalition. Capt. USNG, 1975-87. Mem. ATLA, Maritime Law Assn. (Proctor in Admiralty 1980—). Office: Pitts & Assocs 8866 Gulf Fwy Ste 117 Houston TX 77017-6528

PITTS, JAMES ATWATER, financial executive; b. Greenwich, Conn., Apr. 8, 1940; s. Jeremiah Patrick and Mary Louise (McGregor) P.; m. Noreen Mary Kiggins, July 20, 1963; children: Paul, Andrew, Sarah. BBA with honors, Niagara U., 1962; MBA, U. Conn., 1971. CPA, N.Y. Staff acct. Price Waterhouse, Stamford, Conn., 1962; tax specialist Deloitte Haskins & Sells, Rochester, N.Y., 1965-68; div. contr. Xerox Corp., Stamford, 1968-76; asst. corp. contr. Digital Equipment Corp., Maynard, Mass., 1976-81; v.p., corp. contr. Data Gen. Corp., Westboro, Mass., 1981-86; exec. v.p. fin. adminstrn. and strategic planning Cullinet Software, Inc., Westwood, 1986-88; v.p., chief fin. officer Bain & Co. Inc., Boston, 1988-91; sr. v.p. fin. and adminstrn., treas., CFO Clean Harbors Inc., 1992-96; pres. The Pitts Group, Boston, 1996—; v.p. for fin. and adminstrn. The Boston Found., 1996—. Chmn. Sudbury (Mass.) Town Fin. Com., 1984; v.p., mem. exec. com. Children's Mus. Boston, 1984-96; bd. dirs. Mus. Wharf Inc., 1988-96, Lake Winniepesaukee Assn., Wolfeboro, N.H.; chmn. Sudbury Long Range Capital Expenditures Com., 1981; trustee Lake Regional Conservation Trust, Meridith, N.H. With U.S. Army, 1963-64, USAR, 1965-90, Desert Storm, 1991. Decorated Meritorious Svc. medal, 1991; recipient Internat. Exec. Mgmt. award Internat. Mgmt. Inst. U. Geneva, 1980. Mem. AICPAs, Conn. CPA Soc., N.Y. Soc. CPAs, Fin. Execs. Inst., Harvard Bus. Sch. Assn. Boston (bd. govs. 1992, pres.), Res. Officers Assn. (life), Soc. Mil. Compts., Algonquin Club, Bald Peak Colony Club, Officers Club. Home: 119 Pinckney St Boston MA 02114-3357 Office: The Boston Foundation 24th fl One Boston Pl Boston MA 02108-4405

PITTS, JOE W., III (CHIP PITTS), lawyer, law educator; b. Baton Rouge, Nov. 24, 1960; s. Joe Wise Pitts Jr. and Bobbie (Chachere) Edwards. Cert., Cambridge (Eng.) U., 1980; spl. diploma, Oxford (Eng.) U., 1981; BA, Tulane U., 1982; JD, Stanford U., 1985. Bar: Tex. 1986. Assoc. Legal Resources Ctr., Johannesburg, Republic South Africa, 1984, Carrington Coleman Sloman & Blumenthal, Dallas, 1985-88; vis. asst. prof. law So. Meth. U., Dallas, 1988-89; ptnr. Baker and McKenzie, Dallas, 1989-96; v.p., chief legal officer Nokia, Inc., 1996—; del. UN Commn. on Human Rights, Geneva, 1989, 92-96; U.S. del. to internat. conf. on European security NATO, Rome, 1990. Author numerous articles in field. Bd. dirs. Shakespeare Festival Dallas, 1987-94, pres., 1990-91, chmn., 1991-93; bd. dirs. Proyecto Adelante, 1988—; bd. dirs. Dallas Dem. Forum, 1989-93, sec., 1991-92; chmn. pub. awareness effort Dallas Young Lawyers Constl. Bicentennial Program, 1985-87, bd. dirs., 1987-91; vol. Cath. Charities Dallas, 1987—, North Ctrl. Tex. Legal Svcs., 1985—. Recipient cert. of appreciation Lawyers Against Domestic Violence, Dallas, 1985-87, cert. of recognition North Cen. Tex. Legal Svcs., 1985-87. Fellow Tex. Bar Found.; mem. ABA (vice chmn. sect. of bus. law, young lawyers div. 1986-88, exec. com., internat. law com. 1990—, vice-chair 1991-92, chair 1993—, editor-in-chief law practice notes Barrister Mag. 1988-91, commn. on pub. understanding about law 1989-91), Dallas Bar Assn. (Disting. Pro Bono Svc. award, 1986, 87, 88, 91, coord. immigration amnesty appeals com. 1987-88, chair, minority participation com. 1988-89, Pro Bono Vol. of Yr. 1989, spl. recognition 1990, 92), Tex. Assn. Young Lawyers (internat. law, editorial coms. 1985-91, chair refugee com. 1988-90, co-chmn. internat. law com. 1991-93), Dallas Assn. Young Lawyers (co-chair internat. law com. 1990-92, chair membership com. 1987-88, chair bill of rights com. 1988-89, treas. 1989, v.p. 1989-90), Tex. Accts. and Lawyers for Arts, Dallas Com. Fgn. Rels. (gen. counsel 1987—), Council on Fgn. Relations N.Y. (term mem.), Dallas Council on World Affairs, Dallas Assembly, Crescent Spa Club, Phi Beta Kappa, Pi Sigma Alpha, Omicron Delta Kappa. Democrat. Roman Catholic. Avocations: tennis, piano. Office: Nokia Telecomm Inc 7 Village Cir Ste 100 Westlake TX 76262-8552

PITTS, JOSEPH R., congressman; b. Lexington, Ky., Oct. 10, 1939; s. Joseph S. and Pearl Jackson P.; m. Virginia Pratt, 1961; children: Karen R., Carol J., Daniel J. AB, Asbury Coll., 1961; MEd, West Chester State Coll., 1973. Tchr. Great Valley (Pa.) H.S., 1969-73; rep. dist. 158 State of Pa., 1972-96; mem. 105th Congress from 16th Pa. dist., 1997—; transp. com. State of Pa., 1977-80, appropriations com., 1979-82, rep. policy com., chmn. labor rels. com., transp. and joint legis. budget and fin. coms., chmn. rep. appropriations com., 1989. Decorated Air medal with five oak leaf clusters; recipient Pub. Servant award Chester-Del. Pomona Grange, 1980, Cmty. Leadership award Pa. for Biblical Morality, 1984, Disting. Govt. Svc. award Am. Mushroom Inst., 1985, Defender of Life award Pro Life Coalition S.E. Pa., 1985, William Penn award Pa. FACTS, 1985. Mem. Brandywine Valley Assn., Rotary. Address: 905 Mitchell Farm Ln Kennett Square PA 19348-1319 Office: 504 Cannon Washington DC 20515-3816

PITTS, ROBERT EUGENE, JR., marketing educator, consultant; b. Griffin, Ga., Feb. 12, 1948; s. Robert Eugene and Oree Francis (Brown) P.; m. Cheryl Ann Belew, May 31, 1968. BBA, Ga. State U., 1970, M in Bus. Info. Systems, 1972; PhD, U. S.C., 1977. Account sect. leader Gen. Electric Corp., Atlanta, 1970-72; instr. mktg. Jacksonville (Ala.) State U., 1972-74; assoc. dir. consumer panel U. S.C., Columbia, 1974-77; asst. prof. mktg. U. Notre Dame, South Bend, Ind., 1977-82; assoc. prof. mktg. U. Miss., Oxford, 1982-83, dir. bur. bus. and econ. research, 1983-85; prof., chmn. dept. mktg. DePaul U., Chgo., 1985-97, dir. Kellstadt Ctr. Mktg. Analysis and Planning; dean Coll. Bus. Adminstrn. Creighton U., Omaha, 1997—; cons. in mktg. strategy; expert legal witness in mktg. Author books on bank mktg.; contbr. articles on personal values in mktg. and pub. policy issues to profl. jours. Fellow Am. Mktg. Assn., Assn. Mktg. Sci.; mem. Decision Sci. Inst., So. Mktg. Assn. Avocations: running, akido. Office: Creighton U Omaha NE

PITTS, TERENCE RANDOLPH, curator, museum director; b. St. Louis, Feb. 5, 1950; s. Benjamin Randolph and Barbara Avalon (Gilliam) P.; children: Jacob Richard, Rebecca Suzanne. BA, U. Ill., 1972, MLS, 1974, MA in Art History U. Ariz., 1986. Registrar Ctr. for Creative Photography, Tucson, 1976-77, curator, 1978-88, dir., 1989—; cons. Art and Architecture Thesaurus, Getty Mus., 1984—. Author: (with others) George Fiske: Yosemite Photographer, 1981, Edward Weston: Color Photography; author: exhbn. catalogs: Four Spanish Photographers, 100 Years of Photography in the American West, Photography in the American Grain, Reframing America. NEA fellow, 1983; travel grantee Nat. Mus. Act, 1979, rsch. grantee U. Ariz., 1983.

PITTS, TYRONE S., reverend. Office: Prog Nat Baptist Conv 601 50th St NE Washington DC 20019-5499

PITTS, VIRGINIA M., human resources executive; b. Boston, Nov. 22, 1953; d. Harold Francis and Connie (Caico) Cummings; m. Daniel J. Pitts, Mar. 12, 1977. Student, Northeastern U., 1982-85, Harvard U., 1997—. Adminstrv. asst. J. Baker Inc., Hyde Park, Mass., 1980-82; fin. adminstr., 1982-84, dir. human resources, 1984—, 1st sr. v.p., 1991—; trustee New Eng. Joint Bd. AFL-CIO, Quincy, Mass., 1984-89; guest lectr. Aquinas Jr. Coll.; mem. bd. dirs. Boston Crusaders, Drum & Bugle Corps. Instr. Boston Crusaders Drum and Bugle Corps, other marching bands, Mass., R.I., Maine, N.H., 1973-85; regional v.p. 210 Charitable Assn., Watertown, Mass., 1989-90; bd. dirs. Handi-Kids, Boston Crusaders Drum and Bugle Corps; guest lectr. Aquinas Jr. Coll., Milton, Mass. Mem. Am. Mgmt. Assn., Am. Compensation Assn. (cert. profl.), Soc. Human Resource Mgrs. Avocations: dressage, gardening. Office: J Baker Inc 555 Turnpike St Canton MA 02021-2724

PITYNSKI, ANDRZEJ PIOTR, sculptor; b. Ulanow, Poland, Mar. 15, 1947; naturalized citizen, 1987; s. Aleksander and Stefania (Krupa) P.; m. Christina Teresa Gacek, Aug. 6, 1976; 1 child, Alexander Mark. MFA in Sculpture, Acad. Fine Arts, Cracow, Poland, 1974; postgrad., Art Students League, N.Y., 1975. Cert. tchr., N.J.; supr. modeling, mold, enlarging, resin crafts. Supr. and instr. sculpture Tech. Inst. of Sculpture - Johnson Atelier, Mercerville, N.J., 1979—; instr. sculpture Rider U., Lawrenceville, N.J., 1992—; asst. to sculptor Alexander Ettl, Sculpture House, N.Y., 1975-79;. Bronze/granite monumental sculptures include Katyn-1940, Jersey City, N.J., 1991-92, Pope John Paul II, Manhattan, N.Y., 1991, Ulanow, Poland, 1989, General Anders, Doylestown, Pa., 1995, Father J. Popieluszko, Trenton, N.J., 1987, Avenger, Doylestown, Pa., 1987, Portrait Bust M Curie, 1986, Bayonne, N.J.; aluminum sculpture Partisans, Boston, 1983, Ignacy Paderewski, Cracow, Poland, 1973; exhbn. Mus. of Polish Army, Warsaw, 1995, Contemporary Artists Guild, Lever House, N.Y., 1991, Zacheta Nat. Art Gallery, Warsaw, 1991, Fedn. Internat. De La Medaille/Brit. Mus., London, 1992, Cast Iron Gallery, Soho, N.Y., 1992, Alt. Ext. Gallery, Phila., 1992, Audubon Exhibits-54th Ann. Exhbn., Fed. Hall, N.Y.C., 1996, others. Recipient Polonia Restituta Cross, R.P. London, 1989, Gold Order of Merit, Rep. of Poland, 1990, Cultural award Am. Inst. Polish Culture, Washington, 1992; named Comdr. Order Merit of Republic of Poland, 1996. Fellow Nat. Sculpture Soc.; mem. Allied Artists of Am. (Silver medal of honor 1985, Elliot Liskin Meml. award 1989, Mems. and Assocs. award 1994), Audubon Artists (Gold Medal of Honor 1996), Contemporary Artists Guild, Am. Medallic Sculpture Assn. Republican. Roman Catholic. Avocations: horse jumping, hunting, judo. Office: Johnson Atelier Tech Inst Sculpture 60 Ward Avenue Ext Mercerville NJ 08619-3428

PITZER, KENNETH SANBORN, chemist, educator; b. Pomona, Calif., Jan. 6, 1914; s. Russell K. and Flora (Sanborn) P.; m. Jean Mosher, July 1935; children—Ann, Russell, John. BS, Calif. Inst. Tech., 1935; PhD, U. Calif., 1937; DSc, Wesleyan U., 1962; LLD, U. Calif. at Berkeley, 1963, Mills Coll., 1969. Instr. chemistry U. Calif., 1937-39, asst. prof., 1939-42, asso. prof., 1942-45, prof., 1945-61, asst. dean letters and sci., 1947-48, dean coll. chemistry, 1951-60; pres., prof. chemistry Rice U., Houston, 1961-68, Stanford, Calif., 1968-70; prof. chemistry U. Calif. at Berkeley, 1971—; tech. dir. Md. Rsch. Lab. for OSRD, 1943-44; dir. research U.S. AEC, 1949-51, mem. gen. adv. com., 1958-65, chmn., 1960-62; Centenary lectr. Chem. Soc. Gt. Britain, 1978; mem. adv. bd. U.S. Naval Ordnance Test Sta., 1956-59, chmn., 1958-59; mem. commn. chem. thermo-dynamics Internat. Union Pure and Applied Chemistry, 1953-61; mem. Pres.'s Sci. Adv. Com., 1965-68; dir. Owens-Ill., Inc., 1967-86. Author: (with others) Selected Values of Properties of Hydrocarbons, 1947, Quantum Chemistry, 1953, (with L. Brewer) Thermodynamics, 2d edit., 1961, Activity Coefficients in Electrolyte Solutions, 2d ecit., 1992, Molecular Structure and Statistical Thermodynamics, 1993, Thermodynamics, 3d edit., 1995; editor: Prentice-Hall Chemistry series, 1955-61; contbr. articles to profl. jours. Trustee Pitzer Coll., 1966—; Mem. program com. for phys. scis. Sloan Found., 1955-60. Recipient Precision Sci. Co. award in petroleum chemistry, 1950, Clayton prize Instn. Mech. Engrs., London, 1958, Priestley medal Am. Chem. Soc., 1969, Nat. medal for sci., 1975, Robert A. Welch award, 1984, Clark Kerr award U. Calif., Berkeley, 1991, Robert J. Bernard award, 1996; named to Outstanding Young Men, U.S. Jaycees, 1950; named to Hall of Fame of Alpha Chi Sigma, 1994; Guggenheim fellow, 1951. Fellow Am. Nuclear Soc., Am. Inst. Chemists (Gold Medal award 1976), Am. Acad. Arts and Scis., Am. Phys. Soc.; mem. AAAS, NAS (councilor 1964-67, 73-76), Am. Chem. Soc. (award pure chemistry 1943, Gilbert N. Lewis medal 1965, Williard Gibbs medal 1976), Faraday Soc., Geochem. Soc., Am. Philos. Soc., Chem. Soc. (London), Am. Coun. Edn., Chemists Club (hon.), Bohemian Club, Cosmos Club of Washington. Clubs: Chemists (hon.), Bohemian; Cosmos (Washington). Home: 12 Eagle Hl Kensington CA 94707-1408 Office: U Calif Dept Chemistry Berkeley CA 94720

PITZER, RUSSELL MOSHER, chemistry educator; b. Berkeley, Calif., May 10, 1938; s. Kenneth Sanborn and Jean Elizabeth (Mosher) P.; m. Martha Ann Seares, Sept. 3, 1959; children: Susan M., Kenneth R., David S. BS, Calif. Inst. Tech., 1959; AM, Harvard U., 1961, PhD, 1963. Instr. Calif. Inst. Tech., Pasadena, 1963-66, asst. prof., 1966-68; assoc. prof. Ohio State U., Columbus, 1968-79, prof., 1979—, chmn. dept. chemistry, 1989-94; acting assoc. dir. Ohio Supercondr. Ctr., Columbus, 1986-87; cons. Lawrence Livermore (Calif.) Nat. Lab., 1981-86; trustee Pitzer Coll., Claremont, Calif., 1988—. Contbr. articles to profl. jours. Mem. AAUP, Am. Chem. Soc., Am. Phys. Soc. Office: Ohio State U Dept Chemistry 1o0 W 18th Ave Columbus OH 43210-1106

PITZSCHLER, KATHRYN VAN DUREN, secondary school educator; b. Buffalo, Nov. 22, 1945; d. William and Olive Rasbridge (Decker) Van Duren; m. Robert B. Pitzschler, Aug. 30, 1971; 1 child, Molly Lynn. BA, Bucknell U., 1967; MS, Fairfield (Conn.) U., 1972. Cert. secondary English tchr., Conn. Tchr. English, Trumbull (Conn.) High Sch.; tchr. lang. arts, team leader Hillcrest Mid. Sch., Trumbull; presenter, workshop leader in interdisciplinary teaching; beginning educator support tchr.-mentor, Conn. Mem. NEA, ASCD, Nat. Assn. Secondary Sch. Principals, Nat. Coun. Tchrs. English, Conn. Edn. Assn., Conn. Assn. Curriculum Devel., Trumbull Edn. Assn., Conn. Coun. Tchrs. English, NEATE, Delta Kappa Gamma. Home: 225B Edgemoor Rd Bridgeport CT 06606-2123

PIVEN, FRANCES FOX, political scientist, educator; b. Calgary, Alta., Can., Oct. 10, 1932; came to U.S., 1933, naturalized, 1953; d. Albert and Rachel (Paperny) F.; 1 dau., Sarah. B.A., U. Chgo., 1953, M.A., 1956, Ph.D., 1962; L.H.D. (hon.), Adelphi U., 1985. Mem. faculty Columbia, 1966-72; prof. polit. sci. Boston U., 1972-82, Grad. Ctr., CUNY, 1982—. Co-author: Regulating the Poor: The Functions of Public Welfare, 1971, 2d edit., 1993, The Politics of Turmoil: Essays on Poverty, Race and the Urban Crisis, 1974, Poor People's Movements, 1977, New Class War, 1982, The Mean Season, 1987, Why Americans Don't Vote, 1988; editor: Labor Parties in Post Industrial Societies, 1992. Recipient C. Wright Mills award Soc. Study Social Problems, 1971, Fulbright Disting. Lectureship award U. Bologna, 1990, President's award APHA, 1993, Annual award Nat. Assn. Sec. of State, 1994, Lifetime Achievement award Pol. Sociology Am. Sociological Assn., 1995; Guggenheim fellow, 1973-74; Am. Council Learned Socs. awardee, 1982. Mem. Am. Polit. Sci. Assn. (v.p. 1981-82), Soc. Study Social Problems (pres. 1980-81, Lee founders award 1992), ACLU (dir.). Home: PO Box N Millerton NY 12546 Office: 33 W 42nd St New York NY 10036-8003

PIVEN, PETER ANTHONY, architect, management consultant; b. Bklyn., Jan. 3, 1939; s. William Meyer and Sylvia Lee (Greenberg) P.; m. Caroline Cooper, July 9, 1961; children: Leslie Ann, Joshua Lawrence. A.B., Colgate U., 1960; M.Arch., U. Pa., 1963; M.S., Columbia U., 1964. Diplomate: cert. Nat. Council Archtl. Registration Bds.; registered architect, N.Y., Pa., N.J. Architect Westermann-Miller Assocs., N.Y.C., 1964-66, Bernard Rothzeid, A.I.A., N.Y.C., 1967-68; v.p. Caudill Rowlett Scott, N.Y.C., 1968-72; prin. Geddes Brecher Qualls Cunningham, Phila., 1972-87; pres. The Coxe Group, Inc., Phila., 1980-90, dir., prin. cons., 1980—; adj. prof. U. Pa. Grad. Sch. Fine Arts, 1989—, Rensselaer Poly. Inst. Sch. Architecture, 1994—. Author: Compensation Management: A Guideline for Small Firms, 1982; co-author: Success Strategies for Design Professionals, 1987; contbr. editor Archtl. Record and Design Intelligence; contbg. author: Architects Handbook of Professional Practice, 1994. Mem. N.Y.C. Community Planning Bd., 1969-72. Fellow AIA (chmn. fin. mgmt. com. 1976-80, pres. Phila. chpt. 1980); mem. Phila. C. of C. (dir. 1980-81), The Carpenters Co. of City and County of Phila. (mng. com. 1989-91). Home: 112 N Lambert St Philadelphia PA 19103-1107 Office: The Coxe Group Inc 1218 3rd Ave Seattle WA 98101-3021

PIVER, M. STEVEN, gynecologic oncologist; b. Washington, Sept. 29, 1934; s. Harry Samuel and Sonia (Bard) P.; m. Susan Myers, June 25, 1958; children: Debra Ellen, Carolyn Jan, Kenneth Stuart. BS, Gettysburg Coll., 1957; MD, Temple U., 1961. Diplomate Am. Bd. Ob-Gyn, Am. Coll. Surgeons. Intern Nazareth Hosp., Phila., 1961-62; resident Johns Hopkins U. Hosp., Balt., 1962; resident ob-gyn. Pa. Hosp., U. Pa., Phila., 1965-68; fellow gynecologic oncology U. Tex., Hosp. and Tumor Inst., Houston, 1968-70; asst. prof. gynecologic oncology U. N.C. Sch. Medicine, 1970-71; assoc. chief gynecologic oncology Roswell Park Cancer Inst., Buffalo, 1972-83, founder, dir. Gilda Radner Familial Ovarian Cancer Registry, 1981—, chief gynecologic oncology, 1984—; clin. prof., dir. div. gynecologic oncology SUNY, Buffalo, 1986—. Cons., editor Yearbook of Cancer, 1972-88; assoc. editor Nat. Cancer Inst., PDQ, 1984—; mem. editl. bd. The Female Patient, 1989—, Oncology Reports, 1993—; author: Ovarian Malignancies: Clinical Care of Adults and Adolescents, 1983, Gilda's Disease Sharing Personal Experiences and a Medical Perspective on Ovarian Cancer, 1996, Myths and Facts About Ovarian Cancer, 1997; editor: Ovarian Malignancies: Diagnostic and Therapeutic Advances, 1987, Manual of Gynecologic Oncology/Gynecology, 1989, Conversations About Cancer, 1990, Handbook of Gynecologic Oncology, 1995; contbr. more than 300 articles to profl. jours. Bd. dirs. United Way of Buffalo and Erie County, 1986-91; chmn. bd. trustees D'Youville Coll., Buffalo, 1989—; pres. Friends of Night People, Buffalo, 1988—. Capt. USAF, 1962-64. Hon. fellow Phi Beta Kappa, Gettysburg Coll., 1956, Tex. Assn. Obstetricians and Gynecologists, 1983, Alpha Omega Alpha, Temple U. Sch. Medicine, 1995; named Citizen of Yr., Buffalo News, 1989; recipient YMCA Leadership award Buffalo YMCA, 1990, Brotherhood/Sisterhood Award in Medicine (Western N.Y. Region), NCCJ, 1991, St. Marguerite D'Youville Coll. Community Svc. award, 1992. Fellow ACS, Am. Coll. Obstetricians and Gynecologists; mem. Am. Soc. Clin. Oncology, Soc. Gynecologic Oncologists, Soc. Surg. Oncology, Am. Radium Soc., Phi Beta Kappa, Alpha Omega Alpha. Achievements include documentation of hydroxyurea as a radiation sensitizer in cervix cancer that significantly improves cure rate and that ovarian cancer can be inherited. Home: 315 Lincoln Pky Buffalo NY 14216-3127 Office: Roswell Park Cancer Inst Elm And Carlton St Buffalo NY 14263-0001

PIVIROTTO, RICHARD ROY, former retail executive; b. Youngstown, Ohio, May 26, 1930; s. Arthur M. and Ruth (Erhardt) P.; m. Mary Burchfield, June 27, 1953; children: Mary B., Richard Roy, Susan W., Nancy P., David H., Jennifer P. A.B., Princeton U., 1952; M.B.A., Harvard U., 1954. Pres. Joseph Horne Co., Pitts., 1954-70; vice chmn. Associated Dry Goods Corp., N.Y.C., 1970-72; pres. Associated Dry Goods Corp., 1972-76, chmn. bd., 1976-81, also dir.; bd. dirs. Westinghouse Electric Corp., Pitts., Gen. Am. Investors Co., N.Y.C., N.Y. Life Ins. Co., Gillette Corp., Immunomedics Inc., Morris Plains, N.J. Trustee Princeton U., 1977—; trustee Greenwich Hosp.; bd. dirs. Gen. Theol. Sem., N.Y.C. Served with AUS, 1955-56. Mem. Am. Retail Fedn. (dir. 1968-81). Clubs: Union League, Princeton (N.Y.C.); Duquesne, Rolling Rock, Fox Chapel Golf (Pitts.); Greenwich Country, Field of Greenwich; Bald Peak Colony (Melvin Village, N.H.). Office: 111 Clapboard Ridge Rd Greenwich CT 06830-3405

PIVONKA, LEONARD DANIEL, priest; b. Bryan, Tex., Oct. 19, 1951; s. Herbert Daniel and Geraldine (Schoppe) P. Student, Tex. A&M U., 1969-70, Del Mar Coll., 1970-71; BA, Pontifical Coll. Josephinum, Columbus, Ohio, 1973; MDiv, Josephinum Sch. Theology, Columbus, 1977; JCD, Cath. U. Am., 1982. Ordained priest Roman Cath. Ch., 1977, named monsignor, 1985. Mem. faculty Corpus Christi (Tex.) Minor Sem., 1982-84; adminstr. St. Philip the Apostle Parish, Corpus Christi, 1983-85, pastor, 1985-91; adj. jud. vicar Diocesan Tribunal, Corpus Christi, 1984-88, bishop's sec. for canonical affairs, 1983—; episcopal vicar for synod and coun. Chancery, Corpus Christi, 1985-88, chancellor, 1987-88, jud. vicar Diocesan Tribunal, 1988—; rector Corpus Christi Cathedral, 1991—; mem. adminstrv. coun. Diocese of Corpus Christi, 1985—, Coll. of Consultors, 1985—; chaplain Natural Family Planning Office, Corpus Christi, 1991—; bishop's rep. Spohn Hosp. Coun. on Human Values; treas. Corpus Christi Ministerial Alliance, 1983-84; diocesan chaplain Legion of Mary, 1993—. Avocations: golf, tennis, cycling. Office: Diocese of Corpus Christi 620 Lipan St Corpus Christi TX 78401-2434*

PIZER, DONALD, author, educator; b. N.Y.C., Apr. 5, 1929; s. Morris and Helen (Rosenfeld) P.; m. Carol Hart, Apr. 7, 1966; children—Karin, Ann, Margaret. B.A., UCLA, 1951, M.A., 1952, Ph.D., 1955. Mem. faculty Tulane U., 1957—, prof. English, 1964-72, Pierce Butler prof. English, 1972—, Mellon prof. humanities, 1978-79. Author: Hamlin Garland's Early Work and Career, 1960, Realism and Naturalism in Nineteenth-Century American Literature, 1966, The Novels of Frank Norris, 1966, The Novels of Theodore Dreiser, 1976, Twentieth-Century American Literary Naturalism: An Interpretation, 1982, Dos Passos "USA": A Critical Study, 1988, The Theory and Practice of American Literary Naturalism, 1993, American Expatriate Writing and the Paris Moment, 1996. Served with AUS, 1955-57. Guggenheim fellow, 1962; Am. Council Learned Socs. fellow, 1971-72; Nat. Endowment Humanities fellow, 1978-79. Mem. MLA. Home: 6320 Story St New Orleans LA 70118-6340

PIZER, HOWARD CHARLES, sports and entertainment executive; b. Chgo., Oct. 23, 1941; s. Edwin and Estyr (Seeder) P.; m. Sheila Graff, June 14, 1964; children: Jacqueline, Rachel. B.B.A., U. Wis., 1963; J.D. magna cum laude, Northwestern U., 1966. Assoc. McDermott, Will & Emery, Chgo., 1966-72; ptnr. Katten, Muchin, Zavis, Chgo., 1972-74; exec. v.p., gen. counsel Balcor Co., Skokie, Ill., 1975-80; exec. v.p. Chgo. White Sox, Chgo., 1981—; exec. v.p. United Ctr. Joint Venture. Bd. dirs. Chgo. Conv. and Tourism Bur., Inc., 1983—, Spl. Children's Charities, 1984—, Chgo. Baseball Cancer Charities, 1983—, Near West Side Cmty. Devel. Corp. Mem. Chgo. Bar Assn., Standard Club Chgo., Briarwood County. Home: 300 Euclid Ave Winnetka IL 60093-3606 Office: Chgo White Sox 333 W 35th St Chicago IL 60616-3621

PIZITZ, RICHARD ALAN, retail and real estate group executive; b. Birmingham, Ala., Feb. 24, 1930; s. Isadore and Hortense (Hirsch) P.; m. Joan Black; children: Richard Alan Jr., Jill Carole, Susan Lyn. BA, Washington & Lee U., 1951; MBA, Harvard U., 1953. Mdse. mgr. Pizitz Dept. Stores, Birmingham, 1953-59, v.p., 1959-66, pres., 1966-86, chmn. bd., 1986-87; chmn. Pizitz Mgmt. Group, Birmingham, 1987—. Pres. United Way, Birmingham, 1988, Ala. Commn. on Higher Edn., 1987-95; pres. Better Bus. Bur., Birmingham, 1962; mem. Ala adv. commn. U.S. Commn. on Civil Rights, 1985. Recipient Erskine Ramsay award, 1974; named Mktg. Man of Yr., Am. Mktg. Assn., 1966, Man of Yr., Young Men's Bus. Club, 1970. Mem. Ala. Commn. on Higher Edn., Birmingham C. of C. (pres. 1970), Ala. Retail Assn. (pres. 1965). Avocations: pvt. pilot, skiing, tennis, scuba diving. Home: 2716 Hanover Cir S Birmingham AL 35205-1733 Office: Pizitz Mgmt Group 2140 11th Ave S Birmingham AL 35205-2832

PIZZAGALLI, JAMES, construction executive; b. Burlington, Vt., Nov. 23, 1944; s. Angelo and Theresa (Moalli) P.; m. Judy Rock, June 21, 1969; 1 child, Michael. BS, U. Vt., 1966; JD, Boston U., 1969. Treas. Pizzagalli Constrn. Co., Burlington, Vt., 1969-76, v.p., 1976-91, chmn., chief exec. officer, 1991—; dir. Chittenden Corp., Burlington, 1982—, AGC Edn. Found., Washington, 1992—, Shelburne (Vt.) Mus., 1983-92; life dir. Assn. Gen. Contractors, Washington, 1976—, atty.-at law. Mem. TheMoles, Ethan Allen Club. Republican. Roman Catholic. Home: 158 Harbor Rd Shelburne VT 05482-7004 Office: Pizzagalli Constrn Co PO Box 2009 South Burlington VT 05407

PIZZI, CHARLES PETER, association president; b. Phila., Oct. 1, 1950; s. Charles Ralph and Philomena Ritz (Martella) P.; m. Elise Kathleen Robinson, Aug. 14, 1976; children: Justin, Gabriel, Christian, Keith. BSBA, LaSalle U., 1972; student, Temple U., 1976-78. Client relation rep. Phila. Indsl. Devel. Corp., 1975-77, mktg. dir., 1978-80, v.p., 1981-83; from dep. to dir. commerce City of Philadelphia, 1984-88; v.p. spl. projects Richard I. Rubin & Co., Inc., Phila., 1988-89; pres. Greater Phila. C. of C., 1989—; bd. dirs. Airport Adv. Com., Blue Shield Med. Review Com., Cen. Phila. Devel. Corp., Delaware Valley Indsl. Rsch. Coun., Private Industry Coun., Temple U. Sch. Bus. Mgmt., Southeastern Pa. Transportation Authority, Nat. Constitution Ctr., Maritime Exch., Independence Blue Cross, Internat. Visitors Ctr. Phila. and various others. Bd. dirs. YMCA of Roxborough, Phila., Boy Scouts Am., Phila., Police Athletic League, Phila., United Way, Phila. Sports Congress, Urban League of Phila., Corp. Alliance for Drug Edn., Fairmont Park Hist. Houses Project, Mayoral Residence Com; mem. rep. com. Chmn's. Club Montgomery County, Norristown, Pa., 1990—. Mem. African-Am. Hist. and Cultural Mus. (bd. dirs.), Jaycees, Union League Phila. Office: Greater Phila C of C 200 S Broad St Ste 700 Philadelphia PA 19102-3896*

PIZZO, SALVATORE VINCENT, pathologist; b. Phila., June 22, 1944; s. George J. P. and Aida (Alcaro) Lepore; m. Carol Ann Kurkowski, Dec. 28, 1968 (div. 1987); children: Steven, David, Susan. PhD, Duke U., 1972; BS, St. Joseph's Coll., 1966; MD, Duke U., 1973. Asst. prof. Duke U. Med. Ctr., Durham, N.C., 1976-80, assoc. prof., 1980-85, prof., 1985—, dir. med. scientist tng. program, 1987—, chmn., 1991—; mem., chmn. program rev. com. NIH, Bethesda, Md., 1986-90; vice chmn. Gordon Conf. Proteases, Holderness, N.H., 1990, chmn., 1992-96; cons. in field, 1980—; mem. Cellular and Molecular Basis of Disease Rev. Com., 1992—. Contbr. articles to profl. jours. Grantee NIH, 1976—, Am. Cancer Soc., 1976—. Mem. Am. Heart Assn. (exec. com. Thrombosis coun. 1990, 92), Am. Chem. Soc., Am. Assn. Pathologists (program com. 1985-88, long range planning com. 1990-92), Am. Soc. Biological Chemists, Alpha Sigma Nu, Phi Beta Kappa, Alpha Omega Alpha, Sigma Xi. Achievements include patents in field; research in lipoproteins in coagulation and fibronolysis, a link to atherosclerosis, anticoagulation drug development. Office: Duke U Med Ctr PO Box 3712 Durham NC 27710

PIZZURO, SALVATORE NICHOLAS, special education educator; b. Passaic, N.J., Jan. 25, 1945; s. John G. and Mary F. (Interdonato) P. BA, Jersey City State Coll., 1970, MA, 1973; profl. diploma, Fordham U., 1980; EdD, Columbia U., 1991. Tchr. spl. edn. Garfield (N.J.) Pub. Schs., 1970-71, Lodi (N.J.) Pub. Schs., 1971-75, 76-78; learning cons. Mt. Carmel Guild, Newark, 1976-76; instr. Columbia U., N.Y.C., 1988-91; asst. prof. spl. edn. Jersey City State Coll., 1990—; post-doctoral fellow U. Ky., 1993-94; dir. Learning Consultation Svcs., N.Y.C., 1990—; coord. pre-svcs. program in mental retardation Tchrs. Coll., Columbia U., 1990-91; rsch. assoc. U. Ill., 1991-92; chmn. Early Childhood Inclusion Conf., Phila., 1993; dir. United Learning Consultants, 1994—; chmn. conf. "Assessment: Impact on Svc. Delivery", N.J., 1995; cons. Independent Child Study Teams, Inc., 1995—; mem. task force com. on econ. and ednl. opportunities U.S. Ho. of Reps., 1994-96, chair, cons. Com. Edn. & Workforce, 1997—; chmn. the Future of Edn. in N.J. Conf., 1996. Editor: Learning Consultant Journal, 1995, 96. Chmn. Walk for Hunger, 1979, NE Regional Legis. Coalition, 1984-86, Nat. AD HOC Comm. on the Reauthorization of the Individuals with Disabilities Edn. Act, chmn. Nat. Forum on Reauthorization, 1996, Conf. on Future of Edn. in N.J., 1996—, N.J. Coalition on Study of Sch. Reform, 1996—. Recipient award for dedication to mentally retarded Mt. Carmel Guild, 1972. Mem. Coun. for Exceptional Children, N.J. Coun. for Exceptional Children (pres. 1984-85), N.J. Divsn. on Mental Retardation (pres. 1986-87), Jersey City State Coll. Alumni Assn. (pres. 1974-75), Tchrs. Coll. Christian Fellowship (pres. 1988-90), Rehab. Engring. Soc. N.Am., Correctional Edn. Assn. Roman Catholic. Avocations: writing nonfiction, jogging.

PIZZUTO, DEBRA KAY, secondary school mathematics educator; b. Camden, N.J., Nov. 25, 1957; d. Edward John and Kathryn Mary (Kegolis) Andrews; m. Victor Bruce Pizzuto, Nov. 28, 1981. BA in Bus. Adminstrn., Rutgers U., 1980. Cert. math. tchr., N.J., N.H. Math. tchr. Parkside Jr. High Sch., Manchester, N.H., 1985-87, Cumberland Regional H.S., Seabrook, N.J., 1987-88, St. James High Sch., Carney's Point, N.J., 1988-92, Ocean City (N.J.) High Sch., 1993-96, Atlantic C.C., Mays Landing, N.J., 1996—; ednl. cons. Newshire Inc., Bridgeton, N.J. Author, instr. (video tapes) Algebra One in Superstar Tchr. Series; contbr. articles to profl. jours. Named Superstar Tchr. for H.S. Video Instrn., The Teaching Co. Mem. ASCD, Math. Assn. Am., Nat. Coun. Tchrs. Math. Roman Catholic. Avocations: music, physical fitness, creative writing, theater, nutrition. Office: Atlantic Cmty Coll 5100 Black Horse Pike Mays Landing NJ 08330

PLAA, GABRIEL LEON, toxicologist, educator; b. San Francisco, May 15, 1930; arrived in Can., 1968; s. Jean and Lucienne (Chalopin) P.; m. Colleen Neva Brasefield, May 19, 1951; children: Ernest (dec.), Steven, Kenneth, Gregory, Andrew, John, Denise, David. BS, U. Calif., Berkeley, 1952; PhD, U. Calif., San Francisco, 1958. Diplomate Am. Bd. Toxicology. Asst. toxicologist City/County San Francisco, 1954-58; asst. prof. Sch. Medicine Tulane U., New Orleans, 1958-61; assoc. prof. U. Iowa, Iowa City, 1961-68; prof. U. Montreal, 1968-95, chmn. dept. pharmacology, 1968-80, vice-dean Faculty Medicine, 1982-89, dir. Interuniv. Ctr. Rsch. in Toxicology, 1991-95; ret., 1995, prof. emeritus, 1996; Dorothy Snider disting. lectr. U. Ark., 1995; chmn. Can. Coun. Animal Care, Ottawa, Ont., Can., 1985-86. Editor Toxicology and Applied Pharmacology, 1972-80; contbr. over 200 articles to profl. jours. 1st lt. U.S. Army, 1952-53, Korea. Recipient Thienes award Am. Acad. Clin. Toxicology, 1977. Mem. Am. Soc. Pharmacology, Soc. Toxicology Can. (pres. 1981-83, Henderson award 1969, award of distinction 1994), Pharm. Soc. Can. (pres. 1973-74), Soc. Toxicology (pres. 1983-84, Achievement award 1967, Lehman award 1977, Edn. award 1987, Amb. award 1987, Merit award 1996), Acad. Toxicological Scis. Roman Catholic. Home: 236 Meredith Ave, Dorval, PQ Canada H9S 2Y7 Office: U Montreal Dept Pharmacology, Sta Centre-Ville, PO Box 6128, Montreal, PQ Canada H3C 3J7

PLACIER, PHILIP R., lawyer; b. Chillicothe, Ohio, Mar. 7, 1933; s. Don Harold and Ruth (Hartmann) P.; m. Nancy Kay Young, July 27, 1963; children—David Lane, Thomas Alan, Elizabeth Ann. A.B., Ohio Wesleyan U., 1955; LL.B., U. Mich., 1958. Bar: Calif. 1959. Assoc. Thelen, Marrin, Johnson & Bridges, San Francisco, 1962-69, ptnr., 1970—, chmn. mgmt. com., 1984-92. Contbr. chpt. to book. Elder United Presbyterian Ch., Lafayette, Calif.; trustee San Francisco Theological Seminary. Served to lt. JAGC, USN, 1958-62. Mem. ABA, Calif. State Bar Assn., Orinda County Club (Calif.), World Trade Club (San Francisco). Republican. Avocations: golf; skiing. Office: Thelen Marrin Johnson & Bridges 2 Embarcadero Ctr San Francisco CA 94111-3823

PLACKE, JAMES A(NTHONY), foreign service officer, international affairs consultant; b. Grand Island, Nebr., June 14, 1935; s. Gerhard F. and Florence E. (McCormick) P.; m. Mary Sabina Shea, July 25, 1959; children—Elizabeth, Stephen, Carolyn. B.Sc., U. Nebr., 1957, M.A., 1959. Commd. fgn. service officer Dept. State, 1958; econ. counselor Am. embassy, Tripoli, Libya, 1970-71; fgn. service insp. Dept. State, Washington, 1971-73, dir. office food policy, 1974-76; econ. counselor Am. embassy, Ottawa, Ont., Can., 1977-79; minister Am. embassy, Jidda, Saudi Arabia, 1979-82; dep. asst. sec. Nr. Eastern and South Asian Affairs Bur., Dept. State, Washington, 1982-85, ret., 1986; internat. affairs cons., 1986-90; dir. Cambridge Energy Rsch. Assoc., 1991; del. UN World Food Conf., 1974. Recipient Meritorious Honor award Dept. State, 1969, 71; Presdl. Meritorious Service award, 1985. Office: 1133 Connecticut Ave NW Ste 903 Washington DC 20036-4305

PLACZEK, ADOLF KURT, librarian; b. Vienna, Austria, Mar. 9, 1913; came to U.S., 1940, naturalized, 1943; s. Oswald and Pauline (Selinko) P.; m. Jan Struther, Mar. 1, 1948 (dec. July 1953); m. Laura Beverley Robinson, Jan. 5, 1957. Student, U. Vienna Med. Sch., 1931-34, Inst. Fine Arts, U. Vienna, 1934-38; B.L.S., Columbia U., 1942; diploma of honor, U. Vienna, 1993. Asst. librarian Avery Archtl. Library, Columbia U., 1948-60; Avery librarian Avery Archtl. Library, 1960-80, emeritus, 1980—, adj. prof. architecture, 1971-80, prof. emeritus, 1980—; commr. N.Y.C. Landmarks Preservation Commn., 1984-93. Editor in chief Macmillan Ency. Architects, 1982, Bldgs. of the U.S., Oxford Press, 1984-90; contbr. articles to Columbia Ency., Ency. Brit., also to books and mags. Served with AUS, 1943-46. Decorated Austrian Cross of Honor for Sci. and Art 1st class, 1993; recipient Honor award AIA, 1986. Mem. Soc. Archtl. Historians (sec. 1963-67, dir. 1968-71, 2d v.p. 1974-75, 1st v.p. 1976-77, pres. 1978-80), Am. Council Learned Socs. (del. 1971-74). Home: 176 W 87th St New York NY 10024-2902

PLAEGER, FREDERICK JOSEPH, II, lawyer; b. New Orleans, Sept. 10, 1953; s. Edgar Leonard and Bernice Virginia (Schiwetz) P.; m. Kathleen Helen Dickson, Nov. 19, 1977; children: Douglas A., Catherine E. BS, La. State U., 1976, JD, 1977. Bar: La. 1978, U.S. Dist. Ct. (ea. dist.) La. 1978, U.S. Ct. Appeals (5th cir.) 1981, U.S. Supreme Ct. 1989. Law clk. U.S. Dist. Ct. (ea. dist.) La., New Orleans, 1977-79; assoc. Milling, Benson, Woodward, Hillyer, Pierson & Miller, New Orleans, 1979-85, ptnr., 1985-89; v.p., gen. counsel, corp. sec. La. Land and Exploration Co., New Orleans, 1989—. Bd. dirs. New Orleans Speech and Hearing Ctr., 1985-91, pres., 1988-90; bd. dirs. Children's Oncology Svcs. La. (Ronald McDonald House of New Orleans), 1987-90; selected mem. Met. Area Com. Leadership Forum, 1986; bd. dirs. Soc. Environ. Edn., La. Nature and Sci. Ctr., 1992-94; bd. dirs. New Orleans City Park Assn., 1996—. Recipient Service to Mankind award Sertoma, 1989. Mem. ABA, La. Bar Assn., Am. Corp. Counsel Assn. (bd. dirs. New Orleans chpt. 1995—), Am. Soc. Corp. Secs., Am. Petroleum Inst. (mem. gen. commn. law), Pickwick Club. Republican. Avocations: golf, hunting, fishing. Home: 4632 Neyrey Dr Metairie LA 70002-1423 Office: La Land & Exploration Co 909 Poydras St Ste 3600 New Orleans LA 70112-4000

PLAGENZ, GEORGE RICHARD, minister, journalist, columnist; b. Lakewood, Ohio, Dec. 11, 1923; s. George William and Edith Louise (Fenner) P.; m. Faith Hanna, Sept. 12, 1953 (div.); children—Joel, George William II, Nicole, Sarah. B.A. cum laude, Western Res. U., 1945; S.T.B., Harvard, 1949. Ordained to ministry Unitarian Ch., 1951. Sports writer Cleve. Press, 1943-46; asst. minister King's Chapel, Boston, 1951-54; news broadcaster Radio Sta. WEEI, Boston, 1955-63; writer Boston Sunday Advertiser, 1963-70; religion editor Cleve. Press, 1970-82; syndicated columnist Scripps-Howard Newspapers, 1974-80, Newspaper Enterprise Assn., 1980—. Mem. Beta Theta Pi. Club: Harvard (Boston). Home: 239B E Beck St Columbus OH 43206-1210

PLAGER, S. JAY, federal judge; b. Long Branch, N.J., May 16, 1931; s. A.L. and Clara L. (Matross) P.; children: Anna Katherine, David Alan, Daniel Tyler. A.B., U. N.C., 1952; J.D., U. Fla., 1958; LL.M., Columbia U., 1961. Bar: Fla. 1958, Ill. 1964. Asst. prof. law U. Fla., 1958-62, assoc. prof., 1962-64; assoc. prof. law U. Ill., Champaign-Urbana, 1964-65, prof., 1965-77; dir. Office Environ. and Planning Studies, 1972-74, 75-77; dean, prof. law Ind. U. Sch. Law, Bloomington, 1977-84; prof. law Ind. U. Sch. Law, 1984-90; counselor to undersec. U.S. Dept. Health and Human Svcs., 1986-87; assoc. dir. Office of Mgmt. and Budget Office of Mgmt. and Budget, 1987-88; adminstr. info. and regulatory affairs Exec. Office of the Pres., 1988-89; cir. judge U.S. Ct. Appeals (fed. cir.), 1989—; vis. research prof. law U. Wis., 1967-68; vis. scholar Stanford U., 1984-85. Author: (with others) Water Law and Administration, 1968, Social Justice Through Law-New Approaches in the Law of Property, 1970, (with others) Florida Water Law, 1980. Chmn. Gainesville (Fla.) Planning Commn., 1962-63; mem. Urbana Plan Commn., 1966-70; mem. nat. air pollution manpower devel. adv. com., 1971-75; cons. Ill. Inst. for Environ. Quality, U.S. EPA; chmn. Ill. Task Force on Noise, 1972-76; vice chmn. Nat. Commn. on Jud. Discipline and Removal, 1991-93. With USN, 1952-55. Office: US Ct Appeals for Fed Cir The National Courts Bldg 717 Madison Pl NW Washington DC 20439-0002

PLAGMAN, RALPH, principal. Prin. George Washington High Sch., Cedar Rapids, Iowa. Recipient Blue Ribbon Sch. award Dept. Edn., 1990-91. Office: George Washington High Sch 2205 Forest Dr SE Cedar Rapids IA 52403-1653*

PLAIN, BELVA, writer; b. N.Y.C., Oct. 9, 1919; d. Oscar and Eleanor Offenberg; m. Irving Plain, June 14, 1941 (dec. 1982); 3 children. Grad., Barnard Coll. Author: Evergreen, 1978, Random Winds, 1980, Eden Burning, 1982, Crescent City, 1984, The Golden Cup, 1987, Tapestry, 1988, Blessings, 1989, Harvest, 1990, Treasures, 1992, Whispers, 1993, Daybreak, 1994, The Carousel, 1995, Promises, 1996, Secrecy, 1997. Office: care Delacorte Press 1540 Broadway New York NY 10036-4039

PLAINE, DANIEL J., lawyer; b. Washington, Aug. 23, 1943; s. Herzel H.E. and Norma (Stein) P.; m. Susan Ambrose, Oct. 5, 1985; children: Caroline, Meredith. BA magna cum laude, Williams Coll., 1965; LLB, Cambridge U., Eng., 1967; JD, Yale U., 1970. Bar: D.C. 1970, U.S. Dist. Ct. DC 1970, U.S. Ct. Appeals (D.C. cir.) 1970, U.S. Ct. Appeals (fed. cir.), 1985, U.S. Supreme Ct., 1974. Ptnr. Steptoe & Johnson, Washington, 1970-97, Gibson, Dunn & Crutcher, Washington, 1997—. Marshall scholar, 1967. Mem. ABA, Am. Soc. Internat. Law, Washington Inst. Internat. Law. Office: 1050 Connecticut Ave NW Ste 900 Washington DC 20036-5320

PLAINE, LLOYD LEVA, lawyer; b. Washington, Nov. 3, 1947. BA, U. Pa., 1969; postgrad., Harvard U.; JD, Georgetown U., 1975. Bar: D.C. 1975. Legis. asst. to U.S. Rep. Sidney Yates, 1971-72; with Sutherland, Asbill & Brennan, Washington, 1975-82, ptnr., 1982—. Fellow Am. Bar Found., Am. Coll. Trust and Estate Counsel, Am. Coll. of Tax Counsel; mem. ABA (chmn. real property, probate and trust law sect.). Office: Sutherland Asbill & Brennan 1275 Pennsylvania Ave NW Washington DC 20004-2404

PLAISTED, HARRIS MERRILL, III, real estate executive; b. Portland, Maine, June 3, 1935; s. Harris Merrill and Elizabeth Parsons (Hatch) P.; m. Patricia Walker, Feb. 20, 1982; children: Frederick William II, Parker Bennett; stepchildren: William H. Nau Jr., Mary Beth Nau. BA in Econs., Washington and Lee U., 1957. With Morton G. Thalhimer, Inc., Richmond, Va., 1960-66, v.p., 1966-80, sr. v.p., 1980-86, pres., 1986-92, vice chmn., 1992—; bd. dirs. Morton G. Thalhimer Realty Advisors, Inc., Excel Svcs., Inc., Richmond. Pres. Ridgetop Recreation Assn., 1967, Big Bros. of Richmond, Inc., 1970; bd. dirs. Robert E. Lee coun. Boy Scouts Am., 1981; state dir. Internat. Coun. Shopping Ctrs., 1974-77. Capt. U.S. Army, 1957-59. Mem. Va. Assn. Realtors (bd. dirs. 1973-82), Richmond Bd. Realtors (pres. 1975, Realtor of Yr. 1975), Richmond Real Estate Group (pres. 1987), Richmond Jaycees (life, Key Man Club), Soc. Indsl. and Office Realtors (dist. v.p. 1979-80, regional v.p. 1984-85, Howell H. Watson Disting. Svc. award 1995), Sons of the Revolution (1st v.p. 1997), Ships Watch Assn. (bd. dirs. 1994, pres. 1995), Kiwanis Club Richmond (bd. dirs. 1978-79). Episcopalian. Avocations: golf, sailing. Home: 9013 Wood Sorrel Ct Richmond VA 23229-7072 Office: Morton G Thalhimer Inc 1313 E Main St Richmond VA 23219-3600

PLAISTED, JOAN M., diplomat; b. St. Peter, Minn., Aug. 29, 1945; d. Gerald A. and Lola May (Peters) P. Student, U. Grenoble, France, 1965-66, U. Calif., Berkeley, 1966; BA in Internat. Rels., Am. U., 1967, MA in Asian Studies, 1969; graduate, Nat. War Coll., 1988. Korea desk officer Commerce Dept., Washington, 1969-72, Japan desk officer, 1972-73; commercial officer Am. Embassy, Paris, 1973-78; internat. economist Orgn. Econ. Cooperation & Devel., Paris, 1978-80; econ. officer Am. Consulate Gen., Hong Kong, 1980-83; trade negotiator White House Office of Spl. Trade Rep., Geneva, 1983-85; deputy dir. China desk State Dept., Washington, 1985-87; acting dep. dir., chief econ./comml. sect. Am. Inst. in Taiwan, Taipei, 1988-91; chargé d'affaires, deputy chief of mission Am. Embassy, Rabat, Morocco, 1991-94; dir. Thai and Burma affairs Dept. of State, Washington, 1994-95; sr. advisor U.S. Mission to UN N.Y.C., 1995; amb. to Republic of Marshall Islands and Republic of Kiribati, 1996—. Recipient Lodestar award Am. U., 1993. Mem. Am. Fgn. Svc. Assn., Hong Kong Wine Soc. (founding). Avocations: wine tasting, gastronomy, history, skiing, scuba diving. Address: PO Box 1379 Majuro MH 96960-1379

PLAISTED, ROBERT LEROY, plant breeder, educator; b. Hornell, N.Y., Jan. 1, 1929; s. Robert A. and Eva B. (Gitchell) P.; m. Ellen B. Overbaugh, Feb. 10, 1951; children: Deborah (dec.), Kathleen, Thomas, Diane. B.S., Cornell U., 1950; M.S., Ia. State U., 1954, Ph.D., 1956. Grad. asst. Ia. State U., 1953-56; asst. prof. Cornell U., 1956-60, assoc. prof., 1960-64, prof., 1964-95, prof. emeritus, 1995—. Served with AUS, 1951-53. Mem. European Assn. Potato Research, Potato Assn. Am. (pres. 1971). Home: 536 Ellis Hollow Creek Rd Ithaca NY 14850-9623

PLAKANS, SHELLEY SWIFT, social worker, psychotherapist; b. Boston, Aug. 29, 1943; d. William Nye and Phyllis (Childs) Swift; m. John Joseph Guinan Jr. (div. 1975); children: Ashley, Lindsey Guinan, John Jeffrey, Daniel Plakans; m. John Plakans. AB, Wheaton Coll., 1965; MEd, Fitchburg (Mass.) State Coll., 1977; MSW, Simmons Sch. of Social Work, Boston, 1987. Lic. ind. clin. social worker, Mass.; bd. cert. diplomate. Staff psychologist Ayer (Mass.) Guidance Ctr., 1978-81; substance abuse specialist Family Counseling and Guidance Ctrs., Danvers, Mass., 1990-91; pvt. practice psychotherapy Boston North Shore Assocs., Salem, 1985-90, NEPA, Salem, 1990-94. Mediator Lynn (Mass.) Youth Resource Bur., 1986-87, Marblehead Cmty. Counseling Ctr., 1994-96. Mem. Nat. Assn. Social Workers, Mass. Acad. Clin. Social Work, Inc., Am. Soc. Clin. Hypnosis, Internat. Soc. Clin. Hypnosis. Office: 1 Pleasant Ln Marblehead MA 01945-2341

PLAMONDON, WILLIAM N., rental company executive. Sr. v.p. mktg. Budget Rent A Car Corp., Lisle, Ill., 1982-89, 1989-91, exec. v.p., gen. mgr. N.Am., 1991-97; pres., CEO First Merchant Exemptem Corp., Deerfield, Ill., 1997—. Office: First Merchant Exemptem Corp 570 Lake Cook Rd Ste 126 Deerfield IL 60015*

PLANCHER, ROBERT LAWRENCE, manufacturing company executive; b. N.Y.C., Feb. 21, 1932; s. Murray Leon and Pearl P.; m. Ellen Roslyn, Feb. 14, 1954; children: Kevin, Daryn. B.B.A., CCNY, 1954. With American Brands, Inc., N.Y.C., 1963—; asst. tax dir. American Brands, Inc., 1967, tax dir., 1971, controller, 1978, dir., v.p., controller, 1981-86, sr. v.p., chief acctg. officer, 1986—; bd. dirs. ACCO World Corp., Acushnet Co., Am. Brands Internat. Corp., Am. Tobacco Internat. Corp., Jim Beam Brands Co., Gallaher Ltd., MasterBrand Industries, Inc.; chmn. bd. 1700 Ins. Co. Ltd., dir. JBB Worldwide, Inc.; mem. Mid Atlantic Metro regional adv. bd. Arkwright Mut. Ins. Co. Served with U.S. Army, 1954-56. Mem. Fin. Execs. Inst., Tax Execs. Inst., Inst. Mgmt. Accts. Office: Am Brands Inc 1700 E Putnam Ave Old Greenwich CT 06870-1321

PLANE, DONALD RAY, management science educator; b. Evansville, Ind., July 17, 1938; s. Edward L. and Margaret I. (Downen) P.; m. Rosemary Bieber, Sept. 4, 1961; children: Brian Russell, Dennis Lowell, Margaret Diane. ME, U. Cin., 1961; M.B.A. (NDEA fellow), Ind. U., 1963, D.B.A. (NDEA fellow), 1965. Instr. econs. U.S. Air Force Acad., 1965-67, asst. prof. econs., 1967-68; assoc. prof. mgmt. sci. U. Colo., Boulder, 1968-72; prof. mgmt. sci. and info. systems U. Colo., 1972-84, head div. mgmt. sci., 1976-84; prof. mgmt. sci. Crummer Grad. Sch. Bus., Rollins Coll., Winter Park, Fla., 1984—, pres. Crummer grad. faculty, 1992-93; vis. Fulbright prof. mgmt. sci. U. Nairobi, 1978-79; cons. in field. Co-author: (with E.B. Oppermann) Business and Economic Statistics, 3d edit., 1986; (with J. Dinkel, G. Kochenberger) Management Science: Text and Applications, 1978, Quantitative Tools for Decision Support Using IFPS, 1986, Management Science: A Spreadsheet Approach for Windows, 1996. Served with USAF, 1965-68. Ford Found. fellow, 1965. Research, publs. in field. Home: 980 S Lake Sybelia Dr Maitland FL 32751-5403 Office: Rollins College Crummer Grad Sch Bus Winter Park FL 32789

PLANE, ROBERT ALLEN, academic administrator, chemistry educator, author; b. Evansville, Ill., Sept. 30, 1927; s. Allen George and Altha Margaret (Warren) P.; m. Georia Louise Ames, Dec. 30, 1950 (dec. Oct. 1961); children: David Allen, Martha Lu Plane Deblasio; m. Mary Moore, July 2, 1963; children: Ann Marie, Jennifer Plane Hartman. BA, Evansville Coll., 1948; SM, U. Chgo., 1949, PhD, 1951; DSc (hon.), U. Evansville, 1968, Clarkson U., 1985; LHD, St. Lawrence U., Canton, N.Y., 1986; LLD, Hobart Coll., 1990. Rsch. chemist Oak Ridge Nat. Lab., Tenn., 1951-52; prof., provost Cornell U., Ithaca, N.Y., 1952-74; pres. Clarkson U., Potsdam, N.Y., 1974-85; dir. N.Y. Agr. Expt. Sta., Geneva, N.Y., 1986-90; pres. Wells Coll., Aurora, N.Y., 1991-95. Author: (with M. Sienko) Chemistry, 1957, Physical Inorganic Chemistry, 1963, Chemistry: Principles and Properties; (with R. Hester) Elements of Inorganic Chemistry, 1965. Decorated Outstanding Civilian Svc. medal, US Army. Fellow AAAS; mem. Assn. Ind. Engring. Colls. (pres. 1982-84), Commn. Ind. Coll. U. (chmn. 1976-78). Avocations: wine making, trumpet playing.

PLANGERE, JULES L., III, newspaper company executive; b. Neptune, N.J., Nov. 4, 1944; s. Jules L. and Virginia May (Polhemus) P.; m. Nona Helen Chadwick, Nov. 20, 1971 (div. Mar. 25, 1985). B.A., Lafayette Coll., 1966. Reporter, photographer Asbury Park Press, Asbury Park, N.J., 1970-72, account exec., 1972-74, asst. prodn. mgr., 1974-80, dir. ops., 1980-82, v.p. ops., 1982-85, v.p. pub., 1986-89, exec. v.p., 1989—. Served to lt. comdr. USNR, 1966-69. Mem. N.J. Press Assn. Presbyterian. Home: 2805 Williamsburg Dr Wall NJ 07719-9516 Office: Asbury Pk Press 3601 Hwy 66 PO Box 1550 Neptune NJ 07754

PLANGERE, JULES LEON, JR., media company executive; b. Spring Lake, N.J., Dec. 30, 1920; s. Jules Leon and Jesse Alene (Davidson) P.; student Rutgers U., 1942; m. Jane Wallhauser, Feb. 5, 1978; 1 son, Jules L. III; stepchildren: Mrs. John Bickart, John C. Conover III, Jeffrey Conover. With Asbury Park (N.J.) Press, 1947—, pub., 1977-91, chief exec. officer, 1980-91, chmn. bd., 1980—; former dir. N.J. Bell Telephone Co. Former chmn. bd. trustees Monmouth U., West Long Branch, N.J.; past pres. Welfare Coun. Monmouth County. Lt. U.S. Army, 1942-46. Mem. Asbury Park C. of C. (past pres.), N.J. Press Assn. (past pres.), Am. Newspaper Pubs. Assn., N.J. State C. of C. (bd. dirs.). Clubs: Spring Lake Bath and Tennis, Nassau, Quail Ridge Country, Metedeconk Nat. Golf.

PLANK, BETSY ANN (MRS. SHERMAN V. ROSENFIELD), public relations counsel; b. Tuscaloosa, Ala., Apr. 3, 1924; d. Richard Jeremiah and Bettye (Hood) P.; m. Sherman V. Rosenfield, Apr. 10, 1954. Student, Bethany (W.Va.) Coll., 1940-43; A.B., U. Ala., 1944. Continuity dir. radio sta. KQV, Pitts., 1944-47; account exec. Mitchell McKeown Orgn., Chgo., 1947-54; pub. relations counsel Chgo. chpt. A.R.C., 1954-57; dir. pub. relations Chgo. Council on Fgn. Relations, 1957-58; v.p. Ronald Goodman Pub. Relations Counsel, Chgo., 1958-61; exec. v.p., treas., dir. Daniel J. Edelman, Inc., Chgo., 1961-73; dir. pub. relations planning Am. Tel. & Tel. Co., N.Y.C., 1973-74; asst. v.p. corp. communications Ill. Bell, Chgo., 1974-90; prin. Betsy Plank Pub. Rels., Chgo., 1990—; dep. chmn. VII World Congress on Pub. Rels., 1976; co-chmn. nat. commn. on Pub. Rels. Edn., 1984-86; mem. adv. bd. Ill. Issues. Bd. dirs. United Way Chgo., 1986-90; chmn. Citizenship Coun. Met. Chgo., 1990-96, Betsy Plank chpt. Pub. Rels. Students Soc. Am., No. Ill. U.; trustee Found. for Pub. Rels. Rsch. and Edn., 1975-80; nat. bd. dirs. Girl Scouts U.S.A., 1975-85. Recipient medal of merit Pi Delta Epsilon; named One of World's 40 Leading Pub. Relations Profls., 1984. Fellow Pub. Rels. Soc. Am. (accredited, nat. pres. 1973, chmn. pub. utilities sect. 1977, Outstanding Profl. award 1977, Outstanding Community Svc. award 1989); mem. Student Soc. Am. (co-chair friends of pub. rels. 1981—), Pub. Rels. Clinic (pres. 1979), Publicity Club Chgo. (pres. 1963-64, Outstanding Profl. award 1961), Ill. Coun. on Econ. Edn. (past chmn. bd. trustees), Welfare Pub. Rels. Forum Chgo. (pres. 1966-67), Internat. Pub. Rels. Assn., Chgo. Network (chmn. 1980-81), Nat. Pub. Rels. Coun. (bd. dirs. 1973-75), Arthur W. Page Soc., Union Leaque Club of Chgo., Bon Vivant Soc., Econ. Club Chgo., Zeta Tau Alpha. Presbyterian. Home and Office: 421 W Melrose St Chicago IL 60657-3848

PLANK, WILLIAM BRANDT, minister; b. Fond du Lac, Wis., Apr. 17, 1941; s. Lloyd Thomsen Plank and Helen Frances (Brandt) Plank Moersch; m. Susan Jane Hawthorne, June 29, 1963; children: David Hawthorne, Stephen Brandt, Elizabeth Anne. BA, Carleton Coll., 1963; MDiv, McCormick Theol. Seminary, Chgo., 1966; DMin, McCormick Theol. Seminary, 1986. Ordained minister Presbyn. Ch. Assoc. pastor Glen Avon Presbyn. Ch., Duluth, Minn., 1966-71, Highland Park (Ill.) Presbyterian Ch., 1971-76; pastor First Presbyn. Ch., Kankakee, Ill., 1976-81, Manitowoc, Wis., 1981—; staffing, nominating, evangelism coms., Winnebago Presbytery, N.E. Wis., 1994—, coun. mem., 1994—, moderator, 1986-87. Bd. dirs. Family Svc. Assn., Manitowoc, 1994—; sec./treas. Fairweather Lodge for Mentally Ill, Manitowoc, Wis., 1981—; founding bd. dirs. Peter's Pantry, Manitowoc, 1987-93. Mem. Rotary, Manitowoc County Clergy Assn. Avocations: sailing, travel, reading, cross-country skiing. Home: 715 New York Ave Manitowoc WI 54220-3333 Office: First Presbyterian Ch 502 N 8th St Manitowoc WI 54220-4042

PLANO, RICHARD JAMES, physicist, educator; b. Merrill, Wis., Apr. 15, 1929; s. Victor James and Minnie (Hass) P.; m. Louise Sylvia Grevillius, July 3, 1956; children—Linda Sylvia, Robert James. A.B., U. Chgo., 1949, B.S., 1951, M.S., 1953, Ph.D., 1956. Faculty Columbia, 1956-60; faculty Rutgers U., New Brunswick, N.J., 1960—; prof. physics Rutgers U., 1962-81, prof. II, 1981-97; program officer U.S. Dept. Energy, Germantown, Md. Mem. Am. Inst. Physics, Am. Assn. Physics Tchrs., AAUP. Studies on properties of elementary particles. Home: Apt 734 14337 Long Channel Dr Germantown MD 20874-5415 Office: US Dept Energy Physics Dept ER-223 Germantown MD 20874

PLANT, ALBIN MACDONOUGH, lawyer; b. Balt., July 30, 1937; s. Albin Joseph and Ruth E. (Frech) P.; m. Anne Warwick Brown, June 17, 1961; children: Katherine, Albin MacDonough Jr., Elizabeth Ashby. BA, Princeton U., 1959; LLB, U. Va., 1963; MLA, Johns Hopkins U., 1975.

Bar: Md. 1963, U.S. Dist. Ct. Md. 1963, U.S. Ct. Appeals 1970. Assoc. Semmes, Bowen & Semmes, Balt., 1963-71, ptnr., 1971-91; ptnr. Stewart, Plant & Blumenthal, Balt., 1991—; adj. prof. law U. Balt., 1979, U. Md., 1979-83, 84-85. Co-author Md. Estate Planning, Will Drafting and Estate Administn. Forms Practice Ann. Bd. dirs. Ctr. Stage, T. Rowe Price Spectrum Fund. Mem. Am. Coll. Probate Counsel (regent), Lawyers Roundtable, Md. Club, Wednesday Law Club. Democrat. Office: 7 St Paul St Baltimore MD 21202-1626

PLANT, DAVID WILLIAM, lawyer; b. Ottawa, Ill., Apr. 22, 1931; s. Arthur Percival and Margery Elmina (Flick) P.; children: Susan W. BME, Cornell U., 1953, LLB, 1957. Bar: N.Y. 1957, U.S. Dist. Ct. (ea. and so. dists.) N.Y., U.S. Supreme Ct., 1968, U.S. Patent Office 1982. Assoc. Fish & Neave, N.Y.C., 1957-70; ptnr. Fish & Neave, 1970—, mng. ptnr., 1981-84; domestic and internat. arbitrator, mediator, panel mem., arbitration cons. com. World Intellectual Property Orgn., 1994—; mem. panels of neutrals Internat. C. of C., 1992—, London Ct. Internat. Arbitration, 1992—, ea. dist. N.Y., so. dist. N.Y.; lectr. in field. Contbr. articles to profl. jours. Bd. dirs. Cornell Rsch. Found. Mem. ABA, Assn. of Bar of City of N.Y. (com. on patents 1980-83, chmn. 1983-86, com. on arbitration and alternative dispute resolution 1987-90, 91-94, chmn. 1994—), Am. Arbitration Assn. (various coms. and panels of neutrals), N.Y. Intellectual Property Law Assn. (chmn. arbitration com. 1989-91, bd. dirs. 1994-96), Am. Intellectual Property Law Assn. (chmn. alternative dispute resolution com. 1993-95), Ctr. Pub. Resources (panels of neutrals, co-chmn. tech. com. 1995—), Cornell Law Assn. (exec. com., pres. 1994-96), Lic. Execs. Soc. (co-chmn. alternative dispute resolution com. 1995—). Home: 7 George Langeloh Ct Rye NY 10580-4150 Office: Fish & Neave 49th Flr 1251 Ave of the Americas New York NY 10020

PLANT, FORREST ALBERT, lawyer; b. Sacramento, Dec. 17, 1924; s. Forrest A. and Marie (Phleger) P.; m. Shirley J. Boles, Oct. 15, 1949; children: Forrest Albert, Jr., Randall B., Gregory M., Brian J. AB, U. Calif., Berkeley, 1944, JD, 1949. Bar: Calif. 1950. Ptnr. Diepenbrock, Wulff, Plant & Hannegan, Sacramento, 1950—; prof. law McGeorge Coll. Law, 1952-61; mem. Jud. Coun. State Calif., 1972-76; mem. Calif. Law Revision Commn., 1988-94, chmn., 1988-89. Chmn. bd. editors: Calif. Lawyer, 1981-82. Trustee, dir. Golden Empire coun. Boy Scouts Am., 1963-67; pres. Legal Aid Soc. Sacramento County, 1961-62; former bd. dirs. Sacramento Children's Home; former trustee and mem. exec. com. Sutter Comty. Hosps., Sutter Health Sys.; trustee, pres. Crocker Art Mus. Found., 1994-95, Sacramento Symphony Found., U. Calif.-Berkeley Found., 1980-86; former bd. dirs., v.p. exec. com. Sacramento Symphony Assn.; trustee Calif. Mus. Assn., pres., 1968-69, Sacramento Regional Found., pres., 1996—; bd. visitors Stanford Law Sch., 1971-74; bd. regents U. Calif., 1978-79. With USNR, WWII. Recipient Disting. Svc. award, Boalt Law Sch. Alumni, 1989, Citation award, 1995; U. Calif.-Berkeley fellow. Fellow Am. Bar Found., Am. Coll. Trust and Estate Counsel, Am. Coll. Trial Lawyers (bd. regents 1977-81); mem. State Bar of Calif. (bd. govs. 1968-71, pres. 1970-71), Sacramento County Bar Assn. (pres. 1966, mem. coun.), U. Calif. Alumni Assn. (pres. 1977-79, Alumni citation 1980), Sutter club (past bd. dirs.), Del Paso Country Club, Rotary (past pres., bd. dirs. Sacramento Club, Paul Harris fellow), Phi Beta Kappa. Home: 1515 13th Ave Sacramento CA 95818-4148 Office: 300 Capitol Mall Sacramento CA 95814-4341

PLANT, MARETTA MOORE, public relations and marketing executive; b. Washington, Sept. 4, 1937; d. Henry Edwards and Lucy (Connell) Moore; m. William Voorhees Plant, June 14, 1959; children: Scott Voorhees, Craig Culver, Suzannah Holliday. BS in Bus. Adminstrn., U. Ark., 1959. Owner, mgr. Handcrafts by Maretta, Westfield, N.J., 1966-73; photographer M-R Pictures, Inc., Allendale, N.J., 1973-77; communications asst. United Way-Union County, Elizabeth, N.J., 1977-79; pub. rels. cons. Creative Arts Workshop, Westfield, 1977-81, Coll. Adv. Cons., 1983-89; community rels. coord. Raritan Bay Health Svcs. Corp., Perth Amboy, N.J., 1979-81; dir. pub. rels. St. Elizabeth Hosp., Elizabeth, N.J., 1981-86; dir. mkgt./communications Somerset Med. Ctr., Somerville, N.J., 1986-90; v.p. mktg. and pub. rels. Somerset Med. Ctr., Somerville, 1990—. Trustee Bridgeway House, Elizabeth, 1982-86, Far Hills Race Meeting Assn., N.J., 1989—, pub. rels com. N.J. Hosp. Assn., Princeton, 1982-83, 89-92, coun. auxs., 1988-92, pub. rels. com., 1989-92; committeewoman Union County Rep. Com., Westfield, 1983-85; bd. dirs. pub. affairs com. Morris Mus., Morristown; bd. dirs. communications com. Somerset County United Way, 1992—. Mem. Pub. Rels. Soc. Am., Nat. Fedn. Press Women, N.J. Press Women (chmn. communications contest 1990-92), Am. Soc. Hosp. Mktg. and Pub. Rels. (coun. mem. Region II, membership com.), N.J. Hosp. Mktg. and Pub. Rels. Assn. (corr. sec. 1984-86, pres. 1986-88), Somerset County C. of C. (mag. com. 1988-93), U. Ark. Alumni Assn., Summit-Westfield Assn., Delta Gamma, Coll. Women's (Westfield) Club, Soroptomists (internat., charter). Home: 118 Effingham Pl Westfield NJ 07090-3926 Office: Somerset Med Ctr Rehill Ave Somerville NJ 08876-2546

PLANTE, WILLIAM MADDEN, news correspondent; b. Chgo., Jan. 14, 1938; s. Regis Louis and Jane Elizabeth (Madden) Plante; m. Barbara A. Barnes Orteig, Jan. 18, 1965 (div. 1975); children—Patrick, Michael, Daniel, Christopher, Brian, David; m. Robin L. Smith, May 23, 1987. B.S., Loyola U., 1959; student Columbia U., 1964. Asst. news dir. WISN-TV, Milw., 1960-63; news correspondent CBS News, N.Y.C., Chgo., Washington, 1964—. Bd. trustees Lolyola U. of Chgo. CBS fellow, 1963-64; recipient Emmy award for news coverage Acad. TV Arts and Scis., 1972, 85, 87, Radio News reporting award Overseas Press Club, 70, 75. Mem. Soc. Profl. Journalists, White House Corrs. Assn. Roman Catholic. Avocations: wine, music, running. Office: CBS News 2020 M St NW Washington DC 20036-3304

PLANTS, WALTER DALE, elementary education educator, minister; b. Middlefield, Ohio, June 8, 1942; s. William E. and Hazel A. Plants; m. Sarah A. Gaddis, July 5, 1962; children: Dale Anthony, Jeanette Marie. BD, Azusa Pacific U., 1967; MEd, U. Nev., 1970. Cert. elem. tchr., ednl. adminstr. Elem. tchr. Churchill County Sch. Dist., Fallon, Nev., 1967-69, 70-72, 81—; grad. asst. U. Nev., Reno, 1969-70; tchr. Kingman (Ariz.) Elem. Sch. Dist. #4, 1972-77; head sci. program E. C. Best Elem. Sch., Fallon, 1988—; adj. instr. Ariz. State U., Tempe, 1973-77; cons. sci. Ariz. State Dept. Edn., 1975-77. Bd. dirs. Solar Energy Commn. Mohave County, Ariz., 1974; coord. County Sci. Fair, 1988-93; active Western Regional Sci. Fair Com.; sci. fair coord. Churchill County, 1989-94; mem. com. Regional Sci. Fair, 1992-94. HEW fellow, 1969; NSF grantee, 1973; AIMS Found. scholar, 1988; recipient Ariz. State PTA award, 1977, Ruth Neldon award Ariz. State Dept., 1977, Conservation award Big Sandy Natural Resources Conservation Dist. Ariz., 1976, Community Builder Svc. award Masons, Fallon, 1991, Disting. Leadership award, 1991, 92, 93; named State Tchr. of Yr. Nev. PTA, 1991, Conservation Tchr. of Yr., 1991; named to Congl. Select Edn. panel U.S. Congress, 1993. Mem. NEA, AAAS, Nat. Sci. Tchrs. Assn., Nat. Coun. Tchrs. Math., Internat. Reading Assn., Churchill County Edn. Assn. (Tchr. of Yr. 1989), Internat. Platform Assn., Nat. Arbor Day Found., World Wildlife Fund, Nat. Parks and Conservation Assn., Nat. Audubon Soc., Nev. State Tchrs. of Yr. Assn. (pres. 1994-96, pres. 1996-97), Phi Delta Kappa. Office: EC Best Elem Sch 750 E Williams Ave Fallon NV 89406-3022

PLANTZ, CHRISTINE MARIE, librarian, union officer; b. Moscow, Idaho, July 28, 1946; d. John Albert and Marian Florence (Malm) Holmes; m. Charles Walter Plantz, May 19, 1973. BA, Shimer Coll., 1968; postgrad., U. Chgo. GLS, 1968-72; BS, Chadron State Coll., 1977. Children's libr. Chgo. Pub. Libr., 1969-73; libr. Rushville (Nebr.) Pub. Schs., 1974-77; tchr. Sheridan County Dist. 126, Rushville, 1979; libr. Bur. Indian Affairs, Pine Ridge, S.D., 1980—; tchr. Oglala Lakota Coll., 1994—; pres. local 150 Nat. Fedn. Fed. Employees, Pine Ridge, S.D., 1987-89, 91-92, 95—, sec. BIA coun., 1988-96; owner LaserPress Desktop Pub., Rushville, 1992—; computer instr. Oglala Lakota Coll., Pine Ridge, S.D. Mem. Rushville City Coun., 1986-90, Rushville Pub. Libr. Bd., 1974-82; bd. dirs. Family Rescue Shelter, Gordon, Nebr., 1982-88, Black Hills Girl Scout Coun., Rapid City, S.D., bd. dirs. 1984—, pres. 1995—. Episcopalian. Avocations: computers, reading. Home: PO Box 219 Rushville NE 69360-0219 Office: Laser Press PO Box 219 133 Main St Rushville NE 69360

PLAPP, BRYCE VERNON, biochemistry educator; b. DeKalb, Ill., Sept. 11, 1939; s. Vernon Edgar and Eleanor Barbara (Kautz) P.; m. Rosemary Kuhn, June 13, 1962; children—Brendan Bryce, Laurel Andrea. B.S., Mich. State U., East Lansing, 1961; Ph.D., U. Calif.-Berkeley, 1966. Research assoc. J.W. Goethe U., Frankfurt/Main, Fed. Republic Germany, 1966-68; research assoc. Rockefeller U., N.Y.C., 1968-70; faculty U. Iowa, Iowa City, 1970—, prof. biochemistry, 1979—. Contbr. articles to profl. jours.; mem. editorial bd. Jour. Biol. Chemistry, Archives Biochemistry and Biophysics. Am. Cancer Soc. fellow, 1966-68. Mem. Am. Soc. for Biochemistry and Molecular Biology, Am. Chem. Soc., Sigma Xi. Avocations: travel; sports. Office: U Iowa Dept Biochemistry 4-370 BSB Iowa City IA 52242

PLASIL, FRANZ, physicist; b. Prague, Czechoslovakia, May 17, 1939; came to U.S., 1960; s, Frank and Eva (Wenger) P.; m. Catherine Logan, Feb. 15, 1964 (div. Sept. 1979); 1 child, Maia; m. Carol Baratz, Apr. 12, 1980. BS, Queen Mary Coll., U. London, 1960; PhD, U. Calif., Berkeley, 1964. Chemist Lawrence Berkeley (Calif.) Lab., 1964-65; rsch. assoc. Brookhaven Nat. Lab., Upton, N.Y., 1965-67; rsch. staff physics div. Oak Ridge (Tenn.) Nat. Lab., 1967-78, group leader physics div., 1978-86, sect. head physics div., 1986—. Contbr. articles to Annals of Physics, Phys. Rev., Phys. Rev. Letters. Recipient Alexander von Humboldt award 1985. Fellow Am. Phys. Soc. Achievements include definition of angular-momentum-imposed limits on the stability of rotating nuclei. Home: 964 W Outer Dr Oak Ridge TN 37830-8607 Office: Oak Ridge Nat Lab PO Box 2008 Oak Ridge TN 37831-6372

PLASKETT, THOMAS G., transportation company executive; b. Raytown, Mo., Dec. 24, 1943; s. Warren E. and Frances S. P.; m. Linda Lee Maxey, June 8, 1968; children—Kimberly, Keith. B.I.E., Gen. Motors Inst.; M.B.A., Harvard U. Supr. indsl. engring. Gen. Motors, Flint, Mich., 1968, supt. indsl. engring., 1969-73; sr. staff asst., treas Gen. Motors, N.Y.C., 1973; asst. controller Am. Airlines, N.Y.C., 1974, v.p. mktg. adminstrn., 1975-76, sr. v.p. fin., 1976-80; sr. v.p. mktg. Am. Airlines, Dallas, from 1980; pres., chief exec. officer Continental Airlines Inc., Houston, Tex., until 1988; chmn., chief exec. officer, pres. Pan Am Corp., N.Y.C., 1988-91; mng. dir. Fox Run Capital Assocs., 1991—; dir., interim pres., CEO, acting CFO Greyhound Lines, Inc., Dallas, 1994-95, chmn., dir., 1995—; bd. dirs. Tandy Corp., Ft. Worth, Smart & Final, Inc., L.A. Trustee GMI Engring. and Mgmt. Inst., Flint, Mich. Avocations: golf, skiing, squash. Office: 5215 N O Connor Blvd Ste 1070 Irving TX 75039-3738

PLASKONOS, ANNE, school nurse; b. McAdoo, Pa., June 10, 1917; d. Theodore and Martha (Snihur) P. Diploma in nursing, St. Agnes Hosp., 1939; postgrad., Willis Eye Hosp., Phila., 1948; BS in Edn., U. Pa., 1954; M in Health Edn., Temple U., 1964, postgrad., 1940, 50. RN, Pa. Staff Comty. Disease Hosp., Phila., 1940, Fitzgerald Hosp., Phila., N.D., 1941-44; ensign USNR, Phila., N.C., 1944; staff Vis. Nurse Soc. Phila., 1954-57, U.S. Pub. Health Svc., Whapeton, N.D., 1957-58, Nazareth Hosp., Phila., 1958; staff nurse Sch. Dist. Phila., 1959; ret., 1993. Ensign USN, 1944. Mem. ANA (life), Am. Sch. Health Assn., Temple U. Alumni Assn. (life), St. Agnes Hosp. Alumni Assn. (life), Women in Edn.

PLASTER, GEORGE FRANCIS, Roman Catholic priest; b. Lafayette, Ind., Dec. 6, 1950; s. Robert Lee and Ann Elizabeth (Klinker) P. BS in Econs. and Fin., St. Joseph's Coll., Rensselaer, Ind., 1973; MDiv, Sacred Heart Sch. of Theology, Hales Corners, Wis., 1980. Ordained Roman Cath. Priest, 1980. Bank examiner dept. fin. instns. State of Ind., Indpls., 1973-76; deacon, assoc. pastor St. Patrick Ch., Kokomo, Ind., 1979-82; assoc. pastor Our Lady Mt. Carmel (Ind.), 1982-86, St. Charles Ch., Peru, Ind., 1986-88, St. Joan of Arc Ch., Kokomo, 1988-89; hosp. chaplain St. Vincent's Hosp., Indpls., 1989—; spiritual counselor Jonah Ctr., Wabash, Ind., 1987-88; clin. pastoral educator Ctrl. State Hosp., Indpls., 1989-90, 91-92, 94-95. Mem. Nat. Right to Life, Washington, 1973—. Mem. Nat. Assn. Cath. Chaplains, KC (chaplain 1980-82, 84-85), Indpls. Cursillo (chaplain 1984, 89, 92). Avocation: playing organ and piano. Office: St Vincent Hosp 2001 W 86th St Indianapolis IN 46260-1902

PLAT, RICHARD VERTIN, corporate finance executive; b. San Jose, Calif., July 14, 1929; s. Gaston and Frances (Vertin) P.; children from previous marriage: Julie, Carl, Marsha; m. Janet Toll Davidson, Dec. 19, 1992. BEE, U. Santa Clara, 1951; MBA, Washington U., St. Louis, 1957. Sr. ind. econ. Stanford Rsch. Inst., Menlo Park, Calif., 1959-65; dir. planning Litton Industries, Inc., Beverly Hills, Calif., 1965-70; v.p. Waltham Industries, N.Y.C., 1970-71, Computer Machinery Corp., L.A., 1971-77; exec. v.p. Pacific Scientific Co., Newport Beach, Calif., 1978—; bd. dirs. Powertec Indsl. Corp., Rock Hill, S.C., Automation Intelligence, Inc., Duluth, Ga., High Yield Tech., Inc., Sunnyvale, Calif., Pacific Sci. Ltd., Royce Thompson Ltd., Eng., Pacific Sci. S.A.R.L., France, Pacific Sci. GmbH, Eduard Bautz GmbH, Fed. Republic of Germany, Pacific Sci. Internat., Inc., U.S., V.I. 1st lt. U.S. Army, 1951-54. Mem. Fin. Execs. Inst. (bd. dirs., v.p. 1984—). Republican. Club: Jonathan (L.A.), Balboa Bay (Newport Beach, Calif.). Home: 2027 Bayside Dr Corona Del Mar CA 92625-1847 Office: Pacific Scientific Co 620 Newport Center Dr Newport Beach CA 92660-6420

PLATE, THOMAS GORDON, newspaper columnist, educator; b. N.Y.C., May 17, 1944; s. John William and Irene (Henry) P.; m. Andrea I. Margolis, Sept. 22, 1979; 1 child, Ashley Alexandra. AB, Amherst Coll., 1966; MPA, Princeton U., 1968. Writer Newsweek, N.Y.C., 1968-70; editor Newsday, L.I., N.Y., 1970-72; sr. editor N.Y. Mag., N.Y.C., 1972-75; editor edit. page L.A. Herald Examiner, 1978-82; sr. editor Time Mag., N.Y.C., 1982-83; editor in chief Family Weekly, N.Y.C., 1984-85; editor edit. pages N.Y. Newsday, N.Y.C., 1986-89; editor edit. pages L.A. Times, 1989-95, Times Op-Ed Page columnist, 1995—; adj. prof. UCLA Pub. Policy Sch. and Letters and Scis.; mem. founders bd. UCLA Sch. Pub. Policy. Author: Understanding Doomsday, 1971, Crime Pays!, 1975, Secret Police, 1981; co-author: Commissioner, 1978. Recipient Best Deadline Writing award Am. Soc. Newspaper Editors, 1981, Best Edit. awards L.A. Press Club, 1979, 80, 81, Best Edit. award Calif. Newspaper Pubs. Assn., 1991, 92, 94. Mem. Pacific Coun. on Internat. Rels., Century Assn. (N.Y.C.), Phi Beta Kappa. Avocations: tennis, photography, travel to Asia. Office: LA Times 405 Hilgard Ave Los Angeles CA 90095-9000

PLATER, WILLIAM MARMADUKE, English language educator, academic administrator; b. East St. Louis, Ill., July 26, 1945; s. Everett Marmaduke and Marguerite (McBride) P.; m. Gail Maxwell, Oct. 16, 1971; children: Elizabeth Rachel, David Matthew. BA, U. Ill., 1967, MA in English, 1969, PhD in English, 1973. Asst. dir. Unit One, asst. to dean Coll. Liberal Arts and Scis. U. Ill., Urbana, 1971-72, acting dir. Unit One, 1972-73, asst. dean Coll. Arts and Scis., 1973-74, asst. dir. Sch. Humanities, 1974-77, dir., 1977-83, assoc. coordinator interdisciplinary programs, 1977-83; prof. English, dean Sch. Liberal Arts Ind. U., Indpls., 1983-87; dean of faculties Ind. U.-Purdue U., Indpls., 1987—, exec. vice chancellor, 1988—; cons. in field. Author: The Grim Phoenix: Reconstructing Thomas Pynchon, 1978, also articles, revs., poetry. Bd. dirs. Ind. Com. for Humanities, 1986-92, Ind. Repertory Theatre, 1987-93, Children's Mus., 1992—, U. Ill. YMCA, Urbana, 1982-83, Herron Gallery Contemporary Art, 1987—. Recipient Program Innovation prize Am. Acad. Ednl. Devel., 1982. Mem. MLA, Midwest MLA. Home: 3919 Cooper Ln Indianapolis IN 46228-3136 Office: Ind U-Purdue U Adminstrn Bldg Indianapolis IN 46202

PLATER-ZYBERK, ELIZABETH MARIA, architectural educator; b. Bryn Mawr, Pa., Dec. 20, 1950; d. Josaphat and Maria (Meysztowicz) P.-Z.; m. Andres M. Duany, June 12, 1976. BA in Architecture, Princeton U., 1972; MArch, Yale U., 1974. Registered architect, Fla. Architect, prin. Andres Duany & Elizabeth Plater-Zyberk, Architects, Miami, Fla., 1979—; prof. U. Miami, 1979—; dean Sch. Architecture U. Miami, 1995—. Contbr. numerous articles to profl. jours. and popular publs. Mem. adv. coun. Princeton (N.J.) U. Sch. Architecture, 1982—, trustee 1987-91, 93-2003; mem. vis. com. MIT Sch. Architecture, 1990—. Mem. AIA, Archtl. Club Miami (pres. 1982-87). Office: 1023 SW 25th Ave Miami FL 33135-4824

PLATIKA, DOROS, neurologist; b. Bucharest, Romania, Jan. 31, 1953; came to U.S., 1962; s. Emanuel and Liana (Catsica) P.; m. Patricia Anne Curran, Sept. 10, 1988; children: Christopher Adrian, Alexander Michael. BA in Biology and Psychology, Reed Coll., 1975; MD, SUNY, Stony Brook, 1980. Diplomate Am. Bd. Med. Examiners. Intern in medicine Mass. Gen. Hosp., Boston, 1980-81, resident in medicine, 1981-83, resident in neurology, 1983-86, chief resident in neurology, 1985-86; physician scientist Whitehead Inst. for Biomed. Rsch., MIT, Cambridge, 1986-89; instr. neurology Harvard Med. Sch., Boston, 1986-91; asst. in neurology Mass. Gen. Hosp., Boston, 1986-91; asst. prof. neurology and neurosci. Albert Einstein Coll. Medicine, N.Y.C., 1991-93; exec. v.p. R & D Progenitor, Inc., Columbus, Ohio, 1993-96; pres., CEO Ontogeny, Inc., Cambridge, 1996—; pres. Boston Med. Diagnostics, Inc., 1983-88;. Contbr. articles to Gastroenterology, Procs. NAS USA, Trans. Assn. Am. Physicians, New Biologist, Nature Medicine, Gene Therapy, Annals Neurology, Cell. Recipient 1st prize Rsch. award Boston Soc. Neurology and Psychiatry, 1986; Martin Luther King scholar, 1971, N.Y. State Regents scholar, 1971, Danforth scholar, 1972, John Hairgrove scholar, 1975; grantee NSF, 1974-76. Mem. AMA, AAAS, Am. Acad. Neurology, Soc. for Neurosci., Mass. Gen. Hosp. Soc. Fellows, U.S. Chess Fedn., N.Y. Acad. Scis., Mass. Med. Soc., Phi Beta Kappa. Achievements include patent (with others) for use of immortalized cells of neurons in scientific research; development (with others) of artificial intelligence paradigm for computer aided medical diagnosis, of new treatment for brain tumors; research on effects of 4,4-dichlorobiphenyl on calcium metabolism of Salmonoid fish, on temporal and somatotopic patterns of response in the Nucleus Interpositus of cats and rats to mechanical stimulation of forepaws and hind paws, on the Michigan polybrominated biphenyl contamination, on molecular mechanisms of neuronal development, regeneration and synapse formation, on the development of molecular vectors for gene transfer into neurons and on retroviral vectors for inducible selective ablation of targeted cells. Office: Ontogeny Inc 45 Moulton St Cambridge MA 02138-1118

PLATIS, CHRIS STEVEN, educator; b. East Chicago, Ind., May 21, 1926; s. Sam and Myra (Theodore) P.; m. Jeanette Brown. BS in Phys. Edn., Ind. U., 1955, MS in Edn., 1964, postgrad., 1965-68. Gen. foreman Cast Armor, Inc., East Chicago, 1951-53; tchr. East Chgo. and Ind. Pub. Schs., 1955—; asst. sports editor East Chgo. Calumet News, 1973-78; asst. dir. No. Ind. State Sports Mus., 1984-95. Author: Teaching Kids of Tomorrow, 1978. Master Boy Scouts Am., East Chicago, 1965-87; asst. recreational dir. North Twp., Northern Ind., 1993. With U.S. Army, 1944-46. Named to East Chgo. Hall of Fame All Am. Amateur Baseball Congress, 1955, 56, 57, Ind. Amateur Baseball Hall of Fame, 1962, U.S. Masters Track and Field All Am., 1995, 90 Yr. Greatest Athletes in East Chgo.'s History; recipient 12 league batting titles, 11 MVP awards, 16 times Ind. All State in Baseball, 21 times League Mgr. of Yr., Nat./European Tchr. of Yr., 1984; mem. team won 52 league championships, 53 playoff championships, 39 Ind. State baseball championships, 7 world regional titles, 5 world finalists, 2 runner-up world championships, Nat. C.I.O. baseball championship. Fellow VFW, Am. Legion, Normandy Invasion Club, Nat. Assn. of Basketball Coaches, Nat. Wildlife Assn. Republican. Avocations: reading, writing, baseball, tennis, golf. Home: 427 Fisher St Munster IN 46321-2330

PLATIS, JAMES G., secondary school educator; b. Detroit, Mar. 23, 1927; s. Sam and Myra (Theodore) P.; m. Mary Lou Campbell, Aug. 16, 1974. BS in Physical Edn., Ind. U., 1955, MS in Edn., 1965; postgrad., Ind. State U., 1967. Cert. physical edn. tchr., Ind. Foreman Cast Armor, Inc., East Chicago, Ind., 1951-53, Youngstown Sheet & Tube, East Chicago, 1953-54; dir., tchr. East Chicago Pub. Schs., 1955—; sports editor East Chicago Globe/Calumet News, 1973-78, Herald Newspapers, Merrillville, Ind., 1973-78. Contbr. articles to newspapers, jours. Founder East Chicago Hall of Fame, 1975, Little Olympics, East Chicago, 1956; pres. Ind. Am. Amateur Baseball Congress, 1954-57, commr., 1984-96; dir. No. Ind. State Sports Mus., 1988-97. Cpl. AUS, 1945-47, ETO. Named to Ind. Amateur Baseball Hall of Fame, 1962, East Chicago Hall of Fame, 1976, All-Am. Amateur Baseball Congress, 1955, 56, The Athletic Congress Masters All-Am., 1986, 87, 88, 89, 90, 91, 92, 93, 94, 95, 96; selected to 90 Yr. Greatest Athletes in East Chicago History, Nat. Athletic Congress, 1990; named Amateur Coach of Yr., U.S. Baseball Fedn. Ind., 1990, Amateur Runner-up Coach of Yr., 1988; recipient 29 World and 37 Nat. No. 1 track rankings, Athletic Congress Masters, 1989, 90, 91, 92, 93, 94, 95, 96, 14 League Batting Titles, 12 MV League Players awards; 18 times Ind. all-state team; mem. team won 52 League Championships, 53 Playoff championships, 39 Ind. State Baseball Championships, 7 World Regional Titles, 5 World Finalists, 2 runner-up World Champions, Nat. C.I.O. Baseball Championship; named Athlete of Yr. Ind. Masters Track and Field, 1992, World Sr. Olympic Masters Track & Field Champion, Spain, 6 Gold medals, Fla. Masters Track and Field Athlete of Yr., 1994, 95, 96; recipient 29 Ind. Track and Field Individual medals, 1983-96, 221 All Am. Masters Track and Field Certs., 1986-96, 39 Ill. Grand Prix individual titles, 1989-92, 41 Mid-West Track and Field State medals, 1989-92, 5 Gold medals, Silver medal World Sr. Olympic Masters Track & Field, 1996, Ga., others. Fellow Nat. Assn. Basketball Coaches, Am. Assn. Health, Phys. Edn. and Recreation; mem. Athletic Dirs. Assn. Sportswriters Guild, VFW, Am. Legion. Republican. Avocations: reading, running, baseball, writing. Home: 427 Fisher St Munster IN 46321-2330 Office: E Chgo Pub Schs 2700 Cardinal Dr East Chicago IN 46312-3150

PLATNER, WARREN, architect; b. Balt., June 18, 1919; s. Warren Kelly and Alice Darling (Chapman) P.; m. Joan Payne, 1945; children: Bronson, Joan, Sharon, Madeleine. B.Arch., Cornell U., 1941. Assoc. Eero Saarinen and Assocs. (architects), 1950-65; propr. Warren Platner Assocs. (architects), New Haven, 1965—; vis. lectr. archtl. schs. Prin. works include Kent Meml. Library, Suffield, Conn., 1972, Princeton U. Prospect Center, 1970, MGIC Hdqrs, Milw., 1973, Am. Restaurant, Kansas City, Mo., 1974; malls at Water Tower Pl., Chgo., 1975, Windows on the World, N.Y.C., 1976, Standard Brands Research Center, Wilton, Conn., 1979, Providence Athenaeum, 1980; Sea Containers Hdqrs., London, 1983, Wildflower Restaurant Lodge, Vail, Colo., 1985, Porter, Wright, Morris & Arthur Headqrs., Columbus, Ohio, 1986, Pan Am Bldg. additions, N.Y.C., 1987, ships Fantasia and Fiesta, 1990, Carlyle Hotel additions, 1990, Fair Residence, 1990, Friedman Residence, 1993. Recipient Rome prize architecture, 1955; advanced research Fulbright award architecture, 1955; Graham Found. award advanced studies fine arts, 1962; 1st ann. award Designers Lighting Forum, 1975; Pres.'s fellow R.I. Sch. Design, 1980; Interior Design Hall of Fame award, 1985; also several internat. design awards. Fellow AIA, Am. Acad. in Rome. Address: 18 Mitchell Dr New Haven CT 06511-2516

PLATNICK, NORMAN I., curator, arachnologist; b. Bluefield, W.Va., Dec. 30, 1951; s. Philip and Fannie (Kascenewsky) P.; m. Nancy Stewart Price, June 14, 1970; 1 child, William Durin. BS in Biology, Concord Coll., 1968; MS in Zoology, Mich. State U., 1970; PhD in Biology, Harvard U., 1973. Asst. curator Am. Mus. Natural History, N.Y.C., 1973-77, assoc. curator, 1977-82, curator, 1982—, chmn. dept. entomology, 1987-94; sci. attaché Consulate of Gondwana, N.Y.C., 1976—. Author: Advances in Spider Taxonomy, 1989, 93; co-author: Systematics and Biogeography, 1981; co-editor: Advances in Cladistics, 1983. V.p. Ctr. Internat. de Documentation Arachnologie, 1986-89 (pres. 1995-98). Fellow Willi Hennig Soc. (founder, pres. 1990-92); mem. Am. Arachnological Soc. (charter, membership sec. 1976—). Office: Am Mus Natural History Central Pk W At 79th St W New York NY 10024

PLATOU, JOANNE (DODE), retired museum director; b. Mpls., Jan. 6, 1919; d. Wesley Richmond and Catherine Harriet (Fisher) Pierson; m. Ralph Victor Platou, Jan. 23, 1942 (dec. Sept. 1968); children: Peter Erling, Thomas Stoud, Mary Kirk Platou Marloff. BS, U. Minn., 1939; MFA, Tulane U., 1959. Columnist Mpls. Tribune, 1939-42; med. photographer Ochsner Clinic, New Orleans, 1943-46; tchr. photography Metairie (La.) Pk. Country Day Sch., 1946-51; free lance artist New Orleans, 1953-68; curator edn. New Orleans Mus. Art, 1969-75; chief curator Historic New Orleans Collection, 1976-86, dir., 1986-92, dir. emerita, 1992—; ret., 1992; bd. dirs. Arts Coun. New Orleans, 1972-88, Long Vue House and Gardens, New Orleans, 1982-88; tchr. mus. career course Tulane U., New Orleans, 1983-87. Curator exhbns. The Wit of It, 1972, The Art Works, 1972, The Camera, 1974; author catalogue, curator exhbn. Alfred R. Waud, 1979. NEH grantee, New Orleans Mus. Art, 1975. Mem. Am. Mus. Assn., Friends of the Cabildo, Coll. Art Assn., Am. Assn. State and Local History. Avocations: travel, gardening.

PLATSOUCAS, CHRIS DIMITRIOS, immunologist; b. Athens, Greece, Apr. 17, 1951; came to U.S., 1973; s. Dimitrios Evagelos and Maria

(Tsonidis) P.; m. Emilia L. Oleszak, Oct. 18, 1985. BS, U. Patras (Greece), 1973; postgrad., Purdue U., 1974; PhD, MIT, 1978. Rsch. fellow/assoc. Meml. Sloan-Kettering Cancer Ctr., N.Y.C., 1978-80, asst. mem., 1980-85, asst. prof., 1981-85, head lab. biol. response modifiers, 1981-85; assoc. prof. dept. immunology M.D. Anderson Cancer Ctr., Houston, 1985-89, prof., dep. chmn., 1989-93, Ashbel Smith professorship, 1991-92, H.L. and O. Stringer professorship in cancer rsch., 1992-93; L.H. Carnell prof. and chmn. dept. microbiology, immunology Temple U. Sch. Medicine, Phila., 1993—; biotech. cons., sci. reviewer study sects. NIH, Bethesda, 1982—. Contbr. numerous articles to profl. jours. Nat. Rsch. Svc. award NIH, 1978-79; NIH grantee, 1982—, Am. Cancer Soc. grantee, 1980-91. Mem. Am. Assn. Immunologists, Am. Soc. Hematology, Am. Assn. Biochem & Molecular Biology, Am. Assn. Pathologists. Greek Orthodox. Achievements include patents in field; research on human T cell immunology, on T-cell antigen receptors, on tumor-infiltrating lymphocytes in malignant melanoma and ovarian carcinoma, on lymphoproliferative disorders, on immunoregulatory factors. Office: Temple U Sch Medicine Dept Microbiology and Immunology 3400 N Broad St Philadelphia PA 19140-5104

PLATT, CHARLES ADAMS, architect, planner; b. N.Y.C., May 16, 1932; s. William and Margaret (Littell) P.; m. Joan Mathieson, June 20, 1958; children: Sylvia, Ethan, Virginia L. A.B., Harvard, 1954, M.Arch., 1960. Gen. ptnr. Smotrich & Platt, N.Y.C., 1965-85, Charles A. Platt Ptnrs., N.Y.C., 1985-89; ptnr. Platt Byard Dovell, 1989—; assoc. prof. Columbia U. Grad. Sch. Architecture and Planning, 1985-86. Mem. nat. panel arbitrators Am. Arbitration Assn.; bd. dirs. Pub. Health Research Inst., N.Y.C., 1982-92, The New 42nd Street, 1990—, Municipal Art Soc., N.Y.C., 1966-78, 85—; pres. bd. trustees Augustus St.-Gaudens Meml., 1977-91; commr. N.Y.C. Landmarks Preservation Commn., 1979-84. Recipient Nat. Honor award for excellence in architecture AIA, 1969, Bard award for civic architecture and urban design, 1969, 85, Record Interiors award, 1970, 73, 75, Record House awards, 1971, 78, Et Alia. Mem. AIA, Century Club (N.Y.C.). Home: 1261 Madison Ave New York NY 10128-0569 Office: Platt Byard Dovell Archs 19 Union Sq W New York NY 10003-3304

PLATT, FRANKLIN DEWITT, history educator; b. Marion, La., Nov. 15, 1932; s. Robert Baxter and Ethel Estelle (White) P.; m. Dixie Ferguson, Aug. 4, 1956; 1 dau. Dixie. B.A., La. State U., 1955; Rockefeller Bros. Theol. fellow, Union Theol. Sem., 1955-56; A.M., Washington U., St. Louis, 1963, Ph.D., 1969. Instr. dept. humanities Mich. State U., 1964-69, asst. prof., 1969-72, assoc. prof., 1972-77, prof., 1977-89, asst. chmn. dept. humanities, 1971-78, chmn., 1978-80, prof., 1989-96, prof. emeritus, 1997—. Co-author: The Western Humanities, 1991 (named Best Coll. Textbook Bookbuilders West 1991), Readings in the Western Humanities, 1994. Served with USNR, 1956-60. Home: 1134 Southlawn Ave East Lansing MI 48823-3041 Office: Mich State U Dept History East Lansing MI 48824

PLATT, JAN KAMINIS, county official; b. St. Petersburg, Fla., Sept. 27, 1936; d. Peter Clifton and Adele (Diamond) Kaminis; m. William R. Platt, Feb. 8, 1962; 1 son, Kevin Peter. B.A., Fla. State U., 1958; postgrad. U. Fla. Law Sch., 1958-59, U. Va., 1962, Vanderbilt U., 1964. Pub. sch. tchr. Hillsborough County, Tampa, Fla., 1959-60; field dir. Girl Scouts Suncoast Coun., Tampa, 1960-62; city councilman Tampa City Council, 1974-78; county commr. Hillsborough County, 1978-94, 96—; chmn. Hillsborough County Bd. County commrs., 1980-81, 83-84, ret., 1994; chmn. Tampa Bay Regional Planning Council, 1982; chmn. West Coast Regional Water Supply Authority, Tampa, 1985; chmn. Hillsborough County Council of Govts., 1976, 79; chmn. Sunshine Amendment Drive 7th Congrl. Dist., Tampa, 1976; chmn. Community Action Agy., Tampa, 1980-81, 83-84; chmn. pro tem Tampa Charter Revision Commn., 1975; chmn. Prison Sitting Task Force, Tampa, 1983, Tampa Housing Study Com., 1983, Met. Planning Orgn., Tampa, 1984, Bd. Tax Adjustment, Tampa, 1984; appointee Constitution Revision Commn., Fla., 1977, HRS Dist. IV Adv. Council, Fla.; mem. Hillsborough County Expressway Authority, Taxicab Commn., Ch. Hills Cmty. Youth Coun.; vice chmn. steering com. Nat. Assn. Counties Environ. Task Force; Bd. dirs. March of Dimes, Tampa, The Fla. Orchestra, Tampa, Tampa Bay Sierra, Tampa Audubon; trustee Hillsborough County Hosp. Authority, Tampa, 1984-94; pres. Suncoast Girl Scout Council, Citizens Alert, Tampa, Bay View Garden Club; v.p. Hillsborough County Bar Aux.; mem. adv. bd. Northside Community Mental Health Ctr.: Access House, Tampa; active mem. Arts Council of Tampa-Hillsborough County, 1983-85, Drug Abuse Coordinating Council Orgn., Tampa, Bd. Criminal Justice, Tampa, Fla. Council on Aging, Inebriate Task Force, Tampa, Tampa Downtown Devel. Authority Task Force, Tampa Sports Authority, Tampa Area Mental Health Bd., Children's Study Commn., Manahill Area Agy. on Aging, Tampa, Athena Soc., Tampa Area Com. Fgn. Affairs, LWV. Recipient Athena award Women in Comm., 1976, First Annual Humanitarian award Nat. Orgn. for Prevention of Animal Suffering, 1981, Spessard Holland Meml. award Tampa Bay Com. for Good Govt., 1979, First Lady of Yr. award Beta Sigma Phi, 1980, Women Helping Women award Soroptimist Internat. Tampa, 1983, Eliza Wolff award Tampa United Methodist Ctrs., 1982, Good Govt. award Tampa Jaycees, 1983, Good Govt. award League of Women Voters, 1983. Mem. Am. Judicature Soc., State Assn. County Commrs. Fla. (at-large dir.), AAUW (bd. dirs.), Mortar Bd., Garnet Key, Phi Beta Kappa (pres. local alumni), Phi Kappa Phi. Democrat. Episcopalian. Home: 3531 Village Way Tampa FL 33629-8950 Office: PO Box 1110 Tampa FL 33601-1110

PLATT, JOSEPH BEAVEN, former college president; b. Portland, Oreg., Aug. 12, 1915; s. William Bradbury and Mary (Beaven) P.; m. Jean Ferguson Rusk, Feb. 9, 1946; children: Ann Ferguson Walker, Elizabeth Beaven Garrow. BA, U. Rochester, 1937; PhD, Cornell U., 1942; LLD, U. So. Calif., 1969, Claremont McKenna Coll., 1982; DSc, Harvey Mudd Coll., 1981. Instr. physics U. Rochester, N.Y., 1941-43, from asst. prof. to prof., 1946-56, assoc. chmn. dept. physics, 1954-56; staff mem. radiation lab. MIT, Cambridge, 1943-46; pres. Harvey Mudd Coll., Claremont, Calif., 1956-76, now part-time sr. prof. physics; pres. Claremont U. Ctr., 1976-81; trustee Aerospace Corp., 1972-85, Consortium for Advancement of Pvt. Higher Edn., 1985-92; chief physics br. AEC, 1949-51; cons. U.S. Office Ordnance Rsch., NSF, 1953-56; mem. com. on sci. in UNESCO, NAS-NRC, 1960-62, mem. com. on internat. orgns. and programs, 1962-64, sci. advisor U.S. Del., UNESCO Gen. Conf., Paris, 1960, alt. del., 1962, chmn. Subcom. on Sino-Am. Sci. Cooperation, 1965-79; mem. panel on internat. sci. Pres.'s Sci. Adv. Com., 1961; trustee Analytic Svcs., Inc., 1958-89, chmn., 1961-89; mem. adv. com. on sci. edn. NSF, 1965-70, 72-76, chmn., 1969-70, 73-74, 74-75; bd. dirs. Lincoln Found., 1979-85, Bell & Howell Corp., 1978-88, Am. Mut. Fund, 1981-88, DeVry, Inc., 1984-87, Sigma Rsch., 1983-87, Jacobs Engring. Co., 1978-86. Author: Harvey Mudd College: The First Twenty YEars, 1994. Trustee China Found. for Promotion of Edn. and Culture, 1966—, Carnegie Found. for Advancement Tchg., 1970-78; chmn. select com. Master Plan for Higher Edn. Calif., 1971-73; mem. Carnegie Coun. for Policy Studies in Higher Edn., 1975-80. Fellow Am. Phys. Soc.; mem. IEEE, Automobile Club So. Calif. (bd. dirs. 1973-90, chmn. bd. dirs. 1986-87), Calif. Club, Sunset Club, Twilight Club, Cosmos Club, Bohemian Club, Phi Beta Kappa, Sigma Xi, Phi Kappa Phi. Home: 452 W 11th St Claremont CA 91711-3833

PLATT, LEWIS EMMETT, electronics company executive; b. Johnson City, N.Y., Apr. 11, 1941; s. Norval Lewis and Margaret Dora (Williams) P.; m. Joan Ellen Redmund, Jan. 15, 1983; children: Caryn, Laura, Amanda, Hillary. BME, Cornell U., 1964; MBA, U. Pa., 1966. With Hewlett Packard, Waltham, Mass., 1966-71, engring. mgr., 1971-74, ops. mgr., 1976-77, div. gen. mgr., 1974-80, group gen. mgr., Palo Alto, Calif., 1980-84, v.p., 1983-85, exec. v.p., 1987-92, pres., CEO, chmn., 1993—; dir. Pacific Telesis. Trustee Waltham Hosp., 1978-80, Wharton Sch. Bd. Overseers, 1993; mem. Mid-Peninsula YMCA, 1980—, bd. couns. YMCA-USA, 1993—, Cornell U. Coun., 1992, Computer Sys. Policy Project, 1993, Calif. Bus. Roundtable, 1993, Bus. Coun., 1993, Bay Area Coun., 1993, Bus. Roundtable, 1993; vice chmn. Y Coun., 1989, mem. bd. dirs. Joint Venture, Silicon Valley, 1996. Recipient Red Triangle award Min-Peninsula YMCA, 1992, Internat. Citizens award World Forum Silicon Valley, San Jose, Calif., 1994, outstanding alumnus, Wharton Alumni Honor Roll, Wharton Schl. Business, Univ. Pa., 1994-95, award for bus. excellence U. Calif. Sch. Bus. Adminstrn., 1996, Tree of Life award Jewish Nat. Fund, 1996, Leadership and Vision award San Francisco Chpt. French-Am. C. of C., 1997. Mem. IEEE, Sci. Apparatus Mfg. Assn. (bd. dirs. 1978-80). Office: Hewlett Packard Co 3000 Hanover St Palo Alto CA 94304-1112

PLATT, NICHOLAS, Asian affairs specialist, retired ambassador; b. N.Y.C., Mar. 10, 1936; s. Geoffrey and Helen (Choate) P.; m. Sheila Maynard, June 28, 1957; children: Adam, Oliver, Nicholas. B.A. cum laude, Harvard U., 1957; M.A., Johns Hopkins U., 1959. Commd. fgn. service officer Dept. State, 1959; vice consul Windsor, Ont., Can., 1959-61; Chinese lang. trainee, 1962-63; polit. officer consulate gen. Hong Kong, 1964-68; chief Asian Communist areas div. Bur. Intelligence and Research, Dept. State, Washington, 1969, chief North Asia div., 1970, dept. dir. Exec. Secretariat staff, 1971, dir. staff, 1972-73; chief polit. sect. U.S. Liaison Office, Peking, China, 1973-74; 1st sec. Am. embassy, Tokyo, 1974-77; dir. Office of Japanese Affairs, Dept. State, 1977-78; mem. staff Nat. Security Council, White House, 1978-79; dep. asst. sec. for internat. security affairs Dept. Def., 1980-81; dep. asst. sec. for internat. orgn. affairs Dept. State, 1981-82; amb. Lusaka, Zambia, 1982-84; exec. sec., psl. asst. to sec. state Dept. State, 1985-87; amb. Manila, The Philippines, 1987-91, Pakistan, 1991-92; pres. Asia Soc., N.Y.C., 1992—. Recipient Meritorious award exemplary achievement pub. adminstrn. William A. Jump Found., 1973, Disting. Civilian Svc. medal Dept. Def., 1981, Presdl. Merit award, 1985, 87, Disting. Honor award U.S. Dept. State, 1987, 91, Wilbur Carr award, 1992. Mem. N.Y. Council Fgn. Relations. Clubs: Metropolitan (Washington); Century (N.Y.C.), Union (N.Y.C.). Home: 131 E 69th St New York NY 10021-5158

PLATT, OLIVER, actor. Films include: Crusoe, 1988, Married to the Mob, 1988, Working Girl, 1988, Flatliners, 1990, Postcards from the Edge, 1990, Beethoven, 1992, Diggstown, 1992, Benny & Joon, 1993, Indecent Proposal, 1993, The Temp, 1993, The Three Musketeers, 1993, Tall Tale, 1995, Funny Bones, 1995, Executive Decision, 1996, A Time to Kill, 1996, Venice, 1997, Bulworth, 1997; assoc. prodr. (film) Big Night, 1996. Office: c/o William Morris Agy 151 S El Camino Dr Beverly Hills CA 90212-2704*

PLATT, PETER GODFREY, lawyer; b. Battle Creek, Mich., May 11, 1937; s. Frank Kenneth and Louise Joy (Godfrey) P.; m. Kristine Koch; children: Peter G. Jr., Geoffrey B. BA, Yale U., 1959, JD, 1962. Bar: Calif. 1962. Assoc. Brobeck, Phleger & Harrison, San Francisco, 1962-68, ptnr., 1969-90; ptnr. Coudert Bros., San Francisco, 1990-95, Bangkok, Thailand, 1995—. Trustee Grace Cathedral, San Francisco, 1976—, chmn. bd. trustees, 1985-89; mem. bd. govs. San Francisco Symphony, 1981—, v.p., 1993—; bd. dirs. Arthritis Found., San Francisco, 1983-86; chancellor Episcopal Diocese of Calif., 1989—. Mem. Calif. Bar Assn., San Francisco Bar Assn. Republican. Episcopalian. Clubs: San Francisco Golf, Pacific Union (San Francisco), Burlingame Country (Hillsborough, Calif.) (sec. 1980), Links (N.Y.C.). Avocation: golf. Office: Coudert Bros Ste 3300 Four Embarcadero Ctr San Francisco CA 94111

PLATT, SHERMAN PHELPS, JR., publishing consultant; b. N.Y.C., Mar. 29, 1918; s. Sherman Phelps and Penelope (Sears) P.; m. Leila Bronson, Jan. 11, 1941 (div. 1968); children: Sherman Phelps III, John, Bronson; m. Margaret McClure Smithers, 1968. Grad., Taft Sch., 1936; B.A., Yale, 1940. With Dodd, Mead & Co., N.Y.C., 1940-82, beginning as editor, successively salesman, prodn. mgr., sec., dir., exec. v.p., then pres., until 1982; v.p., dir. Apollo Edits., Inc., N.Y.C., 1962-72; pub. cons., 1982—. Served as 1st lt. inf. U.S. Army, 1943-46. Home: 38 Aylesbury Circle Madison CT 06443-3434

PLATT, THOMAS COLLIER, JR., federal judge; b. N.Y.C., N.Y., May 29, 1925; s. Thomas Collier and Louise Platt; m. Ann Byrd Symington, June 25, 1948; children: Ann Byrd, Charles Collier, Thomas Collier, III, Elizabeth Louise. B.A., Yale U., 1947, LL.B., 1950. Bar: N.Y. 1950. Assoc. Root, Ballantine, Harlan, Bushby & Palmer, N.Y.C., 1950-53; asst. U.S. atty. Bklyn., 1953-56; assoc. Bleakley, Platt, Schmidt, Hart & Fritz, N.Y.C., 1956-60, ptnr., 1960-74; judge U.S. Dist. Ct. (ea. dist.) N.Y., Bklyn., 1974—, chief judge, 1988-95; former dir. Phoenix Mut. Life Ins. Co., RAC Corp., McIntyre Aviation, Inc.; atty. Village of Laurel Hollow, N.Y., 1958-74; acting police justice Village of Lloyd Harbor, N.Y., 1958-63. Alt. del. Republican Nat. Conv., 1964, 68, 72; del. N.Y. State Rep. Conv., 1966; trustee Brooks Sch., North Andover, Mass., 1968-82, pres., 1970-74. Served with USN, 1943-46. Mem. Fed. Judges Assn. (sec., bd. dirs. 1982-91). Episcopalian. Clubs: Phelps Assn. (New Haven) (bd. govs. 1960—); Cold Spring Harbor Beach (N.Y.) (bd. mgrs. 1964-70); Yale of N.Y.C. Office: US Dist Ct Uniondale Ave at Hempstead Tpke Uniondale NY 11553

PLATT, TREVOR CHARLES, oceanographer, scientist; b. Salford, Eng., Aug. 12, 1942; arrived in Can., 1963; s. John and Lily (Hibbert) P.; m. Shubha Sathyendranath, Feb. 24, 1988. BSc, U. Nottingham, U.K., 1963; MA, U. Toronto, Ont., Can., 1965; PhD, Dalhousie U., Halifax, N.S., Can., 1970. Rsch. scientist Bedford Inst. Oceanography, Dartmouth, N.S., 1965-72, chief biol. oceanography, 1972—; chmn. Joint Global Ocean Flux Study, 1991-93. Recipient Rosenstiel medal U. Miami, 1984, A.G. Huntsman medal A.G. Huntsman Found., 1992. Fellow Royal Soc. Can., Acad. Sci. Can.; mem. Am. Soc. Limnology and Oceanography (pres. 1990-92, G.E. Hutchinson medal 1988). Home: 33 Crichton Park Rd, Dartmouth, NS Canada B3A 2N9 Office: Bedford Inst Oceanography, Dartmouth, NS Canada B2Y 4A2

PLATT, WARREN E., lawyer; b. McNary, Ariz., Aug. 5, 1943. BA, Mich. State U., 1965; JD, U. Ariz., 1969. Bar: Ariz. 1969, Calif. 1991, Texas 1993. Atty. Snell & Wilmer, Phoenix. Mng. editor: Ariz. Law Rev., 1968-69. Fellow Am. Coll. Trial Lawyers; mem. Blue Key, Order of Coif, Phi Alpha Delta. Office: Snell & Wilmer One Arizona Ctr Phoenix AZ 85004-0001

PLATT, WILLIAM HENRY, judge; b. Allentown, Pa., Jan. 25, 1940; s. Henry and Genevieve (McElroy) P.; m. Maureen Hart, Nov. 29, 1969; children: Meredith H., William H., James H. AB, Dickinson Coll., 1961; JD, U. Pa., 1964. Bar: Pa. 1967, U.S. Supreme Ct. 1971. Ptnr. Yarus and Platt, Allentown, 1967-77; asst. pub. defender Lehigh County (Pa.), 1972-75, chief pub. defender, 1975-76, dist. atty., 1976-91; ptnr. Eckert, Seamans, Cherin & Mellott, 1991-95; city solicitor City of Allentown, Pa., 1994-95; judge Ct. Common Pleas of Lehigh County, Allentown, 1996—; mem. criminal procedural rules com. Supreme Ct. Pa., 1982-92, chmn., 1986-92. Mem. Gov.'s Trial Ct. Nominating Commn. Lehigh County, 1984-87; mem. Pa. Commn. on Crime and Delinquency Victim Services Adv. Com., 1983-91. Served with M.P., U.S. Army, 1964-66. Mem. ABA, Pa. Bar Assn., Lehigh County Bar Assn., Nat. Assn. Dist. Attys. (state dir. 1982-84), Pa. Assn. Dist. Attys. (pres. 1983-84, exec. com. 1980-86, tng. inst. mem. 1986-91, chmn. 1986-87), Pa. Bar Inst. (bd. dirs. 1989—, treas. 1994-95, sec. 1995-96, v.p. 1996—), Pa. Conf. of State Trial Judges (edn. com. 1997—). Office: Lehigh County Courthouse PO Box 1548 Allentown PA 18105

PLATT, WILLIAM RADY, pathology educator; b. Balt., July 25, 1915; s. Louis Abraham and Ida Selma (Rady) P.; m. Shirley Ades, June 26, 1949 (dec. 1972); children: Karen J., Lois A., James R.; m. Jeanette Krulevitz Fineman, Mar. 4, 1979 (sep. July 1995). BS in Pharmacy, U. Md., 1936, MD, 1940. Diplomate Am. Bd. Pathology. Intern St. Joseph's Hosp., Lexington, Ky., 1940-41; resident in pathology Emory U. Hosp., Atlanta, 1941-44; instr. in pathology Yale U. Sch. Medicine, New Haven, 1944-45, Washington U., St. Louis, 1945-46, U. Pa., Phila., 1948-52; dir. lab. Norton Meml. Hosp., Louisville, 1946-48, West Jersey Hosp., Camden, N.J., 1948-52, Mo. Bapt. Hosp., St. Louis, 1952-76, U.S. Pub. Health Service Hosp., Batl., 1977-81; profl. Southwestern Med. Sch., Dallas, 1976-77, prof., 1976-77; lectr. Johns Hopkins U., Balt., 1977—; profl. Chinese U., Hong Kong, 1985-86. Author: Color Atlas and Textbook of Hematology, 1975, 2d edit., 1979; editor-in-chief Pathology Update, 1972-87. Fellow cytology Cornell U. 1946, radioisotope research AEC, 1947, tropical diseases Tulane U., 1943. Fellow ACP; mem., Coll. Am. Pathologist, Am. Soc. Hematology, Am. Soc. Clin. Pathology, Internat. Acad. Pathology, Rho Chi., Johns Hopkins Club, U. Club. Clubs: Johns Hopkins; Univ. (Balt.). Home and Office: 12 Hamlet Hill Rd Baltimore MD 21210-1501

PLATTHY, JENO, cultural association executive; b. Dunapataj, Hungary, Aug. 13, 1920; s. Joseph K. and Maria (Dobor) P.; m. Carol Louise Abell, Sept. 25, 1976. Diploma, Peter Pazmany U., Budapest, Hungary, 1942; PhD, Ferencz J. U., Kolozsvar, Hungary, 1944; MS, Cath. U., 1965; PhD (hon.), Yangmingshan U., Taiwan, 1975; DLitt (hon.), U. Libre Asie, Philippines, 1977. Lectr. various univs., 1956-59; sec. Internat. Inst. Boston, 1959-62; adminstrv. asst. Trustees of Harvard U., Washington, 1962-85; exec. dir. Fedn. Internat. Poetry Assns., 1976—; pub. New Muses Quar., 1976—. Author: Winter Tunes, 1974, Ch'u Yuan, His Life and Works, 1975, Springtide (opera), 1976, Bamboo, Collected Poems, 1981, The Poems of Jesus, 1982, Holiness in a Worldly Garment, 1984, Ut Pictures Poeta, 1984, European Odes, 1985, The Mythical Poets of Greece, 1985, Book of Dithyrambs, 1986, Asian Elegies, 1987, Space Ecologues, 1988, Cosmograms, 1988, Nova Comoedia, 1988, vols. II-III, 1992, Bartok: A Critical Biography, 1988, Plato: A Critical Biography, 1990, Near-Death Experiences in Antiquity, 1992, Celebration of Life, 1992, Idylls, 1992, Elegies Asiatiques, 1992, Paeans, 1993, Rhapsodies, 1994, Prosodia, 1994, Visions, 1994, Prophecies, 1994, Epyllia, 1994, Budapesttol Tokyoig, 1994, 2d edit., 1995, Walking Two Feet Above the Earth, 1995, Dictionarium Cumanico Hungaricum, 1996, Emblems, 1996, Epodes, 1996, Aeolian Lilts, 1996, Transformations, 1996, Inexpressions, 1996, Songs of the Soul, 1996, Sacrifices, 1996, Gifts with Poetic Horizons, 1997, Imperceptions, Hermeneutics of Poetry, 1997, From Silence to Silence, New Perspectives in Poetry, 1997, numerous others, also translations; editor-in-chief Monumenta Classica Perennia, 1967-84. Named Poet Laureate 2d World Congress of Poets, 1973; recipient Confucius award Chinese Poetry Soc., 1974, Yunus Emre award 12th Internat. Congress of Poets, Istanbul, Turkey, 1991, Jacques Raphael-Leygues prize Société des Poètes Français, 1992, French Ordre des Arts et des Lettres (officer), 1992. Mem. PEN, ASCAP, Internat. Soc. Lit., Die Literarische Union, Internat. Poetry Soc., Acad. Am. Poets, Assn. Lit. Scholars and Critics, 3d Internat. Congress Poets (pres. 1976, poet laureate 1976). Office: Fedn Internat Poetry Assns PO Box 579 Santa Claus IN 47579-0579

PLATTI, RITA JANE, educator, draftsman, author, inventor; b. Stockton, Calif., Aug. 29, 1925; d. Umbert Ferdinand and Concettina Maria (Natoli) Strangio; m. Elvin Carl Platti, July 27, 1955; 1 child, Kimberley Jane. Student, Dominican Coll., 1943-45; AB in Math, U. Pacific, 1947, postgrad., 1947-52, 68. Farmer, almond grower Escalon, Calif., 1943—; tchr. math St. Mary's High Sch., Stockton, 1947-49, 52, 54; chem. analyst Petri Winery, Escalon, 1949; draftsman Kyle Steel Co., Stockton, 1950-52; pvt. practice as draftsman Stockton, 1952-66; tchr. math Montezuma Sch., Stockton, 1956-57, Davis Elem. Sch., Stockton, 1957-58; with rental bus., 1958-81; tchr. math Amos Alonzo Stagg High Sch., 1961-80, Humphreys Coll., 1981-83, Hamilton Jr. High Sch., 1984-90; owner, involved in prodn. and mktg. R.J. Creations, 1991—; farm realtor Century 21, Escalon, Calif., 1996-97; spkr. workshops Stanislaus State U., 1992, Calif. Math. Coun., Fresno State U., 1992, Nat. Sci. Found. Conf., 1993; spkr. math./sci. conf. Calif. State U., Bakerfield, 1994-96; evaluator Math. Framework (K-12) Calif. State Dept. Edn. Author: Math Proficiency Plateaus, 1979, Preparing Fundamentals of The Use of Sound in the Teaching of Mathematics, 1994; author, pub. series, 1979-86; 3 patents in field. Mem. NEA, Calif. Tchrs. Assn. Democrat. Roman Catholic. Avocations: inventing, mathematics theoretical development, poetry, piano, environmental clean up.

PLATTS, FRANCIS HOLBROOK, plastics engineer; b. Brunson, S.C., Sept. 15, 1939; s. Holbrook Trowbridge and Mildred Ruth (Thomar) P.; m. Martha Ann Price, July 1963; children: Martha Susan Platts Gilliam, David Holbrook. BS in Chem. Engring., U. S.C., 1962. Chem. engr. U.S. Naval Weapons Lab., Dahlgren, Va., 1962-64; engr. Westinghouse Electric Corp., Hampton, S.C., 1964-74, sr. engr., 1974-89, mgr. engring. and quality assurance, 1989-91, mgr. design and mktg. svcs., 1991-93, div. engr. mgr., 1993-95; engr. mgr. Internat. Paper Co., Hampton, S.C., 1995—; chmn. NEMA DLATC Engring. Com., Washington, 1991—; mem., chair Color Mktg. Group, Alexandria, Va., 1991—. Pres., mem. Hampton Jaycees, 1964-74; chmn., bd. dirs. Hampton County Watermelon Festival, 1965-76; mem., chmn. blood bank bd. South Atlantic region ARC, Savannah, Ga., 1974-96; mem. Western Carolina Higher Edn. Com., Allendale, 1982—; co-chmn. econ. devel. com. Pro-Hampton County, 1996—. Mem. ASTM (E-5 com. 1972—), Hampton Rotary (sr. mem., pres. 1981, Outstanding Mem. award 1982, Paul Harris fellow), Hampton Gamecock Club (pres. 1966—). Methodist. Achievements include development of decorative high-pressure laminate specialty product, research on color and design trends for interior finish applications; research and development on composites. Office: International Paper Co PO Box 248 Hampton SC 29924-0248

PLATTS, HOWARD GREGORY, scientific/educational organization executive; b. N.Y.C., Aug. 14, 1947; s. Thayer Horton and Anne Elizabeth (Gregory) P.; m. Elizabeth Hertzler Murray, June 7, 1969; children—James Thayer, Christopher Wilke. A.B., Harvard U., 1969; M. Pub. and Pvt. Mgmt., Yale U., 1980. Tchr., Potomac Sch., McLean, Va., 1969-72; investment officer First Am. Bank, Washington, 1972-78; fin. analyst Yale U., New Haven, 1979; fin. asst. to pres. Nat. Geog. Soc., Washington, 1980-82, asst. treas., 1982-91, v.p., treas., 1992—. Treas., bd. dirs. Edes Home Found., Washington, 1975-78; bd. trustees Nat. Presbyn. Sch., Washington, 1988-91; vice chmn., bd. trustees regional blood svcs. ARC, Balt., 1992—; treas., bd. dirs. Friends of Fort Dupont, Washington, 1995—; vice chmn. Decatur House Coun., Washington, 1994—. Mem. Washington Soc. Investment Analysts (pres., bd. dirs. 1985-91), Assn. Investment Mgmt. and Rsch. Clubs: Alfalfa (treas., bd. dirs. 1992—), Alibi (Washington), Bulldog Hockey (treas., bd. dirs. 1993—), Metropolitan (Washington, bd. govs.); Chevy Chase (Md.), Congregational (trustee 1988-91). Home: 5302 Portsmouth Rd Bethesda MD 20816-2929 Office: Nat Geog Soc 1145 17th St NW Washington DC 20036-4701

PLATTS-MILLS, THOMAS ALEXANDER E., immunologist, educator, researcher; b. Colchester, Essex, Eng., Nov. 22, 1941; came to U.S., 1982; s. John Faithful F. and Janet Katherine (Cree) P.-M.; m. Roberta Rosenstock, Apr. 9, 1970; children: Eliza, Timothy, James, Oliver. BA, Balliol Coll., Oxford (Eng.) U., 1963; MB, BChir, Oxford U., 1967; PhD, London U., 1982. Registrar in medicine Bury St. Edmunds, and New Market, Suffolk, Eng., 1968-71; fellow in medicine Johns Hopkins U., Balt., 1971-74; staff mem. Med. Rsch. Coun., U.K., 1976-82; hon. cons. physician Northwick Park Hosp., London, 1978-82; prof. medicine, head div. allergy and clin. immunology U. Va., Charlottesville, 1982—, dir. Asthma and Allergic Diseases Ctr., 1994; mem. immunological scis. study sect. NIH, 1988. Editl. bd. Am. Jour. Respiratory Critical Care Medicine, Clin. and Exptl. Immunology, Clin. Allergy, Jour. Immunological Methods; contbr. articles to profl. jours. Grantee NIH. Fellow Royal Coll. Physicians, Am. Acad. Allergy; mem. Assn. Am. Physicians, Am. Acad. Allergy, Asthma & Immunology (bd. dirs. 1995—), Southeastern Allergy Assn. (Hal Davidson award 1986, pres. 1987-88), Brit. Soc. Allergy and Clin. Immunology. Office: U Va Dept Medicine PO Box 225 Charlottesville VA 22902-0225

PLATZ, TERRANCE OSCAR, utilities company executive; b. Cadillac, Mich., Jan. 20, 1943; s. Jay and Gladys Pearl (Bigelow) P.; m. Nellie Mae Cross, Dec. 15, 1961 (div. Oct. 1977); children: Michael, Christopher, Michelle; m. Dorothy Fay Beasley, Aug. 4, 1984. AS in Electronics Engring. Tech., Pensacola Jr. Coll., 1972. Enlisted USN, 1962, resigned, 1981; adj. instr. in electronics Pensacola (Fla.) Jr. Coll., 1981—; instrument/elec. control technician Escambia County Utilities Authority, Pensacola, 1981-87, instrument/elec. control supr., 1987-94, instrument/elec. mgr., elec. engr., 1994—; instrument controls advisor/cons. to various engring. firms, 1987—. Mem. Instrument Soc. Am. Democrat. Mem. Ch. of God. Achievements include design of cost saving variable speed drive systems, instrument control systems, SCADA systems, wastewater treatment plants, water wells, sewage lift stations, continuous emissions monitoring systems, data acquisition systems. Home: 5045 Bankhead Dr Pensacola FL 32526-9413 Office: Escambia County Utilities Authority 401 W Government St Pensacola FL 32501-5572

PLATZMAN, GEORGE WILLIAM, geophysicist, educator; b. Chgo., Apr. 19, 1920; s. Alfred and Rose I. P.; m. Harriet M. Herschberger, Feb. 19, 1945 (dec. 1985). BS, U. Chgo., 1940, PhD, 1948; MS, U. Ariz., 1941. Instr. U. Chgo., 1942-45, rsch. assoc., 1947-48, faculty, 1949—, head phys. scis. in coll., 1959-60, prof. meteorology, 1960-90, chmn. dept. geophys. scis., 1971-74, emeritus prof., 1990—; cons. Inst. Advanced Study, Princeton, 1950-53. Contbr. articles to profl. jours. Hydrologic engr. C.E., U.S. Army, 1945-46. Guggenheim fellow, 1967-68. Fellow AAAS, Am. Geophys. Union, Am. Meteorol. Soc. (editor jour. 1948-49, chmn. publs. com. 1966-70, Meisinger award 1966). Office: U Chgo Dept Geophys Scis 5734 S Ellis Ave Chicago IL 60637-1434

PLAUD, JOSEPH JULIAN, psychology educator; b. Worcester, Mass., Mar. 25, 1965; s. Henry Emile and Barbara Ann (Perry) P.; m. Christine Marie Therlault, Mar. 14, 1987 (div. Mar. 1990); 1 child, Brianna Marie; m.

Nancy Denise Vogeltanz, Nov. 25, 1994. BA summa cum laude, Clark U., 1987; PhD in Psychology, U. Maine, 1993. Lic. clin. psychologist, N.D. Psychology resident U. Miss. Med. Ctr., Jackson, 1992-93; asst. prof. psychology U. N.D., Grand Forks, 1993—; cons. N.D. Devel. Ctr., Grafton, 1994—. Author: From Behavior Theory to Behavior Therapy, 1997; editor-in-chief Jour. Behavioral Analysis and Therapy; contbr. articles to profl. jours. Lt. Med. Svc. Corps, USNR, 1997. Fellow Behavior Therapy and Rsch. Soc. (clin.); mem. AAAS, Assn. for Advancement of Behavior Therapy, Am. Psychol. Soc., Am. Psychol. Assn., Phi Beta Kappa, Psi Chi. Democrat. Roman Catholic. Home: 1606 S 15th St Grand Forks ND 58201-5326 Office: U ND Dept Psychology PO Box 8380 Grand Forks ND 58202

PLAUT, ERIC ALFRED, retired psychiatrist, educator; b. N.Y.C., Nov. 16, 1927; s. Alfred and Margaret (Blumenfeld) P.; m. Eloine Raab, Sept. 5, 1976. B.S., Columbia U., 1949, M.D., 1953. Diplomate: Am. Bd. Psychiatry and Neurology. Intern Montefiore Hosp., Bronx, N.Y., 1953-54; psychiat. resident State Hosp., Worcester, Mass., 1954-55, Mass. Meml. Hosp., Boston, 1955-57; cons. psychiatrist Mass. Dept. Corrections, 1957; fellow student health psychiatry U. Calif., Berkeley, 1957-58; practice medicine specializing in psychiatry Berkeley, 1958-74; staff psychiatrist Kaiser Hosp., Oakland, Calif., 1958-62, Cowell Meml. Hosp., U. Calif., Berkeley, 1958-62; cons. psychiatrist Bur. Indian Affairs, Dept. Interior, 1967-68; program chief Berkeley Mental Health Services, 1968-71; dep. commr. Ind. Dept. Mental Health, Indpls., 1974-76; commr. Conn. Dept. Mental Health, Hartford, 1976-81; prof. Northwestern U. Med. Sch., Chgo., 1981-93, prof. emeritus, 1994—; asst. clin. prof. psychiatry U. Calif. Med. Sch., San Francisco, 1958-74; asso. clin. prof. psychiatry U. Ind. Med. Sch., Indpls., 1975-76; clin. prof. psychiatry U. Conn. Med. Sch., Farmington, 1978-81, Yale U. Med. Sch., 1979-81; cons. Assembly Sci. Adv. Coun., Calif. Legislature, 1970; chmn. Bay Area region Calif. Conf. Local Mental Health Dirs., 1970-71; gen. ptnr. Vanguard Investments, Berkeley, 1971-78. Author: Grand Opera: Mirror of the Western Mind, 1993; mem. editl. bd. Yale Psychiat. Quar., 1976-81; sect. editor Northeast Univ. Press, 1991—; contbr. articles to profl. jours. Bd. dirs. ACLU, Berkeley, 1960-65; mem. task force on access and barrier Pres.'s Commn. on Mental Health, 1977; mem. psychiatry panel Grad. Med. Edn. Nat. Adv. Com., 1979-81. With USN, 1944-46. Fellow Am. Psychiat. Assn. (cons. task force on govt. rels. 1973-76, chmn. com. public info. 1975-76, mem. com. cert. in adminstrv. psychiatry 1979-82, chmn. task force on problems of Americans overseas 1984-88, chmn. task force on joint meeting with German Psychiat. Soc., 1989-90); mem. com. Chron. Ment. Ill; mem. No. Calif. Psychiat. Soc. (chmn. com. law and legis. 1968-72, fed. legis. rep. 1972-74, councillor 1972-73, pres.-elect 1973-74), Calif. Med. Assn. (alt. del. 1968-71), Alameda-Contra Costa Med. Assn. (chmn. mental health com. 1972), Conn. Med. Soc., Nat. Assn. State Mental Health Program Dirs. (dir.). Address: 912 Michigan Ave Evanston IL 60202-1425

PLAUT, JONATHAN VICTOR, rabbi; b. Chgo., Oct. 7, 1942; s. W. Gunther and Elizabeth (Strauss) P.; m. Carol Ann Fainstein, July 5, 1965; children: Daniel Abraham, Deborah Maxine. BA, Macalester Coll., 1964; postgrad., Hebrew Union Coll., Jerusalem, 1967-68; BHL, Hebrew Union Coll., Cin., 1968, MA, 1970, DHL, 1995; DD, Hebrew Union Coll., 1995. Ordained rabbi, 1970. Rabbi Congregation Beth-El, Windsor, Ont., Can., 1970-84; sr. rabbi Temple Emanu-El, San Jose, Calif., 1985-93; dir. comty. outreach and involvement Jewish Fed. of Met. Detroit, 1993-95; pres. JUP Fund Raising Cons., Inc., Farmington Hills, Mich., 1994—; lectr. Assumption Coll. Sch., 1972-84, St. Clair Coll., 1982-84, U. Windsor, Ont., Can., 1984; adj. asst. prof. Santa Clara U., 1985-93; vis. Rabbinic scholar Temple Beth El, 1993—; pres. JVP Fund Raising Cons., 1994—. Contbg. author: Reform Judaism in America: A Biographical Dictionary and Sourcebook, 1993; editor: Through the Sound of Many Voices, 1982, Jour. Can. Jewish Hist. Soc., 1976-83; also articles; host weekly program Religious Scope, Sta. CBET-TV, Religion in News, Sta. CKWW, 1971-84. Pres. Jewish Nat. Fund Windsor, 1978-81, chmn. bd. dirs., 1981-84; chmn. United Jewish Appeal Windsor, 1981-83, State of Israel Bonds, Windsor, 1980; nat. bd. dirs. Jewish Nat. Fund Can., 1972-84; pres. Reform Rabbis of Can., 1982-84; bd. dirs. Can. Jewish Congress, 1978-84, Jewish Family Svc. Santa Clara County, 1987-90, Jewish Fedn. Greater San Jose, 1986-93; chaplain San Jose Fire Dept., 1987-93; mem. exec. cabinet United Jewish Appeal, Windsor, 1971-84, mem. nat. rabbinic cabinet, 1993-95; mem. exec. com. Windsor Jewish Community Coun., 1970-84, chmn. 1975-84; mem. adv. coun. Riverview unit Windsor Hosp. Ctr., 1972-81; pres. Credit Counselling Svc. Met. Windsor, 1977-79. Honoree Jewish Nat. Fund, 1985. Mem. NCCJ, Can. Jewish Congress (nat. exec. bd. 1978-84), Can. Jewish Hist. Soc. (nat. v.p. 1974-84), Calif. Bd. Rabbis, Rabbinic Assn. Greater San Jose (chmn. 1986-87), Ctrl. Conf. Am. Rabbis, Nat. Assn. Temple Educators. Home & Office: 30208 Kingsway Dr Farmington Hills MI 48331-1648

PLAUT, WOLF GUNTHER, minister, author; b. Muenster, Germany, Nov. 1, 1912; emigrated to U.S., 1935, arrived in Canada, 1961; s. Jonas and Selma (Gumprich) P.; m. Elizabeth Strauss, Nov. 10, 1938; children: Jonathan, Judith. LLB, U. Berlin, 1933, JD, 1934; MHL, Hebrew Union Coll., Cin., 1939, DD, 1964; LLD, U. Toronto, 1978; DLitt, Cleve. Coll. Jewish Studies, 1979; LLD, York U., 1987. Ordained rabbi, 1939. Rabbi B'nai Abraham Zion, Chgo., 1939-48, Mt. Zion Temple, St. Paul, 1948-61; sr. rabbi Holy Blossom Temple, Toronto, Ont., Can., 1961-77; sr. scholar Holy Blossom Temple, 1978—; adj. prof. York U., 1991—. Author: Mount Zion, 1956, The Jews in Minnesota, 1959, The Book of Proverbs: A Commentary, 1961, Judaism and the Scientific Spirit, 1962, The Rise of Reform Judaism, 1963, The Growth of Reform Judaism, 1964, The Case for the chosen People, 1965, Your Neighbour Is a Jew, 1967, Page 2, 1971, Genesis: A Modern Commentary, 1974, Time to Think, 1977, Hanging Threads, 1978, (U.S. title) The Man in the Blue vest, 1980, Numbers: A Modern Commentary, 1979; editor, chief author: The Torah: A Modern Commentary, 1981, 10th edit., 1995, Unfinished Business (autobiography), 1981, Refugee Determination in Canada, 1985, The Letter, 1986, The Magen David: How the Six Pointed Star Became the Jewish Symbol, 1991, The Man Who Would be Messiah, 1988, 2d edit., 1990, Asylum--A Moral Dilemma, 1995, The Haftorah Commentary, 1996, More Unfinished Business, 1997; co-author: The Rabbi's Manual, 1988; editor: Affirmation, 1981-87; co-editor: Teshuvot of the Nineties, 1997; editl. contbr. Toronto Globe and Mail, 1962-94, Can. Jewish News; bibliography pub. in Through the Sound of Many Voices, 1982; contbr. to encys., anthologies, other books, articles to mags., newspapers. Chmn. Minn. Gov.'s Commn. on Ethics in Govt., 1958-61 ; pres. St. Paul Gallery and Sch. Art (name changed to Minn. Mus.), 1953-59, World Federalists Can., 1966-68; nat. pres. Can. Jewish Congress, 1977-80; vice chmn. Ont. Human Rights Commn., 1978-85; bd. govs. World Union for Progressive Judaism, 1970— pres. Central Conf. Am. Rabbis, 1983-85, bd. inquiry human rights cases, 1987—. Capt. AUS, 1943-46. Decorated Bronze Star; named officer Order of Can.; awarded Order of Ont.; Plaut Chair for Project Mgmt. established in his honor at Ben-Gurion U., Israel, 1991, Plaut Manor (pub.-assisted housing project) named in his and his wife's honor, Toronto. Clubs: York Racquets, Oakdale Golf and Country. Office: 1950 Bathurst St, Toronto, ON Canada M5P 3K9

PLAVINSKAYA, ANNA DMITRIEVNA, artist; b. Moscow, Nov. 26, 1960; came to U.S., 1989, naturalized, 1995; d. Dmitri Petrovich and Nina Nicolaevna; m. Gennady Ioffe, Jan 9, 1988 (div. July 1993). Diploma in Costume Design, Theatrical Art Coll., Moscow, 1976-80. Costume designer Evgeny Vahtangov Theater, Moscow, 1980-82; artist freelance Moscow, 1983-89; artist restorator pvt. studio, N.Y.C., 1990-93; artist freelance N.Y.C., 1993—. Exhibited in group shows at art colls., Moscow (hon. mention 1977), Gallery of Moscow Artists, 1983, Ctrl. Exhbn. Hall, Moscow, 1984, 88, Kuznetzky Most Gallery, Moscow, 1985, Tbilisi Acad. of Art, Georgia, 1986, Tallinna Moepaevad '87, Tallinn, Estonia, 1987 (hon. mention), Remizovo St. Gallery, Moscow, 1988, Pushkin Sq. Gallery, Moscow, 1988, The Textile Art Ctr., Chgo., 1991, The Russian Nobility Assn., N.Y.C., 1991, 11th Cleveland Internat. Drawing Biennale, Middlesbrough, Eng., 1993 (2nd prize award), BWA Gallery, Wroclaw, Poland, 1994, BWA Gallery, Lublin, Poland, 1994, EL Gallery, Elblag, Poland, 1994, Tatraniska Gallery, Poprad, Tatry, Slovakia, 1994, State Gallery, Ostrova, Czech Republic, 1994, Arts Botanica '94, Port Royal Mus. Gallery, Naples, Fla., 1994, Art Addiction Gallery, Stockholm, 1996 (hon. mention), 97; represented in permanent collections Cleveland Contemporary Art Collection, Middlesbrough, Eng., Zimmerli Art Mus., Norton T. Dodge Collection, N.J. Russian Orthodox. Avocations: fashion design, antique textile restoration. Home: 815 W 181 St Apt 3E New York NY 10033

PLAVSIC, BRANKO MILENKO, radiology educator; b. Zagreb, Yugoslavia, Croatia, Feb. 14, 1947; came to U.S., 1989; s. Milenko and Nevenka P.; m. Valerie H. Drnovsek, Aug. 26, 1991. MD, U. Zagreb, 1972, MS, 1974, PhD, 1975. Asst. prof. U. Zagreb, 1986, prof. radiology, chief abdominal radiology, 1988; prof. radiology, vice-chmn., dir. abdominal radiol./rsch. Tulane U., New Orleans, 1991—. Co-author: (with A.E. Robinson, R.B. Jeffrey) Gastrointestinal Radiology: A Concise Text, 1992; contbr. articles to profl. jours. Avocations: poetry, music. Home: 4460 Lennox Blvd New Orleans LA 70131-8348 Office: Tulane U Med Ctr Dept Radiology 1430 Tulane Ave New Orleans LA 70112-2699

PLAWECKI, JUDITH ANN, nursing educator; b. East Chicago, Ind., June 5, 1943; d. Joseph Lawrence and Anne Marilyn (Hamnik) Curosh; m. Henry Martin Plawecki, June 10, 1967; children: Martin H., Lawrence H. BS, St. Xavier Coll., Chgo., 1965; MA, U. Iowa, 1971; PhD, 1974. Asst. prof. Mt. Mercy Coll., Cedar Rapids, Iowa, 1971-73; asst. dept. chmn., assoc. prof., 1974-75; assoc. prof. U. Iowa, 1975-76; asst. dean, assoc. prof. U. Minn., 1976-81; acting dean, assoc. dean and prof. U. N.D., Grand Forks, 1981-82, dean and prof. nursing, 1982-83; dean and prof. nursing Lewis U., Romeoville, Ill., 1983-87; dean U. South Fla., Tampa, 1987-95, prof. nursing, 1987—. Univ. Iowa Fellow, 1973. Mem. ANA, AHNA, Nat. League for Nursing, Older Women's League, Sigma Xi, Sigma Phi Omega, Sigma Theta Tau, Phi Lambda Theta. Office: U South Fla Coll Nursing MDC 22 12901 Bruce B Downs Blvd Tampa FL 33612-4742

PLAYER, GARY JIM, professional golfer, businessman, golf course designer; b. Johannesburg, South Africa, Nov. 1, 1935; s. Francis Harry Audley and Muriel (Ferguson) P; m. Vivienne Verwey, Jan. 19, 1957; children: Jennifer, Marc, Wayne, Michele, Theresa, Amanda. Ed., King Edward Sch., Johannesburg; LLD (hon.), St. Andrews U., Scotland, 1995. Profl. golfer, 1953—; joined PGA, 1957—; winner East Rand Open, Republic of South Africa, 1955-56, Egyptian Matchplay, 1955, South African Open, 1956, 60, 65-69, 72, 75-77, 79, 81, Dunlop Tournament, Eng., 1956, Ampol Tournament, Australia, 1956, 58, 61, Australian PGA, 1957, Coughs Harbour Tournament, Australia, 1957-58, Natal Open, South Africa, 1958-60, 62, 66, 68, Ky. Derby Open, 1958, Australian Open, 1958, 62-63, 65, 69-70, 74, Transvaal Open, South Africa, 1959, 60, 62, 63, 66, South African PGA, 1959-60, 69, 79, 82, Western Province Open, South Africa, 1959-60, 68, 71-72, Dunlop Masters, South Africa, 1959-60, 63-64, 67, 71-74, 76-77, Brit. Open, 1959, 68, 74, Victoria Open, Australia, 1959, Masters Tournament, U.S., 1961, 74, 78, Lucky Internat. Open, U.S., 1961, Sunshine Open, U.S., 1961, Yomiuri Open, Japan, 1961, PGA Championship, U.S., 1962, 72, Sponsored 5000, South Africa, 1963, Liquid Air Tournament, South Africa, 1963; winner Richelieu Grand Prix, Capetown, 1963, Johannesburg, 1963; winner San Diego Open, 1963, Pensacola Open, 1964, 500 Festival Open, U.S., 1964, U.S. Open (1st foreigner to win in 45 yrs.), 1965, Piccadilly World Match Play, Eng., 1965, 66, 68, 71, 73, NTL Challenge Cup, Can., 1965, World Series of Golf, U.S., 1965, 68, 72, World Cup Internat., 1965, Australian Wills Masters, 1968, 69, Tournament of Champions, U.S., 1969, 78, Greater Greensboro Open, 1970, Dunlop Internat., Australia, 1970, Gen. Motors Open, South Africa, 1971, 73, 74, 75, 76, Jacksonville Open, 1971, Nat. Airlines Open, U.S., 1971, New Orleans Open, 1972, Japan Airlines Open, 1972, Brazilian Open, 1972, 74, So. Open, U.S., 1973, Rand Internat. Open, South Africa, 1974, Gen. Motors Internat. Classic, South Africa, 1974, Memphis Classic, 1974, Ibergolf Tournament, Spain, 1974, La Manga Tournament, Spain, 1974, Gen. Motors Classic, 1975, ICL Transvaal, South Africa, 1977, World Cup Individual, Philippines, 1977, Houston Open, 1978, Kronenbrau Masters, South Africa, 1979, Sun City, S. Am., 1979, Trophee Boigny, Ivory Coast, 1980, Chilean Open, S. Am., 1980, Australian Tooth Gold Coast Classic, 1981, Johnnie Walker Trophy, Spain, 1984, Quadel Srs. Classic, 1985, PGA Srs. Championship, 1986, 88, 90, Northville Srs., 1987, Sr. Tournament, 1987, U.S. Sr. Open, 1987, 88, Sr. Players Championship, 1990, Aetna Challenge, 1988, Southwestern Bell Classic, 1988, USGA Srs., 1988, Sr. British Open, 1988, 90, Sr. PGA Bank One Classic, 1993, 95; chair Gary Player Group. 3rd man in history to win Grand Slam of Golf; winner over 150 internat. golf tournaments, 22 Sr. Tour tournaments; named Christian Athlete of Yr. So. Bapt. Conv., 1967, Sportsman of the Year in South Africa, 1955, 56, 59, 61, 63, 65, 72, 74, 78, South African Sportsman of the Century, 1990; Richardson award Golf Writers Assn. Am., 1975; named to World Golf Hall of Fame, 1974; hon. mem. R&A, 1994, Skills Challenge, 1994. Avocations: thoroughbred horse breeding, farming, fitness, health, diet. Office: Gary Player Group 3930 Rca Blvd Ste 3001 West Palm Beach FL 33410-4214 Office: PO Box 785629, Sandton 2146, South Africa

PLAYER, THELMA B., librarian; b. Owosso, Mich.; d. Walter B. and Grace (Willoughby) Player; B.A., Western Mich. U., 1954. Reference asst. USAF Aero. Chart & Info. Center, Washington, 1954-57; reference librarian U.S. Navy Hydrographic Office, Suitland, Md., 1957-58; asst. librarian, 1958-59; tech. library br. head U.S. Navy Spl. Project Office, Washington, 1959-68, Strategic Systems Project Office, 1969-76. Mem. ALA, Spl. Libraries Assn., D.C. Library Assn., AAUW, Canterbury Cathedral Trust in Am., Nat. Geneal. Soc., Internat. Soc. Brit. Genealogy and Family History, Ohio Geneal. Soc., Royal Oak Found., Daus. of Union Vets. of Civil War. Episcopalian. Home: 730 24th St NW Washington DC 20037-2543

PLAZEK, DONALD JOHN, materials science educator; b. Milw., Jan. 12, 1931; s. Stanley and Marian (Parker) P.; m. Patricia Lenore Filkins, Oct. 29, 1955; children: Mary, Joseph, Caroline, Daniel, John, David, Anne. BS in Chemistry, U. Wis., 1953, PhD in Phys. Chemistry, 1957. Postdoctoral rsch. fellow U. Wis., Madison, 1957-58; fellow Mellon Inst., Pitts., 1958-67; assoc. prof. materials engring. U. Pitts., 1967-74, prof., 1974-93, prof. emeritus, 1993—; adj. prof. chemistry Carnegie-Mellon U., Pitts., 1987—; mem. adv. bd. Jour. Polymer Sci., 1991—. Assoc. editor Rubber Chemistry and Tech., 1993—; contbr. papers to profl. publs., chpts. to books. Brit. Rsch. Coun. sr. vis. fellow U. Glasgow, Scotland, 1976-77, Japan Soc. for Promotion of Sci. fellow, 1987-88, Bingham medal Soc. of Rheology, 1995. Fellow Am. Phys. Soc.; mem. Am. Chem. Soc. (George Stafford Whitby award for disting. tchg. & rsch. Rubber Divsn. 1993), Soc. Rheology (Bingham Medal, 1995). Avocations: tennis, tropical fish, mushrooms. Office: U Pitts Materials Sci Engring Dept Pittsburgh PA 15261

PLEACHER, DAVID HENRY, secondary school educator; b. Reading, Pa., Dec. 29, 1946; s. John K. and Isabel Kathleen (Moyer) P.; m. Carol Elizabeth Jackson, June 8, 1968; children: Amy Elizabeth, Michael David, Sarah Catherine. BA in Math., Hartwick Coll., 1968; MS in Edn., James Madison U., 1971. Cert. tchr., Va. Tchr. Arlington (Va.) County Pub. Schs., 1968, Fairfax County Pub. Schs., Herndon, Va., 1968-73; tchr., dept. chair Winchester (Va.) City Schs., 1973—; instr. James Madison U., Harrisonburg, Va., 1982-87; lectr., instr. Lord Fairfax C.C., Middletown, Va., 1986-89; project mem. Computer Software Devel. Project, 1985-90; participant Math. Inst. Woodrow Wilson Found., Princeton, 1986. Co-editor: (computer column) Va. Math. Tchr., 1982-84; author computer programs; contbr. articles to profl. jours. Recipient Presdl. award in excellence in math and sci. teaching NSF, Washington, 1985, Homer "Pete" Ice Svc. award Handley High Athletic Dept., 1991, Tandy Tech. Scholars award Tandy Corp./T.C.U., Washington, 1992. Mem. NEA (life), Va. Edn. Assn., Winchester Edn. Assn., Nat. Coun. Tchrs. Math. (presenter at confs.), Va. Coun. Tchrs. Math. (presenter at confs., William Lowry Outstanding Math Tchr. 1987), Valley Va. Coun. Tchrs. Math., Math. Assn. Am., Coun. Presdl. Awardees in Math. Presbyterian. Avocations: model railroading, sports, games, computer programming. Home: 304 Caroline Ave Stephens City VA 22655 Office: John Handley High Sch PO Box 910 Winchester VA 22604-0910

PLEASANT, JAMES SCOTT, lawyer; b. Anniston, Ala., July 14, 1943; s. James C. and Barbara (Scott) P.; m. Susan M. Pleasant, May 17, 1966; children: Deborah Kaye, Carol Ann, Julie Ruth. BS, Oreg. State U., 1965; JD summa cum laude, Williamette U., 1972. Bar: Tex. 1972, U.S. Dist. Ct. (no. dist.) Tex. 1973, U.S. Ct. Appeals (5th cir.) 1975, U.S. Supreme Ct. 1977. Ptnr. Gardere & Wynne LLP, Dallas, 1972—. Mem. Smithsonian Assn., Washington, 1985—, Dallas Mus. of Art, 1987—. Capt. U.S. Army, 1966-69, Vietnam. Mem. ABA (partnership law sect. 1969—), Tex. Bar Assn. (partnership law sect. 1989—), Vietnam Pilots Assn., Dustoff Assn. Office: Gardere & Wynne LLP 1601 Elm St Ste 3000 Dallas TX 75201-4757

PLEASANTS, HENRY, music critic; b. Wayne, Penn., May 12, 1910; s. Henry and Elizabeth Washington (Smith) P.; m. Virginia V. Duffey, Aug. 31, 1940. Student, Phila. Music Acad., Curtis Inst. Music; D.M. (hon.), Curtis Inst. Music, 1977. Music critic Phila. Evening Bulletin, 1930-42; Central European music corr. N.Y. Times, 1945-55; with U.S. Fgn. Service, Munich, 1950-52, Bern, 1952-56, Bonn, 1956-64; London music critic Internat. Herald Tribune, Paris, 1967—; London editor Stereo Review, N.Y.C., 1967—; lectr. in field. Appearances on T.V., U.K., U.S.A., Europe.; Author: The Agony of Modern Music, 1955, Death of a Music?, 1961, The Great Singers, 1966, Serious Music-And All That Jazz!, 1969, The Great American Popular Singers, 1974; translator, editor various books in field; contbr. articles to musical, lit. jours. Served in U.S. Army, 1942-50, Alaska, ETO, NATOUSA. Decorated Bronze Star (twice). Mem. Authors Guild. Home: 95 Roebuck House, Palace St, London SW1E 5BE, England

PLEIN, KATHRYN ANNE, secondary educator; b. Ashland, Wis., Jan. 28, 1945; d. Donald and Frances (Tankersly) Smith; m. Arvid Arthur Plein, Dec. 19, 1970; children: Marty, Michelle. BS in Broadfield Sci., Northland Coll., 1967; MS in Teaching, U. Wis., Superior, 1973. Cert. secondary science tchr., Wis. 7th grade sci. tchr. Wausau (Wis.) Sch. Dist., 1967-73; tchr. John Muir Middle Sch., Wausau, 1977—. Mem. Wis. Soc. Sci. Tchrs., Nat. Sci. Tchr. Assn., AAUW (program v.p. 1995-97, past v.p. membership, pres.-elect 1997—). Roman Catholic. Home: R 8800 Hwy J Schofield WI 54476 Office: John Muir Middle Sch 1400 Stewart Ave Wausau WI 54401-4277

PLEMING-YOCUM, LAURA CHALKER, religion educator; b. Sheridan, Wyo., May 25, 1913; d. Sidney Thomas and Florence Theresa (Woodbury) Chalker; m. Edward Kibbler Pleming, Aug. 25, 1938 (dec. Nov. 1980); children: Edward Kibbler, Rowena Pleming Chamberlin, Sidney Thomas; m. William Lewis Yocum, Dec. 19, 1989 (dec. Apr. 1992). BA, Calif. State U., Long Beach, 1953, MA in Speech and Drama, 1954; postgrad., U. So. Calif., L.A., 1960-63; D Religion, Grad. Sch. Theology, Claremont, Calif., 1968. Internat. lectr. Bibl. studies, 1953—, adult seminar resource person, 1953—; Bibl. lectr. Principia Coll., Elsah, Ill., 1968-90; Bible scholar 1st Ch. of Christ, Scientist, Boston, 1970-75; tchr. adult edn. Principia Coll., summers, 1969-71; tour lectr. to Middle East, 1974—; mem. archaeol. team, Negev, Israel. Author: Triumph of Job, 1979; editor (newsletter) Bibleletter, 1968-84. Mem. AAUP, Am. Acad. Religion, Soc. Bibl. Lit. and Exegesis, Am. Schs. Oriental Rsch., Inst. Mediterranean Studies, Religious Edn. Assn., Internat. Platform Assn., Congress Septuagint and Cognate Studies, Religious Edn. Assn., Zeta Tau Alpha (alumni pres. Long Beach chpt. 1960), Gamma Theta Upsilon (pres. Long Beach chpt. 1952).

PLENTY, ROYAL HOMER, writer; b. Phila., Aug. 28, 1918; s. Royal Homer and Florence (Gehman) P.; m. Evelyn Treaster, Dec. 15, 1945 (dec. 1958); 1 dau., Evelyn Ann; m. Mildred Craig, Sept. 12, 1959 (div. 1970); m. Gladys Ann Muller, Nov. 14, 1970. B.S. in Econs, U. Pa., 1941. Clk. H.M. Byllesby & Co. (investment bankers), 1941; jr. underwriter New Amsterdam Casualty Co., 1941-42; reporter Phila. office Wall St. Jour., 1942-46; mem. staff Phila. Inquirer, 1946-72, financial editor, 1957-72; dir. pub. relations Levitz Furniture Corp., 1972-73; pub. relations account exec. Aitkin-Kynett Co., Inc., Phila., 1973-75; dir. pub. info. Securities Industry Assn., N.Y.C., 1975-77; corporate relations Merrill Lynch & Co., 1977-78; free-lance editor, writer, 1978—. Mem. Phila. Econ. Assn., Phila. Press Assn., Phila. Investment Traders Assn., Sigma Delta Chi. Unitarian. Home: Harrison Towers Apt 7P Somerset NJ 08873

PLESHETTE, SUZANNE, actress, writer; b. N.Y.C., Jan. 31; d. Eugene and Geraldine; m. Thomas Joseph Gallagher III, Mar. 16, 1968. Student, Sch. Performing Arts, Syracuse U., Finch Coll., Neighborhood Playhouse Sch. of Theatre. Founder, prin. The Bedside Manor (later div. of J.P. Stevens). Theatre debut in Truckline Cafe; star in Broadway prodns. Compulsion, The Cold Wind and the Warm, The Golden Fleecing, The Miracle Worker, Special Occasions; star TV series Bob Newhart Show, 1972-78, Suzanne Pleshette is Maggie Briggs, 1984; starred in TV series Bridges to Cross, 1986-87, Nightingales, 1988-89, The Boys Are Back, 1994-95, The Single Guy, 1996-97; star 30 feature films including The Birds, Forty Pounds of Trouble, If It's Tuesday This Must Be Belgium, Nevada Smith, Support Your Local Gunfighter, hot Stuff, Oh God! Book II; TV movies include Flesh and Blood, Starmaker, Fantasies, If Things Were Different, Help-Wanted Male, Dixie Changing Habits, One Cooks, The Other Doesn't, For Love or Money, Kojak, The Belarus file, A Stranger Waits, Alone in the Neon Jungle, Leona Helmsley: The Queen of Mean, 1990, Battling for Baby, 1991-92, A Twist of the Knife, 1993; writer, co-creator, producer two tV series; published author.

PLESKOW, ERIC ROY, motion picture company executive; b. Vienna, Austria; came to U.S., 1939; Film officer U.S. War Dept., 1946-48; asst. gen. mgr. Motion Picture Export Assn., Germany, 1948-50; continental rep. for Sol Lesser Prodns., 1950-51; with United Artists Corp., Far Eastern sales mgr., 1951-52, South African mgr., 1952-53, German mgr., 1953-58, exec. asst. to continental mgr., 1958-59, asst. continental mgr., 1959-60, continental mgr., 1960-62, v.p. in charge fgn. distbn., 1962, exec. v.p., chief operating officer, 1973, pres., chief exec. officer, 1973-78; pres., chief exec. officer Orion Pictures Co., N.Y.C., 1978-82; pres., chief exec. officer Orion Pictures Corp., N.Y.C., 1982-92, also chmn. bd. dirs., until 1992; ptnr. Pleskow/Spikings Partnership, Beverly Hills, Calif., 1992-95; prin. Pleskow Entertainment Inc., Santa Monica, Calif., 1995—. Office: Pleskow Entertainment Inc. 201 Ocean Ave Ste 1501-b Santa Monica CA 90402

PLESS, LAURANCE DAVIDSON, lawyer; b. Jacksonville, Fla., Dec. 22, 1952; s. James William Pless III and Anne (Dodson) Martin; m. Dana Halberg, June 20, 1980; children: Anna Amesbury, William Davidson, Deane Ahlgren. AB cum laude with distinction, Duke U., 1975; JD, U. N.C., Chapel Hill, 1980. Assoc. Neely & Player, P.C., Atlanta, 1980-86, ptnr., 1986-92; ptnr. Welch, Spell, Reemsnyder & Pless, P.C., Atlanta, 1992—. Contbr. articles to profl. jours.; mem. staff N.C. Law Rev. Vol. Saturday Vol. Lawyer's Found., Atlanta, 1980—. Mem. ABA, Lawyer's Club of Atlanta, Atlanta Bar Assn., Capital City Club, Lake Patrun Rabun Assn. Democrat. Episcopalian. Avocations: hiking, tennis, coaching kid's sports, canoeing. Home: 25 Palisades Rd NE Atlanta GA 30309-1530 Office: Welch Spell Reemsnyder & Pless 400 Colony Sq NE Ste 2020 Atlanta GA 30361-6305

PLESS, VERA, mathematics and computer science educator; b. Chgo., Mar. 5, 1931; d. Lyman and Helen (Blinder) Stepen; m. Irwin Pless, June 15, 1952 (div. 1980); children: Naomi, Benjamin, Daniel. PhD, U. Chgo., 1949, MS, 1952; PhD, Northwestern U., 1957. Mathematician USAF, Lincoln, Mass., 1962-72; rsch. assoc. MIT, Cambridge, Mass., 1972-75; prof. math. U. Ill., Chgo., 1975—. Author: The Theory of Error Correcting Codes, 1989; contbr. articles to profl. publs. U. Ill. scholar, 1989-92; recipient Tempo All-Professor Team, Sciences, Chicago Tribune, 1993. Mem. Am. Math. Soc. (chair nominating com. 1984), Math. Assn. Am., IEEE (bd. govs. 1985-89), Assn. Women in Math. Office: UIC MSCS (M/C 249) 851 S Morgan 322 SEO Chicago IL 60607-7045

PLETCHER, DAVID MITCHELL, history educator; b. Faribault, Minn., June 14, 1920; s. Nuba Mitchel and Jean (Hutchinson) P., B.A., U. Chgo., 1941, MA, 1941, PhD, 1946. Asst. U. Chgo., 1943; instr. history U. Iowa, 1944-46; asso. prof. Knox Coll., Galesburg, Ill., 1946-56; asso. prof., then prof. Hamline U., St. Paul, 1956-65; prof. history Ind. U., 1965-90, prof. emeritus, 1990—. Author: Rails, Mines and Progress, Seven American Promoters in Mexico, 1867-1911, 1958, The Awkward Years, American Foreign Relations Under Garfield and Arthur, 1962, The Diplomacy of Annexation, Texas, Oregon and the Mexican War, 1973. Recipient McKnight Found. award, 1962; grantee Social Sci. Research Found., 1950-51, 62-63; grantee Nat. Archives, 1972; Fulbright sr. research fellow, 1953-54. Mem. Orgn. Am. Historians, Am. Hist. Assn. (Albert J. Beveridge award 1957), Soc. Historians Am. Fgn. Relations (v.p. 1979, pres. 1980). Home: 509 N Fess Ave Bloomington IN 47408-3821 Office: Indiana Univ Dept History Ballantine Hall Bloomington IN 47405

PLETCHER, ELDON, editorial cartoonist; b. Goshen, Ind., Sept. 10, 1922; s. Arthur and Dora (Cripe) P.; m. Barbara Jeanne Jones, Jan. 29, 1948; children—Thomas Lee, Ellen Irene. Student, Chgo. Acad. Fine Arts, 1941-42, U. Aberdeen, Scotland, 1945, John Herron Art Sch., Indpls., 1946-47. Editorial cartoonist Sioux City (Iowa) Jour., 1949-66; editorial cartoonist The Times-Picayune, 1966-85; free-lance gag cartoonist Sat. Eve. Post, Rotarian, Nat. Enquirer, other publs. Rep. permanent exhbns., Syracuse U., U. South Miss., U. Cin., Boston Mus. Art, Harry S. Truman Library, Lyndon B. Johnson Library, Wichita State U., John F. Kennedy Libr., Richard M. Nixon Libr. Served with AUS, 1943-46. Recipient Christopher award, 1955, Freedoms Found. award, 12 years. Mem. Assn. Am. Editorial Cartoonists. Democrat. Presbyterian.

PLETCHER, JOHN HAROLD, JR., career officer; b. Findlay, Ohio, May 26, 1945; s. John H. and Bernadette (Gerschutz) P.; m. Phyllis G. Morrin, Jun. 7, 1968; children: Eric, Mary. BS in Aerospace Engring., USAF Acad., 1967; MS in Aerospace Engring., Ill. Inst. Tech., 1969; PhD in Mech. and Aerospace Engring., AF Inst. Tech., 1979. Registered prof. engr., Colo. Commd. 2d lt. USAF, 1967, advanced through grades to col., 1988; pilot 39th Rescue and Recovery Squadron, Cam Ranh AB, Vietnam, 1970-71; pilot and wing air ops. officer 41st Rescue and Recovery Wing, Hickam AFB, Hawaii, 1971-75; assoc. prof. aero., dir. academic ops. USAF Acad., Colorado Springs, Colo., 1978-82; chief systems engr. Aero. Systems Div., Wright Patterson AFB, Ohio, 1982-85; comdr. Frank J. Seiler Rsch. Lab., Colorado Springs, 1985-87; asst. dep. engring. Strategic Def. Initiative, Washington, 1987-90; dir. Armament Directorate, Eglin AFB, Fla., 1990-94; comdr. European Office of Aerospace Rsch. and Devel., London, 1994—. Youth soccer, T-ball coach Dayton, 1982-85. Mem. AIAA, AF Assn., AF Acad. Assn. of Grads. Roman Catholic. Avocations: squash, tennis, chess, gardening, fishing. Home: 7 Manor House Marylebone Rd, London NW1 5NP, England

PLETZ, THOMAS GREGORY, lawyer; b. Toledo, Oct. 3, 1943; s. Francis G. and Virginia (Connell) P.; m. Carol Elizabeth Connolly, June 27, 1969; children: Anne M., John F. BA, U. Notre Dame, 1965; JD, U. Toledo, 1971. Bar: Ohio 1971, U.S. Ct. Appeals (6th cir.) 1978, U.S. Supreme Ct. 1985. Ct. bailiff Lucas County Common Pleas Ct., Toledo, 1967-71; jud. clk. U.S. Dist. Ct. (no. dist.) Ohio, Toledo, 1971-72; assoc. Shumaker, Loop & Kendrick, Toledo, 1972-76, litigation ptnr., 1976—; acting judge Sylvania (Ohio) Mcpl. Ct., 1990—; mem. Ohio Bar Bd. Examiners, 1993—, chmn., 1996-97. mem. Toledo Parish Coun., 1987-93; chmn., trustee Kiroff Trial Adv. Com., Toledo, 1982-91. With USNR, 1965-92; ret. CDR. Recipient Toledo Jr. Bar award, 1995. Mem. ABA, Ohio State Bar Assn., Toledo Bar Assn. (trustee 1981-93), Diocesan Attys. Bar Assn., 6th Cir. Jud. Conf. (life). Roman Catholic. Office: Shumaker Loop & Kendrick 1000 Jackson St Toledo OH 43624-1515

PLEVAN, BETTINA B., lawyer; b. Oceanside, N.Y., Nov. 21, 1945. BA, Wellesley Coll., 1967; JD magna cum laude, Boston U., 1970. Bar: N.Y. 1971, U.S. Supreme Ct. 1977. Mem. Proskauer Rose Goetz & Mendelsohn, N.Y.C. Office: Proskauer Rose Goetz & Mendelsohn 1585 Broadway New York NY 10036-8200

PLIMPTON, CALVIN HASTINGS, physician, university president; b. Boston, Oct. 7, 1918; s. George Arthur and Fanny (Hastings) P.; m. Ruth Talbot, Sept. 6, 1941; children: David, Thomas, George (dec.), Anne, Edward. B.A. cum laude, Amherst Coll., 1939; M.D. cum laude, Harvard, 1943, M.A., 1947; Med. Sci.D., Columbia, 1951; LL.D., Williams Coll., 1960, Wesleyan U., 1961, Doshisha U., Kyoto, Japan, 1962, St. Lawrence U., 1963, Amherst U., 1971; L.H.D., U. Mass., 1962; D.Sc., Rockford Coll., 1962, St. Mary's, 1963, Trinity Coll., 1966, Grinnell (Iowa) Coll., 1967; Litt.D., Am. Internat. Coll., 1965, Mich. State Coll., 1969; DSc, N.Y. Med. Coll., 1986. Diplomate: Nat. Bd. Med. Examiners, Am. Bd. Internal Medicine. Intern, asst. resident, resident medicine Presbyn. Hosp., N.Y.C., 1947-50; asst. attending physician Columbia-Presbyn. Med. Center, 1950-60; asso. medicine (Coll. Phys. and Surg.), 1950-59, asst. prof. clin. medicine, 1959-60; prof. medicine, chmn. dept. Am. U. Beirut, Am. U. Hosp., Beirut, Lebanon, 1957-59; pres. Amherst Coll., 1960-71; pres. Downstate Med. Center, SUNY, 1971-79, dean med. sch., 1971-74, 76-79, prof. medicine, 1971-82, prof. emeritus, 1982—; pres. Am. U., Beirut, 1984-87; vis. prof. Columbia Presbyn. Med. Center, 1976-77. Trustee Am. U., Beirut, 1960-90, trustee emeritus, 1990—, chmn. bd., 1965-82; trustee World Peace Found., 1962-77, Phillips Exeter Acad., 1963-76, Commonwealth Fund, 1962-83, Hampshire Coll., 1963-71, U. Mass., 1962-70, L.I. U., 1972-82, N.Y. Law Sch., 1976-84; mem. Harvard Bd. Overseers, 1969-75. Capt. U.S. Army, 1944-46, ETO. Decorated comdr. Order of Cedars Lebanon; recipient award Nat. Geog. Soc., award New Eng. Soc., John Phillips award Phillip Exeter Acad. Fellow ACP; mem. Am. Acad. Arts and Scis., Coun. Fgn. Rels., Soc. Mayflower Descs., Harvey Soc., Alpha Omega Alpha, Sigma Xi. Clubs: Century, Univ. (N.Y.C.), Charaka (N.Y.C.), Riverdale Yacht (N.Y.C.), Pilgrims (N.Y.C.); Tavern Boston. Home and office: 4600 Palisade Ave Bronx NY 10471-3508

PLIMPTON, GEORGE AMES, writer, editor, television host; b. N.Y.C., Mar. 18, 1927; s. Francis T.P. and Pauline (Ames) P.; m. Freddy Medora Espy, 1968 (div. 1988); children: Medora Ames, Taylor Ames; m. Sarah Whitehead Dudley, 1991; children: Olivia Hartley, Laura Dudley. Student, Phillips Exeter Acad., 1944; A.B., Harvard U., 1948; M.A., Cambridge (Eng.) U., 1952; L.H.D. (hon.), Franklin Pierce Coll., 1968; Litt.D. (hon.), Hobart Smith Coll., 1978, Stonehill Coll., 1982, L.I.U., 1984, U. S.C., 1986, Pine Manor Coll., 1988. Editor in chief Paris Rev., 1953—, Paris Rev. Edits. (subs. Doubleday and Co.), 1965-72; editor-in-chief Paris Rev. Edits. (subs. Brit. Am. Publs.), 1987—; instr. Barnard Coll., 1956-58; assoc. editor Horizon mag., 1959-61; dir. Am. Lit. Anthology program, 1967-71; assoc. editor Harper's mag., 1972-81; contbg. editor Food and Wine Mag., 1978; editorial adv. bd. Realities, 1978; TV host Dupont Plimpton Spls., 1967-69, Greatest Sports Legends, 1979-81, The Ultimate High, 1980, Survival Anglia, 1980—, Writers' Workshop, 1982, Mousterpiece Theater, 1983—, Challenge, 1987; spl. contbr. Sports Illustrated, 1968—; bd. dirs. Int. Film Investors, 1979-82, Leisure Dynamics, 1983-85; curator Tennis Week, 1990—. Author: Rabbit's Umbrella, 1956, Out of My League, 1961, Paper Lion, 1966, The Bogey Man, 1968, Mad Ducks and Bears, 1973, One for the Record, 1974, Shadow-Box, 1976, One More July, 1976, (with Neil Leifer) Sports!, 1978, (with Arnold Roth) A Sports Bestiary, 1982, Fireworks, 1984, Open Net, 1985, The Curious Case of Sidd Finch, 1987, The X-Factor, 1990, The Best of Plimpton, 1990; also numerous articles.; editor; Writers at Work, Vol. 1, 1957, Vol. 11, 1963, Vol. 111, 1967, Vol. IV, 1976, Vol. V, 1981, Vol. VI, 1984, Vol. VII, 1987, Vol. VIII, 1989, Vol. IX, 1992, (with Jean Stein) American Journey: The Times of Robert Kennedy, 1970, Pierre's Book, 1971, The Fancy, 1973, (with Jean Stein) Edie, An American Biography, 1982, (with Christopher Hemphill) D.V., 1984; The Paris Review Anthology, 1989, The Writer's Chapbook, 1989, Women Writers at Work, 1989, Poets at Work, 1989, The Norton Book of Sports, 1992, (with Jean Kennedy Smith) Chronicles of Courage, 1992; contbg. editor Gentlemen's Quar., 1983-85, Smart mag., 1988-90, Esquire mag., 1990. Commr. fireworks, N.Y.C., 1973—; trustee WNET, 1973-81, Nat. Art Mus. Sport, 1967—, Police Athletic League, 1976-90, African Wildlife Leadership Found., 1980—, Guild Hall, East Hampton, 1980—, N.Y. Zool. Soc., 1985—; bd. dirs. Dynamite Mus., Nat. Tennis Found., 1979—, Squaw Valley Center for Written and Dramatic Arts, 1979—, Authors Trust Am., 1979, Friends of the Masai Mara, 1986, Friends of Conservation, 1988—, Roger Tory Peterson Inst., The Carnegie Cook Ctr. for the Arts; chmn. Books Across the Sea, English Speaking Union, 1988—; bd. dirs., pres. N.Y. Philomusica, Pen/Faulkner, 1995; mem. adv. bd. Coordinating Council Lit. Mags., 1979, Yoknapatawpha Press, Am. Chess Found., East Harlem Tutorial, Boy's Harbor. Served to 2d lt. AUS, 1945-48. Assoc. fellow Trumbull Coll., Yale, 1967; recipient Disting. Achievement award U. So. Calif., 1967, Blue Pencil award Columbia Spectator, 1981, Mark Twain award Internat. Platform Assn., 1982, Chancellor's award L.I. U., 1986, l'Ordre des Arts et des Lettres, France, 1994. Mem. NFL Alumni Assn., Am. Pyrotechnics Assn., Pyrotechnics Guild Internat., Explorers Club., Linnean Soc., PEN, Mayflower Descendants Soc. Clubs: Century Assn, Racquet and Tennis, Brook, Piping Rock, Dutch Treat, River, Coffee House, Devon Yacht; Travellers (Paris). Address: Paris Review Inc 541 E 72nd St New York NY 10021-4010*

PLISCHKE, ELMER, political science educator; b. Milw., July 15, 1914; s. Louis and Louise (Peterleus) P.; m. Audrey Alice Siehr, May 30, 1941; children: Lowell Robert, Julianne. Ph.B. cum laude, Marquette U., 1937; M.A., Am. U., 1938; certificate Carnegie summer session internat. law, U. Mich., 1938; Ph.D. (fellow), Clark U., 1943; certificate, Naval Sch. Mil. Govt. and Civil Affairs, Columbia, 1944. Instr. Springfield Coll., 1940; dist. supr., state dir. Wis. Hist. Records Survey, 1940-42; exec. sec. War Records Commn., Wis. Council Def., 1942; asst. prof. DePauw U., 1946-48, U. Md., College Park, 1948-49; assoc. prof. U. Md., 1949-52, prof., 1952-79, prof. emeritus, 1979—, head dept. govt. and politics, 1954-68; adj. prof. Gettysburg (Pa.) Coll., 1979-85; spl. historian Office U.S. High Commr. for Germany, 1950-52; cons. Dept. State, summer 1952; adj. scholar Am. Enterprise Inst. Pub. Policy Research, 1978—; lectr. Air War Coll., Armed Forces Staff Coll., Army War Coll., Def. Intelligence Sch., Indsl. Coll. Armed Forces, Inter-Am. Def. Coll., Nat. War Coll.; lectr. Sr. Officers Seminar Fgn. Service Inst. Dept. State; lectr. Instituto de Altos Estudios Nacionales, Quito, Ecuador.; mem. adv. com. fgn. relations of U.S. Dept. State, 1967-72, chmn., 1969-70; assoc. fellow Gettysburg Coll., 1993—. Author 28 books and monographs including: Conduct of American Diplomacy, 3d edit, 1967, reissued, 1974, (with Robert G. Dixon, Jr.) American Government: Basic Documents and Materials, 1950, reissued, 1971, Berlin: Development of Its Government and Administration, 1952, reissued, 1970, The Allied High Commission for Germany, 1953, International Relations: Basic Documents, rev, 1962, American Foreign Relations: A Bibliography of Official Sources, 1955, reissued, 1966, American Diplomacy: A Bibliography of Biographies, Autobiographies, and Commentaries, 1957, Summit Diplomacy: Personal Diplomacy of the President of the United States, 1958, reissued, 1974, Contemporary Governments of Germany, 1961, rev. edit., 1969, Government and Politics of Contemporary Berlin, 1963, Foreign Relations Decisionmaking: Options Analysis, 1973, United States Diplomats and Their Missions: A Profile of American Diplomatic Emissaries Since 1778, 1975, Microstates in World Affairs: Policy Problems and Options, 1977, Neutralization as an American Strategic Option, 1978, Modern Diplomacy: The Art and the Artisans, 1979, U.S. Foreign Relations: A Guide to Information Sources, 1980, Presidential Diplomacy: A Chronology of Summit Visits, Trips and Meetings, 1986, Diplomat in Chief: The President at the Summit, 1986, Foreign Relations: Analysis of Its Anatomy, 1988, Contemporary United States Foreign Policy: Documents and Commentary, 1991, others; contbr. more than 80 articles to profl. and lit. jours., and encyclopaedias; Americana Ann., 1972-83; also editorials in newspapers; editor, contbr. Systems of Integrating the International Community, 1964; mem. bd. editors Jour. Politics, 1966-68. Served from ensign to lt. USNR, 1943-46; exec. asst., then exec. officer Civil Affairs div., comdr. U.S. Naval Forces for Europe, London, 1944-45; charge de- Nazification policy coordination Office Dir. Polit. Affairs, Office Mil. Govt. for Germany 1945. Recipient research awards U. Md. Gen. Research Bd., 1956, 58, 69; research grantee Earhart Found., 1982-83, 86-87; book Interaction: Foreign Policy and Public Policy (Piper and Terchek) dedicated in honor, 1983; elected knight Mark Twain, Mark Twain Jour., 1970. Mem. AAUP, Am. Soc. Internat. Law, Am. Polit. Sci. Assn. (coun.), D.C. Polit. Sci. Assn. (coun. pres. 1961), So. Polit. Sci. Assn. (coun.), Internat. Studies Assn., Com. Study Diplomacy, Inst. Study Diplomacy, Internat. Torch Club (sec. Gettysburg club 1985-91, archivist 1991—, bd. mem. 1995-97), Eclectic Club, Phi Beta kappa, Phi Kappa Phi, Pi Sigma Alpha, Sigma Tau Delta. Home: 227 Ewell Ave Gettysburg PA 17325-3108

PLISCHKE, LE MOYNE WILFRED, research chemist; b. Greensburg, Pa., Dec. 11, 1922; s. Fred and Ruth Naomi (Rumbaugh) P.; m. Joan Harper, Mar. 11, 1966. BS, Waynesburg Coll., 1948; MS, W.Va. U., 1952. Rsch. chemist U.S. Naval Ordinance Test Sta., China Lake, Calif., 1952-53; asst. prof. chemistry Commonwealth U., Richmond, Va., 1953-54; rsch. chemist E.I. du Pont, Gibbstown, N.J., 1955-57, Monsanto Chem. Co., Pensacola, Fla., 1957—. Mem. Am. Chem. Soc. Achievements include 16 U.S. patents and 48 foreign patents in field. Home: 2100 Club House Dr Lillian AL 36549-5402 Office: Monsanto Co The Chem Group PO Box 97 Gonzalez FL 32560-0097

PLISHNER, MICHAEL JON, lawyer; b. Rockville Center, N.Y., Jan. 22, 1948; s. Meyer J. and Lillian (Gold) P.; m. Rosalind F. Schein, Jan. 26, 1969; children: Aaron, Alexander, Elias. BA summa cum laude, Yale U., 1969, JD, 1972. Bar: Calif. 1972, U.S. Dist. Ct. (no. dist.) Calif. 1972, U.S. Ct. Appeals (9th cir.) 1972. Assoc. McCutchen, Doyle, Brown & Enersen, San Francisco, 1972-79, ptnr., 1979—. Mem. Phi Beta Kappa. Home: 114 St Albans Rd Kensington CA 94708-1035 Office: McCutchen Doyle Brown & Enersen 3 Embarcadero Ctr San Francisco CA 94111-4003

PLISKIN, WILLIAM AARON, physicist; b. Akron, Ohio, Aug. 9, 1920; s. Max and Lena (Slavin) P.; m. Miriam Jaffee, Mar. 15, 1944; children: Karen, Michael, Bina. B.S., Kent State U., 1941; M.S., Ohio U., 1943; Ph.D., Ohio State U., 1949. Rsch. physicist Texaco Rsch. Ctr., Beacon, N.Y., 1949-59; staff physicist IBM, Poughkeepsie, N.Y., 1959-60; adv. physicist IBM, 1960-63; sr. physicist, mgr. IBM, East Fishkill, N.Y., 1964-79; sr. staff mem. IBM, 1979-82, mgr., sr. tech. staff mem., 1982-87, sr. tech. staff mem., 1987-90; cons. characterization and measurement of dielectric films, 1990—. Contbr. numerous articles to profl. jours., chpts. in books; patentee in field. Served to 1st lt. U.S. Army, 1943-46, PTO. Fellow IEEE, Electrochem Soc. (ann. award electronics div. 1973); mem. Am. Phys. Soc., Am. Chem. Soc. (ann. award Mid Hudson sect. 1964), Sigma Xi, Pi Mu Epsilon, Sigma Pi Sigma. Jewish. Home: 31 Greenvale Farms Rd Poughkeepsie NY 12603-4201

PLISKOW, VITA SARI, anesthesiologist; b. Tel Aviv, Israel, Sept. 13, 1942; arrived in Can., 1951; came to U.S., 1967; d. Henry Norman and Renee (Mushkatel) Stahl; m. Raymond Joel Pliskow, June 30, 1968; children: Tia, Kami. MD, U. B.C., Vancouver, 1967. Diplomate Am. Bd. Anesthesiology. Ptnr. Olympic Anesthesia, Bremerton, Wash., 1971-84, pres., anesthesiologist, 1974-84; co-founder Olympic Ambulatory Surgery Ctr., Bremerton, 1977-83; ptnr., anesthesiologist Allenmore Anesthesia Assocs., Tacoma, 1983—; staff anesthesiologist Harrison Meml. Hosp., Bremerton, 1971-95, Allenmore Hosp., Tacoma, 1983—. Trustee Tacoma Youth Symphony Assn., 1994—; active Nat. Coun. Jewish Women, 1972—. Fellow Am. Coll. Anesthesiologists, Am. Coll. Chest Physicians; mem. Am. Soc. Anesthesiologists (del. Wash. State 1987—), Wash. State Med. Assn. (del. Pierce County 1993-94), Wash. State Soc. Anesthesiologists (pres. 1985-87), Pierce County Med. Soc. (sec.-treas. 1992). Avocations: classical music, opera, singing (mezzo soprano). Office: # 109 900 Sheridan Rd Bremerton WA 98310-2701

PLOGER, ROBERT RIIS, retired military officer, engineer; b. Mackay, Idaho, Aug. 12, 1915; s. Robert and Elfrieda (Riis) P.; m. Marguerite Anne Fiehrer, June 13, 1939 (dec. Feb. 1982); children: Wayne David, Robert Riis III, Daniel Bruce, Marguerite Anne, Marianne Ploger Hill, Gregory Fiehrer; m. Jeanne Allys Pray, Nov. 20, 1982. BS, U.S. Mil. Acad., 1939; MS in Engring., Cornell U., 1947; MBA, George Washington U., 1963. Registered civil engr., D.C. Commd. 2d lt. U.S. Army, 1939; served in corps of engrs. U.S. Army, ETO, Okinawa, 1939-65; advanced through grades to maj. gen. U.S. Army, 1966, div. engr. New England div., 1965, comdg. gen. 18th engr. brigade, 1965-66, comdg. gen. engr. command, Vietnam, 1966-67; dir. topography and mil. engring., Office Chief Engrs. U.S. Army, Washington, 1967-70; comdg. gen. Ft. Belvoir and commandant U.S. Army Engr. Sch. Va., 1970-73; ret. U.S. Army, 1973; engr. specialist Bechtel Power Corp., Ann Arbor, 1974-80, mgr. adminstrv. services, 1980-81; counselor SCORE, Ann Arbor, Mich., 1984—; lectr. Indsl. Coll. Armed Forces, 1962-65. Author: Vietnam Studies, U.S. Army Engineers 1965-70; contbr. numerous articles on war and mil. engring. to profl. jours. Chmn. gift com. Class of 1939 50th Reunion of U.S. Mil. Acad., 1985-89. Decorated DSM with oak leaf cluster, Legion of Merit, Silver Star with oak leaf cluster, Bronze Star with oak leaf cluster, Air medal, Purple Heart, Korean Order Mil. Merit Chung Mu, Nat. Order 5th Class Republic of Vietnam; recipient George Washington medal ICAF, 1965, Wheeler medal Soc. Am. Mil. Engrs., 1966, Silver Beaver award Boy Scouts Am., 1973, Médaille du Jubilé, Vire, France, 1994. Fellow Soc. Am. Mil. Engrs.; mem. NSPE (priviliged; chpt. pres. 1979-80), 29th Inf. Divsn. Assn. (Phila. award 1985), West Point Soc. Mich. (pres. 1981-84), SCORE (at-large exec. com. 1991, counselor chpt. 18), Ann Arbor C. of C. (counselor svc. corps ret. execs.), Army Engr. Assn. (life, Silver Order de Fleury medal 1995), SHAPE Officers Assn. (life). Baptist. Avocations: tennis, skiing, sailboarding. Home: 2475 Adare Rd Ann Arbor MI 48104-4021

PLOMP, TEUNIS (TONY PLOMP), minister; b. Rotterdam, The Netherlands, Jan. 28, 1938; arrived in Can., 1951; s. Teunis and Cornelia (Pietersma) P.; m. Margaret Louise Bone, July 21, 1962; children: Jennifer Anne, Deborah Adele. BA, U. B.C. (Can.), Vancouver, 1960; BD, Knox Coll., Toronto, Ont., Can., 1963, DD (hon.), 1988. Ordained to ministry Presbyn. Ch., 1963. Minister Goforth Meml. Presbyn. Ch., Saskatoon, Sask., Can., 1963-68, Richmond (B.C.) Presbyn. Ch., 1968—; clerk Presbytery of Westminster, Vancouver, 1969—; moderator 113th Gen. Assembly Presbyn. Ch. Can., 1987-88, dep. clk., 1987—; chaplain New Haven Correctional Centre, Burnaby, B.C. Contbr. mag. column You Were Asking, 1982-89. Avocations: record collecting, audiophile, biking, swimming. Office: Richmond Presbyn Ch, 7111 #2 Rd, Richmond, BC Canada V7C 3L7

PLONSEY, ROBERT, electrical and biomedical engineer; b. N.Y.C., July 17, 1924; s. Louis B. and Betty (Vinograd) P.; m. Vivian V. Vucker, Oct. 1, 1948; 1 child, Daniel. BEE, Cooper Union, 1943; MSEE, NYU, 1948; PhD, U. Calif., Berkeley, 1955; postgrad. med. sch., Case Western Res. U., 1969-71; D of Technol. Scis., Slovak Acad. Scis., 1995. Registered profl. engr., Ohio. Asst. prof. elec. engring. U. Calif., Berkeley, 1955-57; asst. prof. elec. engring. Case Inst. Tech., Cleve., 1957-60, assoc. prof., 1960-66, prof., 1966-68, dir. bioengring. group, 1962-68; prof. biomed. engring. Sch. Engring. and Sch. Medicine Case Western Res. U., 1968-83, chmn. dept., 1976-80; vis. prof. biomed. engring. Duke U., Durham, N.C., 1980-81, prof., 1983-96, prof. biomed. engring., Hudson prof. engring., 1990-93, Pfizer-Inc.-Edmond T. Pratt Jr. Univ. prof. biomed. engring., 1993-96; Pfizer-Inc.-Edmond T. Pratt Jr. Univ. prof. emeritus Duke U., Durham, 1996—; mem. biomed. fellowships rev. com. NIH, 1966-70; mem. tng. com. Engrs. in Medicine and Biology, 1972-73, cons., 1974—; cons. NSF, 1973-93; mem. internat. sci. adv. com. Ragnar Granit Inst., Tampere (Finland) U. Tech., 1992—; ad hoc mem. sci. adv. com. Whitaker Found., 1989-91. Author: (with R. Collin) Principles and Applications of Electromagnetic Fields, 1961, Bioelectric Phenomena, 1969, (with J. Liebman and P. Gillette) Pediatric Electrocardiography, 1982, (with T. Pilkington) Engineering Contributions to Biophysical Electrocardiography, 1982, (with J. Liebman and Y. Rudy) Pediatric and Fundamental Electrocardiography, (with R.C. Barr) Bioelectricity: A Quantitative Approach, 1988, (with J. Malmivuo) Bioelectromagnetism, 1995; mem. editorial bd. Trans. IEEE, Biomed. Engring, 1965-70; assoc. editor, 1977-79, editorial bd. TIT Jour. 1971-81, Electrocardiology Jour., 1974—, Medical and Biological Engineering and Computing, 1987—; procs. editor Engring. in Medicine and Biology, 17th Ann., Conf., 1965. Mem. com. on electrocardiography Am. Heart Assn., 1976-82; v.p. Your Schs., Cleveland Heights, Ohio, 1968-69, 73-75; provisional trustee Am. Bd. Clin. Engrs., 1973-74, pres. 1975, trustee, 1976-85. With AUS, 1944-46. Recipient sr. postdoctoral award NIH, 1980-81. Fellow AAAS, IEEE (chmn. Cleve. chpt. group on biomed. electronics 1962-63, chmn. publs. com. group on engring. in medicine and biology 1968-70, v.p. adminstrv. com. 1970-72, pres. 1973-74, chmn. fellows com. Engring. in Medicine and Biology Soc. 1986-87-88, v.p. tech. and conf. activities 1991, William S. Morlock award 1979, Centennial medal 1984, co-program chair ann. conf., Paris 1992, chmn. awards com. 1996); mem. AAUP, NAE (bioengring. peer com. 1988-91, chair 1990-91, nominating com. 1991-92, mem. com. 1992-94, program adv. com. 1996—, NRS postdoctoral rsch. associateships evaluation panel 1987-90), Am. Inst. Med. and Biol. Engring. (founding fellow 1992—), Alliance for Engring. in Medicine and Biology (treas. 1976-78), Biomed. Engring. Soc. (bd. dirs. 1975-78, 79-83, pres. 1981-82, chmn. affiliations com. 1987-89, ALZA Disting. lectr. 1988), Am. Physiol. Soc., Am. Soc. Engring. Edn. (bd. dirs. biomed. engring. divsn. 1978-83, chmn. 1982-83). Office: Duke U Dept Biomed Engring Durham NC 27706 *External recognition of success is not nearly so important as the inner awareness of coming to full grips with life, to be fully involved, bending all strengths to fulfill one's goals and philosophies. And of all involvements, those with people are most meaningful (to be aware of and share the feelings of colleagues, students, friends, and family—and to enrich these relationships)—and for me most difficult.*

PLOPPER, CHARLES GEORGE, anatomist, cell biologist; b. Oakland, Calif., June 16, 1944; s. George Eli and Josephine Viola (Gates) P.; m. Suzanne May, Nov. 9, 1969. AB, U. Calif., Davis, 1967, PhD, 1972. Chief. electron microscopy br. U.S. Army Med. Research Nutrition Lab., Denver, 1972-73; vis. scientist Calif. Primate Research Ctr., Davis, 1974-75; chief. electron microscopy div. Letterman Army Inst. Research, San Francisco, 1974-75; asst. prof. U. Hawaii Sch. Medicine, Honolulu, 1975-77; assoc. prof. Kuwait U. Sch. Medicine, 1977-78; sr. staff fellow Nat. Inst. Environ. Health Sci. Research, Triangle Park, N.C., 1978-79; from asst. to assoc. prof. U. Calif. Sch. Vet. Medicine, Davis, 1979-86, dept. chmn., 1984-88; prof. anatomy, physiology and cell biology, Sch. Vet. Medicine U. Calif., Davis, 1986—; mem. study sect. NIH div. Research Grants, Bethesda, Md., 1986-90; Paley vis. prof. Boston U. Sch. Medicine, 1985; vis. pulmonary scholar Duke U., U. N.C., N.C. State U., 1991. Served to capt. U.S. Army, 1972-75. Mem. Am. Soc. Cell Biology, Am. Thoracic Soc., Am. Assn. Antomists, Am. Assn. Pathologists, Anat. Soc. Great Britain and Ireland, Davis Aquatic Masters (bd. dirs. 1993-95). Democrat. Avocations: swimming, hiking, tennis. Home: 511 Hubble St Davis CA 95616-2720 Office: Univ Calif Sch Vet Medicine Dept Anatomy Physiol Cell Biology Davis CA 95616

PLOSSER, CHARLES IRVING, university dean, economics educator; b. Birmingham, Ala., Sept. 19, 1948; s. George Gray and Dorothy (Irving) P.; m. Janet Schwert, June 26, 1976; children: Matthew, Kevin, Allison. B.E. cum laude, Vanderbilt U., 1970; MBA, U. Chgo., 1972, PhD, 1976. Cons. Citicorp Realty Cons., N.Y.C., 1972-73; lectr. Grad. Sch. Bus., U. Chgo., 1975-76; asst. prof. Grad. Sch. Bus. Stanford (Calif.) U., 1976-78; asst. prof. econs. W.E. Simon Grad. Sch. Bus., U. Rochester (N.Y.), 1978-82, assoc. prof., 1982-86, prof., 1986-89; Fred H. Gowen prof. econs. U. Rochester, N.Y., 1989-92, John M. Olin Disting. prof. econs. and pub. policy, 1992—, acting dean W.E. Simon Grad. Sch. Bus., 1990-91, 92-93; dean W.E. Simon Grad. Sch. Bus., 1993—; chmn. bd. Consortium for Grad. Study in Mgmt., 1995-97; bd. dirs. Greater Rochester Health Sys., Inc., 1995—, Rochester Gas & Electric Corp., 1996—, Grad. Mgmt. Admission Coun., 1997—. Editor, Jour. Monetary Econs., 1983—, Carnegie-Rochester Conference Series on Public Policy, 1989—; contbr. articles to profl. jours. 1st lt., U.S. Army, 1972-73. NSF research grantee, 1982, 84. Mem. Am. Econs. Assn., Econometrics Soc., Am. Fin. Assn., Tau Beta Pi, Beta Gamma Sigma. Home: 95 Ambassador Dr Rochester NY 14610-3402 Office: U Rochester Dean Of Simon Grad Sch Rochester NY 14627

PLOTCH, WALTER, management consultant, fund-raising counselor; b. N.Y.C., July 19, 1932; s. Harry and Belle (Lebowsky) P.; AB, Queens Coll., 1957; MA, Harvard U., 1959, postgrad., 1959-62; m. Yvette Gabrielle Lambert, Mar. 15, 1957; children: Allison, Jennifer, Adrienne. Analyst L.F. Rothschild & Co., N.Y.C. and Boston, 1962-64; cmty. cons., 1964-65; edn. dir. for New Eng., Anti-Defamation League of B'nai B'rith, 1965-68, nat. edn. dir., 1968-76; v.p. Brakeley, John Price Jones Inc., N.Y.C., 1976-79, sr. v.p., dir., 1979-89; sr. v.p. The Oram Group, Inc., N.Y.C., 1989-92, exec. v.p.; pres. and CEO Walter Plotch Assocs., Inc., Croton-On-Hudson, N.Y., 1992—; mem. faculty Grad. Sch. Mgmt. and Urban Affairs, New Sch. Social Rsch.; lectr. Harvard U. Grad. Sch. Edn.; cons. Harcourt, Brace, Plenum Pubs. Bd. dirs. Schizophrenia Found., 1975-90; nat. bd. dirs. NCCJ, 1980-84, Nat. Charitable Info. Bur., mem. exec. com., 1986-94. Served with USCGR, 1953-55; Korea. Grantee, U.S. Office Edn., Dept. Labor, N.Y. Coun. Humanities; tchg. fellow Harvard U., 1959-61. Mem. Princeton Club, U. Washington Club, Phi Alpha Theta. Democrat. Jewish. Co-editor: Pluralism in a Democratic Society, 1977; gen. editor: The Job Corps Intergroup Relations Series, 1974; author articles in field, contbg. editor Grants mag., Jour. Sponsored Research 1978-82. Office: 39 Furnace Dock Rd Croton On Hudson NY 10520-1406

PLOTKIN, HARRY MORRIS, lawyer; b. Athol, Mass., May 18, 1913; s. Louis and Fannie (Coffman) P.; m. Esther Lipsez, Dec. 25, 1937; children—Ira L., Judith Deborah (Mrs. Jonathan Wilkenfeld). A.B. magna cum laude, Harvard, 1934, LL.B. magna cum laude, 1937. Bar: Ill. 1937, D.C. 1951. Assoc. firm Topliff & Horween, Chgo., 1937-39; atty. FCC, 1940-51, asst. gen. counsel, 1943-51; ptnr. Arnold, Fortas & Porter, Washington, 1951-56, Arent, Fox, Kintner, Plotkin & Kahn, Washington, 1956-82; of counsel Arent, Fox, Kintner, Plotkin & Kahn, 1983—. Trustee Washington United Jewish Appeal Fedn.. Mem. ABA, Fed. Bar Assn., Fed. Communications Bar Assn., D.C. Bar Assn., Phi Beta Kappa. Clubs: Harvard, Nat.

Lawyers (Washington). Home: 3719 Harrison St NW Washington DC 20015-1815 Office: 1050 Connecticut Ave NW Washington DC 20036

PLOTKIN, IRVING H(ERMAN), economist, consultant; b. Bklyn., July 19, 1941; s. Samuel H. and Dorothy (Falick) P.; BS in Econs., U. Pa., 1963; PhD in Math. Econs., Mass. Inst. Tech., 1968; m. Janet V. Bufe, July 26, 1969; children: Aaron Jacob, Joshua Benjamin. Corp. planning analyst Mobil Oil Co., N.Y.C., 1962-63, Mobil Oil Italiana, Genoa, Italy, 1965; ind. cons. econs. and ops. rsch. to banks, mut. funds, ins. cos. govt. agys., Cambridge, Mass., 1965-68; sr. economist Arthur D. Little, Inc., Cambridge, 1968—; dir. regulation and econs., 1974—, v.p., 1979—; bd. dir. Arthur D. Little Valuation, Inc., 1980—; trustee Arthur D. Little, Inc., ESOP, 1988—; instr. fin. and computer scis. Mass. Inst. Tech., 1965-68; lectr. maj. univs. U.S. and abroad; expert witness U.S. Ho. of Reps. and Senate coms., U.S. Ct. Claims, U.S. Tax Ct. I.C.C., FTC, Fed. Maritime Commn., Fed. Dist. Cts., Fed. Res. Bd., other fed. and state govt. agys., 1967—. NASA fellow, 1963-66, NSF fellow, 1967, Am. Bankers Assn. fellow, 1968. Mem. Am. Econ. Assn., Econometric Soc., Am. Fin. Assn., Beta Gamma Sigma, Pi Gamma Mu, Tau Delta Phi (chpt. pres. 1962-63). Editorial reviewer Jour. Am. Statis. Assn., 1968, Jour. Indsl. Econs., 1968—, Jour. Risk and Ins., 1980—; author: Prices and Profits in the Property and Liability Insurance Industry, 1967, The Consequences of Industrial Regulation on Profitability, Risk Taking, and Innovation, 1969, National Policy, Technology, and Economic Forces Affecting the Industrial Organization of Marine Transportation, 1970, Government Regulation of the Air Freight Industry, 1971, The Private Mortgage Insurance Industry, 1975, On The Theory and Practice of Rate Review and Profit Measurement in Title Insurance, 1978, Torrens in the United States, 1978, Total Rate of Return and the Regulation of Insurance Profits, 1979, Studies on the Impact of Sophisticated Manufacturing Industries on the Economic Development of Puerto Rico, 1981, The Economic Consequences of Controlled Business in the Real Estate Industry, 1981, On the Nature of Captive Insurance, 1984, Economic Foundations of Limited Liability for Nuclear Reactor Accidents, 1985, Transfer Prices, Royalties, and Adam Smith, 1987, Guide to Transfer Pricing Compliance, 1994; contbr. numerous articles to profl. jours. Home: 55 Baskin Rd Lexington MA 02173-6928 Office: 35 Acorn Park Cambridge MA 02140-2301

PLOTKIN, MANUEL D., management consultant, educator, former corporate executive and government official; s. Jacob and Bella (Katz) P.; m. Diane Fern Weiss, Dec. 17, 1967; 1 child, Lori Ann. BS with honors, Northwestern U., 1948; MBA, U. Chgo., 1949. Price economist, survey coordinator U.S. Bur. Labor Statistics, Washington, 1949-51, Chgo., 1951-53; sr. economist Sears Roebuck & Co., Chgo., 1953-61; mgr. market research Sears Roebuck & Co., 1961-66, chief economist, mgr. mktg. rsch., 1966-73, dir. corp. planning and research, 1973-77, exec. corp. planner, 1979-80; dir. U.S. Bur. Census, Washington, 1977-79; v.p., dir. group practice Divsn. Mgmt. Cons. Austin Co., Evanston, Ill., 1981-85; pres. M.D. Plotkin Research & Planning Co., Chgo., 1985—; tchr. statistics Ind. U., 1953-54; tchr. econs. Wilson Jr. Coll., Chgo., 1954-55; tchr. quantitative methods and managerial econs. Northwestern U., 1955-63; tchr. mktg. rsch. and mktg. mgmt. DePaul U., Chgo., 1992-95; mem. Conf. Bd. Mktg. Rsch. Adv. Coun., 1968-77, chmn.-elect, 1977; chmn. adv. com. U.S. Census Bur., 1974-75; trustee Mktg. Sci. Inst., 1968-77; mem. Nat. Commn. Employment and Unemployment Stats., 1978-79, Adv. Coun. Edn. Stats., 1977-79, Interagy. Com. Population Rsch., 1977-79; mem. adv. coun. Kellstadt Ctr., DePaul U., 1987-92; trustee U.S. Travel Data Ctr., 1977-79. Contbr. articles to profl. jours. Served with AUS, 1943-46, ETO. Decorated Bronze Star medal with oak leaf cluster. Mem. Am. Mktg. Assn. (pres. Chgo. 1968-69, nat. dir. 1969-70, nat. v.p. mktg. rsch. 1970-72, nat. v.p. mktg. mgmt. 1981-83, pres., CEO 1985-86), Am. Statis. Assn. (pres. Chgo. 1966-67, Forecasting award 1963), Am. Econ. Assn., Nat. Assn. Bus. Economists, Planning Execs. Inst., World Future Soc., Midwest Planning Assn., U. Ill. Businessmen Rsch. Adv. Group, Chgo. Assn. Commerce and Industry, Beta Gamma Sigma, Alpha Sigma Lambda, Delta Mu Delta. Home and Office: Ste 3910 2650 N Lakeview Ste 3910 Chicago IL 60614-1831

PLOTKIN, MARTIN, retired electrical engineer; b. Bklyn., July 22, 1922; s. David and Tessie (Esris) P.; m. Beverly Ferber, July 2, 1949; 1 child, George Michael. BEE, CCNY, 1943; MEE, Poly. Inst. Bklyn., 1951. Electronic engr. Bendix Aviation Corp., Bklyn., 1943-44; sr. elec. engr. Brookhaven Nat. Lab., Upton, N.Y., 1946-84, ret., 1984, cons., 1986-96. Inventor alternating gradient synchrotron radio frequency system, 1960. Lt. (j.g.) USNR, 1944-46. Fellow IEEE; mem. Nuclear and Plasma Scis. Soc. (pres. 1977-78), Trans. on Med. Imaging (mem. steering com. 1981-90, chmn. steering com. 1981-84, 86-90). Avocations: mineralogy; philately. Home: 117 Clover Dr Massapequa Park NY 11762

PLOTNICK, HARVEY BARRY, publishing executive; b. Detroit, Aug. 5, 1941; s. Isadore and Esther (Sher) P.; m. Susan Regnery, Aug. 16, 1964 (div. Apr. 1977); children: Andrew, Alice; m. Elizabeth Allen, May 2, 1982; children: Teresa, Samuel. B.A., U. Chgo., 1963. Editor Contemporary Books, Inc., Chgo., 1964-66; pres. Contemporary Books, Inc., 1966-94; with Paradigm Holdings, Inc., Chgo., 1994—. Trustee U. Chgo., 1994—. Office: Paradigm Holdings Inc 2 Prudential Plz Ste 1550 Chicago IL 60601-6790

PLOTNICK, ROBERT DAVID, educator, economic consultant; b. Washington, Aug. 3, 1949; s. Theodore and Jean (Hirshfeld) P.; m. Gay Lee Jensen, Dec. 22, 1972. BA, Princeton U., 1971; MA, U. Calif., Berkeley, 1973, PhD, 1976. Research assoc. Inst. Research on Poverty, Madison, Wis., 1973-75; asst. prof. Bates Coll., Lewiston, Maine, 1975-77, Dartmouth Coll., Hanover, N.H., 1977-84; assoc. prof. U. Wash., Seattle, 1984-90, prof., 1990—; assoc. dean, 1990-95, acting dean, 1994-95; vis. scholar Russell Sage Found., 1990, U. New South Wales, 1997; rsch. affiliate Inst. for Rsch. on Poverty, 1989—; cons. Wash. Dept. Social and Health Svcs., Olympia, 1984-86, 90-96; cons. numerous pub. and non-profit orgns. Author: Progress Against Poverty, 1975; also numerous articles. Recipient Teaching Excellence award U. Wash., 1985, 89. Mem. Am. Econ. Assn., Assn. Policy Analysis and Mgmt., Population Assn. Am. Avocations: tennis, hiking, bird watching, scuba. Office: U Wash Grad Sch Pub Affairs Box 353055 Seattle WA 98195-3055

PLOTNIK, ARTHUR, author, editorial consultant; b. White Plains, N.Y., Oct. 1, 1937; s. Michael and Annabelle (Taub) P.; m. Meta Von Borstel, Sept. 6, 1960 (div. 1979); children: Julia Nicole, Katya Michelle.; m. Mary Phelan, Dec. 2, 1983. B.A., State U. N.Y., Binghamton, 1960; M.A., U. Iowa, 1961; M.S. in L.S, Columbia U., 1966. Gen. reporter, reviewer Albany (N.Y.) Times Union, 1963-64; freelance writer, 1964-66; editor Librarians Office, Library of Congress, 1966-69; assoc. editor Wilson Library Bull., Bronx, N.Y., 1969-74; editor-in-chief Am. Libraries, Chgo., 1975-89; assoc. pub. ALA, 1989-97; editl. dir. ALA Editions, 1993-97; writer, editorial cons., 1997—; adj. instr. journalism Columbia Coll., Chgo., 1988-89; speaker in field. Author: The Elements of Editing: A Modern Guide for Editors and Journalists, 1982, Jacob Shallus, Calligrapher of the Constitution, 1987, Honk If You're a Writer, 1992, The Elements of Expression, 1996; also fiction, articles, video scripts, photography; exec. producer Libr. Video mag., 1986-91. Bd. dirs. Am. Book Awards, 1979-82; bd. advs. Univ. Press of Am., 1982—. Served with USAR, 1962-67. Fellow Iowa Writers Workshop Creative Writing, 1961; recipient award Ednl. Press Assn. Am., 1973 (3), 77, 82, 83; cert. of excellence Internat. Reading Assn., 1970, First Pl. award Verbatim essay competition, 1986, award Am. Soc. Bus. Press Editors, 1987. Mem. ALA. Home: 2120 W Pensacola Ave Chicago IL 60618-1718 Office: N E Pub Assocs Literary Agents PO Box 5 Chester CT 06412

PLOTT, CHARLES R., economics educator; b. Frederick, Okla., July 8, 1938; s. James Charles and Flossie Ann (Bowman) P.; m. Marianna Brown Cloninger, May 30, 1961; children: Rebecca Ann, Charles Hugh. BS, Okla. State U., 1961, MS, 1964; PhD, U. Va., 1965; LittD (hon.), Purdue U., 1995; D (hon.), U. Pierre Mendès France, Grenoble, 1996. Asst. prof. econs. Purdue U., 1965-68, assoc. prof., 1968-70; vis. prof. econs. Stanford U., 1968-69; Edward S. Harkness prof. econs. and polit. sci. Calif. Inst. Tech., Pasadena, 1970—, dir. Program for Study of Enterprise and Pub. Policy, 1979—, dir. Lab. for Exptl. Econs. and Polit. Sci., 1987—; vis. prof. law U. So. Calif. Law Ctr., 1976; vis. prof. U. Chgo., 1980; dir. Lee Pharms. Author works in fields of econs., polit. sci., philosophy, exptl. methods, math. methods; contbr. articles to profl. jours.; mem. bd. editors: Social Sci. Rsch., 1976-77, Pub. Choice, 1973—, Jour. Econ. Behavior, 1983—. Named to Coll. Bus. Hall of Fame Okla. State U.; Ford Found. fellow, 1968, Guggenheim fellow, 1981, fellow Ctr. for Advanced Studies in Behavioral Scis., 1981; NSF grantee, 1972, 74, 78, 79, 80, 83, 86, 88, 92, 95. Fellow Am. Acad. Arts and Scis., Econometric Soc., Huntington Library and Art Gallery; mem. Am. Econ. Assn., Econ. Sci. Assn. (pres. 1987), So. Econ. Assn. (mem. exec. com. 1978-79, v.p. 1985-87, pres. 1989-90), Pub. Choice Soc. (pres. 1977-78), Western Econ. Assn. (v.p. 1996-97), Royal Econ. Assn., Am. Polit. Sci. Assn., Econs. Sci. Assn. (pres. 1987-88), Mont Pelerin Soc. Home: 881 El Campo Dr Pasadena CA 91107-5565 Office: Calif Inst Tech Divsn Humanities & Social Scis Pasadena CA 91125

PLOTTEL, JEANINE PARISIER, foreign language educator; b. Paris, Sept. 21, 1934; came to U.S., 1943; m. Roland Plottel, 1956; children: Claudia S., Michael E., Philip B. Baccalauréat lettres, Lycée Français de N.Y., 1952; BA with honors, Barnard Coll., 1954; MA, Columbia U., 1955, PhD with distinction, 1959. Lectr. dept. French and Romance philology Columbia U., N.Y.C., 1955-59; rsch. assoc. fgn. lang. program MLA of Am., N.Y.C., 1959-60; lectr. dept. romance langs. CUNY, N.Y.C., 1960; asst. prof. div. humanities Julliard Sch. Music, N.Y.C., 1960-65; dir. lang. labs. Hunter Coll. CUNY, N.Y.C., 1965-69; asst. prof. dept. romance langs. Hunter Coll. CUNY, N.Y.C., 1965-69, assoc. prof. dept. romance langs., 1969-81, prof. dept. romance langs., 1981—, assoc. prof. French doctoral program grad. sch., univ. ctr., 1980-81, prof. French doctoral program grad. sch., univ. ctr., 1981—; extensive adminstrv. experience in CUNY including chairperson Dept. Romance Langs; bd. dirs. Henry Peyre Inst. Grad. Ctr., CUNY. Author: Les Dialogues de Paul Valéry, 1960; pub., editor N.Y. Literary Forum, 1978-88; contbr. articles to profl. jours., chpts. to books. Pres. Maurice I. Parisier Found., Inc. Named Chevalier des Palmes Acad., 1982; recipient NEH fellowship, 1979; grantee N.Y. Coun. for the Humanities, 1986, Helena Rubenstein Found., 1986, Florence J. Gould Found., 1986, N.Y. Times Found., 1986. Mem. Maison Française (bd. dirs. Columbia U.), Peyre Inst., CUNY. Home: 50 E 77th St Apt 14A New York NY 10021-1836

PLOTZ, CHARLES MINDELL, physician; b. N.Y.C., Dec. 6, 1921; s. Isaac and Rose (Bluestone) P.; m. Lucille Weckstein, Aug. 5, 1945; children: Richard, Thomas, Robert. B.A., Columbia U., 1941, D.Sc., 1951; M.D., L.I. Coll. Medicine, 1944. Diplomate: Am. Bd. Internal Medicine. Intern New Haven Hosp., 1944-45; resident internal medicine Kings County Hosp., 1945-46, Maimonides Hosp., 1948-49; postdoctoral research fellow USPHS, Columbia Coll. Phys. and Surgs., 1949-50; practice medicine, specializing in internal medicine Bklyn., 1950—; chief Arthritis Clinic, attending physician Kings County Hosp. Center, 1950-85; chief L.I. Coll. Hosp. (Arthritis Clinic), 1950-65; asst. attending physician Mt. Sinai Hosp., 1955—; chief Mt. Sinai Hosp. (Arthritis Clinic), 1955-65, Arthritis Clinic, State U., Hosp., 1967-85; asst. physician Columbia-Presbyn. Med. Center, 1949-71; attending physician Bklyn. State Hosp.; dir. ambulatory care Bklyn. Hosp.Ctr., 1991-93; emeritus prof. medicine SUNY, 1991—; professorial lectr. Mt. Sinai Sch. Medicine, 1992—; emeritus prof. in medicine SUNY, 1991—; cons. physician Peninsula Gen. Hosp., Jamaica Hosp.; cons. on rheumatology VA Hosp., Bklyn., L.I. Coll. Hosp.; cons. family practice Luth. Med. Ctr.; vis. cons. internal medicine Jewish Gen. Hosp., Mont., Que., Can., 1965; cons. internal medicine Avicenna Hosp. and Wazir Akbar Hosp., Kabul, Afganistan, 1965; prof. medicine, dir. continuing edn., chmn. dept. family practice SUNY Downstate Med. Ctr., 1967-91, prof. emeritus medicine and family practice, 1991—; Fulbright lectr. U. Paris, 1984, 91; professorial lectr. Mt. Sinai Sch. Medicine, 1992—. Editorial adv. bd.: Pakistan Med. Forum; editor-in-chief: Clin. Rheumatology in Practice, 1981—; editor-in-chief: Advances in Rheumatology, 1986—. Mem. nat. bd. govs. Arthritis Found., 1964-82, bd. govs. N.Y. chpt., 1965—, v.p., 1971-83, trustee, 1977-82, N.Y. chpt. sr. v.p., 1977-82, vice chmn. bd. trustees, 1983-85, 87—, pres., 1985-87; trustee Leo N. Levi Meml. Nat. Arthritis Hosp., Alumni Fund-Alumni Assn. SUNY Downstate Med. Center, Bklyn. Inst. Arts and Scis., Bklyn. Bot. Garden; mem. adv. bd. MEDICO, corp. mem., 1977—; treas. Internat. League Against Rheumatism, 1981-89; trustee Internat. League Against Rheumatism Trust, 1981-89. Served to capt. AUS, 1946-48. WHO fellow U. Negev, 1974; master Am. Coll. Rheumatology, 1991—; recipient Gold medal Am. Coll. Rheumatology, 1992. Master Am. Coll. Rheumatology (Gold medal 1992), fellow ACP, Am. Acad. Family Physicians (charter), N.Y. Acad. Medicine (chmn. edn. com. 1976-78); mem. AMA, (N.Y. chpt.), AAUP, Internat. Soc. for Rheumatic Therapy (chmn. 1987-89), Am. Fedn. Clin. Rsch., Am. Rheumatism Assn. (past sec.-treas.), N.Y. Rheumatism Assn. (past pres., exec. com.), Harvey Soc., (N.Y. chpt.), Kings County med. socs., Bklyn. socs. internal medicine, Soc. Tchrs. Family Medicine, N.Y. State Acads. Family Physicians, Soc. Urban Physicians, Mystery Writers Am., Sigma Xi, Alpha Omega Alpha; hon. mem. Rheumatology Soc. France, Rheumatology Soc. Japan, Rheumatology Soc. Mex., Rheumatology Soc. Brazil, Rheumatology Soc. Yugoslavia, Rheumatology Soc. Norway, Rheumatology Soc. Egypt, Med. Soc. Czechoslovakia. Club: Heights Casino. Home: 184 Columbia Hts Brooklyn NY 11201-2186 also: 450 Clarkson Ave Brooklyn NY 11203-2012

PLOTZ, RICHARD DOUGLAS, pathologist; b. Bklyn., Aug. 15, 1948; s. Charles Mindell and Lucille (Weckstein) P.; m. Judith Anker, Mar. 28, 1971; children: Martha Anne, Michael David. AB cum laude, Harvard U., 1971; MD, U. Pitts., 1977; MPH, Boston U., 1992. Resident Brown U., Providence, 1977-81; staff pathologist Women & Infants Hosp., Providence, 1982-88; med. dir. Corning Metpath (formerly Damon Clin. Lab.), Westwood, Mass., 1988-95, CytoStat, Pawtucket, R.I., 1996—. Del. White Ho. Conf. on Libr. & Info. Svcs., Washington, 1979. Fellow Coll. Am. Pathologists (inspector lab. accreditation program); mem. Am. Soc. Cytopathology, New Eng. Soc. Pathologists, R.I. Med. Soc., R.I. Soc. Pathologists. Democrat. Jewish. Avocation: genealogy. Home: 104 11th St Providence RI 02906-2912 Office: CytoStat 129 School St Pawtucket RI 02860-5305

PLOUGH, CHARLES TOBIAS, JR., retired electronics engineering executive; b. Oakland, Calif., Sept. 7, 1926; s. Charles Tobias Sr. and Miriam Lucille (Miller) P.; m. Jean Elizabeth Rose, June 13, 1950 (div. May 1969); children: Charles III, Cathleen, Mark, Barbara; m. Janet Mary Ansell Lumley, July 5, 1969; children: Mark Ansell Lumley, Simon John Lumley. AB with honors, Amherst Coll., 1950; BSEE with honors, U. Calif., Berkeley, 1953. Mgr. tech. devel. Fairchild Semiconductor, Palo Alto, Calif., 1958-71; v.p. Multi-State Devices, Montreal, Can., 1971-78; mgr. research and devel. Dale Electronics, Norfolk, Nebr., 1978-89, ret., 1989. Patentee in field. Mem. Lions (sec. Norfolk 1982-86); Leader Albuquerque Interfaith 1993—. Avocation: golf. Home: 2030 Quail Run Dr NE Albuquerque NM 87122-1100

PLOURDE, GERARD, company executive; b. Joliette, Que., Can., Feb. 12, 1916; s. Louis-George and Rose de Lima (Jolicoeur) P.; m. Jeannine Martineau, Dec. 4, 1943; children: Monique, Pierre, Marc-André. BA, Brébeuf Coll., 1936; M in Commerce, U. Montreal, Que., 1939, D. Honoris Causa, 1971. Accountant UAP Inc., Montreal, from 1941; pres., gen. mgr. UAP Inc., 1951-70, chmn. bd., chief exec. officer, 1970-80, chmn. bd., 1980-86, hon. dir., 1986—; hon. dir. Molson Cos., Northern Telecom; vice-chmn. bd. Cambior, Inc. Decorated Order of Can. Mem. Soc. Automotive Engrs., Laval-sur-le-Lac Club, Saint Denis Club, Mt. Bruno Country Club. Office: 1010 Sherbrooke W #2012, Montreal, PQ Canada H3A 2R7

PLOWDEN, DAVID, photographer; b. Boston, Oct. 9, 1932; s. Roger and Mary Russell (Butler) P.; m. Pleasance Coggeshall, June 20, 1962 (div. 1976); children: John, Daniel; m. Sandra Oakes Schoellkopf, July 8th, 1977; children: Philip, Karen. BA Econs., Yale U., 1955; pvt. study with Minor White, Rochester, N.Y., 1959-60. Asst. O. Winston Link Studio, N.Y.C., 1958-59, George Meluso Studio, N.Y.C., 1960-62; photographer, writer, 1962—; assoc. prof. Inst. Design, Ill. Inst. Tech., Chgo., 1978-86; lectr. U. Iowa Sch. Journalism, 1985-88; vis. prof. Grand Valley State Univ., 1988-90, 91—; artist-in-residence U. Balt., 1990-91. Author and photographer: Farewell to Steam, 1968, Lincoln and His America, 1970 (Benjamin Barondess award 1971), The Hand of Man on America, 1971, 2d edit, 1974, The Floor of the Sky: the Great Plains, 1972, Bridges: the Spans of North America, 1974, 2d edit. 1984, Commonplace, 1974, Tugboat, 1976 (notable Children's books ALA 1976, Children's Book Showcase 1976), Steel, 1981, An American Chronology, 1982 (Notable Books ALA 1982, Booklist's Best of the 80s 1989), Industrial Landscape, 1985, A Time of Trains, 1987, A Sense of Place, 1988, End of an Era: The Last of the Great Lakes Steamboats, 1992, Small Town America, 1994, Imprints: The Photographs of David Plowden, 1997; co-author, photographer, Nantucket, 1970, Cape May to Montauk, 1973, Desert and Plains, the Mountains and the River, 1975, The Iron Road, 1978 (notable children's books 1978, Honor list Horn Books 1979), Wayne County: the Aesthetic Heritage of a Rural Area, 1979; introduction The Gallery of World Photography/the Country, 1983; commd. illustrator Gems, 1967, The Freeway in the City, 1968, America the Vanishing, 1969, New Jersey, 1977, North Dakota, 1977, Vermont, 1979, New York, 1981, A Place of Sense, 1988; contbr. articles to numerous jours. including Time, Newsweek, Life, Audubon, Fortune; one-man shows include Columbia U., 1965, Smithsonian Instn., 1970, 71, 75, 76, 81, 89, Internat. Ctr. Photography, N.Y., 1976, Witkin Gallery, N.Y.C., 1979, Cin. Art Acad., 1979, The Gilbert Gallery, Chgo., 1980, 81, Chgo. Ctr. Contemporary Photography, 1982, Fed. Hall Mus., N.Y.C., 1982, Calif. Mus. Photography, Riverside, 1982-83, Chgo. Hist. Soc., 1985, Martin Gallery, Washington, 1987, Kunstmuseum, Luzern, Switzerland, 1987, Burchfield Ctr., Buffalo, 1987-88, Iowa State Mus., Des Moines, 1988-89, Catherine Edelman Gallery, Chgo., 1990, Grand Valley State U., 1993, Ewing Gallery, Washington, 1994, Beinecke Rare Book and Manuscript Lib. Yale U., 1997, Albright-Knox Art Gallery, 1997; exhibited in group shows at Met. Mus. Art, N.Y.C., 1967, Kodak Gallery, N.Y.C., 1976, Currier Gallery Art, Manchester, N.H., 1978, Whitney Mus., 1979, Art Inst. Chgo., 1983-86, 87, Witkin Gallery, N.Y.C., 1988, Davenport (Iowa) Mus. Art, 1992, Mus. Contemporary Photography, Chicy, R.I., 1996; represented in permanent collections Art Inst. Chgo., Calif. Mus. Photography, Ctr. Creative Photography, Chgo. Hist. Soc., Libr. Congress, Smithsonian Instn., U. Md., J.B. Speed Mus., Iowa Humanities Bd., Iowa State Hist. Dept., Burchfield Art Ctr., Buffalo and Erie County Hist. Soc., Am. Soc. Media Photographers Archives Internat. Mus. Photography George Eastman House, Internat. Ctr. Photography, Ekstrom Libr. U. Louisville, Beinecke Rare Book and Mauscript Library, Yale U., 1995—, Mus. Contemporary Photography, Chicy, Bayly Mus. U. Va., Charlottesville. John Simon Guggenheim fellow, 1968; grantee N.Y. State Coun. Arts, 1966, 87, Smithsonian Inst., 1970-71, Dept. Transp. and Smithsonian Inst., 1975-76, H. E. Butt Found., 1977, United Bd. Homeland Ministries, 1976, Chgo. Hist. Soc., 1980-84, Seymour H. Knox Found., 1987, Baird Found., 1987, State Hist. Soc. Iowa, 1987-88, Iowa Humanities Bd., 1987-88; recipient Railroad History award, 1989. Mem. Am. Soc. Media Photographers. Home and Office: 609 Cherry St Winnetka IL 60093-2614

PLOWMAN, JACK WESLEY, lawyer; b. Blairsville, Pa., Sept. 12, 1929; s. Ralph Waldo, Sr., and Ethel Beatrice (Nicely) P.; m. Barbara Ellen Brown, Apr. 5, 1952; children: Linda Ellen, Judith Lynn. A.B., U. Pitts., 1951, LL.B. with honors, 1956. Bar: Pa. 1956, U.S. Dist. Ct. (we. dist.) Pa. 1956, U.S. Ct. Appeals 1960, U.S. Supreme Ct. 1978. Assoc. Campbell, Houck & Thomas, Pitts., 1956-57; ptnr. Rose, Houston, Cooper & Schmidt, Pitts., 1957-63, Plowman, Spiegel & Lewis, Pitts., 1963—; adj. prof. Duquesne U. Sch. Law, 1963-70, 83—. Editor-in-chief Pitts. Legal Jour., 1971-81, U. Pitts. Law Rev., 1955-56. Bd. dirs. United Meth. Pub. House, 1984-96, Ward Home for Children, United Meth. Ch. Union, 1977-83, Wesley Inst., 1977-81, Neighborhood Legal Svcs. Assn., 1969-74; chancellor Western Pa. Ann. Conf., United Meth. Ch. Capt. USAF, 1951-53. Fellow Am. Bar Found. (life mem.), Am. Coll. Trial Lawyers, Allegheny County Bar Found. (trustee, sec.); mem. ABA, Pa. Bar Assn., Allegheny County Bar Assn. (pres. 1982), Pa. Bar Inst. (bd. dirs. 1988-92), Am. Law Inst., Supreme Ct. Pa. Hist. Soc. (trustee, pres.). Republican. Home: 1025 Lakemont Dr Pittsburgh PA 15243-1817 Office: Grant Building Fl 2 Pittsburgh PA 15219-2203

PLOWRIGHT, JOAN ANNE, actress; b. Brigg, Lancashire, Eng., Oct. 28, 1929; d. William and Daisy (Burton) P.; m. Roger Gage, 1953 (div.); m. Sir Laurence Olivier, 1961 (dec.); 3 children. Student Old Vic Theatre Sch. Mem. Old Vic Co., toured South Africa, 1952-53; 1st leading role in The Country Wife, London, 1956; mem. English Stage Co., 1956, Nat. Theatre, 1963-74. Appearences include (plays) The Chairs, 1957, The Entertainer, 1958, Major Barbara and Roots, 1959, A Taste of Honey, 1960 (Tony Best Actress award 1960), Uncle Vanya, 1962-64, St. Joan, 1963 (London Evening Standard Best Actress award 1964), Hobson's Choice, 1964, The Master Builder, 1965, Much Ado About Nothing, 1967, Tartuffe, 1967, Three Sisters, 1967, 69, The Advertisement, 1968, 69, Love's Labour's Lost, 1968, 69, The Merchant of Venice, 1970, 71-72, Rules of the Game, 1971-72, Woman Killed with Kindness, 1971-72, Taming of the Shrew, 1972, Doctor's Dilemma, 1972, Rosmersholm, 1973, Saturday Sunday Monday 1973, Eden's End, 1974, The Sea Gull, 1975, The Bed Before Yesterday, 1975 (Variety award 1976), Filumena, 1977 (Soc. West End Theatres Best Actress award 1978), Enjoy, 1980, Who's Afraid of Virginia Woolf?, 1981, Cavell, 1982, The Cherry Orchard, 1983; The Way of the World, 1985, The House of Bernada Alba, 1986-87, Uncle Vanya, 1988, Time and The Conways, 1991, (films) Much Ado About Nothing, 1969, Equus, 1976, Richard Wagner, 1982, Brimstone and Treacle, 1982, Brittania Hospital, 1983, Revolution, 1985, The Dressmaker, 1987, Drowning By Numbers, 1987, The Divider, Conquest of the South Pole, 1989, I Love You To Death, 1990, Avalon, 1990, Enchanted April, 1992 (Acad. award nominee Best Supporting Actress, Golden Globe award 1992), Dennis the Menace, 1993, Last Action Hero, 1993, The Summer House, 1993, Widows' Peak, 1994, Pyromaniacs: A Love Story, 1995, The Grass Harp, 1995, Hotel Sorrento, 1995, Jane Eyre, 1996, Surviving Picasso, 1996, 101 Dalmations, 1996; (TV films) Merchant of Venice, 1973, Daphne, Laureola, 1977, Saturday Sunday Monday, 1977, The Importance of Being Earnest, 1988, The Birthday Party, 1987, House of Bernarda Alba, A Nightingale Sang, 1989, Stalin, 1992 (Golden Globe award 1992, Emmy nomination, Supporting Actress - Miniseries, 1993), A Place for Annie, 1994, On Promised Land, 1994. Office: ICM care Mike Foster, 76 Oxford St, London W1N 0AX, England

PLUCIENNIK, THOMAS CASIMIR, lawyer, former assistant county prosecutor; b. Irvington, N.J., Apr. 8, 1947; s. Casimir Stanley and Helen Victoria (Sienicki) P.; m. Maria Anne Soriano, June 16, 1974. BS in Acctg., Seton Hall U., 1969, JD, 1983; MA in Criminal Justice, CUNY, 1976. Bar: N.J. 1983, U.S. Dist. Ct. N.J. 1983, D.C. 1994, U.S. Supreme Ct. 1995, N.Y. 1996, U.S. Ct. Mil. Appeals, 1996; cert. criminal trial atty., mil. trial atty. Mng. ptnr. Joe Bell's Tavern & Restaurant, Newark, 1979; police officer City of Newark, 1972-79; criminal investigator Essex County Prosecutor, Newark, 1980-84, asst. prosecutor, 1984-88; sr. asst. prosecutor, Warren County, N.J., 1988-89; atty. Voorhees & Acciavatti, Esq., Morristown, N.J., 1989-94; defense atty. Picillo Caruso, 1994-96; assoc. Netchert, Dineen & Hillman, 1996—. cert. instr. N.J. State Police Tng. Commn., Trenton, 1984; mil. instr. N.J. Mil. Acad., Sea Girt, N.J., 1979-81. Committeeman South Orange Republican Club, N.J., 1978-83; treas., founder Tuxedo Park Neighborhood Assn., South Orange, 1977; fin. sec. J. T. Kosciusko Assn., Irvington, N.J., 1979. Served to 1st lt. U.S. Army, 1969-71, maj. (ret.) JAGC, 1985-90. Recipient Class C Commendations, Newark Police Dept., 1973, 74, 75, Command Citations, 1973, 74, 75, 77, 78. Mem. ATLA, Worrall F. Mountain Inn of Ct. (master), N.J. State Bar Assn., N.J. Def. Assn., Morris County Bar Assn., Am. Legion, Officers Club (Sea Girt, N.J.) (pres. 1979-81), South Orange Lions Club, Polish Univ. Club. Republican. Roman Catholic. Home: 11 Laurel Ln Morris Plains NJ 07950-3216

PLUCINSKY, CONSTANCE MARIE, school counselor, supervisor; b. Passaic, N.J., Sept. 17, 1937; d. Stephen and Beatrice (Ruby) Goralski; m. William Plucinsky, June 29, 1957; 1 child, Carolyn. BS, Paterson State Coll., 1959; MA, Seton Hall U., 1970, postgrad., 1975; postgrad., William Paterson Coll., 1989—. Tchr. Garfield (N.J.) Bd. Edn., 1959-61, Paramus (N.J.) Bd. Edn., 1961-71, Bergen Gifted Child Soc., Ridgewood, N.J., 1965-71; guidance counselor grades 9-12 Paramus Bd. Edn., 1971-89, 91—, adminstrv. asst. to supt., 1989-91, counselor, coord. sex equity grades 7-12, 1990—; S.A.T. program supr. Ednl. Testing Svc., Princeton, N.J., 1992—; mem. adv. bd., 1990—, project dir., 1993—. Editor: (newsletter) PEN, 1989-94 (pub. rels. asst., 1991—); author: (brochure) All That You Can BEEEEEE, 1991, 92, 93; contbr. articles to profl. jours. Mem. steering com. Bergen County Intercultural Task Force, 1991—; facilitator trainer Achieving Sex Equity Through Students, 1991—. Named Guidance Counselor of Yr., Bergen County Profl. Guidance Assn., 1989, N.J. Equity Hall of Fame, 1993; recipient N.J. Dept. Edn. Best Practices award Paramus Acad. Sex Equity, 1993-94, Harassment Reduction Project, 1994-95; N.J. Exemplary Equity Program grantee divsn. vocat. edn. N.J. Dept. Edn., 1991-93. Mem. AAUW, N.J. Edn. Assn., Bergen County Profl. Guidance Assn. (exec.

com. 1994, first v.p. 1996—), Edn. Assn. Paramus. Democrat. Roman Catholic. Avocations: equestrian competitive rider, instructor, horse trainer. Home: 1030 Ramapo Valley Rd Mahwah NJ 07430-2413 Office: Paramus High Sch 99 E Century Rd Paramus NJ 07652-4399

PLUFF, STEARNS CHARLES, III, investment banker; b. Biloxi, Miss., Jan. 30, 1953; s. Stearns Charles Jr. and Patricia Elizabeth (Diaz) P.; m. Joan Marie Jay Jones, May 28, 1987; children: Micleah Frances, Ashleigh Nicole. BA, U. Miss., 1975. Supr. Host Internat., New Orleans, 1975-77; contractor Greg Edwards & Co., Falls Church, Va., 1977-80; registered rep. Donald Sheldon & Co., Houston, 1982-85; sr. v.p. GMS Group Inc., Houston, 1985—; dir., sr. v.p. MMP Investments, Inc., Cary, Ill., 1989—; pres. R.P. Telekom U.S.A., Warsaw, 1993—. Vol. Petrosky Elem. Sch., Alief, Tex., 1991—. Mem. Chi Psi. Avocations: world travel, hiking, camping, gardening. Home: GMS Group Inc 15210 La Mancha Houston TX 77083 Office: 5075 Westheimer Rd Ste 1175 Houston TX 77056-5606

PLUIMER, EDWARD J., lawyer; b. Rapid City, S.D., 1949. BA cum laude, U. S.D., 1971; JD cum laude, NYU, 1974. Bar: Minn. 1975. Law clk. to Hon. Robert A. Ainsworth, Jr. U.S. Ct. Appeals (5th cir.), 1974-75; ptnr. Dorsey & Whitney, Mpls.; mem. Minn. Supreme Ct. ADR Task Force, 1988-92. Editor N.Y. U. Law Rev. Mem. Order of the Coif. Office: Dorsey & Whitney LLP 220 S 6th St Minneapolis MN 55402-4502

PLUM, BERNARD MARK, lawyer; b. N.Y.C., Apr. 29, 1952; s. Aaron and Rhoda (Green) P.; m. Sandra M. Rocks, May 25, 1981; children: Benjamin H., Deborah A. BA, NYU, 1973; MA, Columbia U., 1974, MPhil, 1975, JD, 1979. Bar: N.Y. 1980, U.S. Dist. Ct. (so. dist.) N.Y. 1980, U.S. Dist. Ct. (ea. dist.) N.Y. 1981, U.S. Dist. Ct. (no. dist.) N.Y. 1983, U.S. Ct. Appeals (2nd cir.) 1987, U.S. Supreme Ct. 1989. Law clk. U.S. Dist. Ct. (so. dist.) N.Y., N.Y.C., 1979-80; assoc. atty. Proskauer, Rose, Goetz & Mendelsohn, N.Y.C., 1980-87, ptnr., 1987—. Mem. Assn. of Bar of City of N.Y., Fed. Bar Coun. Democrat. Jewish. Home: 300 Riverside Dr New York NY 10025-5279 Office: Proskauer Rose Goetz & Mendelsohn 1585 Broadway New York NY 10036-8200

PLUM, CHARLES WALDEN, retired business executive and educator; b. Circleville, Ohio, Apr. 13, 1914; s. Horace Walden and Anna Frances (Eaton) P.; m. Margaret E. McCollister, Sept. 17, 1939; children: David Walden, Donald Alan (dec.). B.S., Ohio State U., 1936; M.B.A., Case Western Res. U., 1951; postgrad., Advanced Mgmt. Program, Harvard, 1954. CPA, N.Y., Tex. Sr. accountant Coopers and Lybrand, N.Y.C., 1936-42; supr. acctg. Amertorp Corp., Naval Ordnance Plant, St. Louis, 1942-45; various positions to v.p. acctg. and mgmt. systems Standard Oil Co. (Ohio), Cleve., 1945-78; prof. bus. adminstrn. Tex. A&M, College Station, 1978-89; dir., chmn. audit com. Hospitality Motor Inns, Inc., Cleve., 1976-79; sec.-treas., dir., mem. mgmt. com. Am. Assembly Collegiate Schs. Bus., 1977-78; lectr. acctg. Western Res. U., 1946-54; bus. exec. in residence, disting. lectr. Tex. A. and M. U., 1976; Mem. bus. adv. council Kent State U., 1967-77. Mem. AICPA, Fin. Execs. Inst., Am. Petroleum Inst. (chmn. com. on cooperation with AICPA 1955-68), Tex. Soc. CPAs, Sigma Phi Epsilon, Beta Gamma Sigma, Beta Alpha Psi. Home: 5 Forest Dr College Station TX 77840-2321

PLUM, FRED, neurologist; b. Atlantic City, Jan. 10, 1924; s. Fred and Frances (Alexander) P.; children—Michael, Christopher, Carol; m. Susan Butler, Apr. 23, 1990. BA, Dartmouth Coll., 1944, postgrad., 1944-45; MD, Cornell U., 1947; MD (hon.), Karolinska Inst., Stockholm, 1982; DSc (hon.), L.I. U., 1990. Resident N.Y. Hosp., 1947-50, physician to outpatients, 1950-53, neurologist-in-chief, 1963—; instr. neurology Sch. Medicine Cornell U., 1950-53, Anne Parrish Titzell prof. neurology, 1963—, chmn. dept. neurology, 1963—; head neurology sect. U.S. Naval Hosp., St. Albans, N.Y., 1951-53; from asst. prof. to prof. neurology Sch. Medicine U. Wash., 1953-63; vis. scientist U. Lund, Sweden, 1970-71; vis. physician Rockefeller U. Hosp., 1975-85; assoc. neurosci. research program MIT and Rockefeller U., 1977-87; mem. neurology study sect., 1964-68, grad. tng. com., 1959-63, 71, nat. adv. council, 1977-81, Nat. Inst. Neurol., Communicative Disorders and Stroke, 84-86; past pres. McKnight Endowment Fund for Neurosci., 1986-90. Author: Diagnosis of Stupor and Coma, 1966, 3d edit., 1980, Clinical Management of Seizures, 1976, 2d edit., 1983, (with others) Cecil Essentials of Medicine, 1986, 3d edit., 1995; editor, contbg. author: Cecil's Textbook of Medicine, 1968, 2d edit., 1996; chief editor neurology sect. Contemporary Neurology series; editor: Recent Trends in Neurology, 1969, 2d edit., 1989, Brain Dysfunction in Metabolic Disorders, 1974; mem. editorial bd. Archives Neurology, 1958-68; chief editor, 1972-76; founding editor Annals of Neurology, 1977—; contbr. articles to scientific and profl. jours. Mem. Inst. of Medicine, Nat. Acad. Sci., Am. Neurol. Assn. (v.p. 1974-75, pres. 1976-77, Jacoby award 1984), Am. Acad. Neurology (past mem. council), Soc. Neurosci., Am. Soc. Clin. Investigation, Assn. Rsch. Nervous Mental Diseases (pres. 1973, 87), Assn. Am. Physicians, Alpha Omega Alpha; hon. mem. Can., Brit., French, Italian, Swiss neurol. socs. Rsch. in consciousness, coma and stroke. Office: Cornell U Medical Coll 525 E 68th St # A 569 Rm New York NY 10021-4873*

PLUMEZ, JEAN PAUL, advertising agency executive, consultant; b. N.Y.C., Oct. 31, 1939; s. Jean Paul and Marie Antoinette (Compagne) P.; m. Jacqueline Hornor, Feb. 20, 1965; children: Jean Paul, Nicole. B.S. in Chem. Enging., Bucknell U., 1962, B.A. in Chemistry, 1962; M.B.A., U. Pa., 1968. Product engr. Mobil Oil Co., Paulsboro, N.J., 1965-66; account mgr. Dancer Fitzgerald, Sample, Inc., N.Y.C., 1968-86, exec. v.p., 1979-86; pres. Leadership on Paper, Larchmont, N.Y., 1986—; founding ptnr. The Right Direction, 1987—. Served to capt. Signal Corps U.S. Army, 1962-64. Mem. Alpha Chi Sigma, Beta Gamma Sigma, Kappa Delta Rho. Clubs: Larchmont Yacht, Wharton of N.Y., Princeton of N.Y. Home and Office: 90 Beechtree Dr Larchmont NY 10538-1202

PLUMMER, (ARTHUR) CHRISTOPHER (ORME), actor; b. Toronto, Ont., Can., Dec. 13, 1929; s. John and Isabella Mary (Abbott) P.; m. Tammy Grimes (div.); 1 child, Amanda; m. Particia Audrew Lewis, May 4, 1962 (div.); m. Elaine Taylor. Ed. pub. and pvt. schs., Can.; pupil, Iris Warren, C. Herbertcasari. Stage debut in The Rivals with Can. Repertory Theatre, 1950; Broadway debut in Starcross Story, 1954; London debut in Becket, 1961; leading actor Am. Shakespeare Theatre, Stratford, Conn., 1955, Royal Shakespeare Co., London and Stratford, Avon, Eng., 1961-62, Stratford (Ont.) Shakespeare Festival, 1956, 57, 58, 60, 62, 67. Nat. Theatre Co., London; radio roles include Shakespeare, Canada; plays include Home is the Hero, 1954, Twelfth Night, 1954, 70-71, Dark is Light Enough, The Lark, Julius Caesar, The Tempest, 1955, Henry VI, 1956, Hamlet, 1957, Winter's Tale, 1958, Much Ado About Nothing, 1958, J.B., 1958, King John, 1960, Romeo and Juliet, 1960, Richard III, 1961, Arturo Ui, 1963, The Royal Hunt of the Sun, 1965, Antony and Cleopatra, 1967, Danton's Death, 1971, Amphitryon 38, 1971; (musicals) Cyrano, 1973, The Good Doctor, 1973, Love and Master Will, 1975; Othello, 1982, Macbeth, 1988, No Man's Land, 1993, Barrymore, 1996 (Tony award for Best Leading Actor in a Play, 1997); made TV debut 1953; TV prodns. include Little Moon of Alban, Johnny Belinda, 1958, Cyrano de Bergerac, 1962, Oedipus Rex, After the Fall, 1974, The Doll's House, The Prince and the Pauper, Prisoner of Zenda, Hamlet at Elsinore, BBC, 1964, Time Remembered, Capt. Brassbound's Conversion, The Shadow Box, 1981, The Thorn Birds, 1983, Little Gloria-Happy at Last, A Hazard of Hearts, 1987, Crossings, 1986, Danielle Steele's Secrets, 1992, Liar's Edge, 1992; star TV series The Moneychangers, 1977; made film debut in 1957; films include Stage Struck, 1957, Wind Across the Everglades, 1958, The Fall of the Roman Empire, 1963, Inside Daisy Clover, 1965, Sound of Music, 1965, Triple Cross, 1967, Nobody Runs Forever, 1969, The Battle of Britain, 1969, The Royal Hunt of the Sun, 1969, Lock up your Daughters, 1969, The Phyx, 1970, Waterloo, 1971, The Man Who Would Be King, 1975, The Return of the Pink Panther, 1975, Conduct Unbecoming, 1975, International Velvet, 1978, Murder By Decree, 1979, Starcrash, 1979, The Silent Partner, 1979, Hanover Street, 1979, Somewhere in Time, 1980, Eye witness, 1981, The Disappearance, 1981, The Amateur, 1982, Dreamscape, 1984, Ordeal by Innocence, 1984, Lily in Love, 1985, The Boss' Wife, 1986, The Boy In Blue, 1986, An American Tail, 1986 (voice), Souvenir, 1987, Dragnet, 1987, Light Years (voice), 1988, Where the Heart Is, 1989, Fire Head, 1991, Star Trek: VI: The Undiscovered Country, 1991, Rock a Doodle, 1992 (voice), Malcolm X, 1992, Wolf, 1994, Dolores Claiborne, 1994, Twelve Monkeys, 1995. Decorated companion Order of Can., 1968; recipient Theatre World award, 1955, Evening Standard award, 1961, Delia Austrian medal, 1973, 2 Drama Desk awards, 1973, 82, Antoinette Perry award, 1974, Emmy award Nat. Acad. TV Arts and Scis., 1977, Genie award, Can., 1980, Golden Badge of Honor, Austria, 1982, Maple Leaf award Nat. Acad. Arts and Letters. Mem. Theatre's Hall of Fame. Office: ICM care Lou Pitt 8942 Wilshire Blvd Beverly Hills CA 90211-1934*

PLUMMER, DANIEL CLARENCE, III, insurance consultant; b. Chgo., Apr. 30, 1927; s. Daniel C. and Ida May (Hayden) P.; m. Margaret Louise Marshall, Apr. 30, 1955; children: Daniel C., Judith Ann, David Marshall. B.S., Northwestern U., 1950. C.P.A., Ill. Sales rep. Sunbeam Corp., Chgo. and Phila., 1950-51; sr. acct. Touche Ross & Co., Chgo., 1952-56; adminstrv. mgr. Consol. Foundries & Mfg. Corp., Rockford, Ill., 1956-59; dir. internal audit Continental Casualty Co., Chgo., 1959-63; sec.-treas. Moline Malleable Iron Co., St. Charles, Ill., 1963-64; v.p. Allstate Ins. Cos., Northbrook, Ill., 1964-90, ret.; cons. re fin. regulation and mgmt. of insurers Lake Forest, Ill., 1990—; mem. acctg. com. Nat. Assn. Ind. Insurers, 1966-89, chmn., 1984-85; mem. acctg. prins. adv. com. Nat. Assn. Ins. Commrs., 1983-85, emerging acctg. issues com., 1985-93, chmn. data sys. adv. com., 1986-90. Co-author: Property-Liability Insurance Accounting, 1991. Bd. dirs. Chgo. coun. Boy Scouts Am., 1979-87, mem. fin. com., 1979-87, chmn. audit com., 1983-87, mem. exec. com., 1979-81, asst. treas., 1979-81, chmn. ins. com. 1986, adv. bd., 1987-90. With USN, 1945-46. Mem. Ill. Soc. CPAs (chmn. ins. industry com. 1976-77), Torch Lake Yacht Club Mich. Avocations: tennis; sailing; fishing.

PLUMMER, DIRK ARNOLD, professional engineer; b. Stamford, Conn., Apr. 18, 1930; s. Charles Arnold Plummer and Edwina Woodling Johnson; m. Janis Susan Lowery Stuart, Feb. 18, 1967 (div. 1973); 1 child, Julie. B-SChEngr, MIT, 1952; BSEE, U. Calif., Berkeley, 1961; MSEE, Monmouth U., 1995. Cert. nondestructive test examiner of inspectors for radiography, magnetic particle, liquid penetrant and ultrasonic testing methods; cert. comml. pilot. Chem. engr. Foster Wheeler Corp., N.Y.C., 1952; engr. The M.W. Kellogg Co., N.Y.C., 1954; project engr. Am. Machine & Fdry. Co., Greenwich, Conn., 1955-56; devel. engr. Aerojet-Gen. Corp., Azusa, Sacramento, San Ramon, Calif., 1956-61; sr. mem. tech. staff Aerospace Comm. & Controls Divsn. RCA, Burlington, Mass., 1961-62; engr. Elec. Boat Div. Gen. Dynamics Corp., Groton, Conn., 1963; electronics engr. U.S. Civil Svc., various locations, 1963-88; pvt. practice profl. engring. Sea Bright, N.J., 1988—. Contbr. articles to profl. jours. Archtl. control officer Sea Bright Village Assn., 1991. 1st lt. U.S. Army, 1952-54. Recipient Meritorious Svc. medal Pres. of U.S., 1982, Cert. for Commendable Svc. Def. Supply Agy., 1972. Mem. AAAS, NSPE, Soc. Logistics Engrs., AICE (profl. devel. officer 1990), IEEE (chmn. nuclear and plasma sci. chpt. 1990), Am. Phys. Soc., Am. Math. Soc., Math Assn. Am. Home and Office: 45 Village Ln Sea Bright NJ 07760-2233

PLUMMER, EDWARD BRUCE, college librarian; b. Toledo, Feb. 27, 1938; s. Paul Abel and Mabel Bernardine (Wert) P.; m. Mary Louise Girsch, Sept. 9, 1967; children: Andrew Brooks, Jonathan Tad. BA, Ohio Wesleyan U., 1960; MLS, Kent State U., 1967. Tchr., adult tutor Cin. Pub. Schs., 1960-65; dir. br. libr. Kent (Ohio) State U., 1967-70; assoc. dir. Worcester (Mass.) State Coll., 1971-80, dir., libr., 1980-97; assoc. dean Becker Coll., Worcester, 1997—; bd. dirs. Citizens for Edn. Resources, Worcester, 1994; pres. Cen./Western Mass. Automated Resource Sharing, Paxton, Mass., 1991-92; treas. Mass. Coun. Chief Librs. of Pub. Higher Edn. Instn., Amherst, Mass., 1991-93. Author: (book of poetry) Innovations, 1993. Bd. dirs. Talking Books, Worcester, 1991-94, Unitarian Universalist Ch., Worcester, 1991-94; mem. Libr. Pub. Sch. Power Group, Worcester, 1994—; bd. dirs., tutor Literacy Vols. of Am., Worcester, 1989—, del. to nat. conf., 1991; pres. Friends of the Worcester Pub. Libr. Club, 1989-91. Mem. Mass. Libr. Assn., Life Info. for Edn., Ferry Beach Park Assn. (bd. dirs. 1993-96), New England Libr. Assn., Assn. Coll. and Rsch. Librs. New England (city commr. 1995—), Worcester Cultural Commn. (sec. 1996—). Avocations: photography, gardening, painting. Home: 66 Navasota Ave Worcester MA 01602-1119 Office: Becker College Learning Resources Ctr 61 Sever St Worcester MA 01615

PLUMMER, GAYTHER L(YNN), climatologist, ecologist, researcher; b. Indpls., Jan. 27, 1925; s. Conley L. and Rowena H. (Huber) P.; m. H. Eileen Barr, June 3, 1950. BS, Butler U., 1948; MS, Kans. State U., 1950; PhD, Purdue U., 1954. Instr. biology Knox Coll., Galesburg, Ill., 1950-51; naturalist Ind. Dept. Conservation, various locations, 1947-52; asst. prof. biology Antioch Coll., Yellow Springs, Ohio, 1954-55; prof. botany U. Ga., Athens, 1955-95, state climatologist, 1978-95; rsch. fellow Oak Ridge (Tenn.) Inst. Nuclear Studies, 1958-62. Author: Georgia Weather Watchers, 1991, Georgia Temperatures, 1993; cartographer 160 vegetation maps of Ga., 1972-74; editor Ga. Jour. Sci., 1977-84; author over 200 rsch. reports. 2d lt. USAAF, 1943-46. Fellow AAAS; mem. Ecol. Soc. Am., Ind. Acad. Sci., Ga. Acad. Sci., Soil Sci. Soc. Am., Crop Sci. Soc., Agron. Soc. Am., Sigma Xi, Phi Kappa Phi. Achievements include research in droughts in S.E. U.S. relating to astrogeophysical processes via geomagnetics; lightning history in Piedmont for over 70 million years etched in Stone Mountain granite. Office: Ga Climatology Assoc Inc 995 Timothy Rd Athens GA 30606-3838

PLUMMER, MARCIE STERN, real estate broker; b. Plymouth, Mass., Oct. 28, 1950; d. Jacob and Rosalie (Adelman) Stern; m. John Dillon McHugh II, Oct. 8, 1974 (div.); 1 child, Joshua Stern; m. Louis Freeman Plummer Jr., Sept. 25, 1982; children: Jessica Price, Denelle Boothe. BA, Am. Internat. Coll., 1972, MAT in English, 1973, postgrad., 1974; postgrad., U. Conn., 1974; lic. real estate broker, Anthony Sch. Real Estate, Walnut Creek, Calif., 1985. Educator, chair dept. Windsor Locks (Conn.) Sch. Dist., 1972-74; educator, placement dir. Heald Bus. Coll., San Francisco, 1974-77; educator evening and day divs. Diablo Valley Coll., Pleasant Hill, Calif., 1975-77; real estate agt. Morrison Homes, Pleasant Hill, Calif., 1977-78; real estate agt., tract mgr. Dividend Devel., Santa Clara, Calif., 1978-81; real estate agt. Valley Realty, 1981-84; broker, owner Better Homes Realty, 1984-89; real estate broker, owner The Presád Co. Inc. subs. Better Homes Realty, Danville, Calif., 1984-90; owner The Mktg. Group, 1989—; v.p. mktg. Blackpoint Homes, Walnut Creek, Calif., 1997—; v.p., treas. Realty Resource Group, 1996. Better Homes Realty rep. for orgn. of Danville 4th of July Parade, City of Danville, 1984-88; publicist San Ramon Valley Little League, Alamo, Calif., 1986—; active Battered Women's Found., Contra Costa County, Calif., 1986—, Yosemite Fund, 1992—, Safe Home Teen Program, 1991—; active rep. voter registration, Walnut Creek, Calif., 1987—; mem. Civic Arts Coun., Walnut Creek, 1988—; drama coach, dir. Advanced Drama Ensemble, 1993-94. Recipient numerous nat., state and regional awards in field, $400 million closed vol. in real estate sales achievement award, 1991. Mem. AAUW, Bldg. Industry Assn. (Sales vol. award 1978-89), Sales & Mktg. Coun. (sponsor MAME awards banquet 1978-89, Gold sponsor 1986-88), Calif. Assn. Realtors, Contra Costa Bd. Realtors. Jewish. Avocations: playing piano, horseback riding, writing poetry and prose. Home: 123 Erselia Trl Alamo CA 94507-1311 Office: Better Homes Realty PO Box 939 Danville CA 94526-0939

PLUMMER, ORA BEATRICE, nursing educator, trainer; b. Mexia, Tex., May 25, 1940; d. Macie Idella (Echols); B.S. in Nursing, U. N.Mex., 1961; M.S. in Nursing Edn., UCLA, 1966; children—Kimberly, Kevin, Cheryl. Nurses aide Bataan Meml. Meth. Hosp., Albuquerque, 1958-60, staff nurse, 1961-62, 67-68; staff nurse, charge nurse, relief supr. Hollywood (Calif.) Community Hosp., 1962-64; instr. U. N.Mex. Coll. of Nursing, Albuquerque, 1968-69; sr. instr. U. Colo. Sch. Nursing, Denver, 1971-74; asst. prof. U. Colo. Sch. Nursing, Denver, 1974-76; staff assoc. III Western Interstate Commn. for Higher Edn., Boulder, Colo., 1976-78; dir. nursing Garden Manor Nursing Home, Lakewood, Colo., 1978-79; ednl. coordination Colo. Dept. Health, Denver, 1987—. Active Colo. Cluster of Schs.-faculty devel.; mem. adv. bd. Affiliated Children's and Family Services, 1977; mem. state instl. child abuse and neglect adv. com., 1984—; mem. bd. trustee Colo. Acad., 1990—; mem. planning com. State Wide Conf. on Black Health Concerns, 1977; mem. staff devel. com. Western Interstate Commn. for Higher Edn., 1978, minority affairs com., 1978, coordinating com. for baccalaureate program, 1971-76; active minority affairs U. Colo. Med. Center, 1971-72; mem. ednl. resources com. public relations com., rev. com. for reappointment, promotion, and tenure U. Colo. Sch. Nursing, 1971-76; regulatory tng. com., 1989—, gerontol. adv. com., Met. State Coll., 1989-93; expert panel mem. Long Term Care Training Manual, HCFA, Balt., 1989; mem. EDAC com. Colo. Dept. of Health, 1989-96. Mem. NAFE, Am. Soc. Tng. and Devel., Am. Nurses Assn., Colo. Nurses Assn. (affirmative action comm. 1977, 78, 79, 93-96), bd. trusteesColo. Acad., 1990-96, Phi Delta Kappa. Avocation: pub. speaking, training. Contbr. articles in field to profl. jours. Office: 4300 Cherry Creek South Dr Denver CO 80246-1523

PLUMMER, PATRICIA LYNNE MOORE, chemistry and physics educator; b. Tyler, Tex., Feb. 26; d. Robert Lee and Jewell Ovelia (Jones) Moore; m. Otho Raymond Plummer, Apr. 10, 1965; children: Patrick William Otho, Christina Elisa Lynne. BA, Tex. Christian U., Ft. Worth, Tex., 1960; postgrad., U. N.C., 1960-61; PhD, U. Tex., 1964; grad., Bryn Mawr Summer Inst., 1992. Instr., Welch postdoctoral fellow U. Tex., Austin, 1964-66; postdoctoral fellow Dept. Chemistry, U. Ark., Fayetteville, 1966-68; rsch. assoc. Grad. Ctr., Cloud Phys. Rsch., Rolla, Mo., 1968-73; asst. prof. physics U. Mo., Rolla, 1973-77; assoc. dir. Grad. Ctr. Cloud Phys. Rsch., 1977-79, sr. investigator, 1980-85; assoc. prof. physics U. Mo., 1977-85; prof. dept. chemistry and physics U. Mo., Columbia, 1986—; internat. sci. com. Symposium on Chemistry and Physics of Ice, 1982—, vice chair, 1996—, chair of Faculty Sen., 1995-96, pres. U. of Mo. Intercampo Fac. Sen., 1994-95. Assoc. editor Jour. of Colloid and Interface Sci., 1980-83; contbr. articles to profl. jours., chpts. to books. Rsch. grantee IBM, 1990-92, Air Force Office Rsch., 1989-91, NSF, 1976-86, NASA, 1973-78; Air Force Office Rsch. summer fellow, 1988, Bryn Mawr Summer Inst., 1992. Mem. Am. Chem. Soc., Am. Phys. Soc., Am. Geophys. Union, Sigma Xi (past pres.). Democrat. Baptist. Avocations: sailing, gardening, tennis, photography. Office: Univ of Missouri 314 Physics Bldg Columbia MO 65211

PLUMMER, RISQUE WILSON, lawyer; b. Mobile, Ala., Oct. 13, 1910; s. Frederick Harvey and Caroline (Wilson) P.; m. Constance M. Burch, Feb. 21, 1939; children: Risque Wilson Jr., Richard Randolph. J.D., U. Va., 1933. Bar: Va. 1932, Md. 1938. Atty. in charge of litigation HOLC, 1933-38; pvt. practice law, 1938—; counsel U.S. Maritime Commn., 1942; partner firm Griffin & Plummer, 1951-73; counsel O'Connor, Preston, Glenn & Smith, Balt., 1979—; prof. law Am. Inst. Banking, 1948-52. Contbr. articles to profl. jours. Exec. sec. Md. Commn. on Anti-Subversive Activities, 1949-50; co-founder, pres. Roland Park Baseball Leagues, Inc., 1956-57; co-founder, pres. Wyndhurst Improvement Assn., Inc., 1957-59; mem. Selective Service Adv. Bd., 1940-42. Served to lt. USNR, 1943-46, ATO, PTO. Fellow Internat. Acad. Law and Sci.; mem. ABA (council sect. of family law 1966-70), SAR, Md. Bar Assn. (council sect. of family and juvenile law 1968-70), Md. Assn. Trial Lawyers (gov. 1966-67), Bar Assn. Baltimore City (com. on grievances 1966-69, chmn. com. on profl. ethics 1969-70, exec. com. 1969-70), Am. Judicature Soc., Am. Contract Bridge League (Bronze life master, cert. dir., author The Small Club), Soc. Colonial Wars, Delta Tau Delta (pres. U. Va. chpt.), Phi Delta Phi. Episcopalian. Home: Highfield House Unit 512 4000 N Charles St Baltimore MD 21218 Office: Law Bldg 425 St Paul Pl Baltimore MD 21202-2107

PLUMMER, STEVEN TSOSIE, bishop; b. Coalmine, N. Mex., Aug. 14, 1944; m. Catherine B. Tso; children: Brian Tso, Byron Tso, Steven, Jr., Cathlena. Student, San Juan Community Coll., Farmington, N. Mex., Phoenix (Ariz.) Jr. Coll., Ch. Divinity Sch. of the Pacific, San Francisco. Ordained deacon, The Episc. Ch., 1975, priest, 1976. Deacon, priest Good Shepherd Mission, Fort Defiance, Ariz., 1976-77; vicar St. John the Baptizer, Montezuma Creek, Utah, 1977-83; regional vicar for Utah Bluff, Utah, from 1983; consecrated bishop Episc. Ch. in Navajoland, Farmington, N. Mex., 1990; mem. Episc. Council of Indian Ministries. Office: The Episcopal Ch Navajoland Area Mission PO Box 720 Farmington NM 87499-0720 Address: The Episcopal Ch Navajoland Area Mission PO Box 40 Bluff UT 84512

PLUMSTEAD, WILLIAM CHARLES, quality engineer, consultant; b. Two Rivers, Wis., Nov. 2, 1938; m. Peggy Bass, July 19, 1959 (div. July 1968); children: William Jr., Jennifer; m. Vicki Newton, June 27, 1981. Student, U. Fla., 1956-58, Temple U., 1966-72, Albright Coll., 1973-75; BSBA, Calif. Coast U., 1985, MBA, 1989. Registered profl. engr., Calif. V.p. U.S. Testing Co., Inc., Hoboken, N.J., 1963-76; div. mgr. Daniel Internat., Inc., Greenville, S.C., 1976-83; group mgr. Bechtel Group, Inc., San Francisco, 1983-89; prin. engr. Fluor Daniel, Inc., Greenville, 1989-94; pres. Plumstead Quality and Tech. Svcs., Greenville, S.C., 1994—. Author: (with others) Code/Specification Syndrome, 1976, NDT Laboratories Update, 1991, NDT in Construction, 1991, NDT-A Partner in Excellence, 1994; contbr. articles to profl. jours. Bd. dirs. Piedmont Food Bank, 1994-97. Fellow Am. Soc. Nondestructive Testing (coun. chmn. 1985-88, nat. sec., treas. 1992-93, nat. v.p. 1993-94, pres. 1994-95, chmn. bd. dirs. 1995-96); mem. ASTM (sec. 1989-93, vice chmn. 1994-96, chmn. 1996—), Toastmasters Internat. (pres. local chpt. 1990-91, Competent Toastmaster award 1986, Able Toastmaster award 1993). Avocations: sports, wine tasting. Home and Office: Plumstead Quality Tech Svcs 806 Botany Rd Greenville SC 29615-1608

PLUNKERT, DONNA MAE, business owner; b. Pa., Apr. 26, 1951; d. Norman Francis and Rada Mae (Snyder) Dickensheets; m. Bruce Herbert Plunkert, Nov. 2, 1975; 1 child, Gabriel Bruce. Grad., Littlestown (Pa.) H.S., 1969. Sales clk. Colonial Fair, Hanover, Pa., 1970-72, sec., 1972-75; full-time sec. Norm's Auction, Hanover, 1975-79, part-time sec., 1979-84; owner Old Buttermould Patterns Products, Littlestown, 1989—. Reproduced antique buttermolds for gift shops Carroll County Farm Mus., Westminster, Md., Historic Michie Tavern, Charlottesville, Va. Mem. U.S. C. of C., Mus. Store Assn. (assoc.). Mem. Brethren Ch. Avocations: collecting antique buttermoulds presses, country music, playing pool. Home: 315 N Queen St Littlestown PA 17340-1221

PLUNKET, DANIEL CLARK, pediatrician; b. Birmingham, Ala., May 7, 1929; s. Henry Clark and Carolyn Clark (Langford) P.; m. Lillian C. Barrington, Dec. 31, 1971; children: Dennis, Beth, Ann, Brenda, Scott. B.S., Emory U., 1949, M.D., 1952. Diplomate Am. Bd. Pediatrics. Intern Med. Coll. Va. Hosp., Richmond, 1952-53; resident in pediatrics Med. Coll. Va. Hosp., 1953-54, Tripler Army Med. Center, Honolulu, 1958-59, Walter Reed Army Inst., 1962-64; pediatrician, pediatric hematologist/oncologist acad. medicine, chief pediatric service William Beaumont Gen. Hosp., El Paso, Tex., 1959-62; commd. 1st lt. U.S. Army, 1955, advanced through grades to col., 1967; asst. chief dept. pediatrics Letterman Army Med. Center, San Francisco, 1964-65; chmn. dept. pediatrics Fitzsimons Army Med. Center, Denver, 1965-75; prof. pediat. U. Okla. Coll. Medicine, Tulsa, 1975—; sr. assoc. dean for clin. affairs U. Okla. Health Scis. Ctr., Tulsa, 1993—; chmn. dept. pediat. U. Okla. Coll. Medicine, Tulsa, 1975-96; clin. prof. pediatrics U. Colo., Denver, 1974-75. Mem. adv. chmn. March of Dimes, Tulsa chpt., 1975-92; bd. dirs. ARC, Tulsa chpt., 1981—. Decorated Legion of Merit; Walter Reed Inst. Research fellow hematology and research, 1962-64. Mem. Am. Acad. Pediatrics, Am. Pediatric Soc., Am. Soc. Hematology, AMA, So. Soc. Pediatric Rsch. Episcopalian. Home: 2436 E 33rd St Tulsa OK 74105-2316 Office: 2815 S Sheridan Rd Tulsa OK 74129-1013

PLUNKETT, JACK WILLIAM, writer, publisher; b. Dallas, May 17, 1950; s. Ivan Wayne and Waltina Lee (Roark) P.; m. Lynn Ann Richards (div.); 1 child, Jack W. Plunkett Jr.; m. Mary Lee Hartfelder, Dec. 8, 1972 (div.); children: Altus W., Robert L. Pres. Plunkett Properties Corp., Dallas, 1968-74; ind. mktg. cons. Dallas, 1974-83; mgr. ptnr. Brown-Plunkett, Waxahachie, Tex., 1983—; pub. Plunkett Rsch. Ltd. (formerly Corp. Jobs Outlook), Galveston, Tex., 1986—; editor, publisher Dream Trips! Newsletters, Galveston, 1988-96; CEO Cafe Lite Inc., 1990—; spl. cons. Houston Symphony, 1996—, The Odyssey House, Houston, 1997—. Author: The Almanac of American Employers, 1985, 94, 96, 98, Plunkett's Health Care Industry Almanac, 1995, 2d edit., 1997, Plunkett's InfoTech Industry Almanac, 1995, Plunkett's Financial Services Industry Almanac, 1996, Plunkett's Retail Industry Almanac, 1996, Plunkett's Entertainment and Media Industry Almanac, 1997. Chmn. Mayor's Libr. Fundraising Com., Boerne, Tex., 1988-89; founding pres. Greater Boerne Area Econ. Devel. Corp., 1986-87; dir. Boerne Area Cmty. Ctr., 1983-86; area chmn. Lamar Smith for Congress, Boerne, 1986; bd. dirs. Boerne Econ. Devel. Coun., 1992-94, Galveston Hist. Found., 1996—, Sch. of Nursing, U. Tex. Med. Br., 1996—, Strand Theater, 1996—; trustee Galveston County United Way, 1996—; mem. Dickens on the Strand 25th Ann. Com., 1997—; v.p. Houston Symphony Ptnrs., 1997—. Recipient Houston's Singular Best award Cystic

Fibrosis Found., 1997; named outstanding chmn. Boy Scouts Am., 1983, Community Vol. of Yr., Boerne Area C. of C., 1989. Mem. Rotary (pres. Boerne chpt. 1988-89), The Centurions. Republican. Office: Plunkett Rsch Ltd PO Drawer 541737 Houston TX 77554-1737

PLUNKETT, PAUL EDWARD, federal judge; b. Boston, July 9, 1935; s. Paul M. and Mary Cecilia (Erbacher) P.; m. Martha Milan, Sept. 30, 1958; children: Paul Scott, Steven, Andrew, Kevin. BA, Harvard U., 1957, LLB, 1960. Asst. atty. U.S. Atty.'s Office, Chgo., 1963-66; ptnr. Plunkett Nisin et al, Chgo., 1966-78, Mayer Brown & Platt, Chgo., 1960-63, 78-83; judge U.S. Dist. Ct. (no. dist.) Ill., Chgo., 1983—; adj. faculty John Marshall Law Sch., Chgo., 1964-76, 82—, Loyola U. Law Sch., Chgo., 1977-82. Mem. Fed. Bar Assn. Clubs: Legal, Law, Union League (Chgo.). Office: US Dist Ct Everett McKinley Dirksen bldg 219 S Dearborn St Ste 1446 Chicago IL 60604-1705*

PLUNKETT, PHYLLIS JEAN, nursing administrator; b. Owensboro, Ky., Nov. 25, 1953; d. William F. and Fumiko (Komatsu) Anders; m. Richard Orlen Plunkett, Aug. 6, 1976. BSN, U. Evansville, 1975; MSN, Andrews U., 1986, cert. adult nurse practitioner, 1996. Cert. adult nurse practitioner. Nursing supr. St. Joseph's Med. Ctr., South Bend, Ind., 1978-81, head nurse progressive care unit, 1981-85, clin. dir. rehab. ctr., 1985-87; unit dir. surg. nursing Meml. Hosp., South Bend, Ind., 1987-93; dir. med.-surg. patient care ctrs. Meml. Hosp., South Bend, 1993-95, dir. med. and surg. care ctrs., 1995—. Mem. ANA (cert. med.-surg. nursing, cert. in nursing adminstrn.), Sigma Theta Tau. Office: Meml Hosp of South Bend 615 N Michigan St South Bend IN 46601-1033

PLUSK, RONALD FRANK, manufacturing company executive; b. Chgo., Mar. 30, 1933; s. Frank and Ann (Petrauskas) P.; m. Rose Marie Pawlikowski, May 25, 1957; children—Frank A., Ronald S., Cynthia Marie. B.S.C., Loyola U., Chgo., 1954; postgrad., Northwestern U., 1957-59. Mgmt. cons. Peat, Marwick, Mitchell & Co., Chgo., 1963-66; corp. controller Varo, Inc., Garland, Tex., 1966-69; dir. planning and mgmt. systems Rucker Co., Oakland, Calif., 1969-72; dir. ops., audit and systems Rucker Co., 1972-76, v.p. ops., audit and systems, 1976-77; v.p. fin. adminstrn. Rucker Co. (merged with NL Petroleum Svcs. Co.), Houston, 1977-79; v.p. fin., treas. Cobe Labs., Inc., Lakewood, Colo., 1979-92; dir. Ctr. for Hearing Speech and Learning, Denver, 1996—. Contbr. articles to profl. jours. Served to 1st lt. AUS, 1954-56, ETO. Mem. Am. Mgmt. Assn., Planning Execs. Inst., Fin. Execs. Inst. Roman Catholic. Home: 6151 Middlefield Rd Littleton CO 80123-6620

PLUTA, PAUL J., federal agency administrator; b. Carteret, N.J.; m. Jane M. Oakley; children: Christine, Kevin, Brian. BA, USCG Acad., 1967; MSE in Naval Arch. and Marine Engring., U. Mich. Commd. ensign USCG; advanced through grades to rear adm.; asst. engr. USS Chincoteague, USS Minnetonka; staff engr. 8th Dist. Merchant Marine Tech. Office, New Orleans; staff engr. MMT divsn. Coast Guard Hdqs., chief engring. br., chief compliance and enforcement br. Merchant Vessel Inspection Divsn.; chief inspection dept. Marine Safety Office, Balt.; commdg. officer Marine Safety Office, Wilmington, N.C., 1988-91; comdr USCGR Tng. Ctr., Yorktown, Va.; chief staff 9th Coast Guard Dist., Cleve., 1994; dir. Office Intelligence and Security U.S. Dept. Transp., Washington, 1996—. U.S. negotiator UN's Internat. maritime Orgn., London. Decorated Legion of Merit. Office: US Dept Transp Office Intelligence and Security 400 7th St SW Rm 10401 Washington DC 20590*

PLUTA, RYSZARD MAREK, neurosurgeon, scientist; b. Warsaw, Poland, Nov. 19, 1952; came to U.S., 1989; s. Marian and Anastazja (Fornalczyk) P.; m. Agnieszka Zofia Salwa, Sept. 15, 1977; 1 child, Alicja Katarzyna. MD, Warsaw (Poland) Med. Acad., Poland, 1977; PhD, Med. Rsch. Ctr., Warsaw, 1987. Diplomate Nat. Neurosurg. Bd. Examiners. Intern Mcpl. Hosp., Warsaw, 1977-78; resident in neurosurgery Warsaw Med. Acad., 1979-84; attending neurosurgeon Warsaw Acad. Medicine, 1984-87; asst. prof. Warsaw Acad. of Medicine, Poland, 1987-92; vis. scientist NIH, Bethesda, Md., 1989—; Fogarty fellow Nat. Inst. Neurol. Disorders & Stroke, Bethesda, Md., 1989-91; assoc. prof. neurosurgery Polish Acad. Scis., Warsaw, 1996; vis. scientist surg. neurology br. NIH/Nat. Inst. Neurol. Disorders and Stroke, Bethesda, 1989—, animal use com., 1993—, Polish Acad. Scis., 1996. Contbr. articles to profl. jours. Recipient Jerzy & Krystyna Chorobski award Polish Neurosurg. Soc., 1987. Mem. Polish Am. Health Assn. Avocations: trakking, mountain climbing, tennis, skiing. Office: NINDS/NIH Surgical Neurology Br 9000 Rockville Pike B Bethesda MD 20814-1436

PLUTA, STANLEY JOHN, manufacturing project engineer; b. Ware, Mass., Feb. 5, 1966; s. John Henry and Josephine Ann (Wojnicki) Heupel; m. Sandra Akiko Ishizaka. AAS in Aero. Ground Equipment Tech., C.C. of USAF, 1987; BS in Indsl. Tech., So. Ill. U., 1988; MBA, Calif. State U., Long Beach, 1994. Registered profl. engr., Calif. Sort coord. Roadway Package System, L.A., 1989-90; assoc. indsl. engr. Northrop Corp., Hawthorne, Calif., 1990, indsl. engr., 1990-94, sr. indsl. engr., 1994-95; mfg. project engr. Packard-Hughes Interconnect, Irvine, Calif., 1995—. Staff sgt. USAF, 1985-89. Decorated Air Force Commendation medal. Mem. Am. Prodn. and Inventory Control Soc., Inst. Indsl. Engrs. Avocations: bicycling, hiking, reading, computers, photography. Home: 24069 Chateney Ln Murrieta CA 92562 Office: Packard-Hughes Interconnect MS 111 17150 Von Karman Ave Irvine CA 92614-0901

PLYLER, CHRIS PARNELL, dean; b. Washington, Mar. 21, 1951; s. Glenn Parnell and Doris Eleanor (Oswald) P.; m. Allison Rose Lord, Aug. 4, 1979; children: Benjamin, Patrick, Christen. BA, Clemson U., 1973; MEd, U. S.C., 1975; PhD, Fla. State U., 1978. Dir. male housing Coll. Charleston, S.C., 1975-76; asst. to pres. Fla. State U., Tallahassee, 1976-77; asst. to assoc. chancellor faculty and pers. rels. State U. System Fla., Tallahassee, 1977-78; assoc. dean acad. affairs U. S.C.-Salkehatchie, Allendale, 1978-82; dir. grad. regional studies U. S.C., Aiken, 1982-84, assoc. chancellor student svcs., 1984-90; dean U. S.C., Beaufort, 1990—; mem. adv. bd. S.C. Nat. Bank, Aiken, 1988-90, Palmetto Fed. Savs. and Loan Assn. Treas. bd. dirs. ARC, Aiken, 1984-90; bd. dirs. Boys and Girls Club, Beaufort, 1990—, Hitchcock Rehab. Ctr., Aiken, 1988-90. Mem. Am. Assn. for Higher Edn., Nat. Assn. for Student Pers. Adminstrn., S.C. Coll. Pers. Assn., So. Assn. for Coll. Student Affairs, Nat. Inst. Conf. for Regional Campus Adminstrn., Sea Island Rotary, Aiken Sunrise Rotary (bd. dirs. 1986-90), Aiken Sertoma Club, Phi Delta Kappa, Omicron Delta Kappa. Home: U SC Beaufort 370 Cottage Farm Dr Beaufort SC 29902-5968 Office: U SC 801 Carteret St Beaufort SC 29902-4601

PLYLER, JOHN LANEY, JR., healthcare management professional; b. Greenville, S.C., Jan. 31, 1934; s. John Laney and Beatrice Elizabeth (Dennis) P.; m. Caroline Raysor Williams, June 26, 1959; children: Sharon, John III, James (dec.). Student, U.S. Naval Acad., 1953-54; BA, Furman U., 1956; MHA, Duke U., 1970. Prodn. planner J. P. Stevens & Co., Greenville, 1958-65; mgmt. engr., outpatient mgr. Greenville Hosp. Sys., 1967-68; assoc. dir. Cleveland Meml. Hosp., Shelby, N.C., 1970-79; exec. v.p., COO Bapt. Med. Ctr., Oklahoma City, 1979-85; group v.p. SunHealth Alliance, Charlotte, N.C., 1985-86, sr. v.p., 1986-96. 2d lt. U.S. Army, 1957, capt. USAR, 1957-65. Fellow Am. Coll. Healthcare Execs. (mem. ethics com. 1990-93, chair 1992-93), Okla. Hosp. Assn. (mem. coun. on edn.), N.C. Hosp. Assn. (coun. on pers.). Avocations: travel, sailing, photography. Home: PO Box 909 Davidson NC 28036

PNIAKOWSKI, ANDREW FRANK, structural engineer; b. Grodno, Poland, Aug. 18, 1930; s. Josef Leon and Janina (Kodzynski) P.; Diploma Engr., Politechnika Warszawska, 1952; m. Margaret M. Czajkowski, Aug. 15, 1957; 1 dau., Mary. Bridge design and field engr. Govt. of Poland, Ministry of R.R., Warsaw, 1952-57; bridge design engr. Dept. Hwys., of Ont. (Can.), Toronto, 1958-66; sr. structural engr. Sverdrup & Parcel Assos. Inc., Boston, 1967-71; chief structural engr. Louis Berger & Assos. Inc., Needham, Mass., 1972-96; cons. engr. in transp., bridges, hwys., railroads, pub. bldgs., others. Registered profl. engr., Ont., Mass., Maine, N.H. Mem. Am. Inst. Steel Constrn., Am. Concrete Inst., Prestressed Concrete Inst., Assn. Profl. Engrs. of Province Ont. Roman Catholic.

POBINSON, SUZETTE E., airport executive. Dir. Detroit City Airport. Office: Detroit City Airport 11499 Conner St Detroit MI 48213-1206

POBLETE, RITA MARIA BAUTISTA, physician, educator; b. Manila, May 19, 1954; came to U.S., 1980; d. Juan Gonzalez and Rizalina (Bautista) Poblete. BS, U. Philippines, 1974, MD, 1978. Diplomate Am. Bd. Internal Medicine and Infectious Disease. Intern, resident Wayne State U./Detroit Med. Ctr., 1982-85, fellow in infectious disease, 1986-87; fellow in infectious disease Chgo. Med. Sch./VA Hosp., North Chicago, Ill., 1985-86; fellow in spl. immunology U. Miami (Fla.)-Jackson Meml. Hosp., 1987-89; adj. clin. instr. dept. of medicine U. Miami, 1989-90, asst. prof. medicine, 1990-94; infectious disease cons. Cedars Med. Ctr. and Mercy Hosp., Miami, 1994—. Contbr. articles to med. jours. Mem. Am. Soc. for Microbiology, Am. Soc. Internal Medicine, World Found. Successful Women. Avocations: tennis, swimming, playing guitar. Office: Cedars Med Ctr 1295 NW 14th St Ste E Miami FL 33125-1600

POCH, HERBERT EDWARD, pediatrician, educator; b. Elizabeth, N.J., Sept. 4, 1927; s. William and Min (Herman) P.; m. Leila Kosberg, Aug. 27, 1952; children: Bruce Jeffrey, Andrea Susan, Lesley Grace. AB, Columbia U., 1949, MD, 1953. Diplomate Am. Bd. Pediatrics. Intern Kings County Hosp. Ctr., Bklyn., 1953-54; resident Babies Hosp., Columbia-Presbyn. Med. Ctr., N.Y.C., 1954-56; pvt. practice medicine specializing in pediatrics Elizabeth, 1956-92; chmn. dept. pediatrics, 1973-83; pres. med. staff, 1989, attending pediatrician Elizabeth Gen. Med. Ctr., 1973, sr. attending pediatrician, 1990; attending pediatrician St. Elizabeth Hosp., 1968, chmn. dept. pediatrics, 1971-81, attending pediatrician Monmouth Med. Ctr., 1991—, assoc. program dir. pediatrics; instr. pediatrics Columbia U., 1956-72, asst. clin. prof. pediatrics, 1972-91; honorary staff Elizabeth Gen. Med. Ctr., 1993—. With AUS, 1945-46. Fellow Am. Acad. Pediatrics; mem. N.J. Med. Soc., Ambulatory Pediatric Assn. Address: 1175 Ocean Ave Long Branch NJ 07740-4518

POCHI, PETER ERNEST, physician; b. Boston, Mar. 8, 1929; s. Anesti and Alice (Peterson) P.; m. Barbara Orlob, June 11, 1955; children: Alan, Rena. A.B. cum laude, Harvard Coll., 1950; M.D., Boston U., 1955. Diplomate Am. Bd. Dermatology. Intern Boston City Hosp., 1955-56, vis. dermatologist, 1978-91, assoc. dir., 1967-74, 78-84, acting chief dermatology, 1984-85; resident in dermatology Boston U. Hosp., 1958-61, vis. dermatologist, 1977-91, acting chief dermatology, 1984-85; assoc. in medicine Peter Bent Brigham Hosp., Boston, 1972-78; sr. cons. in dermatology Lemuel Shattuck Hosp., Boston, 1975-91; Herbert Mescon prof. dermatology Sch. Medicine, Boston U., 1988-91, prof. emeritus, 1991—, interim chmn. dept. dermatology, 1984-85; cons. med. service in dermatology Boston VA Hosp., 1978-82; lectr. dermatology Sch. Medicine, Tufts U., 1980-91; assoc. staff New Eng. Med. Ctr. Hosp., 1981-91. Assoc. editor: Jour. Investigative Dermatology, 1968-73; contbg. editor: Year Book of Dermatology, 1983-90; mem. editorial bd.: Archives of Dermatology, 1979-84, Jour. Am. Acad. Dermatology, 1981-90; contbr. articles to med. jours. Bd. dirs. Cmty. Music Ctr., 1973-77, corp. mem., 1994—. With USN, 1956-58. USPHS fellow, 1960-62, 62-63; USPHS grantee, 1965-84. Fellow Am. Acad. Dermatology (bd. dirs. 1981-85); mem. Am. Fedn. Clin. Research, AMA, Boston Dermatological Club (sec.-treas. 1967-69), Boston U. Sch. Medicine Alumni Assn. (pres. 1979-80), Boston U. Nat. Alumni Council, Dermatology Found., Evans Med. Found. (dir., sec.), Internat. Soc. Dermatology, Mass. Acad. Dermatology, Mass. Med. Soc. (chmn. sect. dermatology 1977-78), New Eng. Dermatol. Soc., Soc. Investigative Dermatology (bd. dirs. 1976-81, v.p. 1986-87). Home: 333 Commonwealth Ave Boston MA 02115-1931

POCHYLY, DONALD FREDERICK, physician, hospital administrator; b. Chgo., June 3, 1934; s. Frank J. and Vlasta (Bezdek) P.; m. Diane Dilelio, May 11, 1957; children: Christopher, Jonathan, David. M.D., Loyola U., 1959; M.Ed., U. Ill., 1971. Diplomate Am. Bd. Internal Medicine, Am. Bd. Geriatrics. Fellow ACP, 1966-67; asst. prof. med. edn. U. Ill., 1967-72, asso. prof., 1972-74; chmn. dept. health scis. edn. U. of Health Scis., Chgo. Med. Sch., 1975-77, provost, acting pres., 1977-79; prof. clin. medicine Loyola U., Chgo., 1980—; v.p. med. affairs N.W. Community Hosp., Arlington Heights, Ill.; chmn. com. rev. and recognition Am. Coun. Continuing Med. Edn., 1993; cons. Nat. Libr. Medicine, WHO. Contbr. articles to med. jours. Mem. AMA, Ill. Geriatrics Soc. (pres. Chgo. chpt. 1988-89), Ill. Med. Soc., Chgo. Med. Soc., Alpha Omega Alpha. Roman Catholic. Office: Northwest Community Hosp 800 W Central Rd Arlington Heights IL 60005-2349

POCKELL, LESLIE M., publishing company executive; b. Norwalk, Conn., June 19, 1942; s. Abe and Mildred (Shapiro) P.; m. Noriko Maejima, June 23, 1967. AB, Columbia Coll., 1964. Articles editor Avant-Garde Mag., N.Y.C., 1967-70; dir. trade dept. St. Martin's Press, N.Y.C., 1970-84; exec. editor, dir. spl. interest group Doubleday & Co. Inc., N.Y.C., 1984-88; editl. dir. Kodansha Internat., 1988-94; dir. book devel. Book-Of-The-Month Club, Inc., N.Y.C., 1994—; adj. lectr. NYU, 1984-86; mem. adv. com. Small Press Ctr., 1995—. Served with U.S. Army, 1964-67.

POCKER, YESHAYAU, chemistry, biochemistry educator; b. Kishinev, Romania, Oct. 10, 1928; came to U.S., 1961; naturalized, 1967.; s. Benzion Israel and Esther Sarah (Sudit) P.; m. Anna Goldenberg, Aug. 8, 1950; children: Rona, Elon I. MSc, Hebrew U., Jerusalem, 1949; PhD, Univ. Coll., London, Eng., 1953; DSc, U. London, 1960. Rsch. assoc. Weizmann Inst. Sci., Rehovot, Israel, 1949-50; humanitarian trust fellow Univ. Coll., 1951-52, asst. lectr., 1952-54, lectr., 1954-61; vis. assoc. prof. Ind. U., Bloomington, 1960-61; prof. U. Washington, Seattle, 1961—; bicentennial lectr. Mont. State U., Bozeman, 1976; Horizons in Chemistry lectr. U. N.C., Chapel Hill, 1977, guest lectr. U. Kyoto, Japan, 1984; Edward A. Doisy vis. prof. biochemistry St. Louis U. Med. Sch., 1990; plenary lectr. N.Y. Acad. Sci., 1983, Fast Reactions in Biol. Systems, Kyoto, Japan, 1984, NATO, 1989, Consiglio nat. delle Richerche, U. Bari, Italy, 1989, Sigma Tau, Spoleto, Italy, 1990; Internat. lectr. Purdue U., 1990; cons. NIH, 1984, 86, 88; Spl. Topic lectr. on photosynthesis, Leibniz House, Hanover, Fed. Republic Germany, 1991; enzymology, molecular biology lectr., Dublin, Ireland, 1992; 3M lectr., St. Paul, 1996; enzymology, molecular biology, retinal metabolism lectr., Deadwood, S.D., 1996. Mem. editorial adv. bd. Inorganica Chimica Acta-Bioinorganic Chemistry, 1981-89; bd. reviewing editors Sci., 1985—; contbr. numerous articles to profl. jours.; pub. over 220 papers and 12 revs. Numerous awards worldwide, 1983-90. Mem. Royal Soc. Chemistry, Am. Chem. Soc. (nat. spkr. 1970, 74, 84, chmn. Pauling award com. 1978, plaque awards 1970, 74, 84, Outstanding Svc. award 1979, chmn. selection com. Pauling award 1996), Soc. Exptl. Biology, Am. Soc. Biol. Chemists, N.Y. Acad. Scis., Sigma Xi (nat. lectr. 1971). Avocations: Aramaic, etymology, history, philology, poetry. Office: U Wash Dept Chemistry Campus Box 351700 Seattle WA 98195-1700

POCKLINGTON, PETER H., business executive; b. Regina, Sask., Can., Nov. 18, 1941; s. Basil B. and Eileen (Dempsey) P.; m. Eva d. Jack McAvoy, June 2, 1974; 4 children. Pres. Westown Ford, Tilbury, Ont., Can., 1967-69; pres. Chatham, Ont., 1969-71, Edmonton, Alta., Can., 1971-82; chmn. Pocklington Fin. Corp., Edmonton, 1982—; owner, gov. Edmonton Oiler Hockey Club, 1976—; owner Edmonton Trapper Triple A Baseball Club, 1981—; formed Hartford Properties, Inc., 1985, Edmonton, Club Fit Inc., 1990; purchased Superior Furniture Systems Mfg., Inc., 1987, Canbra Foods Ltd., 1988, Green Acre Farms, Sabastool, Miss., 1988, Green Acre Foods Inc., Nacadoches, Tex., 1988. Mem. Mayfair Golf and Country Club, Edmonton Golf and Country Club, Vintage Golf Club, Indian Wells, Calif. Avocations: golf, skiing, fishing. Office: Pocklington Fin Corp Ltd, 2500 Sun Life Pl 10123-99 St, Edmonton, AB Canada T5J 3H1 also: Edmonton Oilers, Edmonton, AB Canada T5B 4M9*

POCOCK, FREDERICK JAMES, environmental scientist, engineer, consultant; b. Canton, Ohio, May 28, 1923; s. Frederick Stanley and Mary Elizabeth (Tinker) P.; m. Lois Jean Rice, Jan. 12, 1952; children—Kathleen Jean, David Walter. B.S. in Chemistry, Mt. Union Coll., 1950; grad., Lincoln Aero Inst., 1942; postgrad., Akron U., 1953. Registered profl. engr., Calif. Aircraft insp. Bell Aircraft Corp., 1942; in tech. sales Republic Steel Corp., 1949-50; with Babcock & Wilcox Co., Alliance, Ohio, 1950-88; sr. scientist Alliance Research Center, 1974-88; cons. water technology. Contbr. articles to profl jours. Past precinct committeeman Louisville Republican Com., Ohio. Served with USAAF, 1943-46. Recipient recognition for 30 yrs. rsch. Ohio Ho. of Reps., 1980, award of merit Internat. Water Conf., 1985; co-recipient Paul Cohen Meml. award, 1993, Engrs. award for disting. svc. Soc. Profl. Engrs., 1987. Fellow ASME (co-recipient Prime Movers award 1962, Disting. Svc. award 1987, Dedicated Svc. award 1987); mem. ASTM, Am. Chem. Soc. (Cert. of Merit 1967), Nat. Assn. Corrosion Engrs. (accredited corrosion specialist).

POCOSKI, DAVID JOHN, cardiologist; b. Waterbury, Conn., July 15, 1945; s. Edward J. and Stella E. (Kolpa) P.; m. Madelyn M. Pocoski, Sept. 25, 1971; 1 child, Sarah C. BAS, U. Conn., 1967; MD magna cum laude, Upstate Med. Ctr., Syracuse, N.Y., 1971. From intern to fellow in cardiology U. Rochester, N.Y.; pres. Osler Clin. of Medicine, Melbourne, Fla., Sez Dines Rehab. Hosp. Commr. Holy Name Jesus Cath. Ch. Maj. USAF, 1974-76. Fellow Am. Coll. Cardiology; mem. AMA. Republican. Roman Catholic. Avocations: music, art, running, community service. Office: 930 S Harbor City Blvd Melbourne FL 32901-1963

PODBERESKY, SAMUEL, lawyer; b. Cremona, Italy, Mar. 16, 1946; came to U.S., 1947; s. Noah and Mina (Milikowsky) P.; m. Rosita Rubinstein, March 8, 1970; children: Daniel J., Michael J. BS in Aeronautical Engring., U. Md., 1967; JD, U. Md., Balt., 1971. Bar: Md. 1972. Flight test engr. Vertol div. Boeing Co., Phila., 1967-68; regulatory atty. FAA, Washington, 1971-78; dep. asst. gen. counsel U.S. Dept. Transp., Washington, 1978-86, asst. gen. counsel aviation enforcement and proceedings, 1986—. Office: US Dept Transp 400 7th St SW Washington DC 20590-0001

PODBOY, ALVIN MICHAEL, JR., lawyer, law library director; b. Cleve., Feb. 10, 1947; s. Alvin Michael and Josephine Esther (Nagode) P.; m. Mary Ann Gloria Esposito, Aug. 21, 1971; children: Allison Marie, Melissa Ann. AB cum laude, Ohio U., 1969; JD, Case Western Res. U., 1972, MLS, 1977. Bar: Ohio 1972, U.S. Dist. Ct. (no. dist.) Ohio 1973, U.S. Supreme Ct. 1992. Assoc. Joseph T. Svete Co. LPA, Chardon, Ohio, 1972-76; dir. pub. services Case Western Res. Sch. Law Libr., Cleve., 1974-77, assoc. law libr., 1977-78; libr. Baker & Hostetler, Cleve., 1978-88, dir. librs., 1988—; instr. Notre Dame Coll. of Ohio, Cleve., 1991—, Am. Inst. Paralegal Studies, Cleve., 1991-96. Bd. overseers Case Western Res. U., 1981-87, mem. vis. com. sch. libr. sci., 1980-86, mem. Westlaw adv. bd., 1987-92, bd. govs. law sch. alumni assn., 1992-95, West's Legal Directory Ohio Adv. Panel, 1990-91; mem. adv. com. West's Info. Innovators Inst., 1995—; chmn. Case Western Res. Libr. Sch. Alumni Fund, 1979-80. Rep. precinct committeeman Cuyahoga County, Cleve., 1981-95, mem. exec. com., 1984-87. 1st lt. USAF, 1972. Mem. ABA, Ohio State Bar Assn. (chmn. libraries com. 1989-91), Cleve. Bar Assn., Am. Assn. Law Librs. (cert., chmn. pvt. law librs. spl. interest sect. 1994-95), Ohio Regional Assn. Law Librs. (pres. 1985), Case Western Res. U. Libr. Sch. Alumni Assn. (pres. 1981), Arnold Air Soc., Am. Legion, Pi Gamma Mu, Phi Alpha Theta. Roman Catholic. Lodge: K.C. Avocations: alpine skiing, boating. Home: 5705 Deer Creek Dr Willoughby OH 44094-4185 Office: Baker & Hostetler 3200 National City Ctr Cleveland OH 44114-3485

PODD, ANN, newspaper editor; b. Buffalo, Jan. 15, 1954; d. Edward and Florence (Bojan) P.; m. Timothy Murray, 1980; children: Laura, Gregory. AB, Syracuse U., 1976; MBA, SUNY, Buffalo, 1981. Reporter AP, 1977; reporter Buffalo Courier-Express, 1977-80, bus. editor, 1980-82; bus. editor Bergen (N.J.) Record, 1982-88; bus. editor New York Daily News, 1988-90, assoc. editor, 1990-92, assoc. editor, dir. human resources, 1992-93; dep. spot news editor Wall St. Jour., N.Y.C., 1994, spot news editor, 1994—. Office: Wall St Journal 200 Liberty St New York NY 10281-1003

PODGORNY, GEORGE, emergency physician; b. Tehran, Iran, Mar. 17, 1934; s. Emanuel and Helen (Parsian) P.; came to U.S., 1954, naturalized, 1973. B.S., Maryville Coll., 1958; postgrad. Bowman Gray Sch. Medicine, 1958; M.D., Wake Forest U., 1962; m. Ernestine Koury, Oct. 20, 1962; children: Adele, Emanuel II, George, Gregory. Intern in surgery N.C. Bapt. Hosp., Winston-Salem, 1962-63, chief resident in gen. surgery, 1966-67, in cardiothoracic surgery, 1967-69; sr. med. examiner Forsyth County, N.C., 1972—; dir. dept. emergency medicine Forsyth Meml. Hosp., Winston-Salem, 1974-80; sec.-treas. Forsyth Emergency Services, Winston-Salem, 1970-80; clin. prof. emergency medicine East Carolina U. Sch. Medicine, Greenville, 1984—, chmn. residency rev. com. on emergency medicine, 1980-88; mem. Accreditation Coun. for Grad. Med. Edn. Dir. Emergency Med. Svcs. Project Region II of N.C., 1975—; chmn. bd. trustees Emergency Medicine Found.; chmn. residency rev. com. emergency medicine Accreditation Coun. Grad. Med. Edn.; founder Western Piedmont Emergency Med. Svcs. Coun., 1973; mem. N.C. Emergency Med. Svcs. Adv. Coun., 1976-81; assoc. prof. clin. surgery Bowman Gray Sch. Medicine, Wake Forest U., Winston-Salem, 1979—. Bd. dirs. Piedmont Health Systems Agy., 1975-84; trustee Forsyth County Hosp., Authority, 1974-75; bd. dirs. N.C. Health Coordinating Coun., 1975-82, Medic Alert Found. Internat. Fellow Internat. Coll. Surgeons, Internat. Coll. Angiology, Royal Soc. Health (Great Britain), Royal Soc. Medicine, Southeastern Surg. Congress; mem. Am. Coll. Emergency Physicians (charter, pres. 1978-79), AMA, (chmn. coun. of sect. emergency medicine 1978-90, alt. del. for Am. Coll. Emergency Physicians, 1990—), Am. Bd. Emergency Medicine (pres. 1976-81). Contbr. articles to profl. publs. on trauma, snake bite and history of medicine; editorial bd. Annals of Emergency Medicine, Med. Meetings. Home and Office: 2115 Georgia Ave Winston Salem NC 27104-1917

PODGORNY, RICHARD JOSEPH, biologist, science administrator; b. Chgo., Jan. 27, 1944; s. Leon and Mary Agatha (Gryzik) P.; m. Dorothy Mary Dorece, June 11, 1966; 1 child, Nicole Marie. BA, St. Mary's Coll., 1966; MS, Am. U., 1971; PhD, Georgetown U., 1975; postgrad., Fed. Exec. Inst., 1989. Quality control supr. Capital Aerosol Packaging Co., Melrose Park, Ill., 1965-66; Peace Corps vol., Adi Teclesan, Ethiopia, 1966-68; sci. dept. chmn. and tchr. Western Sr. High Sch., Washington, 1968-76; dir. marine scis. D.C. Pub. Sch. Systems, 1976-79; mgr. nat. sanctuaries programs U.S. Dept. Commerce, NOAA, Washington, 1979-82, chief user affairs/mktg. unit, external affairs staff, 1983-86, chief internat. affairs Nat. Ocean Service, 1986-94, sr. advisor, pres. Coun. Sustainable Devel., 1994—; U.S. del. to Intergovtl. Oceanographic Commn., 1986—, South Pacific Commn., 1989—; bd. dirs. Pacific Congress Internat., 1987—; lectr. in field; cons. in field. Author: Introduction to Marine Science, 1977; Ocean Ecology, 1978; contbr. articles to profl. jours. Vice pres., bd. dirs. Friends of Arlington County Parks, 1982-86; chmn. bd. dirs. planning com. Burgundy Farm Country Day Sch., Inc., 1980-86. NSF scholar, 1969-71; Georgetown U. fellow, 1972-75; recipient service commendation Emperor Haile Sallassie, 1967. Mem. AAAS, Oceanography Soc., Marine Tech. Soc., Sigma Xi. Roman Catholic. Clubs: Capital Yacht, Skyline Health and Racquet. Home: 4858 28th St S Arlington VA 22206-1370 Office: US Dept Commerce NOAA Office Sustainable Devel Rm 5222 14th St & Constitution Ave NW Washington DC 20011-6930

PODGORSAK, ERVIN B., medical physicist, educator, administrator; b. Vienna, Austria, Sept. 28, 1943; arrived in Slovenia, 1946, came to U.S., 1968, Can., 1973; s. Franc and Gabriella (Cukale) P.; m. Mariana Ambrozic, Oct. 23, 1965; children: Matthew, Gregor. Dipl.Ing. in Physics, U. Ljubljana, Slovenia, 1968; MSc in Physics, U. Wis., 1970, PhD in Physics, 1973. Diplomate Am. Bd. Med. Physics. Rsch. asst. U. Ljubljana, 1965-68, U. Wis., Madison, 1968-73; postdoctoral fellow U. Toronto, Ont., Can., 1973-74; asst. prof. McGill U., Montreal, Que., Can., 1975-79, assoc. prof., 1980-84, prof. med. physics, 1985—, dir. med. physics unit, 1991—; dir. dept. med. physics Montreal Gen. Hosp., 1979—; hon. vis. prof. U. Ljubljana, 1995—; presenter in field. Contbr. over 140 articles to sci. jours., chpts. to books. Fellow Can. Coll. Physicists in Medicine (bd. dirs. 1981-89, v.p. 1984-87, pres. 1987-89), Am. Assn. Physicists in Medicine (bd. dirs. 1990-93, assoc. editor Med. Physics Jour. 1989—, radiother. com. 1994-96); mem. Am. Coll. Med. Physics (bd. chancellors 1997—), Am. Soc. Ther. Radiology and Oncology, Can. Assn. Physicists, Can. Orgn. Med. Physics, Can. Assn. Radiation Oncologists, Can. Radiation Protection Assn., Internat. Stereotactic Radiosurgery Soc. (bd. dirs. 1991-95). Home: 1540 croissant Seville, Brossard, PQ Canada J4X 1J4 Office: Montreal Gen Hosp Dept Med Physics, 1650 Cedar Ave, Montreal, PQ Canada H3G 1A4

PODHORETZ, JOHN, writer, editor; b. N.Y.C., Apr. 18, 1961; s. Norman and Midge (Rosenthal) P.; m. Elisabeth Hickey, 1996. AB, U. Chgo., 1982. Exec. editor news Insight Mag., Washington, 1985-87; contbg. editor U.S.

News and World Report, Washington, 1987-88; speechwriter to Pres. of U.S. White House, Washington, 1988-89; asst. mng. editor Washington Times, 1989-91; sr. fellow Hudson Inst., 1991-94; TV critic N.Y. Post, 1994-95. Author: Hell of a Ride: Backstage at the White House Follies, 1989-1993, 1993; TV critic N.Y. Post, 1994-95; dep. editor The Weekly Standard, 1995—. Recipient J.C. Penney/Mo. award for excellence in feature sects., 1990. Jewish. Office: 1150 17th St NW Ste 505 Washington DC 20036-4621

PODHORETZ, NORMAN, magazine editor, writer; b. Bklyn., Jan. 16, 1930; s. Julius and Helen (Woliner) P.; m. Midge Rosenthal Decter, Oct. 21, 1956; children: Rachel, Naomi, Ruth, John. A.B., Columbia, 1950; B.H.L., Jewish Theol. Sem., 1950, LL.D. (hon.), 1980; B.A. (Kellett fellow), Cambridge (Eng.) U., 1952, M.A., 1957; LHD (hon.), Hamilton Coll., 1969, Yeshiva U., 1991, Boston U., 1995, Adelphi U., 1996. Assoc. editor Commentary, 1956-58, editor in chief, 1960-95, editor-at-large, 1995—; editor in chief Looking Glass Library, 1959-60; sr. fellow Hudson Inst., 1995—; Mem. U. Seminar Am. Civilization, Columbia, 1958. Author: Doings and Undoings, The Fifties and After in American Writing, 1964, Making It, 1968, Breaking Ranks, 1979, The Present Danger, 1980, Why We Were in Vietnam, 1982; The Bloody Crossroads, 1986; editor: The Commentary Reader, 1966. Chmn. new directions adv. com. USIA, 1981-87. Served with AUS, 1953-55. Fulbright fellow, 1950-51. Mem. Coun. on Fgn. Rels.

PODUSKA, JOHN WILLIAM, SR., computer company executive; b. Memphis, Dec. 30, 1937; s. Ben F. and Lily Mae (Reid) P.; m. Susan McElaney, Oct. 1, 1983; 1 child, Lily; children by previous marriage: Alice Casey, Margaret Kay, John Jr., Mary Beth Pandiscio. BS, MS, MIT, 1960, ScD, 1962; LHD (hon.), U. Lowell, 1986. Dir. Honeywell Info. Systems, Cambridge, Mass., 1970-72; v.p. research and devel. Prime Computer, Framingham, Mass., 1972-79; chmn., chief exec. officer, pres. Apollo Computer, Chelmsford, Mass., 1980-85; chmn., chief exec. officer, founder Stellar Computer Inc., Newton, Mass., 1986-89; CEO Stardent Computer, Inc., Newton, 1989-92; chmn. bd. dirs., founder Advanced Visual Systems Inc., Waltham, Mass., 1992—; dir. Safeguard Sci., Pa., Cambridge Tech. Ptnrs., Mass., XLvision, Melbourne, Fla., Union Pacific Resources, Ft. Worth. Trustee Bentley Coll., Rice U., Boston Ballet. Recipient Ah Wang award C. of C., North Middlesex, Mass., 1985; named Man of Yr., Boy Scouts Am., 1983. Fellow IEEE; mem. NAE. Office: Advanced Visual Systems Inc 300 5th Ave Waltham MA 02154-8705

PODWALL, KATHRYN STANLEY, biology educator; b. Chgo., Oct. 14; d. Frank and Marie C. Stanley. BS, U. Ill.; MA, NYU. Prof. biology Nassau C.C., Garden City, N.Y.; developmental reviewer West Ednl. Pub., Amesbury, Mass. and Highland Park, Ill., 1989, 91-92; reviewer AAAS, Washington, 1970—; exec. bd., advisor Women's Faculty Assn., Nassau C.C., 1990—; lectr. in field. Author: Tested Studies for Laboratory Teaching, vol. 5, 1993; editor: (books and cassettes) Rhyming Simon Books and Cassettes, 1990. Mem. AAUW, Nat. Assn. Biology Tchrs., Nat. Sci. Tchrs. Assn., Soc. for Coll. Sci. Tchrs., Am. Women in Sci., Met. Assn. Coll. and Univ. Biologists, Nat. Cathedral Assn., Friends of the Archives, The Xerces Soc., Southampton Colonial Soc., LaSalle County Hist. Soc. (life), Garden City Hist. Soc. (life), Soroptimist Internat. Ams. (charter, Dist. 1 dir. 1994-96, club pres. 1992-94). Avocations: travel, gardening, zoological pursuits. Office: Nassau Community College One Education Dr Garden City NY 11530

POE, DAVID RUSSELL, lawyer; b. Columbia, Mo., Sept. 4, 1948; s. Russell Warren and Chloe Ardith (Prichard) P.; m. Constance Elizabeth Vaught, Aug. 3, 1974; children: Meghan Elizabeth, Michael Lewis. BS in Mechanical and Aerospace Engring., U. Mo., 1970; JD, Duke U., 1974. Bar: N.Y. 1975, N.C. 1977, U.S. Supreme Ct. 1985, D.C. 1991, U.S. Ct. Appeals (1st, 2d, 4th, 6th and D.C. cirs.), U.S. Dist. Ct. (so., ea. dists.) N.Y., U.S. Dist. Ct. (ea. dist.) N.C. Network engr. Southwestern Bell Telephone Co., St. Louis, 1970-71; assoc. LeBoeuf, Lamb, Leiby & MacRae, N.Y.C., 1974-82, ptnr., 1983-89; ptnr. LeBoeuf, Lamb, Leiby & MacRae, Washington, 1989-93, LeBoeuf, Lamb, Greene & MacRae, LLP, Washington, 1994—; adj. faculty Columbus Sch. Law, Cath. U. Am., 1992—. Vestry St. Paul's Ch., Englewood, N.J., 1986-89; legal advisor First Presbyn. Pre-Sch. and Kindergarten, Englewood, 1984-88; vestry St. John's Ch., McLean, Va., 1996—. Mem. ABA (pub. utility sect., chmn. adminstrv. law com. 1988-89, chmn. cable TV com. 1989-92, mem. coun. 1990-93, chmn. publs. com. 1993-95, chmn. ann. mtg. 1997), Fed. Comm. Bar Assn., Fed. Energy Bar Assn. (vice chmn. jud. rev. com. 1994-95, chmn. 1995-96). Home: 1017 Galium Ct Mc Lean VA 22102-1106 Office: LeBoeuf Lamb Greene MacRae 1875 Connecticut Ave NW Washington DC 20009-5728

POE, DOUGLAS ALLAN, lawyer; b. Chicago Heights, Ill., Nov. 14, 1942; s. Armand Leslie and Marcella Elizabeth (Grote) P. BA, DePauw U., 1964; JD, Duke U., 1967; LLM, Yale U., 1968. Bar: Ill. 1967, U.S. Ct. Appeals (4th cir.) 1968, U.S. Supreme Ct. 1972, U.S. Ct. Appeals (7th cir.) 1973. Clk. U.S. Ct. Appeals (4th cir.), Balt., 1968-69; law clk. to Chief Justice Warren E. Burger U.S. Supreme Ct., 1969, to Hon. William J. Brennan, Jr., 1970; assoc. Mayer, Brown & Platt, Chgo., 1970-74, ptnr., 1974—. Mem. ABA, Am. Law Inst., Chgo. Council Lawyers, Order of Coif. Office: Mayer Brown & Platt 190 S La Salle St Chicago IL 60603-3410

POE, H. SADLER, lawyer; b. Rock Hill, S.C., Oct. 17, 1944; s. Alvis Bynum and Frances Guy (Sadler) P.; m. Justina Lasley, Aug. 12, 1972; children: Justina Lasley, Julia Rives, Abigail Sadler. AB, Princeton U., 1967; LLB, U. Va., 1971. Bar: Ga. 1971, U.S. Dist. Ct. (no. dist.) Ga. 1976. Assoc. Alston, Miller & Gaines, Atlanta, 1971-77, ptnr., 1977-82; ptnr. Alston & Bird, Atlanta, 1982—, chmn. bus. and fin. dept., 1988-93; bd. dirs., pres. Hillside, Inc., Atlanta. Presenter in field. Elder Trinity Presbyn. Ch., Atlanta, 1977-80, 92-95; active Leadership Atlanta, 1988, mem. exec. com., 1991-92, 93-94; trustee Ga. Assn. Pastoral Care, Atlanta, 1991-96. Mem. State Bar Ga. (chmn. securities com. 1981-88, chmn. bus. and banking law sect. 1991-92), Am. Coll. Investment Counsel. Avocations: woodworking, water skiing. Office: Alston & Bird One Atlantic Ctr 1201 W Peachtree St NW Atlanta GA 30309-3400

POE, JERRY B., financial educator; b. Springfield, Mo., Oct. 3, 1931; s. Carlyle and Eunice P.; m. Carol J. Mussler, Sept. 9, 1959; children: Cheryl Marie, Jennifer Brenna. A.B., Drury Coll., 1953; M.B.A. (Weinheimer fellow), Washington U., St. Louis, 1957; D.B.A. (Ford Found. fellow), Harvard U., 1963. Instr. U. Ark., spring 1957; indsl. engr. McDonnell Aircraft Corp., St. Louis, 1957; lectr. on fin. Boston U., 1959-61; asst. prof. bus. adminstrn. Drury Coll., 1961-64, assoc. prof., 1964-68, prof., 1968-74; dir. Breech Sch. Bus. Adminstrn., 1968-74; prof. fin. Ariz. State U., 1974—, chmn. dept. fin., 1974-82; vis. prof. Fla. Tech. U., 1971; examiner, commr. North Central Assn. Colls. and Schs.; dir. NDEA Inst. Econs.; cons. in field. Author: Essentials of Finance: An Integrated Approach, 1995, An Introduction to the American Business Enterprise, 1969, 7th rev. edit., 1989, Cases in Financial Management, 1977, 3d rev. edit., 1987. Mem. Regional Manpower Adv. Com.; mem. bus. and profl. adv. council Empire Bank. Served to lt. comdr. USNR, 1953-55. Mem. Fin. Mgmt. Assn., Kappa Alpha, Beta Gamma Sigma, Omicron Delta Kappa. Methodist. Office: Ariz State U Coll Bus Dept Fin Tempe AZ 85287-3906

POE, LUKE HARVEY, JR., lawyer; b. Richmond, Va., Jan. 29, 1916; s. Luke Harvey and Alice Colburn (Reddy) P. BS in Math, U. Va., 1938, JD, 1941; postgrad. (Rhodes scholar), Oxford (Eng.) U., 1939; D.Phil., Christ Ch., 1957. Bar: Va. bar 1940, D.C. bar and D.C. Ct. Appeals bar 1967, U.S. Supreme Ct. bar 1969, Md. bar 1974. Asso. firm Cravath, Swaine & Moore, N.Y.C., 1941-42; tutor St. John's Coll., Annapolis, Md., 1946-50; asst. dean St. John's Coll., 1947-49, tenure tutor, 1953-60, dir. physics and chemistry lab., 1959-60; asst. chmn. Nat. Citizens Com. for Kennedy and Johnson and chmn. Citizens Com., Pres.'s Inaugural Com., 1960-61; asst. to chmn. bd. Aerojet-Gen. Corp., El Monte, Calif., 1961-63; div. pres. Internat. Tech. Assistance and Devel. Co., Washington, 1963-66; ptnr. Howard, Poe & Bastian, Washington, 1966-83; pvt. practice law, 1983—; bd. dirs. First Am. Bank of Md.; cons. Dept. Transp., Dept. State, NEH; lectr. War Coll. of USAF, Gen. Studies program U. Va.; seminar leader Aspen Inst. Humanistic Studies; guest panelist Panel on Sci. and Tech. of Com. on Sci. and Astronautics, U.S. Ho. of Reps., 1970; pres. bd. dirs. Watergate East, Inc., 1976-79, 90-92; organizer U. Va. Unified Liberal Arts Program, 1988—. Author: The Combat History of the Battleship U.S.S. Mississippi, 1947, The Transition From Natural Law to Natural Rights, 1957; (with others) lab. manuals Einstein's Theory of Relativity, 1957, Electro-Magnetic Theory, 1959; editor: (with others) Va. Mag., 1936-38, U. Va. Law Rev., 1940-41. Dean's adv. coun. Lehigh U., 1962-65, mem. Seminar on Sci., Tech. and Pub. Policy, Brookings Instn., 1964-66; coun. on trends and perspectives U.S. C. of C., 1966-69; chmn. bd. Bristol Property Mgmt. and Svcs., Inc., 1967-88; chmn. Annapolis Bd. Zoning Appeals, 1966-75; mem. Annapolis Mayor's Task Force, 1967-74, Md. Gov.'s Commn. on Capital City, 1970-76. Lt. comdr. USNR, 1942-46. Decorated Jhalavada Order of Durbargadh, Dhrangadhara. Mem. Am. Law Inst., AAUP, Raven Soc. (pres.), Soc. of Cincinnati, Sr. Common Room and High Table (Christ Church), Met. Club (Washington), Travellers Club (London), Brook Club (N.Y.C.), New Providence Club (Annapolis), Vincent's Club (Oxford), Phi Beta Kappa, Phi Delta Phi. Episcopalian. Home: 139 Market St Annapolis MD 21401-2628 also: 2500 Virginia Ave NW Washington DC 20037-1901 Office: 2600 Virginia Ave NW Washington DC 20037-1905

POE, ROBERT ALAN, lawyer; b. Bracken County, Ky., Apr. 25, 1951. Student, U. Ky.; BA, Centre Coll., 1973; JD, U. Va., 1976. Bar: Colo. 1976. Mem. Holland & Hart, Denver; adj. prof. taxation U. Denver, 1986-88. Articles editor Va. Law Review, 1974-76. Mem. ABA, Order Coif, Phi Beta Kappa. Office: Holland & Hart 8350 E Crescent Pkwy Ste 200 Englewood CO 80111-2821

POE, WILLIAM FREDERICK, insurance agency executive, former mayor; b. Tampa, Fla., July 22, 1931; s. Fred Holland and Zula Blanche (Willoughby) P.; m. Elizabeth Ann Blackburn, June 21, 1954; children—William, Keren, Janice, Marilyn, Charles. Student, Duke U., 1950; B.S., U. Fla., 1953. Founder, pres. Poe & Assocs. (Ins. Agency), Tampa, 1956-74, chmn., 1979-87, chmn. bd., 1987-93; bd. Poe and Brown, Inc. (formerly Poe & Assocs.), Tampa, 1993—; mayor City of Tampa, 1974-79. Mem. Hillsborough County Port Authority, 1961, chmn., 1963; pres. chpt. ARC, United Way of Greater Tampa. Served with USAF, 1955-56. Mem. Tampa Assn. Ins. Agents, Chief Execs. Orgn. Democrat. Baptist. Club: Yacht. Office: Poe Investments Inc 511 W Bay St Ste 400 Tampa FL 33606-2700

POEHLEIN, GARY WAYNE, chemical engineering educator; b. Tell City, Ind., Oct. 17, 1936; s. Oscar Raymond and Eva Lee (Dickman) P.; m. Sharon Eileen Wood., Jan. 1, 1958; children: Steven Ray, Timothy Wayne, Valorie Ann, Sandra Lee. BSChemE, Purdue U., 1958, MSChemE, 1961, PhD, 1966. Design engr. Proctor & Gamble, Cin., 1958-61; from asst. prof. to assoc. prof. Lehigh U., Bethlehem, Pa., 1965-75, prof. chem. engring., 1975-78, co-dir. emulsion polymers inst., 1973-78; dir. sch. chem. engring. Ga. Inst. Tech., Atlanta, 1978-86, assoc. v.p. rsch., dean grad, studies, 1986-91, v.p. interdisciplinary programs, prof. chem. engring., 1991-95; prof. chem. engring., 1978-96; dir. Chem. and Transport Systems Divsn. NSF, 1996—; bd. dirs. Flexible Products Co., Marietta, Ga. Contbr. over 100 articles to tech. pubs. Mem. sch. bd. Bethlehem Area Sch. Dist., 1969-75. Recipient Honor Scroll award Phila. br. Am. Inst. Chemists, 1977, Mac Pruitt award Coun. for Chem. Rsch., 1989. Fellow AIChE; mem. Am. Chem. Soc., Am. Soc. Engring. Edn., Sigma Xi. Avocations: woodworking, beekeeping. Home: 1121 N Stafford St Arlington VA 22201 Office: NSF 4201 Wilson Blvd Arlington VA 22230-0001

POEHLMANN, CARL JOHN, agronomist, researcher; b. Jamestown, Mo., Jan. 29, 1950; s. Edwin William and Lucille Albina (Neu) P.; m. Linda Kay Garner, Dec. 29, 1973; children: Anthony, Kimberly. BS, U. Mo., 1972, MS, 1978. Farmer Jamestown, Mo., 1972-73; vocat. agrl. tchr. Linn (Mo.) Pub. Schs., 1973-75, Columbia (Mo.) Pub. Schs., 1975-78; dir., mgr. agronomy rsch. ctr. U. Mo., Columbia, 1978—. Mem. Am. Soc. Agronomy (div. A-7 chair 1985-86, bd. mem. 1991-94, cert. crop advisor 1993), Crop Sci. Soc. Am., Soil Sci. Soc. Am., Internat. Assn. Mechanization Field Experiments. Mem. Christian Ch. (Disciples of Christ). Office: U Mo 4968 S Rangeline Rd Columbia MO 65201-8973

POEHLMANN, JOANNA, artist, illustrator, book designer, educator; b. Milw., Sept. 5, 1932; d. Herbert Emil and Lucille (Conover) P. Attended, Layton Sch. Art, 1950-54, K.C. (Mo.) Art Inst., 1954, Marquette U., 1958, U. Wis., 1965, 1985. Assoc. lectr. U. Wis., Milw. Solo exhbns. include (retrospective) Milw. Art Mus., 1966, Bradley Galleries, Milw., 1982, Signature Gallery, John Michael Kohler Art Ctr., Sheboygan, Wis., 1979, 84, Woodland Pattern Book Ctr., Milw., 1988, The Cell Gallery, Rochester, N.Y., 1988, 89, Charles Allis Art Mus., Milw., 1991, Layton Gallery at Cardinal Stritch Coll, Milw., 1993, Univ. Meml. Libr., Madison, Wis., 1993, Wustum Mus. Fine Arts, Racine, Wis., 1994, Villa Terrace Mus., Milw., 1994, U. Western Mich., Kalamazoo, 1994; two-man shows include Bradley Galleries, 1964, 69, 80, 91, Cardinal Stritch Coll., Milw., 1980; invitational group shows include Cudahy Gallery of Wis. Art, Milw. Art Mus., 1962-85, 92, Bradley Galleries, 1967-79, Lakefront Festival of Art, Milw. Art Mus., 1962-63, 70-72, 76-79, Mount Mary Coll., Milw., 1979, 83, Chosy Gallery, 1980, 81, 86, U. Dallas, 1987, Frick Gallery, Tübingen, Germany, 1991, Spertus Mus. Judaica, Chgo., 1986, World Fin. Ctr., N.Y.C., 1992, Istvan Kiraly Muzeum, Budapest, Hungary, 1992, Artspace, Richmond, Va., 1994, Va. Ctr. For Craft Arts, Richmond, 1994, many others; juried group shows include Milw. Art Mus., 1963, 75, 78, Chgo. Art Inst., 1978, 81, Milw. Fine Arts Gallery, 1980, U. Wis. Fine Arts Gallery, Milw., 1980, The West Pub. Co., St. Paul, 1982, Auburn U., 1983, Zaner Gallery, Rochester, N.Y., 1984, Pratt Graphics Ctr., N.Y.C., 1985, Art 54 Gallery, N.Y.C., 1987, Boston Art Inst., 1987, Bradley U., Peoria, Ill., 1989, Wustum Mus. Fine Arts, 1989, 1992, Trenton State Coll., 1991, numerous others; represented in collections including Victoria & Albert Mus., London, N.Y. Pub. Libr., Mus. Kunsthandwerk, Frankfurt, Germany, Milw. Art Mus., Milw. Pub. Libr., U. Dallas, Orchard Corp. Am., St. Louis, Franklin Furnace Archives - Mus. Modern Art, N.Y., McDonald's Corp., GE Med. Systems Bldgs., Waukesha, Goldhirsh Group, Boston, Marquette U.-Haggerty Mus. Art, others; subject of articles; author: Love Letters, Food for Thought, Cancelling Out. Recipient Merit award Art Dir.'s Club, Milw., 1962, 100 Best award, 1967, 100 Best award Milw. Soc. Communicating Arts, 1973, 76, MGIC award Wis. Painters & Sculptors, 1981, Merit award Illustration Milw. Advt. Club, 1983, 2d award Wustum Mus. Fine Arts, 1983, 4th Purchase Prize award McDonald's Fine Art Collection Competition, 1983, Juror's award Zaner Gallery, 1984, Hopper/Koch award Wustum Mus. Fine Arts, 1985, spl. mention, Purchase award Bradley U., 1985, Purchase award Moravian Coll., 1985, Jack Richeson award Wustum Mus. Fine Arts, 1985, Purchase award U. Del., 1986, Strathmore Paper Co. award Wustum Mus. Fine Arts, 1986, Purchase award U. N.Dak., 1987, Award of Excellence miniature art Metro Internat. Competition, N.Y.C., 1987, 3d award Wustum Mus. Fine Arts, 1987, Purchase award U. Dallas, 1988, Award of Excellence Wustum Mus. Fine Arts, 1992, Individual Art fellowship Milw. County, 1993; Arts Midwest/NEA Regional Visual Artist fellow, 1994—. Roman Catholic. Home and Studio: 1231 N Prospect Ave Milwaukee WI 53202-3013

POEL, ROBERT WALTER, air force officer, physician; b. Muskegon, Mich., July 24, 1934; s. Abel John and Fannie M. (Vanderwall) P.; m. Carol Anne Noordeloos, June 24, 1960; children: Kathryn Anne Poel Engle, James Robert, Sharon Kay Poel Thompson. BS, Calvin Coll., 1957; MD, U. Mich., 1959. Diplomate Am. Bd. Surgery. Commd. capt. USAF, 1962, advanced through grades to brig. gen., 1988, ret., 1993; comdr. Hosp. Malmstrom AFB, Great Falls, Mont., 1971-73; dir. profl. svcs. Hdqrs. Tactical Air Command Command Surgeon's Office, Langley AFB, Va., 1973-74; div. chief, med. plans Office of Air Force Surgeon Gen., Wash., 1974-78; comdr. regional hosp. Sheppard AFB, Wichita Falls, Tex., 1978-83; dir. profl. svcs. Office of Air Force Logistics Command Surgeon, Wright-Patterson AFB, Ohio, 1983-85; vice-comdr. Wilford Hall USAF Med. Ctr., San Antonio, 1985-87; chief, quality assurance, dir. plans and resources Air Force Surgeon Gen., Bolling AFB, Washington, 1987-89; hosp. comdr. Malcolm Grow Med. Ctr., Andrews AFB, Washington, 1989-93; med. dir. near south office Meth. Occupational Healthctrs. Inc., Indpls., 1995—; dir. Andrews Fed. Credit Union, 1991-95, vice chmn. bd. dirs., 1992-95. Advisor, bd. regents Uniformed Svcs. U. the Health Scis., Bethesda, Md., 1989-93; mem. pres. coun. Calvin Coll., 1990. Named Disting. alumnus, Calvin Coll., 1990; Paul Harris fellow Rotary Club of Wichita Falls, 1982. Mem. AMA, Assn. Mil. Surgeons of U.S., Am. Coll. Physician Execs. Republican. Home: 12085 Waterford Ln Carmel IN 46033-5501 Office: 1101 Southeastern Ave Indianapolis IN 46202-3946

POEN, MONTE M., history educator, researcher; b. Lake city, Iowa, Nov. 25, 1930; s. John and Garnette (Montgomery) P.; m. Bonnie L. Diehl, July 15, 1952 (div. Feb. 1972); children: John M., Gregory E., Mark A.; m. Kathryn Lomen, May 22, 1982. AA, San Jose (Calif.) City Coll., 1959; BA, San Jose State U., 1961; MA, U. Mo., 1963, PhD, 1967. Instr. U. Mo., Columbia, 1964-66; with No. Ariz. U., Flagstaff, 1966—, prof., 1979-90, regents prof., 1990-96, regents prof. emeritus, 1996—; cons. McFarland papers Earnest W. McFarland Estate, Florence, Ariz., 1987. Author: Harry S. Truman Versus the Medical Lobby, 1979; editor: Strictly Personal & Confidential: Letters Harry Truman Never Mailed, 1982, Letters Home by Harry Truman, 1984. Mem. Coccnino County Dem. Cen. Com., Flagstaff, 1988—. Sgt. USAF, 1950-54, PTO. Truman Libr. Inst. scholar, 1987. Fellow Harry S. Truman Libr. Inst.; mem. Orgn. Am. Historians, Oral History Assn., Ariz. Humanities Coun., Ctr. for Study of the Presidency. Democrat. Avocations: camping, fishing, travel, gardening, hiking. Home: 3703 N Grandview Dr Flagstaff AZ 86004-1601 Office: Dept History No Ariz U Flagstaff AZ 86011

POEPPELMEIER, KENNETH REINHARD, chemistry educator; b. St. Louis, Mo., Oct. 6, 1949. BS in Chemistry, U. Mo., 1971; PhD in Inorganic Chemistry, Iowa State U., 1978. Rsch. chemist, corp. rsch. sci. labs. Exxon Rsch. & Engring. Co., Annandale, N.J., 1978-80, sr. chemist, corp. rsch. sci. labs., 1980-81, staff chemist, corp. rsch. sci. labs., 1981-84, sr. staff chemist, corp. rsch. sci. labs., 1984; assoc. prof. chemistry Northwestern U., Evanston, Ill., 1984-88, assoc. dir. sci. and tech. ctr. for superconductivity, 1989—, prof., 1988—, Dow prof. chemistry, 1992-94; lectr., cons. in field; organizer, chmn. nat. symposium on solid state chemistry of heterogeneous oxide catalysis including new microporous solids ACS, New Orleans, 1987; cons. Exxon Chemicals, Air Products and Chemicals, Inc., Shell, FMC Corp.; assoc. dir. NSF Sci. and Tech. Ctr. for Superconductivity; vice-chair, chair-elect, Gordon Conf. on Solid State Chem. Contbr. articles to numerous chemistry publications; patentee in field. Iowa State U. fellow, 1977-78; Iowa State scholar, 1975-76. Mem. Am. Assn. for the Advancement of Sci., ACS (chmn. Solid State Subdiv. of Div. Inorganic Chemistry 1988-89), AAAS, Am. Phys. Soc., Materials Rsch. Soc., Catalysis Club (Chgo.), Sigma Xi. Office: Northwestern U Dept Chemistry 2145 Sheridan Rd Evanston IL 60208-0834

POESCH, JESSIE JEAN, art historian; b. Postville, Iowa, May 19, 1922; parents: Edward H. and Vina (Meier) P. BA, Antioch Coll., 1944; MA, U. Del., 1956; PhD, U. Pa., 1966. Relief worker Am. Friends Svc. Com., Phila., also, France, Germany, 1946-54; curatorial asst. H.F. DuPont Winterthur (Del.) Mus., 1956-58; from asst. prof. to prof. art history Tulane U., New Orleans, 1963-92, Maxine and Ford Graham chair in fine arts, 1988-92; guest curator "Painting in the South", Va. Mus. Fine Arts, Richmond, 1980-84; curator "Newcomb Pottery: An Enterprise for So. Women, 1895-1940", Newcomb Coll. Tulane U. and Smithsonian Instn. traveling exhbn. svc., 1980-87. Author: Titian Ramsay Peale, 1799-1885, and His Journals of the Wilkes Expedition, 1961, The Art of the Old South: Painting, Sculpture, Architecture and the Products of Craftsmen, 1560-1860, 1983, (with John Cuthbent) David Hunter Strother: "One of the Best Draughtsmen the Country Possesses, 1997; (book/exhbn. catalogue) The Early Furniture of Louisiana, 1972, Newcomb Pottery: An Enterprise for Southern Women 1895-1940, 1984, Will Henry Stevens, 1987; also numerous articles and book revs. Fellow U. Del., 1954-56; Fulbright scholar U. London, 1960-62; NEH grantee, London, 1969-70. Mem. Soc. Archtl. Historians (bd. dirs. 1986-89), Coll. Art Assn., Am. Antiquarian Soc., La. Endowment for the Humanities (bd. dirs. 1984-90, La. Humanist of Yr. 1992), Victorian Soc. Am. (bd. dirs. 1988-92). Office: Tulane U Newcomb Art Dept New Orleans LA 70118

POETTCKER, HENRY, retired seminary president; b. Rudnerweide, Russia, Mar. 27, 1925; s. John and Margaretha (Voth) P.; m. Aganetha Baergen, July 4, 1946; children: Victoria, Ronald, Martin. A.B., Bethel Coll., North Newton, Kans., 1950; B.D., Mennonite Bibl. Sem., Chgo., 1953; Th.D., Princeton Theol. Sem., 1961, converted Ph.D., 1973. Ordained to ministry Mennonite Ch., 1948; instr. Can. Mennonite Bible Coll., Winnipeg, Man., 1954-59; pres. Can. Mennonite Bible Coll., 1959-78; pres. Mennonite Bibl. Sem., Elkhart, Ind., 1978-90, assoc. for devel., 1991-93;, 1993; interim dean Bluffton (Ohio) Coll., 1965-66; vis. lectr. Taiwan Theol. Coll. and Tainan Theol. Coll., Taiwan, 1973-74. Editor: (with Rudy A. Regehr) Call to Faithfulness, 1972, Alumni Bull. Can. Mennonite Bible Coll., 1960-73. Pres. Gen. Conf. Mennonite Ch., Newton, Kans., 1968-74. Mem. Soc. Bibl. Lit. and Exegesis. Home: 80 Plaza Dr Ste 2502, Winnipeg, MB Canada R3T 5S2 *The secret of happiness lies not in doing what one likes, but in liking what one does.*

POFF, RICHARD HARDING, state supreme court justice; b. Radford, Va., Oct. 19, 1923; s. Beecher David and Irene Louise (Nunley) P.; m. Jo Ann R. Topper, June 24, 1945 (dec. Jan. 1978); children: Rebecca, Thomas, Richard Harding; m. Jean Murphy, Oct. 26, 1980. Student, Roanoke Coll., 1941-43; LL.B., U. Va., 1948, LL.D., 1969. Bar: Va. 1947. Partner law firm Dalton, Poff, Turk & Stone, Radford, 1949-70; mem. 83d-92d congresses, 6th Dist. Va.; justice Supreme Ct. Va., 1972-89, sr. justice, 1989—; Vice chmn. Nat. Commn. on Reform Fed. Crime Laws; chmn. Republican Task Force on Crime; sec. Rep. Conf., House Rep. Leadership. Named Va.'s Outstanding Young Man of Year Jr. C. of C., 1954; recipient Nat. Collegiate Athletic Assn. award, 1966, Roanoke Coll. medal, 1967, Distinguished Virginian award Va. Dist. Exchange Clubs, 1970, Presdl. certificate of appreciation for legislative contbn., 1971, legislative citation Assn. Fed. Investigators, 1969, Thomas Jefferson Pub. Sesquicentennial award U. Va., 1969, Japanese Am. Citizens League award, 1972; named to Hall of Fame, Am. Legion Boys State, 1985; fellow Va. Law Found., 1997. Mem. Bar Assn., VFW, Am. Legion, Pi Kappa Phi, Sigma Nu Phi. Clubs: Mason, Moose, Lion. Office: Va Supreme Ct 100 N 9th St Richmond VA 23219-2335 *When you know you are right, fight. When you are in doubt, wait. When you know you are wrong, admit your mistake and correct it.*

POGO, BEATRIZ TERESA GARCIA-TUNON, cell biologist, virologist, educator; b. Buenos Aires, Argentina, Dec. 24, 1932; came to U.S., 1964, naturalized, 1976; d. Dario and Maria Teresa (Vergnory) Garcia-Tunon; m. Angel Oscar Pogo, Jan. 13, 1956; children: Gustavo, Gabriela. B.S., Lycee No. 1, Buenos Aires, 1950; M.D., Sch. Medicine, Buenos Aires, 1956; D.M.Sci., 1961. Intern Univ. Hosp., Buenos Aires, 1956-57; asst. Inst. Histology and Embryology, Buenos Aires U., 1957-59; fellow Sloan Kettering Meml. Hosp., N.Y.C., 1959-60, Rockefeller U., N.Y.C., 1960-61; asst. prof. cell biology Inst. Cell Biology, Cordoba U., Argentina, 1962-64; research assoc. Rockefeller U., N.Y.C., 1964-67; asst. Pub. Health Research Inst., N.Y.C., 1967-69, assoc., 1969-73, assoc. mem, 1973-78; prof. exptl. cell biology and microbiology Mt. Sinai Sch. Medicine, CUNY, 1978—, acting dir. ctr. for exptl. cell biology, 1987-89, prof. neoplastic diseases, 1989—. Contbr. articles to profl. jours. Damon Runyon Fund fellow, 1964-65; grantee Am. Cancer Soc., 1970-73, 79-80, 84-85, 94-95, NIH, 1975—. Fellow N.Y. Acad. Scis.; mem. Am. Assn. for Cancer Rsch., N.Y. Acad. Sci., Am. Soc. Cell Biology, Harvey Soc., Am. Soc. Virology, Assn. for Women in Sci. (v.p. met. N.Y. chpt. 1981-83, pres. 1984-86), Am. Microbiol. Soc., Sigma Xi. Home: 237 Nyac Ave Pelham NY 10803-1907 Office: Mt Sinai Sch Medicine 1 Gustave L Levy Pl New York NY 10029-6504

POGO, GUSTAVE JAVIER, cardiothoracic surgeon; b. Buenos Aires, Feb. 7, 1957; came to U.S., 1964; s. Angel Oscar and Beatriz (Garcia-Tuñon) P.; m. Janis Teitler, Feb. 17, 1983; children: Michael Tyler, Katherine Elizabeth. BA, NYU, 1979, MD, 1983. Gen. surgery resident North Shore Univ. Hosp., Manhasset, N.Y., 1983-88; cardiothoracic surgery resident Mt. Sinai Sch. Medicine, N.Y.C., 1988-91; attending, cardiothoracic surgery North Shore Univ. Hosp., Manhasset, 1991—. Contbr. articles to profl. jours. Fellow ACS, Am. Coll. Chest Physicians, Am. Coll. Cardiology; mem. Soc. Thoracic Surgery. Office: North Shore Univ Hosp 300 Community Dr Manhasset NY 11030-3801

POGREBIN, LETTY COTTIN, writer, lecturer; b. N.Y.C., June 9, 1939; d. Jacob and Cyral (Halpern) Cottin; m. Bertrand B. Pogrebin, Dec. 8, 1963; children: Abigail and Robin (twins), David. A.B. cum laude with spl. distinction in English and Am. Lit, Brandeis U., 1959. V.p. Bernard Geis Assocs. (book pubs.), N.Y.C., 1960-70; columnist The Working Woman column Ladies Home Jour., 1971-81; editor Ms mag., N.Y.C., 1971-87, columnist, editor at large, 1987-89, contbg. editor, 1990—; columnist The

N.Y. Times, Newsday, Washington Post, Moment Mag., Washington, 1990—, Moment Mag., Washington, 1990—; contbg. editor Family Circle, Ms. mag., Tikkun mag.; cons. Free to Be, You and Me projects, 1972—; lectr. women's issues and family politics, changing roles of men and women, friendship in Am., non-sexist child rearing and edn., Judaism and feminism, Mid-East politics. Author: How to Make It in a Man's World, 1970, Getting Yours: How to Make the System Work for the Working Woman, 1975, Growing Up Free, 1980, Stories for Free Children, 1982, Family Politics, 1983, Among Friends, 1986, Deborah, Golda, and Me: Being Female and Jewish in America, 1991, Getting Over Getting Older: An Intimate Journey, 1996; mem. editl. bd. Tikkun Mag., Commonquest mag.; contbr. articles to N.Y. Times, Washington Post, Boston Globe, The Nation, TV Guide, also other mags., newspapers. Sec. bd. Author's Guild; bd. dirs. Ms. Found., Ams. for Peace Now, New Israel Fund, Jewish Fund for Justice, Commn. on Women's Equality, Am. Jewish Congress, PEN Am.; mem. Task Force on Women Fedn. Jewish Philanthropies, Women's Forum. Pointer fellow Yale U., 1982, MacDowell Colony fellow, 1979, 89, 94, Cummington Colony Arts fellow 1985, Edna St. Vincent Millay Colony fellow, 1985; recipient Gloria Steinem Women of Vision award Ms. Found. for Women, 1990, Matrix award Women in Comm., 1981, Abram L. Sachar medal Brandeis U., 1994, Woman of Valor award Jewish Fund for Justice, 1997; named Person of Yr. Fifty-Plus Expo, 1997. Address: 33 W 67th St New York NY 10023-6224

POGUE, JOHN MARSHALL, physician, editor, researcher; b. Washington, Sept. 21, 1945; s. Lloyd Welch and Mary Ellen (Edgerton) P. AB with hons., Princeton U.; MD, Georgetown U. Diplomate Nat. Bd. Med. Examiners. Intern, resident Georgetown U. Hosp., Washington; editor, author Bradford Compact Newsletter, 1983—; historian Gov. Bradford Compact, 1996—. memigner ofcl. flag Gov. William Bradford Flag, 1987 (New Constellation award Nat. Flag Found., 1996); editor, contbr.: Pogue/Pollock/Polk Genealogy as Mirrored in History, From Scotland to Northern Ireland/Ulster, Ohio and Westward, 1990 (recipient 6 awards); asst. editor: Hereditary Soc. Blue Book, 1997—. Fellow Royal Soc. Medicine, Royal Microscopical Soc. Oxford, Royal Statis. Soc., Royal Geog. Soc., Royal Soc. Arts; mem. AMA, Royal Soc. Medicine (cardiothoracic sect.), Am. Heart Assn. (clin. cardiology coun.), Laennec Cardiovascular Sound Soc., Am. Soc. Echocardiography (coun. on cardiac sonography, coun. on intraoperative echocardiography), Internat. Soc. Electrocardiology, Internat. Soc. Heart Rsch. Can., Assn. Am. Med. Colls. (individual), Internat. Soc. Cardiovasc. Ultrasound, Friends of Nat. Libr. Medicine (founding mem.), Friends of McGill U. Osler Med. Libr., Friends of Oxford U. Mus. of History of Sci., Ashmolean Natural History Soc. Oxford, Oxford Hist. Soc., Internat. Shakespeare Assn. Stratford-upon-Avon, Princeton U. Alumni Assn., Gen. Soc. Mayflower Descs. D.C., Order Descs. of Colonial Physicians and Chirurgiens (surgeon gen. 1994—, chmn. hon. membership com. 1994—), The Royal Soc. Medicine Music Club, The Princeton Club (Washington). Avocations: reading Shakespeare, classical music. Home and Office: 5204 Kenwood Ave Chevy Chase MD 20815

POGUE, LLOYD WELCH, lawyer; b. Grant, Iowa, Oct. 21, 1899; s. Leander Welch and Myrtle Viola (Casey) P.; m. Mary Ellen Edgerton, Sept. 8, 1926; children: Richard Welch, William Lloyd, John Marshall. A.B., U. Nebr., 1924; LL.B., U. Mich., 1926; S.J.D., Harvard Law Sch., 1927. Bar: Mass., N.Y., D.C., Ohio, U.S. Supreme Ct. bars. Assoc. Ropes, Gray, Boyden and Perkins, 1927-33; ptnr. firm Searle, James and Crawford, N.Y.C., 1933-38; asst. gen. counsel CAB, 1938-39, gen. counsel, through 1941, chmn. bd., 1942-46; mng. ptnr. Pogue & Neal, Washington, 1946-67; Washington mng. ptnr. Jones, Day, Reavis & Pogue, Washington, 1967-79, ret., 1981; Lindbergh Meml. lectr. Nat. Air and Space Mus., 1991; presenter essay 50th Ann. Internat. Civil Aviation Orgn., Montreal, 1994; spkr. in field. Author: International Civil Air Transport Transition Following WW II, 1979, Pogue/Pollock/Polk Genealogy as Mirrored in History, 1990 (1st pl. in Anna Ford Family history book contest 1991, Nat. Genealogical Soc. award for excellence genealogy and family history 1992, William H. and Benjamin Harrison Book award Coun. Ohio Genealogists 1992, Outstanding Achievement award County and Regional History category Ohio Assn. Hist. Socs. and Mus. 1992, 1st pl. award Iowa Washington County Geneal. Soc. 1994, cert. commendation Am. Assn. State and Local History 1994, 1st place award Lake Havasu Geneal. Soc. 1996); contbr. articles to profl. pubs. Mem. U.S. del. Chgo. Internat. Civil Aviation Conf., 1944; mem. U.S. dels., vice chmn. Bermuda United Kingdom-U.S. Conf., 1946; vice chmn., del. Provisional Assembly Provisional Internat. Civil Aviation Orgn., 1946; del. Internat. Civil Aviation Orgn. Assembly, 1947. With AUS, 1918. Recipient Elder Statesman of Aviation award Nat. Aeronautic Assn., Golden Eagle award Soc. Sr. Aerospace Execs.; fellow Am. Helicopter Soc., Benjamin Franklin fellow Royal Soc. Arts. Fellow Royal Aero. Soc.; mem. AIAA (hon.), Can. Aeronautics and Space Inst., Nat. Aeronautic Assn. (pres. 1947), Nat. Air and Space Soc. (founder), Nat. Geneal. Soc., New Eng. Hist. Geneal. Soc. (life, former trustee), Ohio Geneal. Soc. (life), Md. Geneal. Soc. (life), First Families of Ohio, Helicopter Assn. Internat. (hon. mem. for life), Met. Club, Univ. Club, Wings Club (hon., N.Y.C.), Bohemian Club (San Francisco), Cosmos Club, Masons, Order of the First World War (charter). Home: 5204 Kenwood Ave Bethesda MD 20815-6604 Office: Metropolitan Sq 1450 G St NW Washington DC 20005-2001

POGUE, MARY ELLEN E. (MRS. L. WELCH POGUE), youth and community worker; b. Fremont, Nebr., Oct. 27, 1904; d. Frank E. and Mary (Coe) Edgerton; m. L. Welch Pogue, Sept. 8, 1926; children: Richard Welch, William Lloyd, John Marshall. BFA in Edn. Music, U. Nebr., 1926; studied violin with Harrison Keller, Boston Conservatory of Music, 1926-28, Kemp Stillings Master Class, N.Y.C., 1935-37. Mem. Potomac String Ensemble, Washington, 1939-80. Historian, Gov. William Bradford Compact, 1966—; vice chmn. Montgomery County (Md.) Victory Garden Ctr., 1946-47; pres. Bethesda Community Garden Club, 1947-48; founder Montgomery County YWCA, bd. dirs., 1946-50, 52-55; founder Welcome to Washington Music Group, 1947—; co-founder Group Piano in Montgomery County, Md. schs., 1954. Recipient Gov. William Bradford Compact Cert. of Merit award, 1970, Outstanding Service award Bethesda United Meth. Ch., 1984, Bethesda Cmty. Garden Club award, 1985, 93, Devoted Svc. award D.C. Mayflower Soc., 1985, 89, Welcome to Washington Internat. Club award, 1986. Mem. Soc. Mayflower Descs. D.C. (dir. D.C. 1954—, elder 1971-91, elder emeritus), PEO Sisterhood (pres. 1957-59, charter mem. chpt. R, PEO), Mortar Bd. Alumnae Club (pres. 1965-67, Mortar Bd. award, 1986), Nat. Cap. Area Fedn. Garden Clubs, Bethesda United Meth. Women, Nat. Geneal. Soc., New Eng. Historic Geneal. Soc. (life), Ohio Geneal. Soc. (life), Md. Geneal. Soc., Md. Hist. Soc., Conn. Soc. Genealogists, Pilgrim Soc. (life), Plimoth Plantation, Hereditary Order of Descs. Colonial Govs., Nat. Soc. Magna Charta Dames, Colonial Order of Crown, Sovereign Colonial Soc. Ams. Royal Descent, Order of Descs. Colonial Physicians and Chirurgiens, Nat. Soc. Women Descs. Ancient and Hon. Arty. Co., First Families of Ohio, Sons and Daughters of the Colonial and Antebellum Bench and Bar 1565-1861 (charter mem.), Welcome to Washington Internat. Club, Ind. Agy. Women (assoc.), Capital Speakers Club, The Plantagenet Soc., Soc. Descs. of Knights of the Most Noble Order of the Garter, DAR, Order Ams. Armorial Ancestry, Saybrook Colony Founders Assn. (cert. Descent Richard Edgerton), Soc. Founders of Norwich, Conn., Kenwood Country Club, Alpha Phi, Alpha Rho Tau, Delta Omicron Music (life). Methodist. Compiler, editor: Favorite Menus and Recipes of Mary Edgerton of Aurora, Nebraska, 1963, Family History of Frank Eugene Edgerton and Mary Coe Edgerton of Aurora, Nebraska, 1965. Home: 5204 Kenwood Ave Bethesda MD 20815-6604

POGUE, RICHARD WELCH, lawyer; b. Cambridge, Mass., Apr. 26, 1928; s. Lloyd Welch and Mary Ellen (Edgerton) P.; m. Patricia Ruth Raney, July 10, 1954; children: Mark, Tracy, David. B.A., Cornell U., 1950; J.D., Mich. Law Sch., 1953. Bar: Mich. 1953, Ohio 1957, U.S. Dist. Ct. (no. dist.) Ohio 1960, U.S. Ct. Appeals (6th cir.) 1972, U.S. Ct. Appeals (D.C. and 9th cirs.) 1979. Assoc. Jones, Day, Reavis & Pogue, Cleve., 1957-60, ptnr., 1961—, mng. ptnr., 1984-92, sr. ptnr., 1993-94; sr. advisor Dix & Eaton, Cleve., 1994—; vis. prof. Mich. Law Sch., 1993-95; bd. dirs. Derlan Industries, Toronto, Continental Airlines, Inc., Houston, OHM Corp., Findlay, Ohio, M.A. Hanna Co., Cleve., Redland PLC, Reigate, Eng., Rotek Inc., Aurora, Ohio, Key Corp., Cleve, TRW Inc. Cleve. Chmn. Cleve. Found, 1985-89, Greater Cleve. Roundtable, 1986-89, Greater Cleve. Growth Assn., 1991-93, Univ. Hosps., 1994—, truste 1975—, Cleve. Ballet, 1983-85, United Negro Coll. Fund, Cleve., 1979. Mem. Adminstrv. Conf. U.S., 1974-80; vice chmn. Cleve. Tomorrow, 1988-93, 50 Club Cleve., 1988-89; United Way Cleve., 1989; trustee Case Western Res. U.; active Coun. Fgn. Rels., 1989—, Am./EC Assn. Bus. Adv. Coun., 1988-93; trustee Rock and Roll Hall of Fame and Mus., 1986—; co-chmn 1996 Cleve. Bicentennial Commn., interim chmn. Cleve. Inst. Music, 1994. Army, 1954-57. Recipient Outstanding Alumnus award U. Mich. Club., Cleve., 1983, Torch of Liberty award Anti-Defamation League, 1989, Leadership Cleve. Vol. of Yr. award, 1990, 1st Econ. Devel. Workshop award Nat. Coun. on Urban Econ. Devel., 1992, Humanitarian award Nat. Conf. Christians and Jews, 1992. Mem. ABA (chmn. antitrust sect. 1983-84), Ohio State Bar Assn. (chmn. antitrust sect. 1969-73). Republican. Mem. United Ch. of Christ. Clubs: Bohemian (San Francisco), Soc., Union (Cleve.), Metropolitan (Washington), Links (N.Y.C.).

POGUE, WILLIAM REID, former astronaut, foundation executive, business and aerospace consultant; b. Okemah, Okla., Jan. 23, 1930; s. Alex W. and Margaret (McDow) P.; m. Jean Ann Pogue; children: William Richard, Layna Sue, Thomas Reid. B.S. in Secondary Edn., Okla. Bapt. U., 1951, D.Sc. (hon.), 1974; M.S. in Math., Okla. State U., 1960. Commd. 2d lt. USAF, 1952, advanced through grades to col., 1973; combat fighter pilot Korea, 1953; gunnery instr. Luke AFB, Ariz., 1954; mem. acrobatic team USAF Thunderbirds, Luke AFB and Nellis AFB, Nev., 1955-57; asst. prof. math. USAF Acad., 1960-63; exchange test pilot Brit. Royal Aircraft Establishment, Ministry Aviation, Farnborough, Eng., 1964-65; instr. USAF Aerospace Research Pilots Sch., Edwards AFB, Calif., 1965-66; astronaut NASA Manned Spacecraft Center, Houston, 1966-75; pilot 3d manned visit to Skylab space sta.; now with Vutara Services of Springdale, Ark. Decorated Air medal with oak leaf cluster, Air Force Commendation medal, D.S.M. USAF; named to Five Civilized Tribes Hall of Fame, Choctaw descent; recipient Distinguished Service medal NASA, Collier trophy Nat. Aero. Assn.; Robert H. Goddard medal Nat. Space Club; Gen. Thomas D. White USAF Space Trophy Nat. Geog. Soc.; Halley Astronautics award, 1975; de la Vaalx medal Fedn. Aeronautique Internat., 1974; V.M. Komarov diploma, 1974. Fellow Acad. Arts and Scis. of Okla. State U., Am. Astron. Soc.; mem. Soc. Exptl. Test Pilots, Explorers Club, Sigma Xi, Pi Mu Epsilon. Baptist (deacon). Home: 4 Cromer Dr Bella Vista AR 72715 Office: Vutara Services PO Box 150 Hindsville AR 72738

POHL, ADOLF LEOPOLD, clinical chemist, quality assurance consultant; b. St. Poelten, Austria, Dec. 14, 1936; s. Adolf Theodor and Cornelia Maria Anna (Moerth) P.; m. Ingrid Maria Antonia Payer, Feb. 24, 1962 (div. Dec. 11, 1975); children: Martin, Ulrike; m. Nanako Tanaka, Mar. 14, 1989; 1 child, Anna Yumi. Grad. in classical studies, Stiftsgymnasium Melk, 1954; BSc, U. Vienna, 1957, MSc, 1965, DPhil, 1968. Rsch. asst. med. dept. I U. Vienna Med. Sch., 1967-69, asst. prof., 1969-85, head erythrocyte enzyme lab. med. dept. I, 1969-85, founder tumor marker lab., 1978, head tumor marker lab., 1984-85, assoc. prof. med. dept. I, dept. chemotherapy, 1985-87, assoc. prof. dept. clin. labs., 1987—; quality assurance cons. Med. Pharm. Rsch. Ctr., Vienna, 1993—. Mem. editl. bd. Cancer Molecular Biology Jour., 1994—; contbr. articles to profl. jours., chpts. to books. Recipient Austrian Med. Assn. award, 1969. Mem. Am. Assn. for Clin. Chemistry, N.Y. Acad. Scis., IEEE Computer Soc., Drug Info. Assn. Achievements include discovery in human blood serum of a new ADP-ribosyltransferase, implementation of advanced data analysis in clinical chemistry, detection by new micromethods of phospholipid metabolism in red blood cell membranes and study of its abnormalities in hemolytic anemia; research on serum glycosyltransferases as possible cancer markers and critical analysis of galactosyltransferase heterogeneity; leading of 1st foldboat expedition on Tenojoki, 1st behavioral studies of Thai ferret badger. Avocations: botany and wildlife research, humanitarianism, philosophy, poetry. Home: Lambrechtgasse 3/10, A-1040 Vienna Austria Office: U Hosp Labs, Rummelhardtgasse 4/3, A-1090 Vienna Austria

POHL, FREDERIK, writer; b. N.Y.C., Nov. 26, 1919; s. Fred George and Anna Jane (Mason) P.; m. Carol Ulf, Sept. 15, 1953 (div. 1981); children—Ann, Karen, Frederik, Kathy; m. Elizabeth Anne Hull, July 27, 1984. Editor Popular Pubs., N.Y.C., 1939-43; editor Popular Sci., N.Y.C., 1946-49; freelance writer N.Y.C., 1950-60, 80—; editor Galaxy Pubs., N.Y.C., 1961-69, Bantam Books, N.Y.C., 1973-78. Author: Man Plus, 1977 (Nebula award), Gateway, 1978 (Nebula, Hugo, Campbell awards, Prix Apollo award), Jem, 1979 (Am. Book award), The Years of the City (Campbell award 1985). Served to sgt. USAAF, 1943-45; Italy. Recipient Popular Culture Assn. award, 1982. Fellow AAAS, Brit. Interplanetary Soc.; mem. Sci. Fiction Writers of Am. (pres. 1974-76, Grand Master award 1993), World Sci. Fiction (pres. 1980-82), Authors Guild, N.Y. Acad. Scis., Astron. Soc. Pacific. Democrat. Unitarian. Home: 855 Harvard Dr Palatine IL 60067-7026

POHL, GUNTHER ERICH, retired library administrator; b. Berlin, July 22, 1925; came to U.S., 1927; s. Erich Ernst and Martha (Seidel) P.; m. Dorothy Edna Beck, Aug. 21, 1949; children: Christine, Louise, Elizabeth, Ronald. BA, NYU, 1947, MA, 1950; MLS, Columbia U., 1951. Librarian local history and genealogy div. N.Y. Pub. Library, N.Y.C., 1948-69, chief local history and genealogy div., 1969-80, chief U.S. history and local history and genealogy div., 1980-85; ret. Compiler: N.Y. State Biographical, Genealogical and Portrait Index. Fellow N.Y. Geneal. and Biog. Soc.; mem. ALA (chmn. genealogy com. 1971-73, 76-78, History sect. award 1996), N.Y. Geneal. and Biog. Soc. (libr., trustee 1982-92), Sigma Phi Epsilon (trustee local chpt. 1978—). Republican. Avocations: stamps, opera; collecting New Yorkiana. Home: 24 Walden Pl Great Neck NY 11020

POHL, JOHN HENNING, chemical engineer, consultant; b. Ft. Riley, Kans., May 29, 1944; s. Herbert Otto and Ellen Irene (Henning) P.; m. Judith Lynn Sykes, Aug. 10, 1968; children: J. Otto, Clint. AA, Sacramento City Coll., 1964; BS, U. Calif., Berkeley, 1966; SM, MIT, 1973, DSci, 1976. Inspector constrn. C.O. Henning Cons. Engrs., Sacramento, 1965; engr. E.I. du Pont Nemours, Wilmington, Del., 1966-70; rsch. asst. MIT, Cambridge, 1971-75, lectr., 1975-76; mem. tech. staff Sandia Nat. Labs., Livermore, Calif., 1976-81; dir. fossil fuels Energy and Environ. Rsch., Irvine, Calif., 1981-86; dir. R & D Energy Systems Assocs., Tustin, Calif., 1986-89; sr. scientist energy W.J. Schafer Assocs., Irvine, 1989-91; pres. Energy Internat., Laguna Hills, Calif., 1988—; sr. cons. ESA Engring., Laguna Hills, 1989—; v.p. Advanced Combustion Tech. Co., Hsinchu, Taiwan, 1993-95; v.p. tech. Energeo, Inc., San Mateo, Calif., 1995-96; black coal utilization prof. chem. engring., dir. Black Coal Utilization Rsch. Unit U. Queensland, Brisbane, Australia, 1996—. Contbr. articles to profl. jours.; patentee in field. Treas. Headstart, Cambridge, 1975-76. Recipient Sci. and Tech. Achievement award U.S. EPA, 1987, Best Energy Projects award Energy Commn., Taiwan, coal evaluation, 1989, Low NOx Burner, 1992. Fellow Australian Inst. Energy (bd. dirs. 1996—); mem. ASME (advisor corrosion and deposits com. 1989—, rsch. project subcom. 1994—), AIChE (combustion advisor 1988-92), Am. Flame Rsch. Com., Am. Chem. Soc., Combustion Inst. Western States (mem. exec. com. 1988-95), Combustion Inst. (mem. program subcom. 1976—), Engring. Found. (mem. steering com. on ash deposits 1989—). Home: 26632 Cortina Dr Mission Viejo CA 92691-5429

POHL, PAUL MICHAEL, lawyer; b. Erie, Pa., July 17, 1948; s. Joseph Paul and Mary (Strenio) P.; m. Kaya Lynn Gavriloff, Aug. 13, 1970; children: Thomas Michael, Mary Elizabeth, Michael David. AB, Princeton U., 1970; JD, U. Pitts., 1975. Bar: Pa. 1975, Ohio 1976, U.S. Dist. Ct. (we. dist.) Pa. 1975, U.S. Dist. Ct. (no. dist.) Ohio 1976, U.S. Ct. Appeals (5th cir.) 1980, U.S. Ct. Appeals (11th cir.) 1983, U.S. Ct. Appeals (1st, 3d and 6th cir.) 1993, U.S. Ct. Appeals (D.C. cir.) 1995. Reporter Erie Daily Times, 1970-71; law clk. to presiding justice Pa. Supreme Ct., 1975-76; assoc. Jones, Day, Reavis & Pogue, Cleve., 1976-82, ptnr., 1982—; ptnr.-in-charge Jones, Day, Reavis & Pogue, Pitts., 1989—; guest mem. faculty Sch. Law, Hofstra U., Hempstead, N.Y., 1982, 84; mem. trial advocacy program Sch. Law, Emory U., Atlanta, 1983—; bd. dirs. JURA Corp., Erie, Lord Corp., Cary, N.C. Co-author: Conflicts of Interest—A Trial Lawyers Guide, 1984. Bd. dirs. Franciscan U., Steubenville, Ohio, 1991—, vice chmn., 1994—; bd. dirs. Gannon U., Erie. With USMC, 1971-72. Named one of Cleve.'s 78 Most Interesting People, Cleve. mag., 1978. Mem. Cleve. Bar Assn. (mem. com. task force on violent crime 1983). Roman Catholic. Office: Jones Day Reavis & Pogue 500 Grant St Pittsburgh PA 15219-2502 also: Jones Day Reavis & Pogue 901 Lakeside Ave E Cleveland OH 44114-1116

POHL, ROBERT OTTO, physics educator; b. Gottingen, Germany, Dec. 17, 1929; came to U.S., 1958; s. Robert Wichard and Auguste Eleonore (Madelung) P.; m. Karin Ursula Koehler, May 6, 1961; children: Helen M., Robert S., Otto C. Vordiplom, U. Freiburg, Fed. Rep. Germany, 1951; diploma, U. Erlangen, Fed. Rep. Germany, 1955, Dr. rer. nat., 1957. Asst. U. Erlangen, 1957-58; research assoc. Cornell U., Ithaca, NY, 1958-60, asst. prof., 1960-63, assoc. prof., 1963-68, prof., 1968—; vis. prof. Tech. Hochschule Stuttgart, 1966-67, Tech. U. Munchen, 1973-74, Konstanz U., Regensburg U., 1987-88, all Fed. Republic Germany; vis. scientist Nuc. Research Ctr., Juelich, Fed. Rep. Germany, 1980-81, Hahn-Meitner Inst., Berlin, 1995. Contbr. articles on solid state physics to profl. jours. Recipient Sr. Scientist award Alexander von Humboldt Found., 1980; Guggenheim Found. fellow, 1973, Erskine fellow U. Canterbury, New Zealand, 1988. Fellow AAAS, Am. Inst. Physics (O.E. Buckley award 1985), Internat. Thermal Conductivity Confs. Office: Cornell U Physics Dept Ithaca NY 14853-2501

POHLAD, CARL R., professional baseball team executive, bottling company executive; b. West Des Moines, Iowa. Ed., Gonzaga U. With MEI Diversified, Inc., Mpls., 1959—, chmn. bd., 1976—; pres. Marquette Bank Mpls., N.A., pres., dir.; pres., dir. Bank Shares, Inc.; owner Minn. Twins, 1985—; dir. Meth. Hosp. Adminstrv. Group, T.G.I. Friday's, Tex. Air Corp., Ea. Airlines, Continental Air Lines, Inc., Carlson Cos. Inc. Address: Minnesota Twins Hubert H. Humphrey Metrodome 34 Kirby Puckett Pl Minneapolis MN 55415*

POHLAND, FREDERICK GEORGE, environmental engineering educator, researcher; b. Oconomowoc, Wis., May 3, 1931; s. Arnold Ernest and Eda Karoline (Petermann) P.; m. Virginia Ruth Simmons, Sept. 10, 1966; 1 child, Elizabeth Eda. BS in Civil Engring., Valparaiso U., 1953; MS in Civil Engring., Purdue U., 1958, PhD, 1961; DSc (hon.), Valparaiso U., 1996. Profl. engr.; diplomate Am. Acad. Environ. Engrs. Civil engr. Erie Railroad Co., Huntington, Ind., 1953; preventive medicine specialist U.S. Army, Ft. Bragg, N.C., 1953-56; grad. rsch. asst. Purdue U., West Lafayette, Ind., 1956-61; asst. prof. Ga. Inst. Tech., Atlanta, 1961-64, assoc. prof., 1964-71, prof., 1971-88; Weidlein prof. U. Pitts., 1989—; vis. scholar U. Mich., Ann Arbor, 1967-68; guest prof. Delft U. Tech., Netherlands, 1976-77; mem. sci. adv. bd. EPA, Washington, 1989—, Nat. Inst. for Environ. Renewal, 1995—; mem. sci. adv. com. Gulf Coast Hazardous Substance Rsch. Ctr., Beaumont, Tex., 1989-92, EPRI, Palo Alto, Calif., 1990-94; mem. adv. comm. Purdue U., 1990-94; mem. com. on water rsch., adv. tech. human support in space and on innovative techs. NRC, 1993-96, mem. com. environ. mgmt. techs., 1997—; mem. indsl. adv. com. DOD Advanced Applied Tech. Demonstration Facility, 1994—; co-dir. EPA Ctr. for Groundwater Remediation Tech. Analysis, 1995—. Author: Emerging Technologies in Hazardous Waste Management, 1990, 91, 93, 94, 95, 96, Design of Anaerobic Processes for the Treatment of Industrial and Municipal Waste, 1992; regional editor (jour.) Water Rsch., 1983—, hon. exec. editor Water Rsch., 1994—; author over 130 pubs. in field. Served with U.S. Army, 1953-56. Recipient Harrison Prescott Eddy medal Water Pollution Control Fedn., 1964, Charles Alvin Emerson medal, 1983, Gordon Maskew Fair medal, 1989; recipient Rsch. award Water Pollution Control Assn. Pa., 1991. Fellow ASCE, Am. Acad. Microbiology; mem. AIChE, NSPE, Am. Acad. Environ. Engrs. (diplomate, pres. 1992-93, Stanley E. Kappe award 1995), Assn. Environ. Engring. Profs. (sec.-treas. 1970-71, disting. lectr. 1992), Solid Waste Assn. N.Am. (Lawrence lectr. 1992), Am. Water Works Assn. (life), Nat. Acad. Engring., Am. Chem. Soc., Am. Soc. Microbiology, Ga. Soc. Profl. Engrs., Internat. Assn. on Water Quality, Pa. Soc. Profl. Engrs., Pa. Water and Pollution Control Assn., Sigma Xi, Tau Beta Pi, Chi Epsilon, others. Achievements include major contributions to phase separation in anaerobic treatment processes; originated concept of leachate recirculation for accelerated stabilization in landfill bioreactors. Home: 118 Millstone Ln Pittsburgh PA 15238-1624 Office: U Pitts Dept Civil and Environ Engring Pittsburgh PA 15261

POHLMAN, JAMES ERWIN, lawyer; b. Iowa City, Apr. 10, 1932; s. Erwin Christian and Agnes Freda (Johanns) P.; m. Patricia Anne Likert, Sept. 6, 1958; children: William James, John David, Bruce Likert. AB, Oberlin Coll., 1954; LLB, U. Mich., 1957. Bar: Ohio 1957. Assoc. Wright, Harlor, Purpus, Morris & Arnold, Columbus, Ohio, 1957-62; ptnr. Wright, Harlor, Morris & Arnold, Columbus, 1962-77; ptnr. Porter, Wright, Morris & Arthur, Columbus, 1977—, chmn. litigation dept., 1986—; bd. dirs. Physicians Ins. Co. Ohio, Pickerington. Trustee Oberlin (Ohio) Coll., 1986—, Columbus Children's Hosp., 1976-91; pres. John Frederick Oberlin Soc., 1983-86. Served with Air N.G., 1957-60. Fellow NEH seminar Yale U., summer 1977. Fellow Am. Coll. Trial Lawyers; mem. Am. Soc. Med. Assn. Counsel (pres. 1982-85), Internat. Assn. Def. Counsel (exec. com. 1984-87, sec.-treas. 1993-97), Barristers Soc. (pres Columbus club 1963-66), Sixth Cir. Jud. Conf. (life). Republican. Congregationalist. Clubs: Golf (New Albany, Ohio); Rocky Fork Country (Gahanna, Ohio) (trustee 1980-83). Office: Porter Wright Morris & Arthur 2900 Huntington Ctr Columbus OH 43215

POHLMAN, JANET ELIZABETH, healthcare executive, consultant; b. N.Y.C., Oct. 29, 1938. Diploma in nursing, NYU, 1959, MA, 1981; BA, Queens Coll., 1977; cert. ergonomics in occupl. health, Rutgers U.; cert. EPA hazardous waste mgmt., Harvard U.; cert. advanced safety, Nat. Safety Coun.; cert. radiol. safety tng., Ga. State U.; cert. CPR, emergency cardiac care, Am. Heart Assn.; cert. compliance course for safety officers, U.S. Dept. Labor; cert. asbestos safety tng., N.Y. Dept. Health. RN, N.J., N.Y., Mass.; cert. occupl. health nurse, safety profl., occupl. hearing conservationist. Staff nurse Elmhurst (N.Y.) Gen. Hosp., 1959-63; pvt. practice spl. nurse, 1963-74; occupl. health nurse Allied Stores Corp., Flushing, N.Y., 1974-77; staff nurse N.Y. Telephone, N.Y.C., 1977-79, paramedic svcs. asst. supr., 1979-81, paramed. svcs. supr., 1981-83; assoc. dir. corporate safety and health NYNEX, N.Y.C., 1983-90, dir. paramed. svcs., 1990-95, nurse, claims examienr, 1995-96; claims examiner, grad. nurse County of Essex, Newark, 1996—. Mem. Am. Assn. Occupl. Health Nurses, Greater N.Y. Assn. Occupl. Health Nurses (past dir., sec., past editor newsletter), Am. Soc. Safety Engrs.

POHLMAN, RANDOLPH A., business administration educator, dean; b. Topeka, Jan. 25, 1944; s. Clarence Alvin and Martha Melissa (McElheny) P.; m. Jeanne Lucille Gebhart, Aug. 22, 1965; children—Kristina, Lisa. B.S., Kans. State U., 1967, M.S., 1969; Ph.D., Okla. State U., 1976. Asst. prof., assoc. prof. fin. Kans. State U., Manhattan, 1976-82, assoc. prof., head dept. fin., 1982-84, prof., dean Coll. Bus. Adminstrn., 1984-90; dir. employee devel. Koch Industries, 1990-91, dir. human resources, 1991-95; dean sch. bus. and entrepreneurship Nova Southeastern Univ., Ft. Laud, Fla., 1995—; vis. rsch. scholar UCLA, 1983; holder L.L. McAninch Chair of Entrepreneurship, 1988-90; bd. dirs. Union Nat. Bank, Manhattan, mem. investment com., 1986-87, mem. trust mgmt. com., 1988. Author: International Investment, 1977, Financial Statement Analysis and Forecasting for the Non-Financial Executive, 1990, Understanding the Bottom Line: Finance for Non-financial Managers and Supervisors. Chmn. Kans. State U., United Way, 1982; trustee Meml. Hosp., Manhattan, 1984-90; treas. Kans. State U. Found., 1980-90, mem. investments com., 1988; mem. steering com. Ctr. for Workforce Mgmt.; mem. cost containment roundtable Sedgwick County med. Soc.; mem. bd. dirs. Wichita/Sedgwick County Partnership for Growth Employment and Tng.; mem. Broward Econ. Devel. Coun., 1995; mem. exec. edn. adv. bd. Wharton Sch. Univ. Pa., 1995. With USAF, 1971-73. Recipient Outstanding Tchr. award Coll. of Bus., Kans. State U., 1977, All-Univ. Disting. Tchg. award Kans. State U., 1977, Cutting Edge award selection com. Miami C. of C., 1995-96; investments rsch. grantee Kans. State U., 1978. Mem. Fin. Execs. Inst., Am. Fin. Assn., Am. Econ. Assn., Fin. Mgmt. Assn., Midwest Fin. Assn., Kans. State U. Alumni Assn. (treas. 1980-90, trustee 1983-90, bd. dirs.), Manhattan C. of C. (bd. dirs. 1987-90). Republican. Club: Manhattan Country (bd. dirs. 1983-85). Lodge: Rotary (bd. dirs. Manhattan club, 1986—, pres.-elect Manhattan chpt.). Avocations: golf; guitar playing; reading. Office: Nova Southeastern Univ Sch Bus & Entrepreneurship 3100 SW 9th Ave Fort Lauderdale FL 33315-3025

POHLSANDER, HANS ACHIM, classics educator; b. Celle, Germany, Oct. 10, 1927, came to U.S., 1947, naturalized, 1953; m. Navee Newby, Aug. 20, 1956; children—Dianne, Eileen, Margaret. B.A. with high honors, U. Utah, 1954; M.A., U. Calif.-Berkeley, 1955; Ph.D., U. Mich., 1961. Tchr.

Carmel High Sch., Calif., 1956-58; asst. prof. Washington U., St. Louis, 1961-62; asst. to assoc. prof. SUNY, Albany, 1962-71, prof. classics, 1971-95, prof. religious studies, 1991-95, chmn. dept. classics, 1972-78, prof. emeritus, 1995—; vis. assoc. prof. Am. U. Beirut, 1968-69; vis. prof. Ohio State U., Columbus, 1983-84; lectr. Aegean Inst., Greece, summers 1969, 72, 75, 78, 83, Anatolia Coll., Greece, summer 1981. Pub. Helena: Eurpress and Saint, 1995, The Emperor Constantine, 1996; contbr. articles to profl. jours. Served to cpl. U.S. Army, 1950-52. Grantee NEH, 1979, German Acad. Exchange Service, 1982, Am. Philos. Soc., 1983, 88, Am. Coun. Learned Socs., 1963. Mem. Archaeol. Inst. Am., Am. Philol. Assn., Hagiographic Soc. Home: 52 Wellington Rd Delmar NY 12054-3322 Office: SUNY at Albany Dept Classics 1400 Washington Ave Albany NY 12222-0100

POHOST, GERALD MICHAEL, cardiologist, medical educator; b. Washington, Oct. 27, 1941; married; 3 children. BS, George Washington U., 1963; MD, U. Md., 1967. Diplomate Am. Bd. Internal Medicine, Am. Bd. Cardiovascular Disease, Am. Bd. Nuclear Medicine. Intern Montefiore Hosp. & Med. Ctr., Bronx, N.Y., 1967-68, asst. resident, 1968-69; sr. resident Jacobi Hosp. Albert Einstein Coll. Medicine, Bronx, 1969-70; cardiology resident Montefiore Hosp. & Med. Ctr.; clin. & rsch. fellow in medicine Mass. Gen. Hosp., Boston, 1971-73; rsch. fellow in medicine Harvard Med. Sch., Boston, 1971-73; instr. medicine Harvard Med. Sch., 1974-77, asst. prof., assoc. prof. medicine, 1977-83; with dept. radiology Mass. Gen. Hosp., Boston, 1977-83, asst. gen. med. svcs., 1978-82; prof. medicine, radiology U. Ala., Birmingham, 1983—, Mary Gertrude Waters chair cardiovascular medicine divsn. cardiovascular disease, 1991—; cons. nuclear medicine radiology dept. Mass. Gen. Hosp., 1977-83; dir. ctr. NMR R&D U. Ala. Hosp., Birmingham, 1986—. Sr. editor: Noninvasive Cardiac Imaging, 1983, New Concepts in Cardiac Imaging, 1985, 86, 87, 88, 89, The Principles and Practice of Cardiovascular Imaging, 1991; contbr. more than 400 articles, reviews, book chpts., editls. to profl. jours.; nat. and internat. spkr. in field; mem. editl. bd. Circulation, Jour. Magnetic Resonance in Medicine, Internat. Jour. Cardiology, NMR in BioMedicine, Coronary Artery Disease, others; rsch. interests in radionuclide and nuclear magnetic resonance studies of the heart, myocardial metabolism, cardiac pathophysiology. SCOR grant NIH, 1990—, tng. grant, 1992—, Dept. Energy grant, 1992—, Nat. Ctr. Rsch. Resources, 1992—. Fellow Am. Coll. Cardiology (editl. bd. jour., chmn. cardiac imaging com. 1982-88, current procedural terminology com. 1988—, gov. rels. com. 1989—, trustee 1994—); mem. AMA (chmn. panel nuclear magnetic resonance imaging 1985-88), Am. Fedn. Clin. Rsch., Am. Soc. Clin. Investigations, Am. Assn. Profs., Am. Heart Assn. (fellow coun. clin. cardiology 1975—, Mass. affiliate 1975-83, established investigator 1979-84, Richard and Hinda Rosenthal award for excellence in clin. investigation 1985, chmn. advanced cardiac tech. com. of coun. on clin. cardiology 1981-86, exec. com. 1981—, Ala. affiliate 1983—, long range planning com. 1986-89, chmn. 1989-91, vice chmn. exec. com. coun. clin. cardiology 1988—, nominating com. 1989-91, chmn. 1993—, budget com. 1989-91, chmn. exec. com. 1991-93, immediate past chmn. 1994—, rsch. com. fellow subgroup A 1988-91), Soc. Nuclear Medicine (coun. nuclear Cardiology 1990—), Soc. Magnetic Resonance in Medicine (exec. com. 1987, sci. program com. 1988-89, pres. 1986-87), Nat. Heart, Lung and Blood Inst. (program project rev. com. A 1984-88, cardiovascular and renal study sect. 1991-94, radiol. study sect. 1994—), So. Med. Assn., NIH Reviewers Res., U.S. Nuclear Regulatory Commn. (adv. com. 1984—), Assn. Univ. Cardiologists, Assn. Profs. Cardiology (sec. treas. 1994—), Sigma Xi. Home: 4301 Kennesaw Dr Birmingham AL 35213-3311 Office: U Ala BDB 101 1808 7th Ave S Birmingham AL 35233-1912

POIANI, EILEEN LOUISE, mathematics educator, college administrator, higher education planner; b. Newark, Dec. 17, 1943; d. Hugo Francis and Eileen Louise (Crecca) P. BA in Math., Douglass Coll., 1965; MS in Math., Rutgers U., 1967, PhD in Math., 1971. Teaching asst., grad. preceptor Rutgers U., New Brunswick, N.J., 1966-67; asst. counselor Douglass Coll., New Brunswick, 1967, 69-70; instr. math. St. Peter's Coll., Jersey City, 1967-70, asst. prof., 1970-74, dir. of self-study, 1974-76, assoc. prof., 1974-80, prof., 1980—, asst. to pres., 1976-80; asst. to pres. for planning St. Peter's Coll., 1980—; chairwoman U.S. Commn. on Math. Instrn., NRC of NAS, Washington, 1983-90; founding nat. dir. Women and Math. Lectureship Program, Washington, 1975-81, mem. adv. bd., 1981—; project dir. Consortium for Advancement of Pvt. Higher Edn., Washington, 1986-88; mem. N.J. Math. Coalition, 1991—, Nat. Seminar on Jesuit Higher Edn., 1990-94, mem. strategic planning com. N.J. Assn. Ind. Colls. and Univs., 1990-92; charter trustee Rutgers U., 1992—. Author: (with others) Mathematics Tomorrow, 1981; contbr. articles to profl. jours. Mem. Newark Mus., Nutley (N.J.) Hist. Soc., Friends of Newark Libr.; trustee Nutley Free Pub. Libr., 1974-77, St. Peter's Prep. Sch., Jersey City, 1986-92; active fee arbitration commn. N.J. Supreme Ct., 1983-86, ct. ethics com., 1986-90; U.S. nat. rep. Internat. Congress Math. Edn., Budapest, Hungary, 1988; mem. statewide planning com. NCCJ, 1988-92; chair evaluation teams Mid. States Assn. Coll. and Schs.; mem. U.S. delegation to Internat. Congress on Math; trustee The Cath. Advocate, 1993—. Recipient Douglass Soc. award Douglass Coll., 1982, Outstanding Cmty. Svc. award Christopher Columbus Found., N.J., 1994, Outstanding Svc. award Middle States Assn. Colls. and Schs., 1994, Cert. of Appreciation in Reconition of Outstanding Contbns. as Nat. Dir. of Women and Math. Program, 1993; named Danforth Assoc., Danforth Found., 1972-86. Mem. AAUP, Math. Assn. Am. (bd. dirs. lectureship program, gov. N.J. chpt. 1972-79, chair human resources coun. 1991—, Outstanding Coll. Tchg. award 1993), Am. Math. Soc., Nat. Coun. Tchrs. Math. (spkr. 1974—), Soc. Coll. and Univ. Planning (program com. 1989—, spkr. nat. conf. 1986, 88, 89, 90, judge grad. paper competition), Pi Mu Epsilon (1st woman pres. in 75 yrs. 1987-90, C.C. MacDuffee award for disting. svc. and to math. 1995). Roman Catholic. Avocations: gourmet cook, traveling, biking. Office: St Peter's Coll 2641 Kennedy Blvd Jersey City NJ 07306-5943

POILE, DAVID ROBERT, professional hockey team executive; b. Toronto, Ont., Can., Feb. 14, 1949; s. Norman Robert and Margaret (Elizabeth) P.; m. Elizabeth Ramey, July 4, 1971; children: Brian Robert, Lauren Elizabeth. B.S., Northeastern U., 1971. Asst. mgr. Atlanta Flames, 1971-80, Calgary Flames, Alta., Can., 1980-82; gen. mgr., v.p. Washington Capitals, Landover, MD, 1982—. Office: Washington Capitals Usair Arena 1 Harry S Truman Dr Landover MD 20785-4765*

POINDEXTER, BEVERLY KAY, media and communications professional; b. Noblesville, Ind., Nov. 12, 1949; d. Wayne Francis and Rosalie Christine (Nightenhelser) Hunter; m. Jerry Roger Poindexter, Dec. 7, 1969; children: Nick Ashley, Tracy Lynne, Wendy Dawn, Cory Matthew. Student, Purdue U., Bethany Seminary. Editor Tri Town Topics Newspaper, 1965-69; reporter, photographer Noblesville Daily Ledger, 1969-70; asst. mgr., sales mgr., sports dir. Sta. WHYT Radio, Noblesville, Ind., 1973-79; sales mgr., music dir., DJ, news Sta. WBMP Radio, Elwood, Ind., 1979-88; acct. exec. Stas. WAXT-WHBU Radio, Anderson, Ind., 1988-89; gen. mgr., sales mgr. Sta. WEWZ, Elwood, Ind., 1989-90; now news stringer Sta. WRTV-6, Indpls., Sta. WTHR TV-13, Indpls.; acct. exec. Sta. WLHN Radio, Elwood, Ind.; real estate broker Booker Realty, Cicero, Ind., 1990—. Area rep. Youth for Understanding, 1993-95; Am. Field Svc. liaison, Hamilton County, Ind.; pres. bd. dirs. Hamilton Heights Elem. Football, Arcadia, Ind., 1981-83; founder, chmn. Hamilton Heights Elem. Cheerleaders, Arcadia, 1981-87; youth leader, counselor Ch. of the Brethren, Arcadia, 1991-94; active Ch. of Brethren Women's Fellowship. Mem. Nat. Assn. Realtors, Ind. Assn. Realtors, Met. Indpls. Bd. Realtors. Republican. Avocations: horseback riding, canoeing, swimming, singing, dancing. Home: 14645 E 281st St Atlanta IN 46031-9722 Office: Booker Realty PO Box 437 99 S Peru Cicero IN 46034

POINDEXTER, BUSTER See JOHANSEN, DAVID

POINDEXTER, CHRISTIAN HERNDON, utility company executive; b. Evansville, Ind., Sept. 20, 1938; s. Marlan Glenn and Ellen Mabelle (Sommers) P.; m. Marilyn Ann Mills, June 12, 1960; children: Scott H., Todd S. B.S. in Engring., U.S. Naval Acad., 1960; M.B.A. in Fin., Loyola Coll., Balt., 1976. With Balt. Gas & Electric Co., 1967—, gen. supr. fin. dept., 1976-78, treas., asst. sec., 1978-79, v.p. engring. and constrn., 1980-85; pres., chief exec. officer, dir. Constellation Holdings, Inc. subs. Balt. Gas & Electric Co., 1985-89; vice chmn. bd. Balt. Gas & Electric Co., 1989-93, chmn., CEO, 1993—; chmn. bd., chief exec. officer Constellation Biogas Inc., Constellation Investments Inc., Constellation Properties Inc.; bd. dirs. The KMS Group, Inc., 1986—. Bd. dirs., sec. YMCA of Anne Arundel County, Md., 1985—; bd. dirs., pres. Scholarships for Scholars, Inc.; exec. bd. Balt. Area council Boy Scouts Am.; trustee Md. Acad. Scis., 1984—, Villa Julie Coll., 1986—. Served to lt. USN, 1960-67. Mem. Engring. Soc. Balt., IEEE. Republican. Office: Balt Gas & Electric Co PO Box 1475 Charles Ctr Baltimore MD 21203*

POINDEXTER, KATHLEEN A. KRAUSE, nursing educator, critical care nurse; b. Platteville, Wis., Aug. 30, 1956; d. Gene A. and Catherine E. (Boyle) Gilbertson; m. David L. Poindexter, July 20, 1990; children: Nicholas, Brendon, Ashley, Anna, Steve. BA in Nursing, Coll. of St. Scholastica, Duluth, Minn., 1978; MSN, No. Mich. U., Marquette, 1990. RN, Minn., Mich.; cert. ACLS, BCLS instr.; PALS. Staff nurse pediatrics ICU St. Mary's Med. Ctr., Duluth, 1978-83, head nurse pediatrics/pediatric ICU, 1983-85; clin. III staff nurse ICU/critical care unit Marquette Gen. Hosp., 1985-88; staff nurse critical care unit Bell Meml. Hosp., Ishpeming, Mich., 19909—; assoc. prof. No. Mich. U. Sch. Nursing, Marquette, 1988-96, 1996—; researcher in field. Mem. Coll. Adv. Coun., Faculty Grants Com. No. Mich. U.; advisor, founder No. Mich. U. Practical Nurses Assn.; mem. Alcohol & Drug Abuse Prevention program, Parents Adv. Coun., Marquette Area Pub. Sch. Dist. Recipient Excellence in Edn. award; Exemplary Citizen award, 1995. Mem. AACN (edn. advisor), AAUP (staff coun.), ANA, Am. Heart Assn., Hursing Honor Soc. (sec.), Sigma Theta Tau. Home: 1806 Gray St Marquette MI 49855-1546

POINDEXTER, RICHARD GROVER, minister; b. Carthage, N.C., June 9, 1945; s. Romie Dallas and Mae Ruth (Underwood) P.; m. Glenda Joyce Tudor, Feb. 23, 1968; children: Tonya Joyce, Amanda Caroline. BA in Sociology, N.C. State U., 1967; MDiv., New Orleans Bapt. Theol. Sem., 1973. Ordained to ministry So. Bapt. Conv., 1972. Assoc. pastor, youth dir. Amite Bapt. Ch., Denham Springs, La., 1971-72; Sunday sch. cons. Canal Blvd. Bapt. Ch., New Orleans, 1973; pastor First Bapt. Ch., LaGrange, N.C., 1973-77, Anderson Grove Bapt. Ch., Albemarle, N.C., 1977-86, Rankin Bapt. Ch., Greensboro, N.C., 1986-96, First Bapt. Ch., Haw River, N.C., 1996—; cons. Challenge to Build, Bapt. State Conv. of N.C., Cary, 1977—; mem. Brazil Mission Trip, Piedmont Bapt. Assn., Greensboro, 1989. State chaplain N.C. Army NG, Raleigh, 1996—; trustee Christian Action League N.C., Raleigh, 1985—. Office: First Bapt Ch 508 E Main St Haw River NC 27258-9652

POINDEXTER, WILLIAM MERSEREAU, lawyer; b. Los Angeles, June 16, 1925; s. Robert Wade and Irene M. (Mersereau) P.; m. Cynthia Converse Pastushin, Nov. 10, 1979; children: James Wade, David Graham, Honour Hêlenê, Timothy John. B.A., Yale U., 1946; postgrad., U. Chgo., 1946-47; LL.B., U. Calif., Berkeley, 1949. Bar: Calif. 1952. Practiced in San Francisco, 1952-54, Los Angeles, 1954—; mem. firm Poindexter & Doutre, Inc., 1964—; Pres. Consol. Brazing & Mfg. Co., Riverside, Calif., 1949-52. Pres. South Pasadena-San Marino (Calif.) YMCA, 1963; Mem. San Marino Sch. Bd., 1965-69, pres., 1967; pres. Conf. of Ins. Counsel, 1975. Served with USMCR, 1943. Fellow Am. Coll. Probate Counsel; mem. ABA, L.A. County Bar Assn., State Bar Calif., Yale Club (pres. So. Calif. chpt. 1961), Calif. Lincoln Clubs (downtown pres. 1997—). Republican. Presbyterian. Office: 1 Wilshire Bldg Suite 2420 Los Angeles CA 90017

POINSETT-WHITE, SADIE RUTH, elementary education educator; b. Chgo., May 11, 1934; d. Alexander Abraham and Adele Marie (Prindle) Poinsett; m. Robert Eli White, Sept. 11, 1955; children: Susan Murray, Michael L. White. BS in elem. edn., U. Ill., 1954; MA in early childhood edn., U. Md., 1980. Cert. elem. edn. tchr., Md. Head start tchr. San Bernadino (Calif.) Pub. Sch., 1966, kindergarten tchr., 1967; day care tchr. Kensington (Md.) Day Care, 1970; head start tchr. Montgomery County Pub. Sch., Rockville, Md., 1972-84; kindergarten tchr. Montgomery County Pub. Sch., Silver Spring, Md., 1984—; mem. tchr. evaluation adv. task force Montgomery County Pub. Sch., 1996-97; mem. adv. bd. African Voices project Smithsonian Instn. Nat. Mus. Natural History, 1995—. Mem. adv. bd. Noyes Libr., Kensington, 1980-84, 90-93; mem. NAACP Nat. Black Child Devel. Inc.; mem. Vol. Ptnrship. Montgomery, Inc., United Coun. of African-Am. Orgns. Rsch. fellow U. Md., College Park, 1980. Mem. Nat. Sci. Tchrs. Assn. (conf. presenter 1991-96), Md. State Dept. Edn. (conf. presenter 1991-96), Md. Assn. Sci. Tchrs. (conf. presenter 1991-96), Montgomery County Edn. Assn. (poll vol. 1986—, precinct capt. 1994—), Nat. Coun. Negro Women, Zeta Phi Beta (Basileus 1996). Avocation: 4th degree black belt Tae Kwon Do. Office: Broad Acres Elem Sch 710 Beacon Rd Silver Spring MD 20903-2568

POINTER, PETER LEON, investment executive; b. Erie, Pa., Aug. 3, 1934; s. Leon Royce and Katherine (Hermen) P.; m. Linda Milla Jensen, Sept. 21, 1957; children: Philip Leon, David Andrew. BS in Econs., U. Pa., 1956; MBA, U. Mo., 1968. V.p. Roose-Wade & Co. Inc., Toledo, 1976-78; br. mgr. Wm. C. Roney & Co., Detroit, 1978-79; v.p. Lowe & Assocs., Columbus, Ohio, 1979-88; pres. Pointer Investment Co., Columbus, 1988—; arbitrator Nat. Assn. Security Dealers, Washington, 1987—; adv. com. mem. Dept. Commerce Div. of Securities, Columbus, 1988—. Trustee, sec.-treas. Univ. Urology Ednl. and Rsch. Found., 1993—. Lt. col. USAF, 1956-76. Mem. Brookside Golf and Country Club (treas., trustee 1991-94), Sigma Nu (treas. 1955-56). Republican. Methodist. Avocations: aviation, golf, gardening. Home: 2290 Haverford Rd Columbus OH 43220-4320 Office: Pointer Investment Co 1550 Old Henderson Rd Ste N 152 Columbus OH 43220-3626

POINTER, SAM CLYDE, JR., federal judge; b. Birmingham, Ala., Nov. 15, 1934; s. Sam Clyde and Elizabeth Inzer (Brown) P.; m. Paula Purse, Oct. 18, 1958; children: Minge, Sam Clyde III. A.B., Vanderbilt U., 1955; J.D., U. Ala., 1957; LL.M., NYU, 1958. Bar: Ala. 1957. Ptnr. Brown, Pointer & Pointer, 1958-70; judge U.S. Dist. Ct. (no. dist.) Ala., Birmingham, 1970-82, chief judge, 1982—; judge Temp. Emergency Ct. Appeals, 1980-87; mem. Jud. Panel Multi-dist. Litigation, 1980-87; mem. Jud. Conf. U.S., 1987-90; mem. Jud. Coun. 11th Cir., 1987-90, mem. standing com. on rules, 1988-90, chmn. adv. com. on civil rules, 1990-93. Bd. editors: Manual for Complex Litigation, 1979-91. Mem. ABA, Ala. Bar Assn., Birmingham Bar Assn., Am. Law Inst., Am. Judicature Soc., Farrah Order of Jurisprudence, Phi Beta Kappa. Episcopalian. Office: US Dist Ct 882 US Courthouse 1729 5th Ave N Birmingham AL 35203-2000

POINTON, MARY LOU, special education educator; b. Ft. Smith, Ark., Aug. 1, 1933; d. Clyde Morgan and Rilla Belle (Prater) Dollar; m. Vernie Rodney Pointon, Oct. 24, 1954; children: Pamela Kaye Pointon McDonald, Susan Gail Pointon Friberg. Assoc. BA, Ft. Smith Jr. Coll., 1953; BS Ed in Speech and English, Tex. Tech U., 1962; MEd in Spl. Edn., East Tex. U., 1989. Cert. real estate agt., appraiser Tex. Real Estate Commn. English and drama tchr. Wolforth (Tex.) H.S., 1962-63; drama tchr. Monterrey H.S., Lubbock, Tex., 1963-64; English and history tchr. Meml. Cath. H.S., Enid, Okla., 1964-66; reading and drama tchr., libr. Covington (Okla.) H.S., 1966-68; spl. edn. tchr. drug abuse unit Mercer Island (Wash.) H.S., 1968-69; English, bus. and drama tchr. LaConner (Wash.) H.S., 1969-72; English tchr. Tehran (Iran) Am. Sch., 1972; v.p., dir. tng. and devel. Mary Lou English Tng. Ctr., Tehran, 1972-78; spl. edn. tchr. Mills Elem. Sch., Midlothian, Tex., 1987-88; tchr. learning difference students Fairhill Sch., Dallas, 1988-93; tutor learning difference students Masterpiece Co., Plano, Tex., 1993—; owner, v.p. Masterpiece Real Estate Co., Duncanville, Tex., 1978-89, Masterpiece Co., Plano, Tex., 1993—. Author: Teacher Training Manual/Individual English Training, 1973, also lang. program, 1972-78. V.p. Duncanville C. of C., 1983-85; mem. polit. action com. Dallas Assn. Realtors, 1982-84. Named Outstanding Mem. of Yr. Duncanville C. of C., 1983. Mem. DAR (v.p., founding mem. Duncanville chpt. 1980-88), NAFE, Nat. Safety Assn. Dallas Coop. (outstanding sales team 1994), Nat. Chrysanthemum Soc., N.W. Ark. Chrysanthemum Club (v.p., founding mem. 1988—). Avocations: plants, flowers, music, reading. Home and Office: 2712 S Cypress Plano TX 75075

POINTS, ROY WILSON, municipal official; b. Quincy, Ill., Oct. 21, 1940; s. Jess C. and Gladys (Wilson) P.; m. Karen Lee Olsen, July 23, 1966; children: Eric, Holly. BBA, Culver Stockton Coll., 1968. Tchr., coach Lewis County C-1, Ewing, Mo., 1968-69, Community Unit 3, Camp Point, Ill., 1969-78; real estate salesman Landmark, Quincy, 1978-80; supr. of assessment County of Adams, Quincy, 1980-90; assessor City Twp. of Quincy, 1990—; mem., chmn. Adams County Bd. Rev., 1977-80. Bd. dirs., 1st v.p., sec. Quincy Jaycees, 1970-76, Quincy Rotary East, 1980. Mem. Cert. Ill. Assessing Officers, Internat. Assn. Assessing Officers (cert. ednl. recognition 1988), Ill. Assessors Assn. (bd. dirs. 1992—), Twp. Ofcls. Ill. (bd. dirs. 1995—). Democrat. Avocations: fishing, hunting, jogging, raising cattle. Office: Quincy Twp Assessor City Hall Annex 706 Maine St Quincy IL 62301-4042

POIRIER, FRANK EUGENE, physical anthropology educator; b. Paterson, N.J., Aug. 7, 1940; s. Frank Eugene and Alice (Apelian) P.; m. Darlene Matsko, July 6, 1963; children—Alyson, Sevanne Cara. B.A., Paterson State Coll., Wayne, N.J., 1962; M.A., U. Oreg., 1964, Ph.D., 1967. Asst. prof. dept. psychiatry U. Fla., 1967-68; prof., chair anthropology Ohio State U., Columbus, 1968—. Co-author: Human Evolution in China, 1995, In Search of Ourselves, 5th edit., 1993, An Introduction to Physical Anthropology and the Archaelogical Record, 1982, Understanding Human Evolution, 3d edit., 1993; editor: Primate Socialization, 1972, (with others) Primate Bio-Social Development, 1977; contbr. articles to profl. jours., chpts. to books. Fellow NIH, 1963-67, NIMH, 1969-70, Fulbright, 1986. Mem. AAAS, Internat. Primatological Soc., Am. Assn. Phys. Anthropologists, Current Anthropology, Am. Soc. Primatologists, Explorers Club, Sigma Xi. Democrat. Home: 420 Greenglade Ave Columbus OH 43085-2206 Office: Ohio State U Dept Anthropology 124 W 17th Ave Columbus OH 43210-1316

POIRIER, HELEN VIRGINIA LEONARD, elementary education educator; b. Worcester, Mass., Oct. 2, 1954; d. Robert O'Donnell and Rose C. (Pepper) Leonard; m. Paul Nelson Poirier, Aug. 3, 1985. BS, Worcester State Coll., 1976. Cert. tchr. K-6, reading supr. K-12, adminstrn. K-8. Tchr. grade 5-6 reading and social studies Quabbin Regional Sch. Dist., Oakham, Mass., 1980—. Sec. Local Cable Access Com., Auburn, 1985-92. NEH grantee, 1986; town history grantee Oakham Hist. Soc., 1986, Oakham Hist. Commn., 1986. Mem. Cen. Mass. Coun. Social Studies (bd. dirs., sec. 1986-90, treas. 1990—), Hodges Village Environ. Edn. Assn., Tanheath Hunt Club (pres. 1995-96, sec./newsletter editor 1988-95). Avocations: horseback riding, fox hunting. Office: Oakham Center Sch Deacon Allen Dr Oakham MA 01068

POIRIER, LOUIS JOSEPH, neurology educator; b. Montreal, Que., Can., Dec. 30, 1918; s. Gustave Joseph and Calixta (Brault) P.; m. Liliane Archambault, June 11, 1947; children—Guy, Michel, Louise, Esther. B.Sc., U. Montreal, 1942, M.D., 1947; Ph.D., U. Mich., 1950; D. (hon.), U. Rennes, France, 1973. Asst. prof. U. Montreal, 1950-55, assoc. prof., 1955-58, prof., faculty of medicine, 1958-65; chmn. dept. anatomy Faculty of Medicine, Laval U., Cité Universitaire, Que., 1970-78; prof. exptl. neurology Faculty of Medicine, Laval U., Cité Universitaire, 1970-83; dir. Centre de Research in Neurobiology, Laval U. and Hosp. de l'Enfant-Jesus, 1977-85, prof. emeritus, 1985—. Contbr. articles to profl. jours.; editor the extrapyramidal system and its disorders in: Advances in Neurology, vol. 24, 1979. Pres. Que. Health Scis. Research Council, 1978-81. Decorated officer Order of Can.; recipient Que. sci. award, 1975; Killam commemorative scholar, 1977, 78. Mem. Royal Soc. Belgium (hon.), Neurol. Soc. France (hon.), AAAS, Am. Assn. Anatomists, Am. Physiol. Soc., Soc. for Neuroscis., Internat. Brain Research Orgn. Address: 603 Chemin Caron, Lac Simon, Montpellier, PQ Canada J0V 1M0

POIRIER, RICHARD, English educator, literary critic; b. Gloucester, Mass., Sept. 9, 1925; s. Philip and Annie (Kiley) P. A.B., Amherst Coll., 1949; M.A., Yale U., 1951; Ph.D., Harvard U., 1959; student, U. Paris, France, 1944-45; H.H.D., Amherst Coll., 1978. Mem. faculty Williams Coll., 1950-52, Harvard U., 1953-63; Disting. prof. English Rutgers U., 1963—; bd. dirs., co-founder, chmn. bd. Libr. of Am.; Beckman prof. U. Calif., Berkeley, 1973; chmn. adv. English com. Harvard U., 1988-91; delivered Gauss Seminars, Princeton U., 1990, T.S. Eliot lectures, U. Kent, 1991, Henry James lectures, NYU, 1992. Editor: Partisan Rev, 1963-73, O Henry Prize Stories, 1961-65; editor/founder Raritan Quar., 1981—; author: The Comic Sense of Henry James, 1960, In Defense of Reading, 1962, A World Elsewhere, 1966, The Performing Self, 1971, Norman Mailer, 1973, Robert Frost: The Work of Knowing, 1977, The Renewal of Literature, 1987, Poetry and Pragmatism, 1992; contbr. author numerous articles, revs. to profl. jours. Served with AUS, 1943-46. Recipient achievement award AAAL, 1978, Jay B. Hubbell award, 1988, Lit. Lion award N.Y. Pub. Libr., 1992; Fulbright scholar, Cambridge, Eng., 1952-53; Bollingber fellow, 1962-63, Guggenheim fellow, 1974-75, fellow NEH, 1978-79. Mem. Am. Acad. Arts and Scis., P.E.N. (exec. bd. 1986), PMLA (editorial bd. 1977-79), nominating com. Nat. Medal for Lit., 1986, 87, Nat. Book Critics Cir., 1977-85, Phi Beta Kappa. Club: Century. Home: 104 W 70th St Apt 9B New York NY 10023-4457 Office: Raritan Quarterly Rutgers University 31 Mine St New Brunswick NJ 08901-1111

POIROT, JAMES WESLEY, engineering company executive; b. Douglas, Wyo., 1931; m. Raeda Poirot. BCE, Oreg. State U., 1953. With various constrn. firms, Alaska and Oreg.; with CH2M Hill Inc., 1955, v.p., Seattle and Atlanta, from 1967; chmn. bd. CH2M Hill Ltd., Englewood, Colo., 1983-93; former chmn. Western Regional Coun., Design Profls. Coalition, Accreditation Bd. Engring. and Tech., Indsl. Adv. Coun.; former mem. Oreg. Joint Grad. Schs. Engring., Engring. Coun. Named ENR Constrn. Man of Yr., 1988. Fellow ASCE (pres. 1993-94); mem. Am. Cons. Engrs. Coun. (pres. 1989-90), Am. Acad. Environ. Engrs. (diplomate), Am. Assn. Engring Socs. (vice chmn. 1995), Nat. Acad. Engring. (nat. chmn. engrs. week 1994), World Engring. Partnership for Sustainable Devel. (founding dir.), World Fedn. Engring. Orgns. (com. on tech. transfer, pres. 1995—). Office: CH2M Hill Inc PO Box 22508 Denver CO 80222-0508

POIS, JOSEPH, lawyer, educator; b. N.Y.C., Dec. 25, 1905; s. Adolph and Augusta (Lesser) P.; m. Rose Tomarkin, June 24, 1928 (dec. May 1981); children: Richard Adolph (dec.), Robert August, Marc Howard.; m. Ruth Livingston, Nov. 27, 1983 (div. 1984). A.B., U. Wis., 1926; M.A., U. Chgo., 1927, Ph.D., 1929; J.D., Chgo.-Kent Coll. Law, 1934. Bar: Ill. 1934, Pa. 1978. Staff mem. J.L. Jacobs & Co., Chgo., 1929-35; jr. partner J.L. Jacobs & Co., 1946-47; gen. field supr. Pub. Adminstrn. Service, Chgo., 1935-38; chief adminstrv. studies sect. U.S. Bur. Old Age and Survivors Ins., 1938-39; chief adminstrv. and fiscal reorgn. sect. U.S. Bur. Budget Exec. Office of Pres., 1939-42; dir. finance State of Ill., 1951-53; counsel, asst. to pres., v.p., treas., dir. Signode Corp., 1947-61; prof. U. Pitts., 1961-76, emeritus, 1976—, chmn. dept. pub. adminstrn., 1961-71, asso. dean, 1973-75; dir. Vision Service Plan of Pa., 1984-85; cons. ECA, 1948, Dept. State, 1949, 62-65, U.S. Dept. Def., 1954, Brookings Instn., 1962-63, AID, 1965, Indian Inst. Pub. Adminstrn., 1972, Commn. on Operation Senate, 1976, Pitts. Citizens' Task Force on Refuse Disposal, 1976-78; mem. cons. panel Comptroller Gen. of U.S., 1967-75. Author: The School Board Crisis: a Chicago Case Study, 1964, Financial Administration in the Michigan State Government, 1938, Kentucky, Handbook of Financial Administration, 1937, Public Personnel Administration in the City of Cincinnati, 1936, (with Edward M. Martin and Lyman S. Moore) The Merit System in Illinois, 1935, Watchdog on the Potomac: A Study of the Comptroller General of the United States, 1979; contbg. author: The New Political Economy, 1975, State Audit-Developments in Public Accountability, 1979. Mem. Chgo. Bd. Edn., 1956-61; pres. Chgo. Met. Housing and Planning Council, 1956-57, Immigrants Service League, Chgo., 1960-61; dir. Pitts. Council Pub. Edn., 1965-67; mem. citizens bd. U. Chgo., 1958-78; mem. Pitts. Bd. Pub. Edn., 1973-76; bd. dirs. Pitts. Center for Arts, 1977-85, World Federalist Assn. Pitts., 1984—, Pitts. dist. Zionist Orgn. Am., 1979-81, mem. Hunger Action Coalition, Pitts., 1985-86; mem. Allegheny County Bd. Assistance, 1981-90, chmn. 1981-87. Served from comdr. to capt. USCGR, 1942-46. Decorated Navy Commendation medal; recipient alumni citation for pub. service U. Chgo., 1960; award for pub. service U.S. Gen. Accounting Office, 1971. Mem. ABA, FBA, ASPA (award for pub. svc. Pitts. area chpt. 1995), Am. Polit. Sci. Assn., Ctr. for Study of the Presidency, Govt. Fin. Officers Assn., Fin. Execs. Inst., Inst. Mgmt. Accts., Chgo. Bar Assn., U. Chgo. Alumni Club (pres. Pitts. chpt. 1981-84), Army and Navy Club, Allegheny County Bar Assn., Phi Beta Kappa, Pi Lambda Phi, Phi Delta Phi. Home: 825 Morewood Ave Pittsburgh PA 15213-2950

POISSANT, CHARLES-ALBERT, paper manufacturing company executive; b. Montreal, Sept. 13, 1925; m. Florence Drouin, June 12, 1951; children: Louise, Marc-André Hélène, Isabelle. Chartered acct., U. Montreal, 1953. Chartered acct, Que. Ptnr., pres. Poissant Thibault affiliate Peat Marwick Thorne, Montreal, 1947-87; chmn., CEO Donohue, Inc., Québec City, Que., 1987-92, chmn. bd., 1992—; bd. dirs., mem. exec. com. Quebecor, Inc., Montreal, Les Réseaux Premier Choix, Orchestre Metropolitain; bd. dirs. Found. de l'Universite de Que., Montreal. Author: Taxation in Canada of Non-residents, 1976, Commentary on Canada-Germany Tax Agreement, 1976, How to Think Like a Millionaire, 1985 (transl. into 7 langs.). Mem. Can. Pulp and Paper assn. (bd. dirs., mem. exec. com.), Club St. Denis, Laval sur-le-Lac. Roman Catholic. Avocations: golf, downhill skiing. Home: 333 Somerville, Ahuntsic, PQ Canada H3L 1A4 Office: Donohue Inc, 500 Sherbrooke West 8th Fl, Montreal, PQ Canada H3A 3C6

POITEVENT, EDWARD BUTTS, II, lawyer; b. New Orleans, Oct. 19, 1949; s. Eads and Elizabeth (Schramm) P.; m. Julia Dunbar Baños, Dec. 29, 1972; children: Sarah Dunbar,Elizabeth Grehan, Edward Scott, Mary McCutchen. BA, Tulane U., 1971, JD, 1974. Assoc. Jones, Walker, Waechter, Poitevent, Carrere & Denegre, New Orleans, 1974-79, ptnr., 1979-91; ptnr. Phelps Dunbar, New Orleans, 1991—; mem. ad hoc com. Pipeline div. La. Office of Conservation; mem. adv. coun. La. Mineral Law Inst. Mem. editorial bd. Oil and Gas Law and Taxation Rev.; contbr. articles to profl. jours.; presenter in field. Pres. La. chpt. Leukemia Soc. Am., Inc., New Orleans, 1991; trustee Ea. Mineral Law Found., 1988-93; co-chmn. oil and gas sect. Rocky Mountain Mineral Law Found. 36th Ann. Inst., Santa Fe; trustee-at-large Rocky Mountain Mineral Law Found., 1995—. Mem. ABA (sect. on natural resources, energy and environ. law natural gas and oil coms., litigation sect. energy litigation com., chair program com., editor energy litigation com. newsletter, chair energy litigation com. natural gas mktg. and trans. com., mem. coun. 1994—, mem. nominating com. 1995—, CLE officer 1995—, mem. exec. com. 1996—), La. State Bar Assn., Fed. Energy Bar Assn., Am. Assn. Petroleum Landmen (chair ad hoc com. on model form gas Balancing Agreement). Republican. Roman Catholic. Office: Phelps Dunbar 28th Fl 400 Poydras St Fl 28 New Orleans LA 70130-3245

POJETA, JOHN, JR., geologist; b. N.Y.C., Sept. 9, 1935; s. John and Emilie (Pilat) P.; m. Mary Louise Eberz, June 23, 1957; children: Kim Louise, John Martin. B.S., Capital U., Columbus, Ohio, 1957; M.S., U. Cin., 1961, Ph.D., 1963. Teaching fellow U. Cin., 1957-63; geologist U.S. Geol. Survey, 1963—, chief lower paleozoic studies unit, 1969-74, chief br. paleontology and stratigraphy, 1989-94; assoc. prof., lectr. George Washington U., 1965-74; research assoc. Smithsonian Instn., 1969—; U.S. Geol. Survey-Australian Bur. Mineral Resources exchange scientist, 1974-75. Author papers in field. Pres. Potomac Woods Citizens Assn.; mem. area 4 council Montgomery County (Md.) Bd. Edn.; mem. bd. Citizens for Good Govt.; trustee Paleontol. Research Instn., 1976-85, v.p., 1978-79, pres., 1980-82. Fellow Geol. Soc. Am., AAAS (coun.); mem. Paleontol. Soc. (sec. 1982-88, pres. 1989-90), Assn. Australasian Paleontologists. Home: 1492 Dunster Ln Rockville MD 20854-6119 Office: US Geol Survey Rm E-308 MRC137 Mus Natural History Washington DC 20560

POKELWALDT, ROBERT N., manufacturing company executive; b. North Tonawanda, N.Y.. BS, SUNY, Buffalo, 1960. With York Internat. Corp., 1983—, pres., chief exec. officer, 1991—, now also chmn., dir. Office: York Internat Corp 631 S Richland Ave York PA 17403-3445*

POKEMPNER, JOSEPH KRES, lawyer; b. Monessen, Pa., June 11, 1936; s. Leonard and Ethel Lee (Kres) P.; m. Judith Montague Stephens, Aug. 23, 1970; children: Elizabeth, Jennifer, Amy. AB, Johns Hopkins U., 1957; LLB, U. Md., 1962. Bar: Md. 1962. Law clk. to judge Supreme Bench Balt., 1960-62; field atty. 5th region NLRB, 1962-64; pvt. practice labor law Balt., 1964—; ptnr. Wolf, Pokempner & Hillman, Balt., 1972-86, Whiteford, Taylor & Preston, Balt., 1986—. Contbr. articles to legal jours. Capt. AUS, 1969-74. Mem. ABA, Fed. Bar Assn. (pres. Balt. chpt. 1979-80), Md. Bar Assn., Balt. Bar Assn. (pres. 1984-85), Serjeant's Inn Law Club. Jewish. Home: 1500 Willow Ave Baltimore MD 21204

POKOTILOW, MANNY DAVID, lawyer; b. Patterson, N.J., June 26, 1938; s. Samuel Morris and Ruth (Fuchs) P.; children: Mali, Charyse, Mona, Andrew. BEE, Newark Coll. Enging., 1960; LLB, Am. U., 1964. Bar: Pa. 1964, U.S. Supreme Ct. 1969. Examiner Patent Office, Washington, 1960-64; ptnr. Caesar, Rivise, Bernstein, Cohen & Pokotilow Ltd., Phila., 1965—; lectr. Dickinson Law Sch., various trade assns., expert witness on protection of computer software, patents, trademarks, trade secrets and copyrights; faculty Temple U. Sch. Law, 1985-94. Vol. Support Ctr. for Child Advs., Phila., 1979—; bd. dir., organizer Phila. Bar Assn. 10k Race, Phila., 1980—, Packard Press Road Run Grand Prix, 1986; bd. dirs. Hist. Soc. U.S. Dist. Ct. (ea. dist.) Pa., 1989—. Recipient Chair award for vol. excellence Am. Diabetes Assn., 1991; honored by Support Ctr. for Child Advocates, 1992. Mem. ABA (chmn. proprietary rights in software com., coun. sci. and tech. sect. 1989—), IEEE, Assn. Trial Lawyers Am., Phila. Bar Assn. (bd. govs. 1982-84, chmn. sports and recreation com. 1977—, hon. trustee campaign for qualified judges 1993), Phila. Patent Law Assn. (bd. govs. 1982-84, chmn. fed. practice and procedure com. 1983-88), Phila. Trial Lawyers (chmn. fed. cts. com. 1986-90), Lawyers Club Phila. (bd. govs. 1984-94, chmn. publicity 1994—), Pa. Trial Lawyers, Tau Epsilon Rho (vice chancellor Phila. grad. chpt. 1986-88, chancellor 1988-90). Office: Caesar Rivise Bernstein Cohen & Pokotilow Ltd 1635 Market St Philadelphia PA 19103-2217

POKOTYLO, AUGUST ELMER, government official; b. Dauphin, Man., Can., Aug. 17, 1941. BSc, Royal Mil. Coll., 1963; postgrad., Dalhousie U., 1966-69. Lic. comml. air pilot. Economist Dept. Fin./Treasury Bd., 1970-71, exec. asst., 1971-72, economist, 1972-73; dir. mktg. Dominion-Pegasus Helicopters Ltd., 1973-75; sr. analyst Stats. Can., 1975-76; sr. policy advisor Transport Can., Ottawa, Ont., 1976-81, dir. rwy. freight, 1981-85; dir. gen. rwy. passenger Transport Can., Ottawa, 1985-86, dir. gen. air policy and programs, 1986-90, dir. gen. rsch. and devel., 1990—; Project leader Asia Pacific Eocn. Cooperation study on implementation satellite navigation and comm. systems in region; mem. Rwy. Rsch. Adv. Bd. Can.; mem. exec. com. Can. Strategic Hwy. Rsch. Program; mem. R&D coun. Transp. Assn. Can.; chief del. Can. ICAO Assemblies, 1989, 90; bd. dirs. Can. Inst. Guided Ground Transport, 1982-84. Lt. Royal Can. Navy, 1959-66. Izaak Walton Killam scholar, 1968, Can. Coun. fellow, 1969. Home: 1 Rockfield Crescent, Nepean, ON Canada K2E 5L6

POKRAS, SHEILA FRANCES, judge; b. Newark, Aug. 5, 1935; m. Norman M. Pokras, 1954; children: Allison, Andrea, Larry. Student, Beaver Coll., 1953-54; BS in Edn., Temple U., 1957; JD cum laude, Pepperdine U., 1969. Bar: Calif. 1970, U.S. Dist. Ct. D.C. 1970, U.S. Dist. Ct. Calif. 1970, U.S. Supreme Ct. 1975. Tchr. elem. and secondary schs. Phila. and Newark, 1957-59; pvt. practice law Long Beach, Calif., 1970-78; city councilwoman Lakewood, Calif., 1972-76; judge Long Beach Mcpl. Ct., 1978-80, L.A. Superior Ct., 1980—; supervising judge, 1986; del. Calif. State Dem. Cen. Com., 1975, Calif. State Conv., 1975; mem. Com. on Gender Bias in Calif. Courts, 1986-89. Advisor Jr. League, 1980-85; mem. early childhood adv. bd. Long Beach City Coll.; bd. dirs. Long Beach Alcoholism Coun., 1979-80, Boys and Girls Club Am., 1981-89, Long Beach Symphony, 1985, Jewish Community Fedn., 1982-86, past mem. community rels. com.; active Nat. Women's Polit. Caucus, LWV. Named Woman of Yr. NOW, Long Beach, 1984; recipient Torch of Liberty award B'nai B'rith Anti-Defamation League, 1974; honoree Nat. Conf. Christians and Jews, 1986. Mem. ABA, AAUW, Nat. Assn. Women Judges (dist. supr. 1986), Calif. Bar Assn. (judges div.), Calif. Judges Assn. (mem. ann. seminar com. 1981-89), Mcpl. Cts. Judges Assn. (mem. Marshall com. 1979-80), L.A. County Bar Assn. (judges div., mem. arbitration com.), Women Lawyers Assn., L.A. (judges sect.), Women Lawyers Assn. Long Beach, Long Beach Legal Aid Found. (v.p. 1976-78), Long Beach Bar Assn. (active various coms., bd. govs. 1977-78, Judge of Yr. 1987), Long Beach C. of C. (bd. dirs.). Avocations: swimming, golf, jogging, classical music, movies. Office: So Dist Superior Ct 415 W Ocean Blvd Long Beach CA 90802-4512

POLACCO, PATRICIA, children's author, illustrator. Works include (juveniles) Meteor!, 1987, Rechenka's Eggs, 1988, The Keeping Quilt, 1988, Uncle Vova's Tree, 1989, Boatride with Lillian Two-Blossom, 1989, Thunder Cake, 1990, Just Plain Fancy, 1990, Babushka's Doll, 1990, Some Birthday!, 1991, Appelemando's Dreams, 1991, Picnic at Mudsock Meadow, 1992, Mrs. Katz & Tush, 1992, Chicken Sunday, 1992, The Bee Tree, 1993, Babushka Baba Yaga, 1993, Tikvah Means Hope, 1994, Pink & Say, 1994, My Rotten Readheaded, Older Brother, 1994, Firetalking, 1994, My Ol' Man, 1995, Babushka's Mother Goose, Aunt Chip and the Great Triple Creek Dam Affair, 1995; illustrator: Casey at the Bat, 1992. Office: Putnam Pub Group 200 Madison Ave New York NY 10016-3903*

POLAK, ELIJAH, engineering educator, computer scientist; b. Bialystok, Poland, Aug. 11, 1931; came to U.S., 1957, naturalized, 1977; s. Isaac and Fruma (Friedman) P.; m. Virginia Ann Gray, June 11, 1961; children: Oren, Sharon. B.S.E.E., U. Melbourne, Australia, 1957; M.S.E.E., U. Calif., Berkeley, 1959, Ph.D., 1961. Instrument engr. ICIANZ, Melbourne, Australia, 1956-57; summer student IBM Research Labs., San Jose, Calif., 1959-60; vis. asst. prof. M.I.T., fall 1964; asso. dept elec. engring. and computer scis. U. Calif., Berkeley, 1958-61; asst. prof. elec. engring. and computer scis. U. Calif., 1961-66, asso. prof., 1966-69, prof., 1969-94, prof. Grad. Sch., 1994—. Author: (with L.A. Zadeh) System Theory, 1969, (with E. Wong) Notes for a First Course on Linear Systems, 1970, (with others) Theory of Optimal Control and Mathematical Programming, 1970, Computational Methods in Optimization, 1971, Optimization: Algorithms and Consistent Approximations, 1997. Guggenheim fellow, 1968; U.K. Sci. Research Council sr. fellow, 1972, 76, 79, 82. Fellow IEEE; mem. Soc. Indsl. and Applied Math. (asso. editor Jour. Theory and Applications Optimization 1972—), Soc. Math. Programming. Home: 38 Fairlawn Dr Berkeley CA 94708-2106 Office: U Calif Dept Elec Engring Comp S Berkeley CA 94720

POLAK, JACQUES JACOBUS, economist, foundation administrator; b. Rotterdam, The Netherlands, Apr. 25, 1914; came to U.S., 1940; s. James and Elisabeth F. Polak; m. Josephine Weening, Dec. 21, 1937; children: H. Joost, Willem L. MA in Econs., U. Amsterdam, 1936, PhD in Econs., 1937; PhD in Econs. (hon.), Erasmus U., Rotterdam, 1972. Economist League of Nations, Geneva, Switzerland and Princeton, N.J., 1937-43, Netherlands Embassy, Washington, 1943-44; advisor UN Relief & Rehab. Adminstrn., Washington, 1943-44; from div. chief, asst. dir. to dir. rsch. dept. IMF, Washington, 1947-80, exec. dir., 1981-86; fin. cons. World Bank, Washington, 1987-89, Orgn. Econ. Coop. and Devel., Paris, 1987-89; pres. Per Jacobsson Found., Washington, 1987—; profl. lectr. Johns Hopkins U., Balt., 1949-50, George Washington U., 1950-55. Author: (with J. Tinbergen) The Dynamics of Business Cycles, 1950; author: An International Economic System, 1953, Finanical Policies and Development, 1989, Economic Theory and Financial Policy-The Selected Essays of Jacques J. Polak, 1994; contbr. articles to profl. jours. Fellow Econometric Soc., Royal Netherlands Acad. Sci. (corr.); mem. Cosmos Club (Washington). Home: 3420 Porter St NW Washington DC 20016-3126 Office: care Internat Monetary Fund Washington DC 20431

POLAK, WERNER L., lawyer; b. Bremen, Germany, May 19, 1936; came to U.S., 1946, naturalized, 1955; s. Ludwig and Hilde (Schultz) P.; m. Evelyn F. Ruhmann, June 21, 1959; children—Douglas H., Deborah L. B.A., Columbia U., 1960, LL.B., 1963. Bar: N.Y. 1963. Assoc., Shearman & Sterling, N.Y.C., 1963-72, ptnr., 1972—. Served with U.S. Army, 1954-56. Mem. Trustee Practicing Law Inst. Office: 153 E 53rd St New York NY 10022-4611

POLAKIEWICZ, LEONARD ANTHONY, foreign language and literature educator; b. Kiev, Ukraine, Mar. 30, 1938; came to the U.S., 1950; s. Wladyslaw and Aniela (Ossowska) P.; m. Marianne Helen Swanson, Sept. 7, 1963; children: Barbara, Kathryn, Janet. BS in Russian with distinction, U. Minn., 1964, BA in Internat. Rels., 1964; MA in Russian, U. Wis., 1968; cert. Russian area studies, 1969; PhD in Slavic Langs./Lit., U. Wis., 1978; diploma in Polish Curriculum and Instrn., Curie-Sklodowska U., Lublin, Poland, 1981. Instr. U. Minn., Mpls., 1970-78, asst. prof., 1978-90, assoc. prof., 1990—, dir. Inst. Langs., 1991-93, chair Slavic dept., 1993—; vis. asst. prof. U. London, Eng., fall 1984; dir. U. Minn. Polish Lang. Program, Curie-Sklodowska U., Lublin, Poland, summers 1984-89, dir. Russian Faculty Exch., Herzen Pedagogical U., St. Petersburg, Russia, 1993—; mem. exec. com. Coun. on Internat. Edn., N.Y.C., 1991-94; mem. Russian Lang. Program Acad. Policy Com. CIEE, N.Y.C., 1994—; mem. nat. task force Polish Studies in Am., Ind. U., 1995—; project dir. Nat. Coun. Orgns. of Less Commonly Taught Langs. Polish Lang. Learning Framework, 1995—; dir. U. Minn. Curie Sklodowska U. Faculty Exch., 1988—, U. Minn. Cath. U. of Lublin Faculty Exch., 1995—. Author: Supplemental Materials for First Year Polish, 1991, Supplemental Materials for Fifteen Modern Polish Short Stories, 1994, Directory of US Institutions of Higher Education and Faculty Offering Instruction in Polish Language, Literature and Culture, 1996-97, 1996, Intermediate Polish: Readings and Exercises, 1997; assoc. editor Slavic and East European Jour., 1988-94; editl. bd. The Learning and Tchg. of Slavic Langs. and Cultures: Toward the 21st Century, 1996—. Bd. dirs. Immigration Hist. Rsch. Ctr., Mpls., 1984-89; co-founder Polish-Am. Cultural Inst., Mpls., 1986; mem. gov.'s Commn. on Ea. Europe, St. Paul, 1991. With U.S. Army, 1961-63. Grantee Kościuszko Found., 1981, Coun. for European Studies grantee Columbia U., 1981, 84, 86, Wasie Found. grantee, 1983, IREX Collaborative Activities and New Exchs. grantee, 1984, Ireland Travel grantee Trinity Coll., Dublin, 1984, Bush Found. Rsch. grantee, 1986-87, grantee U.S. Dept. Edn., 1988-91; Fulbright-Hays Group Projects Abroad grantee for Poland, 1989, USIA U. Linkage grantee for Poland, 1989-93, IREX Short Term Travel grantee, 1995, USIA Coll. & U. Affiliations grantee for Poland, 1995—; recipient Polanie Club of the Twin Cities Merit award, 1982, Curie-Sklodowska U. medal for acad. linkage devel., 1992. Mem. Am. Assn. for the Advancement Slavic Studies, Am. Assn. Tchrs. Slavic and East European Langs. and Lits. (com. on testing and profl. devel. 1997—, Excellence in Tchg. in U.S. award 1994), Internat. Czeslaw Milosz Soc. (pres. 1984-85), N.Am. Chekhov Soc., Am. Coun. Tchrs. of Russian, Polish Inst. Arts & Scis. Am. (N.Y.C., Waclaw Lednicki Humanities award com. 1996), Assn. Literary Scholars & Critics, Soc. of Lovers of the Russian Book, Irish Assn. of Russian and East European Studies, Polish Tchrs. Assn. of Am., Polish Studies Assn. Democrat. Roman Catholic. Avocations: reading, philatelics, genealogy, touring, gardening. Home: 466 Oak Creek Drive South Vadnais Heights MN 55127

POLAKOFF, ABE, baritone; b. Bucharest, Rumania; s. Sam and Mary P. Ousherenkova; children: David Fred, Mark Evan, Robert Ira; m. Judyth Kanner, Dec. 5, 1992. Civil engring. student, CCNY; profl. tng. program, Am. Theater Wing, 1952-54; student, N.Y. Coll. Music, 1955-57. Dir. Island Opera Players; opera lectr. Arts Couns. (municipalities and schs.); cantor Progressive Shaari Zedek synagogue, Bklyn., 1972-77, Temple Emanuel, Denver, 1984-94. Debuts include Marcello in La Boheme, Milan, Florence, 1960; leading baritone Zurich Opera, 1961-63, numerous appearances with N.Y. Met. Opera, City Opera N.Y., Phila. Lyric Opera, Pitts. Opera, Seattle Opera, Berlin Deutsche Opera, Frankfurt Opera, Cinn. Opera, Hamburg, Munich Staatsoper, Stuttgart Staatsoper, The Netherlands Opera, Cin. Opera, Kansas City Lyric Opera, Canadian Opera Co., others; soloist with Mex. State Symphony Orch., Kalamazoo Symphony Orch., Winston-Salem (N.C.) Symphony, numerous concert and recital appearances. 1st prize winner Am. Theatre Wing Vocal Profl. Scholarship award, 1954, 1st prize winner Am. Opera Auditions, 1960, Silver medal Vercelli (Italy) Internat. singing contest, 1960; Rockefeller Found. grantee, 1961-62; Bayreuth Festival Masterclass scholar. Mem. Cen. Opera Service, Am. Guild Musical Artists (bd. govs.), Actors Equity Assn. Address: 11132 76th Ave Apt 7H Forest Hills NY 11375-6409

POLAKOFF, MURRAY EMANUEL, university dean, economics and finance educator; b. N.Y.C., Dec. 18, 1922; s. Joseph and Elizabeth (Zimmerman) P.; m. Sheila Doreen Brazil, Dec. 23, 1951; children: Michael Anton, Toni. BA summa cum laude, NYU, 1946; MA, Columbia U., 1951, PhD, 1955. Asst. prof. econs. U. Tex., Austin, 1951-57, assoc. prof. econs., 1957-61; prof. econs. and fin. U. Rochester, N.Y., 1961-63; prof., chmn., vice dean Grad. Sch. Bus. Adminstrn. NYU, 1968-71; leading prof., dean Sch. Mgmt. SUNY, Binghamton, 1971-77; prof. econs. and fin., provost U. Md., College Park, 1977-86, dean, 1986-91, dir. internat. devel. and conflict mgmt., 1991-92, prof. emeritus, 1993—; cons. U.S. House Com. on Banking and Currency, Washington, 1964; lectr. and cons. Brazilian Central Banking, Dept. State, São Paulo, 1966-68; chmn. bd. advisors of joint ventures Cen. Inst. Mathematical and Econ. Modelling of Soviet Acad. Scis., USSR and U. Md., College Park, 1989. Editor, contbg. author: Financial Institutions and Markets, 2d edit., 1981; contbr. articles to profl. jours. Scholar Sch. Law Columbia U., N.Y.C., 1946; Fund for Advancement Edn. faculty grantee, 1955-56; Found. Econ. Edn. fellow, summer 1956; Social Sci. Research Council fellow, 1957; Ford Found. faculty research grantee, 1961-62. Mem. Fin. Mgmt. Assn., Phi Beta Kappa. Jewish. Avocations: squash, theater. Office: Ctr Intl Dev & Conflict Mgmt Univ MD Tydings Hall College Park MD 20742

POLAN, ANNETTE LEWIS, artist, educator; b. Huntington, W.Va., Dec. 8, 1944; d. Lake and Dorothy (Lewis) P.; m. Arthur Lowell Fox Jr., Aug. 31, 1969 (div. 1994); children: Courtney Van Winkle Fox, Arthur Lowell Fox III. 1st degree, Inst. des Profs. de Francaise, Paris, 1965; BA, Hollins Coll., 1967; postgrad., Corcoran Sch. Art, 1968-69. Vis. artist Art Therapy Italia, Vignale, Italy, 1986; dir. summer program La Napoule Art Found., Chateau de la Napoule, France, 1987, 88, 90; guest lectr. China, Japan, 1989, Australia, 1996; prof. Corcoran Sch. Art, Washington, 1974—; chmn. painting dept. Corcoran Coll. Art, Washington, 1991—; dir. Washington Project for the Arts. Illustrator: Say What I Am, 1989, Relearning the Dark, 1991; cover designer Doers of the Word, 1995; portrait commns. include Sandra Day O'Connor, Va. Gov. Gaston Caperton. Bd. dirs. Washington Project for the Arts/Corcoran, 1994—, v.p. 1995—. Mem. Corcoran Faculty Assn. (pres. 1988-89). Avocations: equitation, skiing. Office: Corcoran Sch Art 1680 Wisconsin Ave NW Washington DC 20007-2707

POLAN, MARY LAKE, obstetrics and gynecology educator; b. July 17, 1943. Student, Smith Coll., Paris, 1963-64; BA cum laude, Conn. Coll., 1965; PhD in Biophysics and Biochemistry, Yale U., 1970, MD, 1975. Diplomate Am. Bd. Ob-Gyn., Am. Bd. Reproductive Endocrinology, Nat. Bd. Med. Examiners. Postdoctoral fellow dept. biology, NIH postdoctoral fellow Yale U., New Haven, 1970-72, resident dept. ob-gyn. Sch. Medicine, 1975-78, fellow in oncology, then fellow in endocrinology-infertility, 1978-80, asst. instr., then lectr. molecular biophysics-biochemistry, 1970-72, instr., then asst. prof. ob-gyn., 1978-79, 80-85, assoc. prof., 1985-90; clin. clk. in ob-gyn. and pediat. Radcliffe Infirmary, Oxford (Eng.) U. Med. Sch., 1974; instr. Pahlavi U., Shiraz, Iran, 1978; Katharine Dexter McCormick and Stanley McCormick Meml. prof. Stanford (Calif.) Sch. Medicine, 1990—, chmn. dept. gynecology and obstetrics, 1990—; vis. prof. Hunan Med. Coll., Changsha, China, 1986; mem. med. bd. Yale-China Assn., 1987-90; liaison com. on ethics in modern world Conn. Coll., New London, 1988-90; mem. med. adv. bd. Ova-Med Corp., Palo Alto, Calif., 1992—, Vivus, Menlo Park, Calif., 1993—; bd. dirs. Metra Biosys., Palo Alto, Quidel, San Diego, LipoMatrix, Palo Alto, Stanford Health Svcs., 1994—; mem. reproductive endocrinology study sect. NIH, 1989-90, co-chmn. task force on opportunities for rsch. on woman's health, 1991. Author: Second Seed, 1987; guest editor: Seminars in Reproductive Endocrinology, 1984, Infertility and Reproductive Medicine Clinics of North America: GnRH Analogues, Vol. 4, 1993; editor; (with A.H. DeCherney) Surgery in Reproductive Endocrinology, 1987, (with DeCherney, S. Boyers and R. Lee) Decision Making in Infertility; ad hoc reviewer Jour. Clin. Endocrinology and Metabolism, Fertility and Sterility, Ob-Gyn., also others; contbr. numerous articles to med. jours., chpts. to books. Fellow NRSA, 1981-82; grantee NIRA, 1082-85, HD, 1985-90, NRSA, 1987-88, Johnson & Johnson, 1993-96; scholar Assn. Acad. Health Ctrs., 1993—. Fellow ACOG (PROLOG task force for reproductive endocrinology and infertility 1988-89, rep. to CREOG coun. 1994-97); mem. Am. Fertility Soc., Soc. for Gynecologic Investigation, Soc. for Reproductive Endocrinologists, Am. Gynecologic and Obstetric Soc., Inst. Medicine (com. on rsch. capabilities of acad. depts. ob-gyn. 1990-91, bd. on health scis. policy 1992—), San Francisco Gynecologic Soc., Bay Area Reproductive Endocrine Soc., Phi Beta Kappa. Home: 4251 Manuela Ct Palo Alto CA 94306-3731 Office: Stanford U Sch Medicine 300 Pasteur Dr Rm Hh333 Palo Alto CA 94304-2203*

POLAN, MORRIS, librarian; b. St. Louis, Jan. 24, 1924; s. Jacob and Fannie (Poe) P.; m. Cecelia Hassan, Nov. 16, 1947 (div. 1974); children: Miriam, Ruth. Student, So. Ill. U., 1941-42; B.A., UCLA, 1949; postgrad., 1949-50; M.S. in L.S, U. So. Calif., 1951. Libr. Mcpl. Reference Libr., L.A., 1951-52; serials and reference libr. Hancock Libr. of Biology and Oceanography, U. So. Calif., L.A., 1952-55; periodicals libr. Calif. State U., L.A., 1955, supervising reference libr., 1956-57, chief reader svcs., 1958-64, acting coll. libr., 1965, univ. libr., 1966-89, univ. libr. emeritus, 1989—; libr. and media resources cons., 1990—; publs. coord. Edmund G. "Pat" Brown Inst. Pub. Affairs, 1992-94, pub. affairs and devel. coord., 1995—; univ. adminstr. Ctr. Pub. Resources Calif. State U., 1980-86, mem. chancellor's library adv. com., 1984; lectr. library sci. U. So. Calif., 1967; mem. chancellor's library personnel study com. Calif. State Univs. and Colls., 1969, mem. adv. com. library devel., 1974; chmn. Council Calif. State Univ. and Colls. Library Dirs., 1967-68, 70, 74; Mem. adv. bd. U. So. Calif. Library Sch., 1966-69, Productivity Council of Southwest, 1981-84; mem. library edn. adv. com. U. Calif. System, 1966-70; mem. U. Calif.-Calif. State Univ. and Colls. Task Force on Library Co-op., 1974-76; co-founder Los Angeles Coop. Library Consortium, 1983. Editor: California Librarian, 1971-74. Mem. Com. to Advise Gov. on State Librarian, 1972; mem. planning com. Calif. Library Authority for Systems and Services, 1973-75, adv. council, 1977-80, long range planning group, 1979-81, pres. congress of mems., 1979; mem. adv. bd. Arnold Schoenberg Ins., U. So. Calif., 1974-86, 89-92, Edmund G. (Pat) Brown Inst. Pub. Affairs, 1987-89; exec. com. Roy Harris Archive, 1978-86; mem. Mayor's Blue Ribbon Com. on L.A. Pub. Libr., 1976-77; mem. bd. scholars El Pueblo State Hist. Park, 1978-91; chmn. Calif. del. White House Conf. on Libraries and Info. Services, 1979; bd. dirs. ETHIKON: Inst. Study Ethical Diversity, 1981-88; Calif. state coord. Ctr. for the Book in Library of Congress, 1986-89; mem. adv. com. Ctr. for Study of Media and Values, 1988-90; treas. Frank Casado Meml. Scholarship Fund, 1992-95. With USAF, 1943-46. Mem. ALA, Calif. Library Assn. (pres. 1975, chmn. govt. relations com. 1977). Office: Calif State U 5151 State University Dr Los Angeles CA 90032-4226

POLAN, NANCY MOORE, artist; b. Newark, Ohio; d. William Tracy and Francis (Flesher) Moore; m. Lincoln Milton Polan, Mar. 28, 1934; children: Charles Edwin, William Joseph Marion. AB, Marshall U., 1936. One-man shows include Charleston Art Gallery, 1961, 67, 73, Greenbrier, 1963, Huntington Mus. Art, 1963, 66, 71, N.Y. World's Fair, 1965, W.Va. U., 1966, Carroll Reese Mus., 1967; exhibited in group shows Am. Watercolor Soc., Allied Artists of Am., Nat. Arts Club, 1968-74, 76-77, 86, 87, 91-95, Pa. Acad. Fine Arts, Opening of Creative Arts Center W.Va. U., 1969, Internat. Platform Assn. Art Exhibit, 1968-69, 72-74, 74, 79, 85-86, 88-90, (Gold medal Best of Show 1991, 2d award painting 1994, 1st award watercolor), Allied Artists W.Va., 1968-69, 86, Joan Miro Graphic Traveling Exhbn., Barcelona, Spain, 1970-71, XXI Exhibit Contemporary Art, La Scala, Florence, Italy, 1971, Rassegna Internazionale d'Arte Grafica, Siena, Italy, 1973, 79, 82, Opening of Parkersburg (W.Va.) Art Center, 1975, Art Club Washington, 1992, Pen & Brush, 1992-93, others. Hon. v.p. Centro Studie Scambi Internazionale, Rome, Italy, 1977. Recipient Acad. of Italy with Gold medal, 1979, 86, Norton Meml. award 3d Nat. Jury Show Am. Art, Chautauqua, N.Y., 1960; Purchase prize, Jurors award, Watercolor award Huntington Galleries, 1960, 61, Oil award, 1996; Nat. Arts Club for watercolor, 1969; Gold medal Masters of Modern Art exhbn., La Scala Gallery, Florence, 1975, gold medal Accademia Italia, 1984, 1986, diploma Internat. Com. for World Culture and Arts, 1987, Philip Isenberg Watercolor award Pen & Brush, 1995, many others. Mem. AAUW, DAR, Nat. Mus. Women Artists (charter), Allied Artists W.Va., Internat. Platform Assn. (3rd award-painting in ann. art exhbn. 1977, Gold medal for Best of Show 1991, 1st award for painting 1994), Huntington Mus. Fine Arts (life), Tri-State Arts Assn. (Equal Merit award 1978), Sunrise Found., Composers, Authors, Artists Am., Inc., Pen and Brush, Inc. (Watercolor exhbn. 1993, Grumbacher golden palette mem., Grumbacher award 1978), W.Va. Watercolor Soc. (charter mem.), Nat. Arts Club, Leonardo da Vinci Acad. (Rome), Accademia Italia, Vero Beach Arts Club, Riomar Bay Yacht Club, Guyan Golf and Country Club, Huntington Cotillion (hon., charter mem.), Mass. Hist. Soc. (hon.), Sigma Kappa. Episcopalian. Address (winter): 2106 Club Dr Vero Beach FL 32963 also (summer): 2 Prospect Dr Huntington WV 25701

POLAN-CURTAIN, JODIE LEA, physiologist researcher; b. Galliano, La., Sept. 4, 1963; d. John Lee and Janice Eleanor (Ferris) Polan; m. James Barry Curtain, Sept. 3, 1988; 1 child, Johnna Lela. BS in Biology, U. Tex., San Antonio, 1984, MS in Biology, 1989. Teaching asst. U. Tex., San Antonio, 1989, rsch. assoc. I, 1989-90, teaching assoc., 1990-93, rsch. assoc. II, 1990-93; sr. rsch. asst. U. Tex. Health Sci. Ctr., San Antonio, 1994—. Contbr.

articles to profl. jours. Mem. Soc. Neurosci. Address: 4302 Spiral Creek San Antonio TX 78238

POLAND, PHYLLIS ELAINE, secondary school educator, consultant; b. Norwood, Mass., May 10, 1941; d. Kenneth Gould Vale and Mildred Eloise (Fisk) Arnold; m. Thomas Charles Poland, June 6, 1968 (div. Nov. 1991); 1 child, Sherilyn Ann Poland Colon. AB in Math., Ea. Nazarene Coll., 1963; MS in Math., Nova U., 1986. Cert. secondary tchr., Fla. H.S. math. tchr. Burrillville, R.I., 1963-64; jr. H.S. math. tchr. Quincy, Mass., 1964-65; math. tchr. Seekonk (Mass.) H.S., 1965-68, Howard Jr. H.S., Orlando, Fla., 1968-74, Lake Highland Prep. Sch., Orlando, Fla., 1977-81, Lake Brantley H.S., Altamonte Springs, Fla., 1981—. Mem. coun. Joy Club Ctrl. Nazarene Ch., 1988—, adult edn. sec., 1990—, mem. choir, 1986—. Grantee NSF, 1969, 70, 71, 72. Mem. NEA. Home: 401 Navarre Way Altamonte Springs FL 32714-2224

POLAND, ROBERT PAUL, business educator, consultant; b. Bowling Green, Ohio, July 11, 1925; s. Donovan and Florence (Buck) P. BS, Bowling Green State U., 1949; MA, Columbia U., 1956; PhD, Mich. State U., 1962. Tchr. Mt. Edgecumbe Vocat. Sch., Alaska, 1949-53, Perrysburg High Sch., Ohio, 1954-58; prof. bus. edn. Mich. State U., East Lansing, 1960-90, cons. in field; leader seminars, presentations, workshops and confs. Author: (textbooks) Processing Medical Documents Using WordPerfect, 1995, Gregg Coll. Typing, 1979, 5th edit., 1984, 6th edit., 1989, Gregg College Keyboarding & Document Processing for Microcomputers, 7th edit., 1994, Gregg College Keyboarding & Document Processing for Electronic Typewriters, 7th edit., 1994, A Teaching-Learning System for Business Education, 1986, College Keyboarding and Document Processing for Windows, 8th edit., 1996, (audiovisual programs) Gregg Typing IPM, 1975, 2d edit., 1985; contbr. numerous articles to profl. jours. Served with USN, 1943-46; PTO. Recipient numerous grants in field; recipient John Robert Gregg award, 1986. Mem. Nat. Bus. Edn. Assn. (pres. 1978-79, exec. bd. dirs. 1969-70, 75-76, 77-80, Outstanding Teaching award 1981, Disting. Svc. award 1980), North-Central Bus. Edn. Assn. (pres. 1975, Disting. Svc. award 1972), Internat. Soc. Bus. Edn. (v.p. 1970-74, pres. U.S. chpt. 1967-69, Recognition of Significant Contbns. to internat. bus. edn. U.S. chpt. 1969), Mich. Bus. Edn. Assn. (pres. 1965-66, Recognition award 1970, Disting. Svc. award 1980), Delta Pi Epsilon , Phi Delta Kappa, Pi Omega Pi. Home: 901 N Harrison Rd East Lansing MI 48823-3020

POLANIN, W. RICHARD, engineering educator; b. Chgo., Apr. 14, 1952; s. Walter R. and Marie F. (Zents) P.; m. Terryl Ann Bush, July 22, 1978; children: Joshua R., Bradley J., Krista A. BS, Ill. State U., 1974, MS, 1977; EdD, U. Ill., 1990. Cert. tchr., Ill.; cert. welding insp.; cert. mfg. engr. Classroom tchr. Ill. Valley Cen. High Sch., Chillicothe, 1974-79; prof. mfg. Ill. Cen. Coll., East Peoria, 1979—, v.p. precision laser mfg.; pres. WRP Assocs., Metamora, Ill., 1978—; lectr. Lakeview Mus., Peoria, Ill., 1985-88; mem. adj. faculty Bradley U.; mfg. engr. Nat. Inst. Stds. and Tech.; presenter nat. and internat. confs. Contbr. articles to profl. jours.; tech. reviewer. Mem. citizens adv. bd. Germantown Hills (Ill.) Sch., 1991—. Mem. Am. Welding Soc.-Peoria (chmn. 1987-89), Soc. Mfg. Engrs. (v.p. Peoria sect. 1994—), Am. Soc. for Metals, Ill. Indsl. Edn. Assn. Home: 702 W Bayside Dr Metamora IL 61548-9051 Office: Ill Cen Coll 1 College Dr Peoria IL 61635-0001

POLANSKI, ROMAN, film director, writer, actor; b. Paris, Aug. 18, 1933; s. Ryszard and Bule (Katz-Przedborska) P.; m. Barbara Lass (div.); m. Sharon Tate (dec.); m. Emmanuelle Seigner. Student, Art Sch., Cracow, State Film Coll., Lodz. Appeared in children's radio show The Merry Gang, stage prodn. Son of the Regiment; dir. films Two Men and a Wardrobe, 1958, When Angels Fall, 1958, Le Gros et le Maigre, 1960, Knife in the Water, 1962 (Venice Film Festival award), The Mammals, 1963 (Tours Film Festival award), Repulsion, 1965 (Berlin Film Festival award), Cul-de-Sac, 1966 (Berlin Film Festival award), The Vampire Killers, 1967, Rosemary's Baby, 1968, Macbeth, 1971, What?, 1972, Chinatown, 1974 (Best dir. award Soc. film and TV Arts, Prix Raoul-Levy 1975), The Tenant, 1976, Tess, 1980 (Cesar award), Pirates, 1986, Frantic (also co-writer), 1988, Bitter Moon, 1994, Death and the Maiden, 1994; actor: on stage The Metamorphosis, 1988, in films A Generation, The End of the Night, See You Tomorrow, The Innocent Sorcerers, Two Men and a Wardrobe, The Vampire Killers, What?, The Magic Christian and Andy Warhol's Dracula, Back in the U.S.S.R., A Pure Formality, Chinatown, The Tennant; star, dir. play Amadeus, Warsaw, 1981, Paris, 1982; dir. operas Lulu (Spoleto Festival), 1974, Rigoletto, 1976, Tales of Hoffman, Master Class, 1996-97; author (autobiography): Roman, 1984. Office: ICM 8942 Wilshire Blvd Beverly Hills CA 90211-1934

POLANSKY, LARRY PAUL, court administrator, consultant; b. Blkyn., July 24, 1932; s. Harry and Ida (Gershengoren) P.; m. Eunice Kathryn Neun; children: Steven, Harriet, Bruce. BS in Acctg., Temple U., 1958, JD, 1973. Bar: Pa. 1973, U.S. Dist. Ct. (ea. dist.) Pa. 1973, U.S. Ct. Appeals (3d cir.) 1973, D.C. 1978, U.S. Supreme Ct. 1980. Acct., systems analyst City of Phila., 1956-63; data processing mgr. Jefferson Med. Coll. and Hosp., Phila., 1963-65; systems engr. IBM Corp., Phila., 1965-67; dep. ct. adminstr. Common Pleas Cts. of Phila., 1967-76; dep. state ct. adminstr. Pa. Supreme Ct., Phila., 1976-78; exec. officer D.C. Cts., Washington, 1979-90; presdl. appt. to bd. dirs. State Justice Inst., 1985-89; bd. dirs. Search Group, Inc. Author: A Primer for the Technologically Challenged Judge, 1995; contbr. articles to profl. jours. Served as cpl. U.S. Army, 1951-53, Korea. Fellow Inst. for Ct. Mgmt., Denver, 1984; recipient Reardon award Nat. Ctr. for State Cts., 1982, Disting. Svc. award Nat. Ctr. for State Cts., 1986, Justice Tom C. Clark award Nat. Conf. of Metro. Cts., 1991, award of merit Nat. Assn. Ct. Mgmt., 1996. Mem. ABA (jud. adminstrn. divsn., chmn. tech. com. 1991-93, 95, exec. com. lawyers conf. 1985—, chmn. 1991-92, JAD coun. 1994—), Conf. State Ct. Adminstrn. (bd. dirs. 1980-86, pres. 1984-85). Republican. Jewish. Avocations: tennis, skiing, computers. Home and Office: PO Box 752 Lake Harmony PA 18624-0752

POLANYI, JOHN CHARLES, chemist, educator; b. Jan. 23, 1929; m. Anne Ferrar Davidson, 1958; 2 children. BSc, Manchester (Eng.) U., 1949, MSc, 1950, PhD, 1952, DSc, 1964; DSc (hon.), U. Waterloo, 1970, Meml. U., 1976, McMaster U., 1977, Carleton U., 1981, Harvard U., 1982, Rensselaer U., Brock U., 1984, Lethbridge U., Sherbrooke U., Laval U., Victoria U., Ottawa U., 1987, Manchester U. and York U., Eng., 1988, U. Montreal, Acadia U., 1989, Weizmann Inst., Israel, 1989, U. Bari, Italy, 1990, U. B.C., 1990, McGill U., 1990, Queen's U., 1992, Free U. Berlin, 1993, Laurentian U., 1995, U. Toronto, 1995, U. Liverpool, 1995; LLD (hon.), Trent U., 1977, Dalhousie U., 1983, St. Francis-Xavier U., 1984; LLD (hon.), Concordia U., 1990; LLD (hon.), Calgary U., 1994. Mem. faculty dept. chemistry U. Toronto, Ont., Can., 1956—; prof. U. Toronto, 1962—; William D. Harkins lectr. U. Chgo., 1970; Reilly lectr. U. Notre Dame, 1970; Purves lectr. McGill U., 1971; F.J. Toole lectr. U. N.B., 1974; Philips lectr. Haverford Coll., 1974; Kistiakowsky lectr. Harvard U., 1975; Camille and Henry Dreyfus lectr. U. Kans., 1975; J.W.T. Spinks lectr. U. Sask., Can., 1976; Laird lectr. U. Western Ont., 1976; CIL Disting. lectr. Simon Fraser U., 1977; Gucker lectr. Ind. U., 1977; Jacob Bronowski meml. lectr. U. Toronto, 1978; Hutchinson lectr. U. Rochester, N.Y., 1979; Priestley lectr. Pa. State U., 1980; Barré lectr. U. Montreal, 1982; Sherman Fairchild disting. scholar Calif. Inst. Tech., 1982; Chute lectr. Dalhousie U., 1983; Redman lectr. McMaster U., 1983; Wiegand lectr. U. Toronto, 1984; Edward U. Condon lectr. U. Colo., 1984; John A. Allan lectr. U. Alta., 1984; John E. Willard lectr. U. Wis.; 1984, Owen Holmes lectr. U. Lethbridge, 1985; Walker-Ames prof. U. Wash., 1986, John W. Cowper disting. vis. lectr. U. Buffalo, SUNY, 1986; vis. prof. chemistry Tex. A&M U., 1986; Disting. vis. spkr. U. Calgary, 1987; Morino lectr. U. Japan, 1987; J.T. Wilson lectr. Ontario Sci. Ctr., 1987; Welsh lectr. U. Toronto, 1987; Spiers Meml. lectr. Faraday div. Royal Soc. Chemistry, 1987; Polanyi lectr. Internat. Union Pure & Applied Chemistry, 1988; W.B. Lewis lectr. Atomic Energy of Can. Ltd., 1988; Consol. Bathurst vis. lectr. Concordia U., 1988; Priestman lectr. U. N.B., 1988; Killam lectr. U. Windsor, 1988; Herzberg lectr. Carleton U., 1988; Falconbridge lectr. Laurentian U., 1988; DuPont lectr. Ind. U., 1989, C.R. Mueller lectr. Purdue U., 1989; Luther lectr. U. Regina, 1989; Franklin lectr. Rice U., 1990; Laurier lectr. Wilfred Laurier U., 1990; Pratt lectr. U. Va., 1990; Goodrich lectr. Case Western Res. U., 1990; Phillips lectr. U. Pitts., 1991; Albert Noyes lectr. U. Tex., 1992; John and Lois Dove Meml. lectr. U. Toronto, 1992, Fritz London lectr. Duke U., 1993; Castle lectr. U. South Fla., 1993; Linus Pauling lectr. Calif. Inst. Tech., 1994; Hagey lectr. U. Waterloo, 1995; Larkin Stuart lectr. U. Toronto, 1995; Hungerford lectr., 1995, York Club, 1995; disting. lectr. ser. Meml. U., 1995, John C. Polanyi nobel laureate lectr. U. Toronto, 1995, Floyd E. Bartell Meml. lectr. U. Mich., 1996, Christian Culture award lectr. Assumption U., 1996, Liversidge lectr. U. Sidney, Australia, 1996; dist. scientist lectr. Apotex, Inc., 1996; mem. sci. adv. bd. Max Plank Inst. for Quantum Optics, Fed. Republic Germany, 1982-92; mem. nat. adv. bd. on Sci. and Tech., 1987-89; hon. cons. Inst. Molecular Sci., Okazaki, Japan, 1989-94; bd. dirs. Steacie Inst. Molecular Scis., Ottawa, Can., 1991—; founding mem., pres. Can. Com. of Sci. and Scholars; Beam Disting. vis. prof. U. Iowa, 1992, Charles M. & Martha Hitchcock prof. U. Calif., Berkeley, 1994; Young Meml. visitor Royal Mil. Coll., 1994. Co-editor: (with F.G. Griffiths) The Dangers of Nuclear War, 1979; contbr. articles to jours., mags., newspapers; producer: film Concepts in Reaction Dynamics, 1970. Mem. Queen's Privy Coun. for Can., 1992; bd. dirs. Can. Ctr. for Arms Control and Disarmament; founding mem. Can. Pugwash Com., 1960. Decorated officer Order of Can., companion Order of Can., knight grand cross Order St. John of Jerusalem; recipient Marlow medal Faraday Soc., 1962, Centenary medal Chem. Soc. Gt. Brit., 1965, Noranda award Chem. Inst. Can., 1967, award Brit. Chem. Soc., 1971, Mack award and lectureship Ohio State U., 1969, medal Chem. Inst. Can., 1976, Remsen award and lectureship Am. Chem. Soc., 1978, Nobel Prize in Chemistry, 1986, Izaak Walton Killam Meml. prize, 1988, John C. Polanyi award Can. Soc. Chemistry, 1992, Floyd E. Bartell Meml. lectureship U. Mich., 1996, Liversidge lectureship U. Sydney, Australia, 1996, Christian Culture award and lectureship Assumption U., 1996; co-recipient (with N. Bartlett) Steacie prize, 1965, Wolf prize in chemistry, 1982; named Sloan Found. fellow, 1959-63, Guggenheim fellow, 1979-80 Geoffrey Frew fellow, 1996, Dist. Anniversary fellow Australian Nat. U., 1996. Fellow Royal Soc. Can. (founding mem., pres., com. on scholarly freedom, Marshall Tory medal 1977), Royal Soc. London (Royal medal 1989, Bakerian Lectr. and award 1994), Royal Soc. Edinburgh, Royal Soc. Chemistry (hon., Michael Polanyi medal 1989), Chem. Inst. Can. (hon.); mem. NAS (fgn.), Am. Acad. Arts and Sci. (hon. fgn., mem. com. on internat. security studies), Pontifical Acad. Scis., Rome. Office: U Toronto Dept Chemistry, 80 St George St, Toronto, ON Canada M5S 3H6

POLASCIK, MARY ANN, ophthalmologist; b. Elkhorn, W.Va., Dec. 28, 1940; d. Michael and Elizabeth (Halko) Polascik; BA, Rutgers U., 1967; MD, Pritzker Sch. Medicine, 1971; m. Joseph Elie, Oct. 2, 1973; 1 dau., Laura Elizabeth Polascik. Jr. pharmacologist Ciba Pharm. Co., Summit, N.J., 1961-67; intern Billings Hosp., Chgo., 1971-72; resident in ophthalmology U. Chgo. Hosp., 1972-75; practice medicine specializing in ophthalmology, Dixon, Ill., 1975—; pres. McNichols Clinic, Ltd.; cons. ophthalmology, Jack Mabley Devel. Ctr., 1976-93; mem. staff Katherine Shaw Bethea Hosp. Bd. dirs. Sinnossippi Mental Healh Ctr., 1977-82, Dixon Cmty. Trust Mental Health Ctr., 1989—. Mem. AMA, Ill. Med. Soc., Ill. Assn. Ophthalmology, Am. Assn. Ophthalmology, Alpha Sigma Lambda. Roman Catholic. Club: Galena Territory. Office: 1700 S Galena Ave Dixon IL 61021-9600

POLASEK, EDWARD JOHN, electrical engineer, consultant; b. Cudahy, Wis., Oct. 12, 1927; s. John Vincent and Mary Ann (Totka) P.; m. Alice S. Nee (Harnecki), Aug. 18, 1948. BSEE, Marquette U., 1948. Registered profl. engr., Wis., Fla. Cons. engr. Eau Claire, Wis., Gainesville, Fla., 1955-60, various countries, Korea, Vietnam, Nicaragua, 1960-72; v.p., dir. Finley Engrng. Co., Eau Claire, 1972-78; pres. Chippewa Devel. Co., Eau Claire, 1978-82; planning engr. Harza Engrng. Co. in Cairo, Egypt and Dominican Rep., 1982-86; cons. engr. Gainesville, 1986—; cons. Lake Altoona Rehab. Dist., Eau Claire, 1974. Author: Planning Methods, 1982, Feasibility Study, 1984; editor: Field Engineer's Handbook, 1982. Chmn. Eau Claire chpt. Am. Cancer Soc.; master gardner U. Fla. Ext. Svc., Gainesville, 1990. With USN, 1944-46, PTO. Mem. Nat. Soc. Profl. Engrs. (pres. 1956), IEEE, Audobon Soc., Tau Beta Pi, Eta Kappa Nu. Avocations: mycology, fishing, arts. Home: 8620 NW 13th St # 350 Gainesville FL 32653

POLASKI, ANNE SPENCER, lawyer; b. Pittsfield, Mass., Nov. 13, 1952; d. John Harold and Marjorie Ruth (Hackett) Spencer; m. James Joseph Polaski, Sept. 14, 1985. BA in Psychology, Allegheny Coll., 1974; MSW, U. Pa., 1976; JD, George Washington U., 1979. Bar: D.C. 1979, U.S. Dist. Ct. (D.C. dist.) 1980, U.S. Ct. Appeals (D.C. cir.) 1980, Ill. 1982, U.S. Dist. Ct. (no. dist.) Ill. 1982, U.S. Ct. Appeals (7th cir.) 1982. Law clk. to assoc. judge D.C. Ct., Washington, 1979-80; trial atty. Commodity Futures Trading Commn., Chgo., 1980-84, sr. trial atty., 1984, dep. regional counsel, 1984-88; assoc. Gottlieb and Schwartz, Chgo., 1988-91; staff atty. Chgo. Bd. of Trade, 1991-92, sr. atty., 1992-94, asst. gen. counsel, 1994—. Mem. ABA, Chgo. Bar Assn. Office: Chgo Bd of Trade 141 W Jackson Blvd Chicago IL 60604-2992

POLEDOURIS, BASIL K., composer; b. Kansas City, Mo., Aug. 21, 1945; s. Konstantine John and Helen Poledouris; m. Barbara Renée Godfrey, Aug. 15, 1969; children: Zoë Renée, Alexis Elene. BA in Music and Cinema, U. So. Calif., 1967, postgrad., 1967-69. Intern Am. Film Inst., L.A., 1969; freelance composer Hollywood, Calif., 1970—; pres. Basil Poledouris, Inc., Encino, Calif., 1987—; bd. dirs. Blowtorch Flats, Venice, Calif.; mem. adv. bd. Soc. for Preservation Film Music, L.A., 1985—. Composer music for films 90028, 1971, Extreme Close-Up, 1973, Tintorerra, 1977, Bid Wednesday, 1979, Defiance, 1979, The Blue Lagoon, 1988, The House of God, 1988, Conan the Barbarian, 1981, Summer Lovers, 1982, Making the Grade, 1984, Conan the Destroyer, 1984, Red Dawn, 1984, Protocol, 1984, Flesh and Blood, 1985, Cherry 2000, 1986, Iron Eagle, 1986, Robocop, 1987 (BMI award 1988), No Man's Land, 1987, Split Decisions, 1988, Spellbinder, 1988, Farewell to the King, 1989, Wired, 1989, Hunt for Red October, 1990 (BMI award 1991), Quigley Down Under, 1990, Flight of the Intruder, 1991, White Fang, 1992, Return to the Blue Lagoon, 1991, Harley Davidson and the Marlboro Man, 1991, Robocop III, 1992, Free Willy, 1992 (BMI award 1994, gold record 1994), Hot Shots! Part Deux, 1993, Serial Mom, 1993, On Deadly Ground, 1994, Lassie, 1994, Jungle Book, 1994, Free Willy II, 1995, Under Seige II, 1995, It's My Party, 1995, Celtic Pride, 1996, Amanda, 1996, The War at Home, 1996, Going West, 1996, Breakdown, 1997; composer music for TV films Congratulations It's A Boy, 1973, A Whale for the Killing, 1981, Fire on the Mountain, 1981, Amazons, 1984, Single Women, Single Bars, 1984, Amerika, 1987, Intrigue, 1988, Lonesome Dove, 1989 (Emmy award 1988, BMI award 1989), Nasty Boys, 1989, Lone Justice, 1990, Return to Lonesome Dove, 1993, TV pilots Alfred Hitchcock Presents, 1985, Misfits of Science, 1986, Island Sons, 1987, Murphy's Law, L.A. Takedown, 1989, The Life and Times of Ned Blessing, 1991, Zoya, 1995, Tradition of the Games Opening Ceremonies, 1996 Olympics. Recipient resolution Calif. Legislature, 1990, Orange County Bd. Suprs., 1990, Key to City, Garden Grove City Coun., 1990, Disting. Artist award Calif. State U., Long Beach, 1992. Mem. NARAS, BMI, Am. Fedn. Musicians, Acad. Motion Picture Arts and Scis., Soc. Lyricists and Composers. Avocations: sailing, surfing.

POLEMITOU, OLGA ANDREA, accountant; b. Nicosia, Cyprus, June 28, 1950; d. Takis and Georgia (Nicolaou) Chrysanthou. BA with honors, U. London, 1971; PhD, Ind. U., Bloomington, 1981. CPA, Ind. Asst. productivity officer Internat. Labor Office/Cyprus Productivity Ctr., Nicosia, 1971-74; cons. Arthur Young & Co., N.Y.C., 1981; mgr. Coopers & Lybrand, Newark, 1981-83; dir. Bell Atlantic, Reston, Va., 1983—; chairperson adv. coun. Extended Day Care Community Edn., West Windsor Plainsboro, 1987-88. Contbr. articles to profl. jours. Bus. cons. project bus. Jr. Achievement, Indpls., 1984-85. Mem. NAFE, AICPAs, Nat. Trust for Hist. Preservation, Ind. CPA Soc., N.J. Soc. CPAs (sec. mems. in industry com.), Princeton Network of Profl. Women. Avocations: water skiing, tennis. Home: PO Box 2744 Reston VA 20195-2744 Office: Bell Atlantic Video Svcs Co 1880 Campus Commons Dr Reston VA 20191-1512

POLENSKE, KAREN ROSEL, economics educator; b. Lewiston, Idaho, Mar. 20, 1937; d. Albert T. and Helen M. Polenske. BA in Home Econs., Oreg. State U., 1959; MA in Pub. Adminstrn. and Econs., Syracuse U., 1961; PhD in Econs., Harvard U., 1966. Instr., lectr. Harvard U., Cambridge, Mass., 1966-70, rsch. assoc. econ. rsch. project, 1966-72; sr. visitor faculty of econs. King's Coll., Cambridge U., Cambridge, Eng., 1970-71; assoc. prof. dept. urban studies and planning MIT, Cambridge, Mass., 1972-81, prof. dept. urban studies and planning, 1981—; sr. econs. cons. World Bank (in China), Washington, 1988-90, CMT (in Kuwait), Cambridge, 1987-88, Devel. Alternatives Inc. (in Pakistan), Washington, 1987-88, Asian Devel. Bank (in China), Manila, 1988, 92, Boston Inst. for Developing Econs., Washington, 1990-91, UN Devel. Programme (in India), 1993; del. System of Nat. Accounts Revisions, UN, Vienna, Austria, 1988; vis. scholar exch. program NAS, Beijing, 1986; vis. prof. U. Queensland, Brisbane, Australia, 1983, U. Montpellier, France, 1985, Chinese Acad. Scis., 1988, 90-92, 94, U. Brasilia, 1994, Keio U., 1996; dir. Spl. Program in Urban and Regional Studies (SPURS), 1973-74, 91-94. Co-author: (with mem. of rsch. staff) State Estimates of the Gross National Product, 1947, 58, 63, State Estimates of Technology, 1963; author: The U.S. Multiregional Input-Output Accounts and Model, 1980; editor: Multiregional Input-Output Analysis, 1972, 73; co-editor: (with Jiri V. Skolka) Advances in Input-Output Analysis, 1976, (with Ronald E. Miller, Adam Z. Rose), Frontiers of Input-Output Analysis, 1989, (with Chen Xi Kang) Chinese Economic Planning and Input-Output Analysis, 1991. Mem. Cambridge (Mass.) Com. on the Status of Women, 1978-80. Recipient Walter Isard Disting. Scholar award, 1996; Netherlands Inst. for Advanced Study fellow, 1980. Mem. Am. Econ. Assn., Regional Sci. Assn. (councillor at large 1990-93), Internat. Assn. for Rsch. in Income and Wealth, Internat. Input-Output Assn. (v.p. 1992-96, pres. 1997—). Avocations: birding, photography. Office: MIT 77 Massachusetts Ave Rm 9-535 Cambridge MA 02139-4301

POLENZ, JOANNA MAGDA, psychiatrist; b. Cracow, Poland, Oct. 20, 1936; came to U.S., 1961; d. Mieczyslaw and Nusia (Goldberger) Uberall; m. Daryl Louis Polenz, July 8, 1962 (div. 1991); children: Teresa Ann, Daryl Philip, Elizabeth Sophia. MD, U. Sydney, Australia, 1960; MPH, Columbia U., 1992. Diplomate Am. Bd. Psychiatry and Neurology. Intern Bklyn. Hosp., 1961-62; resident Mt. Sinai Med. Ctr., N.Y.C., 1962-65; ednl. fellow Mt. Sinai Med. Ctr., 1965-66, rsch. assoc., 1966-67; med. dir. Tappan Zee clin. Phelps Meml. Hosp., Tarrytown, N.Y., 1968-71, dir. dept. psychiatry, 1972-77; sr. attending psychiatrist Meml. Hosp. Ctr., 1972-93; pvt. practice Briarcliff Manor, N.Y., 1971-91; physician Joint Commn. Accreditation of Healthcare Orgns., Oakbrook Terrace, Ill., 1993—; lectr. in field. Author: In Defense of marriage, 1981; (with other) Test Your Marriage IQ, 1984, Test Your Success IQ, 1985; contbr. articles to profl. jours.; numerous TV appearances including Phil Donahue, 1988, Oprah Winfrey 1984. Grant Found. grantee, 1970. Fellow Am. psychiatric Assn., Royal Soc. for Health; mem. AMA, N.Y. Acad. Scis., Pan Am. Med. Assn., Westchester Psychiatric Assn. (sec. 1982-85, chair person fellowship com. 1989). Avocations: travel, international affairs. Home: 360 E 88 St Apt 37A New York NY 10128

POLESE, KIM, software company executive. BS, U. Calif., Berkeley; student, U. Wash. Product mgr. Sun Microsys., 1988-95; pres., CEO, co-founder Marimba, Inc., 1996—. Named one of Time Mags. Most Influential Ams. Office: Marimba Inc 445 Sherman Ave Palo Alto CA 94036

POLESKIE, STEPHEN FRANCIS, artist, educator, writer; b. Pringle, Pa., June 3, 1938; s. Stephen Francis and Antoinette Elizabeth (Chludzinski) P.; m. Jeanne Mackin, 1979. B.S., Wilkes Coll., 1959; postgrad., New Sch. for Social Research, 1961. Owner Chiron Press, N.Y.C., 1961-68; instr. Sch. Visual Arts, N.Y.C., 1968; prof. art Cornell U., Ithaca, N.Y., 1969—; vis. critic Pratt Graphic Arts Center, N.Y.C., 1965-68; vis. artist Colgate U., Hamilton, N.Y., 1973, USSR, 1979, Escuela de Bellas Artes, Honduras, 1980, Loughborough Coll. Art and Design, Eng., 1989; vis. prof. U. Calif., Berkeley, 1976. Contbr. short stories to mags.; one-man shows include Louis K. Meisel Gallery, N.Y.C., 1978-80, Galerie Kupinski, Stuttgart, Germany, 1979, Palace of Culture and Sci., Warsaw, Poland, 1979, Sky Art Presentation, MIT, 1981, Am. Ctr., Belgrade, 1981, William and Mary Coll., 1983, McPherson Art Gallery, Victoria, B.C., Can., 1984, Studio D'Ars, Milan, 1985, Gallery Flaviana, Locarno, Switzerland, 1985, Il Salatto Gallery, Como, Italy, 1985, Galleria Schneider, Rome, 1987, Mus. Sztuki Lodz, Poland, 1987, Alternative Mus., Lido di Spina, Italy, 1987, Galerie Klaus Lea, Munich, 1987, Patricia Cerega Gallery, Washington, 1988, Nine Columns Gallery, Palermo, Italy, 1988, John Hansard Gallery, Southampton, Eng., 1989, Quai Art Gallery, Isle of Wight, Eng., 1989, Lee Art Gallery, Clemson (S.C.) U., 1990, Apogeeairway, N.Y.C., 1991, Nine Columns Gallery, Brescia, Italy, 1991, Glenn Curtiss Mus., Hammondsport, N.Y., 1993, Caproni Mus., Trento, Italy, 1995, Temple U., Rome, 1995, Gallery of Modern Art, Maribor, Slovenia, 1995, Palazzo Communale, Todi, Italy, 1995, Palazzo Della Pretura, Piacenza, Italy; works represented in collections at Met. Mus., N.Y.C., Mus. Modern Art, N.Y.C., Victoria and Albert Mus., London, Whitney Mus., N.Y.C., Walker Art Center, Mpls., Tate Gallery, London, Fort Worth Art Center, Nat. Collection, Washington, others. Am. Fedn. of Arts grantee, 1965; Carnegie Found. grantee, 1967; Nat. Endowment for Arts grantee, 1973; N.Y. State Council on Arts grantee, 1973; Creative Artists Public Service Program grantee, 1978; Best Found. grantee, 1985. Mem. Exptl. Aircraft Assn., Aircraft Owners and Pilots Assn., Polish Acad. Sci. and Art, Internat. Aerobatic Club. Home: 306 Stone Quarry Rd Ithaca NY 14850-5308 Office: Cornell U Tjaden Hall Ithaca NY 14853 also: care Richard Curtis Assocs Inc 171 E 74th St New York NY 10021 *I have taken my artwork out of the museums and galleries into the sky. I use an aerobatic bi-plane which I build and fly to make large works in space. The airplane is flown through a series of complex maneuvers while trailing smoke in order to make a four-dimensional piece visible to the spectators for only a few short moments. The work of art has no existence other than in the memory or in documentation.*

POLEVOY, NANCY TALLY, lawyer, social worker, genealogist; b. N.Y.C., May 27, 1944; d. Charles H. and Bernice M. (Gang) Tally; m. Martin D. Polevoy, Mar. 19, 1967; children: Jason Tally, John Gerald. Student, Mt. Holyoke Coll., 1962-64; BA, Barnard Coll., 1966; MS in Social Work, Columbia U., 1968, JD, 1986. Bar: N.Y. 1987. Caseworker unmarried mothers' svc. Louise Wise Svcs., N.Y.C., 1967, caseworker adoption dept., 1969-71; caseworker Youth Consultation Svc., N.Y.C., 1968-69; asst. rsch. scientist, psychiat. social worker dept. child psychiatry NYU Med. Ctr., N.Y.C., 1973-81; adv. ct. apptd. spl. advs. Manhattan Family Ct., N.Y.C., 1981-82; cons. social work, 1981-86; matrimonial assoc. Ballon, Stoll & Itzler, 1987, Herzfeld & Rubin, P.C., 1987-88; pvt. practice, N.Y.C. Contbr. articles on early infantile autism and genealogy to profl. jours. Mem. parents' adv. bd. Riverdale Country Sch., 1988-93; mem. outreach bd. Manhattan divsn. United Jewish Appeal Fedn., 1990-94, exec. bd. Manhattan divsn., 1992-94, mem. met. campaign cabinet, 1994-95; mem. archives com. Ctrl. Synagogue, 1991—, chmn. 1994—; trustee Am. Jewish Hist. Soc., 1992—, asst. treas., 1995—; trustee Jewish Assn. for Svcs. for the Aged, 1996—; bd. dirs. Ctr. for Jewish History. 1996—. Recipient French Govt. prize, 1963. Mem. NASW, Assn. of Bar of City of N.Y., N.Y. State Bar Assn., Acad. Cert. Social Workers, Barnard Coll. Alumni Assn. (v.p. 1966, class pres. of 1966 1996—). Home and Office: 1155 Park Ave New York NY 10128-1209

POLI, KENNETH JOSEPH, editor; b. Bklyn., June 8, 1921; s. Joseph H. and Irene (Seeman) P.; m. Virginia Osk, Dec. 14, 1946; 1 child, Bruce. Student, Goddard Coll., 1938-40. Writer, photographer North Atlantic Area Office ARC, N.Y.C., 1946-49; Editorial cons., 1965—. Author Critical Focus Column, 1972-83; editor: External House Mags., Internat. Nickel Co., N.Y.C., 1949-53, Leica Photography mag., E. Leitz, Inc., N.Y.C., 1953-65; assoc. editor Popular Photography mag., Ziff-Davis Pub. Co., N.Y.C., 1965-69, sr. editor, 1969-70, editor, 1970-83, cons. editor, 1983-87; cons. editor Photography Ann., 35-mm Photography, Photography Directory and Buying Guide, 1970-83; contbr. articles to photog. jours. and encys. With inf. U.S. Army, 1942-45, PTO. Decorated Purple Heart medal. Mem. Am. Photog. Hist. Soc., Photographic Adminstrs., Circle of Confusion, Mensa. Home & Office: 362 Middle Rd Bayport NY 11705-1904

POLI, RINALDO, chemist, researcher and educator; b. Barga, Italy, Aug. 17, 1956; s. Luciano and Ivana (Tognocchi) P.; m. Bénédicte Leurent, Aug. 31, 1985; children: Clementina, Arianna. Laurea, U. Pisa, Italy, 1981; PhD, Scuola Normale Superiore, Pisa, 1985; Dottore di Ricerca, Italian Ministry Edn., Rome, 1987. Rsch. assoc. Tex. A&M U., College Station, 1985-87; asst. prof. U. Md., College Park, 1987-92, assoc. prof., 1992-95, prof., 1995-96; prof. U. de Bourgogne, Dijon, France, 1996—; vis. prof. Technische U. Munich, Garching, Germany, 1993-94, Tokyo Met. U., 1995; cons. W.R. Grace, Columbia, Md., 1991, Shell, HOuston, 1995, 96. Contbr. chpts. to books, articles to profl. jours. Recipient Disting. New Faculty award Camille and Henry Dreyfus Found., 1987, Presdl. Young Investigator award NSF, 1990, award Exxon Edn. Found., 1991, Medaglia Nasini, Soc. Chimica

Italiana; rsch. fellow Alfred P. Sloan Found., 1992, rsch. fellow Alexander von Humboldt Stiftung, 1993. Office: U de Bourgogne, Lab de Synthese et Electrosynthese Orgn, 21100 Dijon France

POLIAKOFF, GARY A., lawyer, educator; b. Greenville, S.C., Nov. 25, 1944; s. Herman and Dorothy (Ravitz) P.; m. Sherri D. Dublin, June 24, 1967; children: Ryan, Keith. BS, U. S.C., 1966; JD, U. Miami, 1969. Bar: Fla. 1969, D.C. 1971. Founding prin., sr. ptnr., pres. Becker & Poliakoff, P.A., Hollywood, Miami, Sarasota, West Palm Beach, Clearwater, Tampa, Naples and Ft. Myers, Boca Raton, Orlando, St. Petersburg, Fla., 1973—; adj. prof. condominium law and practice Nova Southeastern U.; panelist Nat. Confs. Community Assns.; testified before coms. of the U.S. Senate on Condominiums; lectr. ann. condominium seminars Fla. Bar; participant Fla. Law Revision Council; cons. to State Legis. and the White House in drafting Condominium and Coop. Abuse Relief Act, 1980; mem. condominium study commn. State of Fla., 1990; chmn. State of Fla. Advisory Coun. on Condominiums, 1992, 93. Mem. exec. com. Anti-Defamation League So. Region. Mem. Fla. Bar (co-chmn. legis. sub-com. condominium and coop. law), Coll. of Cmty. Assn. Lawyers (bd. govs.), Scribes, Coll. Cmty. Assn. Lawyers (bd. govs.). Author: (with others) Florida Condominium Law and Practice, 1982, The Law of Condominium Operations, 1988; Author: The Law of Condominium Operations, 1988; co-author: Florida Condominium Law and Practice, The Florida Bar Continuing Legal Education, 1982; contbr. articles to the Florida Law Journal and other profl. jours. on condominium law.

POLICANO, ANDREW J., university dean; b. July 4, 1949; m. Susanne Policano; children: Emily, Keith. BS in Math., SUNY, Stony Brook, 1971; MA in Econs., Brown U., 1973, PhD in Econs., 1976. Asst. prof. U. Iowa, Iowa City, 1975-79, assoc. prof. dept. econs., 1979-81, prof., chair dept. econs., 1984-87, sr. assoc. dean academic affairs, 1987-88; prof. dept. econs. Fordham U., N.Y.C., 1981-84, asst. chair, dir. grad. studies, 1982-83; rsch. assoc. Ctr. for Study of Futures Markets Columbia U., N.Y.C., 1982-86; dean divsn. social & behavioral sci. SUNY, 1988-91; dean Sch. Bus. U. Wis., Madison, 1991—; guest prof. Inst. Advanced Studies, Vienna, Austria, 1985; dir. Nat. Guardian Life, Madison, 1991—; mem. Nat. Total Quality Forum Steering Com., Schaumburg, Ill., 1992—, Am. Assembly Collegiate Sch. Bus. Diversity Com., St. Louis, 1993—. Contbr. articles profl. jours. Recipient Disting. Alumnus award SUNY, Stony Brook, 1994. Mem. Rotary. Office: U Wis Sch Bus Grainger Hall 975 University Ave Rm 5110 Madison WI 53706-1324*

POLICINSKI, EUGENE FRANCIS, author, newspaper editor; b. South Bend, Ind., Aug. 31, 1950; s. E.T. and Margaret C. (O'Neill) P.; m. Kathleen Beta O'Donnell Powell, Aug. 19, 1972; children: Ryan, David. Degree in journalism and polit. sci., Ball State U., 1972. Corr. Gannett News Svc., Washington, 1979-82; Washington editor USA Today, Arlington, Va., 1982-83, page one editor, 1983-89, mng. editor sports, 1989-96; spl. asst. to chmn./CEO The Freedom Forum, Arlington, Va., 1996—; host, commentator USA Today Sky Radio, Arlington, 1992-95. Founding editor USA Today Baseball Weekly, 1991. Named one of 100 Most Important People in Sports Sporting News, 1992, 93, 95; inducted into Ball State U. Journalism Hall of Fame, 1989. Mem. Am. Soc. Newspaper Editors (com. chmn. 1989—), Associated Press Sports Editors (com. chmn. 1989-96), Soc. Profl. Journalists. Avocations: sailing, tennis, bicycling.

POLICOFF, LEONARD DAVID, physician, educator; b. Wilmington, Del., Apr. 22, 1918; s. David and Rosalie (Rochkind) P.; m. Naomi Lewis, June 25, 1942; children: Susan, Stephen. B.S., U. Richmond, 1938; M.D., Med. Coll. Va., 1942. Diplomate Am. Bd. Internal Medicine, Am. Bd. Phys. Medicine and Rehab. (mem. 1968-80). Asst. prof. Med. Coll. Va., 1948-55; prof., chmn. dept. phys. medicine and rehab. Albany Med. Coll., Union U., 1955-67, Temple U., Phila., 1967-70; prof., chmn. Hahnemann Med. Coll., Phila., 1970-71; prof. clin. phys. medicine U. Pa.; chmn. dept. rehab. medicine Princeton (N.J.) Hosp., 1971-75, cons., 1975-78; dir. rehab. medicine Somerset Hosp., Somerville, N.J., 1975-78; acting chmn., prof. clin. phys. medicine Rutgers Med. Sch., 1976-78; clin. prof. phys. medicine and rehab. U. Calif.-Davis Sch. Medicine, 1980-86; chmn. dept. rehab. medicine Pacific Med. Center, San Francisco, 1978-81; med. cons. Dept. Health Svcs., State of Calif., 1987-91; chief rehab. medicine svc. VA Med. Ctr., Martinez, Calif., 1983-85; med. dir. Rehab. Ctr., John Muir Meml. Hosp., Walnut Creek, Calif., 1985-87; mem. Bd. Med. Examiners, N.Y. State, 1962-67; chief of staff VA Hosp., Livermore, Calif., 1987-88. Contbr. articles to profl. jours., textbooks. Bd. dirs. Commn. on Edn. in Phys. Medicine and Rehab., 1968-80, com. for Handicapped People-to-People Program, 1967-75. Served to maj. M.C., AUS, 1943-46. Nat. Inst. Neurologic Diseases fellow, 1953-55. Fellow ACP, Am. Acad. Phys. Medicine and Rehab., Am. Acad. Cerebral Palsy; mem. Am. Congress Rehab. Medicine (pres. 1971), Assn. Acad. Physiatrists, AMA (chmn. phys. medicine sect. 1965-66), Phi Beta Kappa, Alpha Omega Alpha, Sigma Zeta. Home: 1304 Henry St Berkeley CA 94709-1929

POLICY, CARMEN A., professional sports team executive; b. Youngstown, Ohio, Jan. 26, 1943; s. Albert and Ruby (Tisone) P.; m. Aug. 8, 1964 (div. Mar. 1989); children: James, Daniel, Edward, Kerry, Kathy; m. Gail Marie Moretti, June 27, 1991. Grad., Youngstown State U., 1963; JD, Georgetown U., 1966. Bar: Ohio 1966, Va. 1966, D.C. 1966. Assoc. Nadler & Nadler, Youngstown, 1966-68; asst. prosecutor City of Youngstown, 1968-69; ptnr. Flask & Policy, Weimer & White, Youngstown, 1969-90; spl. counsel to atty. gen. State of Ohio, 1970-91; v.p., gen. counsel San Francisco 49ers, NFL, 1983-90, pres., 1990—; mem. various coms. NFL, 1990—; bd. dirs. World League Am. Football, N.Y.C., 1991—. Com. mem. various charities, Youngstown, 1969-90, San Francisco, 1990—. Mem. Va. Bar Assn., Ohio Bar Assn., D.C. Bar Assn. Roman Catholic. Avocations: scuba diving, hiking. Home: 1419 Hamilton Ave Palo Alto CA 94301-3150 Office: San Francisco 49ers 4949 Centennial Blvd Santa Clara CA 95054-1229*

POLICY, JOSEPH J., publisher, television producer; b. Youngstown, Ohio, July 12, 1945; s. Vincent James and Anna Marie P.; m. Carole A., May 10, 1969; children: Amy Annette, Holly Anne. BS, U. Md., 1969. Staff TV dir. WDCA-TV, Washington, 1964-68; mgmt. tng. program Triangle Publs., Phila., 1968-72; promo. dir. WFBG-AM-FM-TV, Altoona, Pa., 1972-74, WQXI-TV, Atlanta, 1974-76, WWL-TV, New Orleans, 1976-78; sta. mgr. WPEC-TV, West Palm Beach, Fla., 1978-81; gen. editor Nat. Enquirer, West Palm Beach, Fla., 1981-89; v.p., dir. corp. mktg. Am. Media, West Palm Beach, Fla., 1989—; cons. Coca-Cola, Atlanta, 1972-76, Kearney, Internat., Atlanta, 1972-76, Amiel Industries, Atlanta, 1972-74. Creator/editor: (mags.) Soap Opera Mag., 1991, Country Weekly Mag., 1994, Motor Sport USA, 1997; producer: (TV spl.) Jerry Lee Lewis Live in London, 1986, Prime Time Country: A Country Weekly Tribute, 1995-96, Webmaster, AMI, 1997. With U.S. Army, 1969-72, Far East. Recipient 17 Addy awards Fla. Advt. Assn., 1978-81, BPA Nat. award Broadcast Prom. Assn., 1981, J.R. Stram Grant, U. Md. Mem. Nat. Assn. TV Program Execs., Nat. Acad. TV Arts & Scis., Country Music Assn. Republican. Roman Catholic. Avocations: travel, model railroading, golf. Office: American Media Inc 600 E Coast Ave Lake Worth FL 33464-0001

POLIKOFF, BENET, JR., lawyer; b. Winston-Salem, N.C., Nov. 25, 1936; s. Benet and Margaret (New) P.; m. Jean Troubh, June 26, 1959 (div. Mar. 1971); children—Elisabeth, Benet Steven, Lee; m. Florence Davis, June 11, 1971. BA, Yale U., 1959; LLB, Harvard U., 1962. Ptnr. Marshall, Bratter, Greene, Allison & Tucker, N.Y.C., 1969-82; Ptnr. Rosenman and Colin, N.Y.C., 1982-90, of counsel, 1990—. Mem. Assn. Bar City N.Y. (chmn. real property law com. 1981-84), N.Y. State Bar Assn., Am. Coll. Real Estate Lawyers.

POLIN, ALAN JAY, lawyer; b. N.Y.C., Sept. 5, 1953; s. Mortin and Eleanor (Clarke) P.; m. Sharon Lynn Hirschfeld, Oct. 10, 1976; children: Jay Michael, Meryl Beth. Student, Cornell U., 1971-74; BA cum laude, Seton Hall U., 1978; JD, Nova U., 1981. Bar: Fla. 1981, N.Y. 1990. Assoc. Berryhill, Avery, Williams & Jordan, Esq., Ft. Lauderdale, Fla., 1981-82, Greenspoon & Marder, P.A., Miami, Fla., 1982-83; pvt. practice Ft. Lauderdale, 1983-86; ptnr. Mousaw, Vigdor, Reeves & Hess, Ft. Lauderdale, 1986-90; pvt. practice Coral Springs, Fla., 1990—; adj. faculty mem. Nova U; mem. grievance com. Fla. Bar, 1989-92, vice chair, 1990-91, chair, 1991-92. Chmn. Broward County Crct. Ct. Handbook, 1988; contbr. chpt. to Bridge the Gap Attorney's Handbook, 1987. Dir. Temple Beth Am., Margate, Fla., 1991-93; mem. Anti-Defamation League, Fla. Regional Bd., 1994-96; mem. exec. com. Broward County Dem., 1989-96; vice mayor City of Coral Springs, 1994-96, commr., 1991—; mem. bd. dirs. Fla. Regional Bd. of Anti-Defamation League, 1994—, Children's Cardiac Rsch. Found., Inc., 1996—, Am. Heart Assn., 1997—. Recipient Am. Jurisprudence award Nova U. Law Ctr., 1981. Mem. Fla. Bar Assn. (bd. govs. young lawyers divsn. 1987-89), Broward County Bar Assn. (exec. com. young lawyers sect. 1986-87), North Broward Assn. Realtors, Inc. (affiliate, std. contract forms com. 1989-95, atty./realtor rels. com. 1989-91), Kiwanis (Key Club advisor 1990-91). Office: 3300 N University Dr Ste 601 Coral Springs FL 33065-4132

POLING, KERMIT WILLIAM, minister; b. Elkins, W.Va., Oct. 1, 1941; s. Durward Willis and Della Mae (Boyles) P.; m. Patricia Ann Groves, June 12, 1965; children: David Edward Elson, Mikael Erik. Diploma in Bible, Am. Bible Sch., 1966; BRE, Am. Bible Coll., 1991; BA in Bible, Reed Coll. Religion, 1968; AA, W.Va. U., 1970; ThD, Zion Theol. Sem., 1971; postgrad., Wesley Theol. Sem., 1974; LLD, Geneva Theol. Coll., 1980; DSL (hon.), Berean Christian Coll., 1981; postgrad., Mansfield Coll., U. Oxford, Eng., 1986, 90, 91; D Ecumenical Rsch., St. Ephrem's Inst. for Oriental Studies, 1989; M of Herbology, Emerison Coll., 1994. Ordained to ministry United Meth. Ch., 1967. Pastor Parkersburg-Crossroads (W.Va.) Cir., 1967-70; asst. sec. W.Va. Ann. Conf., 1967-69; pastor Hope-Halleck Morgantown Cir., 1970-76, Trinity-Warren Grafton (W.Va.) Charge, 1976-83, 1st Trinity Pennsboro (W.Va.) Charge, 1983-97, South Parkersburg United Meth. Ch., 1997—; editor local ch. news; instr. Bible Bodkin Bible Inst., 1975-75, United Meth. Lay Acad., 1992—; mem. staff Taylor County Coop. Parish, 1976-83; coord. Hughes River Coop. Parish, 1983-86; mem. chaplains com. Grafton City Hosp., 1976-82; mem. coun. Ctr. d'Etudes et d'Action Oecumeniques, 1972-74. Author: A Crown of Thorns, 1963, A Silver Message, 1964, History of the Halleck Church, 1970, Eastern Rite Catholicism, 1971, From Brahmin to Bishop, 1976, Cult and Occult: Data and Doctrine, 1978, The Value of Religious Education in Ancient Traditional Churches, 1993, Anniversary History of Trinity Church, Pennsboro, 1997; editor: Jane's Heirs; contbr. articles and poems to religious jours. Decorated Royal Afghanistan Order of Crown of Amanullah, Byzantine Order of Leo the Armenian, Order of Polonia Presituta, Mystical Order of St. Peter, knight Grand Cross of the Order of St. Dennis of Zante, 1990; recipient Good Citizenship award Doddridge County, 1954, Silver medal Ordre Universel du Merit Humain, Geneva, 1973, Commendation for Outstanding Achievement in Ministry, Ohio Ho. of Reps., 1988; named Chief of Dynastic Ho. of Polanie-Patrikios, 1988. Mem. SAR, Assn. Bible Tchrs. (founder), Internat. Platform Assn., Sovereign Order St. John Jerusalem, Ritchie County Ministerial Assn. (pres. 1984-97), Order Sacred Cup, Knights of Malta, Order of the Crown of Lauriers. Home: 1820 Mount Vernon Cir Parkersburg WV 26101

POLING, WESLEY HENRY, college president; b. Akron, Ohio, May 22, 1945; s. Elmer Francis and Norma May (Flickinger) P.; m. Carol Ann Young, Aug. 17, 1968; children: Jason Alder, Todd Wesley. BA, Ohio Wesleyan U., 1968; MDiv, Yale U., 1971; PhD, U. Conn., 1983. Dir. parents program Yale U., New Haven, 1971-73, dir. alumni records, 1973-86; v.p. for devel. and alumni rels. Goucher Coll., Towson, Md., 1986-94; pres. Ky. Wesleyan Coll., Owensboro, 1994—; treas. Dist. I CASE, 1985-86, program chair Conf., 1984-85. Chmn. bd. mgr. Ctrl. br. YMCA of New Haven, 1976-83; v.p., treas. Balt. Choral Arts Soc., 1989-93, pres., 1993-94; bd. dirs. Roland Park Place, Balt., 1991-94; mem. Citizens Com. on Edn., Owensboro, 1994—. Berkeley Coll., Yale U. fellow. Mem. Owensboro C. of C. (bd. dirs. 1994-95), Williams Club, Rotary, Phi Delta Kappa. Avocations: squash, running, music. Home: 3100 Frederica St Owensboro KY 42301-6059 Office: Ky Wesleyan Coll PO Box 1039 Owensboro KY 42302-1039

POLINGER, IRIS SANDRA, dermatologist; b. N.Y.C., Feb. 10, 1943; m. Harvey I. Hyman, Feb. 6, 1972. AB, Barnard Coll., 1964; PhD, Johns Hopkins U., 1969; MD, SUNY Downstate, Bklyn., 1975. Diplomate Am. Bd. Dermatology. Teaching positions various schs. including NYU Coll. Dentistry and Harvard Med. Sch., 1969-73; med. intern Baylor Coll. Medicine, 1975-76, resident in dermatology, 1976-79; pvt. practice dermatology Houston, 1979—. Bd. dirs. Ft. Bend County Women's Ctr., Richmond, Tex., 1993—. Mem. Am. Bus. Women's Assn. (chair scholarship com. 1992, 96, chair scholarship event com. 1993—). Office: 4915 S Main St Ste 104 Stafford TX 77477-4601

POLINSKY, JANET NABOICHECK, state official, former state legislator; b. Hartford, Conn., Dec. 6, 1930; d. Louis H. and Lillian S. Naboicheck; BA, U. Conn., 1953; postgrad. Harvard U., 1954; m. Hubert N. Polinsky, Sept. 21, 1958 (div.); children: Gerald, David, Beth. Mem. Waterford 2d Charter Commn. (Conn.), 1967-68, Waterford Conservation Commn., 1968-69; Waterford rep. Town Meeting, 1969-71, SE Conn. Regional Planning Agy., 1971-73; mem. Waterford Planning and Zoning Commn., 1970-76, chmn., 1973-76; mem. Waterford Dem. Town Com., 1976-92, del. State Dem. Conv., 1976, 78, 80, 82, 84, 86, 90, 92; mem. Conn. Ho. of Reps. from 38th Dist., 1977-92, asst. majority leader, 1981-83, chmn. appropriations com., 1983-85, 87-89, ranking mem., 1985-87, minority whip, 1985-86, dep. speaker, 1989-92; dep. commr. dept. adminstrv. svcs., State of Conn., 1993-94, commr., 1994-95, asst. sec. of state, 1995; commr. utilities ctrl. auth. State of Conn., 1995—. Trustee Eugene O'Neill Meml. Theatre Ctr., 1973-76, 81-92; corporator, Lawrence and Meml. Hosps., 1987—; mem. New Eng. Bd. Higher Edn., 1981-83; mem. fiscal affairs com. Eastern Conf. Council of State Govts., 1983-88. Named Woman of Yr., Waterford Jr. Women's Club, 1977, Nehantic Women's Bus. and Profl. Club, 1979, Legislator of Yr., Conn. Library Assn., 1980. Mem. Order Women Legislators, Delta Kappa Gamma (hon.). Home: 15 Gardner Cir New London CT 06320-4314 Office: 10 Franklin Sq New Britain CT 06051-2605

POLIS, MICHAEL PHILIP, university dean; b. N.Y.C., Oct. 24, 1943; s. Max and Sylvia (Goldner) P.; m. Claudette Martin, May 28, 1966; children: Melanie Bobby, Martin Pascal, Karine Melissa. BSEE, U. Fla., 1966; MSEE, Purdue U., West Lafayette, Ind., 1968, PhD, 1972. Grad. instr. elec. engring. Purdue U., West Lafayette, 1966-71; postdoctoral fellow Ecole Polytechnique, Montreal, 1972-73, asst. prof. elec. engring., 1973-74, assoc. prof., 1974-82, prof., 1982-83; program dir. sys. theory NSF, Washington, 1983-87; chmn. dept. elec. and computer engring. Wayne State U., Detroit, 1987-93; dean Sch. Engring. and Computer Sci. Oakland U., Rochester, Mich., 1993—; expert witness various law firms, 1989—; cons. Mich. Bell-Ameritech, Detroit, 1989-95, ICAM Technologies, Inc., Montreal, 1981-83; vis. rsch. assoc. LAAS, Toulouse, France, 1978. Contbr. articles to profl. jours. Mem. IEEE (sr.), IEEE Control Sys. Soc. (bd. govs. 1993-95, Best Paper Trans. on Automatic Control 1974-75, Disting. Mem. 1993, v.p. mem. activities 1990-91, assoc. editor 1981-82). Office: Oakland Univ Sch Engring & Computer Sci Rochester MI 48309

POLISI, JOSEPH W(ILLIAM), academic administrator; b. N.Y.C., Dec. 30, 1947; s. William Charles and Pauline (Kaplan) P.; m. Elizabeth Marlowe. BA in Polit. Sci., U. Conn., 1969; MA in Internat. Relations, Tufts U., 1970, MusM, 1973, M of Mus. Arts, 1975; DMA, Yale U., 1980; DHL (hon.), Ursinus Coll., Collegetown, Pa., 1986; MusD (hon.), Curtis Inst. Music, 1990. Exec. officer Yale Sch. of Music, New Haven, 1976-80; dean of faculty Manhattan Sch. of Music, N.Y.C., 1980-83; dean Coll. Conservatory of Music U. Cin., 1983-84; pres. The Juilliard Sch., N.Y.C., 1984—. Performances as bassoonist throughout the U.S.; contbr. articles to various publs. in U.S. and France. Office: Juilliard Sch Office of the Pres 60 Lincoln Center Plz New York NY 10023-6500*

POLITAN, NICHOLAS H., federal judge; b. Newark, Nov. 13, 1935; m. Marian E. Politan; children: Nicholas H. Jr., Vincent J. Bar: N.J. 1961, U.S. Dist. Ct. N.J. 1961, U.S. Ct. Appeals (2d cir.) 1969, U.S. Ct. Appeals (3d cir.) 1971, U.S. Tax Ct. 1972, U.S. Supreme Ct. 1973. Law clk. to Hon. Gerald McLaughlin U.S. Ct. Appeals (3d cir.), Newark, 1960-61; sr. ptnr. Cecchi and Politan, Lyndhurst, N.J., 1961-64, 72-87; litigation ptnr. Krieger, Chodash & Politan, Jersey City, 1964-72; dir., chmn. exec. com. County Trust Co., Lyndhurst, 1980-87; judge U.S. Dist. Ct. N.J., 1987—; instr. legal rsch. and writing Rutgers U. Law Sch., 1963. Mng. editor Rutgers Law Rev., 1959; contbr. articles to profl. jours. Office: US Dist Ct Box 999 King Bldg Newark NJ 07101-0999

POLITES, MICHAEL EDWARD, aerospace engineer; b. Belleville, Ill., Mar. 19, 1944; s. Matthew Charles and Edith Louise (Schwarz) P. BS in Sys. and Automatic Controls, Washington U., St. Louis, 1967; MSEE, U. Ala., 1971; PhD in Elec. Engring., Vanderbilt U., 1986. Aerospace rsch. engr., guidance, navigation and control sys. NASA/Marshall Space Flt. Ctr. Structures & Dynamics Lab, Huntsville, Ala., 1967-95; supervisory chief, instrumentation and control divsn. Astrionics Lab. NASA/Marshall Space Flight Ctr., Huntsville, Ala., 1995—. 4 patents in field; contbr. numerous articles to profl. jours.; referee various jours. and confs. Recipient 62 NASA awards in the field. Fellow AIAA (assoc., guidance navigation and control tech. com. 1990—, digital avionics tech. com. 1996—); mem. IEEE (sr. Outstanding Engr. Huntsville sect. 1995), ASME, Am. Astronautical Soc. (session co-chmn. 1995 & 97 Guidance and Control Conf.), Mensa, Tau Beta Pi, Eta Kappa Nu, Pi Tau Sigma. Office: NASA Marshall Space Flight Ctr Astronics Lab Huntsville AL 35812

POLITZ, HENRY ANTHONY, federal judge; b. Napoleonville, La., May 9, 1932; s. Anthony and Virginia (Russo) P.; m. Jane Marie Simoneaux, Apr. 29, 1952; children: Nyle, Bennett, Mark, Angela, Scott, Jane, Michael, Henry, Alisa, John, Nina. BA, La. State U., 1958, JD, 1959. Bar: La. 1959. Assoc., then ptnr. firm Booth, Lockard, Jack, Pleasant & LeSage, Shreveport, 1959-79; judge U.S. Ct. Appeals (5th cir.), Shreveport, 1979—, chief judge, 1992—; vis. prof. La. State U. Law Center; bd. dirs. Am. Prepaid Legal Services Inst., 1975—; mem. La. Judiciary Commn., 1978-79; mem. U.S. Jud. Conf., 1992—, exec. com., 1996—. Mem. editl. bd. La. State U. Law Rev., 1958-59. Mem. Shreveport Airport Authority, 1973-79, chmn., 1977; bd. dirs. Rutherford House, Shreveport, 1975—, pres., 1978; pres. Caddo Parish Bd. Election Suprs., 1975-79; mem. Electoral Coll., 1976. Served with USAF, 1951-55. Named Outstanding Young Lawyer in La., 1971, Outstanding Alumnus La. State U. Law Sch., 1991; inducted in La. State U. Hall of Distinction, 1992. Mem. Am. Bar Assn., Am. Judicature Soc., Internat. Soc. Barristers, La. Bar Assn., La. Trial Lawyers Assn., Shreveport Bar Assn., Justinian Soc., K.C., Omicron Delta Kappa. Democrat. Roman Catholic. Office: US Ct Appeals 300 Fannin St Ste 5226 Shreveport LA 71101-3121

POLITZER, HUGH DAVID, physicist, educator; b. N.Y.C., Aug. 31, 1949; s. Alan A. and Valerie T. (Diamant) P. B.S., U. Mich., 1969; Ph.D., Harvard U., 1974. Jr. fellow Harvard U. Soc. Fellows, 1974-77; mem. faculty Calif. Inst. Tech., 1977—, prof. theoretical physics, 1979—, exec. officer for physics, 1986-88. Recipient J.J. Sakurai prize, 1986. Fellow NSF, 1969-74; Sloan Found., 1977-81; Woodrow Wilson grad. fellow, 1969-74, Guggenheim fellow, 1997-98. Mem. Phi Beta Kappa. Address: 452-48 Calif Inst Tech Pasadena CA 91125

POLIVNICK, PAUL, conductor, music director; b. Atlantic City, N.J., July 7, 1947; s. Sidney and Beatrice Ann (Craven) P.; m. Kathleen Lenski, Jan. 19, 1970 (div. 1976); m. Marsha Hooks, June 20, 1980. MusB, Juilliard Sch., N.Y.C., 1969; MusD (hon.), U. Montevallo, 1987. Condr. Debut Orch., L.A., 1969-73; mem. faculty UCLA, 1973-76; assoc. condr. Indpls. Symphony, 1977-80, Milw. Symphony, 1981-85; dir. music Ala. Symphony, Birmingham, 1985-93; music dir. N.H. Music Festival, 1993—; guest condr. various symphony and opera cos., worldwide. Avocations: backpacking, working out, traveling, cooking. Address: care Maxim Gershunoff Attractions Inc PO Box 224055 Hollywood FL 33022*

POLJAK, ROBERTO J(UAN), research director, biotechnology educator; b. Buenos Aires, Argentina, Sept. 17, 1932; s. Giovanni P. and Josephine (Zorzut) P.; m. Mabel Amelia Iglesias, Dec. 28, 1956; children: Leonora, Gustavo. BSc, Coll. Nat. Quilmes, Argentina, 1949; PhD, U. de la Plata, Argentina, 1956. Teaching assoc. Instituto de Fisica, Bariloche, Argentina, 1957; fellow Sch. for Advanced Studies MIT, Boston, 1958-60; postdoctoral fellow Davy Faraday Rsch. Lab., Royal Instn., London, 1960-62; postdoctoral flelow MRC Unit for Molecular Biology, Cambridge, Eng., 1962; asst. prof. biophysics Johns Hopkins Sch. Medicine, Balt., 1962, assoc. prof. biophysics, 1966, prof. biophysics, 1972-81; prof. Institut Pasteur, Paris, 1981-92; dir. rsch. CNRS, Paris, 1981-92; prof., dir. Ctr. Advanced Rsch. in Biotech. U. Md./Nat. Inst. Stds. and Tech., Balt., 1992—; W.H. Elkins prof. U. Md., 1994—. Contbr. about 150 rsch. papers to sci. jours. Recipient Rsch. Career Devel. award USPHS, 1972-77, gold medal Soc. d'Encouragement au Progres, Paris, 1986, Jacques Monod prize Fondation de France, 1986, Disting. Scientist award S.W. Found. for Biomed. Rsch., 1987, Louis Jeantet Found. Medicine prize, Geneva, 1989, Gold medal Jimenez Diaz Found., 1991; Macy Faculty scholar, 1977-78. Mem. European Molecular Biology Orgn., Am. Assn. Immunologists. Office: Ctr for Advanced Rsch Biotech 9600 Gudelsky Dr Rockville MD 20850-3479

POLK, BENJAMIN KAUFFMAN, retired architect, composer, educator; b. Des Moines, May 18, 1916; s. Harry Herndon and Alice (Kauffman) P.; m. Emily Despain Isaacs, Aug. 23, 1946. Student, Amherst Coll., 1933-35, U. Chgo., 1935-36, Iowa State Coll., 1936-38. Ptnr. Polk and Malone, San Francisco, 1948-53; propr. Benjamin Polk, Architect & Planner, New Delhi, Calcutta, Karachi, 1952-64; assoc. W.R. Ewald Jr., Regional Planning, Washington, 1965-66; mem. architecture & planning faculty Calif. Poly. State U., San Luis Obispo, 1966-80; ret., 1980. Author: Architecture and the Spirit of the Place, 1961, Building for South Asia, An Architectural Autobiography, 1992, (with Emily Polk) India Notebook, 1986, (with Seneviratna) Buddhist Monastic Architecture, 1992, A Figure in a Landscape, 1992, Christchurch Priory, Dorset, 1994; Structure for Music and Synthesized Orchestrations, 1995; also booklets, articles; prin. works include Am. Libr., Times of India Press, New Delhi, Jallian Wala Bagh Amritsar India, Utkal U., Orissa, Gwalior Rayons Factories and Town Calicut, Birla Mus., Rajasthan, Woodlands, Calcutta, Palace for the King of Nepal, Buddhist Libr., Rangoon. Vice-pres. Service Civile Internat., East India, 1957-63; advisor Small Wilderness Area Preservation, Calif., 1970-80. Tech. sgt. U.S. Army, 1942-46. Recipient Gold medal Prime Min. of Burma, 1961. Republican. Presbyterian. Avocations: writing, sketching, hiking. Home: 2361 Claranita Ave Los Osos CA 93402-4013 Office: Quaker Gardens 12151 Dale Ave Stanton CA 90680

POLK, CHARLES, electrical engineer, educator, biophysicist; b. Vienna, Austria, Jan. 15, 1920; came to U.S., 1940, naturalized, 1943; s. Heinrich and Amalie (Canar) P.; m. Dorothy R. Lemp, Apr. 27, 1946; children: Dean F., Gerald W. Student, U. Paris-Sorbonne, 1939; BS, Washington U., 1948; MS, U. Pa., 1953, PhD, 1956. Engr. RCA Victor div., Camden, N.J., 1948-52; rsch. and teaching assoc. U. Pa., 1952-57; prof. elec. engring. Drexel Inst. Tech., Phila., 1957-59; tech. staff RCA Labs., Princeton, N.J., 1957-59; prof. elec. engring. U. R.I., 1959-90, prof. emeritus, 1990—, chmn. dept., 1959-79; head elec. scis. and analysis sect. engring. div. NSF, Washington, 1975-76; acting dir. engring. div. NSF, 1976-77; vis. prof. elec. engring. Stanford U., 1968-69, U. Wis., Madison, 1983-84; cons. Oak Ridge Nat. Lab., 1993—. Editor Handbook of Biologial Effects of Electromagnetic Fields; contbr. articles to profl. publs. Mem. R.I. Legis. Commn. on Electricity Rates, 1974-75. With AUS, 1943-46. NSF Superior Accomplishment award, 1977. Fellow IEEE (chmn. Phila. chpt. profl. group antennas and propagation 1954-55, chmn. Providence sect. 1964-65, mem. adminstrn. com., com. on man and radiation 1987-96, chair subcom. biol. effects of power frequency fields 1989-96, engring. in med. and biology soc.); mem. AAAS, AAUP, Am. Geophys. Union (nat. com. on space electricity 1974-75), Am. Soc. for Engring. Edn., N.Y. Acad. Scis., Internat. Sci. Radio Union, Biolelectromagnetics Soc. (pres. 1988-89), Bioelec. Repair and Growth Soc. (coun. mem. 1990-92), Sigma Xi, Tau Beta Pi. Organized 1st microwave closed circuit television link for grad. edn. in U.S., 1962. Home: 53 Springhill Rd Kingston RI 02881-1805

POLK, HIRAM CAREY, JR., surgeon, educator; b. Jackson, Miss., Mar. 23, 1936; s. Hiram Carey and Dorris (Hemby) P.; m. Susan Galandiuk; children: Susan Elizabeth, Hiram Cary. BS, Millsaps Coll., 1956; MD, Harvard U., 1960. Intern Barnes Hosp., St. Louis, 1960-61; resident Barnes Hosp., 1961-65; instr. in surgery Washington U., St. Louis, 1964-65; asst. prof. surgery U. Miami, Fla., 1965-69; assoc. prof. U. Miami, 1969-71; prof. chmn. dept. surgery U. Louisville, 1971—; pres., chmn. bd. Univ. Surg. Assocs., P.S.C., 1971—; chmn. bd. Clin. Services Assn., Inc.; mem. merit rev. bd. for surgery VA, 1983-85. Author: (with H.H. Stone) Contemporary Burn Management, 1971, Hospital-Acquired Infections in Surgery, 1977; (with B. Gardner, H.H. Stone and W.L. Sugg) Basic Surgery, 1978, (with

H.H. Stone and B. Gardner) 2d edit., 1983, 3d edit., 1987, 4th edit., 1992, 5th edit., 1995; (with D.C. Carter) Trauma, 1982; (with J.E. Conte Jr. and L.S. Jacob) Antibiotic Prophylaxis in Surgery: A Comprehensive Review, 1984; (with J.D. Richardson and L.M. Flint Jr.) Trauma: Clinical Care and Pathophysiology, 1987; contbr. numerous articles to profl. publs.; mem. editl. bd. So. Med. Jour., 1970-72, Jour. Surg. Rsch., 1970-72, 75-77, 78-80, Current Problems in Surgery, 1973—, Surgery, 1975-85, Current Surgery, 1977—, Current Surg. Techniques, 1977—, Emergency Surgery: A Weekly Update, 1977—, Collected Letters in Surgery, 1978—, Brit. Jour. Surgery, 1981-94; chief editor Am. Jour. Surgery, 1986—. Bd. govs. Trover Clinic Found., Madisonville, Ky. Mem. ACS (gov. 1972-80, commn. on cancer 1975-80), AMA, Allen O. Whipple Soc. (exec. coun. 1977-80), Am. Assn. Cancer Edn. (exec. coun. 1968-72), Am. Assn. Surgery of Trauma, Am. Burn Assn., Am. Cancer Soc. (pres. Ky. div. 1989-90, nat. del. dir. 1989-92, 93-95), Am. Surg. Assn. (sec. 1984-89), Acad. Surgery (pres. 1975-76), Cen. Surg. Assn., Assn. Am. Med. Colls. (chmn. ad hoc com. on Medicare and Medicaid 1978-79), Collegium Internationale Chirurgiae Digestivae (sec.-treas. 1981-86, pres. 1986-87), Council on Public Higher Edn. (task group on health scis.), Halsted Soc., Jefferson County Med. Soc., Ky. Med. Assn., Ky. Surg. Soc. (pres. 1982-83), Louisville Surg. Soc. (pres. 1989-90), Residency Rev. Com. for Surgery (vice chmn. 1981-83, chmn. 1983-85), Société Internationale de Chirurgie, Soc. Surgery Alimentary Tract (treas. 1975-78, pres. 1985-86), Soc. Clin. Surgery, Soc. Surg. Chairmen, Soc. Surg. Oncology (pres. 1984-85), Soc. Univ. Surgeons (treas. 1971-74, pres. 1979-80), Southeastern Surg. Congress (exec. coun. for Ky. 1985-86, pres. 1994-95), So. Med. Assn. (vice chmn. sect. on surgery 1969-70, chmn. sect. 1972-73, sec. 1970-72, exec. coun. for Ky. 1971-77, 89-90), So. Surg. Assn. (pres. 1988-89), Alpha Omega Alpha. Home: 5609 River Knoll Dr Louisville KY 40222-5846 Office: U Louisville Dept Surgery Louisville KY 40292

POLK, JAMES RAY, journalist; b. Oaktown, Ind., Sept. 12, 1937; s. Raymond S. and Oeta (Fleener) P.; m. Bonnie Becker, Nov. 4, 1962; children: Geoffrey, Amy; m. Cara Bryn Saylor, June 21, 1980; 1 child, Abigail. B.A., Ind. U., 1962. With A.P., Indpls., 1962-65, Milw., 1965, Madison, Wis., 1966-67, Washington, 1967-71; investigative reporter Washington Star, 1971-75; correspondent NBC News, Washington, 1975-92; sr. producer CNN Spl. Assignment, 1992—; pres. Investigative Reporters and Editors, Inc., 1978-80, chmn. bd., 1980-82, nat. coll. chmn., 1983-90. Recipient Raymond Clapper Meml. award, 1972, 74, Pulitzer prize for nat. reporting, 1974, Sigma Delta Chi award, 1974, Nat. Headliner award 2d place, 1994, 96, Emmy award for coverage of Oklahoma City bombing, 1996, Ind. U. Disting. Alumni award; named to Ind. Journalism Hall of Fame, 1994. Mem. Phi Kappa Psi.

POLK, WILLIAM ROE, historian; b. Ft. Worth, Tex., Mar. 7, 1929; m. Joan Alison Cooledge, Dec. 1950; children: Milbry Catherine Polk Bauman, Alison Elizabeth Polk Hoffman; m. Ann Borders Cross, June 9, 1962 (div. Oct. 1979); children: George Washington, Eliza Polk Spence; m. Baroness Elisabeth von Oppenheimer, Dec. 29, 1981. BA with honors, Harvard U., 1951, PhD, 1958; BA with honors, Oxford, Eng., 1955, MA, 1959; LLD (hon.), Lake Forest Coll., 1967. Asst. prof. Harvard Univ., 1956-62; fgn. svc. res. officer class 1, mem. policy planning coun. U.S. State Dept., 1961-65; prof. U. Chgo., 1965-73; pres. Adlai Stevenson Inst., Chgo., 1967-72, Naftex Ltd., Switzerland, 1972-94; chmn. EP Systems, N.Y.C., 1990-93, Chaika Oil Co., London and Moscow, 1993-95; bd. dirs. Hyde Park Bank, Chgo., Microform Data Systems, Arlington Books, Cambridge, Naftex Ltd., Harris & Harris, EP Systems, Chaika Corp., Morrison Internat. Ltd., The Salzburg Seminar; cons. Aetna Life and Casualty, Time Inc., TWA, Crocker Nat. Bank, Wheelabrator Frye Inc., Fuller Petroleum, GTE, Teledyne, J. Henry Schroder, U.K., Power Corp., Can., Allianz Versicherungs A.G., Germany, Volkswagen A.G., Germany, Flughafen Frankfurt Main A.G., Germany, Louis Féraud & Cie, France, UN Stockholm and Vancouver Confs. on the Environment; lectr. in field. Author: What the Arabs Think, 1952, Backdrop to Tragedy, 1957, The Opening of South Lebanon, 1963, The United States and the Arab World, 1965, 2d edit., 1969, 3rd edit., 1975, Passing Brave, 1973, 74, The Golden Ode, 1974, 77, 93, The Elusive Peace, 1979, The Arab World, 1980, The Arab World Today, 1991, The Vence Partitas, 1992, Neighbors and Strangers: The Fundamentals of Foreign Affairs, 1997; editor: The Developmental Revolution, 1963, The Beginnnings of Modernization in the Middle East, 1968; contbr. over 100 articles to books and profl. jours. including Fgn. Affairs, The Atlantic, etc. Dir. The Salzburg Seminar, YMCA C.C., The Middle East Inst., The Adlai Stevenson Inst. Recipient Medal of Honor, Kingdom of Afghanistan, 1967; fellow Rockefeller Found., 1951-55, Ford Found., 1954, Guggenheim Found., 1961. Mem. The Century Assn., Coun. on Fgn. Rels., Middle East Studies Assn. (bd. dirs.), Fed. City Club, The Arts Club, The Cosmos Club, Soc. of the Cin. Democrat. Avocations: exploration, tennis, sailing, gardening. Home: 669 Chemin de la Sine, 06140 Vence France

POLKA, WALTERS S., schools superintendent; b. Niagara Falls, N.Y., Nov. 5, 1945; s. Frank W. and Josephine B. (Ziblut) P.; m. Victoria M. Homiszczak, Aug. 3, 1968; children: Jennifer Marie, Monica Jo. BA, U. Buffalo, 1968; MA, Niagara U., 1970, MS, 1971; EdD, U. Buffalo, 1977; postgrad., Harvard U., 1989-95, Fla. State U., 1993. Cert. sch. dist. adminstr., tchr. social studies, N.Y. Asst. supt. Lewiston-Porter Cen. Schs., Youngstown, N.Y., 1986-90; curriculum coord. Williamsville (N.Y.) Cen. Schs., 1973-86; tchr., high sch. Lewiston-Porter Cen. Schs., 1968-73; supt. Lewiston-Porter Sch. Dist., 1990—; adj. prof. Niagara U., Buffalo State Coll., Medaille Coll., U. Buffalo; curriculum advisor Hudson Inst., 1981-84. Scholar Niagara U. Grad. Sch., 1968-70; Filene Found. fellow Harvard U., summer 1989. Mem. ASCD, Am. Assn. Sch. Adminstrs., Am. Mgmt. Assn., Internat. Soc. Ednl. Planning (pres.), Phi Delta Kappa, Phi Alpha Theta, Pi Lambda Theta. Office: Lewiston-Porter Cen Schs 4061 Creek Rd Youngstown NY 14174-9609

POLK-MATTHEWS, JOSEPHINE ELSEY, school psychologist; b. Roselle, N.J., Sept. 24, 1930; d. Charles Carrington and Olive Mae (Bond) Polk; m. Donald Roger Matthews, Aug. 29, 1959 (div. 1974); children: John Roger, Alison Olivia; m. William Y. Delaney, Sept. 17, 1994. AB, Mt. Holyoke Coll., 1952; credential in occupational therapy, Columbia U., 1954; MA, U. So. Calif., L.A., 1957; Cert. Advanced Study, Harvard U., 1979, MS, 1980; postgrad., Coll. William & Mary, 1995—. Cert. elem. edn. life teaching credential, Calif; cert. ednl. adminstrn. life credential, Calif.; cert. pupil personnel svcs., counseling life credential, sch. psychology credential, Calif.; sch. psychology credential, Nev. Occupational therapist VA Hosp., Northport, N.Y., 1953-55, L.A., 1955-57; health svcs. adminstr. John Wesley County Hosp., L.A., 1957-59; elem. tchr. L.A. (Calif.) City Schs., 1959-60, Santa Clara (Calif.) Unified Sch. Dist., 1960-65, 71-74; asst. prof. Sch. Edn., San Jose (Calif.) State U., 1971; asst. prin. Berryessa Union Sch. Dist., San Jose, Calif., 1974-77, 85-86; ednl. cons. Boston (Mass.) U. Sch. Medicine, 1981-83; asst. prin. Inglewood (Calif.) Unified Sch. Dist., 1986-90; sch. psychologist Clark County Sch. Dist., Las Vegas, 1990-94; contract sch. psychologist Newport News (Va.) Sch. Dist., 1995-96; med. facility developer Commonwealth Mass., Dept. Mental Health, Boston, 1980-81, ednl. liaison, Roxbury Juvenile Ct., 1979. Author: (with others) The New Our Bodies Ourselves, 1983; prodr.: (video) Individualized Rsch., 1971. Commr. Commn. on the Status of Women, Cambridge, Mass., 1981-83; hostess Ctr. for Internat. Visitors, Boston, 1983-84; pers. recruiter L.A. (Calif.) Olympic Organizing Com., 1984; vol. tutor Las Vegas (Nev.) Libr., 1992. Mem. Nat. Assn. Sch. Psychologists, Phi Delta Kappa, Alpha Kappa Alpha, Kappa Delta Pi. Office: Sch Edn Spl Edn PO Box 8795 Williamsburg VA 23187-8795

POLL, HEINZ, choreographer, artistic director; b. Oberhausen, Germany, Mar. 18, 1926; came to U.S., 1964, naturalized, 1975; s. Heinrich and Anna Margareta (Winkels) P. Co-founder, dir. The Dance Inst., U. Akron, 1967-77; founder, artistic dir., choreographer Ohio Ballet, Akron, 1968—; tchr. Chilean Instituto de Extension Musical, 1951-61, N.Y. Nat. Acad., 1965-66. Dancer Göttingen Mcpl. Theatre, 1947-49, Deutsches Theatre Konstanz, 1949-50, East Berlin State Opera, 1950-51, Nat. Ballet Chile, 1951-62, Ballet de la Jeunesse Musicales de France, 1963-64; guest appearances with Nat. Ballet Chile, 1964, Am. Dance Festival, 1965; choreographer works for Nat. Ballet Chile, Paris Festival Ballet, Ballet Jeunesse de la Musicales de France, Nat. Ballet Can., Pa. Ballet, Ohio Ballet, Limon Dance Co. Recipient Ohio Dance award, 1983, 88-89, Achievement Dance award No. Ohio Live Mag., 1985-86, 88-89, 93-94, 94-95, Cleve. Arts prize, 1995; Nat. Endowment for Arts grantee, 1974-75. Mem. NEA (dance panelist 1987-89, 92-93). Office: Ohio Ballet U Akron Akron OH 44325-2501

POLL, MARTIN HARVEY, film producer; b. N.Y.C.; s. David and Fay (Tamber) P.; m. Lee Lindenberg, May 21, 1954 (div. Oct. 10, 1967); children: Mark, Jonathan; m. Gladys Pelitz Jaffe, Oct. 31, 1976; 1 son, Anthony. B.S., Wharton Sch. Bus. U. Pa., 1943. Pres. Inter-Continental TV Films Inc., N.Y.C., 1952; exec. producer Theatre Network TV Inc., N.Y.C., 1953; pres. Gold Medal Studios, Bronx, N.Y., 1954-62; ind. producer, 1962—. (Named Hon. Commr. Motion Picture Arts N.Y.C. 1958, recipient David Di Donatello Best Film Producer award Pres. Italy 1968, N.Y. Film Critics award 1968, Hollywood Fgn. Press Assn. Golden Globe award 1968, Brit. Acad. award 1968); films include Love is a Ball, 1962, Sylvia, 1964, The Appointment, 1968, The Lion in Winter, 1968 (Best Picture award), The Magic Garden of Stanley Sweetheart, 1970, Night Watch, 1972, The Man Who Loved Cat Dancing, 1973, Love and Death, 1975, The Sailor Who Fell From Grace with The Sea, 1976, The Dain Curse, Somebody Killed Her Husband, 1978, Nighthawks, 1981, Arthur the King, 1984, Gimme An F, 1984, Haunted Summer, 1987, My Heroes Have Always Been Cowboys, 1991, (TV miniseries) Diana—Her True Story, 1993. Served with AUS, 1944-47. Mem. Producers Guild of Am., Acad. Motion Picture Arts and Scis., Cinema Circulus, Friends of Library U. So. Calif.

POLL, ROBERT EUGENE, JR., bank executive; b. Urbana, Ill., Apr. 16, 1948; s. Robert E. Sr. and Dorothy (Baker) P.; m. Leslie Tompkins, Aug. 8, 1970 (div. Mar. 1980); m. Virginia O'Donnell, July 17, 1982; children: Alexandra, Bianca, Paulo Felipe Kos. BA, Kenyon Coll., 1970; MBA, Ind. U., 1972. V.p. Chase Manhattan Bank, N.Y.C., 1970-78; assoc. Lazard Freres & Co., N.Y.C., 1978-82, mng. dir., mgr. mcpl. divsn., 1985—; gen. ptnr. William Blair & Co., Chgo., 1982-84; adv. bd. Pub. Fin. Inst., N.Y.C., 1976, Worldvest. Mem. Am. Mktg. Assn., N.Y. Acad. Sci., Am. Assn. Polit. and Social Scis., Acad. Polit. Sci., Chgo. Econ. Forum. Clubs: Tavern (Chgo.); N.Y. Athletic. Office: Lazard Freres & Co 30 Rockefeller Plz New York NY 10112

POLLACK, BRUCE, banker, real estate consultant; b. Bklyn., June 15, 1951; s. Bernard and Grace (Mishanie) P.; children: Gennifer Ellen, Gregory Adam, Erica Dawn. BS, L.I. U., Bklyn., 1973, MBA with honors, 1979. Sr. appraiser Citizens Savs. & Loan Assn., Woodside, N.Y., 1973-77; chief appraiser Walter Oertly Assocs., N.Y.C., 1978, Flushing (N.Y.) Savs. Bank, 1978-81; v.p., real estate specialist Citibank, N.A., N.Y.C., 1981-90; pres. Met. Realty Solutions, Bklyn., 1990—. Contbr. to The Appraisal Jour., Real Estate Rev., Multi-Housing News, other publs. Recipient Pub./Pvt. Partnership award Ocean Pkwy. Community Devel. Corp., 1984, award Consolidated Edison, 1986. Mem. Young Mortgage Bankers Assn., N.Y. State Soc. Real Estate Appraisers, Bklyn. Bd. Realtors (bd. dirs.), Rho Epsilon. Avocations: traveling, sports, reading, numismatics, fishing. Home: 15 Mackay Pl Brooklyn NY 11209-1040 Office: Met Realty Solutions 15 Mackay Pl Brooklyn NY 11209-1040

POLLACK, DANIEL, concert pianist; b. Los Angeles, Jan. 23, 1935. MS in Music, Juilliard Sch., 1957, Acad. Musik, Vienna, Austria, 1958. Asst. prof. U. Hartford, Conn., 1966-70; prof. piano U. So. Calif., Los Angeles, 1971—. Concert performances in U.S., USSR, Europe, Far East, South Am. Recipient prize Internat. Tschaikowsky Piano Competition, Moscow, USSR, 1958; Fulbright grantee, 1957-58; Martha Baird Rockefeller Found. grantee, 1963. Mem. Am. Fedn. Musicians, Kosciuszko Found., Chopin Found., Music Tchrs. Nat. Assn. (nat. exec. bd.). Office: U So Calif Dept Music Los Angeles CA 90089 also: Sheldon Soffer Mgmt Inc 130 W 56th St New York NY 10019*

POLLACK, FLORENCE K.Z., management consultant; b. Washington, Pa.; d. Charles and Ruth (Isaacson) Zaks; divorced; children: Melissa, Stephanie. BA, Flora Stone Mather Coll., Western Res. U., 1961. Pres., CEO Exec. Arrangements, Inc., Cleve., 1978—. Lobbyist Ohio Citizens Com. for Arts, Columbus, 1975-83; mem. Leadership Cleve., 1978-79; trustee jr. com. Cleve. Orch., mem. pub. rels. adv. com.; trustee Great Lakes Theatre Festival, 1989-90; mem. pub. rels. adv. com., Cleve. Ballet, Dance Cleve., Jr. Com. of No. Ohio Opera Assn., Cleve. Opera, Shakers Lakes Regional Nature Ctr., Cleve. Music Sch. Settlement, Playhouse Sq. Cabinet, Cleve. Ctr. Econ. Edn., ARC, Cleve. Conv. and Visitors Bur., domed stadium adv. com.; bd. dirs. ARC, Great Lakes Theatre Festival, City Club of Cleve., Cleve. Ballet. Named Idea Woman of Yr. Cleve. Plain Dealer, 1975, to Au Courrant list Cleve. Mag., 1979, one of Cleve.'s 100 Most Influential Women, 1985, one of 1988 Trendsetters Cleve. Woman mag. Mem. Cleve. Area Meeting Planning, Skating Club, Univ. Club, Women's City Club, Playhouse Club, Shoreby Club. Avocations: arts, travel, reading. Office: Exec Arrangements Inc 13221 Shaker Sq Cleveland OH 44120-2314

POLLACK, GERALD ALEXANDER, economist, government official; b. Vienna, Austria, Jan. 14, 1929; came to U.S. 1938; s. Stephen J. and Tini (Herschel) P.; m. Patricia S. Sisterson; children: Nora S., Carol A. BA, Swarthmore (Pa.) Coll., 1951; MA, MPA, Princeton U., 1953, PhD, 1958. Corp. economist Leeds & Northrup Co., Phila., 1958-62; officer in charge internat. payments U.S. Dept. State, Washington, 1962-63; internat. economist Joint Econ. Com. of Congress, Washington, 1963-65; chief economist Office Spl. Rep. for Trade Negotiations, 1964; dep. asst. sec. U.S. Dept. Commerce, Washington, 1965-68; v.p. Loeb, Rhoades & Co., N.Y.C., 1968-69, Bendix Corp., Southfield, Mich., 1969-70, Citibank, N.Y.C., 1970-71; internat. economist Exxon Corp., N.Y.C., 1971-86; v.p., chief economist Overseas Shipholding Group, N.Y.C., 1986-89; assoc. prof. fin. Pace U., N.Y.C., 1990-94; assoc. dir. for internat. econs. Bur. Econ. Analysis, U.S. Dept. Commerce, 1994—. Contbr. articles to profl. jours. Bd. dirs. Jamaica Estates Assn., 1976-80, Oakwood Sch., Poughkeepsie, N.Y., 1979-89; trustee Lindley Murray Fund, 1990-94; mem. Greenwich Dem. Town Com., 1992-94; clk. Flushing Friends monthly meeting Soc. of Friends, 1990-94. With U.S. Army, 1953-55. Mem. Am. Econ. Assn., Nat. Assn. Bus. Economists, Coun. on Fgn. Rels., Forecasters Club N.Y., Downtown Economists Club, The Nat. Economists Club, Soc. of Friends, Phi Beta Kappa. Soc. of Friends. Avocations: cello, classical music, photography, hiking, bicycling.

POLLACK, GERALD HARVEY, bioengineering educator; b. Bklyn., May 20, 1940; s. Max and Helen (Solomon) P.; m. Sylvia A. Byrne, Aug. 12, 1966 (div. 1982); children: Seth Benjamin, Ethan David, Mia Raphaella. BS, Poly. Inst. Bklyn., 1961; PhD, U. Pa., 1968. Mem. faculty U. Wash. Med. Sch., Seattle, 1968—; prof. bioengrng. U. Wash. Med. Sch., 1977—. Author: Muscles and Molecules: Uncovering the Principles of Biological Motion, 1990 (Excellence award Soc. for Tech. Communication 1992); co-editor: Ballistocardiography and Cardiac Performance, 1967, Cross-bridge Mechanism of Muscle Contraction, 1979, Contractile Mechanisms in Muscle, 1983, Molecular Mechanism of Muscle Contraction, 1988, Mechanism of Sliding in Muscle Contraction, 1993; mem. editorial bd. Jour. Molecular and Cellular Cardiology, 1975-80, Am. Jour. Physiology, 1976-80, Circulation Rsch., 1982-89; contbr. articles to profl. jours. Established investigator Am. Heart Assn., 1974-79. Recipient Kulka award Poly. Inst. Bklyn., 1961; grantee NIH, 1970—; grantee Am. Heart Assn., 1973—; grantee Muscular Dystrophy Assn. Am., 1980. Fellow Am. Inst. Med. and Biol. Engring. (founding); mem. Bioengring. Soc. (dir. 1976-79), Biophys. Soc., Am. Heart Assn. (exec. com. Basic Sci. Coun. 1982-86), Eta Kappa Nu, Tau Beta Pi, Alpha Epsilon Pi. Address: 3714 48th Ave NE Seattle WA 98105-5250

POLLACK, GERALD J., financial executive; b. N.Y.C., Jan. 20, 1942; s. Charles and Reba P.; m. Diane Pollack, Aug. 30, 1964; children: Suzanne, Jennifer, John. BS in Physics, Rensselaer Poly Inst., 1963; MBA, Dartmouth Coll., 1965. Comptroller trainee Exxon Corp., N.Y.C., 1965-67; asst. ops. comptroller Amerada Hess, Woodbridge, N.J., 1967-68; mgr. customer svc. Arthur Young & Co., N.Y.C., 1969-73; dir. mgmt. svc. Arthur Young & Co., Stamford, Conn., 1973-74; v.p., controller Avis Inc., Garden City, L.I., 1975-81; sr. v.p., chief fin. officer Rayonier, Stamford, 1982—. Mem. N.Y. Adv. Bd. Allendale Ins. Co., Fin. Exec. Inst. Office: Rayonier Inc 1177 Summer St Stamford CT 06905-5522

POLLACK, GERALD LESLIE, physicist, educator; b. Bklyn., July 8, 1933; s. Herman and Jennie (Tenenbaum) P.; m. Antoinette Amparo Velasquez, Dec. 22, 1958; children: Harvey Anton, Samuela Juliet, Margolita Mia, Violet Amata. BS, Bklyn. Coll., 1954; Fulbright scholar, U. Gottingen, 1954-55; MS, Calif. Inst. Tech., 1957, PhD, 1962. Physics student trainee Nat. Bur. Standards, Washington, 1954-58, solid state physicist, 1961-65; cons. Nat. Bur. Standards, Boulder, Colo., 1965-70; assoc. prof. dept. physics Mich. State U., East Lansing, 1965-69, prof., 1969—; cons. NRC, Ill. Dept. Nuclear Safety; physicist Naval Med. Rsch. Inst., Bethesda, Md., summer 1979; physicist USAF Sch. Aerospace Medicine, San Antonio, Tex., summer 1987. Contbr. articles to profl. jours. Fellow Am. Phys. Soc.; mem. AAAS, Am. Assn. Physics Tchrs. Office: Mich State U Dept Physics and Astronomy East Lansing MI 48824-1116

POLLACK, HENRY NATHAN, geophysics educator; b. Omaha, July 13, 1936; s. Harold Myron and Sylvia (Chait) P.; m. Lana Beth Schoenberger, Jan. 29, 1963; children—Sara Beth (dec.), John David. A.B., Cornell U., 1958; M.S., U. Nebr., 1960; Ph.D., U. Mich., 1963. Lectr. U. Mich., 1962, asst. prof., asso. prof., prof. geophysics, 1964—, assoc. dean for research, 1982-85, chmn. dept. geol. scis., 1988-91; rsch. fellow Harvard U., 1963-64; sr. lectr. U. Zambia, 1970-71; vis. scientist U. Durham, U. Newcastle-on-Tyne, Eng., 1977-78, U. Western Ont., 1985-86; chmn. Internat. Heat Flow Commn., 1991-95. Fellow AAAS, Geol. Soc. Am.; mem. Am. Geophys. Union. Achievements include research on thermal evolution of the earth, recent climate change. Office: U Mich Dept Geol Scis Ann Arbor MI 48109

POLLACK, HERBERT WILLIAM, electronics executive; b. N.Y.C., Mar. 27, 1927; s. Benjamin and Shirley (Fine) P.; m. Sandra Rowe, March 26, 1950; children: Jill C., Mindy L. BEE, CCNY, 1950; MEE, NYU, 1953. Electronic engr. A.B. Dumont Co., Clifton, N.J., 1950-51; rsch. assoc. NYU, N.Y.C., 1951-54; electronic engr. CBS - Columbia, N.Y.C., 1954-55; v.p., dir. Polarad Electronics Inc., N.Y.C., 1955-65; group div. mgr. Sanders Assocs., Nashua, N.H., 1965-70; chmn., CEO, Parlex Corp., Methuen, Mass., 1970—; pres., dir. Inst. for Interconnecting and Packaging Electronic Cirs., Lincolnwood, Ill., 1984-86. With USN, 1945-46. Fellow IEEE; mem. Tau beta Pi, Eta Kappa Nu. Avocations: reading, music, tennis, golf. Office: Parlex Corp 145 Milk St Methuen MA 01844-4664

POLLACK, IRWIN WILLIAM, psychiatrist, educator; b. Phila., Aug. 14, 1927; s. Nathan and Rose (Bergman) P.; m. Barbara Jean Callaway, Oct. 9, 1988; children from previous marriage: Nathaniel Edward, Joshua Frank, Jonathan Daniel. A.B., Temple U., 1950; M.A., Columbia, 1951; student, U. Pa., 1951-52; M.D., U. Vt., 1956. Diplomate: Am. Bd. Psychiatry and Neurology. Intern Grad. Hosp. U. Pa., 1956-57; asst. resident psychiatry Henry Phipps Psychiat. Clinic (John Hopkins Hosp.), 1957-60; chief resident psychiatry Johns Hopkins Hosp., 1960-61, adminstr. psychosomatic clinic, psychiat. liaison service, 1961-64; psychiatrist-in-chief Sinai Hosp., Balt., 1964-68; mem. faculty psychiatry Coll. Medicine and Dentistry N.J. (Rutgers Med. Sch.), 1968-87, U. Medicine and Dentistry N.J., Robert Wood Johnson Med. Sch., 1987—; asso. prof. psychiatry, 1968-70, prof. psychiatry, 1970—; chmn. dept. Univ. Medicine and Dentistry, prof. neurology, dir. Ctr. for Cognitive Rehab.; exec. dir. Coll. Medicine and Dentistry (Community Mental Health Ctr.), 1970-77. Served with USNR, 1945-46. Fellow Am. Psychiat. Assn. (life); mem. N.J. Psychiat. Assn., Am. Psychosomatic Soc., Am. Congress Rehab. Medicine, Alpha Omega Alpha. Spl. research or problems of time and space perception, psychology of phys. disability, doctor-patient relationships, cognitive retraining of brain-injured persons. Home: 238 Sayre Dr Princeton NJ 08540-5840 Office: Robert Wood Johnson Med Sch U Medicine and Dentistry NJ Hoes Ln Piscataway NJ 08854

POLLACK, JOE, retired newspaper critic and columnist, writer; b. Bklyn., Feb. 3, 1931; s. Samuel H. and Anna (Weisman) P.; m. Joan S., Mar. 6, 1952 (div. 1964); children: Wendy, Dara, Sharon; m. Carol Atchison, Dec. 1, 1964 (dec. 1993); m. Ann Lemons, Nov. 20, 1994. BJ, U. Mo., 1952. Sports writer St. Louis Globe-Democrat, 1955-61; dir. pub. rels. St. Louis Football Cardinals, 1961-72; critic, columnist St. Louis Post-Dispatch, 1972-95; critic Sta. KSDK-TV, St. Louis, 1973-88, Sta. KMOV-TV, St. Louis, 1988-92; commentator Sta. KMOX, St. Louis, 1960-85, Sta. KWMU, St. Louis, 1994—. Author: Joe Pollack's Guide to St. Louis Restaurants, 1988, updated, 1992; contbr. numerous articles to mags. Mem. Am. Theatre Critics Assn., Profl. Football Writers Assn., Am. Soc. Profl. Journalists, Internat. Writers Ctr. (adv. bd. St. Louis). Home: 7417 Oxford Dr Saint Louis MO 63105

POLLACK, JORDAN ELLIS, pharmaceutical company executive; b. N.Y.C., June 16, 1934; s. Irving and Ann Pollack; m. Francine Hornstein, Aug. 23, 1959; children: Robert, Randi. BS in Pharmacy, Columbia U., 1956; MBA in Mktg., Iona Coll., 1971. Registered pharmacist, N.Y., N.J., Fla. Med. rep./market researcher Geigy Pharm., Ardsley, N.Y., 1959-70; account exec. William Douglas McAdams, N.Y.C., 1970-71; account supr. Grey Advt., N.Y.C., 1971-75; account dir. Carrafiello-Diehl Advt., Irvington, N.Y., 1975-79; sr. product mgr. Knoll Pharms., Whippany, N.J., 1979-85, mgr. new product planning, 1985-88, dir. new bus. devel., 1988—. Chmn. Florham Park (N.J.) Airport Adv. Com., 1989—; mem. Florham Park Zoning Bd. of Adjustment, Capital Improvements Com. With U.S. Army, 1957-59. Mem. Pharm. Advt. Coun., Am. Soc. Hosp. Pharmacists, Lic. Exec. Soc. Avocations: walking, softball, swimming. Home: 4 Partridge Ln Florham Park NJ 07932-1728 Office: Knoll Pharm Co 3000 Continental Dr N Budd Lake NJ 07828-1202

POLLACK, JOSEPH, diversified company executive; b. Bklyn., Jan. 7, 1939; s. Soloman and Sophie (Kaufman) P.; m. Larissa Humeniuk, Feb. 27, 1985. BA, Bklyn. Coll., 1960; JD, NYU, 1964, LLM, 1965. Bar: N.Y. 1965. V.p. taxes AMF Inc., White Plains, N.Y., 1965-85; exec. v.p. taxes Grand Met. Inc., Mpls., 1985-93; tax cons. to pvt. clients, 1993-95; group tax dir. Danka PLC, 1995—. Fulbright scholar, 1963. Mem. ABA, N.Y. State Bar Assn., Assn. of Bar of City of N.Y., Order of Coif. Republican. Avocation: landscape gardening. Home: 254 Bridle Path Way Sarasota FL 34241

POLLACK, LOUIS, telecommunications company executive; b. N.Y.C., Nov. 4, 1920; s. Benjamin and Lena (Woloshen) P.; m. Dorothy Silverman, Feb. 4, 1945; children: Annette Pollack Rachlin, Barbara Pollack Held, Lawrence. BEE, CCNY, 1953; postgrad., Stevens Inst. Tech., 1954-55. Registered profl. engr., D.C. Dir. transmission system ops. ITT Fed. Labs., Nutley, N.J., 1943-67; exec. dir. Comsat Labs., Clarksburg, Md., 1967-80; v.p. world systems div. Communications Satellite Corp., Washington, 1980-84; cons. Satellite System design, 1984—; del. XVIII Gen. Assembly Nat. Acad. Sci. Contbr. articles to profl. jours.; patentee in field. Fellow IEEE; mem. AIAA (assoc. fellow), Sigma Xi. Office: 15321 Delphinium Ln Rockville MD 20853-1725

POLLACK, MICHAEL, lawyer; b. N.Y.C., July 14, 1946; s. Irving and Bertha (Horowitz) P.; m. Barbara Linda Shore, Aug. 23, 1970; children: Matthew, Ilana. BEng, Cooper Union, 1967; MS, U. Pa., 1970; JD, Temple U., 1974. Bar: Pa. 1974, U.S. Dist. Ct. (ea. dist.) Pa. 1974. Rsch. scientist Pa. Rsch. Assocs., Phila., 1968-69; engr. GE Co., Valley Forge, Pa., 1969-70, Burroughs Corp., Great Valley, Pa., 1970-71; assoc. Blank, Rome, Comisky & McCauley, Phila., Pa., 1974-82; ptnr. Blank, Rome, Comisky & McCauley, Phila., 1982—; chmn. dept. real estate Blank, Rome, Comisky & McCauley, 1997—; lectr., course planner Pa. Bar Inst., Phila., chmn. real estae dept. Mem. ABA, Pa. Bar Assn., Phila. Bar Assn., Internat. Assn. Attys. and Execs. in Corp. Real Estate, Eta Kappa Nu, Tau Beta Pi. Republican. Avocations: music, tennis. Office: Blank Rome Comisky & McCauley 4 Penn Center Plz Philadelphia PA 19103-2521

POLLACK, MILTON, federal judge; b. N.Y.C., Sept. 29, 1906; s. Julius and Betty (Schwartz) P.; m. Lillian Klein, Dec. 18, 1932 (dec. July 1967); children—Stephanie Pollack Singer, Daniel A.; m. Moselle Baum Erlich, Oct. 24, 1971. A.B., Columbia U., 1927, J.D., 1929. Bar: N.Y. 1930. Assoc. Gilman & Unger, N.Y.C., 1929-38; ptnr. Unger & Pollack, N.Y.C., 1938-44; propr. Milton Pollack, N.Y.C., 1945-67; dist. judge U.S. Dist. Ct. (so. dist.) N.Y., 1967—, sr. status, 1983; mem. com. on ct. adminstrn. Jud. Conf., 1968-87, mem. Jud. Panel on Multi-dist. Litigation, 1983-95. Mem. Prospect Park So. Assn., Bklyn., pres., 1948-50, counsel, 1950-60, bd. dirs., 1945-60; mem. local SSS, 1952-60; chmn. lawyers div. Fedn. Jewish Philanthropies, 1957-61, vice chmn., 1954-57; chmn. lawyers div. Am. Jewish Com., 1964-66, bd. dirs., from 1967; hon. dir. Beth Isreal Hosp.; trustee Temple Emanu-El, from 1977, v.p., from 1978. Recipient Learned Hand award Am. Jewish Com., 1967, Proskauer medal lawyers divsn. Fedn. Jewish Philanthropies,

1968, Disting. Svc. medal N.Y. County Lawyers Assn., 1991, Fordham-Stein Prize award, 1994, Devitt award Disting. Svc. to Justice, 1995; decorated chevalier Legion of Honor (France). Mem. ABA, N.Y. State Bar Assn., Assn. of Bar of City of N.Y., Columbia Law Sch. Alumni Assn. (pres. 1970-72), Harmonie Club (bd. trustees). Office: US Dist Ct US Courthouse Foley Sq New York NY 10007-1501

POLLACK, MURRAY MICHAEL, physician, medical services administrator; b. Bklyn., Nov. 1, 1947; s. Louis R. and Shirley (Schilling) P.; m. Mona Michaels, Dec. 3, 1973; children: Seth, Haley. BA in Biology, U. Rochester, 1970; MD, Albert Einstein Sch. Medicine, 1974. Diplomate Am. Bd. Pediatrics, Am. Bd. Pediatric Critical Care. Intern, then resident in pediatrics Children's Nat. Med. Ctr., Washington, 1974-77, intensivist, 1978-96, dir. health svcs. and clin. rsch., 1990-96, sect. head crit. care medicine, 1995—; chief, critical care medicine, prof. anesthesiology and pediatrics George Washington U. Med. Sch., 1988—; dir. Ctr. Health Svcs. Rsch., Children's Rsch. Inst. Mem. editorial bd. Critical Care Medicine; contbr. articles to profl. jours. PHHS grantee, 1989—, Robert Wood Johnson Found. grantee, 1986-89. Fellow Coll.Critical Care Medicine (faculty, reviewer, moderator 1987—), Nat. Assn. Children's Hosps. (quality com. 1991-95), Am. Bd. Pediatrics (sub-bd. critical care 1991-95). Achievements include research in quantifying the relationship between physiologic instability and mortality risk, reduced risk of death associated with pediatric intensive care, creation of pediatric risk of mortality score. Office: Childrens Nat Med Ctr 111 Michigan Ave NW Washington DC 20010-2916

POLLACK, NORMAN, history educator; b. Bridgeport, Conn., May 29, 1933; s. Benjamin and Mary (Beimel) P.; m. Nancy Bassing, Feb. 2, 1957; 1 son, Peter Franklin. B.A., U. Fla., 1954; M.A., Harvard U., 1957, Ph.D., 1961. Instr. history Yale, 1961-62, asst. prof., 1962-65; asso. prof. Wayne State U., 1965-68; prof. Mich. State U., 1968—. Author: The Populist Response to Industrial America, 1962, The Populist Mind, 1967, The Just Polity, 1987, The Humane Economy, 1990. Guggenheim fellow, 1968-69. Home: 929 Roxburgh Ave East Lansing MI 48823-3130 Office: Dept of History Mich State U East Lansing MI 48824

POLLACK, PAUL ROBERT, airline service company executive; b. N.Y.C., Nov. 17, 1941; s. Harry and Hilda (Tepper) P.; m. Linda Weinstein, Aug. 14, 1965; children: Mark, Melissa. BBA, CCNY, 1962; MBA, L.I. U., Greenvale, N.Y., 1993. CPA, N.Y. Staff acct. Seidman & Seidman, N.Y.C., 1962-68; with Hudson Gen. Corp., Great Neck, N.Y., 1968—, exec. v.p., chief oper. officer, 1990—; pres. Hudson Gen. LLC, 1996—. With U.S. Army, 1962. Mem. AICPA, N.Y. State Soc. CPAs (Haskins award 1966). Office: Hudson Gen Corp 111 Great Neck Rd Great Neck NY 11021-5402

POLLACK, PHYLLIS ADDISON, ballerina; b. Victoria, B.C., Can., Aug. 31, 1919; d. Horace Nowell and Claire Melanie (Morris) Addison; m. Robert Seymour Pollack, Sept. 6, 1941; children: Robert Addison, Gwenda Joyce, Victoria Jean, Phyllis Anne. Student, SUNY, 1941-42, San Mateo Tech. Coll., 1958-62, U. Calif., San Francisco, 1962. Owner, dir. Phyllis Addison Dance Studio, Victoria, 1936-38; ballerina Taynton Dancers/Marcus Show Ballet Troupe, 1939-41, Ballet Russe, 1941; x-ray therapy tech. Meml. Hosp., N.Y.C., 1943-45; corr. fgn. tellers dept. N.C.B., N.Y.C., 1945-46; owner, designer The Dancing Branch Studio, Sonoma, Calif., 1988—; floral designer J. Noblett Gallery, Sonoma, 1988-94. Pres. PTA, 1955-56, 62-63; mem. Assistance League San Mateo, Calif., 1960-70. Mem. Metro. Club, Bay Area Arrangers Guild, Ikebana Internat., San Francisco Garden Club. Democrat. Unitarian. Avocations: dancing, choreography, fashion modelling, photography, reading. Home: 384 Avenida Barbera Sonoma CA 95476-8069

POLLACK, REGINALD MURRAY, painter, sculptor; b. Middle Village, L.I., N.Y., July 29, 1924; m. Kerstin Birgitta Soederlund; children by previous marriage: Jane Olivia, Maia Jaquine. Grad. H.S., High Sch. Music and Art, N.Y.C., 1941; student with, Wallace Harrison, Moses Soyer, Boardman Robinson; student, Academie de la Grande Chaumiere, 1948-52. Occasional asst. to Constantin Brancusi; vis. critic Yale U., 1962-63, Cooper Union, 1963-64; mem. staff Human Rels. Tng. Ctr., UCLA, 1966; artistic dir. The Gallery, Greater Washington Collection Fine Art, Leesburg, Va., 1991-94; chmn. artists adv. com. Loudon Arts Coun., Va., 1990-93. One-man shows include Charles Fourth Gallery, N.Y.C., 1948, Peridot Gallery, 1949, 52, 55-57, 59, 60, 62, 63, 65, 67, 69, Galerie Saint-Placide, Paris, 1952, Dwan Gallery, 1960, Jefferson Gallery, LaJolla, Calif., 1963, 68, 69, Goldwach Gallery, Chgo., 1964, 65, 66, Feliz Landau Gallery, Hollywood, 1963, 65, 67, David Alexander Gallery, 1974, Washington Gallery Arts, 1974, Cosmos Club, Washington, 1976, Washington Project for Arts, 1976, Everhart Mus., Scranton, Pa., 1977, Pa. State U., 1977, Jack Rasmussen gallery, 1978, 79, 80, 81, 82, Art Washington, 1979, 81, Corcoran Mus., 1980, Zenith Gallery, Washington, 1982, Summit Gallery, N.Y., 1982, Tartt Gallery, Washington, 1986, Arctic Images Gallery, Aspen, Colo., 1987, Loudoun County Adminstrn. Bldg., 1988, 95—, Susan Conway Carroll Gallery, Washington, 1990, The Gallery, Leesburg, 1992, Loudoun Valley Vineyard, Waterford, Va., 1992—, Sordoni Art Gallery, Wilkes U., Pa., 1994, The Natural Light Art School Gallery, Leesburg, Va., 1995, George Washington U., Va. Campus, Leesburg; exhibited group shows including Whitney Mus. Am. Art, 1953, 55, 56, 58, 62, U. Nebr., 1951, 56, 57, 60, 63, Chgo. Art Inst., Carnegie, Pitts., Salon du Mai, Paris, U. Ill., Salon des Artistes Independants, Paris, 1955-58, NAS, 1990, NIH, 1990, Elaine Benson Gallery, Bridgehampton, L.I., 1991, Met. Mus. Art, 1997—, numerous others; multi-media theatrical prodns. The War of The Angels, 1974; The Twelve Gifts of Christmas, 1974; commns. include Jacob's Ladder painting, Washington Cathedral, bronze sculpture, The World Bank, awarded to King of Thailand, (TV episode Star Trek) Methusalem Returns, 1968, (laser show) The Crucible, 1996, others; represented in permanent collections, Bezalel Mus., Bklyn. Mus., Collection de L'Etat, France, U. Glasgow, Haifa, Mus. Modern Art, U. Nebr., Newark Mus., Rockefeller Inst., Whitney Mus. Am. Art, Worcester Art Mus., Nat. Mus. Am. Art, Ft. Lauderdale (Fla.) Mus., Loew Mus. U. Miami, Fla., Met. Mus., N.Y., Hirshhorn Mus., Washington, numerous other pub. and pvt. collections.; author and illustrator: The Magician and the Child, 1971; illustrator: Get a Horse (Steven Price), 1974, Visions from the Ramble (John Hollander), 1964, The Quest of the Gole (John Hollander), 1966, O is for Overkill, A Survival Alphabet (Merrill Pollack), 1968, The Blessed Ones (Ulla Isaksson), 1970, Oedipus (Seneca, transl. Ted Hughes), 1973, The Enjoyment of Music (Joseph Machlis). Instr. Quaker Half-way House, Los Angeles, 1968; cons. staff Lighthouse Child Guidance Center Presbyn. Hosp., 1966-69; pvt. instr., 1966-69; vis. artist Materials Research Lab., Pa. State U., 1977; trustee Washington Project for Arts, 1976-80. Served with AUS, 1941-45. Recipient Prix Neumann Paris, 1952, Prix Othon Friesz Paris, mention, 1954, 57, Prix de Peintres Etrangeres, 2d prize Paris Moderne, 1958; Ingram-Merrill Found. grantee, 1964, 70-71; Maurice Fromkis fellow, La Residence, Segovia, Spain, 1953. Address: 16348 Hamilton Sta Rd Waterford VA 20197-9700

POLLACK, ROBERT ELLIOT, biologist, educator; b. Bklyn., Sept. 2, 1940; s. Hyman Ephraim and Molly (Pollack) P.; m. Amy Louise Steinberg, Dec. 23, 1961; 1 child, Marya. BA in Physics, Columbia U., 1961; PhD in Biology, Brandeis U., 1966. Asst. prof. pathology Med. Sch. NYU, N.Y.C., 1969-70; sr. scientist Cold Spring Harbor Lab., N.Y., 1971-75; prof. microbiology Med. Sch., SUNY-Stony Brook, 1975-78; prof. biol. sci. Columbia U., N.Y.C., 1978—; dean Columbia Coll., N.Y.C., 1982-89; bd. dirs., chmn. sci. adv. bd. AMBI, 1994—; instr. Pratt Archtl. Sch., Bklyn., 1970; vis. prof. pharmacology Albert Einstein Coll. Medicine, Bronx, N.Y., 1977-92; lectr. Rosenthal Colloquium, March of Dimes, 1989; McGregory lectr. Colgate U., 1979; du Vigneaud lectr. Med. Sch., Cornell U., 1983. Co-editor: Readings in Mammalian Cell Culture, 1973, 3d rev. edit., 1981, Signs of Life, 1984 (translations in 7 langs., Lionel Trilling award 1995); mng. editor BBA Revs. on Cancer, 1980-86; contbr. numerous rsch. articles on molecular cell biology to profl. jours. Trustee N.Y. Found., 1988-96, Brandeis U., 1989-94, Solomon Schechter Sch. of N.Y.C., 1996—; fellow World Econ. Forum, 1995—; bd. overseers List Coll. of the Jewish theol. Sem. of Am., 1996—; pres. Jewish Campus Life Fund, Columbia U., 1997—. Recipient Rsch. Career Devel. award NIH, 1974, Alexander Hamilton medal, 1989, Lionel Trilling award Columbia U., 1995; NIH spl. fellow Weizmann Inst., Rehovot, Israel, 1970-71; grantee Nat. Cancer Inst., NIH, 1968-92, Am. Cancer Soc., 1985-94; John Simon Guggenheim fellow, 1993. Fellow AAAS; mem. N.Y. Acad. Scis., Am. Soc. Microbiology. Jewish. Office: Columbia U 749 Fairchild Hall 1212 Amsterdam MC 2419 New York NY 10027

POLLACK, RONALD F(RANK), foundation executive, lawyer; b. N.Y.C., Feb. 21, 1944; s. Max Louis and Hanna Esther (Borchardt) Pollack Baruch; m. Rebecca Lucy Bolling, Jan. 8, 1972; children: Sarah Shoshana, Abraham Max, Martin Landrum. B.A., Queens Coll., 1965; J.D., NYU, 1968. Bar: N.Y. 1968, D.C. 1978, U.S. Ct. Appeals (D.C. cir) 1970, U.S. Ct. Appeals (5th cir.) 1971, U.S. Ct. Appeals (6th cir.) 1974, U.S. Supreme Ct. 1973. Atty. Ctr. on Social Welfare Policy and Law, N.Y.C., 1968-73; founder, exec. dir. Food Research and Action Ctr., N.Y.C., 1970-80; dean Antioch Sch. Law, Washington, 1980-83; exec. dir. Families U.S.A., Washington, 1983—, Families U.S.A. Found., Washington, 1983—; sec. treas., bd. dirs. Food Research and Action Ctr., Washington, 1980—; mem. civil legal services D.C. Jud. Conf. Com., 1980-83; appointee Pres.'s Adv. Commn. on Consumer Protection and Quality in the Health Care Industry, 1997. Author: If We Had Ham, We Could Have Ham and Eggs...If We Had Eggs: A Study of the National School Breakfast Program, 1972, Out to Lunch: A Study of USDA's Child Care Feeding and Summer Feeding Programs, 1974; co-author: On the Other Side of Easy Street: Myths and Facts About the Economics of Old Age, 1987. Treas. Jewish Fund for Justice, 1985-88, bd. dirs., 1985-93; bd. dirs. Am. Jewish World Service, Self-Help Community Services, 1974-77; mem. domestic adv. bd., project rev. bd. U.S.A. for Africa/Hands Across Am., 1986-88; v.p. of bd. dirs. Burgundy Farm Country Day Sch., 1988-90, pres. 1990-91; bd. dirs. Americans for Health, 1986-81. Arthur Garfield Hays Civil Liberties fellow, 1967; research fellow Legal Services Corp., Washington, 1978-80.

POLLACK, SEYMOUR VICTOR, computer science educator; b. Bklyn., Aug. 3, 1933; s. Max and Sylvia (Harrison) P.; m. Sydell Altman, Jan. 23, 1955; children: Mark, Sherie. BChemE, Pratt Inst., 1954; MChemE, Bklyn. Poly. Inst., 1960. Lic. chem. engr., Ohio. Engr. Schwarz Labs., Mt. Vernon, N.Y., 1954-55; design engr. Curtiss-Wright, Wood-Ridge, N.J., 1955-57, Fairchild Engines, Deer Park, N.Y., 1957-59, GE, Evendale, Ohio, 1959-62; rsch. assoc. U. Cin., 1962-66; prof. computer sci. Washington U., St. Louis, 1966—; cons. Mo. Auto Club, St. Louis, 1969-82, United Van Lines, Fenton, Mo., 1984-86, Computer Sci. Accreditation Bd., N.Y.C., 1985—. Author: Structured Fortran, 1982, UCSD Pascal, 1984, Studies in Computer Science, 1983, The DOS Book, 1985, Turbo Pascal Programming, 1991; cons. editor Holt Rinehart & Winston, N.Y.C., 1979-86. Bd. dirs. Hillel orgn., Washington U., 1983-84. Recipient Alumni Achievement award Pratt Inst., 1966, Outstanding Teaching award Burlington Northern Found., 1987. Mem. Assn. for Computing Machinery, Am. Assn. for Engring. Edn. Jewish. Avocations: classical and jazz piano, jogging. Office: Campus Box 1045 Washington U Saint Louis MO 63130

POLLACK, SOLOMON ROBERT, bioengineering educator; b. Phila., May 7, 1934; s. Henry and Hannah (Segal) P.; married; children: Michael, Andrea, Carolyn. A.B. in Physics, U. Pa., 1955, M.S., 1957, Ph.D., 1961. Rsch. scientist Univac (div. Sperry Rand), Blue Bell, Pa., 1960-64; asst. prof. dept. materials sci. and engring. U. Pa., Phila., 1964-67; assoc. prof. U. Pa., 1967-75, prof., 1975—, prof., chmn. dept. bioengring., 1977-81, assoc. dean grad. edn. and rsch. (Sch. Engring and Applied Sci.), 1981-86; pres. Cara Corp., Phila., 1971-85, chmn. bd., 1986-90. Editor: (with C. Brighton and J. Black) Electrical Properties of Bone and Cartilage, 1979; editor, contbr. to Ency. of Materials Sci. and Engring, 1981—; contbr. articles to profl. jours. Recipient Lindback award for disting. teaching, 1968, award for disting. rsch. Kappa Delta, 1985, bronze medal in honor of Luigi Galvani for disting. rsch. U. Bologna, 1989, S. Reid Warren award for disting. rsch., 1991, Clemson award for applied rsch., 1993. Fellow Am. Inst. Med. and Biol. Engring (pres. 1st World Congress in Electricity and Magnetism); mem. Soc. for Biomaterials (pres. 1981), Bioelectric Repair and Growth Soc. (pres. 1985), Orthopaedic Rsch. Soc., Bioelectromagnetics Soc., Engring. in Medicine and Biology, Sigma Xi. Jewish. Patentee in field. Home: 115 Westminster Dr North Wales PA 19454-1221 Office: 116 Hayden Hall U Pa Philadelphia PA 19104

POLLACK, STANLEY P., lawyer; b. N.Y.C., Apr. 23, 1928; s. Isidor and Anna (Shulman) P.; m. Susan Aronowitz, June 16, 1974; 1 child, Jane. BA, NYU, 1948; JD, Harvard U., 1951; LLM in Taxation, NYU, 1959. Bar: N.Y. 1951, U.S. Dist. Ct. (so. dist.) N.Y. 1955. Sole practice N.Y.C., 1955-61; v.p., gen. counsel James Talcott, Inc., N.Y.C., 1961-73; sr. exec. v.p. Rosenthal & Rosenthal Inc., N.Y.C., 1973—. Served to j.g. lt. USNR, 1951-54. Mem. Bklyn. Bar Assn. (banking com., bankruptcy com.), Fed. Bar Council, Assn. Comml. Fin. Atty.'s (pres. 1968), Factors Chain Internat. (legal com.). Club: Harvard (N.Y.C.). Home: 6 Peter Cooper Rd New York NY 10010-6701 Office: Rosenthal & Rosenthal Inc 1370 Broadway # 2 New York NY 10018-7302

POLLACK, STEPHEN J., stockbroker; b. N.Y.C., Aug. 25, 1937; s. Harold S. and Gladys H. Pollack; m. Barbara Jane Podgur, May, 1992; B.S. in Econs., U. Pa., 1960. Vice pres. retail sales Drexel Burnham Lambert, N.Y.C., 1960-77; v.p. retail sales, Drexel Burnham Lambert, N.Y.C., 1960-77, 1st v.p. investments Dean Witter Reynolds Inc., N.Y.C., 1978—. pres. Bnai Brith Gothem, N.Y.C.; exec. v.p. Cosmopolitan League of City of Hope; v.p., circle mem. Whitney Mus., N.Y.C.; treas. Sutton Pl. Synagogue, pres. Havurah Group. Served with USAR, 1966. Recipient Double Chai Citation, State of Israel Bonds, 1984; Appreciation award City of Hope, 1984, Kiter Key Club award Franklin Funds, Million Dollar Club Svc. award City of Hope, Bnai Brith Internat. award. Mem. Internat. Assn. Fin. Planners, Assn. Investment Brokers (dir.), Youngmen's Philanthropic League (bd. dirs.), Am. Biog. Inst. (life), Internat. Study & Research Inst, Dean Witter Pres. Club. Jewish. Clubs: Town, Atrium, Schuylkill Country, Wharton Sch., U. Pa., Yale, East River Tennis, Schuylkill Country, Fresh Meadow Country, Matterhorn Sports, East Side Republican, Knickerbocker Republican, Friars, Penn (charter). Home: 245 E 40th St Apt 14E New York NY 10016-1714 Office: Dean Witter Reynolds Inc 900 3rd Ave New York NY 10022-4728

POLLACK, SYDNEY, film director; b. Lafayette, Ind., July 1, 1934; s. David and Rebecca (Miller) P.; m. Claire Griswold, Sept. 22, 1958; children: Steven, Rebecca, Rachel. Grad., Neighborhood Playhouse Theatre Sch., N.Y.C., 1954. Asst. to Sanford Meisner, Neighborhood Playhouse Theatre, 1954, instr. acting, 1954-60; exec. dir. West Coast br. The Actors Studio. Appeared in Broadway prodns.: The Dark Is Light Enough, 1954, A Stone For Danny Fisher, 1955; appeared on live TV programs: Alcoa Presents, others; toured in Stalag 17; dir. TV programs: The Chrysler Theatre, Ben Casey, 1962-63, Something About Lee Wiley, 1963-64; Films include: (dir.) The Slender Thread, 1965, This Property is Condemned, 1966, The Scalphunters, 1968, Castle Keep, 1969, Jeremiah Johnson, 1972, Three Days of the Condor, 1975, The Electric Horseman, 1979, The Firm, 1993; (exec. prodr.) Sense and Sensibility, 1995; (dir., prodr.) They Shoot Horses, Don't They?, 1969, The Way We Were, 1973, The Yakuza, 1975, Bobby Deerfield, 1977, Absence of Malice, 1981, Tootsie, 1982 (also actor), Out of Africa, 1985 (Academy Award for Best Picture and Dir.), Havana, 1990, The Firm, 1993, Sabrina, 1995; (prodr.) Songwriter, 1984, Bright Lights, Big City, 1988, The Fabulous Baker Boys, 1989, Presumed Innocent, 1990; (exec. prodr.) Honeysuckle Rose, 1980, White Palace, 1990, King Ralph, 1991, Dead Again, 1991, Leaving Normal, 1992, Searching for Bobby Fischer, 1993; (actor) The Player, 1992, Death Becomes Her, 1992, Husbands and Wives, 1992, The Firm, 1993. Served with U.S. Army, 1957-59. Recipient Acad. award for best dir. and best picture, 1986. Office: Mirage Enterprises De Mille Bldg # 110 5555 Melrose Ave Los Angeles CA 90038-3112 also: CAA 9830 Wilshire Blvd Beverly Hills CA 90212-1804

POLLACK, SYLVIA BYRNE, educator, researcher, counselor; b. Ithaca, N.Y., Oct. 18, 1940; d. Raymond Tandy and Elsie Frances (Snell) Byrne; divorced; children: Seth Benjamin, Ethan David. BA, Syracuse U., 1962; PhD, U. Pa., 1967; MA, Antioch U., 1993. Instr. Women's Med. Coll. Pa., Phila., 1967-68; rsch. assoc. U. Wash., Seattle, 1968-73, rsch. asst. prof., 1973-77, rsch. assoc. prof., 1977-85, rsch. prof., 1985—, counselor Sch. Nursing, 1993—; asst. mem. Fred Hutchinson Cancer Ctr., Seattle, 1975-79, assoc. mem., 1979-81; mem. study sect. NIH, Washington, 1978-79, 83-85. Contbr. numerous articles to profl. jours.; reviewer for profl. jours. Recipient rsch. grants Am. Cancer Soc., 1969-79, Nat. Health Inst., 1973—, Chugai Pharm. Co., Japan, 1985-91. Mem. Am. Counsel Assn., Am. Assn. Immunologists. Office: U Wash Box 357261 Seattle WA 98195-7261

POLLACK, WILLIAM SHELLEY, psychologist, organizational consultant; b. Bklyn., Nov. 7, 1950; s. Emanuel and Pearl C. (Balcoff) P.; m. Marsha A. Padwa, Nov. 7, 1982; 1 child, Sarah Faye. AB, U. Chgo., 1972; MA, Brandeis U., 1976; postgrad., Boston Psychoanalytic Inst., 1993—; MA, Boston U., 1978, PhD in Clin. Psychology, 1981. Diplomate Am. Bd. Profl. Psychology, Clin. Psychology; nat. register health svc. provider in psychology; lic. psychologist, health provider, Mass.; Qualified Psychologist, Mass. Trainee Boston V.A. Outpatient Clinic, 1977-78; intern Boston U. Med. Ctr., 1978-79; intern McLean Hosp., Belmont, Mass., 1979-80, asst. in psychology, 1980-81, asst. psychologist, 1981-88, assoc. attending psychologist, 1988-90, assoc. psychologist, 1990—; clin. fellow in psychology dept. psychiatry Harvard Med. Sch., Boston, 1979-80, instr. psychology dept. psychiatry, 1981-93, asst. clin. prof. psychology dept. psychiatry, 1994—; clin. assoc. in psychiatry Boston U. Med. Sch., 1980-82; staff psychologist Univ. Hosp., 1980-82; clin. assoc. in psychiatry Mass. Gen. Hosp., Boston, 1992—; lectr. dept. psychology Boston U., 1994; rsch. assoc. Boston U. Pregnancy and Parenthood Project, 1978-81, investigator, 1982—; staff psychologist Psychol. Test Ctr. Boston U. Med. Sch., 1980-81; psychologist in charge North Belknap I, McLean Hosp., 1980-81, Day Program Partial Hosp. Svc., 1981-82, Codman House III, 1982-88, mem. subcom. Patterns of Patient Care Utilization Rev. Com., 1982-88, dir. continuing edn. in psychology, 1982—, registrar APA program in continuing edn., 1982—, mem. edn. and tchg. com., 1983—, chair audio visual task force edn. and tchg. com., 1984, mem. psychiatrist in chief's task force on governance, 1984, interim dir. Inst. Ednl. and Orgnl. Consultation, 1985-86, chair subcom. on media edn. and tchg. com., 1985-87, mem. task force on long term/chronic care dept. psychiatry, 1987-88, chair subcom. on data base, 1987-88, mem. task force on aftercare dept. psychiatry, 1987-88, mem. clin. case conf. com. dept. psychiatry, 1987-88, sr. cons. Rehab. Outpatient Svc., 1987-94, chair continuing edn. com. psychology dept., 1987—, mem., rep. attending psychiatrist and psychologist com., 1989-94, dir. continuing psychology edn. Dept. Continuing Edn. and Postgrad. Edn., 1991—; mem. faculty steering com. psychology internship program McLean Hosp./Harvard Med. Sch, 1983—, mem. psychology internship com., 1983—, mem. com. on continuing med. edn., 1990—, coord. psychology fellowship program, 1991-94, mem. psychology dept. exec. adv. com., 1995—, dir. Ctr. for Men, McLean Hosp., 1994—; supr. med. students, interns and residents; spkr. numerous seminars in field, developer courses of study in field. Co-author: In A Time of Fallen Heroes, Atheneum, 1993, Guilford, 1995, A New Psychology of Men, 1995; mem. editl. bd. Psychotherapy, 1985-94, Jour. Clin. and Consulting Psychology, 1986, Direction in Clin. Psychology, 1990—, Psychotherapy Newsletter, 1994—, Psychoanalysis and Psychotherapy (guest editor 1995), Gender and Psychoanalysis, 1995—; contbr. numerous articles to profl. jours. Psychology rep. Gov.'s Task Force on Stigma, Mass., 1988-92, Mass. Statewide Mental Health Adv. Coun., 1993—; mem. Curriculum Adv. Com. Dept. Mental Health, Mass., 1990—; panel mem. Tech. Consulting Group Harvard Resource-Based Relative Values Scale for Clin. Psychology, 1992—; examiner Am. Bd. Profl. Psychology, 1994—; trustee Boston Psychoanalytic Soc. Inst., 1994—; v.p. McLean Profl. Staff Assn., 1995—. Crown fellow, 1974, NIMH fellow, 1978. Fellow Am. Orthopsychiat. Assn., Mass. Psychol. Assn. (mem. sci. program com., coord. continuing edn. programs 1983, mem. profl. practice com. 1984—, hosp. practice subcom., profl. practice com., mem. state-wide legis. network 1984—, treas. bd. dirs. 1986-88, mem. long-range planning com. 1987—, dir. 1988-95, pres. 1991-93); mem. AAAS, APA (divsn. 12 clin. psychology, divsn. 27 cmty. psychology, divsn. 39 psychoanalysis, divsn. 29 psychothpy 1982—, assoc. program chair divsn. psychotherapy 1987-88, mem. com. continuing edn. sponsor approval 1987-90, chair 1989-90, chair program com. divsn. 29 psychotherapy 1988-90, mem. task force on men's roles and psychotherapy divsn. 29 psychotherapy 1988—, Karl Heiser award 1995—), Soc. Psychotherapy Rsch., Am. Psychoanalytic Assn. (affiliate), Am. Group Psychotherapy Assn., Soc. for Psychol. Study of Men and Masculinity (founder divsn. 51 1990—), Internat. Soc. for Psychoanalytic Study of Orgns., Northeastern Soc. Group Psychotherapy, Phi Beta Kappa. Office: McLean Hosp 115 Mill St Belmont MA 02178-1041

POLLAK, BARTH, mathematics educator; b. Chgo., Aug. 14, 1928; s. Samuel and Esther (Hirschberg) P.; m. Helen Charlotte Schiller, Aug. 22, 1954; children: Martin Russell, Eleanor Susan. BS, Ill. Inst. Tech., 1950, MS, 1951; PhD, Princeton U., 1957. Instr. math. Ill. Inst. Tech., Chgo., 1956-58; asst. prof. Syracuse (N.Y.) U., 1958-63; assoc. prof. U. Notre Dame, Ind., 1963-67, prof., 1967—. Office: U Notre Dame Dept Math Notre Dame IN 46556

POLLAK, CATHY JANE, lawyer; b. Newark, Nov. 15, 1951; d. Seymour and Ruth Norma (Seidler) P.; m. Steven Michael Rosner, Aug. 12, 1976; children: Jessica Dori, Elizabeth Meryl. BA magna cum laude, Cedar Crest Coll., 1973; JD, Rutgers U., 1976. Bar: N.J. 1976, U.S. Dist. Ct. N.J. 1976, N.Y. 1990. Law clk., assoc. atty. O'Brien Daaleman & Liotta, Elizabeth, N.J., 1974-78; assoc. atty., ptnr. Feinberg, Dee & Feinberg, Bayonne, N.J., 1978-84; sr. assoc. Stoldt & Horan, Hackensack, N.J., 1984-93; atty. pvt. practice, Woodcliff Lake, N.J., 1993—; mem. bd. trustees, sec. Bergen County Task Force on Women and Addictions, Paramus, N.J., 1993—; mem. Bergen County Dist. Domestic Violence Legal Advocacy Project, Hackensack, 1993—. Mem. Hebrew sch. exec. com. Temple Beth Or, Washington Twp., N.J., 1993—. mem. sisterhood. Mem. N.J. State Bar Assn. (family law com.), Bergen County Bar Assn. (family law com.). Avocations: reading, dancing. Office: 188 Broadway Woodcliff Lk NJ 07675-8067

POLLAK, EDWARD BARRY, chemical manufacturing company executive; b. N.Y.C., Sept. 6, 1934; s. Ben N. and Harriet E. (Springer) P.; m. Marianne E. Modi, Feb. 27, 1960; children: David, Anne, Kari. BChemE, Cornell U., 1956, MBA, 1957. With Olin Corp., Stamford, Conn., 1957-94, bus. mgr. splty. and consumer products, 1970-72, v.p. Internat. Chems. Group, 1973-76, v.p., gen. mgr. designed products dept., 1976-80, corp. v.p., internat., 1980-86; pres., CEO Olin Hunt Splty. Products, Inc., 1986-93; chmn. OCG Microelectronic Materials Inc., 1991-93; v.p. internat. OSI Spltys. Inc., 1994-97; dir. Etoxyl C.A., Venezuela, Asahi-Olin Ltd., Japan; mem. steering com. internat. affairs group Chem. Mfrs. Assn. 1979-81, SRI adv. coun., 1994—. Bd. dirs. Stamford Symphony, U. Wyo. Inst. for Environment and Natural Resources. Mem. Synthetic Organic Chem. Mfrs. Assn. (gov. 1977-81, v.p. 1978, pres. 1979-80, steering com. internat. affairs group 1979-81), Internat. Isocyanate Inst. (bd. dirs. 1979-81), Cornell Soc. Engrs. (bd. dirs. 1967-72, v.p. 1971-72), Cornell Club For Fairfield County, Japan Soc. Office: Witco Corp 1 American Ln Greenwich CT 06831-2560

POLLAK, HENRY OTTO, retired utility research executive, educator; b. Vienna, Austria, Dec. 13, 1927; came to U.S., 1940, naturalized, 1945; s. Ludwig and Olga (Weil) P.; m. Ida Jeanne Tobias, May 7, 1949; children: Katherine, James. BA, Yale, 1947; MA, Harvard U., 1948, PhD, 1951; DSc, Rose Poly. Inst., 1964; DSc (hon.), Monmouth Coll., 1975, Bowdoin Coll., 1977, Technol. U., Eindhoven, 1981; LLD (hon.), Montclair State Coll., 1984; DSc (hon.), Laval U., Que., 1992. With Bell Telephone Labs., Murray Hill, N.J., 1951-83; mem. tech. staff Bell Telephone Labs., 1951-59, head dept. communications fundamentals II, 1959-61, acting dir. math. and mechanics research center, 1961-62, dir. math. and statistics research center, 1962-83; asst. v.p. math., communications, computer scis. research Bell Communications Research, Morristown, N.J., 1984-86; mem. sch. math. study group, com. on undergrad. program in math. Internat. Commn. on Math. Instrn., 1970-74, 82-86, mem. adv. bd. Unified Sci. and Maths. for Elem. Schs., 1969-77; mem. adv. com. for sci. edn. NSF, 1977-80, 85-89, chmn., 1978-80; program chmn. 4th Internat. Congress Math. edn., 1980; bd. dirs. Math. Inst. Woodrow Wilson Found.; vis. prof. Tchrs. Coll., Columbia U., 1987—. Trustee N.C. Sch. for Sci. and Math, Durham, 1979-89; bd. dirs. COMAP, 1987-96. Mem. Am. Math. Soc., Math. Assn. Am. (pres. 1975-76, Yueh-Gin Gung & Dr. Charles Y. Hu award for Disting. Svc. to Math. 1993), Nat. Coun. Tchrs. Math., Phi Beta Kappa, Sigma Xi. Mem. Christ Ch. Home: 40 Edgewood Rd Summit NJ 07901-3988

POLLAK, JOANNE E., lawyer; b. Cleve., July 16, 1944; m. Mark Pollak, Dec. 26, 1976; children: Elizabeth, Joshua, Rebecca, Benjamin, Jonathan. BA magna cum laude, Dickinson Coll., 1965; JD with honors, U. Md., 1976. Bar: Md. 1976. V.p., gen. counsel The Johns Hopkins Health System Corp., Balt.; assoc., ptnr. and head of health care practice group Piper & Marbury Law Offices, 1976-93. Named One of Mds. Top Women Warfield's Bus. Record, 1996. Office: Johns Hopkins Health System Corp 600 N Wolfe St Baltimore MD 21205-2110

POLLAK, KEVIN, actor. Appeared in films Avalon, 1990, L.A. Story, 1992, Another You, 1991, Ricochet, 1991, A Few Good Men, 1992, Indian Summer, 1993, The Opposite Sex (And How to Live With Them), 1993, Grumpy Old Men, 1993, Clean Slate, 1994, Miami Rhapsody, 1995, The Usual Suspects, 1995, Canadian Bacon, 1995, Casino, 1995, Grumpier Old Men, 1995, House Arrest, 1996, Apt Pupil, 1997. Office: ICM 8942 Wilshire Blvd Beverly Hills CA 90211*

POLLAK, LISA, columnist. Columinist Balt. Sun. Recipient Pulitzer prize for feature writing, 1997. Office: Balt Sun 501 N Calvat St Baltimore MD 21278*

POLLAK, LOUIS HEILPRIN, judge, educator; b. N.Y.C., Dec. 7, 1922; s. Walter and Marion (Heilprin) P.; m. Katherine Weiss, July 25, 1952; children: Nancy, Elizabeth, Susan, Sarah, Deborah. A.B., Harvard, 1943; LL.B., Yale, 1948. Bar: N.Y. bar 1949, Conn. bar 1956, Pa. bar 1976. Law clk. to Justice Rutledge U.S. Supreme Ct., 1948-49; with Paul, Weiss, Rifkind, Wharton & Garrison, N.Y.C., 1949-51; spl. asst. to Amb. Philip C. Jessup State Dept., 1951-53; asst. counsel Amalgmated Clothing Workers Am., 1954-55; mem. faculty Yale Law Sch., 1955-74, dean, 1965-70; Greenfield prof. U. Pa., 1974-78, dean Law Sch., 1975-78, lectr., 1980—; judge U.S. Dist Ct. (ea. dist.), Pa., 1978—; vis. lectr. Howard U. Sch. Law, 1953; vis. prof. U. Mich. Law Sch., 1961, Columbia Law Sch., 1962. Author: The Constitution and the Supreme Court: A Documentary History, 1966. Mem. New Haven Bd. Edn., 1962-68; chmn. Conn. adv. com. U.S. Civil Rights Commn., 1962-63; mem. bd. NAACP Legal Def. Fund, 1960-78, v.p., 1971-78; chmn. New Haven Human Rights Com., 1963-64. Served with AUS, 1943-46. Mem. ABA (chmn. sec. individual rights 1970-71), Assn. Bar City N.Y., Fed. Bar Assn., Phila. Bar Assn., Am. Law Inst. (coun. 1978—). Office: US Dist Ct 13613 US Courthouse 601 Market St Philadelphia PA 19106-1713

POLLAK, MARK, lawyer; b. Paris, July 16, 1947; came to U.S., 1955; s. Joseph and Zofia (Berkowitz) P.; m. Joanne Elizabeth Harris, Dec. 26, 1976; children: Joshua David, Jonathan Stephen, Benjamin Eric, Rebecca Lynn. BA, Bklyn. Coll., 1968; MA in City Planning, U. Pa., 1972, JD, 1972. Bar: Md. 1972. Assoc. Piper & Marbury, Balt., 1972-81, ptnr., 1981—; pres. Balt. Corp. for Housing Partnerships; bd. dirs. Balt. Regional Community Devel. Corp. Bd. dirs. Balt. Children's Mus., Downtown Partnership of Balt., Inc. Mem. ABA, Md. Bar Assn., Am. Coll. Real Estate Lawyers, Am. Planning Assn., Nat. Assn. Bond Lawyers. Office: Piper & Marbury 36 S Charles St Baltimore MD 21201-3020

POLLAK, MARTIN MARSHALL, lawyer, patent development company executive; b. N.Y.C., July 31, 1927; s. Edward and Jennie (Horowitz) P.; m. Ellen R. Spiegel, Sept. 16, 1929; children: David W., Richard M., Barbara S. AB, Syracuse U., 1950; LLB, St. John's U., Bklyn., 1953. Bar: N.Y. 1953, U.S. Dist. Ct. (ea. and so. dists.) N.Y. 1957, U.S. Supreme Ct. 1959. Ptnr. Feldman & Pollak, Attys., N.Y.C., 1953-59; atty. N.Y. State, 1953—; founder, exec. v.p., treas. Nat. Patent Devel. Corp., N.Y.C., 1959—; pres. Internat. Hydron Corp., Woodbury, N.Y., 1981-88; chmn. bd. Interferon Scis. Corp., New Brunswick, N.J., 1981-96, bd. dirs.; trustee Worcester Found. for Exptl. Rsch., Shrewsbury, Mass., 1977—; cons. Allergan Optical Corp., Irvine, Calif., 1988-89; chmn. bd. Czechoslovak-U.S. Econ. Coun., Washington, 1987-96, vice-chmn., 1996—; pres. NPO Trading USA, Inc., N.Y.C., Washington, Prague, Czechoslovakia, 1990—, Am. Drug Co., Washington, N.Y., Moscow, 1993—; bd. dirs. GSE Sys., Inc. With USN, 1945-47. Recipient gold medal Czechoslovakian Rep. C. of C., 1984. Office: Nat Patent Devel Corp 9 W 57th St New York NY 10019 also: Gen Physics Corp 6700 Alexander Bell Dr Columbia MD 21046-2100

POLLAK, NORMAN L., retired accountant; b. Chgo., Aug. 16, 1931; s. Emery and Helen P.; m. Barbara Zeff, Aug. 21, 1955 (div. 1980); children: Martin Joel, Elise Susan McNeal, Rhonda Louise Wilder; m. Sharon Levin, Nov. 12, 1995. BS Sch. Commerce,, Northwestern U., 1955. CPA, Calif.; lic. real estate agt. Calif. Sr. acct., staff acct., 1952-58, pvt. practice, 1958-86; ret. acct., fin. and mgmt. cons., pres. Norman L. Pollak Accountancy Corp., Westlake Village, 1958-86; expert witness on domestic dissolution, 1984-86; lectr. profl. orgns.; bus. mgr. for Steven Martin, Nitty Gritty Dirt Band, 1967-77; acct. for Gregg and Howard Allman, 1967, Marion Ross, 1980s. Former pres. Ventura County Estate Planning Coun., 1975-78, 78-79); founder San Fernando Valley Estate Planning Coun., 1962, chpt. pres., 1964-65; founder Ventura Co. Estate Planning Coun.; chmn. Comm. Contest for Hearing Impaired Optimist Club, emergency com. Disaster Preparedness, Oak Forest Mobile Estates Assn.; compiled disaster preparedness plan; coach Braile Olympics for Blind; mem. Conejo Future Found.; bd. dirs. Oak Forest Homeowners Assn., Honokowai Palms Homeowners Assn.; bd. trustees Westlake Cultural Found.; active sponsor Code 3 for Homeless Children, 1993. Mem. AICPA, Calif. Soc. CPAs (former chmn. San Fernando tech. discussion group 1960-61, former mem. com. on cooperation with credit grantors), Nat. Assn. Accts., Westlake Village C. of C., Northwestern U. Alumni Club, Delta Mu Delta. Home and Office: 143 Sherwood Dr Lake Sherwood CA 91361-4814

POLLAK, RAYMOND, general and transplant surgeon; b. Johannesburg, South Africa, Nov. 12, 1950; came to U.S., 1977; MB BCh, U. Witwatersrand, Johannesburg, 1973. Diplomate Am. Bd. Surgery. Rotating intern Gen. Hosp., Johannesburg, 1974; intern in surgery U. Ill. Hosps. and Clinics, Chgo., 1977-78, resident in surgery; immunology and transplant fellow U. Ill., Chgo., 1982-84, assoc. prof. surgery, chief div. transplant dept. surgery, 1988—; prof. surgery, 1995—. Fellow ACS, Royal Soc. Surgeons (Edinburgh). Office: U Ill Dept Surgery Ste 411 801 S Paulina St M/C 960 Chicago IL 60612-7210

POLLAK, RICHARD, writer, editor; b. Chgo., Apr. 5, 1934; s. Robert and Janet (Spitzer) P.; m. Merle Ann Winer, Mar. 26, 1961 (div. 1979); 1 dau., Amanda.; m. Diane Walsh, Mar. 6, 1982. Student, Knox Coll., 1952-54; B.A. in English, Amherst Coll., 1957. Reporter Worcester (Mass.) Telegram & Gazette, 1957; polit. reporter Evening Sun, Balt., 1959-64; assoc. editor Newsweek, N.Y.C., 1964-67; asst. editor Honolulu Star Bull., 1967-68; freelance writer N.Y.C., 1968-71; co-founder, editor More mag., N.Y.C., 1971-76; lit. editor The Nation, 1980-81, exec. editor, 1988-89; editor-at-large, 1989-95; tchr. Yale U., spring 1977, NYU, fall 1977, 82-86; cons. Ford Found., 1970-72. Author: Up Against Apartheid, 1981, The Episode, 1986, The Creation of Dr. B: A Biography of Bruno Bettelheim, 1997; editor: Stop The Presses, I Want To Get Off!, 1975. Served with AUS, 1957-59. Poynter fellow Yale U., 1977. Mem. Authors Guild. Home and Office: 404 Riverside Dr New York NY 10025-1861

POLLAK, TIM, advertising agency executive. Exec. v.p. Young & Rubicam N.Y., 1987; pres., CEO D,Y&R Worldwide (formerly HDM Worldwide), 1987—; corp. CEO HDM Worldwide; pres., CEO HDM USA, N.Y.C., 1987-90, Young & Rubicam NY, N.Y.C., 1990-91; vice chmn. Young & Rubicam Advt., N.Y.C., 1991—; mem. exec. com., bd. dirs. Young & Rubicam, Inc.; mem. exec. com., bd. dirs. Dentsu, Young & Rubicam. Mem. Internat. Advt. Assn. (pres. N.Y. chpt. 1988-90, mem. worldwide bd. dirs.). Office: Young & Rubicam NY 285 Madison Ave New York NY 10017-6401*

POLLAN, CAROLYN JOAN, state legislator; b. Houston, July 12, 1937; d. Rex and Faith (Basye) Clark; B.S. in Radio and TV, John Brown U., 1959; postgrad. NYU, 1959; PhD in Edn., Walden U., 1993. m. George A. Pollan, Jan. 6, 1962; children—Cee Cee, Todd (dec.), Robert. Mem. Ark. Ho. of Reps., 1974—, now sr. Republican mem., asst. speaker pro-tempore, 1993; apptd. by Gov. numerous coms., comms.; ex-officio mem. Workplace Literacy Project Adv. Bd. U.S. Dept. Labor & Ednl. Testing Svc., 1990-93, Nat. Adult Literacy Survey, 1990-93; del. Am. Soviet Seminar, Am. Council Young Polit. Leaders, Exeter, N.H., 1976; co-developer Total Touch Test; owner Patent Model Mus.. Vice chmn. Ark. Rep. Com., 1972-76; del. Rep. Nat. Conv., 1976; bd. dirs. Ark. Cancer Soc., Ark. Easter Seals Soc.; bd. dirs. Greg Kistler Treatment Center for Physically Handicapped, Ark. Found. Assoc. Colls., 4-H Found. for Sebastian County; trustee John Brown U.; mem. legis. adv. com. So. Regional Edn. Bd., chmn. edn. com. So. Legis. Conf., 1994-96. Recipient Conservation Legislator of Yr. award Ark. Wildlife Fedn., Nat. Wildlife Fedn., Sears Roebuck & Co., 1976, Outstanding State Legislator of Yr. award Ark. Pub. Employees Assn., 1979, Lifetime Mem. award Ark. PTA, 1994, many others; named 1 of 10 Outstanding Legislators, Assembly of Govtl. Employees, 1980, Legislator of Yr., Ark. Human Service Providers Assn., 1982, Citizen of Yr. by Ark. Social Workers, 1993, Outstanding Women in Ark. Politics by Ark. Dem., 1990, One of 10 Top Legislators in 1993 Ark. Dem. Gazette, 1993, one of Top 100 Women in Ark., Ark. Bus. Publ., 1995, 96, 97; voted 1 of Ft. Smith's 10 Most Influential Citizens, S.W. Times Record Readers, 1979. Mem. Ark. Internat. Woman's Forum (founding mem.), Ft. Smith Car Restoration Assn. Baptist. Office: 2201 S 40th St Fort Smith AR 72903-3407

POLLAND, REBECCA ROBBINS, foundation executive; b. Phila., Jan. 11, 1922; d. Louis Aron Jonah and Edith Frances (Kapnek) Robbins; B.A., Bryn Mawr Coll., 1942; M.A., U. Calif., Berkeley, 1957, Ph.D., 1971; m. Harry L. Polland, July 14, 1946 (div. 1979); children: Louise, Margaret, Jonathan. Analyst, cons., commisson mem., local and nat. govt., 1942-82; cons. U.S. Dept. Agr., 1977; lectr. Polit. sci. Sacramento State U., 1975-76; asst. prof. Sonoma State U. (Calif.), 1976-78; asst. prof. Rutgers U., Camden, N.J., 1978-86. Chmn. bd. Frogmore Tobacco Estates Ltd., Zimbabwe; Presdl. appointee Bd. Internat. Food and Agrl. Devel., 1979-82. Exec. trustee J.F. Kapnek Charitable Trust, Phila., 1980—; mem. Berkeley City Commn. on Recreation and Parks, 1970-75; v.p.; mem. White House Conf. Food, Nutrition, Health, 1969, World Food Conf., Rome, 1974. Mem. Am. Polit. Sci. Assn., AAUP, Am. Soc. Public Adminstrn., Am. Soc. Tropical Medicine and Hygiene, Assn. Dirs. Internat. Agrl. Programs Assn. Women in Devel. (founding). Contbr. articles to profl. jours. Home: 220 Locust St Apt 30A Philadelphia PA 19106-3933 also: 1308 Portal Dr Bellingham WA 98226-2447

POLLARA, BERNARD, immunologist, educator, pediatrician; b. Chgo.; s. Joseph and Mamie P. PhB, Northwestern U., 1951, MS, 1954; MD, U. Minn., 1960, PhD, 1963. Intern USPHS Hosp., Seattle, 1960; resident in pediatrics U. Minn. Hosps., 1968-69; rsch. assoc. pediatrics U. Minn., 1960-63, assoc. prof. biochemistry and pediatrics, 1969; prof. pediatrics Albany (N.Y.) Med. Coll., 1969-94, chmn. dept., 1979-93; pediatrician in chief Albany Med. Ctr. Hosp., 1979-93; sabbatical leave, pediatrician Yukon Kuskokwim Regional Hosp., 1992-93; John and Aliese Price prof. pediatrics & adolescent medicine U. South Fla., Tampa, 1994—, head divsn. gen. pediatrics, dept. pediatrics, 1994—; v.p. for rsch. affairs Albany Med. Ctr., 1986-89. Dir. N.Y. State Kidney Disease Inst., 1969-79. With USN, 1945-46. Recipient Acad. Laureate award SUNY, Albany, 1991; Arthritis and Rheumatism Found. fellow, 1961-64. Fellow Am. Acad. Pediats.; mem. AAAS, Am. Assn. Immunologists, Am. Pediat. Soc., Am. Soc. Cell Biology, Clin. Immunology Soc., Sigma Xi, Phi Lambda Upsilon, Alpha Omega Alpha. Office: U South Fla Sch Medicine Dept Pediatrics 17 Davis Blvd Fl 2 Tampa FL 33606-3475

POLLARD, CHARLES WILLIAM, diversified services company executive; b. Chgo., June 8, 1938; s. Charles W. and Ruth Ann (Humphrey) P.; m. Judith Ann, June 8, 1959; children: Julie Ann, Charles W., Brian, Amy. A.B., Wheaton Coll., 1960; J.D., Northwestern U., 1963. Bar: Ill. 1963. Mem. firm Wilson and McIlvaine, 1963-67, Vescelus, Perry & Pollard, Wheaton, Ill., 1968-72; prof., v.p. fin. Wheaton Coll., 1972-77; sr. v.p. ServiceMaster Industries, Downers Grove, Ill., 1977-80, exec. v.p., 1980-81, pres., 1981-83; pres., COO ServiceMaster Industries, 1981-83; pres., CEO ServiceMaster Co., Downers Grove, Ill., 1983-93, chmn. bd. dirs., mem. exec. com., 1994—; bd. dirs. Wheaton Coll., Herman Miller, Inc., Provident Life and Accident Ins. Co. Office: Servicemaster LP 1 ServiceMaster Way 2300 Warrenville Rd Downers Grove IL 60515-1765

POLLARD, DENNIS BERNARD, lawyer, educator; b. Phila., May 12, 1968. BS in Psychology, Pa. State U., 1990; JD, Ohio State U., 1993; postgrad., U. Mich., 1996. Bar: Ohio 1993, U.S. Dist. Ct. (no. dist.) Ohio 1994, U.S. Ct. Appeals (6th cir.) 1994. Staff atty. The Legal Aid Soc. Cleve., 1993-95; atty. student affairs, student life Pa. State U., 1995-96; acad. adminstrv. intern U. Mich. Law Sch., Ann Arbor, 1996-97; asst. dean student affairs U. Tenn. Coll. Law, Knoxville, 1997—. Mem. ABA, Ohio State Bar Assn., Phi Delta Phi. Avocation: biking. Home: 225 Dublin Dr Knoxville TN 37923-5600 Office: U Tenn Coll Law 1505 Cumberland Ave Knoxville TN 37916-3199

POLLARD, FRED DON, finance company executive; b. Proctorsville, Vt., Sept. 15, 1931; s. Bryant Frank and Millie Viola (Brobst) P.; m. Sandra Jean Norton, Oct. 19, 1957; children: Fred Don, Bruce Gardiner, Mark Bryant. BA, Dartmouth Coll., 1953, MBA, 1954. CPA, N.Y. Staff auditor Touche, Niven, Bailey & Smart, Chgo., 1954-55, 57-58; with Hertz Corp., Chgo., 1958-60, London, 1960-62, Paris, France, 1962-64, N.Y.C., 1964-65; European controller Avis Rent A Car, London, 1965-69; internat. treas. Avis Rent A Car, 1969-71; asst. v.p., dir. fin. Avis Rent A Car, Garden City, N.Y., 1971-72; asst. treas. Avis Rent A Car, 1972-75; treas. Garcia Corp., Teaneck, N.J., 1975-78; v.p. fin., treas. Augsbury Orgn., Inc., Ogdensburg, N.Y., 1978-79; sr. v.p. fin., treas. Augsbury Orgn., Inc., 1979-83, also dir.; pres. Corp. Fin. Assocs. No. N.Y., Canton, 1983—, Agrl. Processing Corp., Canton, 1983—; dir. Augsbury Corp., Halco Inc., Montreal, Que., Can., 1978-83, Carlton Holding Co./N.Y. Casualty, Watertown, N.Y., 1978-82, Creg System Inc., Watertown, Whalen, Daley & Looney (CPAs), Ogdenburg, N.Y., 1989—; Mem. adv. bd. Clarkson Sch. Mgmt., Potsdam, N.Y., 1979-83; vis. lectr. sch. of mgmt. Clarkson U., Potsdam, 1986-87; vis. lectr. dept. econs. St. Lawrence U., Canton, N.Y., 1987-88. Exec. bd. Seaway Valley coun. Boy Scouts Am., 1980-86, adv. bd., 1986-95. Served with U.S. Army, 1955-57. Mem. N.Y. State Soc. CPAs, Am. Inst. CPAs., St. Lawrence county C. of C. (bd. dirs. 1997—). Presbyterian. Lodges: Masons; Shriners. Home: Old Stone House 1129 County Route 25 Canton NY 13617-6539 Office: Russell Rd Canton NY 13617

POLLARD, GEORGE MARVIN, economist; b. St. Joseph, Mo., Oct. 5, 1909; s. James Coleman and Ethel (Mallory) P.; m. Jean Mary Campion, Apr. 15, 1939; 1 child, Elizabeth G. A.B., George Washington U., 1934, A.M., 1939; student, Columbia, 1940-41, sch. mil. govt. U. Va., 1944, Stanford, 1944-45. Mem. staff U.S. Dept. Agr., 1928-41, WPB, 1941-43; sr. economist U.S. Dept. Army, 1946-49; internat. economist, 1949-51; fgn. service officer Dept. State, 1955-64, internat. economist, 1951-55, 64—; consul, chief polit. and econ. affairs Am. Consulate Gen., Düsseldorf, Fed. Republic Germany, 1956-58; 1st sec. econ. affairs U.S. Mission to European Communities, Luxembourg, 1958-61; supervisory officer econ. affairs Bur. Internat. Orgn. Affairs, Dept. State, Washington, 1961-63; assigned to Bur. Internat. Commerce, U.S. Dept. Commerce, Washington, 1964-76; Mem. planning and zoning commn., Vienna, Va., 1953-56. Served as lt. USNR, 1943-46; mil. govt. officer Occupation of Japan 1945-46; mem. U.S. rep. Far Eastern Commn. 1947-49, Washington; lt. col. U.S. Army Res., 1949-63; ret. Mem. Phi Theta Kappa, Phi Sigma Kappa, Alpha Kappa Psi. Club: DACOR. Home: 4590 Robinson Place Boulder CO 80301-3143

POLLARD, HARVEY B., physician, neuroscientist; b. San Antonio, May 26, 1943. BA in Biology, Rice U., 1964; MS in Biochemistry, U. Chgo., 1969, MD, 1969, PhD, 1973. Rsch. assoc. NIH-Nat. Inst. Arthritis and Metabolic Diseases, Bethesda, Md., 1969-71, sr. investigator, 1972-74, 1977-75, sect. chief, 1979-81; lab. chief Nat. Inst. Diabetes, Digestive and Kidney Diseases, Bethesda, 1981-96; prof., chair dept. anatomy & cell biology Uniformed Svcs. U. Sch. Medicine, Bethesda, 1997—. Contbr. over 200 articles to profl. jours. With USPHS, 1969-96. Recipient Commendation medal USPHS, 1982, Alumni award for Disting. Svc., U. Chigo. Alumni Assn., 1989, NIH Inventor's award, 1991. Mem. Biophys. Soc., Soc. for Neurosci., Am. Soc. for Pharmacology and Exptl. Therapeutics, Soc. for Cell Biology, Endocrine Soc., Am. Coll. Psychoneuropharmacy, Am. Soc. for Biochemistry and Molecular Biology. Office: USU Sch Med Dept Anatomy & Cell Biol 4301 Jones Bridge Rd Rm B2200 Bethesda MD 20814-4712

POLLARD, HENRY, lawyer; b. N.Y.C., Jan. 10, 1931; s. Charles and Sarah (Lanster) P.; m. Adele Ruth Brodie, June 16, 1954; children: Paul A., Lydia S. AB, CCNY, 1953; JD, Columbia U., 1954. Bar: N.Y. 1954, Calif. 1962. Assoc. Sullivan & Cromwell, N.Y.C., 1954, 56-61; ptnr. Kaplan, Livingston, Goodwin, Berkowitz & Selvin, Beverly Hills, 1962-81, Pollard, Bauman, Slome & McIntosh, Beverly Hills, Calif., 1981-87, Seyfarth, Shaw, Fairweather & Geraldson, L.A., 1987-95; of counsel Oberstein, Kibre & Horwitz, L.A., 1995—; judge pro tem L.A. County Mcpl. Ct.; arbitrator/mediator, mem. large complex case program Am. Arbitration Assn.; arbitrator/mediator Nat. Assn. Securities Dealers, N.Y. Stock Exch., Am. Stock Exch., Pacific Stick Exch., L.A. County Dispute Resolution Svcs.; settlement officer Beverly Hills Mcpl. Ct., 1997—. Editor Columbia U. Law Rev., 1953-54. Served with U.S. Army, 1954-56. Harlan Fiske Stone scholar, 1953-54. Mem. ABA, Calif. Bar Assn., Los Angeles County Bar Assn., Beverly Hills Bar Assn.

POLLARD, JOSEPH AUGUSTINE, advertising and public relations consultant; b. N.Y.C., June 22, 1924; s. Joseph Michael and Mary Theresa (Sheerin) P.; m. Helen Frances O'Neill, Jan. 18, 1947 (dec.); children: Christopher (dec.), Kenneth, Eugene, Daniel, Theresa, Michael; m. 2d, Lee Sharon Rivkins, Jan. 1, 1981. Student Pratt Inst., 1946-50. Advt. mgr. Boston Store, Utica, N.Y., 1951-53; sales promotion dir. Interstate Stores, N.Y., 1954-60, 67-70; v.p. sales Community Discount Stores, Chgo., 1960-63; dir. sales S. Klein, N.Y., 1964-66; v.p. advt. and pub. relations Peoples Drug Stores, Alexandria, Va., 1970-89; ret. Bd. dirs. Lockwood Folly C.C., Holden Beach, N.C. Trustee D.C. divsn. Am. Cancer Soc., 1978-95, pres. 1985-86, nat. del., 1991-92; pres. Modern Retailers Ill., 1962. With USAF, 1943-46, 50-51. Recipient Am. Advt. Fedn. Silver medal award, 1982, St. George's medal Am. Cancer Soc., 1984. Mem. Advt. Club Met. Washington (pres. 1975-76), Country Club of Fairfax (pres. 1994, bd. dirs. 1992-95). Home and Office: 173 Clubhouse Dr SW Supply NC 28462

POLLARD, MORRIS, microbiologist, educator; b. Hartford, Conn., May 24, 1916; s. Harry and Sarah (Hoffman) P.; m. Mildred Klein, Dec. 29, 1938; children: Harvey, Carol, Jonathan. D.V.M., Ohio State U., 1938; M.S., Va. Poly. Inst., 1939; Ph.D. (Nat. Found. Infantile Paralysis fellow), U. Calif.-Berkeley, 1950; D.Sc. (hon.) Miami U., Ohio, 1981. Mem. staff Animal Disease Sta., Nat. Agrl. Research Center, Beltsville, Md., 1939-42; asst. prof. preventive medicine Med. br. U. Tex., Galveston, 1946-48; assoc. prof. U. Tex., 1948-50, prof., 1950-61; prof. biology U. Notre Dame, Ind., 1961-66; prof., chmn. microbiology U. Notre Dame, 1966-81, prof. emeritus, 1981—, dir. Lobund Lab., 1961-85, Coleman dir. Lobund Lab., 1985—; vis. prof. Fed. U. Rio de Janeiro, Brazil, 1977; vis. prof. Katholieke U., Leuven, Belgium, 1981; mem. tng. grant com. NIH, 1965-70; mem. adv. bd. Inst. Lab. Animal Resources NRC, 1965-68; mem. adv. com. microbiology Office Naval Research, 1966-68, chmn., 1968-70; mem. sci. adv. com. United Health Found., 1966-70; cons. U. Tex., M.D. Anderson Hosp. and Tumor Inst., 1958-66; mem. colon cancer com. Nat. Cancer Inst., 1972-76, chmn. tumor immunology com., 1976-79; mem. com. cancer cause and prevention NIH, 1979-81; program rev. com. Argonne Nat. Lab, 1979-85, chmn., 1983-84; lectr. Found. Microbiology, 1978. Editor: Perspectives in Virology Vol. I to XI, 1959-80; contbr. articles to profl. jours. Served from 1st lt. to lt. col. Vet. Corps, AUS, 1942-46. Recipient Disting. Alumnus award Ohio State U., 1979, Army Commendation medal, Presdl. citation; named Hon. Alumnus U. Notre Dame, 1989; McLaughlin Faculty fellow Cambridge U., 1956; Raine Found. prof. U. Western Australia, 1975; vis. scientist Chinese Acad. Med. Scis., 1979, 81; hon. prof. Chinese Acad. Med. Scis., 1982. Mem. Am. Acad. Microbiology (charter), Brazilian Acad. Scis., Soc. Exptl. Biology and Medicine, Am. Soc. Microbiology (Acad. Sci. Achievement award 1990), Am. Soc. Investigative Pathology, Am. Assn. Cancer Rsch., Am. Soc. Lab. Animal Sci., Assn. Gnotobiotics (pres.), Internat. Commn. Lab. Animal Sci., AAAS, Internat. Assn. Gnotobiology (pres.), Internat. Assn. Gnotobiotics (hon. pres. 1987), Sigma Xi, Phi Delta Epsilon (hon.), Phi Zeta (hon.). Home: 3540 Hanover Ct South Bend IN 46614-2331 Office: Lobund Lab Univ of Notre Dame Notre Dame IN 46556

POLLARD, OVERTON PRICE, state agency executive, lawyer; b. Ashland, Va., Mar. 26, 1933; s. James Madison and Annie Elizabeth (Hutchinson) P.; m. Anne Aloysia Meyer, Oct. 1, 1960; children—Mary O., Price, John, Anne, Charles, Andrew, David. AB in Econs., Washington and Lee U., 1954, JD, 1957. Bar: Va. Claims supr. Travelers Ins. Co., Richmond, Va., 1964-67; asst. atty. gen. State of Va., Richmond, 1967, 70-72; spl. asst. Va. Supreme Ct., Richmond, 1968-70; exec. dir. Pub. Defender Commn., Richmond, 1972—; ptnr. Pollard & Boice and predecessor firms, Richmond, 1972-87; bd. govs. Va. Criminal Law Sect., Richmond, 1970-72, 91-93; chmn. prepaid legal services com. Va. State Bar, Richmond, 1982-85; pres. Met. Legal Aid, Richmond, 1978. Del. to State Dem. Cong., Richmond, 1985; mem. Va. Commn. on Family Violence Prevention, 1995. With USN, 1957-59. Recipient service award Criminal Law Bd. of Govs. for Pub. Defender Study, 1971. Mem. ABA, Va. Bar Assn. (chmn. criminal law sect. 1991-93), Richmond Bar Assn., Nat. Legal Aid and Defender Assn. (Reginald Heber Smith award 1991), Va. Bar Assn. (Pro Bono Publico award 1995). Democrat. Baptist. Avocation: fishing. Home: 7726 Sweetbriar Rd Richmond VA 23229 Office: Pub Defender Commn 701 E Franklin St Ste 1416 Richmond VA 23219-2510

POLLARD, SHIRLEY, employment training director, consultant; b. Brunswick City, Va., July 8, 1939; 1 child, Darryl. Degree in bus. adminstrn., Upper Iowa U., 1978. Adminstr. East. Balt. Community Corp.; tng. coord. Balt. County Concentrated Employment Tng. Program; exec. dir. Park Heights Community Corp., Balt.; dir. Linkages, Inc., Balt.; mem. women's and children's adv. coun. Sinai Hosp. Contbr. articles to Afro Am. newspaper. Pres. Park Hts. Cmty. Devel. Corp., United Black Fund, Balt., 1989—, Presdl. Task Force, 1992; active Balt. Urban League, Balt. Welfare Rights Orgn.; founder, pres. Balt. County Polit. Action Coalition, 1982—; founder, dir. Linkages, Inc., 1980; founder, dir. Tng. and Placement Svcs., 1989; active United Svc. Orgn., Md. Minority Contractors Assn., U.S. Civil Rights Mus. and Hall of Fame, Smithsonian Instn.; founder African Am. Culture Ctr.; co-founder Project Lou, Inc.; founder The Afro Fund, Inc.; active Fund for a Free South Africa's Founding Assocs. Leadership Coun., Nat. Women's Hall of Fame, Nat. Abortion Rights Action League, Srs. Coalition, Md. Edn. Coalition, CORE, So. Christian Leadership Conf., Nat. Trust for Hist. Preservation; presdl. appointment Md. Selective Svc. Bd., 1993, Exec. Com. of Am. Friends Svc. Com.; mem. women's adv. coun. Sinai Hosp., 1994—. Recipient Outstanding Achievement award Md. Minority Contractors Assn., Mayor's Citation, Martin Luther King Civil Rights award, 1987, Md. State Dept. Edn. award, 1987, congl. Achievement award, Kool Achiever awards, 1990, Nat. Black Caucus Spl. award, 1990, Congressional Achievement award, 1988, Svc. award The Writers Club, 1991, USO Meritorious Svc. award, 1991, Gov.'s Vol. award, 1992, Acad. of Excellence award, 1992, Signs of Hope award, 1995, Mayor's citation, 1984, Gov.'s citation, 1995, Senatorial award, 1995; recipient Bud Achiever award 1996. Mem. Am. Soc. Pers. Adminstrn., Am. Soc. Health/Manpower/Edn./Tng., Assn. for Providers Employment and Tng., NAACP (founder, pres. Randallstown chpt. 1988-95, Signs of Hope award), Balt. Coun. on Fgn. Affairs, Transafrica, USO, Md. Minority Contractors Assn. (Achievement award 1986, bd. dirs. 1984-89), Smithsonian Assoc., Md. C. of C. (greater Balt. com. 1985). Office: PO Box 32051 Baltimore MD 21282-2051

POLLARD, THOMAS DEAN, cell biologist, educator; b. Pasadena, Calif., July 7, 1942; s. Dean Randall and Florence Alma (Dierker) P.; m. Patricia Elizabeth Snowden, Feb. 7, 1964; children: Katherine, Daniel. BA, Pomona Coll., Claremont, Calif., 1964; MD, Harvard U., 1968. Intern Mass. Gen. Hosp., Boston, 1968-69; staff assoc. NIH, Bethesda, Md., 1969-72; from asst. prof. to assoc. prof. Harvard Med. Sch., Boston, 1972-78; prof., dir. dept. cell biology and anatomy Johns Hopkins Sch. Medicine, Balt., 1977-96; pres. Salk Inst. for Biological Studies, LaJolla, Calif., 1996—; prof. U. Calif., San Diego, 1996—; mem. Commn. on Life Sci., NRC, 1990-97, chair, 1993—; mem. coun. Nat. Inst. Gen. Med. Scis., NIH. Recipient Lewis S. Rosentiel Disting. Work in Basic Med. Rsch. award Brandeis U., 1996; Guggenheim fellow, 1984. Fellow AAAS, Am. Acad. Arts and Scis.; mem. NAS, Am. Soc. Cell Biology (pres. 1987-88, K. R. Porter lectr. 1989), Biophys. Soc. (pres. 1992-93), Marine Biol. Lab. (trustee 1991-97). Office: Salk Inst for Biol Studies Dept Cell Biology-Anatomy 10010 N Torrey Pines Rd La Jolla CA 92037-1002

POLLARD-GOTT, LUCY, writer; b. Endicott, NY, May 20, 1957; d. Frank Trich and Virginia (Claxton) Pollard; m. J. Richard Gott III, June 10, 1978; 1 child, Elizabeth Marjorie. BA summa cum laude, Princeton U., 1978, PhD in Psychology, 1981. Psychology jour. editor Lawrence Erlbaum Assocs., Inc., Mahwah, N.J., 1985-95; writer Carol Pub. Group, N.Y.C., 1995—; admissions cons. Princeton (N.J.) U., 1985-86; abstract preparation cons. ERIC Document Svc., Princeton, 1987. Mem. editl. bd. Discourse Processes, 1983-93; contbr. articles to profl. jours. Nat. Merit scholar, 1974; Pre-doctoral fellow NSF, 1978-81, Postdoctoral fellow USPHS, 1981-82.

Mem. Phi Beta Kappa. Avocation: mandolin. Home and Office: 63 Cartwright Dr Princeton Junction NJ 08550-1934

POLLARO, PAUL PHILIP, artist; b. N.Y.C., Aug. 2, 1921; s. Charles and Maria (Aprile) P.; m. Jo Ann Stover, July 16, 1962 (div. Nov. 1979); children: Lauren, Paul Jr.; m. Laura Clayton, Apr. 2, 1985. Student, Art Students League, 1945-48, Pratt Graphic Ctr., 1972. Instr. painting The New Sch. of Social Rsch., N.Y.C., 1964-69; vis. artist Notre Dame U., South Bend, Ind., 1965-67; asst. prof. art, chmn. art dept. Wagner Coll., Staten Island, N.Y., 1970-73; asst. dir. The MacDowell Colony, Peterborough, N.H., 1973-76; pvt. practice Hancock, N.H., 1976—. One-man shows include Jersey City Mus., N.J., 1966 (second prize), S.I. Mus. Art, N.Y., 1973, Manchester Inst. Arts and Scis., Manchester, N.H., 1970-85, Chryser Mus., Norfolk, Va., 1991, numerous others. Sgt. U.S. Army, 1942-45, PTO. Tiffany Found. grantee, N.Y.C., 1967, N.H. State Coun. Arts grantee, 1985; The MacDowell Colony fellow, 1965-69. Roman Catholic. Home: Norway Hill Hancock NH 03449

POLLEY, EDWARD HERMAN, anatomist, educator; b. Chgo., Sept. 20, 1923; s. Sam and Anna (Revzin) P.; m. Jo Ann Welsh, Aug. 11, 1953; children: Lisa, Eric. B.A., DePauw U., Greencastle, Ind., 1947; M.S., St. Louis U., 1949, Ph.D., 1951. USPHS postdoctoral research fellow Washington U., St. Louis, 1951-53; Instr., then asst. prof. anatomy Hahnemann Med. Coll., Phila., 1953-59; asst. prof., then asso. prof. U. Md. Med. Sch., 1964-70; research biologist Edgewood (Md.) Arsenal, 1959-70; prof. anatomy, neurosurgery and ophthalmology U. Ill. Med. Sch., Chgo., 1970—; vis. prof. dept. pharm. and physiol. scis. U. Chgo., 1979-80. Served to lt. (j.g.) USNR, 1942-46. Mem. Am. Assn. Anatomists, Assn. for Research in Vision and Ophthalmology, AAAS, Am. Soc. Neurosci., Sigma Xi. Club: Cajal. Office: U Ill Dept Anat Cell Biol M/C 512 808 S Wood St Chicago IL 60612-7300

POLLEY, HARVEY LEE, retired missionary and educator; b. Wapato, Wash., Aug. 14, 1924; s. Edward Prestley and Alda June Polley; m. Corinne Weber; children: Catherine, David, Corinne, Robert. BA, Whitworth Coll., Spokane, Wash., 1951; postgrad., East Wash. Coll., 1953, Berkeley Bapt. Div. Sch., 1958-59; MEd, Cen. Wash. Coll., 1958; postgrad., Ecole d'Adminstrn. des Affaires Africaines, Brussels, 1959-60. Tchr. Quincy (Wash.) Pub. Schs., 1953-57, N.W. Christian Schs., Spokane, 1958; missionary Am. Bapt. Fgn. Missionary Soc., Zaire, 1958-89; tchr. Evang. Pedagogical Inst., Kimpese, Zaire, 1961-69, asst. legal rep., dir., prin., supt., 1969-72; dir. BIM Hostel, Kinshasa, Zaire, 1972-73; mem. staff Ctr. for Agrl. Devel. Lusekele, Zaire, 1975-85, dir., 1976-79, 83-85; dir. Plateau Bateke Devel. Program, Kinshasa, 1985-89; ret., 1989. Author: Mpila Kele, a rural development guide written in the Kituba lang., 1989. Mem. Coun. Elders, Kimpese, 1969-72; pres. bd. adminstrn. Vanga (Zaire) Hosp., 1981-83; mem. exec. com. Nat. Human Nutrition Planning Coun. Govt. Zaire-USAID, Kikwit, 1983-85. Home: W2405 W Johansen Rd Spokane WA 99208-9616

POLLEY, RICHARD DONALD, microbiologist, polymer chemist; b. Bklyn., Feb. 23, 1937; s. George Weston and Evelyn (Tuttle) P.; m. Linda R. Radford, Sept. 21, 1991; children from previous marriage: Gordon MacHeath, Jennifer Elizabeth, Tabitha Isabelle, Sean Sullivan; m. Linda R. Radford, 1991. Student, Trinity Coll., 1954-57; BS, BA, Hofstra U., 1960. Asst. advt. mgr. tech. Permatex Chem. Corp., Huntington, N.Y., 1960-61, Sun Chem. Corp., 1961-63; advt. mgr. Celanese Plastics Co., Newark, 1963-67; account dir. McCann Indsl. Tech. Sci. Mktg., N.Y.C., 1967-68, v.p., gen. mgr., Miami, 1968-70; pres. Intercapital Belgium S.A., Brussels, 1970-72; pres., tech. dir. Iodinamics Corp., Lancaster, Pa., El Paso, Tex., 1972-76; tech. dir. Hydrodine Corp., Miami, 1976—, chmn., CEO, 1986—, also bd. dirs.; founder, chmn., CEO, COO, tech. dir. Polymorphic Polymers Corp., Miami, 1978-90; COO, tech. dir. Omnidine Corp., Miami, 1980—, bd. dirs.; pres. Skin Care Labs., Inc., Miami, 1979-90; dir. microbiology, rsch. dir., tech. dir. Pure H2O Biotechnology, Inc., Boca Raton, Fla., 1992—; CEO, tech. dir. Polllabs, São Paulo, Brazil, 1990—; tech. dir. Ecology Tech. do Brasil, São Paulo, 1993—; bd. dirs., tech. dir. Hydrodine Biotech (Far East) Ltd., Bangkok, Thailand and Hong Kong, 1992—; tech. dir., chief scientist Biocer Boreal S.A., Bogotá and Medellín, Colombia, 1995—; chief internat. tech. dir. microbiology Gen. Environ. Sci. Corp., Solon, Ohio, 1993—; chmn. Peer Group Influencers, Ltd., London, also Miami, Fla., 1988—; bd. dirs., v.p. Internat. Airlines, Long Beach, Calif., 1984—; tech. dir. Swiver Corp., Miami, Fla., 1994—; tech. dir., chief scientist, Snowplace Corp., Panama City, Rep. of Panama, 1996—, Infinity Techs., Ltd., Panama City, 1996—; COO, CEO, pres., tech. dir. Aegis Protective Coatings Corp., Miami, Fla., 1996—; overseas dir. Field Iodine Goiter Med. Demonstration Projects, Beth Israel Hosp.-Harvard Med. Sch., 1977—; cons. water microbiology and disinfection control Pan Am. Health Orgn., others. Mem. editorial adv. bd. Chem. Week, 1988; contbr. articles to profl. jours.; patentee in field. Mem. AAAS, Am. Concrete Inst., Water Quality Assn., N.Y. Acad. Scis., Internat. Iodine Inst. (chmn. bd. and tech. dir. 1976—), Associaçao de Ciencia e Tecnologia Ambiental (bd. dirs. São Paulo 1993—). Republican. Office: Hydrodine Corp/Omnidine Corp/Swiver Corp Aegis Protective Coatings 9264 Bay Dr Surfside FL 33154-3026

POLLICOVE, HARVEY MYLES, manufacturing executive; b. Utica, N.Y., May 28, 1944; s. Maxwell Hymen and Carolyn (Vogel) P.; m. Catherine Mary Keady, Aug. 3, 1968; children: Carolyn, Sarah. AAS, Monroe Community Coll., 1968; BS, U. Rochester, 1973. Sr. engr. supr. optics Eastman Kodak Co., Rochester, 1978-82; engring. mgr. optics Eastman Kodak Co., 1982-84, mfg. mgr., 1984-86, mgr. tech. mkts. (internat.), 1986-89; dir. Ctr. for Optics Mfg. U. Rochester, 1989—; U.S. del. (optics) to Internat. Stds. Orgn., 1995—; lectr. in field. Editorial adv. bd. (optics mag. for mfg.) Laser Focus World, 1990—; contbr. articles to profl. jours. Advisor High Tech. of Rochester, 1988-89; advisor tech. applications rev. bd. Strategic Def. Initiative Orgn., 1990-92, Ballistic Missile Def. Orgn., 1993—; industry advisor Monroe C.C., 1986—. Recipient Dept. of Def. Mfg. Tech. Achievement award, 1992. Mem. Am. Precision Optics Mfrs. Assn. (exec. com. 1987—, elected to bd. dirs. 1990-93), Internat. Soc. for Optical Engring., Optical Soc. Am. (hon. mem. Rochester sect. 1996). Home: 177 Georgian Court Rd Rochester NY 14610-3416 Office: U Rochester Ctr for Optics Mfg 240 E River Rd Rochester NY 14623-1212

POLLIHAN, THOMAS HENRY, lawyer; b. St. Louis, Nov. 15, 1949; s. C.H. and Patricia Ann (O'Brien) P.; m. Donna M. Bickhaus, Aug. 25, 1973; 1 child, Emily Christine. BA in Sociology, Quincy U., 1972; JD, U. Notre Dame, 1975; Exec. Masters in Internat. Bus., St. Louis U., 1992. Bar: Mo. 1975, Ill. 1976. Jud. law clk. to judge Mo. Ct. of Appeals, St. Louis, 1975-76; from assoc. to ptnr. Greenfield, Davidson, Mandelstamm & Voorhees, St. Louis, 1976-82; asst. gen. counsel Kellwood Co., St. Louis, 1982-89, gen. counsel, sec., 1989-93, v.p., sec., gen. counsel, 1993—. Trustee Quincy (Ill.) U., 1987-93, pres. alumni bd., 1986-87; pres. S.W. Neighborhood Improvement Assn., St. Louis, 1984, Quincy (Ill.) U. Found., 1993-94; dir., sec. New Piasa Chautauqua, Ill., 1996—. Mem. Bar Assn. Met. St. Louis. Roman Catholic. Avocations: soccer, cycling. Home: 4934 Magnolia Ave Saint Louis MO 63139-1026 Office: Kellwood Co 600 Kellwood Pky Chesterfield MO 63017-5800

POLLIN, ABE, professional basketball team executive, builder; b. Phila., Dec. 3, 1923; s. Morris and Jennie (Sack) P.; m. Irene S. Kerchek, May 27, 1945; children: Robert Norman, James Edward. B.A., George Washington U., 1945; student, U. Md., 1941-44. Engaged in home bldg. bus., 1945—; pres. Abe Pollin Inc., Balt., 1962—; chmn. Balt. Bullets Basketball Club, Inc. (now Washington Bullets), 1964—, Washington Capitals, 1973; dir. County Fed. Savs. & Loan Assn., Rockville, Md. Bd. dirs. United Jewish Appeal, Nat. Jewish Hosp., Jewish Community Center; bd. dirs., adv. com. John F. Kennedy Cultural Center. Mem. Nat. Assn. Home Builders, Asso. Builders and Contractors Md., Washington Bd. Trade. Jewish. Office: Washington Bullets US Air Arena Landover MD 20785 also: Washington Capitals US Air Arena Landover MD 20785*

POLLINGER, WILLIAM JOSHUA, lawyer; b. Passaic, N.J., Dec. 14, 1944; s. Irving R. and Ethel (Groudan) P.; m. Helen Rizzo, May 30, 1977; children: Samantha, Zachary. BA, Rutgers U., 1966; JD, Am. U., 1969. Bar: N.J. 1969, U.S. Dist. Ct. N.J. 1969, N.Y. 1981, U.S. Supreme Ct. 1982, U.S. Ct. Appeals (3d cir.) 1986; cert. Civil Trial Atty. N.J. Supreme Ct., 1983. Assoc. Krieger & Klein, Passaic, 1969-75; ptnr. Delorenzo & Pollinger, Hackensack, N.J., 1975-84; pres. William J. Pollinger, P.A., Hackensack, 1984-88, Pollinger, Fearns & Kemezis, P.A., 1988-90, Pollinger & Fearns, P.A., Hackensack, 1990-92, William J. Pollinger P.A., Hackensack, N.J., 1992—; mem. Bergen County Ethics Com., N.J., 1984-88. Arbitrator Better Bus. Bur. of Bergen and Rockland Counties, Paramus, N.J., 1983-89, Am. Arbitration Assn., 1983—. Assoc. of Yr. award Builders Assn. No. N.J., Paramus, 1981. Mem. N.J. State Bar Assn., Passaic County Bar Assn., Bergen County Bar Assn., Assn. Trial Lawyers Am., Trial Attys. N.J., Am. Arbitration Assn., Def. Research Inst., Phi Delta Phi. Lodge: Masons (past master). Avocation: stamp and coin collecting. Office: 302 Union St Hackensack NJ 07601-4303

POLLINI, FRANCIS, author; b. West Wyoming, Pa., Sept. 9, 1930; s. Sem and Assunta (Ciani) P.; m. Gloria Ann Swann, Sept. 12, 1959; children: Susanne, Lisa. BA in Psychology, Pa. State U., 1951. Author: Night, 1959, Glover, 1965, Excursion, 1966, The Crown, 1967, Three Plays, 1967, Pretty Maids All In a Row, 1968, Dubonnet, 1973, The Hall, 1975. 1st lt. USAF, 1952-57. Home: 14 Oak Ln, Hingham NR9 4JY Norfolk, England

POLLIO, RALPH THOMAS, editor, writer, magazine publishing consultant; b. Bronx, N.Y., Nov. 1, 1948; s. Thomas and Dolores (Miccioli) P.; m. Rita Lucia Napolitano, Sept. 29, 1974; 1 child, Christopher. BCE, Manhattan Coll., 1978; postgrad., Columbia U., 1988—. Founding pub., editor, owner Ea. Basketball Publs., Franklin Square, N.Y., 1975-88; cons., ptnr., founder Ea. Basketball Mag., Rochester, Mich., 1988—; founding pub., owner, editor High School News, 1984, EB News, 1981. Contbr. articles to mags. and profl. jours., 1985—. Sgt. U.S. Army N.G., 1969-74. Mem. U.S. Basketball Writers Assn. (1st Place award for best mag. feature 1984), ASCE, Soc. Profl. Journalists, Sigma Delta Chi, Internat. Soc. Philos. Enquiry, World Lit. Acad., Mag. Pubs. Assn., Am. Soc. Mag. Editors, Mensa, and numerous other high IQ socs. Roman Catholic. Clubs: N.Y. Road Runners (N.Y.C.), Dix Hills Runners. Avocations: running, listening to jazz, gourmet cooking, reading, film. Home: 1201 Hempstead Ave Malverne NY 11565

POLLITT, JEROME JORDAN, art history educator; b. Fair Lawn, N.J., Nov. 26, 1934; s. John Kendall and Doris B. (Jordan) P.; m. Susan Baker Matheson, Feb. 10, 1977. B.A., Yale U., 1957; Ph.D., Columbia U., 1963. Instr. history of art Yale U., New Haven, 1962-64; asst. prof. Yale U., 1964-68, assoc. prof., 1969-73, prof., 1973—, chmn. dept. classics, 1975-77, chmn. dept. history of art, 1981-84, dean, 1986-91. Author: Art and Experience in Classical Greece, 1972, The Ancient View of Greek Art, 1975, Art in the Hellenistic Age, 1986; editor-in-chief: Am. Jour. Archaeology, 1973-77; contbr. articles to profl. jours. Mem. Archaeol. Inst. Am., Coll. Art Assn. Home: 48 Dillon Rd Woodbridge CT 06525-1219 Office: Dept History of Art Yale U PO Box 208272 New Haven CT 06520-8272

POLLITT, KATHA, writer, poet, educator; b. N.Y.C., Oct. 14, 1949; d. Basil Riddiford and Leanora (Levine) P.; div.; 1 child, Sophie Pollitt-Cohen. BA, Harvard U., 1972; MFA, Columbia U., 1975. Lit. editor The Nation, N.Y.C., 1982-84, contbg. editor, 1986-92, assoc. editor, 1992—; jr. fellow council of humanities Princeton (N.J.) U., 1984; lectr. The New Sch., N.Y.C., 1986-90, Poetry Ctr. 92d St. YMHA and YWHA, N.Y.C., 1986-95. Author: Antarctic Traveller, 1982 (Nat. Book Critics Circle award 1983), Reasonable Creatures: Essays on Women and Feminism, 1994; poetry appeared in The New Yorker, The New Republic, Poetry, and others; contbr. articles to jours. Whiting fellow, 1993; recipient I.B. Lavan Younger Poet's award Acad. Am. Poets, 1984; Fulbright grantee, 1985; grantee N.Y. Found. of the Arts, 1987, Nat. Endowment for Arts, 1984; Guggenheim fellow, 1987. Fellow N.Y. Inst. Humanities. Democrat. Home: 317 W 93rd St New York NY 10025-7236

POLLITZER, WILLIAM SPROTT, anatomy educator; b. Charleston, S.C., May 6, 1923; s. Richard Morris and Cora (Sprott) P.; m. Margaret Buhlig, Aug. 29, 1955; children—Virginia, Patricia. A.B., Emory U., 1944, M.A., 1947; Ph.D., Columbia U., 1957. Instr. anatomy U. N.C., Chapel Hill, 1957-59, asst. prof., 1959-67, assoc. prof., 1967-73, prof., 1973-87, emeritus prof., 1987—. Contbr. articles to profl. jours. Served with U.S. Army, 1944-47. Mem. Am. Assn. Phys. Anthropologists (v.p. 1978-79, pres. 1979-81, editor jour. 1970-77), Human Biology Council (pres. 1986-88). Democrat. Avocations: tennis; cycling. Home: 513 Morgan Creek Rd Chapel Hill NC 27514-4931 Office: U NC Dept Cell Biology & Anatomy Chapel Hill NC 27599-7090

POLLOCK, ALEXANDER JOHN, banker; b. Indpls., Jan. 28, 1943; s. Alex S. and Doris L. (VanHorn) P.; m. Anne M. Fryfogle, Jan. 27, 1968; children: Elizabeth, Alexander, Evelyn, James. B.A., Williams Coll., 1965; M.A., U. Chgo., 1966; M.P.A., Princeton U., 1969. Instr. philosophy Lake Forest Coll., (Ill.), 1967; with internat. banking dept. Continental Ill. Nat. Bank, Chgo., 1969-77, v.p., 1977-82, sr. v.p., 1982-85; prin. Nolan Norton & Co., Chgo., 1985-86; chief fin. officer The Marine Corp., Milw., 1986-87; pres. Marine Bank N.A., Milw., 1987; pres., chief exec. officer Community Fed. Savs., St. Louis, 1988-90; vis. scholar Fed. Res. Bank of St. Louis, 1991; pres., CEO Fed. Home Loan Bank Chgo., 1991—; bd. advisors Banking Rsch. Ctr.; bd. dirs. Gt. Lakes Higher Edn. Corp.; exec. com. Internat. Union of Housing Fin. Instns., Success Lab. Inc. Bd. dirs. Great Books Found. Mem. Union League Club, Phi Beta Kappa. Office: Fed Home Loan Bank Chgo 111 E Wacker Dr Chicago IL 60601 *Omnia superans vi rationis et arte loquendi.*

POLLOCK, BRUCE GERALD, lawyer; b. Providence, Feb. 18, 1947; s. Reuben and Stella (Reitman) P.; m. Sheri Barbara Tepper, Dec. 21, 1969; children: Dawn, Meah. BA, U. R.I., 1968; JD, Suffolk U., 1974. Bar: R.I. 1974, U.S. Supreme Ct. 1978, U.S. Dist. Ct. R.I. 1980. Law clk. R.I. Superior Ct., Providence, 1974, adminstrv. asst. to chief justice, 1975; asst. pub. defender R.I. Dept. Pub. Defender, Providence, 1975-80; pvt. practice Warwick and West Warwick, R.I., 1980—; adj. instr. So. N.E. Law Sch., New Bedford, Mass., 1990. Fellow R.I. Bar Found. (bd. dirs. 1990—); mem. ABA, Nat. Conf. Bar Pres., New Eng. Bar Assn. (del. 1991-93), R.I. Bar Assn. (pres. 1992-93, award of merit 1995). Democrat. Avocations: golf, skiing, stained glass craftsman, bicycling. Office: 45 Providence St West Warwick RI 02893-3714

POLLOCK, BRUCE GODFREY, psychiatrist, educator; b. Toronto, Ont., Can., Aug. 18, 1952; s. Ira Justus and Sheila Joy (Godfrey) P.; m. Judith Arluk, May 18, 1982; children: Debra, Ariel. BS, U. Toronto, 1975, MD, 1979; PhD, U. Pitts., 1987. Chief resident Clarke Inst. Psychiatry, Toronto, 1982-83; postdoctoral fellow U. Pitts., 1983-84, asst. prof. dept. psychiatry, 1984-90, assoc. dir. clin. pharmacology dept. psychiatry, 1987-95, assoc. prof. dept. psychiatry and pharmacology, 1990-96, dir. geriatric psychopharm. dept. psychiatry-pharmacology, 1995—, prof. dept. psychiatry, 1996—. Contbr. over 100 articles to profl. jours.; contbg. author books in field. Centennial fellow Med. Rsch. Coun. of Can., Ottawa, 1983, Merck fellow geriatric clin. pharmacology, Am. Fedn. for Aging Rsch., N.Y.C., 1988; recipient acad. award geriatric mental health NIMH, Bethesda, Md., 1992. Fellow Royal Coll. Physicians Can. Home: 7032 Meade Pl Pittsburgh PA 15208 Office: Western Psychiat Inst/Clin 3811 Ohara St Pittsburgh PA 15213-2593

POLLOCK, DAVID, television writer and producer. Writer TV series The New Dick Van Dyke Show, 1972-73, Don Rickles Show, 1972, All in the Family, 1972, Mary Tyler Moore Show, 1972-73, Chico & the Man, 1974, Paul Sand Friends and Lovers, 1974, Hot L Baltimore, 1974-75, That's My Mama, 1974-75, The Carol Burnett Show, 1976-77, Carter Country, 1977, Bonkers, 1977-78, Delta House, 1979, M*A*S*H, 1980-83, Goodnight Beantown, 1983, Steambath, 1984 (Writer's Guild award 1985), One Big Family, 1986-87, Mama's Boy, 1987, Chicken Soup, 1989, Cheers, 1989, Bagdad Cafe, 1990, Growing Pains, 1990-91, Full House, 1991-92, Here and Now, 1992-93, Pride and Joy, 1995; prodr. TV series Frasier, 1994 (Emmy award for outstandi ng comedy series 1995, Geo. Foster Peabody award 1994). Office: care Bernie Weintraub/Valarie Phillips Paradigm 10100 Santa Monica Blvd Los Angeles CA 90067-4003

POLLOCK, EARL EDWARD, lawyer; b. Decatur, Nebr., Feb. 24, 1928; s. Herman and Della (Rosenthal) P.; m. Betty Sokol, Sept. 8, 1951; children: Stephen, Della, Naomi. B.A., U. Minn., 1948; J.D., Northwestern U., 1953; LLD (hon.), Morningside Coll., 1995. Bar: D.C. 1955, Va. 1955, Ill. 1959, U.S. Supreme Ct. 1960. Law clk., chief justices Vinson and Warren, U.S. Supreme Ct. Washington, 1953-55; atty. antitrust div. Dept. Justice, Washington, 1955-56, asst. to solicitor gen., 1956-59; ptnr. Sonnenschein Carlin Nath & Rosenthal, Chgo., 1959—. Trustee Loyola U., Chgo., 1983-92; life trustee Northwestern Meml. Hosp. Mem. Chgo. Bar Assn. (chmn. antitrust law com. 1967-68), ABA (chmn. antitrust law sect. 1979-80), Alumni Assn. Northwestern U. Sch. Law (pres. 1974-75, svc. award 1976). Office: Sonnenschein Nath 233 S Wacker Dr Ste 8000 Chicago IL 60606-6342

POLLOCK, GEORGE HOWARD, psychiatrist, psychoanalyst; b. Chgo., June 19, 1923; s. Harry J. and Belle (Lurie) P.; m. Beverly Yufit, July 3, 1946; children: Beth L. Pollock Ungar, Raphael E., Daniel A., Benjamin B., Naomi R. Pollock Sneider. B.S., U. Ill., 1944, M.D. cum laude, 1945, M.S., 1948, Ph.D., 1951. Diplomate Am. Bd. Psychiatry and Neurology. Intern Cook County Hosp., Chgo., 1945-46; resident Ill. Neuropsychiat. Inst., Chgo., 1948-51; practice medicine, specializing in psychiatry Chgo., 1948-91; clin. assoc. prof. dept. psychiatry Coll. Medicine, U. Ill., 1955-64, clin. prof., 1964-72; prof. psychiatry Northwestern U., 1972-93, Dunbar prof. psychiatry and behavioral scis. emeritus, 1993—, dir. rsch. dept. psychiatry/behavioral scis.m 1988-93, emeritus, 1993—; faculty Inst. for Psychoanalysis, Chgo., 1956-92, asst. dean edn., 1960-67, tng. analyst 1961-92, supervising analyst, 1962-92, dir. rsch., 1963-71, pres., 1971-89; exch. program participant Hampstead Child Therapy Clinic, 1962-63; pres. Ctr. Psychosocial Studies, 1972-90. Chmn. bd. editors Ann. of Psychoanalysis, 1971-89; mem. editorial bd. Jour. Am. Psychoanalytic Assn., 1971-74; mem. editorial bd. sect. psychoanalysis Psychiat. Jour. U. Ottawa Faculty Medicine, 1976—; corr. editor Jour. Geriatric Psychiatry, 1975—; Med. Problems of Performing Artists, Psychoanalytic Edn., Psychoanalytic Psychology, Internat. Forum for Psychoanalysis, Internat. Jour. Behavioral Scis. and the Law, Internat. Psychogeriatrics, Depression and Stress. Mem. med. adv. com. Planned Parenthood Assn., 1966-70; pres. governing bd. Parents Assn. Lab. Schs., U. Chgo., 1966-70; mem. med. adv. coun. Asthma and Allergy Found. for Greater Chgo. Capt. U.S. Army, 1946-48. Commonwealth fellow, 1951; research grantee Founds. Fund for Research in Psychiatry, 1960-65. Fellow Am. Coll. Psychiatrists, Am. Orthopsychiat. Assn., Am. Psychiat. Assn. (treas. 1980-86, pres. 1987-88), Am. Coll. Psychoanalysts (pres. 1985-86); mem. Internat. Psychogeriatrics (mem. editorial bds.), Am. Acad. Polit. and Social Sci., Am. Anthrop. Assn., Nat. Council on Family Relations, AAAS, AAUP, Profs., Am. Electroencephalographic Soc., Am. Heart Assn., Assn. for Research in Nervous and Mental Disease, Soc. for Exptl. Biology and Medicine, Ill., N.Y. acads. scis., Chgo. Psychoanalytic Soc. (pres. 1984-85), Soc. for Gen. Systems Research, AMA, World Med. Assn., Am. Name Soc., Am. Psychoanalytic Assn. (pres. 1974-75), Am. Psychol. Assn., Am. Psychosomatic Soc., Am. Pub. Health Assn., Am. Sociol. Assn., Assn. Am. Med. Colls., Ill. Psychiat. Soc. (pres. 1973-74), Sigma Xi, Alpha Omega Alpha, numerous others. Home: 5759 S Dorchester Ave Chicago IL 60637-1726 Office: 30 N Michigan Ave Chicago IL 60602

POLLOCK, JOHN ALBON, broadcasting and manufacturing company executive; b. Kitchener, Ont., Can., Jan. 18, 1936; s. Carl Arthur and Helen Isabel (Chestnut) P.; m. Joyce Mary Smethurst, Apr. 13, 1963; children—Kimberlee, Kristen, Nichola, Graham. B.A.Sc., U. Toronto, Can., 1959; M.B.A., Harvard U., 1962. Tng. positions Electrohome Ltd., Kitchener, 1962-69, v.p., 1969-71, exec. v.p., 1971-74, pres., 1974-80, chmn., pres., CEO, 1980-92, chmn., CEO, 1992—; bd. dirs. Budd Can. Inc., S.C. Johnson & Sons, Ltd., Can. Gen. Tower, Electrohome Ltd., CTV; past mem. Sci. Coun. Can.. Past chmn. adv. bd. U. Western Ont.; bd. dirs. Trillium Found., Can. Clay and Glass Gallery, Jr. Achievement; past pres. K-W Art Gallery; past mem. bd. govs. U. Waterloo; past chmn. bd. govs. St. John's Sch., Elora; bd. govs. Grand Valley Conservation Found., Freeport Hosp. Mem. XPO Forum Group, Muskoka Lakes Golf and Country Club, Univ. Club Toronto, K-W Gyro Club, Rotary. Office: Electrohome Ltd, 809 Wellington St N, Kitchener, ON Canada N2G 4J6

POLLOCK, JOHN PHLEGER, lawyer; b. Sacramento, Apr. 28, 1920; s. George Gordon and Irma (Phleger) P.; m. Juanita Irene Gossman, Oct. 26, 1945; children: Linda Pollock Harrison, Madeline Pollock Chiotti, John, Gordon. A.B., Stanford U., 1942; J.D., Harvard U., 1948. Bar: Calif. 1949, U.S. Supreme Ct. 1954. Ptnr. Musick, Peeler & Garrett, L.A., 1953-60, Pollock, Williams & Berwanger, L.A., 1960-80; ptnr. Rodi, Pollock, Pettker, Galbraith & Cahill, L.A., 1980-89, of counsel, 1989—. Contbr. articles to profl. publs. Active Boy Scouts Am.; trustee Pitzer Coll., Claremont, Calif., 1968-76, Pacific Legal Found., 1981-91, Fletcher Jones Found., 1969—, Good Hope Med. Found., 1980—. Fellow Am. Coll. Trial Lawyers; mem. ABA, L.A. County Bar Assn. (trustee 1964-66). Home: 30602 Paseo Del Valle Laguna Niguel CA 92677-2317 Office: 801 S Grand Ave Los Angeles CA 90017-4613

POLLOCK, KAREN ANNE, computer analyst; b. Elmhurst, Ill., Sept. 6, 1961; d. Michael Paul and Dorothy Rosella (Foskett) P. BS, Elmhurst Coll., 1984; MS, North Cen. Coll., 1993. Formatter Nat. Data Corp., Lombard, Ill., 1985; computer specialist Dept. VA, Hines, Ill., 1985—. Lutheran. Avocations: cross-stitch, mystery books, bowling, bicycling, softball.

POLLOCK, MARGARET LANDAU PEGGY, elementary school educator; b. Jefferson City, Mo., Oct. 18, 1936; d. William Wold and Grace Elizabeth (Creamer) Anderson; children by previous marriage: Elizabeth, Charles, Christopher, Jeffrey; m. William Whalen Pollock, Jan. 30, 1993. AA, Stephens Coll., 1956; BS in Elem. Edn., U. Mo., Columbia, 1958; MA in Reading Edn., U. Mo., Kansas City, 1987. Cert. elem. tchr., Mo. Kindergarten tchr. Columbia Schs., 1958-59, Moberly (Mo.) Schs., 1960-62; 1st grade tchr. Kansas City Schs., 1962-63; kindergarten tchr. Independence (Mo.) Schs., 1966-75; chpt. I reading specialist Thomas Hart Benton Elem. Sch., Independence, 1975-93; book reviewer Corpus Christi (Tex.) Caller Times, 1994—; children's libr. Corpus Christi Pub. Libr., 1995-97; dir. Johnson City (Tex.) Libr., 1997—; cons., presenter in field. Bd. dirs. Boys and Girls Club, Independence, 1990-93; coord. Independence Reading Fair, 1989-93; coord. books and tutoring Salvation Army, Kansas City, 1990-92. Mem. AAUW, Internat. Reading Assn. (People to People del. to USSR 1991, local v.p. 1990-91, pres. 1991-92), Internat. Platform Assn., Austin Writer's League, Archeol. Inst. Am., Tex. Libr. Assn., Earthwatch, Nature Conservancy, Sierra Club, Phi Kappa Phi, Pi Lambda Theta (pres. Beta Upsilon chpt. 1992-93). Avocations: native American history, rights and education, archeology, reading, travel, conservation. Home: PO Box 482 Johnson City TX 78636

POLLOCK, MICHAEL JEFFREY, periodical editor; b. Elizabeth, N.J., Sept. 8, 1954; s. Leonard D. and Sara (Weiner) P.; m. Karen Zevin, July 31, 1988; children: Jeremy, Leah. BA in English, Rutgers U., 1976, postgrad., 1992—. Reporter The Press of Atlantic City, N.J., 1979-85; assoc. editor editl. page The Press of Atlantic City, 1985-90, editor editl. page, 1990-91; pub. info. officer Casino Control Commn., Atlantic City, 1991-96; editor Gaming Industry Observer, Pleasantville, N.J., 1996—; adj. prof. Richard Stockton Coll., Pomona, N.J., 1993—. Author: Hostage to Fortune: Atlantic City and Casino Gambling, 1987. Chmn. Domestic Affairs Task Force Jewish Cmty. Rels. Coun. Atlantic and Cape May Counties, Bargaintown, N.J., 1993—; trustee Fedn. Jewish Agys. of Atlantic and Cape May Counties, 1995—. Three-time recipient Media award N.J. State Bar Assn., 1981-84; 5-time recipient Journalism award N.J. Press Assn., 1983-91; recipient Editl. Writing award Edn. Writers Assn., 1986. Home: 1 Merridith Ct Northfield NJ 08225-1500 Office: Abarta Metro Pub Washington Ave Pleasantville NJ 08232

POLLOCK, ROBERT ELWOOD, nuclear physicist; b. Regina, Sask., Can., Mar. 2, 1936; s. Elwood Thomas and Harriet Lillian (Rooney) P.; m. Jean Elizabeth Virtue, Sept. 12, 1959; children—Bryan Thomas, Heather Lynn, Jeffrey Parker, Jennifer Lee. B.Sc. (Hons.), U. Man., Can., 1957; M.A., Princeton U., 1959, Ph.D., 1963. Instr. Princeton U., 1961-63; Nat. Research Council Can. postdoctoral fellow Harwell, Eng., 1963-64; asst. prof. Princeton U., 1964-69, research physicist, 1969-70; asso. prof. Ind. U., 1970-73, prof., 1973-84, disting. prof., 1984—, dir. Cyclotron Facility, 1973-79, mem. Nuclear Sci. Adv. Com., 1977-80. Recipient Alexander von Humboldt Sr. U.S. Scientist award, 1985-88. Fellow Am. Phys. Soc.

(Bonner prize 1992). Home: 1261 Winfield Rd Bloomington IN 47401-6147 Office: Ind U Swain Hall Dept Physics Bloomington IN 47405

POLLOCK, ROY VAN HORN, pharmaceutical company animal health researcher; b. Detroit, Dec. 23, 1949; s. Alexander Samuel and Doris Louise (Van Horn) P.; m. Barbara Kathleen James, Aug. 22, 1970; children: Roy Alexander, Irene Eva, Sarah Helen. BA, Williams Coll., 1972; DVM, Cornell U., 1978, PhD, 1981. Asst. dean Coll. Vet. Medicine, Cornell U., Ithaca, N.Y., 1981-85, dir. med. informatics, 1985-89; dir. tech. svcs. SmithKline Beecham Animal Health, Exton, Pa., 1989-93; v.p. strategic product devel. SmithKline Beecham Animal Health, West Chester, Pa., 1993-94; v.p. companion animal divsn. Pfizer Animal Health, West Chester, Pa., 1995—; adj. prof. vet. pathobiology Purdue U., 1990—; cons. Impromed Computer Sys., Oshkosh, Wis., 1989-93; mem. adv. bd. Cornell Feline Health Ctr., 1990—, James A. Baker Inst. Animal Health, 1996—. Author: (with others) Provides Computer Aided Diagnosis, 1987; also articles; editor: Cornell Animal Health Newsletter, 1985-89. Cubmaster local chpt. Boy Scouts Am., Ithaca, 1988-89. Recipient Small Animal Rsch. award Ralston-Purina, 1981; Kellogg Nat. fellow, 1987-90. Mem. AVMA (student advisor 1987-89, Gaines award 1989), N.Y. Acad. Sci., Am. Animal Hosp. Assn. (Veterinarian of Yr. award 1987), Phi Beta Kappa, Phi Zeta. Avocations: photography, creative writing. Office: Pfizer Animal Health 812 Springdale Dr Exton PA 19341-2803

POLLOCK, SHELDON IVAN, language professional, educator; b. Cleve., Feb. 16, 1948; s. Abraham and Elsie (Russ) P.; m. Estera Milman, Dec. 21, 1968 (div. May 1985); children: Nira, Mica; m. Ute Gregorius, 1991. AB, Harvard U., 1971, AM, 1973, PhD, 1975. Instr. Harvard U., Cambridge, Mass., 1974-75; asst. prof. U. Iowa, Iowa City, 1975-79, assoc. prof., 1979-85, prof., 1985-89; George V. Bobrinskoy prof. Sanskrit and Indic Studies U. Chgo., 1989—, chmn. Dept. S. Asian Langs. and Civilizations, 1991—; vis. prof. Collège de France, Paris, 1991; prin. investigator NEH collaborative rsch. project Literay Cultures in History, 1995-98. Author: Aspects of Versification in Sanskrit Lyric Poetry, 1977, Ramayana of Valmiki, Vol. II, 1986, Vol. III, 1991; regional editor: Harper Collins World Reader; contbr. articles to profl. jours. Am. Inst. Indian Studies sr. and short-term fellow, 1979, 84, 87, 94; Maharaja of Cochin Meml. lectr., Sanskrit Coll., Tripunithura, Kerala, 1989. Mem. Am. Oriental Soc., Assn. Asian Studies, Social Sci. Rsch. Coun. (Joint Com. on South Asia 1990-96). Home: 5532 S South Shore Dr Chicago IL 60637-1967 Office: U Chgo Dept South Asian Langs 1130 E 59th St Chicago IL 60637-1539

POLLOCK, STEPHEN MICHAEL, industrial engineering educator, consultant; b. N.Y.C., Feb. 15, 1936; s. Meyer and Frances R. Pollock; m. Bettina Dorn, Nov. 22, 1962; children: Joshua, Aaron, Ethan. B in Engring. Physics, Cornell U., 1958; SM, MIT, 1960, PhD in Physics and Ops. Research, 1964. Mem. tech. staff Arthur D. Little Inc., Cambridge, Mass., 1964-65; asst. prof. Naval Postgrad. Sch., Monterey, Calif., 1965-68, assoc. prof., 1968-69; assoc. prof. U. Mich., Ann Arbor, 1969-73, prof., dept. indsl. and ops. engring., 1974—, chmn. dept., 1980-90; cons. to over 40 orgns. Area editor Ops. Rsch. Jour., 1977-82; sr. editor Inst. Indsl. Engrs. Trans., 1985-89, Army Sci. Bd., 1994—; contbr. more than 60 tech. papers to profl. jours. Fellow, Space Tech. Labs., 1960; sr. fellow NSF, 1975. Fellow AAAS; mem. Inst. Mgmt. Scis., Ops. Research Soc. Am. (pres. 1986-87). Home: 2694 Wayside Dr Ann Arbor MI 48103-2251 Office: U of Mich Dept Indsl Ops Engring Ann Arbor MI 48109-2117

POLLOCK, STEWART GLASSON, state supreme court justice; b. East Orange, N.J., Dec. 21, 1932. BA, Hamilton Coll., 1954, LLD (hon.), 1995; LLB, NYU, 1957; LLM, U. Va., 1988. Bar: N.J. 1958. Asst. U.S. atty. Newark, 1958-60; ptnr. Schenck, Price, Smith & King, Morristown, N.J., 1960-74, 76-78; commr. N.J. Dept. Pub. Utilities; counsel to gov. State of N.J., Trenton, 1978-79; assoc. justice N.J. Supreme Ct., Morristown, 1979—; mem. N.J. Commn. on Investigation, 1976-78; chmn. coordinating coun. on life-sustaining med. treatment decision making Nat. Ctr. for State Cts., 1994—; bd. dirs. Law Ctr. Found., Inst. of Jud. Adminstrn. Assoc. editor N.J. Law Jour.; contbr. articles to legal jours. Trustee Coll. Medicine and Dentistry, N.J., 1976. Mem. ABA (chmn. appellate judges conf. 1991-92), N.J. Bar Assn. (trustee 1973-78), Am. Judicature Soc. (dir. 1984-88), Morris County Bar Assn. (pres. 1973). Office: NJ Supreme Ct Morris County Courthouse Morristown NJ 07963-0900

POLLOCK, WILLIAM JOHN, secondary school administrator; b. N.Y.C., Nov. 25, 1943; s. Edward and Rose (Favero) P.; m. Jennie Ann Taccetta, Jan. 28, 1967; children: John-Paul, Elizabeth. BSEd, CCNY, 1967; MSEd, Trenton State Coll., 1985; EdD, Nova U., 1993; postgrad., Harvard Graduate Sch., 1992. Tchr. N.Y.C. Pub. Schs., 1967-69; tchr. electronics Howell High Sch., Farmingdale, N.J., 1970-85, dept. supr., 1985-89; vice-prin. Monmouth County Vocat. Schs., Middletown, N.J., 1989-90; prin. High Tech. High Sch., Brookdale Community Coll. Campus, Lincroft, N.J., 1990—; pres. suprs.' assn. Freehold (N.J.) Regional High Sch. Dist., 1988-89; pres. exec. bd. Region V Libr. Coop., Freehold, 1989-92. Asst. scout master Jackson (N.J.) area Boy Scouts Am., 1987-92; pres. exec. bd. St. Mary Acad., Lakewood, N.J., 1987-89; mem. Ocean County Agrl. Devel. Bd., Toms River, N.J., 1989—. 1st lt. U.S. Army, 1969-70, Vietnam. Decorated Bronze Star; recipient Geraldine R. Dodge Found. "Dodge Fellow principal award, 1993", N.J.Star Sch.award N.J. State Dept. Edn., 1995, Best Practices award N.J. State Dept. Edn., 1995; named N.J. Prin. of Yr. Met/Life, NAASP. Mem. ASCD, N.J. ASCD (Outstanding Curriculum award 1995), Nat. Assn. Secondary Sch. Prins., Internat. Tech. Edn. Assn., Am. Vocat. Edn. Assn., Prins. and Suprs. Assn., Garden State Prin.'s Ctr. (charter mem.), KC. Avocations: farming, growing Christmas trees, photography, pottery, solar energy. Office: High Tech High Sch PO Box 119 Lincroft NJ 07738-0119

POLLOCK, WILSON F., architectural firm executive. BArch, Pa. State U.; MS in Architecture, Columbia U. Cert. Nat. Coun. Archtl. Registration Bds.; registered architect, 15 states. Formerly with Sert, Jackson Assocs., Cambridge, Mass., Cambridge Seven Assocs., Eshback Pullinger, Phila., Emo Goldfinger, London; founder, pres. ADD Inc., Cambridge; lectr. in field. Prin. works include One Federal Street Renovation, Boston, Hewlett Packard's Med. Products Group Expansion, Andover, Mass., 404 Wyman Street, Waltham, Mass. Bd. trustees Boston Found. for Architects; bd. dirs. Newton Community Devel. Found., Jackson Homestead Mus.; frequent sem. leader Build Boston. Recipient Alumni Achievement award Pa. State U., 1991. Fellow AIA; mem. I.D.R.C., Nat. Assn. Indsl. and Office Parks (assoc.), Boston Soc. Architects (past pres.), Urban Land Inst. Office: ADD Inc 80 Prospect St Cambridge MA 02139-2503*

POLLOCK-O'BRIEN, LOUISE MARY, public relations executive; b. Tarentum, Pa., Mar. 14, 1948; d. Louis P. and Amelia M. (Ballay) Pollock; m. Vincent Miles O'Brien. BS, Ind. U. of Pa., 1970. Tchr. Archbishop Wood High Sch., Warminster, Pa., 1970-75; spokesperson, publicist Calif. Olive Industry, Fresno, 1976-78; account exec. Ketchum Pub. Rels., N.Y.C., 1979-81, account supr., 1982-83, v.p., 1984, v.p., group mgr., 1985-88, sr. v.p., group mgr., 1988-89, assoc. dir., dir. food mktg., sr. v.p., 1990-91; chmn. Aronow & Pollock Communications, Inc., N.Y.C., 1991—; mem. pub. relations adv. com. Mayor's Vol. Action Com., N.Y.C., 1986; mem. food service adv. bd. L.I. City Coll., Bklyn., 1987-88. V.p., fundraiser West 76th St. Block Assn., N.Y.C., 1982. Mem. Internat. Foodservice Editorial Council (v.p., bd. dirs. 1984-85). Avocations: watercolor painting, skiing. Office: Aronow & Pollock Communications Inc 524 Broadway New York NY 10012-4408

POLO, RICHARD JOSEPH, engineering executive; b. Barranquilla, Colombia, Oct. 14, 1936; s. Pedro Pastor and Clotilde (Verano) P.; m. Ana Isabel Cepeda, Feb. 1, 1958; children: Richard J. Jr., James Alan. BCE, NYU, 1957; MS in Structural Engring., Iowa State U., 1963, PhD in Structural and Nuclear Engring., 1971; disting. grad., Command and Gen. Staff Coll., Ft. Leavenworth, Kans., 1970; grad., Inter-Am. Def. Coll., Ft. McNair, Washington, 1977; MBA, Marymount U., 1986. Registered profl. engr., Md., Iowa, Fla., Pa., Conn., N.Y. Commd. 2d lt. U.S. Army, 1957, advanced through grades to col., 1979, various positions, 1957-79; asst. dir. civil works Pacific U.S. Army Office Chief of Engrs., 1979-80; corps engr., engr. brigade comdr. U.S. Army, Ludwigsburg, Fed. Republic Germany, 1980-83; dep. study dir. U.S. Army Office Chief of Staff, Washington, 1984-85; ret. U.S. Army, 1985; v.p. constrn. inspection Kidde Cons. Inc., Balt., 1985, sr. v.p. constrn. inspection, 1986, exec. v.p., 1986-89, corp. sec., 1988-89, also bd. dirs.; v.p. Fla. region CRSS, Miami, 1989-90; CEO, program dir. CRSS/WRJ joint venture, 1989-90; assoc. v.p., dep. divsn. dir. fed. programs Greiner, Inc., Miami, 1991-92; dir. engring. & project ops. CKC (OSC), Miami, 1993-94; dir. L.Am. ops., dir. engring. devel. GeoSyntec Cons., Boca Raton, 1994-96; dir. Miami ops. ICF Kaiser Engrs., Inc., 1996—; pres. Amerint, Miami, 1994—, Am. Enterprises Internat., Inc., Polo Mortgage-Plus, Miami, 1993—; bd. dirs. KCI Holdings, 1988-90. Contbr. articles on mil. and structural engring. to profl. jours. Inventor arcuate space frame. Cmty. comdr. and sr. U.S. rep. Ludwigsburg Mil. Cmty., 1980-83. Decorated Legion of Merit with bronze oak leaf cluster, Bronze Star, others; Fed. Exec. fellow Brookings Institution, 1983-84. Fellow Soc. Am. Mil. Engrs. (bd. dirs. El Paso chpt. 1967-68, pres. Stutttgart chpt. 1980-82); mem. ASCE, NSPE, Md. Soc. Profl. Engrs., Va. Soc. Profl. Engrs. (dir. no. Va. chpt. 1985-89, pres. elect 1988-89), Assn. U.S. Army (pres. Ludwigsburg chpt. 1980-83), Fla. Engring. Soc., Army-Navy Club Coral Gables (dir. 1994—, sec. 1995-96, v.p. 1996—), Greater Miami C. of C. (trustee 1989-92, 97—), Country Club Coral Gables, Rotary, Sigma Xi, Phi Kappa Phi, Tau Beta Pi, Chi Epsilon, Psi Upsilon (pres. Delta chpt. 1956-57). Republican. Roman Catholic. Avocations: model airplanes, racquetball. Home and Office: Amerint/Am Enterprises Int 430 Sunset Rd Miami FL 33143-6339 Office: ICF Kaiser Engrs Inc 3750 NW 87th Ave Miami FL 33178-2421

POLOMÉ, EDGAR CHARLES, foreign language and linguistics educator; b. Brussels, Belgium, July 31, 1920; came to U.S., 1961, naturalized, 1966; s. Marcel Félicien and Berthe (Henry) P.; m. Julia Joséphine Schwindt, June 22, 1944 (dec. May 1975); children: Monique Laure (Mrs. John Ellsworth), André Robert; m. Barbara Baker Harris, July 11, 1980 (div. Jan. 1991); m. Sharon Looper Rankin, Feb. 8, 1991. BA, U. Libre, Brussels, 1941; PhD, Université Libre de Bruxelles, 1949; MA, Cath. U. Louvain, 1943. Prof. Germanic lang. Athénée, 1942-56; prof. Dutch Belgian Nat. Broadcasting Corp., Brussels, 1954-56; prof. linguistics U. Belgian Congo (now Zaire), 1956-61; prof. Germanic, Oriental, African langs. and lits. U. Tex., Austin, 1961—, dir. Ctr. for Asian Studies, 1962-72, Christie and Stanley Adams Jr. Centennial prof. liberal arts, 1984—; chmn. dept. U. Tex., 1969-76. Author: Swahili Language Handbook, 1967, Language in Tanzania, 1980, Language, Society and Paleoculture: Essays, 1982, Essays on Germanic Religion, 1989; editor: Old Norse Literature and Mythology, 1969, The Indo-Europeans in the 4th and 3rd Millennia, 1982, Guide to Language Change, 1990, Reconstructing Languages and Cultures, 1992, Indo European Religion After Dumezil, 1995; co-editor The Jour. Indo-European Studies, 1973—, mng. editor, 1987—; co-editor: The Mankind Quar., 1980—. Served with Belgian Aux. Aerodrome Police, 1945. Fulbright prof. U. Kiel, 1968; Ford Found. team dir. Tanzania survey, 1969-70. Mem. MLA, Linguistics Soc. Am., Am. Oriental Soc., Am. Anthrop. Assn., Philological Assn. (London), Indogermanische Assn., Soc. Linguistica Europea, Soc. Linguistique Paris, Am. Inst. Indian Studies (chmn. lang. com. 1972-78). Home: 2701 Rock Terrace Dr Austin TX 78704-3843 Office: U Tex Dept Germanic Langs EPS 3 102 Austin TX 78712 *Having taught and done research on four continents—Europe, Africa, America and Asia—I feel gratitude that my experience has enabled me to discover the richness of man's intellectual and artistic heritage. It has especially allowed better appreciation of the perennial aesthetic, ethical and social values that make us all part of the great human brotherhood, whatever our language, creed or ethnic background.*

POLON, IRA H., lawyer; b. N.Y.C., Mar. 9, 1943. BA, Lehigh U., 1965; LLB, Columbia U., 1968. Bar: N.Y. 1968, D.C. 1971, U.S. Ct. Appeals (D.C. cir.) 1972. Atty. Dickstein Shapiro Morin and Oshinsky LLP, Washington. Mem. ABA (mem. corporation, banking and bus. law sect.), D.C. Bar, N.Y. State Bar Assn., Bar Assn. D.C. Office: Dickstein Shapiro Morin & Oshinsky LLP 2101 L St NW Washington DC 20037-1526

POLONIS, DOUGLAS HUGH, engineering educator; b. North Vancouver, B.C., Can., Sept. 2, 1928; came to U.S., 1955, naturalized, 1963; s. William and Ada (Burrows) P.; m. Vera Christine Brown, Jan. 30, 1953; children: Steven Philip, Malcolm Eric, Douglas Hugh, Christine Virginia. B.A.Sc., U. B.C., 1951, Ph.D., 1955, M.A.Sc., U. Toronto, 1953. Metall. engr. Steel Co. Can., Hamilton, Ont., 1951-52; mem. faculty U. Wash., Seattle, 1955—; prof. metall. engring., materials sci. & engring. U. Wash., 1962-95, chmn. dept. mining, metall. and ceramic engring., 1969-71, 73-82, prof. emeritus, 1995—; metall. cons., 1955—. Contbr. articles to profl. jours. Fellow Am. Soc. Metals; mem. AIME, Sigma Xi, Tau Beta Pi, Alpha Sigma Mu, Sigma Phi Delta. Home: 19227 46th Ave NE Lake Forest Park WA 98155-2909

POLONSKY, ARTHUR, artist, educator; b. Lynn, Mass., June 6, 1925; s. Benjamin and Celia (Hurwitz) P.; children: Eli, D.L., Gabriel. Diploma with highest honors, Sch. of Mus. Fine Arts, Boston, 1948. Instr. painting dept. Sch. Mus. Fine Arts, Boston, 1950-60; asst. prof. dept. fine arts Brandeis U., 1954-65; assoc. prof. Boston U., 1965-90, prof. emeritus, 1990—. One-man shows include Boris Mirski Gallery, Boston, 1950, 54, 56, 64, Boston Pub. Libr., 1969, 90, 93, 96, Durlacher Gallery, N.Y.C., 1965, Mickelson Gallery, Washington, 1966, 74, Boston Ctr. for Arts, 1983, Starr Gallery, Boston, 1987, Fitchburg Art Mus., 1990; exhibited in group shows including Met. Mus., N.Y.C., 1950, Stedelijk Mus., Amsterdam, The Netherlands, 1950, Carnegie Internat. Expn., 1951, Inst. Contemporary Art, Boston, 1960, Mus. Fine Arts, Boston, 1976, Boston Arts Festival, 1985, Expressionism in Boston, Decordova Mus., Lincoln, Mass., 1986, Decordova Mus., 1987, Palais Univ. de Strasbourg, France, 1992, Boston's Honored Artists, Danforth Mus., Framingham, Mass., 1995; represented in permanent collections Mus. Fine Arts, Boston, Fogg Mus., Harvard U., Addison Gallery of Am. Art, Andover, Mass., Stedelijk Mus., Walker Art Ctr., Mpls. Recipient Louis Comfort Tiffany award for painting, 1951, 1st prize Boston Arts Festival, 1954; European travelling fellow Sch. Mus. Fine Art, Boston, 1948-50. Mem. AAUP, Artists Equity Assn., Inc. (founding, former dir. New Eng. chpt.). Address: 364 Cabot St Newtonville MA 02160-2252

POLOZOLA, FRANK JOSEPH, federal judge; b. Baton Rouge, Jan. 15, 1942; s. Steve A. Sr. and Caroline C. (Lucito) P.; m. Linda Kay White, June 9, 1962; children: Gregory Dean, Sheri Elizabeth, Gordon Damian. Student bus. adminstrn., La. State U., 1959-62, JD, 1965. Bar: La. 1965. Law clk. to U.S. Dist. Ct. Judge E. Gordon West, 1965-66; assoc. Seale, Smith & Phelps, Baton Rouge, 1966-68, ptnr., 1968-73; part-time magistrate U.S. Dist. Ct. (mid. dist.) La., Baton Rouge, 1972-73, magistrate, 1973-80, judge, 1980—; adj. prof. Law Ctr., La. State U., 1977—. Bd. dirs. Cath. High Sch. Mem. FBA, La. Bar Assn., Baton Rouge Bar Assn., Fed. Judges Assn., 5th Cir. Dist. Judges Assn., La. State U. L Club, KC, Omicron Delta Kappa. Roman Catholic. Office: US Dist Ct Russell B Long Fed Bldg & US Courthouse 777 Florida St Ste 313 Baton Rouge LA 70801-1717*

POLSELLI, LINDA MARIE, elementary education educator; b. Providence, R.I., June 13, 1958; d. Anthony Natale and Helen Marie (Magnan) P. BS, R.I. Coll., 1982; MEd, Providence Coll., 1986. Spl. edn. educator Wyman Elem., Warwick, R.I., 1986-91; elem. edn. educator Holliman Elem., Warwick, 1991—; computer software com. Warwick Sch. Dept., mem. math./curriculum revisions com., 1992, report card com., 1995—, tech. adv. bd., 1996—. Adminstr. Warwick Citizens Vol. Assn., Warwick Police Dept., 1983—. Mem. ASCD, Nat. Coun. Tchrs. English, Nat. Coun. Tchrs. Math., Internat. Reading Assn., R.I. Math. Tchrs. Assn., Tchrs. Applying Whole Lang. Roman Catholic. Avocations: travel, guitarist. Home: 128 Cove Ave Warwick RI 02886-5402

POLSKY, DONALD PERRY, architect; b. Milw., Sept. 30, 1928; s. Lew and Dorothy (Geisenfeld) P.; m. Corinne Shirley Neer, Aug. 25, 1957; children: Jeffrey David, Debra Lynn. BArch, U. Nebr., Lincoln, 1951; postgrad., U. So. Calif., 1956, U. Calif., Los Angeles, 1957, U. Nebr., Omaha, 1964, U. Ill., 1965. Project architect Richard Neutra, Architect, Los Angeles, 1953-56, Daniel Dworsky, Architect, Los Angeles, 1956; prin. Polsky, AIA & Assocs., Los Angeles, 1956-62, Omaha, 1964—; dir. dept. architecture MCA, Inc., Universal City, Calif., 1962-64. Prin. works include Mills residence, 1958, apt. bldgs., 1960, Polsky residence, 1961, Milder residence, 1965. Chmn. Design Control 1480 Study Mayor's Riverfront Devel., Omaha, 1969, 71; pres. Swanson Sch. Community Club, Omaha, 1972; mem. Mayor's Adv. Panel Design Services, Omaha, 1974; vice chmn. Omaha Zoning Bd. Appeals, 1976. Recipient archtl. awards Canyon Crier Newspaper, Los Angeles, 1960, House and Home Mag., Santa Barbara, Calif., 1960. Mem. AIA (pres. Omaha chpt. 1968, numerous awards 1956-95), Nebr. Soc. Architects (pres. 1975, award 1965, 87). Office: Donald P Polsky AIA & Assocs 8723 Oak St Omaha NE 68124-3051

POLSKY, MICHAEL PETER, mechanical engineer; b. Kiev, Ukraine, Aug. 5, 1949; s. Peter and Basheva P.; m. Maya, June 28, 1975; children: Alan, Gabriel. BSME, Kiev Poly. Inst., 1973; MBA, U. Chgo., 1987. Registered profl. engr., Ill., Mich. Sr. devel. engr. Indsl. Power Corp., Kiev, Ukraine, 1973-76; mech. engr. Bechtel Power Corp., Ann Arbor, Mich., 1976-78; sr. application engr. Brown Boveri Corp., St. Cloud, Minn., 1978-80; product mgr. congeneration Fluor/Daniel, Chgo., 1980-85; pres. Indeck Energy Svcs., Wheeling, Ill., 1985-90, Polsky Energy Corp., Northbrook, Ill., 1990—; bd. dirs. Ind. Power Producers of N.Y., Albany, 1988-89. Author: Public Utilities Fortnightly, 1985, Power, 1984, 83, Hydrocarbon Processing, 1981, 82; author: (book chpt.) Handbook of Power Plant Engineering, 1991. Mem. ASME, Soc. Energy Engrs. Office: Polsky Energy Corp 650 Dundee Rd Ste 150 Northbrook IL 60062-2753

POLSTON, BARBARA, principal, educational psychologist; b. Litchfield, Ill., Oct. 9, 1943; d. Wilbur Lee and Frances (Leitschuh) P.; children: Charles, Beth, Ann. B of Music Edn., Webster Coll., 1965; MA, St. Louis U., 1985. Cert. elem. tchr., cert. prin., Mo., Wash. Prin. Holy Rosary, Archdiocese of Seattle, Edmonds, Wash., Archdiocese St. Louis, Lady of the Presentation, St. Martin de Porres, Corpus Christi; archdiocesan coord. alternative sch. practices, sch. calendars, multi media and tech., accelerative learning interventions. Mem. Mo. Lead Program, Nat. Yr. Round Edn., Danforth Found. Mem. ASCD, NCEA, Prins. Acad. Mo., Nat. Cath. Prins. Acad., Inst. Responsive Edn., Consortium Responsive Schs.

POLSTON, MARK FRANKLIN, minister; b. Indpls., Feb. 9, 1960; s. Albert Franklin and Mildred (Wiggington) P.; m. Lisa Kaye Polston, July 21, 1984; 1 child, Jordan Franklin. AS, Somerset (Ky.) C. C., 1981; BS, Campbellsville Coll., 1984; JD, Ind. Sch. Law, 1995. Real estate agt. Homestead Real Estate, Somerset, 1978-89; pastor Trace Fork Separate Bapt. Ch., Liberty, Ky., 1979-81, Calvary Separate Bapt. Ch., Nancy, Ky., 1980-84, Harmony Separate Bapt. Ch., Jacksonville, Fla., 1984-85, Fairview Separate Bapt. Ch., Russell Springs, Ky., 1985-89, Calvary Separate Bapt. Ch., Nancy, Ky., 1989-91, Edinburgh (Ind.) Separate Bapt. Ch., 1992—; sales rep. Sentry Ins., Somerset, 1989-91; dep. atty. gen. Ind. Atty. Gen., Indpls., 1992—; clk. Gen. Assn. Separate Bapt., 1988—; bd. dirs. Separate Bapt. Missions., Inc., 1988-92; adj. prof. Ind. Vocat. Tech. Coll., Indpls., 1993—. Home: 787 Kitchen Rd Mooresville IN 46158-8057 Office: Ind Atty Gen 402 W Washington St Indianapolis IN 46204-2739 also: Edinburgh Separate Bapt Ch 1010 S Main St Edinburgh IN 46124-1377

POLSTRA, LARRY JOHN, lawyer; b. Lafayette, Ind., June 28, 1945; s. John Edward and Elizabeth (Vandergraff) P.; m. Joan Marie Blair Rozier, Sept. 2, 1972 (dec.); 1 stepchild, Shawn M. Rozier; m. Barbara Dominy, Mar. 18, 1988; stepchildren: Tobi Shawn Porter, Teri Lane Kelly. BS in Bus. Mgmt., Bob Jones U., 1968; JD, Atlanta Law Sch., 1976, LLM, 1977. Bar: Ga. 1976, U.S. Dist. Ct. (no. dist.) Ga. 1976, U.S. Ct. Appeals (11th cir.) 1990, U.S. Supreme Ct. 1994. Mktg. dir. N.Am. Security, Atlanta, 1972-73; acctg. supr. Allstate Ins. Co., Atlanta, 1973-76; sole practice Atlanta, 1976-77; ptnr. Law Smith (formerly Smith & Polstra), Atlanta, 1977-94, of counsel, 1995; of counsel England & McKnight, 1996—, Hays & Maysilles, P.C., 1997—; arbitrator Fulton County Superior Ct., Atlanta, 1986. Served to 1st lt. USMC, 1968-71, Vietnam. Mem. ATLA, Atlanta Bar Assn., Ga. Assn. Trial Lawyers, Ga. Assn. Criminal Def. Lawyers, Marine Corps Assn. Ga. Lawyers. Avocation: golf. Home: 2081 Hampton Tr Conyers GA 30208

POLUNIN, NICHOLAS, environmentalist, author, editor; b. Checkendon, Oxfordshire, Eng.; s. Vladimir and Elizabeth Violet (Hart) P.; m. Helen Lovat Fraser, 1939 (dec.); 1 child, Michael; m. Helen Eugenie Campbell, Jan. 3, 1948; children: April Xenia, Nicholas V. C., Douglas H. H. Open scholar, Christ Ch., 1928-32; BA (1st class honors), U. Oxford, 1932, MA, 1935, DPhil, 1935, DSc, 1942; MS, Yale U., 1934. Participant or leader numerous sci. expdns., 1930-65, primarily in arctic regions, including Spitsbergen, Greenland, Alaska, Can., East and West Arctic, North Pole; curator, tutor, demonstrator, lectr. various instns., especially Oxford U., 1933-47; vis. prof. botany McGill U., 1946-47, Macdonald prof. botany, 1947-52; Guggenheim fellow, rsch. assoc. Harvard U., 1950-53; earlier fgn. research asso., USAF botanical Ice-island research project dir., lectr. plant sci. Yale, also biology Brandeis U., 1953-55; prof. plant ecology and taxonomy, head dept. botany, dir. U. Herbarium and Botanic Garden, Baghdad, Iraq, 1955-58; guest prof. U. Geneva, 1959-61, 75-76; adviser establishment, planner permanent campus, founding prof. botany, dean faculty sci. U. Ife, Nigeria, 1962-66; founding editor Plant Sci. Monographs and World Crops Books, 1954-78, Biol. Conservation, 1967-74, Environ. Pollution, 1969, Environ. Conservation, 1974-95; chmn. internat. steering com., organizer, editor procs. Internat. Conf. on Environ. Future, Finland, 1971; chmn. internat. steering com., sec. gen., editor procs. 2d Internat. Conf. on Environ. Future, Reykjavik, Iceland, 1977, 3d Internat. Conf. on Environ. Future, Edinburgh, Scotland, 1987; sec.-gen., joint editor procs. 4th Internat. Conf. Environ. Future, Budapest, Hungary, 1990; pres., CEO Found. for Environ. Conservation, 1975—; participant Internat. Bot. Congresses, Stockholm, 1950, Paris, 1954, Edinburgh, 1964, Seattle, 1969, Leningrad, 1975, Sydney, 1981; initiator (pres., CEO) World Council For The Biosphere, 1984—. Author: Russian Waters, 1931, The Isle of Auks, 1932, Botany of the Canadian Eastern Arctic, 3 vols., 1940-48, Arctic Unfolding, 1949, Circumpolar Arctic Flora, 1959, Introduction to Plant Geography and Some Related Sciences, 1960 (various fgn. edits.), Eléments de Géographie Botanique, 1967; editor: The Environmental Future, 1972, Environmental Monographs and Symposia (series), 1979-88, Growth Without Ecodisasters?, 1980, Ecosystem Theory and Application, 1986, (with Sir John Burnett) Maintenance of the Biosphere, 1990, Surviving With The Biosphere, 1993; (with Mohammad Nazim) Environmental Challenges I: From Stockholm to Rio and Beyond, 1993, II: Population and Global Security, 1994, 97; founding chmn. editl. bd. Cambridge Studies in Environ. Policy, 1984—; contbr. articles to various jours. Decorated comdr. of Order Brit. Empire, 1975; recipient undergrad., grad. student scholarships, fellowships, rsch. associateships Yale U., 1933-34, Harvard U., 1936-37, 50-53; Rolleston Meml. prize, 1938; D.S.I.R. spl. investigator, 1938; Leverhulme Rsch. award, 1941; from sr. scholar to sr. rsch. fellow New Coll., Oxford, 1934-47; Guggenheim fellow, 1950-52; recipient Ford Found. award Scandinavia, USSR, 1966-67, Can. Marie-Victorin medal, 1957, Indian Ramdeo medal, 1986, Internat. Sasakawa Environ. prize, 1987, USSR Vernadsky commemoration, 1988, Chinese Academia Sinica medal, 1988, Vernadsky medal USSR Acad. Scis., 1988, 89, Founder's (Zéchenyi) medal Hungarian Acad. Scis., 1990; named to Netherlands Order of the Golden Ark, 1990 (officer), UN Environ. Programme Global 500 Roll of Honour, 1991. Fellow AAAS, Royal Geog. Soc. (life), Royal Hort. Soc. (life), Linnean Soc. London (life), Arctic Inst. N.Am. (life), INSONA (v.p.), NECA (India), Pierson Coll., Yale U. (assoc.); mem. Internat. Soc. Environ. Edn. (life), Internat. Acad. Environment Geneva (conseil de fondation 1992-96), Torrey Bot. Club (life), Bot. Soc. Am. (life), N.Am. Assn. Environ. Edn. (life), Asian Soc. Environ. Protection (life), Sigma Xi, INTECOL, various fgn. and nat. profl. and sci. socs., Harvard Club (N.Y.C.) (life), Field Naturalists' Club (Ottawa) (life), Reform (London) (life), Oxford U. Exploration Club (v.p.). Achievements include confirming existence of Spicer Islands in Foxe Basin and making world's last major land discovery to their East, Can. Arctic, 1946; past rsch. plant life and ecology of arctic, subarctic, and high-altitude regions; present occupation environ. conservation at the global level; initiator of ann. worldwide Biosphere Day, 1991, plans and seeking funds for major Biosphere Fund and Prizes, 1992, Biosphere Clubs, 1993, and plans for planetary econetwork of environmental/conservational watchdogs collated by revived World Coun. for the Biosphere; initiating and editing World Who is Who and Does What in Environment and Conservation, 1st edit. pub. 1997. Address: Found Environ Conservation, 7 Chemin Taverney, 1218 Grand-Saconnex Geneva Switzerland

POLUNSKY, BOB A., movie critic, talk show host; b. San Antonio, Dec. 3, 1931; s. Maurice Bernard and Ethel (Mazur) P.; m. Paulina Norman, June 12, 1960; children: Julianne, Laurianne, Adrianne. BFA, U. Tex., 1953. Traffic mgr. KABC Radio, San Antonio, 1953-55; program dir. KFJZ-TV, Fort Worth, Tex., 1955-57; Yellow Pages sales S.W. Bell Telephone, 1957-60;

sales svc. mgr. KONO/KSAT, San Antonio, 1960-68; sales mgr. KENS-TV, San Antonio, 1968-85; movie critic San Antonio Express-News, 1968-96, KENS-TV and WDAI RAdio, San Antonio, 1968—, Primetime News, 1996—. With U.S. Army, 1950-57. Home: 619 Briar Oak St San Antonio TX 78216-3006 Office: Primetime News Syndicate 8603 Botts St San Antonio TX 78217-6301

POLZIN, JOHN THEODORE, lawyer; b. Rock Island, Ill., Dec. 23, 1919; s. Max August and Charlotte Barbara (Trenkenschuh) P.; m. Helen Louise Hosford, Nov. 27, 1969. A.B., U. Ill., 1941, J.D., 1943. Bar: Ill. 1943. Sole practice, Galva, Ill., 1946-55, Chgo., 1975—; city atty., Galva, 1950-54; assoc. Langner, Parry, Card & Langner, Chgo., 1955-75; lectr. Ill. Inst. for Continuing Legal Edn., 1978. Served to lt. USNR, 1943-46. Mem. ABA, Ill. State Bar Assn. (chmn. patent, trademark and copyright law sect. 1981-82), Patent Law Assn. Chgo. (chmn. fgn. trademark com. 1972, 74). Republican. Home and Office: 1503 Oak Ave Evanston IL 60201-4260

POMBO, RICHARD, congressman, rancher, farmer; b. Tracy, Calif., 1961; m. Annette, 1983; children: Richard Jr., Rena, Rachael. Student, Calif. State U., Pomona, 1981-83. Councilman City of Tracy, 1991-92; mayor pro-tem Tracy City Coun., 1992; mem. 103rd-105th Congresses from 11th Calif. dist., 1993—, chmn. agrl. com., subcom. on livestock, dairy and poultry; mem. Agrl. Com., Resources Com.; chmn. Pvt. Property Rights Task Force, 1993-94, Endangered Species Act Task Force, 1995-96; co-chmn. Spkr.'s Environ. Task Force, 1996. Co-founder San Joaquin County Citizen's Land Alliance, Calif., 1986—; active San Joaquin County Econ. Devel. Assn., Tracy Bus. Improvement Dist., City Coun. (vice chmn. Cmty. Devel. Agy., Cmty. Parks Com., and Waste Mgmt. Com.), San Joaquin County Rep. Ctrl. Com. Mem. Rotary Club. Roman Catholic. Office: US Ho of Reps 1519 Longworth HOB Washington DC 20515-0511

POMERANTZ, CHARLOTTE, writer; b. Bklyn., July 24, 1930; d. Abraham L. and Phyllis (Cohen) P.; m. Carl Marzani, Nov. 12, 1966; children: Gabrielle Rose, Daniel Avram. B.A., Sarah Lawrence Coll., 1953. Children's books include The Bear Who Couldn't Sleep, 1965, The Moon Pony, 1967, Ask the Windy Sea, 1968, Why You Look Like You Whereas I Look Like Me, 1968, The Day They Parachuted Cats on Borneo, 1971 (chosen for Internat. Year of the Child 1977-78), The Princess and the Admiral, 1974 (Jane Addams Children's Book award), The Piggy in the Puddle, 1974 (Featured on Reading Rainbow in Claymation, 1992, NYT Outstanding Picture Book of the Year award 1974), The Ballad of the Long Tailed Rat, 1975, Detective Poufy's First Case, 1976, The Mango Tooth, 1977 (Jr. Literary Guild Selection), The Downtown Fairy Godmother, 1978, The Tamarindo Puppy and Other Poems, 1980 (an ALA Notable Book), Noah's and Namah's Ark, 1980, If I Had a Paka, 1982 (Jane Addams Honor award 1983), Buffy and Albert, 1982, Posy, 1983 (1984 Christopher award), Whiff, Sniff, Nibble and Chew, 1984, Where's the Bear?, 1984, The Half-Birthday Party (Jr. Literary Guild Selection), 1984, All Asleep, 1984, One Duck, Another Duck, 1984, How Many Trucks Can a Tow Truck Tow? (Children's Book of the Year Libr. of Congress 1991) 1987, Timothy Tall Feather, 1987, The Chalk Doll (Top 10 Picture Books of 1989 Boston Globe, Parents Choice award, 1990) 1989, Flap Your Wings and Try, 1989, Serena Katz, 1992, The Outside Dog (One of 100 Books Recommended by the N.Y. Pub. Libr., 1993, ALA Notable) 1993, Halfway to Your House, 1993, Here Come Henny, 1994, Mangaboom, 1997; co-author, lyricist play Eureka!, 1997; author radio play Whiff Sniff Nibble and Chew, 1997; contbr. stories to mags.; spl. editorial asst.: Einstein on Peace, 1960; editor: A Quarter Century of Un-Americana, 1963. Address: 260 W 21st St New York NY 10011

POMERANTZ, JAMES ROBERT, psychology educator, academic admininstrator; b. N.Y.C., Aug. 21, 1946; s. Mihiel Charles and Elizabeth (Solheim) P.; divorced; children: Andrew Emil, William James. BA, U. Mich., 1968; PhD, Yale U., 1974. Prize teaching fellow Yale U., New Haven, 1973-74; asst. prof. psychology Johns Hopkins U., Balt., 1974-77; assoc. prof. SUNY, Buffalo, 1977-83, prof., 1983-88, chmn. dept. psychology, 1986-88, assoc. dean, 1983-86; dean social scis., Elma W. Schneider prof. psychology Rice U., Houston, 1988-95; provost, prof. cognitive and linguistic scis. Brown U., Providence, 1995—; adj. prof. Baylor Coll. Medicine, 1992—. Editor: Perceptual Organization, 1981, The Perception of Structure, 1991. Fellow APA, Am. Psychol. Soc.; mem. Psychonomic Soc. Office: Brown U Provosts Office Box 1892 Providence RI 02912

POMERANTZ, JOHN J., manufacturing executive; b. N.Y.C., July 4, 1933; s. Fred P. and Greta (Grainsky) P.; m. Laura H. Herman; children: Andrea, Susan, Marnie. BS in Econs., U. Pa., 1955. With Leslie Fay Cos., Inc., N.Y.C., 1955—, exec. v.p., 1968-71, pres., 1971-87, chmn., chief exec. officer, 1987—; bd. trustees Fashion Inst. Tech., pres. ednl. found. F.I.T. Bd. dirs. Am. Com. for Shenkar Coll. Textile Tech. and Fashion in Israel, Inc.; founder Albert Einstein Coll. Medicine, N.Y.C., Nat. Jewish Hosp. and Research Ctr., Denver, Israel Bonds Century Club; fundraising com. Am. Cancer Soc.; past chmn. Greater N.Y. Council Boy Scouts Am. Receipient award of Merit, Jack Martin Fund, Champion of Youth award Internat. Officers of B'nai B'rith, Humanitarian award Albert Einstein Coll. Medicine. Clubs: Quaker Ridge (Scarsdale, N.Y.); Palm Beach (Fla.) Country. Office: Leslie Fay Cos 1412 Broadway New York NY 10018-3306

POMERANTZ, MARTIN, chemistry educator, researcher; b. N.Y.C., May 3, 1939; s. Harry and Pauline (Sietz) P.; m. Maxine Miller, June 4, 1961; children: Lee Allan, Wendy Jane, Heidi Lauren. B.S., CCNY, 1959; M.S., Yale U., 1961, Ph.D., 1964. NSF postdoctoral fellow U. Wis.-Madison, 1963-64; asst. prof. Case Western Res. U., Cleve., 1964-69; assoc. prof. chemistry Yeshiva U., N.Y.C., 1969-74; prof. Yeshiva U., 1974-76, chmn. dept., 1971-72, 73-76; prof. chemistry U. Tex.-Arlington, 1976—; co-dir. Ctr. for Advanced Polymer Rsch., 1988-91, dir. Ctr. for Advanced Polymer Rsch., 1991—; vis. assoc. prof. U. Wis.-Madison, 1972; vis. prof. Columbia U., N.Y.C., 1970-75, Ben Gurion U. of the Negev, Beer Sheva, Israel, summers 1981, 85. Contbr. articles to sci. jours. Fellow Alfred P. Sloan Found., 1971-76, NSF and Sterling, 1962-63, Leeds and Northrup Found., 1960-62, Woodrow Wilson fellow, 1959-60; grantee NSF, Robert A. Welch Found., Def. Adv. Rsch. Projects Agy., Air Force Office Sci. Rsch., Dept. Energy, Petroleum Rsch. Fund, Tex. Advanced Tech. program, Tex. Advanced Rsch. program, Disting. Record of Rsch. award U. Tex., Arlington, also others. Mem. Am. Chem. Soc. (Wilfred T. Doherty award Dallas-Fort Worth sect. 1997), Royal Soc. Chemistry, Phi Beta Kappa, Sigma Xi. Home: 5521 Williamstown Rd Dallas TX 75230-2127 Office: U Tex Dept Chemistry & Biochemistry Box 19065 Arlington TX 76019

POMERANTZ, MARVIN, thoracic surgeon; b. Suffern, N.Y., June 16, 1934; s. Julius and Sophie (Luksin) P.; m. Margaret Twigg, Feb. 26, 1966; children: Ben, Julie. AB, Colgate U., 1955; MD, U. Rochester, 1959. Diplomate Nat. Bd. Med. Examiners, Am. Bd. Surgery, Am. Bd. Thoracic Surgery (dir. 1989—). Intern Duke U. Med. Ctr., Durham, N.C., 1959-60, resident, 1960-61, 63-67, instr. surgery, 1966-67; asst. prof. surgery U. Colo. Med. Sch., Denver, 1967-71, assoc. prof. surgery, 1971-74, assoc. clin. prof. surgery, 1974-93, prof. surgery, chief gen. thoracic surgery, 1992—; chief thoracic and cardiovascular surgery Denver Gen. Hosp., 1967-73, asst. dir. surgery, 1967-70, assoc.dir. surgery, 1970-73; pvt. practice Arapahoe CV Assocs., Denver, 1974-92; clin. assoc. surgery br. Nat. Cancer Inst., 1961-63; mem.staff Univ. Hosp., Denver, Denver Gen. Hosp., Rose Med. Ctr., Denver, Denver VA Med. Ctr., Children's Hosp., Denver, U. Colo. Health Sci. Ctr., 1992—, bd. dirs., 1995-97. chmn., 1997, Am. Bd. Thoracic Surgery. Guest editor Chest Surgery Clinics N.Am., 1993; contbr. numerous articles to profl. publs., chpts. to books. Fellow ACS, Am. Coll. Chest Surgeons; mem. AMA, Western Thoracic Surg. Assn. (v.p. 1992, pres. 1993-94, counselor-at-large 1988-90), Am. Assn. Thoracic Surgeons (program com. 1991), Am. Heart Assn. (bd. dirs. Colo. chpt. 1993), Colo. Med. Soc., Denver Acad. Surgery (pres. 1980), Internat. Cardiovascular Soc., Rocky Mtn. Cardiac Surgery Soc., Rocky Mtn. Traumatologic Soc., Soc. Thoracic Surgeons (nomenclature/coding com. 1991-95, standards and ethics com., govt. rels. com., chmn. program com. 1994-95), Soc. Vascular Surgeons, Am. Bd. Thoracic Surgery (vice chmn. 1996—). Office: UCHSC Divsn CTS 4200 E 9th Ave # C310 Denver CO 80220-3706

POMERANTZ, MARVIN ALVIN, container corporation executive; b. Des Moines, Aug. 6, 1930; s. Alex and Minnie (Landy) P.; m. Rose Lee Lipsey, Nov. 12, 1950; children: Sandy Pomerantz, Marcie Kuperman, Vickie Ginsberg, Lori Wolnerman. BS in Commerce, U. Iowa, 1952. Exec. v.p. Midwest Bag Co., Des Moines, 1952-60; founder, pres., gen. mgr. Gt. Plains Bag Corp., Des Moines, 1961-75; v.p. Continental Can Co. Inc., Greenwich, Conn., 1971-75; v.p., gen. mgr. Forest Products Brown Systems Operation (div. Continental Can Co. Inc.), Greenwich, Conn., 1975-77; pres. Diversified Group Internat. Harvester, Chgo., 1980-81, ex. v.p., 1981-82; pres., chmn., chief exec. officer The Mid-Am. Group, Des Moines, 1981—; chmn., chief exec. officer Gaylord Container Corp., Deerfield, Ill., 1986—. Mem. Greater Des Moines Commn.; trustee Drake U., 1978—; pres. Iowa State Bd. Regents, 1987-93, 95-96; mem. U.S. Olympic Budget and Audit Commn., Colorado Springs., Colo., 1989-92. Republican. Avocations: golf, tennis. Office: Gaylord Container Corp 4700 Westown Pkwy Ste 303 West Des Moines IA 50266-6718

POMERANZ, FELIX, accounting educator; b. Vienna, Austria, Mar. 28, 1926; s. Joseph and Irene (Meninger) P.; m. Rita Lewin, June 14, 1953; children: Jeffrey Arthur, Andrew Joseph. BBA, CCNY, 1948; MS, Columbia U., 1949; PhD, U. Birmingham, Eng., 1992. CPA, N.Y., Va., La., N.C.; cert. computer profl., fraud examiner, govt. fin. mgr. Audit staff Coopers & Lybrand, CPAs, N.Y.C., 1949-56; mgr. Marks, Grey & Shron (now Ernst & Young, CPA's), N.Y.C., 1956-58; asst. chief auditor Am.-Standard, N.Y.C., 1958-62; mgr. systems Westvaco Corp., N.Y.C., 1962-66; dir. operational auditing Coopers & Lybrand, CPAs, N.Y.C., 1966-68, ptnr., 1968-85; disting. lectr./dir. Ctr. for Acctg., Auditing, Tax Studies Fla. Internat. U., Miami, 1985-93, prof. acctg., 1993—, assoc. dir. sch. acctg., 1993—, affil. faculty dept. religious studies, 1996—. Author: Managing Capital Budget Projects, 1984; The Successful Audit: New Ways to Reduce Risk Exposure and Increase Efficiency, 1992; co-author: Pensions-An Accounting and Management Guide, 1976; Auditing in the Public Sector: Efficiency, Economy, and Program Results, 1976; Comparative International Auditing Standards, 1985; contbr. articles to profl. jours. Emeritus trustee Nat. Ctr. for Automated Info. Rsch. 1st lt. AUS, 1944-46, 51-52. Recipient Spear Safer Harmon faculty fellow, 1987. Mem. AICPAs, N.Y. State Soc. CPAs, Assn. Systems Mgmt., Acad. Acctg. Historians, Assn. Govt. Accts., N.Y. Acad. Scis., Am. Acctg. Assn., Inter-Am. Acctg. Assn., Assn. Cert. Fraud Examiners, Beta Gamma Sigma, Beta Alpha Psi (Most Disting. and Most Outstanding Prof. awards 1993), Alpha Kappa Psi. Home: 250 Jacaranda Dr Apt 406 Plantation FL 33324-2532 Office: Fla Internat U Sch Acctg University Park Miami FL 33199

POMERENE, JAMES HERBERT, retired computer engineer; b. Yonkers, N.Y., June 22, 1920; s. Joel Pomerene and Elsie Bower; m. Edythe R. Schwenn, Dec. 1, 1944; children: James Bennett, Katherine Ellen, Andrew Thomas Stewart. BSEE, Northwestern U., 1942; postgrad., Princeton U., 1950. Elec. engr. Hazeltine Corp., Little Neck, N.Y., 1942-46; mem. staff electronic computer project Inst. for Advanced Study, Princeton, N.J., 1946-51; chief engr. Inst. for Advanced Study, Princeton, 1951-56; sr. engr. IBM Corp., Poughkeepsie, N.Y., 1956-67; sr. staff mem. IBM Corp., Armonk, N.Y., 1967-76; cons. in field. Patentee in field. IBM fellow T.J. Watson Rsch. Ctr., 1976—. Fellow IEEE (Computer Pioneer award Computer Soc. 1986, Edison medal 1993); mem. NAE, Sigma Xi, Tau Beta Pi. Episcopalian. Home: 403 Bedford Rd N Chappaqua NY 10514-2207

POMEROY, BENJAMIN SHERWOOD, veterinary medicine educator; b. St. Paul, Apr. 24, 1911; s. Benjamin A. and Florence A. (Sherwood) P.; D.V.M., Iowa State U., 1933; M.S., Cornell U., 1934; Ph.D., U. Minn., 1944; m. L. Margaret Lyon, June 25, 1938; children—Benjamin A., Sherwood R., Catherine A., Margaret D. Diagnostician, U. Minn., 1934-38, faculty, 1938-81, prof., 1948-81, prof. emeritus, 1981—, head dept. vet. microbiology and pub. health, 1953-73, assoc. dean, 1970-74, acting dean, 1979-80. Mem. adv. com. FDA; cons. animal scis. div. and animal health div., meat insp. service, animal health service USDA. Republican precinct officer, 1958-60, chmn., 1960-61; chmn. Ramsey County (Minn.) Rep. Com., 1961-65, 4th Congl. Dist., 1961-63, 67-69; mem. Minn. Rep. Central Com., 1961-71; del. Minn. Rep. Conv., 1960-71, 92, 94, 96, Rep. Nat. Conv., 1964. Named Veterinarian of Year in Minn., 1970; recipient Eminent Citizen award St. Anthony Park Legion Post and Aux., 1955, Alumni Merit award, 1975, Stange award, 1977, Disting. Achievement citation, 1981 (all Iowa State U.), Centennial Merit award U. Pa., 1984, Animal Health award USDA, 1986; named to Am. Poultry Hall of Fame, 1977. Fellow Poultry Sci. Assn.; mem. Nat. Turkey Fedn. (life; Research award 1950), Tex. Poultry Assn. (life), Minn. Turkey Growers Assn. (life), Soc. Exptl. Biology and Medicine, Am. Assn. Avian Pathologists (life), Am. Coll. Vet. Microbiologists, Am. Acad. Microbiology, Am. Soc. Microbiology, AVMA (council research 1961-73, Pub. Service award 1980), U.S. Animal Health Assn. (life), Nat. Acad. of Practice, Minn. Vet. Med. Assn. (sec.-treas. 1950-75, pres. 1978-79, Disting. Service award 1980, presdl. award 1992), Sigma Xi, Phi Kappa Phi, Alpha Gamma Rho, Phi Zeta, Gamma Sigma Delta. Presbyterian (elder). Co-author: Diseases and Parasites of Poultry, 1958; contbg. author: Diseases of Poultry, 1972, 78, 84, 91. Home: 1443 Raymond Ave Saint Paul MN 55108-1430

POMEROY, EARL R., congressman, former state insurance commissioner; b. Valley City, N.D., Sept. 2, 1952; s. Ralph and Myrtle Pomeroy; m. Laurie Kirby, Dec. 26, 1986. BA, U. N.D., 1974, JD, 1979. Atty. Sproul, Lenaburg, Fitzner and Walker, Valley City, 1979-84; commr. of ins. State of N.D., Valley City, 1984-92; mem. 103rd Congress from N.D. (at large), Washington, D.C., 1993—; mem. coms.: budget, agriculture. State rep. N.D. Legis. Assembly, 1980-84. Recipient Found. award Rotary, 1975; named Outstanding Young North Dakotan N.D. Jaycees, 1982. Mem. Nat. Assn. of Ins. Commrs. (chmn. midwest zone 1987-88, exec. com. 1987-88), Phi Beta Kappa. Democrat. Presbyterian. Office: US Ho Rep 1533 Longworth Bldg Washington DC 20515-3401*

POMEROY, HARLAN, lawyer; b. Cleve., May 7, 1923; s. Lawrence Alson and Frances (Macdonald) P.; m. Barbara Lesser, Aug. 24, 1962; children: Robert Charles, Caroline Macdonald, Harlan III. BS, Yale U., 1945; LLB, Harvard U., 1948. Bar: Conn. 1949, U.S. Supreme Ct. 1954, U.S. Ct. Appeals (fed. cir.) 1954, Ohio 1958, U.S. Dist. Ct. (no. dist.) Ohio 1958, U.S. Claims Ct. 1958, U.S. Ct. Appeals (6th cir.) 1958, U.S. Tax Ct. 1958, D.C. 1975, Md. 1981, U.S. Dist. Ct. (D.C. dist.) 1984, U.S. Ct. Internat. Trade 1984, U.S. Ct. Appeals (D.C. cir.) 1986; cert. county ct. mediator. Atty. trial sect. tax div. Dept. Justice, Washington, 1952-58; assoc. Baker & Hostetler, Cleve., 1958-62, ptnr., 1962-75; ptnr. Baker & Hostetler, Washington, 1975-92; gen. chmn. Cleve. Tax Inst., 1971; fgn. legal advisor to Romanian Securities Mkts., 1997; mem. neutral roster IRS Mediation Program; lectr. in field. Author: (monographs) The Privatization Process in Bulgaria; Bulgarian Government Structure and Operation-An Overview; contbr. articles to profl. jours. Treas. Shaker Heights (Ohio) Dem. Club, 1960-62; trustee, mem. exec. com. 1st Unitarian Ch. Cleve., 1965-68; trustee River Road Unitarian Ch., 1988-90; gen. counsel, former asst. treas. John Glenn Presdl. Com., 1983-87; participant Vol. Lawyers Project, Legal Counsel for Elderly, Washington, 1983-92; vol. Guardian Ad Litem Program, Sarasota, Fla., 1990-92, GED-H.S. Equivalency Program, Sarasota, 1990-92; participant Guardianship Monitoring program 12th Jud. Cir., Fla., 1996—; vol. exec. fgn. legal advisor Internat. Exec. Svc. Corps. with Privatization Ministry, Prague, Czech Republic, 1994-95; mem. spl. mission to Bulgarian Ministry of Fin., U.S. Dept. Treasury, 1995. Mem. ABA (resident liaison Bulgaria for Ctrl. and East European Law Initiative 1992-93), Am. Arbitration Assn. (arbitrator 1992—), Nat. Assn. of Securities Dealers (arbitrator 1992—), N.Y. Stock Exch. (arbitrator 1995—), Multistate Tax Commn. (arbitrator 1996—), D.C. Bar Assn., Columbia Country Club (Bethesda, Md.), Yale Club, Harvard Club, Ivy League Club of Sarasota. Home: 7336 Villa D Este Dr Sarasota FL 34238-5648 Office: Baker & Hostetler 11th Fl 1050 Connecticut Ave NW Ste 11 Washington DC 20036-5307 also: 3200 National City Ctr Cleveland OH 44414

POMEROY, HORACE BURTON, III, accountant, corporate executive; b. Bronxville, N.Y., July 11, 1937; s. Horace Burton Jr. and Juhn (McCalla) P.; m. Margarita Maria Benavidez, July 14, 1973; children: Josephine, Emily. BS in Bus Adminstrn., U. Ariz., 1964; MBA, Boise State U., 1982. Comml. bank officer Continental Bank, Chgo., 1964-67; cons. Morgan Olmstead Kennedy Gardner, L.A., 1967-74; mgr. cash and banking Morrison Knudsen Corp., Boise, Idaho, 1974-88; rep. Idaho State Legistature Dist. 16, 1988—. With U.S. Army, 1959-60. Mem. NRA, Nat. Assn. Accts., Nat. Corp. Cash Mgrs. Assn., Nat. Philatelic Assn. Republican. Episcopalian. Avocations: stamp collecting, fishing, golf, tennis. Home: 6822 Kingsdale Dr Boise ID 83704-7343 Office: Statehouse Boise ID 83720

POMEROY, KENT LYTLE, physical medicine and rehabilitation physician; b. Phoenix, Apr. 21, 1935; s. Benjamin Kent and LaVerne (Hamblin) P.; m. Karen Jodelle Thomas (dec. Dec. 1962); 1 child, Charlotte Ann; m. Margo Delilah Tuttle, Mar. 27, 1964 (div. Jan. 1990); children: Benjamin Kent II, Janel Elise, Jonathan Barrett, Kimberly Eve, Kathryn M.; m. Brenda Pauline North, Sept. 1, 1990. BS in Phys. Sci., Ariz. State U., 1960; MD, U. Utah, 1963. Diplomate Am. Bd. Phys. Medicine and Rehab., Am. Bd. Pain Medicine. Rotating intern Good Samaritan Hosp., Phoenix, 1963-64; resident in phys. medicine and rehab. Good Samaritan Hosp., 1966-69, asst. tng. dir. Inst. Rehab. Medicine, 1970-74, dir. residency tng., 1974-76, asst. med. dir., 1973-76; dir. Phoenix Phys. Medicine Ctr., 1980-85, Ariz. Found. on Study Pain, Phoenix, 1980-85; pvt. practice, Phoenix and Scottsdale, Ariz., 1985—; lectr. in field. Contbr. articles to med. jours. Leader Theodore Roosevelt coun. Boy Scouts Am.; mem. exec. posse Maricopa County Sheriff's Office, Phoenix, 1981—, posse comdr., 1992-94, qualified armed posseman; mem. med. adv. bd. Grand Canyon-Saguaro chpt. Nat. Found. March of Dimes, 1970-78; missionary, 1955-57. Recipient Scouter's Tng. award Theodore Roosevelt coun. Boy Scouts Am., 1984, Scouter's Woodbadge, 1985. Mem. AMA, Am. Acad. Phys. Medicine and Rehab., Internat. Rehab. Medicine Assn., Am. Assn. Orthopaedic Medicine (co-founder, sec.-treas. 1982-88, pres. 1988-90), Pan Am. Med. Assn. (diplomate), Prolotherapy Assn. (pres. 1981-83), Am. Pain Soc., Western Pain Soc., Am. Assn. for Study Headache, Am. Soc. Addiction Medicine (sec. Ariz. chpt.), Am. Acad. Pain Medicine, Nat. Eagle Scout Assn., Acad. Clin. Neurophysiology, Ariz. Soc. Phys. Medicine (pres. 1977-78), Ariz. Med. Assn., Maricopa County Med. Soc., others, Nat. Sheriff's Assn., Law Enforcement Alliance of Am., Ariz. Narcotic Officers Assn. Mem. LDS Ch. Avocations: camping, drawing, painting, writing, music.

POMEROY, LEE HARRIS, architect; b. N.Y.C., Nov. 19, 1932; s. Alfred and Florence Pomeroy; m. Sarah Pomeroy; children: Jordana, Jeremy, Alexandra. BArch, Rensselaer Poly. Inst., 1955; MArch, Yale U., 1961. Registered architect, N.Y., Conn., Mass., Vt., N.J., Fla., Pa., Maine, Nat. Coun. of Registrators Bd. Architect William Tabler, N.Y.C., 1958-59, The Architects Collaborative, Cambridge, Mass., 1959-60; asst. prof. CCNY, 1962-64; pres. Lee Harris Pomeroy Assocs., N.Y.C., 1965-87; adj. prof. Sch. Architecture, CUNY, 1964-87; prin. solar rsch. group ECOSOL, Conn., Eng., Spain, 1965-84; dir. Project for Pub. Spaces, Inc., N.Y.C., 1982-88; dean's adv. coun. Sch. Architecture, Resselaer Poly, Inst., 1991—, adv. to pres., 1994—. Prin. works include Swiss Bank Tower and Saks Fifth Ave. extension, N.Y.C., restoration of Plaza Hotel, N.Y., Sch. Art and Dance City Coll., N.Y.C., 1989, New Rochelle Pub. Libr., 1980 (AIA-ALA design award 1980, N.Y. State AIA and Urban Design awards 1980), Dutchess County Jail, Poughkeepsie, N.Y. (AIA-ACA design award 1981), HBO Satellite Comm. Ctr., 1983 (N.Y. State AIA design award 1984), Manitou Sta. planned cmty., 1973 (AIA and Progressive Architecture awards 1973), Henry St. studios artists housing (Progressive Architecture mag. design award 1963, AIA design award 1975), Bedford Mews housing (AIA, Owens Corning energy conservation and Record Homes design awards 1980), Fulton Mall, Bklyn., 1985 (City Club N.Y.C. Bard award for design 1985), Trinity Ch. Bridge (AIA design award 1991), Hotel Usixtu, Prague, Czech Republic, Teda Hotel, Tanjin, China, Sch. of Mgmt. and Tech., Rensselaer Polytech. Inst., Troy, N.Y., Reconstruction of Union Square Subway Sta., N.Y. Mem. Cmty. Bd. 5, Midtown Manhattan, N.Y.C., 1980-91; bd. dirs. Bellview Assn., with Bellview Hosp., N.Y.C., 1992—, chmn. strategic planning com. 1st lt. USA Signal Corp., 1955-57. Recipient Mcpl. Arts Soc. award, N.Y.C., 1982; Nat. Endowment for Arts grantee, N.Y.C., 1983. Fellow AIA (bd. dirs. 1979-81); mem. Mcpl. Arts Soc., Regional Plan Assn., Yale Club, Century Club, City Club N.Y. (co-chmn. Bard award program for excellence in urban design 1988-90, 94). Avocations: tennis, photography, travel. Home: 285 Central Park W New York NY 10024-3006 Office: 462 Broadway New York NY 10013-2618

POMEROY, ROBERT CORTTIS, lawyer; b. Syracuse, N.Y., Sept. 17, 1943; s. Stuart E. and Elizabeth (Corttis) P.; m. Sandra Campbell; children: Lisa, Robert Jr., Heather. AB, Hamilton Coll., 1965; LLB, Harvard U., 1968. Bar: Mass. 1968, Fla. 1981. Assoc. Goodwin, Procter & Hoar, Boston, 1968-76, ptnr., 1977—. Mem. Am. Coll. Trust & Estate Counsel. Avocations: skiing, golf, sailing. Home: 3 Pier 7 Charlestown MA 02129 Office: Goodwin Procter & Hoar LLP Exchange Pl Boston MA 02109-2881

POMORSKI, STANISLAW, lawyer, educator; b. Lwow, Poland, Nov. 23, 1934; came to U.S., 1972, naturalized, 1983; s. Juliusz and Maria (Ziemba) P.; m. Patricia Smith; children—Lukasz, Christopher, Maria. M.Law, U. Warsaw, 1956, D.Law, 1968. Law clk., 1958-61; pvt. practice law Warsaw, 1961-64; vis. scholar Harvard U. Law Sch., 1964-66; rsch. assoc. Polish Acad. Scis., 1966-72; mem. faculty Rutgers U. Law Sch., Camden, N.J., 1973—; prof. law Rutgers U. Law Sch., 1977-81, Disting. prof. law, 1981—; fellow Soviet law U., Leyden, Netherlands, 1980-81; trustee Nat. Coun. Soviet and East European Rsch., Washington, 1988-94. Author: American Common Law and the Principle Nullum Crimen Sine Lege, 2d edit, 1975, Restructuring the System of Ownership in the USSR, 1991; co-author: A Profile of the Soviet Constitution of 1977, 1979. Ford Found. fellow, 1972-73. Office: Rutgers U Law Sch 5th And Penn St Camden NJ 08102

POMPADUR, I. MARTIN, communications executive; b. Bklyn., June 25, 1935; s. Jack and Florence (Raitbord) P.; m. Joan Lynn Krassner, Dec. 18, 1960 (div. 1986); children: F. Douglas (dec.), Jana Sue; m. Marian Hackett, Dec. 23, 1987; 1 child, Chelsea Rae. BA, Williams Coll., 1955; LLB, U. Mich., 1958. Bar: Conn. 1958, N.Y. 1961. Atty. ABC-TV Network, N.Y.C., 1960-61, 61-66, chief adminstrv. officer, 1966-68, gen. mgr., 1968-70, v.p. broadcast div., 1970-72, corp. v.p., 1972; pres. ABC Leisure Group I, 1973-75, asst. to pres. parent co., 1975-76; also dir. parent co.; sr. v.p. Ziff Corp., 1977-78, pres., 1978-82; chmn., chief exec. officer GP Sta. Ptnrs., 1982-96; mng. gen. ptnr. TV Sta. Ptnrs., 1982-96; chmn., chief exec. officer PBTV, Inc., 1984—; mng. gen. ptnr. Northeastern TV Investors Ltd. Partnership, 1984—; prin. owner, sec. Caribbean Internat. News Corp., 1985—, also bd. dirs.; CEO, COO RP Media Mgmt., Inc., 1986-93; chief exec. officer ML Media Ptnrs., L.P., 1986—; chief exec. officer, chief oper. officer RP Opportunity Mgmt.; chief exec. officer ML Media Opportunity Ptnrs., L.P., 1988—; prin. shareholder Hispanic Media Inc., 1986-90; prin. shareholder, vice-chmn. Hunter Pub. L.P., 1986-94; co-trustee Lidan Trust, 1983—; atty. Young & Rubicam, Inc., advt. agy., N.Y.C., summer 1961. Mem. Stamford bd. reps., chmn. legis. and rules com., 1959-60. Home: 10 Highland Farm Rd Greenwich CT 06831-2606 Office: RP Cos Inc 350 Park Ave Fl 16 New York NY 10022-6022

POMPEANI, BRUCE PATRICK, television reporter; b. Aliquippa, Pa., Aug. 28, 1962; s. Patsy P. and Virginia Mae (Jula) P.; m. Jana Marie Thomas, June 27, 1986; children: Brock and Brandon (twins), Brett. BA in Broadcast Journalism, Point Park Coll., Pitts., 1984. News anchor, writer Sta. KDKA-TV, Pitts., 1983-85; news anchor, reporter Sta. WTOV-TV, Steubenville, Ohio, 1985-88, Sta. WDTN-TV, Dayton, Ohio, 1988-93, Sta. WPXI-TV, Pitts., 1993-97; Sta. KDKA-TV, Pitts., 1997—. Recipient AP award (2), 1994, Golden Quill award Western Pa. Assn. Broadcasters, 1995. Roman Catholic. Avocation: golf. Home: 4002 Windemere Dr Aliquippa PA 15001 Office: Sta KDKA-TV One Gateway Center Pittsburgh PA 15222

POMPER, PHILIP, history educator; b. Chgo., Apr. 18, 1936; s. Solomon and Rebecca (Fenigstein) P.; m. Alice N. Epstein, Aug. 27, 1961 (div.); children: Erica, Stephen, Karen; m. Emily Meyer, June 26, 1994. B.A., U. Chgo., 1959, M.A., 1961, Ph.D., 1965. Instr. history Wesleyan U., Middletown, Conn., 1964-65, asst. prof., 1965-71, assoc. prof., 1971-76, prof., 1976—, chmn. dept. history, 1981-84; William F. Armstrong prof. history, 1992—. Author: The Russian Revolutionary Intelligentsia, 1970, 2nd edit., 1993, Peter Lavrov and the Russian Revolutionary Movement, 1972, Sergei Nechaev, 1979 (Choice award 1979), The Structure of Mind in History: Five Major Figures in Psychohistory, 1985, Trotsky's Notebooks, 1933-35: Writings on Lenin, Dialectics and Evolutionism, 1986, Lenin, Trotsky, and Stalin: The Intelligentsia and Power, 1990; assoc. editor History and Theory, 1991—; contbr. articles on Russian history and theory of history to profl. jours. Fellow, Ford Found., 1963-64, Social Scis. Rsch. Coun., 1968,

Hoover Instn., 1987, Wilson Ctr., 1988; Russian Rsch. Ctr. scholar, 1987—. Mem. Am. Hist. Assn., Am. Assn. for Advancement Slavic Studies, Conn. Acad. Arts and Scis. Home: 13 Red Orange Rd Middletown CT 06457-4916 Office: History Dept Wesleyan U Middletown CT 06459-0002

POMRANING, GERALD CARLTON, engineering educator; b. Oshkosh, Wis., Feb. 23, 1936; s. Carlton Chester and Lorraine Helen (Volkman) P.; m. Gayle Ann Burkitt, May 27, 1961 (div. 1983); children: Linda Marie, Sandra Lee. BS, U. Wis., 1957; cert., Technische Hogeschool, Delft, Holland, 1958; Ph.D. (NSF fellow), MIT, 1962. Mgr. GE, Pleasanton, Calif., 1962-64; group leader Gen. Atomic Co., La Jolla, Calif., 1964-69; v.p. Sci. Applications, La Jolla, 1969-76; prof. engring. UCLA, 1976—; cons. to govt. and industry. Author: Radiation Hydrodynamics, 1973, Transport in Stochastic Mixtures, 1991; editor: Reactor Physics, 1966; contbr. articles to profl. jours. Fulbright fellow, 1957-58. Fellow AAAS, Am. Nuclear Soc. (Mark Mills award 1963, Arthur Holly Compton award 1997), Am. Phys. Soc.; mem. Math. Assn. Am., Soc. Indsl. Applied Math., Am. Math. Soc., Sigma Xi, Alpha Xi Sigma, Phi Eta Sigma, Phi Kappa Phi, Tau Beta Pi, Phi Lambda Upsilon.

PON-BROWN, KAY MIGYOKU, technical marketing engineer; b. Ft. Lewis, Wash., Mar. 15, 1956; d. Gin Ung and Toyo (China) Pon; m. John Joseph Brown, July 28, 1979; 1 child, J. Jason. BS in Chemistry, U. Idaho, 1978, BA in Zoology, 1978; BS in Math., Boise State U., 1984. Chemist Century Labs., Inc., Boise, Idaho, 1982-84; from customer support specialist to tech. support specialist Learned-Mahn, Inc., Boise, 1984-87; from computer programmer to coord. Idaho Power, Boise, 1987-90, customer solution rep., 1990-92; tech. specialist Hewlett-Packard Co., Boise, 1992-95; engr. tech. mktg. Hewlett Packard Co., Boise, 1995—; cons. Eclipse, Inc., Boise, 1991—, bd. dirs., pres., 1992—, Discovery Ctr. Idaho, Boise, 1991-94. Bd. dirs. Idaho Zool. Soc., Boise, 1986-95, Ada County Divsn. Am. Heart Assn., Boise, 1992-94, divsn. sec., 1992-93; bd. dirs. Jr. League Boise, newsletter com. chair; vol. Am. Cancer Soc., 1990-92; vol. newsletter editor Idaho Soc. Profl. Engrs., 1992-94. 1st Place husband & wife team Royal Victoria Marathon, 1992. Mem. Data Processing Mgmt. Assn. (bd. dirs. 1993-94, newsletter editor 1993-94), Meridian Toastmasters (pres. 1986, dist. 15 best newsletter 1986), Greater Boise Rd. Runners Club (bd. dirs., charter pres. 1993-96, newsletter editor 1994—). Avocations: running, music-flute, bowling, voice. Home: 1350 Nova Ln Meridian ID 83642-6483 Office: Hewlett-Packard Co 11311 Chinden Blvd Boise ID 83714-1021

POND, PATRICIA BROWN, library science educator, university administrator; b. Mankato, Minn., Jan. 17, 1930; d. Patrick H. and Florence M. (Ruehle) Brown; m. Judson S. Pond, Aug. 24, 1959. BA, Coll. St. Catherine, St. Paul, 1952; MA, U. Minn., 1955; PhD, U. Chgo., 1982. Sch. libr. Minn., N.Y., 1952-62; asst. prof. libr. sci. U. Minn., 1962-63; reference libr. U. Mont., 1963-65; asst. prof. U. Oreg., 1967-72, assoc. prof., 1972-77; prof., dept. chair, assoc. dean Sch. Libr. and Info. Sci. U. Pitts., 1977-85. Mem. ALA (life), Phi Beta Kappa, Beta Phi Mu, Delta Phi Lambda, Kappa Gamma Pi. Home: 14740 SW Forest Dr Beaverton OR 97007-5117

POND, PHYLLIS JOAN RUBLE, state legislator; b. Warren, Ind., Oct. 25, 1930; d. Clifford E. and Rosa E. (Hunnicutt) Ruble; m. George W. Pond, June 10, 1951; children: William, Douglas, Jean Ann. BS, Ball State U., Muncie, Ind., 1951; MS, Ind. U., 1963. Tchr. home econs., 1951-54; kindergarten tchr., 1961—; mem. Ind. Ho. of Reps., Indpls., 1978—, majority asst. caucus chmn., vice chmn. ways and means com., 1995. Del. Ind. Rep. Conv., 1976, 80, 84, 86, 88; alt. del. Rep. Nat. Conv., 1980, del., 1996. Mem. AAUW, New Haven Woman's Club. Lutheran.

POND, THOMAS ALEXANDER, physics educator; b. L.A., Dec. 4, 1924; s. Arthur Francis and Florence (Alexander) P.; m. Barbara Eileen Newman, Sept. 6, 1958; children: Arthur Phillip Ward, Florence Alexandra. A.B., Princeton U., 1947, A.M., 1949, Ph.D., 1953. Instr. physics Princeton U., 1951-53; asst. prof., then assoc. prof. physics Washington U., St. Louis, 1953-62; prof. physics SUNY, Stony Brook, 1962-81; prof. emeritus, 1982—; chmn. dept. SUNY, Stony Brook, 1962-68, exec. v.p., 1967-79, acting pres., 1970, 75, 78; prof. physics Rutgers U., New Brunswick, N.J., exec. v.p., chief acad. officer, 1982-91, exec. v.p., chief acad. officer emeritus, 1991—, acting pres., 1990, prof., 1991-97, prof. emeritus, 1997—; Bd. dirs. Action Com. for L.I., 1978-80, Tri-State Regional Planning Commn., 1979-82; trustee Univs. Research Assn., 1985-87; bd. dirs. Fermilab, 1987-89. Served to ensign USNR, 1943-46. Mem. Am. Phys. Soc., Phi Beta Kappa, Sigma Xi. Home: 8 Campbells Brook Rd Whitehouse Station NJ 08889-3344 Office: Rutgers Univ Dept Physics and Astronomy Piscataway NJ 08855-0849

PONDER, ALONZA, church administrator. Vice-chief bishop Ch. of the Living God Exec. Bd. Office: Church of The Living God 5609 N Terry Ave Oklahoma City OK 73111-6866*

PONDER, CATHERINE, clergywoman; b. Hartsville, S.C., Feb. 14, 1927; d. Roy Charles and Kathleen (Parrish) Cook; 1 child, Richard; student U. N.C. Extension, 1946, Worth Bus. Coll., 1948; BS in Edn., Unity Ministerial Sch., 1956. Ordained to ministry, Unity Sch. Christianity, 1958; minister Unity Ch., Birmingham, Ala., 1956-61; founder, minister Unity Ch., Austin, Tex., 1961-69, San Antonio, 1969-73, Palm Desert, Calif., 1973—. Mem. Assn. Unity Chs., Inc. (hon. DD 1976), Internat. New Thought Alliance, Internat. Platform Assn. Clubs: Cardinal (Raleigh, N.C.). Author: The Dynamic Laws of Prosperity, 1962, The Prosperity Secret of the Ages, 1964, The Dynamic Laws of Healing, 1966, The Healing Secret of the Ages, 1967, Pray and Grow Rich, 1968, The Millionaires of Genesis, 1976, The Millionaire Moses, 1977, The Millionaire Joshua, 1978, The Millionaire from Nazareth, 1979, The Secret of Unlimited Prosperity, 1981, Open Your Mind to Receive, 1983, Dare to Prosper!, The Prospering Power of Prayer, 1983, The Prospering Power of Love, 1984, Open Your Mind to Prosperity, 1984, The Dynamic Laws of Prayer, 1987. Office: 73-669 Us Highway 111 Palm Desert CA 92260-4033

PONDER, HERMAN, geologist; b. Light, Ark., Jan. 31, 1928; s. Herman Cook and Sylvia Adell (Cameron) P.; m. Barbara Elaine Sando, May 10, 1947; children: Teresa Elaine, David Mark. BA, U. Mo., 1955, PhD, 1959. Rsch. engr. A.P. Green Refractories Co., Mexico, Mo., 1959-61, lab mgr., 1961-63; project engr., then mgr. mining div. Colo. Sch. Mines Rsch. Inst., Golden, 1963-67, dir. rsch., 1967-70, pres., 1970-85; pres. ATI Exploration, Golden, Colo., 1985-90; chmn. bd. dirs. Analytica, Inc.; v.p. Copper Range Co., White Pine, Mich., 1985-89. Served with USN, 1946-47. Recipient Disting. Alumnus award U. Mo., 1993. Home: PO Box 23268 Silverthorne CO 80498

PONDER, LESTER MCCONNICO, lawyer, educator; b. Walnut Ridge, Ark., Dec. 10, 1912; s. Harry Lee and Clyde (Gant) P.; m. Sallie Mowry Clover, Nov. 7, 1942; children—Melinda, Constance; m. Phyllis Gretchen Harting, Oct. 14, 1978. B.S. summa cum laude in Commerce, Northwestern U., 1934; J.D. with honors, George Washington U., 1938. Bar: Ark. 1937, Ind. 1948. Atty. Ark. Dept. Revenue, Little Rock, 1939-41; atty. IRS, Chgo. and Indpls., 1941-51; ptnr. Barnes & Thornburg and predecessor Barnes, Hickam, Pantzer & Boyd, Indpls., 1952—; adj. prof. Sch. Law, Ind. U., Bloomington, 1951-54, Sch. Law, Ind. U., Indpls., 1954-63; lectr. polit. sci. Ind. U., Indpls., 1982-85. Author: United States Tax Court Practice & Procedure, 1976. Bd. dirs., vice chmn., chmn. Ind. chpt. The Nature Conservancy, 1981-89; mem. adv. coun. Ind. Dept. Natural Resources, 1986—; past bd. mem. Sigma Chi Found. Served with USN, 1942. Fellow Am. Bar Found., Ind. State Bar Found., Ind. Bar Found., Am. Coll. Tax Counsel; mem. ABA (coun., taxation sect. 1970-73, chair sr. lawyers div. 1993-94, adv. coun. Commr. Internal Revenue 1964—), Ind. State Bar Assn., Indpls. Bar Assn., Assn. of Seventh Fed. Cir. Republican. Presbyterian. Club: Meridian Hills Country (Indpls.). Lodge: Rotary (past bd. dirs.). Office: Barnes & Thornburg Merchants Bank Bldg Ste 1313 Indianapolis IN 46204-3506

PONDER, WILLIAM STANLEY, university administrator; b. San Diego, Sept. 12, 1949; s. William Bryant and Mary Louise (Parker) P.; m. Deborah Millot, Dec. 22, 1982 (div. 1989); children: Dana Michelle, Jordan Thomas; m. Mary J. Zodrow, Nov. 4, 1993. BA in Music, San Diego State U., 1972, MS in Counseling, 1983. Tchr. San Diego/Riverside Sch. Dist., 1973-77; dir. tng. Twelfth Night Repertory Co., San Diego, 1977-78; counselor Girls Club of Chula Vista, Calif., 1978-79; v.p. Telesis II of Calif., Inc., San Diego, 1979-83; sr. recruitment officer U. Calif.-Riverside, 1983-86, assoc. dir. Office of Admissions, 1986-91; registrar Shoreline Community Coll., Seattle, Wash., 1991-93, Pierce Coll., 1993—; cons. State of Calif. Health Svc., Sacramento, 1982-83; adj. faculty Riverside Community Coll., 1989—; lectr. Sch. Edn. Calif. State, San Bernardino, 1989-90. Author: Educational Apartheid in a Pluralistic Society, 1995. Commr. City of San Bernardino Bldg. and Safety, 1987-91; mem. planning commn. City of Olympia, Wash., 1996—. Recipient Pub. Svc. award Co. of San Diego, 1984; KPBS TV Svc. award, 1984. Mem. Third World Counselors Assn. (dir. 1983-86), Calif. Articulation Numbering Systems Coun., Western Assn. Coll. Admissions Counselors, Nat. Assn. Coll. Admissions Counselors, Nat. Assn. Coll. Admission Officers (chmn. on minority participation in higher edn.), Am. Assn. Collegiate Registrars and Admissions Officers (profl. access and equity com. 1996-97), Pacific Assn. Collegiate Registrars and Admissions Officers (vice chair Wash. coun. 1996-99, v.p. 1996-97), Rancho Mediterrian Club (Colton, Calif.), Ballys' Pacific West. Democrat. Presbyterian. Avocation: tennis. Home: 1413 20th Ave SE Olympia WA 98501-3095

PONDROM, LEE GIRARD, physicist, educator; b. Dallas, Dec. 26, 1933; s. Levi Girard and Guinevere (Miller) P.; m. Cyrena Jo Norman, Aug. 25, 1961. B.S., So. Meth. U., 1953; M.S., U. Chgo., 1956, Ph.D., 1958. Instr., dept. physics Columbia U., N.Y.C., 1960-63; assoc. prof. dept. physics U. Wis., Madison, 1963-69; prof. physics U. Wis., 1969—, Robert Williams Wood prof., 1992—; mem. high energy adv. com. Brookhaven Nat. Lab., 1973-75, chmn. Associated Universities, Inc., vis. com., 1987; mem. physics adv. com. Fermi Nat. Accelerator Lab., 1979-82, chmn., 1981-82; adv. com. for physics NSF, 1981-84; mem. high energy adv. panel (physics) U.S. Dept. Energy, 1981-84, 87-88, chmn. subcom. on detectors, 1987-88, mem. subpanel on future facilities, high energy physics, 1983, mem. subpanel on future modes of exptl. research in high energy physics, 1987; trustee Univs. Research Assn., 1973-76, 82-85; mem. sci. policy com. Stanford Linear Accelerator Ctr., 1984-88; mem. Internat. Com. Future Accelerators, 1984-90; chmn. Snowmass 1986 Summer Study on the SSC.; chmn. User's Orgn. for the SSC, 1987-89, mem. sci. policy com. SSC Lab., 1992; mem. CDRF awards com. to scientists in former Soviet Union, 1996. Contbr. articles to profl. jours. Served to 1st lt. USAF, 1958-60. J.S. Guggenheim Meml. fellow, 1971-72, Japan Soc. for Promotion of Sci. fellow; recipient Disting. Alumni award So. Meth. U., 1983, W.K.H. Panofsky award Am. Phys. Soc., 1994. Fellow Am. Phys. Soc. (chmn. div. particles and fields 1987, com. on status of women in physics 1989—, chmn. com. to award the Panofsky prize 1991); mem. AAAS, Phi Beta Kappa (pres. Wis. Alpha chpt. 1996-97). Episcopalian. Home: 210 Princeton Ave Madison WI 53705-4077 Office: U Wis Dept Physics Madison WI 53706 *I have been fortunate to pursue a career in research and teaching at a university and at various U.S. national laboratories, where the individual has much freedom to do whatever he or she wants. Close association with many colleagues and my work with younger people in physics have been sources of stimulation.*

PONEMAN, DANIEL BRUCE, lawyer; b. Toledo, Mar. 12, 1956; s. Meyer and Delores Suzanne (Shapiro) P.; m. Susan Anne Danoff, Aug. 12, 1984; children: Claire Gillian, Michael Bruder, William Meyer. AB in Govt. and Econs. magna cum laude, Harvard Coll., 1978; MLitt in Politics, Lincoln Coll., Oxford, Eng., 1981; JD cum laude, Harvard U., 1984. Bar: D.C. 1985, N.Y., 1985. Vis. fellow Internat. Inst. Strategic Studies, London, 1980-81; rsch. fellow ctr. sci. and internat. affairs Kennedy sch. govt. Harvard U., 1981-84; assoc. Covington & Burling, 1985-89; White House fellow U.S. Dept. of Energy, 1989-90; dir. def. policy and arms control NSC, Washington, 1990-93, spl. asst. to the Pres., sr. dir. nonproliferation and export controls, 1993-96; counsel Hogan & Hartson L.L.P., 1996—. Author: Nuclear Power in the Developing World, 1982, Argentina: Democracy on Trial, 1987; contbr. articles to profl. jours. and newspapers including N.Y. Times, Washington Post, L.A. Times, Boston Globe. Grantee Corp. Pub. Broadcasting; Lord Crewe scholar. Mem. D.C. Bar, N.Y. Bar, Coun. Fgn. Rels., Phi Beta Kappa. Home: 2109 Mason Hill Dr Alexandria VA 22306-2416 Office: Hogan & Hartson LLP 555 13th St NW Washington DC 20004-1109

PONITZ, DAVID H., academic administrator; b. Royal Oak, Mich., Jan. 21, 1931; s. Henry John and Jeanette (Bouwman) P.; m. Doris Jean Humes, Aug. 5, 1956; children: Catherine Anne, David Robinson. BA, U. Mich., 1952, MA, 1954; EdD, Harvard U., 1964; hon. degree, U. Dayton. Prin. Waldron (Mich.) Area Schs., 1956-58, supt., 1958-60; cons. Harvard U., Boston Sch. Survey, 1961-63; supt. Freeport (Ill.) Pub. Schs., 1962-65; pres. Freeport C.C., 1962-65, Washtenaw C.C., 1965-75, Sinclair C.C., 1975—; cons. to community colls.; chmn., pres. Ohi Advanced Tech. Ctr. Mem. editorial adv. bd. Nations Schs, 1963-70; chmn. adv. bd. Community Coll. Rev, 1978-89. Past chmn. Dayton Mayor's Coun. on Econ. Devel., 1977-85; mem. Nat. Adv. Coun. on Nursing; former co-chair Performing Arts Edn. Task Force; bd. dirs. Alliance for Edn.; former campaign chmn. Ann Arbor and Dayton United Way; past vice chmn. Dayton Citizens Adv. Coun. for Desegregation Implementation; v.p. Miami Valley Rsch. Park; mem., past chmn. Area Progress Coun., Dayton; bd. dirs. Dayton Devel. Coun.; mem. F.S.B. bd. Citizens Fed. Banks, Universal Energy Systems Bd.; past chmn. Miami Valley Joint Labor/Mgmt. Profls., Area Progress Coun.; chmn. bd. dirs Ctr. Occupational R & D; chmn. Human Svcs. Levy, Tech-Prep Coll. H.S. Consortium; vice chair Miami Valley Rsch. Found.; chmn. bd. dirs. League Innovation C.C.; bd. dirs. Miami Valley Regional Planning Commn. Served with U.S. Army, 1954-56. Named Outstanding Alumnus U. Mich., One of Top 100 Pres. in U.S. Council for Advancement and Support of Edn., Exec. of Yr., Bd. Realtors, Presdl. medallion Patron emeritus Horry-Georgetown Tech. Coll.; recipient Bogie Buster Red Jacket award, 1987, Thomas J. Peters award for Excellence Assn. Community and Jr. Colls. 1988, Marie N. Martin Chief Exec. Officer award, ACCT, 1989, The Living Legend award Martin Luther King Jr. Holiday Celebration Com., 1991, Sinclair Hon. Alumnus award, 1991, India Found. Honor, 1992, Disting. Eagle Scout award Nat. Eagle Scout Assn., 1993, Smitty award, Anti-Defamation award. Mem. Am. Assn. Community and Jr. Colls. (nat. future commn., bd. dirs., chmn. 1988-89), Ohio Tech. and Community Coll. Assn. (pres. 1979-80), Rotary. Methodist. Office: Sinclair Community Coll 4444 W 3rd St Dayton OH 45417

PONITZ, JOHN ALLAN, lawyer; b. Battle Creek, Mich., Sept. 7, 1949; m. Nancy J. Roberts, Aug. 14, 1971; children: Amy, Matthew, Julie. BA, Albion Coll., 1971; JD, Wayne State U., 1974. Bar: Mich. 1974, U.S. Dist. Ct. (ea. dist.) Mich. 1975, (we. dist.) Mich. 1986, U.S. Ct. Appeals (6th cir.) Mich. 1981, U.S. Supreme Ct. 1992. Assoc. McMachan & Kaichen, Birmingham, Mich., 1973-75; atty. Grand Trunk Western R.R., Detroit, 1975-80, sr. trial atty., 1980-89; gen. counsel, 1990-95; ptnr. Hopkins & Sutter, Detroit, 1995—. V.p. Beverly Hills (Mich.) Jaycees, 1981. Served to capt. USAR, 1974-82. Mem. Mich. Bar Assn., Nat. Assn. R.R. Trial Counsel, Oakland County Bar Assn. Lutheran. Avocations: golf, sailing. Office: Hopkins & Sutter 2800 Livernois Rd Ste 220 Troy MI 48083-1215

PONKO, WILLIAM REUBEN, architect; b. Wausau, Wis., Apr. 4, 1948; s. Reuben Harrison and Ora Marie (Ranke) P.; m. Kathleen Ann Hilt, May 5, 1973; children: William Benjamin, Sarah Elizabeth. B.Arch. magna cum laude, U. Notre Dame, 1971. Cert. Nat. Council Archl. Registration Bds. V.p., architect, dir. ednl./instl. specialty LeRoy Troyer & Assocs. (now The Troyer Group), Mishawaka, Ind., 1971—; design instr. dept. architecture U. Notre Dame, 1976; mem. Ind. State Bd. Registration for Architects, 1990—; mem. registration exam com. Nat. Coun. Archtl. Registration Bds., 1992—, vice chair 1996, chair 1997. Leonard M. Anson Meml. scholar, 1966-70. Mem. AIA (gold medal for excellence in archtl. edn. 1971), Ind. Soc. Architects (design excellence award 1978, chpt. pres. 1985). Prin. archtl. works include: St. Peter Luth. Ch., Mishawaka, Ind., 1979, 4 brs. for South Bend Pub. Library, 1983; Edward J. Funk & Sons office bldg., Kentland, Ind., 1976; Music Edn. bldg. Taylor U., Upland, Ind., 1982, Taylor U. Library, carillon tower, 1985, Early Childhood Devel. Ctr. U. Notre Dame, 1994, Convents for Sisters of Holy Cross St. Mary's, Notre Dame, Ind., 1995. Office: The Troyer Group Inc 415 Lincoln Way E Mishawaka IN 46544-2213

PON-SALAZAR, FRANCISCO DEMETRIO, diplomat, educator, deacon, counselor; b. Ica, Peru, July 18, 1951; came to U.S., 1982; s. Alejandro Sen Tac and Demetria (Salazar) P. MPhil, Leopold Franzer U., Innsbruck, Austria, 1977; MA in Hispanic Lit. and Lang., St. Louis U., 1985. Cert. univ. and coll. tchr., Nat. Coun. Peruvian Univs.; cert. adult literacy tchr.; notary pub., State of Mo. Tchr. San Juan Bautista Sch., Puno, Peru, 1972, Jose Toribio Polo High Sch., Ica, 1979-82; prof. Catalina Buendia Pecho Coll., Ica, 1980-82; instr. St. Louis U., 1983-85; asst. of the Consul Fgn. Rels. Consulate of Mex., St. Louis, 1988—; counselor, tutor Christian Bros. Coll., St. Louis, 1984-85; tchr. St. Gabriel's Hall Reformatory, Audubon, Pa., 1985; mentor Youth Svc. Mo./Pub. and Pvt. Ventures, 1992-93. Participant Internat. Alpach (Tirol, Austria) Forum, 1977; asst. scoutmaster Boy Scouts Am., St. Louis, 1990—; vol. State of Mo. Divsn. Youth Svcs. Pub. Pvt. Ventures, 1992-93; mem. adv. bd. Immigration Law Project, Legal Svcs. of Ea. Mo., Inc., St. Louis, 1995—. Mem. Internat. Progress Orgn. of Vienna (Austria), Latin-Am. Soc. of St. Louis U. (v.p. 1983-85), Campus Ministry of Spanish Speaking People, Legal Svcs. of Ea. Mo., Inc. (adv. bd. of the Immigration Project, 1995), Sigma Delta Pi, Alpha Sigma Nu. Avocations: jogging, gymnastics, reading, videos, poetry. Home: 10521 Carroll Wood Way Saint Louis MO 63128-1314 Office: Consulate of Mex 1015 Locust St Ste 922 Saint Louis MO 63101-1323

PONSETI, IGNACIO VIVES, orthopaedic surgery educator; b. Cuidadela, Balearic Islands, Spain, June 3, 1914; s. Miguel and Margarita (Vives) P.; 1 child, William Edward; m. Helena Percas, 1961. BS, U. Barcelona, 1930, MD, 1936, D honoris causa, 1984. Instr. dept. orthopaedic surgery State U. Iowa, 1944-57, prof., 1957—. Author papers on cogenital and developmental skeletal deformities. Capt. M.C. Spanish Army, 1936-39. Recipient Kappa Delta award for orthopaedic rsch., 1955. Mem. Assn. Bone and Joint Surgeons, Am. Acad. Cerebral Palsy, Soc. Exptl. Biology and Medicine, Internat. Coll. Surgeons, N.Y. Acad. Sci., AMA (Ketoen gold medal 1960), Am. Acad. Orthopedic Surgeons, ACS, Am. Orthopedic Assn., Pediatric Orthopaedic Soc. (hon.), Iowa Med. Soc., Orthopedic Rsch. Soc. (Shands award 1975), Sigma Xi, Asociacion Argentina de Cirugia (hon.), Asociacion Balear de Cirugia (hon.), Sociedad de Cirujanos de Chile (hon.), Sociedad Espanola de Cirugia Ortopedica (hon.), Sociedad Brasilera de Ortopedia e Traumatologia (hon.). Home: 110 Oakridge Ave Iowa City IA 52246-2935 Office: Carver Pavilion U Iowa Hosps Iowa City IA 52242

PONSOR, MICHAEL ADRIAN, federal judge; b. Chgo., Aug. 13, 1946; s. Frederick Ward and Helen Yvonne (Richardson) P.; children from previous marriage, Anne, Joseph; 1 stepchild, Christian Walker; m. Nancy L. Coiner, June 30, 1996. BA magna cum laude, Harvard Coll., 1969; BA second class honors, Oxford U., 1971, MA, 1979; JD, Yale U., 1975. Bar: Mass., U.S. Dist. Ct. Mass., U.S. Ct. Appeals (1st cir.), U.S. Supreme Ct. Tchr. Kenya Inst. Administrn., Nairobi, 1967-68; law clk. U.S. Dist. Ct., Boston, 1975-76; assoc. Homans, Hamilton, Dahmen & Lamson, Boston, 1976-78; ptnr. Brown, Hart & Ponsor, Amherst, Mass., 1978-83; U.S. magistrate judge U.S. Dist. Ct., Springfield, Mass., 1984-94, U.S. dist. judge, 1994—; adj. prof. Western N.E. Coll. Sch. Law, Springfield, 1988—, Yale Law Sch., New Haven, 1989-91; presenter in field. Rhodes scholar Oxford U., 1969. Mem. Mass. Bar Assn., Hampshire County Bar Assn., Boston Bar Assn. Office: US Dist Ct 1550 Main St Springfield MA 01103-1422

PONT, JOHN, football coach, educator; b. Canton, Ohio, Nov. 13, 1927; s. Bautista and Susie (Sikurinec) P.; m. H. Sandra Stoutt, June 23, 1956; children: John W., Jennifer Ann, Jeffrey David. BS, Miami U., Oxford, Ohio, 1952, MS, 1956. Profl. football player Can., 1952-53; instr., freshman football and basketball coach Miami U., 1953-55, asst. prof., head football coach, 1955-62; head football coach Yale U., 1963-65; prof., head football coach Ind. U., Bloomington, 1965-73; head coach Northwestern U., Evanston, Ill., 1973-77, athletic dir., 1974-79; head football coach, athletic dir. Hamilton, Ohio; head football coach, tennis coach, asst. athletic dir. Coll. Mt. St. Joseph, Mt. St. Joseph, Ohio; now head football coach Gakusei-Engo-Kai Inc., Tokyo, Japan; agt. Equitable Assurance Soc., U.S., 1981-82; v.p. Fin. Leasing Corp., 1983-85, Splty. Brush, Inc.; athletic dir. Jewish Community Center, Canton, 1953; v.p. NCAA Coun., 1979-80; mem. bd. dirs. Cin. chpt. Nat. Football Found. Hall Of Fame. Mem. Pres.'s Coun. on Phys. Fitness; chmn. Ind. Easter Seal, 1968-69, Ind. div. Cancer Crusade, 1969; bd. dirs. Multiple Sclerosis, N.E. Ill. counc. Boy Scouts Am., Boys Hope. Served with USN, 1945-47. Named Coach of Year Coaches Assn., 1967, Coach of Year Football Writers, 1967, Coach of Yr. Washington Touchdown Club, 1968, Coach of Yr. Walter Camp Found.; recipient Significant Sig award, 1968, Disting. Am. award Nat. Football Found., 1987; charter mem. Miami U. Hall of Fame, 1968; elected Ind. Football Hall of Fame, 1984, Butler County Hall of Fame, 1986, Mid-Am. Conf. Hall of Fame, 1992, Ind. U. Sports Hall of Fame, 1992. Mem. Am. Football Coaches Assn. (chmn. ethics com.), Kusatsu City Football Assn. Japan (hon. chmn.), Am. Legion, Blue Key, Sigma Chi, Phi Epsilon Kappa, Omicron Delta Kappa. Republican. Home: 482 White Oak Dr Oxford OH 45056-9272

PONTE, JAY MICHAEL, research associate in information retrieval; b. Framingham, Mass., Apr. 27, 1965; s. John M. and Mary A. (Scalia) P. BS, Northeastern U., 1993; MS, U. Mass., 1995. Programmer, analyst Perennial Software, Medfield, Mass., 1990-93; rsch. assoc. Ctr. for Intelligent Info. Retrieval, Amherst, Mass., 1993—; computer software cons. Town of Westwood, Mass., 1993. Developer: (computer software) A Hidden Markov Model Based Retargetable Segmentation System for Free Text, 1995, Automatic Identification of Topic Boundaries for Information Retrieval, 1996; contbr. articles to profl. jours. Recipient Sears B. Condit award Northeastern U., 1993; Hodgekinson scholar Northeastern U., 1993. Mem. Assn. for Computing Machinery, Phi Kappa Phi Honor Soc., Golden Key. Avocations: beer and winemaking, martial arts. Office: CIIR LGRC U Mass Amherst MA 01003

PÖNTINEN, PEKKA JUHANI, anesthesiologist, consultant; b. Tampere, Finland, Apr. 5, 1932; s. Otto Edvard and Ellen Margareta (Heiniö) P.; m. Anja Anita Kuukankorpi; children: Anna-Katriina, Juha-Pekka, Riikka-Leena, Hanna-Maaria; m. Irja Tuulikki Ketovuori, Jan. 8, 1976; 1 child, Mika Juhani. B in med., Helsinki U., Finland, 1953; MD, Turku U., Finland, 1957; PhD, Kuopio U., Finland, 1977. Diplomate Finnish Bd. Health Legitimation, Finnish Bd. Anesthesiology. Chief dept. anesthesiology Savonlinna Cen. Hosp., Finland, 1965-69, Kainuu Cen. Hosp., Finland, 1969-75; asst. prof. neurophysiology Kuopio U., Finland, 1974-75; med. dir. Kankaanpää Rehabilitation Ctr., Finland, 1989-92; assoc. prof. anesthesiology Kuopio U., 1978—, Tampere U., Finland, 1980—; chief acupuncture rsch. project Kuopio U., 1976—; cons. dept. neurology Tampere U. Hosp., 1976-93, adv. Ministry of Health & Social Affairs, Helsinki,. 1975—, WHO Com. Standardisation Acupuncture Nomenclature, Geneva, Switzerland, 1989-95uropean Coun. Subcom. Higher Edn., Strassbourg, France, 1990-95. Author: Acupuncture as a Medical Treatment Modality (in Finnish), 1983, Laser as a Medical Treatment Modality (in Finnish), 1988, Low Level Laser as a Medical Treatment Modality (in Swedish), 1991, Low Level Laser Therapy as a Medical Treatment Modality, 1992, Laseracupuncture (in German), 1993; co-author: TENS Transcutaneous Electrical Nerve Stimulation in Pain Treatment (in German), 1992, 2d edit., 1996, Triggerpoints and Triggermechanisms, 1997 (in German), Alternative and Complementary Therapies in Veterinary Medicine (in German), 1997; editor-in-chief Scandinavian Jour. Acupuncture and Electrotherapy, 1987—; editor Acupuncture & Electrotherapeutics Rsch. Internat. Jour., 1981—, AKU, Akupunktur, Theorie und Praxis, 1991—; mem. sci. com. Internat. Jour. Pain Therapy, 1991-95. Recipient German Promotion award Pain Rsch. and Therapy, 1988. Fellow Internat. Coll. Acupuncture & Electro-Therapeutics Rsch. (vice chmn. coun. 1987—), Acupuncture Found. of India (hon.), Am. Acad. Acupuncture (hon.), Am. Coll. Acupuncture (charter); mem. Am. Pain Soc., Am. Soc. Laser Medicine & Surgery, Brit. Med. Acupuncture Soc. (hon.), German Med. Acupuncture Soc. (hon.), Can. Acupuncture Assn. Can. (hon.), Nordic Acupuncture Soc. (pres. 1980-87, 89—, founding), Internat. Assn. Study of Pain (founding), Phys. Medicine Rsch. Found. (intermultidisciplinary bd. dirs. 1995—), N.Y. Acad. Scis., Società Internazionale di Laserterapia Medico Chirugica (v.p. for Finland 1989—), Finnish Soc. Anesthesiologists (v.p. 1970-71, pres. 1972-73), Finnish Med. Acupuncture Soc. (hon.). Avocations: classical music, fishing, gardening, skiing, ice hockey. Home: Pikkusaarenkuja 4B 77, 33410 Tampere Finland

PONTIUS, JAMES WILSON, foundation administrator; b. Orrville, Ohio, Aug. 29, 1916; s. Howard Taggart and Nova Clementine (Mead) P.; m.

Kathryn Jane Sharp, Mar. 12, 1938; children: Howard Garrett, Janne Pettibone, Carolyn Jean, Jon Brewster. BA, Miami U., Oxford, Ohio, 1937. Fin. and taxes GE, Schenectady, N.Y., 1937-47, traveling auditor, 1947-50, cons. electronic data sys., 1953-62; project mgr. internal automation dept. GE, Waynesboro, Va., 1962-64; mgr. advanced info. systems GE, Schenectady, N.Y., 1964-78; retired, 1978; mgr. treasury svcs. GE Supply Corp., Bridgeport, Conn., 1950-53; pres. William Gundry Broughton Charitable Pvt. Found., Inc., Glenville, N.Y., 1992—; mem. adv. com. use of computers in bus. activities U.S. Dept. Def., Washington, 1955-56. Mem. Niskayuna (N.Y.) Sch. Bd., 1965-70, 71-72, 85-86; sec., treas., pres. Schenectady (N.Y.) Rotary Club Found., 1977-80. Republican. Reformed. Avocations: bridge, golf, amateur radio, personal computers, pool. Home: 2009 Garden Dr Niskayuna NY 12309-2309 Office: 133 Saratoga Rd Scotia NY 12302

PONTIUS, PRISCILLA FLOYD, nursing administrator; b. Chattanooga, Aug. 16, 1949; d. Bishop and Edith (Frazier) Floyd; m. William S. Pontius, Oct. 1, 1988; 1 child, Julie Shwiller. AD, Middle Tenn. State U., 1969; BSN, U. Tenn., 1974; MSN, U. Ala., Birmingham, 1983. Resident health care Miami Valley Hosp., Dayton, Ohio, 1983-84; pediatrics supr. Stormont Vail Regional Med. Ctr., Topeka, 1984-86; clin. dir. perinatal So. Hills Med. Ctr., Nashville, 1986-89; dir. maternal/child nursing, adminstr. Children's Hosp. W.Va. Univ. Hosps., Morgantown, 1989—. Recipient Gooche scholarship U. Tenn., Memphis, 1973; named Outstanding Young Women of Am., 1983. Mem. Am. Orgn. Nurse Execs., Am. Coll. Health Care Execs. Home: 3227 Staghorn Ct Marietta GA 30062 Office: Grady Meml Hosp 80 Butler St SE Atlanta GA 30335-3800

PONTIUS, STANLEY N., bank holding company executive; b. Auburn, Ind., Aug. 26, 1946; s. Clayton and Frances (Beuret) P.; m. Cheryl Ann Dawson, Aug. 3, 1968; children: Jarrod B., Dorian K. BS, Ind. U., 1968. Mgmt. trainee Bank One, 1968-73; asst. v.p. Bank One, Cambridge, Ohio, 1973-75; v.p. Bank One, Fremont, Ohio, 1975-79, dir., pres., CEO, 1979-83; pres. Bank One, Marion, Ohio, 1983-84, dir., CEO, 1984-88; dir., CEO Bank One, Mansfield, Ohio, 1988-91; dir., pres., COO 1st Fin. Bancorp, Hamilton, Ohio, 1991, dir., pres., CEO, 1992—; dir., pres., CEO 1st Nat. Banl of Southwestern Ohio, Hamilton, 1991—. bd. trustee, exec. com. Fort Hamilton-Hughes Meml. Hosp., fin. com. Fitton Ctr. for Creative Arts, voting com. Butler County United Way, adv. com. Hamilton City Schs., Hamilton C. of C., bd. dirs. Inroads of Greater Cin.-Dayton, Inc., Ohio Casualty Corp., Fort Hamiliton Health Network. With U.S. Army, 1968-70. Mem. Am. Bankers Coun., Ohio Bankers Assn., Hamilton-Fairfield Arts Assn. Office: 1st Fin Bancorp 300 High St Hamilton OH 45011-6037

PONTY, JEAN-LUC, violinist, composer, producer; b. Avranches, Normandy, France, Sept. 29, 1942; came to U.S., 1973; Grad., Conservatoire National Superieur de Musique, Paris, 1960. Classical violinist to 1964, played with Concerts Lamoureux Symphony Orch.; jazz violinist, Europe, 1964-69, night club and music festivals with George Duke Trio, U.S., 1969, toured with own group, Europe, 1970-72, recorded with Elton John, Honky Chateau, 1972; with Frank Zappa and the Mothers of Invention, 1973, Mahavishnu Orch., 1974-75, pioneer of electric violin, Jazz innovator, headlining internat. concerts with own group since 1975; appearances at music festivals in the U.S. including Meadowbrook, Artpark, Wolf Trap, and in Europe Montreux, North Sea Festival, Paris Jazz Festival; spl. appearance as guest soloist with Montreal Symphony Orch., 1984, Toronto Symphony Orch., 1986, New Japan Philharm., 1987; world tour with Stanley Clarke and Al DiMeola The Rite of Strings, 1994, 95; own-produced albums include: Upon the Wings of Music, Aurora, Imaginary Voyage, Enigm atic Ocean, Cosmic Messenger, Jean-Luc Ponty: Live, Civilized Evil, A Taste for Passion, Mystical Adventures, Individual Choice, Open Mind, Fables, The Gift of Time, Storytelling, Tchokola (with African musicians), No Absolute Time, Live at Chene Park; television appearances include: (with Doug Kershaw and Itzhak Perlman) Fiddlers Three, Soundstage, Rock Concert, The Tonight Show, The Merv Griffin Show, Solid Gold, Pat Sajak Show CNN Entertainment; TV show appearances throughout Europe, Brazil, Chile and Venezuela. Recipient numerous internat. awards. Office: care Gary Kleinman Ste 119 12304 Santa Monica Blvd Los Angeles CA 90025

POOL, MARY JANE, design consultant, writer; d. Earl Lee Pool and Dorothy (Matthews) Evans. Grad., St. de Chantal Acad., 1942; BA in Art with honors, Drury Coll., 1946. Mem. staff Vogue mag., N.Y.C., 1946-68; assoc. merchandising editor Vogue mag., 1948-57, promotion dir., 1958-66, exec. editor, 1966-68; editor House and Garden mag., 1969, editor-in-chief, 1970-80; cons. Baker Furniture Co., 1981-94, Aves Advt., Inc., 1981-94, bd. dirs.; mem. bd. govs. Decorative Arts Trust; past mem. bd. govs. Fashion Group, Inc., N.Y.C. Co-author: The Angel Tree, 1984, The Gardens of Venice, 1989, The Gardens of Florence, 1992, The Angel Tree-A Christmas Celebration, 1993; editor: 20th Century Decorating, Architecture, Gardens, Billy Baldwin Decorates, 26 Easy Little Gardens. Mem. bus. com. N.Y. Zool. Soc., 1979-86; trustee Drury Coll., 1971—; bd. dirs. Isabel O'Neil Found., 1978—. Recipient award Nat. Soc. Interior Designers, Disting. Alumni award Drury Coll., 1961. Address: 1 E 66th St New York NY 10021-5852

POOL, PHILIP BEMIS, JR., investment banker; b. N.Y.C., Apr. 11, 1954; s. Philip B. and Virginia Middleton (French) P.; m. Joan H. Barnes, May 19, 1978; children: Elliott Livingston, Victoria Middleton. BS in Commerce, U. Va., 1976; MBA, Columbia U., 1980. Asst. treas. The Bank of N.Y., N.Y.C., 1976-78; v.p. Kidder Peabody & Co., Inc., N.Y.C., 1980-85; mng. dir. Merrill Lynch & Co., N.Y.C., 1985-94, Donaldson, Lufkin & Jenrette, N.Y.C., 1994—. Mem. Piping Rock Club (gov. 1989—), Meadow Brook Club, Lyford Cay Club, Racquet and Tennis Club. Republican. Episcopalian. Avocations: golf, squash.

POOL, TIMOTHY KEVIN, facilities management consultant; b. Lyons, Kans., Sept. 25, 1954; s. Rubben Roy and Vera Maxine (Vinson) P. BS, Kans. State U., 1977. With F.G. Holl Oil Co., Wichita, Kans., 1972-77; project mgr. The Bunce Corp., St. Louis, 1978-82, Bartex, Inc., Dallas, 1982-84; v.p. corp. real estate Bank Am.-Tex., 1984-94; pres., CEO Facilities Advantage, Inc., Dallas, 1994-95; dir. devel. svcs. Equity Realty & Investment Co., Inc., Colorado Springs, 1995-97; project mgr. Chistofferson Comml. Builders, Inc., 1997—. Mem. Planning Commn., Town of Green Mountain Falls, Colo. Mem. Internat. Facility Mgmt. Assn. (fin. svcs. coun., cert. 1993). Democrat. Christian Ch. Office: Christofferson Comml Builders Inc 1014 N Weber St Colorado Springs CO 80903-2422

POOLE, CECIL F., circuit court judge; b. Birmingham, Ala., 1914; children: Gayle, Patricia. LL.B., U. Mich.; LL.M., Harvard U., 1939. Practice of law San Francisco, former asst. dist. atty., 1951-58; clemency sec. to Gov. Brown of Calif., 1958-61; U.S. atty. No. Dist. Calif., 1961-70; Regents prof. Law U. Calif., Berkeley, 1970; counsel firm Jacobs, Sills & Coblentz, San Francisco, 1970-76; judge U.S. Dist. Ct., No. Dist. Calif., 1976-79, U.S. Ct. of Appeals for 9th Circuit, 1979—; adj. prof. Golden Gate U. Sch. Law, 1953-58; mem. adv. com. Nat. Commn. for Reform Fed. Criminal Laws, 1968-70. Served to 2d lt. AUS, World War II. Mem. ABA (chmn. sect. individual rights 1971-72, ho. of dels. 1972-74), San Francisco Bar Assn. (dir. 1975-76). Office: US Ct Appeals 9th Cir PO Box 193939 San Francisco CA 94119-3939

POOLE, EVA DURAINE, librarian; b. Farrell, Pa., Dec. 20, 1952; d. Leonard Milton and Polly Mae (Flint) Harris; m. Tommy Lynn Cole, May 15, 1970 (div. Sept. 1984); 1 child, Tommy Lynn Cole; m. Earnest Theodore Poole, Sept. 22, 1990; 1 child, Aleece Remelle Poole. BA in LS, Tex. Woman's U., 1974, MLS, 1976; postgrad., U. Houston, 1989. Libr. asst. Emily Fowler Pub. Libr., Denton, Tex., 1970-74; children's libr. Houston Pub. Libr., 1974-75, 1st asst. libr., 1976-77; children's libr. Ector County Libr., Odessa, Tex., 1977-80; head pub. svcs. Lee Davis Libr. San Jacinto Coll., Pasadena, Tex., 1980-84; libr. dir. San Jacinto Coll. South, Houston, 1984-90; libr. svcs. mgr. Emily Fowler Pub. Libr., Denton, 1990-93, interim dir., 1993; dir. libr. svcs. Denton Pub. Librs., Denton, 1993—; mem. Libr. Svcs. Constrn. Act Advisory Coun., 1994-97. Named to Outstanding Young Women of Am., 1991. Mem. ALA (conf. program com. 1994-96), Pub. Libr. Assn., Libr. Adminstrn. and Mgmt. Assn. (program com. 1994-97), Tex. Libr. Assn. (pub. libr. divsn. sec. 1995-96, chair elect 1996-97, chair 1997-98, leadership devel. com. 1995-97, leadership devel. com. chair 1996-97, alumnae 1st class Tex. Accelerated Libr. Leaders 1994, legis. com. 1997-99, Dist. 7 coun. 1996-99), Pub. Libr. Adminstrs. North Tex. (vice chair 1994-95, chair 1995-96), Tex. Mcpl. Libr. Dirs. Assn. (pres. 1995-96, grantee 1993), Denton Rotary Club, Tex. Mcpl. League (bd. dirs. 1997-99). Office: Denton Pub Libr 502 Oakland St Denton TX 76201-3102

POOLE, GALEN VINCENT, surgeon, educator, researcher; b. Pewee Valley, Ky., Apr. 13, 1951; s. Galen Vincent and Audrey (Taylor) P.; m. Carol Ruth Shepherd, Aug. 11, 1974; children: Erin Ruth, Matthew Shepherd. AB, Hanover Coll., 1973; MD, U. Ky., 1978. Diplomate Am. Bd. Surgery; added qualifications in surg. critical care. Intern, resident in surgery Bowman Gray-Wake Forest U., Winston-Salem, N.C., 1978-85; asst. clin. prof. Sch. Medicine U. Ill., Urbana, 1986-89; assoc. prof. Med. Ctr. U. Miss., Jackson, 1989-93, prof. surgery, 1993—. Author: Abdominal Wound Dehiscence, 1987; contbr. more than 70 articles to profl. jours. Chmn. Miss. State Com. on Trauma, Jackson, 1993—; dir. Trauma, Surg., and Critical Care, Jackson, 1989—; mem. adv. coun. Emergency Med. Svcs., Jackson, 1993—. Lt. col. USAFR, 1985-96. Fellow ACS, Southeastern Surg. Congress; mem. Am. Assn. for Surgery of Trauma, Soc. of Univ. Surgeons, Soc. for Surgery of the Alimentary Tract, Soc. for Critical Care Medicine, Alpha Omega Alpha. Home: 145 Summerwood Dr Jackson MS 39208-9075 Office: U Miss Med Ctr Dept Surgery 2500 N State St Jackson MS 39216-4500

POOLE, GORDON LEICESTER, lawyer; b. Mpls., Dec. 25, 1926; s. Arthur Bensell and Mildred Loyal (Wood) P.; m. Lois Claire Teasdale, Oct. 30, 1954; children—David Wilson, Edward Gray, Elisabeth Claire. A.B., Harvard U., 1949, LL.B., 1952. Assoc. Treadwell & Laughlin, San Francisco, 1953-54; assoc. Lillick, McHose & Charles, San Francisco, 1955-63, ptnr., 1963—, mem. exec. com., 1977-81, chmn. mgmt. com., 1981-84, chmn., 1984—. Contbr. articles to profl. jours. Pres. Young Republicans, San Mateo County, Calif., 1958-59; vestryman Trinity Episcopal Parish, Menlo Park, Calif., 1968, 70, 76-78, sr. warden, 1970. Served as sgt. U.S. Army, 1944-47, Korea. Mem. Calif. Bar Assn., San Francisco Bar Assn., Maritime Law Assn. (com. on marine financing), Maritime Adminstrv. Bar Assn., ABA, Mng. Ptnrs. Assn. Clubs: Bohemian, World Trade (San Francisco); Ladera Oaks (Menlo Park). Avocations: stamp collecting; marine paintings, prints and memorabilia. Home: 2280 Stockbridge Ave Woodside ity CA 94062-1130 Office: Lillick & Charles 2 Embarcadero Ctr Ste 2600 San Francisco CA 94111-3900

POOLE, NANCY GEDDES, art gallery curator; b. London, Ont., Can., May 10, 1930; d. John Hardy and Kathleen Edwards (Robinson) G.; m. William Robert Poole, Aug. 15, 1952; 1 child, Andrea Mary. BA, U. Western Ont., 1956, LLD, 1990. Owner, dir. Nancy Poole's Studio, Toronto, Ont., Can., 1969-78; acting dir. London Regional Art Gallery, Ont., Can., 1981—, exec. dir., 1985-89; dir. London Regional Art and Hist. Museums, Ont., Can., 1989-95; chair governing coun. Ont. Coll. Art, 1972-73; bd. dirs. Robarts Rsch. Inst., 1995. Author: The Art of London 1939-1980, 1984; editor Jack Chambers, 1978, The Collection, 1990. Bd. govs. U. Western Ont., 1974-85; bd. dirs. Western Area Youth Svcs., 1996. Fellow Ont. Coll. Art. Office: 420 Fanshawe Park Rd, London, ON Canada N5X 2S9

POOLE, RICHARD WILLIAM, economics educator; b. Oklahoma City, Dec. 4, 1927; s. William Robert and Lois (Spicer) P.; m. Bertha Lynn Mehr, July 28, 1950; children: Richard William, Laura Lynne, Mark Stephen. B.S., U. Okla., 1951, M.B.A., 1952; postgrad., George Washington U., 1957-58; Ph.D., Okla. State U., 1960. Research analyst Okla. Gas & Electric Co., Oklahoma City, 1952- 54; mgr. sci. and mfg. devel. dept. Oklahoma City C. of C., 1954-57; mgr. Office of J.E. Webb, Washington, 1957-58; instr., asst. prof., assoc. prof., prof. econs. Okla. State U., Stillwater, 1960-65; prof. econs., dean Coll. Bus. Adminstrn. Okla. State U., 1965-72, v.p., prof. econs., 1972-88, Regents Disting. Svc. prof., prof. econs., 1988-93, emeritus v.p., dean, Regents Disting. Svc. prof./prof. econ., 1993—; cons. to adminstr. NASA, Washington, 1961-69; adviser subcom. on govt. rsch. U.S. Senate, 1966-69; lectr. Intermediate Sch. Banking, Ops. Mgmt. Sch., Okla. Bankers Assn., 1968-89; lectr. internat. off-campus programs, Okla. City U., 1994-96. Author: (with others) The Oklahoma Economy, 1963, County Building Block Data for Regional Analysis, 1965. Mem. Gov.' Com. on Devel. Ark.-Verdigris Waterway, 1970-71, Gov.'s Five-Yr. Econ. Devel. Plan, 1993; past v.p., bd. dirs., past chmn. Mid-Continent Rsch. and Devel. Coun. 2d lt., arty. U.S. Army, 1946-48. Recipient Delta Sigma Pi Gold Key award Coll. Bus. Adminstrn., U. Okla., 1951, Tchg. award on Am. free enterprise sys. Merrick Found., 1992, Disting. Alumni award Okla. State U., 1995; inductee Coll. Bus. Adminstrn. Hall of Fame, Okla. State U., 1993; named to Stillwater Hall of Fame, Payne County Hist. Soc. and Stillwater C. of C., 1996. Mem. Southwestern Econ. Assn. (past pres.), Am. Assembly Collegiate Schs. Bus. (past bd. dirs.), Nat. Assn. State Univs. and Land Grant Colls. (past chmn. commn. on edn. for bus. professions), Southwestern Bus. Adminstrn. Assn. (past pres.), Okla. C. of C. (past bd. dirs.), Stillwater C. of C. (past bd. dirs. and pres.), Beta Gamma Sigma (past bd. dirs.), Phi Kappa Phi, Phi Eta Sigma, Omicron Delta Kappa. Home: 815 S Shumard Dr Stillwater OK 74074-1136

POOLE, RICHARD WILLIAM, JR., secondary school educator; b. Norman, Okla., Apr. 13, 1951; s. Richrad W. and Lynn (Mehr) P.; m. Sonya Lee, Mar. 20, 1982; 1 child, Amanda Lee. BS in Social Studies, Okla. State U., Stillwater, 1976. Tchr., coach West Jr. H.S., Ponca City, Okla., 1976-80; tchr., coach Ponca City Sr. H.S., 1980-92, Am. history tchr., supr. jr. high athletics, 1992—. Served with USNR, 1969-71, Viet Nam. Mem. Lions Club (tail twister 1992, v.p. 1993, pres. After 5 club 1994), Elks. Democrat. Methodist. Avocations: golf, fishing, country music, reading history books. Home: 1306 El Camino St Ponca City OK 74604-4011

POOLE, ROBERT ANTHONY, journalist; b. St. Austell, Cornwall, Eng., Dec. 17, 1944; arrived in Can., 1977; m. Valerie Avril Taggart, Apr. 14, 1973; children—Claire Lucy, Emma Louise. Irish editor Press Assn., Belfast, Northern Ireland, 1970-77; gen. reporter Calgary Herald, Alta., Can., 1977-79; city editor Calgary Albertan, 1979-80; city editor Calgary Sun, 1980-81, mng. editor, 1981-84, editor-in-chief, 1984-96. Office: Calgary Sun, 2615 12th St NE, Calgary, AB Canada T2E 7W9

POOLE, WILLIAM, economics educator, consultant; b. Wilmington, Del., June 19, 1937; s. William and Louise (Hiller) P.; m. Mary Lynne Ahroon, June 26, 1960; children—William, Lester Allen, Jonathan Carl. AB, Swarthmore Coll., 1959, LLD (hon.), 1989; MBA, U. Chgo., 1963, PhD, 1966. Asst. prof. polit. economy Johns Hopkins U., Balt., 1963-69; professorial lectr. Am. U., Washington, 1970-71; assoc. professorial lectr. George Washington U., Washington, 1971-73; lectr. Georgetown U., Washington, 1972, Harvard U., Cambridge, Mass., 1973; vis. lectr. MIT, Cambridge, 1974, 77; Bank Mees and Hope vis. prof. econs. Erasmus U. Rotterdam, 1991; prof. econs. Brown U., Providence, R.I., 1974, 85—, dir. ctr. for the study fin. markets and insts., 1987-92, prof., chmn. econs. dept., 1981-82, 85-86; economist Bd. Govs. of FRS, Washington, 1964, 1969-70, sr. economist, 1970-74; vis. scholar Fed. Res. Bank, San Francisco, 1977; adviser Fed. Res. Bank, Boston, 1973-74, cons., 1974-81; vis. economist Res. Bank of Australia, 1980-81; mem. Council Econ. Advisers, 1982-85; adj. scholar Cato Inst., 1985—. Mem. Am. Econ. Assn., Am. Fin. Assn. (mem. nominating com. 1979), Western Econ. Assn. (mem. internat. exec. com. 1986-89, mem. nominating com. 1995). Office: Brown U Dept Econs 64 Waterman St Providence RI 02912-9029

POOLE, WILLIAM LANNON, JR., dermatologist; b. Birmingham, Ala., Mar. 28, 1939; s. Wiliam L. Sr. and Mildred (Yates) P.; m. Mary Dudley; children: Shannon, Kimberly, Bill III. MD, U. Ala., 1964. Diplomate Am. Bd. Dermatology. Pvt. practice East Central, Ala. With U.S. Army, Vietnam, 1966-68. Mem. Am. Acad. Dermatology, Am. Soc. Dermatological Surgery, Ala. Dermatology Soc. Avocations: golf, flying, radio, astronomy. Office: Craddock Clinic 308 W Hickory St Sylacauga AL 35150-2914

POOLER, ROSEMARY S., federal judge; b. 1938. BA, Brooklyn Coll., 1959; MA, Univ. of Conn., 1961; JD, Univ. of Mich. Law Sch., 1965. With Crystal, Manes & Rifken, Syracuse, 1966-69, Michaels and Michaels, Syracuse, 1969-72; asst. corp. counsel Dir. of Consumer Affairs Unit, Syracuse, 1972-73; common counsel City of Syracuse N.Y. Public Interest Rsch. Group, 1974-75; chmn., exec. dir. Consumer Protection Bd., 1975-80; commr. N.Y. State Public Services Commn., 1981-86; staff dir. N.Y. State Assembly, Com. on Corps., Authorities and Commns., 1987-94; judge Supreme Ct., 5th Judicial Dist., 1991-94; district judge U.S. Dist. Ct. (N.Y. no. dist.), 2nd circuit, Syracuse, 1994—; vis. prof. of law Syracuse Univ. Coll. of Law, 1987-88; v.p. legal affairs Atlantic States Legal Found., 1989-90. Mem. Onondaga County Bar Assn., N.Y. State Bar Assn., Women's Bar Assn. of the State of N.Y., Assn. of Supreme Ct. Justices of the State of N.Y. Office: Federal Bldg PO Box 7395 100 S Clinton St Rm 1240 Syracuse NY 13261-7395*

POOLEY, BEVERLEY JOHN, law educator, librarian; b. London, Eng., Apr. 4, 1934; came to U.S., 1957; U.S. citizen, 1993; s. William Vincent and Christine Beatrice (Coleman) P.; m. Patricia Joan Ray, June 8, 1958; children—Christopher Jonathan, Rachel Vanessa. BA, Cambridge U., Eng., 1956, LLB, 1957; LLM, U. Mich., Ann Arbor, 1958, SJD, 1961, MLS, 1964. Legis. analyst U. Mich. Law Sch., Ann Arbor, 1958-60; lectr. U. Ghana Law Sch., 1960-62; instr. U. Mich. Law Sch., Ann Arbor, 1962-63, asst. prof., 1963-66, assoc. prof., 1966-70, dir. law library, 1966-84, prof., 1970—, assoc. dean law library, 1984-94. Author: The Evolution of British Planning Legislation, 1960; Planning and Zoning in the United States, 1961. Scholar, King's Coll., Cambridge, Eng., 1956; Blackstone Scholar, Middle Temple, London, 1957. Democrat. Avocations: Acting; musical comedy; food preparation.

POOLEY, JAMES HENRY ANDERSON, lawyer, author; b. Dayton, Ohio, Oct. 4, 1948; s. Howard Carl and Daisy Frances (Lindsley) P.; children by previous marriage: Jefferson Douglas, Christopher James; m. Laura Jean Anderson, Oct. 13, 1984; 1 child, Catherine Lindsley. BA, Lafayette Coll., 1970; JD, Columbia U., 1973. Bar: Calif. 1973, U.S. Dist. Ct. (no. dist.) Calif. 1973, U.S. Ct. Appeals (9th cir.) 1974, U.S. Supreme Ct. 1977, U.S. Dist. Ct. (cen. dist.) Calif. 1978. Assoc. Wilson, Mosher & Sonsini, Palo Alto, Calif., 1973-78; ptnr. Mosher, Pooley & Sullivan, Palo Alto, 1978-88, Graham and James, 1988-93, Fish & Richardson, Menlo Park, 1993—; lectr. Practicing Law Inst., N.Y.C., 1983, 85-86, 88, 95, Santa Clara U. Sch. Law, 1985-87, U. Calif., Boalt Hall Sch. Law, 1997—. Author: Trade Secrets, 1982, Protecting Technology, 1983, Trying the High Technology Case, 1984, Trade Secrets: A Guide to Protecting Proprietary Business Information, 1989, Trade Secret Law and Litigation, 1997; contbr. articles to profl. jours.; editor-in-chief Trade Secret Law Reporter, 1984-85; bd. advisors Santa Clara Computer and High Tech. Law Jour., 1984—; chair Nat. Trade Secret Law Inst., 1994. Arbitrator, spl. master U.S. Dist. Ct. (no. dist.) Calif., Santa Clara County Superior Ct., San Jose, 1979—. Mem. Am. Intellectual Property Lawyers Assn. chmn. trade secrets com. 1996—), Am. Electronics Assn. (chmn. lawyers' com. 1981-82), Internat. Bar Assn., Union Internationale des Avocats. Republican. Office: Fish & Richardson 2200 Sand Hill Rd Ste 100 Menlo Park CA 94025-6936

POOLMAN, JIM, state legislator; b. Fargo, N.D., May 15, 1970; s. Robert Francis and Susan Faye (Brown) P. BBA, U. N.D., 1992, postgrad., 1994—. Sales cons. Straus Co., Grand Forks, N.D., 1987-95; state representative N.D. State Ho. of Reps., 1992—; trust officer First Am. Bank, 1995—. Task force State of N.D., Grand Forks, 1992; mem. United Hosp. Corp. United Health, Grand Forks, 1992—, Presdl. Search Com., U. N.D., 1992; bd. dirs. Red River Red Cross, 1995—. Mem. Toastmasters Internat. (sec.), Phi Delta Theta Alumni (varsity bachelors club scholarship ednl. found. 1992). Republican. Lutheran. Avocations: fishing, water sports, golf. Home: 715 N 42d St # 104B Grand Forks ND 58203-2846

POON, PETER TIN-YAU, engineer, physicist; b. Hengyang, Hunan, China, May 31, 1944; came to U.S., 1967; s. Sam. Chak-Kwong and Lai (Yiu) P.; m. Mable Tsang, Apr. 13, 1974; children: Amy Wei-Ling, Brian Wing-Yan. BS, U. Hong Kong, 1965; MA, Calif. State U., Long Beach, 1969; PhD, U. So. Calif., L.A., 1974. Sr. engr. gasdynamics, planetary probe heat shield design, sys. simulation Jet Propulsion Lab./Calif. Inst. Tech., Pasadena, 1974-77, tech. mgr. advanced solar receiver, task leader advanced solar concentrator, 1978-80, systems engr. mission control and computing ctr. devel., 1981-83; advisor Space Sta. Ada Task, staff mem, task leader software mgmt. and assurance program NASA, 1984-85; mission control ctr. devel. telemetry systems engr. software mgmt. stds., element mgr. NASA software info. sys. Jet Propulsion Lab./Calif. Inst. Tech., Pasadena, 1986-88, systems mgr. for missions to Mars, Comet/Asteroid/Saturn, flight projects interface office, 1988-91, multimission ground systems office mgr. Mission to Mars, 1991-93, telecomm. and mission svcs. mgr. Cassini Mission to Saturn, 1993—; U.S.A. chmn., program com. 2d Internat. Software Engring. Stds. Symposium, Montreal, Can., 1994-95; program com. session chair Software Engring. Stds. Symposium, Brighton, Eng., 1992-93; mem. program com., panel chair 3d Internat. Software Engring. Stds. Symposium, 1995-97; session chair, mem. program com. IEEE Internat. Conf. on Engring. of Complex Computer Systems, Montreal, 1995-96, Como, Italy, 1996-97; mem. Internat. Orgn. for Standardization/Internat. Electrotech. Com./Joint Tech. Com. in Info. Tech. Subcom. Working Group and U.S. Technical Adv. Group, 1995—; U.S. del., Prague, Czech Republic, 1996, Paris, 1996; U.S. del., Walnut Creek, U.S., 1997; program com. mem. 5th Ann. Conf. on Artificial Intelligence and ADA, 1989, 6th Ann Conf. on Artificial Intelligence and ADA, 1990. Author numerous profl. publs. Recipient numerous group awards in field, NASA, 1977-93; represent NASA cert. of recognition, Inventions and Contbns. Bd. Mem. IEEE Software Engring. Stds. (exec. com. 1993—, co-author long range plans and stds. survey 1993), Arcadia Music Club (pres. 1994-95, 1st v.p. 1993-94), Sigma Xi, Eta Kappa Nu, Phi Kappa Phi, Athenaeum. Avocations: music appreciation, hiking, theatre arts. Office: Jet Propulsion Lab Calif Inst Tech Mail Stop 303-402 4800 Oak Grove Dr Pasadena CA 91109-8001

POONS, LARRY, artist; b. Tokyo, Oct. 1, 1937; came to U.S., 1938; Student, New Eng. Conservatory Music, 1955-57, Boston Mus. Fine Arts Sch., 1958. Mem. vis. faculty N.Y. Studio Sch., 1967. Author: The Structure of Color, 1971; exhbns. include, Green Gallery, N.Y.C., 1963-65, Art Inst. Chgo., 1966, Corcoran Gallery Art, Carnegie Inst., 1967, Leo Castelli Gallery, 1967-68, Documenta IV, Kassel, W. Ger., 1968, Whitney Mus. Am. Art Ann., 1968, 72, Lawrence Rubin Gallery, 1970-73, Whitney Biennial, 1973, Knoedler & Co., 1973-78, Knoedler Contemporary Art, N.Y.C., 1974-78, Andre Emmerlich Gallery, N.Y.C., 1979-87, Albright-Knox Art Gallery, Buffalo, 1968, 70, Pasadena Art Mus., 1969, Gallery 99, Bar Harbor Islands, Fla., 1981, Mus. Fine Arts, Boston, 1981-82, Galerie Montaigne, Paris, 1990, Helander Gallery, Palm Beach, Fla., 1990, Salander-O'Reilly Galleries, N.Y.C., 1990, Beverly Hills, Calif., 1990, Berlin, 1990, Gallery Afinsa, Madrid, 1991; represented in permanent collection, Mus. Modern Art, N.Y.C., Allen Meml. Art Mus., Oberlin Coll., Cleve. Mus. Art, Hirschhorn Mus. and Sculpture Garden, Washington, Milw. Art Ctr., Solomon R. Guggenheim Mus., N.Y.C., Tate Gallery, London, Whitney Mus. Am. Art, Met. Mus. Art, Chgo. Art Inst., Denver Mus., Boston Mus. Fine Arts, Albright-Knox Art Gallery, Stedelijk Mus., Amsterdam, Woodward Found., Washington, David Mirvish Gallery, Toronto; artist-in-residence, Inst. Humanistic Studies, Aspen, Colo., 1966-67. Address: PO Box 115 Islamorada FL 33036

POOR, ANNE, artist; b. N.Y.C., Jan. 2, 1918; d. Henry Varnum and Bessie (Breuer) P. Student, Bennington Coll., 1936, 38, Art Students League, 1935, Acad. Julien, Paris. trustee, gov. Skowhegan Sch. Painting and Sculpture, 1947-61, 89, 96; artist corr. WAC, 1943-45. Illustrator: Greece, 1964; works exhibited Am. Brit. Art Ctr., 1944, 45, 48, Maynard Walker Gallery, 1950, Graham Gallery, 1957-59, 62, 68-71, 85, Rockland Ctr. for Arts, West Nyack, N.Y., 1982, 83, Terry Dintefass Gallery, N.Y.C.; executed murals, P.O., Gleason, Tenn., DePew, N.Y., South Solon, Maine, Free Mtg. House, 1957, others; represented permanent collections Whitney Mus., Bklyn. Mus., Wichita Mus., Art Inst. Chgo. Edwin Austin Abbey Meml. fellow, 1948; grantee Nat. Inst. Arts and Letters, 1957; recipient Benjamin Altman 1st prize landscape painting N.A.D., 1971, 86, Childe Hassam award, 1972, 77. Mem. Artists Equity Assn., Nat. Acad. Arts and Letters.

POOR, CLARENCE ALEXANDER, retired physician; b. Ashland, Oreg., Oct. 29, 1911; s. Lester Clarence and Matilda Ellen (Doty) P.; AB, Willamette U., 1932; MD, U. Oreg., 1936. Diplomate Am. Bd. Internal Medicine. Intern U. Wis., Madison, 1936-37, resident in internal medicine, 1937-40, instr. dept. pathology Med. Sch., 1940-41, clin. instr., clin. asst. dept. internal medicine, 1942-44; pvt. practice medicine specializing in internal medicine, Oakland, Calif., 1944-97; mem. emeritus staff Highland Alameda County Hosp., Oakland, 1949—; mem. staff Providence Hosp., Oakland, 1947-97, pres. staff, 1968-69; staff mem. Samuel Meritt Hosp., Oakland, 1958-97; staff mem. Summit Med. Ctr. (merger Providence Hosp. and Samuel Merritt Hosp.), 1991-97; retired, 1997—. Mem. Nat. Coun. on Alcoholism, 1974—, bd. dirs. Bay Area, 1977—. Mem. Am., Calif., Alameda-Contra Costa med. assns., Alameda County Heart Assn. (trustee 1955-62, 72-82, pres. 1960-61), Calif. Heart Assn. (dir. 1962-72), Soc. for Clin. and Exptl. Hypnosis, Am. Soc. Clin. Hypnosis, San Francisco Acad. Hypnosis (dir. 1966—, pres. 1973). Home: 1241 West View Dr Berkeley CA 94705-1650 *Personal philosophy: No matter how easy or how hard the task, the goal is that it be an enjoyment on final review.*

POOR, HAROLD VINCENT, electrical engineering educator; b. Columbus, Ga., Oct. 2, 1951; s. Harold Edgar and Virginia (Hardin) P.; m. Connie Irene Hazelwood, Sept. 1, 1973; children: Kristin Elizabeth, Lauren Alissa. BEE with highest honors, Auburn U., 1972; PhD, Princeton U., 1977. Asst. prof. U. Ill., Urbana, 1977-81, assoc. prof., 1981-84, prof., 1984-90; prof. dept. elec. engring. Princeton (N.J.) U., 1990—; acad. visitor Imperial Coll. London U., 1985; vis. prof. Newcastle (Australia) U., 1987; sr. visiting fellow Imperial Coll., London U., 1993; cons. numerous orgns., 1978—. Author: An Introduction to Signal Detection and Estimation, 1988, 2d edit., 1994; contbr. numerous articles to profl. jours. Grantee NSF, Office of Naval Rsch., Army Rsch. Office, 1978—; recipient Terman award Am. Soc. Engring. Edn., 1992, Centennial certificate Am. Soc. for Engring. Edn., 1993. Fellow IEEE (bd. dirs. 1991-92), AAAS, Acoustical Soc. Am.; mem. Info. Theory Soc. of IEEE (pres. 1990), IEEE Control Sys. Soc. (Disting. Mem. award 1994), Cosmos Club (Washington). Office: Princeton Univ Dept Elec Engring Princeton NJ 08544

POOR, JANET MEAKIN, landscape designer; b. Cin., Nov. 27, 1929; d. Cyrus Lee and Helen Keats (Meakin) Lee-Hofer; m. Edward King Poor III, June 23, 1951; children: Edward King IV, Thomas Meakin. Student, Stephens Coll., 1947-48, U. Cinn., 1949-51, Triton Coll., 1973-76. Pres. Janet Meakin Poor Landscape Design, Winnetka, Ill., 1975—; chmn. bd. dirs. Cgho. Horticultural Soc., Chgo. Botanic Garden. Author, editor: Plants That Merit Attention Vol. I: Trees, 1984; contbr. articles to profl. jours. Participant in longe range planning City of Winnetka, 1978-82, archtl. and environ. bd., 1980-84, beautification commn., 1978-84, garden coun., 1978-82; adv. coun., sec. of agr. Nat. Arboretum, Washington; nat. adv. bd. Filoli, San Francisco; trustee Ctr. Plant Conservation at Mo. Botanical Garden, St. Louis, also mem. exec. com.; mem. adv. coun. The Garden Conservancy, 1989—; trustee Winnetka Congl. Ch., 1978-80. Recipient merit award Hadley Sch. Blind, 1972; named Vol. of Yr. Hadley Sch. Blind. Mem. Chgo. Hort. Soc. (chmn. bd. dirs. 1987-93, medal 1984, gold medal garden design, exec. com., chmn. rsch. com., women's bd., designer herb garden Farwell Gardens at Chgo. Botanic Garden, Hutchinson medal 1994), Am. Hort. Soc. (bd. dirs., Catherine H. Sweeney award 1985), Garden Club Am. (chmn. nat. plant exchange 1980-81, chmn. hort. com. 1981-83, bd. dirs., 1983-85, corresponding sec. 1985-87, Horticulture award Zone X1 1981, Creative Leadership award 1986), Fortnightly Club, Garden Guild (bd. dirs.), Garden Club Am. (v.p. 1987-89, medal awards chmn. 1991-93, Honor medal 1994). Republican. Avocations: gardening, writing, music, hort. rsch., lecturing.

POOR, PETER VARNUM, producer, director; b. N.Y.C., May 17, 1926; s. Henry Varnum and Bessie Breuer (Freedman) P.; m. Eloise Marcovicci Miller, Sept. 27, 1950; children: Candida Eustacia, Anna Maria, Graham Varnum. BA, Harvard U., 1947; postgrad., Centro Sperimentale di Cinematografia, Rome, 1951-52. Prodn. asst. New World Films, N.Y.C., 1948; editor, dir. Willard Pictures, N.Y.C., 1948-51; film editor, dir. and producer CBS News-Airpower, 1954-57, 7 Lively Arts, 1957-58, Twentieth Century, 1958-66, 21st Century, 1966-69, 60 Minutes, 1970-71, CBS Reports, 1971-75; sr. producer NBC News, Monitor, First Camera, White Paper, 1977-87; freelance producer and dir. Crow House Prodns., N.Y.C., 1988—; instr. in TV journalism Fordham U., 1976-78; mem. Screening Com. for Fulbright Grants in Film, TV and Radio, 1965-67, chmn., 1967, 70; adj. assoc. history of documentary Columbia U. Grad. Sch. Journalism, 1987; adj. asst. prof. visual arts NYU, 1991-92. Producer-dir.: (TV documentary films) What's New at School, 1972, The IQ Myth, 1975, The Biggest Lump of Money in the World, 1985, The Japan They Don't Talk About, 1986, Nuclear Power in France, 1987, The Cronkite Report, 1993. Served with USAF, 1944-45. Recipient Emmy award Acad. TV Arts and Sci., 1961, 62, 67, Lasker TV award Lasker Found., 1968, 69, U.S. CEA Forum award, 1967, 87; hon. mention Robert Kennedy Journalism Award in TV, 1976; Fulbright scholar, 1951-52. Mem. Dirs. Guild Am. (coun. 1980-90), Film Editors Union, Writers Guild Am. East. Club: Phoenix S-K (Cambridge, Mass.). Avocations: bicycling, reading, photography, gardening. Home and Office: 1150 5th Ave New York NY 10128-0724

POORE, JAMES ALBERT, III, lawyer; b. Butte, Mont., June 28, 1943; s. James A. Jr. and Jesse (Wild) P.; m. Shelley A. Borgstede, Feb. 12, 1989; children: James IV, Jeffrey. AB, Stanford U., 1965; JD with honors, U. Mont., 1968. Bar: Mont. 1968, U.S. Dist. Ct. Mont. 1968, U.S. Ct. Appeals (9th cir.) 1972, U.S. Supreme Ct. 1973. Assoc. Poore, Poore, McKenzie & Roth, Butte, 1968-74; prin., v.p. Poore, Roth & Robinson, P.C., Butte, 1974-96; ptnr. Knight, Masar & Poore, LLP, Missoula, Mont., 1996Ô; speaker in field. Assoc. editor U. Mont. Law Rev., 1967-68; contbg. editor Product Liability Desk Reference, 1997; contbr. articles to profl. publs. Dist. dir. Boy Scouts Am., S.W. Mont., 1969; dir. YMCA, Butte, 1981-83; founding bd. dirs. Hospice of Butte, 1982-85, Butte Community Theater, 1977-80; pres. Butte Uptown Assn., 1974; dir. Butte Silverbow Am. Cancer Soc. Bd., 1992-95. Fellow Am. Bar Found.; mem. ABA, State Bar Mont., Am. Judicature Soc., Silver Bow Bar Assn., Western Mont. Bar Assn., Phi Delta Phi. Home: 910 Greenough Dr W Missoula MT 59802-3739 Office: Knight Masar & Poore PLLP 300 The Florence 111 N Higgins Ave Missoula MT 59802-4401

POORE, RALPH EZRA, JR., public relations professional; b. Mobile, Ala., Mar. 21, 1951; s. Ralph Ezra Sr. and Beatrice Valara (Pierce) P.; m. Carron Lynn Walker, May 26, 1979 (div. Apr. 1987); 1 child, Ralph Ezra III; m. Becky Jo Johnson, July 27, 1996. BA, U. So. Ala., 1973; MA, U. Ala., Tuscaloosa, 1974. Reporter Fairhope (Ala.) Courier, 1973, George County Times, Lucedale, Miss., 1975; journalism instr. Spring Hill Coll., Mobile, 1975-78; assoc. editor The News-Herald, Chickasaw, Ala., 1978-79; reporter The Mobile Press Register, 1979-84, editorial page editor, 1984-94; editorial page editor The Idaho Statesman, Boise, 1994-96, bus. editor, 1996-97; pub. rels. specialist The Idaho Transp. Dept., Boise, 1997—. Mem. exec. com. Mobile Community Orgn., 1975; bd. dirs. Friends of Mus., Mobile, 1976-78; mem. Mobile Historic Devel. Commn., 1977-79; chmn. bd. dirs. John M. Will Meml. Scholarship Found., Mobile, 1982-84. Recipient Newswriting award Ala. AP, 1981, 83, 90, Community Svc. award, Press Club Mobile, 1979, Commendation award, 1981. Mem. Nat. Conf. Editorial Writers, Soc. Profl. Journalists (pres. Mobile chpt. 1982-83). Methodist. Avocations: triathlete, writing history. Home: 2575 Falling Brook Ln Boise ID 83706 Office: The Idaho Transp Dept PO Box 7129 Boise ID 83707-1120

POORMAN, ROBERT LEWIS, education educator, consultant, academic administrator; b. Germantown, Ohio, Dec. 9, 1926; s. Dale Lowell and Bernice Velma (Krick) P.; m. Lois May Romer, Dec. 26, 1949; children: Paula Beth, Janice Marie, Mark Leon, John Alex, Lisa Ann, Daniel Romer. Student, Ohio Wesleyan U., 1944-45, U. Va., 1945-46; B.S.Ed., Ohio State U., 1948, M.A., 1950; postgrad., U. So. Calif., 1951-53; Ed.D. (Kellogg fellow 1960-62, Disting. Scholar Tuition grantee 1960-62), UCLA, 1964. Tchr., counselor, adminstr., secondary schs. Colo., Mo., Ariz., 1948-57; registrar Phoenix Coll., 1957-60; intern Bakersfield Coll., 1960-63, asst. to pres., 1963-64, asso. dean instrn., 1964-65, dean students, 1965-67; founding pres. Lincoln Land Community Coll., 1967-88, pres. emeritus; edn. cons. MARA of Malaysia, 1983; higher edn. cons. Springfield, Ill., 1988—; interim pres. Parkland Coll., Champaign, Ill., 1989-90; Fulbright lectr., cons. to Lithuania, 1993; vis. assoc. prof. Fla. Internat. U., 1994-95. Contbr. articles to profl. jours. Bd. dirs. (past) United Way of Springfield, bd. dirs. Urban League of Springfield, Good Will Industries of Springfield, Springfield (Ill.) Symphony, Catholic Youth Orgn., Springfield, Gov.'s Prayer Breakfast, Springfield Mental Health, Griffin H.S. Bd., Diocesan Sem.; mem. adv. bd. Sacred Heart Acad., Springfield Commn. on Internat. Visitors, Sisters Cities Assn. Served with USNR, 1944-46. Recipient Midwest region Chief Exec. Officer of Yr. Assn. Community Coll. Trustees, 1988, recognition Ill. Community Coll. Trustees Assn., 1988; named an Outstanding Chief Exec. Officer for Ill. Community Colls. U. Tex. Leadership Program, 1987; Phi Theta Kappa fellow, 1981. Mem. Am. Assn. Community and Jr. Colls., Ill. Council Public Community Coll. Pres. (sec. 1973-74, vice chmn. 1974-75, chmn. 1975-76), Council North Central Community and Jr. Colls. (exec. bd. 1979-81), North Central Assn. (cons., evaluator 1984-88). Republican. Roman Catholic. Home and Office: 2324 Willemoore Ave Springfield IL 62704-4362

POP, IGGY (JAMES NEWELL OSTERBERG), composer, singer, musician; b. Muskegon, Mich., Apr. 21, 1947; s. James Newell and Louella Kristine (Christensen) Osterberg. Student, U. Mich., 1963-64. Drummer, lead singer, composer The Iguanas, 1966-67; lead singer, composer The Stooges, 1967-74; solo artist, 1975—, toured extensively with David Bowie and others. composer music and lyrics for over 90 songs including China Girl (recorded by David Bowie); rec. artist, albums include The Stooges, 1970, Funhouse, 1972, Raw Power, 1973, Kill City, 1976, The Idiot, 1977, Lust for Life, 1977, TV Eye, 1977, New Values, 1979, Soldier, 1980, Party, 1982, Zombie Birdhouse, 1983, Blah, Blah, Blah, 1986, Instinct (Grammy nomination 1988), 1988, BrickXBricks, 1990, ArizonaDream, 1992, American Caesar, 1993, We Are Not Talking About Commercial Shit, 1995, Wake Up Suckers, 1995, Naughty Little Doggie, 1996; has recorded for Elektra, Columbia; RCA, solo albums for Arista, Chrysallis, A&M; guest appearances on television and prodns.; known as Godfather of Punk; appeared in films The Color of Money, Cry-Baby, 1990, Coffey and Cigarettes (Palme d'Or 1993). Named Punk of the Yr. Creem Mag. *

POPCHRISTOV, DAMYAN CHRISTOV, theater director and educator; b. Sofia, Bulgaria, June 25, 1956; came to U.S., 1990; s. Christo Damyanov and Antoinette Ivanova (Popova) P.; m. Olga Lebedeva-Popchristova; 1 child, Antoinette Damyanova. BFA in Acting, Theater Acad. Sofia, 1979, MFA in Directing, 1981. Resident dir. City Theater Haskovo, Bulgaria, 1981-85, City Theater Plovdiv, Bulgaria, 1985-89, Nat. Youth Theater Bulgaria, Sofia, 1989-90; asst. prof. theater Arts Acad. Sofia, 1987-89, assoc. prof., 1989-91; mem. adj. faculty NYU Tisch Sch. Arts, N.Y.C., 1991—; dir. Trinity/LaMaMa N.Y.C. Performing Arts Program, 1994—; guest dir. several theaters, Sofia, Vidin, St. Petersburg, 1981-90; founder, dir. Magic Voices, exptl. theater co., Sofia, 1989-91; vis. prof. U. Tenn., 1990, Columbia U., 1991; vis. prof., theater dir. Trinity Coll., Hartford, Conn., 1992; participant Knoxville (Tenn.) World Theater Festival, 1990, Edmonton (Alta., Can.) Fringe Festival, 1990, Maison des Cultures du Monde, Paris, 1991; mem. bd. new theater com. Internat. Theater Inst., 1985—, pres., 1989—, gen. sec. Bulgarian Ctr., 1987-91. Guest dir. The Last Night of Socrates, 1988, Tale for the Four Hats, 1989, Lattice and Lavage, 1990, The Murderer, 1990, The Underground Man, 1990; founder, dir. internat. festival Theater in a Suitcase, Sofia, 1987—. Office: NYU Tisch Sch Arts 721 Broadway Fl 3 New York NY 10003-6807

POPE, ALEXANDER H., lawyer, former county official; b. N.Y.C., June 4, 1929; s. Clifford H. and Sarah H. (Davis) P.; m. Katherine Mackinlay, Sept. 14, 1985; children by previous marriage: Stephen C., Virginia L., Daniel M. A.B. with honors, U. Chgo., 1948, J.D., 1952. Bar: Ill. 1952, Republic of Korea 1953, Calif. 1955, U.S. Supreme Ct. 1970. Pvt. practice L.A., 1955-77, 87-96; assoc. David Ziskind, L.A., 1955; ptnr. Shadle, Kennedy & Pope, L.A., 1956, Fine & Pope, L.A., 1957-59, 61-77; legis. sec. to gov. State of Calif., 1959-61; county assessor Los Angeles County, L.A., 1978-86; ptnr. Mayer, Brown & Platt, L.A., 1987-88, Barash & Hill, L.A., 1989-92; of counsel Seyforth, Shaw, Fairweather & Geraldson, L.A., 1993-96; exec. dir. Calif. citizens budget commn. Ctr. Govtl. Studies, Los Angeles, 1997—. Pres. Westchester Mental Health Clinic, 1963; nat. bd. mem. Vols. for Stevenson, 1952; vice-chmn. L.A. County Dem. Cen. Com., 1958-59; mem. Calif. Hwy. Commn., 1966-70; mem. L.A. Bd. Airport Commrs., 1973-77, v.p., 1973-75, pres., 1975-76; trustee, sec. L.A. Theatre Ctr., 1984-89. With U.S. Army, 1952-54, Korea. Mem. ACLU, Calif. State Bar Assn. (state and local tax com. 1991—, chair 1993-94), L.A. County Bar Assn. (state and local tax com. 1987—, chair 1995-96), U. Chgo. Alumni Club Greater L.A. (pres. 1970-71), Zero Population Growth, Ams. United, Common Cause, Order of Coif, Phi Beta Kappa. Democrat. Unitarian. Home: Unit 2205 800 W 1st St Los Angeles CA 90012-2412 Office: Calif Citizens Budget Commn 10951 W Pico Blvd Ste 120 Los Angeles CA 90064-2126

POPE, ANDREW JACKSON, JR. (JACK POPE), retired judge; b. Abilene, Tex., Apr. 18, 1913; s. Andrew Jackson and Ruth Adelia (Taylor) P.; m. Allene Esther Nichols, June 11, 1938; children: Andrew Jackson III, Walter Allen. BA, Abilene Christian U., 1934, LLD (hon.), 1980; LLB, U. Tex., 1937; LLD (hon.), Pepperdine U., 1981, St. Mary's U., San Antonio, 1982, Okla. Christian U., 1983. Bar: Tex. 1937. Practice law Corpus Christi, 1937-46; judge 94th Dist. Ct., Corpus Christi, 1946-50; justice Ct. Civil Appeals, San Antonio, 1950-65; justice Supreme Ct. of Tex., Austin, 1965-82, chief justice, 1982-85. Author: John Berry & His Children, 1988; chmn. bd. editors Appellate Procedure in Tex., 1974; author numerous articles in law revs. and profl. jours. Pres. Met. YMCA, San Antonio, 1956-57; chmn. Tex. State Law Libr. Bd., 1973-80; trustee Abilene Christian U., 1958—. Seaman USNR, 1944-46. Recipient Silver Beaver award Alamo council Boy Scouts Am., 1961, Distinguished Eagle award, 1983; Rosewood Gavel award, 1962, St. Thomas More award, St. Mary's U., San Antonio, 1982; Outstanding Alumnus award Abilene Christian U., 1965; Greenhill Jud. award Mcpl. Judges Assn., 1980; Houston Bar Found. citation, 1985; San Antonio Bar Found. award, 1985; Disting. Jurist award Jefferson County Bar, 1985; Outstanding Alumnus award U. Tex. Law Alumni Assn., 1988; George Washington Honor medal Freedom Found., 1988; Disting. Lawyer award Travis County, 1992. Fellow Tex. Bar Found. (Law Rev. award 1979, 80, 81); mem. ABA, State Bar Tex. (pres. jud. sect. 1962, Outstanding Fifty Years Lawyer award 1994), Order of Coif, Nueces County Bar Assn. (pres. 1946), Travis County Bar Assn., Bexar County Bar Assn., Tex. Philos. Soc., Austin Knife and Fork (pres. 1980), Am. Judicature Soc., Tex. State Hist. Assn., Tex. Supreme Ct. Hist. Soc. (v.p.), Sons of Republic of Tex., Christian Chronicle Coun. (chmn.), Masons, K.P. (grand chancellor 1946), Alpha Chi, Phi Delta Phi, Pi Sigma Alpha. Mem. Ch. of Christ. Home: 2803 Stratford Dr Austin TX 78746-4626

POPE, BILL JORDAN, chemical engineering educator, business executive; b. Salt Lake City, Sept. 12, 1922; s. Louis Albert and Ruth (Jordan) P.; m. Margaret McConkie, Sept. 10, 1943; children: Louis, Leslie (Mrs. Alan S. Layton), Kathryn (Mrs. Richard D. Hoopes), Patrice (Mrs. Wayne L. Tew). B.S. in Chem. Engring., U. Utah, 1947; M.S., U. Wash., 1949, Ph.D., 1959. Project chem. engr. Utah Oil Refining Co., 1951-58; mem. faculty Brigham Young U., 1958-59, 62-78, prof. chem. engring., 1962-78, prof. emeritus, 1978—, chmn. dept., 1966-78; prof. chem. engring., acting pres. Abadan (Iran) Inst. Tech., 1959-62; founder, v.p. Megadiamond Corp., Provo, 1966-70, exec. v.p., 1970-73, pres. 1973-78; pres. Megadiamond Industries N.Y., 1976-78; pres. U.S. Synthetic Corp., 1978-92, chmn. bd., 1988—; cons. to industry; specialist in ultra high pressure processes and equipment, diamond synthesis, diamond sintering. Inventor diamond-coated human prosthetic joints. Del. Utah Republican Conv., 1958, 74. Served to 1st lt., C.E. AUS, 1942-46. Research fellow U. Wash., 1947-49; Keysor Chem. Research grantee, 1964-70. Mem. Am. Inst. Chem. Engrs., Am. Chem. Soc., Am. Soc. Profl. Engrs., Am. Soc. Engring. Edn., Utah Acad. Arts and Scis., Utah Soc. Profl. Engrs., Sigma Xi, Tau Beta Pi. Mem. Ch. of Jesus Christ of Latter Day Saints (bishop 1965-72, stake pres., counsellor 1972-76, stake pres. 1976-81, regional rep. 1981-87). Home: 1866 N 1450th E Provo UT 84604

POPE, CARL, professional society administrator. BA summa cum laude, Harvard U., 1967. Vol. Peace Corps, Barhi Barhi, India, 1967-69; with Sierra Club, San Francisco, assoc. conservation dir., polit. dir., conservation dir., exec. dir., 1992—. Bd. dirs. Calif. League of Conservation Voters, 1986-87, exec. dir., 1973-82; bd. dirs. Pub. Voice, 1989, Nat. Clean Air Coalition, Calif. Common Cause, 1976-78, Pub. Interest Econs., Inc., 1973-76, Zero Population Growth, 1972-90, also polit. dir., 1970-73. Office: Sierra Club 730 Polk St San Francisco CA 94109-7813

POPE, DALE ALLEN, investment company executive; b. Racine, Wis., Apr. 11, 1953; s. Warren Edward and Ruth Ann (Adams) P.; m. Colleen Ranee Esson, Aug. 6, 1976; children: Shayna Ranee, Justin Daniel, Evan Hunter. BBA, U. Wis., Eau Claire, 1975; postgrad., U. Wis., Madison, 1976-77. CLU. Estate and ins. planning cons., 1978-81; v.p. Am. Bankers Life, Miami, Fla., 1981-82; pres., COO IFS Capital Corp., North Palm Beach, Fla., 1982-87; founder, pres., CEO Am. Capital Corp., King of Prussia, Pa., 1987—. Mem. Internat. Assn. for Fin. Planning, Internat. Assn. of Registered Fin. Cons., Inc. (charter mem.), Inst. CFPs, Am. Soc. CLU and ChFC, Nat. Assn. Securities Dealers, Inc. (mem. dist. bus. conduct com. 1990-92, bd. arbitrators), Rotary Internat. (dist. gov.'s rep. 1994-95, asst. dist. gov. 1996—, bd. dirs. 1996-97, Paul Harris fellow 1989), Rotary Club of Wayne (past pres., dir. 1993). Avocations: golf, tennis, hunting, fishing. Office: Am Capital Corp 1150 1st Ave Ste 900 Kng Of Prussa PA 19406-1316

POPE, DANIEL JAMES, lawyer; b. Chgo., Nov. 22, 1948. BA, Loyola U., Chgo., 1972; JD cum laude, John Marshall Law Sch., 1975; postgrad., U. Chgo., 1977-78. Bar: Ill. 1975, U.S. Dist. Ct. (no. dist.) Ill. 1982, N.Y. 1983, U.S. Tax Ct. 1985, Tex. 1995, U.S. Supreme Ct. 1995. Corp. trust adminstr. Continental Bank, Chgo., 1972-74; assoc. Haskell & Perrin, Chgo., 1975-77; assoc. Coffield, Ungaretti, Harris & Slavin, Chgo., 1977-81, ptnr., 1981-90, head litigation dept., 1988-90; ptnr. Seyfarth Shaw Fairweather & Geraldson, Chgo., 1990-95, Bell, Boyd & Lloyd, 1996; adj. prof. John Marshall Law Sch., Chgo., 1978-79; appointed panel atty. Fed. Defender Program, Chgo., 1983. Mem. ABA, Ill. Bar Assn., Chgo. Bar Assn. (chmn. aviation law com. 1979, jud. evaluation com. 1982-87), Pub. Interest Law Initiative (dir. 1989-91), Chgo. Athletic Club, Tavern Club, Oak Park Country Club. Home: 146 N Taylor Ave Oak Park IL 60302-2524 Office: Bell Boyd & LLoyd 70 W Madison St Ste 3300 Chicago IL 60602-4243

POPE, DAVID E., geologist, micropaleontologist; b. Forrest City, Ark., Dec. 20, 1920; s. Jesse Ellis and Mary Ruth (Remley) P.; m. Dorothy Angeline Salario, June 8, 1947 (dec. Jan. 1982); children: David Brian, Mark Alan; m. Alice Duke Akins, June 1, 1990. BS, La. State U., 1947, MS, 1948; grad. U.S. Army Command and Gen. Staff Coll., 1967. Paleontologist, Union Producing Co., Houston, 1948-49, New Orleans, 1949-55, dist. paleontologist, New Orleans, 1955-63, Lafayette, La., 1963-67; cons., Lafayette, La., 1967-75; sr. rsch. geologist, La. Geol. Survey, Baton Rouge, 1975—; lectr. La. State U., 1979, 80, N.E. La. U., 1983. Mem. nat. adv. bd. Am. Security Coun., 1983—; bd. dirs. La. State U. Mus. Geosci. Assocs., 1980—, pres. 1981-82, 1987—. Capt. U.S. Army, 1942-46, to lt. col. USAR, 1945-70. Contbr. articles to profl. jours. Decorated Silver Star medal with oak leaf cluster, Purple Heart, Combat Inf. badge. Mem. Am. Assn. Petroleum Geologists (cert., mem. ho. of dels. 1981—), Am. Inst. Profl. Geologists, Gulf Coast sect. SEPM (pres. 1959-60, hon. mem., 1987), New Orleans Geol. Soc. (v.p. 1962-63), Lafayette Geol. Soc., Baton Rouge Geol. Soc. (pres. 1980-81, hon. mem. 1989), Gulf Coast Assn. Geol. Socs. (bd. dirs. 1980-87, historian 1983—, pres. 1985-86), Res. Officers Assn. (life), Mil. Order World Wars, La. State U. Sch. Geology Alumni Assn. (pres. 1958-59, 84-85), La. Petroleum Coun. Home: 12026 Pecan Grove Ct Baton Rouge LA 70810-4835 Office: La Geol Survey Univ Sta PO Box G Baton Rouge LA 70893

POPE, FRED WALLACE, JR., lawyer; b. Sanford, Fla., Feb. 9, 1941; s. Fred Wallace and Dorothy (Marshall) P.; m. Jane Laird Miller, Dec. 27, 1962 (div. Oct. 1986); children: Catherine W., Gregory W.; m. Christine R. Fredrick, Jan. 4, 1991. BA in Polit. Sci., U. Fla., 1962, JD with honors, 1969; AM in Internat. Rels., Boston U., 1965. Bar: Fla. 1970, U.S. Dist. Ct. (so., mid. and no. dists.) Fla., U.S. Supreme Ct. 1975, U.S. Ct. Appeals (11th cir.) 1983. Rsch. aide 2d Dist. Ct. Appeal, Lakeland, Fla., 1970; assoc. Trenam, Simmons, Kemker, Scharf & Barkin, Tampa, Fla., 1970-74; ptnr. Johnson, Blakely, Pope, Bokor, Ruppel & Burns, P.A., Clearwater, Fla., 1974—; dir. Citizens Bank Clearwater, 1986—. Trustee The Fla. Orch., Tampa, 1984—, chmn. bd. trustees, 1991-93; bd. dirs. Pinellas County Arts Coun., Clearwater, 1988-93. Capt. U.S. Army, 1962-67. Mem. ABA (coun. mem. sect. litigation 1983-86, editor, chief Litigation 1979-80), The Fla. Bar (gov. 1982-86), Clearwater Bar Assn. (pres. 1980-81). Office: Johnson Blakely Pope Bokor Ruppel & Burns PA 911 Chestnut St Clearwater FL 33756-5643

POPE, HARRISON GRAHAM, JR., psychiatrist, educator; b. Lynn, Mass., Dec. 26, 1947; s. H. Graham and Alice (Rider) P.; m. Mary M. Quinn, June 7, 1974; children: Kimberly, Hilary, Courtney. AB summa cum laude, Harvard U., 1969, MPH, 1972, MD, 1974. Diplomate Am. Bd. Psychiatry and Neurology. Resident in psychiatry McLean Hosp., Belmont, Mass., 1974-77, clin. rsch. fellow Mailman Rsch. Ctr., 1977-79, asst. psychiatrist, 1979-84, assoc. psychiatrist, 1984-92, psychiatrist, 1992—, chief biol. psychiatry lab., 1984—; Dupont-Warren rsch. fellow Harvard Med. Sch., Boston, 1976-77; instr. psychiatry Harvard Med. Sch., Boston, 1977-82, asst. prof., 1982-85, assoc. prof., 1985—; staff psychiatrist Hampstead (N.H.) Hosp., 1976-80; vis. fellow The Maudsley Hosp., London, 1977, Hôp. Ste. Anne, Paris, 1977; mem. Am. Psychiat. Assn., 1976-80, adv. com. on schizophrenic, paranoid and affective disorders, 1979, adv. com. on preparation of DSM-III-R, 1984, task force on nomenclature and stats., 1979, 84. Author: Voices from the Drug Culture, 1971, The Road East, 1974, (with J.I. Hudson) New Hope for Binge Eaters: Advances in the Understanding and Treatment of Bulimia, 1984; co-editor: The Psychobiology of Bulimia, 1987, Use of Anticonvulsants in Psychiatry: Recent Advances, 1988, Psychology Astray: Fallacies in Studies of "Repressed Memory" and Childhood Trauma, 1997; contbr. numerous papers on biol. psychiatry, with emphasis on diagnosis of psychotic disorders, treatment of mood disorders and eating disorders, and substance abuse, particularly abuse of anabolic steroids by athletes; mem. editl. bd. European Psychiatry, Paris, 1984—, Internat. Jour. of Eating Disorders, 1984—, Jour. Clin. Psychiatry, 1993—. Named one of Outstanding Americans under 40 Esquire mag., 1984; fellow Scottish Rite Schizophrenia Program, No. Masonic Jurisdiction, 1977-81, Charles A. King Trust, Boston, 1977-79. Avocation: weightlifting. Office: McLean Hosp 115 Mill St Belmont MA 02178-1041

POPE, INGRID BLOOMQUIST, sculptor, lecturer, poet; b. Arvika, Sweden, Apr. 2, 1918; came to U.S., 1928; became U.S. citizen.; d. Oscar Emanuel and Gerda (Henningson) Brostrom; m. Howard Richard Bloomquist, Feb. 14, 1941 (dec. Nov. 1982); children: Dennis Howard, Diane Cecile Connelly, Laurel Ann Shields; m. Marvin Hoyle Pope, Mar. 9, 1985. BA cum laude, Manhattanville Coll., 1979, MA in Humanities, 1981; MA in Religion, Yale Div. Sch. Yale U., 1984. lectr. Nat. Assn. Am. Pen Women, Greenwich, Soroptimist Club, Greenwich, Greenwich Travel Club, Ch. Women United Greenwich, 1st Congl. Ch., Scarsdale, N.Y., 2d Congl. Ch., Greenwich, 1st Congl. Ch., Stamford, Conn., 1st Ch. of Round Hill, St. Mary Ch., Greenwich. Exhbns. include Manhattanville Coll., Purchase, N.Y., Yale Div. Sch., Ch. of Sweden in N.Y.C., Greenwich Arts Coun., Greenwich Arts Soc., First Ch. of Round Hill; author: (poems) Musings, 1994. Past bd. dirs. N.Y.C. Mission Soc., Greenwich YWCA, Greenwich Chaplaincy, Greenwich Acad. Mother's Assn.; past trustee First Ch. Round Hill, Greenwich; pres. Ch. Women United, Greenwich, 1989-91. Mem. AAUW, Nat. Assn. Pen Women, English Speaking Union, Yale Club N.Y.C., Nat. Wildflower Assn., Lakeview Club (Austin, Tex.), Acad. Am. Poets, Nat. Mus. of Women in the Arts. Home: 704 Cutlass Austinich TX 78734 also: 538 Round Hill Rd Greenwich CT 06831 *I need to share my feelings deep inside be it in verse or prose or form or line. I need to say it, do it, show, or write and so creatively I try to do my best. I lift up brush and paint a scene, I struggle with a stone or paint in clay or write my verse just as I do today.*

POPE, JESSE CURTIS, theology and religious studies educator; b. Corpus Christi, Tex., Feb. 22, 1955; s. Jesse Rondo and Doris Mae (Whisman) P.; m. Mary Ann Norman, Apr. 17, 1976; children: Jesse Morris, Ashley Elizabeth, Courtney Rebecca, Brianne Leah. AA, Fla. Coll., 1975; BA, Harding U., 1977, MA in Religion, 1978; PhD, Fla. State U., 1990. Min. Ctrl. Ch. of Christ, McAlpin, Fla., 1974-75, Noble Hill Ch. of Christ, Brighton, Mo., 1974, 76, Citizenship Ch. of Christ, McCrory, Ark., 1976-78, Harpersville (Ala.) Ch. of Christ, 1978-81, Moultrie Rd. Ch. of Christ, Thomasville, Ga., 1981-84, Northwood Ch. of Christ, Northport, Ala., 1984-92; min. Carrollwood Ch. of Christ, Tampa, Fla., 1992—, elder, 1994—; prof. Bible Fla. Coll., Temple Terrace, Fla., 1992—; evangelist in field; chmn. profl. devel. com. Fla. Coll., Temple Terrace, 1993—, fin. resources com., 1995—. Contbr. articles to profl. jours. Den leader Boy Scouts Am., Northport, 1986-90, asst. scoutmaster, 1990-92; mem. Nat. Congress Am. Indians,

1993—, Cherokees of S.E. Ala. Named One of Outstanding Young Men of Am., Jaycees, 1980, 84. Mem. Am. Soc. Ch. History, Bibl. Archael. Soc., Soc. Bibl. Lit., Descendants of Mex. War Vets., Evang. Theol. Soc., Sons of Confederate Vets (chaplain 1990-92), Sons of the Republic of Tex. Republican. Ch. of Christ. Avocations: genealogy, hunting, fishing, travel. Home: 9403 Alanbrooke St Temple Terrace FL 33637-4960 Office: Fla Coll 119 Glen Arven Ave Tampa FL 33617

POPE, JOHN CHARLES, airline company executive; b. Newark, Mar. 30, 1949; s. John Aris Coutant and Eleanor Laura (Hillman) P. BA, Yale U., 1971; MBA, Harvard U., 1973. Dir. profit analysis and capital analysis GM, N.Y.C., 1973-77; sr. v.p. fin., treas., chief fin. officer Am. Airlines, Inc., AMR Corp., Dallas-Fort Worth, 1977-88; exec. v.p., chief fin. officer UAL Corp., United Airlines (subs.), Chgo., 1988-91, pres., COO, 1991-94; bd. dirs. Fed. Mogul Corp., Detroit, Wallace Computer Svcs., Inc., Lisle, Ill.; chmn. bd. MotivePower Industries, Inc., Pitts.; bd. trustees, treas. Shedd Aquarium, Chgo. Home: 810 S Ridge Rd Lake Forest IL 60045-2756

POPE, JOHN EDWIN, III, newspaper sports editor; b. Athens, Ga., Apr. 11, 1928; s. Henry Louis and Rose (McAfee) P.; m. Eileen Pope. B.A. in Journalism, U. Ga., 1948. Sports editor Banner-Herald, Athens, Ga., 1943-48; So. sports editor UPI, Atlanta, 1948-50; sports writer Atlanta Constn., 1950-54; exec. sports editor Atlanta Jour., 1954-56; asst. sports editor Miami (Fla.) Herald, 1956-67, sports editor, 1967—. Author: Football's Greatest Coaches, 1956, Baseball's Greatest Managers, 1960, Encyclopedia of American Greyhound Racing, 1963, Ted Williams: The Golden Year, 1970, (with Norm Evans) On the Line, 1976, The Edwin Pope Collection, 1988; contbr. articles to popular mags. and Ency. Brittanica, World Book. Recipient Bill Corum Meml. award Thoroughbred Racing Assn., 1962, top sports column award Nat. Headliners Club, 1962, 79, 86, Eclipse award Thoroughbred Racing Assn., 1986, 82, 86, Red Smith award AP Sports Editors, 1989; named to Internat. Churchmen's Sports Hall of Fame, 1976; recipient Knight-Ridder editl. excellence award Nat. Sportswriters and Sportscasters Assn. Hall of Fame, 1994, Fla. Sports Hall of Fame, 1996. Mem. Profl. Football Writers Am. (pres. 1968-69), Football Writers Assn. Am., Golf Writers Am., U.S. Basketball Writers, Nat. Turf Writers, U.S. Tennis Writers. Presbyterian. Office: Miami Herald 1 Herald Plz Miami FL 33132-1609

POPE, JOHN M., journalist; b. Hattiesburg, Miss., Nov. 5, 1948; s. Paul M. Jr. and Mary Lee (Scott) P.; m. Diana Pinckley, May 19, 1984. BA cum laude, U. Tex., 1970, MA, 1972. Copy editor The States-Item, New Orleans, 1972-73, reporter, 1973-80; reporter The Times-Picayune, New Orleans, 1980-86, med.-health reporter, 1986—. Co-author: American First Ladies: Their Lives and Their Legacy, 1996. Recipient Frank Allen award La.-Miss. AP, 1989, Med. Writing award La. State Med. Soc., 1990. Mem. Soc. Profl. Journalists, Nat. Assn. Sci. Writers, Press Club New Orleans (4 1st pl. awards 1978-87, Alex Waller award 1987), Phi Beta Kappa. Avocations: running, travel, aerobics. Office: The Times-Picayune 3800 Howard Ave New Orleans LA 70140-1002

POPE, KERIG RODGERS, magazine executive; b. Waukesha, Wis., Sept. 30, 1935; s. Kerig James Pope and Mildred (Offerman) Troemel; m. Claudia T. Koralewski, Nov. 1961 (div. 1975); children—Kerig William, Giles Thomas; m. Beth Leslie Kasik, May 24, 1980; children: Kolin Jared, Zoe Alissa. Grad., Art Inst. Chgo., 1958. Designer Jack Denst Wallpaper Designs, Chgo., 1958-60; designer Continental Casualty Ins. Co., Chgo., 1960-62, Leo Burnett Advt. Agy., Chgo., 1962-63; art dir. Mercury Records Corp., Chgo., 1963-66; mng. art dir. Playboy mag., Chgo., 1966—. Exhibited in group shows Whitney Mus. Am. Art, N.Y.C., 1969, Mus. Contemporary Art, Chgo., 1972, Bienal de Sao Paulo, Brazil, 1973, Museo de Arte Moderno, Mexico City, 1974, Nat. Collection Fine Arts, Washington, 1979, Moderno, Mexico City, 1974, Mus. Contemporary Art, Chgo., 1996; represented in permanent collections Nat. Collection Fine Arts, Washington, Mus. Contemporary Art, Chgo., Smart Mus., U. Chgo. Recipient silver medal Communigraphics, N.Y.C., 1971, gold medal, 1971, 72; award of excellence Soc. Publ. Designers, 1979, 4 awards of excellence Design Ann., 1984, Silver medal Illustrators 29, 1986, Silver medal Soc. of Illustrators, 1988. Mem. Soc. Illustrators (gold medal 1981, 84, 91), Art Dirs. Club N.Y., Soc. Typog. Arts, Soc. Publ. Arts (3 Silver awards 1987). Club: Arts (Chgo.). Office: Playboy Enterprises Inc 680 N Lake Shore Dr Chicago IL 60611-4402

POPE, LISTON, JR., writer, journalist; b. New Haven, Dec. 26, 1943; s. Liston and Bennie (Purvis) P. BA in English, Duke U., 1965; postgrad., Sorbonne, Paris, 1965-70, U. Vienna, 1966-67. Probation officer Bronx (N.Y.) Supreme Ct., 1972-73; freelance journalist, 1972—; war correspondent World Coun. of Chs., Beirut, 1978-79, Nat. Cath. News Svc., Managua, Nicaragua, 1983-84; radio prodr. Pacifica Radio, N.Y.C., 1983-90; critic art/lit. Pacifica News, N.Y.C., 1984-89; sr. editor N.A. Gilbert & Sons Publs., 1993—; press agent Liston Pope & Assocs., N.Y.C., 1983-90; media dir. Casa Nicaragua, N.Y.C., 1983-90. Author: Redemption: A Novel of War in Lebanon, 1994, Living Like the Saints: A Novel of Nicaragua, 1996, (plays) Somoza's Niece, 1987, Oratorio, 1987, Canto Epico, 1989. Vis., supporting vol. Meml. Sloan-Kettering, 1972-78; recreation dir., tutor Cath. Guardian Group Home, 1975-90; life skills tchr. Harlem I Men's Shelter, N.Y.C., 1991-93; AIDS support worker St. Vincent's Supportive Care, Bellevue Visitation Program, Bellevue Pediatrics. Recipient Narrative Poetry award N.Y. Poetry Soc., 1972, Grand prize Am. Poetry Assn., 1986, Poetry award Nat. Libr. of Poetry, 1993. Home and Office: 126 W 73rd St Apt 11A New York NY 10023-3031

POPE, MARVIN HOYLE, language educator, writer; b. Durham, N.C., June 23, 1916; s. Charles Edgar and Bessie Cleveland Sorrell Pope; m. Helen Thompson, Sept. 4, 1948 (dec. Feb. 1979); m. Ingrid Brostrom Bloomquist, Mar. 9, 1985. AB, Duke U., 1938, AM, 1939; PhD, Yale U., 1949. Instr. dept. religion Duke U., Durham, 1947-49; asst. prof. Hebrew Yale U., New Haven, 1949-55, assoc. prof., 1955-64, prof. Semitic langs. and lit., 1964-86, prof. emeritus, sr. rsch. scholar, 1986—; Haskell lectr. Oberlin Coll., 1971, vis. lectr. Cath. U. Lublin, Poland, 1977, Fulbright lectr. U. Aleppo, Syria, 1980; Wickenden lectrs. Miami U., Oxford, Ohio, 1982; Fulbright Rsch. scholar Inst. Ugaritforschung U. Muenster, Germany, 1986, 90; Hooker disting. vis. prof. McMaster U., Hamilton, Ont. Can., 1986; dir. Hebrew Union Coll. Bibl. and Archeol. Sch., Jerusalem, 1966-67; trustee Albright Inst. Archeol. Rsch., Jerusalem; fellow Pierson Coll. Yale U. Author: El in the Ugaritic Texts, 1955; The Book of Job, 1973, Song of Songs, 1977 (Nat. Religious Book award 1978), Syrien Die Mythologie der Ugariter und Phoenizier, 1962, Collected Essays, 1994; contbr. articles to scholarly jours. and dictionaries. Mem. Revised Standard Version Bible com. Nat. Coun. Chs., 1960—; mem. First Ch. Round Hill. With USAF, 1941-45, PTO. Nat. Endowment for Humanities Rsch. grantee, 1980—. Mem. Am. Oriental Soc., Am. Schs. Oriental Rsch., Soc. Bibl. Lit., Am. Soc. Study Religions, Columbia U. Seminar for Study of Hebrew Bible, Yale Club, Oriental Club New Haven, Mory's Club, Lakeview Club (Austin, Tex.), Phi Beta Kappa. Home: 704 Cutlass Austin TX 78734 also: 538 Round Hill Rd Greenwich CT 06831

POPE, MICHAEL ARTHUR, lawyer; b. Chgo., June 27, 1944; s. Arthur Wellington and Phyllis Anne (O'Connor) P.; m. Christine Collins, Nov. 19, 1966; children—Jennifer, Amy, Katherine. B.S., Loyola U., Chgo., 1966; J.D. cum laude, Northwestern U., 1969. Bar: Ill. 1969, U.S. Dist. Ct. (no. dist.) Ill. 1969, U.S. Ct. Appeals (7th cir.) 1970, U.S. Supreme Ct. 1980, N.Y. 1985. Teaching asst. U. Ill. Coll. Law, Champaign, 1969-70; assoc. Isham, Lincoln & Beale, Chgo., 1970-76; ptnr. Phelan, Pope & John, Ltd., 1976-90; prin. Pope & John, Ltd., 1990-95; capital ptnr. McDermott Wall & Emory, 1995—; adj. prof. law Chgo.-Kent Law Sch. Ill. Inst. Tech., 1982-85; bd. trustees Nat. Jud. Coll., 1997—; Mem. ABA, Ill. Bar Assn., Chgo. Bar Assn., Am. Bd. Profl. Liability Attys. (pres. 1985-87), Internat. Assn. Def. Counsel (pres. 1993-94), Internat. Soc. Barristers, Am. Coll. Trial Lawyers, Internat. Acad. Trial Lawyers, Am. Law Inst. The Chgo. Club, Skokie Country Club (Glencoe, Ill.), East Bank Club (Chgo.). Office: McDermott Wall & Emery 227 W Monroe St Chicago IL 60606-5016

POPE, MICHAEL THOR, chemistry educator; b. Exeter, Devon, Eng., Apr. 14, 1933; came to U.S. 1962; naturalized, 1992; s. Hector Maurice and Edith Mary (Hewett) P.; m. Ann Mavis Potter, July 12, 1957; children—Gregory, Lucy. B.A., Oxford U., 1954, D.Phil., 1957. Postdoctoral, Boston U., Mass., 1957-59; research chemist Laporte Chems., Luton, Eng., 1959-62; asst. prof. Georgetown U., Washington, 1962-67, assoc. prof., 1967-73, prof., 1973—, dept. chair, 1990-96; vis. prof. Tech. U., Vienna, Austria, 1970-71, Free U. of Berlin, 1979, Northeast Normal U., Changchun, China, 1985, U. Umeå, U. Bielefeld, Germany, 1989; prof. associé U. Pierre et Marie Curie, Paris, 1979. Author: Heteropoly and Isopoly Oxometalates, 1983, Polyoxometalates: From Platonic Solids to Anti-Retroviral Activity, 1994; contbr. articles to profl. publs. Recipient Sr. U.S. Scientist award Alexander von Humboldt Found., 1989-90; Petroleum Research Fund Internat. award fellow, 1970-71; Research grantee Dept. Energy, NSF, NIH, Petroleum Research Fund, Office Naval Research, Army Research Office, Air Force Office of Sci. Research. Mem. Royal Soc. Chemistry (London), Am. Chem. Soc., Sigma Xi (chpt. pres. 1969-70). Episcopalian. Avocations: music, art. Office: Georgetown Univ Chemistry Dept Washington DC 20057-1227

POPE, PRESTON CARLETON, anesthetist, nurse; b. Hartford, Conn., Apr. 8, 1950; s. Preston Louis and Doris Lucinda (Stewart); m. Delair Moses, Aug. 28, 1971; children: Chad, Ryan. Diploma, New Britain Gen. Sch. Nursing, 1972, cert. in anesthesia, 1974. Cert. nurse anesthetist, advanced practice RN; notary pub., Conn., justice of the peace, Conn.; pvt. investigator, Conn.; hypnotherapist; NRA small arms instr.; lic. comml. sea capt., pilot, nuisance wildlife control operator. Staff anesthetist Bristol (Conn.) Hosp., 1974-78; staff anesthetist Harford Hosp., 1978-79, 81—, chief anesthetist, 1987—. Alumni pres. New Britain Sch. Nurse Anesthesia. Capt. USAF, 1979-81. Mem. NRA (life), Am. Assn. Nurse Anesthetists, Nat. Assn. Federally Lic. Firearms Dealers, Boat Owners Assn. Am., Aircraft Owners and Pilots Assn., Nat. Notary Assn. Republican. Avocations: scuba diving, boating, computers, flying, martial arts, weight lifting, target shooting, archery, piano. Home: 102 Simpkins Dr Bristol CT 06010-2688

POPE, RANDALL RAY, retired national park superintendent; b. Durham, Kans., Oct. 15, 1932; s. Reuben S. and Enid Lillian (Powers) P.; m. Kathleen V. Higer, Feb. 23, 1958; children: Mark Randall, Renee Lynn Pope Polenske. BS in Landscape Architecture, Kans. State U., 1959. Cert. landscape arch., Nebr. State Bd. Landscape Archs., 1968. Landscape architect Midwest regional office Nat. Pk. Svc., Omaha, 1959-61, 65-69; pk. landscape architect Grand Teton Nat. Pk. Nat. Pk. Svc., Moose, Wyo., 1961-65; supt. Herbert Hoover Nat. Hist. Site Nat. Pk. Svc., West Branch, Iowa, 1969-71; supt. Ozark Nat. Scenic Riverway Nat. Pk. Svc., Van Buren, Mo., 1971-76; dep. regional dir. Midwest regional office Nat. Pk. Svc., Omaha, 1976-87; supt. Great Smoky Mountains Nat. Pk. Nat. Pk. Svc., Gatlinburg, Tenn., 1987-93; ret., 1993. Counselor Boy Scouts Am., West Branch, Van Buren, 1970-76; bd. dirs. Foothills Land Conservancy, 1994—. With USN, 1951-55. Mem. Am. Soc. Landscape Archs., Rotary (Gatlinburg), Lions (instl. rep. 1970-71, 1st, 2d, 3d v.p., pres. Sunrise club 1986-87), Gamma Sigma Delta. Avocations: hiking, photography, gardening, fishing. Home: 845 Vixen Run Gatlinburg TN 37738-6345

POPE, RICHARD M., rheumatologist; b. Chgo., Jan. 10, 1946. Student, Procopius Coll., 1963-65, U. Ill., 1965-66; MD, Loyola U., 1970. Diplomate Am. Bd. Internal Medicine. Intern in medicine Med. Ctr. Michael Reese Hosp., Chgo., 1970-71, resident in internal medicine, 1971-72; fellow in rheumatology U. Wash., Seattle, 1972-74; asst. clin. prof. medicine U. Hawaii, 1974-77; asst. prof. medicine U. Tex. Health Sci. Ctr., San Antonio, 1976-81, assoc. prof. medicine, 1981-85; assoc. prof. medicine Northwestern U. Med. Sch., 1985-88, prof. medicine, 1988—; attending physician Northwestern Meml. Hosp., Chgo., 1985—, VA Lakeside Med. Ctr., Chgo., 1985—, Rehab. Inst. Chgo., 1985—; chief divsn. rheumatology VA Lakeside Med. Ctr., 1985-91, divsn. arthritis-connective tissue diseases Northwestern U. and Northwestern Meml. Hosp., 1989—, Northwestern Med. Faculty Found., 1989—; mem. program com. Cen. Soc. Clin. Rsch., 1987, cen. region Am. Rheumatism Assn., 1987; mem. sci. com. Ill. chpt. Arthritis Found., 1988-92, bd. dirs., 1990—, mem. chpt. rev. grants subcom., 1983-88, chmn. chpt. rsch. grant subcom., 1986-88, mem. rsch. com., 1986-88; mem. site visit teams NIH, 1986, 87, 89, 96, 97; cons. reviewer VA Merit Rev. Bd., 1984, 87, 91; cons. reviewer Arthritis Soc. Can., 1986, 87; mem. editl. adv. bd. Arthritis and Rheumatism Jour. Lab. and Clin. Medicine, 1992—. Author: (with others) The Science and Practice of Clinical Medicine, 1979, Proceedings of the University of South Florida International Symposium in the Biomedical Sciences, 1984, Concepts in Immunopathology, 1985, Biology Based Immunomodulators in the Therapy of Rheumatic Diseases, 1986, Primer on the Rheumatic Diseases, 1988; contbr. numerous articles to profl. jours. With U.S. Army, 1974-76. Anglo-Am. Rheumatology fellow, 1983. Mem. ACP, Am. Coll. Rheumatology (councillor cen. region coun. 1990-93, program com. 1983-86, 91), Am. Assn. Immunologists, Am. Fedn. Clin. Rsch., Am. Soc. Clin. Investigation, Lupus Found. Ill. (mem. adv. bd. 1990-93), Chgo. Rheumatism Assn. (pres. 1991-93), Cen. Soc. Clin. Investigation, Soc. Irish and Am. Rheumatologists (sec., treas. 1989-93), Univ. Rheumatology Coun. Chgo., Alpha Omega Alpha. Achievements include research in pathophysiology of rheumatoid arthritis, T cell activation, T cell receptor, macrophage gene expression. Office: Northwestern U Multipurpose Arthritis Ctr 303 E Chicago Ave Chicago IL 60611-3008

POPE, ROBERT DANIEL, lawyer; b. Screven, Ga., Nov. 29, 1948; s. Robert Verlyn and Mae (McKey) P.; m. Teresa Ann Mullis, Jan. 26, 1981; children: Robert Daniel Jr., Veronica Teres, Jonathan Chase, Byron Christopher, Jessica Victoria. BS in Criminal Justice magna cum laude, Valdosta (Ga.) State Coll., 1975; JD, John Marshall Law Sch., Savannah, Ga., 1980. Bar: Ga. 1981, U.S. Dist. Ct. (no., mid. and so. dist.) Ga. 1983, U.S. Ct. Appeals Ga. 1982. Pvt. practice Cartersville, 1981—; mem. Valdosta Indigent Def. Atty. Panel, 1981-83, Bartow County Indigent Def. Panel, Cartersville, 1987-91, So. Dist. of Ga. Indigent Def. Panel, Brunswick, 1982-84; mem. Cobb County Cir. Defender's Panel for Indigent Criminal Def., Marietta, Ga., 1986—. Recognized as one of most successful criminal def. lawyers Cobb County Cir. Defenders Office, 1994. Mem. Ga. Assn. Criminal Def. Lawyers, Ga. Bar Assn. (criminal law sect.), Am. Criminal Justice Orgn. (Valdosta chpt. pres. 1974-75). Home: 74 Spruce Ln Cartersville GA 30120 Office: 140 W Cherokee Ave Cartersville GA 30120-3102

POPE, ROBERT DEAN, lawyer; b. Memphis, Mar. 10, 1945; s. Ben Duncan and Phyllis (Drenner) P.; m. Elizabeth Dante Cohen, June 26, 1971; 1 child, Justin Nicholas Nathanson. AB, Princeton U., 1967; Diploma in Hist. Studies, Cambridge U., 1971; JD, Yale U., 1972, PhD, 1976. Bar: Va. 1974, D.C. 1980. Assoc. Hunton & Williams, Richmond, Va., 1974-80; ptnr. Hunton & Williams, Richmond, 1980—; mem. steering com. Bond Attys. Workshop, 1994—. Contbg. author: Disclosure Rules of Counsel in State and Local Government Securities Offerings, 2d edit., 1994. Mem. adv. com. Va. Sec. of Health and Human Svcs. on Continuing Care Legislation, 1992—; mem. Anthony Commn. on Pub. Fin.; adv. coun. dept. history Princeton U., 1987-91; mem. Mcpl. Securities Rulemaking Bd., 1996—. Mem. Govt. Fin. Officers Assn. (com. on govtl. debt and fiscal policy), Va. Bar Assn. (chmn. legal problems of elderly 1982-88), Nat. Assn. Bond Lawyers (treas. 1984-85, sec. 1985-86, pres. 1987-88, bd. dirs. 1982-89, Bernard P. Friel medal for contbns. to pub. fin. 1994), Am. Acad. Hosp. Attys., Yale Law Sch. Assn. (exec. com. 1985-88), Bond Club Va. (bd. dirs. 1990—, v.p. 1993-94, pres. 1994-95), NCCJ (Richmond area bd.), Phi Beta Kappa. Republican. Episcopalian. Avocations: history, golf, music, book reviews. Home: 8707 Ruggles Rd Richmond VA 23229-7918 Office: Hunton & Williams PO Box 1535 951 E Byrd St Richmond VA 23219-4040

POPE, ROBERT E(UGENE), fraternal organization administrator; b. Wellington, Kans., Sept. 10, 1931; s. Samuel E. and Opal Irene (Davis) P. BSChemE with honors, U. Kans., 1952, MS, 1958. Registered profl. engr., Kans. Asst. instr. U. Kans., Lawrence, 1952-56; lab. technician Monsanto Co., St. Louis, 1952; project engr. Mallinckrodt, Inc., St. Louis, 1953-59; traveling sec. Theta Tau, St. Louis, 1959-62, exec. sec., 1963-84, exec. dir., 1984-96, exec. dir. emeritus, 1996—. Author: Years of Progress, 1995; (with C.E. Wales) Designing a Rush Program, 3d edit., 1996; mem. bd. editors (mag.) The Gear of Theta Tau, 1993—, editor-in-chief, 1996—. Carillonneur, Grace United Meth. Ch., St. Louis, 1985—, chmn. adminstrv. coun., 1991-95, trustee, 1997—. Mem. Am. Soc. Assn. Execs., Am. Soc. Engring. Edn., St. Louis Soc. Assn. Execs., Profl. Fraternity Execs. Assn. (charter), Profl. Fraternity Assn. (exec. sec. 1977-86, Disting. Svc. award 1995), Engrs. Club St. Louis, Creve Coeur Country Club, Theta Tau (Alumni Hall of Fame 1988), Tau Beta Pi, Phi Lambda Upsilon, Omicron Delta Kappa. Democrat. United Methodist. Avocations: physical fitness, sports, photography. Address: 13 Sona Ln Saint Louis MO 63141-7742

POPE, SARAH ANN, elementary education educator; b. Granite City, Ill., Dec. 4, 1938; d. Vance Guy and Lily Lovinia (Fischer) Morgan; m. Thomas E. Pope; children: Robert, Susan, James, John, William. BS in Edn., So. Ill. U., Edwardsville, 1970, MS in Edn., 1976. Lang. arts, humanities, sci., English, reading, math. tchr. Madison (Ill.) Community Sch. Dist., 1970—. Co-founder libr. Harris Elem. Sch., 1990. Fellow Old Six Mile Hist. Soc.; mem. Am. Hemerocallis Soc. Avocations: reading, growing flowers, visiting historical sites, swimming. Office: Madison Community Unit Sch 1707 4th St Madison IL 62060-1505

POPE, SHAWN HIDEYOSHI, lawyer; b. Jacksonville, Fla., July 19, 1962; s. Robert George Pope and Michiyo (Nagano) Pope-Griffin. AA with honors, Fla. C.C., Jacksonville, 1983; BBA, U. North Fla., Jacksonville, 1986; JD, Mercer U., Macon, Ga., 1990. Bar: Fla. 1990, U.S. Dist. Ct. (mid. dist.) Fla. 1991, U.S. Ct. Appeals (11th cir.) 1991, U.S. Supreme Ct., 1996. Math. tutor Fla. C.C. of Jax, Jacksonville, 1981-83; heavy equipment operator Sears Roebuck, Jacksonville, 1982-87; actuary technician Am. Heritage Life Ins. Co., Jacksonville, 1986-87; assoc. Boyler, Tanzler & Boyer, P.A., Jacksonville, 1990-91, Penland & Penland, P.A., Jacksonville, 1991-94; pvt. practice Law Office of Shawn H. Pope, Jacksonville, 1994—; pro bono counsel Jax Area Legal Aid, Inc., Jacksonville, 1990—. Coord. United Way, Jacksonville, 1987, Jacksonville Blood Bank, 1986. Mem. ABA, Assn. Trial Lawyers, Assn. Trial Lawyers Am., Acad. Fla. Trial Lawyers, Phi Delta Phi (vice magister). Avocations: surfing, traveling, fishing, reading, foreign langs. Office: 233 E Bay St Ste 615 Jacksonville FL 32202-3447

POPE, STEPHEN BAILEY, engineering educator; b. Nottingham, England, Nov. 26, 1949; came to U.S., 1977; s. Joseph Albert and Evelyn Alice (Gallagher) P.; m. Linda Ann Syatt, Aug. 16, 1979; children: Sarah Evelyn, Samuel Joseph. BS in Engring., Imperial Coll., London, 1971; MS, Imperial Coll., 1972, PhD, 1976; DSc in Engring., U. London, 1986. Rsch. asst. Imperial Coll., London, 1972-77; rsch. fellow Calif. Inst. Tech., Pasadena, 1977-78; asst. prof. MIT, Cambridge, Mass., 1978-81; assoc. prof. MIT, 1981, Cornell U., Ithaca, N.Y., 1982-87; prof. engring. Cornell U., 1987—; cons. GE, Schenectady, N.Y., 1984—, GM, Warren, Mich., 1985—, Allison Engine Co., Indpls., 1986—. Editor: Combustion Theory and Modelling; assoc. editor Physics of Fluids A; contbr. articles to profl. jours. Overseas fellow Churchill Coll, Cambridge, Eng., 1989; awards NSF, Army Rsch. Office, Air Force Office Sci. Rsch., U.S. Dept. Energy. Fellow Am. Phys. Soc., Combustion Inst. Office: Cornell U Upson Hall Ithaca NY 14853

POPE, THEODORE CAMPBELL, JR., utilities executive, consultant; b. Sanford, Fla., Oct. 28, 1932; s. Theodore Campbell and Mary (Cook) P.; m. Edith L. Carlton; children: Theodore, Jeffrey, Laura; m. Jeris Julia Dawson, Nov. 21, 1973. BSME, U. Fla., 1954, MBA, 1959. Registered profl. engr., Fla.; diplomate Am. Acad. Environ. Engrs. Chief mech. engr. Orlando Utilities, 1959-64, plant supt., 1964-67, dir. elec. generation, 1967-70, asst. mgr. elec. ops., 1970-72, mgr water ops., 1972-84, asst. gen. mgr., 1984-86, gen. mgr., 1986-92; pres. Ted Pope Enterprises, Orlando, 1992—. Contbr. articles to profl. jours.; patentee water treatment process. Bd. dirs. United Fund Brevard County; bd. dirs. Econ. Devel. Commn. of Mid-Fla., Orlando; bd. dirs., pres. Ctrl. Fla. Fair; trustee United Arts of Ctrl. Fla. 1st lt. U.S. Army, 1955-57. Recipient Abel Waldman award InterAm. Assn. San. Engrs., 1982. Mem. Am. Water Works Assn. (hon.; Disting. Pub. Svc. award 1991, George Warren Fuller award, chair emeritus Rsch. Found.), Greater Orlando Area C. of C. (pres. 1990-91), Fla. Engring. Soc. (Engr. of Yr.), Fla. Conservation Assn., Rotary Club of Orlando, Smyrna Yacht Club, Country Club of Orlando, Univ. Club, Delta Sigma Pi. Democrat. Avocations: sailing, golfing, travel, hunting, fishing. Home and Office: 39605 Swift Rd Eustis FL 32736-9510

POPE, THOMAS HARRINGTON, JR., lawyer; b. Kinards, S.C., July 28, 1913; s. Thomas H. and Marie (Gary) P.; m. Mary Waties Lumpkin, Jan. 3, 1940; children: Mary Waties (Mrs. Robert H. Kennedy Jr.), Thomas Harrington III, Gary Tusten. A.B., The Citadel, 1935, LL.D., 1977; LL.B., U. S.C., 1938; grad., Command and Gen. Staff Coll., 1951; LL.D., Newberry Coll., 1969. Bar: S.C. 1938, U.S. Supreme Ct. 1962. Practice in Newberry, 1938—; sr. ptnr. Pope and Hudgens, P.A.; spl. circuit judge Richland and Lexington counties, 1955-56; dir. emeritus the Citizens and So. Nat. Bank S.C., Carolina Motor Club; dir. Newberry Fed. Savs. Bank; mem. S.C. Ports Authority, 1957-65; mem. Jud. Coun. S.C., 1957—, chmn., 1979-83; mem. S.C. Archives Commn., 1965-75, vice chmn., 1974-75. Author: The History of Newberry County, South Carolina, Vol. 1, 1973, Vol. 2, 1992; co-author: The History of the 107th Separate Coast Artillery Battalion (AA), 1982. Chmn. Newberry County Sesqui-Centennial Commn., 1939; Mem. S.C. Ho. of Reps. from Newberry County, 1936-40, 45-50, speaker, 1949-50; chmn. S.C. Democratic Party, 1958-60; del. at large Dem. Nat. Conv., 1956, 60; pres. S.C. Dem. Conv., 1958, 62; Mem. S.C. Tricentennial Commn., 1966-71; Trustee U. of South, 1965-70, Newberry Coll., 1965-75; chmn. S.C. Found. Ind. Colls.; bd. visitors The Citadel, 1939-40, 46. Served to lt. col. AUS, 1941-45, ETO; brig. gen. ret. S.C. N.G. Recipient Algernon Sydney Sullivan award Newberry Coll., 1976, Durant Disting. Pub. Svc. award S.C. Bar Found., 1983, The Compleat Lawyer award Law Sch., U. S.C., 1992, U. S.C. Disting. Alumnus, 1994. Fellow Am. Coll. Trial Lawyers, Am. Bar Found., S.C. Bar Found.; mem. ABA, S.C. Bar Assn. (pres. 1964, chmn. exec. com. 1956-58), Newberry County Bar Assn. (pres. 1951), Am. Law Inst. (life), John Belton O'Neall Inn of Ct., So. Hist. Assn., Soc. Colonial Wars, Nat. Trust Historic Preservation (adv. bd. 1967-72), U. S.C. Soc. (curator 1968-72), S.C. Hist. Soc. (curator 1968-74), Newberry County Hist. Soc. (pres. 1966), Mason (grand master S.C. 1958-60, Albert Gallatin Mackey medal Grand Lodge S.C. 1965, Henry Price medal Grand Lodge Mass. 1960), Newberry Country Club, Palmetto Club (Columbia), Pine Tree Hunt Club (Columbia), Phi Beta Kappa, Omicron Delta Kappa, Phi Delta Phi, Phi Kappa Phi, Alpha Tau Omega. Episcopalian (sr. warden 1963-65, 70). Home: 1700 Boundary St Newberry SC 29108-3912 Office: 1508 College St Newberry SC 29108-2749

POPE, TIM LANE, state legislator, consultant; b. Mooresville, Ind., Oct. 2, 1957; s. Eugene L. and Mary L. (Clark) P.; m. LaDonna K. Freeman, Aug. 6, 1976; children: Melissa, Andrea, Erica. Sales mgr. Generay Sales, Martinsville, Ind., 1976-80, Royal Mobile Homes, Oklahoma City, 1980-86; counselor Draughon Coll., Oklahoma City, 1986-88; mem. Okla. Ho. of Reps., Oklahoma City, 1988—. County chmn. Canadian County (Okla.) Reps., 1992; bd. dirs. Mustang (Okla.) Handicapped Assn., 1989-93. Recipient Taxpayers Friend award Okla. Taxpayers Union, 1993. Mem. Mustang Kiwanis. Home: 517 N Lakeside Terrace Mustang OK 73064-9795 Office: 504 State Capital Bldg Oklahoma City OK 73105

POPE, WILLIAM L., lawyer, judge; b. Brownsville, Tex., Nov. 5, 1960; s. William E. and Maria Antonieta P.; m. Sandra Solis, May 16, 1992; children: Ana Lauren, William E.H. AA, Tex. Southmost Coll., 1980; postgrad., U. Tex., 1980-81, Tex. Christian U., 1982, Tex. Coll. Osteo. Medicine, 1982-83; JD, Baylor U., 1986. Bar: Tex. 1986, U.S. Dist. Ct. (so. dist.) Tex. 1988, U.S. Supreme Ct. 1990. Assoc. Adams & Graham, Harlingen, Tex., 1986-91, ptnr., 1991—; mcpl. ct. judge City of La Feria, Tex., 1987—. Mem. ABA, Tex. State Bar Assn., Cameron County Bar Assn. Mem. Ch. of Christ. Office: Adams & Graham L L P PO Box 1429 Harlingen TX 78551-1429

POPEL, ALEKSANDER S., engineering educator; b. Moscow, Oct. 8, 1945; came to U.S., 1975; s. Samson Popel and Mary Gellershtein; m. Natalya Kalnitskaya, Sept. 17, 1966; 1 child, Julie. MS, Moscow State U., 1967, PhD, 1972. Rsch. scientist Inst. Mechanics, Moscow State U., 1970-75; asst. prof. Tulane U., New Orleans, 1976; rsch. assoc. prof. U. Ariz., Tucson, 1976-80; assoc. prof. U. Houston, 1980-84; assoc. prof. Johns Hopkins U., Balt., 1984-88, prof., 1988—. Editor 2 books; contbr. articles to profl. jours. NIH, NSF grantee. Fellow ASME, Am. Inst. Med. & Biol. Engring.; mem AAAS, Biomed. Engring. Soc. (sr.), Am. Physiol. Soc., Soc. for Indsl. and Applied Math. Office: Johns Hopkins U Sch Medicine Dept Biomed Engring Baltimore MD 21205

POPELYUKHIN, ALEKSEY, actuary, researcher; b. Kalarash, Russia, May 16, 1964; came to U.S. 1991; s. Semen and Aleksandra (Stopchik) P.; m.

Valentina Kotova, Dec. 3, 1991; 1 child, Masha. MS in Math., Moscow U., 1985, PhD in Math., 1989; Gold Medal (honor degree), Math. Sch. #2, Kiev, Ukraine, 1980; Red Diploma (honor degree), Moscow U., 1985. Tchr. and methodologist Moscow All-Union Math Sch., 1982-88; supporting profl. Moscow Med.-Biol. Inst., 1984-85; jr. scientist Moscow Lab. of Math. Statistics, 1986-87; jr. rsch. scientist div. math. Moscow State U., 1988-89; asst. prof. math. Kishinev Poly. U., 1989-90, adj. prof., 1990-91; asst. actuary Home Ins. Co., N.Y.C., 1991-93; sr. actuarial asst. Home Ins. Co., N.Y., 1993-94; actuarial analyst, 1994-96; project leader Price Waterhouse LLP, Hartford, Conn., 1995-96, product mgr., 1996-97; mgr. IS Comml. Risk, PC, Stamford, Conn., 1997—; math., olympiad supr. Russian Acad. Sci., Moscow, 1981-86; rschr. Courant Inst. Math. Sci., NYU, 1991-92; cons. Video Internat., Inc., N.Y.C., 1992—, creative dir., Moscow, 1988-91; official developer, plug-in ptnr. Autodesk, Inc., Sausalito, 1994—. Contbr. articles to profl. jours.; screenplay author TV shows on Russian State TV, 1988—; author profl. paper (named Best 1997 Paper by Casualty Actuarial Soc.). Fellow Moscow Math. Soc., Am. Math. Soc.; mem. ACM. Avocations: computer graphics, mathematics. Home: 86 Pine Hill Ave #1 Stamford CT 06906

POPENOE, HUGH LLYWELYN, soils educator; b. Tela, Honduras, Aug. 28, 1929; s. Frederick Wilson and Dorothy (Hughes) P. BS, U. Calif., Davis, 1951; PhD, U. Fla., 1960. Mem. faculty U. Fla., Gainesville, 1960—, dir. ctr. tropical agr., 1965—, dir. internat. programs, 1966-92, dir. Fla. Sea Grant Coll., 1971-81; bd. dirs. Escuela Agricola Panamericana, Zamorano, Honduras, Orgn. Tropical Studies. Contbr. numerous articles to profl. jours. Chari Assn. U.S. Univ. Dirs. Internat. Agrl. Programs, 1969-70, Joint Rsch. Com. Bd. Internat. Food and Agrl. Devel., 1977-82, Joint Com. Agrl. Rsch. and Devel., 1982-86; chair numerous reports Bd. Sci. and Tech. in Devel., 1979-84; trustee Internat. Found. for Sci., Stockholm, 1984-87; mem. sci. liaison officer Internat. Inst. for Tropical Agr., Nigeria, 1983-88; mem. adv. com. internat. programs NSF, 1985-87; bd. dirs. League for Internat. Food Edn., 1976-87. With U.S. Army, 1952-54. Recipient Sci. Pioneer prize Egyptian Vet. Assn. for Buffalo Devel., 1985. Fellow AAAS, Am. Soc. Agronomy, Am. Geog. Soc., Internat. Soil Sci. Soc., Am. Water Buffalo Assn. (pres. 1988—), Cosmos Club. Office: U Fla 3028 McCarty Gainesville FL 32611

POPENOE, JOHN, horticultural consultant, retired botanical garden administrator; b. L.A., Jan. 24, 1929; s. Paul and Betty (Stankowitch) P.; m. Geraldine V. Mann, June 29, 1952; children: Deborah Irene, Natalie, Juanita, Jennifer. B.S., UCLA, 1950; M.S., U. Md., 1952, Ph.D., 1955. Asst. horticulturist U.S. Dept. Agr., Miami, 1955-58; asso. prof. horticulture Ala. Poly. Inst., 1958-59; assoc. horticulturist U. Fla. Subtropical Experiment Sta., 1960-63; dir. Fairchild Tropical Garden, Miami, 1963-91; horticultural cons., 1991—. Served with U.S. Army, 1952-54. Home: 113 Washington St Hancock MD 21750-1127

POPKIN, DAVID RICHARD, academic dean, obstetrician, gynocologist; m. Linda Popkin, 1964; 4 children. BSc in Agr., McGill, 1962, MD, CM, 1966. Head divsn. gynecology and gynecologic oncology Royal Victoria Hosp., Montreal, Can., 1976-82; head dept. ob-gyn. Royal Univ. Hosp. U. Saskatchewan, Saskatoon, Can., 1982-91, assoc. dean postgrad. med. edn. and clin. affairs, 1991-93, dean Coll. Medicine, 1993—. Office: Coll Medicine Health Scis Bldg 107, Wiggins Rd Rm B103, Saskatoon, SK Canada S7N 5E5

POPLE, JOHN ANTHONY, chemistry educator; b. Burnham, Somerset, Eng., Oct. 31, 1925; s. Herbert Keith and Mary Frances (Jones) P.; m. Joy Cynthia, Sept. 22, 1952; children: Hilary Jane, Adrian John, Mark Stephen, Andrew Keith. BA in Math., Cambridge U., Eng., 1946, MA in Math., 1950; PhD in Math., Cambridge U., 1951. Research fellow Trinity Coll., Cambridge U., Eng., 1951-54, lectr. in math., 1954-58; Ford vis. prof. chemistry Carnegie Inst. Tech., Pitts., 1961-62; Carnegie prof. chem. physics Carnegie-Mellon U., Pitts., 1964-74, J.C. Warner prof., 1974-91; prof. Northwestern U., Evanston, Ill., 1986—. Recipient Wolf Found. Chemistry prize, 1992, Kirkwood medal Am. Chem. Soc., 1994, J.O. Hirschfelder Prize in Theoretical Chemistry, Univ. of Wis., Theoretical Chemistry Inst., 1994. Fellow AAAS, Royal Soc. London; mem. NAS (fgn.). Office: Northwestern U Dept Chemistry 2145 Sheridan Rd Evanston IL 60208-0834

POPLER, KENNETH, behavioral healthcare executive, psychologist; b. Bklyn., Nov. 7, 1945; s. Irving and Mildred P.; m. Lois L., Aug. 31, 1969; children: Jonathan, Emily. BA in Psychology, CUNY, 1967; MA in Psychology, New Sch. Social Rsch., N.Y.C., 1969, PhD in Psychology, 1974; MBA, Wagner Coll., 1994. Diplomate Am. Bd. Profl. Psychology. Case worker N.Y.C. Dept. Social Svcs., 1967-70; intern Bklyn. Psychiat. Ctrs., 1970-72; sch. psychologist N.Y.C. Bd. Edn., 1972-73; psychologist Mid Nassau Community Guidance Ctr., Hicksville, N.Y., 1973-77; dir. St. Mary Community Mental Health Ctr., Hoboken, N.J., 1978-81; pres. and CEO Staten Island (N.Y.) Mental Health Soc., Inc., 1981—; psychometrician L.I. Hillside Jewish Med. Ctr., Queens, N.Y., 1972-73; sr. psychologist, dir. psychol. svcs. HHC Gouverneur Hosp., N.Y.C., 1973-78; asst. rsch. scientist N.Y. State Psychiat. Inst., N.Y.C., 1971; vol. rsch. Manhattan Sch. for Seriously Disturbed Children, N.Y.C., 1972-73; instr. CUNY Bklyn. Coll. grad. divsn., 1972-73; pvt. practice, N.Y.C., 1976-85; asst. clin. prof. psychiatry Mt. Sinai Med. Sch., N.Y.C., 1978-95. Apptd. N.Y.C. Cmty. Svcs. Bd., 1984—, alcoholism subcom., 1987-91; pres. Coalition of Voluntary Mental Health Agys., Inc., 1991-94; sec. Head Start Sponsoring Bd. Coun. N.Y.C., 1985-92; chmn. Mental Health Coun. S.I., 1987-89, S.I. United Way Execs. Com., 1985. Mem. Rotary Club of Staten Island, Inc. Office: SI Mental Health Soc Inc 669 Castleton Ave Staten Island NY 10301-2028

POPOFF, FRANK PETER, chemical company executive; b. Sofia, Bulgaria, Oct. 27, 1935; came to U.S., 1940; s. Eftim and Stoyanka (Kossoroff) P.; m. Jean Urse; children: John V., Thomas F., Steven M. B.S. in Chemistry, Ind. U., 1957, M.B.A., 1959. With The Dow Chem. Co., Midland, Mich., 1959—, exec. v.p., 1985-87, dir., pres., chief executive officer, 1987-92; chmn., CEO, dir. Dow Chemical Corp., Midland, Mich., 1992-96, chmn., 1996—; exec. v.p., then pres. Dow Chem. Europe subs., Horgen, Switzerland, 1976-85; bd. dirs. Dow Corning Corp., Am. Express, Chem. Bank & Trust Co., Chem. Fin. Corp., Midland. Mem. dean's adv. coun. Ind. U.; mem. vis. com. U. Mich. Sch. Bus.; mem. Pres.' Commn. Environ. Quality. Recipient Internat. Palladium medal, 1994, Société de Chimie Industrielle (Am. Section). Mem. Chem. Mfrs. Assn. (bd. dirs.), U.S. Coun. for Internat. Bus., Bus. Roundtable, Conf. Bd., Am. Chem. Soc. Office: Dow Chem Co 2030 Dow Ctr Midland MI 48674

POPOFSKY, MELVIN LAURENCE, lawyer; b. Oskaloosa, Iowa, Feb. 16, 1936; s. Samuel and Fannye Charlotte (Rosenthal) P.; m. Linda Jane Seltzer, Nov. 25, 1962; children: Mark Samuel, Kaye Sylvia. BA in History summa cum laude, U. Iowa, 1958; BA in Jurisprudence (first class honors), Oxford U., Eng., 1960; LLB cum laude, Harvard U., 1962. Bar: Calif. 1962. Assoc. Heller, Ehrman, White & McAuliffe, San Francisco, 1962-69, ptnr., 1969—, mem. exec. com., 1980-93, co-chair, 1988-93. Contbr. articles to law jours. Bd. dirs. Mt. Zion Hosp., San Francisco, 1982-88, U.S. Dist. Ct. (no. dist.) Calif. Hist. Soc., 1988—, Jewish Home for Aged, San Francisco, 1989-96, Golden Gate U., 1997—. Rhodes scholar, 1958. Fellow Am. Bar Found., Am. Coll. Trial Lawyers; mem. ABA, Calif. Bar Assn., San Francisco Bar Assn., Bur. Nat. Affairs (adv. bd. antitrust sect.), Calif. Acad. Appellate Lawyers. Democrat. Jewish. Home: 1940 Broadway Apt 10 San Francisco CA 94109-2216 Office: Heller Ehrman 333 Bush St San Francisco CA 94104-2806

POPOV, EGOR PAUL, engineering educator; b. Kiev, Russia, Feb. 19, 1913; s. Paul T. and Zoe (Derabin) P.; m. Irene Zofia Jozefowski, Feb. 18, 1939; children—Katherine, Alexander. BS, U. Calif., 1933; MS, MIT, 1934; PhD, Stanford U., 1946. Registered civil, structural and mech. engr., Calif. Structural engr., bldg. designer L.A., 1935-39; asst. prodn. engr. Southwestern Portland Cement Co., L.A., 1939-42; machine designer Goodyear Tire & Rubber Co., L.A., 1942-43; design engr. Aerojet Corp., Calif., 1943-45; asst. prof. civil engring. U. Calif. at Berkeley, 1946-48, assoc. prof., 1948-53, prof., 1953-83, prof. emeritus, 1983—, chmn. structural engring. and structural mechanics div., dir. structural engring. lab., 1956-60; Miller rsch. prof. Miller Inst. Basic Rsch. in Sci., 1968-69. Author: Mechanics of Materials, 1952, 2d edit., 1976, Introduction to Mechanics of Solids, 1968, Engineering Mechanics of Solids, 1990; Contbr. articles profl. jours. Recipient Disting. Tchr. award U. Calif.-Berkeley, 1976-77, Berkeley citation U. Calif.-Berkeley, 1983, Disting. Lectr. award Earthquake Engring. Rsch. Inst., 1993. Fellow AAAS (assoc.), Am. Concrete Inst.; mem. NAE, Am. Soc. Metals, Internat. Assn. Shell Structures (hon. mem.), ASCE (hon. mem., Ernest E. Howard award 1976, J. James R. Cross medal 1979, 82, Nathan M. Newmark medal 1981, Raymond C. Reese rsch. prize 1986, Norman medal 1987, von Karman medal 1989), Soc. Exptl. Stress Analysis (Hetenyi award 1967, William M. Murray medallion 1986), Am. Soc. Engring. Edn. (Western Electric Fund award 1976-77, Disting. Educator award 1979), Soc. Engring. Sci., Internat. Assn. Bridge and Structural Engring., Am. Inst. Steel Constrn. (adv. com. specifications), Ukrainian Acad. Constrn. (fgn. mem.), Sigma Xi, Chi Epsilon, Tau Beta Pi. Home: 2600 Virginia St # 9 Berkeley CA 94709-1045

POPOVA, NINA, dancer, choreographer, director; b. Novorossisk, USSR, 1922. Ed. in Paris, studied ballet with Olga Preobrajenska, Lubov Egorova, Anatole Vilzak, Anatole Oboukhov, Igor Schwezoff. Ballet debut with Ballet de la Jeunesse, Paris, London, 1937-39; soloist Original Ballet Russe, 1939-41, Ballet Theatre (now Am. Ballet), 1941-42, Ballet Russe de Monte Carlo, 1943, 47, Ballet Alicia Alonso, Cuba; mem. faculty Sch. Performing Arts, N.Y.C., from 1954; later artistic dir. Houston Ballet, 1975; tchr. Nat. Acad. Arts, Champaign, Ill., also N.Y.C., 1975—, now Eglevsky Ballet Sch., L.I.; tchr. ballet Mexico City, Mex.; asst. choreographer mus. comedy Birmingham So. Coll., Ala., 1960; numerous appearances on Broadway stage, TV; former mem. regular cast Your Show of Shows; currently teaching N.Y.C. Address: 33 Adams St Sea Cliff NY 11579-1614

POPOVICI, ADRIAN, law educator; b. Bucharest, Rumania, Sept. 6, 1942; came to Can., 1951; s. Adrian and Alice (Moruzi) P.; children—Adrian, Alexandra. B.A., Stanislas Coll., Montreal, 1959; B.C.L., McGill U., 1962; D.E.S., U. Paris, 1965. Bar: Que. 1963. Prof. law U. Montreal, Que., Can., 1968—. Author: L'Outrage au Tribunal, 1977, La Couleur du Mandat, 1985; editor: Problèmes de Droit Contemporain, 1974. Roman Catholic. Home: 5589 Canterbury, Montreal, PQ Canada H3T 1S8 Office: U Montreal Faculte de Droit, CP 6128 Succursale A, Montreal, PQ Canada H3C 3J7

POPOVICS, SANDOR, civil engineer, educator, researcher; b. Budapest, Hungary, Dec. 24, 1921; came to U.S., 1957; s. Milan and Erzsebet (Droppa) P.; m. Lea M. Virtanen, Aug. 29, 1960; children: John, Lisa. 1st Degree in Civil Engring., Poly. U., Budapest, Hungary, 1944; Advanced Degree in Civil Engring., Poly. U., 1956; PhD, Purdue U., 1961. Registered profl. engr., Ala., Ariz., Pa. Rsch. engr. Met. Lab., Budapest, 1944-48; adj. prof. Tech. Coll., Budapest, 1949-52; rsch. engr., mgr. Inst. for Bldg. Scis., Budapest, 1949-56; grad. asst. Purdue U., Lafayette, Ind., 1957-59; prof. engring. Auburn (Ala.) U., 1959-69; prof. civil engring. No. Ariz. U., Flagstaff, 1968-76; prof. engring. King Abdulazziz U., Jeddah, Saudi Arabia, 1977-78; Samuel S. Baxter prof. civil engring. Drexel U., Phila., 1979-92, rsch. prof., 1992—; pres. Optimum Engring. Rsch. Author: Fundamentals of Pc Concrete, 1982, Concrete Materials, 1992, Strength and Related Properties of Concrete, 1997, others; author more than 200 tech. papers in various langs. Recipient numerous grants and awards. Fellow ASCE (life), Am. Concrete Inst.; mem. ASTM, Ala. Acad. Scis., Ariz. Acad. Scis., Sigma Xi, Chi Epsilon. Avocations: jogging, music, fine art. Home and Office: 283 Congress Ave Lansdowne PA 19050-1206 Office: Drexel U Dept Civil Engring 32nd and Chestnut Philadelphia PA 19104

POPP, CHARLOTTE LOUISE, health development center administrator, nurse; b. Vineland, N.J., July 26, 1946; d. William Henry and Elfriede Marie (Zickler) P. Diploma in Nursing, Luth. Hosp. of Md., Balt., 1967; BA in Health Edn., Rowan U., 1972; MA in Human Devel., Fairleigh-Dickinson U., 1981. Cert. Sch. Nurse, N.J., Health Educator, N.J. Charge nurse Newcomb Hosp., Vineland, N.J., 1967-71; supr. Vineland Rehab. Ctr., 1971-72; charge nurse Bridgeton (N.J.) Hosp., 1972-73; dir. insvc. edn. Millville (N.J.) Hosp., 1973-76; dir. hosp. insvc. edn. Vineland Devel. Ctr. State of N.J., 1976-78, program asst. Vineland Devel. Ctr., 1978-87; dir. habilitation planning services State of N.J., Vineland Devel. Ctr., 1987—, lead program coord. Vineland Devel. Ctr., 1981—; exam proctor State of N.J. Bd. Nursing, Newark, 1973-91. Editorial rev. bd. (jour.) Nursing Update, 1973-77. Instr. basic life support, Am. Heart Assn., bd. dirs. Tri-county chpt., 1979-83, South Jersey chpt., 1983-90. Mem. ANA, N.J. State Nurses Assn., Am. Assn. Mental Retardation, South Jersey Insvc. Exch. (life), Smithsonian Assn., Luth. Hosp. of Md. Alumni Assn., Glassboro State Coll./Rowan U. Alumni Assn., Fairleigh-Dickinson U. Alumni Assn. Lutheran. Avocations: reading, travel, collectable plates, animals, horseracing. Office: Vineland Devel Ctr 1676 E Landis Ave Vineland NJ 08361-2943

POPP, JAMES ALAN, toxicologist, toxicology executive; b. Salem, Ohio, Mar. 13, 1945; s. John W. and Florence H. (Rowley) P.; m. Gloria Jean Paxton, Aug. 20, 1966; 1 child, Candice Renee. DVM summa cum laude, Ohio State U., 1968; PhD, U. Calif., Davis, 1972. Postdoctoral rsch. fellow Temple U. Sch. Medicine, Phila., 1972-74; asst. prof. U. Fla., Gainesville, 1974-78; scientist Chem. Industry Inst. Toxicology, Research Triangle Park, N.C., 1978-84, dept. head, 1984-93, v.p., 1989-93; v.p. Sterling Winthrop Inc., Collegeville, Pa., 1993-94, Sanofi Rsch., Collegeville, Pa., 1994—; mem. bd. sci. counselors Nat. Inst. Environ. Health Scis., Research Triangle Park. Editor mouse liver neoplasia Current Perspectives, 1984, mouse liver carcinogenesis Mechanisms and Species Comparisons, 1990. Recipient George H. Scott award Toxicology Forum, 1992; Borden scholar. Mem. Am. Soc. for Investigative Pathology, Am. Assn. Cancer Rsch., Am. Coll. Vet. Pathologists, Soc. for Toxicology, Soc. Toxicologic Pathologists (pres. 1996-97), Phi Eta Sigma, Phi Zeta, Phi Kappa Phi. Office: Sanofi Rsch PO Box 3026 9 Great Valley Pkwy Malvern PA 19355

POPP, NATHANIEL, bishop; b. Aurora, Ill., June 12, 1940; s. Joseph and Vera (Boytor) P. BA, Ill. Benedictine U., 1962; ThM, Pontifical Gregorian U., 1966. Ordained priest, 1966, bishop, 1980. Asst. priest St. Michael Byz Cath. Ch., Aurora, Ill., 1967; parish priest Holy Cross Romanian Orthodox Ch., Hermitage, Pa., 1975-80; aux. bishop Romanian Orthodox Episcopate of Am., Orthodox Ch. in Am., Jackson, Mich., 1980-84, ruling bishop, 1984—; mem. Holy Synod, Orthodox Ch. in Am., Syosset, N.Y., 1980—; participant Monastic Consultation World Coun. Chs., Cairo, 1979, 7th Assembly, Vancouver, Can., 1983. Author: Holy Icons, 1969; working editor: (monthly newspaper) Solia. Trustee Romanian-Am. Heritage Ctr., Grass Lake, Mich.; chmn. bd. dirs. Congress of Romanian Ams., 1990. Mem. Mineral and Rock Soc. Mich. Home: 2522 Grey Tower Rd Jackson MI 49201-9120 Address: PO Box 309 Grass Lake MI 49240-0309

POPPE, PATRICIA LEE, clinical social worker, consultant; b. Lewiston, Idaho, Feb. 19, 1936; d. Clarence Lee and Emma Lucille (Stephenson) Anderson; m. Stanley Kermit Poppe, June 6, 1956 (div. 1984); children: Stephen Scott, Jeffrey Lee, Julie Anne. BA, Western Wash. U., 1972; MSW, U. Wash., 1976. Pvt. practice Mount Vernon, Wash., 1976—; lectr. Western Wash. U., Bellingham, 1967-72, Skagit Valley Coll., Mount Vernon, 1978—, seminar leader, 1967-72. Vol. probation officer Skagit County Juvenile, Mount Vernon, 1970-71; sec., treas. Skagit Interagency adv. bd., 1970-71. Mem. NASW, Wash. Assn. Social Workers. Democrat. Avocations: writing, hiking, photography, gardening, singing. Office: 1789 N Pamela St Mount Vernon WA 98274-9025

POPPEL, HARVEY LEE, management consultant; b. Bklyn., Dec. 18, 1937; s. Frank M. and Fannie (Axenzow) P.; m. Emily A. Daigneault, Jan. 2, 1959; children: Marc F., Clinton S. BS, Rensselaer Poly. Inst., 1958, MS, 1959. Sr. info. systems analyst Westinghouse Electric Corp., Pitts., 1959-65; mgr. industry systems Western Union, Paramus, N.J., 1965-67; from assoc. to mem. operating coun. Booz, Allen & Hamilton, N.Y.C., 1967-84; pres. Poptech, Inc., Sarasota, Fla., 1984—; bd. dirs. Larscom, Santa Clara, Calif., Cotelligent, San Francisco; mng. dir. Broadview Assocs., Ft. Lee, 1984-96; mem. panel, lectr. on computers, comms. and info. industry; judge Entrepreneur of Yr., 1991, 93, 94, 95, 96. Co-author: Information Technology: The Trillion Dollar Opportunity, 1987; contbr. articles to profl. jours. Mem. Aspen Inst. Fellows, Inst. Mgmt. Cons., Soc. Mgmt. Info. Systems (exec. council), Zeta Psi. Club: Road Runners. Office: 1391 6th St Sarasota FL 34236-4906

POPPEL, SETH RAPHAEL, entrepreneur; b. Bklyn., Mar. 17, 1944; s. Frank M. and Fritzi R. (Axenzow) P.; BS magna cum laude, L.I. U., 1965; MBA, Columbia U., 1967; m. Danine Vokt, Jan. 5, 1974; children: Clarysa, Jared, Stacy. Asst. prof. L.I. U., Greenvale, N.Y., 1967-68; v.p. Synergistic Systems Corp., N.Y.C., 1968-77; v.p., dir. corp. planning Chase Manhattan Corp., N.Y.C., 1977-90; chmn., pres. Am. Vision Ctrs., N.Y.C., 1990-96; owner, pres. Poppel Enterprises, Merrick, N.Y., 1995—; owner harness horses Seth Poppel Stables, 1983—; founder, owner, operator Seth Poppel Yearbook Archives, 1986—. E.I. DuPont fellow, 1965-67, Downie Muir fellow, 1965-66; recipient Claire F. Adler award in math., 1964-65, Mepham High Sch. Hall of Fame award, 1993. Mem. Am. Statis. Assn., Ops. Research Soc. Am., Inst. Mgmt. Sci., Nat. Assn. Bus. Economy, N.Am. Soc. Corp. Planning, U.S. Trotting Assn., Beta Gamma Sigma, Psi Chi, Omega Epsilon. Home and Office: 38 Range Dr Merrick NY 11566-3233

POPPELIERS, JOHN CHARLES, architectural historian; b. Binghamton, N.Y., Oct. 5, 1935; s. Johannes Marinus and Irene (Marx) P.; m. Julia Margaret Tatnell, Dec. 16, 1967. AB, Hamilton Coll., 1957; MA, U. Pa., 1962; PhD, Cath. U. of Am., 1975. Instr. history and English various high schs., Binghamton, Johnson City, 1957-58, 60-62; sr. editor, architectural historian Historic Am. Bldgs. Survey, Dept. Interior, 1962-72, chief, 1972-80; chief ops. and tng. Divsn. Cultural Heritage, Unesco, 1980-86; internat. liaison Officer for Cultural Resources, U.S. Nat. Park Svc., 1986—; rep. for exec. and consultative coms. for internat. campaigns to safeguard Mohenjodaro, Pakistan, Göreme and Istanbul, Turkey, Tyr (Lebanon) UNESCO; rep. Christopher Columbus Quincentenary Commn., U.s. Dept. Interior, 1987-92; curator Smithsonian Traveling Exhbns. on Archtl. History. Author: HABS Massachusetts Catalog, 1965; author: (with Nancy B. Schwartz and S. Allen Chambers) What Style Is It?; contbr. articles to profl. jour.; editor many tech. reports. Fulbright-Hays rsch. grantee, U. Vienna, 1968-69; grad. fellow U. Pa., 1960-62, Catholic U. Am., 1966-68; recipient History Dept. award Hamilton Coll., 1957. Fellow Internat. Coun. on Monuments and Sites (U.S. com. 1990, bd. trustees, asst. sec.-treas.); mem. AIA (cons. mem. com. on historic resources), Nat. Trust for Hist. Preservation, Fulbright Assn., Cosmos Club, Soc. of Arch. Historians (com. on arch. preservation, former pres. Latrobe chpt.), Com. for the Preservation of Architectural Records, Nat. Preservation Inst. (dir. for edn. 1988-92), Nat. Trust Libr. (bd. advisors 1988—), Secular Franciscan Order. Roman Catholic. Avocations: vol. charitable causes, ecology, painting, music. Home: 2939 Van Ness St NW Apt 606 Washington DC 20008-4622 Office: US Nat Park Svc PO Box 37127 Washington DC 20013-7127

POPPEN, ALVIN J., religious organization administrator. Dir., office ministry and pers. svcs. Reformed Ch. in Am., N.Y.C. Office: Reformed Church in Am 475 Riverside Dr Ste 1811 New York NY 10115-0122*

POPPENHAGEN, RONALD WILLIAM, newspaper editor, publishing executive; b. Chgo., Feb. 23, 1948; s. Andrew Charles and Elaine Edith (Larson) P.; m. Judy Diane Wagenblast, July 25, 1981. BA in History and Lit., Augustana Coll., 1970. Reporter Sta. KBUR, Burlington, Iowa, 1970-71, Sta. KROS, Clinton, Iowa, 1971-72; reporter Sta. WDWS, Champaign, Ill., 1972-73, news dir., 1973-77; reporter The Morning Courier, Urbana, Ill., 1977-79; mng. editor The Daily Journal, Wheaton, Ill., 1979-80; met. editor The Southern Illinoisan, Carbondale, Ill., 1980-83; editor Green Bay (Wis.) News Chronicle, 1983-86, editor, general mgr., 1986—; v.p. Wagenblast and Assocs., Green Bay, 1997—. Recipient Best Editls. award Wis. Newspaper Assn., 1985, 86, 93, UPI, 1983-86, Best Local Column award, 1993. Avocation: railroads. Office: Green Bay News Chronicle 133 S Monroe Ave Green Bay WI 54301-4056

POPPENSIEK, GEORGE CHARLES, veterinary scientist, educator; b. N.Y.C., June 18, 1918; s. George Frederick and Emily Amelia (Miller) P.; m. Edith M. Wallace, July 3, 1943; children: Neil Allen, Leslie Marion. Student, Cornell U., 1936-37, M.S., 1951; student, U. Pa., 1937-42, V.M.D., 1942. Diplomate Am. Bd. Microbiology, Am. Coll. Vet. Microbiology (charter), Am. Coll. Vet. Preventive Medicine (hon.). Asst. instr. medicine U. Pa. Sch. Vet. Medicine, 1943; asst. prof. vet. sci. U. Md., 1943-44; head dept. vet. virus vaccine prodn. Lederle Labs. div. Am. Cyanamid Co., 1944-49; dir. diagnostic lab. N.Y. State Coll. Vet. Medicine Cornell U., 1949-51, research assoc. Vet. Virus Research Inst., 1951-55; veterinarian Plum Island Animal Disease Ctr., animal disease and parasite research div. Agrl. Research Service, U.S. Dept. Agr., 1955-56, acting-in-charge diagnostic investigations, 1956-58, charge immunological investigations, 1958-59; dean and prof. microbiology N.Y. State Coll. Vet. Medicine, Cornell U., 1959-74, James Law prof. comparative medicine, 1974-88, dean emeritus, James Law prof. comparative medicine emeritus, 1988—; guest prof. U. Bern, Switzerland, 1975; mem. exam. com. Nat. Bd. Vet. Med. Examiners, 1976-79; bd. dirs. Cornell Research Found., 1963-74; chmn. bd. dirs. Cornell Veterinarian, Inc., 1976-86. Recipient Certificate of Merit award U.S. Dept. Agr., 1958; citation Sch. Vet. Med., U. Pa., 1978, Centennial medals U. Pa., 1984, Ohio State U., 1985; others. Charter fellow Am. Acad. Microbiology; fellow AAAS; charter mem. Am. Soc. Virology; mem. AVMA, N.Y. State Vet. Med. Soc. (disting. life), Am. Bd. Microbiology, U.S. Animal Health Assn., Assn. Am. Vet. Med. Colls. (pres. 1970-71), So. Tier Vet. Med. Assn., Am. Vet. Radiology Soc., Am. Soc. for Microbiology, N.Y. Agrl. Soc. (life), Argentine Nat. Acad. Agronomy and Vet. Medicine (hon.), Societas Polona Medicinae Veterinariae (hon.), Sigma Xi, Phi Kappa Phi, Alpha Psi, Omega Tau Sigma, Phi Zeta. Congregationalist. Home: 122 E Remington Rd Ithaca NY 14850-1456

POPPER, ARTHUR N., zoology educator; b. N.Y.C., May 9, 1943; s. Martin and Evelyn (Levine) P.; m. Helen Apfel, Nov. 30, 1968; children: Michelle, Melissa. BA, NYU, 1964; PhD, CUNY, 1969. Asst. prof. zoology U. Hawaii, Honolulu, 1969-72; assoc. prof. zoology U. Hawaii, 1972-78; assoc. prof. dept. anatomy & cell biology Georgetown U., Washington, 1978-83; prof. dept. anatomy & cell biology Georgetown U., 1983-87; prof., chmn. dept. zoology U. Md., College Park, 1987—. Editor: Comparative Studies of Hearing in Vertebrates, 1980, Hearing and Sound Communication in Fishes, 1981, Sensory Biology of Aquatic Animals, 1988, Evolutionary Biology of Hearing, 1992, Springer Handbook of Auditory Research, 1992—. Recipient Research Career Devel. award NIH, 1978-83. Fellow AAAS, Acoustical Soc.; mem. Soc. for Neurosci., Am. Assn. for Rsch. in Otolaryngology, Internat. Soc. Neurothology, Sigma Xi. Office: U Md Dept Zoology College Park MD 20742

POPPER, ROBERT, law educator, former dean; b. N.Y.C., May 22, 1932; s. Walter G. and Dorothy B. (Kluger) P.; m. Mary Ann Schaefer, July 12, 1963; children: Julianne, Robert Gregory. BS, U. Wis., 1953; LLB, Harvard U., 1956; LLM, NYU, 1963. Bar: N.Y. 1957, U.S. Dist. Ct. (so. dist.) N.Y. 1962, U.S. Ct. Appeals (2d cir.) 1962, U.S. Supreme Ct. 1962, U.S. Dist. Ct. (ea. dist.) N.Y. 1969, U.S. Ct. Appeals (7th cir.) 1970, U.S. Ct. Appeals (8th cir.) 1971, Mo. 1971, U.S. Dist. Ct. (we. dist.) Mo. 1973. Trial atty. criminal br. N.Y.C. Legal Aid Soc., 1960-61; asst. dist. atty. N.Y. County, 1961-64; assoc. Seligson & Morris, N.Y.C., 1964-69; mem. faculty School of Law, U. Mo., Kansas City, 1969-96, prof., 1973-96, acting dean, 1983-84, dean, 1984-93, dean and prof. emeritus, 1996—; cons. and lectr. in field. Author: Post Conviction Remedies in a Nutshell, 1978, De-Nationalizing the Bill of Rights, 1979; contbr. articles to profl. jours. Mem. N.Y. State Bar Assn., Mo. Bar Assn., Kansas City Met. Bar Assn., Mo. Inst. of Justice. Home: 6229 Summit St Kansas City MO 64113 Office: U Mo Kansas City Sch Law 500 E 52nd St Kansas City MO 64110-2467

POPPER, VIRGINIA SOWELL, education educator; b. Macon, Ga., Sept. 10, 1945; d. Clifford E. and Hazel (Lewis) Sowell; m. James Clarence Sikes, June 24, 1967 (div. 1989); children: Zachary Andrew, Cristen Elizabeth; m. Joseph W. Popper, Jr., Dec. 28, 1992. AB, Wesleyan Coll., Macon, 1967; MEd, U. North Fla., 1973; PhD, Ga. State U., 1991. Tchr. 6th grade Jones County Schs., Gray, Ga., 1966-67; tchr. 12th grade Richmond County Schs., Augusta, Ga., 1967-68; guidance counselor Aiken County Schs., North Augusta, S.C., 1968-69, asst. prin., 1969-71; dir. Durham (N.C.) campus Kings Coll., 1974-77; rsch. asst. Ga. Dept. Edn., Atlanta, 1983-85; assoc. prof. Mercer U., Macon, 1989—; tchr. cultural studies exch. program Scinanto Gakuin Coll. of Kitakusha, Japan-Mercer U. Contbg. author: Business in Literature, 1986; contbr. articles, reports to profl. publs. Chmn. Mid. Ga. Regional Libr. System, Macon, 1989-91; bd. dirs. Jr. League Macon, Macon YWCA, Macon Intown, Macon Heritage Found., Bibb County Am.

Cancer Soc., March of Dimes, Macon Ballet, Friends of Libr., Gladys Lasky Weller Scholarship Found., Mayor's Lit. Task Force. Mem. ASCD, Assn. Tchr. Educators, Ga. Coun. Social Studies, Ga. Assn. Ind. Coll. Tchr. Edn., Kappa Delta Lambda, Pi Lambda Theta. Republican. Episcopalian. Home: 798 Saint Andrews Dr Macon GA 31210-4769 Office: Mercer U Sch Edn 1400 Coleman Ave Macon GA 31207-0001

POPPERS, PAUL JULES, anesthesiologist, educator; b. Enschede, Netherlands, June 30, 1929; came to U.S., 1958; naturalized, 1963; s. Meyer and Minca (Ginsburg) P.; m. Ann Feinberg, June 3, 1969; children: David Matthew, Jeremy Samuel. MD, U. Amsterdam, 1955. Diplomate Am. Bd. Anesthesiology. Instr. anesthesiology Columbia U., N.Y.C., 1962-63, assoc., 1963-65, asst. prof. anesthesiology, 1965-71, assoc. prof. anesthesiology, 1971-74; prof., vice chmn. dept. anesthesiology NYU, 1974-79; prof., chmn. dept. anesthesiology SUNY, Stony Brook, 1979—; cons. Brookdale Med. Ctr., Bklyn., 1975—, VA Med. Ctr., Northport, N.Y., 1979—, The N.Y. Hosp. Med. Ctr. of Queens (formerly Booth Meml. Hosp.), Flushing, N.Y., 1979—, L.I. Jewish Med. Ctr., New Hyde Pk., N.Y., 1980—, Ea. L.I. Hosp., Greenport, N.Y., 1995—, Am. Hosp. Paris, 1989-93; cons., lectr. Author: Regional Anesthesia, 1977; editor: Beta Blockade and Anaesthesia, 1979; sect. editor Jour. Clin. Anesthesia, 1990—; mem. editorial bd. Internat. Jour. Clin. Monitoring and Computing, 1990—, Gynecologic and Obstetric Investigation, 1996—; internat. bd. editors Anaesthesiology Digest, 1991-94; contbr. numerous articles to profl. jours. NIH postdoctoral rsch. fellow, 1961; recipient medal Polish Acad. Scis., Poland, 1987, Univ. medal Jagiellonian U., Krakow, Poland, 1987, 1st Sci. award Post-grad. Assembly in Anesthesiology; named Hon. Prof. Anesthesiology, U. Leiden, The Netherlands, 1977. Fellow Am. Coll. Anesthesiology, Am. Coll. Ob-gyns., Royal Soc. Medicine, Post-grad. Assembly in Anesthesiology (hon. chmn. 1989—); mem. Am. Soc. Anesthesiologists, Assn. Univ. Anesthesiologists, Soc. Acad. Anesthesia Chmn., Internat. Anesthesia Rsch. Soc., Soc. Obstetric Anesthesia and Perinatology, Am. Soc. Regional Anesthesia, Jerusalem Acad. Medicine, Am. Soc. Pharmacology and Exptl. Therapeutics, Fedn. Am. Soc. Exptl. Biology, Sigma Xi. Office: SUNY Sch Medicine Health Scis Ctr Stony Brook NY 11794-8480

POPPLER, DORIS SWORDS, lawyer; b. Billings, Mont., Nov. 10, 1924; d. Lloyd William and Edna (Mowre) Swords; m. Louis E. Poppler, June 11, 1949; children: Louis William, Kristine, Mark J., Blaine, Claire, Arminda. Student, U. Minn., 1942-44; JD, Mont. State U., 1948. Bar: Mont. 1948, U.S. Dist. Ct. Mont. 1948, U.S. Ct. Appeals (9th cir.) 1990. Pvt. practice law Billings, 1948-49; sec., treas. Wonderpark Corp., Billings, 1959-62; atty. Yellowstone County Attys. Office, Billings, 1972-75; ptnr. Poppler and Barz, Billings, 1972-79, Davidson, Veeder, Baugh, Broeder and Poppler, Billings, 1979-84, Davidson and Poppler, P.C., Billings, 1984-90; U.S. atty. Dist. of Mont., Billings, 1990-93; field rep. Nat. Indian Gaming Commn., Washington, 1993—. Pres. Jr. League, 1964-65; bd. dirs., pres. Yellowstone County Metre Bd., 1982; trustee Rocky Mt. Coll., 1984-90, mem. nat. adv. bd., 1993—; mem. Mont. Human Rights Commn., 1988-90; bd. dirs. Miss Mont. Pageant, 1995—. Recipient Mont. Salute to Women award, Mont. Woman of Achievent award, 1975, Disting. Svc. award Rocky Mt. Coll., 1990, 1st ann. U. Montana Law Sch. Disting. Female Alumna award, 1996. Mem. AAUW, Mont. Bar Assn., Nat. Assn. Former U.S. Attys., Nat. Rep. Lawyers Assn., Internat. Women's Forum, Yellowstone County Bar Assn. (pres. 1990), Alpha Chi Omega. Republican. Office: Nat Indian Gaming Commn 1441 L St NW Fl 9 Washington DC 20005-3512

POPRAWA, ANDREW, financial services executive, accountant; b. Toronto, Ont., Can., Nov. 13, 1952; s. Mieczyslaw and Wanda (Wolak) P.; m. Rita Poprawa, Oct. 10, 1981; children: Alexandra, Jason. B.Commerce, U. Toronto, 1975. Chartered acct., Can. CEO St. Stanislaus Credit Union, Toronto, 1980-82; dir. Office of Supt. of Fin. Instns. (Can.), Toronto, 1982-92, Ministry of Fin., Province of Ont., Toronto, 1992-93; pres., CEO Depost Ins. Corp. of Ont., Toronto, 1993—. Mem. Inst. Chartered Accts. Ont., Lakeshore Yacht Club, Toronto Bd. of Trade. Roman Catholic. Avocations: sailing, tennis, skiing, hockey. Office: Deposit Insurance Corp of Ontario, 4711 Yonge St #700, Toronto, ON Canada M2N 6K8

PORAD, LAURIE JO, jewelry company official; b. Seattle, Dec. 19, 1951; d. Bernard L. and Francine J. (Harvitz) P. BA, U. Wash., 1974; postgrad., Seattle Pacific U., summers 1975-76. Cert. standard tchr., Wash. Substitute tchr. Issaquah (Wash.) Sch. Dist., 1974-77; with data processing dept. Ben Bridge Jeweler, Seattle, 1977-83, auditing mgr., 1983-87, systems mgr., 1987-92, MIS special project mgr., 1992—; mem. adv. bd. computer sci. dept. Highline C.C., Midway, Wash., 1985—; mem. tech. prep. leadership com., 1993-95. Tchr. religion sch. Temple de Hirsch Sinai, Seattle, 1972-76, 84—, coord. computerized Hebrew learning ctr., 1987-88, coord. of religion sch. city facility, 1988-93, coord. mentor tchr. program, 1993—; tutor Children's Home Soc. Wash., Seattle, 1976-77. Mem. Assn. for Women in Computing (life mem., chmn. chpt. workshop 1985-88, nat. chpts. v.p. 1985-88, nat. pres. 1988-90, nat. chpt. v.p., 1992-93, rep. ind. mems. 1993—). Avocation: travel. Home: 14616 NE 44th St Apt M-2 Bellevue WA 98007-3196 Office: Ben Bridge Jeweler PO Box 1908 Seattle WA 98111-1908

PORAY, JOHN LAWRENCE, professional association executive; b. Rochester, N.Y., Nov. 9, 1955; s. Jack Loysen and Jane Ann (Williams) P.; m. Rebecca Sue Wells, June 16, 1979 (div. Jan. 1993); children: John Lawrence Jr., David Scott. AA in Liberal Arts, Monroe C.C., Rochester, 1975; BA in Human Rels., Salem (W.Va.) Coll., 1977. Sr. dist. exec. Ctrl. Ohio Coun. Boy Scouts Am., Columbus, 1977-83; asst. exec. dir. Columbus Apt. Assn., 1983-88, Apt. Assn. Ind., Indpls., 1988-92; exec. dir. Soc. Broadcast Engrs., Indpls., 1992—. Youth coach Plainfield (Ind.) Optimist Club, 1988-96; moderator 1st Bapt. Ch., Plainfield, 1995-96, facilities coun. chmn., 1997. Mem. Am. Soc. Assn. Execs. (cert.), Ind. Soc. Assn. Execs. Office: Soc Broadcast Engrs Inc 8445 Keystone Xing Ste 140 Indianapolis IN 46240-2454

PORCARO, MICHAEL FRANCIS, advertising agency executive; b. N.Y.C., Apr. 3, 1948; s. Girolamo M. and Marianna (DePasquale) P.; m. Bonnie Kerr, Apr. 7, 1972; children: Sabrina, Jon. BA in English, Rockford (Ill.) Coll., 1969. Broadcaster Sta. KFQD-AM; KENI-AM/TV, Anchorage, 1970-71, Sta. KENI-AM/TV, Anchorage, 1972-73; v.p. ops. Cook Inlet Broadcasters, Anchorage, 1973-74; owner Audio Enterprises, Anchorage, 1974-75; asst. Alaska Pub. Broadcasting Commn., Anchorage, 1975-76; exec. dir. Alaska Pub. Broadcasting Commn., 1976-81; chief exec. officer, ptnr. Porcaro Blankenship Advt. Corp., Anchorage, 1981—; cons. Arco Alaska TV sta., Anchorage, 1981; expert witness U.S. Senate Subcom. on Telecom., Washington, 1978; chmn. citizens adv. com. dept. journalism U. Alaska, 1995-96. Chmn. Municipality of Anchorage Urban Design Commn., 1990-93; mem. mayor's transition team Municipality of Anchorage, 1987-88; bd. dirs. Anchorage Glacier Polits Baseball Club, 1987-88, Anchorage Mus. History and Art, Alaska Ctr. Internat. Bus., 1996, Commonwealth North, 1996, Friends of Alaska Children's Trust, 1996-97, Anchorage Symphony Orch.; chmn. bd. dirs. Brother Francis Shelter for the Homeless, Anchorage, 1993-96; mem. mktg. com. gov.'s transition team, 1995; mem. United Way Anchorage Cabinet, 1996. Recipient Silver Mike award Billboard mag., 1974, Bronze award N.Y. Film Critics, 1981, Best of North award Ad. Fedn. Alaska, 1982—, Addy award, 1985, 91, Grand Addy award 1990, Cable TV Mktg. award 1986; Paul Harris fellow. Mem. Advt. Fedn. Alaska, Anchorage C. of C. (bd. dirs.). Republican. Roman Catholic. Avocations: softball, hockey, travel, fitness. Office: Porcaro Blankenship Advt 433 W 9th Ave Anchorage AK 99501-3519

PORCELLO, LEONARD JOSEPH, engineering research and development executive; b. N.Y.C., Mar. 1, 1934; s. Savior James and Mary Josephine (Bacchi) P.; m. Patricia Lucille Berger, July 7, 1962 (dec. Sept. 1991); children—John Joseph, Thomas Gregory; m. Victoria Roberta Smith, June 21, 1996. B.A. in Physics, Cornell U., 1955; M.S. in Physics, U. Mich., 1957, M.S. in Elec. Engring, 1959, Ph.D. in Elec. Engring, 1963. Research asst. U. Mich., Ann Arbor, 1955-58; instr. elec. engring. U. Mich., 1958-61; research engr. Radar & Optics Lab., 1968-72; asso. dir. Willow Run Labs., 1970-72, asso. prof., 1969-72, prof., 1972-73, adj. prof., 1973-75; dir. radar and optics divsn. Environ. Rsch. Inst. of Mich., Ann Arbor, 1973-76, v.p., 1973-76, trustee, 1975; asst. v.p., mgr. sensor sys. operation Sci. Applications Internat. Corp., Tucson, 1976-79, v.p., 1979-85, corp. v.p., 1985-87, mgr. def. sys. group, 1986-95, sr. v.p., 1987—, dep. mgr. tech. and advanced sys. sector, 1993—, mgr. applied sys. group, 1995—. Bd. dirs. Tucson Jr. Strings, 1977-79, chmn., 1978-79. Fellow IEEE; mem. Optical Soc. Am., AAAS, Sigma Xi, Eta Kappa Nu. Roman Catholic. Research on imaging radar, synthetic aperture radar systems and radar remote sensing. Home: 5072 Grandview Ave Yorba Linda CA 92886 Office: Sci Applications Internat Corp Attn LJ Porcello PO Box 820 Yorba Linda CA 92885-0820

PORCHÉ-BURKE, LISA MARIE, chancellor; b. L.A., Nov. 9, 1954; d. Ralph Antoine and June Yvonne (James) P.; m. Peter A. Burke, Oct. 27, 1984; children: Mallory, Dominique, Lauren. BA in Psychology magna cum laude, U. So. Calif., 1976; MA in Counseling Psychology, U. Notre Dame, 1981, PhD in Psychology, 1983; LLD (hon.), Chgo. Sch. Profl. Psychology, 1994. Tchr. Spanish Pius X High Sch., Downey, Calif., 1976-77; assoc. AVENUES of South Bend (Ind.), Inc., 1981-82; clin. psychology intern Boston U. Sch. Medicine, 1983-84; sch. psychologist Pierce Sch., Brookline, Mass., 1983-84; asst. prof., profl. tng. faculty Calif. Sch. Profl. Psychology, L.A., 1985-87, asst. prof., 1987-90, coord. ethnic minority mental health proficiency, 1987-90, assoc. prof., 1987-90, coord. multicultural cmty./proficiency clin. psychology, 1990-91, chancellor, 1992—; guest lectr. Ind. U., South Bend, 1981; adj. faculty Calif. Sch. Profl. Psychology, 1985, acting provost, 1991-92; cons. Clarke-Porche Constrn. Co., Inc., 1981, Adolscent Sch. Health Program Boston City Hosp., 1983-84, Calif. State Dept. Edn., 1987, The Feilding Inst., Santa Barbara, Calif., 1991; workshop leader Personnel Dept. City of South Bend, 1979; rsch. asst. U. Notre Dame, 1980-81; presenter in field. Contbr. articles to profl. jours. Minority fellow U. Notre Dame, 1977; grad. scholar U. Notre Dame, 1979; recipient Outstanding Young Women Am. award, 1983, Exemplary Profl. Svc. award, 1991. Fellow APA (pub. info. com., 1993-95, mem.-at-large 1987-90, 92-95, treas. 1990—, chair 1985-86, chair fundraising com. 1988-90, midwinter program com. 1989-93, bd. ethnic minority affairs 1987-88, Jack B. Krasner award 1991); mem. Nat. Coun. Sch. Profl. Psychology (nominating com. 1989-90, chair nominating subcom. 1989-90, chair ethnic racial diversity com. 1990-92), Calif. Psuchol. Assn. Found. (bd. dirs. 1992, treas./CEO 1993—), Women Psychology for Legislative Action (bd. dirs. 1992—), Assn. Black Psychologists. Office: Calif Sch Profl Psychology 1000 S Fremont Ave Alhambra CA 91803-4737

PORFILIO, JOHN CARBONE, federal judge; b. Denver, Oct. 14, 1934; s. Edward Alphonso Porfilio and Caroline (Carbone) Moore; m. Joan West, Aug. 1, 1959 (div. 1983); children: Edward Miles, Joseph Arthur, Jeanne Kathrine; m. Theresa Louise Berger, Dec. 28, 1983; 1 stepchild, Katrina Ann Smith. Student, Stanford U., 1952-54; BA, U. Denver, 1956, LLB, 1959. Bar: Colo. 1959, U.S. Supreme Ct. 1965. Asst. atty. gen. State of Colo., Denver, 1962-68, dep. atty. gen., 1968-72, atty. gen., 1972-74; U.S. bankruptcy judge Dist. of Colo., Denver, 1975-82; judge U.S. Dist. Ct. Colo., Denver, 1982-85, U.S. Ct. Appeals (10th cir.), Denver, 1985—; instr. Colo. Law Enforcement Acad., Denver, 1965-70, State Patrol Acad., Denver, 1968-70; guest lectr. U. Denver Coll. Law, 1978. Committeeman Arapahoe County Republican Com., Aurora, Colo., 1968; mgr. Dunbar for Atty. Gen., Denver, 1970. Mem. ABA. Roman Catholic. Office: US Ct Appeals Byron White US Courthouse 1823 Stout St Denver CO 80257-1823

PORGES, WALTER RUDOLF, television news executive; b. Vienna, Nov. 26, 1931; s. Paul and Charlotte (Posamentier) P.; m. Jean Belle Mlotok, Dec. 22, 1953; children: Donald F., Marian E., Lawrence M. B.A., CCNY, 1953. News writer radio sta. WOR, N.Y.C., 1955-56, WCBS Radio and TV, N.Y.C., 1956-57; news writer ABC Radio Network, N.Y.C., 1958-60; news editor ABC Radio Network, 1960-63, asst. dir. radio news, 1963-65; asst. assignment mgr. ABC-TV, 1965-68; asso. producer ABC-TV Evening News, 1968-70, sr. producer, 1973-75; European producer ABC News, London, 1970-73; producer ABC-TV spl. events, N.Y.C., 1975-76; coordinating producer ABC News (Republican Nat. Conv.), 1976; editorial producer, chief writer ABC Evening News, 1976-77, sr. producer, 1977-80; sr. producer ABC World News Tonight, 1978-83; fgn. news dir. ABC News, N.Y.C., 1983-89, v.p. news practices, 1989-93; assoc. Exec. TV, 1993. Served with U.S. Army, 1953-55.

PORIES, WALTER JULIUS, surgeon, educator; b. Munich, Germany, Jan. 18, 1930; came to U.S., 1940; s. Theodore Francis and Frances (Lowin) P.; m. Muriel Helen Aronson, Aug. 18, 1951; children: Susan E., Mary Jane, Carolyn A., Kathy G.; m. Mary Ann Rose McCarthy, June 4, 1977; children: Mary Lisa, Michael McCarthy. BA, Wesleyan U., Middletown, Conn., 1952; MD with honors, U. Rochester, 1955. Diplomate: Am. Bd. Surgery, Am. Bd. Thoracic Surgery. Intern Strong Meml. Hosp., Rochester, N.Y., 1955-56, resident, 1958-62; chmn. dept. surgery Wright-Patterson AFB, Ohio, 1952-67; asst. prof. surgery and oncology U. Rochester, 1967-69; prof. surgery and assoc. chmn. dept. surgery U. Cleve., 1969-77; prof. surgery and biochemistry East Carolina U., Greenville, N.C., 1977—, chmn. dept. surgery, 1977-96; chief surgery Pitt County Meml. Hosp., 1977-96; prof. surgery U. Health Scis. of Uniformed Svcs., 1982—; founder, assoc. dir. Rochester Cancer Ctr., 1967-69; founder, dir. Cleve. Cancer Ctr., 1972-77, Hospice of Cleve., 1975; founder, chmn. bd. Hospice of Greenville, 1981; med. dir. Home Health Care of Greenville, 1978-83; founder, chmn. bd. Ctr. for Creative Living, 1985-91; pres., chmn. Eastern Carolina Health Orgn. and Echo Mgmt. Orgn., 1994—; vis. scholar NIH, 1996. Author: Clinical Applications of Zinc Metabolism, 1974; editor: Operative Surgery series, vols. 1-4, 1979-83, Office Surgery for Family Physicians, 1985; editor in chief Current Surgery, 1990—; editor Nat. Curriculum for Residency in Surgery, 1988—, mem. residency rev. com., 1992—; contbr. articles to profl. jours. Bd. dirs. Boy Scouts Am., Cleve., 1974-77, Greenville Arts Mus., 1980-82; pres., CEO, chmn. bd. dirs. Ea. Carolina Health Orgn. Maj. USAF, 1955-67; col. USAR, 1979-91, comdr. USAF Hosp., Durham, N.C.; activated Desert Shield, 1990. Decorated Legion of Merit; Thorndyke scholar, 1948-51; recipient McLester award USAF, 1966, Miss. Magnolia Cross, 1989, Presdl. citation for Desert Shield, 1994; named to Hon. Order of Ky. Cols., 1965. Fellow ACS, Am. Coll. Cardiology, Am. Coll. Chest Physicians; mem. Soc. for Vascular Surgery, Soc. Surg. Oncology, Soc. Univ. Surgeons, Am. Surg. Assn., Soc. Environ. Geochemistry (past pres.), Residency Rev. Com. for Surgery, So. Surg. Assn., Soc. for Thoracic Surgery, Ea. Carolina Health Orgn. (pres., chmn. bd. 1994—), Assn. Programs Dirs. in Surgery (pres. 1995-96), N.C. Surg. Assn. (pres. 1995-96), Greenville Country Club, Sigma Xi, Phi Kappa Phi. Republican. Roman Catholic. Home: Deep Sun Farm 7464 NC 43 N Macclesfield NC 27852 Office: East Carolina U Dept Surgery Greenville NC 27858

PORILE, NORBERT THOMAS, chemistry educator; b. Vienna, Austria, May 18, 1932; came to U.S., 1947, naturalized, 1952; s. Irving and Emma (Intrator) P.; m. Miriam Eisen, June 16, 1957; 1 son, James. B.A., U. Chgo., 1952, M.S., 1954, Ph.D., 1957. Rsch. assoc. Brookhaven Nat. Lab., Upton, N.Y., 1957-59; assoc. chemist Brookhaven Nat. Lab., 1959-63, chemist, 1963-64; vis. prof. chemistry McGill U., 1963-65; assoc. prof. chemistry Purdue U., West Lafayette, Ind., 1965-69; prof. chemistry Purdue U., 1969—; rsch. collaborator Brookhaven Nat. Lab., Argonne Nat. Lab., Los Alamos Sci. Lab., Lawrence Berkeley Lab.; vis. prof. Facultes des Scis., Orsay, France; fellow Soc. Promotion of Sci. in Japan, Inst. Nuclear Study, U. Kyoto, 1961. Editor: Radiochemistry of the Elements and Radiochemical Techniques, 1986-90. John Simon Guggenheim meml. fellow Institut de Physique Nucleaire Orsay, 1971-72; recipient F.D. Martin Undergrad. Teaching award, 1977; Von Humboldt Sr. U.S. Scientist award Philipps U., Marburg, W. Ger., 1982. Mem. Am. Chem. Soc., Am. Phys. Soc. Office: Purdue U Dept Chemistry Chemistry Bldg Lafayette IN 47907

PORITZ, DEBORAH T., former state attorney general, state judge. Atty. gen. State of N.J., 1994-96; chief justice Supreme Ct. N.J., Trenton, 1996—. Office: Supreme Ct NJ Hughes Justice Complex CN 970 Trenton NJ 08625

PORIZKOVA, PAULINA, model, actress; b. Czechoslovakia, Apr. 9, 1965; came to U.S., 1982; m. Ric Ocasek; 1 child. Ind. model Europe and U.S., 1980-88; became model for Estee Lauder, 1988. Cover girl for numerous mags. including Cosmopolitan, Vogue, Women's Day, Sports Illustrated, Playboy; film acting debut: Anna, 1987, Arizona Dreams, Female Perveserssion, Wedding Bell Blues' also appeared in Portfolio, 1987, Her Alibi, 1989. Office: Elite Model Management Corp 111 E 22nd St Fl 2 New York NY 10010-5400*

POROSOFF, HAROLD, chemist, research and development director; b. Bklyn., Apr. 3, 1946; s. Solomon and Ruth (Goldberg) P.; m. Leslie Pamela Freiman, May 19, 1948; children: Lauren, Stephen, Marc. BS, MIT, 1966; PhD, Brown U., 1970. Various rsch. and mgmt. positions fibers div. Am. Cyanamid Co., Stamford, Conn. and Milton, Fla., 1970-78; various mgmt. positions Shulton Rsch. div. Am. Cyanamid Co., Clifton, N.J., 1978-83, dir., 1983-88; v.p. R & D chem. rsch. divsn. Am. Cyanamid Co., Stamford, 1989-93; v.p. R & D Cytec Industries Inc., Stamford, 1993-95; v.p., chief tech. officer Cytec Industries, Inc., Stamford, 1995—. Patentee in field. Mem. AAAS, Am. Chem. Soc., N.Y. Acad. Scis. Office: Cytec Industries Inc PO Box 60 Stamford CT 06904-0060

PORRECA, BETTY LOU, education educator; b. Cin., Aug. 8, 1927; d. James Long and Hallie Marie (Jacobs) Hackathorn; m. Charles C. Porreca, Aug. 26, 1949 (widowed 1966); 1 child, Zana Sue Porreca Easley. BA, U. Ariz., 1970, MEd, 1973; PhD, Pacific Western U., 1990. Faculty Cochise Coll., Douglas, Ariz., 1973-83, Pima Community Coll., Tucson, 1983—. Author: (poetry) Selected Poems, 1975; contbr. articles to profl. jours. Chairperson Adult Continuing Christian Edn. Catalina Meth. Ch., Tucson, 1990—; vol. Crisis Pregnancy ctr., Tucson, 1989-91. Mem. Modern Lang. Assn., Nat. Coun. Tchrs. English, Pi Lambda Theta. Democrat. Methodist. Avocations: reading, hiking, cooking. Office: Pima Community College 1255 N Stone Ave Tucson AZ 85709-3002

PORRETTA, EMANUELE PETER, retired bank executive; b. N.Y.C., Aug. 4, 1942; s. Joseph Edward and Italia (Sesti) P.; m. Mary Valanzano, Apr. 18, 1964; children: Denise, Robert, Janice. Student, N.Y. Tech. Coll., 1960-61. Transfer clk. Mfrs. Trust Co., N.Y.C., 1961; sr. v.p. U.S. Trust Co. N.Y., N.Y.C., 1984—, sr. v.p., dir. adminstrv. svcs., instn. asst. svcs. divsn., ret., 1996; mem. payment system com. N.Y. Clearing House, 1978-80, chmn. Bank Ops. Conf., 1981-82. Treas. Manalapan, N.J. Rep. campaign, 1980; mem. adv. com. Williams Coll. Exec. Program. Mem. Am. Mgmt. Assn., Am. Bankers Assn. Roman Catholic. Avocations: running, reading, golf.

PORT, ARTHUR TYLER, retired government administrator, lawyer; b. Chgo., Oct. 4, 1916; s. Arthur Christopher and Helen Elizabeth (Brown) P.; m. Aline Helen Gooding, Oct. 21, 1950; children: Cynthia Helen, Christopher Tyler. BA cum laude, Davidson Coll., 1937; JD, Yale U., 1940; LLD, Coll. Advanced Sci., 1962. Bar: N.C. 1940. Law practice Winston-Salem, N.C., 1940-41; radio announcer Sta. WMRF, Lewistown, Pa., 1941-42; civil atty. Judge Adv. div. Hdqrs. European Command, U.S. Army, Frankfurt, Germany, 1946-47; chief policy sect. Mil. Justice Div., 1947-48; legal asst. to spl. advisor to comdr.-in-chief ETO and mil. govt. Germany, 1949; spl. counsel Sec. of Army, 1949-50, spl. asst., 1950-55; dep. dir. office NSC Affairs Office Sec. Def., 1955-56; exec. asst. to asst. sec. def. ISA, 1956-57; dir. office of security policy and dir. indsl. pers. access authorization Office Asst. Sec. Defense, 1957-61; dep. asst. sec. logistics/installatons and logistics Dept. of Army, 1961-67; fgn. ser. res. officer Dept. of State, 1967-73; asst. sec. gen. def. support NATO, Brussels, 1967-73; spl. asst. Asst. Sec. of Army for Energy Policy, 1973-74; dep. for supply, maintenance and transp. Office Asst. Sec. Army, 1974; cons. NATO affairs Stanford Rsch. Inst., Gen. Rsch. Corp., Logistics Mgmt. Inst., 1975-81. With USAAC, 1942-45, USASIGC, 1945-46, ETO, lt. col. USAR, 1946-68. Recipient Meritorious Civilian Svc. award Dept. Army, 1953, decoration for exceptional civilian svc., 1967; Disting. Civilian Svc. award Dept. Def., 1961. Mem. Confrerie de Chevaliers du Tastevin (Cote d'Or, France), Kenwood Golf and Country Club (Bethesda, Md.), Scabbard and Blade, Omicron Delta Kappa, Sigma Upsilon, Eta Sigma Phi, Phi Gamma Delta, Alpha Phi Epsilon. Home: Falcons Landing 20504 Langley Dr Sterling VA 20165-3571

PORT, SIDNEY CHARLES, mathematician, educator; b. Chgo., Nov. 27, 1935; s. Isadore and Sarah (Landy) P.; m. Idelle Jackson, Mar. 24, 1957; children—Ethan, Jonathan, Daniel. A.B., Northwestern U., 1957, M.S., 1958, Ph.D., 1962. Staff mathematician Rand Corp., 1962-66; asso. prof. math. U. Calif. at Los Angeles, 1966-69, prof., 1969—. Author: (with P. Hoel and C. Stone) Probability, Statistics and Stochastic Processes, 1971, (with C. Stone) Brownian Motion and Classical Potential Theory, 1978, Theoretical Probability for Applications, 1993; contbr. articles to profl. jours. Fellow Inst. Math. Statistics; mem. Am. Math. Soc. Home: 680 Kingman Ave Santa Monica CA 90402-1334 Office: Math Dept Univ Calif Los Angeles Los Angeles CA 90024

PORTAL, GILBERT MARCEL ADRIEN, oil company executive; b. Paris, Aug. 2, 1930; came to U.S., 1982; s. Emmanuel Jules and Henriette Josephine (Bonnard) P.; m. Monique Janine Adam, July 12, 1951; children: Dominique, Veronique, Marc-Emmanuel. Baccalaureate, Lycee Charlemagne U., Paris, 1949; Ingenieur Civil des Mines, Sch. of Mines, St. Etienne, 1955; diplome du C.P.A., Ctr. Advanced Bus., Paris, 1969; auditeur 30 eme session IHEDN, Higher Studies Nat. Defense, Paris, 1978. Geophysicist Societe Nationale Elf Aquitaine, Sahara, Algeria, 1957-63; exploration mgr. north sea Societe Nationale Elf Aquitaine, 1963-65, dep. exec. v.p. Europe, 1965-68, dep. exec. v.p. North and South Am., 1968-70; chief exec. officer Societe Nationale Elf Aquitaine, Iraq, 1970-72; dir., chief exec. officer Societe Nationale Elf Aquitaine, Gabon, Africa, 1972-76; dep. exec. v.p. hydrocarbons Societe Nationale Elf Aquitaine, 1976-78, exec. v.p. North Africa, Mid. East, Far East, 1978-82; pres. Elf Aquitaine Petroleum, Houston, 1982-89; chmn., chief exec. officer Elf Exploration, Inc., Houston, 1989-90; sec.-gen. European Petroleum Industry Assn., 1990-95; ptnr. G.M.H. Internat. Oil and Gas Consulting, Paris, 1995—. Served to lt. French Army, 1955-57. Decorated Legion of Honor (France), Nat. Merit Order (France); Equatorial Star (Gabon). Mem. Cercle Royal Gaulois Artistique et Littéraire. Roman Catholic.

PORTALE, CARL, publishing executive. Pub. Elle-Machette Filipacchi Mags., Inc., N.Y.C. Office: ELLE HACHETTE FILIPACCHI MAGAZINES 1633 Broadway Fl 44 New York NY 10019-6708*

PORTE, JOEL MILES, English educator; b. Bklyn., Nov. 13, 1933; s. Jacob I. and Frances (Derison) P.; m. Ilana D'Ancona, June 17, 1962 (div. 1977); 1 child, Susanna Maria; m. Helene Sophrin, Oct. 18, 1985. A.B. magna cum laude, CCNY, 1957; A.M., Harvard U., 1958, Ph.D., 1962. Instr. English Harvard U., Cambridge, Mass., 1962-64, asst. prof., 1964-68, assoc. prof., 1968-69, prof., 1969-82, Bernbaum prof. of lit., 1982-87, chmn. English and Am. Lit. Dept., 1985-87; Frederic J. Whiton prof. of English Cornell U., Ithaca, N.Y., 1987-89, Ernest I. White prof. Am. Studies and Humane Letters, 1989—; vis. lectr. Am. Studies Research Ctr., Hyderabad, India, spring 1976. Author: Emerson and Thoreau: Transcendentalists in Conflict, 1966, The Romance in America: Studies in Cooper, Poe, Hawthorne, Melville and James, 1969, Representative Man: Ralph Waldo Emerson in His Time, 1979, In Respect to Egotism: Studies in American Romantic Writing, 1991; editor: Emerson in His Journals, 1982, Emerson: Prospect and Retrospect, 1982, Emerson: Essays and Lectures, 1983, New Essays on Portrait of a Lady, 1990. Scholar in Residence, Rockefeller Found., Bellagio, Italy, 1979; fellow John Simon Guggenheim Found., 1981-82. Mem. Am. Studies Assn., Am. Lit. Assn., Phi Beta Kappa. Home: 1405 Hanshaw Rd Ithaca NY 14850-2730

PORTENIER, WALTER JAMES, aerospace engineer; b. Davenport, Iowa, Oct. 9, 1927; s. Walter Cleveland and Doris Lucile (Williams) P.; m. Martha L. Dallam, Aug. 26, 1950 (dec. Apr. 1986); children: Andrea Ellen, Renee Suzanne; m. Patty Grosskopf Caldwell, Oct. 3, 1992. B in Aero Engring., U. Minn., 1950; MS in Aero Engring., U. So. Calif., 1958, Engr. in Aerospace Engring., 1969. Sr. engr. aerodynamics N. Am. Aviation, L.A., 1951-61; MTS project engr., mgr. The Aerospace Corp., El Segundo, Calif., 1961-85; instr. U. So. Calif., L.A., 1979; cons. L-Systems, Inc., El Segundo, 1985-89. Pres., bd. dirs. First United Meth. Ch., Santa Monica, Calif., 1988-90; judge, range officer Internat. Shooting Union, 1989—. Recipient Bronze Medal Internat. Shooting Union, 1990. Fellow Am. Inst. Aeronautics and Astronautics (assoc.). Republican. Achievements include discovery of F-100 wing transonic buffet solution, blowing definition and test, design definition and test of area variation, F-108 mach 3 cruise canard and shock lift effectiveness, XB-70 transport wing definition for subsonic lift and supersonic cruise; re-entry systems analysis of vehicle design, payload, observables for systems procurement and technical direction; development of re-entry technology support for nosetip shape change, boundary layer transition, flow field codes, maneuvering technology; DoD-space transportation system support for space transportation system management (program definitions, manpower); launch on demand requirements; support of new booster systems performance options; reliability review of current systems; re-entry systems test in arms control environment; definition of space transportation system DoD reference missions and mission modeling for cost effectivemess, effective V/STOL aircraft implementation options. Home and Office: 2443 La Condessa Dr Los Angeles CA 90049-1221

PORTER, ALAN LESLIE, industrial and systems engineering educator; b. Jersey City, June 22, 1945; s. Leslie Frank and Alice Mae (Kaufman) P.; m. Claudia Loy Ferrey, June 14, 1968; children: Brett, Doug, Lynn. BSChemE, Calif. Inst. Tech., 1967; MS, UCLA, 1968, PhD in Psychology, 1972. Research assoc., asst. prof. program social mgmt. tech. U. Wash., Seattle, 1972-74; asst. prof. indsl. and systems engring. Ga. Inst. Tech., Atlanta, 1975-78, assoc. prof., 1979-85, prof., 1986—, dir., tech. policy and assessment ctr., 1989—; cons. Search Tech., IBM, Coca Cola, Rexam, SAIC, SRI. Author, editor: (with others) A Guidebook for Technology Assessment and Impact Analysis, 1980, Interdisciplinarity, 1986, Impact of Office Automation on Clerical Employment, 1985, Forecasting and Management of Technology, 1991, (with Wm. Read) Information Revolution: Present and Future Consequences, 1997. NSF grantee, 1974-75, 78-86, 89—, Dept. Transp. grantee, 1977-79, Mem. Internat. Assn. Impact Assessment (co-founder, sec. 1981-87, exec. dir. 1987-90, pres. 1995-96), IEEE Systems Man and Cybernetics Soc. (chmn. tech. forecasting com.), Bellcore adv. coun.). Home: 110 Lake Top Ct Roswell GA 30076-3017 Office: Sch Indsl and Systems Engring Ga Tech Atlanta GA 30332

PORTER, ANDREW CALVIN, educational administrator, psychology educator; b. Huntington, Pa., July 10, 1942; s. Rutherford and Grace (Johnson) P.; m. Susan Porter, June 5, 1967; children: Matthew, Anna, John, Joe, Kate. BS, Ind. State U., 1963; MS, U. Wis., 1965, PhD, 1967. Prof., co-dir. inst. rsch. on teaching Mich. State U., East Lansing, 1967-88; assoc. dir. basic skills group Nat. Inst. Edn., Washington, 1975-76; prof. ednl. psychology, dir. Wis. Ctr. Edn. Rsch. U. Wis., Madison, 1988—; vis. asst. prof. Ind. State U., Terre Haute, 1967; mem. adv. bd. Am. Jour. Edn., 1988—; mem. bd. Internat. Studies, Nat. Acad. Scis., Nat. Rsch. Coun., 1993—; chmn. U.S. Dept. Edn., adv. coun. on edn. stats., 1994—. Author: Creating a System of School Process Indicators, 1991. Bd. dirs. Madison Urban League, 1992—. Recipient award Inst. for Sci. Edn., NSF, Ctr. for Policy Rsch. in Edn., Disting. Alumni award Ind. U., 1994. Mem. Am. Ednl. Rsch. Assn. (mem.-at-large), Nat. Coun. Edn. Measurement, Nat. Coun. Tchrs. Math., Psychometric Soc., Nat. Acad. Edn., Phi Delta Kappa (life). Office: U Wis Madison Wis Ctr Edn Rsch 1025 W Johnson St Madison WI 53706-1706

PORTER, ARTHUR T., oncologist, educator; b. June 11, 1956; m. Pamela Porter; 4 children. Student, U. Sierra Leone, 1974-75; BA in Anatomy, Cambridge U., 1978, M.B.B.Chir./M.D., 1980, MA, 1984; DMRT, Royal Coll. Radiologists, Eng., 1985; postgrad., U. Alta., 1984-86; FRCPC, Royal Coll. Physicians and Surgeons, Can., 1986; cert. for physicians mgr. program, U. Toronto, 1990; postgrad., LaSalle U. Lic., bd. cert., Mich., Can., Eng. House physician gen. medicine Norfolk and Norwich Hosp., Eng., 1981; house sugeon gen. surgery New Addenbrookes Hosp., Cambridge, Eng., 1981-82; sr. house officer clin. hematology No. Gen. Hosp., Sheffield, Eng., 1982; sr. house officer gen. medicine Huntington County Hosp., Hinchingbrooke Hosp., Eng., 1982-83; sr. house officer radiotherapy and oncology Norfolk and Norwich Hosp., Norwich, 1983-84; chief resident radiation oncology Cross Cancer Inst., Edmonton, Alta., Can., 1984-86, radiation oncologist, 1986-87, sr. radiation oncologist, 1987; asst. prof. faculty medicine U. Alta., Edmonton, 1987, assoc. clin. prof. dept. surgery faculty medicine, 1988; head divsn. radiation oncology U. Western Ont., London, Can., 1988; cons. radiation oncologist, chief dept. radiation oncology London Regional Cancer Ctr., 1988, program dir. radiation oncology, 1989-91; chmn. dept. oncology Victoria Hosp. Corp., London, 1990; assoc. prof. dept. oncology U. Western Ont., 1990; program dir. radiation oncology Wayne State U., Detroit, 1991-92, prof., chmn. dept. radiation oncology Sch. Medicine, 1991—; chief Gershenson Radiation Oncology Ctr. Harper Hosp., Detroit, 1991—; radiation oncologist-in-chief Detroit Med. Ctr., 1991—; pres., CEO Radiation Oncology R & D Ctr., Detroit, 1991—; dir. multidisciplinary svcs. Meyer L. Prentice Comprehensive Cancer Ctr., Detroit, 1992—; chmn. radiation oncology Grace Hosp., Detroit, 1993—; vis. prof. U. London, Eng., 1990, U. Mich., 1991, U. Ky., 1992, U. Rochester, 1992, U. So. Calif., 1995; cons. neutron therapy Dept. Health Govt. of U.K., 1990; mem. editorial bd. Endocurietherapy/Hyperthermia Oncology, 1991—, Cambridge Cancer Series, 1991—, Baxter Adminstrv. Manual, 1991—, Oncore, 1989-91, Internat. Monitor Oncology, 1992—; mem. genito-urinary com. Radiation Therapy Oncology Group, 1986—, new investigators com., 1986-87, bladder task force, 1986-88, time dose and fractionation, 1987—, large field working group, 1987—, full mem. com., 1987-91, exec. com., 1991; mem. radiation oncology com. Nat. Cancer Inst. Can., 1987-90, radiation quality assurance subcom., 1987-90, G.U. com., 1987-90; prin. investigator Radiation Therapy Oncology Group, U. Alta., 1987-88, U. Western Ont., 1989-91; mem. working group on bladder cancer Internat. Consensus, 1988, working group on prostate cancer, 1988; mem. Can. Uro-Oncology Group, 1990; chmn. brachytherapy subcom. Radiation Therapy Oncology Group, 1990-92, spl. populations com., 1991, systemic radionucleides com., 1991; mem. G.U. com. Southwest Oncology Group, 1991, selection com. Windsor Cancer Ctr., 1992; mem. cancer grant review conf. Nat. Cancer Inst., 1992; mem. NIH Sub-Saharan African Health Rsch. Initiative, 1993; chmn. South Western Ont. Uro-Oncology Group, 1988-91, Profl. Adv. Com. Radiation Oncology, 1990-91, Site Com. for Prostate Cancer, 1990-91; mem. Ont. Commn. Radiation Oncology, 1989-91, Cancer 2000 Com., 1990-91, PET com. Children's Hosp. Mich., 1991—, adv. com. dept. radiology Detroit Receiving Hosp., 1991—; dir. Univ. Physicians, Inc., 1991—; bd. dirs. MLPCCCMD, Biomide Corp., Vetrogen Corp., MedCyc, Med. Knowledge Systems, Am. Cancer Soc.; bd. trustees Fund Med. Rsch. Edn., 1991—, Meyer L. Prentice Comprehensive Cancer Ctr., 1992—; mem. exec. com. Am. Cancer Soc., Wayne County, 1992—; mem. Amersham Internat. Adv. Bd., 1992—; co-chmn. regional adv. bd. Am. Cancer Soc., 1992—, pres., 1994—; mem. Medi-Pysics Adv. Bd., 1992—; pres. Biomide Corp. Bd., 1993—; lectr. in field. Author: (with others) Fundamental Problems in Breast Cancer, 1985, Therapeutic Progress in Urological Cancers, 1988, Proceedings of the Consensus Meeting of the Treatment of Bladder Cancer-1987, 1988, Brachytherapy, 1989, High and Low Dose Rate Brachytherapy, 1989, Brachytherapy of Prostate Cancer, 1991; co-editor Treatment of Cancer, 1991—; assoc. editor Can. Jour. Oncology, 1990—, Antibody and Radiopharmaceuticals, 1992—; contbr. articles to profl. jours. Recipient Nat. award Sierra Leone, 1975-80, Commonwealth Found. scholarship, 1980, Best Doctor in Am. award, 1992, 93, 94, 95, Testimonial Resolution, City of Detroit, 1993. Fellow Am. Coll. Angiology, Detroit Acad. Medicine, Royal Soc. Medicine; mem. AMA (Physicians Recognition award 1986), Am. Soc. Therapeutic Radiation Oncology, Am. Radium Soc., Am. Soc. Clin. Oncology, Am. Coll. Radiation Oncology (chancellor 1994-97), Am. Coll. Oncol. Adminstrs. (pres. 1994-96), Am. Acad. Med. Adminstrs., Am. Endocurietherapy Soc. (pres. 1994-95), Mich. State Med. Soc., Mich. Soc. Therapeutic Radiation Oncology, Mich. Radiol. Soc., Detroit Med. Soc. (Ann. award for Excellence 1993), Wayne County Med. Soc., European Soc. Therapeutic Radiation Oncology, Brit. Inst. Radiology, Can. Oncology Soc., Can. Assn. Radiation Oncology, Royal Coll. Radiologists, Sierra Leone Med. and Dental Assn., Greater Detroit C. of C., Sigma Xi. Achievements include patent in a perineal applicator; research in novel methods in delivery dose, brachytherapy, intraoperative therapy, unsealed source therapy, verification and dosimetry, real time portal imaging, three-dimensional and planning, unsealed source dosimetry, the design of perineal applicators. Office: Radiation Oncology Rsch & Dev Ctr 4201 Saint Antoine St Detroit MI 48201-2153

PORTER, BARBARA, anchorwoman, writer, educator; m. Henry Stroud Elms III; children: Tommy, Dorian. Anchorwoman NBC Radio; tchr. in dramatics and journalism; writer cable TV children's programming. Office: Westwood One Ste 1200 1775 S Jefferson Davis Hwy Arlington VA 22202*

PORTER, BERNARD HARDEN, consulting physicist, author, publisher; b. Porter Settlement, Maine, Feb. 14, 1911; s. Lewis Harden and Etta Flora (Rogers) P.; m. Helen Elaine Hendron, July 15, 1946 (div. Aug. 1947); m. Margaret Eudine Preston, Aug. 27, 1955 (dec. April 1975); m. Lula Mae Blom, Sept. 9, 1976 (div. Nov. 1986). BS, Colby Coll., 1932; MS, Brown U., 1933; DSc (hon.), Inst. Advanced Thinking, Calais, Maine, 1959. Physicist Acheson Colloids Corp., Port Huron, Mich., 1935-40; rsch. physicist Manhattan Dist. Engrs., Princeton, N.J., Berkeley, Calif. and Oak Ridge, 1940-45; cons. physicist San Francisco and Pasadena, Calif., Waldwick, N.J., Rockland, Belfast, Maine, 1945—; chmn. bd. Bern Porter Inc., Pasadena, Rockland, Belfast, 1945—; pres. Bern Porter Books, Pasadena, Rockland, Belfast, 1929—, Bern Porter Internat., Belfast, 1974—; cons. Internat. Exec. Service Corps, 1968, SBA, 1968-88. Author: The 14th of February, 1971, I've Left, 1971, Founds, 1972, Hand Coated Chocolates, 1972, Contemporary Italian Painters, 1973, Trattoria Due Forni, 1973, The Book of Do's, 1974, The Manhattan Telephone Book, 1975, Run-On, 1975, Where, 1975, Selected Founds, 1975, Gee-Whizzles, 1976, Don't Book, 1981, Last Acts, 1985, My, My, 1985, Left Leg, 1988, Neverends, 1988, Numbers, 1989, Sweetend, 1989, Bern Porter and Fa Gaga, 1990, Sounds That Arouse Me, 1992, Less Than Overweight, 1992, Mothering Time, 1993; contbr. numerous articles to profl. jours. Rep. candidate for gov. Maine, 1969; bd. dirs. Inst. Advanced Thinking, Belfast, chmn. bd., 1959—. Recipient awards PEN, 1975, 76, 77, Authors League, 1977; Carnegie author, 1975; diploma merit Centro Studi E Scambi Internazionale, Rome, 1976; Nat. Endowment for Arts lit. award, 1979. Fellow Am. Astronautical Soc., Tech. Pub. Soc., Am. Rocket Soc. (assoc.), Soc. Tech. Writers and Pubs. (assoc.), Internat. Acad. Poets (London, founding); mem. Am. Phys. Soc., Soc. Internat. Devel., Nat. Soc. Programmed Instrn., Fenway Club (Boston), Algonquin Club, St. Andrews Club (N.B., Can.), Phi Beta Kappa, Sigma Xi, Kappa Phi Kappa, Chi Gamma Sigma. Roman Catholic. Address: 50 Salmond St Belfast ME 04915-1316

PORTER, BLAINE ROBERT MILTON, sociology and psychology educator; b. Morgan, Utah, Feb. 24, 1922; s. Brigham Ernest and Edna (Brough) P.; m. Elizabeth Taylor, Sept 27, 1943 (dec.); children: Claudia Black, Roger B., David T., Patricia A. Hintze, Corinna; m. Myrna Katherine Kennedy, Feb. 26, 1988. Student, Utah State U., 1940-41; BS, Brigham Young U., 1947, MA, 1949; PhD (Grant Found. fellow family life edn. 1951-52), Cornell U., 1952. Instr. sociology Iowa State Coll., 1949-51; asst. prof. sociology and child devel. Iowa State U., 1952-55; prof., chmn. dept. human devel. and family relationships Brigham Young U., 1955-65, dean Coll. Family Living, 1966-80, Univ. prof., 1980-87; vis. prof. Fulbright rsch. scholar U. London, 1965-66; vis. prof. U. Wurzberg, 1980, 81, 83; facilitator human rels. workshops for the Human Devel. Inst., Denver, 1988-90. Editor: The Latter-day Saint Family, 1963, rev. edit., 1966; editor quar. jour.: Family Perspective, 1966-82; contbr. articles to profl. jours. Pres. elect Iowa Coun. Family Rels., 1954-55; pres. Utah Coun. Family Rels., 1957-58; chmn. sect. marriage counseling Nat. Coun. Family Rels., 1958-59, bd. dirs., 1957-60, exec. com., 1958-72, pres., 1963-64; bd. dirs. Am. Family Soc., 1975-85. Pilot USAAF, 1942-45. Recipient Prof. of Yr. award Brigham Young U., 1964. Mem. Am. Home Econs. Assn. (vice chmn. sect. family relations and child devel. 1955-56), Am. Sociol. Assn. (sec. sect. on family 1964-67), Am. Assn. Marriage and Family Therapy, Am. Psychol. Assn., Soc. Research in Child Devel., Sigma Xi, Phi Kappa Phi (chpt. pres. 1969-71). Home: 1675 Pine Ln Provo UT 84604-2163 Office: 4505 HBLL Brigham Young U Provo UT 84602

PORTER, BRUCE DOUGLAS, federal agency administrator, educator, writer; b. Albuquerque, Sept. 18, 1952; s. Lyle Kay and Wilma (Holmes) P.; m. Susan Elizabeth Holland, Feb. 2, 1977; children: David William, Christopher Jonathan, Lisa Jeanette, Jennifer Rachel. BA in History, Brigham Young U., 1976; AM in Soviet Studies, Harvard U., 1978, PhD in Polit. Sci., 1979. Sr. rsch. analyst Radio Free Europe/Radio Liberty, Inc., Munich, 1980-83; profl. staff mem. armed svcs. com. U.S. Senate, Washington, 1983-84; sr. analyst Northrop Corp. Analysis Ctr., Washington, 1984-86; exec. dir. Bd. for Internat. Broadcasting, Washington, 1986-90; Bradley sr. rsch. assoc. Harvard U., Cambridge, Mass., 1990-93; assoc. prof. Brigham Young U., Provo, Utah, 1993-95; min. LDS Ch., 1995—. Author: The USSR in Third World Conflicts, 1976, Red Armies in Crisis, 1991, War and the Rise of the State, 1993; co-author: The Polish Drama: 1980-82, 1983; contbr. articles to profl. jours. Lay min. Ch. Jesus Christ Latter-day Saints, bishop, 1985-90, missionary, Düsseldorf, Fed. Republic Germany, 1971-73. Post doctoral fellow Harvard Ctr. for Internat. Affairs, 1979-80, Danforth fellow, 1976-79, David O. McKay scholar Brigham Young U., 1970-71, 74-76; recipient Meritorious Svc. award Pres. of U.S., 1990. Mem. Am. Polit. Sci. Assn., Am. Assn. Advancement Slavic Studies, Internat. Studies Assn. Avocations: swimming, creative writing. Office: Brigham Young U 784 Swkt Provo UT 84602-1130

PORTER, BURTON FREDERICK, philosophy educator, author, dean; b. N.Y.C., June 22, 1936; s. John and Doris (Neloway) P.; m. Susan Jane Porter, May 10, 1966 (div. 1974); 1 child, Anastasia; m. Barbara Taylor Metcalf, Dec. 31, 1980; 1 child, Mark Graham. BA Philosophy cum laude, spl. lit. hons., U. Md., 1959; PhD, St. Andrews U., Scotland, 1968; post-grad., Oxford (Eng.) U. Asst. prof. philosophy U. Md., London, 1966-69; assoc. prof. philosophy King's Coll., Wilkes-Barre, Pa., 1969-71; prof. philosophy, chmn. dept. Russell Sage Coll., Troy, N.Y., 1971-87; prof. philosophy, head dept. humanities-comm. Drexel U., Phila., 1987-91; dean arts and scis. Western New England Coll., Springfield, Mass., 1991—. Author: Deity and Morality, 1968, Philosophy, A Literary and Conceptual Approach, 1974, 80, 95, Personal Philosophy: Perspectives on Living, 1976, The Good Life, Alternatives in Ethics, 1980, 91, 94, Reasons for Living: A Basic Ethics, 1988, Religion and Reason, 1993; also articles and book revs. Named Outstanding Educator of Am., NEA, 1975. Mem. Am. Philos. Assn., MLA. Home: 30 Fearing St Amherst MA 01002-1912 Office: Western New Eng Coll Arts & Scis Dean's Office Springfield MA 01119

PORTER, CHARLES HENRY, photographer; b. Buffalo, N.Y., Mar. 1, 1947; s. Charles Hunt and Jean Grace (Hassler) P.; m. Nora Roxanne Belanger, Nov. 1, 1969; children: Katherine, Elizabeth. BA, Cornell U., 1970. Freelance photographer Poughkeepsie, N.Y., 1973—; chmn. photography dept. Oakwood Sch., Poughkeepsie, N.Y., 1986-92; staff photographer Hudson River Sloop Clearwater, Poughkeepsie, N.Y., 1982—; photographic cons. Vassar Coll., Poughkeepsie, 1986—. Author: (filmstrip series) The Hudson River Series, 1977; contbr. A Sense of Occasion: A Day in the Life of Vassar, 1992. Avocations: playing basketball, collecting CD's and comic books.

PORTER, CHARLES KING, advertising executive; b. Mpls., Oct. 10, 1945; s. King E. and Bernetta Porter Andrews; m. Margit Gammeltoft, Feb. 26, 1972; children: Kristin, Catherine, James. BS in Journalism, U. Minn., 1967. Ptnr. Breen & Porter Co., Miami, Fla., 1974-85; pres. Porter Creative Svcs., Miami, 1985-88, Crispin & Porter Advt., Miami, 1988—; dir. Miami Ad Sch. Trustee Beacon Coun., Miami, 1988—. Recipient Nat. Addy award Am. Advt. Fedn., 1991, 92, Andy award Advt. Club N.Y., 1993, 94. Mem. Am. Assn. Advt Agys. (forum, Nat. A Plus award 1991, 94, 95, 96). Presbyterian. Avocations: skiing, travel, history. Office: Crispin & Porter Advt 2699 S Bayshore Dr Miami FL 33133-5408

PORTER, CLARENCE A., academic dean; b. McAlester, Okla., Mar. 19, 1939; s. Lloyd C. and Myrtle E. (Johnson) P.; children—Richard Alan, Cory Steven. B.S. in Biology, Portland State Coll., 1962; M.S. in Zoology, Oreg. State U., 1964, Ph.D. in Zoology, 1966. Asst. prof. gen. sci. Portland State U., 1966-70, assoc. prof., 1970-72, exec. asst. to pres., 1970-72; asst. v.p. acad. affairs U. N.H., 1972-76; assoc. vice chancellor acad. affairs State Univ. System of Minn., 1977-78; exec. dir. Phyllis Wheatley Community Ctr., Mpls., 1978-82; ednl. cons., Hopkins, Minn., 1982-83; v.p. for acad. affairs Cheyney U. (Pa.), 1983-84; dean Inst. Basic, Applied & Health Scis., Montgomery Coll., Takoma Park, Md., 1984—. Contbr. articles to sci. jours. Bd. dirs. Mpls. Aquatennial, 1980-82, Urban Concerns Workshop Inc., 1979-82, Nat. Coun. Black Am. Affairs, (NE. region, 1995—), Helminthological Soc. Wash., Sigma Xi. Office: Montgomery Coll Inst Natural Scis Takoma Park MD 20912

PORTER, CLOYD ALLEN, state representative; b. Huntley, Ill., May 22, 1935; s. Cecil and Myrtle (Fisher) P.; m. Joan Hawkins, July 25, 1959; children: Ellen, LeeAnn, Jay, Joli. Grad. high sch., Burlington, Wis. Ptnr. Cecil W. Porter & Son Trucking, 1955-70; treas. Burlington Sand and Gravel, 1964-70; owner Cloyd A. Porter Trucking, Burlington, 1970-72; state rep. 43d dist. Wis. State Assembly, Madison, 1972-82; state rep. 66th dist. Wis. State Assembly, 1982—; mem. coun. on recycling, Wis., 1991-94, fire svc. legis. adv. com., 1987-94, legis. coun. com. on fire inspections and fire dues, 1991, legis. coun. spl. com. on emergency med. svcs., 1992-93, mem. joint Com. fins., 1995-98. Contbr. articles to profl. jours. Chmn. Town of Burlington, 1971-75; state and met. affairs chmn. Jaycees, Wis., 1963, state v.p., 1969, adminstrv. asst., 1970, exec. v.p., 1971; mem. Wis. Conservation Congress for Natural Resources Leadership and Support in the State Assembly, 1994. Recipient many awards and honors including being named hon. mem. State Fire Chiefs Assn., Wis., 1992, Guardian of Small Bus., NFIB, Wis., 1991, Friend of Agr., Farm Bur. of Wis., 1992, 94, Friend of Edn. Fair Aid Coalition, 1995, Cert. of Appreciation, Wis. Counties Assn., 1993, award Wis. Sate Fire Chiefs Assn., 1995, Oustanding Legislator Wis. Counties Assn., 1996; named to Vietnam Vets. Am. Legis. All-Star Team Wis. Coun. Vietnam Vets. Am., 1995-97. Mem. Wis. Alliance for Fire Safety. Republican. Roman Catholic. Home: 28322 Durand Ave Burlington WI 53105-9408 Office: State Capitol PO Box 8953 309 North Madison WI 53708

PORTER, DANIEL REED, III, museum director; b. Northampton, Mass., July 2, 1930; s. Daniel Reed and Eleanor (Parsons) P.; m. Joan Joyce Dornfeld, Nov. 22, 1958; children: Leslie Marie, Andrew Gregory. BA, U. Mass., 1952; MA, U. Mich., 1956. Asst. to dir. State Hist. Soc. Wis., Madison, 1956-58; dir. Hist. Soc. York County, Pa., 1958-61; asst. dir., dir. Ohio Hist. Soc., Columbus, 1961-74; exec. dir. Preservation Soc. Newport County, R.I., 1974-78; dir., prof. Cooperstown (N.Y.) Grad. Programs, 1978-82; dir. N.Y. State Hist. Assn. Farmer's Mus. Cooperstown, Cooperstown, 1982-92; hist. preservation officer State of Ohio, Columbus, 1967-74. Editor: N.Y. Heritage, 1984-92; contbr. articles to publs. in field. With U.S. Army, 1952-54, Korea. Recipient Spl. award of Merit Ohio Assn. Hist. Socs., 1970. Mem. Am. Assn. Mus. (accreditation commn. 1982-88, councillor-at-large 1981-84), Am. Assn. State and Local History (coun., Nashville 1971-73, councillor 1985-87). Congregationalist.

PORTER, DARWIN FRED, writer; b. Greensboro, N.C., Sept. 13, 1937; s. Numie Rowan and Hazel Lee (Phillips) P. BA, U. Miami, 1959. Bur. chief Miami Herald, 1959-60; v.p. Haggart Assocs., N.Y.C., 1961-64; editor, author Arthur Frommer Inc., N.Y.C., 1964-67, Frommer/Pasmantier Pub. Corp., N.Y.C., 1967-86, Prentice Hall Press, N.Y.C., 1987-90, Simon & Schuster, N.Y.C., 1991—. Author: Frommer Travel Guides to: England, 1964, Spain, 1966, Scandinavia, 1967, Los Angeles, 1969, London, 1970, Lisbon/Madrid, 1972, Paris, 1972, Morocco, 1974, Rome, 1974, Portugal, 1968, England, 1969, Italy, 1969, Germany, 1970, France, 1970, Caribbean, Bermuda, the Bahamas, 1980, Switzerland, 1984, Austria and Hungary, 1984, Bermuda and the Bahamas, 1985, Scotland and Wales, 1985, the Virgin Islands, 1991, Scotland, 1992, Jamaica/Barbados, 1992, Puerto Rico, 1992, the Caribbean, 1993, Bermuda, 1993, the Bahamas, 1993, Austria, 1993, Madrid & the Costa del Sol, 1993, San Francisco, 1996, California, 1996, Caribbean Cruises, 1996, Caribbean Ports of Call, 1996, Georgia and the Carolinas, 1996, Charleston and Savannah, 1996, Munich and The Bavarian Alps, 1996, Vienna & the Danube, 1996, Guide to Caribbean Cruises, 1997, Frommer's Europe, 1997, Frommer's Venice, 1997, Barcelona, Madrid & Sevilla, 1997; author: (novels) Butterflies in Heat, 1976, Marika, 1977, Venus, 1982. Recipient Silver award Internat. Film and TV Festival N.Y., 1977. Mem. Soc. Am. Travel Writers, Smithsonian Assocs., Nat. Trust for Historic Preservation, Sigma Delta Chi. Home: 75 Saint Marks Pl Staten Island NY 10301-1606

PORTER, DAVID BRUCE, air force officer, behavioral scientist, educator; b. Lexington, Ky., June 17, 1949; m. Sharon Jo Mahood, June 9, 1971; children: David Damien, Kristin Gillian. BS, USAF Acad., 1971; MS, UCLA, 1972; DPhil, Oxford U., 1986. Commd. 2d lt. USAF, 1971, advanced through grades to col., 1993; chief orgnl. maintenance, functional check flight pilot USAF, Hickam AFB, Hawaii, 1973-79; exec. officer USAF, RAF Woodbridge, U.K., 1981-83; instr. behavioral sci., leadership USAF Acad. USAF, Colorado Springs, Colo., 1979-81, assoc. prof., sr. milit. prof., dept. head USAF Acad., 1986—; cons., examiner N. Ctrl. Assn. Colls. and Univs., 1996—. Contbr. to profl. publs. including Jour. Coll. Reading and Learning, Current Psychology Rsch. and Revs., Counseling and Values, Jour. Adult Assessment. Bd. dirs. Citizens Project, Colorado Springs, 1993-95; pres. All Souls Unitarian Ch., 1989-91. Office: USAF Acad Dept Behavioral Sci 6L71 Fairchild Hall Colorado Springs CO 80840

PORTER, DAVID HUGH, pianist, classicist, academic administrator, liberal arts educator; b. N.Y.C., Oct. 29, 1935; s. Hugh B. and Ethel K. (Flentye) P.; m. Laudie Ernestine Dimmette, June 21, 1958 (dec. Nov., 1986); children: Hugh, Everett, Helen, David; m. Helen Louise Nelson, Aug. 24, 1987. BA with highest honors, Swarthmore Coll., 1958; PhD (Danforth Grad. fellow, Woodrow Wilson Grad. fellow), Princeton U., 1962; student, Phila. Conservatory Music, 1955-61. Instr. in classics and music Carleton Coll., Northfield, Minn., 1962-63, asst. prof., 1963-68, assoc. prof., 1968-73, prof., 1973-87, William H. Laird prof. liberal arts, 1974-87, pres. faculty, 1980-82, coll. pres., 1986-87; pres. Skidmore Coll., Saratoga Springs, N.Y., 1987—, prof. classics, 1987—; Phi Beta Kappa vis. lectr., 1979-92, vis. scholar, 1994-95; vis. prof. classics Princeton U., 1986; recitalist, lectr., especially on contemporary music, at colls., univs. throughout U.S., Europe, on radio and TV; bd. dirs. Adirondack Trust Co.; chmn. Hudson-Mohawk Assn., 1990-92. Author: Only Connect: Three Studies in Greek Tragedy, 1987, Horace's Poetic Journey: A Reading of Odes I-III, 1987; editor: Carleton Remembered, 1909-86, 1987, The Not Quite Innocent Bystander: Writings of Edward Steuermann, 1989; contbr. articles on classics, music and edn. to profl. jours. NEH research fellow, 1969-70, 83-84; Am. Council Learned Socs. research fellow, 1976-77. Mem. Am. Philological Assn., Classical Assn. Atlantic States. Democrat. Mem. United Ch. Christ. Avocations: hiking, fishing, reading, collecting rugs and books. Home: 791 N Broadway Saratoga Springs NY 12866-1601 Office: Skidmore Coll Office of Pres Saratoga Springs NY 12866

PORTER, DAVID LINDSEY, history and political science educator, author; b. Holyoke, Mass., Feb. 18, 1941; s. Willis Hubert and Lora Frances (Bowen) P.; m. Marilyn Esther Platt, Nov. 28, 1970; children: Kevin, Andrea. BA magna cum laude, Franklin Coll., 1963; MA, Ohio U., 1965; PhD, Pa. State U., 1970. Asst. prof. history Rensselaer Poly. Inst., Troy, N.Y., 1970-75, co-dir. Am. studies program, 1972-74; ednl. adminstrv. asst. Civil Svc. Office State of N.Y., Troy, 1975-76; asst. prof. history William Penn Coll., Oskaloosa, Iowa, 1976-77, assoc. prof. history, 1977-82, prof. history and polit. sci., 1982-86, Louis Tuttle Shangle prof. history and polit. sci., 1986—, chmn. Sperry & Hutchinson Found. lectureship series, 1980-82; supr. legis. internship program Iowa Gen. Assembly, 1978—, records inventory project Mahaska County, 1978-79, internship program Washington Ctr., 1985—; active Franklin D. Roosevelt Meml. Commn.; chpt. adviser Phi Alpha Theta, 1977—. Author: The Seventy-sixth Congress and World War II, 1939-40, 1979, Congress and the Waning of the New Deal, 1980; contbr. to Dictionary of American Biography, 1981, 88, 94, 95, Directory of Teaching Innovations in History, 1981, The Book of Lists #3, 1983, Biographical Dictionary of Internationalists, 1983, The Hero in Transition, 1983, Herbert Hoover and the Republican Era: A Reconsideration, 1984, The History of Mahaska County, Iowa, 1984, Franklin D. Roosevelt, His Life and Times: An Encyclopedic View, 1985, The Rating Game in American Politics: An Interdisciplinary Approach, 1987, Sport History, 1987, Book of Days, 1988, Sports Encyclopedia North America, 1988, The Harry S. Truman Encyclopedia, 1989, Encyclopedia of Major League Baseball Team Histories: The National League, 1991, Twentieth Century Sports Champions, 1992, Statesmen Who Changed the World, 1993, Ency. Modern Social Issues, 1996, Advanced Placement U.S. History 2, 1996, Encyclopedia of United States Popular Culture, 1997, Encyclopedia of Civil Rights, 1997, Encyclopedia of Propaganda, 1997, Total Padres, 1997; editor, contbr.: Biographical Dictionary of American Sports: vols. Baseball, 1987, Football, 1987, Outdoor Sports, 1988, Basketball and Other Indoor Sports, 1989, 1989-92 Supplement for Baseball, Football, Basketball and Other Sports, 1992, 1992-95, Supplement for Baseball, Football, Basketball and Other Sports, 1995, African-American Sports Greats, 1995; compiler, A Cumulative Index to the Biographical Dictionary of American Sports, 1993; assoc. editor: (with others) American National Biography, 20 vols.; contbr. weekly column to Oskaloosa Herald, 1994—, numerous articles to various dictionaries, directories, encys., jours., revs., newspapers, commentary to Nat. Pub. Radio. Mem. Franklin D. Roosevelt Meml. Commn.; participant Green Bay Packers Project, 1992. Grantee NSF, 1967, NEH, 1974, Rensselaer Poly. Inst., 1974, Eleanor Roosevelt Inst., 1981, William Penn Coll., 1986, 89, 92;

recipient Choice Outstanding Acad. Book awards, 1989. Mem. AAUP, Am. Hist. Assn., Orgn. Am. Historians, N.Am. Soc. for Sport History, Soc. History Am. Fgn. Rels., Ctr. for Study of the Presidency, Soc. Am. Baseball Rsch., Popular Culture Assn., Profl. Football Rschrs. Assn., Coll. Football Rschrs. Assn., Coll. Football Hist. Soc., State Hist. Soc. Iowa, Mahaska County Hist. Soc., Iowa State UN Assn. (chmn. ann. assembly 1982, nat. soc. Disting. Svc. award 1981), Mahaska County UN Assn., Oskaloosa Babe Ruth League (bd. dirs.), Oskaloosa Cmty. Choir, Friends of Oskaloosa Pub. Libr. (mem. nominating com.), Phi Alpha Theta, Kappa Delta Pi. Mem. United Meth. Ch. Home: 2314 Ridgeway Ave Oskaloosa IA 52577-9109 Office: William Penn Coll Dept Social Sci 201 Trueblood Ave Oskaloosa IA 52577-1757

PORTER, DEAN ALLEN, art museum director, art historian, educator; b. Gouverneur, N.Y., June 13, 1939; s. Arnold W. and Gertrude V. Porter; m. Carol DuBrava, July 27, 1963; children: Kellie Ann, Tracie Ann. BA, Harpur Coll., 1961; MA in Art History, SUNY, Binghamton, 1966, PhD in Art History, 1974. curator Art Gallery, U. Notre Dame, 1966-74, dir. Snite Mus. Art, 1974—, prof. art history, 1994—; bd. dirs. Southwest Art History Coun.; mem. mus. coun. Harwood Found., U. N.Mex.; mem. adv. bd. Ind. U. Art Mus.; mem. nat. adv. coun. Valparaiso (Ind.) U. Mus. Art. Samuel H. Kress fellow. Mem. Coll. Art Assn., Am. Assn. Mus., Assn. Art Mus. Dirs. Author exhbn. catalogues, including: Janos Scholz, Musician and Collector, 1980, A Guide to The Snite Museum of Art, 1980, Selected Works from the Snite Museum of Art, 1987, Victor Higgins: An Am. Master, 1990, The Univ. Notre Dame Friends and Alumni Collect: A Sesquicentennial Celebration, 1992. Office: Snite Mus of Art PO Box 368 Notre Dame IN 46556-0368

PORTER, DOUGLAS TAYLOR, athletic administrator; b. Fayetteville, Tenn., Aug. 15, 1928; s. Waudell Phillip and Sophia Mae (Taylor) P.; m. Jean Butcher, Apr. 18, 1953; children: Daria C., Blanche E., Douglas V. BS, Xavier U., 1952; MS, Ind. U., 1960. Asst. football coach St. Augustine High Sch., Memphis, 1955, Xavier U., New Orleans, 1956-60; dir. athletics, head football coach Miss. Vocat. Coll., Itta Bena, Miss., 1960-65; assoc. dir. athletics, coach Grambling (La.) State U., 1966-73; head football coach Howard U., Washington, 1974-78; dir. athletics, head football coach Ft. Valley (Ga.) State Coll., 1979—; pres. Nat. Athletic Steering Com., Ft. Valley, 1990—. Lt. U.S. Army, 1951-54. Recipient Disting. Am. award Mid. Ga. Chpt. Nat. Football Found., 1997; So. Intra Collegiate Athletic Conf. Hall of Fame, 1997. Mem. Am. Alliance of Health, Phys. Edn. and Dance, Nat. Assn. of Collegiate Dirs. of Athletics (inducted Hall of Fame, 1997), Sigma Pi Phi, Alpha Phi Alpha (pres. 1983-87), Phi Delta Kappa. Democrat. Roman Catholic. Avocations: reading, listening to jazz. Home: 107 College Ct Fort Valley GA 31030-3216 Office: Ft Valley State Coll 1005 State College Dr Fort Valley GA 31030-3262

PORTER, DUDLEY, JR., environmentalist, foundation executive, lawyer; b. Paris, Tenn., May 10, 1915; s. Dudley and Mary (Bolling) P.; m. Mary Rhoda Montague, Oct. 21, 1950. Student, Murray (Ky.) State Coll., 1933-34; LL.B., Cumberland U., 1936. Bar: Tenn. 1937. Asst. atty. gen. Tenn., 1937-40; mem. firm Tyne, Peebles, Henry & Tyne, Nashville, 1940-49; with law dept. Nat. Life & Accident Ins. Co., Nasvhille, 1940-49; asso. gen. counsel Nat. Life & Accident Ins. Co., 1948; with Provident Life & Accident Ins. Co., Chattanooga, 1949—; gen. counsel Provident Life & Accident Ins. Co., 1954-72, sr. v.p., 1958-72, sec., 1965-72, vice chmn., sr. counsel, 1972-76; of counsel Chambliss, Bahner, Crutchfield, Gaston & Irvine, Chattanooga, 1977—. Mem. Hamilton County Juvenile Ct. Commn., 1958-64, chmn., 1964; mem. Tenn. Health Planning Council, 1968-76, Tenn. Hist. Commn., 1976-86; trustee Hermitage Assn., Nashville, 1983-90; an incorporator, mem. bd. Sr. Neighbors Chattanooga, 1960-66; vice chmn., trustee Maclellan Charitable Trust. With AUS, 1942-46; judge adv. 100th Inf. Div. ETO. Mem. Am., Tenn., Chattanooga bar assns., Am. Life Conv. (chmn. legal sect. 1958), Assn. Life Ins. Counsel (exec. com. 1970—, pres. 1974-75), Nature Conservancy (life, co-founder and trustee Tenn. chpt.), Sigma Alpha Epsilon. Presbyterian. Clubs: Mountain City (Chattanooga); Belle Meade Country (Nashville). Home: 1125 Healing Springs Rd Elder Mountain Chattanooga TN 37419 Office: 1125 Healing Springs Rd Chattanooga TN 37419-1043 *My environmentalist credo: O Lord, how manifold are thy works! In wisdom hast thou made them all; the earth is full of thy riches. (Psalm 104, verse 24).*

PORTER, DWIGHT JOHNSON, former electric company executive, foreign affairs consultant; b. Shawnee, Okla., Apr. 12, 1916; s. Dwight Ernest and Gertrude (Johnson) P.; m. Adele Ritchie, Oct. 6, 1942; children—Dwight A., James G., Ellen Jean, Barbara Adele, Joan Anne. Ritchie Johnson. A.B., Grinnell Coll., 1938, LL.D., 1968; student, Am. U., 1938-40, 46-48, Nat. War Coll., 1957-58. Govt. intern Nat. Inst. Pub. Affairs, Washington, 1938-39; personnel officer U.S. Housing Authority, 1939-41; exec. officer Dept. Agr., San Francisco, 1941-42; asst. personnel dir. Bd. Econ. Warfare, 1942; dir. adminstrv. services Rural Electrification Adminstrn., 1946-48; mgmt. officer Dept. State, 1948; dep. dir. Displaced Persons Commn., 1949; adminstrv. officer U.S. High Commn., Germany, 1949-54; 1st sec. Am. embassy, London, 1954-56; exec. officer econ. area Dept. State, 1956-57; coordinator Hungarian Refugee Relief, 1957, spl. asst. to dep. under-sec., and under-sec. state, 1958-59; counsellor Am. embassy, Vienna, 1959-62; minister Am. embassy, 1962, dep. chief of mission, 1962-63; asst. sec. of state for adminstrn., 1963-65; ambassador to Lebanon, 1965-70; permanent U.S. rep. IAEA, Vienna, 1970-75; v.p. internat. affairs Westinghouse Electric Corp., Washington, 1975-85; fgn. affairs cons., 1986—. Served to capt. USMCR, 1942-45. Recipient alumni award Grinnell Coll., 1958. Home: 15100 Interlachen Dr Apt 526 Silver Spring MD 20906-5606

PORTER, ELSA ALLGOOD, writer, lecturer; b. Amoy, China, Dec. 19, 1928; d. Roy and Petra (Johnsen) Allgood; m. Raeford B. Liles, Mar. 19, 1949 (div. 1959); children: Barbara, Janet; m. G. Hinckley Porter, Nov. 22, 1962; children: David, Brian, Wendy. BA, Birmingham-So. Coll., 1949; MA, U. Ala., 1959; M in Pub. Adminstrn., Harvard U., 1971; LHD (hon.), U. Ala., 1986. With HEW, Washington, 1960-73; with U.S. CSC, Washington, 1973-77; asst. sec. Dept. Commerce, Washington, 1977-81; disting. practitioner in residence Washington Pub. Affairs Ctr., U. So. Calif., Washington, 1982-84; v.p. R & D The Maccoby Group, Washington, 1990-96; sr. fellow Meridian Internat. Inst., 1990—. Bd. dirs. Delphi Internat. Group, 1981—. Fellow Nat. Acad. Pub. Adminstrs.; mem. Women's Nat. Dem. Club. Home: # 742 2309 SW 1st Ave Apt 742 Portland OR 97201-5008

PORTER, GERALD JOSEPH, mathematician, educator; b. Elizabeth, N.J., Feb. 27, 1937; s. Fred and Tillie Florence (Friedman) P.; m. Judith Deborah Revitch, June 26, 1960; children: Daniel, Rebecca, Michael. AB, Princeton U., 1958; PhD, Cornell U., 1963; MA (hon.), U. Pa., 1971. Instr. MIT, 1963-65; asst. prof. math. U. Pa., Phila., 1965-69; assoc. prof. U. Pa., 1969-75, prof., 1975—, chmn. undergrad. affairs dept. math., 1971-73, assoc. dean computing Sch. Arts and Scis., 1981-91, dir. Interactive Math. Text Project, 1991-96; bd. dirs. Com. Concerned Scientists; chair-elect faculty senate U. Pa., 1992-93, chair, 1993-94, past chair, 1994-95. Author: (with D.R. Hill) Interactive Linear Algebra, 1996. Mem. Dem. Com., Haverford Twp., Pa., 1976-82, ward leader, 1980-84, treas., 1984-87. Postdoctoral fellow Office Naval Rsch., 1965-66. Mem. AAUP, Am. Math. Soc., Math. Assn. Am. (chmn. com. computers in math. edn. 1983-86, chmn. investment com. 1986—, bd. govs. 1980-83, 86—, mem. fin. com. 1986—, exec. com. 1992—, chmn. audit and budget com. 1988-90, 92, treas. 1992—, chair com. on profl. devel. 1995—), Assn. for Women in Math., AAAS, Nat. Assn. Mathematicians, Nat. Coun. Tchrs. Math., Joint Policy Bd. for Math., Am. Math. Assn. of Two Year Colls. Democrat. Jewish. Home: 161 Whitemarsh Rd Ardmore PA 19003-1698 Office: U Pa 4N69 DRL 209 S 33rd St Philadelphia PA 19104

PORTER, GLENN, museum and library administrator; b. New Boston, Tex., Apr. 2, 1944; s. Pat Paul and Mary Lee (Sanders) P.; m. K.T. Wimberly, June 1, 1968 (div. 1986); m. Barbara H. Butler, Dec. 18, 1987. BA, Rice U., 1966; MA, Johns Hopkins U., 1968, PhD, 1970. Asst. prof. bus. history Harvard Bus. Sch., Boston, 1970-76; dir. regional econ. history research ctr. Hagley Mus. & Library, Wilmington, Del., 1976-83, dir., 1984—. Editor Bus. History Rev., 1970-76; editorial bd. Jour. Am. History, 1977-80, Del. History, 1982—, Bus. History Rev., 1983-92; author: (with Harold C. Livesay) Merchants and Manufacturers, 1971; Rise of Big Business, 1860-1910, 1973, rev. edit., 1992, The Workers World at Hagley, 1981; gen. editor: Ency. of Am. Econ. History, 1980, The Papers of John D. Rockefeller, 1991. Mem. cons. com. Nat. Survey of Historic Sites and Bldgs., Washington, 1976-79; council mem. Del. Humanities Council, 1981-83; trustee Worldesign Found., 1993-95, Andalusia Found., 1994—. pres., Ind. Rsch. Librs. Assn, 1994-97; bd. dirs., Nat. Humanities Alliance, 1994-97. Recipient Cultural Achievement award, U.S. Dept. Interior, 1979; NEH grantee, 1977-82, 81-83, 85-92, 93—. Mem. Bus. History Conf. (pres.1987), Soc. for History of Tech., Soc. Archtl. Historians, Independent Rsch. Librs. Assn. (pres. 1994-97), Nat. Humanities Alliance (bd. dirs. 1994-97), Am. Assn. Mus., Mid-Atlantic Assn. Mus., Phi Beta Kappa. Office: Hagley Mus & Libr PO Box 3630 Wilmington DE 19807-0630

PORTER, HELEN VINEY (MRS. LEWIS M. PORTER, JR.), lawyer; b. Logansport, Ind., Sept. 7, 1935; d. Charles Lowry Viney and Florence Helen (Kunkel) V.; m. Lewis Morgan Porter, Jr., Dec. 26, 1966; children: Alicia Michelle, Andrew Morgan. A.B., Ind. U., 1957; J.D., U. Louisville, 1961. Bar: Ind. and Ill. 1961, U.S. Supreme Ct. 1971. Atty. office chief counsel Midwest regional office IRS, Chgo., 1961-73; assoc. regional atty. litigation center Equal Employment Opportunity Commn., Chgo., 1973-74; practice in Northbrook, Ill., 1974-79, 80-86; ptnr. Porter & Andersen, Chgo., 1979-80, Porter & Porter, Northfield, Ill., 1986—; lectr. Law in Am. Found., Chgo., summer, 1973, 74; assoc. prof. No Ill Coll Law (formerly Lewis U. Coll. Law), Glen Ellyn, Ill., 1975-79. Lectr. women's rights and fed. taxation to bar assns., civic groups. Recipient Disting. Alumni award U. Louisville Sch. of Law, 1986, President's award Nat. Assn. of Women Lawyers, 1985. Fellow Am. Bar Found., Ill. State Bar Found.; mem. Women's Bar Assn. Ill. (pres. 1972-73), ABA (chmn. standing com. gavel awards 1983-85, bd. editors jour. 1984-90, mem. standing com. assn. comm. 1990-93), Fed. Bar Assn. (pres. Chgo. chpt. 1974-75), Ill. Bar Assn. (assembly del. 1972-78), Nat. Assn. Women Lawyers (pres. 1973-74). Home and Office: 225 Maple Row Northfield IL 60093-1037

PORTER, HENRY HOMES, JR., investor; b. Chgo., Nov. 13, 1934; s. Henry H. and Mary (Kinney) P.; m. Louisa Catherine Perkins, June 10, 1961; children: Mary Porter Johnson, Catherine. A.B., Yale U., 1956; M.B.A., Harvard U., 1962. With Gen. Mills, Inc., Mpls., 1962-76; asst. treas. Gen. Mills, Inc., 1964-67, treas., 1967-76, v.p. fin., treas., 1969-76; sr. v.p., chief fin. officer, dir. Brown & Williamson Industries, Inc., 1977-79, Batus, Inc., 1980; chmn. bd. Active Ankle Systems, Inc.; bd. dirs. SEI Corp., Dame Inc., Droll Inc., Caldwell & Orkin Funds, Inc., Louisville Nat. Records Mgmt. Corp. Lt. (j.g.) USNR, 1957-60. Home and Office: 5806 River Knoll Dr Louisville KY 40222-5863

PORTER, JACK A., lawyer; b. Lorimor, Iowa, Nov. 20, 1945. BA, U. Iowa, 1967, JD with high distinction, 1969. Bar: Iowa 1969, Wis. 1969, Fla. 1973. Ptnr. in charge Foley & Lardner, West Palm Beach, Fla. Notes and comments editor Iowa Law Review, 1968-69. Mem. Iowa State Bar Assn., State Bar Wis., Fla. Bar, Order Coif, Phi Beta Kappa. Office: Foley & Lardner Phillips Point E Tower 777 S Flagler Dr Ste 200 West Palm Beach FL 33401-6161

PORTER, JACK NUSAN, writer, sociologist, educator; b. Rovno, Ukraine, USSR, Dec. 2, 1944; came to U.S., 1946; s. Irving Puchtik and Faye (Merin) P.; m. Miriam Almuly, Sept. 18, 1977; children: Gabriel, Danielle. Cert., Machon Inst., Jerusalem, 1963; BAS cum laude, U. Wis., Milw., 1967; MA, PhD, Northwestern U., 1971. Rsch. assoc. Harvard U. Ukrainian Rsch. Inst., Cambridge, Mass., 1982-84; pres. The Spencer Group, Newton, Mass., 1984—; exec. dir. The Spencer Sch. Real Estate, Newton, 1986—; dir. The Spencer Inst. for Bus. and Soc., Newton, 1984—; asst. prof. Coll. of Basic Studies Boston U., 1989-90; vis. lectr. Boston U. Met. Coll., 1987, 88, Bryant Coll., Smithfield, R.I., 1991; adj. prof. U. Mass., Lowell, 1994—; adj. prof. sociology Stonehill Coll., Easton, Mass., 1996—; presenter White House Conf. on Family, 1980; mem. Gov. Dukakis' Adv. Coun., 1982-84; panelist on Comparative Genocide, The Oxford (Eng.) Conf., 1988; Boston area coord. Seminars on Zionist Thought, World Zionist Orgn. Author or editor 25 books and anthologies including Confronting History and Holocaust, 1983, Sexual Politics in Nazi Germany, 1991, Kids in Cults, 1977, 85, 94, Jews and the Cults, 1981, Genocide and Human Rights, 1982, Conflict and Conflict Resolution: A Sociological Introduction, 1987, Jewish Radicalism, 1973, Jewish Partisans (2 vols.), 1982, Conflict and Conflict Resolution: A Historical Bibliography, 1982, The Jew as Outsider, 1981, The Sociology of Jewry: A Curriculum Guide, 1992, The Sociology of American Jews: A Critical Anthology, 1980, Forclosed Property (with Gerry Glazer), 1990, The Sociology of the Holocaust: A Curriculum Guide, 1992, The Sociology of Business: A Curriculum Guide, 1992, Holocaust and Genocide: Theories, Cases, Implications, 1997, Women in Chains: Sourcebook on the Agunah, 1996, Holocaustal Suicides: Essays on the Sociology of Genocide, The Death of Sociology, The Holocaust and the Crisis in Modernity, Growing Up in the 50s: A Memoir, others; contbr. chpts. in books, numerous articles and revs. to jours. in field; founder, editor Jour. of the History of Sociology, 1977-85, The Sociology of Bus. Newsletter, 1977-79; mem. editl. bd. Contemporary Jewry, 1995—; dep. editor, dep. pub. Jewish Family and Life, 1997—. Founder Holocaust Survival Video Project, Newton, Mass., 1992—; judge Nat. Jewish Book Awards, 1993-95; mem. Jewish Radical Edn. Project, 1994—. John Atherton fellow Breadloaf Writers Conf., Middlebury, Vt., 1976; recipient Spl. award Boston Police Dept., 1986. Mem. PEN (newsletter com. 1992-95), Am. Sociol. Assn., Ea. Sociol. Soc., New Eng. Soc., Tikkun Assn. Avocations: collecting Jewish baseball cards, reading, spiritual thinking. Home and Office: 8 Burnside Rd Newton Highlands MA 02161-1401 *The older I get, the important things in life are my wife, my children, good health, a few good friends, my brother and sister and Mom, a good meal, and lastly - some money and a little fame. That's all.*

PORTER, JAMES H., chemical engineering executive; b. Port Chester, N.Y., Nov. 11, 1933; s. George James and Josephine (Hall) P.; m. Sandra Adrienne Knox, Sept. 8, 1958 (div. Dec. 1969); children: Michael Brandon, Adrienne Michelle, Lynn Sharon; m. Jennifer Anne Waterhouse, Feb. 26, 1978. BSChemE, Rensselaer Poly. Inst., 1955; ScD, MIT, 1963. Tech. svc. engr. Exxon, Linden, N.J., 1955-58; rsch. engr. Chevron Rsch. Corp., Richmond, Calif., 1963-67; mgr. process design Abcor Inc., Cambridge, Mass., 1967-71; assoc. prof. MIT, Cambridge, 1971-76; v.p. energy div. Energy Resources Co. Inc., Cambridge, 1976-79; pres. Energy and Environ. Engring. Inc., Somerville, Mass., 1979-94; chmn., CEO, 1994—, UV Technologies Inc., 1994—; sci. adv. bd. U.S. EPA, Washington, 1976-83. Author: Chemical Equilibria in C.H.O. Systems, 1976; patentee in field. Bd. dirs. Tisbury Waterways Inc., Vineyard Haven, Mass., 1990, Trustees of Reservation, Boston, 1991, Cambridge Adult Edn. Ctr., Cambridge, 1988, sec., 1991. Mem. Am. Inst. Chem. Engrs., Nat. Orgn. Black Chemists and Chem. Engrs. (pres. 1978-79, bd. dirs., Founders award 1983, Henry Hill lectr. 1995), N.Y. Acad. Scis., Sigma Xi, Pi Delta Epsilon. Avocations: sportsfishing, bridge. Home: PO Box 1131 Vineyard Haven MA 02568-1131

PORTER, JAMES MORRIS, judge; b. Cleve., Sept. 14, 1931; s. Emmett Thomas and Mary (Connell) P.; m. Helen Marie Adams, May 31, 1952; children: James E., Thomas W., William M., Daniel J. A.B., John Carroll U., 1953; J.D., U. Mich., 1957. Bar: Ohio 1957. Assoc. firm M.B. & H.H. Johnson, Cleve., 1957-62, McAfee, Hanning, Newcomer, Hazlett & Wheeler, Cleve., 1962-67; ptnr. firm Squire, Sanders & Dempsey, Cleve., 1967-92; judge Ohio Ct. Appeals, 8th Dist., Cleve., 1993—. 1st lt. U.S. Army, 1953-55. Fellow Am. Coll. Trial Lawyers; mem. Best Lawyers in Am., Union Club, The Club, The Country Club (Cleve.). Republican. Roman Catholic. Office: Lakeside Courthouse Ct Appeals Lakeside Ave Cleveland OH 44113-1082

PORTER, JEANNETTE UPTON, elementary education educator; b. Mpls., Mar. 5, 1938; d. Robert Livingston and Ruby Jeannette (Thomas) Upton; divorced; children: Steven, Fritz, Susan Porter Powell. BS, U. Minn., 1960, Mankato State U., 1968; postgrad., St. Thomas U., 1991. Camp dir. St. Paul's Epsicopal Ch., Mpls., 1956-66; tchr. elem. sch. Bloomington (Minn.) Pub. Schs., 1967—, dir. title I, 1975-82, tchr. spl. assignment of rsch. and devel., 1990-91; team cons. Hillcrest Cmty. Sch., Bloomington, 1990-95; res. tchr. spl. assignment, 1996-97; edn. cons., 1996-97. Tutor Telephone Hot Line Minn. Fedn. Tchrs., Mpls., 1988-92; crisis counselor Neighborhood Improvement Programs, Mpls., 1988-93; adult literacy counselor Right to Read, Mpls., 1987-89; vol. Abbott Northwestern Hosp. Recipient 1st Bank award Mpls., Red Apple award, Mpls., 1988; named Minn. Tchr. of Excellence, 1988, 89. Mem. Assn. Early Childhood Edn. (treas. 1990-94), Bloomington Edn. Found., Delta Kappa Gamma (1st v.p. 1992-93), PEO (past pres. A.C. chpt.). Avocations: fishing, photography, back packing, pottery, music. Home: 4400 W 44th St Saint Louis Park MN 55424-1064

PORTER, JENNIFER MADELEINE, producer, director; b. Milw., Oct. 3, 1962; d. John Hamlin and Helen Meak (Smith) P. BA in Comm., Bowling Green State U., 1984. Audio visual supr. Liberty Mutual Ins. Group, Berwyn, Pa., 1985-88; sr. prodr. audio visual Prudential Ins. Co., Mpls., 1988-93; proprietor Shoot The Moon Prodns., Mound, Minn., 1993-96, Shoot the Moon Prodns., Mpls., 1996—. Prodr., dir., writer: (audio visual programs) Phantom Lake... A Lifetime of Memories, 1991 (Best of Show 1991, Script award Assn. for Multi-Image Internat. 1991), Vision... The Gamma Phi Beta Foundation, 1992 (First Place award 1993), prodr., prodn. coord. Stadium Theatre Experience-College Football Hall of Fame (Silver award Assn. for Multi-Image Internat. 1996). Mentor U. Minn., Mpls., 1989-96; fundraiser Gamma Phi Beta Found. Philanthropy-Spl. Camping for Girls, Minn., Wis., 1991—; chairperson 100th Celebration, Phantom Lake YMCA Camp, Mukwonago, Wis., 1994-96. Mem. Assn. for Multi-Image Internat. (exec. bd. local 1986-88), Gamma Phi Beta (internat. officer, pub. rels. speaker/prodr. 1991—). Avocations: travel, music, sports, camping, canoeing. Home and Office: Shoot The Moon Prodns 4105 Upton Ave S Ste 2 Minneapolis MN 55410-1262

PORTER, JILL, journalist; b. Phila., Aug. 5, 1946; d. Sidney and Mae (Merion) Chalfin; m. Eric Porter, Mar. 7, 1970 (div. 1975); m. Fred Hamilton, Oct. 28, 1983; 1 child, Zachary. BA, Temple U., 1968. Pub. rels. Manning Smith P.R., Phila., 1968-69; reporter Norristown Times Herald, Norristown, Pa., 1969-72, The Trentonian, Trenton, N.J., 1972-75; reporter The Phila. Daily News, Phila., 1975-79, columnist, 1979—; instr. Temple U., 1976-80. Contbr. articles to numerous mags. Vol. Phila. Futures, 1994, 95, 96, Phila. Cares, 1997. Recipient numerous journalism awards. Avocations: reading, gardening. Home: 134 Rolling Rd Bala Cynwyd PA 19004-2113 Office: Phila Newspapers Inc Phila Daily News 400 N Broad St Philadelphia PA 19130-4015

PORTER, JOAN MARGARET, elementary education educator; b. Vernon, Tex., Dec. 25, 1937; d. Elton Lonnie and Clara Pearl (Yeager) Smith; m. Claude Walker Porter, Feb. 13, 1960; children: Jolene Porter Mohindroo, Richard Euin, Vonda Sue, Darla Ailese Porter Blomquist. BA, Wayland Bapt. U., 1960; M in Elem. Edn., Ea. N.Mex. U., 1981, bilingual endorsement, 1982. cert. classroom tchr., N.Mex. ESL tchr. Jefferson Elem. Sch., Lovington, N.Mex., 1979-81, tchr., 1981-82; bilingual tchr. Jefferson Elem. Sch., Lovington, 1982-89, Highland Elem. Sch., Plainview, Tex., 1989-91, 1992-96; vol. tchr. Cert. Adult Literacy, Lovington. Mem. PTA, Assn. Tex. Profl. Educators, Delta Kappa Gamma (profl. affairs com. chmn. 1991), Phi Kappa Phi. Southern Baptist. Home: 205 E Hallie Floydada TX 79235 Office: Campus Press 715 Ash St Plainview TX 79072-7311

PORTER, JOHN EDWARD, congressman; b. Evanston, Ill., June 1, 1935; s. Harry H. and Beatrice V. P.; m. Kathryn Cameron; 5 children. Attended, MIT; BSBA, Northwestern U., 1958; JD with distinction, U. Mich., 1961; DHL, Barat Coll., 1988; LLD (hon.), Kendall Coll., 1992. Bar: Ill. 1961, U.S. Supreme Ct. 1968. Former honor law grad. atty., appellate div. Dept. Justice, Washington; mem. Ill. Ho. of Reps., 1973-79; mem. house appropriations com., subcoms. on labor, health & human svcs., edn., fgn. ops. 96-105th Congresses from 10th Ill. Dist., Ill., 1980—; mem. legis. select com. on aging, 1980-92; founder, co-chmn. Congl. Human Rights Caucus; founder Congl. Coalition on Population and Devel. Past editor: Mich. Law Rev. Recipient Best Legislator award League of Conservation Voters, 1973, Ind. Voters Ill., 1974, Chgo. Crime Commn., 1976, Lorax award Global Tomorrow Coalition, 1989, Spirit of Enterprise award U.S. C. of C., 1988, 89, 90, Golden Bulldog award Watchdogs of the Treasury, 12 times, Taxpayer's Friend award Nat. Taxpayers Union, Taxpayer Superhero award Grace Commn.'s Citizens Against Government Waste. Republican. Office: US Ho of Reps 2373 Rayburn House Bldg Washington DC 20515-1310

PORTER, JOHN FINLEY, JR., physicst, conservationist, retired educator; b. Birmingham, Ala., Aug. 22, 1927; s. John Finley and Janice (Nowell) P.; m. Jacqueline Christine Harbin, Dec. 27, 1949; children: Gayle P. Barnett, John Finley III, Paul William, Adam Michael, David Wade. BS, U. Ala., 1950, MS, 1956; PhD, Johns Hopkins U., 1966. Rsch. staff asst. Radiation Lab., Johns Hopkins U., 1956-59; rsch. assoc. Carlyle Barton Lab. Johns Hopkins U., 1959-66, rsch. scientist, 1966, lectr. elec. engring., 1965-66; assoc. prof. physics U. Ala., Huntsville, 1966-69, chmn. physics faculty, 1968-69, prof., 1969-72; dean faculty U Ala., Hunstville, 1969-70, dean grad. programs and rsch., 1970-72; dep. exec. dir. Ala. Commn. on Higher Edn., 1972-73, exec. dir., 1973-81; vis. prof. adminstrn. and higher edn. U. Ala. Coll. Edn., 1981-83, prof., 1983-92, acting dir. Office Instl. Rsch., 1984-91, dir. Office Instl. Rsch., 1991-92, prof. emeritus, 1992—; cons. Catalyst Rsch. Corp., Balt., Environ. Sci. Svc. Adminstrn., Washington; chmn. State Coun. Grad. Deans, 1971-72; mem. planning bd. Edn. Commn. of States, 1975-77; mem. adv. coun. Ala. Right to Read, 1974-76; mem. Ala. Post Secondary Edn. Planning Commn., 1974-76, Gov.'s Budget Adv. Com., 1976-77. Contbr. articles to profl. jours. Bd. dirs., v.p. Tuscaloosa County Preservation Soc., 1988-89, pres., 1990-91; v.p. Ala. Ornithol. Soc., 1990-91, pres., 1991-93; bd. dirs. Tuscaloosa Audubon Soc., 1989-92, Ala. Coastal Found., 1994—, pres., 1996—; bd. dirs. Mobile Bay Audubon Soc., 1993—; mem. Ala. Audobon Coun., 1990—; pres. Friends of Dauphin Island Audubon Sanctuary Inc., 1992—. Methodist. Home: 1404 Cadillac Ave PO Box 848 Dauphin Island AL 36528-0848

PORTER, JOHN FRANCIS, III, banker; b. Wilmington, Del., Sept. 17, 1934; s. John Francis, Jr. and Eloise Wilhelmina (Berlinger) P.; m. Ann Mayfield, Sept. 8, 1956; children: Leslie Gibson, Nina Porter Winfield, Sophie Porter Rohrer. BA, U. Va., 1956; MBA, U. Del., 1965. With Del. Trust Co., Wilmington, 1958—; asst. treas. Del. Trust Co., 1960-66, sec., 1966-68, v.p., sec., 1968-72, sr. v.p., sec., 1972-75, exec. v.p., 1975-79, pres., 1979-88; chmn., chief exec. officer Del. Trust Co. (nowCoreStates Bank), 1988—; vice chmn. BANKPAC, 1982-86, chmn., 1986-88; mem. Ct. on Judiciary Preliminary Investigatory Com., 1991—. Mem. bank adv. bd. State of Del., 1969-71; mem. Council on Banking for State of Del., 1970—, chmn., 1976—; trustee Alfred I. duPont Testamentary Trust, 1995—, Alfred I. duPont Inst. Nemours Found., 1971-94, chmn. bd. mgrs., 1990-94; chmn. exec. coun. Thomas Jefferson U. Med. Ctr., Del./AIDI Affiliation , 1990-92, mem., 1990—; pres. Wilmington and Brandywine Cemetery, 1974—; bd. dirs., trustee, mem. fin. com. mem. exec. com. Med. Ctr. Del., 1985—; bd. dirs. Penjerdel, 1989—, State v.p., 1990—; bd. gov. Winterthur Corp. Coun., 1989—, chmn., 1993-95; bd. dirs. Nemours Found., 1995—. Capt. arty., U.S. Army, 1957. Mem. Am. Bankers Assn. (govt. rels. coun. 1984-88), Del. Bankers Assn. (pres. 1984-85, bd. dirs. 1981-87), Del. Bus. Roundtable (vice chmn. exec. coun. 1989-92, chmn. 1993-94), Wilmington Country Club (bd. dirs.), Wilmington Club (bd. govs. 1980-89), Vicmead Hunt Club, Nassau Club (Princeton, N.J.). Clubs: Wilmington Country (bd. dir.), Wilmington (bd. govs. 1980-89), Vicmead Hunt; Nassau (Princeton, N.J.). Home: 4821 Kennett Pike Wilmington DE 19807-1813 Office: Del Trust Co 900 N Market St Wilmington DE 19801-3012

PORTER, JOHN ROBERT, art history educator, curator, writer; b. Lévis, Que., Can., Apr. 28, 1949; s. John William and Irène (Bernier) P.; m. Martine Tremblay, July 26, 1975; children: Isabelle, Jean-Olivier. LèsL, Laval U., 1971, Ma, 1972; PhD, U. Montreal, 1982. Asst. curator Can. art Nat. Gallery Can., 1972-78; prof. art history Laval U., 1978—; chief curator Montreal Mus. Fine Arts, 1990-93; dir. Musée du Québec, 1993—; mem. programming and acquisition coms. for various mus. Author various books, catalogues and articles in field. Office: Musée du Que, Parc des Champs-de-Bataille, Quebec, PQ Canada G1R 5H3

PORTER, JOHN ROBERT, JR., space technology company executive, geochemist; b. Oklahoma City, Feb. 27, 1935; s. John Robert and Margaret Florence (Nicholson) P.; m. Amelie Alexanderson Wallace, June 2, 1963; children: Jennifer A. Porter Dowling, Amelie M. BA, Dartmouth Coll., 1957; MS, Okla. U., 1964. Cert. petroleum geologist, Am. Assn. Petroleum Geologists. Analyst CIA, Washington, 1962-66; chief Earth Resources Program NASA, Washington, 1966-69; pres., chmn. Earth Satellite Corp.,

Rockville, Md., 1969—; mem. space applications bd. NRC, Washington, 1983-86, GEOSAT Com., Norman, Okla., 1972—. Trustee Washington Gallery Modern Art, 1966-67. 1st lt. U.S. Army, 1960-62. Mem. Am. Assn. Petroleum Geologists., Chevy Chase Club. Republican. Presbyterian. Avocations: tennis, squash, skiing, jogging. Home: 4000 Cathedral Ave NW # 813 B Washington DC 20016-5272 Office: Earth Satellite Corp 6011 Executive Blvd # 400 Rockville MD 20852-3804

PORTER, JOHN STEPHEN, television executive; b. Avoca, N.Y., Sept. 2, 1932; s. Frank R. and Margaret H. (McGreel) P.; m. Marie C. Eiffert, Sept. 6, 1958; children: Stephen, David, Mark, Kevin, Matthew. B.A. in English, St. John Fisher U., 1958; M.S. in Radio/TV, Syracuse U., 1959; postgrad. in Edn, U. Rochester, 1960-61. Producer, broadcaster weekly news analysis N.Y. State Empire State FM Sch. of Air, 1962-64; producer, narrator weekly series sta. WROC-FM, Rochester, N.Y., 1964-65; pres., gen. mgr. sta. WXXI-TV, Rochester, 1966-69; trustee Eastern Ednl. TV Network, Boston, 1966-68, mem. exec. com., 1967-68, exec. dir., 1969-89, pres., mem. exec. com., 1989-92; pres., mem. exec. com. Am. Program Svc. (formerly Ea. Ednl. TV Network), Boston, 1992—. Served to 1st lt. AUS, 1952-56. Mem. N.Y. State Ednl. Radio/TV Assn. (treas. 1962-64), Pub. TV Sta. Mgrs. New York State (chmn. 1968-69), Nat. Assn. Ednl. Broadcasters (adv. com.). Home: 100 Pond St Apt 82 Cohasset MA 02025-1947

PORTER, JOHN WILSON, education executive; b. Ft. Wayne, Ind., Aug. 13, 1931; 2 children. BA, Albion Coll., 1953; MA, Mich. State U., 1957, PhD, 1962; D in Pub. Adminstrn. (hon.), Albion Coll., 1973; LLD (hon.), Mich. State U., 1977, Cleary Coll., 1987; LHD, Adrian Coll., 1970, U. Detroit, 1979; LLD, Western Mich. U., 1971, Eastern Mich. U., 1975; HHD, Kalamazoo Coll., 1973, Detroit Coll. Bus., 1975, Madonna Coll., Livonia, Mich., 1977; DEd, Detroit Inst. Tech., 1978; AA, Schoolcraft Coll., Livonia, Mich., 1979; DBA, Lawrence Inst. Tech., 1988; LLD, Cleary Coll., 1989. Counselor Lansing (Mich.) Pub. Schs., 1953-58; cons. Mich. Dept. Pub. Instrn., 1958-61; dir. Mich. Higher Edn. Assistance Authority, 1961-65; assoc. supt. for higher edn. Mich. Dept. Edn., 1966-69, state supt. schs., 1969-79; pres. Ea. Mich. U., Ypsilanti, 1979-89; CEO Urban Edn. Alliance Inc., Ann Arbor, Mich., 1988—; v.p. Nat. Bd. for Profl. Teaching Standards, 1989; gen. supt. Detroit Pub. Schs., 1989-91; CEO Urban Edn. Alliance, Inc., Ypsilanti, Mich., 1991—; mem. numerous profl. commns. and bds., 1959—, including; Commn. on Financing Postsecondary Edn., 1972-74, Commn. for Reform Secondary Edn., Kettering Found., 1972-75, Edn. Commn. of States, 1973-79, Nat. Commn. on Performance-Based Edn., 1974-76, Nat. Commn. on Manpower Policy, 1974-79, Mich. Employment and Tng. Svcs. Coun., 1976-79, Nat. Adv. Coun. on Social Security, 1977-79, Commn. on Ednl. Credit, Am. Coun. on Edn., 1977-80; task panel on mental health of family Commn. on Mental Health, 1977-80; mem. Nat. Coun. for Career Edn. (HEW), 1974-76; pres. bd. dirs. Chief State Sch. Officers, 1974-79; pres. Coun. Chief State Sch. Officers, 1977-78; bd. dirs. Comerica Bank; former chmn. bd. Coll. Entrance Exam. Bd., 1984-86. Trustee Nat. Urban League, 1973-79, Charles Stewart Mott Found., 1981—, Albion Coll., 1989—; bd. dirs. Mich. Internat. Council, 1977—, Mich. Congress Parents and Tchrs.; mem. bd. overseers com. for Grad. Sch., Harvard U., 1980-88; mem. edn. com. NAACP; convener goal 6 Nat. Edn. Goals Panel, 1990—; mem. East Lansing Human Relations Commn.; chmn. Am. Assn. State Colls. and U.'s Task Force on Excellence in Edn.; mem. Mich. Martin Luther King, Jr. Holiday Commn., Gov.'s Blue Ribbon Commn. on Welfare Reform; trustee East Lansing Edgewood United Ch.; mem. Catherine McAuley Health Systems Bd., 1990—. Recipient numerous awards including Disting. Svc. award Mich. Congress Parents and Tchrs., 1963, Disting. Svc. award NAACP, Lansing, 1968; cert. of outstanding achievement Delta Kappa chpt. Phi Beta Sigma, 1970; award for disting. svc. Assn. Ind. Colls. and Univs. Mich., 1974; Disting. Alumni award Coll. Edn., Mich. State U., 1974; award for disting. svc. to edn Mich. State U., 1974; Disting. Alumni award, 1979; award for disting. svc. to edn. in Mich. Mich. Assn. Secondary Sch. Prins., 1974; President's award as disting. educator Nat. Alliance Black Sch. Educators, 1977; Marcus Foster Disting. Educator award, 1979; recognition award Mich. Ednl. Rsch. Assn., 1978; recognition award Mich. Assn. Secondary Sch. Prins., 1978; recognition award Mich. Assn. Intermediate Sch. Adminstrs., 1979; recognition award Mich. Assn. Sch. Adminstrs., 1979; Mich. Sch. Bus. Ofcls., 1979; resolution Mich. State Legislature, 1978; Anthony Wayne award Coll. Edn., Wayne State U., 1979; Educator of Decade award Mich. Assn. State and Fed. Program Specialists, 1979; Spirit of Detroit award Detroit City Coun., 1981; Disting. Svc. award Ypsilanti Area C. of C., 1988; Philip A. Hart award Mich. Women's Hall of Fame, 1988; Summit award Greater Detroit C. of C., 1991; Mich. State C. of C. award 1991; inducted Mich. Edn. Hall of Fame, 1992. Mem. Am. Assn. Sch. Adminstrs., Am. Assn. State Colls. and Univs. (president's council, chmn. task force on excellence in edn.), Nat. Measurement Council, NAACP (life), Greater Detroit C. of C. (Summit award 1991), Mich. State C. of C. (Disting. Svc. and Leadership award 1991), Tuskegee Airmen (Disting. Svc. award 1991), Mich. PTA (hon. life), Econ. Club (dir. 1979), Sigma Pi Phi, Phi Delta Kappa. Office: Urban Edn Alliance Inc 2000 N Huron River Dr Ypsilanti MI 48197-1678

PORTER, JUDITH DEBORAH REVITCH, sociologist, educator; b. Phila., Mar. 26, 1940; d. Eugene and Esther (Tulchinsky) Revitch; m. Gerald Joseph Porter, June 26, 1960; children—Daniel, Rebecca, Michael. Student, Vassar Coll., 1958-60; BA, Cornell U., 1962, MA, 1963; PhD, Harvard U., 1967. Lectr. Bryn Mawr (Pa.) Coll., 1966-67, asst. prof., 1967-73, assoc. prof., 1973-79, prof. sociology, 1979—, chair dept. sociology, 1987-93. Author: Black Child, White Child: The Development of Racial Attitudes, 1971; contbr. articles to profl. jours. Committeeperson Haverford Twp. Dem. Party, 1976-96; bd. dirs. Phila. AIDS Fund; vol. Prevention Point Needle Exch. Program, Congreso de Latinos Unidos, Inc.; mem. Mayor's Commn. on Drugs and Alcohol, City of Phila. Recipient Shannon award NIMH, 1992-94; Ford Found. fellow, 1973-74; NSF fellow, 1967. Mem. APHA, Am. Sociol. Assn., Phi Beta Kappa, Phi Kappa Phi. Jewish. Address: 161 Whitemarsh Rd Ardmore PA 19003-1634 Office: Bryn Mawr Coll Dept Sociology Bryn Mawr PA 19010

PORTER, KARL HAMPTON, orchestra musical director, conductor; b. Pitts., Apr. 25, 1939; s. Reginald and Naomi Arzetta (Mitchell) P. Student, Carnegie-Mellon U., 1957-60, Peabody Conservatory, 1960-62, Juilliard Sch. Music, 1962-63, Domaine Sch. Condrs., 1961-63, Am. Symphony Orch. League, Tanglewood, 1962-72; student Polit. Sci., Fordham U., 1978; student Bus. Computer Tng., SUNY, 1986; BA, John Hopkins U., 1987. judge for Congress of Strings, BMI Composers Competition, 1970-74; instr. theory Mt. Morris Park, 1969-73; instr. woodwind L.I. Inst. Music, 1969-75, U. Denver, 1963-64, Coll. New Rochelle, 1980; tchr. bassoon Newark Community Arts Center, 1969-71; instr. music N.Y.C. Tech. Coll., 1972-90; pres. Finale Prodns. Mem. Denver Symphony Orch., 1963-64, Met. Opera Nat. Co., 1965-67, Gil Evans Band, 1967-69, formed, Harlem Youth Symphony, 1968, Harlem Philharmonic Orch., 1969—, New Breed Brass Ensemble, Harlem String Quartet, Harlem Woodwind Quintet, 1970, condr., Balt. Symphony, 1970, mus. dir., condr., Harlem Philharmonic Orch., 1970—, N.Y.C. Housing Authority Orch., 1972-86, Massapequa (N.Y.) Symphony Soc., 1974-80, condr., Park West Symphony, Northeastern Philharmonic of Pa., Scranton Philharmonic, Ridgefield Symphonette, 1971, mus. dir. for Josephine Baker, 1972-75, free lance bassoonist, Am. Symphony, Bklyn. Philharmonic, N.J. Symphony, 1967—; min. of music St. Thomas the Apostle, 1989—; dir. Independence Community Ctr., 1993—; dir. counselor Elmcor Youth Ctr., 1991-93. Mem. nat. adv. bd. Dance Theatre of Harlem, Air Force Assn., Mental Health Assn.; bd. dirs. Empire Trust; hon. bd. dirs. Sickle Cell, Baton Rouge, La.; performing arts coord. Afro-Acad. Cultural Tech. Sci. Olympics; cons. N.Y. State Coun. Arts; dir. Ind. Cmty. Ctr., 1993—; field ops. supr.; U.S. Bur. Census. Recipient Martha Baird Rockefeller Found. grant, 1969, Nat. Endowment grant, 1970. Mem. NAACP, Nat. Soc. Lit. and Arts, N.Y. State Assn. Jr. Colls., Am. Symphony Orch. League, Performing Arts Assn. N.Y., Soc. Black Composers, Nat. Soc. Symphony Condrs. Club: The Bohemians. Home: 425 Central Park W New York NY 10025-4324 Office: PO Box 445 New York NY 10025-0445

PORTER, LAEL FRANCES, communication consultant, educator; b. N.Y.C., July 30, 1932; d. Ronald William Carpenter and Frances Veneranda Fernandez Carpenter; m. Ralph Emmett Porter, June 9, 1954; children: Paula Lee Porter Leggett, Sandra Lynn Livermore. BA in Comm. and Theater, U. Colo., Denver, 1982, MA in Comm. and Theater, 1986. Speech instr. Moultrie, Ga., 1954-55; owner, distributor Lael's Cosmetics & Wigs, Alexandria, Va., 1966-69; sales dept. mgr. May D & F, Denver, 1974-80; instr. comm. U. Colo., Denver, 1987-89, Red Rocks Cmty. Coll., Lakewood, Colo., 1989—; mem. coord. com. Nat. Hispana Roundtable, Denver, 1985; mem. diversity coun. and internat. dimensions Red Rocks C.C., Lakewood, Colo., 1994-96. Mem. bd. dirs. Girls Count, Denver, 1991—, Colo. Statewide Systemic In., Denver, 1994—; mem. adv. bd. Cmty. Liberal Arts & Sci. U. Colo., Denver, 1988-93; mem. utility consumers adv. bd. State of Colo., Denver, 1989-91. Recipient Founding Star award Girls Count, Cert. of Appreciation USAF, 1974, Mack Easton award U. Colo., Denver, 1990. Mem. AAUW (numerous coms. and positions including assn. pub. policy com. 1994—, state pres. 1992-94, named gift award 1991, br. named gift award 1988, br. continuing svc. award 1994), Colo. Speech Comm. Assn., Internat. Soc. Edn., Tng. and Rsch., Latin Am. Rsch. and Svc. Orgn., Western Speech Comm. Assn., Speech Comm. Assn., Leadership Lakewood. Episcopalian. Avocations: swimming, reading, gardening, internet. Home: 2613 S Wadsworth Cir Lakewood CO 80227

PORTER, LILIANA ALICIA, artist, printmaker, photographer; b. Buenos Aires, Argentina, Oct. 6, 1941; came to U.S., 1964, naturalized, 1982; d. Julio and Margarita (Galetar) P.; m. Luis Camnitzer, 1965 (div. 1978); m. Alan B. Wiener, May 28, 1980 (div. 1991). Grad., Nat. Sch. Fine Arts, Argentina, 1963. Co-dir., instr. Studio Camnitzer-Porter summer workshops, Lucca, Italy, 1974, 75, 76, 77; prof. art Queens Coll., N.Y.C., 1991—; adj. lectr. SUNY Coll., Old Westbury, N.Y., 1974-76, Purchase br., 1987; co-dir. Studio Porter-Wiener, N.Y.C., 1979-87. One-woman shows of prints/paintings/photographs include Galeria Artemultiple, Buenos Aires, Argentina, 1977, 78, Galeria Arte Comunale, Adro, Brescia, Italy, 1977, Hundred Acres Gallery, N.Y.C., 1977, Mus. Modern Art, Cali, Colombia, 1978, Center for Interamerican Relations, N.Y.C., 1980, Galeria Arte Nuevo, Buenos Aires, 1980, Barbara Toll Fine Arts, N.Y.C., 1979, 81, 82, 84, Galerie Jolliet, Montreal, 1983, Museo de Arte Contemporaneo, Panama City, Panama, 1984, Dolan/Maxwell Gallery, Phila., 1985, U. Alta., Edmonton, 1985, Dolan/Maxwell Gallery, Phila., 1985, Galería Luigi Marrozzini, San Juan, P.R., 1986, Galería-Taller, Museo de Arte Moderno, Cali, Colombia, 1987, The Space, Boston, 1988, Syracuse U., N.Y., 1990, Steinbaum-Krauss Gallery, N.Y.C., 1993, Galeria Ruth Benzacar, Buenos Aires, 1994, U. Art Gallery, N.Mex. State U., Las Cruces, 1995, Monique Knowlton Gallery, 1996, Ruth Benzecar Gallery, N.Y., 1997; retrospective exhibits 1968-90 Fundacion San Telmo, Buenos Aires, 1990, Museo Nacional de Artes Plasticas, Montevideo, Uruguay, 1991, Centro de Recepciones del Gobierno, San Juan, P.R., 1991, Bronx Mus. Art, N.Y.C., 1992, retrospective exhibit Archer Huntington Art Gallery U. Tex. Austin, 1993; exhibited in group shows at Bonino Gallery, N.Y.C., 1964, N.Y.U., 1968, Inst. Contemporary Art, London, 1969, Paula Cooper Gallery, N.Y.C., 1969, Mus. Modern Art, N.Y.C., 1970, Biblioteque Nat., Paris, 1973, U. Mus., Berkeley, Calif., 1973, Bklyn. Mus., 1974, 75, Paris Biennial, 1975, Whitney Mus. Am. Art, N.Y.C., 1976, Lousiana Mus., Copenhagen, 1976, Fredrick Gallery, Washington, 1976, Australian Nat. Gallery, Sydney, 1977, Center for Interamerican Relations, N.Y.C., 1978, Chateau de L'Hermitage, Belgium, 1978, Mus. Fine Arts, Buenos Aires, 1978, Alternative Center for Internat. Arts, N.Y.C., 1978, Ben Shahn Gallery, N.J., 1979, Everson Mus., Syracuse, N.Y., 1979, Alternative Mus., N.Y.C., 1980, Alt. Mus., N.Y.C., 1981, Bronx Mus. Fine Arts, 1982, Musee d'Art Contemporain, Montreal, 1983, Queens Coll., Flushing, N.Y., 1983, Mus. Modern Art, San Francisco, 1983, Klein Gallery, Chgo., 1983, Cayman Gallery, N.Y.C., 1984, Artist Space, N.Y.C., 1984, U. Park, L.A., 1984, Jersey City Mus., 1986, 93, Hostos C.C., N.Y., 1986, Galeria Epoca, Santiago, Chile, 1986, Centro Wilfredo Lam, Cuba, 1986, Mus. Contemporary Spanish Art, N.Y.C., 1987, U. Tex., Austin, 1987, 88, Bronx Mus. Art, N.Y., 1988, San Diego Mus. Art, 1991, Soho 20, N.Y.C., 1992, 94, MOMA, N.Y.C., 1993, Milw. Art Mus., 1995, Mus. de Art Contemporaneo, Monterrey, Mex., 1996; represented in permanent collections Mus. Phila., Mus. Modern Art, N.Y.C., RCA Corp., N.Y.C., N.Y. Public Library, N.Y.C., La Biblioteque Nationale, Paris, France, Museo del Grabado, Buenos Aires, Museo Universitario, Mexico City, Mexico, Museo de Art Moderno, Cali, Colombia, Museo de Bellas Artes, Caracas, Venezuela, Met. Mus. Art, N.Y.C. Recipient 1st prize Argentinian Art 78 Mus. Fine Arts, Buenos Aires, 1978, Grand Prix XI, Internat. Print Biennial, Cracow, Poland, 1986, 1st prize VII Latin Am. Print Biennial, San Juan, Puerto Rico, 1986; fellow Guggenheim Found., 1980-81, N.Y. Found. for the Arts, 1985. Address: 178 Franklin St 5th Floor New York NY 10013

PORTER, MARIE ANN, neonatal nurse, labor and delivery nurse; b. St. Paul, June 29, 1961; d. Theodore J. Morrison and Betty Ann Verdick; 1 child, Angela. ADN, Columbia Basin Coll., 1988. RN, Wash.; cert. neonatal resusitation, Neonatal Resuscitation Program instr. Staff RN Kennewick (Wash.) Gen. Hosp., 1988-95; legal nurse cons. Richland, Wash., 1995—; owner, pres. Porter Med. Cons.; owner, pres. Porter Med. Conss. Active March of Dimes. Mem. ANA, Nat. Assn. Neonatal Nurses, Tri-Cities Coun. Nursing, Richland C. of C.(amb.).

PORTER, MARSHA KAY, Language professional and educator, English; b. Sacramento, Feb. 7, 1954; d. Charles H. and Eileen J. (Miller) P. BA in English and Edn., Calif. State U., Sacramento, 1976, traffic safety credential, 1979, MA in Ednl. Adminstrn., 1982. Cert. lang. devel. specialist, Calif.; cert. first aid instr. ARC. Bookkeeper Chuck's Parts House, Sacramento, 1969-76; substitute tchr. Sacramento City Unified Sch. Dist., 1976-78; coord. Title I, Joaquin Miller Mid. Sch., Sacramento, 1978-81; tchr. ESL and driver's edn. Hiram Johnson H.S., Sacramento, 1981-85, C.K. McClatchy H.S., Sacramento, 1985—; freelance editor, 1981-87; guest lectr. Nat. U., Sacramento, 1992-93. Co-author film reference book Video Movie Guide, pub. annually; contbr. movie revs., short stories and articles to publs. Vol. instr. CPR and first aid ARC, Sacramento, 1986-92; guest writer United We Stand Calif., Sacramento, 1993-94. Gov.'s scholar State of Calif., 1972. Mem. NEA, Calif. Tchrs. Assn., Calif. Assn. Safety Educators, Calif. Writers, Calif. Writers Assn. (sec. 1987-94, pres. 1996-98), Delta Kappa Gamma. Roman Catholic. Avocations: swimming, helping wounded and/or abandoned animals, acting.

PORTER, MAXIENE HELEN GREVE, civic worker; b. L.A.; d. Henry Chris and Meyerl (Dixon) Greve; student U. So. Calif., 1928; m. Wellington Denny Palmer, Nov. 18, 1928 (dec. Mar. 1933); children: Virginia Palmer Stanhagen, Wellington Denny; m. 2d, Dale R. Porter, May 17, 1941. Accounting clk. Inglewood (Calif.) Sch. System, 1948-51; dep. tax collector City of San Luis Obispo (Calif.), 1963-65; acctg. clk. San Luis Obispo County Schs., 1965-66; asst. innkeeper Holiday Inn, Darien, Conn., 1967, Alexandria, Va.; innkeeper Holiday Inn, Falls Church, Va., 1973—; asst. gen. mgr. Darien Motor Lodge Assos.; tax cons. H & R Block, 1975-79, office mgr., 1976. Officer, Native Daus. Golden West, 1953—, state pres., 1959-60; chmn. various coms. Calif. Fedn. Womens Clubs, 1960-63; v.p. Bus. and Profl. Women, 1936-37; sec. Inglewood Coordinating Coun., 1945-47, pres., 1947-48; pres., various other offices West Ebell Club, L.A., 1947, 60-63; mem. public relations com. YWCA, Fairfax County, Va., 1967-68, Fairfax Hosp. Aux., 1967-68, spl. pub. com. Smithsonian Assn., 1967-68; sec.-treas. Pinecrest Citizens Assn., 1968, v.p., 1974; chmn. finance com. Va. Commn. Status of Women, 1973-75; docent vol. chmn. Green Spring Farm Park, Fairfax County, 1979-80; treas. Greater Falls Church Republican Womens Club, 1968-70, v.p., 1973-74, pres., 1975-76; treas. Va. Fedn. Rep. Women, 1968—, parliamentarian, 1976-80; vice-chmn. Va. Nixon Inaugural Com., 1968-69; treas. Va. Women for Nixon, 1968; mem. Fairfax County Nixon for Pres. Com., co-chmn. Fairfax County Ladies for Lin— Gov.'s Campaign, 1969; mem. Fairfax County Rep. Com., 1968—, dist. chmn., 1974—, sec., 1975-76. Mem. Fairfax County C. of C. (legis., edn., polit. activities coms. 1973-74), Nat. Trust for Historic Preservation, Nat. Hist. Soc., Va., Metro (mem. program com., v.p. 1972-73) motel assns., Am. Mgmt. Assn. Clubs: Toastmistress (treas. No. Va. 1975, organizer, charter pres. Falls Church 1977-78, pres., 1983-84 coun. extension chmn. 1977-78, council treas. 1979-80, council sec. 1980-81, coun. v.p. 1981-82, council pres. 1983-84, parliamentarian 1983-84 editor council newsletter 1978-79, regional awards chmn. 1984-85), Annandale Women's, No. Va. Fedn. Women's (registration chmn. 1980, conservation and energy com., scholarship com. 1982-84, pub. affairs chmn. 1984-86), Nat. Genealogy Soc., Maine Geneal. Soc., Harpswell Sounders, Orr's Island Libr. Assn. (chmn. membership com. 1989-91, editor newsletter 1989-93), Maine Mus. of Art, Maine Maritime Mus. Harpswell Hist. Soc., Merriconeag Grange, Ceres (lectr. 1992-96), Piscataquas Pioneer Soc., 55Plus (sr. concerns com. 1995—), Orr's Island Libr. Assn. (editor newsletter 1990-93, corr. sec. 1995—). Lutheran. Avocation: oil painting. Home: Lane Rd RR1 PO Box 140 Orrs Island ME 04066

PORTER, MICHAEL PELL, lawyer; b. Indpls., Mar. 31, 1940; s. Harold Troxel and Mildred Maxine (Pell) P.; m. Alliene Laura Jenkins, Sept. 23, 1967 (div.); 1 child, Genevieve Natalie, Porter Eason; m. Janet Kay Smith Hayes, Feb. 13, 1983 (div.). Student, DePauw U., 1957-58; BA, Tulane U., 1961, LLB, 1963. Bar: La. 1963, U.S. Ct. Mil. Appeals 1964, N.Y. 1969, Hawaii 1971. Clk. U.S. Ct. Appeals (5th cir.), New Orleans, 1963; assoc. Sullivan & Cromwell, N.Y.C., 1968-71, Cades Schutte Fleming & Wright, Honolulu, 1971-74, ptnr., 1975-94; mem. faculty Addis Ababa (Ethiopia) U. Sch Law, 1995—; legal advisor St. Matthews Anglican Ch. Addis Ababa, 1995—; mem. deans coun. Law Sch. Tulane U., 1981-88; dep. vice chancellor Episcopal Diocese Hawaii, 1980-88, chancellor, 1988-94; chancellor Episcopal Ch., Micronesia, 1988-95. Author: Hawaii Corporation Law & Practice, 1989; Hawaii reporter: State Limited Partnership Laws, 1992-94. Fulbright scholar, 1997-98. Bd. dirs. Jr. Achievement Hawaii, Inc., 1974-84, Inst. Human Svcs., Inc., 1980-88; donor Michael P. Porter Dean's Scholastic award U. Hawaii Law Sch., 1977—; lectorship named in his honor, Addis Abba, Ethiopia, 1994-97; established Michael P. Porter Prizes on Ethnic Harmony and Religious Tolerance in a Dem. Soc. at Addis Ababa, 1995. With JAGC, U.S. Army, 1963-66, Vietnam. Tulane U. fellow, 1981. Mem. ABA, Hawaii State Bar Assn. Republican.

PORTER, PATRICK KEVIN, secondary education educator, administrator; b. Greenfield, Ind., Jan. 17, 1955; s. Herman Monroe and Juanita Helen (Thomas) P.; m. Bonnie Kay Barkdull, July 3, 1988; children: Andrew, Megan, Sean. BS in Teaching, Ball State U., 1977, MA in Teaching, 1981, EdS in Adminstrn., 1991. Cert. tchr., prin., supt., Ind. Tchr., coach Fayetteville Community Sch. Corp., Connersville, Ind., 1977-79, West-Ctrl. Sch. Corp., Anderson, Ind., 1979-87; tchr. Jennings County Sch. Corp., North Vernon, Ind., 1989-90; tchr., coach Bartholomew Consol. Sch. Corp., Columbus, Ind., 1987-89, tchr. sci. and social studies, 1990—; asst. prin. Test, Miss., 1994-96, Richmond (Ind.) High Sch.; asst. dir. Ball State U. Conf. Office, Muncie, Ind., summer 1985, 86; mgr. Halteman Swim Club, 1987, 88. Chmn. adminstrv. bd. East Columbus United Meth. Ch., Columbus, 1990, chmn. pastor parish com., 1991-93. Named to Outstanding Young Men in Am., 1981. Mem. ASCD, Ind. Profl. Educators Inc., Ind. Basketball Coaches Assn., Ind. High Sch. Athletic Assn. (basketball/volleyball ofcl.), NASSP, Ind. Middle Schs. Assn., Blue Key. Avocations: bowling, hunting, fishing, collecting lapel buttons, tennis. Home: 2708 S G St Richmond IN 47374-6557 Office: Richmond High Sch 380 Hub Etchison Pkwy Richmond IN 47374-5339

PORTER, PHILIP THOMAS, retired electrical engineer; b. Clinton, Ky., Mar. 18, 1930; s. Philip Henry and Ruth Frances (Pennebaker) P.; m. Louise Monroe Jett, July 3, 1957; children: Philip C., Sara Shelby Porter Taylor. BA in Physics, Vanderbilt U., 1952, MA in Physics, 1953. Mem. tech. staff Bell Telephone Labs., Murray Hill, N.J., 1953-62; mem. tech. staff Bell Telephone Labs., Holmdel, N.J., 1962-70, supr., 1971-78; supr. Bell Telephone Labs., West Long Branch, N.J., 1979-83; dir. wireless and wireline network compatiblity studies Bell Communications Rsch., Red Bank, N.J., 1984-94; ret., 1994; U.S. del. Consultative Com. for Internat. Radio, Geneva, 1984-93. Contbg. author: Electronics Engineers' Handbook, 1982, History of Science and Technology in the Bell System, 1985, Digital Communications, 1986; patentee in field. Fellow IEEE. Unitarian. Avocations: group singing, bridge, sailing.

PORTER, PHILIP WAYLAND, geography educator; b. Hanover, N.H., July 9, 1928; s. Wayland Robinson and Bertha Maria (LaPlante) P.; m. Patricia Elizabeth Garrigus, Sept. 5, 1950; children: Janet Elizabeth, Sara Louise, Alice Catherine. A.B., Middlebury Coll., 1950; M.A., Syracuse U., 1955; Ph.D., U. London, 1957. Instr. geography U. Minn., Mpls., 1957-58; asst. prof. U. Minn., 1958-64, assoc. prof., 1964-66, prof., 1966—, chmn. dept., 1969-71; asso. to v.p. acad. affairs, also dir. Office Internat. Programs, 1979-83; Mem. geography panel Com. on Space Programs for Earth Observations Nat. Acad. Scis., 1967-71; bd. dirs., liaison officer Midwest Univs. Consortium for Internat. Activities, 1979-83. Contbr. articles, monographs to profl. lit. Served with AUS, 1952-54. Ctrl. Rsch. Fund (London) grantee, 1955-56, NSF grantee, 1961-62, 78-80, 92-93, Social Sci. Rsch. Coun. grantee, 1966-67, Rockfeller Found. grantee, 1969, 71-73, Gen. Svc. Found. grantee, 1981-83, Exxon Edn. Found. grantee, 1983-84, Fulbright grantee, 1992-93; Bush Sabbatical fellow, 1985-86. Mem. Assn. Am. Geographers, Am. Anthrop. Assn., African Studies Assn. Home: 86 Arthur Ave SE Minneapolis MN 55414-3410 Office: U Minn Dept Geography Minneapolis MN 55455

PORTER, RICHARD STERLING, retired metal processing company executive, lawyer; b. Newton, Mass., May 14, 1929; s. William Edwin Jr. and Mabel Elizabeth (Saunders) P.; m. Sara Patten McCrum, June 15, 1955; children: Edwin Ross, John Sterling. AB, Princeton U., 1952; LLB, U. Va., 1957. Various positions Alcan Aluminium Ltd., Montreal, Que. and Cleve., 1957-85; sec., corp. counsel Alcan Aluminium Ltd., Montreal, 1985-88. Served to 1st lt. U.S. Army, 1952-54, Korea. Home: 206 Woodside Rd Brunswick ME 04011-7442

PORTER, ROBERT HUGH, economics educator; b. London, Ont., Can., Jan. 25, 1955; came to U.S., 1976; s. Hugh Donald and Olive Marie (Anderson) P.; m. Therese Jane McGuire, June 20, 1981. BA with honors, U. Western Ont., London, 1976; PhD, Princeton U., 1981. Asst. prof. econs. U. Minn., Mpls., 1980-84; post doctoral fellow Bell Labs., Murray Hill, N.J., 1982-83; assoc. prof. SUNY, Stony Brook, 1984-87; mem. tech. staff Bell Communications Rsch., Morristown, N.J., 1986-88; prof. Northwestern U., Evanston, Ill., 1987—. Mem. bd. editors Am. Econ. Rev., 1987-88, 94-96; assoc. editor Internat. Jour. Indsl. Orgn., 1989-95; co-editor Econometrica, 1988-93, Rand Jour. Econs., 1995—; contbr. articles to profl. jours. NSF grantee, 1985, 88, 93, 97. Fellow Econometric Soc.; mem. Am. Econ. Assn., Can. Econs. Assn., Am. Acad. Arts and Scis. Home: 904 Michigan Ave # 1 Evanston IL 60202-1425 Office: Northwestern U Dept Econs 2003 Sheridan Rd Evanston IL 60208-0826

PORTER, ROGER BLAINE, government official, educator; b. Provo, Utah, June 19, 1946; s. Blaine Robert and Elizabeth M. (Taylor) P.; m. Ann Robinson, Jan. 6, 1972; children: Robert Roger, Stacy Ann, David R., Rachel Elizabeth. BA in History and Polit. Sci., Brigham Young U., 1969; PhB, Oxford U., 1971; MA, Harvard U., 1978, PhD, 1978. Asst. dean, tutor in politics Queen's Coll., Oxford U., 1971-72; spl. asst. to pres. The White House, 1974-77; rsch. assoc. Kennedy Sch. Govt. and Grad. Sch. Bus., Harvard U., 1977-79, asst. prof. pub. policy, 1979-81, assoc. prof., 1981, prof. govt. and bus., 1985—; spl. asst. to Pres. of U.S., 1981-82, dep. asst. to Pres. of U.S., 1982-85; dir. White Ho. Office of Policy Devel., Washington, 1982-85; counselor to sec. U.S. Treasury, 1981-85; exec. sec. Nat. Productivity Adv. Com., 1981-85, Cabinet Coun. on Econ. Affairs, 1981-85, Econ. Policy Coun., 1985; asst. to U.S. Pres. for Econ. and Domestic Policy, 1989-93; exec. sec. Pres.'s Econ. Policy Bd., 1974-77; sr. scholar Woodrow Wilson Internat. Ctr. for Scholars, 1993—; dir. Ctr. for Bus. and Govt. Harvard U., 1995—; mem. Pres.'s Commn. on White House Fellowships, 1976—. Author: Presidential Decision Making, 1980, U.S.-U.S.S.R. Grain Agreement, 1984; asst. editor: Public Policy, 1979-81. Mem. Utahns for Effective Govt., Salt Lake City, 1971-72; mem. Rep. Nat. Com. Econ. Adv. Com., 1977-81. Rhodes scholar, 1969; Woodrow Wilson fellow, 1969; White House fellow, 1974; recipient spl. citation U.S. Sec. Treasury, 1977, Rolex Intercollegiate Tennis Achievement award, 1996; named One of 10 Outstanding Young Men in Am., 1981. Fellow Nat. Acad. Pub. Adminstrn.; mem. Phi Kappa Phi, Pi Sigma Alpha, Phi Eta Sigma, Phi Alpha Theta. Mem. LDS Ch. Avocations: classical music, basketball, tennis, travel. Home: 12 Clifton St Belmont MA 02178-3363 Office: Harvard U Kennedy Sch Govt 79 JFK St Cambridge MA 02138-5801

PORTER, ROGER JOHN, medical research administrator, neurologist, pharmacologist; b. Pitts., Apr. 4, 1942; s. John Keaggy and Margaret (Parker) P.; m. Candace Marie Leland, Feb. 17, 1968; children: David, Stacey. BS, Eckerd Coll., 1964; MD, Duke U., 1968. Diplomate Nat. Bd. Med. Examiners, Am. Bd. Neurology, Am. Bd. Electroencephalography. Intern U. Calif. at San Diego, 1968-69; resident in neurology U. Calif. at San Francisco, 1971-74; fellow Rsch. Tng. Program Duke U., Durham, N.C., 1966-67; staff assoc. sect. epilepsy Nat. Inst. Neurol. Diseases and Stroke, NIH, Bethesda, Md., 1969-71; investigator U. Calif., San Francisco, 1972-73; sr. rsch. assoc. epilepsy br., Neurol. Disorders Program Nat. Inst. Neurol.

and Communicative Disorders and Stroke, NIH, Bethesda, 1974-78, asst. chief epilepsy br., 1977-79, acting chief, 1979-80, acting chief clin. epilepsy sect., IRP, 1979-84, chief epilepsy br., Neurol. Disorders Program, 1980-84, chief med. neurology br. and clin. epilepsy sect. IRP, 1984-87; dep. dir. Nat. Inst. Neurol. Disorders and Stroke, NIH, Bethesda, 1987-92; v.p., clin. pharmacology Wyeth-Ayerst Rsch., Radnor, Pa., 1992—; adj. prof. neurology U. Pa., 1993—; prof. neurology Uniformed Svcs. U. Health Scis., Bethesda, 1980-93, adj. prof. pharmacology, 1982—; cons.-lectr. neurology Nat. Naval Med. Ctr., Bethesda, 1978-93; chmn. White House Subcom. on Brain and Behavioral Scis., 1990-92; scholar-in-residence Assn. Am. Med. Colls., Washington, 1989-90; mem. NIMH/Nat. Inst. Neurol. Disorders and Stroke Coun. of Assembly of Scientists, 1983-86, pres., 1985-86; mem. pharmacy and therapeutics com. NIH, 1977-86, chmn., 1978; mem. instnl. rev. bd. human subjects Nat. Inst. Neurol. Disorders and Stroke, 1984-87, chmn., 1986-87. Author/editor 10 books; mem. editl. bd. Acta Neurologica Scandanavica, Annals of Neurology, Epilepsia; contbr. numerous papers, book chpts., abstracts to profl. publs.; writer, contbr. 5 motion pictures, 1 exhibit. Bd. trustees Eckerd Coll., 1994—. With USPHS, 1969-92. Recipient USPHS Commendation medal, 1977, MacArthur Outstanding Alumnus award Eckerd Coll., 1977, Fulbright Disting. Prof. award, 1985, USPHS Meritorious Svc. medal, 1986, Dept. Def. Meritorious Svc. medal, 1989, Disting. Alumnus award Duke Duke U. Med. Ctr., 1989, USN Commendation medal, 1991, USPHS Disting. Svc. medal, 1991; scholar in residence Assn. Am. Med. Colls., Washington, 1989-90. Fellow Am. Acad. Neurology, Am. Neurol. Assn.; mem. Am. Electroencephalographic Soc., Am. Epilepsy Soc. (pres. 1989-90), Soc. Neurosci., Am. Soc. Clin. Pharmacology and Therapeutics, Am. Soc. Neurologic Investigation (hon.), Internat. League Against Epilepsy (sec.-gen. 1989-93). Home: 461 Timber Ln Devon PA 19333-1232 Office: Wyeth-Ayerst Rsch PO Box 8299 Philadelphia PA 19101-8299

PORTER, ROGER STEPHEN, chemistry educator; b. Windom, Minn., June 2, 1928; s. Sherman Clarence and Cora Ruth (Rogers) P.; m. Catharine Crow, Aug. 3, 1968; children: Margaret Davis, Stephen Cady; children by previous marriage: Laura Jean, Ruth Anne. BS in Chemistry, UCLA, 1950; PhD, U. Wash., 1956; DSc (hon.), U. Mass., 1996. Sr. rsch. assoc. Chevron Rsch. Co., Richmond, Calif., 1956-66; prof., dept. polymer sci. and engring. U. Mass., Amherst, 1966—, head dept., 1966-76, asst. to pres. for rsch., 1979-81; plastics cons. in field; co-dir. NSF Materials Lab., 1972-82; study group head U.S./USSR Commn. on Sci.; com. mem. Nat. Acad. Scis., 1969—; adv. panel NSF; adv. bd. various sci. jours.; lectr. Russian, Brazilian and Romanian acads.; bd. dirs. Plastics Inst. Am.; trustee Gordon Rsch. Conf., chmn. Editor: Polymer Engineering and Science, Polymer Composites; co-editor 14 books. Recipient Polyolefins award Internat. Plastics Edn. award Soc. Plastics Engring., 1977, Internat. award in plastics sci. and engring. Soc. Plastics Engring., 1981, Disting. mem. award Soc. Plastics Engring., 1993, Mettler award, 1983, Bingham medal Soc. Rheology, 1985; named to Plastics Hall of Fame, 1991. Fellow Am. Phys. Soc., N.Am. Thermal Analysis Soc. (pres. 1987); mem. Am. Chem. Soc. (award in plastics 1979), Plastics Acad. (bd. dirs. 1996—), Sigma Xi, Alpha Chi Sigma, Phi Gamma Delta. Home: 220 Rolling Ridge Rd Amherst MA 01002-1423 Office: Univ Mass Polymer Rsch Ctr Amherst MA 01003

PORTER, STEPHEN CUMMINGS, geologist, educator; b. Santa Barbara, Calif., Apr. 18, 1934; s. Lawrence Johnson Porter Jr. and Frances (Cummings) Seger; m. Anne Mary Higgins, Apr. 2, 1959; children: John, Maria, Susannah. BS, Yale U., 1955, MS, 1958, PhD, 1962. Asst. prof. geology U. Wash., Seattle, 1962-66, assoc. prof., 1966-71, prof., 1971—, dir. Quaternary Research Ctr., 1982—; mem. bd. earth scis. Nat. Acad. Sci., Washington, 1983-85; mem. adv. com. divsn. polar programs NSF, Washington, 1983-84; vis. fellow Clare Hall Cambridge (Eng.) U., 1980-81; guest prof. Academia Sinica, People's Republic of China, 1987—; v.p. Internat. Union Quaternary Rsch., 1992-95, pres., 1995—. Co-author: Physical Geology, 1987, The Dynamic Earth, 1989, 92, 95, The Blue Planet, 1995, Environmental Geology, 1996; editor: Late Quaternary Environments of the United States, 1983, Dangerous Earth, 1997; editor Quaternary Rsch., 1976—; assoc. editor Radiocarbon Jour. 1982-89, Am. Jour. Sci., 1997—; mem. editorial bd. Quaternary Sci. Revs., 1988—, Quaternary Internat., 1989—, Quaternary of South Africa and Antarctic Peninsula, 1995—. Served to lt. USNR, 1955-57. Recipient Benjamin Silliman prize Yale U., 1962; Willis M. Tale lectr. So. Meth. U., 1984, S.F. Emmons lectr. Colo. Sci. Soc., 1996; Fulbright Hays sr. rsch. fellow, New Zealand, 1973-74. Fellow Geol. Soc. Am., Arctic Inst. N.Am. (bd. govs.); mem. AAAS, Am. Quaternary Assn. (coun., pres. 1992-94). Avocations: photography, mountaineering. Home: 18034 15th Ave NW Seattle WA 98177-3305 Office: U Wash Quaternary Rsch Ctr PO Box 351360 Seattle WA 98195-1360

PORTER, STEPHEN WINTHROP, stage director; b. Ogdensburg, N.Y., July 24, 1925; s. Charles T. and Anna (Newton) P. B.A., Yale U., 1945, M.F.A., 1948. Asst. prof. English in charge of drama McGill U., Montreal, 1949-56. Stage dir. plays on Broadway Right You Are, Wild Duck, 1966, The Show Off, 1967, The Misanthrope, 1968, 83, The Wrong Way Light Bulb, Private Lives, 1969, Harvey, 1970, The School for Wives, 1971, Captain Brassbound's Conversion, 1972, Don Juan, 1973, Chemin de Fer, 1974, Rules of the Game, 1975, They Knew What They Wanted, 1976, Days in the Trees, 1976, The Importance of Being Earnest, 1977, Tartuffe, 1977, Man and Superman, 1978, Major Barbara, The Man Who Came to Dinner, 1980, You Never Can Tell, 1986, The Devil's Disciple, 1988, The Miser, 1990, Getting Married, 1991. Address: 25 W 54th St New York NY 10019-5404

PORTER, STUART WILLIAMS, investment company executive; b. Detroit, Jan. 11, 1937; s. Stuart Perlee and Alma Bernice (Williams) P.; m. Myrna Marlene Denham, June 27, 1964; children: Stuart, Randall. BS, U. Mich., 1960; MBA, U. Chgo., 1967, postgrad., 1967-68. Investment mgr., prin. Weiss Peck & Greer, 1978—. Chmn. Crusade of Mercy, 1973; chmn. investment com. Presbytery of Chgo. Served with USAF, 1961-62. Recipient Excellence in Bus. and Acctg. award Fin. Exec. Inst., 1966; Am. Acctg. Assn. fellow, 1967. Mem. Midwest Pension Conf., Investment Analysts Soc. Chgo., Assn. Investment Mgmt. Rsch., Inst. Quantitative Rsch. in Fin., Chgo. Quantitative Analysts Soc., Turnberry Country Club, Econ. Club, Haig Point Country Club, Avondale Country Club, Wynstone Golf Club, Beta Gamma Sigma Home: 130 Wyngate Dr Barrington IL 60010-4839 Office: 311 S Wacker Dr Fl 52 Chicago IL 60606-6627

PORTER, TERRY, professional basketball player; b. Milw., Apr. 8, 1963. Student, U. Wis., Stevens Point, 1981-85. With Portland Trail Blazers, 1985—; now with Minnesota Timberwolves, Minneapolis. Recipient Citizenship award, 1993; named to NBA All-Star team, 1991, 93. Holds single game record for most three point field goals without a miss-7, 1992. Office: Minnesota Timberwolves 600 1st Ave N Minneapolis MN 55403-1400*

PORTER, VERNA LOUISE, lawyer; b. L.A., May 31, 1941. B.A., Calif. State U., 1963; JD, Southwestern U., 1977. Bar: Calif. 1977, U.S. Dist. Ct. (cen. dist.) Calif. 1978, U.S. Ct. Appeals (9th cir.) 1978. Ptnr. Eisler & Porter, L.A., 1978-79, mng. ptnr., 1979-86, pvt. practice law, 1986—; judge pro-tempore L.A. Mcpl. Ct., 1983—, L.A. Superior Ct., 1989—, Beverly Hills Mcpl. Ct., 1992—; mem. state of Calif. subcom. on landlord tenant law, panelist conv., mem. real property law sect. Calif. State Bar, 1983; speaker on landlord-tenant law to real estate profls., including San Fernando Bd. Realtors; vol. atty. L.A. County Bar Dispute Resolution, mem. client rels. panel, fee arbitrator. Mem. adv. coun. Freddie Mac Vendor, 1995—. Editl. asst., contbr. Apt. Owner Builder; contbr. to Apt. Bus. Outlook, Real Property News, Apt. Age; mem. World Affairs Coun. Fre Mem. ABA, L.A. County Bar Assn. (client-rels. vol. dispute resolution and fee arbitration, 1981—), L.A. Trial Lawyers Assn., Wilshire Bar Assn., Women Lawyer's Assn., Landlord Trial Lawyers Assn. (founding mem., pres.), Freddie Mac Vendor Adv. Coun., da Camera Soc. Republican. Office: 2500 Wilshire Blvd Fl 1226 Los Angeles CA 90057-4317

PORTER, W. L., bishop. Bishop of Cen. Tenn., Ch. of God in Christ, Memphis. Office: Ch of God in Christ 1235 E Parkway S Memphis TN 38114-6728*

PORTER, WALTER ARTHUR, retired judge; b. Dayton, Ohio, June 6, 1924; s. Claude and Estella (Raymond) P.; m. Patricia Reeves Higdon, Dec. 3, 1947; children—Scott Paul, David Bryant. B.S. in Engring, U. Cin., 1948, LL.B., 1949. Bar: Ohio 1949. Legal dep. Montgomery County Probate Ct., 1949-51; asst. pros. atty. Montgomery County, 1951-56; with Albert H. Scharrer (atty.), Dayton, 1956-61; mem. firm Smith & Schnacke, Dayton, 1962-85; pres. Smith & Schnacke, 1980-85; judge Montgomery County Common Pleas Ct., 1985-95; of counsel Thompson Hine & Flory, Dayton, 1996—. Served with inf. U.S. Army, 1943-45, ETO. Mem. ABA, Ohio Bar Assn. (pres. 1973-74), Dayton Bar Assn., Am. Coll. Trial Lawyers, Am. Coll. Probate Counsel, Phi Alpha Delta, Omicron Delta Kappa. Democrat. Presbyterian. Club: Mason. Home: 785 E Schantz Ave Dayton OH 45419-3818

PORTER, WALTER THOMAS, JR., bank executive; b. Corning, N.Y., Jan. 8, 1934; s. Walter Thomas and Mary Rebecca (Brookes) P.; m. Dixie Jo Thompson, Apr. 3, 1959; children: Kimberlee Paige, Douglas Thompson, Jane-Amy Elizabeth. BS, Rutgers U., 1954; MBA, U. Wash., 1959; PhD, Columbia U., 1964. CPA, Wash., N.Y. Staff cons. Touche Ross & Co., Seattle, 1959-61; NDEA fellow Columbia U., 1961-64; dir. edn. Touche Ross & Co., N.Y.C., 1964-66; assoc. prof. U. Wash., 1966-70, prof., 1970-74; vis. prof. N. European Mgmt. Inst., Oslo, Norway, 1974-75; nat. dir. planning Touche Ross & Co., Seattle, 1975-78, dir. exec. fin. counseling, 1978-84, exec. v.p., mgr. pvt. banking, Rainier Nat. Bank, 1984-87, exec. v.p., mgr. capital mgmt. and pvt. banking, 1987-88, vice chmn. 1988-89; vice chmn. Security Pacific Bank Washington, 1989-92; exec. v.p., mgr. capital mgmt. group Seafirst Bank, Seattle, 1992—; vis. lectr. taxation U. Wash., 1978-85; bd. dirs. AEI, Inc. Mem. Seattle adv. bd. Salvation Army, 1975-83, 89-97, pres. 1993-95; trustee Ryther Child Ctr., 1975-85, pres., 1979-81; trustee Lakeside Sch., 1977-87, pres. 1984-86; trustee Va. Mason Med. Ctr., 1986-97, chair bd. govs. 1994-96; chair Natl. Campaign for Student Athlete U. of Wash., 1995—, Mus. History and Industry, 1982-83. Served with U.S. Army, 1955-57. Author: Auditing Electronic System, 1966; (with William Perry) EDP: Controls and Auditing, 1970, 5th edit., 1987; (with John Burton) Auditing A Conceptual Approach, 1974; (with D. Alkire) Wealth: How to Achieve It, 1976; Touche Ross Guide to Personal Financial Management, 1984, 3d edit., 1989; (with D. Porter) The Personal Financial Planner's Practice Sourcebook, 1986, The Bank of America Guide to Personal Financial Solutions, 1996. Mem. Am. Inst. CPA's. Congregationalist. Club: Wash. Athletic, Sand Point Country, Rainer Club, Sand Point Golf Club. Office: Seafirst Bank PO Box 3586 701 5th Ave 56th Fl Seattle WA 98124

PORTER, WILLIAM L., electrical engineer; b. Leeds, N.D., July 2, 1929; s. Ernest Cecil and Dena Grace (Thompson) P.; m. Mary Lynn Lindsey, Oct. 9, 1948; children: Belinda Joyce, William Harry, Terry Jane, Derek Lewis, Michael Ronald. AA, Springfield Coll., 1960; BSEE, U. Ill., 1963. Registered profl. engr., Ill., Minn,. N.D., S.D. Lineman City Water, Light and Power, Springfield, Ill., 1947-54, troubleshooter, 1954-62, gen. supt. elec. divsn., 1962-76; prin. engr. R.W. Beck and Assocs., Columbus, Nebr., 1976-77; engring. mgr. R.W. Beck and Assocs., Mpls., 1977-80, ptnr., mgr., 1980-90, sr. cons., 1990-97; ret., 1997; speaker on engring. and utilities; cons. to electric utilities. Author numerous engring. reports and engring. and utilities papers. Street light com. chair City of Springfield, 1964, mem. CATV com., 1966; mem. Planning Commn. Spring Park (Minn.), 1978-79; chair environ. quality com. region IV Ill. Soc. Profl. Engrs., chair ethics and practices com. Capital chpt.; mem. tech. adv. com. Fed. Power Commn's Nat. Power Survey; chair engring. and ops. com. Am. Pub. Power Assn., 1967-70, chair power supply planning com., 1973-74. Named Engr. of Yr., Capital chpt. Ill. Soc. Profl. Engrs., 1975. Mem. NSPE, IEEE (chmn. Cen. Ill. sect. 1974-75), Minn. Soc. Profl. Engrs., Cons. Engrs. Coun., Am. Bus. Club, Eta Kappa Nu. Republican. Home: 4349 Channel Rd Spring Park MN 55384-9734

PORTER, WILLIAM LYMAN, architect, educator; b. Poughkeepsie, N.Y., Feb. 19, 1934; s. William Quincy and Lois (Brown) P.; m. Lynn Rogers Porter; children: Quayny Lyman, Zoe Lynn, Eve Lyman. B.A., Yale U., 1955, M.Arch., 1957; Ph.D., MIT, 1969. Designer, job capt. Louis I. Kahn (architect), Phila., 1960-62; urban designer, asst. chief of design Ciudad Guayana project Joint Center for Urban Studies of Harvard and MIT, Caracas, Venezuela, 1962-64; Mellon fellow dept. urban studies and planning MIT, 1964-65; Samuel Stouffer fellow Joint Center for Urban Studies, Harvard and MIT, 1966-67; asst. prof. urban design, depts. architecture and urban studies and planning MIT, 1968-70, assoc. prof. urban design, 1970-71, prof. architecture and planning, 1971—, Norman B. and Muriel Leventhal prof. architecture and planning, 1988—, head. dept. architecture, 1987-91, dean Sch. Architecture and Planning, 1971-81; co-dir. Aga Khan Program for Islamic Architecture Harvard U.-MIT, 1979-85; cons. in field; mem. Nat. Archtl. Accrediting Bd., 1978-80, pres., 1979; mem. Mass. Designer Selection Bd., 1978-79, chmn., 1979; mem. steering com. Aga Khan Award for Architecture, 1977-86, mem. master jury, 1989. Co-founder, co-editor Places: A Quarterly Jour. Environ. Design, 1982-88. Trustee Milton (Mass.) Acad., 1989—; mem. bd. overseers Coll. Fine Arts, U. Pa., 1984-90, Mus. Fine Arts, Boston, 1992-94. Fellow AIA; mem. Boston Soc. Architects (dir. 1969-73, 77-81). Clubs: Harvard Musical Assn. (Boston). Home: 17 Concord Ave Cambridge MA 02138-2321 Office: MIT Sch Architecture & Planning 77 Massachusetts Ave Cambridge MA 02139-4301

PORTER, WILMA JEAN, educational consultant; b. Sylacauga, Ala., May 30, 1931; d. Harrison Samuel and Blanche Leonard Butcher; m. Douglas Taylor Porter, Apr. 18, 1953; children: Daria Cecile, Blanche Evette, Douglas Vincent. BS, Tuskegee U., 1951; MS, Mich. State U., 1966; PhD, Iowa State U., 1980. Asst. dietitian Miss. State Tb Sanatorium, 1951-52; therapeutic dietitian dept. of hosp. City of N.Y., S.I., 1952-53; libr. asst. Mississippi Valley State Coll., Itta Bena, Miss., 1963-65; asst. prof. Grambling (La.) State U., 1966-75, Howard U., Washington, 1976-80; country dir. U.S. Peace Corps, Tonga, 1980-82; asst. dir. internat. programs Ft. Valley (Ga.) Coll., 1983-84, dir. Inst. Advancement, 1984-88; dir. Sch. Home Econs., Tenn. Technol. U., Cookeville, 1989-96; pvt. ednl. cons. Cookeville, 1996—; project dir. Capitol Hill Health and Homemaker, Washington, 1982-83; interim dir. Inst. Advancement Alcorn State U., Lorman, Miss., 1988-89. Author lab. manual for quantity foods, 1977; editor: (cookbook) Some Christmas Foods and Their Origins from Around the World, 1983. Convenor Nat. Issues Forums, Ga. and Tenn., 1985—; citizen participant Nat. Issues Forums Soviet Dialogue, Newport Beach, Calif., 1988; bd. dirs. Leadership Putnam, Cookeville, 1990-94; chmn. Tenn. Technol. U. campaign United Way, 1989; mem. devel. and planning com. Peach County Ft. Valley, 1985-87; mem. Peach County Heart Fund Dr., 1986-88; participant People to People Citizens Amb. program U.S./China Women's Issues Program, 1995. Title III grantee U.S. Dept. Edn., 1986, 87; Tenn. Dept. Human Svcs. grantee, 1993, 94. Mem. AAUW (program chair 1991-92, pres. Cookeville br. 1993-94), Am. Home Econs. Assn., Am. Dietetic Assn., Nat. Coun. Adminstrs. Home Econs., Tenn. Home Econs. Assn., Tenn. Dietetic Assn. Democrat. Roman Catholic. Avocations: writing, vegetable and flower gardening. Home: 512 Fisk Rd Cookeville TN 38501-2925

PORTERFIELD, CHRISTOPHER, magazine editor, writer; b. Weston, W.Va., Apr. 3, 1937; s. James Herman and Irene (Smith) P.; m. Stephanie Brown, Jan. 20, 1962; children: Christopher Brown, Tessa Louise, Kevin Stephenson. BA, Yale U., 1958; MA, Columbia U., 1965. Music critic Time mag., N.Y.C., 1967-69; cultural correspondent Time mag., London, 1969-72; exec. producer Daphne Prodns., N.Y.C., 1974-79; sr. editor Time mag., N.Y.C., 1980-93, asst. mng. editor, 1993—. Co-Author: (with Dick Cavett) (books) Cavett, 1973, Eye on Cavett, 1983; contbr. articles to popular mags. and periodicals, 1975—. Mem. Writer's Guild of Am. Avocations: reading, music, tennis. Home: 315 Central Park W New York NY 10025-7664 Office: Time Mag 1271 Avenue Of The Americas New York NY 10020

PORTERFIELD, CRAIG ALLEN, psychologist, consultant; b. Geneva, N.Y., May 11, 1955; s. Paul Laverne and Elizabeth Louise (Mearns) P.; m. Alta Marie Herring, Aug. 1977; children: Aleine Michelle, Brian Matthew. Student, Sorbonne U., Paris, 1975-76; BA, St. John Fisher Coll., 1977; MA, U. Tex., Austin, 1982, PhD, 1985. Lic. psychologist, N.Y., Del.; cert. sch. psychologist, N.Y. Program evaluation intern Austin Ind. Sch. Dist., 1980, psychol. intern, 1982-83; program evaluator Austin Child Guidance Ctr., 1981-82; evaluation mgr. Child, Inc., Austin, 1981-82; staff therapist Psychotherapy Inst., Austin, 1984-85; consulting psychologist Albany (N.Y.) Psychol. Assocs., 1987-90; staff psychologist Berkshire Farm Ctr. and Svcs. for Youth, Canaan, N.Y., 1985-87, dir. rsch., 1987-90; psychologist Del. Psychiatry Svcs., Dover, 1990-94; sr. psychologist Del. Psychiatry Svcs., Del., 1994-95; pvt. practice psychology Dover and Milford, Del., 1995—; adj. asst. prof. SUNY, Albany, 1986-87, 89-91; psychologist privileges dept. psychiatry Kent Gen. Hosp., Dover, 1990—, Milford Meml. Hosp., 1995—; mem. adv. com. life skills curriculum Lake Forest Sch. Dist., Harrington, Del., 1991; co-founder, advisor Children with Attention Deficit Disorders Kent County, Del., 1991—; active Children with Attention Deficit Disorders State Coun. Del., 1993—. Grantee N.Y State Integrated Task Force on Substance Abuse Programs for Youth, 1988; recipient Presenter of Yr. Del. Coun. on Exceptional Children, 1996. Mem. APA, Nat. Register of Health Svcs. Providers in Psychology, Preservation D el. Avocations: Victorian house restoration, exercise, Zen meditation. Office: PO Box 147 Camden Wyoming DE 19934-0147

PORTERFIELD, JAMES TEMPLE STARKE, business administration educator; b. Annapolis, Md., July 7, 1920; s. Lewis Broughton and Maud Paxton (Starke) P.; m. Betty Gold, Apr. 23, 1949 (dec. 1985); m. Janet Patricia Gardiner Roggeveen, Oct. 5, 1986. AB, U. Calif., Berkeley, 1942; MBA, Stanford U., 1948, PhD, 1955. From asst. to assoc. prof. Harvard U. Bus. Sch., Boston, 1955-59; prof. fin. Stanford (Calif.) U. Grad. Sch. Bus., 1959-79, James Irvin Miller Prof. fin., 1979-90, prof. emeritus, 1990—; prof. IMEDE Mgmt. Devel. Inst., Lausanne, Switzerland, 1962-63. Author: Life Insurance Stocks as Investments, 1955, Investment Decisions and Capital Costs, 1965; co-author: Case Problems in Finance, 1959. Served as lt. USNR, 1941-46. Recipient Salgo Noren award Stanford U., 1966, Richard W. Lyman award Stanford U. Alumni Assn., 1995. Home: 295 Golden Oak Dr Portola Vally CA 94028-7730 Office: Stanford U Grad Sch Bus Stanford CA 94305

PORTERFIELD, NEIL HARRY, landscape architect, educator; b. Murrysville, Pa., Aug. 15, 1936; s. Phil Frank and Alvira Clare (Rea) P.; m. Sandra Jean Beswarick, Aug. 9, 1958; children: Eric Jon, Jennifer Jane, Garrett Andrew. BS in Landscape Architecture, Pa. State U., 1958; M in Landscape Architecture, U. Pa., 1964. Landscape architect Pitts. Dept. Parks and Recreation, 1958-59; land planner Neil H. Porterfield & Assocs., Murrysville, 1961-64; dir. landscape architecture and planning Hellmuth, Obata & Kassabaum, Inc., St. Louis, 1964-70; exec. v.p. HOK Assocs., St. Louis, 1970-72, pres., 1972-85; prin., v.p., dir. Hellmuth, Obata & Kassabaum, Inc., 1977-80, corp. dir. planning, sr. v.p., dir., 1980-85; prof., head dept. landscape architecture Pa. State U., University Park, 1985-93, dean Coll. Arts and Architecture, 1993—; lectr. in field; prof. Washington U., 1979; chmn. Landscape Archtl. Accreditation Bd. Contbr. articles to profl. orgns., anthologies. Bd. dirs. Landscape Architecture Found., 1983-85; adv. coun. Coll. Architecture and Urban Studies, Va. Poly. Inst. and State U., Blacksburg, 1984-86; vice-chmn. The Commn. Fine Arts, Washington, 1985-93. Recipient honor award Married Student Housing, U. Mich., honor award Am. Soc. Landscape Architects, 1969, Merit award Parkside Campus Study U. Wis. at Kenosha, Merit award Am. Soc. Landscape Architects, 1969, Outstanding Alumnus award Coll. Arts and Architecture, Pa. State U., 1983, others. Fellow Am. Soc. Landscape Architects (v.p. 1985-87); mem. Coun. of Edn. Presbyterian. Home: RR 1 Centre Hall PA 16828-9801 Office: Pa State U Coll Arts and Architecture 111 Arts Bldg University Park PA 16802-2900

PORTERFIELD, WILLIAM WENDELL, chemist, educator; b. Winchester, Va., Aug. 24, 1936; s. Donald Kennedy and Adelyn (Miller) P.; m. Dorothy Elizabeth Dail, Aug. 24, 1957; children—Allan Kennedy, Douglas Hunter. B.S., U. N.C., 1957, Ph.D., 1962; M.S., Calif. Inst. Tech., 1960. Sr. research chemist Hercules, Inc., Cumberland, Md., 1962-64; asst. prof. chemistry Hampden-Sydney (Va.) Coll., 1964-65, assoc. prof., 1965-68, prof. chemistry, 1968—, Charles Scott Venable prof. chemistry, 1989—, chmn. natural sci. div., 1973-77, chmn. dept. chemistry, 1982-85, 93—; vis. fellow U. Durham (U.K.), 1984. Author: Concepts of Chemistry, 1972, Inorganic Chemistry, 1984, 2d edit., 1993; contbr. articles to profl. jours. Mem. Am. Chem. Soc., Royal Chem. Soc. (London, Eng.), Phi Beta Kappa. Home: PO Box 697 Hampden Sydney VA 23943

PORTIS, ALAN MARK, physicist, educator; b. Chgo., July 17, 1926; s. Lyon and Ruth (Libman) P.; m. Beverly Aline Portis, Sept. 5, 1948; children: Jonathan Marc, Stephen Compagni, Lori Ann, Eliyahu Shlomo Cohn. Ph.B., U. Chgo., 1948; A.B., U. Calif., Berkeley, 1949, Ph.D., 1953. Mem. faculty U. Pitts., 1953-56; Mem. faculty U. Calif.-Berkeley, 1956—, prof. physics, 1964-95, prof. emeritus, 1995—, asst. to chancellor for research, 1966-67, asso. dean grad. div., 1967-68, dir. Lawrence Hall Sci., 1969-72, univ. ombudsman, 1981-83, 92-94, assoc. dean Coll. Engring., 1983-87, 94-95. Author: Electromagnetic Fields/Sources and Media, 1978, Electrodynamics of High-Temperature Superconductors, 1993; contbg. author: Berkeley Physics Laboratory, 1964, 65, 66, 71. Fulbright fellow, 1961, 67, Guggenheim fellow, 1965, SERC sr. fellow, U.K., 1991-92. Fellow Am. Phys. Soc.; mem. Am. Assn. Physics Tchrs. (Robert Andrews Millikan award 1966).

PORTIS, CHARLES MCCOLL, reporter, writer; b. El Dorado, Ark., Dec. 28, 1933; s. Samuel Palmer and Alice (Waddell) P. BA, U. Ark., 1958. Reporter The Comml. Appeal, Memphis, 1958, Ark. Gazette, Little Rock, 1959-60, N.Y. Herald Tribune, N.Y.C., 1960-64. Author: Norwood, 1966, True Grit, 1968, The Dog of the South, 1979, Masters of Atlantis, 1985, Gringos, 1991. Sgt. USMC, 1952-55, Korea. Presbyterian. Home: 7417 Kingwood Rd Little Rock AR 72207-1734

PORTLAND, CHARLES DENIS, publishing executive; b. N.Y.C., July 11, 1952; s. William and Berta Portela. AAS, CUNY, N.Y.C., 1974; AA, U. Md., 1978, BS, 1979; M in Accounting, U. Okla., 1982; postgrad., Nova U. CPA, Fla. Sr. auditor Arthur Anderson & Co., Oklahoma City, 1982-86; sr. fin. analyst Knight Ridder, Inc., Miami, Fla., 1986-88; special project Miami Herald, Miami, Fla., 1988-89; prin. Denis Portela, CPA, Miami Beach, Fla., 1989-93; founder, pres. Grove Mktg. (dba Charlden Consulting), 1990-95; pub. Portland Pub., Stamford, N.Y., 1997—; cons. Carlson Travel Network, MGM Grand Hotel & Casino, City of Miami, Fla., Microsoft. Author: Portland's Computer Guid., 1996, Personal Computer Reference and Training, 1997. With U.S. Army, 1974-80, Germany, Korea. Mem. AICPA's, Fla. Inst. CPA's, Am. Mgmt. Assn., Governor's Indsl. Dev. Bds. Subcomm. on Computing and Data Communications. Lutheran. Avocation: horticulture. Home: PO Box 267 Stamford NY 12167

PORTMAN, GLENN ARTHUR, lawyer; b. Cleve., Dec. 26, 1949; s. Alvin B. and Lenore (Marsh) P.; m. Katherine Seaborn, Aug. 3, 1974 (div. 1984); m. Susan Newell, Jan. 3, 1987. BA in History, Case Western Res. U., 1968; JD, So. Meth. U., 1975. Bar: Tex. 1975, U.S. Dist. Ct. (no. dist.) Tex. 1975, U.S. Dist. Ct. (so. dist.) Tex. 1983, U.S. Dist. Ct. (we. and ea. dists.) Tex. 1988. Assoc. Johnson, Bromberg & Leeds, Dallas, 1975-80, ptnr., 1980-92; ptnr. Arter, Hadden, Johnson & Bromberg, Dallas, 1992-95, Arter & Hadden, Dallas, 1996—; chmn. bd. dirs. Physicians Regional Hosp., 1994-96; mem. exec. bd. So. Meth. U. Sch. Law, 1994—; lectr. bankruptcy topics South Tex. Coll. Law, State Bar Tex. Asst. editor-in-chief Southwestern Law Jour., 1974-75; contbr. articles to profl. jours. Firm rep. United Way Met. Dallas, 1982-92; treas. Lake Highlands Square Homeowners Assn., 1990-93. Mem. ABA, Am. Bankruptcy Inst., State Bar Tex. Assn., Dallas Bar Assn., So. Meth. U. Law Alumni Assn. (council bd. dirs., v.p. 1980-86, chmn. admissions com., chmn. class agt. program 1986-89, chmn. fund raising 1989-91), 500 Club Inc., Assemblage Club. Republican. Methodist. Home: 9503 Winding Ridge Dr Dallas TX 75238-1451 Office: Arter & Hadden 1717 Main St Ste 4100 Dallas TX 75201-7302

PORTMAN, NANCY ANN, artist, art educator; b. Bath, N.Y., Dec. 10, 1936; d. Lewis Menzo Peck and Neva Irene (Keeler) Wheeler; m. Warren Conrad Portman, Apr. 1, 1961; children: Lorraine Jean Portman, Errol Lawrence. BA with honors, SUNY, New Paltz, 1958; MA with honors, NYU, 1965; postgrad., Coll. New Rochelle, 1982-86, SUNY, Purchase, 1985-90, Pace U., 1990. Permanent tchg. cert., N.Y. Art tchr. Yorktown Ctrl. Schs., Yorktown Heights, N.Y., 1958-60, 61-65, Yorktown Heights, 1971-91; art tchr. Pearl River (N.Y.) Schs., 1960-61. Group shows include Jacksonville Watercolor Soc., St. Augustine Art Assn., Crescdnt Beach Art Gallery. Campaigner for Steve Alexander, State Dist. Atty. Fla., St. Augustine, 1992. Mem. Fla. Watercolor Soc., Jacksonville Watercolor Soc. (chair fall show 1994, co-chair fall show 1995, 1st v.p. and show chmn. 1996-97), St. Augustine Art Assn., Jacksonville Mus., Cummen Mus. Republican. Methodist. Avocations: drawing, photography, reading, sewing, gardening. Home: 3497 Lone Wolf Trail Saint Augustine FL 32086

PORTMAN, RACHEL MARY BERKELEY, composer; b. Eng., Dec. 11, 1960. BA, Oxford Univ. Scores include (films) Sharma and Beyond, 1986, Antonia and Jane, 1991, Life Is Sweet, 1991, Where Angels Fear to Tread, 1991, Rebecca's Daughters, 1992, Used People, 1992, Ethan Frome, 1993, Benny and Joon, 1993, Friends, 1993, The Joy Luck Club, 1993, (TV movies) Young Charlie Chaplin, 1989, The Cloning of Joanna May, 1992, (documentaries) Elizabeth R: A Year In the Life of the Queen, 1992; compositions include Fantasy for Cello and Piano, 1985. Named Composer of Yr. British Film Inst., 1988. Office: The Kraft-Benjamin Agency 345 N Maple Dr Beverly Hills CA 90210-3869*

PORTMAN, ROB, congressman; b. Cin., Dec. 19, 1955; m. Jane Portman; children: Jed, Will. BA, Dartmouth Coll., 1979; JD, U. Mich., 1984. Ptnr. Head & Ritchey, Cin., 1986-89; assoc. counsel to President of U.S., then dep. asst. to President, dir. Office Legis. Affairs White House, Washington, 1989-92; mem. U.S. Del. to UN Subcom. on Human Rights, 1992, 103d-105th Congresses from 2nd Ohio dist., 1993—; mem. ways and means com., mem. Leaders' Econ. Task Force; asst. whip U.S. Ho. of Reps. Bd. trustees Springer Sch., The United Way, Hyde Park Community United Meth. Ch.; founding trustee Cin.-China Sister City Com.; former bd. dirs. United Home Care; vice chmn. Hamilton County George Bush for Pres. Campaign, 1988, 92; chmn. Rep. Early Bird Campaign com., 1992; del. Rep. Nat. Conv., 1988, 92; active Hamilton County Rep. Party Exec. com., Hamilton County Rep. Party Fin. Com. Mem. Cin. World Trade Assn. Office: US Ho of Reps 238 Cannon HOB Washington DC 20515-0509*

PORTNEY, JOSEPH NATHANIEL, aerospace executive; b. L.A., Aug. 15, 1927; s. Marcus and Sarah (Pilson) P.; m. Ina Mae Leibson, June 20, 1959; children: Philip, Jeffrey. BS, U.S. Naval Acad., 1952. Commd. 2d lt. USAF, 1952, advanced through grades to capt., 1956, resigned, 1960; with Litton Systems, Inc., Woodland Hills, Calif., 1960—; project engr. Litton Aero Products, 1967-68; program mgr. Litton Aero Products Litton Systems, Inc., Woodland Hills, 1968-72, advanced program mgr. Guidance and Control Sys., 1972-85, mgr. advanced programs Guidance and Control Sys., 1985—; navigator engr. on 3 historic inertial crossings of the North Pole. Creator solar compass, pilot and navigator calendar. Mem. Inst. of Navigation (v.p. 1988-89, pres. 1989-90), U.S. Naval Acad. Alumni Assn. (trustee 1980-83). Jewish. Avocation: classical piano. Home: 4981 Amigo Ave Tarzana CA 91356-4505 Office: Litton Systems Inc 5500 Canoga Ave Woodland Hills CA 91367-6621

PORTNEY, PAUL R., research and educational organization executive. BA in Econs. and Math., Alma Coll.; PhD in Econs., Northwestern U. Vis. prof. grad. sch. pub. policy U. Calif., Berkeley, 1977-79; chief economist Coun. on Environ. Quality, Exec. Office of Pres., Washington, 1979-80; with Resources for the Future, Washington, 1980—, v.p., dir. Ctr. for Risk Mgmt., Quality of Environment divsn, 1989-95, pres., 1995—; mem. bd. environ. studies and toxicology NAS; mem. panel on contingent valuation NOAA; exec. com. EPA Sci. Adv. Bd., chmn. environ. econs. adv. com.; lectr. in field; vis. lectr. Woodrow Wilson Sch. Pub. and Internat. Affairs, Princeton (N.J.) U., 1992. author: Footing the Bill for Superfund Cleanups: Who Pays and How?, others; contbr. articles to profl. jours. Office: Resources for the Future 1616 P St NW Washington DC 20036-1434

PORTNOY, SARA S., lawyer; b. N.Y.C., Jan. 11, 1926; d. Marcus and Gussie (Raphael) Spiro; m. Alexander Portnoy, Dec. 13, 1959 (dec. 1976); children—William, Lawrence. B.A., Radcliffe Coll., 1946; LL.B., Columbia U., 1949. Bar: N.Y. 1949, U.S. Dist. Ct. (so. dist.) N.Y. 1952, U.S. Dist. Ct. (ea. dist.) N.Y. 1975, U.S. Ct. Appeals (2d cir.) 1975, U.S. Supreme Ct. 1975. Assoc. Seligsberg, Friedman & Berliner, N.Y.C., 1949-51; atty. AT & T, N.Y.C., 1951-61; assoc. Proskauer Rose Goetz & Mendelsohn, N.Y.C., 1974-78, ptnr., 1978-94, retired 1994. Mem. Commn. on Human Rights, White Plains, N.Y., 1973-78; mem. bd. visitors Columbia Law Sch., 1996—; bd. dirs. Legal Aid Soc. of Westchester County, N.Y., 1975-83, Columbia Law Sch. Assn., 1990-94; mem. Pres.'s Coun. Yaddo. Mem. Assn. of Bar of City of N.Y. (chair com. legal support staff 1994). Democrat.

PORTNOY, WILLIAM MANOS, electrical engineering educator; b. Chgo., Oct. 28, 1930; s. Joseph and Bella (Saltzman) P.; m. Alice Catherine Walker, Sept. 9, 1956; children: Catherine Anne, Michael Benjamin. B.S., U. Ill., 1952, M.S., 1952; Ph.D., 1959. Registered profl. engr., Tex. Mem. tech. staff Hughes Aircraft Co., Newport Beach, Calif., 1959-61, Tex. Instruments Inc., Dallas, 1961-67; mem. faculty Tex. Tech. U., Lubbock, 1967—, prof. biomed. engring., 1973-85, prof. physics, 1985—, prof. elec. engring., 1972; adj. assoc. prof. Baylor Coll. Medicine and Inst. Health Svcs. Rsch., Houston, 1969-73; cons. Hughes Rsch. Labs., Malibu, Calif., 1972, NDM Corp., 1974-76, Los Alamos Nat. Lab., 1980-81, 91, Battelle Rsch. Inst., 1980-81, Westinghouse, 1984, SRI Internat., 1986-88, Lawrence Livermore Nat. Lab., 1986-93, W.J. Shafer Assocs., 1988-91, Sandia Nat. Lab., 1989—, Gen. Rsch. Corp., 1990-92, STI Optronics, 1991-92. Contbr. articles to profl. jours.; patentee in field. Bd. dirs. Am. Heart Assn., Lubbock County, 1972-75. Nat. Heart Inst. postdoctoral trainee, 1969; NASA sr. postdoctoral resident, research assoc. Manned Spacecraft Center, Houston, 1968; Fulbright prof., 1975; recipient Abell faculty award, 1984. Fellow IEEE; mem. Am. Soc. Engring. Edn. (Western Electric Fund award for excellence in instrn. engring. students 1980), Am. Phys. Soc., Sigma Xi. Office: Tex Tech U Dept Elec Engring Lubbock TX 79409

PORTOGHESE, PHILIP SALVATORE, medicinal chemist, educator; b. N.Y.C., June 4, 1931; s. Philip A. and Constance (Antonelli) P.; m. Christine L. Phillips, June 11, 1960; children—Stephen, Stuart, Philip. B.S., Columbia U., 1953, M.S., 1958; Ph.D., U. Wis., 1961; Dr. honoris causa, U. Catania, Italy, 1986, Royal Danish Sch. Pharmacy, Copenhagen, 1992. Asst. prof. Coll. Pharmacy, U. Minn., Mpls., 1961-64; assoc. prof. Coll. Pharmacy, U. Minn., 1964-69, prof. medicinal chemistry, 1969—, prof. pharmacology, 1987—, dir. grad. study in medicinal chemistry, 1974-86, head dept., 1974-83; cons. NIMH., 1971-72; mem. med. chemistry B sect. NIH, 1972-76; mem. pharmacology, substance abuse and environ. toxicology interdisciplinary cluster President's Biomed. Research Panel, 1975; mem. expert panel of Flavor and Extract Mfrs. Assn. of U.S., 1984—. Mem. editorial adv. bd. Jour. Med. Chemistry, 1969-71; editor-in-chief, 1972—; mem. editorial adv. bd. Med. Chem. series, 1972—. Served with U.S. Army, 1954-56. Recipient Research Achievement award in med. chemistry Am. Pharm. Assn. Found./Acad. Pharm. Sci., 1980; Ernest H. Volwiler award for outstanding contbns. to pharm. scis. Am. Assn. Colls. of Pharmacy, 1984, N.B. Eddy Meml. award Coll. on Problems of Drug Dependence-NAS NRC, 1991. Fellow AAAS, Acad. Pharm. Scis., Am. Assn. Pharm. Scientists (Rsch. Achievement award 1990); mem. Am. Chem. Soc. (Medicinal Chemistry award 1990, E.E. Smissman-Bristol-Meyers-Squibb award 1991), Am. Soc. Pharm. Exptl. Therapeutics, Internat. Union Pure and Applied Chemistry (commn. on medicinal chemistry 1978-82, internat. com. med. chemistry 1982-85), Soc. Neurosci., Sigma Xi, Rho Chi, Phi Lambda Upsilon. Home: 17 Oriole Ln Saint Paul MN 55127-6334 Office: U Minn Coll of Pharmacy 308 Harvard St SE Minneapolis MN 55455-0353

PORTWAY, PATRICK STEPHEN, telecommunications consulting company executive, telecommunications educator; b. June 18, 1939; s. Christopher Leo and Ceciala (King) P.; m. Malle M. Portway; children by previous marriage: Shawn, Pam, Vicki. BA, U. Cin., 1963; MA, U. Md., 1973; postgrad., Columbia U. Regional ADP coordinator GSA, Washington, 1963-68; mgr. strategic mkt. planning Xerox Corp., 1969-74; mgr. plans and programs System Devel. Corp., 1974-78; fin. indsl. mktg. exec. Satellite Bus. Systems, 1978-80; western regional mgr. Am. Satellite Co., 1980-81; CEO, Applied Bus. Telecomm., Livermore, Calif., 1981—; prof., lectr. Golden Gate U. Grad. Sch., San Francisco, 1983—; pub. mag. Teleconference, 1981—; pub. (newspapers) Discovery Bay, Delta Clippers; prodr. Telecon & Ioccon Confs., 1981—. Author: (with others) Teleconferencing and Distance Learning, 1992, 3d edit. 1997. Presdl. elector Electoral Coll., Va., 1976; candidate Va. State Legislature from 19th Dist., 1971; chmn. Discovery Bay Mcpl. Adv. Coun., 1992-96; mem adv. coun. Discovery Bay Mcpl., 1992-96, chmn. 1992. Served to 1st lt. U.S. Army, 1963-65. Mem. Internat. Teleconferencing Assn. (founder, bd. dirs. 1983-88), Nat. Univ. Teleconferencing Networdk (mem. adv. bd., bd. dirs. 1986-89), U.S. Distance Learning Assn. (founder, exec. dir. 1987—) Electronic Funds Transfer Assn. (founder, bd. dirs. 1980), Satellite Profls., Jaycees charter pres. Chantilly, VA., Disting. Service award Dale City, VA. Club: Commonwealth. Home: 1908 Windward Pt Discovery Bay CA 94514-9510 Office: Applied Bus Telecomm 2600 Kitty Hawk Rd Ste 110 Livermore CA 94550-9625

PORZAK, GLENN E., lawyer; b. Ill., Aug. 22, 1948; m. Judy Lea McGinnis, Dec. 19, 1970; children: Lindsay and Austin. BA with distinction, U. Colo., 1970, JD, 1973. Bar: Colo. 1973. Assoc. Holme Roberts & Owen, Denver, 1973-80, ptnr., 1980-85, mng. ptnr. Boulder office, 1985-95; mng. ptnr. Porzak Browning & Johnson LLP, Boulder, 1996—; bd. dirs. Norwest Bank Boulder, 1993—. Contbr. articles to profl. jours. 1st Lt. U.S. Army, 1970-78. Named Disting. Alumnus U. Colo., 1991. Fellow Explorers Club (bd. dirs. 1995—); mem. Am. Alpine Club (pres. 1988-91), Colo. Mtn. Club (pres. 1983, hon. mem. 1983—), Colo. Outward Bound (trustee 1992—, vice chmn. 1997—), Phi Beta Kappa. Achievements include reaching summit of Mt. Everest, climbing highest peak on all seven continents. Home: 771 7th St Boulder CO 80302-7402 Office: Porzak Browning & Johnson 929 Pearl St Ste 300 Boulder CO 80302-5248

POSAMENTIER, ALFRED STEVEN, mathematics educator, university administrator; b. N.Y.C., N.Y., Oct. 18, 1942; s. Ernest and Alice (Pisk) P.; children: Lisa Joan, David Richard. AB, Hunter Coll., 1964; MA, CCNY, 1966; postgrad., Yeshiva U., N.Y.C., 1967-69; PhD, Fordham U., 1973; Nostrifizierung of Doctorate, U. Vienna, Austria, 1992. Tchr. math Theodore Roosevelt H.S., Bronx, 1964-70; asst. prof. math. edn. CCNY, N.Y.C., 1970-76, assoc. prof., 1977-80, prof., 1981—, dept. chmn. dept. secondary and continuing edn., 1974-80, chmn., 1980-86; assoc. dean Sch. Edn. CCNY, 1986-95; dep. dean Sch. Edn., CCNY, 1995—; dir. select program in sci. and engring. CCNY, 1978—; dir. CCNY, U.K., iniatives program dir., 1983—; dir. Germany/CCNY Exch. Program CCNY, 1985—, dir. Austria/CCNY Exch. Program, 1987—, dir. Czech Republic/CCNY Exch. Program, 1989—, dir. sci. lectr. program, 1981—, dir. Ctr. for Sci. and Maths. Edn., 1986—; chmn. bd. dirs. Salvadori Edn. Ctr. on Built Environ., 1988—; dir. Exxon sponsored early childhood math. specialist tng. program at City Coll., 1988-92; supr. math. and sci. Mamaroneck H.S., N.Y., 1976-79; project dir. Math Proficiency Workshop, Ossining, N.Y., 1976-79, NSF math. devel. program for secondary sch. tchrs. math., 1978-82, N.Y.C., Profl. Preparation of Math. and Sci. Tchrs., 1978-79; project dir. numerous NSF sponsored math./sci. tchr. devel. insts., 1976—; cons. Croft Ednl. Svcs., New London, 1971, N.Y.C. Bd. Edn., 1973-75, N.Y.C. Bd. Edn. Office of Evaluation, 1974-80, N.Y.C. Bd. Edn. Examiners, 1979-92, Ossining Bd. Edn., 1975-83, numerous others; coord. NSF N.E. Resource Ctr. Sci. and Engring., 1980-90; lectr. various convs. and meetings; vis. prof. U. Vienna, Austria, 1985, 87, 88, 90, Tech. U., Berlin, 1989, Tech. U., Vienna, 1993-96, Pedgogical Inst., Vienna, 1993—, Humboldt U., Berlin, 1996. Author: Geometric Constructions, 1973, Geometry, Its Elements and Structure, 1972, rev. edit., 1977, Challenging Problems in Geometry, 2 vols., 1970, Challenging Problems in Algebra, 2 vols., 1970, A Study Guide for the Scholastic Aptitude Test in Math., 1969, 83, Excursions in Advanced Euclidean Geometry, 1980, 2d edit., 1984, Teaching Secondary School Mathematics: Techniques and Enrichment Units, 1981, 3d edit., 1990, 4th edit., 1995, Uncommon Problems for Common Topics in Algebra, 1981, Unusual Problems for Usual Topics in Algebra, 1981, Using Computers in Mathematics, 1983, 2d edit., 1986, Math Motivators: Investigations in Pre-Algebra, 1982, Math Motivators: Investigations in Algebra, 1983, Using Computers: Programming and Problem Solving, 1984, 2d edit., 1989, Advanced Geometric Constructions, 1988, Challenging Problems in Algebra, 1988, 96, Challenging Problems in Geometry, 1988, 96, The Art of Problem Solving: A Resource for the Mathematics Teacher, 1996, Students! Get Ready for Mathematics for SAT-I: Problem Solving Strategies and Practice Tests, 1996, Teachers! Prepare Your Students for Mathematics for SAT-I: Methods and Problem-Solving Strategies, 1996, Deutch-English Mathematik Wörterbuch, 1996. Trustee Demarest Bd. Edn., 1977-80. Decorated Medal of Honor, Austria, 1994; named Tchr. of Yr. CCNY Alumni Assn., 1993; hon. fellow U. South Bank, London, 1988; Fulbright scholar U. Vienna, 1990; recipient Medal of Distinction, City of Vienna, 1996, Medal of Honor, Technische Fachhochschule Berlin, 1996, 1000 Years Austria commemorative medal, Govt. of Austria, 1997. Mem. Math. Assn. Am., Sch. Sci. and Math. Assn., Nat. Coun. Tchrs. Math., (reviewer new publs., referee articles Math. Tchr. Jour.), Assn. Tchrs. Math. N.Y.C. (exec. bd. 1966-67, referee articles assn. jour.), Assn. Tchrs. of Math. of N.Y. State, Assn. Tchrs. Math. N.J. (mem. editl. bd. N.J. Math. Tchr. Jour. 1981-84), Nat. Coun. of Suprs. of Math. Home: 634 Caruso Ln River Vale NJ 07675-6210 Office: CCNY New York NY 10031

POSCH, ROBERT JOHN, JR., lawyer; b. Levittown, N.Y., Feb. 24, 1950; s. Robert John and Maryrose (Finnegan) P.; m. Mary Lou Collins, July 28, 1974; children: Judith Ann, Robert III, Eric. BA, Manhattan Coll., 1972; JD, Hofstra U., 1975, MBA, 1981. Bar: N.Y. 1977, U.S. Ct. Appeals (2d cir.) 1977. Legal asst. Doubleday & Co., Inc., Garden City, N.Y., 1975-77; staff counsel Doubleday & Co., Inc., Garden City, 1977-82, assoc. counsel, 1982-87; sec., counsel Doubleday Book & Music Clubs, Inc., Garden City, 1987-89, v.p. legal affairs, 1989—; instr. Nassau Community Coll., Hempstead, N.Y., 1984—; mem. adv. bd. real estate symposium Hofstra U.; bd. dirs. Crossiys, Inc. Author: Direct Marketer's Legal Adviser, 1983, What Every Manager Needs to Know About Marketing and the Law, 1984, Marketing and the Law, 1988, Cumulative Supplement, 1989, 90, (with others) The Direct Marketing Handbook, 1984, 91; columnist: Direct Marketing, 1981—; contbr. articles to profl. jours.; speaker in field. Mem. ABA, Am. Corp. Counsel Assn. (newsletter editor 1988-92, bd. dirs. Greater N.Y. chpt.), Third Class Mail Assn. (bd. dirs.), Crossings, Inc. (bd. dirs. 1997—), Direct Mktg. Assn. (privacy, use tax and legal lobbying groups, various coms. 1986—), Christian Legal Soc., Nassau Bar Assn. (various coms. 1977—, AAP Postal Affairs), L.I. Assn., N.Y. State Bus. Coun., Alpha Mu Alpha, Beta Gamma Sigma. Republican. Home: 3151 Grand Blvd Baldwin NY 11510-4826 Office: Doubleday Book/Music Clubs 401 Franklin Ave Garden City NY 11530-5943

POSCOVER, MAURY B., lawyer; b. St. Louis, Jan. 13, 1944; s. Edward and Ann (Chapnick) P.; m. Lorraine Wexler, Aug. 14, 1966; children: Michael, Daniel, Joanna. BA, Lehigh U., 1966; JD, Washington U., 1969. Bar: Mo. 1969. Assoc. Husch & Eppenberger, St. Louis, 1969-75, ptnr., 1975—; lectr. Washington U., St. Louis, 1972-79. Editor-in-chief: The Business Lawyer, 1995-96; contbr. articles to profl. jours. Bd. dirs. Childhaven, St. Louis, 1978-92, pres. 1986; pres. Jewish Community Rels. Coun., 1990-92. Mem. ABA (chmn. comml. fin. svcs. com. bus. law sect. coun., chair bus. law sect., editor-in-chief jour.), Bar Assn. Met. St. Louis (pres. 1983-84), Mo. Bar Assn. (bd. govs. 1979-81), Am. Judicature Soc. (dir. 1981-87), Washington U. Alumni Law Assn. (pres. 1980-81), Mo. Athletic Club. Jewish. Office: Husch & Eppenberger 100 N Broadway Ste 1300 Saint Louis MO 63102-2706

POSEN, SUSAN ORZACK, lawyer; b. N.Y.C., Nov. 5, 1945. BA, Sarah Lawrence Coll., 1967; JD, Bklyn. Law Sch., 1978. Bar: N.Y. 1979. Assoc. Stroock & Stroock & Lavan, N.Y.C., 1978-83, 84-86; ptnr. Stroock, Stroock & Lavan, LLP, N.Y.C., 1987—; asst. gen. counsel Cablevision Systems Corp., Woodbury, N.Y., 1983-84. Office: Stroock Stroock & Lavan LLP 180 Maiden Lane New York NY 10038

POSER, CHARLES MARCEL, neurology educator; b. Antwerp, Belgium, Dec. 30, 1923; s. Maurice and Sadye (Gleitsman) P.; m. Joan Doris Crawford, Sept. 3, 1950; children: William John, Nicholas Charles. B.S., CCNY, 1947; M.D., Columbia U., 1951. Diplomate Am. Bd. Psychiatry and Neurology. Resident in neurology Neurol. Inst. Columbia-Presbyn. Med. Center, N.Y., 1952-55; Fulbright scholar Neuropathology Inst. Bunge, Antwerp, Belgium, 1955-56; instr. through assoc. prof. neurology U. Kans. Sch. Medicine, 1955-64; prof., head div. neurology U. Mo. Sch. Medicine, Kansas City, 1964-68; prof., chmn. dept. neurology U. Vt. Coll. Medicine, 1968-81; prof. neurology Boston U. Sch. Medicine, 1981-84, lectr., 1984—; sr. neurologist Beth Israel Hosp.; cons. prof. Tex. Tech. U. Sch. Medicine, Lubbock, 1981-90; neurology lectr. Harvard Med. Sch., 1981-96, vis. prof. neurology, 1996—; neurology lectr. Tufts U. Sch. Medicine, 1982-90; cons. in neurology U.S. Army and U.S. Navy, 1963—; Cross lectr. U. Witwatersrand, Johannesburg, Republic of South Africa, 1990. Editor-in-chief Jour. Tropical and Geog. Neurology, 1989-92, Neurol. Infections and Epidemiology, 1995—; contbr. numerous articles to med. jours. Served with U.S. Army, 1943-46. Decorated officer Order of Leopold II Belgium; recipient Silver Bicentennial medal Coll. of Physicians and Surgeons, 1967; named Luis Guerrero Meml. lectr. U. Santo Tomás, Manila, 1979, Wilder Penfield lectr. Am. U., Beirut, 1983, Salmon James lectr. London Med. Soc., 1987, Kroc lectr. Rush Med. Coll., Chgo., 1987; Wu Ho-Su Meml. Lectr., Taipei, Taiwan, 1994. Fellow ACP, Am. Acad. Neurology, Am. Acad. Pediat., Royal Soc. Medicine (London), Royal Soc. Tropical Medicine and Hygiene (London), Royal Coll. Physicians (Glasgow); hon. fellow Japanese, Belgian, Cuban, French, Icelandic, Filipino, and Columbian socs. neurology, All-Russian Soc. Neurol. Sci., Neurol. Soc. India, Assn. Brit. Neurologists, Dutch Neurol. Soc.; mem. Am. Neurol. Assn. (sr.), Am. Assn. Neuropathologists, Assn. for Rsch. in Nervous and Mental Diseases, Nat. Acad. Medicine Colombia (hon.). Home: 11 Rutland Sq Boston MA 02118-3105 Office: Beth Israel Deaconess Med Ctr East Campus Dept Neurology Harvard Med Sch 330 Brookline Ave Boston MA 02215-5400

POSER, ERNEST GEORGE, psychologist, educator; b. Vienna, Austria, Mar. 2, 1921; emigrated to Can., 1942, naturalized, 1946; s. Paul and Blanche (Furst) P.; m. Maria Jutta Cahn, July 3, 1953; children: Yvonne, Carol, Michael. B.A., Queen's U., Kingston, Ont., 1946, M.A., 1949; Ph.D., U. London, 1952. Diplomate: Am. Bd. Profl. Psychologists; registered psychologist, B.C. Asst. prof. U. N.B., 1946-48; chief psychologist N.B. Dept. Health, 1952-54; prof. psychology McGill U., Montreal, 1954-83; assoc. prof. psychiatry Faculty Medicine McGill U., 1963-83; adj. prof. dept. psychology U. B.C., 1984-95; dir. behavior therapy unit Douglas Hosp. Center, Montreal, 1966-83. Author: Adaptive Learning: Behavior Modification with Children, 1973, Behavior Therapy in Clinical Practice, 1977. hon. fellow Middlesex Hosp., London, 1964. Fellow Canadian Psychol. Assn., Am. Psychol. Assn.

POSER, NORMAN STANLEY, law educator; b. London, May 28, 1928; came to U.S., 1939, naturalized, 1946; s. Jack and Margaret (Salomon) P.; m. Miriam Kugelman, Sept. 1, 1957 (div. 1979); children: Samuel Marc, Susan; m. Judith Eiseman Cohn, Aug. 11, 1985. A.B. cum laude, Harvard U., 1948, LL.B. cum laude, 1958. Bar: N.Y. 1958. Asso. Greenbaum, Wolff & Ernst, N.Y.C., 1958-61; atty. SEC, Washington, 1961-64; asst. dir. div. trading and markets SEC, 1964-67; asso. Rosenman, Colin, Kaye, Petschek, Freund & Emil, N.Y.C., 1967-68; v.p. Am. Stock Exchange, N.Y.C., 1968-72; sr. v.p. Am. Stock Exchange, 1972-75, exec. v.p., 1975-80; adj. prof. law NYU, 1975-80; prof. law Bklyn. Law Sch., 1980—; cons. World Bank, SEC, OAS, various stock exchs.; spl. counsel N.Y. Stock Exch., 1987—. Mem. adv. bd. BNA Securities Regulation & Law Report, 1979—, Rev. Securities and Commodities Regulation, 1975—; author: International Securities Regulation: London's "Big Bang" and the European Securities Markets, 1991, Broker-Dealer Law and Regulation: Private Rights of Action, 1995. Served with U.S. Army, 1951-53. Mem. Am. Law Inst., ABA, N.Y.C. Bar Assn., Nat. Futures Assn. (arbitrator 1987—). Club: Harvard (N.Y.C.). Office: 250 Joralemon St Brooklyn NY 11201-3700

POSEY, CLYDE LEE, business administration and accounting educator; b. Tucumcari, New Mex., Dec. 27, 1940; s. Rollah P. and Opal (Patterson) P.; m. Dora Diane Vassar; children: Amanda Fox, Julia Forsythe, Rebecca; m. Judith James Jerry, July 31, 1991; stepchildren: David Jerry, Georgia Kenyan. BBA, U. Tex., El Paso, 1963; MBA, U. Tex., 1965; postgrad., U. So. Calif., 1968; PhD, Okla. State U., 1978. CPA, Calif., La., Tex. Lab. aide FBI, Washington, 1959-60; acct. Lipson, Cox & Colton (now Deloitte & Touche), El Paso, Tex., 1962; auditor Main & Co. (now KPMG Peat Marwick), El Paso, 1963; teaching asst. U. Tex., Austin, 1963-65; tax cons. Peat, Marwick, Mitchell & Co., Dallas, 1965-66; cons. Roberson, Martin, Horg and Ryckman, Fresno, Calif., 1967; CPA pvt. practice Fresno, Ruston, Calif., La, 1966—; asst. prof. Calif. State U., Fresno, 1966-76; assoc. prof. La. Tech. U., Ruston, 1978-84, prof., 1984—; vis. asst. prof. Ctrl. State U., Edmond, Okla., 1971-72, U. Okla., Norman, 1976-78; cons. J. David Spence Accountancy Corp., Fresno, 1974-76; many coms. at La. Tech. U. including acad. senator, new faculty welcoming com., acctg. scholarship chmn.; faculty senate rep.; Faculty Consortium, St. Charles, Ill., 1993; expert witness Superior Ct. Calif. Contbr. numerous articles to profl. jours., bus. mags., newspapers, also book reviews; presentations to profl. meetings. Past bd. dirs. Goodwill, Inc., Ctrl. Calif.; ch. deacon and mem. many coms.; pres., treas., state scripture coord. Gideons Internat. Ruston Camp; rep. United Way La. Tech. U., Ruston. With USCG, 1965. Recipient El Paso CPA's Outstanding Jr. scholarship, Standard Oil scholarship, Price Waterhouse scholarship, Outstanding Educator award Gamma Beta Phi, 1986. Mem. AICPA, Am. Acctg. Assn. (La. membership com. chmn.), Am. Inst. for Decision Scis. (program com. chmn. acctg. track), Tex. Soc. CPAs, La. Soc. CPAs, Am. Tax Assn. (internat. tax policy subcom.), Beta Gamma Sigma (pres.), Beta Alpha Psi. Baptist. Avocations: triathlons, bicycle racing, golf, tennis, gardening. Home: 2700 Foxxwood Dr Ruston LA 71270-2509 Office: La Tech U CAB 129A Ruston LA 71272

POSEY, ELDON EUGENE, mathematician, educator; b. Oneida, Tenn., Jan. 25, 1921; s. Daniel M. and Eva (Owens) P.; m. Christine K. Johnson, Dec. 25, 1943; children—Margaret Posey McQuain, Daniel Marion. B.S., East Tenn. State U., 1947; M.A., U. Tenn., 1949, Ph.D., 1954. Instr. W.Va. U., 1954-55, asst. prof., 1955-59; asso. prof. Va. Poly. Inst., 1959-61, prof., 1961-64; prof. math. U. N.C., Greensboro, 1964-88, prof. emeritus, 1988—; head dept. math. U. N.C., 1964-80. Served to capt. USAAF, 1941-46. Decorated Air medal with 18 oak leaf clusters, D.F.C., Silver Star, Purple Heart. Mem. Am. Math. Soc., Math. Assn. Am., Sigma Xi, Pi Mu Epsilon. Home: 4311 Dogwood Dr Greensboro NC 27410-5611

POSEY, LORAN MICHAEL, pharmacist, editor; b. Albany, Ga., Aug. 22, 1955; s. Loran Willis and Rubye Jane (Lumpkin) P.; m. Teresa Maria McCoy, June 27, 1975 (div. Mar. 1983); m. Cheryl Ann Emerling, Jan. 31, 1989 (div. Mar. 1997); children: Evan Michael, Alan Michael, Loran Michael. BS in Pharmacy, BS in Microbiology, U. Ga., 1979, postgrad., 1996—. Registered pharmacist, Ga. Sr. editor Am. Soc. Hosp. Pharmacists, Bethesda, Md., 1980-85; pres. PAS Pharmacy/Assn. Svcs., Athens, Ga., 1985-96, PNN Pharmacotherapy News Network, Athens, 1994—, Pharmacy Editl. and News Svcs., Inc., Athens, 1996—; dir. adminstrv. svcs. Ill. Soc. Hosp. Pharmacists, 1986-92, Va. Soc. Hosp. Pharmacists, 1990—; exec. dir. Phi Delta Chi Pharmacy Frat., 1983-96, Ga. Soc. Hosp. Pharmacists, 1993-95. Author: Pharmacy Cadence, 1992; editor: Pharmacotherapy: A Pathophysiologic Approach, 1989, 2d edit., 1992, 3d edit., 1996; editor The Cons. Pharmacist, 1986—, Jour. Managed Care Pharmacy, 1995-96, Jour. of Am. Pharm. Assn., 1997. Mem. Am. Med. Writers Assn. (chpt. pres. 1988-89, Pres.'s award 1988), Profl. Frat. Assn. (com. chair 1986-90), Am. Soc. Assn. Execs., Ill. Coun. Hosp. Pharmacists (hon.), Phi Delta Chi. Avocations: photography, swimming, reading. Office: PENS Pharmacy Editl and News Svcs Inc PO Box 6565 Athens GA 30604

POSHARD, GLENN W., congressman; b. Herald, Ill., Oct. 31, 1945. BA, So. Ill. U., 1970, MS, 1974, PhD, 1984. Tchr. high sch.; asst. dir. then dir. Ill. State Regional Edn. Svc. Ctr.; mem. Ill. State Senate, 1984-88, 101st-105th Congresses from 22nd (now 19th) Ill. Dist., 1989—; ranking minority mem. small bus. subcom. on govt. programs, mem. transp. and infrastructure com. Served with U.S. Army. Democrat. Office: US Ho of Reps 2334 Rayburn HOB Washington DC 20515*

POSIN, DANIEL Q., physics educator, television lecturer; b. Turkestan, Aug. 13, 1909; came to U.S., 1918, naturalized, 1927; s. Abram and Anna (Izritz) P.; m. Frances Schweitzer, 1934; children: Dan, Kathryn. A.B., U. Cal., 1932, A.M., 1934, Ph.D., 1935. Instr. U. Cal., 1932-37; prof. U. Panama, 1937-41; dean natural scis. U. Mont., prof., 1941-44, chmn. dept. physics and math., 1942-44; staff Mass. Inst. Tech., 1944-46; prof. physics, chmn. dept. N.D. State Coll., Fargo, 1946-55; prof. dept. physics DePaul U., 1956-67; prof. phys. sci. dept. Calif. State U., San Francisco, 1967—; chmn. dept. interdisciplinary scis. Calif. State U., 1969—; dir. Schwab Sci. Lecture Series, Atoms for Peace exhibit Mus. Sci. and Industry, Chgo.; Chief cons. Borg Warner Sci. Hall and Allied Chem. Sci. Hall, Times Square; scientific cons. CBS-TV. (Recipient 6 Emmy awards for best educator on TV in Chgo., and best ednl. TV programs). Author: Trigonometria, 1937-41, Fisica Experimental, Fisica, 1937-41, Mendeleyev—The Story of a Great Scientist,

1948, I Have Been to the Village, with Introduction by Einstein, 1948, rev. edit., 1974, Out of This World, 1959, What is a Star, 1961, What is Chemistry, 1961, What is a Dinosaur, 1961, The Marvels of Physics, 1961, Find Out, 1961, Chemistry for the Space Age, 1961, Experiments and Exercises in Chemistry, 1961, What is Matter, 1962, What is Electronic Communication, 1962, What is Energy, Dr. Posin's Giants, 1962, Life Beyond our Planet, 1962, Man and the Sea, 1962, Man and the Earth, 1962, Man and the Jungle, 1962, Man and the Desert, 1962, Science in the Age of Space, 1965, Rockets and Satellites, Our Solar System, The Next Billion Years, 1973; contbr. to: Today's Health; sci. cons.: Compton's Yearbook; contbr. to: feature articles Chgo. Tribune, (book) After Einstein-Remembering Einstein, 1981; co-contbr. to book The Courage to Grow Old, 1989; appearances, CBS Radio-TV, WTTW-WGN-TV, 1956-67, NET; ABC TV series Dr. Posin's Universe. Chmn. edn. com. Chgo. Heart Assn., 1963-67; Trustee Leukemia Soc. James T. Grady award Am. Chem. Soc., 1972. Fellow Am. Phys. Soc.; mem. A.A.A.S., Phi Beta Kappa, Sigma Xi.

POSIN, KATHRYN OLIVE, choreographer; b. Butte, Mont., Mar. 23, 1943; d. Daniel Q. and Frances (Schweitzer) P. BA in Dance, Bennington Coll., 1965; MFA in Interdisciplinary and World Dance, NYU, 1994; studies in composition, 1965-78, studies in ballet, 1965-90, studies in modern dance, 1967-80, studies in Alexander, Feldenkreis Techs., 1989-91; physiotherapy tng. with Marika Molnar, West Side Sports Medicine, 1994. Mem. dance co. Am. Dance Theater at Lincoln Ctr., 1965; dancer Anna Sokolow Dance Co., 1965-73; artistic dir. Kathryn Posin Dance Co., N.Y.C., 1972-91; choreographer Eliot Feld Ballet, N.Y.C., 1978, Netherlands Dance Theater, Den Hague, Switzerland, 1980, Alvin Ailey Am. Dance Theater, N.Y.C., 1980; mem. dance faculty U. Wis., Milw., 1984-86, choreographer, 1984-88; tchr., choreographer UCLA, 1988-90, Trinity Coll., Hartford, Conn., 1990-91; mem. dance faculty, choreographer U. Calif., Santa Barbara, 1986; tchr. dance technique and performance Tchr.'s Coll. Columbia U., spring 1990; tchr. composition and technique Nat. Inst. of Arts, Taiwan, 1991; tchr. ballet Hofstra, U., Hempstead, L.I., 1992; tchr. improvisation and repertory CCNY, 1994; guest educator various univs. and performing cos., 1969-94; participant or spkr. profl. confs. Choreographer (performing cos./orgns.) Cherry Orchard, Lincoln Ctr., N.Y.C., 1978, Ballet West, Salt Lake City, 1981, Ohio Ballet, Akron, 1982, Ballet Pacifica, Laguna Beach, Calif., 1993, others, including The Netherlands Dance Theater, Alvin Ailey Am. Dance Theater, Eliot Feld Ballet, Ohio Ballet, Repertory Dance Theater Utah, Extemporary Dance Co. London, Balletmet, Columbus, Ohio, Milw. Ballet, 1996, Cin. Ballet, 1997; (prin. works) Salvation, Off-Broadway, N.Y.C., 1969, Waves, 1975 (Am. Dance Festival commn.), Lotta, N.Y. Shakespeare Festival, 1979, The Cherry Orchard, N.Y. Shakespeare Festival, 1979, Mary Stuart, Acting Co., 1980, Shady Grove (grantee joint program of Ohio Arts and Humanities Couns. 1991), Later That Day, 1980, The Tempest, Am. Shakespeare Festival, Strratford, Conn., 1982, Midsummer Night's Dream, Arena Stage, Washington, 1982, Boys From Syracuse, Am. Repertory Theater, Harvard U., 1983, The Paper Gramophone, Hartford Stage, 1989, Of Rage and Remembrance, 1990 (Premiere of Yr. in Music and Dance, Milw. Jour.), Stepping Stones, 1993 (co-recipient Meet the Composer/Choreographer award Milw. Ballet 1993), many others; subject of documentary Kathy's Dance. Grantee Guggenheim Found., 1978, N.Y. State Coun. on Arts, 1977, 79, 80, Jerome Robbins Found., 1972; grantee Nat. Endowment for Arts 1981, 82, 85-87, choreography fellow, 1995-96; Doris Humphrey fellow Am. Dance Festival, New London, Conn., 1968; co-recipient Meet the Composer award for Alvin Ailey Repertory Co., 1994. Office: Kathryn Posin Dance Co 20 Bond St New York NY 10012-2406

POSLER, GERRY LYNN, agronomist, educator; b. Cainsville, Mo., July 24, 1942; s. Glen L. and Helen R. (Maroney) P.; m. O. Shirley Weeda, June 23, 1963; children: Mark L., Steven C., Brian D. BS, U. Mo., 1964, MS, 1966; PhD, Iowa State U., 1969. Asst. prof. Western (Macomb) Ill. U., 1969-74; assoc. prof. Kans. State U., Manhattan, 1974-80, prof., 1980—, asst. dept. head, 1982-90, dept. head, 1990—. Contbr. articles to profl. jours. and popular publs., abstracts, book reviews. Fellow Am. Soc. Agronomy, Crop Sci. Soc. Am.; mem. Am. Forage Grassland Coun., Crop Science Soc. Am. (C-3 div. chmn. 1991), Coun. Agrl. Science Tech. (Cornerstone club), Nat. Assn. Colls. Tchrs. Agr. (tchr. fellow award 1978, ensminger interstate dist. teaching award, 1987, north cen. region dir. 1989, v.p. 1990, pres. 1991; life mem.), Kans. Assn. Colls. Tchrs. Agr. (pres. 1983-85), Kans. Forage Grassland Coun. (bd. dirs. 1989-92), Gamma Sigma Delta (Outstanding Faculty award 1991, pres. 1987). Home: 3001 Montana Ct Manhattan KS 66502-2300 Office: Kans State U Dept Agronomy Throckmorton Hall Manhattan KS 66506

POSNER, DONALD, art historian; b. N.Y.C., Aug. 30, 1931; s. Murray and Frances (Teitel) P.; 1 dau., Anne Tyre. A.B., Queens Coll., 1956; M.A., Harvard U., 1957; Ph.D., NYU, 1962. Lectr. Queens Coll., 1957; asst. prof. art history Columbia U., 1961-62; mem. faculty Inst. Fine Arts, NYU, 1962—, Ailsa Mellon Bruce prof. fine arts, 1975—, acting dir. Inst. Fine Arts, 1978-79, now dep. dir.; Robert Sterling Clark prof. Williams Coll., 1973; William R. Kenan, Jr. prof. U. Va., 1976-77; vis. prof. U. Wash., 1991. Author: Annibale Carracci, 1971, Watteau: A Lady at Her Toilet, 1973, Seventeenth and Eighteenth Century Art, 1971, Antoine Watteau, 1984; editor-in-chief: The Art Bull, 1968-71. Served with USAF, 1951-55. Am. Acad. in Rome fellow, 1959-61; Inst. for Advanced Study fellow, 1976; recipient Charles Rufus Morey award, 1972. Mem. Coll. Art Assn. Am. (dir. 1970-74), Am. Soc. 18th Century Studies. Office: Inst Fine Arts 1 E 78th St New York NY 10021-0102

POSNER, EDWARD MARTIN, lawyer; b. Phila., Oct. 20, 1946. BA, Amherst Coll., 1968; JD, Harvard U., 1974. Bar: Pa. 1974. Exec. asst. to sec. of pub. welfare Commonwealth of Pa., Harrisburg, 1971-72; assoc. Drinker, Biddle & Reath, Phila., 1974-80, ptnr., 1980—. Democrat. Avocation: fly fishing. Office: Drinker Biddle & Reath 1345 Chestnut St Philadelphia PA 19107-3426

POSNER, GARY HERBERT, chemist, educator; b. N.Y.C., June 2, 1943; s. Joseph M. and Rose (Klein) P.; children: Joseph, Michael. BA, Brandeis U., 1965; MA, Harvard U., 1965, PhD, 1968. Asst. prof. Johns Hopkins U., Balt., 1969-74, assoc. prof., 1974-79, prof. dept. chemistry, 1979—, Scowe prof. chemistry, 1989—; prof. dept. environ. chemistry Johns Hopkins U., 1982—, chmn. dept. of chemistry, 1987-90; cons. Batelle Meml. Inst., Columbus, Ohio, 1983, S.W. Rsch. Inst., San Antonio, Nova Pharm. Co., Balt.; mem. Fulbright-Hays Adv. Screening Com. in Chemistry, 1978-81; Fulbright lectr. U. Paris, 1976; Michael vis. prof. Weizmann Inst. Sci., Rehovot, Israel, 1983; leader Round Table discussion Welch Found. Conf. Chem. Rsch., Houston, 1973, 83; Plenary lectr. Nobel Symposium on Asymmetric Synthesis, Sweden, 1984. Author: Introduction to Organic Synthesis Using Organocopper Reagents, 1980; mem. editl. bd. Organic Reactions, 1976-89; exec. editor Tetrahedron Reports, 1996. Named Chemist of Yr., State of Md., 1987; fellow Japan Soc. for Promotion Sci., 1991; recipient Johns Hopkins U. Disting. Tchng. award, 1994. Mem. AAAS, Am. Chem. Soc., AAUP, NIH (medicinal chemistry study sect. 1986-89), Phi Beta Kappa. Office: Johns Hopkins U Dept Chemistry 3300 N Charles St Baltimore MD 21218

POSNER, JEROME BEEBE, neurologist, educator; b. Cin., Mar. 20, 1932; s. Philip and Rose (Goldberg) P.; m. Gerta Grunen, Aug. 29, 1954; children: Roslyn, Joel, P.J. BS, U. Wash., 1951, MD, 1955. Intern King County Hosp., Seattle, 1955-56; asst. resident in neurology U. Wash. Affiliated Hosps., Seattle, 1956-59; fellow in neurology U. Wash. Affiliated Hosps., 1958-59; spl. fellow NIH, U. Wash., 1961-63; instr. medicine U. Louisville Sch. Medicine, 1959-61; attending neurologist King County Hosp., 1962-63; asst. prof. neurology Cornell U. Med. Coll., N.Y.C., 1963-67; assoc. prof. Cornell U. Med. Coll., 1967-70, prof., 1970—, vice chmn. dept. neurology, 1978-87; asst. attending neurologist N.Y. Hosp., 1963-67, asso. attending neurologist, 1967-70, attending neurologist, 1970—; asso. Cotzias Lab. of Neuro-Oncology, Sloan Kettering Inst. Cancer Research, N.Y.C., 1967-76; mem. Cotzias Lab. of Neuro-Oncology, Sloan Kettering Inst. Cancer Research, 1976—; chief neuropsychiat. service, attending physician dept. medicine Meml. Hosp. for Cancer and Allied Diseases, 1967-75, attending physician, 1975—, chmn. dept. neurology, 1975-87, 89-97, Cotzias chair neuro-oncology, 1986—; Evelyn Frew clin. rsch. prof. Am. Cancer Soc., 1996—; mem. med. adv. bd. Burke Rehab. Ctr., White Plains, N.Y., 1973—; adj. prof., vis. physician Rockefeller U. and Hosp., N.Y.C., 1973-75; mem. neurology B study sect. NIH, 1972-76. Author: (with F. Plum) Diagnosis of Stupor and Coma, 3d edit., 1980, (with H. Gilbert and L. Weiss) Brain Metastasis, 1980, Neurologic Complications of Cancer, 1995; mem. editorial bd. Archives of Neurology, 1971-76, Annals of Neurology, 1976-80, Am. Jour. Medicine, 1978-93, Neurology, 1992—; contbr. articles to med. jours. Served with M.C. U.S. Army, 1959-61. Fellow AAAS; mem. AMA, Am. Acad. Neurology (Farber Brain Tumor award 1988), Am. Assn. Cancer Rsch., Am. Fedn. Clin. Rsch., Am. Neurol. Assn., Am. Physiol. Soc., Assn. Am. Physicians, Harvey Soc., Inst. Medicine of N.Y. Acad. Scis., Soc. Neurosci., Can. Neurol. Soc. (hon.), Alpha Omega Alpha. Office: Meml Sloan-Kettering Cancer 1275 York Ave New York NY 10021-6007

POSNER, LOUIS JOSEPH, lawyer, accountant; b. N.Y.C., May 29, 1956; s. Alex Pozner and Hilda G. (Gottlieb) Weinberg; m. Betty F. Osin, June 21, 1986; 1 child, Daniel. BS in Acctg., Drexel U., 1979; MS in Taxation, Pace U., 1985; JD, N.Y. Law Sch., 1989. Bar: N.Y. 1990, N.J. 1990, U.S. Dist. Ct. (so. and ea. dists.) N.Y., 1990, D.C. 1991, U.S. Ct. Appeals (2d cir.) 1993, U.S. Supreme Ct. 1994. Auditor Arthur Andersen & Co., CPAs, Phila., 1979-81; tax sr. Kenneth Leventhal & Co., CPAs, N.Y.C., 1981-82; tax mgr. Mann Judd Landau, CPAs, N.Y.C., 1983-86; tax dir. Integrated Resources, Inc., N.Y.C., 1986-89; pvt. practice N.Y.C., 1989—; spkr. in field. Producer, dir. TV show Your Legal Rights. Mem. ABA, AICPA, Assn. Bar City N.Y., N.Y. State Soc. CPA's (tax com. 1985-90, mem. faculty N.Y.C. chpt. Found. for Acctg. Edn. 1989-90), Mensa (coord. spl. interest group N.Y.C. chpt. 1978-90). Home: 300 E 71st St Apt 11J New York NY 10021-5248 Office: 488 Madison Ave Fl 6 New York NY 10022-5702

POSNER, RICHARD ALLEN, federal judge; b. N.Y.C., Jan. 11, 1939; s. Max and Blanche Posner; m. Charlene Ruth Horn, Aug. 13, 1962; children: Kenneth A., Eric A. AB, Yale U., 1959; LLB, Harvard U., 1962; LLD (hon.), Syracuse U., 1986, Duquesne U., 1987, Georgetown U., 1992; Dr. honoris causa, U. Ghent, 1995, Yale U., 1996. Bar: N.Y. 1963, U.S. Supreme Ct. 1966. Law clk. Justice William J. Brennan Jr. U.S. Supreme Ct., Washington, 1962-63; asst. to commr. FTC, Washington, 1963-65; asst. to solicitor gen. U.S. Dept. Justice, Washington, 1965-67; gen. counsel Pres.'s Task Force on Communications Policy, Washington, 1967-68; assoc. prof. Stanford U. Law Sch., Calif., 1968-69; prof. U. Chgo. Law Sch., 1969-78, Lee and Brena Freeman prof., 1978-81, sr. lectr., 1981—; circuit judge U.S. Ct. Appeals (7th cir.), Chgo., 1981—, chief judge, 1993—; research assoc. Nat. Bur. Econ. Research, Cambridge, Mass., 1971-81; pres. Lexecon Inc., Chgo., 1977-81. Author: Antitrust Law: An Economic Perspective, 1976, Economic Analysis of Law, 4th edit., 1992, The Economics of Justice, 1981, The Federal Courts: Crisis and Reform, 1985 (with William M. Landes) The Economic Structure of Tort Law, 1987, Law and Literature: A Misunderstood Relation, 1988, The Problems of Jurisprudence, 1990, Cardozo: A Study in Reputation, 1990, Sex and Reason, 1992, The Essential Holmes, 1992, (with Tomas J. Philipson) Private Choices and Public Health: The AIDS Epidemic in Economic Perspective, 1993, Overcoming Law, 1995, Aging and Old Age, 1995, The Federal Courts: Challenge and Reform, 1996, Law and Legal Theory in England and America, 1996; pres. Harvard Law Rev., 1961-62; editor Jour. Legal Studies, 1972-81. Fellow AAAS, Am. Law Inst., Brit. Acad.; mem. Am. Econ. Assn., Am. Law and econ. Assn. (pres. 1995-96). Office: US Ct Appeals 7th Cir 219 S Dearborn St Chicago IL 60604

POSNER, RONI D., professional organization executive; b. Bklyn.. BA in Secondary Edn. English/Speech, Rider Coll., Trenton, N.J.; MEd in Ednl. Adminstrn., Northeastern U., Boston, EdD in Ednl. Adminstrn.; Cert. Advanced Studies in Adminstrn., Harvard U. Tchr. bus. English Boston Pub. Schs.; asst. to assoc. commr. Mass. State Dept. Occupl. Edn.; coord. fed. projects Franklin (Mass.) Pub. Schs.; asst. exec. dir. for profl. devel. Am. Vocat. Assn.; exec. dir. Women in Comm., Inc.; dir. Fin. Women Internat., Inc.; exec. dir. Inst. for Local Self-Reliance, Washington. Office: Inst for Local Self-Reliance 2425 18th St NW Washington DC 20009-2003

POSNER, ROY EDWARD, finance executive; b. Chgo., Aug. 24, 1933; s. Lew and Julia (Cvetan) P.; m. Donna Lea Williams, June 9, 1956 (div. May 1991); children: Karen Lee, Sheryl Lynn. Student, U. Ill., 1951-53, Internat. Accountants Soc., 1956-59, Loyola U., Chgo., 1959; grad., Advanced Mgmt. Program, Harvard U., 1976. CPA, Ill. Pub. acct. Frank W. Dibble Co., Chgo., 1956-61; supr. Harris, Kerr, Forster & Co. (C.P.A.s), Chgo., 1961-66; with Loews Corp., N.Y.C., 1966—; v.p. fin. svcs., chief fin. officer Loews Corp., 1973-86, sr. v.p., chief fin. officer, 1986—; find. cons. N.Y. Football Giants, Inc., Rutherford, N.J.; bd. dirs. Bulova Italy S.P.A., Milan, Bulova Systems and Instruments Corp., N.Y.C., Loews Hotels Monaco S.A.M., Monte Carlo, Monaco, Loews Internat. Svcs. S.A., Switzerland, G F Corp., Youngstown, Ohio, Taj Mahal Holding Corp., Atlantic City. Mem. editorial com.: Uniform System of Accounting for Hotels, 7th edit. Pres. No. Regional Valley High Sch. Music Parents Assn., 1978-79; trustee Loews Found., N.Y.C. With U.S. Army, 1953-55. Mem. AICPA, Fin. Execs. Inst., Ins. Acctg. and Stats. Assn., Internat. Hospitality Accts. Assn., Am. Hotel and Motel Assn., Ill. Soc. CPAs, N.Y. State CPAs (chmn. com. on hotel restaurant and club acctg. 1980-82), Tri-County Golf Assn. (treas. 1985-88, v.p. 1988-89), Alpine Country Club (bd. govs. 1982-94, exec. com. 1982-90, pres. 1988-90), Delta Tau Delta. Home: 273 Whitman St Haworth NJ 07641-1315 Office: Loews Corp 667 Madison Ave New York NY 10021-8029

POSNER, SIDNEY, advertising executive; b. Syracuse, N.Y., Jan. 14, 1924; s. Harry and Fannie (Hoffman) P.; m. Miriam Frances Kaplowitz, June 8, 1952; children: Steven Charles, Peter Scott, Robert Keith. BS, Syracuse U., 1947. Asst. advt. mgr. Rudolph Bros., Syracuse, 1947-48; copy chief Kaletski Advt. Agy., Syracuse, 1948-50; promotion mgr. Photo Trade News, N.Y.C., 1950-53; asst. to pres. Dobin Advt. Agy., N.Y.C.; pres. S. Posner & Co. Advt. Agy., N.Y.C., 1955-59, Constellation Art Corp., 1959-76, Communicorp, N.Y.C., 1959-76, Bus. Counselors Corp., N.Y.C., 1959-76, Newmark, Posner & Mitchell Inc., N.Y.C., 1959-92, Posner Comm. Inc., Boca Raton, Fla., 1993-94. Office: Posner Comm Assocs Inc 17547 Bocaire Way Boca Raton FL 33487-1109

POSOKHOV, IOURI, ballet dancer, educator; b. Lougansk, Ukraine, July 20, 1964; came to U.S., 1994; s. Mikail and Alla (Korotkova) P.; m. Anna Yurievna Titova, July 9, 1988; 1 child, Danila Yurievich. Student, Choreographic Acad. Bolshoi, Moscow, 1982. Dancer Bolshoi Ballet, 1982-92, mem. corps de ballet, soloist, 1982-87, prin. dancer, 1987-92; prin. dancer Royal Danish Ballet, Copenhagen, 1992-94, San Francisco Ballet, 1994—. Dancer performing in Sleeping Beauty, Swan Lake, Nutcracker, Bayadera, Raymonda,Romeo and Juliet, La Sylphide, Les Sylphides, Prodigal Son, Sirano de Berjerak, Violin Concerto, Mahler 5th Symphony, Somnambula, Sonata, Polaka, Kindertottenlieder, Divertimento # 15, Gizelle, Handel a Celebration, Tzigan, Tchaikovsky Pas de Deux, Tuning Game, Lambarena, The Lesson, In the Night, Maninyas, Rubies, Criss-Cross. Home: 435 9th Ave Apt 4 San Francisco CA 94118-2947 Office: San Francisco Ballet 455 Franklin St San Francisco CA 94102-4438

POSPISIL, GEORGE CURTIS, biomedical research administrator; b. Thomas, Okla., Aug. 8, 1945; s. George Frank and Zelpha Earline (Hensley) P.; children: Heather Elizabeth, Derek Curtis. Student Wheaton Coll., 1963-64; BA, U. Okla., 1968, MA, 1971. Peace Corps tchr., Maseru, Lesotho, Southern Africa, 1973-74; dir. health services fin. project State of Wis., Madison, 1975-76; pub. health advisor USPHS, Rockville, Md., 1972-73, program/policy analyst, 1977-81, contract mgr., 1982-84, program/policy analyst, 1984-86; dir. Services Crime Victims/Witnesses Project, Tioga County, N.Y., 1986—; guest lectr. U. Wis., Summer Inst., Carthage Coll.; analyst biomed. rsch. program NIH, 1989—; sci. editor The Johns Hopkins U. Krieger Mind/Brain Inst., 1993-95; exec. coun. NIH Recreation and Welfare Assn. Mem. Rockville Humanities Commn., 1981-83; spokesperson Neighborhood Planning Com., 1980-82; coordinator mental health svcs. Cuban Refugee Project, Ft. McCoy, Wis., 1980; sec. cmty. adv. com. mental health program Montgomery House, 1982-86; rsch. and tng. adminstr. Cornell U., Ithaca, N.Y., 1986-89; bd. dirs. Family Svc. Montgomery County, 1984-86; legis. fellow U.S. Senate Labor and Human Resources Com./Health Office, 1991; mem. county Spl. Olympics Com., 1982-86; mem. Citizens' Planning Subcom. Carroll County, Md., 1992-93, dep. comdr. CAP squadron; mem. adv. com. Boy Scouts Am. troop 321; bd. dirs. Shepherd's Staff Cmty. Svc. program; mem. Am. Friends Svc. Com.; bd. dirs. Westminster Ch. of the Brethren. Mem. Soc. Rsch. Adminstrs. Editor: Decade of the Brain, 1990, Maximizing Human Potential: Decade of the Brain, 1991. Office: Nat Inst Neurol Disorders NIH 9000 Rockville Pike Rm 8a03 Bethesda MD 20814-1436 *The highest purpose of your business or position is to provide a base to allow you to serve others. When providing basic service, always try to add value to it for the benefit of your client.*

POSPISIL, LEOPOLD JAROSLAV, anthropology and law educator; b. Olomouc, Czechoslovakia, Apr. 26, 1923; came to U.S., 1949, naturalized, 1954; s. Leopold and Ludmila (Petrlak) P.; m. Zdenka Smyd, Jan. 31, 1945; children: Zdenka, Mira. Juris Universae Candidatus, Charles U., Prague, Czechoslovakia, 1947, JD, 1991; BA in Sociology, Willamette U., Salem, Oreg., 1950; MA in Anthropology, U. Oreg., 1952; PhD, Yale U., 1956; ScD (hon.), Willamette U., 1969; PhD (hon.), Charles U., Prague, Czech Rep., 1994. Instr. Yale U., New Haven, 1956-57, asst. prof., 1957-60; asst. curator Peabody Mus., 1956-60, assoc. prof., 1960-65, prof., curator, 1965-93, dir. divsn. anthropology, 1966-93; prof. anthropology, 1965-93, prof. and curator emeritus, 1993—. Author: Kapauku Papuans and Their Law, 1958, Kapauku Papuan Economy, 1963, Kapauku Papuans of West New Guinea, 1963, Anthropology of Law, 1971, Ethnology of Law, 1972, Anthropologie des Rechts, 1981, Obernberg: Quantitative Analysis of a Tyrolean Economy, 1996; contbr. articles to profl. jours. Guggenheim fellow, 1962, NSF fellow, 1962, 64-65, 67-71, NIMH fellow, 1973-79; Social Sci. Rsch. Coun. grantee, 1966. Fellow AAAS, N.Y. Acad. Scis., Am. Anthrop. Assn.; mem. NAS, Conn. Acad. Arts and Scis., Explorers Club, Czechoslovakian Acad. Arts and Scis. (past pres.), Coun. Free Czechoslovakia, Assn. for Polit. and Legal Anthropology (pres.-at-large), Assn. for Social Anthropology in Oceania, Soc. for Econ. Anthropology, Sigma Xi. Home: 554 Orange St New Haven CT 06511-3819 Office: Yale U Dept Anthropology 51 Hillhouse Ave New Haven CT 06511-3703

POSS, JEFFERY SCOTT, architect, educator; b. Harvey, Ill., May 20, 1956. BAS, U. Ill., 1978, MArch, 1980. Intern architect Charles Kober Assocs., Chgo., 1980-81, Skidmore, Owings and Merrill, Chgo., 1981; designer Newman/Lustig and Assocs., Chgo., 1983-84; design assoc. Kevin Roche John Dinkeloo and Assocs., Hamden, Conn., 1985-87; project architect and designer Tai Soo Kim Assocs., Hartford, Conn., 1987-89; pvt. practice Urbana, Ill., 1989—; assoc. prof. U. Ill., Champaign-Urbana, 1989—; invited juror, design work exhibited widely; lectr. in field. Contbr. articles to profl. jours. Recipient First Alt. prize Nat. Inst. for Archtl. Edn., 1981, First Place award Champaign Park Dist./AIA, 1989, Nat. Design award Concrete Steel Reinforcing Inst./AIA, 1992, 2nd Place award for Md. WWII Meml., State of Md., 1996. Mem. AIA (Corp. Ill., Ctrl. Ill. and Champaign-Urbana chpts., Excellence in Edn. Honors award 1993, Ctrl. Ill. award for design excellence, 1993), Am. Soc. Archtl. Perspectives (Excellence in Graphic Representation Architecture award 1990, 93). Office: 909 E Water St Urbana IL 61802-2841

POST, AUGUST ALAN, economist, artist; b. Alhambra, Calif., Sept. 17, 1914; s. Edwin R. and Edna (Stickney) P.; m. Helen E. Wills, Nov. 21, 1940; 1 child, David Wills. AB, Occidental Coll., 1938; student Chouinard Inst. Art, 1938; MA, Princeton, 1940; LLD, Golden Gate U., 1972, Occidental Coll., 1974, Claremont Grad. Sch., 1978. In banking bus., 1933-36; instr. econs. Occidental Coll., 1940-42; asst. prof. Am. U., 1943; economist Dept. State, 1944-45; rsch. dir. Utah Found., 1945-46; chief economist, adminstrv. analyst State of Calif., 1946-50, state legis. analyst, 1950-77; cons. Com. Higher Edn. and State, 1964; mem. Nat. Com. Support of Public Schs., 1967; mem. nat. adv. panel Nat. Center Higher Edn. Mgmt. Systems, 1971-72; chmn. Calif. Gov.'s Commn. on Govt. Reform, 1978; mem. faculty U. So. Calif. Grad. Sch. Pub. Adminstrn., 1978-80; Regents' prof. U. Calif., Davis, 1983, vis. prof., 1984-85; spl. cons. Touche Ross and Co., 1977-87; cons., interim exec. dir. Calif. Commn. for Rev. of Master Plan for Higher Edn., 1985 ; mem. adv. bd. Calif. Tomorrow nat. shows and one-man shows; dir. Crocker Art Gallery Assn., pres., 1966-67. Trustee U. Calif., Berkeley, Art Mus., 1986-91; mem. adv. com. on future ops. Coun. State Govts., 1965; bd. mgrs., pres. YMCA; bd. dirs. Sacramento Civic Ballet Assn.; trustee Calif. Coll. Arts and Crafts, 1982-86; chmn. Calif. State Task Force on Water Future, 1981-82, Sacramento Regional Found., bd. dirs., 1983-91; bd. dirs. Calif. Mus. Assn., pres., 1976-77, Policy Analysis for Calif. Edn., 1985—, Senate Adv. Commn. on Control of Cost of State Govt., 1986—, Pub. Policy Inst. Calif., 1994—; co-chmn. Calif. Citizen's Budget Commn., 1992; chmn. Citizens Commn. on Ballot Initiatives, 1992—, Catalonia Sister State Task Force, 1988—, Commn. on Innovation, Calif. Community Colls., 1992, Judicial Coun. Select com. on Judicial Retirement, 1993—; mem. Supreme Ct. Select com. Judicial Ethics, 1995-96; bd. dirs. Central Valley Found., 1994—. With USNR, 1943-44. Mem. Nat. Acad. Public Adminstrn., Phi Beta Kappa, Kappa Sigma. Home: 1900 Rockwood Dr Sacramento CA 95864-1527

POST, AVERY DENISON, retired church official; b. Norwich, Conn., July 29, 1924; s. John Palmer and Dorothy (Church) P.; m. Margaret Jane Rowland, June 8, 1946; children: Susan Post Ross, Jennifer C., Elizabeth Post Elliott, Anne Post Roy. B.A., Ohio Wesleyan U., 1946; B.D., Yale U., 1949, S.T.M., 1952; L.H.D. (hon.), Lakeland Coll., Sheboygan, Wis., 1977; D.D. (hon.), Chgo. Theol. Sem., 1978, Middlebury Coll. (Vt.), 1978, Defiance Coll. (Ohio), 1979; LL.D. (hon.), Heidelberg Coll. (Ohio), 1982, Chapman Coll.; Litt.D. (hon.), Elmhurst Coll. Ordained to ministry, 1949; pastor chs. in Vt., Ohio, Conn. and N.Y., 1946-63; sr. minister Scarsdale (N.Y.) Congl. Ch., 1963-70; minister, pres. Mass. conf. United Ch. Christ, 1970-77; pres. United Ch. Christ, N.Y.C., 1977-89; mem. central com. World Council Chs., 1978-91; exec. com., bd. govs. Nat. Council Chs., 1977-89; moderator, planning com. 7th Gen. Assembly World Coun. Chs.; lectr. Bible Adelphi Coll., Garden City, N.Y., 1958-59; Luccock lectr. Yale U. Div. Sch., 1961; lectr. homiletics Union Sem., N.Y.C., 1967-69, bd. dirs., 1967-77; trustee Andover Newton Theol. Sem., 1970-80; del. numerous internat. ch. meetings; sr. fellow Hartford Sem., 1989-93. Bd. dirs. Bridges for Peace, 1990-94; exec. dir. Bangor Theol. Sem., Hanover, N.H., 1991-93. With USNR, 1943-45. Decorated Comdr.'s Cross (Federal Republic Germany), 1990; recipient 1st Ecumenical award Mass. Coun. Chs., 1976; Disting. Achievement award Ohio Wesleyan U., 1983. Mem. PTA (life), Randolph Mountain Club (N.H.), Phi Beta Kappa, Omicron Delta Kappa. Democrat. Home: PO Box 344 124 Beaver Meadow Rd Norwich VT 05055

POST, BOYD WALLACE, forester; b. Glouster, Ohio, Oct. 5, 1928; s. Herbert Dwight and Fern Hazel (Wallace) P.; m. Vivian Joan Baker, July 19, 1952; children: Rebecca Jane, Martha Eleanor, Boyd Wallace, Charles Christopher. BS, Ohio U., 1950; M in Forestry, Duke U., 1958, D in Forestry, 1962. Weather observer US Weather Bur., 1948; soil conservationist trainee, Soil Conservation Service USDA, 1948, firefighting laborer Forest Service, 1949; weather observer USAF, 1950, pers. officer, 1952; asst. ranger Ohio Div. Forestry, 1953; asst. prof., asst. forester U. Vermont, Burlington, 1959-67, assoc. prof., assoc. forester, 1967-69; forest biologist CSRS USDA, Washington, 1969-80, 80-81, asst. dept. adminstr., 1981-82, program coordinator, 1982-83, forest biologist, 1984-95; ret., 1995; group leader nat. resources USDA Sci. & Edn. Adminstrn., Washington, 1980; asst. dir. Hawaii Inst. Tropical Agr. & Human Resources, Honolulu, 1983-84. Contbr. articles to profl. jours.; editorial bd. Internat. Jour. Forest Ecology & Mgmt., 1976-90. Co-pres. Juvenile Diabetes Found., N.Va. chpt., 1984-86; scoutmaster Boy Scouts Am., Vienna, Va., 1978-83, asst., 1987-94, chartered orgn. rep., 1994—, dist. activities chmn., 1997—. Fellow AAAS, Soc. Am. Foresters; mem. Internat. Union Foresty Research Orgns., Internat. Soc. Tropical Foresters, Sigma Xi. Lodge: Masons. Avocations: fishing, canoeing, gardening, acting, singing.

POST, DAVID ALAN, broadcast executive, producer; b. N.Y.C., Oct. 20, 1941; s. Emil R. and Ruth (Rosen) P.; m. Arline Goldbrum, June 10, 1962 (div. 1981); children: Randee, Lori, Jill; m. Katlean de Monchy, Dec. 13, 1984. Student, CCNY, 1959-61; grad., Fleigenheimer Ins. Inst., 1961, N.Y. Inst. Fin., 1968. Sales rep. Aetna Life Ins. Casualty, Hartford, Conn., 1961-63; sales mgr. Globe Rubber Products, Phila., 1963-67; ptnr. Zuckerman Smith and Co., N.Y.C., 1968-71; dir. corp. fin. Andersen and Co., N.Y.C., 1971-72; exec. v.p., dir. R.K. Pace Post Investment Bankers, N.Y.C., 1973-76; chmn., chief exec. officer, founder Page Am. Group, Inc., Hackensack, N.J., 1976-86; co-founder, bd. dirs. Cellular Sys. Inc., 1991-92; chmn., founder Channel Am. TV Network, N.Y.C., 1987-96; co-founder Can Do Woman divsn. Can Do Am. TV & Worldwide Web, N.Y.C., 1996—;

founder, chmn. Can Do America, 1996—. Contbr. articles to INC. mag.; creator several TV series. Mem. Nat. Assn. TV Programming Execs. Republican. Jewish. Avocation: writing. Home: 400 E 57th St New York NY 10022-3019 Office: Can Do Woman Divsn Can Do Am TV WW Web 41 Union Sq W Ste 301 New York NY 10023

POST, GAINES, JR., history educator, dean, administrator; b. Madison, Wis., Sept. 22, 1937; s. Gaines and Katherine (Rike) P.; m. Jean Wetherbee Bowers, July 19, 1969; children—Katherine Doris, Daniel Lawrence. B.A., Cornell U., 1959; B.A., Oxford U., 1963; M.A., Stanford U., 1964, Ph.D., 1969. Instr. Stanford U., 1966-69; asst. prof. history U. Tex., Austin, 1969-74, assoc. prof., 1974-83; dean faculty, sr. v.p. Claremont McKenna Coll., Calif., 1983-88, prof., 1988—; exec dir. Rockefeller Found. Commn. on Humanities, 1978-81; fellow Interuniv. Seminar on Armed Forces and Society. Author: The Civil Military Fabric of Weimar Foreign Policy, 1973; (with others) The Humanities in American Life, 1980, Dilemmas of Appeasement: British Deterrence and Defense, 1934-37, 1993; Editor: German Unification: Problems and Prospects, 1992. Mem. exec. com. Forming the Future Project, Austin Ind. Sch. Dist., 1982; mem. Tex. Com. for Humanities, 1981-83; mem. council Calif. Congl. Recognition Program, 1984-88, Calif. Coun. Humanities, 1995—. Rhodes scholar, 1961-63; Am. Council Learned Socs. fellow, 1982-83; Am. Philos. Soc. grantee, 1974. Mem. Community Coll. Humanities Assn. (bd. dirs. 1981-89), Am. Hist. Assn. Home: 850 Columbia Ave Claremont CA 91711-3901 Office: Claremont McKenna Coll Dept History 850 Columbia Ave Claremont CA 91711-3901

POST, GERALD JOSEPH, retired banker, retired air force officer; b. Braintree, Mass., Sept. 27, 1925; s. Robert Z. and Marjorie F. (Dunn) P.; m. Jane Stewart Curry, May 4, 1945; children: Sharyn, Gerald, J., Steven M., Richard J., Sean C., David D., Tracy Post Krupa. M.B.A., U. Chgo., 1958. Commd. 2d lt. U.S. Air Force, 1945, advanced through grades to lt. gen., 1978; comptroller, dir. materiel mgmt. San Antonio Air Materiel Area, 1970-73; dep. chief of Staff for Materiel Mgmt., Wright-Patterson AFB, Ohio, 1973-75; chief of staff Air Force Logistics Command, Wright-Patterson AFB, 1975-77; asst. dep. chief of staff for systems and logistics Hdqrs. USAF, 1977-78, dir. Def. Logistics Agy., 1978-81; ret., 1981; pres. Lackland Nat. Bank, 1981-82. Decorated Def. Disting. Service medal, Legion of Merit with oak leaf cluster, D.F.C., Air medal with 2 oak leaf clusters, others. Mem. Am. Soc. Mil. Comptrollers, Air Force Assn., Am. Inst. Aeros. and Astronautics, Am. Def. Preparedness Assn., Phi Beta Kappa, Beta Gamma Sigma. Home: 12534 Misty Crk San Antonio TX 78232-4629

POST, HOWARD ALLEN, forest industry specialist; b. Mpls., June 14, 1916; s. William Noble and Eva Victoria (Hanson) P.; m. Doloras Clair Nordland, Dec. 6, 1941; children: Philip Noble, Stephen Edward, William Noble, Peter Bentley. BS in Forestry, U. Minn., 1939; MF in Forest Mgmt. and Silviculture, Harvard U., 1942, postgrad., 1994. Forester Colville Indian Reservation, Washington, 1937; with U.S. Forest Svc., various locations, 1939, 64; civil svc. examiner in agriculture and forestry State of Minn., 1939-41; chief materials div. position classifications system War Prodn. Bd., 1942-43; chief China pers. recruitment UN Relief and Rehab. Adminstrn., 1946-47; asst. sec. Soc. Am. Foresters, 1947; adminstrv. forester Minn. and Ont. Paper Co., 1947-57; forester and nat. resources specialist U.S. C. of C., 1957-63; forest industries specialist and team leader Bus. and Def. Svcs. Adminstrn./ Internat. Trade Adminstrn. U.S. Dept. Commerce, Washington, 1965-84; forest industries cons. forest Industries com. on timber valuation and taxation, other Nat. Lumber Mfrs. Assn., 1984—; owner Post Enterprises, Forest Industry Cons.; lectr. in field various univs. U.S. editor World Paper jour. (Britain), Wood Based Panels Internat. column Keeping Posted, 1984—, Xilon Internat. and Perini Jour. (Italy), 1991—; contbr. articles to profl. jours. Com. chmn., scoutmaster, counselor Boy Scouts Am., 1958-80; mem. vestry Episcopal Ch., 1949-57, others. With USAAF, 1943-46, ret., USAFR, 1976. Decorated Air Force Commendation medal; recipient Bronze medal U.S. Dept. Commerce, 1976; named Boy Scouts of Am. Scouter of Yr., 1973. Mem. Tech. Assn. Pulp and Paper Industry, Soc. Am. Foresters, Assn. Cons. Foresters, Ret. Officers Assn., Forest Products Rsch. Soc., Harvard Club (Washington), Mil. Dist. of Washington Club, Nat. Press Club (Harvard group), Am. Legion, Pipers Club Inc., Alpha Zeta. Republican. Home: 6203 Colmac Dr Falls Church VA 22044-1811

POST, MIKE, composer; b. San Fernando Valley, Calif.; children: Jennifer, Aaron. Founder Wellingbrook Singers, First Edition; backup guitar for Dick and Dee, Sammy Davis Jr., Dean Martin; played in Sonny and Cher's band; producer single I Just Dropped In (To See What Condition My Condition Was In); producer/arranger The Mason Williams Phonograph Album (Grammy award); mus. dir. The Andy Williams Show; producer Mac Davis Show; designer various stage shows; composer numerous music scores for TV including (with Pete Carpenter) Toma, The Rockford Files (Grammy award), Baa Baa Black Sheep, Hunter and Magnum P.I., 1968-87, also composer scores for L.A. Law (Grammy award), Doogie Howser, M.D., Wiseguy, Law and Order, Quantum Leap, The-A-Team, The White Shadow, Riptide, Hardcastle & McCormick, Hill Street Blues (Grammy award), Hooperman, Sonny Spoon, The Joan Rivers Show, The Hat Squad, NYPD Blue, NewsRadio; composer TV movies Gidget Gets Married, 1972, The Morning After, 1974, Locusts, 1974, The Invasion of Johnson County, 1976, Scott Free, 1976, Richie Brockelman: Missing 24 Hours, 1976, Dr. Scorpion, 1978, Captain America, 1979, The Night Rider, 1979, Captain America II, 1979, Scouts Honor, 1980, Coach of the Year, 1980, Willi G. Gordon Liddy, 1982, Adam, 1982, Hard Knox, 1984, No Man's Land, 1984, Heart of a Champion, 1985, Stingray, 1985, The Last Precinct, 1986, Adam: His Song Continues, 1986, Destination: America, 1987, Wiseguy, 1987, J.J. Starbuck, 1987, The Ryan White Story, 1989, B.L. Stryker: The Dancer's Touch, 1989, Unspeakable Acts, 1990, Without Her Consent, 1990, The Great Pretender, 1991; (motion pictures) Rabbit Test, 1978, Deep in the Heart, 1981, Running Brave, 1983, Hadley's Rebellion, 1984, Rhinestone, 1984, The River Rat, 1984; producer, arranger, co-writer (with Stephen Geyer) the theme from The Greatest American Hero (Grammy award); music producer, songwriter TV series Cop Rock; arranger various Ray Charles LP's; record producer Dolly Parton's Nine To Five, Peter Allen's I Could've Been A Sailor; album releases include Music from L.A., Law & Otherwise. Established with BMI Found. Pete Carpenter Meml. Fund, 1989. Avocations: golf, running, arm wrestling. Office: c/o Gorfaine Schwartz Agy 3301 Barham Blvd Ste 201 Los Angeles CA 90068-1477 also: Mike Post Prodns 1007 W Olive Ave Burbank CA 91506-2211*

POST, RICHARD BENNETT, retired human resources executive; b. Clyde, Ohio, July 5, 1936; s. Robert Irving and Elinor May (Bennett) P.; m. Nancy Jane Wardlow, Aug. 31, 1956; children: David Bennett, Todd McKinley, Amy Ellen, Brett Richard, Brina Marie. BS in Psychology, Iowa State U., 1958; student, Ohio U., Athens, 1954-56; postgrad., George Washington U., 1959-60, So. Ill. U., Edwardsville, 1972-74. With U.S. Civil Svc. Commn., 1958-79; chief evaluation div. U.S. Civil Svc. Commn., St. Louis, 1967-71; chief staffing div. U.S. Civil Svc. Commn., 1971-74, dep. reg. dir., 1974-79; dep. assoc. dir. staffing U.S. Office Pers. Mgmt., Washington, 1979-81, assoc. dir. staffing, 1982-86; dir. Washington area svc. ctr. U.S. Office Pers. Mgmt., 1986-94; retired, 1994. Recipient Dirs.' Disting. Svc. award U.S. Office Pers. Mgmt., 1986, Dirs.' citation for Exemplary Pub. Svc., 1994. Mem. ASPA, Sr. Execs. Assn. (life), Fed. Exec. Inst. Alumni Assn., Vienna Choral Soc. (pres. 1987-89), Assn. Quality and Participation. Avocations: woodworking, singing, gardening, photography, stamp collecting.

POST, ROBERT CHARLES, law educator; b. Bklyn., Oct. 17, 1947; s. Ted and Thelma (Feifel) P.; m. Fran Layton, Jan. 22, 1981; children: Alexander, Amelia. AB, Harvard U., 1969, PhD, 1980; JD, Yale U., 1977. Bar: D.C. 1979, Calif. 1983. Law clk. to chief judge U.S. Ct. Appeals (D.C. cir.), 1977-78; law clk. to justice William Brennen Jr. U.S. Supreme Ct. D.C., 1978-79; assoc. Williams & Connelly, Washington, 1980-82; acting prof. law U. Calif., Berkeley, 1983-87, prof. law, 1987-94, Alexander F. and May T. Morrison prof. law, 1994—. Editor: Law and the Order of Culture, 1991; author: Constitutional Domains, 1995. Gen. counsel AAUP, 1992-94. Fellow Guggenheim Found., 1990-91, Am. Coun. Gen. Socs., 1990-91. Mem. AAUP, Am. Acad. Arts and Scis., Law & Soc. Assn. Office: U Calif Sch Law Boalt Hall Berkeley CA 94720

POST, ROBERT MORTON, psychiatrist; b. New Haven, Conn., Sept. 16, 1942; s. William B. and Esther (Stolzman) P.; m. Susan Wolf; children: Laura, David. BA, Yale U., 1964; MD, U. Pa., 1968. Resident in psychiatry Mass. Gen. Hosp., Boston, 1969-70; clin. assoc. sect. on psychiatry lab. clin. sci. NIMH, Bethesda, Md., 1970-72, rsch. fellow sect. on psychiatry lab. clin. sci., 1972-73, chief 3-West clin. rsch. unit sect. on psychobiology BPB, 1973-77, chief sect. on psychobiology BPB, 1977-81, chief. biol. psychiatry br., 1981—. Editor: Neurobiology of Mood Disorders, 1984; assoc. editor Psychiatry Rsch. Jour.; editl. bd. Clin. Neuropharmacology, ten other jours. in field; contbr. over 600 articles to profl. jours. With USPHS, 1970-72. Recipient Internat. Anna Monika Psychiat. Rsch. award, 1989. Fellow Am. Coll. Neuropsychopharmacology (Efron Excellence in Rsch. award 1985); mem. Am. Psychiat. Assn. (Found.'s Fund Rsch. award 1983), Soc. Biol. Psychiatry (Bennett Neuropsychiatric Rsch. award 1973), Collegium Internat. Neuro-Psychopharmacologicum. Home: 3502 Turner Ln Chevy Chase MD 20815 Office: NIMH Biol Psychiatry Br Bldg 10 10 Center Dr MSC 1272 Bethesda MD 20892-1272

POST, ROY GRAYSON, nuclear engineering educator; b. Asherton, Tex., June 24, 1923; s. Albert K. and Ruth (Grisham) P.; m. Kate Jordan, Mar. 31, 1946; children: Ruth Jean, Jack K., Carol B., Martha A. BSChemE, U. Tex., 1944, PhD in Chemistry, 1952. Registered profl. nuclear engr., Ariz. Sr. engr. Manhattan Project U. Chgo., 1944-49; sr. engr. Gen. Electric Co., Richland, Wash., 1952-58; sect. head Tex. Instruments, Dallas, 1958-61; prof. nuclear engring. U. Ariz., Tucson, 1961-88, prof. emeritus, 1988—; pres. WM Symposia, Inc., 1992—. Mem. Am. Nuclear Soc. (editor Nuclear Technology Jour. 1969—, sect. chmn. 1986—), Electrochem. Soc. (chmn. Tex. sect. 1960), Am. Inst. Chem. Engrs., AAAS, Sigma Xi. Democrat. Home: PO Box 17690 Tucson AZ 85731-7690 Office: WM Symposia Inc 245 S Plumer Ave Ste 19 Tucson AZ 85719-6347

POSTE, GEORGE HENRY, pharmaceutical company executive; b. Polegate, Sussex, Eng., Apr. 30, 1944; came to U.S., 1972; s. John H. and Kathleen B. (Brooke) P.; m. Mary E. Mudge, Mar. 9, 1968 (div. 1992); 1 child, Eleanor Kathy; m. Linda C. Suhler Lopez, Nov. 21, 1992; stepchildren: John Robert, Lisa Carolyn. DVM, U. Bristol, 1966, PhD, 1969, DSc, 1987, LLD (hon.), 1995. Lectr. Univ. London, 1969-72; assoc. prof. SUNY, Buffalo, 1972-76; prof. pathology Roswell Park Meml. Inst., Buffalo, 1976-80; v.p. rsch. SmithKline Beckman, Phila., 1980-82, v.p. rsch. and devel., 1982-86, v.p. worldwide rsch. and pre-clin. devel., 1987-88, pres. rsch. and devel., 1988-89; pres. rsch. and devel. techs. SmithKline Beecham, King of Prussia, Pa., 1989-90, vice chmn., exec. v.p. rsch. and devel., 1990-91, pres. and chmn. rsch. and devel., 1992—; chief sci. and tech. officer SmithKline Beecham Corp. PLC, King of Prussia, Pa., 1997—, also bd. dirs.; mem. pathology B study sect. NIH, Bethesda, Md., 1978-82; chairperson Gordon Conf., N.H., 1985, 86; pres. coun. U. Tex. M.D. Anderson Cancer Ctr.; mem. adv. coun. Beckman Ctr. for Molecular and Genetic Medicine, Stanford U.; mem. coun. Oxford Internat. Biomedical Centre. Editor: Cell Surface Revs., New Horizons in Therapeutics, Cancer Metastasis Revs., Advanced Drug Delivery Revs., 15 books; contbr. numerous articles to profl. jours. Mem. governing bd. UCLA Symposia, Life Sci. Rsch. Found.; mem. bd. Overseers Sch. Vet. Medicine, U. Penn., Gov.'s adv. com. Sci. and Tech., Pa.; mem. adv. bd. Natural Sci. Assn., U. Pa. Fleming fellow U. Oxford, Eng., 1995; Pitt fellow U. Cambridge, Eng., 1995. Fellow Royal Coll. Veterinary Surgeons, Royal Coll. Pathologists; mem. AAAS, Am. Soc. Cell Biology, Pathol. Soc., Nat. Assn. Biomed. Rsch. (bd. govs. 1984), Univ. Assn. Space Rsch. (mem. coun. 1984), Pharm. Mfrs. Assn. (former chmn. rsch. and devel. section 1988). Avocations: military history, foreign affairs, photography, auto racing. Office: SmithKline Beecham Pharms R & D PO Box 1539 King Of Prussia PA 19406

POSTER, JUNE, performing company executive; b. New York, May 6, 1949. BFA, SUNY, Buffalo, 1970; MA, U. Calif., Berkeley, 1975. Exec. dir. San Francisco Camerawork, 1981-87; dir. devel. Meredith Monk/The House, N.Y.C., 1984-87; dir. fin., domestic booking Merce Cunningham Dance Found., N.Y.C., 1987-90; mng. dir. David Gordon Pick Up co., N.Y.C., 1991-97, Bklyn. Arts & Media Group, 1997—; devel. con. various ind. film projects, N.Y.C., 1991. Office: Brooklyn Arts and Media Group 30 Flatbush Ave Rm 427 Brooklyn NY 11217-1121

POSTER, STEVEN BARRY, cinematographer, photgrapher, publisher, digital imaging consultant; b. Chgo., Mar. 1, 1944; s. David and Lillian Violet (Diamondstone) P. Student, So. Ill. U., 1962-64, L.A. Art Ctr. Coll. Design, 1964-66; BS, Ill. Inst. Tech., 1967. Pres. Posters Internat. Ltd., L.A., 1980. Dir. photography (films) Strange Brew, 1983, Testament, 1984, Heavenly Kid, 1985, Blue City, 1986, The Boy Who Could Fly, 1986, Someone to Watch Over Me, 1986, (Am. Soc. Cinematographers nomination 1987), Big Top Pee Wee, 1987, Next of Kin, 1988, Opportunity Knocks, 1989, Rocky V, 1990, Life Stinks, 1991, Cemetery Club, 1993, Roswell, 1994, Strangers on a Train, 1996, The Color of Justice, 1996, Rocket Man, 1997, UN Chance Sur Deux, 1997. Mem. Am. Soc. Cinematographers (1st v.p.), Leica Hist. Soc. Am., Acad. Motion Picture Arts and Scis., Can. Soc. Cinematographers, Internat. Assn. Panoramic Photographers, Behind the Lens (assoc.), Internat. Alliance of Theatrical and Stage Employees. Democrat. Jewish. Avocations: still photography, computers, bicycles.

POSTERARO, CATHERINE HAMMOND, librarian, gerontology educator; b. Hartford, Conn., Nov. 13, 1946; d. Joseph Francis and Elizabeth Claire (Desmond) Hammond; m. Anthony Francis Posteraro, Jr., June 20, 1970; children: Anthony Francis III, Christopher Clarke. AB, Emmanuel Coll., Boston, 1968; MS, Simmons Coll., 1970; MA, St. Joseph Coll., West Hartford, Conn., 1992. Asst. libr. dir., asst. prof. acad. resources St. Joseph Coll., 1986—, lectr. gerontology, 1991—. Sec., treas. St. Joseph Coll. Faculty Com. of the Whole. Recipient Sister Mary Elizabeth Delice award Inst. Gerontology, St. Joseph Coll., 1992. Mem. ALA, Assn. Coll. and Rsch. Librs. (nat. com. Instrn. for Diverse Population 1994-97, nat. com. continuing edn. com. 1996—), Conn. Libr. Assn., Gerontol. Soc. Am., Sigma Phi Omega (nat. acad. hon. soc. gerontology). Home: 24 Mcdivitt Dr Manchester CT 06040-2240 Office: St Joseph Coll Libr 1678 Asylum Ave Hartford CT 06117-2764

POSTHUMUS, RICHARD EARL, state senator, farmer; b. Hastings, Mich., July 19, 1950; s. Earl Martin and Lola Marie (Wieland) P.; m. Pamela Ann Bartz, June 23, 1972; children—Krista, Lisa, Heather, Bryan. B.S. in Agrl. Econs. and Pub. Affairs Mgmt., Mich. State U., 1972. Exec. v.p. Farmers and Mfrs. Beet Sugar Assn., Saginaw, Mich., 1972-74, Mich. Beef Commn., Lansing, 1974-78; dir. constituent relations Republican Caucus, Mich. Ho. of Reps., 1979-82; self-employed farmer, 1974—. Third vice chmn. Mich. Republican Com., 1971-73; mem. Hope Ch. of the Brethren. Mem. Alpha Gamma Rho. Office: State Senate State Capitol Lansing MI 48909

POSTMA, HERMAN, physicist, consultant; b. Wilmington, N.C., Mar. 29, 1933; s. Gilbert and Sophia Postma; m. Patricia Dunigan, Nov. 25, 1960; children: Peter, Pamela. BS summa cum laude, Duke U., 1955; MS, Harvard U., 1957, PhD, 1959. Registered profl. engr., Calif. Summer staff Oak Ridge Nat. Lab., 1954-57, physicist thermonuclear div., 1959-62, co-leader DCX-1 group, 1962-66, asst. dir. thermonuclear div., 1966, asso. dir. div., 1967, dir. div., 1967-73, dir. nat. lab., from 1974; v.p. Martin Marietta, 1984-88, sr. v.p., 1988-91; vis. scientist FOM-Inst. for Plasma Physics, The Netherlands, 1963; cons. Lab. Laser Energetics, U. Rochester; mem. energy rsch. adv. bd. spl. panel Dept. Energy; bd. dirs. Nashville br. Fed. Res. Bank Atlanta, ICS Corp., PAI Corp., ORAS, Inc., M4 Corp. Mem. editorial bd. Nuclear Fusion, 1968-74; contbr. numerous articles to profl. jours. Bd. dirs. The Nucleus; chmn. bd. trustees Hosp. of Meth. Ch.; mem. adv. bd. Coll. Bus. Adminstrn., U. Tenn., 1976-84, Energy Inst., State of N.C.; bd. dirs., exec. com. Tenn. Tech. Found., 1982-88, Venture Capital Fund; vice chmn., commr. Tenn. Higher Edn. Commn., 1984-92; trustee Duke U., 1987—, Pellissippi State Coll., 1991—; chmn. Meth. Hosp. Found., 1990; mem. adv. bd. Inst. Pub. Policy Vanderbilt U., 1986-88, conf. chmn. 1987. Fellow Am. Phys. Soc. (exec. com. div. plasma physics), AAAS, Am. Nuclear Soc. (dir., chair East Tenn. econ. coun. 1997—); mem. C. of C. (v.p. 1981-83, chmn. 1987), Indsl. Rsch. Inst., Gas Rsch. Inst. (adv. bd. 1986-88), Oak Ridge Rotary (pres. 1996-97), Phi Beta Kappa, Beta Gamma Sigma, Sigma Pi Sigma, Omicron Delta Kappa, Sigma Xi, Pi Mu Epsilon, Phi Eta Sigma. Home and Office: 104 Berea Rd Oak Ridge TN 37830-7829

POSTOL, LAWRENCE PHILIP, lawyer; b. Bridgeport, Conn., Oct. 18, 1951; s. Sidney Samuel and Eunice Ruth (Schine) P.; m. Ellen Margaret Russell, Mar. 22, 1975; children: Raymond Russell, Stephen Russell, Carolyn Russell. BS, Cornell U., 1973, JD, 1976. Bar: Conn. 1976, D.C. 1977, U.S. Dist. Ct. D.C. 1977, U.S. Ct. Appeals (D.C. cir.) 1977, U.S. Supreme Ct. 1980, Va. 1982, U.S. Ct. Appeals (4th cir.) 1982, U.S. Dist. Ct. (ea. dist.) Va. 1985, U.S. Dist. Ct. Md. 1989, U.S. Dist. Ct. Conn. 1990. Assoc. Arent, Fox, Kintner & Plotkin, Washington, 1976-80; assoc. Seyfarth, Shaw, Fairweather & Geraldson, Washington, 1980-83, ptnr., 1985—; assoc. Jones, Day, Reavis and Pogue, Washington, 1983-85; lectr. Loyola U., New Orleans, 1983—, U. Cin., 1987-93; bd. advisers The Environ. Counselor Jour.; spl. counsel Greater Washington Bd. Trade, 1991-93. Author: Legal Guide to Handling Toxic Substances in the Workplace, 1990, Americans with Disabilities Act - A Compliance Manual for Employers, 1993. Jewish. Avocation: sports. Home: 6340 Chowning Pl Mc Lean VA 22101-4129 Office: Seyfarth Shaw Fairweather & Geraldson 815 Connecticut Ave NW Washington DC 20006-4004

POSTON, REBEKAH JANE, lawyer; b. Wabash, Ind., Apr. 20, 1948; d. Bob E. and April (Ogle) P. BS, U. Miami, 1970, JD, 1974. Bar: Fla. 1974, Ohio 1977, U.S. Dist. Ct. (so. and mid. dists.) Fla., U.S. Dist. Ct. (ea. dist.) Wis., U.S. Dist. Ct. (no. dist.) Ohio, U.S.Dist. Ct. (no. dist.) Mich., U.S.Ct. Appeals (5th, 6th, 7th and 11th cirs.). Asst. U.S. atty. U.S. Atty.'s Office, Miami, Fla., 1974-76; spl. atty. organized crime and racketeering sect. Strike Force, Cleve., 1976-78; ptnr. Fine, Jacobson, Schwartz, Nash & Block, Miami, 1978-94, Steel Hector & Davis, Miami, 1994—; adj. prof. U. Miami Law Sch., Coral Gables, 1986; mem. U.S. sentencing guidelines com. So. Dist. of Fla., Miami, 1987-88. Mem. Fla. Bar Assn., Ohio Bar Assn., Nat. Assn. Criminal Def. Attys., Am. Immigration Lawyers Assn., Dade County Bar Assn. Democrat. Lutheran. Avocations: power boat racing, swimming. Home: 1541 Brickell Ave Apt 3706 Miami FL 33129 Office: 200 SE 2nd St Miami FL 33131

POSTON, TOM, actor; b. Columbus, Ohio, Oct. 17, 1927; s. George and Margaret P.; m. Jean Sullivan, 1955; m. Kay Hudson, June 8, 1968; children: Francesca, Hudson, Jason. Student, Bethany Coll., 1938-40. First appeared on stage as a tumbler with The Flying Zebleys; acting and Broadway debuts in Cyrano de Bergerac, 1947; appeared on Broadway, regional theaters, and summer stock; stage appearances include: The Insect Comedy, King Lear, Will Success Spoil Rock Hunter?, Goodbye Again, Best of Burlesque, Romanoff and Juliet, Drink to Me Only, Golden Fleecing, The Conquering Hero, Come Blow Your Horn, Mary, Mary, Forty Carats, But Seriously..., A Funny Thing Happened on the Way to the Forum, The Odd Couple, Bye Bye Birdie, Mother Courage, host WABC-TV series Entertainment, 1955; regular on TV show The Steve Allen Show, 1956-58 (Emmy award for best supporting actor in comedy series 1959); host TV show Split Personality, 1959-60; panelist TV show To Tell the Truth; appeared in TV series On the Rocks, 1975-76, We've Got Each Other, 1977, Mork and Mindy, 1978-82, Newhart, 1982-90, Grace Under Fire, 1993—; numerous TV appearances include The Bob Newhart Show; film appearances include: The Tempest, The City That Never Sleeps, 1953, Zotz, 1962, Soldier in the Rain, 1963, The Old Dark House, 1963, Cold Turkey, 1970, The Happy Hooker, 1975, Rabbit Test, 1978, Up the Academy, 1980, Carbon Copy, 1981. Served with USAAF, World War II. *

POSTON, WALKER SEWARD, II, medical educator, researcher. BA in Biol. Scis., U. Calif., Davis, 1983; PhD, U. Calif., Santa Barbara, 1990. Resident USAF Med. Ctr., Wright-PAtterson AFB, Ohio, 1989-90; dir. psychology svcs., asst. chief mental health svcs. 9th Med. Group, Beale AFB, 1990-92; fellow in behavioral medicine Wilford Hall Med. Ctr., 1992-93; chief health and rehab. psychology svc. Malcolm Grow Med. Ctr., 1993-95, faculty, 1993-95; clin. asst. prof. dept. med. and clin. psychology F. Edward Herbert Sch. Medicine, Bethesda, Md., 1993-95; asst. prof. medicine Baylor Coll. Medicine, Houston, 1995—. Contbr. articles to profl. jours. Recipient Minority Scientist Devel. award Am. Heart Assn., 1995; U. Calif. Doctoral scholars fellow, 1984-85, 85-86, 86-87, 88-89, Clin. fellow Wilford Hall Med. Ctr., Lackland AFB, 1992-93; Nat. Merit scholar, 1979-80. Office: Baylor Coll Medicine Behavior Medicine Rsch Ctr 6535 Fannin MS F-700 Houston TX 77030

POSUNKO, BARBARA, retired elementary education educator; b. Newark, July 17, 1938; d. Joseph and Mary (Prystauk) P. BA, Rutgers U., Newark, 1960; MA, Kean Coll., Union, N.J., 1973; teaching cert., Seton Hall U., Newark, 1966. Cert. elem. tchr., reading specialist, N.J. Social case worker Newark City Hosp., 1960-65; elem. tchr. Plainfield (N.J.) Bd. Edn., 1966; elem., jr. and sr. high sch. tchr. minimum basic skills and reading Sayreville (N.J.) Bd. Edn., 1966-82; tchr. Chpt. I and minimum basic skills Sayreville (N.J.) Bd. Edn., Parlin, 1982-95, cooperating tchr. to student tchrs., 1983-95, coord. testing, 1984-95; ret., 1995; sch. coord. for congressionally mandated study of ednl. growth and opportunity, 1991-95; mem. numerous reading coms. Recipient Outstanding Tchr. award N.J. Gov.'s Tchr. Recognition Program, 1988. Mem. NEA, Internat. Reading Assn., N.J. Reading Assn., N.J. Edn. Assn. Home: 17 Drake Rd Mendham NJ 07945-1805

POSUNKO, LINDA MARY, retired elementary education educator; b. Newark, Dec. 24, 1942; d. Joseph and Mary (Prystauk) P. BA, Newark State Coll., Union, N.J., 1964; MA, Kean Coll., Union, 1974. Cert. permanent elem. tchr., supr., prin., N.J. Elem. tchr. Roselle (N.J.) Bd. Edn., 1964-65; elem. tchr. Garwood (N.J.) Bd. Edn., 1965-92, head tchr., 1974-76, 79-81, head tchr. elem. and early childhood edn., tchr. 1st grade, 1992-95; ret., 1995; cooperating tchr. to student tchrs.; instr. non-English speaking students and children with learning problems; mem. affirmative action, sch. resource coms.; conductor in-svc. workshops on early childhood devel. practices, 1993. Recipient honor cert. Union County Conf. Tchrs. Assn., 1972-73, The Garwood award N.J. Gov.'s Tchr. Recognition Program, 1983, 88, Outstanding Tchr. award N.J. Gov.'s Tchr. Recognition Program, 1988; nominee N.J. Gov.'s Tchr. Recognition award, 1993-94. Mem. ASCD, NEA, Internat. Reading Assn. (bd. dirs. suburban coun.), N.J. Edn. Assn., Garwood Tchrs. Assn. (sec., v.p., pres.), High/Scope Ednl. Found. Home: 17 Drake Rd Mendham NJ 07945-1805

POSVAR, WESLEY WENTZ, university president, educator, consultant; b. Topeka, Sept. 14, 1925; s. Vladimir L. and Marie (Wentz) P.; m. Mildred Miller, Apr. 30, 1950; children: Wesley William, Margot Marina, Lisa Christina. BS, U.S. Mil. Acad., 1946; BA (Rhodes scholar), Oxford U., England, 1951, MA, 1954; MPA, PhD (Littauer fellow), Harvard U., 1964; LLD, LHD, D in Pub. Svc., MIT, 1963-64; rsch. assoc., Center Internat. Studies MIT, 1963-64. Commd. officer USAF; Commd. officer later USAF; fighter test pilot (Air Proving Ground), Fla., 1946-48; pilot (Berlin airlift), 1949; command pilot (S.E. Asia) U.S. Mil. Acad., 1965; mem. long range strategic planning group Hdqrs. USAF, 1954-57; prof. polit. sci., head dept. USAF Acad., 1957-67, brig. gen.; prof. internat. politics U. Pitts., 1967—, pres., 1967-91, pres. emeritus, 1991—; bd. dirs., mutual funds assoc. Federated Investors; exec. com. Allegheny Conf. on Community Devel., 1970-81; founding chmn. Fed. Emergency Mgmt. Adv. Bd., 1978-91, Nat. Adv. Coun. Environ. Policy and Tech., 1986-92; cons. various nat. security agys.; chmn. nat. commns. on emergency telecom., mil. hon. codes, and civil aviation sys. Contbr. articles to books and publs. on mgmt. planning, internat. security, fgn. affairs, higher edn. Trustee Carnegie Endowment for Internat. Peace; adv. trustee RAND Corp.; chmn. bd. trustees Czech Mgmt. Ctr.; dir. U.S. Space Found. Named one of ten outstanding young men U.S. Jr. C. of C., 1959. Mem. Am. Polit. Sci. Assn., Assn. Am. Rhodes Scholars, Internat. Studies Assn. (co-founder, pres. 1961-62), Pa. Assn. Colls. and Univs. (founding mem., pres. 1971-72, 83-84), Am. Coun. on Edn. (co-founder, mem. Bus. Higher Edn. Forum 1978-91, chmn. 1980-81), Internat. Inst. Strategic Studies, Coun. Fgn. Rels., Cosmos Club. Office: Univ Pitts 1202 C L Pittsburgh PA 15260-0001

POTAMKIN, MEYER P., mortgage banker; b. Phila., Nov. 11, 1909; s. Jacob and Ida (Soloman) P.; m. Vivian Orleans, July 27, 1940; children—Macy Ann Potamkin Lasky, Marshall F. Ph.B., Dickinson Coll., 1932; Ed.M., Temple U., 1941; D.F.A., Dickinson Coll., 1972. Social worker, dir. agy. Crime Prevention Assn., Phila., 1935-40; ptnr. Orleans Constrn. Co., Phila., 1940-54; pres. Blvd. Mortgage Co., Phila., 1954—. Pres. Phila. coun. Boys Clubs Am., 1962-82; nat. assoc. Boys Clubs Am., 1972-80; chmn. bd. trustees Camp William Penn, 1964-82; bd. dirs. Glen Mills Sch. for Delinquent Boys, 1960-77, v.p., 1976-77; bd. dirs. Phila. Coll. Art, 1970-75, Phila. Art Commn., 1974-82; mem. Juvenile Task Force Gov.'s

Justice Commn. and L.E.A.A. Coun., 1974-80; bd. dirs. Mann Music Ctr., 1982—, Settlement Music Sch., 1962—; trustee Bklyn. Mus., Crime Prevention Assn. (pres., chmn. bd. trustees 1977-87), Phila. Mus. Art, 1960-75, 1981—, Richmond Coll., Eng., 1982-87; bd. dirs., co-founder Sarah Allen Nursing Home for Blacks; mem. adv. coun. to bd. trustees Dickinson Coll., 1976—; trustee, mem. exec. com. Middle States Assn., 1977-82; bd. dirs. Phila. Ctr. for Older People, 1980-83; pres. Phila. Art Alliance, 1991-92. Recipient AME Mother Bethel award, 1977, Silver Keystone award Boys Clubs Am., 1986, Jewish Basketball League award, 1990, Achievement award Perkiomen Sch., 1990, Alumni award Perkiomen Sch., 1990, Alumni Achievement award Dickinson Coll., 1991, Jewish Basketball Honorable Fenkel award, 1994, Founder's medal Pa. Acad. Fine Arts, 1996; Israel Bond honoree, 1973. Mem. Home Builders Assn., Mortgage Bankers Assn. Am., Phila. Mortgage Bankers Assn. (pres. 1985-86), Pa. Mortgage Bankers Assn. (pres. 1985-86, award 1990), Locust Club, Union League, Bala Golf Club, Squires Golf Club, Friendly Sons of St. Patrick (hon.), Phi Epsilon Pi (bd. trustees found., Achievement award 1967), Zeta Beta Tau (grand coun. v.p. 1978). Office: Blvd Mortgage Co 111 Presidential Blvd Ste 135 Bala Cynwyd PA 19004-1005

POTAMKIN, ROBERT, automotive executive; b. 1946. Grad., U. Pa., 1970, JD, 1972. CEO Potamkin Cos., Miami, Fla., 1972—. Office: 4675 SW 74th St Miami FL 33143-6271*

POTASH, JANE, artist; b. Phila., May 3, 1937; d. Norval and Mary (Fox) Levy; m. Charles Potash, Jan. 21, 1962; children: Andrew Samuel, Dorothy Frances. BA, U. Pa., 1959. One-woman shows include Storelli Gallery, Phila., 1979, Langman Gallery, Jenkintown, Pa., 1979, 81, Phoenix Gallery, N.Y., 1981, A.R.T. Beasley Gallery, San Diego, 1986, Vorpal, N.Y., 1987; exhibited in group shows at Wayne Art Ctr., 1971, Lancaster Summer Arts Festival, 1971, 72, 74, Cooperstown (N.Y.) Nat. Juried Show, 1971, Abington Art Ctr., 1972-74, Phila. Art Alliance, 1975, Allentown Art Mus., 1976, Pa. Acad. Fine Arts, 1978, 80, Butcher and More Gallery, Phila., 1981, Wachs Davis Gallery, Washington, Shayne Gallery, Montreal, Can., 1982, Montreal Mus. Fine Arts, 1982, Source Gallery, San Francisco, 1983, Langman Gallery, 1987, Virginia Miller Gallery, Coral Gables, Fla., 1990; represented in collections at Fox Companies, Blue Cross, Blue Shield of Pa., Subaru, N.J., Nordstrom Stores, Calif., Beaver Ins. Co., San Francisco; represented in pvt. collections in U.S. and Can. Recipient Best of Show award Old York Rd. Avocations: reading, flower arranging, knitting, swimming, opera. Studio: 220 Old York Rd Jenkintown PA 19046-3244

POTASH, JEREMY WARNER, public relations executive; b. Monrovia, Calif., June 30, 1946; d. Fenwick Bryson and Joan Antony (Blair) Warner; m. Stephen Jon Potash, Oct. 19, 1969; 1 child, Aaron Warner. AA, Citrus Coll., 1965; BA, Pomona Coll., 1967. With Forbes Mag., N.Y.C., 1967-69, Japan External Trade Orgn., San Francisco, 1970-75; v.p., co-founder Potash & Co. Pub. Rels., Oakland, Calif., 1980-87; pres. Potash & Co. Pub. Rels., San Francisco, 1987—; founding exec. dir. Calif.-S.E. Asia Bus. Coun., Oakland, 1991—; exec. dir. Customs Brokers and Forwarders Assn., San Francisco, 1990—; adv. bd. Asia Pacific Econ. Rev., 1996—. Editor: Southeast Asia Environmental Directory, 1994; editor: Southeast Asia Infrastructure Directory, 1995-96. Bd. dirs. Judah L. Magnes Mus., Berkeley, 1981-94, co-founder docent program, 1980, pres. Women's Guild, 1980-81; bd. dirs. Temple Sinai, Oakland, 1984-86; pres. East Bay region Women's Am. Orgn. for Rehab. Through Tng., 1985-86. Mem. Am. Soc. Assn. Execs., World Trade Club San Francisco, Oakland Women's Lit. Soc., Book Club Calif. Office: Potash & Co Pub Rels 1946 Embarcadero Oakland CA 94606-5213

POTASH, STEPHEN JON, public relations executive; b. Houston, Feb. 25, 1945; s. Melvin L. and Petrice (Edelstein) P.; m. Jeremy Warner, Oct. 19, 1969; 1 son, Aaron Warner. BA in Internat. Rels., Pomona Coll., 1967. Account exec. Charles von Loewenfeldt, Inc., San Francisco, 1969-74, v.p., 1974-80; founder, pres. Potash & Co., Pub. Rels., Oakland, Calif., 1980-87; cons. APL Ltd. (formerly Am. Pres. Lines, Ltd.), 1979-87, 90—, v.p. corp. comm., APL Ltd., 1987-90; exec. dir. Calif. Coun. Internat. Trade, 1970-87; chmn. Potash & Co., Oakland, 1990—. Bd. dirs. Calif. Coun. Internat. Trade, 1987-94, Calif.-Southeast Asia Bus. Coun., 1992—, Temple Sinai, Oakland, 1979-81, mktg. com. United Way Bay Area. Mem. Pub. Rels. Soc. Am., Commonwealth Club of Calif., World Trade Club San Francisco. Office: Potash & Co Pub Rels 1946 Embarcadero Oakland CA 94606-5213

POTATE, JOHN SPENCER, SR., engineering company executive, consultant; b. Temple, Ga., Mar. 19, 1934; s. Harold Clyde and Eugenia Marie (McClung) P.; m. Barbara Jean Moorefield; children: Pamela, Vivian, Brenda, John Jr. BS in Indsl. Engring., Ga. Inst. Tech., 1959; MS in Aerospace Engring., Fla. Inst. Tech., 1965; MS in Mgmt., MIT, 1975. Program mgr. NASA, Cape Kennedy, Fla., 1961-70; exec. NASA, Washington, 1970-72; exec. Marshall Space Flight Ctr. NASA, Huntsville, Ala., 1973-82; v.p. System Devel. Corp. (now subs. Unisys), Santa Monica, Calif., 1982-84, Unisys, Camarillo, Calif., 1984-89; pres. AC Engring., Huntsville, Ala., 1989-92, ret., 1993; prin. John Potate Assocs., Huntsville, Ala., 1993—. With USCG, 1951-54; engr. USAF, 1959-61. Sloan fellow, MIT, 1972; recipient NASA Exceptional Svc. medal, 1969 (Apollo), NASA Leadership medal, 1980 (shuttle). Home: 1319 Blevins Gap Rd SE Huntsville AL 35802-2709

POTEAT, JAMES DONALD, diaconal minister, retired military officer; b. Spindale, N.C., Feb. 27, 1935; s. Albert Carl and Daliah Elizabeth (Freeman) P.; m. Clara Walker Yelton, Oct. 12, 1957; children: Deborah Poteat Emmons, Clara Poteat Frederick, James Donald Jr., Teresa Poteat Morris. BA disting. mil. graduate, The Citadel, Charleston, S.C., 1957; MA, Kans. State U., 1973; graduate, U.S. Army War Coll., 1980. Ordained to ministry United Meth. Ch. Commd. 2nd lt. U.S. Army, 1957, advanced through grades to col., 1979, ret., 1983; mgmt. cons., 1983-88; pastor's adminstrv. asst. Prospect United Meth. Ch., Covington, Ga., 1988-95. Author: Long Range Planning, Prospect United Methodist Church, 1990, Presidential Decision-Making: Presidents Lincoln and Polk, 1973, others. Decorated Bronze Star medal, three Air medals, Vietnam Cross of Gallantry, three Army Commendation medals with v., Viet Nam Svc. Medal with 3 Campaign Battle Stars. Mem. Ret. Officers Assn., United Meth. Ch. Bus. Adminstrs. Assn. (cert.).

POTEET, DANIEL P(OWELL), II, college provost; b. Dallas, Dec. 22, 1940; s. Daniel Powell and Helene (Van der Veer) P.; m. Nancy Heusinkveld, Mar. 13, 1971; 1 child, Daniel C. BA, Harvard U., 1963; MA, U. Ill., 1965, PhD, 1969. Asst. prof. U. Del., Newark, 1969-76, West Chester (Pa.) State Coll., 1976-77; dean faculty Hampden-Sydney (Va.) Coll., 1978-81, provost, 1981-85; provost Albion (Mich.) Coll., 1985-91, Guilford (N.C.) Coll., 1991—. Co-author: Rise of the Realists, 1979; also articles and revs. Mem. AAUP, Am. Conf. Acad. Deans, Am. Assn. Higher Edn. Episcopalian. Avocation: sailing. Office: Guilford Coll Office of Provost 5800 W Friendly Ave Greensboro NC 27410-4108

POTEET, MARY JANE, computer scientist; b. Raleigh, N.C., May 26, 1946; d. Charles William and Geraldine Lucile (Adams) Hampton; m. William Walter Schubert, Dec. 30, 1967 (div. June 1979); children: Kristen, Stephen, Betsy, Kathryn; m. H. Wesley Poteet, Mar. 21, 1991 (div. Mar. 1996). BA in Math., Park Coll., 1967. Programmer U. Mo. Med. Ctr., Columbia, 1968-72, City and County of Denver, 1979-80; sr. sys. programmer Citicorp Person to Person, Denver, 1980-82; sys. support rep. Software AG, NA, Denver, 1982-83; prin. info. sysm. specialist Idaho Nat. Engring. Lab., EG&G, Idaho Falls, 1983-89; adv. svcs. specialist IBM Profl. Svcs., Albuquerque, 1989-91; field mgr. IBM Svc., Boulder, Colo., 1991-93; project mgr. IBM Cons. & Svcs. SW, Denver, 1993—; presenter career workshop for girls No. Colo. U., Greeley, 1993. Leader Girl Scout Am., Pocatello, Idaho, Columbia, Mo., 1969-79, Idaho Falls, 1986-89, cluster leader, Rigby, Idaho, 1988-89; active Albuquerque Civic Chorus, 1990-91, Luth. Ch. Coun., 1994-96; bd. dirs. LWV, Pocatello, 1977-79, 84-85, pres., 1978-79; bd. dirs. Luth. Ch. Women, Pocatello, 1978-79; youth advisor Luth. Ch., Idaho Falls, 1984-89; tchr. Sunday sch. local ch., Albuquerque, 1990-91; youth com. chair local ch., Boulder, Colo., 1994-96; tchr. 7th and 8th grade Sunday sch., 1993-96, mem. ch. choir, 1995-96. Mem. AAUW. Lutheran. Avocations: youth work, reading, choir, photography. Home: 3916 W 104th Pl Westminster CO 80030-2402

POTEETE, ROBERT ARTHUR, editor; b. Perry, Ark., Aug. 29, 1926; s. Arthur and Ruby (Farish) P.; m. Frances Reynolds, Feb. 15, 1951 (dec. Mar. 1969); children: Anthony R., Julia Anne, Richard A.R. (dec. Sept. 1973). B.A., U. Central Ark., 1948; postgrad., Medill Sch. Journalism, Northwestern U., 1948-49. Reporter Ark. Gazette, 1949; reporter, day city editor, asst. news editor, asst. Sunday editor N.Y. Herald Tribune, 1950-66; mng. editor N.Y. Herald Tribune (European edit.), Paris, 1963-65; sr. editor Saturday Evening Post, N.Y.C., 1966-69; mng. editor, editor Psychology Today, Del Mar, Calif., 1969-73; mng. editor New Publs., Playboy Enterprises, Inc., Chgo., 1973-74; sr. editor Money mag., 1974-76; editor in chief Am. Illustrated mag. USIA, Washington, 1976-91; free-lance editor, writer, 1991—; editorial cons. Episcopal Diocese L.I., Garden City, N.Y., 1967-68. Contbr. articles popular mags. Mem. bd. United Youth Ministry, La Jolla, Cal., 1971-72. Served with U.S. Army, PTO, 1945-46. Recipient Citizens Budget Commn. citation for articles on N.Y.C. govt. purchase of real estate, 1958; named Disting. Alumnus, U. Ctrl. Ark., 1993. Mem. Am. Soc. Mag. Editors, Inner Circle. Home: 30 Julio Dr Apt 509 Shrewsbury MA 01545-3046

POTENTE, EUGENE, JR., interior designer; b. Kenosha. Wis., July 24, 1921; s. Eugene and Suzanne Marie (Schmit) P.; Ph.B., Marquette U., 1943; postgrad. Stanford U., 1943, N.Y. Sch. Interior Design, 1947, DFA Carthage Coll., 1970, DLitt (hon.) Concordia U., 1997; m. Joan Cioffe, Jan. 29, 1946; children: Eugene J., Peter Michael, John Francis, Suzanne Marie. Founder, pres. Studios of Potente, Inc., Kenosha, Wis., 1949—; pres., founder Archtl. Services Assos., Kenosha, 1978—, Bus. Leasing Services of Wis. Inc., 1978—; past nat. pres. Inter-Faith Forum on Religion, Art and Architecture; vice chmn. Wis. State Capitol and Exec. Residence Bd., 1981—. Sec., Kenosha Symphony Assn., 1968-74. Bd. dirs. Ctr. for Religion and the Arts, Wesley Theol. Sem., Washington, 1983-84. Served with AUS, 1943-46. Mem. Am. Soc. Interior Designers (treas., pres. Wis. chpt. 1985-86, 94-95, chmn. nat. pub. svc. 1986), Illuminating Engring. Soc. N.Am., Internat. Inst. Interior Designers, Sigma Delta Chi. Roman Catholic. Lodge: Elks. Home: 8609 2nd Ave Kenosha WI 53143-6511 Office: 914 60th St Kenosha WI 53140-4041

POTENZA, JOSEPH MICHAEL, lawyer; b. Stamford, Conn., June 27, 1947; s. Michael Joseph Sr. and Rose Elizabeth (Coppola) P.; m. Wendy Ann David, Dec. 19, 1971 (div. Jan. 1978); m. Karen Louise Yankee, Jan. 28, 1978; children: Wendy Lynn, Chiara Micol. BSEE cum laude, Rochester Inst. Tech., 1970; JD, Georgetown U., 1975. Bar: Va. 1975, D.C. 1976, U.S. Dist. Ct. D.C., U.S. Ct. Appeals (fed. cir.), U.S. Ct. Appeals (6th cir.), U.S. Supreme Ct. Patent examiner U.S. Patent and Trademark Office, Arlington, Va., 1970-74, law clk. bd. appeals, 1974-75, law clk. to presiding judge, 1975-76; assoc. Banner, Birch, McKie & Beckett, Washington, 1976-80, ptnr., 1980—; adj. prof. Georgetown U. Law Ctr., Washington, 1985—; faculty Nat. Inst. Trial Advocacy--Patent Inst., 1996—. Editor (monographs) Sorting Out Ownership Rights in Intellectual Property, 1980, Recent Developments in Licensing, 1981. Bd. dirs. Found. for a Creative Am., 1991—. Recipient Patent and Trademark Office Superior Performance award Dept. Commerce, 1973-75. Mem. ABA (young lawyers divsn. exec. coun. 1979—, chmn. legis. action com. 1980—, chmn. patent trademark and copyright com. 1977—, house of dels. 1984-86, sci. and tech. sect., coun. mem. 1985—, membership chmn. 1985—, budget co-chmn. 1987—, budget officer 1988—, vice chmn. 1991—, chair elect 1992-93, chair 1993, chair standing com. on pub. oversight, 1996—), IEEE, AAAS (mem. nat. conf. lawyers and scientists), Am. Intellectual Property Law Assn. (chmn. unfair competition com. 1980-81), D.C. Bar Assn. (sec. patent, trademark, copyright sect.), Va. Bar Assn., Wash. Patent Lawyers Club (pres. 1988-89), Am. Inns of Ct. (founding mem. and exec. com. Giles S. Rich 1991—, v.p. 1997), Phi Sigma Kappa, Alpha Sigma (pres. 1979-80), Tau Beta Pi. Home: 1238 Gilman Ct Herndon VA 22070-2418 Office: Banner & Witcoff 1001 G St NW Ste 1100 Washington DC 20001-4545

POTERBA, JAMES MICHAEL, economist, educator; b. Flushing, N.Y., July 13, 1958; s. William Samuel and Margaret Mary (Toale) P.; m. Nancy Lin Rose, June 23, 1984; children: Matthew Robert, Timothy James, Margaret Rose. AB, Harvard U., 1980; MPhil, Oxford U., Eng., 1982, DPhil, 1983. From asst. to assoc. prof. MIT, Cambridge, Mass., 1983-88, prof., 1988—, Mitsui prof., 1996—; dir. pub. econs. rsch. program Nat. Bur. Econ. Rsch., Cambridge, 1990—; fellow Ctr. Advanced Study in Behavioral Scis., 1993-94. Editor: Economic Policy Responses to Global Warning, 1991, International Comparisons of Household Saving, 1994, Housing Markets in the United States and Japan, 1994, Empirical Foundations of Household Taxation, 1996, Jour. Pub. Econs.; contbr. articles to profl. jours. Marshall scholar, 1980-83. Fellow Am. Acad. Arts and Scis., Econometric Soc.; mem. Assn. for Investment Mgmt. and Rsch. (com. on rsch. and edn.), Phi Beta Kappa. Office: MIT 50 Memorial Dr Rm E52-350 Cambridge MA 02142-1347

POTH, STEFAN MICHAEL, retired sales financing company executive; b. Detroit, Dec. 9, 1933; s. Stefan and Anna (Mayer) P.; m. Eileen T. McClimon, May 28, 1966; 1 child, Stefan Michael Jr. Cert. in acctg., Walsh Inst., Detroit, 1954. CPA, Mich.; cert. consumer credit exec. Sr. acct. Lybrand, Ross Bros. & Montgomery, Detroit, 1953-56, 58-61; with Ford Motor Credit Co., Dearborn, Mich., 1961-91; v.p. leasing truck and recreational products and tractor financing Ford Motor Credit Co., Dearborn, 1973-77; v.p. cen. and western U.S. ops. Ford Motor Credit CO., Dearborn, 1977-79; v.p. mktg. and ops. svcs. Ford Motor Credit Co., Dearborn, 1979-85, v.p. bus. planning, 1985-90, v.p. credit policy, 1990-91; bd. dirs. GE Credit Auto Resale Svcs., Inc.; adv. coun. Credit Rsch. Ctr., Krannert Grad. Sch. Mgmt., Purdue U., 1984-91. Chmn. adv. coun. Credit Rsch. Ctr. Krannert Grad. Sch. Mgmt., Purdue U., 1989-90; mem. bd. dirs. Internat. Credit Assoc., 1989-91. With AUS, 1956-58. Roman Catholic. Home: 7230 Mohansic Dr Bloomfield Hills MI 48301-3550

POTLURI, VENKATESWARA RAO, medical facility administrator; b. Krishna Dist., India, Jan. 1, 1955; came to U.S., 1983; s. Venkata Krishnaiah and Bulli Ademma (Koduru) P.; m. Padma Sree Peddu, Dec. 4, 1986; children: Vani, Vamsee Krishna, Varun. BSc, ANR Coll., Gudivada, India, 1975; MSc, AU Coll. Sci. and Tech., Waltair, India, 1977; MPhil, Delhi (India) U., 1979, PhD, 1982. Diplomate Am. Bd. Med. Genetics. Postdoctoral fellow Mt. Sinai Med. Ctr., N.Y.C., 1983-85, vis. asst. prof., 1985-87; lab. dir., adj. mem. med. staff Norwalk (Conn.) Hosp., 1987—. Fellow Am. Coll. Med. Genetics (founding); mem. Am. Soc. Human Genetics, New Eng. Regional Genetics Group. Avocations: classical music, Telugu literature, home improvement. Home: 33 Ledgewood Dr Norwalk CT 06850-1813 Office: Norwalk Hosp Cytogenetic Lab Dept Path Maple St Norwalk CT 06856

POTOCKI, JOSEPH EDMUND, marketing company executive; b. Jersey City, Jan. 31, 1936; s. Joseph and Estelle (Bielski) P.; m. Margaret Mary Shine, May 21, 1960; children: Joseph, Meg, David. BS, Seton Hall U., 1957. Asst. regional sales mgr. Gen. Mills Inc., Valley Stream, N.Y., 1960-67; group mgr. merchandising Warner Lambert Co., Morris Plains, N.J., 1967-74; dir. merchandising svcs. Beatrice Hunt/Wesson, Fullerton, Calif., 1974-81; pres., chief exec. officer Joseph Potocki & Assocs., Irvine, Calif., 1981-92; pres. Mktg. Fulfillment Svcs., Tustin, Calif., 1985-87; chmn. Clarke Hooper Am., 1987-92; sr. exec. Gage Mktg., Newport Beach, 1992—; instr. nat. bus. seminars. Bd. dirs. L.A. Parent Inst. Quality Edn., 1994—. Recipient Mktg. Motivator award L.A. Mktg. Exhbn., 1981, Mktg. Gold medal Am. Mktg. Assn. 1957. Mem. Promotion Mktg. Assn. (chmn. bd. dirs. 1977-79, v.p. West sect. 1980-87, bd. dirs. 1990, chmn. edn. com., Reggie award 1984, 85, 87), Promotion Mktg. Assn. Am. (bd. dirs. exec. com. 1978-87, Chmn.'s Bowl 1979, Named to Chmn.'s Cir. 1986, chmn. basics and advanced edn.), Nat. Premium Sales Execs. (sec. 1985-86, Pres. award 1985, Cert. Incentive Profl. Republican. Roman Catholic. Avocations: sailing, golf, woodworking, travel. Home: Monarch Pointe 22772 Azure Sea Laguna Niguel CA 92677-5439 Office: Gage Mktg Group 3620 Birch St Newport Beach CA 92660-2624

POTOK, CHAIM, author, artist, editor; b. N.Y.C., Feb. 17, 1929; s. Benjamin Max and Mollie (Friedman) P.; m. Adena S. Mosevitzky, June 8, 1958; children: Rena, Naama, Akiva. BA summa cum laude, Yeshiva Coll., 1950; MHL, Jewish Theol. Sem., 1954; PhD, U. Pa., 1965. Ordained rabbi, 1954. Nat. dir. Leaders Tng. Fellowship, 1954-55; dir. Camp Ramah, Ojai, Cal., 1957-59; scholar-in-residence Har Zion Temple, Phila., 1959-63; mem. faculty Tchrs. Inst., Jewish Theol. Sem., 1963-64; editor Jewish Publ. Soc., 1965-74, spl. projects editor, 1974—; vis. prof. U. Pa., 1992, 93, 94, 95, Johns Hopkins U., 1994, 96; vis. lectr. Bryn Mawr Coll., 1985. Author: The Chosen, 1967 (Edward Lewis Wallant award), The Promise, 1969 (Athenaeum award), My Name is Asher Lev, 1972, In The Beginning, 1975, Wanderings, 1978, The Book of Lights, 1981, Davita's Harp, 1985, Tobiasse: Artist in Exile, 1986, The Gift of Asher Lev, 1990 (Nat. Jewish Book award), I Am the Clay, 1992, The Gates of November, 1996, (children's books with Tony Auth) The Tree of Here, 1993, The Sky of Now, 1995, (plays) Out of the Depths, 1990, Sins of the Father, 1991, The Play of Lights, 1992, also short stories; works translated into more than a dozen fgn. langs. Served as chaplain AUS, 1955-57, Korea. Mem. P.E.N., Artists' Equity, Author's Guild, Dramatists Guild, Rabbinical Assembly.

POTRA, FLORIAN ALEXANDER, mathematics educator; b. Cluj, Romania, Dec. 7, 1950; came to the U.S., 1982; s. Ioan and Ana (Popa) P.; m. ELena Lavric, Nov. 15, 1973; 1 child, Valentin. MS, Babes-Bolyai U., Cluj, 1973; PhD, U. Bucharest, 1980. Analyst IPGGH, Bucharest, Romania, 1974-78; researcher INCREST, Bucharest, 1978-82; postdoctoral researcher U. Pitts., 1982-83, asst. prof., 1983-84; assoc. prof. U. Iowa, Iowa City, 1984-90, prof., 1990—; vis. rschr. Lawrence Livermore Nat. Lab., Rice U., U. Catania, Italy, Konrad Zuse Zentrum, Berlin, U. Darmstadt, Germany, 1990, U. Karlsruhe, Germany, 1987-91, Argonne Nat. Lab., 1991, U. Geneva, 1993, U. NSW, Sydney, 1995, U. Rome, 1996, INRIA, France, 1996. Assoc. editor: SIAM Jour. on Optimization, 1991—, Jour. Optimization Theory and Applications, 1991—, Jour. Optimization Methods and Software, 1997—; co-author: Research Notes in Mathematics 103, 1984; contbr. articles to profl. jours. Andrew Mellon fellow, 1982, Old Gold fellow, 1984, James Van Allen fellow in natural scis., 1991; NSF grantee, 1985-87., 94—. Home: 4029 W Overlook Rd NE Iowa City IA 52240-7942 Office: U Iowa Mathematics Iowa City IA 52242

POTSIC, WILLIAM PAUL, physician, educator; b. Berwyn, Ill., May 22, 1943; s. Andrew M. and Estella (Buschak) P.; m. Roberta I. Kite; children: Amie, Jordan. B.S., U. Ill., 1965; M.D. cum laude, Emory U., 1969; postgrad., U. Pa. Intern, resident U. Chgo., 1969-74; practice medicine specializing in pediatric otolaryngology Phila., 1974—; mem. staff Presbyn. Hosp., Pa. Hosp., Children's Seashore House; assoc. prof. otorhinolaryngology and human communication U. Pa., 1974-93, prof. otorhinolaryngology and human communication, 1993—; dir. div. otorhinolaryngology and human communication Children's Hosp., Phila., 1975—; sec.-treas. med. staff Children's Hosp., 1980—, pres. med. staff, 1982-84; vice-chmn. clin. affairs dept. surgery, 1995—. Author book on pediatric otolaryngology; contbr. articles to profl. jours. Recipient 1st prize for clin. research Am. Acad. Ophthalmology and Otolaryngology, 1977; NIH grantee. Mem. AMA, Am. Acad. Otolaryngology Head and Neck Surgery, Am. Laryngology, Otolgy and Rhinology Soc., Am. Coll. Physician Execs., Internat. Acad. Cosmetic Surgery, Pa. Med. Soc., Phila. Coll. Physicians, Phila. County Med. Soc., Phila. Laryngol. Soc. (treas. 1983), Phila. Pediatric Soc., Phila Laryngol. Soc. (pres. 1984), Phila. Soc. Facial Plastic Surgeons, Politzer Soc., Soc. Ear, Nose and Throat Advances in Children (pres. 1983), Am. Soc. Pediatric Otolaryngology (pres. 1991), Soc. Univ. Otolarungologists, Am. Acad. Pediatrics, Alpha Omega Alpha, Phi Chi. Home: 1057 Beaumont Rd Berwyn PA 19312-2007 Office: Children's Hosp Phila 34th And Civic Center Blvd Philadelphia PA 19104

POTT, SANDRA KAY, finance company executive; b. Denver, Apr. 1, 1946; d. Sanford N. and Mary Helen (Davis) Groendyke; m. Joel Frederic Pott, Mar. 7, 1970; children: Eric Christopher, Jessica Elizabeth. BA in English, Ea. Mich. U., 1969. CFP, Mich. Account exec. Dean Witter Reynolds, Troy, Mich., 1984-93, assoc. v.p., 1993—. Mem. AAUW (bd. dirs. 1977-83), Nat. Assn. Women Bus. Owners (bd. dirs. 1994—), Royal Oak League Women Voters (bd. dirs. 1977-83). Office: Dean Witter Reynolds 100 W Big Beaver Rd Ste 500 Troy MI 48084-5283

POTTASH, A. CARTER, psychiatrist, hospital executive; b. Phila., Nov. 30, 1948; s. R. Robert and Elizabeth (Braunschweig) P. BS with high honors, Trinity Coll., Hartford, Conn., 1970; MD, Yale U., 1974. Intern in internal medicine Tufts U. Sch. Medicine, Springfield, Mass., 1974-75; clin. fellow Yale-New Haven Hosp., 1977-78; postdoctoral fellow Yale U., New Haven, 1975-78; med. dir. Psychiatric Diagnostic Labs. Am., Summit, N.J., 1979-83; lectr. in field; cons. in field; vis. prof. St. Elizabeth Med. Ctr., Northeastern Ohio U. Coll Medicine, 1979; clin. prof. NYU, 1989—; pres. Fla. Consultation Svcs., P.A., West Palm Beach, 1992—, Psychiatric Assocs. N.J., P.A., Summit, N.J., 1978-93, Met. Med. Group P.C., N.Y.C., 1981—, So. Fla. Med. Group P.A., Delray Beach, 1984-93, Stony Lodge Hosp., Inc., Briarcliff Manor, N.Y., 1985—, Hampton Med. Group, P.A., Rancocas, N.J., 1986—; exec. med. dir. Fair Oaks Hosp., Summit, 1978-92, The Regent Hosp., N.Y.C., 1981-92, Lake Hosp. of the Palm Beaches, Lake Worth, Fla., 1984-92, Fair Oaks Hosp. at Boca/Delray, Fla., 1984-92, Hampton Hosp., Rancocas, N.J., 1986-95—; chmn. Stony Lodge Hosp., Briarcliff Manor, N.Y., 1985—. Editor Psychiatry Letter, 1980-91; mem. editl. bd. Internat. Jour. Psychiatry in Medicine, 1978-87, The Psychiatric Hosp., 1982—, Jour. Nat. Assn. Pvt. Psychiatric Hosps., 1980-81, Fla. Psychiatry Newsletter, 1992—; reviewer Jour. Nervous and Mental Disorders, Alcoholism, Clin. and Exptl. Rsch., JAMA, Hosp. and Cmty. Psychiatry; contbr. numerous articles to profl. jours. Mem. adv. bd. Mothers for More Halfway Houses, N.Y.C., 1986—; cons. com. on women and alcoholism Jr. League of N.Y.C., 1987; bd. dirs. Met. Soc. Arts, N.Y.C., 1984-87. Fellow Am. Coll. Clin. Pharmacology, Assn. Clin. Scientists, Nat. Acad. Clin. Biochemistry, Am. Psychiat. Assn., The Acad. Medicine N.J.; mem. AMA, Soc. Neurosci., Nat. Acad. Clin. Biochemistry, Palm Beach County Med. Soc., Am. Acad. Clin. Psychiatrists, British Brain Research Assn. (hon.), European Brain and Behavioral Soc. (hon.), Am. Soc. of Addiction Medicine, Am. Academy of Addiction Psychiatry (founding mem. 1987), Am. Psychiatric Assn., Fla. Med. Soc., Palm Beach County Psychiatric Soc., Med. Soc. State N.Y., Med. Soc. N.J., Union County Med. Soc., N.Y. Athletic Club, Canoe Brook Country Club, Beacon Hill Club, Phi Beta Kappa, Delta Phi Alpha. Office: PO Box 511 West Palm Beach FL 33402-0511

POTTER, ALICE CATHERINE, clinical laboratory scientist; b. Oil City, Pa., June 24, 1928; d. Howard Taylor and Hilda Marian (Lewis) P. BA, U. Findlay, 1949; postgrad., Springfield (Ohio) City Hosp., 1949-50. Cert. med. technologist Am. Soc. Clin. Pathologists; cert. clin. lab. scientist. Med. technologist Mercy Hosp., Springfield, 1950-54, Oil City Hosp., 1954-67; staff med. technologist Thomas Jefferson U. Hosp., Phila., 1968-83, sr. med. technologist, 1983-96, retired, 1997. Vol. Acad. Natural Scis., Phila., 1995—. Mem. Am. Soc. Clin. Lab. Scientists, Pa. Soc. Clin. Lab. Scientists (membership chmn. Delaware Valley chpt. 1977-78, chmn. pub. rels. 1982-94, 96-97, bd. dirs. 1989-91, pres.-elect 1991-92, pres. 1992-93, Scrimshaw award 1992). Republican. Avocations: travel, needlework. Home: 1701 Wallace St Philadelphia PA 19130-3312

POTTER, BARRETT GEORGE, historian, educator; b. Cortland, N.Y., Oct. 28, 1929; s. Leo Barrett and Charlotte May (Hazen) P.; B.A., Hobart Coll., 1952, M.S. in Edn., 1955; M.A., Cornell U. 1959; Ph.D. in History, SUNY, Buffalo, 1973; postgrad. SUNY, Cortland, 1952, Syracuse U., 1962; m. Beverly Ann Platts, Aug. 6, 1961; children—Barrett George, Heather Gaye. Instr., Hobart Coll., Geneva, N.Y., 1952-54; lectr. SUNY, New Paltz, 1955-57, summer 1960; high sch. tchr., Bayport, N.Y., 1957-58; asst. mgr. 1000 Acres Ranch Resort, Stony Creek, N.Y., 1958-59; asst. prof. history SUNY Tech. Coll., Alfred, 1959-64, prof., 1965-92, prof. emeritus, 1992—, chmn. dept., 1965-71; teaching asst. SUNY, Buffalo, 1964-65; adj. prof. Elmira Coll., 1978, Rochester Inst. Tech., 1979, Alfred U., 1985, SUNY Tech. Coll., Alfred, 1992-96; tutor Empire State Coll., 1985. Mem. Alfred-Almond Central Sch. Bd. Edn., 1971-74, pres., 1973; trustee Alfred Rural Cemetery Assn., 1973-81, pres., 1979-80; trustee Alfred Hist. Soc., 1974-76, 85-88, Union U. Ch., Alfred 1977-80, Alfred Village, 1987—; acting mayor City of Alfred, 1990-92; vice chmn. Alfred Community Chest, 1983-90. Coe Found. fellow in Am. Studies, 1961. Mem. Am. Fedn. Musicians, Phi Beta Kappa. Republican. Episcopalian. Clubs: Elks, Masons, Foster Lake (exec. com. 1972-74). Contbr. articles to profl. jours. Home: 76 S Main St Alfred NY 14802-1323 Office: Social Science Dept SUNY Alfred NY 14802

POTTER, BLAIR BURNS, editor; b. Spartanburg, S.C., Mar. 11, 1946; d. Leonard Hill and Nancy Milner (Vaughan) Burns; m. Robert Arthur Potter, May 24, 1974; children: Lillian Howard, Gordon Leonard. BA, Hollins Coll., Roanoke, Va., 1968; MA, U. N.C., Chapel Hill, 1971. Editl. asst. Professional Engineer, Washington, 1968-69; manuscript editor Science, Washington, 1970-74; freelance editor, 1974-85; assoc. editor Health Adminstrn. Press/U. Mich., Ann Arbor, 1985-87; freelance editor NAS, Inst. Medicine, Office Tech. Assessment, Washington, 1987-92; assoc. editor Science News, Washington, 1992, mng. editor, 1992—; editl. cons. White House Task Force on Infant Mortality, Washington, 1990, Nat. Commn. on Orphan Diseases, Washington, 1988-89, Nat. Comm. on Children, Washington, 1992-93; lay mem. protocol com. Nat. Heart, Lung and Blood Inst., Bethesda, Md., 1973. Whittaker fellow, 1969-70; Hollins Coll. scholar, 1964-68, English-Speaking Union scholar, 1967. Mem. Nat. Press Club. Avocations: gardening, historic preservation, antique American furniture, sailing. Home: 12 Revell St Annapolis MD 21401 Office: Science News 1719 N St NW Washington DC 20036-2890

POTTER, CLARKSON NOTT, publishing consultant; b. Mendham, N.J., May 17, 1928; s. John Howard Nott and Margaretta (Wood) P.; m. Ruth Delafield, June 14, 1949 (div. Aug. 1965); children—Howard Alonzo, Christian, Margaretta, Edward Eliphalet; m. Pamela Howard, Nov. 26, 1973 (div. Apr. 1976); 1 son, Jack Rohe Howard-Potter; m. Helga Maass, Oct. 31, 1981. B.A., Union Coll., 1950. With Doubleday & Co., N.Y.C., 1950-57; sr. editor, advt. mgr., mng. editor Dial Press, N.Y.C., 1958-59; founder, editor-in-chief Clarkson N. Potter Inc., N.Y.C., 1959-76; dir., editor-in-chief Barre Pub. Co. Inc., Mass., 1974-76; pres. The Brandywine Press, N.Y.C., 1976-80; lit. agt., publishing cons. Jamestown, R.I., 1980-86; pres. The Kestrel Press, Inc., 1992-96; bd. dirs. Beckham House Pubs., Inc., Hampton, Va.; trustee Newport (R.I.) Art Mus., 1994—. Author: Writing for Publication, 1990, Who Does What and Why in Book Publishing, 1990. Mem. Century Club (N.Y.C.), Newport Reading Room. Home and Office: 5 Westwood Rd Jamestown RI 02835-1165

POTTER, CLEMENT DALE, public defender; b. McMinnville, Tenn., Dec. 22, 1955; s. Johnnie H. and Elnora (Harvey) P.; children: Cory, Sarah, John Warren. BS, Middle Tenn. State U., 1984; JD, U. Tenn., 1987; cert., Tenn. Law Enforcement Acad., 1980. Bar: Tenn. 1987, U.S. Dist. Ct. (ea. dist.) Tenn. 1989. Pvt. practice law McMinnville, 1987-89; city judge City of McMinnville, Tenn., 1988-89; pub. defender 31st Dist. State Tenn., McMinnville, 1989—. Asst. to gen. editor Tools for the Ultimate Trial, 1st edit., 1985. Mem. Leadership McMinnville, 1989, chmn., 1995, 96; TSSAA H.S. Football referee, 1988—. Staff sgt. USAF, 1974-80. Named McMinnville Warren County C. of C. Vol. of Yr., 1995; recipient D. Porter Henegar & Fred L. Hoover Sr. Bell Ringer award, 1995. Mem. ABA, Cheer Mental Health Assn. (dir. 1988—, pres. 1991-96), Harmony House Inc. (dir. 1993-95), Noon Exch. Club McMinnville (dir. 1992-94, sec. 1994, pres.-elect 1995, pres. 1996-97), Kiwanis Club of Warren County (pres. 1986-87). Avocations: computers, gardening, coaching youth softball. Office: Pub Defender 31st Dist PO Box 510 314 W Main St Mc Minnville TN 37111

POTTER, CORINNE JEAN, librarian; b. Edmonton, Alta., Can., Feb. 2, 1930; d. Vernon Harcourt and Beatrice A. (Demaray) MacNeill; m. William B. Potter, Aug. 11, 1951 (div. Jan. 1978); children—Caroline, Melanie, Theodore, William, Ellen. B.A., Augustana Coll., 1952; M.S., U. Ill., 1976. Br. librarian Rock Island (Ill.) Pub. Library, 1967-73, children's work supr., 1973-74; dir. St. Ambrose U. Library, Davenport, Iowa, 1978—; chairperson Quad City Library Dir.'s Publicity Com., 1984-88. Chairperson Com. of the Whole for Local Automated Circulation and Online Catalog System, 1989-90. Mem. ALA, Assn. Coll. and Research Libraries (sec., v.p., pres. Iowa chpt. 1979-82), Iowa Library Assn. (com. chmn. 1983-84), Iowa Pvt. Academic Libraries Consortium (sec.-treas. 1986-89), Iowa Oline Computer Libr. Ctr. Users Group (v.p.-pres. elect 1988-89, pres. 1989-90), Zonta Club Quad Cities (chair libr. bldg. com. 1993-94, co-pres. 1994-96). Office: St Ambrose U Libr McMullen Libr 518 W Locust St Davenport IA 52803-2829

POTTER, DAVID SAMUEL, former automotive company executive; b. Seattle, Jan. 16, 1925; children: Diana (Mrs. Paul Bankston), Janice (Mrs. Robert Meadows), Tom, Bill; m. Nancy Shaar, Dec. 1979. B.S., Yale U., 1945; Ph.D., U. Wash., 1951. Mem. staff Applied Physics Lab., U. Wash., 1946-60, asst. dir., 1955-60; with Gen. Motors Corp., 1960-73; chief engr. Milw. ops. GM Delco Electronics div., 1970-73; dir. research and devel. Detroit Diesel Allison div., 1973; asst. sec. for research and devel. Dept. Navy, 1973-74, under sec., 1974-76; v.p. environ. activities staff Gen. Motors Corp., Detroit, 1976-78; v.p. and group exec. public affairs group Gen. Motors Corp., 1978-83, v.p. in charge power products and def. ops. group, 1983-85; ret., 1985; mem. Gov. Calif. Adv. Commn. Ocean Resources, 1964-68; mem. adv. panel Nat. Sea Grant Program, 1966; adv. bd. Naval Postgrad. Sch., Dept. Energy; bd. dirs. Sanders Assocs. Inc., Sci. Applications Internat. Co., John Fluke Mfg. Co., Lockheed Martin Corp. Served to ensign USNR, 1943-46. Mem. Nat. Acad. Engring., NSF, Marine Tech. Soc., Am. Phys. Soc., AIAA, Am. Acoustical Soc., Nat. Oceanographic Assn. (v.p. 1966), Soc. Automotive Engrs. (chmn. tech. bd. 1978-79, dir. 1981-83), Cosmos Club (Washington), Detroit Club, Birmingham Athletic Club (Mich.), Birnam Wood Country Club (Montecito, Calif.), Santa Barbara Club. Research cosmic rays, magnetics, underwater acoustics. Home: 877 Lilac Dr Santa Barbara CA 93108-1438

POTTER, DEBORAH ANN, news correspondent, educator; b. Hagerstown, Md., June 10, 1951; d. Peter R. and H. Louise (McDevitt) P.; m. Robert H. Witten, May 1, 1982; children: Cameron, Evan. BA, U. N.C., 1972; MA, Am. U., 1977. Assignment editor Sta. WMAL-TV, Washington, 1972-73, prodr., 1973-74; reporter Voice of Am., Washington, 1974-77; anchor Sta. KYW, Phila., 1977-78, CBS Radio, N.Y.C., 1978-81; White House corr. CBS News, Washington, 1981-85, state dept. corr., 1985-87, congl. corr., 1987-89, environ. corr., 1989-91; contbg. corr. 48 Hours, 1989-90; host Nightwatch CBS News, Washington, 1991; Washington corr. Cable News Network, Washington, 1991-94; asst. prof. Sch. Comm. Am. U., Washington, 1994-95; dir. Poynter Election Project, St. Petersburg, Fla., 1995—; faculty mem. Poynter Inst. Media Studies. Co-author: Poynter Election Handbook; host (video prodns.) Beyond the Spotted Owl, 1993, Health Beat, 1994, Risk Reporting, 1995, (PBS series) In the Prime, 1996-97. Mem. adv. coun. Environ. Journalism Ctr., Radio and TV News Dirs. Found., Washington, 1994—; lay reader St. Alban's Episc. Ch., Washington, 1988-89. Mem. Radio TV News Dirs. Assn., Soc. of Environ. Journalists, Investigative Reporters and Editors, Assn. for Edn. in Journalism and Mass Comm., U. N.C. Alumni Assn. (bd. dirs. 1990-93, Disting. Young Alumna award 1990). Office: Poynter Institute 801 3rd St S Saint Petersburg FL 33701-4920

POTTER, DELCOUR S., finance company executive; b. 1935. AB, Bowdoin Coll., 1957. With Gen. Electric Corp., N.Y.C., 1957-65, asst. treas., 1965-72; v.p. fin. Chase Manhattan Mortgage and Realty Trust, N.Y.C., 1972-75; sec.-treas. Pvt. Export Funding Corp., N.Y.C., 1975—, chmn., pres., CEO. With U.S. Army, 1958. Office: Private Export Funding Corp 280 Park Ave New York NY 10017-1216

POTTER, ELIZABETH STONE, academic administrator; b. Mount Kisco, N.Y., Oct. 18, 1931; d. Ralph Emerson and Elizabeth (Fleming) Stone; m. Harold David Potter, Aug. 1, 1953; children: David Stone, Nicholas Fleming. BA, Wellesley Coll., 1953. Tchr. Spence Sch., N.Y.C., 1960-62; from audiovisual head to asst. to mid. sch. head Chapin Sch., N.Y.C., 1970—, sci. tchr., sci. coord., 1970—; evaluator NYSAIS, N.Y.C., 1994-95. Mem. NSTA, ATIS. Avocations: reading, skiing, tennis, swimming, gardening. Home: 1160 Fifth Ave New York NY 10029-6936 Office: Chapin Sch 100 E End Ave New York NY 10028-7403

POTTER, EMMA JOSEPHINE HILL, language educator; b. Hackensack, N.J., July 18, 1921; d. James Silas and Martha Loretta (Pyle) Hill; m. James H. Potter, Mar. 26, 1949. AB cum laude with honors in Classics (scholar), Alfred (N.Y.) U., 1943; AM, Johns Hopkins U., 1946. Tchr. Latin, Balt. County Pub. Schs., 1943-44; instr. French, Spanish, Balt. Poly. Inst., 1950-83; instr. Spanish adult edn. classes, 1946-48; treas. Bruno-Potter Inc. Trustee James Harry Potter Gold Medal, ASME. Donor Commemorative plaque in honor of Martha Pyle Hill to Chenango County Coun. Arts, 1996. Mem. Johns Hopkins U., Alfred U. Alumni Assns., Internat. Platform Assn., Clan Hay Soc. Scotland (Am. br.), Johns Hopkins U. Faculty Club. Democrat. Home: 419 3rd Ave Avon By The Sea NJ 07717-1244

POTTER, ERNEST LUTHER, lawyer; b. Anniston, Ala., Apr. 30, 1940; s. Ernest Luther and Dorothy (Stamps) P.; m. Gwyn Johnston, June 28, 1958; children: Bradley S., Lauren D. A.B., U. Ala., 1961, LL.B., 1963, LL.M., 1979. Bar: Ala. 1963, U.S. Dist. Ct. (no. dist.) Ala. 1964, U.S. Ct. Appeals (5th cir.) 1965, U.S. Supreme Ct. 1972, U.S. Ct. Appeals (11th cir.) 1982. Assoc. Burnham & Klinefelter, Anniston, Ala., 1963-64; assoc. Bell, Richardson, Cleary, McLain & Tucker, Huntsville, Ala., 1964-66, ptnr., 1967-70; ptnr. Butler & Potter, Huntsville, 1971-82; pvt. practice, Huntsville, 1983—; bd. dirs. VME Microsystems Internat. Corp., Inc.; mem. faculty Inst. Bus. Law and Polit. Sci., U. Ala.-Huntsville, 1965-67. Contbg. author: Marital Law, 1976, 2d edit. 1985. V.p. No. Ala. Kidney Found., 1976-77; treas. Madison County Dem. Exec. Com., 1974-78; bd. dirs. United Way Madison County, 1982-87, Girls Inc., Huntsville, 1988—, pres., 1991. Mem. Ala. Law Inst., ABA, Ala. Bar Assn., Madison County Bar Assn., Phi Beta Kappa, Order of Coif. Episcopalian. Home: 1284 Becket Dr SE Huntsville AL 35801-1670 Office: 200 Clinton Ave W Huntsville AL 35801-4918

POTTER, JAMES DOUGLAS, pharmacology educator; b. Waterbury, Conn., Sept. 26, 1944; s. Herbert Eugene and Jean Gladys (Troske) P.; m. Priscilla F. Strang, Aug. 9, 1985; children: Liesse, Andrew, Ian Brown. BS, George Washington U., 1965; PhD, U. Conn., 1970; postgrad. (fellow) Boston Biomed. Rsch. Inst., 1970-74. Staff scientist Boston Biomed. Research Inst., 1974-75; assoc. in neurology Harvard U. Med. Sch., 1974-75; asst. prof. cell biophysics Baylor Coll. Medicine, 1975-77; assoc. prof. pharmacology U. Cin., 1977-81, prof., 1981-83; chmn., prof. dept. molecular and cellular pharmacology U. Miami, 1983—; grant reviewer in field. Grantee NIH, 1978-81, 83—, Nat. Heart Lung and Blood Inst., 1978— (Merit award 1989—), Muscular Dystrophy Assn., 1983-94. Fellow Muscular Dystrophy Assn.; mem. AAAS, Am. Chem. Soc., Am. Soc. Pharmacology and Exptl. Therapeutics, Assn. for Med. Sch. Pharmacology (chmn.), Internat. Soc. Heart Rsch., Am. Heart Assn. (established investigator 1974-79), Am. Soc. Biochem. and Molecular Biologists, Cardiac Muscle Soc. (sec.-treas. 1992-94, pres. 1994-96), Biophys. Soc., Sigma Xi. Contbr. articles to profl. jours. Home: 7240 SW 127th St Miami FL 33156-5336 Office: U Miami Sch Medicine Dept of Molecular & Cellular Pharm 1600 NW 10th Ave Miami FL 33136-1015

POTTER, JAMES EARL, retired international hotel management company executive; b. Utica, N.Y., July 25, 1933; s. Earl Moses and Helen May (Cruikshank) P. BS in Hotel Mgmt. with distinction, Cornell U., 1954, postgrad., 1955-56. Owner, propr. Old Drovers Inn, Dover Plains, N.Y., 1956-89; various acctg. positions Inter-Continental Hotels Corp., N.Y.C., 1960-62, fin. dir. for Asia and Pacific, 1963-69; v.p. Overseas Nat. Airways Hotels, N.Y.C., 1969-71; sr. v.p. Inter-Continental Hotels Corp., N.Y.C., 1972-89, London, 1990-92; instr. acctg. Cornell U., Ithaca, N.Y., 1957-59. Author: A Room with a World View, 1996. Trustee Opera Co. Boston, 1978-85; mem. Cornell U. Coun., 1988-91. Mem. Culinary Inst. Am. (trustees com. on acad. policy 1980-90), Met. Opera Club, Cornell Soc. Hotelmen, Cornell Club (N.Y.C.). Presbyterian. Avocation: opera.

POTTER, J(EFFREY) STEWART, property manager; b. Ft. Worth, July 8, 1943; s. Gerald Robert Potter and Marion June (Mustain) Tombler; m. Dianne Eileen Roberb, Dec. 31, 1970 (div. Aug. 1983); 1 child, Christopher Stewart; m. Deborah Ann Blevins, Oct. 20, 1991. AA, San Diego Mesa Coll., 1967. Cert. apartment mgr., apartment property supr., housing adminstr. Sales mgr. Sta. KJLM, La Jolla, Calif., 1964-67; mgr. inflight catering Host Internat., San Diego, 1967-69; lead aircraft refueler Lockheed Co., San Diego, 1969-70; property mgr. Internat. Devel. and Fin Corp., La Jolla, 1970-72; mgr. bus. property BWY Constn. Co., San Diego, 1972-73; mgr. residents Coldwell Banker, San Diego, 1973-74; mgr. Grove Investments, Carlsbad, Calif., 1974-76, Villa Granada, Villa Seville Properties Ltd., Don Cohn, Chula Vista, Calif., 1976-83; gen. mgr. AFL-CIO Bldg. Trades Corp., National City, Calif., 1983—; instr., Cert. Apt. Mgmt. San Diego Apt. Assn. Bd. dirs. San Diego County Apt. Assn., 1995—. Fellow Internat. Platform Assn., Nat. City C. of C., Toastmasters, Founding Families San Diego Hist. Soc., Am. Assn. Retired Persons, San Diego County Apt. Assn. (bd. dirs.), La Jolla Monday Night Club (treas. 1984-89). Roman Catholic. Avocations: golf, tennis, snow skiing. Home: 2550 5th Ave Ste 401 San Diego CA 92103-6622 Office: AFL-CIO Bldg Trades Corp 2323 D Ave National City CA 91950-6730

POTTER, JOHN FRANCIS, surgical oncologist, educator; b. N.Y.C., July 26, 1925; s. John Albert and Isabelle Cecelia (Sullivan) P.; m. Tanya Agnes Kristof, Nov. 19, 1955; children: Tanya Jean, Miriam Isabelle, John Mark. Student, Holy Cross Coll., 1943-45; MD, Georgetown Med. Sch., 1949. Intern Grasslands Hosp., Valhalla, N.Y., 1949-50; resident in surgery Grasslands Hosp., Valhalla, 1949-50, Georgetown U. Hosp., Washington, 1953-56; sr. investigator Nat. Cancer Inst., Bethesda, Md., 1957-60; chief divsn. surg. oncology Georgetown Med. Ctr., Washington, 1960-85; instr, asst.prof., then assoc. prof. surgery Georgetown U. Sch. Medicine, 1957-64, prof., 1969—; dir. Vincent T. Lombardi Cancer Rsch. Ctr., Washington, 1967-87; mem. U.S. Mil. Health Adv. Com. hon. prof. Universidad Cayetano Heredia, Lima, Peru, 1980. Lt. (j.g.) USNR, 1951-53. Recipient Pres.'s medal Georgetown U., 1991. Mem. Soc. Surg. Oncology (rep. adv. bd.), ACS, Assn. Am. Cancer Insts. (v.p. 1985-86, pres. 1986-87, bd. dirs. 1982, chmn. bd. dirs. 1987-88), So. Surg. Assn., Peruvian Cancer Soc. (hon.), Knights of Malta. Office: Georgetown U Med Ctr 3800 Reservoir Rd NW Washington DC 20007-2113

POTTER, JOHN LEITH, mechanical and aerospace engineer, educator, consultant; b. Metz, Mo., Feb. 5, 1923; s. Jay Francis Lee and Pearl Delores (Leeth) P.; m. Dorothy Jean Williams, Dec. 15, 1957; children: Stephen, Anne, Carol. BS in Aerospace Engring., U. Ala., Tuscaloosa, 1944, MS in Engring., 1949; MS in Engring. Mgmt., Vanderbilt U., 1976, PhD in Mech. Engring., 1974. Engr., educator various indsl., ednl. and govt. orgns., 1944-52; chief, flight and aerodyns. lab. Redstone Arsenal, Ala., 1952-56; mgr., div. chief, dep. tech. dir., sr. staff scientist Sverdrup Tech., Inc., Tullahoma, Tenn., 1956-83; research prof. Vanderbilt U., Nashville, 1983-92, prof. emeritus, 1992—; cons. engr. Nashville, 1983—; convener NATO-AGARD, U.S. and Eng., 1980-82, mem. working group, 1984-88; mem. adv. com. Internat. Symposium on Rarefied Gasdynamics, 1970—; invited lectr. USSR Acad. Scis., 1967; mem. NRC com. on assessment nat. aeronautical wind tunnel facilities, 1987-88; mem. NASA working groups, 1987—; mem. Engring. Accreditation Commn., 1985-90. Editor: Rarefied Gas Dynamics, 1977. Contbr. articles to profl. publs., chpts. to books. Chmn. bd. dirs. Coffee County Hist. Soc., Tenn., 1971-72; bd. dirs. Southeastern Amateur Athletic Union, 1972-73; pres. Tullahoma Swim Club, 1972-73, Sheffield Homeowners Assn., Nashville, 1983—. Recipient Outstanding Fellow award U. Ala. Aerospace Engring. Dept., 1987; elected 150th Anniversary Disting. Engring. Fellow U. Ala. Coll. Engring., 1988; USAF Arnold Engring. Devel. Ctr. fellow, 1993. Fellow AIAA (assoc. editor jour. 1970-73, publs. com. 1973-78, assoc. editor Progress in Astronautics and Aeronautics 1981-85, Gen. H.H. Arnold award Tenn. chpt. 1964); mem. Capstone Engring. Soc. (regional bd. dirs. 1972-77), Sigma Xi, Tau Beta Pi, Theta Tau, Pi Tau Sigma, Sigma Gamma Tau. Home: 200 Sheffield Pl Nashville TN 37215-3235 Office: Vanderbilt U Box 1592 Sta B Nashville TN 37235

POTTER, JOHN WILLIAM, federal judge; b. Toledo, Ohio, Oct. 25, 1918; s. Charles and Mary Elizabeth (Baker) P.; m. Phyllis May Bihn, Apr. 14, 1944; children: John William, Carolyn Diane, Kathryn Susan. PhB cum laude, U. Toledo, 1940; JD, U. Mich., 1946. Bar: Ohio 1947. Assoc. Zachman, Boxell, Schroeder & Torbet, Toledo, 1946-51; ptnr. Boxell, Bebout, Torbet & Potter, Toledo, 1951-69; mayor City of Toleao, 1961-67; asst. atty. gen. State of Ohio, 1968-69; judge 6th Dist. Ct. Appeals, 1969-82; judge U.S. Dist. Ct., Toledo, 1982—, sr. judge, 1992—; presenter in field. Sr. editor U. Mich. Law Rev., 1946. Pres. Ohio Mcpl. League, 1965; past assoc. pub. mem. Toledo Labor Mgmt. Commn.; past pres., bd. dirs. Commn. on Rels. with Toledo (Spain); past bd. dirs. Cummings Sch. Toledo Opera Assn., Conlon Ctr.; past trustee Epworth United Meth. Ch.; hon. chmn. Toledo Festival Arts, 1980. Capt. F.A., U.S. Army, 1942-46. Decorated Bronze Star; recipient Leadership award Toledo Bldg. Congress, 1965, Merit award Toledo Bd. Realtors, 1967, Resolution of Recognition award Ohio Ho. of Reps., 1982, award for outstanding rsch. or svc. in law or govt. Ohio State Bar Found., 1995, Outstanding Alumnus award U. Toledo, 1966. Fellow Am. Bar Found., Am. Judicature Soc., 6th Jud. Cir. Dist. Judges Assn., Fed. Judges Assn.; mem. ABA, Ohio Bar Assn. (Outstanding Rsch. award 1995), Toledo Bar Assn. (exec. com. 1962-64, award 1992), Lucas County Bar Assn., Toledo Area C. of C. (v.p. 1973-74), U. Toledo Alumni Assn. (past pres.), Toledo Zool. Soc. (past bd. dirs.), Old Newsboys Club, Toledo Club, Kiwanis (past pres.), Phi Kappa Phi. Home: 2418 Middlesex Dr Toledo OH 43606-3114 Office: US Dist Ct 307 US Courthouse 1716 Spielbusch Ave Toledo OH 43624

POTTER, KARL HARRINGTON, philosophy educator; b. Oakland, Calif., Aug. 19, 1927; s. George Reuben and Mabel (Harrington) P.; m. Antonia Fleak, June 26, 1957; children: David Fleak, Julie Ann. Grad., Taft Sch., 1945; AB, U. Calif. at Berkeley, 1950; MA, Harvard U., 1952, PhD, 1955. Instr. philosophy Carleton Coll., 1955-56; mem. faculty U. Minn., 1956-71, prof. philosophy, 1965-70, chmn. dept., 1964-67, dir., 1967-70; prof. philosophy and South Asian studies U. Wash., Seattle, 1971—, chmn. South Asia program, 1972-86, chmn. dept. philosophy, 1986-91. Author: The Padarthatattvanirupanam of Raghunatha Siromani, 1957, Presuppositions of India's Philosophies, 1963, Ency. of Indian Philosophies, 1970, 77, 81, 94, Guide to Indian Philosophy, 1988. With USNR, 1945-46. Fulbright fellow, India, 1952-53, 59-60, 81, Am. Inst. Indian Studies fellow, India, 1963-64, 95. Mem. Assn. Asian Studies (bd. dirs., mem. South Asia regional coun. 1971-74, chmn. coun. 1972-74), Am. Philos. Assn. Univ. Profs., Am. Oriental Soc., Soc. Asian and Comparative Philosophy (pres. 1968-70). Home: 19548 47th Ave NE Seattle WA 98155-1720 Office: U Washington Dept Philosophy Seattle WA 98105

POTTER, KEVIN, former United States attorney. Former dist. atty. Wood County, Wis.; former chmn. Wis. Labor and Indsl. Review Commn.; U.S. Atty. We. Dist. Wis., Madison, 1991-93; mem. Brennan Steil Basting and MacDougall S.C., Madison, 1993—; former chmn. Wis. Tax Appeals Commn. Office: Brennan Steil et al PO Box 990 433W Washington Ave Ste 100 Madison WI 53701-0990

POTTER, LILLIAN FLORENCE, business executive secretary; b. Montreal, Que., Can., Oct. 19, 1912; came to U.S., 1934; naturalized citizen.; d. Thomas Joseph and Lily Rose (Robertson) Quirk; m. Theodore Edward Potter, July 20, 1932 (dec. Apr. 1980); children: Peter Edward, Stephen Thomas. Grad. high sch., Montreal, 1929, grad., 1931. Sr. sec. S.D. Warren div. Scott Paper Co., Westbrook, Maine, 1955-69, editor indsl. publ. S.D. Warren div., 1969-72; editor Nat. Antiques Rev. mag., Portland, Maine, 1972-77; exec. sec. Humboldt Portland Litho div. Humboldt Nat. Graphics, Inc., Fortuna, Calif., 1977—; free lance writer Guy Gannett Pub. Co., Portland, 1960-64. Author: (children's book) Once Upon an Autumn, 1984 (state 1st pl. award, nat. 3d pl. award), (antiques and collectibles) A Re-Introduction to Silver Overlay on Glass and Ceramics, 1992; co-author: (textbook, tchrs. manual) Foundations of Patient Care, 1981; asst. editor, N.E. dist. The Secretary mag., Profl. Secs. Internat., 1960-62; editor Maine Chpt. Bull., 1963-64. Recipient George Washington Honors medal Freedoms Found., Valley Forge, Pa., 1964, Sec. of Yr. award Portland chpt. Profl. Secs. Internat., 1967, Outstanding Svc. award State of Maine Sesquicentennial, 1970, Outstanding Svc. award Island Pond (Vt.) Hist. Soc. 1978. Mem. Maine Media Women (pres. 1970-71, Woman of Yr. 1973, Communicator of Achievement plaque and prize 1991), Maine Writers and Pubs. Alliance, Woman's Lit. Union, Portland Lyric Theater, Island Pond Hist. Soc., Jones Mus. Glass and Ceramics, Westbrook Woman's Club, OES (past matron, past pres.). Republican. Episcopalian. Avocations: reading, researching, antiques, swimming, gardening. Home: 80 Payson St Portland ME 04102-2851

POTTER, PAUL EDWIN, geologist, educator, consultant; b. Springfield, Ohio, Aug. 30, 1925; s. Edwin Forest and Mabel (Yanser) P. MS in Geology, U. Chgo., 1950, PhD in Geology, 1952; MS in Stats., U. Ill., 1959. Research assoc. Ill. Geol. Survey, Urbana, 1952-54, asst. geologist, 1954-61; assoc. prof. geology Ind. U., Bloomington, 1963-65, prof., 1965-71; prof. U. Cin., 1971-92; rsch. fellow UNESP, Rio Clara, Brazil, 1993-95. Author: Atlas and Glossary of Sedimentry Structures, 1964, Sand and Sandstone, 2d edit., 1987, Paleocurrents and Basin Analysis, 2d edit., 1977, Introduction to Petrography of Fossils, 1971, Sedimentology of Shale, 1980. Served with U.S. Army, 1944-46. Sr. NSF fellow, 1958, Guggenheim fellow, 1961-62; recipient Francis J. Pettijohn Sedimentary medal, 1992. Republican. Office: Geociecias/UNESP, Caixa 178, Rio Claro 13506 CP, Brazil

POTTER, RALPH BENAJAH, JR., theology and social ethics educator; b. Los Angeles, May 19, 1931; s. Ralph Benajah and Vivian Irene MacNabb (Borden) P.; m. Jean Ishbel MacCormick, Aug. 15, 1953; children: Anne Elizabeth, Ralph Andrew, James David, Margaret Jean; m. Christine Iva Mitchell, Aug. 25, 1985 (div. 1995); children: Charles Benajah Mitchell Potter, Christopher Ralph Mitchell Potter. B.A., Occidental Coll., 1952; postgrad., Pacific Sch. Religion, 1952-53; B.D., McCormick Theol. Sem., 1955; Th.D. (Presbyn. Grad. fellow 1958-63, Rockefeller fellow 1961-62, Kent fellow 1963-64), Harvard, 1965. Ordained to ministry Presbyn. Ch., 1955; dir., pastor Clay County Presbyn. Larger Parish, Manchester, Ky., 1955-58; sec. social edn. Bd. Christian Edn., United Presbyn. Ch. in U.S.A., Phila., 1963-65; asst. prof. social ethics Harvard Div. Sch.; mem. Center for Population Studies, Harvard U, Cambridge, Mass., 1965-69; prof. social ethics Harvard Divinity Sch., 1969—; mem., prof., Ctr. for Population Studies, Harvard U., 1969-89; theologian-in-residence Am. Ch. in Paris, 1975; sr. rsch. scholar Kennedy Inst. for Bio-ethics Georgetown U., 1974; assoc. Lowell House, Harvard U.; founding fellow Hastings Ctr. Author: War and Moral Discourse, 1969; contbr. chpts. to The Religious Situation, 1968, 1968, Religion and the Public Order, 1968, Toward a Discipline of Social Ethics, 1972, The Population Crisis and Moral Responsibility, 1973, Community in America, 1988, also scholarly articles. Mem. Soc. Christian Ethics, Soc. for Values in Higher Edn., Société Européene de Culture, Am. Acad. Religion, Tocqueville Soc. Home: 7 Swan St Arlington MA 02174-6507 Office: 45 Francis Ave Cambridge MA 02138-1911

POTTER, ROBERT DANIEL, federal judge; b. Wilmington, N.C., Apr. 4, 1923; s. Elisha Lindsey and Emma Louise (McLean) P.; m. Mary Catherine Neilson, Feb. 13, 1954; children: Robert Daniel, Mary Louise, Catherine Ann. AB in Chemistry, Duke U., 1947, LLB, 1950; LLD (hon.), Sacred Heart Coll., Belmont, N.C., 1982. Bar: N.C. 1951. Pvt. practice law Charlotte, N.C., 1951-81; chief judge U.S. Dist. Ct. (we. dist.) N.C., 1984-91, dist. judge, 1991-94, now sr. judge. Commr. Mecklenburg County, Charlotte, 1966-68. Served to 2d lt. U.S. Army, 1944-47, ETO. Mem. N.C. Bar Assn. Republican. Roman Catholic. Club: Charlotte City. Office: US Courthouse 250 Federal Bldg 401 W Trade St Charlotte NC 28202-1619

POTTER, ROBERT JOSEPH, technical and business executive; b. N.Y.C., Oct. 29, 1932; s Mack and Ida (Bernstein) P.; married; children: Diane Gail, Suzanne Lee, David Craig. BS cum laude, Lafayette Coll., 1954; MA in Physics, U. Rochester, 1957, PhD in Optics, 1960. Cons. ANPA Research Inst., AEC Brookhaven Nat. Lab., RCA Labs., U.S. Naval Research Labs., 1952-60; mgr. optical physics and optical pattern recognition IBM Thomas J. Watson Research Center, Yorktown Heights, N.Y., 1960-65; assoc. dir. Applied Research Lab., Xerox Corp., Rochester, N.Y., 1965-67; v.p. advanced engring. Xerox Corp., 1967-68, v.p. devel. and engring., 1968-69; v.p., gen. mgr. Spl. Products and Systems div. Spl. Products and Sys. divsn. Xerox Corp., Stamford, Conn. and Pasadena, Calif., 1969-71; v.p. info. tech. group Xerox Corp., Rochester, 1971-73; v.p. info. tech. group Xerox Corp., Dallas, 1973-75, pres. Office Sys. divsn., 1975-78; sr. v.p., chief tech. officer Internat. Harvester Co., Chgo., 1978-82; with R.J. Potter & Co., 1983-84; group v.p. integrated office sys. No. Telecom Inc., Richardson, Tex., 1985-87; pres. and CEO Datapoint Corp., San Antonio, 1987-89; pres., CEO R.J. Potter Co., Dallas, 1990—; dir. Molex Inc. Contbr. articles to profl. jours. Trustee Ill. Inst. Tech. Recipient IBM Outstanding Tech. Contbn. award, 1964, Disting. Achievement award Soc. Mfg. Engrs., 1981; Kroner scholar Lafayette Coll., 1954; Disting. Rochester scholar U. Rochester, 1995. Fellow Optical Soc. Am., Am. Phys. Soc., Phi Beta Kappa, Sigma Xi. Office: R J Potter Co 5215 N O Connor Blvd Ste 1110 Irving TX 75039-3739

POTTER, WILLIAM BARTLETT, business executive; b. Washington, Jan. 4, 1938; s. George Holland and Virginia (Bartlett) P.; m. Simone Robert, June 6, 1964; children: Eva Simone, William Bartlett. A.B., Princeton U.,

1960; M.B.A., Emory U., 1962. With Merc.-Safe Deposit & Trust Co., Balt., 1962—; asst. sec., asst. treas. Merc.-Safe Deposit & Trust Co., 1964-66, asst. v.p., 1966-68, v.p., 1968-69, sr. v.p., 1969-76, exec. v.p., 1976; exec. v.p. Preston Trucking Co., 1976-77, pres., 1977-86; chmn., pres. Preston Trucking, 1986-92; Preston Corp., 1986-93, chmn., 1994—. Home: PO Box 870 Trinidad CO 81082-0614

POTTER, WILLIAM BLAKE, language professional, educator; b. Evanston, Ill., Nov. 28, 1955; s. Jack and Jean (Scott) P.; m. Kristin Joan Aspal, Oct., 1993. BA in Drama, N.Mex. State U., 1979; MA in English, CUNY Grad. Ctr., 1990, MPhil, 1996. Adj. prof. English Coll. of Staten Island, N.Y., 1990-92, Wagner Coll., Staten Island, 1993—; active Friday Forum com., CUNY Grad. Ctr., 1990-91. Actor numerous theatrical prodns.; bd. dirs. No Empty Space Theatre, Staten Island, 1987—. Recipient citation for excellence in acting, Am. Coll. Theatre Festival, Dallas/Ft. Worth, 1978, finalist Irene Ryan scholarship, 1978. Mem. U.S. Chess Fedn., ACLU, People for the American Way, Modern Lang. Assn., Mensa. Democrat. Avocations: zoology, chess, weight lifting, classical music, theology.

POTTER, WILLIAM GRAY, JR., library director; b. Duluth, Minn., Feb. 18, 1950; s. William Gray and Kathryn Martha (Scheuer) P.; m. Marsha Ann Munie, Sept. 23, 1982. BA, So. Ill. U., 1973; MLS, U. Ill., 1975, MA, 1975, PhD, 1984. Libr. U. Wis.-Whitewater, 1975-78; asst. dir. gen. svcs. U. Ill.-Urbana, 1978-85; assoc. dean librs. for tech. svcs., automation and systems Ariz. State U., Tempe, 1985-89; dir. librs. U. Ga., Athens, 1989—. Editor: Serials Automation, 1980, Libr. Trends, 1981, Info. Tech. and Librs., 1984-89; mem. editl. bd. Multi-Media Rev., 1989-92, OCLC Micro., 1990—, Libr. Hi-Tech., 1992—, Coll. and Rsch. Libr., 1996—. Contbr. articles to profl. jours. Bd. dirs. Richard B. Russell Found., 1989—, sec., 1990—; mem. adv. com. Ga. Libr. Svcs. and Constrn. Act; bd. trustees OCLC, 1994—; mem. svc. to the citizen com. Ga. Info. Tech. Policy Coun., 1996—. Mem. ALA, Libr. and Info. Tech. Assn. (pres. 1987-88), OCLC Users Coun. (del. 1990-94, pres. 1991-92), IBM (info. steering com. 1994-95, higher edn. adv. coun. 1995-96), Assn. Rsch. Librs. (bd. dirs. 1996—), Beta Phi Mu. Home: 6 Dearing Pl 285 Blue Heron Dr Athens GA 30605 Office: Univ of Georgia Libraries Athens GA 30602

POTTER, WILLIAM JAMES, investment banker; b. Toronto, Aug. 11, 1948; s. William Wakely and Ruby Loretta (Skidmore) P.; m. Linda Lee, Nov. 25, 1972; children: Lisa Michelle, Meredith Lee, Andrew David. AB, Colgate U., 1970; MBA, Harvard U., 1974. With White Weld & Co., Inc., N.Y.C., 1974-75, Toronto Dominion Bank, Toronto (Can.) and N.Y., 1975-78; group mgr. Toronto Dominion Bank, Toronto, 1979-82; 1st v.p. Barclays Bank PLC, N.Y.C., 1982-84; mng. dir. Prudential-Bache Securities, Inc., N.Y.C., 1984-89; pres. Ridgewood Capital Funding Inc., N.Y.C., 1989—, Ridgewood Group Internat. Ltd., N.Y.C., 1989—; advisor Ladenberg Thalman Internat., 1990-92, Laidlaw Holdings, Inc., 1992-93; bd. dirs. 1st Australia Fund Inc., Md., 1st Australia Prime Income Fund Inc., Md., 1st Australia Prime Income Co. Ltd., New Zealand, Impulsora del Fondo Mex., Mexico City, Alexandria Bancorp, Can., Battery Techs. Inc., Can., 1st Commonwealth Fund, Md., Compuflex Inc., Del., Internat. Panorama Resources Inc., Can., Voicenet Inc. Del. Author: Finance for the Minerals Industry, 1985. Bd. dirs. Glen Ridge (N.J.) Community Fund, 1985—; fin. mem. Glen Ridge Congl. Ch., 1985—; trustee Glen Ridge Ednl. Found., 1994—. Mem. Nat. Fgn. Trade Coun. (bd. dirs., chmn. fin. com.), Harvard Club, Williams Club (N.Y.C.), Nat. Club (Toronto), Glen Ridge Country Club (N.J.), Buck Hill Country Club (Pa.), Internat. Platform Assn., Fcon. Club N.Y. Congregationalist. Avocations: golf, tennis. Office: Ridgewood Group Internat Inc 380 Lexington Ave Rm 1511 New York NY 10168-1594

POTTIE, ROSWELL FRANCIS, Canadian federal science and technology consultant; b. St. Peter's, N.S., Can., Oct. 28, 1933; s. John Henry and Margaret Mary (Landry) P.; m. Huguette Lacoste, Aug. 18, 1989; children: Michael F., Gregory J., Lisa M., David S. BS in Chemistry summa cum laude, St. Francis Xavier Univ., 1954; PhD in Chemistry, Notre Dame U., 1958. Postdoctoral fellow Notre Dame (Ind.) U., 1957-58, E.I. Du Pont de Nemours, Inc., Wilmington, Del., 1960-64; postdoctoral fellow NRC Can., Ottawa, 1958-60, research officer, 1964-74, asst. to sr. v.p., 1976-80; Atlantic regional dir. NRC Can., Halifax, N.S., 1980-83; v.p. regional labs. NRC Can., Ottawa, 1983-84, v.p. physical scis. and engring., 1984-86, sr. v.p. labs., 1986-87, exec. v.p., 1987-91; pvt. cons., 1991—; program officer Ministry of State for Sci. and Tech. (secondment), Ottawa, 1974-75; program analyst Treasury Bd. Can. (secondment), Ottawa, 1975-76; bd. govs. Ctr. for Cold Regions Resources Engring., St. John's; mem. N.B. (Can.) Research and Productivity Council, Fredericton, 1981—. Contbr. articles to profl. jours. Coach, exec. baseball, swimming and soccer clubs, Gloucester, Ont., 1970-76; pres. Gloucester Swim Club, 1973-75; sec. exec. North Gloucester Recreation Assn., 1971-74. Recipient Gov. Gen.'s medal, St. Francis Xavier U., 1954. Mem. Can. Research Mgmt. Assn., St. Francis Xavier Alumni Assn. (Ottawa pres. 1970-73), Sigma Xi. Roman Catholic. Avocations: swimming, badminton, carpentry, ancient history. Home: 28 Bellefontaine Ct, Lawrencetown, NS Canada B2Z 1L3

POTTORFF, JO ANN, state legislator; b. Wichita, Kans., Mar. 7, 1936; d. John Edward McCluggage and Helen Elizabeth (Alexander) Ryan; m. Gary Nial Pottorff; children: Michael Lee, Gregory Nial. BA, Kansas State U., 1957; MA, St. Louis U., 1969. Elem. tchr. Pub. Sch., Keats and St. George, 1957-59; cons., elem. specialist Mid Continent Regional Edn. Lab., Kansas City, Mo., 1971-73; cons. Poindexter Assocs., Wichita, 1975; campaign mgr. Garner Shriver Congl. Camp, Wichita, 1976; interim dir. Wichita Area Rape Ctr., 1977; conf. coord. Biomedical Synergistics Inst., Wichita, 1977-79; real estate sales asst. Chester Kappelman Group, Wichita, 1979—; state rep. State of Kans., Topeka, 1985—. Mem. sch. bd. Wichita Pub. Schs., 1977-85; bd. dirs. Edn. Consol. and Improvement Act Adv. com., Kans. Found. for the Handicapped; mem. Children and Youth Adv. com. (bd. dirs.); active Leadership Kans.; chairperson women's network Nat. Conf., State Legislators; mem. Wichita Children's Home Bd. Recipient Disting. Svc. award Kans. Assn. Sch. Bds., 1983, Outstanding Svc. to Sch. Children of Nation award Coun. Urban Bds., 1984, awards Gov.'s Conf. for Prevention of Child Abuse and Neglect, Kans. Assn. Reading. Mem. Leadership Am. Alumnae (bd. dirs., sec.), Found. for Agr. in Classroom (bd. dirs.), Jr. League, Vet. Aux. (pres.), Bd. Nat. State Art Agys., Rotary, Ky. Assn. Rehab. Facilities (Ann. award), Nat. Order Women in Legislature (past bd. dirs.), Rotary, Chi Omega (pres.). Avocations: politics, traveling. Office: Chester Kappelman Group PO Box 8036 Wichita KS 67208-0036

POTTRUCK, DAVID STEVEN, brokerage house executive; b. 1948. BA, U. Pa., 1970, MBA, 1972. Now pres., CEO U.S. Govt., 1972-74; with Arthur Young & Co., 1974-76, sr. cons.; with Citibank N.Am., 1976-81, v.p.; with Shearson/Am. Express, 1981-84, sr. v.p. consumer mktg. and advt.; with Charles Schwab & Co., San Francisco, 1984—; exec. v.p. mktg., br. adminstr. Charles Schwab and Co., Inc.; pres., CEO The Charles Corp., Charles Schwab & Co.; pres., COO The Charles Schwab Corp. Office: Charles Schwab & Co Inc 101 Montgomery St San Francisco CA 94104-4122*

POTTS, ANNIE, actress; b. Nashville, Oct. 28, 1952. Student, Calif. Inst. of Arts; BFA, Stephens Coll. Appeared in films including Corvette Summer, 1978, King of the Gypsies, 1978, Heartaches, 1982, Crime of Passion, 1984, Ghostbusters, 1984, Stick, 1985, Pretty in Pink, 1986, Jumpin' Jack Flash, 1986, Pass the Ammo, 1988, Who's Harry Crumb, 1989, Ghostbusters II, 1989, Texasville, 1990, Breaking the Rules, 1992, Toy Story (voice only) 1995; plays include Richard III, Charley's Aunt, Cymbeline; TV appearances include Black Market Baby, 1977, Flatbed Annie and Sweetie Pie: Lady Truckers, 1979, Cowboy, 1983, Why Me?, 1984, Ladies in Waiting; TV series include Goodtime Girls, 1980, Designing Women, 1986-1993, Love and War, 1993-95 (Emmy nomination, Lead Actress - Comedy Series, 1994), Dangerous Minds, 1996. Spokesperson Women for the Arthritis Found.; mem. aux. bd. MADD. *

POTTS, ANTHONY VINCENT, optometrist, orthokeratologist; b. Detroit, Aug. 10, 1945; m. Susan Claire, July 1, 1967; 1 child, Anthony Christian. Student, Henry Ford Community Coll., 1964-65, Eastern Mich. U., 1965-66; OD, So. Coll. Optometry, 1970; MS in Health Svcs. Mgmt., LaSalle U., 1995. Practice orthokeratology and contact lenses Troy, Mich., 1975—; adj. prof. optometry Ill. Coll. Optometry; lectr., author orthokeratology, contact lenses and astigmatism. Lt. USNR, 1971-73, lt. MSC USNR, 1992—. Fellow Internat. Orthokeratology Soc. (membership chmn. 1976-83, bd. dirs. local chpt. 1976-83, chmn. Internat. Eye Rsch. Found. sect. 1981-83, bd. dirs. nat. chpt. 1985—, adminstrv. dir. nat. chpt. 1985—, chmn. nat. chpt. 1987—), Am. Acad. Optometry, Am. Optometric Assn.; mem. Armed Forces Optometric Soc., Nat. Eye Rsch. Found., Naval Order Am., Assn. of Mil. Surgeons of U.S., Naval Hosp. Great Lakes. Roman Catholic. Office: Med Sq Troy 1575 W Big Beaver Rd Ste 11C Troy MI 48084-3598

POTTS, BARBARA JOYCE, historical society executive; b. L.A., Feb. 18, 1932; d. Theodore Thomas and Helen Mae (Kelley) Elledge; m. Donald A. Potts, Dec. 27, 1953; children: Tedd, Douglas, Dwight, Laura. AA, Graceland Coll., 1951; grad., Radiol. Tech. Sch., 1953; grad. program for sr. execs. in state and local govt., Harvard U., 1989. Radiol. technician Independence (Mo.) Sanitarium and Hosp., 1953, 58-59, Mercy Hosp., Balt., 1954-55; city coun. mem.-at-large City of Independence, 1978-82, mayor, 1982-90; exec. dir. Jackson County Hist. Soc., 1991—; chmn. Mid-Am. Regional Coun., Kansas City, Mo., 1984-85; bd. dirs. Mo. Mcpl. League, Jefferson City, 1982-90, v.p., 1986-87, pres., 1987, 88; chmn. Mo. Commn. on Local Govt. Cooperation, 1985-90. Author: Independence, 1985. Mem. Mo. Gov.'s Conf. Edn., 1976, Independence Charter Rev. Bd., 1977; bd. dirs. Hope House Shelter Abused Women, Independence, 1982—, Vis. Nurses Assn., 1990-93, Mid-Continent Coun. U.S. Girl Scouts, 1991-95; pres. Child Placement Svcs., Independence, 1972-89, Greater Kansas City region NCCJ, 1990—; trustee Independence Regional Health Ctr., 1982-90, 94—, Park Coll., 1989—, chmn. bd. trustees, 1995—; mem. Nat. Women's Polit. Caucus, 1978—; mem. adv. bd. Greater Mo. Focus on Leadership, mem. steering com., 1989—; bd. mem. Independence Cmty. Found., 1990—; bd. mem. Harry S. Truman Libr. Inst., 1995—; trustee Eye Found. Kans. City, 1997—. Recipient George Lehr Meml. award for community svc., 1989, Woman of Achievement award Mid-Continent coun. Girl Scouts U.S.A., 1983, 75th Anniversary Women of Achievement award Mid-Continent coun. Girl Scouts, 1987, Jane Adams award Hope House, 1984, Community Leadership award Comprehensive Mental Health Svcs., Inc., 1984, 90, Graceland Coll. Alumni Disting. Svc. award 1991, Disting. Citizen award Independence C. of C., 1993, Outstanding Community Svc. award Jackson County Inter-Agy. Coun., 1994, Outstanding Cmty. Svc. award Cmty. Svcs. League, 1996; named Friend of Edn. Indpendence NEA, 1990. Mem. LWV (Community Svc. award 1990), Am. Inst. Pub. Svc. (mem. bd. nominators), Nat. Trust for Hist. Preservation. Mem. Reorganized LDS Ch. Home: 18508 E 30th Ter S Independence MO 64057-1904

POTTS, BERNARD, lawyer; b. Balt., Aug. 22, 1915; s. Phillip Louis and Anna (Novey) P.; m. Frieda Hochman, 1949; children: Phillip Louis, Neal Allen, Bryan H., Andrea Maria. ABA, Balt. Coll. Commerce, 1936; LLB, Eastern U., Balt., 1949; JD, U. Balt., Balt., 1950. Bar: Md. 1950. Tax cons. Balt., 1936-49, since practiced in Balt., 1949—; ptnr., sr. counsel Potts & Potts, P.A., Balt., 1975—. Founder, counsel Gamber Community Vol. Fire Co., 1963; founder, pres. Mary Dopkin's Children's Fund, 1950-60; founder Police Cmty. Rels. Coun. Md., 1956; founder, v.p. Boys Town Homes Md., 1965-80; founder, chmn. Accident and Prevention Bur. Md., 1965-75; pres. Safety First Club Md., 1966-68; mem. Md. bd. NCCJ, 1976-80; bd. dirs. NCCJ-Md. Conf. Social Concern, 1976-80; co-founder, co-chmn. Greater Balt. Mental Health Coun., 1980; founder E. Balt. Children's Fund, Coun. Ind. Self-Help, Police Community Rels. Couns., Crime Prevention Bur. Md., 1960-75; founder Md. chpt. Boys & Girls Club Am., 1988; pro bono adviser, bd. dirs. Patterson Emergency Food Ctr. & Soup Kitchen, Bea Gaddy Homes for Homeless Women & Children Inc.; pro bono atty. Trancare, Inc., Md. Vernon Youth Ctr. Served with AUS, 1943. Recipient cert. policy cmty. rels. Mich. State U., 1961, Disting. Citizens award Office Gov. Md., 1971, Presdl. citation Balt. City Coun., 1977, Outstanding Alumnus award Mt. Vernon Law Sch., Eastern U., 1970, Wheel Master's award Metro Civic Assn., 1963, Cert. Appreciation Balt. Police Dept., 1972, Cert. of Appreciation Gov. Schaefer, 1991, Cert. award Balt. City Sheriff, 1994, Cert. of Appreciation and Congratulations, Congressman Ben Cardin, 1994; numerous awards B'nai B'rith, Safety First Club; Bernard Potts Day proclaimed, 1980. Am. Bar Assn., Fed. Bar Assn., Am. Trial Lawyers Assn., Balt. Bar Assn., Met. Civic Assn. Balt. (v.p. 1968-80), Humanitarian Assn. Md. (v.p.), Jewish War Vets. (past post comdr.), Masons, B'nai B'rith (past pres. Balt. 1965, internat. commr. community svcs. 1972—, sec. CVS exec. commn.). Home: 3206 Midfield Rd Baltimore MD 21208-4420 Office: Ste 1102 Court Sq Bldg Baltimore MD 21202

POTTS, CHARLES AARON, management executive, writer; b. Idaho Falls, Idaho, Aug. 28, 1943; s. Verl S. and Sarah (Gray) P.; m. Judith Samimi, 1977 (div. 1986); 1 child, Emily Karen; m. Ann Weatherill, June 19, 1988; 1 child, Natalie Larise. *Charles Potts is 14th generation North American and 5th generation out west. General Robert Caldwell from Warwickshire arrived in Rhode Island in 1653, the first of three generations of generals in the British Army in Potts' Colonial American lineage. Captain Dan Jones, great great grandfather, was with the prophet Joseph Smith when he was martyred. He converted and brought to Utah in 1849 the Welsh choral musicians who began the Mormon Tabernacle Choir. In 1926, Potts' great aunt Stella Gray Evans was the only licensed midwife in Idaho and delivered more than 600 children.* BA in English, Idaho State U., 1965. Lic. real estate broker, Wash. Owner Palouse Mgmt., Inc., Walla Walla, Wash.; founder, dir. Litmus Inc., 1967-77; founding editor COSMEP, Berkeley, Calif., 1968; host poetry radio program Oasis, NPR-KUER, Salt Lake City, 1976-77; N.W. rep. Chinese Computer Communications, Inc., Lansing, Mich., 1988; pres. Tsunami Inc. Author: Blues from Thurston County, 1966, Burning Snake, 1967, The Litmus Papers, 1969, Little Lord Shiva, 1969, Blue Up the Nile, 1972, Wating in Blood, 1973, The Trancemigracion of Menzu, 1973, The Golden Calf, 1975, Charlie Kiot, 1976, The Opium Must Go Thru, 1976, Valga Krusa, 1977, Rocky Mountain Man, 1978, A Rite to the Body, 1989, The Dictatorship of the Environment, 1991, Loading Las Vegas, 1991, How the South Finally Won the Civil War, 1995, 100 Yrs. In Idaho, 1996; columnist (with Kyushu Gleaner) Japan's Polit. Choices, 1995—; pub., editor The Temple, 1997—. Rep. to exec. com. 5th Congl. Dist., Wash. State Dem. Party, 1993-95. Recipient First Place Novel award Manuscript's Internat., 1991, Disting. Profl. Achievement award Idaho State U., 1994. Mem. Italian Heritage Assn. (ice cream chair 1990, award 1993), Pacific N.W. Booksellers Assn., Walla Walla Area C. of C., Downtown W2 Found., Blue Mountain Arts Alliance, Fukuoka Internat. Forum, Chinese Lang. Computer Soc., Soc. Neurolinguistic Programming (master practitioner), Toastmasters. Avocations: tennis, raspberries. Office: Palouse Mgmt 34 S Colville St Walla Walla WA 99362-1920 *Charles Potts is called "An editor and publisher of acumen and flair who consistently showcases works of excellence," in The Selected Essays of Rich Mangelsdorff. Multiple Fulbright and OAS scholar, professor Hugh Fox of Michigan State University published the first full length study of Potts' work through Dustbooks in 1979, The Poetry of Charles Potts. Scott Preston reviewing The Dictatorship of the Environment in Western American Literature called his work "A determined attack on decadence...the real postmodern western American poetry," while Doug Marx, in Writers Northwest said, "In spirit, he is reminiscent of the late, great Thomas McGrath."*

POTTS, DAVID MALCOLM, population specialist, administrator; b. Sunderland, Durham, Eng., Jan. 8, 1935; came to U.S., 1978; s. Ronald Windle and Kathleen Annie (Cole) P.; m. Carolina Merula Deys (div. 1979); children: Oliver, Sarah, Henry; m. Marcia Jaffe (dec. 1993); m. Martha Madison Campbell, Mar. 1995. M.A., St. Catherine's Coll., Cambridge, Eng., 1960; M.B., B.Chir., Univ. Coll. Hosp., London, 1962; Ph.D., Sidney Sussex Coll., Cambridge U., 1965. Intern North Middlesex Hosp., London, 1962-64; fellow Sidney Sussex Coll., Cambridge, 1964-67; med. dir. Internat. Planned Parenthood Fedn., London, 1968-78; pres. Family Health Internat., Research Triangle Park, N.C., 1978-91; Bixby prof. of Fam. Planning and Population U of Calif., Berkeley, Calif., 1991—; dir. Population Services Internat., Washington, Alan Guttmacher Inst., N.Y.C.; Tracey Maund lectr. Women's Hosp., Melbourne, Australia, 1989. Author: Abortion, 1977, Society and Fertility, 1979, Textbook of Contraceptive Practice, 1984, Queen Victoria's Gene, 1995; mem. editl. bd. Jour. Biosocial Sci. Recipient Hugh Moore award Population Crisis Com., 1972. Fellow Zool. Soc. Eng.; mem. Internat. Union for Sci. Study of Population. Avocations: history; writing. Home: 3416 Chris Ln San Mateo CA 94403-3937

POTTS, DOUGLAS GORDON, neuroradiologist; b. New Zealand, Jan. 27, 1927; came to U.S., 1960, naturalized, 1966; s. Leslie Andrew and Vera (Morgan) P.; m. Ann Jean Frank, June 16, 1962; children: David Andrew, Kenneth Morgan, Alison Jean. B.Sc., Canterbury Univ. Coll., Christchurch, New Zealand, 1946; M.B., Ch.B., U. Otago, Dunedin, New Zealand, 1951; M.D., U. New Zealand, 1960. Intern Auckland (New Zealand) Hosp., 1952-53, resident radiology, 1954-57; resident Central Middlesex Hosp., London, Eng., 1957-58; sr. registrar Atkinson Morley's Hosp., London, Eng., 1958-59, Nat. Hosp., London, Eng., 1959-60; radiologist Presbyn. Hosp., N.Y.C., 1960-67, N.Y. Hosp., 1967-85; prof. radiology Cornell U. Med. Coll., 1970-85; prof., chmn. dept. radiology U. Toronto, Ont., Can., 1985-91; ret., 1992. Author: (with Pool) Aneurysms and Arteriovenous Anomalies of the Brain, 1965; editor: (with T.H. Newton) Radiology of the Skull and Brain, Vol. 1, 1971, Vol. 2, 1974, Vol. 3, 1977, Vol. 4, 1978, Vol. 5, 1981, Modern Neuroradiology, Vols. 1 and 2, 1983. Mem. Am. Soc. Neuroradiology (pres. 1970-71).

POTTS, ERWIN REA, newspaper executive; b. Pineville, N.C., Apr. 20, 1932; s. Jennings Bryan and Edith Maxine (Matthews) P.; m. Silvia Antuna Montalbo, Feb. 18, 1961; children: Matthew Kingsley, Jeffrey Manuel, Bryan Erwin (dec.). Student, Mars Hill (N.C.) Jr. Coll., 1950-52; A.B. in Journalism, U. N.C., 1954. Reporter Charlotte News, 1954; Reporter, editor Miami Herald, Miami, Fla., 1958-64; editor, pub. North Dade (Fla.) Jour., 1964-67; asst. mng. editor, city editor Miami Herald, 1967-70; v.p., gen. mgr. Tallahassee Democrat, 1970-73; v.p., gen. mgr. Charlotte (N.C.) Observer, News, 1973-75, asst. mng. editor, 1975—. Bd. dirs. Stanford U. Knight Fellwoships. With USMC, 1955-58. Mem. Newspaper Assn. Am. (bd. dirs., nominating com.), Sacramento Regional Found. (bd. dirs.). Office: Mc Clatchy Newspapers Inc PO Box 15779 2100 Q St Sacramento CA 95816

POTTS, GERALD NEAL, manufacturing company executive; b. Franklin, N.C., Apr. 10, 1933; s. Joseph Thomas and Virgie (Bryant) P.; m. Ann Eliza Underwood, Dec. 21, 1956 (div. 1991); children: Catherine, Thomas, Alice. B.S., U. N.C., 1954; grad., Advanced Mgmt. Program, Harvard, 1973. With Vulcan Mold & Iron Co., Chgo., 1957-59; sales engr. Vulcan Mold & Iron Co., 1959-62; gen. sales mgr. Vulcan Mold & Iron Co., Latrobe, Pa., 1963-65; v.p. sales Vulcan Mold & Iron Co., 1965-68; v.p. Vulcan, Inc., Latrobe, 1968-72; exec. v.p. Vulcan, Inc., 1972-73, pres., 1973-85, chief exec. officer, 1977-85, chmn., 1981-85; group exec. Teledyne Inc., 1985-92; pres. Woodings Verona Tool Works Inc., 1993-97; Active Young Pres.'s Orgn., 1973-83. Bd. dirs. Latrobe Area Hosp., 1967—, chmn., 1985-88; trustee Greater Latrobe Community Chest, 1970-87, pres., 1978-79; adv. bd. U. Pitts. at Greensburg, 1974-80; trustee Seton Hill Coll., Greensburg, 1978-80. Served with AUS, 1954-56. Mem. Laurel Valley Golf Club, Rolling Rock Club, Duquesne Club (Pa.), Masons (32 deg.), Shriners, Chi Phi.

POTTS, JOHN THOMAS, JR., physician, educator; b. Phila., Jan. 19, 1932; married; 3 children. B.A., LaSalle Coll, Phila., 1953; M.D., U. Pa., Phila., 1957. From intern to asst. resident in medicine Mass. Gen. Hosp., Boston, 1957-59; resident Nat. Heart Inst., 1959-60, research fellow in medicine, 1960-63, sr. research staff, 1963-66, head sect. polypeptide hormones, 1966-68; chief endocrine unit Mass. Gen. Hosp., Boston, 1968-81, chief gen med. svc., 1981—; from asst. to assoc. prof. medicine Harvard U. Med. Sch., Boston, 1968-75, prof., 1975-81, Jackson prof. clin. medicine, 1981—; chief endocrine unit Mass. Gen. Hosp., Boston, 1968-81, chief gen. med., 1981-96, dir. rsch., 1996—. Recipient Ernest Oppenheimer award, Andre Lichwitz prize Endocrine Soc., 1968, Fred Conrad Koch award Endocrine Soc., 1991, William F. Neumann award Am. Soc. Bone and Mineral Rsch. Fellow AAA; mem. Am. Soc. Biol. Chemistry, Endocrine Soc. (pres. 1987), Assn. Am. Physicians, Am. Fedn. Clin. Research, Am. Soc. Clin. Investigation, Inst. Medicine. Office: Mass Gen Hosp Med Svcs Fruit St Boston MA 02114-2620

POTTS, KEVIN T., emeritus chemistry educator; b. Sydney, Australia, Oct. 26, 1928; married; children: Mary Ellen, Jeannette, Karen, Susan. B.Sc., U. Sydney, 1950, M.Sc., 1951; D. of Philosophy in Organic Chemistry, Oxford U., Eng., 1954, D.Sc., 1973. Demonstrator chemistry U. Sydney, 1950, teaching fellow, 1951; research asst. organic chemistry Oxford U., 1951-54; scientist Med. Research Council of Eng., 1954-56; research asst. organic chemistry Harvard, 1956-58; lectr. Adelaide, 1958-61; asso. prof. chemistry U. Louisville, 1961-65; assoc. prof. Rensslaer Poly. Inst., 1965-66; prof. chemistry Rensselaer Poly. Inst., 1966-94; prof. emeritus Rensselaer Poly Inst., 1994—; chmn. dept. Rensselaer Poly. Inst., 1973-80. Contbr. articles in field organic chemistry to sci. jours. Grantee Nat. Cancer Inst., Nat. Heart Inst., Dept. Energy, NSF, Am. Chem. Soc.-Petroleum Rsch. Fund. Mem. AAAS, Am. Chem. Soc., Brit. Chem. Soc., Royal Soc. Chemistry. Home: 102 Pelican Cove Sneads Ferry NC 28460-9520 Office: Rennselaer Poly Inst Dept Chemistry 110 Eighth Troy NY 12180

POTTS, RAMSAY DOUGLAS, lawyer, aviator; b. Memphis, Oct. 24, 1916; s. Ramsay Douglas and Ann Clifton (VanDyke) P.; m. Veronica Hamilton Raynor, Dec. 22, 1945 (dec. May 1993); children: Ramsay Douglas, David Hamilton, Lesley Ann, Lindsay Veronica. B.S., U. N.C., 1941; LL.B., Harvard U., 1948. Bar: Tenn. 1948, D.C. 1954, U.S. Supreme Ct. 1957. Commd. 2d lt. USAAF, 1941, advanced through grades to maj. gen. Res., 1961; various combat and operational assignments (8th Air Force and Air Force Res.), 1942-60; chmn. Air Force Res. Policy Com., 1967-68; practice law, Washington, 1955—; spl. asst. to chmn. Nat. Security Resources Bd., 1951; pres. Ind. Mil. Air Transport Assn., 1952-55; ptnr. Shaw, Pittman, Potts & Trowbridge, 1956-86; sr. counsel Shaw, Pittman, Potts & Trowbridge, Washington, 1986—. Publisher: Air Power History, 1989-93; contbr. articles to profl. jours. Mem. State Council Higher Edn. for Va., 1968-71; Trustee Air Force Hist. Found., pres., 1971-75; pres. Washington Area Tennis Patrons Found., 1984-87; trustee emeritus. Physicians for Peace, 199789—. Decorated D.S.C., other combat decorations. Mem. ABA, D.C. Bar Assn., Met. Club (Washington), Harvard Club (N.Y.), Army Navy Country Club (Arlington, Va.), Internat. Lawn Tennis Club (U.S., Gt. Brit., India), Phi Beta Kappa. Home: 2818 27th St N Arlington VA 22207-4921 Office: Shaw Pittman Potts & Trowbridge 2300 N St NW Washington DC 20037-1122

POTTS, ROBERT LESLIE, academic administrator; b. Huntsville, Ala., Jan. 30, 1944; s. Frank Vines and Helen Ruth (Butler) P.; m. Irene Elisabeth Johansson, Aug. 22, 1965; children: Julie Anna, Robert Leslie. Student Newbold Coll., Eng., 1963-64; BA, So. Coll., 1966; JD, U. Ala., 1969; LLM, Harvard U., 1971. Law clk. to chief judge U.S. Dist. Ct. (no. dist.) Ala., 1969-70; researcher Herrick, Smith, Donald, Farley & Ketchum, Boston, 1970-71; lectr. Boston U., 1971, U. Ala., 1973-75, 88; ptnr. Potts & Young, Florence, Ala., 1971-84; gen. counsel U. Ala. System, 1984-89, pres. U. North Ala., 1990—; active Nat. Adv. Com. on Instnl. Quality and Integrity, 1994—; bd. dirs. Bank Ind., Florence, 1975-85; adv. com. Rules Civil Procedure, Ala. Supreme Ct., 1973-88; mem. Ala. Bd. Bar Examiners, 1973-79, chmn., 1983-86; trustee Nat. Conf. Bar Examiners, 1986-96, chmn., 1994-95; trustee Ala. State U., 1976-79, Oakwood Coll., 1978-81; pres. Ala. Higher Edn. Loan Corp., 1988-93. Mem. ABA, Ala. Bar Assn. (pres. young lawyers sect. 1979-80). Contbr. numerous articles to profl. jours., edn. and schs. Office: U North Ala Box 5004 Florence AL 35632

POTTS, SANDRA DELL, elementary education educator; b. Lakeview, Oreg., Aug. 17, 1937; d. George A. and Maxine E. (Withers) Campbell; children: Alexander B. Potts, Casey C. Potts. BA, Chico (Calif.) State U., 1959; postgrad., San Jose State U., Santa Clara U. Elem. tchr. Cupertino (Calif.) Union Sch. Dist., 1959—; tchr. 1st grade parent edn. classes Smart Start and Megaskills Sedgwick Elem. Sch., Cupertino, 1994-97. Recipient Hon. Svc. award PTA; named Tchr. of Yr., Santa Clara County, 1991-92. Mem. NEA, ASCD, Calif. Tchrs. Assn., Cupertino Edn. Assn.

POTTS, STEPHEN DEADERICK, lawyer; b. Memphis, Nov. 20, 1930; s. Ramsay Douglas and Anne (Van Dyke) P.; m. Irene Potter, Mar. 14, 1953; children: Lori Potts-Dupre, Stephen Deaderick Jr., Stacy Potts Krogh. AB, Vanderbilt U., 1952, LLB, 1954. Bar: Tenn. 1954, D.C. 1961. Assoc. Farris, Evans & Evans, Nashville, 1957-61; ptnr. Shaw, Pittman, Potts & Trowbridge, Washington, 1961-90; dir. U.S. Office Gov. Ethics, Washington, 1990—; mem. Pres.'s Coun. on Integrity and Efficiency. Past pres. Washington Tennis Patrons Found., 1970-72, Wood Acres Sch. PTA, 1972. 1st lt. U.S. Army, 1954-57. Mem. ABA, U.S. Supreme Ct. Bar Assn., D.C. Bar Assn., Chevy Chase Club (bd. govs. 1982-86), Met. Club, U.S. Tennis Assn. (bd. dirs., won 5 nat., 1 internat. father/son championships, twice ranked 1st in U.S.). Methodist. Office: Of of Government Ethics 1201 New York Ave NW Washington DC 20005-3917

POTUZNIK, CHARLES LADDY, lawyer; b. Chgo., Feb. 11, 1947; s. Charles William and Laverne Frances (Zdenek) P.; m. Mary Margaret Quady, Jan. 2, 1988; children: Kylie Brommell, Kathryn Mary. BA with high honors, U. Ill., 1969; JD cum laude, Harvard U., 1973. Bar: Minn. 1973. Assoc. Dorsey & Whitney LLP, Mpls., 1973-78, ptnr., 1979—. Mem. Minn. State Bar Assn. (chmn. state securities law subcom., 1987—), Hennepin County Bar Assn., Minn. Securities Adv. Com., Phi Beta Kappa. Mem. Evang. Free Ch. Avocations: hunting, fishing, camping, canoeing, foreign travel. Office: Dorsey & Whitney Pillsbury Ctr S 220 S 6th St Minneapolis MN 55402-4502

POTVIN, ALFRED RAOUL, engineering executive; b. Worcester, Mass., Feb. 5, 1942; s. Alfred Armand and Jacqueline (Morin) P.; m. Janet Holm, Mar. 20, 1965. BEE, Worcester Poly. Inst., 1964; MEE, Stanford U., 1965, Engr. in EE, 1967; MS in Bioengring., U. Mich., 1970, M.S. in Psychology, 1970, PhD in Bioengring., 1971. Registered profl. engr., Tex. Asst. prof. elec. engring. U. Tex., Arlington, 1966-68, assoc. prof. biomed. engring. and elec. engring., 1971-76, prof., 1976-84; chmn. biomed. engring. U. Tex., 1972-84; dir. med. instrumentation systems research div. Eli Lilly & Co., Indpls., 1984-90, dir. tech. assessment and project mgmt., 1990-92; dir. engring., med. devices and diagnostics divsn., 1992-93; prof. elec. engring. Purdue Sch. Engring. and Tech., Ind. U.-Purdue U., Indpls., 1993-96; dean Ind. U.-Purdue U., Indpls., 1993-96; pres. Meeco, Englewood, Fla., 1996—; faculty fellow, life scientist, cons. NASA, Houston, 1972-76, NASA and Moffett Field, 1974-76; clin. prof. biophysics U. Tex. Health Sci. Ctr., Dallas, 1967-84; mem. phys. med. device panel FDA, Washington, 1978-84; mem. adv. bd., reviewer Biomed. Engring. NSF, Washington, 1983-89, 92—; founding dir. Ctr. Advanced Rehab. Engring., 1983-84, mem. adv. bd., 1984-88; mem. adv. bd. Engring. Rsch. Ctrs. NSF, Washington, 1988-92, Biomed. Engr. Worcester Polytech. Inst., Mass., 1987—, Coll. Engrs. Duke U., Durham, N.C., 1987-94, U. Calif., Berkeley, 1989-92, Coll. Engrs. U. Denver, 1990-93, Sch. Engr. and Tech. Ind. U.-Purdue U., Indpls, 1992-93, med. engring. Jet Propulsion Lab., Pasadena, Calif., 1989; chmn. NIH Resource Ctr. Case Western Res. U., Cleve., 1988-96; bd. advisors Sch. of Health and Rehab. Sci., U. Pitts., 1993—; mem. adv. com. NIH, 1993, 95. Author: (with W.W. Tourtellotte) Quantitative Examination of Neurologic Functions, 1985; editl. bd. IEEE Spectrum, 1987-90, 92-95, Biomed. Sci. and Tech., 1990-93; co-editor spl. issue on biosensors IEEE Trans. on Biomed. Engring., 1986, spl. issue on status and future directions in biomed. engring. Medicine and Biol. Mag., 1989; mem. editl. bd. Biomed. Sci. and Tech., 1990-92. Mem. Masthead Property Owners Assn., Indpls., 1984—, Manasota Key Property Owners Assn., Englewood, Fla., 1985—. Recipient Life Scientist award NASA, 1974; spl. fellow NIH, 1968. Fellow IEEE (pres. Engring. in Medicine and Biology Soc. 1983, re-elected 1984, gen. chmn. annual conf. 1982, chmn. health care engring. com. 1986, mem. editorial bd. spectrum 1987-89, 92-94, founding mem. steering com. symposium on computer based med. systems 1988-94, Centennial award 1984, co-editor spl. issue Medicine and Biology, 1989), Am. Inst. Med. and Biol. Engring. (bd. dirs. 1991-94, v.p. pub. awareness 1993-94, elected founding fellow 1992, co-pres. world congress on med. biological engring. in Chgo in the yr. 2000, 1993—), Houston Soc. Engrs. in Medicine and Biology (Career Achievement award 1993), Assn. Advancement of Med. Instrumentation; mem. Am. Soc. Engring. Edn. (chmn. biomed. engring. div. 1979-80), Biomed. Engring. Soc. (sr. mem. 1972-88, chmn. edn. and pub. affairs com. 1979-83), Alliance Engrs. in Medicine and Biology (v.p. nat. affairs 1987-89, pres. 1989-92), Assn. Advancement of Med. Instrumentation, Ind. Elec. Mfg. Assn. (bd. dirs. 1993-96). Avocations: boating, travel, gourmet dining, skiing.

POTVIN, FELIX, professional hockey player; b. Anjou, Que., Canada, July 23, 1971. Goalie Chicoutimi, QMJHL, 1988-91, St. John's, AHL, 1991-92, Toronto Maple Leafs, 1991—. Recipient Goaltender of the Year Award, Can. Hockey League, 1990-91, Hap Emms Mem. Trophy, 1990-91, Jacques Plante Trophy, 1990-91, Shell Cup, 1990-91, Guy Lafleur Trophy, 1990-91, Baz Bastien Trophy, 1991-92, Dudley Garrett Mem. Trophy, 1991-92. All-Star first team goalie, QMJHL, 1990-91, All-Star first team goalie, AHL, 1991-92, All-Rookie Team, NHL, 1992-93. Office: Toronto Maple Leafs, 60 Carlton St, Toronto, ON Canada M5B 1L1*

POTVIN, PIERRE, physiologist, educator; b. Quebec City, Que., Can., Jan. 5, 1932; s. Rosario and Eva (Montreuil) P.; m. Louise Dube, Aug. 31, 1963; children: Aline, Bernard. BA, Laval U., 1950, MD, 1955; PhD, U. Toronto, 1962. Asst. prof. Faculty of Medicine Laval U., Quebec City, 1956-63, assoc. prof., 1963-68, prof., 1968—, vice dean exec., 1977-86, dean, 1986-94; v.p. Internat. Conf. of Deans of French-Speaking Faculties of Medicine, 1990-96; hon. prof. Norman Bethune U. Med. Scis., Changchun, China, 1992. Assoc. editor Modern Medicine Can., 1958-61, Laval Med., 1962-70. Decorated comdr. Ordre Nat. des Palmes académiques (France), officer Ordre Nat. du Lion (Senegal). Fellow Royal Coll. Physicians and Surgeons Can.; mem. Can. Soc. Physiology. Roman Catholic. Avocation: painting. Home: 1915 Bourbonniere, Sillery, PQ Canada G1S 1N3 Office: Laval U Faculty of Medicine, Dept Physiology, Quebec, PQ Canada G1K 7P4

POTVIN, RAYMOND HERVE, sociology educator, author; b. Southbridge, Mass., Oct. 28, 1924; s. Cleophas R. and Eva (Beauvais) P. S.T.B., U. Montreal, 1948; Ph.D., Catholic U. Am., 1958; DHL (hon.), Assumption Coll., 1993. Ordained priest Roman Cath. Ch., 1948; asst. pastor Springfield, Mass., 1948-53; mem. faculty Cath. U., 1958—, prof. sociology, 1967—, chmn. dept., 1968-71, 77-83, asst. acad. v.p. for grad. programs, 1985-88; dir. Inst. Social and Behavioral Research, 1972-74; sr. researcher Boys Town Center, 1974-88; Trustee Population Reference Bur., 1981-87, Center for Applied Research in the Apostolate, 1981-85; Fellow Population Council, 1966-67. Author: (with Charles Westoff) College Women and Fertility Values, 1967, (with Antanas Suziedelis) Seminarians of the Sixties, 1970, Vocational Challenge and Seminary Response, 1971, (with D. Hoge and H. Nelson) Religion and American Youth, 1976, (with Hart Nelsen and Joseph Shields) The Religion of Children, 1977, Seminarians of the Eighties, 1986, (with P. Mucada) Seminary Outcomes: Perseverance and Withdrawal, 1990. Fellow Am. Sociol. Assn., Population Assn.; mem. Soc. Sci. Study of Religion. Office: Cath Univ Dept Sociology Washington DC 20064

POTWIN, JUANITA R., marketing professional, dental hygienist; b. St. Albans, Vt., Oct. 15, 1957; d. Gerald Albert Potwin and Beatrice Julia (Blake) Lamica. Cert. chemistry, N.H. Vo-Tech., Claremont, 1982; AS in Dental Assisting, Champlain Coll., 1984; AS in Dental Hygiene, N.H. Tech. Inst., 1986. Registered dental hygienist ADA. Freelance dental hygienist N.H., 1986—; New Eng. sales dir. Oxyfresh, USA, Spokane, Wash., 1993; exec. sales dir. Oxyfresh, USA, Spokane, 1994-95; N.E. sales dir. Life Sci. Products, St. George, Utah, 1995-96; Ruby sales dir. Life Sci. Products, St. George, 1996-97; exec. mktg. specialist Design 21, Santa Barbara, Calif., 1997—. Mem., supporter Am. Humane Assn., Wold Wildlife Fund, The Wilderness Soc. Scholar Dr. David S. Faigel Meml. Found., 1982. Mem. NAFE, VFW, Am. Legion Aux. Avocations: tennis, travel, golf, photography. Home: 4626 Sierra Madre Santa Barbara CA 93110 Office: Life Sci Products 321 N Mall Dr Saint George UT 84790-7302 Mailing: PO Box 61411 Santa Barbara CA 93160

POUCHE, FREDRICK, state legislator; b. Independence, Mo., Aug. 3, 1945; m. Martha M. Pouche; children: Sean R., Ash Thomas. BA in Bus. Adminstrn. summa cum laude, Park Coll., Parkville, Mo.; MA in Bus. Adminstrn. and Mgmt. magna cum laude, Webster U. Prin. Pouche Corp.; adminstr. labor rels., sr. fin. analyst Trans World Airlines, 1965-84; fee agt. Mo. Dept. Revenue, 1985-89; auditor Platte County, 1989-91; state rep. 30th dist. Mo. Ho. of Reps., 1995-97; candidate Mo. Ho. of Reps., 1982, 86, 88, 94; committeeman Platte County Rep. Com., 1983-84; staff rep. Ashcroft for Gov. Com., 1984; fin. chmn. Platte Rep. Com., 1984-85; dist. chmn. Dole for Pres. Com., 1987-88; Mo. del. Rep. Nat. Conv., 1988; Platte County coord. Roy Blunt for Gov. Com., 1994. Decorated Army Commendation medal with oak leaf cluster (2), others. Mem. KC (# 3430), Northland C. of C., South Platte Rotary Club (Paul Harris fellow), Platte Rep. Assn. Roman Catholic. Office: Mo Ho of Reps Rm 116-5 State Capitol Jefferson City MO 65101

POUGH, FREDERICK HARVEY, mineralogist; b. Bklyn., June 26, 1906; s. Francis H. and Alice H. (Beckler) P.; m. Eleanor C. Hodge, Oct. 14, 1938 (dec. May 1966); children: Frederick Harvey, Barbara Hodge. SB, Harvard, 1928, PhD, 1935; MS, Washington U., 1932; student, Ruperto Carola, Heidelberg, Germany, 1932-33. Asst. curator mineralogy Am. Mus. Natural History, N.Y.C., 1935-40; acting curator Am. Mus. Natural History, 1941, curator, 1942-44, curator phys. geology and mineralogy, 1942-52, cons. mineralogist, 1953-64, 66—; gem cons. Jewelers Circular-Keystone, 1940-85; dir. Santa Barbara Mus. Natural History, 1965-66; pres. Mineralogy, Inc., 1978—. Author: Jewelers Dictionary, 1945, 50, 76, 96, Field Guide to Rocks and Minerals, 1952, 72, 97, All About Volcanoes and Earthquakes, 1953, Hindi translation, 1958, Persian translation, 1959, Bengali translation, 1959, Italian translation, 1960, Arabic translation, 1962, Portuguese translation, 1964, Our Earth, 1961, The Story of Gems and Semi-Precious Stones, 1967, Guide des Roches et Mineraux, 1969, 79, First Guide to Rocks and Minerals, 1991; contbg. editor: Lapidary jour, 1984—. Recipient Bronze medal Royal Geol. Soc., Belgium, 1948, Derby medal Brazilian Geol. Survey, Hanneman award for outstanding contbns. in lit. of mineralogy and gemology, 1988, Mineral. award Carnegie Mus. Nat. History, Pitts., 1989, Lifetime Achievement award Accredited Gemologist Assn., 1993; named Mineralogist of Yr., Am. Fedn. Mineral Soc., 1966. Fellow Mineral Soc. Am., Geol. Soc. Am.; mem. Mineral Soc. Gt. Britain., Gemmological Assn. All Japan (Am. rep. 1985—). Clubs: Harvard (N.Y.C.); Explorers. Address: PO Box 7004 Reno NV 89510-7004

POUL, FRANKLIN, lawyer; b. Phila., Nov. 6, 1924; s. Boris and Anna P.; m. Shirley Weissman, June 26, 1949; children—Leslie Poul Melman, Alan M., Laurie. Student, U. Pa., 1942-43, Haverford Coll., 1943-44; LL.B. cum laude, U. Pa., 1946. Bar: Pa. 1949, U.S. Supreme Ct. 1955. Asso. firm Gray, Anderson, Schaffer & Rome, Phila., 1948-56, Wolf, Block, Schorr and Solis-Cohen, Phila., 1956-60; partner Wolf, Block, Schorr and Solis-Cohen, 1960-93. Bd. dirs. ACLU, Phila., 1955-80, pres., 1975-76. Served with AUS, 1943-46. Mem. ABA, Am. Law Inst., Order of Coif. Office: Wolf Block Shorr & Solis-Cohen 12th Fl Packard Bldg SE Corner 15 Chestnut St Philadelphia PA 19122

POULEUR, HUBERT GUSTAVE, cardiologist; b. Bouffioulx, Belgium, June 6, 1948; m. Michelle Leonet, July 7, 1973; children: Anne-Catherine, Jean-Hubert. MD, U. Louvain, Belgium, 1973, PhD, 1980. Intern, resident, then fellow in internal medicine U. Louvain, Belgium, 1973-77; Pub. Health Service internat. research fellow U. Calif, San Diego, 1977-79; asst. prof. U. Louvain, Brussels, 1979-83, assoc. prof., 1983-91; prof. U. Louvain, Brussels, N.J., 1991-94; assoc. dir. clin. rsch. Pfizer Inc., Groton, Conn., 1993-95; v.p. cardiovascular clin. R&D Bristol-Myers Squibb, Princeton, N.J., 1996—; disting. clin. scientist Syntex Clin. Rsch., Palo Alto, Calif., Maidenhead, U.K., 1988-93. Contbr. numerous sci. articles to profl. jours. Recipient Damman prize Damman Found., 1977, Bekales prize Bekales Found., 1986; Squibb Cardiovascular fellow Belgian Soc. Cardiology, 1982. Fellow Am. Coll. Cardiology; mem. Am. Heart Assn. (fellow Coun. of Circulation, fellow Coun. Clin. Cardiology), Atlantic Salmon Fedn., Trout Unltd. Avocation: fly fishing. Home: 43 Woodlane Rd Lawrenceville NJ 08648

POULIN, CLAUDE, actuarial consultant; b. Montreal, Dec. 9, 1942. BA, U. Montreal, 1963; degree in actuarial sci., Laval U., 1966. Actuarial asst. Sun Life Assurance Co., Montreal, 1966-69; sr. actuarial cons. UAW, Detroit, 1969-80; founder, pres. Poulin Assocs., Inc., Washington, Montreal, 1980—. Commr. Conn. State Employees Retirement Commn., Hartford, 1982—. Fellow Soc. Actuaries, Can. Inst. Actuaries; mem. Hist. Soc. Mus. (gov. 1992-94), Am. Acad. Actuaries, Internat. Actuarial Assn. Avocation: history. Office: Poulin Assocs Inc 1072 30th St NW Washington DC 20007-3822

POULIN, DAVID JAMES, hockey coach; b. Mississauga, Ont., Can., Dec. 17, 1958. Hockey player Phila. Flyers Nat. Hockey League, 1983-90, hockey player Boston Bruins, 1990-93, hockey player Washington Capitals, 1993-95; coach hockey U. Notre Dame, 1995—; played All-Star Game, 1986, 88; capt. Phila. Flyers, 1989-90. Recipient Frank J. Selke Trophy, 1986-87, King Clancy Meml. Trophy, 1992-93. Office: Univ Notre Dame Notre Dame IN 46556

POULIN, THOMAS EDWARD, marine engineer, state legislator, retail business owner; b. Waterville, Maine, Apr. 23, 1956; s. Donald Richard and Beatrice Delores (Berard) P.; m. Kim E. Marston, July 3, 1981; children: Elizabeth, Brittany, Chanelle. BS in Marine Engring., Maine Maritime Acad., 1978; cert. in tchg., U. Maine, Farmington, 1985. Marine engr. Ctrl. Gulf Lines, 1978—; math. tchr. Messalonshee H.S., Oakland, Maine, 1986-90; mem. Maine Ho. of Reps., Oakland and Sidney, 1990—. Mem. budget and adv. coms. Town of Oakland, 1988—. Roman Catholic. Home: R4 Box 1060 Oakland ME 04963-9410

POULIOT, ASSUNTA GALLUCCI, retired business school owner and director; b. West Warwick, R.I., Aug. 14, 1937; d. Michael and Angelina (DeCesare) Gallucci; m. Joseph F. Pouliot Jr., July 4, 1961; children: Brenda, Mark, Jill, Michele. BS, U. R.I., 1959, MS, 1971. Bus. tchr. Cranston High Sch., R.I., 1959-61; bus. dept. chmn. Chariho Regional High Sch., Wood River Junction, R.I., 1961-73; instr. U. R.I., Kingston, 1973-78; founder, dir. Ocean State Bus. Inst., Wakefield, R.I., 1977-95; fin. aid cons., 1995—; dir. Fleet Nat. Bank, 1985-91; bd. mgrs. Bank of New Eng., 1984-85; commr. Accrediting Coun. Ind. Colls. and Schs., 1995—; speaker in field. Pres. St. Francis Women's Club, Wakefield, 1975; sec. St. Francis Parish Coun., Wakefield, 1980; mem. Econ. Devel. Commn., Wakefield, 1981-85; mem. South County Hosp. Corp., Wakefield, 1978—; fin. dir. Bus and Profl. Women's Club, Wakefield, 1982-84; chmn. Ladies Golf Charity, 1985-91; mem. Computer Info. Systems Com., Chariho Regional Career and Tech. Ctr.; Mem. Galilee Beach Club Assn., R.I. Bus. Edn. Assn. (newsletter editor 1979-81), New Eng. Bus. Coll. Assn. (sec. 1984-86, pres. 1985-87), R.I. Assn. Career and Tech. Schs. (treas., bd. dirs. 1979—), Eastern Bus. Edn. Assn. (conf. leader), Nat. Bus. Edn. Assn. (conf. leader), Career Coll. Assn. (conv. speaker, pub. rels. com., govt. rels. com., membership com., key mem., nominating com., evaluator), Assn. Colls. and Schs. (commr. commn. on postsecondary schs. accreditation 1994—, ednl. cons. 1995—), R.I. Women's Golf Assn., Am. Cancer Soc., U. R.I. Alumi Assn. (Excellence Bus. award 1992), Phi Kappa Phi, Delta Pi Epsilon (pres., newsletter editor). Roman Catholic. Club: Point Judith Country (past ladies golf chmn.). Avocations: golf, gardening. Home: 137 Kenyon Ave Wakefield RI 02879-4242 Office: 137 Kenyon Ave Wakefield RI 02879

POULOS, MICHAEL JAMES, insurance company executive; b. Glens Falls, N.Y., Feb. 13, 1931; s. James A. and Mary Poulos; m. Mary Kay Leslie; children: Denise, Peter. BA, Colgate U., 1953; MBA, NYU, 1963. CLU, 1970. With sales and mgmt. U.S. Life Ins. Co., N.Y.C., 1958-70, dir., 1968, mem. exec. com., 1970; with Calif.-Western States Life Ins. Co., Sacramento, 1970-79, pres., chief exec. officer, 1975-79, dir., 1975; with Am. Gen. Corp., Houston, 1979-93, pres., 1981-91; mem. exec. com., dir. Am. Gen. Corp., 1981-93, vice chmn., 1991-93; chmn., CEO, pres. Western Nat. Corp., Houston. Mem. Sam Houston Area coun. Boy Scouts Am. Mem. Am. Soc. CLU's, Nat. Assn. Life Underwriters, Houston Assn. Life Underwriters, Am. Mgmt. Assn., River Oaks Country Club, Univ. Club of N.Y.C. Greek Orthodox. Office: Western National Corp 5555 San Felipe St Ste 900 Houston TX 77056-2725

POULOS-WOOLLEY, PAIGE M., public relations executive; b. Woodland, Calif., Apr. 26, 1958; d. Paul William Jr. and Frances Marie (Gibson) Poulos; m. John Stuart Woolley, Jr., Feb. 3, 1990. Student, U. Calif., Davis 1977-80. Mgr. pub. rels. Somerset Wine Co., N.Y.C. and San Martin, Calif., 1982-88; dir. comm. The Beverage Source, San Francisco, 1988-89, Rutherford (Calif.) Hill Winery, 1989-90; pres. Paige Poulos Comm., Berkeley, Calif., 1990—; founder, chmn. WINECOM, 1992—. Pub. rels. editor: Practical Winery & Vineyards, 1994—; wine editor Focus Mag. Mem. Internat. Assn. Culinary Profls., Pub. Rels. Soc. Am. (bd. dirs. 1993—, sec. 1994, pres. East Bay chpt. 1994-96, editor newsletter food and beverage sect. 1993-95, chmn. food and beverage sect.), Women in Comm., Acad. Wine Comm. (program chair 1994), Internat. Assn. Bus. Communicators, San Francisco Profl. Food Soc. Republican. Episcopalian. Avocations: horseback riding, diving, skiing, wine collecting. Office: Paige Poulos Comm PO Box 8087 Berkeley CA 94707-8087

POULSEN, DENNIS ROBERT, environmentalist; b. Boston, Jan. 17, 1946; s. Stephen Dudley and Dorothy Hope (Davis) P.; m. Bonnie Lou Reed; children: David, Zachery, Patrick. AS in Forestry, U. Mass., Stockbridge-Amherst, 1965; AS in Indsl. Supervision, Chaffey Coll., Alta Loma, Calif., 1977; BS in Bus. Adminstrn., U. Redlands (Calif.), 1979; postgrad., U. Calif., Riverside, 1986, U. Calif., Davis, 1991-93; cert. program, U. Calif., Davis, 1991-94. Cert. environ. profl., registered environ. profl., registered environ. assessor, Calif., cert. hazardous materials mgr., cert. lab. technolgoist; diplomate Inst. Hazardous Materials Mgmt. Water control technician Weyerhaeuser Co. Chem. Lab., Fitchburg, Mass., 1965-69; environ. rsch. technician Kaiser Steel Corp., Fontana, Calif., 1969-78, environ. rsch. engr., 1978-83, asst. environ. dir., 1983-87; mgr. environ. svcs. Calif. Steel Industries Inc., Fontana, 1987—; mem. adv. group Calif. EPA (CAL EPA), 1993—; originator AISE Nat. Environ. Com., Pitts., papers chmn., 1993, com. vice chmn., 1994, chmn., 1995; mem. adv. group Calif. Environ. Protection Agy., 1993—; mem. com. on the environment Am. Iron and Steel Inst., Washington, 1995—; mem. White House Environ. Task Force, 1993; editor-in-chief NAEP News, Washington, 1993—; mem. editl. adv. bd. Indsl. Wastewater Mag., 1993-96; mem. adv. bd. Occupl. Health and Safety Mag., 1993—; mem. U.S. EPA Common Sense Initiative Subcom., Washington, 1994—. Contbr. articles and papers on environmental issues to profl. publs. Del. U.S. Environ. Delegation, Soviet Union, 1990; mem. U.S. Citizens Network of the UN Conf. on Environment and Devel.; del. U.N. Conf. on agenda 21 ethical implications; trustee Acad. Bd. Cert. Environ. Profls.; mem. Hazmat/West Adv. Coun., 1995. Mem. Nat. Assn. Environ. Profls. (cert. rev. bd., mem. internat. com. 1992—, mem. bd. dirs. 1993—, v.p. and mng. dir. 1996—), Air and Water Mgmt. Assn., Nat. Environ. Health Assn., Environ. Info. Assn., Hazardous Materials Control Rsch. Inst., Water Environment Fedn. (groundwater com.), World Safety Orgn. (cert. hazardous materials supr.), Assn. Energy Engrs. (environ. engr.s mgrs. inst., contbg. editor Environ. News 1996—, Environ. Project of Yr. award 1992, Environ. Profl. of Yr. award 1994), Calif. Water Pollution Control Assn., Inst. Hazardous Materials Mgmt., People to People Internat., U. Redlands Alumni Assn. (bd. mem., recipient Gordon Adkins award for profl. achievement 1994). Avocation: travel. Home: 5005 Hedrick Ave Riverside CA 92505-1425 Office: Calif Steel Industries Inc 14000 San Bernardino Ave Fontana CA 92335-5258

POULSEN, LAWRENCE LEROY, research scientist; b. Salmon, Idaho, Nov. 27, 1933; s. William LeRoy and Eva (Martin) P.; m. Maclovia Torres, Feb. 1, 1957; children: William, Nancy, Judith, Doris, Kenneth, Tammy. AA, Riverside City Coll., 1953; BA, U. Calif., Riverside, 1965, DPhil, 1970. Phys. sci. tech. USDA, Riverside, Calif., 1957-65; rsch. assoc. dept. biology Tex. A&M U., College Station, 1969-70; assoc. rsch. scientist Clayton Found., Austin, Tex., 1971-80, rsch. assoc., 1980-89; rsch. assoc. dept. chemistry U. Tex., Austin, 1990—; lectr. and cons. in field. Inventor in field. Bishop LDS Ch., Austin, 1986-91, high counselor, 1991-95; scoutmaster, dist. com. Boy Scouts Am., Austin, 1970-86. Postdoctoral fellow U. Calif., 1965-69, Pub. Health Svc., 1968-69, 71-74, Welch Found., 1969-70. Mem. Am. Soc. Biochemistry and Molecular Biology. Mem. LDS Ch. Avocations: computers, astronomy, genealogy. Home: 6314 Libyan Dr Austin TX 78745 Office: U Tex Dept Chemistry Austin TX 78712

POULSON, RICHARD JASPER METCALFE, lawyer; b. Elizabeth City, N.C., Sept. 4, 1938; s. Richard Jasper and Dorothy (Morse) P.; m. Anne Keenan, Dec. 21, 1963 (div. 1976); m. Anne Dare Wrenn, Sept. 25, 1993. BA, U. Va., 1960; JD, Am. U., 1968; ML in Taxation, Georgetown U., 1970. Bar: Va. 1968, D.C. 1969, U.S. Supreme Ct. 1976. V.p. Am. Security & Trust Co., Washington, 1968-70; assoc. Hogan & Hartson, Washington, 1970-73, ptnr., 1973-94; sr. ptnr. Hogan & Hartson, London, 1990-93; chmn. Rapidan Capital Ptnrs., 1994—; CEO, sr. mng. dir. The Appian Group, Washington, 1995—; adj. prof. Georgetown U. Law Ctr., 1971-78; lectr. Law and Fgn. Svc. Schs. Georgetown U.; internat. advisor in field; active Euro-Arab Conciliation and Arbitration System. Trustee, bd. mgrs., U. Va., Charlottesville, 1992—, v.p., 1994-95, pres., 1995—; dir., chmn. exec. com. Mary & Daniel Loughran Found., Washington, 1976—; chmn., dir. Montpelier Steeplechase Found., Orange, Va., 1991—; chmn., trustee U.S. Rugby Football Found., Boston, 198"—. 1st lt. USAR, 1961-63. Mem. Law Society of England and Wales, Metro. Club, Farmington Country Club, Norfolk Yacht Club, Keswick Country Club. Republican. Episcopalian. Avocations: horseback riding, hunting, steeplechase racing, thoroughbred breeding. Home: Hare Forest Farm Orange VA 22960 Office: The Appian Group 1455 Pennsylvania Ave NW Washington DC 20004-1008

POULSON, ROBERT DEAN, lawyer; b. Valparaiso, Ind., June 10, 1927; s. Frank Ferlin and Esther Marie P.; m. Betty Lou Caroline Mercer, Aug. 19, 1950 (dec.); children: Richard D., Thomas C., John R. LL.B., Drake U., 1953, J.D., 1974. Bar: Iowa 1953, Ill. 1954, Colo. 1957. Staff atty. Texaco, Chgo. and Denver, 1953-59; divisional atty. Superior Oil Co., Denver, 1959-64; of counsel Poulson, Odell & Peterson, Denver, 1995—. Mem. Bow Mar City Council, Colo., 1968-72. Served with USN, 1945-47. Mem. Denver, Arapahoe County (Colo.), Colo., Am. bar assns., Rocky Mountain Mineral Law Found. (pres. 1975-76, trustee 1965—), Rocky Mountain Oil and Gas Assn. (chmn. gen. legal com. 1963-66, trustee 1963—), Ind. Petroleum Assn. Am. (dir.), Phi Alpha Delta. Republican. Methodist. Clubs: Univ. (Denver); Masons. Home: 5455 Lakeshore Dr Littleton CO 80123-1542 Office: 1775 Sherman St Ste 1400 Denver CO 80203-4316

POULTER, CHARLES DALE, chemist, educator, consultant; b. Monroe, La., Aug. 29, 1942; s. Erwin and Mary Helen Poulter; m. Susan Raetzsch, Aug. 24, 1964; children: Mary Christa, Gregory Thomas. BS, La. State U., Baton Rouge, 1964; PhD, U. Calif., Berkeley, 1967. NIH postdoctoral fellow UCLA, 1967-68; asst. prof. chemistry U. Utah, Salt Lake City, 1969-75, assoc. prof., 1975-78, prof., 1978-94, John A. Widtsoe prof. chemistry, 1993-95, chair dept. chemistry, 1995—; cons. Amoco Rsch. Ctr., Naperville, Ill., 1985-90, Merck Sharp & Dohme, Rahway, N.J., 1986-90, Bristol-Myers Squibb, Princeton, N.J., 1989-93, Zeneca Ag Products, Richmond, Calif., 1993-95. Fellow AAAS; mem. Am. Chem. Soc. (organic exec. com. 1983-86, biol. divsn. councillor 1993-97, chair-elect organic divsn. 1997, Ernest Guenther award 1991, Utah award 1992). Office: U Utah Dept Chemistry Salt Lake City UT 84112-1102

POULTON, BRUCE ROBERT, former university chancellor; b. Yonkers, N.Y., Mar. 7, 1927; s. Alfred Vincent and Ella Marie (Scanlon) P.; m. Elizabeth Charlotte Jerothe, Aug. 26, 1950; children: Randall Lee, Jeffrey Jon, Cynthia Sue, Peter Gregory. B.S. with honors, Rutgers U., 1950, M.S., 1952, Ph.D., 1956; LL.D., U. N.H. Research instr., then asst. prof. Rutgers U., 1952-56; assoc. prof., then prof., chmn. dept. animal and vet. sci. U. Maine, 1958-66, dir. Bangor Campus, 1967-68, dean, dir. Coll. Life Scis. and Agr., 1968-71, v.p. research and pub. service, 1971-75; chancellor Univ. System N.H., 1975-82, also trustee; chancellor N.C. State U., Raleigh, 1982-89; vis. prof. Mich. State U., 1966-67; mem. regional adv. com. Farm and Home Administrn.; mem. exec. com., council on research policy and grad. edn. Nat. Assn. State Univs. and Land Grant Colls.; also mem. senate; mem. Gov.'s Econ. Advisory Council, N.H.; mem. selection com. Kellogg Found.; Lectureship in Agr.; chmn. Rhodes scholarship com. for, N.H.; mem. policy devel. com. New Eng. Innovation Group; adv. com. U.S. Command and Gen. Staff Coll. Author articles in field. Bd. dirs. Research Triangle Inst., Microelectronic Ctr., Triangle Univs. Ctr. Advanced Studies, Aubrey Brooks Found. Served with AUS, 1944-46. Am. Council Edn. fellow acad. adminstrn., 1966-67. Mem. Am. Inst. Nutrition, Brit. Nutrition Soc., Fedn. Am. Soc. Exptl. Biology, Am. Soc. Exptl. Biology, Am. Soc. Animal Sci., Am. Dairy Sci. Assn. (past pres. Eastern div.), AAAS, Sigma Xi, Alpha Zeta. Office: NC State U Office of Chancellor Raleigh NC 27695

POULTON, CHARLES EDGAR, natural resources consultant; b. Oakley, Idaho, Aug. 2, 1917; s. Richard and Narrie Jane (Queen) P.; m. Marcile Belle McCoy, Sept. 29, 1939; children: Richard C., Robert J., Mary Jane Poulton Morris, Betty Jean Poulton Strong. B.S. with high honors, U. Idaho, 1939, M.S., 1948; postgrad., Mont. State Coll., 1946-47; Ph.D., Wash. State U., 1955; postdoctoral, U. Calif. at Berkeley, 1967-68. Adminstr., researcher U.S. Forest Service, Western states, 1937-46; dist. forest ranger U.S. Forest Service, 1941-46; cons. forest ecology U.S. Forest Service, Ala., Fla., 1958-59; asst. prof. range mgmt. Mont. State Coll., Bozeman, 1946-47; instr. range mgmt. U. Idaho, Moscow, 1947-49; prof., dir. range mgmt. program Oreg. State U., Corvallis, 1949-70; prof. range ecology Oreg. State U., 1970-73; dir.

Environ. Remote Sensing Applications Lab., 1972-73; dir. range and resource ecology div. Earth Satellite Corp., Berkeley, Calif., 1974-75; sr. officer Rangeland Resources and Pasture, Food and Agr. Orgn. UN, Rome, Italy, 1976-77, 81; Cons., Benton County, Oreg.; (in land use planning), 1972-73, NASA, 1967-71; tng. officer, remote sensing of natural resources NASA-Ames Research Center, 1978-81; cons. natural resource mgmt., bus. devel., 1978—; developed new MS program in interdisciplinary natural resources devel. Asian Inst. of Tech., Bangkok, Thailand, 1986-87, coord. of program, 1987, project work in developing countries. Assoc. editor: Range Mgmt. Jour. Forestry, 1956-62; mem. editorial bd. Ecology, 1965-67; contbr. chpts. to books, articles to profl. jours. Served with USNR, 1945-46. Recipient merit certificate for outstanding service to grassland agr. Am. Grassland Council, 1963. Fellow Soc. Range Mgmt. (charter mem., pres. Pacific N.W. sect. 1962, Outstanding Achievement award 1986, nat. dir. 1965-68, com. on accreditation 1980-8c, chmn. com. on internat. affairs 1983), Soc. Am. Foresters (chmn. range mgmt. div. 1955), Nat. Acad. Sci. (panels 1969, 73-74), Sigma Xi, Phi Eta Sigma, Xi Sigma Pi. Mem. Christian Ch. Home: PO Box 2081 Gresham OR 97030-0601

POULTON, CRAIG KIDD, insurance broker, consultant; b. Salt Lake City, Nov. 22, 1951; s. LaMarr Williams and Marcella (Kidd) P.; m. Diane Adamson, Dec. 28, 1973; children: Brysen, Blake, Marissa, Ashley. BA, U. Utah, 1977. Cert. ins. counselor. V.p. Poulton Insurance Agy., Inc., Salt Lake City, 1977-84, pres., 1984-90; broker Internat. Lines and Comml. Lines, Salt Lake City, 1977—; pres., chmn. Instar Corp., 1988-90, Poulton Assocs., Inc., Salt Lake City, 1990—. Mem. Rep. Presdl. Task Force, 1983—. Paul Harris fellow, 1984. Mem. Profl. Ins. Agts. Am., Ind. Ins. Agts. Assn., Rotary (bd. dirs. Holladay 1985, sec. 1987, v.p. 1987, pres. 1988). Mem. LDS Ch. Avocations: skiing, swimming, bicycling. Office: Poulton Assocs Inc 3785 S 700 E Fl 2D Salt Lake City UT 84106-1183

POUNCEY, PETER RICHARD, academic administrator, classics educator; b. Tsingtao, Shantung, China, Oct. 1, 1937; came to U.S., 1964; s. Cecil Alan and Eugenie Marde (Lintilhac) P.; m. Bethanne McNally, June 25, 1966; 1 son, Christian; m. Susan Rieger, Mar. 21, 1973; 1 dau., Margaret; m. Katherine Dalsimer, June 9, 1990. Lic. Phil., Heythrop Coll., Eng., 1960; B.A., Oxford U., Eng., 1964, M.A., 1967; Ph.D., Columbia U., 1969; AM (hon.), Amherst Coll., 1985; LLD (hon.), Williams Coll., 1985; LHD (hon.), Doshisha U., 1987; LLD (hon.), Wesleyan U., 1989, Amherst (Mass.) Coll., 1995; LHD (hon.), Trinity Coll., 1990. Instr. classics Fordham U., Bronx, N.Y., 1964-67; asst. prof. Columbia U., N.Y.C., 1969-71, dean Columbia Coll., 1972-76, assoc. prof., 1977-83, prof. classics, 1983-84; pres. Amherst (Mass.) Coll., Mass., 1984-94; pres. emeritus Amherst (Mass.) Coll., 1994—, prof. classics, 1994—, Fobes prof. Greek, 1995—; cons. classical lit. Columbia Ency., 1970-73; trustee Columbia Univ. Press, 1972-75. Author: The Necessities of War: A Study of Thucydides' Pessimism, 1980 (Lionel Trilling award 1981). Trustee Brit.-Am. Edn. Found., N.Y.C., 1971-75. Recipient Great Tchr. award Soc. Columbia Grads., 1983. Mem. Am. Philol. Assn., Phi Beta Kappa. *

POUND, E. JEANNE, school psychologist, consultant; b. N.Y.C., Oct. 19, 1949; adopted d. W. James and Thelma (Rendall) P.; div.; 1 child, Courtney Jason Pound. BA in English cum laude, U. Mass., 1971; MS in Social Work, U. Wis., 1973; EdS in Sch. Psychology, U. Ga., 1977. Cert. sch. psychologist, Ga., Mass.; cert. sch. social worker, N.Y. Psychiat. social worker White Mountain Community Mental Health Svcs., Littleton, N.H., 1974; sch. social worker Lake Placid (N.Y.) Ctrl. Schs., 1974-75; sch. psychologist Wilbraham (Mass.) Pub. Schs., 1977-80, Stoneham (Mass). Pub. Schs., 1980-81, Richmond County (Ga.) Pub. Schs., 1981-83, Griffin (Ga.) Regional Ednl. Svc. Agy., 1984-87, Atlanta Pub. Schs., 1987—; evaluator of innovative program grants Ga. State Dept. Edn., Atlanta, 1987—; supr. sch. psychology interns Ga. State U., Atlanta, 1994—; mem. Ga. Adv. Panel Spl. Edn., 1995-98. Author: (chpt.) Children's Needs-Psychological Perspectives ("Children and Prematurity"), 1987. Mem. APA, Nat. Assn. Sch. Psychologists (cert.), Ga. Assn. Sch. Psychologists (regional rep. 1991-93, 97—, chmn. GASP/NASP conv. com. 1995-96, chair awards com. 1996—), Humane Soc. U.S., World Wildlife Fedn., Kappa Delta Pi, Phi Kappa Phi, Phi Delta Kappa. Avocations: snow skiing, water skiing, weight lifting, aerobic exercise, gardening. Home: 150 Bryson Ln Fayetteville GA 30215-5478 Office: Atlanta Pub Schs Office Youth Svcs 978 North Ave NE Atlanta GA 30306-4456

POUND, JOHN BENNETT, lawyer; b. Champaign, Ill., Nov. 17, 1946; s. William R. and Louise Catherine (Kelly) P.; m. Mary Ann Hanson, June 19, 1971; children: Meghan Elizabeth, Matthew Fitzgerald. BA, U. N.Mex., 1968; JD, Boston Coll., 1971. Bar: N. Mex. 1971, U.S. Dist. Ct. N. Mex. 1971, U.S. Ct. Appeals (10th cir.) 1972, U.S. Supreme Ct., 1993. Law clk. to Hon. Oliver Seth, U.S. Ct. Appeals, 10th Cir., Santa Fe, 1971-72; asst. counsel Supreme Ct. Disciplinary Bd., 1977-83, dist. rev. officer, 1984—; mem. Supreme Ct. Com. on Jud. Performance Evaluation, 1983-85; bd. dirs. Archdiocese Santa Fe Cath. Social Svcs., 1995—. Contbr. articles to profl. jours. Pres. bd. dirs. N.Mex. Ind. Coll. Fund, Santa Fe; chmn. N.Mex. Dem. Leadership Coun., 1991—; bd. dirs. Santa Fe Boys Club, 1989-92; rules com. N.Mex. Dem. Party, 1982—; v.p. Los Alamos Nat. Lab. Comm. Coun., 1985-90; fin. chmn. N.Mex. Clinton for Pres. campaign, 1992; co-chmn. Clinton-Gore Re-election Campaign, N.Mex., 1996. Fellow Am. Coll. Trial Lawyers, N.Mex. Bar Found.; mem. ABA, Am. Bd. Trial Advocates, N.Mex. Bar Assn. (health law sect. 1987—), Santa Fe County Bar Assn. Democrat. Roman Catholic. Avocations: history, foreign language, literature, swimming, baseball. Office: Herrera Long & Pound PA PO Box 5098 2200 Brothers Rd Santa Fe NM 87502-5098

POUND, RICHARD WILLIAM DUNCAN, lawyer, accountant; b. St. Catharines, Ont., Can., Mar. 22, 1942; s. William Thomas and Jessie Edith Duncan (Thom) P.; m. Julie Houghton Keith, Nov. 4, 1977. B.Commerce, McGill U., Montreal, 1962, B.C.L., 1967; B.A., Sir George Williams U. (now Concordia U.), Montreal, 1963; PhD (hon.), U.S. Sports Acad., 1989; LLD (hon.), U. Windsor, Can., 1997. Bar: called to Que. bar 1968, Ont. bar, 1980; chartered accountant, 1964. Auditor Riddell, Stead, Graham & Hutchinson, Montreal, 1963-65; law clk., then atty. firm Laing, Weldon, Courtois, Clarkson, Parsons & Tétrault, Montreal, 1965-71; mem. firm Stikeman, Elliott, Montreal, Toronto, Ottawa, Calgary, Vancouver, London, N.Y.C., Hong Kong, Taipei, Budepest, Paris, Washington, 1972—; lectr. taxation McGill U. Faculty Law; lectr. Que. Real Estate Assn.; mem. Ct. of Arbitration of Sport, Lausanne, 1991—; officer Order of Can., officer Order nat. du Quebec, Queen's Coun. Author: Five Rings Over Korea: 1994; editor-in-chief: Doing Business in Canada, Canada Tax Cases, Stikeman Income Tax Act (annotated); editor Pound's Tax Case Notes, Legal Notes, CGA mag. Pres. Canadian Olympic Assn., 1977-82, sec., 1968-76; mem. Internat. Olympic Com., 1978—, exec. bd., 1983-87, 92—, v.p., 1987-91, 1996—; bd. govs. McGill U., 1986—, chmn., 1994—; trustee Martlet Found.; former trustee Stanstead Wesleyan Coll.; chmn. McGill U. Athletic Bd.; chmn. McGill U. Fund Coun. Named to Canadian Swimming Hall of Fame, 1969, Sports Fedn. Can. Hall of Fame, 1976. Mem. Can. Bar Assn., Can. Tax Found., Internat. Fiscal Assn., Internat. Assn. Practicing Lawyers, Can. Squash Racquets Assn., Royal Life Savs. Soc., Alumni Assn. McGill U. (former pres.). Clubs: Montreal Amateur Athletic Assn. (pres. 1987-88), Badminton and Squash (Montreal); Hillside Tennis, Jesters, Mt. Bruno Country. Home: 87 Arlington Ave, Westmount, PQ Canada H3Y 2W5 Office: Ste 4000, 1155 Rene Levesque Blvd W, Montreal, PQ Canada H3B 3V2

POUND, ROBERT VIVIAN, physics educator; b. Ridgeway, Ont., Can., May 16, 1919; came to U.S., 1923, naturalized, 1932; s. Vivian Ellsworth and Gertrude C. (Prout) P.; m. Betty Yde Andersen, June 20, 1941; 1 son, John Andrew. BA, U. Buffalo, 1941; AM (hon.), Harvard Coll., 1950; DSc (hon.), SUNY, Buffalo, 1994. Rsch. physicist Submarine Signal Co., 1941-42; staff mem. Radiation Lab. MIT, Cambridge, 1942-46; Soc. Fellows jr. fellow Harvard U., Cambridge, 1945-48; asst. prof. physics Harvard Coll., Cambridge, 1948-50, assoc. prof., 1950-56, prof., 1956-68; chmn. dept. physics, 1968-72, Mallinckrodt prof. physics, 1968-89, emeritus, 1989—; dir. Physics Lab. Havard U., Cambridge, 1975-83; Fulbright rsch. scholar Oxford (Eng.) U., 1951, vis. rsch. fellow Merton Coll., 1980; Fulbright lectr., Paris, 1958; vis. prof. Coll. de France, 1973; vis. fellow Joint Inst. Lab. Astrophysics, U. Colo., 1979-80; Zernike vis. prof. U. Groningen, The Netherlands, 1982; vis. sr. scientist Brookhaven Nat. Lab., 1986-87; vis. prof. U. Fla., 1987; W.G. Brickwedde lectr. Johns Hopkins U., Balt., 1992; Julian Mack lectr. U. Wis., 1992. Author, editor: Microwave Mixers, 1948; Contbr. articles to profl. jours. Trustee Associated Univs., Inc., 1976—. Recipient B.J. Thompson Meml. award Inst. Radio Engrs., 1948, Eddington medal Royal Astron. Soc., 1965, Nat. Medal Sci., NSF 1990; John Simon Guggenheim fellow,1957-58, 72-73. Fellow AAAS, Am. Phys. Soc., Am. Acad. Arts and Scis.; mem. NAS, French Phys. Soc. (mem coun. 1958-61), Acad. Scis. (France, fgn. assoc.), Phi Beta Kappa, Sigma Xi.

POUNDS, BILLY DEAN, law educator; b. Belmont, Miss., Jan. 23, 1930; s. Seth and Warnie (Wroten) P.; m. Genie Smith, June 22, 1952; children: Nancy Angela Pounds Via, Mary Dean Stone. AA, NE C.C., 1950; BS, Miss. State U., 1952, MS, 1953, EdD, 1968. Tchr. Wheeler (Miss.) High Sch., 1952-53; instr. NE Community Coll., Booneville, Miss., 1953-57; paralegal prof. Miss. U. for Women, Columbus, 1959—, dir. paralegal program, 1983—. Author: A Determination and Appraisal Content of Introduction to Political Science, 1968, History of Republic Party in Mississippi, 1964; co-author: Teaching About Communism, 1977. Pres. Lowndes County (Miss.) Kidney Found., 1970, Lowndes County Cancer Soc., 1972. Capt. USAF, 1957-59. Fellow Miss. State U., 1953; named Faculty Mem. of Yr., Miss. Legis., 1988. Mem. Phi Kappa Phi, Gamma Beta Phi, Kappa Delta Epsilon, Phi Delta Kappa, Phi Alpha Theta, Pi Gamma Mu, Pi Tau Chi. Office: Miss U for Women W Box 551 Columbus MS 39701

POUNDS, GERALD AUTRY, aerospace engineer; b. Boaz, Ala., Mar. 21, 1940; s. C.B. and Pauline (DeBord) P.; m. Linda Lee Lindsey, July 29, 1967; children: Kristina Marie, Alissa Michelle. B in Aerospace Engring., Auburn U., 1963, MS in Aerospace Engring., 1965. With Lockheed Martin Aero. Sys., Marietta, Ga., 1960—, mgr. wind tunnels and aircraft sys. test dept.; lectr. U. Tenn. Space Inst., Tullahoma, 1988-95. Contbr. articles to Jour. Aircraft. Vestry, from jr. warden to sr. warden Christ Episcopal Ch., Kennasaw, Ga., 1974-82; mid. adult retreat coord. Mt. Paran Ch. of God, Atlanta, 1986-91. NSF scholar, 1963-64. Assoc. fellow AIAA (dep. dir. for test, tech. activities com., 1991—, chmn. Atlanta sect.); mem. Supersonic Tunnel Assn. (co. rep.), Subsonic Aerodynamic Testing Assn. (co. rep.). Home: 315 Walton Green Way Kennesaw GA 30144 Office: Lockheed Martin Aero Sys D/73-66 Z-0605 Marietta GA 30063

POUNDS, WILLIAM FRANK, management educator; b. Fayette County, Pa., Apr. 9, 1928; s. Joseph Frank and Helen (Fry) P.; m. Helen Anne Means, Mar. 6, 1954; children: Thomas Mcclure, Julia Elizabeth. B-SChemE, Carnegie Inst. Tech., 1950, MS in Math. Econs., 1959, PhD in Indsl. Adminstrn., 1964. Indsl. engr. Eastman Kodak Co., 1950-51, 55-57; cons. Pitts. Plate Glass Co., 1958-59, from asst. to gen. mgr. Forbes finishes divsn., 1960-61; faculty Sloan Sch. Mgmt., MIT, 196—, prof. mgmt., 1966—, dean, 1966-80; sr. adv. Rockefeller Family and Assocs., 1981-91; bd. dirs. Putnam Funds, Sun Co., Inc., Idexx Labs., Inc., Mgmt. Scis. for Health, Inc., Perseptive Biosystems, Inc.; cons. in field. Trustee Boston Mus. Fine Arts; overseer WGBH Found. Served as aviator lt. (j.g.) USNR, 1951-55. Fellow Am. Acad. Arts and Scis. Home: 83 Cambridge Pkwy # W1205 Cambridge MA 02142-1241 Office: MIT 50 Memorial Dr Cambridge MA 02142-1347

POUNDSTONE, SALLY, library director; m. Robert Bruce Poundstone; children: Nancy Katrina, Holly Megan, Angus Bruce, Alice Heather. BA, U. Ky., 1954, MA in Libr. Sci., 1955. Asst. head ref. dept. Louisville (Ky.) Free Pub. Libr., 1955-59; libr. Folger Shakespeare Libr., Washington, 1959-60; chief acquisition dept. White Plains (N.Y.) Pub. Libr., 1960-62; libr. Bedford Hills (N.Y.) Pub. Elem. Sch., 1965-66; dir. Mamaroneck (N.Y.) Free Libr. and Emelin Theatre, 1966-87, Westport (Conn.) Pub. Libr., 1987—; instr. libr. sci. N.Y. U., 1968-69, Coll. of New Rochelle (N.Y.), 1970-71; adv. coun. mem. Pratt Inst. Grad Sch. of Libr. and Info. Sci., 1978-87; adminstrv. svcs. chmn. N.Y. Met. Ref. and Res. Libr. Agy., 1977-79, bd. trustees, 1979-88, 2d b.p. and chair, 1984-85, pres., 1985-88; planning and devel. com. mem. Bibliomation, Inc., 1988-90; chair Conn. State Adv. Coun. for Libr. Planning and Devel., 1988-90. Pres. Garden Club of Mamaroneck, 1969-70, Larchmont-Mamaroneck Film Coun., 1971-72, Mamaroneck Hist. soc., 1976-77, bd. mem., 1976-87; vice chmn. Village of Upper Nyack Planning Bd., 1988-89; leadership com. and task force mem. Westchester 2,000, 1984-87; com. mem. Rotary Club of Westport, 1987—; active Downtown Westport Adv. Com., 1989-90, Rep. Town. Com., Weston, Conn., 1990-93, Westport Bridge & Traffic Com., 1990—, Honorable Order of Ky. Cols., 1995—, United Way Profl. Adv. Com., 1994—, Westport Telecomm. Com., 1994—, and others. Mem. ALA, Conn. Libr. Assn., Fairfield Libr. Adminstrs. Group, Archons of Colophon, Pub. Libr. Dirs. Assn. Westchester County (various offices and chairs), N.Y. Libr. Assn. (sec. treas. adult libs. assn. 1970-72, pres. pub. libs. sect. 1981-82, chair planning com. 1984-85). Home: 48 Sharp Hill Rd Wilton CT 06897-3531 Office: Westport Lib Assn Arnold Bernhard Plz Westport CT 06880

POURCIAU, LESTER JOHN, librarian; b. Baton Rouge, La., Sept. 6, 1936; s. Lester John and Pearlie M. (Hogan) P.; m. Rebecca Anne Thomas, 1975; 1 son, Lester John III. B.A., La. State U., 1962, M.S., 1964; Ph.D. (Higher Edn. Act fellow), Ind. U., 1975. Asst. reference librarian U. S.C., Columbia, 1963-64; reference librarian Florence County Pub. Library, Florence, S.C., 1964-65; reference services coordinator U. Fla., Gainesville, 1966-67; dir. libraries Memphis State U., 1970—, assoc. v.p. for acad. affairs, dir. libraries, 1987—; chmn. coun. of head librarians State Univ. and C.C. System Tenn., 1980, 87; acad. assoc. Atlantic Coun. of U.S., Memphis State U.; fgn. expert, vis. lectr. Beijing U. of Posts & Telecomms., Beijing Normal U., Peking U., Renmen U., Qinghua U., Chingqing Inst. Posts & Telcomms., Guizhou Normal U., Republic of China, 1993; fgn. expert/vis. lectr. Beijing U. Posts and Telecom, 1993, Beijing Normal U., 1993, Peking U., 1993, RenMen U., 1993, Tsinghua U., 1993, Chongqing Inst. Posts and Telecom., 1993, Guizhou Normal U., 1993; fgn. expert, vis. lectr. Nanjing U. Posts and Telecom., Anhui Normal U., Beijing U. Posts and Telecom., 1994; fg— expert, vis. lectr. Anhui Normal U., Republic of China, 1994. Contbr. articles to profl. jours. Served with USAF, 1955-59. Recipient Adminstrv. Staff award Memphis State U., 1981, Commendation Boy Scouts Am., 1985, Commendation Tenn. Sec. State, 1989, Honor award Tenn. Libr. Assn., 1990; ; named Outstanding Alumnus, La. State U., 1988; named Libr. of Yr., Memphis Libr. Coun., 1989. Mem. Am. Southeastern, Tenn. Libr. Assn., Am. Soc. for Info. Sci., Nat. Assn. Watch and Clock Collectors (chpt. pres. 1983, sec.-treas. 1988, 89), Antique Automobile Am., Mid-Am. Old Time Automobile Assn., Memphis Old Time Car (sec. 1981, pres. 1982, 89), Delta Phi Alpha, Omicron Delta Kappa (Order of Omega), Phi Kappa Phi. Office: Memphis State U U Libr Memphis TN 38152

POUR-EL, MARIAN BOYKAN, mathematician, educator; b. N.Y.C.; d. Joseph and Mattie (Caspe) Boykan; m. Akiva Pour-El; 1 dau., Ina. A.B., Hunter Coll.; A.M., Harvard U., 1951, Ph.D., 1958. Asst. prof. math. Pa. State U., 1958-62, assoc. prof., 1962-64; mem. faculty U. Minn., Mpls., 1964—; prof. math. U. Minn., 1968—; mem. Inst. Advanced Study, Princeton, N.J., 1962-64; mem. coun. Conf. Bd. Math. Scis., 1977-82, trustee, 1978-81, mem. nominating com., 1980-82, chmn., 1981-82; lectr. internat. congresses in logic and computer sci., Eng., 1971, Hungary, 1967, Czechoslovakia, 1973, Germany, 1983, 96, 97, Japan, 1985, 88, China, 1987; lectr. Polish Acad. Sci., 1974; lecture series throughout Fed. Republic of Germany, 1980, 87, 89, 91, Japan, 1985, 87, 90, 93, China, 1987, Sweden, 1983, 94, Finland, 1991, Estonia, 1991, Moscow, 1992, Amsterdam, 1992; mem. Fulbright Com. on Maths., 1986-89. Author: (with I. Richards) Computability in Analysis and Physics, 1989; author numerous articles on mathematical logic (theoretical computer sci.) and applications to mathematical and physical theory. Named to Hunter Coll. Hall of Fame, 1975; NAS grantee, 1966. Fellow AAAS, Japan Soc. for Promotion of Sci.; mem. Am. Math. Soc. (coun. 1980-88, numerous coms., lectr. nat. meeting 1976, also spl. sessions 1971, 78, 82, 84, chmn. spl. sessions on recursion theory 1975, 84), Assn. Symbolic Logic, Math. Assn. Am. (nat. panel vis. lectrs. 1977—, lectr. nat. meetings 1982, 89), Phi Beta Kappa, Sigma Xi, Pi Mu Epsilon, Sigma Pi Sigma. Achievements include research in mathematical logic (theoretical computer science) and in computability and noncomputability in physical theory—wave, heat, potential equations, eigenvalues, eigenvectors. Office: U Minn Sch Math Vincent Hall Minneapolis MN 55455-0488 *In order to practice our careers our family has evolved a pattern of life at variance with the norm. For more than twenty years we have lived apart most of the time. Our strong emotional and personal ties were intensified by this absence of continuous physical nearness. It is my belief that one can succeed personally, socially and professionally without having to accept the constraints of an existing social order.*

POUSSAINT, ALVIN FRANCIS, psychiatrist, educator; b. N.Y.C., May 15, 1934; s. Christopher Thomas V. and Harriet (Johnston) P. BA, Columbia U., 1956; MD, Cornell U., 1960; MS, UCLA, 1964. Intern UCLA Ctr. for Health Sci., 1960-61, resident in psychiatry Neuropsychiat. Inst., 1961-64, chief resident, 1964-65; So. field dir. Med. Com. Human Rights, Jackson, Miss., 1965-66; asst. prof. psychiatry Tufts U. Med. Sch., 1966-69; assoc. prof. psychiatry, assoc. dean students Harvard Med. Sch., 1969-75, 78—, prof. psychiatry, 1993—, dean students, 1975-78; cons. HEW, 1969-73. Author numerous articles in field. Nat. treas. Black Acad. Arts and Letters, 1969-70, Med. Com. Human Rights, 1966—. Recipient Michael Schwerner award, 1968, Am. Black Achievement award in Bus. and the Professions Johnson Pub. Co., Inc., 1986, John Jay award for Disting. Profl. Achievement Columbia Coll., N.Y., 1987, Medgar Evers Medal of Honor Beverly Hills/Hollywood chpt. NAACP, Hollywood, Calif., 1988, and numerous hon. degrees. Fellow AAAS, Am. Orthopsychiatric Assn., Am. Psychiat. Assn. (mem. com. on Black Psychiatrists 1970-75); mem. Nat. Med. Assn., Am. Acad. of Child Psychiatry, Children's Longwood. Office: Judge Baker Ctr 3 Blackfan Circle Ave Boston MA 02115-5794

POUTSMA, MARVIN L., chemical research administrator; b. Grand Rapids, Mich., Aug. 7, 1937; m. Yolanda Arco, July 20, 1968; children: John C., Julie A. BS, Calvin Coll., 1958; PhD, U. Ill., 1962. Staff scientist corp. rsch. Union Carbide, Tarrytown, N.Y., 1961-65, group leader corp. rsch., 1965-68, sr. scientist corp. rsch., 1968-73, sr. group leader corp. rsch., 1972-78; group leader chemistry divsn. Oak Ridge (Tenn.) Nat. Lab., 1978-80, sect. head chemistry divsn., 1980-83, dir. chemistry divsn., 1984-93, dir. chem. & analytical scis. divsn., 1994—. Contbr. chpts. to books and articles to profl. jours. Fellow AAAS; mem. Am. Chem. Soc. Office: Oak Ridge Nat Lab PO Box 2008 Oak Ridge TN 37831-6129

POVICH, DAVID, lawyer; b. Washington, June 8, 1935; s. Shirley Lewis and Ethyl (Friedman) P.; m. Constance Enid Tobriner, June 14, 1959; children: Douglas, Johanna, Judith, Andrew. B.A., Yale U., 1958; LL.B., Columbia U., 1962. Bar: D.C. 1962, U.S. Ct. Appeals (4th cir.) 1980, U.S. Tax Ct. 1981, U.S. Ct. Appeals (5th and 11th cirs.) 1984, U.S. Dist. Ct. Md. Law clk. to assoc. judge D.C. Ct. Appeals, Washington, 1962-63; ptnr. Williams & Connolly, Washington, 1963—, mem. exec. com., 1986-87. Bd. dirs., officer Lisner Home for Aged. Mem. D.C. Bar Assn., ABA, Bar Assn. D.C., Barristers (exec. com. 1992-93). Office: Williams & Connolly 725 12th St NW Washington DC 20005-3901

POVICH, LYNN, journalist, magazine editor; b. Washington, June 4, 1943; d. Shirley and Ethyl (Friedman) P.; m. Stephen B. Shepard, Sept. 16, 1979; children: Sarah, Ned. AB, Vassar Coll., 1965. Rechr., reporter, writer, editor Newsweek Mag., N.Y.C., 1965-91; editor-in-chief Working Woman Mag., N.Y.C., 1991-96; mng. editor, sr. exec. prodr. East coast programming MSNBC Interactive, Secaucus, N.J., 1996—. Recipient Matrix award N.Y. Women in Comms., 1976; named to Acad. of Women Achievers YWCA, 1993. Office: MSNBC Interactive 40 Hartz Way Secaucus NJ 07094-2406

POVICH, (MAURICE) MAURY RICHARD, broadcast journalist, talk show host, television producer; b. Washington, Jan. 17, 1939; s. Shirley and Ethel Povich; m. Constance "Connie" Y. Chung, Dec. 2, 1984; children from previous marriage, Susan, Amy. BA, U. Pa., 1962. Reporter WWDC Radio, Washington, 1962-66; gen. assignment and sports report Sta. WTTG-TV, Washington, 1966; co-anchor Panorama, Washington, 1967-70, host, 1973-76, host and anchor, 1983-86; host People and Povich Sta. WTTG, Washington, 1970-72; news anchor Sta. WMAQ-TV, Chgo., 1977, Sta. KNXT-TV, L.A., 1977-78; anchor Sta. KGO-TV, San Francisco, 1978-79, Sta. KYW-TV, Phila., 1980-83, Sta. WTTG-TV, Washington, 1983-86; host A Current Affair, 1986-90; host, anchor WTTG-TV News, 1983-86; host Maury Povich Show, 1991—; guest on Carol Leiffer show, 1989, Donahue show with Connie Chung, 1989, John MacLaughlin show, 1989, Dick Cavett show, 1989, others; guest speaker Am. Agrl. Editors Assn. Communication Clinic, 1989, ASTA Conf., N.Y.C., 1990, Assn. Broadcast Exec. of Tex., 1990; speaker on tabloid TV, the media and Israel, advertiser blacklists; host Forbes 400, CBS-TV Special, 1992. Author: Current Affairs: A Life on the Edge, 1991. Office: The Maury Povich Show 221 W 26th St New York NY 10001-6703*

POVICH, SHIRLEY LEWIS, columnist, former sports editor; b. Bar Harbor, Maine, July 15, 1905; s. Nathan and Rosa (Orlovich) P.; m. Ethyl Friedman, Feb. 21, 1932; children: David, Maurice R., Lynn. Student, Georgetown U., 1922-24. Reporter Washington Post, 1923-25, sports editor, 1926-33, columnist, 1933-45; war corr. Washington Post, PTO, 1945; columnist Washington Post, 1946—; adj. prof. communications Am. U., 1975—. Author: The Washington Senators, 1954, All These Mornings, 1969; also articles in mags. Recipient citation for outstanding svc. as war correspondent, 1945, Grantland Rice award for sportswriting Nat. Headliners Club, 1964, Red Smith award, 1983, career accomplishment in journalism Nat. Press. Club, 1995; elected to Baseball Hall of Fame, Cooperstown Writers Divsn., 1976. Mem. Baseball Writers Assn. Am. (pres. 1955). Home: 2801 New Mexico Ave NW Washington DC 20007-3921 Office: Washington Post 1515 L St NW Washington DC 20005-1601

POVISH, KENNETH JOSEPH, retired bishop; b. Alpena, Mich., Apr. 19, 1924; s. Joseph Francis and Elizabeth (Jachcik) P. A.B., Sacred Heart Sem., Detroit, 1946; M.A., Cath. U. Am., 1950; postgrad., No. Mich. U., 1961, 63. Ordained priest Roman Catholic Ch., 1950; asst. pastorships, 1950-56; pastor in Port Sanilac Mich., 1956-57, Munger, Mich., 1957-60, Bay City, Mich., 1966-70; dean St. Paul Sem., Saginaw, Mich., 1960-66; vice rector St. Paul Sem., 1962-66; bishop of Crookston Minn., 1970-75; bishop of Lansing Mich., 1975-95; bd. consulators Diocese of Saginaw, 1966-70; instr. Latin and U.S. history St. Paul Sem., 1960-66. Weekly columnist Saginaw and Lansing diocesan newspapers. Bd. dirs. Cath. Charities Diocese Saginaw, 1969-70. Mem. Mich. Hist. Soc., Bay County Hist. Soc., Lions Club, KC (pres. Mich. Cath. Conf. 1985-95), Kiwanis.

POWDERLY, WILLIAM H., III, lawyer; b. Pitts., Feb. 23, 1930. BS, Georgetown U., 1953; LLB, U. Pitts., 1956. Bar: Pa. 1956. Ptnr. Jones, Day, Reavis & Pogue, Pitts. Office: Jones Day Reavis & Pogue 1 Mellon Bank Ctr 500 Grant St Pittsburgh PA 15219-2502

POWELL, ALAN, mechanical engineer, scientist; b. Buxton, Derbyshire, Eng., Feb. 17, 1928; came to U.S., 1956; s. Frank and Gwendolen Marie (Walker) P.; m. June Sinclair, Mar. 28, 1956. Student Buxton Coll., 1939-45; diploma in aeros., Loughborough Coll., 1948; B.Sc. in Engring. with 1st class honors, London U., 1949; honours diploma 1st class, Loughborough Coll., 1949; D.Tech. (hon.), Loughborough U. Tech., 1980; Ph.D., U. Southampton, 1953. Chartered engr. Engr. Percival Aircraft Co., Luton, Eng., 1949-51; research asst. U. Southampton, Eng., 1951-53; lectr. U. Southampton, 1953-56; research fellow Calif. Inst. Tech., Pasadena, 1956-57; engr. Douglas Aircraft Co., 1956; assoc. prof. UCLA, 1957-62, prof. engring., 1962-65, head Aerosonics lab., 1957-65; assoc. tech. dir., head acoustics and vibration lab. David Taylor Model Basin, Dept. Navy, Washington, 1965-66; tech. dir. David Taylor Model Basin, Dept. Navy, 1966-67, David Taylor Naval Ship Research & Devel. Center, Bethesda, Md., 1967-85; mem. Undersea Warfare Research & Devel. Council, 1966-76, chmn., 1971-72; mem. council on Fed. Labs., 1972-85; prof. mech. engring. U. Houston, 1985—, chmn., 1985-87; mem. com. on hearing bioacoustics and biomechs. NAS-NRC, 1961-85, advisor, 1985-95, exec. coun., 1963-65, chmn., 1965-66, mem. naval studies bd. 1990-95; mem. various coms. Naval Studies Bd. and Marine Bd., 1990-96; advisor Chinese U. Devel. Project, 1989-91; cons. Douglas Aircraft Co., various aerospace and acoustics cos., 1956-65; mem. adv. coun. Internat. Towing Tank Conf., 1981-85; mem. advisor U.S.-Japan Program Natural Resources, 1987-90, mem. Marine Facilities Panel. Contbr. articles to profl. jours. Recipient Navy Meritorious Civilian Service award, 1970; Brit. Empire scholar, 1945; named Meritorious Exec. Pres. of U.S., 1982; Capt. Robert Dexter Conrad gold medal for sci. achievement Sec. Navy, 1984. Fellow Royal Aero. Soc. London (Baden-Powell prize 1948, Wilbur Wright prize 1953), Acoustical Soc. Am. (biennial award 1962, assoc. editor Jour. 1962-67, chmn. edn. com. 1964-66, exec. coun. 1966-69, chmn.

medals and awards com. 1978-81, v.p. elect 1981-82, v.p. 1982-83, pres. elect 1989-90, pres. 1990-91, past pres. 1991-92, Silver medal in engring. acoustics 1992, designated Nat. Spkr. in Engring. Acoustics 1994—), Inst. Mech. Engrs., Inst. Acoustics (U.K.); mem. AIAA (assoc. fellow, Aeroacoustics award 1980), ASME (Rayleigh lectr. 1988, Per Brüel Gold medal 1991), Inst. Noise Control Engrs. (initial mem., dir. 1974-77, Disting. lectr. 1975, 83, v.p. 1981-84, bd. cert. 1993), Acoustics, Speech and Signal Processing Soc. (exec. com. 1969-72, awards com. 1971-73, bylaws com. chmn. 1971-73), Am. Soc. Naval Engrs. (life), Am. Acad. Mechanics, Tau Beta Pi (hon. life). Office: U Houston Dept Mech Engring Houston TX 77204-4792

POWELL, ANNE ELIZABETH, editor; b. Cheverly, Md., Nov. 11, 1951; d. Arthur Gorman and Barbara Anne (MacAran) P.; m. John Alan Ebeling Jr., 1972 (div. 1983). BS, U. Md., 1972. Reporter Fayetteville (N.C.) Times, 1973-75; home editor Columbus (Ga.) Ledger-Enquirer, 1976; assoc. editor Builder mag., Washington, 1977-78; architecture editor House Beautiful's Spl. Publs., N.Y.C., 1979-81; editor Traditional Home mag., Des Moines, 1982-87, Mid-Atlantic Country mag., Alexandria, Va., 1987-89; editor in chief publs. Nat. Trust for Hist. Preservation, Washington, 1989-95; editor-in-chief Landscape Architecture Mag., Washington, 1995—. Author: The New England Colonial, 1988. Mem. Nat. Press Club, Am. Soc. Mag. Editors. Home: 707 S Royal St Alexandria VA 22314-4309 Office: Am Soc Landscape Arch 4401 Connecticut Ave NW Washington DC 20008-2322

POWELL, BARRY BRUCE, classicist; b. Sacramento, Apr. 30, 1942; s. Barrett Robert and Anita Louise (Burns) P.; m. Patricia Ann Cox; children: Elena Melissa, Adam Vincent. BA in Classics, U. Calif., Berkeley, 1963, PhD, 1971; MA, Harvard U., 1965. Asst. prof. Northern Ariz. U., Flagstaff, 1970-73; asst. prof. to prof. U. Wis., Madison, 1973—, chmn. dept. classics, 1985-92, chmn. program integrated liberal studies. Author: Composition by Theme in the Odyssey, 1973, Homer and the Origin of the Greek Alphabet, 1991, Classical Myth, 1995, 2nd edit., 1997, New Companion to Homer, 1997; contbr. articles to profl. jours. Woodrow Wilson fellow, 1965. Mem. Am. Philol. Assn., Am. Sch. Classical Studies at Athens (mng. com), Archeol. Inst. of Am., Classical Assn. of Midwest and South, Am. Academy in Rome, Phi Beta Kappa (former pres. Madison chpt.). Home: 1210 Sweetbriar Rd Madison WI 53705-2228 Office: Univ Wis Dept Classics Madison WI 53707

POWELL, BOLLING RAINES, JR., lawyer, educator; b. Florala, Ala., Aug. 10, 1910; s. Bolling Raines and Marie (Arnold) P.; m. Mary Vilette Spaulding, Dec. 10, 1949; children: Bolling Raines, James Spaulding. B.A., Birmingham-So. Coll., 1930; M.A., LL.B., J.D., U. Va., 1934. Asst. prof. law U. Va., 1938-39; partner Paul V. McNutt, Washington and N.Y.C., 1947-50, Powell, Dorsey and Blum, Washington, 1950-62, Powell, Horkan and Powell, Washington, 1962-75; prof. Wythe Sch. Law, Coll. William and Mary, 1969-80; sole practice Gloucester, Va., 1975—; spl. trial counsel to bd. govs. FRS, 1956-62; bd. advisors Ct. Practice Inst., 1973-78. Editor-in-chief: Va. Law Rev., 1934. Chmn. Gloucester United Taxpayers, 1978—; dir. Boy Scouts Am. Fund Raising Campaign, Gloucester County, 1965. Served to lt. col. AUS, 1942-46. Decorated Legion of Merit. Mem. Va. State Bar (bd. govs. adminstrv. law sect.), Ala. Bar Assn., D.C. Bar Assn., ABA, Raven Soc. U. Va., Phi Beta Kappa, Omicron Delta Kappa. Episcopalian. Clubs: Metropolitan (Washington); Farmington Country (Charlottesville, Va.). Home: Warner Hall Plantation Gloucester VA 23061 Office: PO Box 800 Gloucester VA 23061-0800

POWELL, BOONE, JR., hospital administrator; b. Knoxville, Tenn., Feb. 9, 1937; married. BA, Baylor U., 1959; MA, U. Calif., 1960. Adm. intern Marin Gen. Hosp., Greenbrae, Calif., 1959; adm. resident Baptist Meml. Hosp., Memphis, 1960-61; asst. adminstr. Hendrick Med. Ctr., Abilene, Tex., 1961-69, assoc. adminstr., 1969-70, adminstr., 1970-73, pres., 1973-80; pres. Baylor Health Care System, Dallas, 1980—. Contbr. articles to profl. jours. Mem. Am. Coll. Healthcare Execs., Tex. Hosp. Assn. (chair community svc., trustee). Office: Baylor Health Care System 3500 Gaston Ave Dallas TX 75246-2017

POWELL, CAROL ANN, accountant; b. Bklyn., Dec. 5, 1954; d. William Preston and Adelaide Hertha (Sohl) Batty; m. Michael Robert Powell, Jan. 17, 1976; children: Michael David, David Jason. AAS, Delhi Agrl. and Tech. Coll., 1974; BS, Syracuse U., 1975. CPA, N.Y. Sr. acct. Hall & Yann, CPAs, Fayetteville, N.Y., 1975-78; pvt. practice acct. Cold Spring, N.Y., 1979—; adj. tchr. acctg. Onondaga C.C., Syracuse, N.Y., 1977, Dutchess C.C., Poughkeepsie, N.Y., 1982. Den leader Philipstown Pack 137 Boy Scouts Am., Cold Spring, N.Y., 1987-95; treas. Philipstown Little League, Cold Spring, 1990—, Philipstown Babe Ruth League, Cold Spring, 1994. Mem. AICPA, N.Y. State Soc. CPAs. Methodist. Avocations: piano, quilting. Home: PO Box 312 Cold Spring NY 10516-0312 Office: 159 Main St Cold Spring NY 10516-2818

POWELL, CAROL SUE, pediatric special education educator, nursing consultant; b. Phoenix, Nov. 15, 1944; d. Leonard Newson and Rebecca Jane (Housh) Stephens; m. Howard Powell Jr., Aug. 26, 1967; children: Jim, Howard III, Nicole. LPN, Champaign (Ill.) Sch. Practical Nursing, 1965; BA, Ea. Ill. U., 1975, MS in Edn., 1979; ADN, Lincolnland C.C., 1986. RN, Ill.; cert. elem. and secondary edn. tchr., Ill.; qualified mental retardation profl., Ill. Nurse Pattie A. Clay Infirmary, Richmond, Ky., 1966-68, Clark County Hosp., Winchester, Ky., 1968-69, Mattoon (Ill.) Hosp., 1970-77; substitute tchr. Mattoon, Charleston, Findlay, Arcola Schs., 1978-79; spl. edn. and kindergarten tchr. Buda (Ill.) Sch. Dist., 1979-81; staff nurse St. John's Hosp., Springfield, Ill., 1981-87; health svc. supr. Assn. for Retarded Citizens, Springfield, 1987-88; staff nurse St. Vincent's Hosp., Taylorville, Ill., 1988-89; spl. edn. tchr., asst. dir. edn., mental retardation profl. Luth. Social Svcs., Beardstown, Ill., 1989-97. Nurse Shrine Clinics, Springfield, 1989-96, nurse, EMT first aid meets Boy Scouts Am., Springfield, 1988-96. Methodist. Home: 834 Evergreen Dr Chatham IL 62629-1118

POWELL, CAROLYN WILKERSON, music educator; b. Hamburg, Ark., Oct. 9, 1920; d. Claude Kelly and Mildred (Hall) Wilkerson; m. Charles Luke Powell, Dec. 12, 1923; children: Charles Luke Jr., James Davis, Mark Wilkerson, Robert Hall. AB, Cen. Methodist, Fayette, Mo., 1942; MAT, U. N.C., Chapel Hill, 1970. Life Teaching Cert. Mo. Teaching Cert. N.C. Choral dir. Maplewood Richmond Heights Sch., St. Louis, 1943-45; pvt. piano tchr. Greensboro N.C. Area, Greensboro, 1951-63; organist Presbyterian and Methodist Ch., Greensboro, 1950-61; dir. Ch. Youth Choirs, Greensboro, 1958-61; choral and humanities tchr. Page High Sch., Greensboro, 1963-67; choral dir. Githens Jr. High Sch., Durham, N.C., 1967-80; organist St. Peter's Episcopal Ch., Altavista, Va., 1981-83; chmn. Dist. Choral Festival N.C. Dist., 1968-78; accompanist and music dir. Altavista Little Theatre Altavista, Va., 1981-83. Sunday and vacation schs. tchr., organist Grace Meth. Ch., Greensboro; den mother Boy Scouts Am., Greensboro, 1951-57; mem. Chapel Hill Preservation Soc., 1985—; vol., chapel organist, pediat. tutor U. N.C. Hosps., Chapel Hill, 1984-89. Mem. NEA, AAUW, Music Educators Nat. Conf., Am. Organists Guild, Classroom Tchrs. Assn., Ackland Art Mus. Assn., Chapel Hill Preservation Soc., Nat. Federated Music Club Euterpe, Chapel Hill Country Club, U. Woman's Club, The Carolina Club, Delta Kappa Gamma. Avocations: reading, golf, needlework, gardening, travel and antiques. Home: Carol Woods Apt 142 750 Weaver Dairy Rd Chapel Hill NC 27514-1440

POWELL, CHRISTOPHER ROBERT, systems engineer/programmer, computer scientist; b. Summit, N.J., Feb. 2, 1963; s. Robin Powell and Nancy Mae (Spurling) Gould; m. Bonnie Jean Manning, June 10, 1989. BS in Math. and Computer Sci., Clarkson U., 1984; postgrad., Syracuse U., 1988, SUNY, Binghamton, 1990. Sr. assoc. program IBM Corp., Endicott, N.Y., 1984-90; sr. systems analyst/programmer Supercomputer Systems, Inc., Eau Claire, Wis., 1990-93; systems programmer prin. Network Systems Corp./Channel Networking Strategic Bus. Unit, Brooklyn Park, Minn., 1993-96; sys. engring. mgr. Sequent Computer Sys., Eau Claire, Wis., 1996—. Appt. City of Spring Lake Park Energy Commn., 1995; vice chmn. Energy Commn., 1996. Mem. Assn. for Computing Machinery, Nat. Systems Programmers Assn., NSC Leadership Forum, Alpha Phi Omega (torchbearer 1987-97), Pi Mu Epsilon, Pi Delta Epsilon. Democrat. Achievements include assisting in Network Systems registration for ISO 9000; core team leader CPU rsch. and implementation. Home: 3311 W Country Club Ln Altoona WI 54720

POWELL, CLINTON COBB, radiologist, physician, former university administrator; b. Hartford, Conn., Mar. 9, 1918; s. Harry Havey and Nita Florence (Nass) P.; m. Frances Arlene Collins, Apr. 2, 1944; children: Pamela Powell Kellogg, Brenda Joyce, Donna Sue Powell Mason. B.S., Mass. Inst. Tech., 1940; M.D., Boston U., 1944; student, U. Chgo., 1947-48. Diplomate: Am. Bd. Radiology, Nat. Bd. Med. Examiners. Intern U.S. Marine Hosp., Boston, 1944-45; commd. asst. surgeon USPHS, 1946, med. dir., 1956; staff mem. indsl. hygiene research lab. NIH, 1946-47, radiation safety officer, 1948-51; resident radiology USPHS Hosp., Balt., 1951-52; fellow radiology U. Pa. Hosp., 1952-54; staff physician radiation therapy, clin. center NIH, 1954-55; grants analyst, research grants and fellowship br. Nat. Cancer Inst., 1955-56; chief radiol. health med. program, div. spl. health services USPHS, 1956-58; exec. sec. radio and surgery study sect., div. research grants NIH, 1958-59, asst. chief research grants rev. br., div. research grants, 1959-60, dep. chief div., 1960-61; asst. dir. Nat. Inst. Allergy and Infectious Diseases, 1961-62; dir. Nat. Inst. Gen. Med. Scis., NIH, 1962-64; asso. coordinator med. and health scis. U. Calif., 1964-66, coordinator, 1966-71, spl. asst. to pres. for health affairs, 1971-79, spl. asst. emeritus, 1979—; Mem. Internat. Commn. Radiol. Protection, 1965-68; mem. com. Nat. Com. Radiation Protection, 1956-68, exec. com., 1957-67, ad hoc sub-com. wide-spread radioactive contamination, 1958-60, subcom. 1, 1960—; mem. radiol. physics fellowship bd. AEC, 1958-63; com. radiation effects Am. Thoracic Soc., 1957—; com. use radioisotopes in hosps. Am. Hosp. Assn., 1953—; subcom. radiol. health Assn. State and Territorial Health Officers, 1958-66. Contbr. numerous articles profl. jours. Served with USNR, 1945-46. Fellow AAAS; mem. Am. Coll. Radiology (commn. radiol. units, standards and protection 1957—, chmn. com. radiation exposure of women), AMA, Am. Pub. Health Assn. (program area com. radiol. health 1959), Radiol. Soc. N.Am., Radiation Research Soc., Health Physics Soc., Assn. for Acad. Health Centers (dir. 1969-70).

POWELL, COLIN LUTHER, retired military officer, author; b. N.Y.C., Apr. 5, 1937; s. Luther and Maud Ariel (McKoy) P.; m. Alma V. Johnson, Aug. 25, 1962; children: Michael, Linda, Annemarie. B.S., CUNY, 1958; M.B.A., George Washington U., 1971. Commd. 2d lt. U.S. Army, 1958; advanced through grades to gen., 1989; comdr. 2d Brigade, 101st Airborne Div., 1976-77; exec. asst. to sec. Dept. Energy, 1979; sr. mil. asst. to sec. Dept. Def., 1979-81; asst. div. comdr. 4th Inf. Div. Dept. Def., Ft. Carson, Colo., 1981-83; mil. asst. to Sec. of Def. Dept. Def., Washington, 1983-86; assigned to U.S. V Corps, Europe, 1986-87; dep. asst. to the pres. for nat. security affairs The White House, Washington, 1987; asst. to Pres. for nat. security affairs Washington, 1987-89; comdr.-in-chief Forces Command, Ft. McPherson, Ga., 1989-94; chmn. Joint Chiefs of Staff The Pentagon, Washington, 1989-93; ret., 1994. Author: My American Journey, 1995. Decorated Legion of Merit, Bronze Star, Air medal, Purple Heart; The White House fellow, 1972-73; recipient Medal of Freedom (2); named hon. knight comdr. Most Honorable Order of the Bath Queen Elizabeth II, 1993. Mem. Assn. U.S. Army. Episcopalian. Office: 909 N Washington St Ste 767 Alexandria VA 22314-1555

POWELL, DON WATSON, medical educator, physician, physiology researcher; b. Gadsden, Ala., Aug. 29, 1938; s. Gordon C. and Ruth (Bennett) P.; m. Frances N. Rourke; children: Mary Paige, Drew Watson, Shawne Margaret. BS with honors, Auburn U., 1960; MD with highest honors, Med. Coll. Ala., Birmingham, 1963. Diplomate Am. Bd. Internal Medicine, Am. Bd. Gastroenterology. Intern, resident P.B. Brigham Hosp., Boston, 1963-65; resident Yale U. Sch. Med., New Haven, 1968-69, spl. NIH fellow in physiology, 1969-71; asst. prof. medicine U. N.C., Chapel Hill, 1971-74, assoc. prof., 1974-78, prof., 1978-91; chief divsn. digestive diseases U. N.C., 1977-91, dir. Ctr. Gastrointestinal Biol. Diseases, 1985-91, assoc. chmn. clin. affairs dept. medicine, 1989-91; Edward Randall and Edward Randall, Jr. Disting. Chmn., prof. dept. internal medicine, prof. dept. physiology and biophysics Med. br. U. Tex., Galveston, 1991—; cons. WHO, Geneva, 1980-82, Burroughs-Wellcome, Inc., Research Triangle Park, N.C., 1981-82, Hoffman-LaRoche, Inc., Nutley, N.J., 1982—; mem. merit rev. bd. VA, 1977-80; mem. gen. medicine A-2 study sect. NIH, 1985-89, mem. Nat. Inst. Diabetes Digestive and Kidney Diseases Adv. Coun., 1994—; coun., bd. rep. adv. com. to dir.NIH, 1996—. Assoc. editor: Textbook of Gastroenterology, Atlas of Gastroenterology; mem. editl. bd. Am. Jour. Physiology, Gastrointestinal and Liver Physiology, 1979—, Am. Jour. Med. Sci., 1984-92, Regulatory Peptide Letter, 1990—, Annals of Internal Medicine, 1993-96; contbr. over 100 articles to profl. jours. Capt. U.S. Army Med. Corps, 1965-68. Recipient Rsch. Career Devel. award NIH, 1973-78, Merit award, 1987, Outstanding Physician of Yr. award Gulf Coast chpt. Crohn's Colitis Found. Am., 1994. Fellow ACP (mem. med. knowledge self-assessment program VII gastroenterology com. 1983-85); mem. Am. Physiol. Soc., Am. Gastroenterol. Assn. (v.p. 1991-92, pres. 1993-94), Gastroenterology Rsch. Group (chmn. 1988-89), So. Soc. Clin. Investigation, Federated Socs. Gastroenterology and Hepatology (chmn. 1996—), Assn. Am. Physicians, Assn. Prof. Medicine, Am. Clin. and Climatol. Assn. Avocation: singing. Office: U Tex Med Br 4108 John Sealy Annex 301 University Blvd Galveston TX 77555-0567

POWELL, DOUGLAS ROBERT, psychology educator; b. Kalamazoo, Sept. 19, 1948; s. Robert Noel and Vonda Lucile (Warner) P.; m. Barbara Jane Lewellen, Aug. 21, 1971; children: Rachel Mae, Philip Douglas. BA, Western Mich. U., 1970, MA, 1971; PhD, Northwestern U., 1974. Rsch. assoc., dir. program devel. Merrill-Palmer Inst., Detroit, 1974-80; assoc. prof. human devel. Wayne State U., Detroit, 1980-84; prof., head child devel. & family studies Purdue U., West Lafayette, Ind., 1984—; cons. Bush Found., St. Paul, 1982—; mem. tech. resource Nat. Edn. Goals Panel, Washington, 1991-95; mem. nat. adv. com. U. Chgo. Family Support Project, 1995—. Bd. dirs. Tippecanoe County Child Care, Inc., Lafayette, Ind., 1986-88; mem. policy coun. Head Start, Lafayette, 1985-87; mem. standing com. Meth. Children's Village, Detroit, 1981-83. Rsch. grantee Lilly Endowment, Ford Found., Bush Found., Kellogg Found., 1978—; recipient Hoosier Educator of Yr. award Ind. Assn. Edn. Young Children, Indpls., 1990, Mary L. Matthews Outstanding Tchr. award, 1991. Mem. Am. Psychol. Assn., Am. Edn. Rsch. Assn. (chair child devel. group 1992-94), Nat. Assn. Edn. Young Childrem (editor 1985-95), Nat. Coun. Family Rels. Episcopalian. Avocations: music, theatre, gardening. Office: Purdue U CDFS Dept West Lafayette IN 47907

POWELL, DREXEL DWANE, JR., editorial cartoonist; b. Lake Village, Ark., Nov. 7, 1944; s. Drexel Dwane and Minnie Louise (Ruth) P.; m. Janice Sue Lovell, Apr. 10, 1971. B.S. in Agri-Bus, U. Ark. at Monticello, 1970. Cartoonist Sentinel Record, Hot Springs, Ark., 1970-72, San Antonio Light, 1973-74; editorial cartoonist Cin. Enquirer, 1974-75, News and Observer, Raleigh, N.C., 1975—; syndicated L.A. Times Syndicate, 1979—; lectr. in field. Author: Is That All You Do?, 1979, Surely SOMEONE Can Still Sing Bass!, 1981, The Reagan Chronicles, 1987, One Hundred Per Cent Pure Old Jess, 1993; freelance artist; designer book jackets. Served with N.G., 1967-68. Recipient Overseas Press Club citation, 1978, Headliners Club award, 1978; named Disting. Alumnus U. Ark. at Monticello, 1979. Mem. Assn. Am. Editorial Cartoonists. Office: 215 S Mcdowell St Raleigh NC 27601-1331

POWELL, EARL ALEXANDER, III, art museum director; b. Spartanburg, S.C., Oct. 24, 1943; s. Earl Alexander and Elizabeth (Duckworth) P.; m. Nancy Landry Powell, July 17, 1971; children—Cortney, Channing, Sumner. AB with honors, William Coll., 1966; AM, Harvard U., 1970, PhD, 1974. Teaching fellow in fine arts Harvard U., 1970-74; curator, Michener Collection U. Tex., Austin, 1974-76, asst. prof. art history, 1974-76; mus. curator, sr. staff asst. to asst. dir. and chief curator Nat. Gallery Art, Washington, 1976-78, exec. curator, 1979-80; dir. Los Angeles County Mus. Art, 1980-92, Nat. Gallery Art, Washington, 1992—; career advisor Harvard U.; mem. fine arts adv. panel Fed. Res. Bank, Commn. Pres. of White House, Pres.' Commn. on Arts and Humanities, Coun. Arts and Humanities, Fed. Coun. Arts and Humanities, Nat. Portrait Gallery Commn., Scholarly Adv. Coun., Nat. Register Peer Profls. of the GSA Design Excellence Program; mem. nat. adv. bd. O'Keeffe Mus. Author: American Art at Harvard, 1973, Selections from the James Michener Collection, 1975, Abstract Expressionists and Imagists: A Retrospective View, 1976, Milton Avery, 1976, The James A. Michener Collection: Twentieth Century American Painting, catalogue raisonne, 1978, Thomas Cole monograph, 1990. Trustee Pitzer Coll.; mem. vis. com. Williams Coll. Mus. Art. Served with U.S. Navy, 1966-69, comdr. Res., 1976-80. Decorated chevalier Order Arts and Letters, 1985; grand ofcl. Order of the Infante D. Henrique medal, 1995; recipient King Olav medal, 1978, Bicentennial medal Williams Coll., 1995; Harvard U. travelling fellow, 1973-74, Mexican Cultural award, 1996. Mem. Walpole Soc., Am. Assn. Mus. (co-chmn. commn. on mus. for a new century), Am. Assn. Mus. Dirs., Am. Fedn. Arts (trustee), White House Hist. Assn. (trustee), Nat. Trust Hist. Preservation, Thomas Jefferson Meml. Found.

POWELL, EDMUND WILLIAM, lawyer; b. St. Paul, Dec. 23, 1922; s. George L. and Mary (Sexton) P.; m. Ellen M. Williams, May 7, 1949; children—Susan Marie, Sarah Ann, Daniel. Student, St. Thomas Coll., St. Paul, 1941-43, U. Minn., 1943, 46; LL.B., Marquette U., 1948. Bar: Wis. bar 1948. Pvt. practice Milw., 1948—; pres. firm Borgelt, Powell, Peterson & Frauen and predecessors, 1948-90. Served with USNR, 1943-45; to capt. USMCR, 1945-46, 52-53. Fellow Am. Coll. Trial Lawyers; mem. State Bar Wis. (sec. 1964-65, bd. govs. 1961-63, 65-67, sec., dir. ins. sect. 1962-69), Marquette Law Alumni Assn. (pres., dir. 1957-60). Club: Town (Milw.). Home: 4611 N Lake Dr Milwaukee WI 53211-1255 Office: 735 N Water St Milwaukee WI 53202-4100

POWELL, EDWARD LEE, broadcasting company executive; b. Columbus, Ohio, July 3, 1958; s. Louis Andrew and Margaret Letitia (Steen) P.; m. Denise Noel Harlow, July 11, 1981; children: Edward Lee II, Sarah Elizabeth. BS in Bus. Mgmt. and Mktg., Franklin U., 1988. Freelance square dance caller, rec. artist Reynoldsburg, Ohio, 1976—; columnist Columbus Dispatch Newspaper, 1976-79; disc jockey, salesperson Sta. WWWJ, Johnstown, Ohio, 1978-79; disc jockey, ops. dir. Sta. WLGN-AM-FM, Logan, Ohio, 1980-81; disc jockey Sta. WMNI, Columbus, 1980-89, creative dir., disc jockey, 1987-89; disc jockey Sta. WMGG-FM, Columbus, 1986-87; sales assoc. Tom Yontz and Assocs., Eagle Realty, Westerville, Ohio, 1987—; gen. mgr. Radio Sound Network, Columbus, Ohio, 1989-90; prin. Group X, Reynoldsburg, Ohio, 1990—, Radio Cafe Hour/Cafe Prodns. Inc., Branson, Mo., 1993-95; Cons. mktg. and advt. programs, 1984-95, Central Ohio Corp. of Dance Clubs, Columbus, 1982—, direct mail; spokeman, guest on TV; bd. dirs. Y.E.S. (wheelchair) Dancers, Inc., 1986-89, nat. and state square dance conventions, 1976—. Creative dir. advt. campaigns: Levi's, Cavalier; producer, talent advt. campaign Suzuki Motorcycles, 1981 (award of excellence), (record) Phoenix on Her Mind, 1978; author, pub.: So You Want to Be a Caller, 1979; songwriter BMI. Active Ctrl. Ohio Muscular Dystrophy Assn., 1990-92; co-host, organizer Muscular Dystrophy Local Telethon, Beulah Park, Grove City, 1987-89, Reynoldsburg, 1977-80; asst. scoutmaster Boy Scouts Am., 1975-80; hon. dep. sheriff Franklin County, 1988-92. Recipient Eagle Scout award, 1971; Ohio State Life Ins. scholar, 1987, Farmer's Ins. Group scholar, 1986, Honda of Am. Found. scholar, 1986; named one of nation's Top 10 Square Dance Callers, 1979. Mem. Franklin U. Alumni Assn., Columbus Bd. Realtors, Ohio Bd. Realtors, Nat. Bd. Reators, Cen. Ohio Sq. Dancers, Reynoldsburg Promenaders, Muscular Dystrophy Assn.-Cen. Ohio (past bd. dirs.) Franklin U. Top Execs. Club. Avocations: songwriting, entertainment and consumer marketing, recording and production, square dancing. Home: PO Box 40 Reynoldsburg OH 43068-0040 Office: Group X Inc Radiowriters PO Box 65 Reynoldsburg OH 43068-0065 also: Tom Yontz & Assocs/Eagle Realty 180 Allview Rd Westerville OH 43081-2909

POWELL, ERIC KARLTON, lawyer, researcher; b. Parkersburg, W.Va., July 23, 1958; s. James Milton and Sarah Elizabeth (Gates) P. BA in History, W.Va. U., 1980, BSBA, 1981; JD, Western State U., Fullerton, Calif., 1987. Bar: Ga. 1992, W.Va. 1993, U.S. Dist. Ct. (we. dist.) W.Va. 1993. Reference libr. Western State U., 1984; tchr. acctg. Rosary H.S., Fullerton, 1984-85; law clk. Zonni, Ginnochio Taylor, Santa Ana, Calif., 1986-93; temp. law sch. Gibson, Dunn & Crutcher, Irvine, Calif., 1993; pvt. practice, Parkersburg, 1993—. Asst. scoutmaster Boy Scouts Am., Parkersburg, 1981-83. Mem. ABA, ATLA, W.Va. Trial Lawyers Assn., Nat. Eagle Scout Assn., Elks, Delta Theta Phi. Republican. Presbyterian. Avocations: hiking, reading, canoeing, chess, astronomy. Home: 2002 20th St Parkersburg WV 26101-4125 Office: 500 Green St Parkersburg WV 26101-5131

POWELL, ERNESTINE BREISCH, retired lawyer; b. Moundsville, W.Va., Feb. 16, 1906; d. Ernest Elmer and Belle (Wallace) Breisch; student Dayton YMCA Law Sch., 1929; m. Roger K. Powell, Nov. 15, 1935; children—R. Keith (dec.), Diane L.D., Bruce W. Admitted to Ohio bar, 1929; tax analyst tax dept. Wall, Cassell & Groneweg, Dayton, Ohio, 1929-31; practiced law, 1931-42; gen. counsel for Dayton Jobbers and Mfrs. Assn., 1931-41; mem. firm Powell, Powell & Powell, Columbus, Ohio, 1944-86, ret. Ohio chmn. Nat. Woman's Party, Washington, 1950-51, nat. chmn., 1953, hon. nat. chmn. Pres. vol. activities com. Columbus State Sch., 1960-61, mem. bd. trustees, 1957-59. Mem. Nat. Assn. Women Lawyers, Am., Ohio, Columbus bar assns., Nat. Soc. Arts and Letters (pres. Columbus chpt. 1963-64), Nat. Lawyers Club (charter mem.) . Co-author: Tax Ideas, 1955; Estate Tax Techniques, 1956-90. Editor-in-chief: Women Lawyers Jour., 1943-45. Office: 6000 Riverside Dr Apt B308 Dublin OH 43017-2058

POWELL, J. R., lawyer, judge; b. Woodbury, N.J., Feb. 1, 1954; s. Jeremiah Robbins and Elaine Claire (Gardner) P.; m. Dianne M. Gilds, Feb. 20, 1983; children: Sarah Laine, Jillian Ruth. BA summa cum laude, Glassboro (N.J.) State Coll., 1976; JD, Rutgers U., Camden, N.J., 1979. Bar: Pa. 1980, N.J. 1981, U.S. Dist. Ct. N.J. 1981, U.S. Supreme Ct. 1989. Assoc. Falciani, Fletcher, Woodbury, 1980-83, Weber & Marcus, Woodbury, 1983-84; pvt. practice, Woodbury, 1984-95, Pitman, 1995—; mcpl. ct. judge Boroughs of Glassboro, Clayton, Pitman, Paulsboro, Twps. of Harrison and South Harrison, N.J., 1986—, Paulsboro, 1993—, East Greenwich, Greenwich, and Gloucester City, 1996—; instr. Conf. Mcpl. Ct. Judges, Trenton, 1988—, chmn. conf., 1992-94; trustee Gloucester County Bar Found., 1988-94; mcpl. ct. edn. com. N.J. Supreme Ct., Trenton, 1987—, del. Rules of Evidence Conf., New Brunswick, 1992; faculty Nat. Jud. Coll., Reno, 1995—. Author, compiler: Benchbook for Municipal Court Judges, 1992; also articles. Mem. Mantua Twp. Sch. Bd., Barnsboro, N.J., 1984-86; pres. Harrison Twp. Jaycees, Richwood, N.J., 1974-75; trustee Mt. Zion United Meth. Ch., 1988—. With U.S. Army, 1972-74. Mem. Gloucester County Bar Assn. (trustee 1986-94), sec. 1994-95), Gloucester County Mcpl. Judges Assn. (treas., v.p., pres. 1987—). Avocations: golf, reading, music. Office: 708 Lambs Rd Pitman NJ 08071-2038

POWELL, JAMES BOBBITT, biomedical laboratories executive, pathologist; b. Burlington, N.C., Aug. 28, 1938; s. Thomas Edward and Sophia (Sharpe) P.; m. Pamela Oughton, Sept. 12, 1969 (div. Sept. 1979); 1 child, Daphne Oughton; m. Anne Ellington, Oct. 20, 1984; children: James Bobbitt (dec.), John Banks, James Rosser, Helen Bobbitt. BA, Va. Mil. Inst., 1960; MD, Duke U., 1964. Diplomate Am. Bd. Pathology. Intern, Duke U. Med. Ctr., Durham, N.C., 1964-65; resident Cornell Med. Ctr., N.Y.C., 1965-67, Englewood Hosp., N.J., 1967-69; founder Biomed. Labs., Burlington, 1969—; pres. Roche Biomed. Labs., 1982-95, pres., CEO Lab. Corp. Am. Holdings, 1995—, Warren Land Co.; bd. dirs. FirstSouth Bank, Burlington, N.C. Trust Co. Contbr. articles to sci. publs. Trustee Elon Coll. (N.C.), 1981—, N.C. Sch. Sci. and Math.; mem. bd. visitors Duke U. Med. Ctr.; chmn. Alamance Found.; interim bd. edn. Alamance-Burlington, N.C. Served as maj. M.C., U.S. Army, 1969-72. Fellow Am. Soc. Clin. Pathologists, Coll. Am. Pathologists; mem. Alamance Country Club. Republican. Methodist. Avocations: tennis, U.S. military history. Home: 2307 York Rd Burlington NC 27215-3360 Office: LabCorp 358 S Main St Burlington NC 27215-5837

POWELL, JAMES HENRY, lawyer; b. N.Y.C., May 1, 1928; s. Milton Jerome and Doris (Unterberg) P.; m. Connie Lu Egger, Oct. 5, 1958; children: David E., Andrew J., Jeffrey K. AB, Harvard U., 1949; LLB, Yale U., 1952. Bar: N.Y. 1952. Assoc. McLaughlin and Stern, N.Y.C., 1955-69; atty. ABC, N.Y.C., 1969-72; assoc. Fried Frank Harris Shriver & Jacobson, N.Y.C., 1972-76; assoc. Patterson Belknap Webb & Tyler, N.Y.C., 1976-80, ptnr., 1980-95; pvt. practice N.Y.C., 1996—. Mem. exec. com. Lexington Dem. Club, 1961-63. With U.S. Army, 1953-55. Mem. Assn. of Bar of City of N.Y., City Athletic Club N.Y.C. (mem. bd. govs. 1973-81), Phi Beta Kappa. Office: 477 Madison Ave New York NY 10022-5802

POWELL, JAMES KEVIN, financial planner; b. Louisville, July 12, 1959; s. James Alvin and Joyce Marie (Craig) P.; m. Linda Henderson, June 22, 1989; 1 child, Kimberly Pruitt. BS, Cumberland Coll., 1982; diploma in hotel mgmt., Holiday Inn U., 1984. CFP. Gen. mgr. Holiday Inns, Inc., Memphis, 1977-82; area mgr. Servomation Corp., Aiken, S.C., 1983-84; gen. mgr. Restaurant Mgmt. Corp., Augusta, Ga., 1985; fin. planner IDS Fin. Svs., Inc., Augusta, 1986—; fin. cons., host program Sta. WRDW-TV, Augusta, 1988—; CFO Accurate Augusta Reporting, 1990—. Sponsor Childrens Ctr. Med. Coll. Ga., Augusta, 1990—. Mem. Internat. Assn. Fin. Planners (sec. edn. 1990), Inst. CFS, KC. Republican. Roman Catholic. Avocations: reading, fishing, basketball, softball, work. Home: 29 Riverbend Dr Clarks Hill SC 29821-9714 Office: IDS Fin Svcs 801 Broad St Ste 501 Augusta GA 30901-1226

POWELL, JAMES MATTHEW, history educator; b. Cin., June 9, 1930; s. Matthew James and Mary Loretta (Weaver) P.; m. Judith Catherine Davidorf, May 29, 1954 (dec. 1992); children: James, Michael, Mark, Mary Helen, Miriam, John. B.A., Xavier U., Cin., 1953, M.A., 1955; postgrad., U. Cin., 1955-57; Ph.D., Ind. U., 1960. Instr. Kent State U., Ohio, 1959-61; asst. prof. U. Ill., Urbana, 1961-65; asst. prof. Syracuse U., N.Y., 1965-67, assoc. prof., 1967-72, prof. history, 1972—, dir. Ranke Cataloging Project, 1977—; disting. vis. prof. medieval history Rutgers U., New Brunswick, 1996—. Author: Medieval Monarchy and Trade, 1962, Civilization of the West, 1967, Anatomy of a Crusade, 1213-1221, 1986, 2d edit., 1990, Albertanus of Brescia: The Pursuit of Happiness in the Early Thirteenth Century, 1992; translator: Liber Augustalis, 1971; editor: Innocent III: Vicar of Christ or Lord of the World, 1963, revised and enlarged 2d edit., 1994, Medieval Studies, 1976, 2d edit., 1992; (with George G. Iggers) Leopold von Ranke and the Shaping of the Historical Discipline, 1989, Muslims Under Latin Rule, 1100-1300, 1990; contbr. articles to profl. jours. Grantee NEH, 1977-84, 84, Inst. for Advanced Study, Princeton, N.J., 1989-90, Progetto Radici, Brescia, Italy, 1994-95; Fritz Thyssen Stiftung, 1986, 89; recipient John Gilmary Shea prize Am. Cath. Hist. Assn., 1987,. Mem. Am. Hist. Assn., Am. Cath. Hist. Assn., Medieval Acad. Am., Soc. for Italian Hist. Studies (coun. 1976-79, v.p. 1991-92, pres. 1993-95), Midwest Medieval Conf. (pres. 1965-66), Soc. for Study of the Crusades and the Latin East (sec. 1989-95). Democrat. Roman Catholic. Home: 114 Doll Pky Syracuse NY 13214-1428 Office: Syracuse U Maxwell School Syracuse NY 13244 *The good, the beautiful, the true - these are the words of an unchanging quest. They are our noblest.*

POWELL, JOSEPH LESTER (JODY POWELL), public relations executive; b. Vienna, Ga., Sept. 30, 1943; s. Joseph Lester and June Marie (Williamson) P.; m. Nan Sue Jared, Apr. 23, 1966; 1 child, Emily Claire. Student, U.S. Air Force Acad., 1961-64; BA in Polit. Sci., Ga. State U., 1966; post grad., Emory U., 1967-70. Press sec. Gov. Jimmy Carter, Atlanta, 1971-74, 75-76, Pres. Jimmy Carter, Washington, 1977-81; columnist Los Angeles Times Syndicate, 1982-87; news analyst ABC News, Washington, 1982-87; prof. Boston Coll., 1985-86; chmn., CEO Powell Adams & Rinehart, Washington, 1987-91, Powell Tate, Washington, 1991—. Author: The Other Side of the Story, 1984. Baptist. Avocations: golf, tennis, hunting, fishing, Civil War history. Office: Powell Tate 700 13th St NW Fl 10 Washington DC 20005-3960

POWELL, KENNETH EDWARD, investment banker; b. Danville, Va., Oct. 5, 1952; s. Terry Edward and C. Anne (Wooten) P.; m. Cicely Grandin Moorman, Jan. 3, 1976; children: Tanner, Priscilla. Student, Hampden-Sydney Coll., 1971-73; BA in Polit. Sci., U. Colo., 1975; JD, U. Richmond, 1978; LLM in Taxation, Coll. of William and Mary, 1982. Bar: Va. 1978, U.S. Dist. Ct. (ea. dist.) Va. 1979, U.S. Tax Ct. 1980. Ptnr. Maloney, Yeatts & Barr, Richmond, Va., 1978-87; ptnr., owner Hazel & Thomas, P.C., Richmond, 1987-94, mem. bus./tax team, internat. bus. team; v.p. Legg Mason, Richmond, Va., 1994—. Vice chmn. Sci. Mus. Va., Richmond, 1984-91; chmn. Va. Police Found., Inc., 1987; bd. dirs. State Edn. Assistance Authority, 1991—; mem. adv. bd. Va. Opera, 1991—; candidate U.S. Congress, Va., 1986. Recipient Disting. Svc. award Fraternal Order of Police, 1986; named Outstanding Young Man of the Yr., Jaycees, 1981, Outstanding Young Alumni, U. Colo., 1982. Mem. ABA, Va. Bar Assn. (chmn. profl. responsibility com. 1989-92, chmn. com. on legal edn. and admission to the Bar 1991—), Richmond Bar Assn., Richmond C. of C. (bd. dirs. 1988), Va. Econ. Developers Assn. (gen. counsel), Va. Econ. Bridge Initiative. Episcopal. Office: Legg Mason Wood Walker Inc Riverfront Plz East Tower 951 E Byrd St Ste 810 Richmond VA 23219-4039

POWELL, LARRY RANDALL, columnist; b. Texarkana, Tex., Nov. 7, 1948; s. John Calvin and Pearl Mae (Thatcher) P.; m. Martha Jon Muse, Dec. 15, 1991; children: Bret Allen, Bart Randall (twins). AA in Journalism (hon.), Texarkana Community Coll., 1991. Reporter, editor Texarkana Gazette, 1965-68, reporter, asst. mng. editor, 1969-71; sportswriter Shreveport (La.) Times, 1968-69; feature writer Tyler (Tex.) Morning Telegraph, 1969; reporter, editor Fort Worth Press, 1971-75; editor Grand Prairie (Tex.) Daily News, 1975-76; copy editor, page layout editor, nat. editor Dallas Morning News, 1976—, features editor, columnist, 1976—; adj. prof. U. Tex., Arlington, 1982-83. Bd. dirs. Great Pretenders Theatre, Carrollton, Tex., 1981-83, Theatre of the Hill, Cedar Hill, Tex., 1987-88. Recipient 1st pl. headline writing Tex. Gridiron Club, 1974, 1st pl. page one design Tex. UPI Editors Assn., 1980, 3rd pl. sports news reporting, 1975, 2nd pl. page layout, 1975, 2nd pl. page layout Tex. AP Mng. Editors, 1972. Home: 1011 Tarryall Dr Dallas TX 75224-4920 Office: The Dallas Morning News Communications Ctr PO Box 655237 Dallas TX 75265-5237

POWELL, LESLIE CHARLES, JR., obstetrics and gynecology educator; b. Beaumont, Tex., Dec. 13, 1927; s. Leslie Charles and Tillie Bee (Wallace) P.; m. Jeanne LeBarron Gaston, July 30, 1983; children: Jeffrey Johns, Randall Gardner, Daniel Charles, Gerard Paul. B.S., So. Meth. U., 1948; M.D., Johns Hopkins U., 1952. Diplomate: Am. Bd. Ob-Gyn. Intern, then resident U. Tex., Galveston, 1952-55, instr. ob-gyn, 1957-59, asst. prof., 1959-63, assoc. prof., 1963-68, prof., 1968—; cons. Richmond State Sch., 1969—; vis. prof. ob-gyn. Moi U., Eldoret, Kenya, 199-94; vis. prof. ob-gyn. Womens Hosp., Thanh Hoa, Vietnam, 1996. Editorial cons.: Tex. Reports Biology and Medicine, 1975, Psychosomatics, 1977, Tex. Medicine, 1978-88; contbr. articles to profl. jours. Pres. Am. Cancer Soc., Galveston County, 1972-73; dir. S.W. conf. Unitarian Ch. Served with M.C., AUS, 1955-57. Recipient Hannah award Tex. Assn. Ob-Gyn, 1955; research grantee HEW, 1969-71; Fulbright scholar Burma, 1975. Mem. Alpha Tau Omega, Phi Beta Pi. Republican. Home: 1906 Back Bay Dr Galveston TX 77551-1211 Office: 800 Ave B U Tex Med Sch Galveston TX 77550

POWELL, LEWIS FRANKLIN, JR., retired United States supreme court justice; b. Suffolk, Va., Sept. 19, 1907; s. Lewis Franklin and Mary Lewis (Gwathmey) P.; m. Josephine M. Rucker, May 2, 1936 (dec. July 1996); children: Josephine Powell Smith, Ann Pendleton Powell Bowen, Mary Lewis Gwathmey Powell Sumner, Lewis Franklin, III. B.S., Washington and Lee U., 1929, LL.B., 1931, LL.D., 1960; LL.M., Harvard, 1932. Bar: Va. 1931, U.S. Supreme Ct. 1937. Practiced law in Richmond, 1932-71; mem. firm Hunton, Williams, Gay, Powell and Gibson, 1937-71; assoc. justice U.S. Supreme Ct., 1972-87; chmn. emeritus Colonial Williamsburg Found.; mem. Nat. Commn. on Law Enforcement and Adminstrn. Justice, 1965-67, Blue Ribbon Def. Panel to study Def. Dept., 1969-70. Served to col. USAAF, 1942-46, 32 months overseas. Decorated Legion of Merit, Bronze Star; Croix de Guerre with palms (France); Trustee emeritus Washington and Lee U.; hon. bencher Lincoln's Inn. Fellow Am. Bar Found. (pres. 1969-71), Am. Coll. Trial Lawyers (pres. 1969-70); mem. ABA (gov., pres. 1964-65), Va. Bar Assn., Richmond Bar Assn. (pres. 1947-48), Bar Assn. City N.Y., Nat. Legal Aid and Defender Assn. (v.p. 1964-65), Am. Law Inst., Soc. Cin., Sons Colonial Wars, Commonwealth Club (Richmond), Phi Beta Kappa, Phi Delta Phi, Omicron Delta Kappa, Phi Kappa Sigma. Presbyterian. Office: care US Supreme Ct 1 First St NE Washington DC 20543

POWELL, LEWIS FRANKLIN, III, lawyer; b. Richmond, Va., Sept. 14, 1952; s. Lewis F. Jr. and Josephine (Rucker) P.; m. Lisa T. LaFata; children: Emily, Hannah. BA, Washington & Lee U., 1974; JD, U. Va., 1978. Bar: Va. 1978, U.S. Dist. Ct. (ea. and we. dists.) Va. 1979, U.S. Ct. Appeals (4th cir.) 1979, U.S. Ct. Appeals (2d cir.) 1983, U.S. Ct. Appeals (11th cir.) 1992, U.S. Supreme Ct. 1985. Law clk. to judge U.S. Dist. Ct. (ea. dist.), Richmond, 1978-79; from assoc. to ptnr. Hunton & Williams, Richmond, 1979—; pres. young lawyers conf. Va. State Bar, 1986-87. Bd. dirs. William Byrd Cmty. Ho., Richmond, 1982-87, Boys Club of Richmond, 1984-90, Maymont Found., Richmond, 1987-92, St. Christopher's Sch., Richmond, 1989—. Mem. Richmond Bar Assn. (chmn. improvement justice com. 1982-83), 4th Cir. Jud. Conf., Am. Law Inst. Avocations: skiing, mountaineering, backpacking, fishing, duck hunting. Office: Hunton & Williams Riverfront Plz East Tower 951 E Byrd St Richmond VA 23219-4040

POWELL, LINDA RAE, educational healthcare consultant; b. Youngstown, Ohio, Sept. 1, 1947; d. Roger Gene and Beverly (Dahlke) P.; m. James Ronald Taylor, Aug. 14, 1985. BSN, Madonna Coll., 1980; MA in Adult Edn., U. Mich., 1988. RN; cert. profl. healthcare quality. Adminstrv. nurse U. Mich., Ann Arbor, 1970-86; coord. exec. spouse program U. Mich. Bus. Sch., Ann Arbor, 1987, 89, exec. dir. Mich. individual entrepreneurial project, 1986-88, bd. dirs. Mich. Individual Entrepreneurial Project, 1991—; ednl. cons. Quality Mgmt. in Healthcare, Ann Arbor, 1988-91; pres., founder Quality Mgmt. Edn. Cons., Ann Arbor, 1991-96; ret., 1996—; nat. healthcare speaker on quality assessment and improvement. Mag. columnist, 1990-92. Mem. Ronald McDonald House of Ann Arbor, 1988—. Mem. Am. Soc. Healthcare Edn. and Tng., Nat. Assn. Healthcare Quality, Assn. Quality and Participation, Am. Soc. Quality Control, Health Alumni Assn. U. Mich. Avocations: cooking, bicycling, dance. Office: Quality Mgmt Ednl Cons Inc 380 Windycrest Dr Ann Arbor MI 48105-3014

POWELL, MEL, composer; b. N.Y.C., Feb. 12, 1923. Studied piano from age 4; studied composition with Ernst Toch, L.A., 1946-48; with Paul Hindemith, Yale U., from 1948, MusB, 1952. Mem., chmn. faculty composition Yale U., 1957-69; mem. staff, head faculty composition, formerly dean Calif. Inst. Arts, Valencia, provost, 1972-76; now Inst. fellow, Roy E. Disney chair in mus. composition Calif. Inst. Arts, Santa Clarita, Calif. Albums include Six Recent Works, 1982-88, The Return of Mel Powell, 1989; composer: Duplicates: A Concerto for Two Pianos and Orchestra (premier L.A. Philharm. 1990, Pulitzer prize for music 1990), Modules for chamber orch. (recorded L.A. Philharm. 1991), Woodwind Quintet (recorded 1991), Setting for Two Pianos (recorded 1992), Settings for Small Orch., 1992 (commissioned by chamber orchs. of St. Paul, L.A., N.J.), Settings for Guitar (recorded 1993), numerous other compositions; subject of profile in New Yorker mag. Recipient Creative Arts medal Brandeis U., 1989; Pulitzer Prize for music, 1990; Guggenheim fellow; Nat. Inst. Arts and Letters grantee. Mem. Arnold Schoenburg Inst. (hon. life). Office: Calif Arts Inst Dept Composition 24700 Mcbean Pky Santa Clarita CA 91355-2340*

POWELL, MICHAEL ROBERT, biophysicist, physiologist, chemist; b. Detroit, Nov. 23, 1941; s. Herschel Homer and Julia (Dickun) P.; m. Mary Grace Power, Aug. 8, 1964; children: Andrew, Christie, Kevin, Eric. B.S. in Chemistry, Mich. State U., 1963, M.S. in Biophysics, 1966, Ph.D., 1969. Research biophysicist Union Carbide, Tarrytown, N.Y., 1969-75; dir. biophysics dept. Inst. Applied Physiology and Medicine, Seattle, 1975-89, Space Biomedical Rsch. Inst., 1989—; head environ. physiology/biophisics sect. NASA/Johnson Space Ctr., Houston. Mem. Am. Chem. Soc., Biophys. Soc., Am. Physiol. Soc., Aerospace Med. Soc., Undersea Med. Soc. Republican. Roman Catholic. Office: NASA Johnson Space Ctr # SD3 Houston TX 77058

POWELL, MICHAEL VANCE, lawyer; b. San Diego, Sept. 30, 1946; s. Jesse Vance and Mable Louise (Cagle) P.; m. Sarada Marie Hughes, Dec. 23, 1967; children: Marilyn Jean, Michael Benjamin. AB, Davidson Coll., N.C., 1968; MA, U. Tex., 1972, JD with honors, 1974. Bd. cert. civil appellate law Tex. Bd. Legal Specialization. Law clk. to judge U.S. Ct. Appeals (9th cir.), 1974-75; assoc. Rain Harrell Emery Young & Doke, Dallas, 1975-80, ptnr., 1980-87; mem. Locke Purnell Rain Harrell, Dallas, 1987—. Elder St. Barnabas Presbyn. Ch., Richardson, Tex. Avocations: music, travel. Home: 7312 Tophill Ln Dallas TX 75248-5642 Office: Locke Purnell Rain Harrell 2200 Ross Ave Dallas TX 75201

POWELL, MIKE, olympic athlete, track and field; b. Phila., Pa., 1964. Grad., UCLA. Olympic track and field participant Seoul, South Korea, 1988; set world record for long jump at World Track and Field Championships. Tokyo, 1991; Olympic track and field participant Barcelona, Spain, 1992. Recipient Long Jump Silver medal Olympics, Seoul, South Korea, 1988, Long Jump Silver medal Olympics, Barcelona, 1992. Office: Footlocker Track Club 233 Broadway Lbby 4 New York NY 10279-0097*

POWELL, NORBORNE BERKELEY, urologist; b. Montgomery, Ala., July 24, 1914; s. Floyd Berkeley and Eloise (Sadler) P.; m. Elizabeth Mary Balas, Dec. 18, 1939; children—Norborne Berkeley, Barbara Key. M.D., Baylor U., 1938. Diplomate: Am. Bd. Urology. Intern Duke Hosp., Durham, N.C., 1938-39, Charity Hosp., New Orleans, 1939-40; resident Tulane Service, Charity Hosp., 1940-42; practice medicine, specializing in urology Houston, 1942-90; mem. staff Ben Taub Gen. Hosp., Twelve Oaks Hosp., Houston; chief staff Twelve Oaks Hosp., 1974; mem. cons. staff Meth. Hosp., St. Luke's Episc. Hosp.; clin. prof. urology Baylor Coll. Medicine, 1964-90; ret., 1990; Trustee Baylor Med. Found., 1945-55; pres. Twelve Oaks Med. Found., 1976-90. Contbr. articles to profl. jours. Recipient continuing med. edn. award AMA, 1980. Fellow A.C.S., Internat. Coll. Surgeons; mem. Mexican Urol. Assn. (corr.), Am. Urol. Assn. (Sci. Exhbn. 1st prize 1951, continuing med. edn. award 1980), Houston Urol. Soc. (pres. 1955), Can. Urol. Assn. Home: 23 Cedar Cliff Rd Asheville NC 28803-2905

POWELL, REBECCA ANN, secondary school educator; b. Bluffton, Ohio, Oct. 5, 1944; d. Paul Richard and Clara Lucille (Niswander) McDowell; m. William Dean Powell, June 17, 1967; children: Timothy William, Deborah Ann.; AB, Asbury Coll., 1966; MA, Eastern Mich. U., 1978. Cert. tchr. Tchr., history/english Columbus (Ohio) Pub. Schs., 1966-67; tchr., english Lawton (Okla.) Pub. Schs., 1967-68; tchr., social studies Flint (Mich.) Community Schs., 1971-79, Midland (Mich.) Pub. Schs., 1979—; tchr. cons. Mich. Geographic Alliance, 1991—; curriculum developer Midland Pub. Schs., 1985—; insvc. presenter Mich. Coun. for the Social Studies, 1984—; Britton humanities chair Midland County Britton Com., 1992-94. Steering com. mem. Global Emphasis Midland League of Women's Voters, 1992; precinct del. Genessee County, 1974-78. Recipient Apple for the Tchr. award Midland Law Aux., 1988, Fulbright-Hays Seminar Abroad Brazil award Dept. of Edn., 1989, Fulbright-Hays Seminar Abroad Egypt and Zimbabwe award, 1993. Mem. NEA, Nat. Coun. for the Social Studies, Nat. Coun. for Geog. Edn., Mich. Coun. for the Social Studies (dist. rep, awards chair 1983—, Mich Outstanding Social Studies Educator of the Yr. award 1989), Mich. Edn. Assn., Midland City Edn. Assn. (bldg. rep.), Assn. for Supervision and Curriculum Devel. Avocations: traveling, reading, walking, collecting mushrooms and trivets. Office: Midland Pub Schs-Jefferson Intermediate 800 W Chapel Ln Midland MI 48640-2966

POWELL, REBECCA GAETH, education educator; b. Westlake, Ohio, Oct. 23, 1949; d. John Paul and Ione Roxanne (Poad) Gaeth; m. Jerry Wayne Powell, June 14, 1991; children: Justin Matthew (dec.), Ryan Michael. B Music Edn., Coll. of Wooster (Ohio), 1971; MEd, U. N.C., 1976; D in Edn., U. Ky., 1989. Cert. curriculum and instrn. Elem. tchr. Rittman (Ohio) Elem., 1971-72; presch. tchr. YWCA, Durham, N.C., 1974-76; spl. reading tchr. Claxton Elem. Sch., Asheville, N.C., 1977; instr. and dir. reading, cert. program Mars Hill (N.C.) Coll., 1977-80; health educator Hot Springs (N.C.) Health Program, 1984-85; asst. prof. Ky. State U., Frankfort, 1989-93; assoc. prof. Georgetown (Ky.) Coll., 1993—; Ky. primary sch. rschr. U. Ky. Inst. on Edn. Reform, Lexington, 1993—; ednl. cons. Jessamine County Schs., Nicholasville, Ky., 1992-93, Dade County Schs., Miami, Fla., 1995; tchr. educator, trainer, participant pilot project Ky. Tchr. Internship Program, Frankfort, 1990—; chmn. Alliance for Multicultural Edn., Ky., 1993-95; coord. Ctrl. Ky. Whole Lang. Network, 1991-93; mem. Ky. Multicultural Edn. Task Force, 1995. Editor: (monograph series) Alliance for Multicultural Education, 1995—; contbr. articles to profl. jours. Dissertation Year fellow U. Ky., Lexington, 1988-89. Mem. Nat. Assn. Multicultural Edn., Nat. Coun. Tchrs. English, Nat. Conf. Rsch. in English, Am. Ednl. Studies Assn., Ky. Coun. Tchrs. English, Ky. Assn. Tchr. Educators, Alliance for Multicultural Edn. Avocations: reading, golf. Office: Georgetown Coll 400 E College St Georgetown KY 40324-1628

POWELL, RICHARD C., physicist, educator, researcher; b. Lincoln, Nebr., Dec. 20, 1939; s. William Charles and Allis (Conger) P.; m. Gwendolyn Cline Powell, June 24, 1962; children: Douglas W., David M. BS in Engring., U.S. Naval Acad., 1962; MS in Physics, Arizona State U., 1964, PhD in Physics, 1967. Staff scientist Air Force Cambridge Rsch. Labs., Beuford, Mass., 1964-68, Sandia Nat. Lab., Albuquerque, 1968-71; prof. Okla. State U., 1971-92; prof. dir. optical sci. ctr. U. Ariz., Tucson, 1992—; reviewer numerous physics jours. and funding agys.; cons. laser rsch. with several indsl. and govt. agys. Editor-in-chief Jour. Optical Materials, 1992&; patents include Holographic Gratings in Rare Earth Doped Glasses, with Okla. State U., 1988; contbr. numerous articles to profl. jours. Recipient over 40 grants for rsch. support, 1971—. Fellow Am. Phys. Soc. (co-chmn. Internat. Laser Sci. Conf. 1985, chmn. 1986, vice chmn. Topical Group on Laser Sci., 1986, chmn. 1987, APS rep. Joint Coun. on Quantum Electronics, 1986-90), Optical Soc. Am. (mem. bd. dirs. 1993—, mem. program com. OSA Photoacoustic Spectroscopy Mtg., 1979, mem. nom. com. 1982, organizer Laser Tech. Group Session 1985, com. mem. Meggers award, 1986, 89, 90, chmn. program com. CLEO, 1988, mem. book pub. com., 1992—, mem. awards com., 1994—, mem. organizing com. Adv. Solid State Laser Conf., 1992—, OSA rep. Internat. Coun. on Optics, 1994—; mem. IEEE (mem. solid state lasers adv. com., 1987—, program com. mem. Nonlinear Optical Materials Mtg., 1994), Sigma Xi (hon. lectr. 1983-84). Episcopalian. Avocations: skiing, fishing, softball, jogging, hiking.. Office: U Ariz Optical Scis Ctr Tucson AZ 85721

POWELL, RICHARD GORDON, retired lawyer; b. Rochester, N.Y., Jan. 7, 1918. B.S., Harvard U., 1938; LL.B., Columbia U., 1941. Bar: N.Y. 1941, U.S. Supreme Ct. 1955. Assoc. Sullivan & Cromwell, N.Y.C., 1941-52; ptnr. Sullivan & Cromwell, 1952-85. Former mem. bd. mgrs. Englewood (N.J.) Community Chest; trustee, elder 1st Presbyterian Ch. Mem. ABA, Assn. Bar City of N.Y., Am. Law Inst. Home: 200 E 65th St # 33N New York NY 10021-6603

POWELL, RICHARD PITTS, writer; b. Phila., Nov. 28, 1908; s. Richard Percival and Lida Catherine (Pitts) P.; m. Marian Carleton Roberts, Sept. 6, 1932 (dec. Nov. 1979); children: Stephen Barnes, Dorothy Louise; m. Margaret M. Cooper, 1980. Grad., Episcopal Acad., 1926; A.B., Princeton, 1930. Reporter Phila. Evening Ledger, 1930-40; with N.W. Ayer & Son, Phila., 1940-58; mem. pub. relations dept. N.W. Ayer & Son, 1940-42, charge info. services, 1949-58, v.p., 1951-58. Author: mystery books Don't Catch Me, 1943, All Over but the Shooting, 1944, Lay That Pistol Down, 1945, Shoot If You Must, 1946, And Hope to Die, 1947, Shark River, 1950, Shell Game, 1950, A Shot in the Dark, 1952, Say It with Bullets, 1953, False Colors, 1955; novels The Philadelphian, 1957, Pioneer, Go Home, 1959, The Soldier, 1960, I Take This Land, 1963, Daily and Sunday, 1965, Don Quixote, U.S.A, 1966, Tickets to the Devil, 1968, Whom the Gods Would Destroy, 1970, Florida: A Picture Tour, 1972; novel under pen name Jeremy Kirk The Build-Up Boys, 1951; Contbr. short stories, articles, serials to mags. Served as lt. col. AUS, 1942-46; chief news censor 1945, S.W. Pacific Theatre. Home: 1201 Carlene Ave Fort Myers FL 33901-8715

POWELL, ROBERT CHARLES, marriage and family counselor; b. Champaign, Ill., Sept. 19, 1958; s. William York and Betty (Holt) P.; m. Trudy Suedell Graham, May 5, 1986; children: Emily, Amy. BS, We. Ill. U., 1981, MS, 1985. Pvt. practice LaSalle, Ill., 1990—; counselor Luth. Social Svcs., Dixon, Ill., 1994—; founder, leader support group for parents, Peru, Ill., 1990—; co-founder Human Resource Network. Chmn. steering com. Ill. Valley Christian Ch., Peru, 1989-90; bd. dirs. LaSalle County Habitat for Humanity. Mem. AACD, Internat. Assn. Marriage and Family Counselors. Avocations: rock climbing, snow skiing. Office: 2513 5th St Peru IL 61354-2401

POWELL, ROBERT ELLIS, mathematics educator, college dean; b. Lansing Mich., Mar. 16, 1936; s. James Ellis and Mary Frances (Deming) P.; children: Carl Robert, Glenn Arthur, Charles Addison; m. Lisbeth Nilsen, Nov. 21, 1992. B.A., Mich. State U., 1958, M.A., 1959; Ph.D., Lehigh U., 1966. Instr. math. Lehigh U., 1964-66; asst. prof. math. U. Kans., Lawrence, 1966-69; vis. asst. research prof. U. Ky., Lexington, 1967-68; vis. asst. prof. math. Ind. U., Bloomington, summer 1969; assoc. prof. math. Kent State U., Ohio, 1969-74, prof. math., 1974-95; dean grad. coll. Kent State U., 1980-92; prof. math., dean grad. sch., dir. rsch. U. Scranton, Pa., 1995—; bd. dirs. Kent State U. Found., 1981-91, Coun. Grad. Schs., 1990-91; mem. Ohio Bd. Regents' Adv. Com. on Grad. Study, 1980-92, chmn., 1983-84. Co-author: Summability Theory, 1973, rev. edit., 1988, Intuitive Calculus, 1973; contbr. numerous articles to profl. jours. NSF summer grantee, 1964, 65, Fulbright award, 1988. Mem. Math. Assn. Am., Midwest Assn. Grad. Schs. (vice chair 1989-90, chair 1990-91, past chair 1991-92). Home: 3003 Quail Hollow Dr Clarks Summit PA 18411 Office: U Scranton Grad Sch Scranton PA 18510

POWELL, ROBERT EUGENE, computer operator; b. Fairmont, W.V., Mar. 31, 1955; s. Grover E. and Mary Jo (Hart) P. BS, Kent State U., 1980. Clk. Premier Screening, 1987-89; computer operator Sage Computer Svcs., 1989-95. Found mem., treas. Alliance for Mentally Ill; active Pres.'s Com. on Employment People with Disabilities Pres.'s Trophy Candidate for Ohio, 1992. Recipient award of Excellence Ohio Rehab. Assn., 1989, 90, named Internat. Man of Yr., 1992-93. Mem. KC. Democrat. Roman Catholic. Home: 1052 Welton Ave Apt 2 Akron OH 44306-2818

POWELL, SANDRA THERESA, timber company executive; b. Orofino, Idaho, Jan. 9, 1944; s. Harold L. and Margaret E. (Thompson) P. B.S. in Bus./Acctg., U. Idaho, 1966. CPA, Idaho. Acct., Weyerhaeuser Co., Tacoma, Wash., 1966-67; with Potlatch Corp., 1967—, asst. sec., San Francisco, 1981, sec., asst. treas., 1981-89, treas. 1989-92; v.p. fin. svcs., 1993—, sec., 1993-95. Mem. AICPA, Idaho State Bd. Accountancy, Idaho Soc. CPAs. Office: Potlatch Corp PO Box 193591 San Francisco CA 94119-3591

POWELL, SARA JORDAN, musician, religious worker; b. Waller, Tex., Oct. 6, 1938; d. Samuel Arthur and Mable Ruth (Ponder) Jordan; m. John Atkins Powell, June 24, 1967; 1 child, Marc Benet. B.A., Tex. So. U., 1960; M.R.E., U. St. Thomas, Houston, 1979. Tchr., Chgo. Bd. Edn., 1961-68, Houston Ind. Sch. Dist., 1968-73; youth dir. Gospel Music Workshop Am., Detroit, 1972-76; dir. talent and fine arts Ch. of God in Christ, Memphis, 1974—, dir., cons. ch. hist. mus. and fine arts center, 1980—; mem. nat. reference com. One Nation Under God, Virginia Beach, Va., 1979—; regional sponsor Yr. of the Bible, Washington, 1983; soloist Savoy Record Co., 1972-79; counselor Mike Barber Prison Ministries, 1987—. Bd. dirs. talent coordinator Charles Harrison Mason Edn. Found., 1975—; bd. dirs. James Oglethorpe Patterson Fine Arts Scholarships, 1974—; music and talent dir. Juneteenth U.S.A., 1985—; acad. advisor Oral Roberts U., 1991-92. Recipient 1st Pl. award Record Album, Savoy Record Co., 1972. Best Female Vocalist, Gospel Music Workshop Am., 1973, 74, 75, Gold record, 1978; letter of appeciation Cook County Dept. Corrections, Chgo., 1978; Silver Plate award Assembly of God Ch., Calcutta, India, 1978; letter of appreciation for White House performance, Washington, 1979. Mem. Houston PTA, Houston Peoples Workshop (dir. 1981—), Women in Leadership (adv. bd. 1985—).*

POWELL, SHARON LEE, social welfare organization administrator; b. Portland, Oreg., July 25, 1940; d. James Edward Carson and Betty Jane (Singleton) Powell. BS, Oreg. State U., 1962; MEd, Seattle U., 1971. Dir. outdoor edn. Mapleton (Oreg.) Pub. Schs., 1962-63; field dir. Totem Girl Scout Council, Seattle, 1963-68, asst. dir. field services, 1968-70, dir. field services, 1970-72; dir. pub. rels. and program Girl Scout Council of Tropical Fla., Miami, 1972-74; exec. dir. Homestead Girl Scout Council, Lincoln, Nebr., 1974-78, Moingona Girl Scout Coun., Des Moines, 1978—. Pres. agy. dirs. assn. United Way Cen. Iowa, Des Moines, 1987-88, mem. priorities com., 1986-90, chairperson agy. rels., 1994-96, chairperson agy. issues, 1989-90; mem. priority goals task group United Way Found., Des Moines, 1985-92; capt. Drake U. Basketball Ticket Drive, Des Moines, 1983-87; sec. Urbandale Citizens Scholarship Found., 1989-93; mem. ad hoc long-range planning com. Urbandale Schs., 1989, mem. budget rev. task group, mem. year-round sch. task group, 1992-93; mem. gender equity task force State of Iowa, 1993—. Mem. AAUW, Assn. Girl Scouts Execs. (chair nat. conv. 1985-90, nat. bd. dirs. 1985-87, nat. nominating com. 1982-84, nat. treas. 1987-90, nat. pres. 1991-96), Urbandale C. of C. (bd. dirs., chair edn com.), Animal Rescue League of Iowa (bd. dirs. 1992-96, shelter chair 1992—), Des Moines Obedience Tng. Club (pres. 1987-89), Des. Moines Golden Retriever Club (bd. dirs., pres. 1992-94, show chair 1997—), Rotary, Altrusa (treas.

Des Moines chpt. 1983-85, cmty. svc. chair 1986-87), Des Moines Kennel Club. Avocations: wood carving, dog showing, obedience and conformation. Office: Moingona Girl Scout Coun 10715 Hickman Rd Des Moines IA 50322-3733

POWELL, THOMAS EDWARD, III, biological supply company executive, physician; b. Elon College, N.C., Aug. 1, 1936; s. Thomas Edward, Jr., and Sophia Maude (Sharpe) P.; m. Betty Durham Yeager, June 19, 1965; children: Frances Powell Barnes, Thomas Edward IV, Caroline Powell Rogers. AB in Biology, Va. Mil. Inst., 1957; MD, Duke U., 1961; MA, Harvard U., 1966. Surgeon USPHS, 1966-68; co-founder Biomed. Reference Labs., Inc., Burlington, N.C., 1969, exec. v.p., 1969-75, chmn. exec. com., 1979-82, also dir.; exec. v.p. Carolina Biol. Supply Co., Burlington, N.C., 1968-80, chmn., 1977-80, 94—, pres., 1980-94; pres. Wolfe Sales Corp., Burlington, 1980-84, Waubun Labs. Inc., Schriever, La., 1980—, Bobbitt Labs., Inc., Burlington, 1983-94; bd. mgrs. Wachovia Bank and Trust Co. N.A., Burlington. Contbr. articles to profl. jours. Bd. dirs. United Way Alamance County, Burlington, 1968—; bd. dirs. Elon Coll., N.C., 1968—, sec., 1975—; bd. dirs. Am. Cancer Soc., Burlington, 1971-81; bd. dirs. Burlington Day Sch., 1973—, pres., 1974-78, 80-84; bd. dirs. N.C. Citizens for Bus. and Industry, Raleigh, 1983-87, Nat. Found. for Study of Religion and Econs., Greensboro, 1984-88, Blue Ridge Sch., Dyke, Va., 1985-90. Served to capt. USAR, 1957-66. Recipient Citizens Service award Elon Coll. Alumni Assn., 1980. Mem. Assn. Biology Lab. Edn., N.C. Acad. Sci., Alamance-Caswell Med. Soc., N.C. Med. Soc., Assn. Venture Founders, Newcomen Soc. Democrat. Mem. United Ch. of Christ. Clubs: Alamance Country (Burlington); Capital City (Raleigh, N.C.); Congl. Country (Washington); N.C. Country (Pinehurst); Hope Valley Country (Durham, N.C.); Greensboro City.

POWELL, THOMAS ERVIN, consultant, accountant, small business owner; b. Trion, Ga., Mar. 19, 1947; s. Ervin and Myrtice (Wike) P.; m. Lana Lois Lang, June 20, 1976; children: Thomas Christopher, Alissa Lynne, Ashley Beth. BS, U. Ctrl. Fla., 1974, MS, 1977; postgrad. studies, U. Fla., 1979. CPA, Fla.; cert. internal auditor. Pub. acct. KPMG Peat Marwick, Orlando, Fla., 1974-75, Arthur Andersen & Co., Orlando, 1975-77; instr. acctg. U. Ctrl. Fla., Orlando, 1977-81; dir. Inst. Internal Auditors, Altamonte Springs, Fla., 1981-95; pres. The Powell Group, Inc., Windermere, Fla., 1996—; mem. accreditation com. Am. Assembly Collegiate Schs. Bus., 1992-93. Author: Examination Writer's Guide, 1978, rev. edit., 1991, 96; mem. editl. bd. Issues in Acctg. Edn. Jour., 1995—. Vice chmn. audit bd. City of Orlando, 1990-95; treas. Christian Endowment Found., 1996—; chmn. Practice Advising Coun. With USAF, 1967-71. Mem. AICPA, Am. Acctg. Assn. (profl. exam. com. 1986-89, 93—, audit edn. conf. com. 1990-93, mem. profl. rels. com. 1997—, v.p. profl. practices 1994-96, chmn. practice adv. coun. 1996—), Inst. Internal Auditors, Fla. Soc. CPAs (edn. com. 1990-93, legis. com. 1991), Nat. Assn. Corp. Dirs., Beta Alpha Psi (adv. coun. 1993—, Alumnus of Yr. U. Ctrl. Fla. 1992), Beta Gamma Sigma. Republican. Baptist. Avocations: guitar, skiing, photography. Home: 1938 Maple Leaf Dr Windermere FL 34786-8003 Office: The Powell Group Inc PO Box 766 Gotha FL 34734

POWELL, TREVOR JOHN DAVID, archivist; b. Hamilton, Ont., Can., Feb. 3, 1948; s. David Albert and Morvydd Ann May (Williams) P.; m. Marian Jean McKillop, May 1, 1976. BA, U. Sask., Regina, 1971; MA, U. Regina, Sask., Can., 1980. Staff archivist Sask. Archives Bd., Regina, Sask., 1973-80, dir., 1980-86, acting provincial archivist, 1986-87, provincial archivist, 1988—. Co-author: Living Faith: A Pictorial History of Diocese of Qu'Appelle; author: From Tent to Cathedral: A History of St. Paul's Cathedral, Regina. Archivist Diocese of Qu'Appelle, Regina, Sask., 1971—, registrar, 1979—; archivist, eccles. Province of Rupert's Land, Winnipeg, Man., 1988—; mem. adv. coun. Sask. Order of Merit, 1988-95, Sask Honours, 1995—; chair selection com. Sask Vol. medal, 1995-96, Can. 125 medal, 1992. Mem. Soc. Am. Archivists, Can. Hist. Assn., Commonwealth Archivists Assn., Sask. Coun. Archives (sec.-treas. 1987-88, 90-92, pres. 1994-96, Can. Coun. Archives rep. 1994-96), Assn. Can. Archivists (bd. dirs. 1979-81). Anglican. Avocations: gardening, walking, reading, music, bird watching. Home: 241 Orchard Cres, Regina, SK Canada S4S 5B9 Office: Sask Archives Bd, 3303 Hillsdale St-Univ of Regina, Regina, SK Canada S4S 0A2

POWELL, WALTER HECHT, labor arbitrator; b. N.Y.C., Apr. 13, 1915; s. Arthur Lee and Stella (Hecht) P.; m. Dorothy Meyer, Mar. 15, 1945; children: Lawrence L., Alan W., Lesley A., Steven H. BS, NYU, 1938, JD, 1940; MA, U. Pa., 1948. Bar: N.Y. 1940, Pa. 1956. Asst. prof. Temple U., Phila., 1946-51, v.p. for pers. resources, 1973-78; asst. dir. pers. Am. Safety Razor, Kingsbury, Ind., 1951-53; v.p., dir. ops. Internat. Resistance Co., Phila., 1953-69, v.p., dir. indsl. rels., 1956-69; sr. v.p. 1st Pa. Banking & Trust Co., Phila., 1969-73; v.p. human resources Temple U., 1973-77; ind. labor arbitrator Phila., 1978—; mem. panel Am. Arbitration Assn., Fed. Mediation and Conciliation Svc., Pa., N.J. labor rels. bds.; lectr. U. Pitts., Temple U., U. Richmond, Vanderbilt U., Am. U., others.; bd. dirs. Auerbach Corp., Phila. Contbr. book chpts., articles to profl. jours. Commr. Phila. Commn. on Human Rels., 1969—; bd. dirs. Opportunities Industrialization Ctr. Capt. AUS, 1942-46. Recipient award Phila. C. of C., 1968. Mem. Am. Mgmt. Assn. (adv. coun. 1963—), Indsl. Rels. Assn., Indsl. Rels. Rsch. Assn. (pres. local chpt. 1966), Nat. Acad. Arbitrators. Home and Office: 2401 Pennsylvania Ave Ste 9 A 7 Philadelphia PA 19130-3010

POWELL, WILLIAM ARNOLD, JR., retired banker; b. Verbena, Ala., July 7, 1929; s. William Arnold and Sarah Frances (Baxter) P.; m. Barbara Ann O'Donnell, June 16, 1956; children: William Arnold III, Barbara Calhoun, Susan Thomas, Patricia Crain. BSBA, U. Ala., 1953; grad., La. State U. Sch. Banking of South, 1966. With Am. South Bank, N.A., Birmingham, Ala., 1953—, asst. v.p., 1966, v.p., 1967, v.p., br. supr., 1968-72, sr. v.p., br. supr., 1972-73, exec. v.p., 1973-79, pres., 1979-83, vice chmn. bd., 1983-93, also bd. dirs.; pres. AmSouth Bancorp., 1979—; bd. dirs. AmSouth Bank Fla., AmSouth Bancorp. Bd. dirs. United Way Found.; trustee Ala. Hist. Soc., Birmingham Hist. Soc., Ala. Ind. Colls.; bd. visitors U. Ala.; past pres. United Way, campaign chmn., 1987; mem. pres.'s coun. U. Ala., Birmingham; bd. dirs. Warrior-Tombigbee Devel. Assn., Birmingham Mus. Art. Lt. AUS, 1954-56. Mem. Birmingham Area C. of C. (bd. dirs.), The Club, Mountain Brook, Birmingham Country Club, Green Valley Country Club (Birmingham). Home: 2114 Hickory Ridge Cir Birmingham AL 35243-2925

POWELL HILL, DR. QUEEN ELIZABETH T., singer, small business owner; b. San Antonio, Feb. 5, 1954; d. Elijah and Mattie B. Tyler; m. Frederick Powell, Apr. 16, 1977 (div.); children: Frederick Powell, Michael Powell; m. James LaRue Hill, Mar. 10, 1989; 1 child, Victoria Hill. Degree in Applied Science, St. Philip's Coll., 1987, AA, 1989. Lic. fin. broker, real estate investor. Sec. San Antonio Light Newspaper, 1979-80; bus. owner T. Powell Express Co., San Antonio, 1982—; singer pop rock various locations, 1985—; owner Queen Elizabeth Enterprise Global Wealth Builder, San Antonio, 1996—. Author: (song) Just Seeing You, 1985, (book) The Elizabeth Powell Letters, 1992; designer curio dress, 1989; copyright original works as author, 1992. Founder Perfect Abundant Life Mockulisaphen Ch., San Antonio, 1996. Recipient Trophy award for Best Performer Inner City Prodns., 1986, 1st Runner up trophy for performance Elks Lodge, 1990. Mem. Am. Fedn. Musicians, Internat. Platform Assn. Avocations: travel, writing, sewing, singing. Office: T Powell Express Co PO Box 200643 San Antonio TX 78220-0643

POWELSON, MARY VOLIVA, golf course and banquet facility executive; b. Evansville, Ind., Sept. 10, 1954; d. Edward Jr. and Norma Elaine (Koenig) Voliva; m. Kent Howard Powelson, Aug. 4, 1979 (div. 1988); 1 child, Nicholas H. BS, Purdue U., 1976, postgrad., 1979-80; postgrad., U. Evansville, 1977-79, 80-85. Asst. mgr. Paul Harris, Evansville, Ind., 1977-79; speech therapist Dr. Tom Logan, Henderson, Ky., 1979; gen. mgr. Clearcrest Pines, Evansville, 1987—. Exhibited in group shows Evansville Mus. Fine Art, 1983, Ind. Heritage Arts, Nashville, 1984, Brown County Art Guild, Nashville, 1984, Catherine Lorillard Wolfe Art Club, N.Y.C., 1984, Pastel Soc. of Am., N.Y.C., 1984, Oak Meadow Country Club, Evansville, 1991. Mem. Am. Culinary Fedn., Tri-State Chef and Cook's Assn., U.S. Golf Assn., Pastel Soc. of Am., Women in Arts, Gun Club (treas. 1990—). Avocations: Japanese gardening, painting. Office: Clearcrest Pines 10521 Darmstadt Rd Evansville IN 47710-5095

POWER, DENNIS MICHAEL, museum director; b. Pasadena, Calif., Feb. 18, 1941; s. John Dennis and Ruth Augusta (Mott) P.; m. Kristine Moneva Fisher, Feb. 14, 1965 (div. Aug. 1984); children: Michael Lawrence, Matthew David; m. Leslie Gabrielle Baldwin, July 6, 1985; 1 stepchild, Katherine G. Petrosky. BA, Occidental Coll., 1962, MA, 1964; PhD, U. Kans., 1967. Asst. curator ornithology Royal Ont. Mus., Toronto, Can., assoc. curator, 1971-72; asst. prof. zoology U. Toronto, 1967-72; exec. dir. Santa Barbara (Calif.) Mus. Natural History, 1972-94, Oakland Mus. of Calif., 1994—; biol. rschr.; cons. ecology. Editor: The California Islands: Proceedings of a Multidisciplinary Symposium, 1980, Current Ornithology, vol. 6, 1989, vol. 7, 1990, vol. 8, 1991, vol. 9, 1992, vol. 10, 1993, vol. 11, 1993, vol. 12, 1995; contbr. articles to sci. jours. Bd. dirs. Univ. Club Santa Barbara, 1989-92, v.p., 1991-92; bd. dirs. Santa Barbara Chamber Orch., 1990-94, v.p., 1991-94; mem. adv. coun. Santa Cruz Island Found., 1989—; mem. discipline adv. com. for museology Coun. for Internat. Exch. of Scholars, 1991-95. NSF fellow U. Kans., 1967; NRC grantee, 1968-72, 74-78. Fellow Am. Ornithologists Union (life, sec. 1981-83, v.p. 1988-89), Am. Assn. Mus. (mem. coun. 1980-83), Calif. Acad. Scis.; mem. AAAS, Cooper Ornithol. Soc. (bd. dirs. 1976-79, pres. 1978-81, hon. mem. 1993), Calif. Assn. Mus. (bd. dirs. 1981-92, chmn. 1987-89), Western Mus. Conf. (bd. dirs. 1977-83, pres. 1981-83), Am. Soc. Naturalists, Assn. Sci. Mus. Dirs., Ecol. Soc., Am. Soc. Study of Evolution, Soc. Systematic Zoology, Bohemian Club, Sigma Xi. Office: Oakland Mus of California 1000 Oak St Oakland CA 94607-4820

POWER, EDWARD FRANCIS, broadcast executive; b. Norfolk, Va., Oct. 18, 1953; s. Edward Vincent and Elinor (Kuester) P.; m. Marguerite Ulmer, July 25, 1980; children: Edward Graham, Nicholas Conrad. BA, U. Va., 1976, MA, 1978; postgrad., Columbia U., 1979-80. Staff writer The Virginian Pilot/The Ledger-Star, Norfolk, 1983-85, The Phila. Inquirer, 1985-89; from coord. metro editor to dep. mng. editor The Virginian Pilot/The Ledger-Star, 1989—; guest lectr. U. Va., Old Dominion U., Tidewater C.C. Vice-chmn., trustee Va. Ctr. Contemporary Art; bd. dirs. World Affairs Co. Mem. Va. Press Assn. (numerous awards). Avocations: surfing, skiing, sailing, running. Office: Va Pilot/Landmark Comms 150 W Brambleton Ave Norfolk VA 23510-2018

POWER, FRANCIS WILLIAM, newspaper publisher; b. Webster, S.D., Aug. 12, 1925; s. Frank B. and Esther C. (Fowler) P.; m. Margaret Jean Atkinson, Mar. 24, 1951; children: Patricia Ann, John Michael, Kerry Jean. B.B.A., U. N.Mex., 1948. Display advt. sales rep. The Register, Santa Ana, Calif., 1948-51; advt. mgr. Valley Morning Star, Harlingen, Tex., 1951-62; gen. mgr. Pampa (Tex.) Daily News, 1962-69; bus. mgr. Brownsville (Tex.) Herald, 1969-75; pub. The Lima (Ohio) News, 1975-91; v.p. Freedom Comm., Inc., until 1991; ret., 1991. Served with USNR, 1943-46. Roman Catholic. Clubs: Shawnee Country, Rotary, Elks. Office: Freedom Comm Inc 17666 Fitch Irvine CA 92614-6022

POWER, JOHN BRUCE, lawyer; b. Glendale, Calif., Nov. 11, 1936; children by previous marriage: Grant, Mark, Boyd. AB magna cum laude, Occidental Coll., 1958; JD, NYU, 1961; postdoctoral, Columbia U., 1972. Bar: Calif. 1962. Assoc. O'Melveny & Myers, Los Angeles, 1961-70, ptnr., 1970—; resident ptnr. O'Melveny & Myers, Paris, 1973-75; mem. Social Svcs. Commn. City of L.A., 1993, pres., 1993; pres. circle, exec. com. Occidental Coll., 1979-82, 91-94, vice chair, 1992-93, chair, 1993-94. Contbr. articles to jours. Dir. Met. L.A. YMCA, 1988—; mem. bd. mgrs. Stuart Ketchum Downtown YMCA, 1985-92, pres., 1989-90; mem. Los Angeles County Rep. Ctrl. Com., 1962-63; trustee Occidental Coll., 1992—. Root Tilden scholar. Fellow Am. Coll. Comml. Fin. Lawyers; mem. ABA (vice chmn. internat. fin. subcom. 1984-91, comml. fin. svcs. com., com. 3d party legal opinions, bus. law sect.), Am. Bar Found. (life), Calif. Bar Assn. (chmn. partnerships and unincorporated assns. com. 1982-83, chmn. uniform commn. code com. 1984-85, exec. com. 1987-91, treas. bus. law sect. 1988-89, vice chmn. 1989-90, chmn. 1990-91, chmn. coun. sect. chairs 1992-93, liaison to state bar commn. on future of legal profession and state bar), L.A. County Bar Assn. (exec. com. comml. law and bankruptcy sect. 1970-73, 86-89), Internat. Bar Assn., Fin. Lawyers Conf. (bd. govs., dir. 1984-85), Exec. Svc. Corps (sec. 1985—, trustee 1994—), Occidental Coll. Alumni Assn. (pres. 1967-68), Phi Beta Kappa. Office: O'Melveny & Myers 400 S Hope St Los Angeles CA 90071-2801

POWER, JOSEPH EDWARD, lawyer; b. Peoria, Ill., Dec. 2, 1938; s. Joseph Edward and Margaret Elizabeth (Birkett) P.; m. Camille June Repass, Aug. 1, 1964; children—Joseph Edward, David William, James Repass. Student, Knox Coll., Galesburg, Ill., 1956-58; B.A., U. Iowa, 1960, J.D., 1964. Bar: Iowa 1964. Law clk. to judge U.S. Dist. Ct., 1964-65; mem. Bradshaw, Fowler, Proctor & Fairgrave, P.C., Des Moines, 1965—. Bd. dirs. Moingona coun. Girl Scouts U.S.A., 1968-77, pres., 1971-74; mem. Des Moines CSC, 1971-73; bd. dirs. Des Moines United Way, 1976-82, v.p., 1979-81; trustee Am. Inst. Bus., 1987—, chmn., 1992—; bd. dirs. Iowa Law Sch. Found., 1992—, Plymouth Ch. Found., 1991—, Des Moines Found, 1996—; bd. dirs. Iowa Natural Heritage Found., 1995—; mem. Des Moines Civil War Roundtable. Fellow Am. Coll. Trust and Estate Counsel (state chair 1994—), Am. Coll. Real Estate Lawyers; mem. ABA, Iowa Bar Assn. (chmn. probate, property and trust law com. 1983-87), Polk County Bar Assn., Des Moines Estate Planners Forum (pres. 1982-83). Republican. Mem. United Ch. of Christ. Clubs: Des Moines, Rotary. Home: 4244 Foster Dr Des Moines IA 50312-2542 Office: Bradshaw Fowler Proctor & Fairgrave 801 Grand Ave Ste 3700 Des Moines IA 50309-8006

POWER, JULES, television producer; b. Hammond, Ind., Oct. 19, 1921; m. Dorothy Kutchinsky; children—Robert, Robin. Grad. with honors (Hardy scholar in speech and communications), Northwestern U., 1944. chmn. Power-Rector Prodns., Inc.; pres. Jules Power Prodns. Sr. producer AM America, ABC-TV; former producer TV show Watch Mr. Wizard, NBC-TV; exec. producer TV show ABC-TV News and Pub. Affairs; creator, exec. producer TV prodn. Discovery, 1962-71; TV spl. How Life Begins, 1968, The Unseen World, 1970; producer ABC-TV series AM America, 1975; exec. producer TV series Over Easy, Pub. Broadcasting System, 1976-83; sr. program cons. Pub. Broadcasting System, 1987—; producer The Scheme of Things, Disney TV Channel, 1983, ednl. films for ABC-McGraw-Hill, Bits, Bytes and Buzzwords, PBS, 1983, State of the Lang., PBS, 1983; exec producer Take Charge, Pub. Broadcasting System; exec. producer for Mary Martin; author: How Life Begins. Pub. info. advisor Buck Ctr. for Aging Rsch. Served with USAAF, World War II. Recipient 3 network Emmy awards, 11 Emmy nominations; Peabody award (2); Thomas Alva Edison award (3); Ohio State award (6); Am. Film Festival 1st place award (2), Internat. Film and TV Festival award (4); Hammond (Ind.) Ann. Achievement award, 1985. Mem. NATAS (past nat. vice-chmn., past pres. N.Y. chpt.), Writers Guild Am. East, Phi Beta Kappa. Home: 78 Red Hill Cir Belvedere Tiburon CA 94920-1773

POWER, MARK, journalist, photographer, educator; b. Washington, Mar. 6, 1937; s. Francis C. and Mary H. P.; m. Virginia North; children: Nancy, John, Rachel, Shelagh. Student, Bowdoin Coll., 1957, student Art Ctr. Coll. Design, 1960-61. Asst. prof. art Corcoran Sch. Art, Washington, 1971-83, assoc. prof. art, 1983—, prof. art, 1989—; art critic Washington Post, 1974-76, 85-87; lectr. in field. Curatorial work exhbns. include Icon Gallery, 1969-71, Corcoran Gallery Art, Dupont Ctr., Washington, 1972-75, 1985; exhibitor (photographs) one-man shows, Dartmouth Coll., 1967, Corcoran Gallery Art, Washington, 1970, 74, 79, Jefferson Pl. Gallery, Washington, 1974, Columbia (Mo.) Gallery, 1974, Diane Brown Gallery, Washington, 1977, Kathleen Ewing Gallery, Washington, 1978, 85,, 92, 95, Contrast Gallery, London, 1981, Galerie Chambre de la Claire, Paris, 1983, "Un/Common Ground" exhbn. Va. Mus. Fine Art, Richmond, 1996; numerous group shows, permanent collections, Libr. Congress, Smithsonian Instn., Iowa Mus. Art, New Orleans Mus. Art, Balt. Mus. Art, Bibliotheque Nationale, Nat. Mus. Am. Art; contbr. over 100 articles on art, film and photography to newspapers and mags. including Washington Post, Washington Star, Afterimage, Photographies, Art in America, Museum Art, Fotographies Views, San Francisco Camera, Times Lit. Supplement; contbg. editor Photo Rev., Washington Rev. Grantee Va. Mus. of Fine Art, 1995. Mem. Soc. Photog. Educators. Home: 20705 Sycolin Rd Leesburg VA 20175-8918 Office: Corcoran Sch Art 500 17th St NW Washington DC 20006-4804

POWER, MARY SUSAN, political science educator; b. Hazleton, Pa., July 5, 1935; d. Younger L. and Cleo (Boock) P.; 1 dau., Catherine Laverne. B.A., Wells Coll., 1957; postgrad., Exeter U. (Eng.), 1955-56, Yale U., 1958-59; M.A., Stanford U., 1959-60; Ph.D., U. Ill., 1959-61. Asst. prof. Susquehanna U. (Pa.), 1961-64; assoc. prof. U. Ark., Fayetteville, 1965-68; assoc. prof. polit. sci. Ark. State U., State University, 1968-79; prof. Ark. State U., 1979—. Author: Before the Convention, Religion and the Founding Fathers, 1984, Jacques Maritain and the Quest for a New Commonwealth, 1992; contbr. articles to profl. jours. Mem. State com. Ark. Rep. Com., 1968-96, sec., 1978-80; alt. del. Rep. Nat. Conv., 1972, 76, 88; mem. Fed. Edn. Commn. of States, 1982-84, Craighead County Election Commn., 1986-88; chmn. Craighead County GOP, 1986-88, vice chmn., 1990-96; N.E. regional chmn., 1988-96; chmn. Craighead County Sheffield for Gov., 1990; mem. exec. com. Ark. Rep. party, 1990-96, N.E. regional chair, 1988-96; N.E. chair Arkansans for Progress, 1990-96; treas. Women's Soc. Blessed Sacrament Ch., 1996—. Relm Found. fellow, 1960, NSF-Am. Polit. Sci. Assn. fellow, 1963, Nat. Def. Seminar, Nat. War Coll. fellow, 1973, NEH fellow, 1978, Pres.'s fellow Ark. State U., 1988-89. Mem. AAUP (pres. 1983-90, state sec. 1978-80), Ark. Polit. Sci. Assn. (bd. dirs., v.p. 1992-93, pres. 1993-94), Am. Polit. Sci. Assn., So. Polit. Sci. Assn., Phi Sigma Alpha, Phi Gamma Mu, Phi Kappa Phi (pres. 1991). Republican. Roman Catholic. Office: Ark State U Dept Polit Sci State University AR 72467

POWER, THOMAS MICHAEL, economist, educator; b. Milw., May 12, 1940; s. Paul C. and Edith (Thomas) P.; m. Pamela Shore, June 13, 1977; children: Donovan, Kate. BA, Lehigh U., 1962; MA, Princeton U., 1965, PhD, 1971. Instr. Lehigh U., Bethlehem, Pa., 1966-67, Princeton (N.J.) U., 1967-68; from asst. to assoc. prof. U. Mont., Missoula, 1968-78, prof. econ., chmn., 1978—. Author: Economic Value of Quality of Life, 1980, The Economic Pursuit of Quality, 1987, Lost Landscapes and Failed Economies: The Search for an Economic Value of Place, 1996, Environmental Protection and Local Economic Well-Being: The Economic Pursuit of Quality, 1996. Chmn. bd. dirs. Sussex Sch. Bd., Missoula, 1984-93. Woodrow Wilson Nat. fellow, 1963. Mem. Phi Beta Kappa. Avocations: mountaineering, long distance running, skiing. Office: U of Montana Dept Of Econs Missoula MT 59812

POWERS, ANTHONY RICHARD, JR., educational sales professional; b. Chgo., June 14, 1942; s. Anthony Richard and Bernadine Rene (Schwenke) P.; m. Marianne Fugiel, Mar. 15, 1980; children: Kathleen Mary, Anthony Richard III. BA, Quincy Coll., 1964; MS, U. Notre Dame, 1974. Cert. tchr., Ill. Sci. tchr. St. Rene Sch., Chgo., 1964-70; sci. coord. Queen of All Saints Sch., Chgo., 1970-76; sci. and math. product mgr. Ideal Sch. Supply Co., Oak Lawn, Ill., 1976-79, customer svc. mgr., 1980-83, Midwest sales mgr., 1983-85; nat. sales mgr. Ednl. Teaching Aids, Vernon Hills, Ill., 1985-89, v.p., 1989—; lectr., De Lourdes Coll., Des Plaines, Ill., 1970-78; sci. adviser, Archdiocese of Chgo., 1969-76. Author sci. edn. materials. Pres. Orchard Estates Condominium Assn., 1986-87; mem. Vernon Hills Fire and Police Commn., 1995—. Mem. Northeastern Ill. Sci. Assn. (pres. 1970-75), U.S. Golf Assn., Internat. Brotherhood Magicians, K.C. Roman Catholic. Avocations: magic, music, golf. Home: 241 Tally Ho Dr Vernon Hills IL 60061-2900 Office: Ednl Tchg Aids 620 Lakeview Pky Vernon Hills IL 60061-1828

POWERS, BRUCE RAYMOND, author, English language educator, consultant; b. Bklyn., Dec. 10, 1927; s. George Osborne and Gertrude Joan (Bangs) P.; m. Dolores Anne Dawson, July 25, 1969; children: Christopher, Patricia. Student U. Conn., 1947-49; AB, Brown U., 1951, MA, (tuition scholar 61-62), 1965; postgrad. U. Pa., 1961. Announcer/engr. Sta. WNLC, New London, Conn., 1946-47; tng. officer CIA, Dept. Def., 1951-55; TV sales/svc. rep. NBC, 1955; TV news writer and reporter Movietone News, United Press Assns., Inc., 1955-56; asst. to pres. Gotham-Vladimir Advt., Inc., 1956-57; asst. account exec. D'Arcy Advt. Co., 1957-58; asst. campaign dir. Cmty. Counselling Svcs., Inc., 1958-59; fund-raising campaign dir. Tamblyn & Brown, Inc., 1959-60; instr. Brown U., Providence, 1963-65, Ryerson Poly. Inst., Toronto, 1966, Nazareth Coll., Rochester, N.Y., 1966-67; asst. prof. English and communication studies Niagara U., Lewiston, N.Y., 1967-86, assoc. prof., 1986-92, prof. emeritus, 1992, chmn. permanent curriculum com. English dept., 1970-71, dir. Film Repertory Center, 1971-92, dir. communication studies program, 1973-87; producer-mgn. dir. Exptl. Film retrospective, N.Y. State Coun. of the Arts, Buffalo, 1972; narrator (documentary) Niagara: Fading in the Mist, 1996; panelist-judge Artists Com. 2d World Festival of Animated Films, Zagreb, Yugoslavia, 1974; lectr., vis. artist ARTPARK, Lewiston, N.Y., 1975; project dir. Bicentennial Symposium, N.Y. State Am. Revolution Bicentennial Commn., Buffalo, N.Y., 1975-76; research assoc. Center Culture and Tech., U. Toronto, 1977-81; keynote speaker Dupont de Nemours & Co. Health and Safety Conf., Buffalo, 1990; ptnr. Moon Island Documentary Group, 1996—. Co-author (with Marshall McLuhan): The Global Village, Oxford, 1989; editor The Film and Study Guide, 1973-74. Served with USNR, 1945-46, PTO. Recipient Carpenter prize in elocution, Brown U., 1951. Mem. MLA, Broadcast Edn. Assn., Soc. Cinema Studies, Am. Soc. Journalism Sch. Adminstrs., Assn. for Edn. in Journalism and Mass Communication, Internat. Exptl. Film Soc. (founding pres. 1971-73), Western N.Y. Audio-Visual Assn., N.Y. Coll. English Assn., Phi Beta Kappa. Roman Catholic. Home: 915 Sun Valley St North Tonawanda NY 14120-1952 Office: 105 Main St Niagara Falls NY 14303-1111 *All creativity is a search for the survival of the Spirit. It always asks the question - "if I am to die why is my life important?".*

POWERS, CLAUDIA MCKENNA, state government official; b. Key West, Fla., May 28, 1950; d. James Edward and Claudia (Antrim) McKenna; m. Richard Garland Powers, Dec. 27, 1971; children: Gregory, Theodore, Matthew, Thurston. BA in Edn., U. Hawaii, 1972; MA, Columbia U., 1975. Cert. tchr., N.Y. Rep. Greenwich (Conn.) Rep. Town Meeting, 1979-93, sec. bldg. com., 1982-84, sec. legis. com., 1986-88, 90-93; mem. Conn. Ho. of Reps., 1993—, ranking mem. govt. adminstrn. and elections com., 1995-96, asst. minority leader, 1997—. Mem. editorial bd. Greenwich Mag., 1995—. Campaign chmn. Greenwich Rep. Town Com., 1984, 85, chmn., 1986-90; sec. Rep. Round Table, Greenwich, 1988-90; bd. govs. Riverside Assn., Greenwich, 1987-91, sec., 1991-92; class mother Riverside Sch., Greenwich, 1984-90; mem. altar guild Christ Ch., Greenwich, 1990—; adminstrv. coord. Greenwich Teen Ctr., 1990-91; alt. del. Rep. Nat. Conv., New Orleans, 1984—, San Diego, 1996; v.p. LWV of Greenwich, 1990-91; vice chmn. Rep. Bill Rev. Com., 1997—. Episcopalian. Home and Office: 15 Hendrie Ave Riverside CT 06878-1808

POWERS, DAVID RICHARD, educational administrator; b. Cambridge Springs, Pa., Apr. 5, 1939; s. William Herman and Elouise Fancheon (Fink) P.; m. Mary Julia Ferguson, June 11, 1960. Student, Pa. State U., 1957-60; BA, U. Pitts., 1963, MA, 1965, PhD, 1971. Dir. CAS advising ctr. U. Pitts., 1966-68, asst. dean faculty, 1968-70, asst. to chancellor, 1970-76, assoc. provost, 1976-78, vice provost, 1978-79; v.p. for acad. affairs George Mason U., Fairfax, Va., 1979-82; vice chancellor for acad. affairs W.Va. Bd. Regents, Charleston, 1982-88; exec. dir. Minn. Higher Edn. Coord. Bd., St. Paul, 1989-94, Nebr. Coord. Commn. Post-secondary Edn., Lincoln, 1994—. Prin. author: Making Participatory Management Work, 1983, Higher Education in Partnership with Industry, 1988; contbr. articles to Ednl. Record, Adult Learning, Forum for Applied Rsch. on Pub. Policy. Bd. trustees Western Govs. U. Grantee USOE Faculty Seminar, Taiwan, 1967, ARC Ctr. for Edn. & Rsch. with Industry Appalachian Regional Commn., 1983, Republic of China Sino-Am. Seminar, 1985; recipient Award for Acad. Quality W.Va. Coun. Faculty, 1986. Mem. Am. Assn. for Higher Edn., Am. Soc. for Pub. Adminstrn., State Higher Edn. Exec. Officers, Nat. Postsecondary Edn. Coop., Western Coop. Ednl. Telecomm., Civil Air Patrol, Pi Sigma Alpha. Avocation: flying. Home: 1928 High St Lincoln NE 68502-4825 Office: Nebr Coord Comm Post secondary Edn PO Box 95005 Lincoln NE 68509-5005

POWERS, DORIS HURT, retired engineering company executive; b. Indpls., Jan. 17, 1927; d. James Wallace Hurt Sr. and Mildred (Johnson) Devine; m. Patrick W. Powers, Nov. 12, 1950 (dec. 1989); children: Robert W. Powers, Jaye P., Laura S. Powers. Student, So. Meth. U., 1944-45; BS in Engring., Purdue U., 1949; postgrad., U. Tex., W. Tex., 1952-53, Ecole Normale Du Musique, Paris, 1965-68; grad., Harford County Leadership

Acad., 1991. Flight instr. Red Leg Flying Club, El Paso, Lawton, Okla., 1951-57; check pilot Civil Air Patrol, El Paso, Lawton, Okla., 1952-57; ground instr. Civil Air Patrol, Washington, Tex., Okla, 1957-61; exec. v.p. T&E Internat., Inc., Bel Air, Md., 1979-88, pres., 1989-91; exec. v.p. T.E.I.S., Inc., Bel Air, 1979-88, pres., 1989-91; pres. Shielding Technologies, Inc., Bel Air, 1987-95; retired, 1995. Mem. Northeastern Md. Tech. Coun., 1991—; bd. dirs. Leadership Acad., 1991-94. Recipient Svc. award U.S. Army, 1978, Cert. of Appreciation U.S. Army Test and Evaluation Command, 1988, Woman of Distinction award Soroptomist Club, 1996; selected as Old Master Purdue U., 1995. Mem. CAP (lt. maj. 1951-58), Soc. of Women Engrs. (sr., v.p. 1977, treas. 1979, sec. rep. 1986-88, mentor 1986—, speaker 1978—, selected to Coll. of Fellows 1993), Engring. Soc. Balt. (speaker 1980—), 99's (pres. 1951-53), Am. Soc. Indsl. Security, Am. Def. Preparedness Assn., Hartford County Econ. Devel. Coun., Assn. of U.S. Army, Northeastern Md. Tech. Coun. Avocations: ice dancing, music. Home: 11 Glen Gate Ct Bel Air MD 21014

POWERS, DUDLEY, musician; b. Moorhead, Minn., June 25, 1911; s. James Harold and Mary Phoebe (Brainard) P.; m. Dorothy Louise Dasch, May 14, 1935; children: Jean Powers Todd, Eileen Powers Buchanan, Arthur, Anita Powers Palant. Student, Juilliard Mus. Found., 1926-30; MusB, Northwestern U., 1942, MusM, 1945. Cellist Little Symphony of Chgo., 1930-33; cellist Chgo. Symphony, 1933-43, solo cellist, 1943-53; prof. cello Northwestern U., 1931-80; vis. prof. cello U. South Fla., Tampa, 1980-86. Mem. Mischakoff String Quartet, 1935-38, Chgo. Symphony Quartet, 1940-53, Sheridan String Quartet, 1960-72; condr. Youth Symphony Greater Chgo., 1958-80, Eckstein String Quartet, 1972-80; cello recitalist. Home: 5450 Riverfront Dr Apt B Bradenton FL 34208-5236

POWERS, EDWARD ALTON, minister, educator; b. Jamestown, N.Y., Oct. 26, 1927; s. Leslie Edgar and Mabelle Florence (Alton) P.; children: Randall Edward, Christopher Alan, Ann Lynn. BA, Coll. of Wooster, 1948; MDiv, Yale U., 1952; EdD, Columbia U., 1973. Ordained to ministry Congregational Ch., 1951; pastor Hamden, Conn., 1949-53, Pleasant Hill, Ohio, 1953-56; sec. dept. youth work Congl. Christian Ch. Bd. Home Missions, 1956-60; gen. sec. div. Christian edn., bd. home missions Congl. and Christian Chs., 1960-61; div. Christian edn., bd. homeland ministries United Ch. of Christ, 1962-73; gen. sec., div. evangelism, edn., ch. extension United Ch. Bd. Homeland Ministries, 1973-79; mem. faculty Inst. Mgmt. Competency, Am. Mgmt. Assn., N.Y.C., 1980-87; sr. lectr. Grad. Sch. Mgmt. New Sch. for Social Research, 1981—; mem. program bd. div. edn. and ministry Nat. Council Chs., 1963-80; mem. edn. working group World Council Chs.; chmn. Peace Priority Team, United Ch. of Christ, 1970-75, adminstr., editor sexuality study, 1977; ptnr. Cane Powers Cons., and Powers, Wayno & Assocs. Author: Journey Into Faith, 1964, Signs of Shalom, 1973, (with Rey O'Day) Theatre of the Spirit, 1980, In Essentials Unity, 1982, Youth in the Global Village, 1982; also articles. Home: 7 Gramercy Park W Apt 5B New York NY 10003-1759 Office: Graybar Bldg 420 Lexington Ave Rm 300 New York NY 10170-0399

POWERS, EDWARD LATELL, accountant; b. Birmingham, Ala., Jan. 21, 1919; s. Jesse Franklin and Clara (Kircus) P.; m. Frances Gail Watters, Aug. 2, 1939; children: Karen Sue Powers Hoss, Linda Gail Powers Nix. Student, Wayne State U., 1944-45, U. Ala., 1952-53. C.P.A., Ala., N.Y., La., N.C. Accountant So. Cotton Oil Co., Birmingham, 1937-42; examiner pub. accounts Ala. Dept. Examiners Pub. Accounts, 1942; chief accountant Refuge Cotton Oil Co., Columbus, Miss., 1942-43; chief warrant officer, auditor Detroit Ordnance Dist., 1943-46; pub. accountant Screven, Turner & Co., Birmingham, 1946-48, Scarborough, Thomas & Co., Birmingham, 1948-49; sr. ptnr. Blankenship & Powers, Birmingham, 1950-51, Scarborough & Powers, Birmingham, 1951-56; mng. ptnr. Birmingham office, Haskins & Sells (now Deloitte & Touche), 1956-79; Mem., former chmn. Ala. Bd. Pub. Accountancy. Contbr. articles profl. jours. Mem. Mayor's Fact Finding Com., Birmingham, 1964-65; former trustee Bapt. Med.Ctrs.; treas. Lenox Owners Assn. Recipient Army Commendation award Detroit Ordnance Dist., 1945. Mem. AICPA, Ala. Soc. CPAs (past pres.), Soc. States Conf. CPAs (past mem. exec. com.), N.Y. Soc. of CPAs, Beta Alpha Psi. Baptist (deacon). Clubs: Downtown, The Club. Home: 905 Linkside Way Birmingham AL 35242-6430 Office: 3800 Colonnade Pkwy Birmingham AL 35243-2304

POWERS, ELIZABETH WHITMEL, lawyer; b. Charleston, S.C., Dec. 16, 1949; d. Francis Persse and Janes Coleman Cotten (Wham) P.; m. John Campbell Henry, June 11, 1994 (dec. Jan. 1997). AB, Mt. Holyoke Coll., 1971; JD, U. S.C., 1978. Bar: S.C. 1978, N.Y. 1979. Law clk. to justice S.C. Cir. Ct., Columbia; assoc. Reid & Priest, N.Y.C., 1978-86, ptnr., 1986—. Exec. editor S.C. Law Rev., Columbia, 1977-78. Bd. dirs. The Seamen's Ch. Inst., 1996—; vol. N.Y. Jr. League, N.Y.C., 1983—. Mem. ABA, S.C. Bar Assn., Nat. Soc. Colonial Dames of Am. (parliamentarian 1994—), Nat. Soc. Colonial Dames in State of N.Y. (pres. 1992-95), Church Club (v.p. 1992-94). Avocations: bridge, tennis. Office: Reid & Priest 40 W 57th St New York NY 10019-4001

POWERS, ESTHER SAFIR, organizational consultant; b. Tel Aviv, Sept. 1, 1948; arrived in Can., 1953, came to U.S., 1977; d. Nisan and Batia (Epstein) Safir; children: Jared Barnet, Eliott Robert. MusB, McGill U., Montreal, Que., Can., 1969; MusM, Ga. State U., 1982, PhD, 1985. Music tchr. North York Bd. Edn., Toronto, Ont., 1969-77; pres. Ested Mgmt., 1975-77, Mescon Group, Atlanta, 1985-95; cons. PeopleTech, 1995-97; pres., CEO E. Powers & Assocs., Atlanta, 1997—. Contbr. articles to profl. jours., chpt. to book. Pres. bd. dirs. Montessori Sch., Atlanta, 1978; vol. Nat. Coun. Jewish Women, Atlanta, 1990; mem. Ga. Exec. Womens Network; bd. dirs. Ptnrs. Against Domestic Violence, 1994—. Mem. Internat. Soc. for Performance Improvement (pres. Atlanta chpt. 1984-85, conf. mgr. 1983-84, internat. v.p. 1988-90, internat. pres. 1991-92, presdl. citation 1988, presdl. award 1989, leadership award 1990). Avocations: karate, music, bicycling, skiing, reading. Office: E Powers & Assocs 1040 Crown Pointe Pky # 570 Atlanta GA 30338-4777

POWERS, HARRIS PAT, broadcasting executive; b. Junction City, Kans., Oct. 29, 1934; s. Horace Pierce and Margaret (Harris) P.; m. Jerry Biles, Sept. 23, 1976; children: Rebecca, Randal, Mark, Shawn, Shannon, John. BA, Kans. State U., 1956. From salesman to mgr. Sta. KJCK, Junction City, 1957-73; mgr. Sta. KOYY, Eldorado, Kans., 1974-76; pres., CEO Sta. KTPK-FM, Topeka, 1976—; pres., chief exec. officer Stas. KINA and KQNS, Salina, Kans., 1979-87—; mem. bd. pub. adv. coun. Sta. KTWU, Topeka, 1979-87; pres., CEO Twenty First Century Broadcasting, Inc., Topeka, 1994—; bd. dirs. State Savs. & Loan Assn., Topeka; ptnr. Reichs Fgn. Cars and Parts, Topeka and Junction City. Mem. exec. com. Jayhawk Area coun. Boy Scouts Am., 1979-82; bd. dirs. Topeka Big Bros./Big Sisters, local chpt. ARC, Downtown Topeka, Inc.; past chmn. Downtown Topeka, Inc.; mem. Radio-TV-Film Curriculum adv. coun. Kans. U., adv. bd. Channel 11 Pub. TV; bd. dirs. Topeka Community Found., Pub. Schs. Found. Recipient numerous C. of C. and Jaycee awards, Disting. Svc. award Topeka Sales and Mktg. Execs., 1983, Grover Cobb award Kans. U., Silver award Profl. Advt. Club. Mem. Nat. Assn. Broadcasters, Internat. Broadcasters Soc., Mid-Am. Broadcasters (past chmn.), Kans. Assn. Broadcasters (past pres., Disting. Svc. award 1993), Kans. Assn. Commerce and Industry, (pres., bd. dirs. 1980-83), Sales and Mktg. Execs. Internat. (past pres. Topeka chpt.), Greater Topeka C. of C. (past vice chmn. devel. com., past v.p. pub. rels.), Kans. C. of C. (bd. dirs.), Topeka Town Club, Elks, Kiwanis (life mem. found.). Republican. Home and Office: 2120 SW Brooklyn Ave Topeka KS 66611-1612

POWERS, HENRY MARTIN, JR., oil company executive; b. Bath, Maine, July 18, 1932; s. Henry Martin and Eva (Saunders) P.; m. Hepzibah Hinchey Reed, June 20, 1959; children—Henry Martin III, Carlton Reed. B.S., Maine Maritime Acad., 1954. Marine engr. Am. Export Lines, N.Y.C., 1954-58; staff engr. Bull & Roberts Inc., N.Y.C., 1958-59; gen. sales mgr. Williams Bros., Inc., Portland, Maine, 1959-61; v.p. C.H. Sprague & Son Co., Boston, 1961-72; pres. C.H. Sprague & Son Co., 1972—, chmn. bd., 1987—, also bd. dirs.; chmn. Pease Devel. Authority, 1990-93; bd. dirs. Shanley Corp., Strawbery Banke Inc., First N.H. Banks, Seaward Constrn. Co. Vice pres. Seacoast United Fund, 1967-69; chmn. fuels, energy com. New England Council, 1974-75; pres. Portsmouth Council, 1966-67; bd. visitors Maine Maritime Acad. Served to lt. USNR, 1956-58. Mem. Navy League, Mechanic Fire Soc., Algonquin Club (Boston), Cumberland Club (Portland), Masons. Home: 68 River Rd 7 Boat Club Dr Box 261 Stratham NH 03885 Office: C H Sprague & Son Co 1 Parade Mall Portsmouth NH 03801-3749

POWERS, HUGH WILLIAM, newspaper executive; b. Slaton, Tex., Dec. 20, 1926; s. James Jerome and Myrtle (Black) P.; m. Constance Margaret Cornwall, Aug. 30, 1952; children: Nan Margaret, Sarah Ann. Student, W.Va. U., 1943-47. Mng. editor AGC News Svc., Houston, 1949-56; city editor Houston Press, 1956-64; asst. city editor Houston Chronicle, 1964-65, bus. editor, 1965-67, feature editor, 1967-73, assoc. editor, 1973-95; dir. Taping for the Blind, 1995—, v.p., 1997. Mem. Press Club of Houston (pres., dir. 1968-72), Ducks Unltd. (dir. Houston chpt. 1989—, chmn. 1995, Tex. State trustee Nat. Del., 1996—), Phi Kappa Psi. Home: 10818 Hillcroft St Houston TX 77096-6031

POWERS, JAMES FARL, author; b. Jacksonville, Ill., July 8, 1917; s. James Ansbury and Zella (Routzong) P.; m. Elizabeth Alice Wahl, Apr. 22, 1946; children: Katherine, Mary, James, Hugh, Jane. Student, Northwestern U., 1938-40. Instr. writing courses St. John's U., Collegeville, Minn., 1947, 75-93, Marquette U., 1949-51, U. Mich., 1956-57; writer-in-residence Smith Coll., 1965-66. Author: Prince of Darkness and Other Stories, 1947, (short stories) The Presence of Grace, 1956, Morte d'Urban (Nat. Book award 1963, Thormod Monsen award Soc. Midland Authors 1963), 1962, Look How the Fish Live, 1975, (novel) Wheat that Springeth Green, 1988. Decorated Chevalier de l'Ordre des Arts et des Lettres (France); Guggenheim fellow, 1948, Rockefeller fellow, 1954, 57, 67; grantee Am. Acad. of Arts and Letters, 1948. Mem. Am. Acad. of Arts and Letters. Address: Box 5911 Collegeville MN 56321

POWERS, JAMES MATTHEW, neuropathologist; b. Cleve., Sept. 15, 1943; s. Alfred Patrick and Margaret Anne (Gunther) P.; m. Karen P. Smith, 1983; children: Kristin, Scott, Conor. BS in Biology, Manhattan Coll., 1965; MD, U. S.C., Charleston, 1969. Diplomate in anatomic pathology and neuropathology Am. Bd. Pathology. Asst. prof. pathology Med. U. S.C., Charleston, 1973-76; dir. electron micros. lab. VA Hosp., Charleston, 1973-76; assoc. prof. pathology Med. U. S.C., Charleston, 1976-80, prof. pathology, 1980-88; vice chmn. dept. pathology Columbia Coll. Physicians and Surgeons, N.Y.C., 1989-92; assoc. chair of edn., dir. residency tng. program U. Rochester, N.Y., 1994—; prof., dir. neuropathology U. Rochester, 1992—; sec. Biol. Stain Commn., 1994—. Author: (book chpt.) Andersen's Pathology, 10th edit., 1996, (practice guidelines) Archives Pathology and Laboratory Medicine, 1995; mem. editl. bd. Human Pathology, 1991—, Brain Pathology, 1995—, Acta Neuropathologica, 1995—, Biotech. and Histochemistry, 1994—, Modern Pathology, 1996—. Mem. Internat. Soc. Neuropathology (v.p. 1994—), Am. Assn. Neuropathologists (pres. 1993, Moore award 1975, 76, 77, 81), U.S.-Can. Acad. Pathology, Am. Assn. Pathologists. Office: U Rochester Box 626 601 Elmwood Ave Rochester NY 14642

POWERS, JOHN Y., federal judge; b. Lake Orion, Mich., Aug. 1, 1929; s. Henry Stephen and Bertha Mae (Youngerman) P.; m. Barbara Mathilda Levero, Aug. 25, 1958; children: Joshua A., Lucas A., John Matthew, Samuel David. Student, Union U., 1947-48; BA, Vanderbilt U., 1951, LLB, 1953. Bar: Tenn. 1954. Enlisted man U.S. Army, Ft. Holabird, Md., 1954; 1st Lt. Judge Adv. Gen. Corps, Charlottesville, Va., 1955-57; with Claims Divsn. Office of the Judge Advocate General, Ft. Holabird, Md., 1955-57; with Adminstrv. divsn. U.S. Dept. Justice, 1957-58; claims rep. State Farm Ins. Co., Miami, Fla., 1958-59; atty. Spears, Moore, Rebman & Wms, Chattanooga, Tenn., 1959-70; ptnr. Hargraves, Curtis & Powers, Chattanooga, Tenn., 1970-74, Noone, Stringer & Powers, Chattanooga, Tenn., 1974-78, Reingold, Powers & Schulman, Chattanooga, Tenn., 1978-84; U.S. magistrate judge ea. dist. Tenn. U.S. Dist. Ct., Chattanooga, Tenn., 1984—. Mem. Tenn. Bar. Assn., Chatanooga Bar Assn. Office: US District Court US Courthouse 900 Georgia Ave Rm 102 Chattanooga TN 37402-2257

POWERS, MARTHA MARY, nursing consultant, education specialist; b. Medford, Mass., Jan. 8, 1940; d. John Francis and Mary (Denning) P. BS, Boston Coll., 1962; MS in Nursing, Boston U., 1978, EdD in Health Edn., 1985. Mem. faculty Boston Coll. Sch. Nursing; asst. prof. nursing Regis Coll., Weston, Mass.; nursing cons., edn. specialist NIH, Bethesda, Md.; cons. health care NATO, Belgium; coord. curriculum Somerville (Mass.) Hosp. Sch. Nursing; researcher medications, cardiac rehab., interaction analysis and leadership. Author: Health Promotion in Home Nursing: A Teaching Manual, 1986; contbr. articles to profl. jours. Chair nominating com. ARC Boston and Massachussetts Bay, past chmn. nursing and health, specialist home nursing, bd. dirs.; vol. Mass. Assn. Blind. Mem. AAUP, ANA, AACN, Mass. Nurses Assn., Nat. League Nursing, Mass. and R.I. League Nursing , N.Y. Acad. Sci., Assn. Nurse Researchers, Phi Lambda Theta. Home: 29 April Ln Lexington MA 02173-8116

POWERS, MICHAEL KEVIN, architectural and engineering executive; b. Boston, Feb. 3, 1948; s. Albert Thomas and Claire Marie (Sullivan) P.; m. Patricia Marie Collins, July 10, 1971; children: Kristin Michelle, Jennifer Anne. BSCE, Northeastern U., 1971. Registered profl. engr. N.Y., Vt., Minn., Maine, Mass., N.H., Ky., D.C., Pa., R.I. Staff engr. Edwards and Kelcey, Boston, 1967-70; project mgr. DeLeuw Cather & Co., Boston, 1971-80; exec. v.p., dir. engring. Symmes Maini & McKee Assocs., Inc., Cambridge, Mass., 1980—; also bd. dirs. Symmes Maini & McKee Assocs., Inc., Cambridge; guest spkr. Tradeline Forum on Bus. and Tech., Boston, 1986-88, Microcontamination Conf. and Expn., Santa Clara, Calif., 1987, Clean Rooms Conf., Balt., 1995, Santa Clara, 1995, 96, Boston, 1996, Clean Rooms East, Boston, 1996; lectr. facility design MIT, 1989, 92, 93, Wentworth Inst., 1993, 94, Pa. State U., 1995. Contbr. articles to profl. jours. Mem. ASCE, NSPE, Inst. Environ. Scis. (sr.), Mt. River East Condominium Assn. (past trustee). Roman Catholic. Avocations: Alpine skiing, tennis, golf, music. Office: Symmes Maini & McKee Assocs Inc 1000 Massachusetts Ave Cambridge MA 02138-5304

POWERS, NOYES THOMPSON, lawyer; b. New Orleans, Apr. 29, 1929. BA magna cum laude, Duke U., 1951; LLB cum laude, Harvard U., 1954. Asst. to Under Sec. Labor, 1961, dep. solicitor labor, 1962-63; exec. asst. to Sec. of Labor, 1964-65; exec. dir. EEOC, 1965; ptnr. Steptoe & Johnson, Washington, Phoenix, 1966-94; sr. labor counsel Motorola, Inc., Phoenix, 1993—. Mem. ABA (chair pub. utility, comm. and transp. sect. 1994-95). Office: Motorola Inc Corp Law Dept 3102 N 56th St Phoenix AZ 85018-6606

POWERS, PAUL J., manufacturing company executive; b. Boston, Feb. 5, 1935; s. Joseph W. and Mary T. Powers; m. Barbara Ross, June 3, 1961; children: Briana, Gregory, Jeffrey. BA in Econs., Merrimack Coll., 1956; MBA, George Washington U., 1962. Various mfg. and fin. positions with Chrysler Corp., Detroit and overseas, 1963-69; v.p., gen. mgr. Am. Standard, Dearborn, Mich., 1970-78; pres. Abex-Dennison, Columbus, Ohio, 1978-82; group v.p. Comml. Intertech Corp., Youngstown, Ohio, 1982-84, pres., chief ops. officer, 1984-87, chmn., pres., CEO, 1987—; bd. dirs. Ohio Edison Co., Twin Disc, Inc., Global Marine Inc.; chmn. bd. dirs. CUNO, Inc., 1996—. Bd. dirs. Youngstown Symphony, 1984-88. Lt. USNR, 1957-63. Mem. NAM (bd. dirs. 1986-93, 95—), Nat. Fluid Power Assn. (bd. dirs. 1984-87), Mfrs. Alliance (bd. dirs. 1995—), Youngstown Area C. of C. (bd. dirs. 1990—). Office: Comml Intertech Corp 1775 Logan Ave # 239 Youngstown OH 44505-2622

POWERS, PAULINE SMITH, psychiatrist, educator, researcher; b. Sept. 23, 1941; m. Henry P. Powers; children: Jessica, Samantha. AB in Math., Washington U., 1963; MD, U. Iowa, 1971. Med. intern Emanuel Hosp., Portland, Oreg., 1971-72; psychiatry resident U. Iowa, Iowa City, 1972-74, U. Calif., Santa Barbara, 1974-75; from asst. prof. to assoc. prof. psychiatry Coll. Medicine U. So. Fla., Tampa, 1975-85, prof., 1985—, dir. eating disorder program, 1979—, dir. psychosomatic medicine divsn., 1979—. Author: Obesity: The Regulation of Weight, 1980; editor: The Current Treatment of Anorexia Nervosa and Bulimia, 1984. Fellow Am. Psychiat. Assn. (Dorfman Jour. Paper award 1987, Rush Gold Outstanding Exhibit medal 1976); Founding Pres. Acad. Eating Disorders. Office: U So Fla Coll Medicine Dept Psychiatry 3515 E Fletcher Ave Tampa FL 33613-4706

POWERS, RAMON SIDNEY, historical society administrator, historian; b. Gove County, Kans., Sept. 24, 1939; s. Sanford and Gladys Fern (Williams) P.; m. Eva Redin, Apr. 11, 1963; children: Elisabeth, Christina. AB, Ft. Hays (Kans.) State U., 1961, MA, 1963; PhD, U. Kans., 1971. Instr. western civilization U. Kans., Lawrence, 1963-67; asst. prof. history U. Mo., Kansas City, 1967-71; instr. Haskell Indian Jr. Coll., Lawrence, 1971-73; rsch. asst. Kans. Legis. Rsch. Dept., Topeka, 1973-77, rsch. analyst, 1977-78, prin. analyst, 1978-88; asst. exec. dir. Kansas State Hist. Soc., Topeka, 1988, exec. dir., 1988—. Contbr. articles to various jours. Chair Eisenhower Centennial Adv. Com., Topeka, 1988-90, Kans. Antiquities Commn., 1988—, State Records Bd., 1988—, Sante Fe Hist. Trail Adv. Coun.; mem. bd. review Kans. Hist. Sites, 1988—; mem. State Hist. Records Adv. Bd., 1988—, Gov.'s Commn. on Travel and Tourism, 1988—, Kans. Bus. Hall of Fame, 1988-96; mem. bd. dirs. Nat. Conf. of State Historic Preservation Officers, 1991—. Recipient regional award Col. Dames Am., 1965, Disting. Alumni award Ft. Hays State U. and Hays Rotary Club, 1978; travel grantee N.J. Hist. Commn., 1971, summer grantee NEH, 1973. Mem. SAR (Thomas Jefferson chpt.), Am. Assn. State and Local History, Kans. Corral of the Westerns, Kans. History Tchrs. Assn., Western History Assn., Travel Industry Assn. (bd. dirs. 1991-93), Greater Topeka C. of C., Topeka Heritage League, Sat. Night Literary Club. Office: Kans History Ctr 6425 SW 6th Ave Topeka KS 66615-1099

POWERS, RICHARD AUGUSTINE, III, judge; b. Phila., Sept. 22, 1932; s. Richard Augustine and Evelyn Lenore (Clark) P.; m. Helen Regina Penza, Aug. 30, 1958; children: Mary, Helen, Joan, Grace, Patricia, Theodore, Robert. B.S. in Econs., LaSalle Coll., 1958; J.D., Temple U., 1962. Bar: U.S. Dist. Ct. (ea. dist.) Pa. 1962; U.S. Supreme Ct., 1993. Assoc., Leo Francis Doyle, Phila., 1962; law clk. to judges U.S. Dist. Ct. (ea. dist.) Pa., 1962-71; U.S. Magistrate judge U.S. Dist. (ea. dist.) Pa., Phila., 1971—; chief U.S. Magistrate judge, 1994—. lectr. in law Fed. Jud. Center, Washington; lectr. in civil litigation Main Line Paralegal Inst. Contbr. articles to profl. jours. Served with USAR, 1957-63. Recipient award Temple Law Alumni, 1979, LaSalle Law Alumni, 1979. Mem. Nat. Council Fed. Magistrates Judges, Phila. Bar Assn., Pa. Hist. Soc., Genealogical Soc. Pa., Brehon Law Soc., Phila. Museum Art, Smithsonian Contributory Assn., Pa. Hort. Soc., SAR. Roman Catholic. Office: US District Court 3124 US Courthouse Ind Mall W 601 Market St Philadelphia PA 19106-1713

POWERS, RICHARD DANIEL, bank executive; b. Albuquerque, July 11, 1956; s. Richard James and Laura Love (Daniel) P.; m. Savanna Lee Anderson, Aug. 27, 1988; 1 child, Sara Elizabeth. BA, U. State of N.Y., Albany, 1993; MBA, U. Chgo., 1995. Account rep. Covington Knox, Inc., Houston, 1976-78; sales mgr. Morse Realty, Inc., Houston, 1979-86; asst. v.p. Dollar Dry Dock Savs. Bank, White Plains, N.Y., 1986-87; cons. Deloitte & Touche, N.Y.C., 1987; sr. v.p. Gt. Western Mortgage Co., Chatsworth, Calif., 1987-94, Charter One Bank, Cleve., 1994—. Trustee Ohio Mortgage Bankers Assn. With USAF, 1973-75. Mem. Am.'s Cmty. Bankers (mortgage fin. com., secondary market subcom.), Mortgage Bankers Assn., Ohio Mortgage Bankers Assn. (trustee), Bank Adminstrn. Inst., Cleve. Athletic Club, Pine Lake Trout Club. Home: 3108 Royal Oak Ct Westlake OH 44145-3770 Office: Charter One Bank 1215 Superior Ave E Cleveland OH 44114-3249

POWERS, ROBERT DAVID, physician; b. Plainfield, N.J., Nov. 6, 1953; s. John B. and Marian E. (Kuhn) P.; m. Sally Ann Harmet, 1978; children: Alison, Elizabeth, Carolyn. BA, Amherst Coll., 1975; MD, U. Va., 1979. Intern U. Minn., 1979-81; resident U. Va., 1981-83; from asst. to assoc. prof. U. Va., Charlottesville, 1983-94; assoc. prof. U. Conn., Farmington, 1994—; chief dept. emergency medicine, vice chmn. dept. trauma and emergency medicine Hartford (Conn.) Hosp. Fellow ACP, Am. Coll. Emergency Physicians. Office: Hartford Hosp Dept Emergency Medicine Hartford CT 06115

POWERS, RUNA SKÖTTE, artist; b. Anderstorp, Sweden, Oct. 29, 1940; d. Gösta Nils Folke and Kristina Torborg (Andersson) S.; m. David Britton Powers, Mar. 13, 1965; children: Kristina, Davis. Student, Art Inst. So. Calif., 1976-83; BMA, U. So. Calif., 1986. Exhbns. include Newport Festival Arts, Newport Beach, 1980, Costa Mesa Art League, 1980, Orange County Fair, Costa Mesa, 1980, Art Inst. So. Calif., Laguna Beach, 1976-83, Studio Sem Ghelardini, Pietrasanta, Italy, 1983, Design House, Laguna, 1984, Vorpal Gallery, 1983-84, Laguna Beach Mus. Art, 1984, Gallery Sokolov, Laguna Beach, 1985-93, Margareta Sjödin Gallery, Malibu, 1988, Ana Izax Gallery, Beverly Hills, 1988, Envision Art, 1991, Gallery Slottet, Hörle, Sweden, 1990-92, J.F. Kennedy Performing Arts Ctr., Washington, 1991, Internat. Art Expn., L.A., 1985, N.Y., 1986-87, San Bernardino County Mus., 1993. Founder Found. Hörle Manor House, Värnamo, Sweden, 1987—. Avocations: music, reading, cooking, swimming. Home: 1831 Ocean Way Laguna Beach CA 92651-3235 Address: PO Box 2080, S 334 00 Anderstorp Sweden

POWERS, THOMAS EDWARD, managed care executive; b. Miami, Fla., Oct. 18, 1948; s. Samuel Joseph and Marion (Locke) P.; m. Nancy Beekman Mangels, June 19, 1982; children: Thomas Martin, James Michael. BA, Stetson U., 1976; MBA, Barry U., 1992, MHA, 1995. Diplomate Am. Coll. Health Exec. Mgr., account exec. Aetna Life & Casualty, Miami, 1976-92; exec. v.p. Med. Card System, Miami Lakes, Fla., 1992-95; mem. long range planning com. Barry U., Miami. Chmn.'s counsel Miami Heart Inst., 1992; bd. dirs. ARC, Columbus chpt. ARC. Mem. Kiwanis (West Palm Beach, Fla.) (pres. 1982, Kiwanian of Yr. 1978). Republican. Roman Catholic. Avocations: golf, ironman triathlon finisher, commercial pilot.

POWERS, THOMAS MOORE, author; b. N.Y.C., Dec. 12, 1940; s. Joshua Bryant and Susan (Moore) P.; m. Candace Molloy, Aug. 21, 1965; children: Amanda, Susan, Cassandra. B.A., Yale U., 1964. Reporter Rome (Italy) Daily American, 1965-67, U.P.I., N.Y.C., 1967-70; freelance writer, 1970—; contbg. editor The Atlantic mag., L.A. Times Opinion; editor, founding ptnr. Steerforth Press, So. Royalton, Vt., 1993—. Author: Diana: The Making of a Terrorist, 1971, The War at Home, 1973, The Man Who Kept the Secrets: Richard Helms and the CIA, 1979, Thinking About the Next War, 1982, Total War: What It Is, How It Got That Way, 1988, Heisenberg's War: The Secret History of the German Bomb, 1993. Recipient Pulitzer prize for nat. reporting, 1971. Mem. PEN Am. Center, Council on Fgn. Relations. Address: 106 Chelsea St South Royalton VT 05068

POWERS, WILLIAM FRANCIS, automobile manufacturing company executive; b. Phila., Dec. 11, 1940; s. Francis Simpson and Kathryn Emily (Thoroughgood) P.; m. Linda Nell Shelton, Sept.7, 1963; children—Stephen, Leigh. B.S. in Aerospace Engring., U. Fla., 1963; M.S., U. Tex., 1966, Ph.D., 1968. Aerospace engr. NASA Marshall Space Flight Ctr., Huntsville, Ala., 1960-65; faculty mem. U. Mich., Ann Arbor, 1968-79, prof. aerospace engring., 1976-79; research mgr. Ford Motor Co., Dearborn, Mich., 1980-86, rsch. dir., 1986-87, dir. computer ops. N.Am., 1987-89, program mgr., 1989-91, exec dir. rsch., 1991-94, exec. dir info. sys. and rsch., 1994-96, v.p. rsch., 1996— cons. NASA Johnson Space Ctr., Houston, 1971-79, other cos., 1968-79. Contbr. articles to profl. jours. Editor: Astrodynamics, 1975, Jour. Astron. Scis., 1977-80. USSR research exchange scientist U.S. Nat. Acad. Scis., 1976. Fellow AIAA (assoc.), IEEE; mem. ASME, NAE, Soc. Automotive Engrs., Am. Automatic Control Council (v.p. 1986-87, pres. 1988-89), Royal Swedish Acad. Engring. Scis. (fgn.). Home: 3404 E Dobson Ann Arbor MI 48105

POWLEDGE, FRED ARLIUS, freelance writer; b. N.C., Feb. 23, 1935; s. Arlius Raymond and Pauline (Stearns) P.; m. Tabitha Morrison, Dec. 21, 1957; 1 child, Pauline Stearns. AB in English, U. N.C., 1957. Writer, editor AP, New Haven, 1958-60; reporter Atlanta Jour., 1960-63, N.Y. Times, N.Y.C., 1963-66; freelance journalist, 1966—; lectr. New Sch., N.Y.C., 1967-69, 80-82; narrator, co-producer, writer WNET-TV/13, N.Y.C., 1972. Author: Black Power/White Resistance: Notes on the New Civil War, 1967, To Change a Child: A Report on the Institute for Developmental Studies, 1967, Model City: A Test of American Liberalism: One Town's Efforts to Rebuild Itself, 1970, Mud Show: A Circus Season, 1976, Born on the Circus, 1976, The Backpacker's Budget Food Book, 1977, Journeys Through the South, 1979, So You're Adopted: A Book About the Experience of Being Adopted, 1982, Water: The Nature, Uses and Future of Our Most Precious and Abused Resource, 1982, A Forgiving Wind: On Becoming a Sailor,

1983, Fat of the Land, 1984, The New Adoption Maze: And How to Get Through It, 1985, You'll Survive, 1986, Free at Last? The Civil Rights Movement and the People Who Made It, 1991, We Shall Overcome: The Heroes of the Civil Rights Movement, 1993, Working River, 1995. Mem. Bd. Library Trustees, St. Mary's County, Md. With USAR, 1957. Russell Sage fellow Russell Sage Found., 1966-67; travel and study grantee Ford Found., 1971, 93-94. Mem. Nat. Writer's Union, Nat. Assn. Sci. Writers.

POWLEN, DAVID MICHAEL, lawyer; b. Logansport, Ind., May 28, 1953; s. Daniel Thomas and Bertha Frances (Cappa) P.; m. Karen Lamb Gentleman, Aug. 5, 1978 (div. Jan. 1984); 1 child, Brooks Ryan. AB, Harvard U., 1975, JD, 1978. Bar: Ind. 1978, U.S. Dist. Ct. (so. dist.) Ind. 1978, U.S. Ct. Appeals (7th cir.) 1985. Assoc. Barnes & Thornburg, Indpls., 1978-84, ptnr., 1985—, chmn. creditors rights dept. Contbr. articles to profl. jours. Mem. ABA (bus. bankruptcy com., secured creditors and chpt. 11 subcom., comml. fin. svcs. com., creditors rights subcom.), Seventh Cir. Bar Assn., Ind. Bar Assn. (chmn. bankruptcy and creditors rights sect. 1990-91), Indpls. Bar Assn. (chmn. edn. com. 1984, chmn. ct. liaison com. 1985, bankruptcy and comml. law sect.), Am. Bankruptcy Inst. (regional programs and seminars subcom.), Comml. Law League Am. (bankruptcy and insolvency sect.), Harvard Club, Indpls. Sailing Club, Phi Beta Kappa. Republican. Home: 1450 Preston Tr Carmel IN 46032-8971 Office: Barnes & Thornburg 11 S Meridian St Ste 1313 Indianapolis IN 46204-3506

POWNALL, MALCOLM WILMOR, mathematics educator; b. Coatesville, Pa., Jan. 6, 1933; s. Malcolm and Elizabeth (Moore) P.; m. Gertrude Decker, June 3, 1961; children: Joseph, Elizabeth, Kathryn, Thomas. A.B., Princeton U., 1954; M.A., U. Pa., 1958, Ph.D., 1960. Instr. to prof. math. Colgate U., Hamilton, N.Y., 1959—. Author: Prelude to the Calculus, 1967, Functions and Graphs, 1983, Real Analysis, A First Course with Foundations, 1994. Mem. Math. Assn. Am. (exec. dir. com. on undergrad. program 1966-68, chmn. com. on vis. lectrs. and cons. 1969-83). Democrat. Mem. Soc. of Friends. Office: Colgate Univ Dept Math 13 Oak Dr Hamilton NY 13346-1338

POWSNER, EDWARD RAPHAEL, physician; b. N.Y.C., Mar. 17, 1926; m. Rhoda Lee Moscovitz , June 8, 1950; children: Seth, Rachel, Ethan, David. SB in Elec. Engring., MIT, 1948, SM in Biology, 1949; MD, Yale U., 1953; MS in Internal Medicine, Wayne State U., 1957; MHSA, U. Mich. Diplomate Am. Bd. Nuclear Medicine, Am. Bd. Pathology in clin. pathology and anatomic pathology, Am. Bd. Internal Medicine; lic. physician, Mich., Calif., N.Y. Intern Wayne County Gen. Hosp., Eloise, Mich., 1953-54, resident internal medicine, 1954-55; resident internal medicine Detroit Receiving Hosp., 1955-56; fellow in hematology Wayne State U. and Detroit Receiving Hosp., 1957-58; clin. investigator VA Hosp., Allen Park, Mich., 1958-61, chief nuclear medicine svc., 1961-78; dir. clin. labs. Mich. State U., East Lansing, 1978-81; staff pathologist Ingham Med. Ctr., Lansing, Mich., 1978-81; dir. nuclear medicine St. John Hosp., Detroit, 1982-95; rsch. asst. biology MIT, 1948-49, 50; asst. instr. medicine Wayne State U. Coll. Medicine, 1954-56, instr., 1959-61; assoc. prof. pathology Wayne State U. Sch. Medicine, 1961-68, assoc. medicine, 1961, prof. pathology, 1968-78; prof. pathology Mich. State U., 1978-81, assoc. chairperson, 1980-81, clin. prof., 1981-82; chief clin. labs. Detroit Gen. Hosp., 1969-73; chief lab. svcs. Health Care Inst., Wayne State U., 1976-78; mem. adv. coun. Nuclear Medicine Tech. Cert. Bd., 1990-91. Bd. editors Am. Jour. Clin. Pathology, 1963-76, 83-88; author 1 textbook, 10 chpts., 48 peer reviewed papers, 19 abstracts and other publs. With U.S. Army, 1944-47. Mem. AMA (sect. coun. on pathology), Am. Soc. Clin. Pathologists (rep. 1987-89, 93—, govt. rels. com. 1993—, mem. coun. nuclear medicine 1978-82, chmn. 1982-84), Am. Coll. Nuclear Physicians, Am. Soc. Nuclear Cardiology, Coll. Am. Pathologists, Detroit Acad. Medicine, Mich. Soc. Pathologists, Mich. State Med. Soc., Soc. Nuclear Medicine, Washtenaw County Med. Soc., Sigma Xi, Tau Beta Pi. Office: Eastside Nuclear Medicine 18530 Mack Ave Ste 134 Grosse Pointe MI 48236-3223 also: St John Hosp & Med Ctr 22101 Moross Rd Detroit MI 48236-2148

POYNER, JAMES MARION, retired lawyer; b. Raleigh, N.C., Sept. 18, 1914; s. James Marion and Mary (Smedes) P.; m. Florence I Chan, Feb. 24, 1945; children: Susan Poyner Moore, Chan Poyner Pike, Margaret Poyner Galbraith, Edythe Poyner Lumdsen, James Marion III. B.S. in Chem. Engring, N.C. State U., 1935, M.S., 1937; J.D., Duke U., 1940. Bar: N.C. 1940. Pvt. practice Raleigh, 1946-51; ptnr. Poyner, Geraghty, Hartsfield & Townsend, Raleigh, 1951-86; of counsel Poyner & Spruill, Raleigh, 1986-95, ret., 1995; co-founder Cameron-Brown Co. (now 1st Union Mortgage Co.); life dir. 1st Union Corp., 1st Union Nat. Bank; chmn. bd. dirs. Eastern Standard Ins. Co., George Smedes Poyner Founds. Inc. Orch. leader, trombonist, arranger, Jimmy Poyner and His Orch., 1933-38. Mem. N.C. Senate, 1955-59; Past chmn. bd. trustees St. Mary's Coll.; past chmn. bd. World Golf Hall of Fame; past chmn. trustees N.C. Symphony Soc. Served with Chem. Warfare Service, AUS, 1942-46. Decorated Legion of Merit. Mem. ABA, N.C. Bar Assn. (pres. 1967-68, dir. 1963-67), Am. Judicature Soc. (dir. 1973-77), Raleigh C. of C. (past pres.), Phi Kappa Phi. Episcopalian. Home: 710 Smedes Pl Raleigh NC 27605-1141 Office: 3600 Glenwood Ave Raleigh NC 27612-4945

POYNOR, ROBERT ALLEN, JR., guidance counselor; b. Franklin, Tenn., Aug. 2, 1939; s. Robert Allen and Agnes Elizabeth (Gillespie) P.; m. Martha Bellah Stark, July 12, 1996; 1 child, Melissa Dawn Hay. BA, Belmont Coll., Nashville, 1967; MEd, Mid. Tenn. State U., 1972, EdS, 1975; postgrad., Tenn. State U. Cert. elem. tchr., elem. guidance counselor, elem. prin.-advanced, Tenn. Teller, mgmt. trainee Third Nat. Bank, Nashville, 1962-67; employment rep. S.S. Bd. of the S.B.C., Nashville, 1967-68; tchr. Sumner County Bd. Edn., Gallatin, Tenn., 1968-69; asst. sec.-treas., br. mgr. Security Fed. Savs. and Loan Assn., Nashville, 1969-71; tchr. Sumner County Bd. Edn., Gallatin, 1971-79, 83-85, prin., 1979-83, guidance counselor, 1985—; mem. textbook adoption com. Sumner County bd. Edn., 1968-69, mem. gifted com., 1980-82. Charter sec. 100 Oaks Sertoma Club, Nashville, 1970; treas. Am. Savs. and Loan Inst., Nashville, 1970. With U.S. Army, 1957-59, France. Mem. ACA, Tenn. ACA, Tenn. Assn. Counselor Devel., Mid. Tenn. Assn. for Counselor Devel., United Tchg. Profession, Sumner County Elem. Prins. (past pres. 1982-83), Sumner County Edn. Assn. (past pres. 1978-79), Phi Delta Kappa. United Methodist. Avocations: jogging, reading, yard work, spectator sports, art. Home: 288 Indian Lake Rd Hendersonville TN 37075-4344

POYTHRESS, DAVID BRYAN, state commissioner, lawyer; b. Macon, Ga., Oct. 24, 1943; s. John M. and Dorothy (Bayne) P. BA, Emory U., 1964, JD, 1967. Bar: Supreme Ct. Ga. 1967, U.S. Supreme Ct. 1971. Asst. atty. gen. Dept. Law, State of Ga., Atlanta, 1971-72; dep. commr. Ga. Dept. Revenue, Atlanta, 1972-76; commr. Ga. Dept. Med. Assistance, Atlanta, 1976-79; sec. of state State of Ga., Atlanta, 1979-83; ptnr. Kutak Rock & Huie, Atlanta, 1983-84; pvt. practice Atlanta, 1984-86; exec. dir. Ga. Health Network, Atlanta, 1986-89; atty. Chilivis & Grindler, Atlanta, 1989-92; commr. Ga. Dept. Labor, Atlanta, 1992—. With USAF, 1967-71. Mem. State Bar Ga. Democrat. Methodist. Office: Labor Dept 148 Internat Blvd NE Ste 600 Atlanta GA 30303*

POZA, ERNESTO J., business consultant, educator; b. Havana, Cuba, Mar. 27, 1950; came to U.S., 1961; s. Hugo Ernesto and Carmen (Valle) P.; m. Karen Elizabeth Saum, Oct. 14, 1978; 1 child, Kali Jennette. BS in Adminstrv. Sci., Yale U., 1972; MS in Mgmt., MIT, 1974. Personnel mgr. rsch. Sherwin Williams Co., Chgo., 1974-75; orgn. specialist Sherwin Williams Co., Cleve., 1975-77, dir. orgn. planning, 1977-79; pres., sr. mgmt. cons. E.J. Poza Assoc., Cleve., 1979—; prof. Weatherhead Sch. Mgmt. Case We. Res. U., Cleve., 1996—; advisor Family Firm Inst., 1986; bd. dirs. several privately held firms; vis. lectr. Yale U., U. Chile, MIT, Sloan Sch. Mgmt. Author: Smart Growth: Critical Choices for Business Continuity and Prosperity, 1989, A la Sombra del Roble: La Empresa Privada Familiar y Su Continuidad, 1995; mem. editl. bd. Family Bus. REv., 1997—; contbr. articles to profl. jours. Bd. dirs. Neighborhood Health Care, 1980, Family Firm Inst., 1990; mem. program com. United Way, Cleve., 1985, Hispanic Leadership, 1986; founding mem. Family Firm Inst., 1985. Recipient Richard Beckhard Practice award Family Firm Inst., 1996. Mem. Acad. Mgmt. (entrepreneurship div., 1980—, orgn. devel. network, 1975—). Office: EJ Poza Assocs 37300 Jackson Rd Chagrin Falls OH 44022-1922

POZDRO, JOHN WALTER, music educator, composer; b. Chgo., Aug. 14, 1923; s. John and Rose Anna (Mossman) P.; m. Shirley Allison Winans, June 12, 1954; children—John Winans, Nancy Allison. B.M. in Music, Northwestern U.-Evanston, Ill., 1948, M.M. in Music, 1949; Ph.D. in Music, Eastman Sch. Music, 1958. Instr. Iowa State Tchrs. Coll., Cedar Falls, 1949-50; instr. to assoc. prof. U. Kans., Lawrence, 1950-64, prof. music, 1964—; dir. theory and composition U. Kans., 1961—; teaching fellow Eastman Sch. Music, Rochester, NY, 1956-57; chmn. symposium com. U. Kans., Lawrence, 1958-69. Representative works include Third Symphony, 1960, Piano Sonata No. 4, 1976, Malooley & Fear Monster, 1977, Impressions, Winds, Piano, 1984, Tryptich for Carillon, the Spirit of Mt. Oread, 1989. Winds of Autumn, 1996. Served with U.S. Army, 1943-46. Recipient U. Calif. Berkeley medal for Disting. Svc., 1993; grantee Ford Found., 1960, Nat. Endowment Arts, 1976; nominated for Pulitzer prize in Music, 1962. Mem. ASCAP (award 1965-96), Pi Kappa Lambda. Presbyterian. Avocations: golf; photography; reading. Home: 4700 Muirfield Dr Lawrence KS 66047-1820

POZEN, WALTER, lawyer; b. East Orange, N.J., Oct. 17, 1933; s. Irving Joseph and Berte (Protter) P.; m. Elizabeth Klupt, June 19, 1955 (div. 1967); children: Agatha Elizabeth, Jonathan Walter, Thorn Lord; m. Joan Kennan, Apr. 24, 1971 (div. Apr. 1988). B.A., U. Chgo., 1952, grad. student, 1952-53; J.D., 1956. Bar: Md. 1963. With Strasser, Spiegelberg, Fried & Frank, Washington and N.Y.C., 1956-58; mem. campaign staff Harrison A. Williams for U.S. Senator, 1958; legis. counsel Home Rule Com., Inc., Washington, 1959-60; counsel, assoc. dir. Fgn. Policy Clearing House, Washington, 1960-61; asst. to sec. interior, 1961-67; ptnr. Stroock & Stroock & Lavan, N.Y.C., 1967—, in charge Washington office; ofcl. rep. U.S. del. GATT Ministerial Meeting, Geneva, 1963; mem. Gov.'s Commn. on Historic Preservation, Md.; mem. D.C. Bd. Elections and Ethics.; del. Democratic Nat. Conv., 1964, counsel credentials com., 1968; counsel compliance rev. com. Dem. Nat. Com.; vis. prof. Irving B. Harris Sch. Pub. Policy Studies U. Chgo., 1993—. Author: (with Dr. J.H. Cerf) Strategy for the Sixties, 1960; also articles, book reviews. Bd. dirs. Nat. Symphony Orch.; mem. vis. com. Harris Sch. Pub. Policy Studies, U. Chgo. Mem. D.C. Bar Assn., Md. Bar Assn., Harmonie Club, Fed. City Club. Home: 3806 Klingle Pl NW Washington DC 20016-5433 also: PO Box 121 West Halifax VT 05358-0121 Office: Stroock & Stroock & Lavan 1150 17th St NW Ste 600 Washington DC 20036-4620

POZNANSKI, ANDREW KAROL, pediatric radiologist; b. Czestochowa, Poland, Oct. 11, 1931; came to U.S., 1957, naturalized, 1964; s. Edmund Maurycy and Hanna Maria (Ceranka) P.; children: Diana Jean, Suzanne Christine. B.Sc., McGill U., 1952, M.D.C.M., 1956. Diplomate: Am. Bd. Radiology, Royal Coll. Physicians and Surgeons Can. Intern Montreal (Que., Can.) Hosp., 1956-57; resident Henry Ford Hosp., Detroit, 1957-60; staff radiologist Henry Ford Hosp., 1960-68, U. Mich. Med. Center, Ann Arbor, 1968-79; co.-dir. pediatric radiology C.S. Mott Children's Hosp., Ann Arbor, 1971-79; radiologist-in-chief Children's Meml. Hosp., Chgo., 1979—; prof. radiology U. Mich., 1971-79, Northwestern U. Med. Sch., 1979—; bd. dirs. Nat. Coun. on Radiation Protection, 1983-90; mem. Internat. Commn. on Radiologic Protection, 1981-89; mem. adv. panel on radiologic devices FDA, 1975-77, chmn., 1976-77; trustee Am. Bd. Radiology, 1993—. Author: The Hand in Radiologic Diagnosis, 1974, 2d edit., 1983, Practical Approaches to Pediatric Radiology, 1976; bd. editors: Skeletal Radiology, 1975-95, Radiographics, 1980-84, Pediatric Radiology, 1986-91. Fellow Am. Coll. Radiology; mem. AMA, Am. Roentgen Ray Soc. (pres. 1993-94), Soc. Pediatric Radiology (pres. 1980-81), Radiol. Soc. N.Am., Assn. Univ. Radiologists, John Caffey Soc., Am. Assn. Phys. Anthropologists, Internat. Skeletal Soc. (founder, pres. 1992-94), Can. Assn. Radiologists (hon.), Polish Radiol. Soc. (hon.), Teratology Soc., Alpha Omega Alpha. Home: 2400 N Lakeview Ave Chicago IL 60614 Office: Childrens Meml Hosp 2300 N Childrens Plz Chicago IL 60614-3318

POZNIAKOFF, RITA OPPENHEIM, education software consultant; b. Munich, Nov. 19, 1949; (parents Am. citizens); d. Lester and Pearl Tobia (Waldman) Oppenheim; m. Theodore A. Pozniakoff, Dec. 29, 1985. BS, Cen. Mo. State U., 1973. Dept. mgr. Venture Dept. Stores div. May Co., St. Louis, 1973-75; dist. sales mgr. Seven Up Co., St. Louis, 1975-76; account exec. Christmas Club A Corp., Easton, Pa., 1976-83, Bankers Systems Inc., St. Cloud, Minn., 1983-85; edn. svcs. rep. Control Data Corp., Mpls., 1985-86; edn. specialist Radio Shack bus. products Tandy Corp., Ft. Worth, 1986-87, dist. govt. and edn. mktg. mgr., 1987-88, area edn. mktg. mgr., 1988-89; mgr. govt. accounts Grid Systems Corp. div. Tandy Corp., Parsippany, N.J., 1989; sr. account rep. N.Y.C. schs. Unisys Corp., White Plains, N.Y., 1989-90; mktg. mgr. N.Y. schs. Jostens Learning Corp., Phoenix, 1990-92, TRO Learning, Inc., Edina, Minn., 1993-96; govt. and edn. sales mgr. CompUSA, Inc., N.Y.C., 1996—. Republican. Home and Office: 7004 Boulevard East 3 1-C Guttenberg NJ 07093-5029

POZZATTI, RUDY OTTO, artist; b. Telluride, Colo., Jan. 14, 1925; s. Innocente and Mary L. (Mimiolla) P.; m. Dorothy I. Pozzatti, May 20, 1946; children—Valri Marie, Rudy Otto, Gina Maria, Mia Ines, Illica Lara. B.F.A., U. Colo., 1948, M.F.A., 1950, D.H.L., 1973. Mem. faculty dept. art U. Nebr., Lincoln, 1950-52, 53-56; mem. faculty dept. art Ind. U., Bloomington, 1956-91, prof. fine arts, 1964-91, disting. prof., 1975-91; ret., 1991; artist-in-residence Roswell Mus. and Art Ctr. One-man exhbns. include Cleve. Mus. Art, 1955, Whitney Mus. Am. Arts, N.Y.C., 1961, Tyler Sch. Art, Rome, 1969, Sheldon Meml. Art Gallery U. Nebr., 1969, Mitchell Mus. Art, Mt. Vernon, Ill., 4 other sites, 1992-93; represented in permanent collections, Mus. Modern Art, N.Y.C., Libr. Congress, Washington, Art Inst. Chgo., Cleve. Mus. Art. Served with AUS, 1943-46. Recipient George Norlin silver medal U. Colo., 1974; Fulbright grantee, 1952-53, 63-64, grantee U.S. Dept. State, USSR, 1961, Yugoslavia, 1965, Brazil, 1974, Hungary, 1986; grantee Rockefeller Found., Bellagio, Italy, 1995; Guggenheim fellow, 1963-64; Fellow Ford Found., 1963, grantee, Japan, 1981. Mem. Soc. Am. Graphic Artists, Am. Color Print Soc., Coll. Art Assn. (bd. dirs.), Artists Equity Assn., Ind. Acad. (elected). Roman Catholic.

P'POOL, GERALD W., retired manufacturing executive; b. Princeton, Ky., Mar. 1, 1933; s. Herbert Claude and Laura Lucille (Adams) P'P.; m. Peggy Simons (div. Sept. 1960); m. Jo Mercer; children: Deborah, Elisha, Jill. Student, Murray (Ky.) State U., 1951-52. Sales rep. Thomas Industries, Inc., Ky., Tenn., N.C. and Fla., 1956-62; mgr. div. Thomas Industries, Inc., Atlanta, 1964-71; mgr. merchandising Thomas Industries, Inc., Louisville, 1971-72, mgr. nat. sales, 1972-78; pres. Paint Applicators div. Thomas Industries, Inc., Johnson City, Tenn., 1978-81; v.p., group mgr., paint applicator, tool and fastener Benjamin Comml. & Indsl. Lighting Mfg., Johnson City, Tenn., 1981-83; sr. v.p. mktg. Thomas Industries, Inc., Louisville, 1983-84, exec. v.p., 1984-87, exec. v.p., mgr. light group, 1987-88. With USN, 1953-54. Avocations: hunting, fishing. Home: 317 S Jefferson St Princeton KY 42445-2111

PRABHAKAR, ARATI, federal administration research director, electrical engineer; b. New Delhi, Feb. 2, 1959; came to U.S., 1962; d. Jagdish Chandra and Raj (Madan) P. BSEE, Tex. Tech U., 1979; MSEE, Calif. Inst. Tech., 1980, PhD in Applied Physics, 1984; DEng (hon.), Rensselaer Poly. Inst., 1995. Congl. fellow Office Tech. Assessment U.S. Cong., Washington, 1984-86; program mgr. electronic sci. divsn. DARPA, Arlington, Va., 1986-90, dep. dir. defense sci. office, 1990-91, dir. microelectronics tech. office, 1991-93; dir. Nat. Inst. Stds. and Tech., Gaithersburg, Md., 1993-97. Contbr. articles to profl. jours. Rsch. fellow Calif. Inst. Tech., 1979-84, grad. rsch. program for women Bell Labs., 1979, 80; named Disting. Engr. of 1994, Tex. Tech. U.; elected to Tex. Tech. Elec. Engring. Acad., 1994; recipient Disting. Alumni award Calif. Inst. Tech., 1995. Fellow IEEE; mem. Eta Kappa Nu, Tau Beta Pi. Office: Raychem Corp US Dept of Commerce 300 Constitution Dr Menlo Park CA 94025-1140

PRABHUDESAI, MUKUND M., pathology educator, laboratory director, researcher, administrator; b. Lolyem, Goa, India, Mar. 17, 1942; came to U.S., 1967; s. Madhav R. and Kusum M. Prabhudesai; m. Sarita Mukund Usha, Feb. 1, 1972; 1 child, Nitin M. MB, BS (MD), G.S. Med., Bombay, 1967, postgrad., 1973-75. Diplomate Am. Bd. Pathology. Asst. pathologist Fordham Hosp., Bronx, N.Y., 1973-74, assoc. pathologist, 1974-76; assoc. dir. clin. pathology Lincoln Med., Bronx, 1976, dep. dir. pathology, 1977-79; chief pathology and lab. medicine svc., coord. R&D VA Med. Ctr., Danville, Ill., 1979—, dir. electron microscopy lab., 1987—; senator U. Ill. Chgo.; co-investigator U. Ill. Coll. Medicine, Urbana/Champaign, clin. assoc. prof. pathology and medicine Rsch., Rehab., Nutrition, Alcohol, 1982—. Contbr. articles to Am. Jour. Clin. Nutrition, Jour. AMA, Am. Jour. Clin. Pathology. Member Gifted Student Adv. Bd., Danville, 1984-86; v.p. Am. Cancer Soc. Vermilion County chpt., 1982, pres., 1986-88. VA rsch. grantee, 1980-82, 82-85, 83. Fellow Coll. Am. Pathology (inspector 1981—, Ill. state del. to C.A.P. Ho. Dels. 1992—, mem. reference com. 1993); mem. AAAS, Am. Coll. Physician Execs., Ill. State Soc. Pathologists (bd. dirs. 1990—, chmn. membership com. 1990—). Achievements include development of cancer of bladder following portocarval shunting; research in adverse effects of alcohol on lung structure and metabolism; on effects of soy and bran on cholesterol, endocrine response to soy protein, in induction and reversibility of atherosclerosis in trout, effects of ethanol on Vitamin A, lymphatics in atherosclerosis, iron in atherosclerosis, development of dermofluorometer for detection of P.V.D. Office: VA Med Ctr Pathology and Lab Med Svcs 1900 E Main St Danville IL 61832-5100

PRACHT, DRENDA KAY, psychologist; b. Carrollton, Mo., Jan. 15, 1952; d. Ethan Lyle Pracht and Wilma Esteleen (Henderson) Lucas; 1 child, Matthew Kent. BA in Psychology, William Jewell Coll., 1974; MS in Clinical Psychology, Cen. Mo. State U., 1976; postgrad. in clin. psychology, Fielding Inst., Santa Barbara, Calif., 1987—. Lic. psychologist, marriage and family therapist, Minn.; lic. psychologist, Mo., Minn. Therapist Briscoe Carr Cons., Kansas City, Mo., 1978-79; psychologist Crittenton Ctr., Kansas City, 1979-81, Cen. Minn. Mental Health Ctr., St. Cloud, 1981-85, St. Cloud Hosp., 1985-87; gen. practice psychology St. Cloud, 1985-92, Kansas City, 1992—; cons. St. Benedicts Ctr., Country Manor, 1986-92. Mem. Cen. Minn. Child Abuse Team, St. Cloud, 1981-85; bd. dirs. Cen. Minn. Child Care Assn., St. Cloud, 1982-83. Mem. Am. Psychol. Assn., Cen. Minn. Psychol. Assn. (pres. 1984-85), Minn. Lic. Psychologists, Minn. Psychol. Assn., Alpha Delta Pi Aumni Assn. Presbyterian. Avocations: piano, needlework, reading, arts and crafts.

PRADA, GLORIA INES, mathematics and Spanish language educator; b. San Vicente de Chucuri, Colombia, Dec. 2, 1954; came to U.S., 1985; d. Roberto Gomez and Maria Celina (Serrano) Duran; m. Luis Eduardo Prada, June 19, 1975; children: Luis Ricardo, Nicholas. BS in Math., U. Indsl., Santander, Colombia, 1978. Tchr. h.s. math. Santander Sch. Dist., Bucaramanga, 1973-84; tchr. mid. sch. math., mentor tchr. Hayward (Calif.) Unified Sch. Dist., 1989—; pres. Bilingual Adv. Com., Hayward, 1986-89; mem. Gate Task Force, Hayward, 1990-93, Spanish for Educators Alameda County Office Edn., 1995—. Author: Prada's Spanish Course, 1992, Family Math, 1992, Stations on Probabilities, 1994, (math. replacement unit) Success, 1994. Office: Hayward Unified Dist Winton 119 Winton Ave Hayward CA 94544-1413

PRADO, EDWARD CHARLES, federal judge; b. San Antonio, June 7, 1947; s. Edward L. and Bertha (Cadena) P.; m. Maria Anita Jung, Nov. 10, 1973; 1 child, Edward C. AA, San Antonio Coll., 1967; BA, U. Tex., 1969, JD, 1972. Bar: Tex. 1972. Asst. dist. atty. Bexar County Dist. Atty.'s Office, San Antonio, 1972-76; asst. pub. defender U.S. Pub. Defender's Office, San Antonio, 1976-80; judge U.S. Dist. Ct. Tex., San Antonio, 1980; U.S. atty. Dept. Justice, San Antonio, 1980-85; judge U.S. Dist. Ct. (we. dist.) Tex., 1984—. Served to capt. U.S. Army. Named Outstanding Young Lawyer of Bexar County, 1980. Mem. ABA, Tex. Bar Assn., San Antonio Bar Assn., San Antonio Young Lawyers Assn., Fed. Bar Assn. Republican. Roman Catholic. Office: US Courthouse 655 E Durango Blvd San Antonio TX 78206-1102*

PRADO, GERALD M., investment banker; b. Langeloth, Pa., Jan. 19, 1946; s. Caesar S. and Anita A. P.; m. Judith A. Pompe, May 20, 1967; children—Dennis, Eric, Lynn, Christopher. B.A., Washington and Jefferson Coll., 1963-67; M.B.A., U. Pitts., 1983. Sr. acct. Haskins and Sells, Pitts., 1967-72; auditor G.C. Murphy Co., McKeesport, Pa., 1972-76, asst. controller, 1976-78, treas., 1979-80, asst. v.p., treas., 1980-82, v.p., treas., 1982-85; v.p., treas. Russell, Rea & Zappala, Pitts., 1986-87, sr. v.p., 1987-90; pres. Westinghouse Mcht. Banking, Inc., Pitts., 1990-94; prin., co-mgr. Main St. Capital Holdings L.L.C., Pitts., 1994—. Mem. Pa. Inst. CPAs, AICPA, Washington and Jefferson Alumni Assn., Fin. Execs. Inst. Roman Catholic. Home: 205 Overlook Dr McMurray PA 15317-2657 Office: Main St Capital Holdings LLC 135 Technology Dr Ste 501 Canonsburg PA 15317-9549

PRADY, NORMAN, journalist, advertising executive, writer, marketing consultant; b. Detroit, Sept. 19, 1933; s. Calvin and Mildred Prady; m. Susan Frank, July 5, 1959 (div. Nov. 1991); children: William Scott, Anne Elizabeth Prady Sheehan. Student, Wayne State U., 1951-53, Fordham U., 1952. Reporter, feature writer Detroit Times, 1955-60; writer various advt. agys. Detroit, 1960-65, creative dir. various advt. agys., 1965-80; exec. v.p., creative dir., prin. Stone, August & Co., Birmingham, Mich., 1980-84; pres. The Norman Prady Co., Farmington Hills, 1985—; editor, pub. The Riverside Journal, Farmington Hills, 1995—. Contbr. features various newspapers and mags. Bd. dirs. ARC, Detroit, 1983—, exec. com., 1987—, vice-chmn. pub. affairs com., 1986—, fin. devel. com., 1987—.

PRAETORIUS, WILLIAM ALBERT, SR., artist, former advertising and real estate executive; b. Forty-Fort, Pa., Oct. 7, 1924; s. George Albert and Elizabeth (Madden) P.; m. Theresa M. Barnes, June 25, 1949; children: Kathleen Ann, William Albert, Gregg Douglas. Student, Biarittz (France) Am. U., 1945-46, N.Y. U., 1947-48. With L.W. Frohlich Intercon Internat., Inc., 1946-72, sr. v.p., dir. ops., 1969-71, chmn. operating com., 1972; sr. v.p., dir. ops. Deltakos div. J. Walter Thompson Co., N.Y.C., 1972-73; sr. v.p. adminstrn. J.W.T. Affiliated Cos., 1973-75; pres. Healthmark Communications, Inc., N.Y.C., 1975-77; dir. Clause Comml. div. Donald J. Clause, Southampton, N.Y., 1977-78; dir. comml. div. Meadow Real Estate, 1978-86; artist, 1987—. Author, pub.: Concepts in Leadership, 1982; contbr. column to East End Bus. Rev, articles to profl. jours; exhbns. of paintings include East Hampton Town Hall, Edwin Winfield Gallery, Sag Harbor, Guild Hall, East Hampton. Served with AUS, 1943-46. Mem. Barnes Landing Assn. Democrat. Catholic. Home and Studio: 30 Captains Walk East Hampton NY 11937-3169

PRAGER, ALICE HEINECKE, music company executive; b. N.Y.C., Aug. 2, 1930; d. Paul and Ruth (Collin) Heinecke; m. George L. Drescher, 1963. BA, Russell Sage Coll., 1951; postgrad., NYU, 1952-55. V.p. SESAC Inc., N.Y.C., 1956-73, pres., 1973-78, pres., chmn. bd., 1978-92; chmn. bd. Personal Touch, Inc. Mem. Internat. Radio and TV Soc., Am. Inst. of Mgmt., Nat. Acad. Recording Arts and Scis., Country Music Assn. (bd. dirs., 1986, life), Gospel Music Assn. Office: The Personal Touch Inc 68-34 Fleet St Forest Hills NY 11375-5051

PRAGER, DAVID, retired state supreme court chief justice; b. Ft. Scott, Kans., Oct. 30, 1918; s. Walter and Helen (Kishler) P.; m. Dorothy Schroeter, Sept. 8, 1945; children: Diane, David III. AB, U. Kans., 1939, JD, 1942. Bar: Kans. 1942. Practiced in Topeka, 1946-59; dist. judge Shawnee County (Kans.) Dist. Ct., 1959-71; assoc. justice Kans. Supreme Ct., Topeka, 1971-87, chief justice, 1987-88; ret., 1988; lectr. Washburn Law Sch., 1948-68. Served to lt. USNR, 1942-46, ETO, PTO. Mem. Kans. Dist. Judges Assn. (past pres.), Order of Coif, Phi Beta Kappa, Phi Delta Theta, Lions Lodge, Arab Shrine Lodge.

PRAGER, ELLIOT DAVID, surgeon, educator; b. N.Y.C., Sept. 10, 1941; s. Benjamin and Sadye Zelda (Newman) P.; m. Phyllis Damon Warner, July 1, 1967; children: Rebecca, Sarah, Katherine. AB, Dartmouth Coll., 1962; MD, Harvard U., 1966. Diplomate Am. Bd. Surgery, Am. Bd. Colon and Rectal Surgery. Surg. resident Roosevelt Hosp., N.Y.C., 1966-71; colon-rectal fellow Lahey Clinic, Boston, 1971-72; staff surgeon Sansum Clinic, Santa Barbara, Calif., 1974—; dir. colorectal fellowship Sansum Clinic, Santa Barbara, 1982—, chief of surgery, 1986-94; dir. surg. edn. Cottage Hosp., Santa Barbara, 1994—; mem., vice chair Residency Rev. Com., 1992—. Author: (with others) Operative Colorectal Surgery, 1994, Current Therapy in Colon and Rectal Surgery, 1990; contbr. articles to profl. jours. Lt. comdr. USN, 1972-74. Fellow Am. Coll. Surgeons (adv. coun. 1992—), Am. Soc. of Colon and Rectal Surgeons (v.p. 1992, sec. of program dirs., 1990—). Achievements include 5 patents for colostomy control devices. Office: Sansum Clinic 317 W Pueblo St Santa Barbara CA 93105-4355

PRAGER, STEPHEN, chemistry educator; b. Darmstadt, Germany, July 20, 1928; came to U.S., 1941, naturalized, 1950; s. William and Gertrude Ann (Heyer) P.; m. Julianne Heller, June 7, 1948. B.Sc., Brown, 1947; Ph.D., Cornell, 1951. Mem. faculty U. Minn., Mpls., 1952—, assoc. prof. chemistry, 1956-62, prof., 1962-90, prof. emeritus, 1990—; Cons. Union Carbide Corp., Oak Ridge, 1954-74. Asso. editor: Jour. Phys. Chemistry, 1970-79. Fulbright scholar and Guggenheim fellow, 1958, 59; Fulbright lectr. and Guggenheim fellow, 1966-67. Mem. Am. Chem. Soc., Am. Phys. Soc. Home: 3320 Dunlap St N Saint Paul MN 55112-3709 Office: Chemistry Dept U Minn Minneapolis MN 55455

PRAGER, SUSAN WESTERBERG, dean, law educator; b. Sacramento, Dec. 14, 1942; d. Percy Foster Westerberg and Aileen M. (McKinley) P.; m. James Martin Prager, Dec. 14, 1973; children: McKinley Ann, Case Mahone. AB, Stanford U., 1964, MA, 1967; JD, UCLA, 1971. Bar: N.C. 1971, Calif. 1972. Atty. Powe, Porter & Alphin, Durham, N.C., 1971-72; acting prof. law UCLA, 1972-77, prof. Sch. Law, 1977—, Arjay and Frances Fearing Miller prof. of law, 1992—, assoc. dean Sch. Law, 1979-82, dean, 1982—; bd. dirs. Pacific Mut. Life Ins. Co., Newport Beach, Calif. Editor-in-chief, UCLA Law Rev., 1970-71. Trustee Stanford U., 1976-80, 87—. Mem. ABA (council of sect. on legal edn. and admissions to the bar 1983-85), Assn. Am. Law Schs. (pres. 1986), Order of Coif. Office: UCLA Sch Law Box 951476 Los Angeles CA 90095-1476*

PRAH, PAMELA MARIE, journalist; b. Latrobe, Pa., June 22, 1963; d. Lonnie Joseph and Eleanor Ruth (Stefl) P. BS in Journalism, Ohio U., 1985. Assoc. editor McGraw-Hill Pub., Washington, 1986-87; editor Internat. Pubs., Washington, 1987—; staff editor Bur. Nat. Affairs, Washington, 1989-91, 93—; spl. corr. Bur. Nat. Affairs, Heidelberg, Germany, 1991-92; intern 13-30 Pub. Co., Knoxville, Tenn., 1985, Tribune Rev., Greensburg, Pa., 1985, McGraw-Hill World News, London, 1985; editor Athens Mags., 1985, mng. editor, 1984, The Awakening, 1985. Scholar Ohio U., Athens, 1981-85. Mem. Soc. Profl. Jounalists (Washington chpt.), Women Communications, Kappa Tau Alpha. Roman Catholic. Avocations: tennis, reading, theater, travel. Home: # 336 3100 Connecticut Ave NW Washington DC 20008-1419

PRAIRIE, CELIA ESTHER FREDA, biochemistry educator; b. Buenos Aires, Sept. 30, 1940; came to U.S., 1963; d. Rafael Emilio A. and Celia Esther (Seijo) Freda; m. James Roland Prairie, Sept. 19, 1970; children: James Roger, Caryn Elizabeth. BS, U. Buenos Aires, 1961, MS, 1963; PhD, U. Pa., 1967. Fellow Nat. Rsch. Inst., Buenos Aires, 1961-63; rsch. assoc. dept. therapeutic rsch. U. Pa., Phila., 1967-70; postdoctoral rsch. assoc. Lab. Molecular Embryology, Arco Felice, Naples, Italy, 1970; lectr. biology and chemistry depts. Holy Family Coll., Phila., 1974-75, asst. prof. biology dept., 1975-80, assoc. prof., 1980-85, prof. biochemistry, 1985—, chmn. dept. natural scis. and math., 1986-88, acting chmn. biology dept., 1982-86; sr. teaching staff assoc. Marine Biol. Lab., Woods Hole, Mass., 1968-69. Contbr. articles to profl. jours. Bd. dirs. Lower Bucks County Community Ctr., 1970—. Fellow USPHS, 1963-65, U. Pa., 1965-66, Am. Coun. Edn. and Fund for the Improvement of Post Sec. Edn., 1983-84. Mem. AAAS, Nat. Sci. Tchrs. Assn., Am. Inst. Biol. Scis., N.Y. Acad. Scis., Sigma Xi, World Federalist Assn. Democrat. Mem. Religious Soc. of Friends. Avocations: aerobics, yoga, swimming. Home: 31 Fullturn Rd Levittown PA 19056-1924 Office: Holy Family Coll Frankford and Grant Ave Philadelphia PA 19114-2094

PRAKAPAS, EUGENE JOSEPH, art gallery director; b. Lowell, Mass., July 29, 1932; s. Joseph S. Prakapas and Viola Schensnol; m. Dorothy A. Seitner, Dec. 1, 1971. BA, Yale U., 1953; MA, Oxford U., Balliol, 1959. Editor-in-chief, v.p. Trident Press and Pocket Books divsn. Simon & Schuster, Inc., N.Y.C., 1960-70; co-dir. Carus Gallery, N.Y.C., 1973-75; dir. Prakapas Gallery, N.Y.C., 1976—; vis. curator San Francisco Mus. Modern Art, 1986. Author: Bauhaus Photography, 1985. Lt. (s.g.) USNR, 1953-57. Fulbright fellow, 1957-59; Yale U. scholar, 1949-53. Mem. Art Dealers Assn. Am., Assn. Internat. Photography Art Dealers.

PRAKASH, SATYA, biology educator; b. Pilkhuwa, U.P., India, July 8, 1938; came to U.S., 1962; s. Suraj Bali and Atar Kali; m. Louise Burlant; children: Ulka, Ravi, Anita, Sarita. PhD, Washington U., St. Louis, 1966. Asst. prof. biology U. Rochester, N.Y., 1969-74, assoc. prof., 1974-80, prof., 1980-93; prof. U. Tex. Med. Branch, Galveston, 1993—. NIH grantee, 1972—. Mem. Genetics Soc. Am., Am. Soc. Biochemistry and Molecular Biology. Hindu. Office: U Tex Med Branch Sealy Ctr Molecular Sci Galveston TX 77555

PRAMER, DAVID, microbiologist, educator, research administrator; b. Mt. Vernon, N.Y., Mar. 25, 1923; s. Coleman and Ethel (Toback) P.; m. Rhoda Lifschutz, Sept. 6, 1950; children—Andrew, Stacey. Student, St. John's U., 1940, Tex. A&M Coll., 1941; B.S. cum laude, Rutgers U., 1948, Ph.D., 1952. Vis. investigator Butterwich Research Labs., Welwyn, Eng., 1952-54; from asst. to assoc. prof. microbiology Rutgers U., New Brunswick, N.J., 1954-60; prof. Rutgers U., 1960-67, disting. prof., 1967—, dir. biological scis., 1969-73, dir. univ. research, 1973-75, assoc. v.p. research, 1973-80; dir. Waksman Inst. Microbiology, 1980-88, assoc. v.p. corp. liaison, 1988-93; exec. asst. and disting. prof. emeritus, exec. asst. Rutgers U., New Brunswick, N.J., 1993—; cons. various fed. agys., 1965—; dir. New Brunswick Sci. Co., Edison, R&D Coun. of N.J., Nanodyne, Inc., New Brunswick, Organica, Inc., Great Neck, N.Y.; served on numerous chmn., com. and adv. posts. Author: Life in the Soil, 1964, Experimental Soil Microbiology, 1965, The Microbes, 1971, Engineered Organisms in the Environment, 1985; also over 250 articles in profl. jours.; regional editor World Jour. Soil and Biology and Biochemistry; mem. editl. bd. Soil Sci., BioSci., Applied Microbiology and Biotech. Bd. dirs. Library, Highland Park, N.J., 1966-75, chmn., 1976-78; committeeman Democratic Party, Highland Park, 1958-66. Served to cpl. USAF, 1943-46. Fulbright-Hays Sr. Research fellow, 1969. Fellow Am. Acad. Microbiology; mem. Am. Soc. Microbiology, Internat. Commn. Microbial Ecology (chmn.), Internat. Cell Rsch. Orgn., Phi Beta Kappa, Alpha Zeta, Sigma Xi. Jewish. Avocations: jogging, travel. Home: 208 Hampshire Ct Piscataway NJ 08854-6218 Office: Rutgers Univ Office Rsch & Sponsored Programs Adminstrv Svc Bldg Annex II Piscataway NJ 08855-1179

PRAN, DITH, photographer, social activist; b. Cambodia, Sept. 27, 1942; arrived in the U.S., 1979; s. Dith Proeung and Meak Ep; m. Ser Moeun; children: Hemkary, Titonel, Titonath, Titony. Grad. high sch., Cambodia, 1960. Translator U.S. Mil. Assistance Command, 1962-65; asst. to Sydney Schanberg, 1972-76; adminstr. Siem Reap, 1979; apprentice photographer N.Y. Times, 1979-80, photographer, 1980—; advocate Cambodian people, 1984—; goodwill amb. UN; lectr. in field; participant Cambodian Genocide program U.S. Dept. State; mem. Cambodian Documentation Commn. Office: NY Times Photo Desk 229 W 43rd St New York NY 10036-3913

PRANGE, ARTHUR JERGEN, JR., psychiatrist, neurobiologist, educator; b. Grand Rapids, Mich., Sept. 19, 1926; s. Arthur Jergen and Martha Frances (Elliott) P.; m. Sarah Elizabeth Bowen, Feb. 4, 1950; children—Christine Anne, Martha Louise, Laura Beth, David Elliott. B.S., U. Mich., 1947, M.D., 1950. Intern Wayne County Gen. Hosp., Eloise, Mich., 1950-51; resident in psychiatry U. N.C., Chapel Hill, 1954-57; instr. U. N.C., 1957-60, asst. prof., 1960-64, asso. prof., 1964-68, prof. psychiatry, 1968-83, Boshamer prof. psychiatry, 1983—, acting chmn. dept. psychiatry, 1983-85, dir. NIMH Clin. Rsch. Ctr., 1979—; vis. scientist Med. Rsch. Coun. Unit, Epson, Surrey, Eng., 1968-69; chmn. clin. projects rsch. rev. com. HEW, NIMH, 1975-76, chmn. bd. sci. counselors, 1986-87; mem. psychopharmacologic drugs adv. com. HEW, FDA, 1979-82. Editor: The Thyroid Axis, Drugs and Behavior, 74; Contbr. articles to med. jours. Recipient NIMH Career Devel. award 1961-69, Career Scientist award, 1969-95, Gold Medal award Soc. of Biol. Psychiatry, 1992. Fellow Am. Psychiat. Assn. (life, Rsch. in Psychiatry award 1996), Am. Coll. Neuropsychopharmacology (life, pres. 1987, Hoch award 1995); mem. Internat. Soc. Psychoneuroendocrinology (founding mem.), N.C. Neuropsychiat. Assn., Collegium Internationale Neuropsychopharmacologicum, Royal Coll. Psychiatrists (London). Home: 218-6 Conner Dr Chapel Hill NC 27514-7070 Office: Univ NC Sch Medicine Dept Psychiatry Chapel Hill NC 27599-7160

PRANGE, HILMAR WALTER, neurology educator; b. Reichenbach/Eule, Silesia, Germany, Aug. 4, 1944; s. Georg Friedrich Reinhold and Gertrud Wilhelmine (Mueller) P.; m. Carin Juliane Schroeter, Mar. 14, 1970; children: Klaus Richard, Juliane. MD, U. Rostock, Germany, 1969, lic. specialist neurology and psychiatry, 1974; Habilitation, Georg-August U., Goettingen, Germany, 1982. Med. diplomate. Med. resident Regional Hosp., Stralsund, Germany, 1969-71; med. asst. then psychiatrist Univ. Hosp., Rostock, 1971-75; asst. med. dir. Ev. Johannes Hosp., Bielefeld, Germany, 1975-76; head neurologic out-patient clinic Univ. Hosp., Goettingen, Germany, 1976-78, asst. med. dir. dept. neurology, 1979-87, dir. neurological intensive care unit, 1987—. Author: Neurosyphilis, 1987, Infectious Diseases of the Central Nervous System, 1995; editor: CNS Barriers and Modern CSF Diagnostics, 1993; contbr. articles to profl. jours. Grantee Deutsche Forschungsgemeinschaft, German MS Soc. Mem. European Neurological Soc., German Med. Assn. (mem. commn. drug security), European Fedn. Neurological Socs. (sec. scientist panel of infectiology). Lutheran. Avocations: cultural history, sports, jogging, swimming, squash.

PRANGE, ROY LEONARD, JR., lawyer; b. Chgo., Sept. 12, 1945; s. Roy Leonard and Marjorie Rose (Kauppi) P.; m. Carol Lynn Poels, June 5, 1971; children: David, Ellen, Susan. BA, U. Iowa, 1967; MA, Ohio State U., 1968; JD, U. Wis.-Madison, 1975. Bar: Wis. 1975, U.S. Dist. Ct. (we. and ea. dists.) Wis. 1975, U.S. Ct. Appeals (7th cir.) 1978, U.S. Supreme Ct. 1978. Assoc. Ross & Stevens, Svc. Corp., Madison, Wis., 1975-79; ptnr. Ross & Stevens, Svc. Corp., 1979-90, Quarles & Brady, Madison, 1990—; lectr. bankruptcy, debtor-creditor rights, U. Wis., Madison, 1982—. Contbr. Wis. Lawyer's Desk Reference Manual, 1987, Comml. Litigation in Wis. Practice Handbook, 1995. 1st lt. U.S. Army, 1969-72. Fellow Am. Coll. Bankruptcy; mem. ABA, Wis. State Bar (dir. bankruptcy, insolvency, creditors rights sect. 1985-91, chair 1990-92, mem. continuing legal edn. com. 1990-95), Am. Bankruptcy Inst., Dickens Fellowship (v.p. 1980-84). Avocations: running, soccer, karate, golf. Office: Quarles & Brady PO Box 2113 1 S Pinckney St Madison WI 53703

PRANSES, ANTHONY LOUIS, retired electric company executive, organization executive; b. Claracq, France, May 3, 1920; s. Anthony Kasimer and Georgette (Pilon) F.; m. Margaret Louise Hamill, July 24, 1943; children—Anthony Randolph, Terry Jay, Renee Louise. Student, Sorbonne, Paris, France, 1937-39; B.S. in Metall. Engring, Carnegie Inst. Tech., 1942, grad. student, 1946-48. With Westinghouse Electric Corp., 1945-86; mgr. mfg. planning Westinghouse Electric Corp., Lima, Ohio, 1954-57; plant mgr. Westinghouse Electric Corp., Lima, 1958-59, mgr. mfg. services, 1959-72; mgr. mfg. Westinghouse Electric Corp., 1972-80, cons., 1980-86. Joined Am. Youth Hostels, 1935, founder Pitts. council, 1947, pres. council, 1947-50, mem. nat. bd. dirs., 1954-72, Midwest regional v.p., 1957-59, nat. pres., 1959-62, pres. Lima council, 1962-75, 87-91, chmn. nat. bd. dirs., 1963-67. Served to capt., C.E. AUS, 1942- 45. Home: Rural Route 2 6005 Poling Rd Lima OH 45807-9492

PRASAD, ANANDA SHIVA, medical educator; b. Buxar, Bihar, India, Jan. 1, 1928; came to U.S., 1952, naturalized, 1968; s. Radha Krishna and Mahesha (Kaur) Lall; m. Aryabala Ray, Jan. 6, 1952; children: Rita, Sheila, Ashok, Audrey. BSc, Patna (India) Sci. Coll., 1946, MB, BChir, 1951; PhD, U. Minn., 1957. Intern Patna Med. Coll. Hosp., 1951-52; resident St. Paul's Hosp., Dallas, 1952-53, U. Minn., 1953-56, VA Hosp., Mpls., 1956; instr. dept. medicine Univ. Hosp., U. Minn., Mpls., 1957-58; vis. assoc. prof. medicine Shiraz Med. Faculty, Nemazee Hosp., Shiraz, Iran, 1960; asst. prof. medicine and nutrition Vanderbilt U., 1961-63; mem. faculty, dir. div. hematology dept. medicine Wayne State U., Detroit, 1963-84; assoc. prof. Wayne State U., 1964-68, prof., 1968—, dir. research dept. medicine, 1984—; mem. staff Harper-Grace Hosp., VA Hosp., Allen Park, Mich.; mem. trace elements subcom. Food and Nutrition Bd., NRC-Nat. Acad. Scis., 1965-68; chmn. trace elements com. Internat. Union Nutritional Scis.; mem. Am. Bd. Nutrition; pres. Am. Coll. Nutrition, 1991-93. Author: Zinc Metabolism, 1966, Trace Elements in Human Health and Disease, 1976, Trace Elements and Iron in Human Metabolism, 1978, Zinc in Human Nutrition, 1979, Biochemistry of Zinc, 1993; editor: Clinical, Biochemical and Nutritional Aspects of Trace Elements, 1982, Am. Jour. Hematology, Jour. Trace Elements in Exptl. Medicine; editor: Zinc Metabolism, Current Aspects in Health and Disease, 1977; co-editor: Clinical Applications of Recent Advances in Zinc Metabolism, 1982, Zinc Deficiency in Human Subjects, 1983, Essential and Toxic Trace Elements in Human Health and Disease, 1988, Essential and Toxic Trace Elements in Human Health and Disease: An Update, 1993; mem. editorial bd. Jour. Micro Nutrient Analysis, Jour. Am. Coll. Nutrition; contbr. articles to profl. jours., also reviewer. Trustee Detroit Internat. Inst., Detroit Gen. Hosp. Research Corp., 1969-72. Recipient Rsch. Recognition award Wayne State U., 1964, award Am. Coll. Nutrition, 1976, Disting. Faculty Fellowship award Wayne State U., 1986, Acad. Scholars, Wayne State U., 1992, Medal of Honor, City of Lyon, France, 1989; Pfizer scholar, 1955-56. Master Am. Coll. Nutrition; fellow ACP (recipient Mich. Laureate award), AAAS, Am. Inst. Nutrition, Internat. Soc. Hematology; mem. AMA (Goldberger award 1975), Internat. Soc. Trace Element Rsch. in Humans (pres. 1986-92, chmn. steering com. 1985-86, Raulin award 1989), Am. Soc. Clin. Nutrition (awards com. 1969-70), Am. Fedn. Clin. Rsch. (pres. Mich. 1969-70), Am. Inst. Nutrition (trace elements panel), Am. Physiol. Soc. Am. Soc. Clin. Investigation, Am. Soc. Hematology, Assn. Am. Physicians, Ctrl. Soc. Clin. Rsch., Soc. Exptl. Biology and Medicine (Councillor Mich. 1967-71), Wayne County Med. Soc., Internat. Soc. Internal Medicine, Am. Soc. Clin. Nutrition (Robert H. Herman award 1984), Nutrition Soc. India (Gopalan oration award 1988), Cosmos Club (Washington), Sigma Xi. Home: 4710 Cove Rd Orchard Lake MI 48323-3604 Office: Univ Health Ctr 5-C 4201 Saint Antoine St Detroit MI 48201-2153

PRASIL, LINDA ANN, lawyer, writer; b. Chgo., July 27, 1947; d. Joseph J. and Helen Marie (Palucki) P.; m. John T. Rank, July 25, 1970; 1 child, Sean Patrick Prasil Rank. BA in Interdisciplinary Studies, Am. U., Washington, 1974, JD, 1977; MALS, Mundelein Coll., Chgo., 1992. Bar: Ill. 1977. Ind. contractor Baker & McKenzie, Chgo., 1977-78; atty. Pretzel, Stouffer, Nolan & Rooney, Chgo., 1978-79; sole practitioner Lincolnshire, Ill., 1979—; atty. Leonard M. Ring, Chgo., 1982; grader Ill. State Bar Examiners, Chgo., 1978-90; organizer Kennedy for Pres., Chgo., 1979-80, NOW-ERA Ill., Chgo., 1980, Ill. Polit. Action Com., Chgo., 1981. Legal advisor Holy Cross Talk of Town, Deerfield, Ill., 1992-97; tchr. Holy Cross Drug Awareness Program, Deerfield, 1993-94; religious tchr. Holy Cross, Deerfield, 1983-86; chair Northbrook Caucus Com., 1982-83; mem. Citizens' Task Force for Edens-Clavey Rd. Legis. Adv. Com., 1983. Mem. Ill. State Bar Assn., Internat. Alliance of Holistic Lawyers. Avocations: painting, reading, art projects. Office: 35 Keswick Ct Lincolnshire IL 60069-3425

PRATER-FIPPS, EUNICE KAY, educational administrator; b. Cleve., Aug. 22, 1949; d. Jesse and Bertha (McCollum) Prater; m. Theodis Fipps, Apr. 13, 1990. BS, Kent State U., 1974; MEd, Cleve. State U., 1978. Cert. tchr., secondary prin., Ohio. Tchr. bus. edn. Cleve. Pub. Schs., 1974-80, adminstrv. intern, 1980-83, asst. prin., 1983—. Mem. ASCD, Ohio Assn. Secondary Sch. Adminstrs., Cleve. Coun. Adminstrs. and Suprs. Avocations: travel, reading, outdoor activities. Home: 565 Cynthia Ct Richmond Hts OH 44143-2949 Office: Cleve Pub Schs 1380 E 6th St Cleveland OH 44114-1606

PRATHER, DONNA LYNN, psychiatrist; b. Charlotte, N.C., Nov. 4, 1946; d. James Boyd and Ann (Joyner) P. BA, Queens Coll., Charlotte, 1968; MD, U. N.C., 1978. Supr. Meckenburg County Dept. Social Svcs., Charlotte, 1971-74; family practice intern Charlotte Meml. Hosp., 1978-79, resident in family practice, 1979-81; fellow in family medicine U. N.C., Chapel Hill, 1981-82; resident in psychiatry N.C. Meml. Hosp., Chapel Hill, 1982-85; pvt. practice psychiatry Chapel Hill, N.C., 1985—; psychiatrist Person Counceling Ctr., Roxboro, N.C., 1983-92; med. dir. Orange-person-Chatam Mental Health Ctr., Chapel Hill, 1992—; clin. assoc. prof. U. N.C., Chapel Hill, 1985—. Mem. N.C. Psychiat. Assn., N.C. Med. Soc., Am. Psychiat. Assn., N.C. Psychiat. Assn. (chmn., com. for women 1990-91). Avocation: music. Office: The Courtyard Ste 27 Chapel Hill NC 27516-2319

PRATHER, GERALD LUTHER, management consultant, retired air force officer, judge; b. LaGrange, Ga., Apr. 7, 1935; s. Luther Pate and Hazel Belle (McCullough) P.; m. Carolyn Pearson, Nov. 22, 1956; children—Dean Allen, Bryan Pate, Jeri Lynn, Angela. BS.E.E., Auburn U., 1966; M.S. in Mgmt., Air Force Inst. Tech., 1972; postgrad. advanced mgmt., U. Houston, 1978; grad., SQ Officer Sch., Maxwell AFB, 1963, ICAF, Washington, 1974. Enlisted USAF, 1954-56, commd. 2d lt., 1956, advanced through grades to maj. gen., 1981, various assignments as pilot, 1956-68, served in Vietnam, 1967-68; commdr. 1963d Comm. Squadron USAF, Chanute AFB, Ill., 1968-69; comdr. 1918th Comm. Squadron USAF, Scott AFB, Ill., 1969-70; dep. dir. comm.-electronics for 15th Air Force USAF, March AFB, Calif., 1970-72; chief comm. ops. div. hdqrs. USAF, Washington, 1972-75; comdr. strategic comm. div. USAF, Offutt AFB, Nebr., 1975-77; comdr. European Comm. Div. USAF, Ramstein AFB, W. Ger., 1977-80; dir. Command Control, Comm. & Computer Systems, Hdqrs. U.S. Readiness Command USAF, MacDill AFB, Fla., 1980-81; asst. chief of staff of Info. Systems Hdqrs. USAF, Washington, 1981-84; comdr. Air Force Comm. Command USAF, Scott AFB, Ill., 1984-86; ret. USAF, 1986; pvt. practice mgmt. cons. Del Rio, Tex., 1986—; Justice of the Peace Val Verde County, Tex.; lectr. in field; also air traffic controller, parachutist. speech writer Team America 1983 (Freedom Found. nat. award 1984). Scout master Boy Scouts Am., Sacramento, 1963, chmn. com., Sacramento, 1964, cub master, Auburn, Ala., 1965; sponsor Explorer Troop, Boy Scouts Am., Scott AFB, Ill., 1969; alumni Boy Scouts Am., 1984-85; chmn. Amistad Dist. Boy Scouts Am., 1988, chmn. Eagle Scout advancement 1994-96; chmn. Val Verde County United Way campaign, 1989, pres., bd.dirs., 1990. Decorated DSM with oak leaf cluster, Legion of Merit with one oak leaf cluster, DFC, Bronze Star with V device, Air medal with two oak leaf clusters, Republic of Vietnam Gallantry Cross with Palm; recipient Gen. Edwin W. Rawlings award Air Force Inst. Tech., 1972, Comdt.'s award, 1972, also numerous other decorations and awards. Mem. VFW (life), Armed Forces Comm.-Electronics Assn. (assoc. dir. 1984—, internat. v.p. 1982-84, chmn. ethics com. 1982-83, mem. com. 1981-82, Meritorious Gold medal 1976, 83), Air Traffic Control Assn., Soc. Am. Mil. Engrs., Justice of the Peace and Constables Assn., Soc. Logistics Engrs., Telephone Pioneers of Am., Air Force Assn., Air Force Sgts. Assn. (hon.), Non-Commd. Officers Assn. (hon.)m Vietnam Vets. of Am., Ret. Officers Assn., Del Rio C. of C. (bd. dirs. 1990-91, 95-96, v.p. 1991-92, 95-96, pres. 1997), Order of Daedalians, Am. Legion, Lions, Civitan, Del Rio Club (v.p. 1989-90). Avocations: gardening, racquetball, sketching, automotive mechanics, private pilot. Address: HCR 1 Box 7 Del Rio TX 78840-9718

PRATHER, JOHN GIDEON, JR., lawyer; b. Lexington, Ky., Sept. 10, 1946; s. John Gideon Sr. and Marie Jeanette (Moore) P.; m. Hilma Elizabeth Skonberg, Aug. 4, 1973; children: John Hunt, Anna Russell. BS in Acctg., U. Ky., 1968, JD, 1970. Bar: Ky. 1971, U.S. Dist. Ct. (ea. dist.) Ky. 1978, U.S. Dist. Ct. (we. dist.) Ky. 1984, U.S. Ct. Appeals (6th cir.) 1988, U.S. Supreme Ct. 1988. Ptnr., prin. Law Offices John G. Prather, Somerset, Ky., 1972—; bd. dirs. Lawyers Mutual Ins. Co. Ky., 1989—, treas., 1995—. Bd. dirs. United Way, 1978—; mem. state cen. com. Ky. Young. Dems., Frankfort, 1972. Served to 1st lt. USAF, 1971-72, JAG, 1972. Mem. ABA (house dels.), ATLA, Am. Bd. Trial Advs., Am. Coll. Trial Lawyers, Ky. Acad. Trial Attys., Ky. Bar Assn. (ho. of dels. 1984-85, bd. govs. 1985-91, v.p. 1991-92, pres.-elect 1992-93, pres. 1993-94, lectr.), Coun. Sch. Bd. Attys. (state pres., bd. dirs. 1986—, lectr.), Ky. Def. Coun. (bd. dirs. 1987-91), Pulaski County Indsl. Found. (bd. dirs. 1982-95), Phi Delta Phi. Mem. Christian Ch. Avocations: boating, flying. Home: 510 N Main St Somerset KY 42501-1434 Office: PO Box 616 Somerset KY 42502-0616

PRATHER, LENORE LOVING, state supreme court presiding justice; b. West Point, Miss., Sept. 17, 1931; d. Byron Herald and Hattie Hearn (Morris) Loving; m. Robert Brooks Prather, May 30, 1957; children: Pamela, Valerie Jo, Malinda Wayne. B.S., Miss. Univ. Women, 1953; JD, U. Miss., 1955. Bar: Miss. 1955. Practice with B. H. Loving, West Point, 1955-60, sole practice, 1960-62, 65-71, assoc. practice, 1962-65; mcpl. judge City of West Point, 1965-71; chancery ct. judge 14th dist. State of Miss., Columbus, 1971-82; supreme ct. justice State of Miss., Jackson, 1982-92; presiding justice State of Miss., 1993—; v.p. Conf. Local Bar Assn., 1956-58; sec. Clay County Bar Assn., 1956-71. 1st woman in Miss. to become chancery judge, 1971, and supreme ct. justice, 1982. Mem. ABA, Miss. State Bar Assn., Miss. Conf. Judges, DAR, Rotary, Pilot Club, Jr. Aux. Columbus Club. Episcopalian. Office: Miss Supreme Ct PO Box 117 Jackson MS 39205-0117 also: PO Box 903 Columbus MS 39703-0903

PRATHER, WILLIAM C. III, lawyer, writer; b. Toledo, Ill., Feb. 20, 1921; s. Hollie Cartmill and Effie Fern (Deppen) P. BA, U. Ill., 1942, JD, 1947. Bar: Ill. 1947, U.S. Supreme Ct. 1978. Asst. dean U. Ill., 1942-43; atty. First Nat. Bank of Chgo., 1947-51; asst. gen. counsel U.S. Savs. and Loan League, Chgo., 1951-59; gen. counsel U.S. League of Savs. Instns., Chgo., 1959-82, gen. counsel emeritus, 1982—; sole practice, Cumberland County, Ill., 1981—. sem. lectr. in law, banking. Served to lt. Armed Forces, 1943-45. Decorated Bronze Star. Mem. ABA, Internat. Bar Assn., Fed Bar Assn., Ill. Bar. Assn., Chgo. Bar Assn., Union Internat. des Avocats, Nat. Lawyers Club Washington, Cosmos Club., Univ. Club of Chgo., Kiwanis, Mattoon Golf and Country Club, Exeter and County Club (Eng.), Club de Bonmont Melisande (France), Soc. Colonial Wars, Phi Delta Phi, Phi Gamma Delta, Phi Eta Sigma, Phi Alpha Chi. Editor: The Legal Bulletin, 1951-81, The Federal Guide, 1954-81; author: Savings Accounts, 8th edit. 1981; contbr. articles to publs. Home: Applewood Farm PO Box 157 Toledo IL 62468-0157 Office: 738 Courthouse Sq Toledo IL 62468

PRATS, MICHAEL, petroleum engineer, educator; b. Tampa, Fla., Dec. 18, 1925; s. Miguel and Maria (Carbó) P.; m. Mary Blanche Flaherty, Apr. 7, 1951; children: Delicia Anne, Barbara Eileen, Teresa Kaye, Steven Michael. BS in Physics, U. Tex., 1949, MA in Physics, 1951. With Shell Devel. Co., Houston, 1950—, cons. research engr., then sr. research assoc., 1972-89; pres. Michael Prats & Assocs., Houston, 1989—; adj. prof. dept. petroleum engring. U. Tex., Austin, 1991—; participant scientist exchange Royal/Dutch Shell Lab., Amsterdam, The Netherlands, 1954, 55, Shell Internat. Petroleum, The Hague, The Netherlands, 1981, Maraven, S.A., Caracas, Venezuela, 1981-83. Author: Thermal Recovery, 1982, Spanish transl., 1987; contbr. articles to profl. jours.; 21 patents in field. Served to staff sgt. USAAF, 1944-46, PTO. Recipient Diploma of Honor Pi Epsilon Tau, 1986, Disting. Svc. award Rep. Honduras, 1989, Thermal Recovery Disting. Achievement award SPE Thermal Ops. Symposium, 1991, KAPITSA medal Acad. Natural Scis. (Moscow), 1995; named to Internat. Hall of Fame, 1989. Mem. AIME (hon.), NAE, Soc. Petroleum Engrs. (hon., bd. dirs. 1976-79, sr. tech. editor 1987-90, Enhanced Oil Recovery Pioneer 1986, Uren award 1974, Disting. Mem. award 1983, Anthony F. Lucas Gold medal 1993), Soc. Venezolana de Ingenieros de Petroleo, Can. Inst. Mining, Asociacion De Ingenieros Petroleros De Mexico, Mex. Nat. Acad. Engring. (corr.), Acad. Engring. Armenia (fgn. mem.), Russian Acad. Nat. Scis., Pi Epsilon Tau (hon.). Avocation: travel. Address: 2834 Bellefontaine St Houston TX 77025-1610

PRATT, ALBERT, financial consultant, trustee; b. Newton, Mass., May 23, 1911; s. Frederick Sanford and Ella Winifred (Nickerson) P.; m. Alice Mathea Lee, May 24, 1940 (dec. 1976); children: Alice Mathea, Cornelia S., Nina L., Frederick H., Kate Nickerson Pratt Lapping; m. Fanny Gray Little Morgan, Jan. 2, 1977. Grad., Country Day Sch., Newton, 1929; A.B., Harvard, 1933, J.D., 1936. Bar: Mass. bar 1936. With firm Goodwin, Procter & Hoar, Boston, 1936-40; with Paine, Webber, Jackson & Curtis, Inc., Boston, 1946-80; vice chmn. Paine, Webber, Jackson & Curtis, Inc., 1970-76, cons., 1976-80, gen. partner, 1950-54, 57-70, ltd. partner, 1954-57; adv. dir. Blyth, Eastman Paine Webber Inc., Boston, 1980-83; dir., chmn. investment com. Paine Webber Properties, Inc., 1980-84, pres., 1984, cons., 1985—; ptnr. F.S. Pratt & Son, 1946-87; asst. sec. navy, 1954-57; bd. govs. N.Y. Stock Exchange, 1963-66. Pres. United Fund Boston, 1962-64. Served to comdr. USNR, 1940-45. Mem. Investment Bankers Assn. (chmn. N.E. group 1952-53, gov. 1957-60, 64-67, chmn. securities act com. 1959-63, pres. 1965-66), Assn. Harvard Alumni (dir. 1964-70), Boston C. of C. (dir. 1958-61), Assn. Harvard Clubs (pres. 1962-63), Harvard Alumni Assn. (dir. 1958-63), Cruising Club Am., N.Y. Yacht Club, Wianno Club (Osterville, Mass.). Home: Key Largo Anglers Club 50 Clubhouse Rd Key Largo FL 33037-3600 Office: care PaineWebber Properties 265 Franklin St Fl 16 Boston MA 02110-3113

PRATT, ALICE REYNOLDS, retired educational administrator; b. Marietta, Ohio, Oct. 5, 1922; d. Thurman J. and Vera L. (Holdren) Reynolds. BA, U. Okla., 1943. Reporter, high sch. tchr., 1944-50; asst. dir. Houston office Inst. Internat. Edn., 1952-58, dir. office, 1958-87, v.p., 1976-

87, ret. 1987. Decorated Palmes Academiques (France), 1966; Order of Merit (Fed. Republic Germany), 1972; knight Order of Leopold II (Belgium), 1973; named Woman of Yr., Houston Bus. and Profl. Women, 1958; recipient Matrix award Theta Sigma Phi, 1961; Nat. Carnation award Gamma Phi Beta, 1976. Mem. Houston Com. Fgn. Rels., Japan Am. Soc. (Houston), Houston Philos. Soc., Houston-Taipei Soc. (founding mem., pres. 1989-92), Houston-Galveston/Stavanger Sister City Assn. (founding mem.), Sister Cities Internat. (past nat. bd. dirs.), Nat. Coun. Internat. Visitors (past nat. bd. dirs.), Pan Am. Roundtable (bd. dirs.), Inst. Internat. Edn. (bd. dirs. so. regional office),. Houston Forum (past bd. govs.). Republican. Episcopalian.

PRATT, ARTHUR D., printing company executive; b. Indpls., May 7, 1924; s. Arthur D. and Helen L. (Rikhoff) P.; m. Marjorie M. Zwally May 19, 1967 (div. Mar. 1974); m. Amal Marcos, Apr. 11, 1987; children: Margaret, Michael, Sarah, Andrew. Student, Sorbonne U., Paris, 1947. Pres. Found. Internat. Econ. Devel., 1949-56, Life Effectiveness Tng., Indpls., 1969-97, Pratt Printing Co., Indpls., 1972-93. Author: The Party's Over, 1976, Christ and America's Survival, 1977, The Great Idea of God, 1984, How to Help and Understand the Alcoholic, 1987, Christian Revolution, 1996, (poetry) (with Amal Pratt) The Meeting of East and West. Pres. Flynn Christian Fellowship Houses Inc., 1956-94, Cmty. Interfaith Housing Inc., 1966-73, Madras Coun., 1974-79. Mem. Athenaeum Club. Episcopalian. Home: 2621 Sutherland Ave Indianapolis IN 46205-4270 Office: Life Effectiveness Tng 520 E 12th St Indianapolis IN 46202-2630

PRATT, DAN EDWIN, chemistry educator; b. High Point, N.C., Feb. 7, 1924; s. C. Daniel and Carol Druscilla (Wyatt) P.; m. Mana Clariece Peacock, Aug. 29, 1959; 1 child, Mana Lisa. BS, U. Ga., 1950, MS, 1951; PhD (nuclear sci. fellow 1960), Fla. State U., 1962; postgrad. in food sci., U. Mass. Asst. prof. chemistry U. Ga., 1955-61; assoc. prof., research scientist food sci. and nutrition U. Wis., Madison, 1964-69; research scientist, assoc. prof. Purdue U., West Lafayette, Ind., 1969-76, prof. chemistry, 1976-92, prof. emeritus, 1992—; cons. in lipid chemistry, 1992—; vis. prof. food law Emory U., 1954; vis. rsch. scientist Natick R & D Command, 1980; vis. lectr. U. Viscosa, Brazil, 1982, Harvard U., 1980; vis. scientist Am. Oil Chemists, Cannes, France, 1985; vis. rsch. scientist in lipid chemistry FDA, Washington, 1987, lectr., 1988; cons. to food industry, Taiwan, 1981, Nat. Poultry Industry, Lipid Chemistry, 1990; rsch. scientist Am. Oil Chemists, 1992; rsch. com., rep. Inst. Food Technologists, 1986-89. Contbr. numerous articles profl. jours. Del. Internat. Congress Food Scientists, Tokyo, 1978. With USMCR, 1942-45. Recipient Disting. Scientist Research award Ind. Inst. Food Sci., 1982. Fellow Am. Inst. Chemists, Inst. Food Sci. and Tech., Inst. Food Technologists; mem. Nat. Inst. Food Scientists, Am. Acad. Scis., N.Y. Acad. Scis., Sigma Xi, Phi Kappa Phi, Pi Mu Epsilon, Phi Tau Sigma (exec. sec. 1969), Gamma Sigma Delta. Club: Lafayette Toastmasters (pres. 1975). Home: 12734 Hunters Chase St San Antonio TX 78230-1930 Office: Purdue U Dept Foods And Nutriti West Lafayette IN 47906

PRATT, DANA JOSEPH, publishing consultant; b. Cambridge, Mass., Dec. 9, 1926; s. Carroll Cornelius and Marjory (Bates) P.; m. Therese Louis, July 14, 1957; children: Joseph Caldwell, Michael Louis, Benjamin Lyon. B.Naval Sci., Tufts U., 1946, B.A., 1948. Mgmt. trainee N.J. Bell Telephone Co., Newark, 1948-50; sales asst. Princeton U. Press, N.J., 1950-53; sales mgr. U. Ill. Press, Urbana, 1953-55; field cons. Franklin Book Programs, N.Y.C., 1955-59; staff assoc. Am. Book Pubs. Council, N.Y.C., 1959-62; exec. sec. Assn. Am. Univ. Presses, N.Y.C., 1962-66; asst. dir. Yale U. Press, New Haven, 1966-78; dir. pub. Library of Congress, Washington, 1978-93. Contbr. articles to profl. jours. Served as ensign USNR, comdg. officer PC 566, 1946-47. Recipient Award for Superior Svc. Libr. of Congress, 1993. Mem. Washington Book Pubs. (pres. 1984-85), Soc. for Scholarly Pub. (bd. dirs. 1982-86), Washington Map Soc., Washington Rare Book Group. Home and Office: 7514 Old Chester Rd Bethesda MD 20817-6163

PRATT, DAVID TERRY, mechanical engineering educator, combustion researcher; b. Shelley, Idaho, Sept. 14, 1934; s. Eugene Francis and Bernice (Montague) P.; m. Marilyn Jean Thackston, Dec. 22, 1956; children: Douglas Montague, Elizabeth Joann, Brian Stephens. B.Sc. M.E., U. Wash., 1956; M.Sc., U. Calif., Berkeley, 1962, Ph.D., 1968. Asst. prof. marine engring. U.S. Naval Acad., Annapolis, Md., 1961-64; prof. mech. engring., asst. dean Wash. State U., Pullman, 1968-76; prof. mech. engring. U. Utah, Salt Lake City, 1976-78; prof., chmn. mech. engring. and applied mechanics U. Mich., Ann Arbor, 1978-81; prof., chmn. mech. engring. U. Wash., Seattle, 1981-86, prof. mech. engring., 1987-96; research dir. supercomputing Aerojet Propulsion Research Inst., Sacramento, 1986-87. Author (with W.H. Heiser) Hypersonic Airbreathing Propulsion, 1994; editor (with L.D. Smoot) Combustion and Gasification of Pulverized Coal, 1976; contbr. articles to profl. jours. Served to 1st lt. USMC, 1956-60. NSF sci. faculty fellow, 1965-66; Fulbright-Hays sr. research fellow Imperial Coll., 1974-75; David Pierpont Gardner faculty fellow U. Utah, 1976. Mem. ASME, AIAA, Combustion Inst., Am. Soc. Engring. Edn. Lutheran.

PRATT, DIANE ADELE, elementary education educator; b. Battle Creek, Mich., Oct. 24, 1951; d. John Robert and Kathleen Adele (Cooper) Dickert; m. Stephen Howard Pratt, Apr. 29, 1972; children: Eric Stephen, Elizabeth Adele. BS, Western Mich. U., 1972. Cert. elem. tchr., Ohio, Iowa, Mich. Elem. tchr. Berea (Ohio) Cmty. Schs., 1973-76; ednl. cons. Kolbe Products, Inc., Phoenix and Scottsdale, Ariz., 1982-84; tchr. Lemon Tree Nursery Sch., Battle Creek, 1985-88; instr. Jr. Great Books, 1984-87; elem. tchr. Ft. Dodge (Iowa) Cmty. Schs., 1976-78, 90, substitute tchr., 1988-90, middle sch. tchr., 1990—, team leader, 1994—; exec. sec. Born Free Safari Club, Dodgen Industries, Humboldt, Iowa, 1988; advt. exec. Ft. Dodge Today mag., 1989-92; ednl. tutor, Battle Creek, Ft. Dodge, 1986-96; mem. adv. bd. Inst. for Instrn. Svcs., Battle Creek, 1984-88; dir., instr. Battle Creek Presch. Enrichment Program, 1984; chmn. Ft. Dodge Supr.'s Comty. Com. to Study K-8 Curriculum, 1988-89, facilitator K-3 human growth and devel. curriculum, 1989-92; mem. standing com. early childhood needs assessment com. Ft. Dodge Comty. Schs., 1989-95; mem. adv. bd., instr. Kids on Kampus Iowa Cen. C.C., Ft. Dodge, 1990-95; speaker State Conv. Childbirth Educators, Lansing, Mich., 1982; trustee Ft. Dodge Comty. Sch. Found. Bd., 1992—, mem. talented and gifted selection com. Ft. Dodge Comty. Schs., 1993—; mem. pub. rels. com. Ft. Dodge Comty Sch. Dist., 1992-94, mem. ednl. outcomes standing com., 1993-94. Author, editor various newsletters. Mem., past chmn. bd. Christian edn. 1st Bapt. Ch., Ft. Dodge, 1978-79, 89-96, music com., 1992-94, dir. children's choirs, 1988-90, mem. bell choir, 1990-91, ch. sch. supt. 1993-96, pastoral rels. com., 1997—; membership chmn. Battle Creek Parents, 1981-83; neighborhood coord. mothers' march March of Dimes, Battle Creek, 1981-83; troop leader Lakota coun. Girl Scouts U.S., 1988-90; pres. La Mora Park PTA, 1985-87, Phillips Mid Sch. PTA, Ft. Dodge, 1990-91; bd. dirs. Main Stage Players, jr. theater, Ft. Dodge, 1990-91; sec., pres. Jr. Women's Club, Ft. Dodge, 1977-80; mem. kickoff com. United Way, 1991; active Ft. Dodge Athletic Booster Club, 1994—. Recipient Mem. of Yr. award La Mora Park PTA, 1987. Mem. NEA, ASCD, AAUW (sec., pres. Battle Creek br. 1986-88), PEO (N.J. chpt., Ft. Dodge chpt. 1990-94), Iowa Edn. Assn., Ft. Dodge Edn. Assn., Iowa Assn. Middle Level Educators, Iowa Coun. Tchrs. English. Avocations: educational research, cross-country skiing, tennis. Home: 1851 9th Ave N Fort Dodge IA 50501

PRATT, DONALD GEORGE, physician; b. Higgins, Tex., Oct. 19, 1946; s. George Horace and Esta Vici (Barker) P. BS in Biomed. Sci., West Tex. State U., 1970; MD, U. Tex., Galveston, 1974. Diplomate Am. Bd. Family Practice, Am. Bd. Radiology (Radiation Oncology). Intern Scott & White Meml. Hosp., Temple, Tex., 1974-75, resident in gen. surgery and pathology, 1975-77, physician, 1979-83; resident in family practice McLennan County Med. Edn. and Rsch. Found., Waco, Tex., 1977-79; physician Family Practice Assocs., El Paso, Tex., 1983; owner, pvt. contractor Minor Emergency Ctrs., Amarillo, Tex., 1983-85; resident in radiation therapy U. Tex., Galveston, 1985-88; ptnr. Cons. in Radiation Oncology, P.A., Amarillo, 1988—, pres., 1994—; dir. dept. radiation oncology Harrington Cancer Ctr., Amarillo, 1994—; pres. Cons. in Radiation Oncology, 1994—; pres. staff Harrington Cancer Ctr., 1995—; prin. investigator Radiation Oncology Group, 1988-95; pres. of staff Harrington Cancer Ctr., 1995—, also bd. dirs. Mem. AMA, Am. Soc. Therapeutic Radiology and Oncology, Am. Acad. Family Physicians, Tex. Med. Assn., Potter/Randall County Med. Soc., Tex. Radiol. Soc. Home: 3623 Tripp Ave Amarillo TX 79121-1809 Office: Cons Radiation Oncology PA 1600 Coulter Dr Ste 402 Amarillo TX 79106-1721

PRATT, GEORGE CHENEY, law educator, retired federal judge; b. Corning, N.Y., May 22, 1928; s. George Wollage and Muriel (Cheney) P.; m. Carol June Hoffman, Aug. 16, 1952; children: George W., Lise M., Marcia Pratt Burke, William T. BA, Yale U., 1950, JD, 1953. Bar: N.Y. 1953, U.S. Supreme Ct. 1964, U.S. Ct. Appeals 1974. Law clk. to Charles W. Froessel (Judge of N.Y. Ct. Appeals), 1953-55; assoc. then ptnr. Sprague & Stern, Mineola, N.Y., 1956-60; ptnr. Andromidas, Pratt & Pitcher, Mineola, 1960-65, Pratt, Caemmerer & Cleary, Mineola, 1965-75; partner Farrell, Fritz, Pratt, Caemmerer & Cleary, 1975-76; judge U.S. Dist. Ct. (Eastern Dist. of N.Y.), 1976-82, U.S. Circuit Ct. Appeals for 2d circuit (Uniondale), N.Y., 1982-93; sr. circ. judge U.S. Cir. of Appeals for 2d Cir., N.Y., 1993-95; prof. Touro Law Sch., Huntington, N.Y., 1993—; counsel Parnon & Pratt L.L.P., N.Y.C., 1995—. Mem. ABA, N.Y. State Bar Assn., Nassau County Bar Assn., Soc. Am. Law Tchrs. Mem. United Ch. of Christ. Office: Touro Law Ctr 300 Nassau Rd Huntington NY 11743-4346

PRATT, HARRY DAVIS, retired entomologist; b. North Adams, Mass., Apr. 13, 1915; s. Harry Edward and Ethel Mae (Davis) P.; m. Caroline Georgine Kreiss, Apr. 13, 1944 (dec. May 1951); children: Harry Davis Jr., Katherine Maria Pratt Garrison, George Kreiss; m. Dora Belle Ford, Nov. 29, 1952. BS, Mass. State Coll., 1936, MS, 1938; PhD, U. Minn., St. Paul, 1941. Registered profl. entomologist. Asst. entomologist USPHS Malaria Control War Areas, San Juan, P.R., 1942-46; chief med. entomol. lab. USPHS Communicable Disease Ctr., Atlanta, 1946-53, chief insect rodent tr., 1953-63, chief Aedes aegypti control tng., 1964-68; chief insect rodent control tng. Environ. Control Agy., Atlanta, 1968-72; cons., tchr., writer Atlanta, 1972—; spl. cons. Econ. Coop. Administrn., Saigon, Vietnam, 1950, WHO, Geneva, 1966, Kuala Lumpur, Malaysia, 1969. Fellow Entomol. Soc. Am. (life); mem. Am. Mosquito Control Assn. (pres. 1967), Entol. Soc. Washington, Ga. Entomol. Soc. Mem. Christian Ch. (Disciples of Christ). Home: 879 Glen Arden Way NE Atlanta GA 31106-3407

PRATT, JOHN SHERMAN, lawyer; b. Bloomsburg, Pa., Feb. 7, 1952; s. B.D. and Frances Marie (Quinn) P.; m. Teresa Gayle Plemmons, June 14, 1975; children: Andrew, Caroline, Alexander. BS, Clemson U., 1974; JD, Harvard U., 1977. Bar: Ga. 1977, U.S. Dist. Ct. (no. dist.) Ga. 1977, U.S. Patent and Trademark Office 1979, U.S. Ct. Appeals (5th and 11th cirs.) 1981, U.S. Ct. Appeals (fed. cir.) 1985. Ptnr. Kilpatrick Stockton, Atlanta. Bd. dirs. Wesley Woods Geriatric Hosp. at Emory U., Atlanta, 1991, Ga. Biomed. Partnership, Atlanta, 1991-94. Mem. Am. Intellectual Property Law Assn., Licensing Execs. Soc. Avocation: woodworking. Office: Kilpatrick Stockton Ste 2800 1100 Peachtree St NE Atlanta GA 30309-4528

PRATT, JOHN WINSOR, statistics educator; b. Boston, Sept. 11, 1931; s. Frederic Wolsey and Theresa (Winsor) P.; m. Joy A. Wilmunen, Nov. 15, 1958; children: Maria Theresa Winsor, Samuel Frederick Wolsey. AB, Princeton U., 1952; PhD, Stanford U., 1956; MA (hon.), Harvard U., 1966. Rsch. assoc. U. Chgo., 1955-57; mem. faculty Harvard U., Cambridge, Mass., 1957—, prof. bus. adminstrn., 1966—; dir. Social Sci. Rsch. Coun., 1971-76; vis. rsch. prof. Kyoto U., Japan, 1972-73; vis. lectr. Keio U. Bus. Sch., Japan, 1982; Yamaichi vis. prof. fin. Tokyo U., 1989-90; chmn. study group on environment. monitoring NRC, 1975-77, chmn. panel on decennial census methodology NRC, 1983-87, mem. com. nat. stats., 1982-88. Co-author: Introduction to Statistical Decision Theory, 1965, rev. edit., 1995, Social Experimentation: A Method for Planning and Evaluating Social Intervention, 1974, Concepts of Nonparametric Theory, 1981; editor: Statistical and Mathematical Aspects of Pollution Problems, 1974; co-editor: Principals and Agents: The Structure of Business, 1985. Trustee Middlesex Sch., Concord, Mass., 1964-67. Guggenheim fellow, 1971. Fellow AAAS (chmn. sect. U. 1977), Am. Statis. Assn. (editor jour. 1965-69, chmn. bus. and econs. sect. 1983), Inst. Math. Stats., Econometric Soc., Am. Acad. arts and Scis.; mem. Internat. Statis. Inst., Bernoulli Soc. Math. Stats. and Probability, Math. Assn. Am. Home: 2 Gray Gdns E Cambridge MA 02138-1402 Office: Harvard Bus Sch Boston MA 02163

PRATT, JOSEPH HYDE, JR., surgeon; b. Chapel Hill, N.C., Mar. 9, 1911; s. Joseph Hyde and Mary (Bayley) P.; m. Hazel Housman, Dec. 11, 1943; children: Judith Housman, Lisa Mary, Joseph Hyde. AB, U. N.C., 1933; MD, Harvrad U., 1937; MS, U. Minn., 1947. Diplomate Am. Bd. Surgery, Am. Bd. Ob-gyn. Intern Boston City Hosp., 1938-39; fellow surgery Mayo Found., Rochester, Minn., 1940-43; mem. staff Mayo Clinic, Rochester, 1943—, head sect. in surgery, 1945-77, sr. gynecol. surgeon, 1958—; prof. clin. surgery Mayo Grad. Sch. Medicine U. Minn., 1963—; prof. surgery Mayo Med. Sch., 1973—. Contbr. articles to med. jours. Mem. ACS (bd. govs. 1966-71, bd. regents 1971-80), AMA, ACOG, Ctrl. Assn. Ob-Gyn., Minn. Ob-Gyn. Soc., Western Surg. Assn., soc. Vaginal Surgeons (pres. 1979-80), Soc. Pelvic Surgeons (pres. 1968), So. Surg. Assn., Ob-Gyn. Travel Club (pres. 1993—), Sigma Xi, Nu Sigma Nu. Republican. Episcopalian. Home: 1159 Plummer Cir SW Rochester MN 55902-2035 Office: 200 1st St SW Rochester MN 55902-3008

PRATT, KATHERINE MERRICK, environmental consulting company executive; b. Alexandria, Egypt, July 4, 1951; d. Theodore and Bettie (Curland) R.; m. Harry Kenneth Todd (div.); 1 child, Kirsten Todd-Pratt. BBA in Mgmt. Systems, U. Iowa, 1980; postgrad., U. Tex., 1985-87. Program data mgr. Rockwell Internat., Dallas, 1981-85; support coord. GTE Govt. Systems, Taunton, Mass., 1987-89, support engr., 1989-93; pres. Enviro-Logistics Inc., Harwood, Md., 1993—. Recipient Rear Admiral Bernard Eccles award, 1997, Cert. Commendation for Superior Performance as Dist. Dir., 1997. Mem. Soc. Logistics Engrs. (officer, mem. standing com. environ. applications, bd. dirs. New Eng. dist. 1996, dir. New Eng. dist., nat. chpt. newsletter judge), Internat. Soc. Logistics (bd. dirs. Washington chpt. 1997—), U.S. Pony Club (Ctrl. New Eng. championship chairwoman). Avocations: sailing, reading, equitation. Office: Enviro-Logistics Inc 3750 Hardesty Rd Harwood MD 20776-9535

PRATT, LAWRENCE ARTHUR, thoracic surgeon, foreign service officer; b. Paris, Ill., Dec. 20, 1907; s. Luther F. and Katherine (Kaufman) P.; m. Mai Thi NgocSuong, May 7, 1974; children: Elizabeth, Lawrie Porter, D. Jane. B.S., Wayne State U., Detroit, 1930, M.B., M.A., M.D., 1934, M.Ed., 1960; LL.B., Woodrow Wilson Coll. Law, Atlanta, 1943. Diplomate Am. Bd. Surgery, Am. Bd. Thoracic Surgery. Intern Grace Hosp., 1934-35; practice thoracic surgery Detroit, 1935-41, 46-63; attending thoracic surgeon Grace, Detroit Meml. hosps.; courtesy staff St. John's Hosp.; cons. thoracic surgeon Holy Cross, Highland Park Gen. hosps., Detroit; U.S. fgn. svc. officer, 1963—; vis. prof. medicine U. Saigon, Vietnam, 1963-75; med. dir. Urban Health Clinic of Orange County, Calif., 1981—; exec. v.p. Am. Fedn. Med. Ctrs., Inc., 1953-54; chief med. dental edn. divsn. AID/PH, Vietnam; cons. Vietnam Min. Edn., 1974-75; assoc. dean Minh Duc. Med. Sch., Saigon, 1974-75; cons. HEW, 1975-77; spl. asst. HEW (Divsn. Medicine Bur. Health Manpower), 1976; cons., mem. White House Task Force Internat. Health Policy, 1977; mem. World Bank Task Force Internat. Health Policy and Manpower, 1977, U.S. Pub. Health Assn.; leader design team Health Care Program, Mauritania, West Africa, 1978; physician in charge Refugee Transit Camps, Malaysia, 1980; med. dir. Urban Health Clinic, Orange County, Calif., 1981-84, Spl. Disease Specialist 1981—; cons. physician overseas ops. World Cons., Irvine, Calif., 1984-85; cons. to min. health, Rabat, Morocco, 1986; sr. cons. World Care Inc., 1988—; mem. Nat. Coun. for Internat. Health, 1988—; chmn. bd. dirs. Boarne Seven Seas Devel. Corp., 1993—. Author: Total Development for Survival, 1986. bd. dirs. Sun Yet Middle Sch., Zhongshan, Quandong Province, People's Republic of China, 1986—; chmn. bd. 100 For 1 Systems Corp., 1986—. Lt. col., M.C. AUS, 1941-46. Active U.S-Mexican Border Health Assn., 1986—. Recipient Unit citation; medal of Culture and Edn.; medal of Merit Vietnam). Fellow ACS (life), Am. Coll. Chest Physicians; mem. AMA, Mich. Med. Soc., Wayne County Med. Soc., Internat. Bronchoesophagol. Assn. (founder), Am. Bronchoesophagol. Assn., 4th Aux. Surg. Group Assn. (pres. 1955-56), Nat. Coun. on Internat. Health, U.S. Pub. Health Assn., Wayne State U. Med. Alumni Assn. (pres. 1956-57), Ga. Bar Assn. Clubs: Essex Cricket (Eng.); Lambs (N.Y.C.); Scarab (Detroit), Detroit Skating (Detroit); Grosse Pointe Yacht, Grosse Pointe Hunt, Am. Radio Relay League, El Cajon (Calif.) Radio. Home: 2302 Lowell Ln Santa Ana CA 92706-1932

PRATT, LEIGHTON CALVIN, state legislator; b. Hartford, Conn., Apr. 23, 1923; s. Calvin and Jessie (White) P.; m. Sally Burgess, Oct. 21, 1961; children: Randall Leighton, Bruce Charles. BS, U. Vt., 1951; MS, U. R.I., 1953. Plant pathologist Vt. Dept. Agr., Montpelier, 1952-62; tchr. sci. Cabot (Vt.) H.S. and J. H.S., 1962-65; tchr. biology, asst. prin. Newport (Vt.) H.S., 1965-67; tchr. biology North Country Union H.S., Newport, 1967-79; Coos agrl. ext. agt. U. N.H., Durham, 1969-88, prof. emeritus ext. edn., 1988—; mem. N.H. Ho. of Reps., Concord, 1991—. Named hon. state farmer Future Farmers Am., 1986. Mem. Rotary (dir. exch. to Brazil dist. 1986, pres. Lancaster, N.H.), Epsilon Sigma Phi. Republican. Congregationalist. Avocations: travel, gardening. Home: 63 Water St Lancaster NH 03584-1804

PRATT, MICHAEL FRANCIS, physician and surgeon, otolaryngologist; b. Washington, Dec. 14, 1950; s. James William and Eleanor Mary (LeVangie) P.; 1 child, James Michael. BS, U. Md., 1972; MD, U. Md., Balt., 1980. Diplomate Am. Bd. Otolaryngology. Intern Naval Hosp., San Diego, 1980-81, resident in otolaryngology, 1982-86; instr. George Washington U., Washington, 1974-76; from clin. instr. to asst. prof. Med. U. S.C., 1987-89; asst. prof. Ea. Va. Med. Sch., Norfolk, 1989-94, assoc. prof., 1994-96, dir. residency tng., 1989-96, vice chair dept. otolaryngology/head and neck surgery, 1994-95. Editl. reviewer The Laryngoscope Jour., 1994—, Head and Neck Jour., 1994—; contbr. numerous articles to profl. jours.; lyricist In Memorium, 1992; poet: Through the Hourglass, 1996. Bd. dirs. Va. ProMusica, Norfolk, 1991-93; mem. planning com. DePaul Charity Golf Com., Norfolk, 1990-95. Decorated Navy Commendation medal with gold star, Navy Achievement medal with gold star. Fellow ACS, Am. Acad. Facial Plastic and Reconstructive Surgery (Shuster award 1986), Am. Laryngol., Rhinol. and Otol. Soc. (Fowler award 1995), Am. Soc. Head and Neck Surgery, Am. Acad. Otolaryngology/Head and Neck Surgery; mem. Soc. Univ. Otolaryngoly/Head and Neck Surgery, Va. Soc. Otolarynology (bd. dirs. 1994-96). Avocations: golf, running, skiing, tennis, composing poetry and music. Office: Atlanta Ear Nose and Throat Assn #235 5555 Peachtree Dunwoody Rd Atlanta GA 30342

PRATT, MICHAEL THEODORE, book publishing company executive, marketing, sales and publishing specialist; b. Troy, Ohio, May 30, 1943; s. James Alden and Dorothy (Kennedy) P.; m. Helen Diane Biddle, Oct. 24, 1964 (div. Sept. 1983); children: Nicole Christine, Jason Alan. Student, Muskingum Coll., New Concord, Ohio, 1961-62, Ashland Coll., Ohio, 1962-63, Temple U., 1963-64, Wharton Sch. (U. Pa.), 1964. Corp. sr. v.p. Random House, Inc., N.Y.C., 1969-90; pres., chief exec. officer Corinthian Internat., Inc., Spring Valley, N.Y., 1990, also bd. dirs.; sr. v.p. St. Martin's Press, N.Y.C., 1991—; bd. dirs. Shambhala Pubs., Inc., J. Alden Pratt, Inc. Mem. Am. Mgmt. Assn. Democrat. Presbyterian. Club: University (Larchmont, N.Y.). Home: 50 Judges Hollow Rd Fairfield CT 06430-1643 Office: St Martin's Press 175 5th Ave New York NY 10010-7703

PRATT, MURRAY LESTER, information systems specialist; b. Mt. Holly, N.J., Mar. 11, 1956; 8. John N. and Mildred E. P.; m. Sharon Louise Busby, Aug. 13, 1988; children: Kevin Harrison, Brian Gavel, Melissa Anne. BS in Indsl. Engring., Northwestern U., 1976; MS in Computer Sci., Ill. Inst. Tech., Chgo., 1983. Systems analyst Gen. Foods USA, Chgo., 1981-84, systems specialist, 1984-87, computer integrated mfg. mgr., 1987-91; KF logistics systems mgr. Kraft Foods, Northfield, Ill., 1991—. Presbyterian. Avocations: current affairs, tennis, volleyball, hiking. Home: 1241 Swainwood Dr Glenview IL 60025-2839 Office: Kraft Foods Three Lakes Dr NF168 Northfield IL 60093-2753

PRATT, PAUL BERNARD, financial services executive; b. Johnson City, Tenn., Aug. 7, 1946; s. Paul Bernard Pratt and Lois Kathern (Arnold) Thomas; m. Diann Margurite Scroggins, Apr. 2, 1971 (dec.); 1 child, Jennifer Elaine White; m. Patricia Lea Kell Alleman, June 21, 1992 (dec.). BA, Chapman Coll., 1975; MBA, Webster U., 1993; postgrad., Western State U., 1994—. Commd. 2d lt. USMC, 1966, advanced through grades to lt. col., 1983, svc. in RVN, 1969, 70, regimental air officer 2nd Marines, 1977-80, ops. officer MAWTS-1, 1980-83, ops. officer marine corps air sta. Iwakuni SA, 1984-87; asst. dean command and staff coll. USMC, Quantico, Va., 1987-90; dir. morale, welfare and recreation MCAS USMC, El Toro, Calif., 1991-93; ret. USMC, 1993; pres. Success Seminars, Irvine, Calif., 1993—; v.p. ERIC Equities Inc., Santa Ana, Calif., 1993—. Precinct inspector Orange County (Calif.) Voting Commn., 1994; pres. Cath. Parish Coun., Japan, 1986. Recipient Meritorious Svc. medal Pres. of the U.S., 1990, 93. Mem. Internat. Assn. of Fin. Planners. Avocations: running, biking, chess, reading. Office: ERIC Equities Inc 2021 E 4th St Santa Ana CA 92705-3912

PRATT, PHILIP CHASE, pathologist, educator; b. Livermore Falls, Maine, Oct. 19, 1920; s. Harold Sewell and Cora Johnson (Chase) P.; m. Helen Clarke Deitz, Feb. 4, 1945; children: William Clarke (dec.), Charles Chase (dec.). A.B., Bowdoin Coll., 1941; M.D., Johns Hopkins U., 1944. Diplomate: Am. Bd. Pathology. Intern in pathology Johns Hopkins Hosp., 1944-45, asst. resident in pathology, 1945-46; pathologist Saranac Lab., Saranac Lake, N.Y., 1946-52; asst. dir. Saranac Lab., 1952-55; instr. Ohio State U., 1955-57, asst. prof. pathology, 1957-62, assoc. prof., 1962-66; assoc. prof. Duke U. Med. Ctr., 1966-71, prof., 1971-90, prof. emeritus, 1991—. Author: (with V.L. Roggli and S.D. Greenberg) Pathology of Asbestos Related Diseases, 1993; contbr. numerous articles to profl. publs. Fellow Am. Coll. Chest Physicians, Coll. Am. Pathologists; mem. AAAS, Am. Thoracic Soc., Am. Soc. Exptl. Pathology, Am. Assn. Pathologists and Bacteriologists, Internat. Acad. Pathology, Royal Soc. Health. Unitarian. Office: PO Box 3712 Davison Bldg Durham NC 27710 *The innovative idea is the essential commodity of the academic life. Origins of such ideas are varied but for me usually begin with realization that an existing concept does not adequately explain observed phenomena. When direct reasoning does not produce a new, better concept, the problem is put aside. Weeks later a return to the question often promptly reveals a logical new solution which has arisen without conscious effort. Of course, this must then be subjected to investigation to be either confirmed or refuted.*

PRATT, RICHARD HOUGHTON, physics educator; b. N.Y.C., May 5, 1934; s. Karl Chapman and Gertrude (Gennis) P.; m. Elizabeth Ann Glass, Nov. 1, 1958; children—Jonathan Peter, Kathryn Eileen, Mary Caroline, Paul Chapman. A.B., U. Chgo., 1952, S.M., 1955, Ph.D., 1959. Rsch. assoc. Stanford U., 1959-61, asst. prof., 1961-64; assoc. prof. physics U. Pitts., 1964-69, prof., 1969—, acad. dean semester at sea, fall 1984, adminstrv. dean, spring 1990; program dir. theoretical physics NSF, Washington, 1987-89; cons. Lawrence Livermore Nat. Lab.; prin. investigator Dept. Energy, NSF. Fellow Am. Phys. Soc. (chmn. com. internat. sci. affairs 1993), AAAS; mem. Sierra Club (chmn. Pa. chpt. 1976-80, v.p. Appalachian region 1982-84), Internat. Radiation Physics Soc. (sec. 1985—), Phi Beta Kappa, Sigma Xi. Achievements include research in atomic theory, including photoelectric effect, bremsstrahlung, x-ray scattering; applications to atomic processes in plasmas. Home: 1131 Shady Ave Pittsburgh PA 15232-2809

PRATT, RICHARDSON, JR., retired college president; b. N.Y.C., Mar. 25, 1923; s. Richardson and Laura C. (Parsons) P.; m. Mary Esterbrook Offutt, Aug. 12, 1944; children: Laura Pratt Gregg, Thomas R., David. O. A.B., Williams Coll., 1946, LL.D. (hon.), 1978; M.B.A., Harvard U., 1948; LL.D. (hon.), St Joseph, 1984. Econ. analyst, sec. com. on human relations Exxon Co., 1948-52, dist. mktg. mgr., 1953-63, mktg. planning and evaluation, 1964-71; chmn. Charles Pratt & Co., Inc., 1971—; pres. Pratt Inst., Bklyn., 1972-90; bd. dirs. Dime Savs. Bank N.Y., Bklyn. Union Gas Co.; mayor Village of Lloyd Harbor (N.Y.), 1983—. Trustee Near East Found., Fedn. Protestant Welfare Agys.; mem. governing bd. Bklyn. Bot. Gardens, treas., 1996; chmn. bd. dirs. Greenwood Cemetery. With USNR, 1943-46. Presbyterian. Home: 30 Dock Hollow Rd Cold Spring Harbor NY 11724-1002 Office: Charles Pratt & Co Inc 355 Lexington Ave New York NY 10017-6603

PRATT, ROBERT CRANFORD, political scientist, educator; b. Montreal, Que., Can., Oct. 8, 1926; s. Robert Goodwin and Henrietta (Freeman) P.; m. Renate Hecht, July 15, 1956; children: Gerhard, Marcus, Anna. BA, McGill U., Montreal, 1947; postgrad., Inst. Etudes Politique, Paris, 1948; MPhil, Oxford U., Eng., 1952. Lectr. McGill U., 1952-54, 56-58, Makerere U., Uganda, 1954-56; rsch. officer Oxford Inst. Commonwealth Studies, 1958-60;

prin. Univ. Coll., Dar-es-Salaam, Tanzania, 1961-65; chmn. internat. studies program U. Toronto, Ont., Can., 1966-71; prof. polit. sci. U. Toronto, 1966—; spl. asst. to pres., Tanzania, 1965, 69; rsch. fellow Internat. Devel. Rsch. Ctr., 1978; commonwealth vis. prof. U. London, 1979-80; dir. Rsch. Project on Western Mid. Powers and Global Poverty, 1985-89; vis. fellow Devel. Ctr. Orgn. for Econ. Cooperation and Devel., Paris, 1986-87. Author: (with Anthony Low) Buganda and British Overrule, 1960, The Critical Phase in Tanzania, Nyerere and the Emergence of a Socialist Strategy, 1976, Towards Socialism in Tanzania, 1979, (with Robert Matthews) Human Rights in Canadian Foreign Policy, 1988, Internationalism Under Strain: The North-South Policies of Canada, The Netherlands, Norway and Sweden, 1989; (with Roger Hutchinson) Christian Faith and Economic Justice: A Canadian Perspective, 1989); Middle Power Internationalism: The North-South Dimension, 1990, Canadian International Development Assistance Policies: An Appraisal, 1994, 2nd edit., 1996. Rhodes scholar Oxford U., 1952; recipient Killam award Can. Coun., 1968. Fellow Royal Soc. Can.; mem. Can. Polit. Sci. Assn., Can. African Studies Assn. (past pres.), Can. Assn. for Study of Internat. Devel. (mem. exec. coun.), Ecumenical Forum Can. (past chmn.). Mem. New Democratic Party. Mem. United Ch. Canada. Home: 205 Cottingham St, Toronto, ON Canada M4V 1C4 Office: U Toronto, Dept Polit Sci, Toronto, ON Canada M5S 1A1

PRATT, ROBERT WINDSOR, lawyer; b. Findlay, Ohio, Mar. 6, 1950; s. John Windsor and Isabelle (Vance) P.; m. Catherine Camak Baker, Sept. 3, 1977; children: Andrew Windsor, David Camak, James Robert. AB, Wittenberg U., Springfield, Ohio, 1972; JD, Yale U., 1975. Bar: Ill. 1975, U.S. Dist. Ct. (no. dist.) Ill. 1976, U.S. Dist. Ct. (we. dist.) Mich. 1995, U.S. Ct. Appeals (fed. cir.) 1984, U.S. Ct. Appeals (7th cir.) 1996. Assoc. Keck, Mahin & Cate, Chgo., 1975-81, ptnr., 1981—. Bd. dirs. Chgo. region ARC, 1985-96, vice chmn., 1988-92, chmn., 1992-96, bd. dirs. Mid-Am. chpt., 1992-96. Mem. ABA, Chgo. Bar Assn., Yale Club (Chgo.). Office: Keck Mahin & Cate 77 W Wacker Dr Ste 4900 Chicago IL 60601

PRATT, ROSALIE REBOLLO, harpist, educator; b. N.Y.C., Dec. 4, 1933; d. Antonio Ernesto and Eleanor Gertrude (Gibney) Rebollo; Mus.B., Manhattanville Coll., 1954; Mus.M., Pius XII Inst. Fine Arts, Florence, Italy, 1955; Ed.D., Columbia U., 1976; m. George H. Mortimer, Esquire, Apr. 22, 1987; children: Francesca Christina Rebollo-Sborgi, Alessandra Maria Pratt Jones. Prin. harpist N.J. Symphony Orch., 1963-65; soloist Mozart Haydn Festival, Avery Fisher Hall, N.Y.C., 1968; tchr. music public schs., Bloomfield and Montclair, N.J., 1962-73; mem. faculty Montclair State Coll., 1973-79; prof. Brigham Young U., Provo, Utah, 1984—, coord. grad. studies dept. music, 1985-87.; biofeedback and neurofeedback rsch. specialist, 1993—. U.S. chair 1st internat. arts medicine leadership conf., Tokyo Med. Coll., 1993. Co-author: Elementary Music for All Learners, 1980; editor Internat. Jour. Arts Medicine, 1991—, (proceedings) 2d, 3d, 4th Internat. Symposia Music Edn. for Handicapped; contbr. articles to Am. Harp Jour., Music Educators Jour., others. Fulbright grantee, 1979; Myron Taylor scholar, 1954. Mem. Am. Harp Soc. (Outstanding Service award 1973), AAUP (co-chmn. legis. rels. com. N.J. 1978-79), Internat. Soc. Music Edn. (chair commn. music in spl. edn., music therapy, and medicine 1985—), Internat. Soc. Music in Medicine (v.p. 1993—), Internat. Assn. of Music for the Handicapped (co-founder, exec. dir., jour. editor), Coll. Music Soc., Music Educators Nat. Conf., Soc. for Study of Neuronal Regulation, Brigham Young U. Grad. Coun., Phi Kappa Phi, Sigma Alpha Iota. Office: Brigham Young U Harris Fine Arts Ctr Provo UT 84602 *Personal philosophy: I believe in offering my students what I have learned from the educational heroes in my life, the teachers whose example is the reason I prepare my classes carefully and thoughtfully. What I am and what I cherish most in life is also the result of a grandmother and father, neither of whose formal education went beyond the third grade, but whose wisdom was timeless.*

PRATT, SHARON L., secondary and elementary education educator; b. Terrell, Tex., Dec. 5, 1946; d. Cecil and Bobbie Lou (Hodge) Brown; m. John E. Pratt, Aug. 31, 1968; 1 child, Randolph W. BS in Edn., U. North Tex., 1969, MS, 1980; ESL cert., East Tex. U., 1987. Cert. elem., English tchr., reading specialist, ESL tchr., Tex. Tchr. Mesquite (Tex.) Ind. Sch. Dist.; elem. tchr. sci. U.S. Govt., Manama, Bahrain; secondary tchr. McDonald Mid. Sch., Mesquite; tchr. ESL and reading improvement North Mesquite High Sch., 1991-92, 96—; adj. faculty devel. reading Cedar Valley C.C., Lancaster, Tex., 1992-95; secondary tchr. Robert T. Hill Mid. Sch. Dallas Ind. Sch. Dist., 1995-96; ESL and reading tchr. North Mesquite H.S., 1996—; tchr. ESL and adult edn. classes Dallas Ind. Sch. Dist.; instr. ESL class Eastfield Community Coll., Mesquite. Author poems. Mem. TESOL, Internat. Reading Assn., Tex. State Reading Assn. Home: 1001 Villa Siete Mesquite TX 75181-1237 Office: North Mesquite High Sch 18201 Lbj Fwy Mesquite TX 75150-4124

PRATT, SUSAN G., architect; b. Kansas City, Mo., Sept. 24, 1951; d. John Bohman and Alice Marguerite (Harris) Grow; m. W. Scott Pratt; children: David, Alice; stepchildren: David, Laura. BArch, Kans. State U., 1973. Registered architect, Mich., Wis. Project arch. Skidmore Owings & Merrill, Chgo., 1973-78, 83-85; project arch. Murphy/Jahn, Inc., Chgo., 1978-82, 86—, now v.p.; sr. project arch. Froelich & Marik, L.A., 1982-83, Marshall & Brown, Kansas City, 1985-86. Prin. works include New World Ctr., Hong Kong, Group Repertory Theatre, North Hollywood, Calif., Bi State Indsl. Park, Kansas City, Mo., State of Ill. Ctr., Chgo., John Deere Harvester Works Office Facility, Moline, Ill., Two Liberty Pl., Phila., Livingston Pla., Bklyn., North Loop Block 37, Chgo., 1st and Broadway, L.A., Kudamm 119, Berlin, Cologne/Bonn Airport, Cologne, Jeddah Airport, Saudi Arabia, Sony European Hdqs., Berlin, Munich Airport Ctr., 21st Century Tower, Shanghai, China, South Pointe Condominiums, Miami Beach. Mem. First Presbyn. Ch., Evanston, Ill. Mem. AIA (corp. mem.). Presbyterian. Office: Murphy/Jahn 35 E Wacker Dr Chicago IL 60601

PRATT, WILLIAM CROUCH, JR., English language educator, writer; b. Shawnee, Okla., Oct. 5, 1927; s. William Crouch and Irene (Johnston) P.; m. Anne Cullen Rich, Oct. 2, 1954; children: Catherine Cullen, William Stuart, Randall Johnston. B.A., U. Okla., 1949; M.A., Vanderbilt U., 1951, Ph.D., 1957. Rotary Internat. fellow U. Glasgow, Scotland, 1951-52; instr. English Vanderbilt U., 1955-57, Miami U., Oxford, Ohio, 1957-59; asst. prof. Miami U., 1959-64, assoc. prof., dir. Freshman English, 1964-68, prof., 1968—; Fulbright-Hays lectr. Am. lit., prof. Am. lit. Univ. Coll., Dublin, Eire, 1975-76; resident scholar Miami U. European Ctr., Luxembourg, fall 1976; lectr. Yeats Internat. Summer Sch., Sligo, Eire, 1979, 81, 82, 83, James Joyce Summer Sch., Dublin, Ireland, 1996; writer-in-residence Tyrone Guthrie Ctr., County Monaghan, Ireland, summer 1992, 96. Author: The Imagist Poem, 1963, The Fugitive Poets, 1965, rev. edit., 1991, The College Writer, 1969, College Days at Old Miami, 1984, The Influence of French Symbolism on Modern American Poetry, 1985, Miami Poets, 1988, Homage to Imagism, 1992, The Big Ballad Jamboree, 1996, Singing the Chaos: Madness and Wisdom in Modern Poetry, 1996; contbr. essays, translations, poems, revs. to lit. jours., books. Served to lt. USNR, 1953-55. Mem. MLA, Nat. Coun. Tchrs. English (Ohio awards chmn. 1967-69), Coll. Conf. on Composition, Communication, Internat. Contemporary Lit. and Theatre Soc. (program chmn. 1983, 88), Soc. Study So. Lit. (sec. Ezra Pound Internat. Conf. 1993-97), St. George Tucker Soc., Phi Beta Kappa, Sigma Alpha Epsilon, Omicron Delta Kappa. Republican. Home: 212 Oakhill Dr Oxford OH 45056-2710 *True happiness is to live in the understanding of what we love, the pursuit of what we believe in.*

PRATTE, LISE, lawyer, corporate secretary; b. Laval, Que., Can., May 16, 1950. LLB, Laval U., 1976; MBA, Montreal U., Que., Can., 1988. Bar: Que. Asst. sec. Malouf Inquiry Commn. on 21st Olympiad, 1977-79, Des Manoirs Sch. Bd., Terrebonne, Que., 1979-82; legal counsel for various corps., mgmt. cons., 1981-82; corp. sec., legal counsel Can. Arsenals Ltd., Le Gardeur, Que., 1982-85; asst. sec., legal counsel Imasco Ltd., Montreal, 1985-88; corp. sec. Bombardier Inc., Montreal, 1988-96. Bd. dirs. La Fondation de L'Universite Laval. Mem. Can. Bar Assn., Que. Bar Assn., Inst. Chartered Secs. and Adminstrs., Can. Shareholders Svcs. Assn. (bd. dirs.), Am. Soc. Corp. Secs., Order of Chartered Adminstrs. Avocation: management.

PRATTE, LOUIS, judge; b. Quebec City, Que., Can., Nov. 29, 1926; s. Garon and Georgine (Rivard) P.; m. Charlotte Tremblay, July 2, 1953; children—Marie, Francois. Grad. Faculte de droit et des scis economiques, Laval U.; diplome d'etudes superieures en droit prive, U. Paris. Bar: Que. 1950. Mem. trial div. Fed. Ct. Can., 1971-73; judge Fed. Ct. Appeal, Ottawa, Ont., 1973—. Office: Fed Ct Appeal, Kent & Wellington Sts, Ottawa, ON Canada K1A 0H9

PRATTE, ROBERT JOHN, lawyer; b. Victoria, B.C., Can., Feb. 14, 1948; s. Arthur Louis Jr. and Marie Bertha (Latremouille) P.; children from previous marriage: Merie Elise, Jessica Louise, Allison Adele; m. Erica Catherine Street, Oct. 20, 1984; 1 child, Chelsea Nicole. BA, Northwestern U., 1970; JD, Tulane U., 1976. Bar: Minn. 1976. Ptnr. Best & Flanagan, Mpls., 1976-84; ptnr. Briggs & Morgan, Mpls., 1985—, head mortgage banking group. Editor: Mortgage Lending in Minnesota—A Desktop Reference Guide, 1990. Ex-officio mem. Wilderness Inquiry, Minn.; pres. Twin Cities Northwestern U. Alumni Assn., 1978; active Westminster Presbyn. Ch., Mpls. Fellow Am. Coll. Mortgage Attys.; mem. ABA (real estate financing com. real property sect.), Minn. Bar Assn. (banking com.), Hennepin County Bar Assn., Mortgage Bankers Assn. Minn. (chmn. legal issues com. 1989-94), Calhoun Beach Club (exec. mem.), Minnetonka Country Club. Home: 19900 Manor Rd Deephaven MN 55331 Office: Briggs & Morgan 2400 IDS Ctr 80 S 8th St Minneapolis MN 55402-2100 *Undertake with enthusiasm and pursue to completion the tasks that others are unwilling or unable to do. Never be satisfied with mediocrity. Surround yourself with those who are smarter than you; have the patience and judgement to let them succeed. Success can be measured by the hours you spend with your children--reading, fishing, and playing.*

PRATTER, GENE E. K., lawyer; b. Chgo., Feb. 25, 1949; d. Eugene Anthony and Laurel Marilyn (Dauer) Kreyche; m. Robert Lawrence Pratter, Oct. 21, 1978; children: Virginia Paige, Matthew Robert. BA, Stanford U., 1971; JD, U. Pa., 1975. Bar: Pa. 1975, U.S. Dist. Ct. (ea. dist.) Pa. 1975, U.S. Ct. Appeals (3d cir.) 1981. Assoc. Duane, Morris & Heckscher, Phila., 1975-83, ptnr., 1983—; judge pro tem Phila. Ct. Common Pleas, 1994—. Bd. overseers U. Pa. Law Sch., Phila., 1994—, lectr. Ctr. on Professionalism. Fund-raiser U. Pa. Law Sch. Contbr. articles to profl. jours. Mem. ABA (litigation sect. chmn. com. on ethics and professionalism 1995—), Def. Research Inst., Pa. Bar Assn., Phila. Bar Assn., Stanford U. Alumni Club (fund raiser, officer 1976-83). Republican. Roman Catholic. Office: Duane Morris & Heckscher Ste 4200 One Liberty Pl Philadelphia PA 19103

PRAUSNITZ, JOHN MICHAEL, chemical engineer, educator; b. Berlin, Jan. 7, 1928; came to U.S., 1937, naturalized, 1944; s. Paul Georg and Susi Prausnitz; m. Susan Prausnitz, June 10, 1956; children: Stephanie, Mark Robert. B Chem. Engring., Cornell U., 1950; MS, U. Rochester, 1951; Ph.D., Princeton, 1955; Dr. Ing., U. L'Aquila, 1983, Tech. U. Berlin, 1989; DSc, Princeton U., 1995. Mem. faculty U. Calif., Berkeley, 1955—, prof. chem. engring., 1963—; cons. to cryogenic, polymer, petroleum and petrochem. industries. Author: (with others) Computer Calculations for Multicomponent Vapor-Liquid Equilibria, 1967, (with P.L. Chueh) Computer Calculations for High-Pressure Vapor-Liquid Equilibria, 1968, Molecular Thermodynamics of Fluid-Phase Equilibria, 1969, 2d edit., 1986, (with others) Regular and Related Solutions, 1970, Properties of Gases and Liquids, 3d edit., 1977, 4th edit., 1987, Computer Calculations for Multicomponent Vapor-Liquid and Liquid-Liquid Equilibria, 1980; contbr. to profl. jours. Recipient Alexander von Humboldt Sr. Scientist award, 1976, Carl von Linde Gold Meml. medal German Inst. for Cryogenics, 1987, Solvay prize Solvay Found. for Chem. Scis., 1990, Corcoran award Am. Soc. for Engring. Edn., 1991, D.L. Katz award Gas Processors Assn., 1992; named W.K. Lewis lectr. MIT, 1993; Guggenheim fellow, 1962, 73, fellow Inst. Advanced Study, Berlin, 1985; Miller rsch. prof., 1966, 78; Christensen fellow St. Catherine's Coll. Oxford U., 1994, Erskine fellow U. Canterbury Christchurch, New Zealand, 1996. Mem. AIChE (Colburn award 1962, Walker award 1967, Inst. Lectr. award 1994), Am. Chem. Soc. (E.V. Murphree award 1979, Petroleum Chemistry Rsch. award 1995), NAE, NAS, Am. Acad. Arts and Scis. Office: U Calif 308 Gilman Hall Berkeley CA 94720

PRAVEL, BERNARR ROE, lawyer; b. Feb. 10, 1924. BSChemE, Rice U., 1947; JD, George Washington U., 1951. Bar: D.C. 1951, Tex. 1951, U.S. Supreme Ct. 1951. Ptnr. Pravel, Hewitt, Kimball and Krieger, Houston, 1970—. Patent editor George Washington U. Law Rev., 1950. Precinct chmn. Houston Rep. Com., 1972-74. Served to lt. (j.g.) USNR. Fellow Am. Bar Found., Tex. Bar Found.; mem. ABA (chair intellectual property sect. 1991-92), Tex. Bar Assn. (chmn. patent, trademark sect. 1968-69, bd. dirs. 1976-79, Outstanding Contbn. 1982), Nat. Coun. Patent Law (chmn. 1970-71), Am. Intellectual Property Law Assn. (pres. 1983-84), Houston Intellectual Property Law Assn. (pres. 1983-84, Outstanding Svc. award 1986), Order of Coif, Kiwanis, Tau Beta Pi. Home: 10806 Oak Hollow St Houston TX 77024-3017 Office: Pravel Hewitt Kimball and Krieger 1177 West Loop S Fl 10 Houston TX 77027

PRAY, DONALD GEORGE, aerospace engineer; b. Troy, N.Y., Jan. 19, 1928; s. George Emerson and Jansje Cornelia (Ouwejan) P.; m. Betty Ann Williams, Oct. 1, 1950; children: Jennifer Loie, Jonathan Cornelius, Judy Karen, Jeffrey Donald. BA in Physics, Tex. Christian U., 1955; MS in Mech. Engring., So. Meth. U., 1979. Sr. structures engr. Gen. Dynamics Corp., Ft. Worth, 1955-62, 67-84; engring. specialist LTV Astronautics Corp., Dallas, 1962-65, sr. engring. specialist, 1989-91; aero. group engr. space div. Chrysler Corp., New Orleans, 1965-67; V-22 group engr. Bell Helicopter Textron, Ft. Worth, 1984-89; E-3 structural integrity program mgr. Tinker AFB, 1991-95; sr. stress engr. Northrop Grumman Corp., Dallas, 1997—; prin. Donald G. Pray, Cons., Ft. Worth, 1959-61. Contbr. articles to tech. publs. Chmn. bd. trustees Cope Cemetery Assn., Johnson County, Tex., 1987—; corps comdr., v.p. bd. dirs. Masqueraders Drum and Bugle Corps, New Orleans, 1965-67; scoutmaster, cubmaster, explorer advisor, dist. com. chmn. Longhorn coun. Boy Scouts Am., Ft. Worth, 1967-75. Recipient Grand Championship Mardi Gras award, 1966. Mem. ASME, NSPE, NRA, SAR (pres. Van Zandt chpt. Ft. Worth 1996-97, treas. 1997—), Acoustical Soc. Am. (emeritus 1997—), Soc. Mayflower Descendants Tex. (sec. 1983-85, 88-91, gov. 1991-93, dep. gov. gen. 1993—, gen. soc. edn. com. 1990—, chmn. Dallas colony scholarship com. 1988—, gov. Dallas/Ft. Worth colony 1995-97), Ft. Worth Rifle and Pistol Club (marksman 1980), Train Collectors Assn., Ft. Worth Geneal. Soc. (bd. dirs. 1983-84), Internat. Pray Family Assn. (trustee 1996—), Masons, Scottish Rite, Shriners, Sigma Pi Sigma, Pi Mu Epsilon. Baptist. Achievements include analytical engineering contributions to numerous aircraft and spacecraft programs including B-36, B-58, NX-2, Robot, Dynasoar, Scout, Apollo, F/FB-111, F-16, V-22 Osprey, C-17, E-3 AWACS. Home and Office: 3628 Wedgway Dr Fort Worth TX 76133-2135 Home: Lazy Acres Farm 5750 Lazy Bend Rd Brock TX 76066 *Learn what talents you have been blessed with; then exercise them for the betterment of humanity.*

PRAY, LLOYD CHARLES, geologist, educator; b. Chgo., June 25, 1919; s. Allan Theron and Helen (Palmer) P.; m. Carrel Myers, Sept. 14, 1946; children: Lawrence Myers, John Allan, Kenneth Palmer, Douglas Carrel. B.A., Carleton Coll., 1941; M.S., Calif. Inst. Tech., 1943, Ph.D. (NRC fellow 1946-49), 1952. Geologist Magnolia Petroleum Co., summer 1942, U.S. Geol. Survey, 1943-44; hydrographic officer USN, 1944-46; Geologist U.S. Geol. Survey, 1946-56 part time; instr. to assoc. prof. geology Calif. Inst. Tech., 1949-56; sr. research geologist Denver Research Ctr., Marathon Oil Co., 1956-62, research assoc., 1962-68; prof. geology U. Wis., Madison, 1968-88; emeritus prof. geology, 1989—; short course vis. prof. U. Tex., 1964, U. Colo., 1967, U. Miami, 1971, U. Alta., 1969, Colo. Sch. Mines, 1985; vis. scientist Imperial Coll. Sci. and Tech., London, 1977, U. Calif. Santa Cruz, 1987, Nat. Park Svc. Geology panel, 1993. Author articles sedimentary carbonates, the Permian Reef complex, stratigraphy and structural geology So. N.M. and W. Tex., porosity of carbonate facies, Calif. rare earth mineral deposits. Pres. Colo. Diabetes Assn., 1963-67, v.p., 1968; mem. adv. panel earth scis. NSF, 1973-76. Served as hydrographic officer USNR, 1944-46. Named Layman of Year Am. Diabetes Assn., 1968; recipient Disting. Teaching award U. Wis. Madison, 1988; Disting. Achievement citation Carleton Coll., 1991. Fellow Geol. Soc. Am. (rsch. grants com. 1965-67, com. on nominations 1973, com.Penrose medal 1979-81); mem. Am. Assn. Petroleum Geologists (rsch. com. 1958-61, lectr. continuing edn. program 1966-69, Matson trophy 1967, continuing edn. com. 1978-80, disting. lectr. 1986-87, 87-88), Soc. Sedimentary Geologists (hon. life mem. Permian Basin sect., hon. mem. internat. soc., sec.-treas. 1961-63, v.p. 1966-67, pres. 1969-70), Am. Geol. Inst. (edn. com. 1966-68, ho. bd. dels. 1970-72), Phi Beta Kappa. Office: Univ Wis Dept Geology Madison WI 53706

PRAY, RALPH MARBLE, III, lawyer; b. San Diego, June 7, 1938; s. Ralph Marble Jr. and Doris (Thomson) P.; m. Karen L. Pray (div. May 1988); children: Matthew Thomson, Kristen Leigh; m. Sandra Anne Shaw, June 7, 1988. BS, U. Redlands, 1960; JD, U. Calif., San Francisco, 1967. Bar: Calif. 1967, U.S. Dist. Ct. (so. dist.) Calif. 1968, U.S. Supreme Ct. 1972, U.S. Dist. Ct. (ea. dist.) Calif. 1985, U.S. Dist. Ct. (ctrl. dist.) Calif. 1989, U.S. Dist. Ct. (no. dist.) Calif. 1992. Assoc. Gray, Cary, Ware & Friedenrich and predecessor, San Diego, 1967-73, ptnr., 1973—; mem. mgmt. com. Gary, Cary, Ames & Frye, San Diego, 1975-80; arbiter Superior Ct., San Diego, 1984—. Lt. USN, 1960-64. Mem. ABA, SAR, NRA, Calif. Bar Assn., Am. Arbitration Soc. (arbiter), San Diego Zool. Soc., Ducks Unltd., Thurston Soc., Rotary Club of Coronado, Calif., Order of Coif. Republican. Episcopalian. Home: 535 C Ave Coronado CA 92118-1824 Office: Gray Cary Ware & Friedenrich 1700 1st Interstate Plz 401 B St San Diego CA 92101-4223

PRAYSON, ALEX STEPHEN, drafting and mechanical design educator; b. Tulsa, Okla., June 24, 1939; s. Stephen Alexander and Frances Prayson; children: Stephen, David, Timothy, Anthony. AS, Edison Tech., 1967; DC, Cleveland Coll., 1972; AA, Summit U., 1996. Diplomate Am. Bd. Chiropractic Examiners. Owner Prayson Candies Co., Tulsa, 1963-68; cartographer Howard Needles Tammen and Bergendoff, Kansas City, Mo., 1968-71; supr. M. J. Harden Assocs., Kansas City, 1971-81; asst. prof. Tulsa C.C., 1981—; advisor Phi Theta Kappa, Tulsa, 1991—. Author: A Love-Hate Anthology, 1993, Cad Systems Operation, 1996; inventor Taffy-Pull. Mem. selection com. Ahepa Civic Youth Svc. Award, Tulsa, 1992—. Named Most Disting. Regional Advisor, Phi Theta Kappa, Tulsa, 1994-95, Robert Giles Disting. Advisor Internat. award Phi Theta Kappa, 1995-96. Mem. Am. Design and Drafting Assn., Okla. Tech. Soc., Tulsa C.C. Faculty Assn. Avocations: croquet, bridge, travel. Home: 2534 E 20th St Tulsa OK 74104-5810

PRAZNIK, DARREN THOMAS, provincial legislator; b. Selkirk, Canada, May 9, 1961; s. Bernard James and Marjorie Helen (Hargreaves) P. BA, U. Winnipeg, 1982; LLB, U. Manitoba, 1985. Barrister and solicitor, Manitoba, 1986. Articling clk. D'Arcy & Deacon, Winnipeg, Canada, 1985-86; spl. asst. to fed. Min. Health & Welfare, Ottawa, Winnipeg, Canada, 1986-88; mem. legis. assembly Province of Manitoba, 1988—. Mem. Progressive Conservative Party. Roman Catholic. Avocations: model railroading, gardening, reading. Office: Legis Bldg Rm 302, 450 Broadway Ave, Winnipeg, MB Canada R3C 0V8

PREBLE, LAURENCE GEORGE, lawyer; b. Denver, Apr. 24, 1939; s. George Enos and Ruth (Jewett) P.; m. Deborah Joan Horton, Aug. 24, 1963; children—Robin Lee, Randall Laurence. B in Petroleum Refining Engring., Colo. Sch. Mines, 1961; J.D. cum laude, Loyola U., Los Angeles, 1968. Bar: Calif. 1969, N.Y. 1987, U.S. Dist. Ct. (cen. dist.) Calif. 1969, D.C. 1983. Assoc. firm O'Melveny & Myers, Los Angeles, 1968-76; ptnr. O'Melveny & Myers, 1976—; adj. prof. law Southwestern U., 1970-75, Loyola U. of L.A. Sch. Law, 1984-92, Fordham U. Sch. Law, 1992—, Calif. Continuing Edn. of the Bar; lectr., author Practicing Law Inst. Trustee Harvey Mudd Coll., 1991-94, Citizens Bidget Commn. N.Y.C., 1994—. Mem. Los Angeles County Bar Assn. (chmn. real property sect. 1979-80), Calif. Bar Assn. (mem. exec. com. real property sect.), ABA, Am. Coll. Real Estate Lawyers (bd. govs. 1986—), Anglo-Am. Real Property Inst., La Canada-Flintridge C. of C. (pres. 1974-75), Loyola Law Sch. Alumni Assn. (pres. 1978). Office: O'Melveny & Myers 153 E 53rd St Fl 54 New York NY 10022-4611

PREBLE, LOU-ANN M., state legislator; m. Bill Preble. Grad., Tuomey Hosp. Sch. Nursing, 1950, Prima C.C., 1978. RN S.C., 1951-77; physical evaluator Medi-Quik, Tucson, 1978-82; co-owner, mgr. retail apparel store, 1972-75, ret.; mem. Ariz. Ho. of Reps., mem. assignments com. former precinct committeeman, dep. registr.; state committeeman, 1974-92; rep. at large State Exec. Com., 1991-92. Republican. Roman Catholic. Office: House of Representatives 1700 W Washington St Phoenix AZ 85007-2812*

PRECHT, WILLIAM FREDERICK, environmental specialist; b. N.Y.C., Dec. 26, 1956; s. Frederick C. and Ursula I. (Sennholt) P.; m. Joni Ferden, July 27, 1991; children: Lindsey Leona, Chandler Ilsa. BA in Geology, Marine Sci., SUNY, 1978; MS in Earth Sci., Adelphi U., 1981; MA in Marine Geology and Geophysics, U. Miami, 1994; postgrad. in ocean scis., Nova U. Cert. profl. geologist; registered profl. geologist, Pa. Staff geologist Phillips Petroleum Co., Denver, 1981-84; sr. staff geologist Champlin Petroleum Co., Denver, 1984-86; prin. rsch. scientist Reef Resources & Assocs., Billings, Mont., 1986-87; sr. rsch. scientist Reef Resources & Assocs., Miami, Fla., 1987-93; sr. environ. specialist Consulting Engring. & Sci., Miami, 1993-94; environ. dir. Consul-Tech. Engring., Inc., Miami, 1994—; adj. faculty marine scis. Northeastern U., 1987—. Contbr. over 65 articles and abstracts to profl. jours; invited lectr., speaker to over 50 univs. and profl. assns. Pres. Miami Geol. Soc. 1990-91. Recipient fellowship U. Miami, Texaco, 1987-88. Mem. Internat. Soc. for Reef Studies, Soc. for Sedimentary Geology (chmn. carbonate rsch. group 1992-94, Presentation Sci. Excellence award 1985), Am. Assn. Petroleum Geologists (adv. bd. treatise on petroleum geology 1987—, coord. vis. geologists com. 1987—, soc. del. 1990-93), Am. Inst. Profl. Geologists (cert. profl. geologist). Democrat. Achievements include: deciphered the history of reef growth and sea level rise in Belize; investigated the effects of deforestation and runoff on lagoonal reefs in southern Belize; monitors the long term health of Carribean Coral Reefs; designed and implemented large, successful wetland and coral reef restoration projects throughout south Fla. Avocations: fly fishing, baseball, ice hockey, skiing, cycling. Home: 7310 Ponciana Ct Miami Lakes FL 33014 Office: Consul-Tech Engring Inc 10570 NW 27th St # 101 Miami FL 33172-2151

PRECOPIO, FRANK MARIO, chemical company executive; b. Providence, Mar. 12, 1925; s. Domenic and Antonetta (Altomari) P.; m. Rita Marie Carr, Apr. 28, 1956; children—Thomas J., Frank J., Michael J. B.Sc. in Chemistry summa cum laude, Brown U., 1948; Ph.D., Yale U., 1952. Research assoc. Gen. Electric Research Ctr., Schenectady, 1951-55; mgr. research and devel. Gen. Electric Co., Erie, Pa., 1955-61; dir. research and devel. wire and cable dept. Gen. Electric Co., Bridgeport, Conn., 1961-66; v.p. tech. Amchem Products, Ambler, Pa., 1966-83; exec. v.p. Henkel Corp., Ambler, 1983-89; ret., 1989. Patentee in field of organic chemistry and high temperature polymers. Trustee Alfred and Mary Douty Found., Phila., 1972-91, William Jeanes Meml. Library, Whitemarsh, Pa., 1968-74. Served to lt. (j.g.) USNR, 1943-46. Recipient Mordica award Wire Assn. Internat., 1983. Fellow Am. Inst. Chemists; mem. Am. Chem. Soc. (chmn. Erie sect. 1958), Sigma Xi. Republican. Roman Catholic. Avocations: antique pewter collecting; antique furniture refinishing; sailing; gardening.

PRECOURT, GEORGE AUGUSTINE, government official; b. Hartford, Conn., July 26, 1934; s. Charles A. and Antoinette (Gauthier) P.; m. Alma E. Hall, Aug. 28, 1954; children: Debra Ann, Carol Anne, David Charles, Kenneth George. Student, LaSalle U., 1952-55. Prodn. and inventory mgr. Beacon Machine Co., E. Hartford, Conn., 1960-65; purchasing/prodn. control mgr. Redington Counters, Windsor, Conn., 1965-73; gen. mgr. Able Coil & Electronics, Kensington, Conn., 1973-74; chief industries Conn. Svcs. for the Blind, Wethersfield, 1974—, commr., exec. dir., 1989-96; regional dir. Nat. Industry for the Blind, Wayne, N.J., 1983—; chmn. New Eng. Conf. Vending Facility Dirs., 1982—; v.p. sales Bernstein Leibstone Assocs., Inc., N.Y.C.; exec. v.p. Tech. Mktg., Inc., Plantation, Fla. Inventor in field; contbr. articles to profl. jours. Vice chmn. E. Hartford Pub. Bldg. Commn., 1971—; chmn. Dem. Town Com. Dist. 6, E. Hartford, 1970-74; del. Dem. State Conv., 1960. With U.S. Army, 1950-52. Named Lion of the Yr., 1972; Spl. Citation, U.S. Pres., 1974. Mem. Am. Assn. Workers for the Blind, Prodn. and Inventory Control Soc., C. of C., Career Edn. Placement Assn. (bd. dir.), Am. Legion, Lions, Franco War Vets. Episcopalian. Home: 29 Laurel Ter Manchester CT 06040-6833 Office: The Precourt Group 150 N Main St Manchester CT 06040-2003

PREDDY, RAYMOND RANDALL, retired newspaper publisher, educator; b. Texarkana, Ark., Feb. 1, 1940; s. Raymond Watson and Dorothy Belle (Long) P.; m. Sarah Elizabeth Mitchell, Nov. 20, 1965; children: Lewis, Tiffany. B.S., Northwestern U., 1961, M.S. in Journalism, 1962. Copy editor Louisville Courier-Jour., 1965-69; with Dayton (Ohio) Daily News, 1969-74, asst. city editor, 1971, met. editor, 1971-74; systems mgr. Dayton Newspapers, Inc., 1974-76; bus. mgr. Waco (Tex.) Tribune-Herald, 1976-77, asst. pub., 1977-78; pub. Waco Tribune-Herald, 1978-96; part time journalism instr. Baylor U., Waco. Pres. Waco United Way, 1986, Waco Found., 1984-86, Waco Symphony Assn., 1985-86. Served with USN, 1962-65; capt. Res. (ret.). Named Tex. Newspaper Leader of 1994; recipient Pat Taggart award from Tex. Daily Newspaper Assn. Presbyterian. Club: Rotary. Home: PO Box 23021 Waco TX 76702-3021

PREECE, WARREN EVERSLEIGH, editor; b. Norwalk, Conn., Apr. 17, 1921; s. Everett Lowe and Ethel (Miles) P.; m. Deborah Weeks, July 12, 1947; children: Scott Everett, Mark William, Thayer Evelyn. BA cum laude, Dartmouth Coll., 1943; MA, Columbia U., 1947. Instr. English, U. Chgo., 1947-49; reporter Norwalk Hour, 1949-50, writer, copy editor, 1952-56; campaign aide, publicity dir. to U.S. Senator Dodd, 1956-57; exec. sec. bd. editors Ency. Brit., 1957-64, editor, 1964-65, editor-in-chief, 1965-68, gen. editor, 1968-70, editor, 1970-75, vice chmn. bd. editors, 1974-79, bd. editors, 1979—; cons. Center Study Democratic Instns.; Ninth ann. C.N. Williamson lectr. Peabody Coll., Nashville. Author: (with others) The Technological Order, 1962; editor: Encyclopaedia Britannica College Preparatory Series, 1964; bd. editorial advisors Internat. Ency., Tokyo, 1974-88. Bd. dirs., sec. Conn. chpt. ARC, 1955-57; pres. Mass. Protestant Social Svcs. Inc., 1977-78; bd. dirs. Protestant Youth Homes, Baldwinville, Mass., 1976-78; mem. Standing Commn. on Peace with Justice, Episcopal Ch., 1989-94. Served with arty. U.S. Army, 1943-46, 50-52. Mem. Phi Beta Kappa Assos., Phi Beta Kappa, Sigma Nu. Democrat. Episcopalian.

PREEG, ERNEST HENRY, strategic and international studies center executive; b. Englewood, N.J., July 5, 1934; s. Ernest W. and Claudia T. Preeg; m. Florence L. Tate, May 12, 1962; 1 child, Terri E. BS in Marine Transp., N.Y. State Maritime Coll., 1956; MA in Econs., New Sch. for Social Rsch., 1961, PhD, 1964. Officer Mcht. Marine, Am. Export Lines, 1956-61; lectr. econs. Bklyn. Coll., 1962-63; fgn. svc. officer Dept. State, Washington, 1963-88; amb. to Haiti, 1981-83; now William M. Scholl chair internat. bus. Ctr. for Strategic and Internat. Studies, Washington. Author: Traders and Diplomats, 1969, Economic Blocs and U.S. Foreign Policy, 1974, the Evolution of a Revolution, 1981, Haiti and the CBI, 1984, The American Challenge in World Trade, 1988, The Tied Aid and Credit Issue, 1989, Neither Fish Nor Foul: U.S. Economic Aid to the Philippines, 1991, Cuba and the New Caribbean Economic Order, 1993, Trade Policy Ahead, 1995, Traders in a Brave New World, 1995, The Haitan Dilemma, 1996. Coun. Fgn. Rels. fellow, 1967-68. Mem. Am. Fgn. Svc. Assn. Office: CSIS 1800 K St NW Washington DC 20006-2202

PREEG, WILLIAM EDWARD, oil company executive; b. N.Y.C., Oct. 16, 1942; s. Ernest Winfield and Claudia Teresa (Casper) P. BE in Marine Engring., SUNY, 1964; MS in Nuclear Sci. and Engring., Columbia U., 1967, PhD in Nuclear Sci. and Engring., 1970. Project engr. U.S. AEC, N.Y.C., 1964-67; physics specialist Aerojet Nuclear Systems Co., Sacramento, Calif., 1970-71; group leader Los Alamos (N.Mex.) Sci. Lab., 1971-80; dir. fluid-mechanics-nuclear dept. Schlumberger-Doll Rsch., Ridgefield, Conn., 1980-85, v.p., dir. rsch., 1990-94; mgr. nuclear dept. Schlumberger Well Svcs., Houston, 1985-87, v.p. engring., 1987-90; v.p., dir. rsch. Schlumberger Austin Rsch., Austin, 1994—; instr. mech. engring. CCNY, N.Y.C., 1968-70; cons. AEC, Gamma Process Co., Los Alamos Sci. Lab., Lawrence Livermore Lab. Mem. Am. Nuclear Soc., Am. Phys. Soc., Am. Inst. Physics (adv. com on corp. assocs.), Soc. Profl. Well Log Analysts, Soc. Petroleum Engrs. Home: 203 Hurst Creek Rd Austin TX 78734-4223 Office: Schlumberger Austin Rsch 8311 North RR 620 Austin TX 78726

PREER, JEAN LYON, associate dean, information science educator; b. Rochester, N.Y., June 25, 1944; d. Henry Gould and Helen Corinne (McTarnaghan) Lyon; m. James Randolph Preer, June 24, 1967; children: Genevieve, Stephen. BA in History with honors, Swarthmore Coll., 1966; MLS, U. Calif., Berkeley, 1967; JD with highest honors, George Washington U., 1974, PhD, 1980. Bar: D.C. 1975. With Henry E. Huntington Libr., San Marino, Calif., 1967-69; Woodrow Wilson Found. teaching intrn Fed. City Coll., Washington, 1969-70; cons. Inst. for Svcs. to Edn., Silver Spring, Md., 1981-82; vol. edn. divsn. Nat. Archives, Washington, 1981-89; adj. prof. U. D.C., 1984-85; adj. prof. Cath. U. Am., Washington, 1985-87, asst. prof. sch. libr. and info. sci., 1987-92, assoc. prof., 1993—, assoc. dean., 1991-93, 94—, acting dean, 1993-94; adj. assoc. prof. George Washington U., 1985-87. Contbr. articles to profl. jours. Mem. governing bd. Nat. Cathedral Sch., Washington, 1987-91. Fellow Nat. Acad. Edn., 1984-85; grantee Nat. Endowment for Humanities. Mem. Order of Coif, Beta Phi Mu. Home: 2900 Rittenhouse St NW Washington DC 20015-1524 Office: Cath U Am Sch Libr and Info Sci Washington DC 20064

PREER, JOHN RANDOLPH, JR., biology educator; b. Ocala, Fla., Apr. 4, 1918; s. John Randolph Sr. and Ruth (Williams) P.; m. Louise Bertha Brandau; children: James Randolph, Robert William. BS with highest honors, U. Fla., 1939; PhD, Ind. U., 1947. From asst. prof. to assoc. prof. to prof. depts. zoology and biology U. Pa., Phila., 1947-67, chmn. grad. group depts. zoology and biology, 1958-67, admissions officer grad. sch. arts and scis., 1960-61; prof. depts. zoology and biology Ind. U., Bloomington, 1968-77, chmn. dept. biology, 1977-79, disting. prof. depts. zoology and biology, 1977—, disting. prof. emeritus, 1988—. Contbr. 85 articles to profl. jours. and chpts. to books. Served to 1st lt. USAF, 1942-45, ETO. NSF sr. postdoctoral fellow, 1967-68, Guggenheim fellow 1976-77. Mem. AAAS, Nat. Acad. Scis. (elected 1976), Am. Inst. Biol. Scis., Am. Soc. Cell Biology, Am. Soc. Protozoology (pres. 1986-87), Phi Beta Kappa. Democrat. Methodist. Home: 1414 E Maxwell Ln Bloomington IN 47401-5143 Office: Ind Univ care Dept of Biology Bloomington IN 47405

PREGERSON, HARRY, federal judge; b. L.A., Oct. 13, 1923; s. Abraham and Bessie (Rubin) P.; m. Bernardine Seyma Chapkis, June 28, 1947; children: Dean Douglas, Kathryn Ann. B.A., UCLA, 1947; LL.B., U. Calif.-Berkeley, 1950. Bar: Calif. 1951. Pvt. practice Los Angeles, 1951-52; Assoc. Morris D. Coppersmith, 1952; ptnr. Pregerson & Costley, Van Nuys, 1953-65; judge Los Angeles Mcpl. Ct., 1965-66, Los Angeles Superior Ct., 1966-67, U.S. Dist. Ct. Central Dist. Calif., 1967-79, U.S. Ct. Appeals for 9th Circuit, Woodland Hills, 1979—; faculty mem., seminar for newly appointed distr. Judges Fed. Jud. Center, Washington, 1970-72; mem. faculty Am. Soc. Pub. Adminstrn., Inst. for Ct. Mgmt., Denver, 1973—; panelist Fed. Bar Assn., L.A. chpt., 1989, Calif. Continuing Edn. of Bar, 9th Ann. Fed. Practice Inst., San Francisco, 1986, Internat. Acad. Trial Lawyers, L.A., 1983; lect. seminars for newly-appointed Fed. judges, 1970-71. Author over 450 published legal opinions. Mem. Community Rels. Com., Jewish Fedn. Coun., 1984—, Temple Judea, Encino, 1955—; bd. dirs. Marine Corps Res. Toys for Tots Program, 1965—, Greater Los Angeles Partnership for the Homeless, 1988—; bd. trustees Devil Pups Inc., 1988—; adv. bd. Internat. Orphans Inc., 1966—, Jewish Big Brothers Assn., 1970—, Salvation Army, Los Angeles Met. area, 1988—; worked with U.S. Govt. Gen. Svcs. to establish the Bell Shelter for the homeless, the Child Day Care Ctr., the Food Partnership and Westwood Transitional Village, 1988. 1st lt. USMCR, 1944-46. Decorated Purple Heart, Medal of Valor Apache Tribe, 1989; recipient Promotion of Justice Civic award, City of San Fernando, 1965, award San Fernando Valley Jewish Fedn. Coun., 1966, Profl. Achievement award Los Angeles Athletic Club, 1980, Profl. Achievement award UCLA Alumni Assn., 1985, Louis D. Brandeis award Am. Friends of Hebrew U., 1987, award of merit Inner City Law Ctr., 1987, Appreciation award Navajo Nation and USMC for Toys for Tots program, 1987, Humanitarian award Los Angeles Fed. Exec. Bd., 1987-88, Grateful Acknowledgement award Bet Tzedek Legal Svcs., 1988, Commendation award Bd. Suprs. Los Angeles County, 1988, Others award Salvation Army, 1988, numerous others. Mem. ABA (vice-chmn., com. on fed. rules of criminal procedure and evidence sect. of criminal 1972—, panelist Advocacy Inst., Phoenix, 1988), L.A. County Bar Assn., San Fernando Valley Bar Assn. (program chmn. 1964-65), State Bar Calif., Marines Corps Res. Officers Assn. (pres. San Fernando Valley 1966—), DAV (Birmingham chpt.), Am. Legion (Van Nuys Post),. Office: US Ct Appeals 9th Cir 21800 Oxnard St Ste 1140 Woodland Hills CA 91367-3657*

PREHEIM, VERN QUINCY, religious organization administrator, minister; b. Hurley, S.D., June 27, 1935; s. Jacob Roy and Selma (Miller) P.; m. Marion Kathryn Keeney, Aug. 28, 1958; children: Jay, Janette, Beth, Brian, Lorie. AA, Freeman Jr. Coll., 1956; BA, Bethel Coll., 1957; BD, Mennonite Bibl. Sem., 1960. Algeria program dir. Mennonite Cen. Com. Mennonite Ch., Algiers, 1960-62; Peace sec. Gen. Conf. Mennonite Ch., Newton, Kans., 1962-65, gen. sec., 1980-96, dir. Africa and Middle East, 1965-75, Asia dir., 1975-80; mission bd. sec. Gen. Conf. Mennonite Ch., 1968-72, chmn. gen. bd. dirs., 1974-80; coord. resource devel. Mennonite Ctrl. Com., Newton, 1996—. Home: 209 S College Dr Hesston KS 67062 Office: Mennonite Ctrl Com 106 W 24th St N North Newton KS 67117 *To maintain a sense of direction with a vibrant hope in an uncertain world is imperative for the religious community. Our challenge is also to help others find direction and maintain hope.**

PREHLE, TRICIA A., accountant; b. Queens, N.Y., Oct. 17, 1970; d. William G. and Dolores (Cameron) P. BBA in Acctg., CUNY, Baruch Coll., 1992. CPA, N.Y.; cert. mgmt. acct. Fin. analyst Gruntal & Co., Inc., N.Y.C., 1992—. Mgr. Community Tax Aid, Inc., N.Y.C., 1992—. Mem. Inst. Cert. Mgmt. Accts., Sigma Alpha (Delta chpt.). Home: 60-48 69th Ave Flushing NY 11385-5140 Office: Gruntal & Co Inc 14 Wall St New York NY 10005-2101

PREISER, WOLFGANG FRIEDRICH ERNST, architect, educator, consultant, researcher; b. Freiburg, Germany, June 26, 1941; came to U.S., 1967; s. Gerhard Friedrich and Ursula Helene (von Huelsen) P.; m. Cecilia M. Fenoglio, Feb. 16, 1985; children: Johanna, Timothy, Andreas, Nicholas. Student, Vienna Tech. U., 1963; diploma in Engring., Architecture, U. Karlsruhe, 1967; M.Arch., Va. Poly. Inst. and State U., 1969; Ph.D. in Man-Environ. Relations, Pa. State U., 1973. Architect Germany, Austria, Eng., 1960-66; prof. architecture Va. Poly. Inst. and State U., Pa. State U., U. Ill., U. N.Mex., U. Cin., 1970—; research architect constrn. engring. research lab. U.S. Army, 1973-76; co-dir. Inst. Environ. Edn., U. N.Mex., 1976-86; dir. Ctr. for R & D, U. N.Mex., Albuquerque, 1986-90; dir. research Archtl. Research Cons. Inc., 1976—; lectr. ednl., profl. and civic groups worldwide; v.p. faculty club U. N.Mex., 1976-78; pres. Internat. Club, Va. Poly. Inst. and State U., 1968-69. Editor, author 10 books on programming, post-occupancy evaluation and design rsch.; contbr. over 75 articles in field to profl. jours. Trustee Cin. Chamber Orch., 1992—, v.p., 1995—. Recipient Faculty Devel. award for rsch. U. Cin., 1992, Faculty Achievement award, 1995, Pogue/Wheeler Traveling award, 1993, Dean's Spl. award, 1994, Finland's Inst. Tech. award, 1966, awards Am. Iron and Steel Inst., 1968, Progressive Arch. Ann., 1985, 89, undergrad. teaching award U. Ill., 1976, hon. mention 1st Kyoto award Internat. Coun. of Soc. for Indsl. Design, 1979; Fulbright fellow, 1967, 87, Ford Found. fellow, 1968, Nat. Endowment for Arts fellow, 1979, 82; grad. fellow U. Cin., 1996. Mem. Soc. Human Ecology (pres. 1980-86), Environ. Design Research Assn. (vice chmn. 1974-76, sec. 1973-74), Nat. Acad. Scis. (chmn. com. on programming and post-occupancy evaluation, bldg. research bd., 1985-86), Phi Kappa Phi. Research in field. Office: U Cin Coll DAAP Sch Architecture Cincinnati OH 45221-0016

PREISKEL, BARBARA SCOTT, lawyer, association executive; b. Washington, July 6, 1924; d. James and B. Beatrix Scott; m. Robert H. Preiskel, Oct. 28, 1950; children: John S., Richard A. BA, Wellesley Coll., 1945; LLB, Yale U., 1947. Bar: D.C. 1948, N.Y. 1948, U.S. Supreme Ct. 1960. Law clk. U.S. Dist. Ct., Boston, 1948-49; assoc. Poletti, Diamond, Roosevelt, Freidin & Mackay, N.Y.C., 1949-50; assoc. Dwight, Royall, Harris, Hoegel & Caskey, N.Y.C., 1950-54, legal cons., 1954-59; cons. Ford Found. Fund for the Republic, N.Y.C., 1954; dep. atty. Motion Picture Assn. Am., Inc., N.Y.C., 1959-71, v.p., legis. counsel, 1971-77, sr. v.p., gen. atty., 1977-83; pvt. practice N.Y.C., 1983—; bd. dirs. GE, Fairfield, Conn., Textron, Inc., Providence, Am. Stores Co., Salt Lake City, The Washington (D.C.) Post Co. Mem. Pres.'s Commn. on Obscenity and Pornography, 1968-70, Am. Arbitration Assn., 1971-87, N.Y.C. Bd. Ethics, 1976-89, Inst. Civil Justice, 1984-86, Citizens Com. for Children, N.Y.C., 1966-72, 85-91, Child Adoptive Svc. of State Charities Aid Assn., N.Y.C., 1961-68, Hillcrest Ctr. for Children, N.Y.C., 1958-61, Fedn. Protestant Welfare Agys., N.Y.C., 1959-61, 64-92, N.Y. Philharm. Soc., 1971-94, Am. Women's Econ. Devel. Corp., 1981-93, Med. Edn. for South African Blacks, Inc., Washington, 1985-89; bd. dirs. Wiltwyck Sch., N.Y.C., 1968-78, chmn. bd. dirs., 1950, Mass. Mutual Life Ins. Co., Springfield, 1983-97; successor trustee Yale Corp., New Haven, 1977-89; trustee Ford Found., N.Y.C., 1982-94, Am. Mus. of Moving Image, 1986-96, Wellesley Coll., 1988—; mem. distbn. com. N.Y. Cmty. Trust, Inc., N.Y.C. 1978-95, chmn. dist. com. N.Y. Cmty. Trust, 1990-95; chmn. coun. Advisors Hunter Coll. Sch. Social Work, 1985-89; mem. Dumpson chair com., Fordham U., N.Y.C., 1981-89; bd. dirs. Tougaloo Coll. Econ. Devel. Corp., 1991—. Recipient Meritorious award Nat. Assn. Theatre Owners, 1970, 72, Alumni Achievement award Wellesley Coll., 1975, Tribute to Women in Internat. Industry award YWCA, 1984, Elizabeth Cutter Morrow award, 1985, Outstanding Contbrs. award Am. Women's Econ. Devel., 1985, Dirs. Choice award Nat. Women's Econ. Alliance Found., 1989, Keystone award Fedn. Protestant Welfare Agys., 1991, Civic award Citizen's Union of City of N.Y., 1995, Nat. Equal Justice award NAACP, 1996, Dir. of Yr. award Nat. Assn. Corp. Dirs., 1996. Mem. ABA, Assn. of Bar of City of N.Y. (mem. exec. com. 1972-76), ACLU (bd. dirs.), Century Assn., Cosmopolitan Club, Yale Club, Wellesley Club. Episcopalian. Office: 60 E 42nd St New York NY 10165

PREISLER, HARVEY D., medical facility administrator, medical educator; b. N.Y., Feb. 5, 1941; s. Leonard and Estelle Preisler; m. Angela Preisler; children: Sarah, Mark, Vanessa; m. Arza Raza; 1 child, Sheharzad. BA, Bklyn. Coll., 1961; MD, U. Rochester, 1965. Assoc. prof. medicine SUNY, Buffalo, 1974-88; assoc. chief dept. med. oncology Roswell Park Meml. Inst., Buffalo, 1975-82, chief leukemia svcs., 1982-86, acting chief BMT, 1985-87, chief dept. hematology and oncology, 1986-88; head, sec. cell biology and myeloproliferative Buffalo, 1979-82; founder, chmn. Leukemia Intergroup, 1980-89; dir., prof. medicine, chief divsn. hematology Charles M. Barrett C.C., 1989-91; prof. medicine divsn. hematology U. Cin. Med. Ctr., 1989-92; dir. Rush Cancer Inst., chief hematology/oncology, prof. Rush-Presbyn.-St. Luke's Med. Ctr., Chgo., 1992—; founder, chmn. Buffalo Coop. Group of Cmty. Hematologists for Rx Myeloid Diseases, 1977-84, Leukemia Intergroup, 1980-89; chmn. teaching session on acute leukemia Am. Soc. Hematology, 1982-84, co-chmn. session XVIII leukemia and myeloid disorders, 1985. Contbr. articles to profl. jours. Mem. med. adv. bd. Lincoln Park Zoo, Chgo., 1994. Grantee NIH, 1988-89, 89-90, 90-91, 92—. Mem. Internat. Soc. Experimental Hematology, Am. Cancer Soc., Am. Assn. Cancer Rsch., Am. Soc. Clin. Oncology, Cell Kinetics Soc., Soc. Internal Medicine. Office: Rush Cancer Inst 1725 W Harrison St Ste 809 Chicago IL 60612-3832

PREISS, JACK, biochemistry educator; b. Bklyn., June 2, 1932; s. Erool and Gilda (Friedman) P.; children: Jennifer Ellen, Jeremy Oscar, Jessica Michelle. BS in Chemistry, CCNY, 1953; PhD in Biochemistry, Duke U., 1957. Scientist NIH, Bethesda, 1960-62; asst. prof. dept. biochemistry, biophysics U. Calif., Davis, 1962-65, assoc. prof., 1965-68, prof., 1968-85, chair dept. biochemistry, 1971-74, 77-81; prof. dept. biochemistry Mich. State U., East Lansing, 1985—, chair dept., 1985-89; Mem. editorial bd. Jour. Bacteriology, 1969-74, Arch. Biochem. Biophysics, 1969—; mem. editorial bd. Plant Physiology, 1969-74, 77-80, assoc. editor, 1980-92, editor, 1993-95; editor Jour. Biol. Chemistry, 1971-76, 78-83, 94—. Recipient Camille and Henry Dreyfus Disting. scholar award Calif. State U., 1983, Alexander von Humboldt Stiftung Sr. U.S. Scientist award, 1984, Award of Merit, Japanese Soc. Starch Sci., 1992, Disting. Faculty Mem. award Mich. Assn. Governing Bds. of State Univs., 1997, Mich. Scientist of Yr. award Impressions 5 Mus., 1997; Alsberg-Schoch Meml. lectr. Am. Assn. Cereal Chemists, 1990, Nat. Sci. Coun. lectr. Republic of China, 1988; Guggenheim Meml. fellow, 1969-70, Japan Soc. for Promotion of Sci. fellow, 1992-93; grantee NIH, 1963—, NSF, 1978-89, Dept. of Energy, 1993—, USDA, 1988—. Mem. AAAS, Am. Chem. Soc. (Charles Pfizer award in enzyme chemistry 1971), Biochem. Soc., Am. Soc. Biol. Chemists and Molecular Biology, Am. Soc. Microbiologists, Am. Soc. Plant Physiologists, Soc. for Complex Carbohydrates, Protein Soc., Pan Am. Soc. Biochemistry and Molecular Biology (sec. gen. 1994-96, vice chmn. 1997—). Office: Mich State Univ Dept Of Biochemistry East Lansing MI 48824

PREISS-HARRIS, PATRICIA, music educator, composer, pianist; b. N.Y.C., May 19, 1950; d. Fredric H. and Madeline (Robbins) P.; m. Eric A. Lerner, Nov. 1970 (div. 1975); m. William H. Harris, Aug. 13, 1995. BA, Harvard U., 1973; MFA, Calif. Inst. Arts, 1987. Performer, bassist Carla Bley Band, Willow, N.Y., 1977-78; instr. piano, composition The Hall Sch., Pittsfield, Mass., 1983-84; instr. music Santa Monica (Calif.) C.C., 1989; tchr. piano The Hackley Sch., Tarrytown, N.Y., 1991; tchr. piano and composition Fraioli Sch. of Music, Greenwich, Conn., 1991—; accompanist SUNY, Purchase, N.Y., 1991-95; performer, pianist Gary Wofsey Jazz Orchestra, 1996—; pvt. piano tchr., N.Y., Conn., Mass., 1980—; pianist Regency Greenwich Hyatt Hotel, 1995—, performer, solo and ensemble pianist, 1980—. Author: Musical Materials, 1987; composer, performer Jamaica's Album, 1984; composer Messages (piano & flute), 1980, Invocations (women's choir, medieval instruments), 1981, Complete Enlightenment (woodwinds, spkr.), 1986. Performance grantee Cambridge (Mass.) Arts Coun., 1977, Artists grantee No. Berkshire Coun. on Arts, 1983. Home: 162 Toms Rd Stamford CT 06906-1031

PREISTER, DONALD GEORGE, greeting card manufacturer, state senator; b. Columbus, Nebr., Dec. 23, 1946; s. Maurice J. Preister and Leona T. (Dusel) Chereck. BS in Edn., U. Nebr., 1977. Unit dir. Boys' Clubs of Omaha, 1973-83; dep. city clk. City of Omaha, 1984-85; tchr. The Great Peace March, U.S., 1986; founder, owner Joy Creations, Co., Omaha, 1988—; instr. Metro C.C., Omaha, 1979-80. Author: (sect.) Drug Abuse Prevention, 1977. Troop leader Boy Scouts Am., Omaha, 1973-83. Served with U.S. Army, 1966-68, Vietnam. Decorated Bronze Star. Mem. Vets. for Peace, Nebr. Sustainable Agr. Soc., Optimist. Democrat. Roman Catholic. Avocations: gardening, running, horses. Home: 3937 W St Omaha NE 68107-3152 Office: State Capitol Dist # 5 Lincoln NE 68509

PRELL, JOEL JAMES, medical group administrator; b. L.A., Aug. 16, 1944; s. Samuel and Mary Devorah (Schwartz) P.; children: Vanessa S., Matthew. BA, U. So. Calif., L.A., 1967; cert. fin. mgmt., Ohio State U., 1979; M. Pub. Health, UCLA, 1981. Various positions, 1967-72; chief adminstrv. office sr. adminstrv. analyst L.A. County, 1972-73; dep. regional dir. for planning and community rels. L.A. County Dept. Health Svcs. Region, 1973-75; adminstr. ambulatory care L.A. County Harbro Gen. Hosp., 1975-76; assoc. dir. hosp. and clinics ambulatory care svcs. U. Calif.-Irvine Med. Ctr., 1976-78; asst. to the dir. rsch. and analysis unit U. Calif., Davis, 1978-80; v.p. profl. svcs. San Pedro Peninsula Hosp., 1981-84; sr. v.p. South Coast Med. Ctr., 1984-87; pres., CEO Harbor Health Systems, Inc., 1987-90; CEO Santa Monica (Calif.) Plz. Med. Group, Inc., 1990-93; administrator Pathology Cons. Med. Group, Torrance, Calif., 1993—; spl. asst. to the contr. UCLA Hosp. and Clinics, 1980-81, adminstr. emergency medicine ctr., 1981. Mem. Hosp. Coun .So. Calif. (polit. action steering com., chmn. legis. affairs com.), Calif. Hosp. Polit. Action Com. (bd. dirs.), Health Care Execs. So. Calif., UCLA Health Svcs. Adminstrs. Alumni Assn. (pres.), Med. Group Mgmt. Assn., Am. Coll. Health Care Adminstrs., Friends of Westwood. Office: Pathology Cons Med Group 20221 Hamilton Ave Torrance CA 90502-1321

PRELL, MICHAEL JACK, economist; b. Ft. Worth, Nov. 2, 1944; s. Martin and Ruth Dorothy (Sosin) P.; m. Terri Lynne Hume, Nov. 30, 1969; 1 child, Marisa Hume. AB, U. Calif., Berkeley, 1966, MA, 1967, PhD, 1971. Fin. economist Fed. Res. Bank, Kansas City, Mo., 1970-73; with divsn. rsch. and stats. Bd. Govs. of Fed. Res. System, Washington, 1973—; chief capital mkts. sect., 1977-78; assoc. dir. div. rsch. and stats., 1978-83, dep. dir., 1983-87, dir., 1987—; assoc. economist Fed. Open Market Com., 1981-87, economist, 1987—; U.S. del. OECD Com. on Fin. Mkts., Paris, 1982—, chmn., 1997—; bd. dirs. Securities Investor Protection Corp., Washington. Mem. Conf. Bus. Economists (chmn. 1997). Office: Fed Res Bd Rsch & Stats Div 20th St & C St NW Washington DC 20551

PREM, F. HERBERT, JR., lawyer; b. N.Y.C., Jan. 14, 1932; s. F. Herbert and Sybil Gertrude (Nichols) P.; m. Patricia Ryan, Nov. 18, 1978; children from previous marriage: Julia Nichols, F. Herbert III. AB, Yale U., 1953; JD, Harvard U., 1959. Bar: N.Y. 1960. Assoc. Whitman & Ransom, N.Y.C., 1959-66, ptnr., 1967-93, co-chmn. exec. com., 1988-92, chmn., 1993; chmn. Whitman Breed Abbott & Morgan, N.Y.C., 1993—; bd. dirs. Fuji Photo Film U.S.A., Inc., Fuji Med. Sys. U.S.A., Inc., Noritake Co., Inc., Seiko Instruments America, Inc. Bd. dirs. Bagaduce Music Lending Libr., Inc., 1988-95, pres., 1989-93; bd. dirs. Cmty. Action for Legal Svc. Inc., 1967-70, treas., Legal Aid Soc. N.Y.C., 1969-73. Lt. (j.g.) USNR, 1953-56. Mem. ABA, Assn. of Bar of City of N.Y. (sec. 1967-69), N.Y. State Bar Assn., Am. Law Inst., Am. Soc. Internat. Law, Yale Club. Episcopalian. Office: Whitman Breed Abbott & Morgan 200 Park Ave New York NY 10166-0005

PREM, KONALD ARTHUR, physician, educator; b. St. Cloud, Minn., Nov. 6, 1920; s. Joseph E. and Theresa M. (Willing) P.; m. Phyllis Edelbrock, June 14, 1947; children: Mary Kristen, Stephanie, Timothy. B.S., U. Minn., 1947; M.B., 1950, M.D., 1951. Diplomate: Am. Bd. Ob-Gyn (with spl. competence in gynecologic oncology). Intern Mpls. gen. Hosp., 1950-51; fellow dept. obstetrics and gynecology U. Minn., Mpls., 1951-54; instr. U. Minn., 1955-58, asst. prof., 1958-60, assoc. prof., 1960-69, prof., 1969-93; prof. emeritus, 1993—; dir. div. gynecologic oncology U. Minn., 1969-83, head dept. obstetrics and gynecology, 1976-84; prof. dept. surgery, 1993-96. Served to capt. USAR, 1941-46; brig. gen. M.C. USAR (Ret.). Decorated Legion of Merit. Mem. Am. Coll. Ob-Gyn, Am. Gynec. and Obstet. Soc., Central Assn. Ob-Gyn, Hennepin County Med. Soc., Soc. Pelvic Surgeons, Minn. Ob-Gyn Soc., Soc. Gynecologic Oncologists, Internat. Soc. Gynecologic Pathologists, Soc. Gynecologic Surgery, Minn. Acad. Medicine, Am. Radium Soc., Mpls. Surg. Soc., Soc. Med. Cons. to Armed Forces, Am. Assn. Pro-Life Ob-Gyn. Roman Catholic. Home: 15660-16 Place N Plymouth MN 55447-2497 Office: PO Box 395 Mayo Bldg 420 Delaware St SE Minneapolis MN 55455-0374

PREMACK, DAVID, psychologist; b. Aberdeen, S.D., Oct. 26, 1925; s. Leonard B. and Sonja (Liese) P.; m. Ann M. James, Oct. 26, 1951; children: Ben, Lisa, Timothy. BA, U. Minn., 1949, PhD, 1955. Rsch. assoc. Yerkes Labs. Primate Biology, Orange Park, Fla., 1955; rsch. assoc., asst. prof. psychology U. Mo., Columbia, 1956-58; assoc. prof. U. Mo., 1959-62, prof., 1963-64; prof. U. Calif., Santa Barbara, 1965-75; vis. prof. Harvard U., 1970-71; prof. U. Pa., 1975—; artist-in-residence Yaddo, Saratoga Springs, N.Y., 1955; fellow Van Leer Jerusalem Inst., 1980, Inst. for Advanced Study, Berlin, 1985-86; vis. scientist Japan Soc. for Promotion Sci., 1980; univ. rsch. lectr. U. Calif., Santa Barbara, 1973; mem. sci. gov. bd. Fyssen Found., Paris, 1989—; assoc. neurosci. rsch. program, La Jolla, Calif., 1991—. Author: Intelligence in Ape and Man, 1976, (with Ann James Premack) The Mind of an Ape, 1983, Gavagai! Or the Future History of the Animal Language Controversy, 1986 (with Dan Sperber and Ann James Premack) Causal Cognition: A Multidisciplinary Debate, 1995; mem. editorial bd. Jour. Exptl. Psychology: Animal Processes, 1976—, Cognition, 1977—, Brain and Behavior Sci., 1978—, Jour. Cognitive Neurosci. Served with U.S. Army, 1943-46. Ford Found. teaching intern, 1954; USPHS postdoctoral fellow, 1956-59; Social Sci. Research Council fellow, summer 1963; Center for Advanced Study in Behavioral Scis. fellow, 1972-73; Guggenheim fellow, 1979-80; grantee NSF, 1961—, USPHS, 1960-80; recipient Kenneth Craik Research award St. John's Coll.-Cambridge U., 1987, Internat. Sci. prize Fyssen Found., Paris, 1987. Fellow AAAS; mem. Soc. Exptl. Psychologists. Office: 3815 Walnut St Philadelphia PA 19104-3604 also: CREA, Ecole Polytechnique, 1 rue Descartes, 75005 Paris France

PREMO, PAUL MARK, oil company executive; b. Syracuse, N.Y., Nov. 20, 1942; s. Matthias George and Kathryn (Whitbread) P.; m. Mary Catherine Hennessy, June 19, 1965; children—Deborah, Mark. B.S. in Chem. Engring., Manhattan Coll., Riverdale, N.Y., 1964; S.M. in Chem. Engring., MIT, 1965. Chem. engr. Chevron Research, Richmond, Calif., 1965-69; fin. analyst Chevron Corp., San Francisco, 1969-72, coordinator, mgr. supply and distbn., 1972-79; mgr. petroleum regulations Chevron USA, San Francisco, 1979-81, sec.-treas., 1981-85, mgr. property tax adminstrn., 1985-86, mgr. natural gas regulatory affairs, 1986-92; exec. cons. Resource Mgmt. Internat., San Rafael, Calif., 1992-95; v.p. Foster Assoc., Inc., San

Francisco, 1996—; dir. Ky. Agrl. Energy Corp., Franklin. Trustee Calif. Tax Found., 1985—. Mem. Calif. State C. of C. (tax com.), Western Oil and Gas Assn., Am. Petroleum Inst. (property tax com.), Natural Gas Supply Assn., Inst. Property Taxation, Calif. Taxpayers Assn. (bd. dirs. 1985—), MIT Alumni Assn., Commonwealth (San Francisco), Sigma Xi, Tau Beta Pi. Avocations: sailing, investments. Home: 310 Hazel Ave Mill Valley CA 94941-5054 Office: Foster Assocs Inc 120 Montgomery St San Francisco CA 94104-4303

PRENDERGAST, JOHN THOMAS, editor, writer; b. Phila., Feb. 13, 1958; s. John and Margaret (Walsh) P.; m. Carole Robin Bernstein, May 5, 1990. BA, U. Pa., Phila., 1980; MA, John Hopkins U., Balt., 1988. Asst. editor Wharton Mag., Phila., 1982; staff writer U. Pa., Phila., 1982-84; mng. editor Wharton Annual, Phila., 1984; editor Pa. Outlook, Phila., 1984-85; devel. writer Thomas Jefferson U., Phila., 1985-87; assoc. dir. devel. INFORM, Inc., N.Y.C., 1988; mng. editor Civil Engring., N.Y.C., 1989-96; editor Pa. Gazette, Phila., 1996—. Author: (novel) Jump, 1995 (1st Novel award Mid-List Press, 1994). Democrat. Avocations: reading, travel, films. Home: 118 Union St # 12C Brooklyn NY 11231 Office: Pennsylvania Gazette 3533 Locust Walk Philadelphia PA 19104-6226

PRENDERGAST, THOMAS A., investments and management consultant; b. Dec. 10, 1933; m. Mary Alice Peinado; children: Elizabeth Jane, Laura Ann Gordon. BS, Fordham U., 1955; postgrad., U. Tex., El Paso, 1960. CPA, Tex. Pvt. practice acctg., 1957-61; v.p. fin. Farah Mfg., Inc., 1961-71; chmn. bd. Billy the Kid, Inc., 1971-81, Jetco, 1972-74, Fashion Enterprises, Inc., 1982-84; chmn. bd. Air Cargo Equipment Corp., 1983-88, investments, mgmt. cons.; chmn. bd. El Paso Gibson's, Inc., 1988—; chmn. Sunland Audio Ltd. Co., 1994—, N.Am. Bender, Inc., 1995—; chmn. bd. dirs. Baron Chem., Inc., Clinitech, Inc., 1986-91, Steel Corp. Tex., Texzona Industries, Inc., True Blue Sky, Inc.; bd. dirs. APL Corp., DWG Corp., Graniteville Co., Inc., Pa. Engring. Corp., Southeastern Pub. Svc. Co., Wilson Bros., Triarc. Founder, pres. bd. trustees El Paso Community Coll, 1969-82. Office: 3901 N Mesa St Ste 200A El Paso TX 79902-1541

PRENDERGAST, THOMAS FRANCIS, railroad executive; b. Chgo., June 6, 1952; s. Francis V. and Julia M. Prendergast; m. Christine L. Prendergast, Oct. 1, 1994; 1 child, Kelly. BS in Socio-Technol. Sys., U. Ill., Chgo., 1974. Sr. transit planner Chgo. Transit Authority, 1975-77, sys. safety engr., 1977-79; transit safety sys. specialist Fed. Transit Adminstrn., Washington, 1979-82; dir. sys. safety N.Y.C. Transit, 1982-84, asst. v.p. sys. safety, 1984-87, gen. mgr. S.I. divsn., 1987-89, chief elec. officer, 1989-90, sr. v.p. subways, 1990-94; pres. L.I. R.R., Jamaica, 1994—. Office: LIRR Jamaica Station Jamaica NY 11435

PRENG, DAVID EDWARD, management consultant; b. Chgo., Sept. 30, 1946; s. Edward M. and Frances (Maras) P.; m. JoAnne Ferzoco, Dec. 6, 1969; children: Mark, Laura, Stephen, Michael. BS, Marquette U., 1969; MBA, DePaul U., 1973. Supr. Shell Oil Co., Houston and Chgo., 1969-73; controller Litton Office Products, Houston, 1973-74; v.p. Addington & Assocs., Houston, 1974-76; exec. v.p. Mantech S.W., Inc., Houston, 1976-77; sr. asso. Energy div. Korn/Ferry Internat., Houston, 1977-78; v.p. Kors Marlar & Assocs., 1978-80; pres. Preng & Assocs., 1980-85; pres. Preng Zant & Assocs., 1985-87, Preng & Assoc., 1987-97; bd. dirs. Citizens Nat. Bank of Tex., Box Energy Corp., Brit. Am. Bus. Assn. Mem. Sugar Creek Country Club (pres.). Home: 607 Chevy Chase Cir Sugar Land TX 77478-3601

PRENSKY, ARTHUR LAWRENCE, pediatric neurologist, educator; b. N.Y.C., Aug. 31, 1930; s. Herman and Pearl (Newman) P.; m. Sheila Carr, Nov. 13, 1969. A.B., Cornell U., 1951; M.D., N.Y. U., 1955. Diplomate: Am. Bd. Psychiatry and Neurology. Intern Barnes Hosp., St. Louis, 1955-56; resident and research fellow in neurology Harvard U., Mass. Gen. Hosp., Boston, 1959-66; instr. neurology Harvard Med. Sch., 1966-67; mem. faculty Washington U. Sch. Medicine, St. Louis, 1967—; prof. pediatrics and neurology Washington U. Sch. Medicine, to 1975, Allen P. and Josephine B. Green prof. pediatric neurology, 1975—; pediatrician St. Louis Children's Hosp.; neurologist Barnes and Allied Hosps., Jewish Hosp., St. Louis. Author: (with others) Nutrition and the Developing Nervous System, 1975; editor: (with others) Neurological Pathophysiology, 2d edit, 1978, Advances in Neurology, 1976; mem. editorial bd. Pediatric Neurology, 1984-90, Jour. Child Neurology, 1985—. Served with USAF, 1957-59. Fellow Am. Acad. Neurology; mem. Am. Neurol. Assn., Am. Soc. Neurochemistry (mem. council 1973-77), Central Soc. Neurol. Research (pres. 1977-78), Child Neurology Soc. (pres. 1979-80), Am. Pediatric Soc., Internat. Child Neurology Assn., Japanese Soc. Child Neurology, Profs. Child Neurology (pres. 1984-86). Home: 15 Monarch Hill Ct Chesterfield MO 63005-4004 Office: 400 S Kingshighway Blvd Saint Louis MO 63110-1014

PRENTICE, ANN ETHELYND, academic administrator; b. Grafton. Vt., July 19, 1933; d. Homer Orville and Helen (Cooke) Hurlbut; divorced; children: David, Melody, Holly, Wayne. AB, U. Rochester, 1954; MLS, SUNY, Albany, 1964; DLS, Columbia U., 1972; LittD (hon.), Keuka Coll., 1979. Lectr. sch. info. sci. and policy SUNY, Albany, 1971-72, asst. prof., 1972-78; prof., dir. grad. sch. library and info. sci. U. Tenn., Knoxville, 1978-88; assoc. v.p. info. resources U. South Fla., Tampa, 1988-93; dean Coll. of Libr. and Info. Svcs. U. Md., College Park, 1993—, acting asst. v.p. for info. resources, 1994—. Author: Strategies for Survival, Library Financial Management Today, 1979, The Library Trustee, 1973, Public Library Finance, 1977, Financial Planning for Libraries, 1983, 2d edit., 1996, Professional Ethics for Librarians, 1985; editor Pub. Libr. Quar., 1978-81; co-editor: Info. Sci. in its Disciplinary Context, 1990; assoc. editor Library and Info. Sci. Ann., 1987-90. Cons. long-range planning and pers. Knox County Libr. System, 1980, 85-86, Richland County S.C. Libr. System, 1981, Upper Hudson Libr. Fedn., N.Y., State Libr. Ohio, 1986, Am. U., 1996; trustee Hyde Park (N.Y.) Free Libr., treas., 1973-75, pres., 1976; trustee Mid-Hudson Libr. System, Poughkeepsie, N.Y., 1975-78; trustee adv. bd. Hillsborough County Libr., 1991-93. Recipient Disting. Alumni award SUNY, Albany, 1987, Columbia U., 1991. Mem. ALA, CAUSE, Am. Soc. Info. Sci. (exec. bd. 1986-89, conf. chmn. 1989, pres. 1992-93, chmn. info. policy com. 1994-96), Assn. for Libr. and Info. Sci. Edn. (pres. 1986). Office: Univ Md Coll Libr and Info Svcs 4105 Hornbake Bldg College Park MD 20742

PRENTICE, EUGENE MILES, III, lawyer; b. Glen Ridge, N.J., Aug. 27, 1942; s. Eugene Miles and Anna Margaret (Kiernan) P.; m. Katharine Kirby Culbertson, Sept. 18, 1976; children: Eugene Miles IV, Jessie Kirby, John Francis. BA, Washington and Jefferson Coll., Pa., 1964; JD, U. Mich., 1967. Bar: N.Y. 1973, U.S. Dist. Ct. (so. dist.) N.Y. 1973, U.S. Dist. Ct. (ea. dist.) N.Y. 1974, U.S. Ct. Appeals (2d cir.) 1974, N.Y. Supreme Ct. 1973. With Morgan Guaranty Trust, N.Y.C., 1967-68, 71-73; assoc. White & Case, N.Y.C., 1973-78; assoc. Windels, Marx et al, N.Y.C., 1978-80, ptnr., 1980-84; ptnr. Brown & Wood, N.Y.C., 1984-93, Piper & Marbury, N.Y.C., 1993-96; pres. Midland (Tex.) Sports, Inc., 1990—; ptnr. Bryan Cave LLP, N.Y.C., 1996—; bd. dirs. Nat. Life Ins. Co., Montpelier, Vt., Tex. League Profl. Baseball, 1990—. Trustee Vt. Law Sch., 1984—, Washington and Jefferson Coll., Pa., 1985—, Nat. Assn. Profl. Baseball Leagues, 1992—, vice chmn. of bd., 1995—, St. Hilda's and St. Hugh's Sch., N.Y.C., 1993—, pres. of bd., 1995—. Capt. U.S. Army, 1968-70. Mem. ABA, Assn. of Bar of City of N.Y., Links Club, Union League Club, N.Y. Athletic Club, Spring Lake Bath & Tennis Club, Lake Mansfield Trout Club (Vt.). Republican. Home: 34 W 95th St New York NY 10025-6701 Office: Bryan Cave LLP 245 Park Ave New York NY 10167-0002

PRENTICE, JAMES STUART, energy company executive, chemical engineer; b. Louisville, Feb. 4, 1944; s. John Edward and Helen (Staples) P.; m. Mary Joan Kelly, July 24, 1965; children: Holly Michelle, Craig Edward, Brian Andrew. B in Chem. Engring., U. Louisville, 1966; MS, Northwestern U., 1967. Research engr. Esso Research and Engring. Co., Baytown, Tex., 1967-71; engr., supr. ops., mkt. mgr. to plant mgr. No. Petrochem. Co., Morris and Des Plaines, Ill., 1971-82; v.p. mfg. No. Petrochem. Co., Omaha, 1982-85; sr. v.p. corp. planning HNG/Internorth, Omaha, 1985-86; sr. v.p. adminstrn. and human resources Enron Corp., Houston, 1986-87; exec. v.p. Enron Liquid Fuels, Houston, 1987-89; sr. v.p. Enron Gas Pipeline Group, Houston, 1989-93; sr. v.p., chief tech. officer Enron Ops. Corp., Houston, 1993-95, sr. v.p. human resources, 1995-96; pres. Enron Clean Fuels Co., 1996—. Patentee in field. Bd. dirs. St. Joseph Hosp. Found., Child Advocates, Inc. Mem. AIChE, Lakeside Country Club, Petroleum Club of Houston. Roman Catholic. Avocations: tennis, golf. Office: Enron Corp EB 4559 PO Box 1188 Houston TX 77251-1188

PRENTICE, NORMAN MACDONALD, clinical psychologist; b. Yonkers, N.Y., Feb. 25, 1925; s. Lester M. and Islay (Macdonald) P.; m. Marilyn E. Shepherd, Dec. 24, 1953 (dec. July 14, 1979); children: Wendy Elizabeth, Lisa Shepherd; m. Joyce Marie Broyles, June 25, 1987. A.B. in Psychology, Princeton U., 1949; M.A. in Clin. Psychology, Harvard U., 1952, Ph.D., 1956. Diplomate Am. Bd. Profl. Psychology. Research fellow child psychiat. unit Mass. Gen. Hosp., Boston, 1953-55; NIMH fellow Judge Baker Guidance Center, Boston, 1955-57; chief adolescent sect. psychologist Children's Hosp., Boston, 1957-58; staff psychologist to coordinator of training Judge Baker Guidance Center, 1958-65; asso. prof. psychology U. Tex., Austin, 1965-68; prof. psychology and ednl. psychology U. Tex., 1968—, dir. clin. psychology tng. program, 1974-76; cons. VA, 1966-80. Contbr. articles to profl. jours. Bd. dirs. Austin Community Nursery Sch., 1966-69, Austin Child Guidance and Evaluation Ctr., 1981-84; trustee Austin-Travis County Mental Retardation Ctr., 1971-73, Art Inst. Boston, 1968-90. With AUS, 1943-45. Decorated Purple Heart. Fellow APA, Am. Psychol. Soc., Am. Orthopsychiat. Assn. (v.p. 1979-80), Soc. for Personality Assessment; mem. Phi Beta Kappa. Office: U Tex Dept Psychology Austin TX 78712-1157

PRENTICE, TIM, sculptor, architect; b. N.Y.C., Nov. 5, 1930; s. T. Merrill and Theodora (Machado) P.; m. Marie Truesdale Bissell, Aug. 23, 1960; children: Nora L., Phoebe A. B.A., Yale U., 1953, M.Arch., 1960. Gen. partner Prentice & Chan, Ohlhausen, Architects and predecessor, N.Y.C., 1966-74; adj. prof. archtl. design Columbia U., 1974-80. One-man shows include Inst. Architecture and Urban Studies, N.Y.C., 1975, Paul Mellon Arts Ctr., Wallingford, Conn., 1983, Aldrich Mus., Ridgefield, Conn., 1989, Bruce Mus., Greenwich, Conn., 1989, Maxwell Davidson Gallery, N.Y.C., 1990, 94, Mattatuck Mus., Waterbury, Conn., 1990, Neville Sargent Gallery, Chgo., 1991, Maxwell Davidson Gallery, N.Y.C., 1992, 94, 97; group shows New Britain Mus. Am. Art, 1978, Carlson Art Gallery U. Bridgeport, 1978, Indpls. Mus. Art, 1978, Conn. Painting, Drawing and Sculpture Today, 1977, Parsons-Dreyfuss Gallery, N.Y.C., 1980, Am. Acad. and Inst. Arts and Letters, N.Y.C., 1991, Anderson Gallery, 1992, Soma Gallery, San Diego, 1993, Chgo. Cultural Ctr., 1993, Fitchburg (Mass.) Art Mus., 1994, Yale U., New Haven, 1995, Hunner Mus., Chattanooga, Ohio, 1995; kinetic sculpture represented in permanent collections Am. Express Co., N.Y.C., AT&T Long Lines, Bedminster, N.Y., Henry St. Settlement, N.Y.C.; major commns. include CBS Bldg., N.Y.C., 1979, Conn. Natural Gas Co., Hartford, 1980, Mobil Oil, Fairfax, Va., 1982, Tex. Commerce Bank, Houston, 1982, INA CIGNA Corp., Wilmington, Del., 1983, Bank Am. Plaza, N.Y.C., 1984, United Va. Bank, Richmond, 1984, Bradley Internat. Airport, Windsor Locks, Conn., 1987, Hollister Inc., Libertyville, Ill., 1988, Mattatuck Mus., Waterbury, Conn., 1989, Summit Office Bldg., Raleigh, N.C., 1989, Sioux City (Iowa) Pub. Libr., 1990, Tempozan Market Place, Osaka, Japan, 1990, Irving (Tex.) Arts Ctr., 1991, Fed. Res. Bank of N.Y., East Rutherford, N.J., 1992, Math. Lib. Univ. Colo., Boulder, 1992, World Population Coun., N.Y.C., 1993, Peak Galleria, Hong Kong, 1993, Civic Ctr. Torroti, Japan, 1993, Hewlett Packard, Andover, Mass., Nat. Inventors Hall of Fame, 1995, Los Cerritos (Calif.) Ctr., 1995, U. Ctrl. Fla., Orlando, 1996, Wilkes-Barre (Pa.) Gen. Hosp., 1997, others. Served to lt. (j.g.) USNR, 1954-58. Dept. State cultural exchange grantee, 1963-64. Fellow AIA (pres. N.Y. chpt. 1973-74); mem. Nat. Council Archtl. Registration Bds., Mcpl. Arts Soc. N.Y. (pres. 1974-76). Club: Century Assn. Studio: 129 Lake Rd West Cornwall CT 06796-1402

PRENTKE, RICHARD OTTESEN, lawyer; b. Cleve., Sept. 8, 1945; s. Herbert E. and Melva B. (Horbury) P.; m. Susan Ottesen, June 9, 1974; children: Catherine, Elizabeth. BSE, Princeton U., 1967; JD, Harvard U., 1974. Assoc. Perkins Coie, Seattle, 1974-80, ptnr., 1981—, CFO, 1989—. Author: School Construction Law Deskbook, 1989; contbr. articles to profl. jours. Pres., trustee Seattle County Day Sch., 1990—; trustee Pocock Rowing Found., 1996—. With USN, 1967-70. Fellow Leadership Tomorrow, Seattle, 1985-86. Mem. ABA, Wash. State Bar Assn. (mem. jud. screening com. 1985-91, chmn. 1987-91), Seattle-King County Bar Assn. (chmn. jud. task force 1990-93), Am. Arbitration Assn. (arbitrator 1988—), Princeton U. Rowing Assn. (pres. 1993—, trustee 1976—), Rainier Club, Princeton Club Wash. (trustee 1986—, pres. 1990-92), Seattle Tennis Club. Avocations: art, carpentry, travel, rowing, sports. Office: Perkins Coie 1201 3rd Ave Fl 40 Seattle WA 98101-3099

PRENZLOW, ELMER JOHN-CHARLES, JR., minister; b. Norfolk, Nebr., Apr. 4, 1929; s. Elmer Edward and Alvina C. (Henning) P.; m. Karen McHarg DeMoss, July 4, 1980; 1 child, Elmer Carl III. BA, Northwestern Coll., Watertown, Wis., 1950; BD in Theology, WELS Luth. Sem., Mequon, Wis., 1953; MA in English and Philosophy, U. Minn., 1961; MS in Edn. Psychology, U. Wis., 1969; PhD in Psychology and Criminal Justice, Walden U., 1975. Pastor St Paul's Lutheran Ch., Bloomer, Wis., 1953-62; chaplain, instr. U. Wis., Milw., 1962-79; dir. devel. and pub. relations Luth. Ch.-Mo. Synod, Southern Wis. Dist., Milw., 1979-82; major gifts counselor Luth. Ch.-Mo. Synod Internat. Hdqrs., St. Louis, 1982-88; dir. devel. and fin. resources Adult Christian Edn. Found. Bethel Series, Madison, Wis., 1988-89; world relief devel. counselor Luth. Ch.-Mo. Synod Internat. Hdqrs., St. Louis, 1989-94; v.p. major gifts Luth. Ch.-Mo. Synod Found., St. Louis, 1994—; vice chmn. Standing Com. Dept. Campus Ministry Luth. Coun. U.S.A., N.Y., 1964-83; chmn. Milw. Religious Counselors, 1965-72, dept. humanities Spencerian Bus. Coll., 1967-77; v.p. Patricia Stevens Career Coll., bd. dirs. 1978-91; spkr., lectr. in field. Contbr. articles to profl. jours. Mem. Wis. State Legis. Com for Kerner Report, Madison, 1968-69, Nat. Adv. Commn.U.S. Justice Dept. on Law Enforcement standards and goals, Washington, 1971-73, ad hoc com. for establishing U.S. Bur. Prisons Nat. Inst. for Corrections, Washington, 1973-75, 19th congr. dist. Wis. svc. acad. review bd., Milw., 1975-82. Named Outstanding Prof. Spencerian Bus. Coll., Milw., 1972. Mem. Assn. of Luth. Devel. Execs., Optimists, Wis. Club. Republican. Avocations: travel, music, auto racing, golf, fishing. Home: 715 Windy Ridge Dr Ballwin MO 63021-7707 Office: LCMS Internat Ctr 1333 S Kirkwood Rd Saint Louis MO 63122-7226 *Nothing communicates to others what we believe more loudly and effectively than the measure of those principles they witness being personally carried out in our own lives!.*

PREONAS, GEORGE ELIAS, lawyer; b. Dayton, Ohio, Oct. 5, 1943; s. Louis D. and Mary (Drakos) P.; m. Aileen Strike, June 1, 1944; children—Annemarie, Michael, Stephen. B.A., Stanford U., 1965; J.D., U. Mich., 1968. Bar: Ill. 1968, Nev. 1969, Calif. 1974. Ptnr., Seyfarth, Shaw, Fairweather & Geraldson, Los Angeles, 1968—. Mem. Los Angeles County Bar Assn., Calif. Bar Assn., ABA, Ill. Bar Assn., Nev. Bar Assn. Office: Seyfarth Shaw Fairweather 2029 Century Park E Ste 3300 Los Angeles CA 90067-3019

PREPARATA, FRANCO PAOLO, computer science and engineering educator; b. Reggio E, Italy, Dec. 29, 1935; came to U.S., 1965, naturalized, 1977; s. Vincenzo and Stefania P.; m. Rosamaria Cupi, Apr. 30, 1964; children: Paola, Claudia. Dr.Ing., U. Rome, 1959; Libera Docenza, Italian U. System, 1969; Doctorate (hon.), U. Padova (Italy), 1997. System analyst, tech. mgr. Univac, Rome, 1960-63; sr. designer Selenia S.p.A., Rome, 1963-65; professorial staff U. Ill., Urbana, 1965-90, prof. elec. engring. and computer sci., 1970-90; An Wang prof. computer sci. Brown U., Providence, 1991—. Author: (with Raymond T. Yeh) Introduction to Discrete Structures, 1972, Introduction to Computer Engineering, 1985, (with M.I. Shamos) Computational Geometry, 1985; assoc. editor: IEEE Trans. on Computers, 1978-82, also 9 other jours.; contbr. articles to profl. jours. Fellow IEEE (Darlington award 1993), Assn. Computing Machinery. Office: 115 Waterman St Providence RI 02912-9016

PRESANT, SANFORD CALVIN, lawyer, educator, author, lecturer; b. Buffalo, Nov. 15, 1952; s. Allen Norman and Reeta (Coplon) P.; children, Jarrett Matthew, Daniel Michael, and Lauren Carley; BA, Cornell U., 1973; JD cum laude, SUNY-Buffalo, 1976; LLM in Taxation, Georgetown U., N.Y.U., 1981. Bar: N.Y. 1977, D.C. 1977, U.S. Ct. Claims 1978, U.S. Tax Ct. 1977, U.S. Supreme Ct. 1982, Calif. 1992. Staff atty. SEC options task force, Washington, 1976-78; assoc. Barrett Smith Schapiro, N.Y.C., 1978-80, Trubin Sillcocks, N.Y.C., 1980-81; ptnr. Carro, Spanbock, Fass, Geller, Kaster, N.Y.C., 1981-86, Finley, Kumble, Wagner, Heine, Underberg, Manley, Myerson & Casey, N.Y.C., 1987; Kaye, Scholer, Fierman, Hays & Handler, N.Y.C., 1988-95; Battle Bowler LLP, L.A., 1995—; adj. assoc. prof. real estate NYU, 1983—; frequent lectr. in tax law; regular TV appearances on Nightly Business Report, Pub. Broadcasting System, 1986—; co-chmn. NYU Conf. Fed. Taxation of Real Estate Transactions, 1987, 88. Author: (with others) Tax Aspects of Real Investments, 1987, Understanding Estate Partnership Tax Allocations, 1987, Realty Joint Ventures, 1980-86, Tax Sheltered Investments Handbook-Special Update on Tax Reform Act of 1984, Real Estate Syndication Handbook, 1985, Real Estate Syndication Tax Handbook, 1986, The Tax Reform Act of 1986, 1986, The Final Partnership Nonrecourse Debt Allocation Regulations, 1987, Taxation of Real Estate Investments, 1987, Understanding Partnership Tax Allocations, 1987, Tax Aspects of Environmental (Superfund) Settlements, 1994, The Final Regulations Under Section 704(c), 1995, The Proposed Publicly Traded Partnership Regulations, 1995. Kripke Securities law fellow NYU, 1976. Mem. ABA (nat. chmn. audit subcom. of tax sect. partnership com. 1984-86, partnership tax allocation subcom. chmn. 1986-90, nat. chmn. partnership com. 1992-94, chmn. task force publicly traded partnerships 1995—), N.Y. State Bar Assn. (tax sect. partnership com. 1980—), Assn. of Bar of City of N.Y. Republican. Jewish. Office: Battle Fowler LLP 1999 Ave Of Stars Ste 2700 Los Angeles CA 90067-6079

PRESBY, J. THOMAS, financial advisor; b. Newark, Feb. 15, 1940; s. George and Shirley (Kandel) P.; m. Elaine Merle Smith, Aug. 19, 1961; children: Philip, Terry, Mona. BSEE, Rutgers U., 1961; MS in Indsl. Adminstrn., Carnegie-Mellon U., 1963. CPA, Ohio, N.Y. Ptnr. Touche & Ross, N.Y.C., 1972-76; regional ptnr. Touche Ross Internat., Paris, 1976-79, nat. dir. client svcs., 1979-81, exec. dir. internat., 1981-82, ptnr.-in-charge fin. svcs. ctr., 1982-90, mng. ptnr. Ea. Europe, Brussels, 1990-94, chief exec. officer Europe, Paris, 1991-95; COO Deloitte Touche Tohmatsu Internat., N.Y.C., 1995—. Mem. bus. adv. council Grad. Sch. Indsl. Adminstrn., Carnegie-Mellon U., Pitts., 1984—; trustee Rutgers U., New Brunswick, N.J., 1985-90, Coll. Ins., N.Y.C., 1986-89. Mem. AICPA, Ohio Soc. CPAs, N.Y. Soc. CPAs, Harmonie Club, N.Y. Athletic Club. Avocations: antique autos; racquetball; squash, motorcycling. Home: 6 Holton Ln Essex Fells NJ 07021-1709 Office: Deloitte Touche 1633 Broadway New York NY 10019-6708

PRESCHLACK, JOHN EDWARD, management consultant; b. N.Y.C., May 30, 1933; s. William and Anna M. (Hrubesch) P.; m. Lynn A. Stanley, Dec. 29, 1962; children: John Edward Jr., James S., David C. BSEE, MIT, 1954; MBA, Harvard U., 1958. Ptnr. McKinsey & Co., Inc., N.Y.C., London, Düsseldorf, West Germany, 1958-73; pres. ITEK Graphic Products Co., Lexington, Mass., 1973-77; pres., CEO Gen. Binding Corp., Northbrook, Ill., 1977-83; pres. Roberts & Porter, Inc., Des Plaines, Ill., 1984-86; sr. dir. Spencer Stuart, Chgo., 1987-96; chmn., pres. Jepcor, Inc., Lake Bluff, Ill., 1996—; bd. dirs. Blyth Industries, Greenwich, Conn., 1989—. Trustee Chgo. Hort. Soc., 1979—; chmn. Lake Forest (Ill.) Planning Commn., 1982-88; alderman City of Lake Forest, 1989-96; mem. devel. com. MIT, 1986-92. Lt. USAF, 1954-56. Recipient Corp. Leadership award MIT, 1978. Mem. Onwentsia Club, Chgo. Club, John's Island Club. Republican. Roman Catholic. Avocations: tennis, boating, travel. Office: Jepcor Inc 900 N Shore Dr Ste 212 Lake Bluff IL 60044-2225 *Focus on what's right, not who's right; be honest and candid in dealing with others; don't get hung up on who gets credit for what you've done; select and reward outstanding people.*

PRESCOTT, BARBARA LODWICH, educational administrator; b. Chgo., Aug. 15, 1951; d. Edward and Eugenia Lodwich; m. Warren Paul Prescott, Dec. 2, 1979; children: Warren Paul Jr., Ashley Elizabeth. BA, U. Ill., Chgo., 1973, MEd, 1981; MA, U. Wis., 1978; postgrad., Stanford U., 1983-87. Cert. tchr., learning handicapped specialist, cmty. coll. instr., Calif. Grad. rschr. U. Ill., Chgo., 1979-81; learning handicapped specialist St. Paulus Luth. Sch., San Francisco, 1981-83; grad. rsch. asst. Sch. Edn. Stanford (Calif.) U., 1983-87, writing cons. for law students, 1985-86; learning handicapped specialist/lead therapist Gilroy Clinic Speech-Hearing-Learning Ctr., Crippled Children's Soc., Santa Clara, Calif., 1988-89; ednl. dir. Adolescent Intensive Resdl. Svc. Calif. Pacific Med. Ctr., San Francisco, 1989-95; exec. dir. Learning Profiles, South Lake Tahoe, Calif., 1995—; instr. evening San Jose City Coll., 1988-92. Contbr. articles to profl. jours.; author: Proceedings of Internat. Congress of Linguistics, 1987; editor: Proceedings - Forum for Research on Language Issues, 1986; author videotape: Making a Difference in Language and Learning, 1989. Recipient Frederick Bork Teaching Trainee award San Francisco State U., 1983; Ill. State scholar, 1973. Mem. Calif. Assn. Pvt. Specialized Edn. and Svcs., Phi Delta Kappa (v.p. 1984-86), Pi Lambda Theta (sec. 1982-83), Phi Kappa Phi, Alpha Lambda Theta. Home: 1055 Manet Dr Apt 86 Sunnyvale CA 94087-2819 Office: Learning Profiles 2145 Harvard Ave South Lake Tahoe CA 96150-4425

PRESCOTT, JANELLE, medical and surgical nurse; b. Uniontown, Pa., Jan. 5, 1965; d. Robert Lee and Pauline (Marcinek) Smith; m. Marvin Levi Prescott, Oct. 14, 1989; 1 child, Aaron Michael. Diploma, Uniontown Hosp. Sch. Nursing, 1988, Finesse Finishing Sch., Uniontown, 1986. RN, Pa. Nurse Uniontown Hosp., 1988—. Mem. U.S. Friendship Ambs., 1987—. Home: PO Box 1381 Uniontown PA 15401-1381

PRESCOTT, JOHN HERNAGE, aquarium executive; b. Corona, Calif., Mar. 16, 1935; s. Arthur James and Henrietta (Hernage) P.; m. Sandra Baker, Sept. 26, 1985; children by previous marriage—Craig C., Blane R. B.A., UCLA, 1957; postgrad., U. So. Calif., Los Angeles, 1958-60; cert. advanced mgmt. program, Harvard U. Curator Marineland of the Pacific, Palos Verdes, Calif., 1957-70, v.p., 1966-70, gen. mgr., 1970-72; exec. dir., v.p. New Eng. Aquarium, Boston, 1972-95, dir. emeritus, 1995—, life trustee, 1996; corporator Woods Hole (Mass.) Oceanographic Inst., 1976-90; chmn. mem. com. sci. advisers Marine Mammal Commn., Washington, 1977-80; dir. Mus. Inst. Teaching Sci. Boston, 1984-92; chmn. Humpback Whale Recovery Team NOAA, Washington, 1987-93; mem. U.S. del. Internat. Whaling Commn., 1989-94. Author: Aquarium Fishes of the World, 1976. Editor: Georges Bank: Past, Present, Future, 1981, Right Whales: Past and Present Status, 1986. Bd. dirs. Boston Mcpl. Rsch. Bur., 1981-95, Boston Am. Heart Assn., 1983-86, NOAA, Washington, 1987-92; mem. Marine Fisheries Adv. Com., 1991-93, Artery Bus. Com., 1993-95. Recipient commendation for efforts to conserve whales U.S. Ho. of Reps., 1971, Ann. Sci. award for Conservation, Am. Cetacean Soc., 1969. Fellow Am. Assn. Zool. Parks and Aquariums (bd. dirs. 1985-95); mem. AAAS, Soc. Marine Mammalogy, Am. Assn. Mus., Sea Edn. Assn. (trustee 1986-92), Explorers Club (chmn. New Eng. sect. 1981-85). Office: New Eng Aquarium Corp Central Wharf Boston MA 02110-3399

PRESCOTT, JOHN MACK, biochemist, retired university administrator; b. San Marcos, Tex., Jan. 22, 1921; s. John Mack and Maude (Raborn) P.; m. Kathryn Ann Kelly, June 8, 1946; children: Stephen Michael, Donald Wyatt. B.S. in Chemistry, S.W. Tex. State Coll., 1941; M.S. in Biochemistry and Nutrition, Tex. A&M U., 1949; Ph.D. in Biochemistry, U. Wis., 1952. Lab. asst. Dow Chem. Co., Freeport, Tex., 1942-43; faculty Tex. A&M U., College Station, 1946-49, 52-85, prof. biochemistry, 1959-85, dean Coll. Sci., 1970-77, v.p. for acad. affairs, 1977-81, dir. Inst. Occupational and Environ. Medicine, 1981-87, prof. med. biochemistry, 1981-85, prof. emeritus, 1985—, spl. asst. to dep. chancellor for biotech. devel., 1987-88; research asst. U. Wis.-Madison, 1949-51, U. Tex., Austin, 1951-52; vis. prof. Harvard Med. Sch., 1982. Contbr. articles profl. jours. Mem. Tex. Bd. Examiners in Basic Scis., 1974-79, mem. Tex. State Bd. Edn., 1984-88. Served to lt. USAAF, 1943-46; lt. col. USAF Res., 1946-68. Mem. Am. Soc. for Biochemistry and Molecular Biology, Soc. for Exptl. Biology and Medicine, Sigma Xi, Phi Lambda Upsilon. Home: 31 Forest Dr College Station TX 77840-2337

PRESCOTT, PETER SHERWIN, writer; b. N.Y.C., July 15, 1935; s. Orville and Lilias (Ward-Smith) P.; m. Anne Courthope Kirsopp Lake, June 22, 1957; children: David Sherwin, Antonia Courthope. A.B. magna cum laude, Harvard, 1957. Editor E.P. Dutton Co., N.Y.C., 1958-67; lit. editor, syndicated columnist Women's Wear Daily, N.Y.C., 1964-68; mem. faculty Pubs. Sch. for Writers, N.Y.C., 1965-66; lit. editor, columnist Look mag., 1968-71; book critic Newsweek mag., N.Y.C., 1971-91; sr. writer Newsweek mag., 1978-91; lectr. U.S. State Dept., 1978; adj. prof. Grad. Sch. Journalism, Columbia U., 1979-86. Author: A World of Our Own: Notes on Life and Learning in a Boys' Preparatory School, 1970, Soundings:

Encounters with Contemporary Books, 1972, A Darkening Green: Notes from the Silent Generation, 1974, The Child Savers: Juvenile Justice Observed, 1981, Never in Doubt: Critical Essays on American Books, 1972-85, 1986, The Norton Book of American Short Stories, 1988. Mem. Dem. town Com., New Canaan, 1969-72; constable Town of New Canaan, 1969-73; bd. dirs. Authors Guild Found., 1970-95, pres., 1971-93; exec. bd. Authors League Fund, 1st v.p., 1994-97, pres., 1997—. With USAR, 1958-64. Recipient George Polk award criticism, 1978, 1st prize Robert F. Kennedy Book Awards, 1981; fellow Guggenheim Found., 1977, NEH, 1993. Mem. PEN Am. Center (exec. bd. 1974-76), Authors League Am. (exec. bd. 1974-76), Assn. Literary Scholars and Critics, Authors Guild (exec. bd. 1971-91), Nat. Book Critics Circle (exec. bd. 1973-75, 92-93), Century Assn., Harvard Club (N.Y.C.), Phi Beta Kappa. Home and Office: 81 Benedict Hill Rd New Canaan CT 06840-2904

PRESCOTT, RICHARD PAUL, JR., computer company consultant; b. Bloomington, Ill., Apr. 20, 1939; s. Richard Paul Sr. and Kathern Grace (Rhodus) P.; m. Winifred Luce Rockefeller, June 15, 1962 (dec. 1966); children: Paul Luce and Peter Grace (dec.). Bus., Ill. Wesleyan U., 1960; MBA, U. Chgo., 1963; PhD, London Sch. Econ., 1966; lic. real estate sales, Ill. State U., 1992. Systems analyst Honeywell EDP, Chgo., 1963-67; info. specialist IBM, White Plains, N.Y., 1967-68; sr. project dir. United Artists, N.Y.C., 1969-70; info. mgr. Blue Cross Assn., Chgo., 1971-72; software cons. Bloomington, Ill., 1973-92, Referral Co. of McLean County, 1992; founding mem., owner Software Info. Svc. Bd., 1993; cons. Gen. Acct. Office, Washington, Sec. of State, Washington, Econ. Devel. Peru, Lima, 1990—. Author: SSA and Blue Cross Instruction Manual, 1970, (software) Easy Tran-sort, 1971, Operating System, 1974. Mem. Rep. Nat. Com., Pres.'s Conf. Econ. Advisors, 1990—. Comdr. USN, 1963—. Decorated Navy Cross, Silver Star, Purple Heart. Mem. DAV, ACLU, Internat. Platform Assn., Chgo. Econ. Coun., Am. Legion, Smithsonian Inst., Chgo. Art Inst., Bloomington Symphony, Libr. of Congress Assocs. (charter mem.), Mensa, Theta Chi (chpt. pres.). Methodist. Avocations: sailing, collecting U.S. stamps, reading, computers. Home and Office: 1128 N Colton Ave Bloomington IL 61701-1922

PRESCOTT, WILLIAM BRUCE, minister; b. Denver, Dec. 30, 1951; s. William Rex and Betena Naomi (Fletcher) P.; m. D. Kylene Winters, Nov. 24, 1973; children: William Doyle, Candice Joy. BS in Corrections, U. Albuquerque, 1973; MDiv, Southwestern Bapt. Sem., 1978, PhD, 1986. Ordained minister in Bapt. Ch., 1976. Youth minister Sandia Bapt. Ch., Albuquerque, 1974-75; pastor Clairette (Tex.) Bapt. Ch., 1976-79; instr. philosophy and religion Tarrant County Jr. Coll. NW Campus, Ft. Worth, 1984-86; pastor Easthaven Bapt. Ch., Houston, 1987—; adj. prof. Southwestern Bapt. Theol. Sem., HBU Extension, Houston, 1987-90; police chaplain Houston Police Dept., 1987—; trustee S.E. Area Ministries, Houston, 1988—; mem. exec. bd. Union Bapt. Assn., 1987-94, Bapt. Gen. Conv. Tex., 1993—, Tex. Bapts. Committed, 1990—; coord. coun. Coop. Bapt. Fellowship, 1994—, mem. Tex. exec. com., 1996—, Tex. steering com., 1994—; spkr. confs. in field. Book reviewer to Southwestern Jour. Theology; contbr. articles to profl. jours. Served on Bapt. Gen. Conv. Tex. Com. Distinctives Com., 1994—, Exec. Bd. Nominating Com., 1996, Com. on Conv. Arrangements, 1997; CBF Theol. Edn. Ministry Group, 1994-95, Bapt. Principles Ministry Group, 1995—, Adminstrv. Coun. Structure Com., 1996, Adv. Coun., 1996—, Info. Systems Mgmt. Project Team, 1996—, chmn. Bapt. Bapt. Distinctives Partnership Team, 1995—; trustee San Andres U., San Andres Island, San Andres Found. Named one of Outstanding Young Men of Am., Jaycees, 1984. Mem. Am. Acad. Religion, Ams. United for Separation Ch. and State (pres. Houston chpt. 1997—), So. Bapt. Alliance, Baptists Committed, People for the Am. Way, Concord Coalition, Whitsett Soc. Democrat. Home: 2203 Bisontine St Friendswood TX 77546-2391 Office: Easthaven Bapt Ch 9321 Edgebrook St Houston TX 77075-1249

PRESECAN, NICHOLAS LEE, environmental and civil engineer, consultant; b. Indpls., Sept. 4, 1940; s. Nicholas Eli and Dorothy Lee (Moore) P.; m. Joan Westin, Nov. 11, 1940; children: Julie Marie, Mary Lee, Anne Westin. BSCE, Purdue U., 1963; MS in Engring., U. Calif., Berkeley, 1967. Cert. profl. engr., 31 states. Project engr. San Bernardino County (Calif.) Flood Control, 1963, Engring. Sci. Inc., Arcadia, Calif., 1968-70; office mgr. Engring. Sci. Inc., Cleve., 1970-72, v.p., chief engr., 1972-81; v.p. internat. divsn. Engring. Sci. Inc., Arcadia, 1981-84, group v.p., 1984-87; sr. v.p. Engring. Sci. Inc., Pasadena, Calif., 1987—; mem. industry adv. bd. Sch. Engring. and Tech. Calif. State U., L.A., 1986—. Contbr. articles to profl. jours. Commr. Archtl. Commn., Claremont, Calif., 1980-86; councilman Claremont City Coun., 1986-94; mayor City of Claremont, 1989-92; mem. Pasadena Tournament of Roses Assn., 1980—, L.A. 2000 Environ. Com., 1987-88. With USMC, 1963-67. Recipient Disting. Engring. Achievement award Inst. for Advancement of Engring., 1993. Fellow ASCE (mem. internat. adv. com. 1987-90); mem. NSPE, Am. Acad. Environ. Engrs., Am. Water Works Assn. (life), Water Environ. Fedn., Soc. Am. Value Engrs., Rotary. Republican. Avocations: skiing, hiking, fishing, boating, writing. Home: 727 E Alamosa Dr Claremont CA 91711-2008 Office: Parsons Engring Sci Inc 100 W Walnut St Pasadena CA 91124-0001

PRESKA, LORETTA A., federal judge; b. 1949. BA, Coll. St. Rose, 1970; JD, Fordham U., 1973; LLM, NYU, 1978. Assoc. Cahill, Gordon & Reindel, N.Y.C., 1973-82; ptnr. Herzog, Calamari & Gleason, N.Y.C., 1982-92; fed. judge U.S. Dist. Ct. (so. dist.) N.Y., N.Y.C., 1992—. Mem. ABA, N.Y. State Bar Assn., N.Y. County Lawyers Assn., Assn. Bar City N.Y., Fed. Bar Coun., Fordham Law Alumni Assn. (v.p.). Office: US Courthouse 500 Pearl St Rm 1320 New York NY 10007-1316

PRESKA, MARGARET LOUISE ROBINSON, education educator, district service professional; b. Parma, N.Y., Jan. 23, 1938; d. Ralph Craven and Ellen Elvira (Niemi) Robinson; m. Daniel C. Preska, Jan. 24, 1959; children: Robert, William, Ellen Preska Steck. B.S. summa cum laude, SUNY, 1957; M.A., Pa. State U., 1961; Ph.D., Claremont Grad. Sch., 1969; postgrad., Manchester Coll., Oxford U., 1973. Instr. LaVerne (Calif.) Coll., 1968-75, asst. prof., asso. prof., acad. dean, 1972-75; instr. Starr King Sch. for Ministry, Berkeley, Calif., summer, 1975; v.p. acad. affairs, equal opportunity officer Mankato (Minn.) State U., 1975-79, pres., 1979-92; project dir. Kaliningrad (Russia) Mil. Re-Tng., 1992—; disting. svc. prof. Minn. State U., Winona, 1993—, pres. Inst. for Effective Tchg., 1993-96; bd. dirs. No. States Power Co., Norwest Corp., Mankato, Exec. Sports Inc. Pres. Pomona Valley chpt. UN Assn., 1968-69, Unitarian Soc. Pomona Valley, 1968-69, PTA Lincoln Elem. Sch., Pomona, 1973-74, Nat. Camp Fire Boys and Girls, 1986-88; mem. Pomona City Charter Revision Commn., 1972; chmn. The Fielding Inst., Santa Barbara, 1983-86; bd. dirs. Elderhostel Internat., 1983-87, Minn. Agrl. Interpretive Ctr. (Farmam.), 1983-92, Am. Assn. State Colls. and Univs., Moscow on the Mississippi - Minn. Meets the Soviet Union; nat. pres. Campfire, Inc., 1985-87; chmn. Gov.'s Coun. on Youth, Minn., 1983-86, Minn. Edn. Forum, 1984; mem. Gov.'s Commn. on Econ. Future of Minn., 1985—, NCAA Pres. Commn., 1986-92, NCAA Cost Cutting Commn., Minn. Brainpower Compact, 1985; commr. Great Lakes Govs.' Econ. Devel. Coun., 1986, Minn Gov.'s Commn. on Forestry. Carnegie Found. grantee Am. Coun. Edn. Deans Inst., 1974; recipient Outstanding Alumni award Pa. State, Outstanding Alumni award Claremont Grad. Sch., YWCA Leader award 1982, Exch. Club Book of Golden Deeds award, 1987; named One of top 100 alumni, SUNY, 1895-1985, 1985, Hall of Heritage award, 1988, Wohelo Camp Fire award, 1989. Mem. AAUW (pres. Mankato 1990-92), LWV, Women's Econ. Roundtable, St. Paul/Mpls. Com. on Fgn. Rels., Am. Coun. on Edn., Am. Assn. Univ. Adminstrs., Zonta, Rotary, Benedicts Dance Club. Unitarian. Home: 10 Sumner Hills St Mankato MN 56001 Office: Minn State U 457 Gould St Winona MN 55987-2441

PRESLEY, BRIAN, investment company executive; b. Evansville, Ind., Dec. 28, 1941; s. Harry and Ruth P.; B.S. in Bus. Adminstrn., U. Evansville, 1963; M.B.A. Mich. State U., 1964; diploma Wharton Sch., U. Pa., 1995, m. Mary Nell Minyard, Aug. 17, 1972; children: Debra, Cynthia, David, Jeffrey, Clark, Gregory, Steven. Market rsch. analyst Stanley Works, New Britain, Conn., 1964-68; tax shelter coord. F.I. Dupont, Memphis, 1968-73; v.p. Bullington Schas, Memphis, 1973-75; pres., mng. gen. ptnr. Presley Assocs., Memphis, 1965-93; pres., CFO CSG, Inc., Memphis, 1975—; gen. ptnr. various real estate and oil and gas partnerships, 1974-1986; pres. Cooper St. Group Securities, Inc., 1983-86 ; divsn. mgr. Advantage Capital Corp. (divsn. SunAmerica, Inc.), 1986-89, reg. v.p., 1989, CEO 1990-94, mng. dir., mktg. strategist, 1995; pres. Presley Adv. Inc., 1995—, pub. Presley Adv. Letter; instr. fin. divsn. continuing edn. Memphis U. Bd. dirs. Apt. Coun. Tenn., 1980-86, sec.-treas., 1982-83; pres. Memphis Apt. Coun., 1983; mem., U. Evansville Nat. Alumni Bd., 1988-91. Producer 2 daily radio stock market commentary shows, 1988; fin. commentator Sta. WEVU-TV (ABC), Ft. Myers/Naples, 1988-89. Mem. Internat. Assn. Fin. Planners (broker dealer adv. coun., 1993-97), Admirals Club (life, bd. dirs.), Naples Jazz Soc. (bd. dirs.), Naples Sailing and Yacht Club (bd. dirs.), Pi Sigma Epsilon, Beta Gamma Sigma, Tau Kappa Epsilon Alumni Assn. (pres. Memphis area 1979-80). Presbyterian. Host syndicated radio show for sr. citizens, 1979-81. Home: Acorn Ranch 35600 Bermont Rd Punta Gorda FL 33982-9511 Office: 1600 S Federal Hwy Pompano Beach FL 33062-7500

PRESLEY, JOHN WOODROW, academic administrator; b. Jonesboro, Ark., Mar. 24, 1948; s. Marvin Woodrow and Willa Louise (Taylor) P.; m. Katherine Bailey Harrison, Oct. 17, 1978. BSE, Ark. State U., 1970; MA, So. Ill. U., 1972, PhD, 1975; postgrad., Johns Hopkins U., 1976, U. Tex., 1980. Asst. prof. Augusta State U., 1974-77, assoc. prof., 1978-84, prof., 1984-89, chmn. Freshman English, 1974-76, chmn. developmental studies, 1976-78, asst. v.p. for acad. affairs, 1988-89; assoc. dean faculty Lafayette Coll., Easton, Pa., 1989-90, acting provost, dean faculty, 1990-91, assoc. provost, dean faculty, 1991-92; dean Coll. of Arts, Scis. and Letters U. Mich., Dearborn, 1992—; presenter in field. Author: The Robert Graves Letters and Manuscripts at Southern Illinois University, 1976, (with W.M. Dodd) Breakthrough: From Reading to Writing, 1981, To Be Exact: A Handbook for Revision, 1982, (with M.G. Kramer) The Prentice-Hall Workbook for Writers, 1983, 4th edit. (with M.G. Kramer and D. Rigg), 1985, 5th, 1988, 6th, 1990, How Like A Life, 1987, (with N. Prinsky) The World of Work, 1987, (with A.I. Philbin) Technical Communications: Method, Application, Management, 1989; contbg. author: The Prentice-Hall Handbook for Writers, 9th edit., 1985, Sparking Connections: Spoken and Written Communications, 1985, Speech Exercises for Basic Writers and Others, 1987; assoc. editor Gravesiana: The Journal of the Robert Graves Society, 1996—; contbr. articles to profl. jours. NDEA fellow, 1972. Mem. Phi Kappa Phi. Home: 7782 Horsemill Rd Grosse Ile MI 48138-1128 Office: Univ Mich Dearborn 4901 Evergreen Rd Dearborn MI 48128-2406

PRESLEY, PRISCILLA, actress; b. Bklyn., May 24, 1945; m. Elvis Presley, 1967 (div. 1973). Studies with Milton Katselas; student, Steven Peck Theatre Art Sch., Chuck Norris Karate Sch. Prin. Bis and Beau; co-executor Graceland, Memphis. Appearances include (films) The Naked Gun, 1988, The Adventures of Ford Fairlaine, 1990, The Naked Gun 2 1/2, 1991, The Naked Gun 33 1/3, 1994, (TV series) Those Amazing Animals, 1980-81, Dallas, 1983-88, (TV movie) Love Is Forever, 1983; prodr. (TV movie) Elvis and Me, 1988. Office: William Morris 151 S El Camino Dr Beverly Hills CA 90212-2704*

PRESLEY, ROBERT BUEL, state senator; b. Tahlequah, Okla., Dec. 4, 1924; s. Doyle and Annie (Townsend) P.; grad. FBI Nat. Acad., Washington, 1962; student Riverside City Coll., 1960; A.A., UCLA, m. Ahni Ratliff, Aug. 20, 1944; children—Donna Thurber, Marilyn Raphael, Robert Buel. Various positions Riverside County Sheriff's Dept. (Calif.), 1950-62, undersheriff, 1962-74; mem. Calif. Senate, 36th Dist., 1974-94; lectr. ethics. Served with U.S. Army, 1943-46. Decorated Bronze Star. Mem. FBI Nat. Acad. Assn. (pres. Calif. chpt. 1974). Baptist. Clubs: Lions, Elks, Am. Legion, V.F.W., Moose, Riverside County Democratic Century (pres. 1972-73). Home: 5508 Grassy Trail Dr Riverside CA 92504-1251 Office: Office of State Senate 5114 State Capital Sacramento CA 95814

PRESS, AIDA KABATZNICK, former editor, writer; b. Boston, Nov. 18, 1926; m. Newton Press, June 5, 1947; children: David, Dina Press Weber, Benjamin Presskreischer. BA, Radcliffe Coll., 1948. Reporter Waltham (Mass.) News-Tribune, 1960-63; freelance writer, 1960-63; editl. cons. Mass. Dept. Mental Health, Boston, 1966-72; Waltham/Watertown reporter Boston Herald Traveler, 1963-70; dir. news and publs. Harvard Grad. Sch. Design, Cambridge, Mass., 1972-78; publs. editor Radcliffe Coll., Cambridge, 1978-81, dir., editor of publs., 1981-83, editor Radcliffe Quar., 1971-93, dir. pub. info., 1983-93; cons. editor Regis Coll. Alumnae Mag., Weston, Mass., 1994. Editor emerita Radcliffe Quar., 1993—; contbr. articles to newspapers and mags. Recipient Publs. Distinction award Am. Alumni Coun., 1974, Top 5 coll. Mag., Coun. for Advancement and Support of Edn., 1984, Top 10 Univ Mags., 1991, Gold medal Coll. Mags., 1991, Alumnae Achievement award Radcliffe Coll., 1994, Radcliffe Coll. Presdl. Commendation, 1992. Mem. Phi Beta Kappa. Avocations: hiking, playing recorder.

PRESS, CHARLES, retired political science educator; b. St. Louis, Sept. 12, 1922; s. Otto Ernst and Laura (Irion) P.; m. Nancy Miller, June 10, 1950; children: Edward Paul, William David, Thomas Leigh, Laura Mary. Student, Elmhurst (Ill.) Coll.; B of Journalism, U. Mo., 1948; M.A., U. Minn., 1951, Ph.D., 1953. Faculty N.D. Agrl. Coll., 1954-56; dir. Grand Rapids Area Study, 1956-57; with Bur. Govt., U. Wis., 1957-58; faculty Mich. State U., East Lansing, 1958-91; prof. polit. sci. Mich. State U., 1964-91; emeritus, 1991—; chmn. dept. Mich. State U., 1966-73; cons. Mich. Constl. Conv., 1962-63; supr. Ingham County, 1966-72; tchr. summers, London; tchr. U. N.S.W., Sydney, Mich. State U. Author: Main Street Politics, 1962, (with Charles Adrian) The American Government Process, 1965, Governing Urban America, 1968, 5th edit., 1977, American Politics Reappraised, 1974, (with Kenneth VerBurg) States and Community Governments in a Federal System, 1979, 3d edit., 1991, American Policy Studies, 1981, The Political Cartoon, 1982, (with others) Michigan Political Atlas 1984, (with Kenneth VerBurg) American Politicians and Journalists, 1988, (with Kenneth VerBurg) (weekly newspaper column) The Pros and Cons of Politics. Sec. Ingham County Bd. Health, 1983-93; chmn., mem. East Lansing Bd. Rev., 1966-86; bd. dirs. Urban League, 1971-73; mem. East Lansing Housing and Urban Devel. Commn., 1988-93. Served with AUS, 1943-45. Recipient Disting. Prof. award Mich. State U., 1980, Alumni Merit award Elmhurst (Ill.) Coll., 1995. Mem. Am. Polit. Sci. Assn., Midwest Polit. Sci. Assn. (pres. 1974-75), So. Polit. Sci. Assn., Mich. Conf. Polit. Scientists (pres. 1972-73), Nat. Municipal League, B.S.I. Home: 987 Lantern Hill Dr East Lansing MI 48823-2831 Office: Mich State U 315 S Kedzie Hall East Lansing MI 48824-1032

PRESS, EDWARD, consulting physician; b. N.Y.C., May 4, 1913; s. Louis and Anna (Karpas) P.; m. Ruth Scheffer, July 8, 1951; children: Stephen, Phyllis. B.A., Ohio U., 1934; M.D., NYU, 1937; M.P.H., Harvard U., 1947. Diplomate: Am. Bd. Pediatrics, Am. Bd. Preventive Medicine. Intern Beth Israel Hosp., N.Y.C., 1938-40; resident Lincoln Hosp., Bronx, N.Y., 1940; psychiatric resident E.P. Bradley Home, East Providence, R.I., 1940-41; asst. dir. maternal and child health div. W.Va. Health Dept., 1941-42; pediatric cons. Mich. Health Dept., 1946; regional med. dir. U.S. Children's Bur., Chgo., 1947-50; asso. dir. div. services crippled children U. Ill., 1950-55; field dir. Am. Public Health Assn., N.Y.C., 1955-59; dir. Dept. Public Health, Evanston, Ill., 1959-64; med. asst. to dir. Ill. Dept. Public Health, 1964-67; state health officer (Oreg. Health Div.), Portland, 1967-79; public health cons., 1979—; emeritus sec.-treas. Press Internat. Sales Corp., 1978—; asst. prof. preventive medicine U. Ill., 1950-55; asst. prof. pediatrics Northwestern U., 1964-67; clin. prof. pub. health, preventive medicine and pediatrics Med. Sch., Oreg. Health Scis. U., 1967-79, emeritus clin. prof., 1979—; vice chmn. Tech. Adv. Group for Fire Safe Cigarette Act of 1990-93. Mem. editorial adv. com. The Nation's Health, 1989-91; contbr. articles to profl. jours. Organizer Poison Control Ctr., Chgo., 1953; trustee Underwriters' Labs., Inc., 1969-79. Served to maj. USAAF, 1942-46. Recipient Clifford G. Grulee award Am. Acad. Pediatrics, 1961; recognition award Am. Assn. Poison Control Centers, 1975. Mem. AMA, Am. Pub. Health Assn. (founder and pres. Conf. Emeritus Mems. 1986-89, Excellence in Health Admintrn. award 1992), Nat. Soc. Prevention of Blindness, Am. Assn. Public Health Physicians (pres. 1971-72, Bronze medal 1979), Conf. State and Provincial Health Authorities N.Am. (pres. 1971-72), Assn. State and Territorial Health Officers (mem. exec. com. 1972-75, Arthur G. McCormack award 1978), Am. Assn. Sr. Physicians (pres. 1984-86), Oreg. Pub. Health Assn. (Leadership award 1986), Oreg. Med. Assn. (presdl. citation 1980), Portland City Club, Multnomah Athletic Club, Rotary. Home: 2211 SW 1st Ave Apt 905 Portland OR 97201-5013

PRESS, FRANK, geophysicist, educator; b. Bklyn., Dec. 4, 1924; s. Solomon and Dora (Steinholz) P.; m. Billie Kallick, June 9, 1946; children: William Henry, Paula Evelyn. BS, CCNY, 1944, LLD (hon.), 1972; MA, Columbia U., 1946, PhD, 1949; DSc (hon.), 28 univs. Rsch. assoc. Columbia U., 1946-49, instr. geology, 1949-51, asst. prof. geology, 1951-52, assoc. prof., 1952-55; prof. geophysics Calif. Inst. Tech., 1955-65, dir. seismol. lab., 1957-65; prof. geophysics, chmn. dept. earth and planetary scis. MIT, Cambridge, 1965-77, inst. prof., 1981; sci. advisor to pres., dir. Office Sci. and Tech. Policy, Washington, 1977-80; pres. NAS, 1981-93; Cecil & Ida Green sr. fellow Carnegie Inst. of Washington, 1993-97; ptnr. Washington Adv. Group, 1996—; mem. Pres.'s Sci. Adv. Com., 1961-64; mem. Com. on Anticipated Advances in Sci. and Tech., 1974-76; mem. Nat. Sci. Bd., 1970-76; mem. lunar and planetary missions bd. NASA; participant bilateral scis. agreement with Peoples Republic of China and USSR; mem. U.S. delegation to Nuclear Test Ban Negotiations, Geneva and Moscow. Author: (with M. Ewing, W.S. Jardetzky) Propagation of Elastic Waves in Layered Media, 1957, (with R. Siever) Earth, 1986, Understanding Earth, 1997; also over 160 publs.; co-editor: (with R. Siever) Physics and Chemistry of the Earth, 1957—. Decorated Cross of Merit (Germany; Legion of Honor (France); recipient Columbia medal for excellence, 1960, Pub. Svc. award U.S. Dept. Interior, 1972, Gold medal Royal Astron. Soc., 1972, Pub. Svc. medal NASA, 1973, Japan prize Sci. and Tech. Found. Japan, 1993, Pupin medal Columbia U., 1993, Nat. Medal Sci., Pres. of U.S., 1994, Philip Hauge Abelson prize AAAS, 1995; Sherman Fairchild Disting. scholar Calif. Inst. Tech., 1994, Disting. scholar Columbia U., 1995. Mem. NAS, Am. Acad. Arts and Scis., Geol. Soc. Am. (councilor), Am. Geophys. Union (pres. 1973), Soc. Exploration Geophysicists, Seismol. Soc. Am. (pres. 1963), Am. Philos. Soc., French Acad. Scis., Royal Soc. (U.K.), Acad. Scis. of USSR (fgn. mem.), Engring. Acad. Japan (fgn. assoc.). Office: Ste 616 South 2500 Virginia Ave Washington DC 20037-1901

PRESS, JEFFERY BRUCE, chemist; b. Rochester, N.Y., May 24, 1947; s. James Herbert and Mildred (Hau) P.; m. Linda Helen Seghers, Dec. 20, 1976; children: Samantha, Michael. BS, Bucknell U., 1969; PhD, Ohio State U., 1973; postgrad., Harvard U., 1973-75. Rsch. chemist Lederle Labs., Pearl River, N.Y., 1975-77, sr. rsch. chemist, 1977-81, group leader, 1981-83; rsch. mgr. Ortho Pharm. Corp., Raritan, N.J., 1983-89; asst. dir. R.W. Johnson Pharm. Rsch. Inst., Spring House, Pa., 1990-94; v.p., dir. rsch. Emisphere Tech. Inc., Hawthorne, N.Y., 1994-95; v.p. R&D Galenica Pharms., Inc., Frederick, Md., 1996—; treas., sec. Organic Reactions, 1995—. Editor: Organic Reactions, 1983—, Chemtracts Organic 1988—, Current Opinion Therapeutic Patents, 1989—, Analgesia, 1993—; patentee in field; contbr. numerous articles to profl. jours. NIH fellow, 1974. Mem. AAAS, Am. Chem. Soc., N.Y. Acad. Scis., Internat. Soc. Heterocyclic Chemistry, Internat. Pure and Applied Chemistry, Drug Info. Assn., Mid-Atlantic Pharmacology Soc., Drug Info. Assn., Sedgewood Club, Tuxedo Club, Phi Beta Kappa, Sigma Xi, Alpha Chi Sigma. Episcopalian. Avocations: golf, building golf clubs, model railroads. Office: 30 W Patrick St Ste 310 Frederick MD 21701-5655

PRESS, MICHELLE, editor; b. Memphis, Nov. 22, 1940; d. Sam and Rana (Cohen) Appelbaum; m. Robert Press, June 18, 1960 (div. 1965). B.A., New Sch. for Social Research, 1967. Tchr. U.S. Peace Corps, Malawi, Africa, 1962-64; copy editor Japan Quar., Tokyo, 1967-71; asst. editor Am. Scientist, New Haven, 1971-78, mng. editor, 1978-80, editor, 1981-90; mng. editor Scientific American, N.Y.C., 1990—. Office: Scientific American 415 Madison Ave New York NY 10017-1111

PRESS, WILLIAM HENRY, astrophysicist, computer scientist; b. N.Y.C., N.Y., May 23, 1948; s. Frank and Billie (Kallick) P.; m. Margaret Ann Lauritsen, 1969 (div. 1982); 1 dau., Sara Linda; m. Jeffrey Foden Howell, Apr. 19, 1991; 1 son, James Howell. A.B., Harvard Coll., 1969; M.S., Calif. Inst. Tech., 1971, Ph.D., 1972. Asst. prof. theoretical physics Calif. Inst. Tech., 1973-74; asst. prof. physics Princeton (N.J.) U., 1974-76; prof. astronomy and physics Harvard U., Cambridge, Mass., 1976—; chmn. dept. astronomy Harvard U., 1982-85; mem. numerous adv. coms. and panels NSF, NASA, NAS, NRC; vis. mem. Inst. Advanced Study, 1983—; mem. Def. Sci. Bd., 1985-89, sci. adv. com. Packard Found., 1988—, program com. Sloan Found., 1985-91; chmn. adv. bd. NSF Inst. Theoretical Physics, 1986-87; mem. Computer Sci. and Telecomm. Bd., 1991-96; U.S. del. IUPAP Gen. Assembly, 1996; cons. MITRE Corp., 1977—; trustee Inst. Def. Analysis, 1988—, exec. com., 1990—; chief naval ops. Exec. Panel, 1994—. Author: Numerical Recipes, 1986; contbr. articles to profl. jours. Sloan Found. research fellow, 1974-78. Fellow Am. Acad. Arts and Scis., Am. Phys. Soc.; mem. NAS, Am. Astron. Soc. (Helen B. Warner prize 1981), Internat. Astron. Union, Internat. Soc. Relativity and Gravitation, Assn. for Computing Machinery. Office: Harvard U 60 Garden St Cambridge MA 02138-1516

PRESSER, HARRIET BETTY, sociology educator; b. Bklyn., Aug. 29, 1936; d. Phillip Rubinoff and Rose (Gudowitz) Jabish; m. Neil Nathan Presser, Dec. 16, 1956 (div.); 1 child, Sheryl Lynn. BA, George Washington U., 1959; MA, U. N.C., 1962; PhD, U. Calif., Berkeley, 1969. Statistician Bur. Census, Washington, 1959; research assoc. Inst. Life Ins., N.Y.C., 1962-64; lectr. demography U. Sussex, Brighton, England, 1967-68; staff assoc. Population Council, N.Y.C., 1968-69; asst. prof. sociomed. scis. Columbia U., N.Y.C., 1969-73, assoc. prof. sociomed. scis., 1973-76; prof. sociology U. Md., College Park, 1976—, dir. Ctr. on Population, Gender, and Social Inequality,, 1988—, disting. faculty rsch. fellow, 1993-94; fellow in residence Netherlands Inst. for Advanced Study in Humanities & Social Sci., Wassenaar, The Netherlands, 1994-95; fellow Ctr. for Advanced Study in the Behavioral Scis., Stanford, Calif., 1986-87, 91-92; bd. dirs. Population Reference Bur., 1993—; cons. Nat. Inst. for Child Health and Human Devel., 1975—. Editl. bd. Time and Soc., 1991-95, Special Forces, 1984-87, Signs, 1975-85; assoc. editor Jour. Health and Social Behavior, 1975-78. Nat. Inst. for Child Health and Devel. grantee, 1972-78, 83-88, Population Coun. grantee, 1976-79, NSF grantee, 1982-83, 90-94, Rockefeller Found. grantee, 1983-85, 88-94, William and Flora Hewlett Found. grantee, 1989—, Andrew W. Mellon Found. grantee, 1994-95, W. T. Grant Found., 1996—. Mem. Population Assn. Am. (bd. dirs. 1972-75, 2nd v.p. 1983, 1st v.p. 1985, pres.-elect 1988, pres. 1989), Am. Pub. Health Assn. (council mem. population sect. 1976-79), Am. Sociological Assn. (coun. mem. at large 1990-93, chmn., coun. mem. population sect. 1978-83), Sociological Research Assn. (elected). Office: U Md Dept Sociology College Park MD 20742

PRESSER, STANLEY, sociology educator; b. Bklyn., Feb. 18, 1950; s. Sidney and Sydonia (Cohen) P. AB, Brown U., 1971; PhD, U. Mich. 1977. Research investigator Survey Research Ctr. U. Mich., Ann Arbor, 1977-78, head of field office, 1981-83; research assoc. Inst. Research Social Sci.; U. N.C., 1978-81; dir. Detroit Area Study U. Mich., 1983-85; assoc. dir. sociology program NSF, 1985-87, dir., 1987-88; vis. prof. sociology U. Md., College Park, 1988-89, prof. of sociology, dir. Survey Rsch. Ctr., 1989—, dir.joint U Md. and U. Mich. program in Survey Methodology, 1992-96; bd. overseers Nat. Opinion Rsch. Ctr. Gen. Social Survey, 1984-85, 93—; spl. cons. Nat. Econ. Research Assocs., 1986-89; cons. U.S. Dept. Justice, 1995, Dept. of Commerce, 1991, GAO, 1988-89, EOE Commn., 1985, NOAA, 1991-94, State of Alaska Atty. Gen., 1989-92. Co-author: Questions and Answers in Attitude Surveys, 1981, Survey Questions: Handcrafting the Standardized Questionnaire, 1986; editor Pub. Opinion Quar., 1993—; co-editor: Sourcebook of Harris National Surveys, 1981, Survey Rsch. Methods, 1989. Mem. editl. bd. Pub. Opinion Quar., 1983-87 , Sociol. Methods and Research, 1980-83, Social Psychology Quar., 1979-82. Contbr. articles to profl. jours. and books. Fellow Am. Statis. Assn.; mem. Am. Assn. for Pub. Opinion Rsch. (pres. 1993-94). Office: U of Md Survey Rsch Ctr 1103 Art Sociology Building College Park MD 20742-1321

PRESSER, STEPHEN BRUCE, lawyer, educator; b. Chattanooga, Aug. 10, 1946; s. Sidney and Estelle (Shapiro) P.; m. Carole Smith, June 18, 1968 (div. 1987); children: David Carter, Elisabeth Catherine; m. ArLynn Leiber, Dec. 13, 1987; children: Joseph Leiber, Eastman Leiber. A.B., Harvard U., 1968, J.D., 1971. Bar: Mass. 1971, D.C. 1972. Law clk. to Judge Malcolm Richard Wilkey U.S. Ct. Appeals (D.C. cir.), 1971-72; assoc. Wilmer, Cutler & Pickering, Washington, 1972-74; asst. prof. law Rutgers U., Camden, N.J., 1974-76; vis. assoc. prof. U. Va., 1976-77; prof. Northwestern U., Chgo., 1977—, class 1940 rsch. prof., 1992-93, Raoul Berger prof. legal history, 1992—, assoc. dean acad. affairs Sch. Law, 1982-85. Author: (with Jamil S. Zainaldin) Law and Jurisprudence in American History, 1980, 3d edit., 1995,

Studies in the History of the United States Courts of the Third Circuit, 1983, The Original Misunderstanding: The English, The Americans and the Dialetic of Federalist Jurisprudence, 1991, Piercing the Corporate Veil, 1991, revised ann., (with Ralph Ferrara and Meridith Brown) Takeovers: A Strategist's Manual, 2d edit., 1993, Recapturing the Constitution, 1994; assoc. articles editor Guide to American Law, 1985. Mem. acad. adv. bd. Washington Legal Found. Recipient summer stipend NEH, 1975; Fulbright Sr. scholar Univ. Coll., London Sch. Econs. and Polit. Sci., 1983-84, Inst. Advanced Legal Studies, 1996; Adams fellow Inst. U.S. Studies, London, 1996. Mem. Am. Soc. Legal History (bd. dirs. 1979-82), Am. Law Inst., Univ. Club Chgo. (bd. dirs. 1997—), Legal Club Chgo. Home: 1015 Cherry St Winnetka IL 60093-2112 Office: Northwestern U Law Sch 357 E Chicago Ave Chicago IL 60611-3008

PRESSLER, LARRY, senator; b. Humboldt, S.D., Mar. 29, 1942; s. Antone Lewis and Loretta Geneive (Claussen) P.; m. Harriet Dent, 1982; a child, Laura. B.A., U. S.D., 1964; diploma (Rhodes scholar), Oxford U., Eng., 1965; M.A. in Govt., Harvard U., 1971, J.D., 1971. Mem. 94th-95th Congresses from 1st S.D. Dist., 1974-78; mem. U.S. Senate from S.D., 1979-97; U.S. del. Inter-Parliamentary Union for 97th Congress; mem. bd. visitors all mil. svc. academies; chmn. commerce, sci. and transp. coms. U.S. Senate; U.S. Senate subcoms. on aviation, oceans and fisheries, sci., tech. and space; fin. com. mem.; chmn. comms. subcom., 1995-96; small bus. com. mem., 1995-96; mem. spl. com. on aging, 1981-96; mem. fgn. rels. com., 1991-95; congl. del. to UN Gen. Assembly, 1986, 92; mem. U.S. Commn. on Improving the Effectiveness of UN, 1993. Author: U.S. Senators from the Prairie, 1982, Star Wars: The SDI Debates in Congress, 1986. Bd. visitors U.S. Mcht. Marine Acad., 1979, 89-90, USAF Acad., 1987-89, U.S. Mil. Acad., 1993, USCG Acad., 1993; All-Am. del. 4-H agrl. fair, Cairo, 1961. 1st lt. U.S. Army, 1966-68, Vietnam. Recipient Nat. 4-H Citizenship award, 1962, Report to the Pres. 4-H award, 1962, Guardian of Small Bus. award Nat. Fedn. Ind. Bus., 9 times, Golden Bulldog awards Watchdogs of Treasury, 8 times, Sound Dollar awards More Common Sense, 4 times, Spirit of Enterprise awards U.S. C. of C., 8 times, Jefferson award Citizens for Sound Economy; named Taxpayers Friend, Nat. Taxpayers Union, 1989, 93, 95. Mem. Am Assn. Rhodes Scholars, VFW, ABA Phi Beta Kappa. Avocations: golf, tennis, rowing, skiing, horseback riding. Office: 1050 Connecticut Ave NW Washington DC 20036

PRESSLEY, FRED G., JR., lawyer; b. N.Y.C., June 19, 1953; s. Fred G. Sr. and Frances (Sanders) P.; m. Cynthia Denise Hill, Sept. 5, 1981. BA cum laude, Union Coll., 1975; JD, Northwestern U., 1978. Bar: Ohio 1978, U.S. Dist. Ct. (so. dist.) Ohio 1979, U.S. Dist. Ct. (no. dist.) Ohio 1985, U.S. Dist. Ct. (ea. dist.) Wis. 1980, U.S. Ct. Appeals (6th cir.). Assoc. Porter, Wright, Morris & Arthur, Columbus, Ohio, 1978-85, ptnr., 1985—. Bd. dirs. Columbus Area Leadership Program, 1981-84, Franklin County Bd. Mental Retardation and Devel. Disabilities, Columbus, 1989—, Union Coll., Schenectady, N.Y., 1992—. Recipient Civic Achievement award Ohio Ho. of Reps., 1988. Mem. ABA. Avocations: jogging, golf, basketball, military history. Office: Porter Wright Morris & Arthur 41 S High St Columbus OH 43215-6101

PRESSLY, THOMAS JAMES, history educator; b. Troy, Tenn., Jan. 18, 1919; s. James Wallace and Martha Belle (Bittick) P.; m. Lillian Cameron, Apr. 30, 1943; children—Thomas James II, Stephanie (Mrs. Kaoruhiko Suzuki). AB, Harvard U., 1940, AM, 1941, PhD, 1950; LLD (hon.), Whitman Coll., 1981. Instr. history Princeton U., 1946-49; asst. prof. U. Wash., 1949-54, assoc. prof., 1954-60, prof., 1960-87, prof. emeritus, 1987—; vis. assoc. prof. Princeton U., 1953-54, Johns Hopkins U., 1969-70. Author: Americans Interpret Their Civil War, 1954; editor: (with W. H. Scofield) Farm Real Estate Values in the United States, 1965, (with others) American Political Behavior, 1974, Diary of George Templeton Strong (abridged), 1988, (with Glenn M. Linden) Voices From the House Divided, 1995. Served with AUS, 1941-45. Ford Found. Faculty fellow, 1951-52; Center for Advanced Study in Behavioral Scis. fellow, 1955-56. Mem. Am. Hist. Assn., So. Hist. Assn. (editorial bd. Jour. So. History 1973-77), Orgn. Am. Historians. Home: 4545 E Laurel Dr NE Seattle WA 98105-3838 Office: U Wash Dept History Seattle WA 98195

PRESSMAN, GLENN SPENCER, lawyer; b. Phila., May 25, 1952; s. Albert and Elaine (Coffae) P.; m. Laura Feldman, Sept. 5, 1982; children: Alexandra, Daniel. BS, Pa. State U., 1974; JD with honors, Drake U., 1981. Bar: Colo. 1981, U.S. Dist. Ct. Colo. 1981, U.S. Ct. Appeals (10th cir.) 1981. Ptnr. Melat Pressman Ezell & Higbie, Colorado Springs, Colo., 1981—. Recipient Order of the Coif, 1981. Democrat. Jewish. Avocations: skiing, mountain climbing. Office: Melat Pressman Ezell Higbie 711 S Tejon St Colorado Springs CO 80903-4041

PRESSMAN, MICHAEL, film director; b. N.Y.C., July 1, 1950. Ed., Calif. Inst. Arts. Dir.: (films) The Great Texas Dynamite Chase, 1976, The Bad News Bears in Breaking Training, 1977, Boulevard Nights, 1979, Those Lips, Those Eyes, 1980, Some Kind of Hero, 1982, Doctor Detroit, 1983, Teenage Mutant Ninja Turtles II: The Secret of the Oozie, 1991, To Gillian On Her 37th Birthday, 1996; (TV films) Like Mom, Like Me, 1978, The Imposter, 1984, And the Children Shall Lead, 1985, Private Sessions, 1985, Final Jeopardy, 1985, The Christmas Gift, 1986, Haunted By Her Past, 1987, To Heal A Nation, 1988, Shootdown, 1988, Incident at Dark River, 1989, Man Against The Mob: The Chinatown Murders, 1989, Joshua's Heart, 1990, Quicksand: No Escape, 1992, Miracle Child, 1993; co-exec. prod.: (TV series) Picket Fences, 1992— (Emmy award Outstanding Drama Series, 1993); producer, dir.: (pilot) Chicago Hope, 1993. Mem. Dirs. Guild Am. Office: William Morris Agency 151 S El Camino Dr Beverly Hills CA 90212-2704

PRESSMAN, ROBERT, retail executive; b. 1954; s. Fred Pressman. MBA, Boston Univ. With Barney's Inc., 1975—. Office: 575 5th Ave New York NY 10017-2422*

PRESTAGE, JAMES JORDAN, university chancellor; b. Deweyville, Tex., Apr. 29, 1926; s. James J. and Mona (Wilkins) P.; m. Jewel Limar, Aug. 12, 1953; children—Terri, James Grady, Eric, Karen, Jay. B.S. cum laude, So. U., Baton Rouge, 1950; M.S., U. Iowa, 1955, Ph.D., 1959. Instr. biology Prairie View Coll., Tex., 1955-56; asst. prof. So. U., Baton Rouge, 1959, assoc. prof. biology, 1959-61, prof. biology, 1961—, dir. computer sci. ctr., 1968-71, 72-73, dean acad. affairs, v.p. acad. affairs, 1973-81, exec. v.p., 1981-82, chancellor, 1982-85, univ. disting. prof., 1985—; univ. disting. prof. biology Dillard U., New Orleans, 1987—; chair divsn. natural scis. Dillard U., 1990—; asst. dir. La. Coordinating Council for Higher Edn., Baton Rouge, 1971-72; mem. commn. on scholars Ill. Bd. Higher Edn., 1975-82; mem. com. on off-campus instrn. La. Bd. Regents, 1975—; mem. La. Data Processing Council, Baton Rouge, 1979-82; vis. prof. biology Dillard U., New Orleans; trustee Am. Coll. Testing Program, 1983—. Mem. exec. bd. Istrouma council Boy Scouts Am.; vice chmn. bd. trustees Greater Mt. Carmel Baptist Ch., Baton Rouge; bd. dirs. Capital Area United Way, Baton Rouge. Served with USN, 1944-46, 50-52; ETO, Korea. Named Most Outstanding Faculty Mem., So. U., 1966-67; Nat. Med. Fellowships fellow U. Iowa, Iowa City, 1956-59; NIH grantee, 1960-65. Mem. Conf. Acad. Deans So. States. NAACP, Sigma Xi, Alpha Chi, Alpha Phi Alpha (chpt. pres.), Sigma Pi Phi. Democrat. Avocations: fishing; reading; gardening. Home: 2145 77th Ave Baton Rouge LA 70807-5508 Office: PO Box 9222 So Br PO Baton Rouge LA 70813

PRESTAGE, JEWEL LIMAR, political science educator; b. Hutton, La., Aug. 12, 1931; d. Brudis L. and Sallie Bell (Johnson) Limar; m. James J. Prestage, Aug. 12, 1953; children—Terri, James, Eric, Karen, Jay. B.A., So. U., Baton Rouge, 1951; M.A., U. Iowa, 1952, Ph.D., 1954; LHD (hon.), U. D.C., 1994. Assoc. prof. polit. sci. Prairie View (Tex.) Coll., 1954-55, 56; assoc. prof. polit. sci. So. U., 1956-57, 58-62, prof., 1962—, chairperson dept., 1965-83, dean pub. policy and urban affairs, 1983-89; Honors prof. polit. sci. Banneker Honors Coll., Prairie View U., 1989—, dean, 1990—; chmn. La. adv. com. to U.S. Commn. on Civil Rights, 1975-85; mem., chmn. nat. adv. coun. on women's ednl. programs U.S. Dept. Edn., 1980-82; vis. prof. U. Iowa, 1987-88. Author: (with M. Githens) A Portrait of Marginality: Political Behavior of the American Woman, 1976; contbr. articles to profl. jours. Rockefeller fellow, 1951-52; NSF fellow, 1964; Ford Found. postdoctoral fellow, 1969-70. Mem. Am. Polit. Sci. Assn. (v.p. 1974-75), So. Polit. Sci. Assn. (pres. 1975-76), Nat. Conf. Black Polit. Scientists (pres. 1976-77), Nat. Assn. African Am. Honors Programs (pres. 1993-94), Am. Soc. for Pub. Adminstrn. (pres. La. chpt. 1988-89, mem. nat. exec. coun. 1989-90), Links Inc., Alpha Kappa Alpha. Home: 2145 77th Ave Baton Rouge LA 70807-5508 Office: So Univ PO Box 125 Prairie View TX 77446-0125 *Commitments which guide my life are: (1) maximum development of personal potential through pursuit of excellence in all endeavors; (2) fair play, respect, compassion and quest of community in relations with fellow human beings; (3) utilization of personal talents in the interest of removing impediments to the good life "for all persons"; (4) pursuit of truth as the pervasive concern in academia; and (5) transmission of the above as priority goals to all with whom I have contact.*

PRESTBO, JOHN ANDREW, newspaper editor, journalist, author; b. Northwood, N.D., Sept. 26, 1941; s. Oscar Bernt and Jeanne (Schol) P.; m. Darlene Parrish, Aug. 14, 1965; children: Bradford Jonathan, Laura Christine. B.S., Northwestern U., 1963, M.S., 1964. Reporter, writer Wall Street Jour., Chgo., 1964-74; staff editor, Page 1 Wall Street Jour., N.Y.C., 1974-75, commodities editor, 1975-77; bur. chief Wall Street Jour., Cleve., 1977-81; markets editor Wall Street Jour., N.Y.C., 1984—, editor Dow Jones Global Indexes, 1993—; v.p. editorial Dow Jones Radio 2, Inc., Princeton, N.J., 1981-83. Author: Sleuthing, 1976; co-author: (with Frederick C. Klein) News and the Market, 1974, (with Douglas R. Sease) Barron's Guide to Making Investment Decisions, 1994, The Wall Street Jour. Book of Internat. Investing, 1997; editor: This Abundant Land, 1975, Dow Jones Commodities Handbook, 1976-79, The Dow Jones Guide to the World Stock Market, 1994. Served with USAFR, 1966-73. Recipient Econ. Reporting award Ind. Natural Gas Assn., U. Mo., 1967; recipient Achievement-bur. writing award G.M. Loeb, 1968. Home: 14 Charleston Dr Skillman NJ 08558-1801 Office: Wall Street Jour 200 Liberty St New York NY 10281-1003

PRESTIA, MICHAEL ANTHONY, accounting executive; b. S.I., N.Y., Oct. 6, 1931; s. Anthony and Antoinette (Folino) P.; m. Nancy Ferrandino, July 4, 1959 (div. May 1970); 1 child, Anthony; m. Janet Swanson, July 22, 1987. BA, NYU, 1953, MBA, 1956. CPA, N.Y. Sr. accountant Gluckman & Schacht, CPAs, N.Y.C., 1953-60; chief financial officer Franklin Broadcasting Co., N.Y.C., 1960-63; chief accountant asst. to bus. officer, sec. Cooper Union for Advancement Sci. and Art, N.Y.C., 1963-66; bus. officer Inst. Pub. Adminstrn., N.Y.C., 1966-71, controller, 1971-78, treas., 1978-84; cons. taxation and tax planning, 1959—. Served with AUS, 1953-55. Mem. AICPA, N.Y. State Soc. CPAs. Home: 53-06 Francis Lewis Blvd Flushing NY 11364-1633 Office: 445 5th Ave New York NY 10016-0109

PRESTON, ALDA S., academic administrator, nursing educator; b. Kansas City, Kans., Aug. 25, 1949; d. Beryl LeFrance and Vivian Artneal (Wilson) P. Diploma, Bethany Hosp. Sch. Nursing, Kansas City, 1970; BSN, Ft. Hays State U., Hays, Kans., 1972; MA in Curriculum and Instrn., U. Kans., 1981; MSN magna cum laude, U. Mo., Kansas City, 1989; PhD in Ednl. Adminstrn., U. Wis., 1997. RN, Kans., Mo., Wis. DON Hillcrest Manor, Hays, 1971-72; staff nurse various hosps., Met. Kansas City, Kans., 1970-72, 76-87; mem. faculty LPN program Kansas City (Mo.) Bd. Edn., 1976-77; instr. med.-surg. nursing, pediatrics nursing Penn Valley C.C., Kansas City, 1977-90, coord. LPN-ADN bridge program, 1985-89; assoc. dean health, human and protective svcs. div. Madison (Wis.) Area Tech. Coll., 1990—; instr. Cochran Sch. Nursing, Yonkers, N.Y., 1972-76. Historian, reporter Pan Hellenic Coun. Greater Kansas City, 1987-90; treas. no. region Nat. Pan Hellenic Coun., 1988-90. Kellogg fellow League for Innovation in Community Coll., 1992. Mem. ANA, Wis. Nurses Assn., Mo. Assn. Health Occupations Educators (sec., policy com. 1984-87), Am. Assn. Women in Community Colls. (pres., chpt. charter mem.), Mo. Vocat. Assn., Kans. Nurses Assn., Sigma Theta Tau Internat., Delta Sigma Theta (life), Lambda Phi (charter Beta Eta chpt.), Links, Inc.

PRESTON, ANDREW JOSEPH, pharmacist, drug company executive; b. Bklyn., Apr. 19, 1922; s. Charles A. and Josephine (Rizzutto) Pumo; BSc, St. John U., 1943; m. Martha Jeanne Happ, Oct. 10, 1953; children: Andrew Joseph Jr., Charles Richard, Carolyn Louise, Frank Arthur, Joanne Marie, Barbara Jeanne. Cert. bus. intermediary. Mgr. Press Club, Bklyn. Nat. League Baseball Club, 1941-42; purchasing agt. Drug and Pharm. div. Intrassind, Inc., 1947; chief pharmacist Hendershot Pharmacy, Newton, N.J., 1949; agt. Bur. of Narcotics, U.S. Treasury Dept., 1948-49; owner Preston Drug & Surg. Co., Boonton, N.J., 1949-86; CEO Preston Pharmaceutics, Inc., Butler, N.J., 1970-80, Preston Bus. Cons., Inc., Kinnelon, N.J., 1987—; commr. N.J. State Bd. Pharmacy, 1970-72, pres., 1973; organizer State of N.J. Drug Abuse Speakers Program, 1970-76; chmn. Morris County Drug Abuse Coun., 1969-70; lectr. drug abuse and narcotic addiction various community orgns., 1968-78; mem. adv. bd. Nat. Community Bank, Boonton, N.J., 1973. Chmn. bldg. fund com. Riverside Hosp., Boonton, 1963; mem. Morris County (N.J.) Rep. Fin. Com., 1972; pres. Ronald Reagan N.J. Re-Election Adv. Bd., 1984; mem. exec. com. Gov. Tom Kean Annual Ball, 1985-86; chmn. Pharmacists of N.J. for election of Pres. Ford, 1976, Pharmacists for Gov. Tom Kean, 1981-84, N.J. Pharmacists for Reagan/Bush '84; mem. exec. com. Morris County Overall Econ. Devel. Com., 1976-82; chmn. Pharmacists for Fenwick, 1982; v.p. Kinnelon Rep. Club, 1980, Rep. Com., Kinnelon, 1990; adv. com. to Congressman Dean Gallo on Pres. Clinton's Health Security Plan, 1994. Served to lt. (j.g.), USNR, 1943-46. Recipient Bowl Hygeia award Robbins Co., 1969, E.R. Squibb President's award, 1968, N.J. Pharm. Square Club award, 1969. Mem. Am. Pharm. Assn., N.J. Pharm. Assn. (mem. econs. com. 1960-65, pres. 1967-68, Oscar Singer Meml. award 1987, William H. McNeil award 1994), Nat. Assn. of Retail Druggists, Internat. Narcotic Enforcement Officers Assn., N.J. Narcotic Enforcement Officers Assn., Nat. Assn. Realtors, N.J. Assn. Realtors, Morris County Bd. Realtors, Internat. Bus. Brokers Assn. (cert. bus. intermediary), Inst. Bus. Appraisers, Pharmacists Guild Am. (pres. N.Y. div. 1946-47), Pharmacists Guild of N.J., N.J. Public Health Assn., Morris County Pharm. Assn., Morris-Sussex Pharmacists Soc., Am. Legion, St. John's Alumni Assn. Roman Catholic. Clubs: Elks, K.C., Smoke Rise. Contbr. editorials to profl. jours. Home and Office: 568A Pepperidge Tree Ln Kinnelon NJ 07405-2213

PRESTON, FAITH, college president; b. Boston, Sept. 14, 1921; d. Howard Knowlton and Edith Smith (Wilson) P.; m. Winthrop Wadleigh, Dec. 19, 1970. B.A., Boston U., 1944; M.A., 1945; Ed.D., Columbia U. Tchrs. Coll., 1964. Tchr. Georgetown (Mass.) High Sch., 1945-47; tchr. Stoneham (Mass.) High Sch., 1947-50, Endicott Jr. Coll., Beverly, Mass., 1950-53; dir. research P.R. Jr. Coll., 1953-55; dean adminstrn., 1955-63, v.p., 1963-65; pres. White Pines Coll., 1965-91, pres. emerita, 1991—, also life trustee. Author: David and the Handcar, 1950, Jose's Miracle, 1955, The Silver Box, 1979, A Gift of Love, 1994. Mem. bd. incorporators Cath. Med. Ctr., Manchester, N.H., 1978-89; bd. dirs. Caregivers; pres. bd. dirs. N.H. Assn. for Blind; trustee funds Chester Congl. Bapt. Ch., deacon, 1988—. Kellogg fellow, 1964. Mem. Am. Assn. Jr. Colls., Phi Lambda Theta, Kappa Delta Pi, Delta Kappa Gamma. Republican. Clubs: Univ. Women's (London); The College (Boston); Fortnightly. Home: PO Box 25 Chester NH 03036-0025 Office: White Pines Coll Office of the Pres 40 Chester St Chester NH 03036-4305 *I am a teacher, and I yearn to impart a few non-textbook lessons. Two are simply said: care, endure.*

PRESTON, FRANCES WILLIAMS, performing rights organization executive; children: Kirk, David, Donald. Hon. degree, Lincoln (Ill.) Coll.; degree (hon.), Berklee Coll. Musicawd. With BMI (Broadcast Music Inc.), Nashville, 1958—, v.p., 1964-85; sr. v.p. performing rights BMI, N.Y.C., 1985, exec. v.p., chief exec. officer, 1986, pres., chief exec. officer, 1986—, also bd. dirs. Mem. Film, Entertainment and Music Commn. Adv. Council State of Tenn.; founding mem. bd. dirs. Leadership Nashville; past pres. bd. dirs. John Work Meml. Found.; chmn. bd. dirs. Country Music Found., Inc., 1983-85, trustee, past pres., chmn. bldg. com.; mem. Commn. on White House Record Library, Carter adminstrn., Pres.'s Panama Canal Study Com., Carter adminstrn.; bd. dirs. Rock & Roll Hall of Fame; mem. adminstrv. council Confedn. of Internat. Socs. of Authors and Composers; v.p. Nat. Music Council; past bd. dirs. Peabody Awards; hon. trustee Nat. Acad. Popular Music; pres. bd. dirs. T.J. Martell Fedn. for Leukemia, Cancer and AIDS Rsch.; established Frances Williams Preston Rsch. Labs. for T.J. Martell Fedn., 1993. Recipient achievement award Women's Equity Action League, spl. citation award NATAS, Golden Baton award Young Musicians Found., Humanitarian award Internat. Achievement in Arts award, 1995, Creative Achievement award Elaine Kaufman Cultural Ctr., 1996, Lester Sill Humanitarian award, 1996; named one of Am.'s 50 Most Powerful Women Ladies' Home Jour.; named to Country Music Hall of Fame. Mem. Country Music Assn. (life mem. bd. dirs., Irving Waugh Award of Excellence), Nashville Symphony Assn. (past sec., bd. dirs.), NARAS (pres.'s adv. bd., past bd. dirs. Nashville chpt.), Nashville Songwriters Assn. (life mem., bd. dirs.), Gospel Music Assn. (life mem. bd., past chmn., past pres.), Am. Women in Radio and TV (past nat. dir.). Presbyterian. Lodge: Rotary (1st woman mem. Nashville club), Friars Club (Friars Found. Applause award). Office: Broadcast Music Inc 320 W 57th St New York NY 10019-3705

PRESTON, JAMES E., cosmetics company executive; b. 1933. BS, Northwestern U., 1955. With Avon Products, Inc., N.Y.C., 1964—, from mgmt. trainee to dir. sales promotion, 1964-70, dir. personnel, 1970-71, v.p. corp. personnel, 1971-72, from group v.p. mktg. to sr. v.p. field ops. worldwide, 1972-77, exec. v.p., 1977-81, exec. corp. v.p., pres., 1981-88, pres., chief operating officer, 1988-89, chief exec. officer, 1988—, chmn. bd. dirs., 1989—; bd. dirs. ARAMARK Corp., Woolworth Corp. Mem. Reader's Digest Assn. (bd. dirs. 1994). Office: Avon Products Inc 9 W 57th St New York NY 10019

PRESTON, JAMES YOUNG, lawyer; b. Atlanta, Sept. 21, 1937; s. James William and Mary Lou (Young) P.; m. Elizabeth Buxton Gregory, June 13, 1959; children: Elizabeth P. Carr, Mary Lane P. Lennon, James Brenton Preston. BA in English, U. N.C., 1958, JD with high honors, 1961. Bar: N.C. 1961. Assoc. to ptnr. Parker, Poe, Adams & Bernstein L.L.P. and predecessors, Charlotte, N.C., 1961—. Pres. Charlotte Area Fund, 1968, Cmty. Sch. of the Arts, 1976-78; mem. coun. Charlotte/Mecklenburg, Inc., 1986-87, chair The Nat. Conf., Charlotte, 1996—, Wildacres Leadership Initiative, 1994—; vice chair N.C. Dance Theatre, 1995—. Mem. ABA (ho. dels. 1988-92, 95—), N.C. State Bar (pres. 1987-88), Am. Law Inst., Nat. Conf. Bar Presidents (exec. coun. 1989-92), Phi Beta Kappa, Phi Eta Sigma. Democrat. Episcopalian. Avocations: travel, tennis, profl. and civic activities. Office: Parker Poe Adams Bernstein LLP 201 S College St 2500 Charlotte Plz Charlotte NC 28244

PRESTON, LOYCE ELAINE, retired social work educator; b. Texarkana, Ark., Feb. 25, 1929; d. Harvey Martin and Florence (Whitlock) P.; student Texarkana Jr. Coll., 1946-47; B.S., Henderson State Tchrs. Coll., 1950; certificate in social work La. State U., 1952; M.S.W., Columbia U., 1956. Tchr. pub. schs., Dierks, Ark., 1950-51; child welfare worker Ark. Dept. Public Welfare, Clark and Hot Spring counties, 1951-56, child welfare cons., 1956-58; casework dir. Ruth Sch. Girls, Burien, Wash., 1958-60; asst. prof. spl. edn. La. Poly. Inst., Ruston, 1960-63; asst. prof. Northwestern State Coll., Shreveport, La., 1963-73; asst. prof. La. State U., Shreveport, 1973-79; ret., 1979. Chpt. sec. La. Assn. Mental Health, 1965-67, Gov's. adv. council, 1967-70; mem. Mayor's Com. for Community Improvement, 1972-76. Mem. AAUW (dir. Shreveport br. 1963-69), Acad. Cert. Social Workers, Nat. Assn. Social Workers (del. 1964-65, pres. North La. chpt., state-wide com. 1968-69), La Conf. Social Welfare, La. Fedn. Council Exceptional Children (pres. 1970-71), La. Tchrs. Assn. Home: 9609 Hillsboro Dr Shreveport LA 71118-4804

PRESTON, MALCOLM, artist, art critic; b. N.J., May 25, 1919; s. Frank and Anniece (Landau) P.; m. Mary Alice Bales, Nov. 27, 1942; children: Jennifer, Amanda. BS, U. Wis., 1940; MA, Columbia U., 1945, PhD, 1951; student, New Sch. Social Rsch., N.Y.C., 1940-42. Display artist and designer, free lance artist, 1939-41; fellow, asst. instr. painting New Sch. Social Research, 1940-41; high sch. tchr., 1944-49; art supr. Manhasset pub. schs., 1945; part-time instr. Adelphi Coll., 1947; chmn. dept. fine arts Hofstra Coll., 1949-74, prof. fine arts, 1954-74, chmn. div. humanities, 1959-74, coordinator arts, 1961-74; dir. Inst. Arts, 1962-74; art critic Newsday, 1968-86, Boston Herald Traveler, 1970-72. Contbr. articles to newspapers and mags.; radio, television shows Met. area; developed and carried out television series Ford Found. grant, Nat. Ednl. Radio and Television Center, Arts Around Us, Am. Art Today, 1956; one-man shows include Ward Eggleston Gallery, N.Y.C., 1950-51, 54, 56, A.C.A. Gallery, 1959, S.A.G., 1962, Palm Beach, 1968, St. Mary's Coll., 1978, Benson Gallery, 1979, The Gallery, Truro, Mass., 1980, 81, 82, Customs House Gallery, 1984, Country Art Gallery, 1986, Wenniger Gallery, 1988, Elaine Benson Gallery, 1991, Galerie Mourlot, Boston, 1992; group shows include New Art Gallery, 1948-49, Ward Eggleston Gallery, 1949-50, also, L.I. Artists Exhibit, Nat. Water Color Exhibit, San Diego, Am. Artists Assn. Gallery, 1951, Roosevelt Field Art Center, 1957, Art U.S.A., 1958, Hansa Gallery Group Show, 1958, Shore Studio Gallery, Provincetown, 1957-58, Kendall Art Gallery, Wellfleet, Mass., 1974, 75, 76, 77, 78, Roko Gallery, 1978, Himelfarb Gallery, 1978, Linden Gallery, 1981-82, Tower Gallery, 1983, Customs House Gallery, 1983, 84, 85, Grand Central Art Gallery, 1984, 85; work represented in permanent collections: Queens's Mus., Guild Hall Mus., Portland Mus., Cape Cod Mus. Fine Arts, Hofstra U., Living Arts Found., N.Y.C., Islip Art Mus. Served as 2d lt. F.A. AUS, World War II. Lowe Found. research grantee, 1950; Ford Found. grantee, 1958; recipient Emily Lowe award, 1949, 50, 52, 54, 56; 1st prize oil Utica, N.Y.; Shell Research award, 1963. Home: PO Box 182 Truro MA 02666-0182 Office: care Galerie Mourlot 14 Newbury St Boston MA 02116-3201

PRESTON, MARK I., investment company executive; b. Schenectady, May 16, 1938; s. Samuel P. and Fay (Zelig) P.; children: Meredith, Laurence. BS, Syracuse U., 1959. Gen. mgr. AD-Allure Industries Inc., N.Y.C., 1962-64; pres. Marlin Mfg. Corp., 1965-68; acct. exec. Walston, Inc., 1969-72; v.p. DuPont, Walston, Inc., N.Y.C. and Washington, 1973, Legg Mason Wood Walker, Inc., Balt., 1974-81, sr. v.p. mktg., 1981-85, sr. v.p., dir. of sales, 1986-90, sr. v.p., 1991—, also bd. dirs.; bd. dirs. Balt. Opera Co. Pres. Balt. County Gen. Hosp. Found., 1983-84; v.p. Safety First Club Md., 1982-90; trustee Balt. County Gen. Hosp., 1983-88; pres. parent bd. Balt. County Gen. Hosp., 1988-90; bd. dirs. blood svcs. bd. ARC, Md., Balt. Opera Co. Mem. Int. Assn. Fin. Planners (cert.), Sparrows Point Country Club, Bond Club (pres. 1984). Home: 2365 Boston St Baltimore MD 21224-3656 Office: Legg Mason Wood Walker Inc 111 S Calvert St Baltimore MD 21202-6174

PRESTON, RICHARD ARTHUR, historian; b. Middlesbrough, England, Oct. 4, 1910; s. Frank and Florence Rachel (Carter) P.; m. Marjorie Fishwick, Sept. 2, 1939; children—David Frank, Carol Jane, Peter Eric. B.A., Leeds U., 1931, M.A., 1932, Dip.Ed., 1933; Ph.D., Yale U., 1936; LL.D., Royal Mil. Coll. Can., 1977. Mem. faculty U. Toronto, 1936-38, U., Coll. South Wales, 1938-45, U. Toronto, 1945-48; mem. faculty Royal Mil. Coll. Can., Kingston, 1948-65; prof. history Royal Mil. Coll. Can., to 1965, Duke U., Durham, N.C., 1965-80; prof. emeritus Duke U., 1980—, dir. Can. studies, 1973-79. Author: Gorges of Plymouth Fort, 1953, Men in Arms, 1956-91, Royal Fort Frontenac, 1958, Kingston Before the War of 1812, 1958, Canada in World Affairs, 1959-61, 1965, Canada and Imperial Defense, 1967, Canada's R.M.C, 1969, For Friends at Home, 1974, Defence of the Undefended Border, 1977, Perspectives in the History of Military Education and Professionalism, 1980, the Squat Pyramid: Canadian Studies in the U.S, 1980, To Serve Canada, 1991. Served with RAF, 1940-45. Commonwealth Fund fellow, 1933-36; Can. Coun. fellow, 1963-64; Social Sci. Rsch. Coun. fellow, 1963-64; Guggenheim fellow, 1972-73; recipient Achievement award City Kingston, 1959, Can. Confedn. medal, 1967, Queen's Jubilee medal, 1975, Donner medal, 1977, No. Telecom. Internat. Can. Studies award and Gold medal, 1983, Kingston Hist. Soc. Centennial award, 1994. Mem. Can. Hist. Assn. (pres. 1961-62), Assn. Can. Studies U.S. (founding pres. 1971-72), Am. Mil. Inst. Home: 25 Old Oak Ct Durham NC 27705-5644

PRESTON, RICHARD MCKIM, lawyer; b. Balt., June 2, 1947; s. Wilbur Day Jr. and May Virginia (Honemann) P.; m. Trisa Jean Thompson, Apr. 28, 1961. BA, Washington & Lee U., 1969, JD cum laude, 1976; MA cum laude, Fairleigh Dickinson U., 1973. Assoc. vomBaur, Coburn, Simmons & Turtle, Washington, 1976-79; assoc. Seyfarth, Shaw, Fairweather & Geraldson, Washington, 1979-82, ptnr., 1982—; mng. ptnr. Constrn. Group, 1987—. Contbr. articles to profl. publs., chpt. to book. Bd. advisors Jubilee Support Found., Washington, 1989—; mem. Washington & Lee Law Coun., Lexington, Va., 1986-93. Mem. River Bend Golf and Country Club, Sankaty Head Golf Club, Metro. Cub (D.C.). Office: Seyfarth Shaw Fairweather 815 Connecticut Ave NW Washington DC 20006-4004

PRESTON, ROBERT BRUCE, retired lawyer; b. Cleve., Feb. 24, 1926; s. Robert Bruce and Erma May (Hunter) P.; m. Agnes Ellen Stanley, Jan. 29, 1949; children—Robert B., Patricia Ellen Preston Kiefer, Judith Helen Preston Yanover. A.B., Western Res. U., 1950, J.D., 1952. Bar: U.S. Dist. Ct. (no. dist.) Ohio 1953, U.S. Ct. Appeals (6th cir.) 1959, U.S. Supreme Ct. 1964. Assoc. Arter & Hadden, Cleve., 1952-63, ptnr., 1964-93; ret., 1994; dir. Service Stampings Inc., Willoughby, Ohio. Vice pres. Citizens League Cleve., 1965; chmn. Charter Rev. Com., Cleveland Heights, Ohio, 1972; mem. Zoning Bd. Appeals, Cleveland Heights, 1974-76. Mem. Ohio Bar Assn., Greater Cleve. Bar Assn., City Club. Republican. Presbyterian. Avocations: tennis, fishing, travel. Home: 117 Manor Brook Dr South Russell OH 44022-4163 Office: Arter & Hadden 1100 Huntington Bldg Cleveland OH 44115

PRESTON, SAMUEL HULSE, demographer; b. Morrisville, Pa., Dec. 2, 1943; s. Samuel H. and Dora (Berrell) P.; m. Winnifred de Witt, June 19, 1965; children: Samuel, Andrew, Benjamin, Leah. BA in Econs., Amherst Coll., 1965; PhD in Econs., Princeton U., 1968. Asst. prof. demography U. Calif., Berkeley, 1968-72; dir. Ctr. for Demography U. Wash., Seattle, 1972-77; chief, population structure sect. UN, N.Y.C., 1977-79; dir. Population Studies Ctr. U. Pa., Phila., 1979-88. Author: Mortality Patterns in National Populations, 1976, Patterns of Urban and Rural Population Growth, 1980, (with M. Haines) Fatal Years, 1991. Fellow AAAS, Am. Acad. Arts and Scis, Am. Statis. Assn.; mem. NAS, Inst. Medicine, Am. Philos. Soc., Population Assn. Am. (pres. 1984, Irene B. Tauber award for Excellence in Demographic Research 1983), Internat. Union for Sci. Study of Population (council 1981-88). Democrat. Methodist. Home: 234 Walnut Ave Wayne PA 19087-3445 Office: Univ Pa Population Studies Ctr Philadelphia PA 19104

PRESTON, SEYMOUR STOTLER, III, manufacturing company executive; b. Media, Pa., Sept. 11, 1933; s. Seymour Stotler and Mary Alicia (Harper) P.; m. Jean Ellen Holman, Sept. 8, 1956; children: Courtney J., Katherine E., Alicia D., Shelley S. BA, Williams Coll., 1956; MBA, Harvard Coll., 1958. With Pennwalt Corp., Phila., 1961-89; exec. v.p. in charge of chems. and equipment ops., worldwide Pennwalt Corp., 1975-77, pres., COO, 1977-89; pres., CEO Elf Atochem N.Am., Inc. (formerly Atochem N.Am.), Phila., 1990-93; chmn. AAC Engineered Sys. Inc., 1994—; bd. dirs. CoreStates Bank, NA, Scott Specialty Gases, Inc., Albermarle Corp. Trustee Shipley Sch., Bryn Mawr, Pa., 1976-88, Phila. Orch. Assn., 1992-95; trustee Acad. Natural Scis., 1980-95, chmn., 1995—; bd. mgrs. Franklin Inst., Phila., 1980-92; bd. dirs. Lawrenceville (N.J.) Sch., 1982—. 1st lt. USAF, 1958-61. Mem. Soc. for Chem. Industry, Greater Phila. C. of C. (bd. dirs. 1979-94), Radnor Hunt Club (Malvern, Pa.).

PRESTON, THOMAS RONALD, English language educator, researcher; b. Oct. 31, 1936; s. Thomas and Marie Katherine (Nettlow) P.; m. Mary Ruth Atkinson, June 4, 1960; children: Lorel, Mary, Thomas. BA, U. Detroit, 1958; MA, Rice U., 1960, PhD, 1962. Asst. prof. English Duquesne U., Pitts., 1962-63; Asst. prof. English U. Fla., Gainseville, 1963-67; assoc. prof., chmn. dept. Loyola U., New Orleans, 1967-69; prof., chmn. dept. U. Tenn., Chattanooga, 1969-73, U. Wyo., Laramie, 1973-82; prof., dean arts and scis. U. North Tex., Denton, 1982-92; prof. English, 1992—; chmn. Wyo. Council for Humanities, Laramie, 1976-77. Author: Not in Timon's Manner, 1975; editor U. Ga. edit. of Smollett's Humphry Clinker, 1990; contbr. articles on 18th century lit. to profl. jours. Recipient John W. Gardner award Rice U., 1962; George Duke Humphrey award U. Wyo., 1982; NEH grantee, 1979; Am. Council of Learned Socs. grantee, 1980. Mem. South Ctrl. MLA, Am. Soc. for 18th Century Studies, Coll. English Assn., South Ctrl. Soc. for 18th Century Studies (pres. 1986-87). Democrat. Anglican. Home: 11722 S Central Ln Winona TX 75792-6704 Office: U North Tex English Dept Denton TX 76203

PRESTON, WILLIAM HUBBARD, consultant to specialty businesses; b. Bklyn., July 24, 1920; s. Russell Jackson and Mary Louise (Yetman) P.; m. Marcia Whitney Emery, Dec. 18, 1943; children: William Hubbard, Craig Ryder. B.S.M.E. cum laude, Poly. Inst. N.Y., 1942. Asst. supt. Ball & Roller div. SKF Industries, Phila., 1946-51; cons. Booz, Allen & Hamilton, N.Y.C., 1951-53; gen. sales mgr. Joy Mfg. Co., Pitts., 1953-59; exec. v.p. Chase Brass/Kennecott, Waterbury, Conn., 1959-62; pres. Indsl. Group Joy Mfg. Co., Michigan City, Ind., 1962-67, Davis-Standard div., Pawcatuck, Conn., 1967-83; v.p. Crompton & Knowles Corp., N.Y.C., 1967-83; prin. Hubbard Assocs., Hopkinton, Mass., 1983—. Served to lt. (j.g.) USNR, 1943-46. Unitarian. Home: 152 Hayden Rowe St Hopkinton MA 01748-2512

PRESTOWITZ, CLYDE VINCENT, economist, research administrator; b. Wilmington, Del., Sept. 6, 1941; s. Clyde Vincent and Lillian (Lang) P.; m. Carol Ann Jay, Mar. 29, 1964; children: Anne, Clyde, Brian. B.A., Swarthmore Coll., 1963; M.A., U. Hawaii, 1965; M.B.A., U. Pa., 1980. Mgr. market devel. Scott Paper Co., Phila., 1968-72; dir. planning Europe Scott Paper Co., Brussels, 1972-76; v.p. Japan Egon Zehnder Internat., Tokyo, 1976-78; dir. mktg. Am. Can Co., Greenwich, Conn., 1978-79; pres. Prestowitz Assocs., New Canaan, Conn., 1979-81; dep. asst. sec. internat. econ. policy U.S. Dept. Commerce, Washington, 1981-82, acting asst. sec. internat. econ. policy, 1982-83, counselor to sec., 1983-86; Wilson fellow, 1986-87; sr. assoc. Carnegie Endowment for Internat. Peace, Washington, 1987-89; pres. Econ. Strategy Inst., Washington, 1989—; vice-chmn. Pacific Basin Econ. Coun., 1989—; vice chmn., presdl. com. U.S./Pacific Trade and Investment Policy. Republican. Presbyterian. Home: 10420 Masters Ter Potomac MD 20854-3862 Office: Econ Strategy Inst 1401 H St NW Ste 750 Washington DC 20005-2110

PRESTWOOD, ALVIN TENNYSON, lawyer; b. Roeton, Ala., June 18, 1929; s. Garret Felix and Jimmie (Payne) P.; m. Sue Burleson Lee, Nov. 27, 1974; children: Ann Celeste Prestwood Peeples, Alison Bennett, Cynthia Joyce Lee Koplos, William Alvin Lee, Garret Courtney. BS, U. Ala., 1951, LLB, 1956, JD, 1970. Bar: Ala. 1956, U.S. Ct. Appeals (6th and 11th cirs.) 1981, U.S. Supreme Ct. 1972. Law clk. Supreme Ct. Ala., 1956-57; asst. atty. gen. Ala., 1957-59; commr. Ala. Dept. Pensions and Security, 1959-63; pvt. practice Montgomery, Ala., 1963-65, 77-82; ptnr. Volz, Capouano, Wampold, Prestwood & Sansone, 1965-77, Prestwood & Rosser, 1982-85, Capouano, Wampold, Prestwood & Sansone, 1986-94, Volz, Prestwood & Hanan, 1995—; chmn. Gov.'s Com. on White House Conf. on Aging, 1961; mem. adv. com. Dept. Health, Edn. and Welfare, 1962; sec. Nat. Coun. State Pub. Welfare Adminstrs., 1962. Mem. editorial bd. Ala. Law Rev., 1955-56; contbr. articles to profl. jours. Pres. Morningview Sch. P.T.A., 1970; chmn. Am. Nursing Home Assn. Legal Com., 1972; bd. dirs. Montgomery Bapt. Hosp., 1958-65; chmn. bd. mgmt. East Montgomery YMCA, 1969. Served to 1st lt., inf. AUS, 1951-53. Decorated Combat Inf. Badge.; recipient Sigma Delta Kappa Scholastic Achievement award U. Ala. Sch. Law, 1956, Law Day Moot Ct. award U. Ala. Sch. Law, 1956. Mem. ABA (chmn. com. on jud. preformance and conduct 1996, chmn. Judiciary's Image Evaluation Task Force), Ala. Bar Assn. (chmn. adminstrv. law sect. 1972, 78, 83), Montgomery County Bar Assn. (chmn. exec. com. 1971), Farrah Order Jurisprudence, Eleventh Cir. Jud. Conf., Am. Trial Lawyers Assn., Am. Judicature Soc. Home: 1431 Magnolia Ave Montgomery AL 36106-2130 Office: Volz Prestwood & Hanan 350 Adams Ave Montgomery AL 36104-4204

PRESZLER, SHARON MARIE, psychiatric home health nurse; b. L.A.; d. Rudolph Edward Wirth and Bertha Marie (Thornton) Paddock; m. Alan Preszler, Aug. 31, 1966; children: Brent, Alison. BS in Nursing, Loma Linda (Calif.) U., 1963, MS in Marriage and Family Counseling, 1978. RN, Calif., Idaho; cert. pub. health nurse. Team leader med. fl. Loma Linda U. Hosp., 1963-64; office nurse Dr. Lowell Johnson, Redlands, Calif., 1964-65, Dr. H. Glenn Stevens, Loma Linda, 1965-72; team leader women's oncology Loma Linda U. Hosp., 1974-75; pub. health nurse Riverside County Pub. Health, Hemet, Calif., 1975-78; nurse, staff psychologist Dept. Health and Welfare, Idaho Falls, Idaho, 1989-91, Boise, Idaho, 1991-92; psychiat. nurse Cmty. Home Health, Boise, 1992-94, Mercy Home Health & Hospice, Nampa, Idaho, 1995—; hospice nurse, home health nurse Mercy Med. Ctr., 1995—, personal care supr. nurse for medicaid, 1996—; instr. YWCA, Bartlesville, Okla., 1984-88; tchr. Bartlesville Pub. Sch., 1984-88, Heritage Retirement, Boise, 1994. Contbr. to Focus, 1986. Mem. Am. Assn. Marriage and Family Therapy, Sigma Theta Tau. Avocations: reading, tennis.

PRETLOW, THOMAS GARRETT, physician, pathology educator, researcher; b. Warrenton, Va., Dec. 11, 1939; s. William Ribble and May (Tiffany) P.; m. Theresa Pace, June 29, 1963; children: James Michael, Joseph Peter, David Mark. A.B., Oberlin Coll., 1960; M.D., U. Rochester, 1965. Intern, Univ. Hosps., Madison, Wis., 1965-66, fellow McArdle Lab., 1966-67; research assoc. Nat. Cancer Inst., Bethesda, Md., 1967-69; asst. prof. pathology Rutgers Med. Sch., Piscataway, N.J., 1969-70; assoc. prof. pathology, U. Ala., Birmingham, 1971-73, prof. pathology, 1974-83, prof. biochemistry, 1982-83; vis. prof. pathology Harvard Med. Sch., Boston, 1983-84; prof. pathology Case Western Res. U., Cleve., 1983—, prof. oncology, 1987—, prof. environ. health scis., 1991—, prof. urology, 1994—; cons. NIH, Bethesda, 1976-95, Am. Inst. Cancer Rsch., 1995—; mem. editorial bd. Cell Biophysics, Cambridge, Mass., 1978-82. Editor: Cell Separation: Methods and Selected Applications, 5 vols., 1982, 83, 84, 87, Biochemical and Molecular Aspects of Selected Cancers, 2 vols., 1991, 94. Mem. exec. bd. Birmingham council Boy Scouts Am., 1979-83, Greater Cleve. council Boy Scouts Am., 1984-90. Served to lt. comdr. USPHS, 1967-69. Recipient Research Career Devel. award Nat. Cancer Inst., 1973-78; grantee for cancer research. Mem. Am. Assn. Pathologists, Am. Assn. Immunologists, Internat. Acad. Pathology, Am. Soc. Clin. Oncology, Am. Assn. Cancer Research. Club: Serra (pres. Birmingham chpt. 1982-83). Avocations: camping, fishing, Boy Scouts, classical music, biking. Home: 3061 Chadbourne Rd Cleveland OH 44120-2446 Office: Inst of Pathology Case Western Reserve U Cleveland OH 44106

PRETO-RODAS, RICHARD A., foreign language educator; b. N.Y.C., May 30, 1936; s. Manuel and Beatrice Alina (Carvalho) Preto-R. B.A., Fairfield U., 1958; M.A. in Philosophy, Boston Coll., 1960; M.A. in Spanish, U. Mich., 1962, Ph.D. in Romance Langs. (fellow Rackham Sch. Grad. Studies 1965), 1966. Instr. U. Mich., 1964-66; asst. prof. U. Fla., 1966-70; assoc. prof. U. Ill., Urbana-Champaign, 1970-74; prof. U. Ill., 1974-81, chmn. Spanish, Italian, 1978-81; dir. lang. U. South Fla., Tampa, 1981-89, prof. lang., 1989—; cons. MLA; Fulbright vis. prof. comparative lit. Université Stendhal, Grenoble, France, 1994-95. Author: Negritude as A Theme in the Poetry of the Portuguese-Speaking World, 1971, Dialogue and Courtly Lore in Renaissance Portugal, 1971; co-author: Cronicas Brasileiras: A Portuguese Reader, 1980, rev. 1994 as Cronicas Brasileiras, Nova Fase, 40 Historinhas of C.D. de Andrade, 1983; co-editor, contbr: Empire in Transition: The Portuguese World in the Time of Camoes, 1985; contbg. editor: Handbook of Latin American Studies, 1983—; contbg. reviewer World Lit. Today, 1986—. NDEA fellow, 1965. Mem. MLA, Am. Council on Teaching Fgn. Langs., Am. Assn. Tchrs. of Spanish and Portuguese, Phi Beta Kappa. Democrat. Home: 4483 Vieux Carre Cir Tampa FL 33613-3057 Office: CPR-107 U South Fla Tampa FL 33620

PRETTI, BRADFORD JOSEPH, lay worker, insurance company executive; b. Glenwood Springs, Colo., Oct. 11, 1930; s. Joseph John and Ethel Elizabeth (Roe) P.; m. Nancy Ann Clayton, Mar. 30, 1951 (div. 1971); children: Kristi Pretti Micander, Terice Pretti Brownson, Bradford Joseph, Holli Mullins; m. Sarah Jane Rupp, Aug. 8, 1974. BA, U. Colo., 1952. Pres. Pub. Adv. Ins. Com., Chaves County, N.Mex., 1965-72; sr. warden St. Thomas á Beckett Ch., Roswell, N.Mex., 1978-79, St. Andrew's Ch., Roswell, N.Mex., 1991-92; mem. Progam Coun. Diocese of Rio Grande, Albuquerque, 1991-92, mem. Venture in Mission Commn., 1980-84, pres. Standing Commn., 1981-85, chmn. Bishop Search Commn., 1987, dep. to Gen. Conv., 1985-88; Cathedral chpt., 1988-91; pres. Roswell Ins. & Surety Agy., RBS Ins., 1974-93; instr. Ea. N.Mex. U., Roswell, 1970-71. Contbr. articles to jours. in field. Pres. Assurance Home Found., Roswell, 1984—; campaign chmn. United Way of Chaves County, Roswell, 1982, v.p., 1984; bd. dirs. Roswell Hospice Inc., 1984; trustee Roswell Mus. and Art Ctr., 1985, pres. bd. trustees, 1990-92; pres. bd. Roswell Mus. and Art Ctr. Found., 1995; v.p. Sunny Acres, Inc.; chmn. Ea. N.Mex. Med. Ctr. Adv. Coun., 1995. Mem. N.Mex. Ind. Ins. Agts. Assn. (Outstanding Svc. award 1964), Roswell C. of C. (treas. 1984, pres. elect 1985, pres. 1986, Pres.'s Club citation 1983), Mus. Trustees Assn., Am. Contract Bridge League (pres. #382 unit 1965-68, 97—), C Club (Boulder, Colo.). Republican. Episcopalian. Avocation: duplicate bridge. Home: 317 Sherrill Ln Apt 14 Roswell NM 88201-5828 *Without a deep, abiding faith our lives are essentially meaningless.*

PRETTYMAN, ELIJAH BARRETT, JR., lawyer; b. Washington, June 1, 1925; s. Elijah Barrett and Lucy Courtney (Hill) P.; children by previous marriage: Elijah Barrett III, Jill Savage Lukoschek. Grad., St. Albans Sch., Washington, 1943; BA, Yale U., 1949; LLB, U. Va., 1953. Bar: D.C. 1954, U.S. Supreme Ct. 1957. Pvt. practice Washington, 1955—; law clk. to Justices Jackson, Frankfurter and Harlan (U.S. Supreme Ct.), 1953-55; assoc. firm Hogan & Hartson, Washington, 1955-63; partner Hogan & Hartson, 1964—; spl. asst. to Atty. Gen. U.S., 1963, White House, 1963-64; also Pres.'s rep. to Interagy. Com. on Transport Mergers; spl. cons. subcom. to investigate problems connected with refugees and escapees U.S. Senate Judiciary Com., Vietnam, 1967-68; outside cons. to subcom. on oversight and investigations, Ho. of Reps. com. on internal and fgn. commerce, 1978; spl. cons. for ABSCAM investigation to Com. on Standards of Ofcl. Conduct, U.S. Ho. of Reps., 1980-81; trustee emeritus, past mem. exec com. Am. U., Washington; past trustee, mem. exec. com. Washington Journalism Ctr.; past bd. dirs. Nat. Council on Crime and Delinquency; mem. adv. com. Media Law Reporter. Author: Death and the Supreme Court, 1961; Editor: (with William E. Jackson) The Supreme Court in the American System of Government (Justice Robert H. Jackson), 1955; contbr. articles to profl. jours. Past corp. mem. Salvation Army; past mem. adv. com. Procedures of Jud. Coun., D.C.; past mem. adv. bd. Inst. Comm. Law Studies, Cath. U.; bd. govs. St. Albans Sch., 1957-63, 65-72, chmn., 1965-67; past mem. nat. adv. com. Nat. Inst. for Citizen Edn. in Law; mem., bd. dirs., past pres. PEN/Faulkner Found.; v.p., chmn. program com., exec. com. Supreme Ct. Hist. Soc.; mem. internat. adv. group Toshiba Corp.; commr. Jud. Fellows Commn. With AUS, 1943-45. Fellow ABA; mem. Am. Coll. Trial Lawyers, Jud. Conf. D.C. Cir., D.C. Bar Found. (pres. 1983-84), Met. Washington Bd. Trade, D.C. Bar (1st pres. 1972-73, bd. govs. 1973-74), Am. Judicature Soc. (past v.p., exec. com.), Am. Acad. Appellate Lawyers (past pres.), Lawyers Club (past pres.), Vinson Club, Alfalfa Club, Barrister Club, Met. Club, Chevy Chase Club. Methodist (past dir. ch.). Office: Hogan and Hartson Columbia Sq 555 13th St NW Washington DC 20004-1109 Home: 3100 Connecticut Ave NW Washington DC 20008-5148

PREUS, DAVID WALTER, bishop, minister; b. Madison, Wis., May 28, 1922; s. Ove Jacob Hjort and Magdalene (Forde) P.; m. Ann Madsen, June 26, 1951; children: Martha, David, Stephen, Louise, Laura. BA, Luther Coll., Decorah, Iowa, 1943, DD (hon.), 1969; postgrad., U. Minn., 1946-47; BTh, Luther Sem., St. Paul, 1950; postgrad., Union Sem., 1951, Edinburgh U., 1951-52; LLD (hon.), Wagner Coll., 1973, Gettysburg Coll., 1976; DD (hon.), Pacific Luth. Coll., 1974, St. Olaf Coll., 1974, Dana Coll., 1979, Tex. Luth. Coll., 1994; LHD (hon.), Macalester Coll., 1976. Ordained to ministry Luth. Ch., 1950; asst. pastor First Luth. Ch., Brookings, S.D., 1950-51; pastor Trinity Luth. Ch., Vermillion, S.D., 1952-57; campus pastor U. Minn., Mpls., 1957-58; pastor Univ. Luth. Ch. of Hope, Mpls., 1958-73; v.p. Am. Luth. Ch., 1968-73, pres., presiding bishop, 1973-87; exec. dir. Global Mission Inst. Luther Northwestern Theol. Sem., St. Paul; Disting. vis. prof. Luther-Northwestern Sem., St. Paul, 1988-94; Luccock vis. pastor Yale Div. Sch., 1969; chmn. bd. youth activity Am. Luth. Ch., 1960-68; mem. exec. com. Luth. Council U.S.A.; v.p. Luth. World Fedn., 1977-90; mem. cen. com. World Council Chs., 1973-75, 80-90; Luth. del. White House Conf. on Equal Opportunity. Chmn. Greater Mpls. Fair Housing Com., Mpls. Council Chs., 1960-64; Mem. Mpls. Planning Commn., 1965-67; mem. Mpls. Sch. Bd., 1965-74, chmn., 1967-69; mem. Mpls. Bd. Estimate and Taxation, 1968-73, Mpls. Urban Coalition; sr. public adv. U.S. del. Madrid Conf. of Conf. on Security and Cooperation in Europe, 1980-81; bd. dirs. Mpls. Inst. Art, Walker Art Center, Hennepin County United Fund, Ams. for Childrens Relief, Luth. Student Found., Research Council of Gt. City Schs., Urban League, NAACP; bd. regents Augsburg Coll., Mpls. Served with Signal Corps AUS, 1943-46, PTO. Decorated comdr.'s cross Royal Norwegian Order St. Olav, Order of St. George 1st deg. Orthodox Ch. of Georgia (USSR), 1989; recipient Regents medal Augustana Coll., Sioux Falls, S.D., 1973, Torch of Liberty award Anti-Defamation League, 1973, St. Thomas Aquinas award St. Thomas U., Pax Christi award St. John's Univ/. Collegeville, Minn., 1997. Office: 2481 Como Ave Saint Paul MN 55108-1445

PREUSS, ROGER E(MIL), artist; b. Waterville, Minn., Jan. 29, 1922; s. Emil W. and Edna (Rosenau) P.; m. MarDee Ann Germundson, Dec. 31, 1954 (dec. Mar. 1981). Student, Mankato Comml. Coll., Mpls. Sch. Art. instr. seminar Mpls. Coll. Art and Design, Mpls. Inst. Arts Speakers Bur.; former judge ann. Goodyear Nat. Conservation Awards Program; founder U.S. Fed. Roger Preuss Waterfowl Prodn. Area, LeSueur County, Minn., 1997. Painter of nature art; one-man shows include: St. Paul Fine Art Galleries, 1959, Albert Lea Art Center, 1963, Hist. Soc. Mont., Helena, 1964, Bicentennial exhbn., Le Sueur County Hist. Soc. Mus., Elysian, Minn., 1976, Merrill's Gallery of Fine Art, Taos, N.Mex., 1980; exhbns. include: Midwest Wildlife Conf. Exhbn., Kerr's Beverly Hills, Calif., 1947, Laguna Art Mus., Calif., 1947, Joslyn Meml. Mus., Omaha, 1948, Hollywood Fine Arts Center, 1948, Minn. Centennial, 1949, Federated Chaparral Authors, 1951, Nat. Wildlife Art, 1951, 52, N.Am. Wildlife Art, 1952, Ducks Unltd. Waterfowl exhibit, 1953, 54, St. Paul Winter Carnival, 1954, St. Paul Gallery Art Mart, 1954, Harris Fine Arts Center, Provo, Utah, 1969, Galerie Internationale, N.Y.C., 1972, Holy Land Conservation Fund, N.Y.C., 1976, Faribault Art Ctr., 1981, Wildlife Artists of the World Exhbn., Bend, Oreg., 1984, U. Art Mus., U. Minn., Mpls., 1990, Rochester Art Ctr., 1991, Minn. Hist. Soc.-Hill House, 1992, Bemidji Art Ctr., 1992, Jack London Ctr., Dawson City, Yukon Territory, Can., 1992, Weyerhaeuser Meml. Mus., Little Falls, Minn., 1995, Minn. Valley Nat. Wildlife Refuge Ctr., Bloomington, 1995, Sagebrush Artists Exhbn., Klamath Falls, Oreg., 1995; represented in permanent collections: Demarest Meml. Mus., Hackensack, N.J., Smithsonian Instn., N.Y. Jour. Commerce, Mont. Hist. Soc., Inland Bird Banding Assn., Minn. Capitol Bldg., Mont. State U., Wildlife Am. Collection, LeSueur Hist. Soc., Voyageurs Nat. Park Interpretive Ctr., Krause-Hartig VFW Post, Mpls., Nat. Wildlife Fedn. Collection, Minn. Ceremonial House, U.S. Wildlife Svc. Fed. Bldg., Fort Snelling, Minn., Crater Lake Nat. Park Visitors Ctr., VA Hosp., Mpls., Luxton Collection, Banff, Alta., Can., Internat. Inst. Arts, Geneva, Mont. Capitol Bldg., People of Century-Goldblatt Collection, Lyons, Ill., Harlem Savings Collection, N.Y.C., Weisman Art Mus., Mpls., Minn. Vets. Home, Mpls., Blauvelt Art Mus., Oradell, N.J., Roger Preuss Art Collection, Augustana Ctr. for Western Studies, Sioux Falls, S.D., Minn. Mus. Am. Art, St. Paul, U. Minn. Art Mus., C.M. Russell Mus., Great Falls, Mont., others, numerous galleries and pvt. collections; designer: Fed. Duck Stamp, U.S. Dept. Interior, 1949, Commemorative Centennial Pheasant Stamp, 1981, Gold Waterfowl medallion Franklin Mint, 1983, Gold Stamp medallion Wildlife Mint, 1983, 40th Anniversary Commemorative Fed. Duck Stamp etching, 1989; panelist: Sportsman's Roundtable, Sta. WTCN-TV, Mpls. (emeritus), from 1953; author: Is Wildlife Art Recognized Fine Art?, 1986; contbr.: Christmas Echos, 1955, Wing Shooting, Trap & Skeet, 1955, Along the Trout Stream, 1979; contbr. Art Impressions mag., Can., Wildlife Art, U.S.; also illustrations and articles in Nat. Wildlife and over 300 essays on North American animals, others.; assoc. editor: Out-of-Doors mag.; compiler and artist: Outdoor Horizons, 1957, Twilight over the Wilderness, 1972, 60 limited edition prints Wildlife of America, from 1970; contbr. paintings and text Minnesota Today; creator paintings and text Preuss Wildlife Calendar; inventor: paintings and text Wildlife Am. Calendar; featured artist Art West, 1980-84, Wildlife Art; featured in films Your BFA- Care and Maintenance, Black Ducks Along the Border. Del. Nat. Wildlife Conf.; bd. dirs. emeritus Voyageurs Nat. Park Assn., Deep-Portage Conservation Found.; bd. dirs. Wetlands for Wildlife U.S.A.; active Wildlife Am.; co-organizer, v.p., bd. dirs. Minn. Conservation Fedn., 1952-54; mem. U.S. Hospitalized Vets. Venison Program, 1957—; trustee Liberty Bell Edn. Found.; Waseca Arts Coun.; founder, dir. Roger Preuss Conservation Preserve for Study of Nature, 1990—. With USNR, World War II. Recipient Stamp Design award U.S. Fish and Wildlife Svc., 1994, Minn. Outdoor award, 1956, Patron of Conservation award, 1956, award for contbns. conservation Minn. Statehood Centennial Commn., 1958, 1st award Am. Indsl. Devel. Coun., citation of merit VFW, award of merit Mil. Order Cootie, 1963, merit award Minn. Waterfowl Assn., 1976, silver medal Nat. SAR, 1978, Svcs. to Arts and Environ. award Faribault Art Ctr., 1981, Ptnrs. for Wildlife award U.S. Fish and Wildlife Svc., 1994; named Wildlife Conservationist of the Yr., Sears Fund.-Nat. Wildlife Fedn. program, 1966, Am. Bicentennial Wildlife Artist, Am. Heritage Assn., 1976; hon. mem. Ont. Chippewa Nation of Can., 1957; named Knight of Mark Twain for contbns. to Am. art Mark Twain Soc., 1978; named to Water, Woods and Wildlife Hall of Fame, named Dean of Wildfowl Artists, 1981, Hon. Ky. Col.; recipient hon. degree U.S. Vets. Venison program, 1980, Western Am. award significant contbns. to preservation arts and history No. Prairie Plains, Augustana Coll. Ctr. for Western Studies, Sioux Falls, S.D., 1992, Pub. Svc. award for outstanding contbns. to Am. conservation and environ. U.S. Dept. Interior, 1996; named creator first signed, numbered photolithographic print pub. in N.Am., 1959; documented Colorado Springs Fine Arts Ctr., 1993, colleague of Frederick R. Weisman Mus., Mpls., 1994; grantee NEH, 1995, Prairie Lakes Arts Coun., 1995. Fellow Internat. Inst. Arts (life), Soc. Animal Artists (emeritus), N.Am. Mycol. Assn., Nat. Wildlife Fedn. (nat. wildlife week chmn. Minn.), Minn. Ducks Unltd. (bd. dirs. emeritus), Minn. Artists Assn. (v.p., bd. dirs. 1953-59), Outdoor Writers Am. (emeritus), Soc. Artists and Art Dirs. (emeritus), Am. Artists Profl. League (emeritus), Mpls. Soc. Fine Arts, Wildlife Soc., Minn. Mycol. Soc. (pres. emeritus, hon. life mem.), Le Sueur County Hist. Soc. (hon. life mem.), Minn. Conservation Fedn. (hon. life), Wildlife Artists World (charter mem., internat. v.p. 1986—, chmn. fine arts bd.), Internat. Platform Assn. (emeritus), Great Lakes Outdoor Writers (emeritus), The Prairie Chicken Soc. (patron), The Sharp-tailed Grouse Soc. (patron), Mission Oceanic Arctic, 1992, Beaverbrook Club (hon. life), Minn. Press Club (emeritus), Explorers Club (N.Y.C., emeritus). Office: care Wildlife Am PO Box 580004-a Minneapolis MN 55458-0004 Studio: 2224 Grand Ave Minneapolis MN 55405-3412 *With a modicum of natural skills in painting and writing, my basic goal throughout all my work has been to help people appreciate and understand nature. If I as a naturalist am a small voice for our world's waters, woods, and wildlife, if I have influenced many children and adults to become more environment conscious, if my art brings to others a measure of joy, then my best aspirations for my creations have been fulfilled.*

PREUSS, RONALD STEPHEN, lawyer, educator; b. Flint, Mich., Dec. 1, 1935; s. Edward Joseph and Harriette Beckwith (Pease) P.; 1 child, William Stephen. AB, U. Mo., 1958, MA, 1963; JD, St. Louis U., 1973; postdoctoral, Worcester Coll., Oxford, Eng., 1979, U. Calif., Berkeley, 1979, U. Paris, 1984. Bar: Mo. 1973, U.S. Dist. Ct. (ea. and we. dists.) Mo. 1973, U.S. Tax Ct. 1979. From instr. to assoc. prof. English St. Louis Jr. Coll. Dist., 1965—; ptnr. Anderson & Preuss, Clayton, Mo., 1973—. Author: Laudamus Te, 1962, The St. Louis Gourmet. 1979, 86, English Elegies, 1983, Melville: A Psychic Biography, 1984, Theater I, 1987, Letting Go, 1988; editor St. Louis Gourmet Newsletter, 1981-88; co-editor Criterion mag. 1961-62; columnist Capital Courier newspaper 1962-64. Mem. Mo. Bar Assn., Phi Alpha Delta (John L. Sullivan chpt. vice justice 1971-72, justice 1972-73, Eisenhower Commn. 1995). Home: 32 Conway Cove Dr Chesterfield MO 63017-2069 Office: Anderson & Preuss 201 S Central Ave Ste 130 Saint Louis MO 63105-3517

PREUSSER, JOSEPH WILLIAM, academic administrator; b. Petersburg, Nebr., June 18, 1941; s. Louis Henry and Elizabeth Sophia (Oberbrocking) P.; m. Therese Marie Mahoney, Aug. 12, 1967; children: Scott, Michelle, Denise. BA in Social Scis., Wayne State Coll., 1965; MA in Geography, U. Nebr., Omaha, 1971; PhD in Adminstrn., U. Nebr., 1978. Coord. social studies Lewis Cen. Community Sch. Dist., Council bluffs, Iowa, 1967-71; chmn. social sci. div., instr. Platte Jr. Coll., Columbus, Nebr., 1972-73; dean instrn./Platte campus Cen. Community Coll., Columbus, 1973-82, v.p. ednl. planning community edn., pres. Platte campus, 1982-84; pres. Cen. Community Coll., Grand Island, Nebr., 1984—; mem. edit com. devel. Nebr. Tech. Community Coll., 1973-75, sec., , dean instrn., 1974-76, chmn. coun. pres's., 1990-91,; mem. Archdiocese Omaha Bd. Edn., 1980-84; chmn. bd. St. Bonaventure Bd. Edn., 1976-80; pub. speaker in field. Contbr. articles to profl. jours. Bd. dirs. Ctrl. Nebr. Goodwill Industries, Gand island, 1987-95, treas., 1990-91, chmn. 1992; chmn. sustaining membership enrollment campaign Overland Trails Boys Scouts Am., 1990; worker YMCA Fund Drive, Columbus, 1980; mem. Columbus City Planning Commn., 1979-84, chmn., 1981, 82; coach boys baseball and girls softball, Council Bluffs, Columbus and Grand Island, 1968-95. With U.S. Army, 1959-61. Named one Outstanding Young Mem of Am., 1976; recipient Nat. Leadership award U. Tex., 1988-89, Pres. of Yr. award Am. Assn. Women i Comm., 1996. Mem. Am. Assn. Cmty. and Jr. Colls., Am. Voct. Assn., Nebr. Vocat. Assn. (Outstanding Svc. award 1986), Am. Assn. Ret. People, Nat. Coun. Instructional Officers, Nat. Coun. Instructional Adminstrs., Am. Assn. for Women in Cmty. Colls. (Pres. of Yr. 1996), Saddle Club, Rotary, KC, Greater Columbus Area C. of C., Phi Delta Kappa. Democrat. Roman Catholic. Avocations: golfing, gardening, woodworking. *

PREVIN, ANDRE, composer, conductor; b. Berlin, Apr. 6, 1930; came to U.S., 1938, naturalized, 1943; s. Jack and Charlotte (Epstein) P.; m. Mia Farrow, Sept. 10, 1970 (div. 1979); children: Matthew and Sascha (twins), Fletcher, Lark, Daisy; m. Heather Hales, Jan. 1982; 1 child, Lukas. Student, Berlin Conservatory, Paris Conservatory; privately with, Pierre Monteux, Mario Castelnuovo-Tedesco. Mem. faculty Guildhall Sch., London, Curtis Inst., Phila., Berkshire Music Ctr. Rec. artist classical music for RCA, EMI, Phillips, Telarc, Deutsche Gramophone, 1946—; composer chamber music Cello Concerto, Guitar Concerto, piano music, serenades for violin, brass quintet, song cycle on poems by Philip Larkin Every Good Boy Deserves Favour, Principals, Reflections, Piano Concerto, Triolet for Brass Ensemble, Haydn variations for piano solo, 4 lyrics of Toni Morrison for soprano, Cello Sonata, Violin Sonata, Trio for Piano Oboe and Bassoon, Songs of Remembrance (soprano and piano), Sallie Chisum (soprano and orch.), Tango Song and Dance (violin and piano), The Magic Number (soprano and orch.), film scores, 1950-59; condr.-in-chief Houston Symphony, 1967-69; prin. condr. London Symphony Orch., 1968-79, Royal Philharm. Orch., Eng., 1985-91; music dir. L.A. Philharm., 1985-89; condr. laureate London Symphony Orch., 1992—; guest condr. maj. symphony orchs. and festivals in U.S. and Europe including: festivals in Salzburg, Edinburgh, Flanders, Vienna, Osaka, Prague, Berlin, Bergen; music dir. South Bank Music Festival, London, 1972-74, Pitts. Symphony, 1976-84, L.A. Philharmonic, 1984-89; author: Music Face to Face, 1971, Orchestra, 1979, No Minor Chords, 1992. Served with AUS, 1950-51. Knighted (KBE), Her Majesty Queen Elizabeth II, 1996; recipient awards Nat. Grammophone Soc., Acad. Motion Picture Arts and Scis. Mem. Acad. Motion Picture Arts and Scis., Dramatists Guild, Brit. Composers Guild, Nat. Composers and Condrs. League, Degrees Curtis Inst., Royal Acad., Guild Hall Sch./Duquesne U. Address: care Columbia Artists 165 W 57th St New York NY 10019-2201 also: Barbican Centre, Silk St, London England EC2Y8DS

PREVOR, RUTH CLAIRE, psychologist; b. N.Y.C., June 20, 1944; d. Gustav and Greta (Dreifuss) Strauss; m. Sydney Joseph P., July 4, 1963; children: Joy, Grant, Jed. BA, U. P.R., 1966; PhD, Caribbean Ctr. of Postgrad., Studies, San Juan, 1988. Cert. forensic psychologist, critical incident stress debriefing. Asst. dean Caribbean Ctr. of Postgrad. Studies, 1986-87; dir. prenatal edn. Ashford Meml. Hosp., San Juan, 1987; pvt. practice San Juan, 1984—; advisor, field faculty Vt. Coll., Norwich U., 1990-91; trustee Caribbean Ctr. for Advanced Studies, San Juan, Miami, Fla., 1990—. Bd. dirs. Jewish Community Ctr., Miramar, P.R., 1986—, bd. dirs. pre-sch., 1990—; pres. Home and Sch./St. John's Prep., San Juan, 1980-81, P.R. chpt. Hadassah Sch., 1972-74; presdl. adv. com., 1990-92. Mem. Am. Psychol. Assn., Assn. of Psychology of P.R. (hon. award 1984), Caribbean Counselors Assn., Caribe Hilton Club, Nat. Assn. Children with Learning Disabilities, Nat. Register Health Svc. Providers in Psychology. Jewish. Office: Ashford Medical Ctr San Juan PR 00907-1510

PREVOST, EDWARD JAMES, paint manufacturing executive; b. Baie Comeau, Que., Can., May 26, 1941; s. Omer and Jeanne (Ouellet) P.; m. Anna Marie Murphy, June 20, 1964; children: Marc, Louise, Eric. Luc. BA in History with honors, Loyola Coll., Montreal, Que., 1962; MBA, U. Western Ont., London, 1964. Cert. Advt. Agy. Practitioner. Account exec. J. Walter Thompson Co. Ltd., Montreal, 1964-66; successively account exec., account supr., group mgr. and v.p. Cockfield Brown & Co. Ltd., Montreal, 1966-69; gen. mgr. CJRP Radio, Quebec City, 1969-71; exec. v.p., chief operating officer Mut. Broadcasting Ltd., 1971-72, pres., chief operating officer, 1973; exec. v.p. Civitas Corp. Ltd., Montreal, 1973-74, pres., chief exec. officer, 1974-82, also chmn. bd. operating cos., 1974-82; pres., chief exec. officer La Brasserie O'Keefe Limitée, Montreal, 1983-89; sr. v.p. Carling O'Keefe Breweries of Can. Ltd., 1983-89; pres., chief exec. officer, dir. SICO Inc., Longueuil, Can., 1989-91; pres., CEO Para Inc., Brampton, Can., 1991—; bd. dirs. BBM Bur. Broadcasting Measurement, 1971-78; mem. Montreal Bd. Trade; treas., vice chmn.-elect Can. Paint & Coatings Assn., 1994—, chmn., 1995-97. Gov. Can. Advt. Found., 1982; chmn. Telefilm Can., 1983-86; chmn. Montreal Heart Inst. Rsch. Fund, 1979-81, exec. com. 1981-86. Mem. bd. dirs. L'Assn. des Brasseurs du Que. (chmn. 1984-86), Province Que., Can., C. of C., Can. Assn. Broadcasters (dir. 1975, vice Chmn. radio 1976-77, chmn. 1978-79, past chmn., mem. exec. com. 1980-81), Inter-Am. Assn. Broadcasters Uruguay (sec., past treas.), Young Pres. Orgn. (chmn. Que. chpt. 1987), Assn. des MBA du Que. (chmn. 1985-86), Credit Valley Golf and Country Club (Mississauga, Ont.). Clubs: St.-Denis (Montreal), Western Bus. Sch. (Montreal) (founding pres. 1972), Royal Montreal Golf. Office: Para Inc, 11 Kenview Blvd, Brampton, ON Canada L6T 5G5

PREVOZNIK, STEPHEN JOSEPH, anesthesiologist, retired; b. McAdoo, Pa., June 21, 1929; s. John George and Mary Margaret (Ficek) P.; m. Rita Agnes Kellett, Aug. 20, 1955; children—Mary Therese, Stephen Joseph, John Cyril, Michael Edward, Margaret Anne, Rita Marie, Thomas William, Jean Marie. R.N., St. Joseph Hosp. Sch. Nursing, Phila., 1951; B.S., U. Notre Dame, 1955; M.D., U. Pa., 1959. Intern Fitzgerald Mercy Hosp., Darby, Pa., 1959-60; resident in anesthesia U. Pa., Phila., 1960-62; practice medicine specializing in anesthesiology Phila., 1962-94; mem. staff U. Pa. Hosp.; prof. anesthesia U. Pa., 1977-94, dir. clin. activities, 1971-89; ret., 1994; Chmn. Residency Rev. Com. for Anesthesiology, 1991-93. Contbr. to textbooks on anesthesiology. Mem. AMA, Am. Soc. Anesthesiologists, Pa. Soc. Anesthesiologists, Phila. Soc. Anesthesiologists (pres. 1975-77), Internat. Anesthesia Rsch. Soc., Assn. Univ. Anesthesiologists (exec. coun. 1977-79, sec. 1981-84, dir. anesthesiology pain mgmt. program 1992-94). Home: 204 N Concord Ave Havertown PA 19083-5021 *No one does everything by himself; someone is always there to provide a helping hand. As one progresses and matures, he finds many opportunities to repay what he has received. Without this repayment, the chain is broken and that life is without meaning.*

PREWITT, CHARLES THOMPSON, geochemist; b. Lexington, Ky., Mar. 3, 1933; s. John Burton and Margaret (Thompson) P.; m. Gretchen B. Hansen, Jan. 31, 1958; children: Daniel Hansen. SB, MIT, 1955, SM, 1960, PhD, 1962. Research scientist E.I. DuPont De Nemours & Co. Inc., Wilmington, Del., 1962-69; assoc. prof. SUNY, Stony Brook, 1969-71, prof., 1971-86, chmn. dept. earth and space scis., 1977-80; dir. Geophys. Lab., Carnegie Inst. of Washington, 1986—; sec.-treas. U.S. Nat. Com. for Crystallography, Washington, 1983-85; gen. chmn. 14th Meeting of Internat. Mineral. Assn., Stanford, Calif., 1986; chmn. NRC/Nat. Acad. Scis. com. on physics and chemistry of earth materials, 1985-87; mem. bd. govs. Consortium for Advanced Radiation Svcs.; co-dir. NSF Ctr. for High Pressure Rsch., 1991—. Editor: (jour.) Physics and Chemistry of Minerals, 1976-85; contbr. more than 150 articles to profl. jours. Capt. USAR, 1956-65. NATO sr. postdoctoral fellowship, 1975, Churchill overseas fellowship, 1975, Japan Soc. for Promotion of Sci. fellowship, 1983; named Disting. Vis. Prof. Chemistry, Ariz. State U., 1983. Fellow Mineral. Soc. Am. (pres. 1983-84), Am. Geophys. Union; mem. Geol. Soc. Am., Am. Crystallographic Assn., Materials Rsch. Soc., Mineral. Soc. Gt. Britain and Ireland. Home: 2728 Unicorn Ln NW Washington DC 20015-2234 Office: Carnegie Inst Geophys Lab 5251 Broad Branch Rd NW Washington DC 20015-1305

PREWITT, KENNETH, political science educator, foundation executive; b. Alton, Ill., Mar. 16, 1936; s. Carl Kenneth and Louise (Carpenter) P.; children: Jennifer Ann, Geoffrey Douglas. BA, So. Meth. U., 1958; MA, Washington U., St. Louis, 1959; PhD, Stanford U., 1963. Prof. polit. sci. U. Chgo., 1964-80, chmn. dept. polit. sci., 1975-76; dir. Nat. Opinion Research Center, 1976-79; pres. Social Sci. Research Council, N.Y.C., 1979-85, 95—; sr. v.p. Rockefeller Found., N.Y.C., 1985-95; vis. scholar U. Nairobi, Kenya, 1968-71; adj. prof. polit sci. Columbia U., 1980-83; teaching and rsch. Stanford U., 1964-68; cons. Rockefeller Found., Zaire, 1972, Thailand, 1973; chmn. governing bd. Energy Found.; bd. dirs. Washington U., So. Meth. U., Ctr. Advanced Study Behavioral Scis. Author: Political Socialization, 1969, Ruling Elites, 1973, Labyrinths of Democracy, 1973, Introduction to American Government, 1983, 6th edit., 1991. Guggenheim fellow, 1983; fellow Center Advanced Study in Behavioral Scis., 1983. Fellow AAAS, Am. Acad. Arts and Scis. (v.p.); mem. Am. Polit. Sci. Assn. (v.p.), Coun. on Fgn. Rels. Office: Social Sci Rsch Coun 810 7th Ave New York NY 10019-5818

PREWOZNIK, JEROME FRANK, lawyer; b. Detroit, July 15, 1934; s. Frank Joseph and Loretta Ann (Parzych) P.; m. Marilyn Ruth Johnson, 1970; 1 child, Frank Joseph II. AB cum laude, U. Detroit, 1955; JD with distinction, U. Mich., 1958. Bar: Calif. 1959. Pvt. practice, Calif., 1960-91. Served in U.S. Army, 1958-60. Mem. ABA (bus. law sect., law and acctg. com., chmn. auditing standards subcom. 1981-86), State Bar Calif., Order of Coif. Republican. Home and Office: 431 Georgina Ave Santa Monica CA 90402-1909

PREY, BARBARA ERNST, artist; b. Jamaica, N.Y., Apr. 17, 1957; d. Herbert Henry and Margaret (Joubert) Ernst; m. Jeffrey Drew Prey, Jan. 11, 1986; children: Austin William Ernst Prey, Emily Elizabeth Prey. BA with honors, Williams Coll., 1979; MDiv, Harvard U., 1986. Sales staff Tiffany and Co., N.Y.C., summer 1977; summer intern Met. Mus. Art, N.Y.C., summer 1979; personal asst. Prince Albrecht Castell, Castell, Germany, 1980-81; with modern painting dept. Sotheby's Auction House, N.Y.C., 1981-82; sales asst. Marlborough Gallery, N.Y.C., 1982; teaching asst. Boston Coll., 1984, Harvard U., Cambridge, Mass., 1984-85; vis. lectr. Tainan (Taiwan) Coll. and Sem., 1986-87; artist Oyster Bay, N.J., 1987—; art juror Washington and Jefferson Coll., Washington, Pa., 1990; presenter in field. Illustrator: (book) Boys Harbor Cookbook, 1988, A Dream Became You, (4 book series) A City Grows Up, 1991, (cover) Am. Artist Mag., summer 1994; exhibited paintings in group shows including Mus. of Fine Arts, Nassau County, N.Y., 1988, Nat. Arts Club N.Y.C., 1988, Gallery One, Rockland, Maine, 1992, Williams Coll., Williamstown, Mass., 1993, Johnstown (Pa.) Art Mus., 1993, Blair Art Mus., Holidaysburg, Pa., 1993, Phila. Mus. of Art Gallery, 1995, Westmoreland Mus. of Am. Art (Best in Show award), 1996; exhibited in one-woman shows including Harvard-Yale-Princeton Club, Pitts., 1991; represented in many pvt. collections including Pres. and Mrs. George Bush Farnsworth Mus. Art. Class agt. Williams Coll., Williamstown, Mass., 1981-91; bd. mem. Citizens Libr., Washington, 1992-93; active Bethel Presbyn. Ch. Recipient Fulbright scholarship Fulbright Assn., Germany, 1979-80, grant Roothbert Fund, Chataugua, N.Y., 1982-84, Ch. History award Gordon-Conwell Sem., S. Hamilton, Mass., 1984, Henry Luce Found. grant Henry Luce Found., Taiwan, 1986-87. Mem. Pitts. Watercolor Soc. (Jean Thoburn award 1994), Nat. Mus. Women in the Arts. Republican. Avocations: tennis, skiing, bird watching, reading, cross county skiing. Home and Office: 22 Pearl St. Oyster Bay NY 11771

PREY, JEFFREY DREW, minister; b. Pitts., Mar. 10, 1958; s. William Arthur and Shirley Ann Prey; m. Barbara Elizabeth Ernst, Jan. 11, 1986; children: Austin, Emily. Student, Cornell U., 1976; BA, Gordon Coll., 1980; MDiv, Gordon-Conwell Theol. Sem., 1984; DMin, Pitts. Theol. Sem., 1996. Ordained Presbyn. minister. Project mgr. Merritt & Harris Inc., N.Y.C., 1984-86; vis. lectr. Tainan (Taiwan) Theol. Coll. & Sem., 1986-87; pastor Bethel Presbyn. Ch., Prosperity, Pa., 1988-96, First Presbyn. Ch., Oyster Bay, N.Y., 1996—; lectr. New Testament, Waynesburg (Pa.) Coll., 1989-90. Speaker City Mission, Washington, Pa., 1990-93. Republican. Avocations: tennis, swimming, white water rafting. Home: 22 Pearl St Oyster Bay NY 11771 Office: First Presbyn Ch 60 E Main St Oyster Bay NY 11771-2411

PREYER, ROBERT OTTO, English literature educator; b. Greensboro, N.C., Nov. 11, 1922; s. William Yost and Mary Norris (Richardson) P.; m. Renee Haenel, June 14, 1947; children: Jill, Sally, Elizabeth; m. Kathryn Conway Turner, July 19, 1966. Grad., Choate Sch., 1939; student, Davidson Coll., 1939-40; AB, Princeton U., 1945; MA, Columbia U., 1948, PhD, 1954. Instr. Smith Coll., 1948-54; asst. prof. Brandeis U., Waltham, Mass., 1954-55, prof., chmn. dept. English and Am. lit., 1963-66, chmn. faculty senate, 1976-80, dir. univ. studies program, 1979—, prof. emeritus, 1988—; vis. lectr. Amherst Coll., 1952; vis. prof. Freiburg U., Germany, 1956-57; guest prof. Heidelberg U., Germany, 1973-74; bd. dirs. Peidmont Fin. Corp., Richardson Corp., Boston, Blacksides Inc., Boston, Adirondack Conservancy, Earl Warren Legal Tng. Program Inc., N.Y.C.; mem. adv. bd. Eyes on the Prize, TV series, 1985. Author: Bentham, Coleridge and The Science of History, 1958; adv. editor: Victorian Studies, 1961—; editor: Victorian Literature; contbr. essays to profl. jours. Chmn. Mass Civil Liberties Fund, 1987-90; mem. bd. overseers humanities Tufts U., 1989-94; mem. adv. coun. dept. English, Princeton U., 1991—; bd. dirs. Mus. Afro-Am. History, Boston. Ensign USNR, 1940-43, PTO. Mem. MLA, ACLU (bd. dirs.), Legal Def. Found. (nat. bd. dirs. 1990—), Cottage Club, St. Botolph Club, Princeton Club, Keene Valley Country Club. Democrat. Home: 6 Maple Ave Cambridge MA 02139-1116

PREZZANO, WILBUR JOHN, retired photographic products company executive; b. Chappaqua, N.Y., Dec. 18, 1940; s. Wilbur J. and Adelaide J. Prezzano; m. Sheila Neary, Aug. 29, 1964; children: Timothy J., David N., E. Peter. B.S. in Econs., U. Pa., 1962, M.B.A. in Indsl. Mgmt., 1964. Statistician Eastman Kodak Co., Rochester, N.Y., 1965-66, mem. treas.'s staff, 1966-67, fin. analyst, 1967-68, fin. analyst bus. systems markets div., 1968-69, coordinator sales analysis and fin. info. systems, 1969-71, supr. fin. planning analysis, 1971-73, supt. acctg. analysis, 1973, staff asst. to gen. mgr. Customer Equipment Services Div., 1973-76, mgr. field ops., 1976-78, dir. copy products, mgr. field ops., 1978-79, dir. bus. mktg. planning mktg. div., 1979-80, asst. gen. mgr., 1980, v.p., 1980-82, gen. mgr. U.S. mktg. div., 1982-83, group v.p., gen. mgr. mktg., mgr. internat. photog. ops., 1983-84, gen. mgr. photog. products, 1985-90, gen. mgr. internat., 1990-91, pres. health, 1991-94, exec. v.p., chmn. and pres. Kodak greater China region, 1994-96, ret., 1996; bd. dirs. Can. Trust, Toronto, Can., First Fed. Savs. & Loan Assn., Rochester. Mem. Genesee Valley Club (Rochester).

PRIBBLE, EASTON, artist; b. Falmouth, Ky., July 31, 1917; s. Thaddeus Sewell and Louise Ella (Parker) P. Student, U. Cin., 1941. Ind. tchr. N.Y.C., 1950-57; instr. painting and history of art Munson-Williams-Proctor Inst., Utica, N.Y., 1957—; instr. history of art Utica Coll., Syracuse U., 1960-74. One-man exhbns. include Pinacotheca Gallery, N.Y.C., 1947, 48, Alan Gallery, N.Y.C., 1953, 55, 59, Hamilton Coll., Clinton, N.Y., 1975, Munson-Williams-Proctor Inst. Mus. Art, 1957, 76, 82, Kirkland Art Ctr., Clinton, N.Y., 1988, Rome (N.Y.) Art Ctr., 1990; represented in permanent collections Whitney Mus. Am. Art, Hirschorn Mus. and Sulpture Garden, Smithsonian Instn., Parrish Mus., Southampton, N.Y., Munson-Williams-Proctor Inst. Mus. Art., Fallingwater (Frank Lloyd Wright House), Mill Run, Pa., Hudson River Mus., Yonkers, N.Y., Everson Mus., Syracuse, N.Y., Emerson Gallery, Hamilton Coll., The Farnsworth Mus. Art, Rockland, Maine, Colgate U. Art Gallery, Hamilton. Fellow Yaddo, Saratoga Springs, N.Y., 1954, 55, 68. Mem. Artists Equity. Home: 24 Rose Pl Utica NY 13502-5614 Office: Munson-Williams-Proctor Inst 310 Genesee St Utica NY 13502-4764

PRIBLE, LARRY R., insurance company executive; b. 1946. With IBM, Indpls., 1967-79; with Indpls. Life Ins., 1980—, now pres., CEO. Office: Indianapolis Life Ins Co 2960 N Meridian St Indianapolis IN 46208-4715

PRIBRAM, KARL HARRY, psychology educator, brain researcher; b. Feb. 25, 1919. BS, U. Chgo., 1938, MD, 1941; PhD in Psychology (hon.), U. Montreal, Can., 1992; PhD in Philosophy (hon.), U. Bremen, 1996. Diplomate Am. Bd. Neurol. Surgery, Am. Bd. Med. Psychotherapists. Lectr. Yale U., New Haven, 1951-58; dir. psychology Inst. of Living, Hartford, Conn., 1951-58; fellow Ctr. for Advanced Studies in Behavioral Sci., Stanford (Calif.) U., 1958-59, assoc. prof., 1959-62, rsch. career prof., 1962-89, prof. emeritus, 1989—; eminent scholar Radford (Va.) U., 1989—; adjunct prof. U. Tenn., 1993—; vis. scholar, hon. lectr. MIT, 1954, Clark U., 1956, Harvard, 1956, Haverford Coll., 1961, U. So. Calif., 1961, U. Leningrad, 1962, U. Moscow, 1962, Beloit Coll., 1966-67, U. Alberta, Can., 1968, Ctr. for Study Dem. Insts., 1967-75, U. Coll., London, 1972, U. Chgo., 1973, Menninger Sch. Psychiatry, 1973-76, Ohio State U., 1975, Inst. for Higher Studies; vis. lectr. Grass Found., 1977; Phillips lectr., Haverford Coll., 1979; Lashley lectr., Queens Coll., 1979; Pres.' Club lectr., Oakland U., 1980; J.E. Wallace Wallin lectr., Augustana Coll., 1981; Hubert Humphrey lectr, Macalester Coll., 1981; John M. Dorseh lectr. in Psychol. Physiology, Wayne State U., 1983; lectr. Internat. Mgmt. Inst., Geneva, Switzerland, 1987, Texas A&M U., 1987, Inst. Med. Psychol., Naples, 1988; disting. lectr. Second Annual Symposium of the Mind, Arlington, Tex., 1988; hon. lectr. Sirius Seminaries, Paris, 1988, Bielfeld, Germany, 1990; and numerous others. Author: Brain and Behavior, vol. 1-4, 1969, What Makes Man Human, 1971, Languages of the Brain: Experimental Paradoxes and Principles in Neuropsychology, 1971; The Neurosciences: Third Study Program, 1971, Brain and Perception: Holonomy and Structure in Figural Processing, 1991, Rethinking Neural Networks: Quantum Fields and Biological Data, 1993, Origins: Brain and Self Organization, 1994, Scale in Conscious Experience: Is the Brain Too Important to be Left to Specialists to Study?, 1995; editor, mem. consulting bd. Neuropsychologia, Jour. Math. Biology, Internat. Jour. Neurosci., Behavioral and Brain Scis., Jour. Mental Imagery, Jour. Human Movement Studies, Jour. Social and Biol. Structures, ReVision, STSM Quarterly, Indian Jour. Psychophysiology, Interim Jour. Psychology, Internat. Jour. Psychophysiology, Cognition and Brain Theory; contbr. over 170 articles to profl. jours. Recipient Lifetime Rsch. Career award in neurosci. NIH, 1962-89, Humanitarian award INTA, 1980, Realia honor Inst. Advanced Philosophic Rsch., 1986, 93, Outstanding Contbns. award Am. Bd. Med. Psychotherapists, Neural Network Leadership award Internat. Neural Network, 1996. Fellow Am. Acad. Arts and Scis., N.Y. Acad. Scis. (hon. life); mem. AAUP, AMA, AAAS, APA (pres. div. physiol. and comparative psychology 1967-68, pres. div. theoretical and philos. psychology 1979-80), Internat. Neuropsychol. Soc. (founding pres. 1967-69), Internat. Assn. Study of Pain, Soc. Exptl. Psychologists, Am. Psychol. Soc., Am. Psychopathological Assn. (Paul Hoch award 1975), Am. Acad. Psychoanalysis, Soc. Biol. psychiatry (Manfred Sakel award 1976), Soc. Clin. and Exptl. Hypnosis (Henry Guze award 1991), Soc. Neurosci., Profs. For World Peace (pres. 1982-85), Sigma Xi. Home: 102 Dogwood Ln Radford VA 24141-3917 Office: Radford Univ Ctr Brain Rsch Box 6977 Radford VA 24142

PRICE, ALFRED LEE, lawyer, mining company executive; b. Little Rock, May 19, 1935; s. Dewey Ernest and Dorothy Ava (Cooper) P.; m. Magdalena Torres, June 20, 1958; children: Gregory L., Ana Maria. BA, Hendrix Coll., 1956; JD, Tulane U., 1967. Bar: La. 1967, Miss. 1974, D.C. Office mgr., dir. personnel Petroleum Helicopters Co., Lafayette, La. and New Orleans, 1956-67; atty., office mgr. Offshore Navigation and Petroleum Helicopters Co., New Orleans, 1967-74; gen. counsel First Miss. Corp., Jackson, 1974—, corp. sec., 1988-93; commr. Miss. Employment Commn., Brandon. Mem. ABA, La. Bar Assn., Miss. Bar Assn., Hinds County Bar Assn., Miss. Mfrs. Assn. (bd. dirs.), Miss. Econ. Coun. (chmn. tort reform com.), Jackson Country Club, Univ. Club. Methodist.

PRICE, ANNIE LAURIE, senior health program manager; b. Tuskegee Inst., Ala.; d. Edward James and Katie Beatrice (Griffin) Middleton; m. Frederick D. Price, Jr., Feb. 26, 1972; 1 child, Anne Monique. BS in Nursing Edn., Tuskegee Inst.; postgrad., Howard U.; MPA, Am. Univ., 1980; Diploma, Army Mgmt. Staff Coll., 1989. Diplomate Am. Coll. Healthcare Execs.; RN, Ala. Clin. mgr. child health multidisciplinary clinic Prince Georges County Health Dept., Cheverly, Md., 1976-78; occupl. health nurse, liaison Dept. of Health and Human Svcs., Rockville, Md., 1978-80, internat. health analyst spl. projects, tech. asst., 1980-81; program mgr., analyst comml. contracts Dept. of Army, Washington, 1981-86; health program mgr., policy analyst Dept. of the Army Office of the Surgeon Gen., Falls Church, Va., 1986—; faculty mem. worldwide internal rev. confs. Dept. of the Army, Washington, D.C., Tex. and Colo., 1990, 91, 93; faculty nat. healthcare conf. Nat. Managed Healthcare Congress, Washington, 1993; career mentorship program sponsor Dept. of the Army, Washington, 1993-97; presenter, mem. South African Nat. Congress Africare, Washington, 1995; group facilitator Nat. Seminar Wesley Theolog. Sem., Md., 1995. Contbr. articles to profl. jours. Bd. dirs. Music Boosters Assn., Elizabeth Seton H.S., Bladensburg, Md., 1991, 92; chair African activities com. Alpha Kappa Alpha, Washington, 1993, 94; mem. adminstrv. bd. Asbury United Meth. Ch., Washington, 1995-97. Recipient Mayoral Recognition/Cert. for Immunization Campaign, Mayor, Washington, 1992, Adminstr.'s citation The Health Care Financing Adminstrn., 1993, recognition for evaluation of health care contracts Office of Sec. of Def., 1993. Mem. NAFE, Am. Coll. Healthcare Execs., Nat. Capital Healthcare Execs., Dept. of Def. Sr. Profl. Women, Am. Assn. Budget and Program Analysis, Order of Eastern Star, Alpha Kappa Alpha. Methodist. Avocations: theatre, cmty./ch. activities, touring, biking, gardening, reading.

PRICE, B. BYRON, museum director. Dir. Panhandle-Plains Hist. Mus., Canyon, Tex., until 1987; exec. dir. Nat. Cowboy Hall of Fame and Western Heritage Ctr., Oklahoma City, 1987-96, Buffalo Bill Hist. Ctr., Cody, Wyo., 1996—. Office: Buffalo Bill Hist Ctr Cody WY

PRICE, BETTY JEANNE, choirchime soloist, writer; b. Long Beach, Calif., June 12, 1942; d. Grant E. and Miriam A. (Francis) Sickles; m. Harvey H. Price, Aug. 6, 1975; 1 child, Thomas Neil Gering. Degree in Acctg., Northland Pioneer Coll., Show Low, Ariz., 1977. Youth missionary Open Bible Standard Missions, Trinidad, 1958-59; typographer Joel H. Weldon & Assocs., Scottsdale, Ariz., 1980-89; exec. chief acct. Pubs. Devel. Corp., San Diego, 1991-93; coord. music and worship College Ave. Bapt. Ch., San Diego, 1994-95; ChoirChime soloist, 1986—; founder, owner Customized Funding Svcs., San Diego, 1996—. Author: 101 Ways to Fix Broccoli, 1994, ABC's of Abundant Living, 1995; co-author: God's Vitamin C for the Spirit, 1995, Bounce Back, 1997. Mem. Christian Writers Guild, Am. Cash Flow Assn., San Diego Cash Flow Assn. (founder, exec. bd. mem.), Nat. Entrepreneurs Assn., Bus. Incubator Alliance, Econ. Devel. Coun., Am. Soc. Notaries, SCORE, Soroptomist Internat. Home: PO Box 151115 San Diego CA 92175-1115

PRICE, CHARLES EUGENE, lawyer, legal educator; b. Apalachicola, Fla., Mar. 13, 1926; s. Charles Patrick and Lela Frances (Joseph) P.; m. Lennie F. Bryant, Apr. 25, 1947; 1 child, Charles Eugene Jr. (dec.). B.A. Johnson C. Smith Coll., 1946; A.M. Howard U., 1952; LL.B. Am. Law Sch., 1952; postgrad Johns Hopkins U., 1951-52, Boston U., 1956; J.D. John Marshall U., 1967; C.S., Harvard U., 1980. Bar: Ga. 1968, U.S. Dist. Ct. (no. dist.) Ga. 1978. Sole practice, Atlanta, 1967—; prof. John Marshall Law Sch., Atlanta, 1973-76; dean academics Butler Coll., Tyler, Tex., 1950-53, Fla. Meml. Coll., St. Augustine, 1953-55; Ga. staff NAACP, 1955-60; assoc. prof. Morris Brown Coll., Atlanta, 1960—. Author: The Garvey Movement, 1950. Contbr. articles to profl. jours. Presdl. elector Ga. Electoral Coll., 1972; treas. anti-poverty program, Equal Opportunity Authority, Dekalb County, Ga., 1965-70; bd. dirs. Atlanta SBA, 1966-82. Recipient Leadership award Dekalb NAACP, 1962; Leadership award Ga. NAACP, 1964. Mem. Atlanta Gate City, Ga. State Bar Assn., ABA, Smith Alumni Assn., Alpha Phi Alpha, Alpha Kappa Mu. Presbyterian (elder). Club: Harvard (Cambridge, Mass.). Home: 1480 Austin Rd SW Atlanta GA 30331-2204

PRICE, CHARLES H., II, former ambassador; b. Kansas City, Mo., Apr. 1, 1931; s. Charles Harry and Virginia (Ogden) P.; m. Carol Ann Swanson, Jan. 10, 1969; children: Caroline Lee, Melissa Marie, Charles H., C. B., Pickette. Student, U. Mo., 1951-53; LLD (hon.), Westminster Coll., 1984; LLD (honoris causa), U. Mo., 1988; LHD, Baker U., 1991; DSc (hon.), U. Buckingham, Eng., 1993. Chmn. bd., dir. Price Candy Co., Kansas City, 1969-81, Am. Bancorp., Kansas City, 1973-81; chmn., chief exec. officer Am. Bank & Trust Co., Kansas City, 1973-81; Am. ambassador to Belgium Brussels, 1981-83; Am. ambassador to U.K. London, 1983-89; chmn. bd. Americanc, Inc., St. Joseph, Mo., 1989-92, pres., CEO, 1990-92; chmn. bd. Mercantile Bank Kansas City, Mo., 1992-96, bd. dirs., 1996—; bd. dirs. US Industries, Inc., Hanson PLC, London, N.Y. Times Co., Texaco, Inc., 360 Degree Comm., Inc., Kansas City, Mercantile Bancorp, Inc. Bd. dirs. St. Luke's Hosp., Kansas City, 1970-81, hon. dir., 1989—, advisor Heart Inst. com.; bd. dirs. Midwest Rsch. Inst., Kansas City, chmn., 1990-93. Hon. fellow Regent's Coll., London, 1986; recipient William Booth award Salvation Army, 1985, World Citizen of Yr. award Mayor of Kansas City, 1985, Trustee Citation award Midwest Rsch. Inst., 1987, Disting. Svc. award Internat. Rels. Coun., 1989, Mankind award Cystic Fibrosis Found., 1990, Gold Good Citizenship award SAR, 1991, Chancellor's medal U. Mo. Kansas City, 1992, William F. Yates medallion William Jewell Coll., 1996. Mem. Brook Club, Cypress Point Club, Eldorado Country Club, Castle Pines Country Club, Kansas City Country Club, River Club, Swinley Forest Golf Club, White's Club. Republican. Episcopalian. Office: 1 W Armour Blvd Ste 300 Kansas City MO 64111-2087

PRICE, CHARLES STEVEN, lawyer; b. Inglewood, Calif., June 10, 1955; s. Frank Dean Price and Ann (Rounds) Bolling; m. Sandra Helen Laney,

Feb. 26, 1983; children: Katherine Laney, Courtney Ann, Diana Emily. BA, U. Calif., Santa Barbara, 1976; JD, U. Chgo., 1979. Bar: Ariz. 1980, U.S. Dist. Ariz. 1980, U.S. Ct. Appeals (9th cir.) 1982. Assoc. Brown & Bain P.A., Phoenix, Ariz., 1979-85, ptnr., 1985-96; ptnr. Allen & Price P.L.C., Phoenix, Ariz., 1996—. Office: Allen & Price PLC 2850 E Camelback Rd Ste 170 Phoenix AZ 85016-4380

PRICE, CHARLES T., lawyer; b. Lansing, Mich., Feb. 11, 1944. BA, Ohio Wesleyan U., 1966; JD, Harvard U., 1969. Bar: Ohio 1969, U.S. Dist. Ct. (no. dist.) Ohio 1974, U.S. Ct. Appeals (6th cir) 1981, U.S. Supreme Ct. 1982, Ill. 1989. Ptnr. Baker & Hostetler, Cleve.; pres., pub. Chgo. Sun-Times, 1987-88; exec. v.p. Sun-Times Co., 1989-92. Office: Baker & Hostetler 3200 Nat City Ctr 1900 E 9th St Cleveland OH 44114-3401

PRICE, CLIFFORD WARREN, retired metallurgist, researcher; b. Denver, Apr. 22, 1935; s. Warren Wilson and Vivian Fredricka (Cady) P.; m. Carole Joyce Watermon, June 14, 1969; children: Carla Beth, Krista Lynn Kilton. MetE, Colo. Sch. Mines, 1957; MS, Ohio State U., 1970, PhD, 1975. Design engr. Sundstrand Aviation-Denver, 1957-60; materials specialist Denver Rsch. Inst., 1960-63; sr. metallurgist Rocky Flats div. Dow Chem. Co., Golden, Colo., 1963-66; staff metallurgist Battelle Columbus (Ohio) Labs., 1966-75; sr. scientist Owens-Corning Fiberglas, Granville, Ohio, 1975-80; metallurgist Lawrence Livermore (Calif.) Nat. Lab., 1980-93; retired, 1993. Contbr. articles to profl. jours. Battelle Columbus Labs. fellow, 1974-75. Mem. Metall. Soc. AIME, Microscopy Soc. Am. (treas. Denver 1961-62), Am. Soc. for Metals. Achievements include research on electron, scanning probe and optical microscopy, secondary ion mass spectroscopy, deformation, fracture and recrystallization mechanisms in metals, recrystallization kinetics.

PRICE, DALIAS ADOLPH, geography educator; b. Newtonville, Ind., June 28, 1913; s. Fred J. and Rose (Gillam) P.; m. Lillian O. Alexander, May 14, 1943; children—David, Curtis, Kent, Roger. B.A., U. Ill., 1937, M.A., 1938; Ph.D., U. Wis., 1954. Instr. geography U. Ill., 1938-40; acting head dept. S.W. Mo. State Coll., Springfield, 1940-45; asst. U. Wis., 1945-47; assoc. prof. geography So. Ill. U., 1947-58; prof. geography, head dept. Eastern Ill. U., 1958—. Author articles in field. Mem. Wabash Valley Interstate Commn., 1965—; Bd. suprs. Coles County, Ill., 1967, chmn., 1971-72; Bd. dirs. Charleston Community Hosp., 1966—, Inst. Urban and Regional Affairs, 1967—. Recipient Distng. Svc. award Nat. Weather Svc., 1988, 90.; hon. fellow U. Wis., 1953. Mem. AAUP (sec.-treas. Ill. conf. 1958-62), Ill. Geog. Soc. (sec. 1950, chmn. 1951,62, distinguished geographer award 1976), Charleston C. of C. (bd. dirs. 1961-64), Assn. Am. Geographers, Gamma Theta Upsilon. Democrat. Unitarian. Club: Rotarian (pres. Charleston 1965). Home: 517 W Coolidge Ave Charleston IL 61920-3860

PRICE, DANIEL MARTIN, lawyer; b. St. Louis, Aug. 23, 1955; s. Albert and Edith S. (Werner) P.; m. Kim Ellen Heebner, July 15, 1984; children: Emma Rachel, Joseph Armin, Joshua Simon. BA, Haverford Coll., 1977; diploma in law, Cambridge U., 1979; JD, Harvard U., 1981. Bar: D.C. 1981, Pa. 1987. Assoc. Drinker, Biddle & Reath, Phila., 1981-82, 86-89; dep. gen. counsel Office of U.S. Trade Rep., Washington, 1989-92; ptnr. Powell, Goldstein, Frazer & Murphy, Washington, 1992—; atty., adviser Dept. State, Washington, 1982-84; dep. agt. U.S. Iran-U.S. Claims Tribunal, Hague, The Netherlands, 1984-86; lectr. Haverford Coll., 1982. Articles editor Harvard Law Rev., 1980-81; contbr. Am. Jour. Internat. Law, Internat. Lawyer, Internat. Fin. Law Rev., Internat. Banking and Fin. Law. Am. Keasbey scholar Cambridge U., 1977-78. Mem. ABA (co-chmn. trade com. on N.Am. Free Trade Agreement), Internat. Bus. Forum (legal adv. bd. 1987-89), Coun. on Fgn. Rels., Am. Arbitration Assn. (panel arbitrators), Internat. C. of C. (arbitrator 1994-95), Orgn. for Internat. Investment (counsel), Phi Beta Kappa. Office: 1001 Pennsylvania Ave NW Washington DC 20004-2505

PRICE, DAVID, recreational facilities executive; b. 1933. With Am. Golf Corp., Santa Monica, Calif., 1972—, now chief exec. officer; chmn. Nat. Golf Properties, Santa Monica, Calif., 1993—. Office: Am Golf Corp 1633 26th St Santa Monica CA 90404-4023

PRICE, DAVID EUGENE, congressman, educator; b. Johnson City, Tenn., Aug. 17, 1940; s. Albert Lee and Elna (Harrell) P.; m. Lisa Beth Kanwit, July 27, 1968; children: Karen Elizabeth, Michael Edmond. BA, U. N.C., 1961; BD, Yale U., 1964, PhD, 1969. Legis. aide to U.S. senator from Alaska, 1963-67; prof. Duke U., Durham, N.C., 1973-86; mem. 100th-105th Congresses from 4th N.C. dist., Washington, D.C., 1987—; exec. dir. N.C. Dem. Party, Raleigh, 1979-80, chmn., 1983-84, mem. 1983—; staff dir. nat. com. on presdl. nomination Dem. Party, 1981-82. Author: Bringing Back the Parties, The Commerce Committees, Who Makes the Laws, The Congressional Experience: A View From the Hill. Mem. Am. Polit. Sci. Assn., Soc. for Values in Higher Edn., Phi Beta Kappa. Baptist. Lodge: Kiwanis. Avocations: jogging, music. Home: 106 Collums Rd Chapel Hill NC 27514-6610

PRICE, DEBBIE MITCHELL, journalist, newspaper editor; b. Littlefield, Tex., June 3, 1959; d. Horace A. and Diane (Hall) Mitchell; m. Larry C. Price, May 2, 1981. BFA, So. Meth. U., 1980. Reporter Ft. Worth Star-Telegram, 1980-83, 91, Phila. Daily News, 1983-87, Washington Post, 1988-91; columnist Ft. Worth Star-Telegram, 1991-93, exec. editor, 1993—, v.p., 1994-96; suburban reporter Balt. Sun, 1997—; free-lance writer, Phila., 1987-88. Recipient 1st place Gen. Column Writing award Tex. AP Mng. Editors, 1991, 1st place Mag. Writing award Women's Sports Journalism, 1989, 1st place award Chesapeake Bay AP Mng. Editors, 1990. Mem. Am. Soc. Newspaper Editors, Soc. Profl. Journalists (Ft. Worth chpt.). Office: Ft Worth Star-Telegram Inc PO Box 1870 400 W 7th St Fort Worth TX 76102

PRICE, DENNIS LEE, industrial engineer, educator; b. Taber, Alberta, Can., Oct. 24, 1930; s. Walter and Wilma Harlan (Nance) P.; m. Barbara Ann Shelton; children: Denice Lynn Price Thomas, Philip Walter. BA, Bob Jones U., 1952; BD, MA, Am. Bapt. Sem. of the West, Berkeley, Calif., 1955; MA, Calif. State U., Long Beach, 1967; PhD in Indsl. Engring., Tex. A&M U., 1974. Cert. product safety mgr., hazard control mgr., human factors profl. Clergyman Am. Bapt. Conv., Calif., 1953-66; mem. tech. staff autonetics div. Rockwell Internat., Anaheim, Calif., 1966-69; sr. engr. Martin Marietta Aerospace, Orlando, Fla., 1969-72; rsch. assoc. Tex. A&M U., College Station, 1972-74; teaching asst. Calif. State U., Long Beach, 1963-66; asst. prof. dept. indsl. engring. and operations rsch. Va. Poly. Inst. and State U., Blacksburg, 1974-78, assoc. prof. dept. indsl. and systems engring., 1979-83, prof., 1984-95, prof. emeritus, 1996—, dir. safety projects office, 1975-95, coord. Human Factors Engring. Ctr., 1986-95; cons., expert witness in safety engring. and human factors, 1978—; mem. U.S. Nuclear Waste Tech. Rev. Bd., 1989-95; mem. U.S. tech. adv. group Internat. Stds. Tech. Com. 159 Ergonomics, 1987-94; chmn. com. on transp. of hazardous materials NRC, 1981-87; chmn. group 3 coun. emerging issues subcom. Transp. Rsch. Bd., 1987-89; chmn. task force on pipeline safety NAS, 1986. Mem. editorial bd. Human Factors, Santa Monica, Calif., 1989-95; author: (with K.B. Johns, J.W. Bain) Transportation of Hazardous Materials, 1983; contbr. chpts. to books, articles to profl. jours.; reviewer in field. Recipient Disting. Svc. award Nat. Rsch. Coun. NAS, 1987, 89, Outstanding Svc. commendation Transp. Rsch. Bd. NAS, 1981, Jack A. Kraft Innovator award Human Factors and Ergonomics Soc., 1996; grantee NIOSH, Va. Dept. Transp. and Safety, 1977-82, 86-87, IBM, 1981-84, USN Office of Naval Rsch., 1978-80, USN Naval Systems Weapons Command, 1978-79. Mem. Inst. Indsl. Engrs. (sr.), Am. Soc. Safety Engrs. (profl.), Human Factors Soc. (rep. to rev. panel Guideline for the Preparation of Material Safety Data Sheets), Systems Safety Soc. (Educator of Yr. 1993), Alpha Pi Mu. Avocation: flying. Home: 15204 Moonglow Dr Ramona CA 92065 Office: Va Poly Inst and State U Dept Indsl and Systems Engring 302 Whittemore Blacksburg VA 24061

PRICE, DONALD ALBERT, veterinarian, consultant; b. Bridgeport, Ohio, Dec. 25, 1919; s. Arthur David and Louise Ann (Knellinger) P.; m. June Loree Fleming, July 17, 1946; children: Karen Price Privett, Benita Price Esposito, Donna Price Rocap. Grad., Elliott Sch. Bus., 1938; DVM, Ohio State U., 1950. Lic. veterinarian, Ohio, Ill., Tex. Adminstrv. asst. Wheeling (W.Va.) Steel Corp., 1938-41; counselor psychol. dept. Ohio State U., Columbus, 1946-48, lab. asst. vet. parasitology dept., 1948-50; mem. rsch. faculty Tex. A&M U., Sonora, 1950-55; ptnr. San Angelo Vet. Hosp., Tex., 1955-58; assoc. editor AVMA, Chgo., 1958-59, editor-in-chief, 1959-72, exec. v.p., 1972-85; cons., adj. prof. Tex. A&M U., College Station, 1985—. Capt. USAAF, 1941-46. Recipient Disting. Alumnus award Coll. Vet. Medicine, Ohio State U., 1966. Fellow Am. Med. Writers Assn.; mem. AVMA (Svc. Commendation award 1984, Appreciation award, 1984, CEO 1972-85), Ill. Vet. Med. Assn. (hon. life), Mich. Vet. Med. Assn. (hon. life), Tex. Vet. Med. Assn. (disting. life), Am. Equine Practitioners Assn. (hon.), Am. Assn. Sheep and Goat Practioners (hon.), Am. Animal Hosp. Assn. (hon., Merit award 1983), Bexar County Vet. Med. Assn. (hon.), Masons, Phi Eta Sigma, Phi Zeta, Alpha Psi. Republican. Presbyterian. Avocations: woodworking, ranching. Home and Office: Rte 1, Box 174-A Hunt TX 78024

PRICE, DONALD RAY, university official, agricultural engineer; b. Rockville, Ind., July 20, 1939; s. Ernest M. and Violet Noreen (Measel) P.; m. Joyce Ann Gerald, Sept. 14, 1963; children—John Allen, Karen Sue, Kimberly Ann, Daniel Lee. B.S. in Agrl. Engring., Purdue U., 1961, Ph.D. in Agrl. Engring., 1971; M.S. in Agrl. Engring., Cornell U., 1963. Registered profl. engr., Fla. From asst. prof. to prof. Cornell U., Ithaca, N.Y., 1962-80, dir. energy programs, 1975-77, 78-80; program mgr. Dept Energy, Washington, 1977-78, cons.; assoc. dean research U. Fla., Gainesville, 1980-83; dean Grad. Sch., U. Fla., Gainesville, 1983-84; v.p. research U. Fla., Gainesville, 1984—; pres. U. Fla. Research Found., Inc.; chmn. bd. dirs. Progress Research, Inc.; cons. to Pres. Carter, Washington, 1978; bd. dirs. Nat. Food and Engring. Council, Columbia, Mo., 1978-85, S.E. Healthcare Found., Gainesville, Fla., 1985. Contbr. numerous articles on engring. to profl. jours.; patentee mech. device. Mem. Ithaca Sch. Bd., N.Y., 1979-80; deacon Ch. of Christ, Gainesville, Fla., 1983—. Recipient citation Pres. Carter, 1979, Disting. Alumnus award Purdue U., 1990. Fellow Am. Soc. Agrl. Engrs. (dir. 1990, paper awards 1963, 77, 78, Young Engr. of Yr. award 1980); mem. Soc. Research Adminstrs., Nat. Assn. Univ. Research Adminstrs., S.E. Univ. Research Assn., Research Univs. Network. Democrat. Lodge: Rotary. Avocations: tennis, jogging, woodworking. Home: 22415 SW 15th Ave Newberry FL 32669-3205 Office: U Fla 117 Rogers Hall Gainesville FL 32611-2037

PRICE, EDGAR HILLEARY, JR., business consultant; b. Jacksonville, Fla., Jan. 1, 1918; s. Edgar Hilleary and Mary Williams (Phillips) P.; m. Elise Ingram, June 24, 1947; 1 son, Jerald Steven. Student, U. Fla., 1937-38. Mgr. comml. flower farm, 1945-49, Fla. Gladiolus Growers Assn., 1949-55; exec. v.p. Tropicana Products, Inc., Bradenton, Fla., 1955-73, dir. div. govt. and industry regulations, to 1979; dir.; exec. v.p. Indsl. Glass Co., Inc., Bradenton, 1963-73; pres., chmn. bd. Price Co., Inc., Bradenton, cons., 1973—; dir. emeritus F.P.L. Group, Inc.; past chmn. Fla. Citrus Commn., Fla. Gov.'s Freeze Damage Survey Team, Spl. Commn. for Study Abolition Death Penalty; bd. dirs. Fla. Power and Light Co., Fla. Fair Assn., Fla. Citrus Expn., Fla. Fruit and Vegetable Assn.; past chmn. Joint Citrus Legis. Com.; past mem. Fla. Plant Bd., Fla. Bd. Control, Fla. Legis. Coun.; exec. com. Growers and Shippers League Fla., Fla. Agrl. Council, Spl. Health Agrl. Research and Edn.; past pres., chmn. bd. Fla. Hort. Soc. Past chmn., commr. census 12th Jud. Circuit; mem. Gov. Fla. Com. Rehab. Handicapped, Fla. Commn. on Ethics, 1976-77, Presdl. Inaugural Fin. com., 1977, Ea. 5th Circuit U.S. Jud. Nominating Commn., 1977—, Fla. Senate from 36th Dist., 1958-66; past chmn. Manatee County Bd. Sch. Dist. Trustees, Local Housing Authority Bradenton, Bradenton Sub. Std. Housing Bd., Bradenton Charter Adv. Com.; del. Dem. Nat. Conv., 1960, dist. del., 1964; past trustee, mem. exec. com. Stetson U.; former trustee New Coll., Aurora Found. Served to 1st lt. USAAF, 1941-45. Named Boss of Yr., Nat. Secs. Assn., 1959, Man of Yr. for Fla. agr. Progressive Farmer mag., 1919; recipient merit award Am. Flag Assn., 1962, Gamma Sigma Delta, 1965, leadership award Fla. Agrl. Ext. Svc., 1963, Outstanding Senator award Fla. Radio Broadcasters, 1965, Allen Morris award s most valuable mem. Fla. Legislature, 1965, Most Valuable Mem. award Fla. Senate, St. Petersburg Times, 1965, Brotherhood awardSarasota chpt. NCCJ, 1966, Disting. Citizen award Manatee County, 1970, Disting. Alumnus award U. Fla., 1972, Svc. to Mankind award Sertoma Internat., 1976, Goodwill Disting. Citizen award, 1979, Crystal Shield award Salvation Army, 1996; inducted into Fla. Agrl. Hall of Fame, 1992, Tampa Bay Bus. Hall of Fame, 1992. Mem. Fla. C. of C. (bd. dirs. emeritus and past chmn.), Manatee C. of C. (past pres.), Fla. Hort. Soc. (past pres., chmn. bd.), Fla. Flower Assn., ARC Clara Barton Soc., Blue Key (hon.), Omicron Delta Kappa (hon.), Kiwanis (pres. 1955), Sigma Alpha Epsilon. Home: 3009 Riverview Blvd W Bradenton FL 34205-3420 Office: PO Box 9270 Bradenton FL 34206-9270 *The turning point in my life came at the age of 32 when I accepted Jesus Christ as my personal Lord and Saviour. I believe every person should live his life up to the fullest extent of his God-given talents and ability. I think we have a responsibility to "pay our dues" for the privilege of living in a free land by being actively involved in our government.*

PRICE, EDWARD DEAN, federal judge; b. Sanger, Calif., Feb. 12, 1919; s. Earl Trousdale and Daisy Shaw (Biggs) P.; m. Katherine S. Merritt, July 18, 1943; children: Katherine Price O'Brien, Edward M., Jane E. B.A., U. Calif., Berkeley, 1947, LL.B., 1949. Bar: Calif. 1949. Assoc. Cleary & Zeff, Modesto, Calif., 1949-51; assoc. Zeff & Halley, Modesto, Calif., 1951-54; ptnr. Zeff, Halley & Price, Modesto, Calif., 1954-63, Zeff & Price, Modesto, Calif., 1963-65, Price & Martin, Modesto, Calif., 1965-69, Price, Martin & Crabtree, Modesto, Calif., 1969-79; judge U.S. Dist. Ct., Fresno, Calif., 1980-90, sr. judge, 1990—; mem. adv. bd. governing com. Continuing Edn. of Bar, San Francisco, 1963-71, governing bd. Calif. State Bar, 1973-76; v.p. Jud. Council, Calif., 1978-79. Contbr. articles to profl. jours. Served with U.S. Army, 1943-46. Mem. ABA, Am. Coll. Trial Lawyers, Am. Bd. Trial Advocates. Democrat. Methodist. Home: 1012 Wellesley Ave Modesto CA 95350-5042 Office: US Dist Ct 5554 US Courthouse 1130 O St Fresno CA 93721-2201*

PRICE, ELY, dermatologist; b. N.Y.C., Aug. 9, 1932; s. Jacob and Mary (Flattau) P.; m. Ilona Brodie, Apr. 30, 1988; children from previous marriage: Jeremy, Andrew. BS cum laude, CCNY, 1953; AM, Ind. U., 1956; MD, U. Lausanne, Switzerland, 1964. Diplomate Am. Bd. Dermatology. Intern Brookdale Hosp. Med. Ctr., Bklyn., 1964-65, resident internal medicine, 1965-66; fellow Mt. Sinai Hosp., N.Y.C., 1965-66; practice dermatology Bay Ridge Skin and Cancer Dermatology, P.C., Bklyn., 1969—; attending dermatology Bklyn. Hosp., 1985-96; attending-in-charge, head dermatology Maimonides Med. Ctr., Bklyn., 1985—; clin. assoc. prof. dermatology SUNY Sci. Ctr., Bklyn., 1985—; cons. in medicine Luth. Med. Ctr., Bklyn., 1988—; cons. in dermatology Victory Med. Hosp., Bklyn., 1989—. Fellow ACP, Am. Acad. Dermatology, N.Y. Acad. Medicine. Avocation: golf. Home: 674 W Fingerboard Rd Staten Island NY 10305 Office: Bay Ridge Skin & Cancer Dermatology PC 9921 4th Ave Brooklyn NY 11209-8347

PRICE, FRANK, motion picture and television company executive; b. Decatur, Ill., May 17, 1930; s. William F. and Winifred A. (Moran) P.; m. Katherine Huggins, May 15, 1965; children: Stephen, David, Roy, Frank. Student, Mich. State U., 1949-51. Writer, story editor CBS-TV, N.Y.C., 1951-53, Columbia Pictures, Hollywood, Calif., 1953-57, NBC-TV, Hollywood, Calif., 1957-58; producer, writer ZIV-TV, Hollywood, Calif., 1958; producer, writer Universal Television, Universal City, Calif., 1959-64, v.p., 1964-71, sr. v.p., 1971-73, exec. v.p. in charge of production, 1973-74, pres., 1974-78; v.p., dir. MCA, Inc., 1976-78; pres. Columbia Pictures Prodn., 1978-79; chmn., chief exec. officer Columbia Pictures, 1979-84, also bd. dirs.; chmn. MCA Motion Picture Group, 1984-86; chmn., chief exec. officer Price Entertainment Inc., 1987-90; chmn. Columbia Pictures, 1990-91; also bd. dirs. Sony Pictures Entertainment; chmn., chief exec. officer Price Entertainment, 1991—; exec. prodr. The Tuskegee Airmen, 1996. With USN, 1948-49. Recipient Peabody award, 1996, NAACP Image award, 1996. Mem. Writers Guild Am., West. Office: Price Entertainment Inc 23660 Malibu Colony Rd Malibu CA 90265-4637

PRICE, FREDRIC VICTOR, physician, educator, researcher; b. Wilmington, Del., Nov. 4, 1957; s. Martin Burton and Mollie (Saline) P.; m. Ellen S. Wilson, Nov. 30, 1985; children: George, Olivia. BA, Yale U., 1980; MD, U. Louisville, 1986. Diplomate Am. Bd. Ob-Gyn.; cert. gynecologic oncologist. Intern, resident in ob-gyn. U. Pitts., 1986-90; fellow in gynecologic oncology Yale U., New Haven, Conn., 1990-92; asst. prof. U. Pitts., 1993—; attending physician Magee-Womens Hosp., Pitts., 1992—; peer reviewer Obstetrics and Gynecology, L.A., 1996, Gynecologic Oncology, San Diego, 1994—; grant reviewer FDA, Rockville, Md., 1995. Contbr. articles to profl. jours. Felix Rutledge fellow M.D. Anderson Cancer Ctr., Houston, 1989; recipient Clin. Oncology award Am. Cancer Soc., 1991, Bristol-Myers Squibb Clin. Rsch. award Bristol-Myers Oncology, 1995. Fellow Am. Coll. Obstetric Gynecology, ACS; mem. Am. Soc. Clin. Oncology. Office: U Pitts Magee-Womens Hosp 300 Halket St Pittsburgh PA 15213-3108

PRICE, GAIL J. GOODMAN, marriage family, and child therapist, deaf and hearing impaired specialist; b. L.A., July 17, 1950; d. David S. and Ruth M. (Eholnikoff) Goodman; children: Gregory David, Jeffrey Ranen. BA, Calif. State U., Northridge, 1972; MEd, U. Ariz., 1973; postgrad, Chapman U., 1975-77. Lic. marriage, family and child counselor. Tchr. L.A. Unified Sch. Dist., 1973-74; dir. multi-handicapped programs Ennoble Group Homes, Inglewood, Calif., 1979; deaf-blind specialist San Francisco Lighthouse for the Blind, 1979-81; supr. social svcs. Foothill Health and Rehab. Ctr., Sylmer, Calif., 1981-83; dir. counseling ctr. Planned Parenthood of Orange County, Santa Ana, Calif., 1985-88; pvt. practice marriage, family and child counselor Orange, Calif., 1984—. Mem. Nat. Disaster Med. Sys. Disaster Med. Assistance Team CA3. U. Ariz. fellow, 1972-73. Mem. Nat. Assn. Deafness, Calif. Assn. Marriage & Family Therapists, Internat. Soc. for the Study Dissociation, Greater L.A. Coun. Deafness, Kappa Delta Pi. Avocations: edible wild plants, herbal medicine. Home: 13642 Carroll Way Tustin CA 92780-1846 Office: 221 S Glassell St Orange CA 92866-1945

PRICE, GAYL BAADER, residential construction company administrator; b. Gothenburg, Sweden, Mar. 1, 1949; came to U.S., 1951; d. Harold Edgar Anderson and Jeanette Helen (Hallberg) Akeson; m. Daniel J. Baader, Nov. 27, 1971 (div. Sept. 1980); m. Leigh C. Price, Feb. 28, 1983; foster children: Heidi, Heather. BA in Fgn. Lang., U. Ill., 1971. Asst. buyer The Denver, 1971-73, buyer, 1973-75; escrow sec. Transam. Title, Evergreen, Colo., 1975-76, escrow officer, 1976-78, sr. escrow officer, 1978-79, br. mgr., 1979-84; sr. account mgr. Transam. Title, Denver, 1984-87, sales mgr., 1987-91, v.p., 1989-94; cmty. mgr. Village Homes of Colo., Littleton, Colo., 1994—. Vol. Safehouse for Battered Women, Denver, 1986—, Spl. Olympics, 1986—, Adult Learning Source, 1993—, Kids Cure for Cancer, 1994—. Mem. Home Builders Assn. Met. Denver (bd. dirs. 1989-93, exec. com. 1991, assoc. mem. coun. 1988-93, co-chair 1990, chair 1991, Arthur Gaeth Assoc. of Yr. 1989), Sales and Mktg. Coun. Met. Denver (bd. 1986-92, 95—, Major Achievement in Merchandising Excellence chair 1989-90, Most Profl. award 1989, 97, Sales Master award 1995, Silver MAME award 1996, Gold MAME award 1997), Douglas County Econ. Devel., Zonta Club Denver II (charter, pres. 1990, Zontian of Yr. 1988), Colo. Assn. Homebuilders (Assoc. of Yr. 1992). Avocations: cooking, volunteer work, travel. Home: 1975 Linda Ln Evergreen CO 80439 Office: Village Homes 6 W Dry Creek Cir Ste 200 Littleton CO 80120-8031

PRICE, GRIFFITH BALEY, mathematician, educator; b. Brookhaven, Miss., Mar. 14, 1905; s. Walter Edwin and Lucy (Baley) P.; m. Cora Lee Beers, June 18, 1940; children: Cora Lee, Griffith Baley, Lucy Jean, Edwina Clare, Sallie Diane and Doris Joanne (twins). BA, Miss. Coll., 1925; MA, Harvard U., 1928, PhD, 1932; LLD (hon.), Miss. Coll., 1962. Instr. math. Union Coll., Schenectady, N.Y., 1932-33, U. Rochester, N.Y., 1933-36, Brown U., Providence, 1936-37; asst. prof., assoc. prof., then prof. math. U. Kans., Lawrence, 1937-75, prof. emeritus, 1975—, chmn. dept. math., 1951-70; exec. sec. Conf. Bd. Math. Scis., Washington, 1960-62. Author: Linear Equations and Matrices (with others), 1966, Sets, Functions, and Probability (with others), 1968, History of Department of Mathematics of University of Kansas, 1976, Multivariable Analysis, 1984, An Introduction to Multicomplex Spaces and Functions, 1991; contbr. articles to rsch. jours. Civil. ops. analyst USAAF, 1943-45, Eng. Mem. AAAS, Am. Math. Soc. (editor 1950-57), Math. Assn. Am. (pres. 1957-58, award Disting. Svc. 1970), N.Y. Acad. Scis., Cosmos Club, Sigma Xi. Achievements include pioneering development of operations research.

PRICE, GRIFFITH BALEY, JR., lawyer; b. Lawrence, Kans., Aug. 15, 1942; s. Griffith Baley and Cora Lee (Beers) P.; m. Maria Helena Martin, June 29, 1968; children: Andrew Griffith, Alexandra Helena. AB (cum laude), Harvard U., 1964; LLB, NYU, 1967. Bar: N.Y. 1967, U.S. Ct. Appeals (6th cir.) 1975, U.S. Ct. Appeals (2nd cir.) 1978, U.S. Ct. Appeals (3d, 5th and 11th cirs.) 1981, U.S. Ct. Appeals (fed. cir.) 1984, D.C. 1991. Assoc. Dewey, Ballantine, Bushby, Palmer & Wood, N.Y.C., 1967-75; ptnr. Milgrim Thomajan & Lee, N.Y.C., 1976-86; of counsel, ptnr. Finnegan, Henderson, Farabow, Garrett & Dunner, Washington, 1987—; adj. prof., lectr. George Washington U. Law Ctr., Washington, 1989-93; frequent lectr. ABA, Practicing Law Inst., Law & Bus., 1982—. Author: (with others, treatise) Milgrim on Trade Secrets, 1986; contbr. articles to publs. Root-Tilden scholar NYU Law Sch., 1964-67. Mem. ABA (intellectual property sect., com. chmn.), Internat. Trademark Assn. (bd. dirs., com. chmn.), Am. Intellectual Property Law Assn. (com. chmn.), Licensing Execs. Soc., N.Y. Athletic Club, Harvard Club (Washington). Presbyterian. Office: Finnegan Henderson Farabow Garrett & Dunner 1300 I St NW Ste 700 Washington DC 20005-3314

PRICE, HARRISON ALAN, business research company executive; b. Oregon City, Oreg., May 17, 1921; s. Harry I. and Isabel (Esson) P.; m. Anne Shaw, Apr. 29, 1944; children: Bret, David, Dana, Holly. B.S., Calif. Inst. Tech., 1942; M.B.A., Stanford U., 1951. Mgr. econ. research Stanford Research Inst., L.A., 1951-55; gen. mgr. Def. Plant div. Harvey Aluminum, Torrance, Calif., 1955-58; founder, pres. Econ. Research Assocs., West Los Angeles, Calif., 1958-73; sr. v.p., mem. Planning Research Corp., Washington, 1973-76, sr. v.p., chmn. bd. dirs., 1976-78; pres. Harrison Price Co., L.A., 1978—. Trustee Calif. Inst. of Arts. Served with infantry U.S. Army, 1944-46. Club: California. Home: 2141 W Paseo Del Mar San Pedro CA 90732-4556

PRICE, HARRY STEELE, JR., construction materials company executive; b. East Jordan, Mich., Oct. 11, 1910; s. Harry S. and Grace B. (Beers) P.; m. Janet Smith, Apr. 7, 1934; children: Pamela, Harry Steele III, Marlay B. B.S., U. Mich., 1932. Office and field office on heavy constrn. Price Bros. Co., 1932-36, designer, constrn. and operation of gravel plant, 1936-38, in charge concrete sewer and culvert pipe operations, sand and gravel operations, gen. sec., 1938-45, v.p. in charge of pressure pipe div., 1945-67, exec. v.p., 1953-67, chmn., pres., 1967-73, chmn, 1973-80, vice chmn., 1980—. Past commr. Montgomery County Park Dist.; past pres. Dayton Art Inst., past pres. Sinclair Cmty. Coll. Found. Mem. NSPE, ASCE (life), Am. Concrete Pipe Assn. (past pres.), Am. Water Works Assn. (life, past trustee), Little Sturgeon Trout Club. Clubs: Dayton City, Buz-Fuz, Moraine Country, 49 Club, Dayton Raquet; St. Andrews (Delray Beach, Fla.); Wequetonsino Golf Club (Harbor Springs, Mich.). Home: 333 Oakwood Ave Apt 2B Dayton OH 45409-2214 Office: 367 W 2nd St Dayton OH 45402-1432

PRICE, HENRY ESCOE, broadcast executive; b. Jackson, Miss., Oct. 13, 1947; s. Henry E. Price Sr. and Alma Kate (Merrill) Noto; m. Maria Diane Harper, Apr. 8, 1972; children: Henry E. III, Norman Harper. BS in Radio, TV, Film, Journalism, U. So. Miss., 1972. Announcer, news dir. Sta. WROA Radio, Gulfport, Miss., 1967-69; comml. producer Sta. WJTV-TV, Jackson, Miss., 1969-73; prodn. mgr. Sta. WAAY-TV, Huntsville, Ala., 1973-77, Sta. WPEC-TV, West Palm Beach, Fla., 1977-79; dir. promotion Sta. WPTV-TV, Palm Beach, Fla., 1979-81; TV cons. Frank Magid Assoc., Marion, Iowa, 1981-83; dir. advt. and promotion Sta. WJLA-TV, Washington, 1983-84; v.p., dir. programming Sta. WUSA-TV, Gannett TV, Washington, 1984-88; pres., gen. mgr. Sta. WFMY-TV, Gannett TV, Greensboro, N.C., 1988-91, Sta. KARE-TV, Mpls., 1991-9; v.p., gen. mgr. Sta. WBBM-TV, CBS TV Stas., Chgo., 1996—; pres. Carolina News Network, 1988-91. Vice chair, bd. dirs. The Courage Ctr., Mpls.; regional dir. Nat. Conf.; mem. exec. com., bd. dirs. The Minn. Orch.; Pacesetter program chair Mpls. United Way Campaign; active Twin Cities Dunkers, Twin Cities Comm. Coun., 11 Who Care. Mem. Minn. Broadcasters Assn. (bd. dirs.), Greater Mpls. C. of C. (bd. dirs.). Avocations: furniture design and constrn., reading, walking, bicycle riding. Office: Sta WBBM-TV WBBM-TV CBS Television 630 N NcClurg Ct Chicago IL 60611

PRICE, HOWARD CHARLES, chemist; b. South Gibson, Pa., Feb. 26, 1942; s. Howard Thomas and Rachael Emma (Michael) P.; m. Delores Ann

Wilson, July 1, 1967; children: Susanne, Thomas. BS, Dickinson Coll., Carlisle, Pa., 1963; postgrad., Brown U., Providence, 1963-64; PhD, SUNY, Binghamton, 1971. NIH postdoctoral fellow Albert Einstein Coll. Medicine, Bronx, 1970-71; asst. prof. chemistry Marshall U., Huntington, W.Va., 1971-77, assoc. prof., 1978-80; sr. rsch. chemist Adv. Tech. Dept., Zimmer Inc., Warsaw, Ind., 1981-83, rsch. & devel. mgr., 1984-86, rsch. & devel. group mgr., 1987-88; R & D dir. Rsch. Labs., Warsaw, Ind., 1988-90; R & D devel. dir. Advanced Technology Dept., Zimmer Inc., Warsaw, Ind., 1991-92; dir. materials technology divsn. Family Health Internat., Research Triangle Park, N.C., 1992-95; vis. prof. Ohio U., Ironton, 1973-74. Contbr. articles to profl. jours.; author: Pennsylvania Game News, 1982; patentee in field. Band booster Warsaw Community High Sch., 1985-89. 1st lt. U.S. Army, 1964-66. Grantee, Spectroscopy Soc. of Pitts., 1980, Sigma Xi, 1975, NSF and Marshall U., 1973-80. Mem. ASTM, ASM, Am. chem. Soc. (sect. treas. 1975-76), Soc. for Biomaterials, Orthopaedic Rsch. Soc., Soc. Plastics Engrs., N.Y. Acad. Scis., Tissue Engring. Soc., Sigma Xi. Avocations: music, tennis, woodworking, fishing. Home: 1032 Lakeshore Dr Wendell NC 27591-8640 Office: Four M PO Box 549 Wendell NC 27591

PRICE, HUGH B., foundation executive, lawyer; b. Washington, Nov. 22, 1941; s. Kline A. and Charlotte (Schuster) P.; m. Marilyn Lloyd, Dec. 29, 1963; children: Traer, Janeen, Lauren. BA, Amherst Coll., 1963; LLB, Yale U., 1966. Bar: Conn. 1966. Atty. New Haven Legal Assistance Assn., 1966-68; exec. dir. Black Coalition of New Haven, 1968-70; ptnr. Cogen, Holt & Assocs., New Haven, 1970-76; human resources adminstr. City of New Haven, 1977-78; editorial writer N.Y. Times, N.Y.C., 1978-82; sr. v.p. Sta. WNET-TV, N.Y.C., 1982-88; v.p. The Rockefeller Found., N.Y.C., 1988-94; pres. Nat. Urban League, 1994—; lectr. Yale U. Law Sch., New Haven, 1978. Bd. dirs. NAACP Legal Def. & Edn. Fund., N.Y.C., 1986-88, Cooper Union, N.Y.C., 1991—, Rockefeller Bros. Fund., N.Y.C., 1988. Mem. Boule (sire archon 1990-91), The Westchester Clubmen. Avocations: travel, tennis, reading. Home: 21 Trenor Dr New Rochelle NY 10804-3731 Office: Nat Urban League 500 E 62nd St New York NY 10021-8309

PRICE, ILENE ROSENBERG, lawyer; b. Jersey City, July 2, 1951; d. Irwin Daniel and Mildred (Riesberg) Rosenberg; m. Jeffrey Paul Price, Feb. 18, 1973. AB, U. Mich., 1972; JD, U. Pa., 1977. Bar: Pa. 1977, D.C. 1978, U.S. Dist. Ct. D.C. 1979, U.S. Ct. Appeals (D.C. cir.) 1979. Assoc. Haley, Bader & Potts, Washington, 1977-80; staff atty. Mut. Broadcasting System Inc., Arlington, Va., 1980-82, asst. gen. counsel, 1982-85; gen. counsel MultiComm Telecommunications Corp., Arlington, 1985-88; east coast counsel Westwood One, Inc., Arlington, 1988-91; gen. counsel Resource Dynamics Corp., Vienna, Va., 1991—. Mem. Fed. Communications Bar Assn., Wash. Met. Area Corp. Counsel Assn., Women's Bar Assn. D.C. (bd. dirs. 1984-87). Office: Resource Dynamics Corp 8605 Westwood Center Dr Vienna VA 22182-2231

PRICE, JAMES GORDON, physician; b. Brush, Colo., June 20, 1926; s. John Hoover and Rachel Laurette (Dodds) P.; m. Janet Alice McSween, June 19, 1949; children: James Gordon II, Richard Christian, Mary Laurette, Janet Lynn. B.A., U. Colo., 1948, M.D., 1951. Diplomate: Charter diplomate Am. Bd. Family Practice (dir., pres. 1979). Intern Denver Gen. Hosp., 1951-52; practice medicine specializing in family medicine Brush, 1952-78; prof. family practice U. Kans. Med. Ctr., 1978-93; chmn. dept. U. Kans. Med. Center, 1982-90, exec. dean, 1990-93, prof. emeritus in family practice, 1993—; mem. Inst. Medicine, Nat. Acad. Scis., 1973—; med. editor Gen. Learning Corp., 1973-92. Editorial bd.: Med. World News, 1969-79; editor: Am. Acad. Family Physician Home Study Self Assessment Program, 1978-83; contbr.: (column) Your Family Physician, 1973-90. Trustee Family Health Found. Am., 1970-82. Served with USNR, 1943-46. Charter fellow Am. Acad. Family Physicians (pres. 1973); mem. Phi Beta Kappa, Alpha Omega Alpha. Home: 12205 Mohawk Rd Shawnee Mission KS 66209-2137

PRICE, JAMES MELFORD, physician; b. Onalaska, Wis., Apr. 3, 1921; s. Carl Robert and Hazel (Halderson) P.; m. Ethelyn Doreen Lee, Oct. 23, 1943 (div.); children: Alta Lee, Jean Marie, Veda Michele; m. Charlotte E. Schwenk, Sept. 27, 1986; children: Shirley S. Bunn, Cindy S. Davis, Irene S. McCumber. BS in Agr., U. Wis., 1943, MS in Biochemistry, 1944, PhD in Physiology, 1949, MD, 1951. Diplomate Am. Bd. Clin. Nutrition. Intern Cin. Gen. Hosp., 1951-52; mem. faculty U. Wis. Med. Sch., 1952—, prof. clin. oncology, 1959—, Am. Cancer Soc.-Charles S. Hayden Found. prof. surgery in cancer research, 1957—; on leave as dir. exptl. therapy Abbott Labs., 1967—, v.p. exptl. therapy, 1968, v.p. corp. research and exptl. therapy, 1971—, v.p. corp. sci. devel., 1976-78; v.p. med. affairs Norwich-Eaton Pharms., 1978—, v.p. internat. R&D, 1980-82; pres. RADAC Group, Inc., 1982-90, Biogest Products, Inc., 1984-88; mem. metabolism study sect. NIH 1959-62, pathology B study sect., 1964-68; sci. adv. com. PMA Found.; chmn. research adv. com. Ill. Dept. Mental Health; sci. com. Nat. Bladder Cancer program; mem. Drug Research Bd. Nat. Acad. Scis./NRC. Bd. dirs. Grandview Coll., Des Moines, 1977-78. Served with USNR, 1944-45. Fellow Am. Coll. Nutrition, Royal Soc. Medicine London; mem. Am. Soc. Pharmacology and Exptl. Therapeutics, Am. Assn. Cancer Research, Am. Cancer Soc. (com. etiology 1957-61), Pharm. Mfrs. Assn. (chmn. research and devel. sect. 1974-75), Am. Soc. Biol. Chemists, Am. Inst. Nutrition, Am. Soc. Clin. Nutrition, Research Dirs. Assn. Chgo., Soc. Exptl. Biology and Medicine, Soc. Toxicology. Spl. research trytophan metabolism, metabolism vitamin B complex, chem. carcinogenesis; research and devel. pharm., diagnostic and consumer products; licensing and bus. devel. Avocation: pvt. pilot. Home: PO Box 211 Edmeston NY 13335-0211

PRICE, JAMES TUCKER, lawyer; b. Springfield, Mo., June 22, 1955; s. Billy L. and Jeanne Adele (Lancaster) P.; m. Francine Beth Warkow, June 8, 1980; children: Rachel Leah, Ashley Elizabeth. BJ, U. Mo., 1977; JD, Harvard U., 1980. Bar: Mo. 1980. Assoc. firm Spencer, Fane, Britt & Browne, Kansas City, 1980-86; ptnr. Spencer, Fane, Britt & Browne, 1987—; co-chair Brownfields Working Group, 1996—; steering com. Kansas City Bi-State Brownfields Initiative, 1997—. Contbr. to monographs, other legal publs. Mem. ABA (chmn. solid and hazardous waste com. 1990-92, vice chmn. 1985-90, coun. sect. natural resources, energy and environ. law 1992-95, chmn. brownfields task force 1995-97), Mo. Bar Assn., Kansas City Met. Bar Assn. (chmn. environ. law com. 1985-86), Greater Kansas City C. of C. (chmn. energy and environ. com. 1987-89). Office: Spencer Fane Britt & Browne 1000 Walnut St Ste 1400 Kansas City MO 64106-2123

PRICE, JEANNINE ALLEENICA, clinical psychologist, computer consultant; b. Cleve., Oct. 29, 1949; d. Q. Q. and Lisa Denise (Wilson) Ewing; m. T. R. Price, Sept. 2, 1976. BS, Western Res. U., 1969; MS, Vanderbilt U., 1974; MBA, Stanford U., 1985. Cert. alcoholism counselor, Calif. Health Service coordinator Am. Profile, Nashville, 1970-72; exec. dir. Awareness Concept, San Jose, Calif., 1977-80, counselor, 1989—, exec. dir., 1989-90, v.p. Image Makers (formerly Awareness Concepts), 1994—; mgr. employee assistance program Nat. Semiconductor, Santa Clara, Calif., 1980-81; mgmt. cons. employee assistant programs. Mem. Gov.'s Adv. Council Child Devel. Programs. Mem. Am. Bus. Women's Assn., NAFE, AAUW, Coalition Labor Women, Calif. Assn. Alcohol counselors, Almaca. Author: Smile a Little, Cry a Lot, Gifts of Love, Reflection in the Mirror, The Light at the Top of the Mountain, The Dreamer, The Girl I Never Knew, An Act of Love, Walk Toward the Light.

PRICE, JOE (ALLEN), artist, former educator; b. Ferriday, La., Feb. 6, 1935; s. Edward Neill and Margaret (Hester) P. BS, Northwestern U., 1957; postgrad., Art Ctr. Coll., L.A., 1967-68; MA, Stanford U., 1970. Free-lance actor, artist N.Y.C., 1957-60; freelance illustrator, actor, L.A., 1960-68; freelance comml. artist, San Carlos, Calif., 1968-69; package designer Container Corp. Am., Santa Clara, Calif., 1969; prof. studio art and filmmaking, chmn. dept. art Coll. San Mateo, Calif., 1970-94. One-man shows include Richard Sumner Gallery, Palo Alto, Calif., 1975, San Mateo County Cultural Ctr., 1976, 82, Tahir Galleries, New Orleans, 1977, 82, Kerwin Galleries, Burlingame, Calif., 1977, Edits. Gallery, Melbourne, Australia, 1977, Ankrum Gallery, Los Angeles, 1978, 84, Edits. Ltd. West Gallery, San Francisco, 1981, Miriam Perlman Gallery, Chgo., 1982, San Mateo County Arts Council Gallery, 1982, Candy Stick Gallery, Ferndale, Calif., 1984, Assoc. Am. Artists, N.Y.C. and Phila., 1984, Gallery 30, Burlingame, 1991, San Mateo, 1984, Triton Mus. Art, Santa Clara, Calif., 1986, Huntsville (Ala.) Mus. Art, 1987, Gallery 30, San Mateo, 1988-91, Concept Art Gallery, Pitts., 1991, Eleonore Austerer Gallery, San Francisco, 1995; exhibited in groups shows at Berkeley Art Ctr., Calif., 1976, Burlingame Civic Art Gallery, 1976, Syntex Gallery, Palo Alto, Calif., 1977, Gump's Gallery, San Francisco, 1976, 77, Nat. Gallery of Australia, 1978, Sonoma County Gallery, 1979, Gov. Dummer Acad. Art, Byfield, Mass., 1979, Miss. Mus. Art, 1982, C.A.A. Galleries, Chautauqua, N.Y., 1982, Huntsville Mus. Art, 1983, Tahir Gallery, New Orleans, 1983, Hunterdon Art Ctr., N.J., 1984, Editions Galleries, Melbourne, Australia, 1988, Van Stratten Gallery, Chgo., 1988, 6th Internat. Exhbn., Carnegie-Mellon U., Pa., 1988, Forum Gallery, Jamestown, N.Y., 1988, 5th Internat. Biennale Petite Format de Papier, Belgium, 1989, 4th Internat. Biennial Print Exhibit, Taipei Fine Arts Mus., People's Republic China, 1990, Interprint, Lviv '90, USSR, 1990, New Orleans Mus. Art, 1990, Internat. Print Triennale, Cracow, Poland, 1991, 15th Ann. Nat. Invitational Drawing Exhbn. Emporia State U., Kans., 1991, Haggar U. Gallery, U. Dallas, 1991, Directions in Bay Area Printmaking: Three Decades Palo Alto Cultural Ctr., 1992, Am. Prints: Last Half 20th Century, Jane Haslem Gallery, Washington, 1992, Wenniger Graphics, Boston, 1993, Eleonore Austerer Gallery, San Francisco, 1994, Triton Mus. Art, Santa Clara, 1994, Mobile Mus. Art, 1995, Huntsville (Ala.) Mus. Art, 1995, J.J. Brookings Gallery, San Francisco, 1996, Grisham Cornell Gallery, Decatur, Ala., 1996; represented in permanent collections San Francisco Mus. Modern Art, Achenbach Found. Graphic Arts, San Francisco, Phila. Mus. Art, New Orleans Mus. Art, Portland Mus. Art, Maine, The Libr. of Congress, Washington. Huntsville Mus. Art, Midwest Mus. Am. Art, Ind., Cracow Nat. Mus., Poland, Cabo Frio Mus., Brazil, Nat. Mus. Am. Art, Smithsonian Inst., Washington. Recipient Kempshall Clark award Peoria Art Guild, 1981, Paul Lindsay Sample Meml. award 25th Chautauqua Nat. Exhbn. of Am. Art, 1982, 1st Ann. Creative Achievement award Calif. State Legislature/Arts Coun. San Mateo County, 1989. Mem. Am. Color Print Soc., Audubon Artists (Louis Lozowick Meml. award 1978, Silver medal of honor award 1991), Boston Printmakers (Ture Bengtz Meml. award 1987), Calif. Soc. Printmakers (mem. council 1979-81), Los Angeles Printmaking Soc., Phila. Print Club (Lessing J. Rosenwald prize 1979), Arts Council of San Mateo Count, Theta Chi. Democrat. Studio and Office: PO Box 3305 Sonora CA 95370-3305 *Personal philosophy: In being an artist, I do not wish to be just a "recorder" of my time, what I see, what I think. To me, the joy of art is in expressing the love of being an artist, for in loving without shame, without fear, and without doubt one transcends to the moment and speaks with integrity. For the rest of my life I wish to reflect on what life is, and to have the courage to create that which touches not only men's eyes, but their hearts and spirits. I seek the profound truth of what it is to be human and the universal truth of what is means to be creative in expressing the love of being.*

PRICE, JOHN ALEY, lawyer; b. Maryville, Mo., Oct. 7, 1947; s. Donald Leroy and Julia Catherine (Aley) P.; m. Deborah Diadra Gunter, Aug. 12, 1995; children: Theodore John, Joseph Andrew. BS, N.W. Mo. State U., 1969; JD, U. Kans., 1972. Bar: Kans. 1972, U.S. Dist. Ct. Kans. 1972, U.S. Ct. Appeals (10th cir.) 1972, Tex. 1984, U.S. Ct. Appeals (5th cir.) 1984, U.S. Supreme Ct., 1987; cert. civil trial law Tex. Bd. Legal Specialization, 1989—. Law clk. U.S. Dist. Ct. Kans., Wichita, 1972-74; assoc., then ptnr. firm Weeks, Thomas and Lysaught, Kansas City, Kans., 1974-82; ptnr. Winstead, Sechrest & Minick, Dallas, 1982-96, litigation sect. coord., 1990-92, intellectual property sect. litigation coord., 1993-95; gen. counsel Travelhost, Inc., Dallas, 1996—; spl. prosecutor Leavenworth County Dist. Atty., 1970-71, Sedgwick County Dist. Atty., Wichita, Kans., 1971-72. Author: Our Boundless Self (A Call to Awake), 1992, A Gathering of Light: Eternal Wisdom for a Time of Transformation, 1993; co-author: Soular Reunion: Journey to Self, 1997; editor (mag.) Academic Analyst, 1968-69; assoc. editor U. Kans. Law Rev., 1971-72, Dallas Bus. Jour.; author legal publs. Co-dir. Douglas County Legal Aid Soc., Lawrence, Kans., 1971-72; co-pres. Northwood Hills PTA, Dallas, 1984, Westwoood Jr. H.S. PTA, 1989-90; founder New Frontiers Found., 1993; co-founder Wings of Spirit Found., 1994, dir., v.p., 1994—. Mem. ABA, Kans. Bar Assn. (mem. task force for penal reform; Pres.'s Outstanding Svc. award 1981), Tex. Bar Assn., Pro Bono Coll., State Bar Tex., 1992—, World Bus. Acad., Inst. Noetic Scis., UN Assn. (humans rights com. Dallas chpt. 1991-93, bd. dirs. 1991-93), Campaign for the Earth (chpt. coord. Global Report 1991-92, coord. govt. and politics area 1991-92), Blue Key, Order of Coif, Phi Delta Phi, Sigma Tau Gamma (v.p. 1968-69). Mem. Unity Ch. Office: Travelhost Inc 10701 N Stemmons Fwy Dallas TX 75220-2419 *Individually, each person creates his or her reality every moment of existence. Collectively, we hold within ourselves a boundless capacity to co-create a world filled with love, compassion and abundance for all sentient beings. The key to a new order of the ages lies within our own hearts, minds and souls.*

PRICE, JOHN RANDOLPH, writer; b. Alice, Tex., Feb. 12, 1932; s. John Randolph and Eva Mae (Boney) P.; m. Janis Bryant Price, June 20, 1953; children: Susan Lynn, Leslie Anne. BS, U. Houston, 1957. Dir. advt. Gates Radio Corp., Quincy, Ill., 1957-62; v.p. Sander Rodkin, Ltd., Chgo., 1962-64; exec. v.p. Stewart, Price, Tomlin, Inc., Chgo., 1964-67; v.p. Goodwin, Dannenbaum, Littman & Wingfield, Inc., Houston, 1967-70; pres. O'Neill, Price, Anderson, Fouchard, Inc., Houston, 1970-74, John Price & Co., Houston, 1974-79, Arnan, Inc., Austin, 1979-81; chmn. bd. The Quartus Found. Inc., Boerne, Tex., 1981—; adv. bd. Global Family, Inc., Palo Alto, Calif., 1990—; Santi Found., Yucalpa, Calif., 1990—, Unity and Diversity World Coun., Inc., L.A., 1992—. Author: The Superbeings, 1981, The Manifestation Process, 1983, The Planetary Commission, 1984, Practical Spirituality, 1985, With Wings as Eagles, 1987, The Abundance Book, 1987, Prayer, Principles & Power, 1987, A Spiritual Philosophy for the New World, 1990, Empowerment, 1992, The Angels Within Us, 1993, Angel Energy, 1995, Living a Life of Joy, 1997. Chmn. Red Cross Drive, Quincy, Ill., 1960; cons. All Am. City campaign, Quincy, 1962. Staff sgt. USAF, 1952-56. Recipient Joseph S. Cullinan award U. Houston, 1956, Grand Prix Best Consumer Mag. Advt. award, 1970. Mem. Internat. New Thought Alliance (Humanitarian award 1992, Joseph Murphy award 1994). Achievements include organizer of first annual World Peace day on December 31, 1986. Office: The Quartus Found Inc PO Box 1768 Boerne TX 78006

PRICE, JOHN RICHARD, lawyer, law educator; b. Indpls., Nov. 28, 1934; s. Carl Lee and Agnes I. (Douglas) P.; m. Suzanne A. Leslie, June 22, 1963; children—John D., Steven V. B.A. with high honors, U. Fla., 1958; LL.B. with honors, NYU, 1961. Bar: Calif. 1962, Wash. 1977, U.S. Ct. Appeals (9th cir.), U.S. Dist. Ct. (we. dist.) Wash. Assoc. McCutchen, Doyle, Brown & Enersen, San Francisco, 1961-69; prof. law U. Wash., Seattle, 1969-97, dean, 1982-88; of counsel Perkins Coie, Seattle, 1976—. Author: Contemporary Estate Planning, 1983, Price on Contemporary Estate Planning, 1992. Served with U.S. Army, 1953-55. Root-Tilden fellow NYU Sch. Law, 1958-61. Fellow Am. Coll. Trust and Estate Counsel (former regent); mem. ABA, Am. Law Inst., Inst. for Fiscal Studies, Internat. Acad. of Estate and Trust Law, Order of Coif, Phi Beta Kappa. Congregationalist. Home: 3794 NE 97th St Seattle WA 98115-2564 Office: 1201 3d Ave 40th Fl Seattle WA 98101-3099

PRICE, JOHN ROY, JR., financial executive; b. N.Y.C., Dec. 20, 1938; s. John Roy and Pauline Bernice (Milnes) P.; m. Victoria Scott Pohle, Dec. 19, 1970 (div. 1982); 1 child, Matthew Roy; m. Marion Cobb Hardie, Oct. 1, 1988 (div. 1996). B.A., Grinnell Coll., 1960, Queens Coll., Oxford (Eng.) U., 1962; M.A., Queens Coll., Oxford (Eng.) U., 1965; J.D., Harvard U., 1965. Assoc. Casey, Lane & Mittendorf, N.Y.C., 1965-67; v.p. Bedford-Stuyvesant D & S Corp., N.Y.C., 1967-68; spl. asst. to Pres. U.S., Washington, 1969-71; assoc. Donaldson, Lufkin & Jenrette, N.Y.C., 1971-72; v.p. Mfrs. Hanover Trust, N.Y.C., 1972-75; v.p. Mfrs. Hanover Corp., N.Y.C., 1975-80, sr. v.p. non-bank subs., 1980-83, sr. v.p., sec., 1983-87; mng. dir. Mfrs. Hanover Trust Co., 1987-88, Mfrs. Hanover Securities Corp., 1988-92; mng. dir. govt. affairs Chem. Bank, 1992-96, Chase Manhattan, 1996—; bd. dirs. Am. Trust for Oxford, 1990-94, chmn. Cmty. Devel., Inc., Prin. Fin. Group (formerly Bankers Life Co.), Transcell Techs. Corp., Bankers Assn. for Fgn. Trade, 1990-97, pres., 1994-95, Nat. Fgn. Trade Coun., 1991—; pres. Am. for Oxford, 1987—; chmn. local devel. corp. Bklyn. Acad. Music, 1980-82. Nat. chmn. Ripon Soc., 1967-68; trustee Grinnell Coll., 1970—; bd. dirs. New Communities Corp., 1976-77; mem. exec. panel Chief of Naval Ops., 1972-79. Rhodes scholar. Mem. Council Fgn. Relations, Phi Beta Kappa. Club: Harvard (N.Y.C.). Home: 3144 Granite Rd Woodstock MD 21163-1004

PRICE, JONATHAN G., geologist; b. Danville, Pa., Feb. 1, 1950; s. A. Barney and Flora (Best) P.; m. Elisabeth McKinley, June 3, 1972; children: Alexander D., Argenta M. BA in Geology and German, Lehigh U., 1972; MA, U. Calif., Berkeley, 1975, PhD, 1977. Cert. profl. geologist. Geologist Anaconda Copper Co., Yerington, Nev., 1974-75; geologist U.S. Steel Corp., Salt Lake City, 1977, Corpus Christi, 1978-81; rsch. assoc. Bur. Econ. Geology, U. Tex., Austin, 1981-85, rsch. sci., 1984-88, program dir., 1987-88; dir. Tex. Mining & Mineral Resources Rsch. Inst., Austin, 1984-88; dir., state geologist Nev. Bur. Mines & Geology, U. Nev., Reno, 1988-92, 95—; staff dir. Bd. on Earth Scis. & Resources Nat. Rsch. Coun., Washington, 1993-95; asst. prof. Bucknell U., Lewisburg, 1977-78. Author, editor: Igneous Geology of Trans-Pecos Texas, 1986. Vol. instr. CPR and first aid ARC, 1983-95, bd. dirs. Sierra Nev. chpt., 1991-92. German Acad. Exch. Svc. fellow U. Heidelberg, 1972-73; recipient Explorer award Am. Geol. Inst., 1995. Fellow Geol. Soc. Am., Soc. Econ. Geologists; mem. Am. Inst. Profl. Geologists (Nev. sect. pres. 1992, nat. pres. 1997), Mineral. Soc. Am., Phi Beta Kappa. Office: Nev Bur Mines & Geology UNR/MS 178 Reno NV 89557-0088

PRICE, JOSEPH HUBBARD, lawyer; b. Montgomery, Ala., Jan. 31, 1939; s. Aaron Joseph and Minnie Jule (Reynolds) P.; m. Cynthia Winant Ramsey, Sept. 14, 1963 (div. 1980); children—Victoria Reynolds, Ramsey Winant; m. Courtney McFadden, Apr. 26, 1980. A.B., U. Ala., 1961; LL.B., Harvard U., 1964; postgrad. London Sch. Econs., 1964-65. Bar: Ala. 1964, D.C. 1968. Law clerk to justice Hugo L. Black, U.S. Supreme Ct., Washington, 1967-68; assoc. Leva, Hawes, Symington, Martin & Oppenheimer, Washington, 1968-71; v.p. Overseas Pvt. Investment Corp., Washington, 1971-73; ptnr. Leva, Hawes, et. al., Washington, 1973-83, Gibson, Dunn & Crutcher, Washington, 1983—. Mem. CARE Com. Washington; mem. adv. com. Hugo Black Meml. Library, Ashland, Ala. Served to capt. U.S. Army, 1966-67; Vietnam. Decorated Bronze Star; Frank Knox Meml. fellow London Sch. Econs., 1964-65. Mem. ABA, Am. Soc. Internat. Law, Supreme Ct. Hist. Soc., Phi Beta Kappa. Clubs: Metropolitan. Home: 3104 Cathedral Ave NW Washington DC 20008-3419 Office: Gibson Dunn & Crutcher 1050 Connecticut Ave NW Washington DC 20036

PRICE, JOSEPH MICHAEL, lawyer; b. St. Paul, Dec. 2, 1947; s. Leon and Rose (Kaufman) P.; m. Louise Rebecca Braunstein, Dec. 19, 1971; children—Lisa, Laurie, Julie. B.A., U. Minn., 1969, J.D., 1972. Bar: Minn. 1972, U.S. Dist. Ct. Minn. 1974. Ptnr., Faegre & Benson, Mpls., 1972—. Mem. Minn. Bar Assn., Hennepin County Bar Assn. Home: 4407 Country Club Rd Minneapolis MN 55424-1148 Office: Faegre & Benson 2200 Norwest Ctr 90 S 7th St Minneapolis MN 55402-3903

PRICE, KATHLEEN MCCORMICK, book editor, writer; b. Topeka, Kans., Dec. 25, 1932; d. Raymond Chesley and Kathleen (Shoffner) McCormick; m. William Faulkner Black, Aug. 25, 1956 (div. 1961); 1 child, Kathleen Serena; m. William Hillard Price, Aug. 13, 1976. BA, U. Colo., Denver, 1971. Book reviewer Denver Post, 1971-78; book editor San Diego Mag., 1978-92; cons. editor St. John's Cathedral, Denver, 1985-95. Author: There's a Dactyl Under My Foot, 1986, The Lady and the Unicorn, 1994. Dir. Colo. Episcopal Vestment Guild. Mem. PEN, Denver Women's Press Club, Denver County Club, La Garita Club, Phi Beta Kappa. Episcopalian. Home: 27 Crestmoor Dr Denver CO 80220-5853

PRICE, LEONTYNE, concert and opera singer, soprano; b. Laurel, Miss., Feb. 10, 1927; d. James A. and Kate (Baker) P.; m. William Warfield, Aug. 31, 1952 (div. 1973). BA, Central State Coll., Wilberforce, Ohio, 1949, DMus, 1968; student, Juilliard Sch. Music, 1949-52; pupil, Florence Page Kimball; LHD, Dartmouth Coll., 1962, Fordham U., 1969, Yale U., 1979; MusD, Howard U., 1962; Dr. Humanities, Rust Coll., 1968. Profl. opera debut in 4 Saints in 3 Acts, 1952; appeared as Bess in Porgy and Bess, Vienna, Berlin, Paris, London, under auspices U.S. State Dept., also N.Y.C. and U.S. tour, 1952-54; recitalist, soloist with symphonies, U.S., Can., Australia, Europe, 1954—; appeared concerts in India, 1956, 64; soloist, Hollywood Bowl, 1955-59, 66, Berlin Festival, 1960; role as Mme. Lidoine in Dialogues des Carmelites, San Francisco Opera, 1957; opera singer, NBC-TV, 1955-58, 60, 62, 64, San Francisco Opera Co., 1957-59, 60-61, 63, 65, 67, 68, 71, as Aida at La Scala, Milan, 1957, Vienna Staatsoper, 1958, 59-60, 61, Berlin Opera, 1964, Rome Opera, 1966, Paris Opera, 1968, recital, Brussels Internat. Fair, auspices State Dept., 1958, Verona Opera Arena, 1958-59, recitals in Yugoslavia for, State Dept., 1958; rec. artist, RCA-Victor, 1958—, appeared Covent Garden, London, 1958-59, 70, Chgo. Lyric Theatre, 1959, 60, 65, Oakland (Calif.) Symphony, 1980, soloist, Salzburg Festival, 1959-63, Tetro alla Scala, Milano, 1960-61, 63, 67, appeared Met. Opera, N.Y.C., 1961-62, 64, 66, 75, 76; since resident mem., until 1985; soloist, Salzburg Festival, 1950, 60, debut, Teatre Dell'Opera, Rome, 1967, Teatro Colon, Buenos Aires, Argentina, 1969, Hamburg Opera, 1970; recordings include A Christmas Offering with Karajani, God Bless America with Charles Gerhardt, Arias from Don Giovanni, Turandot, Aida, Emani, Messa di Requiem, Trovatore, Live at Ordway, The Prima Donna Collection, A Program of Song with D. Garvey, Right as the Rain with André Previn. Hon. bd. dirs. Campfire Girls; hon. vice-chmn. U.S. com. UNESCO; co-chmn. Rust Coll. Upward Thrust Campaign; trustee Internat. House. Decorated Order at Ment Italy; recipient Merit award for role of Tosca in NBC-TV Opera, Mademoiselle mag., 1955, 20 Grammy awards for classical vocal recs. Nat. Acad. Rec. Arts and Scis., citation YWCA, 1961, Spirit of Achievement award Albert Einstein Coll. Medicine, 1962, Presdl. medal of freedom, 1964, Springarn medal NAACP, 1965, Schwann Catalog award, 1968, Nat. Medal of Arts, 1985, Essence award, 1991, others; named Musician of Year, Mus. Am. mag., 1961. Fellow Am. Acad. Arts and Sci.; mem. AFTRA, Am. Guild Mus. Artists, Actors Equity Assn., Sigma Alpha Iota, Delta Sigma Theta. Office: Columbia Artists Mgmt Inc Walter Divsn 165 W 57th St New York NY 10019-2201 also: 1133 Broadway New York NY 10010-7903*

PRICE, LUCILE BRICKNER BROWN, retired civic worker; b. Decorah, Iowa, May 31, 1902; d. Sidney Eugene and Cora (Drake) Brickner; B.S., Iowa State U., 1925; M.A., Northwestern U., 1940; m. Maynard Wilson Brown, July 2, 1928 (dec. Apr. 1937); m. 2d, Charles Edward Price, Jan. 14, 1961 (dec. Dec. 1983). Asst. dean women Kans. State U., Manhattan, 1925-28; mem. bd. student personnel adminstrn. Northwestern U., 1937-41; personnel research Sears Roebuck & Co., Chgo., 1941-42, overseas club dir. ARC, Eng., Africa, Italy, 1942-45; dir. Child Edn. Found., N.Y.C., 1946-56. Participant 1st and 2d Iowa Humanists Summer Symposiums, 1974, 75. Del. Mid Century White House Conf. on Children and Youth, 1950; mem. com. on program and research of Children's Internat. summer villages, 1952-53; mem. bd. N.E. Iowa Mental Health Ctr., 1959-62, pres. bd., 1960-61; mem. Iowa State Extension Adv. Com., 1973-75; project chmn. Decorah Hist. Dist. (listed Nat. Register Historic Places); trustee Porter House Mus., Decorah, 1966-78, emerita bd. dirs., 1982—; participant N. Cen. Regional Workshop Am. Assn. State and Local History, Mpls., 1975, Midwest Workshop Hist. Preservation and Conservation, Iowa State U., 1976, 77; mem. Winneshiek County (Iowa) Civil Service Commn., 1978-87; rep. Class of 1940 Northwestern U. Sch. Edn. and Social Policy, 1986-88. Recipient Alumni Merit award Iowa State U., 1975, Cert. of Appreciation Iowa State U. Extension, 1988. Mem. Am. Coll. Personnel Assn., (life), ARC Overseas Assn. (life, nat. bd.), AAUW (life, mem. bd. Decorah, Named Gift award 1977), Nat. Assn. Mental Health (del. nat. conf. 1958), Norwegian-Am. Mus. (life, Vesterheim fellow), Internat. Platform Assn., Winneshiek County Hist. Soc. (life, cert. of appreciation 1984), DAR, Luther Coll. Heritage Club (life, pres.'s coun. 1993), Pi Lambda Theta, Chi Omega. Designer, builder house for retirement living. Avocation: remembering WWII. Home: 508 W Broadway St Decorah IA 52101-1704

PRICE, MALCOLM IVAN, podiatrist; b. Clinton, Mass., Dec. 28, 1935; s. Sanford Louis and Lillian (Samels) P.; children: Scott Irwin, Michelle Yvette. BA, Clark U., 1957; D Podiatric Medicine, N.Y. Coll. Podiatric Medicine, 1961. Pvt. practice podiatric medicine Fitchburg, Mass., 1962—. Bd. dris. Soapbox Derby, Fitchburg, 1969-70; coach Biddy League Basketball, Lunenburg, Mass., 1968-78; pres. Little League, Lunenburg, 1970-72. Recipient citation Bd. Registration in Podiatry, 1980, Honor award All Am. Soapbox Derby, inc., 1969-70. Mem. Am. Podiatric Med. Assn., Mass. Podiatry Soc. (bd. dirs. 1970-80), worcester County Podiatric Soc. (pres., sec.), Rotary (dist. vol. chmn.), Shriners, Masons, Elks, Exch. Club of Fitchburg (pres. 1965-66, dist. dir., Exchangite of Yr. 1979-80, Exchangite

Extraordinary 1981-82). Avocations: skiing, swimming, tennis. Home and Office: 79 Prichard St Fitchburg MA 01420-3247

PRICE, MARION WOODROW, journalist; b. Elizabeth City, N.C., Oct. 13, 1914; s. James Asa and Meddie (Divers) P.; m. Mary Dudley Pittman, Aug. 31, 1940; children—Wiley, Dudley, Mary, Catherine. Student, Wake Forest Coll., 1933-34. Reporter Daily Advance, Elizabeth City, 1935-39, Raleigh (N.C.) Times, 1939-41; mng. editor Kannapolis (N.C.) Ind., 1941-42; reporter AP, Raleigh, 1942-43, News and Observer, Raleigh, 1946-57; mng. editor News and Observer, 1957-72; outdoor editor, 1949-76. Mem. Kerr Reservoir Devel. Commn., 1950-52, Cape Hatteras Seashore Commn., 1949-50, N.C. Wildlife Resources Commn., 1977-89; chmn. N.C. Outer Banks Park Commn., 1962-63, N.C. Seashore Commn., 1963-69, N.C. State Ports Authority, 1969-73. Served with USAAF, 1943-45. Mem. AP Mng. Editors Assn., Outdoor Writers Am. Baptist. Home: Old Ferry Dock Rd PO Box 65 Gloucester NC 28528

PRICE, (WILLIAM) MARK, professional basketball player; b. Bartlesville, Okla., Feb. 15, 1964. Student, Ga. Tech. With Dallas Mavericks, 1986; guard Cleve. Cavaliers, 1986-95, Washington Bullets, 1995-96, Golden State Warriors, 1996—. Winner NBA Long Distance Shootout, 1993, 94; named to NBA All-Star team, 1989, 92, 93, 94, NBA First Team, 1993, Dream Team II, 1994. Holder career record for highest free-throw percentages during regular and playoff seasons. Office: Golden State Warriors 1221 Broadway 20th Fl Oakland CA 94612-1918*

PRICE, MICHAEL F., money management executive; b. 1952; div., 3 sons. Graduate, U. Okla., 1975. Rsch. asst., mgr., to CEO Heine Securities, Short Hills, N.J., 1975-97; pres., CEO Franklin Mutual Advs. Inc. (formerly Heine Securities), Short Hills, N.J., 1997—; pres., chmn. bd. dirs. Franklin Mutual Series Fund Inc. Office: Franklin Mutual Advisers Inc 51 John F Kennedy Pkwy Short Hills NJ 07078-2702

PRICE, MICHAEL HOWARD, journalist, critic, composer, cartoonist; b. Amarillo, Tex., Sept. 14, 1947; s. John Andrew and Thelma Adeline (Wilson) P.; m. Christina Renteria, Aug. 31, 1980. BA in Journalism, West Tex. State U., 1970. Edn. writer Amarillo Globe-News, 1968-74, fin. editor, 1974-76, city editor, 1976-77; adminstr. Amarillo Coll., 1977-80; bur. chief Ft. Worth Star-Telegram, 1980-83, features editor, 1983-85, film critic, 1985—; cons. journalism West Tex. State U., Canyon, 1977-90, Tex. Tech U., Lubbock, 1982-85; dirs. The Harvey Group comic-book profls. awards, 1990—. Author: (CD-ROMs) A Century of Fantastic Cinema, 1995, Silver Screen Sensations, 1996, (albums) Cognitive Dissonance, 1994, The Last Temptation of Price, 1995, R. Crumb—The Musical, 1995, Swingmasters Revue, 1995, Claus & Effect, 1996, (books) Forgotten Horrors, 1986, Human Monsters in the Movies, 1994, Krime Duzzin't Pay, 1995, The Guitar in Jazz, 1996, Stitches, 1996, Frights Genuine & Fancied, 1996, (novels) The Prowler, 1989, Carnival of Souls, 1991, Holiday for Screams, 1992; screen actor: Ramming Speed, 1997. Creative dir. Tex. Gridiron Show, Fort Worth, 1984-85, 92-93. Mem. Soc. Profl. Journalists (bd. dirs. 1992-94), Tex. Tornados Blues Hall of Fame, Soc. Film Critics. Address: 7717 Meadowlark Dr Fort Worth TX 76133 *In a career of communication, the conventional wisdom of "writing about what you know" no longer applies. Try "writing about what you want to know," and your progress from that point will astonish you.*

PRICE, (JOHN) NELSON, journalist; b. Augusta, Ga., May 7, 1957; s. John Paul and Joy Gertrude (Scheck) P. BA in Journalism and Psychology, Ind. U., 1978. City hall reporter Lawrence (Kans.) Journal-World, 1978-79; fed. cts. reporter, social issues writer Fort Wayne (Ind.) Journal-Gazette, 1979-80; edn. writer Indpls. News, 1981-85; columnist, feature writer Indpls. Star-News, 1985—; bd. dirs. The Sagamore, Indpls. Contbr. articles to profl. jours. Bd. dirs. Riley Area Revitalization Program, Indpls. Recipient Sagamore of the Wabash award Gov. Ind., 1995, Martin Luther King Jr. award Indpls. Edn. Assn., 1986, Best Sports Writing award Hoosier State Press Assn., 1994, Best Column award, 1994, Best Feature Story award, 1994, Best Personality Profile award, 1994. Mem. Soc. Profl. Journalists (awards), Mental Health Assn. Marion County (awards). Avocations: swimming, theater, travel, Olympic sports. Office: Indianapolis Star-News 307 N Pennsylvania St Indianapolis IN 46204-1811

PRICE, NICK, professional golfer; b. Durban, South Africa, Jan. 28, 1957; m. Sue Price; children: Gregory, Robyn Frances. Winner PGA Championship, 1992, 1994, British Open, 1994, 3rd PGA Tour Money Leader, 1992, PGA Tour Money Leader, 1993, 10 USPGA Tour Victories, 26 World Wide Victories; recipient Vardon Trophy, 1993; named Player of Yr., 1993. Holds PGA Tournament record for lowest score (269), 1994. Address: care PGA Tour 100 Avenue of the Champions Palm Beach Gardens FL 33410-9601*

PRICE, PAUL BUFORD, physicist, educator; b. Memphis, Nov. 8, 1932; s. Paul Buford and Eva (Dupuy) P.; m. JoAnn Margaret Baum, June 28, 1958; children—Paul Buford III, Heather Alynn, Pamela Margaret, Alison Gaynor. BS summa cum laude, Davidson Coll., 1954, DSc, 1973; MS, U. Va., 1956, PhD, 1958. Fulbright scholar U. (Eng.) Bristol, 1958-59; NSF postdoctoral fellow Cambridge (Eng.) U., 1959-60; physicist R&D Ctr. GE, Schenectady, 1960-69; vis. prof. Tata Inst. Fundamental Rsch., Bombay, India, 1965-66; adj. prof. physics Rensselaer Poly. Inst., 1967-68; prof. physics U. Calif., Berkeley, 1969—, chmn. dept. physics, 1987-91, McAdams prof. physics, 1990-92, dean phys. scis., 1992—, dir. Space Scis. Lab., 1979-85; vis. com. Bartol Rsch. Inst., 1991-94; adv. bd. Indian Inst. Astrophysics, Bangalore, 1993-95; cons. to lunar sample analysis planning team NASA; space sci. bd. Nat. Acad. Scis.; vis. prof. U. Rome, 1983, 92; sci. assoc. Ctr. d'Etude Rsch. Nuclear, 1984; Miller rsch. prof. U. Calif., Berkeley, 1972-73; researcher in space and astrophycs, nuclear physics. Author: (with others) Nuclear Tracks in Solids; Contbr. (with others) articles to profl. jours. Regional dir. Calif. Alliance for Minority Participation, 1993—. Recipient Disting. Svc. award Am. Nuclear Soc., 1964, Indsl. Rsch. awards, 1964, 65, E.O. Lawrence Meml. award AEC, 1971, medal for exceptional sci. achievement NASA, 1973; John Simon Guggenheim fellow, 1976-77. Fellow Am. Phys. Soc., Am. Geophys. Union; mem. Nat. Acad. Scis. (chmn. geophysics sect. 1981-84, sec. class phys.-math. scis. 1985-88, chmn. 1988-91).

PRICE, PAUL L., lawyer; b. Chgo., Apr. 21, 1945; s. Walter S. and Lillian (Czerepkowski) L.; m. Dianne L. Olech, June 3, 1967; children: Kristen, Kathryn. BBA, Loyola U., Chgo., 1967; JD with honors, Ill. Inst. Tech., 1971. Bar: Ill. 1971, U.S. Dist. Ct. (no. dist.) Ill., U.S. Ct. Appeals (7th cir.). Tax acct. Arthur Anderson & Co., Chgo., 1970-71; assoc. Doyle & Tarpey, Chgo., 1971-75, Gordon & Assocs., Chgo., 1975-76; from assoc. to ptnr. Pretzel & Stouffer, Chartered, Chgo., 1976-96; ptnr. Price, Tunney, Loughnane, Reiter & Bruton, Chgo., 1996—. Editorial bd. Shepard's Ill. Tort Reporter. With USMC, 1969-70. Fellow Am. Coll. Trial Lawyers; mem. ABA, Ill. Bar Assn., Soc. Trial Lawyers, Ill. Assn. Def. Trial Counsel (pres. 1990-91), Fedn. Ins. and Corp. Counsel (bd. dirs.), Def. Rsch. Inst., Assn. Def. Trial Attys., Ill. Inst. Tech.-Chgo. Kent Coll. Law Alumni Assn. (pres. 1989-90). Roman Catholic. Office: Price Tunney Loughnane Reiter & Bruton 1 S Wacker Dr Ste 2500 Chicago IL 60606-4617

PRICE, PETER WILFRID, ecology educator, researcher; b. London, Apr. 17, 1938; came to U.S., 1971; BSc with honors, U. Wales, Bangor, 1958-62; MSc, U. New Brunswick, Fredericton, 1964; PhD, Cornell U., 1970. Asst. prof. U. Ill., Urbana, 1971-75, assoc. prof., 1975-79; research ecologist Mus. No. Ariz., Flagstaff, 1979-80; assoc. prof. No. Ariz. U., Flagstaff, 1980-85, prof. ecology, 1985-94, Regents' prof., 1994—. Author: Evolutionary Biology of Parasites, 1980, Biological Evolution, 1996, Insect Ecology, 3d edit., 1997; editor: A New Ecology, 1984, Evolutionary Strategies of Parasitic Insects, 1975, Plant-Animal Interactions, 1991, Effects of Resource Distribution on Animal-Plant Interactions, 1991, Population Dynamics, 1995. Guggenheim fellow, 1977-78; Fullbright Sr. scholar, 1993-94. Fellow AAAS, Royal Entomol. Soc. of London; mem. NSF (panel mem. 1978-81, 91-93), Am. Soc. Naturalists, Ecol. Soc. Am. (bd. editors 1973-76), Brit. Ecol. Soc., Ecol. Soc. Am. (Founders Award, 1993). Office: No Ariz U PO Box 5640 Flagstaff AZ 86011-5640

PRICE, REYNOLDS, novelist, poet, playwright, essayist, educator; b. Macon, N.C., Feb. 1, 1933; s. William Solomon and Elizabeth (Rodwell) P. AB summa cum laude (Angier Duke scholar), Duke, 1955; BLitt (Rhodes scholar), Merton Coll., Oxford U., Eng., 1958; LittD, St. Andrews Presbyn. Coll., 1978, Wake Forest U., 1979, Washington and Lee U., 1991; Davidson Coll., 1992; LittD, Elon Coll., 1996. Mem. faculty English Duke U., 1958—; asst. prof., 1961-68, assoc. prof., 1968-72, prof., 1972-77, James B. Duke prof., 1977—, acting chmn., 1983; writer in residence U. N.C., Chapel Hill, 1965, U. Kans., 1967, 69, 80, U.N.C., Greensboro, 1971; Glasgow prof. Washington and Lee U., 1971; faculty Salzburg Seminar, 1977. Author: A Long and Happy Life, 1962, The Names and Faces of Heroes, 1963, A Generous Man, 1966, Love and Work, 1968, Permanent Errors, 1970, Things Themselves, 1972, The Surface of Earth, 1975, Early Dark, 1977, A Palpable God, 1978, The Source of Light, 1981, Vital Provisions, 1982, Private Contentment, 1984, Kate Vaiden, 1986, The Laws of Ice, 1986, A Common Room, 1987, Good Hearts, 1988, Clear Pictures, 1989, The Tongues of Angels, 1990, The Use of Fire, 1990, New Music, 1990, The Foreseeable Future, 1991, Conversations with Reynolds Price, 1991, Blue Calhoun, 1992, Full Moon, 1993, The Collected Stories, 1993, A Whole New Life, 1994, The Promise of Rest, 1995, Three Gospels, 1996, The Collected Poems, 1997, Roxanna Slade. Recipient William Faulkner Found. award notable 1st novel, 1962, Sir Walter Raleigh award, 1962, 76, 81, 84, 86, award Nat. Assn. Ind. Schs., 1964, Roanoke-Chowan Poetry award, 1982; Guggenheim fellow, 1964-65; fellow Nat. Endowment for Arts, 1967-68, lit. adv. panel, 1973-76, chmn., 1976; recipient Nat. Inst. Arts and Letters award, 1971, Bellamann Found. award, 1972, Lillian Smith award, 1976, N.C. award, 1977, Nat. Book Critics Circle award, 1986, Elmer H. Bobst award, 1988, R. Hunt Parker award N.C. Lit. and Hist. Soc., 1991. Mem. Am. Acad. Arts and Letters, Phi Beta Kappa, Phi Delta Theta. Home: PO Box 99014 Durham NC 27708-9014 Office: care Harriet Wasserman Lit Agy Inc 137 E 36th St New York NY 10016-3528

PRICE, RICHARD, anthropologist, author; b. N.Y.C., Nov. 30, 1941; s. George Price and Gertrude (Swee) Jaffe; m. Sally Hamlin, 1963; children: Niko, Leah. AB in History and Lit. magna cum laude, Harvard U., 1963, PhD in Social Anthropology, 1970. From lectr. to assoc. prof. anthropology Yale U., New Haven, 1969-74; prof. anthropology Johns Hopkins U., Balt., 1974-87, chmn. dept., 1974-77, 79-85; Marta Sutton Weeks sr. fellow Stanford Humanities Ctr. Stanford (Calif.) U., 1989-90; fellow Shelby Cullom Davis Ctr. for Hist. Studies, Princeton U., 1992; Rockefeller fellow in humanities U. Fla., 1994; vis. prof. U. Paris, 1985-87, U. Minn., Mpls., 1987-88; George I. Miller vis. scholar U. Ill., 1994; Dittman prof. Am. Studies, anthropology and history Coll. William and Mary, 1994—. Author: Maroon Societies, 1973, Saramaka Social Structure, 1975, The Guiana Maroons, 1976, Afro-American Arts of the Suriname Rain Forest, 1980, First-Time: the Historical Vision of an Afro-American People, 1983, To Slay the Hydra, 1983, Stedman's Narrative of a Five Years Expedition, 1988, Alabi's World, 1990, Two Evenings in Saramaka, 1991, The Birth of African-American Culture, 1992, Stedman's Surinam, 1992, Equatoria, 1992, On the Mall, 1994, Enigma Variations, 1995; editor: GK Hall & Co., Boston, 1980—. Recipient Elsie Clews Parsons prize Am. Folklore Soc., 1984, Albert J. Beveridge award Am. Hist. Assn., 1991, Gordon K. Lewis Mem. award for disting. Caribbean scholarship, 1992, J.I. Staley prize, 1993; NEH grantee, NSF grantee, Fulbright grantee; John Simon Guggenheim Meml. fellow. Fellow Am. Anthrop. Assn., Royal Anthrop. Inst. Gt. Britain and Ireland, Royal Dutch Inst. Anthropology; mem. Am. Ethnological Soc., Phi Beta Kappa. Home: Anse Chaudière, 97217 Anses d'Arlet Martinique Office: Coll William & Mary Dept Anthropology Williamsburg VA 23187

PRICE, RICHARD TAFT, JR., manufacturing company executive; b. San Diego, June 7, 1954; s. Richard Taft and Murial Martha (Weinhold) T. Student, Brigham Young U., 1972-76; BS, Ariz. State U., 1978. Sales mgr. Imperial Metals, L.A., 1978-83; pres. Alumatone, Inc., No. Hollywood, Calif., 1983-88; acquisitions mgr. Calif. Custom Shapes Inc., L.A., 1988-90, pres., 1990—; bd. dirs. IMCOA, Inc., L.A., Calif. Window Corp., Walnut; pres., bd. dirs. Taft Holdings, Inc., Anaheim, Calif., 1995—. Republican. Office: Calif Custom Shapes Inc 1800 E Talbot Way Anaheim CA 92805-6727

PRICE, ROBERT, lawyer, media executive, investment banker; b. N.Y.C., Aug. 27, 1932; s. Solomon and Frances (Berger) P.; m. Margery Beth Wiener, Dec. 18, 1955; children: Eileen Marcia, Steven. AB, NYU, 1953; LLD, Columbia U., 1958. Bar: N.Y. 1958, U.S. Dist. Ct. 1958, U.S. Ct. Appeals 1958, U.S. Supreme Ct 1958, ICC 1958, FCC 1958, IRS 1958. With R.H. Macy & Co., Inc., 1955-58; practiced in N.Y.C., 1958—; law clk. to judge U.S. Dist. Ct. (so. dist.) N.Y., 1958-59; asst. U.S. atty. So. Dist. N.Y., 1959-60; ptnr. Kupferman & Price, 1960-65; dep. mayor N.Y.C., 1965-66; exec. v.p., dir. Dreyfus Corp., N.Y.C., 1966-69; v.p., investment officer Dreyfus Fund, until 1969; gen. ptnr., spl. counsel Lazard, Freres & Co., 1972-82; pres. N.Y. Law Jour., Nat. Law Jour.; pres., treas., dir. Price Communications Corp., 1979—; chmn., pres., dir. PriCellular Corp., 1988—; pres., dir. TLM Corp., 1989—; mem. adv. com. Bankers Trust Co. N.Y.; dir. Holly Sugar Corp., Lane Bryant, Inc., Graphic Scanning Corp.; chmn. N.Y.C. Port Authority Negotiating Com. for World Trade Ctr., 1965-66; spl. counsel N.Y. State Joint Legis. Com. on Ct. Reorgn.; asst. counsel N.Y. State Joint Legis. Com. on N.Y. Banking Laws; rep. of N.Y. State Senate on the Mcpl. Assistance Corp. of N.Y.C., 1996—. Contbr. articles to profl. publs. Trustee CUNY, 1996—; chmn. govt. and civil svc. divsn. United Jewish Appeal Greater N.Y., 1966; co-chmn. met. N.Y. blood drive ARC, 1966; campaign mgr. John V. Lindsay, Campaigns for Congressman, N.Y.C., 1958, 64, for Nelson A. Rockefeller Oreg. Rep. presdl. primary campaign, 1964, Lindsay campaign for mayor, N.Y.C., 1965; del. N.Y. Rep. State Conv., 1962, 66; del. Rep. Nat. Conv., 1988, 96; lectr. Rep. Nat. Com., 1966; bd. dirs. Am. Friends Hebrew U.; past trustee Columbia U. Sch. Pharm. Scis. With U.S. Army, 1953-55. Recipient Yeshiva U. Heritage award, Pub. Svc. award Queens Catholic War Vets. Mem. ABA, FCC Bar Assn., Assn. Bar City N.Y., N.Y. State Dist. Attys. Assn., Coun. Fgn. Rels., Columbia Law Sch. Alumni Assn. (dir.), Scribes, Tau Kappa Alpha. Home: 25 E 86th St New York NY 10028-0553 Office: Price Communications Corp 45 Rockefeller Plz New York NY 10111-0201

PRICE, ROBERT, electronics consultant; b. West Chester, Pa., July 7, 1929; s. Llewellyn Robert and Elise Maclay (Mirkil) P.; m. Jennifer Ann Livingstone Martin, Apr. 19, 1958; children: Stephen Livingstone, Colin Llewellyn, Edmund Hazleton. A.B., Princeton U., 1950; Sc.D. (Indsl. fellow 1950-52), M.I.T., 1953. Engr. Philco Corp., Phila., 1950; mem. staff Lincoln Lab., M.I.T., 1951-65; mgr. Sperry Research Center, Sperry Corp., Sudbury, Mass., 1965-77; staff cons. communication scis. Sperry Research Center, Sperry Corp., 1977-83; chief scientist M/A-COM Govt. Systems Div., Burlington, Mass., 1983-87, cons., 1987-88; cons. scientist Research div. Raytheon Co., Lexington, Mass., 1988-93; pvt. practice cons. Lexington, Mass., 1993—; vis. lectr. U. Calif., Berkeley, 1962-63; adv. council dept. elec. engring. and computer sci. Princeton U., 1971-77; chmn. Mil. Communication Conf. Bd., 1985. Contbr. sci. and hist. articles on spread spectrum techs.; patentee in spread spectrum communications and magnetic recording. Recipient Edwin Howard Armstrong achievement award IEEE Communications Soc., 1981; Fulbright fellow in radio astronomy Australia, 1953-54. Fellow IEEE (gov. info. theory group 1967-70, 77-79); mem. Internat. Union Radio Sci., Nat. Acad. Engring., Franklin Inst., Phi Beta Kappa, Sigma Xi.

PRICE, ROBERT EBEN, judge; b. Waco, Tex., Jan. 13, 1931; s. Robert Eben and Mary Hamilton (Barnett) P.; m. Ann Hodges, June 4, 1954; children—Eben, Mary, Ann, Emily. B.A., So. Methodist U., 1952, J.D., 1954, LL.M., 1972; postgrad., Air War Coll., 1976. Bar: Tex. 1954, U.S. Supreme Ct., U.S. Ct. Mil. Appeals, U.S. Ct. Claims, U.S. Dist. Ct. (no. dist.) Tex. 1954. Mem. firm Taylor, Mizell, Price, Corrigan & Smith, Dallas, 1956-86; judge Dallas County Probate Ct. No. 2, 1986—; lectr. continuing legal edn. program U. Houston Law Found., 1993—; lectr. law So. Meth. U. Law Sch., 1973—, faculty paralegal cert. program Sch. Continuing Edn., 1987—; lectr. practice skills program State Bar Tex., 1974—. Editor-in-chief: Southwestern Law Jour., 1953-54. Trustee and sec. St. Michael and All Angels Found.; bd. dirs. Downtown Ministry, Diocese of Dallas Episcopal; chmn. legis. and legal awareness subcom., vice chmn. Tex. Gov.'s Com. on Employment of Handicapped, 1978-82. Served as legal officer USAF, 1954-56; col. JAGC Res. ret. Fellow Am. Coll. Trust and Estate Counsel (state membership com., fiduciary litigation com.); mem. ABA (nat. conf. spl. ct. judges com. on probate and surrogates cts. 1992—), Nat. Coll. Probate Judges, Coll. of State Bar Tex., Dallas Bar Assn., State Bar Tex. (lectr. profl. devel. program 1988—), Tex. Coll. Probate Judges (mem. faculty), Phi Alpha Delta, Phi Eta Sigma, Phi Delta Theta. Episcopalian. Home: 4300 Arcady Ave Dallas TX 75205-3704 Office: Probate Ct 2 211 Records Bldg 509 Main St Dallas TX 75202-5701

PRICE, ROBERT EDMUNDS, civil engineer; b. Lyndhurst, N.J., Jan. 8, 1926; s. William Evans and Charlotte Ann (Dyson) P.; B.S. in Civil Engring., Dartmouth Coll., 1946; M.S., Princeton U. 1947; m. Margaret Akerman Menard, June 28, 1947; children—Robert Edmunds, Alexander Menard. Mgr., P&S Standard Vacuum Oil Co., N.Y., London and Sumatra, 1947-55; project engr. Metcalf & Eddy, Cons. Engrs., Boston, 1956-59; structural engr. Lummis Co., Cons. Engrs., Newark, 1960-61; mgr. engring. materials Interpace Corp., Wharton, N.J., 1961-78; pres. Openaka Corp., Denville, N.J., 1979—; cons. cement and concrete design and constrn. Mem. Denville Bd. Health, 1963-66, chmn., 1966; mem. Denville Bd. Adjustment, 1966-69. Served with USNR, 1943-46. Registered profl. engr., N.J., Md. Fellow Am. Concrete Inst. (dir. 1981-84); mem. ASTM (chmn. subcom. spl. cements 1976-84, hon. mem. com. C-1), Nat. Assn. Corrosion Engrs. Episcopalian. Home: Lake Openaka Denville NJ 07834 Office: Openaka Corp 565 Openaki Rd Denville NJ 07834-9642

PRICE, ROBERT IRA, coast guard officer; b. N.Y.C., Sept. 22, 1921; s. Alfred and Mary Edna (Schweitzer) P.; m. Virginia Louise Miller, June 20, 1946; children: Andrea Jean, Keven Virginia. B.B.A., CCNY, 1942; B.S., U.S. Coast Guard Acad., 1945; postgrad., M.I.T., 1950-53. Registered profl. engr., D.C. Commd. ensign U.S. Coast Guard, 1945, advanced through grades to vice adm., 1978; asst. chief Mcht. Marine Tech. Div., Washington, 1965-67; chief planning staff Office Mcht. Marine Safety, 1967-71; capt. Port of Phila., 1971-73; chief Office Marine Environ. Washington, 1974-76; comdr. 11th Coast Guard Dist. Long Beach, Calif., 1976-78; comdr. Atlantic Area and 3d Coast Guard Dist. N.Y.C., 1978-81; ret., 1981; sr. v.p. J.J. Henry Co. (marine engrs.), N.Y.C., 1981-86; maritime cons., 1986—; prin. U.S . negotiator to tech. programs Intergovtl. Maritime Consultative Orgn., UN, 1962-71. Contbg. author: Ship Design and Construction, 1980; Contbr. articles to profl. jours. Decorated D.S.M. with gold star, Legion of Merit with gold star, Meritorious Service medal with gold star, Coast Guard Commendation medal. Fellow Royal Instn. Naval Architects, Soc. Naval Architects (Land medalist 1982); mem. Sigma Xi. Clubs: Propeller, Army Navy, N.Y. Yacht.

PRICE, ROBERT STANLEY, lawyer; b. Phila., Jan. 21, 1937; s. Benjamin and Estelle B. (Muchnick) P.; m. Emilie W. Kirschbaum, June 27, 1965; children: Louise W., Marianna R. BA, Kenyon Coll., 1958; LLB, Yale U., 1961. Bar: Pa. 1963, U.S. Dist. Ct. (ea. dist.) Pa. 1963, U.S. Ct. Appeals (3d cir.) 1963, N.Y. 1993. Assoc. Dechert, Price & Rhoads, Phila., 1961-63; asst. tax atty. Smith Kline & French, Phila., 1963-67; tax atty. Pa. Central Transp. Co., Phila., 1967-70; tax counsel IU Internat., Phila., 1970-72; ptnr. Townsend, Elliott & Munson, Phila., 1972-76; ptnr. Pepper, Hamilton & Scheetz, Phila., 1977-86; ptnr. Saul, Ewing, Remick & Saul, 1986-93, spl. cons. 1994—. Served with U.S. Army, 1961-62. Mem. Phila. Bar Assn., Pa. Bar, ABA (tax exempt fin. com.), Alpha Delta Phi Internat. (pres. 1975-78). Club: Racquet of Phila. (v.p. 1987-88). Author ABCs of Industrial Development Bonds, 1981, 5th edit., 1990; contbr. articles to legal jours. Home: 1034 W Upsal St Philadelphia PA 19119-3715 Office: Saul Ewing Remick & Saul 3800 Centre Sq W Philadelphia PA 19102

PRICE, ROBERT SUTER, JR., federal agency administrator; b. Balt., Aug. 31, 1946; s. Robert Suter and Doris Kathryn (Goldstone) P.; m. Edith Anni Katherina Lohmeier, Oct. 29, 1971. BA, Trinity Coll., Hartford, Conn., 1968; MA, George Washington U., 1978. Reporter Hartford Courant, 1967-68; editor AP, Frankfurt, Germany, 1971-73; policy analyst U.S. Dept. Energy, Washington, 1974-81; dept. head, country studies Internat. Energy Agy., Paris, 1981-83; dir. internat. rels. U.S. Dept. Energy, Washington, 1984-96, dir. internat. sci. and tech., 1996—; lectr. Coll. Petroleum Studies, Oxford, Eng., 1990, Indsl. Coll. of the Armed Forces, Washington, 1990-93. Author/editor: Natural Gas Prospects to 2000, 1982; contbr. articles to profl. jours. Mem. Balt. Coun. Fgn. Affairs. With U.S. Army Mil. Intelligence, 1968-71, Germany. Mem. Acad. Polit. Sci., Internat. Assn. Energy Econs. (bd. dirs.), Omicron Delta Epsilon, Pi Sigma Alpha. Democrat. Avocations: woodworking, gardening. Home: 1136 Charing Cross Rd Crofton Chase MD 21114-1357 Office: US Dept Energy 1000 Independence Ave SW Washington DC 20585-0001

PRICE, ROSALIE PETTUS, artist; b. Birmingham, Ala.; d. Erle and Ellelee (Chapman) Pettus; AB, Birmingham-So. Coll., 1935; MA, U. Ala., Tuscaloosa, 1967; m. William Archer Price, Oct. 3, 1936. Instr. Birmingham (Ala.) Mus. Art, 1967-70, Samford U., 1969-70. Painter in watercolors, casein, oil and acrylic; One-man shows include Samford U., 1964, Birmingham Mus. of Art, 1966, 73, 82-83, Town Hall Gallery, 1968, 75, South Central Bell, 1977, Birmingham Southern Coll., 1992, Altamont Sch., 1996; represented in permanent collections Birmingham Mus. Art, Springfield (Mo.) Art Mus., U. Ala. Moody Gallery of Art, many others. Bd. dirs. Birmingham Mus. of Art, 1950-54, vice chmn., 1950-51; bd. trustees Birmingham Music Club, 1956-66, rec. sec., 1958-62. Recipient purchase award Watercolor USA, 1972; named to Watercolor USA Honor Soc., 1986. Mem. Nat. Watercolor Soc., Nat. Soc. Painters in Casein and Acrylic (W. Alden Brown Meml. award 1970, Joseph A. Cain Meml. award 1983), Birmingham Art Assn. (pres. 1947-49, Best Watercolor award 1950, Little House on Linden purchase award 1968), So. Watercolor Soc., Watercolor Soc. Ala. (Lassetter award 1968), La. Watercolor Soc., Pi Beta Phi. Episcopalian. Clubs: Jr. League of Birmingham (chmn. art com. 1947-50), Window Box Garden. Home: 2831 Highland Ave S # 616 Birmingham AL 35205-1801 Office: 2831 Highland Ave S # 616 Birmingham AL 35205-1801

PRICE, SANDRA HOFFMAN, secondary school educator; b. Emden, Ill., July 24, 1935; d. William Frederick and Grace May Hoffman; m. Arthur Elliott Price, Jr., Dec. 27, 1957; 1 child, Anne Marie Price Powell. BS in Math. Tchg., U. Ill., 1957, MA in Math., 1962. Tchr. Ill. Pub. Schs., 1957-69, Libertyville (Ill.) Pub. Sch. Dist. #70, 1970—; adj. staff Coll. Lake County, Grayslake, Ill., 1972-81, Nat.-Louis U., Evanston, Ill., 1996-97; interdisciplinary team leader Highland Sch., Libertyville, 1979-96. Contbr. articles to profl. jours. Pres. Litchfield (Ill.) Women's Club, 1964, Libertyville (Ill.) Edn. Assn., 1979. Univ. scholar-bronze tablet U. Ill., Urbana, 1957; Acad. Yr. fellow NSF, 1961. Mem. Nat. Coun. Tchrs. Math., Phi Beta Kappa, Phi Kappa Phi. Methodist. Office: Libertyville Pub Schs Dist 70 310 W Rockland Rd Libertyville IL 60048-2739

PRICE, SUSAN KAY LIND, employment training organization administrator; b. Burley Cassia, Idaho, Apr. 27, 1958; d. Ray Elden and Melba Jean (Koyle) Lind; m. Randy Sam Price, July 18, 1986; 1 child, Jordan Richard. Student, Brigham Young U., 1976-79, U. Utah, 1983-84; BS magna cum laude, Utah State U., 1988, postgrad., 1991-92; postgrad., So. Calif. U., 1995—. Cert. assertive comm. trainer, Utah State Office Edn.; cert. hypnotist, Am. Coun. Hypnotist Examiners; cert. advanced rapid eye tech. with self discovery processing; cert. core belief therapy. Project coord. single parent/displaced homemaker program Bridgerland Applied Tech. Ctr., Logan; aide, exec. sec., job developer, employment counselor Bear River Assn. of Govt., Logan, Utah; mem. adv. bd. Cmty.-Family Partnership; mem. social work community adv. com., supr. social work practicum, supr. family and human devel. practicum Utah State U.; part-time transitional therapist. Named Outstanding Job Developer, 1987; recipient Master Tchr. award, 1983. Mem. NAFE, Nat. Displaced Homemaker's Network (Utah rep. 1989-93), Box Elder County Self-Sufficiency Coun., Cache County Interagency Coun., Utah Assn. Adult Cmty. and Continuing Edn. (state bd. 1989-92), Bear River Refugee Coun. (sec. 1986-90), Logan Bus. and Profl. Women (Young Careerist 1991), Soroptimist Internat. Home: 376 E 700 S Logan UT 84321-5532

PRICE, THEODORA HADZISTELIOU, individual and family therapist; b. Athens, Greece, Oct. 1, 1938; came to U.S. 1967; d. Ioannis and Evangelia (Emmanuel) Hadzisteliou; m. David C. Long Price, Dec. 26, 1966 (div. 1989); children: Morgan N., Alkes D.L. BA in History/Archaeology, U. Athens, 1961; DPhil, U. Oxford, Eng., 1966; MA in Clin. Social Work, U. Chgo., 1988; Diploma in Piano Teaching, Nat. Conservatory, Athens, 1958. Lic. clin. social worker; bd. cert. diplomate in clin. social work. Mus. asst. and resident tutor U. Sydney, Australia, 1966-67; instr. anthropology Adelphi U., N.Y.C., 1967-68; archaeologist Hebrew Union Coll., Gezer, Israel, 1968; asst. prof. classical archaeology/art U. Chgo., 1968-70; jr. rsch.

fellow Harvard Ctr. Hellenic Studies, Washington, 1970-71; clin. social worker Harbor Light Ctr., Salvation Army, Chgo., 1988-89; therapist Inst. Motivational Devel., Lombard, Ill., 1989-90; caseworker Jewish Family & Community Svc., Chgo., 1989-90; staff therapist Family Svc. Ctrs. of South Cook County, Chicago Heights, 1990-91; pvt. practice child, adolescent, family therapy Bolingbrook, Ill., 1991—; dir. counseling svcs., clin. supr., psychotherapist The Family Link, Inc., Chgo., 1993; staff therapist Cen. Bapt. Family Svcs., Gracell Rehab., Chgo., 1991, 91-92; casework supr., counselor Epilepsy Found. Greater Chgo., Chgo., 1992-93; therapist children, adolescents and families dept. foster care Catholic Charities, Chgo., 1993-94; individual and family therapist South Ctrl. Cmty. Svcs. Individual-Family Counseling Svcs., Chgo., 1994—; lectr. in field; bd. mem., counselor Naperville Sch. for Gifted and Talented, 1982-84. Author: (monograph) Kourotrophos, Cults and Representations of the Greek Nursing Deities, 1978; contbr. articles to profl. jours. Meyerstein Traveling awardee, Oxford, Eng., 1963, 64; Sophocles Venizelos scholar, 1962-65; nominated Internat. Woman of Yr. for 1995-96 Internat. Biog. Ctr., 20th Century Achievement award, 1996. Mem. NASW, Nat. Acad. Clin. Social Workers, Ill. Clin. Social Workers. Avocations: yoga, piano playing, dog training and therapy. Home and Office: 10 Pebble Ct Bolingbrook IL 60440-1557 *Nobody stands alone, for each of us partakes and contributes to universal energy and creation. Every thought or action has progressively timeless impact. Therefore, working in helping people is influencing the flow of creation.*

PRICE, THOMAS BENJAMIN, former textile company executive; b. W. Jefferson, N.C., Aug. 23, 1920; s. Avery Asper and Jenny L. (Goss) P.; m. Judith Ostberg, Jan. 28, 1950; children: Jonathan R., Gregory W., Timothy C. B.S. in Textile Engring., N.C. State U., 1941. With J.P. Stevens & Co., Inc., 1941-83, corp. v.p., 1964-68, pres. Domestics and Allied Products div., 1971-74, corporate group v.p., 1974-83, also dir., mem. exec. com., chmn.'s office. Served to lt. comdr. USNR, World War II, Korean Conflict. Mem. Am. Arbitration Council, Sigma Tau Sigma, Phi Psi. Clubs: Pine Valley (Clementon, N.J.); Royal Poincianna (Naples, Fla.); Lake Sunapee Yacht (New London, N.H.), U.S. Srs. Golf Assn. Home: 530 Turtle Hatch Rd Naples FL 34103-8541 also: PO Box 1245 New London NH 03257-1245

PRICE, THOMAS EMILE, investment company executive; b. Cin., Nov. 4, 1921; s. Edwin Charles and Lillian Elizabeth (Werk) P.; BBA, U. Tex., 1943; postgrad. Harvard U., 1944; m. Lois Margaret Gahr Matthews, Dec. 21, 1970 (dec. Nov. 26, 1988); 1 child by previous marriage, Dorothy Elizabeth Wood Price; stepchildren: Bruce Albert, Mark Frederic, Scott Herbert, Eric William Matthews. Co-founder Price Y Cia, Inc., Cin., 1946—, sec., 1946-75, treas., 1946—, pres., 1975—, also dir.; co-founder Price Paper Products Corp. (merger Price Y Cia, Inc.), Cin., 1956, treas., 1956-75, pres., 1975-90, sec., 1956-75, also dir.; mem. Cin. Regional Export Expansion Com., 1961-63; dir. Cen. Acceptance Corp., 1954-55; founding mem. and dir. Cin. Royals Basketball Club Co., 1959-73. Referee Tri-State Tennis Championships, 1963-68, Western Tennis Championships, 1969-70, Nat. Father-Son Clay Court Championships, 1974—, Tennis Grand Masters Championships, 1975-77, 80; vol. coach Walnut Hills High Sch. Boys Team, Cin., 1970-81; chmn. and coach Greater Cin. Jr. Davis Cup, 1968-78; co-founder Tennis Patrons of Cin., Inc., 1951, trustee, 1951-79, pres., 1958-63, 68; co-founder Greater Cin. Tennis Assn., 1979. Participant in fund raising drives Cin. Boys Amateur Baseball Fund; chmn. Greater Cin. YMCA World Svc. Fund Drive, 1962-64; trustee Cin. World Affairs Inst., 1957-60, gen. chmn., 1959. 1st lt. USAAF, 1943-46; ETO. Elected to Western Hills High Sch. Sport Hall of Honor; named hon. Almaden Grand Master, 1980. Cin. Met. Tennis Tournament renamed Thomas E. Price Cin. Met. Tennis Torunament, 1991. Mem. Cin. World Trade Club (pres. 1959), U.S. Trotting Assn., Cin. Hist. Soc., U.S. Lawn Tennis Assn. (trustee 1959-60, 62-64, chmn. Jr. Davis Cup com. 1960-62, founder of Col. James H. Bishop award 1962), Ohio Valley Tennis Assn. (trustee 1948—, Gillespie award 1957, Dredge award 1973, pres. 1952-53, Tom Price award named in his honor at Jr. Davis Cup 1988), Western Tennis Assn. (trustee 1951—, mem. championships adv. com. 1969-78, pres. 1959-60, Hall of Fame, 1994, Melvin R. Bergman Disting. Svc. award 1979), Greater Cin. Tennis Assn. (named after and recipient of Tom Price award 1989), Assn. Tennis Profls. (nat. championship adv. 1979—), Cin. Country CLub, Univ. Club, Cin. Tennis Club (hon. life, pres. 1957-58, adv. com. 1959—, Founders and Guardians award 1983), Indoor Tennis CLub, Ea. Hills Indoor Tennis Club, Phi Gamma Delta. Republican. Presbyterian. Nationally ranked boys 15, 1936, jr. tennis player, 1939. History columnist Tennis Talk Greater Cin., 1978-80. Home: 3249 Epworth Ave Cincinnati OH 45211-7037 Office: Dixie Terminal Bldg Ste 216 Cincinnati OH 45202-3812 *Personal philosophy: Follow the Ten Commandments and the Golden Rule.*

PRICE, THOMAS FREDERICK, theatre educator; b. Salt Lake City, June 19, 1937; s. Thomas William P. and Caryl Susan Brown; children: Devin, Jennifer. BA in Drama, Pomona Coll., 1960; MA in Theatre, San Francisco State U., 1962; PhD in Drama, Stanford U., 1968. Asst. prof. English U. of the Pacific, Stockton, Calif., 1968-70; asst. prof. drama U.S. Internat. U., Sch. Performing Arts, San Diego, 1970-74; archivist, curator The Philibrick Theatre Libr., Los Altos Hills, Calif., 1975-85; prof. English Tianjin (China) Normal U., 1985-87; adj. prof. theatre So. Oreg. State Coll., Ashland, 1991-92; assoc. prof. English Tanmkang U., Taipei, Taiwan, 1993—; ednl. broadcaster KPFA-FM, L.A., 1960-62, KSRO-FM, Ashland, Oreg., 1990-92. Author: Edward Gordon Craig and the Theatre of the Imagination, 1985, Dramatic Structure and Meaning, 1992; editor: George Colman the Elder: Two Plays; contbr. articles to profl. jours. Mem. Calif. Scholarship Fedn. (hon. life).

PRICE, THOMAS MUNRO, computer consultant; b. Madison, Wis., Oct. 2, 1937; s. John Edward and Georgia Winifred (Day) P.; m. Judith Ann Holm, Aug. 8, 1959; children: Scott Michael, Andrea Lynn. BS, Carroll Coll., Waukesha, Wis., 1959; MS, U. Wis., 1961, PhD, 1964. Prof. math. U. Iowa, 1964-77, U. Wyo., Laramie, 1978-79; computer user cons. U. Wyo., 1979-85, MIS prof., 1985-89; computer cons. Laramie, 1989-93; home rebuilder Pecos, N.Mex., 1994—. Contbr. articles to profl. jours. Home: 17 Crazy Rabbit Dr Santa Fe NM 87505

PRICE, TOM, journalist; b. Pitts., May 26, 1946; s. H. Samuel and Anna Mae (Nicholson) P.; m. Susan Crites; 1 child, Julianna Margaret. BS in Journalism, Ohio U., 1968. Freelance writer, 1973-75; politics writer Dayton (Ohio) Jour. Herald, 1975-82; corr. Washington bur. Cox Newspapers, Washington, 1982-96; freelance writer, 1996—. Co-author: (with Susan Crites Price) The Working Parents Help Book, 1994 (Parent's Choice award, Scholastic Book Club selection), rev. edit., 1996, Working Solutions Internet Column; nat. newspaper columnist Working Parents Lifeline. Presbyterian. Avocations: photography, hiking, travel, reading.

PRICE, TREVOR ROBERT PRYCE, psychiatrist, educator; b. Concord, N.H., Nov. 29, 1943; s. Trevor Alaric and Beatrice (Dinsmore) Price; m. Margaret Ann Bowring, June 8, 1991; children: Meghan Jennifer, Sara Brittany; children by previous marriage: Trevor Breton, Elizabeth Anne. BA, Yale U., 1965; MD, Columbia U., 1969. Diplomate Am. Bd. Psychiatry and Neurology (examiner 1985—), Am. Bd. Internal Medicine, Nat. Bd. Med. Examiners. Intern in medicine Med. Ctr. U. Calif., San Francisco, 1969-70; resident in internal medicine Med. Ctr. of U. Calif., San Francisco, 1972-74; resident in psychiatry Dartmouth Med. Sch., Hanover, N.H., 1974-77, asst. prof., assoc. prof. psychiatry and medicine, 1977-85; assoc. prof., prof. psychiatry U. Pa. Sch. Medicine, Phila., 1985-88; dir. psychiat. in-patient svcs. Hosp. of U. Pa., 1985-88; prof. psychiatry Med. Coll. Pa., Pitts., 1989-90, prof. psychiatry and medicine, 1991-95; tenured prof. psychiatry Med. Coll. Pa., 1993—; chmn. dept. psychiatry Med. Coll. Pa. and Hahnemann U., Allegheny Campus, Pitts., 1989-95, 1995—; sr. assoc. dean Med. Coll. Pa. and Hahnemann U., Pitts., 1993-95; pres. Allegheny Neuropsychiat. Inst. Allegheny Neuropsychiat. Inst., Pitts., 1992-94, exec. dir., 1994—; chmn. Dept. Psychiatry, Med. Coll. Pa. Hahnemann Sch. Medicine, Allegheny U. Health Scis., 1995—; bd. dirs. Coll. Health Consortium, Inc., Phila., 1989-93, Highland Dr. Rsch. and Edn. Found., Yale Club Pitts., Pitts. Psychoanalytic Found.; mem. blue ribbon bd. Alzheimer's Disease Alliance, Western Pa., 1989-97. Mem. editl. bd. Convulsive Therapy, 1984-94, Jour. Neuropsychiatry and Clin. Neurosci., 1992—, Allegheny Gen. Hosp. Jour. Neurosci., 1992—, Seminars in Neuropsychiatry, 1995—; editl. reviewer 14 psychiat. and med. jours., 1978; contbr. chpts. to books and articles in profl. jours. Mem. N.H. Commn. on Laws Effecting Mental Health, 1974-75; bd. dirs. Advanced Studies Program, Friends of St. Paul's Sch., Concord, N.H., 1983-87. Recipient William C. Menninger award Ctrl. Neuropsychiat. Assn., 1977, Faculty Teaching award dept. psychiatry Dartmouth Med. Sch., 1984, Pres. award for Exceptional Achievement AHERF, 1994, numerous grants. Fellow Am. Psychiat. Assn.; mem. Pa. Psychiat. Assn., Am. Coll. Psychiatrists, Am. Assn. Chairmen of Depts. Psychiatry, Soc. Biol. Psychiatry, Am. Neuropsychiat. Assn. (bd. dirs., exec. dir. 1995), Assn. for Acad. Psychiatry, Am. Assn. Dirs. Psychiat. Residency Tng., Assn. Acad. Psychiatry, Assn. Convulsive Therapy, Assn. Medicine and Psychiatry, Yale Club Pitts., H-Y-P Club Pitts. Avocations: fly fishing, tennis, reading, piano. Office: Med Coll Pa Hahnemann Sch of Medicine Dept Psychiatry 320 E North Ave Pittsburgh PA 15212-4756 also: Broad and Vine Sts M/S 403 Philadelphia PA 19102-1192 also: Eastern Pa Psychiat Inst Rm 166 3200 Henry Ave Philadelphia PA 19129 *Life at its best is being continually challenged and fully engaged, yet not self-absorbed.*

PRICE, WILLIAM JAMES, organization executive; b. Alexandria, Ohio, Dec. 3, 1918; s. Lewis J. and Mary (Wright) P.; m. Betty Kistler, Aug. 22, 1943; children—Mary Barbara, Sarah Margaret, Lewis Charles. A.B., Denison U., 1940, Sc.D., 1969; M.S., Rensselaer Poly. Inst., 1941, Ph.D., 1948; DSc (hon.), Denison U., 1969. Research physicist Bendix Aviation Corp., 1942-45, Battelle Meml. Inst., Columbus, Ohio, 1948-50; head dept. physics Air Force Inst. Tech., Dayton, Ohio, 1950-57; chief modern physics br. Aero. Research Lab., Dayton, 1957-59; chief scientist Aero. Research Lab., 1959-63; exec. dir. Air Force Office Sci. Research, 1963-74; mgmt. cons., 1974-78; coordinator World Peacemakers, 1978—; instr. Rensselaer Poly. Inst., 1948; prof. Air Force Inst. Tech., Dayton, Ohio, 1950-57; An organizer Yokefellowship in Nation's Capital, 1964; fed. exec. fellow The Brookings Instn., 1967-68; chmn. Congl. Commn. Govt. Procurement Study Group Research and Devel., 1970-71. Author: Nuclear Radiation Detection, rev. edit, 1964; Co-author: National Security and Christian Faith, 1982, Building Christian Community Pursuing Peace with Justice, 1983, (handbook) World Peacemaker Groups, 1979; Author: also numerous articles. Mem. The Ch. of the Saviour, 1972—; Bd. dirs. Yokefellows Internat., 1967-71, Washington Lift, Inc., 1971-76, World Peacemaker, 1978—. Recipient Alumni citation Denison U., 1965, Outstanding Unit award citation Office Aerospace Research, 1965, Outstanding Unit award citation Air Force Inst. Tech., 1964. Mem. Am. Phys. Soc., A.A.A.S., Phi Beta Kappa, Sigma Xi, Tau Beta Pi (hon.). Home: 11427 Scottsbury Ter Germantown MD 20876-6010

PRICE, WILLIAM JAMES, IV, investment banker; b. Balt., Oct. 6, 1924; s. William James 3d and Frances (Robbins) P.; m. Marjorie Beard, Dec. 6, 1952; children: Marjorie, Jonathan Robbins, William James V, Juliet Robbins. B.S., Yale U., 1949. Propr. Price & Co., 1949-52; with Alex. Brown & Sons, Balt., 1952—, gen. partner, 1959-84, mng. dir., 1984-89; bd. dirs. Alex Brown Cash Res. Fund, chmn., 1981-96; bd. dirs. Boca Rsch., Inc. Trustee Washington Coll., St. Paul's Sch. Served with inf. AUS, 1943-46, ETO. Decorated Bronze Star, Purple Heart with oak leaf cluster, Combat Infantry badge. Mem. Nat. Assn. Securities Dealers (bd. govs. 1964-66, vice chmn. 1966). Home: 6885 N Ocean Blvd Ocean Ridge FL 33435-3342 Office: Alex Brown & Sons Inc 222 Lakeview Ave West Palm Beach FL 33401-6145

PRICE, WILLIAM RAY, JR., state supreme court judge; b. Fairfield, Iowa, Jan. 30, 1952; s. William Ray and Evelyn Jean (Darnell) P.; m. Susan Marie Trainor, Jan. 4, 1975; children: Emily Margret, William Joseph Dodds. BA with high distinction, U. Iowa, 1974; student, Yale U., 1974-75; JD cum laude, Washington and Lee U., 1978. Bar: Mo. 1978, U.S. Dist. Ct. (we. dist.) Mo. 1978, U.S. Ct. Claims 1978, U.S. Ct. Appeals (8th cir.) 1985. Assoc. Lathrop & Norquist, Kansas City, Mo., 1978-84, ptnr., 1984-92, chmn. bus. litigation sect., 1987-88, 90-92, mem. exec. com., 1989-92; judge Supreme Ct. Mo., Jefferson City, 1992—; mem. G.L.V. Zumwalt monitoring com. U.S. Dist. Ct. (we. dist.) Mo., Kansas City. Pres. Kansas City Bd. Police Commrs.; mem. Together Ctr. & Family Devel. Ctr., Kansas City; chmn. merit selection com. U.S. marshal Western Dist. of Mo., Kansas City; bd. dirs. Truman Med. Ctr., Kansas City. Rockefeller fellow, 1974-75; Burks scholar Washington & Lee U., 1976. Mem. Christian Ch. Office: Supreme Ct Mo PO Box 150 Jefferson City MO 65102-0150*

PRICE, WILLIAM S., lawyer; b. Evanston, Ill., May 9, 1942. BSBA, Denver U., 1965; JD cum laude, Northwestern U., 1968. Bar: Ill. 1968. With Bell, Boyd & Lloyd, Chgo. Mem. ABA, Nat. Assn. Bond Lawyers. Office: Bell Boyd & Lloyd 70 W Madison St Chicago IL 60602

PRICE, WAYNE FRANCIS, counseling administrator; b. Bogue, Kans., Feb. 11, 1935; s. William C. and Lena I. (Hecke) P.; m. Alice M. Fitzpatrick, July 25, 1964; children: Wayne F. Jr., Elizabeth Anne. AB, Ft. Hays State U., 1957; MEd, U. N.D., 1963; postgrad., Wayne State U. Nat. cert. counselor; nat. cert. career counselor; nat. cert. sch. counselor; lic. prof. counselor Mich. Counselor Lamphere High Sch., 1963-64, 69-75; asst. prin. Page Jr. High, Madison Heights, Mich., 1964-68; prin. Page Jr. High, Madison Heights, 1968-69; adj. counselor Oakland Community Coll., Bloomfield Hills, Mich., 1969—; dir. guidance Lamphere Schs., Madison Heights, Mich., 1975—; bd. dirs. Haviland Collectors Internat. Contbr. articles to prof. jours. Bd. dirs. Haviland Collectors Internat., 1997—. Mem. ACA, Nat. Assn. Collegiate Registrars and Admission Officers, Assn. for Counselor Edn. and Supervision, Am. Coll. Pers. Assn., Am. Fedn. Tchrs., Am. Sch. Coun. Assn., Am. Vocat. Assn., Assn. for Adult Devel. and Aging, Assn. for Assessment in Counseling, Lamphere Fedn. Tchrs., Mich. Assn. for Adult Devel. and Aging, Mich. Assn. Coll. Admission Counselors, Mich. Counseling Assn., Mich. Assn. for Counselor Edn. and Supervision, Mich. Assn. for Measurement and Evaluation in Guidance (pres.), Mich. Assn. Specialists in Group Work, Mich. Career Devel. Assn. (treas. 1994—), Mich. Coll. Pers. Assn., Mich. Sch. Counselors Assn., Mich. Assn. for Humanistic Edn. and Develop., Mich. Assn. for Multi-Cultural Develop., Nat. Assn. Coll. Admission Counselors, Nat. Career Devel. Assn., Oakland Assn. for Counseling and Devel. (former pres.), Phi Delta Kappa. Office: 610 W 13 Mile Rd Madison Heights MI 48071-1858

PRICER, WILBUR DAVID, electrical engineer; b. Des Moines, July 22, 1935; s. Wilbur Ray and Mary Elizabeth (Berner) P.; m. Nancy Loizeaux, Oct. 10, 1964; children: Douglas, Amy, Timothy, Edward. AB in Physics, Middlebury Coll., 1959; BSEE, MIT, 1959, MSEE, 1959. Engr. IBM Corp., Poughkeepsie, 1959-70, sr. engr., East Fishkill, N.Y., 1970-83, sr. mem. tech. staff, Essex Junction, Vt., 1983—; adj. prof. elec. engring. U. Vt., 1984-90; pres. Solid State Circuits Coun., 1980-81; mem. editl. bd. Spectrum Mag., 1990-92. Editor Jour. of Solid State Circuits, 1983-86. Patentee in field. Fellow, IEEE; mem. Internat. Solid State Circuits Conf. (program chmn. 1976, chmn. 1988-96), program Evaluator Accreditation Bd. for Engring. and Tech., 1990-95, Sigma Xi. Methodist. Home: 5524 Spear St Charlotte VT 05445-9746 Office: IBM Dept M61 Bldg 972-1 Essex Junction VT 05452

PRICHARD, EDGAR ALLEN, lawyer; b. Brockton, Mont., Mar. 6, 1920; s. Clifford B. and Helen (Ouwersloat) P.; m. Nancy M. McCandlish, Apr. 7, 1945; children: Helen Montague (Mrs. Thomas C. Foster), Robert Walton, Thomas Morgan. Student, U. Tulsa, 1937-39, U. Okla., 1940-41; LL.B., U. Va., 1948. Bar: Va. 1947. Ptnr. Boothe, Prichard & Dudley, Fairfax, Va., 1948-87, McGuire, Woods, Battle & Boothe, Fairfax, 1987—; bd. dirs. George Mason Bank Shares, George Mason Bank; bd. editors Va. Law Rev., 1947-48. Mem. gen. bd. Nat. Coun. Chs., 1966-72; councilman City of Fairfax, 1953-64, mayor, 1964-68; chmn. Fairfax Dem. Com., 1962-64, 69-72; mem. Va. Bd. Elections, 1970-75; mem. Lynch Found., pres., 1981-82; trustee Trinity Episcopal Sch. Ministry, 1977—, chmn., 1985-95; bd. visitors George Mason U., 1982-91, rector, 1988-91; chmn. Fairfax Parking Authority, 1991-95; mem. bd. Fairfax Econ. Devel. Authority; mem. George Mason U. Found., pres., 1971-72. Recipient George Mason medal George Mason U., 1995. Fellow ABA, Va. Bar Assn.; mem. Fairfax Bar Assn. (pres. 1964-65), Va. State Bar (v.p. 1969), Am. Law Inst., Diosesan Missionary Soc. Va. (pres. 1986-88), Urban Land Inst., 4th Cir. Jud. Conf., Order of Coif, Raven Soc., Fairfax Racquet Club, Inc. (chmn.), Fairfax Country Club, Spl. Forces Club (London), Lambda Alpha, Lambda Chi Alpha. Episcopalian (lay reader, warden). Home: 3820 Chain Bridge Rd Fairfax VA 22030-3904 Office: McGuire Woods Battle & Boothe 8280 Greensboro Dr Mc Lean VA 22102-3807

PRICHARD, JOHN ROBERT STOBO, academic administrator, law educator; b. London, Jan. 17, 1949; arrived in Can., 1951; s. John Stobo and Joan Suzanne (Webber) P.; m. Ann Elizabeth Wilson, Dec. 19, 1975; children: Wilson, Kenneth, John. Honors Econs. student, Swarthmore Coll., 1967-70; MBA, U. Chgo., 1971; LLB, U. Toronto, Ont., Can., 1975; LLM, Yale U., 1976. Asst. prof. faculty of law U. Toronto, 1976-81, assoc. prof., 1981-88, prof., 1988—, assoc. Ctr. for Indsl. Rels., 1979—, dean faculty of law, 1984-1990, pres. univ., 1990—; vis. assoc. prof. Yale U. Law Sch., New Haven, Conn., 1982-83; vis. prof. Harvard U. Law Sch., Cambridge, Mass., 1983-84; mem. Ont. Law Reform Commn., Toronto, 1986-1990; chmn. Fed., Provincial and Territorial Review of Liability and Compensation on Health Care, Ottawa, Ont., 1987-90. Co-author: Canadian Business Corporations, 1977, Canadian Competition Policy, 1979, Choice of Governing Instrument, 1982; co-author, editor: Public Ownership: The Calculus of Instrument Choice, 1983. Mem. Law Soc. Upper Can. Avocation: children, fishing. Office: U Toronto, 27 Kings College Circle, Toronto, ON Canada M5S 1A1*

PRICKETT, DAVID CLINTON, physician; b. Fairmont, W.Va., Nov. 26, 1918; s. Clinton Evert and Mary Anna (Gottschalk) P.; m. Mary Ellen Holt, June 29, 1940; children: David C., Rebecca Ellen, William Radcliffe, Mary Anne, James Thomas, Sara Elizabeth; m. Pamela S. Blackstone, Nov. 17, 1991. Student Fairmont (W.Va.) State Coll., 1940-42, AB, W.Va. U., 1944; MD, U. Louisville, 1946; MPH, U. Pitts., 1955. pres. Prickett Chem. Co., 1938-43; acct. W.Va. Conservation Commn., Fed. Works Agy., 1941, 42; lab. asst., instr. chemistry, W.Va. U., 1943; intern, Louisville Gen. Hosp., 1947; surg. resident St. Joseph's Hosp., Parkersburg, W.Va., 1948-49; gen. practice, 1949-50, 55-61; physician USAF, N.Mex., 1961-62, U.S. Army, Calif., 1963-64, San Luis Obispo County Hosp., 1965-66, So. Calif. Edison Co., 1981-84; assoc. physician indsl. and gen. practice Los Angeles County, Calif., 1967—; med. dir. S. Gate plant GM, 1969-71; physician staff City of L.A., 1971-76; relief med. practice Appalachia summer seasons, 1977, 1986, 1988-96. Med. Officer USPHS, Navajo Indian Reservation, Tohatchi (N.Mex.) Health Ctr., 1953-55, surgeon, res. officer, 1957-59; pres. W.Va. Pub. Health Assn., 1951-52; local and dist. health officer, W.Va., 1951-53, sec. indsl. and pub. health sect. W.Va. Med. Assn., 1956; dist. health officer Allegheny County, Pa., 1957. Author: The Newer Epidemiology, 1962, rev., 1990, Public Health, A Science Resolvable by Mathematics, 1965. Served to 2d lt. AUS, 1943-46. Dr. Thomas Parran fellow U. Pitts. Sch. Pub. Health, 1955; named to Hon. Order Ky. Cols. Fellow Am. Pub. Health Assn.; mem. SAR, Am. Occupational Med. Assn., Western Occupational Med. Assn., Am. Med. Assn., Calif. Med. Assn., L.A. County Med. Assn., Am. Acad. Family Physicians, Am. Legion, Elks, Phi Chi. Address: PO Box 4032 Whittier CA 90607-4032

PRICKETT, GORDON ODIN, mining, mineral and energy engineer; b. Morris, Minn., Nov. 26, 1935; s. Glenn Irvin and Edna Margaret (Erickson) P.; m. Jean Carolyn Strobush, Oct. 8, 1958; children: Karen Joan Keating, Laura Jean, Glenn Thomas. B Mining Engring., U. Minn., 1958, MS in Mineral Engring. and Econs., 1965. Registered profl. engr., Mo., Ill. U.S. Steel fellow U. Minn., Mpls., 1963-65; rsch. mineral engr. Internat. Minerals & Chem. Corp., Skokie, Ill., 1965-68; mgmt. sci. cons. Computer Mgmt. Cons., Northfield, Ill., 1968-71; mgr. tech. systems Duval Corp., Tucson, Ariz., 1971-77; dir. mgmt. info. systems Arch Mineral Corp., St. Louis, 1977-78; supr. mine planning projects Peabody Coal Co., St. Louis, 1978-82; mgr. elec. tech. transfer, nuclear plant simulator, rsch. Union Electric Co., St. Louis, 1983-95; tech. network advisor GordMett, Ltd., Aitkin, Minn., 1995—; presenter papers at industry confs. Contbr. articles to profl. jours. Co-founder, chmn. Lake Forest-Lake Bluff (Ill.) Com. for Equal Opportunity, 1968-71; com. Confluence St. Louis, 1987-95; bd. dirs., officer ch. bds., polit. twp. orgn. Lake Forest, Tucson, St. Louis, Aitkin, Minn., 1968—. Lt. USN, 1958-63, naval aviator, Cuba; to comdr. USNR, 1963-79. Mem. AIME (chair program com. 1958—), Assn. Quality and Participation (chair programs 1986-90), Norwegian Soc. St. Louis, LWV (charter mem. Brainerd Lakes unit, 1996—), Engrs. Club St. Louis (chair affiliated socs. and pub. affairs. 1987-88, 93-95). Avocations: running, photography, canoeing, Norwegian Singing Club, skiing. Home and Office: Nord Lake HC 5 Box 16CC Aitkin MN 56431

PRIDE, CHARLEY, singer; b. Sledge, Miss., Mar. 18, 1939; m. Rozene Pride, Dec. 28, 1956; children—Kraig, Dion, Angela. Grad. high sch. Formerly with constrn. cos., refining plants; profl. baseball player with Detroit, Memphis Red Sox, Birmingham Black Barons (all Negro Am. League), Los Angeles Angels (Am. League). Appeared with WSM Grand Ole Opry, Nashville, 1967, Lawrence Welk Show, ABC-TV; appeared on Joey Bishop Show, ABC-TV; appeared with Ralph Emery Show, WSM-TV, Nashville; appeared with Syndicated Bill Anderson, Bobby Lord and Wilburn Brothers, Hee Haw, Tom Jones Show, Flip Wilson Show, Johnny Cash Show, numerous other TV shows; recorded for RCA; albums include: Country Charley Pride, Charley Pride Sings Heart Songs, Charley, Happiness, Happiness of Having You, Charley Pride IN Person, Christmas in My Hometown, Did You Think to Pray, Roll on Mississippi, There's a Little Bit of Hank in Me, You're My Jamaica, Best of Charley Pride, The Best There Is, Greatest Hits, Night Games, Power of Love, Country Feelin, Songs of Love, A Sunshiny Day, Charley Pride Live, 1994; recorded songs Kiss an Angel Good Mornin', Snakes Crawl at Night, Let the Chips Fall, Day You Stopped Loving Me, Does My Ring Hurt Your Finger, Let Me Help You Work It Out, Is Anyone Goin' to San Antone, Afraid of Losing You Again, Let Me Live, One of These Days, Whole Lotta Love; (Named Most Promising Male Artist, Country Song Roundup 1967, Male Vocalist of Year, Country Music Assn. 1971, 72, Entertainer of Yr. in Country Music 1971, winner Grammy awards for best scored rec. 1971, for best country vocal 1972, Trendsetter award Billboard 1970, Top Male Vocalist award Cashbox, Photoplay Gold Medal award 1976). Served with U.S. Army, 1956-58. Address: CECCA Prodn PO Box 670507 Dallas TX 75229-0507

PRIDE, DOUGLAS SPENCER, minister; b. Latrobe, Pa., Jan. 13, 1959; s. Spencer MacVeagh and Kathleen (Tidd) P.; m. Elizabeth Armstrong, June 5, 1982; children: Kathryn Elizabeth and Jennifer Suzanne (twins), Pamela Campbell. BA, Westminster Coll., 1980; MDiv, Pitts. Theol. Sem., 1983, DMin, 1993. Ordained to ministry Presbyn. Ch., 1983. Asst. pastor Shadyside Presbyn. Ch., Pitts., 1983-85, assoc. pastor, 1985-91; pastor The Presbyn. Ch. of Clearfield, Clearfield, Pa., 1992—; chaplain palliative care program West Pa. Hosp., 1983-86, Clearfield Hospice, 1992-96; bd. dirs. Krislund Camp and Conf. Ctr., 1993—, chmn., 1994—. Bd. dirs. Theol. Sem., 1983-86; mem. alumni coun. Westminster Coll., New Wilmington, Pa., 1986-90, pres., 1989-90; bd. dirs. Bethesda Ctr., Pitts.; 1st v.p. Spina Bifida Assn., Pitts., 1987-89, pres., 1989-93, bd. dirs., 1984—, sec. bd., 1985-87. Recipient Disting. Alumnus award Westminster Coll., 1996. Mem. Huntingdon Presbytery, Clearfield Curwensville Country Club. Republican. Avocations: tennis, racquetball, reading, bicycling. Home: 2538 Meadow Rd Clearfield PA 16830-1140

PRIDE, MIRIAM R., academic administrator; b. Canton, China, June 6, 1948; d. Richard E. and Martha W. Pride; divorced. Grad., Berea College Found. Sch., 1966, College of Wooster, 1970; MBA, U. Ky., 1989. With sales room Boone Tavern Hotel Berea Coll., Berea, Ky., 1963-70; intern in administrn. in higher edn., head resident College of Wooster, Wooster, Ohio, 1970-72; accounts payable clerk, dir. Boone Tavern Hotel, head resident, dir. student activities Berea Coll., 1972-88; eligibility worker dept. human resources State of Ky., 1975-76; assistantship undergrad. advising coll. bus. U. Ky., 1987-89; asst. to pres. for campus life, v.p. for administrn., pres. Blackburn Coll., Carlinville, Ill., 1989—. Chair United Way Berea, Carlinville, 1989-92; mem. Berea Tourism Commn., Blue Grass Area Devel. Dist., United Way Macoupin Allocation Com., 1989-92; bd. dirs. Girl Scouts, Land of Lincoln, 1993—, fin. chair, 1995—; bd. dirs. Carlinville Area Hosp., 1993—, Assn. Presbyn. Colls. and Univs., Fedn. Ind. Ill. Colls. and Univs., 1993—, Fedn. Ch., 1996—; fin. chair Carlinville Hosp., 1995—. Mem. Carlinville C. of C. (bd. dirs.), Rotary (bd. dirs. 1996—). Mem. Federated Ch. Avocations: reading, walking, knitting. Office: Blackburn Coll Office of the President Carlinville IL 62626

PRIDHAM, THOMAS GRENVILLE, retired research microbiologist; b. Chgo., Oct. 10, 1920; s. Grenville and Gladys Etheral (Sloss) P.; m. Phyllis Sue Hokamp, July 1, 1943 (dec.); children: Pamela Sue, Thomas Foster, Grenville Thomas, Rolf Thomas, Montgomery Thomas; m. Edna Lee Boudreaux, Mar. 6, 1995. BS in Chemistry, U. Ill., 1943, PhD in Bacteriology, 1949. Instr. bacteriology U. Ill., Champaign-Urbana, 1947; rsch.

microbiologist No. Regional Rsch. Lab., USDA, Peoria, Ill., 1948-51, 53-65, U.S. Indsl. Chems., Balt., 1951-52; supr. tech. ops. Acme Vitamins, Inc., Joliet, Ill., 1952-53; sr. rsch. biologist U.S. Borax Rsch. Corp., Anaheim, Calif., 1965-67; supervisory rsch. microbiologist No. Regional Rsch. Ctr. USDA, Peoria, 1967-81, head agrl. rsch. culture collection No. Regional Rsch. Lab., 1967-81; ret., 1981; cons. Mycogen Corp., San Diego, 1985-87; U.S. sr. scientist Fed. Republic Germany, Darmstadt, 1977. Contbg. author: Actinomycetales: The Boundary Microorganisms, 1974, Bergey's Manual of Determinative Bacteriology, 1974, Synopsis and Classification of Living Organisms, 1982; mem. editorial bd. Jour. Antibiotics, 1969-81; contbr. articles to Jour. Bacteriology, Applied Microbiology, Phytopathology, Actinomycetes, Mycologia, Devel. Indsl. Microbiology, Jour. Antibiotics, Internat. Bull. Bacteriological Nomenclature Taxonomy, Antibiotics Ann., Antimicrobial Agts., Chemotherapy, also others. With USNR, 1943-45, with Rsch. Res., 1945-54, lt. ret. Fulbright scholar, Italy, 1952; grantee Soc. Am. Bacteriologists, 1957. Fellow Am. Acad. Microbiology (ASM state network 1991—); mem. Am. Soc. Microbiology (com. mem., workshop presenter), Soc. Indsl. Microbiology, Mycol. Soc. Am., U.S. Fedn. Culture Collections (v.p. 1981). Episcopalian. Achievements include patents in fermentative production of riboflavin and of antibiotics; research in microbial culture collection technology and management, systematics of streptomycetes, industrial microbiology, and air pollution. Home: 38 Mayo Br Prestonsburg KY 41653-8114

PRIDMORE, CHARLES FRANKLIN, JR., mechanical engineer; b. Washington, June 23, 1949; s. Charles F. Pridmore Sr. and Frances Ray (Couch) Soule; m. Mary Ann Meehan, Sept. 22, 1973; children: Colleen Marie, Scott Andrew. AA, Prince Georges C.C., 1987; BS Tech. Mgmt. cum laude, U. Md., 1990. Draftsman Shull Elec. Co., Brentwood, Md., 1972-74; sr. design draftsman Baxter Travenol, Silver Springs, Md., 1975-80; lead elec. designer Niro Atomizer, Columbia, Md., 1980-81; sr. mech. designer Rixon, Silver Spring, 1981-88; assoc. mech. engr. Rixon-Case Comm., Silver Spring, Md., 1981-88; mech. engr. Telecom. Techniques Corp., Germantown, Md., 1988—, sr. mech. engr., 1988-96; consulting engr. various bio-med. devices, Washington, 1988-90; sr. mech. engr. sustaining engring., 1996—. Little league coach South Bowie (Md.) Boys/Girls Clubs, 1990, county baseball coach, 1991-94. With USN, 1968-71, Vietnam. Mem. Soc. Mfg. Engrs. (sr.), Soc. Plastics Engrs., Mason (32 degree, past master Harmony lodge # 17 FAAM Washington), Alpha Sigma Lambda, Phi Kappa Phi. Republican. Southern Baptist. Avocations: hunting, fishing, training labrador retrievers, gardening, travel. Home: 4106 New Haven Dr Bowie MD 20716-1062 Office: Telecom Techniques Corp 20400 Observation Dr Germantown MD 20876-4092

PRIDMORE, ROY DAVIS, government official; b. Gaffney, S.C., May 18, 1925; s. Davis Bailey and Ethel (Hughes) P.; m. Doris Hedy Glatzl, July 16, 1960; children: Lisa Ann, David Michael. Cert., Columbus U., Washington, 1949, Am. Inst., Washington, 1953, U.S. Dept. Agr. Grad. Sch., Washington, 1957. Pers. asst. Dept. Army, Fort Myer, Va., 1955-58; staff asst. D.C. Hwy. Dept., Washington, 1962-67; adminstrv. asst. Dept. Transp., Washington, 1958-62, adminstrv. officer, 1967-94, ret., 1994. Vice pres. Springboard Swim Club, Springfield, Va., 1984-85. Served with U.S. Army, 1946-47; mem. Res. (ret.). Decorated Legion of Merit. Democrat. Roman Catholic. Avocation: swimming, gardening.

PRIEBE, CEDRIC JOSEPH, JR., pediatric surgeon; b. N.Y.C., Feb. 7, 1930; s. Cedric Joseph and Mary Martha (O'Beirne) P.; m. Cynthia Amelia Cali, June 11, 1955; children: Diane Marie, Janice Marie, Cedric Joseph III, Catherine Marie, Michael Stephen, Gregory Paul, Marta Marcella. BS cum laude, Fordham U., 1951; MD, Cornell U., 1955. Surg. resident The Roosevelt Hosp., N.Y.C., 1955-60; pediatric surg. resident Ohio State U., Children's Hosp., Columbus, 1965-67; pediatric surgeon, asst. and assoc. prof. The Roosevelt Hosp., Colombia U., N.Y.C., 1967-79; chief pediatric surgery, prof. surgery La. State U., Charity Hosp., New Orleans, 1979-82, SUNY at Stony Brook, U. Hosp., 1982—; sr. clin. trainee in cancer control NIH, Washington, 1963-65. Editl. cons. Jour. of Pediatric Surgery, Phila., 1994—; author: (with others) Neoplasia in Childhood, 1966; contbr. articles to profl. jours. Maj. USAF, 1956-65. Mem. ACS, Am. Burn Assn., Soc. for Surgery Alimentary Tract, Am. Acad. of Pediatrics (publs. com.), Am. Pediatric Surg. Assn. (membership, by-laws, cancer com. 1970—), Pediatric Oncology Group (cancer control com. 1992—), N.Y. Soc. of Pediatric Surgery (v.p. 1968-79, pres. 1982—). Republican. Roman Catholic. Avocations: tennis, squash racquets, travel. Home: 9 Woodhull Cove Ln Setauket NY 11733 Office: SUNY at Stony Brook HSC T 19 Stony Brook NY 11794-8191

PRIEM, RICHARD GREGORY, writer, information systems executive, entertainment company executive; b. Munich, Sept. 18, 1949; came to U.S., 1953; s. Richard Stanley and Elizabeth Teresa (Thompson) P.; m. Janice Lynne Holland, July 27, 1976; children: Michael John, Matthew Warren (dec.), Kathryn Elizabeth. BS in Radio-TV-Film, U. Tex., 1970; MEd in Ednl. Tech., U. Ga., 1979; postgrad., Coll. William and Mary, 1981-82. Cert. fraud examiner. Radio personality, sales exec. KOKE, Inc., Austin, Tex., 1968-73; commd. 2d lt. U.S. Army, 1973, numerous positions including asst. prof. dept. behavioral scis. and leadership U.S. Mil. Acad., staff officer anti terrorism and inspector gen., 1973-94; exec. v.p. It's Your Party, Herndon, Va., 1992—; dep. divsn. mgr. Sci. Applications Internat. Corp., Vienna, Va., 1994-97; pres., COO Tech., Inc., Centreville, Va., 1997—; cons. Dallas Cowboys Football Club, 1981; scouting coord. Army Football, 1983-85. Contbr. articles to profl. jours. Mem. Assn. Cert. Fraud Examiners, Internat. Soc. for Performance Improvement, Am. Soc. Indsl. Security Internat., Phi Kappa Phi, Kappa Delta Pi. Home: 15386 Twin Creek Ct Centreville VA 20120-3742 Office: Commerce Techs Inc PO Box 221254 Chantilly VA 20153-1254

PRIESAND, SALLY JANE, rabbi; b. Cleve., June 27, 1946; d. Irving Theodore and Rosetta Elizabeth (Welch) P. B.A. in English, U. Cin., 1968; B.Hebrew Letters, Hebrew Union Coll.-Jewish Inst. Religion, 1971, M.A. in Hebrew Letters, 1972; D.H.L. (hon.), Fla. Internat. U., 1973; DD (hon.), Hebrew Union Coll., 1997. Ordained rabbi, 1972. Student rabbi Sinai Temple, Champaign, Ill., 1968, Congregation B'nai Israel, Hattiesburg, Miss., 1969-70, Congregation Shalom, Milw., 1970, Temple Beth Israel, Jackson, Mich., 1970-71; rabbinic intern Isaac M. Wise Temple, Cin., 1971-72; asst. rabbi Stephen Wise Free Synagogue, N.Y.C., 1972-77; assoc. rabbi Stephen Wise Free Synagogue, 1977-79; rabbi Temple Beth El, Elizabeth, N.J., 1979-81, Monmouth Reform Temple, Tinton Falls, N.J., 1981—; chaplain Lenox Hill Hosp., N.Y.C., 1979-81. Author: Judaism and the New Woman, 1975. Mem. commn. on synagogue rels. Fedn. Jewish Philanthropies N.Y., 1972-79, mem. com. on aged commn. synagogue rels., 1972-75; mem. task force on equality of women in Judaism pub. affairs com. N.Y. Fedn. Reform Synagogues, 1972-75; mem. com. on resolutions Ctrl. Conf. Am. Rabbis, 1975-77, com. on cults, 1976-78, admissions com., 1983-89; chmn. Task Force on Women in Rabbinate, 1977-83, chmn. 1977-79, mem. exec. bd., 1977-79, com. on resolutions, 1989-92, chmn. com. conv. program, 1993-96; mem. joint commn. on Jewish edn. Ctrl. Conf. Am. Rabbis-Union Am. Hebrew Congregations, 1974-77; mem. task force on Jewish singles Commn. Synagogue Rels., 1975-77; mem. N.Y. Bd. Rabbis, 1975—, Shore Area Bd. Rabbis, 1981—; mem. interim steering com. Clergy and Laity Concerned, 1979-81; bd. dirs. NCCJ, N.Y.C., 1980-82, Jewish Fedn. Greater Monmouth County, trustee, 1988—; trustee Planned Parenthood of Monmouth County, 1982-90; chair religious affairs com. Brookdale Ctr. for Holocaust Studies, 1983-88; v.p. Interfaith Neighbors, 1988—; mem. UAHC-CCAR Joint Commn. on Synagogue Affiliation, 1992—; bd. govs. Hebrew Union Coll.-Jewish Inst. Religion, 1993—; trustee Union Am. Hebrew Congregations, 1994—. Cited by B'nai Brith Women, 1971; named Woman of Yr. Temple Israel, Columbus, Ohio, 1972, Woman of Yr. Ladies Aux. N.Y. chpt. Jewish War Vets., 1973, Woman for All Seasons N. L.I. region Women's Am. ORT, 1973, Extraordinary Women of Achievement NCCJ, 1978, Woman of Achievement Monmouth County Adv. Commn. on Status Women, 1988; recipient Quality of Life award Dist. One chpt. B'nai B'rith Women, 1973, Medallion Judaic Heritage Soc., 1978, Eleanor Roosevelt Humanities award Women's div. State of Israel Bonds, 1980, Rabbinical award Coun. Jewish Fedn., 1988, Woman of Leadership award Monmouth Coun. Girl Scouts U.S., 1991, The Woman Who Dares award Nat. Coun. Jewish Women, 1993, Women's Studies Disting. Alumnae award Friends of Women's Studies U. Cin., 1997. Mem. Hadassah (life), Ctrl. Conf. Am. Rabbis, NOW, Am. Jewish Congress, Am. Jewish Com., Assn. Reform Zionists Am., Jewish Women Internat. (life), Jewish Peace Fellowship, Women's Rabbinic Network, Nat. Breast Cancer Coalition. Home: 10 Wedgewood Cir Eatontown NJ 07724-1203 Office: 332 Hance Ave Tinton Falls NJ 07724-2730

PRIESMAN, ELINOR LEE SOLL, family dynamics administrator, mediator, educator; b. Mpls., Jan. 19, 1938; d. Arthur and Harriet Lucille (Premack) Soll; m. Ira Morton Priesman, Mar. 30, 1958; children: Phillip Sherman, Artyce-Joy Erin. PhD, Union Inst., 1993. Cert. mediator, Va.; cert. family life educator. Nursery sch. tchr. Jewish Comty. Ctr., Santa Monica, Calif., 1958-59; head tchr. Altrusa Day Nursery, Battle Creek, Mich., 1959-60; prin. Arlington/Fairfax Jewish Ctr., Arlington, Va., 1966-67; tchr. grades 1-10 Congregation Olam Tikvah, Fairfax, Va., 1970-75; dir. Creative Play Nursery Sch., Fairfax, Va., 1970-71; tchr. high sch. Temple Sinai, Washington, Va., 1976-78; prin. Congregation Olam Tikvah, Fairfax, Va., 1975-76; asst. to pres.-emeritus Coun. for Advancement and Support of Edn., McLean, Va., 1987-90; cons. to univ. Union for Experimenting Colls. and Univs., McLean, Va., 1988-90; dir. family dynamics inst. Fairfax; mem. doctoral com. Union Inst., Cin., 1991-92, 93—, acad. waivers com., 1994-96, acad. appeals com., 1996—; faculty mentor Ea. U., Albuquerque, 1993-96. Author: The Empowered Parent, 1993, A New Perspective on Parenting, 1994 (Spanish, Korean translations 1996), A New Perspective on Parenting for Attorneys and Mediators, 1995; editor: Empowered Parenting newsletter, 1991-92. Pres. No. Va. Artistic Skating Club, Manassas, 1983-85; chair edn. com. Olam Tikvah Synagogue, Fairfax. Recipient Pres.'s award Olam Tikvah Synagogue, 1976. Mem. N.Am. Soc. Adlerian Psychology, Nat. Coun. on Family Rels., Children's Rights Coun., Acad. Family Mediators, No. Va. Mediation Svc. (mediator), Hadassah (life, Alexandria chpt. pres. 1966-67, Esther award 1965). Jewish. Office: Family Dynamics Inst 9302 Swinburne Ct Fairfax VA 22031-3027

PRIESS, HOWARD K., II, lawyer; b. Chgo., Jan. 19, 1944. BS, Northwestern U., 1967; JD, Ill. Inst. Tech., 1971. Bar: Ill. 1971. With Tressler, Soderstrom, Maloney & Priess, Chgo. Mem. ABA, Internat. Assn. Defense Counsel, Defense Rsch. Inst., Soc. Trial Lawyers, Fedn. Ins. and Corp. Counsel, Ill. State Bar Assn., Ill. Assn. Defense Trial Lawyers, Chgo. Bar Assn. Office: Tressler Soderstrom Maloney & Priess Sears Tower 22nd Fl 233 S Wacker Dr Chicago IL 60606-6306

PRIEST, GEORGE L., law educator; b. 1947. BA, Yale U., 1969; JD, U. Chgo., 1973. Assoc. prof. U. Puget Sound, Tacoma, 1973-75; law and econ. fellow U. Chgo., 1975-77; prof. U. Buffalo, 1977-80, UCLA, 1980-81, Yale U., New Haven, 1981—; dir. program in civil liability; John M. Olin prof. law and econs., 1986—. Mem. Pres.' Com. on Privatization, 1987-88. Office: PO Box 208215 New Haven CT 06520-8215

PRIEST, HARTWELL WYSE, artist; b. Brantford, Ont., Can., Jan. 1, 1901; d. John Frank Henry and Rachel Thayer (Gavet) Wyse; m. A.J. Gustin Priest, Aug. 4, 1927; children: Paul Lambert, Marianna Thayer. BA, Smith Coll. Former tchr. graphic art Va. Art Inst., Charlottesville; former lectr. on prints and lithography; juror art exhbn. Unitarian Ch., 1993. One-woman shows include Argent Gallery, N.Y.C., 1955, 58, 60, 73, 77, 81, Va., 1969, 71, Nantucket, Mass., 1956, Ft. Lauderdale, Fla. Art Ctr., 1956; Pen & Brush, N.Y.C., 1973, 91, invitational retrospective exhbn. McGuffey Art Ctr., Charlottesville, Va., 1984, Va., N.Y., 1984, 88; work represented in permanent collections Library of Congress Washington, Norton Gallery, Palm Beach, Fla., Soc. Am. Graphic Artists, Hunterdon County Art Ctr., Longwood Coll., Smith Coll., Va. Mus., Richmond, Carnegie Mellon U. and numerous others; solo exhbn. of prints McGuffey Art Ctr., Charlottesville, Va., 1988, 90, 93, Woodstock Artist Gallery, 1990, Soc. Am. Graphic Artists, 1988-89, 92, Bombay, 1989, U. Va. Hosp., 1989, Bergen Mus. Art and Sci., 1991; represented in group shows McGuffey Gallery, 1988, 94, Gallery Show, Richmond, Va., 1988, Nat. Assn. Women Artists, Florence, Italy, 1972, N.Y.C., 1989, 96, ann. show Ojibway Hotel Club, Pointe au Baril, Georgian Bay, Ont., Can., 1991, Soc. Am. Graphic Srts, N.Y.C., 1989, 92, Woodstock, N.Y. Art Assoc., 1990, McGuffey Art Ctr., Charlottesville, Va., 1990, 94, Pen and Brush ann. Graphic Show, N.Y.C., 1991 (award for etching Spring, Ada Rosario Cecere Meml. award), Bergen Mus., N.J., 1991, Ojibway Club, Ont., Can., 1991; Pen and Brush Christmas exhbn., 1994-95, Showing of a Video, Harrisonburg, Va.; represented in traveling group shows Nat. Assn. Women Artists, Puerto Rico, 1987, India, 1989, N.Y.C., 1994; pvt. collection U. Va. Hosp., Charlottesville, 1989; subject of TV documentary Hartwell Priest: Printmaker, 1995. Recipient awards for lithograph Field Flowers, Longwood Coll., 1965, Nat. Assn. Woman Artists, 1965, lithograph West Wind, A Buell award, 1961, print Streets of Silence, T. Giorgi Meml. award, 1973, lithograph Blue Lichen, Pen & Brush, 1984, award for collage, 1985; 1st award for graphics Blue Ridge Art Show, 1985, Gene A. Walker award for print Glacial Rocks, 1986, award for print Blue Ridge Show, 1987, Philip Isenburg award for graphic PreCambrian Rock Pattern, 1988, Ada R. Cecere Meml. award Pen and Brush, 1991, Art award Piedmont Coun. Arts, 1993. Mem. Nat. Assn. Women Artists (Travelling Printmaking Exhbn. 1987-89), Pen and Brush, Soc. Am. Graphic Artists, Washington Print Club, 2d St. Gallery, Charlottesville, McGuffey Art Ctr. Avocations: walking, singing in choir, gardenening, playing Bach and Mozart, playing recorder and piano. Home: 41 Old Farm Rd Charlottesville VA 22903-4725

PRIEST, MELVILLE STANTON, retired consulting hydraulic engineer; b. Cassville, Mo., Oct. 16, 1912; s. William Tolliver and Mildred Alice (Messer) P.; m. Vivian Willingham, Mar. 22, 1941 (dec.); m. Virginia Young, Dec. 16, 1983. BS, U. Mo., 1935; MS, U. Colo., 1943; PhD, U. Mich., 1954. Registered profl. engr., Ala., La., Miss. Jr. engr. U.S. Engrs. Office, 1937-39; from jr. to asst. engr. Bur. Reclamation, 1939-41; from instr. to assoc. prof. civil engring. Cornell U., 1941-55; prof. hydraulics Auburn (Ala.) U., 1955-58, prof. civil engring., head dept., 1958-65; dir. Water Resources Research Inst., Miss. State U., 1965-77; UN adviser on hydraulics, Egypt, 1956, 57, 60; Mem. Ala. Bd. Registration Profl. Engrs., 1962-65. Contbr. articles to profl. jours. Fellow ASCE (pres. Ala. 1962, exec. com., pipeline div. 1971-74), Am. Water Resources Assn. (dir. 1973-75), Sigma Xi, Tau Beta Pi, Chi Epsilon, Pi Mu Epsilon. Address: PO Box 541 Starkville MS 39760-0541

PRIEST, RUTH EMILY, music minister, choir director, composer arranger; b. Detroit, Nov. 7, 1933; d. William and Gertrude Hilda (Stockley) P. Student, Keyboard Studios, Detroit, 1949-52, Wayne State U., Detroit, 1953, 57, Ea. Pentecostal Bible Coll., Peterborough, Ont., Can., 1954-55, Art Ctr. Music Sch., Detroit Inst. Mus. Arts, 1953-54. Legal sec., 1951-90; organist, pianist, vocalist Berea Tabernacle, Detroit, 1943-61; organist Bethany Presbyn. Ch., Ft. Lauderdale, Fla., 1961-67, 69-72; choir dir., organist Bethany Drive-in Ch., Ft. Lauderdale, Fla.; organist First Bapt. Ch., Pompano Beach, Fla., 1967-68, St. Ambrose Episcopal Ch., Ft. Lauderdale, 1969-72; music dir., organist Grace Brethren Ch., Ft. Lauderdale, 1972-75; organist Boca Raton (Fla.) Community Ch., Bibletown, 1975-85; min. music, organist Warrendale Community Ch., Dearborn, Mich., 1985—; ptnr. Miracle Music Enterprises; concert and ch. organist/pianist; organist numerous weddings, city-wide rallies of Detroit and Miami Youth for Christ, Christ for Labor and Mgmt., Holiness Youth Crusade, numerous other civic and religious events; featured weekly as piano soloist and accompanist on Crusade for Christ Telecast, Detroit, 1950-60, CBC-TV, Windsor, Ont., Can.; staff organist Enquire Hotel, Galt Ocean Mile, Ft. Lauderdale, Fla., 1962-67; tchr. piano adult edn. evening sch. program Southfield (Mich.) Pub. Sch. System, 1991—. Ongoing educator in pvt. piano, organ, music theory; Recording artist: Ruth Priest at the Organ, Love Notes from the Heart, Christmas with Ruth. Mem. Am. Guild Organists (past mem. exec. bd. Detroit chpt.). Office: Miracle Music Enterprises 27300 Franklin Rd Ste 214 Southfield MI 48034-2306 *I agree with Martin Luther that music is one of God's greatest gifts to mankind. At a very early age my natural response to life was, and still is, an outflow of love to God through the musical gifts with which He has blessed me.*

PRIEST, SHARON DEVLIN, state official; b. Montreal, Quebec, Can.; m. Bill Priest; 1 child, Adam. Tax preparer, instr. H & R Block, Little Rock, 1976-78; account exec. Greater Little Rock C. of C.; owner, founder Devlin Co.; mem. Little Rock Bd. Dirs., 1986—; vice mayor Little Rock, 1989-91, mayor, 1991-93; Sec. of State State of Arkansas, 1994—; bd. dirs. Invesco Inc., New Futures. Bd. dirs., past pres. Metroplan (Environ. Svc. award 1982), YMCA, Southwest Hosp.; mem. Advt. and Promotion commn., Ark. Internat. Visitors Coun., Pulaski Are Transp. Svc. Policy Com., St. Theresa's Parish Coun., Exec. com. for Ark. Mcpl. League, Nat. League of Cities Trans. and Communications Steering Com. and Policy Com., adv. bd. M.M. Cohn., Little Rock City Beautiful Commn., 1980-86; former bd. dirs. Downtown Partnership, Southwest YMCA, 1984, 86, sec.; former mem. Community Housing Resource Bd., 1984-86, Pub. Facilities Bd. Southwest Hosp., 1985-86, Southwest Merchants' Assn., 1985—, 2d v.p., 1985; chmn. Little Rock Arts and Humanities Promotion Commn.; led petition dr. for appropriation for Fourche Creek Plan 7A. Recipient of the Fighting Back Freedom Fighter award, 1995, recipient of Environ. Svc. award from the Little Rock Metroplan Comm. Mem. Leadership Inst. Alumni Assn. (4 Bernard de la Harpe awards). Selected by Arkansas Business as one of the Top 100 Women in Arkansaa. Office: Office of Secretary of State State Capitol Bldg 256 Little Rock AR 72201*

PRIEST, TROY ALFRED-WILEY, lawyer; b. Balt., Oct. 5, 1968; s. Roy Otis and Sudie Mae (Payton) P.; m. Françoise Borja Santos, Aug. 10, 1991; 1 child, Gabrielle Borja. BA, Brown U., 1990; JD, Northeastern U., 1993. Bar: Md. 1993, D.C. 1994, U.S. Dist. Ct. Md. 1994, U.S. Dist. Ct. D.C. 1995. Law clk. Hon. Annice M. Wagner chief judge D.C. Ct. of Appeals, Washington, 1993-94; assoc. Houston & Howard, Washington, 1994-96, Mason, Ketterman & Morgan, Balt., 1996—; dist. counselor Omega Psi Phi Fraternity, Inc., New Eng., Providence, R.I., 1991-93. Mem. ABA, Nat. Health Lawyers Assn., Nat. Bar Assn., Md. Bar Assn., Bar Assn. D.C., Defense Rsch. Inst. Democrat. Baptist. Home: 1306 Canyon Rd Silver Spring MD 20904 Office: Mason Ketterman & Morgan 300 E Lombard St Ste 1100 Baltimore MD 21202-3228

PRIESTER, HORACE RICHARD, JR., quality assurance professional; b. Charleston, S.C., Nov. 3, 1936; s. Horace Richard and Pearl (Hinely) P.; widowed; children: Horace Richard III, David Eugene, Cheryl Priester Burns; m. Carole Ledford, Aug. 10, 1985; children: Charles Wayne Blackburn Jr., Carl Ashley Blackburn. BS in Chem. Engring., Clemson U., 1958. Asst. chief chemist Savannah (Ga.) Foods & Industries, Inc., 1968-73, chief chemist, 1973-78, chief chemist refineries, 1978-89, corp. dir. quality assurance, 1990—; bd. dirs., lectr. Sugar Processing Rsch. Inst., New Orleans; referee U.S. Nat. Com. on Sugar Analysis, 1990—; mem. U.S. Nat. Com. on Sugar Analysis, 1982—. Founder Savannah chpt. Internat. Christian Bus. Men's Orgn., pres., 1970-73. Mem. U.S. Cane Sugar Refiners Assn. (tech. com.), Sugar Industry Technologists (lectr.), Inst. Food Technologists, Soc. Soft Drink Technologists, Gideons. Southern Baptist. Avocations: computers, travel. Office: Savannah Foods & Industries Inc PO Box 710 Savannah GA 31402-0710

PRIESTLEY, G. T. ERIC, manufacturing company executive; b. Belfast, Northern Ireland, May 7, 1942; came to U.S., 1990; s. Thomas John McKee P.; m. Carol Elizabeth Gingles Nelson, June 8, 1966; children: Peter, Gaye, Simon. BS, Queens U., 1963; postgrad. Bus. Sch., Harvard U., 1989. Sales trainee Burroughs Machines Ltd., 1963-64; dealer, sales devel. Regent Oil Co., 1964-66; ops. mgr. RMC (Ulster) Ltd., 1967-70; distbn. mgr. Bass Charrington, Ireland, 1970-71; dir., gen. mgr. Farrans Ltd., 1971-80; dir., CEO Redland plc/British Fuels/Cawoods, 1980-88; dir. Bowater plc, London, 1988-90; pres., CEO Rexam Inc., Charlotte, N.C., 1990-96; exec. v.p., COO Jefferson Smurfit Corp., St. Louis, 1996—; non-exec. dir. Southwire Inc. Bd. advisors U. N.C., Charlotte. Mem. Moortown Golf Club, Aloha Golf Club, Royal Ulster Yacht Club, Quail Hollow Country Club, Boone Valley Country Club. Home: 9114 Winged Bourne Charlotte NC 28210-5946 also: 144 N Bemiston Ave Clayton MO 63105 Office: Jefferson Smurfit Co 8182 Maryland Ave Saint Louis MO 63105-3786

PRIESTLEY, JASON, actor; b. Vancouver, B.C., Can.. Actor: (TV series) Sister Kate, 1989-90, Beverly Hills 90210, 1990—; (films) Calendar Girl, 1993, Tombstone, 1993, Cold-Blooded, 1995; prodr., dir. episodes TV series Beverly Hills 90210, 1995-96. Office: c/o Wolf Kasteler 132 S Rodeo Dr Ste 300 Beverly Hills CA 90212-2403

PRIEVE, E. ARTHUR, arts administration educator. BBA in Adminstrn. and Art History, U. of Wis., 1959, MBA in Mgmt. and Orgn. Behavior, 1961; DBA in Mgmt. and Psych., George Washington U., Washington, 1965. Asst. dean adminstrv. affairs Sch. Bus. U. Wis., Madison, 1966-69, prof. mgmt. Grad. Sch. Bus., 1969—, dir. exec. MBA program, 1993—; dir. Ctr. For Arts Adminstrn., Madison, 1969—; curriculum cons. for arts adminstrn.; cons. visual, performing and arts svc. orgns.; workshops and presentations on planning, bd. dirs. Mem. Assn. of Arts Adminstrn. Educators (chmn. U.S., Can.). Office: U Wis Ctr Arts Adminstrn 4171 Grainger Hall 975 University Ave Madison WI 53706-1324

PRIGMORE, KATHRYN BRADFORD TYLER, architecture educator, architect; b. St. Albans, N.Y., Nov. 21, 1956; d. Richard Jerome and Shirley Virginia (Neizer) Tyler; m. James Craig Prigmore, June 20, 1986 (div. June 1992); children: Crystal Andrea, Amber Sheriesse. BS in Bldg. Sci., Rensselaer Poly. Inst., 1977, BArch, 1978; MS in Engring., Cath. U. Am., 1981. Registered architect, Va., NCARB. Intern architect VVKR Inc., Alexandria, Va., 1979-82; architect Robert A. Hawthorne, Architects, PC, Washington, 1982; project mgr. Robert Traynham Coles, Architect, PC, Washington, 1982-84; assoc. Segreti Tepper Architects, P.C., Washington, 1984-92; assoc. prof. dept. architecture Howard U., Washington, 1991—, assoc. dean Sch. Architecture and Planning, 1992—; Chair, architect's section, Va. Bd. for Architects, Profl. Engrs., Landscape Architects and Land Surveyors, Nat. Coun. Archtl. Registration Bds., Archtl. Registration Exam and Grading Com.; mem. alumni adv. coun. Sch. Architecture Rensselaer Poly. Inst., 1993—; guest spkr. in field. Contbr. articles to profl. jours. Mem. adv. coun. No. Va. Urban League, 1980-81. Named to Outstanding Young Women in Am., 1983. Mem. AIA (pub. rels. com. Washington chpt. 1983—), AAUW, Nat. Orgn. Minority Archs., Black Women in Architecture and Related Professions (faculty advisor Howard U. chpt. 1992—). Episcopalian. Avocations: writing, gardening. Home: 8911 Union Farm Rd Alexandria VA 22309-3936 Office: Howard U Sch Architecture/Planning 2366 6th St NW Washington DC 20001-2323

PRIGOGINE, VICOMTE ILYA, physics educator; b. Moscow, Russia, Jan. 25, 1917; s. Roman and Julie (Wichmann) P.; m. Marina Prokopowicz, Feb. 25, 1961; children: Yves, Pascal. PhD, Free U. Brussels, 1941; hon. degree, U. Newcastle, Eng., 1966, U. Poitiers, France, 1966, U. Chgo., 1969, U. Bordeaux, France, 1972, U. de Liège, Belgium, 1977, U. Uppsala, Sweden, 1977, U de Droit, D'Economie et des Scis., d'Aix-Marseille, France, 1979, U. Georgetown, 1980, U. Cracovie, Poland, 1981, U. Rio de Janeiro, 1981, Stevens Inst. Tech., Hoboken, 1981, Heriot-Watt U., Scotland, 1985, Universidad Nacional de Educacion a Distancia, Madrid, 1985, U. Francois Rabelais de Tours, 1986, U. Peking, People's Republic of China, 1986, U. Buenos Aires, 1989, U. Cagliari, Sardinia, Italy, 1990, U. Sienne, Italy, 1990; DS (hon.), Gustavus Adolphus Coll., 1990; Membre d'Honneur, l'Academie Nationale d'Argenti, 1990, l'Academie des Sciences Nature, lles de Republique Federale de Russie, 1991; Pres. d'Honneur, l'Acad. Nat. des Scis. de Republique de San Marino, 1991; Membre d'Honneur, l'Academie Chilienne des Scis., 1991, de l'Université de Nice-Sophia-Antipolis, Nice, France, 1991, de l'Univ. Philippines System, Quezon City, 1991, del'Université de Santiago, Chile, del'Université de Tucumán, Argentine, 1991; Docteur Honoris Causa, Université Lomonosov de Moscow, Russie, 1993, L'Univ. de A L.I. Cuza IASI, Iasi, Romania, 1994, U. de San Luis, Argentina, 1994, Institut Nat. Polytechnique, Lorraine, France, 1994, SUNY, Binghamton, 1995, Vrije U. Brussel, Brussels, Belgium, 1995, Internat. Assn. U. Pres., Seoul, 1995, Institut Royal des Elites, Brussels, 1995, U. Valladolid, Espagne, 1995, U. de Valladolid, Spain, 1995; Laurea ad honorem in philosophy, U. degli Studi Inst. Filosofia, Urbino, Italy, 1996; Docteur Honoris Causa, U. Salvador, Buenos Aires, 1996, U. Xanthi, Greece, 1996. Prof. U. Brussels, 1947—; dir. Internat. Insts. Physics and Chemistry, Solvay, Belgium, 1959—; prof. physics and chem. engring. U. Tex., Austin, 1967—; dir. Ilya Prigogine Ctr. for Studies in Statis. Mechanics, Thermodynamics and Complex Systems, U. Tex., Austin, 1967—; hon. prof. U. Nankin, People's Republic of China, 1986, Banaras Hindu U., Varasani, India, 1988; Ashbel Smith regental prof. U. Tex., Austin, 1984—; Dir.'s Disting. visitor Inst. for Advanced Study, Princeton (N.J.) U., 1993; counseiller spl. Commn. des Communautés Européennes, 1993; internat. advisor de l'Internat. Inst. Advanced Studies, Kyoto, 1994; hon. dir. Inst. Internat. Investigaciones Cientficas U. Salvador, 1996; hon. chmn. Inst. Complex Sys., Thrace, Greece, 1996; mem. adv. bd.

Kothari Ctr. Sci., Ethics and Edn. U. Delhi, 1995; mem. Internat. Info. Acad, Moscow, 1996, Académie de Juste-Fautenil J.S. Bach, Madrid, 1996; hon. pres. Ctr. FI No Linear Sistemas Complejos U. Santiago, Chile, 1996—; with Ctr L.Am. Estudios, U. Nacional San Luis, Argentina, 1994, U. Lomonosov, Moscow, 1995, Haute Ecole Libre Tlya Prigogine, Brussels, 1996, Inst. Documentazione Ricerca Sull, Italy, 1996; Ilya Prigogine chair philosophy scis. U. Palermo, Argentina, 1996. Author: (with R. Defay) Traite de Thermodynamique, conformement aux methodes de Gibbs et de De Donder, 1944, 50, Etude Thermodynamique des Phenomenes Irreversibles, 1947, Introduction to Thermodynamics of Irreversible Processes, 1954, 62, 67, translation: Russian, Serbo-Croatian, French, Italian, & Spanish, (with A. Bellemans, V. Mathot) The Molecular Theory of Solutions, 1957, Nonequilibrium Statistical Mechanics, 1962, (with R. Ilerman) Kinetic Theory of Vehicular Traffic, 1971, (with R. Glansdorff) Thermodynamic Theory of Structure, Stability and Fluctuations, 1971, (with G. Nicolis) Self-Organization in Nonequilibrium Systems, 1977, From Being to Becoming-Time and Complexity in Physical Sciences, 1980, French, German, Japanese, Russian, Chinese, Italian, Romanian, & Portuguese edits., (with I. Stengers) Order Out of Chaos, 1983, La Nouvelle Alliance, Les Métamorphoses de la Science, 1979, German, English, Italian, Spanish, Serbo-Croatian, Romanian, Swedish, Dutch, Russian, Japanese, Chinese, Portuguese, Bulgarian, Greek, Korean, & Polish edits., (with G. Nicolis) Die Erforschung des Komplexen, 1987, Exploring Complexity, 1989, Chinese, Russian, Italian, French, Spanish edits., (with I. Stengers) Entre le temps et l'Eternité, 1988, Dutch edit. 1989, Italian edit. 1989, Spanish edit. 1990, Portuguese edit. 1993, Le leggi del Caos, 1993, Das Paradox der Zeit, 1993, (with I. Stengers) Les Lois du Chaos, 1994, Die Gesetze des Chaos, 1995, La Fin des Certitudes, 1996, Spanish, Portuguese, Dutch, English edits., 1997; mem. editl. bd. Ukrainian Phys. Jour., 1990. Mem. sci. adv. bd. Internat. Acad. for Biomed. Drug Rsch., 1990; mem. adv. com. Internat. Coun. Human Duties, U. degli Studi di Trieste, Italy, 1996. Fellow RGK Found. Centennial, U. Tex. 1989-90; decorated comdr. Légion d'Honneur, 1989, France, comdr. de l'Ordre de Leopold, 1968, Médaille de la resistance comdr. de l'Ordre Leopold II, 1961, Grande Croix de l'Ordre de Leopold II, 1977, Médaille Civique de Premiere Classe, 1972, comdr. de l'Ordre National du Mérite, France, 1977, comdr. de l'Ordre des Arts et des Lettres, France, 1984, Titulaire de l' Ordre du Solail Levant, avec Médaille d' Oret d' Argent, Japon, 1990; recipient Prix Franqui, 1955, Prix Solvay, 1965, Nobel prize in chemistry, 1977, Honda Prize, 1983, Rumford gold medal Royal Soc. London, 1976, Karcher medal Am. Crystallographic Assn., 1978, Descartes medal U. Paris, 1979, Prix Umberto Biancamano, 1987, award recipient Gravity Rsch. Found., 1988, Artificial Intelligence Sci. Achievement award Internat. Found. for Artificial Intelligence, 1990, Prix Summa de l'Universite Laval, Can., 1993, Medaille Piotr Kapitza decernee par l'Academie des Scis. Naturelles de Russie, 1996—, Medaille de l'Ecole Normale Superieure, Paris, 1995, Medaille d'honneur de l'Inst. Phys. Chemistry-Polish Acad. Scis., 1996—, others. Fellow NAS India (hon.); mem. Royal Acad. Belgium (pres.), Am. Acad. Sci. (medal 1975), Royal Soc. Scis. Uppsala (Sweden), NAS U.S.A. (fgn. assoc.), Soc. Royale des Scis. Liège Belgium (corr.), Acad. Gottingen Germany, Deutscher Acad. der Naturforscher Leopoldina (Cothenius medal 1970), Osterreichische Acad. der Wissenschaften (corr.), Academie Nationale des Sciences, des Letters et des Arts de Modene (Italy, hon.), Commn. Mondiale de la Culture et du Devel. de l'UNESCO (hon.), Chem. Soc. Poland (hon.), Internat. Soc. Gen. Systems Rsch. (pres.-elect 1988), Royal Soc. Chemistry Belgium (hon.), N.Y. Acad. Sci., Internat. Acad. Philosophy Sci., World Acad. Arts and Scis., World Inst. Sci., Assemblée Européenne Scis. Tech., Communantés Européenne, Étranger Acad. Scis., Internat. Soc. Theoretical Chem. Physics. (mem. hon. bd.), Soc. Coréenne de Chimie (hon.), Conseil Consultatif Sci. Internat. de l'UNESCO, 1996. Address: 67 Ave Fond Roy, 1180 Brussels Belgium U.S. Office: Inst Internat Physics & Chem, Campus Plaine ULB CP231, Bld du Triomphe 1050 Brussels Belgium Office: U Tex of Hou Ilya Prigogine Ctr Studies Statis Mechanics Austin TX 78712

PRIMEAUX, HENRY, III, automotive executive, author, speaker; b. New Orleans, Nov. 16, 1941; s. Henry Jr. and Ethel (Ritter) P.; m. Jane Cathrine Velcich, July 23, 1960; children: Joann Primeaux Longa, Lisa, Henry Joseph. Student, La. State U., New Orleans, 1959-63. Compt. Jimco, New Orleans, 1965-66; owner, mgr. Picone Seafood, New Orleans, 1966-67; v.p. NADW Inc., Metairie, La., 1967-78, Am. Warranty Corp., L.A., 1978-80; pres. F&I Warranty Corp., Arlington, Tex., 1980-87; exec. v.p. F&I Mgmt. Corp., Arlington, 1980-87; pres., chief exec. officer Primco Corp., Arlington, 1987-91; pres. Crown Autoworld Automobile Dealership, Tulsa; cons., corr. Wards Auto Dealer, Detroit, 1987—, weekly TV program Automotive Satellite TV Network; cons. Nissan Motor Co., L.A., 1988-89, Convergent div. Unisys, Hunt Valley, Md., 1988-90; cons. Mercedes-Benz N.Am.; cons. Automatic Data Processing. Writer Auto Age mag.; author: F&I Handbook. Mem. Rep. Task Force, Rep. Senatorial Inner Circle; bd. dirs. Okla. Spl. Olympics, John Starks Found., Tulsa Ballet, Jr. Achievement, YCMA, Boy Scouts U.S., Children's Med. Ctr.; mem. athletic com. Tulsa Pub. Schs.; mem. nat. adv. bd. GM Sch. to Work Initiative; mem. Okla. Boxing Commn., Okla. Sch. to Work Commn. With USN, 1959-61. Mem. Am. Internat. Automobile Dealers Assn., Assn. of F&I Profls. (bd. dirs. 1990—, pres. 1994), Nat. Auto Dealers Assn. (pres. Tulsa chpt. 1994, Time Quality Dealer of Yr. 1994). Roman Catholic. Home: 10504 S Hudson Pl Tulsa OK 74137-7056 Office: Crown AutoWorld 4444 S Sheridan Rd Tulsa OK 74145-1122

PRIMES, ROBERT, cinematographer. Works include: (films) Dr. Heckyl and Mr. Hype, 1980, The Call Me Bruce?, 1982, Crime Wave, 1985, A Great Wall, 1986, 16 Days of Glory, 1986, Bird On a Wire, 1990, The Hard Way, 1991, Aspen Extreme, 1992; (TV movie) My Antonia, 1995 (Emmy award for outstanding individual achievement in cinematography for a mini-series or spl., 1995). Office: c/o Smith Gosnell Nicholson & Assocs PO Box 1166 Pacific Palisades CA 90272*

PRIMM, EARL RUSSELL, III, publishing executive; b. Rhinelander, Wis., Oct. 24, 1958; s. Earl Russell and Betty Joan (Dennis) P. AB in Classics (hon.), Loyola U. Chgo., 1980; MA in Libr. Sci., U. Chgo., 1990. Asst. to edn. dir. J.G. Ferguson Pub. Co., Chgo., 1981-84; prodn. mgr. Joint Commn. on Accreditation of Hosps., Chgo., 1984-85; sr. editor J.G. Ferguson Pub. Co., Chgo., 1985-87; asst. editor U. Chgo. Press., 1987-88; editorial dir. J.G. Ferguson Pub. Co., Chgo., 1988-89; project mgr. Children's Press, Chgo., 1989-92; exec. editor Franklin Watts, Inc., Chgo., N.Y.C., 1992-95; editorial dir. Grolier Children's Pub., Danbury, Conn., 1995—; mem. adv. bd. U. Chgo. Pub. Program, 1990—; judge Lambda Lit. awards, Washington, 1994—. Editorial chief: Career Discovery Encyclopedia, 1990; editor: Civil Rights Movement in America, 2nd edit., 1991, Extraordinary Hispanic Americans, 1991. Mem. crisis counselor Nat. Runaway Switchboard, Chgo., 1985-88; Horizon's hotline counselor, Chgo., 1987-88; bd. dirs. Gerber/Hart Libr. and Archives, Chgo., 1992-94. Named Honors Sr. of Yr., Loyola U. Chgo., 1980; recipient Mertz Latin Scholarship key Loyola U. Chgo., 1980. Mem. Pub. Triangle, Chgo. Book Clinic, Am. Libr. Assn. Democrat. Home: 156 Heatherwood Dr Brookfield CT 06804 Office: Grolier Inc Sherman Twp Danbury CT 06816

PRIMO, JOAN ERWINA, retail and real estate consulting business owner; b. Detroit, Aug. 28, 1959; d. Joseph Carmen and Marie Ann (Nash) P. BA, Wellesley Coll., 1981; MBA, Harvard U., 1985. Acct. exec. Michigan Bell, Detroit, 1981-82, AT&T Info. Sys., Southfield, Mich., 1983; planning analyst Gen. Motors, Detroit, 1984; v.p. Howard L. Green & Assocs., Troy, Mich., 1985-89; prin., founder The Strategic Edge, Inc., Southfield, 1989—. Contbr. articles to profl. jours. Founders soc. mem. Detroit Inst. Arts, 1989—. Mem. Internat. Coun. Shpping Ctrs. (faculty, seminar leader 1987-), Wellesley Club Southeastern Mich. (pres. 1994—), Harvard Bus. Sch. Club Detroit (bd. dirs. 1994—, v.p. 1995—, exec. v.p. 1996—), Ivy Club Detroit (bd. dirs. 1994—, sec. 1995—). Republican. Avocations: antiques, travel, theatre, gourmet cooking. Home: 224 Woodwind Dr Bloomfield Hills MI 48304 Office: The Strategic Edge 24333 Southfield Rd Ste 211 Southfield MI 48075-2849

PRIMOSCH, JAMES THOMAS, music educator, composer, musician; b. Cleve., Oct. 29, 1956; s. Edward Joseph and Rose Marie (Potochar) P.; m. Mary Marguerite Murphy, April 5, 1986. BA in Composition magna cum laude, Cleve. State U., 1978; MA in Composition, U. Pa., 1980; DMA in Composition awarded with distinction, Columbia U., 1988; studied piano privately with Lambert Orkis, Phila., 1978-80; studied composition with John Harbison, Tanglewood, 1984. Asst. prof. music U. Penn., 1988-94, assoc. prof. music, 1994—; grad. assistantships Columbia-Princeton Electronic Music Ctr., 1982-84, 86-87, preceptorship Columbia U., 1984-85; residency Va. Ctr. Creative Arts, 1985, MacDowell Colony, 1988, Bellagio Conf. Ctr., 1992; regional vis. artist Am. Acad. in Rome, 1994; composer in residence Marlboro Music Festival, 1994. Composer of more than 30 compositions and 19 published works; compositions performed by L.A. Philharm., St. Paul Chamber Orch., Cleve. Chamber Symphony, N.Y. New Music Ensemble; compositions performed at Carnegie Hall, Dorothy Chandler Pavilion, Town Hall, Weill (Carnegie) Recital Hall, and many others; reviewer High Performance Rev. Mag., 1987—. Recipient 3rd prize, People's prize Internat. Gaudeamus Competition, The Netherlands, 1977, Helen L. Weiss prize U. Pa., 1979, David Halstead prize U. Penn., 1980, 3rd prize Shreveport Symphony Composer's Competition, 1980-81, John H. Bearns prize, 1981, 1st. prize Holtkamp Organ Composition Contest, 1982, Eda and Boris Rappoport prize Columbia U., 1984, Tanglewood prize in Composition Berkshire Music Ctr., 1984, Cleve. Arts prize, 1992; recipient Mader Meml. Fund Recognition award, 1980, BMI Student Composers award, 1982; New Music Consort Composition Contest winner, 1987, League of Composers ISCM winner, 1988; Fine Arts scholar Cleve. State U., 1974-78, scholar Cleve. Fortnightly Music Club, 1976-78, Arthur Loesser Meml. scholar, 1977-78, Yale Composer's Workshop at Norfolk, 1981, Columbia U. scholar, 1981-82, Charles Ives scholar Am. Acad. Inst. Arts & Letters, 1985; U. fellow U. Penn., 1978-79, Composers Conf. Johnson Vt., 1979, 80, CBS Found. fellow U. Penn., 1979-80, Margaret Lee Crofts fellow Berkshire Music Ctr. Tanglewood, 1984, Guggenheim fellow, 1985, NEA, 1991-92, Goddard Lieberson fellow Am. Acad. Arts and Letters, 1993, Pew fellow in arts, 1996; ASCAP Found. Young Composers grant, 1984, 82, Meet The Composer grant 1980, 82, 85, 87, 89, 90, 94, 96, Am. Music Ctr. Copying Assistance grant, 1985, 90, Penn. Coun. On The Arts, 1990, Presser Found. grant U. Penn. Mem. BMI, Pi Kappa Lambda. Roman Catholic. Avocation: reading.

PRINA, L(OUIS) EDGAR, journalist; b. West New York, N.J., Oct. 7, 1917; s. Louis Edgar and Marion (Duggan) P.; m. Frances Lee Lorick, Feb. 14, 1947; 1 dau., Lee Lorick II. A.B., Syracuse U., 1938, M.A., 1940. Copy editor, asst. night city editor N.Y. Sun, N.Y.C., 1946-48; Washington corr. N.Y. Sun, 1948-50; nat. affairs writer Washington Star, 1950-66; mil. affairs writer/editor Copley News Svc., Washington, 1966-77; bur. chief Copley News Svc., 1977-84, sr. corr., 1984-87; editor Navy mag., Washington, 1961-68; columnist Sea Power mag., 1968—. Author: The Political Virgin, 1958, Flew to South Pole for Overnight Visit, 1966. Served with USN, 1941-46, 51-53; capt. Res. (ret.). Recipient honorable mentionHeywood Broun award, 1956, Disting. Public Svc. award USN, 1965, Alfred Thayer Mahan award Navy League U.S., 1987, Copley Ring of Truth award, 1971, 74-76, 79, 80-81; nominated for Pulitzer Prize (twice). Mem. U.S. Naval Inst., Nat. Press Club (chmn. bd. govs.), White House Corrs. Assn., Explorers Club, Soc. Profl. Journalists (pres. Washington chpt.), Kappa Sigma, Phi Kappa Phi. Roman Catholic. Clubs: Gridiron, Chevy Chase, Met. of Washington. Home: 4813 Quebec St NW Washington DC 20016-3228 Office: The Metro Club National Press Bldg PO Box 47 Washington DC 20006

PRINCE (PRINCE ROGERS NELSON), musician, actor; b. Mpls., June 7, 1958; s. John L. and Mattie D. (Shaw) Nelson; m. Mayte Garcia, 1996; 1 son (dec.). Singer, songwriter, actor. Albums include For You, 1978, Dirty Mind, 1979, Controversy, 1981, 1999, 1983, film star and soundtrack Purple Rain, 1984, Around the World in a Day, 1985 (Best Soul/Rhythm and Blues Album of the Yr., Downbeat readers poll, 1985), Parade, 1986, Sign O' the Times, 1987, Lovesexy, 1988, Batman: Motion Picture Soundtrack, 1989 (Soundtrack of Yr. award Playboy mag. readers' poll, Best Pop/Rock album Downbeat mag. readers' poll), (with the New Power Generation) Diamonds and Pearls, 1991, (symbol as title), 1992, Come, 1994; films include Purple Rain, 1984 (Acad. award for best original score 1985), film star and soundtrack Under the Cherry Moon, 1986, film star and soundtrack Sign O' the Times, 1987; film appearance and soundtrack Graffiti Bridge, 1990; formerly mem. group Prince and the Revolution (Best Soul/Rhythm and Blues Group of Yr. Downbeat mag. readers poll 1985); composer Showgirls, 1995, Girl 6, 1996, Chaos & Disorder, 1996. Recipient 3 Grammy awards, 1985, Am. Music Achievement award for infuence on look and sound of the 80's; named Rhythm and Blues Musician of Yr. Down Beat mag. readers' poll, 1984, 1992. also: Warner Bros Records 75 Rockefeller Plz New York NY 10019*

PRINCE, ALAN THEODORE, former government official, engineering consultant; b. Toronto, Can., Feb. 15, 1915; s. Theodore and Sarah Helena (McMillan) P.; m. Virginia C. Lea, May 30, 1942; children: Linda Lea Prince Anderson, Mary Catherine Prince Kaschub. BA, U. Toronto, 1937, MA, 1938; PhD, U. Chgo., 1941. Registered profl. engr., Ont. With div. chemistry Nat. Research Council Can., Ottawa, 1940-43, Can. Refractories Ltd., Kilmar, Que., 1943-45; lectr. geology U. Man., 1945-46; with Canadian Dept. Mines and Tech. Surveys, 1946-67, dir. water research br., 1965-67; dir. inland waters br. Dept. Environment, 1967-73; asst. dep. minister planning and evaluation Dept. Energy, Mines and Resources, 1973-75; pres. Atomic Energy Control Bd., Ottawa, 1975-79; cons. Fellow Chem. Inst. Can., Mineral. Soc. Am.; mem. Canadian Inst. Mining and Metallurgy, Assn. Profl. Engrs. Ont. Home: 5445 Riverside Dr, PO Box 106, Manotick, ON Canada K4M 1A2

PRINCE, ANDREW STEVEN, lawyer, former government official; b. Bklyn., Oct. 9, 1943; s. Milton S. and Beatrice M. (Ratkin) P.; m. Rochelle Moskowitz, July 4, 1973; children: Brett, Kenneth. B.S., U.S. Naval Acad., 1965; M.B.A., Harvard U., 1974, J.D., 1974. Bar: N.Y. 1975, U.S. Supreme Ct. 1980. Assoc. firm Shearman & Sterling, N.Y.C., 1974-81; dep. asst. sec. Navy Dept., Washington, 1981-86; exec. v.p. fin., gen. counsel Urquhart and Co., Inc., McLean, Va., 1986-94; pres. BretKen Enterprises, McLean, Va., 1994—; sec. Potash Import & Chem. Corp., N.Y.C., 1979-81; mem. panel of arbitrators Am. Arbitration Assn., N.Y.C., 1979—. Bd. dirs. Harvard Coop. Soc., Cambridge, Mass., 1972-74; bd. dirs. USO, Washington, 1982—, N.Y.C., 1979-81. Served with USN, 1965-70; capt. Res. Mem. Harvard Bus. Sch. Club (exec. v.p.), Mil Order World Wars (judge adv.), Naval Acad. Alumni Assn.

PRINCE, DONNA JEAN, artist; b. L.A., Feb. 3, 1954; d. Robert Henry and Anna Marie (Estatico) P.; m. Donald James Molyneux, Sept. 2, 1989. BA with honors, Art Ctr. Coll. of Design, 1989. Key background painter Queen of the Universe Prodn., L.A., 1990, Disney TV Animation, N. Hollywood, 1995—; background painter Turner Publ., Hollywood, Calif., 1991, Hanna Barbera, Hollywood, 1991-92, Rich Animation, Burbank, Calif., 1993-94. Mem. neighborhood activist Friends of Washington Park, Pasadena, 1991-96, workshop presenter Neighborhoods USA Conf. Pasadena, 1994. Recipient Vol. award City of Pasadena Parks & Recs., 1995. Mem. Motion Picture Screen Cartoonists Guild, Friends of Washington Park (pres. 1991-94), Soc. of Illustrators (v.p. 1991). Democrat. Avocations: gardening, traveling, shopping, dancing, interior decorating. Home: 1277 N El Molino Ave Pasadena CA 91104-2839 Office: Disney TV Animation 5200 Lankershim Blvd Ste 600 North Hollywood CA 91601-3100

PRINCE, FRANCES ANNE KIELY, civic worker; b. Toledo, Dec. 20, 1923; d. John Thomas and Frances (Pusteoska) Kiely; m. Richard Edward Prince, Jr., Aug. 27, 1951; children: Anne, Richard III (dec.). Student U. Louisville, 1947-49; AB, Berea Coll., 1951; postgrad., Kent Sch. Social Work, 1951, Creighton U., 1969; MPA, U. Nebr., Omaha, 1978. Instr. flower arranging Western Wyo. Jr. Coll., 1965, 66; editor Nebr. Garden News, 1979-81, 83-90, emeritus, 1990. Author poems. Chmn. Lone Troop coun. Girl Scouts U.S.A., 1954-57, trainer leaders, 1954-68, mem. state camping com., 1959-61, bd. dirs. Wyo. state coun., 1966-69; chmn. Cmty. Improvement, Green River, Wyo., 1959, 63-65, Wyo. Fedn. Women's Clubs State Libr. Svcs., 1966-69; mem. Wyo. State Adv. Bd. on Libr. Inter-Co-op., 1965-69, state libr. bd., 1965-69, Nat. sub com. Commn. on the Bicentennial of the U.S. Constitution, 1986-91; bd. dirs. Sweetwater County Libr. System, 1962-69, pres. bd., 1967-68; adv. coun. Sch. Dist. 66, 1970-79; bd. dirs. Opera Angels, 1971, fund raising chmn., 1971-72, v.p., 1974-80; bd. dirs. Morning Musicale, 1971-82; bazaar com. Children's Hosp., 1970-75; docent Joslyn Art Mus., 1970—; mem. Nebr. Forestry Adv. Bd., 1976—; citizens adv. bd. Met. Area Planning Agy., 1979—; mem. Nebr. Tree-Planting Commn., 1980—; bd. dirs. U.S. Constn. Bicentennial Commn. Nebr., 1986-92, Omaha Commn. on the Bicentennial, 1987-92, Nat. commn. on Bicentennial of U.S. Constitution, 1986-92; bd. dirs. United Ch. Christ, Intermountain, 1963-69, mem. exec. com., 1966-69. Recipient Libr. Svc. award Sweetwater County Library, 1968; Girl Scout Svcs. award, 1967; Conservation award U.S. Forest Service, 1981; Plant Two Trees award, 1981; Nat. Arbor Day award, 1982; Pres. award Nat. coun. of State Garden Clubs, 1986, 87, 89, Joyce Kilmer award Nat. Arbor Day Found., 1990; awards U.S. Constn. Bicentennial Commn. Nebr., 1987, 91, Omaha Commn. on the Bicentennial, 1987, Nat. Bicentennial Leadership award Coun. for Advancement of Citizenship, 1989, Nat. Conservation medal DAR, 1991, George Washington silver award Nat. commn. on Bicentennial of U.S. Constitution, 1992, Mighty Oak award Garden Clubs of Nebr., 1992. Mem. ALA, AAUW (Vol. of Yr. Omaha br. 1989), New Neighbors League (dir. 1969-71), Ikebana Internat., Symphony Guild, Assistance League Omaha, Omaha Playhouse Guild, Nebr. Libr. Assn., Omaha Coun. Garden Clubs (1st v.p. 1972, pres. 1973-75, state bd. dirs. 1979—, mem. nat. council bd. dirs. 1979—, pres. award 1988, 89, 90), Internat. Platform Assn., Internat. Poets Soc. (Disting. mem. 1996), Nat. Trust for Hist. Preservation, Nebr. Flower Show Judges Coun. (chmn. 1995—), Nat. Coun. State Garden Clubs (chmn. arboriculture 1985-90, 93—, chmn. nature conservancy 1991-93), Nebr. Fedn. Garden Clubs (pres. 1978-81), Garden Club (dir. 1970-72, pres. 1972-75). Home: 8909 Broadmoor Dr Omaha NE 68114-4248

PRINCE, FRANK MICHAEL, lawyer; b. Atlanta, Feb. 6, 1946; s. Frank Henry and Madge (Lowe) P.; m. Kathleen McMillan, Jan. 10, 1970; 1 child, Rebekah Kathleen. BA in Polit. Sci., Randolph Macon Coll., 1968; JD, U. Ga., 1977. Bar: Ga. 1977, Tex. 1978, U.S. Dist. Ct. (no. dist.) Tex. 1979, U.S. Ct. Appeals (5th cir.) 1980. Assoc. Carrington, Coleman, Sloman & Blumenthal, Dallas, 1977-84, ptnr., 1984—. Pres. City of Richardson (Tex.) Swimming Assn., 1982-85, chmn., 1986-89; block chmn. YMCA Fund Com., Richardson, 1983-85. Capt. USNR, 1968-96, ret. Mem. ABA, State Bar of Ga., State Bar of Tex. (profl. liability ins. com. 1987-91, adminstr. rules of evidence com. 1988-90, ct. costs & efficiency com. 1989-91, chair 1995-96), Dallas Bar Assn. (awards com. 1979-80), Naval Res. Assn., Law Enforcement Assistance Assn., Order of Barristers, Phi Beta Kappa, Omicron Delta Kappa. Methodist. Avocations: fishing, aerobics. Office: Carrington Coleman Sloman & Blumenthal 200 Crescent Ct Ste 1500 Dallas TX 75201-7839

PRINCE, GARNETT B., JR., business executive; b. Chattanooga, Feb. 1, 1949; w. Garnett B. and Anna Mae (Elrod) P.; m. Deborah Roemer, Jan. 19, 1971 (div.); m. Charlotte V. McCauley, July 23, 1983; children: Shelly McCauley, Becky, Brandon. Student radio and TV broadcasting, Coastal Carolina Community Coll., Jacksonville, N.C., 1971; student, No. Va. Community Coll., Sterling, 1979-80. Dep. ct. clerk Criminal Ct., Chattanooga, 1971-73; dist. field rep. VA, Chattanooga, 1973-76; leadership tng. cons. Nat. Vocat.-Indsl. Clubs Am., Leesburg, Va., 1976-78, dir. tng. and govt. relations, 1978-84; spl. asst. to sec. U.S. Dept. Labor, Washington, 1984-85; dep. asst. sec. for vets. employment and tng. U.S. Dept. Labor, 1985-88; dep. dir. Nat. Drug Policy Bd., Office of Pres., Washington, 1988-89; regional mgr. state govt. affairs Parke-Davis div. Warner-Lambert Co., Atlanta, 1989—; dir. fed. health care policy Warner-Lambert Co., Washington, 1991—, dir. govt. devel., 1995—. Co-author: The Meetings Kit, 1985. Trustee U.S. Internat. Youth Yr. Com., Washington, 1985. Served with USMC, 1967-71. Mem. Mil. Order Purple Heart, DAV, VFW, Am. Legion. Republican. Lodge: Masons. Avocations: golf; bowling; swimming. Home: 17 Uvilla Est Shenandoah Junction WV 25442-9538 Office: 1667 K St NW Ste 1270 Washington DC 20006-1686

PRINCE, GEORGE EDWARD, pediatrician; b. Erwin, N.C., Nov. 25, 1921; s. Hugh Williamson and Helen Herman (Hood) P.; m. Millie Elizabeth Mann, Nov. 26, 1944; children: Helen Elizabeth, Millie Mann, Susan Hood, Mary Lois. MD, Duke U., 1944. Diplomate Am. Bd. Pediatrics, Am. Bd. Med. Examiners. Intern Boston Children's Hosp. Harvard Svc., Boston, 1944-45; resident pediatrics Children's Hosp., Louisville, 1945-47; instr. pediatrics U. Louisville, 1947; founder Gastonia (N.C.) Children's Clinic, 1947, pediatrician, 1947-86; pub. health physician Gaston County Health Dept., Gastonia, N.C., 1986-97, med. dir., 1995-97; chmn. bd. dirs. Carolina State Bank; bd. dirs. So. Nat. Bank, Gastonia, 1979-95, Hospice, Gastonia, 1987-92; organizer, dir. AIDS Adv. Coun., Gaston County, N.C., 1988-94; coord. N.C. chpt. Pediatric Rsch. in Office Setting, 1986-92. Contbr. articles to profl. jours. Mem. Gaston County Human Rels. Com., Gastonia, 1966; mem. Sch. Health Adv. Coun., Gaston County, 1980-97. Maj. USAF, 1955-57. Recipient Balthis Heart Assn. award Gaston County, 1981, Good Ambassador award Health Dept., 1986, Family Adv. award Commn. on the Family, Gaston County, 1995. Fellow Am. Acad. Pediatrics (pres. N.C. chpt. 1984-86); mem. AMA, N.C. Pediatric Soc. (hon., pres. 1970), N.C. Med. Soc., Gaston County Med. Soc. (pres. 1966), Rotary (pres. 1984), County Club (bd. dirs. 1975-76). Democrat. Methodist. Avocations: golf, flying, skiing, sailing, bridge. Home: 2208 Cross Creek Dr Gastonia NC 28056-8808 Office: Gaston County Health Dept 991 Hudson Blvd Gastonia NC 28052-6430

PRINCE, GERALD JOSEPH, Romance languages educator; b. Alexandria, Egypt, Nov. 7, 1942; came to U.S., 1959, naturalized, 1964; s. Tully Rudolph and Marguerite (Bigio) P.; m. Ellen Friedman, June 25, 1967. B.A., Bklyn. Coll., 1963; M.A., U. Fla., 1963; Ph.D., Brown U., 1968. Instr. French lang. U. Pa., Phila., 1967-68, asst. prof., 1968-73, assoc. prof., 1973-81, prof. Romance langs., 1981—, chmn. comparative lit. program, 1984-87; co-dir. Ctr. Cultural Studies, 1987—. Author: Métaphysique et Technique dans l'Oeuvre Romanesque de Sartre, 1968, A Grammar of Stories, 1973, Narratology: The Form and Function of Narrative, 1982, A Dictionary of Narratology, 1987, Narrative as Theme, 1992. Contbr. articles and revs. to scholarly jours. Recipient award of honor, Bklyn. Coll., 1978, Lindback award for excellence in teaching U. Pa., 1974. Mem. MLA, N.E. MLA (officer 1983-86), Am. Comparative Lit. Assn. (adv. bd. 1983-87), Phi Beta Kappa, Phi Kappa Phi, Pi Delta Phi. Office: Ctr Cultural Studies Univ Pa 521 Williams Hall Philadelphia PA 19104

PRINCE, GREGORY SMITH, JR., academic administrator; b. Washington, May 7, 1939; s. Gregory Smith and Margaret (Minor) P.; m. Toni Layton Brewer; children: Tara Wyndom, Gregory S. III. BA, Yale U., 1961, M in Philosophy, 1969, PhD, 1973; cert. in teaching English as a Second Language, Georgetown U., 1961; DHL (hon.), Amherst Coll., 1991, LLD (hon.), 1991. Instr. New Asia Coll., Kowloon, Hong Kong, 1961-62, Chinese U., Kowloon, 1962-63, Yale China Assn., Kowloon, 1961-63, Woodberry Forest (Va.) Sch., 1963-65; dean summer programs Dartmouth Coll., Hanover, N.H., 1970-72, asst. dean faculty, 1972-78, assoc. dean faculty, 1978-89; pres. Hampshire Coll., Amherst, Mass., 1989—; mem. coun. on race and ethnic justice ABA; bd. dirs. Mass Ventures. Producer: (film) A Way of Learning, 1988. Trustee Montshire Mus. Sci., Hanover, 1973-89, Washington Campus, 1978—; trustee, chmn. Univ. Press New England, Hanover, 1983-84; trustee, pres. Yale-China Assn., New Haven, 1969-84; bd. dirs., pres. Five Colls., Inc., Amherst, 1989—; bd. dirs. Mass. Internat. Festival for Arts, 1994—; chmn. bd. dirs. Assn. Ind. Colls. and Univs. Mass., 1994-95; mem. commn. on accreditation Am. Coun. Edn.; bd. dirs. Mass. Nature Conservancy, 1996—. Coe fellow Stanford U., 1965, Woodrow Wilson fellow Yale U., 1966, NDEA fellow, 1967-70. Mem. Internat. Assn. of Chiefs Police Found. (bd. dirs. 1991-95). Democrat. Episcopalian. Home: 15 Middle St Amherst MA 01002-3009 Office: Hampshire Coll 893 West St Amherst MA 01002-3372

PRINCE, HAROLD, theatrical producer; b. N.Y.C., Jan. 30, 1928; s. Milton A. and Blanche (Stern) P.; m. Judith Chaplin, Oct. 26, 1962; children: Charles, Daisy. AB, U. Pa., 1948, DFA (hon.), 1971; LittD, Emerson Coll., 1971. chmn. Performing Arts Libr., N.Y.C. Co-prodr.: Pajama Game, 1954-56 (Antoinette Perry award), Damn Yankees, 1955-57 (Antoinette Perry award), New Girl in Town, 1957-58, West Side Story, 1957-59, A Swim in the Sea, 1958, Fiorello, 1959-61 (Antoinette Perry award, Pulitzer prize), Tenderloin, 1960-61, A Call on Kuprin, 1961, They Might Be Giants, London, 1961, Side by Side by Sondheim, 1977; prodr.: Take Her, She's Mine, 1961-62, A Funny Thing Happened on the Way to the Forum, 1962-64 (Antoinette Perry award), Fiddler on the Roof, 1964-72 (Antoinette Perry award), Poor Bitos, 1964, Flora the Red Menace, 1965; dir., prodr.: She Loves Me, 1963-64, London, 1964, Superman, 1966, Cabaret, 1966-69 (Antoinette Perry award 1968), Zorba, 1968-69, Company, 1970-72 (Antoinette Perry award 1972), A Little Night Music, 1973-74 (Antoinette Perry award 1975), Pacific Overtures, 1976, A Doll's Life, 1982; co-dir., prodr.: Follies, 1971-72 (Tony award for directing), Faust, 1990; co-prodr., dir.: Candide, 1974-75 (Tony award for directing), Merrily We Roll Along, 1981; dir.: A Family Affair, 1962, Baker Street, 1965, Great God Brown, 1972-73, The Visit, 1973-74, Love for Love, 1974-75, Ashmedai, 1976, Some of My Best Friends, 1977, On The Twentieth Century, 1978, La Fanciulla Del West, 1978, Evita, London, 1979, N.Y.C., 1980, L.A., 1982, Australia, 1980, Chgo., 1980, Detroit, 1982, Sweeney Todd, The Demon Barber of Fleet Street, Broadway, 1979, London, 1980, Silverlake, 1980, Willie Stark, 1981, Candide, 1982, 94, 97, Madama Butterfly, 1983, Turandot, 1983, Play Memory, 1984, End of the World, 1984, Grind, 1985, Cabaret Revival, 1987, Roza, 1987, Phantom of the Opera, London, 1986, N.Y.C., (Antoinette Perry award) 1988, Roza, 1987, Cabaret, 1987, Kiss of the Spider Woman, Toronto, 1992, London, 1992, N.Y.C., 1993, Show Boat, Toronto, 1993, N.Y.C., 1994 (Tony award for directing), La Fanciula del West, Don Giovanni, N.Y. City Opera, 1989, Faust, Met. Opera, 1990, The Petrified Prince, 1994, Whistle Down the Wind, 1997, (off broadway) Diamonds, 1984; adapter, dir. (off broadway) Grandchild of Kings, 1992, Whistle Down The Wind, Broadway, 1997, Candide, Broadway, 1997; co-prodr: (films) The Pajama Game, 1957, Damn Yankees, 1958; dir.: (films) Something for Everyone, 1970, A Little Night Music, 1978. Mem. coun. Nat. Endowment Arts; pres. League N.Y. Theatres, 1964-66; chmn. Performing Arts Libr., N.Y.C. Recipient 20 Antoinette Perry (Tony) Meml. awards, Critics Circle awards, Pulitzer prize, 1961, Best Mus. awards London Evening Std., Kennedy Ctr. Honors, 1994. Office: 10 Rockefeller Plz New York NY 10020-1903

PRINCE, JERRY LADD, engineering educator; b. Manchester, Conn., Aug. 10, 1957; s. Ralph Peery and Lela (Ladd) P.; m. Carol Ann Morello, June 12, 1982; children: Emily, Benjamin, Mark, David. SM, MIT, 1982, PhD, 1988. Rsch. asst. MIT, Cambridge, 1979-82; engr. Brigham and Women's Hosp., Boston, 1982-83; teaching asst. MIT, Cambridge, 1983-84, rsch. asst., 1984-88; mem. tech. staff The Analytical Scis. Corp., Reading, Mass., 1988; asst. prof. Johns Hopkins U., Balt., 1989-94, assoc. prof. elec. and computer engring., 1994—. Contbr. articles to profl. jours. Presdl. faculty fellow NSF, 1993. Mem. IEEE (sr., assoc. editor Transactions on Image Processing 1992-95), Sigma Xi. Office: Johns Hopkins Univ 3400 N Charles St Baltimore MD 21218-2608

PRINCE, JOHN LUTHER, III, engineering educator; b. Austin, Tex., Nov. 13, 1941; s. John Luther and Glynda (Chollett) P.; m. Martha Ann Hight, Mar. 4, 1960; children: Cynthia Kay, John Luther IV, Alan Douglas, David William. BSEE, So. Meth. U., 1965; MEE, N.C. State U., 1968, PhD, 1969. Research engr. RTI, Res. Tri. Park, N.C., 1968-70; mem. tech. staff Tex. Instruments, Dallas, 1970-75; from assoc. prof. to prof. Clemson (S.C.) U., 1975-80; dir. R.A. Intermedics, Inc., Freeport, Tex., 1980-83; prof. U. Ariz., Tucson, 1983—; acting dir. packaging scis. Semiconductor Rsch. Corp., 1991-92; cons. numerous semi-conductor and electronics cos., 1983—; dir. Electronic Packaging Lab., 1984-91, Ctr. for Electronic Packaging Rsch., 1991—, SEMATECH Ctr. of Excellence for Contamination and Defect Control, 1988-90. Contbr. articles to profl. jours. Named Ariz. Innovator of the Yr., 1992; NSF fellow, 1965-68. Fellow IEEE; mem. Am. Philatelic Soc. Lutheran. Avocations: stamp collecting, classic cars, motorcycles. Home: 7542 N San Lorenzo Dr Tucson AZ 85704-3141 Office: U Ariz Dept of Engineering Tucson AZ 85721

PRINCE, KENNETH STEPHEN, lawyer; b. Newton, Mass., Jan. 28, 1950; s. Samuel and Edna L. Prince; m. Patricia Denning, Jan. 15, 1977 (dec. Nov. 1985); 1 child, Kenneth Stephen Jr.; m. Jane M. McCabe, Sept. 5, 1987; 1 child, Allison Pamela. BA, U. Pa., 1972; JD, Boston Coll., 1975. Bar: N.Y. 1976, Mass. 1975, U.S. Dist. Ct. (so. and ea. dists.) N.Y. 1978. Assoc. Shearman & Sterling, N.Y.C., 1975-83, ptnr., 1984—; antitrust group practice leader Shearman & Sterling, 1992—. Mem. N.Y. Law Inst. (exec. com. 1984-96), Order of Coif. Office: Shearman & Sterling Citicorp Ctr 153 E 53rd St New York NY 10022-4611

PRINCE, LARRY L., automotive parts and supplies company executive; b. 1937. With Genuine Parts Co., Atlanta, 1958—, v.p., then group v.p., 1977-83, exec. v.p., 1983-86, pres., chief oper. officer, 1986-90, chief exec. officer, 1989—, chmn. bd. dirs., 1990—, also bd. dirs. Office: Genuine Parts Co 2999 Circle 75 Pky NW Atlanta GA 30339-3050*

PRINCE, LEAH FANCHON, art educator and research institute administrator; b. Hartford, Conn., Aug. 12, 1939; d. Meyer and Annie (Forman) Berman; m. Herbert N. Prince, Jan. 30, 1955; children: Daniel L., Richard N., Robert G. Student, U. Conn., 1957-59, Rutgers U., Newark, 1962; BFA, Fairleigh Dickinson U., 1970; postgrad., Caldwell Coll. for Women, 1973-75, Parsons Sch. of Design, N.Y.C., 1978. Cert. tchr. art, N.J. Tchr. art Caldwell-West Caldwell (N.J.) Pub. Schs., 1970-75; pres. Britannia Imports Ltd., Fairfield, N.J., 1979-89; tchr. religious studies Bohrer-Kaufman Hebrew Acad., Randolph, N.J., 1981-82; co-founder and corp. sec. Gibraltar Biol. Labs., Inc., Fairfield, 1970—; dir., co-founder Gibraltar Inst. for Rsch. and Tng., Fairfield, 1984—; cons. Internat. Antiques and Fine Arts Industries, U.K., 1979-89; cons. in art exhibitry Passaic County Coll., Paterson, N.J., 1989-93; art curator Fairleigh Dickinson U., Rutherford, N.J., 1972-74; curator history of design Bloomfield (N.J.) Coll., 1990-91; lectr. nat. meeting Am. Soc. Microbiology, New Orleans, 1989; spkr. in field. Exhibited in group shows at Bloomfield (N.J.) Coll., 1990, Caldwell Coll. Women's Club, N.J., 1991, State Fedn. Women's Clubs Ann. Show, 1992 (1st pl. award 1992), Newark Art Mus., 1992, West (N.J.) Essex Art Assn., 1990, Somerset (N.J.) Art Assn. Ann. Juried Show, 1994, Mortimer Gallery, Gladstone, N.J., 1994, Tewksbury His. Soc. (1st pl. award 1994); one-woman shows include Passaic County Coll., N.J., 1990, Caldwell Coll., N.J., 1990. Chair ann. juried art awards Arts Coun. of Essex Bd. Trustees, Montclair, N.J., 1984-90; chair fundraising Arts Coun. Essex County, N.J., 1989. Recipient 1st place award N.J. Tewksbury Hist. Soc., 1994. Mem. AAUW, Somerset Art Assn., Nat. Mus. of Women in the Arts, Barnegat Light Yacht Club. Republican. Avocations: boating, tennis, the Arts. Home: Mendham Twp 5 Standish Dr Morristown NJ 07960-3224

PRINCE, LESLIE FRANCIS, lobbyist, activist; b. Parika Village, Essequibo, Guyana, Jan. 23, 1950; came ot US, Dec. 1981; s. George Vernon Johnson and Olga Maude (Benjamin) P.; m. Marva Eugene, Oct. 31, 1981; children: Sharon, Natasha, Christie, Tracey, Kimberly. Student, Guyana Youth Corps; graduate, Aeronautical Acad. Rio de Janeiro, Brazil, 1977; Certificate in Spanish, U. Guyana, 1980; AA, Medgar Evers Coll., 1994; student, Hunter Coll., 1996—. Licensed airline pilot, Brazil, US DOT, FAA. Pilot VARIG, British Caledonian Airway, Brazil; cons. Prince Svcs. Internat., Inc. Founder, exec. pres. Guyana Rep. Party, 1985—; established govt. in exile, 1989; official ACTS/VIM com. Episcopal Ch. Archdiocese of Newark, mem. bd., 1995—. Sgt. Guyanese army, 1968. Mem. Guyanese Am. C. of C. (founder, editor newsletter, chmn. 1995—), Rosicrucian Order (lodge custodian 1977). Republican. Avocations: boxing, cricket, car races, motor boat races, airshows. Home: 381 Broad St # A-617 Newark NJ 07104-3363 Office: Guyanese Am C of C 2210 Church Ave Brooklyn NY 11226-3202

PRINCE, MILTON S., investment company executive; b. Bklyn., Jan. 20, 1912; s. Abraham and Frances (Raps) P.; m. Beatrice Ratzkin, Jan. 18, 1942; children: Andrew, Thomas. BS, Carnegie Inst. Tech., 1935; LLB, St. Johns U., Bklyn., 1938, JSD, 1939. Bar: N.Y. 1940, U.S. Dist. Ct. (ea. and so. dists.) N.Y. 1950, U.S. Ct. Mil. Appeals, U.S. Supreme Ct. 1954. Sole practice, Bklyn., 1940-41; mng. ptnr., gen. counsel Prince & Prince, Bklyn., 1946—. Trustee U.S. Naval Acad. Found., Annapolis, Md., 1964—; dir., excom. USO, N.Y.C., 1965—; nat. council mem., Bklyn. council officer, dir. Boy Scouts Am., Irving, Tex. and Bklyn., 1972—; state advisor U.S. Congl. Adv. Bd., 1982-88. Served with USN, 1941-45, to capt. USNR, to rear admiral N.Y. State Naval Militia, 1955—. Recipient USN Disting. Pub. Svc. award, 1972, Shofar award Boy Scouts Am., 1984, Bklyn. citation, 1990; decorated various medals Dept. Def. Mem. Navy League U.S. (nat. dir., officer 1962—), U.S. Naval Inst. (silver), ABA, Mil. Order World Wars (dir., past comdr. 1966-67, Meritorious Achievement award 1964), Naval Order U.S. (ex. com. 1960-88), Salmagundi Club (N.Y.C.), Coasters Harbor Yacht Club (Newport, R.I.), Mcpl. Club, Bklyn. Club, Army-Navy Club (Washington), Rotary. Avocations: sailing, golf, travel, pub. service.

PRINCE, MORTON BRONENBERG, physicist; b. Phila., Apr. 1, 1924; s. David H. and Jennie (Bronenberg) P.; m. Blanche E. Stern, June 15, 1947; 1 child, Judith Ann. A.B., Temple U., 1947; Ph.D., MIT, 1951. Mem. tech. staff Bell Telephone Labs., Inc., Murray Hill, N.J., 1951-56; v.p., gen. mgr. Hoffman Electronics Corp., El Monte, Calif., 1956-61; with electro optical systems div. Xerox, Pasadena, Calif., 1961-69; pres. SSR Instruments Co., Santa Monica, Calif., 1970-74; v.p., gen. mgr. Meret Inc., Santa Monica, 1974-75; with U.S. Dept. Energy, Washington, 1975-93. Contbr. chpts. to books, articles to profl. jours. Served with U.S. Army, 1943-46. Recipient Marconi premium Inst. Radio Engrs., Gt. Britain, 1959, Becquerel prize European Commn., 1994. Fellow IEEE; mem. Am. Phys. Soc., Internat. Solar Energy Soc. Club: Cosmos. Home: 7301 Coventry Ave Apt 601 Elkins Park PA 19027-2953

PRINCE, OLIVER GILBERT, JR., human resources professional; b. Atlanta, Sept. 1, 1953; s. Oliver Gilbert and Bessie Mae (Hutchinson) P.; children: Sara Maria, Oliver Geoffrey. BA, Morehouse Coll., 1975; JD, John Marshall Law Sch., 1981; MBA, Ga. State U., 1987. Asst. mgr. food svc., asst. ops. mgr., then mgr. ops. Six Flags Over Ga., Atlanta, 1975-87; facility analyst CNA Ins. Cos., Chgo., 1987-88, mgr. facility planning and design, 1988-90, mgr. corp. real estate, 1990-92, asst. v.p. corporate real estate, 1992-94, also treas., to 1994; asst. v.p. CNA Cons. Group, 1994-95, v.p. human resources svcs., 1995-97; sr. v.p. human resources The Celtic Group, Chgo., 1997—. Bd. dirs., mem. resource devel. com. Chgo. Coalition for Homeless, 1992; trustee, chmn. long range planning The Asheville (N.C.) Sch., 1994—. Avocations: running, golf, tennis, photography, guitar. Home: 655 W Irving Park Rd Apt 4817 Chicago IL 60613-3138 Office: The Celtic Group Sears Tower 233 S Wacker Dr Ste 700 Chicago IL 60606-6300

PRINCE, ROBB LINCOLN, manufacturing company executive; b. Duluth, Minn., June 30, 1941; s. Milton H. and Katherine (Lincoln) P.; m. Jacqueline H. Marik, June 19, 1965; children: Daniel, Deborah. BA in Econs., Carleton Coll., 1963; MBA in Mktg., U. Pa., 1965. With mktg. planning United Airlines, Chgo., 1965-72; dir. planning Jostens Inc., Mpls., 1973-74, treas., 1975-79, v.p., treas., 1979-95, ret., 1995; dir. FORTIS Mut. Funds, Analysts Internat. Corp. Trustee Hamline U. With USN, 1966-69. Mem. Wharton Alumni Club (bd. dirs.). Office: 5108 Duggan Plz Edina MN 55439-1453

PRINCE, THOMAS RICHARD, accountant, educator; b. New Albany, Miss., Dec. 7, 1934; s. James Thompson and Callie Florence (Howell) P.; m. Eleanor Carol Polkoff, July 14, 1962; children: Thomas Andrew, John Michael, Adrienne Carol. B.S., Miss. State U., 1956, M.S., 1957; Ph.D. in Accountancy, U. Ill., 1962. C.P.A., Ill. Instr. U. Ill., 1960-62; mem. faculty Northwestern U., 1962—, prof. acctg. and info. systems, 1969—, chmn. dept. accounting and info. systems Grad. Sch. Mgmt., 1968-75, prof. health svcs. mgmt., 1980—; cons. in field; dir. Applied Research Systems, Inc. Author: Extension of the Boundaries of Accounting Theory, 1962, Information Systems for Management Planning and Control, 3d edit, 1975, Financial Reporting and Cost Control for Health Care Entities, 1992. Served to 1st lt. AUS, 1957-60. Mem. Am. Accounting Assn., Am. Inst. C.P.A.s, Am. Econ. Assn., Inst. Mgmt. Scis., Fin. Execs. Inst., AAAS, Ill. Soc. C.P.A.s,, Nat. Assn. Accts., Alpha Tau Omega, Phi Kappa Phi, Omicron Delta Kappa, Delta Sigma Pi, Beta Alpha Psi. Congregationalist. Home: 303 Richmond Rd Kenilworth IL 60043-1138 Office: Northwestern U Leverone Hall Evanston IL 60208

PRINCE, WILLIAM J., church officer; m. Evelyn Imel; 1 child. 4th pres. Mt. Vernon Nazarene Coll., 1980-89; pres. So. Nazarene U., 1989; bd. gen. supts. Ch. of the Nazarene, Indpls., 1989—; former supt. Pitts. dist.; pres. European Nazarene Bible Coll., 1970-76; pastor Lone Pine, Reseda and Ventura, Calif., Mpls., and Dayton; min. teaching and preaching missions in Haiti, Guatemala, South Africa, Zambia, Zimbabwe, Swaziland, Kenya; leader preacher missions in Hawaii; participant European Congress on Evangelism, Amsterdam, The Netherlands; speaker to students, Shanghai, 1989; speaker commencement Luzon Nazarene Theol. Sem. Office: Church of Nazarene 6401 Paseo Blvd Kansas City MO 64131-1213*

PRINCE, WILLIAM TALIAFERRO, federal judge; b. Norfolk, Va., Oct. 3, 1929; s. James Edward and Helen Marie (Taliaferro) P.; m. Anne Carroll Hannegan, Apr. 12, 1958; children: Sarah Carroll Prince Pishko, Emily Taliaferro, William Taliaferro, John Hannegan, Anne Martineau, Robert Harrison. Student, Coll. William and Mary, Norfolk, 1947-48, 49-50; AB, Williamsburg, 1955, BCL, 1957, MLT, 1959. Bar: Va. 1957. Lectr. acctg. Coll. William and Mary, 1955-57; lectr. law Marshall-Wythe Sch. Law, 1957-59; assoc. Williams, Kelly & Greer, Norfolk, 1959-63, ptnr., 1963-90; U.S. magistrate judge Eastern Dist. of Va., Norfolk, 1990—; pres. Am. Inn of Ct. XXVII, 1987-89. Bd. editors: The Virginia Lawyer, A Basic Practice Handbook, 1966. Bd. dirs. Madonna Home, Inc., 1978-93, Soc. Alumni of Coll. William and Mary, 1985-88. Fellow Am. Coll. Trial Lawyers, Am. Bar Found., Va. Law found. (bd. dirs. 1976-90); mem. ABA (ho. of dels. 1984-90), Am. Judicature Soc. (bd. dirs. 1984-88), Va. State Bar (coun. 1973-77, exec. com. 1975-80, pres. 1978-79). Roman Catholic. Home: 1227 Graydon Ave Norfolk VA 23507-1006 Office: Walter E Hoffman US Courthouse 600 Granby St Ste 181 Norfolk VA 23510-1915

PRINCIPAL, VICTORIA, actress; b. Fukuoka, Japan, Jan. 3, 1950; d. Victor and Ree (Veal) P.; m. Harry Glassman, 1985. Attended, Miami-Dade Community Coll.; studied acting with Max Croft, Al Sacks and Estelle Harman, Jean Scott, Royal Acad. Dramatic Arts. Worked as model, including TV commls.; appearences include (film) The Life and Times of Judge Roy Bean, 1972, The Naked Ape, 1973, Earthquake, 1974, I Will I Will For Now, 1976, Vigilante Force, 1976; (TV movies) Last Hours Before Morning, 1975, Fantasy Island, 1977, The Night They Stole Miss Beautiful, 1977, Pleasure Palace, 1980, Not Just Another Affair, 1982, Mistress, 1987, The Burden of Proof, 1990, Just Life, 1992, Beyond Obsession, 1994, Dancing in the Dark, 1995, The Abduction, 1996; exec. prodr., actress Naked Lie, 1989, Blind Witness, 1989, Sparks: The Price of Passion, 1990, Don't Touch My Daughter, 1991, Seduction: Three Tales from the Inner Sanctum, 1993, River of Rage: The Taking of Maggie Keene, 1993; exec. prodr. Midnight's Child, 1992; (TV series) Dallas, 1978-87; (theatre) Love Letters, 1990; author: The Body Principal, 1983, The Beauty Principal, 1984, The Diet Principal, 1987. *

PRINCIPE, HELEN MARY, medical case manager; b. Santa Monica, Calif., May 18, 1953; d. William John and Bessie Sylvia (Amsden) McGonagle; 1 child, Francis Edward. AS, Northeastern U., 1978; BSN cum laude, Worcester (Mass.) State Coll., 1981. RN, Mass., Calif. Critical care nurse Mt. Auburn Hosp., Cambridge, Mass.; adminstrv. nurse, critical care nurse, instr. Alta Bates Hosp., Berkeley, Calif.; clin. instr. med.-surg. staff devel., critical care nurse Valley Hosp., Las Vegas, Nev.; med. case mgr., supr. Intracorp, Oakland, Calif.; spl. case cons. Lincoln Nat., Pleasanton, Calif.; with Conservco, Walnut Creek, Calif.; assoc. mgr. PruCare of No. Calif., San Mateo, Calif.; mem. quality assessment and improvement com. Stat Nursing Adv. Bd. Utilization Rev., 1994, rehab. adv. task force Santa Clara Valley (Calif.) Med. Ctr., 1996—. Mem. adv. bd. Bldg. Blocks Pediat. Bldg. Blocks, 1996-97. Mem. AAUW, Rehab. Ins. Nurses Group, Case Mgmt. Soc. Am. (founding pres. No. Calif. chpt., nat. bd. dirs., mem. membership com.), Individual Case Mgmt. Assn.

PRINCZ, JUDITH, publishing executive. BA, Wheaton Coll., 1974. Retail circulation asst. Family Media, 1975-76; asst. mgr. direct mail Redbook, 1977; subscription mgr. Women Sports, 1977; circulation mgr. Sport mag., 1978-79; circulation dir. Weight Watcher's, 1979-83; assoc. pub. Am. Baby mag., N.Y.C., 1983-89, v.p., pub., 1989—; v.p., group pub. Cahners Childcare Group, 1992—. Office: K-111 Family and Leisure 249 W 17th St New York NY 10011-5300

PRINDLE, WILLIAM ROSCOE, consultant, retired glass company executive; b. San Francisco, Dec. 19, 1926; s. Vivian Arthur and Harriette Alnora (Nickerson) P.; m. June Laverne Anderson, June 20, 1947; children—Carol Susan, William Alastair. B.S., U. Calif., Berkeley, 1948, M.S., 1950; Sc.D., M.I.T., 1955. Asst. tech. dir. Hazel-Atlas Glass Co., 1954-56; mgr. research Hazel-Atlas Glass div. Continental Can Co., Wheeling, W.Va., 1956-58, gen. mgr. research and devel., 1959-62; mgr. materials research Am. Optical Co., Southbridge, Mass., 1962-65; v.p. research Southbridge and Framingham, Mass., 1971-76; dir; research Ferro Corp., Cleve., 1966-67, v.p. research, 1967-71; exec. dir. Nat. Materials Adv. Bd., NRC-NAS, Washington, 1976-80; dir. adminstrv. and tech. svcs. R & D div. Corning Glass Works, N.Y., 1980-85, dir. materials rsch., 1985-87; assoc. dir. R & D, Engring. div. Corning Glass Works (now Corning, Inc.), N.Y., 1987-90; div. v.p., assoc. dir. tech. group Corning Inc., N.Y., 1990-92; ret.; pres. XII Internat. Glass Congress, 1980, Internat. Commn. on Glass, 1985-88. Served with U.S. Navy, 1944-46. Named Outstanding Ceramist of New Eng., New Eng. sect. Am. Ceramic Soc., 1974, Toledo Glass and Ceramic award NW Ohio sect., 1986, Albert Victor Bleininger Meml. award Pitts. sect., 1989; Friedberg Meml. lecture Nat. Inst. Ceramic Engrs., 1990. Fellow Am. Ceramic Soc. (disting. life, pres. 1980-81), Soc. Glass Tech., Am. Soc. for Metals Internat.; mem. NAE, AAAS, Cosmos Club (Washington), Sigma Xi, Phi Gamma Delta. Home and Office: 1556 Crestline Dr Santa Barbara CA 93105-4611

PRINE, JOHN, singer, songwriter; b. Maywood, Ill., Oct. 10, 1946. Pres. Oh Boy Records, Nashville. Began performing original compositions, 1969; songs include Paradise, Sam. Stone, Hello in There, Dear Abby; albums include Bruised Orange, Common Sense, Diamonds in the Rough, John Prine, Pink Cadillac, Prime Prine, Storm Windows, Sweet Revenge, Aimless Love, German Afternoons, 1986, John Prine Live, 1988, The Missing Years, 1991 (Grammy award for best contemporary folk rec.), Great Days: The John Pride Anthology, 1993, Lost Dogs & Mixed Blessings, 1995. Served with U.S. Army. Address: Oh Boy Records 33 Music Sq W Ste 102-a Nashville TN 37203-3226*

PRINEAS, RONALD JAMES, epidemiologist, educator; b. Junee, New South Wales, Australia, Sept. 19, 1937; came to U.S., 1973; s. Peter John and Nancy (MacDonald) P.; m. Julienne Swynny, Apr. 21, 1961; children: Matthew Leigh, Anna Mary, John Paul, Miranda Jane. MBBS, U. Sydney, Australia, 1960; PhD, U. London, 1969. Med. house officer Prince Henry Hosp., Sydney, 1961; sr. med. house officer Royal Perth Hosp., Australia, 1962; registrar in medicine Royal Glasgow Infirmary, Scotland, 1963-64; research fellow London Sch. Hygiene and Tropical Medicine, 1964-67, lectr., 1967-68; asst. in medicine U. Melbourne, Australia, 1968-72; prof. epidemiology U. Minn., Mpls., 1973-88, prof. medicine, 1974-88; prof., chair epidemiology and pub. health U Miami, Fla., 1988—, cons. WHO, Geneva, 1976—, Nat. Heart Lung and Blood Inst., 1976—; prin. investigator Nat. Health Lung and Blood Inst., 1973—. Author books, including: Blood Pressure Sounds; Their Measurement and Meaning, 1978; The Minnesota Code Manual of Electrocardiographic Findings, 1982; also numerous articles. Recipient numerous cardiovascular disease research grants and contracts. Mem. Fla. affiliate Am. Heart Assn., Mpls., 1973—, chmn. adv. groups, 1975—. Fellow Royal Coll. Physicians Edinburgh, Am. Coll. Cardiology, Am. Pub. Health Assn., Soc. Epidemiologic Research, Am. Heart Assn. Council on Epidemiology, Internat. Soc. Hypertension, Council on Human Biology, Internat. Soc. Cardiology, Soc. Controlled Clin. Trials, Am. Coll. Epidemiology, Am. Soc. Epidemiology, Internat. Soc. Human Biology; mem. Royal Coll. Physicians London. Avocations: reading, public health policy. Office: U Miami Sch Medicine Dept Epidemiology & Pub Health PO Box 669R Miami FL 33101-0116

PRINGLE, BARBARA CARROLL, state legislator; b. N.Y.C., Apr. 4, 1939; d. Nicholas Robert and Anna Joan (Woloshinovich) Terlesky; m. Richard D. Pringle, Nov. 28, 1959; children: Christopher, Rhonda. Student, Cuyahoga C.C. With Dunn & Bradstreet, 1957-60; precinct committeewoman City of Cleve., 1976-77; elected mem. Cleve. City Coun., 1977-81; mem. Ohio Ho. of Reps., Columbus, 1982—; 20th dist. state ctrl. committeewoman, 1982-92; mem. family svcs. com., ranking mem. econ. devel. & small bus. com., pub. utilities com.; mem. Ohio Children's Trust Fund, Midwestern Legis. Conf. Coun. State Govts.' Com. Status Children. Vol. Cleve. Lupus Steering Com., various community orgns.; charter mem. Statue of Liberty Ellis Island Found. Recipient cert. of appreciation Cleve. Mcpl. Ct., 1977, Exch. Club Bklyn., 1978, Cmty. Recreation Appreciation award City of Cleve., 1978, Key to City of Cleve., 1979, Cleve. Area Soapbox Derby cert., 1976, 77, 81, cert. of appreciation Ward 9 Youth League, 1979-82, No. Ohio Patrolman's Benevolent Assn. award, 1983, Cuyahoga County Firefighters award, 1983, Outstanding Pub. Servant award for Outstanding Svc. to Hispanic Cmty., 1985, Nat. Sr. Citizen Hall of Fame award, 1987, cert. of appreciation Cleve. Coun. Unemployed Workers, 1987, Ohio Farmers Union award, 1990, award of appreciation United Labor Agy., 1993, Susan B. Anthony award, 1995. Mem. Nat. Order Women Legislators, Fedn. Dem. Women of Ohio, Nat. Alliance Czech Catholics, St. Michael Ch. Altar and Rosary Soc., Ward 15 Dem. Club, Polish Falcons. Democrat. Home: 708 Timothy Ln Cleveland OH 44109-3733

PRINGLE, EDWARD E., legal educator, former state supreme court chief justice; b. Chgo., Apr. 12, 1914; s. Abraham J. and Lena (Oher) P.; m. Pauline Judd, Aug. 17, 1941; children: Bruce, Eric. LL.B., U. Colo., 1936, LL.D., 1976; LL.D., U. Denver, 1979. Bar: Colo. Practiced in Denver, 1936-42, 47-57; with fed. govt. service Washington, 1943-47; dist. judge Colo. Dist. Ct., Denver, 1957-61; justice Supreme Ct. Colo., Denver, 1961-79; chief justice Supreme Ct. Colo., 1970-78; dir. research and writing program U. Denver Coll. Law, 1979-90, prof. emeritus, 1990—. Contbr. articles to profl. jours. Bd. dirs. Am. Med. Center, Denver; mem. Nat. Commn. for Establishment of Nat. Inst. Justice. Served with USAAF, 1942. Recipient William Lee Knous award U. Colo. Law Sch., 1975. Mem. Am., Colo., Denver bar assns., Conf. Chief Justices (chmn. 1973-74), Am. Judicature Soc. (Herbert Lincoln Harley award 1973, chmn. bd. 1974-76), Nat. Center State Cts. (pres. 1977-79). Jewish. Club: Masons (33 deg.). Office: U Denver Coll Law 1900 Olive St Denver CO 80220-1857

PRINGLE, LAURENCE PATRICK, writer; b. Rochester, N.Y., Nov. 26, 1935; s. Laurence Erin and Marleah Elizabeth (Rosehill) P.; m. Judith Malanowicz, June 23, 1962 (div. 1970); children: Heidi Elizabeth Jeffrey Laurence, Sean Edmund; m. Susan Deborah Klein, Mar. 13, 1983; children: Jesse Erin, Rebecca Anne. BS in Wildlife Biology, Cornell U., 1958; MS in Wildlife Biology, U. Mass., 1961. Tchr. sci. Lima (N.Y.) Cen. Sch., 1961-62; editor Nature and Sci. mag. Am. Mus. Natural History, N.Y.C., 1963-70; free-lance writer, 1970—; writer-in-residence Kean College, Union, N.J., 1985-86. Author: (children's books) Dinosaurs and Their World, 1968, The Only Earth We Have, 1969, From Field to Forest, 1970, In a Beaver Valley, 1970, One Earth, Many People, 1971, Ecology: Science of Survival, 1971, Cockroaches: Here, There, Everywhere, 1971, From Pond to Prairie, 1972, This Is a River, 1972, Pests and People: The Search for Sensible Pest Control, 1972, Estuaries: Where Rivers Meet the Sea, 1973, Into the Woods: Exploring the Forest Ecosystem, 1973, Follow a Fisher, 1973, Twist, Wiggle and Squirm: A Book about Earthworms, 1973, Recycling Resources, 1974, Energy: Power for People, 1975, City and Suburb: Exploring an Ecosystem, 1975, Chains, Webs and Pyramids: The Flow of Energy in Nature, 1975, Water Plants, 1975, The Minnow Family: Chubs, Dace, Minnows and Shiners, 1987, Listen to the Crows, 1976, Our Hungry Earth: The World Food Crisis, 1976, Death is Natural, 1977, The Hidden World: Life under a Rock, 1977, The Controversial Coyote: Predation, Politics and Ecology, 1977, The Gentle Desert: Exploring an Ecosystem, 1977, Animals and Their Niches: How Species Share Resources, 1977, The Economic Growth Debate: Are There Limits to Growth?, 1978, Dinosaurs and People: Fossils, Facts and Fantasies, 1978, Wild Foods, 1978, Nuclear Power: From Physics to Politics, 1979, Natural Fire: Its Ecology in Forests, 1979, Lives at Stake: The Science and Politics of Environmental Health, 1980, What Shall We Do with the Land?: Choices for America, 1981, Frost Hollows and Other Microclimates, 1981, Vampire Bats, 1982, Water: The Next Great Resource Battle, 1982, Radiation: Waves and Particles/Benefits and Risks, 1983, Wolfman: Exploring the World of Wolves, 1983, Feral: Tame Animals Gone Wild, 1983, The Earth Is Flat—and Other Great Mistakes, 1983, Being a Plant, 1983, Nuclear War: From Hiroshima to Nuclear Winter, 1985, Animals at Play, 1985, Here Come the Killer Bees, 1986, Throwing Things Away: From Middens to Resource Recovery, 1986, Restoring Our Earth, 1987, Home: How Animals Find Comfort and Safety, 1987, Rain of Troubles: The Science and Politics of Acid Rain, 1988, Living in a Risky World, 1989, Nuclear Energy: Troubled Past, Uncertain Future, 1989, Bearman: Exploring the World of Black Bears, 1989, The Animal Rights Controversy, 1989, Saving Our Wildlife, 1990, Global Warming: Assessing the Greenhouse Threat, 1990, The Golden Book of Insects and Spiders, 1990, Killer Bees (rev. edit.) 1991, Batman: Exploring the World of Bats, 1991, Living Treasure: Saving Earth's Threatened Biodiversity, 1991, Antarctica: The Last Unspoiled Continent, 1992, The Golden Book of Volcanoes, Earthquakes, and Powerful Storms, 1992, Chemical and Biological Weapons: The Cruelest Weapons, 1993, Oil Spills: Damage, Recovery, and Prevention, 1993, Jackal Woman: Exploring the World of Jackals, 1993, Scorpion Man: Exploring the World of Scorpions, 1994, Dinosaurs! Strange and Wonderful, 1995, Vanishing Ozone: Protecting Earth from Ultraviolet Radiation, 1995, Coral Reefs: Earth's Undersea Treasures, 1995, Dolphin Man: Exploring the World of Dolphins, 1995, Fire in the Forest: A Cycle of Growth and Renewal, 1995, Taking Care of the Earth: Kids in Action, 1996, Smoking : A Risky Business, 1996, An Extraordinary Life: The Story of a Monarch Butterfly, 1997, Nature! Wild and Wonderful, 1997, Everybody Has a Bellybutton: Your Life Before You Were Born, 1997, Elephant Woman: Cynthia Moss Explores The World of Elephants, 1997, Drinking: A Risky Business, 1997; (fiction) Jesse Builds a Road, 1989, Octopus Hug, 1993, Naming the Cat, 1997; (adult books) Wild River, 1972, Rivers and Lakes, 1985. Recipient Spl. Conservation award Nat. Wildlife Fedn., 1978, Eva L. Gordon award Am. Nature Study Soc., 1983, Honor Book Orbis Pictus award, 1996. Mem. the Authors Guild. Home and Office: PO Box 252 West Nyack NY 10994-0252

PRINGLE, LEWIS GORDON, marketing professional, educator; b. Lansing, Mich., Feb. 13, 1941; s. Gordon Henry and Lucile Roxana (Drake) P.; children: Lewis Gordon Jr., William Davis, Thomas Benjamin. B.A., Harvard U., 1963; M.S., M.I.T., 1965, Ph.D., 1969. Vice pres., dir. mktg. sci. BBDO, Inc., N.Y.C., 1968-73; asst. prof. mktg. Carnegie-Melon U., Pitts., 1973-74; exec. v.p., dir. rsch. svcs., corp. dir. BBDO, Inc., N.Y.C., 1978-91; exec. v.p. BBDO Worldwide, 1986-91; chmn., CEO BBDO Europe, 1986-91, LG Pringle and Assocs., 1992-95; Joseph C. Seibert prof. of mktg. Farmer Sch. Bus. Adminstrn., Miami U., Oxford, Ohio, 1995—. Author numerous articles in field. Active local Boy Scouts Am. Ford Found. fellow, 1967. Fellow Royal Statis. Soc.; mem. Market Rsch. Coun., Am. Psychol. Assn., European Soc. Mktg. and Opinion Rsch., Am. Mktg. Assn., Inst. Ops. Rsch. and Mgmt. Sci. Home: 2858 N Stout Rd Liberty IN 47353 Office: Farmer Sch Bus Adminstrn Miami Univ Oxford OH 45056

PRINGLE, ORAN ALLAN, mechanical and aerospace engineering educator; b. Lawrence, Kan., Sept. 14, 1923; s. Oran Allan and Mae (McClell) P.; m. Billie Hansen, June 25, 1947; children—Allan, Billie, James, Rebecca. B.S. in Mech. Engring, U. Kan., 1947; M.S., U. Wis., 1948, Ph.D., 1967. Registered profl. engr., Mo. Mech. engr. Black and Veatch (cons. engrs.), Kansas City, Mo., 1947-48; engr. Boeing Airplane Co., Wichita, 1952—; prof. U. Mo., Columbia, 1948—. Co-author: Engineering Metallurgy, 1957; contbr. articles to profl. lit. Bd. dirs. United Cerebral Palsy Boone County, Mo. Served with AUS, 1943-45. Ford Found. grantee. Mem. Am. Soc. M.E. (chmn. fastening and joining com., design engring. div.), Sigma Xi. Home: 1820 University Ave Columbia MO 65201-6004 Office: Dept Mech and Aerospace Engring U Mo Columbia MO 65201

PRINGLE, ROBERT MAXWELL, diplomat; b. N.Y.C., Nov. 12, 1936; s. Henry Fowles and Helena Huntington (Smith) P.; m. Barbara Ann Cade, Sept. 26, 1964; children: James Maxwell, Anne Elizabeth. BA, Harvard U., 1958; PhD, Cornell U., 1967. Dir. econ. policy staff Bur. African Affairs Dept. State, 1981-83; dep. chief mission Ouagadougou, Burkina Faso, 1983-85, Port Moresby, Papua New Guinea, 1985-87; ambassador to Mali, 1987-90; dir. cen. African affairs U.S. Dept. State, 1990-93; dir. ecology and terrestrial conservation U.S. Dept. of State, 1993-95; dir. sr. seminar U.S. Dept. State, 1995-96; dep. chief of mission Dept. State, Pretoria, 1996—. Author: Rajahs and Rebels: The Ibans of Sarawak under Brooke Rule, 1970, Indonesia and the Philippines: American Interests in Island Southeast Asia, 1980. Mem. Assn. Asian Studies, African Studies Assn. Avocations: photography, gardening, scuba diving. Home and Office: Embassy-Pretoria Dept State Washington DC 20521-9300

PRINJA, ANIL KANT, nuclear engineering educator; b. Mombasa, Kenya, Apr. 9, 1955; came to U.S., 1980; s. Kapil Dev and Kushal (Dharney) P.; m. Renu Mohan, Sept. 18, 1983; children: Vivek Kapil, Akash Prinja. BSc in Nuclear Engring. with 1st class honors, London U., 1976, PhD in Nuclear Engring., 1980. Asst. rsch. engr. UCLA, 1980-87; asst. prof. nuclear engring. U. N.Mex., Albuquerque, 1987-89, assoc. prof., 1989-95, prof., 1995—; chmn., host Internat. Conf. Transport Theory, 1991, U.S. Edge Plasma Physics: Theory and Applications Workshop, 1993; cons. Sandia Nat. Labs., Albuquerque, 1987—, Sci. Applications Internat., Inc., Albuquerque, 1987—, Los Alamos Nat. Lab., 1989—; vis. prof. dept. reactor physics Chalmers U. Tech., Goteborg, Sweden, 1993, 95; vis. prof. UCLA, 1994. Assoc. editor: Annals of Nuclear Energy; contbr. chpts. to books and articles to profl. jours. Recipient Outstanding Acad. Achievement award Instn. Nuclear Engrs., 1976; grantee Dept. of Energy, Sandia Nat. Lab., Los Alamos Nat. Lab., Culham Labs., U.K., KFA Julich, Germany, 1989—, others. Mem. Am. Phys. Soc., Am. Nuc. Soc., Soc. Indsl. and Applied Math., N.Y. Acad. Scis. Hindu. Avocations: travel, reading. Office: U New Mex 209 Farris Engring Ctr Albuquerque NM 87131

PRINS, DAVID, speech pathologist, educator; b. Herkimer, N.Y., Oct. 4, 1930; s. Tunis W. and Harriet Z. (Baker) P.; m. Gloria B. Fleming, June 4, 1955; children: Leslie, Steven, Douglas, Michael. BA, Central Coll. Iowa, 1952; MA, U. Mich., 1957, PhD, 1961. Tchr. Denison (Iowa) H.S., 1954-55; instr. U. Mich., 1960-63, asst. prof., 1963-66, assoc. prof., 1966-69; asst. dir. U. Mich. Speech and Hearing Camp, 1960-64, dir., 1964-69; dir. program in speech and hearing scis. U. Wash., 1974-75, assoc. prof., 1969-72, prof., 1973-92, chmn. dept. speech and hearing scis., 1975-79, assoc. dean Coll. Arts & Scis., 1979-88, prof. emeritus, 1992—; vis. prof. U. Va. Contbr. articles in field of stuttering and articulation disorders to profl. jours. Served with U.S. Army, 1952-54. Mem. AAAS, Am. Speech and Hearing Assn., Wash. Speech and Hearing Assn., Mich. Speech and Hearing Assn. (past pres.), Phi Beta Kappa, Phi Kappa Phi. Office: U Wash Dept Speech And Scis Seattle WA 98105-6246

PRINS, ROBERT JACK, college administrator; b. Grand Rapids, Mich., Oct. 12, 1932; s. Jacob and Marie (Vanden Brink) P.; m. Ruth Ellen John, Oct. 10, 1950; children: Linda, Douglas, Debra, Nancy, Eric, Sarah. BA, Hope Coll., 1954; DBA, Coll. Emporia, 1974. With Mich. Bell Telephone Co., Detroit area, 1954-66; dir. devel. Bethesda Hosp., Denver, 1966-68; v.p. planning and devel. Park Coll., Parkville, Mo., 1969-70; chief adminstrv. officer Coll. of Emporia, Kans., 1970-75; dir. fin. and devel. The Abbey Sch., Canon City, Colo., 1975-79; dir. devel. Kirksville Coll. Osteo. Medicine, Mo., 1979-84; v.p. devel. McKendree Coll., Lebanon, Ill., 1984-86; pres. Iowa Weslyan Coll., Mt. Pleasant, 1986—; bd. dirs. Iowa Coll. Found., Iowa Commn. on Nat. and Cmty. Svc.; mem., v.p. bd. Pub. Interest Inst., Iowa Assn. Ind. Colls. and Univs.; mem. edn. adv. com. Potomak Internat., Taipei, Taiwan. Mem. Nat. Assn. Ind. Colls. and Univs., Coun. for Advancement and Support of Edn., Mt. Pleasant C. of C. *Education may be the key to opportunity but only solid performance on the job insures success.*

PRINZ, RICHARD ALLEN, surgeon. MD, Loyola U., Chgo., 1972. Diplomate Am. Bd. Surgery, bd. dirs., 1994—. Intern Barnes Hosp., St. Louis, 1972-73, resident in surgery, 1973-74; resident in surgery Loyola U., Chgo., 1974-77, attending surgeon, 1980-93; staff Rush Presbyn.-St. Luke's Med. Ctr., Chgo., 1993—; Helen Shedd Keith prof., chmn. dept. gen. surgery Rush U., Chgo., 1993—. Mem. Am. Surg. Assn., Am. Assn. Endocrine Surgeons (pres. 1996), Midwest Surg. Assn. (pres. 1997), Western Surg. Assn. (treas. 1993—). Office: Rush Presbyn/St Luke Med Ct 810 Professional Bldg 1725 W Harrison St Chicago IL 60612-3828

PRIOR, BOYD THELMAN, management consultant; b. Tacoma, May 7, 1926; s. George Archie and Thelma Mary (Chambers) P. Student, U.S. Naval Acad., 1948-50; BA, Claremont Men's Coll., 1952; MBA, Harvard U., 1954. Sr. v.p., dir. The Lusk Corp., Tucson, 1954-60; v.p. sales & mktg. Horizon Land Corp., Tucson, 1960-62; sr. v.p., dir. Gen. Devel. Corp., Miami, Fla., 1962-71; chmn., pres. Prior Assocs., Phoenix, 1971-74; mgmt. cons., dir. Am. Solar King Corp., Waco, Tex., 1982-85; pvt. practice Kerrville, Tex. and Boca Raton, Fla., 1974-82, Burleson, Tex., 1985; pvt. practice mgmt. cons. Burleson, Dallas/Ft. Worth, Phoenix, Miami, 1985—; cons. Cob Select Sand & Gravel, Inc., 1986—, Resolution Trust, 1989—. Recipient Cert. Appreciation Better Bus. Bur., 1971, 74. Republican. Episcopalian. Home and Office: 221 Meadow Oaks Dr Burleson TX 76028-6515

PRIOR, GARY L., lawyer; b. Niagara Falls, N.Y., June 26, 1943; s. Harold D. and Adeline Thelma (Lee) P.; m. Nancy O'Shaughnessy, Aug. 12, 1975; children: Joseph Lee, Julia Elizabeth. BS, Tulane U., 1965; JD, U. Chgo., 1968. Bar: Ill. 1968, U.S. Dist. Ct. (no. dist.) Ill. 1968, U.S. Ct. Appeals (7th cir.) 1973, U.S. Ct. Appeals (3rd cir.) 1974, U.S. Trial Bar 1983, U.S. Supreme Ct. 1989, U.S. Dist. Ct. (we. dist.) Wis. 1992, U.S. Dist. Ct. (ea. dist.) Wis. 1993. Assoc. Rooks, Pitts & Poust, Chgo., 1968-71; assoc. McDermott, Will & Emery, Chgo., 1971-74, ptnr., 1974—, dir. trial dept. tng., 1980-85, mem. securities approval com., 1986—, mem. nominating com., chmn., 1988-89, partnership com., 1989-92, mem mgmt. com., 1991-93. Mem. Phi Delta Phi. Avocations: farming, sports, family. Home: 1134 W Wrightwood Ave # 2 Chicago IL 60614-1315 Office: McDermott Will & Emery # 3100 227 W Monroe St Ste 3100 Chicago IL 60606-5018

PRIOR, JOHN THOMPSON, pathology educator; b. St. Albans, Vt., July 24, 1948; s. Thomas William and Pauline Agnes Prior; m. Elizabeth Titus Troy, July 24, 1948; children: Anne, Polly, John Jr., Thomas, Jeffrey, Timothy. BS, U. Vt., 1939, MD, 1943. Diplomate Am. bd. Pathology. Resident in pathology Binghamton (N.Y.) City Hosp., 1946-47; fellow in pathology Syracuse (N.Y.) U. Med. Coll., 1947-49; asst. prof. pathology SUNY, Syracuse, 1949-54, assoc. prof., 1954-63, prof., 1963-72, clin. prof. pathology, 1972—; active ARC Blood Bank, Syracuse, 1966-70; pres. N.Y. State Assoc. Lab., Syracuse, 1959-60; med. dir. PSRO Ctrl. N.Y., Syracuse, 1983-84; mem. N.Y. Stat Hosp. Rev. & Planning Assn., Albany, 1980-82; bd. dirs. Am. Med. Peer Rev. Assn., 1985-90. Contbr. articles to profl. jours. Bd. dirs. Lung Assn. Ctrl. N.Y., Syracuse, 1994—. Col. M.C., U.S. Army, 1944-77. Decorated Bronze Star, Silver Star, Legion of Merit, Belgian Croix de Guerre; recipient William Hammond Citation, N.Y. State Jour. Medicine, N.Y.C., 1984, Disting. Alumnus award U. Vt., Burlington, 1994. Mem. Onondaga County Med. Soc. (pres. 1974, disting. svc. award 1981). Avocations: golf, tennis. Home: 4615 Pewter Ln Manlius NY 13104

PRIOR, WILLIAM ALLEN, electronics company executive; b. Benton Harbor, Mich., Jan. 14, 1927; s. Allen Ames and Madeline Isabel (Taylor) P.; m. Nancy Norton Sayles, July 7, 1951 (div. Oct. 1971); children: Stephanie Sayles, Alexandra Taylor, Robert Eames, Eleanor Norton; m. Carol Luise Becker-Ehmck, Oct. 30, 1971; children: Michael Becker-Ehmck, Jeffrey Renner. AB in Physics, Harvard Coll., 1950, MBA, 1954. Salesman IBM, Mineola, L.I., N.Y., 1950-52; sales engr. Lincoln Electric Co., Cleve., 1954-57; ptnr. Hammond Kennedy & Co., N.Y.C., 1957-66; v.p. The Singer Co., N.Y.C., 1967-68; pres. Tansitor Electronics, Bennington, Vt., 1969-71, Aerotron Inc., Raleigh, N.C., 1971-82; v.p. J. Lee Peeler & Co., Durham, N.C., 1986-89; pres. Accudyne, Inc., Raleigh, 1990—; bd. dirs. Carroll's Foods, Warsaw, N.C.; chmn. Royal Blue Capital, Inc., Raleigh. Cpl. USAAF, 1945-46, Germany. Mem. IEEE, North Ridge Country Club (Raleigh), Raleigh Racquet Club, Harvard Club of N.Y.C., 50 Group. Republican. Avocations: tennis, skiing, computer programming. Home: 329 Meeting House Cir Raleigh NC 27615-3133 Office: Accudyne Inc 5800 Mchines Pl Raleigh NC 27616-1839

PRIORE, ROGER L., biostatistics educator, consultant; b. Buffalo, Apr. 21, 1938; s. Anthony J. and Linda M. (DeMarchi) P.; m. Carol A. Cooper, Sept. 3, 1960; children—Howard W., Susan L., John D. B.A., SUNY-Buffalo, 1960, M.S., 1962; Sc.D., Johns Hopkins U., 1965. Jr. cancer research scientist Roswell Park Meml. Inst., Buffalo, 1960-65, sr. cancer research scientist, 1965-67, assoc. cancer research scientist, 1967-69, prin. cancer research scientist, 1974-79, dir. computer sci., 1979-83, dir. dept. biomath., 1983-91, dir. mgmt. info. systems, 1988-91; asst. rsch. prof. SUNY, Buffalo, 1966-68, assoc. rsch. prof., 1968-69, rsch. prof., dir. grad. studies in biometry, 1980-91; rsch. prof. Niagara U., 1968-91; cons. in stats. and computing, 1991—; clin. prof. dept. social and preventive medicine SUNY, Buffalo, 1991—; pres. Compustat Assocs., Inc., Buffalo, 1993—; clin. prof. dept. statistics SUNY, Buffalo, 1995—; cons. Am. Joint Com. on Cancer, 1980-88. Contbr. articles to profl. jours. Mem. Am. Statis. Assn., Soc. for Epidemiol. Rsch., Sigma Xi. Office: 342 Dan Troy Dr Buffalo NY 14221-3514

PRISANT, L(OUIS) MICHAEL, cardiologist; b. Albany, Ga., Dec. 25, 1949; s. Bennie Martin and Mozelle (Cosper) P.; m. Rose Corinth Trincher, June 28, 1975; children: Michelle Elizabeth, Louis Michael. BA, Emory U., 1971; MD, Med. Coll. Ga., 1977. Diplomate Am. Bd. Internal Medicine, Am. Bd. Cardiovascular Diseases, Am. Bd. Geriatric Medicine, Am. Bd. Clin. Pharmacology, Am. Bd. Forensic Medicine, Nat. Bd. Med. Examiners. Intern Med. Coll. Ga., Augusta, 1977-78; resident Med. Coll. Ga., 1978-80; chief med. resident, 1979-80; cardiology fellow Med. Coll. Ga., 1980-82, instr., 1982-83, asst. prof. medicine, 1983-89, assoc. prof. medicine, 1989-94, prof., 1994—, dir. fellowship tng. program, 1996; cons. in field; lectr. in field. Contbr. 97 articles and 89 abstracts to profl. jours., 8 chpts. to books; author of 8 monographs; manuscript reviewer med. jours.; mem. editl. bd. Blood Pressure Monitoring, Cardiovascular Therapeutics, Physicians and Computers. FOE grantee, 1989, Rorer, 1989, Am. Cyanamid, 1988, Sandoz, 1989-93, Merck, 1990-92, Squibb, 1991, Lorex, 1991, NIH, 1991, Lederle, 1993, Ciba-Geigy, 1993. Fellow ACP, Am. Coll. Cardiology, Am. Coll. Clin. Pharmacology, Am. Coll. Chest Physicians, Am. Coll. Forensic Examiners; mem. AMA (Physician's Recognition award 1982-98), AAUP, Am. Fedn. Clin. Rsch., Am. Heart Assn., Am. Soc. Echocardiography, Am. Soc. Hypertension, Am. Soc. Internal Medicine, Internat. Soc. for Hypertension in Blacks, Ga. Heart Assn., Assn. for Advancement Med. Instrumentation, Ga. Med. Care Found., Med. Assn. Ga., Richmond County Med. Soc., Ahlquist Soc. (pres.), AMA Physician, Phi Delta Epsilon, Alpha Phi Omega, Tau Epsilon Phi. Jewish. Avocation: computers. Office: Med Coll Ga Sect Cardiology Rm CK-151 Augusta GA 30912-3150

PRISBREY, REX PRINCE, retired insurance agent, underwriter, consultant; b. Washington, Utah, Mar. 18, 1922; s. Hyrum William and Susan (Prince) P.; m. Pinka Julieta Lucero, Nov. 16, 1943; children: Karol Sue Prisbey Lewallen, Pamela Blanche Prisbrey Ebert, Michael Rex. BA in Acctg., Denver U., 1949. CLU. Ptnr. Allen Stamm & Assocs., home builders, Farmington, N.Mex., 1949-52; acct. Linder Burke & Stevenson, Santa Fe, N.Mex., 1949-52; agt. State Farm Ins. Cos., Farmington, 1952-56; mgr. State Farm Ins. Cos., Phoenix, 1956-60; contractor, agt. State Farm Ins. Cos., Scottsdale, Ariz., 1960—; v.p., treas. Original Curio Store Inc., Santa Fe. Pres. Farmington Jr. C. of C., 1952; v.p. N.Mex. Jr. C. of C., 1953. 1st lt. USAAF, 1941-46, CBI. Decorated DFC, Air medal with oak leaf cluster; recipient Disting. Life Underwriter award Cen. Ariz. Mgrs. Assn., 1979. Mem. Am. Soc. CLU's, Scottsdale Assn. Life Underwriters (pres. 1980-81), Airplane Owners and Pilots Assn., Hump Pilots Assn. (life, speaker at meml. of Hump Flyers, Kunming, China 1993), Pinewood Country Club (bd. dirs., treas., v.p. 1985—), Civitans (pres. Scottsdale 1962-63). Avocations: flying, golf, photography. Home: 4011 N 65th St Scottsdale AZ 85251-4235

PRISCO, FRANK J., psychotherapist; b. N.Y.C.; s. Frank J. and Isabel (Gatano) P.; m. August Frances; children: Frank, Christian, Meredith. BS in History, NYU, 1964, MA in History and Psychology, 1972, PsyD in Psychoanalysis, 1980. Cert. psychoanalyst, cert. med. hypnotherapist. Cons., staff therapist Creedmore Psychiat. Ctr.; faculty Psychanalytic Inst., L.I.; pvt. practice Ctr. for Modern Psychoanalytic Studies. Eucharistic min. Cath. Ch. Recipient Soc. of Emil award. Mem. AAAS, Am. Psychol. Soc., Am. Assn. Guidance and Counseling, N.Y. Acad. Scis., Nat. Assn. Advancement Psychoanalysis, Am. Poetry Assn. (Poet Merit award 1988-90), Soc. Modern Psychoanalysis.

PRISSEL, BARBARA ANN, paralegal, law educator; b. Plum City, Wis., July 7, 1946; d. John Henry and Mary Ann Louise (Dankers) Seipel; m. Stephen Joseph Prissel, Dec. 16, 1967; children: Angela, Benjamin. Graduate with honors, Mpls. Bus. Coll., 1966; student, Moraine Park Tech. Coll., 1983—. Cert. interactive television adult edn. instr. Legal sec. Mott, Grose, Von Holtum & Hefferan, Mpls., 1966-67, Whelan, Morey & Morey Attys. at Law, Durand, Wis., 1967-70, Murry Law Office, River Falls, Wis., 1968-70, Potter, Wefel & Nettesheim, Wisconsin Rapids, Wis., 1970-71; sec. to adminstr. Moraine Park Tech. Coll., Fond du Lac, Wis., 1971-72, instr., 1972—; paralegal Kilgore Law Office, Ripon, Wis., 1985—; chmn. legal adv. com. Moraine Park Tech. Coll., Fond du Lac, Wis., 1985—, mem. adminstrv. assts. adv. com., 1984-86. Contbr. poems to newspapers. Ch. rep. Ch. Women United, Ripon, Wis., 1984-87; pianist Christian Women's Orgn., Ripon, Wis., 1985-95; pianist, organist Our Lady of the Lake Ch., Green Lake, Wis., 1987—; mem. sr. class night parent com. Ripon H.S., 1992-96; mem. parent bd. Young Life Christian Orgn., Ripon, Wis., 1994. Mem. NAFE, Nat. Assn. Legal Secs., Wis. Assn. Legal Secs., Fond du Lac (Wis.) County Legal Secs. Assn. (pres. 1994-95, Legal award of Excellence 1995-96), Legal Secs. Assn. (sec. 1995-96). Roman Catholic. Avocations: teaching and playing piano, creative writing, cooking, swimming, exercising. Home: 129 Wolverton Ave Ripon WI 54971-1144

PRITCHARD, CLAUDIUS HORNBY, JR., retired university president; b. Charleston, W.Va., June 28, 1927; s. Claudius Hornby and Katherine (Ellison) P.; m. Marjorie Walker Pullen, Aug. 9, 1952; children: Virginia Aiken, Katherine Winston, Olivia Reynolds, Claudius V. BA, Hampden-Sydney Coll., 1950; MA, Longwood Coll., 1965; PhD, Fla. State U., 1971. Comml. loan teller Am. Nat. Bank and Trust Co., Danville, Va., 1950-53; asst. cashier Planters Bank & Trust Co., Farmville, Va., 1953-55; asst. to pres. Hampden-Sydney (Va.) Coll., 1955-57, bus. mgr. and treas., 1957-67, v.p. devel., 1967-71; sr. budget analyst-edn. State of Fla., Tallahassee, 1971-72; pres. Sullins Coll., Bristol, Va., 1972-76; v.p. adminstrn. Maryville U., St. Louis, 1976-77, pres., 1977-92, pres. emeritus, 1992—; adv. dir. Commerce Bank of St. Louis, 1982-92. Author: Col. D. Wyatt Aiken (1828-1887) South Carolina's Militant Agrarian, 1970; contbr. articles to profl. jours. Bd. dirs. West St. Louis County YMCA, Chesterfield, Mo., 1985-92; bd. visitors Charleston So. Univ., 1993—. Served with USNR, 1945-46. Fla. State U. fellow, 1969-70, Arthur Vining Davis fellow Am. Council on Edn., 1974. Mem. AAUP, SCV, Am. Assn. Higher Edn., So. Hist. Assn., S.C. Hist. Soc., Mo. Colls. Fund (bd. dirs., chmn. 1987-88), Ind. Colls. and Univs. Mo., Chesterfield C. of C. (pres. 1987, Chesterfield Citizen of Yr. award 1986), SCV, Rotary. Republican. Presbyterian.

PRITCHARD, CONSTANCE JENKINS, human resources organization development trainer; b. Washington, May 6, 1950; d. William Morton and Marguerite Kathleen (Marshall) Jenkins; m. Paul Ralph Pritchard, June 30, 1973; children: Laura, Leslie. BA in English and History, Hiram (Ohio) Coll., 1972; MA in Linguistics, U. S.C., 1978, EdD in Student Pers. Svcs., 1991. Tchr. Sterling High Sch., Somerdale, N.J., 1972-76; instr. U. S.C., Aiken, 1982-93; dir. advisement ctr., 1984-89, asst. dean for career planning, placement and orientation, 1989-93; trainer, cons. Pritchard Group, North Augusta, S.C., 1989—; adminstr. Grace United Meth. Ch., North Augusta, S.C., 1993-97. Scout leader Girl Scouts Am., S.C., 1987-89; trainer Leadership Aiken County, 1991—; bd. dirs. United Way of Aiken County, 1993-96, Aiken County ARC, 1994—. Recipient citation for excellence in career programming Am. Assn. Career Edn., 1992; named Woman of Achievement, Miss. S.C. Pageant, 1993. Mem. Nat. Comty. Leadership Assn., Coll. Placement Coun. (Excellence award 1992, Award for Excellence in Rsch. 1992), Nat. Assn. Acad. Adminstrs. (newsletter editor 1987-89), Student Affairs Profl. Orgn., Cen. Savannah River Area Human Resource Assn. (sec. 1992-93), North Augusta Rotary (Rotarian of Yr. 1990-91), North Augusta C. of C. (bd. dirs. 1995—). Avocations: sailing, reading, family. Office: The Pritchard Group PO Box 6756 North Augusta SC 29861

PRITCHARD, DALTON HAROLD, retired electronics research engineer; b. Crystal Springs, Miss., Sept. 1, 1921; s. Cecil Harold and Marvie Prudence (Lofton) P.; m. Caroline Ann Hnatuk, Apr. 27, 1947; 1 child, Mary Ann Pritchard Poole. B.S.E.E., Miss. State U., 1943; postgrad., Harvard, MIT Radar Sch., 1943-44. Mem. tech. staff RCA Labs., Riverhead, N.Y., 1946-50; mem. tech. staff RCA Labs., Princeton, N.J., 1950-75, fellow tech. staff, 1975-87; session chmn., mem. program com. Internat. Conf. on Consumer Electronics, Chgo., 1980-85. Contbr. articles to profl. jours.; patentee in field. mem. N.J. Gov.'s Sci. Adv. Council, Princeton, 1981-85. Served to capt. U.S. Army Signal Corps. Decorated Bronze Star; recipient Eduard Rhein prize Edward Rhein Found., Berlin, Fed. Republic of Germany, 1980; Disting. Engring. fellow Miss. State U., 1991. Fellow IEEE (Vladimir Zworykin award 1977, David Sarnoff award 1981), Soc. Info. Display, Nat. Assn. Engrs., Nat. Acad. Engring., Sigma Xi, Tau Beta Pi, Kappa Mu Epsilon. Republican. Baptist. Avocations: amatuer radio; tennis. Home: 3 Bent Tree Ln Hilton Head Island SC 29926-1906

PRITCHARD, HUW OWEN, chemist, educator; b. Bangor, Wales, July 23, 1928; s. Owen and Lilian Venetia (McMurray) P.; m. Margaret Ramsden, Nov. 3, 1956; children—Karen, David. B.Sc., U. Manchester, 1948, M.Sc., 1949, Ph.D., 1951, D.Sc., 1964. Asst. lectr. chemistry Manchester (Eng.) U., 1951-54, lectr., 1954-65; prof. chemistry York U., Ont., Can., 1965—. Contbr. articles to profl. jours. Fellow Royal Soc. Can. Office: Chemistry Dept York Univ, Downsview, ON Canada M3J 1P3

PRITCHARD, KATHLEEN JO, not-for-profit association administrator; b. Milw., Feb. 6, 1951; d. Owen J. and Madelon (Coogan) P.; m. William A. Durkin Jr., Oct. 22, 1982; children: Elizabeth Durkin, Christine Durkin, W. Ryan Durkin. BA in Anthropology, U. Wis., Oshkosh, 1973; MA in Pub. Adminstrn., U. Wis., 1980; PhD in Polit. Sci., U. Wis., Milw., 1986. Rsch. analyst Wis. Coun. on Criminal Justice, Madison, 1974-77; planning analyst Wis. Dept. Health and Social Svcs., Madison, 1977-80; assoc. lectr. U. Wis., Milw., 1980-89; vis. asst. prof. Marquette U., Milw., 1986, 90-91; policy cons. dept. adminstrn. City of Milw., 1992; Outcomes Project dir. United Way of Greater Milw., 1992—; faculty advisor Model OAS, UN advisor, Milw., 1986-91; campus rep. spkr. Wis. Inst. for Study of War, Peace and Global Cooperation, Milw., 1989-90; mem. United Way Am. Task Force on Impact, 1995—; instr. Nat. Acad. Volunteerism, 1996. Contbr. articles to profl. jours. Recipient Alice Paul Dissertation award Women's Caucus for Polit. Sci., 1984; Grad. Sch. fellow U. Wis., Milw., 1983, fellow Kenyon Coll. Summer Inst., 1983. Mem. Am. Polit. Sci. Assn., Internat. Polit. Sci. Assn., Phi Kappa Phi (chpt. officer 1989).

PRITCHARD, LLEWELYN G., lawyer; b. N.Y.C., Aug. 13, 1937; s. Llewelyn and Anne Mary (Streib) P.; m. Joan Ashby, June 20, 1959; children: David Ashby, Jennifer Pritchard Vick, Andrew Harrison, William Llewelyn. AB with honors, Drew U., 1958; LLB, Duke U., 1961. Ptnr. Helsell & Fetterman, Seattle. Trustee Allied Arts Found.; pres. Allied Arts Seattle, 1974-76; trustee Meth. Ednl. Found., 1970—, pres., 1991-92; life trustee Patrons of Pacific N.W. Civil, Cultural and Charitable Orgns., 1969—, pres., 1972-73; bd. dirs. Planned Parenthood of Seattle/King County, 1972-78; trustee Seattle Symphony Orch., 1979-81, chmn. bd., 1980-82, hon. trustee; trustee U. Puget Sound., 1972—, mem. exec. com., chmn. bd. visitors to Law Sch., 1984-88; chancellor Pacific N.W. Ann. conf. United Meth. Ch., 1975—. Fellow Am. Bar Found. (life, state chmn. 1988-95); mem. ABA (bd. govs. 1986-89, chmn. program com. 1988-89, exec. com. 1988-89, ho. of Dels. 1979—, nat. dir. young lawyers divsn. 1971, chmn. sect. of individual rights and responsibilities 1975-76, exec. coun. family law sect. 1992—), Wash. State Bar Assn. (bd. govs. King County 1972-75), King County Bar Assn. (chair young lawyers sect. 1970). Avocations: reading, art collector. Home: 5229 140th Ave NE Bellevue WA 98005-1024 Office: Helsell & Fetterman 1500 Puget Sound Plz Seattle WA 98101

PRITCHARD, WILBUR LOUIS, telecommunications engineering executive; b. N.Y.C., May 31, 1923; s. Harmon and Jessie H. (Roth) P.; m. Kathleen H. Moss, Apr. 24, 1949; children: Hugh, Sarah, Ruth. BSEE, CCNY, 1943, ScD (hon.), 1993; postgrad., MIT, 1948-52. Registered profl. engr., Mass., Md. Microwave engr., mgr. Wayland Lab. Raytheon Co., Waltham, Mass., 1946-60; dir. engring. Europe Raytheon Co., Rome, 1960-62; group dir. satellite communication systems Aerospace Corp., El Segundo, Calif., 1962-67; v.p., dir. Comsat Labs., Clarksburg, Md., 1967-73; pres. Fairchild Space & Electronics Co., Germantown, Md., 1973-74, Satellite Systems Engring., Bethesda, Md., 1974-89, SSE Telecom, Inc., Bethesda, 1987-89, Direct Broadcast Satellite Corp., Bethesda, 1982-86, W.L. Pritchard & Co., Inc., Bethesda, 1989—; chmn. panel on broadcast satellites Nat. Acad. Scis., Falmouth, Mass., 1967; mem. space applications bd. Nat. Acad. Engring., Colo., 1968; mem. space applications adv. com. NASA, Washington, 1984, space and earth scis. adv. com., 1984-88, Nat. Acad. Engring. com. on Voice of Am., 1986-89. Author: (with others) China Space Report, 1980, Satellite Communication Systems Engineering, 1986, 2d edit., 1993; contbr. numerous articles to profl. jours.; holder 12 patents. Recipient Systems Command award USAF, 1967, Lloyd V. Berkner Space Utilization award Am. Astronautical Soc., 1983; named to hall of fame Soc. Satellite Profls. Internat., 1997. Fellow IEEE, AIAA (Aerospace Comm. award 1972), Brit. Interplanetary Soc.; mem. Nat. Acad. Engring., Soc. Satellite Profls. Internat. (hall fame 1997), Am. Astronautics Soc. (sr.), Internat. Acad. Astronautics. Home: 9201 Laurel Oak Dr Bethesda MD 20817-1937 Office: WL Pritchard & Co Inc 7315 Wisconsin Ave Ste 520E Bethesda MD 20814-3209

PRITCHARD, WILLIAM ROY, former university system administrator; b. Portage, Wis., Nov. 15, 1924; s. William Roy and Lillian Edith (Roberts) P.; m. Deanna Elaine Pritchard; children: Rosan June, William Roy, Caryl Jean, Alyn Evan, Cynthia Bedeau. Student, U. Wis., 1942-43; D.V.M., Kans. State U., 1946, D.Sc. (hon.), 1970; D.Sc. (hon.), Tufts U., 1988; Ph. D., U. Minn., 1953; J.D., Ind. U., 1957; D.Sc. (hon.), Purdue U., 1977. Asst. prof. U. Wis., 1946-49; asso. prof. U. Minn., 1949-53; prof. Purdue U., 1953-57; prof., head vet. sci. U. Fla., 1957-61; asso. dir. Vet. Med. Research Inst., Ia. State U., 1961-62; prof. U. Calif.-Davis, 1962—, dean Sch. Vet Medicine, 1962-82; asso. dir. Agrl. Expt. Sta., 1962-72; coordinator internat. agrl. programs U. Calif. system, 1977-81; vis. fellow Woodrow Wilson Sch. Pub and Internat. Affairs, Princeton, 1968-69; John Thomson lectr. U. Queensland, 1966; co-dir. nat. veterinary edn. program Duke U., 1987-92; spl. research hemmorrhagic diseases animals. Cons. Dept. Agr., Def. Dept., USPHS, VA, Calif. Dept. Health, FDA, 1962—; bd. cons. agr. Rockefeller Found., 1962-66; nat. med. cons. surgeon gen. USAF, 1962-64; mem. FAO/WHO Expert Panel Vet. Edn., President's Sci. Advisory Com. Panel World Food Supply, 1966-67, President's Sci. Advisory Com. Panel Biology and Med. Sci., 1969-70, Joint Research Com. Bd. Internat. Food and Agr. AID, 1977-81. Served with U.S. Army, 1942-44. Recipient Gov. Fla. award, 1961, Disting. Svc. award Kans. State U., 1963, Outstanding Achievement award U. Minn., 1976, Disting. Pub. Svc. award U. Calif.-Davis, 1991, Gold Headed Cane award Am. Soc. Vet. Epidemiology, 1992. Mem. AAAS, APHA, Am. Vet. Med. Assn. (Internat. Vet. Congress award 1988), Nat. Acad. of Practice in Vet. Medicine (elected 1986), Am. Soc. Vet. Epidemiologists, Conf. of Pub. Health Vets. (hon. life), U.S. Animal Health Assn., Nat. Assn. State Univs. and Land-Grant Colls. (internat. affairs com. 1965-70), Order of Coif, Sigma Xi, Phi Zeta, Gamma Alpha. Home: 2409 Madrid Ct Davis CA 95616-0141

PRITCHARD SCHOCH, TERESA NOREEN, lawyer, law librarian, executive; b. Brackley, Eng., Apr. 2, 1953; came to U.S., Dec. 1953; d. Boston Forrest and Noreen PHyliss (Taylor) P.; m. Claude M. Schoch, 1992. BA magna cum laude, Oakland U., 1974; MLS, Wayne State U., 1976, JD cum laude, 1981. Bar: Fla. 1985, Mich. 1981. Law librarian Honigman Miller Schwartz & Cohn, Detroit, 1979-81; assoc. Honigman, Miller, Schwartz & Cohn, Detroit, 1981-83, Rumberger, Kirk et al, Orlando, Fla., 1984-85; dir. rsch. svcs. Gunster, Yoakley, Criser & Stewart, West Palm Beach, Fla., 1985-91; pres. Pritchard Info., Inc., Palm Beach Gardens, Fla., 1991-92; v.p. Digital Directory Assistance, Bethesda, Md., 1993—. Columnist Online, Database; contbr. articles to profl. jours. Online Authorship award Ifo. Access Co., 1994. Mem. Fla. Bar Assn., Mich. Bar Assn. (judicial and profl. ethics com. 1982-84), Am. Assn. Law Libraries (cert.). Protestant. Avocations: aerobics, gourmet cooking. Office: Digital Lib Sys 6931 Arlington Rd Ste 405 Bethesda MD 20814-5231

PRITCHETT, SAMUEL TRAVIS, finance and insurance educator, researcher; b. Emporia, Va., Dec. 18, 1938; s. Harvey Eugene and Mary (Brown) P.; m. Bertha Yates, Feb. 20, 1960; children: John Travis, Meri Katherine. BSBA, Va. Poly. Inst. and State U., 1960, MSBA, 1967; DBA, Ind. U., 1969. CLU, ChFC, CPCU. Claim rep. Equitable Life Assurance Soc., Richmond, Va., 1960-64, asst. div. claim mgr., 1964-65; asst. prof. bus. adminstrn. U. Richmond, 1969-70; asst. prof. ins. Va. Commonwealth U., Richmond, 1970-72, assoc. prof. ins., 1972-73; assoc. prof. fin. and ins. U. S.C., Columbia, 1973-76, prof. fin. and ins., 1976—, J.H. Fellers prof., 1981-83, W.F. Hipp prof. ins., 1983—, acad. dir. MBA program, 1993-95; vis. prof. ins. Ind. U., Bloomington, 1995-96; chmn. Risk Theory Soc., Columbus, Ohio, 1987-88; acad. dir. internat. exec. devel. program Bamerindus Seguros, Curtiba, Brazil, 1995. Author: Risk Management and Insurance, 7th edit., 1996, Stock Life Insurance Company Profitability, 1986, Individual Annuities as a Source of Retirement Income, 2d edit., 1982, An Economic Analysis of Workers' Compensation in South Carolina, 1994; assoc. editor Jour. Risk and Ins., 1982-86, editor, 1987-91; assoc. editor Fin. Svcs. Rev., 1989-95; asst. editor Jour. Am. Soc. CLU and ChFC, 1993—; mem. acad. rev. bd. Jour. Fin. Planning, 1990-91; mem. editl. bd. Jour. Bus. Rsch., 1976-83, Am. Jour. Small Bus., 1975-79; contbr. articles to profl. jours. Active S.C. Joint Ins. Study Com., 1981-86, 89-95. Mem. Am. Risk and Ins. Assn. (pres. 1980-81), Acad. Fin. Svcs. (pres. 1987-88), So. Risk and Ins. Assn. (pres. 1977-78), Fin. Mgmt. Assn., Profl. Ins. Agts. Found. (named Ins. Educator of Yr. 1989), Beta Gamma Sigma (pres. chpt. 1980-81), Gamma Iota Sigma (nat. trustee 1976-92). Home: 7740 Castleton Ln Columbia SC 29223-2508 Office: U SC Coll Bus Columbia SC 29208 *Apply to others religious values such as honesty, humility, respect, and service. Cultivate a strong work ethic and select admirable mentors.*

PRITCHETT, THOMAS RONALD, retired metal and chemical company executive; b. Colorado City, Tex., Sept. 2, 1925; s. John Thomas and Meddie Omeira (Terry) P.; m. Mary Margaret Hallenbeck, Dec. 23, 1948; children: Rhonda Jean, Thomas Rand, Rebecca Ann. BS in Chemistry and ChemE., U. Tex., 1948, MS, 1949, PhD, 1951. Registered profl. engr. Calif. Rsch. chemist Def. Rsch. Lab., Austin, Tex., 1948-51, Monsanto Chem. Co., Dayton, Ohio, 1951-52; sect. head, rsch. investigator, asst. dir., tech. mgr. Kaiser Aluminum & Chem. Corp., Pleasanton, Calif., 1952-68, v.p., dir. rsch., 1968-89; cons. Alamo, Calif., 1989—. Contbr. articles to profl. jours. Mem. adv. bd. Sch. Engring. U. Calif.-Berkeley. Served with U.S. Army, 1944-46. Fellow Am. Soc. Metals; mem. AIME, Aluminum Assn. (chmn. tech. com. and acad. com.), Nat. Assn. Corrosion Engrs., Am. Chem. Soc., Electrochem. Soc., Materials Properties Council (bd. dirs.), Sigma Xi, Phi Lambda Upsilon. Home and Office: 1430 Laurenita Way Alamo CA 94507-1133

PRITIKIN, DAVID T., lawyer; b. Freeport, Ill., May 2, 1949. BA summa cum laude, Cornell U., 1971; JD magna cum laude, Harvard U., 1974. Bar: Ill. 1974, U.S. Ct. Appeals (9th cir.) 1975, U.S. Ct. Appeals (7th cir.) 1976, U.S. Supreme Ct. 1977, U.S. Ct. Appeals (fed. cir.) 1993. Ptnr. Sidley & Austin, Chgo.

PRITIKIN, JAMES B., lawyer, employee benefits consultant; b. Chgo., Feb. 18, 1939; s. Stan and Anne (Schwartz) P.; m. Barbara Cheryl Demovsky, Apr. 20, 1968 (dec. 1988); children: Gregory, David, Randi; m. Mary Szatkowski, July 7, 1990; 1 child, Peyton. BS, U. Ill., 1961; JD, DePaul U., 1965. Bar: Ill. 1965, U.S. Dist. Ct. (no. dist.) Ill. 1965, U.S. Supreme Ct. 1985; cert. matrimonial arbitrator. Pvt. practice, Chgo., 1965-68, 1984—; ptnr. Sudak, Grubman, Pritikin, Rosenthal & Feldman, Chgo., 1969-80, Pritikin & Sohn, Chgo., 1980-84; pres. Prepaid Benefits Plans Inc., Chgo., 1978—; exec. dir. The Ctr. for Divorce Mediation Ltd. Fellow Internat. Acad. Matrimonial Lawyers, Am. Acad. Matrimonial Lawyers (pres.-elect); mem. ABA, Ill. Bar Assn., Chgo. Bar Assn. (cir. ct. Cook County liaison com.), Chgo. Pub. Schs. Alumni Assn. (v.p. 1984—). Office: 221 N La Salle St Chicago IL 60601

PRITSKER, A. ALAN B., engineering executive, educator; b. Phila., Feb. 5, 1933; s. Robert and Gertrude (Liebowitz) P.; m. Anne Gruner, 1956; children: Caryl DuBrock, Pamela Poteet, Kenneth, Jeffrey. B.S.E.E., Columbia U., 1955, M.S. in Indsl. Engring., 1956; Ph.D., Ohio State U., 1961; DSc (hon.), Ariz. State U., 1992. Registered profl. engr., Tex., Ariz. Engr. Battelle Inst., 1956-62; Prof. engring. Ariz. State U., Tempe, 1962-69; prof. engring. Va. Poly. Inst., Blacksburg, 1969-70; prof. engring. Purdue U., West Lafayette, Ind., 1970-81, adj. prof. engring., 1981—; pres. Pritsker Corp., West Lafayette, 1973-86, 91—, chmn., 1973—; cons. Rand Corp., Gen. Electric Co., Gen. Motors Corp., Bethlehem Steel Co. Author: Simulation With Gasp IV, 1974, Modeling and Analysis Using Q-Gert Networks, 1979, Management Decision Making, 1984, Introduction to Simulation and SLAM II, 1986, 4th edit., 1996, TESS: The Extended Simulation Support System, 1987, SLAM II Network Models for Decision Support, 1994, Papers, Experiences, Perspectives, 1990, Simulation with Visual SLAM and AweSim, 1996. Recipient Gilbreth Indsl. Engring. award Am. Inst. Indsl. Engrs., 1991. Fellow Inst. Indsl. Engrs. (Rsch. and Innovation award 1978, Gilbreth award 1991); mem. NAE, Inst. Mgmt. Scis. (coll. on simulation, Disting. Svc. award 1991), Ops. Rsch. Am. Office: Pritsker Corp PO Box 2413 West Lafayette IN 47906-0413

PRITTS, BRADLEY ARTHUR, JR., management systems consultant; b. Cleve., July 8, 1955; s. Bradley A. and Nannette (Roehm) P.; m. Susan A. Pritts, May 22, 1976. BS, Ohio State U., 1975; MBA, U. Mich., 1982. Cert. quality sys. lead auditor. Acct. mgr. Automatic Data Processing, Ann Arbor, Mich., 1976-79, product trainer, 1979-82; mtkg. rep. Automatic Data Processing, Dearborn, Mich., 1982-83, project mgmt. specialist, 1983-84; tech. mgr. Automatic Data Processing, Southfield, Mich., 1984-85, sr. tech. mgr., 1985-87, sr. product mgr., 1987-88; pvt. practice Ann Arbor, Mich., 1988. Pres. Saline Area Players, 1994-96. Mem. Project Mgmt. Inst., Soc. Mfg. Engrs., U. Mus. Soc., Am. Soc. Quality Control (cert. quality engr., cert. quality control auditor, cert. quality mgr.), Automotive Industry Action Group. Republican. Roman Catholic. Home and Office: 3030 Lexington Dr Ann Arbor MI 48105-1460

PRITTS, KIM DEREK, state conservation officer, writer; b. Connellsville, Pa., Nov. 18, 1953; s. Harold Blaine and Janet Lorraine (Roth) P.; m. Joanna Louise Schlachta, Apr. 1, 1978; children: David, Brent. BS, Pa. State U., 1978. Cert. mcpl. police tng.; cert. conservation officer. Police officer Royersford (Pa.) Police Dept., 1978-81; state conservation officer Pa. Fish and Boat Commn., Lancaster, 1981—; competition judge Ethnic Minorities Screenwriting Competition, L.A., 1992-96; cons., expert Am. Ginseng. Author: The Mystery of Sadler Marsh, 1993, Ginseng: How to Find, Grow, and Use America's Forest Gold, 1995; author: (screenplay) Outlander (Christopher Columbus Discovery award), 1994. Mem. D.U.I. Coun. of Lancaster County. Cpl. USMC, 1972-74. Finalist, Am.'s Best Writing competition The Writers Found., 1994, 95. Mem. Conservation Officers of Pa., N.Am. Wildlife Enforcement Officers Assn., Pa. Sportsmen for the Disabled (Outstanding Svc. award 1992). Mem. Ch. of God. Avocations: hiking, photography.

PRITZ, MICHAEL BURTON, neurological surgeon; b. New Brunswick, N.J., Oct. 8, 1947; s. John Ernest and Helen Violet (Rockoff) P.; m. Edmay Marie Gregorcy, Feb. 18, 1973; children: Edmond Louis, Benjamin David. BS, U. Ill., 1969; PhD, Case Western Res. U., 1973, MD, 1975. Diplomate Am. Bd. Neurol. Surgery. Asst. prof. neurol. surgery U. Calif. Irvine Med. Ctr., Orange, 1981-85, assoc. prof., 1985-93; prof., 1993, U. Calif. Irvine Med. Ctr., Orange, 1993—; prof. sect. neurol. surgery Ind. U. Sch. Medicine, Indpls., 1993—, prof. neurol. surgery, 1993—. Contbr. articles to profl. jours. Recipient Herbert S. Steuer award Case Western Res. U., Cleve., 1975; NSF fellow, 1968; Edmund J. James scholar U. Ill., Champaign, 1968-69. Mem. Soc. Neurosci., Am. Assn. Anatomists, Am. Assn. Neurol. Surgeons, Congress Neurol. Surgeons, Soc. Neurol. Surgeons of Orange County (pres. 1985-86, sec.-treas. 1984-85), Ind. State Neurosurg. Soc. (pres. 1996-98).

PRITZKER, JAY, travel company executive , lawyer; b. Chgo., Aug. 26, 1922; married; children: Tom, John, Dan, Gigi. BS, Northwestern U., 1941, JD, 1947. Bar: Ill. 1947. Ptnr. Pritzker and Pritzker, Chgo., 1947—, Chgo. Mill and Lumber Co., 1948—, Mich.-Calif. Lumber Co., 1951—; chmn., CEO, bd. dirs. Amarillo Gear Co., 1965—; chmn., sec., CEO Marmon Group Inc., 1967—, chmn., sec., chmn. bd. dirs., 1972—; chmn. bd. dirs., CEO Hyatt Corp.; chmn. bd. dirs. Hyatt Corp., Hyatt Internat., Marmon Holdings, Inc.; dir. Berisford plc, Royal Caribbean Cruises Ltd., others. Life trustee Univ. Chgo.; chmn. internat adv. bd. Columbia Univ. Sch. Internat. and Pub. Affairs. Lt. USN, 1942-46. Office: Pritzker and Pritzker 200 W Madison St Ste 3800 Chicago IL 60606-3417*

PRITZKER, LEON, statistician, consultant; b. N.Y.C., June 26, 1922; s. Harry and Sophie (Greene) P.; m. Mary Anne Watts; children: William Earl, David Ronald, Paul Mark, Carol Ann, Phillip Joseph. BS, CCNY, 1942; MA, U. Pa., 1947. Statistician U.S. Bur. of Census, Washington, 1947-61, chief response rsch. br., 1961-67; dir. mktg. info. svcs. Anheuser-Busch Cos., St. Louis, 1967-73, dir. mgmt. systems, 1973-84; exec. v.p., staff ops. Campbell Taggart, Inc., Dallas, 1985-90; cons., 1990—; vis. faculty Case Inst. Tech., Cleve., 1954-55; cons. Cen. Statis. Bur., Govt. Israel, Jerusalem, 1961, Inst. Stats., Govt. Turkey, Ankara, 1967; dir. Med. Alliance, Inc. Contbr. articles to profl. jours. With U.S. Army, 1943-46. Fellow Am. Statis. Assn.; mem. Internat. Assn. Survey Statisticians.

PRITZKER, ROBERT ALAN, manufacturing company executive; b. Chgo., June 30, 1926; s. Abram Nicholas and Fanny (Doppelt) P.; m. Mayari Sargent; children: James, Linda, Karen, Matthew , Liesel. B.S. in Indsl. Engring., Ill. Inst. Tech., Chgo., 1946; postgrad. in bus. adminstrn., U. Ill. Engaged in mfg., 1946—; chief exec. officer, pres., dir. Marmon Corp., Chgo., Marmon Indsl. Corp., Chgo.; pres., dir. The Colson Group, Inc., Marmon Holdings, Inc., Marmon Industries, Inc., Chgo.; bd. dirs. Hyatt Corp., Chgo., Dalfort Corp., Union Tank Car Co.; vis. prof. Oxford U.; chmn. Nat. Assn. Mfrs. Chmn. bd. Pritzker Found., Chgo.; trustee, chmn. Ill. Inst. Tech., Chgo. Symphony Orch.; immediate past chmn. Field Mus. of Natural History; bd. dirs. Rush-Presbyn.-St. Luke's Med. Ctr. Mem. NAE, Nat. Assn. Mfrs. (former chmn.). Office: Marmon Group Inc 225 W Washington St Chicago IL 60606-3418*

PRITZKER, THOMAS JAY, lawyer, business executive; b. Chgo., June 6, 1950; s. Jay Arthur and Marian (Friend) P.; m. Margot Lyn Barrow-Sicree, Sept. 4, 1977; children—Jason, Benjamin, David. BA, Claremont Men's Coll, 1971, MBA, 1972; JD, U. Chgo., 1976. Assoc. Katten, Muchin, Zavis, Pearl and Galler, Chgo., 1976-77; exec. v.p. Hyatt Corp., Chgo., 1977-80, pres., 1980—; chmn. Hyatt Hotels Corp., 1980—; ptnr. Pritzker & Pritzker, Chgo., 1976—; pres. Rosemont Shipping, Chgo., 1980—; chmn. bd. dirs. Health Care Compare Corp., Chgo. Trustee Art Inst. Chgo. 1988—, U. Chgo. Mem. ABA, Ill. Bar Assn., Chgo. Bar Assn., Standard Club, Lake Shore Country Club. Clubs: Standard (Chgo.); Lake Shore Country (Glencoe, Ill.). Office: Hyatt Corp 200 W Madison St Chicago IL 60606-3414

PRIVAT, JEANNETTE MARY, bank librarian; b. Seattle, May 2, 1938; d. Glenn McKenzie and Katherine (VanDerveer) P. BA in Bus. Adminstrn., U. Wash., 1960, MLS, 1969. Asst. libr. United Control Corp., Redmond, Wash., 1960-64, libr., 1964-68; libr. Seattle-First National Bank, Seattle, 1968-75, asst. v.p. and mgr., 1975-93; exec. dir. King County Libr. System Found., Seattle, 1993-95; reference libr. Shoreline (Wash.) Libr., 1994—; mem. vis. com. U. Wash. Grad. Sch. Libr. and Info. Sci., 1981—, chmn., 1991—; mem. adv. bd. extension libr. mgmt. program U. Washington, 1989—. Bd. trustees Northwest Chamber Orch., Seattle, 1986—, pres. 1987-92, exec. com., 1992-95. Named disting. alumnus Wash. Grad. Sch. Libr. and Info. Sci., 1993. Fellow Spl. Librs. Assn. (nat. bd. dirs. 1977-79, various offices 1966-89). Office: Shoreline Library 345 NE 175th St Shoreline WA 98155-3517

PRIVETERA, LORA MARIE, lawyer; b. Toms River, N.J., July 6, 1967; d. Joseph Alfred and Gloria Estelle (Perez) P. BA, Georgian Ct. Coll., 1989; JD, Temple U., 1992. Bar: N.J. 1992, Pa. 1992. Visitation counsellor Ocean County Superior Ct., Toms River, N.J., 1992-93; lawyer Tanner & Tanner, Barnegat, N.J., 1993-95. Mem. ABA. Republican. Roman Catholic. Office: 703 Mill Creek Rd Ste F-2 Manahawkin NJ 08050-3828

PRIVETT, CARYL PENNEY, lawyer; b. Birmingham, Ala., Jan. 7, 1948; d. William Kinnaird Privett and Katherine Speake (Binford) Ennis. BA, Vanderbilt U., 1970; JD, NYU, 1973. Bar: Ala. 1973, U.S. Dist. Ct. (so. dist.) Ala. 1973, U.S. Dist. Ct. (no. dist.) Ala. 1974, U.S. Ct. Appeals (5th cir.) 1974, U.S. Ct. Appeals (11th cir.) 1981. Assoc. Crawford & Blacksher, Mobile, Ala., 1973-74, Adams, Baker & Clemon, Birmingham, 1974-76; asst. U.S. atty. no. dist. Ala. U.S. Atty.'s Office, U.S. Dept. Justice, Birmingham, 1976-92, first asst. U.S. atty., 1992—. Bd. dirs. Legal Aid Soc., Birmingham, 1986-88, pres., 1988; sec., founder Lawyers for Choice, Ala., 1989-92; bd. dirs. Planned Parenthood Ala., Birmingham, v.p., 1986-91; chair domestic violence com. City of Birmingham, 1989-91; sustaining mem. Jr. League Birmingham; active Downtown Dem. Club, Birmingham. Recipient Cert. in Color Photography U. Ala., Birmingham, 1989, Commr.'s Spl. citation Food and Drug Adminstrn.; named one of Outstanding Young Women Am., 1977, 78. Mem. ABA, Fed. Bar Assn. (pres. Birmingham chpt. 1979), Birmingham Bar Assn., Ala. Bar Assn., Downtown Club. Presbyterian. Avocation: photography. Home: 50 Norman Dr Birmingham AL 35213-4310 Office: US Attys Office 1800 5th Ave N Ste 200 Birmingham AL 35203-2112

PRIVO, ALEXANDER, finance educator, department chairman; m. Elena Privo. BS, Touro Coll., N.Y.C., 1982; M Profl. Studies, New Sch. for Social Rsch., N.Y.C., 1985; MS in Edn., CUNY, 1988; PhD in Adminstrn. and Mgmt., Walden U., 1991. Cert. govt. fin. mgr.; cert. secondary tchr. math., ESL, social studies, bus., acctg., Russian, N.y. Dir. acctg. and fin. reporting Assoc. Retail Stores Inc., N.Y.C., 1982-85; tchr. acctg. N.Y.C. Bd. Edn., 1985—; prof., dept. bus. and econs. Touro Coll., 1987—; dean CUNY, 1987-90; chmn. dept. bus. econs. Touro Coll., 1991—; coord. mentoring program CUNY and N.Y.C. Bd. edn., 1985-92; cons. and prof. Russian (former Soviet Union); exec. training program MBA Baruch Coll., CUNY, 1990—; coord. cooperative edn. program NYC BD. Edn./CUNY, 1992—. Curriculum devel. grantee. Mem. ASCD, Am. Acctg. Assn., Assn. Govt. Accts., Nat. Bus. Edn. Assn., Internat. Bus. Edn. Assn., Met. Bus. Edn. Assn., N.Y. Educators (doctorate), Am. Mgmt. Assn., Kappa Delta Pi. Home: 43-33 46th St Apt F15 Sunnyside NY 11104-2036

PRIZER, CHARLES JOHN, chemical company executive; b. Lake Forest, Ill., Apr. 24, 1924; s. Charles Sumner and Josephine Mary (Jansz) P.; m. Dorothy Gore, June 15, 1944; children: John, Sharon Lee, Mark Sumner, Linda Ann. B.S., U. Ill., 1944; M.S., Drexel U., 1956. With Eastman Kodak Co., 1944-46, Edwal Labs., 1946-51; with Rohm & Haas Co., Phila., 1951-85; v.p., dir. N.Am. region Rohm & Haas Co., 1978-83, group v.p. corp. ops., 1983-85; exec. v.p. Clean Sites, Inc., Alexandria, Va., 1986; prin. Mill Creek Co., 1987-93, Prizer & Wilkinson, 1988-93, Dotsu Enterprises, Inc., 1991-93, CJP Enterprises, Inc., 1992—. Mem. Am. Inst. Chem. Engrs., Am. Chem. Soc. Office: 4325 Gulf Of Mexico Dr Unit 307 Longboat Key FL 34228-2418

PRIZZI, JACK ANTHONY, investment banking executive; b. Rochester, N.Y., July 5, 1935; s. Samuel Anthony and Mary Ann (Emanuele) P.; B.S. in Chemistry, Va. Mil. Inst., 1956; M.S. in Phys. Chemistry, U. Va., 1961, M.B.A., 1963; m. Geraldine A. Bias, Feb. 16, 1957 (div. 1971); children—Lynne Marie, Michael Vincent, Karen Annette. Chem. engr. E.I. duPont DeNemours & Co., Inc., Niagara Falls, N.Y., 1956-57; engr. Project Mercury, NASA, 1959; mgr. planning and devel. PPG Industries, Pitts., 1963-68; gen. mgr. Process Components Inc., Norfolk, Va., 1968-70; ptnr. Alan Patricof Assocs., N.Y.C., 1970-74, Beacon Ptnrs., N.Y.C., 1974-76, 77-79, Stuart Bros., N.Y.C., 1976-77; v.p. Walter E. Heller & Co., exec. v.p. Heller Capital Services Inc., N.Y.C., 1979-84; sr. v.p. DnC Am. Banking Corp., N.Y.C., 1984-86; mng. dir. DnC Capital Corp., 1986-89; pres., CEO Jack A. Prizzi & Co., 1989—; spl. ltd. ptnr. Harvest Ptnrs., 1993-97; bd. dirs. Tex. Meridian Resources Corp.; instr. advanced grades N.Y. Power Squadron. Vol. Urban Cons. Group. Served to capt. U.S. Army, 1957-59. Grantee Office Naval Research, 1960, Calif. Research Corp., 1960-61. Mem. Assn. for Corp. Growth, Am. Chem. Soc., Raven Soc., N.Y. Athletic Club. Office: 21 W 58th St Apt 12E New York NY 10019-1634

PRO, PHILIP MARTIN, judge; b. Richmond, Calif., Dec. 12, 1946; s. Leo Martin and Mildred Louise (Beck) P.; m. Dori Sue Hallas, Nov. 13, 1982; 1 child, Brenda Kay. BA, San Francisco State U., 1968; JD Golden Gate U., 1972. Bar: Calif. 1972, Nev. 1973, U.S. Ct. Appeals (9th cir.) 1973, U.S. Dist. Ct. Nev. 1973, U.S. Supreme Ct. 1976. Pub. defender, Las Vegas, 1973-75; asst. U.S. atty., Dist. Nev., Las Vegas, 1975-78; ptnr. Semenza, Murphy & Pro, Reno, 1978-79; dep. atty. gen. State of Nev., Carson City, 1979-80; U.S. magistrate U.S. Dist. Ct. Nev., Las Vegas, 1980-87; U.S. dist. judge, 1987—; instr. Atty. Gen.'s Advocacy Inst., Nat. Inst. Trial Advocacy, 1992; chmn. com. adminstrn. of magistrate judge system Jud. Conf. U.S., 1993—. Bd. dirs. NCCJ, Las Vegas, 1982—, mem. program com. and issues in justice com. Mem. ABA, Fed. Judges Assn. (bd. dirs. 1992—), Nev. State Bar Assn., Calif. State Bar Assn., Nev. Judges Assn. (instr.), Assn. Trial Lawyers Am., Nev. Am. Inn Ct. (pres. 1989—), Ninth Cir. Jury (instructions com.), Nat. Conf. U.S. Magistrates (sec.), Nev. Am. Inn of Ct. (pres. 1989-91). Republican. Episcopalian. Office: US Dist Ct 341 Fed Bldg 300 Las Vegas Bldv S Las Vegas NV 89101

PROBASCO, CALVIN HENRY CHARLES, clergyman, college administrator; b. Petaluma, Calif., Apr. 5, 1926; s. Calvin Warren and Ruth Charlene (Winans) P.; m. Nixie June Farnsworth, Feb. 14, 1947; children—Calvin, Carol, David, Ruth. B.A. cum laude, Biola Bible Coll., La Mirada, Calif., 1953; D.D. (hon.), Talbot Theol. Sem., La Mirada, 1983. Ordained to ministry, 1950. Pastor Sharon Baptist Ch., El Monte, Calif., 1951-58, Carmichael Bible Ch., Calif., 1958—; pres. Sacramento Bible Inst., Carmichael, 1968—. Mem. Ind. Fundamental Chs. Am. (rec. sec. 1978-81, pres. 1981-84, 1st v.p. 1987-88), Delta Epsilon Chi. Republican. Office: Carmichael Bible Ch 7100 Fair Oaks Blvd Carmichael CA 95608

PROBERT, COLIN, advertising executive. Ptnr., pres. Goodby, Silverstein & Ptnrs., San Francisco. Office: Goodby Silverstein & Ptnrs 921 Front St San Francisco CA 94111-1426

PROBERT, WALTER, lawyer, educator; b. Portland, Oreg., Jan. 13, 1925; s. Raymond and Mildred Marie (Pyburn) P.; m. Barbara Louise Stevenson, Mar. 22, 1952; children: Richard Walter, James Stevenson. Student, Alfred U., 1944; B.S., U. Oreg., 1948, J.D., 1951; J.S.D. (Grad. fellow), Yale U., 1957. Bar: Oreg. 1951. Practiced in Portland, 1951-52; asst. prof. Western Res. U., 1953-57, asso. prof., 1957-59; prof. U. Fla., Gainesville, 1959—, endowed prof., 1985-96, titled prof. emeritus, 1996—, prof. law, 1997—; vis. prof. Northwestern U., 1960-61, U. Tex., summer 1970, U. Wash., 1972-73; vis. research prof. U. Denver, 1966-67; lectr. Balliol Coll., Oxford U., 1968; dir. law and social sci. program NSF, 1973-74. Author: Law, Language, and Communication, 1972; faculty editor Western Res. U. Law Rev., 1953-59; contbr. articles to profl. jours. Served with AUS, 1943-47. Recipient grants for law-communication research. Mem. ATLA, Oreg. Bar Assn., Internat. Assn. Philosophy of Law and Social Philosophy, Phi Beta Kappa, Order of Coif, Order of St. Ives, Delta Theta Phi. Home: 1522 SW 35th Pl Gainesville FL 32608-3530

PROBSTEIN, RONALD FILMORE, mechanical engineering educator; b. N.Y.C., Mar. 11, 1928; s. Sidney and Sally (Rosenstein) P.; m. Irene Weindling, July 30, 1950; 1 child, Sidney. BME, NYU, 1948; MSE, Princeton U., 1950, AM, 1951, PhD, 1952; AM (hon.), Brown U., 1957, ScD (hon.), 1997. Rsch. asst. physics N.Y. U., 1946-48, instr. engring. mechanics, 1947-48; rsch. asst. dept. aero. engring. Princeton U., 1948-52, rsch. assoc., 1952-53, asst. prof., 1953-54; asst. prof. divs. engring., applied math. Brown U., 1954-55, assoc. prof., 1955-59, prof., 1959-62; prof. mech. engring. M.I.T., 1962-89, 96—, Ford prof. engring., 1989-96; Disting. prof. engring. U. Utah, 1973; sr. partner Water Purification Assos., Cambridge, 1974-82; chmn. bd. Water Gen. Corp., Cambridge, 1982-83; sr. corp. tech. advisor Foster-Miller, Inc., 1983—; commr. commn. on engring. and tech. systems NRC, 1980-83; sci. advisor to bd. Corrpro Cos., 1993—. Author: Hypersonic Flow Theory, 1959, Hypersonic Flow, Inviscid Flows, 1966, Water in Synthetic Fuel Production, 1978, Synthetic Fuels, 1982, Physicochemical Hydrodynamics, 1989, 2d edit., 1994; editor: Introduction to Hypersonic Flow, 1961, Physics of Shock Waves, 1966, Jour. PhysicoChem. Hydrodynamics, 1987-89; contbr. articles to profl. jours.; patentee in field. Guggenheim fellow, 1960-61; R.F. Probstein Lecture Series in Engring. Sci., MIT, established 1996. Fellow Am. Acad. Arts and Scis. (councilor 1975-79), Am. Phys. Soc., ASME (Freeman award 1971), AIAA, AAAS; mem. NAE, Internat. Acad. Astronautics, Am. Inst. Chem. Engrs. Home: 5 Seaver St Brookline MA 02146-5714 Office: 77 Massachusetts Ave Cambridge MA 02139-4301

PROBUS, MICHAEL MAURICE, JR., lawyer; b. Louisville, Jan. 26, 1963; s. Michael Maurice and Jerilyn Ann (Burks) P.; m. Luz Marie Probus, May 22, 1985; children: Michael Julian, Lauren Michael. BA, U. Dallas, 1985; JD, U. Tex., 1988. Bar: Tex. 1988, U.S. Dist. Ct. (we. dist.) Tex. 1990, U.S. Ct. Appeals (5th cir.) 1993. Jud. law clk. to chief judge U.S. Dist. Ct. Tex., Houston, 1988-90; assoc. Law Offices of Michael A. Wash, Austin, Tex., 1990—. Pro bono atty. Vol. Legal Svcs., Austin, 1994—; active TTLA Advocates, Austin, 1994—. Mem. Tex. Trial Lawyers Assn., Travis County Bar Assn. (mem. CLE com. 1993—). Democrat. Roman Catholic. Office: Law Offices Michael A Wash 600 Congress Ave Ste 3200 Austin TX 78701-3248

PROCHNOW, DOUGLAS LEE, lawyer; b. Omaha, Jan. 9, 1952; s. Albert Delmer and Betty Jean (Wood) P. BA with high distinction, U. Nebr., 1974; JD, Northwestern U., 1977. Bar: Ill. 1977, U.S. Dist. Ct. (no. dist.) Ill. 1977, U.S. Ct. Appeals (7th cir.) 1989. Assoc. Wildman, Harrold, Allen & Dixon, Chgo., 1977-84, ptnr., 1985—. Spl. asst. corp. counsel City of Chgo.,

1986-87. Mem. ABA, Ill. Bar Assn., Chgo. Bar Assn., Assn. Trial Lawyers Am. (assoc.), Ill. Trial Lawyers Assn., Soc. Trial Lawyers, Def. Rsch. Inst., Phi Beta Kappa, Phi Eta Sigma. Home: 1230 N State Pky Apt 6D Chicago IL 60610-2261 Office: Wildman Harrold Allen & Dixon 225 W Wacker Dr Chicago IL 60606-1224

PROCHNOW, HERBERT VICTOR, former government official, banker, author; b. Wilton, Wis., May 19, 1897; s. Adolph and Alvina (Liefke) P.; m. Laura Virginia Stinson, June 12, 1928 (dec. Aug. 1977); 1 child, Herbert Victor. BA, U. Wis., 1921, MA, 1922, LLD, 1956; PhD, Northwestern U., 1947, Northwestern U., 1963; LLD (hon.), LittD, Millikin U., 1952; LLD, Ripon Coll., Wis., 1950, Lake Forest Coll., 1964, Monmouth Coll., 1965, U. N.D., 1966; DHL, Thiel Coll., 1965. Prin. Kendall (Wis.) High Sch.; asst. prof. bus. adminstrn. Ind. U.; advt. mgr. Union Trust Co., Chgo.; officer First Nat. Bank of Chgo., pres., 1962-68, dir., 1960-68, hon. dir., 1968-73; former dir. Carter H. Golembe Assocs., Inc., 1972-76; dir. Banco di Roma, Chgo., 1973-87; columnist Chgo. Tribune, 1968-70; sec. fed. adv. coun. Fed. Res. System, 1945-94; apptd. spl. asst. to sec. of state, 1955, dep. under sec. of state for econ. affairs, 1955-56; alt. gov. for U.S. Internat. Bank and Internat. Monetary Fund, 1955-56; pres. Internat. Monetary Conf., 1968, now cons., hon mem. Co-author: The Next Century Is America's, 1938, Practical Bank Credit, 1963, (with Herbert V. Prochnow, Jr.) A Dictionary of Wit, Wisdom and Satire, 1962, The Public Speaker's Treasure Chest, 1976, rev. edit., 1986, The Successful Toastmaster, 1966, A Treasury of Humorous Quotations, 1969, The Changing World of Banking, 1973, The Toastmaster's Treasure Chest, 1979, rev. edit., 1988, A Treasure Chest of Quotations for All Occasions, 1983; author: Great Stories from Great Lives (an anthology), 1944, Meditations on the Ten Commandments, 1946, The Toastmaster's Handbook, 1949, Term Loans and Theories of Bank Liquidity, 1949, Successful Speakers Handbook, 1951, 1001 Ways to Improve Your Conversations and Speeches, 1952, Meditations on the Beatitudes, 1952, The Speaker's Treasury of Stories for All Occasions, 1953, The Speaker's Handbook of Epigrams and Witticisms, 1955, Speakers Treasury for Sunday School Teachers, 1955, A Treasury of Stories, Illustrations, Epigrams and Quotations for Ministers and Teachers, 1956, The New Guide for Toastmasters, 1956, Meditations on The Lord's Prayer, 1957, The New Speaker's Treasury of Wit and Wisdom, 1958, A Family Treasury of Inspiration and Faith, 1958, The Complete Toastmaster, 1960, Speaker's Book of Illustrations, 1960, 1000 Tips and Quips for Speakers and Toastmasters, 1962, 1400 Ideas for Speakers and Toastmasters, 1964, Tree of Life, 1972, Speaker's Source Book, 1972, A Speaker's Treasury for Educators, Convocation Speakers, 1973, 1,000 Quips, Stories, and Illustrations for All Occasions, 1973, Toastmaster's Quips and Stories and How to Use Them, 1982; editor: American Financial Institutions, 1951, Determining the Business Outlook, 1954, The Federal Reserve System, 1960, World Economic Problems and Policies, 1965, The Five Year Outlook for Interest Rates, 1968, The One-Bank Holding Company, 1969, The Eurodollar, 1970, The Five Year Outlook for Interest Rates in the U.S. and Abroad, 1972, Dilemmas Facing the Nation, 1979, Bank Credit, 1981, Speaker's and Toastmaster's Handbook, 1990, 5100 Quotations for Speakers and Writers, 1992. Mem. O.S.S., 1942-45, U.S. delegation GATT, Geneva, 1956; del. Colombo Conf., Singapore, 1955, OECD, Paris, 1956; former lectr. Loyola U., Ind. U., Northwestern U.; bd. dir. grad. sch. of banking U. of Wis., 1945-81; trustee, cons. McCormick Theol. Sem.; hon. trustee Chgo. Sunday Evening Club. With AEF, 1918-19. Decorated Order of Vasa (Sweden), comdr. Cross Order of Merit (Fed. Republic of Germany).; recipient Bus. Statesmanship award Harvard U. Bus. Sch. Assn. Chgo., 1965, Ayres Leadership award Stonier Grad. Sch. Banking, Rutgers U., 1966, Silver Plaque NCCJ, 1967. Mem. Chgo. Coun. on Fgn. Rels. (pres. 1966-67), Am. Econ. Assn., Chgo. Assn. Commerce and Industry (pres. 1964-65), Rotary, Beta Gamma Sigma (nat. honoree). Clubs: Comml., Glen View; Univ., Chgo., Union League (Chgo.), Bankers (past pres.). Home: 2950 Harrison St Evanston IL 60201-1249 Office: 1 First Natl Plz Chicago IL 60603-2003

PROCHNOW, HERBERT VICTOR, JR., lawyer; b. Evanston, Ill., May 26, 1931; s. Herbert V. and Laura (Stinson) P.; m. Lucia Boyden, Aug. 6, 1966; children: Thomas Herbert, Laura. A.B., Harvard U., 1953, J.D., 1956; A.M., U. Chgo., 1958. Bar: Ill. 1957, U.S. Dist. Ct. (no. dist.) Ill. 1961. With 1st Nat. Bank Chgo., 1958-91, atty., 1961-70, sr. atty., 1971-73, counsel, 1973-91, adminstrv. asst. to chmn. bd., 1978-81; pvt. practice, 1991—. Author: (with Herbert V. Prochnow) A Treasury of Humorous Quotations, 1969, The Changing World of Banking, 1974, The Public Speaker's Treasure Chest, 1986, The Toastmaster's Treasure Chest, 1988; also articles in legal publs. Mem. ABA, Ill. Bar Assn., Chgo. Bar Assn. (chmn. com. internat. law 1970-71), Am. Soc. Internat. Law, Phi Beta Kappa. Clubs: Harvard (N.Y.C.); Chicago (Chgo.), Legal (Chgo.), Law (Chgo.), Onwentsia, Economic (Chgo.), University (Chgo.). Home: 949 Woodbine Pl Lake Forest IL 60045-2275 Office: 155 N Michigan Ave Chicago IL 60601

PROCHNOW, JAMES R., lawyer; b. Hutchinson, Minn., Sept. 22, 1943. BA, Hamline U., 1965; JD, William Mitchell Law Sch., 1969. Bar: Minn. 1969, U.S. Supreme Ct. 1973, Colo. 1975. Staff civil divsn. Dept. Justice, Washington, 1973-74; legal counsel to Pres. The White House, Washington, 1974; ptnr. Baker & Hostetler, Denver, Patton Boggs, 1995—. Editor in chief William Mitchell Opinion, 1968-69; antitrust notes editor The Barrister, 1978-81. 02553627, Denver Bar Assn., Colo. Bar Assn. Office: Patton Boggs 1660 Lincoln St Ste 1975 Denver CO 80264-1901

PROCKOP, DARWIN JOHNSON, biochemist, physician; b. Palmerton, Pa., Aug. 31, 1929; s. John and Sophie (Gurski) P.; m. Elinor Sacks, Apr. 15, 1961; children: Susan Elizabeth, David John. AB, Haverford Coll., 1951; MA, Oxford U., 1953; MD, U. Pa., 1956; PhD, George Washington U., 1962; DSc (hon.), U. Oulu, 1983, U. So. Fla., 1993. Investigator NIH, 1957-61; assoc., asst. prof., asso. prof., prof. medicine and biochemistry U. Pa., Phila., 1961-72; prof., chmn. dept. biochemistry U. Medicine and Dentistry of N.J. (Rutgers Med. Sch.), Piscataway, N.J., 1972-86; prof., chmn. dept. biochemistry and molecular biology Jefferson Med. Coll., Phila., 1986-96; prof., dir. Ctr. for Gene Therapy, Med. Coll. Pa./Hahnemann U., Phila., 1996—; dir. Jefferson Inst. Molecular Medicine, 1986-96. Contbr. articles to profl. jours.; research on collagen. Served with USPHS, 1958-61. Fulbright fellow Oxford U., 1951-53; NIH, grantee, 1961—; recipient Disting. Alumnus award George Wash. U., 1991, U. Pa., 1994. Mem. NAS, Inst. Medicine, Acad. Finland, Am. Soc. Biol. Chemists, Am. Soc. Clin. Investigation, Am. Assn. Physicians, Phi Beta Kappa, Alpha Omega Alpha. Home: 291 Locust St Philadelphia PA 19106-3913 Office: Allegheny U Health Scis MCP Hahnemann Med Sch 15th & Vine St Philadelphia PA 19106

PROCTER, JOHN ERNEST, former publishing company executive; b. Gainesboro, Tenn., July 23, 1918; s. Leon and Mary (Poteet) P.; m. Jane Sprott, May 23, 1941; children: Mary Carol, Valere Kay. Student, Vanderbilt U., 1940-41, U. Miami (also extension div.), 1943-44, U. Tenn., 1946-50; LL.D. (hon.), Ohio No. U., 1971; D.L. (hon.), Ky. Wesleyan Coll., 1981. With Methodist Pub. House, Nashville, 1945-83; v.p., pub. Methodist Pub. House, 1964-70, pres., pub., 1970-83; dir. 3d Nat. Bank, Nashville. Bd. dirs. Tenn Council on Econ. Edn. Served to capt. USAAF and USAF, 1944-45, 50-52. Decorated Certificate of Valor; Air medal with 7 oak leaf clusters; D.F.C. Mem. Adminstrv. Mgmt. Soc. (past pres. Nashville, area. sec.-treas. 1967-68, Merit Key award 1961, Diamond Merit award 1967), Nashville C. of C. (past mem. bd. govs.), Assn. Am. Pubs. (past dir.). Clubs: Golf Club of Tenn., Belle Meade Golf & Country. *The modest success I have achieved is the result of an intense commitment to intellectual honesty, sensitivity to the needs of my associates, the setting of challenging and realistic goals, striving for efficiency by doing things right and being effective by doing the right things, always with faith in myself and my associates.*

PROCTOR, BARBARA GARDNER, advertising agency executive, writer; b. Asheville, N.C.; d. William and Bernice (Baxter) Gardner; B.A. Talladega Coll., 1954; m. Carl L. Proctor, July 20, 1961 (div. Nov. 1963); 1 son, Morgan Eugene. Music critic, contbg. editor Down Beat Mag., Chgo., from 1958; internat. dir. Vee Jay Records, Chgo., 1961-64; copy supr. Post-Keyes-Gardner Advt., Inc., 1965-68, Gene Taylor Assos., 1968-69, North Advt. Agy., 1969-70; contbr. to gen. periodicals, from 1952; founder Proctor & Gardner Advt., Chgo., 1970—, now pres., chief exec. officer. Mem. Chgo. Urban League, Chgo. Econ. Devel. Corp. Bd. dirs. People United to Save Humanity, Better Bus. Bur. Cons. pub. relations and promotion, record industry. Recipient Armstrong Creative Writing award, 1954; awards Chgo. Fedn. Advt. Clubs, N.Y. Art Dirs. Club. Woman's Day; Frederick Douglas Humanitarian award, 1975; named Chgo. Advt. Woman of Year, 1974. Mem. Chgo. Media Women, Nat. Assn. Radio Arts and Sci., Women's Advt. Club, Cosmopolitan C. of C. (dir.), Female Execs. Assn., Internat. Platform Assn., Smithsonian Instn. Assos. Author TV documentary Blues for a Gardenia, 1963. Office: Proctor & Gardner Advt Inc 980 N Michigan Ave Ste 1776 Chicago IL 60611-7503

PROCTOR, CONRAD ARNOLD, physician; b. Ann Arbor, Mich., July 14, 1934; s. Bruce and Luena Marie (Crawford) P.; m. Phyllis Darlene Anderson, June 23, 1956; children: Sharon Darlene Proctor Heimbach, Barbara Jan Brown, David Conrad, Todd Bruce. MD, U. Mich., 1959, MS, 1964. Cert. Am. Bd. Otolaryngology. Intern St. Joseph Mercy Hosp., Ann Arbor, 1959-60; jr. clin. instr. Univ. Hosp., Ann Arbor, 1961-63, sr. clin. instr., 1963-65; chief dept. otolaryngology Munson Army Hosp., Ft. Leavenworth, Kans., 1965-67; mem. attending staff William Beaumont Hosp., Royal Oak, Mich., 1967—; instr. Am. Acad. Otolaryngology, Washington, 1968-82, guest examiner, Chgo., 1978-79; Midwest dir. Macrocellular Cellular Phone Sys., 1990—. Author: Current Therapy in Otolaryngology, 1984-85; (booklet) Dietary Treatment of Meniere's Syndrome, 1983, Hyperinsulinemia and Tinnitus, 1988; (manual) Hereditary Sensorineural Hearing Loss, 1978, Etiology, Treatment of Fluid Retention in Meniere's Syndrome, 1992; (med. jour.) Abnormal Insulin Levels and Vertigo, 1981. Dir. Christian edn. Bloomfield Hills (Mich.) Bapt. Ch., 1969-72, fin. chmn., 1975-78, Sunday sch. tchr., 1967—. Served to capt. U.S. Army, 1965-67. Recipient 1st pl. award for med. rsch. Students Am. Med. Assn., 1959, Merit award Am. Acad. Otolaryngology, 1978; holder 4 world records Internat. Game Fish Assn. Mem. AMA, Mich. State Med. Assn., Oakland County Med. Assn., Am. Bd. Otolaryngology, ACS, Triological Soc., Otosclerosis Study Group, Internat. Game Fish Assn. (Nat. Fresh Wahter Fishing Hall of Fame), Am. Legion, U.S. Tennis Assn., U.S. Golf Assn., Panangling Ltd. (Chgo.), Victors and Presidents Club (Ann Arbor), Audobon Soc., Phi Eta Sigma, Phi Kappa Phi, Phi Beta Kappa. Republican. Avocations: baseball, football, tennis, Arctic exploration, fishing. Home: 1645 Kirkway Ln Bloomfield Hills MI 48302-1360 Office: 3535 W 13 Mile Rd Royal Oak MI 48073-6700

PROCTOR, DONALD FREDERICK, otolaryngology educator, physician; b. Red Bank, N.J., Apr. 19, 1913; s. Frederick R. and Gertrude (Chauncey) P.; m. Janice Carson, June 10, 1937; children: Douglas, Nan. A.B., Johns Hopkins, 1933, M.D., 1937. Diplomate: Am. Bd. Otolaryngology. With otol. lab. Johns Hopkins Hosp., 1937-38, mem. otolaryn. house staff, 1938-40; resident otolaryngology Balt. City Hosps., 1940-41; pvt. practice otolaryngology Balt., 1941-56; asso. prof. otolaryngology Med. Sch., Johns Hopkins, 1946-51, 58-73, prof. anesthesiology, 1951-55, 77-84, asst. prof. physiology, laryngology and otolaryngology, 1955-58, 77-84, prof. laryngology and otology, 1973-84, prof. environ. health sci., 1965-84, prof. emeritus, 1984—, chief bronchoscopic clinic, 1962-66, chief research program air hygiene, dept. environmental medicine, 1955—; with dept. physiology U. Rochester, 1946-47; fellow anesthesiology U. Pa., 1951-52. Author: Anesthesia and Otolaryngology, 1957, Tonsils and Adenoids in Childhood, 1960, Nose Paranasal Sinuses and Ears in Childhood, 1962, Breathing, Speech, and Song, 1980; editor: Respiratory Defense Mechanisms, 1977, The Nose, Upper Airway Physiology and Atmospheric Environment, 1982, A History of Breathing Physiology, 1995; author articles, book chpts. deafness, respiration, air hygiene, air polllution, mucous membrane. Fellow A.C.S., Am. Acad. Otolaryngology; mem. Am. Bronchoesophagol. Assn., Am. Indsl. Hygiene Assn., Air Pollution Control Assn., Am. Physiol. Soc., Phi Beta Pi, Sigma Xi. Club: 14 West Hamilton Street (Balt.). Home: 4300 N Charles St Apt 9-f Baltimore MD 21218-1066

PROCTOR, JOHN FRANKLIN, lawyer; b. Scottsboro, Ala., May 6, 1931; s. James Moody and Lucy (May) P.; m. Anne Esco, Dec. 3, 1988; children from previous marriage: James Moody, Laura. B.S., U. Ala., 1953, LL.B., 1957. Bar: Ala. bar 1957. Asst. atty. gen., 1957-59; pvt. practice Scottsboro, 1959-90; judge Jackson County Ct., 1959-63; pvt. practice, 1963-66, 68-90; judge 9th Jud. Circuit, 1966-68; fed. adminstrv. law judge, 1990—. Served with U.S. Army, 1953-55. Mem. Ala. Bar Assn. (commr. 1979-90), Sigma Chi, Phi Alpha Delta. Methodist. Home: 3110 Olde Towne Ln Chattanooga TN 37415-5903 Office: Office Hearings and Appeals 300 Uplain Bldg Chattanooga TN 37411

PROCTOR, KENNETH DONALD, lawyer; b. Balt., Apr. 28, 1944; s. Kenneth Chauncey and Sarah Elizabeth (Kent) P.; m. Judith Danner Harris, Aug. 2, 1969; children—Kenneth Scott, Kent Harris, Janet Cameron. B.S., Lehigh U., 1966; J.D., U. Md., 1969. Bar: Md. 1969, U.S. Dist. Ct. Md. 1970, U.S. Ct. Appeals (4th cir.) 1980, U.S. Supreme Ct. 1974. Law clk. to presiding judge Md. Ct. Appeals, 1969-70; assoc. Miles & Stockbridge, Balt., 1970-73, 74-76, ptnr., Balt., 1976-81, Towson, Md., 1981-96; asst. atty. gen. Md., Balt., 1973-74; Trustee, Gilman Sch., Balt., 1982-85. Mem. ABA, Md. State Bar Assn., Balt. County Bar Assn. Democrat. Episcopalian. Office: K Donald Proctor PA Ste 505 102 W Pennsylvania Ave Towson MD 21204-4542

PROCTOR, RICHARD J., geologist, consultant; b. L.A., Aug. 2, 1931; s. George Arthur and Margaret Y. (Goodman) P.; m. Ena McLaren, Feb. 12, 1955; children: Mitchell, Jill, Randall. BA, Calif. State U., L.A., 1954; MA, UCLA, 1958. Engring. geologist, Calif.; cert. profl. geologist Am. Inst. Profl. Geologists. Chief geologist Met. Water Dist., L.A., 1958-80; pres., cons. geologist Richard J. Proctor, Inc., Arcadia, Calif., 1980—; vis. assoc. prof. Calif. Inst. Tech., Pasadena, 1975-78. Co-author: Citizens Guide to Geologic Hazards, 1993; editor: Professional Practice Guidelines, 1985, Engineering Geology Practice in Southern California, 1992. Pres., dir. Arcadia Hist. Soc., 1993-96. Fellow Geol. Soc. Am. (Burwell Meml. award 1972); mem. Assn. Engring. Geologists (pres. 1979), Am. Inst. Profl. Geologists (pres. 1989, Van Couvering Meml. award 1990, hon. mem. 1992), Am. Geol. Inst. (sec.-treas. 1979-83).

PROCTOR, RICHARD JEROME, JR., educator, accountant, expert witness; b. N.Y.C., Oct. 6, 1941; s. Richard Jerome and Edith (Decker) P.; m. Elfriede N. Neundorfer, Aug. 19, 1967; children: Courtney, John, David. BS, Columbia U., 1963, MBA, 1970. CPA, N.Y., Conn.; cert. valuation analyst, cert. govt. fin. mgr. Sr. acct. Arthur Anderson, N.Y.C., 1970-72; dir. acctg. N.Y. Stock Exchange, N.Y.C., 1972-75; chief fin. officer Executrans, Greenwich, Conn., 1975-77; dir. planning Irvin Industries, Stamford, Conn., 1977-79; asst. prof. acctg. and taxation U. Hartford (Conn.), 1979-82; prof. and dept. chairperson Ancell Sch. Bus. Western Conn. State U., Danbury, 1983—; pvt. practice, 1979—; cons., expert witness in field. Mem. AICPA, Conn. Soc. CPAs (Disting. Authors award 1983, 92), Nat. Assn. Cert. Valuation Analysts, Inst. Bus. Appraisers, Am. Acctg. Assn., Inst. Mgmt. Accts. Home: 31 Cooper Hill Rd Ridgefield CT 06877-5903 Office: Western Conn State U 181 White St Danbury CT 06810

PROCTOR, RICHARD OWEN, public health administrator, army officer; b. Austin, Tex., Nov. 18, 1935; s. William Owen and Arlene Gertrude (Holdeman) P.; m. Martha June Whitlock, Nov. 19, 1955; children: Tanya Marie, Sheilia Renee, Michael Lee, Terry Glen, Richard Lowell, Roger Owen. BA, Oklahoma City U., 1957; MS, Baylor U. Coll. Medicine, Houston, 1964, MD, 1964; MPH and TM, Tulane U., 1970; diploma, U.S. Army War Coll., 1983. Diplomate Am. Bd. Pediatrics, Am. Bd. Preventive Medicine. Commd. capt. U.S. Army, 1964, advanced through grades to brig. gen.; instr. Imperial Ethiopian Coll. A&M Arts, Alemaya, 1957-59; dep. comdr. U.S. Army Hosp., Kagnew Station, Ethiopia, 1967-69, U.S. Army Med. Lab., Ft. Sam Houston, Tex., 1973-75; instr. U.S. Army Acad. Health Scis., Ft. Sam Houston, 1975-77; surgeon U.S. Army VII Corps, Moeringen, Fed. Republic Germany, 1978-81; prof., chmn., comdt. of students Uniformed Svcs. U. of Health Scis., Bethesda, Md., 1981-82; comdr. Raymond Bliss Army Community Hosp., Ft. Huachuca, Ariz., 1983-85; surgeon U.S. Army Tng. and Doctrine Command, Ft. Monroe, Va., 1985-88; comdg. gen. William Beaumont Army Med. Ctr., El Paso, Tex., 1988-91; dir. pub. health Region 6 Tex. Dept. Health, Houston, 1991-96; rancher, 1985—; cons. WHO/PAHO, Bolivia, 1971; lectr. on medicine, anthropology, theology, history, substance abuse prevention; past adj. or clin. faculty positions Baylor U., Tulane U., U. Tex. Author: (with others) Principles of Pediatrics: Healthcare of the Young, 1978, Current Pediatrics Diagnosis and Treatment, 1978, 80, Primary Pediatric Care, 1987, 2d edit., 1992, Comprehensive Adolescent Health Care, 1992; author multiple articles on viremia with Sabin polio vaccines. Asst. scout master Boy Scouts Am., Bowie, Md., 1971-73; scout committeeman Boy Scouts Am., Moeringen, 1978-81. Decorated D.S.M., Legion of Merit (twice); recipient scholarship Broadhurst Found., Tulsa, 1953-57; rsch. fellow NIH, 1960-61; Tropical Medicine fellow La. State U., 1970. Fellow Am. Acad. Preventive Medicine, Am. Acad. Pediatrics, Royal Soc. Medicine; mem. Assn. Mil. Surgeons of U.S., Nat. Eagle Scout Assn., Tex. Hist. Soc. Methodist. Avocations: conservation, living history. Home: RR 4 Box 1193 Paris TX 75462-9708

PROCTOR, ROBERT SWOPE, retired petroleum company executive; b. Columbus, Ohio, June 15, 1922; s. William Edward and Elsie M. (Swope) P.; m. Mary M. Thornton, Dec. 31, 1945; children: Robert M., Jill, Mary, Ann, Kathleen. MSME, Oreg. State U., 1947. With Standard Oil Co. Calif., Inc., 1947-76; gen. mgr. El Segundo (Calif.) refinery, 1969-71; v.p., dir. Western Operation Inc., San Francisco, 1971-76; v.p. mfg. Chevron U.S.A., San Francisco, 1976-84. Served to 1st lt., C.E. AUS, 1943-45. Mem. Calif. Mfrs. Assn. (dir.). Republican. Home: PO Box 1639 Zephyr Cove NV 89448-1639 *I have been very fortunate in life. I did not set life long goals early in life, rather always tried to develop myself and do the best I could for family, country and community.*

PROCTOR, RONALD EUGENE, academic administrator, educator, consultant; b. Norfolk, Va., Jan. 7, 1947; s. Oliver Watkins and Christine (Eason) P.; m. Sandra Brown, Aug. 27, 1972; 1 child, Kimberle Nichole. BS in History Edn., Hampton Inst., 1968, MA in Ednl. Adminstrn., 1974; EdD in Social Sci. Edn., Rutgers U., 1976. Lectr. Douglass Coll., New Brunswick, N.J., 1974-76; assoc. v.p. acad. affairs Norfolk (Va.) State U., 1976—; auditor Va. Social Sci. Assn., Richmond, 1984-85; v.p. Norfolk State U. Faculty Senate, 1985-86; nat. chmn. Conf. Minority Pub. Adminstrn., Washington, 1993-94. Author econ. impact study Norfolk State U. Rsch. Bull., 1986; co-author article to Va. Social Sci. Jour., 1984; cons. housing history Norfolk: A Historical Account of a Black Community, 1985; researcher agy. report Human Svc. Needs of Portsmouth, Va., 1987. Mem. Virginia Beach (Va.) Community Devel. Corp., 1986; mem. Virginia Beach Tomorrow Task Force, 1986; active Hutton YMCA, 1990, Tidewater Health Care, Virginia Beach, 1993. Capt. U.S. Army, 1969-74. Recipient Rsch. award U.S. Legal Svcs. Corp., Washington, 1982, Inst. Svcs. to Edn., Washington, 1982; named Tchr. of Yr., Norfolk State U., 1984; Pub. Svc. fellow U.S. Dept. Edn., 1991. Mem. ASPA (pres. 1986-87), Kappa Alpha Psi, Hiawatha Social and Beneficial Club, Phi Delta Kappa. Home: 4764 Berrywood Rd Virginia Beach VA 23464-5868 Office: Norfolk State U Office of Acad Affairs 2401 Corprew Ave Norfolk VA 23504-3907

PROCTOR, SAMUEL, history educator; b. Jacksonville, Fla., Mar. 29, 1919; s. Jack and Celia (Schneider) P.; m. Bessie Rubin, Sept. 8, 1948; children: Mark Julian, Alan Lowell. B.A., U. Fla., 1941, M.A., 1942, Ph.D., 1958. Mem. faculty U. Fla., Gainesville, 1946—, prof. history and social scis., 1963-74, disting. service prof. history, 1974—, Julien C. Yonge prof. Fla. history, 1976—, univ. historian, 1953—, dir. oral history program, 1968—; curator History Fla. State Mus.; dir. Doris Duke Southeastern Indian Oral History Program, Ctr. for Study of Fla. History and Humanities. Author: Napoleon Bonaparte Broward, Florida's Fighting Democrat, 1950, Florida Commemorates the Civil War Centennial, 1962, Florida One Hundred Years Ago, 1966, Florida History Preservation Planning, 1971, Gator History: History of the University of Florida, 1986, The University of Florida, 1990, N.B. Broward, 1993; editor, author introduction: Dickison and His Men: Reminiscences of the War in Florida, 1962; series editor: Bicentennial Floridiana Facsimile Series; editor: Eighteenth Century Florida and Its Borderlands, 1975, Eighteenth Century Florida and the Carribean, 1976, Eighteenth Century Florida, Life on the Frontier, 1976, Eighteenth Century Florida and the Revolutionary South, 1977, Eighteenth Century Florida and the Impact of The American Revolution, 1978, Tacachale, Essays on the Indians of Florida and Southeastern Georgia during the Historic Period, Jews of the South; assoc. editor: Fla. Hist. Quar., 1962-64, editor, 1963-93; contbr. articles to profl. jours. Served with U.S. Army, 1943-46. Mem. Fla. Blue Key, Phi Beta Kappa, Tau Epsilon Phi, Pi Kappa Phi, Phi Alpha Theta. Democrat. Jewish. Home: 2235 NW 9th Pl Gainesville FL 32605-5201 Office: Univ Fla Dept History Gainesville FL 32611

PROCTOR, WILLIAM LEE, college president; b. Atlanta, Jan. 27, 1933; s. Samuel Cook and Rose Elizabeth (Nottingham) P.; m. Pamela Evans Duke; children: Samuel Matthews (dec.), Priscilla Nottingham. BS, Fla. State U., 1956, MS, 1964, PhD, 1968. Tchr. Seminole County Pub. Schs., Longwood, Fla., 1956-57, 58-62, Orange County Fla. Pub. Schs., Orlando, Fla., 1957-58; athletic coach Fla. State U., Tallahassee, 1962-65, asst. dean men, 1965-67, grad. fellow, 1967-68; supt. of schs. Rock Hill (S.C.) Sch. Dist. #3, 1968-69; dean of men U. Cen. Fla., Orlando, 1969-71; pres. Flagler Coll., St. Augustine, Fla., 1971—; cons. on higher edn. policy Heritage Found., Washington, 1983—; mem. Commn. on Colls., So. Assn. Colls. and Schs., 1995—. Vice-chmn. Fla. Edn. Stds. Commn., 1995—; bd. dirs. Flagler Health Svcs., Inc., St. Augustine, 1977-95, Penny Farms Retirement Cmty., pres., 1991—; bd. dirs. Fla. Ind. Coll. Fund, Tallahassee, Vickers Landing Retirement Cmty., pres., 1992-95, bd., 1990—; trustee, chmn. Fla. Sch. for Deaf and Blind, St. Augustine, 1984—; mem. adv. coun. Salvation Army, St. Johns County. Recipient Disting. Educator award Fla. State U. Coll. Edn., 1989, Phil Carrol award Soc. for Advancement Mgmt., 1990, Disting. Svc. award Fla. Sch. for Deaf and Blind, 1990, Patrick Henry Medallion patriotic achievement Mil. Order of World Wars, 1991, Stetson S Club Achievement award, 1993; named to Fla. State U. Athletic Hall of Fame, 1988. Mem. Am. Assn. Pres. of Ind. Colls., State Hist. Assn., Ind. Colls. and Univs. of Fla. (legis. chmn. 1974-77, vice chmn. 1976-77, chmn. 1978-79), St. Johns County C. of C. (dir.), Rotary (pres. 1978-79, govs. dist. 697 1988-89). Republican. Presbyterian. Avocations: history, jogging, karate. Office: Flagler Coll Office of the Pres PO Box 1027 Saint Augustine FL 32085-1027

PROCYK, JUDSON M., metropolitan archbishop. Ordained priest, 1957. Bishop Byzantine Catholic Metropolitan Diocese of Pitts., 1994-96; Met. Archbishop Byzantine Metropolitan Archdiocese of Pitts., 1996—. Office: 66 Riverview Ave Pittsburgh PA 15214-2253

PRODAN, JAMES CHRISTIAN, university administrator; b. Columbus, Ohio, Jan. 4, 1947; s. Nicholas Mackley and Muriel Eileen (Bennett) P.; m. Carol Ann Cochran, Mar. 4, 1994; children: Christopher, Tana. BS, Ohio State U., 1969; MMus, Catholic U. Am., 1972; DMA, Ohio State U., 1976. Musician U.S. Army Band, Washington, 1969-72; asst. prof. U. Akron, Ohio, 1975-79; prof. U. N.C., Greensboro, 1979—; assoc. dean sch. music U. N.C., 1989—. Bd. dirs. Vol. Ctr., Greensboro, 1989-95; worship and music com. Christ Luth. Ch., 1988. Mem. Nat. Assn. Schs. Music, Internat. Double Reed Soc. (libr., exec. com.), Am. Fed. Musicians, Nat. Assn. Coll. Wind and Percussion Instrs., Music Educators Nat. Conf., N.C. Music Music Educators Assn., Coll. Music Soc., Music Tchrs. Nat. Assn., Intrnat. Soc. for Music Edn. Republican. Lutheran. Home: 5510 Rutledge Dr Greensboro NC 27455 Office: U NC Greensboro Sch Music Greensboro NC 27412

PROE, JOHN DAVID, business educator, consultant, administrator; b. Passaic, N.J., Dec. 27, 1937; s. John and Mae Barbara (Roehrich) Prokopowicz; m. Betty Jane Patrick, Feb. 23, 1977; children: Celeste, Robert D., Kristin S., Jessica D. B.A., The Citadel, 1959; M.H.A., Baylor U., 1971; Ph.D., U. Iowa, 1977. Commd. 2d lt. inf. U.S. Army, 1959, advanced through grades to maj. med. svc. corps, 1967; assoc. adminstr. Sandia Base Hosp., Albuquerque, 1965-68; sr. med. adv. Region IV RVN, 1968; assoc. adminstr., dir. med. edn. Tripler Med. Ctr., Honolulu, 1970-73; ret., 1973; instr. health planning U. Iowa, Iowa City, 1973-76; assoc. adminstr., asst. to pres. Conemaugh Valley Meml. Hosp., Johnstown, Pa., 1976-78; v.p. Mark Silber Assocs. Ltd., Organizational Psychologists, San Diego, 1978—; dir. Western Pa. Sports Medicine and Rehab. Clinic, Johnstown, 1984—; prof. mgmt. and healthcare adminstrn. Harry F. Byrd Jr. Sch. of Bus. Shenandoah U., Winchester, Va.; bd. dirs. Visual Freedom Ctr., Leesburg, Va., 1996—. Contbr. articles to profl. jours. Decorated Bronze Star, Air medal with two oak leaf clusters; recipient VN Honor medal and cross Gallantry of Palm; USPHS grantee, 1976-77; Nat. Library Medicine grantee, 1977-78. Mem. Am. Coll. Hosp. Adminstrs. (diplomate), Med. Group Mgmt. Assn., John Henry Cardinal Newman Soc., Phi Lambda Theta. Home: 207

Huntfield Ln Charles Town WV 25414-2520 Office: 1460 University Dr Winchester VA 22601-5100

PROEBSTING, EDWARD LOUIS, JR., retired research horticulturist; b. Woodland, Calif., Mar. 2, 1926; s. Edward Louis and Dorothy (Critzer) P.; m. Patricia Jean Connolly, June 28, 1947; children: William Martin, Patricia Louise, Thomas Alan (dec.). BS, U. Calif., Davis, 1948; PhD, Mich. State U., 1951. Asst. horticulturist Wash. State U., Prosser, 1951-57, assoc. horticulturist, 1957-63, horticulturist, 1963-93, supt. Irrigated Agrl. Rsch. and Ext. Ctr., 1990-93; ret., 1993; vis. prof. Cornell U., Ithaca, N.Y., 1966; vis. scientist Hokkaido U., Sapporo, Japan, 1978, Victoria Dept. Agr., Tatura, Australia, 1986—. Contbr. numerous articles to profl. jours. Scoutmaster Boy Scouts Am., Prosser, 1963-76, dist. chmn., 1976-78. Served to lt. USNR, 1943-46, 52-54. Recipient Silver Beaver award Boy Scouts Am.; fellow Japan Soc. Promotion Sci., Sapporo, 1978, Res. Bank. Australia, 1986. Fellow AAAS, Am. Soc. Hort. Sci. (pres. 1983-84, sci. editor jour. 1993—). Methodist. Avocations: backpacking, native plants. Home: 1929 Miller Ave Prosser WA 99350-1532

PROEFROCK, CARL KENNETH, academic medical administrator; b. Curtis, Ill., Mar. 30, 1928; s. Carl Robert and Anna Lorraine (Hagel) P.; m. Margaret Muntz (dec. 1984); children: Philip, Andrew, Elizabeth, Liesl; m. Janelle Dillon, Sept. 8, 1988. BA, Carthage Coll., Kenosha, Wis., 1949; MDiv, Chgo. Luth. Theol. Sem., 1953. Sr. com. orgn. specialist N.Y.C. Housing and Devel. Adminstrn., 1966-68; exec. dir. Model Cities Program, Manchester, n.H., 1968-70, Health Assn. Rochester and Monroe (N.Y.), 1970-73, Mahoning Shenango Area Health Edn. Network, Youngstown, Ohio, 1973-78; spl. asst. to dean Northeastern Ohio Univs. Coll. Medicine, Rootstown, 1978-79; v.p. Med. Coll. Ohio, Toledo, 1979-88, sr. v.p. govtl. affairs, 1988-93; pres. KPA Assocs., Inc., 1993—; v.p. Found. for Applied Rsch., Washington, 1976; chmn. adv. bd. Ohio AHEC, Columbus, 1976; program adminstr. Ohio Statewide Area Health Edn. Ctr., Toledo, 1988-93. Mem. budget allocation com. United Appeal, Youngstown, 1975-78; mem. dist. planning coun. Ohio Dept. Mental Health, Youngstown, 1977-78; chmn. Toledo Area Coun. Tech., 1986. Mem. Nat. Area Health Edn. Ctrs. Assn. (bd. dirs. 1988—), Nat. Assn. Univ. Rsch. Adminstrs., Soc. Rsch. Adminstrs., Internat. Assn. Univ. Rsch. Parks, Soc. Univ. Patent Adminstrs., Nat. Assn. Health Manpower Edn. Systems, Northeastern Ohio Med. Educators Assn. (bd. dirs.), Rotary. Episcopalian. Home: 189 Rose Hill Dr Pawleys Island SC 79585 Office: KPA Assocs PO Box 194 Pawleys Island SC 29585

PROFETA, SALVATORE, JR., chemist; b. Phila., May 1, 1951; m. Catherine Mary Cherry, Sept. 20, 1980; children: Luisa, Theresa. BA, Temple U., 1973; PhD, U. Ga., 1978. Postdoctoral fellow chemistry dept. Fla. State U., Tallahassee, 1979-80; postdoctoral fellow pharm. chemistry dept. U. Calif., San Francisco, 1980-81, teaching fellow, 1981-82; instr. chemistry dept. La. State U., Baton Rouge, 1982-84; sr. scientist Allergan Pharms., Inc., Irvine, Calif., 1984-87; project mgr. computational chemistry Glaxo Rsch. Inst., Research Triangle Park, N.C., 1987-90, head chemistry systems, 1990-93; dir. N.C. Supercomputing Ctr. Rsch. Inst. at MCNC, Research Triangle Park, 1993-95; prin. computational chemist Ceregen/Monsanto, St. Louis, 1996—; cons. CADD-CAMM Smith, Kline & French, Phila., 1980-82, Squibb Rsch. Inst., Princeton, N.J., 1982-84; mem. allocation com. N.C. Supercomputing Ctr., 1989-94. Mem. editorial bd. Jour. Molecular Graphics, 1989—; contbg. editor Chem. Design Automation News, 1991—; contbr. articles to Jour. Am. Chem. Soc. NSF fellow, 1976-78; Petroleum Rsch. Found. grantee, 1984-88. Fellow N.Y. Acad. Scis.; mem. Am. Chem. Soc. Achievements include patents in anticancer drug design; co-author MM1, MM2, MM3 and AMBER molecular mechanical force fields. Office: Ceregen/Monsanto 800 N Lindbergh Blvd # E Saint Louis MO 63141-7843

PROFFIT, WILLIAM ROBERT, orthodontics educator; b. Harnett County, N.C., Apr. 19, 1936; s. Glenn Theodore and Edna Marie (Queener) P.; m. Sara Thomas, Sept. 20, 1953; children: Lola Ann, Edward Thomas, Glenn Theodore. BS, U. N.C., 1956, DDS, 1959; student, Campbell Coll., Buies Creek, N.C., 1952-53; PhD, Med. Coll. Va., 1962; MS, U. Wash., 1963; FDS, Royal Coll. Surgeons, 1990. Am. Bd. Orthodontics. Investigator Nat. Inst. Dental Research, Bethesda, Md., 1963-65; asst. prof. orthodontics U. Ky., Lexington, 1965-68, assoc. prof., 1968-71; prof. U.Ky., Lexington, 1971-73; prof. orthodontics U. Fla., Gainesville, 1973-75; prof., chmn. dept. orthodontics U. N.C., Chapel Hill, 1975—, Kenan prof., 1992; cons. NIH, Bethesda, 1974, 76—. Author: Contemporary Orthodontics, 1986, 2d edit., 1993; co-author: Surgical Correction of Dentofacial Deformity, 1980, Surgical-Orthodontic Treatment, 1990; contbr. articles to sci. jours. Served to lt. comdr. USPHS, 1963-65. Fulbright research scholar U. Adelaide, Australia, 1972. Mem. Am. Assn. Orthodontists (council on research 1970-76), ADA, Internat. Assn. Dental Research, Phi Beta Kappa. Democrat. Presbyterian. Home: 620 Rock Creek Rd Chapel Hill NC 27514-6716 Office: U NC Sch Dentistry Orthodontics Dept Chapel Hill NC 27599

PROFFITT, JOHN RICHARD, business executive, educator; b. Grand Junction, Colo., Sept. 12, 1930; s. Hillus D. and Joy Elaine (Lindsay) P.; m. Claire Boyer Miller, May 8, 1965 (div. 1992); children: Cameron Lindsay, William Boyer. BA in Edn., U. Ky., 1953, MA in Polit. Sci., 1961; postgrad., U. Mich., 1959-65. Asst. dean of men, instr. polit. sci. dept. U. Ky., Lexington, 1957-59; teaching fellow U. Mich., Ann Arbor, 1961-63, 63-65; asst. dir. Nat. Commn. on Accrediting, Washington, 1966-68; dir. accreditation and eligibility staff U.S. Dept. HEW, Washington, 1968-75; dir. div. eligibility and agy. evaluation U.S. HEW, Washington, 1975-80; dir. div. instnl. and state incentive programs U.S. Dept. Edn., Washington, 1980-82; pres. The Clairion Corp., Bethesda, Md., 1982-84, Nat. Asbestos Removal, Inc., Beltsville, Md., 1985-90; pres. Commonwealth Environ. Svcs., Inc., Alexandria, Va., 1987-91, also chmn. bd. dirs.; chmn. Internat. Environ. Engrs., Inc., Alexandria, Va., 1991-92; pres. Canterbury Internat., Vienna, Va., 1992—, Epic, Inc., Bethesda, 1997—; cons. Conn. State Commn. Higher Edn., Hartford, 1967, Am. Coun. Edn., Washington, 1970; cons. U.S. Dept. Hew, 1967, 68; mem. study steering com. Am. Vocat. Assn., Washington, 1968; exec. sec. Nat. Adv. Com. on Accreditation and Instnl. Eligibility, Washington, 1968-80; mem. gen. com. Nat. Study Sch. evaluation, Alexandria, 1970-78; mem. task force Edn. Commn. of the States, Denver, 1972; subcom. chmn. Fed. Interagy. Com. on Edn., Washington, 1974-76; lectr., presenter profl. confs. Co-author: Accreditation and Certification in Relation to Allied Health Manpower, 1971; contbg. author: Health Manpower: Adapting in the Seventies, 1971, Accreditation in Teacher Education, 1975, Transferring Experiential Credit, 1979; contbr. articles to profl. and govtl. agy. publs., 1968-79. v.p., bd. dirs. Nat. Accreditation Coun. for Agys. Serving the Blind, N.Y.C., 1985; pres., chmn. bd. dirs. Found. for Advancement of Quality Svcs. for the Blind, Alexandria, 1988. 1st lt. USAF, 1953-55, Japan and Korea. Higher edn. fellow Univ. Mich., 1959. Mem. Club Internat. (Chgo.), Island Club (Hope Sound, Fla.), Thoroughbred Club Am. (Lexington, Ky.), Tower Club (Vienna, Va.), Sigma Nu. Democrat. Episcopalian. Avocations: conservation, animal welfare, travel, antiques, art. Home: 515 Beall Ave Rockville MD 20350

PROFFITT, KEVIN, archivist; b. Hamilton, Ohio, Dec. 24, 1956; s. Henry C. and Marjorie O. (Elam) P.; m. Joan Moriarity, May 17, 1986. BA, Miami U., Oxford, Ohio, 1979; MA, Wright State U., 1980. Archivist Am. Jewish Archives, Cin., 1981—. Contbr. articles to profl. jours. Mem. Soc. Am. Archivists, Acad. Cert. Archivists (cert.), Midwest Archives Conf., Soc. Ohio Archivists (pres. 1987-89). Office: Am Jewish Archives 3101 Clifton Ave Cincinnati OH 45220-2404

PROFFITT, LAWRENCE ALAN, secondary school educator; b. Encino, Calif., July 1, 1959; s. George Leslie and Cleah (James) Proffitt; m. Melissa Sue. BS, U. Utah, 1982; MA, U. Calif., Riverside, 1988. Cert. tchr., adminstr., Calif. Sterilization technician Deseret Med., Inc., Sandy, Utah, 1977-82; tchr. Jordan Sch. Dist., Sandy, 1982-85, Yucaipa-Calimesa Joint Unified Sch. Dist., Yucaipa, Calif., 1985—; pres. Citrus Belt Uniserv, Rialto, Calif., 1991-94. Named to Outstanding Young Men of Am., 1989. Mem. Calif. Tchrs. Assn. (task force on extremist attacks on edn. 1990—, mem. congl. contact team 1993—), Yucaipa-Calimesa Educators Assn. (fin. dir. 1987, v.p. 1988, pres. 1988—), Yucaipa-Calimesa C. of C. Democrat. Avocations: mechanical-automotive activities, golf, reading. Home: 620 Golden West Dr Redlands CA 92373-6416

PROFFITT, WALDO, JR., newspaper editor; b. Plainview, Tex., Oct. 8, 1924; s. Waldo and Susan Ann (Smith) P.; m. Marjorie Baltzegar, Sept. 14, 1946 (div. 1963); children: Ann Herbert, Deborah, Geoffrey Harrison, Laurence Scott; m. Anne Collier Greene, Feb. 6, 1966; 1 child, Robert Waldo. BA cum laude, Harvard U., 1948. Reporter Bangor (Maine) Commercial, 1948-50; assoc. dir. Harvard News Office, Cambridge, Mass., 1952-54; city editor Charlotte (N.C.) News, 1954-58; mng. editor Journal, Lorain, Ohio, 1958-61; editorial dir. Sarasota (Fla.) Herald-Tribune, 1961-84; editor, 1984—. Lt. U.S. Army, 1943-46, ETO, lt. USAF, 1950-52. Mem. Am. Soc. Newspaper Editors, Fla. Soc. Newspaper Editors (pres. 1978). Democrat. Unitarian. Home: 1581 Hillview Dr Sarasota FL 34239-2047 Office: Sarasota Herald-Tribune PO Box 1719 Sarasota FL 34230-1719

PROFICE, ROSENA MAYBERRY, elementary school educator; b. Natchez, Miss., Oct. 8, 1953; d. Alex Jr. and Louise V. (Fuller) Mayberry; m. Willie Lee Profice, Feb. 12, 1977; children: Jamie Martez, Alesha Shermille. BS in History, Jackson State U., 1974, MS in Elem. Edn., 1975, Edn. Splty. in Elem. Edn., 1977. Cert. elem. reading and social studies tchr., Miss. Tchr. reading Ackerman (Miss.) H.S., 1975-76, North Hazlehurst (Miss.) Elem. Sch., 1976-79; tchr. reading and elem. edn. Natchez-Adams Sch. Sys., Natchez, 1979—. Mem. NEA, Miss. Assn. Educators, Concerned Educators of Black Students, Internat. Reading Assn., Nat. Alliance Black Sch. Educators, Natchez Assn. for the Preservation of Afro-Am. Culture (bd. dirs. 1996-97), Linwood Circle Ruritan Club (bd. dirs. 1992-93, sec. 1994-95), Jackson State U. Alumni Assn., 100 Black Women, Zion Hill #1 Bapt. Ch. Democrat. Baptist. Avocations: reading, travel, shopping. Home: 11 Elbow Ln Natchez MS 39120-5346

PROFT, PAT, screenwriter, film producer; b. Mpls., Apr. 3, 1947; s. Bob and Marguerite Proft; m. Karen Philipp; 1 child, Patrick. Writer: (T.V. series) The Jim Stafford Show, 1975, The Smothers Brothers Show, 1975, When Things Were Rotten, 1975, Cher, 1975-76, Welcome Back Kotter, 1975-79, Van Dyke and Company, 1976 (Emmy award nomination outstanding writing 1976), The Redd Foxx Comedy Hour, 1977-78, The Mary Tyler Moore Comedy Hour, 1979, Detective School, 1979, Police Squad!, 1982, (TV spls.) Bob Hope Special: Bob Hope's Christmas Party, 1975, Cher, 1975, Ringo, 1978, The Roy Clarke Special, 1979, All Commercials: A Steve Martin Special, 1980, Gary Owens All Nonsense News Network, 1982, (TV pilots) Ultra Quiz, 1981, Twilight Theatre II, 1982, High School, U.S.A., 1984, (films) (with Neal Israel) Bachelor Party, 1984, (with Israel and Hugh Wilson) Police Academy, 1984, (with Israel and Peter Torokvei) Real Genius, 1985, (with Jim Abrahams, David Zucker, and Jerry Zucker) The Naked Gun: From the Files of Police Squad!, 1988, (with D. Zucker) Naked Gun 2 1/2: The Smell of Fear, 1991, Brain Donors, 1992, (with D. Zucker and Robert LoCash) Naked Gun 33 1/3: The Final Insult, 1994; writer, exec. prodr.: (films) (with Israel) Moving Violations, 1985, Lucky Stiff, 1989, (with Abrahams) Hot Shots!, 1991, (with Abrahams) Hot Shots! Part Deux, 1993; writer, prodr.: (TV series) Marie, 1980, Buckshot, 1980; tech. advisor: Johnny Dangerously, 1984; appearances include (films) Modern Problems, 1981, Bachelor Party, 1984, (TV series) Madhouse 90, 1972, The Burns and Schreiber Comedy Hour, 1973, Joey & Dad, 1975, Van Dyke and Company, 1976, Detective School, 1979, (TV movies) Fast Friends, 1979, (TV pilots) Twilight Theatre, 1982. *

PROGAR, DOROTHY, retired library director; b. Bruceville, Tex., Sept. 14, 1924; d. Florence Scott and George Thomas Watkins; m. Walter L. Progar, Aug. 3, 1946; 1 child, James Scott. Student, Mich. State U.; BA, Baylor U.; postgrad., Tex. Woman's U. With Waco-McLennan County Libr., 1961-92, circulation libr., 1961-65, young adult libr., 1965-67, ref. libr., 1967-69, asst. dir., 1969-72, assoc. dir., 1972-78, dir. librs., 1978-92. Contbr. articles to profl. jours. Mem. Ctrl. Tex. Lit. Coalition; mem. Strecker Mus. Assocs.; bd. dirs. Heart O'Tex. Fair and Rodeo; mem. adv. bd. Salvation Army; bd. dirs. Dr. Pepper Mus. and Free Enterprise Inst. Recipient Waco-McLennan County Pathfinder in Pub. Svc. award, 1988, Silver Bridge award Cen. Tex. chpt. Pub. Rels. Soc. Am., 1990; Dorothy Progar Day proclaimed by City of Waco, 1986. Mem. ALA, Tex. Libr. Assn. (exec. bd. 1986-89), Tex. Mcpl. Libr. Dirs. Assn. (pres. 1987-88, Libr. Dir. of Yr. award 1989), Baylor Alumni Assn., Friends of Baylor Fine Arts Bd., Advt. Club Waco (Silver Medal award 1988), Rotary. Baptist. Avocations: reading, sports, people. Home: 1800 Trinity Dr Waco TX 76710-2842

PROKASY, WILLIAM FREDERICK, academic administrator; b. Cleve., Nov. 27, 1930; s. William Frederick and Margaret Lovinia (Chapman) P.; children: Kathi Lynn, Cheryl Anne. B.A., Baldwin-Wallace Coll., 1952; M.A., Kent State U., 1954; Ph.D., U. Wis., 1957. Grad. asst. Kent State U., 1953-54; W.A.R.F. fellow U. Wis., 1954-55, teaching asst., 1955-57; asst. prof., then asso. prof. Pa. State U., 1957-66; prof. psychology, chmn. dept. U. Utah, 1966-69, Disting. rsch. prof., 1971-72, dean social and behavioral sci., 1968-70; dean U. Utah (Coll. Social and Behavioral Sci.), 1970-79; acting dean U. Utah (Grad. Sch. Social Work), 1979-80; prof. psychology dean Coll. Liberal Arts and Scis., U. Ill., Champaign-Urbana, 1980-88; prof., v.p. for acad. affairs U. Ga., 1988—; cons. in field. Editor: Classical Conditioning, 1965, (with A.H. Black) Classical Conditioning II, 1971, (with D. Raskin) Electrodermal Responding in Psychological Research, 1973, Psychophysiology, 1974-77; editor (with I. Gormezano and R. Thompson) Classical Conditioning III, 1986; assoc. editor Learning and Motivation, 1969-76; cons. editor Jour. Exptl. Psychology, 1968-80. Del. Utah Dem. Conv., 1968-70, 72-74; trustee Utah Planned Parenthood Assn., 1977-80, Utah bd. dirs. ACLU, 1978-80; v.p., bd. dirs. Champaign-Urbana Symphony, 1986-88; bd. advs. Ga. Mus. of Art, 1989—. NSF sr. postdoctoral fellow, 1963-64, recipient Alumni Merit award Baldwin Wallace Coll., 1992. Fellow AAAS, Am. Psychol. Assn. (chmn. bd. sci. affairs 1977-78, coun. of reps. 1980-86, bd. dirs. 1983-86, bd. edtl. affairs 1993-96); mem. Fedn. Behavioral, Pyschol. and Cognitive Scis. (v.p. 1984-85, pres. 1985-87), coun. of Sci. Soc. Pres.'s (exec. bd. 1987-91, chmn. 1990), Psychonomic Soc., Coun. Rsch. Librs. (bd. dirs. 1990-96), NASULGC (exec. com. coun. on acad. affairs 1995-96), Am. Assn. Higher Edn., Soc. Psychophysiol. Rsch. (bd. dirs. 1978-84, pres. 1982-83), Utah Psychol. Assn. (exec. bd. 1968-70, pres. 1971-72), Assn. Advancement Psychology (bd. dirs. 1982-83), Sigma Xi (pres. U. Utah chpt. 1972-73), Phi Kappa Phi.

PROKOPIS, EMMANUEL CHARLES, computer company executive; b. Peabody, Mass., July 5, 1942; s. Charles Emmanuel and Stevia (Kassotis) P.; m. Mary Catherine Dudeck, Dec. 6, 1969; children: Peter Matthew, Christina Eve. BBA, U. Mass., 1966. Mgr., pricing, budgeting, acctg. The Mitre Corp., Mass., Va., 1969-74; mgr. contracts liaison Pratt & Whitney Aircraft div., Conn., Fla., 1974-78; mgr. fin. planning, corp. office United Techs. Corp., Hartford, Conn., 1978-81; contr. magnet wire and insulation div. United Techs. Corp., Fort Wayne, Ind., 1981-83; v.p. fin., chief fin. officer The Mostek Corp. (subs.) United Techs. Corp., Carrollton, Tex., 1983-85; sr. v.p. fin. and ops., chief fin. officer The Lotus Devel. Corp., Cambridge, Mass., 1985-87; fin. mgr. mfg. and engring. Digital Equipment Corp., 1987-91, v.p. budgeting, 1991-92; exec. v.p. MAST Industries, 1992, Ziff Comm., 1992-93; v.p. corp. contr. Digital Equipment Corp., 1994-96; COO, CFO, treas. IONA Technologies, 1996—. 1st lt. U.S. Army, 1966-69, Vietnam. Decorated Bronze Star. Greek Orthodox.

PROKOPOFF, STEPHEN STEPHEN, art museum director, educator; b. Chgo., Dec. 24, 1929; s. Stephen George and Jadwiga M. (Borejszo) P.; m. Paula M. Delle Donne, Oct. 26, 1957 (div. 1981); children—Alexander, Ilya; m. Lois A. Craig, June 21, 1982. B.A., U. Calif.-Berkeley, 1951, M.A., 1952; Ph.D., NYU, 1962. Dir. Hathorn Gallery, Skidmore Coll., Saratoga Springs, NY, 1966-67; dir. Inst. Contemporary Art, U. Pa., Phila., 1967-71, Mus. Contemporary Art, Chgo., 1971-78, Inst. Contemporary Art, Boston, 1978-82, Krannert Art Mus., U. Ill., Champaign, 1982-92, Univ. Art Mus., U. Iowa, Iowa City, 1992—. Co-author and co-designer (with Joan Siegfried): 19th Century Architecture of Saratoga Springs, New York, 1972 (named 1 of 50 Best Designed Books of Yr.); co-author (with text by Marcel Franciscono) The Modern Dutch Poster: The First Fifty Years, 1986; contbr. articles to art periodicals. Grantee Fulbright, 1956-57, German Govt., 1958, U.S. State Dept., 1974, Am. Council on Germany, 1980, 82. Mem. Coll. Art Assn., Assn. Art Mus., Assn. Art Mus. Dirs. Avocations: music; reading; study of architecture. Home: 200 Ferson Ave Iowa City IA 52246-3507 Office: U Iowa U Art Mus 150 N Riverside Dr Iowa City IA 52246-3536

PROLL, GEORGE SIMON, psychologist; b. Würzburg, Germany, June 30, 1931; s. Jack Ignatz and Irma (Kramer) P.; came to U.S., 1936, naturalized, 1943; B.A., Yale, 1953; M.A., Boston U., 1958, Ph.D., 1962; m. Rita Rosina Rado, Aug. 9, 1954; children—Lauren, Douglas. Intern clin. psychology VA, Brockton, also Bedford, Lowell (all Mass.), 1958-62; dir. dept. psychology, psychologist mental health clinic Trenton Psychiat. Hosp., 1962-67, East Hosp., 1973-75; prin. clin. psychologist Ancora Psychiat. Hosp., 1975—, dir. psychology tng. program, 1980-86; dir. profl. services Youth Reception, Correction Center, Yardville, N.J., 1967-73; pvt. practice clin. psychology, Willingboro, N.J., 1969—. Mem. exec. bd. Psychol. Services Center, Trenton, 1965-66; mem. Drug Study Commn., Willingboro, 1971-72; mem. steering com. Community Mental Health Center, Princeton, N.J., 1973. Served with USN, 1955-57. Winner several chess competitions, including State N.H., 1957, State Mass., 1962, So. N.J., 1971, 74, N.J. Amateur Class A, 1972, South Jersey, 1983, first place, 1984, Chess Trophy U.S. Amateuer Championship, 1990, 94. Mem. Am., N.J. (Burlington County rep. to legis. com. 1968-72), psychol. assns. Club: Cherry Hill (N.J.) Chess. Home: 48 Trebing Ln Twin Hill Park Willingboro NJ 08046 Office: Ancora Psychiat Hosp Hammonton NJ 08037-9699

PROM, STEPHEN GEORGE, lawyer; b. Jacksonville, Fla., July 8, 1954; s. George W. and Bonnie M. (Porter) P.; divorced; children: Ashley Brooke, Aaron Jacob, Adam Glenn. AA in Polit. Sci. with high honors, Fla. Jr. Coll., 1974; BA in Polit. Sci. with high honors, U. Fla., 1977, JD with honors, 1979. Bar: Fla. 1980, U.S. Dist. Ct. (mid. dist.) Fla. 1980, U.S. Dist. Ct. (no. dist.) Fla. 1981, U.S. Tax Ct. 1982, U.S. Ct. Appeals (11th cir.) 1985, U.S. Supreme Ct. 1985. Assoc. Rogers, Towers, Bailey, Jones & Gay, Jacksonville, 1979-83, Foley & Lardner, Jacksonville, 1983-86; ptnr. Christian & Prom, Jacksonville, 1986-87, Prom, Korn & Zehmer, P.A., Jacksonville, 1987-95, Brant, Moore, Macdonald & Wells, P.A., 1995—. Sr. mgmt. editor U. Fla. Law Rev., 1978-79. Mem. Leadership Jacksonville, 1984, Jacksonville Community Coun. Inc., 1985-86; bd. dirs. Mental Health Resource Ctr., Jacksonville, 1984-87, Mental Health Resource Foun., Jacksonville, 1985-87, Mental Health Found., Inc., 1987-89, mem. community bd., 1989-91; bd. dirs. Youth Crisis Ctr., Jacksonville, 1984-86, Young Profls. Bd. Multiple Sclerosis Soc., 1988-89; bd. dirs. The Team, Inc., 1992-94; vol. Jacksonville, Inc., 1993-96, Jacksonville Fund., Inc., 1993-96, Positively Jacksonville!, Inc., 1993-95. Mem. ABA (tax, health law sects.), Fla. Bar Assn. (tax, health law sect., bd. govs. young lawyers sect. 1983-87), Jacksonville Bar Assn. (chmn. health law sect.), Am. Acad. Healthcare Attys., Am. Hosp. Assn., Nat. Health Lawyers Assn., Fla. Acad. Healthcare Attys. (bd. dirs. 1994—), Epping Forest Yacht Club (bd. govs., sail fleet capt.), Ponte Vedra Club, North Fla. Cruising Club, Phi Beta Kappa, Phi Theta Kappa, Phi Kappa Phi. Republican. Baptist. Avocations: sailing, surfing, weightlifting, tennis, jogging. Office: Brant Moore et al 50 N Laura St Jacksonville FL 32202-3664

PROMISEL, NATHAN E., materials scientist, metallurgical engineer; b. Malden, Mass., June 20, 1908; s. Solomon and Lyna (Samwick) P.; m. Evelyn Sarah Davidoff, May, 17, 1931; children: David Mark, Larry Jay. B.S., M.I.T., 1929, M.S., 1930; postgrad., Yale U., 1932-33; D.Engring. (hon.), Mich. Tech. U., 1978. Asst. dir. lab. Internat. Silver Co. Meriden, Conn., 1930-40; chief materials scientist and engr. Navy Dept., Washington, 1940-66; exec. dir. nat. materials adv. bd. Nat. Acad. Scis., Washington, 1966-74; cons. on materials and policy, internationally, Washington, 1974—; mem., chmn. NATO Aerospace Panel, 1959-71; U.S. rep. (materials) OECD, 1967-70; U.S. chmn. U.S./USSR Sci. Exch. Program (materials), 1973-77); hon. guest USSR Acad. Scis.; permanent hon. pres. Internat. Conf. Materials Behavior; mem. Nat. Materials Adv. Bd.; adv. com. Oak Ridge Nat. Lab., Lehigh U., U. Pa., U.S. Navy Dept. Labs., U.S. Congress Office Tech. Assessment. Contbr. 65 articles to profl. publs.; contbr., editor: Advances in Materials Research, 1963, Science and Technology of Refractory Metals, 1964, Science, Technology and Application of Titanium, 1970; other books. Named Nat. Capitol Engr. of Yr. Coun. Engring. and Archtl. Socs., 1974; recipient Outstanding Accomplishment awards Navy Dept., 1955-64, Nat. Materials Advancement award, Fedn. Materials Socs., 1994; annual hon. lectr. Electrochem. Soc., 1970. Fellow AIME (hon. mem., ann. disting. lectr. Metall. Soc. 1984), Soc. Advanced Materials and Process Engring., Am. Soc. Materials Internat. (pres. 1972, hon. mem., Carnegie lectr. 1967, ann. hon. lectr. 1984), Brit. Inst. Materials; mem. NAE, ASTM (hon., ann. disting. lectr. 1964), Fedn. Materials Soc. (pres. 1972-73, 1st Decennial award 1982), Soc. Automotive Engrs. (chmn. aerospace materials divsn. 1959-74), Alpha Sigma Mu (hon.). Inventor in electroplating, 1930-40; metall. devels., 1941-66. Home and Office: Hyatt Classic Residence 8100 Connecticut Ave Apt 1406 Chevy Chase MD 20815-2820 *Ten key words and phrases for a professional career: identified goals, long range vision, can-do attitude, integrity, objectivity, understanding and tolerance, faith and trust, professionalism, dedication and perseverance, sense of humor.*

PROMISLO, DANIEL, lawyer; b. Bryn Mawr, Pa., Nov. 15, 1932; s. Charles and Pearl (Backman) P.; m. Estelle Carasso, June 10, 1961; children: Mark, Jacqueline, Steven. BSBA, Drexel U., 1955; JD magna cum laude, U. Pa., 1966. Bar: Pa. 1966. Pres., owner Hist. Souvenir Co., Phila., 1957—; assoc. Wolf, Block, Schorr & Solis-Cohen, Phila., 1966-70, ptnr., 1977-94, mem. exec. com., 1987-89, of counsel, 1994—; founder, pres. dir. Inst. for Paralegal Tng., Phila., 1970-75, cons., 1975-77. Editor: Corporate Law, 1970, Real Estate Law, 1971, Estates and Trusts, 1971, Civil Litigation, 1972, Employee Benefit Plans, 1973, Criminal Law, 1974; contbr. articles in field to profl. jours. Bd. dirs. Phila. Drama Guild, 1977-95, chmn., 1982-86; bd. dirs. Phila. Israel Econ. Devel. Program, 1983-88, Inst. for Arts in Edn., 1990-93; bd. dirs. WHYY, Inc., 1994—, vice chmn., 1995-96, chmn., 1996—; bd. dirs. U.S. Physicians, Inc., 1995—. Mem. Order of Coif, Blue Key, Phi Kappa Phi. Democrat. Jewish. Avocations: movies, basketball, tennis. Office: Wolf Block Schorr & Solis-Cohen SE Corner 15 Chestnut St Philadelphia PA 19122

PRONOVOST, JEAN, government official; b. Grand' Mère, Que., Can., Apr. 12, 1938; s. Léo and Laurette (Maltais) P.; m. Fauteux France, May 18, 1963; children: Jean-Robert, Pierre, Charles-André. BA in Social Scis., U. Laval, Quebec City, Que., 1961; M in Sociology, U. Laval, Quebec City, Que, 1964; postgrad., Sorbonne U., Paris, 1964-65. Asst. dep. min. planning Ministry Edn., Quebec City, 1980-81, asst. dep. min. adminstrn., 1981-85; asst. dep. min. Ministry Manpower and Income Security, Quebec City, 1985-87, dep. min., 1987-94; dep. min. Ministry Environ. and Wildlife, Quebec City, 1994—. Mem. Inst. Pub. Adminstrn. Can. Home: 3451 Pl Trianon, Sainte-Foy, PQ Canada G1X 2G1 Office: Ministry Environ & Wildlife, 675 Boul Rene-Lévesque 30e, Quebec City, PQ Canada G1R 5V7

PRONZINI, BILL JOHN (WILLIAM PRONZINI), author; b. Petaluma, Calif., Apr. 13, 1943; s. Joseph and Helene (Guder) P.; m. Marcia Muller. Coll. student, 2 years. Author: 50 novels (including under pseudonyms), 4 books of non-fiction, 6 collections of short stories, 1971—; first novel, The Stalker, 1971; editor 80 anthologies; contbr. numerous short stories to publs. Recipient Scroll award, Best First Novel, Mystery Writers Am., 1972, Life Achievement award Pvt. Eye Writers Am., 1987. Democrat. Office: PO Box 2536 Petaluma CA 94953-2536

PROPHETT, ANDREW LEE, political science educator; b. Lynchburg, Va., Mar. 1, 1948; s. Elisha and Evatna (Gilliam) P. BS in History, Hampton U., 1970; MEd in Social Studies, U. Ill., 1972; postgrad., U. Va., 1986-91. Cert. tchr., N.J. and Va. Tchr. U.S. and African history Camden (N.J.) H.S., 1970-85; tchr. social studies Randolph-Henry H.S., Charlotte Court House, Va., 1986—; instr. polit. sci. and African-Am. history Southside Va. C.C., Keysville, 1988—; mem. Campbell County (Va.) Sch. Bd., 1992-95; chmn. edn. com. Staunton River Adv. Commn., Randolph, Va., 1994—; summer participant Armonk Inst. Study Tour of Germany, 1995. Mem. Campbell County Dems., Rustburg, Va., 1986—; pres. Campbell County NAACP, Rustburg, 1992—; mem. youth adv. bd. Gethsemane Presbyn. Ch., Drakes Branch, Va., 1994—, deacon, 1995—, elder, 1997—; mem. study tour of Israel, Va. Dept. Edn., 1997; mem. Campbell County Sch. Bd., 1993-95; session mem. Gethsemane Presbyn. Ch., 1997—. Recipient Excellence in Tchg. award Southside Va. Cmty. Coll., 1994, Tchr. Recognition award Charlotte County Edn. Found., Inc., 1997. Mem. NEA, Va. Edn. Assn., Va. Geog. Soc., Phi Delta Kappa. Democrat. Presbyterian. Home: RR 1 Box 268 Brookneal VA 24528-9631 Office: Randolph-Henry H S PO Box 668 Charlotte Court House VA 23923

PROPST, CATHERINE LAMB, biotechnology company executive; b. Charlotte, N.C., Mar. 10, 1946; d. James Pinckney and Eliza Mayo (Mills) P. BA magna cum laude, Vanderbilt U., 1967; M of Philosophy, Yale U., 1970, PhD, 1973. Head microbiology div. GTE Labs., Waltham, Mass., 1974-77; various mgmt. positions Abbott Labs., North Chgo., Ill., 1977-80; v.p. rsch. and devel. Ayerst Labs., Plainview, N.Y., 1980-83; v.p. rsch. and devel. worldwide Flow Gen. Inc., McLean, Va., 1983-85; pres. and chief exec. officer Affiliated Sci. Inc., Ingleside, Ill., 1985—; vis. prof. genetics U. Ill., Chgo., 1989-90; founder and exec. dir. Ctr. for Biotech., Northwestern U., 1990-95; pres., Ill. Biotechnology Ctr., 1995—; bd. dirs. several cos. Author and editor: Computer-Aided Drug Design, 1989, Nucleic Acid Targeted Drug Design, 1992; contbr. articles to profl. jours. Named to Outstanding Working Women in the U.S., 1982; recipient many sci. and bus. awards. Fellow Soc. Indsl. Microbiology (bd. dirs. 1990-93), Nat. Coun. Biotech Ctrs. (bd. dirs. 1995—); mem. AAAS, Am. Chem. Soc., Nat. Wildlife Fedn., Consortium for Plant Biotech. Rsch. (bd. dirs. 1994—), Phi Beta Kappa, Sigma Xi. Episcopalian. Avocations: horseback riding, skiing, raising German Shephard dogs. Office: Affiliated Sci Inc PO Box 437 Ingleside IL 60041-0437 also: Ill Biotechnology Ctr Chgo Technology Park 2201 W Campbell Park Dr Chicago IL 60612-3547

PROPST, HAROLD DEAN, retired academic administrator; b. Newton, N.C., Feb. 7, 1934; s. Charles Clayton and Sarah Isabel (Hilderbrand) P. B.A., Wake Forest Coll., 1956; M.A., Peabody Coll., 1959, Ph.D., 1964; LL.D., Mercer U., 1985. Tchr. Vandalia Pub. Schs., Ohio, 1959-60; instr. Wake Forest Coll., Winston-Salem, N.C., 1960-61; asst. prof. English, Radford Coll., Va., 1962-64, assoc. prof., 1964-65, prof., 1965-69, chmn. dept. English, 1965-66, 68-69; dean Armstrong State Coll., Savannah, Ga., 1969-76, v.p. for acad. affairs, 1976-79; vice chancellor for acad. devel. Univ. System Ga., Atlanta, 1979-81, exec. vice chancellor, 1981-85, chancellor, 1985-94. Editor: (novel) John Brent, 1970; contbr. articles to profl. jours., monographs, books. Bd. visitors Radford Coll., 1970-74; former pres. bd. Family Counseling Ctr., Savannah; former pres. bd. Family Counseling Ctr., Savannah; former bd. dirs. Savannah Symphony, Savannah Heart Assn., Alliance Theatre, Atlanta; mem. So. Region Edn. Bd., 1985-94; mem. alumni bd. Peabody Coll. Vanderbilt U., 1994; mem. adv. bd. Mars Hill Coll., 1996—. With USN, 1956-58. Fellow Carnegie Found., 1958, Ford Found., 1960; recipient Disting. Alumnus award Wake Forest U., 1986. Mem. Am. Assn. State Colls and Univs. (com. on accreditation 1982-86), Acad. for Ednl. Devel. (study com. on campus govt. 1976-77). Baptist.

PROSCINO, STEVEN VINCENT, food products company executive; b. Phila., Nov. 22, 1954; s. Vincent and Marjorie (Gefrorer) P.; m. Anna Moore, May 31, 1986; children: Matthew, Daniel. BS in Math./Physics, Coll. William and Mary, 1977; BSME, Rensselaer Poly. Inst., 1977; MBA, U. Pa., 1983. Registered profl. engr., Pa. Project mgr. Air Products, Allentown, Pa., 1977-81; dir. MIS/engring. Metal Container Corp. (Anheuser-Busch Cos., Inc.), St. Louis, 1985-94; sr. v.p., gen. mgr. Earthgrains Co., Clayton, Mo., 1994—. Mem. Algonquin Country Club. Avocations: golf, tennis. Office: Earthgrains Co 8400 Maryland Ave Saint Louis MO 63105-3647

PROSKIN, ARNOLD W., state assemblyman, lawyer; b. Albany, N.Y., Apr. 2, 1938; s. Betty (Levin) P.; m. Martha Pollack, June 4, 1960; children: Lisa, Heath, Wendy, Michael. Student, SUNY, Albany, 1961; LLD, Boston Coll., 1964. Bar: N.Y. 1964, U.S. Dist. Ct. (no. dist.) N.Y., U.S. Dist. Ct. (so. dist.) N.Y., U.S. Supreme Ct. 1968. Pvt. practice Albany, N.Y., 1964—; dist. atty. Office of Dist. Atty. Albany County, N.Y., 1969-73; judge Albany County Ct., 1973-76; ptnr. The Proskin Law Firm, Albany, 1976—; mem. N.Y. State Assembly, Albany, 1984-94; mem. judiciary, codes and ethics standing com., guidance standing com., racing and wagering standing com., chmn. steering com. minority conf.; mem. legis. ethics com.; mem. civil practice, property rights, estates and trusts, court ops. and constl. amendments subcoms.; past mem. ins., corps., authorities, commns., election law, labor and housing standing coms. Active Temple Ohav Shalom, Gov. Clinton Coun., Boy Scouts Am. Adv. Bd., Jewish War Vets., Adv. Bd. Barn Raisers. With USN, 1956-58. Recipient N.Y. State Vocat. Schs. award, 1971, Histradrut Pub. Svc. Coun. award, 1973; named Outstanding Young Man of Yr., N.Y. State Jaycees, 1972, Man of Yr., Internat. Order of Alhambra, 1975, Mem. of Yr., Independent Order of Odd Fellows, 1985. Mem. ABA, Am. Judicature Soc., N.Y. State Bar Assn., N.Y. State Dist. Attys. Assn., Saratoga County Bar Assn., Albany Bar Assn., Nat. Dist. Attys. Assn., County Judge's Assn. State N.Y., Am. Legion, B'nai B'rith Gideon Lodge, Masons, Shiners, West Albany Athletic Assn., Latham Area C. of C. Office: The Proskin Law Firm 423 Loudon Rd Albany NY 12211-1722

PROSKY, ROBERT JOSEPH, actor; b. Phila., Dec. 13, 1930; s. Joseph and Helen (Kuhn) Porzuczek; m. Ida Mae Hove, June 4, 1960, children: Stefan, John, Andrew. Student, Temple U., Am. Theatre. Appeared at Arena Stage, Washington, 23 years including roles in Death of a Salesman, Twelfth Night, Enemy of the People, Galileo; appeared on Broadway in Moonchildren, View from the Bridge, Glengarry Glen Ross (Tony award nominee 1985), A Walk in the Woods, 1988 (Tony award nominee 1988, Best Actor award Outer Critics Circle, toured USSR and Lithuania 1989), Camping with Henry and Tim; films include Thief, 1981, Lords of Discipline, 1983, Christine, 1983, The Natural, 1984, Broadcast News, 1987, Outrageous Fortune, 1987, Things Change, 1988, Gremlins II, 1988, Something About Love, 1990, Green Card, 1990, Life in the Food Chain, 1990, Far and Away, 1992, Hoffa, 1992, Life on the High Wire, 1992, Rudy, 1992, Last Action Hero, 1993, Mrs. Doubtfire, 1993, Miracle on 34th Street, 1994, Scarlet Letter, 1995, Dead Man Walking, 1995, The Chamber, 1996, Mad City, 1997; TV appearances include role of Sgt. Jablonski in Hill Street Blues, The Murder of Mary Phagan, 1988, Home Fires Burning, 1988, From the Dead of Night, 1989, Heist, 1989, Dangerous Pursuit, 1990, Johnny Ryan, 1990, The Love She Sought, 1990, Double Edge, 1992, Teamster Boss: The Jackie Presser Story, 1992, narrator Lifestories; mem. first Am. co. to tour Soviet Union, 1972. Joseph Jefferson award nominee, 1985; recipient Drama Desk award, 1985, Helen Hayes award, 1995. *

PROSPERI, DAVID PHILIP, public relations executive; b. Chgo., June 20, 1953. BSBA, U. Ill., 1975; MBA in Internat. Bus., George Washington U., 1983. Moving cons. Fed. Safety Moving & Storage, Elmhurst, Ill., 1975-79; press aide 1980 Reagan for Pres. campaign, Los Angeles, 1979-80, Reagan-Bush Campaign, Alexandria, Va., 1980-81; asst. press sec. to the Pres. White House, Washington, 1981-82; mgr. govt. affairs The Superior Oil Co., Washington, 1982-84; press. sec. U.S. Dept. Energy, Washington, 1985; asst. to sec. dir. pub. affairs U.S. Dept. Interior, Washington, 1985-88; asst. sec. transp. U.S. Dept. Transp., Washington, 1989-90; sr. v.p., asst. to pres. and CEO Chgo. Bd. Trade, 1990-95, sr. v.p., 1995—; prin. Coun. on Excellence in Govt. Bd. dirs. Corp. Pub. Broadcasting, 1992-93. Republican. Roman Catholic. Avocations: basketball, tennis, spending time with family. Office: Chgo Bd Trade 141 W Jackson Blvd Ste 600A Chicago IL 60604-2992

PROSPERI, LOUIS ANTHONY, lawyer; b. Altoona, Pa., Jan. 12, 1954; s. Louis Alfred and Ann Francis (DiDimenico) P.; m. Susan Lynn Irwin, Sept. 14, 1985. BS in Bus. Adminstrn. summa cum laude, Georgetown U., 1975; JD cum laude, Harvard U., 1978. Bar: Pa. 1978, U.S. Dist. Ct. (we. dist.) Pa. 1978, U.S. Ct. Appeals (Fed. cir.) 1985, U.S. Ct. Fed. Claims, 1985, U.S. Tax Ct. 1979. From assoc. to ptnr. Reed, Smith, Shaw & McClay, Pitts., 1978-94; pvt. practice Law Office Louis A. Prosperi, Pitts., 1994—. Mem. Allegheny County Bar Assn., Pitts. Tax Club. Republican. Roman Catholic. Club: Longue Vue (Verona, Pa.). Avocations: golf, tennis, paddle tennis, cross-country skiing. Home: 3036 Grasmere Ave Pittsburgh PA 15216-1862 Office: Law Office of Louis A Prosperi Grant Bldg 310 Grant St Ste 3601 Pittsburgh PA 15219-2301

PROSSER, BRUCE REGINAL, JR. (BO PROSSER), minister, consultant; b. Milledgeville, Ga., Sept. 23, 1953; s. Bruce R. Prosser Sr. and Sarah (Dukes) Ellington; m. Gail Ford, June 26, 1976; children: Jamie Lynn, Katie Beth. BBA, Ga. Coll., 1975; MRE, So. Sem., 1979, MDiv, 1980; postgrad., U. Ga., 1988-89; EdD in Adult Edn., N.C. State U., 1997. Ordained to ministry Hardwick Bapt. Ch., 1978. Assoc. pastor Shepherdville (Ky.) First Bapt. Ch., 1979-82, Cen. Bapt. Ch., Warner Robins, Ga., 1982-84; min. edn., adminstr. First Bapt. Ch., Roswell, Ga., 1984-89; assoc. pastor Forest Hills Bapt. Ch., Raleigh, N.C., 1989-94; min. edn. Providence Baptist Ch., 1995—; mng. ptnr. Creative Consultation Svcs.; chaplain Phi Delta Theta Frat., Ga. Coll., 1974-75, North Roswell PTA, 1985-87; pres. Met. Religious Educators, Atlanta, 1987-88. Author: Promotion Plus!, 1992, (with others) Single Adult Leadership, 1991, Church Administration from A-Z, 1994; contbr. chpts. to books, articles to profl. publs. Assoc. dir. Met. Enlargement Campaign, Atlanta, 1988-89; facilitator N.C. State Leadership Devel. in Creativity, Humor, and Total Quality. Mem. So. Bapt. Religious Edn. Assn. Avocations: motivational speaking, humor, leadership, creativity, organizational development. Office: Providence Baptist Ch 4921 Randolph Rd Charlotte NC 28211-4002 *We have been called by our Divine God to be vessels of his Love, Grace and Redemption. May your day be filled with rainbows and watermelons and blessed with His love and laughter.*

PROSSER, C. LADD, physiology educator, researcher; b. Avon, N.Y., May 12, 1907; s. Clifford James and Izora May (Ladd) P.; m. Hazel Blanchard, Aug. 25, 1934; children—Jane Ellen, Nancy Ladd, Loring Blanchard. A.B., U. Rochester, 1929; Ph.D., Johns Hopkins U., 1932; hon. degree, Clark U., 1975. Asst. prof. physiology Clark U., Worcester, Mass., 1934-39; asst. prof physiology U. Ill., Urbana, 1939-47, assoc. prof. physiology, 1947-52, prof. physiology, 1952-74, prof. emeritus, 1975—; asst. sect. chief Metallurgy Lab. U. Chgo., 1943-46; vis prof. U. Hawaii, U. Wash., U. Mass., Ariz. State U. Author: Adaptational Biology, 1986; author, editor: Comparative Animal Physiology, 1st edit., 1951, 4th edit. 1991; contbr. numerous articles to profl. jours. Guggenheim fellow, 1963-64; Fulbright fellow, 1971-72. Fellow Am. Acad. Arts and Scis.; mem. Nat. Acad. Scis., Soc. Gen. Physiologists (pres. 1958-59), AAAS (v.p. 1960), Am. Soc. Zoologists (pres. 1961), Am. Physiol. Soc. (pres. 1969-70), Bavarian Acad. Sci. Unitarian. Avocations: music; gardening. Home: 101 W Windsor Rd Urbana IL 61801-6663 Office: U Ill 524 Burrill Hall Urbana IL 61801

PROSSER, FRANKLIN PIERCE, computer scientist; b. Atlanta, July 4, 1935; s. Edward Theron and Eunice (McDaniel) P.; m. Brenda Mary Lau, June 16, 1960; children: Edward, Andrea. B.S., Ga. Inst. Tech., 1956, M.S., 1958; Ph.D., Pa. State U., 1961. Prof. computer sci. Ind. U., Bloomington, 1969—; asso. dir. Wrubel Computing Center, 1969-81, chmn. dept. computer sci., 1971-77, 87-93, spl. asst. for acad. computing, 1979-81; v.p. Logic Design, Inc., 1982-92; cons. Lockheed Theoretical Physics Lab., Palo Alto, Calif., 1967. Home: 1200 S Longwood Dr Bloomington IN 47401-6072 Office: Ind U Dept Computer Sci Bloomington IN 47405

PROSSER, JOHN MARTIN, architect, educator, university dean, urban design consultant; b. Wichita, Kans., Dec. 28, 1932; s. Francis Ware and Harriet Corinne (Osborne) P.; m. Judith Adams, Aug. 28, 1954 (dec. 1982); children: Thomas, Anne, Edward; m. Karen Ann Cleary, Dec. 30, 1983; children: Jennifer. B.Arch., U. Kans., 1955; M.Arch., Carnegie Mellon U., 1961. Registered architect, Kans., Colo. Architect, Robinson and Hissem, Wichita, 1954-56, Guirey, Srnka, and Arnold, Phoenix, 1961-62, James Sudler Assocs., Denver, 1962-68; ptnr., architect Nuzum, Prosser and Vetter, Boulder, 1969-73; from asst. prof. to prof. U. Colo., Boulder, Denver, 1968—, acting dean, 1980-84, dean, 1984; dir. environ. design U. Colo., Boulder, 1969-72, dir. urban design, 1972-85; cons. John M. Prosser Assoc., Boulder and Denver, 1974—; vis. prof. urban design Oxford Poly., Eng., 1979; vis. Critic Carnegie Mellon U., U. N.Mex., Colo. Coll.; pres. Denver chpt. AIA, 1983 . Author, narrator PBS TV documentary Cities Are For Kids Too, 1984. Prin. works include (with others) hist. redesign Mus. Western Art, Denver (design honor 1984), Villa Italia, Lakewood, Colo., Denver, Auraria Higher Edn. Ctr., Pueblo C.C. campus plan and new acad. facilities, comprehensive campus plan Denver U., Lamar C.C., Ft. Lewis Coll., Westminster Golf Course Community, Denver Botanic Gardens 20-Yr. Concept Plan, Colo. Coll. Historic Preservation Plan, Commerce City Golf Course Cmty., Fountain Valley Sch., Regional Urban Design and Campus Planning. Bd. dirs. Denver Parks and Recreation Bd., 1987-93; chmn. design rev. bd. Univs. Colo., Boulder, Denver and Colorado Springs, 1981—; mem. archtl. control com. Denver Tech. Ctr., 1984—, Meridian Internat. Bus. Ctr., 1984—, DTC West, 1991—, Denver Internat. Bus. Ctr., 1993—, Nat. Renewable Energy Lab., 1995—; planning cons. Denver Internat. Airport Environs Devel. Projects. Capt. USAF, 1956-59. Co-recipient 2d place nat. award Am. Soc. Interior Designers, 1984, honor award Colo. Soc. Architects, 1984. Mem. Urban Land Inst. Democrat. Club: Denver Country (pres. 1986-87). Avocation: Arlberg Ski. Home: 1620 Monaco Pky Denver CO 80220-1643 Office: U Colo 1200 Larimer St Denver CO 80204-5310

PROSSER, MICHAEL HUBERT, communications educator; b. Indpls., Mar. 29, 1936; s. Marshall Herbert and Clydia Catharine (O'Dea) P.; m. Carol Mary Hegle, Nov. 27, 1958 (div. 1983); children: Michelle Ann Prosser-Evans, Leo Michael, Louis Mark; m. Joan Ann Kirkeby, Dec. 6, 1986. BA, Ball State U., 1958, MA, 1959; PhD, U. Ill., 1964. Tchr. Latin Urbana (Ill.) Jr. High Sch., 1960-63; asst. prof. speech SUNY, Buffalo, 1963-69; assoc. prof. speech Ind. U., Bloomington, 1969-72; prof. rhetoric and comm. U. Va., Charlottesville, 1972—, chair, 1972-77; William A. Kern prof. in comm. Rochester Inst. Tech., 1994—; chair AFS Global Awareness Day, U. Va., 1983-90, RIT Global Awareness Day, 1995-97, Intercultural Comm.; confs. at Rochester Inst. Tech., 1995-97; vis. lectr. comm. Queens Coll. CUNY, 1966, 67; vis. assoc. prof. speech Calif. State U., Hayward, 1971; vis. prof. curriculum Meml. U. Newfoundland, St. John's, 1972, St. Paul U. and U. Ottawa (Can.), 1975; cons. intercultural comm. U.S. Info. Agy., Washington, 1977; disting. vis. prof. speech Kent (Ohio) State U., 1978; Fulbright prof. English, U. Swaziland, Kwalusene, 1990-91, Am. U. of Bulgaria, 1994-95 (declined); fellow New Coll. U. Va., 1992-94; Gannett lectr. Rochester Inst. Tech., 1995, Kern lectr., 1995—. Author: The Cultural Dialogue, 1978 (translated into Japanese 1982); co-author: Diplomatic Discourse: International Conflict at the United Nations: Addresses and Analysis, 1997; editor: An Ethic for Survival, 1969, Sow the Wind, Reap the Whirlwind: Heads of State Address the United Nations (2 vols.), 1970, Intercommunication Among Nations and Peoples, 1973; co-editor: Readings in Classical Rhetoric, 1969, Readings in Medieval Rhetoric, 1973. Mem. Haiti commn. Cath. Diocese Richmond, 1989-93; bd. dirs., v.p. Rochester Assn. UN, 1995-97, pres., 1997-98; pres. Rochester Area Fulbright Chpt., 1995-97; bd. dirs. UN Assn. Rochester. Recipient Disting. Alumnus award Ball State U., 1978. Mem. AAUP, Internat. Soc. for Intercultural Edn., Tng. and Rsch. (pres. 1984-86, Citizen of World 1986, Outstanding Sr. Interculturalist 1990), Internat. Comm. Assn. (v.p., Disting. Svc. award 1978), Speech Communication Assn., Fulbright Assn., Nat. Comm. Assn., Rochester Assn. for UN (bd. dirs., v.p., pres.), Am. Field Svc. (pres. intercultural programs 1982-86, Charlottesville), Assn. for Edn. in Journalism and Mass Media, U.S. Assn. of UN. Democrat. Roman Catholic. Avocations: social justice and peace advocacy, youth, travel. Office: Rochester Inst Tech Coll of Liberal Arts 92 Lomb Memorial Dr Rochester NY 14623-5604

PROSSER, MICHAEL JOSEPH, community college staff member; b. Syracuse, N.Y., May 9, 1948; s. Palmer Adelbert and Viola Mary (Clairmont) P. AA, Riverside (Calif.) City Coll., 1971; BA in History, Calif. State Coll., San Bernardino, 1977; MSLS, U. So. Calif., L.A., 1981. Cert. cmty. coll. instr., librarian, Calif. Libr. clk. Riverside C.C., 1968-81, learning resources asst., 1981—. Author: California and the Pacific Plate: A Bibliography, 1979. Tutor, Queen of Angels Ch., Riverside, 1985—, facilitator/patrons, 1985—. With U.S. Army, 1969-71. Mem. ASCD, Internat. Soc. Poets, Calif. Media Libr. Educators Assn., Calif. Libr. Assn. Democrat. Roman Catholic. Home: 6800 Palos Dr Riverside CA 92503-1330 Office: Riverside Cmty Coll 4800 Magnolia Ave Riverside CA 92506-1242

PROTAS, RON, dance company executive. Gen. dir. Martha Graham Ctr. Contemporary Dance, N.Y.C, assoc. artistic dir.; now artistic dir., exec. dir. Martha Graham Dance Co., N.Y.C. Office: Martha Graham Dance Co 316 E 63rd St New York NY 10021-7702*

PROTEAU, JOCELYN, professional sports team executive. Vice chmn. bd. Montreal Expos. Office: Montreal Expos, 4549 Pierre-de-Coubertin Ave, Montreal, PQ Canada H1V 3N7*

PROTIGAL, STANLEY NATHAN, lawyer; b. Wilmington, Del., June 3, 1950; s. Bernard Protigal. BS in Aircraft Maintenance Engring., Northrop U., 1973; JD, Vt. Law Sch., 1978. Bar: U.S. Patent Office 1977, D.C. 1978. Assoc. Sixbey F. & L., Arlington, Va., 1978-79, atty., 1979-82; patent atty. Allied-Signal Bendix Aerospace, Teterboro, N.J., 1982-88; patent counsel Micron Tech., Inc., Boise, Idaho, 1988-94; pvt. practice Boise, Idaho, 1994-96, Seattle, 1996—. Mem. IEEE, MENSA. Avocations: pvt. pilot, bicycling, skiing.

PROUGH, RUSSELL ALLEN, biochemistry educator; b. Twin Falls, Idaho, Nov. 5, 1943; s. Elza Leroy and Beulah Elsie (Huddleston) P.; M. Betty Marie Ehlers, Dec. 26, 1965; children: Jennifer Sally, Kimberly Marie. BS in Chemistry, Coll. of Idaho, 1965; PhD in Biochemistry and Biophysics, Oreg. State U., 1969. Postdoctoral fellow VA Hosp., Kansas City, Mo., 1969-72; instr. biochemistry U. Tex. Southwestern Med. Sch., Dallas, 1972-73, asst. prof. biochemistry, 1973-77, assoc. prof. biochemistry, 1977-82, prof. biochemistry, 1982-86; prof., chmn. dept. biochemistry U. Louisville Sch. Med., 1986—; mem. NIH Toxicology Study Sect., 1984-88, State of Nebr. Smoking Disease and Cancer Rsch. Program, 1984-91. Assoc. editor Drug Metabolism and Disposition, 1994—. Recipient Rsch. Career Devel. award USPHS. Mem. Am. Soc. Biochemistry and Molecular Biology, Am. Assn. Cancer Rsch., Am. Soc. Pharmacology and Exptl. Therapeutics, Internat. Soc. for Study of Xenobiotics, Sigma Xi. Lutheran. Office: U of Louisville Dept of Biochemistry Louisville KY 40292

PROULX, EDNA ANNIE, writer; b. Norwich, Conn., Aug. 22, 1935; d. George Napolean and Lois Nelly (Gill) Proulx; m. James Hamilton Lang, June 22, 1969 (div. 1990); children: Jonathan Edward Lang, Gillis Crowell Lang, Morgan Hamilton Lang. BA cum laude, U. Vt., 1969; MA, Sir George Williams U., Montreal, Can., 1973; DHL (hon.), U. Maine, 1994. Author: Heart Songs and Other Stories, 1988, Postcards, 1992 (PEN/Faulkner award 1993), The Shipping News, 1993 (Nat. Book award for fiction 1993, Chgo. Tribune Heartland award 1993, Irish Times Internat. Fiction award 1993, Pulitzer Prize for fiction 1994), Accordion Crimes, 1996; contbr. more than 50 articles to mags. and jours. Kress fellow Harvard U., 1974, fellow Vt. Coun. Arts, 1989, NEA, 1991, Guggenheim Found., 1992; rsch. grantee Inter.-U. Ctr., 1975; resident Ucross Found., 1990, 92. Mem. PEN Am. Ctr., Phi Beta Kappa, Phi Alpha Theta. Avocations: canoeing, reading, fishing, carpentry. Office: care Darhansoff Verrill Agy 179 Franklin St New York NY 10013-2857

PROUT, CURTIS, physician; b. Swampscott, Mass., Oct. 13, 1915; s. Henry Byrd and Eloise (Willett) P.; m. Daphne Brooks, June 27, 1939 (div. 1985); children: Diana P. Cherot, Daphne P. Cook, Rosamond P. Warren, Phyllis P. Brosius; m. Diane Neal Emmons, Dec. 7, 1985. AB, Harvard U., 1937, MD, 1941. Diplomate Am. Bd. Internal Medicine. Intern Peter Bent Brigham Hosp., Boston, 1942; resident in internal medicine Johns Hopkins Hosp., Balt., 1943; research fellow Mass. Gen. Hosp., Boston, 1943-45; practice medicine specializing in internal medicine, 1945—; asst. dir. Univ. Health Services Harvard U., Cambridge, Mass., 1961-72; dir. prison health project Office of Econ. Opportunity, 1972-74; asst. dean Harvard Med. Sch., Boston, 1980-94, asst. clin. prof., 1975-82; trustee Humane Soc. of Mass., Boston, 1975-97; bd. dirs. Nat. Commn. on Correctional Health Care, 1980—, chmn., 1990; dir., treas. The Med. Found., Boston, 1980—. Chmn. Bd. Health, Dover, Mass., 1960-75. Fellow ACP, Mass. Med. Soc.; mem. AMA, Am. Clin. and Climatol. Assn., Tavern Club of Boston (pres. 1980-82). Avocations: sailing, writing. Home: 115 School St Manchester MA 01944-1232 Office: 319 Longwood Ave Boston MA 02115-5728

PROUT, GEORGE RUSSELL, JR., medical educator, urologist; b. Boston, July 23, 1924; s. George Russell and Marion (Snow) P.; m. Loa Katherine Wheatley, Oct. 17, 1950; children: George Russell III, Elizabeth Louise. Student, Union Coll., 1943, DSc (hon.), 1990; MD, Albany Med. Coll., 1947, DSc (hon.), 1988; MA (hon.), Harvard U., 1969. Intern Grasslands Hosp., Valhalla, N.Y., 1947-48; resident N.Y. Hosp., N.Y.C., 1952-56; asst. attending physician Meml. Ctr. for Cancer and Allied Disease, N.Y.C., 1956-57; asst. clinician in surgery James Ewing Hosp., N.Y.C., 1956-57; assoc. prof., chmn. div. urology U. Miami, 1957-60; prof., chmn. div. urology Med. Coll. Va., 1960-69; chief urol. svc. Mass. Gen. Hosp., Boston, 1969-89; prof. surgery Harvard Med. Sch., 1969-89; emeritus prof. surgery Harvard Med. Sch., Boston, 1989—; hon. urologist Mass. Gen. Hosp., Boston, 1993—; chmn. Adjuvants in Surg. Treatment of Bladder Cancer; mem. adv. task force to Nat. Cancer Inst., 1968—, expert cons. divsn. surveillance, 1991—, Finland coop. ATBC study, 1991—; chmn. Nat. Bladder Cancer Group, 1973-86. Editor-in-chief Urologic Oncology, 1994—. With USNR, 1950-52. Fellow ACS, Acad. Medicine Toronto (corr.); mem. AMA, AAUP, Am. Urol. Assn., Can. Urol. Assn., Japanese Urol. Soc., Am. Cancer Soc., Soc. Pelvic Surgeons, Soc. Surg. Oncology, Soc. Univ. Urologists, Dallas So. Clin. Soc. (hon.), Am. Assn. Genitourinary Surgeons, Soc. Pediat. Urology, Soc. Urol. Oncology, Soc. Internat. Urologists, Soc. Basic Urol. Rsch., Alpha Omega Alpha. Home and Office: 27 W Prospect Bay Dr Grasonville MD 21638-9668 Winter address: 224 Corsair Rd Marathon FL 33050

PROUT, RALPH EUGENE, physician; b. Los Angeles, Feb. 27, 1933; s. Ralph Byron and Fern (Taylor) P.; m. Joanne Morris, Sept. 17, 1980; children: Michael, Michelle. BA, La Sierra Coll., 1953; MD, Loma Linda U., 1957; D of Nutri-Medicine (hon.), John F. Kennedy Coll., 1987. Diplomate: Nat. Bd. Med. Examiners. Intern Los Angeles County Hosp., 1957-58; resident internal medicine White Meml. Hosp., Los Angeles, 1958-60; resident psychiatry Harding Hosp., Worthington, Ohio, 1960-61; practice medicine specializing in internal medicine Napa, Calif., 1961-63; staff internist Calif. Med. Facility, Vacaville, 1963-68, chief med. officer, 1968-84; chief med. cons. Calif. Dept. Corrections, 1977-86, chief med. services, 1983; med. cons. Wellness Cons., Placerville, Calif., 1986-96; pres. Addiction Medicine Treatment Ctr., Placerville, Calif., 1986-96; instr. Sch. Medicine, Loma Linda U., 1965-66; clin. assoc. U. Calif.-Davis Sch. Medicine, 1978-84; med. cons. Substance Abuse Pine Grove Camp, 1986—; expert witness alcoholism El Dorado (Calif.) Superior Ct., 1994—; pres. Union Am. Physicians and Dentists, Calif. State Employee chpt., 1970-72. Treas. Vacaville Republican Assembly, 1972-75; del. Republican Central Com. Solano County, 1975-78; Bd. dirs. Napa-Solano County United Crusade, Vallejo, Calif., 1969-71, v.p., 1970-71; bd. dirs., co-founder Project Clinic, Vacaville, 1974-77, Home Health Com. Inter-Community Hosp., Fairfield, 1978-80; pres. MotherLode Citizens for Drug-Free Youth, Amador County, 1985—. Named One of Outstanding Young Men of Am., 1968. Mem. AMA, Am. Assn. Sr. Physicians, Internat. Assn. New Sci., Union Concerned Scis., Mother Lode Citizens for Drug-Free Youth, Native Sons of Golden West, Alpha Omega Alpha. Republican. Home and Office: 24405 Shake Ridge Rd Volcano CA 95689-9728 *When we ask better questions, the answers will follow.*

PROUTY, JILL, psychodramatist, psychotherapist; b. Chgo., Oct. 22, 1939; d. Nathan Alfred and Beverly (Bramson) Berkson; m. Robert Howard Winer, July 30, 1961 (div. 1987); children: Garry, Marc, Richard; m. Garry Franklyn Prouty, May 26, 1990. BA, Lake Forest Coll., 1961; MA, Gov. State U., 1973. Cert. trainer, educator, practitioner in psychodrama sociometry and group psychotherapy. Pres. Illiana Psychodrama Inst., Flossmoor, Ill., 1980-90, Fedn. Trainers and Tng. Programs in Psychodrama, 1982-83; psychodramatist Four Winds Hosp., Lemont, Ill., 1990-93, Charter Hosp., Hobart, Ind., 1990-93, Chgo. Osteo. Health Sys., Olympia Fields, 1995-96; adj. prof. Govs. State U., University Park, Ill., 1975-88; internat. cons. Pre-Therapy, Ghent, Belgium, 1988—. Fellow Am. Soc. Group Psychotherapy and Psychodrama; mem. ACA, Nat. Assn. Dual Diagnosed, Nat. Coun. Jewish Women (life). Avocations: reading, collecting matrioshka dolls. Home: 6015 Lakeside Pl Tinley Park IL 60477-1979

PROUTY, NORMAN R., investment banker; b. N.Y.C., Feb. 4, 1939; s. Norman R. and Eleanor (Ryan) P.; m. Alden Finch, July 18, 1964 (div. Mar. 1989); children: Brooks Silliman, Nicholas Alden, Honor Howland; m. Allison LoveJoy Simmons, Jan. 27, 1990; 1 child, Annabel Scarlett LoveJoy. BA, Yale U., 1961. V.p., sr. credit officer Citibank, N.Y.C., 1961-81; gen. ptnr. Lazard Frères & Co., N.Y.C., 1981-95; pres. Brook Capital Corp., Greenwich, Conn., 1996—. Trustee Pitzer Coll., Nature Conservancy of N.Y. State, 1992—; bd. overseers The Claremont Colls., 1990. Mem. Anglers' Club, The Brook, Racquet and Tennis Club, Fishers Island Club. Avocations: fishing, shooting, sailing, tennis. Home: 5 Mountain Wood Dr Greenwich CT 06830-3335

PROVENCHER, ROGER ARTHUR, international consultant; b. Manchester, N.H., June 20, 1923; s. Arthur J. and Rose Albina (Briere) P.; m. Josette Marguerite Camus, Jan. 3, 1946 (dec. 1976); children: Frances Provencher-Kambour, Carl; m. Mary Lou Sack, Mar. 17, 1989. BA, U. N.H., 1949; Doctorat D'Universite', U. Paris, 1950. Joined Dept. State, 1950; asst. commr. gen. Expo 67, Montreal, Que., Can., 1965-67; mgmt. analyst Washington, 1968; assigned to Nat. War Coll., 1969-70; 1st sec., counselor Am. embassy, Moscow, 1970-73; counselor for administrv. affairs Am. embassy, Vientiane, Laos, 1973-74, Tehran, Iran, 1974-77; sr. counsellor Internat. Telecommunication Union, Geneva, 1977-82; mng. dir. Pan African Airlines (Nigeria) Ltd., Lagos, 1962-63. V.p. Rollingwood Community Assn. 1st lt. AUS, 1943-46, ETO. Recipient Meritorious Honor award Dept. State, 1958, 62, also Superior Honor award, 1975. Mem. Nat. War Coll. Alumni Assn., Am. Fgn. Service Assn. (dir.), Lambda Pi. Home and Office: PO Box 326 Ladysmith VA 22501-0326 *A public servant must never forget that his responsibility rests on serving the public. The public have contributed their trust and hope in their investments. Their aspirations must be honored even if at times, physical, ideological, conjugal or other personal stresses invite abdication.*

PROVENSEN, ALICE ROSE TWITCHELL, artist, author; b. Chgo.; d. Jay Horace and Kathryn (Zelanis) Twitchell; m. Martin Provensen, Apr. 17, 1944; 1 child, Karen Anna. Student, Art Inst. of Chgo., 1930-31, U. Calif., L.A., 1939, Art Student League, N.Y., 1940-41; D.H.L. (hon.), Marist Coll., 1986. With Walter Lanz Studios, Los Angeles, 1942-43; OSS, 1944-45. Exhibited (with Martin Provensen) Balt. Mus., 1954, Am. Inst. Graphic Arts, N.Y., 1959, Botolph Group, Boston, 1964; exhibited one person shows: Henry Feiwel Gallery, N.Y.C., 1991, Children's Mus., Washington, 1991, Moscarelle Mus. Art, Williamsburg, Va., 1991; books represented in Fifty Books of Yr. Selections, Am. Inst. Graphic Arts, 1947, 48, 52 (The Charge of the Light Brigade named Best Illustrated Children's Book of the Yr. N.Y. Times 1964, co-recipient Gold medal Soc. Illustrators 1960); author/illustrator: books including Karen's Opposites, 1963, Karen's Curiosity, 1963, What is a Color?, 1967, (with Martin Provensen) Who's In the Egg, 1970, The Provensen Book of Fairy Tales, 1971, Play on Words, 1972, My Little Hen, 1973, Roses are Red, 1973, Our Animal Friends, 1974, The Year at Maple Hill Farm, 1978, A Horse and a Hound, A Goat and a Gander, 1979, An Owl and Three Pussycats, 1981, Town and Country, 1984, Shaker Lane, 1987, The Buck Stops Here, 1990, Punch in New York, 1991 (Best Books N.Y. Times 1991), My Fellow Americans, 1995; illustrator: (with Martin Provensen) children's books including Mother Goose Book, 1976, Old Mother Hubbard, 1977, A Peaceable Kingdom, 1978, The Golden Serpent, 1980, A Visit to William Blake's Inn, 1981, Birds, Beasts and the Third Thing, 1982, The Glorious Flight, 1984 (Caldecott medal 1984), The Voyage of the Ludgate Hill, 1987; also textbooks.

PROVINE, JOHN C., lawyer; b. Asheville, N.C., May 15, 1938; s. Robert Calhoun and Harriet Josephine (Thoms) P.; m. Martha Ann Monson, Aug. 26, 1966 (div. Jan. 1975); m. Nancy Frances Lunsford, Apr. 17, 1976 (div. Mar. 1996); children: Robert, Frances, Harriet. AB, Harvard U., 1960; JD, U. Mich., 1966; MBA, NYU, 1972, LLM in Taxation, 1975. Bar: N.Y., Tenn., U.S. Dist. Ct. (so. and ea. dists.) N.Y., U.S. Ct. Appeals (2nd and 6th cirs.), U.S. Dist. Ct. (mid. dist.) Tenn., U.S. Supreme Ct. From assoc. to ptnr. White & Case, N.Y.C., 1966-74, ptnr., 1974-81, 92-94; ptnr. White & Case, Jakarta and Ankara, 1982-91; counsel Dearborn & Ewing, Nashville, Tenn., 1982. Lt. USN, 1960-63. Mem. ABA, N.Y. Bar Assn., Tenn. Bar Assn., Assn. of Bar of City of N.Y. Avocations: bluegrass music, rural activities. Home and Office: 6630 Manley Ln Brentwood TN 37027-3401

PROVINE, LORRAINE, mathematics educator; b. Altus, Okla., Oct. 6, 1944; d. Claud Edward and Emmie Lorraine (Gasper) Allmon; m. Joe A. Provine, Aug. 14, 1966; children: Sharon Kay, John David. BS, U. Okla., 1966; MS, Okla. State U., 1988. Tchr. math. U.S. Grant High Sch., Oklahoma City Schs., 1966-69; tchr. East Jr. High Sch., Ponca City (Okla.) Schs., 1969-70; tchr. Ponca City High Sch., 1978-79, 81-96; lectr. dept. math. Okla. State U., Stillwater, 1996—. Mem. NEA, Coun. for Exceptional Children, Internat. Soc. Tech. in Edn., Math. Assn. Am., Nat. Coun. Tchrs. Math., Sch. Sci. and Math. Assn., Okla. Edn. Assn., Okla. Coun. Tchrs. Math., Assn. Women in Math., Ponca City Assn. Classroom Tchrs. (treas. 1983-86, 91-96), Okla. Assn. Mothers Clubs (life, state bd. dirs. 1977-87, pres. 1984-85), Delta Kappa Gamma (treas. 1996—). Republican. Baptist. Avocations: reading, knitting, sewing. Home: 1915 Meadowbrook St Ponca City OK 74604-3012 Office: Okla State U Dept Math MS 408 Stillwater OK 74078-1058

PROVORNY, FREDERICK ALAN, lawyer; b. Bklyn., Sept. 7, 1946; s. Daniel and Anna (Wurm) P.; m. Nancy Ileene Wilkins, Nov. 21, 1971; children: Michelle C., Cheryl A., Lisa T., Robert D. BS summa cum laude, NYU, 1966; JD magna cum laude, Columbia U., 1969. Bar: N.Y. 1970, U.S. Supreme Ct. 1973, D.C. 1975, Mo. 1977, Md. 1987, Calif. 1989; CPA, Md., Mo. Law clk. to Judge Harold R. Medina U.S. Ct. Appeals (2d cir.), N.Y.C., 1969-70; asst. prof. law Syracuse (N.Y.) U., 1970-72; assoc. Debevoise, Plimpton, Lyons & Gates, N.Y.C., 1972-75, Cole & Groner P.C., Washington, 1975-76; with Monsanto Co., St. Louis, 1976-86, asst. co. counsel, 1978-86; pvt. practice Washington, 1986-89; ptnr. Provorny & Jacoby, Washington, 1989-91; counsel Shaw, Pittman, Potts & Trowbridge, Washington, 1991-93; ptnr. Tydings & Rosenberg, Balt., 1993-94; pvt. practice Balt., 1994-95, Washington, 1995—; lect. Bklyn Law Sch., 1973-74; adj. prof. U. Balt. Sch. of Law, 1996—; pres. Sci. and Tech. Assocs., Inc., 1986-91. Contbr. articles to profl. jours. Trustee Christian Woman's Benevolent Assn. Youth Home, 1979-83. Mem. ABA, Am. Law Inst., Am. Arbitration Assn. (panel comml. abitrators), Philo-Mt. Sinai Lodge 968, Masons, Beta Gamma Sigma. Jewish. Home: 11803 Kemp Mill Rd Silver Spring MD 20902-1511 Office: 1920 N St NW Ste 650 Washington DC 20036-1619

PROVOST, JAMES H(ARRISON), law educator; b. Washington, Oct. 15, 1939; s. Oscar A. and Mary (Howe) P. BA, Carroll Coll., 1959; STB, U. Louvain (Belgium), 1963, MA, 1963; JCD, Lateran U., Rome, 1967. Chancellor Diocese of Helena, Mont, Roman Cath. Ch. and officialis (presiding judge of Diocesan Tribunal), Helena, 1967-79; prof. canon law Cath. U. Am., 1979—, also chmn. dept. Canon law; exec. coord. Canon Law Soc. Am., Washington, 1980-86. Mng. editor The Twist, 1980—. Mem. Cath. Theol. Soc. Am., Canon Law Soc. Am., Can. Canon Law Soc., Canon Law Soc. Gt. Brit. and Ireland, Canon Law Soc. Australia & New Zealand, Societe Internationale de droit religieuses et comparees, Consociatio Internationalis. Office: Cath U Am Dept of Canon Law Washington DC 20064

PROVOST, THOMAS TAYLOR, dermatology educator, researcher; b. Pitts., Mar. 21, 1938; s. Charles Thomas and Marcelle K. (Taylor) P.; m. Carol Sara Christie, July 2, 1960; children: Charles T., Christie Lynn, Thomas Wright. AB, U. Pitts., 1958, MD, 1962. Intern Mary Hitchcock Meml. Hosp., Hanover, N.H., 1962-63; resident in dermatology Dartmouth Med. Ctr., Hanover, N.H., 1966-67, U. Oreg. Med. Ctr., Portland, 1967-68; fellow in immunology SUNY, Buffalo, 1969-72, asst. prof. dermatology, 1972-75, assoc. prof., 1975-78; assoc. prof. Johns Hopkins U. Med. Sch., Balt., 1978-82, prof., dept. chmn., 1982—. Lt. commdr. USPHS, 1962-64. Mem. Soc. Investigative Dermatology, Soc. Clin. Investigation. Avocation: boating. Office: Johns Hopkins U Sch of Medicine 720 Rutland Ave Baltimore MD 21205-2109

PROVUS, BARBARA LEE, executive search consultant; b. Washington, Nov. 20, 1949; d. Severn and Birdell (Eck) P.; m. Frederick W. Wackerle, Mar. 29, 1985. Student, NYU, 1969-70; BA in Sociology, Russell Sage Coll., 1971; MS in Indsl. Rels., Loyola U., Chgo., 1978; postgrad., Smith Coll., 1971. Sec. Booz, Allen & Hamilton, Chgo., 1973-74, mgr. tng., 1974-77, dir. rsch., 1977-79, cons. search, 1979-80; mgr. mgmt. devel. Federated Dept. Stores, Cin., 1980-82; v.p. Lamalie Assocs., Chgo., 1982-86; prin., founder Sweeney, Shepherd, Bueschel, Provus, Harbert & Mummert, Inc., Chgo., 1986-91; founder Shepherd Bueschel & Provus Inc., Chgo., 1992—. Bd. dirs. Anti-Cruelty Soc., Chgo., 1990—, pres., 1996—. Mem. Assn. Exec. Search Cons. (dir. 1989-92), The Chgo. Network (bd. dirs. 1993—), Econ. Club Chgo. Avocations: collecting rubber bands, modern art, baseball. Home: 3750 N Lake Shore Dr Chicago IL 60613-4238 Office: Shepherd Bueschel & Provus Inc 401 N Michigan Ave Ste 3020 Chicago IL 60611-4257

PROWN, JULES DAVID, art historian educator; b. Freehold, N.J., Mar. 14, 1930; s. Max and Matilda (Cassileth) P.; m. Shirley Ann Martin, June 23, 1956; children: Elizabeth Anderson, David Martin, Jonathan, Peter Cassileth, Sarah Peiter. AB, Lafayette Coll., 1951, DFA (hon.), 1979; AM, U. Del., 1956, Harvard U., 1953; PhD, Harvard U., 1961. Dir. Hist. Soc. Old Newbury, Newburyport, Mass., 1957-58, Old Gaol Mus., York, Maine, 1958-59; asst. to dir. Harvard U., Fogg Art Mus., Cambridge, Mass., 1959-61; instr. to Paul Mellon prof. history of art Yale U., New Haven, 1961—, curator Am. art, 1963-68; vis. lectr. Smith Coll., Northampton, Mass., 1966-67; dir. Yale Ctr. for Brit. Art, New Haven, 1968-76; assoc. dir. Nat. Humanities Inst., New Haven, 1977; trustee Whitney Mus., N.Y.C., 1975-94; mem. editorial adv. bd. Am. Art-Smithsonian, Washington, 1986—, On Common Ground, 1993—; mem. vis. com. Harvard U. Art Museums, 1993—. Author: John Singleton Copley, 2 Vols., 1966, American Painting from Its Beginnings to the Armory Show, 1969, The Architecture of the Yale Center for British Art, 1977, (catalogue) American Art from Alumni Collections, 1968. Recipient George Washington Kidd award Lafayette Coll., 1986. Fellow The Athenaeum of Phila. (hon.); mem. Am. Antiquarian Soc., Coll. Art Assn. (Disting. Tchg. of Art History award 1995), Am. Studies Assn., Conn. Acad. Arts & Scis., Walpole Soc., Royal Soc. Arts. Office: Yale U History of Art Dept 56 High St New Haven CT 06510-2306

PROXMIRE, WILLIAM, former senator; b. Lake Forest, Ill., Nov. 11, 1915; s. Theodore Stanley and Adele (Flanigan) P.; m. Ellen Hodges. Grad., Hill Sch., 1934; B.A., Yale, 1938; M.B.A., Harvard, 1940, M.P.A. in Pub. Adminstrn, 1948. Assemblyman Wis. Legislature, 1951; nominee gov. Wis., 1952, 54, 56; pres. Artcraft Press, Waterloo, Wis., 1953-57; U.S. senator from Wis., 1957-89; former chmn. Sen. Banking, Housing and Urban Affairs com., Cong. JointEcon. com. Author: Can Small Business Survive?, 1964, st of the Big Time Spenders, 1972, You Can Do It, 1977, The Fleecing of America, 1980, Your Joy Ride to Health, 1993. Democrat.

PRSHA, MARIE ALICE, administrator, educator; b. Pitts., Aug. 19, 1927; d. Joseph Albert and Sabina Elizabeth (Rauch) Yoest; m. William John Prsha, July 14, 1951 (wid. Oct. 1977); children: Jon Michael, Mark Steven, Jeffrey Alan, Jeanne-Marie. Grad., Queen of Angels Coll. Nursing, 1950; BS in Health Sci., Chapman U., 1984, MS in Health Adminstrn., 1989. RN, PHN, Calif. Clin. nurse, charge/ob-gyn. Queen of Angels Clinic, L.A., 1950-52; staff nurse Huntington Meml. Hosp., Pasadena, Calif., 1993-94, St. Luke Hosp., Pasadena, 1955-56, La Vina Resp. Disease, Altadena, Calif., 1966; nurse nutritionist, high risk counselor ARC, San Diego, Calif., 1980-91; asst. dir. WIC svcs. ARC, San Diego, 1991-93; nutrition edn. coord. dept. health svcs. County of San Diego WIC Program, 1993-96; asst. program dir. Women, Infants and Children Program San Diego State U., 1996—; mem. adv. bd. Southeast Asian Devel. Disabilities Prevention Program, San Diego, 1993-95. Nurse educator Univ. Calif., San Diego, 1989-90. Recipient scholarship Immaculate Heart Coll., L.A., 1949; traineeship USPHS, San Diego, 1969. Mem. NLN, Am. Pub. Health Assn., Queen of Angels Alumni Assn., Chapman Univ. Alumni Assn. Republican. Roman Catholic. Avocations: reading, poetry, music, personal fitness, aviation. Home: 4872 Dixie Dr San Diego CA 92109-2430 Office: San Diego State U SDSU Found Women Infants and Children Program 7323 Engineer Rd Ste B San Diego CA 92111-1409

PRUCHA, JOHN JAMES, geologist, educator; b. River Falls, Wis., Sept. 22, 1924; s. Edward Joseph and Katharine (Schladweiler) P.; m. Mary Elizabeth Helfrich, June 12, 1948; children—David, Stephen, Katharine, Carol, Mark, Barbara, Margaret, Christopher, Anne, Andrew. Student, Wis. State U., River Falls, 1941-43; Ph.B., U. Wis., 1945, Ph.M., 1946; M.A., Princeton, 1948, Ph.D., 1950. Asst. prof. geology Rutgers U., 1948-51; sr. geologist N.Y. State Geol. Survey, 1951-56; rsch. geologist Shell Devel. Co., 1956-63; prof. geology Syracuse U., 1963-90, prof. emeritus, 1990—, chmn. dept., 1963-70, 88-89, dean Coll. Arts and Scis., 1970-72, vice chancellor acad. affairs, 1972-85; pres. Syracuse U. Press, 1973-85, bd. dirs., 1985-90. Author: Basement Tectonics of Rocky Mountains, 1965, Structural Behavior of Salt, 1967, Stratigraphy and Structure of Southeastern New York, 1959, Fracture Patterns, 1979, Zones of Structural Weakness, 1992, (with Norman A. Foss) Kinnickinnic Years, 1993. Trustee Le Moyne Coll., 1971-78; bd. dirs. Cultural Resources Coun., Syracuse, 1974—, pres., 1978-80; bd. dirs. Everson Mus. Art, Syracuse, 1977-83, v.p., 1980-81; mem. regents vis. com. N.Y. State Mus., 1993—. Recipient John Mason Clarke medal N.Y. State Geol. Survey, 1990. Fellow AAAS, Geol. Soc. Am.; mem. Am. Assn. Petroleum Geologists, Am. Geophys. Union. Home: 112 Ardsley Dr Syracuse NY 13214-2110 Office: Syracuse Univ 204 Heroy Geology Lab Syracuse NY 13244-1070

PRUDEN, ANN LORETTE, chemical engineer, researcher; b. Norfolk, Va., Sept. 3, 1948; d. James Otis and Elora Maie (Bagwell) P.; m. Alan Todd Royer, Aug. 13, 1983; children: James Sebastian Royer, Annabelle Grace Royer. BS in Chemistry, Maryville (Tenn.) Coll., 1970; MA in Chem. Engring., Princeton (N.J.) U., 1978; PhD, 1981. Chemist Mobil Rsch. and Devel. Corp., Princeton, N.J., 1970-73, rsch. chemist, 1973-76, rsch. engr., 1980-86; sr. rsch. engr. Mobil Chem. Co., Princeton, N.J., 1986-92, supr., 1992-97; lab. supr., 1997—; tech. mgmt. team Mobil Chem. Co., Princeton, N.J., 1997—; mem. Quality Director's Network, Indsl. Rsch. Inst., Washington, 1992—. Contbg. author: Photocatalytic Purification and Treatment of Water and Air, 1993; contbr. articles to profl. jours. Fellow Mobil R&D Corp., Princeton, N.J., 1976-79. Mem. ASTM, AIChE, Am. Chemical Soc., Am. Soc. Quality Control. Achievements include research in heterogeneous catalysis, organizational effectiveness. Avocations: gardening, textile handwork, singing. Office: Mobil Chemical Co Rte 27 and Vineyard Rd PO Box 3029 Edison NJ 08818-3029

PRUDEN, JAMES WESLEY, newspaper editor, columnist; b. Jackson, Miss., Dec. 18, 1935; s. James Wesley and Anne (Wilder) P.; m. Ann Fontaine Rice, Oct. 15, 1960 (div. 1961). Student, U. Ark.-Little Rock, Little Rock, 1954-55. Sportswriter Ark. Gazette, Little Rock, 1953, asst. state editor, 1954-56; reporter The Comml. Appeal, Memphis, 1956-63; fgn. corr. The Nat. Observer, Washington, 1963-77; free-lance journalist, 1977-82; chief polit. corr. The Washington Times, 1982-84, dep. mng. editor, 1984-87, mng. editor, 1987-92, editor-in-chief, 1992—. Author: Vietnam: The War, 1965. Ark. del. to Dem. Nat. Conv., L.A., 1960. With USAF, 1957-58, Ark. Air Nat. Guard, 1954-63. Recipient H.L. Mencken prize Balt. Sun, 1991. Mem. Sigma Delta Chi. So. Bapt. Office: The Washington Times 3600 New York Ave NE Washington DC 20002-1947

PRUD'HOMME, ROBERT KRAFFT, chemical engineering educator; b. Sacramento, Jan. 28, 1948; s. Earle Sutter and Adele E. (Wilkens) P.; m. N. Beth Morton, June 2, 1973; children: Wendy A., Graham C., Jodie B. BSChemE, Stanford U., 1969; Grad. Spl. Studies, Harvard U., 1973; PhD ChemE, U. Wis., 1978. Asst. prof. chem. engring. Princeton (N.J.) U., 1978-84, assoc. prof., 1984-91, prof., 1991—; rsch. engr. AT&T Bell Labs, Murray Hill, N.J., 1984-85; bd. dirs. Rheometrics Inc., Piscataway, N.J.; McCabe lectr. Dept. Chem. Engring. N.C. State U. Contbr. articles to profl. jours. Deacon Cornerstone Ch., Hopewell, N.J., 1989-92. Capt. U.S. Army, 1969-73. Decorated Bronze Star, Army Commendation Medal; recipient Presdl. Young Investigator award NSF. Mem. Am. Chem. Soc., Am. Inst. Chem. Engrs. (bd. dirs. material sci. and engring. div. 1982-93), U.S. Soc. Rheology (exec. com. 1989-91), Soc. Petroleum Engrs. Achievements include research in areas of polymer fluid mechanics, polymer characterization and transport phenomena. Office: Princeton U Dept Chem Engring Princeton NJ 08544

PRUETT, JAMES WORRELL, librarian, musicologist; b. Mt. Airy, N.C., Dec. 23, 1932; s. Samuel Richard and Gladys Dorne (Worrell) P.; m. Lilian Maria-Irene Pibernik, July 20, 1957; children—Mark, Ellen. B.A., U. N.C., Chapel Hill, 1955, M.A., 1957, Ph.D., 1962. Mem. faculty U. N.C., Chapel Hill, 1961-87; prof. music U. N.C., 1974-87, music librarian, 1961-76, chmn. dept. music, 1976-86; chief music div. Library of Congress, Washington, 1987-94; vis. prof. U. Toronto, 1976; cons. in music, 1995—. Editor: Studies in the History, Style and Bibliography of Music in Memory of Glen Haydon, 1969; author: Research Guide to Musicology, 1985. Contbr. profl. jours., encys. Newberry Library fellow, summer 1966. Mem. Internat. Musicol. Soc., Am. Musicol. Soc. (chpt. chmn. 1964-66, mem. coun. 1974-77), Music Libr. Assn. (pres. 1973-75, editor jour. 1974-77), Internat. Assn. Music Libraries, Cosmos Club (Washington). Home: 343 Wesley Dr Chapel Hill NC 27516-1520

PRUETT, KYLE DEAN, psychiatrist, writer, educator; b. Raton, N.Mex., Aug. 27, 1943; s. Ozie Douthitt Pruett and Velma Lorraine Smith; children: Elizabeth Storr, Emily Farrar. BA in History, Yale U., 1965; D of Medicine, Tufts U., 1969. Intern Mt. Auburn Hosp.-Harvard U., 1969-70; resident in psychiat. medicine Tufts-New England Med. Ctr., Boston, 1970-72; child psychiatry fellow Child Study Ctr., Yale U., New Haven, 1972-74, asst. clin. prof. psychiatry, 1975-79, assoc. clin. prof., 1979-87, clin. prof., 1987—; dir. child devel. unit Yale U., 1982—; attending physician dept. child psychiatry Yale-New Haven Hosp., 1972—; cons. psychiatrist Guilford (Conn.) Pub. Schs., 1977—; vis. scholar Sch. Medicine, U. Vt., 1987, Sch. Medicine, U. N.Mex., 1988; mem. editorial bd. Med. Problems of Performing Artists jour., 1983—, Good Housekeeping mag., 1987—; bd. dirs. Zero to Three: Nat. Ctr. for Clin. Infant Programs, Washington; cons. CBS News, Lifetime. Author: The Nurturing Father, 1988 (Am. Health Book award 1988); contbr. numerous articles to profl. jours.; host biweekly TV series Your Chid 6 to 12 with Dr. Kule Pruett Lifetime TV, 1993-94. Mem. med. adv. bd. Scholastic, Inc., 1988—, Yale U. Program for Humanities in Medicine, 1989—, World Assn. for Infant Mental Health, 1979—, CBS-TV Family Time, 1989—, Wellesley Child Study Ctr.; prin. tenor Conn. Chancel Opera Co., New Haven, 1983—. Vis. fellow Anna Freud Clinic, London, 1975; recipient Mayoral Citation, City of Indpls., 1987. Mem. Am. Acad. Child and Adolescent Psychiatry, Am. Psychiat. Assn., Soc. for Rsch. in Family Therapy, Physicians for Social Responsibility, Nat. Assn. Physician Broadcasters (CBS news cons. 1989—), Zero to Three (Nat. Ctr. for Clin. Infant Programs pres.-elect 1995—), Yale U. Glee Club Alumni Assn. (pres. 1985-89). Avocations: rowing, sailing, skiing, vocal chamber music, running. Home: 34 York St Ste 3 Guilford CT 06437-2349 Office: Yale Child Study Ctr 333 Cedar St New Haven CT 06510-3206

PRUGH, GEORGE SHIPLEY, lawyer; b. Norfolk, Va., June 1, 1920; s. George Shipley and Florence (Hamilton) P.; m. Katherine Buchanan, Sept. 27, 1942; children: Stephanie Dean, Virginia Patton. A.B., U. Calif., Berkeley, 1941; J.D., U. Calif., San Francisco, 1948; postgrad., Army War Coll., 1961-62; M.A., George Washington U., 1963. Bar: Calif. 1949, U.S. Supreme Ct. 1954. Legal advisor U.S. Mil. Assistance Command, Vietnam, 1964-66; legal adviser U.S. European Command, Stuttgart, Ger., 1966-69; Judge Adv., U.S. Army Europe, Heidelberg, Ger., 1969-71; Judge Adv. Gen. Washington, 1971-75; ret., 1975; prof. law Hastings Coll. Law, U. Calif., San Francisco, 1975-82. Author: (with others) Law at War, 1975; (play) Solferino; contbr. articles to profl. jours. Mem. Sec. Def. Task Force on Racial Discrimination in Adminstrn. Mil. Justice, 1973; mem. U.S. del. Diplomatic Conf. on Law of War, Geneva, 1974, 75. 2d lt. U.S. Army; maj. gen. JAGC, 1971. Decorated D.S.M. with oak leaf cluster, Legion of Merit with oak leaf cluster. Mem. ABA, Am. Judicature Soc., Internat. Soc. Mil. Law and Law of War (hon. pres.), Civil Affairs Assn. (hon. dir.), Selden Soc., Calif. Bar, Order of Coif, Bohemian Club, Army and Navy Club (Washington), Phi Delta Phi. Episcopalian.

PRUGH, WILLIAM BYRON, lawyer; b. Kansas City, Mo., Jan. 3, 1945; s. Byron E. and Helen Prugh; m. Linda Stuart, Aug. 12, 1968; 1 child, K. Niccole. BS, U. Mo., Kansas City, 1966, JD, 1969, LLM in Taxation, 1971. Bar: Mo. 1969, U.S. Tax Ct. 1975, U.S. Supreme Ct. 1975, Kans. 1982. Assoc. Shughart Thomson & Kilroy, P.C., Kansas City, 1969-72, ptnr., dir., 1973—. Author, editor: Missouri Corporation Law and Practice, 1985, Missouri Taxation Law and Practice, 1987. Mem. ABA, Mo. Bar Assn. (chmn. taxation com. 1988-90, chmn. computer tech. com. 1989-91), Kansas City Met. Bar Assn. (chmn. tax com. 1989-90, chmn. computer law com. 1989-91, Pres. award 1988). Republican. Methodist. Office: Shughart Thomson & Kilroy 12 Wyandotte Plz 120 W 12th St Fl 18 Kansas City MO 64105-1917

PRUGOVECKI, EDUARD, mathematical physicist, educator, author; b. Craiova, Romania, Mar. 19, 1937; emigrated to Can., 1965; s. Slavoljub and Helena (Piatkowsky) P.; m. Margaret Rachelle Loveys, July 19, 1973. Dipl. Phys., U. Zagreb, Croatia, 1959; Ph.D., Princeton U., 1964. Rsch. asst. Inst. Ruder Boskovic, Zagreb, 1959-61; rsch. asst. Princeton (N.J.) U., 1961-64, research assoc., 1964-65; postdoctoral fellow Inst. Theoret. Physics, Edmonton, Alta., Can., 1965-67; lectr. U. Alta., Edmonton, 1966-67; asst. prof. math. physics U. Toronto, 1967-69, assoc. prof., 1969-75, prof., 1975-97, prof. emeritus, 1997—; vis. prof. Centre Nat. de Recherche Scientifique, Marseille, France, 1974. Author: monographs Quantum Mechanics in Hilbert Space 1971, 2d rev. edit., 1981, Stochastic Quantum Mechanics and Quantum Spacetime, 1984, 2d rev. edit., 1986, Quantum Geometry, 1992, Principles of Quantum General Relativity, 1995; contbr. articles to profl. jours. Grantee NRC Can., 1971-79; grantee Nat. Sci. and Engring. Research Council, 1980—. Mem. Sci. for Peace. Office: U Toronto, 100 Saint George St, Toronto, ON Canada M5S 1A1

PRUIS, JOHN J., business executive; b. Borculo, Mich., Dec. 13, 1923; s. Ties J. and Trientje (Koop) P.; m. Angeline Rosemary Zull, Sept. 14, 1944; children: David Lofton, Daniel J., Dirk Thomas. B.S., Western Mich. U., 1947; M.A., Northwestern U., 1949, Ph.D., 1951; Litt.D. (hon.), Yeungnam U., Taegu, Korea, Ind. State U.; LL.D. (hon.), Ball State U., U. So. Ind. Tchr. pub. schs. Mich., 1942-43; supervising tchr. Campus Sch., Western Mich. U., 1947-48; instr. speech U. No Ia., 1951-52; from asst. prof. to assoc. prof. speech So. Ill. U., 1952-55; mem. faculty Western Mich. U., 1955-68, sec. bd. trustees, 1964-68, v.p. adminstrn., 1966-68; pres. Ball State U., 1968-78; v.p. corp. rels. Ball Corp., 1978-88; Cons., examiner North Central Assn., 1959-78; also bd. dirs. N. Central Assn. V.p. Country dr. chmn. Kalamazoo Cmty. Chest, 1964; bd. dirs. Kalamazoo chpt. Am. Cancer Soc., 1963-68, Del. County United Way, Muncie Symphony Assn., Ball Meml. Hosp., Big Bros./Big Sisters, Ind. Legal Found.; trustee U. So. Ind., 1985-90; exec. v.p. George and Frances Ball Found. With USNR, 1943-46; capt. Res., ret. Mem. Am. Assn. Higher Edn., Speech Communication Assn., Muncie C. of C., Blue Key, Rotary, Phi Delta Kappa, Omicron Delta Kappa, Beta Gamma Sigma. Presbyterian.

PRUITT, ALBERT W., dean; b. Anderson, S.C., Jan. 1, 1940; s. James Ernest and Jennie L. (Burdette) P.; m. Ellanor Frances Hanson, June 3, 1961; 1 child, Nora Taplin Pruitt Krist. BA, Emory U., 1961, MD, 1965. Mem. pediatrics faculty Emory U. Sch. Medicine, Altanta, 1972-82; chmn. pediatrics Med. Coll. Ga., Augusta, 1982-92; dean. coll. medicine, v.p. med. affairs USA Coll. Medicine, Mobile, Ala., 1992—. Contbr. articles to profl. jours., chpts. to books. Maj. U.S. Army, 1978-80. Fellow Am. Acad. Pediatrics (com. chair), Ga. Acad. Pediatrics (pres.); mem. Alpha Omega Alpha. Episcopalian. Office: U South Ala Coll Medicine CSAB170 307 University Blvd N Mobile AL 36688-3053

PRUITT, ALICE FAY, mathematician, engineer; b. Montgomery, Ala., Dec. 17, 1943; d. Virgil Edwin and Ocie Victoria (Mobley) Maye; m. Mickey Don Pruitt, Nov. 5, 1967; children: Derrell Gene, Christine Marie. BS in Math., U. Ala., Huntsville, 1977; postgrad. in engring., Calif. State U., Northridge, 1978-79. Instr. math. Antelope Valley Coll., Quartz Hill, Calif., 1977-78; space shuttle engr. Rockwell Internat., Palmdale, Calif., 1979-81; programmer, analyst Sci. Support Svcs. Combat Devel. and Experimentation Ctr., Ft. Hunter-Liggett, Calif., 1982-85; sr. engring. specialist Loral Vought Systems Corp., Dallas, 1985-92; dir. concepts and analysis army tactical sys. and tech. Nichols Rsch. Corp., Huntsville, Ala., 1992—. Mem. DeSoto (Tex.) Coun. Cultural Arts, 1987-89. Mem. AAUW (sch. bd. rep. 1982, legal advocacy fund chairperson 1989-91), Toastmasters Internat., Phi Kappa Phi. Republican. Methodist. Avocations: dancing, gourmet cooking. Office: Nichols Rsch Corp PO Box 40002 4040 S Memorial Pkwy Huntsville AL 35815-1502

PRUITT, ANNE LORING, academic administrator, education educator; b. Bainbridge, Ga., Sept. 19, 1929; d. Loring Alphonzo and Anne Lee (Ward) Smith; m. Harold G. Logan; children: Leslie; stepchildren: Dianne, Pamela, Sharon, Ralph Pruitt, Jr., Harold, Minda, Andrew Logan. BS, Howard U., Washington, 1949; MA, Tchrs. Coll. Columbia U., N.Y.C., 1950, EdD, 1964; HumD hon., Ctrl. State U., Wilberforce, Ohio, 1982. Counsel for women Howard U., 1950-52; tchr., dir. guidance Hutto H.S., Bainbridge, 1952-55; dean students Albany State Coll., Ga., 1955-59, Fisk U., Nashville, 1959-61; prof. edn. Case Western Res. U., Cleve., 1963-79; prof. ednl. policy and leadership Ohio State U., Columbus, 1979-95, prof. emeritus, 1995—, assoc. dean Grad. Sch., 1979-84, assoc. provost, 1984-86, dir. Ctr. for Tchg. Excellence, 1986-94; dean in residence Coun. Grad. Schs., Washington, 1994-96, scholar in residence, 1996—; cons. So. Regional Edn. Bd., Atlanta, 1967-78, So. edn. Found., Atlanta, 1978-87. Author: New Students and Coordinated Counseling, 1973, Black Employees in Traditionally White Institutions in the Adams States 1975-77, 1981, In Pursuit of Equality in Higher Education, 1987; co-author: (with Paul Isaac) Student Services for the Changing Graduate Student Population, 1995. Mem. bd. trustees Urban League, Cleve., 1965-71, Ctrl. State U., 1973-82, Case Western Res. U., 1987—, Columbus Area Leadership Program, 1988-91; bd. dirs. ARC, Cleve., 1978-79, Am. West Airlines Found., 1992-95; mem. adv. com. USCG Acad., New London, Conn., 1980-83; Ohio State U. rep. to AAUW, 1989-94; univ. co-chairperson United Way, 1990-91; trustee Marburn Acad., 1991-95; mem. Columbus 1992 Edn. Com., 1988-92; mem. edn. subcom. Columbus Found., 1991-94; mem. exec. com. Renaissance League, 1992-94; mem. vis. panel on rsch., Ednl. Testing Svc., 1996—; mem. Commn. on Future Clemson U., 1997—; bd. dirs. Black Women's Agenda, Inc., 1997—. Recipient Outstanding Alumnus award Howard U. Alumni Assn., 1975; Am. Council on Edn. fellow, 1977; named one of Am.'s Top 100 Black Bus. and Profl. Women Dollars & Sense Mag., 1986; recipient Disting. Affirmative Action award Ohio State U., 1988; named Sr. Scholar Am. Coll. Personnel Assn., 1989, Woman of Achievement award YMCA, 1993. Mem. NSF (mem. com. on equal opportunities in sci. and engring. 1989-95), Am. Coll. Pers. Assn. (pres. 1976-77), Coun. Grad. Schs. in U.S. (chairperson com. on minority grad. edn. 1980-84), Am. Ednl. Rsch. Assn., Ohio Assn. Counselor Edn. (pres. 1966-67), Links Inc., Cosmos Club. Office: Coun Grad Schs 1 Dupont Cir NW Ste 430 Washington DC 20036-1136

PRUITT, BASIL ARTHUR, JR., surgeon, army officer, retired; b. Nyack, N.Y., Aug. 21, 1930; s. Basil Arthur and Myrtle Flo (Knowles) P.; m. Mary Sessions Gibson, Sept. 4, 1954; children: Scott Knowles, Laura Sessions, Jeffrey Hamilton. AB, Harvard U., 1952, postgrad., 1952-53; MD, Tufts U., 1957. Diplomate: Am. Bd. Surgery (bd. dirs. 1982-88). Intern Boston City Hosp., 1957-58, resident in surgery, 1958-59, 61-62; commd. capt., M.C. U.S. Army, 1959, advanced through grades to col., 1972; resident Brooke Gen. Hosp., Ft. Sam Houston, Tex., 1962-64; chief clin. div. Inst. Surg. Rsch., Ft. Sam Houston, Tex., 1965-67; chief profl. services 12th Evacuation Hosp., Vietnam, 1967-68; comdr., dir. U.S. Army Inst. Surg. Research, Brooke Army Med. Center, Ft. Sam Houston, 1968-95; prof. gen. surgery Med. Sch. U. Tex. Health Sci. Ctr., San Antonio, 1996—; prof. surgery U. of the Health Scis., Bethesda, Md., 1978—; mem. surgery, anaesthesiology and trauma study sect. NIH, 1978-82; mem. Shriners Burns Adv. Bd., 1992-95; mem. Shriners Rsch. Adv. Bd., 1995—; mem. rev. bd. for surgery, VA, 1990-93. Author med. books; contr. chpts. to textbooks, articles to profl. jours.; assoc. editor: Jour. Trauma, 1975-94, editor, 1995—; mem. edit. bd.: Archives Surgery, 1981-93, Consultations in Surgery, Correspondence Society of Surgeons, Collected Letters, 1978—, Circulatory Shock, 1985-93, Jour. Burn Care and Rehabilitation, 1984-87, Jour. Investigative Surgery, 1987—, Shock Research, 1993—, Current Opinion in Surgical Infections, 1993—. Decorated Bronze Star, Legion of Merit, Disting. Svc. medal. Fellow ACS (gov. 1973-79, pre and postoperative care com. 1969-79, com. on trauma 1974-84, internat. rels. com. 1983-93, chmn. 1987-89), Am. Coll. Critical Care Medicine; mem. Am. Burn Assn. (pres. 1975-76), Internat. Soc. Burn Injuries (nat. rep. 1974-82, co-chmn. disaster planning com. 1982-86, pres.-elect 1990-94, pres. 1994—), Smoke Burn and Fire Assn. (adv. coun.), Am. Trauma Soc. (dir., pres. Tex. divsn. 1974-75, sec. 1986-88, 2d v.p. 1988-90, pres.-elect 1990-92, pres. 1992-94), Soc. Univ. Surgeons, Am. Surg. Assn. (2d v.p. 1980-81), Tex. Surg. Assn., Western Surg. Assn. (dist. rep. 1984-88, pres. 1993-94), So. Surg. Assn., Halsted Soc. (pres. 1985-86), Am. Assn. Surgery Trauma (recorder 1976-80, pres. 1982-83), Surg. Biol. Club III, Soc. Internat. Surgery, Assn. Acad. Surgery, Surg. Infection Soc. (recorder 1980-84, pres. 1985-86), Internat. Surg. Group, North Am. Burn Soc. (pres. 1993-94), Shock Soc. (clin. counselor 1995—). Home: 402 Tidecrest Dr San Antonio TX 78239-2517 Office: Journal of Trauma 7330 San Pedro Ave Ste 336 San Antonio TX 78216-6250

PRUITT, CHARLES WILLIAM, JR., long term health care executive, educator; b. Jacksonville, Fla., Apr. 10, 1929; s. Charles William and Bertie Lee (Hamm) P. BSBA, U. Fla., 1951, MBA in Mgmt. and Indsl. Rels., 1957; postgrad., Cornell U., 1964, U. Birmingham, Eng., 1981. Grad. assto to dean Grad. Sch., U. Fla., Gainesville, 1953-54, asst. to provost, 1955-57, asst. dir. Univ. Hosp. and Clinic, 1957-65, asst. prof. dept. health and hosp. adminstrn., 1963-65, dir. cmty. svcs. div. Ctr. for Health and Hosp. Adminstrn., 1965-66; pres., CEO, Cathedral Found. Jacksonville, Inc., 1966-73, Urban Jacksonville, Inc., 1968-73; pres. Tremont Mgmt. Co., Dallas, 1973-74; chief adminstrv. and operating officer Trinity Ch., N.Y.C., 1975-79; pres., CEO, bd. dirs. Presbyn. Sr. Care, Pitts., 1979—; speaker, lectr. at numerous local, state and nat. ednl., civic, bus. and govtl. orgns. on gerontol. subjects, 1954—; cons. on elderly housing, long term health care facilities and continuum of care, 1966—; lectr. U. Pitts. Grad. Sch. Pub. Health, 1981—, Carnegie-Mellon U. Sch. Architecture and Grad. Sch. Urban and Pub. Affairs, 1981—, Harvard U. Grad. Sch. Design, 1981—; mem. adv. com. to develop nat. exam. for licensure nursing home adminstrs. Profl. Exam. Svcs., N.Y.C., 1972-82; also others. Trustee Jacksonville Art Mus., 1969-73; pres. Jacksonville Urban Ministry Program, 1971-72, Allegheny Widows' Home Assn., 1983—, Southwestern Pa. Partnership on Aging, 1991—; mem. Alliance on Aging, 1988—; bd. dirs., pres. Ea. Area Adult Svcs., 1987—, pres., 1988—; bd. dirs. Episcopal svcs. ministries Episcopal Diocese of Pitts., 1988-91; mem. com. on aging and continuum of care Hosp. Coun. Western Pa., 1989—; mem. Pa. Health Policy Bd., 1993—; others. 2d lt. USAF, 1951-53; lt. col. USAFR, 1953-79. Sloan fellow, summer 1964. Fellow Am. Coll. Healthcare Execs. (cert., spl. com. to develop program for long term care adminstrs. 1973); mem. Episcopal Soc. for Ministry on Aging (bd. dirs. 1966-89, treas. 1975-82, pres. 1982-86), Fla. Blue Key, Phi Kappa Psi, Alpha Kappa Psi, Beta Theta Pi. Episcopalian. Avocations: travel, exercise, reading, theatre, concerts. Home: 300 Fox Chapel Rd Apt 407 Pittsburgh PA 15238-2326 Office: Presbyn Sr Care 1215 Hulton Rd Oakmont PA 15139-1135

PRUITT, DEAN GARNER, psychologist, educator; b. Phila., Dec. 26, 1930; s. Dudley McConnell and Grace (Garner) P.; m. France Juliard, Dec. 27, 1959; children: Andre Juliard, Paul Dudley, Charles Alexandre. AB, Oberlin Coll., 1952; MS, Yale U., 1954, PhD, 1957. Postdoctoral fellow U. Mich., 1957-59; rsch. assoc. Northwestern U., 1959-61; asst. prof., then assoc. prof. U. Del., 1961-66; assoc. prof., then prof., Disting. prof. SUNY, Buffalo, 1966—, dir. grad. program in social psychology, 1969-73, 76-77, 85-88. Author: Negotiation Behavior, 1981, (with J. Z. Rubin and S.H. Kim) Social Conflict, 1986, 94; (with P.J. Carnevale) Negotiation in Social Conflict, 1993; editor; (with R.C. Snyder) Theory and Research on the Causes of War, 1969, (with K. Kressel) Mediation Research, 1989. Grantee Office Naval Rsch., 1965, NIMH, 1969, NSF, 1969, 74, 76, 80, 83, 86, 88, 93, Guggenheim Found., 1978-79. Fellow APA, Am. Psychol. Soc., Soc. for Psychol. Study Social Issues; mem. Internat. Assn. for Conflict Mgmt. (pres. 1990-92, Lifetime Achievement award 1997), Internat. Soc. Polit. Psychology (v.p. 1984-85, Harold D. Lasswell award 1992), Phi Beta Kappa, Sigma Xi. Home: 9006 Friars Rd Bethesda MD 20817-3320 Office: SUNY Buffalo Dept Psychology Buffalo NY 14260

PRUITT, GEORGE ALBERT, academic administrator; b. Canton, Miss., July 9, 1946; s. Joseph Henry and Lillie Irene (Carmichael) P.; 1 child, Shayla Nicole. BS, Ill. State U., 1968, MS, 1970, DHL (hon.), 1994; PhD, Union Grad. Sch., Cin., 1974; D Pub. Svc. (hon.), Bridgewater State Coll., 1990, MA (hon.), 1990; LLD (hon.), Ill. State U., 1994; DHL honoris causa, SUNY Empire State Coll., 1996. Asst. to v.p. for acad. affairs Ill. State U., Normal, 1968-70, dir. high potential students program, 1968-70; dean students Towson State U., 1970-72; v.p., exec. asst. to pres., assoc. prof. urban affairs Morgan State U., 1972-75; v.p., prof. Tenn. State U., 1975-81; exec. v.p. Council for Advancement Experiential Learning, Columbia, Md., 1981-82; pres. Thomas A. Edison State Coll., Trenton, 1982—; bd. mgrs. Trenton Savs. Bank; mem. commn. on ednl. credit and credentials, labor/higher edn. coun. Am. Coun. on Edn.; advisor group XII, Nat. Fellowship program W.K. Kellogg Found., 1990-94, advisor group XV, 1995—; bd. dirs. SEEDCO; bd. trustees Ctr. for Analysis of Pub. Issues, Princeton, N.J., 1993—; mem. nat. adv. com. on instnl. quality and integrity U.S. Dept. Edn., 1994—. Trustee Union Inst., Cin., Mercer Med. Ctr.; bd. dirs. N.J. Assn. Colls. and Univs., N.J. div. Am. Cancer Soc., 1992—. Recipient Resolution of Commendation Bd., Trustees Morgan State U., 1975, Outstanding Svc. to Edn. award Tenn. State U., 1981, Gubernatorial citation Gov. of Tenn., 1981, Good Guy award George Washington coun. Boy Scouts Am., 1991, Humanitarian award NCCJ, 1992, Educator of Yr. award Black N.J. Mag., 1993, Disting. Alumni award Ill. State U., 1996; apptd. hon. mem. Gen. Assembly Tenn., 1981, hon. mem. U.S. Congress from 5th Tenn. dist., 1981; named ofcr. of the Most Effective Coll. Pres. in U.S., Exxon Edn. Found. Study, 1986; inducted in Coll. of Edn. Hall of Fame, Ill. State U., 1995; named Mercer Co. N.J. Citizen of Yr., Mercer Co. C. of C., 1997. Mem. Coun. for Advancement Exptl. Learning, Am. Assn. State Colls.and Univs., Coun. for Advancement and Support of Edn., Am. Coun. Edn., Mid. States Assn. Colls. and Schs. (accreditation evaluator commn. on higher edn.), Mercer County C. of C. (trustee). Office: Thomas Edison Coll 101 W State St Trenton NJ 08608-1101

PRUITT, THOMAS P., JR., textiles executive; b. 1922. Grad., N.C. State U., 1948; with Springs Mills, 1948-52. With Springs Mills, Lancaster, S.C., 1945-52; with Carolina Mills, Maiden, N.C., 1952—, v.p., now exec. weaving ops. Office: Carolina Mills Inc 618 N Carolina Ave Maiden NC 28650-1100

PRUITT, WILLIAM CHARLES, JR., minister, educator; b. Reed, Okla., May 31, 1926; s. William Charles and Helen Irene (Sanders) P.; m. Ellen Ruth Palmer, Aug. 25, 1953; children: Philip, Suzanne, John. BS, Stephen F. Austin State U., 1956, MEd, 1958; BD, MRE, Bapt. Missionary Assn. Theol. Sem., 1959, DRE, 1963; MLS, East Tex. State U., 1963. Ordained to ministry Bapt. Missionary Assn. Am., 1955. Pastor Mt. Pleasant Bapt. Ch., Bedias, Tex., 1955-60, Calvary Bapt. Ch., Commerce, Tex., 1960-63, Glenfawn Bapt. Ch., Laneville, Tex., 1963-66, New Hope Bapt. Ch., Winkler, Tex., 1966-70, Pleasant Ridge Bapt. Ch., Centerville, Tex., 1970-74, Redland Bapt. Ch., Centerville, 1970-79, Concord (Tex.) Bapt. Ch., 1983—; dir. libr. svc., instr. Bapt. Missionary Assn. Theol. Sem., 1958-67, prof. missions and religious edn., 1967-72; instr. psychology Jacksonville Coll., 1971-76; asst. dir. East Tex. Adult Edn. Coop., 1973-93; supr. Adult Learning Ctr. Rusk State Hosp., 1988-96. Tex. wing chaplain CAP, 1971-77; exec. dir. Armed Forces Chaplaincy Com., Bapt. Missionary Assn. Am., Jacksonville, Tex., 1965-95. Mem. Mil. Chaplains Assn. U.S., Lions. Home: Rte 4 Box 911-A New Caney TX 77357-9804 Office: PO Box 912 Jacksonville TX 75766-0912

PRUNTY, BERT SHERMAN, JR., lawyer; b. Des Moines, Jan. 4, 1924; s. Bert Sherman and Carrie Blanch (Quiner) P.; m. Lois Bernice Cummins, Nov. 27, 1946; children: Randall Charles, Mary Lou, Bert Sherman, III. B.A., Drake U., 1947, J.D., 1950. Bar: Iowa 1950, N.Y. 1972, Maine 1973. Asst. prof. law NYU, 1951-53, assoc. prof., 1953-56, prof., 1956-73, assoc. dean., 1967-73; prof. U. Maine, 1973-79, dean, 1973-78; prof., dean Hastings Sch. Law U. Calif., San Francisco, 1979-87; vis. prof. Duke U., 1978-79, Hebrew U., Jerusalem, 1972—, U. Naples, Italy, 1967—, Tel Aviv U., 1982; cons. to numerous legis. and jud. bodies, N.Y., Maine. Author: Not-for-Profit Corporation Law, 3 vols, 1973; contbr. numerous articles to law jours. Served with U.S. Army, 1943-46. Mem. Am. Law Inst. Office: U Calif Hastings Coll Law 200 Mcallister St San Francisco CA 94102-4707

PRUS, VICTOR MARIUS, architect, urbanist; b. Poland, Apr. 19, 1917; s. Marien Raymond and Susanna (Hoffman) P.; m. Maria Fisz, Sept. 22, 1948. Diploma in architecture, Warsaw Tech. U., 1939; Ing.Arch., M.S., U. Liverpool, 1946. Sr. exec. officer Festival of Britain, London, 1948-51; prin. Victor Prus (Architect), London, 1948-52, Montreal, Que., Can., 1953-76; prin. Victor Prus & Assos. (Architects and Urbanists), Montreal, 1976—; asst. to Buckminster Fuller Princeton U., 1953; vis. prof. McGill U., 1953, 66, 72, Washington U., St. Louis, 1978. Works include New Internat. Airport, Barbados, Montreal Conv. Ctr., Observatory, Mauna Kea, Hawaii, Grand Théâtre de Québec, Conservatory of Music, Montreal Metro stas., Bonaventure, Langelier, Mt. Royal, Brudenell River Resort, P.E.I., Can., Place Longueuil Comml. Centre, Rockland Shopping Centre, Centaur Theatres, Expo '67 Stadium and James Lyng Sch., Montreal. Served with RAF, 1941-45. Decorated Polish Cross of Valour (2); recipient Massey medal, 1961, Can. Architect award, 1971, 1st prize for Que. Performing Arts Centre, 1964, 1st prize for RCAF Meml., 1969, 1st prize for Montreal Congress Center, 1978. Fellow Royal Archtl. Inst. Can., AIA (hon.); mem. Royal Can. Acad. Arts, Royal Inst. Brit. Architects, Can. Inst. Planners. Home and Office: 108 Senneville Rd, Senneville, PQ Canada H9X 1B9

PRUSINER, STANLEY BEN, neurology and biochemistry educator, researcher; b. Des Moines, May 28, 1942; s. Lawrence Albert and Miriam (Spigel) P.; m. Sandra Lee Turk, Oct. 18, 1970; children: Helen Chloe, Leah Anne. AB cum laude, U. Pa., 1964, MD, 1968; PhD (hon.), Hebrew U., Jerusalem, 1995, René Descartes U., Paris, 1996. Diplomate Am. Bd. Neurology. Intern in medicine U. Calif., San Francisco, 1968-69, resident in neurology, 1972-74, asst. prof. neurology, 1974-80, assoc. prof., 1980-84, prof., 1984—, prof. biochemistry, 1988—, acad. senate faculty rsch. lectr., 1989-90; prof. virology U. Calif., Berkeley, 1984—; mem. neurology rev. com. Nat. Inst. Neurol. Disease and Strokes, NIH, Bethesda, Md., 1982-86, 90-92; mem. sci. adv. bd. French Found., L.A., 1985—, chmn. sci. adv. bd., 1996—; mem. sci. rev. com. Alzheimer's Disease Diagnostic Ctr. & Rsch. Grant Program, State of Calif., 1985-89; chmn. sci. adv. bd. Am. Health Assistance Found., Rockville, Md., 1986—. Editor: The Enzymes of Glutamine Metabolism, 1973, Slow Transmissible Diseases of the Nervous System, 2 vols., 1979, Prions--Novel Infectious Pathogens Causing Scrapie and CJD, 1987, Prion Diseases of Humans and Animals, 1992, Molecular and Genetic Basis of Neurologic Disease, 1993, 2d edit., 1997, Prions Prions Prions, 1996—; contbr.more than 200 articles to profl. jours. Mem. adv. bd. Family Survival Project for Adults with Chronic Brain Disorders, San Francisco, 1982—, San Francisco chpt. Alzheimer's Disease and Related Disorder Assn., 1985—. Lt. comdr. USPHS, 1969-72. Recipient Leadership and Excellence for Alzheimer's Disease award NIH, 1990-97, Potamkin prize for Alzheimer's Disease Rsch., 1991, Presl. award, 1993, Med. Rsch. award Met. Life Found., 1992, Christopher Columbus Discovery award NIH and Med. Soc. Genoa, Italy, 1992, Charles A. Dana award for pioneering achievements in health, 1992, Dickson prize for outstanding contbns. to medicine U. Pitts., 1992, Max Planck Rsch. award Alexander von Humboldt Found. and Max Planck Soc., 1992, Gairdner Found. Internat. award, 1993, Disting. Achievement in Neurosci. Rsch. award Bristol-Myers Squibb, 1994, Albert Lasker award for Basic Med. Rsch., 1994, Caledonian Rsch. Found. prize Royal Soc. Edinburgh, 1995, Paul Ehrlich and Ludwig Darmstaedter award Germany, 1995, Paul Hoch award Am. Psychopathol. Assn., 1995, Wolf prize in medicine, 1996, ICN Virology prize, 1996, Victor and Clara Soriano award World Fedn. Neurology, 1996, Pasarow Found. prize in neurosci., 1996, Charles Leopold Mayer prize French Acad. Scis., 1996, Keio Internat. prize for med. rsch., 1996, Baxter award Am. Assn. Med. Colls., 1996; Alfred P. Sloan Rsch. fellow U. Calif., 1976-78; Med. Investigator grantee Howard Hughes Med. Inst., 1976-81; grantee for excellence in neurosci. Senator Jacob Javits Ctr., NIH, 1985-90. Mem. NAS (Inst. Medicine, Richard Lounsbery award for extraordinary achievements in biology and medicine 1993), Am. Acad. Arts and Scis., Am. Acad. Neurology (George Cotzias award for outstanding rsch. 1987, Presdl. award 1993), Am. Assn. Physicians, Am. Soc. Microbiology, Am. Soc. Neurochemistry, Internat. Soc. Neurochemistry, Am. Soc. Virology, Am. Neurol. Assn., Am. Soc. Clin. Investigation, Am. Soc. Cellular Biology, Am. Soc. Molecular Biol. Biochemistry, Protein Soc. (Amgen award 1997), Concordia Argonaut Club.

PRUSOFF, WILLIAM HERMAN, biochemical pharmacologist, educator; b. N.Y.C., June 25, 1920; s. Samuel and Mary (Metrick) P.; m. Brigitte Auerbach, June 19, 1948 (dec. Apr. 1991); children—Alvin Saul, Laura Ann. B.A., U. Miami, Fla., 1941; M.A., Columbia U., 1947, Ph.D., 1949. Research assoc., instr. pharmacology Western Res. U., 1949-53; mem. faculty Yale Med. Sch., 1953—, prof. pharmacology, 1966-90, prof. emeritus. sr. rsch. scientist, 1990—, acting chmn. dept., 1968; cons. in field, 1965—. Mem. Am. Assn. Cancer Rsch., Am. Chem. Soc., Am. Soc. Biol. Chemists, Am. Soc. Pharmacology and Exptl. Therapeutics, Soc. Chinese Bioscientists in Am., Sigma Xi, Internat. Soc. for Antiviral Rsch. Achievements include rsch. in virology, photochemistry, mechanism drug action, synthesis potential drugs; synthesized Idoxuridine; developed (in collaboration with D.T.S. Lin) Stavudine for therapy of AIDS. Home: De Forest Dr Branford CT 06471 Office: Yale U Sch Medicine New Haven CT 06510

PRUSSING, LAUREL LUNT, state official, economist; b. N.Y.C., Feb. 21, 1941; d. Richard Valentine and Maria (Rinaldi) Lunt; m. John Edward Prussing, May 29, 1965; children: Heidi Elizabeth, Erica Stephanie, Victoria Nicole Johanna. AB, Wellesley Coll., 1962; MA, Boston U., 1964; postgrad., U. Calif., San Diego, 1968-69, U. Ill., 1970-76. Economist Arthur D. Little, Cambridge, Mass., 1963-67, U. Ill., Urbana, 1971-72; mem. county bd. Champaign County, Urbana, 1972-76, county auditor, 1976-92; mem. local audit adv. bd. Office Ill. Compt., Chgo., 1984-92. Contbr. to Illinois Local Government: A Handbook, 1990. Founder Com. for Intelligent Tax Reform, Urbana, 1982—, Com. for Elected County Exec., Urbana, 1986—; state rep. 103d dist. Ill. Gen. Assembly, 1993-95; Dem. nominee Ill. 15th dist. U.S. Congress, 1996. Named Best Freshman Legislator Ind. Voters Ill., 1994; recipient Friend of Agriculture award Ill. Farm Bur., 1994; named to Legis. Honor Roll Ill. Environ. Coun., 1994. Mem. LWV, Govt. Fin. Officers Assn., U.S. and Can. (com. on acctg., auditing and fin. reporting 1980-88, Fin. Reporting award 1981-91, Disting. Budget award 1986), Nat. Assn. Local Govt. Auditors (charter), Ill. Assn. County Auditors (pres. 1984-85). Democrat. Home: 2106 Grange Dr Urbana IL 61801-6609

PRUTER, KARL HUGO, bishop; b. Poughkeepsie, N.Y., July 3, 1920; s. William Karl and Katherine (Rehling) P.; m. Nancy Lee Taylor, 1943; children: Hugo Jr., Robert, Karl, Stephen, Maurice, Katherine, Nancy Goodman. B.A., Northeastern U., 1943; M.Div., Lutheran Theol. Sem., Phila., 1945; M.A. in Edn., Roosevelt U., 1963; M.A. in History, Boston U., 1968. Guest lectr. Landerziehungsheim, Stein, West Germany, 1964-65; ordained priest Christ Catholic Ch., 1965; pastor Ch. of the Transfiguration, Boston, 1965-70; bishop Christ Cath. Ch. Author: The Theology of Congregationalism, 1953, The Teachings of the Great Mystics, 1969, A History of the Old Catholic Church, 1973, The People of God, 1975, The Jewish Christians in the United States, 1985. Address: Cathedral Ch Prince of Peace Highlandville MO 65669

PRUTER, MARGARET FRANSON, editor; b. Oak Park, Ill., Jan. 16; d. Frederick G. and Margaret K. (Svoboda) Franson; m. Robert D. Pruter, July 22, 1972; 1 child, Robin. AB, Rosary Coll., 1961; MA, Northwestern U., 1965. Asst. editor Am. People's Ency., Chgo., 1961-62; rsch. assoc. AMA, Chgo., 1962-63; asst. editor New Standard Ency., Chgo., 1964-66, assoc. editor, 1966-75, sr. editor, 1975-96; sr. editor Elmhurst (Ill.) Editl. Svcs., 1996—; exec. dir. Militaria Archives, Elmhurst, Ill., 1972—. Co-author: DuPage Roots, 1985 (Ill. State Hist. Publ. award 1986). Mem. Elmhurst Hist. Commn., 1981—, v.p., 1995—; bd. dirs. DuPage County Hist. Soc., Wheaton, Ill., 1982—, Dupage County Sesquicentennial Com., 1988-89; mem. Friends of Elmhurst Pub. Libr., Elmhurst Art Mus. Found.; bd. dirs. North Ctrl. Coll. Parents Assn., 1995—. Mem. AAUW (bd. dirs. Elmhurst br. 1995—), Orgn. Am. Historians, Nat. Trust Historic Preservation, Am. Studies Assn., Ill. Hist. Soc., Elmhurst Hist. Soc., Chgo. Hist. Soc., Chgo. Architecture Found., Byrd's Nest Chapel Questers (pres. 1992-94), Sisters in Crime, Chgo. Women in Pub., Pi Gamma Mu. Office: Elmhurst Editorial Svcs PO Box 768 Elmhurst IL 60126-3414

PRUYN, WILLIAM J., energy industry executive; b. Boston, Aug. 25, 1922; s. William J. and Ida M. (Langan) P.; m. Mary Anton, May 19, 1945; children: William J., Barbara, Marilyn, Ann Marie, Stephen, Christopher. Student, Bentley Coll., 1939-41, Harvard U., 1944-45, 64; BBA, Northeastern U., 1948. Pub. acct. Meahl, McNamara & Co., 1946-51; with Eastern Gas & Fuel Assocs. (name changed to Eastern Enterprises 1989), Boston, 1951-91, sr. v.p., 1972-76, trustee, 1973—, pres., chief adminstrv. officer, 1976-77, pres., CEO, 1977-85, chmn. bd., CEO, 1986-87, chmn. bd., 1987-91; ret., 1991. Bd. dirs. Med. Found., Inc.; trustee Northeastern U., New Eng. Aquarium; mem. pres.'s adv. council Bentley Coll. Served with USNR. Mem. Corinthian Yacht Club. Home: 8 Walnut St Marblehead MA 01945

PRUZANSKY, JOSHUA MURDOCK, lawyer; b. N.Y.C., Mar. 16, 1940; s. Louis and Rose (Murdock) P.; m. Susan R. Bernstein, Aug. 31, 1980; 1 child, Dina Gabrielle. BA, Columbia Coll., 1960, JD, 1965. Bar: N.Y., 1965, U.S. Dist. Ct. (ea. and so. dists.) N.Y., 1968, U.S. Supreme Ct., 1980. Ptnr. Scheinberg, DePetris & Pruzansky, Riverhead, N.Y., 1965-85, Greshin, Ziegler & Pruzansky, Smithtown, 1985—; mem. exec. coun. N.Y. State Conf. Bar Leaders, 1984—, chmn., 1988-89; mem. grievance com. Appellate Divsn. 10th Judicial Dist., 1992-96; mem. adv. bd. Ticor Title Guarantee Co., 1992—; mem. L.I. adv. bd. Marine Midland Bank, 1995—. Trustee Evan Frankel Found., 1993—, Suffolk Acad. Law, Suffolk County, N.Y., 1979-89. Fellow ABA Found., N.Y. State Bar Found. (bd. dirs. 1994—); mem. ABA (probate and real property sect.), N.Y. State Bar Assn. (ho. dels. 1982—, v.p. 1991-92, 95-96, pres. 1997—, exec. com. 1992—, nominating com. 1986-91, spl. com. women and law 1986-91, task force on small firms 1991—, chair-by-laws com. 1991—, trusts and estates sect.), Suffolk County Bar Assn. (bd. dirs. 1979-89, pres. 1985-86), N.Y. County Lawyers Assn., Nassau County Bar Assn., Suffolk Bar Pac (chmn. 1987-88), Columbia U. Law Alumni Assn Suffolk County (dir. 1989—). Office: Greshin Ziegler & Pruzansky 199 E Main St Smithtown NY 11787-2899

PRYCE, DEBORAH D., congresswoman; b. Warren, Ohio, July 29, 1951. BA cum laude, Ohio State U., 1973; JD with honors, Capital U., 1976. Bar: Ohio 1976. Former asst. city prosecutor, asst. city atty., first asst. city prosecutor Columbus, Ohio; former judge Franklin County Mcpl. Ct., Columbus; mem. 103rd Congress from 15th Ohio dist., Washington, D.C., 1993—; mem. coms. rules. Republican. Presbyterian. Avocation: skiing.

PRYCE, EDWARD LYONS, landscape architect; b. Lake Charles, La., May 26, 1914; s. George Samuel and Dora (Cook) P.; m. Woodia Bernice Smith, Nov. 2, 1940; children—Marilyn C., Joellen G. B.S., Tuskegee Inst., 1937; B.L.A., Ohio State U., 1948; M.S. in Landscape Architecture, U. Calif., Berkeley, 1953. Head dept. ornamental horticulture Tuskegee Inst., 1948-55, supt. of bldgs. and grounds, 1955-69, prof. dept. architecture, 1969-77; pvt. practice landscape architecture Tuskegee, Ala., 1948—; chmn. Ala. State Bd. Examiners for Landscape Architects, 1981—. Mem. Tuskegee City Planning Commn., 1970-76; mem. Tuskegee Model Cities Commn., 1968-72, Ala. State Outdoor Recreation Planning Bd., 1978—. Recipient Alumni Merit award Tuskegee Inst., 1977, Disting. Alumnus award Ohio State U., 1980. Fellow Am. Soc. Landscape Architects. Baptist. Office: PO Box 246 1901 Montgomery Rd Tuskegee AL 36087

PRYCE, JONATHAN, actor; b. North Wales, June 1, 1947. Appearences include (stage) Liverpool Everyman, 1972, Nottinguam Playhouse-Comedians, Comedians, 1977 (Tony award, Theatre World award), Hamlet (Olivier award), Macbeth, Julius Caesar, The Caretaker, 1981, Accidental Death of an Anarchist, 1984, Miss Saigon, 1991 (Tony award), Oliver, 1995; (films) Voyage of the Damned, 1976, Breaking Glass, 1980, Loophole, 1981, Praying Mantis, 1982, The Plowman's Lunch, 1983, Something Wicked This Way Comes, 1983, Brazil, 1985, The Doctor and the Devils, 1985, Haunted Honeymoon, 1986, Jumpin Jack Flash, 1986, Hotel London, 1987, Man On Fire, 1987, The Adventures of Baron Munchausen, 1988, Consuming Passions, 1988, The Rachel Papers, 1989, Glengarry Glen Ross, 1992, The Age of Innocence, 1993, Shopping, 1994, A Business Affair, 1994, Carrington, 1996 (Best Actor award Cannes Film Festival 1995), Evita, 1996, Tomorrow Never Dies, 1997, Regeneration, 1997; (TV movie) Barbarians at the Gate, HBO, 1993 (Emmy nomination, Supporting Actor - Miniseries or Special, 1993), David, 1997. Office: care James Sharkey, 15 Golden Sq 3d Fl, London W1R 3AG, England*

PRYCE, WILLIAM THORNTON, ambassador, executive; b. San Diego, July 19, 1932; s. Roland Fremont and Katharine (Hartmann) P.; m. Joan MacClurg, Mar. 22, 1958; children: Kathy Ellen, Jeffrey Fremont, Scott Fisher. BA, Wesleyan U., 1953; MA, Tufts U., 1954. Joined Fgn. Svc., Dept. State, 1958; spl. asst. to under sec. of state for econ. affairs, asst. sec. for Latin Am. affairs Washington, 1964-65; polit. officer Am. ambassies in Moscow, Panama, Guatemala, 1966-74; dir. Soviet ednl. and cultural programs Dept. State, Washington, 1974-76; exec. asst. to amb.-at-large Ellsworth Bunker Washington, 1977-78; polit. counselor Am. Embassy, Mexico City, 1978-81; dep. chief of mission Am. Embassy, La Paz, Bolivia, 1981-82, Panama City, Panama, 1982-86; alt. U.S. rep. Orgn. Am. States, Washington, 1986-89; spl. asst. to pres. for nat. security affairs NSC, Washington, 1989-92; U.S. amb. to Honduras, 1993-96; v.p. Coun. Ams., Washington, 1997—. Lt. USN, 1955-58. Recipient Meritorious Honor award Dept. State, 1986, Superior Honor award, 1989, Sr. Performance award 1982-87, 89, 90, 92. Mem. Coun. Fgn. Rels., Am. Fgn. Svc. Assn., City Tavern Club. Episcopalian. Home: 8550 Georgetown Pike Mc Lean VA 22102 Office: 1310 G St NW Ste 690 Washington DC 20005-3000

PRYE, ELLEN ROSS, graphic designer; b. Waynesboro, Va., Mar. 12, 1947; d. John Dewey and Betty Lou (Hardman) Ross; m. Warren Douglas Drumheller, June 7, 1969 (div. 1987); children: Amy Heather Drumheller, Warren Daniel Drumheller; m. John Paul Prye, July 24, 1993. BS, James Madison U., 1990. Cert. tchr. art K-12, Va/. Graphic artist The News-Virginian, Waynesboro, 1990-92, advt. prodn./composing mgr., 1992-94; graphic designer The Humphries Press, Inc., Waynesboro, Va., 1994—. Recipient Distinction award Shenandoah Valley Art Ctr., 1989, 1st pl. award for design of newsletter Printing Industries of Va., 1995, 1st pl. for design of brochure, 1995. Mem. Va. Press Assn. (1st pl. color automotive advt. merit cert. 1991, 1st pl. color health, profl. svcs. advt. merit cert. 1991, 1st pl. color food and drugs, variety advt. merit cert. 1993). Baptist. Avocations: ceramics, watercolor, horseback riding. Home: 1830 S Talbott Pl Waynesboro VA 22980-2252 Office: The Humphries Press Inc 1400 Hopeman Pkwy Waynesboro VA 22980-1948

PRYOR, BILL, attorney general; b. Mobile, Ala., Apr. 26, 1962; s. William Holcombe Sr. and Laura Bowles P.; m. Kristan Wilson; children: Caroline Elizabeth, Victoria Camille. B in Legal Studies with honors, Northeast La. U., 1984; JD with honors, Tulane U. Sch. Law, 1987. Law clerk U.S. Ct. of Appeals Fifth Cir.; with Cabaniss, Johnston, Gardner, Dumas & O'Neal, Birmingham, Ala., 1988-91, Walston, Stabler, Wells, Anderson & Bains; dep. atty. gen. State of Ala.; founder Birmingham Federalist Soc., 1989; chair task force on Tobacco Litig. Active Ch. of the Holy Spirit, Montgomery, Ala. *

PRYOR, CAROL GRAHAM, obstetrician, gynecologist; b. Savannah, Ga.; m. Louis O.J. Manganiello, June 11, 1950; children: Carol Helen, Victoria Manganiello Mudano. AB, Ga. Coll., 1943; MD, Med. Coll. Ga., 1947. Rotating intern City Hosps., Balt., 1947-48; asst. resident pathology Baroness Erlanger Hosp., Chattanooga, 1948; intern. obstetrics City Colls., Balt., 1949; coll. physician Ga. State Coll. for Women, Milledgeville, Ga., 1949-50; resident obstetrics City Hosps., Balt., 1950-51; asst. resident gynecology Univ. Hosp., Balt., 1951-52; sr. resident ob-gyn. Univ. Hosp., Augusta, Ga., 1952; pvt. practice ob-gyn. Augusta, 1952—. Mem., former pres. Iris Garden Club, Augusta; mem. coun. on maternal and infant health State of Ga., Atlanta, 1981-90; mem. edn. found. AAUW, 1961-63, state v.p., br. pres., 1963-65. Recipient Cert. of Achievement-Community Leadersip, Ga. div. AAUW, 1982; named Med. Woman of Yr., Ga. br. 51 Am. Med. Women's Assn., 1961. Fellow am. Coll. Surgeons (1st woman mem. Ga. chpt. 1956), Am. Coll. Ob-Gyn.; mem. AMA, Richmond County Med. Soc., So. Med. Assn., So. Surg. Congress, Delta Kappa Gamma. Democrat. Methodist. Office: 2316 Wrightsboro Rd Augusta GA 30904-6220

PRYOR, DAVID HAMPTON, former senator; b. Camden, Ark., Aug. 29, 1934; s. Edgar and Susan (Newton) P.; m. Barbara Lunsford, Nov. 27, 1957; children—David, Mark, Scott. B.A. in Polit. Sci, U. Ark., 1957, LL.B., 1961. Bar: Ark. 1964. Practiced in Camden; mem. firm Pryor and Barnes; founder, pub. Ouachita Citizen newspaper, Camden, 1957-60; mem. Ark. Ho. of Reps., 1961-65, 89th-92d Congresses from 4th Ark. dist.; gov. of Ark., 1974-79, senator from Ark., 1979-96; ranking min. mem. Select Com. On Aging, Nutrition and Forestry Subcom. on Prodn. and Price Competitiveness, Fin. Subcom. on Long Term Growth, Debt. and Deficit Reduction; mem. Govt. Affairs, Sen. Dem. Conf. Com., Sen. Dem. Steering and Coord. Com., Dem. Senatorial Campign Com. Office: US Senate 267 Russell Senate Bldg Washington DC 20510*

PRYOR, DIXIE DARLENE, elementary education educator; b. Anderson, Ind., May 22, 1938; d. Thurman Earle and Alice D. (Watson) Rinker; m. Charles Lee Pryor, Mar. 13, 1958; children: Charles A., Deborah Lee Pryor Evans, Laurinda Ann Pryor Owen. BS, Ball State U., 1967, MEd, 1974. Tchr. Anderson (Ind.) Pub. Schs., 1967-72, Wawasee Cmty. Sch. Corp., Syracuse, Ind., 1972—; bd. dirs. Internat. Palace Sports-Scholarship, North Webster, Ind., chair scholarship com., 1996-97. Bd. dirs. North Webster Day Care, Cardinal Ctr., Inc., Warsaw, Ind. Named Outstanding Mem. Tippkee Reading Coun., 1995, Outstanding Educator Honor Srs., 1995; recipient Ind. State Reading Assn., 1995. Mem. Ind. State Reading Assn. (pres. 1994-95, chair state reading conf. 1996—, outstanding mem. award 1996), Kiwanis (com. chair North Webster 1988—, sec. 1996-97, bd. dirs. 1997—). Republican. Methodist. Avocations: travel, reading. Home: 4630 E Armstrong Rd Leesburg IN 46538-9588

PRYOR, HAROLD S., retired college president; b. Overton County, Tenn., Oct. 3, 1920; s. Hubert S. and Ethel (Stockton) P.; m. LaRue Vaughn, June 26, 1946. B.S., Austin Peay State U., 1946; M.A., George Peabody Coll., 1947; Ed.D., U. Tenn., 1951. Instr. George Peabody Coll., Vanderbilt U., 1946-47, E. Tenn. State U., 1947-49, U. Tenn., Knoxville, 1949-51; head dept. edn. Austin Peay State U., 1952, dir. tchr. edn., 1954-68; pres. Columbia (Tenn.) State Community Coll., 1968-84, now pres. emeritus, 1984—; dir. First Farmers and Merchants Nat. Bank, Columbia, 1970—, First Farmers and Mchts. Corp., 1982—; Columbia State Found., 1971—. Contbr. articles to profl. jours. With U.S. Army, 1943-46. Grantee Dept. Labor; Grantee HEW. Mem. NEA, Tenn. Coll. Assn. (past pres.), Tenn. Edn. Assn., Am. Assn. Higher Edn., Comparative Edn. Soc., Graymere Country Club, Kiwanis, Kappa Delta Pi, Phi Delta Kappa. Democrat. Presbyterian.

PRYOR, HUBERT, editor, writer; b. Buenos Aires, Argentina, Mar. 18, 1916; (parents Am. citizens); s. John W. and Hilda A. (Cowes) P.; m. Ellen M. Ach, 1940 (div. 1959); children: Alan, Gerald, David. Grad., St. George's Coll., Argentina, 1932; student, U. London, Eng., 1934-36. Corr. in S.Am. for United Press, 1937-39; pub. relations rep. Pan Am. Airways in Buenos Aires, 1939-40; reporter N.Y. Herald Tribune, 1940-41; writer, dir. short-wave newsroom CBS, 1941-46; asst. mng. editor Knickerbocker Weekly, 1946-47; sr. editor Look mag., 1947-62; creative supr. Wilson, Haight & Welch (advt.), 1962-63; editor Science Digest, 1963-67; mng. editor Med. World News, 1967; editor NRTA Jour. Modern Maturity, 1967-82; editorial dir. Dynamic Years, 1977-82; publs. coordinator Modern Maturity, Dynamic Years, 1982-84; editorial cons., writer, 1985—. Author: Soul Talk, 1995. Served to lt. USNR, 1943-46. Mem. Am. Soc. Mag. Editors, Author's Guild, Overseas Press Club. Home: 3560 S Ocean Blvd Palm Beach FL 33480-5772

PRYOR, RICHARD, actor, writer; b. Peoria, Ill., Dec. 1, 1940; s. Leroy and Gertrude (Thomas) P.; children: Elizabeth Ann, Richard, Rain, Renee. Grad. high sch. Appeared on: Ed Sullivan, Merv Griffin and Johnny Carson television shows in 1960s; appeared in motion pictures The Busy Body, 1967, The Green Berets, 1968, Wild In The Streets, 1968, The Phynx, 1970, Dynamite Chicken, 1970, Lady Sings the Blues, 1972, Hit, 1973, Wattstax, 1973, The Mack, 1973, Some Call It Loving, 1973, Uptown Saturday Night, 1974, Adios Amigos, 1976, The Bingo Long Travelling All-Stars and Motor Kings, 1976, Car Wash, 1976, Silver Streak, 1976, Greased Lightning, 1977, Which Way is Up?, 1977, Blue Collar, 1978, California Suite, 1978, The Wiz, 1978, Richard Pryor Live in Concert, 1979, The Muppet Movie, 1979, Wholly Moses, 1980, In God We Trust, 1980, Stir Crazy, 1980, Bustin' Loose, 1981, Some Kind of Hero, 1982, The Toy, 1982, Superman III, 1983, Richard Pryor Here and Now, 1983, Brewster's Millions, 1985, Critical Condition, 1987, Moving, 1988, See No Evil, Hear No Evil, 1989, Harlem Nights, 1989, Another You, 1991, Lost Highway, 1996, Mad Dog Time, 1996; writer, producer, dir. Jo Jo Dancer Your Life Is Calling, 1986; writer scripts for Flip Wilson; co-writer TV spls. for Lily Tomlin, 1973 (Emmy award); movie script Blazing Saddles, 1973 (Am. Writers Guild award, Am. Acad. Humor award), Lily, 1974 (Am. Acad. Humor award); recorded That Nigger's Crazy, 1974 (Grammy award, certified Gold and Platinum album), Bicentennial Nigger, 1976 (Grammy award); star Richard Pryor Show, NBC-TV, 1977; owner Richard Pryor Enterprises, Inc., Los Angeles, 1975—. Served with U.S. Army, 1958-60. Mem. Nat. Acad. Rec. Arts and Scis., Writers Guild Am. Office: Indigo Prodns care Edward Astern 16633 Ventura Blvd Ste 1450 Encino CA 91436*

PRYOR, RICHARD WALTER, telecommunications executive, retired air force officer; b. Poplar Bluff, Mo., Nov. 6, 1932; s. Walter V. and Mary (Clifford) P.; m. Barbara LeCompte, Feb. 19, 1955; children: Richard, Susan Davis, Robert, William. B in Gen. Studies, U. Nebr., Omaha, 1972; MA, Webster Coll., St. Louis, 1975; grad., U. No. Colo., 1975. Commd. 2d lt. USAF, 1953, advanced through grades to maj. gen., 1982, ret., 1982, instr. Acad., DVMT engr. space and missile systems, chief of staff Communication Services; mgr. worldwide def. communication system Def. Communications Agy., 1980-81; pres. ITT World Communications, N.Y.C., 1982-84, ITT Indsl. Transmission Co., N.Y.C.; sr. v.p. engring. ops. ITT Communication Services GP; pres., gen. mgr. ITT Christian Rovsing-Copenhagen DK, 1984-86; chmn. Christian-Rovsing Inc., Tulsa; exec. v.p. Electronic Data Systems (EDS) Comm. Corp., Dallas, 1986-89; pres., COO IMM Corp.-Interdigital AMEX, Phila., 1989-92; chmn., CEO. officer Ultranav Corp, Dallas, 1992—; chmn. Prism Video, Dallas, 1994—; pres. Trans-Tech Holdings Corp., Dallas, 1996—; pres., CEO Unison Corp., Dallas, 1996—. Contbr. articles to tech. publs. Assoc. dir. Boy Soucts Am., N.Y.C., 1983. Recipient Cert. of Appreciation Okla. Mental Health Assn., 1979, Kansas City Lions Club, 1974. Mem. Armed Forces Communications and Electronics Assn. (pres. N.Y.C. 1983, nat. dir.), Air Force Assn., Oklahoma City Soc. Profl. Engrs., Canoe Brook Country Club, Army-Navy Club, Phi Alpha Theta. Republican. Roman Catholic. Home: 7802 Mason Dells Dr Dallas TX 75230-6035 Office: 8214 Westchester Dr Dallas TX 75225-6100

PRYOR, WILLIAM AUSTIN, chemistry educator; b. St. Louis, Mar. 10, 1929; s. Saul Arnold and Adeline (Franzel) P. Ph.B., U. Chgo., 1948, B.S., 1951; Ph.D., U. Calif. at Berkeley, 1954. Chemist Calif. Research Corp., Richmond, 1954-60; lectr. U. Calif. at Berkeley, 1956-60; asst. prof. Purdue U., Lafayette, Ind., 1960-63; assoc. prof. La. State U., Baton Rouge, 1963-67; prof. La. State U., 1967-72, Thomas and David Boyd prof. chemistry and biochemistry, 1972—; mem. depts. chemistry and biochemistry Inst. Environ. Studies, La. State U. Med. Ctr., New Orleans; mem. Pennington Biomed. Rsch. Ctr., Baton Rouge; dir. Biodynamics Inst. La. State U., 1985—; vis. prof. Washington U., St. Louis, 1968, UCLA, 1970, U. Calif., Berkeley, 1971, Duke U., 1978, U. Calif., Davis, 1978, U. Calif., San Deigo, 1978, U. Calif., Davis, 1994, Harvard U., 1995, Tufts U., 1995; cons. to chem. co., 1963—. Author: Free Radicals, 1966, (with Melvin Calvin) Organic Chemistry of Life; Free Radicals in Biology, Vols. 1-6, 1976-84, Organic Free Radicals, 1978, Frontiers in Free Radical Chemistry, 1980, Methods in Enzymology, 1984, 90, 94, (with A. T. Diplock, L. J. Macklin, L. Packer) Vitamin E: Biochemistry and Health Implications, 1989, (with J. N. Diana) Tobacco Smoking and Nutrition: Influence of Tobacco-Associated Health Risks, 1993, Vitamin E and the Carotenoids, 1995. Grantee AEC, 1960-64, NIH, 1964—, NSF, 1964—, Air Force Office Sci. Rsch., 1964-68, Dow Chem. Co., 1964—, Du Pont, U.S. Army, 1965-69, Exxon Rsch. and Devel. Co., 1966—, Owens-Corning Fiberglass, 1983—; Disting. Faculty fellow La. State U. Found., 1969, NIH Spl. Postdoctoral fellow, 1970-71, John Simon Guggenheim fellow, 1970-71; recipient Merit award NIH, 1986-96, Harold Harper Meml. award Am. Coun. for Advancement of Medicine, 1987. Fellow Am. Inst. Chemists, AAAS; mem. Am. Chem. Soc. (S.W. sect. award 1975, Petroleum Chemistry award 1980, Southern Chemist award 1983, Charles E. Coates award 1989), Chem. Soc. London (VERIS award for nutrition rsch.), Faraday Soc., Gerontol. Soc., Radiation Rsch. Soc., Am. Aging Assn., Pan-Am. Med. Assn. (hon. life), Soc. for Free Radical Search (founding mem., internat. coun.), Oxygen Soc. (founding mem., pres. 1997—). Patentee in field. Home: 3631 S Lakeshore Dr Baton Rouge LA 70808-3631 Office: La State U Biodynamics Inst 711 Choppin Baton Rouge LA 70803-1800

PRYOR, WILLIAM DANIEL LEE, humanities educator; b. Lakeland, Fla., Oct. 29, 1926; s. Dahl and Lottie Mae (Merchant) P. AB, Fla. So. Coll., 1949; MA, Fla. State U., 1950, PhD, 1959; postgrad. U. N.C., 1952-53. Pvt. art study with Florence Wilde; pvt. voice study with Colin O'More and Anna Kaskas; pvt. piano study with Waldemar Hille and audited piano master classes of Ernst von Dohnányi. Asst. prof. English, dir. drama Bridgewater Coll., 1950-52; vis. instr. English Fla. So. Coll., MacDill Army Air Base, summer 1951; grad. teaching fellow humanities Fla. State U., 1953-55, 57-58; instr. English, U. Houston, University Park, 1955-59, asst. prof., 1959-62, assoc. prof., 1962-71, prof., 1971-97; assoc. editor Forum, 1967, editor, 1967-82; vis. instr. English, Tex. So. U., 1961-63; vis. instr. humanities, govt. U. Tex. Dental Br., Houston, 1962-63; lectr. The Women's Inst., Houston, 1967-72; lectr. humanities series Jewish Community Center, 1972-73; originator, moderator weekly television and radio program The Arts in Houston on Stas. KUHT-TV and KUHF-FM, 1956-57, 58-63. Contbg. author: National Poetry Anthology, 1952, Panorama das Literaturas das Americas, vol. 2, 1958-60; contbr. articles to scholarly jours.; dir. Murder in the Cathedral (T.S. Elliot), U. Houston, 1965; performed in opera as Sir Edgar in Der Junge Lord (Henze), Houston Grand Opera Assn., 1967; played the title role in Aella (Chatterton), Am. premiere, U. Houston, 1970. Bd. dirs. Houston Shakespeare Soc., 1964-67; bd. dirs., program annotator Houston Chamber Orch. Soc., 1964-76; narrator Houston Symphony Orch., Houston Summer Symphony Orch., Houston Chamber Orch., U. Houston Symphony Orch., St. Stephen's Music Festival Symphony Orch., New Harmony, Ind.; narrator world premier of The Bells (Jerry McCathern), 1969, U. Houston Symphony Orch., 1969, Am. premier Symphony No. Seven, Antartica (Vaughn-Williams), Houston Symphony Orch., 1967, L'Histoire du Soldat (Stravinski), U. Houston Symphony Orch., 1957, Am. premier Babar the Elephant (Poulenc-Francais), Houston Chamber Orch., 1967, Le Roi David (Honegger), 1979, Voice of God in opera Noye's Fludde (Britten), St. Stephen's Music Festival, 1981; bd. dirs., program annotator Music Guild, Houston, 1960-67, v.p., 1963-67, adv. bd. 1967-70; bd. dirs. Contemporary Music Soc., Houston, 1958-63; mem.-at-large bd. dirs. Houston Grand Opera Guild, 1966-67; mem. repertory com. Houston Grand Opera Assn. 1967-70; bd. dirs. Houston Grand Opera, 1970-75, adv. bd., 1978-79; mem. cultural adv. com. Jewish Community Center, 1960-66; bd. dirs. Houston Friends Pub. Library, 1962-67, 73-75, 1st v.p., 1963-67; adv. mem. cultural affairs com. Houston C. of C., 1972-75; adv. bd. dirs. The Wilhelm Schole, 1980—, Buffalo Bayou Support Com., 1985-87. Recipient Master Teaching award Coll. Humanities and Fine Arts U. Houston, 1980, Favorite Prof. award Bapt. Student Union, U. of Houston, 1991. Mem. MLA, Coll. English Assn., L'Alliance Francaise, English-Speaking Union, Alumni Assn. Fla. So. Coll., Fla. State U., Am. Assn. U. Profs., South Cen. Modern Lang. Assn., Conf. Editors Learned Jours., Coll. Conf. Tchrs. English, Nat. Council Tchrs. of English, Am. Studies Assn., Phi Beta (patron), Phi Mu Alpha Sinfonia, Alpha Psi Omega, Pi Kappa Alpha, Sigma Tau Delta (cited as an Outstanding Prof. of English U. Houston chpt. 1990), Tau Kappa Alpha, Phi Kappa Phi, Caledonian Club (London). Episcopalian. Avocations: tennis, racquetball, swimming, traveling. Home: 2625 Arbuckle St Houston TX 77005-3929 Office: U Houston English Dept University Park 3801 Cullen Blvd Houston TX 77004-2602 *My commitment is to the humanities. I believe that the most important thing that a teacher can do is to help a student to stand on his/her own intellectual hind legs to help him/her to learn how to acquire facts, to help him/her to learn how to organize and utilize these facts in intelligent, responsible ways.*

PRYSESKI, GARY MICHAEL, secondary school educator; b. Balt., Mar. 15, 1946; s. Charles and Eleanor (Lentowski) P.; m. Joan Cody, June 21, 1969; children: Grant Michael, Charles Cody. BS, Towson State U., 1968; MS, Morgan State U., 1975; cert. in advanced studies, Johns Hopkins U., 1979; EdD, U. Md., 1989. Elem., jr., sr. high, middle sch. tchr., staff devel. specialist in social studies; adminstr. Old Mill High Sch., 1985-88, Wilde Lake Mid. Sch., Columbia, Md., 1988-91, Hammond Mid. Sch., 1991-93; adminstr., staff devel. specialist Mount View Middle Sch., Marriotsville, Md., 1993—; adj. prof. Johns Hopkins U. Mem. NEA, ASCD, Nat. Assn. Secondary Sch. Prins., Md. Assn. Secondary Sch. Prins., Nat. Middle Sch. Assn., Md. Assn. Supervision and Curriculum Devel., Md. Middle Sch. Assn., Md. Tchrs. Assn., Nat. Coun. Social Studies, Am. Ednl. Research Assn., Mont. Hist. Soc., Custer Battlefield Preservation Com., Phi Delta Kappa. Democrat. Roman Catholic. Home: 8 Weston Ct Lutherville Timonium MD 21093-6342 Office: 12101 Woodford Dr Marriottsvl MD 21104-1456

PRYSTOWSKY, HARRY, physician, educator; b. Charleston, S.C., May 18, 1925; s. Moses Manning and Raye (Karesh) P.; m. Rhalda Betsy Bressler, Mar. 8, 1951; children: Michael Wayne, Ray Ellen, Jay Bressler. BS, The Citadel, 1944, DSc (hon.), 1974; MD, Med. Coll. S.C., 1948; LHD (hon.), 1975; DSc (hon.), U. Fla., 1988. Diplomate: Am. Bd. Obstetrics and Gynecology (dir., asso. examiner). Intern Johns Hopkins Hosp. and Med. Sch., 1948-49, resident, 1950-51, 53-55, instr., 1955-56, asst. prof., 1956-58; research fellow U. Cin. Sch. Medicine, 1949; research fellow physiology Yale Med. Sch., 1955-56; prof., chmn. obstetrics and gynecology U. Fla. Coll. Medicine, 1958-73; provost Milton S. Hershey Med. Center, Pa. State U., 1973-84, sr. v.p. health affairs, 1984-86; dean Coll. Medicine, 1973-86; sr. v.p. emeritus health affairs, dean emeritus Pa. State U., 1986—; bd. dirs. STV Group Inc. Contbr. articles to med. jours. Capt., M.C. U.S. Army, 1951-53. Named 1 of 10 Outstanding Young Men Am. U.S. Jaycees; recipient Alumni Centennial award Med. U. S.C. Mem. Soc. Gynecol. Investigation, Am. Assn. Obstetricians and Gynecologists, Am. Gynecol. Soc., Assn. Profs. Gynecology and Obstetrics (pres.), U. Fla. Alumni Assn. (hon.), Pa. State U. Honorary Alumnus award, Alpha Omega Alpha. Home: 8877 Collins Ave Apt 208 Surfside FL 33154-3519

PRYWES, NOAH SHMARYA, computer science educator and researcher; m. Ruth Weinstein; children—Menachem, Daniel, Ron. B.S., Technion, Israel, 1949; M.S. Carnegie Inst. Tech., 1951; Ph.D., Harvard U., 1954. Mgr. dept. Sperry Univac, Phila., 1956—; prof. computer sci. U. Pa., Phila., 1980-85, dir. Shanghai Jiao Tong U. program; founder, pres. Computer Command and Control Co., Phila., 1963—, Comserv Corp., Phila., 1969-73; mem. Navy Audit Adv. Com. Contbr. articles to profl. jours. Fellow IEEE (chmn. various coms.). Jewish. Home: 416 Bryn Mawr Ave Bala Cynwyd PA 19004-2721 Office: U Pa Cis Dept D2 33rd and Walnut Sts Philadelphia PA 19104

PRZELOMSKI, ANASTASIA NEMENYI, retired newspaper editor; b. Cleve., Dec. 11, 1918; d. Ernest Nicholas and Anna (Ress) Nemenyi; m. Edward Adrian Przelomski, July 4, 1946 (dec. July 1995). A.B., Youngstown State U., 1939; M.Ed., U. Pitts., 1942. Tchr. Youngstown Pub. Sch., Ohio, 1939-42; reporter Vindicator, Youngstown, 1942-57, asst. city editor, 1957-73, city editor, 1973-76, mng. editor, 1976-88, ret., 1988. Named Woman of Yr., Youngstown Bus. and Profl. Women's Club, 1977, bus. category Woman of Yr., YWCA, 1986; recipient Community Service award Youngstown Fedn. Women's Clubs, 1981, Woman of Yr. award YWCA, 1983; named to Ohio Woman's Hall of Fame, 1986. Mem. AP Mng. Editors Assn., UPI Ohio Editors Assn. (bd. dirs. 1984-88), Ohio Assn. AP, Ohio Soc. Newspaper Editors, Youngstown State U. Alumni Assn. (trustee 1978-83), Catholic Collegiate Assn., Phi Kappa Phi. Republican. Roman Catholic. Avocations: travel; golf. Home: 4000 Logan Gate Rd Youngstown OH 44505-1773

PRZEMIENIECKI, JANUSZ STANISLAW, engineering executive, former government senior executive and college dean; b. Lipno, Poland, Jan. 30, 1927; came to U.S., 1961, naturalized, 1967; s. Leon and Maria (Sarnacka) P.; m. Stefania (Fiona) Rudnicka, July 17, 1954; children: Anita, Christopher. BS, U. London, 1949, PhD, 1958; diploma in Aeros., Imperial Coll. Sci. and Tech., 1953; DSc in Engring., U. London, 1988. Registered profl. engr., Ohio. Head structural R & D sect. Bristol Aircraft Ltd., Eng., 1954-61; from assoc. prof. to prof. mechanics Sch. Engring., Air Force Inst. Tech., Wright-Patterson AFB, Ohio, 1961-66; from asst. dean, assoc. dean rsch. to dean Sch. Engring., Air Force Inst. Tech., 1966-89, sr. dean, 1970-95; pres. Astra Technologies, Inc., Fla., 1996—; cons. in field. Author: Theory of Matrix Structural Analysis, 1968, Mathematical Methods in Defense Analyses, 1990, Defense Analyses Software, 1991; assoc. editor: Jour. Aircraft, 1970-71; editl. bd.: Internat. Jour. Numerical Methods in Engring., 1969-75; editor: Mechanics of Structural Systems (textbook series) 1973-89; editor: Critical Technologies for Nat. Defense, 1991, Acquisition of Defense Systems, 1993; contbr. articles to profl. jours. Chmn. bd. trustees The Air Force Inst. Tech. Found., Ohio, 1987-88, trustee, 1993-95; trustee Engring. and Sci. Found. of Dayton, 1984-95. Decorated Polish Underground Army Cross, Warsaw Uprising Cross, Armed Forces medal; recipient USAF superior performance award, 1965, exceptional civilian svc. decoration, 1978, Presdl. rank of Meritorious Exec., 1981, Disting. Exec., 1982, Outstanding Engr. award Dayton Engring. and Sci. Found., 1986, Outstanding Civilian Svc. medal, 1995, Comdrs. Cross of the Polonia Restituta Order by Pres. of Poland, 1995, Disting. Svc. award, Am. Insts. of Polish Culture, 1997. Fellow Royal Aeros. Soc. (Usborne Meml. prize 1959), AIAA (editor-in-chief ednl. series 1981—, Pendray medal 1992), City and Guilds of London Inst.; mem. Am. Soc. Engring. Edn., Ohio Acad. Sci., Polish Inst. Arts and Scis., Tau Beta Pi. Home: 510 Pennyroyal Pl Venice FL 34293-7233

PRZYBYLOWICZ, EDWIN PAUL, chemical company executive, research director; b. Detroit, June 29, 1933; s. Ignacy and Antonette Olga (Krezalek) P.; m. Roberta Richardson, June 5, 1954; children: Christine, Margaret, Paul, Sue, Anne, Thomas, Catherine, James, Elizabeth, Sara, Edward. BS in Chemistry, U. Mich., 1953; PhD in Analytical Chemistry, MIT, 1956. Research chemist, lab. head. Eastman Kodak Co., Rochester, N.Y., 1956-68, asst. div. head, 1969-74, tech. asst. to dir. of research labs., 1974-75, dir. photographic program devel., 1975-77, asst. dir. research labs., 1977-81, program mgr. copy products, 1981-83, asst. dir. research labs., 1983-85, dir. research, 1985-91; cons. Eastman Kodak Co., Rochester, 1991-93; dir. Ctr. Imaging Sci. Rochester Inst. Tech., 1994-96; acad. assignment Nat. Bur. Standards, Washington and MIT, Cambridge, 1968-69; mem. U.S.-Polish Joint Commn. for Cooperation in Sci. and Tech., Nat. Rsch. Coun. Adv. Panel on Cen. Europe, numerous coms. in field; seminar speaker MIT Sloan Sch.; workshop facilitatator Insl. Rsch. Inst.; bd. dirs. Cytologics, more. Co-Author: Activation Analysis with Neutron Generators, 1973, Chem. Analysis, A Series of Monographs on Analytical Chemistry and Its Applications, 1973; patentee in field. Pres. Webster Bd. (N.Y.) Edn., 1965-72; bd. dirs. St. Paul's Ch. Bd., Webster, 1980-85. Eastman Kodak fellow MIT, 1955; recipient Moses Gomberg Prize in Chemistry U. Mich., 1953, Disting. Alumni award, 1994; Civic award in Sci. and Tech. Greater Rochester Area C. of C., 1993, Leo East award Engr. of Yr. Rochester Engring. Soc., 1990. Mem. AAAS, Am. Chem. Soc., Nat. Acad. Engring., Indsl. Rsch. Inst., Soc. Imaging Sci. and Tech. (hon.). Republican. Roman Catholic. Avocations: tennis, sailing, cross-country skiing, woodworking, geneology. Home: 1219 Crown Point Dr Webster NY 14580-9532 Office: Rochester Inst Tech Ctr for Imaging Science 54 Lomb Memorial Dr Rochester NY 14623-5604

PRZYBYLSKI, SANDRA MARIE, speech pathologist; b. Berwyn, Ill.; d. Raymond and Julie Marie (Vocelka) Hammers; m. James Przybylski; children: Eric, Sara. BS, U. Iowa, 1968; MA, U. Ill., 1971. Cert. clin. speech pathologist; speech/lang., educable mentally retarded education, learning disabilites and elem. tchr., life, Mo. Speech, lang. pathologist LaPlata (Mo.) Sch. Dist., 1974-87, Maysville (Mo.) Sch. Dist., 1990-92, Bucklin (Mo.) Sch. Dist., 1992—. Named to Disting. Svc. Registry-Speech and Hearing, 1990. Mem. Am. Speech, Lang., Hearing Assn., Autism Soc. Am., Mo. State Tchrs. Assn., Mo. Speech, Lang. and Hearing Assn.

PSALTIS, JOHN COSTAS, retired manufacturing company executive; b. Drama, Greece, Jan. 5, 1940; came to U.S., 1955; naturalized, 1961; s. Costas Dimitriou and Kay Psaltis; m. Dorothy May Coons, Sept. 18, 1961; children: Costas John, Kay Joanne. BSBA, Loyola U., Chgo., 1971; diploma corp. fin. mgmt, Harvard U., 1979, postgrad. internat. sr. mgrs. program, 1981. With Molex Inc., mfrs. electronic connectors, Lisle, Ill., 1973-96; contr. internat. ops. Molex Inc., 1973-78, mem. corp. mgmt. com., 1978-91; mem. corp. exec. com., 1991-96; treas. Molex Inc., 1978-79, v.p., treas., 1982-94, corp. v.p., treas., CFO, 1994-96, pres. for Americas, 1982-87, treas., bd. dirs. Molex Internat. Inc., 1979-96; sec.-treas., dir. Molex Far East Svcs. Ltd.; sec-treas. Molex Electronics Ltd.; sec., dir. Molex Electronics Ltd. U.K., Molex Euorpean Svcs. Ltd.; bd. dirs. Molex Japan, Molex Singapore Pte. Ltd., Molex Italia Spa, Molex Korea Co. Ltd., Molex Malaysia Ltd.; auditor Touche Ross & Co., 1971-72, sr. auditor, 1972-73. Mem. adv. com. Inst. for Internat. Mktg., Ill. Benedictine Coll. With USAR, 1958-66. Mem. Fin. Execs. Inst., Am. Mgmt. Assn. (fin. coun., briefing adv. bd.), Leading CFO's, Strategic Planning Inst., Pers. Inventory Mgmt. Sys. (coun. on value for 90's), Chicagoland C. of C. (bd. dirs. 1989-95, exec. com., v.p. world trade div. 1994, past chmn. fin. and audit com.). Office: 2222 Wellington Ave Lisle IL 60532-3820

PSATHAS, GEORGE, sociologist, educator; b. New Haven, Feb. 22, 1929; s. Milton Emanuel and Melpa (Joannides) P.; m. Irma M. Amatruda, Feb. 5, 1951; children: Christine Ann, David George, Anthony Paul. BA, Yale U., 1950; MA, U. Mich., 1951; PhD, Yale U., 1956; diploma, N.E. Sch. Photography, 1979. Instr. to asst. prof. Ind. U., Bloomington, 1955-63; lectr. Harvard U., Cambridge, Mass., 1961-62; assoc. prof. Washington U.,

St. Louis, 1963-68, rsch. assoc. Social Sci. Inst., 1963-68; program dir. community mental health tng. program NIMH/Washington U., 1966-68; prof. sociology Boston U., 1968—, acting chair, 1968-69; assoc. chair Boston U., Mass., 1969-70, 76-78, chair, 1984-85; dir. Ctr. for Applied Social Sci. Boston U., 1970-73, co-dir. post-doctoral rsch. tng. program in sociology and mental health Nat. Inst. Mental Health, 1976-79; co-dir. Sociology and Health Svcs. Rsch. Tng. Program NCHSR and Boston (Mass.) U., 1970-78; vis. lectr. MRC Med. Sociology-U. Aberdeen, Scotland, 1974, U. Colo., 1963, U. London, 1973, U. Bologna, 1996; vis. prof. Panteios Sch. Polit. Sci., Athens, 1982, Internat. U. Japan, Yamato-Machi, 1988, Doshisha U., Kyoto, Japan, 1989; Brit. Acad. vis. prof. U. Manchester, Eng., 1996; guest prof. Inst. for Human Scis., Vienna, 1996; chair Mass. Interdisciplinary Discourse Analysis seminar, 1989-95; cons. NSF, 1978, 79, 89, 94, 95, Rsch. Coun. Can., 1983-84, Social Sci. Rsch. Coun. Eng., 1981-82; active Ctr. Advanced Rsch. in Phenomenology, 1980—; presenter 70 presentations at profl. and scholarly socs. Editor: Phenomenological Sociology, 1973, Everyday Language, 1979, Interaction Competence, 1990, Situated Order, 1994; co-editor: Alfred Schutz Collected Papers, IV, 1996; editor-in-chief: Human Studies, Boston, 1978—; assoc. editor Social Problems, 1958-61, Visual Sociology, 1993—; author: Student Nurse in Diploma School of Nursing, 1968, Phenomenology & Sociology, 1989, Conversation Analysis, 1995; cons. editor Temple Univ. Press, Kluwer Academic Pubs., Qualitative Sociology; author 11 book chpts.; contbr. over 60 articles to profl. jours. Cons. Human Rels. Lab., Boston, Bethel, St. Louis, 1967, 69, Sch. for the Blind, Kallithea, Athens, Greece, 1982; tng. dirs. com. Nat. Ctr. for Health Svcs. Rsch., Washington, 1971-73; bd. dirs. Carroll Ctr. for the Blind, Newton, Mass., 1974-79. Named Post-Doctoral fellow NIMH Dept. Social Rels., Harvard U., Cambridge, 1961-62; recipient Sci. Faculty Devel. award NSF, 1978-79, Fulbright grant Fulbright Commn., Greece and Turkey, 1982, Brit Acad. grant, 1996. Mem. AAUP (sec. 1977-79, v.p. Boston U. chpt. 1979-80), Am. Sociol. Assn., Ea. Sociol. Assn., Internat. Visual Sociology Assn., Internat. Inst. for Ethnomethodology (chair 1990—), Soc. for Phenomenology & Existential Philosophy, Soc. for Phenomenology and Human Scis. (co-chair 1981-85, exec. com. 1993-97), Soc. Study Social Problems (treas., bus. mgr. 1959-61). Home: 150 Mt Vernon St Newtonville MA 02160 Office: Sociology Dept Boston Univ Boston MA 02215

PSILLOS, SUSAN ROSE, artist, educator; b. Bethpage, N.Y., Feb. 15, 1960; d. Reginald and Gloria Barbara Psillos; 1 child, Jennifer Rose. Student, Alfred U., 1978-80; Teaching Degree in Art, L.I. U., Southampton, 1996. Substitute tchr. art Shoreham-Wading River Schs., Shoreham, N.Y., 1992—; tchr. arts and crafts Round-out S.W.R. Sch., Shoreham, 1995-96; guest speaker in field. Exhibited sculpture at Smithtown (N.Y.) Mus., 1995, 96-97, Bellemeade Gallery, 1992; exhibited paintings at Ambiente Gallery, 1991-92, Smithtown Twsp. Art Mus., 1995, 96. Advisor Partnership for Survival, Smithtown, 1991—; bd. dirs., pub. rels. person Sexual Abuse Survivors, Smithtown,1991—. Recipient Art Judge's award Parrish Art Mus., 1976, Outstanding award Sch. Visual Arts, 1976, Profl. Recognition Day award, 1996, Child Abuse & Neglect Family Violence Vol. award Town of Brookhaven. Mem. NOW, Artist Support Group. Avocations: cooking, gardening, fine arts, painting, sculpture.

PSOMIADES, HARRY JOHN, political science educator; b. Boston, Sept. 8, 1928; s. John and Koula (Yalmanides) P.; m. Dorothy Smith, Aug. 18, 1962 (dec. Aug. 27, 1984); children—Kathy Alexis, Christine Anne. B.A., Boston U., 1953; M.Internat. Affairs, Columbia U., 1955; cert., Middle East Inst., 1956, Ph.D. (Ford Found. fellow), 1962; Litt.D. (hon.), Holy Cross/Hellenic Coll., 1985. Lectr. govt. Columbia U., 1959-65, asst. dean Grad. Sch. Internat. Affairs, 1959-65, dir. Carnegie Endowment Fellowships in Diplomacy, 1959-71; assoc. prof. polit. sci. Queens Coll., City U. N.Y., 1965-69, prof., 1970—, chmn. dept. polit. sci., 1967-71, dep. exec. officer Ph.D. program in polit. sci., 1975-76, program dir. seminar on the modern Greek state, 1976—; dir. Center Byzantine and Modern Greek Studies, 1976—; cons. faculty U.S. Army Command and Gen. Staff Coll., 1968-86; U.S. Dept. State Fgn. Service Inst., 1968-71; mem. screening com. Fgn. Area Fellowships Program for Asia and Middle East Joint Com., Social Sci. Research Council and Am. Council Learned Socs., 1967-69. Author: Greece and Turkey: Mutual Economic Interests, 1964, (with Thomas Spelios) A Pictorial History of the Greeks, 1967, The Eastern Question: The Last Phase, 1968, (with T.A. Couloumbis) Foreign Interference in Greek Politics: An Historical Perspective, 1976, (with A. Scourby) The Greek American Community in Transition, 1982, (with R.S. Orfanos) Education and Greek Americans: Process and Prospects, 1987, (with S. Thomadakes) Greece, The New Europe and the Changing International Order, 1993; editor: Jour. Modern Hellenism, 1984—; contbr. articles to profl. jours. Served with U.S. Army, 1946-50; to col. USAR, 1950-83. Hon. fellow Soc. Macedonian Studies, Thessaloniki, Greece, 1970—; named Comdr. Order of Honor The Republic of Greece, 1996. Fellow Middle East Studies Assn. N.Am.; mem. Am. Polit. Sci. Assn., Middle East Inst., Modern Greek Studies Assn. (mem. exec. com. 1972-76), Phi Beta Kappa. Greek Orthodox. Home: 440 Riverside Dr New York NY 10027-6828 Office: Dept Polit Sci Queens Coll Flushing NY 11367

PSUTY, NORBERT PHILLIP, marine sciences educator; b. Hamtramck, Mich., June 13, 1937; s. Phillip and Jessie (Proszykowski) P.; m. Sylvia Helen Zurinsky, June 13, 1959; children: Eric Anthony, Scott Patrick, Ross Phillip. BS, Wayne State U., 1959; MS, Miami U., Oxford, Ohio, 1960; PhD, La. State U., 1966. Rsch. assoc. Coastal Studies Inst., La. State U., Baton Rouge, 1962-64; instr. dept. geography and dept. geology U. Miami, Coral Gables, Fla., 1964-65; asst. prof. geography U. Wis., Madison, 1965-69; assoc. prof. geography and geol. scis. Rutgers U., New Brunswick, N.J., 1969-73, prof., 1973—, chmn. dept. marine and coastal scis., 1991—, dir. Marine Scis. Ctr., 1972-76, dir. Ctr. for Coastal and Environ. Studies, 1976-90; assoc. dir. Inst. Marine and Coastal Scis., New Brunswick, N.J., 1990—; mem. sci. com. Thalassas, Vigo, Spain, 1985—. Co-author: Living with the New Jersey Shore, 1986, Coastal Dunes, 1990; mem. editorial bd Coastal Mgmt., 1981—, Jour. Coastal Rsch., 1987—; editl. bd. Jour. of Coastal Conservation, 1996—; contbr. numerous articles to scholarly jours., chpts. to books, monographs. Mem. Water Policy Bd., East Brunswick, N.J., 1981-83, N.J. Shoreline Adv. Bd., Trenton, 1984-86; chmn. N.J. Gov.'s Sea Level Rise Com., Trenton, 1987-90; mem. N.J. State Beach Erosion Commn., 1994—; referee U.S.A Volleyball, Nat. Assn. of Girls and Women in Sports. Recipient Disting. Pub. Svc. award Pres. of Rutgers U. 1988; numerous grants including NSF, Nat. Park Svc., EPA, Office Naval Rsch., Nat. Sea Grant Program, NOAA, 1961—. Mem. AAAS, Assn. Am. Geographers (Honors award 1993), Coastal Soc. (pres. 1980-82), Internat. Geog. Union (vice chair commn. on coastal environ. 1988-92, chmn. commn. on coastal systems, 1992-96, editor newsletter 1984-96), N.J. Acad. Sci. (pres. 1982). Avocations: gardening, reading. Office: Rutgers U Inst Marine & Coastal Scis Cook Campus New Brunswick NJ 08903

PTAK, FRANK S., manufacturing executive; b. Chgo., Apr. 23, 1943; s. Frank J. and Stella R. (Los) P.; m. Karen M. Novoselsky, May 2, 1971; children: Jeffrey B., Jacquelyn F., Russell E. BS, De Paul U., 1965. CPA, Ill. Sr. auditor Arthur Young & Co., Chgo., 1965-69; sr. rsch. cons. Kemper Fin. Svcs., Chgo., 1969-71; asst. sec., mgr. acquisitions Sara Lee Corp., Chgo., 1971-73, asst. treas., 1973-74, asst. to chmn., 1974, v.p. planning, 1974-75; bus. devel. mgr. ITW Conex, Des Plaines, Ill., 1975-77; mktg. mgr. ITW Shakeproof, Elgin, Ill., 1977-78, group pres., 1977-78; group pres. ITW Metal Components Cos., Glenview, Ill., 1978-91; exec. v.p. Global Automotive Components ITW Corp., Glenview, 1991-95, vice-chmn., 1996—. Patentee in field. Mem. AICPA, Assn. Corp. Growth, ITW Patent Soc. Jewish. Home: 849 Edgewood Ct Highland Park IL 60035-3714 Office: ITW Corp 3600 W Lake Ave Glenview IL 60025-1215

PTAK, JOHN ANTHONY, talent agent; b. San Diego, Sept. 23, 1942; s. John and Doris Elizabeth P.; m. Margaret Elizabeth Black, May 21, 1981; 1 child, Hillary Elizabeth. BA, UCLA, 1967. Theatre mgr., booker Walter Reade Orgn., Beverly Hills, Calif., 1967-69; adminstrv. exec. Am. Film Inst., Beverly Hills, 1968-70; talent agent Internat. Famous Agy. (now ICM), L.A., 1971-75, William Morris Agy., Beverly Hills, 1976-91, Creative Artists Agy., Beverly Hills, 1991—; cons. Nat. Endowment for Arts, Washington, 1980—; co-chmn. Am. Film Inst. Ctr. for Film & Video Preservation, L.A., 1991—; mem. Nat. Film Preservation Bd., Washington, 1992—. Bd. dirs. Motion Pictures and T.V. Fund Found., 1996—, Nat. Film Preservation Found., 1997—. Avocations: tennis, travel. Office: Creative Artists Agy 9830 Wilshire Blvd Beverly Hills CA 90212-1804

PTASHNE, MARK STEVEN, biochemistry educator; b. Chgo., June 5, 1940; s. Fred and Mildred P. BA, Reed Coll., 1961; PhD, Harvard U., 1968. Lectr. biochemistry Harvard U., Cambridge, Mass., 1968-71, prof., 1971—, chmn. dept. biochemistry and molecular biology, 1980-83, Herchel Smith prof. of molecular biology, 1993—; Feodor Lynen lectr. U. Miami, Fla., 1988. Author: A Genetic Switch, 1986; contbr. numerous articles to sci. jours. Recipient Eli Lilly award, 1975, prix. Charles-Leopold Mayer Acad. des Scis., Inst. de France, 1977, Louisa Gross Horwitz prize Bd. Trustees Columbia U., 1985, Gairdner Found. Internat. award, 1985; co-recipient Ledle award Harvard U., 1986, GM Sloan prize, 1990. Fellow N.Y. Acad. Sci., Am. Acad. Sci.; mem. NAS, Fedn. Am. Scis. (bd. sponsors 1981). Avocations: opera, classical music. Office: Harvard U Dept Molecular & Cellular Biology 7 Divinity Ave Cambridge MA 02138-2019

PTASZKOWSKI, STANLEY EDWARD, JR., civil engineer, structural engineer; b. N.Y.C., June 11, 1943; s. Stanley Edward and Elsie Helena (Heihs) P. AAS, Acad. Aeronautics, Flushing, N.Y., 1967; BS in Civil Engring., U. Mo., 1975. Registered profl. engr., Tex., profl. sanitarian, Tex. Engr. Brown & Root, Inc., Houston, Tex., 1975-79; sr. engr. Marathon Marine Engring. Co., Houston, 1979-84, Gen. Dynamics, Ft. Worth, 1984-91, Bridgefarmer & Assocs., Dallas, 1991-93; prin. Pasko Consultants, Arlington, Tex., 1993—; sr. site constrn. engr. Raytheon Svc. Co., Ft. Worth, 1994—. Mem. NSPE, Tex. Soc. Profl. Engrs., Soc. Profl. Bldg. Designers (cons., sec.). Lutheran. Avocations: lic. pvt. pilot, golf, racquet ball. Home: 2002 Park Hill Dr Arlington TX 76012

PUCEL, ROBERT ALBIN, electronics research engineer; b. Ely, Minn., Dec. 27, 1926; s. Joseph and Theresa (Francel) P.; m. Catherine Ann Silva, June 30, 1952; children: Robert W., James J., Valerie A., Marc R., David J. BS, MIT, 1951, MS, 1951, DSc, 1955. With rsch. div. Research div. Raytheon Co., Lexington, Mass., 1955-93; staff mem. microwave tube group Research div. Raytheon Co., 1951-55, solid state physics group, 1955-65, project mgr. microwave semicondr. group, 1965-70, cons. to microwave semicondr. group, 1970-74, cons. scientist semicondr. group, 1974-93; pres. RCP Cons., Needham, Mass., 1994—; lectr. on monolithic microwave integrated circuits. Editor: Monolithic Microwave Integrated Circuits, 1985; contbg. author: Advances in Electronics and Electron Physics, vol. 38, 1975, Gallium Arsenide Technology, 1985. Served with USNR, 1945-46. Recipient Excellence in Technology award Raytheon, 1988. Fellow IEEE (life); mem. Microwave Theory and Techniques Soc. (editorial rev. bd., nat. lectr. 1980-81, Microwave prize 1976, Microwave Career award 1990), Nat. Acad. Engring., Electron Devices Soc. Inventor low-distortion FET; co-inventor Spacistor, Overlay FET. Office: RCP Cons 427 South St Needham MA 02192-2761

PUCHTLER, HOLDE, histochemist, pathologist, educator; b. Kleinlosnitz, Germany, Jan. 1, 1920; came to U.S., 1955; d. Gottfried and Gunda (Thoma) P. Cand. med., U. Würzburg, 1944; Md, U. Köln, 1949; MD, U. Köln, Germany, 1951. Rsch. assoc. U. Köln, 1949-51, resident in pathology, 1951-55; rsch. fellow Damon Runyon Found., Montreal, Que., Can., 1955-58; rsch. assoc. Med. Coll. Ga., Augusta, 1959-60, asst. rsch. prof., 1960-62, assoc. rsch. prof., 1962-68, prof., 1968-90, prof. emerita, 1990—. Assoc. editor Jour. Histotech., 1982-94; mem. editorial bd. Histochemistry, 1977-90. Honored at Symposium on Connective Tissues in Arterial and Pulmonary Diseases, 1980. Fellow Am. Inst. Chemists, Royal Microscopical Soc.; mem. Royal Soc. Chemistry, Am. Chem. Soc., Histochem. Soc. Gesellschaft Histochemie, Anatomische Gesellschaft, Ga. Soc. Histotech. (hon.). Achievements include development of new techniques for light, polarization, visible and infrared flourescence based on theoretical and physical chemistry and x-ray diffraction data; demonstration of relations between dye configurations and selective affinity for certain components of human tissues, such as collagens, elastin, myosins, neurofibrils, and amyloids; application of molecular orbital theories to histochemistry. Avocations: archeology, history of science, folk medicine, comparative religion. Office: Med Coll Ga Dept Pathology Augusta GA 30912

PUCIE, CHARLES R., JR., public affairs executive; b. Asheville, N.C., Oct. 8, 1943. BSFS in Internat. Affairs, Georgetown U., 1965. Fin. analyst Chase Manhattan Bank, 1969-70; account exec. Doremus, 1970-73, v.p., 1973-80; sr. v.p., regional mgr. Doremus, Washington, 1980-85; sr. v.p., group dir., internat. counseling Hill and Knowlton, 1986-90, exec. v.p., 1991; founder, CEO Capitoline Internat. Group, Washington, 1991—; chmn., CEO C.I.H. Ltd., 1992—; CEO Capitoline/MS&L, G.P., 1994—. Capt., aviator U.S. Army, 1966-69, Vietnam. Office: Capitoline/MS&L GP 1615 L St NW Washington DC 20036-5610

PUCK, THEODORE THOMAS, geneticist, biophysicist, educator; b. Chgo., Sept. 24, 1916; s. Joseph and Bessie (Shapiro) Puckowitz; m. Mary Hill, Apr. 17, 1946; children: Stirling, Jennifer, Laurel. B.S., U. Chgo., 1937, Ph.D., 1940. Mem. commn. airborne infections Office Surgeon Gen., Army Epidemiol. Bd., 1944-46; asst. prof. depts. medicine and biochemistry U. Chgo., 1945-47; sr. fellow Am. Cancer Soc., Calif. Inst. Tech., Pasadena, 1947-48; prof. biophysics U. Colo. Med. Sch., 1948—, chmn. dept., 1948-67, disting. prof., 1986—; founder, dir. Eleanor Roosevelt Inst. Cancer Research, 1962-95; Disting. research prof. Am. Cancer Soc., 1966—; nat. lectr. Sigma Xi, 1975-76. Author: The Mammalian Cell as a Microorganism: Genetic and Biochemical Studies in Vitro, 1972. Mem. Commn. on Physicians for the Future. Recipient Albert Lasker award, 1958, Borden award med. rsch., 1959, Louisa Gross Horwitz prize, 1973, Gordon Wilson medal Am. Clin. and Climatol. Assn., 1977, award Environ. Mutagen Soc., 1981, E.B. Wilson medal Am. Soc. Cell Biology, 1984, Bonfils-Stanton award in sci., 1984, U. Colo. Disting. Prof. award, 1987, Henry M. Porter medal, 1992; named to The Colo. 100, Historic Denver, 1992; Heritage Found. scholar, 1983; Phi Beta Kappa scholar, 1985; Fogarty Internat. scholar NIH, 1997. Fellow Am. Acad. Arts and Scis.; mem. Am. Soc. Human Genetics, Am. Chem. Soc., Soc. Exptl. Biology and Medicine, AAAS (Phi Beta Kappa award and lectr. 1983), Am. Assn. Immunologists, Radiation Research Soc., Biophys. Soc., Genetics Soc. Am., Nat. Acad. Sci., Tissue Culture Assn. (Hon. award 1987), Paideia Group, Santa Fe Inst. Sci. Bd., Phi Beta Kappa, Sigma Xi. Achievements include pioneering contributions to establishment of somatic cell approaches to mammalian cell genetics, to the identification and classification of the human chromosomes; measurement of mutation in mammalian cells; demonstration of the camp-induced reverse transformation reaction and the genome exposure defect in cancer; development of quantitative approaches to mammalian cell radiobiology. Office: Eleanor Roosevelt Inst Cancer Rsch 1899 Gaylord St Denver CO 80206-1210 *Our age is threatened by distorted emphasis on power, material wealth, and competitiveness, and by an explosive increase in population which exceeds our traditional regulative capacities. But it also holds promise for new and profound understanding of ourselves - of our basic human biological intellectual and emotional needs. There is room for hope.*

PUCKET, SUSAN, newspaper editor. Exec. food editor features desk Atlanta Jour. and Constn. Office: Atlanta Jour and Constn 72 Marietta St NW Atlanta GA 30303-2804*

PUCKETT, ALLEN WEARE, health care information systems executive; b. Pasadena, Calif., Mar. 17, 1942; s. Allen Emerson Puckett and Betty Jane (Howlett) Ward; m. Joan Adrienne Roth, Apr. 10, 1965 (div. 1980); children: Glenn A., Tod A.; m. Laura Treadgold, July 10, 1992. BS, U. Calif., Berkeley, 1963; JD, Harvard U., 1966. Bar: Calif. 1966. Prin. McKinsey & Co., San Francisco, 1966-78; pres. Atman Corp., San Francisco, 1979-83; v.p. VWR Sci., San Francisco, 1980-83, Univar Corp., Seattle, 1984-85; sr. v.p. fin. VWR Corp., Seattle, 1986-90, Momentum Distbn. Inc., Seattle, 1990; v.p. cen. ops. Eldec Corp., Lynnwood, 1990-92; exec. v.p., CEO Phycom Corp., 1993—. Recipient Nathan Burkan prize ASCAP, 1966. Mem. Wash. Athletic Club. Democrat. Avocations: skiing, scuba diving, music. Home: 1624 38th Ave E Seattle WA 98112-3134 Office: Phycom Corp 3380-146th Pl SE Bellevue WA 98007

PUCKETT, C. LIN, plastic surgeon, educator; b. Burlington, N.C., Oct. 19, 1940; s. Harry W. and Lula C. Puckett; m. Florence Elizabeth Loy, June 18, 1961 (div. 1976); children: Loy C., Lisa A., Leslie A.; m. Patricia Louise Wells, June 17, 1984 (div. 1994); 1 child, Henry James; m. Theresa G. Teel, Nov. 24, 1995. MD, Bowman Gray Sch. Medicine, 1966. Assoc. in surgery Duke U. Med. Ctr., Durham, N.C., 1971-73; assoc. prof., head div. plastic surgery U. Mo. Med. Ctr., Columbia, 1976-81; prof., head attending plastic surgeon U. Mo. Med. Ctr., Truman VA Hosp., Columbia, 1982—. Contbr. numerous articles to profl. jours. Fellow ACS (gov. 1992); mem. AMA, Am. Assn. Hand Surgery (bd. dirs. 1982-84, chmn. nominating com. 1985, v.p. 1987, pres.-elect 1988, pres. 1988—), Am. Assn. Plastic Surgeons (trustee 1995), Am. Cleft Palate Assn., Am. Soc. Plastic and Reconstructive Surgeons Inc. (bd. dirs. 1985—, asst. sec. 1988, trustee 1990, chmn. bd. trustees 1992, parlamentarian 1993, historian 1994, sec. 1995, v.p. 1997—), Am. Bd. Plastic Surgery (cert., bd. dirs. 1988-94, chmn. 1993-94), Am. Soc. Surgery of the Hand, Am. Trauma Soc., Internat. Microsurg. Soc., Mo. Chpt. ACS, Plastic Surgery Rsch. Coun., So. Med. Assn., Assn. Acad. Chmn. Plastic Surgery (bd. dirs. 1985—, pres. 1987-88), Sigma Xi, Alpha Omega Alpha. Republican. Avocation: breeding Quarter horses, angus cattle. Office: U Mo Med Ctr Dept Plastic Surgery 1 Hospital Dr # M349 Columbia MO 65201-5276

PUCKETT, CARLISSA ROSEANN, non-profit association executive; b. Effingham, Ill., Jan. 21, 1951; d. Carl Winston and Flora Pauline (Cox) Browning; m. Steve Dawson Puckett, Oct. 27, 1973; children: Heather Nicole, Adam Dawson, Christopher Alex. AS, Lake Land Jr. Coll., Mattoon, Ill., 1972; BA, Ea. Ill. U., 1976; MS, So. Ill. U., 1986. Child care aide Assn. Retarded Citizens Effingham County, Effingham, 1972-74, asst. supr. devel. work activities, 1975-77, residential coord., 1981-84, residential dir., case coord. dir. family support, 1984-88; owner, mgr. Denim's Inn, Effingham, 1977-81; coord. housing Ill. Dept. Mental Health and Devel. Disabilities, Springfield, 1988-89, coord. Community Integrated Living Arrangements, 1989-90; bur. chief Bur. Resource Design, Springfield, 1990-91, Bur. Devel. Field Svcs., 1991-93; exec. dir. Springfield Assn. for Retarded Citizens Inc., 1993—. Named Bus. and Profl. Woman of Yr., Effingham County Jr. Women's Club, 1986. Mem. Am. Assn. on Mental Retardation (membership com. Ill. chpt. 1992—, bd. dirs. 1995—), Assn. for Retarded Citizens, Sons and Daus. of Pearl Harbor Survivors (charter, pres. Ill. chpt. 1993-95), Rotary (fellowship dir. 1995-96, club svc. dir. 1997-98), Women in Mgmt. Women of Achievement-Not-for-Profit, Phi Kappa Phi. Avocations: family activities, swimming, sewing, reading. Home: 2516 Kipling Dr Springfield IL 62707-7247 Office: Springfield Assn Retarded Citizens Inc One SPARCenter Plz 232 N Bruns Ln Springfield IL 62702-4613

PUCKETT, ELIZABETH ANN, law librarian, law educator; b. Evansville, Ind., Nov. 10, 1943; d. Buell Charles and Lula Ruth (Gray) P.; m. Joel E. Hendricks, June 1, 1964 (div. June 1973); 1 child, Andrew Charles; m. Thomas A. Wilson, July 19, 1985. BS in Edn., Eastern Ill. U., 1964; JD, U. Ill., 1977, MS in L.S., 1977. Bar: Kans. 1978, Ill. 1979. Acquisitions/reader services librarian U. Kans. Law Library, Lawrence, 1978-79; asst. reader services librarian So. Ill. U. Law Library, Carbondale, 1979-81, reader services librarian, 1981-83; assoc. dir. Northwestern U. Law Library, Chgo., 1983-86, co-acting dir., 1986-87; dir./assoc. prof. South Tex. Coll. Law Library, Houston, 1987-89; dir./prof. South Tex. Coll. Law Libr., Houston, 1990-94, U. Ga. Law Libr., Athens, 1994—. Co-author: Evaluation of System-Provided Library Services to State Correctional Centers in Illinois, 1983; co-editor Uniform Commercial Code: Confidential Drafts, 1993. Mem. ABA, Am. Assn. Law Librs. (mem. exec. bd. 1993-96). Avocations: reading, antiques. Office: U Georgia Law Libr Athens GA 30602-6018

PUCKETT, HOYLE BROOKS, agricultural engineer, research scientist, consultant; b. Jesup, Ga., Oct. 15, 1925; s. Lawrence Parham and Martha Isabella (Mizell) P.; m. Faye Eloise Bowden, June 22, 1945; children: Carol P. Keeley, Hoyle B. Jr., Kristina P. Berbaum. BS in Agrl. Engring., U. Ga., 1948; MS in Agrl. Engring., Mich. State U., 1949; student, Ga. Inst. Tech., 1964-65. reg. profl. engr. Ill. Rsch. engr. GS 7-9 USDA/ARS, Oxford, N.C., 1949-55; res. engr. GS 11-13 USDA/ARS, Urbana, Ill., 1955-68, res. ldr. GS 14-15, 1968-85; ret., 1985; engring. cons. pvt. practice, Champaign, Ill., 1985—. Fellow Am. Soc. Agrl. Engrs.; mem. Exchange Club of Urbana. Home: 407 W University Ave Apt 104 Champaign IL 61820-3914

PUCKETT, JAMES MANUEL, JR., genealogist; b. Oakman, Ga., Dec. 8, 1916; s. James Manuel and Alma (Willkie) P.; student West Ga. Coll., Emory U.; m. Robbie Horton, Sept. 13, 1944; 1 son, James William (dec.). Retail mcht., 1937-42; with Treasury Dept., 1944-53; public acct., 1955-60; feature writer Ga. Geneal. Soc. quar., 1965-75; genealogist, lectr., 1965—. Mayor of Oakman, 1940-42. Served with USNR, 1942-44. Fellow Ancient Monument Soc., Heraldry Soc., Am. Coll. Genealogists; mem. SAR, Am. Coll. Heraldy, Archaeol. Inst. Am., Sons Confederate Vets., Ga. Hist. Soc., Order Stars and Bars (Ga. comdr. 1966-70), Nat. Hi. Soc., So. Hist. Soc., Am. Hist. Assn., Orgn. Am. Historians, Ctr. for Study of the Presidency, Internat. Platform Assn., Ga. Geneal. Soc., Nat. Geneal. Soc., Nat. Mus. Am. Indian (charter), Civil War Trust (charter). Home: 1563 Runnymeade NE Atlanta GA 30319-2130

PUCKETT, KIRBY, professional baseball team executive, former player; b. Chgo., Mar. 14, 1961; s. Catherine Puckett; m. Tonya Hudson; children: Catherine, Kirby, Jr. Student, Bradley U., Ill., Triton Coll., Ill. Baseball player Minnesota Twins, Mpls., 1982-96; exec. v.p. Minnesota Twins, 1996—. Author: I Love This Game!, 1993, Be The Best You Can Be, 1993. Founder, benefactor Kirby Puckett Eight-Ball Invitational to benefit Children's Heart Fund, United Way. Recipient All-Star Most Valuable Player award, 1993, Gold Glove award, 1986-89, 1991-92, Silver Slugger award, 1986-89, 92, 94, All-Star team, 1986-94; named to Sporting News All-Star Team, 1986-89, 92, 94, Am. League All-Star Team, 1986-89, Am. League Batting Champion, 1989, Minn. Twins Most Valuable Player 1985, 86, 88, 89, 92; named Calif. League Player of the Yr., 1983, Most Valuable Player, Am. League Championship Series, 1991, Best Hitter and Most Exciting Player, Baseball America, 1992; inducted Triton Coll. Hall of Fame, 1993. Mem. Alexis de Tocqueville Soc. Achievements include: led Major League in hits 1988-92, highest batting average among active batters 1988-92, seasons with 200 or more hits: 1986-89, 92. Office: Minnesota Twins Hubert H Humphrey Metrodome 34 Kirby Pucket Pl Minneapolis MN 55415-1517*

PUCKETT, RICHARD EDWARD, artist, consultant, retired recreation executive; b. Klamath Falls, Oreg., Sept. 9, 1932; s. Vernon Elijah and Leona Belle (Clevenger) P.; m. Velma Faye Hamrick, Apr. 14, 1957 (dec. 1985); children: Katherine Michelle Briggs, Deborah Alison Bolinger, Susan Lin Rowland, Gregory Richard. Student So. Oreg. Coll. Edn., 1951-56, Lake Forest Coll., 1957-58; Hartnell Jr. Coll., 1960-70; B.A., U. San Francisco, 1978. Acting arts and crafts dir., Fort Leonard Wood, Mo., 1956-57; arts and crafts dir., asst. spl. svcs. officer, mus. dir., Fort Sheridan, Ill., 1957-59; arts and crafts dir., Fort Irwin, Calif., 1959-60, Fort Ord, Calif., 1960-86; dir. arts and crafts br. Art Gallery, Arts and Crafts Center Materials Sales Store, 1960; opening dir. Presidio Monterey Army Mus., 1968; dir. Model Army Arts and Crafts Program. Recipient First Place, Dept. Army and U.S. Army Forces Command awards for programming and publicity, 1979-81, 83-85, 1st and 3d place sculpture awards Monterey County Fair Fine Arts Exhibit, 1979, Comdrs. medal civilian svcs., 1986, other awards, Golden Acad. award, Internat. Man of Yr. award, 1991-92. Mem. Monterey Peninsula Art Assn., Salinas Fine Arts Assn., Rogue Valley Art Assn., Fort Ord Alumni Assn. One-man shows: Seaside City Hall, 1975, Fort Ord Arts and Crafts Center Gallery, 1967, 73, 79, 81, 84, 86, Presidio of Monterey Art Gallery, 1979, Rogue Valley Art Assn., Salinas Valley Art Gallery; Glass on Holiday, Gatlinburg, Tenn., 1981, 82; exhbns. in Mo., Ill., and pvt. collections; designed and opened first Ft. Sheridan Army Mus., Presidio of Monterey Mus. Home: 110 Ashland Ave Medford OR 97504-7523 also: 1152 Jean Ave Salinas CA 93905-3321

PUCKETT, ROBERT HUGH, political scientist, educator; b. Kansas City, Mo., July 16, 1935; s. John William and Marjorie (Shirlaw) P.; m. Barbara Ann Chandley, Dec. 23, 1964; 1 child, Sarah Anne. BA, De Pauw U., 1957; MA, U. Chgo., 1958, PhD, 1961. Asst. prof. polit. sci. Mary Washington Coll., Fredericksburg, Va., 1961-63; vis. scholar, postdoctoral fellow social sci. rsch. coun. MIT, Cambridge, 1963-64; asst. prof. govt. and fgn. affairs U. Va., Charlottesville, 1964-66; asst. prof. social sci. Mich. State U., East Lansing, 1966-68; prof. polit. sci. Ind. State U., Terre Haute, 1968—; cons. in field.; cons. Rand Corp., 1962, U.S. Army, 1985-89, U.S. Dept. Edn., 1987-88, USN, 1990-95; del. Ind. Gov.'s Conf. on Librs. and Info. Svcs., 1990. Author: America Faces the World: Isolationist Ideology in American Foreign Policy, 1972, (with Oscar H. Rechtschaffer) Reflections on Space, 1964, The United States and Northeast Asia, 1993; contbr. articles to polit. sci. jours. Bd. dirs. So. Ind. Health Sys. Agy., 1978-81; adv. com. U.S.

Army Command and Gen. Staff Coll., 1985-89; mem. Pres.'s Commn. on White House Fellowships, 1990-93; bd. advisors to pres. Naval War Coll., 1990-95. Mem. Am. Polit. Sci. Assn., Indpls. Com. Fgn. Rels., Midwest Polit. Sci. Assn., Internat. Studies Assn., Ind. Consortium for Security Studies, Ind. Acad. Social Scis., Ind. Polit. Sci. Assn. (v.p. 1977-79), Coun. Fgn. Rels., Ind. Coun. on World Affairs, Inter-Univ. Seminar on Armed Forces and Soc., Japan-Am. Soc. Ind., Nat. Strategy Forum, DePauw U. Alumni Assn., Econ. Club Indpls., Columbia Club (Indpls.), MVP Club (Terre Haute), Phi Bata Kappa, Sigma Iota Rho, Phi Eta Sigma, Pi Sigma Alpha, Pi Kappa Alpha, Alpha Phi Omega. Home: 122 Marigold Dr Terre Haute IN 47803-1538 Office: Dept Polit Sci Ind State U Terre Haute IN 47809

PUCKETT, STANLEY ALLEN, consultant, realtor, marketing-management educator; b. Dayton, Ohio, July 21, 1951; s. Russell Elwood and Dorothy Christine (Hoskins) P.; m. Kum Cha Pak, July 28, 1986; children: Thomas Abraham, Jacqueline Sue. BGS, U. Ky., 1974; MSM, Troy State U., Eng., 1983; PhD, Sussex Coll., Eng., 1987. Asst. prof. mktg. Lamar U., Beaumont, Tex., 1987-88; asst. prof. mgmt. Grambling (La.) State U., 1988-93; realtor Tourtelor Bros., Inc., St. Petersburg, Fla., 1994-95, 97—, Century 21 Am. Dream Realty, Inc., St. Petersburg, 1995-96; mainframe cons. Decision Cons., Inc., Clearwater, Fla., 1997—; edn. cons. Hyndai Mgmt. Devel. Inst., I-chon, Korea, 1986-87; bus. cons. NAF Contracting Office, Ft. Polk, La., 1990; free enterprise fellow Students in Free Enterprise, Inc., Springfield, Mo., 1989-90; admissions liaison USAF Acad., Colorado Springs, Colo., 1989-96; adj. prof. Union Inst. Grad. Sch., Tampa Coll., U. South Fla. Author: Social Marketing, 1988; contbg. author: Great Ideas for Teaching Marketing, 1991; editor chpts.: History of the 8th Air Force, 1986, 87-88, 89-92, History of U.S. Central Command, 1992-94. Lt. col. USAFR, 1975-96, ret. Named to Honorable Order of Ky. Colonels, 1974. Mem. Am. Assn. Individual Investors, Ret. Officers Assn., Air Force Assn.,. Republican. Mem. Christian Ch. (Disciples of Christ). Avocations: flying, computers, investing, golf, consulting. Home: 4500 15th Ave N Saint Petersburg FL 33713-5234 Office: Decision Cons Inc 13535 Feather Sound Dr Clearwater FL 34624

PUCKETTE, STEPHEN ELLIOTT, mathematics educator, mathematician; b. Ridgewood, N.J., Oct. 18, 1927; s. Charles McDonald and Elizabeth Argyle (Gettys) P.; m. Upshur Smith, June 22, 1957; children: Robert B. E., Miller S., Emily E., Charles McD., Charlotte Elliott. BS, U. of the South, 1949; MS, Yale U., 1950, MA, 1951, PhD, 1957. Asst. prof. math. U. of the South, Sewanee, Tenn., 1956-64; vis. asst. prof. math. U. Ga., Athens, 1962-63; assoc. prof. math. U. Ky., Lexington, 1966-69; dean of arts and scis., prof. U. of the South, Sewanee, Tenn., 1969-79; prof. associé U. Nationale, Cote d'Ivoire, Côté d'Ivoire, Ivory Coast, 1979-80; prof. math. U. of the South, Sewanee, Tenn., 1980-93, prof. emeritus, 1993—; vis. prof. U. N.C., Chapel Hill, 1986-87; vis. lectr. Math. Assn. Am., Washington DC, 1967-77. NSF faculty fellow, Yale U., 1964-65; Fulbright scholar (France), 1952-53; Fulbright lectr. (Ivory Coast), 1979-80. Mem. Am. Math. Soc., Societé Mathématique de France, Deutsche Mathematiker-Vereinigung, London Math. Soc. Democrat. Episcopalian. Home: Morgan's Steep Sewanee TN 37375 Office: Univ of the South Math Dept Sewanee TN 37375

PUCKO, DIANE BOWLES, public relations executive; b. Wyndotte, Mich., Aug. 15, 1940; d. Mervin Arthur and Bernice Letitia (Shelly) Bowles; m. Raymond J. Pucko, May 22, 1965; children: Todd Anthony, Gregory Bowles. BA in Sociology, Bucknell U., Lewisburg, Pa., 1962. Accredited in pub. rels. Asst. to pub. rels. dir. Edward C. Michener Assocs., Inc., Harrisburg, Pa., 1962-65; advt./pub. rels. coord. Superior Switchboard & Devices, Canton, Ohio, 1965-66; editorial dir. women's svc. Hutchins Advt. Co., Inc., Rochester, N.Y., 1966-71; pres. Editorial Communications, Rochester and Elyria, Ohio, 1971-77; mgr. advt. and sales promotion Tappan Air Conditioning, Elyria, 1977-80; mgr. pub. affairs Kaiser Permanente Med. Care Program, Cleve., 1980-85; corp. dir. pub. affairs Keystone Health Plans, Inc., Camp Hill, Pa., 1985-86; v.p., dir. client planning Young-Liggett-Stashower, Cleve., 1986; v.p., dir. pub. rels. Marcus Pub. Rels., Cleve., 1987-91; sr. v.p. Proconsul, Cleve., 1991-95, also bd. dirs.; sr. ptnr. pub. rels. Poppe Tyson, Cleve., 1995-96; managing dir. Bozell PR, Cleve., 1996—; mgr., role model Women in Mgmt. Field Placement program, Cleve. State U., 1983-92; prof. advisor, pub. rels. adv. bd. Pub. Rels. Student Soc. Am., Kent State U., 1988—. Bd. trustees, mem. exec. com., chmn. pub. rels. adv. com. Ronald MacDonald House of Cleve., 1993—; bd. dirs., chmn. pub. rels. com. Assn. Retarded Citizens, Cleve., 1987-91; mem. pub. rels.-mktg. com. Beech Brook, 1996—. Recipient Woman Profl. Excellence award YMCA, 1984, MacEachern award Acad. Hosp. Pub. Rels., 1985, Bell Ringer award Cmty. Rels. Report, 1985, Bronze Quill Excellence award Internat. Assn. Bus. Communicators, 1992, 93, Cleve. Comms. award Women in Comms. Internat., 1993, 95, Tower award Bus./Profl. Advt. Assn., 1993, 95, Creativity in Pub. Rels. award, 1994, Silver Screen award U.S. Internat. Film & Video Festival, 1995, Silver Quill Excellence award Internat. Assn. Bus. Communicators, 1995, Internat. Assn. Bus. Communicators. Fellow Pub. Rels. Soc. Am. (bd. dirs. 1983-85, 86-94, officer 1991-95, mem. counselors acad. 1996—, Silver Anvil award 1985, Mktg./Consumer Rels. award East Ctrl. dist. 1992, 95, Lighthouse award 1995); mem. Press Club Cleve. (bd. dirs. 1989-96, v.p. 1990-96), Cleve. Advt. Club, Women's City Club Cleve. Republican. Methodist. Avocation: soccer. Home: 656 University Ave Elyria OH 44035-7239

PUDDINGTON, IRA EDWIN, chemist; b. Clifton, N.B., Can., Jan. 8, 1911; s. Charles Edwin and Elizabeth (Currie) P.; m. Hazel Jean Duncan, Aug. 27, 1936; 1 child, James Donald. B.S., Mt. Allison U., Sackville, N.B., Can., 1933, D.Sc. (hon.), 1967; M.S., McGill U., Montreal, Que., Can., 1936, Ph.D., 1938; D.Sc. (hon.), Carleton U., Ottawa, Ont., Can., 1975, Meml. U., St. John's, Nfld., Can., 1977. Chemist Nat. Research Council Can., Ottawa, 1938-52, dir. div. chemistry, 1952-75. Contbr. numerous articles to profl. jours.; patentee (over 50) in field. Fellow Am. Inst. Chemists (Pioneer award 1984), Royal Soc. Can., Chem. Inst. Can. (pres. 1967-68, Montreal medal 1971); mem. Am. Chem. Soc., Can. Soc. Chem. Engring. (R.S. Jane award 1975). Mem. United Ch. of Can. Avocations: sailing; gardening. Home: 2324 Alta Vista Dr, Ottawa, ON Canada K1H 7M7 Office: Nat Research Council Can, Div Chemistry, Ottawa, ON Canada K1A 0R9

PUDER, JANICE, special education educator; b. Phila., Apr. 6, 1950; d. Allen Thrasher and Dorothy Ruth (Mathis) P.; foster child: Corienna Gallagher. AA, Pasadena (Calif.) City Coll., 1970; BA, U. Calif., Chico, 1973; postgrad., U. Calif., U. Pacific, 1973-74, 82; MA in Spl. Edn., Santa Clara U., 1996. Cert. elem./secondary edn. tchr., spl. edn., Calif.; cert. early childhood intervention. Tchr. New Covenant Christian H.S., Palo Alto, Calif., 1977-81; spl. edn. tchr. Sunnyvale (Calif.) Christian Jr. and Sr. H.S., 1981-82; adapted phys. edn. and cons. to spl. edn. local plan area 3 Santa Clara County Office Edn., 1983-92, adapted phys. edn. specialist, 1992—. Vol. Christian Counseling. Mem. PEO. Avocations: Bible study, reading, sports, advocate for foster daughter. Home: 575 Tyndall St # 6 Los Altos CA 94022

PUDLO, FRANCES THERESA, real estate company administrator; b. Hartford, Conn., Jan. 17, 1948; d. Alexander and Eve Antoinette (Paczkowski) P. AS in Secretarial Sci., U. Hartford, 1974. Sec. United Techs. Corp., East Hartford, Conn., 1966-74; asst., sec. Richard M. Bissell, Jr., Farmington, Conn., 1974-94; adminstrv. officer DeWolfe New Eng., Avon, Conn., 1994—. Co-author: Reflections of a Cold Warrior: From Yalta to the Bay of Pigs, 1996. Bd. dirs. Friends of Hill-Stead Mus., Farmington, Conn., 1994—; mem. World Affairs Coun., 1996—. Avocations: reading, cooking, gardening, ancient history, travel. Home: 63 Lafayette Ave East Hartford CT 06118-2628

PUENTE, TITO ANTHONY, orchestra leader, composer, arranger; b. N.Y.C., Apr. 20, 1923; s. Ernest Anthony and Ercilia (Ortiz) P.; m. Margaret Asencio, Oct. 19, 1963; children: Ronald, Audrey, Tito Anthony. Student, Julliard Conservatory Music, N.Y. Sch. Music, Schillinger System; MusD (hon.), SUNY, Albany, 1987. Orch. leader appearing in numerous night clubs and ballrooms, throughout U.S., 1949—; appeared in Woody Allen's Radio Days, John Candy's Armed & Dangerous, 1986-87; recorded 96 albums; appeared in concert Red Sea Jazz Festival, Israel, all major jazz festivals, including Montreaux, Monterey, Munich, North Sea, others, Tribute in P.R., 1986, Los Angeles Ford Theatre Tribute, 1987; composer Para Los Rumberos, 1960, Oye Como Va, 1962, numerous other works recorded with Dizzy Gillespie, Lionel Hampton, George Shearing, Woody Herman, other major jazz artists; sold out performance Radio City Music Hall & Apollo Theatre, 1986; appeared Madison Square Garden, N.Y.C., 1986, Los Angeles Amphitheatre, 1986, on Bill Cosby Show, 1987, Regis Philbin, Bill Boggs shows, 1987; guest artist with Bklyn. Philharmonic Symphony Orch., N.Y. and Phila., 1987. Founder T. Puente Scholarship fund, 1980. Served with USN, 1942-45. Recipient Bronze medallion City of N.Y., 1969, Key to City Los Angeles, 1976, Key to City of Chgo., 1985, Key to City of Miami, 1986; named Musician of Month on several occasions by Downbeat, Metronome, Playboy and trade mags., 1950's; named King of Latin Music, La Prensa newspaper, 1955; his band named Best Latin Am. Orch. New York Daily News, 1977; recipient 6 Grammy nominations, Grammy award, 1978, 83, 85, 90; N.Y. Music award, 1986. Office: Thomas Cassidy Inc 11761 E Speedway Blvd Tucson AZ 85748-2017*

PUERNER, JOHN, newspaper publishing executive. V.p., dir. mktg. and devel. Chgo. Tribune; now pres., pub. The Orlando Sentinel, Fla., 1993—. Office: The Orlando Sentinel 633 N Orange Ave Orlando FL 32801-1300*

PUESCHEL, SIEGFRIED M., pediatrician, educator; b. Waldenburg, Germany, July 28, 1931; came to U.S., 1961; naturalized, 1971; widowed. Student, Braunschweig Coll., Germany, 1953-55, Leibniz Coll., Tubingen, Germany, 1955-56, U. Tubingen, Germany, 1955-57, Free U., Berlin, 1957-58, U. Freiburg, Germany, 1958; MD summa cum laude, Med. Acad., Dusseldorf, Germany, 1960; MPH, Harvard U., 1967; PhD, U. R.I., 1985; JD, So. New Eng. Sch. Law, 1996. Diplomate Am. Bd. Pediatrics, Am. Bd. Med. Genetics. Intern Mercer Hosp., Trenton, N.J., 1961-62; jr. resident in pediatrics Children's Hosp., Honolulu, 1962-63; asst. resident in pediatrics Children's Hosp. Med. Ctr., Boston, 1963-64, asst. in mental retardation, 1967-68, assoc. in mental retardation, 1968-75, dir. Down Syndrome Program, 1970-75, dir. PKU Clinic, 1972-75; sr. resident in pediatrics Montreal Children's Hosp., 1964-65, fellow in biochemical genetics/metabolism, 1965-66; assoc. physician R.I. Hosp., Providence, 1975-79, dir. child devel. ctr., 1975-94, dir. PKU and Amino Acid Program, 1975—, dir. Down Syndrome Program, 1978—, physician, 1979—; instr. pediatrics Harvard U., Cambridge, Mass., 1968-74, asst. prof. in pediatrics, 1974-75, lectr. in pediatrics, 1975—; asst. prof. in pediatrics Brown U., Providence, 1975-77, assoc. prof. in pediatrics, 1977-85, prof. in pediatrics, 1985—; consulting pediatrician Waltham (Mass.) Hosp., 1968-75; cons. in genetics Lying in Hosp., Boston, 1969-75, Women and Infants Hosp., Providence, 1975—; cons. Devel. Evaluation Clinic Children's Hosp. Med. Ctr., Boston, 1975—; mem. prevention of mental retardation com. Internat. League of Socs. for Persons with Mental Handicaps; mem. rsch., prevention and program svc. com. Assn. for Retarded Citizens U.S.; mem. nat. conf. on rsch. perspectives in down syndrome Nat. Inst. Child Health and Rehab. Svcs.; mem. state-of-the-art conf. on down syndrome Office Spl. Edn. and Rehab. Svcs. U.S. Dept. Edn.; mem. nat. adv. child health and human devel. coun. NIH, Washington; mem. sub-com. on tng., edn. and quality assurance-tech. assistance Devel. Disabilities Coun., R.I.; mem. med. adv. com. Spl. Olympics. Author chpts. to books; mem. editl. bd. Down Syndrome Papers and Abstracts for Profls., Exceptional Parents, Down's Syndrome: Rsch. and Practice; reviewer numerous jours.; contbr. articles to profl. jours. Grantee Mass. Dept. Health, 1968, Vigneron Meml. Fund, 1984-85, Charlotte Taylor Fund, 1985-86, Dept. Health and Human Svcs., 1982-86, March of Dimes Nat. Found., 1987-89, Sigma-Tau Pharm., Inc., 1990-93; recipient Recongnition award March of Dimes, 1976, Recognition award Blackstone Valley chpt. R.I. Assn. for Retarded Citizens, 1979, Fogarty Founders award, 1988, Edn. award Muscular Dystrophy Assn., 1985, 86, Muscular Dystrophy Tchg. award, 1988, Recognition award Devel. Ctr. for Handicapped Personsn-Utah State U., 1986, Down Syndrome Assn. of Greater Cin. award, 1986, Colegion John Langdown Down award Mexico City, 1987, Disting. Rsch. award Assn. for Retarded Citizens of U.S., 1990, Conn. Down Syndrome Assn. award, 1991, Sindrome de Down award Asociación Down de Monterrey (Mexico), 1994. Fellow Am. Acad. Pediatrics, Am. Coll. Med. Genetics (founder); mem. AAAS, Am. Assn. Mental Retardation (Profl. Contbn. award 1991), Am. Acad. Cerebral Palsy and Devel. Medicine, Am. Pediatric Soc., Am. Soc. Human Genetics, Nat. Down Syndrome Congress (past pres., Recognition for Disting. Svc. award 1980, Mid-Hudson Valley award 1983, Achievement in Rsch. award 1988, Outstanding Physician award 1991), N.Y. Acad. Sci., R.I. Med. Soc., New Eng. Regional Genetics Group, Soc. Inherited Metabolic Disorders, Down Syndrome Soc. R.I. (award 1985), Assn. for Children with Down Syndrome (bd. dirs.). Office: RI Hosp Child Devel Ctr 593 Eddy St Providence RI 02903-4923

PUFFER, RICHARD JUDSON, retired college chancellor; b. Chgo., Aug. 20, 1931; s. Noble Judson and Lillian Katherine (Olson) P.; m. Alison Foster Cope, June 28, 1952; children—Lynn, Mark, Andrew. Ph.B., Ill. Wesleyan U., 1953; M.S. in Edn, Ill. State U., 1962; PhD (Roy Clark Meml. scholar), Northwestern U., 1967. Asst. plant supt. J.A. Olson Co., Winona, Miss., 1957-59; tchr. Leroy Community Unit Dist. (Ill.), 1959-60; tchr., prin. Community Unit, Dist. 7, Lexington, Ill., 1960-62; asst. county supt. schs. Cook County, Ill., 1962-65; dean arts and scis. Kirkwood Community Coll., Cedar Rapids, Iowa, 1967-69; v.p. Black Hawk Coll., Moline, Ill., 1969-77; pres. Black Hawk Coll., 1977-82, chancellor, 1982-87; pres. The Ark Computer Ctr., 1989-92; dir. W. Ctrl. Ill. Ednl. TV Corp., Springfield, Ill., 1977-87; cons. examiner North Central Assn., 1978-87. Editor: Cook County Ednl. Digest, 1962-65. Bd. dirs. Cedar Rapids Symphony, 1967-69, United Way of Rock Island and Scott Counties, Ill., 1978-80, Unitarian Universalist Dist. Mich.; sec., treas. Ill. Ednl. Retirement Cts., 1987-91; vice-chmn. Illini Hosp. Bd., 1988-93, chmn., 1993-95; bd. dirs. Illowa coun. Boy Scouts Am., 1979-83, v.p., 1981-83. With USNR, 1953-57. Mem. Rotary (pres. 1975-76, East Moline, Ill.), Green Medallion, Blue Key, Phi Delta Kappa, Pi Gamma Mu. Home and Office: 6191 Grace Ave Ludington MI 49431-9639

PUGAY, JEFFREY IBANEZ, mechanical engineer; b. San Francisco, June 26, 1958; s. Herminio Salazar and Petronila (Ibanez) P. BSME, U. Calif., Berkeley, 1981, MSME, 1982; MBA, Pepperdine U., 1986, MS in Tech. Mgmt., 1991. Registered profl. engr., Calif. Engring. asst. Lawrence Berkeley Nat. Lab., 1978-80; assoc. tech. staff Aerospace Corp., L.A., 1981; tech. staff Hughes Space & Comm. Co., El Segundo, Calif., 1982-85, from project engr. to project mgr., 1985-95; mgr. spaceway program mktg. Hughes Comm. Inc., Long Beach, Calif., 1995-97, dir. bus. devel., 1997—. Active ARC Emergency Svcs. White House Fellow regional finalist, 1991, 92. Mem. ASME, Soc. Competitor Intelligence Profls., Am. Mgmt. Assn., L.A. World Affairs Coun., Make A Wish Found., Pi Tau Sigma, Delta Mu Delta. Republican. Roman Catholic. Avocations: racquetball, scuba diving, sailing, backpacking, volleyball. Home: 8180 Manitoba St Apt 120 Playa Del Rey CA 90293-8651 Office: Hughes Comms Inc PO Box 9712 Long Beach CA 90810-9928

PUGH, DOROTHY GUNTHER, ballet company executive; b. Memphis, May 8, 1951. Grad. magna cum laude, Vanderbilt U., 1973; studied with Raymond Clay, studied with Donna Carver, studied with David Howard; student, Royal Acad. Dancing, London. Founder, artistic dir. Ballet Memphis. Mem. AIDS Consortium Com.; mem. fine arts com. St. Agnes Acad. Recipient Woman of Achievement award for Initiative, 1987; featured as one of city's influential citizens in Memphis Mag. Office: Ballet Memphis 4569 Summer Ave Memphis TN 38122

PUGH, EMERSON WILLIAM, electrical engineer; b. Pasadena, Calif., May 1, 1929; s. Emerson Martindale and Ruth Hazel (Edgin) P.; m. Elizabeth Burnam Russell; children: William Russell, Sarah Elizabeth, David Emerson. BS in Physics, Carnegie Mellon U., 1951, PhD in Physics, 1956. Asst. prof. physics Carnegie Mellon U., Pitts., 1956-57; with IBM, 1957-93, rsch. staff mem. rsch. div., Poughkeepsie, N.Y., 1957-61, engring. mgr. components div., 1962-65, group dir. data processing group, Harrison, N.Y., 1965-66, dir. tech. planning rsch. div., Yorktown Heights, N.Y., 1966-68, asst. to v.p. IBM Corp., Armonk, N.Y., 1968-71, rsch. mgr. rsch. div., Yorktown Heights, 1971-85, mgr. tech. history, 1985-93; vis. scientist IBM Lab., Zurich, Switzerland, 1961-62; mem. United Engring. Trustees Bd., N.Y.C., 1986-92; mem. Engring. Soc. Libr. Bd., N.Y.C., 1986-89; trustee Chalres Babbage Found., 1990—. Author: Principles of Electricity and Magnetism, 1960, Memories That Shaped an Industry, 1984, IBM's Early Computers, 1986, IBM's 360 and Early 370 Systems, 1991, Building IBM, 1995; also articles; 10 patents. Fellow IEEE (v.p. 1986-87, pres. 1989, chmn. friends com. Ctr. for History Elec. Engring. 1991-94, chmn. history com. 1995—, dir. found. bd. 1996—), AAAS, Am. Phys. Soc. Home: 3 Rock St Cold Spring NY 10516-2911

PUGH, GEORGE WILLARD, law educator; b. Napoleonville, La., Aug. 17, 1925; s. William Whitmell and Evelyn (Foley) P.; m. Jean Earle Hemphill, Sept. 6, 1952; children: William Whitmell III, George Willard, David Nicholls, James Hemphill. B.A., La. State U., 1947, J.D., 1950; J.S.D., Yale U., 1952; Dr. h.c., U. Aix-Marseille III, France, 1984. Bar: La. 1950. Instr. La. State U. Law Sch., 1950, mem. faculty, 1952-94, prof. law, 1959-94, Julius B. Nachman prof. law, 1984-94; prof. law emeritus, 1994—; faculty summer session abroad U. Thessaloniki Greece summer 1974, Aix-en-Provence, France, 1985; mem. faculty summer program U. San Diego, Paris, 1977; part-time rsch. cons. La. State Law Inst., 1953-54; 1st jud. adminstr. Jud. Coun. Supreme Ct. La., 1954-56; vis. prof. U. Tex., summer 1961; vis. Doherty prof. law U. Va., 1966-67; mem. faculty orientation program in Am. law Assn. Am. Law Schs., 1968, law teaching clinic, summer 1969; vis. prof. U. Aix-Marseille III, France, 1983, fall 1987, U. Catholique de Louvain, Belgium, fall 1987; cons. La. State U.S. Vietnam Legal Adminstrn. Project, 1969. Author: Louisiana Evidence Law, 1974, supplement, 1978; co-author: Cases and Materials on the Adminstration of Criminal Justice, 2d edit., 1969, Handbook on Louisiana Evidence Law, 1989, 9th edit., 1997; coord., reporter Code of Evidence for La., 1981-95. Bd. dirs. Legal Aid Soc. Baton Rouge, 1965-89, chmn., 1963-64; adv. bd. St. Alban's Episcopal Student Ctr., La. State U., 1965-68, 70-72. Served with AUS, World War II. Fellow Comparative Study Adminstrn. Justice, 1962-65. Mem. Am., La., Baton Rouge bar assns., Order of Coif, Omicron Delta Kappa, Lambda Chi Alpha. Democrat. Episcopalian. Home: 167 Sunset Blvd Baton Rouge LA 70808-5073

PUGH, GRACE HUNTLEY, artist; b. Schenectady, N.Y., Sept. 25, 1912; d. Grant and Grace La Vallée (Lake) Huntley; m. Cresson Pugh, Sept. 21, 1940; 1 child, Gigi Grace Huntley Pugh Sundstrom. Student, Wellesley Coll., 1930-32; BA, Barnard Coll., 1934; postgrad., Nat. Acad. Design, 1934-36, Art Students League, 1938. Head art dept., artist in residence Briarcliff Jr. Coll., Briarcliff Manor, N.Y., 1936-40; mem. staff directions in Am. painting exhibit Carnegie Inst., Pitts., 1942-44; asst. art dir. Young & Rubicam Inc., N.Y.C., 1946-50; painting instr. Westchester County Workshop, White Plains, N.Y., 1961-63; chair fine arts and exhbn. Mamaroneck (N.Y.) Libr., 1950-88; co-chair Emelin Theatre Street Fair, Mamaroneck, 1975-81; fine arts advisor, artist in residence Village of Mamaroneck, 1977—. Exhibited oil and watercolor paintings in numerous group and one-woman shows including Nat. Acad. Design, N.Y.C., 1957, N.Y. State Painters, N.Y. State bldg. in World's Fair, 1965, Franklin & Marshall Colls., 1974, Carnegie Inst., 1950, Canton Art Inst., Ohio, 1995, Canton (Ohio) Art Inst., 1995, Kinderhook (N.Y.) Lib., 1971 many others; Editor Mamaroneck Historical Society Newsletter, 1980—. Charter pres. Mamaroneck Hist. Soc., 1980-82, trustee emerita, 1980—; 1st chair Landmarks Adv. Com. Village of Mamaroneck, 1982-92, co-chair cherry blossom festival centennial com., 1993—; trustee Friends of Wildlife Sanctuary, Rye, N.Y., 1990—; founding pres. Mamaroneck Artists Guild, 1953-55; founding sec. Westchester Soc. Archeol. Inst. of Am., 1976-78. Day named in her honor Village of Mamaroneck, 1982, 91. Mem. Am. Watercolor Soc., Rockport Art Assn. (Longfellow award 1944), Federated Conservationists of Westchester County (Cert. of Appreciation 1991), DAR (conservation chair 1982-88, mus. chair 1997—). Republican. Episcopalian. Avocations: swimming, gardening, community service, research, sailing. Home: 823 Stuart Ave Mamaroneck NY 10543-4122

PUGH, JOYE JEFFRIES, educational administrator; b. Ocilla, Ga., Jan. 23, 1957; d. Claude Bert and Stella Elizabeth (Paulk) Jeffries; m. Melville Eugene Pugh, Sept. 21, 1985. AS in Pre-law, S. Ga. Coll., 1978; BS in Edn., Valdosta State Coll., 1980, MEd in Psychology, Guidance and Counseling, 1981; EdD in Adminstrn., Nova U., Ft. Lauderdale, Fla., 1992. Cert. tchr., adminstr., supr., Ga. Pers. adminstr. TRW, Inc., Douglas, Ga., 1981-83; recreation dir. Ocilla (Ga.), Irwin Recreation Dept., 1983-84; exec. dir. Sunny Dale Tng. Ctr., Inc., Ocilla, 1984-96; pres. and registered agt. Irwin County Resources, Inc., Ocilla, 1988-97, Camelot Ct., Inc., 1994-97. Contbr. articles on handicapped achievements to newspapers, mags. (Ga. Spl. Olympics News Media award, 1987, Assn. for Retarded Citizens News Media award, 1988). Mem. adv. bd. Area 12 Spl. Olympics, Douglas, Ga., 1984-88; pres. Irwin County Spl. Olympics, 1984-97, mem. adv. task force Spl. Olympics Internat. for 6-7 yr. olds, 1995—; bd. dirs. Ga. Spl. Olympics, 1995-98, mem. comm. and mktg. com., 1995-96, mem. nominations com., 1997—; exec. dir., fund raising chmn. Irwin Assn. for Retarded Citizens, Ocilla, 1984-97; arts and crafts chmn. Ga. Sweet Tater Trot 5k/1 Mile Rd. Races, 1993-97; founder, chmn. Joseph Mascolo Celebrity Events, 1985—. Recipient Spirit of Spl. Olympics award Ga. Spl. Olymics, Atlanta, 1986, Cmty. Svc. award Ga. Assn. for Retarded Citizens, Atlanta, 1987, Govs.' Vol. award Ga. Vol. Awards, Atlanta, 1988, Presdl. Sports award AAU, Indpls., 1988, Humanitarian award Sunny Dale Tng. Ctr., Inc., Ocilla, 1988, Golden Poet award New Am. Poetry Anthology, 1988, Outstanding Coach-Athlete Choice award Sunny Dale Spl. Olympics, Ocilla, 1992, Dist. Coach award, 1993, Outstanding Unified Sports Ptnr. of Yr. award, 1995, Coach of Yr. award, 1996; carried Olympic Torch, Ocilla, Ga., 1996; Ga. Spl. Olympics State Gold medalist Golf Unified Team, 1996, State Silver medalist Unified Table Tennis Team, 1996, State Bronze medalist Master's Unified Softball Team, 1995. Mem. DAR, Mut. Unidentified Flying Object Network (Ga. state sect. dir., asst. state dir.), Ga. State Assn. for Retarded Citizens, Ctrs. Dirs. Ga., Ocilla Rotary Club (program dir. 1995-97, bd. dirs. 1995-97, sec. 1996-97), Sunny Dale Unified Track Club (founder 1991), Sunny Dale Ensemble (founder), Ocilla/Irwin County C. of C., Irwin Assn. Retarded Citizens Inc. Baptist. Avocations: playing musical instruments, jet skiing, weight lifting, dancing, singing. Home: 201 Lakeside Cir Douglas GA 31535

PUGH, KEITH E., JR., lawyer; b. L.A., Mar. 17, 1937; s. Keith Emerson and Serena (Reynolds) P.; m. Kathleen Perry, Aug. 28, 1958 (div. Mar. 1973); children—Linda, Lisa, Scott; m. Pamela Carolyn Winberry, May 20, 1973; children—Alexander, Caroline. Student, Principia Coll., 1955-58; J.D., U. So. Calif., 1962. Bar: Calif. 1962, D.C. 1969, U.S. Supreme Ct. 1976, U.S. Ct. Internat. Trade 1983, U.S. Ct. Appeals (fed. cir.) 1994. Dep. atty. gen. antitrust sect. Office Calif. Atty. Gen., San Francisco, 1962-65; assoc. Broad, Busterud & Khourie, San Francisco, 1965-66, Office Joseph Alioto, San Francisco, 1966-68, Howrey & Simon, Washington, 1968-69; ptnr. Howrey & Simon, 1970—, also mem. mgmt., 1980—. Mem. ABA, Fed. Cir. Bar Assn., State Bar Calif., D.C. Bar Assn., Annapolis Yacht Club, Capitol City Club, Ocean Reef Club, Phi Delta Phi. Avocation: boating. Home: 3939 Fordham Rd NW Washington DC 20016-1937 Office: Howrey & Simon 1299 Pennsylvania Ave NW Washington DC 20004-2400

PUGH, LAWRENCE R., apparel executive; b. Jan. 22, 1933; m. Jean Pugh; 2 children. Grad., Colby Coll., 1956. Div. sales mgr. Borden Inc., 1958-66; product mgr., gen. mktg. mgr. Hamilton Beach Co., 1966-70; dir. mktg. Ampex Corp., 1970-72; group pres. Beatrice Foods Co., 1972-80; pres. V.F. Corp., Wyomissing, Pa., 1980-83, chmn., chief exec. officer, 1983-96; chmn. bd. V.F. Corp., Wyomissing, 1996—. Office: VF Corp 1047 N Park Rd Wyomissing PA 19610-1339*

PUGH, MARION STIRLING, archaeologist, author; b. Middletown, N.Y., May 12, 1911; d. Louis and Lena May (Randall) Illig; m. Matthew Williams Stirling, Dec. 11, 1933 (dec. 1975); children: Matthew Williams, Jr. (dec.), Ariana Stirling Withers; m. John Ramsey Pugh, Aug. 7, 1977 (dec. Mar. 1994). BS, Rider Coll., 1930; postgrad. George Washington U., 1931-33. Office sec. Bur. Am. Ethnology, Smithsonian Instn., Washington, 1931-33; archaeologist with Matthew W. Stirling, Fla., 1934-38, Smithsonian Instn.-Nat. Geog. Soc. archeol. expdn. Mex., 1939-46, Panama, 1948-53, Ecuador, 1957, Costa Rica, 1962. Author: (with Matthew Stirling) Tarqui, an Early Site in Manabi, Ecuador, 1962, El Limon, an Early Tomb Site in Cocle Province, Panama, 1963, Archaeological Notes on Almirante Bay, Bocas del Toro, Panama, 1963, The Archeology of Taboga, Uraba and Taboguilla Islands, Panama, 1963; contbr. articles to Nat. Geog. mag. and Ames. mag. Trustee The Textile Mus., Washington, 1968—, pres. 1984-87. Co-recipient Franklyn L. Burr award Nat. Geog. Soc., 1941, Dist. Svc. medal Peruvian Embassy, 1985. Fellow Am. Anthrop. Assn., Gen. Div. Anthropology; mem. Am. Ethnol. Soc., Soc. Latin Am. Anthropology, Washington

Anthrop. Soc., Washington Acad. Sci., Soc. Woman Geographers (pres. 1960-63, 69-72, mem. exec. council 1954-74, Gold medal 1975). Avocations: swimming, textiles. Home: 20351 Airmont Rd Round Hill VA 20141

PUGH, RICHARD CRAWFORD, lawyer; b. Phila., Apr. 28, 1929; s. William and Myrtle P.; m. Nanette Bannen, Feb. 27, 1954; children: Richard Crawford, Andrew Lembert, Catherine Elizabeth. AB summa cum laude, Dartmouth Coll., 1951; BA in Jurisprudence, Oxford (Eng.) U., 1953; LLB, Columbia U., 1958. Bar: N.Y. 1958. Assoc. firm Cleary, Gottlieb, Steen & Hamilton, N.Y.C., 1958-61; ptnr. Cleary, Gottlieb, Steen & Hamilton, 1969-89, counsel, 1989—; disting. prof. law U. San Diego, 1989—; mem. faculty Law Sch. Columbia U., 1961-89, prof., 1964-69, adj. prof., 1969-89; lectr. Columbia-Amsterdam-Leyden (Netherlands) summer program Am. law, 1963, 79; dep. asst. atty. gen. tax div. U.S. Dept. Justice, 1966-68; Cons. fiscal and fin. br. UN Secretariat, 1962, 64. Editor: Columbia Law Rev., 1957-58; editor: (with W. Friedmann) Legal Aspects of Foreign Investment, 1959, (with others) International Law, 1993, Taxation of International Transactions, 1996, Taxation of Business Enterprises, 1995. Served with USNR, 1954-56. Rhodes scholar, 1953. Mem. ABA, Am. Law Inst., Am. Coll. Tax Counsel, Am. Soc. Internat. Law, Internat. Fiscal Assn. (pres. U.S. br. 1978-79). Home: 7335 Encelia Dr La Jolla CA 92037-5729 Office: Univ San Diego Sch Law Alcala Park San Diego CA 92110-2429

PUGH, RODERICK WELLINGTON, psychologist, educator; b. Richmond, Ky., June 1, 1919; s. George Wilmer and Lena Bernetta (White) P.; m. Harriet Elizabeth Rogers, Aug. 29, 1953 (div. 1955). B.A., Fisk U., 1940; M.A., Ohio State U., 1941; Ph.D., U. Chgo., 1949. Diplomate: Am. Bd. Profl. Psychology. Instr. Albany (Ga.) State Coll., 1941-43; psychology trainee VA, Chgo., 1947-49; lectr. Roosevelt U., Chgo., 1951-54; staff clin. psychologist VA Hosp., Hines, Ill., 1950-54, asst. chief psychologist for psychotherapy, 1954-58, chief clin. psychology sect., 1958-60, supervising psychologist, coord. psychol. internship tng., 1960-66; pvt. practice clin. psychology Chgo., 1958—; assoc. prof. psychology Loyola U., Chgo., 1966-73, prof., 1973-88, emeritus prof. psychology, 1989—; Cons. St. Mary of the Lake Sem., Niles, Ill., 1965-66, Ill. Div. Vocational Rehab., 1965-82, Center for Inner City Studies, Northeastern State U., Chgo., 1966-67, VA Psychology Tng. Program, 1966—, Am. Psychol. Assn. and Nat. Inst. Mental Health Vis. Psychologists Program, 1966-89; juvenile problems research rev. com. NIMH, 1970-74; cons. Center for Minority Group Mental Health Programs, 1975-77, cons. psychology edn. br., 1978-82; lectr. U. Ibadan, Nigeria, 1978; Mem. profl. adv. com. Div. Mental Health, City of Chgo., 1979-82; mem. adv. com. U.S. Army Command and Gen. Staff Coll., 1981-83. Author: Psychology and the Black Experience, 1972; Contbr.: chpt. in Black Psychology, 1972; Cons. editor: Contemporary Psychology, 1975-79; contbr. articles to profl. jours. Sec. bd. trustees Fisk U., 1968-78. Served to 2d lt. AUS, 1943-46, ETO. Vis. scholar Fisk U., 1966, vis. prof. in psychology, 1994. Fellow Am. Psychol. Soc., Am. Psychol. Assn. (nat. adv. panel to Civilian Health and Med. Program of Uniformed Services 1980-83, joint coun. on profl. edn. in psychology 1988-90); mem. Midwestern Psychol. Assn., Ill. Psychol. Assn. (chmn. legis. com. 1961, council mem. 1960-62, Disting. Psychologist award 1988), Soc. for Psychol. Study Social Issues, Assn. Behavior Analysis, AAUP, Sigma Xi, Alpha Phi Alpha, Psi Chi. Home: 5201 S Cornell Ave Chicago IL 60615-4207 Office: 30 N Michigan Ave Chicago IL 60602 also: Loyola U 6525 N Sheridan Rd Chicago IL 60626-5311

PUGH, THOMAS DOERING, architecture educator; b. Jacksonville, Fla., May 27, 1948; s. William Edward Jr. and Lina Lillian (Doering) P.; m. Virginia Margaret McRae, June 14, 1972; children: Rachel McRae, Jordan Faith, Nathan Calder. B in Design, U. Fla., 1971, MA in Architecture, 1974. Asst. prof. architecture U. Ark., Fayetteville, 1976-78; pres. Thomas D. Pugh Constrn. Co., Inc., Fayetteville, Ark., 1978-87; assoc. prof. Fla. A&M U. Sch. Architecture, Tallahassee, 1987—; interim dir. Inst. Bldg. Scis. Fla. Argl. and Mech. U., Tallahassee, 1991-93, dir., 1993—; vis. rsch. fellow Tech. U. Eindhoven, The Netherlands, 1993-94; chmn. radon adv. bd. Fla. State U. Sys., 1988-94; mem. Fla. Coordinating Coun. on Radon Protection; juror Progressive Arch.-AIA Nat. Archtl. Rsch. Awards, 1995; mem. rsch. policy bd. AIA/Assn. Collegiate Schs. of Arch., 1996—; mem. edn. com. Odyssey Sci. Ctr., Tallahassee, 1995—. Bd. dir. Tallahassee Habitat for Humanity, 1987-92; crew leader Habitat for Humanity Internat., Americus, Ga., 1988, 90. Recipient Bronze medal Fla. Assn. AIA, Gainesville, 1975; Named Vol. of Yr. Tallahassee Dem. and Vol. Tallahassee, Inc., 1991. Mem. ASCE (sec. spl. task com. radon mitigation 1990-91), Assn. Collegiate Schs. Architecture (coun. on archtl. rsch. 1994). Democrat. Lutheran. Avocations: sailing, woodworking. Office: Fla A&M Univ Sch Architecture 1936 S Martin Luther King Jr B Tallahassee FL 32301-4257

PUGH, THOMAS WILFRED, lawyer; b. St. Paul, Minn., Aug. 3, 1949; s. Thomas Leslie and Joann Marie (Tauer) P.; m. Susan Elizabeth Beattie, Sept. 12, 1971; children: Aimee Elizabeth, Douglas Thomas. AB cum laude, Dartmouth Coll., 1971; JD cum laude, U. Minn., 1976. Assoc. Thuet & Lynch, South St. Paul, 1976-79; ptnr. Thuet, Lynch & Pugh, South St. Paul, 1980-85; atty., pres. Thuet, Pugh & Rogosheske, Ltd., South St. Paul, 1986—; mem. Minn. Ho. of Reps., St. Paul, 1989—; mem. Supreme Ct. Task Force Conciliation Ct., St. Paul, 1992, Dakota County Tech. Coll. Adv. Bd., 1991—. Bd. dirs. Wakota Arena, South St. Paul, 1984-87; pres. Luther Meml. Ch., South St. Paul, 1983-84. Daniel Webster scholar Dartmouth Coll., 1970, Rufus Choate scholar, 1971. Mem. Minn. State Bar Assn., 1st Dist. Bar Assn., Ducks Unltd., Pheasants Forever, South St. Paul C. of C. (local issues chair 1982, Dedicated Svc. award 1983), South St. Paul Jaycees (pres. 1978-79, Key award 1979), Lions. Lutheran. Avocations: tennis, golf, hunting, fishing, reading. Office: Thuet Pugh & Rogosheske 833 Southview Blvd South Saint Paul MN 55075-2237

PUGH, WILLIAM WHITMELL HILL, lawyer; b. Baton Rouge, La., June 25, 1954; s. George Willard and Jean (Hemphill) P.; m. Beth Smith, Mar. 12, 1983; children: Brendan Kelly, Bryan Clayton, Katharine Elaine. BA, U. Va., 1976; JD, La. State U., 1979. Bar: La. 1979, U.S. Supreme Ct. 1986, U.S. Ct. Appeals (5th and 11th cirs.) 1983. Law clk. to presiding justice U.S. Ct. Appeals (5th cir.), New Orleans, 1979-80. Editor-in-chief La. Law Rev., 1978-79. Mem. Maritime Law Assn., La. Assn. Def. Counsel, La. State Bar Assn., La. State Law Inst. (young lawyers rep. 1988-91, mem. 1992—). Office: Liskow & Lewis One Shell Sq 50th Fl New Orleans LA 70139-5001

PUGLIESE, KAREN OLSEN, freelance public relations counsel; b. S.I., N.Y., Aug. 20, 1963; d. Harold Birger and Janet Mildred (Cronk) Olsen; m. John Michael Pugliese Jr., Oct. 21, 1989; 1 child, Emily Olsen. BA in Polit. Sci., Union Coll., 1985. Asst. editor Food Mgmt. mag., N.Y.C., 1985-86; account exec. Edelman Pub. Rels., N.Y.C., 1986-87; account exec., sr. v.p., group dir. Creamer Dickson Basford, N.Y.C., 1987-96; freelance pub. rels. counsel, Darien, Conn., 1996—. Recipient Gold Quill, Internat. Assn. Bus. Communicators, 1991, award Internat. Pub. Rels. Soc., 1993, Creativity in Pub. Rels., Inside PR, 1993. Republican. Avocations: tennis, reading, walking.

PUGLIESE, MARIA ALESSANDRA, psychiatrist; b. Phila., Sept. 16, 1948; d. Peter Francis and Ida Agnes (Rosa) P.; m. J. Paul Hieble, Sept. 14, 1985; children: Helen Elisa Hieble, Jesse Paul Hieble. BS, Chestnut Hill Coll., 1970; MD, U. Pa., 1974. Diplomate Am. Bd. Psychiatry and Neurology; with added qualifications in addiction psychiatry. Intern in pediatrics Children's Hosp. of Phila., 1974-75; resident in psychiatry Inst. Pa. Hosp., Phila., 1975-78, attending psychiatrist, 1978-97; attending psychiatrist Malvern (Pa.) Inst., 1982—, Pa. Hosp., 1997—. Office: 111 N 49th St Philadelphia PA 19139-2718

PUGLIESE, ROBERT FRANCIS, lawyer, business executive; b. West Pittston, Pa., Jan. 15, 1933. BS, U. Scranton, 1954; LLB, Georgetown U., 1957, LLM, 1959; grad. advanced mgmt. program Harvard U., 1976. Bar: D.C. 1957, U.S. Dist. Ct. 1957, U.S. Ct. Claims 1958, U.S. Tax Ct. 1957, U.S. Ct. Appeals 1957. Assoc. Hedrick & Lane, Washington, 1957-60; tax counsel Westinghouse Electric Corp., Pitts., 1961-70, gen. tax counsel, 1970-75, v.p., gen. tax counsel, 1975-76, v.p., gen. counsel, sec., 1976-86, sr. v.p., 1987, exec. v.p., 1988-92; spl. counsel Eckert, Seamans, Cherin & Mellott, Pitts., 1993—; bd. dirs. OCWEN Asset Investment Corp. Mem. exec. com. U. Scranton; bd. dirs. St. Clair Meml. Hosp. Mem. Assn. Gen. Counsel. Office: Eckert Seamans Cherin & Mellott 600 Grant St Ste 42 Pittsburgh PA 15219-2703

PUGLISI, PHILIP JAMES, electrical engineer; b. Paterson, N.J., Feb. 26, 1943; s. Philip James and Josephine Theresa (Guido) P.; children: Brent, Tara. BEE, Poly. U., 1971; MEE, Stanford U., 1972. Researcher, mem. staff Bell Telephone Labs., Whippanny, N.J., 1967-77; chief engr. Dionex Corp., Sunnyvale, Calif., 1977-80; engrng. supr. AT&T Microelectronics, Lees Summit, Mo., 1980-83, with semiconductor design dept., 1983-86, mktg. mgr., 1986-91; dir. engrng. PPG Biomed. Systems, Lenexa, Kans., 1991-93; product mgr.- optics AT&T (now Lucent Techs.), Lee's Summit, Mo., 1993-96; global product mgr. optical connectors AT&T, Lee's Summit, Mo., 1994-96; exec. recruiter tech. Aureus Group, Omaha, 1997—; mem. exec. com. Optical Data Link Forum, Murry Hill, N.J., 1987-91; cons. for optical interconnection. Contbr. articles to profl. jours. Organizing parent Dist. and State Music Festival, Springfield & Columbia, Mo., 1984-88; bd. dirs. Dist. Water Com., Grovespring, Mo., 1987-88; scoutmaster Boy Scouts Am., Bonny Doon, Calif., 1976-79. With USN, 1960-64. Mem. ISHM, Electronic Industries Assn. (mem. optical comm. com. 1987-91). Avocations: pocket billiards, home computing, carpentry, Shared Heart Foundation, country dancing. Home: 405 Cline St Pleasant Hill MO 64080-1805 Office: Aureus Group 1126 S 72nd St Omaha NE 68124-1605

PUGSLEY, FRANK BURRUSS, lawyer; b. Kansas City, Mo., Apr. 3, 1920; s. Charles Silvey and Emma (Burruss) P.; m. Aline East, May 7, 1943; children—John, Susan Pugsley Patterson, Nancy Pugsley Young. B.S. in Mech. Engring, U. Tex., Austin, 1942; J.D., DePaul U., Chgo., 1950. Bar: Ill. 1950, Tex. 1953, U.S. Supreme Ct. 1960. Engr. Gen. Electric Co., Schenectady, 1946-50; patent atty. Gen. Electric Co., 1950-52; assoc. Baker & Botts, Houston, 1952-60; ptnr. Baker & Botts, 1960-84, sr. ptnr., 1974-84; lectr. Southwestern Legal Found., Practising Law Inst., Bur. Nat. Affairs Conf. Contbr. articles to legal jours. Trustee West Univ. Methodist Ch., Houston, 1959-65; bd. dirs. St. Stephens Episcopal Day Sch., 1960-62; adminstrv. bd. St. Luke's United Meth. Ch., 1981-83. Served to lt. USNR, 1942-46. Fellow Tex. Bar Found.; mem. ABA (chmn. intellectual property law sec. 1980-81), Am. Intellectual Property Law Assn. (pres. 1966-67), Tex. Bar Assn. (chmn. intellectual property law sect. 1960-61), Houston Bar Assn., Petroleum Club, Frisch Auf! Valley Country Club, Friars. Home: 3602 Nottingham St Houston TX 77005-2221 Office: 3000 One Shell Plz Houston TX 77002

PUGSLEY, ROBERT ADRIAN, legal educator; b. Mineola, N.Y., Dec. 27, 1946; s. Irvin Harold and Mary Catherine (Brusselars) P. BA, SUNY-Stony Brook, 1968; JD, NYU, 1975, LLM in Criminal Justice, 1977. Instr. sociology New Sch. Social Rsch., N.Y.C., 1969-71; coordinator Peace Edn. programs The Christophers, N.Y.C., 1971-78; assoc. prof. law Southwestern U., L.A., 1978-81, prof., 1981—; adj. asst. prof. criminology and criminal justice Southampton Coll.-Long Island U., 1975-76; acting dep. dir. Criminal Law Edn. and Rsch. Ctr., NYU, 1983-86; bd. advisors Ctr. Legal Edn. CCNY-CUNY, 1978, Sta. KPFK-FM, 1985-86; founder, coordinator The Wednesday Evening Soc., L.A., 1979-86; vis. prof. Jacob D. Fuchsberg Law Ctr. Touro Coll., L.I., N.Y., summers 1988, 89; lectr. in criminal law and procedure Legal Edn. Conf. Ctr., L.A., 1982-96; lectr. Comparative Criminal Law and Procedure Inst., U. B.C., Vancouver, summer, 1994; lectr. legal profl. responsibility West Bar Rev. Faculty, Calif., 1996—; legal analyst/commentator for print and electronic media, 1992—. Creative advisor Christopher Closeup (nationally syndicated pub. svc. TV program), 1975-83; host Earth Alert, Cable TV, 1983-87; producer, moderator (pub. affairs discussion program) Inside L.A., Sta. KPFK-FM, 1979-86, Open Jour. program, Sta. KPFK-FM, 1991-94; contbr. articles to legal jours. Founding mem. Southwestern U. Pub. Interest Law com., 1992—; mem. L.A. County Bar Assn. Adv. Com. on Alcohol & Drug Abuse, 1991-95, co-chair, 1993-95; mem. exec. com. non-govtl. orgns. UN Office of Pub. Info., 1977; mem. issues task force L.A. Conservancy, 1980-81, seminar for law tchrs. NEH UCLA, 1979; co-convener So. Calif. Coalition Against Death Penalty, 1981-83, convener, 1983-84; mem. death penalty com. Lawyer's Support Group, Amnesty Internat. U.S.A.; founding mem. Ch.-State Coun., L.A., 1984-88. Robert Marshall fellow Criminal Law Edn. and Rsch. Ctr., NYU Sch. Law, 1976-78; bd. dirs. Equal Rights Sentencing Found., 1983-85, Earth Alert Inc., 1984-87; mem. adv. bd. First Amendment Info. Resources Ctr., Grad. Sch. of Libr. and Info. Sci., UCLA, 1990—; mem. coun. Friends UCLA Libr., 1993—, pres., 1996—. Mem. Am. Legal Studies Assn., Am. Soc. Polit. and Legal Philosophy, Assn. Am. Law Schs., Inst. Soc. Ethics and Life Scis., Soc. Am. Law Tchrs., Internat. Platform Assn., The Scribes. Democrat. Roman Catholic. Office: Southwestern U Sch Law 675 S Westmoreland Ave Rm 410 Los Angeles CA 90005-3905 Address: PO Box 440 East Hampton NY 11937

PUHALA, JAMES JOSEPH, lawyer; b. Pitts., Sept. 5, 1942; s. Leo Andrew and Agnes (Ruglovsky) P.; m. Linda Sue Lash, Oct. 1, 1977; children: Stephen, Susan, Matthew. BBA, U. Dayton, 1964; MBA, U. Pitts., 1965; JD, Duquesne U., 1974. Bar: Pa. 1974, U.S. Dist. Ct. (we. dist.) Pa. 1974. Mgr. internat. taxes Dravo Corp., Pitts., 1974-79, sr. counsel, 1979-86, group gen. counsel, 1986-87, v.p., gen. counsel, sec., 1987—. Decorated D.F.C., Bronze Star. Mem. Am. Corp. Counsel Assn., Allegheny County Bar Assn. Home: 1061 Lindendale Dr Pittsburgh PA 15243 Office: Dravo Corp 3600 One Oliver Plaza Pittsburgh PA 15222-2682

PULANCO, TONYA BETH, special education educator; b. Portland, Oreg., Apr. 17, 1933; d. Anthony Lorenzo and Adelfa Elizabeth (Dewey) P. BA, San Jose State U., 1955; MA, Columbia U., 1966. Occupl. therapist Langley Porter Hosp., San Francisco, 1958-60; writer ednl. sub-contracts Columbia U., N.Y.C., 1961-64; from tchr. to dir. edn. Gateway Sch. N.Y., N.Y.C., 1965—. Mem. Assn. for Children with Learning Disabilities, Am. Occupl. Therapy Assn., Japanese Am. Citizens League. Avocations: tap dancing, walkathons, silversmithing, jazz, opera. Office: Gateway Sch NY 921 Madison Ave New York NY 10021-3508

PULASKI, CHARLES ALEXANDER, JR., lawyer; b. Flushing, N.Y., Oct. 22, 1941; s. Charles Alexander and Mary Ann (Spencer) P.; m. Linda Shannon Holden, Aug. 16, 1965; 1 child, Alison. BA in Econs., Yale U., 1964, LLB, 1967. Bar: Conn. 1968, U.S. Dist. Ct. Conn. 1968, U.S. Ct. Appeals (2d cir.) 1968, Iowa 1974, U.S. Dist. Ct. (no. and so. dists.) Iowa 1975, U.S. Ct. Appeals (8th cir.) 1975, Ariz. 1986, U.S. Dist. Ct. Ariz. 1986, U.S. Supreme Ct. 1970. Prof. law U. Iowa, 1975-80, Ariz. State U., Tempe, 1980-88; assoc. Snell & Wilmer, Phoenix, 1986-87; ptnr. Snell & Wilmer, 1988--. Author: Criminal Procedure Case Book, 1982, also numerous articles in law revs. Recipient Kalven award, Law and Soc. Assn., 1987. Mem. ABA, Ariz. Bar Assn., Am. Coll. Tax Counsel. Office: Snell & Wilmer 1 Arizona Ctr Phoenix AZ 85004

PULASKI, LORI JAYE, career officer; b. Madison, Wis., June 22, 1962; d. Stanley Harold and Phyllis Mabel (Billock) P.; m. Joseph Kawika Kim, Sept. 14, 1986 (div. Aug. 1991). BS, USAF Acad., 1984; MA in Aero. Sci., Embry Riddle Aero. U., 1995. Commd. 2d lt. USAF, 1984, advanced through grades to maj., 1996; evaluator, instr. pilot USAF, Carswell AFB, Tex., 1986-92; flight safety officer USAF, Edwards AFB, Calif., 1992-95, evaluator, instr. pilot, 1992-95; command flight safety officer Hqrs. Air Combat Command USAF, Langley AFB, Va., 1995—. Avocations: flying, skiing, scuba diving, bicycling. Home: 106 Derosa Dr Hampton VA 23666

PULCRANO, DAN MICHAEL, newspaper and online services executive; b. New Brunswick, N.J., Oct. 1, 1958; s. Charles A. and Edith (Tanner) Ostern. BA in Journalism and Newspaper Mgmt., U. Calif., Santa Cruz, 1980. Reporter Santa Barbara (Calif.) News & Rev., 1978; asst. to pub. L.A. Weekly, 1978, 79; editor, pub. Santa Cruz (Calif.) Weekly, 1981, Los Gatos (Calif.) Weekly, 1982-84; editor Metro, San Jose, Calif., 1985-93, 95—; exec. editor Los Gatos Weekly-Times, Saratoga News, Willow Glen Resident, Cupertino Courier, Sunnvale Sun, Metro Santa Cruz, San Francisco Met., Sonoma County Independent, 1990—; pres., CEO Metro Pub., Inc., San Jose, 1992—, Virtual Valley, Inc., San Jose, 1993—; pres. Boulevards New Media Inc., 1996—. Founding pres., bd. mem. San Jose Downtown Assn., 1986-95. Recipient Disting. Svc. award Oakes Coll., 1980; named Dist. Honoree City of San Jose, Dist. 3, 1989. Mem. Calif. Free Press Assn. (pres. 1991-92, bd. dirs.), Assn. Alternative Newspapers (v.p. 1993-94, bd. dirs.s 1993-95), Rotary. Avocations: gardening, bicycling, travel, photography. Home: PO Box 7 San Jose CA 95103-0007 Office: Metro Newspapers 550 S 1st St San Jose CA 95113-2806

PULEO, FRANK CHARLES, lawyer; b. Montclair, N.J., Nov. 25, 1945; s. Frank and Kathren (Despenzerie) P.; m. Alice Kathren Leek, June 1, 1968; children—Frank C., Richard James. B.S.E., Princeton U., 1967; J.D., N.Y.U., 1970. Bar: N.Y., 1971. Ptnr., Milbank, Tweed, Hadley & McCloy, N.Y.C., 1970—. Mem. ABA (mem. com. on fed. regulation securities), N.Y. State Bar Assn. Office: Milbank Tweed Hadley & McCloy 1 Chase Manhattan Plz New York NY 10005-1401

PULGRAM, ERNST, linguist, philologist, Romance and classical linguistics educator, writer; b. Vienna, Austria, Sept. 18, 1915; came to U.S. 1939, naturalized 1943; s. Sigmund and Gisela (Bauer) P.; m. Frances McSparran, Nov. 29, 1985. Dr. Phil. in Romance and Classical Philology, U. Vienna, 1947, Dr. phil. honoris causa, 1990; PhD in Comparative Linguistics, Harvard U., 1946. Asst. prof. Union Coll., Schenectady, N.Y., 1946; asst. prof. U. Mich., Ann Arbor, 1948-51, assoc. prof., 1951-56, prof., 1956—, H. Keniston disting. prof. romance and classical linguistics, 1979-86, prof. emeritus, 1986—; vis. prof. U. Florence, Italy, 1956-57, U. Cologne, Germany, 1970, U. Heidelberg, Germany, 1972, U. Regensburg, Germany, 1975, U. Vienna, 1977, Internat. Christian U., Tokyo, 1982, U. Innsbruck, Austria, 1983. U. Munich, Germany, 1987; lectr. numerous univs., internat. linguistic congresses; cons. Sch. Langs. and Linguistics, Georgetown U., Washington. Author: Theory of Names, 1951, The Tongues of Italy, 1958, Introduction to Spectrography of Speech, 1959, Syllable, Word, Nexus, Cursus, 1970, Latin-Romance Phonology, Prosodics and Metrics, 1975, Italic, Latin, Italian: 600 B.C.-A.D. 1250, 1978, Practicing Linguist, Essays 1950-1985 (2 vols.), 1986; editor: Studies Presented to Joshua Whatmough, 1957, Romanitas: Studies in Romance Linguistics, 1984; contbr. articles to profl. jours.; author revs.; mem. editorial bd. Current Issues in Linguistic Theory (Amsterdam), Mich. Germanic Studies, Jour. Linguistics and Philology, Mediteranean Language Rev. Served to pvt. inf. U.S. Army, 1942-44; PTO. fellow Am. Council of Learned Socs., 1951-52, 59-60, Guggenheim Found., 1954-55, 62-63; recipient Henry Russell award U. Mich., 1951, Festschrift, Amsterdam, 1980. Mem. Linguistic Soc. Am. (exec. com., com. on appointment of hon. mems., program com.), Internat. Linguistic Assn., Internat. Phonetics Assn., Linguistic Assn. Can. and the U.S. (founding mem., pres. 1978-79). Avocations: collecting drawings and watercolors; hiking; swimming. Home: 1050 Wall St Ann Arbor MI 48105-1974

PULGRAM, WILLIAM LEOPOLD, architect, space designer; b. Vienna, Austria, Jan. 1, 1921; came to U.S., 1940; s. Sigmund and Gisela (Bauer) P.; married, Jan. 12, 1952; children: Deirdre, Laurence, Anthony, Christopher. BS, Ga. Inst. Tech., 1949, BArch, 1950; postgrad., Ecole des Beaux Arts, Fontainebleau, France, 1951. Archtl. designer various firms, Atlanta, 1951-58; assoc., chief interior design FABR&P, Atlanta, 1958-63; exec. v.p., gen. mgr. Associated Space Design Inc., Atlanta, 1963-70, pres., chief exec. officer, 1971-85, chmn., chief exec. officer, 1985-86, chmn. emeritus, 1986-88; architect, cons. Atlanta, 1988—; cons. UN, 1986; com. mem. NAS, 1980-84; lectr. at colls., univs., U.S. and abroad. Author: Designing the Automated Office, 1984, Japanese transl., 1985; contbr. articles to jours. in field. Mem., lectr. High Mus. Art, Atlanta, 1970—. With U.S. Army, 1943-46. Named to Hall of Fame, Interior Design mag., 1986. Fellow AIA (chmn. interiors 1978-84, archt. res. coun. AIA Found. 1983-85); mem. Architects, Designers and Planners for Social Responsibility (nat. bd. dirs. 1989-93), Am. Soc. Interior Designers, Atlanta C. of C., Atlanta City Club, Lake Lanier Sailing Club. Mem. Unitarian Universalist Ch. Home and Office: W L Pulgram FAIA Cons 4317 E Conway Dr NW Atlanta GA 30327-3528

PULHAMUS, MARLENE LOUISE, retired elementary school educator; b. Paterson, N.J., Sept. 11, 1937; d. David Weeder and Elfrieda (Ehler) Wemmell; m. Aaron R. Pulhamus, Aug. 20, 1960; children: Steven, Thomas, Nancy. Student, Trenton State U., 1957; BS, William Paterson U., 1959; postgrad., Rutgers U., 1992. Cert. elem. tchr., N.J. Kindergarten tchr. Wayne (N.J.) Bd. Edn., 1959-63; kindergarten tchr. Paterson Bd. Edn., 1974-75, 2d grade tchr., 1975-81; basic skills instr. Paterson Pub. Schs., 1981—, tchr. accelerated program 1st grade, 1992—; trainer for insvc. groups of learning ctrs. and math. with manipulatives for local pub. schs., trainer for local pub. schs. Contbr. Lessons 4Mat in Action, 3d edit., 4Mat: A Quest for Wholeness, 1977. Pres. Friends of Eisenhower Libr., Totowa, N.J., 1975-77; coord. ch. sch. Preakness Reformed Ch., Wayne, 1990—. Recipient Gov.'s award for tchg. excellence State of N.J. Commn. Edn., 1991, 4Mation program award, 1994. Mem. ASCD, NEA, AAUW, Nat. Coun. Tchrs. Math., Nat. Assn. for Edn. Young Children, N.J. Edn. Assn., Passaic County Edn. Assn., Paterson Edn. Assn. (mem. exec. bd., 1985-89, legis. chmn. 1986-89). Home: 47 Easedale Rd Wayne NJ 07470-2486 Office: Paterson Pub. Sch # 3 448 Main St Paterson NJ 07501-2818

PULIAFITO, CARMEN ANTHONY, ophthalmologist, laser researcher; b. Buffalo, Jan. 5, 1951; s. Dominic F. and Marie A. (Nigro) P.; m. Janet H. Pine, May 19, 1979. AB cum laude, Harvard Coll., 1973, MD magna cum laude, 1978; postgrad., U. Pa. Diplomate Am. Bd. Ophthalmology. Intern Faulkner Hosp., Tufts U. Sch. Medicine, 1978-79; resident Mass. Eye and Ear Infirmary, Boston, 1979-82, retina fellow, 1982-83; instr. Harvard Med. Sch., Boston, 1983-85, asst. prof., 1985-89, assoc. prof., 1989-91; dir. divsn. continuing edn. dept. ophthalmology Harvard Med. Sch., 1989-91; vis. scientist MIT Regional Laser Ctr., Cambridge, 1982—, asst. prof. health scis. and tech. program, 1987-89, assoc. prof., 1989-91; mem. staff Mass. Eye and Ear Infirmary, Boston, 1983; dir. Morse Laser Ctr., Mass. Eye and Ear Infirmary, 1986-91, dir. New Eng. Eye Ctr., 1991—; prof., chmn. dept. ophthalmology Tufts U. Sch. Medicine, 1991—; adj. prof. biomed. engring. Tufts U., 1991—; chmn. med. bd. New Eng. Med. Ctr. Hosps., 1994—, ophthalmologist in chief, 1991—; assoc. examiner Am. Bd. Ophthalmology, 1990—. Author: (with D. Albert) Foundations of Ophthalmic Pathology, 1979, (with R. Steinert) Principles and Practice of Ophthalmic YAG Laser Surgery, 1984, Lasers in Surgery and Medicine: Principles and Practice, 1996, (with M.R. Hee, J.S. Schuman and J.G. Fujimoto) Optical Coherence Tomography of Ocular Diseases, 1996, (with E. Reichel) Atlas of Indocyanine Green Angiography, 1996; editor-in-chief Lasers in Surgery and Medicine, 1987-95, Ophthalmic Surgery and Lasers, 1995—; contbr. about 100 articles to profl. jours. Pres. Am. Soc. for Laser Medicine and Surgery, 1994-95; v.p. Mass. Soc. Eye Physicians and Surgeons, 1994-96; assoc. examiner Am. Bd. Ophthalmology, 1990—; retina trustee Assn. Rsch. in Vision and Ophthalmology, 1995—. Recipient Richard and Hinda Rosenthal award in visual scis., 1994, Man of Vision award Boston Aid to the Blind, 1993, Leon Goldman award Biomed. Optics Soc., 1993, I Migliori award Pirandello Lyceum of Mass., 1994. Fellow Am. Acad. Ophthalmology, Am. Soc. for Laser Medicine and Surgery (pres. 1994-95); mem. Mass. Soc. Eye Physicians and Surgeons (v.p. 1994-96). Roman Catholic. Home: 69 Pigeon Hill Rd Weston MA 02193-1641 Office: New Eng Eye Ctr PO Box 450 750 Washington St Boston MA 02111-1533*

PULIDO, MIGUEL LAZARO, marketing professional; b. Havana, Cuba, Dec. 17, 1934; s. Jose Fabriciano and Maria Dolores (Perez) P.; m. Janie Ham, Nov. 28, 1980; 1 child, Michael James. AE, Sugar Techs., Havana U., 1956; MS, La. State U., 1961, PhD, 1965; completed Exec. Program, U. Va., 1986. Agrl. engr. Agrl. and Indsl. Bank Cuba, Havana, 1956-58, mgr. agrl. and eastern devel. div., 1958-59; agrl. engr. Productora Superfosfatos, Havana, 1959-60; asst. mgr. Tech. Svcs. div. Velsicol Chem. Co., Chgo., 1965-67; v.p. internat. mktg. Buckman Labs., Memphis, 1985—. Editor Jour. Fitopatologia, 1969-74; contbr. articles to profl. jours. Fellow Pan Am. U., 1960-62. Mem. AAAS, Am. Phytopathol. Soc., Weed Sci. Soc., Plant Growth Regulator Soc., Biol. Soc., Internat. Sugarcane Techs. Soc., Tech. Assn. Pulp and Paper Industry. Republican. Office: Buckman Labs Internat Inc 1256 N Mclean Blvd Memphis TN 38108-1241

PULITZER, EMILY S. RAUH (MRS. JOSEPH PULITZER, JR.), art consultant; b. Cin., July 23, 1933; d. Frederick and Harriet (Frank) Rauh. AB, Bryn Mawr Coll., 1955; student, Ecole du Louvre, Paris, France, 1955-56; MA, Harvard U., 1963. Mem. staff Cin. Art Mus., 1956-57; asst. curator drawings Fogg Art Mus., Harvard, 1957-64, asst. to dir., 1962-63; curator City Art Mus., St. Louis, 1964-73; mem. painting and sculpture com. Mus. Modern Art, 1975—; chmn. visual arts com. Mo. Arts Council, 1976-81; co-chmn. fellows Fogg Art Mus., 1978—; mem. bd. Inst. Mus. Services,

1979-84; commr. St. Louis Art Mus., 1981-88, vice chmn., 1988; chair collections com. Harvard U. Arts Museums, 1992—; bd. dirs. Pulitzer Pub. Co. Bd. dirs. Forum, St. Louis, 1980—, pres., 1990-94; bd. dirs. Mark Rothko Found., 1976-88, Grand Ctr., 1993-95, St. Louis Symphony Orch., 1994—; bd. dirs. arts in transit com. Bi-State Devel. Agy., vice-chmn., 1987—; mem. Leadership St. Louis, 1990-91; mem. overseers com. to visit Harvard Art Mus., 1990—; trustee Mus. Modern Art, 1994—. Mem. Am. Fedn. Arts (dir. 1976-89), St. Louis Mercantile Libr. Assn. (bd. dirs. 1987-93), Women's Forum of Mo. Home: 4903 Pershing Ave Saint Louis MO 63108-1201

PULITZER, MICHAEL EDGAR, publishing executive; b. St. Louis, Feb. 23, 1930; s. Joseph and Elizabeth (Edgar) P.; m. Cecille Stell Eisenbeis, Apr. 28, 1970; children: Michael Edgar, Elizabeth E. Voges, Robert S., Frederick D., Catherine D. Culver, Christina H. Eisenbeis, Mark C. Eisenbeis, William H. Eisenbeis. Grad., St. Mark's Sch., Southborough, Mass., 1947; AB, Harvard U., 1951, LLB, 1954. Bar: Mass. 1954. Assoc. Warner, Stackpole, Stetson & Bradlee, Boston, 1954-56; reporter Louisville Courier Jour., 1956-60; reporter, news editor, asst. mng. editor St. Louis Post-Dispatch, 1960-71, assoc. editor, 1978-79; pub. Ariz. Daily Star, Tucson, 1971—; pres. chief operating officer Pulitzer Pub. Co. (and subs.), 1979-84, vice chmn., 1984-86, pres., chmn., 1986—, also bd. dirs., chief exec. officer, 1988—. Trustee St. Louis U., 1989—. Clubs: St. Louis Country; Mountain Oyster (Tucson). Office: Pulitzer Pub Co 900 N Tucker Blvd Saint Louis MO 63101-1069*

PULITZER, ROSLYN K., social worker, psychotherapist; b. Bronx, N.Y., Apr. 25, 1930; d. George and Laura Eleanor (Holtz) P. BS in Human Devel. and Life Cycle, SUNY, N.Y.C., 1983; MSW, Fordham U., 1987; postgrad., Masterson Inst., N.Y.C., 1991. cert. in psychoanalytic psychotherapy of the personality disorders, Masterson Inst., N.Y.C.; lic. clin. social worker, N.Y. Clinic dir. Resources Counseling and Psychotherapy Ctr., N.Y.C., 1985-89; social worker, clin. supr. methadone maintenance treatment program Beth Israel Med. Ctr., N.Y.C., 1989—; cons. therapist, clin. supr. Identity House, N.Y.C., 1980—, exec. dir., 1985, clin. dir., 1993-94. Mem. regional adv. coun. N.Y. State Div. Human Rights, N.Y.C., 1975-76; mem. Community Bd. 6, N.Y.C., 1978-81; founder, legis. chmn. N.Y. State Women's Polit. Caucus, 1978-80. Mem. NASW, Acad. Cert. Social Workers, Soc. Masterson Inst., N.Y. Milton Erickson Soc. for Psychotherapy and Hypnosis (cert.). Avocations: photography, snorkeling. Home: 110 Bank St Apt 5F New York NY 10014-2171

PULLEN, EDWIN WESLEY, anatomist, university dean; b. Flushing, N.Y., June 2, 1923; s. Edwin Leeson and Henrietta Esther (Treharne) P.; m. Ruthann Chambers, Sept. 7, 1946; children—Wayne, Jeffrey, Susan, Kimberly. A.B. (Pres.'s scholar), Colgate U., 1943; M.S., U. Mass., 1948; Ph.D. (DuPont fellow), U. Va., 1953. Instr. anatomy U. Va., 1951-53, asst. prof., 1953-57, asso. prof., 1957-73, prof., 1973-91; assoc. dean U. Va. (Sch. Medicine), 1974-91, ret., 1991—. Served with USNR, 1943-46. Mem. Am. Assn. Anatomists, AAAS, Sigma Xi. Home: 2700 Magnolia Dr Charlottesville VA 22901-2019

PULLEN, KEATS A., JR., electronics engineer; b. Onawa, Iowa, Nov. 12, 1916; s. Keats A. and Mabel Jeannette (Faus) P.; m. Phyllis Kouwenhoven, Jan. 6, 1945; children: Peter K., Paul V., Keats A. 3d, Andrew W., Victoria F. B.S. in Physics, Calif. Inst. Tech., 1939; Dr.Engring., Johns Hopkins U. Registered profl. engr., Md. Electronic research engr. Ballistic Research Labs., Aberdeen Proving Ground, Md., 1946-78; electronic engr. Army Material Systems Analysis Activity, Aberdeen Proving Ground, 1978-90; cons. engr., 1990—. Author 9 books; Contbr. articles to profl. jours. Recipient Marconi Meml. award Vet. Wireless Operator's Assn., 1982. Fellow IEEE (officer Balt. sect. 1962-66); mem. Am. Def. Preparedness Assn., Assn. U.S. Army, Armed Forces Communications and Electronics Assn. (ex-pres. Aberdeen chpt.), Am. Assn. of Concerned Engrs. (bd. dirs.), Sigma Xi. Episcopalian. Home: 2807 Jerusalem Rd Kingsville MD 21087-1098

PULLEN, MARGARET I., genetic physicist; b. Nebr., Sept. 13, 1950; d. Robert and Martha (Holtort) P. AA, Stephens Coll., 1971; BA in Internat. Rels., Econs., Bus. & Trade, U. Colo., 1975; BS in Physics, Northeastern U., 1983; MS in Physics, Tufts U., 1984; postgrad., U. Calif., 1984-86. Mathematician Lawrence Livermore Lab., Calif., 1987; entrepreneur Evergreen Applied Rsch. Inc., 1988—; mem. Biotechnology Roundtable, Denver, 1987—; cons. in field, 1988—. Vol. Nat. Sports Ctr. for the Physically Disabled, Winter Park, Colo., 1988-92. Tufts U. grantee, U. Colo. grantee; Nat. Sci. fellow; Stephens scholar, Perry Mansfield Ctr. for the Preforming Arts scholar. Mem. Am. Phys. Soc. Office: Evergreen Applied Rsch Inc PO Box 1551 Aspen CO 81612

PULLEN, PENNY LYNNE, non-profit administrator, former state legislator; b. Buffalo, Mar. 2, 1947; d. John William and Alice Nettie (McConkey) P.; BA in Speech, U. Ill., 1969. TV technician Office Instructional Resources, U. Ill., 1966-68; community newspaper reporter Des Plaines (Ill.) Pub. Co., 1967-72; legislative asst. to Ill. legislators, 1968-77; mem. Ill. Ho. of Reps., 1977-93, chmn. ho. exec. com., 1981-82, minority whip, 1983-87, asst. minority leader, 1987-93; pres., founder Life Advocacy Resource Project, 1992—; exec. dir. Ill. Family Inst., 1993-94; dir. Legal Svcs. Corp., 1989-93; mem. Pres.'s Commn. on AIDS Epidemic, 1987-88; mem. Ill. Goodwill Del. to Republic of China, 1987. Del. Atlantic Alliance Young Polit. Leaders, Brussels, 1977, Rep. Nat. Conv, 1984; mem. Republican Nat. Com., 1984-88; summit conf. observer as mem. adhoc Women for SDI, Geneva, 1985; former mem. Maine Twp. Mental Health Assn.; pres. Maine Twp. Rep. Women's Club, 1997—; active Nat. Coun. Ednl. Rsch., 1983-88. Recipient George Washington Honor medal Freedoms Found., 1978, Dwight Eisenhower Freedom medal Chgo. Captive Nations Com., 1977, Outstanding Legislator awards Ill. Press Assn., Ill. Podiatry Soc., Ill. Coroners Assn., Ill. County Clks. Assn., Ill. Hosp. Assn., Ill. Health Care Assn.; named Ill. Young Republican, 1968, Outstanding Young Person, Park Ridge Jaycees, 1981, One of 10 Outstanding Young Persons, Ill. Jaycees, 1981. Mem. Am. Legis. Exchange Council (dir. 1977-91, exec. com. 1978-83, 2d vice chmn. 1980-83), DAR. Lodge: Kiwanis.

PULLEN, RICHARD OWEN, lawyer, communications company executive; b. New Orleans, Nov. 6, 1944; s. Roscoe LeRoy and Gwendolen Sophia Ellen (Williams) P.; m. Frances G. Eisenstein, Jan. 24, 1976 (div. 1986). B.A. in Econs., Whitman Coll., 1967; J.D., Duke U., 1972. Bar: D.C. 1973. Fin. mgmt. trainee Gen. Electric Co., Lynn, Mass., 1967-69; sr. atty. domestic facilities div. Common Carrier Bur., FCC, Washington, 1972-79, atty. advisor Office of Opinions and Rev., 1979-81; chmn. definitions and terminology of joint industry, govt. com. for preparation of U.S. Proposals 1977 Broadcasting Satellite World Adminstrv. Radio Conf.; v.p. Washington office Contemporary Comm. Corp., New Rochelle, N.Y., 1981-91; v.p., gen. counsel Comm. Innovations Corp., New Rochelle, 1991—. With USCGR, 1967-75. Mem. ABA, Fed. Comm. Bar Assn., Fed. Bar Assn., Internat. Platform Assn. Republican. Unitarian.

PULLEYBLANK, EDWIN GEORGE, history educator emeritus, linguist; b. Calgary, Alta., Can., Aug. 7, 1922; s. W. George E. and Ruth Elizabeth (Willoughby) P.; m. Winona Ruth Relyea, July 17, 1945 (dec. Jan. 1978); children: David Edwin, Barbara Jill, Marcia Ruth. B.A., U. Alta., 1942; Ph.D., U. London, 1951. Research officer Nat. Research Council, Ottawa, 1943-46; lectr. Sch. Oriental and African studies U. London, 1948-53; prof. Chinese U. Cambridge, 1953-66; prof. Asian studies U. B.C., 1966-87, prof. emeritus, 1988—, head dept., 1968-75; editorial adviser Ency. Brit. Author: The Background of the Rebellion of An Lu-shan, 1955, Middle Chinese, 1984, Lexicon of Reconstructed Pronunciation in Early Middle Chinese, Late Middle Chinese and Early Mandarin, 1991, Outline of Classical Chinese Grammar; editor: (with W.G. Beasley) Historians of China and Japan, 1961; contbr. articles to profl. jours. Fellow Royal Soc. Can.; mem. Royal Asiatic Soc. (coun. 1956-59), Philol. Soc. London (coun. 1961-66), Assn. Asian Studies (dir. 1969-73), Can. Liguistic Assn., Can. Soc. Asian Studies (pres. 1971-74), Am. Oriental Soc. (pres. 1990-91), Internat. Assn. of Chinse nguistics (pres. 1995-96). Office: U BC, Dept Asian Studies, Vancouver, Canada V6T 1Z1

PULLIAM, BRENDA JANE, secondary school educator; b. Griffin, Ga., Jan. 28, 1941; d. Delmus Lawton and Eva Jane (Cobb) P. BA, Mercer U., 1963; MA in Teaching, Converse Coll., 1972; EdD, Nova U., 1993; postgrad., U. Toulouse, France. Cert. secondary tchr., Ga. Tchr. French Jonesboro (Ga.) H.S., 1963—, chair fgn. lang. dept., 1970—; co-founder KPS Leadership Specialists, 1993—; correlator Harcourt Brace Jovanovich, 1989; speaker So. Conf. Lang. Teaching, 1993, adv. bd. Contbr. articles to profl. jours.; contbr. ednl. papers to ERIC. Chair citizen exchs. Atlanta-Toulouse Sister Cities, 1987—, tour leader, 1989, 94; interpreter Travelers Aid Met. Atlanta, 1989—. Grantee NDEA, 1963; recipient STAR Tchr. award, 1983. Mem. NEA, Am. Coun. Teaching Fgn. Langs., Am. Assn. Tchrs. French, Ga. Assn. Educators, Fgn. Lang. Assn. Ga., Clayton County Edn. Assn., So. Conf. Lang. Teaching. Baptist. Avocations: piano, traveling, writing, reading, gardening. Home: 9261 Brave Ct Jonesboro GA 30236-5110 Office: Jonesboro High School 7728 Mount Zion Blvd Jonesboro GA 30236-2441

PULLIAM, EUGENE SMITH, newspaper publisher; b. Atchison, Kans., Sept. 7, 1914; s. Eugene Collins and Myrta (Smith) P.; m. Jane Bleecker, May 29, 1943; children: Myrta, Russell, Deborah. A.B., DePauw U., 1935, LL.D., 1973. Reporter, UP, Chgo., Detroit, Buffalo, 1935-36; news editor Radio Sta. WIRE, Indpls., 1937-41; city editor Indpls. Star, 1947-48; mng. editor Indpls. News, 1948-62; asst. publisher Indpls. Star and News, 1962-76; pres. Phoenix Newspapers, 1979-97; exec. v.p. Central Newspapers, Indpls., 1979—. With USNR, 1942-46. Mem. Am. Soc. Newspaper Editors, Am. Newspaper Pubs. Assn. Found. (past pres.), Soc. Profl. Journalists, Delta Kappa Epsilon. Club: Crooked Stick Golf. Office: Indpls Star Indpls Newspapers Inc 307 N Pennsylvania St Indianapolis IN 46204-1811 also: Phoenix Newspapers Inc 200 E Van Buren St Phoenix AZ 85004-2227

PULLIAM, FREDERICK CAMERON, educational administrator; b. Mesa, Ariz., Jan. 5, 1936; s. Fredrick Posy and Nathana Laura (Cameron) P.; AA., Hannibal LaGrange Coll., 1955; AB, Grand Canyon Coll., 1958; M.Ed., U. Mo., Columbia, 1966, Ed.S., 1976, EdD, 1981; m. Deborah Jean Botts, June 1, 1979; 1 child, Sarah Elizabeth; children by previous marriage: Cameron Dale, Joy Renee. tchr., Centerview (Mo.) Public Schs., 1958-59; ordained to ministry So. Baptist Conv., 1955; minister Bethel Bapt. Ch., Kansas City, Mo., 1959-61; adminstr. Fiti'uta, Manu'a sch., Am. Samoa, 1966-68; cons. in fin. Mo. State Tchrs. Assn., Columbia, 1969-79; supt. schs. Midway Heights C-VII, Columbia, 1979-83; dir. elem. edn. Brentwood Pub. Schs. (Mo.), 1983-90; founder, coordinator Mo. Computer-Using Educators Conf., 1982-84; contbg. writer St. Louis Computing News, 1984-95; adj. asst. prof. ednl. studies U. Mo., St. Louis, 1986-90; assoc. prof. edn. Mo. So. State Coll., 1990—, dir. clinical and field experiences in tchr. edu., Mo. So. State Coll., 1994—; adj. assoc. prof. grad. studies Southwest Baptist Univ., 1991-96; cons. sch. fin., curriculum improvement. Mem. Columbia Am. Revolution Bicentennial Commn. Inst. Devel. Ednl. Activity fellow, 1969, 78-84. Mem. Am. Assn. of Colls. for Tchr. Edn., Assn. Childhood Edn. Internat. Nat. Assn. Supervision and Curriculum Devel. (bd. dirs. 1984-90),Mo. Gov's. Transition Team (edn. adv. com. 1992-93), Phi Delta Kappa (chpt. pres.). Contbr. articles to profl. jours. Home: 2140 Kayla Ln Mount Vernon MO 65712-1243 Office: Mo So State Coll 224 Taylor Hall Joplin MO 64801-1595

PULLIAM, JAMES MICHAEL, military career officer; b. Maxton, N.C., May 23, 1946; s. Henry Delos and Ruby Hazel (Mills) P.; m. Patricia Ann Harbuck, Mar. 8, 1969; children: Christopher Michael, James Aaron. BS in Phys. Edn., Wake Forest U., 1968; MPA, Shippensburg State U., 1988. Commd. 2nd lt. U.S. Army, 1968, advanced through grades to col.; infantry advisor Mil. Assistance Command, Trang Bang, Vietnam, 1971; staff officer Pentagon, Washington, 1983; battalion comdr. 52d Aviation Battalion, Seoul, South Korea, 1984-86; brigage comdr. Aviation Brigade, 2nd Infantry Divsn., Camp Stanley, South Korea, 1989-91; chief of staff Combined Field Army, Ouijongbu, South Korea, 1992; comdr. Readiness Group Atlanta, Forest Park, Ga., 1995—; mem. total quality mgmt. exec. coun. U.S. Army Forces Command, Atlanta, 1992-94. Decorated Bronze Star, U.S. Army, Republic of Vietnam, 1971, Purple Heart, U.S. Army, Republic of Vietnam, 1971, Meritorious Svc. medal with 3 oak leaf clusters U.S. Army, 1979-84, Legion of Merit with 2 oak leaf clusters U.S. Army, 1987, 92, 95. Mem. Assn. of the U.S. Army (mem. exec. bd. 1992-93), Army Aviation Assn. Am. (v.p. Morning Calm chpt. 1984, 86, 89-91, 20 Yr. pin 1992), Clayton County C. of C. (mem. mil. affairs com. 1995—). Avocations: golf, softball, running, weightlifting. Office: Readiness Group Atlanta Bldg 207A Fort Gillem Forest Park GA 30050-5000

PULLING, RONALD WILSON, SR., aviation systems planner, civil engineer, consultant; b. L.A., Oct. 30, 1919; s. Albert Elmer and Mary (Porter) P.; m. Florence Dorothy Rooke, June 24, 1945 (dec.); children: Mary Anna, Ronald Jr. (dec.), William; m. Florence Marie MacIntyre, Oct. 19, 1996. BSCE, U. Calif., Berkeley, 1940; PFPA, Princeton U., 1963-64; PhD (hon.), Sierra Madre City Coll., 1981. Registered profl. engr., Calif., Fla., Hawaii, Md., Va. Civil engr. CAA, Honolulu, 1943-51; chief facility materials div. CAA, Oklahoma City, 1951-63; chief airport planning div. FAA, Washington, 1964-66, dep. dir. Office of Policy, 1966-68, dep. assoc. adminstr. for plans, 1968-73; sr. v.p. William L. Pereira Assoc., Washington, 1973-74; staff cons. TAMS Cons. Inc., Washington, 1975—; pres. Ronald W. Pulling Assoc., Alexandria, 1976—; v.p. United Global Airlines, Sierra Madre, Calif., 1984—. Author: (with others) Airport Economic Planning, 1971, Airport Planning, 1972; contbr. articles to profl. jours.; corr. Sierra Madre News, 1988-94. Recipient Meritorious Svc. award FAA, 1971, Disting. Career Svc. award, 1973. Fellow ASCE (James Laurie prize 1981); mem. NAE (elected), Transp. Rsch. Bd. (Disting. Svc. award 1984), Am. Planning Assn., Am. Inst. Cert. Planners (cert.), Springfield (Va.) Golf Club, Nat. Aviation Club. Episcopalian. Avocations: golf, creative writing, travel. Home: 4809 Polk Ave Alexandria VA 22304-2257 Office: R W Pulling Assoc PO Box 9526 Alexandria VA 22304-0526

PULLING, THOMAS LEFFINGWELL, investment advisor; b. N.Y.C., May 1, 1939; s. T.J. Edward and Lucy (Leffingwell) P.; m. Lisa Canby, Sept. 14, 1962 (div. 1968); children: Elizabeth, Edward L.; m. Sheila Sonne, Mar. 12, 1970 (div. 1980);children: Victoria, Diana, Christopher; m. Eileen Kingsbury-Smith, Dec. 21, 1989. BA cum laude, Princeton U., 1961. Asst. treas. J.P. Morgan & Co. Inc., N.Y.C., 1962-68; v.p. N.Y. Securities Co., N.Y.C., 1968-71, L.M. Rosenthal & Co., N.Y.C., 1971-76; mng. dir. Smith Barney (formerly Shearson Lehman Hutton), N.Y.C., 1977—; CEO Smith Barney Investment ADvisors, 1985—. Bd. dirs. Henry Luce Found., 1988—, Woodlawn Cemetery, 1980—; trustee South St. Seaport Mus., Long Island U., 1994—. with USMC, 1962-67. Mem. Century Assn., Pilgrims of the U.S. (N.Y.C.), Piping Rock Club (Locust Valley, N.Y.), Surf Club (Miami, Fla.), Univ. Club (N.Y.C.). Republican. Episcopalian. Home: 34 Yellow Cote Rd Oyster Bay NY 11771-4111 Office: Smith Barney 388 Greenwich St New York NY 10013-2375

PULLMAN, BILL, actor; b. Hornell, N.Y., 1953; m. Tamara Pullman, 3 children. Attended, SUNY, Oneonta; MFA, U. Mass., Amherst. theatre instr. Mont. State U., Bozeman. Actor: (theatre) The Rover, 1981, Ah, Wilderness!, 1983, The Old Flag, 1983, Dramathon '84, 1984, Curse of the Starving Class, 1985, All My Sons, 1986, Barabbas, 1986, Nanawatai, 1986, Demon Wine, 1988, Control Freaks, 1993, (films) Ruthless People, 1986, Spaceballs, 1987, The Serpent and the Rainbow, 1988, Rocket Gibraltar, 1988, The Accidental Tourist, 1989, Cold Feet, 1989, Brain Dead, 1989, Sibling Rivalry, 1990, Going Under, 1991, Bright Angel, 1991, Newsies, 1992, A League of Their Own, 1992, Singles, 1992, Sommersby, 1993, Sleepless in Seattle, 1993, Malice, 1993, Mr. Jones, 1993, The Favor, 1994, Wyatt Earp, 1994, While You Were Sleeping, 1995, Casper, 1995, Mr. Wrong, 1996, Independence Day, 1996, Lost Highway, 1997, The End of Violence, 1997, (TV movies) Home Fires Burning, 1989, Crazy in Love, 1992, The Last Seduction, 1994, Mistrial, 1996. Office: UTA 9560 Wilshire Blvd Fl 5 Beverly Hills CA 90212-2401

PULLMAN, MAYNARD EDWARD, biochemist; b. Chgo., Oct. 26, 1927; s. Harry and Gertrude (Atlas) P.; m. E. Phyllis Light, Sept. 12, 1948; children: H. Cydney, B. Valerie, Jacky Leigh. B.S., U. Ill., 1948, M.S., 1950; Ph.D. (NIH fellow), Johns Hopkins U., 1953. Fellow in pediatrics Johns Hopkins Hosp., 1953-54; asst. Pub. Health Rsch. Inst., City N.Y., 1954-56; assoc. Pub. Health Rsch. Inst., 1956-61, assoc. mem., 1961-65, mem., 1965-89, chief, 1973-87, assoc. dir., 1983-89; sr. rsch. scientist Coll. Physicians and Surgeons Columbia U., 1989-92; vis. prof. biochemistry U. São Paulo (Brazil) Sch. Medicine, 1963-64; research assoc. prof. biochemistry Sch. Medicine NYU, 1966-76, research prof., 1976-90; biochemistry study section mem. NIH, 1969-73. Editorial bd.: Jour. Biol. Chemistry, 1967-71, 78-80. NIH grantee, 1956-85; Shubert Found. grantee, 1972-74. Fellow N.Y. Acad. Scis.; mem. AAAS, Am. Soc. Biol. Chemistry and Molecular Biology, Brit. Biochem. Soc., Am. Chem. Soc. Home and Office: 338 Archer St Freeport NY 11520-4233

PULLMAN, PHILIP NICHOLAS, author, educator; b. Norwich, Norfolk, Eng., Oct. 19, 1946; s. Alfred Outram and Audrey Evelyn (Merrifield) P.; m. Judith Speller, Aug. 15, 1970; children: James, Thomas. BA, Oxford U., 1968. Tchr. Oxfordshire Edn. Authority, Oxford, Eng., 1972-88; lectr. Westminster Coll., Oxford, 1988—. Author: The Ruby in the Smoke, 1987 (Internat. Reading Assn. best book award 1988), Shadow in the North, 1988, The Tiger in the Well, 1991, Spring-Heeled Jack, 1991, The Broken Bridge, 1992, The White Mercedes, 1993, The Golden Compass (Guardian Children's Fiction award 1996, Carnegie medal 1996). Avocations: music, drawing. Home: 24 Templar Rd, Oxford OX2 8LT, England

PULSIFER, EDGAR DARLING, leasing service and sales executive; b. Natick, Mass., Jan. 11, 1934; s. Howard George and Elvie Marion (Morris) P.; m. Alice Minarik, Feb. 16, 1957 (div. Oct. 1979); children: Mark Edgar, Audrey Carol, Lee Howard; m. Barbara Ann Chuhak, Apr. 19, 1980. BSEE, MIT, 1955. With sales and service dept. Beckman Instruments, Fullerton, Calif., 1956-59; regional sales mgr. Hewlett Packard, Palo Alto, Calif., 1959-72, Gen. Automation, Anaheim, Calif., 1973-74; exec. v.p. Systems Mktg., Elk Grove Vlg., Ill., 1975-79; pres. Consol. Funding, Mt. Prospect, Ill., 1979—. Served as 1st lt. U.S. Army, 1956. Mem. MENSA, Coast Guard Auxiliary. Republican. Episcopalian. Clubs: North Shore Country (Glenview, Ill.), Itasca (Ill.) Country. Avocations: coins, stamps, curling, scuba diving, golf. Home: 370 Dulles Rd Des Plaines IL 60016-2755 Office: Consol Funding Corp P O Box 801 Mount Prospect IL 60056-0801

PUMPER, ROBERT WILLIAM, microbiologist; b. Clinton, Iowa, Sept. 12, 1921; s. William R. and Kathrine M. (Anderson) P.; m. Ruth J. Larkin, June 24, 1951; 1 son. Mark. B.A., U. Iowa, 1951, M.S., 1953, Ph.D., 1955. Diplomate: Am. Soc. Microbiology. Asst. prof. Hahnemann Med. Coll., Phila., 1955-57; prof. microbiology U. Ill. Med. Sch., Chgo., 1957—, Raymond B. Allen Med. lectr., 1970, 74, 76, 87. Co-author: Essentials of Medical Virology; contbr. articles to profl. jours. Served with USAAF, 1942-46. Recipient Chancellors' award U. Ill., Bombeck award for excellence in med. edn., 1992. Mem. Tissue Culture Assn., Sigma Xi, Phi Rho Sigma. Lutheran. Home: 18417 Argyle Ave Homewood IL 60430-3007 Office: U Ill Med Sch Dept Microbiology 808 S Wood St Chicago IL 60612-7300

PUMPHREY, JANET KAY, editor; b. Balt., June 18, 1946; d. John Henry and Elsie May (Keefer) P. AA in Secondary Edn., Anne Arundel C.C., Arnold, Md., 1967, AA in Bus. and Pub. Adminstrn., 1976. Office mgr. Anne Arundel C.C., 1964—; mng. editor Am. Polygraph Assn., Severna Park, Md., 1973—; archives dir. Am. Polygraph Assn., Severna Park, 1973—; owner JKP Publ. Svcs., 1990—; dir. Am. Polygraph Assn. Reference Svc., 1995—. Editor: (with Albert D. Snyder) Ten Years of Polygraph, 1984, (with Norman Ansley) Justice and the Polygraph, 1985, 2d edit., 1996, A House Full of Love, 1990, Mama, There's A Mouse in My House, 1996. Mem. Rep. Nat. Sustaining Com. Mem. NAFE, Am. Polygraph Assn. (hon.), Md. Polygraph Assn. (affiliate), Anne Arundel County Hist. Soc., Alumni Assn. Anne Arundel Community Coll. Republican. Methodist. Avocations: travel, poetry, gardening, mystery writer. Home: 3 Kimberly Ct Severna Park MD 21146-3703 Office: JKP Pub Svcs PO Box 1535 Severna Park MD 21146-8535

PUNCH, JERRY, sports reporter. Grad. magna cum laude, N.C. State U., 1975; MD, Wake Forest U., 1979. Dir. emergency room svcs. Meml. Hosp.-Flagler, Bunnell, Fla.; substitute track announcer Hickory, N.C., 1975-79; announcer NASCAR Motor Racing Network, 1979-82; announcer WTBS-TV, 1982-87, ABC, 1987—; pit reporter NASCAR ESPN, 1984—, coll. football sideline reporter, 1989—. Recipient outstanding performance award USAF, 1989, outstanding youth alumnus award N.C. State U., 1989; named NASCAR Team Player of Yr., 1990. Office: ESPN ESPN Plaza Bristol CT 06010

PUOTINEN, ARTHUR EDWIN, college president, clergyman; b. Crystal Falls, Mich., Sept. 7, 1941; s. Kaleva Weikko and Ines Pauline (Maki) P.; m. Judith Cathleen Kapoun, Aug. 8, 1964; children: Anne, Marjetta, Sara. AA, Suomi Coll., 1961; BA, Augustana Coll., Rock Island, Ill., 1963; MDiv, Luth. Sch. Theology, Chgo., 1967; MA, U. Chgo., 1969, PhD, 1973; MBA, Wake Forest U., 1984. Pastor Trinity Luth. Ch., Chgo., 1968-70; asst. prof. religion Cen. Mich. U., Mt. Pleasant, 1971-74; dean faculty Suomi Coll., Hancock, Mich., 1974-78; v.p. acad. affairs Lenoir-Rhyne Coll., Hickory, N.C., 1978-83; assoc. dean acad. affairs Roanoke Coll., Salem, Va., 1983-84; exec. dir. Luth. Ednl. Conf. of N.Am., Washington, 1984-88; pres. Grand View Coll., Des Moines, 1988-96; v.p., provost Suomi Coll., Hancock, Mich., 1996—; pastor S.E. Northern Great Lakes Synod, Evang.-Luth. Ch. Am. Author: Finnish Radicals..., 1979; contbr. articles to books and jours. Grantee NEH, U.S. Dept. Edn. Democrat. Avocations: jogging, reading, travel. Home: 1404 Sugar Maple Lane Houghton MI 49931 Office: Suomi Coll 600 Quincy St Hancock MI 49930-1806

PUPELLO, DENNIS FRANK, cardiac surgeon, educator; b. Tampa, Fla., May 31, 1939; s. Frank and Grace Ann (Torres) P.; m. Lisa Valerie Acuri, Feb. 23, 1991; children: Ariel, Alana, Alexa, Angela, Dennis, Frank, Bradford, Derek. BS in Biology, U. Tampa, 1961, postgrad., 1962, DSc, 1988; MD, U. Fla., 1967. Diplomate Am. Bd. Surgery. Intern Stanford U. Hosp., Palo Alto, Calif., 1967-68, resident in cardiovasc. surgery, 1968-72; dir. cardiac surgery Tampa (Fla.) Gen. Hosp., 1972-82; chief dept. cardiac surgery St. Joseph's Hosp., Tampa, 1985—; chief cardiac surgery Blake Meml. Hosp., Brandenton, Fla., 1988—, Wuesthoff Hosp., Rockledge, Fla., 1991—; clin. asst. prof. sugery Univ. S. Fla., 1974—; mem. courtesy staff Tampa Gen. Hosp., 1982—, Meml. Hosp. Tampa, 1982—, Univ. Cmty. Hosp., Tampa, 1982—; mem. consulting staff MacDill AFB Regional Hosp., Tampa, 1982—, Women's Hosp. Tampa, 1982—; dir. cardiac surgery program St. Joseph's Hosp., Tampa, 1983-84. Author: (chpt.) Valvular Heart Disease, 1995; contbr. articles to profl. jours. Capt. USAR. Fellow Am. Coll. Cardiology, Am. Coll. Chest Physicians; mem. AMA, Internat. Assn. Biol. Implants, Fla. Med. Assn., Fla. Heart Assn. (mem. rsch. com. 1973, mem. com. CPR 1974), Fla. Soc. Thoracic and Cardiovasc. Surgeons (sec., treas. 1984, pres. 1986-87, chmn. membership com. 1991-95), Hillsborough County Med. Assn., Hillsborough County Heart Assn. (bd. dirs. 1973, chmn. profl. edn. com. 1977), Mantee County Med. Assn., Alpha Omega Alpha. Avocations: scuba diving, pianist, boating. Office: Pupello Bessone Glaterer & Lopez 2814 W Virginia Ave Tampa FL 33607-6330

PURAVS, JOHN ANDRIS, journalist; b. Ruckersdorf, Germany, Feb. 23, 1945; s. Janis Alfreds and Alma Otilija (Grundulis) P.; m. Trudi Ann Tiedeman, July 2, 1966 (div. Feb. 1982). BA, U. Mich., 1966. Reporter Saginaw (Mich.) News, 1966-78, suburban editor, 1978-79, editorial editor, 1979—, chmn. editorial bd., 1981—; commentator Sta. WUCM-TV, Univ. Ctr., Mich. Contbr. articles to profl. jours. Mem. adv. bd. Saginaw Valley State U. Coll. Edn., 1991—. 1st lt. U.S. Army, 1967-69, Vietnam. Medill fellow Northwestern U., 1970; Regents-Alumni scholar U. Mich., 1962-66, Chgo. House Coun., 1963-64; recipient over 40 journalism awards. Mem. Soc. Profl. Journalists, Am. Coun. on Germany (McCloy fellow 1980, Haus Rissen fellow 1982, del. German-Am. Biennial Conf. 1989), Saginaw Valley Press Club (pres. 1976), Nat. Conf. Editl. Writers (group chmn. 1991), Latvian Club Saginaw. Avocations: sports, history, geo-politics. Home: 3925 Cabaret Trl W Apt 4 Saginaw MI 48603-2205 Office: Saginaw News 203 S Washington Ave Saginaw MI 48607-1244

PURCELL, ANN RUSHING, state legislator, office manager medical business; b. Reidsville, Ga., May 12, 1945; d. William Robert and Katie (Dasher) Rushing; m. Dent Wiley Purcell, May 26, 1966; children: Edwin Wiley, Mieke Ann, Mikki Marie. BS in Edn., Ga. So. Coll., 1966. Cert. secondary tchr. Tchr. math. Evans (Ga.) High Sch., 1966-68; tchr. math., earth and sci. Beaumont Jr. High Sch., Lexington, Ky., 1969-70; substitute tchr. Tallahassee, Fla., 1970's; agt. Noblin Realty, Tallahassee, 1970's; office mgr. Radiation Therapy Assocs., PC, Savannah, Ga., 1979—; state legislator Ho. of Reps. Ga. Gen. Assembly, Atlanta, 1991—. Author: Purcells of South

Georgia and Other Related Families, 1976. Bd. dirs. Med. Assn. Ga. Polit. Action Com., Atlanta, 1988-89, Girl Scout Coun. Savannah, 1991-93, Ga. So. U. Found., 1992—; mem. adv. com. Effingham County Extension Svc., 1992—; fin. chmn. State YMCA, 1991—; bd. adv. Claxton Youth Detnetion Ctr. Recipient Friend of Medicine award Med. Assn. Ga., 1991, 93, 94, 96, Guardian of Small Bus. award Nat. Fedn. Ind. Bus., 1992, 94, 96, Commendation cert. Ga. Emergency Mgmt. Agy., 1995; named Georgia's Legislator of the Yr., Ga. Sch. Councilors Assn., 1996. Mem. Aux. to the Med. Assn. Ga. (pres. 1985), Aux. to the Ga. Med. Soc. (pres. 1981-82), Ga. Salzburger Soc., Effingham County Pub. Officials Assn., Rotary Internat., Ga. Peace Officers Assn. (hon.). Democrat. Methodist. Avocations: painting, genealogy, fishing. Home: 410 Willowpeg Way Rincon GA 31326-9111 Office: State Capitol SW Ste 401 Atlanta GA 30334-1600

PURCELL, BRADFORD MOORE, publishing company executive; b. Garden City, N.Y., Oct. 1, 1929; s. William Lawrence and Margaret (Moore) P.; m. Louise Rauth, July 10, 1954; children: Margaret, Philip, Mark, Louisa, Christopher. B.A., Williams Coll., 1951; M.B.A., Columbia U., 1957. Sr. v.p. devel. McGraw Hill, Inc., 1976-79, sr. v.p., 1979-81, group v.p. tng. systems, 1981-83, sr. v.p. mktg., 1983-85; pres. W.H. Smith Pubs Inc., N.Y.C., 1985-91; Rsch. Books Inc., 1992. Served to 1st lt. USAF, 1951-53. Home: RR 3 21-31 Croton Lake Rd Katonah NY 10536 Office: Rsch Books Inc 38 Academy St # 1507 Madison CT 06443-2611

PURCELL, DALE, college president, consultant; b. Baxley, Ga., Oct. 20, 1919; s. John Groce and Agnes (Moody) P.; m. Edna Jean Rowell, Aug. 2, 1944; children: David Scott, Steven Dale, Pamela Jean; m. Mary Louise Gerlinger, Aug. 26, 1962; adopted children: Amelia Allerton, Jon Allerton. B.A., U. Redlands, 1948, M.A., 1949; postgrad., Northwestern U., 1951-52; LL.D., Lindenwood Colls., 1974. Topographer U.S. E.D., 1939; U.S. counter-intelligence agt., 1940-42; assoc. prof. Ottawa U., 1953-54, asst. to pres., 1954-58; gen. sec. Earlham Coll., 1958-61; dir. devel. U. So. Fla., 1961-63; pres. MITAC, Inc., Beverly Hills, Calif., 1961-72; exec. dir. Cancer Research Center, Columbia, Mo., 1963-65; pres. Westminster Coll., Fulton, Mo., 1973-76, Dale Purcell Assocs., 1972-92, Westminster Coll., Fulton, Mo., 1973-76; a founding dir. Am. Sports Medicine Inst., Birmingham, Ala., 1987-92; chmn. Corp. Health Solutions, Arlington, Tex., 1988—; rep. consolidated clients Hughston Sports Medicine Found., Columbus, Ga., Berry Coll., Mt. Berry, Ga., Hope Coll., Holland, Mich., William Woods Coll., Fulton, Mo., Eureka (Ill.) Coll., Cranbrook Insts., Bloomfield Hills, Mich., Penrose Hosp., Colorado Springs, Colo., Northwestern Coll., Orange City, Iowa, Centro Medico Docente, Caracas, Venezuela, Wayland Acad., Beaver Dam, Wis., Cen. Coll., Pella, Iowa, U. of Stirling, Scotland, U. Ottawa, Ont., Can., Washington & Lee U., Lexington, Va., Taylor U., Upland, Ind., Menninger Found., Topeka, Kans., Ill. Wesleyan U., Bloomington, Cox Med. Systems, Springfield, Mo., Nat. Council Family Rels. Mpls., Stephens Coll., Columbia, Mo., Hist. Savannah Found., Ga. Bd. visitors Berry Coll. Capt. USMCR, 1942-46, 52-53. Recipient Disting. Achievement award Berry Coll., 1974, medal Pres. of China, 1945, medal Pres. of Korea, 1953. Mem. Pi Kappa Delta (Alpha chpt.). Presbyterian (elder 1964—). Clubs: St. Louis (Clayton), Univ. (St. Louis and N.Y.C.), Litchfield County Ct. Home: Woodlands 120 Belden St Falls Village CT 06031

PURCELL, GEORGE RICHARD, artist, postal employee; b. Clayton, N.Y., May 4, 1921; s. George Thomas and Katherine Eileen (Eagan) P.; m. Mary Sutter, Apr. 3, 1961. BS, Niagara U., 1947; postgrad., Syracuse U., 1952-53, 55-56. With Eagan Real Estate, Syracuse, 1948-49; claims interviewer N.Y. State Div. Unemployment Ins., 1949-50, 52; with U.S. Postal Service, Syracuse, 1957—, cert. classifier of mails, 1975-77, with registry dept., 1977—; tutor philosophy, 1971—. Exhibited in Central N.Y. Art Open, 1981, Drake Gallery, Fayetteville, N.Y., 1982, Assoc. Artists Gallery, Syracuse, 1983, 91, Fayetteville Art Festival, 1984, Recreation Generation Art Exhibit, 1982—, DeWitt (N.Y.) Libr., 1986-94, N.Y. State Fair, 1990, Art Telauc WCNY-TV, Syracuse, N.Y., 1990—, Cazenovia Coll. Art Auction, 1994. Founder, pres. Syracuse chpt. Cath. Med. Mission Bd., 1973-76, rep., 1976—; del. Predsl. Trust, 1992; senator of high chamber Internat. Parliament for Safety and Peace, also dep. of assembly; active Cath. Near-East Welfare Assn., Book Mission Program, New Mems. Art Show Manlius Libr., 1991, Rep. Nat. Com., Heritage Found, Washington. Decorated Legion de L'Aigle de mer, Order of Holy Cross of Jerusalem, Order Knight Templars of Jerusalem, knight Order of Holy Grail, knight Lofsensischen Ursinius Orden, baron Royal Order of Bohemian Crown. Served with U.S. Army, 1943-46. N.Y. State War Service scholar, 1955. Fellow Australian Inst. Co-ordinated Rsch. (life); mem. Am. Biog. Inst. (life assoc., rsch. bd. advisors nat. div.), Internat. Soc. Neoplatonic Studies, World Jewish Congress, Soc. Ancient Greek Philosophy, Inst. des Hautes Etudes, Alliance Universelle pour La Paix (hon. prof.), Osterrichische Albert Sweitzer Gesselshaft, Lofsensischen Ursinius Orden (knight), Internat. Parliament for Safety and Peace (senator high chamber dept. mem. assembly), German Order of the Holy Grail (knight), Heritage Found., Acad. Maison Des Internationale Intellectuels, Australian Inst. of Co-Ordinated Rsch. (life fellow), Contemporary Personalities. Roman Catholic.

PURCELL, JAMES FRANCIS, former utility executive, consultant; b. Miles City, Mont., May 13, 1920; s. Robert E. and Mary A. (Hickey) P.; m. Dorothy Marie Abel, Nov. 4, 1944; children—Angela, Ann, Alicia, Anita, Alanna, James Francis, Andrea, Adria, Michael, Gregory, Amara. A.B. magna cum laude, U. Notre Dame, 1942; MBA, Harvard U., 1943. With McGraw-Hill Pub. Co., N.Y.C., 1946-48; dir. public relations Am. Maize Products Co., N.Y.C., 1948-51; public relations cons. Selvage & Lee, Chgo., 1951-53; with No. Ind. Public Service Co., Hammond, 1953—, v.p. public relations, 1961-75, sr. v.p., 1975-84, bd. dirs., chmn. environ. and consumer affairs com.; owner, pres. James F. Purcell and Assocs., 1984—. Chmn. bd. govs. Our Lady of Mercy Hosp., Dyer, Ind., 1979-83; past chmn. Hammond Community Chest drive; past mem. nat. president's council St. Mary's (Ind.) Coll.; bd. dirs. Catholic Charities, 1965-85; chmn. bd. dirs. Bishop Noll Found., 1988-90. Served to lt. USNR, 1943-46. Named Man of Year Notre Dame U., 1967. Mem. Pub. Rels. Soc. Am. (past pres. Hoosier chpt.), N.W. Ind. Assn. Commerce and Industry (v.p., dir. 1979-83), Newcomen Soc. N. Am., Briar Ridge Country Club (Schererville), Serra Club (past pres. Calumet region), Notre Dame Club, Harvard U. Bus. Sch. Club of Chgo. Office: 2842 45th St Highland IN 46322-2905

PURCELL, JAMES NELSON, JR., international organization administrator; b. Nashville, July 16, 1938; s. James Nelson and Mary Helen P.; m. Walda Jean Primm, July 16, 1961; children: Deirdre Ann, Carole Elizabeth. B.A. in Polit. Sci., Furman U., 1961; M.P.A. (Maxwell Grad. Sch. fellow), Syracuse U., 1962. Mgmt. intern U.S. AEC, N.Y.C., Washington, Oak Ridge, 1962; budget analyst U.S. AEC, Oak Ridge, Washington, 1962-66; mgmt. analyst AID, State Dept., Washington, 1966-68; budget preparation specialist Office Mgmt. and Budget/Exec. Office of the Pres., 1968-69, dept. chief budget preparation, 1969-72; sr. budget examiner Internat. Ednl. Exch. program Office of Pres., 1972-74; chief Justice-Treasury br. Office Mgmt. and Budget/Exec. Office of the Pres., 1974-76; chief resources programming and mgmt. div. Bur. Ednl. and Cultural Affairs, Dept. State, Washington, 1976-77; exec. dir. Bur. Adminstrn., Dept. State, Washington, 1978-79; dep. asst. sec. Bur. Refugee Programs, Dept. State, Washington, 1979-82, dir., 1982-87; dir. gen. Internat. Orgn. for Migration, Geneva, 1988—. Mem. Am. Soc. Pub. Adminstrn. Home: 6 Chateau-Banquet, CH-1202 Geneva Switzerland Office: IOM/Case postale 71, 17 Rt des Morillons, 1211 Geneva 19, Switzerland

PURCELL, JOHN F., lawyer; b. Bellingham, Wash., Apr. 25, 1954. AB with honors, Stanford U., 1976; JD, Lewis and Clark Coll., 1980. Bar: Oreg. 1980. Ptnr. Miller, Nash, Wiener, Hager & Carlsen, Portland. Mem. Oreg. State Bar. Office: Miller Nash Wiener Hager & Carlsen 111 SW 5th Ave Portland OR 97204-3604

PURCELL, KENNETH, psychology educator, university dean; b. N.Y.C., Oct. 21, 1928; s. Herman and Ann (Bulkin) P.; m. Claire Dickson Kepler, Dec. 17, 1949 (div. Dec. 1986); children: Kathleen Ann, Andrew Kepler; m. Marjorie Bayes, Jan. 17, 1987. B.A., Ph.D., U. Nebr. Asst. prof. U. Ky., 1956-58; dir. behavior sci. div. Children's Asthma Research Inst.; asst. prof. U. Colo. Med. Center, 1958-68; prof., dir. clin. tng. psychology U. Mass., 1968-69, chmn. dept. psychology, 1969-70; prof. psychology, chmn. dept. U. Denver, 1970—, dean Coll. Arts and Scis., 1976-84, prof. psychology, 1984—. Author papers in field. Served to 2d lt. AUS, 1953-56. Fellow Am. Psychol. Assn., Soc. Research Child Devel., AAAS, Colo. Psychol. Assn. (dir. 1962-64). Home: 3759 E Noble Rd Littleton CO 80122-2042 Office: Univ Denver Coll Arts And Scis Denver CO 80208

PURCELL, LEE, actress, producer; b. N.C., June 15, 1957; divorced; 1 child, Dylan D. Purcell. Studies with Margot Lister, London; studies with Milton Katselas, Jeff Corey, U.S. Co-owner Silver Strand Entertainment; co-owner Silver Strand Entertainment (film and TV prodn.). Appeared in (films) Adam at 6 A.M., 1970, The Toy Factory, 1971, Dirty Little Billy, 1972, Kid Blue, 1973, Mr. Majestyx, 1974, Almost Summer, Big Wednesday, 1978, Stir Crazy, 1980, Valley Girl, Eddie Macon's Run, 1983, Laura's Dream, 1986, Airplane II, 1989, Trackers, 1990, The Joke, 1994, (TV) Highjack, 1973, Stranger in Our House, 1978, Howard, The Amazing Mr. Hughes, 1979, Kenny Rogers as the Gambler, 1980, Killing At Hell's Gate, 1981, My Wicked Wicked Ways: The Legend of Errol Flynn, 1986, Betrayal of Innocence, 1989, Long Road Home (Emmy nominee Lead Actress-Special), 1991, To Heal a Nation, 1992, Dazzle, 1994, Secret Sins of the Father (Emmy nominee Supporting Actress-Special), 1994, Due South (recurring role), 1995, (stage) One Flew Over the Cuckoo's Nest, Richard III, A Streetcar Named Desire, The Taming of the Shrew, A Midsummer's Night Dream. Recipient Bronze Star Halo Career Achievement award So. Calif. Motion Picture Council, 1985, Golden Star Halo award, 1986, Silver Medal award N.Y. Film and TV Festival, 1987. Mem. Actors' Equity Assn., Screen Actors Guild, AFTRA, Acad. Motion Picture Arts and Scis., Acad. TV Arts And Scis. Avocations: writing, collecting antiques and art. Office: PO Box 12581 La Crescenta CA 91224-5581 Office: PO Box 12581 La Crescenta CA 91224-5581

PURCELL, MARY LOUISE GERLINGER, educator; b. Thief River Falls, Minn., July 17, 1923; d. Charles and Lajla (Dale) Gerlinger; student Yankton Coll., 1941-45, Yale Div. Sch., 1949-50, NYU, summer 1949; MA (alumni fellow), Tchrs. Coll. Columbia, 1959, EdD, 1963; m. Walter A. Kuyawski, June 9, 1950 (dec. July 1954); children: Amelia Allerton, Jon Allerton; m. 2d, Dale Purcell, Aug. 26, 1962. Teen-age program dir., YWCA, New Haven, 1945-52; dir. program in family rels., asst. prof. sociology and psychology Earlham Coll., Richmond, Ind., 1959-62, conf. coord. undergrad. edn. for women, 1962; chmn. div. home and community Stephens Coll., Columbia, Mo., 1962-73, chmn. family and community studies, 1962-78, dir. Learning Unltd., continuing edn. for women, 1974-78, developer course The Contemporary Am. Woman, 1962, cons., 1962; prof., Auburn (Ala.) U., 1978-88, prof. emerita, 1988—, head dept. family and child devel., 1978-84, spl. asst. to v.p. acad. affairs, 1985-86. chmn. search com. for v.p. acad. affairs, 1984; vis. prof. Ind. U. Summer Sch., 1970. Cons. student personnel svcs., Trenton (N.J.) State Coll., 1958-59, 61. Recipient Alumni Achievement award Yankton Coll., 1975. Mem. AAUW, Am. Home Econs. Assn. (bd. dirs. 1967-69, chair 1st subject matter unit 1969, family relations and child devel. sect. 1986-89), Groves Conf. on Family, Nat. Council Family Relations (dir., chmn.-elect affiliated councils, 1981-82, chmn., 1982-84, nat. program chmn. 1977, chmn. film awards com., chmn. spl. emphases sect., bd. dirs., Ernest G. Osborne award for excellence in teaching 1979), Housetonic Camera Club (co-pres. 1996—), Delta Kappa Gamma. Presbyterian. Contbr. articles to coll. bulls., jours. Home: 120 Belden St Falls Village CT 06031-1124

PURCELL, PATRICK B., motion picture company executive; b. Dublin, Ireland, Mar. 16, 1943; s. James P. and Rita (Donohoe) P.; m. Simone Gros-Long, Feb. 1, 1968; children: Alexander J., Christopher P., Benjamin J. Student, Staffordshire Coll. Commerce, 1964-66; M.B.A., Fordham U., 1973. CPA, Calif. Various positions in pub. and pvt. acctg. Eng. and U.S., 1960-70; with Paramount Pictures Corp., N.Y.C., Los Angeles, 1970—, v.p. fin., 1980—83, exec. v.p. fin. and adminstrn., 1983-89, exec. v.p., chief fin. and adminstrv. officer, 1989—. Fellow Chartered Assn. Cert. Accts.; mem. AICPA, Calif. Soc. CPAs, Fin. Execs. Inst., Chartered Inst. Taxation. Roman Catholic. Club: Jonathan. Home: 1449 Capri Dr Pacific Palisades CA 90272-2706 Office: Paramount Pictures 5555 Melrose Ave Los Angeles CA 90038-3112

PURCELL, PATRICK JOSEPH, newspaper publisher; b. N.Y.C., Nov. 9, 1947; s. Patrick Joseph and Sarah (Muller) P.; m. Maureen T. Shuart, Aug. 8, 1970; children: Kathleen, Erin, Patrick, Kerry. B.B.A., St. John's U., 1969; M.B.A., Hofstra U., 1977. Various supr. positions N.Y. Daily News, N.Y.C., 1969-80; assoc. pub. Village Voice, N.Y.C., 1980-82; v.p. advt. N.Y. Post, N.Y.C., 1982-83; v.p. sales and mktg. Skyband Inc., N.Y.C., 1983; pres., pub. Boston Herald, 1984—, owner, 1994—; pub. The N.Y. Post, 1986-88; exec. v.p. News Am./Newspapers, 1986-90, pres., 1990-93, CEO, 1993-94; East Coast pres. Am. Ireland Fund, 1996—; bd. dirs. Bay Bank, MetroWest Sub. Regional Bd., The Genesis Fund. Bd. dirs. NCCJ, Boston, 1984-86, Boy Scouts Am., Boston, 1984-85, Cath. Charitable Bur., Boston, 1984-86, John F. Kennedy Found.; mem. Greater Boston Assn. Retarded Citizens, 1984-86; chmn. Boston Against Drugs, 1988—; mem. White House Conf. for a Drug Free Am., 1987—. Mem. Boston Better Bus. Bur., Am. Newspaper Pub. Assn., New Eng. Newspaper Assn., Boston C. of C. (bd. dirs. 1984-86), Downtown Crossing Assn. (bd. dirs.). Roman Catholic. Clubs: Publicity, Ad (Boston). Avocations: jogging; skiing. Office: Boston Herald 1 Herald St Boston MA 02118-2200*

PURCELL, PHILIP JAMES, financial services company executive; b. Salt Lake City, Sept. 5, 1943; m. Anne Marie Mc Namara, Apr. 2, 1964. B.B.A., U. Notre Dame, 1964; M.Sc. in Econs., London Sch. Econs. and Polit. Sci., U. London, 1966; M.B.A., U. Chgo., 1967. Mng. dir., cons. McKinsey & Co., Inc., Chgo., 1967-78; v.p. planning and adminstrn. Sears, Roebuck and Co., Chgo., 1978-82; from pres., CEO, to chmn., CEO Dean Witter Discover & Co., N.Y.C., 1982—; also bd. dirs. Dean Witter InterCapital Inc., N.Y.C.; bd. dirs. Dean Witter Realty Inc., Dean Witter Reynolds, Inc., N.Y. Stock Exchange, SPS Payment Systems Inc., Transaction Svcs. Inc.; mem. coun. Grad. Sch. Bus., Univ. Chgo.; chmn. Discover Card Svcs. Inc.; chmn., CEO Novus Credit Svcs. Inc. Bd. trustees U. Notre Dame Bus. Sch., Ind. Served with USNR. Roman Catholic. Clubs: Economic of Chgo., The Chgo. Office: Dean Witter/Discover 2 World Trade Ctr New York NY 10048-0203

PURCELL, RICHARD FICK, lawyer, food companies advisor and counsel; b. Washington, Apr. 19, 1924; s. Richard J. and Clara A. (Fick) P.; m. Judith Wyckoff, Nov. 28, 1964; children: Richard Wyckoff, Edward Thomas, Carolyn Elizabeth P. Reichenbach. BA, George Washington U., 1948; MA, Columbia U., 1949; cert., U. Fribourg (Switzerland), 1949; LLB, Harvard U., 1952; grad., Command and Gen. Staff Coll., Ft. Leavenworth, Kans., 1970, Indsl. Coll. Armed Forces, 1971. Bar: D.C. 1953, Mass. 1953, Minn. 1953, N.Y. 1954, U.S. Ct. Appeals (D.C. and 2d cirs.) 1954, U.S. Dist. Ct. D.C. 1954, U.S. Dist. Ct. (so. and ea. dists.) N.Y. 1954, U.S. Ct. Mil. Appeals 1954, U.S. Supreme Ct. 1963, U.S. Ct. Appeals (3rd cir.) 1996. Assoc. Shearman & Sterling, N.Y.C., 1954-74; v.p., dep. gen. counsel 1st Nat. City Bank (now Citibank N.A.), N.Y.C., 1974-75; sr. v.p., gen. counsel The Connell Co. and related cos., Westfield, N.J., 1975-93; food co. cons. and counsel, 1993—; bd. dirs. Combined Life Ins. Co., N.Y., 1973—, Connell Co. and related cos., 1975-86. Author: Government Administration of Wage Incentives in Wartime, 1949, Church and State in Colonial Connecticut, 1953; contbr. to Cath. Ency., legal and banking jours.; law editor (Banking Law Jour.), 1965-67; mem. adv. bd. Letter of Credit Update, 1987—. Lt. col. F.A., U.S. Army, 1943-46, 52-53, PTO, ETO. Mem. ABA (task force on study and revision of UCC Article 5), D.C. Bar Assn., Minn. Territorial Pioneers, Mil. Order of World Wars, Army and Navy Club (Washington), Harvard Club (N.Y.C.), Harvard Law Alumni (life), Lincoln's Inn (Cambridge). Republican. Roman Catholic. Office: PO Box 257 Oldwick NJ 08858-0257

PURCELL, ROBERT HARRY, virologist; b. Keokuk, Iowa, Dec. 19, 1935; s. Edward Harold and Elsie Thelma (Melzl) P.; m. Carol Joan Moody, June 11, 1961; children: David Edward, John Leslie. BA in Chemistry, Okla. State U., 1957; MS Biochemistry, Baylor U., 1960; MD, Duke U., 1962. Intern in pediatrics Duke U. Hosp., Durham, N.C., 1962-63; officer USPHS, 1963, advanced through grades to med. dir. (O-6), 1974; with Epidemic Intelligence Svc., Communicable Disease Ctr. Atlanta; assigned to vaccine br. Nat. Inst. Allergy and Infectious Diseases, Bethesda, Md., 1963-65; sr. surgeon Lab. Infectious Diseases, NIH, Bethesda, Md., 1965-69, med. officer, 1969-72, med. dir., 1972-74, head hepatitis viruses sect., 1974—; organizer, invited participant, speaker numerous nat. and internat. symposia, confs., workshops, meetings; temporary advisor WHO, 1967—; expert cons. in hepatitis U.S.—China, U.S.—Taiwan, U.S.—Japan, U.S.—Russia, U.S.—India, U.S.—Pakistan Bilateral Sci. Agreements; lectr. various virology classes. Mem. editl. bd. and/or reviewer Am. Jour. Epidemiology, Gastroenterology, Hepatology, Infection and Immunity, Jour. Clin. Microbiology, Jour. Infectious Diseases, Jour. Med. Virology, Jour. Nat. Cancer Inst., Nature, Sci.; contbr. over 500 articles to profl. jours., chpts. to books; numerous patents in field. Decorated D.S.M.; recipient Superior Svc. award USPHS, 1972, Meritorious Svc. medal USPHS, 1974, Gorgas medal, 1977, Disting. Alumni award Duke U. Sch. Medicine, 1978, Eppinger prize 5th Internat. FALK Symposium on Virus and Liver, Switzerland, 1979, Medal of City of Turin, Italy, 1983, Gold medal Can. Liver Found., 1984, Inventor's Incentive award U.S. Commerce Dept., 1984; fellowships Baylor U., 1959-60, Duke U., 1960-62; named to Alumni Hall of Fame East Okla. State Coll., 1996. Fellow Washington Acad. Scis.; mem. Am. Epidemiology Soc., Am. Soc. Microbiology, Am. Soc. Virology, Am. Acad. Microbiology, AAAS, Soc. Epidemiol. Rsch., Infectious Diseases Soc. Am. (Squibb award 1980), N.Y. Acad. Scis., Am. Soc. Clin. Investigation, Assn. Am. Physicians, Am. Coll. Epidemiology, Am. Assn. Study of Liver Diseases, Internat. Assn. Study and Prevention Virus Associated Cancers, Internat. Assn. Biol. Standardization, Internat. Assn. Study Liver, Soc. Exptl. Biology and Medicine (Disting. Scientist award 1986), Nat. Acad. Scis. Office: NIH Lab Infectious Diseases NIH Bldg 7 Rm 202 7 Center Dr MSC 0740 Bethesda MD 20892-0740

PURCELL, STEVEN RICHARD, international management consultant, engineer, economist. B of Mech. and Indsl. Engring., NYU Coll. Engring., 1950; MS in Indsl. Engring., Columbia U., 1951; EdM, Harvard U., 1968. Registered profl. engr., Can. Lectr. engring. NYU Coll. Engring., N.Y.C., 1948-50; gen. mgr. Dapol Plastics Co., Inc., Boston, 1956-58; gen. div. mgr. Am. Cyanamid Co., Sanford, Maine, 1958-61; sr. prin., mgmt. cons. investment banking Purcell & Assocs., N.Y.C., 1961-66; prof., chmn. Bristol Coll., Fall River, Mass., 1966-68; assoc. dean grad. faculty adminstrv. studies York U., Toronto, Ont., Can., 1969-71; chief economist Dept. Manpower and Immigration, Ottawa, Ont., Can., 1970-71; cons. Treasury Bd., Ottawa, 1971-72; dir. urban and internat. environ. policy Ministry of State for Urban Affairs Internat. Activities, Ottawa, 1973-74; mem. com. on challenges of modern soc. NATO, Ottawa, 1973-74; mem. sci., econ. policy com. OECD UN, Ottawa, 1973-74; prof. Grad. Sch. Bus. Adminstrn. and Econs. Algonquin Coll., Ottawa, 1974-76; advisor, cons. House of Commons, 1976-77; sr. prin. Purcell & Assocs., Internat. Mgmt. Cons., Washington, 1977-80, chmn., CEO, 1981—; chmn., CEO Phoenix Internat. Capital Associates, Washington, 1981—; exec. dir. nat. coastal zone mgmt. adv. com. NOAA U.S. Dept. Commerce, Washington, 1980-81; profl. lectr. Northeastern U. Grad. Sch. Bus. Adminstrn., Boston, 1953-56, U. Toronto, 1968-69, George Washington U. Grad. Sch. Bus. Adminstrn., Washington, 1979; vis. prof. Rensselaer Poly. Inst. Advanced Mgmt. Program, 1967, U. Ottawa Grad. Sch. Bus. Adminstrn., 1971-74; lectr. Council for Internat. Progress in Mgmt., N.Y.C., 1960, Royal Bank Can. Mgmt. Assn., Toronto, Ont., 1970; corp. appointment cons. Harvard U., Cambridge, Mass., 1967-68; cons. Govt. Venezuela, 1967-68, Can. Inst. Bankers, Toronto, 1969-70; internat. sr. adviser NASA, 1985-86, mem. nat. adv. bd. Ctr. for Nat. Policy; dir. Rental Resource Corp., 1986-89. Contbr. articles on indsl. orgn., sci. policy and fin. to profl. jours. Lt. AC, USNR, 1943-46. Mem. UN Assn., Soc. for Advancement of Mgmt. (pres. 1949-50, leadership award 1950), Tau Beta Pi, Alpha Pi Mu (v.p. 1949-50), Columbia Univ. Club (Washington, trustee 1982-84, chmn., sr. trustee 1984-85), Harvard Univ. Club. Office: 12904 Mayflower Ln Bowie MD 20720-3368

PURCELL, STUART MCLEOD, III, financial planner; b. Santa Monica, Calif., Feb. 16, 1944; s. Stuart McLeod Jr. and Carol (Howe) P. AA, Santa Monica City Coll., 1964; BS, Calif. State U., Northridge, 1967; grad., CPA Advanced Personal Fin. Planning Curriculum, San Francisco, 1985. CPA, Calif.; CFP. Sr. acct. Pannell Kerr Forster, San Francisco, 1970-73; fin. cons. Purcell Fin. Services, San Francisco, 1973-74, San Rafael, Calif., 1980-81; controller Decimus Corp., San Francisco, 1974-76, Grubb & Ellis Co., Oakland, Calif., 1976-78, Marwais Steel Co., Richmond, Calif., 1979-80; owner, fin. counselor Purcell Wealth Mgmt., San Rafael, 1981—; guest lectr. Golden Gate U., San Francisco, 1985—; leader ednl. workshops, Larkspur, Calif., 1984; speaker Commonwealth Club Calif., 1989, 91. Contbr. articles to newspapers and profl. jours. Treas. Salvation Army, San Rafael-San Anselmo-Fairfax, Calif., 1987—; chmn. fin. planners div. United Way Marin County, Calif., 1984; mem. fundraising com. Marin County March of Dimes, 1987—, Marin County Arthritis Found., 1988—; mem. Marin Estate Planning Council. Served to lt. (j.g.) USNR, 1968-76. Named Eagle Scout, 1959, Best Fin. Advisor Marin County Independent-Jour. newspaper, 1987, Top Producer Unimarc, 1986; recipient Outstanding Achievement award United Way, 1984; named to The Registry of Fin. Planning Practitioners, 1987. Mem. AICPA, Calif. Soc. CPAs, Nat. Speakers Assn., Internat. Assn. for Fin. Planners (exec. dir. North Bay chpt., San Francisco 1984), Internat. Soc. Pre-Retired Planners, Soc. CPA-Fin. Planners (dist. membership chmn. San Francisco 1986), Registry Fin. Planning Practitioners, Sigma Alpha Epsilon. Presbyterian. Avocations: travel, auto racing, skiing, gardening. Home: 45 Vineyard Dr San Rafael CA 94901-1228 Office: Purcell Wealth Mgmt 1811 Grand Ave Ste B San Rafael CA 94901-1925

PURCELL, WILLIAM PAXSON, III, association administrator; b. Phila., Oct. 25, 1953; s. William Paxson Jr. and Mary (Hamilton) P.; m. Deborah Lee Miller, Aug. 9, 1986; 1 child, Jesse Miller. AB, Hamilton Coll., 1976; JD, Vanderbilt U., 1979. Bar: Tenn. 1979, U.S. Ct. Appeals (6th cir.) 1985, U.S. Supreme Ct. 1986. Staff atty. West Tenn. Legal Svcs., Jackson, Tenn., 1979-81; asst. pub. defender Metro Pub. Defender, Nashville, Tenn., 1981-84, sr. asst. pub. defender, 1984-85; assoc. Lionel R. Barrett, P.C., Nashville, 1985-86; ptnr. Farmer, Berry & Purcell, Nashville, 1986-90; mem. Tenn. Ho. of Reps., Nashville, 1986-96, also majority leader, 1990-96; dir. child and family policy ctr. Vanderbilt Inst. for Pub. Policy Studies, Vanderbilt U., Nashville, 1996—; chmn. select com. on children and youth Tenn. Gen. Assembly, 1989-96; exec. dir. Vanderbilt Legal Aid Soc., 1978-79; chmn. NCSL Assembly of State Issues, 1995; chmn. policy makers' program adv. bd. Danforth Found. Mem. exec. com. exec. com. 6th dist. Dems., Nashville, 1986-88, mem. Tenn. Statee Gen. Assembly, Nashville, 1986-96, Majority leader, 1990-96, chmn. human svcs.com. Nat. Conf. State Legislatures, Washington, 1993; mem. Dem. Nat. Com. exec. com., 1994-97; chmn. Dem. Legislative Campaign Com., 1994-96. Toll fellow Coun. State Govts., 1988; named Legislator of Yr. Dist. Attys.' Gen. Conf. 1989, Tenn. Conservation League, 1991. Mem. ABA, Tenn. Acad. Pediatricians, Tenn. Bar Assn., Nashville Bar Assn., Dem. Legis. Leaders Assn. (chmn. 1994—). Methodist. Home: 1207 18th Ave S Nashville TN 37212

PURCIFULL, DAN ELWOOD, plant virologist, educator; b. Woodland, Calif., July 1, 1935; s. Ernest Lee and Virginia (Margaroli) P.; m. Marcia Ann Weatherby, Sept. 7, 1966; children: Scott, Douglas. B.S., U. Calif., Davis, 1957, M.S., 1959, Ph.D., 1964. Asst. prof. plant pathology U. Fla., Gainesville, 1964-69; assoc. prof. U. Fla., 1969-75, prof., 1975—; dept. grad. coord., 1988-91; mem. plant virus subcom. Internat. Com. for Taxonomy of Viruses, 1973-75, mem. potyvirus study group, 1987-93; mem. plant virology adv. com. Am. Type Culture Collection, 1993-96; mem. Internat. Legume Virus Working Group. Assoc. editor Phytopathology, 1971-73, Plant Disease, 1987-89; contbr. articles to profl. jours. Mem. Morningside Nature Center Commn., City of Gainesville, 1978-81, treas., 1981. Served with U.S. Army, 1957. Fellow AAAS, Am. Phytopathol Soc. (Lee Hutchins award 1981, Ruth Allen award 1992); mem. Fla. State Hort. Soc., N.Y. Acad. Sci., Am. Soc. Virology, Sigma Xi, Gamma Sigma Delta. Home: 3106 NW 1st Ave Gainesville FL 32607-2504

PURCIFULL, ROBERT OTIS, insurance company executive; b. Grinnell, Iowa, July 1, 1932; s. Chauncey O. and Mildred E. (Clendenen) P.; m. Mary G. White, Sept. 12, 1953; children: Jane, Robert Otis, Patricia, Elizabeth. B.A., Grinnell Coll., 1954. C.L.U. With Occidental Life Ins. Co., Calif., 1960-78; 1st. v.p. charge agys. Occidental Life Ins. Co., Los Angeles, 1968-71; exec. v.p. sales Occidental Life Ins. Co., 1971-76; pres., chief exec. officer Transmerica Ins. Mgmt., Inc., Los Angeles, 1972-78, Countrywide Life Ins. Co., Los Angeles, 1973-76; dir. Countrywide Life Ins. Co., 1973-78; chmn. bd., pres. Plaza Ins. Sales Inc., San Francisco; pres., chief exec. officer Occidental Life of Can., 1977-78; pres., chief operating officer, dir. Penn Mut. Life Ins. Co., Phila., 1979-80; sr. v.p. life divsn. Am.

Gen. Corp., 1981-82; pres. Lincoln Am. Life Ins. Co., Am. Gen. Life Ins. Co. Del., Am. Gen. Life Ins. Co. Tex., Am. Amicable Life Ins. Co., Pioneer Am., 1982-84; vice chmn. Pioneer Security Life Ins. Co., 1982-84; pres., CEO Gulf Life Ins. Co., Interstate Fire Co., Jacksonville, Fla., 1984-88, also dir.; pres. Am. Gen. Group Ins. Co. Fla., 1986-89; vice chmn. Gulf Life Ins. Co., 1988-91; chmn., CEO ROP & Assocs. Past pres. Vols. of Am., L.A.; councilman City of Upper Arlington, Ohio, 1962-66; trustee Life Underwriters Tng. Coun., Washington, 1975-78; campaign chmn. Jacksonville United Way, 1988, 89, chmn., 1989-90; pres. Jacksonville Univ. Coun., 1992, 93; pres. Jacksonville Symphony Orch., 1993-94; chmn. bus. adv. coun. U. North Fla.; bd. dirs. Acordia Benefits Fla., 1993-96. Mem. Life Ins. Mktg. and Rsch. Assn. (bd. dirs. 1982-85). Home: 12285 Fairway Pointe Row San Diego CA 92128

PURCUPILE, JOHN STEPHEN, lawyer; b. Ventura, Calif., Nov. 8, 1954; s. John Charles and Sylvia Marie (Pilgrim) P.; m. Anna Marie Leone, June 20, 1981; children: John Justin, Jessica Marie. BA, Case Western Reserve U., 1980; JD, Duquesne U., 1983. Bar: Pa. 1983, U.S. Dist. Ct. (we. dist.) Pa. 1983, U.S. Supreme Ct. 1987. Lawyer Stone & Stone, Pitts., 1983-85; law clk. Ct. of Common Pleas Hon. Livingstone M. Johnson, Pitts., 1985-88; lawyer Egler, Garrett & Egler, Pitts., 1988—. Home: 335 Kennedy Rd Prospect PA 16052 Office: Egler Garrett & Egler 428 Forbes Ave Pittsburgh PA 15219-1603

PURDES, ALICE MARIE, adult education educator, retired; b. St. Louis, Jan. 8, 1931; d. Joseph Louis and Angeline Cecilia (Mozier) P. AA, Belleville Area Coll., 1951; BS, Ill. State U., Normal, 1953, MS, 1954; cert., Sorbonne U., Paris, 1964; PhD, Fla. State U., Tallahassee, 1976. Cert. in music edn., elem. edn., secondary edn., adult edn. Teaching/grad. asst. Ill. State U., 1953-54; music supr. Princeton (Ill.) Pub. Schs., 1954-55; music dir. Venice (Ill.) Pub. Schs., 1955-72, secondary vocal music dir., 1955-72; coord. literacy program Venice-Lincoln Tech. Ctr., 1983-86, chair lang. arts dept., 1983—; retired; tchr. in space candidate, 1985. Mem. St. Louis chpt. World Affairs Coun., UN Assn., Nat. Mus. of Women in the Arts, Humane Soc. of Am.; charter mem. St. Louis Sci. Ctr., Harry S. Truman Inst.; contbr. Old Six Mile Mus., 1981, Midland Repertory Players, Alton, Ill., 1991; chair Cystic Fibrosis Spring Bike-A-Thon, Madison, Ill., 1981, Granite City, Ill., 1985. Recipient gold medal Nat Senior Olympics, 1989, Senior World Games, 1992, several scholarships. Mem. AAUW, Music Educators Nat. Conf., Ill. Music Educators Assn., Am. Choral Dirs. Assn., Fla. State Alumni Assn., Ill. Adult and Continuing Educators Assn., Am. Fedn. Tchrs. (pres. 1957-58), Western Cath. Union, Croation Fraternal Union, Nat. Space Soc., Travelers Abroad (pres. 1966-68, 89—), Internat. Platform Assn., Archaeol. Inst. Am., Friends St. Louis Art Mus., St. Louis Numis. Assn. Madison Rotary Club (internat. amb., Humanitarian award 1975), Slavic and East European Friends (life), Lovejoy Libr. Friends, Ill. State U. Alumnia Assn. Roman Catholic. Avocations: bowling, travel. Home: PO Box 274 Madison IL 62060-0274

PURDOM, PAUL WALTON, JR., computer scientist; b. Atlanta, Apr. 5, 1940; s. Paul Walton and Bettie (Miller) P.; m. Donna Armstrong; children—Barbara, Linda, Paul. B.S., Calif. Inst. Tech., 1961, M.S., 1962, Ph.D., 1966. Asst. prof. computer sci. U. Wis.-Madison, 1965-70, asst. prof., 1970-71; mem. tech. staff Bell Telephone Labs., Naperville, Ill., 1970-71; assoc. prof., chmn. computer sci. dept. Ind. U., Bloomington, 1977-82, prof. computer sci., 1982—; grant researcher FAW, Ulm, Germany. Author: (with Cynthia Brown) The Analysis of Algorithms; assoc. editor: Computer Surveys; contbr. articles to profl. jours. NSF grantee, 1979, 81, 83, 92, 94. Mem. AAAS, Soc. for Indsl. and Applied Math., Assn. Computing Machinery, Sigma Xi. Democrat. Methodist. Home: 2212 S Belhaven Ct Bloomington IN 47401-6803 Office: Ind U Dept Computer Science 215 Lindley Hall Bloomington IN 47405-4101

PURDOM, THOMAS JAMES, lawyer; b. Seymour, Tex., Apr. 7, 1937; s. Thomas Exer and Juanita Florida (Kuykendall) P.; m. Betty Marie Shoemaker, May 31, 1969; 1 son, James Robert. Student, U. Syracuse, 1956-57, U. Md., 1958-59; BA, Tex. Tech. Coll., 1962; JD, Georgetown U., 1966. Bar: Tex. 1966, U.S. Supreme Ct. 1978, U.S. Ct. Appeals (5th cir.) 1983. Ptnr. Griffith & Purdom, Lubbock, Tex., 1966-67; asst. dist. atty. 72d Jud. Dist., Lubbock, 1967-68; county atty. Lubbock County, Tex., 1968-72; pres. Purdom Law Offices, P.C. and predecessor firms, Lubbock, Tex., 1972—; mem. com. for Vol. 5 pattern jury charges, 1988-97. Author: West's Texas Forms Vols. 16, 17, 18, 1984-96; (with others) Family Law, Texas Practice and Procedure,, 1981. Served with USAF, 1956-60. Fellow Tex. Bar Found.; mem ABA, Lubbock County Bar Assn. (bd. dirs. 1970), State Bar Assn. Tex. (sec. family law sect. 1974-75, chmn. family law sect. 1975-77, mem. examining commn. for family law specialization), Am. Acad. Matrimonial Lawyers (cert. family law, Tex. bd. legal specialization), Tex. Assn. Def. Counsel, Delta Theta Phi. Democrat. Baptist. Home: 3619 55th St Lubbock TX 79413-4713 Office: Purdom Law Offices PC 1801 Avenue Q Lubbock TX 79401-4826

PURDY, ALAN HARRIS, biomedical engineer; b. Mt. Clemens, Mich., Dec. 13, 1923; s. Harry Martin and Elinor (Harris) P.; m. Anna Elizabeth Sohn, Aug. 16, 1968 (dec.); children: Catherine, Charles, Susan, Harry; m. Margaret Josephine Kelly, Mar. 5, 1997. BSME, U. Miami, 1954; MS in Physiology, UCLA, 1967; PhD in Engring., U. Mo., 1970. Cert. clin. engr., Washington. Project engr. in acoustics Arvin Industries, Columbus, Ind., 1954-56, AC Spark Plug Co., Flint, Mich., 1956-60; asst. prof. engring. Calif. Poly. U., Pomona, 1960-62; assoc. dir. biomed. engring. U. Mo., Columbia, 1967-71; dep. assoc. dir., assoc. dir. Nat. Inst. for Occupational Safety and Health, Rockville, Md., 1971-81; scientist, biomed. engr. Nat. Inst. for Occupational Safety and Health, Cin., 1983-86; asst. dir. Fla. Inst. Oceanography, St. Petersburg, 1981-83; pres. Alpha Beta R & D Corp., Cape Coral, Fla., 1986—; cons. Smithy Muffler Corp., L.A., 1961-62, Statham Instruments, L.A., 1966; cons. faculty, Tex. Tech. U., Lubbock, 1972-73; lectr. U. Cin., 1980. Patentee in diving, acoustical and occupational safety fields. Pilot CG Aux., Ft. Myers, Fla., 1989—; mem. Dem. Exec. Com., Lee County, 1989—. With USAF, 1942-43. Nat. Heart Inst. spl. fellow, 1963-67; Fulbright scholar, Yugoslavia, 1984. Mem. Acoustical Soc. Am., Biomed. Engring. Soc., Am. Inst. Physics, Exptl. Aircraft Assn., Aircraft Owners and Pilots Assn., DAV. Democrat. Home and Office: 5228 SW 5th Pl Cape Coral FL 33914-6504

PURDY, ALAN MACGREGOR, financial executive; b. Iowa City, Iowa, Apr. 23, 1940; s. Rob Roy MacGregor and Frances Norrine (Edwards) P.; m. Sarah Lane Robins, June 13, 1964; children—William Wallace, John Alan, Tammi Ann. A.B., Duke U., 1962; M.B.A., Wharton Sch. Fin. and Commerce, U. Pa., 1968. Bus. analyst Gen. Mills, Inc., Mpls., 1968-71; sr. fin. analyst Dayton Hudson Corp., Mpls., 1972-73, mgr. capital expenditure analysis, 1973, dir. corp. analysis, 1973-75, dir. planning and analysis, 1975-77; v.p., treas. Fleming Cos., Inc., Oklahoma City, 1977-81; v.p. fin., chief fin. officer John A. Brown Co. (subs. Dayton Hudson Corp.), Oklahoma City, 1981-83; sr. v.p., chief fin. officer B. Dalton Co. (subs. Dayton Hudson Corp.), Mpls., 1983-86, Robinson's of Fla.(subs. May Co.), St. Petersburg, 1986-87, Miller's Outpost (subs. Am. Retail Group), Ontario, Calif., 1988-92, Builders Emporium (subs. Collins and Aikman Group), Irvine, Calif., 1993; Remedy Temp, San Juan Capistrano, Calif., 1994—. Served with USN, 1962-66. Home: 2190 Hillview Dr Laguna Beach CA 92651-2211 Office: Remedy Temp 32122 Camino Capistrano San Juan Capistrano CA 92675-3717

PURDY, DAVID LAWRENCE, biotechnical company executive; b. N.Y.C., Sept. 18, 1928; s. Earl and Mabel (Roberts) P.; m. Margaret Helen Rye, July 7, 1951; children: Susan Lee, John F. (dec.), Ross David (dec.), Thomas Griffith. BSME, Cornell U., 1951; degree in advanced & creative engring., GE, 1955, degree in prof. bus. mgmt., 1956. Devel. engr. GE, Valley Forge, Pa., 1953-64; mgr. energy conversion divsn. Nuclear Materials and Equipment Corp. (acquired by ARCO), Apollo, Pa., 1964-69, Atlantic Richfield Corp., Apollo, 1969-72; founder, pres., chmn. Biocontrol Tech., Inc., Indiana, 1972—; chmn., treas. Diasense, Inc., Indiana, 1989—. Contbr. over 22 articles to profl. jours. 1st lt. USAF, 1961-63. Fellow ASME (life); mem. AAAS, Am. Diabetes Assn. Achievements include patents for generator of electrical energy by radioisotope thermoelectric conversion, for radioisotope powered cardiac pacemaker, for radioisotope powered artificial heart, for thermoelectric apparatus for high thermoelectric efficiency by cascading materials, for method of metals joining and articles produced by such method - brazing copper to tungsten, for thermoelectric apparatus for high thermoelectric efficiency by cascading materials, for generator of electrical energy by radioisotope thermoelectric conversion, for rate responsive pacemaker, for artificial pancreas, for noninvasive glucose sensor for multi-leaflet heart valve. Office: Biocontrol Tech Inc 300 Indian Springs Rd Indiana PA 15701-9704

PURDY, DENNIS GENE, insurance company executive, education consultant; b. Detroit, June 12, 1946; s. Culver and Tessie (Gillette) P.; m. Ardyce Maxine Wilcox, Aug. 9, 1969; children: Krista Rochelle, Steven Dennis. BS in Edn., Wayne State U., 1969; CLU, Am. Coll., Bryn Mawr, Pa., 1981; ChFC, Am. Coll., 1984. Cert. life underwriter tng. coun. fellow, 1989. Claims adjustor State Farm Ins., Southfield, Mich., 1969-71; pvt. practice Northville, Mich., 1971-73; claims rep. Farmers Ins. Co., Southfield, 1973-76; asst. tng. mgr. Farmers Ins. Co., Aurora, Ill., 1976-78; life tng. mgr. Ohio State Life Ins., Columbus, 1978-80; sales adminstrn. mgr. Farmers Ins. Co., Columbus, 1980-81, life tng. rep., 1981-86, life mktg. specialist, 1986-94, sr. claims rep., 1994—; continuing edn. coord. for state of Ind., Farmers Ins. Group, Dublin, Ohio, 1990—; mem. pre-lic. adv. bd. State of Ohio, Columbus, 1992, mem. exam. rev. bd., 1992; field faculty mem. Life Underwriters Tng. Coun. Contbr. articles for internal publ., 1980—. Pres. Columbus Barbershop Chorus, 1989-90, v.p., 1991-92. Named Man of Yr. Columbus Barbershop Chorus, 1990. Mem. Nat. Assn. Life Underwriters, Am. Soc. CLUs and ChFCs., Columbus Assn. Life Underwriters. Avocations: music, swimming. Home and Office: 2129 Shirlene Dr Grove City OH 43123-4008

PURDY, JAMES, writer; b. 1923. Ed., Spain. Editor, other positions Cuba, Mexico. Author: Don't Call Me by My Right Name, 1956; 63, Dream Palace, 1956, 1980, Color of Darkness, 1957, Malcolm, 1959, 1980, paperback, 1987, The Nephew, 1960, , 1980, paperback, 1987, (play) Children is All, 1962, Cabot Wright Begins, 1964, Eustace Chisholm and The Works, 1967, An Oyster is A Wealthy Beast, 1967, Mr. Evening, 1968, Jeremy's Version, 1970, On the Rebound, 1970, (poems) The Running Sun, 1971, Collected Poems, 1990, (novel) I am Elijah Thrush, 1971; Sunshine is an Only Child, 1973, Sleepers in Moon Crowned Valleys, The House of the Solitary Maggot, 1974, Island Avenue, 1997, (play) Foment, 1997, (selected stories) Color of Darkness, Children is All, The Candles of Your Eyes, 1991, (fairy tale) Kitty Blue, 1993 (Eng. edit. The Netherlands); (novel) In a Shallow Grave, 1976; (plays and stories) A Day After the Fair, 1977; (recordings) Eventide, 63; Dream Palace, 1968, 1980; (novel) Narrow Rooms, 1978; (poetry) I Will Arrest the Bird that has No Light, 1978, Lessons and Complaints, 1978; Sleep Tight, 1978, Proud Flesh, 4 short plays, 1980; (novel) Mourners Below, 1981, The Berry-Picker, 1981, Scrap of Paper, 1981, Dawn, 1985, The Brooklyn Branding Parlors, 1986; (novel) On Glory's Course, 1983, (poems) Don't Let the Snow Fall, 1985, Are You in the Winter Tree?, 1987, (novel) In the Hollow of His Hand, 1986, (collected stories) The Candles of your Eyes, 1987, Garments the Living Wear, 1989, (fiction) Reaching Rose, 1994, (play) Ruthanna Elder, 1989; subject of book: James Purdy (Stephen D. Adams), 1976, Collected Poems, 1990, (plays) In The Night of Time and Four Other Plays, 1992, A Day After the Fair, 1993, (novel) Out With The Stars, 1992, In the Night of Time and Four Other Plays, 1992, (plays) Foment, 1994, Brice, 1994, Where Quentin Goes, 1994; intro. to Weymouth Sands (by John Cowper POWYS); contbr. article to Life Mag., 1965. Recipient Morton Dauwen Zabel Fiction award Am. Acad. Arts and Letters, 1993, Oscar Williams and Gene Durwood award for poetry and art, 1995; subject of The Not-Right House, Essays on the Books of James Purdy (Bettina Schwarzschild), 1969-70. Address: 236 Henry St Brooklyn NY 11201-4280

PURDY, KEVIN M., estate planner; b. Escondido, Calif., Jan. 26, 1952; s. Kenneth C. and Helen M. (Moore) P.; m. Janice M. Cook, May 12, 1982. BA in Philosophy, Psychology, U. Redlands, 1974. CFP. Pres. Timeline Pub., San Diego, Calif., 1980-90; estate planner CIGNA Fin. Advisors, San Diego, Calif., 1990—; pub. speaker. Author: A Brief History of the Earth and Mankind, 1986, A Brief History of Mankind, 1987. Fundraiser San Diego Hist. Soc., 1993-94. Avocations: photography, music, travel, investment analysis. Office: CIGNA Fin Advisers 4275 Executive Sq Ste 400 La Jolla CA 92037-1476

PURDY, SHERRY MARIE, lawyer; b. Billings, Mont., Mar. 12, 1960. Student, U. Mont., 1978-80; BS, Mont. State U., Billings, 1983; JD, Willamette U., 1987. Bar: Colo. 1987, U.S. Dist. Ct. Colo. 1987. Assoc. Holland & Hart, Denver, 1987-90; sr. atty. Atlantic Richfield Co., Denver, 1990-96; gen. counsel Terranext, Inc., Lakewood, Colo., 1996—. Contbr. articles to profl. jours. Mem. ABA, Colo. Bar Assn., Colo. Women's Bar Assn., Colo. Hazardous Waste Mgmt. Soc. (program com. chair 1989-90, v.p. 1990-91), Denver Bar Assn. Office: Terranext Inc Union Tower Ste 1000 165 S Union Blvd Lakewood CO 80228

PURDY, TEDDY GEORGE, JR., programmer, analyst, researcher, consultant; b. Leadville, Colo., May 11, 1954; s. Teddy George and Geneva Ruth Purdy; m. Karen Ann Puleo, May 28, 1977 (div. Dec. 19, 1983); children: Christopher, Sarah. Student, Colo. U., 1972-75. Free-lance programmer/analyst Boulder, Colo., 1975-84; pres., treas. IBEX Bus. Systems, Leadville, 1984—; cons. Carlson Promotions, Mpls., 1987-91, Unidata, Inc., Denver, 1992, Household Fin., Chesapeake, Va., 1992—, Focus Tech., Dallas, 1992—. Avocations: geology, biking, hiking, books, music.

PURDY, WILLIAM CROSSLEY, chemist, educator; b. Bklyn., Sept. 14, 1930; s. John Earl and Virginia (Clark) P.; m. Myrna Mae Moman, June 17, 1953; children—Robert Bruce (dec.), Richard Scott, Lisa Patrice, Diana Lori. B.A., Amherst Coll., 1951; Ph.D., MIT, 1955. Instr. U. Conn., Storrs, 1955-58; faculty U. Md., College Park, 1958-76, prof. chemistry, 1964-76, head div. analytical chemistry, 1968-76; prof. chemistry McGill U., 1976-86, assoc. in medicine, 1976—, Sir William Macdonald prof. chemistry, 1986—, assoc. vice prin. (acad.), 1986-91; vis. prof. Institut für Ernährungswissenschaft, Justus Liebig-Universität, Giessen, Germany, 1965-66; nat. lectr. Am. Assn. Clin. Chemistry, 1971; Fisher Sci. Lecture award Chem. Inst. Can., 1982; cons. Surg. Gen., U.S. Army, 1959-75; sci. adviser Balt. dist. FDA. Author: Electro-analytical Methods in Biochemistry, 1965, also numerous articles; mem. bd. editors Clin. Chemistry, 1971-80, Anal. Letters, 1979-95, Anal. Chim. Acta, 1979-84, Clin. Biochemistry, 1983-91, Pure and Applied Chemistry, 1983-91; adv. bd. editors Analytical Chemistry, 1971-73. Bd. govs. Trafalgar Sch. Girls, Montreal, 1980-90, chmn., 1983-87; bd. trustees Trafalgar-Ross Found., Montreal, 1983-90, chmn., 1983-87. Fellow Nat. Acad. Clin. Biochemistry, Royal Soc. Chemistry (London), Chem. Inst. Can., Can. Acad. Clin. Biochemistry; mem. Am. Chem. Soc., Am. Assn. Clin. Chemistry (Outstanding Contbns. to Clin. Chemistry award 1984), Can. Soc. Clin. Chemists (Outstanding Contbr. through Rsch award, 1990), Sigma Xi. Achievements include research in application of modern analytical methods to biochem. and clin. systems, separation sci., electroanalytical chemistry. Home: 4854 Cote des Neiges #503, Montreal, PQ Canada H3V 1G7 Office: McGill U, 801 Sherbrooke St W, Montreal, PQ Canada H3A 2K6

PURI, MADAN LAL, mathematics educator; b. Sialkot, Feb. 20, 1929; came to U.S., 1957, naturalized, 1973; s. Ganesh Das and S. V. P.; m. Uma Kapur, Aug. 24, 1962; 3 children. B.A., Punjab U., India, 1948, M.A., 1950, D.Sc., 1975; Ph.D., U. Calif. at Berkeley, 1962. Head dept. math. D.A.V. Coll., Punjab U., 1955-57; instr. U. Colo., 1957-58; teaching asst., research asst., jr. research statistician U. Calif. at Berkeley, 1958-62; asst. prof., assoc. prof. math. Courant Inst., N.Y. U., 1962-68; vis. asso. prof. U. N.C., summers 1966-67; prof. math. Ind. U., Bloomington, 1968—; guest prof. stats. U. Gottingen, West Germany, 1972, Alexander von Humboldt guest prof., 1974-75; guest prof. U. Dortmund, West Germany, 1972, Technische Hochschule Aachen, West Germany, 1973, U. Goteborg, Chalmers U. Tech., both Sweden, 1974; vis. prof. U. Auckland, N.Z., 1977, U. Calif., Irvine, 1978, U. Wash., Seattle, 1978-79, U. Bern (Switzerland), 1982, Va. Poly. Inst., 1988; disting. visitor London Sch. Econs. and Polit. Sci., 1991; vis. prof. U. Göttingen, Germany, 1991, June-July 1992; rsch. fellow Katholieke U., Nijmegen, The Netherlands, 1992; vis. prof. U. Des Scis. et Tech. de Lille, France, 1994, U. Basel, Switzerland, 1995—, U. New South Wales, Australia, 1996. Co-author: Non Parametric Methods in Multivariate Analysis, 1971, Non Parametric Methods in General Linear Models, 1985. Editor Statochastic Process and Related Topics, 1975, Statistical Inference and Related Topics, 1975, Non Parametric Techniques in Statistical Inference, 1970; co-editor: Nonparametric Statistical Inference, Vols. I and II, 1982, New Perspectives in Theoretical and Applied Statistics, 1987, Mathematical Statistics and Probability Theory, Vol. A, 1987, Statistical Sciences and Data Analysis, 1993, Recent Advances in Statistics and Probability, 1994. Recipient Sr. U.S. Scientist award, Humboldt Preis, 1974-75, 83. Fellow Royal Statis. Soc., Inst. Math. Statistics, Am. Statis. Assn.; mem. Math. Assn. Am., Internat. Statis. Inst., Bernoulli Soc. Math. Stats. and Probability. Office: Ind U Dept Math Rawles Hall Bloomington IN 47405

PURKERSON, MABEL LOUISE, physician, physiologist, educator; b. Goldville, S.C., Apr. 3, 1931; d. James Clifton and Louise (Smith) P. AB, Erskine Coll., 1951; MD, U. S.C., Charleston, 1956. Diplomate Am. Bd. Pediat. Instr. pediat. Washington U. Sch. Med., St. Louis, 1961-67, instr. medicine, 1966-67, asst. prof. pediat., 1967—, asst. prof. medicine, 1967-76, assoc. prof. medicine, 1976-89, prof., 1989—, assoc. dean curriculum, 1976-94; assoc. dean acad. projects, 1994—; cons. in field. Editl. bd. Jour. Am. Kidney Diseases, 1981-87 ; contbr. articles to profl. jours. USPHS spl. fellow, 1971-72. Bd. counselors Erskine Coll., 1971—. Mem. Am. Heart Assn. (exec. com. 1973-81), Coun. on the Kidney, Am. Physiol. Soc., Am. Soc. Nephrology, Internat. Soc. Nephrology, Central Soc. Clin. Rsch., Am. Soc. Renal Biochemistry and Metabolism, Sigma Xi (chpt. sec. 1974-76). Avocations: traveling; gardening; photography. Home: 20 Haven View Dr Saint Louis MO 63141-7902 Office: Washington U Sch Medicine Renal Div Dept 660 S Euclid Ave St Box 8132 Saint Louis MO 63110

PURL, O. THOMAS, retired electronics company executive; b. East St. Louis, Ill., June 5, 1924; s. Ruthford Keith and Muriel Agnes (Thompson) P.; m. Martha Elaine Smalley, Feb. 21, 1948; children—Thomas Keith, Jeanne Marie Purl Elder. B.S., U. Ill., 1948, U. Ill., 1951; M.S., U. Ill., 1952, Ph.D., 1955. Head high-power traveling wave tube sect., mem. tech. staff Hughes Research Lab., Culver City, Calif., 1955-58; sect. head, dept. mgr., group v.p., v.p. shareholder relations and planning coordination Watkins-Johnson Co., Palo Alto, Calif., 1958-86. Contbr. articles to profl. jours. Chmn. career guidance com. Santa Clara Valley Joint Engring. Council, 1971-73; bd. dirs. Jr. Achievement of Santa Clara County, 1975-79. Served to 1st lt. USAAF, 1943-46. Fellow IEEE (chmn. Santa Clara Valley subsect. 1972); mem. Sigma Xi, Eta Kappa Nu, Phi Kappa Phi, Sigma Tau. Club: Commonwealth of Calif. Patentee in field. Home: 466 La Mesa Portola Valley CA 94028

PURNELL, CHARLES GILES, lawyer; b. Dallas, Aug. 16, 1921; s. Charles Stewart and Ginevra (Locke) P.; m. Jane Carter; children: Mimi, Sarah Elizabeth, Charles H., John W. Student Rice Inst., 1938-39; BA, U. Tex., 1941; student Harvard Bus. Sch., 1942; LLB, Yale U., 1947. Bar: Tex. 1948. Ptnr. Locke, Purnell, Boren, Laney & Neely, Dallas, 1947-89, Locke, Purnell, Rain & Harrell, 1989-90, of counsel, 1990—; exec. asst. to Gov. of Tex., Austin, 1973-75. Bd. dirs. Trinity River Authority of Tex., 1975-81; vice chmn. Tex. Energy Adv. Council, 1974. Served to lt. U.S. Navy, 1942-45; PTO. Mem. ABA, Tex. Bar Assn., Tex. Bar Found. Episcopalian. Clubs: Yale, Dallas Country, Dallas Petroleum, La Jolla (Calif.) Beach and Tennis. Home: # 1 Saint Laurent Place Dallas TX 75225 Office: Locke Purnell Rain Harrell 2200 Ross Ave Ste 2200 Dallas TX 75201-2748

PURNELL, MAURICE EUGENE, JR., lawyer; b. Dallas, Feb. 17, 1940; s. Maurice Eugene Sr. and Marjorie (Maillot) P.; m. Diane Blake, Aug. 19, 1966; children: Maurice Eugene III, Blake Maillot. BA, Washington and Lee U., 1961; MBA, U. Pa., 1963; LLB, So. Meth. U., 1966. Bar: Tex. 1966. Ptnr. Locke, Purnell, Boren, Laney & Neely, Dallas, 1966-87; shareholder Locke Purnell Rain Harrell P.C., Dallas, 1987—; bd. dirs. Leggett & Platt, Inc. Bd. dirs. Dallas Summer Musicals. Mem. ABA, Tex. Bar Assn., Dallas Bar Assn. Am. Judicature Soc., Dallas C. of C, Brook Hollow Golf Club. Home: 4409 S Versailles Ave Dallas TX 75205-3012 Office: Locke Purnell Rain Harrell PC 2200 Ross Ave Ste 2200 Dallas TX 75201-2748

PURPURA, DOMINICK P., neuroscientist, university dean; b. N.Y.C., Apr. 2, 1927; m. Florence Williams, 1948; children—Craig, Kent, Keith, Allyson. A.B., Columbia U., 1949; M.D., Harvard U., 1953. Intern Presbyn Hosp., N.Y.C., 1953-54; asst. resident in neurology Neurol. Inst., N.Y.C., 1954-55; Prof., chmn. dept. anatomy Albert Einstein Coll. Medicine, Yeshiva U., N.Y.C., 1967-74, sci. dir. Kennedy Ctr., 1969-72, dir. Kennedy Ctr., 1972-82, prof., chmn. dept. neurosci., 1974-82, dean, 1984—; dean Stanford U., Calif., 1982-84; mem. neurophysiol. panel Internat. Brain Rsch. Orgn., pres. 1987—; v.p. med. affairs UNESCO, 1961—; chmn. internat. congress com. Internat. Brain Rsch. Orgn./World Found. Neuroscientists, 1983—. Mem. editorial bd. Brain Rsch., 1965—, editor-in-chief, 1975—; editor-in-chief Brain Rsch. Revs., 1975—, Developmental Brain Rsch., 1981—, Molecular Brain Rsch., 1985—, Cognitive Brain Rsch., 1991—. Served with USNR, 1945-47. Fellow N.Y. Acad. Scis.; mem. Inst. Medicine of Nat. Acad. Scis., Nat. Acad. Scis., Am. Acad. Neurology, Am. Assn. Anatomists, Am. Assn. Neurol. Surgeons, Am. Epilepsy Soc., Am. Physiol. Soc., Assn. Research in Nervous and Mental Disease, Soc. Neurosci., Sigma Xi. Office: Yeshiva U Albert Einstein Coll Medicine 1300 Morris Park Ave Bronx NY 10461-1926

PURPURA, PETER JOSEPH, museum curator, exhibition designer; b. Bklyn., Nov. 29, 1939; s. Salvatore and Vincenza (Scozzari) P. B in Indsl. Design, Pratt Inst., 1962. Package designer Walter Dorwin Teague Assocs., N.Y.C., 1961-65; exhibit designer Will Burtin, Inc., N.Y.C., 1965-69; sr. exhibits designer Corning Glass Works, N.Y., 1969-71; assoc. exhibits dir. Met. Mus. Art, N.Y.C., 1971-72; exhibits dir. Mus. Sci., Boston, 1972-74; curator, dir. Explorers Hall, Nat. Geographic Soc., Washington, 1974-82; pres. Purpura & Kisner Inc., N.Y.C., 1983—; vis. design instr. Cornell U., 1971; lectr. Parsons Sch. Design, 1988, Phila. U. for Arts, 1992, 93, 94, 95, 96; exhibn. design mgr. Forbes Mag., N.Y., 1996—. Recipient Gold medal award Internat. Film and TV Festival of N.Y., 1973, Edison award for excellence GE, 1985. Mem. Indsl. Designers Soc. Am. (v.p. Mid Atlantic chpt. 1978); Am. Assn. Museums. Office: Purpura & Kisner 142 E Court St Doylestown PA 18901-4338

PURSE, CHARLES ROE, real estate investment company executive; b. Redhill, Surrey, Eng., May 19, 1960; came to U.S., 1960.; s. James Nathanial II and Rolande Marie-Louise (Redon) P.; m. Carole Lynn Sadler, July 5, 1986; children: Hayley Elizabeth, Cameron James. BA, Dartmouth Coll., 1982; MBA, Northwestern U., 1985. Account officer Northern Trust Bank, Chgo., 1982-85; asst. v.p. Citicorp Real Estate, Inc., Chgo., 1985-88; v.p. Citibank, Ltd., Sydney, Australia, 1988-91, Citibank Realty Investment Advisors, N.Y.C., 1991-94; sr. v.p. The Yarmouth Group, N.Y.C., 1994-96; mng. dir. DRA Advisors Inc., N.Y.C., 1996—. V.p., bd. dirs. Perrot Meml. Libr., Old Greenwich, Conn., 1993. Mem. Nat. Assn. Comml. Real Estate Investment Fiduciaries, Pension Real Estate Assn., The Country Club (Cleve.), Cromer Golf Club (Sydney, Australia), The Hillsboro Club (Hillsboro Beach, Fla.), Fox Meadow Tennis Club (Scarsdale, N.Y.). Republican. Avocations: golf, photography, skiing, tennis. Office: DRA Advisors Inc 18th Fl 1180 Ave of the Americas New York NY 10036-8401

PURSELL, CARROLL WIRTH, history educator; b. Visalia, Calif., Sept. 4, 1932; s. Carroll Wirth and Ruth Irene (Crowell) P.; m. Joan Young, Jan. 28, 1956 (dec. 1985); children: Rebecca Elizabeth, Matthew Carroll; m. Angela Woollacott, Dec. 20, 1986. B.A., U. Calif., Berkeley, 1956, Ph.D., 1962; M.A., U. Del., 1958. Asst. prof. history Case Inst. Tech., Cleve., 1963-65; asst. prof. U. Calif., Santa Barbara, 1965-69; asso. prof. U. Calif., 1969-76, prof., 1976-88; Adeline Barry Davee Disting. prof. history Case Western Res. U., Cleve., 1988—; Mellon prof. Lehigh U., Bethlehem, Pa., 1974-76; vis. research scholar Smithsonian Instn., 1970. Author: Early Stationary Steam Engines in America, 1969, Military Industrial Complex, 1972, From Conservation to Ecology, 1973, White Heat, 1994, The Machine in America, 1995. Fellow AAAS; mem. Soc. History of Tech. (pres. 1990-92, Leonardo da Vinci medal 1991, pres. internat. com. for history of tech. 1997—), Orgn. Am. Historians, Am. Hist. Assn., Phi Beta Kappa. Democrat. Office: Case Western Res U Dept History Cleveland OH 44106

PURSER, DONALD JOSEPH, lawyer; b. Chgo., Apr. 21, 1954; s. Donald Cornelius and Mary Alice (Fashingbauer) P.; m. Anne E. Wegner, Aug. 20,

1976. BS, U. Utah, 1975; MS, Reid Coll., 1976; JD, George Mason U., 1980; postdoctoral, Georgetown U., 1981. Bar: Va. 1980, U.S. Tax Ct. 1980, U.S. Ct. Appeals (4th and 10th cirs.) 1980, Utah 1981, U.S. Supreme Ct, 1987; diplomate Nat. Bd. Trial Advocacy. Spl. agt. U.S. Dept. of State, Washington, 1976-80; law clk. to judge U.S. Dist. Ct., Alexandria, Va., 1980-81; assoc. Richards, Brandt, Miller & Nelson, Salt Lake City, 1981-83; sole practice Salt Lake City, 1983-85; ptnr. Fowler & Purser, Salt Lake City, 1985-87, Purser & Edwards LLC, Salt Lake City, 1987—; judge pro tem Salt Lake County Cir. Ct., 1981-85; adj. faculty U. Phoenix, Salt Lake City, 1984—; advance staff office of v.p. of U.S., Washington, 1986; bd. dirs. Ameralix Risk Retention Group Chgo., Am. Western Life Ins. Co., Tarzana, Calif.; chmn. Rep. Congl. Dist. Utah. Active fin. com. Snelgrove for Congress campaign, 1988. Capt. JAGC, USAR. Mem. ABA (litigation sect., torts and ins. practice sect.), Am. Bd. Trial Advocates, Am. Inn of Ct. II (barrister), Phi Delta Theta, Delta Theta Pi. Republican. Roman Catholic. Clubs: Blue Goose (Salt Lake City), Utah Elephant Lodge: K.C. Avocations: skiing, stock market, reading, Aikido. Home: 3054 E Kennedy Dr Salt Lake City UT 84108 Office: Donald J. Purser and Assocs 236 3rd Ave # D Salt Lake City UT 84103-2471

PURSEY, DEREK LINDSAY, physics educator; b. Glasgow, Scotland, Oct. 22, 1927; came to U.S., 1964; s. Henry Edwin and Margaret Martin (Lindsay) P.; m. Barbara Ann Parker, Aug. 4, 1962; 1 child, John. BS, U. Glasgow, 1948, PhD, 1952. Asst. lectr. theoretical physics King's Coll., London, 1951-54; lectr. math. physics U. Edinburgh, Scotland, 1954-59; vis. lectr. UCLA, 1959-60; mem. sch. math. Inst. for Advanced Studies Princeton U., 1960-61; lectr. in theoretical physics U. Glasgow, Scotland, 1961-64; vis. prof. Iowa State U., Ames, 1964-65, prof. physics, 1965-93, emeritus prof. physics, 1993—. Contbr. articles to profl. jours. Fellow Royal Soc. Edinburgh, Am. Phys. Soc.; mem. Am. Assn. Assn. Advancement Sci., Sigma Xi. Democrat. Presbyterian. Avocations: church-related activities; photography; music; reading; wilderness camping.

PURSLEY, MICHAEL BADER, electrical engineering educator, communications systems research and consulting; b. Winchester, Ind., Aug. 10, 1945; s. Bader E. and Evelyn L. (Bennett) P.; m. Lou Ann Hinchman, July 6, 1968; 1 child, Jessica Ann. B.S., Purdue U., 1967, M.S., 1968; Ph.D., U. So. Calif., 1974. Mem. tech. staff Hughes Aircraft Co., Los Angeles, 1967; engr. Northrop Co., Hawthorne, Calif., 1968; staff engr. Hughes Aircraft Co., Los Angeles, 1968-74; acting asst. prof. UCLA, 1974; asst. prof., then assoc. prof. elec. engring. U. Ill., Urbana, 1974-80, prof., 1980-93; Holcombe prof. elec. and computer engring. Clemson (S.C.) U., 1992—; assoc. Ctr. Advanced Study, 1980-81; vis. prof. UCLA, 1985; cons. U.S. Army, Huntsville, Ala., 1977, Ft. Monmouth, N.J., 1983-86, 91; cons. ITT, Ft. Wayne, Ind., 1979—; pres. SIGCOM, Inc., 1986-90; prin. scientist Techno-Scis. Inc., 1990—. Contbr. chpts. to books. Recipient Fred W. Ellersick award Comms. Soc., 1996. Fellow IEEE (pres. info. theory group 1983, Centennial medal 1984); mem. Inst. Math. Stats. Office: Clemson U 102 Riggs Hall Box 340915 Clemson SC 29634-0915

PURSWELL, BEVERLY JEAN, veterinary medicine educator, theriogenologist; b. Atlanta; d. Henry D. and Frances (Martin) P.; m. C.M. Wall, Jan. 1, 1990. DVM, U. Ga., 1977, MS, 1981, PhD, 1985. Equine vet., 1977-79; theriogenology resident Medical Microbiology, 1979-85; assoc. prof. vet. medicine Va. Poly. Inst. and State U., Blacksburg, 1985—. Mem. AVMA, Soc. for Theriogenology (bd. dirs. 1989—, sec.-treas., v.p. 1992-93, pres. 1993-94), Va. Vet. Med. Assn. (bd. dirs. 1990-96, v.p. 1996-97). Avocations: dressage, livestock breeding. Office: Va Poly Inst and State U Coll Vet Medicine Duck Pond Rd Blacksburg VA 24061

PURTELL, LAWRENCE ROBERT, lawyer; b. Quincy, Mass., May 2, 1947; s. Lawrence Joseph and Louise Maria (Loria) P.; m. Cheryl Lynn Tymon, Aug. 3, 1968; children: Lisa Ann, Susan Elizabeth. AB, Villanova U., 1969; JD, Columbia U., 1972. Bar: N.Y. 1973, N.J. 1978, Conn. 1988. Assoc. White & Case, N.Y.C., 1972-73; judge advocate USMC, Washington, 1973-76; assoc. White & Case, N.Y.C., 1977-79; corp. counsel Great Atlantic & Pacific Tea Co., Montvale, N.J., 1979-81; asst. gen. counsel United Techs. Corp., Hartford, Conn., 1981-84, assoc. gen. counsel, 1984-92, sec., gen. counsel, 1989-92; v.p., gen. counsel and sec. Carrier Corp., 1992-93; sr. v.p., gen. counsel and corp. sec. Mc Dermott Internat., New Orleans, La., 1993-96; sr. v.p., gen. counsel Koch Industries, Wichita, Kans., 1996—. Capt. USMC, 1973-76. Roman Catholic. Avocations: running. Home: 8911 Summerfield St Wichita KS 67206-3318 Office: Koch Industries Inc PO Box 2256 Wichita KS 67201

PURTLE, JOHN INGRAM, lawyer, former state supreme court justice; b. Enola, Ark., Sept. 7, 1923; s. John Wesley and Edna Gertrude (Ingram) P.; m. Marian Ruth White, Dec. 31, 1951; children: Jeffrey, Lisa K. Student, U. Central Ark., 1946-47; LLB, U. Ark., Fayetteville, 1950. Bar: Ark. 1950, U.S. Dist. Ct. (ea. dist.) Ark. 1950. Pvt. practice Conway, Ark., 1950-53, Little Rock, 1953-78; mem. Ark. State Legislature, 1951-52, 69-70; assoc. justice Ark. Supreme Ct., 1979-90; ret. N000, Little Rock, Ark., 1990; pvt. practice Little Rock, Ark., 1990—. Tchr., deacon Baptist Ch. Served with U.S. Army, 1940-45. Mem. ABA, Ark. Bar Assn., Am. Judicature Soc., Ark. Jud. Council. Democrat.

PURVES, WILLIAM KIRKWOOD, biologist, educator; b. Sacramento, Calif., Oct. 28, 1934; s. William Kirkwood and Dorothy (Brandenburger) P.; m. Jean McCauley, June 9, 1959; 1 son, David William. B.S., Calif. Inst. Tech., 1956; M.S., Yale U., 1957, Ph.D., 1959. NSF postdoctoral fellow U. Tubingen, Fed. Republic Germany, 1959-60; Nat. Cancer Inst. postdoctoral fellow UCLA, 1960-61; asst. prof. botany U. Calif., Santa Barbara, 1961-65; assoc. prof. biochemistry U. Calif., 1965-70, prof. biology, 1970-73, chmn. dept. biol. scis., 1972-73; prof. biology, head biol. sci. group U. Conn., Storrs, 1973-77; Stuart Mudd prof. biology Harvey Mudd Coll., Claremont, Calif., 1977-95, prof. emeritus, 1996—, chmn. dept. biol., 1985-95; chmn. dept. computer sci. Harvey Mudd Coll., 1985-90; adj. prof. plant physiology U. Calif., Riverside, 1979-85; vis. fellow computer sci. Yale U., 1983-84; vis. scholar Northwestern U., 1991. Author: Life, the Science of Biology, 1983, 4th edit., 1995. NSF sr. postdoctoral fellow U. London, 1967; NSF sr. postdoctoral fellow Harvard U., 1968; NSF rsch. grantee, 1962-83. Fellow AAAS; mem. Am. Soc. Plant Physiologists, Sigma Xi. Home: 2817 N Mountain Ave Claremont CA 91711-1550 Office: Harvey Mudd Coll 301 E 12th St Claremont CA 91711-5901

PURVIS, GEORGE FRANK, JR., life insurance company executive; b. Rayville, La., Nov. 22, 1914; s. George Frank and Ann Mamie (Womble) P.; m. Virginia Winston Wendt, May 16, 1942; children: Virginia Reese (Mrs. William H. Freshwater), Winston Wendt, George Frank III. AA, Kemper Mil. Sch., 1932; LLB, La. State U., 1935. Bar: La. bar 1935. Sole practice Rayville, 1935-37; atty. Office Sec. State State of La., Baton Rouge, 1937-41; also dep. ins. commr. State of La., 1945-49; atty. La. Ins. Dept., also spl. asst. to atty. gen., 1937-41; with Pan-Am. Life Ins. Co., New Orleans, 1949—, exec. v.p., 1962-64, pres., chief exec. officer, 1964—, chmn. bd., 1969—, also bd. dirs.; pres., bd. dirs. Compania de Seguros Panamericana, S.Am.; pres. Pan-Am. de Colombia Compania de Seguros de Vida, S.A.; chmn., bd. govs. Internat. Ins. Seminars, Inc., 1984—; mem. Industry Sector Adv. Com. for Trade Policy Matters, 1986; lectr. ins. law Tulane U., New Orleans, 1949-56; bd. dirs. 1st Nat. Bank Commerce in New ORleans, Republic Airlines, Inc., 1st Commerce Corp., So. Airlines-Republic Airlines, Pan Am de Mex. Cos. de Seguros Sobre la Vida, S.A., 1964-88; dir. Northwest Airlines, 1986-87. Compiler, author: Louisiana Insurance Code, 1948; contbr. articles to profl. jours. Chmn. big donors com. New Orleans Christmas Seal Campaign, 1961, gen. campaign chmn., 1962, chmn. profl. group VIII, 1963; vice chmn. New Orleans United Fund campaign, 1965, gen. chmn., 1967; pres. Tb Assn. Greater New Orleans, 1967, La. State U. Found., 1967, YMCA, New Orleans, 1968—, Internat. House, 1977, Met. Area Com., 1979; geog. chmn. U.S. Savs. Bond Campaign, Greater New Orleans, 1971; mem. Bd. City Park Commrs., 1965-79, mem. bd. commrs. Port of New Orleans, 1979—, pres. bd. commrs., 1982; chmn. S.S. Huebner Found. Ins. Edn., 1977—, Bus. Task Force on Edn., Inc., 1980—; mem. adv. bd. Bapt. Hosp., 1985—, Salvation Army, 1986—; bd. dirs. Family Svc. Soc. New Orleans, Council for a Better La., New Orleans Philharm. Symphony Soc., Summer Pop Concerts, Bur. Govt. Rsch. New Orleans; mem. Govs. Cost Control Comm., 1981-89; trustee Greater New Orleans Found., 1987—, chmn. bd. trustees La. Ind. Coll. Fund Inc., 1987-88, mem. 1987—. Served with USNR, 1941-45. Decorated Order of Vasco Nunez de Balboa (Panama); named Alumnus of Yr., La. State U., 1975, role model Young Leadership Coun., 1993; recipient award Inst. for Human Understanding, 1975, Weiss Meml. award, 1976, Vol. Activist award, 1978, award of excellence Greater New Orleans Fedn. Chs., 1983, Disting. Svc. award Navy League, 1983, Humanitarian award Nat. Jewish Hosp./Nat. Asthma Ctr., 1984, internat. ins. award Internat. Ins. Adv. Coun., 1986, 1st ann. award for outstanding efforts in promoting trade with L.Am., Rotary Club, 1987, Hall of Fame award La. State U., 1987, Man of Yr. award Fedn. Ins. and Corp. Counsel, 1988, Integritas Vitae award Loyola U. of South, 1991, Bus. Hall of Fame award Jr. Achievement, 1993, cert. of appreciation La. Air N.G., 1995; selected role model Young Bus. Leadership Coun., 1993; honored as a founding mem. in Soc. of St. Ignatius, Loyola U., 1996. Mem. ABA, La. Bar Assn., La. Law Inst., Am. Judicature Soc., Assn. Life Ins. Counsel, Am. Life Conv. (past chmn. legal sect., exec. com., v.p. La., chmn. 1972), Health Ins. Assn. Am. (dir., chmn. 1970), Ins. Econs. Soc. Am. (chmn. 1980-81), La. Assn. Legal Res. Life Ins. Cos. (pres. 1963-68), New Orleans Assn. Life Underwriters (award for Loyal and Unselfish Service to the Ins. Industry 1987), Internat. Trade Adminstrn. (industry sector and functional adv. coms. for trade policy matters), C. of C. Greater New Orleans Area (dir., pres. 1970), Phi Delta Phi, Omicron Delta Kappa, Delta Kappa Epsilon. Episcopalian. Home: 5501 Dayna Ct New Orleans LA 70124-1042

PURVIS, HOYT HUGHES, political scientist, academic administrator, educator; b. Jonesboro, Ark., Nov. 7, 1939; s. Hoyt Somervell and Jane (Hughes) P.; children: Pamela R., Camille C. BJ, U. Tex., 1961, MJ, 1963; postgrad., U. Nancy, France, 1962-63, Vanderbilt U., Nashville, 1963-64. Researcher/writer So. Edn. Reporting Svc., Nashville, 1963-64; reporter Houston Chronicle, 1964-65; press sec., spl. asst. Sen. J.W. Fulbright, Washington, 1967-74; dir. pubs. and lectr. LBJ Sch. Pub. Affairs, U. Tex., Austin, 1974-76; fgn./def. advisor and dep. staff dir. Sen. Majority Leader and Sen. Dem. Policy Com., Washington, 1977-80; sr. rsch. fellow LBJ Sch. Pub. Affairs, U. Tex., 1980-82; dir. and prof. Fulbright Inst. Internat. Rels., U. Ark., Fayetteville, 1982—. Author: Interdependence, 1992; co-author: Legistling Foreign Policy, 1984, Seoul & Washington, 1993; editor: The Presidency and the Press, 1976, The Press: Free and Responsible?, 1982; co-editor: Old Myths and New Realities in U.S.-Soviet Relations, 1990. Mem. adv. coun. Sci. Info. Liaison Office, Ark. Gen. Assembly, Little Rock, 1984-96; chmn. Fayetteville City Cable Bd., 1991-93; apptd. J. Wm. Fulbright Fgn. Scholarship Bd., 1994—, vice chair, 1995, chmn., 1996—. Rotary fellow, 1962-63, others; recipient Fulbright Coll. Master Tchr. award, Disting. Faculty Achievement award U. Ark. Alumni Assn. Mem. Internat. Studies Assn. (regional v.p. 1984-86), Am. Polit. Sci. Assn., Assn. for Edn. in Journalism and Mass Communication, Phi Beta Delta, Delta Phi Alpha. Methodist. Home: PO Box 1872 Fayetteville AR 72702-1872 Office: Fulbright Inst Internat Rels 722 W Maple St Fayetteville AR 72701-3229

PURVIS, JOHN ANDERSON, lawyer; b. Greeley, Colo., Aug. 31, 1942; s. Virgil J. and Emma Lou (Anderson) P.; m. Charlotte Johnson, Apr. 3, 1976; 1 child, Whitney; children by previous marriage: Jennifer, Matt. B.A. cum laude, Harvard U., 1965; J.D., U. Colo., 1968. Bar: Colo. 1968, U.S. Dist. Ct. Colo. 1968, U.S. Ct. Appeals (10th cir.) 1978, U.S. Ct. Claims, 1980. Dep. dist. atty. Boulder, Colo., 1968-69; asst. dir. and dir. legal aid U. Colo. Sch. Law, 1969; assoc. Williams, Taussig & Trine, Boulder, 1969; head Boulder office Colo. Pub. Defender System, 1970-72; assoc. and ptnr. Hutchinson, Black, Hill, Buchanan & Cook, Boulder, 1972-85; ptnr. Purvis, Gray, Schuetze and Gordon, 1985—; acting Colo. State Pub. Defender, 1978; adj. prof. law U. Colo., 1981, 84-88, 94, others; lectr. in field. Chmn., Colo. Pub. Defender Commn., 1979-89; mem. nominating commn. Colo. Supreme Ct., 1984-90; mem. com. on conduct U.S. Dist. Ct., 1993—, chmn., 1996—; chmn. Boulder County Criminal Justice Com., 1975-81, Boulder County Manpower Coun., 1977-78. Recipient Ames award Harvard U., 1964; Outstanding Young Lawyer award Colo. Bar Assn., 1978. Mem. Internat. Soc. Barristers, Am. Coll. of Trial Lawyers, Colo. Bar Assn. (chair litigation sect. 1994-95), Boulder County Bar Assn., Colo. Trial Lawyers Assn., Am. Trial Lawyers Assn., Trial Lawyers for Pub. Justice. Democrat. Address: 1050 Walnut St Ste 501 Boulder CO 80302-5144

PURYEAR, ALVIN NELSON, management educator; b. Fayetteville, N.C., Apr. 6, 1937; s. Byron Nelson and Gladys (Bizzell) P.; m. Catherine Paulette Wiggins, Aug. 30, 1962; children: Pamela, Susan, Karen. B.A., Yale U., 1960; M.B.A., Columbia U., 1962, Ph.D., 1966. Employee relations adviser Mobil Oil Corp., N.Y.C., 1965-66; fin. analyst Mobil Oil Corp., 1966-67; specialist computational systems Allied Chem. Corp., 1967-68; asso. prof. Grad. Sch. Bus. Adminstrn. Rutgers U., Newark, 1968-69; asso. prof. mgmt. Bernard M. Baruch Coll., N.Y.C., 1970-72; prof. mgmt. Bernard M. Baruch Coll., 1972—, chmn. dept., 1978-79, dean coll., 1972-75, dir. Baruch/Cornell Indsl. and Labor Relations program, 1977-81; v.p. for orgn. and mgmt. Ford Found., 1980-82; 1st dep. comptroller City of N.Y., 1983-85; chmn. bd. Broadcast Capital Fund Inc., 1993-95; bd. dirs. Green Point Fin. Corp., Bank of Tokyo, Mitsubishi Trust; trustee Greenpoint Savs. Bank, 1992—. Co-author: Black Enterprise, Inc, 1973; also articles. Trustee Barber-Scotia Coll., 1977-82, Loyola coll., Balt., 1976-82, Riverdale Country Sch., Bronx, 1980-92, chmn. bd., 1987-89, Grad. Sch. Polit. Mgmt., 1987-95, Pitts. Theol. Sem., 1989-92, 96—, Yale U., New Haven, 1994-96, Cmty. Svc. Soc. of N.Y., 1997—; bd. dirs. Program Agy. United Presbyn. Ch., 1976-88, pres. 1983-86, Presbyn. Ch. U.S.A., 1987-97, chmn. 1991-93; chmn. Presbyn. Investment and Loan Corp., 1996—, Yale Alumni Fund, 1977-82. John Hay Whitney fellow, 1960-61; Samuel Bronfman fellow, 1960-62. Mem. Acad. Mgmt., Assn. Yale Alumni (vice chmn. 1984-86, chmn. 1986-88), Am. Mgmt. Assn., Smithsonian Nat. Bd., Internat. Coun. Bus. Opportunity (bd. dirs.). Presbyn. (elder).

PURYEAR, JAMES BURTON, college administrator; b. Jackson, Miss., Sept. 2, 1938; s. Harry Henton and Doris (Smith) P.; m. Joan Copeland, June 13, 1965; children: John James, Jeffrey Burton, Joel Harry. BS, Miss. State U., 1960, MEd, 1961; PhD, Fla. State U., 1969. Lic. profl. counselor, Ga. Assoc. dir. YMCA Miss. State U., Starkville, 1962-64; dir. YMCA, Starkville, Miss., 1964-65; dir. fin. aid Fla. State U., Tallahassee, 1967-69; asst. dir. student affairs Med. Coll. of Ga., Augusta, 1969-70, dir. student affairs, 1970-86, v.p. student affairs, 1986—. Adv. bd. mem. Ga. Fed. Bank, Augusta, 1978-85; chmn. bd. First Bapt. Ch., Augusta, 1978-80; pres. Learning Disabilities Assn., Augusta, 1987, PTA, 1994, Band Assn.; bd. dirs. Augusta Tng. Shop for Handicapped, 1994—; exec. bd. mem. Boy Scouts Am. Yearbook Dedication MCG Student Yearbook, 1975; scholar Med. Coll. Ga., 1988; recipient Svc. to Mankind award Sertoma, 1988. Mem. Nat. Assn. Student Pers. (S.E. regional bd. 1985), Am. Coll. Pers. Assn., So. Assn. Coll. Student Affairs, Rotary (pres. 1978, dist. lt. gov., Paul Harris fellow 1985). Baptist. Avocations: golf, photography, scouting. Office: Student Affairs Med Coll Ga Augusta GA 30912

PURYEAR, JOAN COPELAND, English language educator; b. Columbus, Miss., May 10, 1944; d. John Thomas and Mamie (Cunningham) Copeland.; m. James Burton Puryear, June 13, 1965; children: John James, Jeffrey Burton, Joel Harry. BA summa cum laude, Miss. State U., Starkville, 1965; MA, Fla. State U., 1969; EdD, U. Ga., 1987. Cert. tchr., Ga. English instr. Fla. State U., Tallahassee, 1965-69, Augusta (Ga.) Coll., 1987-88; head English dept. Augusta Tech. Inst., 1989-93, chairperson gen. edn. and devel. studies, 1993-96, mem. dean's coun., mgmt. team and grant proposal team, 1994—, dean allied health scis., gen. edn. and devel. studies, 1997; chmn. State Exec. Bd. English, Ga., 1990-92, East Ctrl. Consortium English, Ga., 1990-92; mem. Augusta Tech. Inst. Tech. Com., 1990—; chmn. Capital Funds Raising Family Campaign, Augusta Tech. Inst., vice chmn. Capital Fund Raising Cmty. Campaign; mem. and co-chmn. Continuous Improvement Coun., 1996—, Augusta Tech. Inst.; facilitator Total Quality Mgmt. Tech. Tng.; mem. exec. steering com. Continuous Improvement Coun.; chmn. editing com. Augusta Tech. Inst. Self Study, 1992-93, chmn. long range planning goals and objectives com., 1994. Mem. Cmtys. in Schs., 1996—; trustee Augusta Tech. Inst. Found. Bd., 1996—; co-pres. Davidson Fine Arts Sch. PTA, 1995, co-pres. bd. assn., 1996; pres. Med. Coll. Spouse's Club, Augusta, 1972; dir. Women's Mission Orgn., First Bapt. Ch., Augusta, 1982, dir. Youth Sunday Sch., 1992—, chmn. 175th Anniversary, 1992, deacon, 1996—, mem. ministerial adv. com. Mem. Modern Lang. Assn., Nat. Coun. Tchrs., Am. Vocat. Assn., Ga. Vocat. Assn., So. Assn. Colls. (accreditation team 1994), Phi Theta Kappa (adv. 1992—, Horizon award for outstanding advisor). Baptist. Avocations: flower arranging, home decorating, reading, traveling. Office: Augusta Tech Inst 3116 Deans Bridge Rd Augusta GA 30906-3375

PUSATERI, JAMES ANTHONY, judge; b. Kansas City, Mo., May 20, 1938; s. James A. and Madeline (LaSalle) P.; m. Jacqueline D. Ashburne, Sept. 1, 1962; children—James A., Mark C., Danielle L. B.A., U. Kans., 1960, LL.B., 1963. Bar: Kans. 1963, U.S. Dist. Ct. Kans. 1963, U.S. Ct. Appeals (10th cir.) 1964. Assoc. Payne, Jones, Chartered, Olathe, Kans., 1963-65; assoc. James Cashin, Prairie Village, Kans., 1965-69; asst. U.S. atty. Dept. Justice, Kansas City, Kans., 1969-76; judge U.S. Bankruptcy Ct. Dist. Kans., Topeka, 1976—. Mem. Prairie Village City Council, 1967-69. Mem. Kans. Bar Assn., Topeka Bar Assn., Nat. Conf. Bankruptcy Judges, Am. Bankruptcy Inst. Office: US Dist Ct 444 SE Quincy St Topeka KS 66683

PUSATERI, LAWRENCE XAVIER, lawyer; b. Oak Park, Ill., May 25, 1931; s. Lawrence E. and Josephine (Romano) P.; m. Eve M. Graf, July 9, 1956; children: Joanne, Lawrence F., Paul L., Mary Ann, Eva. JD summa cum laude, DePaul U., 1953. Bar: Ill. 1953. Asst. state's atty. Cook County, 1957-59; ptnr. Newton, Wilhelm, Pusateri & Naborowski, Chgo., 1959-77; justice Ill. appellate ct., Chgo., 1977-78; ptnr. Peterson, Ross, Schloerb & Seidel, Chgo., 1978-95; of counsel Peterson & Ross, 1996—; pres. Conf. Consumer Fin. Law, 1984-92, chmn. gov. com., 1993—; mem. Ill. Supreme Ct. Com. on Pattern Jury Instrns., 1981-96; mem. U.S. Senate Jud. Nominations Commn. State Ill., 1993, 95; exec. dir. State of Ill. Jud. Inquiry Bd., 1995-96; mem. Merit Selection Panel for U.S. Magistrate; lectr. law DePaul U., Chgo., 1962, Columbia U., N.Y.C., 1965, Marquette U., Milw., 1962-82, Northwestern U. Law Sch., Def. Counsel Inst., 1969-70; apptd. by U.S. Senator Paul Simon to Merit Screening Com. Fed. Judges, U.S. Atty. and U.S. Marshal, 1993, others; mem. task force indigent appellate def. Cook County Jud. Adv. Coun., 1992—; mem. Ill. Gen. Assembly, 1964-68. Contbr. articles to profl. jours. Chmn. Ill. Crime Investigating Commn. 1967-68, chmn. Ill. Parole and Pardon Bd., 1969-70; bd. dirs. Ill. Law Enforcement Commn., 1970-72; chmn. Com. on Correctional Facilities and Services; exec. v.p. and gen. counsel Ill. Fin. Svcs. Assn., 1980-95; chmn. law forum Am. Fin. Svcs. Assn., 1975-76; mem. spl. commn. on adminstrn. of justice in Cook County, Ill. (Greylord Com.) 1984-90, bd. dirs. Chgo. Crime Commn., 1986-91; mem. Ill. Supreme Ct. Spl. Commn. on the Adminstrn. of Justice, Ill. Supreme Ct. Appointment, 1991. Served to capt. JAGC, AUS, 1955-58. Named One of Ten Outstanding Young Men in Chgo., Chgo. Jr. Assn. Commerce and Industry, 1960, 65; recipient Outstanding Legislator award Ill. Gen. Assembly, 1966. Mem. ABA (chmn. consumer fin. svcs. 1975—, ho. dels. 1981-90, judicial adminstrn. divsn. 1980—, mem. exec. com. lawyer's conf. 1994—, mem. bench and bar rels. com. 1994-96, mem. adv. com. to Ill. State Del., Jud. Adminstrn. Divsn. in Recognition of Leadership in Improvement of Adminstrn. of Justice award 1993), Ill. State Bar Assn. (pres. 1975-76, com. on fed. jud. and related appointments; Abraham Lincoln Legal Writing award 1959, mem. adv. com., state del., 1994—, bd. dirs.), Chgo. Bar Assn. (bd. mgrs. 1965-66), Fred B. Snite Found. (sec., counsel 1976-90), Gertrude and Walter Swanson Found. (sole trustee), Mid-Am. Club Chgo. Republican. Roman Catholic.

PUSCH, WILLIAM GERARD, lawyer; b. La Porte, Ind., Jan. 29, 1935; s. William C. and Margaret (Elshout) P.; m. Mikellanne Peet, June 1, 1963; children: Jeffrey, Gregory, Anne. BA with honors, U. Mich., 1957; JD, Stanford U., 1960. Bar: Wash. 1961, U.S. Dist. Ct. (we. dist.) Wash. 1961. Ptnr. Davis Wright Tremaine (and predecessor firms), Seattle, 1961—. Editor: Wash. Partnership Law, 1981-84; bd. editors: Stanford Law Rev., 1959-60. Mem. ABA, Wash. State Bar Assn. (chair partnership law com., 1988—, exec. com. bus. law sect.), Seattle-King County Bar Assn., Order of Coif. Avocations: gardening, fishing, golf. Home: 8434 W Mercer Way Mercer Island WA 98040-5633 Office: Davis Wright Tremaine 2600 Century Sq 1501 4th Ave Seattle WA 98101-1662

PUSCHECK, HERBERT CHARLES, social sciences educator; b. Marshfield, Wis., July 14, 1936; s. Herbert and Ella (Sanger) P.; m. Elizabeth, Oct. 17, 1959; children: Elizabeth E. and Lisa Marie. BS in Gen. Engring., U.S. Mil. Acad., 1958; MS in Elec. Engring., Purdue U., 1964, PhD in Ops. Rsch., 1969. Officer U.S. Army, various cites, 1958-78; dir. spl. studies Office of Sec. Def., Washington, 1974-78, dep. asst. sec. def., 1987-94; prof. Nat. Def. U., Washington, 1979; assoc. dir. Selective Svc. System Hdqrs., Washington, 1980-82; asst. chief staff Army Materiel Command, Alexandria, Va., 1983-86; army chair Def. Systems Mgmt. Coll., Ft. Belvoir, Va., 1986-87; prof. pub. and internat. affairs George Mason Univ., Fairfax, 1994—; pres. H & BI (investments), Alexandria, 1985—. Contbr. articles to profl. jours. Co-chmn. Mt. Vernon Coun., Fairfax, Va., 1977-79. Recipient Meritorious Achievment award Pres., 1989. Mem. Mil. Ops. Rsch. Soc. (v.p. 1972-74, sponsor 1988-94). Avocations: sailing, hiking, fly fishing. Home: 8106 W Boulevard Dr Alexandria VA 22308-1711

PUSCHEL, PHILIP P., textiles executive; m. Roberta J. Green. AB, Hamilton Coll., 1960; MBA, Stanford U., 1962. V.p. F Schumacher & Co., N.Y.C., 1971, pres., CEO, 1981, chmn. bd., CEO officer, 1989—. With USN, 1962-65. Office: F Schumacher & Co 79 Madison Ave New York NY 10016-7802

PUSCHETT, JULES B., medical educator, neprhrologist, researcher; b. Hazelton, Pa., Mar. 13, 1934; m. Diane Puschett; children: Mitchell, Lynne. BA magna cum laude, Lehigh U., 1955; MD, U. Pa., 1959. Intern Jackson Meml. Hosp., Miami, 1959-60; resident, fellow endrocrinology and metabolism Univ. Hosp., Balt., 1963-66; postdoctoral fellow in medicine NIH Inst. Arthritis and Metabolic Disease, Bethesda, Md., 1966-68; fellow, renal-electrolyte sect. U. Pa. Sch. Medicine, Phila., 1966-68; rsch. assoc. VA Hosp., Phila., 1968-70, staff to chief renal-electrolyte sect. dept. medicine, 1968-73, clin. investigator, 1970-73; head renal-electrolyte divsn. Allegheny Gen. Hosp., Pitts., 1973-78; dir. renal-electrolyte divsn. fellowship tng. program U. Pitts. Sch. Medicine, 1976-78; chief renal-electrolyte divsn. dept. medicine U. Ark. for Med. Scis., Little Rock, 1979-80, U. Pitts. Sch. Medicine, 1980-90; interim chief sect. nephrology dept. medicine Tulane U. Sch. Medicine, New Orleans, 1990-92; chmn. dept. medicine Tulane U. Sch. Medicine, New Orleans, 1990—, asst. dean network affairs, 1996—; instr. medicine U. Pa. Sch. Medicine 1967-79, assoc. in medicine 1969-70, asst. prof. medicine 1970-73; clin. assoc. prof. medicine U. Pitts. Med. Sch. 1973-78; prof. medicine U. Ark. Med. Scis. 1979-80; prof. medicine U. Pitts. Sch. Medicine 1980-90; prof. medicine Tulane U. Sch. Medicine 1990—. Editor: The Diuretic Manual, 1984, Diuretics: chemistry, Pharmacology and Clinical Applications, 1984, Disorders of Fluid and Electrolyte Balance: diagnosis and Management, 1985, Diuretics II: Chemistry, Pharmacology and Clinical Applications, 1986, Diuretics III, 1989, Diuretics IV, 1993; contbr. over 170 articles to profl. jours.; spkr. and presenter in field; editl. bd. Am. Jour. Med. Scis., Am. Jour. Nephrology (sect. editor Physiology for the Nephrologist), Cardiovasc. Risk Factors, Internat. Jour. Artificial Organs, Southern Med. Jour. Chmn. 1st Ann. Kidney Ball, Nat. Kidney Found. of Western Pa., 1988, chmn. 2d Ann. Kidney Ball, 1989. With USN 1960-63. Coxe Meml. schlar, Lehigh U., 1951; named Outstanding Tchr. Yr., Owl Club, Tulane U., 1991, 94. Fellow ACP; mem. AMA, AAAS, Am. Fedn. Clin. Rsch., Am. Soc. Artificial Internal Orgnas. Am. Soc. Nephrology (chmn. audit com. 1992), Nat. Kidney Found. (pub. policy com. 1989, vol. svc. award 1990), Internat. Soc. Nephrology, Am. Heart Assn. Coun. on the Kidney in Cardiovasc. Disease (chmn. subcom. on scientific confs. 1991-92, exec. com. 1991-95, long-range planning com. 1992—), Am. Heart Assn. Coun. for High Blood Pressure Rsch., Am. Physiol. Soc., Fedn. Am. Socs. for Exptl. Biology, Am. Geriat. Soc., Ctrl. Soc. for Clin. Rsch., Soc. for Exptl. Biology and Medicine, Am. Soc. Clin. Pharmacology and Therapeutics, Am. Coll. Clin. Pharmacology, Endocrine Soc., Am. Soc. Renal Biochemistry and Metabolism, Am. Soc. Hypertension (Outstanding Tchr. Yr. 1986), Internat. Soc. Nutrition and Metabolism in Renal Disease, Am. Soc. Bone and Mineral Rsch., European Dialysis and Transplant Assn., Nat. Kidney Found. of Western Pa. (med. adv. com. 1981, chmn. 1981-83, Gift of Life award 1991), Nat. Kidney Found. of La. (mem.-at-large, trustee 1991), So. Med. Assn., So. Soc. Clin. Investigation (councilor 1992-94, sec.-treas. 1994-95), La. State Med. Soc., Orleans Parish Med. Soc. (membership com. 1993, long-range planning com. 1993), La. Soc. Internal Medicine, S.E. Clin. Club, Midwestern Salt and Water Club, Phi Beta Kappa, Alpha Epsilon Delta. Office: Tulane Univ Sch Medicine Dept Medicine SL 12 1430 Tulane Ave New Orleans LA 70112-2699

PUSEY, WILLIAM ANDERSON, lawyer; b. Richmond, Va., Mar. 17, 1936; s. Paul H. and Vernelle (Barnes) P.; m. Patricia Powell, Sept. 3, 1960; children: Patricia Brent, William A. Jr., Margaret Glen. AB, Princeton U., 1958; JD, U. Va., 1962. Bar: Calif. 1963, Va. 1964, D.C. 1987. Assoc. McCutchen, Brown, et al, San Francisco, 1962-63; dep. dist. atty. Alameda County, Oakland, Calif., 1963-64; assoc., counsel Hunton & Williams, Washington, Fairfax and Richmond, Va., 1964—; trustee Ea. Mineral Law Found., Morgantown, W.Va., 1985—, pres., 1987-88. Chmn. bd. dirs. Presbyn. Sch. Christian Edn., Richmond, 1984-85. Mem. Nat. Coal Coun., Order of Coif, Phi Beta Kappa, Omicron Delta Kappa. Home: 3910 N Glebe Rd Arlington VA 22207-4221 Office: Hunton & Williams 1900 K St NW Washington DC 20006-1110

PUSHINSKY, JON, lawyer; b. N.Y.C., May 30, 1954; s. Paul and Harriet (Rosenberg) P.; m. M. Jean Clickner, July 31, 1982; children: Matthew Clickner-Pushinsky, Jeremy Clickner-Pushinsky. BA, U. Pa., 1976, MA, 1976; JD, U. Pitts., 1979. Bar: Pa. 1979, U.S. Dist. Ct. (we. dist.) Pa. 1979, U.S. Ct. Appeals (3rd cir.) 1980, U.S. Supreme Ct. 1988. Staff counsel W.Va. Legal Svcs. Plan, Wheeling, 1979-80; pvt. practice Pitts., 1980—. Dem. candidate Superior Ct. Pa., 1993, 95; solicitor Cmty. Human Svcs. Corp., Pitts., 1992—; consulting lawyer ARC-Allegheny, Pitts., 1981—. Recipient Civil Libertarian award ACLU of Pa., 1994, Cmty. Citation of Merit Allegheny County Mental Health/Mental Retardation Bd., 1992, Cert. Appreciation Pitts. Commn. on Human Rels., 1992. Mem. Pa. Trial Lawyers Assn., Allegheny County Bar Assn. (appellate practice com., civil rights com.). Democrat. Avocations: reading, hiking, movies. Office: 429 4th Ave Pittsburgh PA 15219-1503

PUSHKAREV, BORIS S., research foundation director, writer; b. Prague, Czechoslovakia, Oct. 22, 1929; came to U.S., 1949, naturalized, 1954; s. Sergei G. and Julie T. (Popov) P.; B.Arch., Yale U., 1954, M.C.P., 1957; m. Iraida Vandellos Legky, Oct. 20, 1973; Instr. city planning Yale U., New Haven, 1957-61; chief planner Regional Plan Assn., N.Y.C., 1961-69, v.p. research, 1969-89, sr. v.p., 1989-90; adj. assoc. prof. N.Y.U., 1967-79; chmn. Russian Research Found. for Study of Alternatives to Soviet Policy, 1981—. Bd. dirs. Russian Solidarists; lectr. New Humanitarian U., Moscow, 1993—. Recipient Nat. Book award (with C. Tunnard), 1964. Mem. Am. Assn. for Advancement of Slavic Studies, editorial bd. POSSEV. Russian Orthodox. Author: (with Christopher Tunnard) Man-Made America, 1963; (with Jeffrey Zupan) Urban Space for Pedestrians, 1975, Public Transportation and Land Use Policy, 1977; Urban Rail in America, 1982, Russia and the Experience of the West, 1995; contbr. articles to profl. jours. Home: 300 Winston Dr Cliffside Park NJ 07010-3236

PUSKAR, MILAN, pharmaceuticals executive; b. 1935. Grad., Youngstown State U., 1961. V.p. Mylan Pharm. Inc., 1961-72; divsn. v.p. ICN Pharms., Inc., 1972-75; pres. Mylan Lab. Inc., 1976—; vice chmn. bd. dirs. Mylan Lab. Inc., 1980-93, chmn. bd., CEO, 1993—. Office: Mylan Labs Inc 1030 Century Bldg Pittsburgh PA 15222

PUSTILNIK, DAVID DANIEL, lawyer; b. N.Y.C., Mar. 10, 1931; s. Philip and Belle (Gerberholtz) P.; m. Helen Jean Todd, Aug. 15, 1959; children: Palma Elyse, Leslie Royce, Bradley Todd. BS, NYU, 1952, JD, 1958, LLM, 1959; postgrad., Air War Coll., 1976. Bar: N.Y. 1959, U.S. Supreme Ct. 1962, Conn. 1964. Legis. tax atty. legis. and regulations div. Office Chief Counsel, IRS, Washington, 1959-63; atty. Travelers Ins. Co., Hartford, Conn., 1963-68; assoc. counsel Travelers Ins. Co., Hartford, 1968-73, counsel, 1973-75, assoc. gen. counsel, 1975-87, dep. gen. counsel, 1987-93; mem. adv. coun. Hartford Inst. on Ins. Taxation, 1978-93, vice chmn., 1991-92, chmn., 1992-93. Grad. editor NYU Tax Law Rev., 1958-59. Trustee Hartford Coll. for Women, 1985-91; life sponsor Am. Tax Policy Inst. Served to col. USAFR. Kenneson fellow NYU, 1958-59. Fellow Am. Coll. Tax Counsel; mem. ABA (chmn. ins. cos. com. 1976-78), Am. Coun. Life Ins. (chmn. co. tax com. 1982-84), Am. Ins. Assn. (chmn. tax com. 1979-81), Assn. Life Ins. Counsel (chmn. tax sect. 1991-93), Twentieth Century Club, Sea Pines Country Club. Democrat. Jewish.

PUSTILNIK, JEAN TODD, elementary education educator; b. Ranger, Tex., Dec. 12, 1932; d. Lonnie Elvin and Frances Elvira (Lee) Todd; m. David Daniel Pustilnik, Aug. 15, 1959; children: Palma Elyse, Leslie Royce, Bradley Todd. BA, U. Okla., 1954; MA, St. Joseph Coll., West Hartford, Conn., 1983. Asst. buyer Foley's, Houston, 1954-58; buyer Kerr's, Oklahoma City, 1958-59; mgr. Woodward & Lothrup, Washington, 1959-61; instr. M. Webster Jr. Coll., Washington, 1961-63; tchr. West Hartford (Conn.) Bd. Edn., 1974-92; instr. St. Joseph Coll., 1976—; curriculum creator Conn. Home Econs. Dept., Middletown, 1985-88. Mem. Am.Home Econs. Assn., Hadassh (pres. 1967-71), Sea Pines Country Club. Home: 60 N Sea Pines Dr Hilton Head Island SC 29928-6007

PUSTILNIK, SEYMOUR W., mathematics educator, education educator; b. N.Y.C., Apr. 3, 1927; s. Morris and Susan Pustilnik; m. Phyllis Lampert, Apr. 8, 1962; children: Michael, Susan. BA in Math., U. Mich., 1948; MA in Math., Bowling Green State U., 1950. Grad. asst. math. Bowling Green (Ohio) State U., 1948-49; assoc. prof. math. CUNY, 1956-86; asst. prof. math. edn. NYU, N.Y.C., 1988-90; owner SWP Co., Brooklyn, N.Y. Author, editor (pamphlet) Rehabilitation and Redevelopment: A Plan to Rehabilitate the Homeless Men on the Cooper Square Site through Urban Renewal, 1961. Mem. Cmty. Sch. Bd., Dist. 13, Bklyn., 1973-77; chmn. Com. for Coop. of Parents, Tchrs., and Prin., Bklyn., 1973-77, Com. for Kindergarten through 6th Grade P.S. 8, Bklyn., 1972-76. Mem. MLA (presenter), Am. Math. Soc. (presenter), Nat. Coun. Tchrs. Math., Math. Assn. Am. (presenter), Soc. Lit. and Sci. (presenter), Soc. Utopian Studies (presenter), Learning Styles Network, N.Y. State Math. Assn. of 2-Yr. Colls., Melus, Soc. for Study of Multi-Ethnic Lit. (presenter), MLA (presenter). Avocations: literary criticism, theater, educational games. Home: 140 Cadman Plz W Brooklyn NY 11201-1852

PUTCHAKAYALA, HARI BABU, engineering company executive; b. Maddirala, India, July 15, 1949; came to the U.S., 1978; s. Seshadri Chowdary and Sambrajyam (Penubothu) P.; m. Vijay Lakshmi, Aug. 9, 1976; children: Sashi Manohar, Gopi Krishna. BS in Chem. Engring., REC, Warangal, India, 1971; MS, BITS, Pilani, India, 1974; PhD, IIT, New Delhi, 1978. Registerd profl. engr., Mich., Md., Calif., Pa., Mo. Trainee Fertilizer Corp., Bombay, 1971; environ. engr. Madison Madison Internat., Detroit, 1978-81, project coord., 1981-84, project mgr., 1984-89, v.p., 1990—, total quality officer, 1995—, also bd. dirs.; bd. dirs. Spack Inc., Bloomfield Hills, Mich. Contbr. articles to Canadian Jour. Chem. Engring. Rsch. fellow Univ. Grants Commn., 1974-78; recipient Cert. Boiler Efficiency Inst., 1981, U. Wis., 1986, 1992, Mich. State U., 1989, Ctr. for Hazardous Materials Rsch., 1990. Mem. AICE, NSPE, Am. Soc. for Quality Control, Am. Cons. Engrs. Coun., Project Mgmt. Inst. Achievements include development of design modification for incineration plants, O&M manuals for numerous water and wastewater facilities; design of wastewater treatment systems; research into energy and value engineering studies; capital improvement programs for public schools. Home: 654 Fox River Dr Bloomfield Hills MI 48304-1012 Office: Madison Internat 1420 Washington Blvd Detroit MI 48226-1716

PUTH, JOHN WELLS, consulting company executive; b. Orange, N.J., Mar. 14, 1929; s. Leonard G. and Elizabeth R. (Wells) P.; m. Betsey Leeds Tait, Mar.1, 1952; children: David Wells, Jonathan Craig, Alison Leeds. BS cum laude, Lehigh U., 1952. Dir. mktg. Purolator Products, Rahway, N.J., 1955-61; pres., chief exec. officer Bridgeport (Conn.) Hardware Mfg. Co. subs. Purolator, 1962-65; group v.p. H.K. Porter Co., Pitts., 1965-72; pres., CEO Disston Inc., Pitts., 1972-75, Vapor Corp., Niles, Ill., 1975-83; chmn., pres., CEO Clevite Industries Inc., Glenview, Ill., 1983-89; pres. JW Puth Assocs., Skokie, Ill., 1989—; bd. dirs. L.B. Foster, Pitts., A.M. Castle & Co., Franklin Park, Ill., Lindberg Corp., Chgo., V.J. Growers Inc., Apopka, Fla., Sys. Software Assocs., Chgo., U.S. Freightways, Inc., Rosemont, Ill., George W. Schmidt Inc., Niles, Ill., Allied Products Corp., Chgo., Golder, Thomas Cressy & Funds, Chgo., Brockway Std., Atlanta, Am. Acads., Cary, Ill. Chmn. bd. trustees Hadley Sch. for Blind, Winnetka, Ill., 1982-84; trustee Lehigh U., Kenilworth Union Ch.; bd. dirs. Iaccoca Inst. With U.S. Army, 1946-47, PTO. Mem. Chgo. Club, Econ. Club, Comml. Club, Indian Hill Country Club, Old Elm Club, Loblolly Pines Club. Republican. Presbyterian. Home: 180 De Windt Rd Winnetka IL 60093-3744

PUTHENVEETIL, JOS ANTHONY, laboratory executive; b. Cochin, Kerala, India, Apr. 2, 1947; came to U.S., 1972; s. Peter Joseph and Angela (Thengaparackal) P.; m. Tresa Joseph Maliekal, Apr. 14, 1973; children: Peter, Marietta, Joseph. BS, Kerala U., India, 1969; BBA, Northwestern Bus. Coll., 1973. Lab. technologist United Med. Lab., Chgo., 1973-74; lab. adminstr. Westlawn Med. Lab., Chgo., 1974-76; pres. Roseland Med. Lab., Chgo., 1976-77; v.p. Foster Western Med. Lab., Chgo., 1977—; pres., CEO Med. World Lab., River Forest, Ill., 1984—; chmn. Pro-Vet Labs., River Forest; bd. dris., exec. v.p. Superior Printed Circuits, Inc., Wheeling, Ill.; Oak Brook, Ill., 1981—, Promed Mgmt., Inc., River Forest; bd. dirs. Shogun Diapers Pvt. Ltd., Bombay, Golden Shrimp Hatchery, Inc., Cochin, India. Founder, chmn. Care and Share, USA, River Forest, 1989; pres. Indo-Am. Friendship Soc., Westmont, 1981; chmn. Nat. South Asian AIDS Orgn., River Forest, 1992. Named Businessman of Yr. Indo-Am. Forum, 1989; recipient Son of India, Indian Christian Assn., 1992, Community Svc. award Fedn. of Christians, 1990, Svc. Excellence award Cen. Wis.-Indians, 1990; Paul Harris fellow Rotary Internat., 1990. Avocations: tennis, writing, speaking, charitable work, community service. Home: 209 Roslyn Rd Oak Brook IL 60521-2516 Office: Med World Lab Inc 7716 Madison St River Forest IL 60305-2102

PUTHOFF, FRANCIS URBAN, insurance salesman; b. Minster, Ohio, Mar. 2, 1922; s. Bernard Leo and Bertha Eliz (Menker) P.; m. Freda Althea Foster, Sept. 20, 1947; children: Francis C., Patricia J., Mary L., Donna M., Frederick U., Teresa A. BS in Health and Phys. Edn., Ohio State U., 1949, MA, 1952; postgrad., Bryn Mawr (Pa.) Coll., 1974, Sinclair Coll., Dayton, Ohio, 1976, U. Dayton, 1960. CLU. Tchr. Vandalia-Butler High Sch., Vandalia, Ohio, 1949-56, St. Christopher's Cath. Sch., Vandalia, 1958-61; salesman Ohio Nat. Life Ins. Co., Cin., 1953-91; gen. agt. Ohio Nat. Life Ins. Co., Dayton, Ohio, 1985-91. Editor: Career Counseling in a Horse Stable, 1984, Paths of Heritage, 1986; author: My Homeland, 1996. Rep. to sister city Ft. Loramie H.S. of 1940, Germany; pres. Ft. Loromie Future Farmers of Am., 1940, St. Christopher Ch. Soc., Vandalia, 1959. Lt. col. USAR; ret. Decorated Bronze Star, Arrowhead. Mem. Nat. Assn. Life Underwriters, Dayton Assn. Life Underwriters, lMillion Dollar Round Table (assoc.), St. Christopher Holy Name Club (pres.), St. Christopher Bldg. Club (pres.). Republican. Roman Catholic. Avocation: writing. Home: 8725 Haloran Ln Dayton OH 45414-2407 Office: Ohio Nat Life Ins Co 237 Williams St Cincinnati OH 45215-4603

PUTKA, ANDREW CHARLES, lawyer; b. Cleve., Nov. 14, 1926; s. Andrew George and Lillian M. (Koryta) P. Student, John Carroll U., 1944, U.S. Naval Acad., 1945-46; A.B., Adelbert Coll., Western Res. U., 1949; J.D., Western Res. U., 1952. Bar: Ohio 1952. Practice law Cleve.; instr. govt. Notre Dame Coll.; v.p. Koryta Bros. Coal Co., Cleve., 1952-56; supt. div. bldg. and loan assns. Ohio Dept. Commerce, 1959-63; pres., chmn. bd., chief exec. officer Am. Nat. Bank, Parma, Ohio, 1963-69; dir. fin. City of Cleve., 1971-74; dir. port control, 1974-78; dir. Cleve. Hopkins Internat. Airport, 1974-78. Mem. Ohio Ho. of Reps., 1953-56, Ohio Senate, 1957-58; dep. auditor, acting sec. Cuyahoga County Bd. Revision, 1970-71; mem. exec. com. Cuyahoga County Democratic Com., 1973-81, Assn. Ind. Colls. and Univs. Ohio, 1983-89; bd. govs. Sch. Law, Western Res. U., 1953-56; mem. exec. com. World Service Student Fund, 1950-52; U.S. rep. Internat. Pax Romana Congress, Amsterdam, 1950, Toronto, 1952; mem. lay advisory bd. Notre Dame Coll., 1968-90, trustee, 1990-93, hon. trustee, 1993—; mem. adv. bd. St. Andrew's Abbey, 1976-88 ; trustee Case-Western Res. U., Newman Found. No. Ohio, 1980-93, hon. trustee, 1993—; 1st v.p. First Cath. Slovak Union of U.S., 1977-80; pres. USO Council of Cuyahoga County, 1980-83. Voted an outstanding legislator Ohio Press Corrs., 1953; named to All-Star Legislative team Ohio Newspaper Corrs., 1955; named one of Fabulous Clevelanders Cleve. Plain Dealer, John Henry Newman honor Soc. Mem. Cuyahoga County, Cleve. Bar Assn., Nat. Assn. State Savs. and Loan Suprs. (past nat. pres.), U.S. Savs. and Loan League (mem. legis com, 1960-63), Am. Legion, Ohio Mcpl. League (bd. trustees 1973), Parma C. of C. (bd. dirs., treas. 1965-67), Newman Fedn. (past nat. pres.), NCCJ, Catholic Lawyers Guild (treas.), Am. Ohio Bankers Assn., Am. Inst. Banking, Adelbert Alumni Assn. (exec. com.), Cathedral Latin Alumni Assn. (trustee 1952—), Internat. Order of Alhambra (internat. parliamentarian 1971—, past grand comdr., supreme advocate 1973), Amvets, KC, Pi Kappa Alpha, Delta Theta Phi (past. pres. Cleve. alumni senate, master inspector 1975). Home: 28 Pond Dr Cleveland OH 44116-1062

PUTMAN, DALE CORNELIUS, management consultant, lawyer; b. Ponca, Nebr., Apr. 29, 1927; s. Merle H. and Catherine V. (Sheahan) P.; m. Alice Anselmi, Sept. 8, 1951; children: Mark, Lee, Neil, Bruce, Kirk, Nancy, Wendy. B.S., U. Nebr., 1949, LL.B., 1951. Bar: Nebr. 1951, Iowa 1951, Mo. 1977. Mgr. Interstate Assn. Credit Mgmt., Sioux City, Iowa, 1951-52; sec., legal counsel Metz Baking Co., Sioux City, 1953-66; v.p. Metz Baking Co., 1966-69, exec. v.p., 1969-72, pres., 1972-76; chief operating officer Interstate Brands Corp., Kansas City, Mo., 1976-77; pres., dir. Interstate Brands Corp., 1977-80, pres., chief exec. officer, 1980-84; chmn., chief exec. officer, pres., dir. Interstate Bakeries (formerly DPF, Inc.), 1980-84; pvt. practice mgmt. cons., 1984—. Served with U.S. Army, 1945-46. Knight, Order of the Holy Sepulchre of Jerusalem. Republican. Roman Catholic. Home: 8405 Reinhardt Ln Shawnee Mission KS 66206-1316

PUTMAN, ROBERT DEAN, golf course architect; b. Wallace, Idaho, Dec. 18, 1924; m. Sally Harmon, 1945; 3 children. Grad., Fresno State Coll. Art dir. Sta. KJEO-TV, Fresno, Calif. Prin. works include Arvin Mcpl. Golf Course, Wasco, Calif., Madera (Calif.) Mcpl. Golf Course, Rancho Canada Golf Course, Carmel Valley, Calif., La Manga Golf Couse, Costa Blanca, Spain, Monterey (Calif.) Country Club Shore Course, San Joaquin Country Club, Fresno, Visalia (Calif.) Mcpl. Golf Course, River Island Golf Course, Poterville, Calif., Kings River Country Club, Kingsburg, Calif. Office: Robert Dean Putman GCA 5644 N Briarwood Ave Fresno CA 93711-2501*

PUTMAN, ALLAN RAY, association executive; b. Melrose, Mass., July 16, 1920; s. Carl Eugene and Alice (Atwood); B.S. in Econs., U. Pa., 1942; m. Marion S. Witmer, Aug. 8, 1942 (dec. Mar. 1993); children—Judith H. (Mrs. Martin Kaliski), Robert W., Victoria, Christian; m. Ann K. Mossman, Sept. 10, 1994. Mem. exec. staff Am. Electroplaters Soc., 1946-49; asst. exec. sec., pub. mag. Tool Engr., Am. Soc. Tool and Mfg. Engrs., 1949-59; mng. dir. ASM Internat., Materials Park, Ohio, 1959-84, sr. mng. dir., 1983-85; sec.-gen. World Materials Congress, 1986—; pres. Nat. Assn. Exhibit Mgrs., 1955, Council Engring. and Sci. Soc. Execs., 1958; mgr. Am. Soc. Metals Found. Edn. and Research, 1963-85. Bd. govs., treas., pres. Cape Cod Conservatory of Music and Arts; bd. govs. Cape Cod symphony Orch. Served to capt. USAAF, 1942-46. Mem. ASTM, Am. Soc. Assn. Execs. (past dir.), Cleve. Conv. and Visitors Bur. (past dir.), Pres.'s Assn., Am. Mgmt. Assn., Metal Properties Council (past dir.), Franklin Inst., Internat., Am. Iron and Steel Inst., S.E. Asia Iron and Steel inst., Metals Soc. (London) (hon.), Am. Assn. Cost Engrs., Associacao Brasileira de Metais, Italian Soc. of Metallurgy, Chinese Soc. Metals, German Soc. Metals, Australasian Inst. Metals, Am. Nuclear Soc., Soc. Automotive Engrs., Soc. Mfg. Engrs., AAAS, Cyrogenic Soc., Soc. for Advancement Materials and Process Engring., Am. Soc. for Engring. Edn., Iron and Steel Inst. Japan (hon.), Nat. Sci. Tchrs. Assn. (life), Metall. Soc., Greater Cleve. Growth Assn., Buckeye Trail Assn., Country Club (Pepper Pike, Ohio), Appalachian Mountain Club, Horseshoe Trail Club, Univ. Club (Washington), Orleans Yacht Club (bd. dirs.), Rotary (sec.). Home: 17 Pride's Path PO Box 2772 Orleans MA 02653 Office: ASM Internat Materials Park OH 44073

PUTNAM, FRANK WILLIAM, biochemistry and immunology educator; b. New Britain, Conn., Aug. 3, 1917; s. Frank and Henrietta (Holzmann) P.; m. Dorothy Alice Linder, Nov. 18, 1942; children—Frank William, Beverly Susan. B.A., Wesleyan U., Middletown, Conn., 1939, M.A., 1940; Ph.D., U. Minn., 1942; M.A. (hon.), Cambridge (Eng.) U., 1973. Instr., research asso. Duke U. Med. Sch., 1942-46; biochemist CWS, Camp Detrick, Md., 1946; asst. prof. U. Chgo., then assoc. prof. biochemistry, 1947-55; Lasdon research fellow Cambridge U., 1952-53; prof. biochemistry, head dept. U. Fla., 1955-65; prof. biology, dir. div. biol. scis. Ind. U., Bloomington, 1965-69; prof. molecular biology and zoology Ind. U., 1972-74, disting. prof. molecular biology and biochemistry, 1974-88, prof. emeritus, 1989—; bd. visitors Duke U. Med. Center, 1970-75; chmn. com. nomenclature of human immunoglobulins Internat. Union Immunol. Socs., 1971-76; chmn. basic sci. rev. bd. VA, 1972-76; chmn. cancer cause and prevention adv. com. Nat. Cancer Inst., 1974-75; sci. adv. com. Papanicolaou Cancer Research Inst., 1976-82; research rev. com. ARC, 1973-77; sci. com. Brussels Colloquium on Protides of Biol. Fluids, 1970-90; chmn. virus cancer program adv. com. Nat. Cancer Inst., 1975-77; sr. med. adv. group VA, 1976-80; council div. biol. scis. and Pritzker Med. Sch., U. Chgo., 1977-87; chmn. Assembly Life Scis. Nat. Acad. Scis., 1977-81; mem. U.S. Nat. Com. Biochemistry, 1973-79; pres. sci. adv. com. G.E.R.M.I., Lyon, France, 1981-87. Co-author, editor: The Plasma Proteins, vol. 1, Isolation, Characterization and Function, 1960, vol. 2, Biosynthesis, Metabolism, Alterations in Disease, 1960, The Plasma Proteins, 2d edit., Structure, Function, and Genetic Control, Vol. 1, 1975. Vol. 2, 1975, Vol. 3, 1977, Vol. 4, 1984, Vol. 5, 1987; mem. editorial bd. Archives of Biochemistry and Biophysics, 1954-59, Science, 1968-82, Immunochemistry, 1972-75, Biomed. News, 1969-73, Fedn. Proc, 1958-63; Author numerous research papers. Trustee Argonne Univs. Assn., 1981-82; bd. govs. U. Chgo. Argonne Nat. Lab., 1983-89, chmn. Sci. and tech. com., 1983-87; bd. dirs. Radiation Research Found., 1981-87. Markle scholar med. scis., 1950-56; Guggenheim fellow, 1970; fellow Churchill Coll., Cambridge U., 1973—; recipient Distinguished award teaching and research Wesleyan U., 1964, Distinguished Service award in medicine U. Chgo., 1968; Outstanding Achievement award U. Minn., 1974. Fellow AAAS, N.Y. Acad. Scis.; mem. Nat. Acad. Scis., Am. Acad. Arts and Scis. (Midwest council 1975-84), Pan-Am. Assn. Biomed. Scis. (sec.-gen. 1975-78), Japan Electrophoresis Soc. (hon.), Am. Inst. Biol. Scis. (life), Am. Soc. Biol. Chemists (sec. 1958-63), Soc. Exptl. Biology and Medicine, Am. Assn. Immunologists, Am. Chem. Soc. (chmn. div. biol. chemistry 1966-67), Soc. Peruana de Patologia (hon.), Fedn. Socs. Exptl. Biology (chmn. secs. com. 1958-63), Protein Soc., Internat. Soc. Thrombosis Haemostasis, Phi Beta Kappa, Sigma Xi, Phi Lambda Upsilon, Delta Sigma Rho. Club: Cosmos. Address: 5025 E Heritage Woods Rd Bloomington IN 47401-9314

PUTNAM, FREDERICK WARREN, JR., bishop; b. Red Wing, Minn., June 17, 1917; s. Frederick W. and Margaret (Bunting) P.; m. Helen Kathryn Prouse, Sept. 24, 1942; children: James Douglas, John Frederick, Andrew Warren. B.A., U. Minn., 1939; M.Div., Seabury-Western Theol. Sem., 1942, D.D., 1963; postgrad., State U. Iowa, 1946-47. Ordained to ministry Episcopal Ch. as deacon, priest, 1942. Pastor in Windom and Worthington, Minn., 1942-43, Iowa City, 1943-47, Evanston, Ill., 1947-59, Wichita, Kans., 1960-63; Episc. chaplain State U. Iowa, 1943-47; suffragan bishop Episcopal Diocese, Okla., 1963-79; bishop Episcopal Ch. in Navajoland, 1979-83; asst. bishop Diocese of Minn., 1983-89, 96-97; acting rector St. George's Episcopal, Pearl Harbor, Hawaii, 1984-85, 96, St. Clement's, Honolulu, 1986, St. John's, Kula, Maui, Hawaii, 1988, St. Elizabeth's, Honolulu, 1990; interim rector St. Stephen's Episcopal Ch., Edina, Minn., 1991-92, Trinity Episcopal Ch., Pocatello, Idaho, 1994; vis. bishop Diocese of N.J., 1995; bd. dirs. Kiyosoto Ednl. Experiment Program, 1954-91, v.p., 1989-91; cons. Oklahoma City Community Relation Commn., 1966-70; Pres. Okla. Conf. Religion and Race, 1963-67; v.p. Greater Oklahoma City Council Chs., 1966-67; nat. chaplain Brotherhood of St. Andrew, 1967-79, mem. brotherhood legion, 1972—; priest assoc. Order Holy Cross, 1942—; exec. com. Conf. Diocesan Execs., 1969-76, pres., 1972-74; mem. Okla. Commn. United Ministries in Higher Edn., 1970-79, pres., 1973-75; mem. nat. com. on Indian work Episc. Ch., 1977-80; chaplain Okla. Assn. Alcoholism and Alcohol Abuse, 1974-78; hon. life mem. Oklahoma City and County Criminal Justice Council, 1978—; Bechtel lectr. U. Denver, 1966. Editor: (pub.) Sharers Mag., 1957-63; contbr. articles to profl. publs. Founder, pres. Oklahoma City Met. Alliance for Safer City, 1971-78; Trustee Seabury-Western Theol. Sem., 1959-65, Episcopal Theol. Sem. Southwest, 1966-69, St. Simeon's Episcopal Home, 1963-79, St. Crispins Episcopal Conf. Center, 1963-79, Casady Sch., 1963-79, Holland Hall Sch., 1963-79, Episcopal Soc. Cultural and Racial Unity, 1967-70; trustee Neighborhood Services Orgn., treas., 1969; founder, 1st pres. Friends of Wichita Pub. Library, 1962; bd. dirs. Minn. Photographic Exbn.; chmn. Mpls.-St. Paul Internat. Photographic Exhbn., 1987, 89; State Bd. Minn. Common Cause, 1989—, state chmn., 1993-95—. Recipient Disting. Service award Evanston Jr. C. of C., 1952; Merit award Photog. Soc. Am. Fellow Coll. Preachers; mem. ACLU, Assoc. Parishes (pres. 1960-64), Mpls. Soc. Fine Arts (mem. photo coun.), Photog. Soc. Am., Am. Com. for KEEP (v.p. 1961-70, 90), Walker Art Ctr., Sierra Club, Met. Sr. Fedn., Audubon Club, Am. Assn. Ret. Persons, Minn. Hort. Soc., Hist. Soc. Episcopal Ch., Archaeol. Conservancy, Ancient Bibl. Manuscripts Ctr., Claremont, Calif., World Future Soc., Photographic Soc. Am. (assoc. 1989—, mem. v.p., 1995-97—), Twin Cities Assn. Camera Clubs (v.p. 1987), U. Minn. Alumni Assn., Minn. Hist. Soc., St. Paul Camera Club, Crosstown Camera Club, N.Am. Rights Fund., People for the Am. Way, Episcopal Peace Fellowship, Amnesty Internat., Greenpeace, Liturgical Conf., Living Ch. Found., Worldwatch Inst., Clan Douglas Soc., Northwest Racquet and Swim Club, Explorers Club, Phi Kappa Psi. Clubs: Normandale Tennis and Swim. Home: 5229 Meadow Rdg Edina MN 55439-1412

PUTNAM, GEORGE W., JR., army officer; b. Ft. Fairfield, Maine, May 5, 1920; s. George W. and Rae B. (Merrithew) P.; m. Elaine Anderson (dec. 1973); m. Claudine Mahin (div. 1995); m. Helen Guerin, 1995; children: James M., J. Glenn; stepchildren: Philip Mahin, Leslie Mahin. Served as enlisted man U.S. Army, 1941-42, commd. 2d lt., 1942, advanced through grades to maj. gen., 1970; comdg. gen. (1st Cavalry Div.), Vietnam, 1970-71; dir. Mil. Personnel Mgmt., Hdqrs. Dept. Army, Washington, 1971-75; comdg. gen. U.S. Army So. European Task Force, Vicenza, Italy, 1975-77, U.S. Army Phys. Disability Agy., Washington, 1977-81; ret. U.S. Army, 1981; dir. Army Coun. Rev. Bds., 1977-81; pres. Nat. Capital Retiree Coun., 1982-85. Internat. judge 5th and 6th World Helicopter Championships, 1986, 89, 94, chief judge 7th World Championship, 1992; U.S. mem. Internat. Helicopter com. Fedn. Aeronautique Internationale, 1988-91, 93-95; bd. dirs. Army Aviation Mus. Found., 1987—, pres., 1993-96; chmn. bd. trustees Army Aviation Hall of Fame, 1996—. Inducted Army Aviation Hall of Fame, 1980. Mem. Nat. Aero. Assn. (sr. v.p. 1991-95, sr. v.p. Fedn. Aero. Internat. affairs 1995—, U.S. v.p. 1995—), Army Aviation Assn. Am. (sr. v.p., pres. 1983-87, pres. scholarship found. 1991-93), Helicopter Club Am. (pres. 1988-90). Home: 4106 N Richmond St Arlington VA 22207

PUTNAM, J. STEPHEN, financial executive; m. Pamela Schirmer; 3 children. BA, Bowdoin Coll., 1965. Pres. Robert Thomas Securities, Inc., St. Petersburg, Fla.; sr. v.p. Raymond James & Assocs., Inc.; bd. dirs., exec. v.p. Raymond James Fin., Inc.; treas. Meerschaert Mut. Fund; v.p., bd. dirs. F.L. Putnam Securities. Bd. dirs., former chmn. bd. St. Joseph's Coll., North Windham, Maine; bd. dirs., chmn. Citizens Scholarship Found. Am., Inc.; pres. Palm Harbor (Fla.) Cmty. Svc. Agy. Decorated Bronze Star, Army Commendation medal. Mem. NASD (by-laws and spl. com. to investigate investment adv. regulation), Fla. Securities Dealers Assn. (bd. dirs.), Youth Soccer Assn. Office: Robert Thomas Securities Inc 880 Carillon Pky Saint Petersburg FL 33716-1102

PUTNAM, LINDA LEE, communication educator, researcher; b. Frederick, Okla., Aug. 10, 1945; d. Allard Warren and Etta Wanona (Tucker) Loutherback; m. Thomas Milton Putnam III, Mar. 28, 1970; 1 child, Ashley Ann. BA, Hardin-Simmons U., 1967; MA, U. Wis., 1968; PhD, U. Minn., 1977. Instr. U. Mass., Amherst, 1968-69; instr., chair dept. speech-theatre Normandale Community Coll., Bloomington, Minn., 1969-77; prof. communication Purdue U., West Lafayette, Ind., 1977-93; dept. head Tex. A & M Univ., 1993—; vis. scholar Stanford U., U. Calif.-Berkeley, San Francisco, 1984, Harvard U.-Harvard Negotiation Project, 1992. Editor: Communication and Organization, 1983(Best Publ. award 1985), Handbook of Organizational Communication, 1987 (Best Publ. award 1988), Communication and Negotiation, 1992. Del. Dem. State Conv., Mpls., 1972-74; treas. local dist. Dem. Farm Labor Party, Mpls., 1973-74, co-chairperson, 1974-75; block chair Am. Can. Soc. Fund Raiser, West Lafayette, 1986-87. Recipient AMOCO Teaching award Purdue U., 1986, Andersch award Ohio U., 1991, Disting. Alumni award Hardin-Simmons U., 1991, Charles H. Woolbert Rsch. award Speech Comm. Assn., 1993. Fellow Internat. Comm. Assn. (chair 1986-88, orgn. com. divsn. 1995); mem. Acad. Mgmt. (chair power negotiation, conflict mgmt. com. 1989-91), Speech Comm. Assn. (mem. at large 1984-87), Ctrl. States Speech Assn. (sec. comm. theory com. 1978-79, Scholar Showcase award 1989), Internat. Assn. for Conflict Mgmt. (bd. dirs. 1990-92, pres. 1994). Avocation: cooking. *In an age when change is inevitable, we often fear and try to avoid the unknown. In our drive for security, we forget that one of our richest blessings is change—the change that preserves diversity and the balance of power.*

PUTNAM, MICHAEL COURTNEY JENKINS, classics educator; b. Springfield, Mass., Sept. 20, 1933; s. Roger Lowell and Caroline (Jenkins) P. AB, Harvard U., 1954, AM, 1956, PhD, 1959; LLD (hon.), Lawrence U., 1985. Instr. classics Smith Coll., Northampton, Mass., 1959-60; faculty classics Brown U., Providence, 1960—; prof. Brown U., 1967—, chmn., 1968, 70-72, 77-78, 1994-95, prof. comparative lit., 1980—, MacMillan prof. of classics, 1985—; acting dir. Ctr. for Hellenic Studies, Harvard U., 1961-62, sr. fellow, 1971-86; Townsend prof. classics Cornell U., 1985; Mellon prof.-in-charge Am. Acad. in Rome, 1989-91; scholar in residence Am. Acad. in Rome, 1969-70, mem. classical jury, 1982-83, trustee, 1991—; assoc. univ. seminar on classical civilization Columbia U., N.Y.C., 1972—; mem. cath. Commn. on Intellectual and Cultural Affairs, 1969—; mem. adv. coun. dept. classics Princeton U., 1981-87, chmn., 1983-87; cons. Am. Coun. Learned Socs., 1987-89; mem. Inst. for Advanced Study, 1987-88; vis. scholar Phi Beta Kappa, 1994-95; councillor Assn. of Lit. Scholars and Critics, 1996—. Author: The Poetry of the Aeneid, 1965, Virgil's Pastoral Art, 1970, Tibullus: A Commentary, 1973, Virgil's Poem of the Earth, 1979, Essays on Latin Lyric, Elegy and Epic, 1982, Artifices of Eternity: Horace's Fourth Book of Odes, 1986, Virgil's Aeneid: Interpretation and Influence, 1995; contbr. articles to profl. jours. Sole trustee Lowell Obs., Flagstaff, Ariz., 1967-87, bd. advisors, 1987—; trustee Bay Chamber Concerts, Camden, Maine, 1972-88, incorporator, 1988-94; mem. bd. cons. Portsmouth Abbey Sch., 1985-89; hon. sec. Keats-Shelley Meml. Assn., Rome, 1989-91. Rome Prize fellow Am. Acad. in Rome, 1963-64; Guggenheim Meml. fellow, 1966-67; sr. fellow NEH, 1973-74, cons. 1974-78, 87—; Am. Council Learned Soc. fellow, 1983-84. Fellow Am. Acad. Arts and Scis.; mem. Am. Philol. Assn. (bd. dirs. 1972-75, mem. com. on award of merit 1975-78, chmn. 1977-78, 1st v.p. 1981, pres. 1982, del. Am. Coun. Learned Socs. 1984-87, Charles J. Goodwin award of merit 1971), Archaeol. Inst. Am., Classical Assn. New Eng., Medieval Acad. Am., Vergilian Soc. Am. (trustee 1969-73, v.p. 1974-76), Accademia Nazionale Virgiliana, Acad. Lit. Studies, Art Club. Office: Brown U Dept Classics Providence RI 02912

PUTNAM, PAUL ADIN, retired government agency official; b. Springfield, Vt., July 12, 1930; s. Horace Adin and Beatrice Nellie (Baldwin) P.; m. Elsie Mae (Ramseyer) June 12, 1956; children: Pamela Ann, Penelope Jayne, Adin Tyler II, Paula Anna. B.S., U. Vt., 1952; M.S., Wash. State U., 1954; Ph.D., Cornell U., 1957. Research animal scientist Agrl. Research Service, USDA, Beltsville, Md., 1957-66, investigation leader beef cattle nutrition, 1966-68, chief beef cattle research br., 1968-72; asst. dir. Beltsville Agrl. Research Ctr., 1972-80, dir., 1980-84; dir. cen. plains area Ames, Iowa, 1984-87; assoc. dir. mid. south area Stoneville, Miss., 1987-88, dir. mid south area, 1988-94. Contbr. articles to profl. jours. Recipient Kidder medal U. Vt.; Outstanding Performance awards USDA, also cert. merit; Danforth fellow; Borden fellow; Purina Research fellow. Fellow AAAS (rep. sect. O), Am. Soc. Animal Sci. (pres., North Atlantic sect., chmn. various coms., N.E. sect. Disting. Service award); mem. Am. Dairy Sci. Assn., Orgn. Profl. Employees USDA (pres. Beltsville chpt.), Council for Agrl. Sci. and Tech. Home: 36 Putnam Rd Springfield VT 05156-9115

PUTNAM, PETER BROCK, author, lecturer; b. Georgia, June 11, 1920; s. Brock and Margaret (Faber) P.; m. Durinda Dobbins, Aug. 12, 1944; children: Brock II, Barbara Durinda, John Gerry. Grad., Hill Sch., 1938; B.A., Princeton, 1942, Ph.D., 1950. Lectr. history Princeton, 1950-55; v.p. Unitarian Universalist Assn., 1965-67; cons. recording for the blind and dyslexic, 1988—. Author: Keep Your Head Up, Mr. Putnam, 1952, Seven Britons in Imperial Russia, 1952, Cast off the Darkness, 1957, Triumph of the Seeing Eye, 1962, Peter, the Revolutionary Tsar, 1973, Love in the Lead, 1979; Translator: (Marc Bloch): Apologie Pour l'Histoire, 1953. Pres. Chapin Sch., 1961-63; exec. com. Princeton Alumni Coun., 1972-76; bd. dirs. Recording for Blind, 1955—, pres., 1976-80; bd. dirs. Mass. Assn. Blind, 1967-71, Star Island Corp.; pres. Unitarian Ch., 1954-57; bd. dirs. Lucerna Fund, 1976—; trustee Seeing Eye, 1981-90; trustee Continental Assn. Funeral and Meml. Socs., 1983-89; pres. Meml. Soc. Fund, 1983-87, Talking Books for Hosps., 1983-87. Mem. Author's League, Princeton Meml. Assn. (bd. dirs. 1956—, pres. 1988—). Clubs: Cottage, Princeton Triangle (trustee 1962-87), Nassau Club. Home: 48 Roper Rd Princeton NJ 08540-4070 *The fear of uncertainty is the principal fear from which all others flow. It is always necessary to act on insufficient evidence. The acceptance of uncertainty is a major step on the road to maturity. A sense of humor is indispensable.*

PUTNAM, RICHARD JOHNSON, federal judge; b. Abbeville, La., Sept. 27, 1913; s. Robert Emmett and Mathilde (Young) P.; m. Dorethea Gooch, Jan. 27, 1940; children: Richard Johnson, Claude Robert, Mary Stacy, Cynthia Anne. BS cum laude, Springhill Coll., Mobile, 1934; LLB, Loyola U., New Orleans, 1937. Bar: La. 1937. Pvt. practice law Abbeville, 1937-54; dist. atty. 15th Jud. Dist., La., 1948-54; judge 15th Jud. Dist. Ct., La., 1954-61; dist. judge U.S. Dist. Ct. (we. dist.) La., 1961-75; sr. U.S. dist. judge, 1975—; temporary judge U.S. Ct. Appeals for 5th cir., 1983; rep. fed. cts. Coun. La. Law Inst., 1976-89, sr. mem. inst. coun., 1989—; liaison judge for we. dist. 5th Cir. Archives - Hist. Com. , 1980; chmn. sr. judges adv. bd. Fed. Judges Assn., 1983—. Served from ensign to lt. USNR, 1942-45. Recipient Student Coun. Key Loyola U., 1937. Mem. Dist. Judges Assn., ABA, La. Bar Assn., Fifth Cir. Dist. Judges Assn., Am. Legion, VFW, St. Thomas Moore Soc. (Svc. award 1937), Delta Theta Phi. Lodge: KC. Office: US Dist Ct 300 Fed Bldg 705 Jefferson St Lafayette LA 70501-6936*

PUTNAM, ROBERT E., writer, editor; b. Mt. Sterling, Ill., Sept. 13, 1933; s. John Harold and Florence Pauline (Curran) P.; m. Linda J. Wiant, Aug. 30, 1960; children: Justine, Robbie, Dylan. B.A., U. Ill., 1959; M.A., Roosevelt U., 1969. Asso. engr. Western Electric Co., Chgo., 1960-62; with Am. Tech. Pubs., Inc., Chgo., 1964—; editor-in-chief Am. Tech. Pubs., Inc., 1973—, v.p. editorial, 1980-82. Author: Fundamentals of Carpentry, 1967, Concrete Block Construction, 3d edit, 1973, Bricklaying Skill and Practice, 3d edit, 1974, Architectural and Building Trades Dictionary, 3d edit, 1974, Fundamentals of Carpentry: Tools, Materials and Practices, 5th edit, 1977, Basic Blueprint Reading: Residential, 1980, Builder's Comprehensive Dictionary, 1984, 89, Construction Blueprint Reading, 1985, Building Trades Blueprint Reading, 1985; Welding Print Reading, 1986, Motorcycle Operation and Service, 1986, Masonry, 1988. Served with U.S. Army, 1953-55. Mem. Am. Welding Soc., Am. Soc. Tng. and Devel., Am. Soc. for Quality Control, Nat. Soc. Performance and Instrn. (Chgo. chpt.). Home: 256 Lester Rd Park Forest IL 60466-2039

PUTNAM, RUTH ANNA, philosopher, educator; b. Berlin, Germany, Sept. 20, 1927; d. Martin and Marie (Kohn) Hall; m. Hilary W. Putnam, Aug. 11, 1962; children: Samuel, Joshua, Maxima. BS in Chemistry, UCLA, 1954, PhD in Philosophy, 1962. Instr. Philosophy UCLA, 1957-59; acting asst. prof. U. Oreg., 1959-62; from lectr. to prof. Wellesley (Mass.) Coll., 1963—, chair dept. Philosophy, 1979-82, 91-93; dir. summer seminar NEH, 1986, 89; mem. extramural grad. fellowships Wellesley Coll., faculty benefits com., com. budget, academic review bd., taskforce on affirmative action, bd. of admissions; presenter in field. Editor: Cambridge Companion to William James, 1997; contbr. chpts. to books, articles to profl. jours., encyclopedias. Mem. Am. Philos. Assn. (program com. ea. divsn. 1977). Jewish. Office: Wellesley Coll 106 Central St Wellesley MA 02181-8203

PUTNAM, TERRY MICHAEL, federal judge; b. Albany, Ga., June 7, 1954; s. Thomas Arnold and Betty Lavonia (Taylor) P.; m. Leigh Ann Smith, Aug. 20, 1983; 1 child, Thomas, Amelia. BA, U. Ala., 1976, JD, 1979. Bar: Ala. 1979, U.S. Dist. Ct. (no. dist.) Ala. 1980, U.S. Ct. Appeals (5th cir.) 1980, U.S. Ct. Appeals (11th cir.) 1981, U.S. Supreme Ct. 1985. Assoc. Potts, Young & Blasingame, Florence, Ala., 1979-83; ptnr. Potts, Young, Blasingame & Putnam, Florence, 1983-86; U.S. magistrate judge U.S. Dist. Ct. (no. dist.) Ala., Birmingham, 1987—; lectr. continuing legal edn. Ala. Bar Inst., 1985, 88, 90, 92, Cumberland Sch. Law, 1993. Mem. ABA, Fed. Magistrate Judges Assn., Order of Coif, Phi Beta Kappa. Democrat. Avocations: sailing, reading. Office: 268 US Courthouse 1729 5th Ave N Birmingham AL 35203-2000

PUTNAM, WILLIAM LOWELL, science association administrator; b. Springfield, Mass., Oct. 25, 1924; s. Roger Lowell and Caroline Piatt (Jenkins) P.; m. Joan Fitzgerald, Sept. 29, 1951 (dec. April 1993); children: Katherine Elizabeth, W. Lowell. Grad., Harvard Coll., 1945. With Springfield C. of C., 1950-52; founder, chmn. Springfield TV Corp., 1952-84; with Carroll Travel Bur., 1984—; vice chmn. Assn. Maximum Svc. Telecasters, 1975-84; sec.-treas. NBC Affiliates, 1980-83. Sole trustee Lowell Obs., Flagstaff, Ariz.; chmn. Springfield Pk. Commn., 1991-95. 1st lt. U.S. Army, 1943-45. Decorated Silver Star, Bronze Star, Purple Heart. Mem. Assn. Canadian Mountain Guides (hon.), Alpine Club Can. (hon.), Appalachian Mountain Club (hon.), Am. Alpine Club (pres. 1974-76, treas. 1977-91, hon.), Am. Mountain Guides Assn. (dir.), Internat. Union Alpine Clubs (Am. del., v.p.). Avocation: alpinism. Office: Lowell Obs Flagstaff AZ 86001

PUTNEY, JOHN ALDEN, JR., insurance company executive; b. Bklyn., Mar. 5, 1939; s. John Alden and Anne Marie (Davenport) P.; m. Theresa Rose DeFrisco, Feb. 9, 1964; children: Angela, Alexander. B.S. cum laude in Math, St. John's U., 1960. Systems engr. IBM, N.Y.C., 1961-64; mktg. rep. IBM, 1964-66; cons. Topas Computer Corp., N.Y.C., 1966-67; dir., v.p., sec. Topas Computer Corp., 1967-70; with Tchrs. Ins. and Annuity Assn., N.Y.C., 1971—, v.p., 1977-79, sr. v.p., 1979-80, exec. v.p., 1980—, office and info. systems area mgr., 1979-87, mgr. ops. support area, 1987-95, mgr. pension and annuity svc. area, 1995—. Served with USMC, 1960. Home: 9 Concord Ave Larchmont NY 10538-3105 Office: Tchrs Ins & Annuity Assn 730 3rd Ave New York NY 10017-3206

PUTNEY, MARK WILLIAM, lawyer, utility executive; b. Marshalltown, Iowa, Jan. 25, 1929; s. Lawrence Charles and Geneva (Eldridge) P.; m. Ray Ann Bartnek, May 25, 1962; children: Andi Bartnek, William Bradford, Blake Reinhart. BA, U. Iowa, 1951, JD, 1957. Bar: Iowa 1957, U.S. Supreme Ct. 1960. Ptnr. Bradshaw, Fowler, Proctor & Fairgrave, Des Moines, 1961-72, of counsel, 1992-94; chmn., CEO. Bradford & Blake Ltd., Dakota Dunes, S.D., 1992—; pres., chmn., chief exec. officer Iowa Resources, Inc.,, 1984-90; chmn., chief exec. officer Iowa Power & Light Co., 1984-90, Iowa Gas Co.,, 1984-85, Midwest Resources Inc., 1990-92. Civilian aide to Sec. Army for Iowa, 1975-77; bd. dirs. Greater Des Moines YMCA, 1976-86, Boys' Home Iowa, 1982-86, Hoover Presdl. Libr. Assn., 1983—, U. Iowa Found., 1984—, Edison Electric Inst., 1986-89; bd. dirs. Greater Des Moines Com., 1984—, pres. 1988; bd. dirs. Assoc. Edison Illuminating Cos., 1988-93, pres., 1991-92; chmn. Iowa Com. Employer Support of Guard and Res., 1979-86; bd. dirs. Des Moines Devel. Corp., 1984-92, chmn., 1989-90. With USAF, 1951-53. Recipient Disting. Alumnus award U. Iowa, 1995. Mem. Iowa Utility Assn. (chmn. 1989, dir.), Des Moines Club (pres. 1977), Desert Forest Golf Club (Carefree, Ariz.), Masons, Shriners, Delta Chi, Phi Delta Phi. Republican. Episcopalian. Home: 600 Stevens Port Dr Dakota Dunes SD 57049-5149

PUTNEY, PAUL WILLIAM, lawyer; b. Phila., Feb. 6, 1940; s. R. Emerson and Dorothea (Schulz) P.; m. Joan E. High, June 9, 1961; children: Joanna E., Andrew E. AB, Princeton U., 1962; JD, Harvard U., 1965. BarP Pa. 1965, U.S. Dist. Ct. (ea. dist.) Pa. 1966, U.S. Supreme Ct. 1977, N.Y. 1988. Assoc. Dechert Price & Rhoads, Phila., 1965-73, ptnr., 1973-74, 77-87; mng. ptnr. Dechert Price & Rhoads, N.Y.C., 1987-94; chmn. trust and estates dept., 1994—; dep. chief broadcast bur. FCC, Washington, 1974-77; chmn. Phila. Presbytery Homes, Inc., 1987-93. Mem. ABA (past chair com. fin. planning for bus. owners, task force on legal fin. planning of real property, trust and probate sect.). Office: Dechert Price & Rhoads 4000 Bell Atlantic Tower 1717 Arch St Philadelphia PA 19103-2713

PUTTER, IRVING, French language educator; b. N.Y.C., Dec. 3, 1917; s. Joseph and Anna (Schrank) P.; children—Paul Stephen, Candace Anne Putter. B.A., CCNY, 1938; M.A., State U. Iowa, 1941; Ph.D., Yale U., 1949. Mem. faculty U. Calif.-Berkeley, 1947-88; prof. French U. Calif. at Berkeley, 1961-88, chmn. dept., 1968-71, humanities research fellow, 1971-72, 78-79, 84-85. Author: Leconte de Lisle and His Contemporaries, 1951, The Pessimism of Leconte de Lisle: Sources and Evolution, 1954, The Pessimism of Leconte de Lisle: The Work and The Time, 1961, La Dernière Illusion de Leconte de Lisle: Lettres Inédites a Emilie Leforestier, 1968; also numerous articles.; editor, translator: Chateaubriand: Atala, René, 1952. Guggenheim fellow, 1955-56; Fulbright fellow, 1955-56. Home: 115 St James Dr Piedmont CA 94611-3603

PUTTERMAN, FLORENCE GRACE, artist, printmaker; b. N.Y.C., Apr. 14, 1927; d. Nathan and Jean (Feldman) Hirsch; m. Saul Putterman, Dec. 19, 1947. BS, NYU, 1947; MFA, Pa. State U., 1973. Founder, pres. Arts Unlimited, Selinsgrove, Pa., 1969—; curator Milton Shoe Collection, 1970—; artist in residence Title III Program Cultural Enrichment in Schs. Program, 1969-70; instr. Lycoming Coll., Williamsport, Pa., 1972-74, Susquehanna U., Selinsgrove, PA, 1984—. Exhibited one-woman shows, Everson Mus., Syracuse, N.Y., 1976, Hagerstown, Md., 1978, Stuhr Mus., Grand Island, N.B., 1979, Muhlenburg Ctr. for the Arts, Pa., 1985, Harmon Gallery, Fla., 1985, The State Mus. of Pa., 1985-86, Segal Gallery, N.Y., 1986, Canton Inst. Fine Arts, Ohio, 1986, Fla. Biennial Polk Mus., Lakeland, Fla., 1987, 89, Artists Choose Artists, Tampa Mus., 1987, Auburn Works on Paper, 1987, Ala., Ruth Volid Gallery, Chgo., 1989, Polk Mus. Art, Lakeland, Fla., 1989, Lowe Gallery, Atlanta, 1990, Mickelson Gallery, Washington, 1990, Palmer Mus., Pa. State U., 1990, Payne Gallery, Moravian Coll., 1991, Everhart Mus., Scranton, Pa., 1991, Lowe Gallery, L.A., 1992, Center Gallery, Bucknell U., Pa., 1993, Lore Degenstein Gallery, Susquehanna U., Selinsgrove, Pa., 1993, Lowe Gallery, Atlanta, 1993, Donn Roll Gallery, Sarasota, Fla., Gallery 10, Washington, Donn Roll Contemporary, Sarasota, Fla., 1996, Grand Central Gallery, Tampa Fla., 1997, Walter Wickiser Gallery, N.Y., Hodges-Taylor Gallery, Charlotte N.C.; group shows include Libr. Congress, Soc. Am. Graphic Artists, Ball State Drawing Ann., Muncie, Ind., Arts Club N.Y., Colorprint, U.S.A., Smithsonian Traveling Exhbn., Boston Printmakers, N.C. Print & Drawing, Chautauqua Nat., U. Dallas Nat. Print Invitational, Segal Gallery, Rutgers Drawing, Polk Mus., Tampa Mus., Sichaun Fine Art Inst., Mickelson Gallery, Harmon Gallery, Mus. Art U. Ariz., 1988, U. Del., Newark, 1988 Mid Am. Biennial, Owensboro Mus. Art, VCCA Exhbn. Mcpl. Gallery, Regensburg, Federal Republic of Germany, 1989, Erie (Pa.) Art Mus., 1990, 1990 twenty year survey Palmer Mus., Pa. State U., Univ. Park, Payne Gallery Moravian Coll., Bethlehem, Pa., 1991, Everhart Mus., Scranton, Pa., 1991, U. Del. Biennial, Phila. Watercolor Soc., Noyes Mus., N.J., 1992, Erie (Pa.) Mus., 1991, Mus. Fine Arts, Hanoi, 1991, Spanish Embassy, Madrid, 1992, Anita Shapolsky Gallery, N.Y., 1990, American Women's Artists, Foster Harman Gallery Sarasota, Fla., 1993, Humphrey Gallery, N.Y., 1992, Anita Shapolsky Gallery, N.Y., 1993, Fla. Printmakers, Miami, 1993, Fla. Artists Ringling Mus., 1994, Walter Wickiser Gallery, N.Y., 1995. Recipient award Silvermine Guild Conn. Appalachian Corridors, Arena, 1976, Gold medal of honor Audubon Artists ann. competition, Whitehead award Boston Printmakers, 1985, Shellenberg award Artists Equity, 1985, award N.C. Print & Drawing, 1985, award Chautauqua Nat., 1985, Johnson & Johnson award 3rd Ann. Nat. Printmaking Coun. of N.J., 1985, Purchase award N.J. State Mus., 1987, Disting. Alumni award Pa. State U. Sch. Arts & Architecture, 1988, Ethel Klassen Meml. award Fla. Artists Group, 1992, Earl Horter award Phila. Watercolor Club, 1992, award of excellence, 1995, Stella Drabkin Meml. award Colorprint Soc., Award for Excellence Phila. Watercolor Club, 1996, Elizabeth Morse Meml. award Fla. Artists Group, 1996, Daniel Serra Y Navas Meml. award Audubon Artists, N.Y., 1996; Va. Ctr. for the Creative Arts fellow, 1983-84; Nat. Endowment Arts grantee. Mem. Soc. Am. Graphic Artists (v.p.), Nat. Assn. of Women Artists (Nat. Medal of Honor, Elizabeth Blake award). Home: 220 Morningside Dr Sarasota FL 34236-1113 *I examine the world through painting. I consider the act of art a spiritual experience. My work is informed by nature and visually recalled and then made permanent on paper or canvas. Maintaining a feeling of being in harmony with the world allows for periods of quiet meditation and creativity.*

PUTTERMAN, LOUIS G., economics educator; b. N.Y.C., Apr. 27, 1952; s. Milton and Eileen L. (Goldstein) P.; (div.); 1 child, Laura Lee; m. Vivian Tseng, Apr. 5, 1981; children: Serena Rose, Mark Isaac. BA summa cum laude, Columbia U., 1976; MA in Internat. Relations, Yale U., 1978, PhD in Econs., 1980; MA (hon.), Brown U., 1983. From asst. prof. to prof. econs. Brown U., R.I., 1980—; rsch. assoc., Ctr. for East Asian Rsch. Harvard U., Cambridge, Mass., 1987-93. Author: Peasants, Collectives and Choice, 1986, Division of Labor and Welfare, 1990, Continuity and Change in China's Rural Development: Collective and Reform Eras in Perspective, 1993; co-author: Economics of Cooperation and the Labor-Managed Economy, 1987; editor: The Economic Nature of the Firm, 1986, 2d edit., 1996, State and Market in Development: Synergy or Rivalry, 1992; mem. editl. bd. Modern China, 1990—, Comparative Economic Studies, 1991-93, Annals of Public and Cooperative Economics, 1992—, Jour. Comparative Econs., 1989-91, 97—; assoc. editor Pacific Econ. Rev., 1996—. Recipient Sloan Rsch. fellow, Alfred P. Sloan Found., 1983, Fellow in Chinese Studies, Wang Inst., 1986, Am. Coun. Learned Socs., 1997. Mem. Am. Economic Assn., Assn. for Comparative Economic Studies, Phi Beta Kappa. Office: Brown U Dept Econs 64 Waterman St Providence RI 02912-9029

PUTTNAM, SIR DAVID TERENCE, film producer; b. London, Feb. 25, 1941; s. Leonard Arthur and Marie Beatrix P.; m. Patricia Mary Jones, 1961; two children. LLD (hon.) Bristol (Eng.) U., 1983; DLitt (hon.) Leicester U., 1986, Leeds U., 1992, U. Bradford, 1993. Knighted, 1995. With advt. firms, 1958-66; photographer's agt., 1966-68; film producer, 1968—. Chmn., Columbia Pictures, 1986-88. Producer films including That'll Be the Day, 1971, Mahler, 1973, Bugsy Malone, 1975, The Duellists (Spl. Jury prize Cannes 1977), 1977, Midnight Express, 1977 (2 Acad. awards), Chariots of Fire (4 Acad. awards and 3 BAFTA awards including Best Film award 1981, 4 Oscars including Best Picture), Local Hero, 1982, The Killing Fields, 1984 (3 Am. Acad. awards, 8 Brit. Acad. awards, BAFTA award for Best Picture), Cal, 1984, The Mission, 1986 (Palme d'Or 1986, Acad. award), Memphis Belle, 1990, Meeting Venus, 1991, Being Human, 1992, War of the Buttons, 1993, The Burning Season, 1994 (Golden Globe award best film for TV), Le Confessional, 1995. Chmn ITEL; founder, pres. Atelier du Cinema European; vis. prof. films Bristol U.; dir. Anglia TV. Survival Anglia; trustee Nat. Energy Found., Sci. Mus. (Benjamin Franklin award 1996) 1996; hon. fellow The Chartered Soc. Designers; hon. fellow Manchester Polytechnic; chmn. Nat. Mus. Photography, film and TV adv. com. Decorated Officier dans l'Ordre des Arts et des Lettres, 1986; comdr. of the Most Excellent Order of the Brit. Empire, 1982, Kt., 1995; recipient Michael Balcon award for Outstanding Contbn. Brit. Film Industry, BAFTA, 1982, Benjamin Franklin medal, 1996, Crystal award World Econ. Forum, 1997. Fellow Royal Soc. Arts, Royal Photographic Soc., Royal Geog. Soc. Address: 13/15 Queen's Gate Pl Mews, London SW7 5BG, England

PUTZEL, CONSTANCE KELLNER, lawyer; b. Balt., Sept. 5, 1922; d. William Stummer and Corinne (Strauss) Kellner; m. William L. Putzel, Aug. 28, 1945; 1 son, Arthur William. A.B., Goucher Coll., 1942; LL.B., U. Md., 1945, J.D., 1969. Bar: Md. 1945. Social worker Balt. Dept. Pub. Welfare, 1945-46; atty. New Amsterdam Casualty Co., Balt., 1947; staff atty. Legal Aid Bur., Balt., 1947-49; mem. Putzel & Putzel, P.A., Balt., 1950-89; sole practitioner Balt., 1989—; instr. U. Balt. Sch. Law, 1975-77, Goucher Coll., 1976-77; chmn. character com. Ct. Appeals for 3d Cir., 1976—. Author: Divorce Organization System, 1984, 3d edit., 1993, Representing the Older Client in Divorce, 1992. Mem. Md. Com. on Status of Women, 1972-76; mem. Com. to Implement ERA, 1973-76; Pres. U. Md. Law Alumni Assn., 1978; bd. dirs. Legal Aid Bur., 1951-52, 71-73, chmn. elder issues com. Fellow Am. Acad. Matrimonial Lawyers; mem. ABA (sr. lawyers divsn., mem. coun., editl. bd. Experience), Md. Bar Assn. (bd. govs. 1972-73, chmn. family law sect. 1978-79). Home: 8207 Spring Bottom Way Baltimore MD 21208-1859 Office: 29 W Susquehanna Ave Baltimore MD 21204-5201

PUTZEL, MICHAEL, journalist, consultant; b. Washington, Sept. 16, 1942; s. Max and Nell (Converse) P.; m. Ann Blackman, Feb. 23, 1974; children: Leila Elizabeth, Christof Blackman. BA, UNC in Polit. Sci., 1967. Reporter Charleston (W.Va.) Gazette, 1963-66; newsman AP, Raleigh, N.C., 1967-68, N.Y.C., 1968-69; war corr. AP, Vietnam, 1969-72; reporter AP, Washington, 1972-79; asst. metro editor Washington Post, Washington, 1979; White House corr. AP, Washington, 1979-84; chief White House corr. AP, 1984-87; chief of bur. AP, Moscow, 1987-90; diplomatic corr. AP, Washington, 1990-91; Washington bureau chief Boston Globe, 1991-92; White House corr. Boston Globe, Washington, 1993-94; columnist "Plugged In", 1994-95; founder, CEO Trysail, Inc., Washington, 1996—. With USAR, 1964-65. Recipient AP Mgn. Editors citation, 1975, 81, Merriman Smith Meml. award White House Corr. Assn., 1986. Home: 4938 Quebec St NW Washington DC 20016-3231 Office: Trysail Inc 1155 Connecticut Ave NW Ste 300 Washington DC 20036-4327

PUTZELL, EDWIN JOSEPH, JR., lawyer, mayor; b. Birmingham, Ala., Sept. 29, 1913; s. Edwin Joseph and Celeste (Joseph) P.; children: Cynthia Putzell Reidy, Edwin Joseph III; m. Dorothy Corcoran Waters, Aug. 5, 1967. AB, Tulane U., 1935; LLB, Harvard U., 1938. Bar: N.Y. 1939, Mo. 1947, U.S. Supreme Ct. 1945. Atty. Donovan, Leisure, Newton & Lumbard, N.Y.C. and Washington, 1937-42; asst. dir., exec. officer Office of Strategic Svcs., 1942-45; asst. treas. Monsanto Co., St. Louis, 1945-46, asst. sec., atty., 1946-51, sec., 1951-77, dir. law dept., 1953-68, v.p., gen. counsel, 1963-77; ptnr. Coburn, Croft, Shepherd, Herzog & Putzell, St. Louis, 1977-79; of counsel Coburn, Croft & Putzell St. Louis, 1979-96; mayor City of Naples, Fla., 1986-90; of counsel Thompson & Coburn, St. Louis, 1996—. Dir. St. Louis Symphony Soc., 1955-69; pres. The Conservancy, Inc., 1981-85, chmn. bd. dirs., 1984-85; vice chmn. St. Louis County Bd. Police Commrs., 1964-72, Big Cypress Basin Bd., South Fla. Water Mgmt. Dist., 1985-86; pres. Social Planning Coun., St. Louis, 1954-57; chmn. Naples Airport Authority, 1979-83, 94—; vice chmn. Westminster Coll., 1976-79; chmn. Sta. KETC-TV, St. Louis, 1977-79; trustee St. Luke's Hosp., 1973-79; bd. dirs. Hospice of Naples, Cmty. Found. Collier County, The Moorings, Inc., Collier/Naplescape, Inc. Mem. ABA, Mo. Bar Assn., St. Louis Bar Assn., Am. Soc. Corp. Secs. (pres. 1968-69), Assn. Gen. Counsel, Bogey Club, Noonday Club, Port Royal Club, Hole in the Wall Golf Club, Naples Area C. of C., Naples Yacht Club, Phi Beta Kappa, Delta Sigma Phi. Episcopalian. Home: 1285 Gulf Shore Blvd N Naples FL 34102-4911

PUYAU, FRANCIS ALBERT, physician, radiology educator; b. New Orleans, Dec. 1, 1928; s. Frank Albert and Rose Sue (Jones) P.; m. Geraldine Sally diBenedetto, June 6, 1951; children: Michael, Stephen, Jeanne Marie, Julie, Melissa. B.S., Notre Dame U., 1948; M.D., La. State U., 1952. Diplomate Am. Bd. Pediatrics, Am. Bd. Pediatric Cardiology, Am. Bd. Radiology. Intern Charity Hosp., New Orleans, 1952-53; resident in pediatrics Charity Hosp., 1955-57; instr. pediatrics La. State U. Sch. Medicine, New Orleans, 1957-59; asst. prof. La. State U. Sch. Medicine, 1959-61, clin. asso. prof., 1968-71, prof. radiology and pediatrics, 1971-74, acting head dept. radiology, 1971-72, head dept., 1972-74; asst. prof. pediatrics Vanderbilt U., 1961-68; fellow dept. diagnostic radiology Charity Hosp., New Orleans, 1968-70; prof. radiology and pediat. Tulane U. Sch. Medicine, New Orleans, 1974—, prof. medicine, 1974-95; acting chmn. dept. pediatrics Tulane U. Sch. Medicine, 1976-78; cons. St. Tammany Hosps., Covington, La., 1968-81; dir. cardiac catherization lab. dept. cardiology Charity Hosp., New Orleans, 1970-85; staff radiologist Our Lady of the Lake Regional Med. Ctr., Baton Rouge, 1986-93; mem. staff Hotel Dieu, New Orleans, 1973-80; head x-ray dept. Children's Hosp. of New Orleans, 1976-82. Contbr. articles to med. jours. Served with USPHS, 1953-55. Fellow Am. Coll. Cardiology, Am. Coll. Radiology; mem. East Baton Rouge Med. Soc., So. Soc. Pediatric Research, Am. Coll. Radiology, La. Radiology Soc., New Orleans Radiology Soc. (pres. 1985), New Orleans Pediatric Soc., Soc. Chmn. Acad. Radiology Depts., Radiol. Soc. N.Am., Am. Roentgen Ray Soc., Assn. Univ. Radiologists, Southern Yacht Club (New Orleans), Alpha Omega Alpha. Roman Catholic. Home: 458 Shady Lake Pky Baton Rouge LA 70810-4322 Office: Tulane U Med Ctr Dept Radiology 1415 Tulane Ave New Orleans LA 70112-2605

PUZDER, ANDREW F., lawyer; b. Cleve., July 11, 1950; s. Andrew F. and Winifried M. Puzder; m. Deanna L. Descher, Sept. 26, 1987. BA, Cleve. State U., 1975; JD, Washington U., 1978. Gen. counsel, exec. v.p. Fidelity Nat. Fin., Inc., CKE Restaurants, Inc. Editor Washington U. Law Quarterly, 1977-78. Author of law upheld by U.S. Supreme Ct. in Webster v. Reproductive Health Svcs., 1989; founding dir. Common Ground Network for Life and Choice, 1993. Mem. State Bar Nev., The Mo. Bar, State Bar Calif., Phi Alpha Theta. Address: 17911 Von Karman Ave #300 Irvine CA 92714-6253

PUZO, MARIO, author; b. N.Y.C., Oct. 15, 1920; s. Antonio and Maria (Le Conti) P.; m. Erika Lina Broske, 1946; children: Anthony, Joey, Dorothy, Virginia, Eugene. Student, New Sch. for Social Research, Columbia U. Lit. reviewer various mags.; former civil service employee; former editor Male Mag. Author: The Dark Arena, 1955, The Fortunate Pilgrim, 1964, The Runaway Summer of Davie Shaw, 1966, The Godfather,

1969, The Godfather Papers and Other Confessions, 1972, Inside Las Vegas, 1977, Fools Die, 1978, The Sicilian, 1984, The Fourth K, 1991, The Last Don, 1996; screenwriter: (with Francis Ford Coppola) The Godfather, 1972 (Academy award best adapted screenplay 1972, Screen award Writers Guild Am. West 1972, Golden Globe award best screenplay 1973), (with Coppola) The Godfather, Part II, 1974 (Academy award best adapted screeplay 1974, Screen award Writers Guild Am. West 1974), (with George Fox) Earthquake, 1974, (with Robert Benton, David Newman, and Leslie Newman) Superman, 1978, (with D. Newman and L. Newman) Superman II, 1981, (with Coppola and William Kennedy) The Cotton Club, 1984, (with Coppola) The Godfather, Part III, 1990 (Golden Globe award best screenplay 1990), (with John Briley and Cary Bates) Christopher Columbus: The Discovery, 1992. Office: Greenberg Glusker Fields Claman & Machtinger 1900 Avenue Of The Stars Los Angeles CA 90067-4301*

PYATT, EVERETT ARNO, government official; b. Kansas City, Mo., July 22, 1939; s. Arno Doyne and Myrl Elizabeth (Osborn) P.; m. Susan Evelyn Kristal, Sept. 28, 1968; children: Jennifer, Laura, Jeffrey. B.E., B.S., Yale U., 1962; M.B.A., U. Pa., 1977. Staff engr. office dir. def. research and devel. Office Sec. Def., Dept. Def., Washington, 1962-72; dir. acquisition planning Office Asst. Sec. Def. for Program Analysis and Evaluation, 1972-75; dir. logistics resources Office Asst. Sec. Def. for Installations and Logistics, 1975-77; prin. dep. asst. sec. for logistics Dept. Navy, Washington, 1977-79, prin. dep. asst. sec. for shipbldg. and logistics, 1981-84; asst. sec. for shipbldg. and logistics Dept. Navy, 1984-89; exec. advisor Coopers & Lybrand, 1989—; pres. EV Ventures; dep. chief fin. officer Dept. Energy, 1979-81; dir. Dept. Energy (Office of Alcohol Fuels), 1980. Recipient Disting. Civilian Svc. medal USN, 1980-81, 87, Superior Civilian Svc. medal, 1981, Outstanding Svc. medal Dept. Energy, 1981, Pres.'s award of meritorious excellence, 1983, Disting. Civilian Pub. Svc. award Dept. Def., 1989; Office of Sec. Def. fellow, 1975-77. Mem. IEEE. Club: Yale. Home: 4560 25th Rd N Arlington VA 22207-4147 Office: Coopers & Lybrand 1530 Wilson Blvd Arlington VA 22209-2447

PYATT, KEDAR DAVIS, JR., research and development company executive; b. Wadesboro, N.C., May 20, 1933; s. Kedar D. and Frances (Hales) P.; m. Mary Mackenzie, June 2, 1956; children: Geoffrey, Kira, David, Rebecca. BS in Physics, Duke U., 1955; PhD in Physics, Yale U., 1960. With Gen. Atomic, San Diego, 1959-67; sr. v.p. Fed. divsn. Maxwell Techs., San Diego, 1967—. Recipient Exceptional Pub. Svc. medal Dept. Def., 1985, Lifetime Achievement medal DSWA, 1997. Office: Fed Divsn Maxwell Techs 8888 Balboa Ave San Diego CA 92123-1506

PYATT, LEO ANTHONY, real estate broker; b. Key Port, N.J., Oct. 20, 1925; s. Ralph James and Anna Regina (Kussmaul) P.; m. Geraldine Genevive Gibb, May 31, 1947; children: Steven Lee, Rebecca Lynn. Student, Franklin U., 1947-49. Salesperson Standard Oil Co., Columbus, Ohio, 1947-49, Borden Dairy Co., Columbus, 1950-57, Frito-Lay, Inc., Columbus, 1958-74; sec., treas. Snack Time, Inc., Columbus, 1974-75; agt. N. NE Realty Co., Columbus, 1976-86; owner-broker Pyatt's Rose Realty Co., Columbus, 1986—. Presiding judge County Rep. Party, Franklin County, 1991; mem. Citizens for an Alternative Tax System. With USN, 1943-46, PTO. Decorated Air medal, Philippine Liberation award. Republican. Roman Catholic. Avocations: writing, travel, hiking, reading. Home: 4400 Wanda Lane Rd Columbus OH 43224-1026 Office: Pyatts Rose Realty Co 4400 Wanda Lane Rd Columbus OH 43224-1026

PYDYNKOWSKY, JOAN ANNE, journalist; b. Ft. Riley, Kans., Oct. 2, 1951; d. Fredrick Albert and Mary Elizabeth (O'Connor) Gadwell; m. Michael Stanley Pydyknowsky, Mar. 14, 1981; children: Deborah Findley, Alexandra Pydynkowsky, Royce. BA in Journalism, U. Ctrl. Okla., 1991, MEd in Journalism, 1993. Trust clk. Ill. Nat. Bank, Rockford, 1974-75; engring. aide Barber Colman, Rockford, 1976-77; draftsperson Gen. Web, Rockford, 1979-80, Keeson, Ltd., Rockford, 1981; editor Oklahoma City Marriage Encounter, 1988-89, 94-95; humor columnist UCO Vista, Edmond, Okla., 1990-91; city editor Guthrie (Okla.) Daily Leader, 1991-92; substitute tchr. Edmond (Okla.) Pub. Schs., 1993-94; with N.W. News, Piedmont, Okla., 1994-95, South Oklahoma City Leader, 1995-96; staff writer, columnist, reporter, photographer N.W. News, Piedmont-Surrey Gazette, Okarche Chieftain, Piedmont, 1996-97; city editor Okarche Chieftain, Piedmont, 1996-97; staff writer, columnist, photographer El Reno (Okla.) Tribune, 1997—; copywriter, cons., Edmond, 1991—, photographer, 1990—, cartoonist, 1984—, humorist, 1990—; columnist, contbg. writer N.W. News, Piedmont, Okla., 1994-95; reporter and assoc. editor: All About Kids/South Oklahoma City Leader, 1995-96. Asst. leader Boy Scouts Am., Edmond, 1993-95; league coach Young Am. Bowling Alliance, Edmond, 1993-97; counselor Oklahoma City YWCA Rape Crisis, 1986-88; mem. Tiaras Jr. Women's Honor Soc., 1990-91; mem. selection com. Okla. Journalism Hall of Fame, 1990. Recipient awards State Fair of Okla., 1983-96, Feature Writing award Okla. chpt. Soc. Profl. Journalists, 1992-93, six awards, 1995-96; first place Feature Writing award, State Fair of Okla. Better Newspaper Contest, 1995. Mem. Soc. Profl. Journalists (pres. U. Ctrl. Okla. chpt. 1990, treas. 1989, 91), Kappa Tau Alpha. Roman Catholic. Avocations: writing, photography, horsemanship, arts, martial arts. Home: 301 Reynolds Rd Edmond OK 73013-5121

PYE, GORDON BRUCE, economist; b. Oak Park, Ill., Oct. 30, 1933; s. Harold Charles and Florence Martha P. B.S. in Chem. Engring, M.I.T., 1955, Ph.D. in Econs, 1963. Asst. prof. bus. adminstrn. U. Calif., Berkeley, 1963-66; assoc. prof. U. Calif., 1966-69, prof., 1969-72; econ. cons. Standard Oil Co. Calif. (name changed to Chevron Corp.), San Francisco, 1972-74; v.p., sr. economist Irving Trust Co., N.Y.C., 1974-78, sr. v.p., mgr. econ. research and planning div., 1978-89; prin. Gordon B. Pye Assocs., N.Y.C., 1990—. Assoc. editor: Fin. Analysts Jour, 1972-89. Mem. Forecasters Club N.Y. (pres. 1980-81). Home: 230 E 50th St New York NY 10022-7702

PYE, LENWOOD DAVID, materials science educator, researcher, consultant; b. Little Falls, N.Y., May 16, 1937; s. Lenwood George and Elizabeth Marie Pye; m. Constance Lee Lanphere, Sept. 6, 1958; children: DeAnn, Lorie, Lisa, Brien. BS, Alfred U., 1959, PhD, 1968. Rsch. engr. PPG Industries, Pitts., 1959-60; rsch. scientist Bausch & Lomb, Rochester, N.Y., 1960-61, 62-64; prof. glass sci. N.Y. State Coll. Ceramics Alfred U., 1968—, dean N.Y. State Coll. Ceramics, 1996—, dir. Inst. Glass Sci. and Engring., 1984-96, dir. Industry-Univ. Ctr. Glass Rsch., 1986-96; pres. Internat. Commn. on Glass, 1997—; bd. dirs. Alfred Tech. Resources, Inc., Schott Glass Technologies; dir. Paul Vicker Gardner Glass Ctr. 1st lt. U.S. Army, 1960-62. Recipient Dominick Labino lectr. award 1995, Phoenix award as Glassman of Yr., 1996. Mem. Acad. Ceramics, Am. Ceramics Soc., Optical Soc. Am., U.K. Soc. Glass Tech., Can. Ceramic Soc., German Soc. Glass Technology (hon.), Acad. Ceramics. Office: Alfred U Office of Dean NY State Coll Ceramics 2 Pine St Alfred NY 14802-1214

PYE, LUCIAN WILMOT, political science educator; b. Shansi, China, Oct. 21, 1921; s. Watts Orson and Gertrude (Chaney) P.; m. Mary Toombs Waddill, Dec. 24, 1944; children: Evelyn, L. Christopher, Virginia. B.A., Carleton Coll., 1943; M.A., Yale U., 1949, Ph.D., 1951. Instr., then asst. prof. polit. sci. Washington U., St. Louis, 1949-52; research assoc. Yale U., 1951-52, Princeton, 1952-56; vis. lectr. Columbia U., 1956; mem. faculty Mass. Inst. Tech., 1956-92, prof. polit. sci., 1960-92, Ford prof., 1972-92, chmn. sect., 1961-63; sr. staff mem. Mass. Inst. Tech. (Center Internat. Studies), 1956—; vis. assoc. prof. Yale U., 1959-61; vis. prof. George Washington U., 1993, Balliol Coll., Oxford U., 1994, Fletcher Sch., Tufts U., 1994; chmn. com. comparative politics Social Sci. Rsch. Coun., 1963-73; mem. adv. com. adminstr. AID, 1961-68; cons. Dept. State, 1962-68, NSC, 1968—; trustee Asia Found., 1963—; gov. East-West Ctr., Honolulu, 1976-80; bd. dirs., v.p. Nat. Com. U.S.-China Rels. Author: Guerrilla Communism in Malaya, 1956, Politics, Personality and Nation Building, 1961, Aspects of Political Developments, 1966, Southeast Asia's Political Systems, 1967, The Spirit of Chinese Politics, 1968, Warlord Politics, 1971, China: An Introduction, 1972, Mao Tse-tung: The Man in The Leader, 1976, Dynamics of Chinese Politics, 1982, Asian Power and Politics, 1985; co-author: The Politics of the Developing Areas, 1960, The Emerging Nations, 1961; Editor: Communications and Political Development, 1963, Political Culture and Political Development, 1965, Political Science and Area Studies, 1975. Served as 1st lt. USMCR, 1945-46. Fellow Center Advanced Study Behavioral Scis., 1963. Fellow Am. Acad. Arts and Scis., Am. Philos. Soc.; mem. Assn. Asian Studies (dir.), Am. Polit. Sci. Assn. (dir., pres. 1989), Council Fgn. Relations (dir.), Asia Soc. (dir.), Pilgrim Soc., Phi Beta Kappa. Unitarian. Club: Cosmos. Home: 72 Fletcher Rd Belmont MA 02178-2017 Office: Mass Inst Tech Dept Polit Sci Cambridge MA 02139

PYERITZ, REED EDWIN, medical geneticist, educator, research director; b. Pitts., Nov. 2, 1947; s. Paul L. and Ida Mae (Meier) P.; m. Jane Ellen Tumpson, May 28, 1972; 2 children. SB in Chemistry, U. Del., 1968; AM, Harvard U., 1971, PhD in Biochemistry, 1972, MD, 1975. Diplomate Am. Bd. Internal Medicine, Am. Bd. Med. Genetics. Intern Peter Bent Brigham Hosp., Boston, 1975-76, resident, 1976-77; resident Johns Hopkins Hosp., Balt., 1977-78; from instr. to prof. medicine and pediatrics Sch. Medicine, Johns Hopkins U. Balt., 1978-93, chair dept. human genetics, prof. human genetics, medicine and pediatrics, 1994—, MCP Hahnemann Sch. Med.; dir. Inst. Med. Genetics Allegheny U. Health Sci., 1993—; dir. Ctr. for Med. Genetics, Allegheny Gen. Hosp., 1995—; chief physician Md. Athletic Commn., Balt., 1978-93; med. adv. bd. Nat. Marfan Found., N.Y.C., 1982—, chmn. 1982-93; med. dir. Alliance of Genetic Support Groups, 1994—; mem. rsch. adv. bd. Nat. Orgn. Rare Disorders, 1989—; mem. rsch. adv. com. Am. Heart Assn., 1996—. Co-editor Principles and Practice of Medical Genetics; mem. editorial bd. New Eng. Jour. Medicine (1993-97); contbr. numerous articles to profl. publs. NIH Grantee. Fellow ACP, Am. Coll. Med. Genetics (dir. 1992-94, pres.-elect 1995-96, pres. 1997-98); mem. Am. Soc. Human Genetics (chair program com. 1994-95), Am. Heart Assn., AAAS, Hastings Ctr. Office: Allegheny Univ Health Sci 320 E North Ave Pittsburgh PA 15212-4756

PYFER, JOHN FREDERICK, JR., lawyer; b. Lancaster, Pa., July 25, 1946; s. John Frederick and Myrtle Ann (Greiner) P.; m. Carol Trice, Nov. 25, 1970; children: John Frederick III, Carol Lee. Grad. cum laude, Peddie Sch., 1965; BA in Polit. Sci. and Econs., Haverford Coll., 1969; JD, Vanderbilt U., 1972. Bar: Pa. 1972, U.S. Dist. Ct. (ea. dist.) Pa. 1973, U.S. Tax Ct. 1975, U.S. Supreme Ct. 1975, U.S. Dist. Ct. (mid. dist.) Pa. 1984, U.S. Ct. Appeals (3d cir.) 1986. Law clk. to presiding justice Ct. Common Pleas, Lancaster, Pa., 1972-74; assoc. Xakellis, Perezous & Mongiovi, 1972-76; founding ptnr. Allison & Pyfer, Lancaster, 1976-85, pres. Pyfer & Assocs., 1986-88, Pyfer & Reese, 1988—; prof. para-legal tng. Pa. State Extension Service, 1989-93; fed. ct. mediator, 1992—. Pres. Lancaster-Lebanon Coun. Boy Scouts Am. 1989-93, coun. commr. 1987-89, mem. nat. com., 1996—, Eagle Scout with 3 palms, God and Country award, God and Svc. award, Wood Badge, Scouter's Key, Vigil Honor, Order of Arrow, Disting. Commnr. award, Silver Beaver award, West fellow 1910 Soc., Nat. Jamboree, 1960, 64, 85, 89, 93, 97, World Jamboree, 1967, 87, 95, Japan Jamboree, 1990, Can. Jamboree, 1993; bd. dirs. World of Scouting Mus. Fellow Am. Bd. Criminal Lawyers, Lancaster Heritage Ctr.; mem. ABA (First prize Howard C. Schwab Nat. Essay Contest in Writing, 1972), ATLA, Nat. Assn. Criminal Def. Lawyers, Pa. Trial Lawyers Assn., Pa. Criminal Def. Lawyers Assn., Am. Arbitration Assn., Pa. Bar Assn., Lancaster Bar Assn., Inns Ct. (founder, pres. W. Hensel Brown, 1993-94), Christian Lawyers Soc., SAR. Republican. United Ch. of Christ (elder, pres. 1989, 95). Clubs: Lions (pres. 1980-82) (Willow Street, Pa.); Masons (Lancaster). Contbr. articles to law revs., law treatises. Home: 1100 Little Brook Rd Lancaster PA 17603-6116 Office: Pyfer & Reese 128 N Lime St Lancaster PA 17602-2951

PYKE, JOHN SECREST, JR., lawyer, polymers company executive; b. Lakewood, Ohio, July 11, 1938; s. John S. and Elma B. Pyke; student Haverford Coll., 1956-58; BA, Columbia Coll., 1960, postgrad. Columbia Sch. Grad. Faculties, 1960-61; JD, Columbia Law Sch., 1964; m. Judith A., Dec. 26, 1970; 1 child, John Secrest, III. Bar: N.Y. 1965. Assoc. firm Townsend & Lewis (now Thacher, Proffit & Wood), N.Y.C., 1964-68; atty. M.A. Hanna Co., Cleve., 1968—, sec., 1973—, v.p., gen. counsel, 1979—. Trustee, Western Res. Acad., Hudson, Ohio, 1976—. Mem. ABA, Assn. Bar City N.Y., Am. Soc. Corp. Secs., Am. Corp. Counsel Assn., Union Club, Clifton Club, Cleve. Yachting Club. Author: Landmark Preservation, 1969, 2d edit., 1972. Office: MA Hanna Co 200 Public Sq Ste 36-5000 Cleveland OH 44114-2301

PYKE, RONALD, mathematics educator; b. Hamilton, Ont., Can., Nov. 24, 1931; s. Harold and Grace Carter (Digby) P.; m. Gladys Mary Davey, Dec. 19, 1953; children: Darlene, Brian, Ronald, Gordon. BA (hon.), McMaster U., 1953; MS, U. Wash., 1955, PhD, 1956. Asst. prof. Stanford U., Calif., 1956-58; asst. prof. Columbia U., N.Y.C., 1958-60; prof. math. U. Wash., Seattle, 1960—; vis. prof. U. Cambridge, Eng., 1964-65, Imperial Coll., London, 1970-71, Colo. State U., Ft. Collins, 1979, Technion, Israel, 1988, 90, 92; pres. Inst. Math. Stats., 1986-87; mem. bd. math. scis. NRC/NAS, 1984-88, chmn. com. applications and theoretical stats., 1985-88. Editor Ann. Prob., 1972-75; contbr. articles to profl. jours. NSF grantee, 1961-91. Fellow Internat. Statis. Inst. (v.p. 1989-91), Am. Statis. Assn., Inst. Math. Stats. (pres. 1986-87); mem. Bernoulli Soc., Statis. Soc. of Can. Office: U Washington Dept Math Box 354350 Seattle WA 98195-4350

PYKE, THOMAS NICHOLAS, JR., government science and engineering administrator; b. Washington, July 16, 1942; s. Thomas Nicholas and Pauline Marie (Pingitore) P.; m. Carol June Renville, June 22, 1968; children—Christopher Renville, Alexander Nicholas. BS, Carnegie Inst. Tech., 1964; MS in Engring., U. Pa., 1965. Electronic engr. Nat. Bur. Standards, Gaithersburg, Md., 1964-69, chief computer networking sect., 1969-75, chief computer systems engring. div., 1975-79, dir. ctr. for computer systems engring., 1979-81, dir. ctr. programming sci. and tech., 1981-86; asst. adminstr. for satellite and info. services NOAA, Washington, 1986-92, dir. high performance computing and comm., 1992—; dir. The Globe Program The White House, Washington, 1994—; organizer profl. computer confs., 1970-86; mem. Presdl. Adv. Com. on Networking Structure and Function, 1980, Interagy. com. on Info. Resources Mgmt., 1983-84, bd. dirs., 1984-87, vice chmn. 1986-87 (Exec. Excellence award 1991), chmn. Interagy. Working Group on Data Mgmt. for Global Change, 1987-93; speaker in field. Editorial bd. Computer Networks Jour., 1976-86; contbr. articles to profl. jours. Bd. dirs. Glebe Commons Assn., Arlington, Va., 1976-79, v.p., 1977-79; chmn. Student Congress, Carnegie Inst. Tech., 1963-64; mem. Task Force on Computers in Schs., Arlington, 1982-85; pres. PTA, Arlington, 1983-84. Recipient silver medal Dept. Commerce, 1973, gold medal, 1995; award for exemplary achievement in pub. adminstrn. William A. Jump Found., 1975, 76, Presdl. Rank award of Meritorious Exec., 1988; Westinghouse scholar Carnegie Inst. Tech., 1960-64; Ford Found. fellow U. Pa., 1964-66. Fellow Washington Acad. Scis. (Engring. Sci. award 1974); mem. Am. Fedn. Info. Processing Socs. (bd. dirs. 1974-76), IEEE (sr. mem.), Computer Soc. of IEEE (bd. govs. 1971-73, 75-77, vice chmn. tech. com. on personal computing 1982-86, chmn. 1986-87), AAAS, Assn. Computing Machinery, Sigma Xi, Eta Kappa Nu, Omicron Delta Kappa, Pi Kappa Alpha (chpt. v.p. 1963-64). Episcopalian. Office: The Globe Program 744 Jackson Pl NW Washington DC 20503-0003

PYLE, DONALD ALAN, music educator, tenor; b. Ridgewood, N.J., Jan. 12, 1933; s. Aime A. and Muriel Ann (Barbour) P.; m. Barbara Jean Sly, July 6, 1961 (dec.); m. 2d, Virginia R. Tinker, June 4, 1968. Student Juilliard Sch. Music, 1956-59; B.A. in Vocal Performance, U. So. Fla., 1969; Mus. M., Mus. D., Fla. State U., 1972. Mem. company South Shore Music Circus, Cohassett, Mass., 1958-59; tenor soloist John Harms Chorus, St. Michael's Episcopal Ch., Juilliard Opera Theatre, N.Y.C., Temple Bethel, Englewood, N.J., St. Leo Coll., Dade City, Fla., 1956-61; teaching asst. Fla. State U., Tallahassee, 1969-71, adj. faculty, 1971-72; instr. U. Mo.-Columbia, 1972-76, acting dean, Swinney Conservatory Music, Central Meth. Coll., Fayette, Mo., 1976-77, dean, prof. voice, 1977-90; asst. dean. Sch. Fine Arts, U. Conn., 1990-93, assoc. dean, 1994—; tenor soloist numerous U.S. colls. and univs.; tenor soloist world premiers Songs from the Ark, The Labyrinth, Of Mice and Men; performances include: Strauss's Ariadne Auf Naxos, Bacchus, Verdi Requiem, Otello, Rigoletto, Duke, Bizet's Carmen, Don Jose, Handel's Acis & Galatea, Massanet's Le Cid, Flotow's Martha, Lionel, Purcell's Dido & Aeneas, Puccini's Turandot, Calaf, Rossini's Stabat Mater, Bach's St. Matthew's Passion, Mendelsohn's The Elijah and Les Troyens (under Sir Thomas Beecham); recordings for Koch Recordings Internat., RCA. Served to sgt. USMC, 1951-54. U. So. Fla. scholar, 1966. Mem. Nat. Assn. Tchrs. Singing, Nat. Assn. Schs. Music, Blue Key, Gold Key, Phi Delta Kappa, Omicron Delta Kappa, Phi Mu Alpha, Pi Kappa Lambda, Phi Kappa Phi. Roman Catholic.

PYLE, GERALD FREDRIC, medical geographer, educator; b. Akron, Ohio, Dec. 22, 1937; s. Russell Roy and Ruth (Martin) P.; m. Carole Wood, Aug. 29, 1959; children: Eric, Frances. BA, Kent State U., 1963; MA, U. Chgo., 1968, PhD, 1970. Cartographer, Rand McNally, Chgo., 1962-64; research geographer Ency. Britannica, Chgo., 1964-65; cartographer U. Chgo., 1965-70; asst. to full prof. U. Akron, Ohio, 1970-80; prof. geography and earth sci. U. N.C., Charlotte, 1980—; prof. health promotion, 1995—; vis. fellow Macquarie U., Sydney, Australia, 1988; research dir. Center for Urban Studies, Akron, 1973-80; tech. dir. Akron Area Census File, 1974-80; vis. scholar U. S.C., 1977. Author: Heart Disease, Cancer and Stroke in Chicago, 1971, Spatial Dynamics of Crime, 1974, Applied Medical Geography, 1979, Diffusion of Influenza: Patterns and Paradigms, 1986, (with Shannon and Bashshur) The Geography of AIDS, 1990, (with Shannon) Medical Atlas of the Twentieth Century, 1993; sr. editor Med. Geography, Social Sci. and Medicine, 1977-84; book rev. editor Social Sci. and Medicine, 1990—. Recipient Scholars medal First Citizen's Bank, 1992. Grantee Ill. Regional Med., 1969, Law Enforcement Adminstrn. Agy., 1972, 74, NSF, 1979, 82, Nat. Geog. Soc., 1988, NRC, 1995. Fellow Ohio Acad. Sci.; mem. Assn. Am. Geographers (Rsch. Honors S.E. divsn. 1994), Nat. Council Geog. Edn., Phi Kappa Phi. Democrat. Anglican. Current work: Continued research in spatial diffusion of infectious diseases and the location of health care delivery facilities. Subspecialty: Regional epidemiology. Home: 9801 Belt Rd Midland NC 28107-9057 Office: U NC Coll Nursing & Health Profs 9201 University City Blvd Charlotte NC 28223-0001

PYLE, JERRY, automotive executive. Pres. Gulf States Toyota, Houston, 1981—, now CEO. Office: Gulf States Toyota PO Box 40306 7701 Wilshire Pl Houston TX 77240-0306*

PYLE, KENNETH BIRGER, historian, educator; b. Bellefonte, Pa., Apr. 20, 1936; s. Hugh Gillespie and Beatrice Ingeborg (Petterson) P.; m. Anne Hamilton Henszey, Dec. 22, 1960; children: William Henszey, Anne Hamilton. AB magna cum laude, Harvard U., 1958; PhD, Johns Hopkins U., 1965. Asst. prof. U. Wash., 1965-69, assoc. prof., 1969-75, prof. history and Asian studies, 1975—, dir. Henry M. Jackson Sch. Internat. Studies, 1978-88; pres. Nat. Bur. Asian Rsch., 1988—; vice chmn. Japan-U.S. Friendship Commn., 1989-92, chmn., 1992-95; co-chmn. Joint Com. on U.S.-Japan Cultural and Ednl. Coop., 1992-95; vis. lectr. history Stanford U., 1964-65; vis. assoc. prof. history Yale U., 1969-70. Author: The New Generation in Meiji, Japan, 1969, The Making of Modern Japan, 1978, rev. edit., 1996; editor: The Trade Crisis: How Will Japan Respond?, 1987, The Japanese Question: Power and Purpose in a New Era, 1992, rev. edit., 1996; founding editor Jour. Japanese Studies, 1974-86, chmn. editl. bd., 1987-89, assoc. editor, 1989—. Bd. dirs. Maure and Mike Mansfield Found., 1979-88; bd. govs. Henry M. Jackson Found., 1983—; adv. bd. Japan Found., 1989—, Japan-Am. Student Conf., 1991—. Ford Found. fellow, 1961-64; Fulbright-Hays fellow, 1970-71; Social Sci. Research Council-Am. Council Learned Socs. fellow, 1970-73, 77, 83-84. Mem. Assn. Asian Studies, Am. Hist. Assn., Coun. Fgn. Rels. Presbyterian. Home: 8416 Midland Rd Medina WA 98039-5336 Office: Henry M Jackson Sch Internat Studies U Wash Seattle WA 98195

PYLE, LUTHER ARNOLD, lawyer; b. Pontotoc County, Miss., Dec. 5, 1912; s. Thomas Luther and Lillie Dean (Reynolds) P.; m. Elizabeth McWillie Browne, Aug. 9, 1941; children—William A., Robert Bradford, Ben Cameron. LL.B., Cumberland U., 1936, J.D., 1960. Bar: Miss. 1936, D.C. 1974, U.S. Dist. Ct. (no. dist.) Miss. 1936, U.S. Dist. Ct. (so. dist.) Miss. 1946, U.S. Ct. Apls. (5th cir.) 1946, U.S. Ct. Appeals (11th cir.) 1981, U.S. Supreme Ct. 1959. Sole practice, New Albany, Miss., 1936-42; pros. atty. Union County, Miss., 1940-42; assoc. Cameron & Wills, Jackson, Miss., 1946-52; chancellor 5th chancery ct. dist. Miss., 1952-58; ptnr. Watkins, Pyle, Ludlam, Winter & Stennis, Jackson, 1958-80; ptnr. Barnett, Alagia & Pyle, Jackson, 1981-83; of counsel Pyle, Dreher, Mills & Dye, 1993—; participant World Law Conf., Manila, 1977, Madrid, 1979; bd. dirs. Miss. Bar Commn., 1959-63. Mem. exec. bd. Andrew Jackson council Boy Scouts Am., 1946; bd. govs. Jackson Little Theatre, 1964-67; pres. Jackson Jr. C. of C., 1949; chmn. downtown div. United Givers, Mental Health Assn. Served to lt. col. JAG Corps, U.S. Army, 1942-46. Recipient Silver Beaver award Boy Scouts Am. Fellow Miss. Bar Found.; mem. Fed. Bar Assn., ABA (chmn. continuing legal edn. 1958-74), Am. Judicature Soc. (dir.), Hinds County Bar Assn., Miss. Bar Assn. (chmn. jud. adminstrn. com. 1966-70), U.S. Supreme Ct. Hist. Soc., U.S. C. of C., Jackson C. of C. (dir. 1960-63), Miss. Dept. Res. Officers Assn. (pres. 1950), Am. Legion (past comdr.). Episcopalian. Clubs: University (dir. 1972-92), Jackson Country, Annandale Golf. Contbr. articles to profl. jours. Home: 1803 E Northside Dr Jackson MS 39211-6029

PYLE, ROBERT MILNER, JR., financial services company executive; b. Orange, N.J., Oct. 24, 1938; s. Robert M. and Dorothy (Collings) P.; m. C. Page Neville, May 31, 1969; children: Cynthia Neville, Laura Collings. BA, Williams Coll., 1960; JD, U. Va., 1963. Bar: N.Y. 1964. Assoc. Mudge Rose Guthrie & Alexander, N.Y.C., 1963-68; with Studebaker-Worthington, Inc., N.Y.C., 1968-77; sec. Studebaker-Worthington, Inc., 1972-76, assoc. gen. counsel, 1974-77; with Singer Co., N.Y.C., 1977-79; corp. counsel, asst. to sec. Singer Co., 1977-78, sr. corp. counsel, asst to sec., 1979; v.p., counsel Am. Soc. Corp. Secs., Inc., N.Y.C., 1979-89, v.p., sec., counsel, 1989-91; v.p., sr. asst. sec. Am. Express Co., N.Y.C., 1991-96, cons., 1997—; Career counseling rep. for Williams Coll., 1977—. Trustee Pingry Sch., Martinsville, N.J., 1972-74; trustee Arts Coun. Suburban Essex Inc., 1979-84, chmn. bd., 1981-84; bd. govs. Colonial Dances, Ltd., N.Y.C., 1970-74; bd. dirs. Millburn-Short Hills Hist. Soc., 1985-90, v.p., 1985-87; trustee Suburban Cmty. Music Ctr., 1985-87. Mem. ABA, Assn. Bar City N.Y., Am. Soc. Corp. Secs. (hon.), Pingry Sch. Alumni Assn. (pres. 1972-74, bd. dirs. 1966-78, cert. of merit 1968), Pilgrims U.S., Met. Squash Racquets Assn. (past treas.), Racquet and Tennis Club, Bay Head Yacht Club (N.J.), Short Hills Club, Sigma Phi, Delta Theta Phi, Pi Delta Epsilon. Republican. Episcopalian. Office: Am Express Tower World Fin Ctr New York NY 10285-5003

PYLE, ROBERT NOBLE, public relations executive; b. Wilmington, Del., Oct. 23, 1926; s. Joseph Lybr and LaVerne Ruth (Noble) P.; m. Claire Thoron; children: Robert Noble Jr., Mark C., Nicholas A., Lovis P. Crosier, Sarah L. B.A., Dickinson Coll., 1948; postgrad., Wharton Sch., U. Pa., 1949, U. Minn. Pres. Robert N. Pyle, Inc., Wilmington, 1949-52; adminstrv. asst. to U.S. Congress, Washington, 1952-63; bus. and polit. cons. and lobbyist Robert N. Pyle & Assoc., Washington, 1970—; pres. Ind. Bakers Assn., 1981—; sec./treas. Bulgarian Am. Bus. Ctr. Contbr. numerous articles to profl. jours.; reporter covering Nurnburg Trials, Paris Peace Conf. for, Stars & Stripes, Europe, 1946. Part-time field man Rep. Nat. Congl. Com., 1959-74; Selective Service Bd.; Served with U.S. Army, 1945-46, ETO. Mem. City Tavern Club, Nat. Press Club, Kenwood Golf & Country Club. Presbyterian. Home: 2613 Dumbarton St NW Washington DC 20007-3103 Office: 1223 Potomac St NW Washington DC 20007-3212

PYLE, THOMAS ALTON, instructional television and motion picture executive; b. Phoenix, Sept. 8, 1933; s. Thomas Virgil and Evelyn B. (Redden) P.; m. Victoria K. Bileck, Apr. 21, 1957; children: Pamela V., Brett T. BA, Ariz. State U., 1956. Freelance unit mgr. theatrical motion picture industry, N.Y.C. and L.A., 1956-60; v.p. sales Depicto Films Corp., N.Y.C., 1960-65; prodr. John Sutherland Prodns., N.Y.C. and L.A., 1965-67; v.p. mktg. Audio Prodns. Ednl. Svcs., N.Y.C., 1967-71; exec. v.p. Data Plex Systems, N.Y.C., 1971-74; divsn. pres., exec. prodr. Sterling Inst. Video Prodns., Washington, 1974-80; pres. Applied Video Concepts, Inc., Washington, 1980-83; pres., CEO, Nat. Sci. Ctr. Found., Burke, Va., 1983-85; CEO, Network for Instrnl. TV, Inc., Reston, Va., 1987—; active in new bus. and project fundraising; mem. bd. dirs. Nat. ITFS Assoc., So. Fla. Instrnl. TV, Delaware Valley (Del.) Ednl. Telecomms. Network, Inc., Instrnl. Opportunities Inc., St. Louis; cons. Wireless Cable Industry, 1993—. Writer, dir., producer film on Pres. John F. Kennedy, 1962; producer film biography on Pres. Lyndon B. Johnson, 1964. V.p. Dexter Park Assn., Spring Valley, N.Y., 1968-74, Solaridge Cluster Assn., Reston, Va., 1990. Recipient 27 awards from nat. and internat. film and video festivals, also 2 Commendation awards White House, 1970, 2 Acad. award nominations. Mem. AAAS, Internat. Platform Assn., N.Y. Acad. of Scis. Republican. Methodist. Avocation: photography. Office: Network Instructional TV 11490 Commerce Park Dr Ste 110 Reston VA 20191-1532

PYLE, WILLIAM CARMODY, human resource management educator, researcher; b. Indpls., Nov. 28, 1939; s. William Branham and Florence Evelyn (Carmody) P.; m. Barbara Bostian, Aug. 1978 (div. 1982); stepchildren: Lori Weaver, Jeffrey Bostian, Kyle Bostian; 1 foster child, Ramin Sobhian. BBA, U. Notre Dame, 1961; MBA, Butler U., 1962; PhD, U. Mich., 1971. Rsch. fellow U. Mich., Ann Arbor, 1967-69, rsch. assoc., 1969-72, dir. human resource acctg. program, 1972-74; assoc. prof. indsl. rels., dir. human resource rsch. program U. Minn., Mpls., 1974-78; dir. Human Resource Rsch. Ctr., U. Mass., Amherst, 1978-86; prof. mgmt. Eckerd Coll., St. Petersburg, Fla., 1986-90, Holder prof. mgmt. and internat. bus., 1990—, founding dir., chmn., 1986—; cons. to over 100 Fortune 500 firms, 1970—. Contbr. articles to profl. jours. 1st lt. USAF, 1962-65. Recipient award for outstanding contbn. to field of human resource mgmt. Am. Soc. for Pers. Adminstrn., 1971. Mem. Bahai Faith. Achievements include director of research project to implement first human resource accounting system. Avocations: classical music, reading. Home: 6600 Sunset Way Unit 520-b Saint Pete Bch FL 33706-2157 Office: Eckerd Coll Human Resource Inst 4200 54th Ave S Saint Petersburg FL 33711-4744

PYLES, CAROL DELONG, dean, consultant, educator; b. Oil City, Pa., Apr. 6, 1948; d. William J. and Doris (Gresh) DeLong; m. Richard Pyles, Mar. 26, 1980; 1 child, Whitney Dawn. BS, Alderson-Broaddus Coll., Philippi, W.Va., 1966-70; MS in Nursing, Tex. Woman's U., 1982-85; MA, W. Va. U., 1972-73, EdD, 1974-80. RN, W.Va., Tex., Fla.; cert. health edn. specialist; lic. profl. counselor, Tex., Okla.; nat. cert. counselor. Instr. nursing Fairmont (W.Va.) State Coll., 1971-73, asst. prof. nursing edn., 1973-76, asst. dean Com. Coll., 1976-78, prof. nursing, chmn. divsn. health careers, 1978-81; cons., adj. faculty Salem Coll., Clarksburg, W.Va., 1978-81; officer Allied Health Houston Com. Coll. System, 1981-83, chmn. divsn. sales, mktg. & mgmt., 1983-85; dean Coll. Spl. Arts & Scis., prof. health edn. adminstrn. Cen. State U., Edmond, Okla., 1985-87; dean Coll. of Health, Phys. Edn. & Recreation Ea. Ill. U., Charleston, 1987-91, prof. health studies, 1987-91; dean, prof. med. ctr. campus Miami-Dade (Fla.) C.C., 1991—; bd. dirs. Dade County Area Health Edn. Ctr., Inc.; treas. bd. dirs. Nat. Network for Health Career Programs in Two Yr. Colls.; pres. cons. seminar devel., P & P Assoc., Inc., Houston; coun. pvt. practice for marriage, life crises, behavior & image problems. Author: articles for Issues in Higher Edn. Mem. South Fla. Health Planning Coun., Indigent Health Care Task Force, Met. Dade County, Fla., Dade County Area Health Edn. Ctr., Inc.; chmn. Indsl. Commn., Charleston (Ill.) Recreation Ctr., 1989; bd. dirs. ARC, East Coles County chpt., Reg. United Way, Coalition Against Domestic Violence, Am. Cancer Soc. Named Personality of Am. 1986, Outstanding Young Leader in Allied Health, 1984, Most Outstanding Young Women of Am., 1983; recipient Svc. award Am. Cancer Soc., 1984. Mem. Am. Coun. Edn., Nat. Identification Program, Am. Cancer Soc., Am. Assn. Coll. for Tchrs. Edn. Inst. Rep., Assn. Schs. Allied Health Professions, Fla. Assn. Community Colls., Alliance of 100 (Fla. Hosp. Assn.), Rotary Internat., Sigma Theta Tau. Avocations: water & snow skiing, bridge, sailing, golf, tennis. Office: Miami Dade Community Coll Med Ctr Campus 950 NW 20th Med Ctr Miami FL 33127-4693

PYLES, RODNEY ALLEN, archivist, county official; b. Morgantown, W.Va., June 21, 1945; s. Melford John and Luci L. (Scarcella) P.; m. Carol Louise Wrobleski, May 20, 1972; 1 child, Janessa Louise. B.A., M.A. (Benedum scholar 1966-67, grad. research asst. 1967-68, grad. teaching fellow 1968-69), W.Va. U., 1967, 69. Instr. polit. sci. Alderson-Broaddus Coll., Philippi, W.Va., 1969-71; asst. curator W.Va. U. Library, 1971-77; dir. archives and history div. W.Va. Dept. Culture and History, 1977-85; dep. chief Assessor's Office Monongalia County, 1985-88; assessor Monongalia County, 1989—. Mng. editor: W.Va. History quar, 1977-85. Mem. Morgantown (W.Va.) Dem. exec. com., 1966-69, Monongalia County (W.Va.) Dem. exec. com., 1972-74; mem. Morgantown Libr. Bd., 1988-91; pres. Morgantown Hist. Landmarks Commn., 1986—. Mem. Soc. Am. Archivists, Mid-Atlantic Regional Archives Conf., W.Va. Hist. Soc. (exec. sec. 1977-90), W.Va. Libr. Assn., Am. Assn. State and Local History (state awards chmn. 1980-85, state membership com. 1981-87), Monongalia Hist. Soc. (pres. 1986-88), W.Va. Polit. Sci. Assn. (treas. 1991—), W.Va. Assessors' Assn. (pres. 1992-93), KC (pres. bowling league 1995-96, 4th deg., faithful capt. 1996—), Sons of Italy (treas. 1995—). Roman Catholic. Home: 536 Harvard Ave Morgantown WV 26505-2157 Office: County Court House Rm 215 Morgantown WV 26505

PYLIPOW, STANLEY ROSS, retired manufacturing company executive; b. Coudersport, Pa., Apr. 4, 1936; s. Stanley Edward and Helen L. (Haskins) P.; m. Phyllis Beverly Moore, Dec. 1, 1956; children—David, James, Vicky, Kenneth, Sandra. B.B.A. in Acctg. cum laude, St. Bonaventure U., 1957. Various fin. positions Chicopee Mfg., New Brunswick, N.J., 1957-65; various positions to v.p., gen. mgr. Domestic Coatings div. Mobil Chem. Co., N.Y.C., 1965-73; asst. corp. controller Monsanto Co., St. Louis, 1974-76; controller, dir. planning Monsanto Comml. Products, St. Louis, 1976-79; sr. v.p., chief fin. officer Fisher Controls Internat., Inc., St. Louis, 1979-92; ret., 1992; bd. dirs. RBA Group; mem. Acctg. Edn. Change Commn., 1992-96; bd. dirs. Liguori Publs. Treas., City of Town and Country, Mo., 1980-84; bd. dirs. Ecumenical Housing Prodn. Corp., St. Louis, 1980-90; sr. warden St. Peter's Episcopal Ch., St. Louis, 1984-87. Served to 1st lt., U.S. Army, 1958. Named Exec. of Yr., Profl. Secs. Internat., 1982. Mem. Inst. Mgmt. Accts. (chmn. com. chpt. ops. 1984-86, rsch. com. 1986-87, v.p. 1983-84, exec. com. 1988-90, pres. 1990-91, chmn. 1991-92), Fin. Execs. Inst., Bellerive Country Club. Republican. Avocations: golf, fitness, spectator sports. Home: 14006 Baywood Village Dr Chesterfield MO 63017

PYM, BRUCE MICHAEL, lawyer; b. Alameda, Calif., Sept. 29, 1942; s. Leonard A. and Willamay (Strandberg) P. B.B.A., U. Wash., 1964, J.D., 1967. Bar: Wash. 1967, U.S. Dist. Ct. (we. dist.) Wash. 1968, U.S. Ct. Appeals (9th cir.) 1968, U.S. Tax Ct. 1969, U.S. Supreme Ct. 1971. Law clk. Wash. State Supreme Ct., Olympia, 1967-68; assoc. Graham & Dunn, Seattle, 1968-73, shareholder, 1973-92; ptnr. Heller, Ehrman, White & McAuliffe, Seattle, 1992—; mng. ptnr. Northwest Offices, 1994—. Bd. dirs. United Way of King County, 1986-92, chmn., 1990. Mem. ABA, Wash. State Bar Assn., King County Bar Assn. (pres. 1984-85). Office: Heller Ehrman White & McAuliffe 701 5th Ave Ste 6100 Seattle WA 98104-7016

PYNCHON, THOMAS RUGGLES, JR., author; b. Glen Cove, N.Y., May 8, 1937; s. Thomas R. Pynchon. BA, Cornell U., 1958. Former editorial writer Boeing Aircraft Co., Seattle. Author: V, 1963 (William Faulkner novel award 1963), The Crying of Lot 49, 1966 (Rosenthal Found. award Nat. Inst. Arts and Letters 1967), Gravity's Rainbow, 1973 (Nat. Book award 1974), Slow Learner, 1984, Vineland, 1989, Deadly Sins, 1994; contbr. short stories to publs. including N.Y. Times Mag., N.Y. Times Book Rev., Cornell Writer, Saturday Evening Post, Kenyon Rev. Served with USNR. Recipient Howells medal Nat. Inst. and Am. Acad. Arts and Letters, 1975. Office: Little Brown & Co 34 Beacon St Boston MA 02108-1415

PYNE, FREDERICK WALLACE, genealogist, clergyman, retired civil engineer, retired mathematics educator; b. El Paso, Tex., Aug. 19, 1926; s. Frederick Cruger and Helen Louise (Wallace) P.; m. Jo Ann Rammes, July 18, 1952; children: Stephen VanRensselaer, Anne Wallace, Elizabeth Glover, Mary Clinton. BS in Civil Engring., Tri-State U., 1951; MS in Engring., Johns Hopkins U., 1966. Profl. engr., Md., Pa. Del., N.Y.; registered land surveyor; registered sanitarian; ordained priest Episcopal Ch. (traditional), 1993; certified genealogist. Mcpl. engr., 1951-54; hwy. engr., pub. health engr., chief engr. State of Md., Balt., 1951-81; civil engr., biomedical engr. Dept. Def., Frederick, Md., 1981-88; adj. prof. math. Frederick C.C., 1988-94; priest Episcopal Ch. (traditional). Author: The John Pyne Family in America, 1992. County surveyor Carroll County, Md., 1966-74; scout commr. Boy Scouts Am., Carroll and Frederick Counties, 1956—. Lt. inf. U.S. Army, 1944-51. Named Disting. Commr. Boy Scouts Am., 1993. Fellow ASCE, Am. Coll. Genealogists; mem. Am. Acad. Environ. Engrs. (diplomate), Md. Soc. Surveyors (bd. dirs. 1972-78); life mem. SAR (Md. state registrar 1994—), Descs. Signers Declaration Independence (pres.-gen. 1975-78), Soc. Colonial Wars, Mayflower Soc. Republican. Avocations: history, languages, stamp collecting. Home: 7997 Windsail Ct Frederick MD 21701-9304

PYTELL, ROBERT HENRY, lawyer, former judge; b. Detroit, Sept. 27, 1926; s. Henry Carl and Helen (Zielinski) P.; m. Laurie Mazur, June 2, 1956; children: Mary Beth, Mark Henry, Robert Michael. JD, U. Detroit, 1951. Bar: Mich. 1952. Prin. R.H. Pytell & Assocs., P.C., Detroit, 1952—; asst. U.S. atty. Ea. Dist. Mich., 1962-65; judge Mcpl. Ct., Grosse Pointe Farms, Mich., 1967-85. With USNR, 1945-46. Mem. Nat. Acad. Elder Law Attys., Am. Coll. Trust and Estate Coun., Comml. Law League Am., Crescent Sail Yacht Club (Grosse Pointe), Delta Theta Phi. Roman Catholic. Office: 18580 Mack Ave Grosse Pointe MI 48236-3251

PYTTE, AGNAR, academic administrator; b. Kongsberg, Norway, Dec. 23, 1932; came to U.S., 1949, naturalized, 1965; s. Ole and Edith (Christiansen) P.; m. Anah Currie Loeb, June 18, 1955; children: Anders H., Anthony M., Alyson C. A.B., Princeton U., 1953; A.M., Harvard U., 1954, Ph.D., 1958. Mem. faculty Dartmouth Coll., 1958-87, prof. physics, 1967-87, chmn. dept. physics and astronomy, 1971-75, assoc. dean faculty, 1975-78, dean grad. studies, 1975-78, provost, 1982-87; pres. Case Western Res. U., Cleve., 1987—; researcher in plasma physics; mem. Project Matterhorn, Princeton, 1959-60, U. Brussels, 1966-67, Princeton U., 1978-79; bd. dirs. Goodyear Tire & Rubber Co.; A.O. Smith Corp. Bd. dirs. Sherman Fairchild Found. Inc., 1987—, Cleve. Growth Assn.; bd. trustees Univs. Rsch. Assn., Ohio Aerospace Inst., Cleve. Inst. Music, Cleve. Orch. Mem. Am. Phys. Soc., Ohio Sci. and Tech. Coun., Cleve. Roundtable, Cleve. Tech. Leadership Coun., Phi Beta Kappa, Sigma Xi. Office: Case Western Res U Office of Pres Cleveland OH 44106

QASIM, SYED REAZUL, civil engineering educator, researcher; b. Allahabad, India, Dec. 1, 1938; came to U.S., 1960; s. Syed Zamir and Fakhira (Begum) Q.; m. Mujtaba Rizvi, Dec. 17, 1966; children: Zeba Saira, Saba Bano. BCE, Aligarh (India) Muslim U., 1957; MCE, W.Va. U., 1962, PhD in Environ. Engring., 1965. Registered profl. engr., Tex., Ohio. Sr. lectr. Allahabad Agrl. Inst., 1958-59; asst. dist. engr. Allahabad Mcpl. Corp., 1959-60; pool officer Indian Agrl. Rsch. Inst., New Delhi, 1965-66; design civil engr. Alden E. Stilson and Assocs., Columbus, Ohio, 1966-68; sr. civil engr. Battelle Meml. Inst., Columbus, 1968-70; assoc. prof. Poly. Inst. Bklyn., 1970-73; assoc. prof. U. Tex., Arlington, 1973-78, prof. civil engring., 1978—; cons. Chiang, Patel & Yerby, Inc., Dallas, 1981—, Gutierrez, Smouse, Wilmut & Assocs., Dallas, 1984—, Kuwait Inst. for Sci. Rsch., 1992, Hong Kong Rsch. Coun., 1994—; TOKTEN (Transfer of Knowledge through Expatriate Nats.) cons. to UN Devel. Program, 1992. Author: Wastewater Treatment Plants: Planning, Design and Operation, 1994, Sanitary Landfill Leachate: Generation, Control and Treatment, 1994; contbr. articles to profl. jours. Recipient Halliburton award U. Tex. Arlington Coll. Engring., 1988-89, Disting. Rsch. award U. Tex. Arlington, 1990-91; Fulbright scholar India, 1986. Mem. ASCE, NSPE (chmn. awards com. 1969-70), Water Environ. Fedn., Am. Water Works Assn., Assn. of Environ. Engring. Profs., Tech. Transfer Soc., Sigma Xi, Chi Epsilon, Tau Beta Pi. Home: 907 Leslie Dr Arlington TX 76012-4109 Office: U Tex at Arlington Dept Civil Engring Box 19308 Arlington TX 76019

QIAN, JIN, law librarian; b. Shanghai, China; came to the U.S., 1987; s. Bingchun and Shiyi Qian. BA, Shanghai Tchrs. U., ;, 1981; MA, Fordham U., 1988; MLS, St. John's U., 1990. Libr. trainee N.Y. Pub. Libr., N.Y.C., 1988; reference asst. N.Y. Hist. Soc., N.Y.C., 1989-90; asst. libr. Wilson, Elser et al., N.Y.C., 1990-92, head libr., 1992—. Presdl. scholar Fordham U., 1987. Mem. Law Libr. Assn. Greater N.Y., Am. Assn. Law Librs., Spl. Librs. Assn., ALA. Home: PO Box 811 New York NY 10163 Office: Wilson Elser & Moskowitz 150 E 42nd St New York NY 10017-5612

QIAO, LIANG, physician; b. Tanghe, China, Oct. 20, 1962; s. Wancheng and Wenfang (Zhao) Q.; m. Wei Liu, July 14, 1986; 1 child, George Z. MD, Sun Yat-sen U. of Med. Sci., Guangzhou Guangdong, China, 1983, MS in Pathology, 1988. Resident physician Henan Med. U., Zhengzhou, China, 1983-85; fellow in pathology Sun Yat-sen U. of Med. Sci., Guangzhou, China, 1985-88; attending physician Henan Med. U., Zhengzhou, China, 1988-90; vis. scholar SUNY at Stony Brook, 1990-91; rsch. assoc. Meml. Sloan-Kettering Cancer Ctr., N.Y.C., 1991-92; physician, rsch. assoc. N.Y. Med. Coll., Valhalla, N.Y., 1992-93, Cornell Med. Coll., N.Y.C., 1993-96; physician N.Y. Meth. Hosp., Bklyn., 1996—. Apptd. editor Chinese Jour. of Gastroenterology and Hepatology, 1994—; contbr. rsch. articles to Leukemia Rsch., Urological Rsch. and other profl. jours. Mem. Am. Assn. for Cancer Rsch., Internat. Soc. Analytical Cytology, Histochem. Soc. Achievements include rsch. in Suramin affects proliferation of prostate cancer; rsch. on proliferation antigen expression on leukemia and status of prostate cancer; research on HLA expression on thyroid carcinoma, NSAIDs and colon cancer, sulindac inhibited proliferation of colon cancer, aspirin induced HLA-DR expression in colon cancer, aspirin induced apoptosis in colon cancer cells. Office: NY Meth Hosp Dept Medicine 506 6th St Brooklyn NY 11215-3609

QUAAL, WARD LOUIS, broadcast executive; b. Ishpeming, Mich., Apr. 7, 1919; s. Sigfred Emil and Alma Charlotte (Larson) Q.; m. Dorothy J. Graham, Mar. 9, 1944; children: Graham Ward, Jennifer Anne. A.B., U. Mich., 1941; LL.D. (hon.), Mundelein Coll., 1962, No. Mich. U., 1967; D.Pub. Service, Elmhurst Coll., 1967; D.H.L. (hon.), Lincoln Coll., 1968, DePaul U., 1974. Announcer-writer Sta. WBEO (now sta. WDMJ), Marquette, Mich., 1936-37; announcer, writer, producer Sta. WJR, Detroit, 1937-41; spl. events announcer-producer WGN, Chgo., 1941-42, asst. to gen. mgr., 1945-49; exec. dir. Clear Channel Broadcasting Service, Washington, 1949-52, pres., chief exec. officer, 1964-74; v.p., asst. gen. mgr. Crosley Broadcasting Corp., Cin., 1952-56; v.p., gen. mgr., mem. bd. WGN Inc., Chgo., 1956; exec. v.p., then pres. WGN Continental Broadcasting Co. (now Tribune Broadcasting Co.), 1960-75; pres. Ward L. Quaal Co., 1975—; dir. Tribune Co., 1961-75; dir., mem. exec. com. U.S. Satellite Broadcasting Co., 1982—; bd. dirs. Christine Valmy Inc., Nat. Press Found., chmn. exec. com., dir. WLW Radio Inc., Cin., 1975-81; co-founder, dir. Universal Resources Inc., 1961-86; mem. FCC Adv. Com. on Advanced TV Sys., 1988-96. Author: (with others) Broadcast Management, 1968, rev. edit., 1979, new edit. 1997; co-prodr. (Broadway play) Teddy and Alice, 1988. Mem., Hoover Commn. Exec. Br. Task Force, 1949-59; mem. U.S.-Japan Cultural Exchange Commn., 1960-70; mem. Pres.'s Council Phys. Fitness and Sports, 1983-93; bd. dirs. Farm Found., 1963-73; bd. trustees Hollywood (Calif.) Mus., 1964-78, MacCormac Jr. Coll., Chgo., 1974-80; chmn. exec. com. Council for TV Devel., 1969-72; mem. bus. adv. coun. Chgo. Urban League, 1964-74; bd. dirs. Broadcasters Found., Internat. Radio and TV Found., Sears Roebuck Found., 1970-73; trustee Mundelein Coll., 1962-72, Hillsdale Coll., 1966-72. Served as lt. USNR, 1942-45. Recipient Disting. Bd. Gov.'s award Nat. Acad. TV Arts and Scis., 1966, 87, Freedoms Found. award, Valley Forge, 1966, 68, 70, Disting. Alumnus award U. Mich., 1967, Loyola U. Key, 1970, Advt. Man of Yr. Gold medallion, Chgo. Advt. Club, 1968, Disting. Svc. award Nat. Assn. Broadcasters, 1973, Ill. Broadcaster of Yr. award, 1973, Press Vet. of Yr. award, 1973, Comm.award of distinction Brandeis U., 1973, Founder & Leadership award Broadcast Pioneers Libr., 1991; first recipient Sterling Medal, Barren Found., 1985, Lifetime Achievement award in broadcasting Ill. Broadcasters Assn., 1989; 1st person named to Better Bus. Bur. Hall of Fame, Council of Better Bus. Burs. Inc., 1975; named Radio Man of Yr. Am. Coll. Radio, Arts, Crafts & Scis., 1961, Laureate in Order of Lincoln, Lincoln Acad. Ill., 1965, Communicator of Yr., Jewish United Fund, 1969, Advt. Club Man of Yr., 1973; named to Broadcasting mag. Hall Fame, 1991, Delta Tau Delta Disting. Svc. Chpt., 1970. Mem. NATAS (bd. govs. 1966-76, Silver Circle award 1993), Nat. Press Found. (bd. dirs. 1991—), Nat. Assn. Broadcasters (bd. dirs. 1952-56), Fed. Comm. Bar Assn., Broadcast Music Inc. (bd. dirs. 1953-70), Assn. Maximum Svc. Telecasters Inc. (bd. dirs. 1952-72), Broadcast Pioneers (pres., bd. dirs. 1962-73), Broadcast Pioneers Libr. (pres. 1981-84), Broadcast Pioneers Ednl. Fund Inc., Broadcasters Found. (chmn. bd. 1996—). Office: Ward L Quaal Co 401 N Michigan Ave Ste 3140 Chicago IL 60611-4251

QUACKENBUSH, JUSTIN LOWE, federal judge; b. Spokane, Wash., Oct. 3, 1929; s. Carl Clifford and Marian Huldah (Lowe) Q.; m. Marie McAtee; children: Karl Justin, Kathleen Marie, Robert Craig. BA, U. Idaho, 1951; LLB, Gonzaga U., Spokane, 1957. Bar: Wash. 1957. Dep. pros. atty. Spokane County, 1957-59; ptnr. Quackenbush, Dean, Bailey & Henderson, Spokane, 1959-80; dist. judge U.S. Dist. Ct. (ea. dist.) Wash., Spokane, 1980—, now sr. judge; part-time instr. Gonzaga U. Law Sch., 1960-67. Chmn. Spokane County Planning Commn., 1969-73. Served with USN, 1951-54. Mem. ABA, Wash. Bar Assn., Spokane County Bar Assn. (trustee 1976-78), Internat. Footprint Assn. (nat. pres. 1967), Spokane C. of C. (trustee, exec. com. 1978-79). Episcopalian. Club: Spokane Country. Lodge: Shriners. Office: US Dist Ct PO Box 1432 Spokane WA 99210-1432

QUACKENBUSH, MARGERY CLOUSER, psychoanalyst, administrator; b. Reading, Pa., Apr. 30, 1938; d. Carl Brumbach and Katherine Elvina (Althouse) Clouser; m. Robert Mead Quackenbush, July 3, 1971; 1 child, Piet Robert. BA, Pratt Inst., 1960; MA, Calif. Grad. Inst., 1982. Cert. in psychoanalysis Ctr. for Modern Psychoanalytic Studies. Instr. Pratt Inst., Bklyn., 1978-79, Fash. Inst. of Tech., N.Y.C., 1980-81; counselor Wiltwyck, Bronx Ctr., 1981-82; adminstr. Nat. Assn. for Advancement of Psychoanalysis, N.Y.C., 1982—; pvt. practice in psychoanalysis N.Y.C., 1980—. Mem. Lenox Hill Dem. Club, N.Y.C., 1993-95; spkr. various community groups, 1991-95. Recipient Maison Blanche award, 1959, Miriam Berkman Spotnitz award, 1992. Mem. Nat. Assn. for Advancement of Psychoanalysis, Nat. Soc. DAR, Alumni Assn. of the Ctr. for Modern Psych. Studies (sec. 1992-94, Alumni Assn. program dir., v.p. 1995-96). Democrat. Avocations: reading, writing, golf, horseback riding. Home: 460 E 79th St Apt 14E New York NY 10021-1447 Office: Nat Assn Advancement Psychoanalysis 80 8th Ave # 1501 New York NY 10011-5126

QUACKENBUSH, ROBERT DEAN, management consultant; b. Lansing, Mich., Oct. 12, 1947; s. Gerald G. and Margaret Lee (McLean) Q.; m. Donna Jean Cleary, Aug. 4, 1976; children: Dana McLean, Grant Robert. BA, Elmhurst Coll., 1969; postgrad., John Marshall Law Sch., 1969, 71. Mgmt. cons. Nineveh, Pa., 1982—; instr. Washington and Jefferson Coll., 1982-85. Author: Lake Lauzon, 1991. With U.S. Army, 1970-71, Vietnam. Mem. Anawana Club. Avocations: fishing, snorkeling, travel. Home and Office: PO Box 14 Nineveh PA 15353-0014

QUACKENBUSH, ROBERT MEAD, artist, author, psychoanalyst; b. Hollywood, Calif., July 23, 1929; s. Roy Maynard and Virginia (Arbogast) Q.; m. Margery Clouser, July 3, 1971; 1 child: Piet Robert. Bachelor Profl. Arts, Art Ctr. Coll. of Design, Pasadena, Calif., 1956; grad., Ctr. Modern Psychoanalytic Studies, N.Y.C., 1991; MSW, Fordham U., 1994. Art dir. Scandinavian Airlines System, N.Y.C. and Stockholm, 1956-61; pvt. practice N.Y.C., 1961—; psychoanalyst New Hope Guild Ctrs. for Emotionally Disturbed Children, Bklyn., 1994—; educator Robert Quackenbush Studios, N.Y.C.; lectr. U.S., Europe, Middle East and South Am.; TV performer Ednl. TV; mem. faculty N.J. Ctr. for Modern Psychoanalysis. Author/artist over 160 books for young readers including Old MacDonald Had A Farm, 1972, Clementine, 1974, There'll Be a Hot Time in the Old Town Tonight, 1974, Pop! Goes the Weasel and Yankee Doodle, 1976, The Holiday Song Book, 1977, Along Came the Model T! How Henry Ford Put the World on Wheels, 1978, Who Threw That Pie?, The Birth of Comedy Movie, 1979, Henry's Awful Mistake, 1980, Piet Potter's First Case, 1980, The Boy Who Waited for Santa Claus, 1981, Detective Mole Mystery Series (winner Edgar Allen Poe Spl. award 1982), Henry's Important Date, 1981, No Mouse for Me, 1981, Here a Plant, There a Plant, Everywhere a Plant, Plant! The Story of Luther Burbank, 1982, Henry Babysits, 1983, I Don't Want to Go, I Don't Know How to Act, 1983, Taxi to Intrigue, 1984, Who Said There's No Man on the Moon? The Story of Jules Verne, 1985, Who Let Muddy Boots into the House? The Story of Andrew Jackson, 1986, Mouse Feathers, 1988, Danger in Tibet, 1989, Robert Quackenbush's Treasury of Humor, 1990, Benjamin Franklin and His Friends, 1991, Evil Under the Sean, 1992, James Madison & Dolly Madison and Their Times, 1993, Arthur Ashe and His Match with History, 1994, Clara Barton and Her Victory Over Fear, 1995, Batbaby, 1997, (under pen name Richard Gobbletree) Treasure Hunt, 1997; prodr.: TV series Dear Mr. Quackenbush and The Great American Storybook for Educational Television; films include American Songfest, 1978, Beth B's Visiting Desire, 1997. With U.S. Army 1951-53. Recipient 2 Citations for outstanding Troop Info. & Edn. instrn. from commdg. gen. 31st Inf. Divsn. 1953, 3 time winner Am. Flag Inst. award for outstanding contbn. to field of children's lit., 1976, 77, 81, Edgar Allen Poe Spl. award, 1982. Mem. Mystery Writers of Am., Authors' Guild, Authors' League of Am., Holland Soc. of N.Y., Nat. Assn. for Advancement of Psychoanalysis (trustee, v.p. pub. info., founder and chair Gradiva awards), Soc. Modern Psychoanalysts (cert.). Avocations: travel, antique restoration. Home: 460 E 79th St Apt 14E New York NY 10021-1445 Office: Robert Quackenbush Studios 223 E 78th St New York NY 10021-1222 *Humor became a key to survival in my family when I was growing up during the depression and World War II. Thus humor became the keynote of all the books I wrote - I want young readers to know that as long as we keep our sense of humor, our spirits cannot be crushed.*

QUACKENBUSH, ROGER E., retired secondary school educator; b. Cooperstown, N.Y., Jan. 22, 1940; s. Eugene W. and Marion I. (Clark) Q.; m. Cathy E. Quackenbush, Mar. 31, 1973; children: Michele, Stacey, Thomas. BS, SUNY, Albany, 1961, MS, 1966; PhD, Columbia Pacific U., San Rafael, Calif., 1984; postgrad., numerous univs. Cert. permanent biology and gen. sci. tchr., N.Y. Tchr. gen. sci. and math Troy (N.Y.) Pub. Sch. System, 1961-64; tchr. earth sci. and biology Schuylerville (N.Y.) Cen. H.S., 1964-66; tchr. biology Bethlehem Cen. H.S., Delmar, N.Y., 1966-95; cons. advanced placement biology Niskayuna (N.Y.) H.S., 1995-96; instr. anatomy and physiology lab. Russell Sage Coll., Troy, N.Y., 1996—; mentor student tchrs., 1968-90; instr. Tchr. Expectation Student Achievement program, 1985-91; lectr. on marine mammals SUNY, Albany, 1986; instr. DNA Sci. and Tech. for high sch. students SUNY, Albany, 1996; lectr. on whales; workshop leader on use microcomputers in classroom; former mem. Mid States Commn. on Evaluation Local High Schs.; past mem. adv. bd. Upstate N.Y. Jr. Sci. and Humanities Symposium; test writer Regents biology exams. N.Y. State Dept. Edn.; presenter/cons. N.Y. State Edn. Dept. alt. assessment writer's workshop, 1994; leader, naturalist for whale watch trips and Kenya safaris; workshop presenter for DNA-molecular biology lab. techniques; workshop presenter on the use of the Tex. Instruments calculator and the Calculator Based Lab. sys. in the sci. classroom; mem. Select Seminar on Evaluating Tchrs., 1985; mem. Wells Conf. Regents Biology Syllabus Revision, 1991; faculty cons. AP Biology reading Coll. Bd. Advanced Placement Program, 1997; cons. DNA molecular biology technology Greater Capital Region Tchr. Ctr., 1988-97. Editor/writer of alternative assessments for N.Y. State Edn. Dept., 1993-94; contbr. numerous articles to profl. jours.; author: Swahili Phrasebook, 1993. Hon. admisssions liaison officer USAF Acad., 1988. Recipient Excellence in Tchg. award, 1989, letter of commendation U. Chgo., 1978, MIT, 1985, U.S. Army, 1989, Tufts U., 1990, 94, Tchr. of Yr. award, Tufts U., 1985, Golub Tchr.-Scholar award SUNY, 1991, 96; Chpt. II grantee N.Y. State Dept. Edn., 1987, NSF grantee, 1965, 67, 68, 72, 87, 90, Future Directions, 1990, Greenwall Found., 1993, hon. mention Tandy Tech. Scholar award, 1994, Tandy Tech. Scholar prize for excellence in sci. tchg., 1995, Outstanding Tchr award U. Chgo., 1995; named Hon. Grad. Marshal, 1991, 94, hon. N.Y. State Biology Mentor, 1995. Mem. NEA, Nat. Assn. Biology Tchrs., BALSA, Soc. Marine Mammalogy, Am. Cetacean Soc., Cetacean Soc. Internat., Sci. Tchrs. Assn. N.Y. State (past sect. dir., past state bd. dirs.), NEA of N.Y., Phi Delta Kappa. Home: 25 Robinhood Rd Albany NY 12203-5133

QUADE, QUENTIN LON, political science educator; b. Ft. Dodge, Ia., Jan. 28, 1933; s. Louis Anton and Vera (Chrisman) Q.; m. Phyllis F. Fleskes, Jan. 2, 1954; children: Zachary, Christopher, Matthew, Stephanie, Leslie. B.S., Creighton U., 1957; M.A., Notre Dame U., 1958, Ph.D., 1965. Instr. polit. sci. St. Louis U., 1959-61; faculty polit. sci. Marquette U., Milw., 1961—, prof., 1968—, Raynor prof. polit. sci., 1991—, dean Grad. Sch., 1968, assoc. acad. v.p., grad. dean, 1970-72, acad. v.p., 1972-74, exec. v.p., 1974-90; dir. Ctr. for Parental Freedom in Edn., 1992—. Author: U.S. and Wars of National Liberation, 1966, (with T.J. Bennett) American Politics: Responsible and Efffective?, 1969, Pope and Revolution, 1982, Paths to Parental Freedom and School Choice, 1995, Financing Education: The Struggle Between Governmental Monopoly and Parental Freedom, 1996. Served with USAF, 1950-53. Roman Catholic. Home: 7326 Maple Ter Milwaukee WI 53213-3153 Office: 615 N 11th St Milwaukee WI 53233-2305 *Love the truth. Know the good. Do it.*

QUADE, VICTORIA CATHERINE, editor, writer; b. Chgo., Aug. 15, 1953; d. Victor and Virginia (Uryasz) Q.; m. Charles J. White III, Feb. 15, 1986 (div. Aug. 1996); children: Michael, David, Catherine. BS in Journalism, No. Ill. U., 1974. Staff reporter news divsn. The News-Tribune, LaSalle, Ill., 1975-77; staff writer news divsn. The News-Sun, Waukegan, Ill.,

1977-81; staff writer ABA Jour., Chgo., 1981-85; mng. editor ABA Press, Chgo., 1985-90, editor, 1990—, sr. editor, 1994—. Author: (poetry) Rain and Other Poems, 1976, Laughing Eyes, 1979, Two Under the Covers, 1981; playwright: Late Nite Catechism: Saints, Sisters & Ejaculation, 1993, (with Maripat Donovan) Room for Advancement, 1994, Mr. Nanny, 1996; editor Human Rights mag.; contbr. to numerous anthologies and publs. Recipient numerous awards from Soc. Nat. Assn. Publs., AP, UPI. Mem. Am. Soc. Bus. Press Editors (award), Chgo. Newspaper Guild (award), Am. Soc. Assn. Execs. (Gold Circle award 1989, 90). Avocations: traveling, photography. Office: ABA 750 N Lake Shore Dr Chicago IL 60611-4403

QUADER, PATRICIA ANN, elementary education educator; b. Pitts., Sept. 9, 1941; d. Andrew and Julia Supira; m. Walter Anthony Quader, Jan. 15, 1966. BA, Carlow Coll., 1963; MEd, U. Pitts., 1967. Cert. elem. tchr., supt., Pa. Tchr. Diocese of Pitts., 1963-64; tutor Pitts. Tchrs. Tutoring Svc., 1964-65; intern tchr. Burrell Sch. Dist., Lower Burrell, Pa., 1966; tchr. Kiski Area Sch. Dist., Vandergrift, Pa., 1966-91; computer, libr. skills tchr. Vandergrift Elem. Sch., North Washington Elem. Schs., 1991—; instr. Pa. State U., New Kensington, 1970-72; in-svc. instr. in computer literacy Kiski Area Sch. Dist., 1985-91, 95-96, edited K-3 computer skills curriculum. Co-author: 4th and 5th grade computer literacy curricula for Kiski Sch. Dist.; editor Kiski Area K-6 Computer Skills Curriculum, 1991—. Chmn. Bell-Avon PTA, Salina, Pa., 1988-91. Recipient scholarship Carlow Coll., 1959. Mem. NEA, ASCD, Pa. State Edn. Assn., Kiski Area Edn. Assn., Phi Delta Kappa. Democrat. Roman Catholic. Avocations: mystery novels, computer games. Office: Vandergrift Elem Sch 420 Franklin Ave Vandergrift PA 15690-1311

QUADRACCI, HARRY V., printing company executive, lawyer; b. 1936. JD, Columbia U., 1959. Assoc. N.Y.C., Milw., 1961-71; corp. counsel W.A. Krueger Co., Brookfield, Wis., 1961-71; pres. Quad Graphics, Inc., Pewaukee, Wis., 1971—. Office: Quad Graphics Inc W224n3322 Duplainville Rd Pewaukee WI 53072-4137*

QUADT, RAYMOND ADOLPH, metallurgist, cement company executive; b. Perth Amboy, N.J., Apr. 16, 1916; s. Adolph and Florence (MacCracken) Q.; 1 child, Brian. B.S., Rutgers U., 1939; M.A., Columbia U., 1943; M.S., Stevens Inst. Tech., 1948. Tchr. high sch. Plainfield, N.J., 1939-42; research metallurgist Am. Smelting & Refining Co., Barber, N.J., 1942-48; dir. aluminum devel. Am. Smelting & Refining Co., 1948-50; v.p. Hunter Douglas Corp., Riverside, Calif., 1950-57; v.p. research and devel. Bridgeport Brass Co., 1958-60, v.p. spl. metals, 1962-63; v.p. Nat. Distillers and Chem. Corp., N.Y.C., 1963—; chmn. bd. Loud Co., Pomona, Calif., 1963—; pres., gen. mgr. Reactive Metals Inc., 1960-62; v.p., gen. mgr. Pascoe Steel Corp., Pomona, 1965-73; pres. Phoenix Cement Co., 1973-80, cons., 1980-83; chmn. bd. Trendex, Inc., Phoenix, 1983-87, Mesco, Phoenix, 1983-88; vice chmn. Sunstate Bancshares Inc., Casa Grande, Ariz., 1982; bd. dirs. Republic Nat. Bank, Phoenix, 1982—; chmn. Express Delivery, Phoenix, 1991-94, Mariah Internat., Inc., Phoenix, 1992-93; v.p., sec. Ariz. Custom Motorcoaches, Mesa, Ariz., 1995-96. Mem. Am. Soc. Metals, Pomona C. of C. (pres. 1970), Phi Beta Kappa. Home and Office: 6454 S Willow Dr Tempe AZ 85283-3968

QUAID, DENNIS, actor; b. Houston, Apr. 9, 1954; s. William Rudy and Juanita B. Q.; m. Meg Ryan, 1991; 1 child, Jack Henry. Student, U. Houston, 1972-75. Appearances include (film) Crazy Mama, 1975, I Never Promised You A Rosegarden, 1977, Sept. 30, 1955, 1977, Our Winning Season, 1978, The Seniors, 1978, Breaking Away, 1979, G.O.R.P., 1980, The Long Riders, 1980, Caveman, 1981, All Night Long, 1981, The Night the Lights Went Out in Georgia, 1981, Tough Enough, 1983, Jaws 3-D, 1983, The Right Stuff, 1983, Dreamscape, 1984, Enemy Mine, 1985, Innerspace, 1987, The Big Easy, 1987, Suspect, 1987, D.O.A., 1988, Everybody's All-American, 1988, Great Balls of Fire, 1989, Postcards from the Edge, 1990, Come See the Paradise, 1990, Undercover Blues, 1993, Wilder Napalm, 1993, Flesh and Bone, 1993, Wyatt Earp, 1994, Something to Talk About, 1995, Dragonheart, 1996, Criminal Element, 1997, Going West, 1997; (theatre) The Last of the Knucklemen, 1983, True West, 1984, (TV movies) Are You In the House Alone?, 1978, Amateur Night at the Dixie Bar and Grill, 1979, Bill, 1981, Johnny Belinda, 1982, Bill: On His Own, 1983. *An artist must take chances in performing his craft. If he is to succeed he must be willing to fall flat on his face.*

QUAIFE, MARJORIE CLIFT, nursing educator; b. Syracuse, N.Y., Aug. 21. Diploma in Nursing with honors, Auburn Meml. Hosp; BS, Columbia U., 1962, MA, 1978. Cert. orthopaedic nurse; cert. in nursing continuing edn. and staff devel.; BLS instr. Staff instr. Columbia Presbyn. Hosp., N.Y.C.; content expert for computer assisted instrn. program-ctrl. venous catheters. Contbr. articles to numreous profl. publs. Mem. ANA, N.Y. State Nurses Assn., Nat. Assn. Orthopaedic Nurses, Nat. Assn. Nursing Staff Devel., Nat. Assn. Vascular Access Networks, Intravenous Nurses Soc., Sigma Theta Tau.

QUAIL, BEVERLY J., lawyer; b. Glendale, Calif., June 19, 1949; d. John Henry and Dorothy Marie (Sanblom) Q.; m. Timothy D. Roble; children: Benjamin W., Elizabeth L. BA magna cum laude, U. So. Calif., 1971; JD, U. Denver, 1974. Bar: Colo. 1974. Dir. Dufford & Brown, P.C., Denver, 1975-95; ptnr. Ballard Spahr Andrews & Ingersoll, Denver, 1996—; broker Colo. Assn. Realtors, 1982—; lectr. continuing legal edn. Colo.; v.p., bd. mem. Girls Club Denver, 1984-87; bd. dirs. Swedish Hosp. Found., Legal Aid of Colo. Found., Central City Opera House Assn. Mem. ABA (chmn. real property litigation and dispute resolution com., coun. real property, probate & trust sect. 1990-95, co-chair membership com. 1993-95, sec. 95-96, sect. vice chair 1996—), Am. Coll. Real Estate Lawyers (bd. govs. 1990-95, treas. 95-96), Colo. Real Estate Council, Castle Pines Golf Club, Cherry Hills Country Club (Denver), Phi Beta Kappa. Author Colo. Real Estate Forms-Practice, Real Property Practice & Litigation; editor newsletter The Colo. Lawyer, 1983-87; contbr. articles to profl. jours. Office: Ballard Spahr Andrews & Ingersoll 1225 17th St Ste 2300 Denver CO 80202-5534

QUAIN, MITCHELL I., investment executive; b. N.Y.C., Nov. 15, 1951; m. Cherie Quain; children: Sam, Rhonda, Jacob, Samuel, Michelle. BSEE, U. Pa., 1973; MBA, Harvard U., 1975. CFA. Mng. dir., founder indsl. mfg. group Schroder Wertheim & Co., N.Y.C., 1975—; bd. dirs. Allied Products Corp., Mech. Dynamics, Inc., Strategic Distbn., Inc., DeCrane Aircraft Holdings, Inc., Roller Bearings Corp. Mem. bd. overseers Sch. Engring. & Applied Scis., U. Pa.; trustee St. Lukes Acad. Office: Schroder Wertheim and Co 787 7th Ave New York NY 10019-6018

QUAINTON, ANTHONY CECIL EDEN, diplomat; b. Seattle, Apr. 4, 1934; s. Cecil Eden and Marjorie Josephine (Oates) Q.; m. Susan Long, Aug. 7, 1958; children: Katherine, Eden, Elizabeth. B.A., Princeton U., 1955; B.Litt., Oxford (Eng.) U., 1958. Research fellow St. Antony's Coll., Oxford, 1958-59; with Fgn. Service, State Dept., 1959—; vice consul Sydney, Australia, 1960-62; Urdu lang. trainee, 1962-63; 2d sec., econ. officer Am. embassy, Karachi, Pakistan, 1963-64, Rawalpindi, Pakistan, 1964-66; 2d sec., polit. officer Am. embassy, New Delhi, 1966-69; sr. polit. officer for India Dept. State, Washington, 1969-72; 1st sec. Am. embassy, Paris, 1972-73; counselor, dep. chief mission Am. embassy, Kathmandu, Nepal, 1973-76; ambassador to Central African Empire, Bangui, 1976-78, Nicaragua, Managua, 1982-84, Kuwait, 1984-87; dir. Office for Combatting Terrorism, Dept. State, Washington, 1978-81; dep. insp. gen. Dept. State, 1987-89; ambassador Peru, 1989-92; asst. sec. of state for diplomatic security Dept. State, Washington, 1992-95, dir. gen. fgn. svc., 1995—. English Speaking Union fellow, 1951-52; Marshall scholar, 1955-58; recipient Rivkin award, 1972, Herter award, 1984. Mem. Am. Fgn. Svc. Assn., Lions Internat., Met. Club, Phi Beta Kappa. Home: 3424 Porter St NW Washington DC 20016-3126 Office: Dept State M/DGP Rm 6218 2201 C St NW Washington DC 20520-0001

QUALE, JOHN CARTER, lawyer; b. Boston, Aug. 16, 1946; s. Andrew C. and Luella (Meland) Q.; m. Diane Zipursky, Jan. 19, 1992; children: Virginia Ann, Jane Harris, John Andrew; stepchildren: Rachel Goldman, Alisa Goldman. AB cum laude, Harvard U., 1968, JD cum laude, 1971. Bar: Mass. 1971, D.C. 1972. Assoc. Kirkland & Ellis, Washington, 1971-78, ptnr., 1978-83; ptnr. Wiley, Rein & Fielding, Washington, 1983-96, Skadden, Arps, Slate, Meagher & Flom L.L.P., Washington, 1996—; Spkr. mass media trade groups. Contbr. articles to profl. jours. Trustee Fed. Comm. Bar Assn. Found., 1992-93. Mem. ABA, Fed. Comm. Bar Assn. (treas. 1982-83, mem. exec. com. 1993—), Barristers, Met. Club. Office: Skadden Arps Slate et al 1440 New York Ave NW Washington DC 20005-2111

QUALLEY, CHARLES ALBERT, fine arts educator; b. Creston, Iowa, Mar. 19, 1930; s. Albert Olaf and Cleora (Dietrick) Q.; m. Betty Jean Griffith, Nov. 26, 1954; children: Janet Lynn, John Stuart. B.F.A., Drake U., 1952; M.A., U. Iowa, 1956, M.F.A., 1958; Ed.D., Ill. State U., 1967. Art tchr. Des Moines Pub. Schs., 1952,, 54-55; critic art tchr. U. Iowa, 1955-57; prof. fine arts U. Colo., Boulder, 1958-90, prof. emeritus, 1990—; chmn. dept. fine arts U. Colo., 1968-71, assoc. chmn., 1981-82; vis. prof. Inst. for Shipboard Edn., semester at sea, 1979, Ill. State U., 1985. Author: Safety in the Art Room, 1986; contbg. editor Sch. Arts, 1978-85, mem. editorial adv. bd., 1985-87; author column Safetypoint, 1981-85. Served with AUS, 1952-54, Korea. Mem. Nat. Art Edn. Assn. (v.p. 1980-82, pres. 1987-89, dir. conv. svcs. 1990—, fellow 1990—, Art Educator of Yr. 1993), Nat. Art Edn. Found. (trustee 1987—, chair bd. trustees 1996—), Colo. Art Edn. Assn. (editor 1965-67, 75, pres. 1976-78), Delta Phi Delta, Omicron Delta Kappa, Pi Kappa Delta. Home: 409 Fillmore Ct Louisville CO 80027-2273

QUALLS, CHARLES WAYNE, JR., veterinary pathology educator; b. Oklahoma City, Feb. 8, 1949; s. Charles Wayne and Mary Opal (Howard) Q.; m. Cheryl Lynn Lightfoot, Aug. 9, 1969; children: Kerry Lynn, Julie Elizabeth. BS, Okla. State U., 1971, DVM, 1973; PhD, U. Calif., Davis, 1980. Diplomate Am. Coll. Vet. Pathologists. Postdoctoral fellow U. Calif., Davis, 1973-77; asst. prof. La. State U., Baton Rouge, 1977-82; assoc. prof. Okla. State U., Stillwater, 1982-87, prof. vet. pathology, 1988—, acting head dept. vet. pathology, 1991-92, coord. grad. instrn. Coll. Vet. Medicine, 1996—. Mem. editl. bd. Jour. Toxicology and Environ. Health, Vet. Pathology, Bull. Environ. Toxicology; contbr. articles to profl. jours., chpts. to books. Grantee Dept. of Def., U.S. Army Rsch. and Engring. Program, others. Mem AVMA (student sponsor 1983—), Soc. Toxicologic Pathologists, Soc. Toxicology, Phi Kappa Phi, Phi Zeta. Home: 3118 Timberlake Stillwater OK 74075-9999 Office: Okla State U Dept Vet Pathology Stillwater OK 74078

QUALLS, JUNE CAROL, elementary education educator; b. Ft. Worth, June 22, 1954; d. Earl Clayton and Viola Maurine (McFaul) Irvin; m. Richard Eugene Qualls, Apr. 20, 1984. BS, Tarleton State Coll., 1976; MEd, East Tex. State U., 1979, cert. in spl. edn., 1992, cert. in ednl. diagnostics, 1993. Cert. elem. tchr., Tex. Tchr. kindergarten Elisha M. Pease Elem. Sch., Dallas, 1979-80, 87-91, Mt. Auburn Elem. Sch., Dallas, 1983-84; tchr. jr. high sch. Maypearl (Tex.) Ind. Sch. Dist., 1980-83; edn. specialist Alaska Headstart-Rural Cap, Anchorage, 1984-85; multi-level tchr. Tom Thumb Montessori Sch., Anchorage, 1985-87; tchr. 2d grade John Neely Bryan Elem. Sch., Dallas, 1991-92; tchr. kindergarten, chairperson kindergarten John Q. Adams Elem. Sch., Dallas, 1993-94, mentor tchr., 1993-94, tchr. spl. edn. resource/content mastery, 1995—; mentor tchr. Elisha M. Pease Elem. Sch., 1989-90; math. coord. Maypearl Jr. H.S., 1980-83. Contbg. writer curriculum materials for gifted edn. Mem. Internat. Reading Assn., Tex. State Reading Assn., Ellis County Reading Assn., Parent-Tchr. Orgn., Greenpeace, Coun. for Exceptional Children. Avocations: scuba diving, camping, archaelogical interests. Office: Dallas Ind Sch Dist JQ Adams Elem Sch 8329 Lake June Rd Dallas TX 75217-2169

QUALLS, ROBERT L., manufacturing executive, banker, former state official, educator; b. Burnsville, Miss., Nov. 6, 1933; s. Wes E. and Letha (Parker) Q.; m. Carolyn Morgan, Feb. 10, 1979 (dec. July 1996); 1 child, Stephanie Elizabeth. BS, Miss. State U., 1954, MS, 1958; PhD, La. State U., 1962; LLD, Whitworth Coll., 1974; DBA (hon.), U. of the Ozarks, 1984. Prof., chmn. div. econs. and bus. Belhaven Coll., Jackson, Miss., 1962-66; asst. to pres. Belhaven Coll., 1965-66; asst. prof. finance Miss. State U., State College, 1967-69, adj. prof., 1969-73; sr. v.p., chmn. venture com. Bank of Miss., Tupelo, 1969-73; v.p. Wesleyan Coll., Macon, Ga., 1974; pres. U. of the Ozarks, Clarksville, Ark., 1974-79; mem. cabinet Bill Clinton Gov. of Ark., 1979-80; exec. v.p. Boatmen's Bank of Ark., Little Rock, 1980-85; chmn., CEO, dir. NationsBank (formerly Boatmen's), Harrison, Ark., 1985-86; pres., dir. First Bank Fin. Services, Inc., 1980-85, Advt. Assocs., Inc., 1980-85; pres., chief oper. officer Baldor Electric Co., Ft. Smith, Ark., 1986—, CEO, 1992; mktg. cons. Ill. Central Industries, Chgo., 1964; mem. faculty, thesis examiner Stonier Grad. Sch. Banking, Rutgers U., 1973-86; mem. faculty Miss. Sch. Banking, U. Miss., 1973-78; course coordinator Sch. Banking of the South, La. State U., 1978-88, Banking Sch., Duke U., 1977; lectr. Southwestern Sch. Banking, So. Meth. U., 1983; adj. prof. bus. adminstrn. U. Central Ark., 1985-86. Author: Entrepreneurial Wit and Wisdom, 1986; co-author: Strategic Planning for Colleges and Universities: A Systems Approach to Planning and Resource Allocation, 1979; mem. editorial adv. bd.: Bank Mktg. Mag., 1984-86. Chmn. cmty. svc. and continuing edn. com. Tupelo Cmty. Devel. Found., 1972-73; mem. Miss. 4-H adv. coun., 1969; active Boys Scouts Am.; mem. Lee County Dem. Exec. Com., 1973-74; trustee Wal-Mart Found., 1975-79, Oklahoma City U., 1990-95; trustee, mem. exec. com. U. Ozarks, 1982-88; mem. Pres.'s Roundtable U. Ctrl. Ark., 1982-87; mem. exec. com. Coll. Bus. Adv. Bd., U. Ark., Little Rock, 1980-85; bd. dirs. U. Ark. Med. Sch. Found., 1991—, Ark. Inst., 1991-94. Lt. AUS, 1954-56. Found. for Econ. Edn. fellow, 1964; Ford Found. faculty research fellow Vanderbilt U., 1963-64; recipient Pillar of Progress award Johnson County, 1977. Mem. Am. Bankers Assn. (mktg. planning and rsch. com. 1972-73), Ark. Coun. Ind. Colls. and Univs. (chmn. 1978-79), Johnson County C. of C. (pres. 1977), Fort Smith C. of C. (dir. 1995—), Blue Key, Omicron Delta Kappa, Delta Sigma Pi, Sigma Phi Epsilon (citation 1977), Masons (32 deg.), Clarksville Rotary (pres. 1979). Presbyterian. Office: Baldor Electric Co 5711 S 7th St Fort Smith AR 72901-8394

QUALLS, ROXANNE, mayor. Former exec. dir. Women Helping Women; former dir. No. Ky. Rape Crisis Ctr.; former dir. Cin. office Ohio Citizen Action; councilwoman City of Cin., 1991-93, mayor, 1993—; former chairperson Cin. City Council's Intergovtl. Affairs and Environment Com.; former vice chairperson Community Devel., Housing and Zoning Com.; 2d v.p. OKI Regional Coun. Govts.; mem. Gov.'s Commn. on Storage and Use of Toxic and Hazardous Materials, Solid Waste Adv. Com. of State of Ohio, Gov.'s Waste Minimization Task Force; former chair bd. commrs. Cin. Met. Housing Authority; bd. dirs. Shuttlesworth Housing Found. Hon. chair Friends of Women's Studies; mem. Jr. League Adv. Coun. Recipient Woman of Distinction award Girl Scouts U.S., 1992, Woman of Distinction award Soroptomists, 1993, Outstanding Achievement award Cin. Woman's Polit. Caucus, 1993. Office: City Hall 801 Plum St Ste 150 Cincinnati OH 45202-5704*

QUALSET, CALVIN O., agronomy educator; b. Newman Grove, Nebr., Apr. 24, 1937; s. Herman Qualset and Adeline (Hanson) Vakoc; m. Kathleen Boehler; children: Douglas, Cheryl, Gary. BS, U. Nebr., 1958; MS, U. Calif., Davis, 1960, PhD, 1964. Asst. prof. U. Tenn., Knoxville, 1964-67; from asst. prof. to assoc. prof. U. Calif., Davis, 1967, prof., 1973-94, prof. emeritus, 1994—, chmn. dept. agronomy and range sci., 1975-81, 91-94, assoc. dean coll. agrl. and environ. sci., 1981-86; dir. Genetic Resources Conservation Program, Davis, 1985—; sci, liaison officer U.S. Agy. Internat. Devel., Washington, 1985-93, mem. rsch. adv. com., 1989-92; mem. nat. plant genetic resources bd. USDA, Washington, 1982-88. Contbr. over 180 articles to profl. jours. Fulbright fellow, Australia, 1976, Yugoslavia, 1984. Fellow AAAS (chmn. agr. sect. 1992), Am. Soc. Agronomy (pres. 1994); mem. Soc. Conservation Biology, Soc. Econ. Botany, Genetic Soc. Am., Crop Sci. Soc. Am. (pres. 1989). Achievements include development of 10 cultivars of wheat, oat triticale. Office: Genetic Res Conserv Prog Univ of Calif Davis CA 95616

QUANDT, RICHARD EMERIC, economics educator; b. Budapest, Hungary, June 1, 1930; came to U.S., 1949, naturalized, 1954; s. Richard F. and Elisabeth (Toth) Q.; m. Jean H. Briggs, Aug. 6, 1955; 1 son, Stephen. BA, Princeton U., 1952; MA, Harvard U., 1955, PhD, 1957; Dr. Econs. (hon.), Budapest U. Econs. Scis., 1991, Kossuth Lajos U., Hungary, 1994, Gödöllö Agrl. U., 1995, Comenius U., Slovakia, 1996; DrLaws (hon.), Queens U., Can., 1996. Mem. faculty Princeton U., 1956-95, prof. econs., 1964-95, prof. emeritus, sr. rsch. economist, 1995—, Hughes-Rogers prof. econs., 1976-95; prof. emeritus, 1995—; chmn. dept. Princeton U., 1968-71, 85-88; dir. Fin. Rsch. Ctr., 1982-95; rsch. prof. Ford Found., 1967-68; prof. emeritus, sr. rsch. economist Princeton U., 1995—; cons. Alderson Assocs., 1959-61; sr. cons. Mathematica, Inc., 1961-67; cons. Internat. Air Transport Assn., 1974-75, N.Y. Stock Exch., 1976-77, N.Y. State Dept. Edn., 1978; adviser Am.-Hungarian Found., 1977-78; editorial advisor Holt, Rinehart & Winston, 1968-72; fin. adviser Inst. for Rsch. in History, 1986; sr. advisor Andrew W. Mellon Found., 1989—; mem. adv. coun. Budapest U. Econ. Scis., 1992-93; vis. prof. Birkbeck Coll., 1981, U. Leicester, 1989-92; mem. Census Adv. Com., 1983-86; mem. adv. com. Coll. Fin. and Acctg., Budapest, 1993-94. Author: (with J. M. Henderson) Microeconomic Theory: A Mathematical Approach, 1958, 2d edit., 1971, 3d edit., 1980, (with W.L. Thorp) The New Inflation, 1959, (with B.G. Malkiel) Strategies and Rational Decisions in the Securities Option Market, 1969; editor: The Demand for Travel: Theory and Measurement, 1970; (with S.M. Goldfeld) Nonlinear Methods in Econometrics, 1972, Studies in Nonlinear Estimation, 1976; (with P. Asch) Racetrack Betting: The Professor's Guide to Strategies, 1986, (with M. Peston) Prices, Competition and Equilibrium, 1986, The Econometrics of Disequilibrium, 1988, (with H.S. Rosen) The Conflict Between Equilibrium and Disequilibrium Theories, 1988; also numerous articles; editorial bd.: Applied Econs., Econs. of Planning, Rev. Econ. and Stats., 1980-91; assoc. editor: Econometrica, 1976-80, Jour. Am. Statis. Assn, 1974-80, Bell Jour. Econs., Jour. of Comparative Econs., 1988-91, Empirica, 1988-93. Trustee Corvina Found., 1992—. Recipient merit citation Jagiellonian U., Poland, 1991, gold medal Eötvös Lóránd U., Budapest, 1991, Order of Merit, Govt. of Republic of Hungary; Guggenheim fellow, 1958-59; McCosh fellow, 1964; NSF sr. postdoctoral fellow, 1971-72. Fellow Am. Statis. Assn., Econometric Soc. (mem. coun. 1985-88), Am. Acad. Arts and Scis.; mem. Am. Econ. Assn., Am. Philos. Soc., Hungarian Librs. Assn. (hon.). Home: 162 Springdale Rd Princeton NJ 08540-4948 Office: Princeton U Fin Rsch Ctr Dept Econs Princeton NJ 08544

QUANDT, WILLIAM BAUER, political scientist; b. Los Angeles, Nov. 23, 1941; s. William Carl and Dorothy Elaine (Bauer) Q.; m. Anna Spitzer, June 21, 1964 (div. 1980); m. Helena Cobban, Apr. 21, 1984; 1 child, Lorna. B.A., Stanford U., 1963; Ph.D., MIT, 1968. Researcher Rand Corp., Santa Monica, Calif., 1968-72; staff mem. Nat. Security Council, Washington, 1972-74, sr. staff mem., 1977-79; assoc. prof. U. Pa., Phila., 1974-76; sr. fellow Brookings Instn., Washington, 1979-94; prof. govt. and fgn. affairs U. Va., Charlottesville, 1994—; sr. assoc., Cambridge Energy Research Assocs., Mass., 1983—. Author: Revolution and Political Leadership: Algeria, 1954-68, The Politics of Palestinian Nationalism, 1973, Decade of Decisions, 1977, Saudi Arabia in the 1980's, 1981, Camp David: Peacemaking and Politics, 1986, The United States and Egypt, 1990, Peace Process, 1993. Social Scis. Research Council fellow, 1966; Council Fgn. Relations fellow, 1972; NDEA fellow, 1963. Mem. Council Fgn. Relations, Middle East Inst., Middle East Studies Assn. (pres. 1987-88). Avocations: tennis; travel; photography. Home: 2318 44th St NW Washington DC 20007-1101 Office: U Va Dept Govt and Fgn Affairs Cabell Hall 255 Charlottesville VA 22901

QUANN, JOAN LOUISE, English language educator, real estate broker; b. Phila., Oct. 14, 1935; d. John Joseph and Pauline Cecelia (Karpink) Q. Diploma, U. Paris, 1963; BA in French, U. Pa., 1976; grad., Temple U. Real Estate Inst., 1988; MEd, Temple U, 1994. Lic. real estate broker. Exec. sec. to chief fgn. corr. Newsweek, Inc., Paris, 1964-70; internat. editorial asst. Newsweek, Inc., N.Y.C., 1971-73; exec. sec., adminstrv. asst. Richard I. Rubin & Co., Inc., Phila., 1977-91; tchr. French and English to speakers of other langs. The Sch. Dist. of Phila., Bd. Edn., 1991—. Judge of elections City of Phila., 1977-81. Mem. AAUW (2d v.p. membership 1985-87), bd. dirs., corr. sec. 1987-91, fin. com. 1993), Alliance Francaise, La Societe Francophone Arts et Loisirs (bd. dirs. 1988—), Pa. Acad. Fine Arts, MLA of Phila. and Vicinity, ACTFL. Republican. Roman Catholic. Avocations: art history, reading, swimming, travel. Office: Sch Dist of Phila Bd Edn 21st St S Of The Pky S Philadelphia PA 19103

QUANT, HAROLD EDWARD, financial services company executive, rancher; b. Aug. 21, 1948; s. Harold Atwell and Dorothy Ann Quant; m. Michelle Bumpers, June 27, 1982; children: Andrew, Angela, Emily. BSBA, San Jose State U., 1976. Account exec. Dun & Bradstreet, San Jose, Calif., 1970-81; pres. Telecredit Collection Svcs., Inc., L.A., 1981-85; v.p. FCA, Arlington, Tex., 1986-90; pres., CEO Creditwatch, Inc., Arlington, 1990—, chmn. bd. dirs. Sgt. USMC, 1965-70, Vietnam. Decorated Bronze Star, Purple Heart. Mem. City Club. Republican. Mem. United Ch. of God. Avocation: horses. Office: Creditwatch Inc 1200 E Copeland Rd Ste 400 Arlington TX 76011-4938

QUARLES, CARROLL ADAIR, JR., physicist, educator; b. Abilene, Tex., Nov. 24, 1938; s. Carroll Adair and Marguerite Marie (Vollmers) Q.; m. Sonja Gale Bandy, May 14, 1971; children: Jennifer Anne, John Patrick. BA, Tex. Christian U., 1960; PhD, Princeton U., 1964. Rsch. physicist Brookhaven Nat. Lab., Upton, N.Y., 1964-67; mem. faculty Tex. Christian U., Ft.Worth, 1967—; assoc. prof. physics Tex. Christian U., Ft. Worth, 1970-76; prof. Tex. Christian U., Ft.Worth, 1976—; W.A. Moncrief Jr. prof. physics Tex. Christian U., 1986—; chmn. dept. physics Tex. Christian U., Ft. Worth, 1978-84, 96—; assoc. dean Coll. Arts and Scis. Tex. Christian U., Ft.Worth, 1974-78. Contbr. articles to profl. jours. Mem. AAAS, Am. Phys. Soc. (sec.-treas. Tex. sect. 1993—), Am. Assn. Physics Tchrs. (pres. Tex. sect. 1984), Sigma Xi, Phi Beta Kappa (pres. Delta of Tex. chpt. 1982-84), Alpha Chi, Pi Mu Epsilon. Roman Catholic. Office: Tex Christian U Dept Physics Fort Worth TX 76129

QUARLES, JAMES CLIV, law educator; b. Charlottesville, Va., Mar. 18, 1921; s. James Cliv and Lucy (Sinclair) Q.; m. Prudence White, Sept. 1, 1944 (dec.); children: Rebecca Wayne (Mrs. Douglas S. McLeod), James Peyton, Christopher Sinclair.; m. Audrey Clark Keeter, June 10, 1983. B.A., U. Va., 1942, LL.B., 1945. Bar: Va. 1944, Ga. 1955. Law clk. U.S. circuit judge, 1945-47; instr. law Walter F. George Sch. Law, Mercer U., 1947-48, asst. prof., 1948-49, asso. prof., 1949-52, prof., 1952-69, acting dean, 1950-51, 56-58, dean, 1958-69; prof. law U. Fla., Gainesville, 1969-96, prof. emeritus, 1997; Exec. dir. Fla. Law Revision Commn., 1969-71; chmn. research group Ga. Criminal Law Study Com., 1961-66; Mem. Gainesville Human Relations Adv. Bd., 1972-85, chmn., 1975-77, 81-83; bd. dirs. Macon Legal Aid Soc., 1956-60; mediator State Atty.'s Citizen Dispute Resolution Program, 1983—. Editor: Cases and Materials on Florida Constitutional Law, 1977; contbr. articles to legal publs. Mem. ABA; Ga. Bar Assn.; Macon Bar Assn.; Mem. Am. Law Inst., State U. System Law Faculty Assn. (pres. 1975—), Order Coif, Raven Soc., Pi Delta Epsilon. Democrat. Presbyn. Home: 9519 NW 27th Pl Gainesville FL 32606-5179

QUARLES, JAMES LINWOOD, III, lawyer; b. Huntington, W.Va., Oct. 12, 1946; s. James Linwood Jr. and Beatrice (Hardwick) Q.; m. Sharon Taft, Dec. 20, 1969; children: Jessica, Matthew. BS cum laude, Denison U., 1968; JD cum laude, Harvard U., 1972. Bar: Mass. 1974, U.S. Dist. Ct. Mass. 1975, U.S. Ct. Appeals (D.C. cir.) 1975, U.S. Ct. Appeals (6th cir.) 1979, U.S. Supreme Ct. 1980, D.C. 1981, U.S. Ct. Appeals (2d cir.) 1981, U.S. Ct. Appeals (1st and 4th cirs.) 1983, Md. 1985. Law clk. to presiding justice U.S. Dist. Ct. Md., Balt., 1972-73; with Watergate Spl. Pros. Force, Washington, 1973-75; from assoc. to sr. ptnr. Hale and Dorr, Boston and Washington, 1975—. Mem. Am. Law Inst. Democrat. Office: Hale & Dorr 1455 Pennsylvania Ave NW Washington DC 20004-1008

QUARLES, PEGGY DELORES, secondary school educator; b. Dalton, Ga., July 14, 1947; d. Henry Lemuel and Mae Bradford (Hester) Q. BA, Trevecca Nazarene Coll., 1969; MEd, U. Ga., 1981; EdS, West Ga. Coll., 1987. English tchr. Darlington County Schs., Lamar, S.C., 1969-78, Murray County Schs., Chatsworth, Ga., 1978—; mem. Shakespeare Inst., NEH, Washington, 1985, Writing Inst., Boulder, Colo., 1988, Italian Renaissance Inst., Del., Ohio and Florence, Italy, 1990, Women in Renaissance Inst., Richmond, Va., 1992. Vol. ARC, 1987—; mem. Dalton Little Theater, 1980—; bd. dirs. Friends of Libr., 1989-92. Named Tchr. of Yr., Murray County Bd. Edn., 1989. Mem. NEA, Nat. Coun. Tchrs. English, Ga. Coun. Tchrs. English (H.S. English Tchr. of Yr. 1994-95), Carpet Capital Running Club (pres. 1980-82, v.p. 1993-94), Lesche Literary Club. Avocations: running, travel, cooking, reading, attending plays.

QUARTARARO, PHIL, recording industry executive. Pres., CEO, CHB Virgin Records Am. Inc. Office: Virgin Records Am Inc 338 N Foothill Rd Beverly Hills CA 90210-3608*

QUARTERMAN, CYNTHIA LOUISE, lawyer; b. Savannah, Ga., Apr. 6, 1961; d. Rudolph V. and Bernice Q.; m. Pantelis Michalopoulos, Nov. 2, 1993. BS, Northwestern U., 1983; JD, Columbia U., 1987. Atty. Benson & McKay, Kansas City, 1987-88, Steptoe & Johnson, Washington, 1989-93; dep. dir. Minerals Mgmt. Svc., Dept. Interior, Washington, 1993-95, dir., 1995—. Mem. ABA (vice chair programs litigation sect. 1993-94). Home: 1337 21st St NW Washington DC 20036-1503 Office: Dept Interior 1849 C St NW Washington DC 20240-0001

QUARTON, WILLIAM BARLOW, broadcasting company executive; b. Algona, Iowa, Mar. 27, 1903; s. William B. and Ella B. (Reaser) Q.; m. Elnora Bierkamp, Aug. 24, 1935; 1 dau., Diane (Mrs. Waldo F. Geiger). Student, U. Iowa, 1921-22, George Washington U., 1923-25. Joined radio sta. KWCR, Cedar Rapids, Iowa, 1931; comml. mgr. radio sta. WMT, 1936, gen. mgr., 1943; exec. v.p. Am. Broadcasting Stas., Inc., 1959-68, chmn., 1968-70; chmn. bd. KWMT Inc., Ft. Dodge, Iowa, 1968-88, Cable Communications Iowa, Inc., 1971-83; pres. WMT-TV, Inc., 1959-68; chmn. adv. bd. CBS-TV Affiliates, 1960; Mem. bd. Iowa Ednl. Broadcasting Network, 1967-77; bd. govs. Pub. Broadcasting Service, 1973-78. Trustee Coe Coll., 1946-78; trustee, mem. exec. com. Herbert Hoover Presdl. Library; bd. regents State Iowa, 1965-71. Mem. Cedar Rapids C. of C. (pres. 1944), Nat. Assn. Broadcasters (chmn. TV bd. 1962-63, chmn. joint bd. 1963-64). Clubs: Ft. Lauderdale Country (Fla.), Coral Ridge Yacht (Ft. Lauderdale); Cedar Rapids Country. Lodge: Rotary. Home: 134 Kyrie SE Cedar Rapids IA 52403-1712 Office: 1810 I E Tower Cedar Rapids IA 52401

QUATE, CALVIN FORREST, engineering educator; b. Baker, Nev., Dec. 7, 1923; s. Graham Shepard and Margie (Lake) Q.; m. Dorothy Marshall, June 28, 1945 (div. 1985); children: Robin, Claudia, Holly, Rhodalee; m. Arnice Streit, Jan., 1987. B.S. in Elec. Engring, U. Utah, 1944; Ph.D., Stanford U., 1950. Mem. tech. staff Bell Telephone Labs., Murray Hill, N.J., 1949-58; dir. research Sandia Corp., Albuquerque, 1959-60, v.p. research, 1960-61; prof. dept. applied physics and elec. engring. Stanford (Calif.) U., 1961-95, chmn. applied physics, 1969-72, 78-81, Leland T. Edwards prof. engring., 1986—, assoc. dean Sch. Humanities and Scis., 1972-74, 82-83, rsch. prof. dept. elec. engring., 1995—; sr. rsch. fellow Xerox Rsch. Ctr., Palo Alto, Calif., 1984-94. Served as lt. (j.g.) USNR, 1944-46. Recipient Rank prize for Opto-electronics, 1982, Pres.'s Nat. medal of Sci. 1992. Fellow IEEE (medal of honor 1988), Am. Acad. Arts and Scis., Acoustical Soc.; mem. NAE, NAS, Am. Phys. Soc., Royal Microscop. Soc. (hon.), Royal Soc. (fgn. mem.), Sigma Xi, Tau Beta Pi. Office: Stanford University E L Ginzton Lab Stanford CA 94305-4085

QUATTRONE-CARROLL, DIANE ROSE, clinical social worker; b. N.Y.C., July 18, 1949; d. Mario Anthony and Filomena (Serpico) Quattrone; m. Rene Eugene Carroll Jr., June 7, 1980; children: Jenna Cristine, Jonathan Rene. BA cum laude, Bklyn. Coll., 1971; MSW, Rutgers U., 1974. Lic. marriage and family counselor, lic. clin. social worker, N.J.; bd. cert. diplomate in clin. social work. Clin. social worker, field instr. Essex County Guidance Ctr., East Orange, N.J., 1974-82; exec. dir. Psychotherapy Info. and Referral Svc., Madison, N.J., 1982-87; pvt. practice Sparta, N.J., 1982—. Nat. Assn. Social Workers. Avocation: travel.

QUAY, THOMAS EMERY, lawyer; b. Cleve., Apr. 3, 1934; s. Harold Emery and Esther Ann (Thomas) Q.; divorced; children: Martha Wyndham, Glynis Cobb, Eliza Emery; m. Winnifred B. Cutler, May 13, 1989. A.B. in Humanities magna cum laude (Univ. scholar), Princeton U., 1956; LL.B. (Univ. scholar), U. Pa., 1963. Bar: Pa. 1964. Assoc. Pepper, Hamilton & Scheetz, Phila., 1963-65; with William H. Rorer, Inc., Ft. Washington, Pa., 1965—; sec., counsel William H. Rorer, Inc., 1974-79, v.p., gen. counsel, sec., 1979-88; v.p. legal planning and adminstrn. Rorer Group, 1988-90; counsel Reed Smith Shaw and McClay, Phila., 1991-93; v.p., gen. counsel Athena Inst., Haverford, Pa., 1993—. Bd. dirs. Main Line YMCA, Ardmore, Pa., 1971-73, chmn. bd., 1972-73; editor 10th Reunion Book Princeton Class of 1956, 1966, 25th Reunion Book, 1981—, class sec., 1966-71, class v.p., 1971-81, pres., 1981-86. Lt. (j.g.) USNR, 1957-60. Recipient Svc. Commendation Main Line YMCA, 1973. Mem. ABA, Pa. Bar Assn., Phila. Bar Assn., Pharm. Mfrs. Assn. (chmn. law sect. 1983), Pa. Biotech. Assn. (chmn. legis. com., mem. exec. com. 1991-93), Phila. Drug Exch. (chmn. legis. com. 1975-78), Cannon Club of Princeton U., Sharswood Law Club of U. Pa., Princeton Club of Phila. Democrat. Presbyterian. Office: 1211 Braefield Rd Chester Springs PA 19425-1912

QUAYLE, JAMES DANFORTH, former vice president United States, entrepreneur; b. Indpls., Feb. 4, 1947; s. James C. and Corinne (Pulliam) Q.; m. Marilyn Tucker, Nov. 18, 1972; children: Tucker Danforth, Benjamin Eugene, Mary Corinne. BS in Polit. Sci., DePauw U., Greencastle, Ind., 1969; JD, Ind. U., 1974. Bar: Ind. 1974. Ct. reporter, pressman Huntington (Ind.) Herald-Press, 1965-69, assoc. pub., gen. mgr., 1974-76; with consumer protection divn. Office Atty. Gen., State of Ind., 1970-71; adminstrv. asst. to gov. State of Ind., 1971-73; dir. Ind. Inheritance Tax Div., 1973-74; tchr. bus. law Huntington Coll., 1975; mem. 95th-96th Congresses from 4th Dist. Ind.; U.S. Senator from Ind., 1981-89, V.P. of U.S., 1989-93; author, speaker, corp. bds.; disting. vis. prof. Am. Grad. Sch. Internat. Mgmt., 1997. Author: Standing Firm, 1994, The American Family, 1996. Chmn. Campaign Am., 1995—. Capt. Ind. Army N.G., 1970-76. Mem. Huntington Bar Assn., Hoosier State Press Assn., Huntington C. of C. Club: Rotary. Office: 6263 N Scottsdale Rd Ste 292 Scottsdale AZ 85250-5402

QUAYLE, MARILYN TUCKER, lawyer, wife of former vice president of United States; b. 1949; d. Warren and Mary Alice Tucker; m. J. Danforth Quayle, Nov. 18, 1972; children: Tucker, Benjamin, Corinne. BA in Polit. Sci., Purdue U., 1971; JD, Ind. U., 1974. Pvt. practice atty. Huntington, Ind., 1974-77; ptnr. Krieg, DeVault, Alexander & Capehart, Indpls., 1993—. Author: (with Nancy T. Northcott) Embrace the Serpent, 1992, The Campaign, 1996. Office: Krieg DeVault Alexander & Capehart 1 Indiana Sq Ste 2800 Indianapolis IN 46204-2017 Office: Champion Amer Arizona 6263 N Scottsdale Rd Ste 292 Scottsdale AZ 85250-5402*

QUAYTMAN, HARVEY, painter; b. Far Rockaway, N.Y., 1937. Student, Syracuse U., 1955-57; BFA, Tufts U., 1959, Sch. of Mus. of Fine Arts, Boston, 1959; grad. cert., Tufts U., 1959. One-man shows include AIA Gallery, London, 1962, Ward-Nasse Gallery, Boston, 1964, Royal Marks Gallery, N.Y., 1966, Contemporary Arts Mus., Houston, 1967, 73, Paula Cooper Art Gallery, 1969, 71, Onnasch Galerie, Cologne, Germany, 1971, Galerie Ostergren, Malmo, Sweden, 1973, Henri 2, Washington, 1973, Cunningham Ward Gallery, 1974, David McKee Gallery, N.Y., 1975, 77, 78, 80, 82, 84, 86, 87, 91, 93, 94, 96, Nina Nielsen Gallery, Boston, 1976, 78, 80, 83, 86, 89, 93, 94, 95, Galerie Arnesen, Copenhagen, Galerie Nordenhake, Stockholm, 1982, 86, 87, 90, 96, Galerie Engstrom, Stockholm, 1982, Storrer Gallery, Zurich, 1983, Galleria Katarina, Helsinki, Finland, 1984, Dolan/Maxwell Gallery, Phila., 1987, Hoffman/Borman Gallery, L.A., 1988, Persons & Lindell Gallery, Helsinki, 1990, Gilbert Brownstone Gallery, Paris, 1990, Tony Oliver Gallery, Melbourne, Australia, 1990, Art Gallery New South Wales, Sydney, Australia, 1991, Haines Gallery, San Francisco, 1994, 95, Room NYC, 1995, Henie-Onstad Art Ctr., Oslo, 1996, Riis Gallery, Oslo, 1996, Art Soc., Trondheim, Norway, 1996; group exhbns. include Paula Cooper Gallery, 1968, 69, 70, 71, 73, The Jewish Mus., N.Y.C., 1969, Akron Art Inst., 1969, Art Inst. Chgo., 1972, Poindexter Gallery, N.Y.C., 1973, Phyllis Kind Gallery, N.Y.C., 1973, Power Gallery Contemporary Art, Sydney, 1973, Balt. Mus. Art, 1974, Albright-Knox Art Gallery, Buffalo, 1974, Inst. Contemporary Art, Boston, 1974, High Mus. Art, Atlanta, 1974, 76, PSI, Queens, N.Y., 1977, Mus. Modern Art, N.Y.C., 1978, 87-88, Nina Nielsen Gallery, Boston, 1979, 84, 90, Gallerie Schlegl, Zurich, 1979, Grand Palais, Paris, 1980, Axiom Gallery, Melbourne, 1981, Israel Mus., Jerusalem, 1982, Weatherspoon Art Gallery, Greensboro, N.C., 1982, Jersey City Mus., 1983, Galerie Norballe, Copenhagen, 1983, Harvard U., 1983, Hokkaido (Japan) Mus. Modern Art, 1984, Galerie Grafiart, Turku, Finland, 1984, Hill Gallery, Birmingham, Mich., 1985, 94, Jay Gorney Modern Art, N.Y.C., 1985, Pamela Auchincloss Gallery, Santa Barbara, Calif., 1986, Asher/Faure Gallery, L.A., 1987, Corcoran Bienvale, Washington, 1987, Ateneum, Helsinki, Finland, 1987, Dart Gallery, Chgo., 1988, Germans Van Eck Gallery, N.Y.C., 1989, Ljubjana Bienale 18, Yugoslavia, 1989, Tony Oliver Gallery, 1992, Rose Art Mus., Waltham, Mass., Ark. Art Ctr., Little Rock, Galerie Denis Cade, N.Y., 1994, Tel Aviv Mus. Art, 1994, Henie-Onstaad Ctr., Oslo, 1994, The Painting Ctr., N.Y., 1994, Bill Maynes Contemporary Art, N.Y., 1994, Haines Gallery, San Francisco, 1994, Stephen Wirtz Gallery, 1995; public collections include Mus. Modern Art, N.Y.C., Tate Gallery, London, Whitney Mus. Am. Art, N.Y.C., Corcoran Gallery Art, Washington, Mus. Fine Arts, Boston, Henie-Onstad Mus., Oslo, Israel Mus., Jerusalem, Kuntsthalle Malmo, Sweden, Mus. Contemporary Art, Helsinki, Allen Meml. Art Mus., Oberlin, Ohio, Del. Art Mus., Wilmington, Denver Mus. Art, Fogg Art Mus., Cambridge, Mass., High Art Mus., Atlanta, Houston Mus. Fine Arts, Lannan Mus., L.A., The Lousiana Mus., Humlebaeck, Denmark, Newberger Mus., Purchase, N.Y., Nat. Gallery Art, Canberra, Australia, Nat. Gallery Art, Wellington, New Zealand, Pasadena (Calif.) Art Mus., Pori Mus., Finland, Rose Art Mus., Waltham, Mass., Tel Aviv Mus., Va. Mus. Fine Arts, Richmond, Worcester (Mass.) Mus. Art., Henie-Onstad Art Ctr., Oslo, Queensland Art Gallery, Australia, Cleve. Ctr. for Contemporary Art, The Phillips Collection, Washington.., Bill Maynes Contemporary Art, N.Y., Haines Gallery, San Francisco, Stephen Wirtz Gallery, Phillips Collection, Washington D.C. Grantee: CAPS, 1972, 75, Elizabeth Found. for the Arts, 1994; Guggenheim fellow, 1979, 85, Artist's fellow NEA, 1983. Mem. NAD. Avocation: early 20th century model airplane building. Home: 119 W 71st St New York NY 10023

QUEBE, JERRY LEE, architect; b. Indpls., Nov. 7, 1942; s. Charlie Christopher and Katheryn Rosella (Hankins) Q.; m. Mary Lee Darby (div.); children: Chad, Tara; m. Julie Ann Gordon (div.); 1 child, Dana Ann; m. Lisbeth Jane Gray, Mar. 16, 1986. BArch, Iowa State U., 1965. Registered architect, Ill., Calif. Mem. staff Hansen Lind Meyer, Iowa City, 1965-70, assoc., 1970-74, prin., 1975-77; prin., v.p. Hansen Lind Meyer, Chgo., 1977-86; exec. v.p. VVKR, Inc., Alexandria, Va., 1986-93; prin., sr. v.p. Perkins & Will, Chgo., 1994-96, also bd. dirs.; sr. v.p. RTKL Assocs. Inc., Chgo., 1996—; chmn. Cedar Rapids/Iowa City Architects Council, 1974. Author: Drafting Practices Manual, 1978; contbr. articles to profl. jours. Pres. bd. dirs. Mental Health Assn. of Greater Chgo., 1990-95. Fellow AIA; mem. Am. Hosp. Assn., Chgo. Health Exec. Forum, Forum for Health Care Planning (bd. dirs. 1992—). Avocations: photography, scuba diving, sports car racing. Home: 1908 N Sedgwick St Chicago IL 60614-5410 Office: RTKL Assocs Inc 515 N State St Ste 2640 Chicago IL 60610-4361

QUEBEDEAUX, BRUNO, horticulture and plant physiology educator; b. Arnandville, La., June 8, 1941; s. Bruno Sr. and Iola (Guidry) Q.; m. Maureen Fahey, Aug. 13, 1966; children: Mark E., Annette M., Michael J., Adele M. BS, La. State U., 1962, MS, 1963; PhD, Cornell U., 1968. Horticulturist Tex. A&M U., College Station, 1963-65; rsch. scientist E.I. du Pont de Nemours & Co., Wilmington, Del., 1968-80; team leader/COP U.S. AID Contract, Mauritania, 1980-83; chmn. dept. horticulture U. Md., College Park, 1983-90, prof., 1983—; sci. advisor USDA Plant Genome Rsch. Program, Washington, 1989-96. Assoc. editor Crop Sci. Soc. Am., Madison, Wis., 1979-82; editor: Horticulture and Human Health, 1988; author: (publ.) Oxygen: New Factor Controlling Reproductive Growth, 1973. Bd. dirs. League of Internat. Food Edn., Washington, 1987-90; sch. bd. chmn. Internat. Sch. Nauakchott, Mauritania, 1980-82; asst. scout master Boy Scouts Am., Wilmington, 1978-80; bd. dirs. Chapelcroft Civic Assn., Wilmington, 1978-80, v.p., 1975-77. Recipient Merit award USDA/ARS Nat. Resources, 1989. Fellow Am. Soc. Hort. Sci. (v.p. internat. merit 1988-89, L. Ware award 1962); mem. Am. Soc. Plant Physiology (pres. 1989-90, pres. Washington sect. 1990-91), Am. Soc. Agronomy (assoc. editor 1979-82), N.Y. Acad. Sci., Alpha Zeta. Achievements include patents for Method of Increasing Sugar Content in Crops, for Carbomoyl Phosphonate as Plant Growth Regulators, for Ureidotriazoles as Cytokinins and Yield Increasing Agents for Crop Plants, for Ureidotriazoles as Cytokinins and Plant Antisenescence Agents, for Selected Amidoxy Compounds as Flower Preservatives; research on oxygen regulation of plant growth. Home: 2417 Laurelwood Ter Silver Spring MD 20905-6419 Office: U Md/Dept Natural Resource Scis and Landscape Arch College Park MD 20742-5611

QUEEN, EVELYN E. CRAWFORD, judge, law educator; b. Albany, N.Y., Apr. 6, 1945; d. Iris (Jackson) Crawford; m. Charles A. Queen, Mar. 6, 1971; children: Angelia, George. BS, Howard U., 1968, JD, 1975. Bar: N.Y. 1976, D.C. 1977, U.S. Ct. Appeals (D.C. cir.) 1977, U.S. Dist. Ct. (D.C. dist.) 1978, U.S. Supreme Ct. 1980. Park ranger Nat. Park Svc., Washington, 1968-69; pers. specialist NIH, Bethesda, Md., 1969-75; staff atty. Met. Life Ins. Co., N.Y.C., 1975-76; atty. advisor Maritime Adminstrn.-U.S., Washington, 1976-78; asst. U.S. atty.-D.C. Justice Dept., Washington, 1978-81; hearing commr. D.C. Superior Ct., Washington, 1981-86, judge, 1986—; adj. law prof. Howard U., 1988, D.C. Sch. Law, 1993, 94. Recipient spl. achievement awards HEW, 1975, certs. of appreciation and placques Dept. Justice, 1981, Trefoil award Hudson Valley coun. Girl Scouts U.S.A., 1988. Mem. ABA, Nat. Bar Assn., Nat. Assn. Women Judges, Washington Bar Assn. Office: DC Superior Ct 500 Indiana Ave NW Washington DC 20001-2131

QUEEN, SANDY (SANDRA JANE QUEEN), psychologist, trainer, small business owner; b. Washington, Jan. 25, 1946; d. Ralph Edward and Nettie Mae (Peeler) Bort; m. Roy Queen (div. 1973); children: David Brice, Lara Renee, Wendy Joy. BS in Psychology summa cum laude, Towson State U., 1975. Mem. staff social svc. dept. St. Joseph Hosp., Towson, Md., 1973-76; outreach dir. St. Joseph Hosp., Towson, 1980-82; legal rsch. aide, office mgr. Ellin and Assocs., Balt., 1976-77; mkt. mgr. east coast Nat. Med. Cons., Kansas City, Mo., 1977-80; owner, dir. Lifeworks, Columbia, Md., 1982—; wellness coord. St. Anthony Sch., Balt., 1975—, Goucher Coll., 1981-87, Nat. Wellness Conf., Stevens Point, Wis., 1982—, Nat. Humor Conf., 1996; adv. coun. Gov.'s Coun. on Physical Fitness, Balt. 1990—; cons.Ministry of Sport and Recreation, Australia, 1991—, Singpore Kidney Found. Author: Wellness for Children, 1982, Wellness for Youth, 1992, vol. II, 1993; (curriculi) Well and Wonderful, 1982, Child Abuse Resistance, 1985. Chmn. edn. com. Nat. Cancer Soc., Towson, 1981-83, pub. info. com. Am. Heart Assn., Balt., 1982-83; race dir. Am. Heart Assn., Balt., 1982-84; commr. Gov's Coun. on Physical Fitness, Balt., 1984-90; mem. Md. Wellness Com., Balt., 1991—; owner Lifeline Publs., 1993. Recipient Spl. Svc. award, Jaycees of Md., 1982, Am. Heart Assn., 1983. Democrat. Baptist. Avocation: marathon running (6). Office: Lifeworks PO Box 2668 Columbia MD 21045-1668

QUEENAN, JOHN THOMAS, obstetrician, gynecologist, educator; b. Aurora, Ill., June 4, 1933; s. John William and Alice Margaret (Thomas) Q.; m. Carrie Ethel Neher, June 15, 1957; children: John Thomas Jr., Carrie Lynne. BS cum laude, U. Notre Dame, 1954; MD, Cornell U., 1958. Diplomate Am. Bd. Ob-Gyn., Am. Bd. Maternal-Fetal Medicine. Intern, Bellevue Hosp., N.Y.C., 1958-59; resident N.Y. Hosp., 1959-62; instr. Cornell U., 1962-65, clin. asst. prof. ob-gyn, 1965-70, assoc. prof., 1970-72; prof. ob-gyn, chmn. dept. ob-gyn U. Louisville, 1972-80; chief ob-gyn. Norton-Children's Hosps., Louisville Gen. Hosp., 1972-82; prof., chmn. dept. ob-gyn Georgetown U., 1980—, obstetrician and gynecologist-in-chief Georgetown U. Hosp., 1980—; spl. adv. ob-gyn devices panel FDA, 1978—. Bd. dirs. ARC, Greenwich, Conn., 1970-72. Fellow Am. Gynecol. and Obstet. Soc., Royal Coll. Ob-Gyn. (ad eundum); mem. Am. Coll. Obstetricians and Gynecologists, ACS, Am. Fertility Soc., Nat. Perinatal Assn. (pres. 1976-78), So. Perinatal Assn. (pres. 1975), Royal Soc. Medicine, Round Hill Club (Greenwich), Cosmos Club (Washington), Chevy Chase Club (Md.), Edgartown Yacht Club (Mass.), Alpha Omega Alpha. Author: Modern Management of the Rh Problem, 1977; Management of High Risk Pregnancy, 1980, 2d edit., 1985, 3d edit., 94; (with Carrie N. Queenan) A New Life, 1980, 2d edit., 1986, (with Kimberly K. Leslie) Preconceptions: Preparation for Pregnancy, 1989; editor: (with John C. Hobbins) Protocols for High Risk Pregnancies, 1982, 3d edit., 1995; editor-in-chief Contemporary Ob-Gyn, 1973—. Home: 3257 N St NW Washington DC 20007-2845 Office: Georgetown U Hosp 3800 Reservoir Rd NW Washington DC 20007-2113

QUEENAN, JOSEPH MARTIN, JR., writer, magazine editor; b. Phila., Nov. 3, 1950; s. Joseph M. and Agnes Catherine (McNulty) Q.; m. Francesca Jane Spinner, Jan. 7, 1977; children: Bridget Noelle, Gordon Pasha. B.A., St. Joseph's U., 1972. Editor in chief Uncle Sam Mag., N.Y.C., 1981-82; mng. editor Moneysworth, Am. Bus., N.Y.C., 1982-83; editor in chief Am. Bus., Moneysworth, Better Living, N.Y.C., 1983-86; staffwriter Barron's, 1987-89; sr. editor Forbes Mag., N.Y.C., 1989; freelance writer, 1989—. Author: Imperial Caddy, 1992, If You're Talking to Me Your Career Must Be in Trouble, 1994, The Unkindest Cut, 1996; dir. (film) 12 Steps to Death, 1995. Democrat. Roman Catholic.

QUEEN LATIFA See OWENS, DANA

QUEHL, GARY HOWARD, association executive, consultant; b. Green Bay, Wis., Mar. 25, 1938; s. Howard and Virginia Babcock (Dunning) Q.; children: Scott Boyer, Catherine Mary. BA, Carroll Coll., 1960; MS, Ind. U., 1962, EdD, 1965; LHD (hon.), Buena Vista Coll., 1977, Davis and Elkins Coll., 1979; EdD (hon.), Columbia Coll., S.C., 1987. Asst. dean students Wis. State U., 1962; asst. dean coll. Wittenberg U., 1965-76; v.p., dean coll. Lindenwood Colls., St. Charles, Mo., 1967-70; exec. dir. Coll. Center of the Finger Lakes, Corning, N.Y., 1970-74; pres. Council of Ind. Colls., Washington, 1974-86, Council for Advancement and Support of Edn., Washington, 1986-90, Quehl Assocs., Quehl Group, Lafayette, Calif., 1990—; cons. in field, 1990—. Editor, author books in field. Mem. secretariat Nat. Center for Higher Edn.; bd. dirs. Carroll Coll., Muskingum Coll., Elmira Coll., Nat. Assn. Ind. Colls. and Univs., ind. sector, Cornell Coll. Mem. Am. Council Edn., Am. Conf. Acad. Deans, Nat. Panel for Women in Higher Edn., North Central Assn. Acad. Deans (past pres.). Mem. United Ch. Christ.

QUELER, EVE, conductor; b. N.Y.C.. Student, Mannes Coll. Music, CCNY. Music dir. Opera Orchestra of N.Y. Music staff N.Y.C. Opera, 1958-70; assoc. condr. Ft. Wayne (Ind.) Philharm., 1970-71; founder, music dir. Opera Orch., N.Y., 1968; condr. Lake George Opera Festival, Glen Falls, N.Y., 1971-72, Oberlin (Ohio) Music Festival, 1972, Romantic Festival, Indpls., 1972, Mostly Mozart Festival, Lincoln Center, 1972, New Philharmonia, London, 1974, Teatro Liceu, Barcelona, 1974, 77, San Antonio Symphony, 1975; guest condr. Paris Radio Orch., 1972, P.R. Symphony Orch., 1975, 77, Mich. Chamber Orch., 1975, Phila. Orch., 1976, Montreal Symphony, 1977, Cleve. Orch., 1977 (Recipient Martha Baird Rockefeller Fund for Music award 1968, named Musician of Month Mus. Am. Mag. 1972), N.Y.C. Opera, 1978, Opera Las Palmas, 1978, Opera de Nice, 1979, Nat. Theatre of Prague, 1980, Opera Caracas, Venezuela, 1981, San Diego Opera, 1984, Australian Opera, Sydney, 1985, Kirov Opera, St, Petersburg, Russia, 1993, Hamburg Opera, Germany, 1994, Pretoria, South Africa, 1995, Hamilton, Ont., 1995; Opei Bonn, 1994, 95, 96; recording CBS Masterworks, 1974, 76, Hungaroton Records, 1982-85. Office: care Alix Barthelmes Manager Opera Orchestra NY 239 W 72nd St Frnt 2R New York NY 10023-2734

QUELLE, FREDERICK WILLIAM, JR., physicist; b. Chgo., Sept. 4, 1934; s. Fred William and Viola Mildred (Miller) Q.; m. Claudia Jean Suba, June 18, 1961 (div. 1979); children: Frederick William, Goeffrey William. B.S., Ill. Inst. Tech., 1955; M.A., Harvard U., 1957, Ph.D., 1964. Staff mem. Lincoln Labs., Lexington, Mass., 1955-61; mem. solid state and molecular theory group M.I.T., Cambridge, 1958-63; physicist Office Naval Research, Boston, 1961—; pres. Tech. Engring. Devel. Co., Cohasset, Mass., 1978—; head ONR laser team, 1968-78, SHAD Space Navigation Team, 1979—; Navy mem. Adv. Group on Electronic Devices, 1975-80; mem. Exploratory Research and Devel. Com., 1980-89. Contbr. articles in field to profl. jours. Gen. Communication Co. fellow Harvard U., 1955. Mem. Am. Phys. Soc., Sigma Xi, Sigma Pi Sigma. Patentee in field. Home: 120 Nichols Rd Cohasset MA 02025-1146 Office: 495 Summer St Boston MA 02210-2109 *The name of the game is to cover as much unplowed ground and tread on as much snow where no man has ever walked as one can in his lifetime.*

QUELLER, FRED, lawyer; b. N.Y.C., July 10, 1932; s. Victor and Helen (Cenzer) Q.; m. Stephanie Tarler, Aug. 29, 1965; children: Jessica, Danielle. BA, CCNY, 1954; JD, NYU, 1956. Bar: N.Y. 1956, U.S. Dist. Ct. (so. and ea. dists.) N.Y. 1958, U.S. Supreme Ct. 1960, U.S. Ct. Appeals (2d cir.) 1967, Fla. 1980; cert. diplomate civil trial advocacy Nat. Bd. Trial Advocacy, cert. adv. Am. Bd. Trial Advs. Sole practice, N.Y.C., 1956-70; ptnr. Queller & Fisher, N.Y.C., 1970—, now sr. ptnr.; lectr. N.Y. County Lawyers Assn., Practicing Law Inst., Med. Soc. State of N.Y., N.Y. Women's Bar Assn., Victims for Victims, Council of N.Y. Law Assocs., Bklyn. Coll. Inst. for Retired Profls. and Execs., Nassau Acad. Law, Mt. Sinai Med. Ctr., 1975-91, App. Divsn. of the Supreme Ct. State of N.Y. 2d Judicial Dept., Violent Crimes Compensation bd. of N.J.; The Coll. of Ins., Transamerica Ins. Co., Park Slope Sr. Ctr., Touro Coll. Jacob D. Fuchsberg Sch. of Law; panelist Med. Malpractice Panel of Supreme Ct. State of N.Y., County of N.Y. 1973-91; arbitrator Compulsory Arbitration Service of State of N.Y., 1st Jud. Dept., 1975-91; co-chmn. jud. screening com. of lawyers' com., 1979; adminstrv. sec. ad hoc com. for Preservation of an Elected Judiciary, 1977-80; counsel com. for elected judiciary, 1981-84; mem. coordinating council on lawyer competence of Conf. of Chief Justices, 1983-84. Contbr. articles to profl. jours. Chmn. Big Apple Pothole and Sidewalk Protection Corp., 1982-83, pres. 1984-87. Mem. Am. Soc. Legal and Indsl. Medicine, Assn. Bar City of N.Y., Bronx Bar Assn., Am. Bd. Trial Advs. (lectr., pres. N.Y. chpt. 1988-90, vice-chmn. N.Y. Am. Bd. Trial Advs. Key Person Com. 1995), N.Y. State Bar Assn. (com. on automobile liability 1981-93, com. on products liability ins. 1986-93, torts reparation com. 1983-93), ABA (trial techniques com. 1984), Fla. Bar Assn., Met. Women's Bar Assn. (bd. dirs. 1975-83, lectr. 1975-87, treas. 1978-80, v.p. 1980-81), N.Y. Criminal and Civil Cts. Bar Assn., Bklyn. and Manhattan Trial Counsel Assn., N.Y. County Lawyers Assn., Bklyn. Bar Assn., Judiciary/Trial Lawyers Joint Com. of O.C.A., Trial Lawyers for Pub. Justice, N.Y. State Trial Lawyers Inst. (dean 1988-95), N.Y. State Trial Lawyers Assn. (bd. dirs. 1970—, 86-93, lectr. 1975—, v.p. 1980-83, pres. 1984-86, chmn. products liability com. 1980-81, chmn. brief bank com. 1982-84, chmn. expert bank com. 1982-84, nominating com. 1986-95, Pres.'s award 1986, Disting. Service award 1986), Assn. Trial Lawyers of City N.Y. (bd. dirs. 1975—), Assn. Trial Lawyers Am., Nat. Judicature Soc., Nat. Coalition Victims Attys. and Cons., Nat. Adv. Coun., Nat. Com. for Furtherance Jewish Edn. (bd. dirs. 1980-95, Man of Yr. 1984), Inst. Jewish Humanities (bd. dirs. 1985—, Humanitarian award 1988), Jewish Trial Lawyer's Guild (gov. 1977—), Lawyers Polit. Action Com. (trustee 1984-86), NYU Law Rev. Alumni Assn., Assoc. editor NYU Law Rev., 1955-56. Office: Queller & Fisher 110 Wall St New York NY 10005-3801

QUELLMALZ, HENRY, printing company executive; b. Balt., May 18, 1915; s. Frederick and Edith Margaret (Shaw) Q.; m. Marion Agar Lynch, Aug. 2, 1940; children: Lynn Quellmalz Johnson, Susan Quellmalz Mastan, Jane Quellmalz Carey. . BA with high honors, Princeton U., 1937. Pres. Princeton Advt. Agy., 1936-37; dir. pers. Macy's Men's Store, 1938-40; asst. mgr. Fowlers Dept. Store, Glens Falls, N.Y., 1940-41; pers. dir. U.S. Army Post Exchs., Ft. Meade, Md., 1941-44; with Boyd Printing Co., Albany, N.Y., 1944—, pres., 1952-84, chmn. bd., 1984—; v.p. Q Corp. U.S.; agt. for WHO publs., 1965—. Campaign chmn. ARC, Albany, 1956, 57; bd. govs. Doane Stuart Sch., Albany, 1977-79, treas. bd., 1977-78; vice chmn. Family Svc. Assn. Am. Salute to Families, 1979—, Nat. UN Day com., 1980-82; mem. adv. bd. Ind. Coll. Fund of N.Y., 1971-91, corp. trustees, 1992—; bd. dirs. Am. Assn. World Health, 1977-82, Combined Health Appeal of Capitol Dist., Inc., 1984, Camelot Home for Boys, 1975; trustee St. Peter's Hosp. Found., Albany, 1982—, asst. sec., 1987-89, chmn. bd. dirs., 1989-91. With AUS, 1943. Recipient Pres.'s award Am. Assn. Mental Deficiency, 1976; 25 Yrs. Svc. award N.Y. State Bar Assn., 1983, 34 Yrs. Svc. Award Am. Sociol. Assn., 1985. Mem. Albany Area C. of C., Printing Industry Am. Assn. East Ctrl. N.Y. (pres. 1958), Ft. Orange Club, Hudson Mohawk Assn. of Colls. and Univs. (Spl. award for svcs. 1995, Sr. Svcs. of Albany 3rd Age Achievement award for Bus. 1996). Democrat. Episcopalian. Home: 1 Park Hill Dr Apt 6 Albany NY 12204-2142 Office: 49 Sheridan Ave Albany NY 12210-2735

QUELLO, JAMES HENRY, government official; b. Laurium, Mich., Apr. 21, 1914; s. Bartholomew and Mary Katherine (Cochis) Q.; m. Mary Elizabeth Butler, Sept. 14, 1937; children: James Michael, Richard Butler. BA, Mich. State U., 1935, D of Humanities (hon.), 1977; D of Pub. Svc. (hon.), No. Mich. U., 1975. V.p., sta. mgr. Goodwill Stas., Inc., Detroit, 1947-72; v.p. Capital Cities Communications Corp., 1968; commr. FCC, Washington, 1974—; communications cons., Detroit, 1972-74; commr.

FCC, Washington, 1974—; commr. Detroit Housing and Urban Renewal Commn., 1951-72. Contbr. articles to mags., newspapers. Bd. dirs. Greater Detroit Hosp. Assn.; trustee Mich. Vet. Trust Fund; mem. Gov.'s Spl. Commn. on Urban Problems, Mich., Gov.'s Spl. Study Com. on Legis. Compensation, Mayor's Com. on Human Relations; bd. dirs. Am. Negro Emancipation Centennial; mem. exec. bd. Boy Scouts Am.; TV-radio chmn. United Found. Lt. col. AUS, 1940-45. Decorated Bronze Star with oak leaf cluster, Croix de Guerre (France); recipient Internat. Pres.'s award Nat. Assn. TV Program Execs., 1985, Silver Satellite award Am. Women in Radio and TV, 1988, 93, Sol Taishoff award Washington Area Broadcasters Assn., 1989, 93, Pub. Svc. award Fed. Comm. Bar Assn., 1993, Disting. Svc. award Media Inst., 1993, Golden Eagle Amb. award Pa. Assn. Broadcasters, 1993, Disting. Alumni award Mich. State U., Club Dir. award Detroit Adcraft Club, 1993, L.I. Coalition for Fair Broadcasting award, 1993, Nat. Disting. Svc. award Nat. Assn. Pub. TV, 1993, Obie award Ohio Ednl. TV Stas., 1993, Gold Eagle Leadership award Wireless Cable Assn. Internat., 1993, Pres. award Alaska Broadcasting Assn., 1994, Chmn. award Nat. Religious Broadcasters, 1994, Ga. Broadcasters award Broadcasters of Am., 1994, 1st Amendment award Radio & TV News Dirs. Found., 1994. Mem. Nat. Assn. Broadcaster (mem. gov. liaison com. 1964-72, Keystone award 1990, Disting. Svc. award 1994, Honor award for protecting the technical integrity of radio and TV 1994, Broadcasting Cable Hall of Fame, 1995, Nat. Radio Hall of Fame 1996), Mich. Assn. Broadcasters (pres. 1958, legis. chmn. 1959-72, dir., Outstanding Mich. Citizen 1989, Pioneer award 1994), Greater Detroit Bd. Commerce, Adcraft (Detroit), Detroit Athletic, Army and Navy Country Club, Nat. Press Club (Washington), Sigma Alpha Epsilon. Clubs: Adcraft (Detroit); Detroit Athletic, Army and Navy Country; Nat. Press (Washington). Office: FCC 1919 M St NW Washington DC 20036-3521

QUENCER, ROBERT MOORE, neuroradiologist, researcher; b. Jersey City, Nov. 14, 1937; s. Arthur Bauer and Isabell (Moore) Q.; m. Christine F. Thomas, Sept. 16, 1972; children: Kevin, Keith. BS, Cornell U., 1959, MS, 1963; MD, SUNY, Syracuse, 1967. Diplomate Am. Bd. Radiology, Nat. Bd. Med. Examiners; cert. of added qualifications in neuroradiology. Intern Jackson Meml. Hosp., Miami, Fla., 1967-68; resident in radiology Columbia U., N.Y.C., 1968-71, fellow in neuroradiology, 1971-72; asst. prof. Downstate Med. Ctr., Bklyn., 1972-76; assoc. prof. U. Miami, 1976-79, prof., 1979-92, chmn., prof., 1992—, chief sect. neuroradiology, 1976-86, dir. divsn. magnetic resonance imaging, 1986-92; vis. prof. U. Tenn. Coll. Medicine, Memphis, 1982, Downstate Med. Ctr. Coll. Medicine, Bklyn., 1992, U. Vt. Coll. Medicine, Burlington, 1983, N.Y. Med. Coll., Valhalla, 1984, U. Va. Sch. Medicine, Charlottesville, 1984, U. Ky. Sch. Medicine, Lexington, 1985, Yale U. Sch. Medicine, New Haven, 1986, Columbia U. Sch. Medicine, N.Y.C., 1986, The Mayo Clinic & Found., Rochester, Minn., 1987, Med. Coll. Va., Richmond, 1988, U. Pa. Sch. Medicine, Phila., 1988, Harvard U. Sch. Medicine/Mass. Gen. Hosp., Boston, 1989, U. Conn., Farmington, 1990, Kumamoto, Japan, 1993, U. Man., Can., 1992, Mich. State U., 1996, Mt. Sinai Med. Ctr., 1997; Phaler lectr. Phila. Roentgen Soc., 1995; dir. programs in dept. radiology U. Miami Sch. Medicine, 1984, 86, Med. Coll. Wis., Tucson, 1990, 92, Kauai, Hawaii, 1991, Whistler, B.C., 1990; guest lectr. at ASEAN Congress of Radiology, Malaysia, 1992, Royal Australia Radiology Soc., Brisbane, 1993, Brazilian Congress Neurology, 1996, N.Y. Roentgen Soc., 1997; adv. cons. NIH, 1987, 90; sci. merit reviewer V.A., 1987; presenter, lectr. in field. Author: Neurosonography, 1988; dep. editor Am. Jour. Neuroradiology, 1984-96, editor-in-chief, 1998— ; assoc. editor for neuroimaging Yearbook of Neurology and Neurosurgery, 1991—; book reviewer Am. Jour. Neuroradiology, 1984—, Paraplegia, 1989—, Radiographics, 1991—, Pediatrics, 1993—; mem. editorial bd. Jour. Clin. Neuro-Ophthalmology, 1980—; contbr. articles to profl. jours. Pres. Am. Soc. Neuroadiology, 1994-95; prin. investigator NIH Grant on imaging/pathology of spinal cord injury. Lt. (j.g.) USN, 1959-61. Fellow Am. Coll. Radiology, Am. Soc. Neuroradiology (pres. 1994-95, program com. 1985-89, 92, editl. com. 1984—, publs. com. 1984—); mem. AMA, Radiol. Soc. N.Am. (program subcom. on neuroradiology 1990-94), Southeastern Neuroradiol. Soc. (founder, pres. 1980-81, examiner for bd. certification in radiology and neuroradiology), Dade County Med. Assn., Soc. Chmn. Acad. Radiology Depts., Fla. Radiol. Soc. (magnetic resonance com. 1991-92), Alpha Omega Alpha. Avocations: golf, travel. Office: U Miami 1150 NW 14th St Miami FL 33136-2137

QUENNELL, NICHOLAS, landscape architect, educator; b. London, Sept. 30, 1935; s. Cecil William and Beatrice Irene Quennell; m. Grace Tankersley, Apr. 30, 1983. AA, Archtl. Assn., London, 1957; MLA, Harvard U., 1969. Registered architect, N.Y., Pa., N.J., Conn., U.K.; registered landscape architect, N.Y., N.J., Conn., Mass., N.C. Architect London County Coun., 1959-61, Jose Luis Sert, Cambridge, Mass., 1961-62, Lawrence Halprin & Assocs., San Francisco, 1962-65, Vollmer Assocs., N.Y.C., 1965-68; prin. Nicholas Quennell Assocs., N.Y.C., 1968-79, Quennell Rothschild Assocs., N.Y.C., 1979—; v.p. The Mcpl. Art Soc. (dir. 1978-85), N.Y.C., 1985-92, dir. The Archtl. League, N.Y.C., 1984-89. Bd. dirs. nat. Assn. for Olmsted Pks., Washington, 1988-90, chmn., 1990-93; mem. Art Commn. of City of N.Y., 1992—, pres., 1993—. Fellow Am. Soc. of Landscape Architects; mem. Century Assn. Office: Quennell Rothschild Assocs 118 W 22nd St New York NY 10011-2416

QUENNEVILLE, KATHLEEN, lawyer; b. Mt. Clemens, Mich., July 31, 1953; d. Marcel J. and Patricia (Armstrong) Q.;. BA, Mich. State U., 1975; JD, Golden Gate U., 1979. Bar: Calif. 1980. Atty. Wells Fargo Bank, San Francisco, 1980-81; staff counsel Calif. State Banking Dept., San Francisco, 1981-83; assoc. Manatt, Phelps, Rothenburg & Tunney, Los Angeles, 1983-84; v.p., assoc. gen. counsel Bank of Calif., San Francisco, 1984-96; gen. counsel The Mechanics Bank, Richmond, Calif., 1996—. Asst treas. AIDS Legal Referral Panel of the San Francisco Bay Area, 1986-92. Mem. Calif. State Bar Assn. (bus. law sect. corp. law depts. com. 1988-90), Calif. Bankers Assn. (chair regulatory compliance com. 1994-96, legal affairs com. 1996—). Office: The Mechanics Bank 3170 Hilltop Mall Rd Richmond CA 94806-1921

QUENON, ROBERT HAGERTY, retired mining consultant and holding company executive; b. Clarksburg, W.Va., Aug. 2, 1928; s. Ernest Leonard and Josephine (Hagerty) Q.; m. Jean Bowling, Aug. 8, 1953; children: Evan, Ann, Richard. B.S. in Mining Engring., W.Va. U., 1951; LL.B., George Washington U., 1964; PhD (hon.), U. Mo., 1979, Blackburn Coll., 1983, W.Va. U., 1988. Mine supt. Consol. Coal Co., Fairmont, W.Va., 1956-61; mgr. deep mines Pittston Co., Dante, Va., 1964-66; gen. mgr. Riverton Coal Co., Crown Hill, W.Va., 1966-67; mgr. ops. coal and shale oil dept. Exxon Co., Houston, 1967; pres. Monterey Coal Co., Houston, 1969-76; sr. v.p. Carter Oil Co., Houston, 1976-77; exec. v.p. Peabody Coal Co., St. Louis, 1977-78; pres., chief exec. officer Peabody Coal Co., 1978-83; pres., chief exec. officer Peabody Holding Co., Inc., St. Louis, 1983-90, chmn., 1990-91; bd. dirs. Newmont Gold Co., Denver, Union Electric Co., St. Louis, Laclede Steel Co., St. Louis; bd. dirs., chmn. Fed. Res. Bank St. Louis, 1993-95, dep. chmn., 1990-92; mem. coal industry adv. bd. Internat. Energy Agy., 1980—, bd. chmn., 1984-90; chmn. Bituminous Coal Operator's Assn., 1980-83, 89-91. Trustee Blackburn Coll., Carlinville, Ill., 1975-83, St. Louis U., 1981-91; pres. St. Louis Art Mus., 1985-88. Served with AUS, 1946-47. Recipient Eavenson award Soc. Mining, Metallurgy, and Exploration, 1994. Mem. Am. Mining Congress (vice-chmn. 1980-91), Nat. Coal Assn. (chmn. bd. 1978-80), U.S. C. of C. (dir. 1982-88). Office: PO Box 11328 Saint Louis MO 63105-0128

QUERY, JOY MARVES NEALE, medical sociology educator; b. Worcestershire, Eng.; came to U.S., 1952; d. Samuel and Dorree (Oakley) Neale; children: Jonathan, Margo, Evan. A.B., Drake U., 1954, M.A., 1955; postgrad., U. Syracuse, 1955-56; Ph.D., U. Ky., 1960. Tchr. secondary schs. Staffordshire, Eng., 1947-52; dep. prin. Smethwich Hall Girls' Sch., Staffordshire, 1948-52; instr. U. Ky., 1956-57, asst. prof., 1960; assoc. prof. sociology Transylvania Coll., Lexington, Ky., 1961-66; assoc. prof. N.D. State U., Fargo, 1966-68; prof. sociology and psychology N.D. State U., 1969-75, also chmn. sociology and psychology depts., 1969-70, chmn. sociology and anthropology dept., 1968-73; prof. div. psychiatry behavioral sci., dept. neurosci. U. N.D. Sch. Medicine, Fargo, 1975-89, prof. emeritus, 1989—; on sabbatical leave Yale U., 1974-75; coord. AIDS Edn. State Program NIMH, 1989-93. Mem. bd. adv. editors Sociological Inquiry jour., 1987-93; contbr. articles and papers to profl. jours. Field dir. Girl Scouts U.S.A., 1953-55; mem. Lexington Civil Rights Commn., 1960-66; bd. dirs. Fargo-Moorhead Family Service Agy., 1967-70; mem. Mayor's Coordinating Council for Youth, Fargo-Moorhead, 1976—; pres. Hospice of Red River Valley, 1986-87 (Svc. award 1987). Named Profl. Woman of Yr. Fargo-Moorhead YWCA, 1981, Disting. Lectr. of Yr., N.D. State U., 1991, Outstanding Educator U. N.D. Sch. Medicine Class of 1992; recipient Burlington No. award, 1987, Alumni award U. Ky., 1988, Disting. Svc. award Gt. Plains Sociol. Assn., 1988; Joy M. Query scholarship at N.D. State U., U. N.D. Coll. Medicine created in her honor, 1987. Fellow Internat. Assn. Social Psychiatry; mem. AAUP, Am. Sociol. Asns., N.D. Mental Health Assn. (pres. Red River Valley chpt., Heritage award 1987), midwest Sociol. Soc. (dir. 1970-73, 75-78, mem. standards, tng. and employment com. 1988-89), Alpha Kappa Delta. Unitarian. Home: 1202 Oak St Fargo ND 58102-2707 Office: U ND Sch Medicine 1919 Elm St Fargo ND 58102-2416

QUESENBERRY, KENNETH HAYS, agronomy educator; b. Springfield, Tenn., Feb. 28, 1947; s. James William and Cora Geneva (Moore) Q.; m. Joyce Ann Kaze, July 28, 1947; children: James Kenneth, Kendra Joyce. BS, Western Ky. U., 1969; PhD U. Ky., 1975. D. F. Jones predoctoral fellow U. Ky., Lexington, 1972-75; asst. prof. U. Fla., Gainesville, 1975-80, assoc. prof. agronomy, 1980-86, prof. agronomy, 1986—; Contbr. articles to profl. jours. Chair So. Pasture and Forage Crop Improvement Conf., 1991. Served with U.S. Army, 1969-71, Vietnam. Fellow Am. Soc. Agronomy, Crop Sci. Soc. Am. (chair divsn. C-8 1993-94) . Democrat. Avocations: sports, antique furniture refinishing. Achievements include rsch. in germplasm enhancement of forages with release of four cultivars of tropical grasses and two clovers and genetic transformation of clovers; specialist trifolium species germplasm. Office: Univ Fla PO Box 110500 Gainesville FL 32611-0500

QUESNEL, GREGORY L., transportation company executive; b. Woodburn, Oreg., May 24, 1948. BA in Finance, U. Oregon; MA in Bus. Adminstrn., U. Portland; grad. Exec. Program in Bus. Adminstrn., Columbia U. Dir. fin. acctg. Consolidated Freightways, Portland, 1975-78, dir. mgmt. and cost acctg., 1978-86; fin. officer CF MotorFreight, Consolidated Freightways, Portland, 1986-89; v.p. acctg. Emery Worldwide, Consolidated Freightways, Scranton, Pa., 1989-91; exec. v.p., CFO CNF Transp. Inc., Palo Alto, Calif., 1991—. Mem. Fin. Exec. Inst., Chief Fin. Execs. (conf. bds. coun., conf. bds. coun. of fin. execs.).

QUEST, JAMES HOWARD, marketing executive; b. Johnstown, Pa., June 21, 1934; s. Norris R.D.O. and Edna Jane (Nichols) Q.; m. Sarah Jo Ames, June 11, 1960 (dec. 1973); m. Leslie Reiman; children: Daniel, Anna, Benjamin. BS in Hotel Adminstrn., Cornell U., 1956. Brand mgr. Procter & Gamble, Cin., 1956-60; v.p. SSC&B Advt., N.Y.C., 1961-64; group product dir. Pfizer Consumer Products, N.Y.C., 1964-67; v.p. Am. Home Products, N.Y.C., 1967-71, RS&L Advt., N.Y.C., 1971-75; sr. v.p., mem. bd. dirs. The Marschalk Co., Advt., N.Y.C., 1975-80; chmn., chief exec. officer Posey & Quest Advt., Greenwich, Conn., 1980-90; exec. v.p. TBWA Advt., N.Y.C., 1990-95; CEO Quest Assoc. LTD., Stamford, Conn., 1995—; spkr. AAAA, N.Y.C., 1985-87, Assn. Nat. Advertisers, 1987-89; guest lectr. Cornell Sch. Hotel Adminstrn., 1985. Author: (with others) Developing New Products, 1980, Executive Chess, 1987. Bd. dirs., exec. com. Children of Alcoholics Found., N.Y.C., 1987-96; mem. Cornell U. Coun.; bd. dirs. Stamford Symphony; v.p. Cornell Class of 1956. With U.S. Army, 1956-58. Mem. Cornell Soc. Hotelmen, Cornell Club (N.Y.C.), Woodway Country Club, Darien, Conn. Avocations: tennis, golf., travel, writing. Home: 14 Alfred Ln Stamford CT 06902-1238 Office: Quest Assocs Ltd PO Box 3005 Stamford CT 06905-0005

QUESTEL, MAE, actress; b. Bronx, N.Y., Sept. 13, 1908; d. Simon and Frieda (Glauberman) Q.; m. Leo Balkin, Dec. 22, 1930 (dec.); children: Robert (dec.), Richard; m. Jack E. Shelby, Nov. 19, 1970. Student in drama, J.G. Geiger, N.Y.C., 1916-24; scholar, Theatre Guild, N.Y.C., 1923, Columbia U., 1949, Theatre Wing, 1951. Appeared in vaudeville at, Palace Theatre, 1930, on RKO theater circuit, 1931-38; radio shows include Betty Boops Frolics, NBC, 1932; cartoon voices Betty Boop, 1931—, Olive Oyl, 1933—, Mr. Bugs Goes to Town, 1934, Little Audrey, 1946; TV cartoon Winky Dink and You, 1956-60, Popeye (as Olive Oyl), 1981; stage appearances include Dr. Social, 1948, A Majority of One, 1959-61, Come Blow Your Horn, 1963, Enter Laughing, 1963, Bajour, 1964, The Warm Peninsula, 1966, Walk Like A Lion, 1969, Barrel Full of Pennies, 1970, Where Have You Been, Billy Boy, 1969, Betty Boop—60 Yrs., N.Y.C., 1990, Betty Boop (Olive Oyl), U. Nebr., Lincoln, 1990; appeared: films A Majority of One, 1961, It's Only Money, 1962, Funny Girl, 1967, Move, 1969, Zelig, 1983, Hot Resorts, 1984, Who Framed Roger Rabbit?, 1988, New York Stories: A Trilogy, 1988-89, Christmas Vacation, 1989; TV spokeswoman for Scott Paper Co. as Aunt Bluebell films, 1971-78; other commls. include Playtex, 1970-72, Romilar, 1970-72, Folger's Coffee, 1970-72, Speidel Watch Bands, 1980, S.O.S, 1981, Parker Bros. video game Popeye, 1983-84; soap opera Somerset, 1976-77, All My Children, 1983; other TV appearances include Good Morning America, 1980, Good Day Show, 1980, Picture Pages, 1981, Entertainment Tonight, Joan Rivers and Her Friends; also numerous recs. including Good Ship Lollipop; (Troupers award for outstanding contbn. to entertainment 1979, Annie award Internat. Animated Film Soc. 1979). Named Living Legend NYU Sch. Social Work, 1979. Mem. Screen Actors Guild, AFTRA, Actors Equity Assn., Nat. Acad. TV Arts and Scis. (award 1978), Hadassah. Clubs: Troupers (award 1963), Variety. Mae Questel Day named by City of Indpls., 1968. Home: 27 E 65th St Apt 7C New York NY 10021-6556 *My mother was a singer and a mimic - took me to the theater when I was about 3 yrs. old - performed in school and for many charities - always wanted to entertain - at seventeen won a "Betty Boop" contest. I have never turned down anything - performed on radio, tv, soap, theater and movies - always acted - because I just love show business.**

QUESTER, GEORGE HERMAN, political science educator; b. Bklyn., July 14, 1936; s. Jacob George and Elizabeth (Mattern) Q.; m. Aline Marie Olson, June 20, 1964; children: Theodore, Amanda. A.B., Columbia U., 1958; M.A., Harvard U., 1964, Ph.D., 1965. Instr., then asst. prof. govt. Harvard U., 1965-70; assoc. prof. govt. Cornell U., 1970-73, prof., 1973-82; prof. polit. sci. U. Md., College Park, 1982—; vis. prof. U.S. Naval Acad., Annapolis, Md., 1991-93. Author: Deterrence Before Hiroshima, 1966, Nuclear Diplomacy, 1970, The Politics of Nuclear Proliferation, 1973, The Continuing Problem of International Relations, 1974, Offense and Defense in the International System, 1977, American Foreign Policy: The Lost Consensus, 1982, The Future of Nuclear Deterrence, 1986, The International Politics of Television, 1990. Served with USAF, 1958-61. Fellow Center Advanced Study Behavioral Scis., 1974-75. Mem. Council Fgn. Relations, Inst. Strategic Studies, Am. Polit. Sci. Assn. Home: 5124 37th St N Arlington VA 22207-1862 Office: Univ Md 2181 Lefrak Hall College Park MD 20742-8200

QUETGLAS, MOLL JUAN, plastic and maxillofacial surgeon; b. Cuidadela, Menorca, Spain, Feb. 11, 1922; s. Honesto Quetglas Montserrat and Catalina Moll Coll; m. Conception Marimon Alvarez; children: Juan, Alfonso, Carlos. Degree, U. Barcelona, Spain, 1945; MD, U. Madrid, 1970. Diplomate Bd. Plastic Surgery, Bd. Maxillofacial Surgery and Plastic and Reconstructive Surgery, Bd. Gen. Surgery and Traumatology. Gen. practice medicine Mahon, Spain, 1945-52; resident in gen. surgery Madrid, 1953-55; head surg. svc. Mil. Hosp., Larache, Morocco, 1955-59, Tenerife, Canary Island, 1960-61; head surg. svc. Social Security, Madrid, 1962-84; head plastic surgery svc. Ctrl. Mils. Hosp., Madrid, 1962-87; prof. U. Madrid, 1978-87; dir. hosps. Social Security, 1968-71; mem. exec. com. I.S.A.P.S., 1975-76; prof. anatomy Med. Sch., Salamanca (Spain) U., 1972; asst. plastic surgery svc. Walter Reed Hosp., Washington, 1969. Author: Brief Handbook of Plastic and Aesthetic Surgery of the Face, 1971; co-author: Treatise of Medical Rehabilitation, 1967, 2d edit., 1970, Iberoamerican Text of Plastic Surgery, 1986, 2d edit., 1994, Art of Aesthetic Plastic Surgery, 1989, Ualoracion de las Secuelas Traumaticas en el Aparato Locomotor, 1995, Rehabilitacion Media-Editorial Masson, 1996; dir., founder Spanish Jour. Plastic Surgery, 1968-76; hon. dir. Jour. Plastic Jour., 1983; editor: Facial Traumatology, 1983; dir. Jour. Ibero-L.Am. Jour. Plastic Surgery, 1975—; contbr. over 100 articles to med. jours. Col. M.C., Spanish Army, 1987. Recipient Ex-Combatiente, Donador de Sangre, Cruz de San Hermenegildo, Placa de San Hermenegildo, Cruz del Merito Militar, Spanish Army Min., medal Complutense U. Madrid. Mem. Internat. Confedn. Plastic Surgery, Spanish Soc. Plastic Surgery (mem. exec. com. 1969-71, pres. 1972-74), Plastic Surgery Soc. Ecuador (hon.), Plastic Surgery Soc. Argentina (hon.), Plastic Surgery Soc. Chile (hon.), Spanish Soc. Traumatology, Assn. Mil. Plastic Surgeons, Assn. Mil. Surgeons, Acad. Surgery Madrid, N.Y. Acad. Scis., Helenic Soc. Plastic Reconstructive Surgery.

QUEVEDO, HECTOR ADOLF, operations research analyst, environmental scientist; b. Juarez, Mex., June 25, 1940; came to U.S., 1973; s. Robert and Margaret (Urias) Quevedo Endlich; m. Gloria Guijarro, June 2, 1971; children: Gloria, Hector. BA, U. Tex., El Paso, 1966; MS in Environ. Scis., U. Okla., 1972, PhD in Environ. Scis., 1977. Part-time instr. maths. U. Tex., El Paso, 1977-80; environ. engr. El Paso Natural Gas Co., 1978-79; systems analyst U.S. Army, White Sands Missile Range, N.Mex., 1980-84, Ft. Bliss, Tex., 1985—. Democrat. Avocations: classical music, reading, outdoor recreation, writing books, playing dominoes. Home: 11148 Voyager Cove St El Paso TX 79936-3007

QUIAT, GERALD M., lawyer; b. Denver, Jan. 9, 1924; s. Ira L. and Esther (Greenblatt) Q.; m. Roberta M. Nicholson, Sept. 26, 1962; children: James M., Audrey R., Melinda A., Daniel P., Ilana L., Leonard E. AA, U. Calif., Berkeley, 1942; AB, LLB, U. Denver, 1948, changed to JD, 1970. Bar: Colo. 1948, Fed. Ct. 1948, U.S. Dist. Ct. Colo. 1948, U.S. Ct. Appeals (10th cir.) 1948, U.S. Surpeme Ct. 1970. Dep. dist. atty. County of Denver, Colo., 1949-52; partner firm Quiat, Seeman & Quiat, Denver, 1952-67, Quiat & Quiat (later changed to Quiat, Bucholtz & Bull, P.C.), 1968; pres. Quiat, Bucholtz & Bull & Laff, P.C. (and predecessors), Denver, 1968-85; pvt. practice Denver, 1985—; bd. dirs., chmn. audit com. Guaranty Bank & Trust Co., Denver; past bd. dirs. and chmn. bd. ROMED, RMD, Inc. Past trustee Holding Co., Rose Med. Ctr., Denver, pres., chmn. bd. dirs., 1976-79; mem. Colo. Civil Rights Com., 1963-71, chmn., 1966-67, 69-70, hearing officer, 1963-71; bd. dirs. Am. Cancer Rsch. Ctr., Denver, chmn. bd., 1991-93; chmn. bd. Am. Med. Ctr., 1993-95; mem. nat. civil rights com., hon. mem. nat. exec. com., hon. nat. commr. Anti-Defamation League, B'nai B'rith, mem. exec. com., chmn. bd. Mountain States region, 1980-82. With inf. U.S. Army, 1942-45. Decorated Combat Infantry Badge, Bronze Star. Mem. ABA, Colo. Bar Assn., Colo. Trial Lawyers Assn. (pres. 1970-71), Am. Legion (comdr. Leyden-Chiles-Wickersham post 1 1955-56, past judge adv. Colo. dept.). Home: 8130 Lt Wm Clark Rd Parker CO 80134 Office: Penthouse Suite 1720 S Bellaire St Denver CO 80222-4304

QUIBAN, ESTELITA CABRERA, controller; b. Manila, Sept. 3, 1938; came to U.S., 1969; d. Apolonio and Regina (Lacasmana) Cabrera; m. Teodoro Quiban Jr., June 20, 1964; children: Erwin James, Theodelinde, Joyce Ann, Rina Francis. Assoc. Bus., Phillipine Coll. Commerce, Manila, 1956; BS in Acctg., Far Ea. U., Manila, 1958. Cost acct. Associated Pharms., Manila, 1959-65; chief acct. Allied Travels, Manila, 1965-69; acct. Allied Outlets, San Francisco, 1969-70, Chalet 21, San Francisco, 1970-75; head acct. Anna Millers Inc., San Francisco, 1976-81, contr., 1981—; v.p. Pacific Outlets Inc., San Francisco, 1985—; corp. sec. Anna Millers Inc., San Francisco, 1989—; trustee Anna Millers Pension Plan, San Francisco, 1990—. Treas. St. Augustine Choralle, 1990-92. Democrat. Roman Catholic. Avocations: reading, travel, camping, singing. Home: 2926 Dublin Dr South San Francisco CA 94080-5522 Office: Anna Millers Inc 86 Dorman Ave San Francisco CA 94124-1807

QUICK, ALBERT THOMAS, law educator, university dean; b. BattleCreek, Mich., June 28, 1939; s. Robert and Vera Quick; m. Brenda Jones; children: Lori, Traci, Becki, Breton, Regan, Leigh. BA, U. Ariz., 1962; MA, Cen. Mich. U., 1964; JD, Wayne State U., 1967; LLM, Tulane U., 1974. Bar: Mich. 1968, Ky. 1987. Asst. prosecutor Calhoun County, Marshall, Mich., 1968-69; assoc. Hatch & Hatch, Marshall, 1969-70; asst. prof. U. Maine, Augusta, 1970-73; prof. law U. Louisville, 1974-87, spl. asst. to univ. provost, 1983-87; dean, prof. law Ohio No. U., Ada, 1987-95; prof. law, dean U. Toledo, Ohio, 1995—. Co-author: Update Federal Rules of Criminal Procedure; contbr. articles to profl. jours. Recipient Medallion of Justice Nat. Bar Assn., 1995. Mem. ABA, Assn. Am. Law Schs. (criminal justice sect.), Ky. State Bar Assn., Mich. State Bar Assn., Willis Soc., Ohio State Bar Assn., Toledo Bar Assn., Rotary, Phi Kappa Phi. Episcopalian. Avocations: racquetball, tennis, art, reading. Office: Univ Toledo Coll Law 2801 W Bancroft St Toledo OH 43606-3328

QUICK, EDWARD RAYMOND, museum director, educator; b. L.A., Mar. 22, 1943; s. Donald Russell Quick and Gertrude Ruth (Albin) Thornbrough; m. Ruth Ann Lessig; children: Jeannette Lee, Russell Raymond. BA, U. Calif., Santa Barbara, 1970, MA, 1977. Adminstr. supr. Civil Service, Santa Ana, Calif., 1971-75; sr. computer operator Santa Barbara Rsch. Ctr., 1975-77; asst. collections curator Santa Barbara Mus. Art, 1977-78; collections mgr. Montgomery (Ala.) Mus. Fine Arts, 1978-80; asst. dir. Joslyn Art Mus., Omaha, 1980-85; dir. Sheldon Swope Art Mus., Terre Haute, Ind., 1985-95, Berman Mus., Anniston, Ala., 1995—; adv. Ind. Arts Commn., Indpls., 1986-91; mem. Arts in Pub. Places Commn., Terre Haute, Ind., 1986-93; pres. Friends Vigo County Pub. Libr., 1988-95, treas., 1990-93. Author: Code of Practice for Couriering Museum Objects, 1985, Gilbert Brown Wilson and Herman Melville's "Moby Dick", 1993, The American West in the Berman Collections, 1997; co-author: Registrars in Record, 1987. Bd. dirs. Vol. Action Ctr., Terre Haute, 1987-90, Terre Haute Cmty. Relief Effort for Environ. and Civic Spirit, 1989. With USAF, 1961-65, Air N.G., 1979-96. Mem. Am. Assn. Mus. (adv. 1994—, mgmt. and long-range planning com. 1994—), Assn. Ind. Mus., Am. Assn. State and Local History, Internat. Coun. Mus., Rotary Internat., Kiwanis Internat., Alpha Gamma Sigma. Republican. Avocation: museum administrative research. Office: Berman Mus 840 Museum Dr PO Box 2245 Anniston AL 36202-6261

QUICK, JERRY RAY, academic administrator; b. Gosport, Ind., July 3, 1939; s. Waldo C. and M. Marguerite (Goss) Q.; m. Elizabeth Ahlemeyer, June 10, 1962; children: Patrick, Andrew. BS, Ind. State U., 1961; MS, Ind. U., 1965. Tchr., coach MSD Washington Twp., Indpls., 1961-63; assoc. dir. housing Ind. State U., Terre Haute, 1963-75; asst. v.p. Ctrl. Mich. U., Mt. Pleasant, 1975-85; assoc. vice chancellor for bus. Vanderbilt U., Nashville, 1985-89; v.p. fin. and adminstrn. U. Ala., Huntsville, 1989—; mem. task force U.S. Dept. Edn., Washington, 1981-84; mem. accreditation teams So. Assn. Colls. and Schs., 1993—. Contbr. articles to profl. jours. and chpts. to books. Bd. dirs. Better Bus. Bur., Nashville, 1988-89; active Mayor's Commn. on Efficiency, Nashville, 1989. Mem. Nat. Assn. Coll. and Univ. Bus. Officers (editl. bd. 1987-92), So. Assn. Coll. and Univ. Bus. Officers, Nat. Assn. Coll. Aux. Svcs., Ala. Assn. Coll. and Univ. Bus. Officers, Assn. Coll. and Univ. Housing Officers (pres. 1979-80), Huntsville C. of C., Huntsville Rotary Club. Avocations: farming, collecting and restoring antiques, travel, microcomputers. Home: 2513 Garth Rd SE Huntsville AL 35801-1422 Office: U Ala Huntsville MDH 131 Huntsville AL 35899

QUICK, LISA R., accountant, scheduler; b. Baytown, Tex., Aug. 14, 1964; d. Bob R. Allen and H. Ruth (Reeder) Allen; m. Terry K. Quick, Oct. 5, 1991. AA in Bus. Adminstrn., Lee Coll., 1985; BBA in Gen. Bus., U. Houston-Clear Lake, 1987, BS in Finance, 1994. Accounts receivable supr. D.E. Harvey Builders, Inc., Houston, 1988-89; document controller Brown & Root, Inc., Houston, 1989-90, cost engr., 1990-94, internal auditor, 1994-95, acct., scheduler, 1996—. Mem. NAFE. Methodist. Avocation: cross stitch. Office: Brown & Root Inc PO Box 3 Houston TX 77001

QUICK, NORMAN, bishop. Bishop of R.I. Ch. of God in Christ, Bklyn. *

QUICK, THOMAS CLARKSON, brokerage house executive; b. Westbury, N.Y., Feb. 26, 1955; s. Leslie Charles and Regina (Clarkson) Q. BS in Bus., Fairfield U., 1977. Br. mgr. Quick & Reilly Inc., Palm Beach, Fla., 1977-81; dir. The Quick & Reilly Group, N.Y.C., 1981—; v.p. Quick & Reilly Inc., Palm Beach, 1981-86; pres., dir. Quick & Reilly Inc., N.Y.C., 1986—, also bd. dirs.; trustee Security Industry Found. for Econ. Edn., Securities Industry Inst. Trustee Nat. Corp. Theater Fund, Trustee, U.S. Com., Trustee Alcoholism Coun. of N.Y.C; mem. investment adv. bd. and endowment com. St. Jude Children's Rsch. Hosp., Memphis, 1986—; chmn. com. Wall Street Friends of St. Jude Children's Rsch. Hosp., 1979—, mem. endowment com. Mem. The Investment Assn. N.Y., N.Y. Stock Exch., Securities and Industry Assn. (econ. edn. com.), Am. Assn. of Sovereign Mil., Order of Malta, Young Pres.'s Orgn., Univ. Club, Friendly Sons of St. Patrick, Apawamis Country Club (Rye, N.Y.), The Beach Club (Palm Beach, Fla.), Fairfield U. Adv. Coun., Chgo. Athletic Club., New York Yacht Club.

Home: 30 Sutton Pl New York NY 10022 Office: Quick & Reilly Inc 26 Broadway New York NY 10004-1703

QUICK, VALERIE ANNE, sonographer; b. Alta., Can., Feb. 14, 1952; came to U.S., 1953; d. Kenneth Conrad and Kathryn (Maller) Bjorge. Grad. high sch., Salinas, Calif. Registered adult and pediatric echocardiographer, abdomen, small parts and ob-gyn sonographer; registered cardiovasc. technician, registered diagnostic cardiac sonographer. Chief EKG technician Natividad Med. Ctr., Salinas, 1978-81, chief ultrasound dept., 1981-94, chief cardiac echo lab., 1995—. Mem. Am. Inst. Ultrasound in Medicine, Am. Soc. Echocardiography, Nat. Soc. for Cardiopulmonary Technicians, Soc. Pediat. ECHO, Soc. Diagnostic Med. Sonographers, Am. Heart Assn., Am. Registry Diagnostic Med. Sonographers. Avocations: reading, photography, travel. Office: PO Box 6694 Salinas CA 93912-6694

QUICK, WILLIAM THOMAS, author, consultant; b. Muncie, Ind., May 30, 1946; s. Clifford Willett and Della May (Ellis) Q. Student, Ind. U., 1964-66. Pres. Iceberg Prodns., San Francisco, 1986—. Author: Dreams of Flesh and Sand, 1988, Dreams of God and Men, 1989, Yesterday's Pawn, 1989, Systems, 1989, Singularities, 1990, (as Quentin Thomas) Chains of Light, 1992, Ascensions, 1997, (as Margaret Allan) The Mammoth Stone, 1993, Keeper of the Stone, 1994, The Last Mammoth, 1995, Spirits Walking Woman, 1997, (as W.T. Quick) Star Control: Interbellum, 1996, American Gothic: Family, 1996, (with William Shatner) Quest for Tomorrow: Delta Search, 1997, Quest for Tomorrow: In Alien Hands, 1997. Mem. Sci. Fiction and Fantasy Writers Am., The Authors Guild. Home and Office: 1558 Leavenworth St San Francisco CA 94109-3220

QUIE, PAUL GERHARDT, physician, educator; b. Dennison, Minn., Feb. 3, 1925; s. Albert Knute and Nettie Marie (Jacobson) Q.; m. Elizabeth Holmes, Aug. 10, 1951; children: Katie, Bill, Paul, David. B.A., St. Olaf Coll., 1949; M.D., Yale U., 1953; PhD (hon.), U. Lund, 1993. Diplomate Am. Bd. Pediatrics, Nat. Bd. Med. Examiners (mem.). Intern Hennepin County Hosp., 1953-54; pediatric resident U. Minn. Hosps., 1957-59; mem. faculty U. Minn. Med. Sch., 1959—, prof. pediatrics, 1968—, prof. microbiology, 1974—; assoc. dean of students, 1992—; Am. Legion meml. heart research prof. U. Minn. Med. Sch., 1974-91, Regents prof., 1991, interim dir. Ctr. for Biomed. Ethics, 1985-86; attending physician Hennepin County Hosp., 1959-91; cons. U. Minn. Nursery Sch., 1959-91; chief of staff U. Minn. Hosp., 1979-84; vis. physician Radcliffe Infirmary, Oxford, Eng., 1971-72; mem. Adv. Allergy and Infectious Disease Coun., 1976-80; mem. pediat. com. NRC, 1978; mem. bd. sci. counselors Gamble Inst., 1985-90; vis. prof. U. Bergen, 1991; hon. prof. U. Hong Kong Med. Sch., 1995; vis. prof. pediat. Chubu Hosp., Nagasaki, Japan, 1996. Mem. editorial bd. Pediatrics, 1970-76, Rev. Infectious Diseases, 1989-92. Served with USNR, 1954-57; med. officer. Recipient E. Mead-Johnson award Am. Acad. Pediatrics, 1971; Guggenheim fellow, 1971-72; John and Mary R. Markle scholar, 1960-65; Alexander Von Humbolt fellow, 1986. Mem. Inst. Medicine of NAS, N.W. Pediatrics Soc., Minn. Med. Found. (pres. 1986-88), Am. Fedn. Clin. Rsch., Am. Soc. Microbiology, Infectious Diseases Soc. Am. (coun. 1977-82, pres. 1985, Bristol award 1994), Soc. Pediatric Rsch., Am. Pediatric Soc. (coun. 1976-83, pres. 1987-88), Am. Soc. Clin. Investigation, Minn. Acad. Pediatrics, Am. Acad. Pediatrics, Assn. Am. Physicians, Minn. Acad. Medicine (pres. 1993-94). Research in function of human leukocytes. Home: 2154 Commonwealth Ave Saint Paul MN 55108-1717 Office: U Minn Hosp PO Box 483 Minneapolis MN 55440-0483

QUIGLEY, JACK ALLEN, service company executive; b. Bloomington, Ill., Apr. 11, 1914; s. Thomas M. and Margaret (Brown) Q.; m. Eleanor T. Steen, Nov. 17, 1946 (dec. 1996); children: J. Timothy, J. William, Margaret, Richard A. B.S., Northwestern U., 1935. With Means Services, Inc., 1935—, personnel dir., 1935-37, div. mgr., 1937-41, gen. mgr., 1946-48, v.p., dir., 1948-50, pres., dir., 1950-72, chmn. bd., chief exec. officer, 1972-96; cons. Aramark Uniform Svcs., 1981—; Co-chmn. First and Second Internat. Linen Supply Congresses, 1959, 62; founder, chmn. Chgo. Pres.'s Orgn., 1966-68, Young Pres.'s Orgn., 1951-62. Served with USAF, World War II. Mem. Linen Supply Assn. Am. (pres. 1955-57, founder chmn. rsch. group 1957-60), Chief Execs. Forum, Royal Poinciana Golf Club (Naples, Fla.). Home: 114 Moorings Park Dr Apt A-812 Naples FL 34105-2151 *Died, March 26, 1996.*

QUIGLEY, JEROME HAROLD, management consultant; b. Green Bay, Wis., Apr. 19, 1925; s. Harold D. and Mabel (Hansen) Q.; BS, St. Norbert Coll., 1951; m. Lorraine A. Rocheleau, May 3, 1947; children: Kathy, Ross, Michael, Daniel, Mary Beth, Andrew, Maureen. Personnel adminstr. Gen. Motors Corp., 1959-64; dir. indsl. rels. Raytheon Co., Santa Barbara, Calif., 1964-67; dir. personnel U. Calif., Santa Barbara, 1967-72; corp. dir. indsl. rels. Gen. Rsch. Corp., 1972-73; dir. indsl. rels. ISS Sperry Univac, 1973-75; corp. dir. indsl. rels. Four-Phase Systems, Inc., Cupertino, Calif., 1975; sr. v.p. human resources UNC, Annapolis, Md., 1975-86; pres. Profl. Guidance Assocs. Inc., 1986—. Aviator with U.S. Navy, 1943-47. Mem. Am. Electronics Assn., Assn. Former Intelligence Officers, Machinery and Allied Products Inst., Assn. Naval Aviation, Tailhook Assn., Ariz. County Atty.'s and Sheriff's Assn., Ariz. County Attys. and Sheriffs Assn., Marines' Meml. Assn., Ret. Officers Assn., AVCAD/NAVCAD Assn., Navy Aviation Mus. Found., Navy League, Scottsdale Radisson Racquet Club. Republican. Roman Catholic. Office: Profl Guidance Assocs Inc 7789 E Joshua Tree Ln Scottsdale AZ 85250-7962

QUIGLEY, JOHN BERNARD, law educator; b. St. Louis, Oct. 1, 1940; s. John Bernard and Ruth Rosina (Schieber) Q. BA, Harvard U., 1962, MA, LLB, 1966. Bar: Ohio 1973, Mass. 1967, U.S. Dist. Ct. (so. dist.) Ohio 1976, U.S. Ct. Appeals (6th cir.) 1986, U.S. Supreme Ct. 1989. Research assoc. Harvard U. Law Sch., Cambridge, Mass., 1967-69; prof. law Ohio State U., Columbus, 1969—. Author: Basic Laws on the Structure of the Soviet State, 1969, The Soviet Foreign Trade Monopoly, 1974, Palestine and Israel: A Challenge to Justice, 1990, The Ruses for War: American Interventionism since World War II, 1992. Mem. Nat. Lawyers Guild (v.p. 1977-79), Am. Soc. Internat. Law, AAUP. Avocations: tennis, speed skating, violin. Office: Ohio State U Coll. of Law Coll of Law 55 W 12th Ave Columbus OH 43210-1338

QUIGLEY, JOHN JOSEPH, special education educator; b. Auburn, N.Y., May 28, 1946; s. Thomas Edward and Mary Agnes (Brechue) Q.; m. Nancy Louise Crehan, June 7, 1969 (div. 1979); 1 child, Kris Renae. BS, U. Cen. Mich., 1970; MA, U. No. Colo., 1976. Cert. tchr., spl. edn. tchr., Fla. Tchr. of socially maladjusted Dade County Schs., Miami, Fla., 1970-71, tchr. of trainable mentally handicapped, 1971-74, tchr. profoundly mentally handicapped, 1974-75, tchr. multiply handicapped, hearing impaired, 1975-77, tchr. hearing-impaired total communication, 1977—; tchr. Habilitation for the Handicapped, Miami, 1972-81; cons. in trainable mentally handicapped curriculum devel., Duval County, Fla., 1973; master tchr. assoc. Gulfstream Elem. Sch., 1984-87; impact tchr. developer Dade Pub. Edn./Nat. Tchr. Network, 1991-92; adj. prof. U. Miami, 1991-92. Mem. Fla. Educators of Hearing Impaired, United Tchrs. Dade, Deaf Svc. Bur. Home: 10776 N Kendall Dr # 1 Miami FL 33176-1484 Office: Gulfstream Elem Sch 20900 SW 97th Ave Miami FL 33189-2354

QUIGLEY, JOHN MICHAEL, economist, educator; b. N.Y.C., Feb. 12, 1942. B.S. with distinction, U.S. Air Force Acad., 1964; M.Sc. with honors, U. Stockholm, Sweden, 1965; A.M., Harvard U., 1971, Ph.D., 1972. Commd. 2d lt. USAF, 1964, advanced through grades to capt., 1968; asst. prof. econs. Yale U., 1972-74, assoc. prof., 1974-81; prof. pub. policy U. Calif., Berkeley, 1979—, prof. econs., 1981—, chmn. dept. econs., 1992-95; vis. prof. econs. and stats. U. Gothenberg, 1978; cons. numerous govt. agys. and pvt. firms; econometrician Hdqrs. U.S. Air Force, Pentagon, 1965-68; research assoc. Nat. Bur. Econ. Research, N.Y.C., 1968-78; mem. com. on nat. urban policy NAS, 1985-93. Author, editor, contbr. articles to profl. jours.; editor in chief Reg. Sci. and Urban Econs., 1987—; mem. editorial bd. Land Econs., 1974-81, Jour. Urban Econs., 1978-93, Coun. on Pub. Policy and Mgmt., 1979—, AREUEA Jour., 1985—, Property Tax Jour., 1990—, Jour. Housing Econs., 1990—. Fulbright scholar, 1964-65; fellow NSF, 1968-69, Woodrow Wilson, 1968-71, Harvard IBM, 1969-71, NDEA, 1969-71, Thord-Gray Am. Scandinavian Found. 1971-72, Social Sci. Research Council, 1971-72. Mem. Am. Econ. Assn., Econometric Soc., Regional Sci. Assn. (bd. dirs. 1986—), Nat. Tax Assn., Assn. for Pub. Policy and Mgmt. (bd. dirs. 1986-89, v.p. 1987-89), Am. Real Estate and Urban Econs. Assn. (bd. dirs. 1987—, pres. 1995—). Home: 875 Hilldale Ave Berkeley CA 94708-1319 Office: U Calif 2607 Hearst Ave Berkeley CA 94709-1005

QUIGLEY, LEONARD VINCENT, lawyer; b. Kansas City, Mo., June 21, 1933; s. Joseph Vincent and Rosemary (Cannon) Q.; m. Lynn Mathis Pfohl, May 23, 1964; children: Leonard Matthew, Cannon Louise, Daniel Pfohl, Megan Mathis. A.B., Coll. Holy Cross, 1953; LL.B. magna cum laude, Harvard U., 1959; LL.M. in Internat. Law, NYU, 1962. Bar: N.Y. 1960. Assoc. Cravath, Swaine & Moore, N.Y.C., 1959-67; ptnr. Paul, Weiss, Rifkind, Wharton & Garrison, N.Y.C., 1968—; gen. counsel Archaeol. Inst. Am., Boston. Served to lt. USN, 1953-56. Mem. ABA, Can. Bar Assn., N.Y. State Bar, Coun. Fgn. Rels., Assn. Bar City N.Y., Harvard Club (N.Y.C.), West Side Tennis Club (Forest Hills, N.Y.).

QUIGLEY, MARTIN SCHOFIELD, publishing company executive, educator; b. Chgo., Nov. 24, 1917; s. Martin Joseph and Gertrude Margaret (Schofield) Q.; m. Katherine J. Dunphy, July 2, 1946; children: Martin, Elin, William, Kevin, Karen, Patricia, John, Mary Katherine, Peter. AB magna cum laude, Georgetown U., 1939; MA, Columbia U., 1973, EdD, 1975. Reporter Motion Picture Herald, N.Y.C. and Hollywood, Calif., 1939-41; with overseas br. OWI, 1942; secret war work U.S. Govt., 1943-45; various editorial and mgmt. posts Quigley Pub. Co., Inc., N.Y.C., 1946—; pres. Quigley Pub. Co., Inc., 1964—; staff, dept. higher and adult edn. Tchrs. Coll., 1974-75; prof. higher edn. grad. courses Baruch Coll. CUNY, 1977-89; prof. higher edn. grad. courses Tchrs. Coll. Columbia U., 1979-80, 90; prof. higher edn. grad. courses Seton Hall U., 1981-82; pres. QWS, Inc., 1975-80; ednl. cons.; cons. supt. schs. N.Y. Archdiocese, 1962-70. Author: Great Gaels, 1944, 2d edit. 1997, Roman Notes, 1946, Magic Shadows--the story of the origin of motion pictures, 1948, Government Relations of Five Universities in Washington, D.C., 1975, Peace Without Hiroshima-Secret Action at the Vatican in Spring of 1945, 1991, First Century of Film, 1995; co-author: Catholic Action in Practice, 1962, Films in America, 1969; editor: New Screen Techniques, 1953. Pres. N.Y. Christian Family Movement, 1960-62, mem. nat. exec. com., 1960-65; founder, chmn. N.Y. Ind. Schs. Opportunity Project, 1965-77; pres. Found. Internat. Coop., 1960-65; bd. dirs. Will Rogers Inst., Motion Picture Pioneers; treas. Religious Edn. Assn. U.S. and Can., 1975-81, chmn., 1981-84; trustee Village of Larchmont, N.Y., 1977-79, mayor, 1980-84; mem. Laymen's Nat. Bible Assn., 1981—; trustee Am. Bible Soc., 1984—; bd. dirs. William J. Donovan Meml. Found., 1994—. Roman Catholic. Club: Larchmont Yacht. Home: 8 Pheasant Run Larchmont NY 10538-3423 Office: 159 W 53rd St New York NY 10019-6005

QUIGLEY, PHILIP J., telecommunications industry executive; b. 1943. With Advanced Mobile Phone Svc. Inc., 1982-84, v.p., gen. mgr., Pacific region; with Pac Tel Mobile Access, 1984-86, pres., chief exec. officer; with Pac Tel Personal Communications, 1986-87, pres., chief exec. officer; exec. v.p., chief oper. officer Pac Tel Corp., 1987; with Pacific Bell, San Francisco, 1987—; now chmn., pres., chief exec. officer Pacific Telesis Group, San Francisco; pres. Pacific Bell, 1987-94. Office: Pacific Telesis 130 Kearny St San Francisco CA 94108

QUIGLEY, ROBERT CHARLES, insurance industry consultant; b. Phila., Feb. 2, 1949; s. James and Kathrine Regina (Kinckiner) Q.; m. Barbara Jeanne Browne, Apr. 17, 1971; children: Robert J., Michael J., Brian A., Jason T. BS in Acctg., Pa. State U., 1970. CPA, Pa. Sr. acct. Touche Ross & Co., Phila., 1970-72; dir. acctg. policy and rsch. Ins. Co. of N.Am., Phila., 1972-81; asst. treas. Reliance Ins. Co., Phila., 1981-85; v.p., treas. Mutual Fire Marine and Inland Ins. Co., Phila., 1985-86; owner Quigley & Assocs., Hatboro, Pa., 1987—; team leader accreditation Nat. Assn. of Ins. Commrs., Kansas City, 1992—. Author: (with others) Property and Liability Insurance Accounting, 5th edit., 1991. With USMCR, 1967. Mem. AICPA, Soc. of Ins. Fin. Mgmt., Am. Arbitration Assn. (panelist 1987—). Republican. Presbyterian. Avocations: family, reading, investments. Office: PO Box 147 20 N York Rd Hatboro PA 19040-3201

QUIGLEY, THOMAS J., lawyer; b. Mt. Carmel, Pa., July 22, 1923; s. James S. and Helen C. (Laughlin) Q.; m. Joan R. Reifke, Aug. 11, 1956; children: Thomas J., Jr., Joan E., James S. AB, Bucknell U., 1947; LLB, Yale U., 1950. Bar: Ohio, U.S. Dist. Ct. Ohio, U.S. Ct. Appeals (6th and D.C. cirs.). With Squire, Sanders & Dempsey, 1950—, adminstr. labor dept., 1971-80, mng. ptnr., Washington, 1980-85; nat. vice chmn., 1985-86; nat. chmn., 1986-90. Immediate past pres., dir. exec. com. Nat. Symphony Orch., nat. trustee Musical Arts Assn. Cleve.; bd. dirs. Call for Action, Belgian Am. C. of C. 1st lt. USAAF, 1942-45. Decorated D.F.C., Air medal with oak leaf cluster, Belgium's Order of the Crown. Mem. ABA, Ohio Bar Assn., D.C. Bar Assn., Cleve. Bar Assn., Yale Law Sch. Alumni. Assn., Case-Western Res. Univ. Law Sch. (vis. com.). Roman Catholic. Clubs: Yale (N.Y.C.), Edgartown Yacht (Mass.), Chevy Chase, Metropolitan (Wash.). Office: Squire Sanders & Dempsey PO Box 407 1201 Pennsylvania Ave NW Washington DC 20004 also: Soc Ctr Bldg Cleveland OH 44114

QUIJADA, ANGÉLICA MARÍA, elementary educator; b. Tijuana, Mex., Mar. 22, 1963; came to U.S., 1967; d. Juan José and Paula (Magallanes) Q. AA, L.A. Harbor Coll., Wilmington, Calif., 1985; BA, Calif. State U., Carson, 1990, MA, 1993. Tchr. asst., tutor L.A. Harbor Coll., 1982-85; elem. tchr. asst., tutor Ambler Avenue Sch., Carson, 1985-90; bilingual elem. tchr. Hooper Avenue Sch., L.A., 1991—; stakeholder Instrnl. Transformation Team, 1995-96; mem. pupil quality rev. team, 1995-96; co-chair local sch. leadership coun., 1996—; mentor Latino Tchr. Project, U. So. Calif., 1993—; mem. coordinated compliance rev. team Hooper Ave. Elem. Sch., 1996—. counselor Pathfinders, Carson Seventh Day Adventist Ch., 1980; treas. Carson Spanish Seventh-Day Adventist Ch., 1994; pianist Harbor City Seventh Day Adventist Ch.; Jefferson cluster tchr. trainer dist. stds. LAVSD, 1996—, early literacy, 1997—. Mem. TESOL, United Tchrs. L.A. (co-chair 1994, chpt. chair 1995—). Democrat. Avocations: playing piano, photography, reading, playing softball, drawing. Home: 320 E 181st St Carson CA 90746-1815

QUILICO, LOUIS, baritone; b. Montreal, Jan. 14, 1925; s. Louis and Jeanne (Gravel) Q.; m. Lina Pezzolongo, Oct. 30, 1949 (dec. Sept. 1991); children: Donna Maria, Gino; m. Christina Petrowska, Nov. 30, 1993; children: Alexandra Dominique, Dominique Brigent. Studied, Conservaatoire Province Que., Mannes Coll. Music, N.Y.C., Conservatoir de Santa Cecilia, Rome. Prof. U. Toronto, Ont., Acad. Vocal Art, Phila. Operatic debut in La Traviata, N.Y.C. Opera, 1956; performed with major opera cos. including Royal Opera, Covent Garden, Staatsoper, Opera Nat. de Belgique, L'Opera de Quebec, Canadian Opera Co., Bolshoi Opera, Opera Co. of Phila., San Francisco Opera, Seattle Opera, San Diego Opera, Opera Soc. of Washington (D.C.), many others; created numerous roles; resident mem., Met. Opera, (Winner Nos Futurs Étoiles, Montreal 1953, Met. Opera Audition of the Air 1955). Named Esquire Montreal Expo, 1967; decorated companion Order of Can.; celebration for 25 years at Met. Opera. Roman Catholic. Office: care Robert Lombardo Assocs One Harkness Plaza 61 W 62nd St Apt 6F New York NY 10023-7017 also: Ann Summers Int, Box 188 Station A, Toronto, ON Canada M5W 1B2

QUILLEN, CECIL DYER, JR., lawyer, consultant; b. Kingsport, Tenn., Jan. 21, 1937; s. Cecil D. and Mary Louise (Carter) Q.; m. Vicey Ann Childress, Apr. 1, 1961; children: Cecil D., Ann C. BS, Va. Poly. Inst., 1958; LLB, U. Va., 1962. Bar: Va. 1962, N.Y. 1963, Tenn. 1974. Atty. patent dept. Eastman Kodak Co., Rochester, N.Y., 1962-65, atty. patent sect. Tenn. Eastman Co. (div. Eastman Kodak), Kingsport, Tenn., 1965-69, mgr., 1969-72, mgr. licensing, 1972-74, sec. and asst. chief counsel, 1974-76, dir. patent litigation Eastman Kodak, 1976-82, dir. antitrust litigation Eastman Kodak, 1978-82, v.p. and chief counsel Tenn. Eastman, 1983-85, v.p., and assoc. gen. counsel Eastman Kodak, 1986, sr. v.p., gen. counsel, dir., 1986-92; sr. adv., Putnam, Hayes & Bartlett, Inc., Washington, 1992—. Mem. ABA, Va. State Bar, Am. Intellectual Property Law Assn., Va. Poly. Inst. Com. of 100, Assn. of Gen. Counsel.

QUILLEN, JAMES HENRY (JIMMY QUILLEN), former congressman; b. Wayland, Va., Jan. 11, 1916; s. John A. and Hannah (Chapman) Q.; m. Cecile Cox, Aug. 9, 1952. Ed. high sch.; LL.D. (hon.), Milligan Coll., Tenn., 1978. With Kingsport Press, 1934-35, Kingsport Times, 1935-36; founder newspaper Kingsport Mirror (semi-weekly), 1936, pub., 1936-39; founder Johnson City (Tenn.) Times, 1939, pub., 1939-44; pub. Johnson City (Tenn.) Times (converted to daily), 1940; Mem. Tenn. Ho. of Reps., 1954-62, minority leader, 1959-60, mem. legislative council, 1957, 59, 61, mem. rules com., subcom. legis. process, Rep. chmn. emeritus; mem. U.S. Congress from Tenn., 1963-96. Served to lt. USNR, 1942-46. Mem. Am. Legion, VFW, C. of C. Republican. Methodist. Clubs: Lions, Ridgefields Country (Kingsport); Capitol Hill (Washington). Office: US Ho Reps 102 Cannon Ho Office Bldg Washington DC 20515*

QUILLEN, MARY ANN, university administrator, consultant; b. Md., Dec. 10, 1947; 1 child, Jessica. BS, Del. State U., 1977; Cert. Spl. Edn., Pa. State U., 1981; MS, U. Pa., 1991. Spl. edn. tchr. Wordsworth Acad., Ft. Washington, Pa., 1979-82; tchr. specialist Rens, Inc., Langhorne, Pa., 1982-83; area rep. Pa. State U., King of Prussia, 1983-85; dir. continuing edn. Ea. Montgomery County AVTS, Willow Grove, Pa., 1985-93; mgr. Drexel U., Phila., 1993—; con. in field. Chair Montgomery County Commn. on Women and Families, Norristown, Pa., 1992—; coord. Domestic Violence Forum for Montgomery County, Norristown, 1994—. Mem. ASTD, AAUW, Pa. Assn. for Adult and Continuing Edn., U. Pa. Alumni Assn. (dir. comm. com. 1993—). Avocations: gourmet cooking, gardening, reading. Home: 1000 Valley Forge Cir #1103 King Of Prussia PA 19406

QUILLEN, WILLIAM TATEM, judge, lawyer, educator; b. Camden, N.J., Jan. 15, 1935; s. Robert James and Gladys Collings (Tatem) Q.; m. Marcia Everhart Stirling, June 27, 1959; children: Carol Everhart, Tracey Tatem. B.A., Williams Coll., 1956; LL.B., Harvard U., 1959; LL.M., U. Va., 1982. Bar: Del. 1959. Assoc. Richards, Layton & Finger, Wilmington, Del., 1963-64; adminstrv. asst. to Gov. of Del., 1965; assoc. judge Superior Ct. of Del., 1966-73; chancellor State of Del., 1973-76; sr. v.p. Wilmington Trust Co., 1976-78; justice Supreme Ct. of Del., 1978-83; ptnr. Potter Anderson & Corroon, Wilmington, 1983-86; gen. counsel, v.p. Howard Hughes Med. Inst., 1986-91; sec. of state State of Del., Dover, 1993-94; assoc. judge Superior Ct. Del., Wilmington, 1994—; mem. adj. faculty Widener U. Sch. Law, Wilmington, 1976-83, 85-86, 95—, disting. vis. prof. law, 1992-94. Trustee Widener U., 1979-91; Democratic candidate for gov. Del., 1984. Served with JAGC, USAF, 1959-62. Mem. Am. Bar Assn., Del. State Bar Assn., Phi Beta Kappa. Democrat. Presbyterian. Club: Wilmington.

QUILLIAN, WARREN WILSON, II, pediatrician, educator; b. Miami, Fla., Jan. 21, 1936; s. Warren Wilson and Rosabel (Brown) Q.; m. Sallie Ruth Creel, July 26, 1958; children: Rutledge, Ruth, Warren C., Frances. MD, Emory U., 1961. Diplomate Am. Bd. Pediat. (examiner 1966—, bd. dirs. 1974-80, 1992—, treas. 1978, v.p. 1979, pres. 1980). Intern in pediatrics Vandertilt U., Nashville, 1961-62; resident Children's Hosp. Med. Ctr., Harvard U., Boston, 1962-63; chief resident Grady Meml. Hosp., Emory U., Atlanta, 1963-64; pvt. practice, Coral Gables, Fla., 1966; instr., asst. clin. prof., assoc. clin. prof., now clin. prof. pediat. U. Miami Med. Sch., 1966—; active staff, bd. dirs. Miami Children's Hosp.; active staff Jackson Meml. Hosp.; chief pediat. Doctors' Hosp.; mem. courtesy staff Mercy Hosp., Bapt. Hosp., South Miami Hosp., Cedars of Lebanon Hosp.; chmn. health adv. com. Dade County Schs.; bd. dirs., v.p. Am. Bd. Pediat. Found., 1991—; mem. adv. bd. McGlannon Sch.; cons. Fla. Div. Med. Svcs.; bd. dirs. Bank Coral Gables. Contbr. articles to med. jours. Hon. bd. dirs. Soc. for Abused Children of Children's Home Soc., Miami, 1980-84; mem. Coral Gables Code Enforcement Bd., 1986-88; team-sch. physician Coral Gables Sr. H.G., 1980-88; bd. dirs. Dade County March of Dimes, Miami, 1968-72; bd. advisors Dade County Assn. Retarded Children, 1968-76; trustee Emory U., 1991—; mem. coun. ministries, youth coord., mem. fin. com., Sunday sch. tchr. United Meth. Ch. Coral Gables, 1966—; mem. parrish rels. com.; mem. bd. advisors The Growing Place. Capt. M.C., U.S. Army, 1964-66. Recipient citation of merit Emory U., 1980, alumni commendation Miami Children's Hosp., 1983, Teaching award U. Miami Sch. Medicine, 1995; named CGHS Athletic Hall of Fame, 1996. Fellow Am. Acad. Pediat.; mem. AMA, Fla. Med. Assn. (sch. health com.), Fla. Pediatric Soc. (past chmn. sch. health com.), So. Med. Assn., Dade County Med. Assn. (sch. health com., continuing edn. com.), Empirical Soc. (past pres.), So. Soc. for Pediatric Rsch., So. Perinatal Soc., Greater Miami Pediatric Soc. (past pres., chmn. legis. and sch. health com.), Miami Med. Forum (past pres., Maxwell Cup 1985), Alpha Omega Alpha, Omicron Delta Kappa, Alpha Epsilon Upsilon, Phi Delta Theta. Democrat. Avocations: fishing, golf. Office: 305 Granello Ave Coral Gables FL 33146-1806

QUILLIAN, WILLIAM FLETCHER, JR., retired banker, former college president; b. Nashville, Apr. 13, 1913; s. William Fletcher and Nonie (Acree) Q.; m. Margaret Hannah Weigle, June 15, 1940; children—William Fletcher III, Anne Acree, Katherine, Robert. A.B., Emory U., 1935, Litt.D. (hon.), 1959; B.D., Yale, 1938, Ph.D., 1943; postgrad., U. Edinburgh, 1938-39, U. Basel, 1939; Day fellow from, Yale, 1938-39; Rosenwald fellow, 1940-41; LL.D., Ohio Wesleyan U., 1952, Hampden-Sydney Coll., 1978, Randolph-Macon Coll., 1967; D.H.L., Randolph-Macon Woman's Coll., 1978. Ordained to ministry Meth. Ch., 1942. Student asst. Stamford (Conn.) Presbyn Ch., 1936-38; del. Gen. Com. of World Student Christian Fedn., Bievres, France, 1938; discussion leader World Conf. Christian Youth, Amsterdam, Holland, 1939; pastor Clarendon (Vt.) Community Ch., summer 1940; asst. prof. philosophy Gettysburg Coll., 1941-43, prof., 1943-45; prof. philosophy Ohio Wesleyan U., 1945-52; pres. Randolph Macon Woman's Coll., 1952-78; pres. emeritus Randolph Macon Woman's Coll., 1978—; sr. v.p. Central Fidelity Bank, 1978-88; exec. dir. Greater Lynchburg (Va.) Community Trust, 1988—; v.p., bd. dirs. Pride of Virginia Meats, Inc.; tchr. Garrett Biblical Inst., summer 1951. Author: The Moral Theory of Evolutionary Naturalism, 1945, Evolution and Moral Theory in America, Evolutionary Thought in America, 1950; Contbr. articles to philos. and religious jours. Pres. bd. dirs. United Way Cen. Va., campaign chmn., 1987; bd. dirs. Alpha Tau Omega Found., Lynchburg Gen. Hosp.; hon. life trustee Va. Found. Ind. Colls., pres., 1958-61. Mem. Assn. Va. Colls. (past pres.), So. U. Conf. (pres. 1967-68), So. Assn. Colls. for Women (pres. 1956), Nat. Assn. United Methodist Colls. and Univs. (pres. 1973), Am. Philos. Assn., Soc. for Values in Higher Edn. (mem. central com. 1945-48, chmn. 1947-48), Nat. Assn. Bibl. Instrs., AAUP, Greater Lynchburg C. of C. (dir. pres. 1979-80), Phi Beta Kappa, Omicron Delta Kappa, Alpha Tau Omega (dir. found.). Home: 1407 Club Dr Lynchburg VA 24503-2503 Office: Central Fidelity Bank 828 Main St Lynchburg VA 24504-1522

QUILLIGAN, EDWARD JAMES, obstetrician, gynecologist, educator; b. Cleve., June 18, 1925; s. James Joseph and Maude Elvira (Ryan) Q.; m. Betty Jane Cleaton, Dec. 14, 1946; children—Bruce, Jay, Carol, Christopher, Linda, Ted. B.A., Ohio State U., 1951, M.D., 1951; M.A. (hon.), Yale, 1967. Intern Ohio State U. Hosp., 1951-52, resident, 1952-54; resident Western Res. U. Hosps., 1954-56; asst. prof. obstetrics and gynecology Western Res. U., 1957-63, prof., 1963-65; prof. obstetrics and gynecology UCLA, 1965-66; prof., chmn. dept. Ob-Gyn Yale U., 1966-69; prof., chmn. dept. Ob-Gyn U. So. Calif., 1969-78, asso. v.p. med. affairs, 1978-79; prof. Ob-Gyn. U. Calif., Irvine, 1980-83, vice chancellor health affairs, dean Sch. Medicine, 1987-89; prof., chmn. ob.-gyn. dept. U. Wis., 1983-85; prof., chmn. Ob-Gyn Davis Med. Ctr. U. Calif., Sacramento, 1985-87; vice chancellor Health Scis., dean Coll. Med. U. Calif., Irvine, 1987-89, prof. ob-gyn, 1987-94, prof. emeritus ob-gyn., 1994; exec. dir. med. edn. Long Beach (Calif.) Meml. Health Svcs., 1995—. Contbr. articles to med. jours.; co-editor-in-chief: Am. Jour. Obstetrics and Gynecology. Served to 2d lt. AUS, 1944-46. Recipient Centennial award Ohio State U., 1970. Mem. Soc. Gynecologic Investigation, Am. Gynecol. Soc., Am. Coll. Obstetics and Gynecology, Sigma Xi. Home: 24 Urey Ct Irvine CA 92612-4045 Office: UC Irvine Med Ctr Dept Ob-Gyn Bldg 40 101 The City Dr S Orange CA 92868-3201

QUIMBY, FRED WILLIAM, pathology educator, veterinarian; b. Providence, Sept. 19, 1945; s. Edward Harold and Isabel (Barber) Q.; m. Cynthia Claire Connelly, Aug. 21, 1965; children—Kelly Ann, Cynthia Jane. V.M.D., U. Pa., 1970, Ph.D., 1974. Diplomate Am. Coll. Lab. Animal Medicine. Hematology fellow New Eng. Med. Ctr., Boston, 1974-75, instr. pathology, 1975-76, asst. prof., 1976-79; assoc. prof. pathology Cornell Med. Coll., N.Y.C., 1979-92, prof. pathology, 1993—; assoc. prof. N.Y. State Vet. Coll., Ithaca, 1979-93, prof. pathology, 1993—; dir. lab. animal medicine Tufts-New Eng. Med. Ctr., Boston, 1975-79; dir. Ctr. Rsch. Animal Resources, Cornell U., Ithaca, 1979—. Editor: Clinical Chemistry of Laboratory Animals, 1988, Animal Welfare, 1992, Lab. Animal Sci., 1992-

93, consulting editor, 1993-95; chmn. editorial bd. ILAr News, 1988-91; contbr. 100 sci. papers and abstracts. Greenfield Trust scholar, 1966-70; N.H. Rural Rehab. Corp. scholar, 1966-70; U. Pa. scholar, 1969-70. Mem. AVMA (Charles River prize 1995), Am. Assn. Lab. Animal Sci. (pres. Northeast br. 1978-79; B. Trum award 1979), World Vet. Assn. (sec. exec. com. animal welfare 1990-96). Episcopalian. Home: 115 Terrace View Dr Ithaca NY 14850-6256 Office: NYSCVM Cornell U 221 Vrt Ithaca NY 14853

QUIMBY, ROBERT SHERMAN, retired humanities educator; b. St. Albans, Vt., Feb. 20, 1916; s. Christopher Sherman and Lura Mae (Wills) Q.; m. Shirley Lenore Lay, Oct. 19, 1957. B.S. in Edn, U. Vt., 1937, M.A., 1938; Ph.D., Columbia U., 1952; postgrad., Am. Sch. Classical Studies, Athens, Greece, 1958. Teaching asst. in history U. Vt., Burlington, 1938-39, 41-42; instr. history U. Vt., 1942-44, Cornell U., Ithaca, N.Y., 1944-45; instr. history of civilization Mich. State U., East Lansing, 1945-52; asst. prof. humanities Mich. State U., 1952-59, asso. prof., 1959-68, prof., 1968-81, prof. emeritus of humanities, 1981—; Mem. Mich. Commn. of United Ministries in Higher Edn., 1970-87, sec., 1975-77. Author: The Background of Napoleonic Warfare; contbr. articles to profl. jours. and encys. George Ellis fellow Columbia U., 1939-41. Mem. Mich. Hist. Soc., U.S. Naval Inst., Rwy. and Locomotive Hist. Soc. Republican. Episcopalian. Club: University. Address: 145 Columbia Ave Apt 207 Holland MI 49423-2983 Address (winter): 3400 S Ironwood Dr Lot 379 Apache Junction AZ 85220-7114

QUIN, JOSEPH MARVIN, oil company executive; b. Vicksburg, Miss., Aug. 18, 1947; s. Billy Henry Quin and Cele (Burdette) Peterson; m. Terry Gage, June 12, 1973; children—William C., Elizabeth G. B.B.A., U. Miss., 1969; M.B.A., U. Va., 1972. Dir. planning and devel. Ashland Chem. Co., Dublin, Ohio, 1978-81, adminstrv. v.p., 1981-83; treas. Ashland Inc., 1983-87; adminstrv. v.p. fin., treas. Ashland Inc., Ky., 1987-92, sr. v.p., CFO, 1992—; bd. dirs. Ashland Coal, Inc., Ky. Electric Steel, Inc. Episcopalian. Office: Ashland Inc PO Box 391 Ashland KY 41105-0391

QUIN, LOUIS DUBOSE, chemist, educator; b. Charleston, S.C., Mar. 5, 1928; s. Louis DuBose and Olga vonOven (Jatho) Q.; children: Gordon, Howard, Carol. B.S., The Citadel, 1947; M.A., U. N.C., 1949, Ph.D., 1952. Research chemist Am. Cyanamid Co., Stamford, Conn., 1949-50; research project leader FMC Corp., South Charleston, W.Va., 1952-54, 56; mem. faculty dept. chemistry Duke U., Durham, N.C., 1956-86; prof. Duke U., 1967-81, James B. Duke prof. chemistry, 1981-86, chmn. dept., 1970-76; prof. chemistry U. Mass., Amherst, 1986-96, prof. emeritus, 1996—, head dept., 1986-94; adj. prof., disting. vis. prof. chemistry U. N.C., Wilmington, 1996—; Mem. Durham Human Relations Commn., 1978-81. Author: Heterocyclic Chemistry of Phosphorus, 1981, (with J.G. Verkade) Phosphorus-31 NMR Spectroscopy in Stereochemical Analysis, 1987, Phosphorus-31 NMR Spectral Properties in Compound Characterization and Structural Analysis, 1994;. Served to 1st lt. U.S. Army, 1954-56. Fellow AAAS; mem. Am. Chem. Soc. Office: U NC Dept Chemistry Wilmington NC 20000

QUINBY, WILLIAM ALBERT, lawyer, mediator, arbitrator; b. Oakland, Calif., May 28, 1941; s. George W. and Marge (Diaz) Q.; m. Marion Bach, Nov. 27, 1964; 1 child, Michelle Kathleen. BA, Harvard U., 1963; JD, U. Calif., San Francisco, 1967. Bar: Calif. 1967. V.p., dir., shareholder Crosby, Heafey, Roach & May, Oakland, Calif., 1967-96; mediator, arbitrator Am. Arbitration Assn. and AAA Ctr. for Mediation, San Francisco, 1996—; bd. dirs. Haws Drinking Faucet Co., Berkeley, Calif.; mem. faculty Hastings Coll. Advocacy, San Francisco, 1980, instr. Boalt Hall Sch. Law, 1997; co-moderator Counsel Connect's Calif. ADR Discussion Group; lectr. currents devels. in banking arbitration and mediation; mem. fellowship rev. com. HEW; mem. panel disting. neutrals Ctr. for Pub. Resources, Inc.; mem. mediation panel Nat. Assn. Securities Dealers; trustee Nat. Pre-Suit Mediation Program. Author: Six Reasons--Besides Time and Money--to Mediate Rather Than Litigate, Why Health Care Parties Should Mediate Rather Than Litigate, Starting an ADR Practice Group in a Law Firm, Mediation Process Can Amicably Solve Business Disputes and Not a Gold Rush (But Silver, Maybe), ADR Practice in a Large Law Firm Produces No Overnight Bonanzas, Making The Most of Mediation (Effective Mediation Advocacy). Bd. dirs. Big Bros. East Bay, Oakland, 1983-87, Easter Seals Soc. East Bay, 1973, Oakland East Bay Symphony; chmn. bd. dirs. Bay Area Tumor Inst. Scholar Harvard U., 1962-63. Mem. ABA, ATLA, Calif. Bar Assn., Alameda County Bar Assn., Calif. Bus. Trial Lawyers Assn., Am. Arbitration Assn. (large, complex case panel, comml. mediation and arbitration panels), Oakland C. of C. (bd. dirs., exec. com.), Alameda County Barristers Club (bd. dirs., pres. 1972), Harvard Club, San Francisco Calimari Club, Lakeview Club, Bohemian Club. Republican. Avocations: running, skiing, tennis, travel, gardening. Office: Crosby Heafey Roach & May 1999 Harrison St Oakland CA 94612-3520

QUINE, WILLARD VAN ORMAN, philosophy educator; b. Akron, Ohio, June 25, 1908; s. Cloyd Robert and Hattie Ellis (Van Orman) Q.; m. Naomi Ann Clayton, Sept. 19, 1930; children: Elizabeth Roberts, Norma; m. Marjorie Boynton, Sept. 2, 1948; children: Douglas Boynton, Margaret McGovern. AB in Math. summa cum laude, Oberlin Coll., 1930, LittD (hon.), 1955; AM in Philosophy, Harvard U., 1931, PhD, 1932, LLD (hon.), 1979; MA, Oxford U., 1953, LittD (hon.), 1970; LittD (hon.), Ohio State U., 1957; hon. doctorate, U. Lille, France, 1965, Uppsala U., Sweden, 1980, U. Berne, Switzerland, 1982, U. Granada, Spain, 1986; LittD (hon.), Akron U., 1965, Washington U., St. Louis, 1966, Temple U., 1970, Cambridge (Eng.) U., 1978, Syracuse U., 1981; LHD (hon.), U. Chgo., 1967, Ripon Coll., 1983, Adelphi U., 1989. Instr., tutor philosophy Harvard U., Cambridge, Mass., 1936-41, assoc. prof., 1941-48, prof., 1948—, Edgar Pierce prof. philosophy, 1955-78, chmn. dept. philosophy, 1952-53; vis. prof. U. Sao Paulo, Brazil, 1942, Rockefeller U., 1968, Coll. de France, 1969; George Eastman vis. prof. Oxford U., 1953-54, U. Tokyo, 1959; mem. Inst. Advanced Study, Princeton U., 1956-57; Gavin David Young lectr. in philosophy U. Adelaide, Australia, 1959; Paul Carus lectr. Am. Philos. Assn., 1971; Hagerstrom lectr. U. Uppsala, Sweden, 1973; Ferrater Mora lectr., Gerona, Spain, 1990. Author: A System of Logistic, 1934, Mathematical Logic, 1940, Elementary Logic, 1941, O Sentido da Nova Logica, 1944, Methods of Logic, 1950, From a Logical Point of View, 1953, Word and Object, 1960, Set Theory and Its Logic, 1963, The Ways of Paradox, 1966, Selected Logic Papers, 1966, Ontological Relativity, 1969, Philosophy of Logic, 1970, (with J.S. Ullian) The Web of Belief, 1970, The Roots of Reference, 1974, Theories and things, 1981, The Time of My Life, 1985, Quiddities, 1987, La Scienza e i Dati di Senso, 1987, Pursuit of Truth, 1989, The Logic of Sequences, 1990, From Stimulus to Science, 1995; co-author: Philosophical Essays for A.N. Whitehead, 1936; Philosophy of A.N. Whitehead, 1941; Philosophy of Rudolf Carnap, 1963; Words and Objections, 1969, Aspectos de la Filosofia de W.V. Quine, 1975, Philosophy of W.V. Quine, 1986, Symposio Quine, 1988, Perspectives on Quine, 1989; also articles. Served to lt. comdr. USNR, 1942-46. Recipient Nicholas Murray Butler Gold medal Columbia U., 1970, Frantisek Polacky gold medal, Czech Republic, 1991, Charles U. silver medal, Prague, 1993, Rolf Schock prize in philosophy, Sweden, 1993, Kyoto prize in creative arts and moral scis., 1996; Harvard U. Soc. Fellows jr. fellow, 1933-36, sr. fellow, 1948-78; univ. scholar Harvard U.; James Walker fellow Harvard U.; Sheldon traveling fellow, Europe, 1932-33; Rockefeller fellow, Bellagio, 1975; fellow Ctr. Advanced Study Behavioral Scis., 1958-59, Ctr. Advanced Studies, Wesleyan U., 1965; Sir Henry Savile fellow Merton Coll., Oxford, 1973-74. Fellow Am. Philos. Soc., Brit. Acad. (corr.); mem. Am. Philos. Assn. (pres. East div. 1957), Assn. Symbolic Logic (pres. 1953-56), Am. Acad. Arts and Scis., Nat. Acad. Scis., Institut de France (corr.), Norwegian Acad., Institut Internat. de Philosophie, Instituto Brasileiro de Filosofia (corr.), Academie Internationale de la Philosophie de Sci., Phi Beta Kappa. Office: Harvard U Dept Philosophy Emerson Hall Cambridge MA 02138

QUINLAN, GUY CHRISTIAN, lawyer; b. Cambridge, Mass., Oct. 28, 1939; s. Guy Thomas and Yvonne (Carver) Q.; m. Mary-Ella Holst, Apr. 18, 1987. AB, Harvard Coll., 1960, JD, Harvard U., 1963. Bar: N.Y. 1964, U.S. Dist. Ct. (so. and ea. dists.) N.Y. 1965, U.S. Ct. Appeals (2d cir.) 1967, U.S. Supreme Ct. 1969, U.S. Ct. Appeals (8th cir.) 1973, (10th cir.) 1977, (4th cir.) 1993, (11th cir.) 1995, U.S. Tax Ct. 1977. Assoc. Rogers & Wells, N.Y.C., 1963-70, ptnr., 1970-90, of counsel, 1991—. Past pres. Unitarian Universalist Svc. Com., Yorkville Common Pantry; past pres. Unitarian Universalist Dist. of Met. N.Y.; mem. adv. council on ministerial studies Harvard U. Div. Sch. Mem. ABA, N.Y. State Bar Assn., Fed. Bar Coun., Am. Judicature Soc., Am. Assn. Internat. Commn. Jurists, Lawyers Alliance for World Security. Democrat. Club: Harvard (N.Y.C.). Office: Rogers & Wells 200 Park Ave New York NY 10166-0005

QUINLAN, J(OSEPH) MICHAEL, lawyer; b. Rockville Centre, N.Y., Nov. 2, 1941; s. Joseph Charles Quinlan and Harriet Veronica (Gorman) Greene; m. Agnes Mary Quinlan, May 5, 1973; children: Kara Ann, Kristen Mary. BS. in Social Sci., Fairfield U., 1963; JD, Fordham U., 1966; LLM, George Washington U., 1970. Bar: N.Y. 1966, D.C. 1967, Va. 1993, U.S. Ct. Mil. Appeals 1967, U.S. Supreme Ct. 1970. Exec. asst. to warden U.S. Penitentiary, Leavenworth, Kans., 1973-74; of counsel N.E. region U.S. Bur. Prisons, Phila., 1974-75, exec. asst. to dir., Washington, 1975-78; supt. Fed. Prison Camp, Eglin AFB, Fla., 1978-80; warden Fed. Correctional Inst., Otisville, N.Y., 1980-85; dep. asst. dir. U.S. Bur. Prisons, Washington, 1985-86, dep. dir., 1986-87; dir. U.S. Bur. Prisons, 1987-92; dir. strategic planning, Corrections Corp. Am., 1993—, dir., bd. dirs. United Kingdom Detention Svcs., London. 1st vice chmn. bd. dirs. Horton Meml. Hosp., Middletown, N.Y., 1982-85; criminal justice cons. Lt. Col. USAFR, 1966-93. Recipient SES Presdl. Disting. Rank award, 1988, SES Presdl. Meritorious Rank award, 1991, Exceptional Leadership award U.S. Atty. Gen., 1991, Nat. Pub. Svc. award Nat. Acad. Pub. Adminstrn./Am. Soc. Pub. Adminstrn., 1992, John Marshall award Dept. Justice, 1993. Fellow Nat. Acad. Pub. Adminstrn.; mem. ABA (corrections and sentencing com. 1985—, Am. Correctional Assn. (mem. prison industries com.), Nat. Com. Comm. Corrections, N.Y. Bar Assn., D.C. Bar Assn., Va. Bar Assn. Roman Catholic. Avocations: reading, family activities.

QUINLAN, KATHLEEN, actress; b. Pasadena, Calif., Nov. 19, 1954. Actress: (theatre) Taken in Marriage, 1979 (Theatre World award 1979), Accent on Youth, 1983, Les Liaisons Dangereuses, 1988, (feature films) One is a Lonely Number, 1972, American Graffiti, 1973, Lifeguard, 1976, Airport '77, 1977, I Never Promised You a Rose Garden, 1977, The Promise, 1979, The Runner Stumbles, 1979, Sunday Lovers, 1981, Hanky Panky, 1982, Independence Day, 1982, Twilight Zone: The Movie, 1983, The Last Winter, 1983, Warning Sign, 1985, Wild Thing, 1987, Sunset, 1988, Clara's Heart, 1988, The Doors, 1991, Trial by Jury, 1994, Apollo 13, 1995 (Acad. award nominee for best actress 1996); (TV movies) Can Ellen Be Saved?, 1974, Lucas Tanner, 1974, Where Have All the People Gone?, 1974, The Missing Are Deadly, 1975, The Turning Point of Jim Malloy, 1975, The Abduction of Saint Anne, 1975, Little Ladies of the Night, 1977, She's in the Army Now, 1981, When She Says No, 1984, Blackout, 1985, Children of the Night, 1985, Dreams Lost, Dreams Found, 1987, Trapped, 1989, The Operation, 1990, Strays, 1991, An American Story, 1992, Stolen Babies, 1993, Last Light, 1993, Perfect Alibi, 1994, Breakdown, 1996. Mem. Actors' Equity Assn., Screen Actors Guild.

QUINLAN, MARY LOU, advertising executive. CEO, pres. N.Y.C. office N.W. Ayers & Ptnrs., N.Y.C. Office: NW Ayer & Ptnrs 825 8th Ave New York NY 10019-7416*

QUINLAN, MICHAEL ROBERT, fast food franchise company executive; b. Chgo., Dec. 9, 1944; s. Robert Joseph and Kathryn (Koerner) Q.; m. Marilyn DeLashmutt, Apr. 23, 1966; children: Kevin, Michael. BS, Loyola U., Chgo., 1967, MBA, 1970. With McDonald's Corp., Oak Brook, Ill., 1966—, v.p., 1974-76, sr. v.p., 1976-78, exec. v.p., 1978-79, chief ops. officer, 1979-80, pres. McDonald's U.S.A., 1980-82, pres., 1982-89, chief oper. officer, 1982-87, chief exec. officer, 1987—, chmn., 1989—, also bd. dirs. Republican. Roman Catholic. Clubs: Butterfield Country, Oakbrook Handball-Racquetball. Office: McDonald's Corp 1 Kroc Dr Oak Brook IL 60523-2275*

QUINN, ANDREW PETER, JR., lawyer, insurance executive; b. Providence, Oct. 22, 1923; s. Andrew Peter and Margaret (Canning) Q.; m. Sara G. Bullard, May 30, 1952; 1 child, Emily H. AB, Brown U., 1945; LLB, Yale U., 1950. Bar: R.I. 1949, Mass. 1960, U.S. Tax Ct. 1960, U.S. Supreme Ct. 1986. Pvt. practice Providence, 1950-59, Springfield, Mass., 1959-88; ptnr. Letts & Quinn, 1950-59; with Mass. Mut. Life Ins. Co., 1959-88, exec. v.p., gen. counsel, 1971-88; of counsel Day, Berry & Howard, Hartford, Conn. and Boston, 1988—; pres., trustee MML Series Investment Fund, 1971-88; bd. dirs. Sargasso Mut. Ins. Co., Ltd., 1986-95, pres., 1986-89, chmn. bd. dirs., 1989-93. Trustee, MacDuffie Sch., 1974-87, chmn. bd., 1978-85; trustee Baystate Med., Springfield, 1977-80. Lt. (j.g.) USNR, 1944-46. Mem. ABA (co-chmn. nat. conf. lawyers and life ins. cos. 1973), Assn. Life Ins. Counsel (pres. 1983-84), Am. Coun. Life Ins. (chmn. legal sect. 1971), Life Ins. Assn. Mass. (chmn. exec. com. 1975-77), Brown U. Alumni Assn. (bd. dirs. 1969-72), N.Y. Yacht club, Longmeadow Country Club, Dunes Club, Hillsboro Club, Conn. Valley Brown U. (past pres.). Home: 306 Ellington Rd Longmeadow MA 01106-1559 Office: Day Berry & Howard City Pl Hartford CT 06103-3499

QUINN, ANTHONY RUDOLPH OAXACA, actor, writer, artist; b. Chihuahua, Mexico, Apr. 21, 1915; naturalized, 1947; s. Frank and Nellie (Oaxaca) Q.; m. Katherine de Mille, Oct. 2, 1937 (div.); children: Christina, Kathleen, Duncan, Valentina; m. Iolanda Addolori, Jan. 1966; children: Francesco, Daniele, Lorenzo. Student pub. schs. Actor in plays including Clean Beds, 1936, Gentleman from Athens, 1947, Street Car Named Desire, Let Me Hear the Melody, Beckett, 1961, Tchin-Tchin, 1963, Zorba, 1983-86; has appeared in over 200 motion pictures including Guadalcanal Diary, 1943, Buffalo Bill, 1944, Irish Eyes are Smiling, 1944, China Sky, 1945, Back to Bataan, 1945, Where Do We Go From Here?, 1945, Tycoon, 1947, The Brave Bulls, 1951, Mask of the Avenger, 1951, World in his Arm, 1952, Against all Flags, 1952, Viva Zapata (Acad. award 1952), Ride Vaquero, 1953, City Beneath the Sea, 1953, Seminole, 1953, Blowing Wild, 1953, East of Sumatra, 1953, Long Wait, 1954, Magnificent Matador, 1955, Ulysses, 1955, Naked Street, 1955, Seven Cities of Gold, 1955, Lust for Life, (Acad. award best supporting actor 1956), La Strada, 1954, Man from Del Rio, 1956, Wild the Wind, 1957, Attila the Hun, 1958, The Wild Party, 1956, The Ride Back, 1957, The Hunchback of Notre Dame, 1957, The River's Edge, 1957, Hot Spell, 1958, Heller with a Gun, Savage Innocents, 1959, The Black Orchid, 1958, Last Train From Gun Hill, 1958, Warlock, 1959, Heller in Pink Tights, 1960, Portrait in Black, 1960, Guns of Navarrone, 1961, Becket, 1961, Barabbas, 1962, Lawrence of Arabia, 1962, Requiem for a Heavyweight, 1963, The Visit, 1963, Behold a Pale Horse, 1964, Zorba the Greek, 1964, High Wind in Jamaica, 1965, Guns for San Sebastian, 1968, The Shoes of the Fisherman, 1968, The Secret of Santa Vittoria, 1969, A Dream of Kings, 1969, Flap, 1970, A Walk in Spring Rain, 1970, R.P.M., 1970, The City, 1971, Jesus of Nazareth, 1971, Across 110th Street, 1972, Arruza, Deaf Smith and Johnny Ears, 1973, The Don Is Dead, 1973, Mohammed Messenger of God, 1977, Caravans, 1978, The Children of Sanchez, 1978, The Greek Tycoon, 1978, The Inheritance, 1978, The Passage, 1979, Lion of the Desert, 1981, High Roll, 1981, Valentina, 1984, The Salamander, 1984, Treasure Island, 1986, Stradivarius, 1987, Revenge, 1990, Ghosts Can't Do It, 1990, A Star for Two, 1990, Jungle Fever, 1990, Only the Lonely, 1991, Mobsters, 1991, The Last Action Hero, 1993, Somebody to Love, 1994, A Walk in the Clouds, 1995, Project Mankind, 1996, Il Sindaco, 1996, Seven Servants, 1996; appeared in TV prodns. of The Life of Christ, Onassis: The Richest Man in the World, 1988, Old Man and the Sea, 1990, This Can't Be Love, 1994, Gotti, 1996; script writer: Metro-Goldwyn-Mayer prodn. The Farm; author: The Original Sin, 1972, Self-Portrait, 1995; artist 13 major exhbns. oil paintings, sculptures and serigraphs, Hawaii, 1982, 87, San Francisco, 1983, N.Y.C., 1984, 89, San Antonio, 1984, Houston, 1984, Washington, 1985, Beverly Hills, Calif., 1986, Mexico City, 1990, Paris, 1990, Zurich, Switzerland, 1990, Vienna, Austria, 1991, Buenos Aires, 1992, Las Vegas, 1993. Address: 420 Poppasquash Rd Bristol RI 02809

QUINN, ART JAY, veterinarian, retired educator; b. Bennington, Kans., Aug. 2, 1936; s. Arthur Jess and Edith Mae (Reigle) Q. BS, Kans. State U., 1959, DVM, 1961. Diplomate Am. Coll. Vet. Ophthalmologists. Pvt. practice Albuquerque, 1961-75; field rep. Am. Animal Hosp. Assn., Denver, 1968-69; prof. Coll. Vet. Medicine, Okla. State U., Stillwater, 1975-95; prof. emeritus Coll. Vet. Medicine, Okla. State U., 1995—. Contbr. articles to profl. jours. Capt. U.S. Army, 1962-64. Recipient Kans. Vet. Med. Assn. Small Animal Proficiency award, 1961, Upjohn award, 1961, AAHA Western Region Practitioner award, 1993; Sarkey Found. grantee, 1981. Mem. AVMA, Am. Animal Hosp. Assn., Am. Coll. Vet. Ophthalmologists, North Ctrl. Okla. Vet. Med. Assn. Democrat. Home: 210 Diamond Head Dr Sand Springs OK 74063-5309 Office: Okla State U Coll Vet Medicine Stillwater OK 74078

QUINN, BETTY NYE, former classics educator; b. Buffalo, Mar. 22, 1921; d. Fritz Arthur and Alma (Svenson) Hedberg; A.B., Mt. Holyoke Coll., 1941; A.M., Bryn Mawr Coll., 1942, Ph.D., 1944; m. John F. Quinn, Sept. 21, 1950. Analyst, U.S. Army, 1944-46, CIA, 1947; instr., asst. prof. Vassar Coll., Poughkeepsie, N.Y., 1948-59, dir. pub. relations, 1952-59, assoc. prof., 1959-68; prof. classics Mt. Holyoke Coll., South Hadley, Mass., 1968-91, prof. emeritus, 1991—. Am. Acad. Rome fellow, 1942-43; Am. Philos. Soc. grantee, 1952. Mem. Am. Philos. Assn., Mediaeval Acad. Am., Classics Assn. New Eng. (pres. 1970-71) Vergilian Soc. Am. Republican. Lutheran. Home: 27 W Parkview Dr South Hadley MA 01075-2164

QUINN, BOB, professional baseball team executive. Sr. adv. baseball ops. San Francisco Giants. Office: San Francisco Giants Candlestick Park San Francisco CA 94124*

QUINN, CHARLES NICHOLAS, journalist; b. Utica, N.Y., July 28, 1930; s. Charles Dunaway and Elsa (Zarth) Q.; children—Diana David, Ben, Jane. B.A., Cornell U., 1951; M.S., Columbia U. Sch. Journalism, 1954. Reporter Providence Jour., 1954-56, N.Y. Herald Tribune, 1956-62; corr. NBC News, N.Y.C., 1962-66, Washington, 1966-71, Rome, 1971-74; mng. editor, chief corr. NBC Radio News, Washington, 1978-80; corr. Ind. Network News, Washington, 1980-81; electronic media rep. Am. Petroleum Inst., Washington, 1981-91. Reported on hunger in U.S. on: Huntley-Brinkley Report, (co-recipient Emmy 1969). Served with arty. U.S. Army, 1951-53. Mem. Nat. Press Club (bd. govs. 1990-91).

QUINN, CHARLES NORMAN, lawyer; b. Abington, Pa., Nov. 5, 1943; s. Charles Ransom and Lela Josephine (Cooper) Q.; m. Mary Bernadette Bradley, Oct. 4, 1975 (div. Oct. 1976); m. Vicki Lou Erickson Heinze, Nov. 11, 1978; stepchildren: Scott L., Kymbra Lynn. BSME, Purdue U., 1965; ME, Pa. State U., 1970; JD, Villanova (Pa.) U., 1973. Bar: U.S. Dist. Ct. (ea. dist) Pa. 1974, U.S. Ct. Appeals (fed. cir.) 1984. Systems engr. GE Co., King of Prussia, Pa., 1965-70; atty. Paul and Paul, Phila., 1973-75, Penwalt Corp., Phila., 1976-80, A.R. Miller, P.C., Phila., 1981-85; ptnr. Miller & Quinn, Phila., 1986-91; atty., of counsel Dann Dorfman Herrell & Skill, Phila., 1992—. Contbr. articles to profl. jours. Mem. ABA, Phila. Patent Law Assn. (treas. 1980-83, gov. 1987-89), Phila. Intellectual Property Law Assn., Am. Intellectual Property Law Assn., Phila. Bar Assn. Avocations: golf, classical music, personal computers. Home: 617 Marydell Dr West Chester PA 19380-6328 Office: Dann Dorfman Herrell & Skillman 1601 Market St Ste 720 Philadelphia PA 19103-2337

QUINN, DENNIS B., English language and literature educator; b. Bklyn., Oct. 3, 1928; s. Herbert John and Thelma Leona (Warren) Q.; m. Eva M. Jensen, Aug. 13, 1952; children—Timothy, Monica, Alison. Student, Creighton U., 1948-50; B.A. in English, U. Wis., 1951, M.A. in English, 1952, Ph.D. in English, 1958. Instr. English U. Kans., Lawrence, 1956-60, asst. prof. English, 1960-64, assoc. prof. English, 1964-68, prof. English, 1968—, dir. Pearson Coll., 1968-75, dir. integrated humanities program, 1971-79. Contbr. articles on Medieval and Renaissance literature and children's literature to profl. jours. Served with U.S. Army, 1946-48; Japan. Recipient student Fulbright award, Leiden, The Netherlands, 1955-56, research Fulbright award, Salamanca, Spain, 1962-63; H. Bernard Fink Outstanding Tchr. award U. Kans., 1965, H.O.P.E. Teaching award, 1969; NEH grantee, 1971. Roman Catholic. Avocations: gardening, travel. Home: 1102 W 25th St Lawrence KS 66046-4441 Office: Univ Kansas Dept English Lawrence KS 66045

QUINN, EDWARD J., broadcasting company executive. BS in Speech, U. Wis. Gen. sales mgr. WTMJ-TV, Milw.; v.p., gen. mgr. KTNV-TV, Las Vegas, WVUE-TV, New Orleans; gen. mgr. KGTV, v.p. McGraw-Hill Broadcasting Co., San Diego, 1986-96, pres., 1996—; bd. govs. ABC TV Affiliates Assn.; pres.'s adv. bd. San Diego State U.; chmn. San Diego Baha Comms. Coun. Recipient George Walker Smith humanitarian award San Diego Coalition for Equality, medal of honor DAR, disting. svc. award Soc. Profl. Journalists, golden mike award Radio and TV News Dirs. Assn. So. Calif., Emmy award NATAS. Office: McGraw-Hill Broadcasting Co PO Box 85347 San Diego CA 82186-5347

QUINN, EUGENE FREDERICK, government official, clergyman; b. Oil City, Pa., Sept. 16, 1935; s. Frederick Anthony and Wilma (Scott) Q.; m. Charlotte Alison Smith, Aug. 25, 1965; children: Christopher Edward Vermilye, Alison Moore. AB, Allegheny Coll., 1957; MA in African studies, UCLA, 1966, MA in History, 1969, PhD in History, 1970; diploma in theol. studies, Va. Theol. Sem., 1974. Ordained to ministry Episcopal Ch. U.S.A., 1975. Info. officer Am. Embassy, Rabat, Morocco, 1958-59; cultural affairs officer Am. Embassy, Port-au-Prince, Haiti, 1959-61; country pub. affairs officer Ouagadougou, Upper Volta, 1961-63; field rep. Joint U.S. Affairs Office, Saigon, Vietnam, 1964-66; country pub. affairs officer Am. embassy, Yaounde, Cameroun, 1966-68; counselor embassy for press and cultural affairs Am. embassy, Prague, Czechoslovakia, 1975-78; apptd. career mem. Sr. Fgn. Service with class of counselor, 1981, minister-counselor, 1986; dir. fgn. service personnel Voice of Am., Washington, 1981-83; dep. asst. sec. pub. affairs Dept. Transp., 1983-85; dir. Office Pub. Affairs Voice of Am., 1985-86; internat. coord. for Bicentennial U.S. Constn., dir.'s office U.S. Info. Agy., 1986-91; cons. internat. affairs, 1992—; dir. rule of law programs, conf. on security and cooperation in Europe, Office of Dem. Instns. and Human Rights, Warsaw, 1993-95. Author: Federalist Papers' Reader, 1992, To Heal the Earth, 1994, Democracy at Dawn, a Personal Memoir of Poland and Points East, 1993-95, Human Rights and You, 1997; editor: Diplomacy for the Seventies, 1969; mem. editl. bd. Fgn. Svc. Jour., 1972-75, Dept. State Open Forum Jour., 1982-83; contbr. articles to profl. jours., chpts. to books. Trustee N.J. Ednl. Consortium, 1970-72; coord. USIA Yorktown Bicentennial Activities, 1981; assisting clergyman St. Columba Ch., Washington, 1973-75, 78-81, Nat. Cathedral, Washington, 1981-82, 95, Grace Ch., Silver Spring, Md., 1981-82, Epiphany Ch., Washington, 1983, 86-92; chaplain Anglo-Am. Diplomatic Cmty., Prague, 1975-78, Warsaw, 1993-95; vicar St. James Ch., Bowie, Md., 1983-84; rector Christ Ch., Accokeek, Md., 1985, St. John's Ch., Pomonkey, Md.; assisting clergyman All Saints Ch., Chevy Chase, Md., 1981-82, 86-90; interim pastor Ch. of Holy Communion, Washington, 1992-93; chair environ. com. Episcopal Diocese of Washington Peace Commn., 1991-92; mem. Environ. Stewardship Team, Episcopal Ch., 1992-95. Recipient Meritorious Honor award USIA, 1964, 66, 85; Merit medal Republic of Vietnam, 1965, medal of honor, 1966. Club: Cosmos (Washington). Home and Office: 5702 Kirkside Dr Chevy Chase MD 20815-7116

QUINN, FRANCIS A., bishop; b. L.A., Sept. 11, 1921. Ed., St. Joseph's Coll., Mountain View, Calif., St. Patrick's Sem., Menlo Park, Calif., Cath. U., Washington, U. Calif., Berkeley. Ordained priest Roman Cath. Ch., 1946; ordained titular bishop of Numana and aux. bishop of San Francisco, 1978; bishop Diocese of Sacramento, 1979-94, bishop emeritus, 1994—. Office: 2110 Broadway Sacramento CA 95818-2518

QUINN, FRANCIS F., lawyer; b. Phila., Jan. 22, 1946. AB, St. Joseph's U., 1967; JD, U. Pa., 1971. Bar: Pa. 1972. Law clk. to Hon. Daniel H. Huyett III U.S. Dist. Ct. (ea. dist.) Pa., 1971-73; atty. Lavin, Coleman, O'Neill, Ricci, Finarelli & Gray, Phila. Mem. ABA, Phila. Bar Assn., Def. Rsch. and Trial Lawyers Assn., Phila. Assn. Def. Counsel. Office: Lavin Coleman Finarelli & Gray Penn Mutual Tower 510 Walnut St Ste 1000 Philadelphia PA 19106-3619

QUINN, FRANCIS XAVIER, arbitrator and mediator, author, lecturer; b. Dunmore, Pa., June 9, 1932; s. Frank T. and Alice B. (Maher) Q.; m. Marlene Stoker Quinn; children: Kimberly, Catherine, Cameron, Lindsay, Megan. AB, Fordham U., 1956, MA, 1958; STB, Woodstock Coll., 1964; MSIR, Loyola U., Chgo., 1966; PhD in Indsl. Rels., Calif. Western U., 1966. Assoc. dir. St. Joseph's Coll. Inst. Indsl. Rels., Phila., 1966-68; Manpower fellow Temple U., 1969-74, asst. to dean Sch. Bus. Adminstrn., 1972-78; arbitrator Fed. Mediation and Conciliation Svc., Nat. Mediation Bd., Am.

Arbitration Assn., Nat. Assn. Railroad Referees, Dem. Nat. Steering Com.; apptd. to Rail Emergency Bd., 1975, to Fgn. Service Grievance Bd., 1976, 78, 80—; chmn. Hall of Fame com. Internat. Police Assn., 1990—, Tulsa City-County Mayor's Task Force to Combat Homelessness, 1991-92; mem. exec. bd. Tulsa Met. Ministries, 1990-92, Labor-Religion Coun. Okla., 1990—. Named Tchr. of Yr., Freedom Found., 1959; recipient Human Rels. award City of Phila., others. Mem. Nat. Acad. Arbitrators (chair SW Region 1995—), Indsl. Rels. Rsch. Assn., Assn. for Social Econs., Soc. for Dispute Resolution, Am. Arbitration Assn. (arbitrator), Internat. Soc. Labor Law and Social Security, Internat. Ombudsman Inst. Democrat. Author: The Ethical Aftermath of Automation, Ethics and Advertising, Population Ethics, The Evolving Role of Women in the World of Work, Developing Community Responsibility. Editor: The Ethical Aftermath Series; contbr. articles to profl. jours. Home: 230 Hazel Blvd Tulsa OK 74114-3926

QUINN, JACK, congressman, English language educator, sports coach; b. South Buffalo, N.Y., 1951; s. Jack Sr. and Norma Ide Q.; m. Mary Beth McAndrews, 1974; children: Jack III, Kara. BA, Siena Coll.; MA in Edn., SUNY, Buffalo. English language tchr. Orchard Park (N.Y.) Schs.; town councilman Town of Hamburg, N.Y.; also town supv. Town of Hamburg; mem. 103d-105th Congresses from 30th N.Y. Dist., 1993—; mem. transp. and infrastructure com., mem. vet. affairs com., mem. congl. reform task force, mem. joint econ. com. Recipient Humanitarian award Erie County for the Disabled, Pub. Svc. award Niagara Frontier Parks and Recreation Soc., Disting. Grad. award Nat. Cath. Elem. Schs. Assn., Bronze Good Citizen medal SAR, New Horizons award Drug Edn. of Internat. Assn. of Lions Club, Red, White and Blue award Am. Legion of N.Y., Honor medal Hilbert Coll., Fin. Reporting award Govt. Fin. Officer's Assn., Disting. Career Svc. award Siena Coll., 1995. Mem. Hamburg C. of C., Greater Buffalo C. of C., Buffalo KC, Hamburg Kiwanis Club. Republican. Roman Catholic. Office: US Ho Reps 331 Cannon HOB Washington DC 20515-3230*

QUINN, JACK J., professional hockey team executive; b. Boston; s. John Quinn; m. Connie Quinn; children: Beth, Kay, Connie, John. Exec. v.p. St. Louis Blues, 1983-86, pres., 1986-95, chrm., ceo, 1995—. Office: St Louis Blues Kiel Ctr 1401 Clark Ave Saint Louis MO 63103-2700*

QUINN, JAMES W., lawyer; b. Bronxville, N.Y., Oct. 1, 1945; s. James Joseph Quinn and Marie Joan (Blossy) Tisi; m. Kathleen Manning, Kellianne, Christopher, Tierney, Kerrin. AB cum laude, U. Notre Dame, 1967; JD, Fordham U., 1971. Bar: N.Y. 1972, U.S. Dist. Ct. (so. and ea. dists.) N.Y. 1973, U.S. Ct. Appeals (2nd cir.) 1976, U.S. Supreme Ct. 1984, U.S. Ct. Appeals (3rd, 7th and 9th cirs.) 1985, U.S. Ct. Appeals (8th cir.) 1991. Assoc. Weil, Gotshal & Manges, N.Y.C., 1971-77, 78-79, ptnr., 1979—; ptnr. Fleisher & Quinn, N.Y.C., 1977-78; adj. assoc. prof. law Fordham U., N.Y.C., 1985-87. Editor Fordham U. Law Rev., 1969-71; contbr. articles to legal jours. Mem. ABA (litigation sect., co-chmn. subcom. alternate means of dispute resolution of com. corp. counsel, program chmn. trial practice com., sports and entertainment forum), Assn. of Bar of City of N.Y. (com. of state jurisdiction, com. on entertainment sports, com. on anti-trust regulation, chmn. sports law com.). Home: 1 Maple Way Armonk NY 10504-2602

QUINN, JANE, journalist; b. San Antonio, Tex., Oct. 5, 1916; d. James Edward and Willie Stell (Mitchell) Q. BA, Fla. State U., 1938; MS in Social Work, Cath. U. of Am., 1945. Reporter St. Augustine (Fla.) Record, 1938-41; journalist, editl. staff The Fla. Cath. for Diocese of St. Augustine, 1940-68, The Fla. Cath., St. Augustine, 1940—, The Fla. Cath. for Diocese of Orlando, Fla., 1968—; archivist Diocese of Orlando, 1988—. Author: Minorcans in Florida, 1975, Story of a Nun: Jeanie Gordon Brown, 1979, others; contbr. articles to profl. jours. Recipient Papal award Pro Ecclesia et Pontifice, 1979, citation Cath. Press Assn. of U.S. and Can., 1994. Fellow Orlando Interfaith Sponsoring Com.; mem. DAR, Assocs. of Josephite Nuns, Orlando Diocesan Coun. Cath. Women (hon. life), Assocs. of Cath. Diocesan Archivists, St. Joseph Alumni Assn., Alpha Xi Delta. Roman Catholic. Avocations: reading biographies, Florida history books, collecting US commemoratives. Office: Diocese of Orlando 421 E Robinson St Orlando FL 32801-1916

QUINN, JANE BRYANT, journalist, writer; b. Niagara Falls, N.Y., Feb. 5, 1939; d. Frank Leonard and Ada (Laurie) Bryant; m. David Conrad Quinn, June 10, 1967; children—Matthew Alexander, Justin Bryant. B.A. magna cum laude, Middlebury Coll., 1960. Assoc. editor Insiders Newsletter, N.Y.C., 1962-65, co-editor, 1966-67; sr. editor Cowles Book Co., N.Y.C., 1968; editor-in-chief Bus. Week Letter, N.Y.C., 1969-73, gen. mgr., 1973-74; syndicated financial columnist Washington Post Writers Group, 1974—; contbr. fin. column to Women's Day mag., 1974-95; contbr. fin. column Good Housekeeping, 1995—; contbr. NBC News and Info. Service, 1976-77; bus. corr. WCBS-TV, N.Y.C., 1979, CBS-TV News, 1980-87, ABC-TV Home Show, 1991-93; contbg. editor Newsweek mag., 1978—; host PBS personal fin. series Take Charge!, 1988. Author: Everyone's Money Book, 1979, 2d edit., 1980, Making the Most of Your Money, 1991, 2d edit., 1997, A Hole in the Market, 1994; contbr. Quicken Financial Planner, 1995. Mem. Phi Beta Kappa. Office: Newsweek Inc 251 W 57th St New York NY 10019-1802

QUINN, JANITA SUE, city secretary; b. Breckenridge, Tex., Apr. 14, 1950; d. Doyle Dean and Peggy Joyce (Melton) Allen; m. John Lloyd Rippy, June 27, 1969 (div. Mar. 1976); children: Johna DeAnn, Jason Allen; m. Ervel Royce Quinn, Jan. 31, 1987; stepchildren: Amy Talitha, Jason Ervel. Student, Odessa (Tex.) Jr. Coll., 1968-70, U. Tex. of Permian Basin, Odessa, 1978-79, 85-86. Tex. Registered Mcpl. Clk., 1996. New accts. clk. State Nat. Bank, Odessa, Tex., 1975-76; accts. receivable clk. Woolley Tool Corp., Odessa, Tex., 1976-78; data entry operator M-Bank, Odessa, Tex., 1978-79; asst. county treas. Ector County, Odessa, Tex., 1979-83, county treas., 1983-88; office mgr., co-owner Nat. Filter Svc., Inc., San Antonio, 1988-91; temporary employment Kelly Temporary Svcs., Abilene, Tex., 1991; sec. Pride Refining, Inc., Abilene, Tex., 1991-93; city sec. City of Eastland, Tex., 1993—. Mem., treas., bd. dirs. Family Outreach Svc. Taylor County; vol. tchr. Parenting for Parents and Adolescents; recorder, del. West Tex. Corridor II Com., Eastland and Dallas, 1993; county del. Taylor County Dem. Party, Dallas, 1991; charter mem. Bluebonnet chpt. City Secs. Region 6 Group, 1994-96, pres., 1994-96; alt. delegate to the Tex. Midwest Cmty. Network, 1995-97. Named Outstanding Mcpl. Clk., Bluebonnet Chpt. Mcpl. Clks./Secs., 1995. Mem. Tex. Mcpl. Clks. Assn., Bluebonnet Chpt. Mcpl. Clks. (founder, pres. 1994-95, 95-96, immediate past pres. 1996-97), County Treas. Alumni Assn. (recorder 1991-93), Rotary Interant. Democrat. Ch. of Christ. Avocations: teaching parenting classes, knitting, golfing, gen. craft painting. Office: City of Eastland 416 S Seaman St Eastland TX 76448-2750

QUINN, JARUS WILLIAM, physicist, former association executive; b. West Grove, Pa., Aug. 25, 1930; s. William G. and Ellen C. (DuRoss) Q.; m. Margaret M. McNerney, June 27, 1953; children: J. Kevin, Megan, Jennifer, Colin, Kristin. BS, St. Joseph's Coll., 1952; postgrad., Johns Hopkins U., 1952-55; PhD, Cath. U. Am., 1964. Rsch. assoc. physics Johns Hopkins U., 1954-55; staff scientist Rsch. Inst. Advanced Study, 1956-57; rsch. assoc. physics Cath. U. Am., 1958-60, instr., 1961-64, asst. prof., 1965-69; exec. dir. Optical Soc. Am., Washington, 1969-93; governing bd. Am. Inst. Physics, 1973-94; pres. Stellar Focus, Sunnyvale, Calif., 1994-95. Bd. govs. Am. Assn. Engring. Socs., 1990-93. Fellow Optical Soc. Am. (Distinguished Service Award, 1993), mem. Am. Phys. Soc., Am. Soc. Assn. Execs., Coun. Engring. and Sci. Soc. Execs. Home: 357 Fearrington Post Pittsboro NC 27312-8517

QUINN, JOHN ALBERT, chemical engineering educator; b. Springfield, Ill., Sept. 3, 1932; s. Edward Joseph and Marie (Von De Bur) Q.; m. Frances Wilkie Daly, June 22, 1957; children: Sarah D., Rebecca V., John E. BSChemE, U. Ill., 1954; PhDChemE, Princeton U., 1959. Mem. faculty chem. engring. U. Ill., Urbana, 1958-70; prof. U. Pa., Phila., 1971—, Robert D. Bent prof., 1978—, chmn. dept. chem. engring., 1980-85; vis. prof. Imperial Coll. U. London, 1965-66; vis. scientist MIT, 1980; vis. prof. U. Rome/La Sapienza, 1992; mem. sci. adv. bds. Sepracor, Inc., Marlborough, Mass., 1984—, Whitaker Found., Mechanicsburg, Pa., 1987—; Mason lectr. Stanford U., 1981; Katz lectr. U. Mich., 1985; Reilly lectr. U. Notre Dame, 1987. Contbr. articles to profl. pubs.; editl. advisor Jour. Membrane Sci., 1975—, Indsl. and Chem. Engring. Rsch., 1987-88, Revs. in Chem. Engring., 1980—; pioneer rschr. on mass transfer and interfacial phenomena. Sr. postdoctoral fellow NSF, 1965-66; Sherman Fairchild scholar Calif. Inst. Tech., 1985. Fellow AAAS, Am. Inst. Med. and Biol. Engring.; mem. NAE, AIChE (Allan P. Colburn award 1966, Alpha Chi Sigma award 1978), Am. Acad. Arts and Scis., Am. Chem. Soc., Internat. Soc. Oxygen Transport to Tissue, Sigma X, Phi Lambda Upsilon, Tau Beta Pi. Home: 275 E Wynnewood Rd Merion Station PA 19066-1627 Office: Univ Pa Towne Bldg 220 S 33rd St Philadelphia PA 19104-6315

QUINN, JOHN COLLINS, publishing executive, newspaper editor; b. Providence, Oct. 24, 1925; s. John A. and Kathryn H. (Collins) Q.; m. Lois R. Richardson, June 20, 1953; children: John Collins, Lo-anne, Richard B., Christopher A. A.B., Providence Coll., 1945; M.S., Columbia U. Sch. Journalism, 1946. Successively copy boy, reporter, asst. city editor, Washington corr., asst. mng. editor, day mng. editor Providence Jour.-Bull., 1943-66; with Gannett Co. Inc., Rochester, N.Y., 1966-90; exec. editor Rochester Democrat & Chronicle, Times-Union, 1966-71; gen. mgr. Gannett News Service, 1967-80, pres., 1980-88, v.p. parent co., 1971-75, sr. v.p. news and info., 1975-80, sr. v.p., chief news exec. parent co., editor USA TODAY, 1983-89; exec. v.p. Gannett Co., Arlington, Va., 1983-90; trustee Gannett Found., Arlington, 1988-91; trustee, dep. chmn. Freedom Forum, Arlington, 1991—. Named to R.I. Hall of Fame, 1975, Editor of Yr. Nat. Press Found., 1986; recipient William Allen White citation, 1987, Women in Communications Headliner award, 1986; Paul Miller/Okla. State U. medallion, 1988. Mem. AP Mng. Editors (past dir., nat. pres. 1973-74), Am. Soc. Newspaper Editors (dir., chmn. editorial bd., chmn. conv. program, nat. pres. 1982-83). Roman Catholic. Home: 365 S Atlantic Ave Cocoa Beach FL 32931-2719 Office: Freedom Forum 1101 Wilson Blvd Arlington VA 22209-2248

QUINN, JOHN MICHAEL, physicist, geophysicist; b. Denver, May 8, 1946; s. Leonard Simon and Winifred Ruth (Doolan) Q.; m. Pamela Dagmar Shield, May 28, 1983. BS in Physics, U. Va., 1968; MS in Physics, U. Colo., 1982. Physicist U.S. Naval Rsch. Lab., Washington, 1967-73; prin. engr. Singer Simulation Products, Silver Spring, Md., 1973-74; rsch. physicist U.S. Naval Rsch. Lab, Washington, 1979-80; geophysicist U.S. Naval Oceanog. Office, Stennis Space Ctr., Miss., 1974-79, 82-85, geophysicist, mathematician, 1985—; investigator Polar Orbiting Geomagnetic Survey Experiment, 1990—; prin. investigator Def. Meteorol. Satellite Program Polar Orbiting Geomagnetic Survey Ext., 1991—; chmn. com. on earth and planetary geomagnetic survey satellites Internat. Assn. Geomagnetism and Aeronomy, 1991—, mem. internat. geomagnetic ref. field com., 1989—. Author: Epoch World Geomagnetic Model, 1985, 90, 95. With U.S. Army, 1968-71. Mem. Am. Geophys. Union, Am. Math. Soc., European Geophys. Soc., Math. Assn. Am. Achievements include creation of official Department of Defense world magnetic models which are used by military and civilian agencies for navigational purposes and basic rsch. of the earth's magnetic field; project coord. USN Project MAGNET; developed specialized remote geomagnetic sensing/modeling techniques to detect, in the lithosphere above the Curie isotherm, magnetization due to meteorite impact shocks and plate tectonic stresses, a technique which has implications with respect to earthquake and nuclear explosion monitoring. Home: 2732 S Braun Way Lakewood CO 80228-4954 Office: US Geog Survey Magnetics Group 966 Federal Blvd Denver CO 80204-3215

QUINN, JOHN R., archbishop; b. Riverside, Calif., Mar. 28, 1929; s. Ralph J. and Elizabeth (Carroll) Q. Student, St. Francis Sem., Immaculate Heart Sem., San Diego, 1947-48; Ph.B., Gregorian U., Rome, 1950, Licentiate in Sacred Theology, 1954, S.T.L., 1954. Ordained priest Roman Cath. Ch., 1953, as bishop, 1967. Assoc. pastor St. George Ch., Ontario, Calif., 1954-55; prof. theology Immaculate Heart Sem., San Diego, 1955-62, vice rector, 1960-62; pres. St. Francis Coll. Sem., El Cajon, Calif., 1962-64; rector Immaculate Heart Sem., 1964-68; aux. bishop, vicar gen. San Diego, 1967-72; bishop Oklahoma City, 1972-73, archbishop, 1973-77; archbishop San Francisco, 1977-95; provost U. San Diego, 1968-72; pastor St. Therese Parish, San Diego, 1969; apptd. consultor to Sacred Congregation for the Clergy in Rome, 1971; pres. Nat. Conf. Cath. Bishops, 1977-80, chmn. Com. of Liturgy; chmn. com. on Family Life U.S. Cath. Conf.; chmn. Bishops' Com. on Pastoral Rsch. and Practices, Bishops' Com. on Doctrine; mem. Bishops' Com. on Sems., Pontifical Commn., Seattle, 1987-88, Bishops' Com. for Pro-Life Activies, 1989—; apptd. pontifical del. for religious in U.S., 1983; pres. Calif. Cath. Conf., 1985; mem. Synod of Bishops, Rome, 1994; chmn. Nat. Conf. Cath. Bishops Com. on Doctrine, 1994—; vis. fellow Campion Hall, U. Oxford, 1996. Trustee U. San Diego, 1991-93. Mem. Cath. Theol. Soc. Am., Canon Law Soc. Am., Am. Cath. Hist. Soc. Address: 445 Church St San Francisco CA 94114-1720

QUINN, MICHAEL DESMOND, diversified financial services executive; b. Balt., Sept. 4, 1936; s. Michael Joseph and Gladys (Baldwin) Q.; m. Mary Annette McHenry, Apr. 11, 1961; children: Cailin A., Maureen K., Patricia B., Marianne P. BA, U. Md., 1970. With Weaver Bros., Inc. of Md., Balt., 1960—, investment v.p., corporate dir. interim loan dept., 1978-86; chmn. bd. Wye Mortgage Co., L.P., 1977—, Christiana Capital Group, Inc.; chmn., chief exec. officer Alliance Recovery Group, Inc., 1990—, Estate Trust Co., Inc.; faculty evening coll. Johns Hopkins U., Essex Community Coll., 1967—. Mem. gov.'s task force Md. Housing Ins. Fund; mem. Md. Health Claims Arbitration Panel; bd. visitors U. Md.; dist. adv. coun. U.S. Small Bus. Adminstrn. With USN, 1956-58. Mem. Md. Mortgage Bankers Assn. (pres. bd. govs.), Real Estate Bd. Greater Balt. (bd. dirs.), Home Builders Assn. Md., Md. Bankers Assn., Balt. Econ. Soc., N.Am. Soc. Corp. Planning, Greater Balt. Com., Ancient Order Hibernians, Balt Jr. Assn. Commerce (Richard Troja Meml. award 1967, Outstanding Young Man of Balt. 1969), Balt. County C. of C. (bd. dirs.). Home: 8207 Robin Hood Ct Baltimore MD 21204-1900 Office: 7400 York Rd Ste 300 Baltimore MD 21204-7502

QUINN, PAT MALOY, engineering company executive; b. Clay Ctr., Kans., May 28, 1932; s. Lawrence Maloy and Lois Shouse (Benjimen) Q.; m. Virginia Lois White, June 1, 1957; children: Michael Maloy, Jennifer Quinn Williams, Patrick Maloy, Amy Anne. BA in Literature, Kans. State U., 1954, BS in Civil Engring., 1960. Licensed engr. Civil engr. Schuab-Eaton, Manhattan, Kans., 1957-66; civil engr. Louis Berger Internat., East Orange, N.J., 1966—, v.p., 1976-84; chief structural engr. Louis Berger Internat., Thailand, 1966-68; chief engr. Louis Berger Internat., Indonesia, 1968-72; project mgr. Louis Berger Internat., Peru, 1973, The Philippines, 1974; v.p. Louis Berger Internat., Iran, 1974-76; group v.p., ptnr. Louis Berger Internat., Washington, 1984—. 1st lt. U.S. Army, 1954-57, Germany. Mem. ASCE, ASME, NSPE. Office: Louis Berger Internat 1819 H St NE Ste 900 Washington DC 20002-4017

QUINN, PATRICK, tranportation executive. Pres., co-chmn. U.S Xpress Enterprises, Inc., Chattanooga, Tenn., 1985—. Office: US Xpress Enterprises Inc 2931 S Market St Chattanooga TN 37410-1037

QUINN, PATRICK MICHAEL, wholesale food executive; b. Grand Rapids, Mich., Mar. 5, 1934; s. Robert George and Albertine Frances (Kolzinski) Q.; m. Rita Lee Ronan, Aug 6, 1955; children: Suzanne, Brian, Karen, Timothy, Catherine, Patricia. BSBA, Aquinas Coll., 1958. Sales mgr. Nabisco, Inc., Grand Rapids, 1958-73; exec. v.p. D&W Food Ctrs., Grand Rapids, 1973-85; pres., chief exec. officer Spartan Stores, Inc., Grand Rapids, 1985—; bd. dirs. Aquinas Coll., Grand Rapids; adv. bd. N. Am. Wholesale Grocers Assn., Falls Church, Va. Chmn. United Way Appeal, Grand Rapids, 1988. With U.S. Army, 1953-55. Mem. Nat. Grocers Assn. (vice chmn., bd. dirs. 1983—, chmn. 1989). Roman Catholic. Avocations: reading, hunting, fishing, golf. Office: Spartan Stores Inc 850 76th St SW Grand Rapids MI 49518

QUINN, PHILIP LAWRENCE, philosophy educator; b. Long Branch, N.J., June 22, 1940; s. Joseph Lawrence and Gertrude (Brown) Q. AB, Georgetown U., 1962; MS, U. Del., 1967; MA, U. Pitts., 1968, PhD, 1970; MA (hon.), Brown U., 1972. Asst. prof. philosophy Brown U., Providence, R.I., 1969-72, assoc. prof. philosophy, 1972-78, prof. philosophy, 1978-85, William Herbert Perry Faunce prof. philosophy, 1982-85; John A. O'Brien prof. philosophy U. Notre Dame, South Bend, Ind., 1985—. Author: (book) Divine Command and Moral Requirements, 1978; editor Faith and Philosophy, 1990-95; co-editor: A Companion to Philosophy of Religion, 1997; contbr. articles to profl. jours. Fulbright fellow, 1962-63; Danforth fellow, 1967-69. Mem. Am Philos. Assn. (sec., treas. ea. divsn. 1982-85, chmn. career opportunities com. 1985-90, exec. com. ctrl. divsn. 1987-90, v.p. ctrl. divsn. 1993-94, pres. 1994-95, chair ctrl. divsn. nominating com. 1995-96, acting chair Nat. Bd. of Officers 1995-96, chair 1996-99), Philosophy of Sci. Assn. (nominating com. 1984-86), Soc. Christian Philosophers (exec. com. 1981-84), N.Y. Acad. Scis. Roman Catholic. Avocations: reading, swimming, film, theatre. Home: 1645 W Turtle Creek Dr South Bend IN 46637-5660 Office: Univ Notre Dame Dept Philosophy Notre Dame IN 46556

QUINN, RICHARD KENDALL, environmental engineer; b. Cleve., July 15, 1957; s. William Jerome and Nancy Drysdale (Kendall) Q.; m. Ann Marie (Beebe), Jan. 28, 1984; children: Ryan K., Eric E., Margaret A., Emily E. BS in Civil Engring., U. Mich., 1979; BS in Geology, Colo. Sch. Mines, 1981; M Environ. Engring., Iowa State U., 1989. Registered profl. engr., Colo., Nebr., Mich., Ill., Minn., Ind., N.C. Geophysic surveyor Shell Oil Co., Denver, 1980-84; profl. engr., environ. engr. Camp Dresser & McKee Engring., Denver, 1985-91; engr. Harco Tech. Corp., Schaumburg, Ill., 1991-92, Walker divsn. Chgo. Bridge & Iron, Aurora, Ill., 1992-94; sr. v.p. Tonka Equipment Co., Plymouth, Minn., 1994—; sec./treas. Minn. sect. Water Pollution Control Agy., 1995, pres. elect, 1996-97. Cons. Iowa Community Devel. Block Grants, Des Moines, 1988—; active Big Bros. Assn. Grantee Iowa Engring. Soc., 1989. Mem. ASCE (chpt. sec. 1986-87), NSPE (edn. and coll. rels. com.), Am. Pub. Works Assn. (chpt. sect. 1987—), Am. Water Works Assn., Water Pollution Control Fedn., Am. Soc. Mil. Engrs., Iowa Engring. Soc., Ill. Engring. Soc., N.C. Engring. Soc., Mich. Engring. Soc., Nat. Assn. Corrosion Engrs., CSWEA Minn. sect. (pres. 1996—), Ctrl. State Water Pollution Control Assn. (sec.-treas.), Minn. Engring. Soc. Republican. Roman Catholic. Avocations: golf, hockey, flying, baseball, basketball. Home: 9176 Yates Bay Ct Brooklyn Park MN 55443-1629 Office: Tonka Equipment Co 13305 Water Tower Cir Plymouth MN 55441-3803

QUINN, ROBERT HENRY, surgeon, medical school administrator; b. Omaha, July 3, 1919; s. Henry Thomas and Esther Mary (Hecklin) Q.; m. Ruth Elizabeth Binder, Aug. 1, 1942; children: Karen, Terrence, Thomas, Lisa. B.S., Creighton U., 1941, M.D., 1943. Intern St. Joseph's Hosp., Denver, 1943; resident in ob-gyn Northwestern U., 1946-47, Luth. Deaconess Hosp., Chgo., 1948; gen. practice medicine Sioux Falls, S.D., 1946-54; surgery fellow Ochsner Clinic, New Orleans, 1954-58; practice medicine specializing in surgery Sioux Falls, S.D., 1958-75; asso. dean U. S.D. Sch. Medicine, Sioux Falls, 1974-81; prof., chmn. div. surgery U. S.D. Sch. Medicine, 1977-82, v.p., dean, 1982-87, acting chmn. dept. surgery, 1982-89, prof. surgery emeritus, 1989—; chief staff McKennan Hosp., Sioux Falls, 1966; assoc. dean West River Campus, 1987-89; mem. adv. bd. clin. fellowship Bush Found., 1983-88. Bd. dirs. Karl Mundt Found., 1970—, McCrossan Boys Ranch, 1985—, Rapid City Regional Eye Inst. Found., 1987. Served with M.C., USNR, 1943-46. Recipient Disting. Service award U. S.D., 1978, Alumni Merit award Sch. Medicine Creighton U., 1985. Mem. AMA (mem. council on continuing physician edn. 1978-81, cert. of appreciation ho. of dels. 1971-75), ACS, Assn. Surg. Chmn., Ochsner Surg. Soc., S.D. State Med. Assn. (pres. 1969-70), Alpha Omega Alpha. Republican. Roman Catholic. Club: Rotary. Home: 110 Fairway Dr Spearfish SD 57783-3109 Office: 3526 5th St Ste 200 Rapid City SD 57701

QUINN, THOMAS JOSEPH, lawyer; b. Worcester, Mass., May 26, 1954; s. John Peter and Winifred Agnes (McDonough) Q.; children: Meghan, Conor, Alexander. BA summa cum laude, St. Francis Coll., Biddeford, Maine, 1975; JD, U. Notre Dame, 1978. Bar: Maine 1978, Mass. 1979, U.S. Dist. Ct. Maine 1978, U.S. Ct. Appeals (1st cir.) 1991. Rsch. asst. to prof. Alan Dershowitz Harvard Law Sch., Cambridge, Mass., 1977; law clk. to Hon. Charles A. Pomeroy Supreme Jud. Ct. of Maine, Portland, 1978-79; assoc., ptnr. Douglas, Whiting, Quinn & Denham, Portland, 1979-93; ptnr. Beals & Quinn, Portland, 1993—; instr. U. So. Maine, Portland, 1982-86. Author: (screenplay) Choice of Law, 1992; notes editor, author Jour. of Legislation, 1978-79; contbg. author Maine Lawyers Rev. Mem. City of Portland Historic Preservation Com., 1993-95. Mem. Am. Bd. Trial Advocates, Maine Bar Assn., Cumberland County Bar Assn., Maine Trial Lawyers Assn., Million Dollar Advocates Forum. Avocations: painting, travel, writing. Home: 415 Brighton Ave Portland ME 04102-2326 Office: Beals & Quinn 77 Middle St Portland ME 04101-4214

QUINN, TIMOTHY CHARLES, JR., lawyer; b. Caro, Mich., Mar. 3, 1936; s. Timothy Charles and Jessie (Brown) Q.; m. Linda Ricci, June 21, 1958; children: Gina M., Samantha E., Timothy Charles III. BA, U. Mich., 1960; JD, Columbia U., 1963. Bar: N.Y. 1963, U.S. Dist. Ct. (so. and ea. dists.) N.Y. 1965, U.S. Ct. Appeals (2d cir.) 1967. Assoc. Clark, Carr & Ellis, N.Y.C., 1963-69, Casey, Tyre, Wallace & Bannerman, N.Y.C., 1969-71, Arsham & Keenan, N.Y.C., 1971; assoc. Conboy, Hewitt, O'Brien & Boradman, N.Y.C., 1972-74, ptnr., 1975-83, mem. exec. com., 1981-83; ptnr. Quinn, Cohen, Shields & Bock, N.Y.C., 1983-88, Quinn & Suhr, White Plains, N.Y., 1988-95, Quinn, Marantis & Rosenberg, White Plains, N.Y., 1995-97, Dickerson & Reilly, N.Y.C., 1997—; arbitrator N.Y.C. Civil Ct., 1982-88 , Am. Arbitration Assn., N.Y.C., 1966—, 9th Jud. Dist., 1988—. Mem. ABA, N.Y. State Bar Assn., Westchester County Bar Assn., Assn. of Bar of City of N.Y., N.Y. State Trial Lawyers Assn., Nat. Assn. R.R. Trial Counsel, Conf. Freight Loss and Damage Counsel, N.Y. Law Inst., Def. Rsch. Inst., Westchester Country Club. Avocation: golf. Home: 34 Pinehurst Dr Purchase NY 10577-1307 Office: Dickerson & Reilly 780 3rd Ave New York NY 10017-2024

QUINN, WILLIAM FRANCIS, lawyer; b. Rochester, N.Y., July 13, 1919; s. Charles Alvin and Elizabeth (Dorrity) Q.; m. Nancy Ellen Witbeck, July 11, 1942; children: William Francis, Stephen Desford, Timothy Charles, Christopher Thomas, Ann Cecily, Mary Kaiulani, Gregory Anthony. B.S. summa cum laude, St. Louis U., 1940; LL.B. cum laude, Harvard U., 1947. Bar: Hawaii 1948. Ptnr. Robertson, Castle & Anthony, Honolulu, 1947-57; gov. Ter. of Hawaii, 1957-59, state Hawaii, 1959-62; partner Quinn & Moore, Honolulu, 1962-64; exec. v.p. Dole Co., Honolulu., 1964-65; pres. Dole Co., 1965-72; ptnr. Jenks, Kidwell, Goodsill & Anderson, Honolulu, 1972-73, Goodsill Anderson & Quinn, 1973-82, Goodsill Anderson Quinn & Stifel, 1982-91; mem. sr. adv. bd. 9th Cir. Jud. Coun. Served with USNR, 1942-46. Decorated knight of Holy Sepulchre Order. Republican. Roman Catholic. Clubs: Waialae Country, Pacific (Honolulu). Home: 1365 Laukahi St Honolulu HI 96821-1407 Office: Alii Place 1099 Alakea St Ste 1800 Honolulu HI 96813-4500

QUINN, WILLIAM WILSON, army officer, manufacturing executive; b. Crisfield, Md., Nov. 1, 1907; s. William Samuel and Alice (Wilson) Q.; m. Bette Williams, Dec. 16, 1939; children: Sally, Donna, William Wilson. Student, St. John's Coll., Annapolis, Md., 1927-29; B.S., U.S. Mil. Acad., 1933; postgrad., Inf. Sch., Ft. Benning, Ga., 1938-39, Command and Staff Sch., Ft. Leavenworth, Kans., 1941, Nat. War Coll., Washington, 1948-49. Commd. 2d lt. inf. U.S. Army, 1933, advanced through grades to lt. gen., 1961; co. comdr. inf., 1933-36; provost marshal city of Manila, 1937-38; assigned G-2 IV Corps, 1943-44, G-2 7th Army Invasion S. France, 1944-45; dir. Strategic Service Unit, 1946-47, G-2 X Corps, Inchon Landing, Inchon Landing, Korea, 1950; comdg. officer 7th Inf. Div. 17th Inf. Regt., Korea, 1951; office Chief of Staff U.S. Army, 1952; asst. divsn. comdr. 47th Inf. Div., 1953; chief Army sect. Joint U.S. Mil. Adv. Group to Greece, 1953-55; asst. divsn. comdr. 9th Inf. Div., Germany, 1955-56; comdg. gen. Ft. Carson, Colo., 1956; comdg. gen. 4th Inf. Div. Ft. Lewis, Washington, 1957; chief pub. info. Dept. Army, 1960-61; dep. dir. Def. Intelligence Agy., 1961-64; comdg. gen. 7th U.S. Army Germany, 1964-66; ret., 1966; v.p. Martin Marietta Corp., Washington, 1966-72; pres. Quinn Assos., Washington, 1972—. Author articles. Vice chmn. Goldwater Edn. Found. Decorated D.S.M. with cluster, Silver Star, Legion of Merit with cluster, Air medal with clusters, Purple Heart, Bronze star with V device, Officer, Legion of Honor, France; recipient Presdl. Unit citation, Korea, Das. Grosse Verdienstkreuz mit Stern, Germany. Mem. SAR, Army Navy Club, Chevy Chase Club, Bohemian Club of San Francisco, Kappa Alpha. Episcopalian. Address: 900 N Taylor St Arlington VA 22203

QUINN, YVONNE SUSAN, lawyer; b. Spring Valley, Ill., May 13, 1951; d. Robert Leslie and Shirley Eilene (Morse) Q.; m. Ronald S. Rolfe, Sept. 1, 1979. BA, U. Ill., 1973; JD, U. Mich., 1976, MA in Econs., 1977. Bar: N.Y. 1978, U.S. Dist. Ct. (ea. and so. dists.) N.Y. 1978, U.S. Ct. Appeals

(3d, 5th, 9th, 10th and D.C. cirs.) 1982, U.S. Ct. Appeals (2d cir.) 1992, U.S. Ct. Appeals (4th cir.) 1994, U.S. Supreme Ct. 1982. Assoc. Cravath, Swaine & Moore, N.Y.C., 1977-80; assoc. Sullivan & Cromwell, N.Y.C., 1980-84, ptnr., 1984—. Mem. ABA, Assn. of Bar of City of N.Y., India House Club. Office: Sullivan & Cromwell 125 Broad St New York NY 10004-2400

QUINNAN, GERALD VINCENT, JR., medical educator; b. Boston, Sept. 7, 1947; s. Gerald Vincent and Mary (Lally) Q.; children: Kevin, Kylie, Kathleen, John, Gerald; m. Leigh A. Sawyer. AB in Chemistry, Coll. Holy Cross, 1969; MD cum laude, St. Louis U., 1973. Diplomate Am. Bd. Internal Medicine. Intern, resident, fellow Boston U. Med. Ctr., 1973-77; med. officer Bur. Biologics, USPHS, Bethesda, Md., 1977; advanced through grades to asst. surgeon gen. USPHS, 1992; dir. herpes virus br., dep. dir. div. virology Bur. Biologics, Bethesda, 1980-81; dir. div. virology Ctr. for Drugs and Biologics, Bethesda, 1981-88; dep. dir. Ctr. Biologics Evaluation and Rsch., Bethesda, 1988-93, acting dir., 1990-92; prof. uniformed svcs. U. Health Scis., Bethesda, 1993—. Contbr. chpts. to books, numerous articles to profl. jours.; editl. bd./reviewer several jours. Fellow Infectious Diseases Soc. Am.; mem. AAAS, Am. Soc. for Microbiology, Am. Soc. for Clin. Investigation, Sigma Xi, Alpha Omega Alpha. Roman Catholic. Office: Uniformed Svcs U Hlth Scis Div Tropical PH 4301 Jones Bridge Rd Bethesda MD 20814-4712

QUINNELL, BRUCE ANDREW, retail book chain executive; b. Washington, Jan. 6, 1949; s. Robert Kay and Marion Louise (Moseley) Q.; m. Aug. 31, 1972 (div. June 1986); children: Paul David, Andrea Carolyn; m. Marcia Melodie Mundie. BS in Acctg., Va. Poly. Inst. and State U., 1971, MA in Acctg., 1972. CPA, Ohio, Mo., Tex., Tenn. Sr. auditor Ernst & Whinney, Columbus, Ohio, 1972-75; treas., chief fin. officer Midway Ford Truck Ctr., Kansas City, Mo., 1975-82; sr. v.p., chief fin. officer Rsch. Health Svcs., Kansas City, 1982-85; sr. v.p. VHA Enterprises Inc., Irving, Tex., 1985-87; v.p., treas., chief fin. officer Dollar Gen. Corp., Nashville, 1987-92; exec. v.p. Pace Membership Warehouse, Englewood, Colo., 1992-93; exec. v.p., COO Walden Book Co., Stamford, Conn., 1993, pres., 1994-97; pres. Borders Group, Inc., Ann Arbor, Mich., 1997—. Bd. dirs. Advs. Tenn. State U. Coll. Bus., Nashville, 1991-92, Jr. Achievement Mid. Tenn., 1992; mem. adv. coun. Reading Is Fundamental. Mem. Fin. Execs. Inst., Am. Inst. CPA'S, Nat. Investor Rels. Inst. Republican. Lutheran. Avocations: racquetball, golf, scuba diving. Office: Borders Group Inc 100 Phoenix Dr PO Box 996 Ann Arbor MI 48106-9700

QUINN-KERINS, CATHERINE, psychologist; b. Neptune, N.J., Mar. 12, 1951; d. James R. and Jane (Forman) Quinn; m. Daniel Kerins, Jan. 14, 1978; children: Katie, Amanda, Benjamin. BA magna cum laude, Fairleigh Dickinson U., 1973; postgrad., Hahneman Med. Coll., 1974-75; MEd, U. Del., 1975; PhD, U. Pa., 1983. Lic. psychologist, Pa. Treatment coord., psychologist St. Gabriel's Hall, Audubon, Pa., 1975-86; clin. psychologist InterPsych Assocs., King of Prussia, Pa., 1985-87; full-time ind. practice Audubon, 1987—; mem. allied health staff Phoenixville (Pa.) Hosp., 1990—; mem. part-time faculty dept. psychology Neuman Coll., Aston, Pa., 1977. V.p. Montessori Children's House of Valley Forge, Wayne, Pa., 1985-87. Mem. APA, Am. Assn. Anxiety Disorders, Obsessive Compulsive Found., Phi Omega Epsilon, Phi Zeta Kappa, Psi Chi. Avocations: spending time with her children, walking on the beach, artwork, reading. Home: 2018 Blackbird Cir Norristown PA 19403-1845 Office: 2605 Egypt Rd Norristown PA 19403-2317

QUINSLER, WILLIAM THOMSON, retired investment advisor; b. Watertown, Mass., June 21, 1924; s. Phillips Brooks and Eleanor (Macurdy) Q.; m. Barbara Jean Faust, June 15, 1957; children: William Thomson, Jr., Harry Faust, Catharine Marten Quinsler Örn. B.S. in Elec. Engring., U. Ariz., 1950. Registered profl. engr., Ariz. Engr. Ariz. Pub. Service Co., Phoenix, 1950-53; staff cons. treasury dept. Ariz. Pub. Service Co., 1953, supr. treasury dept., 1954, mgr. fin. services, 1955-62, asst. treas., 1962-69, sec., asst. treas., 1969-83; founding dir. Utility Svcs. Ins. Co. Ltd., Hamilton, Bermuda, 1970-84; pres., chief oper. officer Utility Svcs. Ins. Co. Ltd., 1982-84; trustee Tax-Free Trust of Ariz., 1986—, chmn. audit com., 1992—. Mem. adv. bd. Apache Nat. Forest Service; mem. Phoenix Symphony Assn. Served with USAAF, 1943-46. Mem. IEEE, NSPE, Ariz. Soc. Profl. Engrs., Am., Pacific Coast gas assns., Am. Soc. Corp. Secs., Pacific Coast Electric Assn., C. of C., Ariz. Cattle Growers Assn., Greenlee County Cattle Growers Assn., Phoenix Soc. Fin. Analysts (past pres. and dir.). Home and Office: 5428 E Calle Del Medio Phoenix AZ 85018-4530

QUINSON, BRUNO ANDRE, publishing executive; b. Norwich, Conn., Jan. 1, 1938; s. Louis Jean and Suzanne Marie (Richard) Q.; m. Mary Ann Goodman, May 3, 1980; children by previous marriage: Timothy Bruno, Marc Albert (dec.), Christopher Louis; stepchildren: J. Geoffrey Taylor, Luke J. Taylor, Adam J. Taylor, Joshua P. Taylor. BA, Williams Coll., 1958; postgrad., NYU, 1960-61. Product mgr. Simon & Schuster, N.Y.C., 1960-65; pub., gen. mgr. Golden Press (div. Western Pub. Co., Inc.), 1965-70; pres. Larousse & Co., Inc., N.Y.C., 1970-82, also bd. dirs.; pres. trade and reference div. Macmillan Pub. Co., N.Y.C., 1982-88; pres., chief exec. officer Henry Holt & Co. Inc., N.Y.C., 1988-96; bd. dirs. The Frost Place, Music & More, Henry Holt & Co., Inc., N.Y.C.; bd. dirs. Fitzhenry & Whiteside, The Voyager Co., Nat. Book Found., chmn., 1993-96; treas. Columbia Univ. Press, 1994—; mem. exec. bd. MacMillan Ltd., 1995-96. Bd. dirs. Rye (N.Y.) Art Ctr., treas., 1973-74; bd. dirs. Northside Ctr. for Child Devel., 1981-89, chmn., 1987-89, mem. adv. bd., 1990—; bd. dirs. 1115 Fifth Ave. Corp., 1983-94, 96—; bd. dirs. Lycee Francais de New York, 1994-96, bd. dirs. Vol. Cons. Group, 1997. Decorated chevalier des Arts et Letters (France). Mem. Am. Assn. Pubs. (bd. dirs. 1991-95), Century Assn., Manhattan Theater Club (bd. dirs. 1991—), Norfolk Country Club, The River Club. Office: Henry Holt & Co Inc 115 W 18th St New York NY 10011-4113

QUINT, ARNOLD HARRIS, lawyer; b. Boston, Jan. 3, 1942; s. Milton and Esther (Kirshen) Q.; m. Susan Arenson, July 23, 1967; children: Edward, Michael. AB, Haverford (Pa.) Coll., 1963; LLB, Yale U., 1966. Bar: D.C. 1967. Supervisory atty. Fed. Power Commn., Washington, 1967-70; assoc. Hunton & Williams, Washington, 1970-74, ptnr., 1974—. Mem. ABA, Fed. Energy Bar Assn. (com. chmn. 1979-83, bd. dirs. 1989-92). Office: Hunton & Williams 1900 K St NW Washington DC 20006-1110

QUINT, BERT, journalist; b. N.Y.C., Sept. 22, 1930; s. George and Sadye (Slonim) Q.; m. Diane Frances Schwab, Apr. 10, 1975; children: Lara Gabrielle, Amy Frances. BS, NYU, 1952. Reporter Worcester (Mass.) Telegram, 1952-53, AP, 1953-54, N.Y. Herald Tribune, 1956-58; mag. editor, free lance corr. N.Y. Herald Tribune, Wall Street Jour., CBS News, others, Mexico City, 1958-65; corr. CBS News, 1965-93; adj. prof. broadcast journalism U. Colo., Boulder, 1993—; journalist/anchor/writer TV Quint Colo. Inc. Recipient Radio Reporting award Overseas Press Club, 1971. Mem. Soc. Profl. Journalists, Fgn. Corr. Assn. Mex. (pres.). Home and Office: 539 Bari Ct Boulder CO 80303-4312

QUINT, IRA, retail executive; b. N.Y.C., May 29, 1930; s. Theodore Isaac and Rebecca (Ginandes) Q.; m. Carol Ann Goldsmith (div. Feb. 1984); children: Susan Amy, Stephanie Ann. B.S., NYU, 1951; M.B.A., Harvard U., 1954. Group nat. mdse. mgr. Sears Roebuck & Co., Chgo., 1954-78; pres. Colonial Corp. Am., N.Y.C., 1978-79; pres., CEO Venture Stores, St. Louis, 1979-81; exec. v.p. Montgomery Ward, Chgo., 1981-85; pres. Lane Bryant Stores, N.Y.C., 1985-90; pres., chief exec. officer Conston Corp., Phila., 1990-92; pres. Quint Consultancy, N.Y.C., 1992—. Club: Harvard (N.Y.C.). Home and Office: 130 E 67th St New York NY 10021-6136

QUINTANA, JOSE BOOTH, health care executive; b. Coral Gables, Fla., July 13, 1946; s. Jose Luis and Carmen Elaine (Booth) Q.; m. Mary Jo Gregg, Sept. 7, 1968; children: Stephanie Elizabeth, Meredith Caroline. BSBA, U. Fla., 1968; MHA, Duke U., 1974; PhD, U. Ala., 1984. Commd. 2d lt. USAF, 1969, advanced through grades to lt. col., 1985, resigned, 1989; dir. pers. and adminstrv. svcs. USAF Regional Hosp., March AFB, Calif., 1969-71, adminstrv. asst. hosp. svcs., 1971-72; adminstr. USAF Hosp., Ubon Royal Thai Air Base, Thailand, 1974, Kunsan Air Base, South Korea, 1974-75; dir. pers. and adminstrv. svcs. USAF Regional Hosp., Maxwell AFB, Ala., 1975, dir. patent info., 1975-76, dir. med. resource mgmt., 1976-78; chief med. readiness ops. divsn. Office of Surgeon, USAF in Europe, Ramstein AFB, West Germany, 1978-81; strategic planner, health affairs and plans divsn. Office Air Force Surgeon Gen., Bolling AFB, Washington, 1984-86, sr. health rsch. analyst, directorate med. plans and resources, 1986-89; health svcs. rsch. and devel. coord., rsch. svc. VA Med. Ctr., Birmingham, Ala., 1989—, exec. asst. to dir. (quality), 1991—, acute care mgr. surg. svc., 1997—; asst. prof. dept. health svcs. adminstrn. U. Ala., Birmingham, 1989—; lectr. in field. Contbr. articles to profl. jours. Fellow ACHE; mem. Am. Soc. Quality Control (mem. edn. com. 1993), Ala. Hosp. Assn. (mem. quality innovation com. 1992—), Assn. Health Svcs. Rsch., Assn. Univ. Programs in Health Adminstrn., Acad. Mgmt., Phi Kappa Phi, Beta Gamma Sigma. Republican. Southern Baptist. Avocations: computers, bridge, bible study. Office: U Ala Dept Health Svcs Adminstrn 1675 University Blvd # 512 Webb Birmingham AL 35233

QUINTANA, SAMMY J., lawyer; b. Santa Fe, Mar. 15, 1949; s. Genaro and Mary (Sena) Q.; m. Patricia Lujan, June 5, 1971; children: Paul, Ana Maria. BA, U. N.Mex., 1971, JD, 1974. U.S. Dist. Ct. Asst. atty. gen. Atty. Gen. N.Mex., Santa Fe, 1978-80; asst. dist. atty. Dist. Atty. Santa Fe, 1980-84; dep. dist. atty. Dist. Atty. Taos, N.Mex., 1984-91; chief pub. defender Pub. Defender N.Mex., Santa Fe, 1991-95; Bd. dirs. N.Mex. Bd. Bar Examiners, Santa Fe, 1987-94. Mem. sch. bd. Pojoaque (N.Mex.) Valley Schs., 1977—; bd. dirs. Gov's. Mental Health Planning Coun., Santa Fe, 1991-95, Nat. Sch. Bds. Assn., Alexandria, Va., 1990—, sec./treas., 1993-94; bd. dirs. exec. com. N.Mex. Sch. Bds. Assn., Santa Fe, 1986—, pres., 1995-96. Recipient Outstanding Sch. Bd. Mem. award N.Mex. Sch. Bds. Assn., 1987, Outstanding Svc. award Nat. Sch. Bds. Assn., 1991. Mem. N.Mex. Bar Assn., Nat. Assn. Criminal Def. Laywers. Democrat. Roman Catholic. Avocations: golf, bowling, softball, hiking. Home: 14-A County Rd 113-A Santa Fe NM 87501-8301 Office: Simons Caddy & Friedman LLP PO Box 4160 Santa Fe NM 87502

QUINTERO, JOSE, theatrical director; b. Panama City, Panama, Oct. 15, 1924; s. Carlos Rivira and Consuelo (Palmerola) de Q. Student, Goodman Theater, Chgo., 1934-35, U. So. Calif. and L.A. City Coll., 1948. Producer, dir. Circle in the Square Theatre, N.Y.C., 1951-63; instr. Fla. State U., U. Houston. Producer, dir.; (plays) Desire Under the Elms, Cradle Song, La Ronde, The Iceman Cometh, The Girl on the Via Flaminia, Summer and Smoke, The King and the Duke, Burning Bright, Yerma, Dark of the Moon, The Balcony, Our Town, Plays for Bleecker Street, (Broadway plays) A Moon for the Misbegotten (Tony award), The Innkeepers, Portrait of a Lady, Gabrielle, In the Summer House, The Girl on the Via Flaminia, The Skin of Our Teeth, Long Days Journey into Night, A Touch of the Poet, Look We've Come Through, Great Day in the Morning, Strange Interlude, Diamond Orchid, Anna Christie, Faith Healer, Clothes for a Summer Hotel, Welded, 1981, Cat On A Hot Tin Roof, 1984, Long Days Journey Into Night, 1987, Private Lives, 1990, Our Town, 1993, others, (film) The Roman Spring of Mrs. Stone, 1961, (TV movies) Hughie, Medea, Our Town; dir. Eugene O'Neill play for Nat. Pub. Radio, 1988/93. Decorated Cabellero de la Order de Vasco Nunez de Balboa; recipient spl. citation La Asamblea Nacional de Panama, Drama Desk award, Tony award, Page One award, Disting. Artist award, 1985, L.A. Drama Circle award, O'Neill Gold Medal award, 1988, South Ea. Theatre Conf. award for life achievement; named to Theatre Hall of Fame. Mem. Dirs. Guild Am., Soc. Stage Dirs. and Choreographers, Am. Fellows of Theatre. Address: The Lantz Office 888 7th Ave Ste 2500 New York NY 10106*

QUINTERO, RONALD GARY, management consultant; b. Detroit, Jan. 5, 1954; s. John Urdiales and Jean Lorraine (Morton) Q.; m. Barbara Kay McDaniel, June 15, 1985; children: Jean Marie, Alexandra Lisa. AB, Lafayette Coll., 1975; MS, NYU, 1976, APC, 1978. CPA, CFA, CFP, cert. mgmt. acct., cert. fraud examiner, cert. insolvency and reorgn. acct., cert. turnaround profl. Sr. mgr. Peat, Marwick, Mitchell & Co., N.Y.C., 1975-85; workout cons. Zolfo, Cooper & Co., N.Y.C., 1985-87; assoc. Bear, Stearns & Co., Inc., N.Y.C., 1987-88; prin. R. G. Quintero & Co., N.Y.C., 1988—; mng. dir. Chartered Capital Advisers, Inc., N.Y.C., 1988—; adj. prof. New Sch. for Social Rsch., N.Y.C., 1983-85; internat. lectr.; adj. prof. N.Y. Inst. Fin., N.Y.C., 1988—; instr. Ctr. for Profl. Edn., Berwyn, Pa., 1991—. Author: (book and cassette) Mergers and Acquisitions, 1990; contbg. author several books; contbr. articles to profl. jours.; creator: Quintero Index of Bankrupt Stocks. Mem. AICPAs, Am. Bankruptcy Inst., N.Y. Soc. CPAs (chmn. com. 1990-91, Max Block Disting. Article award 1990, Outstanding Discussion Leader 1991), Turnaround Mgmt. Assn. (bd. dirs., exec. com.). Avocations: squash, softball, running, computers, reading. Office: R G Quintero & Co 145 4th Ave New York NY 10003-4906

QUINTIERE, GARY G., lawyer; b. Passaic, N.J., Nov. 26, 1944; s. Benjamin and Sadie (Riotto) Q.; m. Judy Rosenthal, Aug. 16, 1966; children: Karen, Geoffrey. AB in Govt., Lafayette Coll., 1966; JD, George Washington U., 1969. Law clk. to Judge Philip Nichols, Jr. U.S. Ct. Appeals (Fed. cir.), Washington, 1969-70; from assoc. to ptnr. Miller & Chevalier, Washington, 1970-85; ptnr. Morgan, Lewis & Bockius, Washington, 1985—. Mem. ABA, D.C. Bar Assn., Va. Bar Assn. Avocations: tennis, skiing, golf. Home: 14 Mercy Ct Potomac MD 20854-4540 Office: Morgan Lewis & Bockius 1800 M St NW Washington DC 20036-5802

QUINTON, PAUL MARQUIS, physiology educator, researcher; b. Houston, Tex., Sept. 17, 1944; s. Curtis Lincoln and Mercedes Genale (Danley) Q.; m. Liesbet Joris, Dec. 31, 1992; 1 child, Marquis. BA, U. Tex., 1967; PhD, Rice U., 1971. Asst. prof. physiology and medicine UCLA Med. Sch., 1975-79; asst. prof. biomed. scis. U. Calif., Riverside, 1979-81, assoc. prof., 1981-84, prof., 1984— prof. Pediatrics, UCSD, 1997—; assoc. prof. physiology UCLA, 1981-91. Assoc. ed. Am. Journal Physiology: Cell Biology (Bethesda), assoc. ed. Experimental Physiology (Cambridge). Recipient Rsch. Career Devel. award NIH, 1978, Paul di Sant'Agnese Disting. Sci. Achievement award Nat. Cystic Fibrosis Found., 1991, Joseph Levy Meml. award Internat. Cystic Fibrosis (Mucovisidosis) Assn., 1994. Office: U Calif Sch Medicine 9500 Gilman Dr La Jolla CA 92093-5003

QUINTOS, ELIAS RILLORAZA, cardiac surgeon, thoracic surgeon; b. Manila, Apr. 29, 1955; s. Melanio and Aurora (Rilloraza) Q.; m. Augusta Madarang, Mar. 17, 1985; children: Melanie, Amanda, Elias Joseph. BS in Biochemistry, SUNY, Stony Brook, 1977; MD, Tulane U., 1982. Diplomate Am. Bd. Thoracic Surgery, Am. Bd. Surgery. Resident in surgery SUNY, Stony Brook, 1982-87; resident in thoracic surgery SUNY, Syracuse, 1987-89; cardiac surgeon Arnot-Ogden Med. Ctr., Elmira, N.Y., 1989-91; resident in surgery Orlando (Fla.) Regional med. Ctr., 1991-92, asst. dir. surg. edn. and thoracic surgery attending, 1992-93; cardiac surgeon Arnot-Ogden Med. Ctr., 1993—. Recipient Attending Surgeon of Yr. award, 1992-93, Physician Recognition award AMA, 1994—. Fellow Am. Coll. Surgeons, Am. Coll. Chest Physicians, Am. Coll. Cardiology; mem. Soc. Thoracic Surgeons, Upstate Soc. Thoracic Surgeons, Med. Soc. State of N.Y. Roman Catholic. Avocations: tennis, boating, skiing. Office: Ctrl NY Cardiac Sug Group 600 Ivy St Ste 101 Elmira NY 14905-1627

QUIRANTES, ALBERT M., lawyer; b. Cuba, Jan. 25, 1963; came to U.S., 1966; s. Alberto adn Haydee (Mendez) Q. B in Bus., U. Miami, Fla., 1984; JD, U. Fla., 1987. Bar: Fla. 1988, U.S. Dist. Ct. (so. dist.) Fla. 1990, U.S. Dist. Ct. (mid. dist.) Fla. 1990, U.S. Ct. Appeals (11th cir.) 1990, U.S. Supreme Ct. 1991, U.S. Dist. Ct. Ariz. 1991. Pub. defender Ct. 8th cir., Gainsville, Fla., 1988-89; pvt. practice Miami, Fla., 1989—; sr. ptnr. Ticket Law Ctr., P.A., Miami, Fla., 1990—. Mem. Fla. Traffic Ct. Rules Com., Tallahassee, 1991—. Mem. Fla. Assn. Criminal Def. Attys., Dade Bar (cts. com. 1992—, criminal cts. com. 1992—), Latin C. of C., Jaycees. Home and Office: 1800 NW 7th St Miami FL 33125-3504

QUIRICO, FRANCIS JOSEPH, retired state supreme court justice; b. Pittsfield, Mass., Feb. 18, 1911; s. Luigi and Lucia (Giovanetti) Q. LL.B., Northeastern U., 1932, LL.D., 1970; J.D. (hon.), Suffolk U., 1971; LL.D. (hon.), Am. Internat. U., 1974, New Eng. Sch. Law, 1975, Western New Eng. Coll., Springfield, Mass., 1981, North Adams (Mass.) State Coll., 1981. Bar: Mass. 1932, U.S. Ct. Appeals (1st cir.), U.S. Supreme Ct. 1939. Pvt. practice law Pittsfield, 1932-56, city solicitor, 1948-52; justice Superior Ct. Mass., 1956-69, Supreme Jud. Ct. Mass., 1969-81; recalled to active service with Superior Ct., 1981-86, Appeals Ct., 1986-87. Served with USAAF, 1942-46. Mem. Berkshire County Bar Assn., Am. Law Inst., Am. Legion. Roman Catholic. *

QUIRING, FRANK STANLEY, chemist, educator; b. Goessel, Kans., Sept. 2, 1927; s. Henry and Helen (Lehrman) Q.; m. Evelyn Ruth Wiebe, Aug. 16, 1950; children: Samuel, Sherwood, Natalie, Powell. BA, Bethel Coll., 1950; MA, U. Kans., 1957. Cert. tchr. Kans., Mo. Tchr. sci. Coldwater (Kans.) High Sch., 1950-51, Pretty Prairie (Kans.) High Sch., 1952-55; tchr. chem. Wyandotte High Sch., Kansas City, Kans., 1955-59, Clayton (Mo.) High Sch., 1959-91; lab. dir. NSF Summer Insts. Hope Coll., Holland, Mich., 1964-92; rsch. assoc. Washington U., St. Louis, 1967-68; rsch. chemist Monsanto U., St. Louis, 1976-77, 84-85; cons. Coll. Bd. Adv. Placement Divsn., Princeton, N.J., 1966—, Ohaus Corp., Florham Park, N.J., 1986-90. Contbr. articles to profl. jours. With USN, 1945-46. Recipient Presdl. award NSF, 1984, Catalyst award Chem. Mfgs. Assn., 1973; Tandy Corp. Tech. scholar, 1990. Mem. NEA (pres. Clayton chpt. 1965-66), Am. Chem. Assn. (pres. St. Louis chpt. 1970-71), Am. Chem. Soc. (Conant award 1969), Nat. Sci. Tchrs. Assn. Mennonite. Avocations: hiking, tennis, church choir. Home: 32 Regal Crescent St North Newton KS 67117-8039

QUIRK, FRANK JOSEPH, management consulting company executive; b. N.Y.C., Feb. 27, 1941; s. Frank J. and Madeline B. Quirk; BA, Cornell U., 1962, MBA, 1964; m. Betty Josephine Mauldin, Jan. 7, 1967; children: Laura Josephine, Katherine Elizabeth. Assoc., Booz, Allen & Hamilton, Inc., Chgo. and Washington, 1967-72; exec. v.p. Macro Internat., Inc., Silver Spring, Md., 1972-79, pres., CEO, 1980—. Bd. dirs. Profl. Svcs. Coun. Served to capt. U.S. Army, 1964-66. Club: Belle Haven Country. Home: 2110 Foresthill Rd Alexandria VA 22307-1128 Office: Macro Internat Inc 11785 Beltsville Dr Beltsville MD 20705-3121

QUIRK, JOHN JAMES, investment company executive; b. N.Y.C., July 10, 1943; s. Francis J. and Madeline A. (Meizinger) Q.; m. Kathryn Anne O'Brien, Mar. 21, 1963; children: John James, Ashlin Carter, Merritt Andrew. B.A., Georgetown U., 1965; M.B.A., U. Va., 1967. Asst. treas., mgr. corp. fin. dept. W.R. Grace & Co., N.Y.C., 1967-74; asst. v.p., asst. treas. City Investing Co., N.Y.C., 1974-77; v.p., treas. City Investing Co., 1978-81, sr. v.p., treas., 1982-85; chmn. bd. Quirk Carson Peppet Inc., 1985—; dir. Global Union Bank, N.Y.C., Entertainment Completions Inc., Haywood & Co., Environmental Opportunities Fund., Ltd. Clubs: Racquet and Tennis; Wee Burn (Conn.). Home: 445 Hollow Tree Ridge Rd Darien CT 06820-3030 Office: 126 E 56th St New York NY 10022-3613

QUIRK, KENNETH PAUL, accountant; b. Lake Charles, La., Aug. 29, 1953; s. Charles Patrick and Helen (Lejeune) Q.; m. Teresa Ann Tucker, Mar. 26, 1982 (div. Mar. 1988); 1 child, Heather Marie. BS in Acctg., McNeese State U., 1978; postgrad. MBA on-line, U. Phoenix, 1995—. CPA, La. Staff acct. Quirk, Cargile, Hicks & Reddin, Lake Charles, 1979-80, Browning-Ferris Industries, Lake Charles, 1980-81, La. Savs. Assn., Lake Charles, 1981-90, Calcasieu Marine Nat. Bank, Lake Charles, 1990-96, Hibernia Nat. Bank, Lake Charles, 1996—. Author fin. acctg. software sys. Mem. Young Men's Bus. Club, Lake Charles, 1986-90, Girl Scouts U.S., Lake Charles, 1989-90. Mem. AICPA, Soc. La. CPAs, Assn. for Computing Machinery, Computer Soc. IEEE, Kiwanis. Republican. Episcopalian. Avocations: jazz drumming, geneaology.

QUIRK, PETER RICHARD, engineering company executive; b. New Orleans, Dec. 28, 1936; s. Andrew John and Elise (Richard) Q.; m. Marilyn Ann Montalban, Aug. 16, 1958; children: Karen, Cheryl, Brian, Kathleen, Aimee, Elizabeth. BS, La. State U., 1959. Registered profl. engr., La. Sr. staff engr. Continental Oil Co., Ponca City, Okla., 1959-64; pres. Walk, Haydel & Assocs. Inc., New Orleans, 1964—, now pres. and CEO; mem. Bur. Govtl. Rsch., Natural Gas Assn. of New Orleans, 1991—. Active World Trade Ctr., 1972—; bd. dirs. Closer Walk Ministries, 1984—, Covenant Ho. New Orleans, 1989—, Met. Area Com., 1989—, La. State U. Found., 1989—, Phi Kappa Theta Nat. Found., 1990—, Cath. Found., 1993—, Xavier U., 1995—; chair bd. dirs. United Way of Greater New Orleans, 1996, chmn. gen. campaign, 1991, co-chair Day of Caring, 1995; bd. dirs. U. New Orleans Higher Edn. Coun., 1992—; mem. adv. bd. U. New Orleans Ctr. for Energy Resources Mgmt., 1992—; chair exec. com. Archbishop's Cmty. Appeal, 1993—, Daughters of Charity Health Svc., 1996—; chair Cystic Fibrosis Found. Ann. Walk, 1993. 2d lt. C.E., AUS, 1960. Recipient A.E. Wilder Jr. award Cons. Engr. Coun. L.A., 1989, Vol. Activist award, 1993, Man of Achievement award Phi Kappa Theta Nat. Found., 1991, Order St. Louis award. Mem. Instrument Soc. Am., NSPE, Constrn. Mgmt. Assn. Am. (bd. dirs. 1987-90), La. Engring. Soc., Am. Cons. Engrs. Council (trustee polit. action com. 1984-90, fellow 1988, Cmty. Svc. award 1996), Cons. Engrs. Council La. (pres. 1982-83), New Orleans and River Region C. of C., La. Chem. Industry Alliance, Greater New Orleans Bus. Roundtable, Paper Industry Mgmt. Assn., Phi Kappa Theta. Republican. Roman Catholic. Clubs: Serra (New Orleans pres. 1986, 94-95), Engineers (New Orleans pres. 1984-85). Home: 1201 Beverly Gardens Dr Metairie LA 70002-1903 Office: Walk Haydel & Assocs Inc 600 Carondelet St New Orleans LA 70130-3511

QUIRKE, LILLIAN MARY, retired art educator; b. West Haven, Conn., Oct. 1, 1928; d. Mortimer Francis and Ellen Louise (Bird) Q. BS, BA, So. Conn. U., 1950; MA, Long Beach State U., 1953; EdD, Columbia U., 1963. Cert. elem. and art tchr., Conn., Calif. Tchr. Long Beach (Calif.) Pub. Schs., 1950-54; jr. high art tchr. Army Dependents Sch., Frankfurt, Germany, 1954-55; art tchr. Navy Dependents Sch., Naples, Italy, 1955-56; art instr. So. Conn. U., New Haven, 1956-64, Foothill C.C., Los Altos, Calif., 1964-67; from art instr. to prof. DeAnza C.C., Cupertino, Calif., 1967-88; adj. prof. Queens (N.Y.) Coll., 1990-91. Author: The Rug Book, 1979; contbr. articles to profl. jours.; mem. editl. bd. Art Edn. mag., 1985-87. Active Dem. and Rep. Ctrl. Coms., San Jose, Calif., 1968-71; mem. arts rev. com. Cupertino Pub. Libr., 1977-81. Title IV grantee, 1967, grantee State of Calif., 1968, NDEA grantee U.S. Office Edn., 1966. Mem. Nat. Art Edn. Assn. (life, sec. Pacific chpt. 1954—, founder higher edn. sect. 1973), Calif. Art Edn. Assn. (rsch. chair 1969-72), Artists and Tech. (bd. dirs. 1984-88), Fla. Shore and Beach Preservation Assn. (founding bd. dirs. St. Johns First Coast chpt. 1996, sec.-treas. 1996-97). Avocations: quilting, boating, cooking, computer graphics. Home: 5916 Rio Royalle Rd Saint Augustine FL 32084-7304

QUISENBERRY, NANCY LOU, university administrator, educator; b. Washington, Ind., Jan. 29, 1938; d. Joseph Franklin and Maud Helen (Fitch) Forbes; m. James D. Quisenberry, Feb. 6, 1960; 1 child, James Paul. BS in Home Econs., Ind. State Tchrs. Coll., 1960, MS in Home Econs., 1962; EdD, Ind. U., 1971. Cert. tchr., Ind. Home economics tchr. Honey Creek High Sch., Terre Haute, Ind., 1961-62; third grade tchr. Indpls. Pub. Sch., 1962-64; sustitute tchr. Dep. of Def., Baumholder, Fed. Republic Germany, 1964-65; first grade tchr. Wayne Twp. Schs., Indpls., 1966-67; assoc. faculty lang. arts Purdue U., Ind. U., Indpls., spring 1970; prof. curriculum and instruction So. Ill. U., Carbondale, 1971—, assoc. dean Coll. of Edn., 1976—, interim dean, 1996-97; cons. U. N.C., Durham, 1977, Ministry Edn., Bangkok, Thailand, 1980, 84, DePaul U., 1990; dir. tech. and tng. assistance grant Head Start-OCD, Carbondale, 1972-74, Cameroon project USAID, Carbondale, 1984-86; mem. Ill. State Tchr. Certification Bd., 1981-84, 84-87. Co-author: Early Childhood Education Programs: Developmental Objectives and Their Use, 1975, Play as Development, 1978. Chair candidacy com. Ctrl. So. Ill. Synod Evang. Luth. Ch. Am., Springfield, 1987-90, sec. multisynodical com., Chgo., 1987-90, synod coun., 1992-95; pres. Epiphany Luth. Ch. Coun., Carbondale, 1984-85, 89-92, 94—; bd. dirs. Jackson County YMCA, 1988. Recipient Dare To Be Great award Ill. Women Adminstrs. and So. Ill. Region III. Women Adminstrs., 1989, Woman of Distinction award, So. Ill. U., 1992; grantee Bur. Educationally Handicapped, 1979-82, 90-95. Mem. Internat. Coun. on Edn. for Teaching (bd. dirs. 1988—, N.Am. v.p. 1992-94), Assn. Childhood Edn. Internat. (chair tchr. edn. com. 1989-93, folio rev. coord. elem. edn. 1989—), Nat. Coun. for Accreditation Tchr. Edn. (bd. examiners 1987—, new profl. tchr. project elem. edn. stds. drafting com. 1992—), Am. Assn. Colls. for Tchr. Edn. (chair adv. coun. state reps. 1987-88, bd. dirs. 1986-88, 91-94), Ill. Assn. Colls. for Tchr. Edn. (pres. 1984-86), Assn. Tchr. Educators (chairperson com. racism from a healing perspective, 1995—). Avocations: gardening, organ, flute, sewing, walking. Home: 3208 W Kent Dr Carbondale IL 62901-1917 Office: So Ill U Coll Edn Carbondale IL 62901-4624

QUIST, GORDON JAY, federal judge; b. Grand Rapids, Mich., Nov. 12, 1937; s. George J. and Ida F. (Hoekstra) Q.; m. Jane Capito, Mar. 10, 1962;

children: Scot D., George J., Susan E., Martha J., Peter K. BA, Mich. State U., 1959; JD with honors, George Washington U., 1962. Bar: D.C. 1962, Ill. 1964, U.S. Dist. Ct. (no. dist.) Ill. 1964, U.S. Supreme Ct. 1965, Mich. 1967, U.S. Dist. Ct. (we. dist.) Mich. 1967, U.S. Ct. Appeals (6th cir.) 1967. Assoc. Hollabaugh & Jacobs, Washington, 1962-64, Sonnenschein, Carlin, Nath & Rosenthal, Chgo., 1964-66; assoc. Miller, Johnson, Snell & Cummiskey, Grand Rapids, 1967-72, ptnr., 1972-92, mng. ptnr., 1986-92; judge U.S. Dist. Ct. (we. dist.) Mich., Grand Rapids, 1992—. Bd. dirs. Wedgewood Acres-Ch. Youth Home, 1968-74, Mary Free Bed Hosp., 1979-88, Christian Ref. Pubis., 1968-78, 82-88, Opera Grand Rapids, 1986-92, Mary Free Bed Brace Shop, 1988-92, Better Bus. Bur., 1972-80, Calvin Theol. Sem., 1992-93; bd. dirs. Indian Trails Camp, 1970-78, 82-88, pres., 1978, 88. Mem. Am. Indicature Soc., Mich. State Bar Assn., Univ. Club Grand Rapids, Order of Coif. Avocations: reading, travel. Office: 482 Ford Fed Courthouse 110 Michigan St NW Grand Rapids MI 49503-2313

QUITTELL, FREDERIC CHARLES, personnel and labor relations executive; b. Bronxville, N.Y., Apr. 22, 1948; m. Andrea Quittell. BSBA, Babson Coll., 1970; paralegal cert., Long Island U., 1978; A in Risk Mgmt., Ins. Inst. Am., 1990. Sales rep. Met. Life, New Rochelle, N.Y., 1973-78; rep. Profl. Indusl. Plan Assn., White Plains, N.Y., 1978-80; risk mgr. Daytop Village, N.Y.C., 1980-89, City of Norwalk, Conn., 1989-91; dir. personnel and labor rels. City of Norwalk, 1991—. Mem. Conn. Pub. Risk and Ins. Mgmt. Assn. (bd. dirs.). Avocation: swimming. Office: City of Norwalk 125 East Ave Norwalk CT 06851-5702

QUON, MICHAEL JAMES, medical scientist, physician; b. Oakland, Calif., Apr. 26, 1960; s. Jimmie Earl and Helen (Tang) Q.; m. Huison Kim, June 22, 1985; children: Hana, James. BS in Biomed. Engring., Northwestern U., 1982, PhD in Biomed. Engring., 1987, MD, 1988. Diplomate Nat. Bd. Med. Examiners, Am. Bd. Internal Medicine. Resident in internal medicine U. Chgo., 1988-90; fellow in endocrinology NIH, Bethesda, Md., 1990-93, sr. clin. investigator, 1993-95, sr. investigator Nat. Heart, Lung and Blood Inst., 1995—. Contbr. over 40 articles to profl. jours. Comdr. USPHS, 1990—. Mem. Am. Diabetes Assn. (Rsch. award grant 1994—), Am. Coll. Physicians, Am. Heart Assn., Coun. for High Blood Pressure, Juvenile Diabetes Found. Internat. Avocations: piano, violin. Office: NIH NHLBI HEB Bldg 10 Rm 8C-103 Bethesda MD 20892

QURAISHI, MARGHOOB A., management consultant; b. Jaipur, India, July 15, 1931; s. Nazir A. Quraishi and Khudija B. Khan; married; 4 children. B of Commerce, U. Karachi, Pakistan, 1955, postgrad., 1956; cert. in bus. fin., indsl. mgmt. & rels., McGill U., Montreal, Que., 1958; MBA, Stanford U., 1959. Rsch. economist Riches Rsch., Inc., 1960-61; acct., auditor Webb & Webb, CPAs, 1961-62; contr., adminstrv. asst. to pres. Capcom, 1963; v.p., sr. cons. CPM Internat., Inc., 1964-65; mgr., contr. Woodside Homes, 1965-66; founder, pres. Associated Mgmt. Systems, Palo Alto, Calif., 1966—; guest speaker, tchr. in field. Author numerous publs. in field. Mem. Inst. Mgmt. Cons., Am. Arbitration Assn., Am. Mgmt. Assn., Am. Mktg. Assn., Am. Soc. Appraisers. Office: Associated Mgmt Systems 974 Commercial St Ste A Palo Alto CA 94303-4907

QURAISHI, MOHAMMED SAYEED, health scientist, administrator; b. Jodhpur, India, June 23, 1924; came to U.S., 1946, naturalized, 1973; s. Mohammed Latif and Akhtar Jahan Q.; m. Akhtar Imtiaz, Nov. 12, 1953; children: Rana, Naveed, Sabah. B.Sc., St. John's Coll., 1942; M.Sc., Aligarh Muslim U., 1944; Ph.D., U. Mass., 1948. Sr. mem. UN, WHO Team to Bangladesh, 1949-51; entomologist Malaria Inst. Pakistan, 1951-55; sr. rsch. officer Pakistan Council Sci. and Indsl. Rsch., 1955-60; sr. sci. officer Pakistan AEC, 1960-64; assoc. prof. entomology U. Man., 1964-66; assoc. prof. entomology N.D. State U., Fargo, 1966-70, prof., 1970-74; chief scientist biology N.Y. State Sci. Svc., Albany, 1974-75; entomologist, toxicologist, chief pest control and consultation sect. NIH, Bethesda, Md., 1976-84; health scientist adminstr., exec. sec. microbiology and infectious disease rsch. com. Nat. Inst. Allergy and Infectious Diseases, Bethesda, Md., 1984-88, sci. rev. adminstr. spl. revs., 1988—; sr. scientist Cen. Treaty Orgn., Inst. Nuclear Sci., Tehran, Iran, 1960-64; program mgr. interdepartmental contract Project THEMIS, Dept. Def., 1968-74; vis. scientist Harvard Sch. of Pub. Health, 1995. Author: Biochemical Insect Control: Its Impact on Economy, Environment and Natural Selection, 1977; mem. editorial bd. Jour. Environ. Toxicology and Chemistry, 1981-84; author numerous sci. papers. Chmn. NIH Asian-Am. Cultural Assn., 1980-81. Recipient Sustained High Quality Performance award, 1980, Merit Pay Performance awards, 1984, 86, 87, Recognition and Appreciation of Spl. Achievement award NIH, 1988, Spl. Recognition award for Svcs. to NIH, Asian Am. Cultural Com., 1989, Appreciation in Recognition of Outstanding Support for Combined Fed. Campaign, 1991. Mem. Am. Chem. Soc., Soc. Environ. Toxicology and Chemistry (mem. publs. com. in charge spl. publs. 1982-84), Sigma Xi, Phi Kappa Phi. Home: 19813 Cochrane Way Gaithersburg MD 20879-1637 Office: NIH Rm 4C22 Solar Bldg 6003 Executive Blvd Bethesda MD 20892

QURAISHI, NISAR ALI, internist; b. Rawalpindi, Punjab, Pakistan, May 15, 1946; came to U.S., 1970; s. Jehan Dad and Sahib Jan (Qureshi) Q.; m. Shahida Parveen, June 25, 1970; children—Abid, Zahid. M.B., B.S. Dacca (Pakistan) Med. Coll., 1969. Diplomate Am. Bd. Internal Medicine. House surgeon Dacca Med. Coll., 1969, sr. house physician, 1969-70; intern Beekman Downtown Hosp., N.Y.C., 1970-71, resident, 1971-74; assoc. attending N.Y. Infirmary-Beekman Downtown Hosp., N.Y.C., 1982—; physician in charge exercise EKG, Mobil Oil Corp., N.Y.C., 1977-86; clin. asst. prof. medicine N.Y. Med. Coll., 1996—; attending physician St. Vincent's Hosp. and Med. Ctr. of N.Y., 1996—. Mem. N.Y. County Med. Soc., N.Y. State Med. Soc., AMA, ACP, Am. Soc. Internal Medicine. Office: 303 Greenwich St New York NY 10013-3801 also: 1 Chopin Ct Jersey City NJ 07302-3240

QUREISHI, A. SALAM, computer software and services company executive; b. Aligarh, India, July 1, 1936; s. M.A. Jabbar and Saira (Sattar) Q.; m. Naheed Fatima; children: Lubna, Leila. BS in Physics and Math., Aligarth U., India, 1954; MS in Stats., Patna U., India, 1957. Mgr. applications IBM Corp., Palo Alto, Calif., 1961-67; founder, pres., chmn. bd. Optimum Sys., Inc., Palo Alto, Calif., 1967-71; chmn. bd. Sysorex Internat., Inc., Mountain View, Calif., 1972—. Republican. Home: 925 Mountain Home Rd Redwood City CA 94062-2519 Office: Sysorex Internat Inc 225 E Middlefield Rd Mountain View CA 94043-3909

QUTUB, MUSA YACUB, hydrogeologist, educator, consultant; b. Jerusalem, June 2, 1940; came to U.S., 1960; s. Yacub and Sarah Qutub; married; children: Hanhia, Jennan, Sarmad, Muntaser, Aya, Saif, Tasneem. B.A. in Geology, Simpson Coll., Indianola, Iowa, 1964; M.S. in Hydrogeology, Colo. State U., 1966; Ph.D in Water Resources, Iowa State U. Sci. and Tech., 1969. Instr. earth sci. Iowa State U., Ames, 1966-69; from asst. prof. to prof. Northeastern Ill., Chgo., 1969-80, prof. geography and environ. studies, 1980—; cons. hydrogeology, Des Plaines, Ill., 1970—; sr. adviser Saudi Arabian Ministry Planning, Riyadh, 1977-78; leader U.S. environ. sci. del. to People's Republic of China, 1984; pres., founder Islamic Info. Ctr. Am. Author: Secondarty Environmental Science Methods, 1973; contbr. numerous articles to profl. jours.; editor Environ. Resource, Directory Environ. Educators and Cons. World. NSF grantee, 1970-71, 71-72, 72-73, 75, 76, Hew grantee, 1974, grantee Ill. Dept. Edn., 1970. Mem. AAAS, NSF (cons.), Am. Waterworks Assn., Am. Men and Women Sci., Nat. Assn. Geology Tchrs. (pres. central sect. 1974), Environ. Sci. Inst. (edn. com.), Internat. Assn. Advancement of Earth and Environ Sci. (pres. 1975—, founder), Ill. Earth Sci. Edn. (pres. 1971-73, founder), Phi Delta Kappa. Muslim. Avocations: tennis, track, cross country, soccer.

RAAB, G. KIRK, biotechnology company executive; b. N.Y.C., Sept. 27, 1935; s. George Rufus and Ann Maria (Wood) R.; m. Mollie Elizabeth Painter, Dec. 6, 1986; children; Julia Woodson, Dean Kirk; children from previous marriage: Kristina Elizabeth, Alyson Ann, Michael George. B.A. with honors, Colgate U., 1959. With Pfizer Inc., 1959-65; gen. mgr. A.H. Robins Co., Mex., 1965-68; v.p. Latin Am. Beecham Group Ltd., 1968-75; v.p. Latin Am., then exec. v.p. internat. Abbott Labs., North Chicago, Ill., 1975-79, corp. group v.p., 1980-81, pres., COO, dir., 1981-85; pres., COO Genentech Inc., San Francisco, 1985—, pres., CEO, 1985-95; chmn., bd. dirs. various biotech. cos. Trustee Colgate U. San Francisco Symphony, KQED; bd. dirs. Found. Nat. Sci. and Tech. medals, Oclassen Pharms. Inc., Shaman Pharms. Inc. Address: 999 Mountain Home Rd Woodside CA 94062-2519

RAAB, HARRY FREDERICK, JR., physicist; b. Johnstown, Pa., May 9, 1926; s. Harry Frederick and Marjorie Eleanor (Stiff) R.; m. Phebe Ann Duerr, June 16, 1951; children: Constance Diane, Harry Frederick, Cynthia Ann Raab Morgenthaler. Student Navy Electronics Tech. Sch., 1944-45; SB and SM E.E., MIT, 1951; postgrad. Oak Ridge Sch. Reactor Tech., 1954-55. Reactor control engr. Bettis Atomic Power Lab. Westinghouse Electric Corp., West Mifflin, 1951-54, mgr. surface ship physics, 1955-62, mgr. light water breeder reactor physics, 1962-72; chief physicist Navy Nuc. Propulsion Directorate, Washington, 1972-95; retired 1995. Patentee light water breeder reactor. Active Laymen's Missionary League, Episc. Diocese of Pitts., 1957-72; lay eucharistic min. and lector Episc. Ch. of the Good Shepherd, Burke, Va., 1972—, Sunday Sch. tchr., 1957-72, dir. liturgy, 1987—, stewardship chmn., 1979-82, 84, 92-93, chmn. presch. bd., 1994—, healing ministry, 1989—, sr. warden, 1983, 85, 97; mem. stewardship com. Diocese of Va., 1983—, chmn. stewardship, 1995—; chaplain for mentally retarded No. Va. Tng. Ctr., 1983—; bd. dirs. Phoenix Cmty. Svcs., 1995—; lay chaplain Fairfax Hosp., 1995—. With USNR, 1944-46, PTO. Fellow Am. Nuc. Soc.; mem. Internat. Platform Assn., Sigma Xi, Tau Beta Pi, Eta Kappa Nu. Republican. Lodge: Masons. Home: 8202 Ector Ct Annandale VA 22003-1342 *Always treat others with respect. Strive for excellence. Always act with honestyand integrity. Remember Henry Ford's observation: "If you say that you can, or if you say you cannot, you are right."*

RAAB, HERBERT NORMAN, retail executive; b. N.Y.C., Nov. 7, 1925; s. Jacob and Pauline (Neuwirth) R.; m. Blanche Muriel Levin, Jan. 27, 1952 (dec. Mar. 1981); children: Nancy Renée, James Harris; m. Carmen Sandra Fernandez, Aug. 17, 1986. AB, Harvard U., 1947; postgrad., Harvard U. Bus. Sch., 1947-48, Seton Hall U. Law Sch., 1972-75. V.p. Bamberger Div. R.H. Macy Inc., N.Y.C., 1968-75, v.p., 1975-78; pres. and chief exec. officer W&J Sloane, N.Y.C., 1978-80; pvt. practice cons. N.Y.C., 1980-84; sr. v.p. Wayside Furniture Co., Milford, Conn., 1984-90; adj. prof. U. Bridgeport (Conn.), 1986-91. Jewish.

RAAB, IRA JERRY, lawyer, judge; b. N.Y.C., June 20, 1935; s. Benjamin and Fannie (Kirschner) R.; divorced; children: Michael, Shelley; m. Katie Rachel McKeever, June 30, 1979 (div. 1991); children: Julie, Jennifer, Joseph; m. Gloria Silverman, Nov. 7, 1996; children: Jill, Todd, John. BBA, CCNY, 1955; JD, Bklyn. Law Sch., 1957; MPA, NYU, 1959, postgrad., 1961; MS in Pub. Adminstrn., L.I. U., 1961; MBA, Adelphi U., 1990. Bar: N.Y. 1958, U.S. Dist. Ct. (so. and ea. dists.) N.Y. 1960, U.S. Supreme Ct. 1967, U.S. Tax Ct. 1976, U.S. Ct. Appeals (2d cir.) 1977. Pvt. practice Woodmere, N.Y., 1958-96; agt. Westchester County Soc. Prevention of Cruelty to Children, White Plains, N.Y., 1958; counsel Dept. Correction City of N.Y., 1959, trial commr. Dept. Correction, 1976, asst. corp. counsel Tort divsn., 1963-70; staff counsel SBA, N.Y.C., 1961-63; counsel Investigation Com. on Willowbrook State Sch., Boro Hall, S.I., N.Y., 1970; gen. counsel Richmond County Soc. Prevention of Cruelty to Children, Boro Hall, 1970-81; pro bono counsel N.Y.C. Patrolmen's Benevolent Assn., 1974-81; rep. to UN Internat. Criminal Ct., 1977-78; arbitrator Small Claims Ct. Day Cts., N.Y.C., 1970-96; arbitrator L.I. Better Bus. Bur., 1976-93; arbitrator Nassau County Dist. Ct., 1978-93, arbitrator Small Claims Ct., 1978-96; spl. master N.Y. County Supreme Ct., 1977-96; judge N.Y.C. Parking Violations Bur., 1991-93; small claims arbitrator N.Y.C. Civil Ct., 1970-96, U.S. Dist. Ct. (ea. dist.) N.Y., 1986-96; small claims arbitrary Nassau County Dist. Ct., 1970-96; lectr. comty. and ednl. orgns.; instr. paralegal course Lawrence Sch. Dist., N.Y., 1982-84. Chmn. Businessmen's Luncheon Club, Wall St. Synagogue, 1968-79; sec. Cmty. Mediation Ctr., Suffolk County, 1978-80, exec. v.p., 1980-81; vice chmn. Woodmere Inc., Com., 1980-81; mem. adv. bd. Nassau Expressway Com., 1979-80; bd. dirs. Woodmere Mchts. Assn., 1979-80, v.p., 1979-83, chmn., 1984-93; candidate for dist. ct. judge Nassau County, 1987, 88, 89, 91, 93, 94; candidate for supreme ct. justice Nassau and Suffolk Counties, 1995; elected judge Nassau County Dist. Ct., 1997—. Recipient Consumer Protection award FTC, 1974, 76, 79, Recognition award Pres. Ronald Reagan, 1986, Man of Yr. award L.I. Coun. of Chambers, 1987. Mem. ABA (chmn. cts. and comty. com. 1988-93, exec. com. jud. adminstrn. divsn. lawyers conf. 1989-95), Am. Judges Assn. (nat. treas. 1978-82, 82-83, 89-96, chmn. civil ct. ops. com. 1975-76, chmn. ednl. film com. 1974-77, editl. bd. Ct. Rev. mag. 1975-79, 82-86, chmn. spkrs. bur. com. 1976-77, chmn. legis. com. 1983-95, chmn. resolutions com. 1995—, historian 1988—, William H. Burnett award 1983), Am. Judges Found. (pres. 1977-79, chmn. bd. trustees 1979-83, treas. 1974-75, 76-77, trustee 1983—), Assn. Arbitrators of Civil Ct. City of N.Y. (past pres.), N.Y. State Bar Assn. (sec. dist., city town and villages cts. com.), Nassau County Bar Assn. (criminal cts. com., matrimonial and family ct. com., ct. com., ethics com.), Profl. Group Legal Svc. Assn. (past pres.), Internat. Assn. Jewish Lawyers and Jurists (com. to draft Internat. Bill of Rights to Privacy 1982, coun. 1981-95, bd. govs. 1984-95, adv. bd. comty. dispute ctr. 1979-81), K.P. (past chancellor comdr.). Democrat. Home: 375 Westwood Rd Woodmere NY 11598-1624

RAAB, LAWRENCE EDWARD, English educator; b. Pittsfield, Mass., May 8, 1946; s. Edward Louis and Marjorie (Young) R.; m. Judith Ann Michaels, Dec. 29, 1968; 1 child, Jennifer Caroline. BA, Middlebury Coll., 1968; MA, Syracuse U., 1972. Lectr. Am. U., Washington, 1970-71; jr. fellow U. Mich. Soc. Fellows, Ann Arbor, 1973-76; prof. English Williams Coll., Williamstown, Mass., 1976—. Author: (poems) Mysteries of the Horizon, 1972, The Collector of Cold Weather, 1976, Other Children, 1987, What We Don't Know About Each Other, 1993 (National Book award nominee, 1993). Creative Writing fellow Nat. Endowment Arts, 1972, 84; recipient Bess Hokin prize Poetry mag., 1983; residencies at Yaddo, 1979-80, 82, 84, 86-90, 94, MacDowell Colony, 1993, 95. Office: Williams Coll English Dept Williamstown MA 01267

RAAB, SELWYN, journalist; b. N.Y.C., June 26, 1934; s. William and Berdie (Glantz) R.; m. Helene Lurie, Dec. 25, 1963; 1 dau., Marian. B.A., Coll. City N.Y., 1956. Reporter N.Y. World-Telegram and Sun, N.Y.C., 1960-66; producer, news editor NBC-TV News, N.Y.C., 1966-71; exec. producer WNET-News, N.Y.C., 1971-74; reporter New York Times, 1974—. Author: Justice in the Back Room, 1967; co-author: Mob Laywer, 1994. Recipient award for best mag. consumer protection article U. Mo. Sch. Journalism, 1969, Deadline awards for excellence in television reporting Sigma Delta Chi, 1971, 73, 1st prize for excellence in television reporting N.Y. State A.P., 1973, Best Television Reporting award N.Y. Press Club, 1973, Heywood Broun Meml. award, 1974, Page One award Newspaper Guild of New York, 1975, Best Feature Story award N.Y. Press Club, 1984, N.Y.C. Patrolmen's Benevolent Assn. award, 1985. Office: NY Times 229 W 43rd St New York NY 10036-3913

RAAB, SHELDON, lawyer, Bklyn. Nov. 30, 1937; s. Morris and Eva (Shereshevsky) R.; m. Judith Deutsch, Dec. 15, 1963; children: Michael Kenneth, Elisabeth Louise, Andrew John. AB, Columbia U., 1958; LLB cum laude, Harvard U., 1961. Bar: N.Y. 1961, U.S. Ct. Appeals (2d cir.) 1963, U.S. Dist. Ct. (so. and ea. dists.) 1967. Dep. asst. atty. gen. State of N.Y., 1961-63, asst. atty gen., 1963-64; assoc. Fried, Frank, Harris, Shriver & Jacobson and predecessor firm, N.Y.C., 1964-69, ptnr., 1970-81, inc. ptnr., 1981—. Mem. exec. com. lawyers' div. United Jewish Appeal, 1982—. Mem. ABA, Am. Law Inst., N.Y. State Bar Assn. (trial lawyers sect. 1968—), Assn. of Bar of City of N.Y. (adminstrv. law com. 1968-71, spl. com. electric power and environment 1971-73, chmn. energy com. 1974-79, fed. cts. com. 1981-84, state superior cts. juris. com. 1985-88). Democrat. Office: Fried Frank Harris Shriver & Jacobson 1 New York Plz New York NY 10004

RAABE, WILLIAM ALAN, tax author and educator; b. Milw., Dec. 14, 1953; s. William Arthur and Shirley (Semmann) R.; m. Mary Jane Swiggum, Aug. 7, 1976 (div. July 1984); m. Nancy Elizabeth Miller, Mar. 1989; children: Margaret Elisabeth, Martin William. BS, Carroll Coll., 1975; MAS, U. Ill., 1976, PhD, 1979. Wis. Disting. prof. U. Wis., Milw., 1979-96; tax edn. cons. Price Waterhouse, N.Y.C., 1990—; prof. Samford U., Birmingham, Ala., 1997—; vis. assoc. prof. Ariz. State U., Tempe, 1985; vis. faculty Ernst. & Young, N.Y.C., 1990—, Calif. CPA Found., 1986, AICPA, 1984—; developer Estate Tax Planner, McGraw Hill Software, N.Y.C., 1980-88; expert witness, 1985—. Author West's Federal Taxation, 1985—, West's Federal Tax Research, 1986—, Income Shifting After Tax Reform, 1987, Multistate Corporate Tax Guide, 1985—; contbr. articles to profl. jours. Bd. dirs., pres. Luth. High Sch. Assn. Milw., 1991-96, Bethesda Luth. Home, Watertown, Wis., 1989-91, Concord Chamber Orch., Milw., 1983-88; mem. Econ. Devel. Com., Wauwatosa, Wis., 1986-89; faculty athletic rep. to NCAA from U. Wis. Milw., 1990-96; mem. Milw. Symphony Chorus, Master Singers of Milw., Sanford Master Singers, Sanford Die Kantorei. Fellow Am. Acctg. Assn., Nat. Ctr. for Tax Edn. and Rsch.; mem. U. Wis. Milw. Tax Assn. (bd. dirs. 1981-96), Wis. Inst. CPAs (Educator of Yr. 1987). Office: Samford Univ Sch of Bus 800 Lakeshore Dr Birmingham AL 35229-0001

RAAD, VIRGINIA, pianist, lecturer; b. Salem, W.Va., Aug. 13, 1925; d. Joseph M. and Martha (Joseph) R. BA in Art History, Wellesley Coll., 1947; spl. student, New Eng. Conservatory Music, 1947-48; diplôme, Ecole Normale de Musique, Paris, 1950; Doctorate with honors (French Govt. grantee 1950-52, 54-55), U. Paris, 1955; student, Alfred Cortot, Jeanne Blancard, Berthe Bert, Jacques Chailley. Artist in residence Salem (W.Va.) Coll., 1957-70; ind. concert pianist, 1960—; musician in residence N.C. Arts Council, at community colls., 1971-72; adjudicator Nat. Guild Piano Tchrs., Nat. Fedn. Music Clubs; panelist, grant reviewer NEH, 1978-84, 92—; mem. com. Nat. Endowment Arts, 1978; Am. rep. Debussy Centennial Colloque, Paris, 1962. Perfomances, concerts, lectrs. master classes at West Ga. Coll., Carrollton, La Grange (Ga.) Coll., Columbus (Ga.) Coll., Young Harris (Ga.) Coll., U. Fla., Gainesville, Norton Gallery, Palm Beach, Fla., Alliance Française de Rollins Coll., Winter Park, Fla., Dixon Gallery and Gardens, Memphis, St. Jude Children's Rsch. Hosp., Memphis, Cleveland (Tenn.) State C.C., Sampson Tech. Inst., Clinton, N.C., Wayne C.C., Goldsboro, N.C., Brevard (N.C.) Coll., Ctrl. (S.C.) Wesleyan Coll., Ky. Wesleyan Coll., Owensboro, Berea (Ky.), Coll., Alice Lloyd Coll., Pippa Passes, Ky., Coll. of William and Mary, Williamsburg, Va., Eastern Mennonite Coll., Harrisonburg, Va., The Phillips Gallery, Washington, Trinity Coll., Washington, Manhattanville Coll., Purchase, N.Y., Elmira (N.Y.) Coll., Fordham U., N.Y.C., The Piano Tchrs. Congress of N.Y., Middlebury (Vt.) Coll., St. Anselm's Coll., Manchester, N.H., Mount St. Mary's Coll., Hooksett, N.H., Wellesley (Mass.) Coll., Curry Coll., Milton, Mass., So. Conn. State U., New Haven, Slippery Rock (Pa.) U., Seton Hill Coll., Greensboro, Pa., Alliance Française de Pitts. and U. Piits., Channel 13 WQED (PBS) Pitts., Lincoln U., Oxford, Pa., The Grier Sch., Tyrone, Pa., Mount de Chantal Acad., Wheeling W.V.a, Wheeling Jesuit Coll., among other colls. and univs.; contbg. author: Debussy et l'Evolution de la Musique au XX Siècle, 1965; author: The Pianistic Sonority of Claude Debussy, 1994; recording artist: EDUCO, 1995—; contbr. articles to profl. jours. Active Amnesty Internat. Urgent Action Network; alumna regional representative Wellesley Coll. Named Outstanding W.Va. Woman Educator Delta Kappa Gamma, 1965; included in Schlesinger Library on History of Women in Am. Radcliffe Coll., 1967; grantee Govt. France, Am. Coun. Learned Socs. Mem. Soc. Française de Musicologie, Am. Musicol. Soc. (regional officer 1960-65), Am. Coll. Musicians, Am. Soc. for Aesthetics (grant reviewer), Internat. Musicol. Soc., Music Tchrs. Nat. Assn. (adjudicator, musicology program chair 1983-87), W.Va. Music Tchrs. Assn., Coll. Music Soc., Alpha Delta Kappa (hon.). Republican. Roman Catholic. Avocations: hiking, gardening, birding. Address: 60 Terrace Ave Salem WV 26426-1116 *Whether on the concert stage or in the classroom, I am a teacher with the desire to enlarge each person's vision in the arts.*

RAAFLAUB, KURT ARNOLD, classics educator; b. Buea, Cameroon, Feb. 15, 1941; s. Fritz and Heidi (Ninck) R.; m. Deborah Dickmann Boedeker, July 14, 1978. MA, U. Basel, Switzerland, 1967, PhD, 1970. Asst. prof. ancient history Free U. Berlin, 1972-78; asst. prof. ancient history Brown U., Providence, 1978-80, assoc. prof. classics and history, 1980-83, prof., 1983—, John Rowe Workman Disting. prof. classics and humanistic tradition, 1989-92, chmn. dept. classics, 1984-89; co-dir. Ctr. for Hellenic Studies, Washington, 1992—. Author: Dignitatis Contentio, 1974, Die Entdeckung der Freiheit, 1985; co-author: Studien zum Attischen Seebund, 1984, Aspects of Athenian Democracy, 1990; editor or co-editor: Social Struggles in Archaic Rome, 1986, Between Republic and Empire: Interpretations of Augustus and His Principate, 1990, Athens and Rome, Florence and Venice: City-States in Classical Antiquity and Medieval Italy, 1991, Anfänge politischen Denkens in der Antike: Die nahöstlichen Kulturen und die Griechen, 1993, Studies in the Ancient Greek Polis, 1995, More Studies in the Ancient Greek Polis, 1996, Democracy 2500: Questions and Challenges, 1997; contbr. articles to profl. jours. Mem. Historisches Kolleg Munich, 1989-90. Am. Coun. Learned Socs. fellow, 1983-84, Ctr. for Hellenic Studies fellow, 1976-77, NEH fellow, 1989; faculty fellow U. New England, Armidale, Australia, 1996. Mem. Philol. Assn., Assn. Ancient Historians, Am. Inst. Archaeology. Avocation: music. Home and Office: Ctr Hellenic Studies 3100 Whitehaven St NW Washington DC 20008-3614

RAASCH, ERNEST MARTIN, company executive; b. Norfolk, Nebr., May 15, 1927; s. Ernest Carl and Esther Eleanor (Martin) R.; m. Helen Veronica Gillespie, Dec. 15, 1973. Student, NYU, Columbia U. Pres. Dixon Co. Ltd., Newmarket, Can., 1967-69; v.p. mktg. Joseph Dixon Crucible Co., Jersey City, 1962-69; dir. mktg./gen. mgr. Borden Chem., N.Y.C., 1969-71; pres., chief operating officer Swingline Co., div. SWL Inc., L.I.C., 1971-75; exec. v.p. Swingline Co., div. SWL Inc., 1975-78, pres., chief exec. officer, 1978-80; pres., chief exec. officer Gesistner Corp., Yonkers, N.Y, 1980-84; exec. v.p., chief operating officer Codenoll Tech. Corp., Yonkers, 1984-87; pres., chief exec. officer SRS/C-Tech Inc., N.Y.C., 1987-92; bd. dirs. Exercycle Inc., Woonsocket, R.I., 1984—, SRS/C Tech. Inc., Acquivest Inc., Framingham, Mass., 1987-91; pres., CEO G-Tech Inc., Alpine, N.J., 1992—, Networking Comms., Inc., Tenafly, N.J., 1992-95; exec. v.p., COO, Bay Colony, Inc., Nisswa, Minn., 1991—. Contbr. articles to profl. jours.; patentee in field. Trustee The Hudson River Mus., Yonkers, 1982-84. Named Man of the Yr., Office Product Mfrs. Assn., 1980. Mem. Soc. Mfg. Engrs., Nat. Indsl. Conf. Bd., Sales/Mktg. Execs. of N.Y. (bd. dirs. 1984—), N.Y. Athletic Club. Lutheran. Avocations: skiing, sailing, writing. Office: SRS/C Tech Inc 330 7th Ave New York NY 10001-5010

RAASH, KATHLEEN FORECKI, artist; b. Milw., Sept. 12, 1950; d. Harry and Marion Matilda (Schwabe) Forecki; m. Gary John Raash, June 13, 1987. BS, U. Wis., Eau Claire, 1972; MFA, U. Wis., Milw., 1978. One-, two- and three-person shows include Sight 225 Gallery, Milw., 1979, 81, Nicolet Coll., Phinelander, Wis., 1981, Messing Gallery, St. Louis, 1982, Arts Consortium, Cin., 1982, Ctr. Gallery, Madison, Wis., 1982, Otteson Theatre Gallery, Waukesha, Wis., 1982, Foster Gallery, Eau Claire, 1984, Duluth (Minn.) Art Inst., 1984, West Bend (Wis.) Gallery of Fine Arts, 1987, U. Wis.-Waukesha Fine Arts Gallery, 1988, Marion Art Gallery, Milw., 1990, Layton Honor Gallery, Milw., 1991, West Bend Art Mus., 1995, Gwenda Jay Gallery, Chgo., 1995, Wis. Acad., Madison, 1996; exhibited in group shows at River Edge Galleries, Wis., 1990, 91, 94, 95, Peltz Gallery, Milw., 1990, 91, 92, 93, 94, 96, Minnetonka Ctr. Arts, Wayzata, Minn., 1996; represented in permanent collections United Bank and Trust of Madison, Fine Arts Gallery U. Wis., Miller Brewing Co., Independence Bank Waukesha, U. Wis. Home and Studio: W 1630 Bear Trail Rd Gleason WI 54435

RABAGO, KARL ROGER, lawyer; b. Landstuhl, Germany, Nov. 5, 1957; (parents Am. citizens); s. Rogerio I. and Christa J. (Ubelhor) R.; m. Pamela Houston, June 9, 1979; children: Timothy K., Troy R., Kara R. BBA in Bus. Mgmt., Tex. A&M U., 1977; JD with honors, U. Tex., 1984; LLM in Mil. Law, U.S. Army JAG Sch., Charlottesville, Va., 1988; LLM in Environ. Law, Pace U., 1990. Bar: Tex. 1984, U.S. Ct. Mil. Appeals 1985. Commd. 2d lt. U.S. Army, 1977, advanced through grades to maj., 1989; officer 2d Squadron, 9th Armored Cav., 24th Inf. Div., Ft. Stewart, Ga., 1978-81; trial counsel 5th Inf. Div., Ft. Polk, La., 1984-86, def. counsel, 1986-87; asst. prof. law U.S. Mil. Acad., West Point, N.Y., 1988-90; resigned, 1990; assoc. prof. U. Houston Law Ctr., 1990-92; commr. Pub. Utility Commn. Tex., Austin, 1992-94; dept. asst. sec. U.S. Dept. Energy, Washington, 1995-96; energy program mgr. Environ. Def. Fund, Austin, 1996—. Democrat. Roman Catholic. Office: Environ Def Fund 44 East Ave Ste 304 Austin TX 78701-4334

RABASSA, GREGORY, Romance languages educator, translator, poet; b. Yonkers, N.Y., Mar. 9, 1922; married 1966. A.B., Dartmouth Coll., 1945, Litt.D. hon., 1982; M.A., Columbia U., 1947, Ph.D. in Portuguese, 1954.

Instr. Spanish Columbia U., 1947-52, assoc., 1952-58, asst. prof., 1958-63, assoc. prof. Spanish and Portuguese, 1963-68; prof. Romance langs. Queens Coll., CUNY Grad. Sch., Flushing, N.Y., 1968-86; Disting. prof. Queens Coll., CUNY Grad. Sch., 1986—; assoc. editor Odyssey Rev., 1961-64. Contbr. articles to profl. jours. Staff sgt. OSS, 1942-45. Decorated Croce al Merito di Guerra (Italy), Order of San Carlos (Colombia); recipient Nat. Book award for transl., 1967, transl. prize PEN Am. Ctr., 1977, Gode award Am. Transl. Assn., 1980, PEN transl. medal, 1982, arts award N.Y. Gov., 1985, transl. prize Wheatland Found., 1988, lit. award Am. Acad. and Inst. Arts and Letters, 1989, presdl. medal Dartmouth Coll., 1991, Ivan Sandrof award The Nat. Book Critics Cir., 1993, Lit. Lion award N.Y. Pub. Libr., 1993, Mellon Humanities award Loyola U., Chgo., 1995, Gabriela Mistral prize, Chile, 1996; Fulbright-Hays fellow, 1965-66, NEH fellow, 1979-80, Guggenheim fellow, 1988-89. Mem. Renaissance Soc. Am., MLA, Am. Assn. Tchrs. Spanish and Portuguese, Latin Am. Studies Assn., Am. Lit. Translators Assn., Hispanic Soc. Am., PEN Club, Phi Beta Kappa. Office: Dept of Hispanic Langs & Lits CUNY Queens College Flushing NY 11367

RABB, BRUCE, lawyer; b. Cambridge, Mass., Oct. 4, 1941; s. Maxwell M. and Ruth (Cryden) R.; m. Harriet Rachel Schaffer, Jan. 4, 1970; children: Alexander Charles, Katherine Anne. AB, Harvard U., 1962; Cert. d'Etudes Politiques, Institut d'Etudes Politiques, Paris, 1963; LLB, Columbia U., 1966. Bar: N.Y. 1966. Law clk. to judge U.S. Ct. Appeals (5th cir.), 1966-67; assoc. Stroock & Stroock & Lavan, N.Y.C., 1967-68, 71-75, ptnr., 1976-91; ptnr. Kramer, Levin, Naftalis & Frankel, N.Y.C., 1991—; staff asst. to Pres. U.S., 1969-70; vice-chmn. Lawyers Com. Human Rights, 1977-95, nat. coun., 1996—; bd. dirs. Chiquita Italia, SpA; supr. bd. dirs. Agora-Gazeta, sp.zo.o., 1993—, Agora-Druk, sp.zo.o., 1995—; pub. mem. Adminstrv. Conf. U.S., 1982-86, 89-92, spl. counsel, 1986-88. sec. Lehrman Inst., 1978-88; bd. dirs. Citizens Union of N.Y., 1981-87, 88-94, 95—, Am. Friends of Alliance Israelite Universelle, 1987—, Human Rights Watch, 1987—; mem. Human Rights Watch/Ams., 1982—, Human Rights Watch/Helsinki, 1985—, Fund for Free Expression, 1987—, Human Rights Watch/Middle East, 1989—, vice chmn., 1990—; mem. internat. adv. com. Internat. Parliamentary Group for Human Rights in the Soviet Union, 1984-88, Prin. of the Coun. for Excellence in Govt., 1990—; adv. coun. Doctors of the World USA, 1996—. Mem. ABA (adv. panel Internat. Human Rights Trial Observer project), Am. Law Inst., Assn. of Bar of City of N.Y. (fed. legis., internat. law chair 1992-95, internat. human rights, civil rights, legal edn. and admission to bar, internat. trade coms., coun. on fgn. affairs), Harvard Club N.Y.C., Met. Club of Washington. Office: Kramer Levin et al 919 3rd Ave New York NY 10022

RABB, GEORGE BERNARD, zoologist; b. Charleston, S.C., Jan. 2, 1930; s. Joseph and Teresa C. (Redmond) R.; m. Mary Sughrue, June 10, 1953. BS, Coll. Charleston, 1951, LHD (hon.), 1995; MA, U. Mich., 1952, PhD, 1957. Teaching fellow zoology U. Mich., 1954-56; curator, coord. rsch. Chgo. Zool. Park, Brookfield., Ill., 1956-64; assoc. dir. rsch. and edn. Chgo. Zool. Park, 1964-75, dep. dir., 1969-75, dir., 1976—; rsch. assoc. Field Mus. Natural History, 1965—; lectr. dept. biology U. Chgo., 1965-89; mem. Com. on Evolution Biology, 1969—; pres. Chgo. Zool. Soc., 1976—; mem. steering com. Species Survival Commn., Internat. Union Conservation of Nature, 1983—, vice chmn. for N.Am., 1986-88, dep. chmn., 1987-89, chmn., 1989-96, vice chmn. comms., 1997—; chmn. policy adv. group Internat. Species Info. System, 1974-89, chmn. bd., 1989-92; mem. bd. dirs. Ill. State Mus., 1994—. Fellow AAAS; mem. Am. Soc. Ichthyologists and Herpetologists (pres. 1978), Herpetologists League, Soc. Systematic Zoology, Soc. Mammalogists, Soc. Study Evolution, Ecol. Soc. Am., Soc. Conservation Biology (council mem. 1986), Am. Soc. Zoologists, Soc. Study Animal Behavior, Am. Assn. Museums, Am. Soc. Naturalists, Am. Assn. Zool. Parks and Aquariums (dir. 1979-80), Internat. Union Dirs. Zool. Gardens, Am. Com. Internat. Conservation (chmn. 1987—), Chgo. Coun. Fgn. Relations (Chgo. com.), Sigma Xi. Club: Economic (Chgo.), Tavern. Office: Brookfield Zoo 3300 Golf Rd Brookfield IL 60513-1060

RABB, HARRIET SCHAFFER, lawyer, educator; b. Houston, Sept. 12, 1941; d. Samuel S. and Helen G. Schaffer; m. Bruce Rabb, Jan. 4, 1970; children: Alexander, Katherine. BA in Govt., Barnard Coll., 1963; JD, Columbia U., 1966. Bar: N.Y. 1966, U.S. Supreme Ct. 1969, D.C. 1970. Instr. seminar on constl. litigation Rutgers Law Sch., 1966-67; staff atty. Center for Constl. Rights, 1966-69; spl. counsel to commr. consumer affairs N.Y.C. Dept. Consumer Affairs, 1969-70; sr. staff atty. Stern Community Law Firm, Washington, 1970-71; asst. dean urban affairs Law Sch., Columbia U., N.Y.C., 1971-84, prof. law, dir. clin. edn., 1984—; George M. Jaffen prof. law and social responsibility Law Sch., Columbia U., 1991—, vice dean, 1992—; gen. counsel Dept. Health and Human Svcs., Washington, 1993—; mem. faculty employment and tng. policy Harvard Summer Inst., Cambridge, Mass., 1975-79. Author: (with Agid, Cooper and Rubin) Fair Employment Litigation Manual, 1975, (with Cooper and Rubin) Fair Employment Litigation, 1975. Bd. dirs. Ford Found., 1977-89, N.Y. Civil Liberties Union, 1972-83, Lawyers Com. for Civil Rights Under Law, 1978-86, Legal Def. Fund NAACP, 1978-93, Mex. Am. Legal Def. and Edn. Fund, 1986-90, Legal Aid Soc., 1990-93; mem. exec. com. Human Rights Watch, 1991-93; trustee Trinity Episcopal Sch. Corp., 1991-93. Office: Dept Health and Human Svcs 200 Independence Ave SW Rm 722A Washington DC 20201-0004

RABB, MAXWELL M., lawyer, former ambassador; b. Boston, Sept. 28, 1910; s. Solomon and Rose (Kostick) R.; m. Ruth Criedenberg, Nov. 2, 1939; children: Bruce, Sheila Rabb Weidenfeld, Emily Rabb Livingston, Priscilla Rabb Ayres. AB, Harvard U., 1932, LLB, 1935; LLD (hon.), Wilberforce U., 1957; DHL (hon.), Mt. St. Mary's Coll., 1983; LLB (hon.), Pepperdine U., 1985, St. Thomas U., 1986; DHL (hon.), Hebrew Union Coll., 1990. Bar: Mass. 1935, N.Y. 1958. Mem. firm Rabb & Rabb, Boston, 1935-37; adminstrv. asst. to U.S. Senator H.C. Lodge Jr., Mass., 1937-43; adminstrv. asst. U.S. Senator Sinclair Weeks, Mass., 1944; legal and legis. cons. Sec. Navy Forestal, 1946; practice law Boston, 1946-51; cons. U.S. Senate Rules Com., 1952; presdl. asst. to Pres. Eisenhower, sec. to Cabinet, 1953-59; partner Stroock & Stroock & Lavan, N.Y.C., 1959-81, of counsel, 1989-91; of counsel Kramer, Levin, Natalis, Nessen, Kamin & Frankel, N.Y.C., 1991—; amb. to Italy, 1981-89; bd. dirs. Sterling Nat. Bank, MIC Industries, Data Software Sys. Inc., Alusit Internat. Corp., Liberty Cable Co., Inc. Exec. asst. campaign mgr. Eisenhower presdl. campaign, 1951-52; del. Republican Nat. Conv., 1952, 56, 76, 80; mem. exec. com. U.S. Commn. for UNESCO, 1959-60; chmn. U.S. del. UNESCO conf., Paris, 1958; mem. Coun. on Fgn. Rels., 1978—; pres. Congregation Emanu-El, N.Y.C., 1973-81; mem. bd. advisors John F. Kennedy Sch. Govt., Harvard U.; trustee Cardinals Cooke and O'Connor Inner City Scholarship Fund, The Lighthouse, 1995—, N.Y. Med. Coll., Eisenhower Inst., Annenberg Inst., John Cabot U., Italy, George Marshall Meml. Found.; mem. bd. mgrs. Seamen's Ch. Inst.; mem. presdl. adv. panel on South Asian Relief assistance, 1971; mem. panel conciliators World Bank Internat. Ctr. for Settlement of Investment Disputes, 1967-73, U.S. rep., 1974-77; mem. Presdl. Commn. on Income Maintenance Programs, 1968-69; mem. bd. trustees N.Y. Med. Coll., hon. chmn. bd. Am. Friends of Alliance Israelite Universelle; vice chmn. United Cerebral Palsy, Inc., Nat. Com. on Am. Fgn. Policy, Coun. for U.S. and Italy; mem. adv. bd. Auburn U. Served as lt. amphibious corps USNR, 1944-46. Decorated Commendation Ribbon, commendatore Order of Merit, 1958, Grand Cross ofOrder of Merit (Italy), 1982; Grand Cross of Order of Malta, 1989. Mem. ABA, Am. Law Inst., Amb.'s Club of Reps. Abroad (hon. chmn.), Harvard Club (N.Y.C.), Harmonie Club (N.Y.C.), Army and Navy Club (Washington), Met. Club (Washington). Home: 480 Park Ave New York NY 10022-1613 also: Wilson Hill Rd Colrain MA 01340 Office: Kramer Levin Natalis et al 919 3rd Ave New York NY 10022

RABB, THEODORE K., historian, educator; b. Teplice-Sanov, Czechoslovakia, Mar. 5, 1937; came to U.S., 1956, naturalized, 1978; s. Oskar Kwasnik and Rose (Oliner) Rabinowicz; m. Tamar Miriam Janowsky, June 7, 1959; children: Susannah Rabb Bailin, Jonathan Richard, Jeremy David. B.A., Queen's Coll. Oxford U., Eng., 1958; M.A., Queen's Coll. Oxford U., 1962, Princeton U., 1960; Ph.D., Princeton U., 1961. Instr. Stanford U., 1961-62; instr. Northwestern U., 1962-63; asst. prof. Harvard U., 1963-67; mem. faculty Princeton U., 1967—, prof. history, 1976—; vis. assoc. prof. Johns Hopkins U., 1969, SUNY-Binghamton, 1973-74; visitor Inst. Advanced Studies, Princeton, 1973, 82; mem. nat. bd. cons. NEH, Nat. Coun. History Edn. (chair); N.J. Com. for Humanities (chair); chief historian Renaissance Television Series; bd. dirs. Humanities West; cons. in field. Author: The Thirty Years War, 2d edit, 1972, Enterprise and Empire, 1967, The Struggle for Stability in Early Modern Europe, 1975, The Origins of Modern Nations, 1981, Renaissance Lives: Portraits of an Age, 1993, Origins of the Modern West, 1993; co-author: The Western Experience, 6th edit., 1994, Peoples and Nations, 1982; editor: Jour. Interdisciplinary History, 1970—; co-editor: Action and Conviction in Early Modern Europe, 1969, The Family in History, 1973, Marriage and Fertility, 1981, Industrialization and Urbanization, 1981, Climate and History, 1981, The New History, 1982, Hunger and History, 1985, Population and Economy, 1986, Art and History, 1988, La Fame nella storia, 1991, Origin and Prevention of Major Wars, 1988. Bd. govs. Hebrew U. Fellow and/or grantee Folger Shakespeare Library, Am. Philos. Soc., Social Sci. Research Council, Am. Council Learned Socs., Guggenheim Found., NEH. Mem. Am. Hist. Assn. (chmn. com. quantitative rsch. history, chmn. nominating com.), Social Sci. History Assn. (exec. com., treas.), Am. Assn. Advancement Humanities (dir., sec.-treas.), Nat. Coun. History Stds., C.C. Humanities Assn. (steering com.), Royal Hist. Soc., Internat. Commn. History Parliamentary and Rep. Instns., Renaissance Soc. Am., Hakluyt Soc., Nat. Coun. History Edn. (chair), Historians Early Modern Europe, Conf. Brit. Studies. Office: Princeton University History Dept Princeton NJ 08544

RABBAT, GUY, electronics company executive, inventor; b. Cairo, Jan. 30, 1943; came to U.S., 1972; s. Victor and Alice R.; m. Elfriede Freitag, Aug. 3, 1968; children: Ralph, Shirley; m. Nadia Kobinger, Feb. 8, 1992. Baccalaureate, France; BS, Queens U., Eng., 1967, MS, 1969, PhD in Elec. Engring. with honors, 1971. Design supr. Siemens AG, Germany, 1964-68; asst. lectr. Queens U., Eng., 1968-72; dir. ops. IBM, 1972-84; v.p. Austin ops., CAE system div. Tektronix, 1984-86; head elec. engring. GM Corp., Mich., 1986-87; pres., chief exec. officer Modular Computer Systems, Inc. (MODCOMP), Ft. Lauderdale, Fla., 1987-92; mng. dir., exec. bd. dirs. Rank Xerox, Ltd., Welwyn Garden City, Herts, England, 1992-96; corp. v.p. Gen. Elec. Co., Milw., 1996—; chief tech. officer, chief info. officer Gen. Elec. Med. Sys., Milw., 1996—; chmn. Internat. IEEE Conf. on Cirs. and Computers, 1980, Internat. IEEE Conf. on Computer Design, 1983; bd. dirs. indsl. affiliates Mich. State U., 1986-88; pres. Am. Automation Assn., 1984-86. Author: Hardware and Software Concepts in VLSI, 1983, Advanced Semiconductor Technology and Computer Systems, 1988; contbr. numerous scis. tech. papers; patentee in field. Fellow Inst. Elec. Engrs. England (chartered engr.), IEEE (editor-in-chief, chmn . editorial bd. Circuits and Devices Magazine 1984-86, recipient invention and outstanding contbn. awards), Royal Engring. Coun. (London). Avocations: history, archeology, poetry, jogging. Home: 1025 N Kings Way Dr Waukesha WI 53188 Office: GE Med Sys PO Box 414 Milwaukee WI 53201-0414

RABBITT, EDWARD THOMAS, singer, songwriter; b. Bklyn., Nov. 27, 1941; m. Janine Girardi; children: Demelza Anne, Timmy (dec.), Thomas Edward. Nightclub and concert singer, 1962—; founder Hare Trigger band, composer more than 300 songs, including Kentucky Rain, 1970, Pure Love, 1974, Drivin' My Life Away, 1980, I Love a Rainy Night; recs. of own compositions include: Two Dollars in the Jukebox, Forgive and Forget, Rocky Mountain Music, Drinkin' My Baby Off My Mind; recorded albums: Horizon, 1981 (2 Gold Album awards.), Best of Eddie Rabbitt, Step by Step, 1981, Rabbitt Trax, 1985, The Best Year of My Life, 1985, I Wanna Dance with You, 1987, Greatest Country Hits, 1991. Office: Moress Nanas Shea Entertainment 1209 16th Ave S Nashville TN 37212-2901

RABE, DAVID WILLIAM, playwright; b. Dubuque, Iowa, Mar. 10, 1940; s. William and Ruth (McCormick) R.; m. Elizabeth Pan, 1969 (div.); 1 child; m. Jill Clayburgh, Mar. 1979. BA in English, Loras Coll., 1962; MA, Villanova U., 1968. Feature writer Register, New Haven, 1969-70; asst. prof. Villanova U., 1970-72. Author: (plays) The Basic Training of Pavlo Hummel, 1971 (Obie award disting. playwriting 1971, Drama Desk award 1971, Drama Guild award 1971), Sticks and Bones, 1971 (Elizabeth Hull-Kate Warriner award Dramatists Guild 1971, Variety Poll award 1971, Outer Critics' Circle award 1972, Tony award best play 1972, N.Y. Drama Critics' Circle citation 1972), The Orphan, 1973, In the Boom Boom Room, 1974, Burning, 1974, Streamers, 1976 (N.Y. Drama Critics' Circle award best Am. play 1976), Goose and Tomtom, 1976, Hurlyburly, 1985, Those the River Keeps, 1990, Crossing Guard, 1994, (screenplays) I'm Dancing as Fast as I Can, 1982, Streamers, 1983, Casualties of War, 1989, State of Grace, 1990, The Firm, 1993, (novel) Recital of the Dog, 1992. With U.S. Army, 1965-67. Recipient AP award, 1970, Am. Acad. Arts and Letters award, 1974, Nat. Inst. and Am. Acad. award, 1976; Rockefeller Found. grantee, 1969; Guggenheim fellow, 1976. Address: care United Talent Agy 9560 Wilshire Blvd 5th Flr Beverly Hills CA 90212*

RABE, ELIZABETH ROZINA, hair stylist, horse breeder; b. Granby, Quebec, Canada, Sept. 28, 1953; d. John J. and Christina Maria (De Vaal) Gluck; m. Oct. 21, 1972 (div. 1981); children: Diana Marie Claire, Michelle Diane. Diploma in hairstyling, Art Inst. Film hairstylist Internat. Alliance Theatrical, Stage Employees and Moving Pictures Machine Operators Local 706, L.A., 1977-94. Recipient Design Patent hock support horse brace U.S. Design Patent Office, Washington, 1994. Home: 522 W Stocker St Apt 1 Glendale CA 91202-2299

RABE, LAURA MAE, mathematician, educator; b. Cin., May 28, 1945; d. Howard Lawrence and Alberta Catherine (Held) R. BS, U. Cin., 1967, MS, 1972, supr. cert., 1982. Tchr. Colerain H.S., Cin., 1967—, chairperson math. dept., 1980—; presenter grant writing workshop Miami U., Oxford, Ohio, 1994; presenter in field. Named Hixon Tchr. of Yr., 1996; grantee GTE, 1994-95, NSF, 1980, Dartmouth Univ., 1995, 96; Tandy Tech. scholar, 1995-96. Mem. NEA, Nat. Coun. Tchrs. Math., Ohio Coun. Tchrs. Math., Greater Cin. Coun. Tchrs. Math. Roman Catholic. Avocations: travel, camping, water skiing, snow skiing, photography. Office: Colerain HS 8801 Cheviot Rd Cincinnati OH 45251-5907

RABEL, ED, news correspondent. BA in Political Sci., Morris Harvey Coll., 1963; LHD (Hon.), U. Charleston, 1985. Dir., anchor CBS Affiliate-WCHS-TV, 1962-66; chief so. correspondent CBS, 1967-70; war correspondent CBS, Saigon, 1970-71; middle east correspondent CBS, Tel Aviv, 1971-73; roving correspondent CBS, Atlanta, Ga., 1973-81; nat. correspondent CBS Evening News, N.Y., 1981-85; sr. correspondent NBC Nightly News, Wash., 1985-88; chief Latin Am. correspondent NBC Nightly News, Miami, 1988-89; sr. correspondent NBC Nightly News, Wash., 1989-93; Pentagon correspondent NBC Evening News, Wash., 1993—; trustee bd. dirs. U. Charleston. Recipient News and Documentary Emmy award, CBS Evening News, 1981, CBS Reports, 1981, George Polk award, 1982, three time Emmy nominee, CBS Sunday Morning, Communication award Nat. Easter Seal Soc., 1990. Home: 507 Scenic Way Great Falls VA 22066-3011 Office: NBC News Washington Bur 4001 Nebraska Ave NW Washington DC 20016-2733

RABEN, NINA, molecular biologist, biochemist; b. Moscow, Russia, Jan. 13, 1945; came to the U.S., 1987; d. Anatoly S. and Liza M. (Vinogradsky) R.; m. Mark Belenky, Sept. 23, 1966; 1 child, Masha Belenky. MD, 1st Moscow (Russia) Med. Inst., 1967; PhD in Biochemistry, USSR Acad. Med. Sci., Moscow, 1973. Rschr. USSR Surgery Ctr., Moscow, 1968-73, sr. investigator, 1973-79; vis. assoc. Nat. Inst. of Diabetes, Digestive and Kidney Diseases, Bethesda, Md., 1987-90; vis. scientist Nat. Inst. of Arthritis and Musculoskeletal Diseases, Bethesda, 1990-94; rsch. chemist NIAMS, NIH, Bethesda, 1994—. Contbr. articles to profl. jours.; patentee in field. Mem. AAAS. Jewish. Home: 5455 Grove Ridge Way Rockville MD 20852 Office: NIAMS NIH 9000 Rockville Pike Bethesda MD 20814-1436

RABENSTEIN, DALLAS LEROY, chemistry educator; b. Portland, Oreg., June 13, 1942; 8. Melvin Leroy and Rose Marie (Nelson) R.; m. Gloria Carolyn Duncan, Aug. 30, 1964; children: Mark, Lisa. BS, U. Wash., 1964; PhD, U. Wis., 1968. Lectr. U. Wis., Madison, 1967-68; research chemist Chevron Research Co., Richmond, Calif., 1968-69; from asst. prof. to prof. chemistry U. Alta., Edmonton, Can., 1969-85; prof. U. Calif., Riverside, 1985—, chmn. chemistry dept., 1989-92, dean Coll. Natural and Agrl. Scis., 1993-94; vis. prof. U. Oxford, 1976-77, U. Western Ont., 1982; McElvain lectr. U. Wis., 1981; Dow lectr. U. B.C., 1988; Eli Lilly lectr., Ind. U., 1993. Contbr. articles to profl. jours. NIH and NSF grantee. Fellow AAAS, Chem. Inst. Can. (Fisher Sci. Lecture award 1984); mem. Am. Chem. Soc., Internat. Soc. Magnetic Resource. Avocations: reading, gardening, music. Home: 5162 Palisade Cir Riverside CA 92506-1521 Office: U Calif Dept Chemistry Riverside CA 92521

RABER, MARTIN, health facility administrator, medical educator; b. N.Y.C., Mar. 29, 1947; married. BA, Washington U., St. Louis, 1968; MD magna cum laude, Cath. U. Louvain, Belgium, 1975; postgrad., Rice U., 1992. Diplomate Am. Bd. Internal Medicine, Am. Bd. Med. Oncology. Intern Dalhousie U., Halifax, N.S., Can., 1974-75, resident internal medicine, 1975-78; chief med. resident Dalhousie U., Halifax, N.S., 1978-80; fellow dept. devel. therapeutics M.D. Anderson Hosp. and Tumor Inst., Houston, 1978-80, assoc. internist, 1985-92, assoc. prof. medicine divsn. medicine, 1985-92; asst. prof. medicine dept. internal medicine U. Tex. Med. Sch., Houston, 1980-84, assoc. prof. medicine divsn. hematology/oncology, 1984-85; attending physician Hermann Hosp., Houston, 1980—; internist, prof. medicine M.D. Anderson Cancer Ctr., 1992—; chief sect. gen. oncology U. Tex. M.D. Anderson Cancer Ctr., 1985-92, chief sect. gen. med. oncology, 1992-93, dir. Office Clin. Trials Adminstrn., 1986-95, acting head divsn. medicine, 1993-94, assoc. v.p. for patient care, 1992-94, chmn. dept. clin. investigation divsn. medicine, 1993-94, assoc. med. dir. outreach corp., 1994-96, med. dir. managed care, 1994-96, physician-in-chief, 1994-96, ex officio mem. pres.' exec. bd., 1996—; dir. house staff tng. dept. internal medicine U. Tex. Med. Sch., 1981-85; lectr., cons. in field. Editor Cancer Bull., Tex. Medicine, Cancer Bull., Conquest; mem. editl. adv. bd. Oncology and Biotech. News; guest editor Cancer Update series Tex. Medicine; contbr. numerous articles to profl. jours. Fellow ACP, Royal Coll. Physicians (cert. in internal medicine); mem. Am. Soc. Clin. Oncologists (program com. 1992, oncology tng. com. 1992—, vice chmn. 1994, chmn. 1995), Am. Assn. Cancer Rsch., Soc. Analytical Cytology, N.Y. Acad. Scis., So. Med. Assn. (editor Dial Access cancer sect.), Tex. Med. Assn. (mem. com. on cancer 1988), Harris County Med. Soc. Home: 4812 Florence Bellaire TX 77401 Office: U Tex MD Anderson Cancer Ctr 1515 Holcombe Blvd # 318 Houston TX 77030-4009

RABER, MARVIN, retired utility company executive, consultant; b. Bklyn., Aug. 3, 1937; s. Robert Abraham and Claire (Miller) R.; m. Miriam Lewin, Dec. 18, 1960; children: Steven, Suzanne Beth. BChemE, Poly. Inst. Bklyn., 1958; MChemE, NYU, 1963. Registered profl. engr., N.Y., Md. Engr. Nuclear Devel. Corp. Am./United Nuclear Corp., White Plains, N.Y., 1958-66; section chief, v.p. subs. Hittman Corp. (Hittman Nuclear & Devel. Corp.), Columbia, Md., 1966-70; sect. mgr. Combustion Engring., Inc., Windsor, Conn., 1970-78; v.p. strategic planning Gen. Pub. Utilities Corp., Parsippany, N.J., 1978-95; ret., 1995; founder Raber Cons., Randolph, N.J., 1995—. Co-patentee subcooled liquid inlet fog cooled nuclear reactor, 1965, reactor power reduction system and method, 1978. Mem. Am. Mgmt. Assn., The Strategic Leadership Forum, Am. Nuclear Soc., Inst. Mgmt. Cons. Jewish. Avocation: boating. Home: 5 Bayberry Ln Randolph NJ 07869-3801

RABIDEAU, MARGARET CATHERINE, media center director; b. Chgo., Nov. 24, 1930; d. Nicholas and Mary Agnes (Burke) Oberle; m. Gerald Thomas Rabideau, Nov. 27, 1954; children: Mary, Margaret, Michelle, Gregory, Marsha, Grant. BA cum laude, U. Toledo, 1952, MA in Ednl. Media Tech., 1978. Cert. tchr. K-12 media tech., supr. ednl. media, tchr. English and journalism, specialist in edn. Asst. dir. pub. rels. U. Toledo, 1952-55; publicity writer United Way, Toledo, 1974-75; tchr. Toledo Pub. Schs., 1975-80, libr., media specialist, 1980-90; dir. media svcs. Sylvania (Ohio) Schs., 1990—; task force to evaluate coll. programs Ohio Dept. Edn., 1987; on-site evaluation team, Hiram Coll., Ohio, 1991; north ctrl. evaluation team Northwestern Ohio, 1985—. Citizen task force Toledo/Lucas County Libr., Ohio, 1991, mem. friends of the libr., 1990—; task force Sta. WGTE-TV PBS Sta., Toledo, 1993; mem. strategic plan com. Sylvania Schs., 1997—; instr. U. Toledo, 1990. Mem. ALA, U. Toledo Alumni Assn., Ohio Ednl. Libr. Media Assn. (N.W. dir. 1993—, vocat. dir. 1985-89, Libr. Media Specialist of Yr. 1993), Am. Ednl. Comm. and Tech., Maumee Valley Computer Assn. (task force), Phi Delta Kappa (Outstanding Newsletter Nat. award 1990, pres. Toledo chpt.). Avocations: running, travelling, cross stitching. Home: 1038 Olson St Toledo OH 43612-2828 Office: Sylvania Schs 6850 Monroe St Sylvania OH 43560-1922

RABIDEAU, PETER WAYNE, university dean, chemistry educator; b. Johnstown, Pa., Mar. 4, 1940; s. Peter Nelson and Monica (Smalley) R.; m. Therese Charlene Newquist, Sept. 1, 1962 (div.); children—Steven, Michael, Christine, Susan; m. Jennifer Lee Mooney, Nov. 15, 1986; children: Mark, Leah. B.S., Loyola U., Chgo., 1964; M.S., Case Inst. Tech., Cleve., 1967; Ph.D., Case Western Res U, Cleve., 1968. Postdoctoral asst. U. Chgo., 1968-69, instr., 1969-70; asst. prof. Ind. U.-Purdue U., Indpls., 1970-73, assoc. prof., 1973-76, prof., 1976-90, chmn. dept. chemistry, 1985-90; dean Coll. Basic Scis. La. State U., Baton Rouge, 1990—; program officer NSF, 1988-89. Contbr. numerous articles to profl. jours. Recipient research award Purdue Sch. Sci. at Indpls., 1982. Mem. AAAS, Am. Chem. Soc. (chmn. Ind. sect. 1974, councilor 1981-90). Home: 15160 Old Oak Ave Baton Rouge LA 70810-5546 Office: La State U Office of the Dean 338 Choppin Baton Rouge LA 70803

RABIL, ALBERT, JR., humanities educator; b. Rocky Mount, N.C., May 8, 1934; s. Albert and Sophie Mae (Safy) R.; m. Janet Spain, Aug. 29, 1956; children—Albert, III, J. Alison. B.A., Duke U., 1957; M.Div., Union Theol. Sem., 1960; Ph.D., Columbia U., 1964. Instr. religion Trinity Coll., Hartford, Conn., 1964-65, asst. prof., 1965-68; asst. prof. hist. theology Chgo. Theol. Sem., 1969-71; assoc. prof. SUNY-Old Westbury, 1971-74, prof., 1974-77, disting. teaching prof. humanities, 1977—; program dir. NEH Summer Inst., 1992, 94, 95, 96. Author: Merleau-Ponty, 1967 (Ansley award 1964), Erasmus and the New Testament, 1972, Laura Cereta, 1981, (with others) Her Immaculate Hand, 1983, Erasmus' Paraphrases of Romans and Galatians, 1983, Erasmus' Annotations on Romans, 1994; editor: Renaissance Humanism (3 vols.), 1988; editor, translator: Knowledge, Goodness, and Power, 1991, Henricus Cornelius Agrippa Declamation on the Nobility and Preeminence of the Female Sex, 1996; co-editor Renaissance Quarterly, 1992-97; series co-editor The Other Voice in Early Modern Europe, 1993—; editorial bd. Soundings: An Interdisciplinary Jour., 1992-94. Travelling fellow Union Theol. Sem., 1960, Soc. for Values in Higher Edn., 1961; grantee. Fulbright Found., 1961, NEH, 1974, 81, 94. Mem. Erasmus Rotterdam Soc. (mem. editorial bd. 1980—), Soc. for Values in Higher Edn. (bd. dirs. 1981-90, 94—), Renaissance Soc. Am. (bd. dirs. 1991-97). Democrat. Home: 324 Post Ave Apt 9H Westbury NY 11590-2249 Office: SUNY PO Box 210 Old Westbury NY 11568-0210

RABIL, MITCHELL JOSEPH, lawyer; b. Smithfield, N.C., Sept. 19, 1931; s. Albert G. and Eva (Nassif) R.; BS, Wake Forest Coll., 1953; LLB, Georgetown U., 1961; m. Antoinette M. Olivry, Nov. 25, 1956 (div. Oct. 1986); children: Elizabeth, Nathalie, Marcus, Gregory; m. Dolores E. Bleam, Jan. 21, 1989; children: Susan Starr Vermes, Scott Starr. Bar: N.C. 1961, N.J. 1967, D.C. 1980, Pa. 1981, U.S. Tax Ct. 1962, U.S. Supreme Ct. 1979. Supervisory acct. GAO, Washington, 1956-60; fin. analyst, staff acct. SEC, Washington, 1960-62; tax atty. Office Chief Counsel, IRS, Phila. and N.Y.C., 1962-66; assoc. Archer, Greiner, Hunter & Read, Camden, N.J., 1966-71; ptnr. Myers, Matteo, Rabil, Norcross & Landgraf, Cherry Hill, N.J., 1971-89, Montgomery, McCracken, Walker and Rhoads, Cherry Hill, 1989-95; sole stockholder, pres. Mitchell J. Rabil & Assocs., P.A., 1995—. Mcpl. chmn. Riverton (N.J.) Rep. Com., 1976-83; chmn. area 2 Burlington County Rep. Com., 1976-82; bd. dirs. The Archway Programs, Inc., 1988—, West Jersey Chamber Music Soc., 1990-91, Zurbrugg Meml. Hosp., 1991-93; mem. N.J. New Capital Sources Bd., 1996—. Served with AUS, 1953-55. C.P.A., N.J., N.C. Mem. Am. Bar Assn., AICPA, N.J. Bar Assn., Phila. Bar Assn., N.J. Soc. CPAs, Am. Assoc. Atty. CPAs (bd. dirs. sec. Delaware Valley, Greater Phila.; chpt. founder, past pres.), Cherry Hill C. of C. (bd. dirs. 1990-94), World Affairs Council Phila., Union League (Phila.), Riverton Country Club, Rotary Club (Cherry Hill, N.J. past pres. 1980-81, past dir.). Roman Catholic. Home: 107 Wayside Ct Delran NJ 08075-2000 Office: Rabil & Assoc PA 1010 Kings Hwy S Ste B Cherry Hill NJ 08034-2524

RABIN, ALAN ABRAHAM, economics educator; b. N.Y.C., June 16, 1947; s. Sidney and Claire R. B.A., Hamilton Coll., 1969; Ph.D., U. Va., 1977. NSF trainee U. Va., 1970-71, 71-72; intern Coun. Econ. Advisors, 1971; asst. prof. Calif. State U.-Northridge, 1973-74, Georgetown U., Washington, summer 1975; asst. prof. econs. U. Tenn.-Chattanooga, 1977-81, assoc. prof.,

1981-86, prof., 1986—. Contbr. articles to profl. jours. NDEA fellow, 1969-70; U. Tenn.-Chattanooga faculty research grantee, 1982. Mem. Am. Econ. Assn., So. Econ. Assn., Atlantic Econ. Soc., We. Econ. Assn., U. Tenn. Chattanooga Council Scholars, Omicron Delta Epsilon. Jewish. Avocations: sports; stamp collecting; bridge. Home: 409 Cameron Cir Apt 806 Chattanooga TN 37402-1513 Office: U Tenn-Chattanooga Dept Economics Chattanooga TN 37403

RABIN, BRUCE STUART, immunologist, physician, educator; b. Buffalo, Jan. 25, 1941; s. Eli and Dorothy R.; children: Andrew L., Alison J. B.A., Case Western Res. U., 1962; M.D., SUNY, Buffalo, 1969, Ph.D. (NIH predoctoral fellow, 1967), 1969. Diplomate Am. Bd. Med. Lab. Immunology. Asst. prof. pathology SUNY and Ctr. for Immunology, Buffalo, 1970-72; asst. prof. pathology Sch. Medicine, U. Pitts., 1972-76, assoc. prof. pathology, 1976-86, prof. pathology, 1986—, prof. psychiatry, 1987—, dir. Brain, Behavior and Immunity Ctr., 1989—; dir. div. clin. immunopathology Univ. Health Ctr. of Pitts., 1972—, med. dir. clin. lab. svcs., 1985—; interim chmn. dept. pathology, U. Pitts. Sch. Medicine, 1990-91; mem. merit rev. bd. for immunology VA Central Office, 1980-83; mem. study sect. NIMH, 1988-91. Assoc. editor Clin. Immunology Newsletter, 1980, Brain Behavior and Immunity, Clin. Immunology and Immunopathology; contbr. sci. papers in field to profl. publs. NIH research grantee, 1973—. Mem. AAAS, Pitts. Pathology Soc., Am. Assn. Pathologists, Acad. Clin. Lab. Physicians and Scientists, Am. Acad. Allergy, Am. Assn. Immunologists, Am. Assn. Clin. Histocompatibility Testing, Am. Soc. Clin. Pathologists (clin. immunopathology coun. 1978-84, editor Clin. Immunology Check Sample Program), Am. Acad. Microbiology (com. on postdoctoral edn. 1980), Assn. Med. Lab. Immunologists (pres. 1988), Psychoneuroimmunology Rsch. Soc. (pres. 1995). Home: 318 Schenley Rd Pittsburgh PA 15217-1173 Office: Presbyn-U Hosp Clin Immunopathology DeSoto & O'Hara Sts Pittsburgh PA 15213-2582

RABIN, HERBERT, physics educator, university official; b. Milw., Nov. 14, 1928; 2 children. B.S., U. Wis., 1950; M.S., U. Ill., 1951; Ph.D. in Physics, U. Md., 1959. Physicist elec. div. U.S. Naval Research Lab., 1952-54, physicist solid state physics div., 1954-62, head radiation effects sect. optical materials br., 1962-67, head quantum optics sect., applied optics br., 1967-68, head quantum optics br., 1968-71, asso. dir. research for space sci. and tech., 1971-77, asso. dir. research for space and communication sci. and tech., 1977-79; dep. asst. sec. of Navy for research, applied and space tech. Office of Navy Secretariat, Washington, 1979-83; dir. engring. research ctr., prof. elec. engring., assoc. dean Coll. Engring., U. Md., College Park, 1983—; vis. scientist Technisch Hochschule, Stuttgart, Germany, 1960-61; mem. staff physics dept. George Washington U., 1955-73; cons. Sch. Engring. of Sao Carlos, U. Sao Paulo, Brazil, 1964, 70. Contbr. articles to tech. jours.; patentee in field. Recipient Meritorious Civilian Svc. award USN, 1969, Disting. Civilian Svc. award, 1976, 93; Disting. Civilian Svc. award Dept. Def., 1979, cert. of commendation NASA, 1986, Centennial medal U. Md. Coll. Engring., 1994. Fellow Am. Phys. Soc., AAAS, Optical Soc. Am., AIAA; mem. IEEE (sr. mem.), Brazilian Acad. Scis. (corr.). Home: 7109 Radnor Rd Bethesda MD 20817-6332 Office: U Md Engring Rsch Ctr College Park MD 20742

RABIN, JACK, lawyer; b. Bklyn., Aug. 19, 1930; s. Leo and Bertha R.; m. Roberta Edith Libson, Oct. 25, 1953; children: Keith Warren, Michael Jay, Adam Douglas. Student Bklyn. Coll., 1948-50; LLB, Bklyn. Law Sch., 1953. Bar: N.Y. 1953, U.S. Ct. Mil. Appeals 1955, U.S. Dist. Ct. (so. and ea. dists.) N.Y. 1957, U.S. Tax Ct. 1960, U.S. Ct. Claims 1964, U.S. Supreme Ct. 1964, U.S. Ct. Appeals (2d cir.) 1968. Ptnr. Hoffberg, Rabin & Engler and predecessor firms, N.Y.C., 1968-82, Javits, Hinckley, Rabin & Engler, N.Y.C., 1982-84, Phillips, Nizer, Benjamin, Krim & Ballon, N.Y.C., 1984-94, counsel 1994—; arbitrator gen. comml. and constrn. panel Am. Arbitration Assn., 1968—; instr. Real Estate Inst., NYU, 1976-78; ct. apptd. mediator U.S. Dist. Ct. (so. dist.), N.Y., 1994—. Assoc. editor Bklyn Law Rev., 1952, editor-in-chief, 1953, also author law rev. note. Served to 1st lt. JAGC, U.S. Army, 1954-57, col. Res., ret., 1983.. Mem. N.Y. State Bar Assn., Res. Officers Assn. U.S. (pres. Rockland County chpt. 1967-68), B'nai B'rith (pres. New City, N.Y. 1965-66). Jewish. Home: Box 233 Goshen CT 06756-0233 Office: Phillips Nizer Benjamin Krim & Ballon 666 5th Ave New York NY 10103-0001

RABIN, MONROE STEPHEN ZANE, physicist; b. Bklyn., Dec. 19, 1939; s. Louis and Helen (Haspel) R.; m. Joan Greenblatt, Feb. 27, 1965; children: Elaine Judith, Carolyn Sandra. AB, Columbia Coll., 1961; PhD, Rutgers, 1967. Physicist Lawrence Berkeley (Calif.) Lab., 1967-72; assoc. prof. physics U. Mass., Amherst, 1972-81, prof. physics, 1981—; vis. physicist Stanford Linear Accelerator Ctr., Palo Alto, Calif., 1979-80; vis. scholar in Physics Dept. Harvard U., Cambridge, Mass., 1986-87; Soriano scholar in radiol. physics, radiation therapy dept. Mass. Gen. Hosp., Boston, 1986-87; mem. oversight panel Proton Therapy Med. Facility, Mass. Gen. Hosp., Boston, 1991-96. Contbr. articles to Physical Rev., Physical Rev. Letters, Physics Letters, Nuclear Instruments and Methods. Mem. Am. Phys. Soc., Sigma Xi. Achievements include research in experimental elementary particle physics, medical physics (cancer therapy using accelerated protons) and heavy-ion physics. Home: 21 Atwater Cir Amherst MA 01002-3205 Office: U Mass Dept Physics & Astronomy Amherst MA 01003

RABINER, LAWRENCE RICHARD, electrical engineer; b. Bklyn., Sept. 28, 1943; s. Nathan Marcus and Gloria Hannah (Bodinger) R.; m. Suzanne Login, June 23, 1968; children—Sheri Lynn, Wendi Beth, Joni Elizabeth. B.S., MIT, 1964, M.S., 1964, Ph.D., 1967. Mem. tech. staff AT&T Bell Labs., Murray Hill, N.J., 1967-70, supr. human machine voice communications group, 1971-85, head speech rsch. dept., 1985-90, dir. info. principles rsch. lab., 1990-95, v.p. user experience rsch. divsn., 1995-96; v.p. Speech and Image Processing Svcs., 1995—. Author: Theory and Application of Digital Signal Processing, 1975, Digital Speech Processing, 1979, Multirate Digital Signal Processing, 1983, Fundamentals of Speech Recognition, 1993. Bd. dirs. Summit Jewish Community Ctr., N.J., 1985-90. Fellow NAE, NAS, IEEE (pres. ASSP Soc. 1974-75, Piori award 1980), Soc. award 1980, Centennial award 1984), Acoustical Soc. Am. (Biennial award 1974, v.p. 1994-95). Republican. Jewish. Avocations: stamp collecting, bridge, racquetball. Home: 58 Sherbrook Dr Berkeley Heights NJ 07922-2346

RABINOVICH, RAQUEL, painter, sculptor; b. Buenos Aires, Argentina, Mar. 30, 1929, came to U.S., 1967, naturalized, 1973; d. Enrique Rabinovich and Julia Dinitz; m. Jose Luis Reissig, Feb. 14, 1956 (div. 1981); children—Celia Karen, Pedro Dario, Nora Vivian. Student U. Córdoba, Argentina, 1950-53, Sorbonne, Paris, 1957, U. Edinburgh, Scotland, 1958-59; lectr. Whitney Mus., 1983-86, Marymount Manhattan Coll., 1984-90. Exhbns. include Hecksher Mus., Huntington, N.Y., 1974, Susan Caldwell Gallery, N.Y.C., 1975, CUNY Grad. Ctr., 1978, The Jewish Mus. Sculpture Ct., N.Y.C., 1979, Ctr. Inter-Am. Rels., 1983, Bronx Mus. Arts, N.Y.C., 1986, Fordham U. Lincoln Ctr., N.Y.C., 1985, Ams. Soc., 1990, Erik Stark Gallery, 1991, Montgomery Ctr., 1992, Trans-Hudson Gallery, 1993, Noyes Mus., 1994, Nelson Atkins Mus. Art, 1995, Intar Gallery, N.Y.C., 1996, U. Tex. Art Mus., 1997, Trans Hudson Gallery, N.Y.C., 1997, others; represented in collections World Bank Fine Art Collection, Washington, Univ. Art Mus., Austin, Cin. Art Mus., Walker Art Ctr., others. NEA fellow, 1991-92; grantee N.Y. State Coun. Arts, 1995—. Avocations: travel, music. Home and Studio: 141 Lamoree Rd Rhinebeck NY 12572-3013

RABINOVICH, SERGIO, physician, educator; b. Lima, Peru, Apr. 8, 1928; m. Nelly; children—Gina, Sergio, Norca, Egla. M.D., San Fernando Med. Sch., U. San Marcos, Lima, Peru, 1953. Intern San Fernando Med. Sch., U. San Marcos, Lima, 1947-54; resident in medicine Grasslands Hosp., Valhalla, N.Y., 1954-57, Henry Ford Hosp., Detroit; prof., head dept. internal medicine U. Arequipa Med. Sch., 1960-61; asst. prof. dept. internal medicine U. Iowa, Iowa City, 1963-65; asst. prof. U. Iowa, 1965-69; attending physician and cons. VA Hosp., Iowa City, 1965-73; assoc. prof. U. Iowa, 1969-73; prof., chief dept. medicine div. infectious disease So. Ill. U. Sch. Medicine, Springfield, 1973-96; prof., chmn. dept. medicine So. Ill. U. Sch. Medicine, 1974-88, pres. Faculty Coun., 1992-93. Author: (with I.M. Smith, S.T. Donta) Antibiotics and Infection, 1974. Fellow ACP, Infectious Disease Soc. Am.; mem. AMA, Am. Soc. Microbiology, N.Y. Acad. Sci., Am. Fedn. Clin. Research, AAAS, Am. Thoracic Soc., Ill. Thoracic Soc. (pres. 1978-79), Central Soc. Clin. Research, Sigma Xi. Office: So Ill U Sch Medicine 800 N Rutledge St Springfield IL 62702-4911

RABINOVITCH, BENTON SEYMOUR, chemist, educator emeritus; b. Montreal, Que., Can., Feb. 19, 1919; came to U.S., 1946; s. Samuel and Rachel (Schachter) R.; m. Marilyn Werby, Sept. 18, 1949; children—Peter Samuel, Ruth Anne, Judith Nancy, Frank Benjamin; m. Flora Reitman, 1980. BSc, McGill U., 1939, PhD, 1942; DSc (hon.), Technion Inst., Haifa, 1991. Postdoctoral fellow Harvard, 1946-48; mem. faculty U. Wash., Seattle, 1948—, prof. chemistry, 1957—, prof. chemistry emeritus, 1985—; Cons. and/or mem. sci. adv. panels, coms. NSF, Nat. Acad. Scis.-NRC; adv. com. phys. chemistry Nat. Bur. Standards. Former editor: Ann. Rev. Phys. Chemistry; mem. editorial bd.: Internat. Jour. Chem. Kinetics, Rev. of Chem. Intermediates, Jour. Phys. Chemistry, J. Am. Chem. Soc. (assoc. editor). Served to capt. Canadian Army, 1942-46, ETO. Nat. Research Council Can. fellow, 1940-42; Royal Soc. Can. Research fellow, 1946-47; Milton Research fellow Harvard, 1948; Guggenheim fellow, 1961; vis. fellow Trinity Coll., Oxford, 1971; Recipient Sigma Xi award for original research, Debye award in phys. chemistry, 1984, Polanyi medal Royal Soc. Chemistry. Fellow Am. Phys. Soc., Am. Acad. Arts and Scis., Royal Soc. London; mem. Am. Chem. Soc. (past chmn. Puget Sound sect., past chmn. phys. chemistry div., editor jour.), Faraday Soc. Spl. research Unimolecular gas phase reaction. Home: 12530 42nd Ave NE Seattle WA 98125-4621

RABINOVITZ, JASON, film and television consultant; b. Boston, Aug. 17, 1921; s. Morris J. and Martha (Leavitt) R.; m. Frieda Pearlson, July 18, 1948; children: Abby, Judith, Daniel, Jonathan. B.A. magna cum laude, Harvard U., 1943, M.B.A. with distinction, 1948. With Chase Nat. Bank, N.Y.C., 1948-49; asst. to sec.-treas. United Paramount Theatres, Inc., N.Y.C., 1949-53; dir. Microwave Assocs., Burlington, Mass., 1952-54; asst. controller ABC, N.Y.C., 1953-56; adminstrv. v.p. ABC-TV Network, N.Y.C., 1956-57; with Metro-Goldwyn-Mayer, Inc., N.Y.C., 1957-69; treas., CFO Metro-Goldwyn-Mayer, Inc., 1963, financial v.p., 1967-69; dir., exec. v.p., gen. mgr. Ency. Brit. Ednl. Corp., Chgo., 1971-73; sr. v.p., gen. mgr. Am. Film Theatre, N.Y.C., 1974-75; v.p., asst. to pres. Metro-Goldwyn-Mayer, Inc., Culver City, Calif., 1976-79; v.p. fin. Metro-Goldwyn-Mayer, Inc., 1979-83; sr. v.p. fin. and corp. adminstrn. MGM/UA Entertainment Co., 1983-84; cons. motion picture and TV, 1984—; dir. Pacific Rim Entertainment, 1993-95. Capt. 1942-46. Decorated Bronze Star. Mem. Phi Beta Kappa, Phi Eta Sigma. Home: 1675 Stone Canyon Rd Los Angeles CA 90077-1912

RABINOVITZ, JOEL, lawyer, educator; b. 1939. A.B., Cornell U., 1960; LL.B., Harvard U., 1963. Bar: N.Y. 1963, Calif. 1981. Asst. prof. U. Fla., Gainesville, 1966-68; vis. assoc. prof. UCLA, 1968-69, acting prof., 1969-72, prof., 1972-79; ptnr. with Irell & Manella, L.A., 1981—; vis. prof., NYU, 1976; dep. Internat. Tax Counsel, Dept. Treasury, 1980-81. Office: UCLA Law Sch 405 Hilgard Ave Los Angeles CA 90095-9000 Office: Irell & Manella 1800 Avenue Of The Stars Los Angeles CA 90067-4212

RABINOW, JACOB, electrical engineer, consultant; b. Kharkov, Russia, Jan. 8, 1910; came to U.S., 1921, naturalized, 1930; s. Aaron and Helen (Flesher) Rabinovich; m. Gladys Lieder, Sept. 26, 1943; children: Jean Ellen, Clare Lynn. B.S. in Elec. Engring, Coll. City N.Y., 1933, E.E., 1934; D.H.L. (hon.), Towson State U., 1983. Radio serviceman N.Y.C., 1934-38; mech. engr. Nat. Bur. Standards, Washington, 1938-54; pres. Rabinow Engring. Co., Washington, 1954-64; v.p. Control Data Corp., Washington, 1964-72; research engr. Nat. Bur. Standards, 1972-89; cons. Inst. Standards and Tech., Gaithersburg, Md., 1989—; Regent's lectr. U. Calif.-Berkeley, 1972; lectr., cons. in field. Author. Recipient Pres.'s Certificate of Merit, 1948; certificate appreciation War Dept., 1949; Exceptional Service award Dept. Commerce, 1949; Edward Longstreth medal Franklin Inst., 1959; Jeffersom medal N.J. Patent Law Assn., 1973; named Scientist of Yr. Indsl. R&D mag., 1980. Fellow IEEE (Harry Diamond award 1977), AAAS; mem. Nat. Acad. Engring., Philos. Soc. Washington, Audio Engring. Soc., Sigma Xi. Club: Cosmos (Washington). Patentee in field. Home: 6920 Selkirk Dr Bethesda MD 20817-4750 Office: Inst Standards and Tech Gaithersburg MD 20899 *I believe that inventions enrich both the material wealth and the cultural life of a nation and the world. Being a product of original thought, they are an art form and should be supported as such.*

RABINOWITCH, DAVID GEORGE, sculptor; b. Toronto, Ont., Can., Mar. 6, 1943; came to U.S., 1972; s. Joseph and Ruthe (Calverley) R.; m. Sheila Martin, June 1966 (div. 1981); m. Catrina Neiman, Mar. 14, 1983. BS, U. Western Ont., London, 1966. Instr. sculpture Yale U., New Haven, 1974-75; prof. sculpture Staatliche Kunstakademie Düsseldorf, Germany, 1984—; sculptor in residence Atelier Calder, Saché, France, 1994. Sculptures include Box Troughs, 1963, Fluid Sheet Pieces, 1964, Gravitational Vehicles, 1965, Tubers and Wood Constructions, 1966-67, Phantoms, 1967, Sectioned Mass Constructions, 1968, Metrical Constructions, 1973—, Tyndale Constructions, 1974—, Construction of Vision Drawings, 1969—, Ottonian Drawings, 1977—, Collinasca Cycle (Woodcuts), 1991-92. Recipient CAPS award N.Y. State Coun., 1974, Lynch-Staunton award of distinction Can. Coun., Ottawa, Ont., 1977; J.S. Guggenheim Meml. Found. fellow, N.Y.C., 1975, Nat. Endowment Arts fellow, Washington, 1986-87. Mem. Royal Can. Acad. Arts and Scis. Avocations: music. Studio: 175 E 2nd St # 5C New York NY 10009

RABINOWITZ, HOWARD K., physician, educator; b. Pitts., Sept. 25, 1946; s. Mac and Anne (Morgan) R.; m. Carol A. Gelles, Feb. 4, 1968; children: Elyse, Daniel J. Student, Rutgers Coll., 1964-67; MD, U. Pitts., 1971. Diplomate Am. Bd. Family Practice, Am. Bd. Pediatrics. From instr. to assoc. prof. Dept. Family Medicine Jefferson Med. Coll., Phila., 1976-90, vice chmn., 1990-95; prof., 1990—; bd. dirs. Am. Bd. Family Practice, Lexington, Ky., pres., 1992-93. Contbr. articles to profl. jours. With USPHS, 1972-74. RWJ Health Policy fellow, 1993-94. Fellow Phila. Coll. Physicians; mem. AMA, Soc. Tchrs. Family Medicine, Am. Acad. Family Physicians. Office: Jefferson Medical College Dept Family Medicine 1015 Walnut St Ste 401 Philadelphia PA 19107-5005

RABINOWITZ, JACK GRANT, radiologist, educator; b. Monticello, N.Y., July 9, 1927; s. Abraham and Bessie (Sussman) R.; m. Rica Gedalia Arnon, Oct. 19, 1972; children—Antoine, Anne, Pierre, Yaron, Tal. B.A., UCLA, 1949; M.D., U. Berne, Switzerland, 1955. Diplomate: Am. Bd. Radiology. Intern Kings County Hosp., Bklyn., 1955-56; resident Kings County Hosp., 1956-59; instr. radiology Downstate Med. Center, Bklyn., 1960-61; asst. prof. radiology Downstate Med. Center, 1967-70, prof. radiology, 1970-73; asst. radiologist Mt. Sinai Sch. Medicine, N.Y.C., 1962-65; asst. prof. radiology Mt. Sinai Sch. Medicine, 1965-66, asso. prof. radiology, 1966-67, prof., chmn. dept. radiology, 1978-95, prof., 1995—; asso. attending radiologist Mt. Sinai Hosp., N.Y.C., 1965-67, dir. radiology, 1978—; radiologist-in-chief Bklyn.-Cumberland Med. Center, Bklyn., 1967-70; dir. diagnostic radiology Kings County Hosp. Center, Bklyn., 1970-73; prof., chmn. dept. diagnostic radiology U. Tenn., Memphis, 1973-78; cons. in radiology VA Hosp., Bronx, N.Y. Author: Pediatric Radiology, 1978, Radiology for the Primary and Emergency Care of Physicians, 1981. Fellow Am. Coll. Radiology; mem. Radiol. Soc. N. Am., Am. Roentgen Ray Soc., Assn. Univ. Radiologists, AMA, Soc. Chmn. Acad. Radiology Depts., Tenn. Radiol. Soc., Tenn. Med. Soc., Memphis and Shelby County Med. Soc., Memphis Roentgen Soc. Office: Mt Sinai Hosp 1 Gustave L Levy Pl New York NY 10029-6504

RABINOWITZ, MAYER ELYA, librarian, educator; b. N.Y.C., Jan. 31, 1939; s. Simcha Rabinowitz and Dvora (Resnikoff) Masovetsky; m. Renah Lee Levine, June 16, 1965; children: Adi, Dalya, Ayelet. BA, B in Hebrew Lit., Yeshiva U., 1960, MA, 1961; M in Hebrew Lit., Jewish Theol. Sem., 1965, PhD, 1974. Ordained rabbi, 1967. Instr. Jewish Theol. Sem., N.Y.C., 1970-74, asst. prof., 1974-76, dean students Tchrs. Inst., 1974-76, assoc. prof., 1976—, assoc. dean grad sch., 1976-79, dean grad. sch., 1979-88, libr., 1988—; mem. com. on Jewish law and standards Rabbinical Assembly, N.Y.C., 1978—; chair Joint Bet Din Conservative Movement, N.Y.C., 1990—. Author: Sefer Hamordekhai Gittin, 1990, Sefer Hemordekhai Megillah, 1997; contbr. articles to profl. jours. Mem. Assn. Jewish Studies, Assn. Jewish Librs. Office: Jewish Theol Sem 3080 Broadway New York NY 10027-4650

RABINOWITZ, SAMUEL NATHAN, lawyer; b. Hazleton, Pa., Sept. 16, 1932; s. Morris M. and Bodia (Janowitz) R.; m. Barbara G. Cohen, Mar. 27, 1955; children—Fredric E., Mark I., Joshua A. BA, Pa. State U., 1955; JD, Temple U., 1959. Bar: D.C. 1959, Pa. 1960. Agt. IRS, Phila., 1956-60; sole practice Phila., 1960-61; ptnr. Blank, Rome, Comisky & McCauley, Phila., 1961—; mem. trust com. Continental Bank, Phila., 1983-91; faculty Temple U. Sch. Law. Contbr. articles to profl. jours. Active Phila. Friends Boys Town Jerusalem; bd. dirs. Jerusalem Soc. Boys Town, Phila. Friends of Ben Gurion U. the Negev, Jewish Nat. Fund Coun., Phila.; bd. dirs., pres. Jewish Cmty. Ctrs. Greater Phila.; past chmn. Albert Einstein Soc. Albert Einstein Med. Ctr., past trustee; trustee Jewish Fedn. Phila. (officer Fedn. Endowments Corp.). Fellow Am. Coll. Trust and Estate Counsel; mem. ABA, Pa. Bar Assn., Phila. Bar Assn. (chmn. probate and trust sect. 1985-86), Green Valley Country Club, Elkview Country Club, Locust Club, Pyramid Club, Golden Slipper, B'nai B'rith, Maccabi/USA Sports for Israel (exec. com., counsel). Home: 1161 Norsam Rd Gladwyne PA 19035-1419 Office: Blank Rome Comisky et al 1200 Four Penn Ctr Plz Philadelphia PA 19103

RABINOWITZ, STANLEY SAMUEL, rabbi; b. Duluth, Minn., June 8, 1917; S. Jacob Mier and Rose (Zeichik) R.; m. Anita Bryna Lifson, June 24, 1945; children: Nathaniel Herz, Sharon Deborah, Judith Leah. B.A., State U. Iowa, 1939; M.A., Yale U., 1950; M. Hebrew Lit., Jewish Theol. Sem., 1944, Doctor Hebrew Lit., 1971. Ordained rabbi, 1943; dir. United Synagogue, N.Y.C., 1943-46; rabbi B'nai Jacob Synagogue, New Haven, Conn., 1946-53, Adath Jeshurun Synagogue, Mpls., 1953-60; rabbi Adas Israel Synagogue, Washington, 1960-86, rabbi emeritus, 1986—; v.p. Rabbinical Assembly, N.Y.C., 1974-76, pres., 1976-78; vice chmn. B'nai B'rith Youth Commn., 1965-76; pres. Mercaz, 1977-83. Club: Cosmos (Washington). Home: 3115 Normanstone Ter NW Washington DC 20008-2732 Office: Adas Israel Synagogue 2850 Quebec St NW Washington DC 20008-5200

RABINOWITZ, STUART, law educator, dean. BA cum laude, CCNY, 1966; JD magna cum laude, Columbia U., 1969. Bar: N.Y. 1970. Assoc. in law Sch. Law Columbia U., N.Y.C., 1969-71; assoc. litigation dept. Rosenman, Colin, Kaye, Petschek, Freund & Emil, N.Y.C., 1971-72; asst. prof. law Hofstra U. Sch. Law, Hempstead, N.Y., 1972-75, assoc. prof. law, 1975-83, prof. law, 1983—, Alexander M. Bickel Disting. prof. law, 1985—, assoc. dean, 1976-79, vice dean, 1982-86, dean, 1989—, chair local budget adv. com.; pvt. cons., 1972-89. Commr. Nassau County Commn. on Govt. Revision, 1993—. Recipient UJA Fedn. Leadership award, Disting. Svc. in the Cause of Justice award Legal Aid Soc., 1995, Martin Luther King Living the Dream award Equal Opportunity Commn., 1995. Mem. ABA, Am. Arbitration Assn. (mem. adv. com.), Fund for Modern Cts. (bd. dirs.), Am. Law Inst., N.Y. State Bar Assn., Nassau County Bar Assn. (proclamation for outstanding svc. to both the legal profession and the cmty. 1991), Suffolk County Bar Assn., Inns of Ct., Phi Beta Kappa. Office: Hofstra U Sch Law 121 Hofstra Univ Hempstead NY 11550-1090

RABINS, MICHAEL JEROME, mechanical engineer, educator; b. N.Y.C., Feb. 24, 1932; s. Herman and Ida (Olinsky) R.; m. Joan Rose, Apr. 6, 1956; children: Andrew, Evan, Alexandra. BS, MIT, 1953; MS, Carnegie Inst. Tech., 1954; PhD, U. Wis., 1959. Lic. engr., Calif., Tex. Asst. prof. U. Wis., Madison, 1959-60; asst. prof. NYU, N.Y.C., 1960-64, assoc. prof., 1964-70; prof. Polytechnic Inst. N.Y., Bklyn., 1970-75; dir. Office Univ. Rsch., U.S. Dept. Transp., Washington, 1975-77; chmn. mech. engring. dept. Wayne State U., Detroit, 1977-85, assoc. dean, 1985-87; prof. mech. engring., head dept. Tex. A&M U., College Station, 1987-89; TEES rsch. prof., 1989-91; dir. engring. ethics & professionalism program Tex. A&M U., College Station, 1992—. Author: Controls and Dynamics Systems Response, 1970, Introducing Systems and Controls, 1974, Engineering Ethics: Concepts and Cases, 1995, Practicing Engineering Ethics, 1997. Chmn. Detroit 3 Ctr. Transp. Com., 1977-87. Recipient Superior Svc. award Dept. Transp., Washington, 1976, Cert. of Merit, Mayor of Detroit, 1980. Fellow ASME (exec. com., chmn., editor jour., v.p. 1985-87, bd. govs. 1989-90, com. on program rev. 1992-96, Disting. Svc. award 1974, Leadership award 1996); mem. Am. Soc. Engring. Edn. (projects bd. 1987-90), Am. Automatic Control Coun. (pres. 1984-86, Edn. award 1991). Avocations: reading, Chinese cooking, stained glass, classical music. Office: Tex A&M U Mech Engring Dept College Station TX 77843

RABJOHN, NORMAN, chemistry educator emeritus; b. Rochester, N.Y., May 1, 1915; s. Alfred Augustus and Elizabeth Mary (Hooper) R.; m. Dora I. Taylor, Sept. 9, 1943; 1 son, James Norman. B.S., U. Rochester, 1937; M.S., U. Ill., 1939, Ph.D., 1942. Instr. chemistry U. Ill., Champaign-Urbana, 1942-44; research Goodyear Tire, Akron, Ohio, 1944-48; from assoc. prof. to prof. chemistry U. Mo., Columbia, 1948-83; prof. emeritus, 1983—. Mem. editorial bd.: Organic Syntheses, 1960—; assoc. editor: Chem. Revs., 1965-67. Fellow AAAS; mem. Am. Chem. Soc. (chmn. council com. publs. 1970-71), Phi Beta Kappa, Sigma Xi, Phi Lambda Upsilon, Alpha Chi Sigma. Home: 100 E Ridgeley Rd Columbia MO 65203-3530

RABKIN, MITCHELL THORNTON, physician, hospital administrator, educator; b. Boston, Nov. 27, 1930; s. Morris Aaron and Esther (Quint) R.; m. Adrienne M. Najarian, June 24, 1956; children: Julia Margaret, David Gregory. AB magna cum laude, Harvard U., 1951, MD cum laude, 1955; DSc (hon.), Brandeis U., 1983; DPharm (hon.), Mass. Coll. Pharmacy, 1983; DSc (hon.), Curry Coll., 1989, Northeastern U., 1994; DHumLet (hon.), Salem (Mass.) State Coll., 1995. Intern Mass. Gen. Hosp., Boston, 1955-56; resident in internal medicine Mass. Gen. Hosp., 1956-57, 59-60, chief resident, 1962, mem. staff, 1963-72, bd. consultation, 1972-80, hon. physician, 1981—; clin. fellow NIH, Bethesda, Md., 1957-59; gen. dir. Beth Israel Hosp., Boston, 1966-80, pres., 1980-96; CEO CareGroup, Boston, 1996—; assoc. prof. medicine Harvard U., 1969-70, assoc. prof., 1971-83, prof., 1983—; mem. Health Care Adv. Coun. U.S. Gen. Acctg. Office, 1991-96. Served with USPHS, 1957-59. Fellow ACP, AAAS; mem. Am. Fedn. Clin. Rsch., Mass. Med. Soc., Soc. Med. Adminstrs., Assn. Am. Med. Colls. (chmn. coun. tchg. hosps. 1996-97), Conf. Boston Teaching Hosps. (past chmn.), Inst. Medicine, NAS, Century Assn. (N.Y.C.), Harvard Club of Boston. Jewish. Office: CareGroup 375 Longwood Ave Boston MA 02215-5328

RABÓ, JULE ANTHONY, chemical researcher, consultant; b. Budapest, Hungary; came to U.S., 1957; m. Sheelagh Ennis; children: Benedict, Sebastian. BSChemE, Poly. U., Budapest, 1946, DSc in Chemistry, 1949, D honoris causa, 1986. From asst. prof. to assoc. prof. Poly U., Budapest, 1946-54; assoc. dir. Hydrocarbon Rsch. Inst., Budapest, 1951-56; rsch. assoc. Union Carbide Corp., Buffalo, 1957-60; rsch. mgr. Union Carbide Corp., Tarrytown, N.Y., 1960-72, corp. fellow, 1969-82, sr. corp. rsch. fellow, 1982—; sr. corp. rsch. fellow UOP, Tarrytown, 1988—; cons. in chemsitry and catalysis, Armonk, N.Y.; former mem. adv. bd. Ctr. for Advanced Materials, Lawrence-Berkeley Lab.; mem. adv. bd. dept. chemistry Lehigh U. Author: Zeolite Chemistry and Catalysts; former mem. editorial bd. Jour. Catalysis, Applied Catalysis; contbr. articles to profl. jours.; patentee in field. Recipient Kossuth award Govt. of Hungary, 1953, Excellence in Catalysis award N.Y. Catalysis Soc., 1982, Humboldt award, Fed. Republic of Germany, 1990. Mem. Am. Chem. Soc. (E.V. Murphree award 1988), Am. Catalysis Soc. (Eugene J. Houdry award 1989), Hungarian Acad. Sci. (Varga medal 1991), Am. Inst. Chemists (Chem. Pioneer award 1993).

RABON, RONALD RAY, retail jewelry store chain executive; b. Dothan, Ala., Apr. 27, 1955; s. Billy R. and Mary E. (Bruner) R.; m. E. Marie Hall, Oct. 25, 1974 (div. Sept. 1985); 1 child, Courtney Marie; m. Sheri L. Smith, Dec. 28, 1989; 1 child, Skylar Nicole. AS, Wallace Community Coll., Dothan, 1975. Cert. in diamond grading and evaluation Gemologist Inst. Am. Payroll clk., ironworker Daniels Constrn., Dothan, 1973-75; estate planner R&R Ins. Agy., Dothan, 1975-76; v.p. merchandising Wilbro Co. Inc., Dothan, 1976-84; owner, pres. Courtney's Jewelers Inc., Dothan, 1984-87, Knight DetectivE Agy., Dothan, 1986-88; sr. merchandiser Reliable Stores Inc., Columbia, Md., 1988-89; dir. merchandising Glennpeter Jewelers, Schenectady, 1989-91, v.p. merchandising, 1991-92, sr. v.p. adminstrn., 1992-96; chief fin. adminstr. Bailey's Jewelers, Rocky Mount, N.C., 1996—. Lt. gov. Ala. dist. Circle K Internat., 1974-75, gov., 1975-76. Recipient awards U.S. Jaycees, Circle K Internat.; named Outstanding Young Men of Am., 1977. Mem. Nat. Assn. Jewelry Appraisers (charter). Republican. Baptist. Avocations: reading, music, computer programming.

Home: 2805 Wellington Rocky Mount NC 27803 Office: Bailey's Jewelers 117 Winstead Ave Rocky Mount NC 27804

RABON, WILLIAM JAMES, JR., architect; b. Marion, S.C., Feb. 7, 1931; s. William James and Beatrice (Baker) R; m. Martha Ann Hibbitts, Mar. 7, 1987. BS in Arch., Clemson (S.C.) Coll., 1951; BArch, N.C. State Coll., 1955; MArch, MIT, 1956. Registered architect, Calif., Ky., N.C., Ohio, Pa., Ga. Designer archtl. firms in N.Y.C. and Birmingham, Mich., 1958-61; designer, assoc. John Carl Warnecke and Assocs., San Francisco, 1961-63, 64-66, Keyes, Lethbridge and Condon, Washington, 1966-68; prin. archtl. ptnr. A.M. Kinney Assocs. and William J. Rabon, Cin., 1968-85; v.p., dir. archtl. design A.M. Kinney, Inc., Cin., 1977-85; v.p., dir. programming svcs. Design Art Corp., 1977-85; sr. architect. John Portman & Assocs., Atlanta, 1985-88; dir. architectural design Robert and Co., Atlanta, 1988-89; studio dir., design prin. Carlson Assocs., Atlanta, 1990-93; prin. Rosser Internat., 1993-97, William Rabon, Architect, 1995—; lectr. U. Calif., Berkeley, 1963-65; asst. prof. archtl. design Cath. U. Am., 1967-68. Prin. works include Kaiser Tech. Ctr., Pleasanton, Calif. (Rsch. Devel. Lab. of Yr. award), 1970, Clermont Nat. Bank, Milford, Ohio, 1971, Pavilion bldg. Children's Hosp. Med. Ctr., Cin. (Cin. AIA design award), 1973, EG&G, Hydrospace, Inc., Rockville, Md. (Potomac Valley AIA design award), 1970, Mead Johnson Park, Evansville, Ind. (Rsch. Devel. Lab. of Yr. merit award), 1973, Hamilton County Vocat. Sch., Cin., 1972, hdqrs. lab. EPA, Cin., 1975, Arapahoe Chem. Co. Rsch. Ctr., Boulder, Colo. (Rsch. Devel. Lab. of Yr. award 1976, Concrete Reinforced Steel Inst. Nat. Design award, Regional AIA Design award), 1976, corp. hdqrs. Ohio River Co., Cin., 1977, Children's Hosp. Therapy Ctr., Cin. (Cin. AIA design award 1978, award of merit Am. Wood Council 1981), VA Hosp. addition, Cin. (Cin. ASHRAE Design award 1980), NALCO Chem. Co. Rsch. Ctr., Naperville, Ill. (Ohio and Cin. AIA design awards 1980, 81), 1980, Proctor & Gamble-Winton Hill Tunnel, Cin. (Ohio AIA design award), 1978, Toyota Regional Ctr., Blue Ash, Ohio (Ohio AIA and Ohio Masonry Council combined design award 1981), planning cons. Nat. Bur. Standards, Republic of China, 1982, East and West fleet hdqrs. and Data Ctr. Libras of Royal Saudi Arabian Navy, 1985, corp. hdqrs. The Drackett Co., Cin., 1983, corp. hdqrs. Brown & Williamson, Louisville, 1984, Inst. Paper Sci. and Tech., Atlanta, 1989, 93, Animal Sci. Complex, Athens, Ga., 1996. 1st lt. AUS, 1951-53, Korea. Decorated Silver Star, Bronze Star with V device, Bronze Star, Purple Heart with bronze cluster; MIT Grad. Sch. scholar, 1956; Fulbright scholar, Italy, 1957-58. Mem. AIA, Nat. Council Archtl. Registration Bds. Office: William Rabon Architect 5290 W Bank Dr Marietta GA 30068-1701

RABOSKY, JOSEPH GEORGE, engineering consulting company executive; b. Sewickley, Pa., May 20, 1944; s. Mary Helen (Mayer) Rabosky; m. Suzanne Lazzelle, Aug. 23, 1969. BS, Pa. State U., 1966; MS in Engring., W.Va. U., 1969, MSCE, 1973; PhD, U. Pitts., 1984. Registered profl. engr., Pa., Tenn., W.Va., Mo., Ohio. Project engr. Chester Engrs., Coraopolis, Pa., 1969-70, mgr., 1989-92; project mgr. Calgon Corp., Pitts., 1970-73, sect. leader, 1979-85, mktg. mgr., 1985-86; sr. environ. specialist Mobay Chem. Corp., Pitts., 1975-79; project engr. Morris Knowles, Inc., Pitts., 1973-74; project mgr. Penn Environ. Cons., 1974-75; engring. mgr. Baker/TSA, Inc., Pitts., 1986-89; pres. AquaTerra, Inc., Moon Twp., Pa., 1992-95, Rabosky & Assocs., Moon Township, Pa., 1995—; adj. prof. U. Pitts., 1985-88, Pa. State U.-Beaver, McKeesport and New Kensington campuses, 1985—. Bd. dirs. Moon Twp. Mcpl. Authority, 1980-89. Mem. ASCE, Am. Acad. Engrs. (diplomate, waste water), Water Environ. Fedn., Pa. Water Environ. Assn. (chmn. rsch. com. 1984-89, 91-92, mem. program com. 1984-89, mem. long planning com. 1993-95, officer 1994—, pres. 1996-97), Western Pa. Water Pollution Control Assn. (officer, pres. 1992-93), Internat. Water Conf. (mem. exec. bd. 1989-94, gen. chmn. 1992-93). Home: 104 Wynview Dr Moon Township PA 15108-1033

RABSON, ALAN SAUL, physician, educator; b. N.Y.C., July 1, 1926; s. Abraham and Florence (Shulman) R.; m. Ruth L. Kirschstein, June 11, 1950; 1 son, Arnold B. BA, U. Rochester, 1948; MD, SUNY, Bklyn., 1950. Intern Mass. Meml. Hosp., Boston, 1951-52; resident in pathology NYU Hosp., 1952-54, USPHS Hosp., New Orleans, 1954-55; pathologist Nat. Cancer Inst., Bethesda, Md., 1955—; prof. pathology Georgetown U. Med. Sch., 1974—, Uniformed Services U. Health Scis., 1978—, George Washington U., 1978—. Contbr. articles to med. jours. Mem. Am. Assn. Pathologists, Phi Beta Kappa, Sigma Xi, Alpha Omega Alpha. Address: NIH-National Cancer Institute Bldg 31-Cancer Biology 9000 Rockville Pike Bethesda MD 20892-0001

RABSON, ROBERT, plant physiologist, retired science administrator; b. Bklyn., Mar. 4, 1926; s. Samuel and Rose (Strauss) R.; m. Eileen K. Rabson, Aug. 27, 1950; children: Michael, Barbra, Laurel. BS, Cornell U., 1951, PhD, 1956. Rsch. assoc. biolog. div. Oak Ridge (Tenn.) Nat. Lab., 1956-58; asst. prof. U. Houston, 1958-62, assoc. prof., 1962-63; biochemist civ. biology and medicine AEC, Washington, 1963-67, asst. br. chief, 1967-73; first officer plant breeding and genetics sect. FAO/IAEA, Vienna, Austria, 1973-76; mem. divsn. biomed. and environ. sci. Energy Rsch. & Devel. Dept. Energy, 1976-79; dir. div. energy bioscis. Dept. Energy, Washington, 1979-95; mem. adv. bd. Rsch. Sch. Biol. Sci. Australian Nat. U., 1991-95. Mem. plant scis. adv. bd. McKnight Found., Mpls., 1981-92. With U.S. Army, 1944-46, PTO, ETO. Fellow AAAS; mem. Am. Soc. Plant Physiologists (chmn. publ. com. 1984-86, treas. 1988-91, Adolph Gude award 1986).

RABSTEJNEK, GEORGE JOHN, executive; b. Queens, N.Y., June 14, 1932; s. George John and Rose Anna (Krasa) R.; m. Patsy Kidd, July 17, 1964; 1 child, Marley Ann. B in Indsl. Engring., Ga. Inst. Tech., 1954; postgrad., U. Conn. Sch. Law, 1960, NYU Sch. Bus., 1965-69; advanced mgmt. program, Harvard U., 1975. Dir. material mgmt. svcs. divsn. Harbridge House, Inc., Boston, 1965-69, v.p., group head, 1969-75, exec. v.p., 1975-76, pres., 1976-83, CEO, 1983-92, chmn., 1983-93, ret., 1993; chmn. bd. dirs. R.P.W., Inc., Bluelight, Inc.; mem. exec. com. Keck Neural Prothesis Rsch. Ctr. Contbr. articles to profl. jours. Vice chmn. World Affairs Coun. Boston, 1988, pres., 1984-87; trustee Internat. Coord. Coun., Boston, 1984—; trustee Mass. Eye and Ear Infirmary, Boston, 1984—, vice chmn. bd. dirs.; mem. Draper Labs. Corp., 1994; mem. adv. bd. Town of Cohasset, Mass., 1975; chmn. nat. adv. bd. Ga. Inst. Tech., 1991-92; mem. exec. adv. bd. Ivan Allen Coll.; mem. bd. visitors Northeastern U.; bd. dirs. Ctr. for Tech. Commercialization. Comdr. USNR, 1958-75, ret. Recipient Disting. Alumni award Sch. Indsl. and Sys. Engring., Ga. Inst. Tech., named to Acad. Disting. Engring. Alumni. Mem. Am. Inst. Indsl. Engrs., Nat. Security Indsl. Assn. (v.p. 1987—), Nat. Def. Transp. Assn. (Def. Transp. award 1980), Assn. Naval Aviators, Navy League, Reynolds Soc. (chmn.), Nat. Security Industry Assn. (trustee 1990-93), Harvard Club, Algonquin Club (Boston), Cohasset Golf Club (Mass.), Cohasset Yacht Club, Cohasset Tennis and Squash Club, Mill Reef Club, Antigua, B.W.I., Comml. Club, F St. Club (Washington), Phi Kappa Sigma. Republican. Unitarian. Home: 181 Border St Cohasset MA 02025-2043

RABUCK, DONNA FONTANAROSE, English educator; b. Edison, N.J., Aug. 2, 1954; d. Arthur Thomas and Shirley Gertrude (Golub) Fontanarose; m. John Frederick Rabuck, July, 28, 1973; 1 child, Miranda Rose. BA in Eng., Rutgers U., 1976, MA in Eng. Lit., 1980, PhD in Eng. Lit., 1990. Prof. writing Pima C. C., Tucson, 1981-86; asst. dir. writing skills program U. Ariz., Tucson, 1983—; asst. dir. summer inst. writing U. Ariz., Tucson, 1985—, asst. dir. grad. writing inst., 1996—; adj. faculty Pima C. C., Tucson, 1992-95. Author: The Other Side of Silence: Performing Heroinism in the Victorian Novel, 1990, Writing Ctr. Perspectives, 1995; editor: Writing is Thinking: Collected Writings of the Summer Inst., 1985—. Founder, pres. Miles East-West Neighborhood Assn., Tucson, 1983—; dir. Ctr. for Sacred Feminine, Tucson, 1995—; program coord. U. Ariz. Arts and Scis. Minority Retention Program, 1988-93. Rutgers alumni scholar, 1972-76; Bevier fellow Rutgers U., 1976-78. Mem. Intercollegiate Writing Com. (task force), Commn. Cultural Thinking (task force), Nat. Coun. Tchrs. Eng. Avocations: feminist scholarship, women's rituals, yoga, hiking, meditation. Home: 1115 N Camino Mira Flores Tucson AZ 85745 Office: Univ Ariz Writing Skills Program 1201 E Helen St Tucson AZ 85719-4407

RABUN, JOHN BREWTON, JR., criminal justice agency administrator; b. Augusta, Ga. Nov. 16, 1946; s. John Brewton and Alsie Imor (Bateman) R.; m. Anna Betsy Park, Dec. 27, 1967; children: Kerry Kristin, John Candler. B.A., Mercer U., 1967; postgrad. So. Bapt. Theol. Sem., 1967-70; M.S. in Social Work, U. Louisville, 1971. Cert. social worker, Ky., D.C. Exec. dir. Ky. Civil Liberties Union, Louisville, 1971-72; dir. Community Residential Treatment Services, Louisville, 1973-78; program mgr. Field Services, Louisville, 1978-80; program mgr. Exploited and Missing Child Unit, Louisville, 1980-84; v.p., chief oper. officer Nat. Ctr. for Missing & Exploited Children, Washington, 1984—; mem. Alderman's Task Force on Social Svcs., Louisville, 1982, Mayor's City Youth Commn., Louisville, 1983-84; trainer and/or cons. to numerous agys. in U.S., U.K., Can., Mex., Belgium, The Netherlands. Contbr. articles to criminal justice and healthcare publs. and books. Recipient Key to City of Louisville, 1983, Disting. Alumnus award U. Louisville, 1985, Russell L. Colling lit. award Internat. Assn. for Healthcare Security and Safety, 1991, Russell Colling Lit. award Internat. Assn. for Healthcare Security and Safety, 1991; named hon. chief of police, City of Louisville, 1982. Mem. ACLU, Nat. Assn. Social Workers, Nat. Sheriff's Assn., Nat. Coun. Juvenile and Family Ct. Judges, Internat. Juvenile Officers Assn., Acad. Cert. Social Workers, Internat. Assn. Chiefs of Police. Baptist (deacon). Avocations: photography, hunting, fishing, Internet. Home: 13519 Oak Ivy Ln Fairfax VA 22033-1230 Office: Nat Ctr for Missing and Exploited Children 2101 Wilson Blvd Ste 550 Arlington VA 22201-3062

RABUNSKI, ALAN E., lawyer; b. N.Y.C., Jan. 18, 1948; s. Leo and Noima (Alperovich) R.; m. Jean Scheinberg, Oct. 31, 1976; children: Jonathan Sandler, Benjamin Jacob. BA, CUNY, 1971; JD with honors, John Marshall Law Sch., 1975; LLM in Taxation, NYU, 1978. Bar: N.Y. 1975, Ill. 1975, U.S. Tax Ct. 1981. Law clk. Hon. Allan Stouder Ill. Appellate Ct., Kankakee, 1975-76; pvt. practice law N.Y.C., 1976-94; ptnr. Rabunski & Katz, LLP, N.Y.C., 1994—; lectr. NYU Sch. of Continuing Edn., N.Y.C., 1985-89; lectr. in field. Coach Little League, Larchmont, N.Y., 1988-91; mem. Bd. Assessment Rev., Larchmont, 1992-94; arbitrator Civil Ct. of City of N.Y. Mem. ABA, N.Y. State Bar Assn. (trusts and estates law sect. com. taxation, tax sect. com. on estates, trusts, practice and procedure). Home: 72 Pinebrook Dr Larchmont NY 10538 Office: Rabunski & Katz LLP 630 3d Ave New York NY 10017

RABUSKA, MICHÈLE JOANNE, valuation analyst; b. Waterbury, Conn., Dec. 6, 1963; d. Peter Constantine and Joan Elfreida (Bergstrom) R. BA in Govt., Wesleyan U., 1995; MA in Econs., Trinity Coll., Hartford, Conn., 1997. With bus. office St. Francis Hosp. and Med. Ctr., Hartford, Conn., 1990-93; customer rels. specialist St. Francis Hosp. and Med. Ctr., Hartford, 1993-96; valuation analyst Valuation & Fin. Strategies, LLC, Farmington, Conn., 1996—; adminstrv. support, personal computer trainer, cons. The 1000 Corp., Hartford, 1993-94; cons. St. Francis Hosp. Profl. Svcs., 1995. Election pollwatcher Hartford Courant newspaper, 1992—; mem. Pub. Concern Found., Washington, 1993-94, Amnesty Internat., 1989—. Grantee State of Conn., 1993, 94; scholar Wesleyan U., 1993, 94, Etherington scholar Wesleyan U., 1993, 94. Mem. St. Francis Hosp. Women's Aux., We Adopt Greyhounds, Phi Theta Kappa, Alpha Zeta Psi. Democrat. Russian Orthodox. Avocations: glass etching and jewelry making, print-making, inline skating. Home: 47 Congress St Hartford CT 06114-1025 Office: Valuation & Fin Strategies LLC 195 Farmington Ave Farmington CT 06032-1700

RABUZZI, DANIEL D., medical educator; b. Pitts., June 19, 1935; s. Daniel Ralph and Victoria (Bruni) R.; m. Kathryn Allen, June 11, 1958; children: Daniel, Matthew, Douglas. AB, Harvard Coll., 1957; MD, U. Pa., 1961. Diplomate Am. Bd. Otolaryngology. Instr. otolaryngology U. Md., Balt., 1967-68; asst. prof. SUNY, Syracuse, 1968-71, assoc. prof., 1971-77, prof., 1977-81, clin. prof. otolaryngology, 1984—; prof., chmn. N.Y. Med. Coll. and N.Y. Eye & Ear Infirmary, N.Y.C., 1981-84; pres. St. Joseph's Hops. Med. Staff, Syracuse, 1990-92; med. dir. Harrison Surgery Ctr., 1996—. Contbr. 54 articles to profl. jours. and chpts. to books. Capt. U.S. Army, 1966-68. Fellow ACS; mem. Am. Soc. Head and Neck Surgery, Am. Acad. Otoloaryngology, Am. Cancer Soc. (pres. County unit 1978-80), Onondaga County Med. Soc. (pres. 1987-88). Avocations: Roman archeology, European travel, golfing, historical readings. Office: Ctrl NY Ear Nose & Throat Cons 1100 E Genesee St Syracuse NY 13210-1912

RABY, WILLIAM LOUIS, author; b. Chgo., July 16, 1927; s. Gustave E. and Helen (Burgess) R.; m. Norma Claire Schreiner, Sept. 8, 1956; children: Burgess, Marianne, Marlene. BSBA, Northwestern U., 1949; MBA, U. Ariz., 1961, PhD, 1971. Ptnr. VAR CPA Firms, 1950-76, Touche Ross & Co., N.Y.C., 1977-87; pres. Ariz. State Bd. Accountancy, 1993-94; mem. Ariz. State Bd. Tax Appeals, 1994—, chmn., 1997—; prof. acctg. emeritus Ariz. State U.; columnist Tax Notes mag., Arlington, Va., 1990—; cons. on video and audio tax edn. tapes Bisk Pub. Co., 1992—. Author: The Income Tax and Business Decisions, 1964, Building and Maintaining a Successful Tax Practice, 1964, The Reluctant Taxpayer, 1970, Tax Practice Management, 1974, Introduction to Federal Taxation, annually, 1980-91, Tax Practice Management: Client Servicing, 1986; editor: Raby Report on Tax Practice, 1986-96, PPC Guide To Successful Tax Practice, 1991; mem. editorial adv. bd. Taxation for Accountants, The Tax Adviser; contbr. articles to profl. jours. Mem. AICPA (chmn. fed. tax divsn. 1980-83, v.p. 1983-84, coun. 1983-90), Tax Ct. Bar. Presbyterian (elder, chmn. adv. coun. on ch. and soc. 1979-81). Office: PO Box 26846 Tempe AZ 85285-6846

RACCAH, DOMINIQUE MARCELLE, publisher; b. Paris, Aug. 24, 1956; arrived in U.S., 1964; d. Paul Mordechai and Colette Bracha (Madar) R.; m. Raymond W. Bennett, Aug. 20, 1980; children: Marie, Lyron, Doran. BA, U. Ill., Chgo., 1978; MS, U. Ill., Champaign-Urbana, 1981. Research analyst Leo Burnett Advt., Chgo., 1980-81, research supr., 1981-84, assoc. research dir., 1984-87; pub., owner Sourcebooks, Inc., Naperville, Ill., 1987—; co-CEO Login Pubs. Consortium, Chgo., 1990—. Author Financial Sourcebooks' Sources, 1987. Mem. Pubs. Mktg. Assn., Am. Booksellers Assn. Democrat. Jewish. Avocations: photography, writing, history. Home: 26 N Webster St Naperville IL 60540-4527 Office: Sourcebooks Inc 121 N Washington St Naperville IL 60540-4548

RACE, GEORGE JUSTICE, pathology educator; b. Everman, Tex., Mar. 2, 1926; s. Claude Ernest and Lila Eunice (Bunch) R.; m. Annette Isabelle Rinker, Dec. 21, 1946; children: George William Daryl, Jonathan Clark, Mark Christopher, Jennifer Anne (dec.), Elizabeth Margaret Rinker. M.D., U. Tex., Southwestern Med. Sch., 1947; M.S. in Pub. Health, U. N.C., 1953; Ph.D. in Ultrastructural Anatomy and Microbiology, Baylor U., 1969. Intern Duke Hosp., 1947-48, asst. resident pathology, 1951-53; intern Boston City Hosp., 1948-49; asst. pathologist Peter Bent Brigham Hosp., Boston, 1953-54; pathologist St. Anthony's Hosp., St. Petersburg, Fla., 1954-55; staff pathologist Children's Med. Center, Dallas, 1955-59; dir. labs. Baylor U. Med. Center, Dallas, 1959-86; chief dept. pathology Baylor U. Med. Center, 1959-86, vice chmn. exec. com. med. bd., 1970-72; cons. pathologist VA Hosp., Dallas, 1955-71; adj. prof. anthropology and biology So. Meth. U., Dallas, 1969; instr. pathology Duke, 1951-53, Harvard Med. Sch., 1953-54; asst. prof. pathology U. Tex. Southwestern Med. Sch., 1955-58, clin. assoc. prof., 1958-64, clin. prof., 1964-72, prof., 1973-94, prof. emeritus, 1994—, dir. Cancer Center, 1973-76, assoc. dean for continuing edn., 1973-94, emeritus assoc. dean, 1994—; pathologist-in-chief Baylor U. Med. Ctr., 1959-86, prof. biomed. studies Baylor Grad. sch., 1989-94; chmn. Baylor Rsch. Found., 1986-89; prof. microbiology Baylor Coll. Dentistry, 1962-68, prof. pathology, 1964-68, prof., chmn. dept. pathology 1969-73, dean A. Webb Roberts Continuing Edn., 1973-94; spl. advisor on human and animal diseases to gov. State of Tex., 1979-83. Editor: Laboratory Medicine (4 vols.), 1973, 10th edit., 1983; Contbr. articles to profl. jours., chpts. to textbooks. Pres., Tex. div. Am. Cancer Soc., 1970; chmn. Gov.'s Task Force on Higher Edn., 1981. Served with AUS, 1944-46; flight surgeon USAF, 1948-51, Korea. Decorated Air medal. Fellow Coll. Am. Pathologists, Am. Soc. Clin. Pathologists, AAAS; mem. AMA (chmn. multiple discipline research forum 1969), Am. Assn. Pathologists, Internat. Acad. Pathology, Am. Assn. Med. Colls., Explorer's Club (dir., v.p. 1993—), Sigma Xi. Home: 3429 Beverly Dr Dallas TX 75205-2928

RACHANOW, GERALD MARVIN, pharmacist, lawyer; b. Balt., Aug. 7, 1942; s. Louis and Lillyan (Binstock) R.; m. Sally Davis, July 26, 1964; children: Mindy, Shelly, Gary. BS in Pharmacy, U. Md., 1965; JD, U. Balt., 1972. Bar: Md. 1973, U.S. Dist. Ct. Md. 1977, U.S. Supreme Ct. 1977. Consumer safety officer FDA, Rockville, Md., 1973-96, dep. dir. divsn. OTC drug evaluation, 1978-96, regulatory counsel divsn. OTC drug products, 1996—; ptnr. Rachanow & Wolfson, Randallstown, Md., 1975—; contbr. fed. drug law exam. Nat. Assn. Bds. Pharmacy, 1985. Contbr. articles to profl. jours. Bd. dirs. parent tchr. student orgn. Md. Sch. for Blind, Balt., 1985—; mem. Community Living for Multihandicapped Blind, Balt., 1984—, adv., 1984—, Spina Bifida Assn. Md., Balt., 1985—. Fellow Am. Soc. Pharmacy Law; mem. ABA, Soc. FDA Pharmacists, Heuisler Honor Soc. Avocations: chess, stamp and coin collecting, sports. Home: 8817 Allenswood Rd Randallstown MD 21133-4111 Office: US FDA 5600 Fishers Ln Rockville MD 20857-0001

RACHELEFSKY, GARY S., medical educator; b. N.Y.C., 1942. Intern Bellevue Hosp. Ctr., N.Y.C., 1967-68; resident in pediatrics Johns Hopkins Hosp., 1968-70, Ctr. Disease Control, 1970-72; fellow UCLA Med. Ctr., 1972-74; clin. prof., assoc. dir. A/I Tng. Program UCLA. Mem. Am. Acad. Allergy, Asthma and Immunology (bd. dirs., pres.). Office: 11620 Wilshire Blvd Ste 200 Los Angeles CA 90025-1767

RACHIE, CYRUS, lawyer; b. Willmar, Minn., Sept. 5, 1908; s. Elias and Amanda (Lien) R.; m. Helen Evelyn Duncanson, Nov. 25, 1936; children: John Burton Rachie, Janice Carolyn MacKinnon, Elisabeth Dorthea Becker. Student, U. Minn., 1927-28; JD, George Washington U., 1932, William Mitchell Coll. Law, 1934. Bar: Minn. 1934, U.S. Supreme Ct. Atty. Minn. Hwy. Dept., 1934-43; spl. asst. atty. gen. Minn., 1946-50; counsel Luth. Brotherhood (fraternal life ins. co.), 1950-61; pvt. practice law Mpls., 1961-62; v.p., counsel Gamble-Skogmo, Inc., Mpls., 1962-64; v.p., gen. counsel Aid Assn. Lutherans, Appleton, Wis., 1964-70; sr. v.p., gen. counsel Aid Assn. Lutherans, 1970-73; with Rachie & Rachie, 1973-83; pvt. practice, 1983—; part-time spl. master Minn. 4th Jud. Dist., 1977—. Councillor Nat. Luth. Coun., 1959-66, sec., 1962-64, mem. exec. com., 1965-66; United Luth. Ch. in Am. del. to 4th Assembly Luth. World Fedn., Helsinki, 1963; past pres. Luth. Welfare Soc. Minn.; past chmn. Mpls. Mayor's Coun. on Human Rels.; chmn. finance United Fund drive, 1967-68; past mem. bd. dirs. Mpls. YMCA; trustee emeritus William Mitchell Coll. Law Augsburg Coll. With USNR, 1943-46. Recipient Disting. Alumnus award William Mitchell Coll. Law, 1987. Mem. ABA Minn. Bar Assn., Am. Legion, Minn. Fraternal Congress (past pres.). Lutheran. Club: Rotarian. Home: 7500 York Ave S Apt 101 Minneapolis MN 55435-4736 *I always try to keep in mind that the Christian Cross consists of both vertical and horizontal lines. The vertical is the longest line and represents a direct line from all of us on the bottom to God on the top and we must commune with Him. The horizontal represents an encompassing line that takes in all of mankind. If my life activities do not include the implementation of both lines of the cross, I will not have a balanced and Christian life.*

RACHLEFF, OWEN SPENCER (OWEN SPENCER RACKLEFF), actor, author; b. N.Y.C., July 16, 1934; s. Harold Kirman and Theresa (Friedman) R. BFA, Columbia, 1956; MA, London U., 1959. Editor Harry N. Abrams, Inc., Am. Heritage Co.; asst. prof. humanities N.Y. U., 1962-74. Profl. actor (theater prodns.) Catsplay, 1978, The Lesson, 1978, Arms and the Man, 1980, Escoffier: King of Chefs, 1981-96, A New Way to Pay Old Debts, Enter Laughing, 1984, The Imaginary Invalid, 1985, The Jew of Malta, 1987, Sunday Promenade, 1989, Variations Without Fugue, 1992, Impropriety, 1995; (films) The Dain Curse, 1977, Question of Honor, 1981, Murder of Mary Phagan, 1988; (TV shows) The Bloodhound Gang, Ryan's Hope, All My Children; author: Rembrandt's Life of Christ, 1968, Young Israel, 1969, Great Bible Stories and Master Paintings, 1970, The Occult Conceit, 1971, Sky Diamonds, 1973, Secrets of Superstitions, 1976, Exploring the Bible, 1981, The Occult in Art, 1990; (plays) Javelin, 1966, Uncle Money, 1980, Escoffier: King of Chefs, 1982, Tosca '43, 1984, The Fabulous La Fontaine, 1990; (novels) Eric's Image, 1982, Enigma, 1988. MacDowell Colony fellow, 1970. Mem. Actors Equity Assn., Screen Actors Guild, AFTRA, Dramatists Guild. Home and Office: 135 E 71st St New York NY 10021-4258 *It's a lucky man who has a goal and is not sidetracked. Personally, I was fooled into looking for comfort and security while in my twenties. As a result, a dream I'd cherished of a life in the theatre grew dim; dim, but not extinguished. At age 42 I opted for myself and pursued the dream.*

RACHLIN, HARVEY BRANT, author; b. Phila., June 23, 1951; s. Philip and Mazie (Drucker) R.; m. Marla Sivak Goldwert, June 28, 1987; 1 child, Glenn. BA in Biology, Hofstra U., Hempstead, N.Y., 1973. With music pub. cos., 1973—; owner Western Hemisphere Music Co., Ellipsis Music Mgmt. Co., Manhasset Hills, N.Y., 1975—, pres. 1982-92; faculty Five Towns Coll., Seaford, N.Y., 1978-84. Author: The Songwriter's Handbook, 1977 (N.Y. Pub. Libr. Book for Teen Age 1979-82); The Encyclopedia of the Music Business, 1981 (Outstanding Reference Source, Libr. Jour., 1981, ASCAP-Deems Taylor award 1982); Love Grams, 1983; The Money Encyclopedia, 1984 (Outstanding Fin. Reference Book, Libr. Jour., 1984, Ency. Britannica Home Libr. selection); The Kennedys: A Chronological History 1823—, 1986; The Songwriter's and Musician's Guide to Making Great Demos, 1988 (N.Y. Pub. Libr. Book for Teen Age 1989); The Making of a Cop, 1991, The Songwriter's Workshop, 1991, The TV and Movie Business: An Encyclopedia of Careers, Technologies, and Practices, 1991, The Making of a Detective, 1995, Lucy's Bones, Sacred Stones, and Einstein's Brain, 1996 (History Book Club); free-lance music journalist; contbr. Law and Order Mag., 1992—, Songwriter's Market 1979, 80, 87, 92; guest on The Dinah Shore Show, 1978, The Sally Jessy Raphael Show, 1993, The Late Late Show, 1996; compositions performed L.I. Mandolin and Guitar Orch., 1988. Recipient Outstanding Reference Book Yr. Am. Libr. Assn., 1981, Outstanding Reference Book Yr. Libr. Jour., 1984, Profiled in The New York Times, 1996, Newsday, 1996, The Sarasota Herald-Tribune, 1996, The Coral Springs Forum, 1997, The Boston Herald, 1997. Mem. ASCAP, Am. Guild Authors and Composers, L.I. Songwriters Workshop (bd. dirs.). Home: 878 Warner Rd Valley Stream NY 11580-1526

RACHLIN, LAUREN DAVID, lawyer; b. Buffalo, Feb. 6, 1929; s. Harry A. and Thelma (Goldberg) R.; m. Jean K. Rachlin, June 27, 1954; children: Laura Gail, Ellen Joan, James N. BS, U. Buffalo, 1948; JD, Harvard U., 1951. Bar: N.Y. 1952, U.S. Dist. Ct. (no. and we. dists.) N.Y. 1952, U.S. Supreme Ct. 1958, U.S. Ct. Appeals (2nd cir.) 1967, U.S. Tax Ct. 1952, U.S. Ct. Internat. Trade 1978. Ptnr. Rachlin & Rachlin, Buffalo, 1952-81; sr. ptnr. Kavinoky & Cook, Buffalo, 1981—; lectr. in inernat. law and trade; U.S. appointee to Bi-nat. Dispute Settlement Panel created under U.S.-Can. Free Trade Agreement, 1989-93; U.S. appointee N. Am. Free Trade Agreement Bi-Nat. Dispute Settlement Panel, 1994-96; arbitrator Internat. C. of C., Am. Arbitration Assn. U.S. del. to UN Human Rights Commn., 1970; cons. to temporary commn. N.Y. State Constl. Conv.; mem. Erie County Charter Rev. Commn.; mem.-at-large U.S. Nat. Commn. for UNESCO, 1972-76, chmn. human rights task force; mem. industry functional adv. com. Customs for Trade Policy Matters of U.S. Dept. Commerce, Office U.S. Trade Rep., 1987—. Mem. ABA (fgn. investment in U.S. real estate com., internat. bus. law com., subcom. on trade import), N.Y. State Bar Assn. (founding chmn. internat. sect. 1987-89, chmn. internat. divsn. 1989-94), World Arbitration Inst. (adv. bd., bd. dirs.), Am. Assn. Exporters & Importers (various coms.), Internat. Law Assn., Am. Soc. Internat. Law, Internat. Bar Assn., U.S. Inst. Human Rights (adv. coun.), Customs and Internat. Trade Bar Assn., Erie County Bar Assn., Union Internationale des Advocats. Office: Kavinoky & Cook 120 Delaware Ave Buffalo NY 14202-2704

RACHLIN, STEPHEN LEONARD, psychiatrist; b. N.Y.C., Mar. 6, 1939; s. Murray and Sophie (Rodnitsky) R.; m. Florence Einsidler, Nov. 22, 1962; children: Michael Ira, Robert Alan. BA, NYU, 1959; MD, Albert Einstein Coll. Medicine, 1963. Diplomate Nat. Bd. Med. Examiners, Am. Bd. Forensic Psychiatry, Am. Bd. Psychiatry and Neurology with added qualifications in forensic psychiatry. Internship UCLA, 1963-64; resident, chief resident in psychiatry Mt. Sinai Hosp., N.Y., 1964-67; staff psychiatrist Bronx Psychiat. Ctr., Bronx, N.Y., 1969-72; asst. chief svc. Bronx Psychiat. Ctr., 1970-72, chief svc., 1972-74; dep. dir. Meyer-Manhattan Psychiat. Ctr., N.Y.C., 1974-76; acting dir. Meyer-Manhattan Psychiat. Ctr., 1976-77; dep. dir. Manhattan Psychiat. Ctr., N.Y.C., 1977; clin. dir. dept. psychiatry & psychology Nassau County Med. Ctr., E. Meadow, N.Y., 1978-80; assoc. chmn. dept. psychiatry & psychology Nassau County Med. Ctr., 1979-80, chmn. dept. psychiatry & psychology, 1980-94; clin. dir. Meadowview Psychiat. Hosp., Secaucus, N.J., 1997—; assoc. prof. clin. psychiatry sch. medicine SUNY, Stony Brook, 1978-87, prof. clin. psychiatry, 1987-94; spl.

prof. law Hofstra U., Hempstead, N.Y., 1983-95. Editor in chief Psychiat. Quar., 1990—; assoc. editor Bull. of the Am. Acad. of Psychiatry & the Law, 1989—; contbr. articles to profl. jours. Lt. comdr. USNR, 1967-69. Mem. Am. Psychiat. Assn. (chmn. com. adminstrv. psychiatry 1987-92, mem. assembly 1991-94, mem. com. confidentiality 1993-96), N.Y. State Psychiat. Assn. (chmn. com. on pub. psychiatry 1986-94), Am. Assn. Psychiat. Adminstrs. (pres. 1989-90), Am. Acad. Psychiatry and Law (pres. tri-state chpt. 1988-90), Am. Assn. Gen. Hosp. Psychiatrists (pres. 1993-94), Am. Bd. Forensic Psychiatry (dir. 1990-94, treas. 1992-93), Am. Hosp. Assn. (gov. coun. sect. psychiat. and substance abuse 1991-92), Hosp. Assn. N.Y. State (chmn. mental health 1992, 93). Office: Meadowville Psychiat Hosp Secaucus NJ 07094 Office: Meadowview Psychiat Hosp Secaucus NJ 07094-2605

RACHLIN, WILLIAM SELIG, surgeon; b. Hartford, Conn., May 13, 1929; s. Irving I. and Rose (Szke) R.; m. Joy B. Loitman; children: Faye, Marge. AB, Princeton U., 1948; MD, Harvard Med. Sch., 1952. Diplomate Am. Bd. Surgery. Intern in surgery Beth Israel Hosp., Boston, 1952-53, asst. resident in surgery, 1953-54, 58-59, chief resident in surgery, 1959-60; pvt. practice surgery Brookline, Mass., 1960—. Capt. USAF, 1954-56. Fellow ACS, Am. Coll. Gastroenterology; mem. Mass. Med. Soc. (trustee 1980—), Norfolk Dist. Med. Soc. (pres. 1977-79). Democrat. Jewish. Office: 1 Brookline Pl Ste 302 Brookline MA 02146-7224

RACHMAN, BRADLEY SCOTT, chiropractic physician; b. Reading, Pa., July 23, 1961; s. Roger Stuart Rachman and Lanie Brenda (Chertok) Stuart; m. Amy Sue Rachman, Oct. 14, 1994; children: Nicole, Carly, Mackie. D of Chiropractic, Palmer U., 1986. Diplomate Nat. Bd. Chiropractic Examiners. Asst. dir. student affairs Palmer U., Davenport, Iowa, 1984-86; dir. Rachman Chiropractic, Ft. Myers, Fla., 1986—; dir. Multi-Disciplinary Symposium, Sanibel, Fla., 1989—; keynote speaker Am. Holistic Nurses Assn., Gainsville, Fla., 1988. Author: American Red Cross-Backtalk, 1987; (textbook) Peripheral Neurology Workbook, 1986. Dir. spinal health program ARC, Ft. Myers, 1987, also bd. dirs. H. Neilsen scholar, 1985. Mem. Fla. Chiropractic Assn. (dir. 1990-92), Tri-County Chiropractic Soc. (pres. 1990-91). Home: 8721 Cajuput Cv Fort Myers FL 33919-1843 Office: Rachman Chiropractic 12734 Kenwood Ln Ste 84 Fort Myers FL 33907-5638

RACHOFSKY, DAVID J., lawyer; b. Oceanside, N.Y., Nov. 17, 1936; s. Lester M. and Marjorie A.; m. Faith Allen; children: Robert, Patricia, Edward. BSEE, MIT, 1958; JD, Temple U., 1968. Bar: Pa., U.S. Dist. Ct. (ea. dist.) Pa., U.S. Tax. Ct., U.S. Ct. Fed. Claims, Pa. Supreme Ct. 1968. Ptnr. Dechert Price & Rhoads, Phila., 1968—; lectr. law Temple U. Law Sch., 1976—. Contbr. articles to profl. jours. With USAF, 1969-72. Mem. ABA, Phila. Bar Assn., Internat. Fiscal Assn. (chmn. mid-Atlantic region 1985-87, mem. coun. 1986-92, v.p., sec. 1992-96, exec. v.p. 1996—), Internat. Bus. Forum (tax sect. coun.). Office: Dechert Price & Rhoads 1717 Arch St Philadelphia PA 19103-2713

RACHOW, LOUIS A(UGUST), librarian; b. Shickley, Nebr., Jan. 21, 1927; s. John Louis and Mable (Dondlinger) R. B.S., York Coll., 1949; M.S. in L.S., Columbia U., 1959. Librarian York Coll., Nebr., 1949-54; instr. library asst. Queens Coll., N.Y.C., 1956-57; serials acquisition asst. Columbia U. Law Library, N.Y.C., 1957-58; asst. librarian Univ. Club, N.Y.C., 1958-62; librarian Hampden-Booth Theatre Library at the Players, N.Y.C., 1962-86, curator, 1986-88; library dir. Internat. Theatre Inst. U.S., N.Y.C., 1989—; cons. theatre sect. U. Calif., San Diego, new campuses program, 1964, Music Ctr. Operating Archives, Los Angeles, 1985; mem. library adv. bd. Eugene O'Neill Meml. Theatre Center, 1966—. Editor, compiler: Guide to Performing Arts, 1968; assoc. editor Am. Notes and Queries, 1971-74, asst. editor, 1967-71; mem. editorial adv. bd. Nat. Dir. for Performing Arts and Civic Ctrs.; editor Performing Arts series Gale Info. Guide, 1976-83, Theatre and Performing Arts Collections, 1981; contbr. articles and revs. to profl. jours. Mem. adv. bd. Am. Theatre Co., OKC Theatre Prodns. Served with AUS, 1954-56. Mem. Theatre Libr. Assn. (rec. sec. 1966-67, pres. 1967-72, 81-83, v.p. 1976-80, editor Broadside 1973-81), ALA, Spl. Librs. Assn. (sec.-treas. mus. group N.Y.C. chpt. 1964-66), N.Y. Libr. Club (pres. 1979-80), Am. Theatre Assn., New Drama Forum Assn. (pres. 1983-86), Am. Soc. Theatre Rsch., N.Y. Tech. Svcs. Librs., Archons of Colophon (convener 1982-83), Episcopal Actors Guild Am. (bd. dirs. 1976—), Drama Desk, Broadway Theatre Inst. Outer Critics Circle, Players Club. Home: 528 W 114th St New York NY 10025-7841 Office: Internat Theatre Inst/US 47 Great Jones St New York NY 10012-1118

RACHOW, SHARON DIANNE, realtor; b. St. Joseph, Mo., Apr. 12, 1939; d. Norman DeLos Zancker and Sylvia Lavina (Hawkins) Trouel; m. Thomas Eugene Rachow, Oct. 22, 1968. Student, So. Ill. U., 1969-72. Sec. Westab, Inc. (now Mead), St. Joseph, 1957-60, Seitz Packing Co., St. Joseph, 1960-66; exec. asst. to v.p., gen. mgr. Kansas City (Mo.) Chiefs, 1972; co-owner, mgr. Pool 'N Patio Plus, St. Joseph, 1973-84; realtor Coldwell Banker Gen. Realtors, St. Joseph, 1984-93, RE/MAX, 1993—. Trustee Nat. Multiple Sclerosis Soc., Mid Am. chpt., Midland M.S. Express Br., 1993-97. Mem. St. Joseph Regional Bd. Realtors (mem. Multi-List com. 1993-94, mem. forms com. 1994-97, dir. 1994, Top Residential Sales award 1986, grad. Realtor Inst. 1986, cert. residential specialist 1987), Million Dollar Club (life), Re/Max 100% Club (referrral and relocations cert. 1991), St. Joseph Regional Bd. Realtors-Chmn.'s Club, Real Estate Buyer's Agt. Coun. Republican. Lutheran. Home: 4211 Country Ln Saint Joseph MO 64506-2454 Office: RE/MAX of St Joseph Inc 1119 N Woodbine Rd Saint Joseph MO 64506-2434

RACHWALSKI, FRANK JOSEPH, JR., financial executive; b. Chgo., Mar. 26, 1945; s. Frank Joseph and Julia Alice (Cwikowski) R.; children: Mark, Karla, Brian. B.B.A., Loyola U., Chgo., 1967, M.B.A., 1969. Chartered fin. analyst. Systems analyst N. Am. Life/U.S. Life, Chgo., 1963-73; portfolio mgr. Zurich Kemper Investments, Chgo., 1973—; sr. v.p. Zurich Kemper Investments, Inc., Chgo., 1979—; v.p. Kemper Investors Life Ins. Co., Chgo., and subs. cos., Cash Equivalent Fund Inc., Chgo. Mem. Investment Analyst Soc. Chgo. Roman Catholic. Club: River Forest Country Club. Avocations: tennis, exercise, golf. Home: 380 S Kenilworth Ave Elmhurst IL 60126-3927 Office: Zurich Kemper Investments 120 S La Salle St Fl 21 Chicago IL 60603

RACICOT, MARC F., governor; b. Thompson Falls, Mont., July 24, 1948; s. William E. and Patricia E. (Bentley) R.; m. Theresa J. Barber, July 25, 1970; children: Ann, Timothy, Mary Catherine, Theresa, Joseph. BA, Carroll Coll., Helena, Mont., 1970; JD, U. Mont., 1973; postgrad., U. Va., 1973, Cornell U., 1977. Bar: Mont. 1973. With U.S. Army, 1973-76; advanced through grades to capt., 1973; legal assistance officer U.S. Army, Ft. Lewis, Wash., 1973; chief trial counsel U.S. Army, Kaiserslautern, Fed. Republic of Germany, 1975-76; resigned, 1976; dep. county atty. Missoula (Mont.) County, 1976-77; bur. chief County Prosecutor Svcs. Bur., Helena, Mont., 1977-89; asst. atty. gen. State of Mont., Helena, 1977-89; spl. prosecutor for the Atty. Gen.'s Office State of Mont., atty. gen., 1989-93, gov., 1993—. Founder Missoula Drug Treatment Program, 1977; active United Way, Helena; bd. visitors U. Mont. Sch. Law. Inducted into Basketball Hall of Fame Carroll Coll., 1982. Mem. Mont. Bar Assn., Carroll Coll. Century Club. Republican. Roman Catholic. Office: State Capitol RM 204 Helena MT 59620

RACINE, BRIAN STANLEY, telecommunications executive; b. Orange, N.J., Apr. 17, 1963; s. Franklin Louis R. and Joan Ann Pfeiffer. BA, Belmont Abbey Coll., 1986. Customer support rep. BTI, Raleigh, 1992-93, major acct. rep., 1993, project leader, 1993-96; project mgr. Fujitsu Network Comms., Raleigh, 1996—. Mem. AAAS, IEEE, Engring. Mgmt. Soc., Comms. Soc., Profl. Comm. Soc. Democrat. Roman Catholic. Avocations: skiing, golf. Home: 3210 J Walnut Creek Pkwy Raleigh NC 27606 Office: Fujitsu Network Comms 4403 Bland Rd Raleigh NC 27609-6288

RACINE, DOUG, state official; b. Burlington, Vt., Oct. 7, 1952; m. Roberta A. Harold. AB, Princeton U., 1974. U.S. senator from Vt., 1983-92; v.p. Racine's Jeep, Eagle, Isuzu, Inc. Office: Office of the Lt Gov 203 State Capitol Salt Lake City UT 84114*

RACINE, RENE, academic administrator, astronomer; b. Quebec City, Can., Oct. 16, 1939; married; two children. BA, Laval U., 1958, BSc, 1963; MA, U. Toronto, 1965, PhD, 1967. Carnegie fellow Hale Obs., Calif., 1967-69; from asst. prof. to assoc. prof. astronomy U. Toronto, 1969-76; prof. U. Montreal, 1976-97, prof. emeritus, 1997—; dir. Can.-France-Haw Tel Corp., 1980-84, Observatory Astron., Mont Megantic, 1976-80, 84-97. Mem. Am. Astron. Soc., Can. Astron. Soc. (pres. 1974-76). Achievements include research in galactic structure, galaxies, open and globular clusters, optical instrumentation/telescopes. Office: U Montreal Dept Physics, PO Box 6128 Sta Ctr Ville, Montreal, PQ Canada H3C 3J7

RACITI, CHERIE, artist; b. Chgo., June 17, 1942; d. Russell J. and Jacque (Crimmins) R. Student, Memphis Coll. Art, 1963-65; B.A. in Art, San Francisco State U., 1968; M.F.A., Mills Coll., 1979. Assoc. prof. art San Francisco State U., 1984-89, prof., 1989—; lectr. Calif. State U., Hayward, 1974, San Francisco Art Inst., 1978; mem. artist com. San Francisco Art Inst., 1974-85, sec., 1980-81. One woman show U. Calif., Berkeley, 1972, Nicholas Wilder Gallery, Los Angeles, 1975, San Francisco Art Inst., 1977, Marianne Deson Gallery, Chgo., 1980, Site 375, San Francisco, 1989, Reese Bullen Gallery, Humboldt State U., Arcata, Calif., 1990; group shows include Whitney Mus. Art, 1975, San Francisco Sci. Fiction, The Clocktower, N.Y.C., Otis-Parsons Gallery, Los Angeles, 1984-85, San Francisco Art Inst., 1985, Artists Space, N.Y.C., 1988, Angles Gallery, Santa Monica, 1987, Terrain Gallery, San Francisco, 1992, Ctr. for the Arts, San Francisco, 1993. Bd. dirs. New Langton Arts, 1988-92. Eureka fellow Fleishhacker Found., San Francisco; recipient Adaline Kent award San Francisco Art Inst., 1976, Djerassi resident, 1994, Tyrone Guthrie Ctr. resident, Ireland, 1995. Office: San Francisco State U Art Dept 1600 Holloway Ave San Francisco CA 94132-1722

RACKLEFF, OWEN SPENCER See RACHLEFF, OWEN SPENCER

RACKOW, JULIAN PAUL, lawyer; b. Phila., Dec. 16, 1941; s. Lawrence Lionel and Blanche (Wachman) R.; m. Paulette Schorr, June 23, 1963; children: Jeffrey A., Andrea B. AB, Cornell U., 1963; JD, Harvard U., 1966. Bar: Pa. 1966, U.S. Dist. Ct. (ea. dist.) Pa. 1966. Assoc. atty. Goodis, Greenfield, Narin & Mann, Phila., 1966-69; ptnr., co-chmn. dept. real estate Blank, Rome, Comisky & McCauley, Phila., 1970—. Sec., mem. exec. com., bd. dirs. Ctrl. Phila. Devel. Corp., 1990—, pres. 1996—. Mem. Pa. Bar Assn., Phila. Bar Assn., Harvard Law Sch. Assn. Phila. (v.p., exec. com. 1991—). Avocations: tennis, travel, piano. Office: Blank Rome Comisky & McCauley 4 Penn Center Plz Fl 1200 Philadelphia PA 19103-2512

RACLIN, ERNESTINE MORRIS, banker; b. South Bend, Ind., Oct. 25, 1927; d. Ernest M. and Ella L. Morris; m. O.C. Carmichael, Jr., Sept. 28, 1946; children: Carmen Carmichael Murphy, O.C., III, Ernestine Carmichael Nickle, Stanley Clark; m. Robert L. Raclin, July 22, 1977. Student, St. Mary's Coll., South Bend, 1947; LL.D. (hon.), U. Notre Dame, 1978, Ind. State U., 1981; L.H.D. (hon.), Converse Coll., 1974; D (hon.), Vincennes U., 1987, U. So. Ind., 1988; D in Tech. (hon.), Purdue U., 1992. Chmn. 1st Source Corp., 1976, South Bend, Ind.; Chmn. 1st Source Bank; former bd. dirs. First Chgo. Corp., First Nat. Bank Chgo.; bd. dirs. No. Ind. Pub. Service Co. Trustee U. Notre Dame, 1973—; bd. govs. United Way Am., 1973-80; adv. bd. Ind. U. South Bend; bd. dirs. Mich. Public Broadcasting, United Way of Ind.; bd. dirs., former chmn. Project Future, Ind. Acad. Bd. Regents; mem. nat. fin. com. George Bush for Pres., steering com., co-chair Ind. fin. com. Bush/Quayle, 1992. Recipient E.M. Morris Meml. award Ind. Acad., Community Service award St. Mary's Coll., Ivy Tech's Excellence in Edn. award, Edmund F. Ball award Ind. Pub. Broadcasting Soc., Castaldi award United Way Ind., Top Vol. award United Way Ind., 1987, Helping Hands award Hospice of St. Joseph County. Mem. St. Joseph County C. of C. South Bend (dir. 1977— , chmn.-elect 1986, Woman of Yr. award 1970, Disting. Bus. Leader award, 1993), Ind. State C. of C. (mem. edn. task force). Republican. Presbyterian. Clubs: Summit (South Bend); Ocean (Delray Beach, Fla.); Signal Point (Niles, Mich.), Audubon (Naples, Fla.), Collier's Res. Country (Naples). Office: 1st Source Corp PO Box 1602 South Bend IN 46634-1602

RACZKIEWICZ, PAUL EDWARD, hospital administrator; b. Lockport, N.Y., June 17, 1944; s. Edward Paul and Helen (Lentivech) R.; m. Rosemary Raczkiewicz, Jan. 16, 1973; children: Ann, Edward, Ellen. AA, Niagara County C.C., 1965; BS, SUNY, Brockport, 1968; Master in Hosp. and Health Care Adminstrn., St. Louis U., 1973. Dir. profl. svcs. Alton (Ill.) Meml. Hosp., 1973; v.p., corp. officer St. Elizabeth Hosp., Granite City, Ill., 1973-86; exec. v.p. St. Elizabeth Med. Ctr., Granite City, 1986—; pres., chief exec. officer St. Elizabeth Captive Med. Ins. Co.; v.p. Providence Mgmt. and Mktg. Svcs., Provide Med. Equipment Supply Co.; pres.-elect HAMSTL, Hosp. Industry Data Inst., bd. dirs. HIDI Ill. State rep. for HAMSTL; mem. adv. com., adv. bd. regional incinerator project Shared Resource Enterprises (HAMSTL). Past pres. bd. Tri-Cities Area United Way; mem. quality measurement tech. com. St. Louis Bus. Coalition. With U.S. Army, 1969-71. Fellow Am. Coll. Healthcare Execs.; Ill. Hosp. Assn. (past pres. region 4, cost containment coun., coun. institutional regulation), Assn. Ind. Hosps., Southwestern Ill. Indsl. Assn. (govt. affairs com.). Office: St Elizabeth Medical Ct 2100 Madison Ave Granite City IL 62040-4701

RADA, ALEXANDER, university official; b. Kvasy, Czechoslovakia, Mar. 28, 1923; s. Frantisek and Anna (Tonnkova) R.; came to U.S., 1954, naturalized, 1959; M.S., U. Tech. Coll. of Prague, 1948; postgrad. Va. Poly. Inst., 1956-59, St. Clara U., 1966-67; Ed.D., U. Pacific, 1975; m. Ingeborg Solveig Blakstad, Aug. 8, 1953; children: Alexander Sverre, Frank Thore, David Harald. Head prodn. planning dept. Mine & Iron Corp., Kolin, Czechoslovakia, 1941-42; mgr. experimenting and testing dept. Avia Aircraft, Prague, 1943-45; sec.-gen. Central Bldg. Office, Prague, 1948; head metal courses dept. Internat. Tech. Sch. of UN, Grafenaschau, W.Ger., 1949-50; works mgr. Igref A/S, Oslo, 1950-51; cons. engr., chief sect. machines Steel Products Ltd., Oslo, 1951-54; chief engr., plant supr. Nelson J. Pepin & Co., Lowell, Mass., 1954-55; sr. project engr., mfg. supt. Celanese Corp. Am., Narrows, Va., 1955-60; mgr. mfg., facilities and maint. FMC Corp., San Jose, Calif., 1960-62; mgr. adminstrn. Sylvania Electronic Systems, Santa Cruz, Calif., 1962-72; asst. to pres., devel. officer Napa (Calif.) Coll., 1972-88; chief exec. officer NAVCO Pacific Devel. Corp., Napa, 1984-91; pres. NAVCO Calif. Co., 1991—; prof. indsl. mgmt. Cabrillo Coll., Aptos, Calif., 1963-72; mgmt. and engring. cons., 1972—. Pres. ARC, Santa Cruz, 1965-72, bd. dirs., pres., Napa, 1977-88; mem. Nat. Def. Exec. Res., U.S. Dept. Commerce, Washington, 1966—, chmn. No. Calif. region 9, 1981-88; mem. President's Export Council-DEC, San Francisco, 1982—. Recipient Meritorious Service citation ARC, 1972, Etoile Civique l'Ordre de l'Etoile Civique, French Acad., 1985; registered profl. engr., Calif. Mem. NSPE, Calif. Soc. Profl. Engrs., Am. Def. Preparedness Assn., Assn. Calif. Community Coll. Adminstrs., Nat. Assn. Corp. Dirs., World Affairs Council No. Calif., Phi Delta Kappa. Editor-in-chief Our Youth, 1945-48; co-editor (with P. Boulden) Innovative Management Concepts, 1967. Home and Office: 1019 Ross Cir Napa CA 94558-2118

RADANOVICH, GEORGE P., congressman. BS in Agr. Bus. Mgmt., Calif. State Polytechnic U., 1978. Pres. Radanovich Winery, Mariposa, Calif., 1982—; county supr., 1986-87; chair County Planning Commn., 1988-92; mem. U.S. Ho. of Reps., 104th Congress, Washington, 1995—; mem. Budget Com., Resources Com., subcoms. Water & Power Resources, Nat. Parks, Forests & Lands. U.S. Ho. of Reps., 104th Congress, mem. Resources Com. Task Force on Endangered Species. Mem. Calif. Agrl. Leadership Program Class XXI, Rotary (Paul Harris Fellowship). Office: US House Reps 213 Cannon Bldg Washington DC 20515-0519

RADCLIFF, WILLIAM FRANKLIN, lawyer; b. Fredericksburg, Ind., May 21, 1922; s. Samuel Pearl and Hester Susan (Sherwood) R.; m. Elizabeth Louise Doeller Haines, May 15, 1982; children—Forrest Lee, Stephanie Anne; foster children—Cheryl Lynn, Sandra Lee, Richard Alan, Lezlie Laverne; stepchildren—Mark David, Laura Louise, Pamela Lynn, Veronica Leigh. B.A., Yale U., 1948; J.D., Ind. U., 1951. Bar: Ind. 1951. With DeFur, Voran, Hanley, Radcliff & Reed and predecessors, Muncie, Ind., 1951—, ptnr., 1954—; dir., mem. exec. com. Am. Nat. Bank and Trust Co., Muncie . Author: Sherman Minton: Indiana's Supreme Court Justice, 1996, Sagamore of the Wabash. Pres. Delaware County Mental Health Assn., 1962-63; founding mem. Ind. Mental Health Meml. Found., 1962, sec., 1962-84; bd. dirs. Delaware County Cancer Soc.; trustee Acad. Community Leadership. Served with AUS, 1940-46, PTO. Mem. ABA, Ind. Bar Assn., Muncie Bar Assn., Muncie-Delaware County C. of C. (pres. 1972-73). Clubs: Muncie Tennis and Country (bd. dirs., sec.), Muncie, Delaware Country (pres. 1972-73), Exchange (pres. 1962) (Muncie). Lodge: Masons. Home: 1809 N Winthrop Rd Muncie IN 47304-2532 Office: 201 E Jackson St Muncie IN 47305-2832 *Be yourself. Do not try to be someone else. Use your God given talents to the best of your ability and be content with the success that such effort brings.*

RADCLIFFE, GEORGE GROVE, retired life insurance company executive; b. Balt., Nov. 12, 1924; s. George G. and Elsie (Winter) R.; m. Bettie Howell, Feb. 10, 1951 (div.); 1 child, Cynthia; m. Kathleen Moore Smith, 1991. B.A., Johns Hopkins U., 1947; grad. Advanced Mgmt. Program,, Harvard U. Grad. Sch. Bus. Adminstrn., 1962. With Balt. Life Ins. Co., 1947-89, v.p. treas., 1963-69, exec. v.p., 1969-72, pres., 1972-89, chief exec. officer, 1974-89, chmn. bd., 1980-89, pres., 1981-86, ret., 1989; dir., 1989—, EA Engring. Sci. and Tech., Inc. Chmn. bd. trustees Johns Hopkins U., 1984-90, trustee, 1975-93, trustee emeritus, 1993—. Mem. Johns Hopkins Club, Maryland Club (Balt.), Tre Avon Yacht Club, Talbot Country Club, Delta Upsilon. Methodist. Home and Office: PO Box 98 Oxford MD 21654-0166

RADCLIFFE, GERALD EUGENE, judge, lawyer; b. Chillicothe, Ohio, Feb. 19, 1923; s. Maurice Gerald and Mary Ellen (Wills) R.; children: Jerilynn K. Radcliffe Ross, Pamela J. Radcliffe Dunn. BA, Ohio U., 1948; JD, U. Cin., 1950. Bar: Ohio 1950, U.S. Dist. Ct. 1951, U.S. Supreme Ct. 1957. Sole practice, Chillicothe, 1950-66; asst. pros. atty. Ross County, Ohio, 1966-70; acting mcpl. judge Chillicothe Mcpl. Ct., 1970-72; judge probate, juvenile divs. Ross County Ct., Chillicothe, 1973-96; mem. rules adv. com. Ohio Supreme Ct., 1984; mem. Ohio Legis. Oversite com., 1974-81; trustee Ohio Jud. Coll., 1980-87. Editor Cin. Law Rev., 1949-50. Co-author: Constitutional Law, 1979. Contbr. articles to profl. jours. Project dir. South Central Ohio Regional Juvenile Detention Ctr., 1971-72; co-founder, developer Roweton Family Complex; co-chmn. Chillicothe United Way Fund Campaign, 1972; mem., chmn. Adv. Coun. of Gov. Dept. Youth Svcs., 1983-89; mem. N.W. Ordinance and U.S. Constn. Bicentennial Com., 1993-96. Recipient Superior Jud. award Ohio Supreme Ct., 1976-82, Meritorious Service award Probate Ct. Judges Ohio, 1984-89, Commendation 118th Ohio Senate, 1990, Gov's. Spl. Recognition Svc. and Leadership to Youth Svcs. Adv. Coun., 1990, Nat. Commendation Ohio Conf. Nat. Assn. Blacks in Criminal Justice; Dirs. award Ohio Dept. Youth Svcs., 1984, Silver Helmet award for Americanism Nat. Amvets, 1992, Disting. Alumni award Chillicothe Bd. Edn., 1996; named Outstanding Citizen Chillicothe Edn. Assn., 1987, Outstanding Citizen of Yr. Jr. C. of C., 1972. Mem. Ohio Juvenile Judges Assn., (pres. 1983-84), Nat. Coun. Juvenile and Family Ct. Judges (trustee 1982-84, 93-95, chmn. govtl. rels. com., recipient Meritorious Svc. award 1988, Kendall L. Lingle award 1996), Nat. Ctr. Juvenile Justice (bd. fellows 1995—), Ohio Jud. Conf., Ohio State Bar Assn. Democrat. Lodges: Kiwanis (lt. gov. 1983-84, Ohio Statehood Achievement award 1979), Ohio State Bar Assn., Masons. Avocation: golf. Office: Common Pleas Ct Probate Div Ross County Courthouse Chillicothe OH 45601

RADCLIFFE, REDONIA WHEELER (DONNIE RADCLIFFE), journalist, author; b. Republican City, Nebr.; d. Donnel F. and Lois (Woolman) Wheeler; m. Robert C. Radcliffe, 1957; 1 son, M. Donnel Nunes. B.A., San Jose (Calif.) State U., 1951. Reporter, women's editor, county editor The Salinas Californian, 1951-59; free-lance writer Europe, 1959-66; reporter Washington Star, 1967-72; reporter, columnist Washington Post, 1972-95. Author: Simply Barbara Bush: A Portrait of America's Candid First Lady, 1989, Hillary Rodham Clinton: A First Lady for Our Time, 1993; contbr.: The Fall of a President, 1974, Guide to Washington, 1989. Trustee Calvert County (Md.) Libr. Bd. Address: 2795 Spout Ln Lusby MD 20657-2989

RADDING, ANDREW, lawyer; b. N.Y.C., Nov. 30, 1944; m. Bonnie A. Levinson, Oct. 7, 1972; children: Judith Lynne, Joshua David. BBA, CCNY-Baruch Sch., 1965; JD, Boston U., 1968. Bar: N.Y. 1968, Md. 1977, D.C. 1977, U.S. Supreme Ct. Grad. fellow Northwestern U. Sch. Law, 1968-69; asst. csl. U.S. Ho. of Reps. Select Com. on Crime, 1969-72; asst. U.S. atty. for Dist. Md., 1972-77; ptnr. Francomano, Radding & Mannes, Balt., 1977-80, Burke, Gerber, Wilen, Francomano & Radding, Balt., 1980-85, Blades & Rosenfeld P.A., Balt., 1985—; mem. adj. faculty clin. practice skills, criminal law, fed. criminal practice U. Balt. Sch. Law, 1980—; mem. trial experience com. U.S. Dist. ct., 1986-88; apptd. by gov. State Adminstrv. Bd. of Election Laws, 1995-96. Bd. dirs. Copper Hill Condominium, 1979-82, pres., 1981-82; subcom. Md. Republican Conv., 1981; sen. C.M. Mathias Jud. Selection com., 1986, chmn. U.S. Dist. Ct. Bicentennial Program, 1989-90. Mem. ABA, Md. Bar Assn., Balt. City Bar Assn. (jud. selection com. 1990-92, 94—, chmn. 1996—), Fed. Bar Assn. (Balt. chpt. pres. 1986-87), Balt. City Bar Assn. (jud. selection com. 1990-92, 94—, chmn. 1996—, ethics com. 1991-92), U.S. Atty. Alumni Assn. Md. (pres. 1978—), Md. Inst. Continuing Profl. Edn. for Lawyers (bd. govs. 1987-92, inquiry panel atty. grievance com. 1991—), Am. Arbitration Assn. (arbitrator), U.S. Arbitration and Mediation (mediator). Republican. Jewish. Avocations: playing tennis, baseball. Office: Blades & Rosenfeld PA 20 S Charles St Baltimore MD 21201-3220

RADEBOLDT-DALY, KAREN ELAINE, medical nurse; b. Bklyn., Mar. 3, 1944; d. Harry Phillip and Lillian Florence (Renton) McAney; m. Richard William Radeboldt, Aug. 19, 1968 (dec. Aug. 1985); children: Karyn, Kellianne, Kimberly, Kristi-Jo, Richard; m. William J. Daly, Sr., Jan. 22, 1995. Lic. practical nurse, Wyckoff Heights Sch. Nursing, Bklyn., 1968; RN, Orange County C.C., Middletown, N.Y., 1990. LPN, N.Y., RN, N.Y.; cert. med.-surg. nurse, N.Y. Nurses aide, lic. practical nurse Wyckoff Heights Hosp., Bklyn., 1967-90; staff nurse, med.-surg. nurse Westchester Med. Ctr., Valhalla, N.Y., 1990-96, staff nurse, trauma unit, 1996—. Mem. Am. Jour. Nursing. Adventist. Avocations: reading, sewing, bowling, walking, motorcycle riding. Home: 101 Daly Rd Middletown NY 10940 Office: Westchester Med Ctr Valhalla NY 10595

RADEKA, VELJKO, electronics engineer; b. Zagreb, Yugoslavia, Nov. 21, 1930; came to U.S., 1962; s. Milan and Neda Radeka; m. Jelena Horvat, May 17, 1958; children: Dejan, Dina. Diploma Engr., U. Zagreb, 1955, D. Engring. Scis., 1961. Scientist Inst. Ruder Boskovic, Zagreb, 1955-62, 64-66; scientist Brookhaven Nat. Lab., Upton, N.Y., 1962-64, 66-72; sr. scientist, head instrumentation div. Brookhaven Nat. Lab., 1972—. Contbr. in field. Fellow IEEE: mem Am. Phys. Soc., Nuclear and Plasma Physics Soc., Bellport Bay Yacht Club. Home: 29 Academy Ln Bellport NY 11713-2742 Office: Brookhaven Nat Lab Upton NY 11973

RADEL, EVA, pediatrician, hematologist; b. Vienna, Austria, Apr. 10, 1934; came to U.S., 1939; d. Ernest O. and Marian (Feiks) Grossman; m. Stanley Robert Radel, May 31, 1954; children: Carol, Laura. AB, N.Y. U., 1954, MD, 1958. Pediatric intern, resident Bronx Mcpl. Hosp. Ctr., 1958-61; pediatric hematology rsch. fellow Albert Einstein Coll. Medicine, Bronx, 1961-63; pediatric hematologist, head pediatric hematology Morrisania city Hosp., Bronx, 1963-76; assoc. dir. pediatrics North Cen. Bronx Hosp., 1978-82; attending physician pediatric hemetology out patients Montefiore Med. Ctr., Bronx, 1965-79, svc. head pediatric hematology-oncology, 1979—; head pediatric hematology North Cen. Bronx Hosp., 1976—; responsible investigator Children's Cancer Study Group, 1980—; dir. pediatric hematology-oncology Albert Einstein Coll. Medicine, Bronx, 1981—. Fellow Am. Acad Pediatrics; mem. Am. Soc. Hematology, Am. Soc. Pediatric Hematology-Oncology, Soc. for the Study of Blood. Office: Dept Pediatrics Montefiore Med Ctr 111 E 210th St Bronx NY 10467-2401

RADELL, NICHOLAS JOHN, management consultant; b. South Range, Mich., Sept. 2, 1930; s. Nicholas and Anna (Pekkala) R.; m. Jennifer L. Beemer, May 19, 1989; childrenfrom previous marriage: Susan Diane, Sally Anne, Nicholas Steven; stepchildren: Andrew Justin Beemer, Shana Kristen Beemer. B.S., U. Mich., 1952, M.B.A., 1956. C.P.A., Mich. registered profl. engr., Mich. Application engr. Square D Co., Detroit, 1954-55; mem. firm Touche, Ross, Bailey & Smart (C.P.A.'s), Detroit, 1956-61; with Cresap, McCormick & Paget Inc., Chgo., 1961-83, ptnr., 1967-69, v.p., dir., 1969-82, region mgr., 1971-82; v.p., dir. Cresap, a Towers Perrin Co., 1983-90; chmn.

Towers Perrin Australia, 1989-90; v.p. Mercer Mgmt. Consulting, Chgo., 1991-95; pres. NJR Assoc., Inc., 1996—. Contbg. author: Handbook of Process Planning and Estimating, 1962, Scientific Inventory Management, 1963, Introduction to Manufacturing Management, 1969, Managing Radical Change, 1995. Bd. dirs. Chgo. Conv. and Tourism Bur., 1983, U. Mich. Alumni Assn., 1989. 1st lt. USAF, 1952-54. Fellow Inst. Prodn. Engrs. U.K. (hon.); mem. Soc. Mfg. Engrs. (bd. dirs., nat. v.p. 1971, pres. 1973), Am. Assn. Engring. Socs. (chmn. 1984), Inst. Indsl. Engrs., Chgo. Club, Mid-Day Club, Met. Club, Phi Gamma Delta. Presbyterian. Home: 1230 Sunset Rd Winnetka IL 60093-3628

RADEMACHER, RICHARD JOSEPH, librarian; b. Kaukauna, Wis., Aug. 20, 1937; s. Joseph Benjamin and Anna (Wyuts) R.; m. Mary Jane Liethen, Feb. 12, 1966; children: Alicia Mary, Ann Marie, Amy Rose. A.B., Ripon Coll., 1959; M.S., Library Sch. U. Wis., 1961. Dir. Kaukauna Public Library, 1964-66, Eau Claire (Wis.) Public Library, 1966-69; librarian Salt Lake City Public Library, 1969-76; dir. Wichita (Kans.) Public Library, 1976—. Bd. dirs. Salt Lake Art Center, Reading Room for the Blind.; mem. Kans. Com. for the Humanities, 1977-82; mem. exec. bd. Wichita Girl Scouts, 1977—. Served with AUS, 1962-64. Mem. ALA; Mem. Mountain Plains Library Assn. (sect. chmn.); mem. Kans. Library Assn. (pres. 1982-83); Mem. Wichita Library Assn. Office: Wichita Pub Libr 223 S Main St Wichita KS 67202-3715*

RADEMAKER, STEPHEN GEOFFREY, lawyer; b. Balt., July 18, 1959; s. Thomas Joseph and Ruth Virginia (Wentz) R.; m. Danielle Pletka; children: Andrew, Olivia. BA with Highest Distinction, U. Va., 1981, JD, 1984, MA in Fgn. Affairs, 1985. Bar: Va. 1984, D.C. 1985. Assoc. Covington & Burling, Washington, 1984-86; law clk. to Hon. James L. Buckley U.S. Ct. Appeals (D.C. cir.), Washington, 1986; counsel to vice chmn. U.S. Internat. Trade Commn., Washington, 1986-87; spl. asst. to asst. sec. for Inter-Am. affairs Dept. State, Washington, 1987-89; assoc. counsel to Pres. of U.S. and dep. legal advisor to NSC, Washington, 1989-92; gen. counsel Peace Corps, Washington, 1992-93; Rep. chief counsel Com. Fgn. Affairs U.S. Ho. of Reps., Washington, 1993-95, chief counsel Com. Internat. Rels., 1995—. Recipient Raven award U. Va.,1984; S. Philip Heiner scholar U. Va., 1983. Mem. ABA (U.S. Govt. liaison for sect. internat. law and practice), Va. Bar Assn., D.C. Bar Assn., Phi Beta Kappa, Omicron Delta Kappa. Republican. Lutheran. Avocations: skiing, cycling, scuba diving. Office: US House Reps 2170 Rayburn St Com Internat Rels Washington DC 20515

RADEN, LOUIS, tape and label corporation executive; b. Detroit, June 17, 1929; s. Harry M. and Joan (Morris) R.; m. Mary K. Knowlton, June 18, 1949; children: Louis III, Pamela (Mrs. T.W. Rea III), Jacqueline. BA, Trinity Coll., 1951; postgrad. NYU, 1952. With Time, Inc., 1951-52; with Quaker Chem. Corp., 1952-63, sales mgr., 1957-63; exec. v.p. Gen. Tape & Supply, Inc., Detroit, 1963-68, pres., chmn. bd., 1969—; pres. Mich. Gun Clubs, 1973-77; pres. L.R. Properties, Inc., Detroit, 1995—. Detroit County Day Sch. Varsity Soccer Coach, 1965-1969. Fifth reunion chmn. Trinity Coll., 1956, pres. Mich. alumni, 1965-72, sec. Class of 1951, 81-86, pres. 1986-91, The McCook Fellow Soc.; trustee, v.p. Mich. Diocese Episcopal Ch., 1980-82, mem. urban evaluation com., 1975-78, chmn. urban evaluation com., 1978, chmn. urban affairs com., 1977-79; vice chmn., bd. dirs. Robert H. Whitaker Sch. Theology, 1983-85; vice chmn. Mich. Diocese Econ. Justice Commn., 1989—, bd. dirs. Poverty and Social Reform Inst., 1992—; founding sponsor World Golf Hall of Fame; mem. Founders Soc. Detroit Inst. Arts; trustee Mich. Housing Trust Fund, 1993—. Recipient Person of Yr. award Mich. Diocese Econ. Justice Commn., 1994; inductee Hall of Fame Robert H. Whitaker Sch. Theology, 1996. Mem. NRA (life), Nat. Skeet Shooting Assn. (life, nat. dir. 1977-79, 5 Man Team World Champion award 1977, pres. coun.), Mich. Skeet Assn. (all state team 1975-80, inductee Hall of Fame 1994), Greater Detroit Bd. Commerce, Automotive Industry Action Group, Mich. C. of C., U.S. C. of C., Greater Hartford Jaycees (exec. v.p. 1955-57, Key Man award 1957), Theta Xi (life, Disting. Service award 1957, alumni pres. 1952-57, regional dir. 1954-57). Republican. Clubs: Detroit Golf, Detroit Gun (sec. bd. dirs., 1996—), Katke-Cousins Golf, Midland Country, Black Hawk Indians, Pinehurst Country; Oakland U. Pres.'s, Round Table, Detroit Sportsmen's Congress. Home: 1133 Ivyglen Cir Bloomfield Hills MI 48304-1236 Office: Gen Tape & Supply Inc PO Box 5018 Southfield MI 48086-5018

RADER, DOTSON CARLYLE, author, journalist; b. Minn., July 25, 1941; s. Paul Carlyle and Lois (Schacht) R. Student, Columbia, 1962-68. Editor Defiance: A Radical Rev. (Warner Communications, Inc.), 1969-71; contbg. editor Evergreen Rev., 1969-73, Esquire, N.Y.C., 1973-77, N.Y. mag., 1977-80; cons. Nat. Com. for Lit. Arts at Lincoln Center, N.Y.C., 1980—; Mem. sponsoring bd. New Politics, 1972—; host Free Time Show, WNET-TV, N.Y.C., 1972-73. Author: I Ain't Marchin' Anymore!, 1969, Government Inspected Meat and Other Fun Summer Things, 1971, Blood Dues, 1973, Tennessee: Cry of the Heart; An Intimate Memoir of Tennessee Williams, 1985; screenplay The Bronze Lily, 1974, The Dream's on Me: A Love Story, 1976, Miracle, 1978; novel Beau Monde, 1981; play (with Mike Miller) Shattered Glass, 1990; contbg. editor Parade Mag., 1984—. Mem. Student Peace Union, 1961-63, Students for a Democratic Soc., 1964-69, War Resisters League, 1970—; pres. Humanitas, Columbia, 1963-67; vice chmn. Peoples Coalition for Peace and Justice, 1972. Named hon. ambassador State of W. Va., 1982; recipient award for nat. journalism Odyssey Inst., 1982, Spl. Olympics award for nat. journalism Joseph P. Kennedy Found., 1985. Mem. PEN, Overseas Press Club, The Dramatists Guild.

RADER, I. A., electronic components manufacturing company executive. Chmn., Allen-Bradley Co., Milw. Office: Bradley Found Inc 777 E Wisconsin Ave Ste 2285 Milwaukee WI 53202-5302

RADER, LOUIS T., corporation executive, educator; b. Frank, Can., Aug. 24, 1911; came to U.S., 1934, naturalized, 1940; s. Italo and Louise (Bonamico) R.; m. Constance Wayland, Sept. 10, 1938; children—Louis Albert, John Newton. B.S., U. B.C., 1933; Ph.D. in Elec. Engring, Calif. Inst. Tech., 1938. Engr. Gen. Electric Co., 1937-45; prof., head dept. elec. engring. Ill. Inst. Tech., 1945-47; with Gen. Electric Co., 1947-59, gen. mgr. splty. control div., 1951-59; v.p., dir. ITT, N.Y.C., 1959-61; group v.p. U.S. Commercial, 1961—; pres. Univac div. Sperry Rand Corp., N.Y.C., 1962-64; v.p., gen. mgr. Indsl. Process Control div. Gen. Electric Co., N.Y.C., 1964-69; prof. elec. engring. U. Va., 1969-82, prof. emeritus, 1982—, prof., Grad. Sch. Bus., 1969-82; vis. com. div. engring. and applied sci. Calif. Inst. Tech., 1968-75. Recipient Alumni distinguished service award Calif. Inst. Tech., 1966; Va. Engring. Found. award, 1982. Fellow IEEE; mem. Am. Soc. Engring. Edn., Nat. Acad. Engring., Sigma Xi, Tau Beta Pi, Beta Gamma Sigma, Eta Kappa Nu, Omicron Delta Kappa. Home: PO Box 1721 Waynesboro VA 22980 Office: U Va Prof Emeritus Darden Grad Sch Bus PO Box 6550 Charlottesville VA 22906-6550

RADER, PAUL ALEXANDER, minister, administrator; b. N.Y.C., Mar. 4, 1934; s. Lyell M. and Gladys Mina (Damon) R.; m. Kay Fuller, May 29, 1956; children: Edith Jeanne, James Paul, Jennifer Kay. BA, Asbury Coll., Wilmore, Ky., 1956; BD, Asbury Theol. Sem., 1959; LLD (hon.), Asbury Coll., Wilmore, Ky., 1984; ThM, So. Bapt. Theol. Sem., Louisville, 1961; D Missiology, Fuller Theol. Sem., 1973. Ordained to ministry Salvation Army, 1961. Tng. prin. The Salvation Army, Seoul, 1973-74, edn. sec., 1974-77, chief sec., 1979-83; tng. prin. The Salvation Army, Suffern, N.Y., 1983-86; divisional comdr. for Ea. Pa. and Del. The Salvation Army, Phila., 1986-88; chief sec. ea. ter. The Salvation Army, N.Y.C., 1988; territorial comdr. U.S.A. western ter. The Salvation Army, Rancho Palos Verdes, Calif., 1989—; adj. prof. Seoul Theol. Sem., 1980-82; trustee Asian Ctr. for Theol. Studies and Mission, 1980-83, Asbury Coll., 1988—; pres. The Salvation Army Calif. Corp., Rancho Palos Verdes, 1989—. Recipient Alumnus A award Asbury Coll., 1982, Disting. Alumni award Asbury Theol. Sem., 1989; Paul Harris fellow Rotary Internat., 1989. Mem. Am. Soc. Missiology, Internat. Assn. Mission Studies. Office: The Salvation Army 639 Sabrina Way Vista CA 92084-6264*

RADER, RALPH TERRANCE, lawyer; b. Clarksburg, W.Va., Dec. 5, 1947; s. Ralph Coolidge and Jeanne (Cover) R.; m. Rebecca Jo Vorderman, Mar. 22, 1969; children: Melissa Michelle, Allison Suzanne. BSME, Va. Poly. Inst., 1970; JD, Am. U., Washington, 1974. Bar: Va. 1975, U.S. Ct. Customs and Patent Appeals 1977, U.S. Dist. Ct. (ea. dist.) Mich. 1978, Mich. 1979, U.S. Ct. Appeals (6th cir.) 1979, U.S. Dist. Ct. (we. dist.) Mich. 1981, U.S. Ct. Appeals (fed. cir.) 1983. Supervisory patent examiner U.S. Patent Office, Washington, 1970-77; patent atty., ptnr. Cullen, Sloman, Cantor, Grauer, Scott & Rutherford, Detroit, 1977-88; ptnr., Dykema, Gossett, 1989-96; ptnr. Rader, Fishman & Grauer, 1996—. Contbr. articles to profl. jours. Mem. adminstrv. bd. First United Methodist Ch., Birmingham, Mich., 1980—. With U.S. Army, 1970-76. Recipient Superior Performance award U.S. Patent Office, Washington, 1971-77. Mem. Am. Patent Law Assn., ABA, Mich. Patent Law Assn., Mich. Bar. (mem. governing council patent trademark and copyright law sect. 1981-84), Engring. Soc. Detroit, Masons, Tau Beta Pi, Pi Tau Sigma, Phi Kappa Phi. Methodist. Home: 4713 Riverchase Dr Troy MI 48098-4186 Office: Rader Fishman & Grauer 1533 N Woodward Ave Ste 140 Bloomfield Hills MI 48304-2862

RADER, RANDALL RAY, federal judge; b. 1949. BA magna cum laude, 1974; JD with honors, George Washington U., 1978. Bar: D.C., U.S. Ct. Appeals (fed. cir.) 1990, U.S. Claims Ct., U.S. Supreme Ct. Legis. asst. to Congresswoman Virginia Smith U.S. Ho. of Reps., 1975-78; mem. staff Ways and Means Com. U.S. Ho. Reps., 1978-81; chief counsel subcom. on Constn. U.S. Senate Judiciary Com., chief counsel, staff dir. subcom. on patents, copyrights and trademarks, 1981-87; counsel to Senator Orrin Hatch, 1981-88; judge U.S. Ct. Claims, Washington, 1988-90, U.S. Ct. Appeals (fed. cir.), Washington, 1990—; lectr. patent law U. Va. Sch. Law, trial advocacy George Washington U. Nat. Law Ctr. Contbr. articles to prof. jours.; co-editor: Criminal Justice Reform, 1983. Mem. Fed. Bar Assn. Office: US Ct Appeals Fed Cir 717 Madison Pl NW Ste 913 Washington DC 20439-0002

RADER, STEVEN PALMER, lawyer; b. Charlotte, N.C., Dec. 30, 1952; s. Alvin Marion Jr. and Shirley Ninabelle (Palmer) R. AB, Duke U., 1975; postgrad., Stetson U., 1975-76; JD, Wake Forest U., 1978. Bar: N.C. 1978, U.S. Dist. Ct. (ea. dist.) N.C. 1979. Assoc. Wilkinson and Vosburgh, Washington, N.C., 1978-81; pvt. practice Washington, 1981-88; spl. asst. to sec. N.C. Dept. Human Resources, Raleigh, 1988-89, asst. dir. office legal affairs, 1989-91, gen. counsel, 1991-93; ptnr. Wilkinson & Rader, P.A., Washington, 1993—; commr. Nat. Conf. Commrs. on Uniform State Laws, 1985-93; gen. counsel N.C. Rep. Party, 1992—. Mem., sec. City of Washington Human Rels. Coun., 1981-83; chmn. Beaufort County Rep. party, Washington, 1983-87, 1st Congl. Dist. Rep. party, N.C., 1985-92; v.p. East Main St. Area Neighborhood Assn., 1983-85; del. Rep. Nat. Conv., 1984, 88, 92. Mem. N.C. State Bar, 2d Jud. Dist. Bar, Beaufort County Hist. Soc. (v.p. 1981-85, pres. 1985-86). Lutheran. Avocations: boating, classic automobiles, travel. Home: PO Box 1901 Washington NC 27889-1901 Office: Wilkinson & Rader PA PO Box 732 Washington NC 27889-0732

RADEST, HOWARD BERNARD, clergyman, educator; b. N.Y.C., June 29, 1928; s. Louis and Gussie (Permison) R.; m. Rita Stollman, Dec. 22, 1951; children: Robert, Michael. A.B., Columbia U., 1949, Ph.D., 1971; M.A. (Hillman fellow 1950), New Sch. Social Research, 1951. Dir. youth activities N.Y. Soc. Ethical Culture, 1955-56; leader Ethical Culture Soc. Bergen County, Teaneck, N.J., 1956-64, Ethical Culture Movement, 1956—; mem. Coun. Ethical Leaders, 1958—; exec. dir. Am. Ethical Union, N.Y.C., 1964-70; asso. prof. philosophy Ramapo Coll., N.J., 1971-73; prof. Ramapo Coll., 1973-79; dir. Ethical Culture Schs., 1979-91; adj. prof. philosophy U. S.C., Beaufort, 1991—; co-chmn., sec. gen. Internat. Humanist and Ethical Union, 1970-86, bd. trustees, 1986—; assoc. Am. Civilization Seminar Columbia U., chmn. moral edn. seminar, 1983-91; adv. bd. NBC, 1988-94; dir. Camp Elliott, Jeffersonville, N.Y., 1963, 64; dean Humanist Inst., 1982-92; dean emeritus; cons. state based programs NEH, Beaufort Meml. Hosp., 1994—, Hilton Head Hosp., 1994—; mem. assessment com. Vols. in Medicine, 1994—. Author: Understanding Ethical Religion, 1958, On Life and Meaning, 1963, Toward Common Ground, 1969, To Seek a Humane World, 1971, Can We Teach Ethics, 1989, The Devil and Secular Humanism, 1990, Community Service Encounter with Strangers, 1992, Humanism with a Human Face, 1996, Felix Adler: An Ethical Culture, 1997; also articles; editor: Ramapo Papers, 1976-79, International Humanism; edtl. bd. Religious Humanism, Free Inquiry, The Humanist. Mem. bd. Encampment for Citizenship, 1963-71, Mental Health Assn. Bergen County, Bergen Co. Mental Health Bd., 1964-67, Assn. Moral Edn., 1986-94; mem. bd. past treas., v.p. N.J. Welfare Conf., 1958-64; mem. bd., past pres. Health and Welfare Coun. Bergen County, 1956-64; bd. mgrs. Bergen Pines County Hosp., 1966-70; Bergen County (N.J.) Mem. Democratic Com., 1970-71. Served with AUS, 1953-55. Mem. AAUP (treas. N.J. coun. 1973-74), Com. Sane Nuclear Policy (sponsor N.J.), Am. Assn. UN, Am. Philos. Assn., Soc. Advancement Am. Philosophy, N.Am. Com. Humanism (trustee 1985—), S.C. Philos. Assn., Grad. Faculties Alumni Columbia U. (trustee 1989-91), Network Progressive Educators (steering com. 1988-91), Phi Beta Kappa. Home: 108 Devil's Elbow Ln Hilton Head Island SC 29926

RADEWAGEN, FRED, publisher, organization executive; b. Louisville, Mar. 20, 1944; s. Hobart Fred and Mildred Lillian (Carlsen) R.; m. Amata Catherine Coleman, Dec. 4, 1971; children—Erika Catherine, Mark Peter, Kirsten Alexandra. BA, Northwestern U., 1966; MS, Georgetown U., 1968. Rsch. asst. Republican Nat. Com., Washington, 1967-68; dir. mgmt. services Republican Presdl. Campaign and Inaugural Com., Washington, 1968-69; liaison officer Trust Terr. Washington, 1969-71; staff coordinator for territorial affairs Dept. Interior, Washington, 1971-75; assoc. dir. govtl. and polit. participation programs C. of C. U.S., 1975-76, dir., 1976-79; dir. resource devel. Rep. Govs. Assn., Washington, 1979-81; dir. state and fed. relations Rep. Govs. Assn., 1981-82; Washington rep. Gov. of Am. Samoa, 1982-85, 89-93; pub. Washington Pacific Report, 1982—; dir. Pacific Islands Washington office, 1984—; rep. Cook Islands, Washington, 1986-89; pres. Washington and Pacific Assocs., 1975-84; staff exec. Bus. Alliance for Congl. Action, 1974-77; lectr. Insts. for Orgn. Mgmt., 1977-79; exec. dir. Nat. Chamber Alliance for Politics, 1977-79; mem. U.S. del. UN Trusteeship Coun., 1972, advisor U.S. del. to Com. of Twenty-Four, 1982-83; mem. Am. Samoa dels. to South Pacific Conf., 1982-83, 89, 91, Post-Forum Dialogue, 1991, UN Conf. on Environment and Devel., 1992; del. Am. Coun. Young Polit. Leaders, 1982-83, mem. coun., 1984—; exec. dir. U.S.- New Zealand Coun., 1995, sr. v.p., 1996-97. Mem. Alexandria Rep. City Com., 1979-80; del. Va. Rep. State Conv., 1981, 89, 93, 94; participant Rep. Nat. Convs., 1968, 80, 84, 88, 92, 96; past mem. Christian edn. com. Westminster Presbyn. Ch. Mem. Northwestern U. Alumni Assn. (past Washington bd. govs.), Washington Roundtable for Asian/Pacific Press, Nat. Capital Interfrat. Forum (past pres.), Nat. Eagle Scout Assn. (life), Mensa, Delta Tau Delta (past pres. Washington alumni). Clubs: Ill. State Soc. (past v.p.), Capitol Hill (life), Circumnavigators. Home: 103 E Luray Ave Alexandria VA 22301-2027 also: 1245 Taft Ave Berkeley IL 60163-1043 also: 1019 3rd St Rehoboth Beach DE 19971-1503 Office: PO Box 26142 Alexandria VA 22313-6142

RADFORD, DIANE MARY, surgeon, surgical oncologist; b. Irvine, Ayrshire, Scotland, Nov. 14, 1957; came to U.S., 1985; d. Sidney and Mary Margery (Parr) R. BSc with honors, Glasgow U., Scotland, 1978, MBChB, 1981; MD, Glasgow U., 1991. Jr. house officer Gartravel Gen. Hosp., Glasgow, 1981-82, Monklands Dist. Gen. Hosp., Airdrie, Scotland, 1982; sr. house officer Western Infirmary, Glasgow, 1982-83, Royal Infirmary, Edinburgh, Scotland, 1983-84; registrar Crosshouse Hosp., Kilmarnock, Scotland, 1984-85; fellow in surg. oncology Roswell Park Meml. Inst., Buffalo, 1985-87; resident in surg. St. Louis U. Hosp., 1987-91; instr. in surgery Wash. U., St. Louis, 1991-92; asst. prof. surgery Washington U., St. Louis, 1992-96; mem. Parkcrest Surg. Assocs., St. Louis, 1996—. Contbr. articles to profl. jours. Recipient 1st prize residents competition Mo. chpt. ACS, 1989. Fellow Am. Coll. Surgeons (bd. cert. gen. surgery), Royal Coll. Surgeons (Edinburgh); mem. Brit. Assn. Surg. Oncology, Am. Assn. Cancer Rsch., Assn. Acad. Surgery, Mo. State Med. Assn., Mo. Acad. Sci., St. Louis Met. Med. Soc., Roswell Pk. Surg. Soc. Office: 675 Old Ballas Rd Saint Louis MO 63141-7011

RADFORD, LINDA ROBERTSON, psychologist; b. Winnipeg, Man., Can., Nov. 6, 1944; came to U.S., 1954; d. William and Edith Aileen (Wheatley) Robertson; 1 child, Drew Richard; m. Richard D. Polley, Sept. 21, 1991. BA, Seattle Pacific U., 1970; MEd, U. Wash., 1972, PhD, 1980. Lic. psychologist, Fla.; cert. clin. hypnotherapist. Dir. support svcs. Highline-West Seattle Mental Health Clinic, 1973-75; rsch. asst. in human affairs Battelle, Seattle, 1976-80, rsch. scientist, 1982-87; sr. cons. Martin Simmonds Assoc., Seattle, 1980-82; pres., owner R.R. Assocs., Seattle and Miami, 1982—; pres. PGI Inc., Miami and London, 1989—; pvt. clin. psychologist Bay Harbor Island, Fla., 1991—, West Palm Beach, Fla., 1991—; chmn., chief exec. officer Swiver Corp., North Miami, Fla., 1994—; chair Swiver Corp., 1994—; vis. sr. assoc. Joint Ctr. for Environ. and Urban Problems, North Miami, Fla., 1986-88; cons. Health Ministry Govt. Thailand, Bangkok, 1989—. Contbr. articles to profl. jours. Community Mental Health Ctr fellow, Seattle, 1972-73. Mem. Am. Psychol. Assn., Am. Soc. Clin. Hypnosis, N.Y. Acad. of Sci. Avocations: tennis, music, snorkeling, racquetball, fishing. Home: 9264 Bay Dr Surfside FL 33154-3026 Office: 1160 Kane Concourse Ste 401 Bal Harbour FL 33154-2020 also: Ste 680 1645 Palm Beach Lakes Blvd West Palm Beach FL 33409

RADHARAMANAN, RAMACHANDRAN, mechanical and industrial engineering educator; b. Mailam, Tamil Nadu, India, Dec. 4, 1948; s. Balakrishnan and Rajasekari (Sabapathi) Ramachandran; m. Jeyalakshmi Bhaskaran, Feb. 16, 1981; children: Radharamanan Balachandran, Radharamanan Kamalakannan. BE in Mech. Engring., Madras (India) U., 1970, MS in Prodn. Engring., 1973; PhD in Prodn. Engring., Katholieke U., Leuven, Belgium, 1977. Prof. Mech. Engring. and Indsl. Engring. Fed. U., Santa Maria, Brazil, 1977-84; assoc. prof. Indsl. Engring. U. Utah, 1984-86; assoc. prof. mech. engring. San Diego (Calif.) State U., 1986-89; acting dir. Indsl. Engring. Marquette U., Milw., 1989-90, assoc. prof. Indsl. Engring., 1990-91, dir. Advanced Mfg. Ctr., 1991-95; prof., rschr. Indsl. Engring. Fed. U., Santa Maria, Brazil, 1995—; coord. internat. exch. program Fed. U. Rio Grande do Sul, Brazil, 1989—, vis. scholar, 1989-91; coord. internat. exch. program Fed. U. Santa Maria, Brazil, 1991—, vis. scholar, 1992-94; coord. internat. exch. program U. Vale do Rio dos Sinos, 1991—, Cath. U. Rio Grande do Sul, 1991—; coord. internat. exch. program Fed. U. Santa Catarina, Florianopolis, Brazil, 1992—, vis. scholar, 1993; vis. scholar Inst. Tech. Bandung, Indonesia, 1992; rsch. assoc. AFOSR program Wright Lab, Ohio, 1994. Editor Proceedings Second Internat. Conf. on Robotics and Factories of the Future, 1988. Fellow Internat. Soc. for Productivity Enhancement; mem. ASME, Am. Soc. for Engring. Edn., Soc. Mfg. Engrs. (exec. bd. Milw. chpt. 4, 1990—, faculty adviser 1991-95, President's award 1992, Outstanding Faculty Advisor award 1993), Inst. Indsl. Engrs., Am. Soc. Quality Control, Inst. Mgmt. and Mktg. Sci. Hindu. Avocations: reading, swimming, gardening, travel, basketball. Home: 4360 W Tesch Ave Greenfield WI 53220-2768 Office: Fed U Santa Maria, Santa Maria Brazil 97119

RADI, DORINDA RUDY, health facility administrator; b. Washington, Sept. 2, 1953; d. Lester Eugene and Grace Marie (Crim) Rudy; m. Michael J. Radi, July 11, 1994; 1 child, Jenny Marie LaBelle. RN, Jackson Meml. Hosp., Miami, Fla., 1974; BA in Psychology, U. Ctrl. Fla., Orlando, 1986; MBA, Rollins Coll., Winter Park, Fla., 1988. RN, Fla. Nursing supr. surgery George Washington U. Hosp., Washington, 1980-82; head nurse surgery Orlando Regional Health Care Sys., 1982-85, dir. ctrl. supply, 1985-87, project leader MIS, 1987, adminstrv. dir., 1988-93, corp. dir., 1993-95; COO Cmty. Healthcare Sys., Maitland, Fla., 1995—; nat. adv. bd. MediQual, Mass., 1994-96; cons., spkr. in field. Bd. dirs. orientation tng. Vol. Ctr. Ctrl. Fla., 1991. Brecht scholar Jackson Meml. Hosp. Sch. Nursing, 1971; recipient Presdl. Sports award Pres. George Bush, 1992, Nat. Partnership award Nat. Managed Healthcare Congress, 1996, Quality award Ctrl. Fla. Healthcare Coalition, 1996. Mem. Alliance Healthcare Mktg. Strategy, Am. Mktg. Assn., Healthcare Fin. Mgmt. Assn. (advanced), Fla. Exec. Women, Fla. Hosp. Assn. Republican. Presbyterian. Avocations: computers, gardening, reading. Office: Cmty Health Care Sys Inc 2301 Lucien Way Ste 440 Maitland FL 32751-7025

RADICE, ANNE-IMELDA, museum director; b. Buffalo, Feb. 29, 1948; d. Lawrence and Anne (Marino) R. AB, Wheaton Coll., 1969; MA, Villa SchiFanoia, Florence, Italy, 1971; PhD, U. N.C., 1976; MBA, Am. U., 1984. Asst. curator Nat. Gallery of Art, Washington, 1972-76; archtl. historian U.S. Capitol, Washington, 1976-80, curator Office of Architect, 1980-85; dir. Nat. Mus. Women in the Arts, 1985-89; chief div. of creative arts USIA, 1989-91; sr. dep. chmn. Nat. Endowment for Arts, Washington, 1991-92; acting chmn., 1992-93; exec. v.p. Gray & Co. II, Miami, Fla., 1993; prodr. World Affairs TV Prodn., 1994; assoc. producer Think Tank, 1994; chief spl. projects, confidential adviser Courtney Sale Ross, 1994-96; v.p., COO ICL Internat., 1996—; cons. in pub. rels. and TV, 1994—. Contbr. articles to profl. jours.

RADIGAN, FRANK XAVIER, pharmaceutical company executive; b. Paterson, N.J., Apr. 13, 1933; s. John Joseph and Susan Clair (Brett) R.; m. Julia Lou Smith, Aug. 27, 1960 (div. Nov. 1988); children: Francis Gregory, Patricia Louise, Brett Frasier; m. Carol E. Berkley, June 26, 1992; children: Dana, Traci. AB in Sociology, Seton Hall U., 1955; MBA Mktg., U. Hartford, 1968. Asst. mgr. Beneficial Fin. Co., Newark, 1955-57; hosp. rep. Becton-Dickinson Co., Rutherford, N.J., 1957-58; dist. mgr. Merck Sharp & Dohme, West Point, Pa., 1958—. Chmn. St. John the Baptist Social Justice, New Freedom, Pa., 1981-85; mem. Passaic County Dem. Com., 1985-86. Capt. USAR, 1956. Mem. Am. Mktg. Assn., Md. Pharmacists Assn. (chmn. indsl. rels. com.), W.Va. Pharm. Soc., Balt. Pharm. Assn. (hon. pres. 1989), Hopewell Fish and Game Assn., Bon Air Country Club, Elk, Lion (pres. Glen Rock 1975-76, 86-88). Roman Catholic. Avocation: horsebreeding. Home and Office: 2440 Bradenbaugh Rd White Hall MD 21161-9661

RADIGAN, JOSEPH RICHARD, human resources executive; b. N.Y.C., Apr. 9, 1939; s. Joseph Anthony and Mae Cecilia (Holden) R.; m. Margaret Mary Krug, Apr. 23, 1962; children—Kateri, Laureen, Kenneth. BA, Fordham Coll., 1961; MA, Fordham U., 1962; grad. advanced mgmt. program, Harvard U., 1982; grad., Air War Coll., 1982, Navy War Coll., 1989. Mgr. employee relations Gen. Electric Co., N.Y.C., 1965-79; cons. orgn. planning Gen. Electric Co., Fairfield, Conn., 1981-83; dir. orgn. and mgmt. Kennecott Co., Stamford, Conn., 1979-81; sr. v.p. human resources Donaldson, Lufkin & Jenrette Inc., N.Y.C., 1983-86, The Equitable, N.Y.C., 1986-90; sr. v.p., gen. mgr. Manchester Co., N.Y.C., 1991-92; pres. Cove Communications, 1991-92; sr. v.p. human resource Blue Cross/Blue Shield Ga., 1993—. Mem. Cardinal's Com. of Laity. 1st lt. U.S. Army, 1962-65, col. USAR. Mem. Wall Street Pers. Mgrs. Assn. (sec. 1984-85), Knights of Malta. Republican. Roman Catholic. Home: 6 Cardinal Ln Westport CT 06880-1714

RADIN, ALEX, former association executive, consultant; b. Chattanooga, June 14, 1921; s. Joseph and Mollie (Pernat) R.; m. Sara Leah Gordon, Sept. 6, 1943 (dec. Nov. 20, 1964); children—Jay Jacob, William Gordon m. Carol Nita Schuman, Sept. 21, 1979. B.A., U. Chattanooga, 1948. Reporter Chattanooga Times, Chattanooga, 1938-42; adminstrv. asst. Office of Price Adminstrn., Washington, 1942-43; adminstrv. analyst Dept. of State, Washington, 1945-48; asst. to gen. mgr. Am. Pub. Power Assn., Washington, 1948-51, exec. dir., 1951-86; pres. Radin & Assocs. Inc., 1986—; cons. U.S. Senate Com. on Interior and Insular Affairs, Washington, 1959; mem. exec. com. Am. Nuclear Energy Coun., Washington, 1973-88; v.p. Consumer Fedn. Am., Washington, 1978-86; mem. So. States Energy Bd.'s Adv. Com. on TVA, 1986-87; chmn. Monitored Retrievable Storage Rev. Commn., 1988-89; rep., sec. U.S. Dept. Energy, Independent Mgmt. and Fin. Rev. of Yucca Mt. (Nev.) Project, 1994-95; mem. adv. bd. Ford Found. Energy Policy Project, 1973-74. Columnist, Pub. Power Mag.; contbr. articles to newspapers and mags. Mem. adv. bd. Dance Theatre of Harlem, N.Y.C., 1985—. Recipient Leland Olds award Western States Water and Power Consumers Conf., 1970, Philip Hart Disting. Consumer Svc. award Consumer Fedn. Am., 1985, Alex Radin Disting. Svc. award Am. Pub. Power Assn., 1986. Democrat. Jewish. Club: Nat. Press. Avocations: photography; music; art; hiking. Home: 2510 Virginia Ave NW Apt 610N Washington DC 20037-1904 Office: Radin & Assocs Inc 1200 New Hampshire Ave NW Washington DC 20036-6802

RADINSKY, ALLAN MICHAEL, human services adminstrator, behavior consultant, mental health services professional; b. Canonsburg, Pa., Feb. 28, 1950; s. Andrew Michael and Joanna Delores (Retzel) R.; m. Sophia Beckich, Oct. 7, 1978; 1 child, Brian Scott. BA, Wittenberg U., 1972; MEd, U. Pitts., 1973, PhD, 1984. Tchr. spl. edn. Western State Sch. and Hosp., Canonsburg, 1972, Canon-McMillan Sch. Dist., Canonsburg, 1973-75; program dir., corp. v.p. Citizen Care, Inc. Robinson Devel. Ctr., McKees Rocks, Pa., 1975-82; assoc. dir. psychology, adminstr. active treatment program Polk (Pa.) Ctr., 1984-85; psychology discipline coord. Western Ctr.,

Canonsburg, 1985-86, 87-88, acting facility dir., 1986-87; facility dir. Rosewood Ctr., Owings Mills, Md., 1988-92, regional dir., 1989-91; dir. cmty. based programs Nat. Ctr. on Instns. and Alternatives, Balt., 1992; exec. dir., corp. pres. Human Svcs. Assocs., Inc., Pitts., 1992-96; clin. dir. Starflight Enterprises, Inc., Columbia, Md., 1997—; pres., bd. dirs. Quality of Life Assocs., Inc.; corp. v.p., mem. bd. dirs., dir. of program and clin. svcs. Other Options, Inc., 1996-97; co-founder, v.p., clin. dir. Comprehensive Rehab. Sys., Inc., 1997—. Mem. Am. Assn. on Mental Deficiency, Coun. for Exceptional Children, Assn. for Person with Severe Handicaps. Avocations: readin, swimming, cross country skiing. Home: 5501 Harvest Scene Columbia MD 21044 Office: 5570 Sterrett Pl Ste 310 Columbia MD 21044

RADKE, JAN RODGER, pulmonologist, hospital program administrator; b. Detroit, Nov. 16, 1942; s. Edward V. and Dorothy M. Radke; m. Judith Hogan, June 20, 1987; children: Jennifer, John, Colin, Cameron. BS, Mich. State U., 1965; MD, U. Wis., 1969. Diplomate Am. Bd. Internal Medicine, Am. Bd. Pulmonary Disease. Intern Henry Food Hosp., 1969-70, resident internal medicine, 1970-71, resident, 1974-75, chief med. resident internal medicine, 1975-76, fellow pulmonary/critical care, 1977-78; v.p. satellite program Henry Ford Health Systems, Detroit, 1989; assoc. v.p. ambulatory program, assoc. prof. medicine Loyola U. Med. Ctr., Maywood, Ill., 1990-93, v.p. health care svcs., 1993-96; pres., CEO Univ. Care Plus, 1996—; exec. dir. med. svcs. R & D plan and ambulatory care U. Tex. Med. Sch. and Hermann Hosp., Houston, 1996—. Lt. comdr. USNR, 1971-73. Fellow ACP, Am. Coll. Chest Physicians; mem. Am. Thoracic Soc., Am. Coll. Physician Execs. Avocation: bird watching. Office: U Tex Med Sch Hermann Profl Bld 6410 Fannin St Houston TX 77030-3000

RADKE, RODNEY OWEN, agricultural research executive, consultant, research biologist; b. Ripon, Wis., Feb. 5, 1942; s. Edward Ludwig and Vera Ione (Phillips) R.; m. Jean Marie Rutsch, Sept. 1, 1963; children: Cheryl Lynn, Lisa Diane, Daniel E. BS, U. Wis., 1963, MS, 1965, PhD, 1967. Cert. environ. insp. Rsch. sci. Monsanto Agrl. Co., St. Louis, 1969-75, sr. research group leader, 1975-79, research mgr. 1979-81, mgr. research, 1981-93; pvt. practice cons., 1993—. Contbr. articles to profl. jours. Served to capt. U.S. Army, 1967-69. Mem. Weed Sci. Soc. Am., North Ctrl. Weed Sci. Soc., Environ. Assessment Assn. Lutheran. Club: First Capitol Soccer (coach 1981-92) (St. Charles). Avocations: power boating; soccer; gardening; woodshop. Home and Office: 1119 Grand Prix Dr Saint Charles MO 63303-6313

RADKOWSKY, KAREN, advertising/marketing research executive; b. Washington, Nov. 8, 1957; d. Lawrence and Florence (Kramer) R. BA, Columbia U., 1979. Rsch. analyst Cosmair, Inc., N.Y.C., 1979-82, sr. rsch. analyst, 1982-84; asst. rsch. mgr. Am. Express Co., N.Y.C., 1984-85; account rsch. mgr. BBDO, Inc., N.Y.C., 1985-88, v.p., assoc. rsch. dir., 1988-94, sr. v.p., assoc. rsch. dir., 1994-95; sr. v.p., rsch. dir. BBDO N.Y., N.Y.C., 1995—.

RADLER, FRANKLIN DAVID, publishing holding company executive; b. Montreal, Que., Can., June 3, 1942; m. Rona Lassner, Mar. 26, 1972; children: Melanie, Melissa. MBA, Queen's U., Can., 1967. Pres., chief oper. officer, dir. Hollinger Inc., Toronto; exec. v.p. Argus Corp. Ltd., Toronto; chmn. Am. Pub. Co., Jerusalem Post Ltd., Palestine Post Ltd. Office: Hollinger Inc, 1827 W 5th Ave, Vancouver, BC Canada V6J 1P5 also: Hollinger Inc, 10 Toronto St, Toronto, ON Canada M5C 2B7*

RADLEY, VIRGINIA LOUISE, humanities educator; b. Marion, N.Y., Aug. 12, 1927; d. Howard James and Lula (Ferris) R. B.A., Russell Sage Coll., 1949, L.H.D., 1981; M.A., U. Rochester, 1952; M.S., Syracuse U., 1957, Ph.D., 1958. Instr. English Chatham (Va.) Hall, 1952-55; asst. dean students, asst. prof. English Goucher Coll., 1957-59; dean freshmen, asst. prof. English Russell Sage Coll., 1959-60, assoc. dean, assoc. prof. English, 1960-61, prof. chmn. dept., 1961-69; dean coll., prof. English Nazareth Coll., Rochester, N.Y., 1969-73; provost for undergrad. edn., central adminstrn. SUNY, Albany, 1973-74; exec. v.p., provost Coll. Arts and Scis., SUNY, Oswego, 1974-76; acting pres. Coll. Arts and Scis., SUNY, 1976-78; pres. SUNY, Oswego, 1978-88; prof. English and Humanities SUNY, 1988-93; scholar-in-residence Russell Sage Coll., 1993—; vis. prof. Syracuse U., summer 1957-59, Nazareth Coll., summer 1965; cons. N.Y. State Dept. Edn.; chmn. commn. on women Am. Coun. on Edn., 1978-81, sr. assoc. Office of Women, 1990—; trustee Marymount Manhattan Coll., 1988-90; mem. commn. on higher edn. Middle States Assn., 1979-86; disting vis. prof. Russell Sage Coll., 1994-95. Author: Samuel Taylor Coleridge, 1966, Elizabeth Barrett Browning, 1972, also articles. Mem. MLA (chmn. regional sect. Romanticisn 1969), English Inst., Pi Lambda Theta. Republican. Home: 75 Plank Rd Poestenkill NY 12140-1706

RADLOFF, ROBERT ALBERT, real estate executive; b. Chgo., Mar. 30, 1947; s. Henry O. and Virginia G. (Grothus) R.; m. Ann Macy Beha, June 21, 1975; children: Macy, Allison. BS in Fin., Boston U., 1969. V.p. Kuras & Co., Inc., Boston, 1971-76; sr. v.p. Boston Co. Real Estate Counsel, Inc., 1976-81, pres., 1981-89, chmn., 1989-91; real estate investments counselor Boston, 1991—; bd. dirs. Boston Pvt. Bank and Trust Co. Bd. dirs. First Night, Boston, 1990, Mass. Cultural Coun., 1992, Friends of Vieilles Maison Francais, 1992; trustee Isabella Stewart Gardner Mus., 1995; overseer Children's Hosp., WGBH Ednl. Found. Mem. Am. Soc. Real Estate Counselors (cert.), Somerset Club. Avocations: art, tennis, travel. Office: 33 Kingston St Boston MA 02111-2208

RADLOFF, WILLIAM HAMILTON, editor, writer; b. Milw., Mar. 5, 1914; s. Alfred Carl and Florence (Hamilton) R.; m. Mary Ellen Borgman, Nov. 10, 1940; children: Thomas M., Susan M. BA, Ripon Coll., 1936. Reporter, writer Milw. Sentinel, 1937-42; reporter, writer Milw. Jour., 1946-49, asst. city editor, 1949-60, asst. feature editor, 1960-61, feature editor, 1961-69; asst. story editor 20th Century Fox Film Corp., L.A., 1969-72; freelance writer, poet L.A., 1972—. Author, editor numerous news and feature articles. Lt. U.S. Army, Counter Intelligence, 1942-46, PTO. Recipient Letter of Commendation, Japanese Occupation. Home: 313 S Anita Ave Los Angeles CA 90049-3805

RADMER, MICHAEL JOHN, lawyer, educator; b. Wisconsin Rapids, Wis., Apr. 28, 1945; s. Donald Richard and Thelma Loretta (Donahue) R.; children from previous marriage: Christina Nicole, Ryan Michael; m. Laurie J. Anshus, Dec. 22, 1983; 1 child, Michael John. B.S., Northwestern U., Evanston, Ill., 1967; J.D., Harvard U., 1970. Bar: Minn. 1970. Assoc. Dorsey & Whitney, Mpls., 1970-75, ptnr., 1976—; lectr. law Hamline U. Law Sch., St. Paul, 1981-84; gen. counsel, rep., sec. 150 federally registered investment cos., Mpls. and St. Paul, 1977—. Contbr. articles to legal jours. Active legal work Hennepin County Legal Advice Clinic, Mpls., 1971—. Mem. ABA, Minn. Bar Assn., Hennepin County Bar Assn. Club: Mpls. Athletic. Home: 4329 E Lake Harriet Pky Minneapolis MN 55409-1725 Office: Dorsey & Whitney Pillsbury Ctr S 220 S 6th St Minneapolis MN 55402-4502 *A key to a successful and happy life is achieving a balance. Intellectual, academic and vocational goals are important, but their pursuit should be balanced with ample time spent with family and friends, travel and enjoying reading, music, art and sports. Don't be afraid to try something new; realize that education should be a lifelong pursuit. Much frustration can be avoided by realizing that life is full of trade-offs. You can't experience the joy of raising children and have the complete freedom of the child-free. Finally, while you should strive for perfection, be content with less. We are only human, and live in an imperfect, yet wonderful, world.*

RADNER, ROY, economist, educator, researcher; b. Chgo., June 29, 1927; s. Samuel and Ella (Kulansky) R.; m. Virginia L. Honoski, July 26, 1949 (dec. Apr. 1976); children: Hilary A., Erica H. (dec.), Amy E., Ephraim L.; m. Charlotte Virginia Kuh, Jan. 22, 1978. PhB with honors, U. Chgo, 1945, BS in Math., 1950, MS in Math., 1951, PhD in Math. Stats., 1956. Rsch. asst. Cowles Commn. for Rsch. in Econs. U. Chgo., 1951, rsch. assoc., 1951-54, asst. prof., 1954-55; mem. Cowles Found. for Rsch. in Econs. Yale U., New Haven, 1955-57, asst. prof. econs., 1955-57; assoc. prof. econs. and stats. U. Calif., Berkeley, 1957-61, prof. econs. and stats., 1961-79, chmn. dept. econs., 1966-69; Taussig prof. econs. Harvard U., Cambridge, Mass., 1977-78, vis. prof. Kennedy Sch. Govt., 1978-79; mem. tech. staff AT&T Bell Labs, Murray Hill, N.J., 1979-84, disting. mem. tech. staff, 1985-95; rsch. prof. econs. NYU, N.Y.C., 1983-95, prof. econs. and info. sys., 1995-96, L.N. Stern Sch. prof. bus., 1996—; mem. com. on fundamental rsch. relevant to edn. NRC-NAS, 1976-77, mem. commn. on human resources, 1976-79; mem. assembly of behavioral and social scis. NRC, 1979-82, mem. com. on risk and decision making, 1980-81, mem. working group on basic rsch. in behavioral and social scis., 1985-86; mem. panel on contingent valuation methodology NOAA, U.S. Dept. Commerce, 1992-93; mem. steering com. Enjeux et Procedures de Decentralization Commisariat du Plan, Paris, 1992—; active Com. on Prevention of Nuclear War, also various other profl. coms., bds., panels. Author: (books, monographs) Notes on Theory of Economic Planning, 1963, (with D. Jorgenson and J.J. McCall) Optimal Replacement Policy, 1967, (with J. Marshack) Economic Theory of Teams, 1972, (with L.S. Miller) Demand and Supply in U.S. Higher Education, 1975, (with C.V. Kuh) Mathematicians in Academia, 1980; also articles on econ. theory, orgn. theory, econs. of edn.; co-editor: Decision and Organization, 1972, Education as an Industry, 1976, Information, Incentives and Economic Mechanisms, 1987, Perspectives on Deterrence, 1989, Bargaining with Incomplete Information, 1992; assoc. editor Mgmt. Sci., 1959-70, Econometrica, 1961-68, Jour. Econ. Theory, 1968—, Am. Econ. Rev., 1970-82, Games and Econ. Behavior, Econ. Theory, Econ. Design, Rev. Acctg. Studies. 2d lt. U.S. Army, 1945-48, PTO. William Cook scholar U. Chgo., 1944-45; fellow Ctr. Advanced Study in Behavioral Scis., Stanford, Calif., 1955-56, Guggenheim Found. fellow, 1961-62, 65-66, overseas fellow Churchill Coll., Cambridge U., Eng., 1969-70, 89. Fellow AAAS (disting. fellow), Econometric Soc. (v.p. 1970-72, pres. 1972-73), Am. Acad. Arts and Scis., Am. Econ. Assn. (disting. fellow); mem. NAS (chair econ. sect. 1994—), Inst. Math. Stats. Avocations: music, backpacking, cross-country skiing. Home: 3203 Davenport St Washington DC 20008 Office: Stern Sch Business NYU MEC 9-68 44 W 4th St New York NY 10012-1106

RADNER, SIDNEY HOLLIS, retired rug company executive; b. Holyoke, Mass., Dec. 8, 1919; s. William I. Radner; m. Helen Jane Cohen, Dec. 12, 1946; children: William Marc, Richard Scott. Student, Yale U., 1941. Ret. pres. Am. Rug Co., Holyoke; lectr., cons., investigator on crooked gambling, U.S. Armed Forces, FBI, Govt. of Can., state and mcpl. police squads; dir. Houdini Magical Hall of Fame, Niagara Falls, Ont., Can.; dir., organizer Annual Ofcl. Houdini Seance. Author: Radner on Poker, Radner on Dice, Radner on Roulette and Casino Games, How to Detect Card Sharks; contbr. articles to profl. jours.; appeared in First TV series Turn of A Card, 1953, BBC Omnibus: Houdini, 1971, CNN, 1993, 94, Tonight Show, 1956, Today Show, Merv Griffin Show, CNBC, PBS, CBC, In Search Of..., First TV series exposing crooked gambling techniques, 1956; cons., maj. participant Houdini TV spl. A&E, 1996, Discovery Channel documentary, 1997. Past pres. Holyoke C. of C.; co-founder Volleyball Hall of Fame; past bd. dirs. Greater Springfield (Mass.) Better Bus. Bur.; hon. curator, dir. Houdini Hist. Ctr., Appleton, Wis. Served with criminal investigation divsn. U S. Army, 1942-46. Mem. Soc. Am. Magicians (occult investigation com.), Internat. Brotherhood Magicians, Magic Circle London (mem. Inner Magic Circle), Magicians Guild (charter), Magic Collector's Assn. (charter, Honor award 1992), Am. Platform Assn., Houdini Club Wis. (hon.), Nat. Assn. Bunco Investigators, Profls. Against Confidence Crime, China-Burma-India Vets. Assn. (life), Rotary, Masons, Shriners. Jewish. Home: 1050 Northampton St Holyoke MA 01040-1321 Office: 1594 Dwight St Holyoke MA 01040-2356

RADNOFSKY, BARBARA A., lawyer, mediator/arbitrator; b. Broomall, Pa., July 8, 1956; m. Daniel Edward Supkis Jr.; children: Danielle Esther, Max David, Michaela Sarah. BA magna cum laude, U. Houston, 1976; JD with honors, U. Tex., 1979. Bar: Tex. Assoc. Vinson & Elkins, L.L.P., Houston, 1979-87, ptnr., 1987—; mem. faculty intensive trial advocacy programs U. Tex. Sch. Law, Internat. Acad. Trial Lawyers; spkr. in field; mediator/arbitrator in field; mem. Disting. Panel of Neutrals of Ctr. for Pub. Resources. Contbr. articles to profl. jours. Albert Jones scholar U. Tex. Sch. Law; named Outstanding Young Lawyer Tex., Tex. Young Lawyers Assn., 1988-89. Mem. ABA (chmn. Nat. Trial Competition 1983), Tex. Young Lawyers Assn. (Outstanding Young Lawyer Tex. 1988-89), Nat. Health Lawyers Assn. Avocations: sailing, ballet, modern dance, basketball. Office: Vinson & Elkins 3300 First City Tower 1001 Fannin St Houston TX 77002-6706

RADNOR, ALAN T., lawyer; b. Cleve., Mar. 10, 1946; s. Robert Clark and Rose (Chester) R.; m. Carol Sue Hirsch, June 22, 1969; children: Melanie, Joshua, Joanna. B.A., Kenyon Coll., 1967; M.S. in Anatomy, Ohio State U., 1969, J.D., 1972. Bar: Ohio 1972. Ptnr., Vorys, Sater, Seymour & Pease, Columbus, Ohio, 1972—; adj. prof. law Ohio State U., Columbus, 1979—. Contbr. articles to profl. jours. Bd. dirs., trustee Congregation Tifereth Israel, Columbus, 1975—, 1st v.p., 1983-85, pres., 1985-87; trustee Columbus Mus. Art, 1995. Named Boss of Yr., Columbus Assn. Legal Secs., 1983. Mem. ABA, Ohio State Bar Assn., Columbus Bar Assn. (chmn. dr.-lawyer com. 1979-80), Columbus Def. Assn. (pres. 1980-81), Def. Research Inst., Internat. Assn. Def. Counsel, Ohio Hosp. Assn. Democrat. Jewish. Avocations: reading; sculpture. Home: 400 S Columbia Ave Columbus OH 43209-1629 Office: Vorys Sater Seymour & Pease 52 E Gay St PO Box 1008 Columbus OH 43216-1008

RADOCK, MICHAEL, foundation executive; b. Belle Vernon, Pa., July 17, 1917; s. Nicholas M. and Pauline (Radich) R.; m. Helen Adelaide Hower, Sept. 2, 1944; children: Robert Hower, William Michael. AB magna cum laude, Westminster Coll., New Wilmington, Pa., 1942, LittD (hon.), 1965; MS in Journalism, Northwestern U., 1946; postgrad., Case Western Res. U., 1950-52. Reporter Fayette City (Pa.) Jour., 1937-39; corr. for Pa. newspapers, 1937-39; reporter, sports editor Charleroi (Pa.) Daily Mail, 1942; dir. news bur., asst. prof. journalism Westminster Coll., 1942-45; dir. pub. relations, prof. journalism Kent (Ohio) State U., 1945-53; with corp. pub. relations Ford Motor Co., Dearborn, Mich., 1953-61; established Inst. for Pub. Rels. Kent (Ohio) State U., 1947; v.p. univ. relations, prof. journalism U. Mich., Ann Arbor, 1961-81; sr. v.p. devel. and univ. relations, prof. journalism U. So. Calif., Los Angeles, 1981-82; v.p. resource devel. Aspen Inst. Humanistic Studies, N.Y.C., 1982-83; advisor to pres. C.S. Mott Found., Flint, Mich., 1983-90, cons., 1990—; mem. faculty Harvard U. Inst. in Ednl. Mgmt., 1972, 73, Williamsburg Devel. Inst., 1979-81; vis. prof. journalism U. Wyo., Laramie, 1952, U. Kent, Canterbury, Eng., 1989; trustee Westminster Coll., 1972-82; mem. adv. bd. Pub. Rels. News; cons. NSF, 1972-73; mem. adv. bd. Chronicle of Non-Profit Enterprise, 1990—. Contbr. Handbook of Institutional Advancement, 1977, (books) Lesly's Public Relations Handbook, 1978, Public Relations Career Directory, 1987, 88, 89, 93, 95, Lesly's Handbook of Public Relations and Communications, 1990. Mem. Fulbright Bd. Fgn. Scholarships, Washington, 1972-74; mem. exec. bd. U. Mich., 1979-81, mem. bd. in control of intracollegiate athletics, 1961-81; trustee Glacier Hills Retirement Ctr., Ann Arbor, 1988-93, Ann Arbor Area Cmty. Found., 1989-92, Mich. Hist. Ctr. Found., 1990—; chmn. White House Sci. and Tech. Adv. Com. on Black Colls., Washington, 1986-88. Recipient Disting. Service award Kent State U., 1965, Frank Ashmore award for disting. service to edn. Am. Coll. Pub. Relations Assn., 1968-69; Disting. Service award for leadership in institutional advancement for minority colls. and univs., 1980. Fellow Pub. Rels. Soc. Am. (accredited); mem. Inst. for Pub. Rels. Rsch. and Edn. (bd. trustees 1980-84), Soc. of Profl. Journalists, Nat. Soc. Fund Raising Execs., Higher Edn. Roundtable. Republican. Presbyterian. Home: 851 Greenhills Dr Ann Arbor MI 48105-2719

RADOFF, LEONARD IRVING, librarian, consultant; b. Houston, Jan. 9, 1927; s. Morris Aaron and Jenny (Goldberg) R.; m. Lisel Ruth Ephraim, July 25, 1953; 1 child, Lesley Radoff Rappaport. B.A., Rice U., Houston, 1949; M.L.S., U. Tex., Austin, 1965. Cert. secondary sch. tchr., Tex. Tchr. math Aldine Ind. Sch. Dist., Houston, 1959-61, sch. librarian, 1961-63; head pub. services Abilene Pub. Library, Tex., 1964-65; library dir. Pasadena Pub. Library, Tex., 1966-70; chief br. services Houston Pub. Library, 1971-92, ret., 1992; library bldg. cons. Houston, 1975—. Treas. Literacy Vol. Am., Houston, 1984-85; mem. Northside Interests, Houston, 1982-85. Served with USN, 1945-46. Hoenthal scholar, 1948. Mem. Tex. Library Assn., ALA, Freedom to Read Found., Houston Great Books Council (leader trainer 1953-59, pres. 1967-69). Avocations: tutoring; listening to music; stamp collecting. Home: 4013 Gano St Houston TX 77009-4119

RADOJCSICS, ANNE PARSONS, librarian; b. Mansfield, Ohio, Mar. 23, 1929; d. Richard Walbridge Parsons and Iva Pearl (Ruth) Kemp; m. Joseph Michael Radojcsics, July 8, 1950; children: Kurt Joseph, Jo Anne Radojcsics Kent. Diploma, Bethel Woman's Coll., Hopkinsville, Ky., 1949; BS, Miss. State U., 1972, MEd, 1974. Cert. secondary tchr., Miss. Chemist Humphries Borg-Warner Co., Mansfield, 1950-53; asst. reference libr. Mansfield Pub. Libr., 1953-59; libr. media specialist Verona (Miss.) Sch., 1970-92, supr. Verona computer lab., 1983-92; libr. media specialist Pierce St. Elem. Sch., Miss., 1992-95; ret., 1995; libr. Saints Libr., Tupelo, Miss., 1995—; supr. libr. Guntown (Miss.) Scho., 1988-92; chmn. assessment project Miss. Libr. Miss. Dept. Edn., Jacson, 1986-92; coord. region I Miss. Conf. on Libr. and Info. Svc., 1990; mem. Miss. Edn. TV Adv. Coun., 1985-89; cons. content instrnl. prodn. libr. rsch. skills Miss. Ednl. TV., 1995; Equity Adv. Coun. Itawamta Comm. Coll., Tupelo, 1995—. Author: Clay Tablets to Media Centers: Library Development from Ancient to Modern Times, 1975; (tchr. guide) Media Mania, 1996 Mississippi Educational TV. Bd. dirs., past pres. SAFE, Inc., Tupelo, Miss., 1978-92, bd. dirs. emeritus, 1992—; mem. Lee County Adult Lit. Task Force, Tupelo, 1987-90; schs. chmn. Target Tupelo, 1981-85. Recipient Ed Ransdell Instructional TV award, 1991, Woman of Achievement Equity Program award, 1996. Mem. AAUW (pres. Tupelo chpt. 1977-81, 1993-97, Miss. divsn. 1984-86)), Miss. Profl. Educators, Mississippians for Ednl. Broadcasting, Miss. Ednl. Computer Assn., Miss. Libr. Assn. (project chmn. com. on. sch. librs. 1989, awards chmn. 1987-88, ednl. comml. and tech. roundtable chair 1993), Miss. Profl. Educators Tupelo/Lee County (treas. 1993-95, pres. 1995-97), Apple Computer User Group (co-organizer). Democrat. Episcopalian. Avocations: reading, church music and liturgy, quilt making. Home: Carr Vista 105 Michael St Tupelo MS 38801-8608

RADOMSKI, JACK LONDON, toxicology consultant; b. Milw., Dec. 10, 1920; s. Joseph Elwood and Evelyn (Hansen) R.; BS, U. Wis., 1942; PhD, George Washington U., 1950; m. Margery Dodge, Feb. 1, 1947 (div. Nov. 1970); m. Teresa Pascual, Feb. 19, 1971; children—Mark, Linda, Eric, Janet, Mayte. Chemist, Gen. Aniline & Film Corp., Binghamton, N.Y. 1942-44; pharmacologist FDA, Washington, 1944-52, acting chief acute toxicity br., 1952-53; prof. pharmacology U. Miami, Coral Gables, Fla., 1953-82; pres. Covington Tech. Services, Andalusia, Ala., 1982-88; pvt. practice cons. in toxicology, Hudson, Fla., 1988—; cons. WHO, IARC, GAO, EPA, HEW, NIOSH. Contbr. articles to profl. jours. Recipient Spl. award Commr. FDA, 1952; diplomate in gen. toxicology Acad. Toxicol. Scis., 1982. Mem. Am. Soc. Pharmacology and Exptl. Therapeutics, Soc. Toxicology, Am. Assn. Cancer Research, N.Y. Acad. Scis., Am. Bd. Forensic Examiners. Home and Office: 6432 Driftwood Dr Port Richey FL 34667-1018 *The single most important thing in life is to make a continuous, intensive effort to comprehend things as they really are, as distinct from as we wish them to be. Failure to perceive the world and everything in it accurately and objectively, admittedly a difficult and frequently fearful task, causes untold misery and misfortune to individuals, organizations and nations. Success in all endeavors is in direct proportion to the degree we achieve this goal.*

RADUAZO, ANTHONY F., lawyer; b. Portsmouth, N.H., Oct. 16, 1945; s. Anthony and Geraldine (Huntress) R.; m. Elizabeth A. Raduazo; children: Ann M., Phillip A. BA in Liberal Arts, Ctrl. Mich. U., 1967; JD, Detroit Coll., 1974. Bar: Mich. 1974, U.S. Dist. Ct. (ea. dist.) Mich. 1978, U.S. Dist. Ct. (we. dist.) Mich. 1983, U.S. Ct. Appeals (6th cir.) 1983. Tchr., coach Plymouth (N.H.) Pub. Schs., 1967-68, Raymond (N.H.) Pub. Schs., 1968-69; sales staff Addison Wesley Pub. Co., Menlo Park, Calif., 1969-70; mktg. supr. Addison Wesley Pub. Co., Menlo Park, 1970-71; asst. prosecuting atty. Washtenaw County Mich., Ann Arbor, 1974-78; asst. city atty. City of Jackson, Mich., 1979-81, city atty., 1981—. Treas. Jackson (Mich.) County Rep. Com., 1987-88, 91-93, vice chair, 1989-91. Mem. Mich. Assn. Mcpl. Attys. (pres. 1993-95), Mich. Pub. Risk and Ins. Mgmt. Assn. (pres. 1985-86), Mich. Mcpl. League Legal Def. Fund (chair 1993-95). Office: City Attys Office 161 W Michigan Ave Jackson MI 49201-1303

RADWICK, MELISSA JANE, elementary counselor; b. Memphis, Nov. 26, 1954; d. Nelson Arthur and Mary Jane (Loss) Haas; m. Douglas Martin, Oct. 23, 1976; children: Nathan, Eric. BA in Elem. Edn., Mich. State U., 1975; MA in Health Edn., U. Mich., 1981; counseling endorsement, Ctrl. Mich. U. 6th grade tchr. North Branch (Mich.) Schs., 1976-93, elem. counselor, 1993—; student asst. coord. North Br. Schs., 1991-93, Ruth Fox. Mid. Sch., 1996, coord. parent class, 1991—, chmn. cmty. teen, 1993—; county schs. rep. Continuum Care Com., Lapeer, Mich., 1992-93. Active Lapeer County Strong Family/ Safe Children com., 1996—. Grantee Genesee Intermediate Dist., 1991, 93—. Mem. AAUW, PEO. Republican. Lutheran. Avocations: coaching soccer and baseball, reading, traveling, cross-country skiing. Home: 8635 Gera Rd Birch Run MI 48415-9717

RADZINOWICZ, MARY ANN, language educator; b. Champaign, Ill., Apr. 18, 1925; d. Arthur Seymour and Ann (Stacy) Nevins; m. Leon Radzinowicz, June 16, 1958 (div. 1978); children: Ann Stacy Radzinowicz Prior, William Francis Henry. BA, Radcliffe Coll., 1945; MA, Columbia U., 1947, PhD, 1953; MA (hon.), U. Cambridge, Eng., 1960. Prof. Vassar Coll., Poughkeepsie, N.Y., 1947-50, 52-59, Girton Coll., Cambridge, Eng., 1960-80, U. Cambridge, 1973-80, Cornell U., Ithaca, N.Y., 1980-90; Jacob Gould Schurman prof. English emeritus Cornell U., Ithaca, 1990—; mem. adv. bd. 2d, 3d, 4th Internat. Milton Symposia, 1985—. Author: Toward Samson Agonistes, 1978 (Hanford prize 1979), Milton's Epics and Psalms, 1989, Milton and the Tragic Women of Genesis, 1995 (Hanford prize); editor American Colonial Prose, 1984, Paradise Lost, Book VIII, 1974; mem. editorial bd. Milton Quarterly, 1981—, Christianity and Literature, 1989—. Mem. MLA, Renaissance Soc. Am., Milton Soc. Am. (honored scholar 1987), John Donne Soc. Home: Ballyconry House, Ballyvaughan County Clare Ireland Office: Cornell U Dept English Lit Ithaca NY 14850

RAE, BARBARA JOYCE, former employee placement company executive; b. Prince George, B.C., Can., May 17, 1930; d. Alfred and Lottie Kathleen (Davis) Holmwood; m. George Suart, Feb. 14, 1984; children: Jamie, Glenn, John. MBA, Simon Fraser U., Burnaby, B.C., 1975. Chmn., CEO Adia Can., Ltd., Vancouver, B.C., 1953-95; also bd. dirs.; bd. dirs. Can. Imperial Bank Commerce, Grosvenor Internat. Ltd., B.C. Telephone Co., B.C. Telecom, Noranda, Inc., Xerox Can. Ltd.; dir. Can. Inst. Adv. Rsch., 1995—, KTCS Pub. Broadcasting; bd. govs. Multiple Sclerosis Soc., 1995—; mem. Fed. Task Force on Future of Can. Fin. Svcs. Sector; chmn. B.C. Women's Hosp. Found., 1994—. Chancellor Simon Fraser U., 1987-93; mem. Jud. Appts. Com., B.C., 1988-90; commr. Triennial Commn. on Judges Salaries and Benefits; mem. adv. coun. Imagine Campaign, 1988-95; mem. Premier's Econ. Adv. Coun., B.C., 1987-91; mem. Price Minister's Com. on Sci. and Tech., B.C., 1989-94; gen. chmn. United Way Lower Mainland, 1987, Salvation Army Red Shield Vancouver Campaign, 1986; bd. dirs. Vancouver Bd. Trade, 1972-76; nat. co-chmn. Can. Coun. Christians and Jews. Decorated Order of Can., Order of B.C.; recipient Outstanding Alumnae award Simon Fraser U., 1985, Disting. Alumni Svc. award, 1995, Bus. Women of Yr. award Vancouver YWCA, 1986, West Vancouver Achievers award, 1987, B.C. Entrepreneur of Yr. award, 1987, Nat. Vol. award, 1990, Can. Woman Entrepreneur B.C. award, 1992. Home: 2206 Folkestone Way #3, West Vancouver, BC Canada V7S 2X7

RAE, JOHN JOSEPH, lawyer; b. Battle Creek, Mich., Sept. 11, 1935; s. James Gordon and Mary Kathryn (McGrail) R.; m. Patricia Ann Rae, Dec. 30, 1961; children: Elizabeth, Susan, Mary. BS in Social Sci. cum laude, John Carroll U., Cleve., 1957; JD, DePaul U., Chgo., 1961. Bar: Ill. 1961, Mich. 1965. Assoc. McDermott, Will & Emery, Chgo., 1961-65; pvt. practice Battle Creek, Mich., 1965-75; pros. atty. Calhoun County, Marshall, Mich., 1975-76; city atty. City of Midland, Mich., 1977-95; mem. State Bar Ethics Com., Lansing, Mich., 1994. Editor Calhoun County Bar Assn. Newsletter; contbr. articles to profl. jours. Chairperson bd. trustees Mid-Mich. Dispute Resolution Ctr., Saginaw, 1995. Capt. U.S. Army, 1959-69. Mem. State Bar Mich., Midland County Bar Assn. Roman Catholic. Avocations: reading, music.

RAE, MATTHEW SANDERSON, JR., lawyer; b. Pitts., Sept. 12, 1922; s. Matthew Sanderson and Olive (Waite) R.; m. Janet Hettman, May 2, 1953; children: Mary-Anna, Margaret Rae Mallory, Janet S. Rae Dupree. AB, Duke, 1946, LLB, 1947; postgrad., Stanford U., 1951. Bar: Md. 1948, Calif. 1951. Asst. to dean Duke Sch. Law, Durham, N.C., 1947-48; assoc. Karl F. Steinmann, Balt., 1948-49, Guthrie, Darling & Shattuck, L.A., 1953-54; nat. field rep. Phi Alpha Delta Law Frat., L.A., 1949-51; research atty. Calif.

Supreme Ct., San Francisco, 1951-52; ptnr. Darling, Hall & Rae (and predecessor firms), L.A., 1955—; mem. Calif. Commn. Uniform State Laws, 1985—, chmn., 1993-94; chmn. drafting com. for revision Uniform Prin. and Income Act of Nat. Conf., 1991—, Probate and Mental Health Task Force, Jud. Coun. Calif., 1996—. Vice pres. L.A. County Rep. Assembly, 1959-64; mem. L.A. County Rep. Ctrl. Com., 1960-64, 77-90, exec. com., 1977-90; vice chmn. 17th Congl. Dist., 1960-62, 28th Congl. Dist., 1962-64; chmn. 46th Assy. Dist., 1962-64, 27th Senatorial Dist., 1977-85, 29th Senatorial Dist., 1985-90; mem. Calif. Rep. State Ctrl. Com., 1966—, exec. com., 1966-67; pres. Calif. Rep. League, 1966-67; trustee Rep. Assocs., 1979-94, pres., 1983-85, chmn. bd. dirs., 1985-87. 2d lt. USAAF, WWII. Fellow Am. Coll. Trust and Estate Counsel; academician Internat. Acad. Estate and Trust Law (exec. coun. 1974-78); mem. ABA, L.A. County Bar Assn. (chmn. probate and trust law com. 1964-66, chmn. legis. com. 1980-86, chmn. program com. 1981-82, chmn. membership retention com. 1982-83, trustee 1983-85, dir. Bar Found., 1987-93, Arthur K. Marshall award probate and trust law sect. 1984, Shattuck-Price Meml. award 1990), South Bay Bar Assn., State Bar of Calif. (chmn. state bar jour. com. 1970-71, probate com. 1974-75; exec. com. estate planning trust and probate law sect. 1977-83, chmn. legis. com. 1977-89; co-chmn. 1991-92; probate law cons. group Calif. Bd. Legal Specialization 1977-88; chmn. conf. dels. resolutions com. 1987, exec. com. conf. dels. 1987-90), Lawyers Club L.A. (bd. govs. 1981-87, 1st v.p. 1982-83), Am. Legion (comdr. Allied post 1969-70), Legion Lex (bd. dirs. 1964—, pres. 1969-71), Air Force Assn., Aircraft Owners and Pilots Assn., Town Hall (gov. 1970-78, pres. 1975), World Affairs Coun., Internat. Platform Assn., Breakfast Club (law, pres. 1989-90), Commonwealth Club, Chancery Club (pres. 1996-97), Rotary, Phi Beta Kappa (councilor Alpha Assn. 1983—, pres. 1996), Omicron Delta Kappa, Phi Alpha Delta (suprem e justice 1972-74, elected to Disting. Svc. chpt. 1978), Sigma Nu. Presbyterian. Home: 600 John St Manhattan Beach CA 90266-5837 Office: Darling Hall & Rae 777 S Figueroa St Fl 37 Los Angeles CA 90017-5800

RAEBER, JOHN ARTHUR, architect, construction specifier consultant; b. St. Louis, Nov. 24, 1947; s. Arthur William and Marie (Laux) R. AA, Jefferson Coll., 1968; AB, Washington U., 1970, MArch, 1973. Registered architect, Calif., Mo.; cert. constrn. specifier; cert. Nat. Coun. Arch. Specification writer Hellmuth, Obata & Kassabaum, St. Louis, 1973-78, constrn. administr., 1978-79; mgr. of specifications Gensler & Assocs., San Francisco, 1979-82; ind. constrn. specifier San Francisco, 1982—; adj. prof. architecture Calif. Coll. Arts and Crafts, San Francisco, 1986—; access code advisor Constrn. Industry & Owners, 1982—; spkr., instr. seminars orgns., univs., 1982—; mem. Calif. State Bldg. Standards Commn. Accessibility Adv. Panel, Sacramento, 1981, Calif. Subcom. Rights of Disabled Adv. Panel, Sacramento, 1993; cons. Nat. Inst. Bldg. Scis., 1996—. Author: CAL/ABL: Interpretative Manual to California's Access Barriers Laws, 1982; co-author: (with Peter S. Hopf) Access for the Handicapped, 1984; columnist Constrn. Specifier Mag., 1988-95. Vol. Calif. Office Emergency Svcs. Safety Assessment, Sacramento, 1991—. Fellow AIA (San Francisco chpt. codes com., Calif. coun. codes and standards com., nat. masterspec rev. com. 1982-84, nat. codes com. corr.), Contrns. Specifications Inst. (cert., columnist newsletter San Francisco chpt. 1984-95, Ben John Small award for Outstanding Stature as practicing specifications writer 1994, pres. St. Louis chpt. 1978-79, pres. San Francisco chpt. 1993-94, tech. com., edn. com., publs. com., Specifications Proficiency award San Francisco chpt. 1989, Tech. Commendation award 1987); mem. Specifications Cons. in Ind. Practice (nat. pres. 1990-92, nat. sec./treas. 1988-90), Internat. Conf. Bldg. Officials, Phi Theta Kappa. Avocations: history, anthropology, sci. fiction. Home and Office: 888 Farrell W 606 San Francisco CA 94109

RAEBURN, ANDREW HARVEY, performing arts association executive, record producer; b. London, July 22, 1933; arrived in U.S., 1964, Can., 1993; s. Walter Augustus Leopold and Dora Adelaide Harvey (Williams) R. BA in History, King's Coll., Cambridge U., Eng., 1958; MA, King's Coll., Camridge U., Eng., 1962. Mus. dir. Argo Record Co., London, 1959-64; asst. to music dir., program editor Boston Symphony Orch., 1964-73; dir. artists and repertory New World Records, N.Y.C., 1975-79; artistic adminstr. Detroit Symphony Orch., 1979-82; exec. dir. Van Cliburn Found. Inc., Ft. Worth, 1982-85; performing arts cons., 1985-93; exec. v.p. The Peter Pan Children's Fund, 1990-91; exec. dir. Esther Honens Internat. Piano Competition Found., 1993-95, pres., 1995—; cons. music; radio and TV commentator; mem. faculty Boston U., 1966-67; condr. New World String Orch., 1978. Author record liner notes, Argo, RCA, Time-Life records, 1960-79, program notes, Boston Symphony Orch., 1968-73. Served with Royal Arty. Brit. Army, 1952-55. Home: Apt 406, 929 18th Ave SW, Calgary AB, AB Canada T2T 0H2 Office: 116 8th Ave SE 3rd Fl, Calgary, AB Canada T2G OK6

RAEBURN, JOHN HAY, English language educator; b. Indpls., July 18, 1941; s. Gordon Maurice and Katherine (Calwell) R.; m. Gillian Kimble, Aug. 18, 1963 (div. July 1979); children—Daniel Kennedy, Nicholas Kimble; m. Kathleen Kamerick, July 5, 1986. A.B. with honors, Ind. U., 1963; A.M., U. Pa., 1964, Ph.D., 1969. Asst. prof. U. Mich., Ann Arbor, 1967-74; vis. lectr. U. Iowa, Iowa City, 1974-75, assoc. prof., 1976-83, prof. English, 1983—; chmn. Am. Studies dept., 1983-85, 94—; chmn. English dept. U. Iowa, Iowa City, 1985-91; assoc. prof. U. Louisville, 1975-76. Author: Fame Became of Him: Hemingway as Public Writer, 1984; editor: (with others) Frank Capra: The Man and His Films, 1975. Mem. Am. Studies Assn. Democrat. Home: 321 Hutchinson Ave Iowa City IA 52246-2407 Office: U Iowa Dept Am Studies Dept English 202 Jefferson Building Iowa City IA 52242-1418

RAEDER, MYRNA SHARON, lawyer, educator; b. N.Y.C., Feb. 4, 1947; d. Samuel and Estelle (Auslander) R.; m. Terry Oliver Kelly, July 13, 1975; children: Thomas Oliver, Michael Lawrence. BA, Hunter Coll., 1968; JD, NYU, 1971; LLM, Georgetown U., 1975. Bar: N.Y. 1972, D.C. 1972, Calif. 1972. Spl. asst. U.S. atty. U.S. Atty.'s Office, Washington, 1972-73; asst. prof. U. San Francisco Sch. Law, 1973-75; assoc. O'Melveny & Myers, L.A., 1975-79; assoc. prof. Southwestern U. Sch. Law, L.A., 1979-82, prof., 1983—, Irwin R. Buchalter prof. law, 1990; mem. faculty Nat. Judicial Coll., 1993—. Prettyman fellow Georgetown Law Ctr., Washington, 1971-73. Author: Federal Pretrial Practice, 2d edit., 1995, ALI, 1989. Fellow Am. Bar Found.; mem. ABA (chmn. com. on fed. rules and criminal procedure criminal justice sect. 1987-93, vice-chair pubs. criminal justice sect. 1994-96, vice chair planning, criminal justice sect., 1996-97, trial evidence com. litigation sect. 1980—, adv. to nat. conf. commrs. uniform state laws drafting com. uniform rules of evidence 1996-97), Assn. Am. Law Schs. (chair elect evidence sect. 1996, chair 1997, com. on sects. 1984-87, chairperson women in legal edn. sect. 1982), Nat. Assn. Women Lawyers (bd. dirs. 1991—, pres.-elect 1993, pres. 1994-96), Women Lawyers Assn. L.A. (bd. dirs., coord. mothers support group 1987-96), Order of Coif, Phi Beta Kappa. Office: Southwestern U Sch Law 675 S Westmoreland Ave Los Angeles CA 90005-3905

RAEL, HENRY SYLVESTER, retired health administrator, financial and management consultant; b. Pueblo, Colo., Oct. 2, 1928; s. Daniel and Grace (Abeyta) R.; m. Helen Warner Loring Brace, June 30, 1956 (dec. Aug. 1980); children: Henry Sylvester Jr., Loring Victoria. AB, U. So. Colo., 1955; BA in Bus Adminstrn., U. Denver, 1957, MBA, 1958. Sr. boys counselor Denver Juvenile Hall, 1955-58; adminstrv. asst. to pres. Stanley Aviation Corp., Denver, 1958-61; Titan III budget and fin. control supr. Martin Marietta Corp., Denver, 1961-65; mgmt. adv. services officer U. Colo. Med. Center, Denver, 1965-72; v.p. fin., treas. Loretto Heights Coll., Denver, 1972-73; dir. fin. and adminstrn. Colo. Found. for Med. Care, 1973-86, Tri-County Health Dept., Denver, 1986-96; fin. cons., Denver, 1996—; instr. fin. mgmt., mem. fin. com. Am. Assn. Profl. Standards Rev. Orgn., 1980-85; speaker systems devel., design assns., univs., 1967-71. Mem. budget lay adv. com. Park Hill Elem. Sch., Denver, 1967-68, chmn., 1968-69; vol. worker Boy and Girl Scouts, 1967-73; bd. dirs. Community Arts Symphony, 1981-83, 85-87; controller St. John's Episcopal Cathedral, 1982-83; charter mem. Pueblo (Colo.) Coll. Young Democrats, 1954-55; block worker Republican party, Denver, 1965-68, precinct committeeman, 1978-84 ; trustee Van Nattan Scholarship Fund, 1974-96; bd. dirs. Vis. Nurse Assn., 1977-84, treas., 1982-84. Served with USAF, 1947-53; res. 1954-61. Recipient Disting. Service award Denver Astron. Soc., 1968, Citation Chamberlin Obs., 1985; Stanley Aviation masters scholar, 1957; Ballard scholar, 1956. Mem. Assn. Systems Mgmt. (pres. 1971-72), Hosp. Systems Mgmt. Soc., Budget Execs Inst. (v.p. chpt. 1964-65, sec. 1963-64), Colo. Pub. Employees Retirement Assn. (bd. dirs. 1993), Denver Astron. Soc. (pres. 1965-66, bd. dirs. 1982-94), Am. Assn. Founds. for Med. Care (fin. com. 1981-82), Nat. Astronomers Assn. (exec. bd. 1965—). Epsilon Xi, Delta Psi Omega. Episcopalian. Home: 7755 E Quincy Ave # 57 T-8 Denver CO 80237

RAEMER, HAROLD ROY, electrical engineering educator; b. Chgo., Apr. 26, 1924; s. Leo and Fannie (Marx) R.; m. Paulyne Barkin, Dec. 21, 1947; children: Daniel, Liane, Diane. B.S., Northwestern U., 1948, M.S., 1949, Ph.D., 1959. Teaching asst. Northwestern U., 1950-52; physicist Bendix Research Labs., Detroit, 1952-55; staff engr. Cook Research Labs., Chgo., 1955-60; sr. engrng. specialist Sylvania Applied Research Lab., Waltham, Mass., 1960-63; assoc. prof. elec. engrng. Northeastern U., Boston, 1963-65, prof., 1965—, chmn. dept., 1976-77, acting chmn., 1982-84, Snell prof. engrng., 1986-93; prof. emeritus, 1994—; vis. lectr. Harvard U., 1962, hon. research assoc., 1972-73; vis. scientist MIT, 1984-85; cons. in field. Author: Statistical Communication: Theory and Applications, 1969, Radar Systems Principles, 1996; contbr. articles to profl. jours. Served with USAAF, 1943-46. Mem. IEEE (sr.), AAAS, Am. Soc. for Engring. Edn., Sigma Xi, Pi Mu Epsilon, Eta Kappa Nu, Tau Beta Pi. Home: 1200 Noanett Needham MA 02194-2442 Office: Dept Elec and Computer Engring Northeastern U Boston MA 02115

RAETZ, CHRISTIAN R. H., biochemistry educator; b. Berlin, Germany, Nov. 17, 1946. B.S. in Chemistry, Yale U., 1967; M.D., Harvard U., 1973, Ph.D., %. House officer Peter Bent Brigham Hosp., Boston, 1973-74; research assoc. Nat. Inst. Gen. Med. Scis., USPHS, Bethesda, Md., 1974-76; asst. prof. biochemistry U. Wis.-Madison, 1976-79, assoc. prof., 1979-82, prof., dir. Ctr. for Membrane Biosynthesis Research, 1982-95; chmn. biochemistry dept. Duke U., 1995—; mem. biochemistry study sect. NIH. Contbr. numerous articles to profl. jours. Mem. editorial bd. Jour. Biol. Chemistry. Recipient James Tolbert Shipley Research prize Harvard U. Med. Sch., 1973, Harry and Evelyn Steenbock Career Advancement award, 1976, Research Career Devel. award NIH, 1978-83, Dreyfus Tchr.-Scholar award, 1979; H. I. Romnes Faculty fellow U. Wis., 1984; NIH grantee. Mem. Am. Soc. Biol. Chemists, Japanese Soc. Promotion Sci., Phi Beta Kappa, Alpha Omega Alpha. Office: Duk U Dept Biochemistry Box 3711 DUMC Durham NC 27710*

RAEUCHLE, JOHN STEVEN, computer analyst; b. Washington, Sept. 21, 1955; s. Richard Frank and Ruth Darlene (Fulton) R. BS, Tex. Christian, 1978. Programmer Tex. Christian U., Fort Worth, 1976-78, Warrex Computer Sys., Ft. Worth, 1978-79; sys. programmer Tandy Data Processing, Ft. Worth, 1979-84; sr. programmer, analyst Commodity News Svcs., Leawood, Kans., 1984-86, Logica Data Archs., St. Louis, 1986-89; computer analyst Credit Sys., Inc., St. Louis, 1989-95; software engr. Master Card Internat., St. Louis, 1995—. Mem. St. Louis Ambassadors, 1989—; active Boy Scouts Am., 1964—. Recipient awrd of merit Boy Scouts Am., Commrs. Key, 1982. Mem. St. Louis Jaycees Found. (treas. 1990-94, sec. 1994-96, pres. 1996—), Mo. Jr. C. of C. Internat. Senate (treas. 1997—), Mo. Jaycees (state officer 1989-94), Kansas City Jaycees (bd. dirs. 1985-87), Kansas City Jaycees Found., St. Louis Jr. C. of C. (pres. 1988-89). Democrat. Methodist. Avocations: camping, bowling, hiking. Home: 52 Country Creek Dr Saint Peters MO 63376-3041 Office: Master Card Internat 12115 Lackland Rd Saint Louis MO 63146

RAFAEL, RUTH KELSON, archivist, librarian, consultant; b. Wilmington, N.C., Oct. 28, 1929; d. Benjamin and Jeanette (Spicer) Kelson; m. Richard Vernon Rafael, Aug. 26, 1951; children: Barbara Martinez Yates, Brenda Elaine. BA, San Francisco State U., 1953, MA, 1954; MLS, U. Calif.-Berkeley, 1968. Cert. archivist, 1989. Tchr. San Francisco Unified Sch. Dist., 1956-57; libr. Congregation Beth Sholom, San Francisco, 1965-83; archivist Western Jewish History Ctr. of Judah L. Magnes Mus., Berkeley, Calif., 1968, head archivist, libr., curator of exhibits, 1969-94; cons. NEH, Washington, NHPRC, Congregation Sherith Israel, San Francisco, Mount Zion Hosp., San Francisco, Benjamin Swig archives project, San Francisco, Koret Found., Camp Swig, Saratoga, Calif.; project dir. Ethnicity in Calif. Agriculture, 1989, San Francisco Jews of European Origin, 1880-1940, an oral history project, 1976; curator exhibits Western U.S. Jewry. Author: Continuum, San Francisco Jews of Eastern European Origin, 1880-1940, 1976, rev. edit., 1977; (with Davies and Woogmaster) poetry book Relatively Speaking, 1981; Western Jewish History Center: Archival and Oral History Collections, Judah L. Magnes Meml. Mus., 1987; contbg. editor Western States Jewish History, 1979—. Mem. exec. bd. Bay Area Library Info. Network, 1986-88. NEH grantee, 1985. Mem. Calif. Libr. Assn., Soc. Am. Archivists, Acad. Cert. Archivists.

RAFAJKO, ROBERT RICHARD, medical research company executive; b. Chgo., Sept. 3, 1931; s. Edward Michael and Mildred Eleanor (Simo) R.; m. Mary Ann Filipi, June 24, 1954 (div. 1979); children: Rorie Rae, Ronald Raymond, Robin Rene, Rod Richard, Rebecca Rae.; m. Anne Thorne Sloan, Jan. 26, 1982; 1 son, Andrew Sloan. BA, Coe Coll., 1953; MS, U. Iowa, 1958, PhD, 1960. Research assoc. Merck Sharp and Dohme, West Point, Pa., 1960-61; research scientist Microbiol. Assos., Bethesda, Md., 1961-66; v.p., gen. mgr. Med. Research Cons., Rockville, Md., 1966-69; v.p. research and devel. N. Am. Biols., Rockville, 1969-74; pres. Biofluids, Inc., Rockville, 1974—; pres. Tysan Serum, Inc., Rockville, 1974—, Kytaron Inc, Rockville, 1987—; breeder thoroughbred horses, 1980—. Contbr. 23 articles to profl. jours. Chmn. PVAAU Swimming Program, Washington, Md. and Va., 1973-76; bd. dirs. Montgomery County Swim League, Montgomery County, Md., 1968-76. Served with USAF, 1954-55. Mem. AAAS, N.Y. Acad. Scis., Am. Soc. Microbiology, Tissue Culture Assn., Am. Horse Council, Horsemans Benevolent and Protective Assn. Republican. Presbyterian. Avocations: scuba diving, photography, collecting stamps, travel. Home: 12053 Wetherfield Ln Potomac MD 20854 Office: Biofluids Inc 1146 Taft St Rockville MD 20850-1310

RAFEEDIE, EDWARD, federal judge; b. Orange, N.J., Jan. 6, 1929; s. Fred and Nabeeha (Hishmeh) R.; m. Ruth Alice Horton, Oct. 8, 1961; children: Fredrick Alexander, Jennifer Ann. BS in Law, U. So. Calif., 1957, JD, 1959; LLD (hon.), Pepperdine U., 1978. Bar: Calif. 1960. Pvt. practice Santa Monica, Calif., 1960-69; mcpl. ct. judge Santa Monica Jud. Dist., Santa Monica, 1969-71; judge Superior Ct. State of Calif., L.A., 1971-82; dist. judge U.S. Dist. Court (cen. dist.) Calif., L.A., 1982—. With U.S. Army, 1950-52, Korea. Office: US Dist Ct RM 244P 312 N Spring St Ste 244P Los Angeles CA 90012-4704

RAFELSON, BOB, film director; b. N.Y.C., 1933. Dir.: (films) Head, 1968, Five Easy Pieces, 1970 (Acad. award nomination for best picture), The King of Marvin Gardens, 1972, Stay Hungry, 1976, The Postman Always Rings Twice, 1981, Black Widow, 1987, Mountains of the Moon, 1990, Man Trouble, 1992, Blood and Wine, 1997; (short films) Wet, 1993, Armed Response, 1994, (rock video - Lionel Ricie) All Night Long, 1983; author: (TV series) Play of the Week; creator (TV series) The Monkees; dir. (series) The Painted Word, (film) Blood and Wine, 1997. Recipient N.Y. Film Critics award for Five Easy Pieces, 1970.

RAFELSON, MAX EMANUEL, JR., biochemist, medical school administrator; b. Detroit, June 17, 1921; s. Max Emanuel and Lillian (Kay) R.; m. Trudy Diane Hellem, Mar. 31, 1973; children—Mark Thomas, Anne Elizabeth. B.S., U. Mich., 1943; Ph.D., U. So. Cal., 1951. Postdoctoral rsch. fellow U. Stockholm, Sweden, 1951-52; asst. prof. biol. chemistry U. Ill. Coll. Medicine, Chgo., 1953-55, assoc. prof., 1955-60, prof., 1961-70; assoc. dean biol. and behavioral scis. Rush Med. Coll., Rush-Presbyn.-St. Luke's Med. Center, 1970-71, v.p. info. scis., 1971-77, v.p., 1972—; prof. biochemistry Rush Med. Coll., 1972-90, prof. and chmn. emeritus, 1990—; John W. and Helen H. Watzek meml. chmn. biochemistry Presbyn.-St. Lukes Hosp., Chgo., 1961-70; vis. prof. U. Paris, France, 1960, 77-78, U. Ulm, Fed. Republic Germany, 1986; assoc. mem. commn. influenza Dept. Def., 1961—. Author: Basic Biochemistry, 1965, 68, 71, 80, Concise Biochemistry, 1996; contbr. articles on biochemistry, blood platelets, viruses, protein structure, endothelial cells and metabolism to profl. publs. Served with USNR, 1943-46. Mem. Am. Soc. Biol. Chemists, Biochem. Soc. (London), Am. Chem. Soc., AAAS, Nat. Acad. Clin. Biochemistry, Société de Chemie Biologique, Sigma Xi. Home: 2246 N Seminary Ave Chicago IL 60614-3507 Office: Rush-Presbyn-St Luke's Med Ctr 1653 W Congress Pky Chicago IL 60612-3833

RAFFA, JEAN BENEDICT, author, educator; b. Lansing, Mich., Apr. 23, 1943; d. Ernest Raymond and Verna Lois (Borst) Benedict; m. Frederick Anthony Raffa, June 15, 1964; children: Juliette Louise, Matthew Benedict. BS, Fla. State U., 1964, MS, 1968; EdD, U. Fla., 1982. Tchr. Leon County Sch. Sys., Tallahassee, Fla., 1964-69; coord. children's programming WFTV, Orlando, Fla., 1978-80; cons. edn. Tchr. Edn. Ctr. U. Ctrl. Fla., Orlando, 1980-89; writer Orlando, Fla., 1989—; instr. Disney Inst., Orlando, Fla., 1996; adj. instr. U. Cen. Fla., 1977-85; vis. asst. prof. Stetson U., DeLand, Fla., 1988-89; cons. Lang. Arts Curriculum Com. Orange County Sch. Sys., 1983; CEO Inner World Encounters, Orlando, 1995—. Author: Introduction to Television Literacy, 1989, The Bridge to Wholeness: A Feminine Alternative to the Hero Myth, 1992, Dream Theatres of the Soul: Empowering the Feminine Through Jungian Dreamwork, 1994; contbr. articles to profl. jours., articles and meditations to religious jours. Mistress of ceremonies Young Authors' Conf., Orange and Volusia County Sch. Sys., 1984-85; cons. Young Authors' Conf. Orange and Seminole County Sch. Sys., 1985-89; judge Volusia County Pub. Schs. Poetry Contest, 1983, 84, Seminole County Pub. Schs. Lit. Mag., 1985-89; pres. Maitland (Fla.) Jr. H.S. PTA, 1986-87; pres., bd. dirs. Canterbury Retreat and Conf. Ctr. Episcopal Diocese Ctrl. Fla., 1988-90; chair edn. commn. Episcopal Ch. of the Good Shepherd, 1986-89; sr. warden Vestry of Episcopal Ch. of the Good Shepherd, 1988. Mem. Kappa Delta Pi, Phi Delta Kappa. Democrat. Avocations: antiques, horseback riding, travel, reading. Office: 17 S Osceola Ave Ste 200 Orlando FL 32801-2828

RAFFAY, STEPHEN JOSEPH, manufacturing company executive; b. McAdoo, Pa., Oct. 25, 1927; s. Stephen John and Stephanie (Severa) R.; m. Audree Eugenia Kuehne, Sept. 12, 1953; children: Andrea, Stephen, Leslie. B.A., Columbia, 1950, M.S., 1951. C.P.A., N.Y. Sr. accountant Arthur Andersen & Co., N.Y.C., 1951-56; asst. controller Emhart Corp., Farmington, Conn., 1956-61, asst. treas., 1961-63, treas., 1963-67, v.p. internat., 1967-72, v.p., group pres., 1972-79, exec. v.p., 1979-84, vice chmn., chief adminstrv. officer, 1984-87, dir., 1980-87; sr. v.p. Dexter Corp., Windsor Locks, Conn., 1987-90; bd. dirs. Reflexite Corp., Fresnel Optics, Inc., Schaar Inds., Inc., United Plumbing Tech., Inc., Trust Co. Conn., Rossi Enterprises, Inc. Bd. dirs. Hartford Symphony Soc. With AUS, 1946-47. Mem. AICPA, Conn. Soc. CPAs. Office: 93 Westmont St West Hartford CT 06117-2929

RAFFEL, JEFFREY ALLEN, urban affairs educator; b. Bklyn., June 19, 1945; s. George A. and Renee (Lane) R.; m. Joanne Ruth Traum, Aug. 27, 1966; children: Allison, Lori, Kenneth. AB, U. Rochester, 1966; PhD, MIT, 1972. Asst. prof. U. Del., Newark, 1971-76, assoc. prof., 1976-82, dir. M Pub. Adminstrn. program, 1980-86, prof., 1982—, chair pub. mgmt. faculty, 1994-97; acting assoc. dean Coll. Urban Affairs and Pub. Policy U. Del., 1989; chair pub. mgmt. faculty U. Del., Newark, 1994—, dir. sch. urban affairs and pub. policy, 1997—; pub. svc. fellow, spl. asst. to gov. for intergovtl. rels. State of Del., 1979-80; chair urban ednl. policy group Nat. Assn. State Univs. and Land Grant Colls., 1987-93; mem. state supt.'s adv. com. on tchr. recruitment, Del., 1988-91. Author: Politics of School Desegregation, 1980; co-author: Systematic Analysis of University Libraries, 1969, Selling Cities: Attracting Homebuyers Through Schools and Housing Programs, 1995; mem. editl. bd. Pub. Productivity Rev., N.Y.C., 1984—; contbr. articles to urban affairs publs. Treas. Nottingham Swim Club, Inc., Newark, 1985-88; co-chair Gov.'s Task Force on Enhancing Ednl. Dollar, 1986-87; chair long-range planning com. and membership com. Delmarva coun. Boy Scouts Am., 1988-89; mem. Gov.'s Sch. Reform Partnership, Del, 1990—. Recipient cert. of recognition, NCCJ Greater Wilmington, 1980, numerous profl. and civic awards. Mem. ACLU (Del. chpt. sec. 1992—), Del. Assn. Pub. Adminstrn. (pres. 1981-82), Am. Soc. Pub. Adminstrn., Am. Edn. Rsch. Assn. Avocations: golf, reading. Home: 4 High Pond Dr Newark DE 19711-2597 Office: U Del Coll Urban Affairs Pub Policy Newark DE 19716

RAFFEL, LEROY B., real estate development company executive; b. Zanesville, Ohio, Mar. 13, 1927; s. Jacob E. and Anne M. (Oliker) R.; m. Shirley Balbot, Sept. 11, 1949; children: Kenneth, Janet, James, Nancy. B.S., U. Pa., 1949. Pres. Raffel Bros., Inc., Youngstown, Ohio, 1949-78; ret., 1978; pres. York Mahoning Co., Youngstown, 1950-64, Arby's, Inc., Youngstown, 1964-70; chmn. bd. Arby's, Inc., 1971-79; ret., 1979; pres. Brom Equity Devel., Inc., Miami, Fla., 1979—. Served with USNR, 1945-46. Home: 2141 NE 190th Ter North Miami Beach FL 33179-4352 Office: Brom Equity Devel Inc # 207 1380 NE Miami Gardens Dr Miami FL 33179-4709

RAFFERTY, BRIAN JOSEPH, investor relations consultant; b. Washington, Sept. 1, 1957; s. James Francis and Betty Jane (Finney) R.; m. Helen Marie Glancy, Oct. 10, 1986. BA in Philosophy, Georgetown U., 1979. Clk. Corcoran, Youngman & Rowe, Washington, 1977-80; account exec. Ogilvie Talyor Assocs., Inc., N.Y.C., 1980-82; ptnr. Taylor, Rafferty Assoc. Inc., N.Y.C., 1983—. Mem. N.Y. Soc. Security Analysts, Nat. Investor Rels. Inst. Avocations: flying, martial arts. Office: Taylor Rafferty Assocs 205 Lexington Ave New York NY 10016-6022

RAFFERTY, JAMES GERARD, lawyer; b. Boston, July 9, 1951; s. James John and Helen Christine (Kennedy) R.; m. Rhonda Beth Friedman, May 17, 1981; children: Jessica Faith, Evan Louis Quinn. BA, Brown U., 1974; MA, Princeton U., 1980; JD, Georgetown U., 1984. Bar: Md. 1985, D.C. 1985, U.S. Tax Ct. 1988, U.S. Ct. Appeals (4th cir.) 1989, U.S. Ct. Appeals (3d cir.) 1992. Assoc. Piper & Marbury, Washington, 1984-91, Pepper, Hamilton & Scheetz, Washington, 1991-92; founding ptnr. Harkins Cunningham, Washington, 1992—. Contbr. articles to legal jours. Mem. ABA (chmn. com. on affiliated and related corps. tax sect. 1994-95). Roman Catholic. Avocation: golf. Office: Harkins & Cunningham 1300 19th St NW Ste 600 Washington DC 20036-1625

RAFFERTY, NANCY SCHWARZ, anatomy educator; b. Jamaica, N.Y., June 11, 1930; d. Franklin and Louise (Barry) Schwarz; m. Keen Alexander Rafferty, Aug. 7, 1953; children: Burns Arthur, Katherine Louisa. B.S., Queens Coll., 1952; M.S., U. Ill., 1953, Ph.D., 1958. Instr. anatomy Johns Hopkins U., 1963-66, asst. prof., 1966-70; asst. prof. anatomy Northwestern U., Chgo., 1970-72; asso. prof. Northwestern U., 1972-76, prof., 1976-94, prof. emeritus, 1994—; corp. mem., gen. libr. reader Marine Biol. Lab., Woods Hole, Mass. Contbr. articles on cell biology of the crystalline lens to profl. jours. USPHS fellow, 1958-63; USPHS grantee. Mem. Assn. Research in Vision and Ophthalmology, Internat. Soc. for Eye Research, Am. Assn. Anatomists, AAAS, Am. Soc. Cell Biology, Visual Scis. (study sect. of NIH), Sigma Xi, Phi Sigma. Home: 59 Harbor Hill Rd Woods Hole MA 02543-1219 Office: Marine Biol Lab Woods Hole MA 02543

RAFFERTY, WILLIAM BERNARD, lawyer; b. Balt., May 15, 1912; s. John Patrick and Dorothy Amalye (Hartje) R.; m. Elizabeth Catherine Henkel, Dec. 26, 1938; children: Patricia Carol Buchan, Susan Elizabeth Magri, Dorothy Lee Schultz. AB with honors, U. Md., 1934, LLB with honors, 1936. Bar: Md. 1936, U.S. Supreme Ct. 1942. Ptnr. Miles & Stockbridge (and predecessor firms), Balt., 1936-41, ptnr., 1941-92, of counsel, 1992-94, ret., 1994; bd. dirs. Fidelity Fed. Savs. and Loan Assn., Henkel-Harris Co. Inc., Rolling Road Realty Co., Balt., 1975—; lectr. pub. utility law U. Balt. Law Sch., 1951-56. Pres., Roland Park Civic League, 1954-57. Fellow Md. Bar Found.; mem. Wednesday Law Club (pres. 1953), Merchants. Democrat. Presbyterian. Home: 9 Midvale Rd Baltimore MD 21210-2113 Office: Miles & Stockbridge 10 Light St Baltimore MD 21202-1435

RAFFI (RAFFI CAVOUKIAN), folksinger, children's entertainer; b. Cairo, July 8, 1948. Attended, U. Toronto. Recordings include: Singable Songs for the Very Young, 1976, More SIngable Songs for the Very Young, 1977, Love Light, 1977, The Corner Grocery Store, 1979, Baby Beluga, 1980, Rise and Sun, 1982, Raffi's Christmas Album, 1983, One Light One Sun, 1985, Everything Grows, 1987, Raffi in Concert with the Rise and Shine Band, 1989, Evergreen, Everblue: An Ecology Album for the '90's, 1990; Broadway appearances: A Family Concert, 1993, Bananaphone, 1994; videos: A Young Children's Concert with Raffi, 1985, Raffi and the Rise and Shine Band, 1988; author: Down By the Bay, 1988, Shake My Sillies Out, 1988, Baby Beluga, 1990, (with Debi Pike) Like Me and You, 1994. Recipient Order of Can., 1983, Parents' Choice award Parents' Choice Mag.,. Office:

Troubadour Records Ltd, 1075 Cambie St, Vancouver, BC Canada V6B 5L7*

RAFFIN, THOMAS A., physician; b. San Francisco, Jan. 25, 1947; s. Bennett L. and Carolyn M. Raffin; m. Michele Raffin, June 19, 1987; children: Elizabeth S., Ross Daniel, Jake Bennett, Nicholas Ethan. AB in Biol. Sci., Stanford Med. Sch., 1968, MD, 1973. Diplomate Am. Bd. Pulmonary Medicine, Am. Bd. Internal Medicine (also in Critical Care Medicine). Intern Peter Bent Brigham Hosp., 1973-75; fellow in respiratory medicine sch. medicine Stanford U., Stanford, Calif., 1975-78, med. fiberoptic bronchoscopy service dir. med. ctr., 1978—, acting asst. prof. sch. medicine, 1978-80, assoc. dir. med. ctr. intensive care units, med. dir. dept. respiratory therapy hosp., 1978—, assoc. prof. medicine sch. medicine, 1986-95, acting chief div. respiratory medicine, 1988—; chief div. pulmonary and critical care Stanford U., 1990—, prof. medicine sch. of medicine, 1995—; co-dir. Stanford U. Ctr. for Biomed. Ethics, 1989—; chmn. ethics com. Stanford U. Med. Ctr., 1987—. Author: Intensive Care: Facing the Critical Choices, 1988; contbr. articles to profl. jours. V.p. lung cancer com., No. Calif. Oncology Group, 1983-85; com. mem. NIH Workshop, 1984. Recipient Henry J. Kaiser Found. award, 1981, 84, 88, Arthur L. Bloomfield award, 1981. Fellow ACP (rep. coun. subsplty. socs. 1986), Am. Coll. Chest Physicians (program com. mem. 1985—); mem. AAAS, Am. Fedn. for Clin. Rsch., Am. Thoracic Soc., Santa Clara County Lung Assn. and Med. Soc., Calif. Med. Assn. (chmn. sect. chest diseases 1984-85), Soc. for Critical Care Medicine, Calif. Thoracic Soc. Jewish. Avocations: painting, gardening. Home: 13468 Three Forks Ln Los Altos CA 94022-2432 Office: Stanford U Med Ctr Dept Medicine Div Pul & Crit Care Med # H3151 Stanford CA 94305

RAFFO, SUSAN HENNEY, elementary education educator; b. Kendallville, Ind., Feb. 14, 1945; d. Gordon Theron and Sue (Kizer) Henney; m. Lawrence Albert Raffo, Feb. 19, 1977; children: Timothy, Kathleen. BS in Elem. Edn., Ball State U., 1967; M in Spl. Edn., San Francisco State U., 1972. Cert. elem. tchr., Calif. Tchr. East Noble Sch. Corp., Kendallville, Ind., 1967-68, Burlingame (Calif.) Sch. Dist., 1968—; master tchr. San Francisco State U., 1970-95, Coll. Notre Dame, Belmont, Calif., 1980-95, instr. edn. dept., 1996—. Registrar AYSO, Burlingame, 1987-94; bd. dirs. Burlingame Cmty. Edn. Found., 1989-95, sec., 1992-94. Recipient Svc. award PTA, 1989, J. Russell Kent award for innovative programs San Mateo County Sch. Bds. Assn., 1993; named Tchr. of Yr., Lions Club, 1993. Mem. Calif. Reading Assn., Alpha Delta Kappa. Avocations: reading, fabric arts, golf. Office: Franklin Sch 2385 Trousdale Dr Burlingame GA 94010-5704

RAFKIN, ALAN, television and film director; b. N.Y.C., July 23, 1928; s. Victor and Til (Bernstein) R.; children—Dru, Leigh Ann. B.S., Syracuse U., 1950. guest lectr. Bowling Green State U., 1975. Actor Robert Q. Lewis TV Show, 1955, daytime shows, CBS-TV; dir. Verdict is Yours, 1960, Mary Tyler Moore Show, 1970-71, Sanford and Son, 1972, Bob Newhart Show, 1972-73, Rhoda, 1973, Let's Switch, 1975, MASH, 1976-77, Love, American Style, 1970-71, Laverne & Shirley, 1977-83; TV movie: One Day at a Time: Barbara's Crisis, 1981-82; films include Ski Party, 1965, The Ghost and Mr. Chicken, 1966, The Ride to Hangman's Tree, 1967, Nobody's Perfect, 1968, The Shakiest Gun in the West, 1968, Angel in my Pocket, 1969, How to Frame a Figg, 1971. Served with U.S. Army, 1950-52. Democrat. Jewish. also: Grey Entertainment 9150 Wilshire Blvd Beverly Hills CA 90212*

RAFSHOON, GERALD MONROE, communications executive; b. N.Y.C., Jan. 11, 1934; s. Jack and Helen (Goodman) R.; m. Eden White Donohue, Mar. 3, 1978; children by previous marriage: Susan, Patricia, Janet, Scott. B.J., U. Tex., 1955. Copywriter Rich's Dept. Store, Atlanta, 1959; Southeastern advt. and publicity mgr. 20th Century Fox Film Corp., Atlanta, 1959-62; nat. advt. mgr. 20th Century Fox, N.Y.C., 1962-63; pres. Gerald Rafshoon Advt., Inc., Atlanta, 1963-77; chmn. bd. Gerald Rafshoon Advt., Inc., 1977-78; asst. to pres. U.S. for communications White House Washington, 1978-79; media and communications dir. Carter Presdl. Campaign, 1976, Carter Re-election Campaign, 1980; pres. Rafshoon Communications, Washington, 1980-88, Rafshoon Prodns., Washington, 1981-88, Consol. Prodns., Inc., Washington, 1988-91; vice-chmn. Consol. Entertainment, Inc., L.A., 1988-91; pres. Gerald Rafshoon Prodn., 1991—; guest scholar Brookings Instn., Washington, 1991—. Exec. prodr. TV spl. and movies including: The Atlanta Child Murders (CBS-TV), 1985, Circle of Violence (CBS-TV), 1986, The Nightmare Years (TNT), 1989, Bob Hope 75th Birthday Spl. (NBC-TV), 1977, Iran (TNT), 1990, Abraham (TNT), 1993, Jacob (TNT), 1994, Joseph (TNT), 1995 (Emmy for Best Miniseries NATAS 1995), Moses (TNT), 1996 (Emmy nomination for best miniseries 1996), Samson and Delilah, 1996, David, 1997, The Very Best Men, 1997; ind. film prodn., 1991—. Trustee Kennedy Center for Performing Arts. Served to lt. USN, 1955-58. Office: 1775 Massachusetts Ave NW Washington DC 20036-2188

RAFTERY, BILL, basketball analyst; b. Mar. 19, 1942. BA in History, LaSalle U.; MEd, Seton Hall U. Head coach Seton Hall U., 1970-81; coll. basketball analyst ESPN, 1980—; coll. basketball analyst NBC, 1981-82, CBS, 1982—; cons. coll. athletics, corp. rels. Meadowlands Sports Complex, East Rutherford, N.J.; co-owner Doyle & Raftery restaurant, 1991—. Named coach of the year N.J. Basketball Writer's Assn., 1979. Office: ESPN ESPN Plaza Bristol CT 06010

RAGAN, BETTY SAPP, artist, educator; b. Birmingham, Ala., Mar. 15, 1937; d. Robert William and Emma Mildred (O'Neal) Sapp; m. Thaxton Drew Ragan, Apr. 1958 (div. Aug. 1986); 1 child, Robert McClearan. BA cum laude, Birmingham-So. Coll., 1958; student, Allegheny Coll., 1971-72, Auburn U., 1980-83; MFA, Pratt Inst., 1985. Teachng asst. Pratt Inst., Bklyn., 1985; vis. asst. prof. dept. art Auburn U., 1985-89; asst. prof. dept. art U. Puget Sound, 1989-91, assoc. prof. photography and printmaking, dept. art, 1992—; panel moderator Soc. for Photo Edn. N.W., Tacoma, 1993; co-curator But Is It Art, Tacoma, 1993. Exhibited photography in solo shows at Maude Kerns Gallery, Eugene, Oreg., 1995, Helen Smith Gallery, Green River C.C., Auburn, Wash., 1996, others; group shows include Hanson Gallery, New Orleans, 1980, Montgomery (Ala.) Mus. Fine Arts, 1981, Ga. State U., Atlanta, 1981, Park Ave Atrium, N.Y.C., 1985, Carnegie Art Ctr., Walla Walla, Wash., 1990, Definitive Image Gallery, Seattle, 1992, Seattle Ctr. Pavilion, 1993, San Diego Art Inst., 1993, Eagle Gallery, Murray, Ky., 1994, B St. Pier Gallery, San Diego, 1995, numerous others; artist/photographer various collage series; co-curator But Is It Art?, Tacoma, 1993. Recipient numerous awards for art including Merit award Fine Arts Mus. of the South, Mobile, 1983, Dirk Andrew Phibbs Rsch. award U. Puget Sound, Tacoma, 1994. Mem. Soc. for Photog. Edn., Soc. Photog. Edn./N.W. (sec. 1990-93), Artist Trust, Women's Caucus for Art, Coll. Art Assn., Seattle Women's Caucus for Art. Unitarian. Avocations: entomology, hiking, gardening, existential philosophy. Office: U Puget Sound Dept Art 1500 N Warner St Tacoma WA 98416-0001

RAGAN, CHARLES RANSOM, lawyer; b. N.Y.C., Aug. 13, 1947; s. Charles Alexander Jr. and Josephine Forbes (Parker) R.; m. Barbara Thiel McMahon, Aug. 30, 1969; children: Alexandra Watson, Madeline McCue. AB, Princeton U., 1969; JD, Fordham U., 1974. Bar: N.Y. 1975, U.S. Ct. Appeals (3d cir.) 1975, Calif. 1976, U.S. Ct. Appeals (9th cir.) 1976, U.S. Dist. Ct. (no. dist.) Calif. 1976, U.S. Supreme Ct. 1981, U.S. Dist. Ct. (so. dist.) N.Y. 1982, U.S. Ct. Appeals (2d cir.) 1984. Law clk. to Hon. R.J. Aldisert U.S. Ct. Appeals (3rd cir.), 1974-76; assoc. Pillsbury, Madison & Sutro, San Francisco, 1976-81, ptnr., 1982—; mem. exec. com. 9th Cir. Judicial Conf., 1987-91; mem. Civil Justice Reform Act Adv. Group, No. Dist. Calif., 1995—. Contbr. articles to profl. jours. Mem. Inst. Transnational Arbitration (bd. dirs., advisor), San Francisco Bar Assn. (chair feds. cts. 1982-89). Avocations: biking, swimming, spectator sports. Office: Pillsbury Madison & Sutro 235 Montgomery St San Francisco CA 94104-2902

RAGAN, DAVID, publishing company executive; b. Jackson, Tenn., Aug. 26, 1925; s. Amos and Esther Lee (Tacker) R.; m. Violet Claire Sills, Dec. 27, 1948; children—David Nathaniel, Sarah Sills, Jennifer Leigh. B.A. in English, Union U., Jackson, 1947; M. Theatre Arts, Calif. Sch. Theatre, 1950. Radio writer Grand Central Sta., 1950; syndicated columnist Hollywood South Side, 1951; mng. editor Tele-Views mag., 1952; free-lance writer, 1952-57, 74-77, 82—; editor TV and Movie Screen Sterling Group, Inc., N.Y.C., 1957-61; mng. editor Motion Picture mag. Fawcett Pub. Co., N.Y.C., 1961-64; editor TV Radio Mirror, Macfadden-Bartell Pub. Co., N.Y.C., 1964-71; pub., editorial dir. Movie Digest, Words and Music, Planet mags. Nat. Periodical Publs. (Warner Communications), N.Y.C., 1971-74; editorial dir. Photoplay, Motion Picture, TV Mirror mags.; Macfadden Women's Group, N.Y.C., 1977-79; entertainment editor Globe Nat. Weekly, N.Y.C., 1979-82. Author: Who's Who in Hollywood 1900-1976, 1977, Movie Stars of the '30s, 1985, Movie Stars of the '40s, 1985, Mel Gibson: An Intimate Biography, 1985, Who's Who in Hollywood: The Largest Cast of Film Personalities Ever Assembled, rev., 1992; co-author: Richard Pryor: This Cat's Got Nine Lives, 1982; contbr. articles to profl. jours. Served with U.S. Army, 1952-54. Mem. Screen Actors Guild, TV Acad., Alpha Tau Omega, Tau Kappa Alpha. Republican. Presbyterian. Home: 1230 Park Ave New York NY 10128-1724

RAGAN, JAMES THOMAS, communications executive; b. San Diego, Mar. 15, 1929; m. Susan Held, Nov. 9, 1957; children: James, Maria, Carey, Andrew. BA, Oxford U., Eng., 1951, MA, 1955. With Gen. Electric Co., 1954-69; pres., chief operating officer Athena Communications Corp. subs. Gulf & Western Industries, Inc., N.Y.C., 1969-74; v.p. broadcast services Western Union Telegraph Co., 1974-76, v.p. satellite services, 1976-82, pres. Western Union personal communications corp., v.p. communication systems group, 1982-85; pres. Associated Info. Services Corp., 1985-86, Bunting, Inc., 1985-86; ptnr. Pierce Kennedy Hearth, 1988-91; CEO Nat. Lang. Assocs. Lanarea Pub., Guilford, Conn., 1990—. Patentee recreational sports equipment; author: The Ultimate Diet, The First Alaskans, A Guide to the Geography of the Native Languages, Cultures, Their Communities, and Populations, 1996. Pres. Wilton (Conn.) Pop Warner Football League, 1972-73. Served with USMCR, 1952-54, maj. (ret.). Mem. Sachem's Head Assn. (v.p., pres., treas.), Sachem's Head Yacht Club (Guilford, Conn.), Madison (Conn.) Winter Club (pres.). Clubs: Racquet and Tennis (N.Y.C.); Sachem's Head Yacht (Guilford, Conn.); Madison Winter (pres.). Home: 630 Colonial Rd Guilford CT 06437-3139 Office: Nat Lang Assocs PO Box 442 Guilford CT 06437-0442

RAGANS, ROSALIND DOROTHY, textbook author, retired art educator; b. Brooklyn, N.Y., Feb. 28, 1933; d. Sidney Guy Gordon and Beatrice (Zuckerman) Safier; m. John Franklin Ragans, July 31, 1965; 1 child, John Lee. BFA, CUNY-Hunter Coll., 1955; MEd, Ga. So. Coll., 1967; EdD, U. Ga., 1971. Cert. tchr. art, Ga. Tchr. art Union City (N.J.) Bd. Edn., 1956-62; tchr. 1st grade Chatham Bd. Edn., Savannah, Ga., 1962-64; instr. art Ga. So. U., Statesboro, 1964-69, asst. prof., 1969-76, assoc. prof., 1976-89, prof. emeritus, 1989—; keynote speaker art edn. confs., Ind., 1987, 88, Ark., Wis., 1989, Md., 1990, others. Author: (textbooks) ArtTalk, 1988, 2d edit., 1994, Exploring Art, 1990, Understanding Art, 1990, 2d edit., 1997, (with others) Art Connections K-5, 1997. Mem. Nat. Assn. Educators (life), Ga. Assn. Educators (life), Nat. Art Edn. Assn. (Southeastern Art Educator of Yr. 1991, Nat. Art Educator of Yr. 1992), Ga. Art Edn. Assn. (Ga. Art Educator of Yr. 1990), Pilot Club Internat. (Ga. dist., Ga. Profl. Handicapped Woman of Yr. 1988). Jewish. Avocation: painting. Home: 198 Wendwood Dr Statesboro GA 30458-5467

RAGATZ, THOMAS GEORGE, lawyer; b. Madison, Wis., Feb. 18, 1934; s. Wilmer Leroy and Rosanna (Kindschi) R.; m. Karen Christensen, Dec. 19, 1965; children—Thomas Rolf, William Leslie, Erik Douglas. BBA, U. Wis.-Madison, 1957, LLB, 1961. Bar: Wis. 1961, U.S. Dist. Ct. (ea. and we. dists.) Wis. 1961, U.S. Tax Ct. 1963, U.S. Ct. Appeals (7th cir.) 1965, U.S. Supreme Ct. 1968; CPA, Wis. Staff acct. Peat, Marwick, Mitchell & Co., Mpls., 1958; instr. Sch. Bus., U. Wis.-Madison, 1958-60, formerly lectr. in acctg. and law Law Sch. U. Wis.; law clk. Wis. Supreme Ct. , 1961-62; assoc. Boardman Suhr Curry & Field, Madison, 1962-64, ptnr., 1965-78; ptnr. Foley & Lardner, Madison, 1978—, mgr. ptnr., 1984-93; dir. Sub-Zero Freezer Co., Inc., Wis. Tales & Trails, Inc., Acme Equipment Corp., Mortenson, Matzell & Meldrem, Inc., More Than Computers, Inc., Norman Bassett Found.; dir., past pres. Wis. Amateur Sports Corp.; lectr. seminars on tax subjects. Editor in chief Wis. Law Rev., 1960-61; chmn. Nat. Conf. Law Revs., 1960-61; author: The Ragatz History, 1989; contbr. articles to profl. jours. Formerly dir. United Way, Meth. Hosp. Found.; mem. U. Wis. Found., United Way of Dane County; chmn. site selection com. U. Wis. Hosp.; bd. regents U. Wis., panel provision of legal svcs.; former moderator 1st Congl. Ch.; past pres. First Congl. Ch. Found.; bd. dirs. Met. YMCA, Madison, 1983-90, YMCA Found.; pres. Bus. & Edn. Partnership, 1983-89, also bd. dirs. Fellow Am. Bar Found.; mem. ABA, Seventh Cir. Bar Assn., Wis. Bar Found., State Bar Wis. (sec. 1969-70, bd. govs. 1971-75, chmn. fin. com. 1975-80, chmn. tax sect., chmn. spl. com. on econs., chmn. svcs. for lawyers com.), Dane County Bar Assn. (pres. 1978-79, chmn. jud. qualification com., sec.), Am. Judicature Soc., Wis. Inst. CPAs, Madison Club (pres. 1980-81), Order of Coif, Bascom Hill Soc., Beta Gamma Sigma, Sigma Chi, Order of Constantine. Republican. Home: 3334 Lake Mendota Dr Madison WI 53705-1469 Office: Foley & Lardner 150 E Gilman St PO Box 1497 Madison WI 53701-1497 also: Foley & Lardner 1st Wisconsin Ctr 777 E Wisconsin Ave Milwaukee WI 53202-5302

RAGENT, BORIS, physicist; b. Cleve., Mar. 2, 1924; s. Samuel and Bertha (Lev) R.; m. Dorothy Kohn, Sept. 11, 1949; children—David Stefan, Lawrence Stanton, Jesse Ron. Student, Ohio State U., 1941-44; B.S.E.E., Marquette U., 1944; Ph.D. in Physics, U. Calif., Berkeley, 1953. Registered profl. engr., Calif. Engr. Victoreen Instrument Co., Cleve., 1946-48; engr., physicist Radiation Lab., U. Calif., Berkeley, 1948-53; physicist Livermore, 1953-56, Broadview Research Corp., Burlingame, Calif., 1956-59, Vidya div. Itek Corp., Palo Alto, Calif., 1959-66, Ames Research Ctr., NASA, Moffett Field, Calif., 1966-87, San Jose (Calif.) State U. Found., 1987—; lectr. Stanford U., U. Calif. Extension. Served in USNR, 1944-46. Mem. AAAS, Am. Phys. Soc., Optical Soc. Am., Am. Geophys. Union, Sigma Xi. Office: Ames Research Ctr NASA Mail Stop 245-1 Moffett Field CA 94035

RAGGI, REENA, federal judge; b. Jersey City, May 11, 1951. BA, Wellesley Coll., 1973; JD, Harvard U., 1976. Bar: N.Y. 1977. U.S. atty. Dept. Justice, Bklyn., 1986; ptnr. Windels, Marx, Davies & Ives, N.Y.C., 1987; judge U.S. Dist. Ct. (ea. dist.) N.Y., Bklyn., 1987—. Office: US Courthouse 225 Cadman Plz E Brooklyn NY 11201-1818

RAGGIO, KENNETH GAYLORD, lawyer, mediator; b. Dallas, Oct. 18, 1949; s. Grier H. and Louise (Ballerstedt) R.; m. Patricia Thornbury, June 28, 1980; children: Jeffrey, Michael. BA, U. Tex., Austin, 1971, JD, 1974. BarL Tex. 1974, U.S. Dist Ct. (no. dist.) Tex. 1974. Pvt. practice Austin, 1974-76; shareholder Raggio & Raggio, Inc., Dallas, 1977—; speaker, lectr. in field of tracing and characterization of property, and applying tech. to clients cases; mediator for family law cases. Contbr. to profl. publs. Recipient Cici Simon Meml. award Children's Rights Coun., 1993. Mem. ABA (chair family law sect. 1991-92, spl. com. on project 2000, 1991—), Tex. Bar Found., Am. Acad. Matrimonial Lawyers, Internat. Acad. Matrimonial Lawyers, Tex. Acad. Family Law Specialists, State Bar Tex., Dallas Bar Assn. (chair family law sect. 1980-81). Office: Raggio & Raggio Inc 3316 Oak Grove Ave Dallas TX 75204-2365

RAGGIO, LOUISE BALLERSTEDT, lawyer; b. Austin, Tex., June 15, 1919; d. Louis F. and Hilma (Lindgren) Ballerstedt; m. Grier H. Raggio, Apr. 19, 1941; children: Grier, Thomas, Kenneth. B.A., U. Tex., 1939; student, Am. U. Washington, 1939-40; J.D., So. Methodist U., 1952. Bar: Tex. 1952, U.S. Dist. Ct. (no. dist.) Tex. 1958. Intern Nat. Inst. Pub. Affairs, Washington, 1939-40; asst. dist. atty. Dallas County, Tex., 1954-56; shareholder Raggio and Raggio, 1956—. Sec. Gov.'s Commn. on Status of Women, 1970-71; trustee Tex. Bar Found., 1982-86, chmn., 1984-85, chmn. fellows, 1993—, Dallas Women's Found., 1993—, Nat. Conf. Bar Founds., 1986-92. Recipient Zonta award, Bus. and Profl. Women's Club award, So. Meth. U. Alumni award, Woman of Yr. award Tex. Fedn. Bus. and Profl. Women's Clubs, 1985, award Internat. Women's Forum, 1990, Disting. Law Alumni award So. Meth. U., 1992; Disting. Trial Lawyer award, 1993, Outstanding Trial Lawyer award Dallas Bar Assn., 1993, Pacemaker award Nat. Bus. Women Owners Assn., 1994, Thomas Jefferson award ACLU, 1994, Courage award Women Journalists North Tex., 1995; inducted into Tex. Women's Hall of Fame, 1985. Fellow Am. Bar Found.; mem. ABA (chmn. family sect. 1975-76, Best Woman Lawyer award 1995), LWV (pres. Austin 1945-46), State Bar Tex. (chmn. family law sect. 1965-67, dir. 1979-82, citation for law reform 1967, Pres.'s award 1987, Sarah T. Hughes award 1993), Dallas Bar Found. (pres. fellow com. 1991), Am. Acad. Matrimonial Lawyers (gov. 1973-81, trustee found. 1992—), Bus. and Profl. Women's Club (pres. Town North 1958-59), Phi Beta Kappa (pres. Dallas chpt. 1970-71, 90-92). Unitarian. Home: 3561 Colgate Ave Dallas TX 75225-5010 Office: Raggio and Raggio 3316 Oak Grove Ave Dallas TX 75204-2365 *All things are possible in our expanding universe if we can tune in to the infinite power available to all of us. Our ancestors concentrated on the problems—let us be a part of the solutions so desperately needed in our complex and troubled world.*

RAGGIO, WILLIAM JOHN, state senator, lawyer; b. Reno, Oct. 30, 1926; s. William John and Clara M. (Cardelli) R.; student La. Poly. Inst., 1944-45, U. Okla., 1945-46; BA, U. Nev., 1948; JD, U. Cal. at Hastings, 1951; m. Dorothy Brigman, August 15, 1948; children: Leslie Ann, Tracy Lynn, Mark William. Bar: Nev. 1951, U.S. Supreme Ct. 1959. Atty., Reno and Las Vegas; asst. dist. atty. Washoe County, Nev., 1952-58, dist. atty., 1958-71; ptnr. firm Wiener, Goldwater, Galatz & Raggio, Ltd., 1971-72, Raggio, Walker & Wooster Reno and Las Vegas, 1974-78, Raggio, Wooster & Lindell, 1978-92, sr. ptnr. Vargas & Bartlett, 1992—; mem. Nev. Senate, 1973—, minority floor leader, 1977-81, 82-87, 91, majority flr. leader, 1987—; mem. legis. commn., vice chmn. criminal law and adminstrn. com. Council State Govts., 1972-75; bd. dirs. Am. Savs. & Loan Assn.; v.p., dir. Santa Fe Gaming Corp., Casino Properties, Inc., Sahara Las Vegas, Inc. Adv. bd. Salvation Army, Reno; mem. Nev. Am. Revolutionary Bicentennial Commn., 1975-81; mem. Republican State Cen. Com. Bd. dirs. YMCA, Reno chpt. NCCJ, Salvation Army; past nat. chmn., current dir. Am. Legislative Exchange Council, dir. Sierra Health Svcs.; trustee Nat. Dist. Attys. Found. (vice chmn. 1962-65); trustee Community Action Program Washoe County. Republican candidate for U.S. Senate, 1970. Served with USNR, 1944-46; to 2d lt. USMCR, 1946-47. Named Young Man of Yr., Reno-Sparks Jr. C. of C., 1959; recipient Disting. Nevadan award, 1968, Fellows award The Salvation Army, Torch of Liberty award The Anti-Defamation League, SIR award Assoc. Gen. Contractors, 1995. Fellow Am. Bd. Criminal Lawyers (v.p. 1978—); mem. ABA (state chmn. jr. bar conf. 1957-60, ho. dels.) Am. Judicature Soc., Navy League, Air Force Assn., Nat. (nat. pres. 1967-68; named Outstanding Prosecutor 1965), Nev. State (sec. 1959, pres. 1960-63) Dist. Attys. Assn., NCCJ (Brotherhood award 1965), Nev. Peace Officers Assn., Internat. Assn. Chiefs Police, Am. Legion, Elks, Lion Club, Prospectors Club, Alpha Tau Omega, Phi Alpha Delta. Republican. Roman Catholic. Home: PO Box 281 Reno NV 89504-0281

RAGHAVAN, DEREK, oncology and medical educator; b. Buenos Aires, Aug. 11, 1949; came to U.S., 1991; m. Patricia Harrison, Jan. 4, 1979; 2 children. MB, BS with honors, Sydney U., 1974; PhD, London U., 1984. Cert. Royal Australian Coll. Physicians, Fgn. Lic. Exam Coun., Ednl. Coun. Fgn. Med. Grads., Gen. Med. Coun. (U.K.), NSW Med. Bd. (Australia). Resident, registrar Royal Prince Alfred Hosp., Sydney, 1974-77; lectr., sr. registrar Royal Marsden Hosp., London, 1978-80; rsch. fellow Ludwig Inst. Cancer Rsch., London, 1978-80; med. rsch. specialist U. Minn., Mpls., 1980-81; sr. specialist med. oncology Royal Prince Alfred Hosp., Sydney, 1981-91; prof., chief solid tumor oncology and investigational therapeutics Roswell Park Cancer Inst. and SUNY, Buffalo, 1991—; pres. med. staff Roswell Park Cancer Inst., Buffalo, 1995-96; chair VA Merit Rev. Bd. in Oncology, 1996-97; mem. oncology drug adv. com. FDA, 1996—; chair cancer clin. investigations review com. Nat. Cancer Inst., 1996—; prof. medicine SUNY, Buffalo, 1991—, prof. urology, 1996—. Editor: The Management of Bladder Cancer, 1988, Textbook of Uncommon Cancer, 1988, Principles and Practice of Genitourinary Oncology, 1996; mng. editor Urologic Oncology, 1995—, assoc. editor Clin. Cancer Rsch., 1996—; mem. editl. bd. Jour. Clin. Oncology, 1990-94, European Jour. Cancer, The Prostate, The Breast, Prostate Cancer, Advances in Oncology; bd. cons. Jour. Urology, 1996—; contbr. numerous articles to profl. jours. Rsch. grantee Nat. Health and Med. Rsch. Coun., Australia, 1983-90; traveling fellow NSW Cancer Coun., Sydney, 1978; named Hospice Physician of Yr., Hospice of Buffalo, 1994. Fellow ACP, Royal Australian Coll. Physicians (chair specialist adv. com. in med. oncology 1988-90); mem. Am. Soc. Clin. Oncology, Am. Assn. Cancer Rsch., Soc. Urologic Oncology, Med. Oncology Group Australia (chmn. 1988-90), Sydney U. Med. Soc. (pres. 1974). Avocations: tennis, squash. Office: Roswell Park Cancer Inst Divsn Medicine Buffalo NY 14263-0001

RAGINSKY, NINA, artist; b. Montreal, Apr. 14, 1941; d. Bernard Boris and Helen Theresa R.; 1 child, Sofia Katrina. BA, Rutgers U., 1962; studied painting with, Roy Lichtenstein; studied sculpture with, George Segal; studied Art History with Allan Kaprow, Rutgers U. Freelance photographer Nat. Film Bd., Ottawa, Ont., Can., 1963-81; instr. metaphysics Emily Car Coll. Art, Vancouver, B.C., Can., 1973-81; painter Salt Spring Island, B.C., 1989—; sr. artist, jury Can. Coun.; selected Can. rep. in Sweden for Sweden Now Mag., 1979; tchr., lectr. in field, 1973—. One woman shows include Vancouver Art Gallery, Victoria Art Gallery, Edmonton Art Gallery, Art Gallery Ont., San Francisco Mus. Art, Acadia U., Nancy Hoffman Gallery, N.Y.C., Meml. U. Newfoundland Art Gallery; exhibited in group shows at Rutgers U., 1962, Montreal Mus. Fine Arts, 1963, Nat. Film Bd., Ottawa, 1964, 65, 67, 70, 71, 76, 77, Internat. Salon Photography, Bordeaux, France, 1968, Nat. Gallery Ottawa, 1968, Eastman House Rochester, N.Y., 1969, Vancouver Art Gallery, 1973, 80, Mural for Conf. Ctr. Ottawa, 1973, Field Mus., Chgo., 1976, Edmonton Art Gallery, 1978, 79, Walter Philips Gallery, 1979, Glenbow Mus. Gallery, 1979, Harbour Front Community Gallery, 1980, Hamilton Art Gallery, 1980, Musée Maisil de St. Lambert, 1981, Mendel Art Gallery, 1981, Dunlop Art Gallery, Regina, Can., 1981; represented in permanent collections Nat. Film Bd. Stills divsn., Ottawa, Ont., Banff (Alta.) Sch. Fine Arts, Nat Gallery Ottawa, Can., George Eastman House, Wadsworth Atheneum, Edmonton Art Gallery, various pvt. collections. Bd. dirs. Island Watch, Salt Spring Island, B.C., 1993; founder, coord. Salt Spring Island Ecosys. Stewardship Project, 1993; founder, coord. Salt Spring Island Waterbird Watch Collective, 1994—. Decorated officer Order of Can.; recipient Kees Vermeer award for edn. and conservation, 1997. Mem. Royal Can. Acad. Arts. Avocations: gardening, birding, subject of numerous publs. Home and Office: 272 Beddis Rd, Salt Spring Island, BC Canada V8K 2J1

RAGLAND, CARROLL ANN, law educator, judicial officer; b. New Orleans, Nov. 28, 1946; d. Herbert Eugene Watson and Mary May (LeCompte) Leathers; children: Robert A. Sinex, Jr., Stacie Bateman, Joy Montgomery. JD, San Francisco Law Sch., 1980. Bar: Calif. 1980, U.S. Supreme Ct. 1993. Pvt. practice Santa Rosa, Calif., 1980-85; child custody mediator Sonoma County Superior Ct., Santa Rosa, 1985-86; chief dep. county counsel Butte County Counsel, Oroville, Calif., 1986-87; chief dep. dist. atty. Butte County Dist. Atty., Oroville, 1987-95; referee Shasta County Superior Ct., Redding, Calif., 1995-96; commr. Shasta County Superior Ct., Redding, 1996—; dean faculty, law prof. Calif. No. Sch. of Law, Chico, 1987—; instr. Shasta Coll., 1996—. Commr. Yuba County Juvenile Justice and Delinquency Prevention Commn., Marysville, Calif., 1993-94. Fellow Lawyers in Mensa. Avocations: scuba diving, reading, crossword puzzles. Office: Shasta County Superior Ct 1431 Market St Redding CA 96001-1026

RAGLAND, JACK WHITNEY, artist; b. El Monte, Calif., Feb. 25, 1938; s. Jack Rider and Dorsey (Whitney) R.; m. Marilee J. Weaver, July 31, 1969; children—Roxanne, Natasha. B.A., Ariz. State U., 1960, M.A., 1964; postgrad., UCLA, 1961-64. Grad. asst. tchr. Ariz. State U., 1960-61; grad. teaching asst. UCLA, 1961-64; head art dept. Simpson Coll., Indianola, Iowa, 1964-76; demonstrator Nat. Art Materials Trade Assn., Denver, 1993, Pasadena Conv. Ctr., 1994. One-man shows include Kleine Gallery, Vienna, Austria, Billy Son Gallery, Coralville, Iowa, Tamarack Gallery, Stillwater, Minn., Percival Galleries, Des Moines, Simpson Coll., Internat. Art Svc., Pan Pacific Hotel, San Diego, Lakes Art Center, Okaboji, Iowa, Greenstone Ct. Collection, Fallbrook, Calif., Santa Barbara (Calif.) Art Co.; exhibited in group shows, Lyn Kottler Gallery, N.Y.C., Phoenix Art Mus., Tucson Festival Art, Talisman Gallery, Bartlesville, Okla., Exhibiting Artists Fedn., Poultney, Vt., Des Moines Art Center, Danskin Gallery, Palm Desert, Calif., Joslyn Mus. Art, Omaha, Lagerquist Gallery, Atlanta, Glez-Harkins Gallery, Palm Desert, Calif., Cabrillo Art Ctr., Point Loma, Calif., San Diego, NAMTA Art Show, San Francisco, 1995, Eagle Gallery, La Jolla, Calif., Tirage Gallery, Alta Dena, Calif., Polson Gallery, Pasadena, Show Case Houses, Pasadena, Rancho Santa Fe, Calif., 1995, 96, 97; represented in permanent collections, Albertina Museum, Vienna, Kunsthaus, Basel, Switzerland, Bibliothèque National, Paris, Los Angeles County Mus., Simpson Coll., Phoenix Art Mus., Ariz. State collection, Graphische Bundes Versuchsanstalt, Vienna, Austria, also pvt. collections, works include stained glass windows, Meth. Ch., Perry, Iowa.; works reproduced Applause mag, 1971, New Woman mag, 1974, Artists of Cen. and No. Calif., Vol. II, San Diego Better Homes and Gardens Lifestyles mag., 1995, San Diego Decorating mag., 1995, Pasadena Showcase House Design Mag., 1995, San Diego Decor and Style, 1996, Sci. of Mind Mag., 1997. Recipient grand purchase prize Ariz. Ann. Art Show, 1961, 1st prize in prints Iowa State Fair, 1974, 1st prize So. Calif. Expn., Del Mar; featured in Am. Artist mag. Oct. 1993. Home: 5490 Rainbow Heights Rd Fallbrook CA 92028-9619 *To capture the spiritual essence of a subject through form and color is the goal of my art.*

RAGLAND, TERRY EUGENE, emergency physician; b. Greensboro, N.C., June 14, 1944; s. Terry Porter and Virginia Lucile (Stowe) R.; m. Marguerite Elizabeth Morton, May 15, 1976; children: Kenneth John McConnell, Ryan Lee Ragland. Student, Cen. Mich. U., 1962-66; MD, U. Mich., 1970. Diplomate Am. Bd. Internal Medicine, Am. Bd. Emergency Medicine. Intern St. Joseph Mercy Hosp., Ann Arbor, Mich., 1970-71, internal medicine resident, 1974-77, chief resident internal medicine, 1975-76; emergency physician St. Joseph Mercy Hosp., Ann Arbor, 1977—; med. dir. emergency ctr. St Joseph Mercy Hosp., Ann Arbor, 1985-97; clin. asst. prof. U. Mich., Ann Arbor, 1981—; chief of staff St. Joseph Mercy Hosp., 1996-97; pres., CEO Secure Care, Inc., 1992—; pres. Huron Valley Phys. Assn., 1997—; examiner Am. Bd. Emergency Medicine, 1983—; med. dir. Life Support Services, Ann Arbor, 1983—. Contbr. chpts. to book. Bd. dirs. Emergency Physicians Med. Group, Ann Arbor. Lt. USN, 1972-74. Fellow Am. Coll. Emergency Physicians; mem. Am. Coll. Physicians, Nat. Assn. Emergency Med. Technicians, Mich. State Med. Soc. (alt. del. 1982-84, 89-90, del. 1991-94), Mich. Emergency Med. Technicians Assn., Washtenaw County Med. Soc. (pres. 1993—). Democrat. Avocations: trout fishing, gardening, skiing.

RAGLE, GEORGE ANN, accountant; b. Detroit, Dec. 21, 1946; d. Joseph Theodore and Josephine Theresa (Mastrogiovanni) Gibson; m. James Albert, Sept. 3, 1976; children: Gina Ann, Jeffrey Allen. Assoc. Bus., Oakland C.C., Farmington Hills, Mich., 1974; B Accountancy, Walsh Coll., Troy, Mich., 1975; MBA, Ctrl. Mich. U., 1981. Cert. sch. bus. adminstr., Mich. Tax analyst Burroughs Corp., Detroit, 1976, Robillard & Joyce, St. Clair Shores, Mich., 1977-78; acctg. mgr. Baker Driveaway, Bloomfield Hills, Mich., 1978-79; staff acct. Macomb County Contr., Mt. Clemens, Mich., 1979-80; sr. acct. Macomb Intermediate Sch. Dist., Mt. Clemens, 1980-86; dir. bus. Mt. Clemens Community Schs., 1986-88, Pinconning (Mich.) Area Sch., 1988-90; dir. bus. and pers. St. Clair Intermediate Sch. Dist., Port Huron, Mich., 1990—. Bd. officer, treas. Fraser (Mich.) Pub. Schs. Bd. Edn., 1984-88; mem. Anchor Bay Schs. Bd. Edn., New Baltimore, Mich., 1991-95, treas., 1991-92, 94-95. Mem. Assn. Sch. Bus. Ofcls., Mich. Sch. Bus. Ofcls., Mich. Assn. Sch. Pers. Adminstrs., Macomb/St. Clair Sch. Bus. Ofcls. Avocation: gourmet cooking. Home: 52134 Charleston Ln New Baltimore MI 48047-1191 Office: St Clair Intermediate Sch Dist 499 Range Rd Port Huron MI 48061

RAGNO, NANCY NICKELL, educational writer; b. Phila., Sept. 2, 1938; d. Paul Eugene and Sara Jane (Mensch) Nickell; m. Joseph Diego Ragno, Aug. 25, 1961; 1 child, Michelle Angela. BA, Lebanon Valley Coll., 1960; MA, NYU, 1968. Cert. tchr., N.J. Tchr. N.J. pub. schs., 1961-68; project editor Prentice-Hall, Inc., Englewood Cliffs, N.J., 1968-70, Harcourt Brace Jovanovich, N.Y.C., 1970-72; sr. editor Silver Burdett Co., Morristown, N.J., 1972-76; editor, writer Houghton Mifflin Co., Boston, 1976-77; sr. editor J.B. Lippincott Co., Phila., 1977-79; sr. author Silver Burdett Ginn, Morristown, 1984—. Author: (textbook series) Silver Burdett English, 1984, World of Language, 1992, (sound filmstrip) The City and the Modern Writer, 1970, Buying on the Installment Plan, 1974. Bassoonist Harrisburg (Pa.) Symphony Orch., 1959, Plainfield (N.J.) Symphony Orch., 1976, Somerset (N.J.) County Orch., 1989, Princeton (N.J.) Community Orch., 1992. Mem. ASCD, Nat. Coun. Tchrs. English, Internat. Reading Assn., Am. Soc. Journalists and Authors, Textbook Authors Assn., Authors Guild, U.S. Power Squadron. Democrat. Mem. Ch. of Christ. Avocations: music, writing, boating. Home: 38 Tortoise Ln Tequesta FL 33469

RAGO, ANN D'AMICO, public relations professional, educator; b. Pitts., Aug. 24, 1957; d. Jack and Florence (Zappa) D'Amico; m. John Thomas Rago, Aug. 31, 1984; children: Annie J., Emily J. BA, Duquesne U., Pitts., 1979, MA, 1987. From communications assoc. to dir. pub. relations Duquesne U., 1979-89, coord. univ. relations, 1989-93, exec. dir. pub. affairs, 1993—, adj. prof. comm. Editor University Record, 1989 (silver medal). Bd. dirs. Support, Pitts., 1989-91; sch. dir. Carlynton Sch. Bd., Pitts., 1989-93, pres. sch. bd., 1990. Recipient Gold award for publs./external prospectus 9th Ann. Admissions Advt. Awards, 1994, Gold award for Total Pub. Rels. Campaign, 10th Ann. Admissions Advt. Awards, 1995, Gold award for Total Pub. Rels. Campaign, 11th Ann. Admissions Awards, 1996, 1st Place award in Category 35, Internal Pub. Rels. Campaign, Pitts. chpt. Women in Comm., Inc., 1996. Mem. Pub. Rels. Soc. Am. (1st place award 1993), Internat. Assn. Bus. Communicators (award of excellence 1991, award of honor 1993, award of merit 1994), Am. Mgmt. Assn., Press Club Western Pa., Sigma Delta Chi. Office: Duquesne U 600 Forbes Ave Pub Affairs Office Pittsburgh PA 15282

RAGON, ROBERT RONALD, clergyman; b. Flintstone, Ga., Sept. 10, 1939; s. Robert Emmett and Frances Cora (Stoner) R.; m. Judith Ann Ward, Apr. 27, 1962; children: Ronald Russell, Regina Renee. BS, U. Chattanooga, 1962; BDiv, MDiv, Columbia Theol. Sem., Decatur, Ga., 1967. Ordained to ministry Presbyn. Ch., 1967. Pastor Trion (Ga.) Presbyn. Ch., 1967-72; dir., pastor Chattooga County Presbyn. Ministries, Trion, 1971-72; pastor Brainerd Presbyn. Ch., Chattanooga, 1972—; moderator Knoxville Presbytery, 1979-80; founder An Order of Slaves of Christ, Chattanooga, 1970; stated clk. Presbytery of S.E., 1990-93, moderator, 1995-96. Author: Covenant Agreement: O.S.C., 1970, The Journey, 1990. Trustee King Coll., Bristol, Tenn., 1983-86. Mem. Masons (Ga. chaplain 1980), KT (sec. 1991), Shriners, Kiwanis (bd. dirs. Chattanooga 1986-90). Republican. Avocation: investments. Home: 4229 Happy Valley Rd Flintstone GA 30725-2222 Office: Brainerd Presbyterian Church 1624 Jenkins Rd Chattanooga TN 37421-3249

RAGONE, DAVID VINCENT, former university president; b. N.Y.C., May 16, 1930; s. Armando Frederick and Mary (Napier) R.; m. Katherine H. Spaulding, Dec. 18, 1954; children: Christine M., Peter V. S.B., MIT, 1951, S.M., 1952, Sc.D., 1953. Asst. prof. chem. and metall. engring. U. Mich., Ann Arbor, 1953-57, assoc. prof., 1957-61, prof., 1961-62; asst. dir. John J. Hopkins Lab for Pure and Applied Sci., also chmn. metallurgy dept. Gen. Atomic div. Gen Dynamics, La Jolla, 1962-67; Alcoa prof. metallurgy Carnegie-Mellon U., Pitts., 1967-69; assoc. dean Carnegie-Mellon U. (Sch. Urban and Pub. Affairs), 1969-70; dean Thayer Sch. of Engring., Dartmouth Coll., 1970-72, Coll. Engring., U. Mich., 1972-80; pres. Case Western Res. U., Cleve., 1980-87; vis. prof., dept. materials sci. and engring. MIT, Cambridge, 1987-88, sr. lectr. dept. materials sci. and engring., 1988—; gen. ptnr. Ampersand Splty. Materials Ventures, 1988-92; ptnr. Ampersand Specialty Materials Ventures, 1992—; trustee Mitre Corp.; bd. dirs. Cabot Corp., Sifco Inc. Mem. Nat. Sci. Bd., 1978-84; mem. tech adv. bd. U.S. Dept. Commerce, 1967-75; chmn. adv. com. advanced auto power systems Council on Environ. Quality, 1971-75; Trustee Henry Luce Found. Named Outstanding Young Engr., Engring. Soc. Detroit, 1957. Mem. Univ. Club (N.Y.C.), Longwood Cricket Club (Boston), Sigma Xi, Tau Beta Pi. Office: MIT Dept Materials Sci Engring Rm 8-403 Cambridge MA 02139

RAGSDALE, CARL VANDYKE, motion picture producer; b. Illmo, Mo., May 16, 1925; s. Vandyke and Iona Lee (Bledsoe) R.; m. Diane E. Ringrose, Sept. 18, 1976; children: John Sheldon, Susan Lee. Student, Wash. U., 1942-43; BA, Denison U., 1950. Commd. ensign USN, 1945, advanced through grades to capt., 1972; ops. officer on staff comdr. in-chief Pacific, 1945; officer-in-charge Western Pacific Fleet Camera Party, 1946-47; capt. Res., 1954-85; photo officer USS Eldorado, Korea, 1950-52; dir.-prodr. USN Photo Ctr., 1952-53; comdg. officer Naval Res. Combat Camera Group—Atlantic, 1972-74; comdg. officer Naval Res. Office Info., N.Y.C., 1975-76, Houston, 1977-83; v.p. Depicto Films Inc., N.Y.C., 1954-62; pres. Carl Ragsdale Assocs. Inc., Houston and N.Y.C., 1962—. Producer films including A Year Towards Tomorrow, 1966, While I Run This Race, 1967. Vice chmn. USS San Jacinto Com., 1987; chmn. USS Houston (CA30) Found., 1991—. Decorated Navy Commendation medal with Gold star, Navy Meritorious Svc. medal; recipient Oscar award Acad. Motion Picture Arts and scis., 1966, nomination, 1967, Silver Anvil award Pub. Rels. Soc. Am., 1983, Meritorious Pub. Svc. award, U.S. Navy, 1995. Mem. Dirs. Guild Am., Naval Res. Assn., Naval Order of U.S. (founder Tex. commandery), Am. Legion, DAV, Naval Aviation Commandery, Navy League, Inst. Diving, Underwater Photog. Soc., Soc. Motion Picture and TV Engrs., Houston C. of C., Mil. Affairs Com., N.Y. Athletic Club, Bentwater Country Club, Masons, Shriners. Republican.

RAGSDALE, GEORGE ROBINSON, lawyer; b. Raleigh, N.C., Mar. 26, 1936; s. George Young and Susan (Jolly) R.; m. Adora Prevost, Oct. 20, 1962; children: John Robinson, George Young II, Adora P. AB, U. N.C., 1958, LLB, 1961. Asst. to chief counsel U.S. Senate Subcom. on Constnl. Rights, Washington, 1961-62; law ptnr. Bailey & Ragsdale, Raleigh, 1962-65; legal counsel to Dan K. Moore, Gov. of N.C., Raleigh, 1965-68; judge Superior Ct. of N.C., Raleigh, 1968-70; ptnr. Moore, Ragsdale, Liggett, Ray & Foley, Raleigh, 1970-86, LeBoeuf, Lamb, Leiby & MacRae, Raleigh, 1987-93, Ragsdale, Liggett & Foley, 1994—; lectr. N.C. Assn. Def. Counsel. Trustee U. N.C., Chapel Hill, 1979-87, vice-chmn. bd. trustees, 1983-84, chmn., 1984-85; trustee U. N.C. Endowment, 1980—, chmn., 1984-85; bd. dirs. U. N.C. Instnl. Devel. Found., Inc., 1985—, U. N.C.-Chapel Hill Found.; bd. visitors U. N.C., The Ednl. Found., Inc. Mem. ABA, N.C. Bar Assn., Wake County Bar Assn., Assn. Bar of City of N.Y., Def. Rsch. Inst., Raleigh C. of C., Kiwanis, Sphinx Club of Raleigh, Terpsichorean Club, Raleigh Execs. Club, Carolina Country Club, Laurel Ridge Country Club. Episcopalian. Office: Ragsdale Liggett & Foley 2840 Plaza Pl PO Box 31507 Raleigh NC 27622

RAGSDALE, KEITH ELLEN, nurse, educator, administrator; b. Austin, Tex., Dec. 27, 1949; d. Kenneth B. and Janet (Dittlinger) R. AAS, Del Mar Coll., 1971; BS, Purdue U., 1973; MS, U. Colo., 1974; EdD, Nova Southeastern U., 1994. Asst. prof. rsch. and mgmt. U. So. Miss., Hattiesburg, 1974-75; asst. prof. community health Tex. Christian U., Ft. Worth, 1975-78; assoc. prof., acting asst. dean U. N.D., Grand Forks, 1978-79; chair divsn. nursing and allied health Austin C.C., 1982-95, dir. acad. support, 1995—. Contbr. articles to profl. publs. Mem. Nat. League for Nursing (v.p. Tex. chpt.), World Future Soc., Tex. Assn. ADN's (chmn. legis. com.), Tex. Deans and Dirs., Tex. Jr. Coll. Tchrs. Assn., Sigma Theta Tau. Home: Rte 1 1300 Cardinal Dr Paige TX 78659-9742 Office: Austin CC 1020 Grove Blvd Austin TX 78741-3337

RAGSDALE, REX H., health facility administrator, physician; b. Henderson, Ky., July 31, 1957; s. Carl Wilkes and Sue Ann (Hart) R.; m. Sally E.; children: Leslie D'Anne, Kellen Edward. BSBA, U. Evansville, 1979; MD, St. Louis U., 1982. Diplomate Am. Bd. Family Practice. Resident St. Mary's Med. Ctr., Evansville, Ind., 1982-85; pvt. practice Newburgh, Ind., 1985-89; v.p. med. affairs Deaconess Hosp., Evansville, 1989—; bd. dirs. Ohio Valley Hospice, Evansville, 1990—, Impact Ministries Healthcare Ctr., Evansville, 1991-93; mem. VHA Nat. Physician Leadership Coun., 1993—. Pres. 1st Dist. Med. Soc., Evansville, 1993-94; state del. Ind. State Med. Assn., Indpls., 1992—; med. advisor United Parents Support for Downs Syndrome, Newburgh, 1990, 91, 92; med. dir. Arts coun. Fun Run, Evansville, 1988. Mem. AMA, Am. Coll. Physician Execs., Am. Acad. Family Practice, Aircraft Owners and Pilots Assn., Phi Mu Alpha. Avocations: flying, fishing, golf. Office: Deaconess Hosp Inc 600 Mary St Evansville IN 47747-0001

RAGSDALE, RICHARD ELLIOT, healthcare management executive; b. St. Louis, Dec. 20, 1943; s. Billie Oscar and Isabelle (Roques) R.; m. Anne Elizabeth Ward, Aug. 20, 1968; children: Richard, Kevin, Bethany. BBA, Ohio U., 1965; M in Internat. Commerce, Thunderbird Grad. Sch. Internat. Mgmt., 1968. Asst. treas. Chase Manhattan Bank, N.Y.C., 1968-73; v.p., treas. Hosp. Affiliates Internat., Nashville, 1973-80; v.p., treas., chief fin. officer INA Health Care Group, Dallas, 1980-81; sr. v.p., chief fin. officer, dir. Republic Health Corp., Dallas, 1981-83, sr. exec. v.p., dir., 1983-85; chmn. Community Health Systems Inc., Brentwood, Tenn., 1985—, Great No. Health Mgmt., Ltd., London, 1986-89; bd. dirs. RehabCare Group, Inc., St. Louis; chmn. ProMed Co., Inc. Ft. Worth, Tex., 1994—. Coach Spring Valley Athletic Assn., Dallas, 1985; trustee Watkins Inst., 1988-94; trustee Benton Hall Sch., 1988—, chair, 1991—; trustee Maryville Coll., 1990—, chair, 1992—. Recipient Thunderbird Disting Alumni award Entrepreneurship, 1990, Jonas Meyer Disting. Alumni award, 1993. Mem. Fedn. Am. Hosps. (legis. commn. 1984-95). Republican. Avocations: SCUBA diving, drag racing. Office: Community Health Systems Inc 155 Franklin Rd Ste 400 Brentwood TN 37027-4646

RAGUCCI, JOHN ALBERT, family practice physician; b. Medford, Mass., Feb. 8, 1960; s. Emilio A. and Ann Marie (Russo) R.; m. Kristin A. Spiro, Oct. 26, 1991; 1 child, Rachel K. BS in Biology cum laude, Boston Coll., 1982; MS in Health Sci., Northeastern U., 1985; MD, Tufts U., 1991. Diplomate Am. Bd. Family Medicine, Nat. Bd. Med. Examiners. Resident in family medicine Brown U./Meml. Hosp., Pawtucket, R.I., 1991-94, asst. chief resident for scheduling, 1993-94, asst. instr. in family medicine, 1993-94; mem. staff Norwood Hosp./Neponset Valley Health System, 1993-94; mem. staff Dept. Family Practice Beverly Hosp., 1994—; substitute tchr. Newton Cath. H.S., 1984-85; tchg. fellow Northeastern U., 1982-83, tchg. asst. microbiology labs., 1983-84; instr. microbiology Emmanuel Coll., New Eng. Bapt. Hosp. Sch. Nursing, 1985, 86, Anna Maria Coll., Malden Hosp. Sch. Nursing, 1986, 87, Middlesex C.C., 1985, 88; instr. anatomy and physiology dept. clin. lab. scis. U. Lowell, 1986; preceptor/tchg. attending physician Beverly Hosp. Family Practice Residency; presenter in field. Vol. mgr. Little League Baseball, 1977-81; vol. recreational program for retarded children, 1976-78. Mem. AMA, Mass. Med. Soc., Am. Acad. Family Physicians, Soc. Tchrs. of Family Medicine, Nat. Assn. Residents and Interns, Mass. Chess Fedn., U.S. Chess Fedn., Sierra Club, Planetary Soc., Alpha Omega Alpha, Phi Sigma. Avocations: golf, tennis, astronomy, chess.

RAGUSEA, STEPHEN ANTHONY, psychologist, educator; b. N.Y.C., Mar. 26, 1947; s. Anthony S. and Marie (Giampietro) R.; m. Kathleen Fox, Aug. 14, 1971; children: Anthony, Adam. AA, Nassau Coll., Garden City, N.Y., 1967; BS, Bowling Green (Ohio) State U., 1969; D of Psychology, Baylor U., Waco, Tex., 1980. Lic. psychologist, Pa.; diplomate Am. Bd. Profl. Psychology in Family Psychology, Am. Bd. Profl. Neuropsychology. Tchr. Dayton (Ohio) then Cedar Rapids (Iowa) Community Schs., 1969-76; mem. cons. team for local sch. system Waco, Tex., 1976-77; therapist Meth. Home Children's Guidance Ctr., Waco, 1977-79, Heart of Tex. Mental Health/Mental Retardation Ctr., Waco, 1977-79; intern in psychol. svcs. Norristown (Pa.) State Hosp., 1979-80; cons. Altoona (Pa.) Hosp. Community Mental Health Ctr., 1981-82; interim dir. psychol. svcs. Nittany Valley Rehab. Hosp. for Spl. Svcs., Pleasant Gap, Pa., 1983-84; pres., chief exec. officer Centre Valley Mgmt., Inc., 1981-85; exec. dir. Psychol. Forensics, P.C., State College, Pa., 1984—; clin. dir. The Medows Psychiat. Ctr., 1984-85; psychologist, dir. ops. Child, Adult, & Family Psychol. Ctr., State College, 1980—; asst. prof. Dept. Individual and Family Studies, Pa. State Univ.; adj. faculty dept. psychology Pa. State U.; mem. cons. psychol. staff The Meadows Psychiat. Ctr.; psychol. staff rep. to med. staff, mem. allied staff Centre Community Hosp.; bd. dirs. Penn PsyPac; numerous presentations in field. Fellow Am. Coll. Forensic Psychology, Cen. Pa. Psychol. Assn. (past-pres., chmn. profl. affairs com.), Pa. Psychol. Assn. (past-pres. clin. div., chmn. hosp. practice com., fellow and pres. 1993-94); mem. Am. Psychol. Assn. (del. from Pa. Coun. Reps. 1994—), Am. Soc. Clin. Hypnosis, Nat. Acad. Neuropsychologists.

RAHAL, PARAMVIR SINGH, physician; b. Jalandhar, Punjab, India, Feb. 14, 1964; came to U.S., 1991; s Shangara Singh and Joginder (Kaur) R.; m. Simrita Minhas, Jan. 7, 1990; 1 child, Harman K. Diploma in pre-med., Guru Nanak Dev U., Amritsar, India, 1981; MD, Med. Coll., Amritsar, 1986. Diplomate Am. Bd. Internal Medicine; lic. physician, Calif., Mich., Punjab. House officer dept. medicine and surgery Med. Coll., Amritsar, 1987-88; med. officer Ruby Nelson Hosp., Jalandhar, Punjab, India, 1990-91; intern U. Louisville, Ky., 1991-92; resident in internal medicine U. Louisville, 1992-94; fellow in gastroenterology Providence Hosp. and Med. Ctrs., Southfield, Mich., 1994-96; gastroenterologist Kaiser Permanente, Bakersfield, 1996—; presenter in field. Contbr. articles and abstracts to publs. Mem. AMA, ACP, Am. Coll. Gastroenterology, Am. Gastroent. Assn., Ky. Med. Assn. Avocations: music, driving, reading, family gatherings. Home: 1417 Galliard Ct Bakersfield CA 93312

RAHAL, ROBERT W., automotive company executive; b. Medina, Ohio, Jan. 10, 1953; s. Michael G. and Barbara (Woodward) R.; m. Deborah Ann Kuhl, Nov. 16, 1980; children: Michaela, Jarrad, Graham. BA in History, Denison U., Granville, Ohio, 1975. Profl. race car driver, 1982—; owner Bobby Rahal, Inc., Dublin, Ohio, 1988—. Hon. chmn. Easter Seals, Cen. Ohio, Columbus, 1985—; chmn. Children's Hosp., Columbus, 1988—; trustee Columbus Zoo, 1986—. Winner numerous car races including the Indianapolis 500, 1986; named CART champion, 1986, 87, 92. Avocations: golf, antiques, antique cars, reading. Office: Bobby Rahal Inc PO Box 39 Hilliard OH 43026-0039*

RAHALL, NICK JOE, II (NICK RAHALL), congressman; b. Beckley, W.Va., May 20, 1949; s. N. Joe and Alice Rahall; children: Rebecca Ashley, Nick Joe III, Suzanne Nicole. BA, Duke U., 1971. Staff asst. U.S. Senator Robert C. Byrd, 1971-74; sales rep. Sta. WWNR, Beckley, 1974; pres. Mountaineer Travel Co., Beckley, 1975-77, W.Va. Broadcasting, 1980—; mem. 95th-105th Congresses from 4th (now 3rd) W.Va. dist., Washington, 1977—; mem. transp. and infrastructure com. with subcom. on aviation, surface transp., water resources and environ., mem. resources com. with subcom. on energy and mineral resources; bd. dirs. Rahall Comm. Corp. Del. Dem. Nat. Conv., 1972, 74, 78, 80, 84, 88, 92; W.Va. chmn. March of Dimes, 1979; mem. profl. adv. bd. Alsac-St. Jude Children's Rsch. Hosp. Named Young Man of Year, Beckley Jaycees, 1972; Outstanding Young Man in W.Va., W.Va. Jaycees, 1977; recipient Achievement award Logan Cripple Children Soc., 1978; Citizenship award K.C., 1978, Disting. Svc. award Am. Fedn. Govt. Employees W.Va., 1984, Young Dem. of Yr. Dem. Nat. Conv., 1980, Outfitter of Yr. Profl. Outfitters, 1987, Seneca award Sierra Club 1988, River Conservation award Am. River 1988; named Coal Man of Yr. Coal Industry News, 1979, W.Va. Son of Yr., W.Va. Soc. of Washington, 1996. Mem. NAACP, NRA, Elks, Moose, Masons (33d degree) Shriners. Presbyterian. Office: US Ho of Reps 2307 Rayburn HOB Washington DC 20515-4803

RAHE, MARIBETH SEMBACH, bank executive; b. Evanston, Ill., Oct. 3, 1948; d. Daniel F. and Boysie (Beebe) Sembach; m. Martin E. Rahe, May 31, 1975. BA, Bowling Green State U., 1970; postgrad., Ohio State U., 1970-72; MA in Internat. Mgmt., Am. Grad. Sch. Internat. Mgmt., 1974. Internat. banking officer Harris Bank, Chgo., 1974-77; asst. v.p. Harris Bank, London, 1977-80; v.p. Morgan Guaranty Trust Co., London, 1980-83, N.Y.C., 1983-84; sr. rep. Sparebanken Oslo Akershus, N.Y.C., 1984-85; v.p. Morgan Guaranty Trust Co., N.Y.C., 1985-87, J.P. Morgan Investment Mgmt., N.Y.C., 1987-88; sr. v.p. Harris Bank, Chgo., 1988-91, dept. exec., 1991-94, sr. exec. v.p., 1994-95, vice chmn. bd., 1995—; bd. dirs. Harris Bankcorp., Trustmark Ins. Co. Bd. dirs. Children's Meml. Hosp., Rush Presbyn. Hosp., U. Chgo.; trustee Ill. Inst. Tech., MasterCard Internat. Recipient Outstanding Alumni award Am. Grad. Sch., 1991. Mem. Am. Bankers Assn. (vice chmn. 1991-92, chmn. 1992-93, exec. com. pvt. banking, banking advisor 1993—), Com. of 200, Econ. Club, Chgo. Women's Network, Chgo. Club. Republican. Lutheran. Office: Harris Trust & Savs Bank 111 W Monroe St Chicago IL 60603

RAHE, RICHARD HENRY, psychiatrist, educator; b. Seattle, May 28, 1936; s. Henry Joseph and Delora Lee (Laube) R.; m. Laurie Ann Davies, Nov. 24, 1960 (div. Dec. 1990); children: Richard Bradley, Annika Lee. Student, Princeton U., 1954-57; MD, U. Wash., 1961. Diplomate Am. Bd. Psychiatry and Neurology. Chief resident in psychiatry U. Wash. Sch. Medicine, Seattle, 1965; rsch. psychiatrist USN, San Diego, 1965-75; commdg. officer Naval Health Rsch. Ctr., San Diego, 1976-80; exec. officer Long Beach (Calif.) Naval Hosp., 1980-82; commdg. officer Guam Naval Hosp., Agana, 1982-84; prof. psychiatry U.S. Univ. Health Scis. Mil. Med. Sch., Bethesda, Md., 1984-86, U. Nev. Sch. Medicine, Reno, 1986—; dir. Mil. Stress Studies Ctr., Bethesda, 1984-86, Nev. Stress Ctr. Vets. Affairs Med. Ctr., Reno, 1986—. Contbr. numerous articles to sci. jours., chpts. to books; photographer prints and video. Dir. Nev. Mental Health Inst., Sparks, 1991-94. Capt. USN, 1965-86. Recipient Humanitarian award Vietnamese Refugee Com., 1974, Dept. of State award for treatment of Am. hostages held in Iran, 1981. Fellow Am. Psychiat. Assn.; mem. Am. Psychosomatic Soc. (past pres.), World Psychiat. Assn. (past. pres. mil. sect.). Avocations: hiking, skiing, swimming. Home: 638 Saint Lawrence Ave Reno NV 89509-1440 Office: VA Med Ctr Code 151-C 1000 Locust St Reno NV 89520-0102

RAHHAL, DONALD K., obstetrician, gynecologist; b. Clinton, Okla., 1942. MD, U. Okla. Coll. Medicine, 1971. Diplomate Am. Bd. Ob.-Gyn. (bd. dirs.). Resident Indiana U. Hosp., Indpls., 1971-74; obstetrician-gynecologist Mercy Health Ctr., Okla. City, 1981—, Deaconess Hosp., Okla. City, 1981—; clin. prof. U. Okla. Coll. Medicine, Okla. City, 1981—. Mem. ACOG, AMA, Am. Bd. Med. Specialties (del.), Coll. Acad. Obstetricians, Gynecologists., dir. Am. bd. ObGyn., 1992—. Office: 4200 W Memorial Rd Ste 410 Oklahoma City OK 73120-8305

RAHILL, MARGARET FISH, retired museum curator; b. Milw., Feb. 21, 1919; d. Joseph Benedict and Margaret (Scherdan) Schmidt; m. William James Fish, Nov. 14, 1941 (dec. Jan. 1945); 1 child, Mary Fish Arcuri; m. Frank M. Rahill, Mar. 14, 1951 (dec. Oct. 1986); children: Marguerite Rahill-Dunlap, Laura Rahill Maramba. BA, U. Wis., 1958; student, Mt. Mary Coll., 1958. With pub. rels. Blackland Army Air Base, Waco, Tex., 1942-43; reporter, art critic Milw. Sentinel, 1945-62; with pub. rels. dept. Milw. Art Mus., 1962-63, Layton Sch. Art, Milw., 1965-68, Bel Canto Chorus, Milw., 1965-68; curator in charge Charles Allis Art Mus., Milw., 1968-91; prin. Book Bay, Milw., 1962-72; vis. instr. journalism Marquette U., Milw., 1972-73; mem. organizing com. Florentine Opera Club, 1962, with pub. rels. dept. 1962-65, Bel Canto Chorus, 1966-68; mem. organizing com. Wis. Chamber Orch., Milw., 1975-76; v.p. art, councillor-at-large Wis. Acad. Sci. Arts and Letters, Madison, 1981-85; juror numerous art competitions, Wis., 1962-91. Contbr. articles to profl. jours. Active City of Milw. Art Commn., 1982-90, pres., 1984-85. Recipient Gridirm award Milw. Press Club, 1955, 57, 59, 60, Community Svc. award Milw. Art Commn., 1976, Ann. Bookfellows award Milw. Pub. Libr., 1977, Devel. award Milw. County Hist. Soc., 1982, Promotion of Hispanic Culture award Centro de la Communidad Unida, 1988. Mem. Wis. Painters and Sculptors (hon.), Wis. Crafts Coun. (hon.). Roman Catholic. Avocations: Oriental art studies, child care, reading. Home: 4801 Connecticut Ave NW Apt 302 Washington DC 20008-2203

RAHL, LESLIE LYNN, risk advisor, entrepreneur; b. N.Y.C., May 16, 1950; d. Myron and Esther (Botwin) Horwitz; m. Jeffrey Mark Lynn, Dec. 20, 1969 (div. 1981); m. J. Andrew Rahl Jr., Apr. 30, 1989; 1 child, Kevin; stepchildren: Kaitlin, Stephen. SB, MIT, 1971, MBA, 1972. V.p. swaps and derivatives Citibank, N.Y.C., 1972-91; pres. Leslie Rahl Assocs., N.Y.C., 1991-94; co-prin. Capital Market Risk Advisors, N.Y.C., 1994—; presenter in field. Contbr. articles to profl. jours. Recipient On the Rise award Fortune; One of Top 50 Women in Fin. Euromoney, 1997. Mem. Internat. Assn. Fin. Engrs. (bd. dirs. 1993—), Madison Beach Club. Avocation: wine tasting. Office: Capital Market Risk Advisors 565 5th Ave New York NY 10017-2413

RAHM, DAVID ALAN, lawyer; b. Passaic, N.J., Apr. 18, 1941; s. Hans Emil and Alicia Katherine (Onuf) R.; m. Susan Eileen Berkman, Nov. 23, 1972; children: Katherine Berkman, William David. AB, Princeton U., 1962; JD, Yale U., 1965. Bar: N.Y. 1966, D.C. 1986. Assoc. Paul, Weiss, Rifkind & Wharton, N.Y.C., 1965-66, 1968-69; asst. counsel N.Y. State Urban Devel. Corp., N.Y.C., 1969-72, assoc. counsel, 1972-75; counsel real estate div. Internat. Paper Co., N.Y.C., 1975-80; ptnr. Stroock & Stroock & Lavan, N.Y.C., 1980-83, sr. ptnr., 1984—; mem. legis. com. Real Estate Bd. N.Y., 1988-92; lectr. Old Dominion Coll., Norfolk, Va., 1967-68, NYU, 1986—; mem. editl. bd. Comml. Leasing Law and Strategy, 1988-95; mem. N.Y.C. bd. advisors Commonwealth Land Title Ins. Co., 1996—. Contbr. articles to profl. jours. Fund raiser corp. com. N.Y. Philharm., N.Y.C., 1980-84; trustee Manhattan Sch. Music, 1989—, treas., 1991-94, chmn., 1994—. Mem. ABA (comml. leasing com. 1987-88, 94—, pub./pvt. devel. com. 1989—, real property sect.), Assn. of Bar of City of N.Y. (housing and urban devel. com. 1977-80, 81-84, real property com. 1989-92), Princeton

Club. Democrat. Presbyterian. Avocations: music, reading, travel. Office: Stroock Stroock & Lavan 180 Maiden Ln New York NY 10038-4925

RAHM, SUSAN BERKMAN, lawyer; b. Pitts., June 25, 1943; d. Allen Hugh and Selma (Wiener) Berkman; m. David Alan Rahm, Nov. 23, 1972; children: Katherine, William. BA with honors, Wellesley Coll., 1965; postgrad., Harvard U., 1966-68; JD, NYU, 1973. Bar: N.Y. 1974, D.C. 1988. Assoc. Marshall, Bratter, Greene, Allison & Tucker, N.Y.C., 1973-81, ptnr., 1981-82; ptnr. Kaye, Scholer, Fierman, Hays & Handler, N.Y.C., 1982—, chair real estate dept., 1993—; N.Y. adv. bd., Chgo. Title Ins. Co., 1995. Editor: New York Real Property Service, 1987. Bd. dirs. Girls Inc., 1989-93; mem. aux. bd. Mt. Sinai Hosp., N.Y.C., 1976-78. Recipient cert. of outstanding svc. D.C. Redevel. Land Agy., 1969, She Knows Where She's Going award Girls' Clubs of Am., 1987. Mem. ABA, Assn. of Bar of City of N.Y., N.Y. Bar Assn. (real property law com., co-chmn. real-estate devel. 1987-91), Am. Coll. Real Estate Lawwyers, Comml. Real Estate Women N.Y. (bd. dirs. 1988-94), v.p. 1988-91, pres. 1991-93). Office: Kaye Scholer Fierman Hays & Handler 425 Park Ave New York NY 10022-3506

RAHMAN, MUHAMMAD ABDUR, mechanical engineer; b. Sylhet, Assam, India, Mar. 1, 1930; came to U.S., 1950; s. Haji Sajjad Ali Khan and Momotaj Khanom. BSME, U. Toledo, 1953, MSME, 1968; PhD in Engring., Calif. Coast U., 1985. Registered profl. engr., Calif. Mech. design engr. various cons. firms, L.A., 1955-61; aerospace engr. Douglas Aircraft Co., Santa Monica, Calif., 1962-63, N.Am. Aviation, Inc., L.A., 1963-64, NASA Manned Spacecraft Ctr., Houston, 1964-70; safety engr. U.S. Dept. Labor, OSHA, Washington, 1975-86; invention researcher Arlington, Va., 1987—; Contbr. articles to profl. jours. Mem. N.Y. Acad. Scis. Democrat. Islam. Achievements include patent for solar energy collector, supersonic MHD generator system; copyrights for hypothesis on unified field theory and creation of the universe, on the mechanism of superconductivity, a note of caution for superconductivity in reference to permeability and permitivity, concentration on suggesting methods to build superconductors and biomedical engineering instrumentation for cancer in particular, others. Home and Office: 1805 Crystal Dr # 1013-s Arlington VA 22202-4402

RAHMAN, RAFIQ UR, oncologist, educator; b. Mirali, Pakistan, Mar. 3, 1957; came to U.S., 1985; s. Rakhman and Bibi (Sana) Gul; m. Shamim Ara Bangash; children: Maryam, Hassan, Haider. BS, MB, U. Peshawar, Pakistan, 1980. Bd. cert. internal medicine, med. oncology; lic. physician Pa., Ala., Ky. House officer in internal medicine Khyber Teaching Hosp.-U. Peshawar, Pakistan, 1980-81, house officer in gen. surgery, 1981, jr. registrar med. ICU, 1983-84; jr. registrar internal medicine Khyber Teaching Hosp., 1981-82; sr. registrar internal medicine Khyber Teaching Hosp.-Lady Reading Hosp. & Postgrad. Inst., Peshawar, 1984-85; Audrey Meyer Mars fellow in med. oncology Roswell Park Cancer Inst., Buffalo, 1985-86; resident in internal medicine SUNY-Buffalo Gen. Hosp.-Erie County Med. Ctr.-VA Med. Ctr., 1986-88; chief resident in internal medicine SUNY-Buffalo-Erie County Med. Ctr., 1988; fellow in hematology and med. oncology SUNY-Buffalo-Roswell Park Cancer Inst., 1989-90; hematologist, med. oncologist Daniel Boone Clinic and Harlan A.R.H., 1991-92; clin. asst. prof. medicine U. Ky., 1991—; attending physician, hematology/med. oncologist Hardin Meml. Hosp., Elizabethtown, 1993—, chief medicine, 1996; tchr. med. students Med. Sch., SUNY; participant CALGB protocol studies Roswell Park Cancer Inst., investigator. Editor English sect. Cenna mag. Cenna; contbr. articles to profl. jours. Mem. Pakistan Med. & Dental Coun., Ky. Med. Assn., Harlan County Med. Soc., Hardin-LaRue County Med. Soc. Avocations: traveling, aeromodeling, swimming, studying political science and history. Home: 400 Briarwood Cir Elizabethtown KY 42701-6915 Office: 1107 Woodland Dr Ste 105 Elizabethtown KY 42701-2789

RAHMAN, YUEH-ERH, biologist; b. Kwangtung, China, June 10, 1928; came to U.S., 1960; d. Khon and Kwei-Phan (Chan) Li; m. Aneesur Rahman, Nov. 3, 1956; 1 dau., Aneesa. B.S., U. Paris, 1950; M.D. magna cum laude, U. Louvain, Belgium, 1956. Clin. and postdoctoral research fellow Louvain U., 1956-60; mem. staff Argonne (Ill.) Nat. Lab., 1960-72, biologist, 1972-81, sr. biologist, 1981-85; prof. pharmaceutics Coll. Pharmacy, U. Minn., Mpls., 1985—, dir. grad. studies, pharmaceutics, 1989-92, head dept. pharmaceutics, 1991-96; vis. scientist State U. Utrecht, Netherlands, 1968-69; adj. prof. No. Ill. U., DeKalb, 1971-85; cons. NIH.; mem. com. of rev. group, div. research grants NIH, 1979-83. Author. Recipient IR-100 award, 1976; grantee Nat. Cancer Inst., Nat. Inst. Arthritis, Metabolic and Digestive Diseases. Fellow Am. Assn. Pharm. Scientists; mem. AAAS, Am. Soc. Cell Biology, N.Y. Acad. Scis., Radiation Rsch. Soc., Assn. for Women in Sci. (1st pres. Chgo. area chpt. 1978-79). Unitarian. Patentee in field. Home: 902 Dartmouth Pl SE Minneapolis MN 55414-3158 Office: Coll Pharmacy U Minn Minneapolis MN 55455

RAHN, ALVIN ALBERT, former banker; b. St. Paul, Apr. 8, 1925; s. Albert and Manda (Lau) R.; m. Helen Lyngen, June 10, 1950; children: Jennifer, Karen, Paul. B.B.A., U. Minn., 1949; postgrad., Stonier Sch. Banking, 1968. C.P.A., Minn. With income tax div. Minn. Dept. Taxation, 1949-61, asst. dir., 1957-61; with 1st Bank System Inc., Mpls., 1961-85; treas. 1st Bank System Inc., 1969-85, chief fin. officer, 1973-74, sr. v.p., 1974-85. Served with USNR, 1943-46. Mem. Am. Inst. C.P.A.s, Minn. Soc. C.P.A.s, Fin. Execs. Inst. Home: 5601 Dewey Hill Rd Minneapolis MN 55439-1919

RAHR, STEWART, health medical products executive; b. 1946. BA, N.Y. Univ., 1968. CEO Kinray, pres., 1978, sole stockholder, 1984. Office: 15235 10th Ave Whitestone NY 11357-1233*

RAIBLE, PETER SPILMAN, minister; b. Peterborough, N.H., Nov. 22, 1929; s. Robert Jules and Mildred (Galt) R.; m. Dee Dee Rainbow, June 18, 1976 (div. 1968); children: Stephen M., Robin S., Robert R., Deborah R.; m. Marcia McClellan Barton, June 5, 1987. PhB, U. Chgo., 1949; BA, U. Calif., Berkeley, 1952; MDiv, Starr King Sch. Ministry, 1953, D in Sacred Theology (hon.), 1974. Ordained to ministry Unitarian Ch. Asst. minister First Unitarian Ch., Providence, 1953-55; minister Unitarian Ch., Lincoln, Nebr., 1955-61, Univ. Unitarian Ch., Seattle, 1961—; bd. pres. Starr King Sch., Berkeley, 1967-68; mem. exec. com. Coun. Chs., Seattle, 1982-88; adj. prof. Meadville Lombard, 1987-88, N.W. Theol. Union, 1989, Seattle U., 1995. Author: How to Case a Church, 1982, Manual for Ordination Installation Services, 1984; book editor: Jour. Liberal Ministry, 1965-71; editor UU Polity Manual, 1992. Bd. dirs. Coun. Planning Affiliates, Seattle, 1969-73, Wash. State chpt. ACLU, Seattle, 1963-67; chmn. ministerial adv. com. Planned Parenthood Ctr., Seattle, 1963-68; pres. UN Assn., Lincoln, 1959-61. Cpl. USAF, 1948-49. Merrill fellow Harvard U., Cambridge, Mass., 1972. Mem. Unitarian Universalist Ministers Assn. (pres. 1973-75), Pacific N.W. Dist. Unitarian Universalist Assn. (exec. 1962-64, pres. 1985-87, mem. commn. on appraisal 1977-81), Unitarian Universalist Ptnr. Ch. Coun. (pres. 1995—). Office: U Unitarian Ch 6556 35th Ave NE Seattle WA 98115-7332

RAICHLE, ELAINE LUCAS, retired art educator; b. Fremont, Nebr., Dec. 14, 1915; d. Arthur Wilson and Lily Kathryn (Christensen) Lucas; m. Donald Roderick Raichle, Dec. 15, 1942; children: Douglas, Donald, Alan, Lynne. BA, Midland Coll., 1939; MA, Columbia U., 1949, EdD, 1955. Cert. fine arts tchr., Nebr. Elem. tchr. Cedar Bluffs (Nebr.) Sch., 1934-35, Garden City (Nebr.) Sch., 1935-36; primary tchr. Fremont Pub. Schs., 1936-39, supr. art, 1939-42; art tchr. Irvington (N.J.) High Sch., 1951-53; supr. art edn. Irvington Pub. Schs., 1953-87; mem. bd. trustees Classroom Renaissance N.J. Dept. Edn., Trenton, 1968-72; founder, trustee N.J. Sch. Arts, Trenton, 1980—; advisor art dept. Kean. Coll. N.J., Union, 1974—. Co-editor: Art Education Issues, 1989, History of Art Educators of New Jersey, 1990, The Year of Crafts, 1994, Art: A Cultural Connection, 1995, Art History: Our Heritage, 1996; contbr. numerous articles to profl. jours. Founder, pres. Irvington Symphony Orch., 1968-87; founder, trustee Irvington Cultural Com., 1968-87; co-founder Arts Adminstrs., N.J., 1968; designer Teen Arts N.J., 1970. Lt. (s.g.) USN, 1942-44. Named Citizen of Yr. Irvington C. of C., 1988; recipient Art awards Gov. N.J., 1989, 91. Fellow N.J. Art Edn. Assn. (disting.); mem. Nat. Art Edn. Assn. (N.J. Art Educator of Yr. 1990, Art Adminstr. eastern divsn. 1991), N.J. Congress Parents and Tchrs. (arts chmn. 1966-74, life), Art Educators N.J. (chmn. speakers com. 1988-95, Disting. Art Educator award 1990), Getty Confs. Art Edn., N.J. Coun. on Edn., Ret. Art Educators N.J. (founder), Nat. Ret. Art Educators (treas. 1991-96), Arts Alliance in Edn., Hands and Minds Inst. Avocations: theater, gardening, bridge, travel. Home: 43 Meadow Lks # 08 Hightstown NJ 08520-3342

RAICHLE, MARCUS EDWARD, radiology, neurology educator; b. Hoquiam, Wash., Mar. 15, 1937; m. Mary Elizabeth Rupert, 1964; children: Marcus Edward, Timothy Stephen, Sarah Elizabeth, Katherine Ann. BS, U. Wash., 1960, MD, 1964. Diplomate Am. Bd. Psychiatry and Neurology. Intern Balt. City Hosps., 1964-65, resident, 1965-66; asst. neurologist N.Y. Hosp. Cornell Med. Ctr., N.Y.C., 1966-68, neurologist, chief resident, 1968-69; clin. instr. dept. medicine divsn. neurosci. U. Tex. Med. Sch., San Antonio, 1969-70; rsch. instr. Washington U. Sch. Med., St. Louis, 1971-72, from asst. prof. neurology to assoc. prof. neurology, 1972-78, from asst. prof. radiology (radiation scis.) to assoc. prof. radiology Edward Mallinckrodt Inst. Radiology, 1972-79, from asst. prof. to assoc. prof. biomedical engring., 1974-79, prof. neurology, 1978—, prof. radiology Edward Mallinckrodt Inst. Radiology, 1979—, prof. biomedical engring., 1979—; instr. dept. neurology Cornell U. Med. Coll., N.Y.C., 1968-69; asst. neurologist Barnes Hosp., St. Louis, 1971-75, assoc. neurologist, 1975-78, neurologist, 1978—; cons. neurologist St. Louis Children's Hosp., 1975—; neurologist Jewish Hosp., St. Louis, 1984—, St. Louis Regional Hosp., 1985—; mem. neurology study sect. A NIH, 1975-79; mem. com. cerebrovascular diseases Nat. Inst. Neurol. Diseases and Stroke, long range planning effort, 1978, basic sci. task force, 1978; mem ad hoc adv. panel, Nat. Inst. Neurol. Diseases and Stroke, 1983, chmn. PET grants spl. rev. com., 1983, chmn. brain imaging ctrs. spl. rev. com., 1985; mem. adv. bd. McDonnell-Pew Program cognitive neuroscience, 1989; other coms. Editorial bds. Stroke, 1974-82, Neurology, 1976-82, Annals of Neurology, 1979-86, Journal Cerebral Blood Flow and Metabolism, 1983-86, dep. chief editor, 1981-83, Brain, 1985-90, Human Neurobiology, 1985-87, Brain Research, 1985-90, Synapse, 1987-90, Journal Neuroscience, 1989—, Journal Cognitive Neuroscience, 1989—, Cerebral Cortex, 1990—, Journal Nuclear Medicine, 1990—, Biological Psychiatry, 1993—, Learning and Memory, 1993—; over 120 pub. papers; contbr. over 75 book chpts., revs. Major USAF, 1969-71. Recipient numerous awards, lectrs., fellows; sr. McDonnell fellow McDonnell Ctr. Studies Higher Brain Function, Washington U., St. Louis, 1982—. Mem. AAAS, Am. Heart Assn. (stroke coun. 1974—, cardiovascular D rsch. study com. 1975-78, Academia Rodinensis Pro Remediatione (acting), Am. Acad. Neurology, Am. Neurological Assn. (councillor 1986-88, nom. com. 1990-91), Am. Physiological Soc., Assn. Rsch. Nervous and Mental Disease, Birmingham Med. Rsch. Expeditionary Soc., Explorers Club (N.Y.), Internat. Soc. Cerebral Blood Flow and Metabolism (sec. 1985-89, pres. elect 1989-91, pres. 1991-93), Inst. Medicine/NAS, Internat. Double Reed Soc., Soc. Neuroscience (pub. rels. com. 1988—), St. Louis Soc. Neurological Scis., Soc. Nuclear Medicine. *

RAIDER, LOUIS, physician, radiologist; b. Chattanooga, Sept. 7, 1913; s. Leaha Reevin; m. Emma Silberstein, Oct. 19, 1940; children: Lynne Dianne, David Bernard, Paula Raider Olichney. BS, Bklyn. Coll., 1935; MD, Dalhousie U., 1941. Diplomate, cert. Am. Bd. Radiology. Intern Met. Hosp., N.Y.C., 1940-41, resident in radiology, 1941-42; resident in radiation therapy Bellevue Hosp., N.Y.C., 1942-43; fellow in cancer therapy NIH, N.Y.C., 1943-44; chief of radiology Vets. Hosp., New Orleans, 1947-50; radiologist, chief radiology Providence Hosp., Mobile, Ala., 1950-76; clin. prof. Med. Sch. U. South Ala., Mobile, 1987—. Contbr. articles to profl. jours. Maj. AUS, 1944-47. Fellow Am. Coll. Radiology, Am. Coll. Chest Physicians; mem. Radiol. Soc. N.Am., Am. Roentgen Ray Soc., AMA, Ala. Acad. Radiology (pres. 1970-71, Silver medal 1989), So. Med. Assn. (chmn. sect. radiology 1973-74), Soc. Thoracic Radiology, So. Radiol. Conf., Am. Soc. Emergency Radiology. Democrat. Jewish. Home: 1801 S Indian Creek Dr Mobile AL 36607-2309 Office: Hosp U South Ala 2451 Fillingim St Mobile AL 36617-2238

RAIJMAN, ISAAC, gastroenterologist, endoscopist, educator; b. Empalme, Sonora, Mex., July 6, 1959; came to U.S., 1985; s. Jose and Amalia (Langsam) R. MD, Nat. Autonomous U., Mexico City, 1985; postgrad., Nat. U. Houston, U. Wis., 1985. Diplomate Am. Bd. Internal Medicine, Am. Bd. Gastroenterology. Resident in medicine Mt. Sinai Hosp., Milw., 1986-88, chief resident, 1989; clin. fellow in therapeutic endoscopy Wellesley Hosp., Toronto, Ont., Can., 1992-93; rsch. fellow in gastroenterology U. Tex., Houston, 1989-90, clin. fellow, 1990-92, asst. prof. medicine, 1993—, dir. therapeutic endoscopy, 1993—, asst. prof. M.D. Anderson Cancer Ctr., 1993—. Author: Pancreas, 1993, Bockus Textbook of Gastroenterology, 1993; also numerous articles. Mem. Am. Coll. Gastroenterology, Am. Gastroenterology Assn., Internat. Assn. Pancreatology, Am. Soc. Gastrointestinal Endoscopy, Am. Soc. Internal Medicine. Avocation: painting. Office: Therap and Diag Gastro Assocs PA 1200 Binz Suite 480 Houston TX 77004

RAIKES, CHARLES FITZGERALD, retired lawyer; b. Mpls., Oct. 6, 1930; s. Arthur FitzGerald and Margaret (Hawthorne) R.; m. Antonia Raikes, Dec. 20, 1969; children: Jennifer Catherine, Victoria Samantha. B.A., Washington U., 1952; M.A., Harvard U., 1955, LL.B., 1958. Bar: N.Y. State 1959. Assoc. White & Case, N.Y.C., 1958-69; assoc. gen. counsel Dun & Bradstreet, Inc., N.Y.C., 1969-72; v.p., gen. counsel Dun & Bradstreet, Inc., 1972-73; v.p., gen. counsel The Dun & Bradstreet Corp., N.Y.C., 1973-76, sr. v.p., gen. counsel, 1976-94, of counsel, 1994-95; ret., 1995; cons. Bd. Govs. Fed. Reserve System, 1958-95. Served with U.S. Army, 1952-54. Woodrow Wilson fellow, 1952. Mem. Assn. Bar City of N.Y., Harvard Club, Sky Club, Phi Beta Kappa. Home: 26 Crooked Trl Rowayton CT 06853-1106

RAIKLEN, HAROLD, aerospace engineering consultant; b. Boston, June 7, 1920; s. Michael Isaac and Jennie Zelda (Jaffee) R.; m. Shirley Gesetz, Nov. 24, 1954; children: David R., Margery Claire. B, MIT, 1947, M, 1949. Dir. electronics and electrics Rockwell, El Segundo, Calif.; v.p. program mgr. Saturn II Rockwell, Downey and Seal Beach, Calif., 1965-70; v.p. rsch. and engring. Rockwell, Downey, Calif., 1970-72; v.p. B-1 bomber engring. Rockwell, El Segundo, Calif., 1972-80, v.p. strategic aircraft, 1980-82; amateur anthropoligist, Long Beach, Calif., 1982—. Contbr. articles to profl. jours.; co-patentee in anti-skid sys. Co-recipient Collier trophy USAF, 1976, Pub. Svc. award NASA, 1969. Fellow AIAA (assoc., Aircraft Design award 1979); mem. IEEE (life), Old Crows Assn., China Burma India Veterans Assn., Pi Tau Sigma, Tau Beta Pi, Phi Kappa Phi. Home and Office: 4300 Cerritos Ave Long Beach CA 90807-2462

RAILTON, WILLIAM SCOTT, lawyer; b. Newark, July 30, 1935; s. William Scott and Carolyn Elizabeth (Guiberson) R.; m. Karen Elizabeth Walsh, Mar. 31, 1979; 1 son, William August; children by previous marriage: William Scott, Anne Greenwood. BSEE, U. Wash., 1962; JD with honors, George Washington U., 1965. Bar: D.C. 1966, Md. 1966, Va. 1993, U.S. Patent Office 1966. Assoc., then ptnr. Kemon, Palmer & Estabrook, Washington, 1966-70; sr. trial atty. Dept. Labor, Washington, 1970-71, asst. counsel for trial litigation, 1971-72; chief counsel U.S. Occupational Safety and Health Rev. Commn., Washington, 1972-77; acting gen. counsel U.S. Occupational Safety and Health Rev. Commn., 1975-77; ptnr. Reed, Smith, Shaw & McClay, Pitts., 1977—; lectr. George Washington U. Law Sch., 1977-79, seminar chmn. Occupational Safety and Health Act, Govt. Inst., 1979-96; lectr. Practicing Law Inst., 1976-79. Author: (legal handbooks) The Examination System and the Backlog, 1965, The OSHA General Duty Clause, 1977, The OSHA Health Standards, 1977; OSHA Compliance Handbook, 1992; contbg. author: Occupational Safety and Health Law, 1988, 93. Regional chmn. Montgomery County (Md.) Republican party, 1968-70; pres. Montgomery Sq. Citizens Assn., 1970-71; bd. dirs., pres. Foxvale Farms Homeowners Assn., 1979-82; pres. Orchards on the Potomac Homeowners Assn., 1990-92; dir. Great Falls Hist. Soc., 1991-94; scoutmaster Troop 55 Boy Scouts Am., 1993—. With USMC, 1953-58. Recipient Meritorious Achievement medal Dept. Labor, 1972, Outstanding Service award OSHA Rev. Commn., 1977. Mem. ABA (mgmt. co-chmn. occupational safety and health law com. 1995—), Md. Bar Assn., Va. Bar Assn., Bar Assn. D.C. (vice chmn. young lawyers sect. 1971), Order of Coif, Sigma Phi Epsilon, Phi Delta Phi. Home: 10102 Walker Lake Dr Great Falls VA 22066-3502 also: East Tower 1301 K St NW #1100 Washington DC 20005 *Lawsuits are won by pre-trial preparation. A litigator should be candid with his clients and honest in his dealings with associates, opponents and the courts; an attorney should also volunteer his service to the community of which he is a part.*

RAIMI, BURTON LOUIS, lawyer; b. Detroit, May 5, 1938; s. Irving and Rae (Abel) R.; m. Judith Morse, Mar. 31, 1963 (div. Mar. 1985); children: Diane L., and Matthew D. BA, Brandeis U., 1960; JD with honors, U. Mich., 1963; LLM, George Washington U., 1964. Bar: Mich. 1963, D.C. 1964, Fla. 1991; U.S. Ct. Appeals (4th, 7th, 8th, 9th, 10th and D.C. cirs.). Atty. NLRB, Washington, 1964-69; assoc. Morgan, Lewis & Bockius, Washington, 1969-71; dep. gen. counsel FDIC, Washington, 1971-78; ptnr. Rosenman and Colin, Washington, 1978-86, Dechert Price & Rhoads, Washington, 1986-93; shareholder McCaffrey & Raimi, P.A., Naples and Sarasota, Fla., 1994—; speaker various insts. Mem. ABA (chmn. bank receiverships subcom. of banking com.), D.C. Bar Assn. (past chmn. banking law com., com. on interest on lawyers trust accounts), Fla. Bar. Avocations: sailing, travel, golf, fishing. Home: 4452 Staghorn Ln Sarasota FL 34238-5626 Office: McCaffrey & Raimi PA 1800 2nd St Ste 753 Sarasota FL 34236-5900

RAIMI, SAMUEL M., film director; b. Royal Oak, Mich., Oct. 23, 1959; s. Leonard Ronald and Celia Barbara (Abrams) R. Student in humanities study, Mich. State U., East Lansing, 1977-79. V.p. Renaissance Pictures, Ferndale, Mich., 1979—. Writer, dir. (films) Evil Dead, 1981, Crimewave, 1985 (Best Dir. award 1986), Evil Dead II, 1986, Darkman, 1990, Army of Darkness: Evil Dead 3, 1993; co-writer: (screenplay) The Hudsucker Proxy, 1994; prodr. Hard Target, 1993, Timecop, 1994; dir. (film) The Quick and the Dead, 1995; appeared in films Spies Like Us, 1985, Thou Shall Not Kill...Except, 1987, Maniac Cop, 1988, Miller's Crossing, 1990, Innocent Blood, 1992, Intruder, 1994, Terminal Force, 1995; appeared on TV Journey to the Center of the Earth, 1993, Body Bags, 1993, The Stand, 1994; prodr., writer Mantis, 1993; exec. prodr. syndicated TV series The Legendary Journeys of Hercules, 1994-97, Xena: Warrior Princess, 1995-97, (series) American Gothic, 1995-96, Spy Game, 1997—. Recipient Best Horror Film, Knokke'heist Film Festival Belgium, 1982, Best Horror Film and Best Spl. Effects, Sitges Film Festival, Spain, 1982, 1st Prize of the Critics, 1st Prize of the Pub., Paris Festival Sci. Fiction, Fantasy and Horror, 1983, Best Horror Film of Yr., Fangoria Mag., 1983. Mem. Mich. State U. Soc. for Creative Film Making (founder, pres. 1978, 79), Calif. Rare Fruit Growers. Office: ICM 8942 Wilshire Blvd Beverly Hills CA 90211-1934

RAIMO, BERNARD, JR. (BERNIE RAIMO), lawyer; b. Kansas City, Mo., May 29, 1944; m. Sharon Marie Brady, Aug. 23, 1974; children: Sarah Elizabeth, Peter Bernard. BA, U. Notre Dame, 1965, MA, U. Md., 1967; JD with honors, George Washington U., 1972. Bar: D.C. Staff asst. to Sen. Stuart Symington Mo., 1968-72; asst. corp. counsel Washington, 1972-76; legis. analyst Am. Petroleum Inst., 1976-78; counsel Permanent Select Com. Intelligence U.S. Ho. Reps., Washington, 1978-91, chief counsel Ho. Com. Standards of Official Conduct, 1991-95; minority counsel Ho. Com. Standards of Official Conduct, 1995-97; counsel to Dem. leader U.S. Ho. of Reps., 1997—. Office: Office of the Dem Leader H-204 The Capitol Washington DC 20515

RAIMONDI, ALBERT ANTHONY, mechanical engineer; b. Plymouth, Mass., Mar. 29, 1925; s. William and Amelia (Taddia) R. B.S., Tufts U., 1945; M.S., U. Pitts., 1963, Ph.D. in Mech. Engring, 1968. Rsch. engr. Westinghouse Rsch. Labs., Pitts., 1945-68; mgr. lubrication mechanics Westinghouse Rsch. Labs., 1968-85, mgr. tribology and exptl. mechanics, 1978-90, cons. engr. mechanics and tribology dept., 1990—. Contbr.: Am. Soc. Lubrication Engr. Handbook, 1968, 84; editor: jours. Am. Soc. Lubrication Engrs, 1971-76; assoc. editor: Trans. Am. Soc. Lubrication Engrs., 1960-71; Contbr. articles to profl. jours. Fellow Soc. for Tribologists and Lubrication Engrs. (Hunt award 1959, nat. award 1968, Westinghouse Maj. Innovation award 1990). Home: 125 8th St Turtle Creek PA 15145-1805 Office: Westinghouse Sci & Tech Ctr 1310 Beulah Rd Pittsburgh PA 15235-5068

RAIMONDI, RUGGERO, opera singer; b. Bologna, Italy, Oct. 3, 1941; m. Isabel Maier, 1987. Studies with, Teresa Pediconi, Rome, Armando Piervenanzi. Debut in La Boheme, Spoleto, Italy, 1964; singer in major houses, Europe and U.S.; Met. debut in Ernani, N.Y.C., 1970; favorite roles include Don Giovanni, Philip II, Boris and Don Quichotte; recorded Verdi Requiem, Vespri Siciliani, La Boheme, Aida, Attila, Don Carlos, Macbeth, Simon Boccanegra, Don Giovanni, Boris Godunov, Tosca, Turandot, Barbiere di Siviglia, Mosè, Nozze di Figaro, Italiana in Algieri, Cenerentola, Il Viaggio A Reims; appeared in films Don Giovanni (Joseph Losey), 1978, Six Characters in Search of a Singer (Maurice Bejart), 1983, Carmen (Francesco Rosi), 1986, others; opera prodn. since, 1986—. Decorated Officier des Arts et Lettres, Chevalier de l'Ordre de Malte, Grand Ufficiale della Repubblica Italiana, Citizen of Honor, City of Athens, Greece. Office: 140 bis rue Lecourbe, F-75015 Paris France

RAIMONDO, LOUIS JOHN, psychiatrist; b. N.Y.C., Jan. 9, 1959; s. Louis John and Josephine Anne (Christiano) R. BS, Fordham U., 1981; MD, SUNY at Buffalo, 1985. Diplomate Nat. Bd. Med. Examiners. Resident psychiatry N.Y. Med. Coll. Consortium at Westchester, Valhalla, N.Y., 1985-89; staff psychiatrist Danbury (Conn.) Hosp., 1987-89, Westch County Crisis Intervention Svcs., Valhalla, 1989-90; clin. asst. prof. psychiatry N.Y. Med. Coll., Valhalla, 1990—; med. staff Columbia Med. Ctr., Halifax Med. Ctr., Meml. Hosp., Daytona Beach, Fla., 1989—, Atlantic Shores Hosp., 1990-94; chief of staff Atlantic Shores Hosp., Ormond Beach, Fla., 1993-94; psychiat. med. dir. Columbia Home Health Care, Ormond Beach, Fla., 1994—; med. dir. partial hospitalization programs Quality Life Ctr., Daytona Beach/West Volusia, 1994—; med. dir. Columbia Behavioral Health Unit, 1996—; speaker and cons. in field. Recipient Clin. Excellence in Psychiatry award Sandoz Corp., 1989. Mem. AMA, Am. Psychiat. Assn. (conv. presenter), Fla. Med. Assn., Volusia County Med. Soc., Am. Acad. Forensic Examiners (bd. cert.), Fla. Psychiat. Soc., Phi Beta Kappa. Home: 103 Sand Dunes Dr Ormond Beach FL 32176-2183 Office: East Coast Ctr Psychiatry 595 W Granada Blvd Ste 2E Ormond Beach FL 32174-5190

RAINA, RAJESH, computer engineer; b. New Delhi, Oct. 17, 1963; came to U.S., 1984; s. Niranjan Nath and Durga Raina; m. Karuna Sazawal, Mar. 6, 1993; 1 child, Aiyesha. BTech in Electronics/Elec. Comm. Engring, Indian Inst. Tech., Kharagpur, 1984; MSEE, Mich. Tech. U., 1986; PhDEE, Duke U., 1991. Sr. engr. Digital Equipment Corp., Hudson, Mass., 1991-94; prin. staff engr., project leader, scientist Somerset Design Ctr.-Motorola Inc., Austin, Tex., 1994—; session chair, moderator, panelist Design Automation Conf., 1996, Internat. Conf. on Computer Design, 1996, Motorola 10x Cycle-Time Reduction Conf., 1996, Internat. High-Level Design Validation and Test Workshop, 1996, 97. Referee, reviewer Internat. Test Conf., 1991—, IEEE Transactions on Cirs. and Systems, 1991—, Design Automation Conf., 1996—; contbr. articles to profl. jours. including Internat. Jour. of Computer and Elec. Engring., 1987, Internat. Test Conf., 1989, Internat. Symposium on Fault-Tolerant Computing, 1991, Design Automation Conf., 1996, Design SuperCon, 1997. Tchr. Durham Edn. Vols., Duke U., Durham, N.C., 1986-87; mem. Habitat for Humanity, Hudson, 1991. Summer rsch. fellowship Duke U., 1987, 89, Grad. sch. conf. travel fellowship, 1989. Mem. Sigma Xi. Achievements include development of prototype of programmable fault-tolerant clock receiver, VLSI chip; use of non-linear feedback shift registeres in signature analysis; method and apparatus for improved testability of scan-based circuits; design verification and testability of very high speed microprocessors. Office: Motorola Inc Somerset Design Ctr Mail Drop 0E70 6200 Bridgepoint Pkwy # 4 Austin TX 78730

RAINBOLT, JOHN VERNON, II, lawyer; b. Cordell, Okla., May 24, 1939; s. John Vernon (Mike) and Mary Alice (Power) R.; m. Janice Glaub, Oct. 2, 1976; children—John Vernon, III, Sara McLain, Charles Joseph. B.A., Okla. U., 1961, LL.B., 1964; postgrad. George Washington U. 1971-73. Bar: Okla. 1964, D.C. 1971, U.S. Supreme Ct. 1971. Legis. counsel, adminstrv. asst. U.S. Rep. Graham Purcell, Washington, 1967-72; counsel agr. com. U.S. Ho. of Reps., Washington, 1972-74, chief counsel, 1975; commr. Commodity Futures Trading Commn., Washington, 1975-78; sole practice, Washington, 1978—; ptnr. Miles & Stockbridge, Washington, 1982-86; advisor agr. policy Tokyo Roundtable White House, 1978-81; mem. Adminstrn. Conf., U.S., 1976-79; mem. CFTC Adv. Com. on Regulatory Coord. Author and draftsman Commodity Futures Trading Commn. Act, 1974; contbr. articles to legal jours. Served to 1st lt. Inf., U.S. Army, 1964-67. Vice chmn. Commodity Futures Trading Commn., 1975-78. Mem. ABA (chmn. subcom. on fgn. markets and traders 1982-85, chmn. subcom. internat. issues 1996-97), U.S. Futures Industry Assn. (assoc., internat. com.,

Japan chpt.), Vietnam Vets. Amputation. Clubs: Commodity of Washington. Office: Rainbow Law Office 1200 G St NW Ste 800 Washington DC 20005-3814

RAINER, JAMES W., JR., bank executive; b. 1943; married. BA, Auburn U., 1965. Exec. v.p. South Trust Corp., 1965—. 1st lt. USAF. Office: SouthTrust Corp 112 N 20th St PO Box 2554 Birmingham AL 35290 also: 420 N 20th St PO Box 2554 Birmingham AL 35290

RAINER, JOHN DAVID, psychiatrist, educator; b. N.Y.C., July 13, 1921; s. Louis W. and Daisy (Harris) Rosen; m. Barbara Antin, Dec. 23, 1944; children: Jeff, Peter. AB, Columbia Coll., N.Y.C., 1941; MA, Columbia U., 1944, MD, 1951; DLitt (hon.), Gallaudet U., 1968. Rotating intern Mt. Sinai Hosp., N.Y.C., 1951-52; resident psychiatry N.Y. State Psychiat. Inst., N.Y.C., 1952-55; rsch. assoc. in psychiatry Columbia U., N.Y.C., 1956-59; asst. clin. prof. psychiatry Columbia U., 1959-67; chief psychiat. rsch. (genetics) N.Y. State Psychiat. Inst., N.Y.C., 1965-91; assoc. clin. prof. psychiatry Columbia U., N.Y.C., 1967-70; assoc. prof. clin. psychiatry Columbia U., 1970-72, prof. clin. psychiatry, 1972—; tng. and supervising analyst Columbia Psychoanalytic Ctr., N.Y.C., 1972—; attending psychiatrist Presbyterian Hosp., N.Y.C., 1972—. Editorial bd. mem. Am. Annals of the Deaf, Neuropsychobiology, Jour. Preventive Psychiatry; contbr. over 150 articles to profl. jours. Pres. Lake Isle Civic Assn., Eastchester, N.Y., 1989-91. With U.S. Army, 1945-46. Recipient Samuelson award N.Y. League for Hard of Hearing, 1974. Fellow Am. Psychiat. Assn. (life), Am. Psychoanalytic Assn. (life), Am. Coll. Psychoanalysts; mem. Am. Soc. Human Genetics, Am. Psychopathol. Assn. (life), Eastern Psychiat. Rsch. Assn. (pres. 1971-73), Westchester Psychoanalytic Soc. (pres. 1975-76), Phi Beta Kappa, Alpha Omega Alpha. Achievements include establishment of first psychiatric program for deaf people. Home: 9 Innisfree Pl Eastchester NY 10707-1207 Office: NY State Psychiat Inst 722 W 168th St New York NY 10032-2603

RAINER, REX KELLY, civil engineer, educator; b. Montgomery, Ala., July 17, 1924; s. Kelly Kenyon and Pearl (Jones) R.; m. Betty Ann Page, Aug. 28, 1945; children: Rex Kelly, John Kenyon. B.S., Auburn (Ala.) U., 1944, M.S., 1946; Ph.D., Okla. State U., 1967. Asst. engr. L. & N. R.R. Co., Cin., 1944-45; design engr. Polglaze & Basenberg, Birmingham, Ala., 1945-51; pres., chmn. Rainer Co., Inc., Orlando, Fla., 1951-62; prof. civil engring. Auburn U., 1962-67, head civil engring. dept., 1967; exec. v.p., 1980; hwy. dir. State of Ala., 1979-80, fin. dir., 1981-82; spl. asst. to gov. of Ala., 1981-82; dir. Office for Advancement Devel. Industry U. Ala., Birmingham, 1982-86; pres., cons. engr. Rex K. Rainer, Inc., 1982—; cons. to ins. cos., constrn. engring. firms; mem. Ala. Bd. Registration Profl. Engrs. and Land Surveyors, 1977-89. Contbr. articles to profl. jours. Mem. Municipal Planning Bd., 1963-65, Indsl. Park Devel. Bd., 1969-71, So. Regional Edn. Bd., 1982-86. Served with AUS, 1943. Fellow ASCE (sec., treas. 1970, pres. Ala. chpt. 1976-77, chmn. Constrn. Rsch. Coun., chmn. hwy. div. publs. com.; Civil Govt. award 1981); mem. Assn. Gen. Contractors Am. (bd. dirs. 1955), Am. Soc. for Engring. Edn. (chmn. constrn. engring. com.), Am. Pub. Works Assn., Phi Kappa Phi, Tau Beta Pi, Chi Epsilon. Home: 901 Ogletree Rd Auburn AL 36830-7207

RAINER, WILLIAM GERALD, cardiac surgeon; b. Gordo, Ala., Nov. 13, 1927; s. Jamie Flournoy and Lula (Davis) R.; m. Lois Sayre, Oct. 7, 1950; children: Vickie, Bill, Julia, Leslie. Student, Emory U., Atlanta, Ga., 1943-44, U. Ala., 1944-45; MD, U. Tenn., Memphis, 1948; MS in Surgery, U. Colo., Denver, 1958. Diplomate Am. Bd. Surgery, Am. Bd. Thoracic Surgery. Intern Wesley Hosp., Chgo., 1949; gen. practice medicine Blue Island, Ill., 1950-52; resident Denver VA Hosp., 1954-59; practice medicine specializing in cardiac surgery Denver, 1960—; bd. dirs. St. Joseph Hosp. Found., Denver. Contbr. articles to profl. jours. Lt. U.S. Army, 1952-54. Decorated Bronze Star; recipient Disting. Alumnus award U. Tenn. Health Sci. Ctr., 1992. Mem. Soc. Thoracic Surgeons (sec. 1980-85, pres. 1989), Colo. Med. Soc. (pres. 1984-85), Denver Med. Soc. (pres. 1984), Am. Coll. Chest Physicians (pres. 1984), Am. Bd. Thoracic Surgeons (bd. dirs. 1982-88), Am. Surg. Assn., Am. Assn. Thoracic Surgery, Societé Internationale de Chirugie, Denver Athletic Club. Avocations: photography, traveling. Office: 2005 Franklin St Ste 380 Denver CO 80205-5404

RAINES, CHARLOTTE AUSTINE BUTLER, artist, poet; b. Sullivan, Ill., July 1, 1922; d. Donald Malone and Charlotte (Wimp) Butler; m. Irving Isaack Raines, Sept. 26, 1941; children: Robin Raines Collison, Kerry Raines Lydon. BA in Studio Arts magna cum laude, U. Md., 1966. One-woman show at Castle Theatre, 1988, C.T.V. Awards Hall, Md., 1993; exhbd. in numerous group shows including Corcoran Gallery, 1980, Md.'s Best Exhbn., 1986, Md. State House, 1990, four-artist video documentary, 1992, U. Md. Univ.-Coll. Gallery, 1996; artist publ. cover Writers' Ctr., 1997; represented in various pvt. collections and permanent collection at U. Md. Univ.-Coll.; selected works in U.S. Dept. State Arts in Embassies Program; contbr. poems to lit. publs. Mem. Artists Equity Assn., Writers' Ctr., Phi Kappa Phi. Avocations: piano, jogging, gardening. Studio: 4103 Longfellow St Hyattsville MD 20781-1748

RAINES, FRANKLIN DELANO, investment banker; b. Seattle, Jan. 14, 1949; s. Delno Thomas and Ida Mae (Fortson R.; m. Wendy Farrow, Sept. 11, 1982; children: Laura Farrow, Andrea Landon. BA magna cum laude, Harvard U., 1971, JD cum laude, 1976; postgrad., Oxford U., 1971-73. Assoc. dir. Seattle Model Cities Program, 1972-73; assoc. Preston, Thorgrimson, Ellis, Holman & Fletcher, Seattle, 1976-77; asst. dir. White House Domestic Policy Staff, Washington, 1977-78; assoc. dir. U.S. Office of Mgmt. and Budget, Washington, 1978-79; v.p. Lazard, Freres & Co., N.Y.C., 1979-82, sr. v.p., 1983-84, gen. ptnr., 1985-90; ltd. ptnr., 1990-91; vice chmn. Fed. Nat. Mortgage Assn., Washington, 1991-96; dir. Office Mgmt. and Budget, 1996—. Mem. bd. overseers Harvard U.; trustee U. Puget Sound, German Marshall Fund of U.S., French-Am. Found., Am. Mus. Natural History, Mitre Corp.; mem. Nat. Adv. Coun. Edn. Disadvantaged Children, N.Y.C. Commn. on Early Childhood Edn., White House Confs. on Children and Youth, N.Y. Gov.'s Task Force on Poverty and Welfare Reform, Commn. on Behavioral and Social Scis.; bd. dirs. Ctr. Law and Social Policy, Am. Inst. Rsch., Washington, Black Student Fund, Washington, Nat. Inst. Dispute Resolution. Rhodes scholar, 1971. Mem. AAAS, Coun. Fgn. Rels., Nat. Acad. Social Ins., Washington State Bar Assn., D.C. Bar Assn. Avocations: running, tennis. Office: Office Mgmt and Budget Old Exec Office Bldg Washington DC 20016-2806*

RAINES, HOWELL HIRAM, newspaper editor, journalist; b. Birmingham, Ala., Feb. 5, 1943; s. W.S. and Bertha Estelle (Walker) R.; m. Laure Susan Woodley, Mar. 22, 1969 (div.); children: Ben Hayes, Jeffrey Howell. BA, Birmingham So. Coll., 1964; MA, U. Ala., 1973. Reporter Birmingham Post-Herald, 1964-65, Sta. WBRC-TV, Birmingham, 1965-67, Tuscaloosa (Ala.) News, 1968-69, Birmingham News, 1970-71; polit. editor Atlanta Constitution, 1971-74, St. Petersburg (Fla.) Times, 1976-78; Atlanta bur. chief N.Y. Times, 1978-80, White Ho. corr., 1980-82, nat. polit. corr., 1982-84, dep. Washington editor, 1985-86, London bur. chief, 1987-88, Washington editor, 1988-92; editl. page editor N.Y. Times, N.Y.C., 1993—. Author: Whiskey Man, 1977, My Soul is Rested, 1977, Fly Fishing Through the Midlife Crisis, 1993. Recipient Pulitzer Prize for feature writing, 1992. Office: NY Times 229 W 43rd St New York NY 10036-3913

RAINES, JEFF, biomedical scientist, medical research director; b. N.Y.C., Sept. 5, 1943; s. Otis J. and Mildred C. (Wetzler) R.; BSME, Clemson U., 1965; MME, U. Fla., 1967; MD Harvard U., 1968; PhD in Biomed. Engring. (NIH fellow), MIT, 1972; children: Gretchen Christena, Victoria Jean. Mem. staff MIT, Cambridge, 1968-70; biophysicist dept. surgery Mass. Gen. Hosp., Boston, 1972-77, dir. Vascular Lab., 1972-77; instr. surgery Harvard Med. Sch., Boston, 1973-77; preceptor Harvard/MIT Sch. Health Scis., 1976-77; rsch. dir., dir. Vascular Lab., Miami (Fla.) Heart Inst., Miami Beach, 1977-88; adj. prof. bioengring. U. Miami, Coral Gables, 1977—; prof. surgery U. Miami (Fla.) Sch. Medicine, 1977—, prin. investigator series NIH programs and pharm. firms, 1977—; Harvard Travelling fellow lectr. in Europe, 1975. Recipient Apollo Achievement award NASA, 1969. Fellow Am. Coll. Cardiology, Am. Coll. of Radiology, Am. Assn. of Physicists in Medicine; mem. Biomed. Engring. Soc., Instrument Soc. Am., Am. Heart Assn., Internat. Cardiovasc. Soc., Cardiovasc. Sys. Dynamics Soc. (founding mem., editor 1976—, pres. 1980-82), New England Cardiovasc. Soc., AAAS, ASME, Kiwanis, Sigma Xi, Tau Beta Pi. Republican. Presbyterian. Clubs: La Gorce Country, Harvard, MIT. Contbr. numerous articles on biomechanics, cardiovasc. diagnosis, dynamics and instrumentation to sci. jours.; patentee med. devices; developer math. models of arterial hemodynamics and clin. use of autotransfusion. Home: 6820 Granada Blvd Coral Gables FL 33146 Office: Univ Miami Dept Surgery R-310 1611 NW 12th Ave Miami FL 33136-1005

RAINES, TIMOTHY, professional baseball player; b. Sanford, Fla., Sept. 16, 1959; m. Virginia Raines; children: Tim Jr., André Darrell. Baseball player Montreal Expos, 1977-90, Chgo. White Sox, 1990-95, N.Y. Yankees, 1996—; mem. Nat. League All-Star Team, 1981-87. Recipient Silver Slugger award 1986, Sporting News Gold Shoe award, 1984; named Minor League Player of the Yr. The Sporting News, 1980, Nat. League Batting Champion, 1986; named to Sporting News Nat. League Rookie of Yr., 1981, Sporting News All-Star Team, 1983, 86, Nat. League Stolen Base Leader, 1981-84, N.L. All-Star Game, 1981-87 (named MVP 1987). Office: N.Y. Yankees E 161st St and River Ave Bronx NY 10451*

RAINESS, ALAN EDWARD, psychiatrist; b. N.Y.C., Sept. 24, 1935; s. George W. and Ida Rainess; m. Alice Maree Haber, June 5, 1968; children: Alice Jeanne Rainess Kules, James Alan (dec.). AB, Columbia Coll., 1957; MD, U. Paris, 1965. Diplomate Am. Bd. Psychiatry and Neurology. Intern Meadowbrook Hosp., East Meadow, L.I., 1965-66; resident in psychiatry N.Y. VA Hosp., N.Y.C., 1966-67; teaching fellow in psychiatry Harvard Med. Sch., Boston, 1967; chief resident in psychiatry Boston City Hosp., 1967; resident in psychiatry Walter Reed Med. Ctr., Washington, 1970-72; clin. dir. St. Elizabeth's Hosp., Washington, 1973-76; asst. chief psychiatry Andrews AFB Hosp., Camp Springs, Md., 1976-80, chief neurology, 1989-91; resident in neurology Wilford Hall USAF Med. Ctr., San Antonio, 1980-83; chief medicine and neuropsychiatry Air Univ. Hosp., Maxwell AFB, Ala., 1983-89, chief neurology, 1991-94; psychiatrist Manhattan Psychiat. Ctr., N.Y.C., 1994—; asst. clin. prof. psychiatry Georgetown U. Med. Sch., Washington, 1974-79, NYU Sch. Medicine, 1997—; assoc. prof. neurology and asst. prof. psychiatry Uniformed Svcs. U. Health Scis., Bethesda, Md., 1989-94. Maj. U.S. Army, 1968-73, col. USAF, 1976-94, ret. Fellow Am. Psychiat. Assn.; mem. Am. Soc. Psychoanalytic Physicians (pres. N.Y. chpt. 1996), Masons. Home: 345 E 93rd St Apt 22H New York NY 10128-5522 Office: Manhattan Psychiat Ctr New York NY 10035

RAINEY, CLAUDE GLADWIN, retired health care executive; b. Enloe, Tex., Apr. 21, 1923; s. Claude C. and Pauline (Whitlock) R.; m. Peggy Ballard, July 27, 1947; children—Kathy Suzanne, David Claude, Mark Jeffery, Joel Allen, Peggy Jan, Susan Elise. Student pub. health and adminstrv. medicine, Columbia U., 1961-62. Med. adminstrv., officer dept. medicine and surgery VA, Temple, Tex., 1946-51; med. adminstrv., officer dept. medicine and surgery VA, Muskogee, Okla., 1951-56; med. adminstr. Fite Clinic, Lakeland Med. Ctr., Muskogee, Okla., 1956-59; hosp. adminstr. M.-K.-T. R.R. Employees Hosp. Assn., Denison, Tex., 1959-62, also sec., treas. trustee; hosp. adminstr., cons. Denison Hosp. Authority, Meml. Hosp., 1962-66; adminstr. Seton Hosp., Austin, Tex., 1966-74; exec. v.p. Fort Worth Osteo. Hosp., 1974-83; pres. Health Care of Tex., Inc., Fort Worth, 1983-88, ret. Pres. North Grayson County chpt. Am. Cancer Soc., 1960-66, bd. dirs., Tex., 1961—. Served with USNR, 1942-46. Fellow Am. Coll. Hosp. Adminstrs., Am. Coll. Osteo. Hosp. Adminstrs. (award of merit 1984); mem. Am. Hosp. Assn., Tex. Hosp. Assn., Am. Osteo. Hosp. Assn. (Disting. Service award 1985).

RAINEY, GORDON FRYER, JR., lawyer; b. Oklahoma City, Apr. 26, 1940; s. Gordon F. and Esther (Bliss) R.; m. Selina Norman, Aug. 3, 1968; children—Kate, Melissa, Gordon III. B.A. in English, U. Va., 1962, LL.B., 1967. Bar: Okla. 1967, Va. 1968. Assoc. Rainey, Flynn, Wallace, Ross & Cooper, Oklahoma City, 1967-68; assoc. Hunton & Williams, Richmond, Va., 1968-75, ptnr., 1975—; chmn. of exec. com. Hunton & Williams; bd. dirs. Bon Secours Richmond Health Sys., Inc.; dir. Crestar Fin. Corp., Crestar Bank, Weidmuller North Am., Inc., Health Corp. of Va., Meml. Regional Med. Ctr., Inc.; bd. mgrs. U. Va. Alumni Assn.; trustee Ch. Schs. Diocese Va., Colonial Williamsburg Found., Va. Found. Ind. Colls.; campaign chmn. United Way of Greater Richmond, 1982, trustee, 1981-84; bd. dirs., past pres. Sheltering Arms Hosp., 1984; trustee Sheltering Arms Found.; chmn. Gov.'s Econ. Devel. Adv. Coun. Dist. 12; mem. Gov.'s Blue Ribbon Strike Force Commn. on Govtl. Reform, Bd. Housing & Cmty. Devel.; past mem. bd. govs. St. Catherine's Sch.; past chmn. bd. dirs. Leadership Met. Richmond; mem. Mayor's Emergency Shelter Task Force, 1981; past pres., bd. dirs. Met. Bus. Found. Served to 1st lt. U.S. Army, 1962-64, Korea. Recipient Communication and Leadership award Toastmasters Internat., 1983. Mem. ABA (sect. on bus. law, banking law com., mem. com. on devel. in investment services), Richmond Metro C. of C. (bd. dirs., past chmn.). Republican. Episcopalian. Clubs: Forum (Richmond, Va.). Office: Hunton & Williams Riverfront Plz East Tower 951 E Byrd St Richmond VA 23219-4040

RAINEY, JEAN OSGOOD, public relations executive; b. Lansing, Mich., Apr. 5, 1925; d. Earle Victor and Blanche Mae (Eberly) Osgood; m. John Larimer Rainey, Nov. 29, 1957 (dec. Oct. 1991); children: Cynthia, John Larimer, Ruth. Grad., Lansing Bus. U., 1942. Pub. rels. dir. Nat. Assn. Food Chains, Washington, 1954-59; v.p. pub. rels. Manchester Orgns., Washington, 1959-61; ptnr. Rainey, McEnroe & Manning, Washington, 1962-73; v.p. Manning, Selvage & Lee, Washington, 1973-79, pres. Washington div., 1979-84, sr. counsellor, 1985—; owner Jean Rainey Assocs., Washington, 1986-87; sr. v.p. Daniel J. Edelman Inc., 1987-96; owner Jean Rainey Assocs., Washington, 1996—; bd. chmn. Windward Mortgage, 1997—. Author: How to Shop for Food, 1972. Pres. Hyde Home and Sch. Assn., Washington, 1969-71; co-chmn. Nat. Com. for Reelection of the Pres., 1972; chmn. bd. trustees St. John's Presch., 1996—; pres. Sherwood Forest Endowment Fund, 1995—. Mem. Pub. Rels. Soc. Am. (accredited), Am. Women in Radio and TV (pres. Washington chpt. 1962-63, mem. nat. bd. 1963-65), Am. News Women's Club (pres. 1973-75). Republican. Episcopalian. Club: City Tavern. Home: Apt 250B 4000 Cathedral Ave NW Washington DC 20016-5249 Office: PO Box 251 Main Lobby W 4000 Cathedral Ave NW Washington DC 20016

RAINEY, JOHN DAVID, federal judge; b. Freeport, Tex., Feb. 10, 1945; s. Frank Anson and Jewel Lorene (Hortman) R.; m. Judy Davis, Aug. 17, 1968; children, John David Jr., Jacob Matthew, Craig Thomas. BBA, So. Meth. U., 1967, JD, 1972. Bar: Tex. 1972, U.S. Dist. Ct. (no. dist.) Tex. 1974, U.S. Tax Ct. 1974, U.S. Ct. Appeals (5th cir.) 1981, U.S. Supreme Ct. 1981, U.S. Dist. Ct. (so. dist.) Tex. 1986. Assoc. Taylor, Mizell, Price, Corrigan & Smith, Dallas, 1973-79; ptnr. Gilbert, Gilbert & Rainey, Angleton, Tex., 1979-82, Rainey & LeBoeuf, Angleton, 1982-86; judge 149th Dist. Ct., Brazoria County, Tex., 1987-90, U.S. Dist. Ct. (so. dist.) Tex., 1990—; bd. dirs. Angleton Bank of Commerce. Mem. City of Angleton Planning and Zoning Commn., 1981-84; mem. Angleton Charter Rev. Commn., 1984, chmn. 1982. Served with U.S. Army, 1969-70. Mem. ABA, State Bar Tex., Brazoria County Bar Assn. (pres. 1983-84). Methodist. Lodge: Lions (pres. Angleton 1986-87). Avocations: hunting, fishing, woodworking. Office: US Dist Ct 515 Rusk St Ste 8613 Houston TX 77002-2603

RAINEY, JOHN MARK, administrator; b. Laurel, Miss., Mar. 16, 1947; s. Eleanor I. Rainey; children: Trisha, Kelly, Christopher, Heather, Melissa. BFA, U. So. Miss., 1972; M of Edni. Adminstrn., Ctrl. Mich. U., 1976; postgrad., Western Mich. U., 1994—. Instr. vocat. media, broadcasting, asst. prin. Sch. Dist. of the City of Saginaw, Mich., 1976-77, specialist, media and publ. svcs., 1977-79; prin., coord. of media and printing svcs. Salina elem. Sch. Dist. of the City of Saginaw, 1979-80, coord. media and publ. svcs., 1980-84, supr. Saginaw pub. schs. media ctr., 1984-92; dir. regional ednl. media ctr. and instrn. ctr. Kalamazoo Valley Intermediate Sch. Dist., 1992—; adj. prof. Ctrl. Mich. U., Mt. Pleasant, 1989—, Western Mich. U., Kalamazoo, 1992—; bd. dirs. TeleCity USA, Kalamazoo, 1994—, Community Cable Access, Kalamazoo, 1994—. Author: (manual) Critical Viewing Skills/Television, Copyright Manual for Educators, HyperCard for the Teacher, Macintosh Basics-Your Recipe for the Macintosh computer. Bd. dirs. Pub. Awareness Com. Saginaw Community Found., 1990-92; commr. Saginaw City Human Rels. Commn., 1990-92. With USAF, 1965-69. Recipient Outstanding Secondary Educator of Am. award, 1974. Mem. AAUW, ASCD, Nat. Staff Devel. Coun., Assn. for Ednl. Comm. and Tech. (pres. 1992-93, Richard B. Lewis Meml. award 1991), Action for Children's TV, Phi Delta Kappa (Leadership award 1991). Office: Kalamazoo Valley Intermed Sch Dist 1819 E Milham Rd Portage MI 49002-3035

RAINEY, KENNETH TYLER, English language educator; b. Memphis, Feb. 27, 1936; s. Andrew Laughlin Jr. and Gracie Ruth (Mullins) R.; m. Elaine Fitts, Jan. 1, 1960; children: Kenneth Tyler Jr., Timothy Andrew, Kevin Laughlin. BA, Miss. Coll., Clinton, 1958; AM, U. Mich., 1959; ThD, New Orleans Bapt. Sem., 1966; PhD, Ohio State U., 1976. Asst. prof. Eng. Miss. Coll., Clinton, 1965-70, Ohio State U., Lima, 1977-83, U. Memphis, 1983-89; prof. Humanities and tech. comm. So. Poly. State U., Marietta, Ga., 1989-97, disting. prof. of tchg. and learning, 1997—; cons. in field; vis. prof. Magdeburg, Germany, 1997. Contbr. articles to profl. jours. Woodrow Wilson fellow, 1958-59; Nat. Endowment Humanities grantee, 1981-82. Fellow Soc. Tech. Comm. (assoc.), Nat. Coun. Tchrs. English (conf. coll. composition and comm.), Assn. Tchrs. Tech. Writing. Baptist. Avocation: gourmet cooking. Home: 1194 Robert Ln Marietta GA 30062 Office: So Poly State U 1100 S Marietta Pkwy SE Marietta GA 30060-2855

RAINEY, WILLIAM E., II, medical educator. BS in Biology, U. North Tex., 1980, MS in Biology, 1981; PhD in Cell Biology, U. Tex., Dallas, 1985. Assoc. prof. ob-gyn. U. Tex. Southwestern Med. Ctr.; vis. scientist Flinders Med. Ctr., Adelaide, Australia, 1995. Grantee NIH, Am. Heart Assn.; Given Inst. Pathobiology fellow, 1984, Noble Found. fellow, 1984-85, Fogarty Internat. fellow, 1987-88. Mem. Fedn. Am. Socs. for Exptl. Biology, Endocrine Soc., Soc. Gynecol. Investigation. Office: U Tex SW Med Ctr Dept Ob-Gyn 5323 Harry Hines Blvd Dallas TX 75235-7208

RAINEY, WILLIAM JOEL, lawyer; b. Flint, Mich., Oct. 11, 1946; s. Ralph Jefferson and Elsie Matilda (Erickson) R.; m. Cynthia Hetsko, June 15, 1968; children: Joel Michael, Allison Elizabeth. AB, Harvard U., 1968; JD, U. Mich., 1971. Bar: N.Y. 1973, Wash. 1977, Ariz. 1987, Mass. 1992, Kans. 1997, U.S. Dist. Ct. (so. and ea. dists.) N.Y. 1973, U.S. Ct. Appeals (2nd cir.) N.Y. 1973, U.S. Dist. Ct. (we. dist.) Wash. 1977, U.S. Supreme Ct. 1976, U.S. Ct. Appeals (9th cir.) Wash. 1978, U.S. Dist. Ct. Ariz. 1987, U.S. Dist. Ct. Mass. 1992, U.S. Ct. Appeals (1st cir.) Mass. 1992. Assoc. atty. Curtis, Mallet-Prevost, Colt & Mosle, N.Y.C., 1971-76; atty., asst. corp. sec. Weyerhaeuser Co., Tacoma, Wash., 1976-85; v.p., corp. sec., gen. counsel Southwest Forest Industries Inc., Phoenix, 1985-87; sr. v.p., corp. sec., gen. counsel Valley Nat. Corp. and Valley Nat. Bank, Phoenix, 1987-91; v.p., gen. counsel Cabot Corp., Boston, 1991-93; exec. v.p., gen. coun., corp. sec. Fourth Fin. Corp., Wichita, Kans., 1994-96; sr. v.p., gen. counsel, corp. sec. Payless Shoe Source, Inc., Topeka, 1996—. Editor U. Mich. Jour. Law Reform, 1970-71. Bd. dirs. Big Bros./Big Sisters, 1994-96, Topeka Symphony Orch., 1997—. Maj. USAR, 1970-91. Mem. ABA (chmn. task force 1984-91), Wash. State Bar Assn., State Bar of Ariz., Assn. Bank Holding Cos. (steering com. 1989-91, chmn. lawyers com. 1990-91), Harvard Club of Phoenix (bd. dirs. 1989-91). Avocations: backpacking, running, fishing. Home: 901 Deer Run Dr Lawrence KS 66049-4708 Office: Payless Shoe Source Inc PO Box 1189 Topeka KS 66601-1189

RAINIER, ROBERT PAUL, publisher; b. Adrian, Mich., Oct. 19, 1940; s. Paul Leslie and Mildred Sofia (Magdefrau) R.; m. Dorothy Krauss, May 28, 1966; children: Michele Carole, Kenneth Charles. BA, Northwestern U., 1962, MA, 1964. Various positions with mktg. and sales dept. Times Mirror/McGraw Hill Book Co., N.Y.C., 1964-70, sponsoring editor coll. div., 1970-74, editor in chief humanities, 1974-79; pub. engring. coll. dept. Holt-Rinehart and Winston, N.Y.C., 1979-80, editor in chief, sci. and engring., 1980-81, pub. humanities, 1981-83, v.p., editor in chief, 1983-84; v.p., editor in chief CBS Coll. Pub., N.Y.C., 1984-86; dir. publs. AICPA, N.Y.C., 1986-96, pub., 1996—. Vestryman St. Johns Episcopal Ch., Larchmont, N.Y., 1987-90, fundraiser, 1988-89. Staff sgt. N.Y. N.G., 1964-70. Mem. The Dessoff Choirs (treas. 1993-96, bd. dirs. 1993—), Soc. Nat. Assn. Publs. (bd. dirs. 1988-94, pres. 1992-93). Democrat. Episcopalian. Avocations: music, sports. Home: 21 Summit Ave Larchmont NY 10538-2913

RAINS, EUGENE CHARLES, brokerage house executive; b. N.Y.C., Sept. 24, 1940; s. Charles William and Louise Theresa (Nold) R.; m. Jane Margaret Micucci, Nov. 28, 1964; children—Ellen, David, Mark. B.S., Fordham U., 1962; M.B.A., U. Pa., 1964. Security analyst trainee Merrill, Lynch Pierce Fenner & Smith, N.Y.C., 1963-65; ptnr. Brown Bros. Harriman & Co., N.Y.C., 1965—, also bd. dirs.; chmn. bd. dirs. Jefferson Ins. Co. N.Y., Monticello Ins. Co. Trustee St. Vincents Hosp., N.Y.C., Fordham U., N.Y.C., Cath. Health Care Network, Xavier H.S., N.Y.C. Robert Brunner Found. Mem. Inst. Chartered Fin. Analysts, Down Town Assn. (N.Y.C.), Knights of Malta, Harbour Ridge Golf Club (Palm City, Fla.). Republican. Roman Catholic. Avocations: fishing; trap and skeet shooting. Office: Brown Bros Harriman & Co 59 Wall St New York NY 10005-2808

RAINS, GLORIA CANN, environmentalist company executive; b. Atlanta, Feb. 12, 1928; d. Norman Douglas and Jane (McCurdy) Cann; m. John H. Rains Jr., Jan. 15, 1946 (dec. 1983); children: Michael W., Gordon C., Deborah C., John H. III. Freelance writer, cons. Palmetto, 1976—; chmn. ManaSota-88, Inc., Palmetto, 1976—; producer, host ManaSota-88 and the Environ., Brandenton, Fla., 1989-91; pres. ManaSota-88 Inc., Palmetto, 1991—; pres., bd. dirs. Environ. Confedn. S.W. Fla., Ft. Myers, 1976-85; bd. dirs., sec. Fla. div. Izaak Walter League of Am., Palmetto, 1976-80, Manatee chpt., Bradenton, 1976-80. Chmn. natural resources com. Manatee LWV, 1988-89; mem. Gov.'s Phospate Related Radiation Task Force, Fla., 1980-84, Gov.'s Hazardous Waste Policy Adv. Com., Fla., 1983-85, Gov.'s Local Govt. Study Commn., Mantee County, Fla., 1976-77, Mantaee County Pollution Control Bd., 1985-91. Mem. Air & Waste Mgmt. Assn., AAAS, Nat. Coalition Against the Misuse of Pesticides, Save Our Bays (bd. dirs. 1991), Pub. Citizen, Tampa Bay Nat. Estuary Com. Democrat. Home: 5314 Baystate Rd Palmetto FL 34221-8756

RAINS, MARY JO, banker; b. Konawa, Okla., Oct. 27, 1935; d. Albert Wood and Mary Leona (Winfield) Starns; m. Billy Z. Rains, June 17, 1956; 1 child, Nicky Z. Student Okla. Sch. Banking, 1969, Seminole Jr. Coll., 1970-72, E. Central State U., 1978-79, Okla. State U., 1987, Pontotoc County Adult Vocat. Tech. Ctr., 1987; diploma Am. Inst. Banking, 1981, 83. Acctg. divsn. Universal C.I.T., Oklahoma City, 1953-56; cashier Okla. State Bank (name changed to Bancfirst), Konawa, 1957-89, sr. v.p., 1989-95, sr. v.p., br. mgr. 1995—. Sec. 1st Baptist Ch., Konawa, 1969-79, mem. budgeting com., 1982-92, chmn. fin. com., 1994. Mem. Okla. Bankers Assn. (dir. women's div. 1974-76), Konawa C. of C., Am. Legion., Order Eastern Star. Home: RR 2 Box 28 Konawa OK 74849-9704 Office: PO Box 156 Konawa OK 74849-0156

RAINS, MERRITT NEAL, lawyer; b. Burlington, Iowa, July 26, 1943; s. Merritt and Lucille (Lepper) R.; m. Jean Baldwin, July 26, 1980 (div. 1995); children: Robert Baldwin, Kathleen Kellogg. B.A. in Polit. Sci. with honors, U. Iowa, 1965; J.D., Northwestern U., 1968. Bar: Ohio 1968. Assoc. Arter & Hadden, Cleve., 1968-76, ptnr., 1976—, mem. exec. com., 1981—, mem. mgmt. com., 1987-90, mng. ptnr., 1990-92; master bencher Inns of Ct., 1990—; lectr. on profl. topics, including alternative dispute resolution, distbn. law, litigation practice and procedure, and antitrust. Contbr. articles to profl. jours. Former trustee Legal Aid Soc. Cleve.; trustee Cleve. Play House, mem. adv. coun., 1988—; trustee Citizens League Greater Cleve., Cleve. Art Assn. With U.S. Army, 1968-70. Fellow Am. Bar Found.; mem. ABA, Ohio Bar Assn., Bar Assn. Greater Cleve. (chmn. young lawyers sect. 1975-76, recipient cert. merit 1975), Def. Rsch. Inst., Internat. Assn. Def. Counsel, Ohio Assn. Civil Trial Attys., Union Club, Cleve. Skating Club, Cleve. Play House Club, City Club, Print Club, Rowfant Club, Phi Beta Kappa, Omicron Delta Kappa, Phi Delta Phi. Home: 12546 Cedar Rd Cleveland Heights OH 44106-3294 Office: Arter & Hadden 1100 Huntington Bldg Cleveland OH 44115

RAINWATER, R. STEVEN, systems engineer; b. Tyler, Tex., Dec. 13, 1962; s. Clois Miles and Nancy Jane Rainwater; m. Susan C. Chance, May 11, 1991. AA, Northlake Coll., Irving, Tex., 1981-83; student, U. Tex., 1983-88. Programmer Profl. Info. Libr., Dallas, Tex., 1984-89; systems engr. Kimball Computer Video Tech., Irving, Tex., 1989-91; pres. Network Cybernetics Corp., Irving, 1992—; cons. Chaparal Steel Inc., Midlothian, Tex., 1988-89; sys. operator The Interocitor BBS, Irving, 1990—. Author computer software. Mem. Soc. Motion Picture and TV Engrs. Avocation: artificial intelligence rsch. Home: 2821 Vassar Dr Irving TX 75062-4575 Office: Network Cybernetics Corp Ste 202 4201 Wingren Rd Irving TX 75062-2763

RAINWATER, RICHARD, financial consultant, investor; b. Ft. Worth. BA in Math., U. Tex., 1966; MBA in Fin. and Mktg., Stanford U., 1968. With Goldman, Sachs & Co., N.Y.C., Dallas; chief fin. arch. Bass Orgn., Ft. Worth, 1970-86; ind. investor Ft. Worth, 1986-94; founder, chmn. bd. Crescent Real Estate Equities, Inc., Ft. Worth, 1994—; chief investor Mesa Inc., 1994—; spkr. Harvard Bus. Sch., Stanford U., U. Tex. Bus. Sch. Appeared on cover of Bus. Week mag., Oct. 1986; recipient Man of Yr. award, 1989, Kupfer Disting. Exec. award Tex. A&M U., 1991, Golden Plate award Am. Acad. Achievement, 1992. Office: Rainwater Inc 777 Main St Ste 2700 Fort Worth TX 76102-5331

RAIRDIN, CRAIG ALLEN, software company executive, software developer; b. Cedar Rapids, Iowa, Oct. 23, 1959; s. Ernie W. and Sherryl E. (Asklund) R.; m. Johnna L. Miller, Jan. 9, 1982. BS in Computer Sci. with distinction, U. Iowa, 1981. Software engr. Rockwell Internat., Cedar Rapids, 1982-88; div. dir. Parsons Tech., Cedar Rapids, 1988-90, v.p., 1990—; cons. Creative Computer Systems, Cedar Rapids, 1987-90. Author: (software) Juliet, 1987, Quick Verse, 1988, Bible Illustrator, 1990, Standard Template for Electronic Publishing (STEP), 1995. Chmn. Area Liaison Com., Campus Bible Fellowship, Iowa City, 1983-90; precinct chmn. Linn. County Rep. Party, Cedar Rapids, 1986-90; founder Bible Software Industry Standards Group, 1995. Mem. Iowa Home Educators Assn. Republican. Baptist. Avocations: church, amatuer radio, flying.

RAISBECK, GORDON, systems engineer; b. N.Y.C., May 4, 1925; s. Milton Joseph and Marcelle (Ellinger) R.; m. Barbara Wiener, Dec. 22, 1948; children: Michael Norbert, Lucy Margaret, Alison Jane, Timothy Gordon, James Gregory. Rhodes scholar, Oxford (Eng.) U., 1947-48; B.A., Stanford U., 1944; Ph.D., MIT, 1949. Registered profl. engr., Mass., Maine. Instr. M.I.T., Cambridge, 1948-49; mem. tech. staff Bell Telephone Labs., Inc., Murray Hill, N.J., 1949-61; dir. transmission line research Bell Telephone Labs., Inc. (now Lucent), 1954-61; mem. profl. staff research and devel. Advanced Research Projects Agy., Washington, 1959-60; mem. profl. staff Arthur D. Little, Inc., Cambridge, 1961-86; dir. systems engring. Arthur D. Little, Inc., 1966-70, dir. phys. systems research, 1970-75, v.p. systems engring., 1973-86 , part-time 1982-86; cons. mgmt. of technol. innovation, 1982—; instr. Drew U., Stanford U., MIT. Contbr. articles to profl. jours.; author: Information Theory: An Introduction for Engineers and Scientists, 1964. Served to lt. (j.g.) USNR, 1944-46, ATO, PTO. Rhodes scholar, 1947. Fellow IEEE, Acoustical Soc. Am.; mem. Oceanic Engring. Soc. IEEE (sec. 1988-92), Engring. Mgmt. Soc. IEEE, N.Y. Acad. Scis., New Coll. Soc., Math. Assn. Am., Oxford Soc., Inst. Ops. Rsch. and the Mgmt. Scis., Assn. Am. Rhodes Scholars, Amateur Chamber Music Players, Chamber Music Am., Sigma Xi. Democrat. Episcopalian. Patentee in field (22). Home and Office: 40 Deering St Portland ME 04101-2212 also: Blanche Rd, RR #1 Barrington, Cape Negro, NS Canada B0W 1E0

RAISBECK, JAMES DAVID, engineering company executive; b. Milw., Sept. 29, 1936; m. Sherry Raisbeck; 1 child, Jennifer Lee; stepchildren: Eric Valpey, Laura Valpey. BS in Aerodynamics, Purdue U., 1961. Rsch. aerodynamist Boeing Comml. Airplane Co., Seattle, 1961-66; new airplane and rsch. outplant mgr. Boeing Airplane Co., Wright-Patterson AFB, Ohio, 1966-68; program mgr. comml. STOL airplane programs Boeing Co., 1968-69; pres., CEO Robertson Aircraft Corp., Seattle, 1969-73; v.p. tech. Am. Jet Industries, Van Nuys, Calif., 1973-74; CEO Raisbeck Group, San Antonio and Seattle, 1974-80, Raisbeck Engring., Inc., Seattle, 1980—. Named Disting. Engring. Alumnus 1979, Purdue U. Fellow AIAA (assoc.); mem. Soc. Automotive Engrs., NBAA, Purdue U. Alumni Assn., Tau Beta Pi, Phi Eta Sigma, Sigma Gamma Tau. Achievements include numerous patents in aircraft design. Office: Raisbeck Engring Inc 4411 S Ryan Way Seattle WA 98178-2083

RAISER, MARY M., chief of protocol; b. Buffalo, Aug. 5, 1942; d. Robert and Eleanor (Verduin) Millonzi; m. Charles Victor Raiser II, Sept. 7, 1963 (dec. July 1992); 1 child, Mary van Schuyler. Student, Smith Coll., 1960-63; BS in Edn., U. Va., 1964; MA, SUNY, Buffalo, 1978; postgrad., George Washington U., 1990—. Tchr. grade 5 Pub. Sch. #56, 1965-66; tchr. grades 5-8 Emwood Franklin Sch., Buffalo, 1973-75; regional dir. western N.Y. office Sen. Daniel P. Moynihan, Buffalo, 1977-79; spl. asst. Sen. Daniel P. Moynihan, Washington, 1979-81; chief of protocol to U.S. Pres., v.p., sec. of state Dept. State and White House, Washington, 1993—. Founder Smith Coll. Club Scholarship; pres. Del. Assn., 1971; chair Quality of Life Task Force, Com. Alternative Forms of Govt., Buffalo, 1976; chair vols. D.C. chpt. ARC, 1985-86, bd. dirs., 1986-90, chair comm. com., 1986-90, mem. mgmt. com. D.C. chpt.; bd. dirs. Cmty. Mus. Sch., Buffalo, 1967-70, Jr. Group, Albright-Knox Gallery, Buffalo, 1967-70, Sasha Bruce House, Washington, 1981-83, Higher Achievement Program, Washington, 1989-90, Ellington Fund of Duke Ellington Sch. for the Arts D.C. Pub. Performing Arts H.S., 1989-92, Nat. Symphony Orch., 1992—; participant, fundraiser local and statewide elections Buffalo, 1970-92; fundraiser Dem. Nat. Com., Congressmen Matsui, LaFalce, Dicks, Nowak, Sens. Gore, Robb, others, 1970-92; mem. fin. com. Moynihan for Sen., 1981-82; mem. arrangements com. Dem. Nat. Conv., 1984, mem. site selection com., 1987-88; mem. Albert Gore Jr. Presdl. Fin. Com., 1987-88; chair devel. com., bd. dirs. Women's Campaign Fund, 1988-90, Dem. chair, 1990-93; founder women's coun. Dem. Senatorial Campaign Com., 1992—. Episcopalian. Office: Office of Protocol Dept State 2201 C St NW Rm 1232 Washington DC 20520-0001

RAISH, DAVID LANGDON, lawyer; b. Cleve., Mar. 12, 1947; s. John E. Raish and Roslyn V. (Skeels) Pettibone; m. Roslyn Anne Dinnick, Sept. 12, 1969; children: David Jr., Anne, Julia. BA, Yale U., 1969; JD, Harvard U., 1973. Bar: Mass. 1975, D.C. 1981. Law clk. to hon. James R. Browning U.S. Ct. Appeals-9th Cir., San Francisco, 1973-74; assoc. Ropes & Gray, Boston, 1974-82, ptnr., 1982—; mem. Com. on U.S. Activities of Foreigners and Tax Treaties, ABA Tax sect. 1981—, chair, 1991-93, mem. employee benefits com., 1993—. Author: Cafeteria Plans, 1985, Cash or Deferred Arrangements, 1986, Compensation and Benefits for Key Employees of Tax-Exempt Organizations, 1995; editor Tax Highlights Boston Bar Assn., 1985-93; bd. advisors Jour. Taxation of Employee Benefits. Tenor Tanglewood Festival Chorus. Office: Ropes & Gray One International Pl Boston MA 02110

RAISIAN, JOHN, university institute director, economist; b. Conneaut, Ohio, July 30, 1949; s. Ernest James and Ruby Lee (Owens) R.; m. Joyce Ann Klak, Aug. 17, 1984; children: Alison Kathleen, Sarah Elizabeth. BA, Ohio U., 1971; PhD, UCLA, 1978; LLD (hon.), Albertson Coll. Idaho, 1995. Rsch. assoc. Human Resources Rsch. Ctr., U. So. Calif., L.A., 1972-73; cons. Rand Corp., Santa Monica, Calif., 1974-75, 76; vis. asst. prof. econs. U. Wash., Seattle, 1975-76; asst. prof. econs. U. Houston, 1976-80; sr. economist Office Rsch. and Evaluation, U.S. Bur. Labor Stats., Washington, 1980-81; spl. asst. for econ. policy Office Asst. Sc. for Policy, U.S. Dept. Labor, Washington, 1981-83, dir. rsch. and tech. support, 1981-84; pres. Unicon Rsch. Corp., L.A., 1984-86; sr. fellow Hoover Instn., Stanford, Calif., 1986—, assoc. dir., dep. dir., 1986-90, dir., 1990—; exec. dir. Presdl. Task Force on Food Assistance, Washington, 1983-84. Mem. editorial bd. Jour. Labor Rsch., 1983—; contbr. articles to profl. jours. Advisor Nat. Coun. on Handicapped, Washington, 1985-86, Nat. Commn. on Employment Policy, Washington, 1987-88; chmn. minimum wage bd. Calif. Indsl. Welfare Commn., 1987; mem. nat. adv.com. Student Fin. Assistance, Washington, 1987-89; corp. mem. Blue Shield Calif., 1994-96; bd. dirs. Sentinel Groups Fund, Inc., 1997—; mem. Pacific Coun. Internat. Policy, nat. adv. bd. City Innovation. Recipient Best Publ. of Yr. award Econ. Inquiry, Western Econ. Assn., 1979, Disting. Teaching award U. Houston Coll. Social Scis., 1980, Disting. Svc. award U.S. Dept. Labor, 1983; predoctoral fellow Rand Corp., 1976. Mem. Am. Econs. Assn., Western Econ. Assn. (chmn. nominating com. 1992), Commonwealth Club of Calif., World Affairs Coun., Mont Pelerin Soc., Coun. on Fgn. Rels., Nat. Assn. Scholars, Phi Beta Kappa. Republican. Avocations: wine collecting, sports enthusiast. Office: Stanford U Hoover Hoover Inst War-Revolution Stanford CA 94305-6010

RAISIG, PAUL JONES, JR., lawyer; b. Jamestown, N.Y., June 21, 1932; s. Paul Jones and Marian Elizabeth (Christian) R.; m. Carolyn Virginia Sides, June 12, 1955; children: Dawn Virginia, Paul Christian, Anne Sibley. B.G.E., U. Nebr., 1961; M.B.A., U. Ala., 1965; JD, Campbell U., 1989. Bar: N.C., 1989, D.C. 1991, U.S. Supreme Ct. 1992. Commd. 2d lt. U.S. Army, 1953, advanced through grades to col., 1973, ret., 1977, served in Vietnam, 1963, btn. comdr., Vietnam, 1968; dep. dir. U.S. Army Reorganization, 1973; v.p. Armed Forces Relief and Benefit Assn., Washington, 1977-79; sr. cons. Dept. Def., Washington, 1979-80; exec. dir. Am. Fedn. Info. Processing Socs., Arlington, Va., 1980-84; v.p., dir. Designs, Ltd., Alexandria, Va., 1985-86; ptnr. Barrington, Herndon & Raisig, P.A., Fayetteville, N.C., 1989-92; adj. prof. bus. law and bus. mgmt. Campbell U., 1992-97; cons. in field. Decorated Legion of Merit (4), Bronze Star medal (2), Air medal (7), Purple Heart (2), Meritorious Service medal, Army Commendation medal with V Device (3). Mem. U.S. Council for World Communications, Beta Gamma Sigma. Home and Office: Buffalo Lake 7612 Mallard Dr Sanford NC 27330-8444 *As we go about climbing the mountains in our lives, we must always remember to take the high road - for that is the only way to truly reach the top.*

RAISLER, KENNETH MARK, lawyer; b. New Rochelle, N.Y., May 15, 1951; s. Herbert A. and Norma (Glaubach) R.; m. Sara Ann Kelsey, June 11, 1978; children: Caroline Elisabeth, Katharine Kelsey, David Mark. BSBA, Yale Coll., 1973; JD, NYU, 1976. Bar: N.Y. 1977, D.C. 1977, U.S. Dist. Ct. (so. dist.) N.Y. 1977, U.S. Dist. Ct. D.C. 1977, U.S. Ct. Appeals (2d cir.) 1977, U.S. Ct. Appeals (D.C. cir.) 1977, U.S. Ct. Appeals (7th cir.) 1982, U.S. Ct. Appeals (10th cir.) 1983, U.S. Supreme Ct. 1985. Law clk. U.S. Dist. Ct. (so. dist.) N.Y., N.Y.C., 1976-77; asst. U.S. atty., Washington, 1977-82; dep. gen. counsel Commodity Futures Trading Commn., Washington, 1982-83, gen. counsel, 1983-87; ptnr. Rogers & Wells, N.Y.C., 1987-92, Sullivan & Cromwell, N.Y.C., 1992—. Mem. Assn. of Bar of City of N.Y. (chair futures regulation com. 1988-91). Office: Sullivan & Cromwell 125 Broad St New York NY 10004-2400

RAISZ, LAWRENCE GIDEON, medical educator, consultant; b. N.Y.C., Nov. 13, 1925; s. Erwin Joseph and Marie Georgette (Patai) R.; s. Helen Martin, June 5, 1948; children: Stephen, Matthew, Jonathan, Katherine, Nicholas. Student, Harvard U., 1943, MD, 1947; DOdontology (hon.), U. Umea, Sweden, 1990. Diplomate Am. Bd. Internal Medicine, Nat. Bd. Med. Examiners. Intern Harvard Med. Svc., Boston City Hosp., 1947-48; resident in medicine Cushing VA Hosp., 1950, Boston VA Hosp., 1952-54; asst. and instr. in physiology NYU-Bellevue Med. Ctr., 1948-50; asst. and instr. in medicine sch. medicine Boston U., 1953-56; chief renal sect. Boston VA Hosp., 1954-56; asst. chief radioisotope svc. Syracuse VA Hosp., 1956-57; asst. prof. medicine Coll. Medicine SUNY, Syracuse, 1956-61; assoc. prof. pharmacology and medicine Sch. Medicine U. Rochester, 1961-66, assoc. prof. medicine Sch. Medicine, 1966-68, prof. pharmacology, toxicology, and medicine Sch. Medicine, 1966-74, chief div. of clin. pharmacology Sch. Medicine, 1961-74; prof. medicine, head div. of endocrinology and metabolism Sch. Medicine U. Conn., Farmington, 1974—; program dir. Gen. Clin. Rsch. Ctr. U. Conn Health Ctr., Farmington, 1993—; sr. assoc. physician Strong Meml. Hosp., Rochester, 1961-68, physician, 1968-74; acting chmn. dept. pharmacology Sch. Medicine, U. Rochester, 1962-63, vis. prof. pharmacology, toxicology and medicine Sch. Medicine and Dentistry, 1974-76; vis. assoc. prof. pharmacology Sch. Medicine Stanford U., 1966; vis. prof. Coll. Medicine U. Lagos, Nigeria, 1973; mem. gen. B study sect. NIH, 1986-88; mem. subspecialty bd. on endocrinology and metabolism Am. Bd. Internal Medicine, 1990—; mem. U.S.-Japan Malnutrition Panel, 1985-91; clin. investigator Syracuse VA Hosp., 1957-60; William N. Creasy Vis. Prof. Clin. Pharmacology Med. Sch. Dartmouth Coll., 1977; chmn. Gordon Conf. on Bones and Teeth, 1980; Edwin B. Astwood lectr. Endocrine Soc., 1983. Mem. numerous editorial bds.; contbr. more than 300 articles to profl. jours. With USNR, 1943-45; capt. AUS, 1950-52. Spl. Rsch. fellow Nat. Inst. Arthritis and Metabolic Disease, Strangeways Rsch. Lab., 1960-61, Nat. Inst. Dental Rsch. NIH, 1971-72; Burroughs-Wellcome scholar in Clin. Pharmacology, 1963-68; recipient Prix Andre Lichtwitz, 1980, Class of 1947 Disting. Prof. award Med. Sch. U. Wis., 1988. Mem. AAAS, Am. Fedn. for Clin. Rsch., Am. Soc. for Clin. Investigation, Am. Soc. for Pharmacology and Exptl. Therapeutics, Endocrine Soc., Assn. Am. Physicians, Conn. Endocrine Soc. (pres. 1976), Am. Soc. for Bone and Mineral Rsch. (pres. 1980-81, William F. Neuman award 1986), Conn. Acad. Sci. and Engring., Sigma Xi. Avocations: travel, skiing, wind surfing. Home: 118 Waterville Rd Farmington CT 06032-1624 Office: U Conn Health Ctr 263 Farmington Ave Farmington CT 06030-0001

RAITT, BONNIE LYNN, blues singer, guitarist; b. Burbank, Calif., Nov. 8, 1949. Student, Radcliffe Coll. Performer blues clubs, East Coast; concert tours in Britain, 1976, 77; albums include Bonnie Raitt, 1971, Give It Up, 1972, Takin' My Time, 1973, Streetlights, 1974, Home Plate, 1975, Sweet Forgiveness, 1977, The Glow, 1979, Green Light, 1982, Nine Lives, 1986, Nick of Time, 1989 (Grammys 1990, Rock-Best Vocal Performance, Female, Pop-Best Vocal Performance, Female, Album of Yr.), I'm in the Mood (with John Lee Hooker) (Grammy 1990, Blues-Best Traditional Record), The Bonnie Raitt Collection, 1990, Luck of the Draw, 1991 (Grammy 1992, Rock-Best Vocal Performance, Female, Grammy for Best Duet with Delbert McClinton), Longing In Their Hearts, 1994 (Grammy award Best Pop Album), Road Tested, 1996; songs include Something to Talk About (Grammy 1992, Best Pop Vocal Performance, Female), Good Man, Good Woman (with Delbert McClinton) (Grammy 1992, Rock-Best Vocal by a Duo or Group). Recipient numerous Grammy nominations, four Grammy awards 1990, three Grammy awards 1992, 94. Office: PO Box 626 Los Angeles CA 90078-0626

RAJAB, MOHAMMAD HASAN, biostatistician, educator; b. Oct. 8, 1955; married; 2 children. BS in Agrl. Scis., Damascus (Syria) U., 1976; MS in Quantitative Genetics, Tex. A&M U., 1983, MS in Stats., 1987, PhD in Quantitative Genetics, 1987. Instr. Coll. Agr., Damascus (Syria) U., 1976-80, asst. prof. quanititative genetics, 1987-90; tchg. asst. dept. stats. Coll. Sci., Tex. A&M U., College Station, 1986-87; vis. asst. prof. Tex. A&M U., College Station, 1990; rsch. sci. dept. stats. Coll. Sci., Tex. A&M U., College Station, 1990-93, asst. prof. dept. psychiatry-behavioral scis. Coll. Medicine, 1993—; vis. asst. prof. Inst. für Tierenranhrung, U. Bonn, Bermany, 1990; co-investigator Coordinating Ctr. Partial Hospitalization of High-Rise Suicidal Youth Study, NIH, 1990-94, statistician ctrl. vein occlusion study, 1994—; epidemiologist biostats. dept. Scott and White Hosp., Temple, Tex., 1993—; presenter in field. Contbr. articles to profl. jours. Acad. scholar USAID, 1980; recipient Govt. award Damascus U., 1976. Mem. Am. Statis. Assn., Soc. Clin. Trials, Sigma Xi. Office: Texas A&M U Health Sci Ctr Biostatistics 2401 S 31st St Temple TX 76508-0001 also: Scott and White Biostats Dept 2401 S 31st St Temple TX 76508-0001

RAJAKARUNA, LALITH ASOKA, civil engineer; b. Pannala, Srilanka, Aug. 25, 1958; came to U.S., 1985; s. Weerathilaka and Padma (Wickramanayaka) R.; m. Janitha Munaweera, Sept. 25, 1985; children: Reginald, Ashley, Keith. BS in Civil Engring., U. Moratuwa, 1984; MS in Civil Engring., Poly. U., N.Y., 1991. Lic. Profl. Engr., N.Y. State. Civil engr. Colombo Internat. Airport, Srilanka, 1984-85; assoc. of firm, chief engr. Ettlinger & Ettlinger, P.C., Staten Island, N.Y., 1985-93; pres. Rajakaruna & Ettlinger, cons. engrs. and land surveyor, P.C., Staten Island, 1993—; adj. prof. Coll. Staten Island, Staten Island, N.Y., 1992—, Poly. U., Bklyn., 1994—; dir. profl. engring. rev. course Am. Soc. Civil Engrs., N.Y., 1992—, chmn. edn. com., 1994—. V.p. Asian Am. Coalition of S.I., 1996—. Mem. NSPE, Asian Am. Coalition S.I., N.Y. (v.p.). Home: 32 Endor Ave Staten Island NY 10301-4610 Office: Rajakaruna & Ettlinger PO Box 030304 Staten Island NY 10303-0304

RAJAN, FRED E. N., clergy member, church administrator. Exec. dir. Commn. for Multicultural Ministries of the Evangelical Lutheran Church in America, Chicago, Ill. Office: Evangelical Lutheran Church Am 8765 W Higgins Rd Chicago IL 60631-4101*

RAJANI, PREM RAJARAM, transportation company financial executive; b. Bombay, Nov. 9, 1949; came to U.S., 1973; s. Rajaram N. and Devibai Rajani; m. Rekha Rohera, Apr. 21, 1977; children: Anand, Harshada. B Tech., Indian Inst. Tech., Bombay, 1973; MBA in Acctg. and Fin., Columbia U., 1975. Sr. ops. auditor Pfizer, Inc., N.Y.C., 1975-78; sr. projects fin. analyst Sea-Land Industries subs. RJR, Edison, N.J., 1978-80, fin. mgr. joint ventures, 1980-81, mgr. corp. planning and analysis, 1981-84; mgr. corp. fin. Sea-Land Corp., Edison, 1984-87; asst. treas.-internat. Sea-Land Svc. Inc. subs. CSX Corp., Edison, 1987-88, asst. treas.-domestic, 1988, staff v.p., treas., 1988-94, staff v.p. fin. and planning Americas, 1994—. Mem. Nat. Assn. Corp. Treas., Soc. Internat. Treas. Office: Sea-Land Svc Inc 6000 Carnegie Blvd Charlotte NC 28209-4637

RAJESHWAR, KRISHNAN, chemist, educator; b. Trivandrum, India, Apr. 15, 1949; m. Rohini Chidambaram, 1977; children: Reena, Rebecca. BSc, U. Col, India, 1969; postgrad., Indian Inst. Technol. Sci., 1971, PhD in Chemistry, 1974. From asst. to assoc. prof. chemistry U. Tex., Arlington, 1983-89, prof. chemistry, 1989—; rsch. chemist Prods Formulation Group Foseco Internat., India, 1974-75, rsch. fellow in chemistry St. Francis, Xavier U., Can., 1975-76; rsch. fellow Colo. State U., 1976-78, vis. asst. prof., 1978-79, sr. rsch. assoc., 1979-83; cons. U. Wyo Rsch. Corp. & Forensic Labs., Edwards Aerospace Inc., Tex. Mem. Am. Chem. Soc. (Wilfred T. Doherty award 1994), Electrochem. Soc. Achievements include research in charge storage and transport mechanisms in a variety of metals, semiconductors and polymers, environmental electrochemistry and photoelectrochemistry. Office: U Texas Dept Chemistry & Biochemistry PO Box 19065 Arlington TX 76019

RAJKUMAR, AJAY, computer scientist, consultant; b. Jagadhri, Haryana, India, Aug. 4, 1962; came to the U.S., 1990; s. Rajkumar and Pushpa Rajkumar; m. Aradhana Goel, Feb. 9, 1996. BSc in Math. with honors, U. Delhi, India, 1984; M in Computer Applications, U. Poona, Pune, India, 1987; MS in Computer Sci., Utah State U., 1992; postgrad., NYU. Rsch. engr. Uptron India Ltd., Lucknow, India, 1987-90, Vigyan Inc., Hampton, Va., 1991-92; cons. AT&T Bell Labs., Murray Hill, N.J., 1993-95, mem. tech. staff, 1995-96; mem. tech. staff Lucent Tech., Bell Labs. Innovations, 1996, cons., 1997. Grantee NASA-Goddard Space Flight Ctr., Hampton, 1992, Dept of Energy, Hampton, 1992. Mem. Assn. for Computing Machinery. Avocations: hiking, traveling, reading. Office: NYU 715 Broadway # 1205 New York NY 10003-6806

RAJLICH, VACLAV THOMAS, computer science educator, researcher, consultant; b. Prague, Czech Republic, May 3, 1939; came to U.S., 1980; s. Vaclav and Marie (Janovska) R.; m. Ivana m. Bartova, Aug. 6, 1968; children: Vasik, Paul, John, Luke. MS, Czech Tech. U., Prague, 1962; PhD, Case Western Res. U., 1971. Rsch. engr. Rsch. Inst. for Math. Machines, Prague, 1963-67, scientist, 1971-75, mgr., 1975-79; vis. assoc. prof. computer sci. Calif. State U., Fullerton, 1980-81; assoc. prof. computer and communication sci. U. Mich., Ann Arbor, 1982-85; prof. Wayne State U., Detroit, 1985—, chair dept. computer sci., 1985-90; vis. scientist Carnegie-Mellon U., Pitts., 1987, Harvard U., Cambridge, Mass., 1988. Contbr. articles to profl. jours. Recipient Chrysler Challenge Fund, 1988. Mem. Computer Soc. of IEEE, Assn. for Computing Machinery. Roman Catholic. Achievements include development of tools for software maintenance, program comprehension, software design methods, and parallel grammars. Office: Wayne State U Dept Computer Sci Detroit MI 48202

RAJOTTE, RAY V., biomedical engineer, researcher; b. Wainwright, Alta., Can., Dec. 5, 1942; s. Sam and Bernadette (Tremblay) R.; m. Gloria A. Yackimetz, Aug. 20, 1966; children: Brian, Michael, Monique. RT, No. Alta. Inst. Tech., 1965; BSc in Elec. Engring., U. Alta., 1971, MSc in Elec. Engring., 1973, PhD in Biomed. Engring., 1975. Postdoctoral fellow U. Alta. Dept. Medicine, Edmonton, 1975-76, Oak Ridge (Tenn.) Nat. Lab., 1976-77, Washington U., St. Louis, 1977, UCLA, 1977; rsch. assoc. dept. medicine U. Alta., Edmonton, 1977-79, asst. prof. dept. medicine, 1979-82, asst. prof. dept. medicine & surgery, 1983-84, assoc. prof., 1984-88, prof., 1988—; dir. Islet Cel Transplant Lab. U. Alta., 1982—, Divsn. Exptl. Surgery U. Alta., 1988-96; assoc. dir. Surg.-Med. Rsch. Inst. U. Alta., 1984-87, dir., 1987—; co-dir. Juvenile Diabetes Fund Diabetes Interdisciplinary Rsch. Program U. Alta., 1992—. Co-editor: The Immunology of Diabetes Mellitus, 1986; mem. adv. bd. Diabetologia jour., 1993—; author over 350 publs. in field; contbr. 18 chpts. to books. Mem. Cell Transplantation Soc. (founding mem., councillor 1991—), Internat. Pancreas and Islet Transplant Assn. (founding mem., treas. 1991—), Can. Transplantation Soc. (Western councillor 1992-93), European Assn. for Study of Diabetes, Assn. Profl. Engrs., Geologists & Geophysicists Alta., Soc. Cryobiology, Am. Diabetes Assn., Can. Soc. Clin. Investigation, N.Y. Acad. Sci., Transplantation Soc., Can. Diabetes Assn., Acad. Surg. Rsch., Internat. Diabetes Fedn. Achievements include patent for glucose sensor. Office: U Alta, Surgical-Med Rsch Inst, Edmonton, AB Canada T6G 2N8

RAJSKI, PEGGY, film director, film producer; b. Stevens Point, Wis.. Attended, U. Wis. Films include: (prodn. mgr.): Lianna, 1982, Almost You, 1984; (prodr., prodn. mgr.) The Brother From Another Planet, 1984, Matewan, 1987, (co-prodr., prodn. mgr.) Eight Men Out, 1988; (co-prodr.) The Grifters, 1990, (prodr.) Little Man Tate, 1991 (also 2nd. unit dir.), Used People, 1992, Home for the Holidays, 1995; (prodr. video) Bruce Springsteen's Glory Days; (dir.) Trevor, 1994 (Acad. award for Best Live Action Short Film).

RAJUR, SHARANABASAVA BASAPPA, chemistry educator, researcher; b. Benakanhal, India, June 1, 1956; came to U.S., 1987; s. Basappa and Basamma Rajur; m. Krupa Sharanabasava Mensinkal, June 30, 1990; children, Vinaya S., Naveen S. PhD, Karanatak U., Dharwad, India, 1987. Rsch. asst. Karnatak U., 1984-85; lectr. organic chemistry Kittle Coll., Dharwad, 1985-86; asst. prof. Coll. of Pharmacy, Dharwad, 1986-87; rsch. assoc. U. Tex. Southwestern Med. Ctr., Dallas, 1987-90, Boston Coll., 1990-93; rsch. scientist Millipore Corp., Bedford, Mass., 1993-94; profl. researcher, group leader Boston Coll., 1994-95; instr. Mass. Gen. Hosp., Boston, 1995—. Reviewer Jour. Pharm. Scis., 1990-93; contbr. articles to profl. jours. Recipient grant Dept. Mental Health Clinics, 1988-89. Mem. AAAS, Am. Chem. Soc., Indian Chem. Soc. Hindu. Achievements include patent for developing FMOC protected peptide nucleic acid (PNA) derivatives. Avocations: tennis, swimming, skiing. Home: 157 Chestnut St Foxboro MA 02035 Office: Mass Gen Hosp Shriners Burns Inst/Harvard 1400 West One Kendall Sq Cambridge MA 02139

RAKEL, ROBERT EDWIN, physician, educator; b. Cin., July 13, 1932; s. Edwin J. and Elsie (Machino) R.; m. Peggy Klare; children: Barbara, Cindy, Linda, David. BS in Zoology, U. Cin., 1954, MD, 1958. Diplomate: Charter diplomate Am. Bd. Family Practice (v.p., dir.). Intern St. Mary's Hosp., Cin., 1958-59; resident in internal medicine USPHS Hosp., Seattle, 1959-61; resident in gen. practice Monterey County Hosp., Salinas, Calif., 1961-62; practice medicine Newport Beach, Calif., 1962-69; chmn. family practice program U. Calif., Irvine, 1969-71; prof., head dept. family practice U. Iowa, 1971-85; assoc. dean acad. and clin. affairs, Richard M. Kleberg, Sr. prof., chmn. dept. family medicine Baylor Coll. Medicine, Houston, 1985-97; dir. family practice residency program Hoag Meml. Hosp., Newport Beach, 1969-71; med. staff Mercy Hosp., Iowa City, 1971-85; chief family practice service St. Luke's Episc. Hosp., The Meth. Hosp., Houston, 1985-97; trustee The Hospice of Tex. Med. Ctr., 1986-97, Inst. of Religion Tex. Author: Selected References in Family Medicine, 1973, (with H.F. Conn & T.W. Johnson) Family Practice, 1973, (with H.F. Conn.) Textbook of Family Practice, 1978, editor 3d edit., 1984, 5th edit., 1995, Principles of Family Medicine, 1977; author foreword Neurology for the Everyday Practice of Medicine, R.G. Feldman, 1984; contbr. Dictionary of Am. Med. Biography Vols. I and II, 1984; editor: Conn's Current Therapy, 1984—, Yearbook of Family Practice, 1977-90, (series) Procedures for Your Practice Patient Care, Vol. 18, Essentials of Family Practice, 1992, Saunders Manual Med. Practice, 1996; mem. 13 editorial bds. med. jours.; contbr. articles to med. jours.; contbr. Encyclopedia Britannica, 1995. Served with USPHS, 1959-61. Recipient Mead-Johnson Scholar award in Gen. Practice, 1971. Fellow Am. Acad. Family Physicians (pres. Orange County chpt. Calif. 1969, commn. on edn. 1970-76, Thomas W. Johnson award 1973); mem. AMA (sect. on med. schs. 1985-97, gov. council of sect. 1986-88), Tex. Med. Assn., Am. Bd. Family Practice (bd. dirs. 1973-79, v.p. 1977-79, chmn. exam. com. 1974-79, recert. com. 1973-79, others), Am. Bd. Med. Spltys. (com. splty. evaluation 1978-81), Nat. Bd. Med. Examiners (bd. dirs. 1975-79), Soc. Tchrs. Family Medicine (dir. 1971-79, sec. 1971-73), Council Acad. Socs., Assn. Am. Med. Colls., History of Medicine Soc. (founder, chmn. U. Iowa 1978-85, founder, chmn. Baylor Coll. Medicine 1986—), Am. Osler Soc. (bd. dirs. 1989—, pres. 1994), Cosmos Club. Home: 2420 Underwood St Houston TX 77030-3506 Office: Baylor Coll Medicine 1 Baylor Plz Houston TX 77030-3411

RAKES, GANAS KAYE, finance and banking educator; b. Floyd, Va., May 2, 1938; s. Samuel D. and Ocie J. (Peters) R.; m. Mary Ann Simmons, Oct. 1, 1961; 1 child, Sabrina Darrow. BS, Va. Tech., 1960, MS, 1964; D of Bus. Adminstrn., Washington U., St. Louis, 1971. Assoc. prof. commerce U. Va., Charlottesville, 1968-80; O'Bleness prof. fin. and banking Ohio U., Athens, 1980—; chmn. fin. dept. Coll. of Bus. Adminstrn., 1983—; bd. dirs. Caldwell Savs. and Loan Co.; pres. bd. dirs. Enterprise Devel. Corp. Contbr. articles to profl. jours. Served to 1st lt. U.S. Army, 1961-63. Mem. Fin. Mgmt. Assn., Midwestern Bus. Adminstrs. Assn., Eastern Fin. Assn., Rotary, Reynolds Nat. Club. Republican. Episcopalian. Avocation: sailing. Office: Ohio U Dept of Fin Athens OH 45701

RAKIC, PASKO, neuroscientist, educator; b. Ruma, Yugoslavia, May 15, 1933; came to U.S., 1969; m. Patricia Goldman, 1969. MD, U. Belgrade, Yugoslavia, 1959, ScD in Neuroembryology, 1969. With inst. path. physiology Med. Sch. U. Belgrade, 1959-61, resident in neurosurgery, 1961-62; NIH research fellow neuropathology Harvard Med. Sch., Boston, 1962-66; asst. prof. Inst. Biol. Rsch., Belgrade, 1967-68; from asst. prof. to assoc. prof. neuropathology and neuroscience Harvard Med. Sch., 1969-77; prof. neurosci. Yale Med. Sch., New Haven, 1977-78, Dorys McConnell Duberg prof. neurosci., 1978—, also chmn. neurobiology sect. Author of 200 sci. papers and gen. books on brain orgn. and devel. Recipient Henry Gray award Am. Assn. Anatomists, 1996. Mem. NAS, Am. Acad. Arts and Sci., Soc. Neurosci. (pres. 1996), Am. Phys. Soc. (Lashley award 1986, Fyssen internat. sci. prize 1992). Office: Yale U Sch Medicine Sect Neurobiology 333 Cedar St New Haven CT 06510-3206

RAKITA, LOUIS, cardiologist, educator; b. Montreal, Que., Can., July 2, 1922; came to U.S., 1951, naturalized, 1962; s. S. and Rose (Weinman) R.; m. G. Blanche Michlin, Dec. 4, 1945; 1 son, Robert M. B.A., Sir George Williams Coll., Montreal, 1942; M.D., C.M., McGill U., 1949. Diplomate: Am. Bd. Internal Medicine. Intern Montreal Gen. Hosp., 1949-50; resident in medicine Jewish Gen. Hosp., Montreal, 1950-51; fellow in medicine Alton Ochsner Med. Found., New Orleans, 1951-52; chief resident in medicine Cleve. City Hosp., 1952-53, Am. Heart Assn. fellow, 1954-55; Am. Heart Assn. fellow Inst. for Med. Research, Cedars of Lebanon Hosp., Los Angeles, 1953-54; practice medicine specializing in internal medicine and cardiology Cleve., 1954—; instr. medicine Western Res. U., Cleve., 1954-55; sr. instr. Western Res. U., 1955-57, asst. prof., 1957-61, asso. prof., 1961-71; asst. vis. physician Cleve. City Hosp., 1954-57, vis. physician, 1957—; advanced fellow Cleve. Met. Gen. Hosp., 1959-61, dir. cardiology, 1966-87, immediate past dir., div. cardiology, 1987—; asso. div. of research in med. edn. Case Western Res. U., Cleve., 1969-75; prof. medicine Case Western Res. U., 1971-93, prof. emeritus medicine, 1993; chmn. Phase IIA Cardiovascular com. Case Western Res. U., 1965-70, Faculty Senate Subcom. for Devel. and Evaluation of Ednl. Methods, 1969, chmn. Univ. Com. on Ednl. Planning, 1971-73, Faculty Coun. Sch. Medicine, 1979-80, Faculty Coun. Steering Com. Sch. Medicine, 1979-80, mem. bd. trustees Com. on Univ. Plans, 1971-73, Faculty Senate, Exec. Coun.; cons. in cardiology Luth. Med. Ctr., Cleve., 1970—, Crile VA Hosp., Cleve., 1969—; vis. cardiologist Sunny Acres Hosp., Cleve., 1973—; cardiologist rep. of del. to USSR, 1973. Author: (with M. Broder) Cardiac Arrhythmias, 1970, (with M. Kaplan) Immunological Diseases, 1972; Contbr. (with M. Kaplan) articles on cardiovascular diseases to profl. publs. Served with RCAF, 1942-45. Recipient Research Career Devel. award USPHS, 1962-69. Fellow ACP (Laureate award Ohio chpt. 1992), Am. Coll. Cardiology, Royal Coll. Physicians and Surgeons Can. (cert.), Am. Heart Assn. (mem. exec. com. N.E. Ohio chpt. 1972—, trustee 1969—, pres. N.E. Ohio chpt. 1972-74, coun. on clin. cardiology 1972—, chmn. various coms., v.p. North Ctrl. Region 1985-86, bd. dirs. 1985-86, hon. life trustee Northeast Ohio affiliate, vice chmn. task force on product licensing feasibility 1987—, Award of Merit 1987, Gold Heart award 1989); mem. AAUP, Am. Fedn. Clin. Rsch., Ctrl. Soc. Clin. Rsch., Soc. Exptl. Biology and Medicine, Cleve. Med. Libr. Assn. (trustee 1972—), Nat. Bd. Med. Examiners, The Press of Case Western Res. U. (adv. com. 1970), Nat. Heart and Lung Inst., Nat. Insts. Health (left ventricular assist device clin. trial program divsn. extramural affairs, data rev. bd. 1981—, adv. com. med. devices applications program 1971-75), Sigma Xi. Home: 24151 S Woodland Rd Cleveland OH 44122-3315 Office: 2500 Metrohealth Dr Cleveland OH 44109-1900

RAKOFF, JED SAUL, federal judge, author; b. Phila., Aug. 1, 1943; s. Abraham Edward and Doris Tobiah (Michell) R.; m. Ann Rosenberg, Aug. 4, 1974; children: Jena Lynn, Elana Beth, Keira Jan. BA, Swarthmore Coll., 1964; MPhil, Balliol Coll., Oxford U., Eng., 1966; JD, Harvard U., 1969. Bar: N.Y. 1971, D.C. 1983, U.S. Supreme Ct. 1986. Law clk. U.S. Ct. Appeals (3rd cir.), Phila., 1969-70; assoc. Debevoise, Plimpton, Lyons & Gates, N.Y.C., 1970-73; asst. U.S. atty. So. Dist. N.Y., N.Y.C., 1973-80, chief bus. and securities fraud prosecutions U.S. Atty.'s Office, 1978-80; ptnr. Mudge Rose Guthrie Alexander & Ferdon, N.Y.C., 1980-90, Fried Frank Harris Shriver & Jacobson, N.Y.C., 1990-96; judge U.S. Dist. Ct. (so. dist.) N.Y., 1996—; lectr. in law Columbia Law Sch., 1988—. Author: (with S. Arkin et al) Business Crime, 6 vols., 1982, Criminal Defense Techniques, 6 vols., 1982, (with H. Goldstein) RICO: Civil and Criminal Law and Strategy, 1989, (with L. Blumkin and R. Sauber) Corporate Sentencing Guidelines,: Compliance and Mitigation, 1993; editor-in-chief Bus. Crimes Bull., 1994-95; columnist N.Y. Law Jour., 1985-95; contbr. numerous articles to law revs. Mem. exec. bd. N.Y. chpt. Am. Jewish Com., 1971-95. Fellow Am. Coll. Trial Lawyers (chmn. N.Y. State 1993-94), Am. Bd. Criminal Lawyers; mem. ABA, N.Y. State Bar Assn., Assn. of Bar of City of N.Y. (chmn. criminal law com. 1986-89), Fed. Bar Coun., N.Y. Coun. Def. Lawyers (dir. 1990-94). Democrat. Jewish. Office: U.S. Courthouse 500 Pearl St Rm 750 New York NY 10007-1316

RAKOFF, VIVIAN MORRIS, psychiatrist, writer; b. Capetown, South Africa, Apr. 28, 1928; s. David Wilfred and Bertha Lillian (Woolf) R.; m. Gina Shochat, Nov. 27, 1959; children: Simon, Ruth, David. B.A., U. Capetown, 1947, M.A. with 1st class honors, 1949; M.B.B.S., U. London, 1957; diploma psychiat. medicine, McGill U., 1963. Intern St. Charles Hosp., London, 1957, Victoria Hosp., Capetown, 1958; resident Groote Schuur Hosp., Capetown, 1959-61, Jewish Gen. Hosp., Montreal, 1961-62, Verdun Protestant Hosp., Montreal, 1961-62; staff psychiatrist Jewish Gen. Hosp., Montreal, 1963-66, dir. research psychiatry, 1967-68; dir. postgrad. edn. dept. psychiatry U. Toronto, Ont, Can, 1968-75; prof. psychiat. edn. U. Toronto, Ont., Can., 1975-80, prof., chmn. dept. psychiatry, 1980-90; prof. emeritus U. Toronto, 1990—; head dept. psychiatry Sunnybrook Hosp., Toronto, 1978-80; dir., psychiatrist-in-chief Clarke Inst. Psychiatry, Toronto, 1980-90. Author: plays Nonquasi, 1967; Mandelstam's Witness, 1975; editor: Psychiatric Diagnosis, 1977, A Method of Psychiatry, 1979. Fellow Royal Coll. Physicians and Surgeons, Am. Psychiat. Assn., Am. Coll. Psychiatrists; mem. Sigma Xi. Jewish. Office: Clarke Inst Psychiatry, 250 College St, Toronto, ON Canada M5T 1R8

RAKOLTA, JOHN, construction company executive; b. 1923. Student, U. Detroit. With Walbridge Aldinger Co., Livonia, Mich., 1945—, sec., treas., 1955-70, pres., treas., 1970-78, pres., 1978-80, now chmn. bd. dirs., 1980—. Office: Walbridge Aldinger Co 613 Abbott St Detroit MI 48226-2513*

RAKOV, BARBARA STREEM, marketing executive; b. Bklyn., Jan. 4, 1946; d. Harold B. and Claire (Colbert) Streem; m. Harris J. Rakov, Nov. 20, 1970 (div. Mar. 1972). BS, Boston U., 1967; postgrad. NYU, 1972-74. Market rsch. analyst, product mgr., mktg. mgr. J.B. Williams, N.Y.C., 1967-77; mktg. mgr. Del Labs., Farmingdale, N.Y., 1977-78; product mgr., sr. product mgr., asst. to office of pres., dir. mktg. and sales Benelux countries, v.p. group mktg., dir., dir. new products, v.p. bus. devel. Joseph E. Seagram & Sons, 1978-90; pres. BSR Assocs., N.Y.C., 1990-92; v.p. mktg. Del Labs., 1992-94; v.p. mktg. Tsumura Internat., Secaucus, N.J., 1994-96; v.p. Disneymktg. Franco Mfg. Co., Inc., Metuchen, N.J., 1996—. Mem. L'Ordre des Coteaux de Champagne, Les Gastronomes de la Mer, Am. Mgmt. Assn. Avocations: tennis, skiing, squash, reading, water skiing. Office: Franco Mfg Co Inc 555 Prospect St Metuchen NJ 08840-2271

RAKOVE, JACK NORMAN, history educator; b. Chgo., June 4, 1947; s. Milton Leon and Shirley (Bloom) R.; m. Helen Scharf, June 22, 1969; children: Robert, Daniel. AB, Haverford Coll., 1968; PhD, Harvard U., 1975. Asst. prof. history Colgate U., Hamilton, N.Y., 1975-80; from asst. to assoc. prof. history Stanford (Calif.) U., 1980-90, prof., 1990—, Coe prof. history and Am. studies, 1996—. Author: Beginnings of National Politics, 1979, James Madison & The Creation of the American Republic, 1990, Original Meanings, 1996 (Pulitzer prize for History, 1997); editor: Interpreting the Consitution, 1990. Commr. Calif. Bicentennial Commn., 1986-87. With U.S. Army Res. NEH fellow, 1985-86, Stanford Humanities Ctr. fellow, 1988-89. Mem. Am. Hist. Assn., Orgn. Am. Historians, Soc. Am. Historians, Am. Polit. Sci. Assn. Office: Stanford Univ Dept History Stanford CA 94305-2024

RAKOWER, JOEL A., business appraiser, litigation consultant; b. 1958. BA in Acctg., U. South Fla., 1980. CPA, N.Y., Fla. Ptnr. Goodman, Rakower & Agiato, Commack, N.Y., 1989-93; pres. Rakower Fin. Appraisal Svcs. Ltd., Commack, 1993—; testified as expert witness numerous times in N.Y. and Conn.; lectr., seminar presenter to profl. and ednl. orgns. Author: Enhanced Earning Capacity: Understanding the Computations, 1993, Quantifying Celebrity Status, 1995; contbr. articles to profl. jours. Mem. Nat. Assn. Cert. Fraud Examiners (cert.), Fla. Inst. CPAs, Am. Soc. Appraisers, Inst. Bus. Appraisers, N.Y. State Soc. CPAs, Nat. Assn. Forensic Economists. Office: Rakower Fin Appraisal Svcs 366 Veterans Memorial Hwy Commack NY 11725-4333

RAKOWICZ-SZULCZYNSKA, EVA MARIA, molecular oncologist; b. Poznan, Poland, Nov. 22, 1951; came to U.S., 1984; d. Tadeusz and Wieslawa Maria (Hankiewicz) Rakowicz; divorced; 1 child, Adriana Maria. MS in Biochemistry, A. Mickiewicz U., Poznan, 1974; PhD in Biochemistry, Acad. Medicine, Poznan, 1977, DMS in Human Genetics & Molecular Biol., 1981. Asst. prof. Inst. Human Genetics, Poznan, 1978-82, assoc. dir., 1982-86, assoc. prof., 1982-89; assoc. scientist, lab. head Wistar Inst., Phila., 1984-90, rsch. asst. prof., 1991-92; assoc. prof. ob/gyn. U. Nebr. Med. Ctr., Omaha, 1992—, assoc. prof. Eppley Inst., 1993-96, assoc. prof. biochemistry, 1995—; mem. Eppley Cancer Ctr., Omaha, 1995—. Author: Nuclear Localization of Growth Factors and of Monoclonal Antibodies, 1993; contbr. 60 articles to Am. Jour. Pathology, Carcinogenesis, others. Grantee Nebr. Dept. Health, 1993-95, Elsou U. Pardee Found., 1993-94, Olson Ctr. for Women's Health, 1993—. Mem. AAAS, Am. Assn. Cancer Rsch., Am. Assn. Microbiology, Internat. Soc. for Preventive Oncology, Am. Assn. Clin. Chemistry, N.Y. Acad. Scis. Roman Catholic. Achievements include patents for Methods for Detecting Growth Factor Receptor Expression, Methods for Screening Monoclonal Antibodies for Therapeutic Use; patent pending for diagnosis and therapy of breast and gynecological cancer. Office: U Nebr Med Ctr Dept Ob/Gyn 600 S 42nd St Omaha NE 68198-1002

RALEIGH, CECIL BARING, geophysicist; b. Little Rock, Aug. 11, 1934; s. Cecil Baring and Lucile Nell (Stewart) R.; m. Diane Lauster, July 17, 1982; children: Alison, Marianne, Lawrence, David. B.A., Pomona (Calif.) Coll., 1956; M.A., Claremont (Calif.) Grad. Sch., 1958; Ph.D., UCLA, 1963. Fellow Research Sch. Phys. Sci., Australian Nat. U., Canberra, 1963-66; geophysicist U.S. Geol. Survey, Menlo Park, Calif., 1966-80; program mgr. for earthquake prediction research program U.S. Geol. Survey, 1980-81; dir. Lamont-Doherty Geol. Obs. and prof. geol. scis. Columbia U., Palisades, N.Y., 1981-89; dean Sch. Ocean and Earth Sci. and Tech. U. Hawaii, Honolulu, 1989—; CEO Ctr. for a Sustainable Future, Inc., 1996—; mem. Gov.'s Task Force on Sci. Tech., 1996—; mem. NAS/NRC Ocean Studies Bd.; chmn. NAS/NRC Yucca Mountain Panel; bd. dirs. JOI, Inc., High Tech. Devel. Corp. Author papers control earthquakes, rheology of the mantle, mechanics of faulting, crystal plasticity. Recipient Interdisciplinary award U.S. Nat. Com. Rock Mechanics, 1969, 74; Meritorious Service award Dept. Interior, 1974; Barrows Dist. Alumnus award Pomona Coll. Fellow Am. Geophys. Union, Geol. Soc. Am. Democrat. Inventor formation fracturing method. Office: U Hawaii Sch Ocean Earth Sci & Tech Honolulu HI 96822

RALIS, PARASKEVY, art educator, artist; b. N.Y.C., Sept. 16, 1951; d. Harry and Katerina (Koumi) R. AA, Miami-Dade Community Coll., 1970; BFA, Fla. Internat. U., 1973; MS, Nova U., 1977. Tchr. Miami (Fla.) Park Elem. Sch., 1973-80; instr. visual arts, photography Am. Sr. High Sch., 1980-81; tchr. Holmes Elem. Sch., 1981-84, Horace Mann Jr. High Sch., 1983-85; instr. magnet program visual arts, photography R.R. Moton South Ctr. for the Expressive Arts, 1984—, head dept. fine arts spl. area, 1986-89, 93-94, magnet lead tchr., 1992-93; magnet dept. head R.R. Moton South Ctr. for the Expressive Arts, Miami, 1993-94; chairperson grant writing com. R.R. Moton Expressive Arts Ctr., 1990; mem. SBM Sch. Cadre, 1993-94, R.R. Moton's Sch. Based Mgmt. Cadre, 1994-95. Prin. works include Twenty-First M. Allen Hortt Meml. Exhbn., Contemporary Reflections of the 19th Century, 1979, Media Plus, 1980, Inception, 1981, Artspace, 1982, Class Impressions, 1983, Southern Exposure, 1986; exhibited in group shows at Met. Mus. Art and Art Ctr./Coral Gables, Fla., 1986, Broward C.C. Fine Arts Gallery, 1985, Mus. Art, Ft. Lauderdale, 1979, 84, North Miami Mus. and Art Ctr., 1983, Fla. Internat. U., 1980, Nat. Exhibit Am. Art, Chautauqua, N.Y., 1985, Images I Miami Dade C.C., 1988, Omni Internat. Mall Artworks Gallery, 1990, 91, 92, The Ctr. for Visual Comms., 1993, Sheldon Lurie Art Against AIDS Auction IV, Biltmore Hotel, Coral Gables, Fla., 1994, Rex Art Tchrs. Exhibit, 1996, Jacqueline Hinchey Sipes Invitational Art Exhibit, Miami, 1996; inventor first art game in U.S. History, 1978; Photog. of James Brown, 1981. Mem. Dade County Art Tchrs. Assn. (bd. dirs., publicity chmn., Pres.'s award 1984), Fla. Art Educators Assn. (presenter 1994), United Tchrs. of Dade (liaison to Dade Art Educators Assn. 1981-94, 95—, arts advocacy chair for Dade Art Educators 1996—), Fla. Art Edn. Assn. (chair photography com. conv. 1990), Dade Art Educators (pres. (1996-98). Greek Orthodox. Home: 798 NE 71st St Miami FL 33138-5718 Office: RR Moton S Ctr for Excellence 18050 Homestead Ave Exp Arts Ctr Miami FL 33157-5529

RALL, DAVID PLATT, pharmacologist, environmentalist; b. Aurora, Ill., Aug. 3, 1926; s. Edward Everett and Nell (Platt) R.; children: Jonathan D., Catharyn E.; m. Mary Gloria Monteiro, Apr. 22, 1989. BS, North Ctrl. Coll., Naperville, Ill., 1946; MS, Northwestern U., 1948, MD, PhD, 1951. Intern Bellevue Hosp., N.Y.C., 1952-53; officer USPHS, 1953-90, asst. surgeon gen., 1971-90; sr. investigator Lab. Chem. Pharmacology, Nat. Cancer Inst., NIH, Bethesda, Md., 1953-55, Clin. Pharmacology and Exptl. Therapeutics Service, 1956-58, head service, 1958-63; chief Clin. Pharmacology and Exptl. Therapeutics Service (Lab. Chem. Pharmacology), 1963-69; assoc. sci. dir. for exptl. therapeutics Nat. Cancer Inst., 1966-71; dir. Nat. Inst. Environ. Health Scis., 1971-90, dir. Nat. Toxicology Program, 1978-90; adj. prof. pharmacology U. N.C., Chapel Hill, 1972-90, Foreign Sociology NAS Inst. Medicine, 1994—. Trustee Environ. Def. Fund, 1991—; treas. Ramazzini Soc., 1992—. Fellow AAAS; mem. Am. Assn. Cancer Rsch., Am. Soc. Clin. Investigation, Am. Soc. Pharmacology and Exptl. Therapeutics, Inst. Medicine, Soc. Toxicology. Home and Office: 5302 Reno Rd NW Washington DC 20015-1908

RALL, JOSEPH EDWARD, physician; b. Naperville, Ill., Feb. 3, 1920; s. Edward Everett and Nell (Platt) R.; m. Caroline Domm, Sept. 28, 1944 (dec. Apr. 1976); children: Priscilla, Edward Christian. B.A., North Central Coll., 1940, D.Sc. (hon.), 1966; M.S., Northwestern U., 1944, M.D., 1945; Ph.D., U. Minn., 1952; Dr. honoris causa, Faculty of Medicine, Free U. Brussels, Belgium, 1975; M.D. (hon.), U. Naples, 1985. Assoc. mem. Sloan Kettering Inst., N.Y.C., 1950-55; chief clin. endocrinology br. Nat. Inst. Arthritis, Metabolism and Digestive Diseases, NIH, 1955-62; dir. intramural research Nat. Inst. Arthritis, Diabetes, Digestive and Kidney Diseases, 1962-83; dep. dir. intramural research NIH, 1983-91; sr. investigator Nat. Inst. Diabetes and Digestive and Kidney Diseases, NIH, 1991; scientist emeritus NIH, 1995; mem. NRC, 1960-65. Author numerous articles, chpts. in books on thyroid gland and radiation. Chmn. Coun. of Scientists for Internat. Human Frontier Sci. Program, 1989-93. Served to capt. M.C. AUS, 1946-48. Recipient Van Meter prize Am. Goiter Assn., 1950, Fleming award, 1959, Outstanding Achievement award Mayo Clinic and U. Minn., 1964; Disting. Service award Am. Thyroid Assn., 1967; Disting. Service award HEW, 1968, Disting. Exec. rank, sr. exec. service, 1980, R.H. Williams Disting. Leadership award in endocrinology, 1983, Disting. Achievement award N.Y. Hosp., Cornell Med. Ctr., 1987; named Outstanding Alumnus N. Central Coll., 1966. Mem. NAS, AAAS, Am. Acad. Arts and Scis., Am. Soc. Clin. Investigation, Am. Phys. Soc., Endocrine Soc., Assn. Am. Physicians, Societe de Biologie (France), Royal Acad. Medicine (Brussels). Home: 3947 Baltimore St Kensington MD 20895-3913 Office: NIH Bldg 10 Rm 8N307 Bethesda MD 20892

RALL, LLOYD LOUIS, civil engineer; b. Galesville, Wis., Dec. 7, 1916; s. Louis A. and Anna (Kienzle) R.; m. Mary Moller, July 12, 1952; children: Lauris, David, Christopher, Jonathan. BCE, U. Wis., 1940. Commd. 2d lt. U.S. Army, 1940, advanced through grades to col., 1972, engr. forward area strategic air force, 1944-45, ret., 1977; chief construct divsn. Far East forces U.S. Army, Tokyo, 1945-47; engr., mem. mil. survey mission U.S. Army, Turkey, 1947; with office joint chiefs of staff U.S. Army, Washington, 1947-49, exec. officer R&D office chief engrs., 1949-51; asst. dist. engr. U.S. Army, Seattle, 1952-54; dept. engr. Comm. Zone U.S. Army, France, 1954-56; commanding officer 540th combat engr. group U.S. Army, 1956-57, prof. mil. sci. and tactics Mo. Sch. Mines and Metallurgy, 1957-60; dep. dir. topography office chief engrs. U.S. Army, Washington, 1960-64; dir. geographic intelligence and mapping U.S. Army, Ft. Belvoir, Va., 1964-66, dep. asst. dir. defense intelligence mapping, 1966-69, asst. dir. defense intelligence agy. mapping and charting, 1969-72; dir. Washington ops. Itek Optical Systems, Washington, 1977-91; mem. nat. tech. adv. com. Antarctica Mapping, 1960-64. Decorated Legion of Merit with oak leaf cluster, Bronze star. Home: 301 Cloverway Alexandria VA 22314-4817

RALLI, CONSTANTINE PANDIA, lawyer; b. Bronxville, N.Y., Apr. 6, 1948; s. Pandia C. and Mary (Motter) R.; m. Alison Rhoads, Aug. 11, 1973; children: Pandia C., Christopher A. BA, Middlebury Coll., 1970; JD, Fordham U., 1973; LLM in Taxation, NYU, 1986. Bar: N.Y. 1974, U.S. Ct. Appeals (2nd cir.) 1974, U.S. Dist. Ct. (so. and ea. dists.) N.Y. 1975, U.S. Tax Ct. 1977, Fla. 1985, Conn. 1985, U.S. Dist. Ct. Conn. 1987. Assoc. Davis Polk & Wardwell, N.Y.C., 1973-81; ptnr. Hall, McNicol, Hamilton & Clark, N.Y.C., 1981-88, LeBoeuf, Lamb, Greene & MacRae, N.Y.C., 1988—; sec., bd. dirs. Fairfield-Maxwell Ltd., Campo Tankers SA, N.Y.C., 1987-95. Bd. dirs. Samaritan Counseling Ctr., Rye, N.Y., 1987-90, Rye Free Reading Room, 1990-93, Rye Presbyn. Ch., 1986-89. Mem. Union Club, Am. Yacht Club, Ekwanok Country Club (Manchester, Vt.). Republican. Presbyterian. Home: 11 Rockridge Rd Rye NY 10580-4130 Office: LeBoeuf Lamb Greene & MacRae 125 W 55th St New York NY 10019-5369 also: 411 Pequot Ave Southport CT 06880

RALLS, KATHERINE, zoologist; b. Oakland, Calif., Mar. 21, 1939; d. Alvin Wallingsford and Ruth (McQueen) Smith; m. Kenneth M. Ralls, June 1958 (div. Sept. 1968); children: Robin, Tamsen, Kristin. AB, Stanford U., 1960, MA, Radcliffe Coll., 1962; PhD, Harvard U., 1965. Guest investigator Rockefeller U., N.Y.C., 1968-70, adj. asst. prof. biology, 1970-76; asst. prof. Sarah Lawrence Coll., Bronxville, N.Y., 1970-73; rsch. zoologist Inst. Rsch. in Animal Behavior, N.Y. Zool. Soc., 1970-73; zoologist Nat. Zool. Park, Smithsonian Instn., 1976—; mem. psychobiology adv. panel NSF, 1982-83; mem. sea otter recovery team U.S. Fish and Wildlife Svc., 1989—, mem. Calif. condor recovery team, 1990—; apptd. Hawaiian monk seal recovery team Nat. Marine Fisheries Svc., 1997. Mem. editorial bd. Signs, 1975-78; contbr. articles to profl. jours. Radcliffe Inst. fellow, 1973-74, Smithsonian Instn. fellow, 1973-76. Fellow AAAS, Animal Behavior Soc.; mem. Am. Soc. Mammalogists (bd. dirs. 1984-87, 2d v.p. 1990-91, 92, C. Hart Merriam award 1996), Internat. Union Conservation of Nature and Natural Resources (captive breeding specialist group 1979—, otter specialist group 1989—), Am. Assn. Zool. Pks. and Aquaria (species survival plan subcom. 1981-88), Soc. Marine Mammalogy (editorial bd., book rev. editor Marine Mammal Sci. 1983-89), Soc. Conservation Biology (bd. govs. 1985-90, Edward T. LaRoe award 1996), Animal Behavior Soc., Assn. Women in Sci., Wildlife Soc. Achievements include research in relationship between mammalian social behavior and other aspects of mammalian biology, conservation biology, genetic problems of small populations, and threatened and endangered mammals. Office: Nat Zoo Smithsonian Instn Washington DC 20008

RALPH, DAVID CLINTON, communications educator; b. Muskogee, Okla., Jan. 12, 1922; s. Earl Clinton and Rea Jane (Potter) R.; m. Kathryn Juanita Wicklund, Nov. 29, 1947; children: David Randall, Steven Wicklund. AA, Muskogee Jr. Coll., 1941; BS in Theatre, Northwestern U., 1947, MA in Theatre, 1948, PhD in Speech, 1953. Lectr. Ind. U., Hammond, 1947-48; instr. speech U. Mo., Columbia, 1948-53; tchr. debate-forensics summer program for high sch. students Northwestern U., Evanston, Ill., 1949-51; asst. prof. speech Mich. State U., East Lansing, 1953-57, assoc. prof., 1957-64, prof. speech and theatre, 1964-68, prof. communication, 1968—, dir. communication undergrad. program, 1968-88; cons. on pub. speaking, 1948—. Co-author: Group Discussion, 1954, 2d edit., 1956, Principles of Speaking, 1962, 3d edit., 1975; contbr. articles to profl. jours., chpts. to books. Coach Jr. League Boys' Baseball, Lansing, Mich., 1958-74; mem. civilian aux. to Lansing Fire Dept., 1987—. Lt. USNR, 1942-46, PTO, ETO. Named Hon. State Farmer, Future Farmers Am., 1965; recipient Community Svc. award Mich. State U. Sr. Class Coun., 1979, Outstanding Faculty award, 1987, 91; Teaching Excellence award State of Mich., 1990. Mem. AAUP, Speech Communication Assn., Internat. Communication Assn., Cen. States Communication Assn., Golden Key (hon., faculty advisor), Omicron Delta Kappa. Democrat. Methodist. Avocation: model trains and fire engines. Office: Mich State U Dept Communication East Lansing MI 48824

RALSTON, ANTHONY, computer scientist, mathematician, educator; b. N.Y.C., Dec. 24, 1930; s. Alfred Joseph and Ruth (Bien) R.; m. Jayne Madeleine Rosenthal, Feb. 14, 1958; children: Jonathan, Geoffrey, Steven, Elizabeth. BS, MIT, 1952, PhD, 1956. Mem. tech. staff Bell Tel. Labs., 1956-59; lectr. U. Leeds, 1959-60; mgr. tech. computing Am. Cyanamid Co., 1960-61; assoc. prof. math. Stevens Inst. Tech., 1961-64, prof., 1964-65; dir. computer services SUNY, Buffalo, 1965-70, prof., 1965-95; chmn. dept. computer sci. SUNY, 1967-80; prof. emeritus SUNY, Buffalo, 1995—; bd. examiners Grad. Record Exam in Computer Sci., 1976-82; mem. computer sci. and tech. bd. NRC, 1976-79, math. sci. edn. bd., 1985-89; acad. visitor Imperial Coll., London, 1995—. Author: A First Course in Numerical Analysis, 1965, 2d edit., 1978, Introduction to Programming and Computer Science, 1971, Discrete Algorithmic Mathematics, 1991, Algorithma, 1997; editor: Ency. of Computer Science, 1976, 2d edit., 1982, 3d edit., 1992, ABACUS, 1983-88; co-editor: Mathematical Methods for Digital Computers, Vol. 1, 1960, Vol. 2, 1967, Vol. 3, 1977, The Influence of Computers and Informatics in Mathematics and Its Teaching, 1993. 2d lt. U.S. Army, 1957. Fellow AAAS, Royal Soc. of Arts, Assn. Computing Machinery (pres. 1972-74, mem. coun. 1968-76, Disting. Svc. award 1982); mem. Math. Assn. Am. (bd. govs. 1984-87), Am. Fedn. Info. Processing Soc. (pres. 1975-76), Com. Concerned Scientists (bd. dirs.). Home: Flat 4, 58 Prince Consort Rd, London SW7 2BA, England

RALSTON, HENRY JAMES, III, neurobiologist, anatomist, educator; b. Berkeley, Calif., Mar. 12, 1935; s. Henry James and Sue Harris (Mahnke) R.; m. Diane Cornelia Daly, Oct. 29, 1960; children: Rachel Anne, Amy Sue. BA, U. Calif., Berkeley, 1956, MD, 1959. Intern Mt. Sinai Hosp., N.Y.C., 1959-60; resident in medicine U. Calif., San Francisco, 1960-61, prof., 1973—, chmn. dept. anatomy, 1973—, chair acad. senate, 1986-88; spl. postdoctoral fellow Univ. Coll., London, 1963-65, Univ. lectr., 1981; asst. prof. anatomy Stanford (Calif.) U., 1965-69; assoc. prof. U. Wis., Madison, 1969-73; cons. NIH; mem. com. for future of anat. scis., Macy Found., 1977-80; vis. prof. French Med. Rsch. Inst.-INSERM, Paris, 1981-82; chair step I U.S. Med. Lic. Examination Com. Nat. Bd. Med. Examiners, 1992-96. With M.C. U.S. Army, 1961-63. Recipient Henry J. Kaiser award for excellence in tchg., 1978, Jacob Javits Neurosci. Investigator award NIH, 1988-95; USPHS grantee, 1966—. Mem. AAAS, Soc. Neurosci., Soc. Study Pain, Am. Pain Soc., Am. Assn. Anatomists (pres. 1987-88, chair publs. com. 1989-91, Henry Gray award 1996), Anat. Assn. Gt. Britain, Anat. Assn. Gt. Britain, Alpha Omega Alpha. Research in field of organization of mammalian nervous system studied by electron microscopy, mechanisms subserving pain in animals and humans. Office: U Calif Dept Anatomy PO Box 0452 San Francisco CA 94143

RALSTON, JOANNE SMOOT, public relations counseling firm executive; b. Phoenix, May 13, 1939; d. A. Glen and Virginia (Lee) Smoot; m. W. Hamilton Weigelt, Aug. 15, 1991. B.A. in Journalism, Ariz. State U., 1960. Reporter, The Ariz. Republic, Phoenix, 1960-62; co-owner, pub. relations dir. The Patton Agy., Phoenix, 1962-71; founder, pres., owner Joanne Ralston & Assocs., Inc., Phoenix, 1971-87, 92—; pres. Nelson Ralston Robb Comm., Phoenix, 1987-91; pres. Joanne Ralston & Assoc., Inc., Scottsdale, Ariz., 1992—. Contbr. articles to profl. jours. Bd. dirs. Ariz. Parklands Found., 1984-86, Gov.'s Council on Health, Phys. Fitness and Sports, 1984-86; task force mem. Water and Natural Resources Council, Phoenix, 1984-86; mem. Ariz. Republican Caucus, 1984—, others. Recipient Lulu' awards (36) Los Angeles Advt. Women, 1964—, Gold Quill (2) Internat. Assn. Bus. Communicators, Excellence awards Fin. World mag., 1982-93, others; named to Walter Cronkite Sch. Journalism Hall of Fame, Coll. Pub. Programs Ariz. State U., 1987; name one of 25 Most Influential Arizonians, Phoenix Mag., 1991. Mem. Pub. Relations Soc. Am. (counselor sect.), Internat. Assn. Bus. Communicators, Phoenix Press Club (pres. bd.), Investor Rels. Inst., Phoenix Met. C. of C. (bd. dirs. 1977-84, 85-91), Phoenix Country Club. Republican. Avocations: horses, skiing. Office: 5725 N Scottsdale Rd C 105 Scottsdale AZ 85253-3664

RALSTON, JOSEPH W., career officer; b. Hopkinsville, Ky., Nov. 4, 1943; m. Diane Dougherty; children: Christopher, Paige, David, Sarah. Grad., Miami (Ohio) U., 1965; M in Pers. Mgmt., Ctrl. Mich. U.; student, Army Command and Gen. Staff Coll., Nat. War Coll. at Fort McNair, Harvard U. Mem. reserve officer tng. program USAF, 1965, advanced through grades to vice-chmn. of the Joint Chiefs of Staff, 1996—; chmn. Joint Requirements Oversight Coun., Planning, Programming and Budgeting Sys.; vice-chmn. Defense Acquisition Bd.; active Nat. Security Coun. Deputies Com., Nuclear Weapons Coun. Nation's second highest ranking mil. officer. Office: Joint Chiefs Staff The Pentagon Washington DC 20318*

RALSTON, LENORE DALE, academic policy and program analyst; b. Oakland, Calif., Feb. 21, 1949; d. Leonard Earnest and Emily Allison (Hudnut) R. BA in Anthropology, U. Calif., Berkeley, 1971, MPH in Behavioral Sci., 1981; MA in Anthropology, Bryn Mawr Coll., 1973, PhD in Anthropology, 1980. Asst. rschr. anthropology inst. internat. studies U. Calif., Berkeley, 1979-82, rsch. assoc. Latin Am. Study Ctr., 1982-83, acad. asst. to dean Sch. of Optometry, 1990-95, prin. policy analyst, chancellor's office, 1995—; assoc. scientist, rsch. adminstr. Med. Rsch. Inst., San Francisco, 1982-85; cons. health sci. Berkeley, 1986-90; mem. fin. bd. Med. Rsch. Inst., 1983-84; speaker in field. Co-author: Voluntary Effects in Decentralized Management, 1983; contbr. articles to profl. jours. Commr. Cmty. Health Adv. Com., Berkeley, 1988-90; vice chair, commr. Cmty. Health Commn., Berkeley, 1990-93; mem. bd. safety com. Miles, Inc., Berkeley, 1992—. Grantee Nat. Rsch. Svc. Award, WHO, NIMH, NSF. Fellow Applied Anthropology Assn.; mem. APHA, Am. Anthropology Assn., Sigma Xi. Home: 1232 Carlotta Ave Berkeley CA 94707-2707

RALSTON, LUCY VIRGINIA GORDON, artist; b. Washington, Sept. 9, 1926; d. Byron Brown and Lucy (Virginia (Gordon) R. Grad., Finch Jr. Coll., 1942; student, Parsons Sch. Design; studied with, Leon Kroll. Freelance artist Tiffany and Co., 1947-48; designer U.S.S. Constution book Am. Bible Soc. and John Jay and Eliza Jane Watson Found. for presentation Bibles to grads. U.S. Naval Acad., USCG Acad., Marchant Marine Acad., 1953—; art tchr. Sr. Citizens of Pelham, 1948-50. One-woman show Pelham (N.Y.) Meml. High Sch., 1939; exhibited in group shows Westchester Fedn. Women's Clubs, Bronxville, N.Y., 1954, Mt. Vernon (N.Y.) Art Assn., 1955, Allied Artists Am., N.Y.C., 1955, others; represented in permanent collections Assn. Jr. Leagues Am., N.Y.C. and tour U.S. and Can., John Jay and Eliza Jane Watson Found., Elizabeth, N.J.; executed mural at Westchester Restaurant, Mamaroneck, N.Y.; commd. portraits of Princess Anne and Prince Charles of Eng., Brit. Am. Soc. Vol. numerous civic orgns., 1942-45. Recipient Popular prize Manor Club, 1947, 48, 2d prize, 1958, 1st prize for graphic art, 1957; Popular prize Westchester Assn. Women's Clubs, 1951, Mt. Vernon Art Assn., 1954, 2d prize Met. Mus., Pelham, 1969. Mem. DAR (registrar Knapp chpt. 1961-63, rec. sec. Anne Hutchinson chpt. 1989—), Jr. League Pelham, Daus. of Cin. (registrar 1973-78), Colonial Soc. Ams. Royal Descent, Nat. Soc. Magna Carta Dames, Colonial Soc. Descs. Knights of Garter, Colonial Order Crown, Huguenot Soc. Am., Welcome to Washington Internat. Club. Republican. Episcopalian. Avocations: raising purebred dogs, swimming, sailing. Home and Studio: 4784 Boston Post Rd Pelham NY 10803

RALSTON, RICHARD H., lawyer; b. L.A., Sept. 28, 1942. BA, U. Kans., 1965; JD, U. Mo., Kansas City, 1969. Bar: Mo. 1969, U.S. Dist. Ct. (we. dist.) Mo., U.S. Ct. Appeals (8th cir.). Law clerk to Hon. Elmo B. Hunter U.S. Dist. Ct. (we. dist.) Mo., 1968-72, U.S. magistrate judge, 1976-88; prof. law Creighton U., 1972-76; mem. Polsinelli, White, Vardeman & Shalton, Kansas City, Mo.; adj. prof. law U. Mo. Kansas City, 1977-79; chmn. subcom. on patterned civil jury instructions U.S. Ct. Appeals (8th cir.), 1986—. Editor-in-chief U. Mo. Kansas City Law Rev., 1968-69; contbr. articles to profl. jours. Mem. ABA (chmn. state membership com. 1988—), Mo. Bar (chmn. fed. practice com. 1988-92), Kansas City Met. Bar Assn., Ross T. Roberts Inn Ct. (master 1986-91), Phi Delta Phi. Office: Polsinelli White Vardeman & Shalton 700 W 47th St Ste 1000 Kansas City MO 64112-1805

RAM, CHITTA VENKATA, physician; b. Machilipatnam, India, Oct. 24, 1948; s. Chitta M. Row and Chitta (Cheruvu) Sarojini; m. Ashalata Ram, Feb. 17, 1979; children: Gita, Radha. B.Sci, Marathwada U., Aurangabad, India, 1966; MD, Osmania U., Hyderabad, India, 1972. Diplomate Am. Bd. Internal Medicine. Resident in internal medicine Brown U., R.I. Hosp., Providence, 1974-76; fellow in hypertension Hosp. U. Pa., Phila., 1976-77; faculty assoc. U. Tex. Southwestern Med. Ctr., Dallas, 1977-78, asst. prof., 1978-83, assoc. prof., 1983-89; prof., 1989—; dir. hypertension clinic Parkland Meml. Hosp., Dallas, hypertension unit St. Paul Med. Ctr., Dallas, dir. continuing med. edn. dept., 1996—, chmn. instnl. rev. com., 1996—, pres. med. staff, 1997—. Contbr. numerous articles to profl. jours. and chpts. to textbooks; editl. cons., reviewer numerous nat. and internat. jours. and pubs. Pres. Tex. IndoAm. Physician Soc., Dallas, 1988; trustee Dallas/Ft. Worth Hindu Temple Soc., Dallas, 1988. Named Outstanding Tchr. St. Paul Med. Ctr., 1982; recipient Mother of India award, 1992. Fellow ACP, Am. Coll. Cardiology, Am. Coll. Chest Physicians (regent), Am. Coll. Clin. Pharmacology; mem. Am. Assn. Physicians from India (pres.-elect 1994-95, pres. 1995-96), Tex. Indo-Am. Physicians Soc. Office: St Paul Med Ctr 5939 Harry Hines Blvd Ste 600 Dallas TX 75235-6243

RAMACHANDRAN, VENKATANARAYANA DEEKSHIT, electrical engineering educator; b. Mysore, India, May 3, 1934; s. K.C. Venkatanarayana Deekshit and Subbamma Deekshit R.; m. Kamala Visweswaraiya, June 12, 1960; 1 child, Ravi P. BS, U. Mysore, 1953; B in Engring., Indian Inst. Sci., Bangalore, 1956, M in Electronics, 1958, PhD, 1965. Registered profl. engr. Sr. research asst. Indian Inst. Sci., 1958-59, lectr., 1959-66; asst. prof. N.S. Tech. Coll., Halifax, Can., 1966-69; prof. elec. engring. Concordia U. (formerly Sir George Williams Univ.), Halifax, Can., 1971—; acting chmn. dept. elec. and computer engring. Montreal, various times; grad. program dir. dept., 1969-84; adj. prof. U. Windsor, Ont., Can., 1983—, Ecole Tech. Superieure U. Quebec, Montreal, 1989—; mem. program com. Internat. Symposium on Operator Theory of Networks and Systems, 1975; vice chmn. Internat. Symposium on Circuits and Systems IEEE, Montreal, 1984, mem. tech. program com., 1987; internat. coordinator Internat. Conf. on Computers, Systems and Signal Processing, Indian Inst. Sci., 1984. Author papers in profl. jours., over 125 papers presented to confs., others. Named to Order of Engrs. of Que.; recipient Merit award Concordia Council on Student Life, 1981-82, Outstanding Contbn. award Engring. and Computer Sci. Assn., Concordia U., 1996. Fellow Inst. Electronics and Telecomms. India (edit. bd. jour. 1986), Inst. Engrs. India, Inst. Elec. Engrs. Eng., Engring. Inst. Can. (sec. Montreal chpt. 1979-80, centennial bd. 1983-84), IEEE; mem. Circuits and Systems chpt. IEEE (chmn. Montreal sect. 1978-84), Can. Soc. Elec. Engrs. (editor jour. 1983-85, editor bull. 1981-83), Am. Soc. Engring. Edn. (chmn. awards com. St. Lawrence chpt. 1987-88, Western Elec. Fund award 1983, Myril B. Reed Best Rsch. Paper award 1984, Outstanding Svc. 1993). Office: Concordia U Faculty of Engring, 1455 de Maisonneuve Blvd W, Montreal, PQ Canada H3G 1M8

RAMADHYANI, SATISH, mechanical engineering educator; b. Bangalore, Karnataka, India, Aug. 1, 1949; came to U.S., 1975; s. K. R. Keshavachar and Padma (Iyengar) R.; m. Rachel B. Sparrow, June 17, 1979. B of Tech., Indian Inst. of Tech., Madras, India, 1971; MS, U. Minn., 1977, PhD, 1979. Asst. engr. devel. Motor Industries Co., Bangalore, 1971-75; asst. prof. Dept. Mech. Engring., Tufts U., Medford, Mass., 1979-83; asst. prof. Sch. of Mech. Engring., Purdue U., West Lafayette, Ind., 1983-86, assoc. prof., 1986-91, prof., 1991—, dir. grad. studies in mech. engring., 1996—; expert cons. Teltech, Inc., Mpls., 1990—; expert reviewer numerous profl. jours. and funding agys., 1979—. Assoc. tech. editor ASME Jour. of Heat Transfer; mem. edtl. adv. bd. Internat. Jour. for Numerical Heat Transfer; contbr. over 60 articles to profl. jours. Recipient Pres. of India Gold Medal Govt. India, 1971. Mem. AIAA, ASME (mem. heat transfer div. K-6), Am. Soc. of Engring. Educators, Phi Kappa Phi, Tau Beta Pi, Sigma Xi. Achievements include development of new finite-element and finite-volume computational techniques for heat transfer and fluid flow problems, liquid immersion cooling technology for high-speed digital computers, mathematical models to predict performance of industrial furnaces. Office: Purdue U Sch Of Mech Engring West Lafayette IN 47907

RAMAGE, JAMES EVERETT, JR., respiratory and critical care physician, educator; b. Downers Grove, Ill., Dec. 15, 1944; s. James Everett and Patsy Eva (Huggins) R.; m. Patricia Lee Kraemer, Apr. 9, 1984; children: Mollie, Maxwell, Spencer. BS in Biology, Stanford U., 1977; MD, Duke U., 1981. Cert. Am. Bd. Internal Medicine. Intern Emory U., Atlanta, 1981-82, resident, 1982-84; fellow Duke U., Durham, N.C., 1984-87; clinician Med. Assocs. of Savannah, Ga., 1987-96, Savannah Ctr. for Respiratory and Critical Care Medicine, 1996—; med. dir. Med. ICU Meml. Med. Ctr., Savannah, 1990—. Contbr. rsch. papers to med. jours. Fellow ACP, Am. Coll. Chest Physicians; mem. Am. Thoracic Soc. (health care policy com. 1992-93), Ga. Thoracic Soc. (chmn. clin. practice com. 1993—), Phi Beta Kappa. Office: Savannah Ctr for Respiratory and Critical Care Medicine 4750 Waters Ave Ste 301 Savannah GA 31404-6268

RAMAGE, MARTIS DONALD, JR., banker; b. Tupelo, Miss., Oct. 6, 1957; s. Martis Donald and Helen Frances (Estes) R. AA, Itawamba Jr. Coll., Fulton, Miss., 1978; BBA in Banking and Fin., U. Miss., 1980; grad., Mid South Sch. of Banking, 1989. Mgmt. trainee Peoples Bank & Trust Co., Tupelo, 1981-82, asst. cashier, 1983-89, asst. v.p., 1989-90, v.p., 1990-93, 1st v.p., 1993—; sec. Peoples Holding Co., 1993-96, v.p., 1996—. Author: Our Ramage Family, 1986, Mississippi Society SAR 1909-1993, Tupelo, Mississippi, Tornado 1936, 1997; co-editor: The Peoples Bank & Trust Co-In Partnership with the Community, 1989; editor N.E. Miss. Hist. Geneal. Soc. Quar. Sec., treas. United Way of Greater Lee County, Tupelo, 1988-89, Leadership Lee; pres. Friends of Lee County Libr., 1995-97; bd. dirs. Brice's Battlefield Commn., Inc., 1995—; trustee Miss. Dept. Archives and History, 1996—; chmn. Christmas Festival Com., Tupelo, 1990-91. Mem. SAR (trustee 1992-94, pres. Miss. 1991-92, v.p. 1994—, Silver Good Citizenship medal 1990), SCV, Mil. Order of Stars and Bars, Am. Inst. Banking (pres. Tupelo chpt. 1986-87), Ole Miss. Alumni Assn. (bd. dirs. 1991-94), Tupelo Luncheon Civitan Club, Masons, Bank Adm. Inst. (North Miss. chpt. pres. 1994-95, v.p. 1990-94), Tupelo Artists Guild (bd. dirs., sec. 1996—), Miss. Hist. Soc. (bd. dirs. 1995-97), Itawamba Jr. Coll. Alumni Assn. (pres. 1982-83). Home: 4218 Ridgemont Dr Belden MS 38826-9785 Office: Peoples Bank & Trust Co 209 Troy St Tupelo MS 38801-4827

RAMAKRISHNAN, VENKATASWAMY, civil engineer, educator; b. Coimbatore, India, Feb. 27, 1929; came to U.S., 1969, naturalized, 1981; s. Venkataswamy and Kondammal (Krishnaswamy) R.; m. Vijayalakshmi Unnava, Nov. 7, 1962; children: Aravind, Anand. B.Engring., U. Madras, 1952, D.S.S., 1953; D.I.C. in Hydropower and Concrete Tech, Imperial Coll., London, 1957; Ph.D., Univ. Coll., U. London, 1960. From lectr. to prof. civil engring., head dept. P.S.G. Coll. Tech., U. Madras, 1952-69; vis. prof. S.D. Sch. Mines and Tech., Rapid City, 1969-70, prof. civil engring., 1970—, dir. concrete tech. research, 1970-71, head grad. div. structural mechanic and concrete tech., 1971—; program coordinator materials engring. and sci. Ph.D. program S.D. Sch. Mines and Tech., —, 1985-86; disting. prof. S.D. Sch. Mines and Tech., Rapid City, 1996—. Author: Ultimate Strength Design for Structural Concrete, 1969; also over 200 articles. Recipient Outstanding Prof. award S.D. Sch. Mines and Tech., 1980, 1st Rsch. award, 1994; Colombo Plan fellow, 1955-60. Mem. Internat. Assn. Bridge and Structural Engring., ASCE (vice chmn. constrn. div. publs. com. 1974), Am. Concrete Inst. (chmn. subcom. gen. considerations for founds., chmn. com. 214 on evaluation of strength test results, sec.-treas. Dakota chpt. 1974-79, v.p. 1980, pres. 1981), Instn. Hwy. Engrs., Transp. Rsch. Bd. (chmn. com. on admixtures and curing, chmn. com. on mech. properties concrete), Am. Soc. Engring. Edn., NSPE, Internat. Coun. Gap-Graded Concrete Rsch. and Application, Sigma Xi. Address: 1809 Sheridan Lake Rd Rapid City SD 57702-4219 *To me, success is a coin with hard work on one side and perseverance with devotion on the other. No matter what—head or tails—the message is the same: keep on working. Goals in my life were pursuit of truth and beauty. The structures I have created, and my writings based on research have given me greater satisfaction than any wealth, position, or power.*

RAMALEY, JUDITH AITKEN, academic administrator, endocrinologist; b. Vincennes, Ind., Jan. 11, 1941; d. Robert Henry and Mary Krebs (McCullough) Aitken; m. Robert Folk Ramaley, Mar. 1966 (div. 1976); children: Alan Aitken, Andrew Folk. BA, Swarthmore Coll., 1963; PhD, UCLA, 1966; postgrad., Ind. U., 1967-69. Rsch. assoc., lectr. Ind. U., Bloomington, 1967-68, asst. prof. dept. anatomy and physiology, 1969-72; asst. prof. dept. physiology and biophysics U. Nebr. Med. Ctr., Omaha, 1972-74, assoc. prof., 1974-78, prof., 1978-82, assoc. dean for rsch. and devel., 1979-81; asst. v.p. for acad. affairs U. Nebr., Lincoln, 1980-82; prof. biol. scis. SUNY, Albany, N.Y., 1982-87, v.p. for acad. affairs, 1982-85, acting pres., 1984, exec. v.p. for acad. affairs, 1985-87; exec. vice chancellor U. Kans., Lawrence, 1987-90; pres. Portland (Oreg.) State U., 1990—; mem. endocrinology study sect. NIH, 1981-84; cons.-evaluator North Cen. Accreditation, 1978-82, 89-90; mem. regulatory panel NSF, 1979-82; mem. Ill. Commn. Scholars, 1980-90; adv. com. Bank of Am.; mem. ACE Commn. on Govt. Rels. Co-author: Progesterone Function: Molecular and Biochemical Aspects, 1972; Essentials of Histology, 8th edit., 1979; editor: Covert Discrimination, Women in the Sciences, 1978; contbr. articles to profl. jours. Bd. dirs. Family Svc. of Omaha, 1979-82, Albany Symphony Orch., 1984-87, mem. exec. com., 1986-87, 2d v.p., mem. exec. com., 1986-87, Capital Repertory Co., 1986-89, Assn. Portland Progress, 1990—, City Club of Portland, 1991-92, Metro Family Svcs., 1993—, Campbell Inst. for Children, Portland Met. Sports Authority, 1994; vice-chair Ore. Campus Compact (exec. com. 1996—), nat. adv. coun. Sch.-Work Opportunities, 1996—; bd. dirs. NCAA Pres. Commn., 1991, chair divsn. II subcom., 1994, mem. joint policy bd., 1994; chmn. bd. dirs. Albany Water Fin. Authority, 1987; mem. exec. com. United Way Douglas County, 1989-90; mem. adv. bd. Emily Taylor Women's Resource Ctr., U. Kans., 1988-90; mem. Silicon Prairie Tech. Assn., 1989-90, Portland Opera Bd., 1991-92, Portland Leaders Roundtable, 1991—; mem. bd. devel. com. United Way of Columbia-Willamette, 1991—; active Ore. Women's Forum, 1991—, Portland Met. Sports Authority; progress bd. Portland-Multnomah County, 1993—. NSF grantee, 1969-71, 71-77, 75-82, 77-80, 80-83. Fellow AAAS; mem. Nat. Assn. State Univs. and Land Grant Colls. (exec. com., mem. senate 1986-88, vice chair commn. urban agenda 1992—), Assn. Am. Colls. and Univs. (bd. dirs. 1995—), ACE commn. govt. rels., Kellogg Commn. on future of state and land-grant univs.; mem. Endocrine Soc. (chmn. edn. com. 1980-85), Soc. Study Reprodn. (treas. 1983-85), Soc. for Neurosci., Am. Physiol. Soc., Am. Coun. on Edn. (chmn. commn. on women in higher edn. 1987-88), Assn. Portland Progress (bd. dirs.), Portland C. of C. (bd. dirs. 1995), Western Assn. of Schs. and Colls. (commr. 1994). Office: Portland State U Office of the President PO Box 751 Portland OR 97207-0751

RAMANARAYANAN, MADHAVA PRABHU, science administrator, researcher, educator; b. Varapuzha, Kerala, India, Feb. 5, 1945; came to U.S., 1972; s. Srinivasa Madhava and Priyothama (Shenoy) Prabhu; m. Leelavati Murthy, Sept. 2, 1972; children: Malini, Ananth. BS, American Coll., Madurai, India, 1964, MS, 1966; PhD, Indian Inst. Sci., Bangalore, India, 1972. Post-doctoral research worker dept. biochemistry Coll. Physicians and Surgeons of Columbia U., N.Y.C., 1972-75; staff assoc. Inst. Cancer Research, Columbia U., N.Y.C., 1975-81; dir. research & devel. Diagnostic Reagent Tech., Teaneck, N.J., 1981-85; v.p. research & devel. Visual Diagnostics, Inc., Teaneck, 1985-88; pres. Windsor Park Labs., Inc., Teaneck, 1988—; lectr., instr. postgrad. courses Am. Acad. Otolaryngic Allergy. Contbr. sci. articles to profl. jours. Fellow Am. Inst. Chemists, Nat. Acad. Clin. Biochemistry; mem. N.Y. Acad. Scis., Am. Chem. Soc., Internat. Union Pure and Applied Chemistry, Am. Assn. for Clin. Chemistry.

RAMANATHAN, KAVASSERI VAIDIANATHA, accounting educator, researcher, consultant; b. Trichur, Kerala, India, Nov. 26, 1932; came to U.S., 1966; s. Kavasseri Viswanatha and Saraswathy (Apathira) Vaidianathan; m. Rajalakshmi Ramanathan, Apr. 22, 1959; 1 dau., Saraswathy. B.Com., Calcutta U., India, 1954; M.B.A., Northwestern U., 1962, Ph.D., 1970. Systems mgr. Philips India Ltd., Calcutta, 1955-59; prof. acctg. Indian Inst. Mgmt., Ahmedabad, 1963-66; assoc. prof. acctg. U. Wash., Seattle, 1969-79, prof. acctg., 1979—, chmn. exec. M.B.A. program, 1982-86; dir. Russian programs, 1992-95; vis. scientist Battelle Meml. Inst., Seattle, 1974-77; vis. prof. Harvard U., Cambridge, Mass., 1979-80; vis. fellow Australian Nat. U., Canberra, 1983, Monash U., Australia, 1983; vis. prof. NYU, N.Y.C., 1986-87, U. Auckland, 1992. Author: Management Control in Nonprofit Organizations, 1982; editor: Accounting for Managerial Decision Making, 1974, Readings in Management Control in Nonprofit Organizations, 1982. Adviser Sandeepany West, Piercy, Calif., 1981-82; bd. dirs. Arsha Vidya Pitam, Los Gatos, Calif., 1982—; pres. Ragamala, Seattle; founder, chmn. Hindu Temple & Community Ctr. Pacific N.W., Seattle, 1988—. Fulbright scholar Calcutta, 1960-63. Fellow Indian Inst. of Cost and Works Accts.; mem. Am. Acctg. Assn. , Fin. Execs. Inst., Inst. of Mgmt. Accts. Home: 19311 63rd Ave NE Seattle WA 98155-3331 Office: Univ Wash Dj 10 Dept Acctg # 10 Seattle WA 98195

RAMANI, RAJA VENKAT, mining engineering educator; b. Madras, India, Aug. 4, 1938; came to U.S., 1966; s. Natesa and Meenakshi (Srinivasan) Rajaraman; m. Geetha V. Chalam, July 9, 1972; children: Deepak, Gautam. BSc with honors, Indian Sch. Mines, Dhanbad, Bihar, 1962, DSc (hon.), 1997; MS, Pa. State U., 1968, PhD, 1970. Registered profl. engr., Pa., 1971; lic. first class mine mgr., 1965. Mining engr., mgr. Andrew Yule & Co., Asansol, West Bengal, India, 1962-66; grad. asst. Pa. State U., University Park, 1966-70, asst. prof., 1970-74, assoc. prof., 1974-78, prof. mining engring., 1978—, chmn. mineral engring. mgmt. sect., 1974—, head dept. mineral engring., 1987—; chmn. com. post-disaster survival/rescue NAS, Washington, 1979-81; cons. UN, UN Devel. Program, Dept. Econ. and Social Devel., N.Y.C., 1983-97; cons., expert panels U.S. Dept. Labor, 1979, 92, 96, HHS, 1977, 92, U.S. Dept. State, 1986, 87, U.S. Dept. Interior, 1995, Dept. Environ. Resources, Commonwealth of Pa., 1990, 92; co-dir. Generic Mineral Tech. Ctr. on Respirable Dust, U.S. Bur. Mines, 1983—, Nat. Mines/Land Reclamation Ctr., 1988—, Std. Oil Ctr. of Excellence on Longwall Tech., 1983-89; presenter in field. Sect. editor, author: Computer Methods for the Eighties, 1979, SME Mining Engineering Handbook, 1992; editor State-of-the-Art in Longwall-Shortwall Mining, 1981, Longwall Thick Seam Mining, 1988. Computers in Mineral Industry, 1994. Recipient Disting. Alumni award Indian Sch. Mines, Dhanbad, 1978, Ednl. Excellence award Pitts. Coal Mining Inst., 1986, Environ. Conservation award AIME, N.Y.C., 1990, Howard N. Eavenson award SME/AIME, N.Y.C., 1991, Robert Stefanko Best Paper award, 1993, Coal Divsn. Disting. Svc. award, 1993, Howard L. Hartman award, 1997, Percy H. Nicholls award AIME/ASME Joint Soc., 1994; Fulbright scholar to Soviet Union Coun. Internat. Exch. of Scholars, Washington, , 1989-90; Henry Krumb lectr. AIME, 1994. Mem. Internat. Coun. for Application of Computers in the Mineral Industry (chmn. 1984-87, Disting. Achievement award 1989), Soc. Mining, Metall. and Exploration (Disting. Mem. 1989, pres. 1995), Mine Ventillation Soc. South Africa, Inst. for Ops. Rsch. and Mgmt. Scis. Achievements include research in health, safety, environmental and productivity aspects in underground and surface mining engineering. Home: 285 Oakley Dr State College PA 16803-1349 Office: Dept Mineral Engring Pa State U University Park PA 16802

RAMANUJA, TERALANDUR KRISHNASWAMY, structural engineer; b. Mysore, Mysore, India, June 23, 1941; came to U.S., 1967, naturalized, 1979; s. Teralandur R. and Padmammal Krishnaswamy; m. Jayalakshmi Ramanuja, Jan. 18, 1971; children: Srinivasan, Rekha. BSCE, U. Mysore, 1962; MS in Structural Engring., U. Notre Dame, 1969. Registered profl. engr., Ill., Mich., Ind., N.Y. Sub-divisional officer Mil. Engring. Svcs., Bangalore, India, 1962-67; structural engr. Clyde E. Williams and Assocs., South Bend, Ind., 1969-73; head structural engring. dept. Ayres, Lewis, Norris & May, Cons. Engrs., Ann Arbor, Mich., 1973-76; sr. project mgr. Johnson & Anderson Cons. Engrs., Pontiac, Mich., 1976-78; supr. Bechtel Power Corp., Ann Arbor, 1978-85; supr. Shoreham Nuclear Power Sta. Lilco, N.Y.C., 1985-89; supervising engr. Clinton (Ill.) Power Sta. Ill. Power Co., 1989—. Fellow ASCE; mem. Am. Concrete Inst.; mem. Chi Epsilon. Achievements include structural and foundation design of facilities for fossil and nuclear power plants, water/waste treatment plants, petrochemical plants, pulp and paper mills and for heavy equipment/machinery for these plants; seismic and dynamic analysis of structures, systems and components in nuclear power plants. Home: 2006 Hidden Lake Rd Bloomington IL 61704-7283 Office: Ill Power Co Clinton Power Sta PO Box 678 Clinton IL 61727-0678

RAMAPRASAD, SUBBARAYA, medical educator; b. Mysore, India, May 20, 1954; came to the U.S., 1980, naturalized, 1993; s. Puttaniah and Sharadamma Subbaraya; m. Padma, Sept. 28, 1987; 1 child, Sanjay. PhD, Indian Inst. Sci., 1979. Instr. U. Ark. Med. Scis., Little Rock, 1989-91, asst. prof., 1991-94, assoc. prof., 1995—. Contbr. articles to profl. jours. Grantee NIMH, 1994, Ark. Sci. Tech. Authority, 1991, 95. Mem. Internat. Soc. Magnetic Resonance Medicine, N.Y. Acad. Sci., Soc. PHotooptical Instrumentation Engrs., Sigma Xi. Hindu. Avocation: photography. Home: 5 Sams Cove Little Rock AR 72212 Office: U Ark Med Sci Dept Radiol 4301 W Markham St Little Rock AR 72205-7101

RAMATY, REUVEN ROBERT, physicist, researcher; b. Timisoara, Rumania, Feb. 25, 1937; came to U.S., 1963; s. Nikolas and Elizabeth (Markowitz) Reiter; m. Vera Marie Klein, Aug. 8, 1961; children: Daphne, Deborah. BSc, Tel-Aviv (Israel) U., Israel, 1961; PhD, UCLA, 1966. Rsch. assoc. UCLA, 1966-67; rsch. assoc. NASA/Goddard Space Flight Ctr., Greenbelt, Md., 1967-69, astrophysicist, 1969-80, head Theory Office, 1980-93, sr. scientist, 1993—; adj. prof. U. Md., College Park, 1983—; orgnizer several internat. confs. Contbr. over 200 articles and papers to sci. jours. Fellow Am. Phys. Soc. (chmn. div. cosmic physics 1977-78, councilor div. astrophysics 1985-89); mem. Am. Astron. Soc. (chmn. div. high energy astrophysics 1984-85), Internat. Astron. Union. Achievements include research in the origin of the elements, the origin of cosmic rays and high energy processes in solar flares. Avocations: linguistics, foreign languages, history, geography. Office: Goddard Space Flight Ctr Greenbelt MD 20771

RAMBERG, WALTER DODD, architect; b. Charlotte, N.C., Feb. 17, 1932; s. Walter Gustav Charles and Julia Elisabeth (Lineberger) R.; m. Lucinda Jenifer Ballard, Nov. 25, 1961 (dec. 1989); children: Lucinda E.G., Jenny S.F., Julia E.L.; m. Seska Peck Dunne, Sept. 14, 1996. B.A., Yale U., 1953, M.Arch., 1956. Fulbright fellow Kyoto (Japan) U., 1956-58; apprentice architect Paul Rudolph, New Haven, 1958-61; project designer Meyer & Ayers, Balt., 1961-63; partner Howe & Ramberg, Washington, 1963-65; prin. Walter Dodd Ramberg (Architect), Washington, 1965—; prof. architecture Cath. U. Am., 1977—; mem. design adv. panel Balt. Dept. Housing and Community, 1973—; mem. bd. architecture rev. Baltimore County, 1986-89. Designer: N.W. Balt. High Sch, 1963 (P.A. Excellence in Design award); architect: Bridge for Washington Cathedral, 1965 (Excellence in Design award Washington Bd. Trade, AIA), Kidder Guest House, 1965 (1st Honor award Balt. AIA), Azrael House, 1969 (Honor award Balt. AIA), Cutts House, 1973 (Honor award Balt. AIA), Woody House, 1975 (Merit award Balt. AIA), Lineberger Meml. Library, 1976 (Merit award Nat. AIA, ALA); contbr. articles to profl. publs. Served to lt. USCGR, 1958-59. Mem. AIA (corp.), AAUP, Soc. Archtl. Historians. Episcopalian. Club: Met. (Washington). Home: 1651 Belfast Rd Sparks MD 21152-9788 Office: 1830 T St NW Washington DC 20009-7138

RAMBO, A. TERRY, anthropologist, research program director; b. San Francisco, Apr. 3, 1940; s. Arthur Ira Rambo and Dorothy V. (Miller) Schlee; m. Dawn Jean Bowman, Jan. 24, 1971 (dec. July 1987); children: Charmaine Malia, Claire Norani. AB in Anthropology with distinction, U. Mich., 1963; MA in Anthropology, Am. U., 1969; PhD in Anthropology, U. Hawaii, 1972. Rsch. scientist Human Scis. Rsch., Inc., McLean, Va., 1964-69; acting asst. prof. anthropology U. Hawaii, 1971-72; asst. prof. anthropology Wash. State U., 1972-73; vis. prof. social sci. Grad. Sch. Politics and Econs., Dalat U., Saigon, Vietnam, 1973-75; lectr. dept. anthropology and sociology U. Malaya, 1975-80; sr. fellow, coord. program on renewable resources mgmt. East-West Ctr. Environ. and Policy Inst., Honolulu, 1980-92; dir. program on environ., coord. Indochina initiative East-West Ctr., Honolulu, 1992-97, sr. fellow, program on environment, 1997—; bd. dirs. S.E. Asian Univs. Agroecosystem Network; cons. in field. Author: Primitive Polluters, 1985, Comparison of Peasant Social Systems of Northern and Southern Vietnam, 1973; co-editor: An Introduction to Human Ecology Research on Agricultural Systems in Southeast Asia, 1984, Cultural Values and Human Ecology in Southeast Asia, 1985, Ethnic Diversity and the Control of Natural Resources in Southeast Asia, 1988, Agroecosystems of the Midlands of Northern Vietnam: A Report on a Preliminary Human Ecology Field Study of Three Districts in Vinh Phu Province, 1990, Environment, Natural Resources, and the Future Development of Laos and Vietnam: Papers from a Seminar, 1991, Profiles in Cultural Evolution, 1991, The Challenges of Vietnam's Reconstruction, 1992, Too Many People, Too Little Land: The Human Ecology of a Wet Rice-Growing Village in the Red River Delta of Vietnam, 1993, The Challenges of Highland Development in Vietnam, 1995, Some Issues of Human Ecology in Vietnam (in Vietnamese), 1995, Red Books, Green Hills: The Impact of Economic Reform on Restoration Ecology in the Midlands of Northern Vietnam, 1996; also reports, papers, monographs, procs. in field; contbr. articles to profl. publs., chpts. to books. Grantee Asia Soc./SEADAG, 1969-70, U. Malaya, 1976-79, Ford Found., 1978-79, 84, 85-87, 87-89, 91-93, 95-96, 96—, U. Hawaii East-West Ctr., 1981-82, 84-85, Rockefeller Bros. Fund, 1988-89, 90-92, 94-95, 97—, MacArthur Found., 1990-91, 91-93, 93-95, 96—, Luce Found., 1995-96; Nat. Def. Fgn. Lang. fellow 1970-71, Ford Found. S.E. Asia rsch. fellow, 1972, 73-74, 75-76. Avocations: gardening, backpacking, reading. Office: East-West Ctr Program on Environment 1601 E West Rd Honolulu HI 96848-1601

RAMBO, SYLVIA H., federal judge; b. Royersford, Pa., Apr. 17, 1936; d. Granville A. and Hilda E. (Leonhardt) R.; m. George F. Douglas, Jr., Aug. 1, 1970. BA, Dickinson Coll., 1958; JD, Dickinson Sch Law, 1962; LLD (hon.), Wilson Coll., 1980, Dickinson Sch. Law, 1993, Dickinson Coll., 1994, Shippensburg U., 1996. Bar: Pa. 1962. Atty. trust dept. Bank of Del., Wilmington, 1962-63; pvt. practice Carlisle, 1963-76; from public defender to chief public defender Cumberland County, Pa., 1974-76; judge Ct. Common Pleas, Cumberland County, 1976-78, U.S. Dist. Ct. (mid. dist.) Pa., Harrisburg, 1979-92; chief judge U.S. Dist. Ct. (mid. dist.) Pa., Pa. & Md., 1992—; asst. prof., adj. prof. law Dickinson Sch. Law, 1974-76. Mem. Nat. Assn. Women Judges, Phi Alpha Delta. Democrat. Presbyterian. Office: US Dist Ct Federal Bldg PO Box 868 Harrisburg PA 17108-0868

RAMBO, WAYNE HERBERT, English language and education educator; b. Camden, N.J., Aug. 1, 1947; s. Herbert Jordan and Gladys Marie (Savage) R.; m. Alice Carolyn Huber, Nov. 3, 1944; children: Theodore Yung-Kyo, Faith Yung Gin. BA, Clearwater Christian Coll., 1969; MA, Glassboro State Coll., 1976; EdD, Temple U., 1982. Cert. sch. adminstr., Pa. Elem. prin. Phila. Assn. Christian Schs., 1969-72, dir. pub. rels., 1972-75; teaching asst. Temple U., Phila., 1975-79; rsch. grants analyst Inst. Exptl. Psychiatry, Phila., 1979—; prof. English, acad. skills Camden County Coll., Blackwood, N.J., 1986—; prof. humanities, social sci., biometrics Med. Coll. Allegheny-Hahnemann U., Phila., 1990—; adj. prof. comm. Rowan U., Glassboro, N.J., 1990—, Gloucester County Coll., Sewell, N.J., 1995—; adj. prof. speech and English, Salem (N.J.) Coll., 1991—; cons. Ednl. Testing Svc., Princeton, N.J., 1989—, N.J. Dept. Higher Edn., Trenton, 1991, N.J. Divsn. Vocat. Edn., Trenton, 1981-82; adj. prof. composition and lit. Hahnemann U., Phila., 1994—; co-founder Camden County Adj. Fedn., 1994. Author: Developing Critical Thinking Skills Through Reading and Writing: Expanding Bloom's Taxonomy to Differentiate Between Consumptive and Productive Cognitive Behavior, 1982, Gunning Rambo Readability Writability, 1994; contbg. author: Paragraphy and Essays, 1993; author symposium in field. 1st pres. Marie J. Carrol Found., Merchantville, N.J., 1984; bd. dirs. Merchantville Bd. Edn., 1979—, pres., 1989-92. Avocations: restoration of historical homes, building trades, travel. Home: 37 Rogers Ave Merchantville NJ 08109-2528 Office: Inst for Exptl Psychiatry 111 N 49th St Philadelphia PA 19139-2718

RAMER, BRUCE M., lawyer; b. Teaneck, N.J., Aug. 2, 1933; s. Sidney and Anne S. (Strassman) R.; children: Gregg B., Marc K., Neal I. BA, Princeton U., 1955; LLB, Harvard U., 1958. Bar: Calif. 1963, N.J. 1958. Assoc., Morrison, Lloyd & Griggs, Hackensack, N.J., 1959-60; ptnr. Gang, Tyre, Ramer & Brown, Inc., L.A., 1963—; bd. dirs. Home Shopping Network, Inc., Inc. Exec. dir. Entertainment Law Inst., Law Ctr. of U. So. Calif.; bd. of councilors Law Ctr. U. So. Calif.; past pres. L.A. chpt.; chmn., nat. bd. govs. Am. Jewish Com., nat. v.p., 1982-88, pres. L.A. chpt., 1980-83, chair Western region, 1984-86, comty. svc. award, 1987; chmn. Asia Pacific Rim Inst.; trustee Loyola Marymount U., L.A. Children's Mus., 1986-89; vice chair United Way, 1991-93, corp. bd. dirs., 1981-93, chair coun. pres. 1989-90, mem. cmty. issues coun., 1989-90, chair discretionary fund distbn. com., 1987-89; bd. dirs., chair Geffen Playhouse, bd. dirs. L.A. Urban League, 1987-93, 96—, Jewish Fedn. Coun. of Greater L.A. (mem. Cmty. Rels. com., bd. dirs., exec. com.), Jewish TV Network, Sta. KCET-TV; mem., bd. dirs. Rebuild L.A.; bd. govs. Calif. Cmty. Found.; recipient Ann. Brotherhood award NCCJs, 1990; mem. Fellows of Am. Bar Found. Pvt. U.S. Army, 1958-59, 2d lt., 1961-62. Mem. ABA, L.A. County Bar Assn., Calif. Bar Assn., Beverly Hills Bar Assn. (Exec. Dirs. award 1988, Entertainment Lawyer of Yr. award 1996), L.A. Copyright Soc. (pres. 1974-75), Calif. Copyright Conf. (pres. 1973-74), Princeton Club (pres. 1975-78). Office: Gang Tyre Ramer & Brown Inc 132 S Rodeo Dr Beverly Hills CA 90212-2403

RAMER, HAL REED, academic administrator; b. Kenton, Tenn., June 8, 1923; s. Claude Orion and Dixie Clayton (Carroll) R. BS, George Peabody Coll., 1947; MSW, U. Tenn., 1952; PhD, Ohio State U., 1963. Asst. dean men Ohio State U., Columbus, 1953-58, dir. internat. house, 1958-60, staff asst. to pres., 1960-62; asst. commr. State Dept. Edn., Nashville, 1963-70; founding pres. Vol. State C.C., Gallatin, Tenn., 1970—; bd. dirs. Sumner Regional Health Sys., Inc. Mem. adv. bd. First Union Bank Mid. Tenn., Hendersonville, Tenn., com. March of Dimes, Gallatin; trustee Nashville United Way, 1970s; bd. advisors Aquinas Coll., Nashville, 1967—; bd. dirs. Y.M.C.A.; former chmn. Tenn. Fulbright-Hays Sch. Commn. With USAAF, 1943-45; col. Tenn. Def. Force. Recipient Distinctive Svc. award Devel. Coun. Peabody Coll., Nashville, 1960s, Distinguished Svc. award Tenn. Dept. Edn., 1970, Outstanding Leader award Vanderbilt U. chpt. Phi Delta Kappa, 1987, Gov.'s Svc. award State of Tenn., 1993, Sertoma Club Svc. to Mankind award, 1995-96, Disting. Alumnus award Peabody Coll., 1996; named Rotarian of the Yr., 1979; Paul Harris fellow Rotary Internat., 1981. Mem. Am. Legion, Coun. Pres. C.Cs. (chmn. state Tenn. 1988-89), Tenn. Coll. Assn. (pres. 1985-86), Nat. Alumni Assn. Peabody Coll. (pres. 1970-71, bd. trustees), Tenn. Acad. Sci., Tenn. and Sumner Co. Hist. Socs. (bd. dirs.), English Speaking Union Internat. (Nashville chpt.), So. Assn. Colls. and Schs., Univ. Club Nashville, Gallatin and Hendersonville C. of C., Torch Club Internat., Alpha Tau Omega, Kappa Phi Kappa, Alpha Phi Omega, Phi Delta Kappa. Methodist. Avocations: antique cars, photography. Home: 120 Abbottsford Nashville TN 37215-2440 Office: Vol State CC Office of Pres 1480 Nashville Pike Gallatin TN 37066-3148

RAMER, JAMES LEROY, civil engineer; b. Marshalltown, Iowa, Dec. 7, 1935; s. LeRoy Frederick and Irene (Wengert) R.; m. Jacqueline L. Orr, Dec. 15, 1957; children: Sarah T., Robert H., Eric A., Susan L. Student U. Iowa, 1953-57; MCE, Washington U., St. Louis, 1976, MA in Polit. Sci., 1978; postgrad. U. Mo., Columbia, 1984—. Registered profl. engr., land surveyor. Civil and constrn. engr. U.S. Army C.E., Tulsa, 1960-63; civil and relocations engr. U.S. State Dept., Del Rio, Tex., 1964; project engr. H. B. Zachry Co., San Antonio, 1965-66; civil and constrn. engr. U.S. Army C.E., St. Louis, 1967-76, tech. advisor for planning and nat. hydropower coordinator, 1976-78, project mgr. for EPA constrn. grants, Milw., 1978-80; chief architecture and engring. HUD, Indpls., 1980-81; civil design and pavements engr. Whiteman AFB, Mo., 1982-86, project mgr. maintenance, 1993—; soil and pavements engr. Hdqtrs. Mil. Airlift Command, Scott AFB, Ill., 1986-88; project manager AF-1 maintenance hangar; cattle and grain farmer, 1982—; pvt. practice civil-mech. engr., constrn. mgmt., estimating, cost analysis, cash flow, project scheduling, expert witness, Fortuna, Mo., 1988—, chief construction inspector divsn. Design and Construction, State of Mo., 1992-93; adj. faculty civil engring. Washington U., 1968-78, U. Wis., Milw., 1978-80. Ga. Mil. Coll., Whiteman AFB., Longview Coll., Kansas City; adj. research engr. U. Mo., Columbia, 1985-86. Author tech. writing operation and maintenance manuals, fin. reports and environ. control plans,designs & builds tech. & indsl. models; holder 25 U.S. patents in diverse art, 9 copyrights. Achievements include developer solar waterstill, deep shaft hydropower concept. Mem. ASCE, NSPE, AAUP, Soc. Am. Mil. Engrs. Lutheran. Club: Optimists Internat. Home: RR 1 Box 50-aa Fortuna MO 65034-9720

RAMER, LAWRENCE JEROME, corporation executive; b. Bayonne, N.J., July 29, 1928; s. Sidney and Anne (Strassman) R.; m. Ina Lee Brown, June 30, 1957; children: Stephanie Beryl, Susan Meredith, Douglas Strassman. B.A. in Econs, Lafayette Coll., 1950; M.B.A., Harvard U., 1957; LLD (hon.), Lafayette Coll., 1992. Sales rep., then v.p. United Sheet Metal Co., Bayonne, 1953-55; with Am. Cement Corp., 1957-64; v.p. mktg. div. Riverside Cement Co., 1960-62, v.p. mktg. parent co., 1962-64; vice chmn. bd., chief exec. officer Clavier Corp., N.Y.C., 1965-66; exec. v.p., vice chmn. bd. Pacific Western Industries, Los Angeles, 1966-70; pres., chief exec. officer Nat. Portland Cement Co. Fla., 1975-89; chmn. bd. Sutro Partners, Inc., Los Angeles, 1977-89, Somerset Mgmt. Group, 1975-92, Luminall Paints Inc., Los Angeles, 1972-95; chmn. bd., chief exec. officer Bruning Paint Co., Balt., 1979—, Pacific Coast Cement Co., Los Angeles, 1979-90; pres., chief exec. officer Ramer Equities, Inc., 1990—; chmn. Lawrence J. Ramer Family Found., 1986—; bd. dirs. Orbis Internat., N.Y.C., The Music Ctr., L.A., Music Ctr. Operating Co., L.A., Canyon Ranch, Tucson, Music Ctr. Found., L.A.; chmn. bd. dirs. Ctr. Theatre Group-Taper Ahmanson Theatres, L.A. Chmn. bd. trustees Lafayette Coll., Easton, Pa.; trustee, chmn. bd. trustees Calif. Inst. Arts, Valencia, Calif.; bd. dirs. Non-Traditional Casting Project, N.Y.; nat. bd. govs. Am. Jewish Com., N.Y. Office: Ramer Equities Inc 1999 Ave Of Stars Ste 1090 Los Angeles CA 90067-6034

RAMER, WINNIFRED ROBISON, school nurse; b. Duluth, Minn., Jan. 25, 1933; d. Thomas Jefferson and Mable Jeanette (Thorstad) Robison; m. Louis William Ramer, July 30, 1954; children: Jan Carol, Leigh Ellen, Linda Jeanette, Anna Lynn. Diploma, St. Luke's Sch. Nursing, 1954; BS in Health Arts, Coll. of St. Francis, Joliet, Ill., 1980. RN, Minn., Ind. Staff nurse St. Luke's Hosp., Duluth, 1954; pediatric nurse Davis Clinic, Marion, Ind., 1955-57; surg. charge nurse Ball Meml. Hosp., Muncie, Ind., 1957-59; mem. I.V. team Cmty. Hosp., Indpls., 1960-64; pvt. duty nurse Hancock County Meml. Hosp., Greenfield, Ind., 1965-74; sch. nurse, health coord. Warren Ctrl. H.S., Indpls., 1974—; staff nurse detox unit Fairbanks Hosp., Indpls., 1991—; dir. nursing Fairbanks Hosp, Indpls., 1996—; camp nurse MW Lodge, Three Lakes, Wis., summers, 1971-88. Mem. AIDS adv. bd., curriculum rev. bd., OSHA stds. policy originator Met. Sch. Dist. Warren Twp., Indpls. (mem. Townshipwide Exposure Control Compliance com.). Mem. Nat. Assn. Sch. Nursing (dist. rep. 1987-89). Presbyterian. Avocations: sewing, riding, breeding show horses. Home: 7908 Bellwood Dr Indianapolis IN 46226-6307 Office: Warren Ctrl HS 9500 E 16th St Indianapolis IN 46229-2008 also: Fairbanks Hosp Inc 8102 Clearvista Pkwy Indianapolis IN 46256

RAMESH, KALAHASTI SUBRAHMANYAM, materials scientist; b. Tiruchi, Madras, India, Mar. 22, 1949; s. Subrahmanyam Veeraragaviah and Kuntala (Chinnaswami) Kalahasti; m. Atsumi Yoshida Ramesh, Jan. 30, 1990; children: Siva, Arjun. MS in Ceramic Engring., Benaras Hindu U., India, 1973; D in Engring., Tokyo Inst. Tech., 1986. Asst. rsch. mgr. Steel Authority India Ltd., Ranchi, Bihar, 1979-80; lectr. dept. ceramic engring. Benaras U., Varanasi, India, 1980-82; tech. mgr. ceramics div. TYK Corp., Tokyo, 1986-89; mgr. rsch. and devel. Mer Corp., Tuscon, Ariz., 1989; prin. scientist Battelle meml. Inst., Columbus, Ohio, 1989-93; sr. sci. Pacific N.W. Lab., Richland, Wash., 1993—; adv. Internat. Bus. Svc., Tokyo, 1988-89; cons. HTP Inc., Sharon, Pa., 1989—, Pierce Leslie Cashew & Coffee Ltd., 1997—, Hi-Tech Internat. Cons., 1997—; mem. U.S. Dept. Energy Ceramics Adv. Com., Washington, 1991—; tech. dir. XTALONIX, Inc., Columbus, Ohio, 1993—; mem. Boreskov Meml. Conf. Catalyst and Catalysis Sci. and Engring., Russia, 1997. Panel mem. NSF on Materials and Mechanics, 1995. Mombusho rsch. fellow Ministry Edn. Japan, 1982-84, Max Planck Soc. fellow, 1989. Fellow Indian Inst. Ceramics, Inst. Ceramics U.K.; mem. Japan India Assn., Found. for Indsl. Rsch. (expert), N.Y. Acad. Scis. Hindu. Achievements include development of several ceramic refractories for iron, steel, catalysis material and catalytic combustion and gas turbine/enbine applications. Home: 100 Hillview Dr Richland WA 99352-9668 Office: Hi Tech Internat Cons 100 Hillview Dr Richland WA 99352-9668

RAMETTE, RICHARD WALES, chemistry educator; b. Hartford, Conn., Oct. 9, 1927; s. Joel Edward and Grace Margaret (Wales) R.; m. Lenora Kathryn Kelleher, Aug., 21, 1949; children: Cheryl Lee, James Edward, John Richard, David Joel, William Michael. BA, Wesleyan U., Middletown, Conn., 1950; PhD, U. Minn., 1954. Prof. chemistry Carleton Coll., Northfield, Minn., 1954-90, Laurence M. Gould prof. chemistry, 1971-90, prof. emeritus, 1990—; sci. advisor FDA, Mpls., 1969-80. Author: Chemical Equilibrium and Analysis, 1981. Asst. scoutmaster Boy Scouts Am., Northfield, 1968-73; calligraphy instr. Northfield Arts Guild, 1974-80. Served with USN, 1946-48. Recipient Chemistry Teaching award Mfg. Chemists, 1966, Analytical Chemistry Teaching award Am. Chem. Soc., 1991, Disting. Alumnus award Wesleyan U., 1995. Home: 765 W Fountain Creek Dr Green Valley AZ 85614

RAMEY, CARL ROBERT, lawyer; b. Binghamton, N.Y., Feb. 15, 1941; s. Clinton W. and Hester May (Wisdom) R.; m. Maryan Sitzenkopf, Aug. 11, 1962 (dir. Sept. 1987); children: Mark Alan, Christian David; m. Karen Reichard, Nov. 28, 1987. AB, Marietta Coll., 1962; MA, Mich. State U., 1964; JD, George Washington U., 1967. Bar: D.C. 1968, U.S. Dist. Ct. D.C. 1968, U.S. Ct. Appeals (2d, 3d, 4th, 5th, 7th and 9th cirs.), U.S. Supreme Ct. 1972. Assoc. McKenna, Wilkinson & Kittner, Washington, 1967-71, ptnr., 1971-86; ptnr. Wiley, Rein & Fielding, Washington, 1986—. Contbr. articles to profl. jours., chpt. to Copyright Law Symposium, 1969; editorial staff George Washington Law Rev., 1965-67. Recipient First Prize award Nat. Nathan Burkan Meml. Writing Competition, ASCAP, 1969. Mem. ABA, Fed. Communications Bar Assn. (treas. 1977-78, co-chair editl. adv. bd. Fed. Comms. Law Jour. 1993-96), D.C. Bar Assn. Republican. Episcopalian. Avocations: skiing, tennis, boating, biking. Office: Wiley Rein & Fielding 1776 K St NW Washington DC 20006-2304

RAMEY, CECIL EDWARD, JR., lawyer; b. Shreveport, La., Nov. 9, 1923; s. Cecil Edward and Blanche (Gwin) R.; m. Betty Loper, June 15, 1945; children—Martha L., L. Christine, Stephen E. BS summa cum laude, Centenary Coll., 1943; LLB, Yale U., 1949; postgrad., Tulane U., 1950-51. Bar: Wis. 1949, La. 1951. Assoc. Miller, Mack & Fairchild, Milw., 1949-50; mem. faculty Tulane U., 1950-54; assoc. Hargrove, Guyton, Van Hook and Hargrove, Shreveport, 1954-56, ptnr., 1956-63; ptnr. Hargrove, Guyton, Van Hook and Ramey, Shreveport, 1963-73; ptnr. Hargrove, Guyton, Ramey and Barlow, Shreveport, 1973-89, of counsel, 1989-94; of counsel Barlow and Hardtner, L.C., Shreveport, 1994—; adj. prof. Centenary Coll., 1992—. Former chmn. Citizens Capital Improvements com. City of Shreveport; former mem. governing bd. Shreveport YMCA; former chmn. bd. trustees Broadmoor Meth. Ch., Shreveport, chmn. bd. stewards; former bd. dirs., former chmn. Shreveport-Bossier Found.; former trustee Centenary Coll. With AC, U.S. Army, 1943-46. Named Shreveport's Outstanding Young Man of Yr., 1956, Mr. Shreveport, 1968; recipient Clyde E. Fant Meml. award community service United Way, 1979. Fellow Am. Coll. Trust and Estate Counsel; mem. ABA, La. Bar Assn., Shreveport Bar Assn., La. Law Inst., Shreveport C. of C. (pres. 1974), Centenary Coll. Alumni Assn. (past pres.), Shreveport Club, Order of Coif, Phi Delta Phi, Kappa Sigma. Club: Shreveport. Home: RR 1 Box 873 C Karnack TX 75661-9801 Office: Barlow and Hardtner LC 401 Edwards St Shreveport LA 71101-3289

RAMEY, CRAIG T., psychology educator. BA in Psychology, W.Va. U., 1965; MA in Psychology, 1967, PhD in Devel. Psychology, 1969; postdoctoral in Devel. Psychology, U. Calif., Berkeley, 1969. Asst. prof. psychology Wayne State U., 1969-71; assoc. prof., dept psychology U. N.C., Chapel Hill, 1971-78; sr. investigator, dir. infant rsch. Frank Porter Graham Child Devel. Ctr., U. N.C., Chapel Hill, 1971-74, dir. rsch., 1975-89, assoc. dir., 1978-89; prof. psychology U. N.C., Chapel Hill, 1979-90, prof. pediatrics, Sch. Medicine, 1984-90; dir. Civitan Internat. Rsch. Ctr., U. Ala., Birmingham, 1990—, Sparks Ctr. for Devel. and Learning Disorders, U. Ala., Birmingham, 1990—; prof., depts. psychology, pediatrics and pub. health U. Ala., Birmingham, 1990—. Contbr. to profl. jours. including Journal of the American Medical Association, American Journal of Public Health, Am. Psychologist, Educational Psychology. Office: University of Alabama Dept Psychology 1717 7th Ave S Birmingham AL 35294-0001

RAMEY, DENNY L., bar association executive director; b. Portsmouth, Ohio, Feb. 22, 1947; s. Howard Leroy and Norma Wylodine (Richards) R.; m. Jeannine Gayle Dunmyer, Sept. 24, 1971 (div. Nov. 1991); children: Elizabeth Michelle, Brian Michael. BBA, Ohio U., 1970; MBA, Capital U., 1976. Cert. assn. exec. Adminstrv. mgr. Transit Warehouse div. Elston Richards Storage Co., Columbus, Ohio, 1970-73; mgr. continuing profl. edn. Ohio Soc. CPA's, Columbus, 1973-79; exec. dir. Engrs. Found. of Ohio, Columbus, 1979-80; asst. exec. Ohio State Bar Assn., Columbus, 1980-86, exec. dir., sec., treas., 1986—; treas., exec. com., bd. dirs. Ohio Bar Liability Ins. Co., Columbus, 1986—; treas. Ohio State Bar Found., 1986—; treas. Ohio Legal Ctr. Ins., Columbus, 1988-91; sec. Ohio Printing Co., Ltd., 1991; v.p. Osbanet, Inc., 1993—. Mem. Nat. Assn. Bar Execs. (chmn. various coms.), Am. Soc. Assn. Execs., Ohio Soc. Assn. Execs., Heritage Golf Club, The Player's Club. Methodist. Avocations: tennis, golf, sports, music, wine appreciation. Office: Ohio State Bar Assn 1700 Lake Shore Dr PO Box 16562 Columbus OH 43216-6562

RAMEY, DRUCILLA STENDER, legal association executive; b. 1946. BA, Radcliffe Coll.; JD, Yale U. Bar: Calif. 1972. Exec. dir. Bar Assn. San Francisco. Office: 465 California St Ste 1100 San Francisco CA 94104-1804

RAMEY, JAMES MELTON, chemist; b. Waco, Tex., Sept. 1, 1928; s. Ernest Sylvester and Audrey Lee (McCasland) R.; m. Frankie Jo Montomery, Aug. 23, 1952; children: Marlana Ramey Valdez, James Monte Ramey, Douglas Dwain Ramey, Susan Elizabeth Ramey Attebery, Angela Dawn Ramey. BS, Southwestern U., 1949. Cert. product safety profl., profl. source for safety cons. Chemist Celanese Chem. Co., Bishop, Tex., 1954-57, group leader, spl. problems lab., 1957-60, dir. spl. problems lab., 1960-67; dir. quality assurance to dir. product standards Celanese Chem. Co., N.Y.C., 1967-76, dir. indsl. hygiene and toxicology, 1976-78; corp. dir. of product safety Celanese Corp., N.Y.C., 1978-83, dir. safety, 1983-85, dir. environ. health and safety audit program, 1985-87; dir. environ. health and safety audit programs Hoechst Celanese Corp., Somerville, N.J., 1987-88; cons. environ. health scis. Horseshoe Bay, Tex., 1988—; chmn. bd. Formaldehyde Inst., Washington, 1978-82, chmn. OSHA com. SOCMA, Washington, 1978-84; mem. environ. audit roundtable, Washington, 1985-88. Contbr. chpt. on quality control to Ency. Chem. Process and Design, 1980; contbr. articles to profl. jours.; patentee in field. Adv. Jesse Owens Found., N.Y., 1982-88; del. Tex. Dem. Conv., Tex., 1964-68; v.p. Internat. Amateur Athletic Assn., N.Y., 1982-88; bd. dirs. Property Owners Assn., Horseshoe Bay, 1991-94; mem. Horseshoe Bay Chapel Choir, 1992-94; mem. PLAN. Fellow Am. Inst. Chemists; mem. Bishop C. of C. (pres. 1965-66). Methodist. Achievements include development of health surveillance and info. systems for Celanese Chem. Co., one of first comprehensive product safety programs in chemical industry and charter mem. of product safety forum, one of first comprehensive environ. health audit programs. Home and Office: PO Box 8634 Horseshoe Bay TX 78657-9211

RAMEY, REBECCA ANN, elementary education educator; b. Dayton, Ohio, Jan. 27, 1948; d. Donald Smith and Margaret Jeanne (Cross) Ingabrand; divorced; 1 child, Joshua David. BS, Miami U., Oxford, Ohio, 1970, MEd in Adminstrn., 1978. Cert. permanent tchr., prin., Ohio. Tchr. social studies and lang. arts Springboro (Ohio) Community Schs., 1970—; dept. head Clearcreek Elem. Sch., Springboro, 1991—. Choir dir. 1st Bapt. Ch., Franklin, Ohio, 1985—, chmn. bd. Christian edn., 1991-96; sec. exec. bd. Tamarack Swim Club, Springboro, 1990-96, Springboro Band Boosters Assn., 1992. Named Worker of Yr., 1st Bapt. Ch., 1992. Mem. NEA, Ohio Edn. Assn., Springboro Edn. Assn., Order Ea. Star (past matron 1973, 84), Ladies Oriental Shrine N.Am. Republican. Avocations: music, reading, needlework. Home: 205 Foliage Ln Springboro OH 45066-9312 Office: Clearcreek Elem Sch 750 S Main St Springboro OH 45066-1424

RAMEY, SAMUEL EDWARD, bass soloist; b. Colby, Kans., Mar. 28, 1942; s. Robert Guy and Grace Irene (Mallory) R.; m. Carrie Tanate, Jan. 10, 1970. Student, Kans. State U., 1960-62; B.Mus., Wichita State U., 1968. Debut in Carmen, N.Y.C. Opera, 1973, leading bass, 1973—, European debut, Glyndebourne Festival, 1976, debut, Hamburg Staatsoper, 1978, Paris Opera, 1979, Houston Grand Opera, 1975, San Francisco Opera, 1978, Chgo. Lyric Opera, 1979, Festival International Aix-en-Provence, 1979, 80, Teatro della Scala, 1981, Vienna Staatsoper, 1981, in Rinaldo, Met. Opera, 1984; recording artist opera and oratorio, Philips, Angel, RCA, Deutsche Grammophone, London, CBS Records. Named Kansan of the Year Native Sons and Daughters of Kansas, 1994. Office: Columbia Artists Mgmt Inc Arbib Div 165 W 57th St New York NY 10019-2201*

RAMIREZ, CARLOS DAVID, publisher; b. San Juan, P.R., Aug. 19, 1946; s. Carlos David and Maria (Melendez) R.; children: Christine, David. AAS, CCNY, 1969, BBA, 1972; PhD, Pace U., 1995. Asst. controller TRW, London Am. Mktg. Corp. (Midland Bank), Meridien Mktg. Corp.; dep. dir. fin. svcs. ITM Group, N.Y.C., 1980; controller El Diario-La Prensa, N.Y.C., 1981—; pres., pubr. El Diario-La Prensa, 1984—; exec. v.p. Latin Comm. Group Inc.; mem. bd. dirs. and sec. Latin Comm. Arcup, Inc. Mem. El Museo del Barrio; trustee Pace U., Partnership for a Drug-Free Am. Mem. N.Y. Press Club, Am. Newspapers Pubs. Assn., , Nat. Assn. Hispanic Journalists, Nat. Assn. Hispanic Pubs., N.Y. C. of C. (bd. dirs.), Nat. Advt. Bur., Nat. Hispanic Coalition. Roman Catholic. Office: El Diario La Presna 143 Varick St New York NY 10013-1106

RAMIREZ, GLORIA MARIA, physician; b. Mayagüez, P.R., Apr. 14, 1953; d. Jose Ramirez and Gloria E. (Baez-Murphy) Ruiz; stepfather Ismael Ruiz; m. Bruce William Konrad, Mar. 31, 1951. BS, U. P.R., Mayaguez, 1973; MT, Inst. Health Labs., Rio Piedras, P.R., 1974; MD, San Juan Bautista Med. Sch., 1981. Lic. physician, N.Y., Va. Med. technologist Inst. Health Labs., Rio Piedras, 1974-77; intern Bronx-Lebanon Hosp., 1981-82; resident in internal medicine St. Barnabas Hosp., Bronx, 1982-84; chief resident Bronx-Lebanon Hosp., 1984-85, fellow in hematology, 1985-86; fellow in hematology/oncology L.I. Coll. Hosp., Bklyn., 1986-88, attending physician in ambulatory surgery/med., 1988-89; internist Family Care Group Practice/St. Luke's Roosevelt Hosp., N.Y.C., 1989-94; hematologist Sickle Cell program/St. Luke's Roosevelt Hosp., 1989—. Contbr. articles to profl. jours. Vol. counselor Hole in the Wall Gang Camp, Ashford, Conn., 1989-96. Mem. AMA, Am. Soc. Hematology, Am. Women's Med. Assn., Spanish Am. Med. Soc., P.R. Coll. Med. Technologists. Avocations: photography, hiking, travel, crafts. Office: St Lukes-Roosevelt Hosp Sickle Cell Program 1111 Amsterdam Ave New York NY 10025-1716

RAMIREZ, JANICE L., assistant school superintendent; b. Dodge City, Kans., July 16, 1947; d. Chris William and Lois (Moore) Langvardt; 1 child, Jessica. BS, Emporia State U., 1969, MA, 1970; PhD, Kans. State U., 1982. Div. prin. Highland Park High Sch./Topeka (Kans.) pub. schs.; prin. Topeka pub. schs.; prin. Mesa (Ariz.) pub. schs., asst. supt.; mem. mid. level task force Ariz. Dept. Edn. Contbr. articles to profl. jours. Recipient Kamelot award; named one of Top 100 Bus. Women in Ariz., Today's Ariz. Woman Success Mag., 1996-97. Mem. Am. Assn. Sch. Pers. Adminstrs., Ariz. Sch. Pers. Adminstrs. Assn., Nat. Assn. Ednl. Negotiators, Kans. Assn. for Middle Level Edn., Nat. Mid. Sch. Assn., Ariz. Hispanic Sch. Adminstrs. Assn., Pi Gamma Mu, Phi Delta Phi, Delta Kappa Gamma, Phi Delta Kappa. Office: 546 N Stapley Dr Mesa AZ 85203-7204

RAMIREZ, JULIO JESUS, neuroscientist; b. Bridgeport, Conn., Dec. 25, 1955; s. Julio Pastor and Elia Rosa (Cortes) R. BS in Psychology magna cum laude, Fairfield U., 1977; MA, Clark U., 1980, PhD in Biopsychology, 1983. Asst. prof. Coll. of St. Benedict, St. Joseph, Minn., 1981-85; vis. scientist MIT, Cambridge, Mass., 1985-86; asst. prof. Davidson (N.C.) Coll., 1986-89, assoc. prof. dept. psychology, 1989-96, prof. dept. psychology, 1996—; vis. scientist Centre Nationale de Recherche Scientifique, Strasbourg, France, summer 1982, U. Va., Charlottesville, summers 1983-92, 96, Ludwig-Maximillians-Universitat, Munich, Summer 1988, Yale U., New Haven, spring 1991; cons. dept. neurosci. U. Va., Charlottesville, 1983-92, 96; panelist NSF, 1991-95, chair, 1994-95; panelist NIMH, 1992—, chair, 1995—; pres., co-founder Faculty for Undergrad. Neurosci., 1991-94. Contbr. articles to profl. publs. Mem. Habitat for Humanity, Davidson, 1989—, Union Concerned Scientist, Cambridge, 1987—; mem. adv. action com. Project Kaleidoscope, Washington, 1993-97. Named N.C. Prof. of Yr., Nat. Gold Medalist Coun. for Advancement and Support of Edn., 1989, MacArthur Asst. Prof., 1986-89; recipient rsch. award Nat. Inst. Mental Health, 1992, NSF, 1991, Nat. Inst. Neurol. Disorders and Stroke, 1987, 93, N.C. Bd. Sci. & Tech., 1987. Mem. AAAS, APA, Am. Psychol. Soc., Coun. on Undergrad Rsch. (councilor 1992-97), Soc. Neurosci. Democrat. Achievements include demonstration that lesion-induced axonal sprouting may contribute to recovery of function after central nervous system injury. Home: PO Box 26 Davidson NC 28036-0026 Office: Davidson Coll Dept Psychology Davidson NC 28036

RAMIREZ, MANUEL ARISTIDES (MANNY RAMIREZ), professional baseball player; b. Santo Domingo, Dominican Republic, May 30, 1972. Grad. high sch., N.Y.C. Outfielder Cleve. Indians, 1993—. Named to The Sporting News Am. League Silver Slugger Team, 1995, mem. Am. League All-Star Team, 1995. Mem. Cleve. Indians Am. League Champions, 1995. Office: Cleveland Indians 2401 Ontario St Cleveland OH 44115-4003*

RAMIREZ, MARIA FIORINI, economist, investment advisor; b. Naples, Italy, Jan. 1, 1948; came to U.S., 1961; d. Fernando and Clelia Ambrosio Fiorini; m. George M. Ramirez, 1973. BBA, Pace U., 1972, postgrad., 1974-76. Analyst Meinhard-CIT Comml. Fin., N.Y.C., 1967-68; credit analyst Am. Express Internat. Bank, N.Y.C., 1968-72; credit mgr. Banca Nazionale del Lavoro, N.Y.C., 1972-73; credit mgr., asst. v.p. Merrill Lynch G.S.I., 1973-74, economist, 1974—, v.p., sr. money market economist Merrill Lynch Econs. Inc., 1981-84; sr. v.p., sr. money market economist Becker Paribas Inc., N.Y.C., 1984; corp. first v.p., money market economist Drexel Burnham Lambert Inc., N.Y.C., 1984-86, mng. dir., chief money market economist, 1986—; pres. Maria Ramirez Capital Cons. Inc. (subs. Hancock Freedom), N.Y.C., 1990—; pres. and CEO Maria Fiorini Ramirez, Inc., 1992—; bd. dirs. various orgns. Roman Catholic. Home: PO Box 992 Belcher Ln Far Hills NJ 07931 Office: 1 World Fin Ctr 200 Liberty St Fl 4 New York NY 10281-1003

RAMIREZ, MARIO EFRAIN, physician; b. Roma, Tex., Apr. 3, 1926; s. Efren M. and Carmen (Hinojosa) R.; m. Sarah B. Aycock, Nov. 25, 1949; children: Mario, Patricia Ann, Norman Michael, Jaime Eduardo, Roberto Luis. Student, U. Tex., 1942-45; MD, U. Tenn., 1948. Diplomate Am. Bd. Family Physicians. Intern Shreveport (La.) Charity Hosp., 1949; resident; practice medicine specializing in family practice Shreveport (La.) Charity Hosp., Roma; pvt. family practice Roma, 1950-75, Rio Grande City, Tex., 1975-93; owner, adminstr. Ramirez Meml. Hosp., Roma, 1958-75; assoc. med. dir. South Tex. Blue Cross Blue Shield Tex., McAllen, 1993-95. County judge Starr County, Rio Grande City, 1969-78; chmn. South Tex. Devel. Coun., 1975-76, Tri-County Cmty. Action Coun., 1971-78; mem. coordinated bd. Tex. Colls. and Univs., 1979-85; mem. devel. bd. U. Tex., 1986—; presdl. appointee bd. regents Uniformed Svcs. U. Tex. Health Scis., 1985-92; mem. bd. regents U. Tex. Sys., 1989-95, vice chmn. bd., 1991-92. Recipient Spl. citation Surgeon Gen., 1967, Disting. Alumnus award U. Tex., 1975, 78, Achievement award Lab World, 1978, Presdl. citation U. Tex., 1979, Outstanding Alumnus award U. Tenn., 1991; named Family Dr. of Yr., Good Housekeeping mag. and Am. Acad. Family Physicians, 1978, Border Texan of the Yr., 1995; honoree Founder's Day for contbns. to higher edn. U. Tex. Pan Am., 1989. Fellow Am. Acad. Family Physicians; mem. AMA (vice chmn. com. health care of poor 1971-75, Benjamin Rush Bicentennial award 1976, Council of Med. Services 1985-94), Tex. Med. Assn. (chmn. com. health care of poor 1971, Disting. Service award 1972, pres. 1979-80), Tex. Acad. Family Physicians (v.p. 1973, pres. 1975, Distinguished Service award 1967, Outstanding Leadership award 1975-76, v.p. Valley chpt. 1960-61, pres. 1961-62), Hidalgo-Starr Counties Med. Soc. (pres. 1964). Clubs: Lions, K.C, Rotary, Alhambra. Address: 212 W Pine Ridge Ln Mcallen TX 78503

RAMIREZ, MARTIN RUBEN, engineer, educator, administrator, consultant; b. San Luis Potosi, Mex., Aug. 17, 1962; s. Victorio Niño and Concepcion (Zuñiga) R.; m. Maureen Therese McDermott, July 27, 1991. BS in Civil Engring., Northwestern U., 1984, MS, 1986, PhD in Theoretical and Applied Mechanics, 1991. Asst. to v.p. engring. Perkins & Will, Chgo.; cons. engr. Alfred Benesch & Co., Chgo., 1985-86, Teng & Assocs., Chgo.; asst. prof. engring. Johns Hopkins U., Balt., 1990-94; cons., dir. curriculum and learning assessment IMSA, Aurora, Ill., 1996—; cons. Wiss-Jenney Elstner, Northbrook, Ill., 1985-86, Mitsubishi Heavy Industries, Hunt Valley, Md., 1994 Synthesis NSF Coalition, U. Calif. Berkeley; founder, Dir. program on engring. edn. Johns Hopkins U., 1993. Reviewer for several jours.; editor Needs Database. Recipient Fazlur Khan Meml. prize, 1986, Young Investigator award NSF, 1993; Lilly fellow, 1992; NSF grad. fellow, 1985. Mem. ASCD, ASCE (assoc.), ASME, Am. Soc. Engring. Edn. (chair Frontiers in Edn. Conf. 1993), U.S. Assn. for Computational Mechanics, IEEE Computer Soc., Am. Acad. Mechanics, Tau Beta Pi. Avocations: bicycling, music. Office: IMSA 1500 Sullivan Rd Aurora IL 60506-1067

RAMIREZ, MICHAEL P., editorial cartoonist; b. Tokyo; s. Ireneo Edward and Fumiko Maria R. Syndicated cartoonist Copley News Svc., 1986—; cartoonist The Comml. Appeal, Memphis, 1990—. Recipient Pulitzer Prize for editorial cartooning, 1994. Office: The Commercial Appeal 495 Union Ave Memphis TN 38103-3242*

RAMIREZ, RICARDO, bishop; b. Bay City, Tex., Sept. 12, 1936; s. Natividad and Maria (Espinosa) R. B.A., U. St. Thomas, Houston, 1959; M.A., U. Detroit, 1968; Diploma in Pastoral Studies, East Asian Pastoral Inst., Manila, 1973-74. Ordained priest Roman Catholic Ch., 1966; missionary Basilian Fathers, Mex., 1968-76; exec. v.p. Mexican Am. Cultural Ctr., San Antonio, 1976-81; aux. bishop Archdiocese of San Antonio, 1981-82; bishop Diocese of Las Cruces, N.M., 1982—; cons. U.S. Bishop's Com. on Liturgy, from 1981; advisor U.S. Bishop's Com. on Hispanic Affairs, from 1981. Author: Fiesta, Worship and Family, 1981. Mem. N.Am. Acad. on Liturgy, Hispanic Liturgical Inst., Padres Asociada Derechos Religiosos Educativos y Sociales. Lodges: K.C; Holy Order Knights of Holy Sepulcher. Office: Diocese of Las Cruces 1280 Med Park Dr Las Cruces NM 88005-3239*

RAMIREZ, TINA, artistic director; b. Caracas, Venezuela; d. Gloria Maria Cestero and Jose Ramirez Gaonita. Studied dance with Lola Bravo, Alexandra Danilova, Anna Sokolow. Toured with Federico Rey Dance Co.; founder, artistic dir. Ballet Hispanico, N.Y.C., 1970—; panelist NEA, N.Y. Sate Coun. on Arts; mem. advisory panel N.Y.C. Dept. Cultural Affairs; bd. dirs. Dance Theater Workshop. Appearances include (Broadway) Kismet, Lute Song, (TV) Man of La Mancha. Recipient Arts and Culture Honor award Mayor of N.Y.C., 1983, Ethnic New Yorker award N.Y.C., 1986, Gov.'s Arts award N.Y. State Gov. Mario Cuomo, 1987; honoree Nat. Puerto Rican Forum, Hispanic Inst. for Performing Arts. Office: Ballet Hispanico 167 W 89th St New York NY 10024-1901*

RAMIREZ-RIVERA, JOSE, physician; b. Mayaguez, P.R., June 26, 1929; S. Jesus Ramirez and Nieves Rivera; m. Leila Suner, May 14, 1971; children: Federico, Steven, Sally, Juliette, Natasha, Leila. B.A., Johns Hopkins U., 1949; M.D., Yale U., 1953. Diplomate Am. Bd. Internal Medicine. Intern U. Md. Hosp., 1953-54; resident in medicine Univ. Hosp., Balt., 1954-55, fellow in hematology, 1958-59, resident, 1959; staff physician VA Hosp., Balt., 1960-67; assoc. chief of staff VA Hosp., 1962-68; asst. in medicine Johns Hopkins U., 1960-67, instr. in medicine, 1967-68; asst. prof. medicine U. Md., 1961-68; assoc. prof. Duke U., Durham, N.C., 1966-70; dir. med. edn. and clin. investigation Western Region P.R., 1970-80; chief medicine Mayaguez (P.R.) Med. Ctr., 1971-82; prof. medicine U. P.R., San Juan, 1974—, dir. univ. med. svcs. Med. Sci. Campus, 1982-86; dir. Rincon Rural Health Project, 1975-82, assoc. chief staff for edn. VA Med. Ctr., San Juan, 1990-92. Contbr. articles to med. jours. Bd. dirs. Soc. Edn. Suroeste. With USPHS, 1955-57. Fellow ACP (pres. P.R. chpt. 1986-88), Royal Soc. Medicine (London), Coll. Chest Physicians; mem. Am. Fedn. Clin. Rsch., P.R. Lung Assn. (bd. dirs. 1975-80), Soc. Autores Puertorriguenos, PEN Club, Alliance Francaise of P.R. (v.p. 1995-96, pres. 1996—). Roman Catholic. Office: Dept Vets Affairs Med Ctr One Veterans Pla San Juan PR 00927-5800

RAMIS, HAROLD ALLEN, film director, screenwriter, actor; b. Chgo., Nov. 21, 1944; s. Nathan and Ruth (Cokee) R.; m. Erica Mann; children: Violet, Julian, Daniel. B.A., Washington U., St. Louis, 1966; ArtsD (hon.), Washington U., 1993. Assoc. editor Playboy mag., 1968-70; actor, writer Second City, Chgo., 1970-73, Nat. Lampoon Radio Hour, Lampoon Show, 1974-75; actor, head writer SCTV, 1977-78; producer, head writer Rodney Dangerfield Show, ABC-TV, 1982. Screenwriter (with Douglas Kenny and Chris Miller) National Lampoon's Animal House, 1978, (with Janice Allen, Len Blum and Dan Goldberg) Meatballs, 1979, (with Douglas Kenny, Brian Doyle-Murray) Caddyshack, 1980, (with Len Blum and Dan Goldberg) Stripes, 1981, (with Dan Aykroyd) Ghostbusters, 1984, (with Brian Doyle-Murray) Club Paradise, 1986; co-screenwriter (with Peter Torokvei) Armed and Dangerous, 1986; writer (with Dan Akroyd) Ghostbusters II, 1989; dir. feature films: Caddyshack, 1980, National Lampoon's Vacation, 1983, Club Paradise, 1986; exec. producer, co-screenwriter (with Rodney Dangerfield) Back to School, 1986; film appearances include: Stripes, 1981, Ghostbusters, 1984, Baby Boom, 1987, Stealing Home, 1988, Ghostbusters II, 1989; dir., exec. producer, co-writer Groundhog Day, 1993; dir., co-prodr. Stuart Saves His Family, 1995, Multiplicity, 1996. Mem. AFTRA, Screen Actors Guild, Writers Guild Am., Dirs. Guild Am.

RAMLER, SIEGFRIED, educator; b. Vienna, Austria, Oct. 30, 1924; s. Lazar and Eugenia Ramler; m. Piilani Andrietta Ahuna, Jan. 27, 1948; children: David K., Dita L., Laurence K., Malia R. Diplôme supérieur, U. Paris, 1958; MA, U. Hawaii, 1961. Interpreter Internat. Mil. Tribunal, Nuremberg, Germany, 1945-46, chief interpreting br., 1946-49; chair fgn. lang. dept. Punahou Sch., Honolulu, 1951-71, dir. instnl. svcs., 1971-91, dir. Wo Internat. Ctr., 1990-95; exec. dir. Found. for Study in Hawaii and Abroad, Honolulu, 1969-90; vis. fellow East-West Ctr., 1995—; chmn. adv. bd. Pacific Basin Consortium, Hawaii, 1997—. Contbr. articles to profl. publs. Sec., bd. dirs. crown Prince Akihito Scholarship Found., 1989—. Decorated medal Freedom Found., 1958, Order of the Palmes Académiques, French Govt., 1964, Order of the Sacred Treasure, Japanese Govt., 1992, Ordre National du Mérite, French Govt., 1993. Mem. ASCD, Internat./Global Edn. Com. (chair nat. adv. com. 1987-93), Japan-Am. Soc. Hawaii (pres. 1986-87, program chmn. 1975-94, Alliance Française of Hawaii (pres. and founder 1961, bd. dirs. 1992—). Avocations: running, travel, swimming. Home: 921 Maunawili Cir Kailua HI 96734-4620 Office: East West Ctr 1777 E West Rd Honolulu HI 96822-2323

RAMM, DOUGLAS ROBERT, psychologist; b. New Haven, Dec. 11, 1949; s. Robert Frederick and Gladys (Torgrimson) R. B.A., Ithaca Coll., 1972; M.A., Duquesne U., 1974; Ph.D., 1979; m. Barbara Stephens, Aug. 10, 1974; children—Jennifer, Jessica. Staff psychologist Westmoreland Hosp, Greensburg, Pa., 1976-79; chief clin. psychologist, dir. child and adolescent psychiat. services Westmoreland Hosp., Greensburg, 1979-82; pvt. practice, Greensburg, 1980—; pres. Ethics, Inc., Ctr. for Sci. Study of Values and Morality, 1995—; cons. U. Pitts., Pa. Bur. Vocat. Rehab., Westmoreland County Ct. of Common Pleas; past pres. Mental Health Assn. Westmoreland County. Author: Clinically Formulated Principles of Morality, 1996. Mem. ASCD, Am. Psychol. Assn., Am. Philos. Assn., Pa. Psychol. Assn., Soc. Personality Assessment, Nat. Acad. Neuropsychologists, Am. Bd. Med. Psychotherapists, N.Y. Acad. Scis., Nat. Register Health Svc. Providers in Psychology, Am. Coll. Forensics Examiners (diplomate), Soc. Bus. Ethics. Methodist. Home: 225 Humphrey Rd Greensburg PA 15601-4571 Office: 1717 Penn Ave Apt 327 Pittsburgh PA 15221-2655

RAMMING, MICHAEL ALEXANDER, school system administrator; b. St. Louis, Feb. 4, 1940; s. William Alexander and Emily Louise (Reingruber) R.; m. Susan Ray Oliver, July 9, 1962; children: Michael Murray, Todd Alexander. BS, Centenary Coll., 1963; MA, Washington U., St. Louis, 1968. Cert. adminstr. secondary schs., Mo. Teacher and coach Ladue Sch. Dist., St. Louis, 1963-88, adminstr., 1988—. Vol. Sr. Olympics, St. Louis, 1992, 93. Mem. Nat. Assn. Secondary Sch. Prins., Mo. Assn. Secondary Sch. Prins., Nat. Interscholastic Athletic Adminstrs. Assn., Mo. Interscholastic Athletic Adminstrs. Assn. (25 Yr. Svc. award). Avocations: tennis, walking, travel. Home: 13309 Kings Glen Dr Saint Louis MO 63131-1022 Office: Ladue Horton Watkins High Sch 1201 S Warson Rd Saint Louis MO 63124-1266 *As I look back I feel that participation in sports as a player, coach, and fan provided me with a wealth of leadership, community building, daring, sharing, and the ability to accept success and failure.*

RAMO, SIMON, engineering executive; b. Salt Lake City, May 7, 1913; s. Benjamin and Clara (Trestman) R.; m. Virginia Smith, July 25, 1937; children: James Brian, Alan Martin. BS, U. Utah, 1933, DSc (hon.), 1961; PhD, Calif. Inst. Tech., 1936; DEng (hon.), Case Western Res. U., 1960, U. Mich., 1966, Poly. Inst. N.Y., 1971; DSc (hon.), Union Coll., 1963, Worcester Polytechnic Inst., 1968, U. Akron, 1969, Cleve. State U., 1976; LLD (hon.), Carnegie-Mellon U., 1970, U. So. Calif., 1972, Gonzaga U., 1983, Occidental Coll., 1984, Claremont U., 1985. With Gen. Electric Co., 1936-46; v.p. ops. Hughes Aircraft Co., 1946-53; with Ramo-Woolridge Corp., 1953-58, Ramo-Wooldridge Corp., 1954-58; dir. TRW Inc., 1954-85, exec. v.p., 1958-61, vice chmn. bd., 1961-78, chmn. exec. com., 1969-78, cons., 1978—; pres. The Bunker-Ramo Corp., 1964-66; chmn. bd. TRW-Fujitsu Co., 1980-83; bd. dirs. Arco Power Techs.; vis. prof. mgmt. sci. Calif. Inst. Tech., 1978—; Regents lectr. UCLA, 1981-82, U. Calif. at Santa Cruz, 1978-79; chmn. Center for Study Am. Experience, U. So. Calif., 1978-80; Faculty fellow John F. Kennedy Sch. Govt., Harvard U., 1980-84; mem. White House Energy Research and Devel. Adv. Council, 1973-75; mem. adv. com. on sci. and fgn. affairs U.S. State Dept., 1973-75; chmn. Pres.'s Com. on Sci. and Tech., 1976-77; mem. adv. council to Sec. Commerce, 1976-77, Gen. Atomics Corp., 1988—, Aurora Capital Ptnrs., 1991—, Chartwell Investments, 1992—; co-chmn. Transition Task Force on Sci. and Tech. for Pres.-elect Reagan; mem. roster consultants to adminstr. ERDA, 1976-77; bd. advisors for sci. and tech. Republic of China, 1981-84; chmn. bd. Aetna, Jacobs & Ramo Venture Capital, 1987-90, Allenwood Ventures Inc., 1987—. Author: The Business of Science, 1988, other sci., engring. and mgmt. books. Bd. dirs. L.A. World Affairs Coun. 1973-85, Mus. Ctr. Found., L.A., L.A. Philharm. Assn., 1981-84; life trustee Calif. Inst. Tech., Nat. Symphony Orch. Assn., 1973-83; trustee emeritus Calif. State Univs.; bd. visitors UCLA Sch. Medicine, 1980—; bd. dirs. W.M. Keck Found., 1983—; bd. govs. Performing Arts Coun. Mus. Ctr. L.A., pres., 1976-77. Recipient award IAS, 1956; award Am. Inst. Elec. Engrs., 1959; award Arnold Air Soc., 1960; Am. Acad. Achievement award, 1964; award Am. Iron and Steel Inst., 1968; Disting. Svc. medal Armed Forces Communication and Electronics Assn., 1970; medal of achievement WEMA, 1970; awards U. So. Calif., 1971, 79; Kayan medal Columbia U., 1972; award Am. Cons. Engrs. Coun., 1974; medal Franklin Inst., 1978; award Harvard Bus. Sch. Assn., 1979; award Nat. Medal Sci., 1979; Disting. Alumnus award U. Utah, 1981; UCLA medal, 1982; Presdl. Medal of Freedom, 1983; named to Bus. Hall of Fame, 1984; recipient Aesculapian award UCLA, 1984, Durand medal AAIA, 1984, John Fritz medal, 1986, Henry Townley Heald award Ill. Inst. Tech., 1988, Nat. Engring. award Am. Assn. Engring. Socs., 1988, Franklin-Jefferson medal, 1988, Howard Hughes Meml. award, 1989. Fellow IEEE (Electronic Achievement award 1953, Golden Omega award 1975, Founders medal 1980, Centennial medal 1984), Am. Acad. Arts and Scis., Am. Acad. Polit. Sci.; mem. N.Y. Acad. Scis., Nat. Acad. Engring. (founder, coun. mem. Bueche award), Nat. Acad. Scis., Am. Phys. Soc., Am. Philos. Soc., Inst. Advancement Engring., Coun. Fgn. Rels., Pacific Coun. Internat. Policy, Internat. Acad. Astronautics, Eta Kappa Nu (eminent mem. award 1966), Theta Tau (Hall of Fame laureate). Office: 9200 W Sunset Blvd Ste 801 Los Angeles CA 90069-3603

RAMO, VIRGINIA M. SMITH, civic worker; b. Yonkers, N.Y.; d. Abraham Harold and Freda (Kasnetz) Smith; B.S. in Edn., U. So. Calif., DHL (hon.), 1978; m. Simon Ramo; children—James Brian, Alan Martin. Nat. co-chmn. ann. giving U. So. Calif., 1968-70, vice chmn., trustee, 1971—, co-chmn. bd. councilors Sch. Performing Arts, 1975-76, co-chmn. bd. councillors Schs. Med. and Engring.; vice-chmn. bd. overseers Hebrew Union Coll., 1972-75; bd. dirs. The Muses of Calif. Mus. Sci. and industry, UCLA Affiliates, Estelle Doheny Eye Found., U. So. Calif. Sch. Medicine; adv. council Los Angeles County Heart Assn., chmn. com. to endow Chair in cardiology at U. So. Calif.; vice-chmn., bd. dirs. Friends of Library U. So. Calif.; bd. dirs., nat. pres. Achievement Rewards for Coll. Scientists Found., 1975-77; bd. dirs. Les Dames Los Angeles, Community TV So. Calif.; bd. dirs., v.p. Founders Los Angeles Music Center; v.p. Los Angeles Music Center Opera Assn.; v.p. corp. bd. United Way; v.p. Blue Ribbon-400 Performing Arts Council; chmn. com. to endow chair in gerontology U. So. Calif.; vice chmn. campaign Doheny Eye Inst., 1986. Recipient Service award Friends of Libraries, 1974, Nat. Community Service award Alpha Epsilon Phi, 1975, Disting. Service award Am. Heart Assn. 1978, Service award U. So. Calif., Spl. award U. So. Calif. Music Alumni Assn., 1979, Life Achievement award Mannequins of Los Angeles Assistance League, 1979, Woman of Yr. award PanHellenic Assn., 1981, Disting. Service award U. So. Calif. Sch. Medicine, 1981, U. So. Calif. Town and Gown Recognition award, 1986, Asa V. Call Achievement award U. So. Calif., 1986, Phi Kappa Phi scholarship award U. So. Calif., 1986, Vision award Luminaires of Doheny Eye Inst., 1994. Mem. UCLA Med. Aux., U. So. Calif. Pres.'s Circle, Commerce Assos. U. So. Calif., Cedars of Lebanon Hosp. Women's Guild (dir. 1967-68), Blue Key, Skull and Dagger.

RAMOS, ALBERT A., electrical engineer; b. L.A., Feb. 28, 1927; s. Jesus D. and Carmen F. (Fontes) R.; B.S. in Elec. Engring., U. So. Calif., 1950, M.S. in Systems Mgmt., 1972; Ph.D., U.S. Internat. U., 1975; m. Joan C. Pailing, Sept. 23, 1950; children—Albert A., Richard R., James J., Katherine. With guided missile test group Hughes Aircraft Co., 1950-60; with TRW DSG, 1960-91, sr. staff engr. Norton AFB, San Bernardino, Calif., 1969-91, ret., 1991. Served with USNR, 1945-46. Registered profl. engr., Calif. Mem. IEEE, NSPE, Air Force Assn., Mexican-Am. Engring. Soc., Mexican-Am. Profl. Mgmt. Assn. (mem. administering commn. dept. community svcs.), Sigma Phi Delta, Eta Kappa Nu, Tau Beta Pi. Home: 8937 Napoli Dr Las Vegas NV 89117-1182

RAMOS, CARLOS E., law educator; b. Caguas, P.R., Oct. 20, 1952; s. Francisco E. and Olga (Gonzalez) R.; m. Lesbia Hernandez, July 30, 1988; children: Carlos Francisco, Isabel Maria, Macarena. BA, U. P.R., 1974, JD, 1978; diploma, U. Stockholm, 1975; LLM, U. Calif., Berkeley, 1987. Bar: P.R. 1978, U.S. Dist. Ct. P.R. 1978, U.S. Ct. Appeals (1st cir.) 1979. Staff atty. P.R. Legal Svcs., San Juan, P.R., 1978-79; asst. prof. law InterAm. U. P.R., San Juan, 1979-86, assoc. prof., 1986-93, dean, prof. law, 1993—; exec. dir. Santurce Law Firm, San Juan, 1983-86. Co-author: Derecho Constitucional de Puerto Rico y los Estados Unidos, 1990. Mem. ABA, ATLA, Am. Judicature Soc., P.R. Bar Assn. Office: InterAm U PR Sch Law Office of Dean PO Box 9023863 San Juan PR 00902

RAMOS, ELEANOR LACSON, transplant nephrologist; b. Quezon City, The Philippines, Mar. 26, 1956; d. Pol and Evelyn (Lacson) Ramos. BS, Tufts U., 1977; MD, Tufts Med. Sch., Boston, 1981. Diplomate Am. Bd. Internal Medicine, Am. Bd. Nephrology. Resident in internal medicine New Eng. Med. Ctr., Boston, 1981-84; fellow in nephrology Brigham and Women's Hosp., Boston, 1984-88, med. dir. renal transplant svc., 1988-90; med. dir. renal transplant svc. U. Fla., Gainesville, 1990-94; assoc. dir. immunology clin. rsch. Bristol-Myers Squibb Pharm. Rsch. Inst., Wallingford, Conn., 1994-96; asst. clin. prof. medicine Yale U., 1995-96; dir. med. rsch. Roche Global Devel., Palo Alto, Calif., 1996—. Mem. Am. Soc. Transplant Physicians (chairperson patient care and edn. com. 1994-95, clin. practice guideline com., Young Investigator award 1988), Am. Soc. Nephrology, Internat. Soc. Nephrology, Transplantation Soc., Alpha Omega Alpha, United Network for Organ Sharing (patient affairs com.).

RAMOS, GERARDO ERNESTO, Spanish teacher; b. Manizales, Colombia, Mar. 1, 1953; came to U.S., 1980; s. Gerardo and Magalena (Marin) R. BA, U. Caldas, 1979; PhD, CUNY, 1994. H.S. tchr. Inst. Universitario, Manizales, 1974-80; asst. Spanish tchr. Orono H.S., Mpls., 1980-81; Spanish tchr. Inlingua Sch. Langs., N.Y.C., 1982-83, Dewey H.S., Bklyn., 1983—. Author: (translator) Columbian Dialectology, Contribution to the Study of Slang in Colombia-Caldas and Its Slang. Mem. MLA, N.Y. State Bilingual Edn.

RAMOS, MANUEL ANTONIO, JR., pulmonologist; b. Lima, Peru, Dec. 17, 1959; arrived in U.S., 1962; s. Manuel and Rosa (Palao) R. BS with Hons., cum laude, U. Miami, 1980; MD, Tulane U., 1984. Diplomate Am. Bd. Internal Medicine, diplomate Subspecialty of Pulmonary Disease. Intern Tulane Hosps., New Orleans, 1984-85; resident in medicine Jackson Meml. Hosp., Miami, Fla., 1985-87, fellow in pulmonology, 1987-90; pvt. practice in pulmonology Plantation, Fla., 1990—; sec. dept. medicine Plantation Gen. Hosp. Contbr. articles to profl. jours. Active Archbishops of Miami Charity Drive Guild. Fellow Am. Coll. Chest Physicians; mem. AMA (Physicians Recognition award 1990, 95), ACP, Am. Thoracic Soc., Am. Soc. Internal Medicine, Broward County Med. Assn. (Salvation Army Clinic, Ft. Lauderdale 1991—), Plantation C. of C. Avocations: tennis, basketball. Office: 7050 NW 4th St Ste 301 Plantation FL 33317-2247

RAMOS, MELVIN JOHN, artist, educator; b. Sacramento, July 24, 1935; s. Clifton John and Agnes (Enos) R.; m. Lolita Alice Helmers, Aug. 14, 1955; children: Bradley, Scot, Rochelle. B.A., Calif. State U.-Sacramento, 1957, M.A., 1958. Tchr. Elk Grove High Sch., (Calif.), 1957-60, Mira Loma High Sch., Sacramento, 1960-66; prof. art Calif. State U.-Hayward, 1966—. Exhibited one man shows, Louis Meisel Gallery, N.Y.C., 1974, 76, 81, 85, 89, Mus. Haus Lange, 1975, Oakland Mus., 1977, Rose Art Mus., 1980, group shows, Whitney Mus., N.Y.C., 1969, 78, 83, Bklyn Mus., 1970, Mus. Modern Art, N.Y.C., 1970; Ludwig Mus. Cologne, 1992, Mus. of Cont. Art La., 1993; represented in permanent collections, San Francisco Mus. Modern Art, Oakland Mus., Indpls. Mus., Mus. Modern Art, N.Y.C., Crystler Mus., Va., Smithsonian Instn., Washington, Guggenheim Mus., N.Y.C., Nat. Gallery, Washington, Kunsthaus, Darmstadt, W.Ger., Whitney Mus. Am. Art; author: Mel Ramos: Watercolors, 1979. Democrat. Roman Catholic. Home: 5941 Ocean View Dr Oakland CA 94618-1842 Office: 25800 Hillary St Hayward CA 94542

RAMOS, RAUL, surgeon; b. Sabinas, Coahulla, Mex., Oct. 30, 1942; s. Raul and Carmen (Lopez) R.; m. Hilda Mazquiz de Ramos, Mar. 1, 1992; children by previous marriage: Raul, Maria, Ana, Veronica. MD, U. Nuevo Leon, Mex., 1966. Diplomate Am. Bd. Surgery, Am. Bd. Colon and Rectal Surgery. Intern Bapt. Meml. Hosp., San Antonio, 1966-67, mem. active staff, chmn. dept. surgery, 1983-84, 89-90; clin. asst. prof. surgery U. Tex. Health Sci. Ctr., San Antonio, 1973-78, head divns. proctology, 1973—, clin. assoc. prof. surgery, 1978-89, dir. residency program colon and rectal surgery, 1979-82, clin. prof. surgery, 1989—; mem. active staff Santa Rosa Med. Ctr., S.W. Tex. Meth. Hosp., Audie Murphy Meml. VA Hosp., San Antonio Humana Hosp., St. Luth's Luth. Hosp., Bexar County Hosp. Dist.; vis. prof. U. Nuevo Leon, Monterrey , Mex., 1976, 80, Assemblea Nacional de Cirjuanos, Mexico City, 1976, Mil. Med. Sch., Mexico City, 1980, 81, Socieda Mex. Cirjanos Puebla, 1990, Loyola Univ., 1992, U. Guanajuato, mex., 1992, Institutos Technologico Estudios Superiores en Monterrey, 1993; examiner Am. Bd. Surgery, 1990; presenter numerous seminars. Mem. AMA, ACS, Am. Soc. Colon and Rectal Surgeons (mem. coun. 1981-82), Tex. Med. Assn., Tex. Soc. Colon and Rectal Surgeons (pres. 1977, 78), Tex. Soc. Colo-Rectal Surgeons (sec. 1977)Associacion de Cirujanos de Noreste A.C., Sociedad Colombiana de Gastroenterologia, Sociedad Colombiana de Cirujanos de Colon y Recto, Sociedad Chilena de Cirugia, Sociedad Chilena de Proctologia, Sociedad mexicana de Cirjuanos de Colon y Recto, Collegium Internatcionale Chirurgia Digestivae, Internat. Soc. Univ. Colon and Rectal Surgeons, So. Med. Assn. (v.p. sect. colo-rectal surgery 1979, chmn. 1980, sec. 1981, 82, 83), Priestly Surg. Soc., Bexar County Med. Soc. (bd. dirs. 1990-92, chmn. exhibits com.), Gen. Surg. Soc. San Antonio (v.p. 1979, pres. 1980), Sociedad Medica Hispano-Americano de Tejas (sec. 1979, pres. 1986), San Antonio Surg. Soc. (pres. 1986-87), Aust Soc., Mayo Alumni. Avocations: tennis, golf, reading. Office: Colon and Rectal Assocs San Antonio 7950 Floyd Curl Dr Ste 101 San Antonio TX 78229-3916

RAMOS, ROSE MARY, elementary education educator; b. San Antonio, Aug. 8, 1942; d. Henry Barbosa and Bertha Alice (Cuellar) Gonzalez; m. Jesus Ramos Jr., Sept. 11, 1965; children: Rebecca Anne, Veronica Anne. BS in Elem. Edn., Our Lady of Lake U., San Antonio, 1965; MA in Edn., U. Houston, 1992. Cert. elem. educator, kindergarten, reading specialist, bilingual and ESL. Tchr. San Antonio Ind. Sch. Dist., 1965-89, Ft. Bend County (Tex.) Ind. Sch. Dist., 1989—; acad. adv. com. Ft. Bend I.S.D., 1996. Mem. Nat. Space Soc., Tex. State Reading Assn., Greater Houston Area Reading Assn., San Antonio Conservation Soc., Internat. Reading Assn. Democrat. Roman Catholic. Avocations: reading, life sciences, writing. Home: 3614 Belle Grove Ln Sugar Land TX 77479-2257

RAMOS-CANO, HAZEL BALATERO, caterer owner, innkeeper, entrepreneur; b. Davao City, Mindanao, Philippines, Sept. 2, 1936; came to U. S., 1960.; d. Mauricio C. and Felicidad (Balatero) Ramos; m. William Harold Snyder, Feb. 17, 1964 (div. 1981); children: John Byron, Snyder, Jennifer Ruth; m. Nelson Allen Blue, May 30, 1986 (div. 1990); m. A. Richard Cano, June 25, 1994. BA in Social Work, U. Philippines, Quezon City, 1958; MA in Sociology, Pa. State U., 1963, postgrad., 1966-67. Cert. exec. chef, Am. Culinary Fedn. Faculty, tng. staff Peace Corps Philippine Project, University Park, Pa., 1961-63; sociology instr. Albright Coll. Sociology Dept., Reading, Pa., 1963-64; research asst. Meth. Ch. U.S.A., State College, Pa., 1965-66; research asst. dept. child devel. & family relations Pa. State U., University Park, Pa., 1966-67; exec. dir. Presbyn. Urban Coun. Raleigh Halifax Ct. Child Care and Family Svc. Ctr., 1973-79; early childhood educator Learning Together, Inc., Raleigh, 1982-83; loan mortgage specialist Raleigh Savings & Loan, 1983-84; restaurant owner, mgr. Hazel's on Hargett, Raleigh, 1985-86; admissions coord., social worker Brian Corp. Nursing Home, Raleigh, 1986-88, food svc. dir., 1989-90; regional dir. La Petite Acad., Raleigh, 1989-90; asst. food svc. mgr. Granville Towers, Chapel Hill, N.C., 1990-92; mgr. trainee Child Nutrition Svcs. Wake County Pub. Sch. System, Raleigh, N.C., 1993-94; food svc. dir. S.W. Va. 4-H Ednl. Conf. Ctr., Abingdon, 1994-95; caterer, owner The Eclectic Chef's Catering, 1995—; innkeeper, owner Love House Bed and Breakfast, 1996—; cooking instr. Wake Cmty. Tech. Coll., Raleigh, 1986-92; freelance caterer, 1964-95; chair Internat. Cooking Demonstrations Raleigh Internat. Festival, 1990-93. Pres. Wake County Day Care United Coun., 1974-75, N.C. Assn. Edn. Young Children (Raleigh Chpt.), 1975-76; bd. mem. Project Enlightenment Wake County Pub. Schs., 1976-77; various positions Pines of Carolina Girl Scout Council, 1976-85; chmn. Philippine Health and Medical Aid Com., Phil-Am Assn. Raleigh 1985-88 (publicity chmn.); elder Trinity Presbyn. Ch., Raleigh, 1979-81, bd. deacons, 1993-94; elder, session mem. Sinking Spring Presbyn. Ch., 1997—; treas. Abingdon Newcomers Club, 1997—. Recipient Juliette Low Girl Scout Internat. award, 1953, Rockefeller grant Rockefeller Found., 1958-59, Ramon Magsaysay Presidential award, Philippine Leadership Youth Movement, 1957; Gov.'s Cert. Appreciation State N.C., 1990, Raleigh Mayor's award Quality Childcare Svcs., 1990. Mem. Am. Culinary Fedn., Presby. Women, Raleigh, (historian 1975-76), Penn State Dames (pres. 1968-69). Democrat. Office: Love House Bed & Breakfast 210 E Valley St Abingdon VA 24210

RAMSAUR, ALLAN FIELDS, lawyer, lobbyist; b. Rocky Mount, NC, Dec. 30, 1951; s. Carl Hamilton and Celestine (Fields) R.; m. Jimmie Lynn Brewer, Sept. 2, 1972; children: Katherine Celeste, Benjamin Allan. BA in Polit. Sci., Lambuth Coll., 1974; JD, U. Tenn., 1977. Bar: Tenn. 1977. Staff atty. Tenn. Dept. Mental Health, Nashville, 1977-80; dir. Tenn. Assn. Legal Services, Nashville, 1980-86; campaign dir. Steve Cobb, Nashville, 1986; exec. dir. Nashville Bar Assn., 1986—. Pres. Woodland-in-Waverly Neighborhood Assn., Nashville, 1985; bd. dirs. SAGA, Nashville, 1984-86, Bethlehem Center, Nashville, 1990— (sec. 1992). Recipient Leadership Nashville award, 1988. Mem. ABA (liaison to standing com. on legal aid and indigent defendants 1984-86, spl. com. on prepaid legal svcs. 1988-89, standing com. on lawyer referral and info. svc. 1990-92), Nat. Assn. Bar Execs. (chair edn. com.), Tenn. Bar Assn. (pres. young lawyers divsn. 1985-86), Nat. Legal Aid and Defender Assn. (chmn. legis com. 1984-86), Nashville Bar Assn. (exec. dir. 1986—). Democrat. Methodist. Home: 1417 Beddington Park Nashville TN 37215-5815

RAMSAY, DAVID LESLIE, physician, dermatologist, medical educator; b. Rochester, N.Y., Apr. 25, 1943; s. Joseph Walter and Jean (Eastwood) R. AB in English with honors, Ind. U., 1965, MD, 1969; MEd, U. Ill., 1973. Diplomate Am. Bd. Dermatology. Assoc. faculty mem. Ind. U., Indpls., 1965-69; intern in medicine George Washington U. Med. Ctr., 1969-70; resident in dermatology NYU Med. Ctr., 1970-73; dir. dermatology residency tng. Nat. Naval Med. Ctr., Bethesda, Md., 1973-75; asst. prof. medicine Georgetown U., Washington, 1974-75; asst. prof. dermatology NYU, 1974-78, assoc. prof. dermatology, 1978-95, prof. dermatology, 1995—, senator, 1986-94, pres. faculty coun., 1988-90, dir. ednl. affairs dermatology, 1975—, dir. cutaneous lymphoma sect., 1975—. Author: Simulations in Dermatology, 1974; contbg. author: Adolescent Dermatology, Basic Mechanisms of Physiologic and Aberrant Lymphoproliferation in the Skin, Hematology and Oncology Clinics in North America; contbr. more than 25 articles to profl. jours. Pres., bd. dirs. One Fifth Ave. Apt. Corp., N.Y.C., 1978-80; trustee Bklyn. Acad. Music, 1989—. Lt. comdr. USN, 1973-75. NIH fellow U. Ill., 1972-73. Fellow ACP, Internat. Soc. Cutaneous Lymphomas, Am. Acad. Dermatology; mem. Am. Dermatologic Assn. Roman Catholic. Avocations: collecting visual art, swimming, reading. Home: One Fifth Ave New York NY 10003 Office: NYU Med Ctr 530 5th Ave New York NY 10036-5101

RAMSAY, DONALD ALLAN, physical chemist; b. London, July 11, 1922; s. Norman and Thirza Elizabeth (Beckley) R.; m. Nancy Brayshaw, June 8, 1946; children: Shirley Margaret, Wendy Kathleen, Catharine Jean, Linda Mary. BA, Cambridge (Eng.) U., 1943, MA, 1947, PhD, 1947, ScD, 1976; D honoris causa, U. Reims, France, 1969; Filosofie hedersdoktor, U. Stockholm, Sweden, 1982. With divs. chemistry Nat. Research Council Can., Ottawa, Ont., 1947-49; with divs. physics Nat. Research Council Can., 1949-75; with Herzberg Inst. Astrophysics, 1975-87, sr. research officer, 1961-68, prin. research officer, 1968-87; vis. prof. U. Minn., 1964, U. Orsay, 1966, U. Stockholm, 1967, 71, 74, U. Calif., Irvine, 1970, U. Sao Paulo, 1972, 78, U. Bologna, 1973, U. Western Australia, 1976, Australian Nat. U., 1976, Tex. Christian U., 1988, U. Wuppertal, Germany, 1988, U. Canterbury, Christchurch, New Zealand, 1996, U. Ulm, Germany, 1992, 96, 97; guest worker Steacie Inst. Molecular Scis. Editor: (with J. Hinze) Selected Works of Robert S. Mulliken, 1975; contbr. numerous articles on molecular spectra and molecular structure to profl. jours. Recipient commemorative medal for 125th anniversary Confederation Can., 1992, Alexander von Humboldt Rsch. award, 1993-95; decorated Queen Elizabeth Silver Jubilee medal. Fellow Royal Soc. London, Royal Soc. Can. (hon. treas. 1976-79, 88-91, Centennial medal 1982), Am. Phys. Soc., Chem. Inst. Can. (Chem. Inst. Can. medal 1992). Mem. United Ch. of Canada (organist 1954-97). Club: Leander (Henley-on-Thames, Eng.). Home: 1578 Drake Ave, Ottawa, ON Canada K1G 0L8 Office: Nat Research Council, 100 Sussex Dr, Ottawa, ON Canada K1A 0R6

RAMSAY, ERNEST CANADAY, lawyer; b. Statesboro, Ga., Feb. 14, 1939; s. Ernest Francis and Miriam Carolyn (Canaday) R.; m. Barbara Ann Gazaway, Dec. 18, 1960; children: Elizabeth Kennerly, Lydia Katherine. Student, Ga. Tech., 1957; AB, Mercer U., Macon, Ga., 1961; JD, Mercer U., 1963. Bar: Ga. 1964. Assoc. Bryan, Carter, Ansley & Smith, Atlanta, 1963-65; ptnr. Carley & Ramsay, Decatur, Ga., 1965-69; assoc. Hansell & Post, Atlanta, 1969-74, mng. ptnr., 1974-89; mng. ptnr. Ramsay & Calloway, Atlanta, 1989—; bd. dirs. Attys.' Title Guaranty Fund, Inc., Cartersville, Ga., 1974-93. Mem. Atlanta Bar Assn. (real property law sect. 1979—), State Bar Ga. (real property law sect. chmn. 1971-72), Decatur-DeKalb Bar Assn. (real estate sect. chmn. 1973-74)., Ravinia Club (Atlanta), DeKalb Hist. Soc. (pres. 1973-75). Office: Ramsay Title Group LLC 6400 Atlantic Blvd Ste 170 Norcross GA 30071-1214

RAMSAY, GUSTAVUS REMAK, actor; b. Balt., Feb. 2, 1937; s. John Breckinridge and Caroline V. (Remak) R. BA, Princeton U., 1958. Appeared in plays Hang Down Your Head and Die, 1964, Half A Sixpence, 1965, Lovely Ladies, Kind Gentlemen, Sheep on the Runway, 1970, On the Town, 1971, The Real Inspector Hound, After Magritte, 1972, Jumpers, 1974, Private Lives, 1975, Landscape of the Body, Dirty Linen, 1977, The Rear Column, 1978, All's Well That Ends Well, 1978, Every Good Boy Deserves Favor, 1980, Save Grand Central, 1980, The Winslow Boy, 1980-81, The Dining Room, 1982, as St. John Quartermaine in Quartermaine's Terms, 1983— (Obie award), Woman in Mind, 1988, The Devil's Disciple, 1988, Love Letters, 1989, Prin, 1990, Nick & Nora, 1991, St. Joan, 1993, The Moliere Comedies, 1995, The Heiress, 1995, Misalliance, 1997; appeared in movies The Tiger Makes Out, The Stepford Wives, The Great Gatsby, The Front, Class, Simon, The House on Carroll Street, Mr. and Mrs. Bridge, Shadows and Fog, King of the Hill, Addicted to Love; TV movies The Dining Room, Heartbreak House, Kennedy, Liberty, Concealed Enemies, Dream House, Mellon, Lincoln and Seward, Dead Ahead: The Exxon Valdez Disaster, Truman. With U.S. Army, 1959-62. Democrat. Presbyterian. Home: 115 Central Park W New York NY 10023-4153

RAMSAY, JOHN BARADA, research chemist, educator; b. Phoenix, Dec. 28, 1929; s. John A. and Helen G. Ramsay; m. Barbara Ann Hilsenhoff, Apr. 18, 1953; children: Bryan J., Kathleen L., Carol A., David A. BS in Chemistry, Tex. Western U., 1950; PhD in Analytical Chemistry, U. Wis., 1954. Mem. staff Los Alamos Nat. Lab., 1954-70, 73-95; assoc. prof. Coll. Petroleum and Minerals, Dhahran, Saudi Arabia, 1970-73; cons. U.S. Navy, USAF, 1980—; adj. prof. U. N.Mex., Los Alamos, 1980-85, Comforce 1995—. Author sci. articles. Recipient award of excellence U.S. Dept. Energy, 1984, 92. Mem. N.Mex. Acad. Sci. (pres. 1988), Am. Inst. Archeol. (chpt. pres. 1979, 96, 97), Nat. Ski Patrol (appt. 7651), Westerners Internat. (chpt. pres. 1988-90), Sigma Xi. Democrat. Home: 6 Erie Ln Los Alamos NM 87544-3810

RAMSAY, JOHN T., professional basketball team coach; b. Phila., Feb. 21, 1925; m. Jean Ramsay; 5 children. Student, St. Joseph's Coll., 1949; MS, U. Pa., 1952, EdD, 1963. Coach St. Joseph's Coll., Phila., 1955-66, Phila. 76ers (Nat. Basketball Assn.), 1968-72, Buffalo Braves, 1972-76, Portland (Oreg.) Trail Blazers, 1976-86, Ind. Pacers, Indpls., 1986-88; commentator, basketball analyst ESPN, Bristol, Conn. Coached winning team Nat. Basketball Assn. Championship, 1977. Office: care ESPN ESPN Plaza Bristol CT 06010*

RAMSAY, KARIN KINSEY, publisher, educator; b. Brownwood, Tex., Aug. 10, 1930; d. Kirby Luther and Ina Rebecca (Wood) Kinsey; m. Jack Cummins Ramsay Jr., Aug. 31, 1951; children: Annetta Jean, Robin Andrew. BA, Trinity U., 1951. Cert. assoc. ch. edn., 1980. Youth coord. Covenant Presbyn. Ch., Carrollton, Tex., 1961-76; dir. ch. edn. Northminster Presbyn. Ch., Dallas, 1976-80, Univ. Presbyn. Ch., Chapel Hill, N.C., 1987-90, Oak Grove Presbyn. Ch., Bloomington, Minn., 1990-93; coord. ecum. ministry Flood Relief for Iowa, Des Moines, 1993; program coord. 1st Presbyn. Ch., Green Bay, Wis., 1994-95; publicity & tour dir. Hist. Resources Press, Green Bay, 1994—; dir. Godspell tour Covenant Presbyn. Ch., 1972-75; mem. Presbytery Candidates Com., Dallas, 1977-82, Presbytery Exams. Com. Dallas, 1979-81; clk. coun. New Hope Presbytery, Rocky Mount, N.C., 1989-90; creator, dir. Thee Holy Fools mime/musical group and This Is Me retreats. Author: Ramsay's Resources, 1983—; contbr. articles to jours. in field. Design cons. Brookhaven Hosp. Chapel, Dallas, 1977-78; elder Presbyn. Ch. U.S.A., 1982—; coord. Lifeline Emergency Response, Dallas, 1982-84. Mem. Internat. Platform Assn. *Yesterday taught me the lessons which made today possible. Today is the challenging link between yesterday and tomorrow. Tomorrow is an opportunity built on the foundation of today. Today is special.*

RAMSAY, LOUIS LAFAYETTE, JR., lawyer, banker; b. Fordyce, Ark., Oct. 11, 1918; s. Louis Lafayette and Carmile (Jones) R.; m. Joy Bond, Oct. 3, 1945; children: Joy Blankenship, Richard Louis. JD, U. Ark., 1947; LLD (hon.), U. Ark., Fayetteville, 1988, U. Ark., Pine Bluff, 1992. Bar: Ark. 1947, U.S. Dist. Ct. Ark. 1947, U.S. Ct. Appeals (8th cir.) 1948, U.S. Supreme Ct. 1952. Sr. counsel Ramsay, Bridgforth, Harrelson & Starling and predecessor firm Ramsay, Cox, Lile, Bridgforth, Gilbert, Harrelson & Starling, Pine Bluff, Ark., 1948—; pres. Simmons First Nat. Bank, Pine Bluff, Ark., 1970-78, CEO, chmn. bd. dirs., 1978-83; chmn. exec. com., bd. dirs. Blue Cross-Blue Shield of Ark., Usable Life Ins. Co.; chmn. exec. com. Simmons First Nat. Corp. Mem. bd. Econ. Devel. Alliance of Jefferson County; mem. ofcl. bd. First United Meth. Ch. With USAF, 1942-45, maj. Res., 1945-49. Recipient Disting. Alumnus award U. Ark., 1982, Outstanding Lawyer award Ark. Bar Assn./Ark. Bar Found., 1966, 87. Mem. ABA (mem. spl. com. on presdl. inability and vice presdl. vacancy 1966), Ark. Bar Assn. (pres. 1963-64), Ark. Bar Found. (pres. 1960-61, Joint Bar Assn.,-Bar Found. Outstanding Lawyer award 1966, Lawyer Citizen award 1987), Ark. Bankers Assn. (pres. 1980-81), Pine Bluff C. of C. (pres. 1968), Rotary (pres. Pine Bluff 1954-55). Methodist. Office: Ramsay Bridgforth Harrelson & Starling PO Box 8509 Pine Bluff AR 71611-8509

RAMSAY, ROBERT HENRY, investment manager; b. Atchison, Kans., June 18, 1925; s. Ronald and Dorcas (Carlisle) R.; m. Margaret Packard, Aug. 16, 1952 (dec. Dec. 1989); children: Margaret R. Gray, William P., David C.; m. Carolyn McKillop, Dec. 8, 1991. BS in Aeronautical Engring., U. Kans., 1945; M in Retailing, U. Pitts., 1948. Br. mgr. Boettcher & Co., Grand Junction, Colo., 1956-65, Colorado Springs, Colo., 1965-71; pres. Robert H. Ramsay Fin. Svcs., Colorado Springs, 1971-74, Ramsay & Ellsworth, Inc., Colorado Springs, 1974-87, Ramsay Investment Counsel Inc., Colorado Springs, 1987—; bd. dirs. Norwest Bank of Colorado Springs. Bd. dirs. Colorado Springs Sch., Colo. Outward bound Sch. Mem. Rotary Club of Colorado Springs. Avocations: skiing, bicycling. Office: Ramsay Investment Counsel Inc 2 N Cascade Ave Ste 810 Colorado Springs CO 80903-1627

RAMSAY, WILLIAM CHARLES, writer; b. N.Y.C., Nov. 6, 1930; s. Claude Barnett and Myrtle Marie (Scott) R.; m. Charlotte Appleton Kidder, June 10, 1988 (dec. Sept. 1995); children from previous marriages: Alice, John, Carol Ramsay Scott, David. BA in English Lit., U. Colo., 1952; MA in Physics, UCLA, 1957, PhD in Physics, 1962. NFS postdoctoral fellow U. Calif., San Diego, 1962-64; asst. prof. U. Calif., Santa Barbara, 1964-67; tech. mgr. Systems Assocs., Inc., Long Beach, Calif., 1967-72; sr. environ. economist U.S. AEC, Bethesda, Md., 1972-75; tech. adviser U.S. Nuclear Regulatory Agy., Washington, 1975-76; sr. fellow Resources for the Future, Washington, 1976-83, Ctr. for Strategic and Internat. Studies, Washington, 1983-85; sr. staff officer NAS, Washington, 1985-86; freelance writer, editor, publ. Washington, 1986—; cons. Vols. in Tech. Assistance, Arlington, Va., 1987-90, Internat. Resources Group, Washington, 1991; treas., bd. dirs. Jordan Conservation and Rsch. Ctr., Inc. Author: Unpaid Costs of Electrical Energy, 1979, Bicenergy and Economic Development, 1985; co-author: Managing the Environment, 1972, Energy in America's Future, 1979; editor, pub. Fiction-Online (electronic lit. jour.). Mem. adv. bd. Nat. Zoo, Washington. Buenos Aires Convention fellow, 1952, NSF fellow, 1962; NATO scholar, 1960, 62. Mem. Am. Phys. Soc., Am. Astron. Soc., Internat. Assn. Energy Economists, Washington Ind. Writers, Writers' Ctr. (bd. dirs.). Avocations: piano, musical composition. Home and Office: 2930 Foxhall Rd NW Washington DC 20016-3429

RAMSBY, MARK DELIVAN, lighting designer and consultant; b. Portland, Oreg., Nov. 20, 1947; s. Marshall Delivan and Verna Pansy (Culver) R.; divorced; children: Aaron Delivan, Venessa Mercedes. Student, Portland (Oreg.) State U., 1966-67. With C.E.D., Portland, 1970-75; minority ptnr. The Light Source, Portland, 1975-78, pres., 1978-87; prin. Illume Lighting Design, Portland, 1987-90; ptnr. Ramsby, Dupuy & Seats, Inc., Portland, 1990-91; dir. lighting design PAE Cons. Engrs., Inc., Portland, 1991—; pvt. practice cons. Portland, 1979—. Recipient Top 100 Outstanding Achievement award Metalux Lighting, 1981-85, 100% award, 1985, Edwin F. Guth award of merit, 1990, Edison award of excellence, 1990, Edwin F. Guth award of excellence, 1993, 94, Paul Waterbury award of Merit, 1995. Mem. Illuminating Engring. Soc. Am. (sec.-treas. Oreg. sect. 1978-79, Oreg. Section and Regional and Internat. awards 1989, 90, 93, 94, Lighting Design awards), Internat. Assn. Lighting Designers. Republican. Lutheran. Avocations: lighting design, historical restoration, flyfishing, downhill skiing. Office: PAE Cons Engrs 808 SW 3rd Ave Ste 300 Portland OR 97204-2426

RAMSDELL, RICHARD ADONIRAM, marine engineer; b. Hartford, Conn., Feb. 28, 1953; s. Robert Allen and Irene Ella (Lewis) R.; m. Vicki Lynn Pepin, July 1, 1978 (div. Mar. 1984); children: Eric Charles, Ryan Amber; m. Beverly Jane Tenken; children: Alexander Richard, Matthew Robin. BS in Marine Engring., Maine Maritime Acad., 1975. Plant operator Ga. Pacific, Woodland, Maine, 1975-77; 2d asst. engr. Farrell Lines, Inc., N.Y.C., 1977-83; steam plant foreman Jackson Lab., Bar Harbor, Maine, 1984-86; plant operator Babcock-Ultrapower Jonesboro, Maine, 1986-90; results, environ. engr. Maine Power Svcs., Bangor, 1990-92; plant engr. Babcock-Ultrapower West Enfield, Maine, 1992-95, Ebensburg (Pa.) Power Co., 1995—. Mem. Assn. Energy Engrs. Office: Ebensburg Power Co PO Box 845 Ebensburg PA 15931

RAMSDEN, LINDA GISELE, lawyer; b. Lewiston, Maine, July 19, 1969; d. Donald Jean and Rita Lorraine (Lemieux) Rossignol; m. Matthew Edmund Ramsden, Aug. 13, 1994. Student, Bristol (Eng.) U., 1989-90; BA cum laude, Colby Coll., 1991; JD cum laude, U. Maine, 1994. Bar: Mass. 1995, U.S. Dist. Ct. Mass. 1995. Prearraignment screening vol. Maine Pretrial Svcs., Portland, 1991-92; law clk. U.S. Atty., Dist. of Maine, 1993; legal intern Gardner, Gardner and Murphy, Saco, Maine, 1993-94; ptnr. Hoffman and Ramsden, LLP, Boston, 1995—. Mem. ACLU, ABA, Mass. Bar Assn., Boston Bar Assn., Phi Beta Kappa, Nat. Polit. Honor Soc. Democrat. Roman Catholic. Avocations: traveling, skiing, golfing. Home: 15 Howitt Rd Boston MA 02132 Office: Hoffman & Ramsden LLP Ste 715 Six Beacon St Boston MA 02108

RAMSDEN, NORMA LA VONNE HUBER, nurse; b. Lewiston, Idaho, Aug. 1, 1921; d. Lawrence Henry and Gertrude Melissa (Ryder) Huber; m. John Burton Wormell, Nov. 18, 1942 (div. 1950); m. Everett Glenn Ramsden, Dec. 25, 1957; 1 child, Valerie Ann Ramsden Brooks. Diploma in nursing, St. Joseph's Hosp., Lewiston, 1952. Psychiatric nurse Oreg. State Hosp., Salem, 1952-57; clin. instr. Idaho State Hosp., Orofino, Idaho, 1957-58; night nurse ICU Tri State Hosp., Clarkston, Wash., 1969-94; ret., 1994, Rogers Counseling Ctr., Clarkston, 1994; adv. bd. Rogers Counseling Ctr., Clarkston, 1969—. Leader Camp Fire Girls Am., 1958-61, 69-71; Episcopalian vestry, 1992—, fellowship chmn., 1994—; vol. Interlink, 1994—. Recipient Woman Achievement award Altrusa Club, 1985. Mem. Am. Nurses Assn., Anatone Grange, Pollyette (pres., sec., treas.). Avocations: hiking, sewing, oil painting, gardening. Home: 817 Highland Ave Clarkston WA 99403-2760

RAMSEY, BILL (WILLIAM MCCREERY), singer, actor, composer-lyricist, television executive; b. Cin., Apr. 17, 1931; s. William McCreery II and Olivia (James) R.; m. Erica Moeckli, Dec. 14, 1962 (div. Feb. 1982); 1 son, Joachim.; m. Petra Bock, Aug. 3, 1983. Student, Yale U., 1949-51, Goethe U., Frankfurt/Main, Germany, 1955, 57, U. Cin., 1956-57. guest prof. vocal jazz and presentation in pop and jazz program Hamburg U. Music and Drama, Hamburg, 1983-86. Partime profl. singer, 1949; appeared on Horace Heidt show, Hollywood, Calif., 1951, Eddie Fisher tour, Europe, 1953, Raymond Burr tour, Europe and North Africa, 1954, series jazz concerts, Germany and Am., 1953-55; 1st American to appear at German Jazz Festival, 1955, 1st American jazz vocalist after war to tour Yugoslavia, 1955, 1st TV portrait, Frankfurt/Main, 1955, 1st films in Baden-Baden, Munich, Hamburg, 1955; full-time profl. jazz and pop vocalist, 1957—, numerous recs.; actor numerous films, TV shows; songwriting, disc jockey work with Radio Luxembourg, Europawelle Saar, Radio Salzburg; 1st American jazz singer to tour Poland after war, also appearances Polish Jazz Festival, 1957, 67, Czek Jazz Festival, 1966; 1st pop record hit German version of Purple People Eater, 1958; program dir. Televico AG, Zurich/Gockhausen, Swiss TV and Film Prodn. Co., 1968-72, rec. artist for Polydor, Electrolia, Columbia, Cornet, Warner Bros., Stockfish, Ariola, Dino, Bear Family; in addition to singing, TV moderator on all three German Programs as well as in Austria since 1970. With USAF, 1951-55. Recipient top positions in various jazz polls. Mem. German Authors and Composers Soc. Address: Elbchaussee 118, D-22763 Hamburg Germany

RAMSEY, CHARLES EUGENE, sociologist, educator; b. Paragon, Ind., Apr. 24, 1923; s. Sarcefield Dodson and Stella (Goss) R.; m. Alberta Mae Jordan, July 19, 1943; children—James D., Charles W., Jane E., Suzanne. B.S., Ind. State Tchrs. Coll., 1947; M.S., U. Wis., 1950, Ph.D., 1952. Faculty U. Wis., 1951-52, U. Minn., 1952-54, Cornell U., 1954-62, Colo. State U., 1962-65; prof. sociology U. Minn., Mpls., 1965-77; chmn. dept. sociology U. Tex., Arlington, 1977-83; vis. prof. Inter-Am. Instn. Agrl. Sci., Costa Rica, 1961, Exptl. Sta., U. P.R., 1961-62; research cons. to various univs., agys. Author: (with Lowry Nelson and Cooley Verner) Community Structure and Change, 1960, (with David Gottlieb) The American Adolescent, 1965, Understanding the Deprived Child, S.R.A, 1967, Problems of Youth, 1967, (with D.J. McCarty) The School Managers: Power and Conflict in American Public Education, 1971, (with William A. Stacey) Social Statistics, 1992; also articles. Mem. Am. Sociol. Assn., Rural Sociol. Soc., Sigma Xi. Developed and tested theory of variations in community power structure, types of sch. bds., and roles of sch. supt., developed method of comparative measurement of level of living for different countries. Home: 1102 De Pauw Dr Arlington TX 76012-5339 Office: U Tex Dept Sociology Arlington TX

RAMSEY, DAN STEVEN, foundation and organization administrator; b. Rockford, Ill., Apr. 15, 1949; s. Marvin Eugene and Clara Judith (Johnson) R.; m. Martha Duffy, Dec. 30, 1972; 1 child, Sara Judith. BA, Rockford Coll., 1971. Admissions rep., resident dir. Rockford (Ill.) Coll., 1970-74; dir. admissions Centenary Coll., Shreveport, La., 1974-77; dir. admissions Nichols Coll., Dudley, Mass., 1977-80, dir. inst. advancement, 1980-86; dir. devel. New Britain (Conn.) Gen. Hosp., 1986-88; dean of coll. advancement Post Coll., Waterbury, Conn., 1988-89; v.p. inst. advancement LeMoyne Coll., Syracuse, N.Y., 1989-93; pres. The Ramsey Group, DeWitt, N.Y., 1980—; exec. dir. The Loretto Found., Syracuse, 1994-96; v.p. for advancement Syracuse Cmty. Health Ctr., 1996—; comm. cons. C.W. Beggs & Assoc., Rockford, Ill., 1970, writer, fund raising cons. G. Frederick Co., bd. mem. R. M. Jones & Co., Bristol, Conn., 1978-82, pres., CEO The Ramsey Group, DeWitt, 1980—. Author: Introduction To Fund Raising, 1993, Giving It Away in America, 1995. Com. mem. Manlius Pebble Hill Sch., DeWitt, 1991-96; bd. dirs. Child and Family Svc. of Ctrl. N.Y., 1994-96, Frank Hiscock Legal Aid Soc., 1994-96, bd. dirs. Leadership Greater Syracuse Alumni Assn. Mem. Nat. Soc. of Fund Raising Exec., Assn. for Healthcare Philanthropy, Greater Syracuse C. of C. Republican. Avocations: sailing, computers, cooking, fishing, camping. Home: 313 Lansdowne Rd Syracuse NY 13214 Office: The Ramsey Group 313 Lansdowne Rd Syracuse NY 13214-2128

RAMSEY, DAVID ALLEN, psychologist; b. Huntington, W.Va., Sept. 11, 1934; s. Cecil Lyle and Henrietta Margaret R.; B.A., Marshall U., 1956; M.S., W.Va. U., 1957; Ph.D., C.U., 1983. Clin. psychologist Huntington (W.Va.) Psychiat. Hosp., 1958-63; coordinator of evaluative services Vocat. Rehab. Center, Pitts., 1963-67; asst. dir. edn. and tng. Research and Tng. Center, U. Pitts., 1967-69; dir. personnel devel. corp. office Am. Insts. for Research, Pitts., 1969-72; rehab. services coordinator Pioneer Center, Pitts., 1972-76; pvt. practice psychol. evaluation, Pitts., 1976—; supr. outpatient services S.W. Communities Mental Health, Pitts., 1981—; cons. in field. Served with U.S. Army, 1957-58. Diplomate Am. Bd. Med. Psychotherapists; lic. psychologist, Pa. Mem. Am. Psychol. Assn. Home: 1254 Shadycrest Dr Pittsburgh PA 15216-3018 Office: Birmingham Towers Ste 200 21st and Wharton Sts Pittsburgh PA 15203

RAMSEY, DAVID SELMER, retired hospital executive; b. Mpls., Feb. 19, 1931; s. Selmer A. and Esther D. (Dahl) R.; m. Elinor Corfield, Aug. 15, 1953; children—Scott, Stewart, Thomas. B.S., U. Mich., 1953, M.S. in Microbiology, 1954, M.H.A., 1962. Research asst. Detroit Inst. Cancer Research, 1954-60; asst. adminstr. Harper Hosp., Detroit, 1962-68; assoc. adminstr. Harper Hosp., 1968-72; exec. v.p. Iowa Meth. Med. Ctr., Des Moines, 1972-83; pres. Iowa Meth. Med. Ctr., 1983-93, Iowa Health Sys., 1993-95. Avocations: golf; tennis; photography. Home: 25213 Quail Haven Dr Rio Verde AZ 85263

RAMSEY, FORREST GLADSTONE, JR., engineering company executive; b. Wichita, Kans., Oct. 25, 1930; s. Forrest Gladstone and Anastasia Ruth (Linot) R.; m. Gwendolyn Moreton, June 22, 1953 (div. Jan. 1982); children: Deborah Jenkins, Rebecca Johnson, Susan Klopp, Diane Hayes, Forrest G. III, Mark, Kenneth; m. Carmen Bergen, Apr. 30, 1988. BS in Engring., U.S. Naval Acad., 1952; postgrad., Wichita State U., 1957-58, U. Colo., 1958-64. Commd. ensign USN, 1952, res., 1957; planner, engr. Boeing Corp., Wichita, Kans., 1957-58; engr., logistician Martin-Marietta, Denver, 1959-65; div. dir. Computer Scis., Washington, 1965-73; program dir. Systems Cons., Washington, 1973-76; CEO Am. Sys. Corp., Washington, 1976-92, chmn., bd. dirs., 1992—. Mem. Profl. Svcs. Coun. (vice chmn. 1990), Naval Submarine League (bd. dirs. 1982-90). Roman Catholic. Home: 8 Hidden Vly Palmyra VA 22963-9500

RAMSEY, FRANK, retired basketball player; b. Corydon, Ky., July 13, 1931. Grad., U. Ly., 1954. Basketball player Boston Celtics. Named to Basketball Hall of Fame, 1981; selected All-Southeastern Conf. Team, NCAA All-Am. Team; mem. NBA Championship Team. Office: c/o Basketball Hall Fame PO Box 179 Springfield MA 01101-0179

RAMSEY, FRANK ALLEN, veterinarian, retired army officer; b. Rocksprings, Tex., May 1, 1929; s. Reynolds Allen and June (Burdette) R.; m. Lucette C. Reboul, Jan. 1958; children: Randal R., Ramsay A.; m. 2d, Mary Lou Cain, June 1991. D.V.M., Tex. A & M U., 1954; grad., U.S. Army Command and Gen. Staff Coll., 1965, U.S. Army War Coll., 1972. Commd. 1st. lt. U.S. Army Vet. Corps, 1955, advanced through grades to brig. gen., 1980; chief vet. service Ft. Leonard Wood, Mo., 1958-61; acad. vet. U.S. Mil. Acad., West Point, N.Y., 1962-64; vet. staff officer U.S. Army Combat Devel. Command Med. Service, Ft. Sam Houston, Tex., 1965-67; asst. chief profl. programming and planning br. Office Surgeon Gen., Washington, 1967-68, chief profl. programming and planning br., 1968-71, chief food inspection policy office, 1972-73, sr. vet. staff officer, 1973-77; asst. chief of staff Vet. Service, 7th Med. Command, Army Europe and 7th Army, Heidelberg, W. Ger., 1977-80; asst. for vet. services to surgeon gen. and chief U.S. Army Vet. Corps, Hdqrs. Dept. Army, Washington, 1980-85; ret., 1985. Decorated Army Commendation medal, Legion of Merit with oak leaf cluster, D.S.M. Mem. AVMA, Assn. Fed. Veterinarians, Assn. Mil. Surgeons U.S., Assn. Equine Practitioners, Am. Assn. Food Hygiene Veterinarians, Conf. Pub. Health Veterinarians, Tex. Vet. Med. Assn. Presbyterian. Lodge: Masons (32 degree). Home: 8 El Norte Cir Uvalde TX 78801-4021

RAMSEY, HENRY, JR., university official, lawyer, retired judge; b. Florence, S.C., Jan. 22, 1934; s. Henry Ramsey and Mary Ann Brunson; reared by Charles Arthur and and Nellie Tillman; m. Evelyn Yvonne Lewis, June 11, 1961 (div. Sept. 1967); children: Charles, Githaiga, Robert, Ismail; m. Eleanor Mason Ramsey, Sept. 7, 1969; children: Yetunde, Abeni. Student, Howard U.; BA, U. Calif., Riverside, 1960; LLB, U. Calif., 1963; student Inst. Edn. Mgmt., Harvard U., 1992; LLD (hon.), William Mitchell Coll. Law, 1996. Bar: Calif., 1964, U.S. Supreme Ct., 1967. Dep. dist. atty. Contra Costa County, Calif., 1964-65; pvt. practice Ramsey & Rosenthal, Richmond, Calif., 1965-71; prof. law U. Calif., Berkeley, 1971-80; judge Superior Court County of Alameda State Calif., Oakland, 1980-90; dean Sch. Law, Howard U., Washington, 1990-96, v.p. for legal affairs, acting gen. counsel, 1994-95; vis. prof. law U. Tex., Austin, 1977, U. Colo., Boulder, 1977-78, Am. Indian Law Ctr., U. N.Mex., 1980; mem., pres. Coun. Legal Edn., Opportunity, Washington, 1987-93; chair Law Sch. Admission Coun.-Bar Passage Rate Study Group, 1990-93; mem. Fellows of Am. Bar Found. Adv. Rsch. Com., 1995—; mem. Coun. for Ct. Excellence, D.C. Jury Project, 1996—; panelist Washington, D.C. region Ctr. for Pub. Resources, Institute for Dispute Resolution. Mem. City Coun. Berkeley, 1973-77, Criminal Justice Planning Bd., County of Alameda, 1973-76; trustee City of Berkeley Libr., 1973-74, Fibreboard Asbestos Compensation Trust, 1994—; bd. dirs. Redevel. Agy., Berkeley, 1971-73. With USAF, 1951-55. Recipient Jefferson Jurist award Calif. Assoc. Black Lawyers, 1986, Disting. Alumnus award U. Calif., 1987, Disting. Svc. award Wiley Manuel Law Found., 1987. Mem. ABA (mem. sect. legal edn. and admissions to bar 1982—, chair 1991-92, mem. standards rev. com. 1992-95), Nat. bar Assn., Nat. Ctr. State Cts. (mem. commn. trial ct. performance stds. 1987-95, Dist. Svc. award 1990), Am. Law Inst., Am. Judicature Soc., Calif. Judges Assn., Cosmos Club, Fed. City Club, Alpha Phi Alpha. Democrat. Avocations: cooking, reading, gardening, travel.

RAMSEY, IRA CLAYTON, retired pipeline company executive; b. Quitman, Ga., May 13, 1931; s. James Redding and Ruth Frances (Treadaway) R.; m. Marianne Vinzant, Dec. 23, 1962; children: Clayton Hamilton, Robin Leigh. BBA, U. Ga., Atlanta, 1954; LLB, Atlanta Law Sch., 1950; postgrad., U. Tex., 1968, U. Pitts., 1973. With Plantation Pipe Line Co., Atlanta, 1948-96, asst. sec., 1967-70, treas., contr., 1970-90, v.p. fin., 1990-96. Trustee Ga. Found. for Ind. Colls.; trustee, treas. KingsBridge Retirement Ctr., Inc. Baptist. Home: 780 Wesley Oak Rd NW Atlanta GA 30328-4738

RAMSEY, JACKSON EUGENE, management educator; b. Cin., Dec. 20, 1938; s. Leonard Pershing and Edna Willa (Blakeman) R.; m. Inez Mae Linn, Apr. 22, 1961; children: John Earl, James Leonard. BS in Metall. Engring., U. Cin., 1961; MBA, SUNY-Buffalo, 1969, PhD, 1975. Registered profl. engr., Va., Ohio. Welding engr. Gen. Electric Co., Cin., 1961-62, Westinghouse-Bettis Lab., Pitts., 1962-66; prodn. control mgr. Columbus-McKinnon Corp., Buffalo, 1966-71; asst. prof. mgmt. SUNY, Buffalo, 1971-73; prof. mgmt. James Madison U., Harrisonburg, Va., 1973—, provost; cons. in field. Chmn. Harrisonburg Reps., 1978-86, vice chmn., 1974-78; vice chmn. 6th Dist. Rep. Com., 1984-94. Served with USMCR, 1956-62. Named Outstanding Young Scholar, Xerox Corp., 1976. Mem. Acad. of Mgmt., Am. Inst. for Decision Scis., Inst. of Mgmt. Sci., Am. Soc. for Metals, Nat. Soc. Profl. Engrs. Republican. Baptist. Author: R D Strategic Decision Criteria, 1986; Handbook for Professional Managers, 1985; Budgeting Basics, 1985; Library Planning and Budgeting, 1986. Contbr. articles to profl. jours. Home: 282 Franklin St Harrisonburg VA 22801-4019 Office: James Madison U Coll Intergrated Sci & Tech Harrisonburg VA 22807

RAMSEY, JAROLD WILLIAM, English language educator, author; b. Bend, Oreg., Sept. 1, 1937; s. Augustus S. and Wilma E. (Mendenhall) R.; m. Dorothy Ann Quinn, Aug. 16, 1959; children: Kate, Sophia, John. B.A. with honors, U. Oreg., 1959; Ph. D., U. Wash., 1966. Acting instr. U. Wash., Seattle, 1963-65; asst. prof. English U. Rochester, (N.Y.), 1965-70, assoc. prof., 1970-81; prof. U. Rochester, (N.Y.), 1981—, dir. undergrad. rsch., 1990—; vis. prof. English U. Victoria, B.C., Can., 1974, 75-76; dir. NEH summer seminars on Indian lit., 1985, 88. Author: The Space Between Us, 1970, Love in an Earthquake, 1973 (Lillian Fairchild award 1973), Dermographia, 1982, Reading the Fire, 1983, Hand-shadows, 1989, (play) Coyote Goes Upriver, premier 1985, (cantata) (with Samuel Adler) The Lodge of Shadows, premiere 1988; editor: Coyote Was Going There, 1977, Nehalem Tillamook Tales, 1990, The Stories We Tell: Oregon Folk Literature (with Suzi Jones), 1994. Recipient Don Walker award Western Am. Lit., 1979, Borestone Mount Found. Best Poems award, 1972, 75, 76; Helen Bullis prize, 1984, Poetry prize Quar. Rev., 1989; Alumni Achievement award U. Oreg. Alumni Assn, 1990; Nat. Endowment Arts writing grantee, 1974, 76; Ingram Merrill Found. writing grantee, 1976. Mem. MLA (chair com. on lits. and langs. of Am. 1991-92), Assn. Study Am. Indian Lit. (pres. 1981), Am. Folklore Soc., Phi Beta Kappa. Democrat. Home: 519 Wellington Ave Rochester NY 14619-1828 Office: U Rochester English Dept Rochester NY 14619

RAMSEY, JERRY VIRGIL, educator, financial planner, radio broadcaster; b. Tacoma, July 24, 1940; s. Virgil Emory and Winifred Victoria (Carothers) R.; m. Elaine Sigrid Perdue, June 24, 1967; 1 child, Jason Perdue. BA in Elem. Edn., U. Puget Sound, 1967; MEd in Tchr. Tng. and Curriculum Devel., U. Wash., 1971; PhD in Econ. Geography Curriculum, Columbia Pacific U., 1985. Tchr. Tacoma Pub. Schs., 1967-95; fin. planner Primerica Corp., Tacoma, 1986-90, Waddell & Reed, Inc., Tacoma, 1990-93; N.Am. Mgmt., 1993-96; real estate investor, CEO Ramsey Properties, Gig Harbor, Wash., 1970—; radio broadcaster KGHP, KJUN/The Country Club Network, KMAS, 1990-96, KGY, 1996—; study skills specialist Sylvan Learning Ctr., 1995—; lectr. Pacific Luth. U., Tacoma, 1972-86. Precinct committeeman Pierce County Rep. Com., Tacoma, 1968-78, 95—; mem. steering com. Peninsula Neighborhood Assn., Gig Harbor, Wash., 1991-92; mem. Fort Nisqually Hist. Site Adv. Coun., 1996—. With USAF, 1959-62. Recipient Golden Acorn award PTA, 1975, Meritorious Teaching award Nat. Coun. Geog. Edn., 1978, achievement award Rep. Nat. Com., 1985; grantee U.S. Office Edn., 1971. Mem. NEA (life), Knife and Fork Club (pres. 1983), Kiwanis (pres. Tacoma 1976), Phi Delta Kappa. Methodist. Avocation: real estate investing, management and education. Office: Ramsey Properties PO Box 1311 Gig Harbor WA 98335-3311

RAMSEY, JOHN ARTHUR, lawyer; b. San Diego, Apr. 1, 1942; s. Wilbert Lewis and Lillian (Anderson) R.; m. Nikki Ann Ramsey, Feb. 9, 1943; children: John William, Bret Anderson, Heather Nichole. AB, San Diego State U., 1965; JD, Calif. Western Sch. Law, 1969. Bar: Colo. 1969, Tex. 1978. Assoc., Henry, Cockrell, Quinn & Creighton, 1969-72; atty. Texaco Inc., 1972-80, asst. to pres. Texaco U.S.A., 1980-81, asst. to div. v.p., Houston, 1981-82, div. atty., Denver, 1982-88; ptnr. Holland & Hart, 1989—. Bd. dirs. Selective Service, Englewood, Colo., 1972-76; chmn. council Bethany Lutheran Ch., Englewood, 1976. Mem. ABA (vice chmn. oil, natural gas exploration and prodn. com. sect. natural resource law 1983-88, chmn. 1989—, coun. sect. natural resources, energy and environ. law 1993). Republican. Editor-in-chief: Calif. Western Law Rev., 1969. Office: Holland & Hart Ste 200 8350 E Crescent Pkwy Englewood CO 80111

RAMSEY, JOHN HANSBERRY, executive search firm executive, investment banker; b. Scranton, Pa., May 4, 1941; s. Robert Martin and Elizabeth Mary (Durrick) R.; children: Mark Joseph, Craig Andrew, Alison Dianne. B.S., Tufts U., 1963; M.B.A. with distinction, Harvard U., 1968. Commd. 2d lt. USAF, 1963, advanced through grades to maj., 1971, resigned, 1972; sr. v.p., treas., chief fin. officer Union Commerce Corp./ Bank, Cleve., 1972-81; sr. v.p. devel. Am. Savs. and Loan Assn. of Fla., 1982-84; co-founder, pres. Mark Stanley & Co., Miami, Fla., 1983—; co-founder EMA Ptnrs. Internat., 1988—; treas., dir. Union Commerce Leasing Corp., 1974-75; treas. Union Capital Mgmt. Corp., 1974-75. Participant Leadership Cleve., 1980-81; co-fin. chmn. Cuyahoga County George Bush for Pres. Campaign, 1980; trustee mem. Beacon Council. Decorated Bronze Star, AF Commendation Medal. Mem. Fin. Execs. Inst., Greater Miami C. of C., Venture Coun. Forum, Harvard Club N.Y., Harvard Bus. Sch. So. Fla. Republican. Office: Mark Stanley & Co PO Box 149071 Coral Gables FL 33114-9071

RAMSEY, KATHLEEN SOMMER, toxicologist; b. Port Washington, Wis., June 2, 1947; d. Harrison Wilson and June Kathleen (Hansen) S.; m. Glenn A. Ramsey, Oct. 4, 1975; 1 child, David A. BA, Ripon Coll., 1969; PhD, U. Iowa, 1973. Diplomate Am. Bd. Toxicology. Rsch. assoc. U. Wis., Milw., 1969; instr. Baylor Coll. Medicine, Houston, 1973-74, USPHS rsch. fellow, 1974-76; rsch. chemist Shell Devel. Co., Houston, 1976-77; toxicologist Shell Oil Co., Houston, 1977-80; dir., cons. toxicologist Toxicon Corp., Magnolia, Tex., 1980—; mem. nat. adv. rsch. resources coun. NIH, Bethesda, Md., 1974-78; bd. dirs. Reid Road Mcpl. Utility Dist., Houston, 1982-95; guest lectr. U. Tex. Sch. Pub. Health, Houston. Contbr. articles to profl. jours. Paramedic Cy-Fair Vol. Fire Dept., Houston, 1983-87; dir. Harvest Bend Home Owners Assn., Houston, 1984-86. U. Iowa grad. fellow, Iowa City, 1969-73; recipient Nat. Rsch. Svc. award NIH, Bethesda, 1975. Mem. Am. Coll. Toxicology, Assn. Water (bd. dirs.), Am. Chem. Soc., Nat. Sci. Tchrs.' Assn. Office: Toxicon Corp 26535 Fm 2978 Rd Magnolia TX 77354-3035

RAMSEY, LLOYD BRINKLEY, retired savings and loan executive, retired army officer; b. Somerset, Ky., May 29, 1918; s. William Harold and Mary Ella (Barnett) R.; m. Glenda Burton, Feb. 22, 1941; children: Lloyd Ann (Mrs. Kyle D. Wallace), Larry Burton, Judi Carol (Mrs. David E. Derr). A.B., U. Ky., 1940; postgrad., Yale U., 1946, Command and Gen. Staff Coll., Ft. Leavenworth, Kans., 1949-50, U.S. Army War Coll., Carlisle Barracks, Pa., 1953-54, Harvard, 1961. Commd. 2d lt. U.S. Army, 1940, advanced through grades to maj. gen., 1968; bn. comdr. 7th Inf., 3d Inf. Div., 1944-45; instr. Inf. Sch., Ft. Benning, Ga., 1946-49; assigned Office G-2 Dept. Army Gen. Staff, 1950-53; sec. joint staff UN Far East Command, 1954-57; comdg. officer 1st Inf. Brigade, 1957-58; with Office Chief Legis. Liaison, Dept. Army Gen. Staff, 1960-63, Office Asst. Chief Staff Force Devel., 1963-64; dep. comdr. St. Leonard Wood, Mo., 1964-65; dep. chief information, 1966-67; div. comdr. Am. 23d Div., Vietnam, 1969-70; provost marshall gen. Army, Washington, 1970-74; ret. Army, 1974; chmn. bd. McLean Savs. & Loan Assn., Va., 1974-88. Decorated D.S.M. with oak leaf cluster, Silver Star medal with two oak leaf clusters, Legion of Merit with oak leaf cluster, D.F.C., Bronze Star medal with three oak leaf clusters, Air medal with 16 oak leaf clusters, Army Commendation medal with oak leaf cluster, Purple Heart with four oak leaf clusters, Combat Inf. badge; mem. Order Brit. Empire; Croix de Guerre France; Vietnamese Nat. Order; Vietnamese Armed Forces Honor medal; Vietnamese Gallantry Cross with palm. Mem. Sigma Chi, Omicron Delta Kappa. Baptist. Home: 6451 Dryden Dr Mc Lean VA 22101-4625 *Accept a man for what he is, not for what you want him to be.*

RAMSEY, LYNN ALLISON, public relations executive; b. Phila., July 31, 1944; d. Charles Edward and Edna Berry (Whetstone) R. Student, Inst. European Studies, Vienna, Austria, 1964-65; BA, Boston U., 1967. Copy editor Am. Heritage Pub. Co., N.Y.C., 1969-71; prodr., writer Rick Carrier Film Prodns., N.Y.C., 1971-72; mng. editor New Ingenue mag., N.Y.C., 1973-75; freelance writer N.Y.C., 1975-80; mgr. pub. rels. Cunningham and Walsh (acquired by Ayer Pub. Rels. 1987), N.Y.C., 1981—; v.p., mgr. Ayer Pub. Rels., N.Y.C., 1988-95; pres., CEO Jewelry Info. Ctr., N.Y.C., 1995—. Author: Gigolos; The World's Best-Kept Men, 1978; photographer: FLY: The Complete Book of Sky Sailing, 1974; contbr. articles to profl. jours. Mem. Fgn. Policy Assn. 1982-87, Chelsea Cmty. Ch. Bd., 1996—; sec. U.S.A. Bald Eagle Command, 1975—. Mem. Pub. Rels. Soc. Am. (accredited, bd. dirs. N.Y. chpt. 1993-95), The Fashion Group, Women's Jewelry Assn. (bd. dirs. 1993—, Award for Excellence 1993). Avocations: cross-country skiing, traveling, cooking, reading.

RAMSEY, MARJORIE ELIZABETH, early childhood education educator; b. Kimball, Minn., May 25, 1921; d. William Emil and Emma Edith (Ryti) Leppa; children: Rebecca, Cynthia. B.S., St. Cloud State Coll., 1955, M.S., 1957; Ed.D. (Ford Found. fellow), George Peabody Coll., 1961. Tchr., prin., vis. lectr. Minn., 1940-57; asst. prof. St. Cloud State Coll., Minn., 1957-59; supr. edn. Montgomery County, Md., 1961-64; research assoc. George Peabody Coll., Nashville, 1964-68; supr. Vanderbilt U., Nashville, 1964-69; assoc. prof. early childhood edn. Kent (Ohio) State U., 1969-73, prof., 1973-79, dean student pers. Coll. Edn., 1973-79; head div. edn., dir. tchr. edn. Ga. Southwestern Coll., Americus, 1979-89, Ga. Adv. Coun. Edn., 1983-89. Author: Music: A Way of Life for the Young Child, 1978, 4th edit., 1991, Kindergarten: Programs and Practices, 1980; contbr. articles to profl. jours. Mem. AAUW, Edn. Internat. (publs. com. 1980-86), Mid-South Writers Assn. Home: 242 S Reese St Memphis TN 38111-4517

RAMSEY, NANCY LOCKWOOD, nursing educator; b. L.A., Jan. 26, 1943; d. Jack Thanke and Virginia Lee (Slaughter) Lockwood; m. Gordon S. Ramsey, June 24, 1972; children: Douglas Lockwood, Kathryn Anne. BSN, Loma Linda U., 1966; MS in Nursing, Duke U., 1969; postgrad., Calif. State U., L.A., 1974. Staff nurse various hosps., 1966-82, 91-92; clin. instr. Azusa (Calif.)-Pacific U., 1966-93; instr. U. N.C., Chapel Hill, Calif. State U., L.A.; acting dir. nursing edn. Children's Hosp. L.A.; prof. nursing L.A. City Coll., East L.A. Coll., Monterey Park, Calif.; instr. pediatric nursing State Bd. Rev. Classes, L.A. and San Francisco; instr. statewide nursing program Calif. State U., Dominguez Hills. Author, editor: Child and Family Concepts of Nursing Practice, 1982, 87; contbr. articles to profl. jours. Mem. Sigma Theta Tau. Home: 1561 Berenice Dr Brea CA 92821 Office: East LA Coll Dept Nursing 1301 Cesar Chavez Monterey Park CA 91754-6099

RAMSEY, NORMAN F., physicist, educator; b. Washington, Aug. 27, 1915; s. Norman F. and Minna (Bauer) R.; m. Elinor Jameson, June 3, 1940 (dec. Dec. 1983); children: Margaret, Patricia, Janet, Winifred; m. Ellie Welch, May 11, 1985. AB, Columbia U., 1935; BA, Cambridge (Eng.) U., 1937, MA, 1941, DSc, 1954; PhD, Columbia U., 1940; MA (hon.), Harvard U., 1947; DSc (hon.), Case Western Res. U., 1968, Middlebury Coll., 1969, Oxford (Eng.) U., 1973; DCL (hon.), Oxford (Eng.) U., 1990; DSc (hon.), Rockefeller U., 1986, U. Chgo., 1989, U. Sussex, 1990, U. Houston, 1991, Carleton Coll., 1991, Lake Forest Coll., 1992, U. Mich., 1993, Phila. Coll. Pharmacy & Sci., 1995. Kellett fellow Columbia U., 1935-37, Tyndall fellow, 1938-39; Carnegie fellow Carnegie Inst. Washington, 1939-40; assoc. U. Ill., 1940-42; asst. prof. Columbia U., 1942-46; assoc. MIT Radiation Lab., 1940-43; cons. Nat. Def. Research Com., 1940-45; expert cons. sec. of war, 1942-45; group leader, assoc. div. head Los Alamos Lab., 1943-45; assoc. prof. Columbia U., 1945-47; head physics dept. Brookhaven Nat. Lab. of AEC, 1946-47; assoc. prof. physics Harvard U., 1947-50, prof. physics, 1950-66, Higgins prof. physics, 1966-86, Higins prof. emeritus, 1986—; sr. fellow Harvard Soc. of Fellows, 1970—; Eastman prof. Oxford U., 1973-74; Luce prof. cosmology Mt. Holyoke Coll., 1982-83; prof. U. Va., 1983-84; dir. Harvard Nuclear Lab., 1948-50, 52-53, Varlan Assos., 1963-66; mem. Air Forces Sci. Adv. Com., 1947-54; sci. adviser NATO, 1958-59; mem. Dept. Def. Panel Atomic Energy; exec. com. Cambridge Electron Accelerator and gen. adv. com. AEC. Author: Nuclear Moments and Statistics, 1953, Nuclear Two Body Problems, 1953, Molecular Beams, 1956, 85, Quick Calculus, 1965; contbr.: articles Phys. Rev.; other sci. jours. on nuclear physics, molecular beam experiments, radar, nuclear magnetic moments, radiofrequency spectroscopy, masers, nucleon scattering. Trustee Asso. Univs., Inc., Brookhaven Nat. Lab., Carnegie Endowment Internat. Peace, 1962-85, Rockefeller U., 1977-90; pres. Univs. Research Assocs., Inc., 1966-72, 73-81, pres. emeritus, 1981—. Recipient Presdl. Order of Merit for radar devel. work, 1947, E.O. Lawrence and AEC, 1960, Columbia award for excellence in sci., 1980, medal of honor IEEE, 1983, Rabi prize, 1985, Monte Ferst award, 185, Compton medal, 1985, Rumford premium, 1985, Oersted medal, 1988, Nat. medal of Sci., 1988, Nobel prize for Physics, 1989, Pupin medal Columbia Engring. Sch. Alumni Assn., 1992, Sci. for Peace prize, 1992, Einstein medal, 1993, Vannevar Bush award, 1995, Alexander Hamilton award, 1995; Guggenheim fellow Oxford U., 1954-55. Fellow Am. Acad. Sci., Am. Phys. Soc. (coun. 1956-60, pres. 1978-79, Davisson-Germer prize 1974); mem. NAS, French Acad. Sci., Am. Philos. Assn., AAAS (chmn. physics sect. 1977), Am. Inst. Physics (chmn. bd. govs. 1980-87), Phi Beta Kappa (senator 1979-88, v.p. 1982-85, pres. 1985-88), Sigma Xi. Home: 24 Monmouth Ct Brookline MA 02146-5634 Office: Harvard U Lyman Physics Lab Cambridge MA 02138

RAMSEY, PAUL GLENN, internist; b. Pitts., 1949. MD, Harvard U., 1975. Diplomate Am. Bd. Internal Medicine. Intern Cambridge Hosp., 1975-76; resident in medicine Mass. Gen. Hosp., Boston, 1976-78; resident in medicine U. Wash., Seattle, 1980-81, fellow infectious diseases, 1978-80, prof., 1991—, chmn. dept. medicine, 1992—; physician-in-chief U. Wash. Med. Ctr., 1992—. Mem. ACP, AFCR, AAP, AAAS, APM, SGIM. Office: U Wash Hosp RG-20 Dept Medicine Seattle WA 98165

RAMSEY, PETER CHRISTIE, bank executive; b. N.Y.C., Oct. 1, 1942; s. Norman Carnegie and Rosalie Amelia (Christie) R.; m. Maryalice Ives, Nov. 15, 1969. BA, Brown U., 1964. Mgmt. trainee Irving Trust Co., N.Y.C., 1965-67; account exec. Hayden Stone, N.Y.C., 1967-72; regional sales mgr. Autex, Inc., Chgo., 1972-78; v.p. Chase Manhattan, N.Y.C., 1978—. Mem. coun. of chairs YMCA Greater N.Y., N.Y.C., 1987-90; chmn. bd. mgrs. McBurney YMCA, N.Y.C., 1980-92. Mem. Brown U. Club. Home: 345 E 80th St New York NY 10021-0644

RAMSEY, ROBERT LEE, judge, lawyer; b. Glen. Allen, Va., Jan. 9, 1929; s. Hubert Smith and Louise Estelle (Ennis) R.; m. Dorothea Catherine Cherubini, Mar. 28, 1958 (div. 1972); children: Craig John, Matthew Lee, Scott Garrett; m. Lynn Marie Giubbini, July 15, 1978. BA, Hofstra U., 1954; LLB, Union U., 1957, JD, 1968; MPA, SUNY-Albany, 1966; LLM, So. Meth. U., 1969. Bar: N.Y. 1958, Tex. 1970, Calif. 1990. Assoc. Kouray & Kouray, Schenectady, 1957-60; spl. agt. FBI, U.S. Dept. Justice, Washington, 1960-64; asst. atty. gen. State of N.Y., Albany, 1964-65; ptnr. Kalteux & Ramsey, Schenectady, 1965-68; chief asst. dist. atty. Schenectady County, N.Y., 1965-68; asst. gen. counsel Internat. Air Transport Assn., Montreal, Que., Can., 1969-70; sr. atty. Air Transport Assn. Am., Washington, 1970; sole practice Dallas, 1970-76; adminstrv. law judge U.S. Dept. Labor, San Francisco, 1976-77; adminstrv. law judge U.S. Dept. Labor, Washington, 1977-81, chmn., chief adminstrv. appeals judge Benefits Rev. Bd., 1981-88; adminstrv. law judge U.S. Dept. Labor, San Francisco, 1988-89; ptnr. Mullen & Filippi, San Francisco, 1989-91; adminstrv. law Judge Calif. Pub. Utilities Commn., San Francisco, 1991—; mem. adj. faculty So. Meth. U. Sch. Law, 1970-75;. Served with USMC, 1946-48, 50-52. Mem. ABA, State Bar Tex., State Bar Calif., Fed. Adminstrv. Law Judges Conf. Republican. Presbyterian. Home: 4725 Fairway Dr Rohnert Park CA 94928-1304 Office: Calif Pub Utilities Commn 505 Van Ness Ave San Francisco CA 94102-3214

RAMSEY, SANDRA LYNN, psychotherapist; b. Camp LeJeune, N.C., Feb. 7, 1951; d. Robert A. and Lola J. (Hann) R.; m. Edward G. Schmidt, July 9, 1988 (div. 1997); children: Seth, Sarah, Anna, Rachel. Student, U. Calif., Long Beach, 1969-70, Orange Coast Coll., Costa Mesa, Calif., 1971-72; BA in Psychology with distinction, U. Nebr., 1987, MA in Counseling Psychology, 1989. Vol. coord., client adv. Rape/Spouse Abuse Crisis Ctr., Lincoln, 1989-90; mental health therapist Health Am., HMO, Lincoln, 1991-94; pvt. practice, Lincoln, 1994—; adj. faculty S.E. Cmty. Coll; contract therapist Lincoln Pediatric Group, 1990-91, Family Svc. Assn., Lincoln, 1990-91, Cmty. Preservation Assocs., Lincoln, 1991-94. Mem. Nebr. Domestic Violence Sexual Assault Coalition; vol. ARC Disaster Mental Health Svcs.; mem., vol. Nebr. Critical Incident Stress Debriefing team. Portenier scholar U. Nebr., 1986-87. Mem. APA (assoc., divsn. 50 addictions), Am. Assn. Sex Educators, Counselors and Therapists, Assn. Pvt. Practice Therapists, Nebr. Assn. for Counseling and Devel., Sex Info. and Edn. Coun. of the U.S., Am. Mental Health Counselors Assn. (clin.), Golden Key, Am. Assn. Marriage and Family Therapists, Psi Chi. Avocations: gardening, reading, travel, pvt. pilot.

RAMSEY, STEPHEN DOUGLAS, lawyer, environmental manager; b. Oklahoma City, Okla., May 10, 1947; s. Oliver F. and Gladys O'Neil (Smith) R.; m. Abigail Havens, June 11, 1977 (div. 1983); 1 child, Andrew Havens; m. Ann Jones, Nov. 4, 1990. AB, Princeton U., 1969; JD, U. Tex., 1978. Assoc. Coffee, Goldston & Bradshaw, Austin, Tex., 1972-77; atty. U.S. Dept. Justice, Washington, 1978-79, asst. chief pollution control sect., land and nat. resourses div., 1979-80, chief environ. enforcement sect., 1980-85; ptnr. Sidley & Austin, 1985-90; v.p. corp. environ. programs GE, 1990—. Author: Superfund Handbook, 1985. Mem. com. to nominate alumni trustees Princeton U., (N.J.), 1977-80; pub. weigher Travis County, Austin, Tex., 1972-74; bd. dirs. Clean Sites, Inc., 1991—, Environ. Law Inst., 1993—, Inst. For Sustainable Cmty, 1995—, Keystone Ctr., 1995—. Recipient Atty. Gen. Disting. Svc. award Dept. Justice, 1983. Mem. ABA (nat. resources and adminstrv. law sects., chmn. environ. values subcom.), Tex. Bar Assn., D.C. Bar Assn. Democrat. Baptist.

RAMSEY, WILLIAM DALE, JR., marketing and technology consultant; b. Indpls., Apr. 14, 1936; s. William Dale and Laura Jane (Stout) R.; m. Mary Alice Ihnet, Aug. 9, 1969; children: Robin, Scott, Kimberly, Jennifer. AB in Econs., Bowdoin Coll., 1958. With Shell Oil Co., 1958-95, salesman, Albany, N.Y., 1960, merchandising rep., Milton, N.Y., 1961-63, real estate and mktg. investments rep., Jacksonville, Fla., 1963-65, dist. sales supr., St. Paul, 1965-67, employee relations rep., Chgo., 1967-69, spl. assignment mktg. sfaff-adminstrn., N.Y.C., recruitment mgr., Chgo., 1970-72, sales mgr., Chgo., 1973-75, sales mgr., Detroit, 1975-79, dist. mgr. N.J. and Pa., Newark, 1979-84, Mid-Atlantic dist. mgr. (Md., D.C., Va.) 1984-87, econ. advisor head office, Houston, 1987-89; mgr. mktg. concepts head office, Houston, 1989-94, mgr. tech. head office, Houston, 1994-95, prin. Ramsey Cons., 1995—; dir. N.Am. Fin. Services, 1971-72; lectr., speaker on energy, radio, TV, appearances, 1972—; guest lectr. on bus. five univs., 1967-72; v.p., dir. Malibu East Corp., 1973-74; prin. Robotics Rsch. Consortium, 1991—; mem. Am. Right of Way Assn., 1963-65. James Bowdoin scholar Bowdoin Coll., 1958. Active Chgo. Urban League, 1971-75; mem. program com., bus. adv. council Nat. Rep. Congl. Com., 1981-87, rep. nat. com., 1994—, nat. Rep. senatorial com., 1997—; mem. Rep. senatorial adv. com., Gov.'s Council on Tourism and Commerce, Minn., 1965-67; mem. Founders Soc., Detroit Inst. Arts, 1978-80; bd. dirs. N.J. Symphony Orch. Corp., 1981-85. Capt. U.S. Army, 1958-60. Mem. Internat. Svc. Robot Assn., N.J. Petroleum Council (exec. com. 1979-84 vice chmn. 1982-84), Midwest Coll. Placement Assn., Md. Petroleum Council (exec. com. 1984-87). Presbyterian. Clubs: Ponte Vedra (Fla.); Bowdoin Alumni (Houston); Morris County (N.J.) Golf; Kingwood (Tex.) Country, Houston Soc. Club; Bethesda (Md.) Country. Author: Corp. Recruitment and Employee Relations Organizational Effectiveness Study, 1969; Inventor 6 patents pending. Office: Ramsey Consulting PO Box 251 Kingwood TX 77339

RAMSEY, WILLIAM EDWARD, retired naval officer, space systems executive; b. San Diego, Sept. 7, 1931; s. Paul Hubert and Isabelle (Turton) R.; m. Peggy Scott Booth, Oct. 23, 1954; children—Timothy Scott, William Blake, Christopher Booth. B.S., U.S. Naval Acad., 1953. Commd. ensign U.S. Navy, 1953, advanced through grades to vice adm., 1985; comdg. officer USS Pensacola, Little Creek, Va., 1972-73; instr. Naval War Coll., Newport, R.I., 1973-75; comdg. officer in USS Dwight D. Eisenhower, Norfolk, Va., 1975-79; comdr. Carrier Group One, Coronado, Calif., 1979-81; dir. Navy space systems div. Dept. Navy, Washington, 1981-85; dept. comdr.-in-chief U.S. Space Command, Peterson AFB, Colo., 1985-89; ret. U.S. Space Command, 1989; v.p., dir. space systems div. CTA, Inc., Rockville, Md., 1989—, also dir. corp. bus. devel. Decorated Bronze star, Air medal (11), Navy Commendation medal (3), Legion of Merit (2), Def. Disting. Svc. medal. Fellow Assn. Naval Aviation (trustee), Daedelian Soc., Soc. Exptl. Test

Pilots; mem. Am. Inst. Aeros. and Astronautics, Tailhook Soc., Nat. Sec. Indsl. Assn., Armed Forces Commmunications and Elect. Assn. Episcopalian. Club: Nat. Space (bd. govs. 1983—). Avocations: golf; tennis. Home: 825 Bayshore Dr # 1300 Pensacola FL 32507 Office: CTA Inc Space Systems Dv Rockville MD 20852

RAMSEY, WILLIAM RAY, professional society administrator; b. Minerva, Ohio, Aug. 25, 1926; s. Carl Andrew and Alwilda Pauline (Foss) R.; m. Betty Jane Hawkins, Dec. 2, 1950 (dec. Dec. 1975); children: Thomas, Kevin (dec.), Mary Joanne, Robert, Matthew; m. Linda Rae Foss, May 14, 1977; 1 stepchild, Jeffrey Chambers. B.S., Mt. Union Coll., 1948; postgrad., Kent State U., 1948; M.H.A., Washington U., St. Louis, 1950; postgrad. in health systems mgmt, Harvard Bus. Sch., 1974. Exec. sec. King County Med. Soc., Seattle, 1953-61; field rep. AMA, Chgo., 1961-64; asst. dir. div. field service AMA, 1964-68; exec. dir. Am. Soc. Internal Medicine, San Francisco, 1968-78; exec. v.p. Am. Soc. Internal Medicine, Washington, 1978-85; ret., 1985. Served with USAAF, 1944; with USAF, 1950-53. Mem. Am. Assn. Med. Soc. Execs. (dir. 1978-81). Home: 16055 Volz Rd Moores Hill IN 47032-9428

RAMSEYER, J. MARK, law educator; b. 1954. BA, Goshen Coll., 1976; AM, Mich. U., 1978; JD, Harvard U., 1982. Bar: Ill. 1983. Law clk. to Hon. S. Breyer U.S. Ct. Appeals (1st cir.), Boston, 1982-83; assoc. Sidley & Austin, Chgo., 1983-85; acting prof. UCLA, 1986-89, prof., 1989-92; prof. U. Chgo. Law Sch., 1992—. Office: U Chgo Law Sch 111 E 60th St Chicago IL 60637-2105

RAMSEY-GOLDMAN, ROSALIND, physician; b. N.Y.C., Mar. 22, 1954; d. Abraham L. and Miriam (Colen) Goldman; m. Glenn Ramsey, June 29,1 975; children: Ethan Ramsey, Caitlin Ramsey. BA, Case Western Res. U., 1975, MD, 1978; MPH, U. Pitts., 1988, DPH, 1992. Med. resident U. Rochester (N.Y.), 1978-81; chief resident Rochester Gen. Hosp., 1981-82; staff physician Univ. Health Svc., Rochester, 1982-83; rheumatology fellow U. Pitts., 1983-86, instr. medicine, 1986-87, asst. prof., 1987-91, co-dir. Lupus Treatment and Diagnostic Ctr., 1987-91; asst. prof. medicine Northwestern U., Chgo., 1991-96; assoc. prof. medicine Northwestern U., 1996—; dir. Chgo. Lupus Registry, Northwestern U., Chgo., 1991—. Contbr. rsch. articles to profl. jours. Recipient Finkelstein award Hershey (Pa.) Med. Ctr., 1986. Fellow Am. Coll. Rheumatology; mem. Am. Coll. Physicians, Soc. for Epidemiologic Rsch., Ctrl. Soc. Clin. Rsch. Office: Northwestern U Ward 3-315 303 E Chicago Ave Chicago IL 60611-3008

RAMSIER, PAUL, composer, psychotherapist; b. Louisville, Ky., Sept. 23, 1927; s. Paul and Lucie (Herrmann) R. PhD., N.Y.U., 1972; MSW, SUNY, Stony Brook, 1976. Composer N.Y.C., 1950—, psychotherapist in pvt. practice, 1977—; adj. prof. music N.Y.U., 1970—. Composer numerous musical compositions including Divertimento Concertante on a Theme of Couperin, 1965, Road to Hamelin, 1978, Eusebius Revisited, 1980, Silent Movie, 1985, Zoo of Dreams, 1994, Stargazer, 1995; pub. Boosey and Hawkes. Huntington Hartford fellow, 1960, MacDowell fellow, 1963, Yaddo fellow, 1970; NEA grantee, 1975; recipient Disting. Alumnus award U. Louisville, 1983, Composer award Internat. Soc. Bassists, 1995. Mem. ASCAP. Home and Office: 210 Riverside Dr New York NY 10025-6802

RAMSTAD, JIM, congressman, lawyer; b. Jamestown, N.D., May 6, 1946; s. Marvin Joseph and Della Mae (Fode) R. BA, U. Minn., 1968; JD with honors, George Washington U., 1973. Bar: N.D. 1973, D.C. 1973, U.S. Supreme Ct. 1976, Minn., 1979. Adminstrv. asst. to speaker Minn. Ho. Reps., 1969; spl. asst. to Congressman Tom Kleppe, 1970; pvt. practice law, Jamestown, 1973, Washington, 1974-1978, Mpls., 1978-90; mem. Minn. Senate, 1981-90, asst. minority leader, 1983-87; mem. 102nd-103rd Congresses from 3rd Minn. dist., 1990—; adj. prof. Am. U., Washington, 1975-78. Bd. dirs. Children's Heart Fund, Lake Country Food Bank. Served as 1st lt. U.S. Army Res., 1968-74. Mem. Minn. Bar Assn., D.C. Bar Assn., N.D. Bar Assn., Hennepin County Bar Assn., U. Minn. Alumni Assn. (nat. dir.), Am. Legion, Wayzata C. of C., TwinWest C. of C., U. Minn. Alumni Club (past pres. Washington), Lions, Phi Beta Kappa, Phi Delta Theta. Republican. Office: 103 Cannon Bldg Ofc Bldg Washington DC 20515-2303

RAMUS, JOSEPH S., marine biologist; b. Grosse Pointe Farms, Mich., May 7, 1940; married; three children. AB, U. Calif., Berkeley, 1963, PhD in Botany, 1968. From asst. prof. to assoc. prof. biology Yale U., New Haven, 1968-78; from assoc. prof. to prof., asst. dir. marine lab. Duke U., Beaufort, 1978-90; dir. marine lab. Duke U., Beaufort, N.C., 1990—. Mem. AAUP, Am. Soc. Limnology & Oceanology, Phycol. Soc. Am., Am. Geophys. Union. Office: Duke U Marine Lab Marine Lab 135 Duke Marine Lab Rd Beaufort NC 28516-8648 Office: Duke U Marine Lab Piver's Island Beaufort NC 28516

RAN, SHULAMIT, composer; b. Tel Aviv, Oct. 21, 1949; came to U.S., 1963; m. Abraham Lotan, 1986. Studied composition with, Paul Ben-Haim, Norman Dello, Joio, Ralph Shapey; student, Mannes Coll. Music, N.Y.C., 1963-67. With dept. music U. Chgo., 1973—, William H. Colvin prof. music; composer-in-residence Chgo. Symphony Orch., 1990-97, Lyric Opera of Chgo., 1994-97. Compositions include 10 Children's Scenes, 1967, Structures, 1968, 7 Japanese Love Poems, 1968, Hatzvi Israel Eulogy, 1969, O the Chimneys, 1969, Concert Piece for piano and orch., 1970, 3 Fantasy Pieces for Cello and Piano, 1972, Ensembles for 17, 1975, Double Vision, 1976, Hyperbolae for Piano, 1976, For an Actor: Monologue for Clarinet, 1978, Apprehensions, 1979, Private Game, 1979, Fantasy-Variations for Cello, 1980, A Prayer, 1982, Verticals for piano, 1982, String Quartet No. 1, 1984, (for woodwind quintet) Concerto da Camera I, 1985, Amichai Songs, 1985, Concerto for Orchestra, 1986, (for clarinet, string quartet and piano) Concerto da Camera II, 1987, East Wind, 1987, String Quartet No. 2, 1988-89, Symphony, 1989-90, Mirage, 1990, Inscriptions for solo violin, 1991, Chicago Skyline for brass and percussion, 1991, Legends for Orch., 1992-93, Invocation, 1994, Yearning for violin and string orch., 1995; commd. pieces include for Am. Composers Orch., Phila. Orch., Chgo. Symphony, Chamber Soc. of Lincoln Ctr., Mendelssohn String quartet, Da Capo Chamber Players, Sta. WFMT, Between Two Worlds (The Dybbuk), 1995-97, Lyric Opera Chgo.; composer and soloist for 1st performances Capriccio, 1963, Symphonic Poem, 1967, Concert Piece, 1971. Recipient Acad. Inst. Arts and Letters award, 1989, Pulitzer prize for music, 1991, Friedheim award for orchestral music Kennedy Ctr., 1992; Guggenheim fellow, 1977, 90. Office: U Chgo Dept Music 1010 E 59th St Chicago IL 60637-1512

RANALD, MARGARET LOFTUS, English literature educator, author; b. Auckland, N.Z., Sept. 5, 1927; came to U.S., 1952; d. Leonard R. and Geraldine (McGrath) Loftus; m. Ralph Arthur Ranald, Feb. 26, 1955; 1 child, Caroline Margaret. AB, U. N.Z., Wellington, 1949, MA honors, 1951; MA, UCLA, 1954, PhD, 1958. Jr. asst. Dept. Prime Min. Govt. N.Z., Wellington, 1944-52; asst. to sec. Princeton (N.J.) U., 1956-57; from instr. to asst. prof. Temple U., Phila., 1957-61; from asst. prof. to prof. CUNY, N.Y.C., 1961—; assoc. bibliographer MLA, N.Y.C., 1958—; mem. assoc. faculty, mem. adv. com. Columbia U., N.Y.C., 1976—; vis. prof. UCLA, 1970-85, tchg. asst., 1953-55. Author: The Eugene O'Neill Companion, 1984, Shakespeare and his Social Context, 1987, John Webster, 1989; assoc. editor (book series): International Bibliography of Theatre, 1985—. Fulbright fellow, 1952-54; sr. fellow Folger Shakespeare Libr., 1970-72. Mem. MLA, Am. Soc. Theatre Rsch. (exec. sec., v.p. 1976-83), Eugene O'Neill Soc. (pres., mem. coun., pres.), Shakespeare Soc. Am. (former rsch. asst.), Princeton Club N.Y. Avocations: music, drama, theatrical history, travel. Office: CUNY 65-30 Kissena Blvd Flushing NY 11367

RANALD, RALPH ARTHUR, government official, educator; b. N.Y.C., Nov. 25, 1930; s. Josef A. and Pearl R.; AB, UCLA, 1952, MA, 1954; AM, Princeton U., 1958; postgrad. (Carnegie fellow) Law Sch., Harvard U., 1961-62, 76-77, grad. Exec. Program in Nat. and Internat. Security, 1978; PhD, Princeton U., 1962; JD, Fordham U., 1997; m. Margaret Florence Loftus, Feb. 26, 1955; 1 dau., Caroline. Teaching asst. UCLA, 1952-54; univ. fellow, rsch. asst. Princeton (N.J.) U., 1956-59; asst. prof. Fordham U. Grad. Sch., N.Y.C., 1959-65; asst. dean acad. affairs, prof. Coll. Arts and Scis., NYU, N.Y.C., 1965-69; prof. CUNY, 1969—; spl. policy asst. HEW, Washington, 1968-69, Office of Mgmt. and Budget, 1976-77; sr. cons. U.S. Dept. Def., 1969-70, 77-78; mem. staffs Dept. Def. and Army Gen. Staff, U.S. Govt. Long Com., 1989, U.S. Dept. Def., 1995-96; vis. prof. and cons. univs. including U. So. Calif., summers 1968-74, Calif. State U., UCLA, summer 1985. Treas. N.Y. State Com. for Pub. Higher Edn., 1975-78, mem. com., 1970—. 1st lt. U.S. Army, 1953-56, to col., 1977-78, res., 1978—. Recipient U.S. Legion of Merit, 1983. Sr. fellow Am. Soc. Pub. Adminstrn. (selection com. for fellows, 1970-74); mem. Res. Officers Assn. U.S. (life), Harvard U. Law Sch. Assn., Assn. of Princeton U. Grad. Alumni, U.S. Army War Coll. Alumni Assn., John F. Kennedy Sch. of Govt. Alumni Assn., Princeton Club of N.Y., Army and Navy Club, Phi Beta Kappa. Author: Management Development in Government, 1979, George Orwell, 1965; contbr. reports, articles to publs. in law, govt. and edn. Home and Office: 239 Central Park West New York NY 10024-6038

RANBERG, CHUCK ALAN, television writer, producer. BA, U. Calif., Santa Cruz, 1977. Writer (TV series) Kate and Allie, 1986-89, Working it Out, 1991, Baby Talk, 1991-92; co-prodr. (TV series) Frasier, 1993 (Emmy awards for Outstanding Comedy Series 1995, 96). Office: c/o Writers Guild Am 8955 Beverly Blvd West Hollywood CA 90048-2420

RANCE, QUENTIN E., interior designer; b. St. Albans, Eng., Mar. 22, 1935; came to U.S., 1981.; s. Herbert Leonard and Irene Ann (Haynes) R.; m. India Adams, May 17, 1974. Grad., Eastbourne (Eng.) Sch. Art, 1960. Soft furnishings buyer Dickeson & French Ltd., Eastbourne, 1960-61, outside sales mgr., 1961-62; design dir. Laszlo Hoenig, Ltd., London, 1962-73; mng. dir. Quentin Rance Interiors Ltd., London, 1973-81; pres. Quentin Rance Enterprises, Inc., Encino, Calif., 1981—. Works featured in Designers West, 1983, Design House Rev., 1983, Profiles mag., 1987, Nat. Assn. Mirror Mfrs. Jour., 1988, Designer Specifier, 1990. Mem. Founders for Diabetic Research/City of Hope. Served with RAF, 1953-55. Recipient Hon. Mention award Nat. Assn. Mirror Mfrs., 1987, 1st Pl. Nat. Pub. Svc. award, Designer Specifier, 1990. Fellow Chartered Soc. Designers (Eng.); mem. Am. Soc. Interior Designers (profl., chpt. bd. dirs. 1983-87, 89-91, chmn. Avanti 1983-85, admissions chmn. 1985—, Presdl. citations 1984, 87, 91, 95), Knights of Vine. Avocations: bicycling, antiques, fine wines, philately, theatre. Home and Office: 18005 Rancho St Encino CA 91316-4214 *Personal philosophy: Good design is always there to be seen, there to be appreciated, and there for expanding one's own boundaries of creativity.*

RANCK, EDNA RUNNELS, academic administrator, researcher; b. Waterville, Maine, Aug. 24, 1935; d. Everett Elias and Edna May (King) Runnels; m. James Gilmour Ranck, June 30, 1971 (dec. May 1979); children: Matthew, Christopher, Joshua Duggan; m. Martin Fleischer, Apr. 19, 1982; stepchildren: Christina, Laura Ranck. BA cum laude, Fla. State U., Tallahassee, 1957; MDiv magna cum laude, Drew U. Theol. Sch., Madison, N.J., 1971, MEd in Edn. Adminstrn., 1978; EdD in Curriculum and Teaching, Columbia U. Tchrs. Coll., N.Y.C., 1986. Dir. Collinsville Child Care Ctr., Morristown, N.J., 1971-78; exec. dir. Children's Svcs. Morris County, Morristown, N.J., 1980-84; co-mgr. N.J. Child Care Clearinghouse, Trenton; coord. N.J. Child Care Adv. Coun., Trenton, 1987-92; dir. N.J. Office Child Care Devel., Trenton, 1992; child care coord. N.J. Dept. Human Svcs., Trenton, 1992—; mem. adj. faculty Kean Coll. N.J., Union, 1983; dir. Sprout House Preschool, Chatham, N.J., 1984-87; mem. Morris County Human Svcs. Adv. Coun., Morristown, N.J., 1986-87. Author: Dodge Foundation Project, 1984, Young Children, 1987, Our History, Our Vision: A History of the National Association of Child Care Rsource and Referral Agencies, 1997; contbr. articles to profl. jours. Mem. exec. bd. Drew U. Alumni Assn. Theol. Sch., 1986-92; mem. Drew U. Alumni Study Commn., 1993, Non-Govt. Orgn. rep. to UN Internat. Fedn. Educative Cmtys., 1992—. Recipient Volpe Commitment in Child Care award, N.J. Child Care Assn., 1991. Mem. Child Care Action Campaign Panel, N.J. Assn. Infant Mental Health (bd. dirs.), Acad. Child and Youth Care Workers, N.J. Assn. Infant Mental Health (bd. dirs.), Phi Beta Kappa, Pi Sigma Alpha. republican. United Methodist. Avocations: writing, travel, swimming, clothing design. Home: 15 Rosedale Ave Madison NJ 07940-2148 Office: NJ Dept Human Svcs 222 S Warren St # N700 Trenton NJ 08608-2306

RANCOURT, JAMES DANIEL, optical engineer. BA in Physics, Bowdoin Coll., 1963; MS in Physics, Carnegie Tech., 1965; PhD in Optical Scis., U. Ariz., 1974. Engr. Itek Corp., Lexington, Mass., 1965-69; rsch. assoc. U. Ariz., Tucson, 1969-74; engr. OCLI, Santa Rosa, Calif., 1974-95, chief scientist, 1996—. Author: Optical Thin Films Users Handbook, 1987; patentee in field. Fellow Optical Soc. Am. Achievements include 13 patents. Office: 2789 Northpoint Pkwy Santa Rosa CA 95407-7350

RAND, CALVIN GORDON, arts and education producer and consultant; b. Buffalo, May 15, 1929; s. George Franklin and Isabel (Williams) R.; m. Patricia Clemens Andrew, Aug. 18, 1951; children—Robin, Melissa, Jennifer, Lucinda, Elizabeth. B.A., Princeton U., 1951; M.A., Columbia U., 1954; Dr of Letters (hon.), York U., Can., 1984. Head history dept. Riverdale Sch., N.Y.C., 1955-60; lectr. philosophy SUNY-Buffalo, 1961-68, acting dir. cultural affairs, 1968-71; founder, pres. The Niagara Inst., Niagara-on-the-Lake, Can., 1971-79; pres. Am. Acad. in Rome, N.Y.C., 1980-84; ind. producer, theatre and film cons., N.Y.C., 1985-90; founding chmn., dir. Shaw Festival Theatre, Niagara-on-the-Lake, 1964-78,. bd. govs., 1979—; trustee Playwrights Horizons Theatre, N.Y.C., 1982-92; bd. dirs. Niagara Inst.; pres. Arts in Edn. Inst.; mem. N.Y. State Coun. on Arts, 1978-82, Arts Coun. Western N.Y., 1987-93; chmn. World Ency. Contemporary Theater; chmn. arts coun. SUNY, Buffalo, 1987-94, adj. prof. theater, 1988—. Contbr. articles to profl. jours. Bd. dirs. Burchfield-Penney Art Ctr., Buffalo, 1991—, Irish Classical Theater, 1993—; trustee Albright-Knox Gallery, Buffalo, 1976-80, 84-88, 90-94. Recipient spl. citation Ont. Arts Coun., 1976, Fellowship Fund award Niagara Inst., 1980, Centennial Arts award Nichols Sch., 1992; named Man of Yr., Coun. World Affairs, 1976, Buffalo Courier Express, 1976, Arts Patron of Yr., Western N.Y. Arts Coun. and C. of C., 1989; Vanier Coll. fellow York U., Walter B. Cooke award, 1997, Disting Non-Alumni, Sunny, Buffalo. Mem. Players Club, Princeton Club, Saturn Club. Home and office: 930 Fifth Ave New York NY 10021-2651

RAND, DUNCAN D., librarian; b. Biggar, Sask., Can., Oct. 28, 1940; s. Dawson Ellis and Elizabeth Edna (Gabie) R.; m. Nancy Jean Daugherty, Sept. 7, 1963; children: Jacqueline Nancy, Duncan Dawson, Thomas Nelson, John David, Jennifer Nancy. B.A., U. Sask., 1963; B.L.S., McGill U., 1964. Young adult librarian Regina Pub. Library, Sask., 1964-65; coordinator library services Regina Separate Sch. Bd., 1965-68; asst. chief librarian Regina Pub. Library, 1968-71; dep. dir. London Pub. Library and Art Mus., 1971-73, acting dir., 1973-74; chief librarian Lethbridge Pub. Library, Alta., 1974—; dir. So. Alta. Art Gallery. Editor: Sask. Geneal. Soc. Bull, 1968-71. Vice pres. Alta. council Boy Scouts. Mem. Libr. Assn. Alta (dir., pres. 1986-87), Can. Libr. Assn. (dir.), Can. Assn. Pub. Librs. (chair 1976-77), Sask. Geneal. Soc. (pres.), Assn. Profl. Librs. of Lethbridge (chmn. 1982-84), So. Alta. Regional Info. Network (chmn. 1996—), Samaritans (bd. dirs. 1993—), Allied Arts Coun. (bd. dirs. 1993—), Southern Alberta Regional Info. Network (chmn.), Rotary, Ipalosh (archivist, sec. 1980-94). Office: 810 5th Ave S, Lethbridge, AB Canada T1J 4C4

RAND, HARRY ISRAEL, lawyer; b. N.Y.C., July 27, 1912; s. Samuel and Rose (Hirth) R.; m. Anna Tulman, Oct. 22, 1938; children: Steven, Deborah, Naomi. BS, CCNY, 1932; JD, NYU, 1936. Bar: N.Y. 1936, U.S. Supreme Ct. 1943, D.C. 1947, U.S. Dist. Cts. (so. and ea. dists.) N.Y. 1959, 60, U.S. Ct. Appeals (2d cir.) 1966. Atty. U.S. Pub. Works Adminstrn., 1938-39, U.S. Dept. Interior, 1939-43, U.S. Dept. Justice, 1943-48; pvt. practice Washington, 1948-58; mem. Weisman, Celler, Allan, Spett & Sheinberg, N.Y.C., 1959-67, Botein, Hays & Sklar, N.Y.C., 1967-89; counsel Herrick, Feinstein, N.Y.C., 1990—. Mem. Assn. of Bar of City of N.Y., Am. Law Inst. Home: 66 Hillandale Rd Westport CT 06880-5319 also: 320 W 86th St New York NY 10024-3139 Office: Herrick Feinstein LLP Two Park Ave New York NY 10016

RAND, HARRY ZVI, art historian, poet; b. N.Y.C., Jan. 10, 1947; m. Jennifer Rand; 1 child, Leah Zoë. BA, CCNY, 1969; AM, Harvard U., 1971, PhD, 1974. Contbg. editor Arts mag., N.Y.C., 1975-91, 1975—; assoc. curator Nat. Mus. Am. Art, Washington, 1977-79, curator, 1979-93, chmn. dept., 1978-84, sr. curator, 1993-97; curator cultural history Nat. Mus. Am. Hist., Smithsonian Inst., Washington, 1997—; adv. bd. mem. Awards in Visual Arts, Winston-Salem, N.C., 1982-92, Austrian Internat. Art Inst., 1989—; arts advisor Virlane Found., New Orleans, 1980—; cons. NAS, 1983, Cosanti Found., 1989—, Exodus Found., 1992—, World Econ. Forum, 1992-94, World Bank, 1994—. Co-author: The Genius of American Painting, 1973, Still Working, 1993, Vincent Pepi, 1995; author: Seymour Lipton, 1979, Arshile Gorky, 1981, 91, Recent Trends in Collecting, 1982, The Beginning of Things, 1983, Martha Jackson Meml. Collection, 1985, Der Maler Hundertwasser, 1986, Manet's Contemplation at the Gare Saint-Lazare, 1987, paperback edit. 1991, Paul Manship, 1989, Julian Stanczak, 1990, Hundertwasser, 1991, 92, Jochen Seidel, 1992, Color, 1993, The Clouds, 1996; hon. editor Leonardo mag., 1993—; patentee in field. N.Y. State Regents scholar, 1965-68; travelling fellow Harvard U., 1973, Andrew W. Mellon Found. fellow, 1976-77; Rockefeller Found. devel. grantee, 1982-83, Rsch. Opportunities grantee Smithsonian Instn., 1985, 86, 87, 88, 89, 90, 91, 92, 94, 95, Spl. Scholarly Studies grantee, 1987—, Ednl. Outreach grantee, 1995. Fellow Explorers Club; mem. World Art Coun. (steering com. Geneva 1992—), World Soc. to Stop Trade Stolen Art (bd. dirs. 1994—). Home: 5511 Greystone St Chevy Chase MD 20815-5556 Office: Nat Mus Am Art MRC 210 8th and G Sts NW Washington DC 20560

RAND, JOELLA MAE, nursing educator, counselor; b. Akron, Ohio, July 9, 1932; d. Harry S. and Elizabeth May (Miller) Halberg; m. Martin Rand; children: Craig, Debbi Stark. BSN, U. Akron, 1961, MEd in Guidance, 1968; PhD in Higher Edn. Adminstrn., Syracuse U., 1981. Staff nurse Akron Gen. Hosp., 1953-54; staff-head nurse-instr. Summit County Receiving, Cuyahoga Falls, Ohio, 1954-56; head nurse psychiat. unit Akron Gen. Hosp., 1956-57; instr. psychiatric nursing Summit County Receiving, Cuyahoga Falls, 1957-61; head nurse, in-service instr. Willard (N.Y.) State Hosp., 1961-62; asst. prof. Alfred (N.Y.) U., 1962-76, assoc. prof., assoc. dean, 1976-78, acting dean, 1978-79, dean, 1979-90, dean coll. profl. studies, 1990-91, prof. counseling, 1991—; cons. N.Y. State Regents Program for Non-Collegiate Sponsored Instrn., 1984; cons. collegiate programs N.Y. State Dept. Edn., 1985, Elmira Coll., 1991, U. Rochester, 1992-93; accreditation visitor Nat. League for Nursing, 1984-92; ednl. cons. Willard Psychiat. Hosp., 1992-93; mem. profl. practice exam. subcom. Regents Coll., 1990-95. Recipient Teaching Excellence award Alfred U., 1977, Mary E. Gladwin Outstanding Alumni award Akron U. Coll. Nursing, 1983, Alfred Alumni Friends award, 1989, Grand Marshall commencement Alfred U., 1993. Mem. Am. Counseling Assn., N.Y. State Counseling Assn. (v.p. elect profl. svcs. 1995-96, v.p. profl. svcs. 1996-97), N.Y. State Coun. of Deans (treas. 1984-88), Genesee Regional Consortium (v.p.), Western N.Y. League Nursing (bd. dirs. 1991-93), Genesee Valley Edn. Com. (chair 1984-86), Sigma Theta Tau (treas. Alfred chpt. 1984-85). Avocations: boating, fishing, public speaking in areas of family and child abuse. Office: Alfred U 343 Myers Hall Alfred NY 14802

RAND, KATHY SUE, public relations executive; b. Miami Beach, Fla., Feb. 24, 1945; d. William R. and Rose (Lasser) R.; m. Peter C. Ritsos, Feb. 19, 1982. BA, Mich. State U., 1965; M in Mgmt., Northwestern U., 1980. Asst. editor Lyons & Carnahan, Chgo., 1967-68; mng. editor Cahners Pub. Co., Chgo., 1968-71; pub. rels. writer Super Market Inst., Chgo., 1972-73; account supr. Pub. Communications Inc., Chgo., 1973-77; divisional mgr. pub. rels. Quaker Oats Co., Chgo., 1977-82; exec. v.p., dep. gen. mgr. Golin/Harris Communications, Chgo., 1982-90; exec. v.p. Lesnik Pub. Rels., Northbrook, Ill., 1990-91; mng. dir. Manning, Selvage & Lee, Chgo., 1991—. Dir. midwest region NOW, 1972-74; mem. Kellogg Alumni Adv. Bd.; bd. dirs. Jr. Achievement of Chgo. Mem. Pub. Rels. Soc. Am. (Silver Anvil award 1986, 87), Pub. Club Chgo. (Golden Trumpet awards 1982-87, 90, 94, 95), Northwestern Club Chgo., Kellogg Alumni Club, Beta Gamma Sigma. Home: 400 Riverwoods Rd Lake Forest IL 60045-2547

RAND, LAWRENCE ANTHONY, investor and financial relations executive; b. Bklyn., Nov. 19, 1942; s. Gerald M. and Elaine Shirley (Borenstein); m. Madelon L., July 4, 1942; children: Allan, Joshua, Emily. AB with honors, Brown U., 1964; MA, NYU, 1965, postgrad., 1966-67. Lectr. NYU, 1967, CUNY, 1968; analyst CIA, Langley, Va., 1967-68; account supr. Ruder & Finn Inc., N.Y.C., 1968-71; co-founder, sr. v.p. Kekst & Co., N.Y.C., 1971—, also bd. dirs.; chmn., bd. dirs. ALS Assn., L.A., 1987-92. Chmn. ethics com. Village of Rye Brook, N.Y. Mem. City Athletic Club, Brown U. Club, Bailiwick Club (Greenwich, Conn.). Office: Kekst & Co 437 Madison Ave New York NY 10022-7001

RAND, LEON, academic administrator; b. Boston, Oct. 8, 1930; s. Max B. and Ricka (Muscanto) Rakisky; m. Marian L. Newton, Aug. 29, 1959; children: Debra Ruth, Paul Martin, Marta Leah. B.S., Northeastern U., 1953; M.A., U. Tex., 1956, Ph.D., 1958. Postdoctoral fellow Purdue U., 1958-59; asst. prof. to prof. U. Detroit, 1959-68; prof., chmn. dept. chemistry Youngstown (Ohio) State U., 1968-74, dean grad. studies and research, 1974-81, acting acad. v.p., 1980; vice chancellor acad. affairs Pembroke (N.C.) State U., 1981-85; chancellor Ind. U.-S.E., New Albany, 1986-96; chancellor emeritus Ind. U., 1996—; spl. asst. to chancellor IUPUI, 1996—; bd. dirs. INB Banking Co., Jeffersonville, Ind, Jewish Hosp., Louisville, Ky., 1991—. Bd. dirs., mem. exec. com. Louisville (Ind.) Area chpt. ARC; bd. dirs. Floyd Meml. Hosp., New Albany, 1987-90. Mem. Am. Chem. Soc., Am. Inst. Chemists, Metroversity (bd. dirs.), Sigma Xi, Phi Kappa Phi. Home: 1785 Arrowwood Dr Carmel IN 46033 Office: Office of Chancellor 355 Lansing St Indianapolis IN 46202-2815

RAND, PETER ANDERS, architect; b. Hibbing, Minn., Jan. 8, 1944; s. Sidney Anders and Dorothy Alice (Holm) R.; m. Nancy Ann Straus, Oct. 21, 1967; children—Amy, Dorothy. B.A., St. Olaf Coll., 1966; cert. Oslo Internat. Summer Sch., Norway, 1964; student U. Minn. Sch. Architecture, 1969-72. Registered architect, Minn. Designer, architect, dir. pub. relations Setter, Leach & Lindstrom, Inc., Mpls., 1972-78; dir. bus. devel. and head Eden Prairie Office, Archtl. Design Group, Inc., Minn., 1979-80; dir. mktg. and publs. Minn. Soc. AIA, 1981-82, exec. dir., 1982-85, exec. v.p./CEO, 1986—; pub. Architecture Minn. mag.; cons., archtl. designer. Bd. dirs. Project for Pride in Living, 1979-88, chmn. 1980-86; trustee Bethlehem Luth. Ch., 1980-86, chmn. bd. trustees, 1985, chmn. com. on worship, 1993-96, mem. ch. coun., 1993-96; mem. Minn. Ch. Ctr. Commn., 1981-89, chmn., 1985-88; sec. Council of Component Execs. of AIA, 1987, 92; bd. dirs. Minn. Council of Chs. 1985-89, sec. 1989, Mpls. Council of Chs., 1985-88, Arts Midwest, 1987-96, treas. 1989, v.p. 1990-91, chmn., 1992-93; bd. dirs. Nordic Ctr., 1989-96, Preservation Alliance of Minn., 1995—. Served with U.S. Army, 1966-69. Fellow AIA (jour. honor award 1981, Nat. Svc. award 1993); mem. MSAADA Architects & Engrs. (bd. dirs. 1994—), Minn. Soc. AIA, Nat. Trust Hist. Preservation, Torske Klubben. Home: 1728 Humboldt Ave S Minneapolis MN 55403-2809 Office: 275 Market St Ste 54 Minneapolis MN 55405-1621

RAND, PETER W., environmental health researcher; b. Boston, Oct. 16, 1929; m. Alice Hildreth Rand. AB, Harvard U., 1951, MD, 1955. Intern Maine Med. Ctr., Portland, 1955-56, resident internal medicine, 1956-57, 59-60, dir. rsch. dept., 1965-82, med. rsch. com., 1974-97, assoc. v.p. for rsch., 1989-95; asst. clin. prof. medicine U. Vt. Coll. Medicine, 1972—. Mem. Am. Fedn. Clin. Rsch., Am. Physiol. Soc., Entomol. Soc. Am., Health Physics Soc. Office: ME Med Ctr Rsch Inst 125 John Roberts Rd Ste 5 S Portland ME 04106-3295

RAND, PHILLIP GORDON, chemist; b. Meredith, N.H., Nov. 5, 1934; s. Roger Orville and Mary Isabel (Gordon) R.; m. Lela Joyce Magouirk, Aug. 14, 1955; children: Bruce Edward, Brenda Lea, Steven Alan. B.A., John Brown U., 1956; M.S., U. Wyo., 1958; Ph.D., Purdue U., 1963. With Miles Labs., Elkhart, Ind., 1963-89; prin. rsch. scientist Miles Labs., 1978-83, sr. devel. scientist, 1983-89; sales rep. Crain Industries, 1990-92; quality control technician Ross Labs., 1992-94; sr. scientist Environ. Test Systems, 1994—. Mem. Am. Chem. Soc. Republican. Methodist. Clubs: Toastmasters, Gideons. Patentee in field. Home: 1320 W Lexington Ave Elkhart IN 46514-2048

RAND, ROBERT WHEELER, neurosurgeon, educator; b. L.A., Jan. 28, 1923; s. Carl W. and Catherine (Humphrey) R.; m. Helen L. Pierce, Dec. 17, 1949; children: Carl W., Richard P. Student, Harvard U., 1940-42, UCLA, 1942-44; MD, U. So. Calif., 1947; MS, U. Mich., 1951, PhD in Anatomy, 1952; JD, U. West L.A., 1974. Intern, resident in neurosurgery U. Mich., Ann Arbor, 1947-52; from instr. to prof. neurol. surgery UCLA, 1953-89; expert witness malpractice cases Superior Ct. Author: Spinal Cord Tumors in Childhood, 1960, Microneurosurgery, 3d edit., 1985; contbr. articles to profl. jours.; inventor neuropledgets, thermomagnetic surgery coil system, microballoon for aneurysm occlusion, Malcolm-Rand graphite cranial frame, cobalt scalpel. Lt. comdr. USNR, 1943-46, 54-56. Recipient Profl. award UCLA, 1973. Fellow ACS; mem. AMA, Calif. Med. Assn., L.A. County Med. Assn., Am. Surg. Assn., Internat. Coll. Surgeons, Am. Assn. Neurol. Surgeons, Assn. Neurol. Surgeons, Soc. Neurol. Surgeons, Western Neurosurg. Soc., L.A. Country Club. Office: John Wayne Inst St John's Hosp 2200 Santa Monica Blvd Santa Monica CA 90404-2302

RAND, SHARON KAY, elementary education educator; b. Carlisle, Pa., Sept. 5, 1947; d. Charles Eugene and Pauline B. (Wheeler) Caldwell; m. David Foster, Jan. 13, 1968; children: Kelly Ann, Neal Patrick (dec.). BSEd, Shippensburg U., 1969, MEd, 1973. Tchr. grade one Big Spring Sch. Dist., Newville, Pa., 1969-79, tchr. grade three, 1979-93, lead tchr. process writing, 1986—; staff developer Big Spring Sch. Dist., 1992—; instrnl. support tchr. Big Spring Sch. Dist., Newville, Pa., 1993—. Mem. Big Spring Area Women's Club, Newville, 1977-95, pres., 1986-88. Recipient Outstanding Tchr. award Shippensburg U. Study Coun., 1993. Mem. NEA, ASCD, Pa. State Edn. Assn., Big Spring Edn. Assn. (pres. 1994-96, v.p. 1996—), Phi Delta Kappa, Delta Kappa Gamma. Presbyterian. Home: 38 Parsonage St Newville PA 17241-1314 Office: Oakflat Elem/Big Spring Dist 45 Mount Rock Rd Newville PA 17241-9412

RAND, SIDNEY ANDERS, retired college administrator; b. Eldred, Minn., May 9, 1916; s. Charles William and Ida Alice (Pedersen) R.; m. Dorothy Alice Holm, Sept. 1, 1942 (dec. Jan. 1974); children: Peter Anders, Mary Alice; m. Lois Schiager Ekeren, Nov. 23, 1974. BA, Concordia Coll., Moorhead, Minn., 1938, DD (hon.), 1956; degree in theology, Luther Sem., St. Paul, 1943; LHD (hon.), Colo. Coll., 1976; LLD (hon.), Carleton Coll., 1980, St. Olaf Coll., 1980, Coll. of St. Scholastica, 1985; DTh (hon.), St. John's U., 1980; LHD (hon.), Augustana Coll., 1988. Faculty Concordia Coll., Moorhead, Minn., 1945-51; pres. Waldorf Coll., Forest City, Iowa, 1951-56; exec. dir. coll. edn. Am. Luth. Ch., Mpls., 1956-63; pres. St. Olaf Coll., Northfield, Minn., 1963-80; U.S. ambassador to Norway, Oslo, 1980-81; pres. Augustana Coll., Sioux Falls, S.D., 1986-87, 92-93, Suomi Coll., Hancock, Mich., 1990-91; sr. cons. Minn. Pvt. Coll. Council, St. Paul, 1981-87. Pastor Nashwauk (Minn.) Luth. Ch., 1943-45; pres. Fund for Theol. Edn., Princeton, N.J., 1984-87; mem. Gov.'s Tax Commn., Minn., 1984-85; chmn. Minn. Citizens for Ct. Reform, 1984-87. Decorated Comdr. Norwegian Order of Merit, 1986, comdr. Norwegian Order of Merit with cross, 1996; named Knight 1st Class Order of St. Olaf Kingdom of Norway, 1974; recipient Wittenberg award, 1996. Mem. AIA (hon.), Phi Beta Kappa, Torske Klubben Club. Home: 19 S 1st St Apt 907B Minneapolis MN 55401-1808

RAND, WILLIAM, lawyer, former state justice; b. N.Y.C., Oct. 11, 1926; s. William and Barbara (Burr) R.; married; children: Alicia, Carley Coudert, William Coudert, Paula Burr. AB, Harvard U., 1948; LLB, Columbia U., 1951. Bar: N.Y. 1951, U.S. Dist. Ct. N.Y. 1951, U.S. Supreme Ct., 1958, U.S. Ct. Appeals (2d cir.) 1961, U.S. Ct. Appeals (4th cir.) 1985. Asst. dist. atty. New York County, 1954-59; asst. counsel to gov. of State of N.Y., 1959-60; assoc. Coudert Bros., N.Y.C., 1961-62, ptnr., 1963—; justice N.Y. County Supreme Ct., 1962; justice Village of Cove Neck, Oyster Bay, N.Y., 1974—. Mem. exec. com. New York County Reps., 1968-72. Served with USN, 1944-46, PTO. Clubs: Piping Rock (Locust Valley, N.Y.); Seawanhaka Corinthian Yacht (Oyster Bay); Racquet and Tennis (N.Y.C.). Home: 73 Cove Neck Rd Oyster Bay NY 11771-1821 Office: Coudert Bros 1114 Avenue Of The Americas New York NY 10036-7703

RAND, WILLIAM MEDDEN, biostatistics educator; b. Seneca Falls, N.Y., June 26, 1938; s. Austin Loomer and Rheua Vaughn (Medden) R.; m. Patricia Ann Gooding, Oct. 7, 1967; 1 child, Toby Stewart. BA, Ind. U., 1959; MA, Brandeis U., 1961; PhD, UCLA, 1969. Rsch. engr. Jet Propulsion Lab., Pasadena, Calif., 1962-65; rsch. assoc. U. So. Calif., L.A., 1965-67; asst. prof. MIT, Cambridge, 1969-74, assoc. prof., 1974-76, lectr., 1976-88; prof. biostats. Tufts U. Sch. Medicine, Boston, 1988—, dir. biometry div., 1988—; prof. veterinary medicine Tufts U., Boston, 1995—; rsch. coord. world hunger program UN U., Tokyo, 1979-82. Editor: Protein-Energy Requirement Studies in Developing Countries, 1984, Food Composition Data, 1987. Mem. Am. Statis. Assn., Biometric Soc., Am. Inst. Nutrition, Am. Soc. for Clin. Nutrition. Home: 17 Belmont St Newton MA 02158 Office: Tufts U Sch Medicine 136 Harrison Ave Boston MA 02111-1817

RANDA, RUDOLPH THOMAS, judge; b. Milw., July 25, 1940; s. Rudolph Frank and Clara Paula (Kojis) R.; m. Melinda Nancy Matera, Jan. 15, 1977; children—Rudolph Daniel, Daniel Anthony. B.S., U. Wis.-Milw., 1963; J.D., U. Wis.-Madison, 1966. Bar: Wis. 1966, U.S. Dist. Ct. (ea. and we. dists.) Wis., 1966, U.S. Ct. Appeals (7th cir.) 1973, U.S. Supreme Ct. 1973. Sole practice, Milw., 1966-67; prin. city atty. Office Milw. City Atty., 1970-75; judge Milw. Mcpl. Ct., 1975-79, Milwaukee County Circuit Ct., 1979-81, 1982-92, Appellate Ct., Madison, Wis., 1981-82; federal judge U.S. Dist. Ct. (ea. dist.) Wis., 1992—; chmn. Wis. Impact, Milw., 1980—; lectr. Marquette U. Law Sch., Milw., 1980—. Served to capt. U.S. Army, 1967-69, Vietnam. Decorated Bronze Star medal. Mem. Milw. Bar Assn., Wis. Bar Assn., Trial Judges Wis., Am. Legion (adjutant Milw. 1980), Thomas More Lawyers Soc. (former pres. Milw.), Milw. Hist. Soc., Phi Alpha Theta. Roman Catholic. Office: US Courthouse 517 E Wisconsin Ave Rm 247 Milwaukee WI 53202-4504

RANDALL, CHANDLER CORYDON, church rector; b. Ann Arbor, Mich., Jan. 22, 1935; s. Frederick Stewart and Madeline Leta (Snow) R.; m. Marian Archias Montgomery, July 2, 1960; children: Sarah Archais, Elizabeth Leggett, Rebekah Stewart. AB in History, U. Mich., 1957; S.T.B. in Theology, Berkeley Divinity at Yale U., 1960; PhD in Hebraic Studies, Hebrew Union Coll., 1969; D.D. (honoris causa), Berkeley Divinity at Yale U., 1985. Rector St. Paul's Episcopal Ch., Richmond, Ind., 1967-71; rector Trinity Episcopal Ch., Ft. Wayne, Ind., 1971-88, St. Peter's Episcopal Ch., Del Mar, Calif., 1988—; bd. dirs. Living Ch. Found., Milw.; bibl. theologian Episcopal Ch. Stewardship, N.Y.C., 1985; alumni coun. Berkeley Divinity at Yale, New Haven, Conn., 1981-87; bishop's cabinet Diocese of No. Ind., South Bend, 1983-87. Author: Satire in the Bible, 1969, An Approach to Biblical Satire, 1990; contbr. articles to profl. jours. Founder Canterbury Sch., Ft. Wayne, 1977; commr. Ind. Jud. Qualifications Commn., Indpls., 1981-87; pres. Ft. Wayne Plan Commn., 1977; bd. dirs. Ft. Wayne Park Found., 1983-88; platform com. Ind. Republican Party, Indpls., 1974. Recipient Disting. Svc. medal U. Mich., 1981, Scheuer scholar Hebrew Union Coll., 1963-66, Liberty Bell award Ft. Wayne Bar Assn., 1988; named Sagamore of the Wabash, Gov. Ind., 1987. Mem. Am. Schs. Oriental Research, Yale U. Alumni Club (pres. 1982-88), Quest Club (pres.), Rotary Club, Chi Psi (nat. chaplain 1982). Republican. Avocations: college recruiting, genealogy. Office: St Peters Episcopal Church PO Box 336 Del Mar CA 92014-0336

RANDALL, CLAIRE, church executive; b. Dallas, Oct. 15, 1919; d. Arthur Godfrey and Annie Laura (Fulton) R. A.A., Schreiner Coll., 1948; BA, Scarritt Coll., 1950; DD (hon.), Berkeley Sem., Yale U., 1974; LHD (hon.), Austin Coll., 1982; LLD, Notre Dame U., 1984. Assoc. missionary edn. Bd. World Missions Presbyterian Ch., U.S., Nashville, 1949-57; dir. art Gen. Council Presbyterian Ch., U.S., Atlanta, 1957-61; dir. Christian World Mission, program dir., assoc. dir. Ch. Women United, N.Y.C., 1962-73; gen. sec. Nat. Coun. Ch. of Christ in U.S.A., N.Y.C., 1974-84, ret., 1985; nat. pres. Ch. Women United, N.Y.C., 1988-92. Mem. Nat. Commn. on Internat. Women's Yr., 1975-77, Martin Luther King Jr. Fed. Holiday Commn., 1985. Recipient Woman of Yr. in Religion award Heritage Soc., 1977; Empire State Woman of Yr. in Religion award State of N.Y., 1984; medal Order of St. Vladimir, Russian Orthodox Ch., 1984. Democrat. Episcopalian. Avocations: golf, swimming; painting; reading; music. Home: 13427 W Countryside Dr Sun City West AZ 85375-4711

RANDALL, CLIFFORD WENDELL, civil engineer; b. Somerset, Ky., May 1, 1936; s. William Lesbert and Geneva (James) R.; m. Phyllis Amis, Aug. 15, 1959; children: Andrew Amis, William Otis. B.S. in Civil Engring., U. Ky., 1959, M.S. in San. Engring., 1963; Ph.D. (AEC trainee 1963-65), U. Tex., 1966. Asst. prof. civil engring. U. Tex., Arlington, 1965-68; mem. faculty Va. Poly. Inst. and State U., 1968—, prof. civil engring., 1972—, Charles Lunsford prof., 1981—; vis. prof. U. Cape Town, South Africa, 1983; chmn. environ. engring. and scis. program Va. Poly. Inst. and State U., 1979—; lectr. Shanghai Archtl. and Mcpl. Engring. Inst., Wuhan Tech. U., 1987; dir. Occoquan Watershed Monitoring Program, 1971—; mem. U.S. nat. com. Internat. Water Quality, 1976-88, chair 1986-88, mem. 1992 Biennial Conf. Com., chair conf. arrangements, Washington; tng. grant cons. EPA, 1970-71; cons. to industry, 1969—; WHO cons. to Nat. Environ. Engring. Rsch. Inst. India, 1983-84; gov. appointee sci. and tech. adv. com. EPA Chesapeake Bay Restoration Project, 1984—, chmn. 1993—. Author tech. papers in field; co-author: Biological Process Design for Wastewater Treatment, 1980, Stormwater Management in Urbanizing Areas, 1983, Design and Retrofit of Wastewater Treatment Plants for Biological Nutrient Removal, 1992. Troop com. chmn. local Boy Scouts Am., 1978-82, chmn. dist. Camporee com., 1977; camp pres. Gideons Internat., 1976-78, 80, 95—, state cabinet mem., 1985-88; vice moderator Highlands Bapt. Assn., 1980-81, moderator, 1982-83; mem. bd. deacons Blacksburg Bapt. Ch., 1971-74, 79-82, chmn., 1974. Lt. U.S. Coast and Godetic Survey, 1959-62. Ford Found. fellow, 1964-65; recipient citation Engring. News-Record, 1988, Disting. Svc. award U.S. nat. com. Internat. Assn. Water Quality, 1989, Salute to Excellence Gov. of Md., 1994, Pub. Svc. award Va. Tech., 1996, Mathias medal for sci. excellence Chesapeake Rsch. Consortium and the Sea Grant Offices of Md. and Va., 1996; named Conservationist of Yr. Chesapeake Bay Found., 1986;. Mem. ASCE (chmn. water resources mgmt. com. 1977, environ. engring. rsch. coun. 1989-90, svc. award 1978, 80, meritorious tech. paper award 1969), Am. Water Works Assn. (cert. recognition for acad. excellence 1980, 89), Water Environ. Fedn. (bd. dirs. 1981-84, Morgan cert. of merit for full scale rsch. 1982, Bedell award 1983, svc. award 1984), Internat. Assn. Water Quality (Mem. gov. bd. 1986-88, USA rep. on sci. and tech. com. 1994—, mem. nutrient removal specialist group mgmt. com. 1990—, chmn. 1994—), Va. Water Environment Assn. (v.p. 1974-75, pres. 1975-76), Assn. Environ. Engring. Profs. (sec.-treas. 1979-80, bd. dirs. 1978-80, 93—, v.p. 1994-95, pres. 1995-96, past pres. 1996-97). Home: 1302 Crestview Dr Blacksburg VA 24060-5609 Office: Va Poly Inst & State U Dept Civil Engring 330 Norris Hall Blacksburg VA 24061

RANDALL, DAVID JOHN, physiologist, zoologist, educator; b. London, Sept. 15, 1938. BSc, U. Southampton, 1960, PhD, 1963, FRSC, 1981. From asst. to assoc. prof. U. B.C., 1963-73, prof. zoology, 1973—, assoc. dean grad. studies, 1990-96; vis. lectr. Bristol U., 1968-69; vis. sci. Marine Labs U. Tex., 1970, Zool. Sta., Naples, Italy, 1973; NATO vis. sci. Acadia U., 1975, Marine Lab U. Tex., 1977; chief sci. Alpha Helix Amazon Expedition, 1976; mem. adv. bd. J. Comp Physiology, 1977-92, J. Exp. Biol., 1981-84; chmn. animal biol. comt. Nat. Res. Coun., Can., 1974; vis. prof. U. Nairobi, 1988, George Washington U., 1988-89; concurrent prof. Nanjing U., China, 1993—; external examiner U. Singapore, 1990-91. Assoc. editor: Marine Behavior Physiology. Recipient Award of Excellence Am. Fisheries Soc., 1994. Fellow Royal Soc. Can.; mem. Can. Soc. Zoologists (Fry medal 1993), Soc. Exp. Biologists. Office: U BC, Dept Zoology 6270 Unv Blvd, Vancouver, BC Canada V6T 1Z4

RANDALL, ELIZABETH ELLEN, press clippings company executive; b. Maple Hill, Kans., Mar. 21, 1915; d. Edwin and Ann (Scott) Sage; m. George Albert Randall, May 29, 1941; children: Cheryl Ann, Rebecca Lynn. Student, Kans. State U., 1932-34. Tchr. elem. sch Maple Hill, Kans., 1932-34, Dover, Kans., 1934-46; reader Luce Press Clippings, Topeka, 1959-63, supr., 1964, office mgr., 1964-97, sr. staff advisor, 1997—. Tchr. Jr. High Ch. Sch., 1949-61; mem. pastoral com. Dover Federated Ch., 1991—. Mem. Dover 4-H Club (leader 1960-62), Dover Rebekah Lodge, Eastern Star, Am. Leg. Aux., Disabled Am. Vets. Aux., 14th Armored Divsn. Aux. Democrat. Avocations: collecting antiques, plates and dolls, needlework. Home: 5731 SW 22nd Ter Topeka KS 66614-1831 Office: Luce Press Clippings 912 S Kansas Ave Topeka KS 66612-1211

RANDALL, FRANCIS BALLARD, historian, educator, writer; b. N.Y.C., Dec. 17, 1931; s. John Herman, Jr. and Mercedes (Moritz) R.; m. Laura Regina Rosenbaum, June 11, 1957; children: David R., Ariane R. B.A., Amherst Coll., 1952; M.A., Columbia, 1954, Ph.D., 1960. Instr. history Amherst Coll., 1956-59; instr., asst. prof. history Columbia, 1959-61, vis. prof., 1967-68; mem. humanities faculty Sarah Lawrence Coll., Bronxville, N.Y., 1961—, chmn., 1985-89; trustee Sarah Lawrence Coll., 1971-76. Author: (with others) Essays in Russian and Soviet History, 1963, Stalin's Russia, an Historical Reconsideration, 1965, N.G. Chernyshevskii, 1967, Vissarion Belinskii, 1987. Freedom rider civil disobedience to racism, 1961, war draft resistance arrests, 1967, 70. Fulbright fellow for study in India, 1965; Wye fellow, 1986. Mem. Am. Hist. Assn., Am. Assn. for Advancement Slavic Studies, Am. Assn. U. Profs. (chpt. chmn. 1966-69), Phi Beta Kappa, Sigma Xi. Home: 425 Riverside Dr # 10I New York NY 10025-7730 Office: Humanities Dept Sarah Lawrence Coll Bronxville NY 10708

RANDALL, FRANKIE, professional boxer; b. Fort Pierce, Fla., Sept. 25, 1961. Named WBA Jr. Welterweight Champion, 1996. Achievements include record of 53 wins, 4 losses, and one tie, with 40 knock-outs. Office: c/o Consejo Mundial de Boxeo, Genova 33 Oespacho # 503, 06600 Mexico City Mexico

RANDALL, GENE, news correspondent, anchor; b. Port Chester, N.Y., Jan. 10, 1942; m. Susan Biggs; children: Christopher, Gina, Dominic. BA in English, Georgetown U., 1964. Anchor, corr. Sta. WLWT, Cin., 1966-71; anchor Sta. WTVC, Chattanooga, 1972-74; corr., anchor Sta. KTVI, St. Louis, 1974-76, Sta. WMAQ-TV, Chgo., 1976-80; bur. chief/corr. NBC, Moscow, 1980-83; nat. corr. CNN, Washington, 1983—. Recipient Emmy awards for Best TV Talk Show, 1975, Best Spot News Story, 1976, U.S. Operation in Somalia, 1993, DuPont award, 1993. Office: CNN Bldg Wash Bureau 820 1st St NE Washington DC 20002-4243

RANDALL, GERALD J., insurance company executive; b. Sparta, Wis., Mar. 6, 1931; s. Jean Oliver and Mabel E. (Olson) R.; m. Beverly J. Gehrig, Apr. 23, 1955; children: Robin Jean, Scott Gerald, Susan Kay. BBA, U. Wis., 1954, JD, 1957. Bar: Wis., U.S. Supreme Ct.; CLU, ChFC. With Conn. Mutual Life Ins. Co., Hartford, 1957-61, asst. counsel advanced sales, 1961-69, asst. v.p. advanced sales, 1969-70, 2d v.p. advanced sales, 1970-73, v.p. pension divsn., 1973-80, sr. v.p., 1980-81; pres. Diversified Ins. Svcs. Am., Inc. subs. Conn. Mutual Life Ins. Co., 1981-84; pres. Conn. Mutual Fin. Svcs., Inc. subs. Conn. Mutual Life Ins. Co., 1984-88, sr. v.p. advanced sales SBU, 1988-94; broker Mass. Mutual Life Ins. Co., Glastonbury, Conn., 1994—; instr. CLU dip. courses U. Conn., 1965-72; founder, charter mem., pres. Estate & Bus. Planning Coun. Hartford, 1969-70; mem. exec. program Dartmouth Coll., 1973, Columbia U., 1988; chmn. pension com. Am. Coun. Life Ins., 1976. Contbr. articles to profl. jours. Mem. Jaycees, 1960-65; bd. dirs. Hartford Better Bus. Bureau, 1981-84, greater Hartford YMCA, 1989-94. 1st Lt. U.S. Army, 1955-56. Recipient CLU Inst. scholarship, 1971. Mem. ABA, Wis. Bar Assn., Hartford Life Underwriters Assn., Estate & Bus. Planning Coun. Hartford, Life Ins. Mgmt. Rsch. Assn. (chmn. advanced sales com. 1978-79), Gen. Agents and Mgrs. Assn., Assn. Advanced Life Underwriting, Hartford Club. Republican. Congregationalist. Avocations: antique cars, travel, jogging, antique watch collecting. Home: 178 Tall Timbers Rd Glastonbury CT 06033-3351 Office: Mass Mut Life Ins Co 178 Tall Timbers Rd Glastonbury CT 06033-3351

RANDALL, JOHN ALBERT, III, elementary and secondary education educator; b. Great Lakes, Ill., Dec. 2, 1951; s. John Albert Jr. and Barbara Blanche (Coen) R.; m. Jerri Lynn Nesmith, Aug. 10, 1985; 1 child, John Albert IV. BA in Psychology, Loma Linda U., 1974; MA in Edn., Calif. State Poly. U., 1981; MBA, Nat. U., 1982. Cert. tchr. Prof. L.A. City Coll., Fuji, Japan, 1979-80; educator Perris (Calif.) Union High Sch. Dist., 1989-91, Val Verde Unified Sch. Dist., Moreno Valley, Calif., 1991-96, Perris (Calif.) Union H.S. Dist., 1996—; site rep. Perris Tchr.'s Assn., 1990-91; mem. Year Round Sch. Task Force, Perris, 1990-91; chairperson Disaster Com., Rancho Verde High Sch., Moreno Valley, 1991-92. Author: Motor Developmental Skills, 1981. Mem. Community Action Com., Montclair, Calif., Am. Legion; active Boy Scouts Am. Lt. Col. USMCR, 1976—. Decorated Navy Commendation Medal. Mem. NEA, Calif. Tchr.'s Assn., Nat. Coun. for Social Studies, Marine Corps Res. Officers Assn. (life), Nat. U. Alumni Assn. (life), Eagle Scout Assn. (life). Avocations: family, running, bicycling. Home: 30756 Sky Terrace Dr Temecula CA 92592-3255

RANDALL, KARL W., aviation executive, lawyer; b. Mount Pleasant, Mich., Feb. 12, 1951; s. Herbert J. and Wilma E. (Worstell) R.; m. Natalie Kilmer Randall, Dec. 17, 1971; children: Adam B., Kara J. AA, Mich. Christian Coll., Rochester, 1971; BA, Oakland U., Rochester, 1977; JD, Wayne State U. Law Sch., Detroit, 1981. Bar: Mich., 1981, U.S. Dist. Ct., 1981, U.S. Ct. Appeals, 1983; cert. airport mgr., Mich., 1993. Quality controller Stacey and BOL corp., Pontiac, Mich., 1971-72; engring. tech. Oakland Co. Drain Comm., Pontiac, 1972-83; sr. asst. corp. counsel Oakland County Corp. Counsel, Pontiac, 1983-93; mgr. aviation Oakland County Internat. Airport, Waterford, Mich., 1993—; dir. Integrity Jour., Mount Pleasant, 1980—, Oakland County Coord. Child Care Coun., Waterford, 1992—. Author, editor: (religious jour.) Integrity, 1982, 94-95. Mem. Rep. Com. Oakland County, 1988—, Exec. Club Oakland County, 1993—. Mem. Mich. Assn. Airport Execs. (exec.). Republican. Mem. Ch. of Christ. Avocations: physical fitness, jogging, golf, piano. Office: Oakland County International Airport 6500 Highland Rd Waterford MI 48327-1649

RANDALL, LILIAN MARIA CHARLOTTE, museum curator; b. Berlin, Feb. 1, 1931; came to U.S., 1938; d. Frederick Henry and Elizabeth Agnes (Ziegler) Cramer; m. Richard Harding Randall, Apr. 11, 1953; children: Christopher, Julia, Katharine. BA cum laude, Mount Holyoke Coll., 1950; MA, Radcliffe Coll., 1951, PhD, 1955; LHD (hon.), Towson State U., 1993. Asst. dir. Md. State Arts Coun., 1972-73; curator manuscripts and rare books Walters Art Gallery, Balt., 1974-85, rsch. curator manuscripts, 1985-95; rsch. cons., 1995-97; vis. lectr. dept. art history Johns Hopkins U., 1964-68; hon. vis. lectr. U. Mich., Ann Arbor; lectr. in field. Author: Images in the Margins of Gothic Manuscripts, 1966; co-editor: Gatherings in Honor of Dorothy Miner, 1974, The Diary of George A. Lucas: An American Art Agent in Paris, 1909-1957, 1979, Illuminated Manuscripts: Masterpieces in Miniature, 1984, Medieval and Renaissance Manuscripts in the Walters Art Gallery, Vol. I, France, 875-1420, 1989, Vol. II, France, 1420-1540, 1992, Vol. III, Belgium, 1250-1530, 1997; contbr. numerous articles to profl. jours. Mem. Williston Libr. com., 1988-89; reviewer, panelist NEH, 1980—. Grantee AAUW, 1953-54, ACLS, 1960, 65, Bunting Inst., 1961-63, Ford Found., 1967-69, Am. Philos. Soc., 1971, NEA, 1975, Samuel H. Kress Found., 1979, 81-84, NEH, 1977-84, 89—; grantee publ. subsidy Md. State Arts Coun., 1972, Mcpl. Art Soc. Balt., 1972, Andrew W. Mellon Found., 1988, Getty Grant program, 1990-92, NEA Mus. program, 1992-93; recipient Festschrift, Walters Art Gallery, ed. Elizabeth Burin, 1996. Fellow Medieval Acad. Am. (libr. preservation com., various coms. 1985-87, 90-93); mem. Internat. Ctr. Medieval Art (bd. dirs. 1978-82, 96—), Coll. Art Assn. (Arthur Kingsley Porter prize 1957), Balt. Bibliophiles (bd. dirs. 1966-80, pres. 1980-83), Pyramid Atlantic (bd. dirs. 1985-88), Phi Beta Kappa, Grolier Club. Home: 301 Kendall Rd Baltimore MD 21210-2562

RANDALL, LINDA LEA, biochemist, educator; b. Montclair, N.J., Aug. 7, 1946; d. Lowell Neal and Helen (Watts) R.; m. Gerald Lee Hazelbauer, Aug. 29, 1970. BS, Colo. State U., 1968; PhD, U. Wis., 1971. Postdoctoral fellow Inst. Pasteur, Paris, 1971-73; asst. prof. Uppsala (Sweden) U., 1975-81; assoc. prof. Washington State U., Pullman, 1981-83, prof. biochemistry, 1983—; guest scientist Wallenberg Lab., Uppsala U., 1973-75; study section NIH, 1984-88. Mem. edtl. bd. Jour. of Bacteriology, 1982-96; co-editor: Virus Receptors Part I, 1980; contbr. articles to profl. jours. Recipient Eli Lilly Award in Microbiology and Immunology, Am. Soc. Microbiology, Am. Assn. Immunologists, Am. Soc. Exptl. Pathology, 1984, Faculty Excellence Award in Rsch., Washington State U., 1988, Disting. Faculty Address, 1990, Parke-Davis award, 1995. Fellow Am. Acad. Microbiology; mem. AAAS, Am. Microbiol. Soc., Am. Soc. Biol. Chemists, Protein Soc. Avocation: dancing. Office: Washington State U. Biochemistry Biophysic Dept PO Box 644660 Pullman WA 99164-4660

RANDALL, MALCOM, health care administrator; b. East St. Louis, Ill., Aug. 9, 1916; s. John Leeper and Merle Dorothy Randall; m. Christine Sheppard, Nov. 10, 1972. A.B., McKendree Coll., 1939; M.H.A., St. Louis U., 1955; D of Pub. Svc. with honors, U. Fla., 1996. Chief br. office VA, St. Louis, 1946-49, asst. area dir. area office, 1949-53; spl. asst. to dir. VA Hosp., St. Louis, 1953-56; hosp. adminstr. VA Hosp., Spokane, Wash., 1956-57, Chgo., 1957-58, Indpls., 1958-60, Wood, Wis., 1960-64; hosp. dir. VA Hosp., Miles City, Mont., 1964-66; med. ctr. dir. and med. dist. dir. VA, Gainesville, Fla., 1966—; regional rep. VA, Gainesville, 1991—; prof. health and hosp. adminstrn. U. Fla., Gainesville, 1966—; pres. N. Cen. Fla. Health Planning Council; mem. Fla. State Health Planning Council; chmn. Gov.'s Commn. on Alzheimer's Disease; mem. Alachua County Emergency Med. Svcs. Coun.; bd. dirs. emeritus 1st Union Nat. Bank Fla., Regional Med. Programs; mem. editorial bd. Jour. Am. Coll. Health Care Execs.; cons. on health care Univ. Clin. Ctr., Ljubljana, Slovenia, 1982—, Ministry of Health, Hungary and Med. U. Debrecen, 1989—. Contbr. numerous articles to profl. jours. Bd. dirs. Civitan Regional Blood Ctr., Gainesville, 1970. Served to capt. USN, 1942-46. Recipient Presdl. Rank award Pres. U.S., 1983, Meritorious Svc. award U. Fla., 1984, Exceptional Svc. award, 1985, Exec. Performance award, 1986, all VA; named Citizen of Yr., Gainesville, 1977. Fellow Am. Coll. Health Care Execs. (council regents, VA liaison); mem. Inst. Medicine, Nat. Acad. Sci., Assn. Am. Med. Colls. (bd. dirs., council tchg. hosps.), Am. Health Planning Assn. (bd. dirs.), Am. Hosp. Assn. (governing council met. and fed. hosp. sect.). Club: Heritage. Lodge: Rotary. Home: 1617 NW 19th Cir Gainesville FL 32605-4092 Office: VA Med Ctr Archer Rd Gainesville FL 32608 *A core set of values should be the base for all of your activities, both professional and personal.*

RANDALL, NEIL WARREN, gastroenterologist; b. White Plains, N.Y., Mar. 24, 1957; s. Leroy Bruce and Libby Cynthia (Brandt) R.; m. Linda Ilene Zell, Oct. 31, 1992. BA, U. Va., 1978; MD, U. Md., 1983. Diplomate Am. Bd. Internal Medicine with subspecialty in gastroenterology, geriatrics. Resident in internal medicine Ochsner Clinic, New Orleans, 1983-86; fellow in gastroenterology Tufts U., Boston, 1986-88; staff gastroenterologist Cleve. Clinic Fla., Fort Lauderdale, 1988-92, Geisinger Clinic, Danville, Pa., 1992—; Fellow ACP, Am. Coll. Gastroenterology; mem. Am. Gastroent. Assn., Am. Soc for Gastroent. Endoscopy. Avocations: Theatre, Travel, Wine. Office: Geisinger Med Ctr Dept Gastroenterology Danville PA 17822

RANDALL, PRISCILLA RICHMOND, travel executive; b. Arlington, Mass., Mar. 19, 1926; d. Harold Bours and Florence (Hoefler) Richmond; m. Raymond Victor Randall, Mar. 2, 1946; children: Raymond Richmond, Priscilla Randall Middleton, Susan Randall Geery. Student, Wellesley Coll., 1943-44; Assoc., Garland Coll., 1946; student, Winona State U., 1977-81. Pub. relations dir. Rochester Meth. Hosp., Rochester, Minn., 1960-69; dir. pub relations Sheraton Rochester, 1969-71; pres. Med. Charters, Rochester, 1970-75, Ideas Unltd., Rochester, 1969-77; chief exec. officer Randall Travel, Rochester, 1977-89; pres. Randall Travel Delray, Delray Beach, Fla., 1989—; pres. Bar Harbour Apts. Inc., Delray Beach, 1989. Editor, Inside Story, 1960-69, Rochester Meth. Hosp. News, 1960-69; producer Priscilla's World, 1972-75. Pres. Rochester Meth. Hosp. Aux., 1957-59, Downtown Bus. Assn., Rochester, 1985; treas. Class of 1947 Wellesley (Mass.) Coll., 1997—. Recipient Woman of Achievement Bus. YWCA, Rochester, 1983, Golden Door Knob, Bus. and Prfl. Women, Rochester, 1979. Mem. Inst. Cert. Travel Agts. (life), Assn. Retail Travel Agts. (life, nat. bd. 1988-90, sec. to bd. 1988-90, sec.-treas. Arlington, Va. nat. bd. 1990), Am. Soc. Travel Agts., Pacific Area Travel Agts., Minn. Exec. Women in Travel, Cruise Line Internat. Assn. (master cruise counselor), Women's Golf Com. Little Club (Gulfstream, Fla.) (sec.), Hibiscus Garden Club (Delray Beach, Fla.) (pres.). Avocation: travel writing. Home: 86 Macfarlane Dr Apt 2C Delray Beach FL 33483-6901 Office: Randall Travel Delray Inc 1118 E Atlantic Ave Delray Beach FL 33483-6936

RANDALL, RICHARD HARDING, JR., art gallery director; b. Balt., Jan. 31, 1926; s. Richard Harding and Mary Scott (Buzby) R.; m. Lilian M.C. Cramer, Apr. 11, 1953; children: Christopher, Julia, Katherine. AB, Princeton U., 1950; MA, Harvard U., 1951. Asst. and assoc. curator medieval art The Cloisters, N.Y.C., 1953-59; asst. curator decorative arts Mus. Fine Arts, Boston, 1959-64; asst. dir. Walters Art Gallery, Balt., 1964-65, dir., 1965-81, curator medieval art, 1981-85; vis. prof. medieval art Columbia U., 1955. Author: A Cloisters Bestiary, 1960, American Furniture, 1965, Masterpieces of Ivory, 1985, The Golden Age of Ivory, 1993. With armored divsn. AUS, 1944-46, ETO. Mem. Walpole Soc., Colonial Soc., Armor and Arms Club (N.Y.C.), South River Club (Annapolis, Md.).

RANDALL, RICHARD RAINIER, geographer; b. Toledo, July 21, 1925; s. Robert Henry and Maree (Gard) R.; m. Patricia Lee Spencer, June 9, 1962;

children: Allison Maree, Susan Rebecca, Richard Rainier Jr. BA, George Washington U., 1949, MA, 1950; PhD, Clark U., 1955; postgrad., Graz U., Austria. Geog. analyst U.S. Govt., Washington, 1955-61; Washington rep. Rand McNally & Co., Washington, 1961-72; owner Randall Assocs., Washington, 1972-73; exec. sec. U.S. Bd. Geog. Names, Washington, 1973-93; geographer Def. Mapping Agy., Washington, 1973-93; ret., 1993, cons. on geog. names,, 1993—; convenor UN Working Group on Undersea and Maritime Feature Names, 1975-84; mem., prin. U.S. tech. advisor U.S. and U.K. Conf. on Geog. Names, 1976, 79, 81, 84, 86, 88, 92; dep. head U.S. del. UN Conf. on Geog. Names, 1977, 87, head, 1982, 92; 1st v.p. of 6th UN Conf. '92; prin. U.S. expert UN Group Experts on Geog. Names, 1975, 77, 79, 82, 84, 86, 87, 89, 92; pres. com. on geog. terminology Pan Am. Inst. Geography and History, 1973-77, pres. working group on geog. names and gazetters, 1981-94. Contbr. articles to profl. jours.; inventor flexible fishhook. V.p. North Cleveland Park Citizens Assn., Washington, 1968. With U.S. Army, 1943-46, ETO. Fulbright scholar, NRC, Austria, 1953-54. Mem. Am. Congress on Surveying and Mapping (dir. cartography divsn. 1973-75, dir. press rels. 1961-72, program dir. cartography divsn. ann. meeting 1967), Am. Geog. Soc., Assn. Am. Geographers (chmn. Mid-Atlantic divsn. 1978, dir. press rels. ann. conf. 1968), Am. Names Soc., Am. Austrian Soc. (v.p. 1955-57), Explorers Club, Cosmos Club. Republican.

RANDALL, ROBERT L(EE), ecological economist; b. Aberdeen, S.D., Dec. 28, 1936; creHarry Eugene and Juanita Alice (Barstow) R. MS in Phys. Chemistry, U. Chgo., 1960, MBA, 1963. Market devel. chemist E.I. du Pont de Nemours & Co., Inc., Wilmington, Del., 1963-65; chem. economist Battelle Meml. Inst., Columbus, Ohio, 1965-68; mgr. market and econ. rsch. Kennecott Copper Corp., N.Y.C., 1968-74, economist, 1974-79, dir. new bus. venture devel., 1979-81; pres., mng. dir. R.L. Randall Assocs., Inc., 1981—; economist U.S. Internat. Trade Commn., Washington, 1983—; founder, pres., exec. dir. The RainForest ReGeneration Inst., 1986—; indsl. panel policy rev. of effect of regulation on innovation and U.S.-internat. competetion U.S. Dept. Commerce, 1980-81; participant preparatory com. UN Conf. on Environ. and Devel., Rio de Janeiro, 1991; del. observer internat. negotiating com. Framework Conv. on Climate Change, 1991—. Contbr. articles to profl. jours.; contbg. author: Computer Methods for the '80's. Mem. Gay Activists Alliance, N.Y.C., 1971-75, chmn. state and fed. legislation com., 1975. Mem. AAAS (organizer ann. meeting Tropical Forest Regeneration Symposium), AIME (econs. coun. sec. mineral econ. subsect.), Am. Econ. Assn., Am. Statis. Assn., Am. Chem. Soc., Soc. Mining Engrs., Chemists Club of N.Y.C., Metall. Soc., N.Y. Acad. Scis., Nat. Econs. Club Washington (sec., reporter), Assn. Environ. and Resource Economists; Wanderbirds Hiking Club (hike leader, treas.), Capital Hiking Club (hike leader, Washington). Home: 1727 Massachusetts Ave NW Washington DC 20036-2153 Office: US Internat Trade Com 500 E St SW Washington DC 20024-2760 *Like thousands of organizations around the world, The RainForest ReGeneration Institute is trying to find a practical and effective way forward, through United Nations-sponsored treaty negotiations, appropriate national actions, and imaginative project work, on the ground, in local communities. Tropical rainforests must have recognizable community value if they are to be viable. Global value is not enough for the conservation of the tropical rainforests. Ultimate wisdom does not reside in any individual or organization. All must work together through every available forum and mechanism, and to create new modalities where those presently in existence are inadequate or ineffective.*

RANDALL, ROBERT QUENTIN, nursery executive; b. Jacksonville, Ill., May 1, 1945; s. William Orlando and Agnes Johanna (Bruins) R.; m. Catherine Horn, Dec. 27, 1969. BS in Biology, Ill. Coll., 1967. Lab. technician Passavant Meml. Hosp., Jacksonville, 1966-68; sect. head in viral prodn. Beecham Labs., Whitehall, Ill., 1968-79, safety dir., animal welfare dir., 1970-79; prin. Jacksonville Landscape Nursery, 1979-89, nurseryman, 1989-95; ret., 1995. Contbr. articles on birding to topical publs. Sec. Jacksonville Theatre Guild; elder, deacon, trustee 1st Presbyn. Ch., Jacksonville, Ill. Coll. Jacksonville area Alumni Assoc., 1989; bd. dirs. Friends of the Libr., 1991-95; mem. Ill. Coll. Blue Ribbon Task Force, 1995-96. Mem. Jacksonville Kiwanis (bd. dirs. 1986-87), Morgan County Audubon Soc. (treas. 1989-91, pres. 1991-94), Ill. Audubon Soc. (bd. dirs.), Jacksonville Symphony Soc. (bd. dirs. 1994—, pres. 1996-97). Avocations: birding, tennis, wildlife photography, travel, reading. Home: 11 Pitner Pl Jacksonville IL 62650-2266 Office: Jacksonville Landscape Nursery RR 5 Jacksonville IL 62650-9805

RANDALL, ROGER DAVID, publishing executive; b. St. Charles, Minn., Dec. 24, 1953; s. Curtis Clark and Virginia Mae (Tollefson) R.; BA, Morningside Coll., 1976; m. Mary Barnard, Aug. 25, 1979; children: Sara Louise, Clark Robinson. Advt. dir. Nutra-Flo Chem. Co., Kay Dee Feed Co., Sioux City, Iowa, 1976-78; agrl. account svc. Lewis & Gilman, Phila., 1978-80, Creswell, Munsell, Fultz & Zirbel, Cedar Rapids, Iowa, 1980-81, Richardson, Myers & Donofrio,Inc. Balt., 1981-84; mktg. mgr. Farm Jour., Inc., Phila., 1984-85, v.p., 1986-89, sr. v.p., pub., 1989-95, pres., 1995—, also bd. dirs; mem. bus. adv. com. Nat. Assn. Conser. Dist. Bd. dirs. Planned Parenthood Sioux City, 1977-78, Iowa Planned Parenthood Fedn., 1978, Sioux City Pub. Mus., 1977-78; trustee Old 1st Reformed Ch., 1994-95; mem. Acad. Nat. Scis. Mem. Nat. Agri-Mktg. Assn. (pres. Chesapeake chpt. 1984, nat. awards agri. excellence 1988, exec. com. 1990-92, sec.-treas. 1992-93), Franklin Inst., Phila. Mus. Art, Phila. Zool. Soc., Queen Village Neighbors Assn. (dir., treas 1987-90, pres. 1994-95). United Ch. of Christ. Home: 1 Christian St # 7 Philadelphia PA 19147 Office: Farm Jour Ctr Sq West #2800 1500 Market St Philadelphia PA 19102

RANDALL, RONALD FISHER, grocery store chain executive; b. Sioux City, Iowa, June 25, 1934; s. F. Dwain and J. Gale (Fisher) R.; m. Lavonne E. Woltoff, Dec. 27, 1961 (dec. May 1966); children—DaLinda, Ronald; m. Charlys Fern Stewart, Mar. 7, 1969. B.S. in Engring., U.S. Naval Acad., 1958. Dir. ops. Randall Stores, Mitchell, S.D., 1958-72, pres., 1972-81, pres., chmn. bd., 1981—; pres. Coca-Cola Bottling Co. of Central S.D. Inc., Mitchell; dir. Comml. Bank, Mitchell, Dakota Mfg. Inc., Mitchell. Clubs: Interlachen Country (Mpls.); Minnehaha Country (Sioux Falls, S.D.). Office: Randall Stores Inc PO Box 1200 Mitchell SD 57301-1019*

RANDALL, TONY (LEONARD ROSENBERG), actor; b. Tulsa, Feb. 26, 1920; m. Florence Gibbs (dec.), m.Heather Harlan; 1 child, Julia Laurette. Student, Northwestern U., Columbia; studies, Neighborhood Playhouse Sch. of Theater, N.Y.C. Founder, artistic dir. Nat. Actors' Theatre, N.Y.C. Appearances include: (theatre) Circle of Chalk, 1941, Candida, 1941, The Corn is Green, 1942, The Barretts of Wimpole St., 1947, Antony and Cleopatra, 1948, Caesar and Cleopatra, 1950, Oh Men, Oh Women, 1954, Inherit the Wind, 1955-56, Oh Captain, 1958, UTBU, 1966, Two Into One, 1988, M. Butterfly, 1989, A Little Hotel on the Side, 1992, Three Men on a Horse, 1993, The Government Inspector, 1994, tour with Jack Klugman The Odd Couple, 1994; (tv) Mr. Peepers, 1952-55, Max Liebman Spectaculars, Tonight Show, 1956, The Odd Couple, 1970-75, also The Tony Randall Show, 1976-77, Love Sydney, 1981-83; (motion pictures) Oh Men, Oh Women, 1957, Will Success Spoil Rock Hunter, 1957, The Mating Game, 1959, Pillow Talk, 1959, Let's Make Love 1960, Lover Come Back, 1962, Bang, Bang, You're Dead, 1966, Huckleberry Finn, 1974, Scavenger Hunt, 1979, Foolin' Around, 1980, The King of Comedy, 1983, My Little Pony, 1986, That's Adequate, It Had to Be You; appeared in TV movies: Kate Bliss and the Ticker Tape Kid, 1978, Sidney Shorr: A Girl's Best Friend, 1981, Off Sides, 1984, The Man in the Brown Suit, 1989, The Odd Couple Returns, 1993; author: (with Michael Mindlin) Which Reminds Me, 1989. Served from pvt. to 1st lt. Signal Corps, AUS, 1942-46. Recipient Emmy award for The Odd Couple 1975. Office: care Nat Actors' Theatre 1560 Broadway Ste 409 New York NY 10036-1525*

RANDALL, VERNELLIA, lawyer, nurse, educator; b. Gladewater, Tex., Mar. 6, 1948; d. Ernest and Pauline (Hall) R.; children: Tshaka, Issa. AA, Amarillo (Tex.) Coll., 1968; BS, U. Tex., 1972; MSN, U. Wash., 1978; JD, Lewis and Clark Coll., 1987. Bar: Oreg. 1987. Prof. torts, health care law, women and the law, race/racism U. Dayton, Ohio, 1990, dir. acad. excellence program, 1994—; assoc. Bullivant, Houser, Bailey, Pendergrass & Hoffman, Portland, Oreg., 1987-90; adj. prof. law Lewis and Clark Coll., 1988-90, Wright State Med. Sch., 1990—; vis. prof. Seattle U., 1995. Bd. dirs. Oreg. Legal Svcs., 1988-90, Oreg. Chpt. Am. Heart Assn., 1988-90. Mem. ABA (vice chmn. health ins. com. 1988-90, young lawyers health com. religious non-profit orgn.), ANA, Am. Health Care Assn., Am. Assn. Law Schs. (sec. sect. on health care law 1995, sec., chair sect. law and medicine 1996, exec. com. sect. on tchg. methods), Oreg. Bar Assn., Assn. Oreg. Black Attys., Oreg. Women Lawyers (bd. dirs. 1989-90), Multnomah County Bar Assn. (status of women com.), Thurgood Marshall Legal Soc. (continuing edn. chair 1992). Avocation: computers. Office: U Dayton Sch Law 300 College Park Ave Dayton OH 45469-0001

RANDALL, WILLIAM B., manufacturing company executive; b. Phila., Jan. 8, 1921; s. Albert and Ann (Fine) R.; m. Geraldine Kempson, Aug. 10, 1943; children: Robert, Erica Lynn, Lisa. Student, Rider Coll., Trenton, N.J., 1940-41. Gen. Sales mgr. Lowres Optical Mfg. Co., Newark, 1946-49; pres., founder Rand Sales Co., N.Y.C., 1949-58; gen. mgr. Sea & Ski Co. div. Botany Industries, Inc., Millbrae, Calif., 1958-61; pres., dir. Botany Industries, Inc., 1961-66, v.p., 1961-65; pres. Renauld of France, Reno, 1967-68; chmn. bd. Renauld Internat., Reading, Pa., 1963-65; pres., chief operating officer Renauld Internat., Ltd., Burlingame and Reno, 1966-67; pres., chmn. bd. Randall Internat., Ltd., 1967-68; sr. exec. v.p. Forty-two Prods. Ltd., 1969-71; pres. Exec. Products Internat. Ltd., 1969-71, New Product Devel. Ctr., Carlsbad, Calif., 1971—; pres. Internat. Concept Ctr. Exec. Products Internat. Ltd., Irvine, 1971—, pres. Sun Research Ctr., 1974—; pres. La Costa Products Internat., 1975-86; mng. dir. merchandising La Costa Hotel and Spa, 1986-88; pres., chief exec. officer Randall Internat., Carlsbad, 1989—; bd. dirs. Bank of La Costa, Garden Botanika. Served to 1st lt., navigator USAAF, 1942-45. Mem. Am. Mgmt. Assn., Nat. Wholesale Druggists Assn., Nat. Assn. Chain Drug Stores, Hon. Order Ky. Cols., Baja Beach and Tennis Club (bd. dirs.). Home: 7150 Arenal Ln Carlsbad CA 92009-6701 *I play to win. I like to win. And I hate good losers.*

RANDALL, WILLIAM SEYMOUR, leasing company executive; b. Champaign, Ill., July 5, 1933; s. Glenn S. and Audrey H. (Honnold) R.; m. Sharon Larsen; children: Steve, Cathy, Mike, Jennifer. B.S., Ind. State U., 1959. Controller Amana Refrigeration Co., Iowa, 1966-70; div. controller Trane Co., Clarksville, Tenn., 1970-74; corporate controller Trane Co., La Crosse, Wis., 1974-79; v.p., chief fin. officer Sta-Rite Industries, Milw., 1979-82; pres., owner Profl. Staff Resources, Inc., Milw., 1982—. Served with AUS, 1953-55. Mem. Financial Execs. Inst. Lodge: Rotary. Home: 13365 Tulane St Brookfield WI 53005-7141 Office: 14430 W Bluemound Rd Ste 103 Milwaukee WI 53226

RANDAZZO, ANTHONY, dancer; b. Ann Arbor, Mich.. Student, Nat. Ballet Can. Mem. Nat. Ballet of Can.; soloist San Francisco Ballet, 1987-88, prin. dancer, 1988—. Performances with San Francisco Ballet include The Sleeping Beauty, Swan Lake, Handel—A Celebration, Ballet d'Isoline, Valses Poeticos, Intimate Voices, La Fille Mal Gardee, The Four Temperaments, Symphony in C, Theme and Variations, Ballo dell Regina, Glinka Pas de Trois, Duo Concertant, Forgotton Land, The Comfort Zone, Dream of Harmony, Nutcracker, In The Middle, Somewhat elevated, Stravinsky Violin Concerto, Terra Firma, Dance House, Sonata, Romeo and Juliet, New Sleep, Rodeo, Connotations, Rodin, La Sylphike, Variations de Ballet, Krazy Kat, Harvest Moon, The Wonder Fantasy; ballets with other cos., including Etudes, Nutcracker, Napoli, Don Juan, Don Quixote, The Merry Widow. Office: 133 W 71st St New York NY 10023 also: San Francisco Ballet 455 Franklin St San Francisco CA 94102-4438*

RANDEL, RONALD DEAN, physiologist, educator; b. Lewis, Kan., May 22, 1938; s. Emery Howard and Pauline (Mahan) R.; m. Colleen Kay O'Brien, Sept. 4, 1966; 1 child, Lowell Warren. BS in Animal Sci., Washington State U., 1965; PhD in Animal Physiology, Purdue U., 1971. Research fellow Purdue U., West Lafayette, Ind., 1965-71; visiting scientist U.S. Range Livestock Experiment Station, Miles City, Mont., 1971-72; research physiologist USDA, Agrl. Rsch. Svc., Miles City, 1972-74; assoc. prof. Texas A & M U., Overton, Tex., 1974-78, prof., 1978—; cooperating scientist USDA-Office Internat. Coop. and Devel./Taiwan Livestock Rsch. Inst., Ping Tung, 1987—; presenter in field. Mem. editl. bd. Jour. Animal Sci., 1990-93, 95—, Theriogeneology, 1994—; contbr. numerous papers to profl. jours., 2 chpts. to books, also numerous paper presentations, misc. papers, and symposia. Adult leader 4-H, Rusk County Riding Club Overton, 1981-90. With USN, 1958-62. Named Alpha Zeta agrl. hon. Wash. State U., 1964, Phi Kappa Phi scholastic hon. Wash. State U., 1964, Sigma Xi rsch. hon. Purdue U., 1970, Award in Excellence for Rsch. Tex. A&M U., 1987, 90, Svc. award Dept. Animal Sci., 1994; sr. Fulbright rsch. fellow James Cook U. of N. Queensland, Townsville, Australia, 1984; Donald Henry Barron lectr., 1995. Mem. Am. Soc. of Animal Sci. (Physiology and Endocrinology award 1996), Soc. for the Study of Reproduction, Assn. Latino Americana de Prodn. Animal, Reproductive Performance of Domestic Ruminants (W-112Reg. Proj. Com.; pres. 1986). Protestant. Home: 604 W Patricia Dr Overton TX 75684-1526 Office: Tex A&M U Agrl Rsch & Extension Drawer E Overton TX 75684

RANDELL, RICHARD C., mathematics educator; b. Fairfield, Iowa, Aug. 23, 1946; m. Linda Randell; children: John, Alex. BS, U. Iowa, 1968; MS, U. Wis., 1971; PhD, 1973. Asst. prof. U. Mich., Ann Arbor, 1973-79; vis. mem. Inst. Advanced Study, Princeton, N.J., 1976-78; asst., assoc. prof. U. Okla., Norman, 1979-81, U. Iowa, 1981-87; prof., 1987—, dept. chair, 1991-94; mem., governing bd. Iowa Math. Coalition, Cedar Falls, 1990-95. Editor, author: Singularities, 1989; contbr. articles to profl. jours. recipient Rsch. grants U.S. Nat. Sci. Found., 1974-87. Mem. Am. Math. Soc. Office: Dept Math University of Iowa Iowa City IA 52242

RANDELS, ED LEE, lawyer; b. Albuquerque, Nov. 17, 1953; s. James L. and Betty J. (Ridgeway) R.; m. Kathryn J. Eddleman, July 11, 1975; children: Nancy L, Joshua L. BA, Mid-Am. Nazarene Coll., Olathe, Kans., 1975; JD, U. Kans., 1982. Bar: Kans. 1982, U.S. Dist. Ct. Kans. 1982, U.S. Ct. Appeals (10 cir.) 1994. Asst. county atty. Montgomery County, Indpendence, Kans., 1982-85, Miami County, Paola, Kans., 1985-86; asst. city atty. City of Wichita, Kans., 1986-92; asst. county counselor Sedgwick County, Wichita, Kans., 1992—; law day dir. Miami County Bar Assn., Paola, Kans., 1985-86. Contbr. articles to profl. jours. Mem. ABA, Kans. Bar Assn., Wichita Bar Assn., Christian Legal Soc. Republican. Nazarene. Office: Sedgwick County Counselor 525 N Main St Ste 359 Wichita KS 67203-3703

RANDHAWA, BIKKAR SINGH, psychologist, educator; b. Jullundur, India, June 14, 1933; came to Can., 1961, naturalized, 1966; s. Pritam S. and Sawaran K. (Basakhi) R.; m. Leona Emily Bujnowski, Oct. 8, 1966; children—Jason, Lisa. BA in Math., Panjab U., 1954, BT in Edn., 1955, MA in History, 1959; BEd, U. Alta., Can., 1963; MEd in Measurement and Evaluation, U Toronto, 1967, PhD, 1969. Registered psychologist. Tchr. secondary sch. math. Panjab, 1955-61; asst. headmaster, then headmaster, 1955-61; tchr. high sch. math. and sci. Beaver County, Riley, Alta., 1964-65, Camrose County, Alta., 1961-64; tchr. high sch. math. and sci. Edmonton (Alta.) Public Schs., 1965-67; tutor in math. for social sci. Ont. Inst. Studies in Edn., Toronto, 1968-69; mem. faculty U. Sask., Saskatoon, 1969-76, 77—; prof. ednl. psychology U. Sask., 1977—, asst. dean research and field services, 1982-87; prof., coord. Visual Scholars' Program, U. Iowa, 1976-77; cons. in field. Contbr. articles profl. jours. Fellow APA, Am. Psychol. Soc. (charter), Can. Psychol. Assn.; mem. Am. Ednl. Rsch. Assn., Can. Ednl. Rsch. Assn. (pres. 1997—), Can. Soc. Study Edn., Sask. Psychol. Assn., Phi Delta Kappa (pres. Saskatoon chpt. 1971, 85). Home: 510 Forsyth Crescent, Saskatoon, SK Canada S7N 4H8 Office: U Sask, 3117 Edn Bldg 28 Campus Dr, Saskatoon, SK Canada S7N OX1

RANDI, JAMES (RANDALL JAMES HAMILTON ZWINGE), magician, writer, educator; b. Toronto, Aug. 7, 1928; naturalized U.S. citizen, 1987; s. George Randall and Marie Alice (Paradis) Zwinge. Student, Oakwood Collegiate Inst., Toronto, 1940-45; LittD (hon.), U. Indpls., 1995. Internationally known conjuror; regent's lectr. UCLA, 1984; skeptical lectr. on paranormal subjects. Author: The Magic of Uri Geller, 1975 (with Bert Sugar) Houdini, His Life and Art, 1978, Flim-Flam, 1982, Test Your ESP Potential, 1983, The Faith Healers, 1987, The Magic World of the Amazing Randi, 1989, The Mask of Nostradamus, 1990, James Randi: Psychic Investigator, 1991, Conjuring, 1992, An Encyclopedia of Claims, Frauds, and Hoaxes of the Occult and Supernatural, 1995; host TV spls. Recipient Blackstone award Internat. Platform Assn., 1983, 87, Forum award Am. Phys. Soc., 1988, Nat. Consumer Svc. award Nat. Coun. Against Health Fraud, 1988, Gold medal U. Ghent, Belgium, 1989, Humanist Disting. Svc. award Am. Humanist Assn., 1990, medal with golden wreath Hungarian Soc. for Dissemination of Scientific Knowledge, 1992; MacArthur Found. fellow, 1986, Spl. fellow Acad. Magical Arts and Scis., 1987; inducted into Soc. Am. Magicians Hall of Fame, 1988. Founding fellow Com. for Scientific Investigation of Claims of the Paranormal (exec. bd. dirs. 1973-91). Performed at White House, 1974. Home: 12000 NW 8th St Fort Lauderdale FL 33325-1406 Office: James Randi Ednl Found 201 SE 12th St Fort Lauderdale FL 33316-1815 *Irrationalism and the anti-science movement continue to grow, fed by the irresponsible media. Quack medicine, Creation "Science," TV psychics and other pseudo-scientific matters are heedlessly and increasingly embraced by the public. We must reach out to our youth and develop in them a respect for critical thinking. Acceptance of every opinion as valid, of "politically correct" attitudes as standards, and of unquestioning belief in obviously crackpot notions have brought us to a crisis in education. We need to adopt higher standards for our young people in respect to critical thinking.*

RANDINELLI, TRACEY ANNE, magazine editor; b. Morristown, N.J., Apr. 6, 1963; d. Andrew R. and Patricia Ann (Brenner) R. BA in Comm., U. Del., 1985. Copywriter Macy's N.J., Newark, 1985-86; edit. asst. Globe Comms. Corp., N.Y.C., 1986-87; from asst. editor to assoc. editor Scholastic Math and DynaMath Mags. Scholastic, Inc., N.Y.C., 1987-89, editor Scholastic Math Mag., 1989-95; mng. editor Zig Zag Mag. Games Pub. Group, N.Y.C., 1995; sr. editor 321 Contact Mag. Children's Television Workshop, N.Y.C., 1996—. Mem. Soc. Children's Book Writers, Ednl. Press Assn. Am. (Disting. Achievement award feature articles divsn. 1991, 95, cover design 1996).

RANDLE, JOHN, professional football player; b. Hearne, Tex., Jan. 12, 1967. Student, Trinity Valley C.C., Tex., Tex. A&I U. Defensive tackle Minn. Vikings, 1990—. Selected to Pro Bowl, 1993, 94; named to The Sporting News NFL All-Pro Team, 1994. Achievements tied AFC record for most sacks, 1994. Office: c/o Minn Vikings 9520 Viking Dr Eden Prairie MN 55344-3825*

RANDLE, ROLINDA CAROL, elementary education educator; b. Fort Worth, Nov. 3, 1959; d. John Arthur and Ann Junette (Jones) Richards; m. Joseph L. Randle, June 12, 1982; children: Joseph Jr., Jennifer Michelle, Ja'Lissa Maurnice. BS in Edn., Tex. Christian U., 1982; postgrad., Tarleton State U. Cert. elem. edn., English, mid-mgmt., Tex. 2d grade tchr. Sunset Valley Elem. Sch., Austin, Tex., 1982-84; 6th grade tchr. Rosemont Middle Sch., Fort Worth, 1985-87; 6th grade tchr., adminstrv. intern Meadowbrook Middle Sch., Fort Worth, 1987—; mem. site-based decision making team Rosemont Middle Sch., 1985-87, Meadowbrook Middle Sch., 1987-90, mem. leadership team, 1994—, mem. tech. com., 1991—; indsl. tech. trainer Fort Worth Ind. Sch. Dist., 1994—; owner, pres., CEO Triple J Enterprises; exec. distbr. ShapeRite Concepts, Ltd. Fellow Summer Writing Inst; mem. ASCD, NEA, United Educators Assn., Jack-n-Jill of Am. Inc., Ft. Worth Classroom Tchr. Assn., Tex. State Tchr. Assn., Delta Sigma Theta. Mem. Ch. of Christ. Avocations: reading, computers, family activities. Home: 4733 Leonard St Fort Worth TX 76119-7540

RANDLETT, MARY WILLIS, photographer; b. Seattle, May 5, 1924; d. Cecil Durand and Elizabeth (Bayley) Willis; m. Herbert B. Randlett, Oct. 19, 1950 (div.); children—Robert, Mary Ann, Peter, Susan. B.A., Whitman Coll., Walla Walla, Wash., 1947. Freelance photographer, 1949—; one-person shows include Seattle Sci. Center, 1971, Western Wash. State U., 1971, Seattle Art Mus., 1971, Art Gallery of Greater Victoria, 1972, Alaska State Mus., 1972, State Capitol Mus., 1983, Whatcom Mus. History and Art, Bellingham, Wash., 1986, Janet Huston Gallery, LaConner, Wash., 1990, Gov.'s Gallery, Office of Gov., Olympia, Wash., 1991, Stonington Gallery, Seattle, 1992, Valley Mus. Art, LaConner, 1992, Grad. Sch. Design Dept. Landscapde Architecture Harvard U., Cambridge, Mass., 1996, others; group shows: Am. Soc. Mag. Photographers, 1970, Whatcom Mus., Bellingham, Wash., Henry Gallery, Seattle, 1971, 74, Royal Photog. Soc., 1979, Heard Mus., Phoenix, 1979, Gov.'s Invitational State Capital Mus., Olympia, Wash., 1983, Helmi: Interpretations N.W. Indian Art State Capital Mus., 1984, The Small Show Santa Fe Ctr. for Photography, 1987, Wash. State Capital Mus., 1988, Wash. State Capital Mus., Olympia, 1988, 89, 93, Tacoma (Wash.) Art Mus., 1989, Helen Day Art Ctr., Stowe, Vt., 1989, Valley Mus. Northwest Art, LaConner, 1991, Allen Libr. U. Wash., Seattle, 1991, Wing Luke Asian Mus., Seattle, 1991, Cheney Cowles Mus., Spokane, 1991, Security Pacific Gallery, Seattle, 1992, Benham Gallery, Seattle, 1993, Stonington Gallery, 1993, Rainier Club, Seattle, 1994, Valley Mus. of Northwest Art, La Conner, Wash., 1994, Port Angeles Fine Arts Ctr., Port Angeles, Wash., 1994, Mus. History and Industry, Seattle, 1994, Whatcom Mus., Bellingham, Wash., 1994, Pacific Northwest Annual Bellevue Art Mus., Wash., 1995, Skagit Valley Hist. Mus., LaConner, Wash., 1995, Mus. Northwest Art, LaConner, 1996, Seattle Art Mus., 1996-97, and numerous others; works represented in permanent collections Met. Mus., Nat. Collection of Fine Arts, Nat. Portrait Gallery, Washington State Library, Manuscript div. U. Wash., Pacific Northwest Bell, Seattle, Swedish Med. Center, Seattle, Whatcom Mus., Bellingham, Henry Gallery, Seattle, Wash. State Capitol Mus., Olympia, Phillips Collection, Washington; works appeared in books: The Master and His Fish (Roderick Haig-Brown), 1982; Theodore Roethke: The Journey to I and Otherwise (Neal Bowers), 1982; Mountain in the Clouds (Bruce Brown), 1982; Masonry in Architecture (Louis Redstone), 1982; Writings and Reflections from the World of Roderick Haig-Brown), 1982; Pike Place Market (Alice Shorett and Murray Morgan), 1982; The Dancing Blanket, (Cheryl Samuel), 1982, Collected Poems of Theodore Roethke, 1982; Spires of Form (Victor Scheffer), 1983; Assault on Mount Helicon (Mary Barnard), 1983; New as a Wave (Eve Triem), 1983; Sketchbook: A Memoir of the '30's and the Northwest School (William Cumming), 1983; Good Intentions (Jane Adams), 1985; Blackbirds of the Americas (Gordon Orians and Tony Angell), 1985; Historic Preservation in Seattle (Larry Kreisman), 1985; Down Town Seattle Walking Tours (Mary Randlett and Carol Tobin), 1986; Seattle, the Seattle Book, 1986; When Orchids were Flowers (Kate Knap Johnson), 1986, Jacob Lawrence, American Painter, (Ellen Wheat), 1986, Manic Power: Robert Lowell and His Circle, (Jeffrey Meyers), 1987, The Isamu Noguchi Garden Museum, (Isamu Noguchi), 1987, Washington's Audacious State Capitol and its Builders, (Norman Johnston), 1988, The Bloedel Reserve: Gardens in the Forest, (Lawrence Kreisman), 1988, Washingtonians: A Biographical Portrait of the State on the Occasion of its Centennial, 1988, Directory of Literary Biography: Canadian Writers 1920-59, 2d series, 1989, Crafts of America, 1989, The Lone Tree Tragedy (Bruce Brown), 1989, Northwest Coast Handbook of North American Indians, 1990, Dancing on the Rim of the World, 1990, Openings, Original Essays by Contemporary Soviet and American Writers (eds. Robert Atwan, Valeri Vinokurov), 1990, George Tsutakawa (Martha Kingsbury), 1990, Contemporary American Poetry (ed. Al Polin Jr.), 1991, Natural History of Puget Sound Country (Arthur Kruckberg), 1991, Bones (Joyce Thompson), 1991, Cebu (Peter Basho), 1991, Catalogue of Historic Preservation Publications, 1992, Art in Seattle's Public Places (James Rupp), 1992, The Olympic Rainforest (Ruth Kirk with Jerry Franklin), 1992, Steelhead Fly Fishing, (Trey Combs), 1992, Illustrated Guidelines for Rehabilitation Historic Buildings, 1993, A History of African American Artists (Bearden and Henderson), 1994, Childrens Literature Review Vol. 1, 1994, Invisible Gardens: The Search for Modernism the American Landscape (Walker and Simo), 1994, Seeing Seattle (Roger Sale), 1994, Reaching Home (Jay and Matson), 1994, Redesigning the American Lawn: A Search for Environmental Harmony (Gordone Geballe, Diana Balmari and F. Herbert Bormann), 1995, Reaching Home: Pacific Salmon, Pacific People (Foves, Jay and Matson), 1995, Carl F. Gould: A Life in Architecture and the Arts (T. William Booth and William H. Wuksib), 1995, and numerous others; works also appeared in newspapers and mags. Nat. Endowment for Arts grantee, 1976; recipient Wash. State Gov.'s award for spl. commendation for contbns. in field of photography, 1983, Individual Artist award King County Arts Commn., 1989. Mem. Am. Soc. Mag. Photographers. Home: PO Box 10536 Bainbridge Island WA 98110

RANDMAN, BARRY I., real estate developer; b. Cin., Apr. 1, 1958; s. David I. and Marilyn June (Garfinkel) F. BBA in Fin., U. Denver, 1980. With acctg. dept. Rookwood Pottery & Celestial Restaurants, Cin., 1976-80; asst. to pres., head mktg. and real estate branching Great Am. Banks Inc., Miami, 1980-83; pres. Tower Mgmt. Inc., Cin., 1983-85, bd. dirs.; pres. Ohio Jet Svcs. Inc., Cin., 1983-85; v.p. Home State Fin. Svcs. Inc., Cin., 1984-85;

pres. East Hill Devel. Corp., Cin., 1985—, B.I.R. Properties Inc., Cin., 1985—; pres. Golden Devel. Corp., 1988-91, SRB Food Corp., 1988-92, Scarborough Devel. Corp., 1989, Redmont Devel Corp., 1990—, Eastridge, Inc., 1993—. Mem. Jewish Welfare Fund, Cin., 1980. Avocations: skiing, tennis, gardening. Home: 2840 Ambleside Pl Cincinnati OH 45208-3357 Office: 2321 Kemper Ln Cincinnati OH 45206-2610

RANDOLPH, ARTHUR RAYMOND, federal judge, lawyer; b. Riverside, N.J., Nov. 1, 1943; m. Eileen J. O'Connor, May 18, 1984; children from previous marriage: John Trevor, Cynthia Lee. BS, Drexel U., 1966; JD summa cum laude, U. Pa., 1969. Bar: Calif. 1970, D.C. 1973, U.S. Supreme Ct. 1973. Law clk. to hon. judge Henry J. Friendly U.S. Ct. Appeals, 2d Cir., N.Y.C., 1969-70; asst. to solicitor gen. U.S. Dept. Justice, Washington, 1970-73, dep. solicitor gen., 1975-77; ptnr. Sharp, Randolph & Green, Washington, 1977-83, Randolph & Truitt, Washington, 1983-87, Pepper, Hamilton & Scheetz, Washington, 1987-90; judge U.S. Ct. Appeals (D.C. cir.), Washington, 1990—; spl. asst. atty. gen. State of Mont., 1983-90, State of N.Mex., 1985-90, State of Utah, 1986-90; mem. adv. panel Fed. Cts. Study Com., 1989-90; spl. counsel Com. on Stds. of Ofcl. Conduct, U.S. Ho. of Reps., 1979-80; adj. prof. law Georgetown U. Law Ctr., 1974-78; exec. sec. Atty. Gen.'s Com. on Reform of Fed. Jud. System, 1975-77; mem. com. on Fed. Rules of Evidence U.S. Justice Dept., 1972; chmn. Com. on Govtl. Structures, McLean, Va., 1973-74; adj. prof. law sch. George Mason U., 1992; mem. com. codes conduct Jud. Conf. U.S., 1993—, chmn., 1995—. Recipient Spl. Achievement award U.S. Dept. Justice, 1971. Mem. Am. Law Inst., Calif. Bar Assn., D.C. Bar Assn., Order of Coif. Office: US Ct Appeals 333 Constitution Ave NW Washington DC 20001-2802

RANDOLPH, CARL LOWELL, chemical company executive; b. Pasadena, Calif., May 30, 1922; s. Carl L. and Lulu (McBride) R.; m. Jane Taber, June 25, 1943; children—Margaret, Stephen. B.A., Whittier Coll., 1943; M.S., U. So. Calif., 1947, Ph.D., 1949; LL.D. (hon.), Whittier Coll., 1982; D. Pub. Service (hon.), U. Alaska, 1983. Prin. chemist Aerojet-Gen. Corp., 1949-57; v.p. U.S. Borax Research Corp., Anaheim, Calif., 1957-63; asst. to pres. U.S. Borax & Chem. Corp., Los Angeles, 1963-66; v.p. U.S. Borax & Chem. Corp., 1966-68, exec. v.p., 1968-69, pres., 1969-86, vice chmn., 1983-87. Trustee, chmn. bd. Whittier Coll., emeritus, 1969—; bd. dirs., chmn., Ind. Colls. So. Calif., 1982—. Served from ensign to lt. (j.g.) USNR, 1944-46. Mem. Phi Beta Kappa, Sigma Xi. Home: 1407 Seaview Way Anacortes WA 98221-9794

RANDOLPH, DAVID, conductor; b. N.Y.C., Dec. 21, 1914; s. Morris and Elsie (Goodman) R.; m. Mildred Greenberg, July 18, 1948. BS, CCNY, 1936; MA, Tchrs. Coll., Columbia U., 1941. Music specialist OWI, N.Y.C., 1943-47; adj. prof. music NYU, 1948-85, Mostly Mozart course, 1976-85; lectr. Town Hall, N.Y.C., 1955-60, Columbia U., 1957, Cosmopolitan Club, N.Y.C., 1962-63; pre-concert lectr. N.Y. Philharm., Avery Fisher Hall, 1964-86,Cleve. Orch., 1981, Vienna Symphony Orch., 1988; tchr. conducting Dalcroze Sch., 1948-49; music commentator Little Orch. Soc. Concerts and Broadcasts, 1950-62, Met. Opera Intermission Broadcasts; intermission commentator Lewisohn Stadium Concert Broadcasts, 1952-58; vis. prof. music SUNY, New Paltz, 1970-72, Fordham U., 1972-73; lectr. New Sch. for Social Rsch., 1973-90, IBM, N.Y.C., 1978-86, Beethoven Soc., 1977, 83; prof. music Montclair State Coll., Upper Montclair, N.J., 1973-87; guest condr. Rockland County (N.Y.) Ann. Choral Festival, 1972, 73; adviser film Music to Live By, mem. N.J. Arts Coun., 1967-70; mem. music com. Gov. N.J.'s Commn. to Study Arts, 1965; honored guest Handel Festival, Halle, Germany, 1991. Condr. Randolph Singers, 1944-62 (appeared on NBC Today, and Tonight Shows), United Choral Soc., 1961-86, N.J. Ballet Orch., 1977, 83, Masterwork Chamber Orch., 1982, 83, The Philharmonia Orch. in Brahms' Requiem, London, 1988, Barge Concert, N.Y.C., 1987, 89; guest condr., Conn. Symphony Orch., 1961; condr. concert tour Spain with Am. choruses and Radio TV Orch. of Moscow, 1992; music annotator, CBS, N.Y.C., 1947-48; yearly choral seminar leader Mohonk Mountain House, 1986-95; music dir., condr. Masterwork Chorus and Orch., 1955-93, St. Cecilia Chorus and Orch., N.Y.C., 1965—; numerous performances at Carnegie Hall, Avery Fisher Hall, Lincoln Ctr., Kennedy Ctr. including Brahms' Requiem, Schicksalslied, Mozart's Requiem, C Minor Mass, Beethoven's Missa Solemnis, Bach's Mass in B Minor, St. John Passion, St. Matthew Passion, Christmas Oratorio, Magnificat, Vaughan Williams' A Sea Symphony, Dona Nobis Pacem, Mass in G Minor, Hodie, Verdi's Requiem, Four Sacred Pieces, Mendelssohn's Elijah, Die erste Walpurgisnacht, Poulenc's Gloria, Dvorak's Requiem, Kodaly's Te Deum, Berlioz' Requiem, Cherubini's requiem, Schubert"s Masses 5 and 6, Zelenka's Missa Dei Patris, Israel in Egypt including 168 complete performances of Handel's Messiah, others; broadcaster: David Randolph Concerts, WNYC and numerous radio stas. of Nat. Assn. Ednl. Broadcasters, 1946-79, Young Audience telecasts, CBS-TV, 1958-59, series of candid rehearsals of Bach's Mass in B minor, PBS, 1965; host: weekly broadcasts Lincoln Ctr. Spotlight, Sta. WQXR, N.Y.C., 1966-67; regular guest critic First Hearing program Sta. WQXR, N.Y.C., and 68 other stas., 1986—; author: This Is Music, 1964, numerous album jacket notes; editor: David Randolph Choral Series; writer, narrator: Instruments of the Orchestra, 1958, compact disc 95, Stereo Review's Guide to Understanding Music, 1973; music critic, High Fidelity Mag., 1952-57; composer: A Song for Humanity, 1968, Andante for Strings, Edward; contbg. author: The N.Y. Times Guide to Listening Pleasure, 1968; Recs. for Columbia, Vanguard, Westminster, Concert Hall Soc., Esoteric records; analyzed Mendelssohn's Symphony No. 3 on records for Book of Month Club. Recipient 1st award for edn. by radio Ohio State Inst., 1948, 50, 51, Sylvania TV award, 1959, Disting. Alumni award Columbia U., 1982, cert. of appreciation Mayor of City of N.Y. at Carnegie Hall, 1991, Townsend Harris medal CCNY, 1996; St. Cecilia Chorus endowed David Randolph Disting. Artist-in-Residence program at New Sch. in N.Y., 1996. Home: 420 E 86th St Apt 4-C New York NY 10028-6450

RANDOLPH, HARRY FRANKLIN, III, health facility administrator, physician assistant; b. Vallejo, Calif., Nov. 5, 1946; s. Harry Franklin Jr. and Viola Vinnie (Snyder) R.; m. Candice Patricia Garrison, Dec. 30, 1970; 1 child, Brandon Todd. BS in Zoology, San Diego State U., 1969; BS, Baylor Coll. Med., 1977. Cert. physician asst., Nat. Commn. Cert. Physician Assts. Staff rsch. assoc. U. Calif. San Diego, La Jolla, 1969-72; med. mach. Technitian VA Hosp., San Diego, 1972-75; physician asst. So. Calif. Permenente Med. Group, San Diego, 1977-79, Mt. Health Ctr., Boulevard, Calif., 1979-81, So. Calif. HMO, San Diego, 1981-82, Scripps Clin. Med. Group, La Jolla, 1982—; chief physician extender sect. Scripps Clin. Med. Group, La Jolla, 1991—, expert witness/pysician asst. practice, 1992—, chief physician assts. Green Hosp., 1994—; med. legal cons. Contbr. articles to profl. jours.; editor Surg. Physician Asst., 1994-97. Mem. Health Sys. Agency Sub-area Coun. VI, El Cajon, Calif., 1980-81, San Diego Zool. Soc., 1985—. Fellow Am. Acad Physician Assts., Am. Assn. Surgical Physician Assts. (treas. 1994-96), Calif. Acad. Physician Assts. (dir. at large 1984, chmn. continuing med. edn. com. 1984-86, v.p. 1985, chmn. prof. practice com. 1996, 97, Outstanding Achievement award 1985, Outstanding Svc. award, 1994). Democrat. Avocations: camping, gardening, mountain biking, hiking. Office: Scripps Clin Med Group Mail Drop MS 213 10666 N Torrey Pines Rd La Jolla CA 92037-1027

RANDOLPH, JACKSON HAROLD, utility company executive; b. Cin., Nov. 17, 1930; s. Dward Bradley and Cora Belle (Puckett) R.; m. Angelina Losito, June 20, 1958; children: Terri, Patti, Todd, Craig. B.B.A., U. Cin., 1958, M.B.A., 1968. C.P.A., Ohio. Acct. Arthur Andersen & Co., Cin., 1958-59; with Cin. Gas & Electric Co., 1959—, v.p. fin. and corp. affairs, 1981-85, exec. v.p., 1985-86, chmn., pres., chief exec. officer, 1986—, also dir.; chmn., CEO CINergy Corp., 1994—; also pres. Union Light Heat and Power Co., Covington, Ky.; bd. dirs. Cen. Trust Bank, N.A., Cin. Fin. Corp., PNC Corp.; CEO CINergy Corp., 1994-95, chmn., 1995—. V.p., bd. dirs. Gen. Protestant Orphan Home, Cin., 1981-86; treas., bd. dirs. Cin. chpt. ARC, 1975—; mem. adv. com. Catherine Booth Home, 1980—, Dan Beard council Boy Scouts Am., 1985. Served with USN, 1951-55. Mem. Cin. Country Club, Queen City Club, Met. Club, Bankers Club, Delta Sigma Pi, Phi Eta Sigma, Beta Gamma Sigma. Home: 414 Bishopsbridge Dr Cincinnati OH 45255-3900 Office: CINergy Corp 139 E 4th St Cincinnati OH 45202-4003 also: Union Light Heat & Power Co 107 Brent Spence Sq Covington KY 41011-1433

RANDOLPH, JENNINGS, JR. (JAY RANDOLPH), sportscaster; b. Cumberland, Md., Sept. 19, 1934; s. Jennings and Mary Katherine (Babb) R.; m. Sue Henderson, May 28, 1966; children: Jennings, Brian Robert, Rebecca Sue. B.A., Salem (W.Va.) Coll., 1963. Sports and promotion dir. Sta. WHAR, Clarksburg, W.Va., 1958-61; sportscaster Sta. KLIF, Dallas, 1963-66; Sta. KMOX, St. Louis, 1966-68; with Sta. KSDK-TV, St. Louis, 1968—; sports dir. Sta. KSDK-TV, 1968-88, spl. sports corr., 1988—, also on nationally televised broadcasts for various sports events.; TV announcer Fla. Marlins Baseball Club, Ft. Lauderdale, 1993—; TV announcer St. Louis Cardinals, 1970-87, Cin. Reds., 1988; mem. NBC's broadcast staff for 1988 Olympics, Seoul, Korea and 1992 Summer Games, Barcelona, Spain; host nationally syndicated The Golf Show. Trustee Salem Coll., 1976-89. With U.S. Army, 1954-56. Inducted into Boys and Girls Clubs of Am. Hall of Fame, 1990. Mem. Nat. Assn. Sportscasters, Delta Tau Delta. Amateur golf champion. Office: The Fla Marlins 2267 NE 199th St Miami FL 33180

RANDOLPH, JOE WAYNE, machine manufacturing executive, stock broker; b. Madisonville, Ky., Aug. 5, 1938; s. Albert Clay and Helen (Brown) R.; m. Mary Ann Rabenau, July 20, 1963; children: Ann E., Charles J. BS, Murray State U., 1962, MS, 1964; MBA, Washington U./ Lindenwood Coll., 1978. High sch. tchr. Benton (Ky.) Sch. System, 1962-64, St. Charles (Mo.) Sch. System, 1964-65; mfg. mgr. Sunnen Products Co., St. Louis, 1967-96; stock broker Linsco/Pvt. Ledger Securities, Washington, Mo., 1996—. 1st lt. U.S. Army, 1965. Named Col., Hon. Order of Ky. Cols., 1990. Mem. AAIM Mgmt. Assn. (prodn. exec. round table, leader 1984—), Elks. Avocations: golf, fishing, travel, hunting. Home: 5700 Highway T Augusta MO 63332-1419 Office: 317 Elm St Washington MO 63090-2328

RANDOLPH, JUDSON GRAVES, pediatric surgeon; b. Macon, Ga., July 19, 1927; s. Milton Fitz and Abigail Theresa (Graves) R.; m. Susan Comfort Adams, June 14, 1952; children: Somers, Garrett, Judson, Adam, Comfort. BA, Vanderbilt U., 1950, MD, 1953. Intern in surgery U. Rochester, N.Y., 1953-54; asst. resident in pathology Vanderbilt U., 1954-55; asst. resident, then sr. resident in surgery Mass. Gen. Hosp., Boston, 1956-58; asst. resident in surgery Children's Hosp., Boston, 1955-56, sr. resident, then chief resident, 1958-61, asst. surgeon, 1961-63; teaching fellow to instr. surgery Med. Sch. Harvard U., 1960-63; jr. assoc. in surgery Peter Bent Brigham Hosp., Boston, 1961-63; surgeon-in-chief Children's Hosp., Washington, 1964-91; mem. faculty Med. Sch. George Washington U., 1964-91, prof. surgery and child health, 1968-91; prof. surgery Meharry Med. Coll., 1992-96; cons. Nat. Naval Med. Ctr., NIH, Walter Reed Army Med. Ctr.; trustee Children's Hosp. Nat. Med. Ctr., 1972-84, Vanderbilt U., 1980—. Editor: Pediatric Surgery, 3d edit., 2 vols., 1979, 4th edit., 2 vols., 1985, The Injured Child, 1980; mem. editl. bd. Surgery, 1978-92; contbr. numerous articles to med. jours. With USNR, 1945-46, PTO. Mem. ACS (gov. 1969-75), AMA, Am. Acad. Pediats. (chmn. exec. com. surg. sect. 1974-75), Am. Assn. Thoracic Surgery, Am. Pediat. Surg. Assn. (gov. 1980—, pres. 1984), Washington Acad. Surgery (pres. 1989), Soc. U. Surgeons, Am. Surg. Assn., So. Surg. Assn., Am. Bd. Surgery (bd. dirs. 1973-79, diplomate), Alpha Omega Alpha (faculty), Cosmos Club (Washington). Methodist.

RANDOLPH, KEVIN H., marketing executive; b. Seattle, July 6, 1949; s. Howard Amos and Betty Elaine (Leahy) R.; m. Deborah Lou Newell, Sept. 18, 1976; children: Heather, Lyndsay. BA, Wash. State U., 1972. Mgr. Computers for Mktg., L.A., 1972-74; data processing mgr. Parker Rsch., Pasadena, Calif., 1974-77; prin. Randolph & Assocs., L.A., 1977-79; v.p. Bank Am. Corp., San Francisco, 1979-87, Interactive Network, Mountain View, Calif., 1987-91; sr. v.p. ICTV, Santa Clara, Calif., 1991-93; pres. Interactive Enterprises, San Ramon, Calif., 1993—; v.p. U.S. West Mrg., Inc., Benicia, Calif., 1993-94; exec. v.p., COO Interactive Video Enterprises, Inc., San Ramon, 1994-95; cons. Randolph Home Ctr., Ephrata, Wash., 1972—. Mem. Am. Mktg. Assn., Am. Mgmt. Assn. Home: 170 Edinburgh Cir Danville CA 94526-2906

RANDOLPH, LILLIAN LARSON, medical association executive; b. Spokane, Wash., May 3, 1932; d. Charles P. and Juanita S. (Parrish) Larson; m. Philip L. Randolph, Nov. 12, 1952; children: Marcus, Andrew. BA, U. Wash., 1954, MA, 1956; PhD, U. Calif., Berkeley, 1966; EdD, N.Mex. State U., 1979. Researcher U. Wash., Seattle, 1954-59; asst. prof. Calif. State U., Hayward, 1964-68, U. Tex., El Paso, 1972-74; dir. S.W. Conservatory of Music, El Paso, 1972-74; adj. prof. Loyola U. and DePaul U., Chgo., 1974-78; asst. prof. DeVry Inst. Tech., Lombard, Ill., 1982-84; mgr. AMA, Chgo., 1985—; cons. Weber Co., Chgo., 1979-85. Author: Fundamentals of Government Organizations, 1971, Third Party Settlement of Disputes, 1973. Mem. AAUP, Phi Beta Kappa. Home: 408 W Wilshire Dr Wilmette IL 60091-3154

RANDOLPH, NANCY ADELE, nutritionist, consultant; b. St. Louis, Sept. 7, 1941; d. Robert Andrew and Mary Jane (Hilliker) R.; m. John Reginald Randolph-Swainson, Sept. 16, 1989. BS, U. Ariz., 1963; MEd, Boston U., 1971; postgrad., Harvard U., 1983. Intern instn. adminstrn. Mills Coll., Oakland, Calif., 1963-64; staff dietitian St. Lukes Hosp., St. Louis, 1964-65; clin. dietitian New England Deaconess Hosp., Boston, 1965-66; dietitian mgr. The Seiler Corp., Waltham, Mass., 1966-67; instr., acting dir. Whidden Hosp. Sch. Nursing, Everett, Mass., 1967-72; instr. nutrition Northeastern U. Coll. Nursing, Boston, 1972; renal/rsch. dietitian Lemuel Shattuck Hosp., Jamaica Plain, Mass., 1979-81; New England regional dietitian coord. Beverly Enterprises, Virginia Beach, Va., 1985-88; state nutritionist, surveyor Mass. Dept. Pub. Health/Health Care Quality, Boston, 1988-89; cons. nutritionist Randolph Assocs., West Palm Beach and Sarasota, Fla., 1990—; cons. dietitian Jewish Rehab Ctr., Swampscott, Mass., 1972-79, Lenox Hill Rehab. Ctr., Lynn, Mass., 1972-79, Jesmond Nursing Home, Nahant, Mass., 1972-88, numerous other health care facilities in New England, 1972-88. Mem. Am. Dietetic Assn. (cert.), Fla. Dietetic Assn., Cons. Nutritionists Practice Group, Cons. Dietitians in Health Care.

RANDOLPH, ROBERT DEWITT, lawyer; b. Sligo, Pa., Mar. 6, 1929; s. DeWitt Lyman and Hazel Irene (McCall) R.; m. Betty Ann McElhattan, May 8, 1953 (dec. Aug. 1979); children: Douglas, Andrew; m. Susan Denise Hopkins, Oct. 15, 1988. BA, Westminster Coll., 1951; LLB, Harvard U., 1957. Bar: Ohio 1958, Pa. 1960, U.S. Supreme Ct. 1981. Assoc. Buckingham, Doolittle & Burroughs, Akron, Ohio, 1957-59, Rose, Houston, Cooper & Schmidt, Pitts., 1959-60, 61-65; fgn. svc. officer U.S. Dept. State, Washington, 1960-61; ptnr. Houston, Cooper, Spear & German, Pitts., 1965-70, Randolph & O'Connor, Pitts., 1970-74, Buchanan Ingersoll P.C., Pitts., 1974-93. Pres. Assn. Retarded Citizens Allegheny, Pitts., 1990-92. With U.S. Army, 1951-54. Mem. Duquesne Club, St. Clair Country Club. Democrat. Presbyterian. Avocations: golf, skiing. Home: 750 Washington Rd Pittsburgh PA 15228

RANDOLPH, ROBERT LEE, economist, educator; b. East St. Louis, Ill., Jan. 2, 1926; s. John Andrew and Willye (Smith) R.; m. Patricia Smith, June 13, 1954 (div. 1986); 1 dau., Heather Elizabeth. A.B., DePauw U., Greencastle, Ind., 1948; M.S., U. Ill., Urbana, 1954, Ph.D., 1958; postdoctoral student, Case Western Res. U., 1960, U. Mich., 1962. From instr. to assoc. prof. econs. Springfield (Mass.) Coll., 1958-65, chmn. dept., 1960-63, dir. eve. and summer schs., 1960-64; dep. exec. dir. Equal Employment Opportunity Commn., Washington, 1967-68; dep. assoc. dir. Job Corps, 1965-67; exec. v.p. Chgo. State U., 1969-73; pres. Westfield (Mass.) Coll., 1973-79; vice-chancellor Mass. State Coll. System, 1979-81; pres. Ala. State U., 1981-83; prof. econs. U. Montevallo, Ala., 1983-86; pres. Randolph Assocs., Birmingham, Ala., Boston, 1983-91, Hyannis, Mass., 1991—; pres. State C.C., East St. Louis, Ill., 1993-95; cons. to industry. Author articles, monographs. Vice pres. Springfield Urban League, 1962-66; bd. dirs. Wesson Hosp., Springfield, Holyoke (Mass.) Hosp., Sickle-Cell Anemia Found.; mem. Cape Cod Commn., 1996—. Served to lt. (j.g.) USNR, 1943-45, 50-51. Decorated Bronze Star; recipient Danforth Found. award, 1943; Republic Steel Found. award, 1961; Vice Pres.'s award excellence pub. service U.S. Govt., 1967; Outstanding Alumni award Lincoln High Sch., E. St. Louis, 1973, Alumni Svc. award U. Ill., 1990, DePauw U., 1991; Navy V-12 scholar, 1943-45; State of Ill. scholar, 1952-56; Bailey fellow, 1957-58, Carnegie fellow, 1962. Mem. Am. Assn. State Colls. and Univs. (chmn. personnel com. 1974-75), Am. Assn. Polit. and Social Scis., Am. Econ. Assn., Phi Delta Kappa, Alpha Phi Omega, Kappa Alpha Psi. Clubs: Quandrangle (Chgo.), Internat. (Washington), Cape (Cape Cod). Home: 101 John Joseph Rd Harwich MA 02645-2822

RANDOLPH, SCOTT HOWARD, chemical company executive; b. Chgo., May 8, 1962; s. Robert David and Jeannette Dominica R.; m. Constance Lynn Randolph; children: Ryan Scott, Janelle Marie. BS, U.S. Naval Acad., 1984; MBA, George Washington U., 1985. Cert. mgmt. acct. Commd. ensign USN, 1984, advanced through grades to lt., 1989, ret., 1989; fin. analyst Gen. Chem. Corp., Parsippany, N.J., 1989; asst. contr. Gen. Chem. Corp., Green River, Wyo., 1989-91; contr. N.Am. Chem. Co., Trona, Calif., 1991-93; v.p. fin. and adminstrn. Harris Chem. Group, London, 1993-95; v.p. strategic planning and devel. Harris Chem. Group, Overland Park, Kans., 1995—. Judge ann. student speakers program Lyons Club, Trona, 1992. Mem. Inst. Mgmt. Accts., Sigma Iota Epsilon, Omicron Delta Epsilon, Beta Gamma Sigma, Phi Kappa Phi. Avocations: basketball, tennis, travel, softball. Office: Harris Chem Group Inc 8300 College Blvd Overland Park KS 66210-1841

RANDOM, IDA, production designer. Art dir.: (films) On Golden Pond, 1981, Partners, 1982, Frances, 1982; prodn. designer: (TV movies) The Kid from Nowhere, 1982, First Flight, 1989, (films) The Big Chill, 1983, Irreconcilable Differences, 1984, Body Double, 1984, Silverado, 1985, About Last Night..., 1986, Throw Momma from the Train, 1987, Who's That Girl?, 1987, Rainman, 1988 (Academy award nomination best art direction 1988), The War of the Roses, 1989, How I Got into College, 1989, Defending Your Life, 1991, Hoffa, 1992, Housesitter, 1992, Wyatt Earp, 1994. Office: care Spyros Skouras Skouras Agency 725 Arizona Ave Ste 406 Santa Monica CA 90401-1736*

RANDS, BERNARD, composer, educator; b. Sheffield, Eng., Mar. 2, 1934. B.Music, U. Wales, 1956, M.Music, 1958; pvt. student composition, 1958-62; MusD (hon.), U. Sheffield, U.K., 1996. Former concert performer Europe, Australia and U.S.; co-founding artistic dir. Contemp Music. Fest, Calif. Inst. Arts; lectr. U. Wales, 1960-66; vis. fellow Princeton U., N.J., 1966-67; mem. faculty music, Granada fellow creative arts York U., 1968-75; composer in residence U. Ill, 1967-68; fellow creative arts Brasenose Coll., Oxford U., Eng., 1972-73; prof. music U. Calif.-San Diego, 1975-85, founder, conductor SONOR; prof. music Boston U., 1985-89, Harvard U., 1989—; composer in residence Phila. Orch., 1989-96. Compositions include Actions for Six, 1963, Wildtrack 1, 2 & 3, 1969-75, Mésalliance, 1972, AUM, 1974, Madrigali, 1977, déjà, 1979, Obbligato, 1980, Canti Lunatici, 1980/81, Canti del Sole for tenor and orch., 1982/83 (Pulitzer prize 1984), Le Tambourin: Sts. #1 and 2, 1984, Hiraeth for cello and orch., 1987, Ceremonial II, 1988, "...in the receding mist...", 1988, "...among the voices...", 1988, "...body and shadow...", 1989, Bells, 1989, Canti dell' Eclisse for bass and orch., 1991, Canti d'Amor, 1991, "...where the murmurs die...", 1991-92, Symphony, 1994, Canzoni per Orch., 1995. Harkness Internat. fellow Commonwealth Fund N.Y., 1966; grantee Nat. Endowment Arts, 1977, 81, 86, 89, 91, 93; recipient Calif. Arts Council award, 1978, 92, Koussevitzky award, 1984, 94, Barlow award, 1994. Office: Harvard U Dept Music Cambridge MA 02138*

RANDZA, JASON MICHAEL, engineer; b. Ellwood City, Pa., June 18, 1963; s. Frank Anthony and Jean Ann (Tracy) R. BS in Aerospace Engring., Pa. State U., 1985; postgrad., Camp Cmty. Coll. Cert. pvt. pilot. Engr. Atlantic Rsch. Corp., Gainesville, Va., 1985-90; control rm. operator Hadson Power #11, Franklin, Va., 1991; tng. coord. LG&E Westmoreland Southampton, Franklin, Va., 1991-96, plant engr., 1996-97, team leader, 1997—; process engr. SONY Electronics, Mt. Pleasant, Pa., 1997—. Mem. AIAA, Nat. Assn. Rocketry, Pa. State U. Alumni Assn., Tripoli Rocketry Assn., Cousteau Soc., Am. Kitefliers Assn., Tau Beta Pi, Sigma Gamma Tau. Republican. Roman Catholic. Avocations: rocketry, hang gliding, kite flying, weight training, aerobics. Home: 504 Fairlane Blvd New Galilee PA 16141

RANGAN, CHAKRAVARTHI RAVI, environmental engineer; b. Madras, India, June 9, 1956; came to U.S., 1988; s. Chakravarthi and Tara Rangan; m. Rashmi Mishra, Nov. 8, 1981; 1 child, Artika. BS, Directorate Marine Engring., Calcutta, 1977; MS, U. Del., 1990. Profl. engr., Del. Jr. engr. Seven Seas Transp., Bombay, 1977-80; 1st engr. Garware Shipping Corp., Bombay, 1980-83; chief engr. Tolani Shipping Co., Bombay, 1985-88; from environ. engr. I to environ. engr. IV Del. Dept. Natural Resources & Environ. Control, New Castle, 1990—. Recipient Gov.'s award for excellence in state govt. Mem. ASTM (subcom. 1993—), Inst. Engrs. India, Inst. Marine Engrs. India, Inst. Engrs. U.K., Nat. Assn. Corrosion Engrs. (cert. cathodic protection splst., Gov.'s award for excellence 1996). Avocations: automobile repair, woodworking. Home: 114 Cardiff Ct W Newark DE 19711 Office: Del Dept Natural Resources& Environ Control 715 Grantham Ln New Castle DE 19720-4801

RANGEL, CHARLES BERNARD, congressman; b. Harlem, N.Y., June 11, 1930; s. Ralph and Blanche (Wharton) R.; m. Alma Carter, July 26, 1964; children: Steven, Alicia. BS, NYU, 1957; JD, St. John's U. Sch. Law, 1960; LLD (hon.), Wagner Coll., 1982, Atlanta U., 1983, St. John's U., Mt. Sinai Sch. Medicine, NYU, Howard U., 1988, Hofstra U., 1989. Bar: N.Y. 1960. Asst. U.S. atty. So. Dist. N.Y., 1961-62; mem. N.Y. State Assembly, 1966-70, 92nd-105th Congressess from 19th (now 15th) N.Y. dist., Washington, D.C., 1971—; mem. Ways and Means Com., subcom. on trade, subcom on human resources; mem. Joint Com. on Taxation. Served with AUS, 1948-52, Korea. Decorated Bronze Star, Purple Heart (U.S.); Korean presdl. citations. Home: 40 W 135th St New York NY 10037-2504 Office: US Ho of Reps 2354 Rayburn Ho Office Bldg Washington DC 20515*

RANGELL, LEO, psychiatrist, psychoanalyst; b. N.Y.C., Oct. 1, 1913; s. Morris and Pauline (Kaiser) R.; m. Anita J. Buchwald, Feb. 22, 1939; children: Judith Ellen, Susan Roberta, Richard Neal, Paul Charles. AB, Columbia, 1933; MD, U. Chgo., 1937. Diplomate Am. Bd. Neurology and Psychiatry, 1943. Intern Bklyn. Jewish Hosp., 1937-39; resident neurology Montefiore Hosp., N.Y.C., 1939; resident psychiatry Grasslands Hosp., Valhalla, N.Y., 1940, N.Y. State Psychiat. Inst. and Hosp., N.Y.C., 1941; pvt. practice neurology and psychiatry N.Y.C., 1942-43; instr. neurology Columbia U. Coll. Physicians and Surgeons, 1942-46; Stroock rsch. fellow neuropsychiatry Montefiore Hosp., 1942-43; psychoanalytic tng. N.Y. Psychoanalytic Inst., later L.A. Psychoanalytic Inst., 1941-49; tng. analyst L.A. Psychoanalytic Inst., 1956—, dir. extension divsn., 1956-57, mem. bd. trustees, 1958—; pvt. practice psychoanalysis and neuropsychiatry Beverly Hills and L.A., 1946—; cons. Reiss-Davis Clinic Child Guidance, L.A., 1953-65; clin. prof. psychiatry Sch. Medicine UCLA, 1953—; clin. prof. psychiatry/psychoanalysis U. Calif., San Francisco, 1976—; fellow Ctr. Advanced Study Behavioral Scis., Stanford, 1962-63, Ctr. Advanced Psychoanalytic Studies, Princeton, N.J., 1962-70, Ctr. Advanced Psychoanalytic Studies, Aspen, Colo., 1970, 86; John B. Turner vis. prof. psychiatry Columbia U. Psychoanalytic Clinic for Tng. and Rsch., N.Y.C., 1971-72. Mem. editl. bd. Israel Annals Psychiatry and Related Disciplines, 1973—, Jour. Phila. Psychoanalytic Assn., Rev. Psychoanalytic Books, 1980—; contbr. numerous articles to profl. jours. Pres. bd. dirs. Westwood Hosp., L.A., 1959-60. Maj. M.C., USAAF, 1943-46. Guggenheim fellow, 1971-72; Recipient Internat. Clin. Essay prize Brit. Inst. Psychoanalysis, 1951, 53, Disting. Alumni award U. Chgo. Sch. Medicine, 1987, Sigourney Hon. award, 1991. Mem. Am. Psychoanalytic Assn. (pres. 1961-62, 66-67, bd. editors 1956-60, 62-66, 76-79, cons. 1979-81, 82-84, Edn. award Phila. chpt. 1978, Jour. award 1981, Hartmann award N.Y. chpt. 1985), L.A. Psychoanalytic Soc. (pres. 1956-58, 64-65, hon. mem. 1980—), Internat. Psychoanalytic Assn. (v.p. 1967-69, pres. 1969-71, 71-73, hon. v.p. 1994—), Am. Psychiat. Assn., So. Calif. Psychiat. Assn. (pres. 1955-56), So. Calif. Psychoanalytic Soc. (hon. mem. 1986), Peruvian Psychoanalytic Soc. (hon. mem. 1987). Home and Office: 456 N Carmelina Ave Los Angeles CA 90049-2704 also: Spindrift Rd Carmel Hglds CA 93923

RANIS, GUSTAV, economist, educator; b. Darmstadt, Germany, Oct. 24, 1929; s. Max and Bettina (Goldschmidt) R.; m. Ray Lee Finkelstein, June 15, 1958; children: Michael Bruce, Alan Jonathan, Bettina Suzanne. BA summa cum laude, Brandeis U., 1952, hon. degree, 1982; MA, Yale U., 1953, PhD, 1956. Asst. adminstr. program and policy AID/Dept. of State, 1965-67; dir. Econ. Growth Ctr. Yale U., New Haven, 1967-75, prof. econs., 1964—, Frank Altschul prof. internat. econs., 1981—; dir. Yale Ctr. Internat. and Area Studies, 1996—; Ford Found. vis. prof. U. De Los Andes,

Bogota, Colombia, 1976-77; Ford Found. faculty fellow Colegio de Mex., 1971-72; fellow Inst. for Advanced Study, Berlin, 1993-94; cons. World Bank, AID, Ford Found., ILO, FAO, Inter-Am. Devel. Bank. Author: (with John Fei) Development of the Labor Surplus Economy: Theory and Policy, 1964, (with Fei and Shirley Kuo) Growth with Equity: The Taiwan Case, 1979, (with Keijiro Otsuka and Gary Saxonhouse) Comparative Technology Choice in Development, 1988, (with F. Stewart and E. Angeles-Reyes) Linkages in Developing Economies: A Philippine Study, 1990, (with S.A. Mahmood) Political Economy of Development Policy Change, 1992; editor: Taiwan: From Developing to Mature Economy, 1992, En Route to Modern Economic Growth: Latin America in the 1990s, 1994; co-editor: The State of Development Economics, 1988, Science and Technology: Lessons for Development Policy, 1990. Trustee Brandeis U., 1967-93, chmn. acad. affairs com., 1986-93. Social Sci. Rsch. Coun. fellow, Japan, 1955-56. Mem. Am. Econ. Assn., Coun. Fgn. Rels., Overseas Develop. Coun. (mem. adv. com.). Home: 7 Mulberry Rd Woodbridge CT 06525-1716 Office: Yale U Econ Growth Ctr 27 Hillhouse Ave New Haven CT 06511-3703

RANK, EVERETT GEORGE, government official; b. Fresno, Calif., Dec. 1, 1921; s. Everett George and Evelyn Lydia (Dawson) R.; m. Evelyn Ingeborg Karschen, Apr. 30, 1948; children—Patricia, Judy, Ginny. Student pub. sch., Clovis, Calif. Farmer Fresno, 1946-81; chmn. Fresno County Agrl. Stblzn. and Conservation Service, 1959-69, Calif. Agrl. Stblzn. and Conservation Service, Berkeley, 1969-73; western regional dir. Agrl. Stblzn. and Conservation Service, Dept. Agr., Washington, 1974-76, adminstr., 1981-86. Pres. Clovis Unified Sch. Bd., 1959-72; bd. govs. U. Calif.-Fresno, 1977-81. Served with USN, 1941-45, PTO. Mem. Masons (32 degree), Shriners. Republican. Baptist. Avocation: golf. Home: 11868 Old Friant Rd Fresno CA 93720-9701

RANK, LARRY GENE, management consultant; b. Auburn, Ind., July 14, 1935; s. Lloyd R. Rank and Elizabeth M. (Williamson) Jackson; m. Bette Whitehurst, May 2, 1959; children: Kevin, Karen. Grad., Am. Inst. Banking, 1962, U. Balt., 1969, Grad. Sch. Banking, Brown U., 1975, Nat. Council Savs. Instns., 1985. Asst. treas. Provident Savs. Bank, Balt., 1967-70, v.p., 1975-76, treas., v.p., 1976-79, sr. v.p., treas., 1979-82; exec. v.p. Provident Bank Md., Balt., 1982-85, pres., chief operating officer, 1985-90; dir. Provident Bank Md., 1984-90; mng. dir. Jannotta, Bray & Assocs. Inc., Balt., 1991-92; exec. dir. Big Bros. and Big Sisters Ctrl. Md. Inc., 1993-96; bd. dirs. Raise, Inc., One to One. Bd. dirs. Children's Cancer Found., Inc., Balt., 1984-90, Balt. chpt. ARC, 1990-92, bd. dirs., 1984—; divsn. chmn. United Way of Ctrl. Md., Balt., 1984-85, group chair, chair pub. sector mktg. com., Mktg. Task Force, bd. dirs., 1991-93; blood chmn. ARC, 1984-87, bd. dirs., first vice chair, 1988-89, Balt. Regional chpt., mem. campaign cabinet, hon. chmn 1988 ARC Humanitarian Award Dinner; chair Gov.'s Vol. Awards Selection com., 1989; chmn. Am. Heart Assn.-Heart Ball, 1989, bd. dirs. Am. Heart Assn., 1989-95, treas. 1992-94; mem. Vol. Coun. on EqualOpportunity; bd. trustees Md. Banking Sch., chmn. bd. trustees; chmn. bd. Neighborhood Housing Svcs., 1990; mem. 1988 Com. for a Capital Affair; bd. dirs. Balt. Goodwill Industries, 1989—, 1st vice chmn., 1992; trustee Northwest Hosp. Ctr., 1988, exec. com., 1989-95, chair capital campaign, 1990—, sec., 1992, 1st v.p. 1992-94, vice-chmn. bd., 1996—; exec. dir. Big Bros./Big Sisters of Ctrl. Md., 1993-96, bd. dirs., 1993-97. Mem. Nat. Coun. Savs. Instns. (mem. ecn. com. 1984-85), Assn. Corp. Growth (pres. 1985-86), Assn. Balt. Area Grantmakers, Am. Inst. Banking (chmn. sr. exec. commn. 1989), Md. Hosp. Assn. (mem. PAC com.), Deacon Club, Wake Forest Wildcat Club, Villanova Club, Hunt Valley Golf Club, Camden Club. Lutheran. Avocations: golf, sports, books, travel.

RANKAITIS, SUSAN, artist; b. Cambridge, Mass., Sept. 10, 1949; d. Alfred Edward and Isabel (Shimkus) Rankaitis; m. Robbert Flick, June 5, 1976. B.F.A. in Painting, U. Ill., 1971; M.F.A. in Visual Arts, U. So. Calif., 1977. Rsch. asst., art dir. Plato Lab., U. Ill., Urbana, 1971-75; art instr. Orange Coast Coll., Costa Mesa, Calif., 1977-83; chair dept. art Chapman Coll., Orange, Calif., 1983-90; Fletcher Jones chair in art Scripps Coll., Claremont, Calif., 1990—; represented by Robert Mann Gallery, N.Y.C.; overview panelist visual arts Nat. Endowment for Arts, 1983, 84. One-woman shows include Los Angeles County Mus. Art, 1983, Internat. Mus. Photography, George Eastman House, 1983, Gallery Min. Tokyo, 1988, Ruth Bloom Gallery, Santa Monica, 1989, 90, 92, Schneider Mus., Portland, Ore., 1990; Ctr. for Creative Photography, 1991, Robert Mann Gallery, N.Y.C., 1994, Mus. Contemporary Photography, Chgo., 1994; represented in permanent collections U. N.Mex. Art, Santa Monica Coll., Ctr. for Creative Photography, Mus. Modern Art, Santa Barbara Mus. Art, Los Angeles County Mus. Art, Mpls. Inst. Arts, San Francisco Mus. Modern Art, Mus. Modern Art, Lodz, Poland, Princeton U. Art Mus., Stanford U. Art Mus., Contemporary Art Mus., Honolulu, Mus. Contemporary Photography, others. Active art auction Venice Family Clinic, 1980—. Nat. Endowment for Arts fellow, 1980, 88, U.S./France fellow, 1989, Agnes Bourne fellow in painting and photography Djerassi Found., 1989; recipient Graves award in Humanities, 1985. Mem. Coll. Art Assn., Los Angeles County Mus. Art, Santa Monica Mus. Art. Studio: Studio 5 1403 S Santa Fe Ave Los Angeles CA 90021-2500

RANKIN, ALFRED MARSHALL, JR., business executive; b. Cleve., Oct. 8, 1941; s. Alfred Marshall and Clara Louise (Taplin) R.; m. Victoire Conley Griffin, June 3, 1967; children: Helen P., Clara T. BA in Econs. magna cum laude, Yale U., 1963, JD, 1966. Mgmt. cons. McKinsey & Co., Inc., Cleve., 1970-73; with Eaton Corp., Cleve., 1974-81, pres. materials handling group, 1981-83, pres. indsl. group, 1984-86, exec. v.p., 1986, vice chmn., chief oper. officer, 1986-89; pres., COO NACCO Industries, Inc., Cleve., 1989-91, pres., CEO, 1991-94, also bd. dirs., chmn., pres., CEO, 1994—, chmn., 1994—; bd. dirs. B.F. Goodrich Co., The Std. Products Co., Vanguard Group. Former pres., trustee Hathaway Brown Sch.; trustee The Cleve. Found., Univ. Hosps. Cleve., Mus. Arts Assn., Univ. Circle, Inc., Cleve. Mus. Art, Greater Cleve. Growth Assn., John Huntington Art Trust, Cleve. Tomorrow; past chairperson The Cleve. Found. Mem. Ohio Bar Assn. Republican. Clubs: Chagrin Valley Hunt, Union, Tavern, Pepper Pike, Kirtland Country (Cleve.); Rolling Rock (Ligonier, Pa.); Met. (Washington). Office: NACCO Industries Inc Ste 300 5875 Landerbrook Dr Mayfield Heights OH 44124

RANKIN, ARTHUR DAVID, paper company executive; b. Bklyn., July 5, 1936; s. David Emerson and Elizabeth Howe (Smart) R.; m. Judith Ann Clark, Sept. 6, 1958; children: Debi Lynn Murlowski, Kristen Lori. B-SChemE, 5-Yr. Cert. Pulp and Paper, U. Maine, Orono, 1960, MS in Pulp and Paper, 1960. Tech. svc. engr. Mead Corp., Chillicothe, Ohio, 1960-65; product engr. Jones div. Beloit Corp., Dalton, Mass., 1965-69; tech. asst. paper supt. Crown Zellerbach St. Francisville, La., 1969-71; stock prep. supr. Crown Zellerbach, St. Francisville, La., 1971-74; paper machine supt. Appleton Papers, Inc., Combined Locks, Wis., 1974-84, steps project coord., 1984-85, sr. paper machine supt., 1986-88, sr. prodn. assoc., 1988-90, edn. and mill planning mgr., 1991-95, tech. and devel. mgr. Coated Free Sheet divsn., 1995—; instr. video U. Wis., Stevens Point, 1988, 89. Officer Jaycees, Waverly, Ohio, 1960-63, Chillicothe, Ohio, 1963-65, Pittsfield, Mass., 1965-69; bd. dirs. acad. adv. coun. U. Minn. Paper Sci. Sch., Mpls., 1988—; bd. dirs. U. Minn. Paper, 1988—; acad. adv. coun. paper sci. U. Wis., Stevens Point, 1987—, bd. dirs., 1990—. Mem. ASTM, TAPPI, Nat. Paper Indsl. Mgmt. Assn. (bd. dirs. 1988, pres. 1993, treas. 1994—, Del Boutin award 1995), North Ctrl. Paper Indsl. Mgmt. Assn. (bd. dirs. 1977—). Republican. Congregationalist. Avocations: reading, golf, YMCA fitness center, wine collecting and study. Home: 1408 S Lee St Appleton WI 54915-3824

RANKIN, CLYDE EVAN, III, lawyer; b. Phila., July 3, 1950; s. Clyde Evan, Jr. and Mary E. (Peluso) R. A.B., Princeton U., 1972; J.D., Columbia U., 1975; postgrad. Hague Acad. Internat. Law, 1975. Bar: N.Y., N.J., D.C., U.S. Supreme Ct. Law clk. to judge U.S. Dist. Ct. So. Dist. N.Y., 1975-77; assoc. Debevoise, Plimpton, Lyons & Gates, N.Y.C., 1977-79; assoc. Coudert Bros., N.Y.C., 1979-83, ptnr., 1984—. Trustee The Rensselaerville (N.Y.) Inst., 1989—, Coun. on Fgn. Rels., 1996—. Stone scholar, 1974. Mem. ABA, Assn. of Bar of City of N.Y., N.Y. State Bar Assn., D.C. Bar Assn., N.J. Bar Assn. Roman Catholic. Club: Amateur Comedy (N.Y.C.). Contbr. article to legal jour. Office: Coudert Bros 1114 Avenue Of The Americas New York NY 10036-7703

RANKIN, ELIZABETH ANNE DESALVO, nurse, psychotherapist, educator, consultant; b. Wurtzburg, Germany, Sept. 30, 1948; d. William Joseph and Elizabeth Agnes (Faraci) DeSalvo; m. Richard Forrest Rankin, June 5, 1971; children: William Alvin, David Michael. BSN, U. Md., Balt., 1970, MS, 1972; PhD., U. Md., College Park, 1979. Cert. health edn. specialist, specialist stress mgmt. edn., master hypnotherapist, master practitioner neurolinguistic programmer, nonaquatic exercise instrn.; cert. Nat. Bd. Cert. Clin. Hypnotherapists. Prof. U. Md.; mem. dept. psychiat. mental health/community health nursing U. Md. at Balt. Sch. Nursing, dir. div. bus. and industry; prof. U. Md.; cns. Ctr. for Alternative Medicine, Pain Rsch. and Evaluation; cons. various publs. Co-author of books; contbr. chpts. to books, articles to profl. jours.; editor: Network Independent Study; mem. editl. bd. Md. Nurse, Delmarva Found. Newsletter. Advisor U. Md. chpt. Nat. Student Nurses Assn. Recipient Twila Stinecker Leadership award, 1987, Leadership Excellence award Md. Assn. Nursing Students, 1990-92. Mem. ANA, Md. Nursing Assn. (bd. dirs., exec. com., 2d v.p., appointments mgr.), U. Md. Assn. Nursing Students (chpt. Nat. Student Nurses Assn. advisor), Nat. Coun. Family Rels., Coun. Nurse Rschrs., Nat. Assn. Cert. Health Educators (charter), Am. Assn. Profl. Hypnotherapists, Milton H. Erickson Found., Washington Soc. Clin. Hypnosis, Aquatic Exercise Assn., Capital Area Roundtable on Informatics in Nursing, Sigma Theta Tau, Phi Epsilon Alpha, Phi Kappa Phi, Alpha Xi Delta.

RANKIN, HAYWOOD FORNEY, diplomat; b. Washington, July 31, 1946; s. Forney Anderson and Jean Smith (Cantrell) R.; m. Sabine Irmgard Schmid, Aug. 5, 1982; children: Johanna, Susanna. AB in Sociology, U. N.C., 1968, JD, 1971; BS in Geology, Oxford U., Eng., 1982. Bar: N.C. 1971. Law clk. to chief justice N.C. Supreme Ct., Raleigh, 1971-72; vice consul Am. Consulate Gen., Tangier, Morocco, 1973-75; consul Am. Consulate Gen., Port Said, Egypt, 1977-79; polit. analyst Bureau Intelligence and Rsch. Dept. State, Washington, 1982-84; polit. officer Am. Embassy, Damascus, Syria, 1984-86; chief polit. sect. Am. Embassy, Baghdad, Iraq, 1986-88; dep. chief mission Am. Embassy, Muscat, Oman, 1989-92, Algiers, Algeria, 1992-94; dep. dir. Office Near East South Asia Bur. Intelligence & Rsch., Washington, 1994-95, dir., 1995-96; polit.-econ. counsellor Am. Embassy, Abidjan, Côte d'Ivoire, 1996—. Recipient Meritorious Honor award, 1986, Superior Honor award, 1992. Democrat. Presbyterian. Avocations: travel, photography. Home: 144 Redlair Ln Gastonia NC 28056 Office: Am Embassy Abidjan Dept State Washington DC 20521-2010

RANKIN, JACQUELINE ANNETTE, communications expert, educator; b. Omaha, Nebr., May 19, 1925; d. Arthur C. and Virdie (Gillispie) R. BA, Calif. State U., L.A., 1964, MA, 1966; MS in Mgmt., Calif. State U., Fullerton, 1977; EdD, U. LaVerne, Calif., 1981. Tchr. Rowland High Sch., La Habra, Calif., 1964-66, Lowell High Sch., La Habra, Calif., 1966-69, Pomona (Calif.) High Sch., 1969-75; program asst. Pomona Adult Sch., 1975-82; dir. Child Abuse Prevention Program, 1985-86; exec. dir. child abuse prevention Calif. Dept. Pub. Svc., 1985-87; instr. Ind. U., Purdue U. Ind., 1993; assoc. prof. speech Ball State U., Muncie, Ind., 1993-94; instr. No. Va. U., 1994—, trainer Loudoun campus, 1996; faculty evening divsn. Mt. San Antonio C.C., 1966-72; asst. prof. speech Ball State U., Muncie, Ind., 1993; instr. No. Va. U., Alexandria, Annandale, Manassas, Woodbridge, 1995—; assoc. faculty dept. comm. and theatre, Ind. U., Purdue U., Indpls., 1993; trainer internat. convs., sales groups, staffs of hosps., others; spkr., writer, trainer, lectr., cons. in field. Columnist, Jackie's World, Topics Newspapers, Indpls.; author: Body Language: First Impressions, Body Language in Negotiations and Sales, Body Language in Love & Romance; contbr. articles to profl. jours. Mem. Fairfax County Dem. Com.; mem. adv. coun., mem. nat. capital chpt. bd. dirs. ARC. Mem. Internat. Platform Assn., Pi Lambda Theta, Phi Delta Kappa. Home and Office: 7006 Elkton Dr Springfield VA 22152-3330

RANKIN, JAMES WINTON, lawyer; b. Norfolk, Va., Sept. 9, 1943; s. Winton Blair and Edith (Griffin) R.; m. Donna Lee Carpenter, June 25, 1966 (dec.); children—Thomas James, William Joseph, Elizabeth Jeanne; m. JoAnne Katherine Murray, Feb. 11, 1978. A.B. magna cum laude, Oberlin Coll., 1965; J.D. cum laude, U. Chgo., 1968. Bar: Ill. 1968, U.S. Dist. Ct. (no. dist.) Ill. 1969, U.S. Ct. Appeals (7th cir.) 1971, U.S. Ct. Appeals (5th cir.) 1979, U.S. Supreme Ct. 1975, Calif. 1986. Law clk. U.S. Dist. Ct. (no. dist.) Ill., 1968-69; assoc. Kirkland & Ellis, Chgo., 1969-73, ptnr., 1973—. Mem. ABA, Order of Coif, Mid-Am. Club, Univ. Club, Mich. Shores Club, Kenilworth Club, Ephriam Yacht Club. Presbyterian. Home: 633 Kenilworth Ave Kenilworth IL 60043-1070 Office: Kirkland & Ellis 200 E Randolph St Chicago IL 60601-6436

RANKIN, ROBERT, retired educational foundation executive; b. Des Moines, Sept. 14, 1915; s. Wiley Strange and Estelle Blanche (Renne) R.; m. Martha Jean Roberts, Sept. 7, 1940; children: Mary Renne (Mrs. Joseph L. Sturdevant Jr.), Margaret Lloyd, Wiley Robert, William Roberts. B.A., U. Iowa, 1937; B.D., Yale, 1940, M.A., 1942; D.D. (hon.), Lindenwood Coll., St. Charles, Mo., 1964, Northland Coll., Ashland, Wis., 1981; D.H.L. (hon.), U. So. Calif., 1967. Ordained to ministry Methodist Ch., 1944, United Ch. Christ, 1960; minister Sunnyvale, Calif., 1942-44; campus minister, lectr. religion, dir. YMCA Oberlin Coll., 1946-51; chaplain, assoc. prof. religion Claremont Colls., 1951-58; exec. dir. Rockefeller Bros. Theol. Fellowship Program, Princeton, N.J., 1954-55; assoc. dir. Danforth Found., St. Louis, 1958-66; v.p. Danforth Found., 1966-80, dir. programs campus ministry, 1958-80, assoc. program, 1958-75; cons. Fund Theol. Edn., Lilly Endowment, Pres.'s Commn. on Campus Unrest; chmn. St. Louis Met. Conf. Edn. Culturally Disadvantaged, 1962; cons. to bd. dirs. Nat. Inst. for Campus Ministry, 1974-83; mem. St. Louis region selection panel White House fellows, 1975, 77, chmn., 1978; mem. Nat. Commn. Higher Edn., United Meth. Ch., 1975-77; chmn. exec. com. Wingspread Conf., 1969-73. Author, editor: The Recovery of Spirit in Higher Education, 1980; author articles, chpts. in books; edit. adv. bd. Religion and Intellectual Life, 1984—. Trustee Sch. Theology at Claremont, 1955-59, advisor, 1985—, Am. Friends of Wilton Park, 1975, Healing Community St. Louis, 1976-81, Claremont, 1984-90, Nat. Task Force for Disability and the Art, 1978-81, Evangelicals for Social Action; mem. Com. on Disability City of Claremont; resident Pilgrim Place, Claremont, 1981; advisor Pilgrim Festival, 1983—, Pilgrim Aquatic Fitness Ctr., 1993—. Recipient E. Harris Harbison hon. award for gifted teaching, 1970; Fellow Wilton Park Conf., Sussex, Eng.; Fellow Soc. Values Higher Edn. Mem. Nat. Assn. Coll. and Univ. Chaplains, Assn. for Religion and Intellectual Life, Nat. Campus Ministry Assn., Am. Friends Svc. Com., Am. Assn. UN, Am. Acad. Religion, Am. Assn. for Higher Edn., ACLU, NAACP, Sigma Chi, Univ. Claremont Club. Mem. United Ch. of Christ. Home: 627 Leyden Ln Claremont CA 91711-4236

RANKIN, ROBERT ARTHUR, journalist; b. Richmond, Va., May 31, 1949; s. Arthur Norton and Martha Louise (Rountree) R.; m. Janis Johnson, May 11, 1979; 1 child, Benjamin John. BA in Polit. Sci., Randolph Macon Coll., 1971; MA in Govt., U. Va., 1974. Reporter Richmond News Leader, Va., 1972-75; reporter Congl. Quar., Washington, 1975-78; editorial writer Miami Herald, Fla., 1980-85, Phila. Inquirer, 1985-87; nat. corr. Washington bur. Knight Ridder Newspapers, 1987—. V.p. Civic Assn. Hollin Hills, Alexandria, Va., 1991-92. Co-recipient Pulitzer prize for editorial writing 1983, Olive Branch award N.Y.U. Ctr. for War, Peace and The News Media, 1990; recipient 1st prize Va. Press Assn., 1974; best editorial award Phila. chpt. Sigma Delta Chi, 1987; Walter Bagehot fellow Columbia U., 1978-79. Mem. White House Corres. Assn. (bd. govs., 1996-97), Nat. Press Club. Office: Knight Ridder Newspapers 700 National Press Building Washington DC 20045-1701

RANKIN, SCOTT DAVID, artist, educator; b. Newark, Mar. 21, 1954; s. Clymont J. and Jean L. (Lane) R.; m. Linda K. Piemonte, Sept. 3, 1989. BFA, Tyler Sch. of Art, Phila., 1976; MFA, UCLA, 1980. Asst. prof. U. Iowa, Iowa City, 1985-86, U. Chgo., 1986-94; assoc. prof. Ill. State U., Normal, 1994—; video cons. Math. Edn. Rsch. Project, L.A., 1991-93, 3d ann. math. and sci. study UCLA dept. psychology, 1994-95. Prodr., dir.: (videotapes) Fugue, 1985, This and that (version 1), 1987, (version 2), 1990, The Pure, 1993, Flow, 1997. Regional media arts fellow Nat. Endowment for Arts, 1984, visual artist's fellow Ill. Arts Coun., 1989, 90, visual artist's fellow Nat. Endowment for Arts, 1990, 93.

RANKIN, TERESA P. FRONCEK, insurance educator, consultant, former state agency administrator; b. Camp Lejeune, N.C., May 5, 1952; d. Richard A. and Carol Ann (Leverenz) Froncek; m. Robert W. Rankin, Dec. 22, 1978. BA, Ariz. State U., 1974; JD, U. Ariz., 1979. Chartered property casualty underwriter. Atty. Smith & Gamble, Carson City, Nev., 1979-80; dep. legis. counsel Legis. Counsel Bur., Carson City, 1981-83; chief ins. asst. Nev. Ins. Divsn., Carson City, 1984-91, commr. ins., 1991-95. Recipient Recognition award U. Nev. Las Vegas-Inst. Ins. & Risk Mgmt., 1993. Mem. Nat. Assn. Ins. Commrs., Reno Jaquar Club (bd. dirs. 1986-95). Avocations: collecting English cars, quilting. Home and Office: 4221 Tara St Carson City NV 89706-1333

RANKIN, WILLIAM BROWN, II, airport administrator. BS in Aviation Mgmt., Mid. Tenn. State U.; MS in Aviation Mgmt., Embry-Riddle U. Airport mgr. Smith-Reynolds Airport, Winston-Salem, N.C., 1974-85; airport dir. Cedar Rapids (Iowa) Regional Airport, 1985-89; mgr. ops. divsn. Washington Nat. Airport, 1989-94; dir. aviation El Paso (Tex.) Internat. Airport, 1994—. Dir. El Paso Conv. and Tourism Bd.; past dir. Cedar Rapids Conv. and Vis. Bur., Greater Downtown Assn. Cedar Rapids, Auburn U. Scholarship Com. Mem. Am. Assn. Airport Execs. (accredited), S.E. Airport Mgrs. Assn., N.C. Assn. Airports (past dir.). Office: El Paso Internat Airport 6701 Convair Rd El Paso TX 79925-1029

RANKIN, WILLIAM PARKMAN, educator, former publishing company executive; b. Boston, Feb. 6, 1917; s. George William and Bertha W. (Clowe) R.; m. Ruth E. Gerard, Sept. 12, 1942; children: Douglas W., Joan W. BS, Syracuse U., 1941; MBA, NYU, 1949, PhD, 1979. Sales exec. Redbook mag., N.Y.C., 1945-49; sales exec. This Week mag., N.Y.C., 1949-55, adminstrv. exec., 1955-60, v.p., 1957-60, v.p., dir. advt. sales, sales devel. dir., 1960-63, exec. v.p., 1963-69; gen. exec. newspaper div. Time Inc., N.Y.C., 1969-70; gen. mgr. feature svc. Newsweek, Inc., N.Y.C., 1970-74, fin. and ins. advt. mgr., 1974-81; prof., asst. to the dir. Walter Cronkite Sch. Journalism and Telecommunication, Ariz. State U., Tempe, 1981—; lectr. Syracuse U., NYU, Berkeley Sch. Author: Selling Retail Advertising, 1944; The Technique of Selling Magazine Advertising, 1949; Business Management of Consumer Magazines, 1980, 2 ed. 1984, The Practice of Newspaper Management, 1986. Mem. Dutch Treat Club. Home: 1220 E Krista Way Tempe AZ 85284-1545 also: Rustics Rd Bomoseen VT 05732 Office: Ariz State U Walter Cronkite Sch Journalism/Telecom Tempe AZ 85287-1305

RANKIN-SMITH, PAMELA, photographer; b. Kansas City, Kans., Jan. 12, 1918; d. Dexter Leon and Ruth Dee (Millard) Rankin; m. George W. Witcher, 1943 (div. 1945); 1 child, Vann Leigh Witcher; m. A. Arthur Smith, 1968 (dec. 1968). Diploma, Dallas Little Theater, 1936; student, U. Tex., 1937-41; lic. in real estate, New Sch., N.Y.C., 1954; cert., Sogetsu Sch. Ikebana, N.Y.C., 1954-96. Real estate agt. N.Y.C., 1989-97; flower arranger Ikebana Flowers The Met. Mus. Art, Patrons Lounge, N.Y.C., 1989-97. Author: Perfectly Candid, 1994; one-woman photography shows include Soho/Stieglitz Gallery, N.Y.C., 1978, La Galerie, Paris, 1979, Donnell Libr., N.Y.C., 1979, Fed. Hall, N.Y.C., 1978, Nikon House, N.Y.C., 1980, Overseas Press Club, N.Y.C., 1980, Le Gallery, Kent, Conn., 1981, Camera Club N.Y., N.Y.C., 1985. Mem. PEN, Photographic Adminstrs., Inc., Actors Equity Assn., Am. Soc. Media Photographers Ikebana Internat., Nat. Guild Decoupeurs, Mcpl. Art Soc., Nat. Arts Club, Camera Club N.Y., Circle of Confusion. Avocations: oriental painting, decoupage, calligraphy, ikebana. Home: 150 E 69th St New York NY 10021-5704

RANNEY, (JOSEPH) AUSTIN, political science educator; b. Cortland, N.Y., Sept. 23, 1920; s. Frank Addison and Florence Edith (Ranney) R.; m. Elizabeth Mackay (div. Oct. 1975); m. Nancy Boland; children: Joseph, Douglas, Gordon, David. BS, Northwestern U., 1941, LLD (hon.), 1995; MA, U. Oreg., 1943; PhD, Yale U., 1948, DSS (hon.), 1985; LLD (hon.), SUNY, 1986, Northwestern U., 1995. Statistician Douglas Aircraft Corp., Chgo., 1942-44; instr. Yale U., New Haven, 1945-47; from instr. to prof. U. Ill., Urbana, 1947-63; prof. U. Wis., Madison, 1963-76; resident scholar Am. Enterprise Inst., Washington, 1976-86; prof. U. Calif., Berkeley, 1986-91, prof. emeritus, 1991—, chmn. dept. polit. sci., 1987-90. Author: The Doctrine of Responsible Party Government, 1954, Governing, 1958, Curing the Mischiefs of Faction, 1975, Channels of Power, 1983. Mem. Presdl.-Congl. Commn. on Polit. Activity Govtl. Employers, Washington, 1967-68, Dem. Nat. Com. Commn. on Party Structure, Washington, 1969-72, Commn. on Presdl. Debates, Washington, 1980-88; chmn. Gov.'s Commn. on Registration and Voting Participation, Madison, Wis., 1964, social sci. rsch. coun. Com. on Govtl. Processes, 1964-71, coun. on social scis. policy Yale U., 1983-88. Recipient Wilbur Lucius Cross medal Yale U. Grad. Sch., 1977; sr. rsch. fellow NSF, 1970, John Simon Guggenheim fellow, 1974, fellow Ctr. for Advanced Study in Behavioral Scis., 1978. Mem. Am. Polit. Sci. Assn. (pres. 1975-76), Am. Acad. Arts and Scis. (v.p. 1981-84). Home: 990 Regal Rd Berkeley CA 94708-1430 Office: Univ Calif Dept Polit Sci Berkeley CA 94720

RANNEY, CARLETON DAVID, plant pathology researcher, administrator; b. Jackson, Minn., Jan. 23, 1928; s. Carleton Oran and Ada Elizabeth (Harriman) R.; m. Mary Kathryn Ransleben, July 16, 1949; children: David Clayton, Mary Elizabeth. AA, Chaffey Jr. Coll., Ontario, Calif., 1952; BS, Tex. A&M U., 1954, MS, 1955, PhD, 1959. Plant pathologist Crops Rsch. Div. Agrl. Rsch. Svc. USDA, College Station, Tex., 1955-58, Stoneville, Miss., 1958-70; investigations leader Crops Rsch. Div. Agrl. Rsch. Svc. USDA, Beltsville, Md., 1970-72; area dir. Ala. No. Miss. area Agrl. Rsch. Svc. USDA, Starkville, Miss., 1973-78; area dir. Delta States area Agrl. Rsch. Svc. USDA, Stoneville, Miss., 1978-84; area dir. Mid-South area Agrl. Rsch. Svc. USDA, Stoneville, 1984-87; asst. dir. Miss. Agrl. and Forestry Exptl. Stas., Stoneville, 1987-94, head Delta br. sta., 1987-94, emeritus plant pathologist, 1994—; adj. prof. agronomy Miss. State U., 1970-94; sr. exec. svc. USDA, Stoneville, Miss., 1984-87; adv. bd. Belt Wide Meetings Nat. Cotton Coun., Memphis, Tenn., 1987-96. Contbr. articles to profl. jours. Sect. advisor SE2 Order of Arrow, Boy Scouts Am., Miss. and West Tenn., 1973-83; pres. Delta Area coun. Boy Scouts Am., Clarksdale, Miss., 1990-91, Leland Habitat for Humanity, 1995—. Recipient Silver Beaver Boy Scouts Am., 1981, Disting. Svc. Order of Arrow, 1983. Mem. Agron. Soc. Am., Nat. Cotton Disease Coun. (sec. 1959-60, chmn. 1961-62), Lions (pres. Leland club 1995-96), Sigma Xi, Alpha Zeta, Phi Kappa Phi. Methodist. Achievements include development of fungicide control seedling diseases; definition of relationship of microclimate to boll rot of cotton; development of non-mercurial seed treatments. Office: Delta Rsch & Ext Ctr PO Box 197 Stoneville MS 38776-0197

RANNEY, GEORGE ALFRED, lawyer, former steel company executive; b. Chgo., May 30, 1912; s. George Alfred and Cornelia (Williams) R.; m. Nora Ryerson, June 18, 1938 (dec. Mar. 1987); children: George Alfred, Edward R., David M., Nancy R. (Mrs. David F. Levi). A.B., Yale, 1934, LL.B., 1939. Bar: Ill. 1939. Mem. firm Sidley, Austin, Burgess & Smith, Chgo., 1939-62; v.p., gen. counsel Inland Steel Co., Chgo., 62-68; sr. v.p. Inland Steel Co., 1968-71, vice chmn., 1971-77, also dir. Trustee U. Chgo. Served as 1st lt. AUS, 1942-45. Mem. Am., Ill., Chgo. bar assns. Episcopalian. Home: 17370 W Casey Rd Libertyville IL 60048-9748

RANNEY, HELEN MARGARET, physician, educator; b. Summer Hill, N.Y., Apr. 12, 1920; d. Arthur C. and Alesia (Toolan) R. AB, Barnard Coll., 1941; MD, Columbia U., 1947; ScD, U. S.C., 1979, SUNY, Albany, 1996. Diplomate: Am. Bd. Internal Medicine. Intern Presbyn. Hosp., N.Y.C., 1947-48, resident, 1948-50, asst. physician, 1954-60; practice medicine specializing in internal medicine, hematology N.Y.C., 1954-70; instr. Coll. Phys. and Surg. Columbia, N.Y.C., 1954-60; assoc. prof. medicine Albert Einstein Coll. Medicine, N.Y.C., 1960-64, prof. medicine, 1965-70; prof. medicine SUNY, Buffalo, 1970-73; prof. medicine U. Calif., San Diego, 1973-90, chmn. dept. medicine, 1973-86, Disting. physician vet. adminstr., 1986-91; mem. staff Alliance Pharm. Corp., San Diego, 1991—. Master ACP; fellow AAAS; mem. NAS, Inst. Medicine, Am. Soc. for Clin. Investigation, Am. Soc. Hematology, Harvey Soc., Am. Assn. Physicians, Am. Acad. Arts and Scis., Phi Beta Kappa, Sigma Xi, Alpha Omega Alpha. Office: Alliance Pharm Corp 3040 Science Park Rd San Diego CA 92121-1102

RANNEY, MARY ELIZABETH, business executive; b. Louisville, Nov. 10, 1928; d. James William and Erna Marie Katerina (Hansen) Connell; m. Glen Royal Ranney, July 26, 1947; children: Darleen Diane Ranney Bowie, Nancy Elizabeth Ranney Pieratt. Student, Monmouth Coll., 1946-47. Cert. profl. sec., nursing asst. Nursing asst. Monmouth (Ill.) Hosp., 1957-63; asst. in fin. Bd. Pub. Instrn. Collier County, Naples, Fla., 1964-68; sec. 1st Nat. Bank,

Bonita Springs, Fla., 1969-71; founder, dir. Planned Parenthood, Naples, 1972-76; writer Am. Hibiscus Soc., 1977-82; owner Tree Gallery, Naples and Ft. Myers, 1983—; tchr., seedling judge Am. Hibiscus Soc., 1977-79. Author: (brochure) Abortion, 1976; solo performance Fiddler on the Roof, 1976. Chair Fla. Assn. for Repeal Abortion Laws, Lee and Collier County, 1972; founder Abortion Referral Svc. S.W. Fla., 1972-75; founder, dir. Accordion Band, Naples, 1974-79, Floridian Accordion Band, Ft. Myers, 1989-91; founding officer Naples Concert Band, 1972-79; sponsor Am. hibiscus shows, Naples, 1973-81. Recipient Prominent Woman of Cmty. award Naples Star, 1977, 78, 79, Mover of 70's award Naples NOW Mag., 1980, Shaker, Mover and Star award Naples NOW Mag., 1983, Life Work Feature award Naples Star, 1981, Great Achiever award Naples Star, 1982. Mem. NOW (charter nat. pres. 1975-77), Am. Hibiscus Soc. (life, founder Ranney chpt. 1973—, editor Show Chair Manual 1979, Judges Manual 1980, Pres. Svc. award 1979, Hibiscus of Yr. 1980, 82), Meml. Soc. S.W. Fla. (pres. 1975-77). Democrat. Avocations: musician, seamstress, biker, walker, dancer. Home: 3164 Palm Beach Blvd Fort Myers FL 33916-1579

RANNEY, MAURICE WILLIAM, chemical company executive; b. Buffalo, Jan. 13, 1934; s. Maurice Lynford and Helen Hart (Birdsall) R.; m. Theresa Ann Berthot, Oct. 24, 1953 (div. 1974); children: William, Linda, Laurel, James; m. Elisa Ramirez Villegas, Dec. 21, 1974; 1 stepchild, Elisa. BS in Chemistry, Niagara U., 1957, MS in Organic Chemistry, 1959; PhD in Phys. Organic Chemistry, Fordham U., 1967. Group leader, tech. mgr. Union Carbide Corp., Tarrytown, N.Y., 1957-75; gen. mgr. Union Carbide Japan KK, 1976-80; exec. v.p. Showa Union Gosei Co., Ltd., 1976-80; rep. dir. Union Carbide Svcs. Eastern Ltd., 1976-80; dir. Nippon Unicar Co., Ltd., 1976-80, Union Showa KK, 1976-80; pres. Union Carbide Formosa Co., Ltd., Hong Kong, Tokyo, 1980-82; bus. dir. Union Carbide Eastern, Inc., Tokyo, 1982-85; pres., rep. dir. Union Carbide Japan KK, 1986-94; pres. Union Indsl. Gas Corp.; rep. dir. Oriental Union Chem. Corp., 1980-82; mng. dir. Nippon Unicar Co., Ltd., 1982-85; v.p. internat. Union Carbide Chems. and Plastics Co., 1986-94; vice chmn., rep. dir. Nippon Unicar, 1986-95; pres. Nihon Parylene, 1992-94, pres. Internat. Partnerships, 1995; dir. Seaforms, Inc., 1995, Accu-Search, 1995. Author: Flame Retardant Textiles, 1970, Power Coatings, 1971, Synthetic Lubricants, 1972, New Curing Techniques, 1976, Fuel Additives, 1976, Durable Press Fabrics, 1976, Silicones, Vols. I, II, 1977, Reinforced Plastics and Elastomers, 1978, Offshore Oil Technology, 1979, Oil Shale and Tar Sands, 1980, Primary Electrochemical Cell Technology, 1981; contbr. articles to profl. jours. Union Carbide fellow, Mellon Inst. Indsl. Rsch., 1958-60. Achievements include numerous patents in field. Home: # 6 Cotton Hall Ln Hilton Head Island SC 29938

RANNEY, RICHARD RAYMOND, dental educator, researcher; b. Atlanta, July 11, 1939; s. Russell Ballou and Maureen Joan (Bannon) R.; m. Beverly Anne Toton, June 10, 1961 (div.); children—Christine Marie, Kathleen Anne; m. 2d, Patricia Marie DeNoto, Feb. 22, 1969; children—Maureen Frances, Russell Christopher. D.D.S., U. Iowa, 1963; M.S., U. Rochester, 1969; D (hon.), U. Buenos Aires, 1995. Asst. prof. periodontology U. Oreg., 1969-72; assoc. prof. periodontics Va. Commonwealth U., Richmond, 1972-78, prof., 1978-86, dir. grad. periodontics, 1972-76, chmn. dept. periodontics, 1974-77, asst. dean research and grad. affairs, 1977-84, asst. dean research, 1984-86; dir. Clin. Research Ctr. for Periodontal Diseases, 1978-86. Served with USPHS, 1963-66. Nat. Inst. Dental Research grantee, 1970-86; prof. Sch. of Dentistry, U. Ala., Birmingham, 1986-91, dean, 1986-89; prof., dean U. Md., Balt., 1991—. Fellow AAAS, Internat. Coll. Dentists, Am. Coll. Dentists; mem. ADA, Am. Acad. Periodontology, Internat. Assn. Dental Research (pres. 1995-96, basic research in periodontology award 1985), Am. Assn. Dental Rsch. (pres. 1990-91), Am. Assn. Dental Schs., Am. Soc. Microbiology, Sigma Xi, Omicron Kappa Upsilon. Contbr. chpts. to books, articles to profl. jours. Office: U Md 666 W Baltimore St Baltimore MD 21201-1510

RANONE, JOHN LOUIS, school board executive; b. N.Y.C., July 7, 1940; s. Michael Nicholas and Josephine Clara (Iannone) R.; m. Carolyn Margaret Smith, June 13, 1964; children: Michelle Mary, Margaret Anne. AA in data processing, Fairleigh Dickinson, 1960; BA in Elem. Edn., Jersey City State Coll., 1964; AA/Classroom Renaissance, Montclair State Coll., 1969; MA in Adminstrn., Monmouth Coll., 1974. Cert. elem. tchr., adminstr., sex edn., classroom renaissance. Teaching prin. Hollie M. Davis Sch., River Edge, N.J., 1972-77; prin. Lincoln Sch., Ridgefield Park (N.J.) Bd. Edn., 1977-89; dir. curriculum and instruction Ridgefield Park Bd. Edn., 1989—; cons., lectr., N.J. State Dept. Edn., Trenton, 1974—; chmn. N.J. State Adv. Council, Trenton, 1976—; lectr. Jersey City State Coll., 1979—; rep. U.S. Council for Individually Guided Edn., Atlanta, 1979-87; bd. trustees for teacher edn. Felician Coll. Trustee River Edge Pub. Libr., 1978-85. Recipient Outstanding Svc. award, Cath. Youth Orgn., Newark. 1965, Bergen County Outstanding Tchr. award, PTA, 1971, Child Assault Prevention award, N.J. State Dept. Edn., 1988, Halls Motor Co. scholarship, Jersey City, N.J., 1958-59; named to Edn. at the Met., Met. Opera Co., N.Y.C., Workshop Series I, 1988. Mem. Assn. Supervision and Curriculum Devel., Prins. and Suprs. Assn., River Edge Edn. Assn. (pres. 1974-76, v.p. 1972-74), Ridgefield Park Adminstr. Assn. (treas. 1981—), River Edge Dem. Club, Friends of the Libr. Roman Catholic. Avocations: travel, reading, ceramic, collector. Home: 490 Windsor Rd River Edge NJ 07661-1834 Office: Ridgefield Park Bd Edn Ridgefield Park NJ 07660

RANSDELL, TOD ELLIOT, pharmaceutical, parenteral and in vitro diagnostics validation specialist; b. Imperial, Nebr., May 17, 1953; s. Merrill Guy and Rosalie E. Ransdell. BS in Botany, Mont. State U., Bozeman, 1977. Police officer Dillon (Mont.) Police Dept., 1979-80; dept. mgr. Woolco, Bozeman, Mont., 1980-83; lab. coord. Skyland Sci. Svcs., Inc., Bozeman, Mont., 1983-86; sales assoc. S&P Office Supply, Bozeman, Mont., 1986-87; validation specialist Skyland Sci. Svcs., Inc., Bozeman, Mont., 1987-92, sr. validation specialist, 1992; sr. validation specialist Genetic Systems Corp., Redmond, Wash., 1992—; cons. Skyland Sci. Svcs., Inc., Bozeman, Mont., 1987-92. Bd. advisors Jour. Validation Tech., 1996—. Order of Arrow, brotherhood, chpt. chief Boy Scouts Am. (life rank), 1973; pres. Bozeman (Mont.) Jaycees, 1983, 85, Crime Stoppers, 1982; mem. Benevolent and Prtective Order of the Elks, Bozeman, Mont. 1989-94. Mem. NRA, Orgn. Regulatory and Clin. Assocs., Union of Concerned Scientists, Inst. Validation Tech., Parenteral Drug Assn., Bozeman Jr. C. of C., Internat. Soc. Pharm. Engring., Nature Conservancy, Greenpeace, Nat. Pks. and Conservation Assn., Seattle Mountaineers. Office: Genetic Systems Corp Sanofi Diagnostics Pasteur 6565 185th Ave NE Redmond WA 98052-5039

RANSIL, BERNARD J(EROME), research physician, methodologist, consultant, educator; b. Pitts., Nov. 15, 1929; s. Raymond Augustine and Louise Mary (Berhalter) R. BS, Duquesne U., 1951; PhD in Phys. Chemistry, Cath. U. Am., 1955; MD, U. Chgo., 1964. NRC-NAS postdoctoral fellow Nat. Bur. Stds., Washington, 1955-56; cons. heat div. thermodynamics sect. Nat. Bur. Standards, Washington, 1956-62; cons. NASA exobiology project, Washington, 1962-68; rsch. assoc. and dir. diatomic molecule project, Lab. Molecular Structure and Spectra, physics dept. U. Chgo., 1956-63; intern Harbor Gen. Hosp., UCLA, Torrance, 1964-65, Guggenheim fellow, 1965-66; from rsch. assoc. in medicine to assoc. prof. in medicine Harvard Med. Sch., Boston, 1966-96; from rsch. assoc. and clin. fellow to clin. assoc. Harvard II and IV Med. Svcs., 1966-74; core lab. scientist Clin. Rsch. Ctr. Thorndike Meml. Lab Boston City Hosp., Boston, 1966-74; asst. physician Beth Israel Hosp., Boston, 1974-96, sr. physician, 1996—; dir. Core Lab. Clin. Rsch. Ctr., 1974-89, Data Analysis Lab., 1989-94; with rsch. ops. Beth Israel Hosp., Boston, 1994-96; rsch. assoc., cons. computational statistics Dept. Neurology Beth Israel Deaconess Med. Ctr., Boston, 1996—; statis. computing cons. Boston City Hosp and Beth Israel Hosp., 1966-96; cons. Prophet project NIH, Bethesda, Md., 1971-88, exec. com., 1986-91, Howard Hughes Med. Inst., Boston, 1979-80, Coop. Cataract Rsch. Group, Boston, 1981-83, Mass. Alzheimer's Disease Rsch. Ctr., 1992-94; guest lectr. med. ethics Seton Hall U., 1970—; vis. scientist Rockefeller U., 1985, Scripps Rsch. Found., 1986, Calif. State U., 1986, U. Pitts. Med. Sch., 1987. Author: Abortion, 1969, Background to Abortion, 1979; editor: Life of a Scientist: Autobiography of Robert S. Mulliken, 1989, (videocassettes) Elements of Statistics and Data Analysis, 1985; contbr. biography of R.S. Mulliken to Nobel Laureates in Chemistry, 1973; contbr. numerous articles on computational chemistry, med. topics, computational stats. to sci. jours., also book revs. to Boston Globe, other periodicals, essays and poetry to The Critic. Recipient alumni rsch. award Cath. U. Am., 1969, Duquesne U. centennial award, 1978. Mem. numerous profl. socs. Home: 226 Calumet St Boston MA 02120-3303

RANSOHOFF, RICHARD MILTON, neurologist, researcher; b. Cin., Aug. 18, 1946; s. Jerry Nathan and Sue (Westheimer) R.; m. Margaret Seidler, Mar. 26, 1988; children: Amy Julia, Lena Jane. BA, Bard Coll., 1968; MD, Case Western Reserve U., 1978. Diplomate Am. Bd. Psychiatry and Neurology, Am. Bd. Internal Medicine. Resident in internal medicine Mt. Sinai Hosp., Cleve., 1978-81; resident in neurology The Cleve. Clinic Found., 1981-83, chief resident in neurology, 1983-84, mem. assoc. staff in neurology 1984-93, mem. asst. staff in molecular biology Rsch. Inst., 1989-94, mem. staff neurology dept., 1993—, mem. assoc. staff in molecular biology Rsch. Inst., 1994—, mem. assoc. staff in neuroscis. Rsch. Inst., 1994—; postdoctoral fellow in molecular biology Case Western Reserve U., Cleve., 1984-89; mem. neurology C study sect., Washington, 1995—; adj. prof. dept. biology Cleve. State U., 1994—. Editor: Cytokines in the CNS, 1996; assoc. editor: Jour. Immunology, 1996—; contbr. articles to profl. jours. Chair profl. adv. com. Nat. Multiple Sclerosis Soc., Northeast Ohio, 1985-95, trustee, 1985—, mem. med. adv. bd. Nat. Multiple Sclerosis Soc., N.Y.C. 1996—. Grantee NIH, Washington, 1988, Harry Weaver Neurosci. scholar Nat. Multiple Sclerosis Soc., N.Y.C., 1987-92; recipient Physicians Rsch. Tng. award Am. Cancer Soc., N.Y.C., 1984-86, Clin. Investigator Devel. award Nat. Inst. Neurol. and Communicative Diseases and Stroke, Washington, 1988-93. Mem. Am. Neurol. Assn. (mem. sci. program com. 1996—), Am. Assn. Neurology. Office: Rsch Inst NC-30 Cleve Clinic Found 9500 Euclid Ave Cleveland OH 44195-0001

RANSOM, BILL, author; b. Puyallup, Wash., June 6, 1945; s. Bert and LaVerne (Marcoe) R.; m. Kathy Ann Potocki, June 17, 1967 (div.); 1 child, Hali Kalae. Student, Wash. State U., 1963-65, U. Puget Sound, 1965-67; BA in English and Sociology Edn., U. Wash., 1970; postgrad., U. Nev., 1970-72. Nat. Endowment for Arts and Wash. State Arts Commn. poet-in-residence Tacoma and Port Townsend, Wash., 1972-75; Manpower Tng. Act master poet for Wash. and Colo., 1974; instr. writing So Utah U, Cedar City; dir. Port Townsend Writer's Conf., 1973-77; instr. So. Utah U. Author: Finding True North, 1974 (Nat. Book award and Pulitzer prize nominee 1974), Last Rites, 1978; author: (chapbook) Waving Arms At The Blind, 1975, (novel with Frank Herbert) The Jesus Incident, 1979, (chapbook) The Single Man Looks at Winter, 1983, Last Call, 1984, (novels with Frank Herbert) The Lazarus Effect, 1982, The Ascension Factor, 1988, (novels) Jaguar, 1990, Viravax, 1993, Learning the Ropes, 1995, Burn, 1995; author documentary of Artists-in-Schs. Program, Look: Listen, 1975; co-author (screen adaptations) Viravax, 1996, Jaguar, 1996; freelance journalist, Ctrl. Am., 1982-84; contbr. articles, stories, poems to mags., newspapers. Mem. PEN (selected stories for syndicated fiction project 1983, 85), AAUW, Sci. Fiction and Fantasy Writers Am., Poets & Writers, Inc., Associated Writing Programs. Office: PO Box 284 Grayland WA 98547-0284

RANSOM, BRIAN CHARLES, artist, educator, musician, composer; b. Portland, Oreg., Sept. 27, 1954; s. James Charles Willis and Margret Marie (Wallace) R.; m. Emily Lucile Phelps, June 21, 1982 (div. Oct. 1987); children: Willis, Stefan, Jacob; m. Amanda Marie Donta, June 3, 1995. Student, U. Puget Sound, 1972-73, R.I. Sch. Design, Providence, 1973-74; BFA in Visual Art, N.Y. State Coll. Ceramics, Alfred, 1978; MA in Ceramics/Anthropology, U. Tulsa, 1984; MFA in Sculpture, Claremont (Calif.) Grad. Sch., 1985. Tchr. U. Tulsa, 1983-84, Pitzer Coll., Claremont, 1984-85, UCLA, Westwood, Calif., 1988-89, Chaffey Coll., Rancho Cucamonga, Calif., 1990-95, Scripps Coll., Claremont, 1991; artist in residence/ceramics Tierra Del Sol, Claremont, 1992-95; asst. prof. ceramics Eckerd Coll., St. Petersburg, Fla., 1995—; condr. various workshops and lectrs. Founder, creator The Ceramic Ensemble, 1986; one-person shows include Maude Kerns Gallery, Eugene, Oreg., 1981, Courtyard Gallery, Portland, Oreg., 1982, Whitebird Gallery, Cannon Beach, Oreg., 1982, U. Tulsa, 984, Claremont Grad. Sch., 1985, New Harmony (Ind.) Gallery of Contemporary Art, 1986, Lawrence Gallery, Portland, 1986, Nexus Gallery, Phila., 1987, Norra Eccles Mus. Art, Logan, Utah, 1987, Cera Cossa Coll., Ridgecrest, Calif., 1989, Couturier Gallery, L.A., 1989, 90, 94, Art Space, Winnipeg, Man., Can., 991, Conejo Valley Art Mus., Thousand Oaks, Calif., 1991, Mendecine Arts Ctr., Calif., 1995; exhibited in group shows at Portland Art Mus., 1973, Devo Gallery, Portland, 1980, Johnson Atilier Art Ctr., Tulsa, 1983, Hansen Howard Gallery, Ashland, Oreg., 1985, Scripps Coll., Claremont, 1986, Reflections Gallery, La Mesa, Calif., 1986, Contemporary Crafts Gallery, Portland, 1987, Oreg. Sch. Arts and Crafts, Portland, 1988, Wita Gardner Gallery, San Diego, 1988, Faith Nightingale Gallery, San Diego, 1990, Irvine (Calif.) Fine Arts Ctr., 1992, Hollywood (Calif.) Bowl Mus., 1992, El Camino Coll., Torrence, Calif., 1994, Wabash Coll., Crawfordsville, Ind., 1994, Mus. Nebr. Art, Kearny, 1997, Tustin (Calif.) Renaissance Gallery, 1997; represented in permanent collections Everson Mus., N.Y. State Coll. Ceramics Alfred U. Mus.,; recs.: Between Two Worlds, 1986, Try to Tell Fish About Water, 1986, The Destroyer, 1987, Echoes, 1989, Tales of the Human Dawn, 1990, Sounding Clay, 1990, At Home with Mother Earth, 1994, Internal Medicine, 1995. Recipient Fulbright/Hayes Congl. fellowship, 1978-79, Oreg. Arts Commn. fellowship, 1982, rsch. fellowship U. Tulsa, 1985, COGS fellowship Claremont Grad. Sch., 1985, fellowship in sculpture Nat. Endowment Arts, 1986, Artist in Residence fellowship Calif. Arts Coun., 1992-95; named Emerging Artist Nat. Ceramic Educators' Conf. Am., 1986. Mem. Coll. Art Assn., Sierra Club. Avocations: bicycling, sailing, hiking, camping. Office: Art Dept 4200 54th Ave S Saint Petersburg FL 33711-4744

RANSOM, CHRISTINA ROXANE, librarian; b. N.Y.C., Oct. 28, 1951; d. Roy Martin Palhof and Virginia O'Brien Starr; m. Eddie Darden (div.); 1 child, Shani Aisha Darden; m. Stanley Austin Ransom, Jr., Nov. 27, 1980; children: Sarah, Austin, Rebecca. BA in Chemistry, Bard Coll., 1973; MLS, Columbia U., 1974; postgrad., Sage Coll., 1994—. Libr. asst. Libr. of Bard Coll., Annandale-on-Hudson, N.Y., 1969-73, Columbia U. Law Libr. and Libr. Svc. Libr., N.Y.C., 1973-74, Winthrop, Stimson, Putnam & Roberts, N.Y.C., 1974-76; tax libr. White & Case, N.Y.C., 1976-78; libr. cons. Corning (N.Y.) Glass, 1978; info. scientist Wyeth-Ayerst Labs., Rouses Point, N.Y., 1979-84; med. libr. CVPH Med. Ctr., Plattsburgh, N.Y., 1984—; libr. skills instr. SUNY Plattsburgh, N.Y., 1981-82; trustee North Country Reference and Rsch. Resources, Canton, N.Y., 1982-83; mem. trres., sec., v.p., pres. No. N.Y. Health Info. Coop., 1979-89. Recipient North Country Regional Centennial Coms. Excellence in Librarianship award New York Libr. Assn., 1990. Mem. Med. Libr. Assn., Friends of the Nat. Libr. Medicine, No. Adirondack Libr. Assn. Home: 39 Broad St Plattsburgh NY 12901-3447 Office: CVPH Med Ctr 75 Beekman St Plattsburgh NY 12901-1438

RANSOM, CLIFTON LOUIS, JR., lawyer, real estate investor; b. Houston, May 25, 1935; s. Clifton Louis and Birdelle (Wykoff) R.; m. Dorothy Ellen Peterson, Dec. 25, 1974. BS in Math., Tex. So. U., 1956; BA in Philosophy, St. Joseph's Coll., Rensselaer, Ind., 1964; MA in Bibl. Theology, St. Louis U., 1970; JD, Tex. So. U., 1974; LLM in Taxation, Washington Law Sch., Salt Lake City, 1991. Bar: Tex. 1974, U.S. Dist. Ct. (so. dist.) Tex. 1976, U.S. Ct. Appeals (5h cir.) 1980, U.S. Supreme Ct. 1980, U.S. Tax Ct. 1991; ordained priest Roman Cath. Ch., 1968. Priest Diocese of Galveston-Houston, 1968-74; atty. Tex. Welfare Dept., Houston, 1975-80, Gulf Coast Legal Found., Houston, 1980—. Bd. dirs. Hope Is Victory AIDS Found., Houston, 1993—. Lt. (j.g.) USN, 1957-60. Democrat. Home: 3919 Point Clear Dr Missouri City TX 77459-3710 Office: Gulf Coast Legal Found 1415 Fannin St Ste 200 Houston TX 77002-7644

RANSOM, DAVID MICHAEL, diplomat; b. St. Louis, Nov. 23, 1938; s. Clifford Fredic and Inez Natalie (Green) R.; m. Marjorie Ann (Marilley) Ransom; children: Elizabeth Inez, Katherine Hope, Sarah Grace. AB, Princeton U., 1960; MA, Johns Hopkins Sch. of Advanced Internat. Studies, 1962; student, The Nat. War Coll., 1982-83. With U.S. Dept. State, Yemen, Iran, Lebanon, Saudi Arabia, 1965-71; nat. security coun. staff White House U.S. Dept. State, Washington, 1971-73; dep. chief mission-Am. Embassy Sanaa U.S. Dept. State, Yemen Arab Rep., 1975-78; dir., dept. dir. near east divsn. internat. security affairs Office of Sec. of Def., U.S. Dept. of Def., Washington, 1978-82; dep. chief of mission-Am. Embassy Abu Dhabi U.S. Dept. State, United Arab Emirates, 1983-85; dep. chief of mission-Am. Embassy Damascus U.S. Dept. State, Syria, 1985-88; country dir. Arabian Peninsula-Near East bureau U.S. Dept. State, Washington, 1988-90, country dir. Greece, Turkey, Cyprus-European bureau, 1990-93; Am. ambassador to State of Bahrain-Am. Embassy Manama U.S. Dept. State, 1994. 1st lt. inf. USMC, 1962-65. Mem. Met. Club (Washington). Episcopalian. Avocations: scuba diving, canoeing, skiing. Office: Bahrain Am Embassy FPO AE 09834-5100

RANSOM, EVELYN NAILL, language educator, linguist; b. Memphis, Apr. 20, 1938; d. Charles Rhea and Evelyn (Goodlander) Naill Ransom; m. Gunter Heinz Hiller, June 7, 1960 (div. Mar. 1964). AA, Mt. Vernon Jr. Coll., 1958; BA, Newcomb Coll., 1960; MA, N.Mex. Highlands U., 1965; PhD, U. Ill., 1974. Cert. secondary tchr., N.Mex. Instr. Berlitz Sch. Langs., New Orleans, 1961; tchr. MillerWall Elem. Sch., Harvey, L.A., 1961-62; teaching asst. N.Mex. Highlands U., Las Vegas, 1963-64; instr. U. Wyo., Laramie, 1965-66; teaching asst. U. Ill., Urbana, 1966-70; prof. English lang. Ea. Ill. U., Charleston, 1970-93; vis. prof. in linguistics No. Ariz. U., Flagstaff, 1990-91, adj. faculty, 1993-94; adj. faculty Ariz. State U., Tempe, 1995—; referee Pretext: Jour. of Lang. and Lit., Ill., 1981; co-chair roundtable Internat. Congress of Linguistics, 1987; linguistics del. People to People, Moscow, St. Petersburg, Prague, 1993; dissertation reader SUNY, Buffalo, 1982; vis. scholar UCLA, 1977; conductor workshop LSA summer inst. Author: Complementation: Its Meanings and Forms, 1986; contbr. articles to profl. publs. Organizer Prairie Women's Cir., Champaign, 1981-83. Nat. Def. Fgn. Lang. fellow, 1969; grantee Ea. Ill. U., 1982, 87, 88, NSF, 1988. Mem. Linguistic Soc. Am., Linguistic Assn. S.W. Avocations: computer applications for the humanities, chess, motorhoming. Home: 201 E Southern Ave # 135 Apache Junction AZ 85219-3740

RANSOM, JEREMY, ballet dancer; b. St. Catharines, Ont.. Grad., Nat. Ballet Sch. With Nat. Ballet Canada, Toronto, Ont., 1980—, 2d soloist, 1984-85, 1st soloist, 1985-90, prin. dancer, 1990—; performed with Zurich Ballet, Switzerland, 1986-87, Australian Ballet. Created roles in David Allan's Occasion, Capriccio, Etc!; Glen Tetley's Alice; James Kudelka's The Actress, The Miraculous Mandarin; also L'Ile Inconnue, Oiseaux Exotiques. Office: National Ballet of Canada, 470 Queens Quay W, Toronto, ON Canada M5V 3K4*

RANSOM, KEVIN RENARD DORTCH, investment banker; b. Detroit, Sept. 24, 1964; s. Donald Lewis and Etta Mae (Dortch) R. B in Econs., Morehouse Coll., 1988. Fin. analyst Goldman Sachs & Co., N.Y.C., 1987-88, Merrill Lynch & Co., N.Y.C., 1988-89; freelance journalist KDR & Assocs., N.Y.C., 1989-90; fiscal analyst Mich. State Legislature, Lansing, 1990-92; dir. fiscal analysis Detroit City Coun., 1992-95; v.p. First of Mich. Investment Bank, Detroit, 1995—; cons. Lansing C.C., 1990—. Editor: Neighborhood Economic Development Strategies, 1990. Mem. Dem. Nat. Com. Mem. Nat. Assn. Securities Profls., Morehouse Nat. Alumni Assn., Kappa Alpha Psi. Democrat. Baptist. Avocations: weight lifting, basketball. Home: 100 Riverfront Park # 1507 Detroit MI 48226

RANSOM, MARGARET PALMQUIST, public relations executive; b. Davenport, Iowa, Aug. 13, 1935; d. Herman Philip and Margaret (Burchell) Palmquist; m. David Duane Ransom, July 16, 1960; 1 child, David Burke. BA in Speech and English, Augustana Coll., 1957. Tchr. speech and English Beloit (Wis.) High Sch., 1957-59; tchr. English Lake Forest (Ill.) High Sch., 1959-60, Warren High Sch., Gurnee, Ill., 1960-62, 64-66; asst. to dean Grad. Sch. Bowling Green (Ohio) State U., 1963; freelance writer Coll. Bd. Examinations, 1966; market rsch. analyst Kitchens of Sara Lee, Deerfield, Ill., 1972-74; pub. affairs mgr. Sara Lee Bakery, Deerfield, 1975-89; sr. cons. Ransom Pub. Svc. Cons., Libertyville, Ill., 1990-94; cons. Olsten Staffing Svcs., Chgo., 1994-96, Kelly Svcs. Chgo. Region, 1996—; judge nat. competitions Pub. Rels. Soc. Am., 1986-89; spkr. on motivation and orgn.; chmn. employer coun. Ill. Dept. Employment Security, 1995-96; cons. Kelly Svcs., 1996—. Bd. dirs. Early Childhood Adv. Coun., Northeastern Ill. State U., 1989-91; mem. Main St. Libertyville com., 1990-92; creator Job Market Place '96, Lake County. Recipient Ill. Citizens Svc. medal, 1993. Mem. AAUW, Bus. and Profl. Women Lake County, Mortar Bd. Avocations: computer science, reading, original art. Office: 1037 Mayfair Dr Libertyville IL 60048-3548 *This is the day the Lord has made. Let us rejoice and be glad. Carpe diem!.*

RANSOM, NANCY ALDERMAN, sociology and women's studies educator, university administrator; b. New Haven, Feb. 25, 1929; d. Samuel Bennett and Florence (Opper) Alderman; m. Harry Howe Ransom, July 6, 1951; children—Jenny Alderman, Katherine Marie, William Henry Howe. B.A., Vassar Coll., 1950; postgrad. Columbia U., 1951, U. Leeds (Eng.), 1977-78; M.A., Vanderbilt U., 1971; EdD, Vanderbilt U., 1988. Lectr. sociology U. Tenn.-Nashville, 1971-76; grant writer Vanderbilt U., Nashville, 1976-77, dir. Women's Ctr., 1978—, instr. sociology, 1972, 74, lectr. sociology and women's studies, 1983, 90—; speaker profl. meetings. Vol. counselor family planning Planned Parenthood Assn. of Nashville, 1973-77, bd. dirs., 1978-89, adv. coun., 1989—, v.p., 1981—, pres., 1987-89; bd. dirs. Sr. Citizens, Inc., 1996—; mem. planning com. ACE/ACE nat. identification program Women in Higher Edn., 1984-92. Recipient Woman of Achievement award Middle Tenn. State U., 1996; Columbia U. residential fellow, 1951; Vanderbilt U. fellow, 1971. Mem. AAUW, NOW, Am. Sociol. Assn., Nat. Women's Studies Assn., Southeastern Women's Studies Assn., Nat. Women's Polit. Caucus, LWV, Cable Club, Phi Beta Kappa (v.p. Alpha of Tenn. 1994-95, pres. 95—). Office: Vanderbilt U PO Box 1513 Nashville TN 37235

RANSOM, PERRY SYLVESTER, civil engineer; b. Atlanta, July 3, 1929; s. Perry Sylvester and Eva James (Smith) R.; m. Wilma Ruth Cone, June 1, 1951; children: Beverly Kay, Barbara Ann. BSCE, Auburn U., 1958. Registered profl. engr., La., Miss., Ala.; cert. land surveyor, La., Miss. Asst. timekeeper Swift & Co., Montgomery, Ala., 1947-51; trainman Atlantic Coast Line RR, Montgomery, 1951-58; lab. mgr. A.W. Williams Inspection Co., Mobile, Ala., 1958-60; owner, CEO Cons. Engrs., Inc., Biloxi, Miss., 1960—. Mem. Civitan Club, Mobile, 1959, Rotary Internat., Moss Point, Miss., 1965; pres. Gulf Coast chpt. Miss. Engring. Soc., Biloxi, 1965-66, chmn. Pepp sect., Jackson, 1967-68; bd. dirs. Miss. sect. ASCE, Jackson, 1972-74. With U.S. Army, 1951-53. Named Boss of Yr., Miss. Nat. Sec. Assn., 1975-76, for Outstanding Svc., Miss. Engring. Soc., 1966, Outstanding Supporter, Boys Clubs Am., Biloxi, 1991; recipient Cert. of Appreciation, Boys Clubs Am., Biloxi, 1990. Mem. Miss. Cons. Engrs. Coun., Aircraft Owners and Pilots Assn., VFW (Merit/Disting. Svc. 1989), Masons (life). Republican. Baptist. Home: 711 Twin Oaks Dr Ocean Springs MS 39564-4221 Office: Cons Engrs Inc 430 Caillavet St Biloxi MS 39530-2050

RANSOM, RICHARD EDWARD, retired state supreme court justice; b. Hampton, Iowa, Dec. 9, 1932. BA, U. N.Mex., 1954; LLB, Georgetown U., 1959. Bar: N.Mex. 1959, D.C. 1959. Trial lawyer Albuquerque, 1959-86; justice N.Mex. Supreme Ct., Santa Fe, 1987-97; chief justice N. Mex. Supreme Ct., 1992-94, sr. justice, 1994-97. 1st lt. USMC, 1954-56. Fellow Am. Coll. Trial Lawyers, Internat. Soc. Barristers, Internat. Acad. Trial Lawyers. Office: PO Drawer D Albuquerque NM 87103

RANSOM, WILLIAM HARRISON, lawyer; b. Flint, Mich., Aug. 15, 1938; s. Earl Jarvis and Aileen (Halpin) R.; m. Marilyn Jean Novotny, Aug. 27, 1960; children: Nancy Aileen Maggard, Andrew William, Elizabeth Hope. BA in Econs., U. Mich., 1960, JD, 1963. Bar: Ohio, 1964. Assoc. Squire, Sanders & Dempsey, Cleve., 1964-74, ptnr., 1974-91, counsel, 1992—. Mem. ABA (tax sect. benefits com.), Ohio Bar Assn., Cleve. Bar Assn. Office: Squire Sanders & Dempsey 4900 Key Tower 127 Public Sq Cleveland OH 44114-1216

RANSOME, ERNEST LESLIE, III, retail company executive; b. Riverton, N.J.; s. Percy A. and Clarice (Frishmuth) R.; m. Nancy Ellis Clark, Aug. 16, 1947 (div. Jan. 1984); children: Leslie Ransome Hudson, Elizabeth Ransome, Jane Ransome Bromley; m. Myradean Alcott, Feb. 12, 1984. AB in Econs., Princeton U., 1947. Ins. exec. Johnson & Higgins, Phila., 1947-48; asst. to dean Princeton (N.J.) U., 1948-50; asst. treas. Giles & Ransome, Bensalem, Pa., 1950-55; v.p. adminstrn. Giles & Ransome, Bensalem, 1955-69, exec. v.p., 1969-82, vice chmn., 1982-88, chmn. bd., 1988—; v.p. Ransome Airlines, Bensalem, Pa., 1966-86; with Mannington Mills, Salem, N.J., chmn., 1991-92; bd. dirs. Sun Source, Phila. Mem. Zoning Bd. Borough of Riverton, N.J., 1965-69; bd. trustees Riverton Library, 1959-79; campaign chmn. Zurbrugg Hosp., Riverside, N.J., 1971. 2d lt. USMC, 1944-46. Mem.

Pine Valley Golf Club (pres. 1977-88, chmn. 1988—), Royal and Ancient Golf Club (St. Andrews, Scotland). Republican. Episcopalian. Avocation: golf.

RANTA, RICHARD ROBERT, university dean; b. Virginia, Minn., Nov. 18, 1943; s. V. Robert and Bernice (Smith) R.; 1 child, Erick H.; m. Carol Crown. AS, Hibbing (Minn.) Community Coll., 1963; BS, U. Minn., 1965; MA, Cornell U., 1967; PhD, U. Iowa, 1974. Floor dir. Sta. KDAL-TV, Duluth, Minn., 1964-65; asst. prof. U. Va., Charlottesville, 1969-72; asst. prof. U. Memphis, 1972-75, assoc. prof., 1975-91, prof., 1991—, interim dean Univ. Coll., 1975, asst. v.p. academic affairs, 1976-78, dean Coll. Comm. and Fine Arts, 1977—; gen. mgr. High Water Records, Memphis, 1980—; bd. dirs. Concerts Internat., Memphis, pres., 1988-90; TV cons., free-lance producer, 1973—. Assoc. prodr.: (TV program) Nat. Arthritis Telethon, 1985-90; Rec. Acad. graphics and prodn. coord. Grammy Awards TV program, 1983—; author articles in Communication Adminstrn. Bull., 1977—, editl. bd., 1991—, exec. com., 1996—. Chmn., v.p. Tenn. Humanities Coun., Nashville, 1980-82; v.p. Memphis Devel. Found., 1983-86; bd. dirs. Leadership Memphis, 1987-90, 94—, chmn. mktg. com., 1987-90, chmn. selection com., 1994-95; bd. dirs. Life Blood, Memphis, 1984-92; treas. Memphis-Shelby County Film, Tape and Music Commn., 1986—; mem. adv. com. Tenn. Film, Entertainment and Music Commn., Nashville, 1987—, chmn., 1993-95; chmn. bd. dirs. Crime Stoppers Memphis Assn., 1993-95; chmn. Memphis Arts Festival, 1992-94. Recipient Edn. Operational Models grant Ednl. Testing Svc., 1975, Communication Lab. grant HEW, 1976, Disting. Alumnus award Minn. Cmty. Coll. System, 1984, Alumni Cmty. Svc. award Leadership Memphis, 1997; named to Recording Hall of Fame Selection panel, Nat. Rec. Acad., L.A., 1986—. Mem. NARAS (v.p. 1986-88, 92-93, chmn. edn. com. 1983—, trustee 1982-86, 88-92, 93—, pres. Memphis chpt. 1984-86, bd. govs. 1978—), So. States Comm. Assn. (pres. 1987-88, fin. bd. 1985-87, 93-95, exec. dir. 1995—), Tenn. Speech Comm. Assn. (pres. 1986-87, editor Communicator 1993—), Speech Comm. Assn. (vice chmn., then chmn. exptl. learning com. 1979-83, mem. fin. and adminstrn. coms. 1989-93, chmn. fin. com. 1991-93), So. Arts Fedn. (bd. dirs. 1994—), Internat. Coun. Fine Arts Deans (parliamentarian 1996—), Tenn. Arts and Scis. Deans Assn. (chair 1997—), Delta Sailing Assn. Club (sec. 1984—). Avocations: sailing, tennis, photography. Office: U Memphis Coll Communication & Fine Arts Memphis TN 38152-6546

RANTS, CAROLYN JEAN, college official; b. Hastings, Nebr., Oct. 3, 1936; d. John Leon and Christine (Helzer) Halloran; m. Marvin L. Rants, June 1, 1957 (div. July 1984); children: Christopher Charles, Douglas John. Student, Hastings Coll., 1954-56; BS, U. Omaha, 1960; MEd, U. Nebr., 1968; EdD, U. S.D., 1982. Tchr. elem. Ogallala (Nebr.) Community Sch., 1956-58, Omaha Pub. Schs., 1958-60, Hastings Pub. Schs., 1960-64, Grosse Pointe (Mich.) Community Schs., 1964-67; asst. prof., instr. Morningside Coll., Sioux City, Iowa, 1974-82, dean for student devel., 1982-84, v.p. for student affairs, 1984-94, interim v.p. for acad. affairs, 1992-94, v.p. enrollment and student svcs., 1994-96, v.p. adminstrn., 1996—. Mem. new agy. com., chmn. fund distbn. and resource deployment com. United Way, Sioux City, 1987-94, co-chair, United Way Day of Caring, 1996; mem. Iowa Civil Rights Commn., 1989—; bd. dirs. Leadership Sioux City, 1988-93, pres., 1992-93; bd. dirs. Siouxland Y, Sioux City, 1985-90, pres., 1988; bd. dirs. Girls, Inc., 1995—, Work Activity Co., 1996—; mem. Vision 2020 Cmty. Planning Task Force, 1990-92. Mem. Iowa Women in Ednl. Leadership (pres. Sioux City chpt. 1986), Nat. Assn. Student Pers. Adminstrs.(region IV-E adv. bd.), Nat. Assn. for Women Deans, Adminstrs. and Counselors, Iowa Student Pers. Adminstr. (chmn. profl. devel. Iowa chpt. 1988-89, pres. 1991-92, Disting. Svc. award 1995), AAUW (corp. rep., coll./univ. rep. 1994-96), P.E.O. (pres. Sioux City chpt., Tri-State Women's Bus. Conf. (treas., planning com. Sioux City chpt. 1987-89), Quota Club (com. chmn. Sioux City 1987-89, v.p. 1992-94, pres. 1994-95, Siouxland Woman of Yr. award 1988), Sertoma (officer, bd. govs., regional dir.), Omicron Delta Kappa (faculty dir. province X 1996—), Delta Kappa Gamma (state 1st v.p. 1993-95, state pres. 1995—). Republican. Methodist. Avocations: handbells, cross-stitching. Home: 2904 S Cedar St # 4 Sioux City IA 51106-4246 Office: Morningside Coll 1501 Morningside Ave Sioux City IA 51106-1717

RANU, HARCHARAN SINGH, biomedical scientist, administrator, orthopaedic biomechanics educator; b. Lyallpur, India; came to U.S., 1976; s. Jodh Singh and Harnam Kaur R. BSc, Leicester Poly., Eng., 1963; MSc, U. Surrey, Guilford, Eng., 1967, Cambridge (Eng.) U., 1972; PhD, Middlesex Hosp. Med. Sch. and Poly. of Cen. London, 1975; diploma, MIT, 1984. Chartered engr., Eng. Med. scientist Nat. Inst. Med. Rsch. of the Med. Rsch. Coun., London, 1967-70; rsch. fellow Middlesex Hosp. Med. Sch. and Poly. of Cen. London, 1971-76; rsch. scientist Plastics Rsch. Assn. of Great Britain, Shawbury, Eng., 1977; asst. prof. Wayne State U., Detroit, 1977-81; prof. biomed. engring./orthopaedic biomechanics biomaterials La. Tech. U., Ruston, 1982—; prof., chmn. dept. biomechanics N.Y. Coll. Osteo. Medicine, Old Westbury, 1989-93; prof., asst. to pres. and dir. doctoral program Life Coll., Marietta, Ga., 1993—; dir. tng. Rehab. Rsch. and Devel. Ctr., 1983-85; mem. La. Tech. U. Libr. Com., 1983-85; chmn. design competition Assn. Biomed. Engrs.; mem. steering com. So. Biomed. Engring. Confs., 1983—; chmn. tech. in health care conf. U. Cambridge, 1985; chmn. Internat. Symposium on Bioengring., Calcutta, India, 1985; dir. orthopaedic biomechanics rsch. labs., staff Nassau County Med. Ctr., Long Island, 1989—; prof., asst. to pres., dir. doctoral program Life Coll., Marietta, Ga., 1993—; mem. biomed. engring. faculty com. La. Tech. U., faculty com., rsch. awards com., grad. studies com., grad. faculty, acad. bd. dirs; vis. scientist Dryburn Hosp., Durham, Eng., 1985-87, cons., 1988—; vis. prof. U. Istanbul, 1982, Lab. de Recherch Orthopediques, Paris, 1985—, Kings Coll. Med. Sch. U. London, 1989—, Indian Inst. Tech., New Delhi, Postgrad Inst. Med. Edn. and Rsch., Chandigarh, India, 1989—, Inst. Biol. Physics USSR Acad. Sci., Moscow, 1990, Polytech. Ctrl. London, 1991—; adj. prof. Coll. Physicians and Surgeons Columbia U., N.Y.C., 1988—, Inst. Biol. Physics USSR Acad. Sci., Moscow, 1990, N.Y. Coll. Podiatric Medicine, 1991—, CUNY, 1992—; cons. Lincoln Gen. Hosp., Ruston, La., 1982-85, La. State U. Med. Ctr., Shreveport, 1982—, St. Luke's and Roosevelt Hosp. Ctr., N.Y., 1988—, Foot Clinics N.Y., 1991—, Vets. Affairs Med. Ctr., N.Y., 1992—, various biomed. rsch. & legal corps., U.S., United Kingdom; mem. media resource svc. Inst. Pub. Info., N.Y., 1989—; med. scientist, cons. NATO, 1982—; presenter, lectr., dir. organizer numerous sci. orgns. and nat. & internat. confs.; external examiner for doctoral candidates All India Inst. Med. Scis., New Delhi, Indian Inst. of Tech., New Delhi, Banaras Hindu U., Varanasi, India, 1994—. Author: Rheological Behavior of Articular Cartiliage Under Tensile Loads, 1967, Effects of Ionizing Radiation on the Mechanical Properties of Skin, 1975, Effects of Fractionated Doses of X-irradiation on the Mechanical Properties of Skin--A Long Term Study, 1980, Effects of Ionizing Radiation on the Structure & Physical Properties of the Skin, 1983, 3-D Model of Vertebra for Spinal Surgery, 1985, Application of Carbon Fibers in Orthopaedic Surgery, 1985, Relation Between Metal Corrosion & Electrical Polarization, 1989, The Distribution of Stresses in the Human Lumbar Spine, 1989, Medical Devices & Orthopaedic Implants in the United States, 1989, Spinal Surgery by Modeling, 1989, Multipoint Determination of Pressure-Volume Curves in Human Intervertebral Discs, 1993, Evaluation of Volume-Pressure Relationship in Lumbar Discs Using Model and Experimental Studies, 1994, A Mechanism of Laser Nuclectomy, 1994, Microminiaturization in Laser Surgery in Vivo Intradiscal Pressure Measurements in Lumbar Intervertebral Discs, 1994, An Experimental and Mathematical Simulation of Fracture of Human Bone Due to Jumping, 1994; editor The Lower Extremity, 1993—; guest editor IEEE Engring. in Medicine & Biology, 1991; mem. editorial bd. Med. Instrumentation, 1988—, Jour. Biomed. Instrumentation & Tech., 1988—, Jour. Med. Engring. & Tech., 1989—, Jour. Med. Design & Material, 1990—, Jour. Long-Term Effects Med. Implants, 1991—, Biomed. Sci. & Tech., 1991—; reviewer Jour. Biomechanics, 1981—, Clin. Biomechanics, 1984—, Jour. Biomed. Engring., 1981, Phys. Therapy, 1990—, IEEE Biomed. Transactions, 1991—, Jour. Engring. in Medicine, 1989—; contbr. articles to profl. jours. Faculty advisor India Students Assn. Wayne State U., 1980. Recipient Edwin Tate award U. Surrey, 1968, Third Internat. Olympic Com. World Congress On Sprots Scis. award, Atlanta, 1995; numerous rsch. grants. Fellow ASME (bioengring. com. 1990—, award L.I. chpt. 1991), Biol. Engring. Soc. (London) (President's prize 1984), Instn. Mech. Engrs. (chmn. revv. bd. for corp. memberships, James Clayton awards 1974-76); mem. Am. Soc. Biomechanics (edn. com. 1990—), Orthopaedic Rsch. Soc., Biomed. Engring. Soc., India Assn., India Assn. North La. Sikh. Research includes microfracture simulation of human vertebrae under compressive loading, laserectomy of the human nucleus pulposus and its effect on the intradiscal pressure, pressure-volume relation in human intervertebral discs, in vitro and in vivo intradiscal pressure measurements before and after laserectomy of the human nucleus pulposus, gait analysis of a diabetic foot. Office: Sch of Grad Studies Life Coll Marietta GA 30060

RANUM, OREST ALLEN, historian, educator; b. Lyle, Minn., Feb. 18, 1933; s. Luther George and Nada (Chaffee) R.; m. Patricia McGroder, July 4, 1955; children—Kristin, Marcus. B.A., Macalester Coll., St. Paul, 1955; M.A., U. Minn., 1957, Ph.D., 1961. Asst. prof. U. So. Calif., 1960-61, Columbia U., N.Y.C., 1961-63; assoc. prof. Columbia U., 1963-69; prof. history Johns Hopkins U., Balt., 1969—; mem., chmn. GRE Ednl. Testing Service, Princeton, 1973-78. Author: Richelieu and Councilors, 1963; Paris, Age of Absolutism, 1968; Artisans of Glory, 1981, The Fronde, 1993. Recipient Bronze medal City of Tours, France, 1980. Mem. Am. Hist. Assn., Soc. French Hist. Studies, Inst. de France (corr.), Académie des Sciences Morales et Politiques (Paris; corr. 1989), Société de l'Histoire de France, Collège de France (internat. chair 1994-95). Home: 208 Ridgewood Rd Baltimore MD 21210-2539 Office: History Dept Johns Hopkins U Baltimore MD 21218

RANZAHUER, GUILLERMO GONZALEZ, bishop; b. Huatusco, Veracruz, Mex., Mar. 12, 1928; s. Edmundo Ranzahuer Cárcamo. Ordained priest Roman Cath. Ch., 1951; consecrated bishop of Diocese of San Andres Tuxtla, 1969. Office: Constitucion Y Morelos, San Andres Tuxtla, Veracruz CP 95700, Mexico*

RAO, ABDUL SOHAIL, transplant immunologist, researcher; b. Karachi, Sind, Pakistan, Jan. 1, 1958; came to U.S., 1981; s. Majid Khan and Saeeda Majid (Fareed) R.; m. Rukhsana Sohail Bukhari, Oct. 12, 1983; children: Rida, Raoul, Rameez. MD, Dow Med. Coll., Karachi, 1983; MA, Boston U., 1990; DPhil, U. Oxford, Eng., 1993. Instr. Dow Med. Coll., 1983-85, Aga Khan U., Karachi, 1985-87; rsch. fellow Harvard Med. Sch., Boston, 1989-90; clin. instr. U. Oxford, 1990-92; dir. sect. of med. informatics Thomas E. Starzl Transplantation Inst., Pitts., 1993—, dir. sect. of cellular transplantation, 1995—; assoc. dir. translational rsch. Thomas E. Starzl Transplantation Inst., 1994—, dir. rsch. adminstrn., 1994—, vice chair protocol com., 1994—; mem. exec. com. Pitts. Transplantation Inst., 1994—; asst. prof. U. Pitts., 1993—; prof. ad honorarium U. Antioquia, Medellin, Columbia, 1995—; sci. mem. Pitts. Cancer Inst., 1994—. Contbr. articles to profl. jours. Rsch. grantee British VC Com., 1990-92, BenVenue Pharm., 1994-96, Cancer Rsch. Treatment Found., 1996—, NIH, 1996—. Mem. AAAS, British Soc. Immunology, British Transplantation Soc., Pakistan Physiol. Soc., Pakistan Med. Assn., Cell Transplantation Soc., Transplantation Soc., Am. Soc. Transplant Surgeons, Am. Soc. Transplant Physicians. Home: 5256 Forbes Ave Pittsburgh PA 15217 Office: Pitts Transplantation Inst 200 Lothrop St Pittsburgh PA 15213-2546

RAO, CALYAMPUDI RADHAKRISHNA, mathematics and statistics educator; b. Hadagili, India, Sept. 10, 1920, came to U.S., 1978, naturalized, 1983; s. Calyampudi Doraswamy and Arcot Laxmikantamma Naidu; m. Bhargavi Swarnapuri, Sept. 9, 1948; children—Tejaswini, Veerendra. Ph.D., Cambridge U., Eng., 1948, Sc.D., 1965; D.Sc. (hon.), Andhra U., 1967, Delhi U., 1973, Osmania U., 1977, Hyderabad U., 1991, Venkateswara U., 1995, Indian Stat. Inst., 1989, Colo. State U., 1990, Ohio State U., 1979, Athens U., Greece, 1976, Leningrad U., USSR, 1970, Philippines U., 1983, Tampere U., Finland, 1985, Poznan U., Poland, 1991, Slovak Acad. Scis., 1994, Barcelona U., 1995, Munich U., 1995, Guelph U., 1996, Waterloo U., Can., 1997. Dir. research Indian Statistical Inst., India, 1964-72, dir., sec., 1972-78; prof. U. Pitts., 1979-87; nat. prof., India, 1987—. Contbr. articles to profl. jours. Author: Linear Statistical Inference and Its Applications, 1965; Advanced Statistical Methods in Biometric Research, 1952; Computers and the Future of Human Soc., 1970; (with R.K. Mukherji and J.C. Trevor) Ancient Inhabitants of Jebel Moya, 1955; (with P.C. Mahalanobis and D.N. Majumdar) Anthropometric Survey of the United Provinces, 1941; A Statistical Study, 1950; (with D.N. Majumdar) Race Elements of Bengal, A Quantitative Study, 1958 (with Mitra) Generalized Inverse of Matrices and its Applications, 1971, (with Kagan and Linnik) Characterization Problems of Mathematical Statistics, 1972 (with Kleffe) Estimation of Variance Components and its Applications, 1988, Statistics and Truth, 1989 (with Shanbhag) Choquet-Deny Type Functional Equations with Applications to Scholastic Models, 1994, (with Toutenburg) Linear Models: Least Squares and Alternatives, 1995; Chief editor Jour. Multiple Analysis, 1988—. Recipient Gold medal Calcutta U., 1943; Shanti Swarup award Council Scientific and Indsl. Research, 1963; Guy medal Royal Statistical Soc., Eng., 1965; Padma Bhushan award Govt. India, 1968, Megnadh Saha medal Indian Nat. Sci. Acad., 1969; J.C. Bose gold medal, 1975, S.S. Wilks medal, 1989, Mahalanobes medal, 1996. Fellow Royal Soc., Am. Acad. Arts and Sci., Internat. Biometric Soc. (pres. 1974-75, v.p. 1975-76, hon. mem. 1986), Indian Nat. Sci. Acad. (v.p. 1973-75), Inst. Math. Stats. (pres. 1976-77), Andhra Pradesh Acad. Scis., Royal Statis. Soc., Am. Statis. Assn., Internat. Econometric Soc. (hon.), Indian Acad. Scis., Third World Acad. Scis. (founder 1983), King's Coll. (hon. life); mem. Internat. Statis. Inst. (hon., pres. 1977-79), Indian Econometric Soc. (pres. 1971-76, chmn. 1977-95), Forum for Interdisciplinary Math. (pres. 1982-84), Nat. Acad. Scis., Sankhya (co-editor 1964-72, editor 1972—). Home: 826 W Aaron Dr State College PA 16803 Office: Pa State U University Park PA 16802

RAO, DABEERU C., epidemiologist; b. Santhabommali, India, Apr. 6, 1946; came to U.S., 1972; s. Ramarao Patnaik and Venkataratnam (Raghupatruni) R.; m. Sarada Patnaik, 1974; children: Ravi, Lakshmi. BS in Stats., Indian Statis. Inst., Calcutta, 1967, MS, 1968, PhD, 1971. Research fellow U. Sheffield, Eng., 1971-72; asst. prof., geneticist U. Hawaii, Honolulu, 1972-78, assoc. prof.-geneticist, 1978-80; assoc. prof., dir. div. biostats. Washington U. Med. Sch., St. Louis, 1980-82, prof. depts. biostats., psychiatry and genetics, 1982—, adj. prof. math., 1982—, dir. div. biostats., 1980—. Author: A Source Book for Linkage in Man, 1979, Methods in Genetic Epidemiology, 1983, Genetic Epidemiology of Coronary Heart Disease, 1984; editor-in-chief Genetic Epidemiology jour., 1984-91; contbr. articles to profl. jours. Grantee NIH, 1978—. Mem. Am. Statis. Assn., Am. Soc. Human Genetics, Internat. Genetic Epidemiology Soc. (pres. 1996), Behavior Genetics Assn., Soc. Epidemiol. Res., Biom. Soc. Office: Washington U Sch Medicine Div Biostatistics 660 S Euclid Ave Saint Louis MO 63110-1010

RAO, DESIRAJU BHAVANARAYANA, meteorologist, oceanographer, educator; b. Visakhapatnam, India, Dec. 8, 1936; came to U.S., 1960, naturalized, 1974; s. Desiraju Sreeramulu and Desiraju Hanumayamma Adavikolanu; m. Padmavati Kavuru; children: Desiraju Pramila, Desiraju Kavitha. B.Sc., Andhra U., Waltair, India, 1956, M.Sc., 1959; M.S., U. Chgo., 1962, Ph.D., 1965. Rsch. scholar Indian Naval Phys. Labs., Cochin, 1959-60; postdoctoral fellow Nat. Center Atmospheric Rsch., Boulder, Colo., 1965-67; rsch. scientist marine scis. br. Can. Dept. Energy, Mines and Resources, Ottawa, Ont., 1967-68; asst. prof. atmospheric sci. Colo. State U., Ft. Collins, 1968-71; assoc. prof. energetics, also Center Gt. Lakes Studies, U. Wis.-Milw., 1971-74, prof., 1974-76; head phys. limnology and meteorology group Gt. Lakes Environ. Rsch. Lab., NOAA, Ann Arbor, Mich., 1975-80; adj. prof. limnology and meteorology U. Mich., Ann Arbor, 1977-80; head oceans and ice br. Lab. for Atmospheric Sci., Goddard Space Flight Ctr., NASA, Greenbelt, Md., 1980-84; chief marine prediction br. Nat. Meteorol. Ctr., NOAA, Washington, 1984-95; chief Ocean Modeling Br., Nat. Ctrs. Environ. Prediction NOAA, Washington, 1995—; adj. prof. meteorology U. Md., College Park, 1981—; cons. in field. Contbr. articles on atmospheric, oceanic and lake dynamics to sci. jours. Fellow Am. Meteorol. Soc. (v.p. Denver chpt. 1969-70); Mem. Am. Soc. Limnology and Oceanography, AAAS, Internat. Water Resources Assn. (charter), Am. Geophys. Union, Internat. Assn. for Gt. Lakes Research, The Oceanography Soc. (charter), Sigma Xi. Home: 13101 Hugo Pl Silver Spring MD 20906-5916 Office: 5200 Auth Rd Rm 209 Suitland MD 20746-4304

RAO, NANNAPANENI NARAYANA, electrical engineer; b. Kakumanu, Andhra Pradesh, India; m. Sarojini Jonnalagadda, June 10, 1955; children: Vanaja, Durgaprasad, Hariprasad. BSc in Physics, U. Madras, India, 1952; DMIT in Electronics, Madras Inst. Tech., 1955; MSEE, U. Wash., 1960, PhD in Elec. Engring, 1965. Acting instr. elec. engring. U. Wash., 1960-64, acting asst. prof., 1964-65; asst. prof. elec. engring. U. Ill., Urbana, 1965-69; asso. prof. U. Ill., 1969-75, prof., 1975—, assoc. head elec. and computer engring., 1987—; cons. Fakultas Teknik, Univ. Indonesia, Jakarta, 1985-86, 87. Author: Basic Electromagnetics with Applications, 1972, Elements of Engineering Electromagnetics, 4th edit., 1994; contbr. numerous articles to profl. jours. Recipient Engring. award Telugu Assn. N.Am., 1983, Fakultas Teknik award Universitatas Indonesia, 1986. Fellow IEEE (Undergrad. Teaching award 1994); mem. Am. Soc. Engring. Edn. (AT&T Found. award for excellence in instrn. engring. students 1991), Internat. Union Radio Sci. (U.S. Commn. G). Activities include rsch. carried out in the general area of ionospheric propagation. Home: 2509 S Lynn St Urbana IL 61801-6841 Office: U Ill Dept Elec & Computer Engring 1406 W Green St Urbana IL 61801-2918

RAO, POTARAZU KRISHNA, government executive; b. Andhra Pradesh, India, Mar. 26, 1930; s. Satyanarayana and Annapoorna (Mullapudi) P.; m. Rukmani Krutivinti, Aug. 5, 1954; children: Ramanarayan, Sreedhar. BS, Andhra U., 1950, MS, 1952; MS, Fla. State U., 1957; PhD, NYU, 1968. Meteorologist Can. Meteorol. Svc., Montreal, Can., 1960-61; rsch. phys. scientist Nat. Oceanic and Atmospheric Adminstrn./Nat. Environ. Satellite Data and Info. Svc., Washington, 1961-74, chief atmospheric energetics br., acting dir., 1976-80, chief satellite applications lab., 1980-86, dir. office of rsch. and applications, 1986-96; chief scientist for satellite and info. svcs. Nat. Oceanic and Atmospheric Adminstrn., Washington, 1996—; program dir., weather modification NSF, Washington, 1971-72; advisor on satellite programs World Meteorological Orgn., Geneva, 1974-76; bd. dirs. Nat. Oceanic and Atmospheric Adminstrn. Climate and Global Change Program, Washington; adv. bd. Coop. Inst. for Rsch. in Atmospheres, Ft. Collins, Colo., 1986—. Editor: Weather Satellites, 1990; contbr. articles to profl. jours. Founder, trustee Sri Siva Vishnu Temple, Lanham, Md. Fellow Am. Meteorol. Soc., Royal Meteorol. Soc. (U.K.), N.Y. Acad. Scis. Hindu. Avocations: tennis, photography. Home: 15824 Buena Vista Dr Rockville MD 20855 Office: NESDIS/NOAA Science Ctr 4700 Silver Hill Rd Washington DC 20233-9909

RAO, SETHURAMIAH LAKSHMINARAYANA, demographer, United Nations official; b. Mysore, Karnataka, India, Apr. 28, 1942; came to U.S., 1967; s. Ramakrishniah Sethuramiah and Bhageerathi; m. Sudha Bagur Viswanath, Aug. 1, 1971; children: Rekha, Kumar. MSc, U. Mysore, 1963; MPH, U. N.C., 1968; cert., U. Mich., 1969; PhD, U. Pa., 1971. Cert. DTRC Dombay. Asst. prof. Brown U., Providence, 1971-73; UN adviser Govt. of Sri Lanka, Colombo, 1974-77; chief population and devel. UN Population Fund, N.Y.C., 1978-82, chief policy br., 1982-90; country dir. UN Population Fund, Addis Ababa, Ethiopia, 1991-92; dep. dir. info. & extern rels. UN Population Fund, N.Y.C., 1992-95, dir. tech. and evaluation divsn., 1996—; sec. UN Population Fund segment of UN Devel. Program/UN Population Fund exec. bd.; leader UN tech. missions to several countries. Author: Socio-Religious Factors in Fertility, 1973; co-author: Population Problems of Sri Lanka, 1977, Population Program Experience, 1991; contbr. articles to profl. jours. V.p. Mysore Self Reliance Assn., Mangalore, 1963-65, Indo-Am. Forum for Polit. Edn., N.Y., 1989-90; founder, pres. New Eng. Kannada Koota, Providence, 1972-73. Recipient several acad. honors and gold medals, U. Pa., 1971, U. Mysore, 1961, 63. Mem. Delta Omega, Internat. Union for the Scientific Study of Population. Avocations: traveling, debate, bridge playing. Home: 143 Nelson Rd Scarsdale NY 10583-5811 Office: UN Population Fund 220 E 42nd St New York NY 10017-5806

RAPAPORT, FELIX THEODOSIUS, surgeon, editor, researcher, educator; b. Munich, Germany, Sept. 27, 1929; s. Max W. and Adelaide (Rathaus) R.; m. Margaret Birsner, Dec. 14, 1969; children: Max, Benjamin, Simon, Michel, Adelaide. AB, NYU, 1951, MD, 1954. Diplomate Am. Bd. Surgery. Intern Mt. Sinai Hosp., N.Y.C., 1955-56; resident, chief resident NYU Surg. Services, 1958-62, USPHS postdoctoral fellow in pathology, 1956; exec. officer Naval Med. Rsch. Unit No. 1, U. Calif., Berkeley, 1956-58; trainee in allergy and infectious diseases NYU, 1958-61; head, transplantation and immunology div. NYU Surg. Svcs., 1965-77; dir. rsch. Inst. Reconstrn. and Plastic Surgery, NYU, 1965-77; assoc. prof. surgery NYU Med. Ctr., 1965-70, prof., 1970-77; prof. surgery, prof. pathology, dir. transplantation svc. SUNY, Stony Brook, 1977-95, disting. prof., 1995—, chmn. dept. surgery, 1989-91; guest investigator Hosp. St. Louis, Paris, 1963-79; Claude Bernard vis. prof. exptl. medicine Coll. de France, Paris, 1985; sr. attendingsurgeon SUNY Hosp., 1980—, surgeon-in-chief, 1989-91; pres. bd. dirs. regional N.Y. Transplant Program, 1977-89; cons. VA Hosp., N.Y.C., 1963-77, Northport, N.Y., 1977—; adv. panel on medicine and dentistry U.S. Office of Naval Res., 1974-78; adv. com. NIAID, 1964-68; merit review bd. immunology V.A. Dept. of Medicine and Surgery, 1974-78. Editor in chief Transplantation Proc., 1968—; assoc. editor Am. Jour. Kidney Diseases, 1981-86, Am. Jour. Craniofacial Genetics and Developmental Biology, 1980-85, Cellular Immunology, 1980-97; contbr. over 500 articles to profl. jours.; author, editor 20 books on transplantation. Bd. dirs. United Network for Organ Sharing, 1986-88. Served to lt. comdr. M.C. USNR, 1956-58. Decorated comdr. Order Sci. Merit, chevalier Ordre National du Merite, France, 1970, officer Legion of Honor (France), 1990; recipient Gold medal Societe d'Encouragement au Bien, 1979, Gold medal City of Paris, France, 1980, Commandeur Ordre des Palmes Academiques, France, 1981, Samuel L. Kountz award Howard U., 1989, Lester Hoenig award Nat. Kidney Found., 1990, Sol Berson award NYU, 1990, Disting. Achievement in Med. Scis. award Touro Coll. B. Levine Sch. Health Scis., 1991, USPHS Res. Career Devel. award, NIAID, 1961-62, Career Scientst award Health Rsch. Coun., 1963-72, Maimonides Physician award, new Skwere Institutions, 1995. Mem. ACS, French Acad. Scis., Soc. Univ. Surgeons, N.Y. Surg. Soc., Am. Burn Assn., Am. Surg. Assn., Am. Assn. Immunologists, Soc. Exptl. Biology and Medicine, Harvey Soc., Am. Soc. Transplant Surgeons, Am. Soc. Transplant Physicians, Soc. for Organ Sharing (hon. pres.), Am. Assn. Clin. Histocompatibility Testing, Internat. Soc. Exptl. Hematology, Transplantation Soc. (founding sec., v.p., treas., councillor, historian, pres. 1986-88), Alpha Omega Alpha. Jewish. Current Work: induction of specific tolerance to major transplantable organs in man; research concerned with effects of irradiation and bone marrow transplantation in the production of host unresponsiveness to tissue allografts. Office: SUNY Stony Brook Dept Surgery Health Sc Ctr Stony Brook NY 11794

RAPAPORT, MICHAEL, actor. Appeared in films Zebrahead, 1992, Point of No Return, 1993, Poetic Justice, 1993, Money for Nothing, 1993, True Romance, 1993, The Scout, 1994, Higher Learning, 1994, Kiss of Death, 1995, Mighty Aphrodite, 1995, Beautiful Girls, 1996, The Pallbearer, 1996, Copland, 1997, Kicked in the Head, 1997, Metro, 1997. Office: Innovative Artists Talent Agy 1999 Ave of Stars Ste 2850 Los Angeles CA 90067*

RAPAPORT, RITA, artist, sculpture, painter; b. N.Y.C., May 25, 1918; d. Mandel E. and Birdie (Shapiro) Cohen; m. Alexander Rapaport, Oct. 13, 1940 (widowed June 1983); children: Anne, Marshall, Judith; m. Leon L. Wolfe, Mar. 15, 1986. BA, N.Y.U., 1940. artist-in-residence Westchester Holocaust Commn. Manhatanville Coll. Purchase N.Y., 1990—. Prin. works include Gate of Remembrance, 1992. Mem. Nat. Orgn. Women, Dem. Party, B'nai Brith Haddassah, Mamaroneck Artists Guild, Hudson River Mus., Metro. Mus., Hudson River Contemporary Artists, Jewish Mus. N.Y., Nat. Holocaust Mus. Jewish. Avocations: swimming, photography, gardening, interior decorating. Home: 15 Tompkins Rd Scarsdale NY 10583

RAPER, CHARLES ALBERT, retired management consultant; b. Charleston, W.Va., Aug. 18, 1926; s. Kenneth B. and Louise (Williams) R.; m. Margaret Ann Weers, Dec. 26, 1947; children: Kathleen, Josephine, Charles. Student, Okla. State U., 1945; B.S., U. Ill., 1949. Sales mgr. Meyer Furnace Co., Peoria, Ill., 1949-54; v.p. mktg. Master Consol., Inc., Dayton, Ohio, 1954-61; mgmt. cons. McKinsey & Co., Inc., Chgo., 1961-67; v.p. mktg. Gen. Portland Inc., Dallas, 1967-69; pres. Gen. Portland Inc., 1969-75, also dir.; v.p., gen. mgr. Scholl Inc., Chgo., 1975-81; pres. Oxford Group of Sara Lee, 1981-84; mgmt. cons. McKinsey & Co., 1984—. Vice chmn. devel. bd. U. Tex. at Dallas; exec. bd. Circle 10 council Boy Scouts Am. Served with USNR, 1944-46. Mem. Dallas C. of C. (chmn. bd. dirs. 1974—), Sales Execs. Club, Cherokee Country Club, Chattooga Club, Atlanta Mellett Club (pres.), Phi Gamma Delta. Methodist. Home: 301 Townsend Pl NW Atlanta GA 30327-3035

RAPER, WILLIAM BURKETTE, retired college president; b. nr. Wilson, N.C., Sept. 10, 1927; s. William Cecil and Beulah Maybelle (Davis) R.; m. Rose Mallard, Aug. 19, 1951; children: Olivia, Kristie, Burkette, Elizabeth, Stephen, Laura. AB, Duke U., 1947, MDiv, 1951; MS (Kellogg fellow), Fla. State U., 1962; LLD, Atlantic Christian Coll. (now Barton Coll.), 1960. Ordained to ministry Free Will Baptist Ch., 1946; pastor Hull Rd. Free Will Bapt. Ch., Snow Hill, N.C., 1951-55; pres. Mt. Olive (N.C.) Coll., 1954-95, ret., 1995; dir. Wachovia Bank and Trust Co.; promotional dir. Free Will Bapt. State Conv. N.C., 1953-54; pres. council Ch.-Related Colls. N.C., 1966-67; mem. N.C. Edn. Assistance Authority, 1972-76; sec. Ind. Coll. Fund of N.C., 1976-78; Mem. N.C. Gov.'s Com. on Hwy. Traffic Safety, 1968; regional coordinator U.S. Office Edn. Program with Developing Instns., 1968-70; dir. Edn. Professions Devel. Act Grant for Strengthening Devel. in Pvt. Two-Year Colls., 1970-72; trustee N.C. Coll. Found., 1977-94; adv. com. Ind. Coll. Presidents, U. N.C. Recipient Disting. Service award Mt. Olive Jr. C. of C., 1961; named N.C. Young Man of Year, 1961. Mem. Am. Assn. Community and Jr. Colls. (commn. on legislation 1963-66, cons. 1968-71, chmn. commn. on student personnel 1970-71), N.C. Assn. Ind. Colls. and Univs. (exec. com. 1967-70, 76-77, 83-85), N.C. Assn. Colls. and Univs. (pres. 1969-70), Masons. Democrat. Office: Mt Olive Coll Office of Pres Emeritus Mount Olive NC 28365

RAPER, WILLIAM CRANFORD, lawyer; b. Asheville, N.C., Aug. 17, 1946; s. James Sidney and Kathryn (Cranford) R.; m. Patricia Dotson, Sept. 28, 1974; children: Kimber-leigh, Heather, James. AB, U. N.C., 1968; JD, Vanderbilt U., 1972. Bar: N.C. 1972, U.S. Ct. Appeals (4th cir.) 1972, U.S. Supreme Ct. 1977, U.S. Ct. Appeals (fed. cir.) 1985. Law clk. to Senator Sam Ervin Jr. Washington, 1971; law clk. to presiding justice U.S. Ct. Appeals (4th cir.), Richmond, Va., 1972-73; ptnr. Womble, Carlyle, Sandridge & Rice, Winston-Salem, N.C., 1974—. Mem. ABA, N.C. Bar Assn., N.C. Assn. of Def. Attys. (charter). Office: Womble Carlyle Sandridge & Rice 3300 One First Union Ctr 301 S College St Charlotte NC 28202-6000

RAPHAEL, ALBERT ASH, JR., lawyer; b. N.Y.C., June 4, 1925; s. Albert Ash and Clare (Schindler) R.; m. Dorothy Buck, Oct. 7, 1960; 1 child, Bruce William. A.B., Yale U., 1947; LL.D., Harvard U., 1950. Bar: N.Y. 1950, Vt. 1972. Mem. firm Gallert, Hilborn & Raphael, N.Y.C., 1950-60, Alter, Lefevre, Raphael, Lowry, and Gould, N.Y.C., 1960-78; individual practice Waitsfield, Vt., 1972-86, 95—; ptnr. Raphael and Ware, Waitsfield, 1986-95; Dir. various real estate cos. Mem. bd. zoning appeals, Waitsfield, 1974-83, selectman, 1976-82, chmn. bd. selectmen, 1981-82. Mem. Waitsfield Planning Commn., 1996—. Served with F.A., AUS, 1943-46. Mem. Vt. Bar Assn., Assn. of Bar of City of N.Y. Home: PO Box 1149 Waitsfield VT 05673-1149 Office: PO Box 1149 Raphael Rd Waitsfield VT 05673

RAPHAEL, COLEMAN, business consultant; b. N.Y.C., Sept. 16, 1925; s. Morris and Adella (Leav) R.; m. Sylvia Moskowitz, Feb. 28, 1948; children—Hollis, Gordon. B.Civil Engring., CCNY, 1945; M.C.E., Poly. Inst. Bklyn., 1951, Ph.D. in Applied Mechanics, 1965. Structural research engr., test research engr. Republic Aviation Corp., 1945-47; instr. mech. engring. Pratt Inst., Bklyn., 1947-51; from sr. research engr. to mgr. space systems div. Republic Aviation Corp., 1951-65; gen. mgr. space and electronics systems div., then v.p. Fairchild Hiller Corp., Germantown, Md., 1965-70; with Atlantic Rsch. Corp., Alexandria, Va., 1970-86, chmn. bd., 1980-86; chmn. bd. SJI Industries, 1968-70; dean bus. sch. George Mason U., Fairfax, Va., 1986-91; ret., 1991; bd. mem., prin. owner Applied Bus. Systems, Bethesda, Md., 1990—; bd. dirs. ENVIPCO (chmn. 1995), Fairfax, Va.; founder, chmn. Night Owl Security, Landover, Md., Geico, Chevy Chase, Md., 1981-92; mem. engring. adv. com. Montgomery Coll., Md., 1968-69, George Washington U., 1977-82; mem. Gov. Va. Task Force Nuclear Power Plants, 1969; chmn. energy com. Gov. Md. Sci. Adv. Coun., 1974-76; bd. visitors U. Pitts., 1980-82. Author textbook, papers, reports in field. Chmn. U.S. Bond drive, Alexandria, 1975-76; chmn. adv. com. Montgomery County Bldg. Codes, 1976-77. Recipient Citizenship award Montgomery County Press Assn., 1967, Disting. Service award Montgomery County C. of C., 1969, Disting. Citizenship award State of Md., 1970. Mem. AIAA (chmn. mgmt. com. 1976), Aircraft Industries Assn., Nat. Space Club, disting Alumus, Poly. Inst. of Bklyn., 1982. Home: 508 Hermleigh Rd Silver Spring MD 20902-1608

RAPHAEL, FREDERIC MICHAEL, author; b. Chgo., Aug. 14, 1931; s. Cedric Michael and Irene (Mauser) R.; m. Sylvia Betty Glatt, Jan. 17, 1955; children: Paul Simon, Sarah Natasha, Stephen Matthew Joshua. M.A. (Major Open scholar), St. John's Coll., Cambridge (Eng.) U., 1954. Author: (novels) Obbligato, 1956, The Earlson Way, 1958, The Limits of Love, 1960, A Wild Surmise, 1961, The Graduate Wife, 1962, The Trouble with England, 1962, Lindmann, 1963, Darling, 1965, Orchestra and Beginners, 1967, Like Men Betrayed, 1970, Who Were You With Last Night?, 1971, April, June and November, 1972, Richard's Things, 1973, California Time, 1975, The Glittering Prizes, 1976, Heaven and Earth, 1984, After the War, 1988, A Double Life, 1993, Old Scores, 1995; short stories Sleeps Six, 1979, Oxbridge Blues, 1980, Think of England, 1986, The Hidden I, 1990, The Latin Lover, 1994, Old Scores, 1995; screenplays Nothing But the Best, 1964, Darling, 1965, Two For the Road, 1967, Far From the Madding Crowd, 1967, A Severed Head, 1971, Daisy Miller, 1973, The Glittering Prizes, 1976, Rogue Male, 1976, Something's Wrong, 1978, Oresteia of Aeschylus, 1978, The Best of Friends, 1980, School Play, 1980, Richard's Things, 1981, Oxbridge Blues, 1984, After The War, 1989, (dir.) The Man in the Brooks Brothers Shirt, (Ace award best film on cable TV) 1990, Armed Response, 1995 (cinema and/or TV) Nothing But the Best, 1964 (Best Comedy Screenplay award Writers' Guild of U.K.), Darling, 1965, (U.S. Academy award, Best Original Screenplay Original British Academy and Writers' Guild of U.K.), Two For the Road, 1967 (nom. for Oscar, Best Screenplay Original), Far From the Maddening Crowd, 1968, A Severed Head, 1971, Daisy Miller, 1973, The Glittering Prizes, 1976 (Writer of the Yr. award Royal TV Soc.), Rogue Male, 1976, The Best of Friends and Sch. Play, 1980, Richard's Things, 1981, Oxbridge Blues, 1984; (criticism) Somerset Maugham and His World, 1977, Byron, 1982, Euripides' Medea, 1995; translator (with Kenneth McLeish) book revs. The Poems of Catullus, 1978, The Oresteia of Aeschylus, 1979, Aeschulus Complete Plays, 1991, Of Gods and Men, 1993; editor: Bookmarks, 1975, Cracks In The Ice (Views & Reviews), 1978, A List of Books, 1981; screenwriter, dir. Recipient Oscar award for original screenplay Darling, 1966, Ace awards 1987, 92, Brit. Acad. award, 1966; named Writer of Yr. Royal TV Soc., 1976. Fellow Royal Soc. Lit. Address: Lagardelle, St Laurent-la-Vallée, 24170 Belves France

RAPHAEL, LOUISE ARAKELIAN, mathematician, educator; b. N.Y.C., Oct. 24, 1937; d. Aristakes and Antionette (Sudbeaz) Arakelian; m. Robert Barnett Raphael, June 12, 1966 (div. 1985); children: Therese Denise, Marc Philippe. BS in Math., St. John's U., 1959; MS in Math., Cath. U., Washington, 1962; PhD in Math, Cath. U., 1967. Asst. prof. math. Howard U., Washington, 1966-70, vis. prof., 1981-82, assoc. prof., 1982-86, prof., 1986—; assoc. prof. Clark Coll., Atlanta, 1971-79, prof., 1979-82; vis. assoc. prof. MIT, Cambridge, 1977-78, vis. prof., 1989-90; vis. mem. Courant Inst. Math. Scis., NYU, 1996-97. Contbr. over 40 rsch. articles to profl. jours. Program dir. NSF, Washington, 1986-88; acting adminstrv. officer Conf. Bd. Math. Scis., 1985-86. Grantee NSF, 1975-76, 79-81, 89-91, Army Rsch. Office, 1981-89, Air Force Sci. Rsch., 1981-82, 91-95, Nat. Security Agy., 1994-96. Mem. Am. Math. Soc. (com. mem.), Math. Assn. Am. (chmn. minorities in math. task force 1988, 1st v.p. 1996—), Soc. Indsl. and Applied Math., Sigma Xi. Democrat. Roman Catholic. Office: Howard U Dept Math Washington DC 20059

RAPHAEL, SALLY JESSY, talk-show host; b. Easton, Pa., Feb. 25, 1942; children: Allison (dec.), Andrea; m. Karl Soderlund; 2 step-daughters, 1 adopted son, also foster children. BFA, Columbia U. Anchored radio program Jr. High Sch. News WFAS-AM, White Plains, N.Y., 1955; host of cooking program WAPA-TV, San Juan, P.R., 1965-67; radio and television broadcaster Miami and Ft. Lauderdale, Fla., 1969-74; host Sta. WMCA-Radio, N.Y.C., 1976-81; talk show host NBC Talk-net, N.Y.C., 1982-88, ABC Talkradio, N.Y.C., 1988-91; syndicated TV talk-show host N.Y.C., 1983—; part-time owner of a perfume factory, 1964-68; owner of an art gallery, 1964-69; owner, The Wine Press, N.Y.C., 1979-83; ind. producer TV films, 1991;. Author: (with M.J. Boyer) Finding Love, 1984, (with Pam Proctor) Sally: Unconventional Success, 1980; film appearances include: Resident Alien, 1990, The Addams Family, 1991, The Associate, 1996, Meet Wally Sparks, 1996; TV appearances include: Murphy Brown, Dave's World, The Nanny, The Tonight Show, Nightline, Diagnosis Murder, Conspiracy of Silence, Touched By An Angel, Sabrina the Teenage Witch, John LaRoquette Show; co-exec. producer (mini-series) The 3rd Twin, 1997. Recipient Bronze medal, Internat. Film & Television Festival of NY, 1985; Emmy award as outstanding talk-show host, daytime, 1988, 89. Office: Universal TV 515 W 57th St New York NY 10019-2901

RAPHAEL-HOWELL, FRANCES JAYNE, clinical psychologist; b. Alexandria, Va., Apr. 26, 1945; d. Robert Arthur and Isabelle Georgiana (Francis) Raphael; m. Frederick Alfred Howell, June 14, 1977; children: Robert, Carolyn, Cheryl. BS in Psychology, Howard U., 1971; MA in Clin. Psychology, Clark U., 1976, PhD, 1992; pre-doctoral intern, Children's Hosp. Med. Ctr., Boston, 1974-75. Diplomate Am. Bd. Forensic Examiners; cert. clin. psychologist; play therapist and supr. Assn. for Play Therapy. Spl. edn. tchr. Boston U. Mini Sch., 1975-76; instr. psychopathology U. Mass., Boston, 1976; psychologist Boston U. Med. Ctr., 1976-77; psychologist cons. Head Start, Boston, 1977; psychologist Montgomery County Pub. Schs., 1978; clin. psychologist D.C. Pub. Schs., Washington, 1978-91, supr. psychol. svcs., 1991-93; dir. Title I Pupil Pers. Svcs., Washington, 1993-96; instr. urban edn. Grad. Sch. George Washington U., 1995—; instr. play therapy Trinity U., 1996; presentations at confs. and workshops. Bd. dirs. Washington Humane Soc. Harvard U. fellow, 1974-75. Mem. APA (div. Clin. Psychology), Assn. for Play Therapy, Inc. (registered supr), D.C. Assn. for Sch. Psychologists. Democrat. Methodist. Home: 3010 W St SE Washington DC 20020-3361

RAPHAELSON, JOEL, retired advertising agency executive; b. N.Y.C., Sept. 27, 1928; s. Samson and Dorothy (Wegman) R.; m. Mary Kathryn Hartigan, Aug. 20, 1960; children: Matthew, Katherine, Paul. B.A., Harvard U., 1949. Copywriter Macy's, N.Y.C., 1950-51, BBDO, N.Y.C., 1953-58; with Ogilvy & Mather, Inc., N.Y.C., 1958-94, v.p., joint copy chief, 1964-66, dir., 1968-75, mem. exec. com., 1970-75; creative cons. Ogilvy & Mather, Inc., Europe, 1975-76; exec. creative dir. Ogilvy & Mather, Inc., Chgo., 1976-82; sr. v.p. internat. creative svcs. Ogilvy & Mather Worldwide, 1982-92, spl. assignments as editor, writer, speechwriter, cons., 1993-94, ret., 1995; lectr. bus. writing Am. Assn. Advt. Agys., other bus. orgns. Author: (with Kenneth Roman) How To Write Better, 1978, Writing That Works, 1981, rev. expanded edit., 1992; editor: The Unpublished David Ogilvy, 1986, Viewpoint (co. jour.), 1983-94. Cons. Lyric Opera Chgo., Snake River Inst., Jackson Hole, Wyo., Exec. Svc. Corps, Chgo. Home: 20 E Cedar St Chicago IL 60611-1149

RAPHEL, ROBIN, federal official; b. Vancouver, Wash., Sept. 16, 1947; m. Leonard Arthur Ashton; 2 children. BA, U. Wash.; Diploma in Hist. Studies, Cambridge U., Eng.; MA, U. Md. Lectr. history Damavand Coll., Tehran, Iran; analyst CIA; with Fgn. Svc., 1977, Islamabad, Pakistan, 1977-78; with office investment affairs bur. econs. Dept. of State, 1978-80, staff asst. to asst. sec. Near East and South Asian affairs, 1980-81, econ. officer Israel desk, 1981-82, spl. asst. to under sec. polit. affairs, 1982-84; 1st sec. polit. affairs London, 1984-88; polit. counselor Pretoria, South Africa, 1988-91, New Delhi, 1991-93; asst. sec. South Asian affairs Dept. of State, Washington, 1993—. Mem. Am. Econ. Assn., Am. Fgn. Svc. Assn., Phi Beta Kappa. Office: S Asian Affairs 2201 C St NW Washington DC 20520-0001*

RAPIER, PASCAL MORAN, chemical engineer, physicist; b. Atlanta, Jan. 11, 1914; s. Paul Edward and Mary Clare (Moran) R.; m. Martha Elizabeth Doyle, May 19, 1945; children: Caroline Elizabeth, Paul Doyle, Mollie Clare, John Lawrence, James Andrew. BSChemE, Ga. Inst. Tech., 1939; MS in Theoretical Physics, U. Nev., 1959; postgrad., U. Calif., Berkeley, 1961. Registered profl. engr., Calif., N.J. Plant engr. Archer-Daniels-Midland, Pensacola, Fla., 1940-42; group supr. Dicalite div. Grefco, Los Angeles, 1943-54; process engr. Celatom div. Eagle Picher, Reno, Nev., 1955-57; project mgr., assoc. research engr. U. Calif. Field Sta., Richmond, 1959-62; project mgr. sea water conversion Bechtel Corp., San Francisco, 1962-66; sr. supervising chem. engr. Burns & Roe, Oradell, N.J., 1966-74; cons. engr. Kenite Corp., Scarsdale, N.Y., Rees Blowpipe, Berkeley, 1960-66; sr. cons. engr. Sanderson & Porter, N.Y.C., 1975-77; staff scientist III Lawrence Berkeley Lab., 1977-84; bd. dirs. Newtonian Sci. Found.; v.p. Calif. Rep. Assembly, 1964-65; discoverer phenomena faster than light, origin of cosmic rays and galactic red shifts. Contbr. articles to profl. jours.; patentee agts. to render non-polar solvents electrically conductive, direct-contact geothermal energy recovery devices; contbr. Marks' Standard Handbook for Mechanical Engineers, 10th edit., 1996. Mem. Am. Inst. Chem. Engrs., Gideons Internat., Lions Internat., Corvallis, Sigma Pi Sigma. Home: 8015 NW Ridgewood Dr Corvallis OR 97330-3026 *Personal philosophy: Adopt a primary causal principle in your life and your work will not go unrewarded. Seek a guiding principle for your life, and find your efforts well rewarded.*

RAPIN, ISABELLE, physician; b. Lausanne, Switzerland, Dec. 4, 1927; d. Rene and Mary Coe (Reeves) R.; m. Harold Oaklander, Apr. 5, 1959; children: Anne Louise, Christine, Stephen, Peter. Physician's Diploma. Faculte de Medicine, U. Lausanne, 1952, Doctorate in Medicine, 1955. Diplomate Am. Bd. Psychiatry and Neurology. Intern in pediatrics N.Y. U. Bellevue Med. Center, 1953-54; resident in neurology Neurol. Inst. of N.Y., Columbia-Presbyn. Med. Center, 1954-57, fellow in child neurology, 1957-58; mem. faculty Albert Einstein Coll. Medicine, Bronx, N.Y., 1958—; prof. neurology and pediatrics Albert Einstein Coll. Medicine, 1972—; attending neurologist and child neurologist Einstein Affiliated Hosps., Bronx.; Mem. Nat. Adv. Neurol. and Communicative Disorders and Stroke Coun., NIH, 1984-88. Contbr. chpts. to books, articles to med. jours. Recipient award Conf. Ednl. Adminstrs. Serving the Deaf, 1988. Fellow Am. Acad. Neurology (exec. bd. 1995—); mem. AAAS, Internat. Child Neurology Assn. (sec.-gen. 1979-82, v.p. 1982-86, Frank R. Ford lectr. 1990), Am. Neurol. Assn. (v.p. 1982-83), Child Neurology Soc. (Hower award 1987), Internat. Neuropsychology Soc., N.Y. Acad. Scis., Assn. for Rsch. in Nervous and Mental Diseases (v.p. 1986). Office: Albert Einstein Coll Medicine 1410 Pelham Pky S Bronx NY 10461-1101

RAPKE, JACK, agent. Co-head of motion picture divsn., then co-chmn. Creative Artists Agy., Beverly Hills, Calif. Office: Creative Artists Agy 9830 Wilshire Blvd Beverly Hills CA 90212-1804

RAPKIN, JEROME, defense industry executive; b. Wilmington, Del., Aug. 1, 1929; s. Harry and Ida (Hermann) R.; B.S. in Marine Engring., U.S. Naval Acad., 1952; M.S. in E.E., U.S. Naval Postgrad. Sch., 1959; postgrad. Armed Forces Staff Coll., 1965, Catholic U. Am., 1978; m. Janet Vansant, Nov. 4, 1954; children—Keith, Leigh, Paige. Commd. ensign U.S. Navy, 1952, advanced through grades to capt., 1979; dir. Surface Warfare Systems Naval Sea Systems Command, Washington, 1974-75; comdr. Destroyer Squadron 26 Surface Force Atlantic, Norfolk, Va., 1975-78; head surface to surface warfare, chief naval ops., Washington, 1978; dir. programs and budget Chief Naval Material, Washington, 1979; v.p. engring. devel. Ocean Systems div. Gould, Inc., Cleve., 1979-83; head combat systems VSE Corp., 1983-85; v.p. def. systems Dynamac, 1985-88; sr. v.p., COO CASDE Corp., 1988-91; sr. v.p. Simms Industries, Inc., 1991-94; pres., CEO Breakwater Devel. Co., Inc., 1994—. Decorated Navy Meritorious Service medal, Navy Commendation medal with gold star; recipient Surpior Pub. Svc. award Sec. Navy. Mem. Navy League U.S. (nat. treas. 1987-92, nat. v.p. fin. 1992-95, nat. v.p. pub. rels. 1995—), U.S. Naval Inst., Am. Soc. Naval Engrs., Surface Navy Assn. Office: 3139 Catrina Ln Annapolis MD 21403-4341

RAPOPORT, ANATOL, peace studies educator, mathematical biologist; b. Lozovaya, Russia, May 22, 1911; emigrated to U.S., 1922, naturalized, 1928; s. Boris and Adel (Rapoport) R.; m. Gwen Goodrich, Jan. 29, 1949; children: Anya, Alexander, Charles Anthony. PhD, U. Chgo., 1941; DHL, U. Western Mich., 1971; LLD, U. Toronto, 1986; DS, Royal Mil. Coll. Can., 1995; Ehrendoktor, U. Bern, Switzerland, 1995. Faculty dept. math. Ill. Inst. Tech., 1946-47; com. math. biology U. Chgo., 1947-54; fellow Ctr. Advanced Study Behavioral Scis., Stanford, 1954-55; asso. prof. Mental Health Research Inst., prof. math. biology U. Mich., 1955-70; prof. psychology and math. U. Toronto, 1970-80; dir. Inst. for Advanced Studies, Vienna, 1980-83; prof. peace studies U. Toronto, 1984—. Author: Science and the Goals of Man, 1950, Operational Philosophy, 1953, Fights, Games, and Debates, 1960, Strategy and Conscience, 1964, Prisoner's Dilemma, 1965, Two-Person Game Theory, 1966, N Person Game Theory, 1970, The Big Two, 1971, Conflict in Man Made Environment, 1974, Semantics, 1975, The 2 x 2 Game, 1976, Mathematische Methoden in den Sozialwissenschaften, 1980, Mathematical Models in the Social and Behavioral Sciences, 1983, General System Theory, 1986, The Origins of Violence, 1989, Decision Theory and Decision Behavior, 1989, Canada and the World, 1992, Peace: An Idea Whose Time Has Come, 1992, Gewissheiten and Zweifel, 1994; editor General Systems, 1956-77. Served to capt. USAAF, 1942-46. Fellow Am. Acad. Arts and Scis.; mem. Am. Math. Soc., Internat. Soc. Gen. Semantics (pres. 1953-55), Canadian Peace Research and Edn. Assn. (pres. 1972-75), Soc. for Gen. Systems Research (pres. 1965-66), Sci. for Peace (pres. 1984-86). Home: 38 Wychwood Park, Toronto, ON Canada M6G 2V5

RAPOPORT, BERNARD, life insurance company executive; b. San Antonio, July 17, 1917; s. David and Riva (Feldman) R.; m. Audre Jean Newman, Feb. 15, 1942; 1 child, Ronald B. B.A., U. Tex.-Austin, 1939. Chmn. bd., chief exec. officer Am. Income Life Ins. Co., Waco, Tex., 1951—; chmn. bd. regents U. Tex., 1991; apptd. by pres. adv. com. for trade policy and negotiations, 1994—. Mem. Nat. Council on Crime and Delinquency, San Francisco, 1979—, Jerusalem Found., N.Y.C., 1979—, Hebrew Union Coll., Cin., 1980—, Union Am. Hebrew Congregations, 1981—; Nat. Hispanic Ctr. for Advanced Studies and Policy Analysis, Oakland, Calif., 1981—; assoc. mem. U. Cancer Found., Houston, 1976—, Jt. Ctr. Polit. and Econ. Studies, 1987—; appointed mem. Adv. Com. for Trade Policy and Negotiation; chmn. United Negro Coll. Fund, Waco, 1979-80, United Way of Waco, 1982-83; trustee Paul Quinn Coll., Waco, 1963-90, Boy's Club, Waco, 1982—; chmn. bd. regents U. Tex., 1991-97. Fellow City of Jerusalem., 1994. Democrat. Jewish. Club: Brazos. Avocations: tennis; politics; reading. Home: 2332 Wendy Ln Waco TX 76710-2011 Office: Am Income Life Ins Co PO Box 2608 Waco TX 76797

RAPOPORT, BERNARD ROBERT, lawyer; b. N.Y.C., Jan. 18, 1919; s. Max and Rose (Gerard) R.; m. Robyrta Wechter, May 31, 1959; 1 son: Michael. AB, Cornell U., 1939, JD, 1941. Bar: N.Y. 1941, Fed. Ct. (so. dist.) 1946. Assoc. firm Proskauer, Rose, Goetz, Mendelsohn, N.Y.C., 1941-50; gen. counsel M. Lowenstein Corp., N.Y.C., 1950-86, bd. dirs., 1961-86, treas., 1975-86, sec., 1970-86; dir., treas., sec. Leon Lowenstein Found. Served to capt. Signal Corps, U.S. Army, 1942-45. Mem. ABA, Assn. of Bar of City of N.Y. Address: 910 5th Ave New York NY 10021-4155

RAPOPORT, DAVID E., lawyer; b. Chgo., May 27, 1956; s. Morris H. and Ruth (Tecktiel) R.; m. Andrea Gail Albun; children: Alyson Faith, Steven Andrew. BS in Fin., No. Ill. U., 1978; JD with high honors, Ill. Inst. Tech., 1981; cert. in trial work Lawyers Postgrad. Inst., Chgo., 1984; cert. civil trial specialist Nat. Bd. Trial Adv., 1991. Bar: Ill. 1981, Wis. 1995, U.S. Dist. Ct. (no. dist.) Ill. 1981, U.S. Dist. Ct. (trial bar) Ill. 1993, U.S. Dist. Ct. (so. and cent. dists.), U.S. Ct. Appeals (7th cir.) 1981, U.S. Ct. Appeals (4th cir.) 1996. Litigation clk. Steinberg, Polacek & Goodman, Chgo., 1979-81; assoc. Katz, Friedman, Schur and Eagle, Chgo., 1981-90, ptnr., 1990, Baizer & Rapoport, Chgo., Highland Park, Ill., 1990-95; founding ptnr. Rapoport & Kupets Law Offices, 1995—; instr. legal writing Ill. Inst. Tech.-Kent Coll. Law, Chgo., 1981, guest lectr., 1985—; instr. Ill. Inst. CLE, 1995—; arbitrator Cir. Ct. Cook County, Ill., Million Dollar Advocates Forum, 1995—; mem. plaintiff's steering com. In Air Disaster at Charlotte Douglas Airport, 1994; bd. dirs. Congregation Beth Judea, Long Grove, Ill. Fellow Roscoe Pound Found.; mem. ABA, Am. Trial Lawyers Assn., Assn. Trial Lawyers of Am., Ill. Bar Assn., Ill. Trial Lawyers Assn., Chgo. Bar Assn. (mem. workers compensation com. 1981—, tort litigation com. 1982—), Ill. Inst. for Continuing Legal Edn., Trial Lawyers for Pub. Justice, Trial Lawyers for Civil Justice, Lake County Bar Assn. Contbr. chpt. to book. Office: Rapoport & Kupets Law Offices 77 W Washington St Fl 20 Chicago IL 60602-2801 also: O'Hare Internat Ctr 10275 W Higgins Rd Ste 370 Rosemont IL 60018-5625

RAPOPORT, JUDITH, psychiatrist; b. N.Y.C., July 12, 1933; d. Louis and Minna (Enteen) Livant; m. Stanley Rapoport, June 25, 1961; children: Stuart, Erik. BA, Swarthmore Coll., 1955; MD, Harvard U., 1959. Lic. psychiatrist. Cons., child psychiatrist NIMH/St. Elizabeth's Hosp., Washington, 1969-72; clin. asst. prof. Georgetown U. Med. Sch., Washington, 1972-82, clin. assoc. prof., 1982-85, clin. prof. psychiat., 1985—; med. officer biol. psychiatry br. NIMH, Bethesda, Md., 1976-78, chief, child mental illness unit, biol. psychiat. br., 1979-82, chief, child psychiatry lab. of clin. scis., 1982-84, chief, child psychiatry div. intramural rsch. programs, 1984—; prof. psychiatry George Washington U. Sch. Med., Washington, 1979—; prof. pediatrics Georgetown U., Washington, 1985—; cons. in field. Author: (non-fiction) The Boy Who Couldn't Stop Washing, 1989 (best seller literary guild selection 1989), Childhood Obsessive Compulsive Disorder, 1989. Fellow Am. Psychiat. Assn., Am. Acad. Child Psychiat.; mem. D.C. Psychiat. Assn., Inst. Medicine. Home: 3010 44th Pl NW Washington DC 20016-3557 Office: NIMH Bldg 10 Rm 6N240 Bethesda MD 20892

RAPOPORT, MILES S., state official; m. Sandra Luciano; children: Jeff, Ross. BA in Polit. Sci., NYU, 1971. Exec. dir. Conn. Citizen Action Group, 1979-84; mem. Conn. Ho. of Reps., asst. majority leader, 1987-92, house chmn. govt. adminstrn. and elections com., mem. fin., revenue and bonding com.; sec. of state State of Conn., 1994—. Address: 30 Montclair Dr West Hartford CT 06107-1246 Office: State Capitol # 104 Hartford CT 06106*

RAPOPORT, ROBERT MORTON, medical educator; b. Oakland, Calif., Nov. 20, 1952; married; 2 children. BA in Biological Scis., U. Calif., Santa Barbara, 1974; PhD in Pharmacology, U. Calif., L.A., 1980; postdoc. studies in Pharmacology, U. Va., 1980-81, Stanford U., 1981-83. Rsch. pharmacologist VA Med. Ctr., Palo Alto, Calif., 1983-84, Cin., 1984—; asst. prof. dept. pharmacology and cell biophysics U. Cin., 1984-91, assoc. prof., 1991—; asst. dir. med. pharmacology, 1994; spkr. in field. Reviewer manuscripts. various jours., grants various assns.; contbr. over 100 articles to profl. publs. Grantee U. Calif., 1977, VA, 1983-86, 85-86, 87-90, NIH, 1985-87, 88-93, Am. Heart Assn. S.W. Ohio, 1985-86, 86-87, 88-89, 89-91, 91-92, U. Cin., 1985-86, Am. Heart Assn., 1987-90, 1995—, Veterans Affairs, 1994-95, 95—, Univ. Rsch. Coun., 1994-95, Parke-Davis, 1994, 95; recipient Rsch. Career Devel. award, 1986-91. Office: Dept Pharmacology Univ Cincinnati 231 Bethesda Ave Cincinnati OH 45229-2827

RAPOPORT, RONALD JON, journalist; b. Detroit, Aug. 14, 1940; s. Daniel B. and Shirley G.; m. Joan Zucker, Sept. 2, 1968; children—Rebecca, Julie. B.A., Stanford U., 1962; M.S., Columbia U., 1963. Reporter Mpls. Star, 1963-65; asso. editor Sport mag., 1965-66; sports reporter AP, N.Y.C., San Francisco, 1966-70, Los Angeles Times, 1970-77; sports columnist Chgo. Sun-Times, 1977-88, Los Angeles Daily News, 1988-95; sports commentator Weekend Edit. Nat. Pub. Radio, 1986—; dep. sports editor Chgo. Sun-Times, 1996—. Author: (with Chip Oliver) High for the Game, 1971, (with Stan Love) Love in the NBA, 1975, (with Jim McGregor) Called for Travelling, 1979; editor: A Kind of Grace: A Treasury of Sportswriting by Women, 1994. Served with U.S. Army Res., 1963. Address: 3150 N Lake Shore Dr Chicago IL 60657

RAPOPORT, SONYA, artist; b. Boston; d. Louis Aaron and Ida Tina (Axelrod) Goldberg; m. Henry Rapoport; children—Hava Rapoport de Feres, David, Robert. Student Mass. Coll. Art, 1941-42; B.A., NYU, 1945; M.A., U. Calif.-Berkeley, 1949. One woman shows Calif. Palace of Legion of Honor, 1963, Peabody Mus., Harvard U., 1978, N.Y.C. Pub. Library, 1979, New Sch. Social Research, N.Y.C., 1981, NYU Grad. Sch. Bus. Adminstrn., 1982, Sarah Lawrence Coll., Bronxville, N.Y., 1984, Kuopio Mus., Finland, 1992; group shows include Union Gallery San Jose State U., Calif., 1979, Ctr. for Visual Arts, Oakland, Calif., 1979, Walker Art Ctr., Mpls., 1981, Nat. Library, Madrid, 1982, SUNY Library, Purchase, 1983, Otis Art Inst. of Parsons Sch. of Design, Los Angeles, 1984, Cleve. Inst. Art, 1984, FISEA93, 95, 96, Digital Salon, 1965, 66, Copenhagen Film Festival, 1996, 4th Internat. Symposium on Electronic Art, Mpls.also others; respresented in permanent collections Stedelijk Mus., Amsterdam, Indpls. Mus. Art, Grey Art Gallery, NYU, San Francisco Mus. Modern Art, San Jose State U. Found.-Union Gallery, Crocker Art Mus., Sacramento, Hall of Justice, Hayward, Calif.; book artist Shoe-Field, Chinese Connections, About Me, Objects on My Dresser, (interactive books) Gateway to Your Ka, Your Fate is in Your Feet, Digital Mudra2; producer A Shoe-In, Biorhythm, Coping with Sexual Jealousy, (computer assisted interactive installations) The Animated Soul, Digital Mudra, Transgenic Bagel; contbr. to profl. publs. Web Art Works for Internet, 1995, 96, Smell Your Destiny, Brutal Myths. Home: 6 Hillcrest Ct Berkeley CA 94705-2805

RAPP, CHARLES WARREN, computer scientist, researcher; b. Evanston, Ill., Nov. 30, 1961; s. Daniel Warren and Eunice Marie (Gockel) R. BS in Math. and Computer Sci., U. Ill., Chgo., 1984; MS in Computer Sci., Oreg. State U., 1986. Mem. tech. staff AT&T Bell Labs., Naperville, Ill., 1984-90; cons. BALR Corp., Oak Brook, Ill., 1990-91; sr. devel. engr. Clear Comm., Lincolnshire, Ill., 1991—. Author: (chpt.) Current Trends in SNePS, 1990. Mem. Assn. for Computing Machinery, Am. Assn. Artificial Intelligence. Republican. Lutheran. Office: Clear Comm Corp 100 Tri-State Internat Lincolnshire IL 60069

RAPP, FRED, virologist; b. Fulda, Germany, Mar. 13, 1929; came to U.S., 1936, naturalized, 1945; s. Albert and Rita (Hain) R.; children: Stanley I., Richard J., Kenneth A.; m. Pamela A. Miles, Aug. 28, 1988. BS, Bklyn. Coll., 1951; MS, Albany Med. Coll., Union U., 1956; PhD, U. So. Calif., 1958. Jr. bacteriologist to bacteriologist divsn. labs. and rsch. N.Y. State Dept. Health, 1952-55; from teaching asst. to instr. dept. med. microbiology Sch. Medicine U. So. Calif., 1956-59; cons. supervisory microbiologist Hosp. Spl. Surgery, N.Y.C., 1959-62; also virologist div. pathology Philip D. Wilson Research Found., N.Y.C.; asst. prof. microbiology and immunology Cornell U. Med. Coll., N.Y.C., 1961-62; assoc. prof. Baylor U. Sch. Medicine, Houston, 1962-66, prof., 1966-69; prof., chmn. dept. microbiology and immunology Pa. State U. Coll. Medicine, Hershey, Pa., 1969-90; Evan Pugh prof. microbiology Pa. State U. Coll. Medicine, University Park, 1978-90, prof. emeritus, 1990—, assoc. provost, dean health affairs, 1973-80, sr. mem. grad. faculty, assoc. dean acad. affairs, research and grad. studies, 1987-90, professor emeritus, 1990—; researh career prof. of virology Am. Cancer Soc., 1966-69, prof. virology, 1977-90; dir. Coll. Med. Pa. State U. (Specialized Cancer Research Ctr.), 1973-84; mem. del. on viral oncology, U.S./USSR Joint Com. Health Cooperation; chmn., Gordon Rsch. Conf. in Cancer, 1975; virology Task Force, 1976-79; chmn. Atlantic Coast Tumor Virology Group, Nat. Cancer Insts. Health, 1971-77; mem. council for projection and analysis Am. Cancer Soc., 1976-80; chmn. standards and exam. com. on virology Am. Bd. Med. Microbiology, 1977, 80; chmn. subsect. on virology program com. Am. Assn. Cancer Research, 1978-79; mem. adv. council virology div. Internat. Union Microbiol. Socs., 1978-84; referee Macy Faculty Scholar Award Program, 1979-81; mem. programme com. Fifth Internat. Congress for Virology, Strasbourg, France, 1981; mem. basic cancer rsch. group U.S.-France Agreement for Cooperation in Cancer Research, 1980-84; mem. organizing com. Internat. Workshop on Herpes viruses, Bologna, Italy, 1980-81, NATO Internat. Advanced Study Inst., Corfu Island, Greece, 1981; mem. Herpes viruses Study Group, 1981-84; mem. sci. adv. com. Wilmot Fellowship Program, U. Rochester Med. Ctr., 1981-90 ; mem. scientific rev. com. Hubert H. Humphrey Cancer Research Ctr., Boston U., 1981; mem. fin. com. Am. Soc. Virology, 1982-89, mem. council, 1984-88; mem. adv. com. persistent virus-host interactions research program R.J. Reynolds Scientific Bd./Wistar Inst., 1983-90; mem. med. adv. bd. Herpes Resource Ctr., Am. Social Health Assn., 1983-90; bd. dirs. U.S.-Japan Found. Biomedicine, 1983-90; mem. council Soc. Exptl. Biology and Medicine, 1983-87; mem. scientific adv. com. Internat. Assn. Study and Prevention of Virus-Associated Cancers, 1983-90; mem. Basil O'Connor Starter Research Adv. Com., 1984-90; mem. council for research and clin. investigation awards Am. Cancer Soc., 1984-90; mem. recombinant DNA adv. com. NIH, 1984-87; mem. outstanding investigator grant rev. com. Nat. Cancer Inst., 1984-90; mem. organizing com. Fourth Symposium Sapporo Cancer Seminar, Japan, 1984, Second Internat. Conf. Immunobiology and Prophylaxis of Human Herpes virus Infections, Ft. Lauderdale, Fl., 1984-85, Internat. Congress of Virology, Sendai, Japan, 1984; mem. internat. sci. com. Internat. Meeting on Adv. in Virology, Catania, Italy, 1984-85; mem. adv. bd. Cancer Info., Dissemination and Analysis Ctr. Carcinogenesis and Cancer Biology, 1984-89; mem. internat. programme com. 7th Internat. Congress of Virology, Edmonton, Can., 1985-87; councilor div. DNA viruses Am. Soc. Microbiology, 1985-87; mem. adv. com. rsch. on etiology, diagnosis, natural history, prevention and therapy of multiple sclerosis Nat. Multiple Sclerosis Soc., 1985-89; mem. sci. adv. bd. Tampa Bay Rsch. Inst., 1985-91; mem. sci. adv. coun. Pitts. Ctr. AIDS Rsch. U. Pitts., 1988; mem. recombinant DNA adv. com. Working Group on Transgenic Animals NIH, 1988; mem. adv. com. 15th Internat. Herpes Virus Workshop, Washington, 1989-90. Sect. editor on oncology: Intervirology, 1972-84, assoc. editor, 1978-84, editor-in-chief, 1985-90; adv. bd. Archives Virology, 1976-81; editorial bd. Jour. Immunology, 1966-73, Jour. Virology, 1968-88; assoc. editor Cancer Research, 1972-79; editorial bd. Virology, 1979-83, editor, 1983-90; mem. adv. bd. Ency. Americana, 1992—. Recipient 1st CIBA-Geigy Drew award for biomed. research, 1977, Nat. award for teaching excellence in microbiology, U. Medicine and Dentistry N.J. Med. Sch., 1988; Wellcome vis. professorship in microbiology, 1989-90; Disting. fellow Inst. Advanced Biotech., 1991. Mem. AAAS, AAUP, Am. Acad. Microbiology (fellow, diplomate), Soc. Microbiology (mem. com. med. microbiology and immunology, bd. pub. sci. affairs 1979-88, chmn. DNA viruses div. 1981-82, divsn. councilor DNA viruses), Am. Soc. Virology (chmn. fin. com. 1987-88, emeritus 1991), Am. Assn. Immunologists, The Harvey Soc., Soc. Exptl. Biology and Medicine (emeritus 1993), Am. Assn. Cancer Rsch. (emeritus 1991), Assn. Med. Sch. Microbiology Chmn. (pres. 1980-81), Seven Seas Cruising Assn. (assoc. 1987-91, commodore 1991—), Sigma Xi (Monie A. Ferst award 1990, nat. lectr. 1977-79), Alpha Omega Alpha. Home: 65 Governors Harbor Hilton Head Island SC 29926

RAPP, GEORGE ROBERT, JR. (RIP RAPP), geology and archeology educator; b. Toledo, Sept. 19, 1930; s. George Robert and Gladys Mae (Warner) R.; m. Jeannette Messner, June 15, 1956; children: Kathryn, Karen. BA, U. Minn., 1952; PhD, Pa. State U., 1960. Asst. then assoc. prof. S.D. Sch. Mines, Rapid City, 1957-65; assoc. prof. U. Minn., Mpls., 1965-75; prof. geology and archeology U. Minn., Duluth, 1975-95, dean Coll. Letters and Sci., 1975-84, dean Coll. Sci. and Engring., 1984-89, dir. Archeometry Lab., 1975—; Regents' prof. geoarchaeology, 1995—; prof. Ctr. for Ancient Studies, U. Minn., Mpls., 1970-93, prof. interdisciplinary archaeol. studies, 1993—, Regents' prof. geoarchaeology, 1995—; cons. USIA, Westinghouse Corp., Exxon Corp., Ford Found. Author, editor: Excavations at Nichoria, 1978, Troy: Archeological Geology, 1982, Archeological Geology, 1985, Excavations at Tel Michal, 1989, Encyclopedia of Minerals, 1989, Phytolith Systematics, 1992; mem. editorial bd. Jour. Field Archeology, 1976-85, Jour. Archeol. Sci., 1977-79, Geoarcheology Jour., 1984—, Am. Jour. Archeology, 1985-92. NSF postdoctoral fellow, 1963-64, Fulbright-Hayes sr. rsch. fellow, 1972-73. Fellow AAAS (chmn. sect. E, 1987-88, nat. coun. 1992-95), Geol. Soc. Am. (Archeol. Geology award 1983), Mineral. Soc. Am.; mem. Nat. Assn. Geology Tchrs. (pres. 1986-89), Soc. for Archeol. Sci. (pres. 1983-84), Assn. Field Archeology (pres. 1979-81), Archaeol. Inst. Am. (Pomerance medal 1988), Sigma Xi (bd. dirs. 1990—). Avocation: classical music, archaeological excavations in Greece, Turkey, Cyprus, Israel. Office: U Minn-Duluth Archaeometry Lab Duluth MN 55812

RAPP, GERALD DUANE, lawyer, manufacturing company executive; b. Berwyn, Nebr., July 19, 1933; s. Kenneth P. and Mildred (Price) R.; children: Gerald Duane Jr., Gregory T., Amy Frances Wanzek. B.S., U. Mo., 1955; J.D., U. Mich., 1958. Bar: Ohio bar 1959. Practice in Dayton, 1960—; ptnr. Smith & Schnacke, 1963-70; asst. gen. counsel Mead Corp., Dayton, 1970, v.p. human resources and legal affairs, 1973, v.p., corp. sec., 1975, v.p., gen. counsel, corp. sec., 1976, v.p., gen. counsel, 1979, sr. v.p., gen. counsel, 1981-91, counsel to bd. dirs., 1991-92; of counsel Bieser, Greer & Landis, 1992—; pres. R-J Holding Co., Weber Canyon Ranch, Inc. Sr. editor U. Mich. Law Rev., 1957-58. Past chmn. Oakwood Youth Commn.; past v.p., bd. dirs. Big Bros. Greater Dayton; mem. pres.'s visitors com. U. Mich. Law Sch.; past trustee Urbana Coll.; past pres., trustee Ohio Ctr. Leadership Studies, Robert K. Greenleaf Ctr., Indpls.; past pres. bd. trustees Dayton and Montgomery County Pub. Libr.; past. mem. bd. visitors Law Schs. of Dayton. 1st lt. U.S. Army, 1958-60. Mem. ABA, Ohio Bar Assn., Dayton Bar Assn., Moraine Country Club, Dayton Racquet Club, Dayton Lawyers Club, Met. Club Washington, Phi Kappa Psi, Phi Delta Phi, Beta Gamma Sigma. Presbyterian. Office: Bieser Greer & Landis 400 National City Ctr Dayton OH 45402-1908

RAPP, JAMES ALLEN, marketing executive; b. St. Louis, Dec. 30, 1946; s. William Albert and Catherine C. (Book) R.; m. Ester Liselotte Nelson, May 26, 1979 (div. 1992); m. Janet Critchley, Feb. 24, 1996. Student, St. John's U., Collegeville, Minn., 1965-66; BA, Benedictine Colls., Atchison, Kans., 1969; MBA, Wake Forest U., 1993. Editor Apt. Living mag., St. Louis, 1972-73; mng. editor Daily Record, New Orleans, 1973-74; dir. mktg., devel. Sta. WYES, New Orleans, 1974-78; dir. mktg. services Stewart Enterprises Inc., New Orleans, 1978-85; v.p. Perez Corp., New Orleans, 1985-86; prin. J.A. Rapp & Assocs., 1987-88; dir. mktg. comm. ISA, Raleigh, N.C., 1988-95; ops. mgr. direct mktg. IBM, Phoenix, 1995-96; mgr. N.Am. bus. planning and analysis, direct mktg. IBM, White Plains, N.Y., 1996—. Editor: Metairie Cemetery, An Historical Memoir, 1983 (Anvil award). Chmn. community bd. Boys Clubs of New Orleans, 1985-86; chmn. programming com., bd. dirs. Cultural Communications, Inc., 1987-88; devel. advisor New Orleans Opera Assn., 1983-85. Mem. Pub. Rels. Soc. Am. (Anvil award 1983), Am. Mktg. Assn., Direct Mktg. Assn., Am. Soc. Assn. Execs. Avocations: writing music, writing prose and poetry, languages, fencing. Home: 18 Oenoke Pl # 6 Stamford CT 06907

RAPP, ROBERT ANTHONY, metallurgical engineering educator, consultant; b. Lafayette, Ind., Feb. 21, 1934; s. Frank J. and Goldie M. (Royer) R.; m. Heidi B. Sartorius, June 3, 1960; children: Kathleen Rapp Raynaud, Thomas, Stephen, Stephanie Rapp Surface. BSMetE, Purdue U., 1956; MSMetE, Carnegie Inst. Tech., 1959, PhDMetE, 1960; D (hon.), Inst. Polytech., Toulouse, France, 1995. Asst. prof. metall. engring. Ohio State U., Columbus, 1963-66, assoc. prof., 1966-69, prof., 1969—, M.G. Fontana prof., 1988—, Univ. prof., 1989-95; disting. univ. prof. emeritus, 1995—; cons. KB Alloys; vis. prof. Ecole Nat. Superior d'Electrochimie, Grenoble, France, 1972-73, U. Paris-Sud, Orsay, 1985-86, Ecole Nat. Superior de Chimie, Toulouse, France, 1985-86, U. New South Wales, Australia, 1987; Acta/Scripta Metallurgica lectr., 1991; rsch. metallurgist WPAFB, Ohio, 1960-63. Editor: Techniques of Metals Research, vol. IV, 1982, High Temperature Corrosion, 1984; translator Metallic Corrosion (Kaesche), 1986; bd. rev. jour. Oxid. Metals; contbr. numerous articles to profl. jours. Recipient Disting. Engring. Alumnus award Purdue U., 1988, B.F. Goodrich Collegiate Inventor's award, 1991, 92, Ulrick Evans award Brit. Inst. Corrosion, 1992; Guggenheim fellow, 1972; Fulbright scholar Max Planck Inst. Phys. Chemistry, 1959-60. Fellow Am. Soc. Metals Internat. (B. Stoughton award 1968, Howe gold medal 1974), Mining Metals and Materials Soc., Electrochem. Soc. (HTM Divsn. Outstanding Achievement award 1992), Nat. Assn. Corrosion Engrs. (W.R. Whitney award 1986), French Soc. Metals and Materials (hon.), Chevalier des Palmes Acad. Lutheran. Home: 1379 Southport Dr Columbus OH 43235-7649

RAPP, ROBERT NEIL, lawyer; b. Erie, Pa., Sept. 10, 1947; m. Sally K. Meder; 1 child: Jeffrey David. BA, Case Western Res. U., 1969, JD, 1972; MBA, Cleve. State U., 1989. Bar: Ohio 1972, U.S. dist. Ct. (no. dist.) Ohio 1973, U.S. Ct. Appeals (6th crct.) 1981, U.S. Supreme Ct. 1980. Assoc. Metzenbaum, Gaines & Stern, Co., L.P.A., Cleve., 1972-75; ptnr. Calfee, Halter & Griswold, Cleve., 1975—; adj. prof. law Case Western Res. U., 1975-78, 94—, Cleve. Marshall Coll. Law, Cleve. State U., 1976-82; disting. lawyer-in-residence Cornell U. Law Sch., 1993; mem. legal adv. bd. Nat. Assn. Securities Dealers, 1992-96, arbitrator; mem. market ops. rev. com. Nasdaq Stock Market, 1996—; arbitrator Nat. Futures Assn.; ind. arbitrator securities and futures law matters. Contbr. numerous articles to law jours. Mem. ABA (sect. bus. law: mem. com. fed. regulation of securities, subcom. broker-dealer regulation, sect. litigation: mem. com. securities litigation), Am. Arbitration Assn. (securities arbitrator, mem. comml. adv. coun. Cleve. region), Ohio State Bar Assn. (elected mem. coun. dels. 1976-82, corp. law com. 1980—), Cleve. Bar Assn. (chmn. young lawyers sect. 1976-77), assoc. mem. cert. grievance com., sect. securities law: exec. coun. 1980-85, chmn. govt. liaison com. 1980-81). Office: Calfee Halter & Griswold 1400 McDonald Investment Ct Cleveland OH 44114-2688

RAPP, STEPHEN JOHN, United States attorney; b. Waterloo, Iowa, Jan. 26, 1949; s. Spurgeon John and Beverly (Leckington) R.; m. Donna J.E. Maier, 1981; children: Alexander, Stephanie. AB cum laude, Harvard U., 1970; JD with honors, Drake U., 1973. Bar: Iowa 1974, U.S. Dist. Ct. (no. and so. dists.) Iowa 1978, U.S. Ct. Appeals (8th cir.) 1979, U.S. Supreme Ct. 1979. Rsch. asst. Office of U.S. Senator Birch Bayh, Ind., 1970; community program asst. HUD, Chgo., 1971; mem. Iowa Ho. Reps., 1972-74, 79-83, Coun. to Majority Caucus, Iowa Ho. Reps., 1975; staff dir., counsel subcom. on juvenile delinquency U.S. Senate, Washington, 1977-78; ptnr. Rapp & Gilliam, Waterloo, 1979-83; pvt. practice Waterloo, 1983—; U.S. atty. U.S. Dist. Ct. (no. dist.) Iowa, 1993—. Del., mem. com. Dem. Nat. Conv., 1976, 80, 84, 88; mem. Dem. Nat. Adv. Com. on Econ., 1982-84, chmn. Black Hawk Dem. Com., 1986-91; mem. Iowa Dem. Com., 1990-93, chair 2d C.D. Dem. Com., 1991-93. Mem. ABA, Iowa Bar Assn., Order of Coif. Methodist. Home: 219 Highland Blvd Waterloo IA 50703-4229

RAPPACH, NORMA JEANNE, health occupations educator; b. Hastings, Pa., Mar. 7, 1938; d. James Eugene and Katherine Luella (Lear) Fairbanks; m. James Davis Mrus, June 30, 1959 (div. Aug. 1978); children: Timothy James, Susan Marie Mrus Hughes, Joseph Michael; m. Ronald Michael Rappach, Aug. 9, 1979; stepchildren: Kelley Rae, Lynn Rae Rappach Paris. Diploma, Trumbull Meml. Sch. Nursing, 1959; cert. EMT/paramedic, Cuyahoga C.C., 1978; AAS with honors, Kent State U., 1983, vocat. tchr. cert., 1996; BSN magna cum laude, Youngstown State U., 1986. RN, Ohio; cert. diversified health occupations instr., Ohio. Pediatric staff nurse Trumbull Meml. Hosp., Warren, Ohio, 1960-62, part-time pvt. duty nurse, 1969-71; geriatric staff nurse Meadows Manor, Terre Haute, Ind., 1965-66; Vocat. Tchr.; substitute sch. nurse Howland Local Schs., Warren, 1972-78; cert. emergency med. instr. Ohio Dept. Edn., Columbus, 1973-78; substitute indsl. nurse Packard Electric divsn. GM, Warren, 1974-76; sch. nurse Lordstown Local Schs., Warren, 1978-93; diversified health occupations instr. Gordon D. James Career Ctr., Lordstown Schs., Warren, 1993—; part-time nurse obstetrical office, Warren, 1961-73; part-time gen. office nurse, Warren, 1960-72; part-time geriatric nurse Gillette's Nursing, Warren, 1972-74; instr. nurse aid tng. Ohio Bd. Nursing, 1993—. Adviser Teen Inst. for Alcohol Abuse, Warren, 1981; county emergency med. coord. Trumbull County, Warren, 1976-77; pres. Trumbull County Emergency Med. Com., 1976-77; HIV/AIDS coord. Lordstown Local Schs., 1985-93, mem. diversified health adv. bd., 1990—; vol. nurse, 1st aid/CPR/HIV-AIDS instr., ARC, Warren, 1990—; parish nurse Blessed Sacrament Ch., Warren, 1992-94. Named Profl. Woman of Yr., Trumbull County Fair, 1977, Hon. Firewoman, Howland Twp. Fire Dept., 1978, Vocat. Citizenship award Omicron Tau Theta chpt. Kent State U., 1995; nursing scholar Warren Kiwanis Club, 1956. Mem. Am. Fedn. Tchrs., Ohio Vocat. Assn. Avocations: reading, computers, crafts.

RAPPAPORT, CHARLES OWEN, lawyer; b. N.Y.C., May 15, 1950; s. Edward and Edith (Novick) R.; m. Valerie B. Ackerman, Oct. 11, 1987; children: Emily Randle, Sarah Elisabeth. BA, Columbia U., 1970; JD, NYU, 1975. Bar: N.Y. 1976. Assoc. Simpson, Thacher & Bartlett, N.Y.C., 1975-82, ptnr., 1982—. Home: 26 N Moore St Apt 4W New York NY 10013-2461 Office: Simpson Thacher & Bartlett 425 Lexington Ave New York NY 10017-3903

RAPPAPORT, GARY BURTON, defense equipment and software company executive; b. Mpls., Apr. 27, 1937; s. Max and Beatrice (Berkinsky) R.; m. Susan Heller, Nov. 26, 1961; children: Debra Lynn, Melissa Ellen. B.S., U. Pa., 1959. Asst. to pres. Napco Industries, Inc., Hopkins, Minn., 1959-61, v.p., 1961-65, exec. v.p., 1964-65, pres., 1965-74, chmn. bd., chief exec. officer, 1974-84; chmn. bd., chief exec. officer Venturian Corp., Hopkins, 1984—; dir. La Maur, Inc., Mpls., 1980-87. Chmn. bd. govs. Mt. Sinai Hosp., Mpls., 1979-81. Served with Air N.G., 1960-64. Jewish. Office: 11111 Excelsior Blvd Hopkins MN 55343-3434

RAPPAPORT, LAWRENCE, plant physiology and horticulture educator; b. N.Y.C., May 28, 1928; s. Aaron and Elsie R.; m. Norma, Nov. 21, 1953; children: Meryl, Debra Kramer, Craig. BS in Horticulture, U. Idaho, 1950; MS in Horticulture, Mich. State Coll., 1951; PhD in Horticulture, Mich. State U., 1956. Lectr. U. Calif., Davis, 1956-67, jr. olericulturist dept. vegetable crops, 1956-58, asst. olericulturist, 1958-63, assoc. olericulturist, 1963-67, prof., 1968—, prof. emeritus, 1991—, dir. plant growth lab., 1975-78, chairperson dept. vegetable crops, 1978-84; vis. scientist Calif. Inst. Tech., 1958; co-dir. Horticulture Subproject, Calif./Egypt project, 1978-82. Contbr. articles to profl. jours. 1st pres. Davis Human Rels. Coun., 1964-66; v.p. Jewish Fedn. Sacramento, 1969; pres. Jewish Fellowship, Davis, 1985-89. Sgt. maj. U.S. Army, 1952-53, Korea. Decorated Bronze star; Guggenheim Found. fellow, 1963, Fulbright fellow, 1964, USPHS Spl. fellow, 1970, Am. Soc. Horticulture Sci. fellow, 1987, Sir Frederick McMaster fellow, 1991. Achievements include discovery of evidence for gibberellin-binding protein in plants; evidence for the signal hypothesis operating in plants, positive evidence for phytochrome-mediated gibberellin metabolism and stem growth; isolation of somaclonal variants of celery bearing stable resistance to Fusarium oxysporum f. sp. apii. Home: 637 Elmwood Dr Davis CA 95616-3514 Office: U Calif Dept Vegetable Crops Asmundson Hall Rm 210 Davis CA 95616

RAPPAPORT, MARTIN PAUL, internist, nephrologist, educator; b. Bronx, N.Y., Apr. 25, 1935; s. Joseph and Anne (Kramer) R.; BS, Tulane U., 1957, MD, 1960; m. Bethany Ann Mitchell; children: Karen, Steven. Intern, Charity Hosp. of La., New Orleans, 1960-61, resident in internal medicine, 1961-64; pvt. practice medicine specializing in internal medicine and nephrology, Seabrook, Tex., 1968-72, Webster, Tex., 1972—; mem. courtesy staff Mainland Ctr. Hosp. (formerly Galveston County Meml. Hosp.), Houston, 1968-96, Bapt. Meml. System, 1969-72, 88—; mem. staff Clear Lake Regional Med. Ctr., 1972—; cons. staff St. Mary's Hosp., 1973-79; cons. nephrology St. John's Hosp., Nassau Bay, Tex.; fellow in nephrology Northwestern U. Med. Sch., Chgo., 1968; clin. asst. prof. in medicine and nephrology U. Tex., Galveston, 1969—; lectr. emergency med. technician course, 1974-76; adviser on respiratory therapy program Alvin (Tex.) Jr. Coll., 1976-82; cons. nephrology USPHS, 1979-80. Served to capt. M.C., U.S. Army, 1961-67. Diplomate Am. Bd. Internal Medicine, Nat. Bd. Med. Examiners. Fellow ACP, Am. Coll. Chest Physicians; mem. Internat., Am. Socs. Nephrology, So. Med. Assn., Tex. Med. Assn., Tex. Soc. Internal Medicine (bd. govs. 1994-96), Am. Soc. Artificial Internal Organs, Tex. Acad. Internal Medicine, Harris County Med. Soc., Am. Geriatrics Soc., Bay Area Heart Assn. (bd. govs. 1969-75), Clear Lake C. of C., Phi Delta Epsilon, Alpha Epsilon Pi, Tulane Alumni Assn. Lodge: Rotary. Home: 1818 Linfield Way Houston TX 77058-2324 Office: PO Box 57609 Webster TX 77598-7609

RAPPAPORT, STUART R., lawyer; b. Detroit, Apr. 13, 1935; s. Reuben and Zella (Golechen) R.; m. Anne M. Plotnick; children: Douglas, Erica Rappaport Witt. BA in History, U. Mich., 1956; JD, Harvard U., 1959. Bar: Calif. 1962. Trial lawyer, chief trials, bur. chief, chief. asst. pub. defender L.A. County Pub. Defender's Office, L.A., 1962-87; pub. defender Santa Clara County, San Jose, Calif., 1987-95; mem. standing adv. com. on criminal law Jud. Coun. Calif., San Francisco, 1993—; mem. discipline evaluation com. State Bar of Calif. Contbr. articles to profl. jours. Recipient Lifetime Achievement award Calif. Attys. for Criminal Justice. Mem. Calif. Pub. Defenders Asn. (pres. 1982-83, Lifetime Achievement award), L.A. County Pub. Defenders Assn. (pres.). Democrat. Jewish. Address: PO Box 960 Mendocino CA 95460-0960

RAPPAPORT, THEODORE SCOTT, electrical engineering educator; b. Bklyn., Nov. 26, 1960; s. Eugene and Carol Ann (Cooper) R.; m. Brenda Marie Velasquez, May 30, 1981; children: Matthew B., Natalie M., Jennifer L. BSEE, Purdue U., 1982, MSEE, 1984, PhD, 1987. Registered profl. engr., Va. Engring. coop. Magnavox Govt./Ind. Elec. Co., Fort Wayne, Ind., 1980-81; engr. Harris Corp., Melbourne, Fla., 1983, systems engr., 1986; rsch., teaching asst. Purdue U., West Lafayette, Ind., 1982-87; prof. Va. Poly. Inst. and State U., Blacksburg, 1992—; founding dir. Mobile & Portable Radio Rsch. Corp.; cons. Ralph M. Parsons Co., Pansonic, Inc., Ericsson/GE Mobile Comm. Co-author, co-editor 6 books on wireless personal comm. including Wireless Communications, Cellular Raido and Personal Communications; contbr. articles to profl. jours. V.p. Gilbert Linkous Elem. Sch. PTA, Blacksburg, 1990-91; exec. com., asst. den leader Boy Scouts of Am., Blacksburg, 1992. Named Marconi Young scientist IEEE, 1990, one of Young Men of Am., 1988, Pres. Faculty fellow NSF, 1992. Fellow Radio Club Am. (dir.); mem. NSPE, IEEE (sr. mem., developer first wireless textbook and learning program 1995), Am. Radio Relay League, Am. Soc. Engring. Edn. Achievements include patents in Tunable Discone Antenna, computer-based bit error simulation for digital wireless communications, real-time DSP receivers.

RAPPEPORT, IRA J., lawyer; b. Phila., Jan. 13, 1954. BA with honors, Washington U., 1975; JD with honors, Villanova U., 1978. Bar: Calif. 1978. Assoc. Pillstory Madison & Sutro, 1978-83; assoc. Memel, Jacobs, Pietro & Gersh, 1983-85, ptnr., 1985-87; ptnr. McDermott, Will & Emory, L.A., 1987—. Mng. editor Villanova Law Rev., 1977-78. Recipient Scribes award Villanova Sch. Law, 1978. Mem. Am. Acad. Hosp. Attys., L.A. County Bar Assn. (mem. healthcare law sect.), Beverly Hills Bar Assn. (mem. healthcare law sect.), Century City Bar Assn. (mem. healthcare law sect.), Nat. Health Lawyers Assn., Calif. Soc. Healthcare Attys. Office: McDermott Will & Emery 2049 Century Park E Fl 34 Los Angeles CA 90067-3101

RAPPLEYE, RICHARD KENT, financial executive, consultant, educator; b. Oswego, N.Y., Aug. 10, 1940; s. Robert Edward and Evelyn Margaret (Hammond) R.; m. Karen Tobe Greenberg, Sept. 7, 1963; children: Matthew Walker, Elizabeth Marion. AB, Miami U., Oxford, Ohio, 1962; postgrad. Boston U., 1962-63; MBA, U. Pa., 1964; postgrad. DePaul U., 1965-66. CPA, Ill. Auditor DeLoitte Haskins & Sells, Chgo., 1962-67, mgmt. cons., 1967-71; controller, United Dairy Industry Assn., Rosemont, Ill., 1971, dir. fin. and adminstrn., 1971-73, exec. v.p., 1973-74; asst. to exec. v.p. Florists' Transworld Delivery, Southfield, Mich., 1974-75, group dir. fin. and adminstrn., 1975-80; asst. treas. Erb Lumber Co., Birmingham, Mich., 1980, v.p. fin., chief fin. officer, 1981-83; v.p., sec.-treas. C.S. Mott Found., Flint, Mich., 1983—; lectr. U. Mich., Flint, 1987-91; cons. in field; instr. Oakland U., Rochester, Mich., 1981-83; bd. dirs. Treas. Council Mich. Founds, 1986-92, 96—. Mem. AICPAs, Mich. Assn. CPAs. Unitarian. Lodge: Masons, Rotary. Home: 503 Arlington St Birmingham MI 48009-1639 Office: CS Mott Found 503 S Saginaw St Flint MI 48502-1807

RAPSON, RICHARD L., history educator; b. N.Y.C., Mar. 8, 1937; s. Louis and Grace Lillian (Levenkind) R.; m. Susan Burns, Feb. 22, 1975 (div. June 1981); m. Elaine Catherine Hatfield, June 15, 1982; 1 child, Kim Elizabeth. BA, Amherst Coll., 1958; PhD, Columbia U., 1966. Asst. prof. Amherst (Mass.) Coll., 1960-61, Stanford (Calif.) U., 1961-65; from assoc. prof. to prof. history U. Hawaii, Honolulu, 1965—, founder, dir. New Coll., 1968-73; bd. dirs. Semester at Sea, U. Pittsburgh, 1979—; psychotherapist, Honolulu, 1982—. Author: Indivisualism and Conformity in the American Character, 1967, Britons View America, 1971, The Cult of Youth, 1972, Major Interpretations of the American Past, 1978, Denials of Doubt, 1980, Cultural Pluralism in Hawaii, 1981, American Yearnings, 1989; co-author: (with Elaine Hatfield) Love, Sex and Intimacy: Their Psychology, Biology and History, 1993, Emotional Contagion, 1994, Love and Sex: Cross-Cultural Perspectives, 1995; mem. editl. bd. Univ. Press Am., 1981—. Woodrow Wilson fellow, Wilson Found., Princeton, 1960; Edward Perkins scholar, Columbia U., 1961; Danforth tchr., Danforth Found., St. Louis, 1965; recipient E. Harris Harbison for Gifted Teaching award, Danforth Found., 1973, Outstanding Tchr. award Stanford U. 25th Reunion Class, 1992. Mem. Am. Hist. Assn., Orgn. Am. Hist., Nat. Womens Hist. Project, Phi Beta Kappa, Outrigger Canoe Club, Honolulu Club. Avocations: squash, travel, classical music. Office: U Hawaii Dept History 2530 Dole St Honolulu HI 96822-2303

RARICH, ANNE LIPPITT, management and organizational development consultant; b. New Haven, Conn., Apr. 8, 1943; d. Gordon L. and Phyllis (Parker) Lippitt; m. Thomas D. Rarich, June 26, 1965; children: Kirsten Ruth, Diana Lynn. BA, Baldwin-Wallace Coll., Berea, Ohio; MEd, Springfield (Mass.) Coll. NLP practitioner. Field dir. Mystic Side G.S. Coun., Medford, Mass., 1965-67; field dir., trainer Shabonee G.S. Coun., Moline, Ill., 1967-69; prin. Learning Exch., Concord, Mass., 1976—; v.p. mktg. and sales orgn. Renewal Inc., 1980-84; human resources devel. Digital Equipment Corp., Maynard, Mass., 1986-91; dir. human resource devel. Liberty Mutual Ins., Boston, 1992-94; field mgr. Carlson Learning Co., Mpls., 1989—; leadership devel. for bd. Mass. League Women Voters, Boston, 1983-85; presenter in field. Contbg. author: When the Canary Stops Singing, Women's Perspective on Transforming Business, 1993, Open Letter to Our Daughters, 1997. Pres. League of Women Voters, Concord, 1979-81; chmn. sch. com., Concord, 1983-89, Edn. Collaborative of Greater Boston,

1985-86; founder, past pres. Network for Women's Lives, Concord, 1991-95; bd. dirs. New Eng. Women's Fund, 1997. Recipient Outstanding Working Woman award Working Woman Mag., 1980, Boston YMCA, 1981. Mem. ASTD (v.p. 1979-81), World Bus. Coord. (program coord. 1990-92), Soc. for Human Resource Planning. Mem. UCC Ch. Home: 315 College Rd Concord MA 01742-5418 Office: Learning Exchg 315 College Rd Concord MA 01742-5418

RARIDON, RICHARD JAY, computer specialist; b. Newton, Iowa, Oct. 25, 1931; s. Jack Allison and Letha Helen (Woods) R.; m. Mona Marie Herndon, May 28, 1956; children—Susan Gayle, Ann Chaney. B.A., Grinnell Coll., 1953; M.A., Vanderbilt U., 1955, Ph.D., 1959. Assoc. prof. phys. sci. Memphis State U., 1958-62; research scientist Oak Ridge Nat. Lab., 1962-92; cons. ORNL, fusion energy divsn., 1992—; environ. specialist Coop. Sci. Edn. Center, Oak Ridge, 1971-72. Contbr. articles to profl. jours. Radiol. Physics fellow AEC, 1953-55. Fellow AAAS, Tenn. Acad. Sci. (pres. 1971); mem. Assn. Acads. Sci. (sec.-treas. 1972-76, pres. 1977), Sigma Xi. Home: 111 Columbia Dr Oak Ridge TN 37830 Office: Oak Ridge Nat Lab Oak Ridge TN 37831-8071

RASCH, ELLEN MYRBERG, cell biology educator; b. Chicago Heights, Ill., Jan. 31, 1927; d. Arthur August and Helen Catherine (Stelle) Myrberg; m. Robert W. E. Rasch, June 17, 1950; 1 son, Martin Karl. PhB with honors, U. Chgo., 1945, BS in Biol. Sci., 1947, MS in Botany, 1948, PhD, 1950. Asst. histologist Am. Meat Inst. Found., Chgo., 1950-51; USPHS postdoctoral fellow U. Chgo., 1951-53, rsch. assoc. dept. zoology, 1954-59; rsch. assoc. Marquette U., Milw., 1962-65, assoc. prof. biology, 1965-68, prof. biology, 1968-75, Wehr Disting. prof. biophysics, 1975-78; rsch. prof. biophysics East Tenn. State U., James H. Quillen Coll. Medicine, Johnson City, 1978-94, interim chmn. dept. cellular biophysics, 1986-94, prof. anatomy and cell biology, 1994—. Mem. Wis. Bd. Basic Sci. Examiners, 1971-75, sec. bd., 1973-75. Recipient Post-doctoral fellowship USPHS, 1951-53, Research Career Devel. award, 1967-72; Teaching Excellence and Disting. award Marquette U., 1975; Kreeger-Wolf vis. disting. prof. in biol. sci. Northwestern U., 1979. Mem. Royal Microscopic Soc., Am. Soc. Cell Biology, Am. Soc. Zoologists, Am. Soc. Ichthyologists and Herpetologists, The Histochem. Soc., Phi Beta Kappa, Sigma Xi. Contbr. articles to various publs. Home: 1504 Chickees St Johnson City TN 37604-7103 Office: East Tenn State Univ Dept Anatomy & Cell Biology PO Box 70 421 Johnson City TN 37614-0421

RASCH, STUART GARY, emergency physician; b. Rochester, N.Y., Aug. 2, 1958; s. Stanley Alvin and Lore (Mane) R.; m. Carolynn Gold; 1 child, Erica Danielle. BS in Biology, SUNY, New Paltz, 1980; MD, St. George's U., Grenada, West Indies, 1988. Emergency med. technician II The N.Y. Hosp./Empire State Ambulance, N.Y.C., 1977-82; computer cons. Goldman Sachs & Co., N.Y.C., 1986-87; intern, resident Maimonides Med. Ctr., Bklyn., 1988-90; resident in Emergency Medicine The Greenwich (Conn.) Hosp., 1990—; physician Emergency dept. The Nyack (N.Y.) Hospital/ Rockland Critical Care, 1991—; tchg. asst., vis. prof. internal medicine St. George's U. Sch. Medicine, Grenada, 1990—. Mem. postal adv. com. U.S. Postal Svc., Pearl River, N.Y.; police surgeon Pearl River Fire Dept. Mem. AMA, Conn. Med. Soc., Fairfield County Med. Soc., Rockland County Med. Soc., N.Y. State Med. Soc. Avocation: computers. Home: 40 Sickletown Rd Pearl River NY 10965-2858

RASCHE, ROBERT HAROLD, economics educator; b. New Haven, June 29, 1941; s. Harold A. and Elsa (Bloomquist) R.; m. Dorothy Anita Bensen, Dec. 28, 1963; children: Jeanette Dorothy, Karl Robert. B.A., Yale U., 1963; A.M., U. Mich., 1965, Ph.D., 1966. Asst. prof. U. Pa., Phila., 1966-72; assoc. prof. econs. Mich. State U., East Lansing, 1972-75, prof., 1975—; vis. scholar St. Louis Fed. Res., 1971-72, 76-77, 94—, San Francisco Fed. Res., 1985, Bank of Japan, Tokyo, 1990; disting. vis. prof. econs. Ariz. State U., Tempe, 1986; rsch. assoc. Nat. Bur. Econ. Rsch., Cambridge, Mass., 1982-91; mem. Mich. Gov. Coun. Econ. Advisers, 1992-96; mem. Shadow Open Market Com., 1973—. Mem. Am. Econs. Assn. Lutheran. Home: 1736 Hitching Post Rd East Lansing MI 48823-2144 Office: Mich State U Dept Econs East Lansing MI 48824-1038

RASCOE, PAUL STEPHEN, librarian, researcher; b. Corpus Christi, Tex., July 7, 1954; s. Stephen Thomas and Barbara Jean (Butler) R. BA, U. Tex., Arlington, 1975, U. Tex., Austin, 1976; M Libr. Info. Sci., U. Tex., Austin, 1983; MA, U. London, 1977. Govt. documents and electronic info. svcs. libr. U. Tex., Austin, 1985—, libr., 1978-85; dir. rsch. Weissmann Travel Reports, Austin, 1990-96. Avocation: travel. Office: U Tex Austin Documents Collection Gen Librs PCL 2.400 Austin TX 78713-7330

RASCÓN, ARMANDO, artist; b. Calexico, Calif., Dec. 9, 1956; s. Reynoldo and Maria (Herrera) R. BFA Coll. Creative Studies, U. Calif., Santa Barbara, 1979. Owner Terrain Gallery, San Francisco, 1988—; mem. artist's com. San Francisco Art Inst., 1988-90; guest faculty dept. art U. Calif., Davis, 1988, Calif. Coll. Arts and Crafts, Oakland, 1991, dept. art practice U. Calif., Berkeley, 1995; co-juror McMilan award, San Francisco Art Inst., 1993; Intersection for the Arts, San Francisco, 1993; juror, panelist Artist Trust Fellowship Grants, Visual Arts, Seattle, 1994; lectr. N.Y. Mus. Modern Art, 1995; panelist LEF Found. Orgn. Grants, Cambridge, Mass., 1996, Nev. State Coun. on the Arts Grants, Carson City, 1996, 97, San Diego Mus. Contemporary Art, 1997; presenter various lectrs., panels, workshops, confs. Bd. dirs. New Langton Arts, San Francisco, 1988-92; vice-chair Art Commn. City of San Francisco, 1997. Recipient Hazel S. Lagerson scholarship U. Calif., Santa Barbara, 1975, fellowship grant in painting Nat. Endowment for Arts, Washington, 1987, Adaline Kent award San Francisco Art Inst., 1994, Goldie award in visual art San Francisco Bay Guardian, 1994. Home & Office: 165 Jessie St Ste 2 San Francisco CA 94105-4008

RASHAD, AHMAD (BOBBY MOORE), sports broadcaster, former professional football player; b. Portland, Oreg., Nov. 19, 1949; m. Phylicia Allen; 1 child, Condola Phylea. Student, U. Oreg. With St. Louis Cardinals, 1972-73, Buffalo Bills, 1974-76, Seattle Seahawks, 1976, Minn. Vikings, 1976-82; sports broadcaster NBC, N.Y.C., 1982—; played in Pro Bowl (Nat. Football League All-Star Game), 1979. Author: Vikes, Mikes and Something on the Backside, 1988. Named to Nat. Football Conf. All-Star Team Sporting News, 1978, 79. Office: care NBC Sports 30 Rockefeller Plz New York NY 10112*

RASHBA, EMMANUEL IOSIF, physicist, educator; b. Kiev, Ukraine, Oct. 30, 1927; came to U.S., 1991; s. Iosif Ovsei and Rosalia (Mirkine) R.; m. Erna Kelman, July 13, 1957; 1 child, Julia. Diploma with Honor, U. Kiev, Ukraine, 1949; PhD, Ukrainian Acad. Scis., 1956; DSc, Ioffe Inst. Physics and Tech., Leningrad, 1963. Jr. and sr. scientist Inst. of Physics Ukrainian Acad. of Scis., Kiev, Ukraine, 1954-60; head theoretical divsn. Inst. of Semiconductors Ukrainian Acad. of Scis., Kiev, 1960-66; head divsn. of theory of semiconductors, prin. scientist Landau Inst. for Theoretical Physics, Acad. Sci. of Russia, Moscow, 1966—; prof. Moscow Inst. for Physics and Tech., 1967-82; rsch. prof. dept. physics U. Utah, Salt Lake City, 1992—; vis. scholar CNRS, Grenoble, France, 1987, U. Stuttgart, Germany, 1988, U. Warsaw, Poland, 1989, Inst. for Sci. Interchange, Torino, Italy, 1990, Internat. Ctr. for Theoretical Physics, Trieste, Italy, 1990, Racah Inst. for Physics, Hebrew U., Jerusalem, 1991, CUNY, 1991-92, Dartmouth Coll., N.H., 1997. Co-author: Collection of Problems in Physics, 1978, 2d edit., 1987, English edit., 1986, Japanese edit., 1989; Spectroscopy of Molecular Excitons, Russian edit. 1981, English edit. 1985; assoc. editor Jour. Luminescence, 1985—; editl. bd. Letters to the Jour. of Exptl. and Theoretical Physics, 1967-88; contbr. numerous sci. and rev. articles to profl. jours. Recipient Lenin prize in sci. Sci. Govt. of USSR, 1966, A.F. Ioffe prize Acad. of Scis. of the USSR, 1987. Fellow Am. Phys. Soc. Achievements include research on electron theory of solids, especially prediction of electric-dipole spin resonance, giant oscillator strengths, and coexistence of free and self-trapped states; initiation of mechanics of growing elastic bodies in civil engineering, initiating mechanics of growing elastic bodies in civil engineering. Office: U Utah Dept of Physics 201 J Fletcher Bldg Salt Lake City UT 84112

RASHER, GEORGE JOSEPH, entrepreneur, business owner; b. Northridge, Calif., Apr. 18, 1956; s. Clarence Emerson and Berta (Sturm) R.; m. Kim Eileen Abel, Mar. 27, 1978. BA in Radio, TV & Film with highest honors, Calif. State U., Northridge, 1978; MBA magna cum laude, Pepperdine U., 1981. Account exec. various advt. agys., L.A., 1978-81; product mgr. Mattel Electronics, Hawthorne, Calif., 1981-83; dir. product mktg. Epson Am., Torrance, Calif., 1983-90; v.p. sales and mktg. Parana Supplies Corp., Torrance, 1990-93; founder Cabrillo East Media Corp., Santa Barbara, Calif., 1993—; mem. AT&T Creative Alliance Program, Oracle New Media Program; ptnr. Netscape Alliance; SUN catalyst developer, SGI Affiliate Plus. Mem. Am. Motor Cyclist Assn., Apple Multimedia Program. Avocations: motorcycle riding, photography, basketball. Office: Cabrillo East Media Corp 610 Anacapa St Santa Barbara CA 93101-1615

RASHID, HARUN UR, philosopher, educational administrator; b. Bakshimul, Comilla, Bangladesh, Oct. 6, 1954; came to U.S., 1984; s. Ali Akber and Johra Begum; m. Jaha Afroz Sayeeda, June 10, 1979; children: Mashiyat, Anira. BA with honors, U. Dacca, Bangladesh, 1977, MA, 1978; MA, U. Waterloo, Ontario, Can., 1984; PhD, Wayne State U., 1993. Adminstrv. cert., Mich. Grad. teaching asst. U. Waterloo, Ontario, 1983-84; adj. grad. faculty Wayne State U., Detroit, 1990—, instr. performance learning sys., 1994—, mem. adj. grad. faculty Sch. of Edn., 1996—; asst. prof. philosophy Marygrove Coll., 1993—; asst. dir. Master in the Art of Tchg. Marygrove Coll., Detroit, 1995—; philosophy lectr. U. Dacca, 1980-83, U. Chittagong, Bangladesh, 1978-80; cons. on critical thinking Wayne State U. Sch. Edn., Detroit, 1986—. Author: (with others) Effective Secondary Teaching, 1989. U. Waterloo scholar, Ontario, 1983-84, Merit scholar U. Dacca, 1973-77, Residential scholar Bd. Edn., Comilla, 1971-73. Mem. Am. Philos. Assn., Philosophy Edn. Soc. Avocations: reading, reasoning, music, travel, public speaking. Home: 20462 Glenmore Ave Redford MI 48240-1040 Office: Marygrove Coll Master in the Art Tchg 8425 W Mcnichols Rd Detroit MI 48221-2546

RASHID, KAMAL A., program director, researcher; b. Sulaimania, Kurdistan, Iraq, Sept. 11, 1944; came to U.S., 1972; s. Ahmad Rashid and Habiba M. Muhiedin; m. Afifa B. Sabir, May 23, 1970; children: Niaz K., Neian K., Suzanne K. BS, U. Baghdad, Iraq, 1965; MS, Pa. State U., 1974, PhD, 1978. Lab. instr. U. Baghdad, Iraq, 1966-72; mem. faculty U. Basrah, Iraq, 1978-80, U. Sulaimania, Iraq, 1980-83; sr. rsch. assoc., vis. prof. Pa. State U., University Park, 1983—, rsch. assoc. prof., 1992—; dir. Biotech. Tng. Program program Pa. State U., 1989—, dir. summer symposium molecular biology, 1991—; v.p. Cogenic Inc., State College, Pa., 1989-90; cons., spkr. biotech. tng. program developer. Contbr. articles to profl. jours. Iraqi Ministry Higher Edn. scholar. Mem. Am. Chem. Soc., Environ. Mutagen Soc., Pa. Biotech. Assn. (mem. edn. com.), Rotary. Avocations: travel, swimming, reading. Home: 100 Berwick Dr Boalsburg PA 16827-1611 Office: Pa State U 203 S Frear University Park PA 16807

RASHKIN, MITCHELL CARL, internist, pulmonary medicine specialist; b. N.Y.C., June 1, 1951; m. Karen B. Ohlbaum, Aug. 8, 1982. BS in Computer Sci., U. Mich., 1973, MD, 1977. Diplomate Am. Bd. Internal Medicine, subspecialty Pulmonary Disease, Nat. Bd. Med. Examiners; cert. in critical care medicine Am. Bd. Internal Medicine; insr. Advanced Cardiac Life Support. Intern U. Cin. Med. Ctr., 1977-78, resident, 1978-80, fellowship in pulmonary medicine, 1980-82, dir. med. intensive care unit, 1982—, program dir. critical care medicine, 1989-95, co-dir. pulmonary care unit, 1990-93, dir. respiratory therapy, 1993—, dir med. stepdown unit, 1993—, asst. prof. medicine, 1982-89, assoc. prof. medicine, 1989—; asst. prof. clin. emergency medicine U. Cin. Hosps., 1988-90, assoc. prof. 1990—; fellowship dir. Pulmonary/Critical Care U. Cin. Med. Ctr., 1995—; mem. numerous hosp. coms. including pharmacy and therapeutics sub com. Respiratory Drugs Com., 1987-88, Hosp. Computer Adv. Com., 1989-94, Search Com. Clin. Nurse Specialist Critical Care, 1992, MICU head nurse search com., 1993, Intensive Care Unit Forms Com, 1993-94, Hosp. Cost Reduction Project, 1994-95, Sedation Policy Task Force, 1994; chmn. quality assurance program Dept. Internal Medicine, 1987-91, Subcom. on Resident Tng., 1986, Task Force on Critical Care Tng., 1987, Med. Intensive Care Unit Com., 1992—. Contbr. articles to profl. jours., abstracts and presentations to sci. publs. and internat. med. confs.; guest reviewer Chest, 1987—, Archives Internal Medicine, 1991—. Mem. State of Ohio Intensive Care Quality of Care Com., 1995; mem. Am. Lung Assn. Ohio (exec. com. 1987-88). Fellow Am. Coll. Physicians, Am. Coll. Chest Physicians; mem. Am. Thoracic Soc., Ohio Thoracic Soc. (program planning com. 1982-83, chmn. 1985-86, profl. edn. and rsch. awards com. 1985, v.p. 1985-86, pres.-elect 1986-87, pres. 1987-88, chmn. nominating com. 1988-89, membership com. 1994, mem. at large 1996). Office: U Cin Med Ctr PO Box 670564 231 Bethesda Ave Rm 6004 Cincinnati OH 45229-2827

RASHKIND, PAUL MICHAEL, lawyer; b. Jamaica, N.Y., May 21, 1950; s. Murray and Norma (Dorfman) Weinstein; m. Robin Shane, Dec. 20, 1975; children: Adam Charles, Noah Hamilton, Jennifer Elizabeth. AA, Miami-Dade Jr. Coll., 1970; BBA, U. Miami, Coral Gables Fla., 1972, JD, 1975. Bar: Fla. 1975, D.C. 1981, N.Y. 1981, U.S. Dist. Ct. (so. dist.) Fla. 1975, U.S. Ct. Appeals (5th cir.) 1976, U.S. Supreme Ct. 1978, U.S. Dist. Ct. (mid. dist.) Fla. 1979, U.S. Ct. Appeals (2d and 11th cirs.) 1981, U.S. Ct. Appeals (4th and 6th cirs.) 1986, U.S. Dist. Ct. (no. dist.) Fla. 1987, U.S. Dist. Ct. (no dist.) Calif. 1989; diplomate Nat. Bd. Trial Advocacy-Criminal Law, bd. cert. Criminal Trial Law, Fla. Bar. Asst. state atty. Dade County State Attys. Office, Miami, Fla., 1975-78, chief asst. state atty. in charge of appeals, 1977-78; atty. Sams, Gerstein & Ward, P.A., Miami, 1978-83; ptnr. Bailey, Gerstein, Rashkind & Dresnick, Miami, 1983-92, supr. asst. Fed. Defender Chief of Appeals, Miami, 1992—; spl. master Ct. Appointment, Miami, 1982-83; arbitrator Dade County Jail Inmates Grievance Program, Miami, 1981-92; mem. Fla. Bar Unauthorized Practice of Law Com. C, 11th Jud. Cir., Miami, 1980-84, Fed. Ct. Practice Com., 1992—. Contbr. articles on ethics and criminal law to profl. jours. Pres., bd. dirs. Lindgren Homeowners Assn., Miami, Fla., 1981-86. Fellow Am. Bd. Criminal Lawyers (bd. govs. 1980-86; mem. ABA (ethics com. criminal justice sect. 1979-92, vice chmn. 1985-87, chmn. 1987-89, ethics advisor to chair, 1992—), Fla. Bar Assn. (commn. on Lawyer professionalism 1988-89, criminal law cert. com. 1989-94, standing com. on professionalism 1989-94), N.Y. Bar Assn., D.C. Bar Assn., Dade County Bar Assn., Assn. Trial Lawyers Am., Acad. Fla. Trial Lawyers (chmn. criminal law sect. 1985-86, diplomate 1986—), Nat. Assn. Criminal Def. Lawyers, Soc. Bar and Gavel, Iron Arrow, Hon. Order Ky. Cols., Omicron Delta Kappa, Delta Sigma Rho-Tau Kappa Alpha, Pi Sigma Alpha, Phi Rho Pi, Delta Theta Phi. Democrat. Jewish. Office: Fed Pub Defender's Office SD FL 150 W Flagler St Ste 1500 Miami FL 33130-1555

RASI, HUMBERTO MARIO, educational administrator, editor, minister; b. Buenos Aires, Argentina, Mar. 23, 1935; came to U.S., 1962, naturalized, 1968; s. Mario and Gertrudis Frida (Heyde) R.; m. Julia Cuchma, Feb. 28, 1957; children—Leroy Mario, Sylvia Beatrice. B.A., Instituto Superior del Profesorado, Buenos Aires, 1960; M.A., San Jose State U., 1966; Ph.D., Stanford U., 1971. Ordained to ministry Seventh-day Adventist Ch., 1980. Mem. faculty Instituto Florida, Buenos Aires, 1957-61; asst. editor Pacific Press Publ. Assn., Mountain View, Calif., 1962-66; asst. prof., assoc. prof. modern langs. Andrews U., 1969-76, prof., dean Sch. Grad. Studies, 1976-78; chief editor internat. publs. Pacific Press Publ. Assn., 1978-83, v.p. editorial devel., 1984-86; assoc. world dir. edn. Gen. Conf. Seventh-day Adventists, Silver Spring, Md., 1987-90, world dir. edn., 1990—; exec. dir. Inst. for Christian Teaching, 1987—; bd. dirs. Andrews U., Loma Linda U., Adventist Internat. Inst. Advanced Studies. Author: The Life of Jesus, 3 vols., 1984-85; contbg. editor Handbook of L.Am. studies, Libr. of Congress, 1972-82; gen. editor Comentario Biblico Adventista, 7 vols., 1978-90; co-editor: Meeting the Secular Mind, 1985; editor Coll. and Univ. Dialogue, 1989—, editor-in-chief, 1996—; compiler Christ in the Classroom, 17 vols., 1991—; also articles on modern Hispanic lit. and religious trends. NEH postdoctoral fellow Johns Hopkins U., 1975-76. Mem. Instituto Internacional de Literatura Iberoamericana. Office: 12501 Old Columbia Pike Silver Spring MD 20904-6601

RASIN, RUDOLPH STEPHEN, corporate executive; b. Newark, July 5, 1930; s. Simon Walter and Anna Rasin; m. Joy Kennedy Peterkin, Apr. 11, 1959; children: Rudolph Stephen, James Stenning, Jennifer Shaw Dennistion. B.A., Rutgers Coll., 1953; postgrad., Columbia, 1958-59. Mgr. Miles Labs., Inc., 1959-61; devel. mgr. Gen. Foods Corp., White Plains, N.Y., 1961-62; asst. to pres., chmn. Morton Internat. Inc., Chgo., 1962-72; pres. Rasin Corp., Chgo., 1971—; bd. dirs. Federated Foods Inc. Bd. dirs. Ctr. for Def. Info., 1972—, English Speaking Union, Ct. Theatre. Served with USAF, 1954-56. Mem. Hinsdale Golf Club, Mid Am. Club (Chgo.), Lake Geneva Country Club, Williams Coll. Club (N.Y.C.), Chgo. Club. Republican. Mem. United Ch. of Christ. Home: 328 E 8th St Hinsdale IL 60521-4504 Office: One First Nat Plz Ste 2690 One First Nat. Plz Ste Chicago IL 60603

RASKIN, EDWIN BERNER, real estate executive; b. Savannah, Ga., Mar. 19, 1919; s. Isaac and Hannah (Berner) R.; m. Rebecca Kornman, Nov. 13, 1946; children: Susan, Joan. B.B.A., Tulane U., 1940. Cert. property mgr., counselor of real estate, Inst. Real Estate Mgmt. Pres., Superior Shoe Co. and Nat. Shoe Co., Savannah, Ga., 1946-50; pres. A.L. Kornman Co., Nashville, 1947-54; from pres. to sr. chmn. Edwin B. Raskin Co., Nashville, 1954—. Served to capt. USAAF, 1942-46. Mem. Nashville Bd. Realtors, Tenn. Assn. Realtors, Nat. Assn. Real Estate Bds., Inst. Real Estate Mgmt. (past pres. middle Tenn. chpt.). Club: Old Natchez (Nashville), Hillwood Country Club (Nashville). Lodge: Rotary. Home: 419 Ellendale Ave Nashville TN 37205-3401 Office: Edwin B Raskin Co 5210 Maryland Way Brentwood TN 37027-5015

RASKIN, FRED CHARLES, transportation and utility holding company executive; b. N.Y.C., Sept. 11, 1948; s. Harry and Isabel (Wexler) R.; m. Lorraine Mary Sabourin, Apr. 25, 1974; children: Elizabeth Harris, Alexander Eastwood. BS, Syracuse U., 1970; JD, NYU, 1973. Bar: R.I. 1973, Mass. 1974; CPA, Ohio. Assoc. counsel Fleet Nat. Bank, Providence, 1973-75, Bank of Boston, 1975-78; asst. gen. counsel Ea. Enterprises, Boston, 1978-79, treas., 1979-81, v.p., treas., 1981-84; sr. v.p. fin. Ea. Assoc. Coal Co., Pitts., 1984-87; exec. v.p. Midland Enterprises, Inc., Cin., 1987-90, pres., 1991—; Dept. of Energy Nat. Coal coun. Mem. Fin. Execs. Inst., Treas.' Office: Midland Enterprises Inc 300 Pike St Cincinnati OH 45202-4222

RASKIN, MICHAEL A., retail company executive; b. N.J., Feb. 26, 1925; s. Harry and Elizabeth Rose (Furstenberg) R.; m. Mary Bonetta Whalen, June 12, 1948; children: Robin Raskin Crowell, Hillary Raskin Maass, Mary Allison Sullivan. A.B., Pa. State Coll., 1947; M.B.A., Columbia U., 1948. With Abraham & Straus, 1949-65; successively mdse. v.p., dir. stores, sr. v.p. Abercrombie & Fitch, N.Y.C., 1966-68; exec. v.p. Dayton's div. Dayton Hudson Corp.; pres. Jos. Magnin Co., San Francisco, 1978—; chmn., CEO, bd. dirs. Imnar Corp., San Francisco, Info. Please; chmn. exec. com. Acajoe Internat.; bd. dirs. Fortune Almac, Canterbury Cuisine, Cultural Devel. Assocs., HELP Inc., Express Yourself Through Art, Inc., Munsingwear, Inc., B&B Acceptance Corp. Bd. dirs. Amyotrophic Lateral Sclerosis Assn.

RASKIN, NOEL MICHAEL, thoracic surgeon; b. Bklyn., May 29, 1947; s. Rubin and Pauline (Sturm) R.; m. Deborah M. Axelrod, Feb. 27, 1987; children: Max, Ben. BA, NYU, 1969; MD, N.Y. Med. Coll., 1977. Intern St. Vincent's Hosp., N.Y.C., 1977-78; resident SUNY, Stony Brook, 1978-82; fellow in cardio-thoracic surgery U. Miami, Fla., 1982-84, fellow in thoracic oncology, 1984-85; attending surgeon Beth Israel Med. Ctr. and Cabrini Med. Ctr., N.Y.C., 1985—; chief thoracic surgery Cabrini Med. Ctr.; thoracic surgeon Kriser Lung Cancer Ctr., N.Y.C., 1989; attending surgeon Dover (N.J.) Gen. Hosp., 1989-91; surgeon pvt. practice N.Y.C., 1992—. Fellow ACS, Am. Coll. Chest Physicians; mem. AMA, Soc. Thoracic Surgeons, Gen. Thoracic Surg. Club. Office: 41 5th Ave New York NY 10003-4319

RASKIND, LEO JOSEPH, law educator; b. Newark, Nov. 2, 1919; s. Isaac and Fannie (Michelson) R.; m. Mollie Gordon, June 14, 1948; children—Carol Inge, John Richard. A.B., UCLA, 1942; M.A., U. Wash., 1949; Ph.D. (Fulbright fellow), London Sch. Econs., 1952; LL.B., Yale, 1955. Faculty Stanford Law Sch., 1955-56; lectr., research asso. Yale Law Sch., 1956-58; faculty Vanderbilt Law Sch., 1958-64, Ohio State U. Coll. of Law, 1964-70, U. Minn., 1970-90; vis. tchr. NYU, 1964, 83, U. Tex., 1964, U. Utah, 1967, So. Meth. U., 1973, U. N.C., 1978, Lyon III, 1984, Kiel U., 1988; vis. prof. Bklyn. Law Sch., 1991-94, Coll. Law, U. Tenn. Knoxville, 1994, Law Sch., U. Calif., Davis, 1995, Bklyn. Law Sch., 1991-96. Co-author: Casebook Corporate Taxation, 1978, Casebook Antitrust Law, 1997; mem. adv. bd. BNA jour. Served to capt. AUS, 1942-46. Mem. Am. Law Inst. Office: Bklyn Law Sch 250 Joralemon St Brooklyn NY 11201-3700

RASKY, HARRY, producer, director, writer; b. Toronto, Ont., Can., May 9, 1928; emigrated to U.S., 1955; s. Louis Leib and Pearl (Krazner) R.; m. Ruth Arlene Werkhoven, Mar. 21, 1965; children: Holly Laura, Adam Louis. BA, U. Toronto, 1949, LLD, 1984. Reporter No. Daily News, Kirkland Lake, Ont., 1949; news editor-producer Sta. CHUM, Toronto, 1950, Sta. CKEY, 1951-52; co-founder new documentary dept. CBC, 1952-55; assoc. editor Saturday Night Mag., 1955; producer-dir-writer Columbia Broadcasting Corp., 1955-60, NBC-TV, N.Y.C., 1960-61, ABC-TV, N.Y.C., 1963-69, CBC-TV, Toronto, 1971-78; pres. Harry Rasky Prodns., N.Y.C. and Toronto, 1971—, Maragall Prodns., Toronto, 1978—; guest lectr. film and TV at various univs., colls. Creator: Raskymentary (recipient numerous awards, including Emmy award 1978, 86, San Francisco Film Festival award 1978, Grand prize N.Y. TV-Film Festival 1978, Jerusalem medal 1975); numerous films include Travels Through Life with Leacock, 1976, The Peking Man Mystery, 1978, Arthur Miller on Home Ground, 1979, (TV film) Hall of Kings (Emmy award, 1965); producer, dir., writer: numerous films including Next Year in Jerusalem, 1973, The Wit and World of G. Bernard Shaw, 1974, Tennessee Williams South, 1975, Homage to Chagall-The Colours of Love, 1977 (200 internat. prizes including Oscar nomination, Emmy 1986), Stratasphere, The Mystery of Henry Moore, Karsh: The Searching Eye; play Tiger Tale, 1978, The War Against The Indians, 1992 (Humanities Prize, Great Plains Film Festival, Lincoln, Nebr., Golden Hugo award Chgo. Film Festival), Prophecy, 1994 (Golden Angel award, honored by Smithsonian, Jerusalem Found.), William Hutt: A Fortunate Man, 1997; author: memoirs Nobody Swings on Sunday—The Many Lives of Harry Rasky, 1980, Tennessee Williams a Portrait in Laughter and Lamentation, 1986, Karsh: The Searching Eye, 1986, To Mend the World, 1987, Stratas: An affectionate tribute, 1988, Degas co-prodn. Met. Mus. of N.Y., 1988, The Great Teacher, 1989, Robertson Davies-The Magic Season, 1989; 19 hour retrospective of his films on Rasky's Gallery: Poets, Painters, Singers and Saints, CBC, 1988, The War Against the Indians, 1993 (12 Internat. awards, adopted Huron Nation title Keeper of teh Flame. Mem. YMCA; mem. adv. coun. Univ. Coll./U. Toronto. Recipient honors City of Venice, Italy, 1970, Golden Eagle, Grand prize N.Y. Intenat. TV and Film Festival of N.Y., 1977, Cert. of Merit, Acad. Motion Picture Arts and Scis., 1984, Red Ribbon, Am. Assn. Film and Video, N.Y.C., 1988, Blue Ribbon, Am. Film Festival, Emmy award, 1990, Moscow award for cultural contbn. to 20th Century USSR, 1991, Retrospective of Films, 1990, Golden Hugo award Chgo. Film Festival, 1993; named Best Non-Fiction Dir., Dirs. Guild Am., N.Y.C. and L.A., 1988, hon. Mayor N.Y.C., 1977, City of Toronto, 1979; Harry Rasky Day named in his honor, City of Toronto, 1988; Moscow Film Festival honoree, 1991; adopted by Huron Indians, named Keeper of the Spirit, adopted by Ojibway Tribe, named Mountain Eagle. Mem. Writers Guild Am. (best non-fiction dir. 1986), Dirs. Guild Am., Writers Union Can., Am., Acad. TV Arts and Scis., Assn. Can. TV and Radio Artists, Producers Assn. Can., Acad. Motion Picture Arts and Scis., Overseas Press Club, Acad. of Can. TV and Film Can. (lifetime achievement award 1992), PEN (Toronto), Nat. Arts Club. Jewish. Avocations: swimming, lecturing. Home: 15 Gregory Ave, Toronto, ON Canada M4W 2X7 Office: care CBC, Box 500 Terminal A, Toronto, ON Canada M5W 1E6 *I have tried to find the positive forces in life and out of them create works of art of a lasting nature with the idea of improving the lives of others. This, plus the adventure of passing on the tradition of my father and his, is my life.*

RASLEAR, THOMAS GREGORY, psychologist; b. N.Y.C., Nov. 25, 1947; s. John W. and Catherine (Turchin) R.; m. Lois T. Keck, Aug. 7, 1971. BS, CCNY, 1969; PhD, Brown U., 1974. Asst. prof. Wilkes Coll., Wilkes-Barre, Pa., 1975-79; rsch. psychologist Walter Reed Amy Inst. Rsch., Washington, 1979-89, sr. rsch. psychologist, 1989-93; engring. psychologist Fed. R.R. Adminstrn., Washington, 1993—; lectr., presenter in field. Bd. editors Jour. of the Exptl. Analysis of Behaviour, 1989-92; author numerous publs. in field including Proceedings of the XXIV Internat. Congress of Psychology, Vol. 6: Learning; co-author: Understanding Economic Behavior, Animal Learning and Behaviour, 16, Physiology and Behavior, 43, others; contbr. articles to profl. jours.; guest reviewer Jour. of Exptl. Psychology:

Animal Behavior Processes, Animal Learning and Behavior, Jour. of Comparative Psychology. Maj. U.S. Army, 1979-89. Rsch. fellow USPHS, 1970-72, N.Y. State Regents fellow, 1969-70. Mem. IEEE, Am. Psychol. Soc. (charter), Am. Psychol. Assn., Acoustical Soc. Am., Ea. Psychol. Assn., AAAS, Sigma Xi, Phi Beta Kappa. Achievements include development and validation of procedures for measuring subjective magnitudes in non-verbal subjects, including non-human animals; testing for toxic effects of drugs and electromagnetic radiation in non-humans; management of research projects on human factors and safety in railroad operations. Home: 1408 Woodman Ave Silver Spring MD 20902-3905 Office: Fed RR Adminstrn Office of Rsch and Devel RDV-32 400 7th St SW Washington DC 20590-0001

RASMASON, FREDERICK C., III, emergency nurse; b. Evergreen Park, Ill., May 10, 1958; s. Frederick C. Jr. and Kathleen M. R.; m. Concepcion A. Rasmason, Nov. 14, 1981; children: F. Charlie IV, Randy. Diploma, Clin. Specialist Sch., 1977; BS in Nursing, Chgo. State U., 1988; MS in Human Svc. Adminstrn., Spertus Coll., 1997. RN, Ill.; CEN; cert. TNS, ACLS, PALS, emergency dept. nursing. Staff nurse Holy Family Hosp., Des Plaines, Ill., Mt. Sinai Med. Ctr., Chgo., King Drew Med. Ctr., Calif.; emergency dpet. staff Provident Hosp. Cook County, Chgo. Sgt. U.S. Army, 1976-82, 86-88. Named Nightingale Soc. Honors Mem.; recipient U.S. Achievement Acad. Scholastic All-Am. award, U.S. Achievement Acad. Nat. Collegiate Nursing award. Mem. Am. Assn. Critical Care Nurses, Emergency Nurses Assn., Ill. Nurses Assn. Home: 13260 Windward Trl Orland Park IL 60462-1860

RASMUSON, BRENT (JACOBSEN), photographer, graphic artist; b. Logan, Utah, Nov. 28, 1950; s. Eleroy West and Fae (Jacobsen) R.; m. Tess Bullen, Sept. 30, 1981; children: John, Mark, Lisa. Grad. auto repair and painting sch., Utah State U. Pre-press supr. Herald Printing Co., Logan, 1969-79; profl. drummer, 1971-75; owner Valley Automotive Specialties, 1971-76; exec. sec. Herald Printing Co., 1979-89; owner Brent Rasmuson Photography, Smithfield, Utah, 1986—, Brent Rasmuson Temple Photographs, Smithfield, 1996—. Author photo prints of LDS temples: Logan, 1987, 96, Manti, 1989, Jordan River, 1989, 96, Provo, 1990, Mesa, Ariz., 1990, 96, Boise, Idaho, 1990, 96, Salt Lake LDS Temple, 1990, 96, Idaho Falls, 1991, 96, St. George, 1991, 96, Portland, Oreg., 1991, 96, L.A., 1991, 96, Las Vegas, Nev., 1991, Seattle, 1992, Oakland, Calif., 1993, 96, Ogden, 1996; author photo print: Statue of Angel Moroni, 1994; author photos used to make neckties and watch dials of LDS temples: Salt Lake, Manti, Logan, L.A., Oakland, Seattle, Las Vegas, Mesa, Portland, St. George, Jordan River, scenic tie Mammoth Hot Springs in Yellowstone Park, 1995; landscape scenic photographs featured in Best of Photography Ann., 1987, 88, 89, also in calendars and book covers. Mem. Internat. Platform Assn., Assoc. Photographers Internat., Internat. Freelance Photographers Orgn., Nat. Trust Hist. Preservation. Republican. Mem. LDS Ch. Avocations: landscape design, gardening, audio and video recording and mixing, reading, traveling. Home and Office: 40 N 200 E Smithfield UT 84335-1543

RASMUSON, ELMER EDWIN, banker, former mayor; b. Yakutat, Alaska, Feb. 15, 1909; s. Edward Anton and Jenny (Olson) R.; m. Lile Vivian Bernard, Oct. 27, 1939 (dec. 1960); children: Edward Bernard, Lile Muchmore (Mrs. John Gibbons, Jr.), Judy Ann; m. Col. Mary Louise Milligan, Nov. 4, 1961. BS magna cum laude, Harvard U., 1930, AM, 1935; student, U. Grenoble, 1930; LLD, U. Alaska, 1970, Alaska Pacific U., 1993. C.P.A., N.Y., Tex., Alaska. Chief accountant Nat. Investors Corp., N.Y.C., 1933-35; prin. Arthur Andersen & Co., N.Y.C., 1935-43; pres. Nat. Bank of Alaska, 1943-65, chmn. bd., 1966-74, chmn. exec. com., 1975-82, now chmn. emeritus; mayor City of Anchorage, 1964-67, dir., emeritus and cons., 1989; civilian aide from Alaska to sec. army, 1959-67; Swedish consul Alaska, 1955-77; Chmn. Rasmuson Found.; Rep. nominee U.S. Senate from Alaska, 1968; U.S. commr. Internat. N. Pacific Fisheries Commn., 1969-84; mem. Nat. Marine Fisheries Adv. Com., 1974-77, North Pacific Fishery Mgmt. Council, 1976-77, U.S. Arctic Research Commn., 1984-92. Mem. City Coun. Anchorage, 1945, chmn. city planning commn., 1950-53; pres. Alaska coun. Boy Scouts Am., 1953; regent U. Alaska, 1950-69; trustee King's Lake Camp, Inc., 1944—, Alaska Permanent Fund Corp., 1980-82; bd. dirs. Nat. Mus. Natural History Smithsonian Inst. 1994-97. Decorated knight first class Order of Vasa, comdr. Sweden; recipient silver Antelope award Boy Scouts Am., Japanese citation Order of the Sacred Treasure, Gold and Silver Star, 1988; outstanding civilian service medal U.S. Army; Alaskan of Year award, 1976. Mem. Pioneers Alaska, Alaska Bankers Assn. (past pres.), Defense Orientation Conf. Assn., NAACP, Alaska Native Brotherhood, Explorers Club, Phi Beta Kappa. Republican. Presbyn. Clubs: Masons, Elks, Anchorage Rotary (past pres.); Harvard (N.Y.C.; Boston); Wash. Athletic (Seattle), Seattle Yacht (Seattle), Rainier (Seattle); Thunderbird Country (Palm Desert, Calif.); Bohemian (San Francisco); Eldorado Country (Indian Wells, Calif.); Boone & Crockett. Home: PO Box 100600 Anchorage AK 99510-0600

RASMUSSEN, ALICE CALL, nursing educator; b. Grand Rapids, Mich., Dec. 16, 1947; d. Amon Burton and Jessie Pearl (Dann) Call; m. Charles P. Rasmussen, Apr. 16, 1972. BSN, Andrews U., 1971; MSN, Med. Coll. Ga., 1977; postgrad., Ferris State U., 1990. Staff nurse Lockwood-MacDonald Hosp., Petoskey, Mich., 1971-72; instr. Lake Michigan Coll., Benton Harbor, Mich., 1973-86; nursing coord. Lake Mich. Coll., Benton Harbor, Mich., 1986—; Mem. Mich. Bd. Nursing. Mem. AAUW, NAFE, Mich. League for Nursing, Mich. Coun. Nursing Edn. Adminstrs., Nat. Ordn. ADN, Mich. Assn. Women in Edn., S.W. Mich. Nurse Educator Network, Sigma Theta Tau. Home: 9088 4th St Berrien Springs MI 49103-1637 Office: Lake Mich Coll 2755 E Napier Ave Benton Harbor MI 49022-1881

RASMUSSEN, DAVID TAB, physical anthropology educator; b. Salt Lake City, June 17, 1958; s. David Irvin and Deon (Robison) R. BA, Colo. Coll., 1980; PhD, Duke U., 1986. Rsch. assoc. Duke Primate Ctr., Durham, N.C., 1986-87; vis. asst. prof. Rice U., Houston, 1987-88; asst. prof. UCLA, 1988-91; asst. prof. phys. anthropology Washington U., St. Louis, 1991-93, assoc. prof., 1993—, grad. coord. dept. anthropology, 1993-96; rsch. assoc. Los Angeles County Mus., L.A., 1989—, Carnegie Mus., Pitts.; condr. paleontol. fieldwork in Africa and N.Am. Editor: Origin and Evolution of Humans and Humanness, 1993; contbr. numerous articles to sci. jours. Achievements include finding fossils of early primates from 30 to 50 million years old; research on anthropoid origins, on mammal and bird evolution. Avocations: birding, mountain climbing, canoeing. Office: Washington U Dept Anthropology Saint Louis MO 63130-4862

RASMUSSEN, DENNIS LOY, sales and marketing executive; b. Green Bay, Wis., Oct. 12, 1940; s. Maurice G. and Irene Rose (Heitzke) R.; m. Janet A. Meyer, June 1959 (div. June 1973); 1 child, Anne E. Rusnak; m. Susan J. Duncan, July 4, 1991. BA cum laude, St. Norbert Coll., De Pere, Wis., 1966. Sales promotion mgr. Tape Inc., Green Bay, Wis., 1966-69; program sales mgr. Xerox Corp., Stamford, Conn., 1969-78; regional v.p. Foremost Guaranty Corp., Madison, Wis., 1978-82; mgr. tng. and devel. Gates Rubber Co., Denver, 1982-84; v.p. mktg. Holy Cross Health System Corp., South Bend, Ind., 1985-87, Globe Security Systems Corp., Phila., 1987-88, U. Tex. M.D. Anderson Cancer Ctr., Houston, 1988-90; nat. sales mgr. Referral Systems Group, Sacramento, 1990-91; pres. Rasmussen Consulting, 1990-92; with AVP Tng. and Devel. Chase Home Mortgage Corp., Tampa, Fla., 1992-93; dir. sales Express Pharmacy Svcs., TMESYS, Tampa, 1994-95. With U.S. Army, 1959-62. Mem. Am. Mgmt. Assn., Am. Soc. Tng. and Devel., Am. Mktg. Assn. (exec.), Am. Coll. Healthcare Execs. Republican. Roman Catholic. Avocations: golf, fishing, collections, reading, jogging, cycling.

RASMUSSEN, GAIL MAUREEN, critical care nurse; b. Can., Feb. 22, 1941; d. Thomas Alfred and Bernice Hilda (Sayler) Salisbury; m. Byron Karl Rasmussen, June 28, 1964; children: Stephen, Carla, Wade, Gregory. AS, Riverside City Coll., 1961; BSN, U. Phoenix, 1987; MS in Health Professions Edn., Western U Health Scis., 1991. RN, Calif.; CCRN. Staff nurse Meml. Med. Ctr., Long Beach, Calif., 1961-63, UCLA Med. Ctr., 1963-64; clin. nurse critical care unit Intercomty. Med. Ctr. (name changed to Citrus Valley Health Ptnrs.- Intercomty. Campus), Covina, Calif., 1964-71, 78-95, 96; instr. ACLS, Los Angeles County, 1991—. Mem. AACN.

RASMUSSEN, GUNNAR, engineer; b. Esbjerg, Denmark, Nov. 23, 1925; s. Karl Sigurd and Frederikke Valentine (Gjerulff) R.; m. Hanna Hertz, June 27, 1973; children: Jan, Lise, Per, Thue. Student, Aarhus Teknikum, Denmark, 1950. Mgr. quality control Brüel and Kjaer, Nerum, Denmark, 1950-54, with devel. div., 1955-69, with product planning div., 1969-74, with innovation div., 1975-93; engr. GRAS Sound and Vibration, Vedbaek, Denmark, 1993—; lectr. Danish Tech. U., Copenhagen, 1974-79, Med. Air Force Acad., Jegersborg, Denmark, 1978-79; examiner Danish Engring. Acad., Copenhagen, 1972—, Chalmers Tech. U., Gothenburg, Sweden, 1984-85. Editor: Intensity Measurements, 1989; inventor measurement microphones, accelerometers; contbr. articles to profl. jours. Chairman Audio Engring. Soc. Denmark, Cophenhagen, 1976. Recipient Danish Design prize for microphones, 1962, medal for contbn. to intensity techniques SETIM, 1990. Fellow Acoustical Soc. Am., Can. Acoustical Soc., Danish Medico Tech. Soc.; mem. Internat. Union Pure and Applied Physics (vice chmn. internat. commn. on accoustics), Danish Acoustical Soc. (bd. dirs.), Internat. Electronical Commn., Internat. Orgn. for Standarization. Home: Hojbjerggardsvej 15, 2840 Holte Denmark Office: GRAS Sound & Vibration, Skelstedet 10 B, DK-2950 Vedbaek Denmark

RASMUSSEN, HARRY PAUL, horticulture and landscape educator; b. Tremonton, Utah, July 18, 1939; s. Peter Y. and Lorna (Nielsen) R.; m. Mary Jane Dalley, Sept. 4, 1959; children—Randy Paul, Lorianne, Trent Dalley, Rachelle. A.S., Coll. of So. Utah, 1959; B.S., Utah State U., 1961; M.S., Mich. State U., 1962, Ph.D., 1965. Research scientist Conn. Agr. Expt. Sta., New Haven, 1965-66; researcher, instr. Mich. State U., East Lansing, 1966-81; chmn. dept. horticulture and landscape architecture Wash. State U., Pullman, 1981-88; dir. Utah Agrl. Expt. Sta., Utah State U., 1988—; assoc. v.p. Utah State U., Logan, 1992—. Contbr. articles to profl. jours., chpts. to books. Mem. bd. control YMCA, Lansing, Mich., 1976; mem. council Boy Scouts Am., Lansing, 1980; stake pres. Ch. of Jesus Christ of Latter-day Saints, Lansing, 1973-81. NDEA fellow, 1961-65. Fellow Am. Soc. Horticulture Sci.; mem. AAAS, Scanning Electron Microscopy (chmn. plant sect. 1976-83, chmn. exptl. sta. com. on orgn. and policy 1996-97). Home: 1949 N 950 E Logan UT 84341-1813 Office: Utah State U 235 Agr Sci Bldg Logan UT 84322

RASMUSSEN, HOWARD, medical educator, medical institute executive; b. Harrisburg, Pa., Mar. 1, 1925; s. Frederick and Faith (Elliott) R.; m. Jane Claire Spence, June 10, 1950; children: Gail, Paul, Jane, Craig. AB in Chemistry and Physics, Gettysburg Coll., 1948; MD, Harvard U., 1952; PhD in Biochemistry and Physiology, Rockefeller U., 1959; DSc, Gettysburg Coll., 1964. Asst. prof. physiology Rockefeller U., N.Y.C., 1959-61; assoc. prof. biochemistry U. Wis., Madison, 1961-64; prof. sch. medicine U. Pa., Phila., 1964-75, Benjamin Rush prof. biochemistry, 1964-75, prof. biochemistry and biophysics, 1964-76, chmn. dept. biochemistry, 1964-70, prof. pediatrics, 1975-76; Guggenheim fellow Cambridge U., 1971-72; prof. medicine and cell biology sch. medicine Yale U., New Haven, 1976-93; prof. medicine, surgery, cell biology, anatomy Med. Coll. Ga., Augusta, 1993—; dir. SCOT Urolithiasis Ctr., Sch. Medicine, Yale U., 1977-82, chief divsn. endocrinology, 1980-86, dir. med. scientist tng. program, 1983-91; dir. Inst. for Molecular Medicine and Genetics, Med. Coll. Ga., 1993—; Wellcome vis. prof. U. Va., Richmond, 1988; Klenk lectr. U. Koln, West Germany, 1989; Lily lectr. XI Internat. Conf. Calcium Regulation, Florence, Italy, 1992. Author: Calcium and cAMP as Synarchic Messengers, 1981, The Physiological and Cellular Basis of Metabolic Bone Disease, 1984. Bd. trustees Gettysburg Coll., 1985-93. Staff sgt. U.S. Army, 1942-44. Recipient Cotlove award Acad. Clin. Lab. Physicians and Scientists, 1993, Andre Lichtwitz prize, 1971. Fellow AAAS. Avocations: opera, hiking. Office: Med Coll Ga 1120 15th St CB-2803 Augusta GA 30912

RASMUSSEN, JOHN OSCAR, nuclear scientist; b. St. Petersburg, Fla., Aug. 8, 1926; s. John Oscar and Hazel (Ormsby) R.; m. Louise Brooks, Aug. 27, 1950; children—Nancy, Jane, David, Stephen. B.S., Calif. Inst. Tech., 1948; Ph.D., U. Calif. at Berkeley, 1952; M.A. (hon.), Yale U., 1969. Mem. faculty dept. chemistry U. Calif., Berkeley, 1952-68, 73-91, prof. chemistry, 1971-91, ret., 1991, mem. research staff, 1952-68; sr. rsch. assoc. Lawrence Berkeley Nat. Lab., 1972—; prof. chemistry Yale U. 1969-73; asso. dir. Yale Heavy Ion Accelerator Lab., 1970-73; vis. research prof. Nobel Inst. Physics, Stockholm, 1953; vis. prof. Inst. Nuclear Sci. U. Tokyo, 1974, Fudan U., Shanghai, 1979, hon. prof., 1984. Contbr. articles on radioactivity, nuclear models, heavy ion reactions. Served with USN, 1944-46. Recipient E.O. Lawrence Meml. award AEC, 1967; NSF sr. postdoctoral fellow Niels Bohr Inst., Copenhagen, 1961-62, NORDITA fellow, 1979, Guggenheim Meml. fellow, 1973, Alexander von Humboldt sr. rsch. fellow Tech. U. Munich, 1991. Fellow Am. Phys. Soc., AAAS; mem. Am. Chem. Soc. (Nuclear Applications in Chemistry award 1976), Fedn. Am. Scientists (chmn. 1969). Office: Lawrence Berkeley Lab MS 70A # 3307 Berkeley CA 94720

RASMUSSEN, KATHLEEN MAHER, nutritional sciences educator; b. Dayton, Ohio, Mar. 1, 1948. AB, Brown U., 1970; MSc, Harvard U., 1975, DSc, 1978. Registered dietitian. Tchr. sci. Cape Elem. Sch., Buxton, N.C., 1971-72; analytical chemist Berkeley Machine Works, Foundry Co., Norfolk, Va., 1972-73; rsch. assoc. dept. nutrition Harvard U., Boston, 1978; instr. div. nutritional scis. Cornell U., Ithaca, N.Y., 1981-83, asst. prof., 1983-88, assoc. prof., 1988-96, assoc. dir. grad. affairs, 1992-95, prof., 1996—; com. mem. NAS, Washington, 1988—; Pew faculty scholar in nutrition Nat. Ctr. Sci. Rsch., Meudon-Bellevue, France, 1989-90. NIH trainee, 1974-80; NIH grantee, 1984-90, 87—, 93—, various other grants and awards, 1982-85, 88-89, 89-92, 92-94, 93-96. Mem. Am. Inst. Nutrition, Am. Soc. Clin. Nutrition, Brit. Nutrition Soc., Internat. Soc. for Rsch. in Human Milk and Lactation. Office: Cornell U Div Nutritional Sci 111 Savage Hall Ithaca NY 14853-6301

RASMUSSEN, NEIL WOODLAND, insurance agent; b. Portland, Oreg., Sept. 14, 1926; s. Ernest Roy and Lulu Mildred (Woodland) R.; m. Mary Ann Cannon, Aug. 10, 1957; children: Kirk, Sally, P. Cannon, Eric (dec.). BA, Stanford U., 1949. Registered mut. funds rep. Warehouseman Consol. Supply Co., Portland, Oreg., 1949-50, sales rep., 1955-56; sales rep. Consol. Supply Co., Eugene, Oreg., 1950-52; sales rep. Consol. Supply Co., Salem, Oreg., 1956-64, br. mgr., 1964-82; agt. life and health ins. N.Y. Life Ins. Co., Salem, 1982—. Lt. Cmdr. USN, 1952-55; officer U.S. Selective Svc. Res., 1969-73. Recipient Nat. Quality award Nat. Assn. Life Underwriters, 1986-88. Mem. Salem Assn. Life Underwriters, Res. Officers Assn. (bd. dirs. 1988-91, v.p. 1988-91), Rotary (bd. dirs. East Salem 1980-83, sr. active mem. 1990-92, Paul Harris fellow). Republican. Episcopalian. Avocations: golf, fishing, camping. Office: NY Life Ins Co 530 Center St NE Salem OR 97301-3744

RASMUSSEN, RICHARD ROBERT, lawyer; b. Chgo., July 5, 1946; s. Robert Kersten Rasmussen and Marisa Bruna Batistoni; children: Kathryn, William. BS, U. Oreg., 1970, JD, 1973. Bar: Oreg. 1973. Atty. U.S. Bancorp, Portland, Oreg., 1973-83, 95—, v.p. law div., 1983-87, mgr. law div., 1983-95, sr. v.p., 1987-95, mgr. corp. sec. div., 1990-94. Mem. editorial bd. Oreg. Bus. Law Digest, 1979-81, Oreg. Debtor/Creditor newsletter, 1980-84; contbr. articles to profl. jours. Chmn. mgmt. com. YMCA of Columbia-Willamette, Portland, 1978-79; bd. dirs. Camp Fire, 1988-89, v.p., 1990-91; bd. dirs. Portland Repertory Theatre, 1994-96. Mem. Oreg. State Bar Assn. (chmn. corp. counsel com. 1979-81, debtor/creditor sect. 1982-83; sec. com. on sects. 1982-83), ABA, Multnomah County Bar Assn., Am. Bankers Assn. (bank counsel com. 1996—), Beta Gamma Sigma. Club: Founder's (Portland). Avocations: mountaineering, white-water rafting, tennis, basketball. Office: US Bancorp Law Div 111 SW 5th Ave Portland OR 97204-3604

RASMUSSEN, WAYNE ROGER, law educator, consultant; b. Sioux Falls, S.D., May 8, 1936; s. Ezra Christian and Loretta Mae Belle (Schlafer) R.; m. Carol Joy Longsdorf Prue, June 4, 1960 (div. May 1973); children: Joy, Corbin; m. Mary Dee Fowlkes, May 20, 1973; children: Thomas, Frances, Heather. BA, ThB, St. Paul Bible Coll., 1963; JD, John Marshall Law Sch., Atlanta, 1989. Bar: Ga. 1989, Calif. 1992; CPCU. Claims adjuster Travelers Ins. Co., St. Paul, 1966-70; claims supr. Travelers Ins. Co., Washington, 1970-72; asst. mgr. claims Travelers Ins. Co., Atlanta, 1972-77; asst. v.p. Continental Ins. Co., N.Y.C., 1977-82; mgr. state claims Continental Ins. Co., Charlotte, N.C., 1982-86; pvt. practice, Atlanta, 1989—; prof. law John Marshall Law Sch., 1989—; ins. cons., Atlanta, 1990—. Aux. police officer N.Y. Police Dept., N.Y.C., 1978-82. With USAF, 1954-58. Named Outstanding Prof. of Yr., John Marshall Law Sch., 1992. Mem. Soc. of CPCU (treas. 1980), Soc. of CLU. Avocations: skiing, walking.

RASMUSSON, GARY HENRY, medicinal chemist; b. Clark, S.D., Aug. 2, 1936; s. Rudolf M. and Alice Ernestine (Henry) R.; m. Nancy Elaine Torkelson, June 7, 1958; children: Randall, Korise, Tamara, Todd. BA, St. Olaf Coll., 1958; PhD, MIT, 1962. Postdoctoral fellow Stanford U., Palo Alto, Calif., 1962-64; sr. chemist Merck, Sharp & Dohme Rsch. Labs., Rahway, N.J., 1964-72, rsch. fellow, 1972-77, sr. rsch. fellow, 1977-85, sr. investigator, 1985-94; v.p. chemistry Biofor, Inc., Waverly, Pa., 1996; cons. synthetic and medicinal chemistry, 1996—. Medicinal discovery new type drug 5alpha reductase inhibitors, 1986. Named Inventor of Yr. Intellectual Property Owners, Washington, 1993. Mem. AAAS, Am. Chem. Soc. Lutheran.

RASOR, DINA LYNN, investigator, journalist; b. Downey, Calif., Mar. 21, 1956; d. Ned Shaurer and Genevieve Mercia (Eads) R.; m. Thomas Taylor Lawson, Oct. 4, 1980. BA in Polit. Sci., U. Calif., Berkeley, 1978. Editorial asst. ABC News, Washington, 1978-79; researcher Pres.'s Commn. on Coal, Washington, 1979; legis. asst. Nat. Taxpayers Union, Washington, 1979-81; founder, dir. Project on Mil. Procurement, Washington, 1981-89; investigative reporter Lawson-Rasor Assocs., El Cerrito, Calif., 1990-92; pres., CEO, investigator Bauman & Rasor Group, El Cerrito, Calif., 1993—. Author: The Pentagon Underground, 1985; editor: More Bucks, Less Bang, 1983; contbr. articles to profl. jours. Recipient Sigma Delta Chi Outstanding Leadership award Soc. Profl. Journalists, 1986; named to register Esquire Mag., 1986, Nat. Jour., 1986. Mem. United Ch. Christ.

RASPORICH, ANTHONY WALTER, university dean; b. Port Arthur, Ont., Can., Jan. 9, 1940; s. Milan and Sophia (Grgurich) R.; m. Beverly Jean Matson. BA, Queen's U., Kingston, Ontario, 1962, MA, 1965; PhD, U. Man., Winnipeg, 1970. Tchr. Kingston Bd. Edn., 1962-63; prof. history U. of Calgary, Alta., 1966—, dean social scis. faculty, 1986-94. Author: For a Better Life, 1982, Oil and Gas in Western Canada 1900-80, 1985; editor: The Making of the Modern West, 1984; co-editor: Canadian Ethnic Studies, 1980-96, Sports in the West, 1990. C.D. Howe postdoctoral fellow, fellow Assn. Univs. Colls. Can., Thunder Bay, Ontario, 1970, Vis. Can. Studies, Sussex, Eng., 1979, Killam Found., Calgary, 1979, Social Scis. Human Rsch. Coun., Ottawa, Can., 1981. Mem. Canada Ethnic Studies Assn., Can. Hist. Assn. Office: U Calgary, Dept History, Calgary, AB Canada T2N 1N4

RASSBACH, HERBERT DAVID, marketing executive; b. Glen Ridge, N.J., Mar. 23, 1944; s. Merrill Augustus and Ruth Bruce (Sims) R.; m. Sherry Miriam Reichel, July 14, 1974. BS, Del. State Coll., 1971; MBA, Drexel U., 1979. Prodn. planning mgr. Standard Brands Chem. Industries, Edison, N.J., 1971-74; order fulfillment mgr. P Q Corp., Valley Forge, Pa., 1974-77, mkt. devel. project mgr., 1977-82; market mgr. Willson Safety Products, Reading, Pa., 1983-85; pres. HDR Group, mktg. and mgmt. cons., Wayne, Pa., 1986—; guest speaker Wharton Sch. U. Pa., 1988, Temple U., Phila., 1989, Wharton Club, 1995. Committeeman Upper Merion Twp., Pa., 1977; Media Comms. bd., Upper Merion Twp., 1989, vice chmn., 1990, 92-97, chmn., 1991. Mem. Drexel U. Alumni Assn. (v.p. Montgomery County chpt. 1988-91), Alpha Kappa Mu, Delta Mu Delta. Democrat. Avocations: golf, tennis, racquetball, travel, American History, arts. Home: 635 Mallard Rd Wayne PA 19087-2346 Office: HDR Group PO Box 904 Valley Forge PA 19482-0904

RASSMAN, JOEL H., real estate company executive, accountant; b. N.Y.C., May 16, 1945. BBA, CUNY, 1967. CPA, N.Y. Mng. dir. Ernst & Young, N.Y.C., 1967-73; ptnr. Kenneth Leventhal & Co. (now Ernst & Young), N.Y.C., 1973-84; sr. v.p., CFO, bd. dirs. Toll Bros., Inc., Huntingdon Valley, Pa., 1984—. Mem. AICPA, N.Y. State Soc. CPA's.

RAST, WALTER, JR., hydrologist, water quality management; b. San Antonio, Jan. 14, 1944; s. Walter and Jane Irene (Tudyk) R.; m. Claudia Leigh Jones, July 16, 1971; children: Margaret Amanda, Elizabeth Miranda. BA in Zoology, U. Tex., Austin, 1970; MS in Molecular Biology, U. Tex., Richardson, 1974, MS in Environ. Sci., 1976, PhD in Environ. Sci., 1978. Limnologist Gt. Lakes Regional Office, Internat. Joint Commn., Windsor, Ont., Can., 1977-79; environ. advisor U.S. Hdqrs. sect. Internat. Joint Commn., Washington, 1979-82; rsch. hydrologist U.S. Geol. Survey, Sacramento, 1982-86, Austin, 1986-92; chief freshwater unit UNEP, Nairobi, Kenya, 1992-95, dep. dir. water br., 1996—; adj. prof. dept. biology Wayne State U., Detroit, 1978-79; adj. prof. dept. aquatic biology S.W. Tex. State U., San Marcos, 1992—; mem. core editorial group program on man and biosphere UNESCO, 1982-89, chmn. sci. adv. com., 1988—; instr. Austin Community Coll., 1989—; reviewer sci. books and films AAAS, Washington, 1989—. Co-author: Control of Eutrophication of Lakes and Reservoirs, 1989; co-editor: Phosphorus Management Strategies for Lakes, 1979; mem. editorial bd. Internat. Jour. Devel., 1993—; contbr. articles to sci. jours. Scholar Richardson Environ. Action League, 1976-77. Mem. N.Am. Lake Mgmt. Soc. (co-chmn. scholarship com. 1988—, mem. internat. com. and lake cert. com. 1988—, tech. chmn. 9th internat. symposium 1989), Am. Soc. Limnology and Oceanography, Internat. Soc. Applied and Theoretical Limnology. Roman Catholic. Avocations: jogging, model railroads, piano, reading, amateur politics. *One of the most difficult things for a person to do is undertake necessary and even unpleasant tasks, at the same time others are content to offer excuses as to why they cannot be done. Fortunately, a sufficient number of people display this virtue to make it all worthwhile.*

RASTINEJAD, FRAYDOON, biophysicist, structural biologist, educator; b. Tehran, Iran, Dec. 29, 1965; came to U.S., 1975; s. Shahriar and Irantaj (Pourmostadam) R. BA, Northwestern U., 1987; PhD, U. Pa., 1992. NIH postdoctoral fellow Yale U., New Haven, 1992-95; asst. prof. U. Va., Charlottesville, 1995—. NSF predoctoral fellow, 1988-91. Achievements include research in X-ray crystallography of protein-DNA complexes, structural determinants of protein-DNA and protein-protein interactions. Home: Box 448 1300 Jefferson Park Ave Charlottesville VA 22903-3363 Office: U Va Dept Pharmacology Jordan Hall Box 448 Charlottesville VA 22908

RASTOGI, ANIL KUMAR, medical device manufacturer executive; b. India, July 13, 1942; came to U.S., 1969, naturalized, 1978; s. R.S. and K.V. Rastogi; m. Anjali Capur, Mar. 18, 1970; children: Priya, Sonya. B.S. with honors, Lucknow U., 1963, M.S., 1964; Ph.D. in Polymer Sci., McGill U., 1969. Mem. staff Owens-Corning Tech. Ctr., Granville, Ohio, 1969-87; lab. supr. Owens-Corning Tech. Ctr., 1975-76; lab. mgr. materials tech. labs Ownes-Corning Tech. Ctr., Granville, Ohio, 1976-79; lab. mgr. product devel. labs. Owens-Corning Tech. Ctr., Granville, Ohio, 1979-80, research dir., 1980-83, dir. corp. diversification portfolio, 1983-87; v.p. Mead Imaging, Miamisburg, Ohio, 1987-89; pres. Mead Cycolor Div., Dayton, Ohio, 1989-92; v.p., gen. mgr.infusion systems div. Pharmacia Deltec, Inc., St. Paul, 1992-93; exec. v.p. Pharmacia Deltec, Inc., 1993-94; COO SIMS Deltec, Inc., St. Paul, 1994-95; pres., COO Sabratek Corp., Niles, Ill., 1995—; mem. adv. bd. Central Ohio Tech. Coll.; lectr., cons. in field. Author of 15 bus. and tech. publs.; patentee in field. Bd. dirs. Licking County Family Services Assn.; bd. dirs. Tech. Alliance of Central Ohio; v.p. local United Way; bd. dirs. and treas. Columbus Bus. Tech. Ctr.; mem. Overview Adv. Com. Strategic Hwy. Research Program. Fellow NRC Can., 1966-69. Mem. AAAS, Am. Mgmt. Assn., Am. Chem. Soc., Soc. Plastics Engrs., Comml. Devel. Assn., Med. Alley (bd. dirs.), Health Ind. Mfrs. Assn., Nat. Infusion Therapy Alliance (bd. dirs.), Sigma Xi. Club: Toastmasters (past pres.). Lodge: Rotary. Home: 107 S Old Wilke Rd Apt 406 Arlington Heights IL 60005-2978 Office: Sabratek Corp 5601 W Howard St Niles IL 60714-4011

RATAJ, EDWARD WILLIAM, lawyer; b. St. Louis, Oct. 14, 1947; m. Elizabeth Spalding, July 4, 1970; children: Edward, Suzanne, Anne, Thomas, Charles. BS in Acctg., St. Louis U., 1969, JD, 1972. Assoc. Bryan, Cave, McPheeters & McRoberts, St. Louis, 1972-82, ptnr., 1983—. Office: Bryan Cave McPheeters & McRoberts 1 Metropolitan Sq Saint Louis MO 63102-2733

RATAJ, ELIZABETH ANN, artist; b. Flint, Mich., Oct. 3, 1943; d. Lloyd Milton Clem and Mildred (Lamrock) Clem-Taylor; m. David Henry Rataj, Oct. 17, 1970. BA, Bob Jones U., 1966; BFA, U. Iowa, 1987. Educator Oscoda (Mich.) Area Schs., 1966-71, 73-83, Ft. Wayne (Ind.) Pub. Schs.,

1971-72, St. Louis Pub. Schs., 1983-85. Represented in permanent collections Mich. Edn. Assn., Lansing, 1978, Munson Williams Proctor Mus., Utica, N.Y., 1989, Jesse Besser Mus., Alpena, Mich., 1993, Austin Peay State U., Clarksville, Tenn., 1997; two-person shows include The Art Ctr., Mount Clemens, Mich., 1996; group shows include Mus. Modern Art Miami, 1993, San Bernardino County Mus., Redlands, Calif., 1995, 96, Austin Peay State U., Clarksville, Tenn., 1995, The Art Ctr., Mount Clemens, Mich., 1996, San Bernardino County Mus., Rolands, Calif., 1995, 96, Women's Caucus for Art, Nat. 25th Anniversary Exhbn., 1997, Artemisia Gallery, Chgo., 1997. Mem. Delta Kappa Gamma (1978-82, 86-87, 76-87), Nat. Mus. of Women in the Arts (charter).

RATAJSKI, MAGDA ANNE, public relations executive; b. Hampshire, Farnborough, Eng., Dec. 20, 1950; came to U.S., 1957; d. James May and Halina K. (Podlewski) R. BA, Marquette U., 1972; MA, Georgetown U., 1979; grad. Advanced Mgmt. Program, Harvard U., 1992. Asst. to v.p. pub. affairs Norfolk and Western Ry. Co., Washington, 1976-77, rep. pub. affairs, 1977-80, asst. v.p. pub. affairs, 1980-82; asst. v.p. pub. affairs Norfolk So. Corp., Washington, 1982-84; v.p. pub. rels. Norfolk (Va.) So. Corp., 1984-96; with MarassCo., Virginia Beach, Va., 1997—; vice chmn. bd. dirs. exec. com. Sta. WHRO Pub. TV and Radio, Norfolk. Mem. exec. adv. coun. Coll. Bus. and Pub. Adminstrn., Old Dominion U., Norfolk, 1986—; chmn. Va. Waterfront Adv. Coun.; mem. Bus. Com. Arts, Inc., N.Y. Mem. R.R. Pub. Rels. Assn., Assn. R.R. Advt. and Mktg., Pub. Rels. Soc. Am., Hampton Roads C. of C. (bd. dirs. 1985, pub. info. com.), Am. Coun. R.R. Women, Arthur W. Page Soc., Mid-Atlantic Arts Found. (bd. dirs.), Pub. Rels. Seminar, Nat. Dem. Club (Washington), The Harbor Club, 116 Club (Washington). Office: MarassCo 2244 Widgeon Ln Virginia Beach VA 23456-4634

RATCLIFF, CARTER GOODRICH, writer, art critic, poet; b. Seattle, Aug. 20, 1941; s. Francis Kenneth and Marian Elizabeth (Carter) R.; m. Phyllis Derfner, Jan. 28, 1976. BA, U. Chgo., 1963. Dir. poetry workshop St. Mark's Poetry Project, N.Y.C., 1969-70; editorial assoc. Artnews, N.Y.C., 1969-72; advisory editor Art Internat., Lugano, Switzerland, 1970-75; instr. modern and contemporary art and art theory The Sch. of Visual Arts, N.Y.C., 1972-83; instr. modern and contemporary art Phila. Coll. of Art, 1973; instr. art history NYU Sch. of Continuing Edn., 1973-75; contbg. editor Saturday Review, N.Y.C., 1980-82, Art in America, N.Y.C., 1976—; mem. editorial adv. com. Sculpture, Washington, 1992—; via. prof. post-war Am. art SUNY, Purchase, 1983-84; vis. prof. modern and contemporary art and art theory Pratt Inst., Bkyn., 1984-85; vis. prof. art criticism and theory Hunter Coll., CUNY, 1985-86, 95-96. Author: (books, poetry), Fever Coast, 1973, Give Me Tomorrow, 1983; (books) John Singer Sargent, 1982, Andy Warhol, 1983, Robert Longo, 1985, Komar and Melamid, 1989, Gilbert and George: The Singing Sculpture, 1993, Jackson Pollock, 1996; (catlog essays) Joseph Cornell, 1980, Willem de Kooning: The North Atlantic Light, 1983, Sean Scully, 1993, Ellsworth Kelly, 1996; contbr. over 350 articles on art to magazines and catalogs including The Times Literary Supplement, The L.A. Times Book Review, Art in America, Art Internat., Artnews, Architectrual Forum; lectr. at many instns. including Met. Mus., N.Y.C., Mus. Modern Art, N.Y.C., Whitney Mus. of Am. Art, Pratt Inst., U. So. Calif., U. Chgo., Detroit Inst. of Art, San Francisco Art Inst. Recipient of the Frank Jewett Mather award for art criticism Coll. Art Assn., 1987; Poets Found. grantee, 1969, NEA Arts Critics grantee, 1972, 76; Guggenheim fellow, 1976. Home and Office: 26 Beaver St New York NY 10004-2311

RATCLIFF, JAMES LEWIS, administrator; b. Indpls., Mar. 3, 1946; s. Perry Albert and Viola Ruth (Hall) R.; m. Carol Rocklin Kay, Dec. 24, 1984 (dec.); m. Barbara Marie Montgomery, Aug. 31, 1995. Student, Raymond Coll.; B of History, Polit. Sci., Utah State U., 1968; MA in History, Wash. State U., 1972, PhD, 1976. Dir. Ctr. for the Study of Higher Edn. Pa. State U., University Pk.; prof., leader higher edn. section Iowa State U., Ames; assoc. prof. Fla. Atlantic U., Boca Raton; asst. prof. Wash. State U., Pullman. Author: Assessment and Curriculum Reform, 1992, Community Colleges, 1994, Postsecondary Education, 1995, (with J. Gaff) A Handbook of Undergraduate Curriculum, 1996. U.S. Dept. Edn. grantee. Mem. AAAS, Am. Assn. Community Jr. Colls., Assn. Study Higher Edn. (bd. dirs.), Coun. Universities Colls. (past pres., bd. dirs.), European Assn. for Inst. Rsch.,Consortium Higher Edn. Rschs., Phi Delta Kappa, Phi Kappa Phi, Phi Alpha Theta.

RATH, ALAN T., sculptor; b. Cin., Nov. 25, 1959; s. George and Carolyn R. BSEE, MIT, 1982. One-man exhbns. include San Jose (Calif.) Art Mus., 1990, Dorothy Goldeen Gallery, Santa Monica, Calif., 1990, 92, Walker Art Ctr., Mpls., 1991, Mus. Contemporary Art, Chgo., 1991, Carl Solway Gallery, Cin., 1991, Inst. Contemporary Mus., Honolulu, 1992, Ctr. Fine Art, Miami, Fla., 1992, Galerie Hans Mayer, Dusseldorf, Germany, 1992, Hiroshima (Japan) City Mus. Contemporary Art, 1994, Worcester (Mass.) Art Mus., 1994, John Weber Gallery, N.Y.C., 1994, Haines Gallery, San Francisco, 1995, 96, Contemporary Art Mus., Houston, 1995, Aspen Art Mus., Colo., 1996; group exhbns. include Visiona, Zurich, 1989, Arc Electronics, Linz, Austria, 1989, L.A. Contemporary Exhbns., 1989, Mus. Folkwang, Essen, Germany, 1989, Cite des Arts et des Nouvelles Technologies, Montreal, 1990, Stadtmuseum Siegburg, Siegburg, Germany, 1990, San Francisco Mus. Modern Art, 1990, 95, Denver ArtMus., 1991, Whitney Am. Art, N.Y.C., 1991, Alvar Alto Mus., Jyvaskyla, Finland, 1992, Internat. Ctr. Photography, N.Y.C., 1992, Padiglione d'Arte Contemporanea, Ferrara, Italy, 1992, John Weber Gallery, N.Y.C., 1993, Spiral Art Ctr., Tokyo, 1994, Aldrich Mus. of Contemporary Art, Ridgefield, Conn., 1995, Olso Gallery, Espo Finland, 1996, LaLonja, Palma de Malloren, Spain, 1996. Grantee NEA, 1988; Guggenheim fellow, 1994. Office: IKON 830 E 15th St Oakland CA 94606-3631

RATH, BERNARD EMIL, trade association executive; b. Arnstein, Fed. Republic of Germany, Oct. 9, 1949; arrived in Can., 1952; U.S. resident, 1985; s. Rudolph and Elfriede (Kraft) R.; m. Susan Elaine Garner, July 8, 1972; children: Vanessa, Andrew, Lauren. BA in Polit. Sci., McMaster U., Can., 1972, BA in Phys. Edn., 1972; Diploma Edn., U. Western Ont., Can., 1973. Sales rep. Doubleday Pubs., Toronto, Ont., Can., 1973-75; sales mgr. Macmillian Pubs., Toronto, Ont., Can., 1975-77, nat. sales mgr., 1977-79; exec. dir. Can. Booksellers, Toronto, 1979-83, Am. Booksellers Assn., N.Y.C., 1984-96; pres. Libris, 1997—, Westchester Holdings Inc., 1997—; pres. Booksellers Order Service, N.Y.C., 1984—. Contbr. articles to profl. jours. Am. Soc. Assn. Execs. Home: 33 Chester Ct Cortlandt Manor NY 10566

RATH, HOWARD GRANT, JR., lawyer; b. L.A., Sept. 2, 1931; s. Howard Grant and Helen (Cowell) R.; m. Peyton McComb, Sept. 13, 1958 (dec. Apr. 1984); children: Parthenia Peyton, Francis Cowell; m. Dorothy Moser, Aug. 29, 1986. BS, U. Calif., 1953; JD, U. So. Calif., 1958. Bar: Calif. 1959, U.S. Dist. Ct. (cen. dist.) Calif., 1959, U.S. Ct. Claims 1974, U.S. Tax Ct. 1960. Assoc. O'Melveny & Myers, L.A., 1959-66; tax counsel, dir. tax adminstrn., asst. treas. Northrop Corp. L.A., 1966-74; sr. tax ptnr. Macdonald, Halsted & Laybourne, L.A., 1974-86, Hill & Weiss, L.A., 1986-90; ptnr. Lewis, D'Amato, Brisbois & Bisgaard, L.A., 1990—; dir. Rath Packing Co., Waterloo, Iowa, 1966-81. 1st lt. U.S. Army, 1953-55. Mem. ABA, State Bar Calif., L.A. County Bar Assn., Order of Coif, Phi Beta Kappa. Republican. Episcopalian. Club: Valley Hunt (pres. 1981-82). Office: Lewis D'Amato Brisbois & Bisgaard 221 N Figueroa St Ste 1200 Los Angeles CA 90012-2646

RATH, R. JOHN, historian, educator; b. St. Francis, Kans., Dec. 12, 1910; s. John and Barbara (Schauer) R.; m. Isabel Jones, June 26, 1937; children: Laurens John (dec.), Donald (dec.), Isabel Ferguson. A.B., U. Kans., 1932; A.M., U. Calif., Berkeley, 1934; Ph.D., Columbia U., 1941. Instr. history U. Ark., 1936-37, summer vis. prof., 1947; pre-doctoral field fellow Social Sci. Research Council in Austria and Italy, 1937-38; instr. history Coll. Puget Sound, Tacoma, Wash., 1938-39; head dept. history and polit. sci. Lindenwood Coll., St. Charles, Mo., 1939-41; assoc. prof. history Miss. State Coll. for Women, 1941-43; chief bur. documentary evidence UNRRA Bur. Documents and Tracing, U.S. Zone of Ger., 1945-46; asst. prof. history U. Ga., 1946-47; assoc. prof. history, assoc. editor Jour. Central European Affairs, U. Colo., 1947-51, vis. prof., summer 1958; prof. history U. Tex., Austin, 1951-63; prof. history, chmn. dept. history and polit. sci. Rice U., 1963-68, Mary Gibbs Jones prof., 1968-80, prof. emeritus, 1980—; prof. history U. Minn., Mpls., 1980-85; vis. prof. U. Wis., 1955, Duke U., 1963; Guggenheim fellow in Italy, 1956-57. Author: The Fall of the Napoleonic Kingdom of Italy, 1941, The Viennese Revolution 1948, 1957, L'amministrazione austriaca nel Lombardo Veneto, 1814-21, 1959, The Austrian Provisional Regime in Lombardy Venetia, 1969, The Deterioration of Democracy in Austria, 1927-1992, 1996, The Molding of Engelbert Dellfuss as an Agrarian Reformer, 1997; contbg. author: The Fate of East Central Europe (editor Stephen Kertesz), 1956, East Central Europe and the World (edited S. Kertesz), 1962; also Ency. Americana; founder, editor: Austrian History Newsletter, 1960-63, Austrian History Yearbook, 1965-82; contbr. Die Aufloesung des Habsburgerreiches, 1970, Native Fascism in the Successor States, 1971, Beitraege zur Zeitgeschichte, 1976, The Austrian Socialist Experiment, 1985, The Mirror of History, 1988, Austria, 1938-88, 1995. Served in AUS, 1943-45. Recipient 1st class Austrian Cross of Honor in arts and scis., 1963. Mem. Am. Hist. Soc. (com. internat. activities 1960-66, exec. com. modern European history sect. 1963-66), So. Hist. Soc. (chmn. European sect. 1961-62, exec. coun. 1965-68), Soc. Italian Hist. Studies (Sr. Scholar Citation 1984), Conf. Ctrl. European History (nat. exec. bd. 1959-61, chmn. 1970, com. on Austrian history 1957-68, 70-81, exec. sec. 1957-68), Am. Assn. Study of Hungarian History (chmn. 1978), Southwestern Social Sci. Assn. (pres. 1976-77), Austrian Acad. Sci. (corr.), Deputazione di Storia Patria par le Venezie (corr.), Phi Beta Kappa. Home: 5015 35th Ave S Apt 130 Minneapolis MN 55417-1562

RATH, THOMAS DAVID, lawyer, former state attorney general; b. East Orange, N.J., June 1, 1945; s. Harvey and Helen R.; m. Christine Casey, Dec. 18, 1971; children—Erin, Timothy. A.B., Dartmouth Coll., 1967; J.D., Georgetown U., 1971. Bar: N.J. 1971, N.H. 1972, U.S. Supreme Ct. 1978. Law clk. Judge Clarkson Fisher, U.S. Dist. Ct. N.J., 1971-72; atty. criminal div. Office of Atty. Gen., State of N.H., 1972-73; asst. atty. gen. Office of Atty. Gen., 1973-76, dep. atty. gen., 1976-78, atty. gen., 1978-80; ptnr. Orr & Reno, P.A., Concord, 1980-87, Rath & Young, P.A., Concord, 1987-91; founding ptnr. Rath, Young, Pignatelli & Oyer, P.A., Concord, 1991—; polit. analyst WHDH-TV, Boston, WGBH Pub. TV, Boston, WENH, N.H. Pub. TV, WBUR-Boston Radio; chief strategist Alexander for Pres.; vice chmn. of bd. Primary Bank, 1995; pres. Play Ball, N.H., 1994—; commentator, polit. analyst WMUR-TV and Yankee Network. Host State of the State, Yankee Cable Network; co-host Close-Up, WMUR-TV. Chmn. campaign Warren B. Rudman for U.S. Senate, 1980, 86; bd. overseers Aquinas House, Dartmouth Coll., com. on trustees Rockefeller Ctr. Bd. Visitors; bd. oversers Dartmouth Med. Sch.; nat. dir. Baker Exploratory Com., 1986-87; sec. bd. trustees Concord Hosp.; treas. N.H. Rep. party, 1981-93; trustee DWC, 1981-87, chmn., 1982-86; mem. Baker Exploratory Com., 1986-87; trustee Concord Hosp., 1980-86; sr. nat. cons. Dole for Pres.; del. Rep. Nat. Conv., 1984, 88, 92, rules com., 1988, 92, N.H. committeeman, 1996—; Rep. nat. committeeman State of N.H., 1996; bd. dirs. New Eng. Coun., 1997. Mem. Nat. Assn. Attys. Gen. (vice-chmn. Eastern region, vice chmn. standing com. on energy), N.H. Bar Assn. (Spl. Pres. award 1992). Roman Catholic. Club: Dartmouth Coll. (v.p. Merrimack County). Office: Rath Young and Pignatelli One Capital Plaza PO Box 1500 Concord NH 03302-1500

RATHBONE, PERRY TOWNSEND, art museum director; b. Germantown, Pa., July 3, 1911; s. Howard Betts and Beatrice (Connely) R.; m. Euretta de Cosson, Feb. 10, 1945; children: Peter Betts, Eliza, Belinda. A.B., Harvard U., 1933, postgrad., 1933-34; Arts D., Washington U., St. Louis, 1958; L.H.D., Northeastern U., 1960, Suffolk U., Williams Coll., 1970; A.F.D., Bates Coll., 1964, Boston Coll., 1970, R.I. Sch. Design, 1982. Co-dir. Harvard Soc. Contemporary Art, 1931-33; ednl. asst. Detroit Inst. Arts, 1934-36; instr. fine arts Wayne U., Detroit; curator Alger House (suburban br. Detroit Inst. Arts) and gen. rsch. asst. to Dir. Valentiner, 1936-39; asst. to Dir. Valentiner (dir. gen. masterpieces of art), N.Y. World's Fair; later dir.); dir. City Art Mus., St. Louis, 1940-55; dir. Mus. Fine Arts, Boston, 1954-72; dir. Mus. Fine Arts, 1955-72, dir. emeritus, cons., 1972—; dir. Christie's USA, 1973-77; sr. v.p., dir. Christie's Internat., 1977-86; cons. to Christie's Internat., 1987—; Pres. St. Louis Art Commn., 1940-55, St. Louis Little Symphony, 1950-55; adviser council Harvard Found. for Advanced Study and Research, 1953-58; mem. vis. com. Fogg Art Mus., Harvard, 1955-66; mem. U.S. nat. commn. Internat. Council of Museums; adviser program for humanities Ford Found., 1957-73; adviser art com. Chase Manhattan Bank, 1958-76; pres. Met. Boston Arts Center, Inc., 1958-61, chmn. bd., 1961-72; mem. Rockefeller Panel on Performing Arts, 1963-64, Skowhegan Sch. Painting and Sculpture, 1965-77; fine arts vis. com. R.I. Sch. Design, 1966-68, trustee, 1969-74; adviser Urasenke Found., Kyoto, Japan, 1974—; vice chmn. Mass. Art Commn.; v.p. Cosmopolitan Art Found., 1974-13 ; mem. Cambridge Arts Council, 1978-79, 79—. Author: Charles Wimar, 1946, Max Beckmann, 1948, Mississippi Panorama, 1950, Westward the Way, 1954, Lee Gatch, 1960, (with Peter Selz) Max Beckmann, 1964, Handbook of the Forsyth Wickes Collection, 1968, Museum of Fine Arts, Boston, Western Art, 1971, Andrew Wyeth (in Japanese), 1974; also numerous articles in mus. bulls. and art jours.; Contbr. to: (with Peter Selz) Great Drawings of All Times, 1962, The Arts and Public Policy in the U.S., chpt. 3, 1984. Mem. bd. overseers Brandeis U., Strawbery Banke, Inc.; trustee Am. Fedn. Arts, 1959-79, New Eng. Conservatory of Music, 1960-80, Boston Arts Festival, Cape Cod Art Assn., Internat. Exhbns. Found., 1965-81, Royal Oak Found., 1974-92, Opera Co. of Boston, 1976-90. Lt. comdr. USNR, 1942-45, PTO. Decorated chevalier Légion d'Honneur; Benjamin Franklin fellow Royal Soc. Art; fellow R.I. Sch. Design, 1981. Mem. Am. Assn. Mus. (v.p. 1960—, coun.), St. Louis Round Table, Mass. Hist. Soc., Colonial Soc. Mass., Assn. Art Mus. Dirs. (pres. 1959-60, 69-70, trustee 1969-72), Am. Acad. Arts and Scis., Royal Art Soc. London, Phi Beta Kappa (hon. Harvard chpt.), Century Club (N.Y.C.), Tavern Club (Boston), Odd Volumes Club (Boston), Harvard Club (Boston). Episcopalian. Home: Univ Green 130 Mount Auburn St Apt 506 Cambridge MA 02138-5779

RATHBONE, SUSAN WU, social services administrator; b. Hofei, Anhwei, China, Oct. 29, 1922; came to U.S., 1946; d. Chung Liu and Jin Ban (Gung) Wu; m. Frank Harold Rathbone, Aug. 20, 1945; children: Frank, Edward George. BA, CUNY, 1984. Tchr. Second Sch., Chungking, China, 1941-42; founder Chinese-Am. Bus. Women's Assn., Flushing, N.Y., 1990; founder, chair Chinese Immigrants Soc. Inc., Flushing, N.Y., 1984—, Queens Chinese Woman's Assn., Flushing, N.Y., 1984—. Editor Women's Voice mag., 1995—. Recipient Susan B. Anthony award NOW, 1987, Ethnic New Yorker award City of N.Y., 1984, Cmty. Svc. award NAACP, 1994, Gov.'s Woman of Distinction award N.Y. State, 1994. Mem. Anhui Provincial Assn. (founder, hon. life pres.), Nat. Women's Polit. Caucus, Univ. Women. Avocation: writing. Home: 26-10 Union St Flushing NY 11354 Office: 135-17 40th Rd PO Box 1656 Flushing NY 11354

RATHBUN, JOHN WILBERT, American studies educator; b. Sioux City, Iowa, Oct. 24, 1924; s. Wilbert W. and Paulina Amanda (Baldes) R.; m. Mary Regina Walsh, Aug. 2, 1947 (div. Sept. 19, 1985); children: Mary Walsh, John Philip. Ph.B., Marquette U., Milw., 1951, M.A., 1952; Ph.D., U. Wis., 1956. Mem. faculty Calif. State U., Los Angeles, 1956—; prof. English/Am. studies Calif. State U., 1959—, chmn. dept. Am. studies, 1969-75, prof. emeritus, 1991—. Author: American Literary Criticism, 1800-1860, vol. 1, 1979, (with Harry Hayden Clark) American Literary Criticism, 1860-1905, vol. 2, 1979, Literature and Literary Analysis, 1983; (with Monica Grecu) American Literary Critics and Scholars, 1800-1850, vol. 1, 1987, 1850-1880, vol. 2, 1880-1900, 1988, vol. 3, 1988; contbr. articles to profl. jours. Served with AUS, 1943-46. Recipient Service citation Calif. State U., Los Angeles, 1977, Univ. Meritorious Achievement award, 1986; Fulbright fellow Romania, 1979-81. Mem. Am. Studies Assn. (council 1974), So. Calif. Am. Studies Assn. (pres. 1973), Coll. English Assn. So. Calif. (pres. 1966-67), MLA. Democrat. Office: 5151 State University Dr Los Angeles CA 90032-4226

RATHER, DAN, broadcast journalist; b. Wharton, Tex., Oct. 31, 1931; m. Jean Goebel; children: Dawn Robin, Danjack. B.A. in Journalism, Sam Houston State Coll., Huntsville, Tex., 1953; student, U. Houston, South Tex. Sch. Law. Instr. journalism Sam Houston State Coll., for 1 year; later worked for U.P.I. and Houston Chronicle; with CBS; joined staff of radio Sta. KTRH (CBS affiliate), Houston; staying about 4 years as news writer, reporter, and later, as news dir.; became dir. news and pub. affairs with CBS Houston TV affiliate KHOU-TV, in the late 1950's; became White House corr., 1964; and then transferred to overseas burs., including chief of London bur., 1965-66, then worked in Vietnam, returned to White House position in fall of 1966; appearing nightly on segments of CBS Evening News; became anchorman-corr. for CBS Reports, 1974-75; co-editor 60 Minutes, CBS-TV, 1975-81; anchorman Dan Rather Reporting, CBS Radio Network, 1977—; anchorman, mng. editor CBS Evening News with Dan Rather, 1981—; co-editor show Who's Who, CBS-TV, 1977; anchor 48 Hours, 1986—; anchored numerous CBS News spl. programs. Author: (with Gary Gates) The Palace Guard, 1974, (with Mickey Herskowitz) The Camera Never Blinks, 1977, The Camera Never Blinks Twice: The Further Adventures of a Television Journalist, 1994, (with Peter Wyden) Memoirs, I Remember, 1991; editor Our Times, 1994. Recipient numerous Emmy awards; honors include dedication of Dan Rather Comm. Bldg., classroom facility Sam Houston State U., Huntsville, Tex. Office: CBS News 524 W 57th St New York NY 10019-2902

RATHER, LUCIA PORCHER JOHNSON, library administrator; b. Durham, N.C., Sept. 12, 1934; d. Cecil Slayton and Lucia Lockwood (Porcher) Johnson; m. John Carson Rather, July 11, 1964; children: Susan Wright, Bruce Carson. Student, Westhampton Coll., 1951-53; A.B. in History, U. N.C., 1955, M.S. in Library Sci., 1957; PhD in History, George Washington U., 1994. Cataloger Library of Congress, Washington, 1957-64; bibliographer Library of Congress, 1964-66, systems analyst, 1966-70; group head MARC Devel. Office, 1970-73, asst. chief, 1973-76, acting chief, 1976-77, dir. for cataloging, 1976-91; Chmn. standing com. on cataloguing Internat. Fedn. Library Assns., 1976-81; sec. Working Group on Content Designators, 1972-77; chmn. Working Group on Corp. Headings, 1978-79, Internat. ISBD Rev. Com., 1981-87. Co-author: the MARC II Format, 1968. Recipient Libr. Congress Disting. Svc. award, 1991, Disting. Alumnus award U. N.C. Sch. Libr. and Info. Sci., 1992. Mem. ALA (Margaret Mann award 1985, Melvil Dewey award 1991), Phi Beta Kappa. Democrat. Presbyterian. Home: 10308 Montgomery Ave Kensington MD 20895-3327

RATHI, MANOHAR LAL, pediatrician, neonatologist; b. Beawar, Rajasthan, India, Dec. 25, 1933; came to U.S. 1969; s. Bagtawarmal and Sitadevi (Laddha) R.; m. Kamla Jajoo, Feb. 21, 1960; children: Sanjeev A., Rajeev. M.B.B.S., Rajasthan U., 1961. Diplomate Am. Bd. Pediats., sub-bd. Neonatal Perinatal Medicine; lic. physician, N.Y., Ill., Calif. Resident house physician internal medicine Meml. Hosp., Darlington, U.K., 1963-64; resident sr. house physician pediatrics Gen. Hosp., Oldham, U.K., 1964-65; dir. perinatal medicine, attending pediatrician Christ Hosp. Perinatal Ctr., Oak Lawn, Ill., 1974—; assoc. prof. pediatrics Rush Med. Coll., Chgo., 1979—; cons. obstetrician Christ Hosp., Oak Lawn, 1976—; cons. neonatologist Little Co. of Mary Hosp., Evergreen Park, Ill., 1972—, Palos Community Hosp., Palos Heights, Ill., 1978—, Silver Cross Hosp., Joliet, Ill., 1989—; cons./lectr. in field. Contbr. articles to profl. jours.; editor: Clinical Aspects of Perinatal Medicine, 1984, Vol. I, 1985, Vol. II, 1986, Current Perinatology, 1989, Vol. II, 1990; editor with others: Perinatal Medicine Vol. I, 1978, Vol. I, 1980, Vol. II, 1982. Hummell Found. grantee, 1976-77, WyethLab grantee, 1977-78; recipient Physicians Recognition award AMA, 1971-74, 91-92, Outstanding New Citizen's award State of Ill., 1978, Asian Human Svcs. of Chgo., 1988, Nitric Oxide Study by Ohmeda, 1994-95. Fellow Am. Acad. Pediats. (perinatal sect., Ill. chpt. treas. 1994-96); mem. AMA, Chgo. Med. Soc., Ill. Med. Soc., Chgo. Pediat. Soc., Med. Soc. County of Kings Bklyn., N.Y. Acad. Scis., Am. Thoracic Soc., Soc. Critical Care Medicine. Republican. Hindu. Office: Christ Hosp & Med Ctr 4440 W 95th St Ste N232 Oak Lawn IL 60453-2600

RATHINAVELU, MADI, manufacturing executive; b. Pondicherry, India, Dec. 18, 1958; came to U.S., 1982; s. Rathinavelu Viswanathan and Subbulakshmi Rathinavelu; m. Kaliani, Mar. 24, 1990. B in Engring. with honors, U. Madras, 1982; MS in Mech. Engring., Ohio U., 1984; MBA, Gannon U., 1994. Mechanical engr. Corry (Pa.) Mfg. Co., 1984-86, engring. mgr., 1986-87; v.p., gen. mgr. Corry (Pa.) Laser Technology, Inc., 1987—. Mem. Am. Soc. for Mechanical Engrs., Soc. Automotive Engrs., Am. Soc. Metals Internat. (exec. com. 1988-90). Avocations: astronomy, gardening, travel. Office: Corry Laser Technology Inc 414 W Main St Corry PA 16407-1728

RATHJENS, GEORGE WILLIAM, political scientist, educator; b. Fairbanks, Alaska, June 28, 1925; s. George William and Jennie (Hansen) R.; m. Lucy van Buttingha Wichers, Apr. 5, 1950; children: Jacqueline, Leslie, Peter. B.S., Yale U., 1946; Ph.D., U. Calif., Berkeley, 1951. Instr. chemistry Columbia U., 1950-53; staff weapons systems evaluation group Dept. Def., 1953-58; research fellow Harvard U., 1958-59; staff spl. asst. to Pres. U.S. for sci. and tech., 1959-60; chief scientist Advanced Research Projects Agy., Dept. Def., 1961, dep. dir., 1961-62; dep. asst. dir. U.S. ACDA, 1962-64, spl. asst. to dir., 1964-65; dir. weapons systems evaluation div. Inst. Def. Analyses, 1965-68; prof. dept. polit. sci. MIT, 1968—. Fellow Am. Acad. Arts and Scis.; mem. Coun. for Livable World (bd. dirs.), Fedn. Am. Scientists (sponsor), Coun. Fgn. Rels., Inst. Strategic Studies. Office: Mass Inst Tech 77 Massachusetts Ave Cambridge MA 02139-4301

RATHKE, DALE LAWRENCE, community organizer and financial analyst; b. Rangely, Colo., Mar. 16, 1950; s. Edmann Jacob and Cornelia Ruth (Ratliff) R. BA, Yale U., 1971; MA, Princeton U., 1974, ABD, 1977. Dir. internal ops. Assn. of Cmty. Orgns. for Reform Now (ACORN), New Orleans, 1977—; CFO Citizens' Cons. Inc., New Orleans, 1979—; fin. dir. ACORN Housing Corp., New Orleans, 1984—; pres., sec.-treas. Broad St. Corp., New Orleans, 1986—, Elysian Fields Corp., New Orleans, 1986—, Greenwell Springs Corp., New Orleans, 1989—, ACORN Fund, Inc., New Orleans, 1991—, ACORN Beneficial Assn., Inc., New Orleans, 1991—. Pres., sec.-treas. Assn. for Rights of Citizens, New Orleans, 1980—, ACORN Cultural Trust, Inc., 1988—; active Overture to Cultural Season, 1987—, New Orleans Mus. Art, 1990—. Mem. Yale Club of N.Y.C., Princeton Club of N.Y.C. Avocations: 18th century French furniture, English country homes. Office: ACORN 1024 Elysian Fields Ave New Orleans LA 70117-8402

RATHKE, DIETER B., construction company executive. Pres. Philipp Holzmann U.S.A. Ltd., Charlotte, N.C., also bd. dirs.; atty.-in-fact Philipp Holzmann USA, Inc., Wilmington, Del.; chmn. bd. Regent Ptnrs., Inc., Atlanta, Hebel S.E., Atlanta; bd. dirs. Germania Am., Inc., Atlanta. Bd. dirs. various cmty. assns. Office: Philipp Holzmann USA Inc 6060 Ja Jones Dr Charlotte NC 28287-0001

RATHKE, SHEILA WELLS, advertising and public relations executive; b. Columbia, S.C., Aug. 9, 1943; d. Walter John and Betty Marie (McLaughlin) Wells; m. David Bray Rathke, Sept. 1966 (div. Apr. 1977); 1 child, Erinn Michele. BA summa cum laude, U. Pitts., 1976, postgrad., 1976-77. Loan coord. Equibank, Pitts., 1961-65; office mgr. U.S. Steel Corp., Pitts., 1966-70; various account and mgmt. positions Burson-Marsteller, Pitts., 1977-87, exec. v.p., gen. mgr., 1987-94; CEO Can. ops. Burson-Marsteller, Toronto, Montreal, Ottawa, Vancouver, 1994-96; sr. v.p., dir. corp. devel. Young and Rubicam, Inc., N.Y.C., 1996—; instr. Slippery Rock Coll., Pitts., 1984-85; adviser Exec. Report Mag., Pitts., 1986-88. Trustee U. Pitts., 1976-80; mem. alumni bd. dirs., trustee Robert Morris Coll., 1992-95; bd. dirs. Vocat. Rehab. Ctr., 1987-93, Freewheelers, 1989-92, Pitts. Hist. Soc., River City Brass Band. Named Disting. Alumnus, U. Pitts., 1992. Mem. Female Execs. Am., Am. Assn. Advt. Agys. (chair ea. region 1994-95), Pitts. Advt. Club (bd. dirs. 1988-91, pres. 1990), Alpha Sigma Lambda (charter). Avocations: skiing, reading, gardening, traveling, music. Home: 330 E 38th St New York NY 10016-2759 Office: Young and Rubicam Inc 285 Madison Ave New York NY 10017-6401

RATHMAN, WILLIAM ERNEST, lawyer, minister; b. Middletown, Ohio, Jan. 10, 1927; s. Ernest Daniel and Marguerite (Sebald) R.; m. Constance Schedler, Nov. 28, 1958; children: Marchie, William E. Jr. Grad., Phillips Exeter Acad., 1944; BA, Kenyon Coll., 1948; postgrad., Harvard U., 1950, Ohio State U. Coll. of Law, 1951, United Theol. Seminary, Dayton, Ohio, 1975. Bar: Ohio 1952; ordained to ministry Episc. Ch., 1975. Pvt. practice law Middletown, Ohio, 1952-78; sr. ptnr. Rathman, Elliott & Boyd, Middletown, 1979-84, Rathman, Combs, Schaefer, Valen & Kaup, Middletown, 1985-88, Rathman, Combs, Schaefer & Kaup, Middletown, 1989-95; of counsel Combs & Schaefer, 1995—; spl. counsel to County of Butler, 1956-64, City of Middletown, 1965-66, Ohio Atty. Gen., 1967-69; acting judge Middletown Mcpl. Ct., 1969-74. Pres. Middletown Community Found., 1972-76, Middletown Chamber Found., 1977-80, Butler County Park

Commn., 1986-90; trustee-at-large Ohio Found. of Ind. Colls., Columbus, 1972-90; trustee, mem. exec. com. Middletown United Way, 1963-90; trustee Middleton Req. Hosp. Found., 1986-90; adv. bd. Middletown campus Miami U., 1984-90. With USN, 1944-46, capt. USAF, 1959, comdr. Am. Legion, 1965. Named Exec. Yr., Middletown chpt. Nat. Secs. Assn., 1969; recipient Outstanding Community Svc. award Middletown post Am. Legion, 1975, Outstanding Svc. award Parstoral Counselling Svc., 1983, Vol. of Yr. award Middletown Area United Way, 1986. Fellow Am. Coll. Trust and Estate Counsel; mem. ABA (estate tax com. 1966-69), Ohio Bar Assn. (coun. dels. 1980-93), Butler County Bar Assn. (pres. 1980), Middletown Bar Assn. (pres. 1967), Fed. Bar Assn. (pres. Cin. chpt. 1975), Ohio State Bar Found. (trustee 1992-96, Ohio Supreme Ct. bd. of commrs. on grievances and discipline 1996—), Jefferson Lodge, Browns Run Country Club, Masons (master 1959-60), Scottish Rite Valley of Cin. (treas. 1986, 33rd degree mason 1988—, chmn. bd. 1990). Episcopalian. Home: 501 Thornhill Ln Middletown OH 45042-3750 Office: Combs and Schaefer Law Firm 1081 N University Blvd Ste B Middletown OH 45042-3363

RATHMANN, PEGGY, author, illustrator; b. St. Paul. BA in Psychology, U. Minn.; student, Am. Acad. Chgo., Atelier Lack, Mpls., Otis Parsons Sch. Design, L.A. Author: Ruby the Copycat (Most Promising New Author Cuffie award Pubs. Weekly 1991), Good Night, Gorilla (ALA Notable Children's Book 1994), Officer Buckle and Gloria (Caldecott medal 1996); illustrator: Bootsie Barker Bites, 1992. Office: Putnam Berkley Group 200 Madison Ave New York NY 10016-3903

RATHMELL, SANDRA LEE, women's health nurse; b. St. Louis, Apr. 3, 1944; d. Charles Chester and Estelle Lucille (Simon) Dunham; m. Thomas S. Rathmell, Sept. 17, 1965 (div. May 1990); children: John Thomas, Tamara Lynn. Diploma, St. Luke's Hosp., 1965. RN, Ariz., Mo., Del. Staff nurse Dover (Del.) AFB Hosp., 1966-68, Luth. Med. Ctr., St. Louis, 1975-82, Maricopa Med. Ctr., Phoenix, 1982-84, Chandler (Ariz.) Regional Hosp., 1984-96; instr. hosp. postpartum classes, St. Louis, Phoenix. Mem. St. Luke's Alumni Assn.

RATHORE, NAEEM GUL, retired United Nations official; b. Lahore, Punjab, Pakistan, Nov. 21, 1931; arrived in country, 1950; s. Jalaluddin and Zohra (Butt) R.; m. Carol Salima, Sept. 19, 1951; 1 child, Amna Elona. BS, Mich. U., 1952; MA in Polit. Sci., Columbia U., 1955, PhD in Internat. Affairs, 1965. Dir. personnel and adminstrn. UNRWA, Beirut, 1975-76; exec. sec. Internat. Civil Svc. Commn. UN, N.Y.C., 1980-81, sec. First Com., 1980-84, asst. dir. Office Under-Sec. Gen./Dept. Polit. Affairs, 1984-87, chief Div. of Palestinian Rights, 1987-89; spl. advisor, spkr. Punjab Assembly, Pakistan, 1994-95; coord. Pakistan Expatriates in UN Systems UN, N.Y.C., 1992—, adviser to the Pakistan amb., and permanent rep. of Pakistan, 1994—; corporator Emerson Hosp., Concord, Mass., 1996—; lectr. Pakistan studies NEar and Mid. E. Inst., Columbia U., N.Y., 1954-55; prof., head dept. internat. affairs U. Islamabad, 1974; active numerous coms., panels and task forces with Office of Human Resources Mgmt., UN, including chmn. N.Y. Gen. Svc. Classification Appeals and Rev. Com., 1986-92; pres. FICSA, 1971-74; chmn. UN staff com., 1971-74; active External Exam. in Polit. Affairs (France, Japan, others); counselor, Minuteman Regional Program, Serving Health Info. Needs of Elders, Mass. Exec. Office of Elder Affairs, 1996—. Author: In Defense of the International Civil Service: Statements and Submission, 1974, United Nations Secretariat: Problems and Prospects, 1974, other publs. in field; contbr. articles to profl. jours. Mem. Fedn. of Nat. Civil Svcs. (pres. 1971-74). Muslim. Avocations: reading, writing newspaper columns, horseback riding, scuba diving, swimming. Home: 1305 Elm St Concord MA 01742-2103

RATHWELL, PETER JOHN, lawyer; b. Windsor, Ont., Can., Aug. 20, 1943; came to U.S., 1947; s. Harold Wilfred and Jean Isabel (Lucas) R.; m. Ann Wickstrom Williams, Sept. 10, 1977; 1 child, James Michael. BA, U. Ariz., 1965, JD, 1968. Bar: Ariz. 1968. Assoc. Boettcher, Crowder & Schoolitz, Scottsdale, Ariz., 1972-73; ptnr. Snell & Wilmer, Phoenix, 1973—; seminar lectr. Nat. Bus. Inst. Inc., 1987-90, Ariz. Ann. Bankruptcy Symposium, 1995, 97. Mem. exec. com. Jr. Achievement Ctrl. Ariz., Phoenix, 1980-92; chmn. scholarship fund St. Mary H.S., 1982-91; mem., chmn. Phoenix Parks Bd., 1982-87; trustee Orme Sch., 1991—, chair devel. com., 1994-97; treas. Smith Scholarship Trust U. Ariz. Law Sch., 1985—. Capt. JAGC, USAF, 1969-72. Fellow State Bar Ariz. Found. (founding mem.), Maricopa County Bar Found. (founding mem.); mem. Am. Bankruptcy Inst., Ariz. Bar Assn. (chmn. discipline hearing com. 1987-93, mem. bankruptcy sect.), S.W. Bankruptcy Conf. (bd. advisors 1995—), Maricopa County Bar Assn. (seminar lectr. 1987), Comml. Law League Am., Phoenix Zoo Wildest Club in Town (founding mem. 1972). Republican. Avocations: fishing, raising cattle, riding, stamp collecting. Home: 4523 E Mountain View Rd Phoenix AZ 85028-5213 Office: Snell & Wilmer 1 Arizona Ctr Phoenix AZ 85004

RATIGAN, HUGH LEWIS, middle school and elementary school educator; b. Rochester, N.Y., Apr. 28, 1946; s. Lewis Bernard and Julia (Berle) R.; m. Norma Ruth Townsend, Aug. 7, 1971; children: Lorrie Ann, Noreen Ruth. BS, SUNY, Brockport, 1968, MS in Zoology, 1973, CAS in Adminstrn., 1977; EdD, U. Sarasota, 1986. Cert. tchr. biology N-12, adminstrn. Sci. tchr. middle sch. Hilton (N.Y.) Cen. Sch. Dist., 1968—. Editor, art illustrator Art Corner newsletter Rochester Seneca park Zoo 1 Soc., 1987-90, 92—; contbr. articles to profl. jours.; author booklets. Mem. Rochester Theatre Organ Soc. 9v.p. 1986-89, pres. 1989-96). Roman Catholic. Avocations: drawing, painting, playing piano and pipe organ, canoeing, walking. Home: 95 Brook St Hilton NY 14468-1201

RATKOWSKI, DONALD J., mechanical engineer, consultant; b. Cleve., July 29, 1938; m. Joyce Ellen Kotlarczyk, July 15, 1961; children: Rhonda, Tamyra, Cheryl, Randall. Student, Ariz. State U.; AAS, Alliance Coll., 1959, DSc (hon.), 1986. Sr. project engr. semiconductor products div. Motorola, 1960-70, 75-77; v.p. engring. Danker & Wohlk, 1970-75; founder, pres. Paragon Optical Inc., 1976-90; exec. v.p. Pilkinton Vision Care, 1987-90, cons., 1990-91; pres. DJR Resources Inc., Chandler, Ariz., 1990—; mem. adv. bd. Am. Sec. Coun., 1988-89; mem. steering com. Optometry Coll., Marcinkowski Acad. Medicine, Poland, 1989-91; founder Rigid Gas Permeable Lens Inst., 1985; speaker Nat. Contact Lens Examiners, 1984-91. Contbr. articles to profl. jours.; patentee in field. Sustaining mem. Rep. Nat. Com., 1983-90; mem. U.S. Congl. Adv. Bd., 1990. Recipient Alumnus of Yr. award Alliance Coll., 1985. Mem. Opticians Assn. Am. (assoc. mem. adv. coun. 1987-88), Contact Lens Soc. Am. (bd. dirs. 1986-88, founder scholarship program 1988, hon. chmn. steering com. edn. fund 1989-91), Contact Lens Mfrs. Assn. chmn. external communication com. 1981-90, bd. dirs. 1982-84, Trailblazer award 1987, program chmn. 1989-90, Leonardo DaVinci award 1990), Ariz. Soc. Plastic Engrs. bd. dirs. 1976-78, 83, v.p. 1980-81, pres. 1981-82), Sigma Tau Gamma (Outstanding Alumni award 1985). Home: 31 E Oakwood Hills Dr Chandler AZ 85248-6200 Office: DJR Resources Inc 574 E Alamo Dr Ste 60 Chandler AZ 85225-1225

RATLIFF, CHARLES EDWARD, JR., economics educator; b. Morven, N.C., Oct. 13, 1926; s. Charles Edward and Mary Katherine (Liles) R.; m. Mary Virginia Heilig, Dec. 8, 1945; children: Alice Ann, Katherine Virginia, John Charles. B.S., Davidson Coll., 1947; A.M., Duke U., 1951, Ph.D., 1955; postgrad., U. N.C., Harvard, Columbia. Instr. econs. and bus. Davidson Coll., 1947-48, asst. prof., 1948-49; scholar econs. Duke, 1949-51; mem. faculty Davidson (N.C.) Coll., 1951—, prof., 1960—, chmn. dept. econs., 1966-83, Charles A. Dana prof., 1967-77, William R. Kenan prof., 1977-92, prof. emeritus, 1992—; prof. econs. Forman Christian Coll., Lahore, Pakistan, 1963-66, 69-70; summer vis. prof. U. N.C. at Charlotte, 1958, 60, Appalachian State U., 1962, Punjab U., Pakistan, 1963-64, Kinnaird Coll., Pakistan, 1965, Fin. Svcs. Acad., Pakistan, 1966, NDEA Inst. in Asian History, 1968; lectr. U.S. Cultural Affairs Office, East and West Pakistan, 1969-70. Author: Interstate Apportionment of Business Income for State Income Tax Purposes, 1962, A World Development Fund, 1987, Economics at Davidson: A Sesquicentennial History, 1987; co-author textbooks and monographs; contbg. author: Dictionary of the Social Sciences, Distinguished Teachers on Effective Teaching, 1986, Those Who Teach, 1988, Britain-USA: A Survey in Key Words, 1991; mem. editorial bd. Growth and Change: A Journal of Urban and Regional Policy, 1993—; contbr. articles to profl. jours. Mem. Mayor's Com. on Affordable Housing, Davidson, 1996—, Mayor's Com. Comty. Rels., Davidson, 1973-80, chmn., 1973-78; mem. Mecklenburg County Housing and Devel. Commn., 1975-81; mem. exec. com. Mecklenburg Dem. Com., 1967-69, precinct com., 1967-69, 72-74, 79—, issues com., 1979—, nat. bd. dirs. Rural Advancement Fund Nat. Sharecroppers Fund, Inc., 1978-94, exec. com., 1981-94, treas., 1981-94; mem. Mecklenburg County Comty. and Rural Devel. Exec. Com., 1981—; bd. dirs. Bread for the World, Inc., 1983-84, Pines Retirement Comty., 1990—, Crisis Assistance Ministry, 1992-96, Davidson Coll. Devel. Corp., 1992-95, Our Towns Habitat for Humanity, 1996—, Davidson Coll. Alumni Assn., 1997—; bd. advisors Mecklenburg Ministries, 1992—. Ford Found. rsch. grantee, 1960-61, Fulbright-Hays grantee, 1973; rsch. fellow Inter-Univ. Com. Econ. Rsch. on South, 1960-61; recipient Thomas Jefferson award Davidson Coll., 1972, Gold medalist Prof. of Yr. award Coun. Advancement and Support of Edn., 1985, Tchg. Excellence and Campus Leadership award Sear Roebuck Found., 1991, Hunter-Hamilton Love of Tchr. award, 1992. Mem. AAUP, So. Econ. Assn. (exec. com. 1961-63, v.p. 1975-76, N.C. corr. So. Econ. Jour.), Am. Econ. Assn., So. Fin. Assn. (exec. com. 1966-68), Nat. Tax Assn. (chmn. interstate allocation and apportionment of bus. income com. 1972-74), Assn. Asian Studies, Fulbright Alumni Assn., Old Catawba Soc., Phi Beta Kappa, Omicron Delta Kappa (Teaching award 1991). Home: 301 Pinecrest St PO Box 597 Davidson NC 28036-0597

RATLIFF, FLOYD, biophysics educator, scientist; b. La Junta, Colo., May 1, 1919; s. Charles Frederick and Alice (Hubbard) R.; m. Orma Vernon Priddy, June 10, 1942; 1 child, Merry Alice. BA magna cum laude, Colo. Coll., 1947, DSc (hon.), 1975; MS, Brown U., 1949, PhD, 1950; NRC postdoctoral fellow, Johns Hopkins, 1950-51. Instr., then asst. prof. Harvard U., 1951-54; assoc. Rockefeller Inst., 1954-58; mem. faculty Rockefeller U., 1958-89, prof. biophysics and physiol. psychology, 1966-89, prof. emeritus, 1989—, head lab. biophysics, 1974-86; pres. Harry Frank Guggenheim Found., N.Y.C., 1983-89, bd. dirs., 1983—; rsch. assoc. Sch. Am. Rsch., Santa Fe, N.Mex., 1989—; cons. to govt., 1957-89, to John D. and Catherine T. MacArthur Found., 1986. Author: Mach Bands: Quantitative Studies on Neural Networks in the Retina, 1965, Paul Signac and Color in Neo-Impressionism, 1992, also articles; editor: Studies on Excitation and Inhibition in the Retina, 1974; editorial bd.: Jour. Gen. Physiology, 1969-86. Bd. dirs. Esperanza, Santa Fe, 1990-93, pres., 1992-93. Served to 1st lt. AUS, 1941-45, ETO. Decorated Bronze Star; recipient Howard Crosby Warren medal Soc. Exptl. Psychologists, 1966; Edgar D. Tillyer medal Optical Soc. Am., 1976; medal for disting. service Brown U., 1980; Pisart Vision award N.Y. Assn. for Blind, 1983. Fellow AAAS; mem. NAS, Am. Inst. Physics, Am. Psychol. Assn. (disting. sci. contbn. award 1984), Am. Psychol. Soc. (William James fellow 1989), Manhattan Philos. Soc., Internat. Brain Rsch. Orgh., Am. Philos. Soc., China Inst. Am., Oriental Ceramic Soc. (London), Oriental Ceramic Soc. (Hong Kong), 20th Century Chinese Ceramic Soc., Asia Soc., Japan Soc., Phi Beta Kappa, Sigma Xi. Home: 2215 Calle Cacique Santa Fe NM 87505-4944

RATLIFF, GERALD LEE, dean, speech and theater educator; b. Middletown, Ohio, Oct. 23, 1944; s. Ray and Peggy (Donisi) R. BA magna cum laude, Georgetown (Ky.) Coll., 1967; MA, U. Cin., 1970; PhD, Bowling Green (Ohio) State U., 1975. Area head English theatre Glenville State Coll., 1970-72; prof., chair theatre Montclair State Coll., Upper Montclair, N.J., 1975-92; dean Sch. Fine and Performing Arts Ind.-Purdue U., Ft. Wayne, Ind., 1993-95; dean Coll. Arts and Architecture Mont. State U., Bozeman, Mont., 1995—; feature writer Lexington (Ky.) Herald-News, 1967-68. Author: Beginning Scene Study: Aristophanes to Albee, 1980, Speech and Drama Club Activities, 1982, Oedipus Trilogy, 1984, Combating Stagefright, 1985, Playscript Interpretation and Production, 1985, (Machiavelli's) The Prince, 1986, (with Suzanne Trauth) Introduction to Musical Theatre, 1986, Playing Scenes: A Sourcebook for Performance, 1993, Playing Contemporary Scenes: A Sourcebook for Performance, 1996; contbr. articles and revs. to profl. jours. Exec. coun. mem. Assn. for Commn. Adminstrn., 1995—; bd. dirs. Am. Conf. Acad. Deans. Fulbright scholar, 1989; recipient Nat. Medallion of Honor award Theta Alpha Phi, 1989; Alumni Assn. faculty rsch. grantee, 1980, 83, 86. Mem. Speech Communication Assn. (legis. coun. 1987-88, chair theatre div. 1986-87), Am. Assn. Theatre in Secondary Edn. (nat. bd. dirs. 1986-87), Secondary Sch. Theatre Assn. (nat. bd. dirs. 1983-86), Internat. Arts Assn. (v.p. 1975-76), Eastern Communication Assn. (exec. sec. 1986-89, 1st v.p. elect 1989, exec. com. 1986—, pres. 1991, Disting. Svc. award 1993), Theta Alpha Phi (nat. pres. 1984-87, nat. coun. 1979-82, 84-87). Avocations: writing, softball. Home: 2 Morningside Dr Potsdam NY 13676

RATLIFF, LOIS L., secondary school educator; b. Anson County, N.C., May 8, 1951; d. Walter A. and Corine S. Ratliff. BS, Bennett Coll., Greensboro, N.C., 1971; MS, N.C. A&T State U., 1974. Cert. tchr., N.C., S.C. Instr. biology Paine Coll., Augusta, Ga., 1976-78, Livingston Coll., Salisbury, N.C., 1979-80; tchr. chemistry Florence (S.C.) Sch. Dist. 1, 1980-85; tchr. phys. sci. Union County Schs., Monroe, N.C., 1985-86; tchr. chemistry Myers Park High Sch., Charlotte, N.C., 1986-89; tchr. phys. sci. Darlington (S.C.) Schs., 1989-96; tchr. chemistry Union County Schs., Monroe, N.C., 1996—; advisor Jr. Acad. Sci.; mem. evaluation team Nat. Assn. State Dept. Tchr. Edn. Evaluation Com. Mem. NEA, ASCD, NSTA.

RATLIFF, LOUIS JACKSON, JR., mathematics educator; b. Cedar Rapids, Iowa, Sept. 1, 1931; s. Louis Jackson and Ruth Sara (Sidlinger) R. BA, State U. Iowa, 1953, MA, 1958, PhD, 1961. Lectr. Ind. U., Bloomington, 1961-63, U. Calif., Riverside, 1963-64; asst. prof. math. U. Calif., 1964-67, assoc. prof., 1967-69, prof., 1969—. Author: Chain Conjectures in Ring Theory, 1978; assoc. editor Procs. of AMS, 1987-92, Comm. in Algebra, 1990-95; contbr. articles to profl. jours. 1st lt. USAF, 1953-57. NSF fellow, 1960-62, grantee, 1965-69, 71-88; recipient Disting. Teaching award, U. Calif.-Riverside, 1983. Mem. Am. Math. Soc., Phi Beta Kappa. Democrat. Seventh Day Adventist. Home: 22344 San Joaquin Dr W Canyon Lake CA 92587 Office: U Calif Dept Math Riverside CA 92521

RATLIFF, ROBERT BARNS, JR., mechanical engineer; b. Narrows, Va., Oct. 24, 1950; s. Robert Barns and Rosemary (Simpson) R.; m. Marsha Meredith, Aug. 19, 1972; children: Lori Ann, Robert Barns III, Heather Michelle. BSME, Va. Tech, 1973. Registered profl. engr., N.C. Distbn. engr. Duke Power Co., Winston-Salem, N.C., 1973-76; distbn. svc. engr. Duke Power Co., Charlotte, N.C., 1976-77; supt. engring. Duke Power Co., Lenoir, N.C., 1977-79; gen. mgr. Floyd S. Pike Elec. Contractor, Inc., Mt. Airy, N.C., 1979-86, asst. v.p., 1986-90, v.p., 1990-91, exec. v.p., 1991—. Mem. exec. coun. Old Hickory Coun. of Boy Scouts, Winston-Salem, 1985; mem. C. of C., Mt. Airy, 1992; mem. adminstrv. bd. Ctrl. United Meth. Ch., Mt. Airy, 1992; bd. dirs. N.C. FREE, John Locke Found. Mem. NSPE, Profl. Engrs. N.C., Internat. Soc. Arboriculture, Internat. Platform Soc., Mt. Airy C. of C. Methodist. Office: Floyd S Pike Contractor Inc PO Box 868 Mount Airy NC 27030-3850

RATNER, BUDDY DENNIS, bioengineer, educator; b. Bklyn., Jan. 19, 1947; s. Philip and Ruth Ratner; m. Teri Ruth Stoller, July 7, 1968; 1 child, Daniel Martin. BS in Chemistry, Bklyn. Coll., 1967; PhD in Polymer Chemistry, Polytech. Inst. Bklyn., 1972. Postdoctoral fellow U. Wash., Seattle, 1972-73, from rsch. assoc. to assoc. prof., 1973-86, prof., 1986—; dir. Nat. ESCA and Surface Analysis Ctr., Seattle, 1984-96; dir. U. Washington Engineered Biomaterials NSF Engring. Rsch. Ctr., 1996—. Editor: Surface Characterization of Biomaterials, 1989, Plasmas and Polymers, 1994—, Biomaterials Science, 1996, Biomaterials Science: An Introduction to Materials in Medicine, 1996, Characterization of Polymeric Biomaterials, 1997; mem. editl. bds. 9 jours. and book series; contbr. more than 270 articles to profl. jours. Recipient faculty achievement/outstanding rsch. award Burlington Resources Found., 1990, Perkin Elmer Phys. Electronics award for excellence in surface sci.; grantee NIH. Fellow AAAS, Am. Inst. Med. Biol. Engring. (founder), Am. Vacuum Soc.; mem. AIChE, Adhesion Soc., Am. Chem. Soc., Internat. Soc. Contact Lens Rsch., Materials Rsch. Soc., Soc. for Biomaterials (pres. 1991, 92, Clemson award 1989, fellow 1994). Achievements include 10 patents in field. Office: U Wash Dept Chem Engring PO Box 351750 Seattle WA 98195

RATNER, DAVID LOUIS, legal educator; b. London, Sept. 2, 1931. AB magna cum laude, Harvard U., 1952, LLB magna cum laude, 1955. Bar: N.Y. 1955. Assoc. Sullivan & Cromwell, N.Y.C., 1955-64; assoc. prof. Cornell Law Sch., Ithaca, N.Y., 1964-68, prof., 1968-82; prof. law U. San Francisco Law Sch., 1982—, dean, 1982-89; exec. asst. to chmn. SEC, Washington, 1966-68; chief counsel Securities Industry Study, Senate Banking Com., Washington, 1971-73; vis. prof. Stanford (Calif.) U., 1974, Ariz. State U., Tempe, 1974, U. San Francisco, 1980, Georgetown U., Washington, 1989-90, U. Calif., Hastings, San Francisco, 1992; mem. Larkspur (Calif.) Planning Commn., 1992—. Fulbright scholar Monash U., Australia, 1981. Author: Securities Regulation; Cases and Materials, 5th edit., 1996, Securities Regulation in a Nutshell, 5th edit., 1996, Institutional Investors: Teaching Materials, 1978. Fellow Royal Soc. Arts (London); mem. Am. Law Inst., Cosmos Club (Washington), Phi Beta Kappa. Home: 84 Polhemus Way Larkspur CA 94939-1928 Office: U San Francisco Law Sch 2130 Fulton St San Francisco CA 94117-1080

RATNER, ELLEN FAITH, radio talk show host, writer; b. Cleve., Aug. 28, 1951; d. Harry Ramer and Anne Spott. BA, Goddard Coll., 1974; EdM, Harvard U., 1978. Coord. women's svcs. Homophile Comty. Health Svc., Boston, 1971-73; co-dir., co-founder Boundaries Therapy Ctr., Acton, Mass., 1973-86; dir. psychiat. day treatment program South Shore Mental Health Ctr., Quincy, Mass., 1974-81; v.p. rsch., devel. and svc., dir. ARC Rsch. Found. Addiction Recovery Corp., Rockville, Mass., 1986-90; health care cons., dir. Found. for Addiction Rsch., 1990-94; pres. Talk Radio News Svc., White House corr. Good Day USA "The Washington Reality Check", Washington, 1991—; pres. Talk Radio News Svc. White House corr. Good Day USA "Washington Day", 1995; tchr. Curry Coll., Milton, Mass., 1979-80; cons. program devel. Addiction Recovery Corp., 1984-86; developer, planner The Art's in Mileau Treatment of Phychiatric Outpatients, Quincy, 1980, New Eng.'s first conf. on Chem. Dependency and AIDS, 1988. Author: The Other Side of the Family: A Book for Recovery from Abuse, Incest and Neglect, 1990; appeared on nat. TV and radio shows including C-SPAN, The Oprah Winfrey Show, CNN, Nat. Empowerment TV, others; mem. adv. bd. The Counselor Mag., 1987-90. Bd. trustees, mem. exec. com., vis. com. presdl. search com. Goddard Col., Plainfield, Vt. 1977-81; bd. trustees Samaritan Coll., L.A., 1988-90; bd. dirs. Nat. Lesbian and Gay Health Found., Washington, 1985-92, pres., exec. com., program com., program chair; v.p. Harry Ratner Human Svcs. Fund, Cleve., 1991—; mem. adv. bd. Women of Washington, Inc., 1992—; bd. dirs. Theater Chamber Players, Kennedy Ctr., Washington, 1988-91, An Uncommon Legacy Found., N.Y.C., 1993—, The Ctr. for Spiritual Enlightment, Falls Church, Va., 1994—. Recipient Comty. Svc. award Lesbian and Gay Counseling Svc., Boston, 1985, The Addams-Brown award Nat. Lesbian and Gay Health Found., 1993. Mem. Nat. Assn. Radio Talk Show Hosts, Mass. Assn. Day treatment Adminstrs. (chair regulations and standards com. 1979-81), Lily Dale Assembly. Democrat. Jewish. Avocation: writing works on spiritualism. Office: Talk Radio News Svc 2514 Mill Rd NW Washington DC 20007-2950*

RATNER, GERALD, lawyer; b. Chgo., Dec. 17, 1913; s. Peter I. and Sarah (Soreson) R.; m. Eunice Payton, June 18, 1948. PhB, U. Chgo., 1935, JD cum laude, 1937. Bar: Ill. 1937. Since practiced in Chgo.; sr. ptnr. Gould & Ratner and predecessor firm, 1949—; officer Henry Crown & Co., CC Industries, Inc., Material Svc. Corp., Freeman United Coal Mining Co., Mineral and Land Resources Corp.; lectr., writer on real estate law. Capt. AUS, 1942-46. Mem. ABA, Ill. Bar Assn., Chgo. Bar Assn., Order of Coif, U. Chgo. Pres. Coun. and Endowment Assn., Phi Beta Kappa. Home: 180 E Pearson St Apt 6205 Chicago IL 60611-1525 Office: 222 N La Salle St Chicago IL 60601-1002

RATNER, HAROLD, pediatrician, educator; b. Bklyn., June 19, 1927; s. George and Bertha (Silverman) R.; BS, Coll. City N.Y., 1948; MD, Chgo. Med. Sch., 1952; m. Lillian Gross, Feb. 4, 1961; children—Sanford Miles, Marcia Ellen. Intern, Jewish Hosp., Med. Center Bklyn., 1952-53, resident in pediatrics, 1953-55; practice medicine specializing in pediatrics, Bklyn.; clin. instr. pediatrics SUNY Downstate Med. Center, N.Y.C., 1955-67, clin. asst. prof., 1967-69, clin. assoc. prof., 1969-87; lectr. pediatrics, 1987—; chief of pediatrics Greenpoint Hosp., Bklyn., 1967-80, pres. med. staff, 1970-71, 74-80; dir. ambulatory services Woodhull Med. and Mental Health Center, Bklyn., 1980-83; clin. assoc. prof. pediatrics SUNY-Bklyn., 1983-87, lectr., 1987—; clin. assoc. prof. pediatrics, N.Y.U., 1987-90, 97—, clin. assoc. prof. psychiatry, 1997—; med. specialist Nathan Kline Inst. for Psychiat. Research, Orangeburg, N.Y., Rockland Psychiat. Ctr., Orangeburg, N.Y., 1986-88, unit chief med. services, 1988-90; assoc. clin. dir. and dir. medicine Manhattan Psychiat. Ctr., N.Y.C., 1990—; mem. adv. council to pres. N.Y.C. Health and Hosp. Corp., 1970-71, 74-80, 81-83, sec., 1975, v.p., 1976-80; mem. med. bd., dir. Camp Sussex, camp for underprivileged children; bd. dirs. Kings County Health Care Rev. Orgn., Bklyn., 1976-84, past co-chmn. hosp. rev. com., continuing med. edn., med. care evaluation com. Trustee Village of Saddle Rock (N.Y.), 1980—. Served with AUS, 1945-47. Diplomate Nat. Bd. Med. Examiners, Am. Bd. Pediatrics. Fellow Am. Pediatric Soc., Am. Soc. Clin. Hypnosis, Bklyn. Pediatric Soc., Kings County Med. Soc., Royal Soc. Health; mem. AMA, Soc. Clin. and Exptl. Hypnosis, Am. Pub. Health Assn., Am. Soc. Clin. Hypnosis, N.Y. State Soc. Clin. Hypnosis, Kings County Med. Soc., Pan-Am. Med. Socs. Democrat. Jewish. Contbr. articles to med. jours. Home: 55 Blue Bird Dr Great Neck NY 11023-1001

RATNER, JAMES HENRY, dermatologist; b. El Paso, Tex., Mar. 31, 1945; s. Alfred A. and Adalaide M. (Moye) R.; m. Janice Dimenstein, June 30, 1968; children: Derek J., Andrea E. BS, Yale U., 1967; MD, Baylor U., 1971. Diplomate Am. Bd. Dermatology, Am. Bd. Pathology in Dermatopathology. Intern in internal medicine St. Luke's Epsicopal Hosp., Houston, Tex., 1971-72; resident in dermatology Dartmouth Med. Sch. Affiliated Hosps., Hamover, N.H., 1972-75; chief of dermatology U.S. Army Hosp., Ft. Polk, La., 1976-77; pvt. practice in dermatology Amherst, Mass., 1977—. Bd. dirs. Amherst (Mass.) Youth Hockey Assn., 1985-91, Greater Springfield (Mass.) Jr. Amateur Hockey Assn., 1989-91. Major, U.S. Army, 1976-77. Fellow Am. Acad. Dermatology, Mass. Acad. Dermatology (bd. dirs. 1989-93); mem. New Eng. Dermatol. Assn., Internat. Soc. Dermatology, Mass. Med. Soc. (alt. exec. councilor 1983-84), So. Med. Assn. Office: 196 N Pleasant St Amherst MA 01002-1721

RATNER, MARK ALAN, chemistry educator; b. Cleve., Dec. 8, 1942; s. Max and Betty (Wohlvert) R.; m. Nancy Ball, June 19, 1969; children—Stacy, Daniel. A.B., Harvard U., 1964; Ph.D., Northwestern U., 1969; Amanuensis (hon.), Aarhus U., Denmark, 1970; Akad Rat (hon.), Tech. U., Munich, W. Ger., 1971. Asst. prof. NYU, 1971-75; prof. chemistry Northwestern U., Evanston, Ill., 1975—, Dow rsch. prof., 1988-90; cons. U.S. Army, Huntsville, Ala., 1973-75; lectr. IBM, Yorktown Heights, N.Y., 1973; dir. Electrochem. Industries, Israel, 1980—; assoc. dean arts and scis. Northwestern U., Evanston, 1980-84; vis. prof. Rush Presbyn. Sch. Medicine, 1990—. Contbr. numerous articles and manuscripts to profl. jours. Bd. dirs. Hillel Found., Evanston, 1984—; bd. govs. Tel-Aviv U., 1996—, Hebrew U. Jerusalem, 1996—. Fellow A.P. Sloan Found., 1973-76, Inst. Advanced Study, Israel, 1979. Fellow AAAS, Am. Phys. Soc.; mem. Am. Chem. Soc., Rumplestiltskin Soc., Sigma Xi. Jewish. Avocations: scientific education; canoeing; conservation. Home: 615 Greenleaf Ave Glencoe IL 60022-1745 Office: Northwestern U Chemistry Dept 2145 Sheridan Rd Evanston IL 60208-0834

RATNER, STEVEN A., television broadcast executive; b. Irvington, N.J., Oct. 6, 1954; s. Irwin and Carol (Tallin) R.; m. Amy Grantonic; children: Ben, Sam. BA, Boston U., 1976. From videographer, editor, promotion mgr. to dir. creative svcs. WLVI-TV, Boston, 1977—. Recipient Emmy award for lighting, 1987, Emmy award for promotion, 1989, Emmy award for set design, 1990, Emmy award for promo, 1991, 93, Telly award for Promo, 1994, others. Mem. New England Advt. Club, New England Broadcasters Assn. Office: WLVI-TV 75 Morrissey Blvd Boston MA 02125-3316

RATNOFF, OSCAR DAVIS, physician, educator; b. N.Y.C., Aug. 23, 1916; s. Hyman L. and Ethel (Davis) R.; m. Marian Foreman, Mar. 31, 1945; children: William Davis, Martha. AB, Columbia U., 1936, MD, 1939; LLD (hon.), U. Aberdeen, 1981; ScD (hon.), Case Western Res. U., 1996. Intern Johns Hopkins Hosp., Balt., 1939-40; Austin fellow in physiology Harvard Med. Sch., Boston, 1940-41; asst. resident Montefiore Hosp., N.Y.C., 1942; resident Goldwater Meml. Hosp., N.Y.C., 1942-43; asst. in medicine Columbia Coll. Physicians and Surgeons, N.Y.C., 1942-46; fellow in medicine Johns Hopkins, 1946-48, instr. medicine, 1948-50, instr. bacteriology, 1949-50; asst. prof. medicine Western Res. U., Cleve., 1950-56; assoc. prof. Case Western Res. U., 1956-61, prof., 1961—; asst. physician Univ. Hosp., Cleve., 1952-56; assoc. physician Univ. Hosp., 1956-67, physician, 1967—. Author: Bleeding Syndromes, 1960; mem. editorial bd. Jour. Lab. Clin. Medicine, 1956-62, assoc. editor, 1986-91, bd. rev. editors 1991-95, editl. adv. bd. 1995—; editor: Treatment of Hemorrhagic Disorders, 1968, (with C. D. Forbes) Disorders of Hemostasis, 1984, 3d edit., 1996; mem. editorial bd. Circulation, 1961-65, Blood, 1963-69, 78-81, Am. Jour. Physiology, 1966-72, Jour. Applied Physiology, 1966-72, Jour. Lipid Rsch., 1967-69, Jour. Clin. Investigation, 1969-71, Circulation Rsch., 1970-75, Annals Internal Medicine, 1973-76, Perspectives in Biology and Medicine, 1974—, Thrombosis Rsch., 1981-84, Jour. Urology, 1981-88, Internat. Jour. Hematology, 1991—; contbr. articles to med. jours. Career investigator Am. Heart Assn., 1960-86. Served to maj. M.C., 1943-46, Ind. Recipient Henry Moses award Montefiore Hosp., 1949, Disting. Achievement award Modern Medicine, 1967, James F. Mitchell award, 1971, Murray Thelin award Nat. Hemophilia Found., 1971, H.P. Smith award Am. Soc. Clin. Pathology, 1975, Joseph Mather Smith prize Columbia Coll. Physicians and Surgeons, 1976, Disting. Achievemtn in Med. Sci. award U. Hosps. of Cleve, 1992, Saltzman award Mt. Sinai Hosp. of Cleve., 1994; named to Heart Hall of Fame, N.E. Ohio Heart Assn., 1989. Master ACP (John Phillips award 1974); fellow AAAS; mem. NAS (Kovalenko award 1985), AMA, Am. Fedn. Clin. Rsch., Soc. Scholars Johns Hopkins U., Am. Soc. Clin. Investigation, Ctrl. Soc. Clin. Rsch. (Disting. Svc. award 1992), Assn. Am. Physicians (Kober lectr. 1985, Kober medal 1988), Am. Soc. Hematology (Dameshek award 1972), Internat. Soc. Hematology, Internat. Soc. Thrombosis (Grant award 1981, spl. award 1993), Am. Physiol. Soc., Am. Soc. Biol. Chemists. Home: 2916 Sedgewick Rd Cleveland OH 44120-1840 Office: Univ Hosps of Cleve Dept Medicine Cleveland OH 44106

RATNY, RUTH LUCILLE, publishing company executive, writer; b. Chgo., Dec. 8, 1937; d. Herman Joseph and Bertha (Levy) R. Student, De Paul U., 1950-54. Creative v.p. Niles Communications Ctrs., Chgo., 1954-64; prin. Ruth L. Ratny Mktg. Communications, Chgo., 1964-69; owner Screen mag., Chgo., 1979—; bd. dirs. Ind. Feature Project/Midwest. Bd. dirs. Chgo. Internat. Film Festival. Named Advt. Women of Yr., 1979, Midwest Advt. Person of Yr., 1979; recipient Recognition award Chgo. Coalition, 1983, Clio awards, 1960-61, Women in Film's Recognition award, 1993. Mem. Women in Film, Women's Advt. Club, Pearl S. Buck Found. Mem. Christian Sci. Ch.

RATTAZZI, SERENA, art museum and association administrator; b. Taranto, Italy, Aug. 20, 1935; came to U.S., 1969; d. Umberto and Ligetta (Maresca) Bardelli; m. Mario Cristiano Rattazzi, Jan. 15, 1962; 1 child, Claudia. BA, Liceo Umberto I, Naples. Italy, 1953; MSW, U. Naples, 1958; postgrad. in legal problems of mus. adminstrn., Am. Legal Inst., ABA, 1985, 86, 87, 89. Pub. rels., publs. asst. Albright-Knox Art Gallery, Buffalo, 1974-76, coord. pub. rels., 1976-82, asst. dir. for adminstrn., 1982-84; asst. dir. for adminstrn. The Bklyn. Mus., 1984-85, vice dir. for adminstrn., 1985-89, assoc. dir., 1989-90; dir. Am. Fedn. Arts, N.Y.C., 1990—; adv. bd. The Pitts. Ctr. for Arts, 1989-92, A.I.R. Gallery, N.Y.C., 1990-93; field reviewer Inst. Mus. Svcs., Washington, 1990; adv. coun. dept. art history and archaeology Columbia Univ., 1992—. Mem. ArtTable Inc. (bd. dirs. 1986-88, pres. 1986-88), Am. Assn. Museums (standing profl. com. on pub. rels. mgmt. 1978-82, bd. 1990—). Avocation: reading. Office: Am Fedn Arts 41 E 65th St New York NY 10021-6508

RATTHAHAO, SISOUPHANH, minister. Dir. Lao Ministry Dist. of the Christian and Missionary Alliance. Office: 226 Longford Ct Elgin IL 60120-4652*

RATTI, RONALD ANDREW, economics educator; b. Neath, West Glamorgan, Wales, Oct. 10, 1948; came to U.S., 1970; s. Ronald Rudolph and Janet (Marshall) R. BA, U. Lancaster, 1970; MA, Case Western Res. U., 1972; PhD, So. Meth. U., 1975. Asst. prof. to assoc. prof. U. Mo., Columbia, 1975-85, prof. econs., 1985—, chmn. dept., 1982-89; vis. scholar Fed. Res. Bank Kansas City, Mo., 1978, Fed. Res. Bank St. Louis., 1984-85; acad. visitor London Sch. Econs., 1985; vis. Fulbright prof. Korea U., Seoul, 1996. Contbr. articles to profl. jours. Office: U Mo Dept Econs 118 Profl Bldg Columbia MO 65211

RATTLE, SIMON, conductor; b. Liverpool, Eng., 1955. Studied conducting and piano, Royal Acad. Music; PhD (hon.), Birmingham U., 1985. At age 15 occasional percussion player Royal Liverpool Philharm. Orch.; prin. condr., artistic adviser City of Birmingham Symphony Orch., 1980-91, mus. dir., 1990—; prin. guest condr. L.A. Philharm. Orch., 1981-93, Orch. of the Age of Enlightenment, 1992—, Rotterdam Philharm. Orch., 1981-84; prin. condr. London Choral Soc., 1979-84; assoc. condr. Royal Liverpool Philharm. Orch., 1977-80, BBC Scottish Symphony Orch., 1977-80; artistic dir. South Bank Summer Music, 1981-83; asst. condr. Bournemouth Symphony Orch. and Bournemouth Sinfonietta, 1974-76; debut at Glyndebourne Festival Opera, 1977, appeared regularly since; debuts at Boston Symphony Orch., 1983, English Nat. Opera, 1985, Berlin Philharmonic, 1987, Los Angeles Opera, 1988, Royal Opera House, 1990, Vienna Philharmonic, 1993, Philadelphia Orchestra, 1993. Decorated comdr. Brit. Empire, knight Brit. Empire; Officier des Arts et des Lettres (France); recipient 1st prize John Player Internat. Condrs. Competition, 1974, Edison award, 1987, Gramophone Record of Yr., 1988, Gramophone Opera award, 1989, Internat. Record Critics award, 1990, Grand Prix in Honorem de l'Academie Charles Cros, 1990, Artist of Yr. Gramophone award, 1993, 95, Montblanc de la Culture prize, Paris, 1993, Officier des arts et Lettres, 1995, Shakespeare prize Toepfer Found. of Hamburg, 1996. Office: care Harold Holt Ltd, 31 Sinclair Rd, London W14 ONS, England also: Frank Salomon Assoc 201 W 54th St Apt 4C New York NY 10019-5521

RATTLEY, JESSIE MENIFIELD, former mayor, educator; b. Birmingham, Ala., May 4, 1929; d. Alonzo and Altona (Cochran) Menifield; m. Robert L. Rattley; children: Florence, Robin. BS in Bus. Edn.with hons., Hampton U., 1951; postgrad., Hampton Inst., 1962, IBM Data Processing Sch., 1960, LaSalle Extension U., 1955. Tchr. Huntington High Sch., Newport News, Va., 1951-52; owner, operator Peninsula Bus. Coll., Newport News, 1952-85; hosp. adminstr. Newport News Gen. Hosp., from 1986; fellow Inst. Politics John F. Kennedy Sch. Govt. Harvard U., 1990; sr. lectr. polit. sci. Hampton U.; elected mayor of Newport News, 1986-90. Mem. Nat. League Cities, bd. dirs., 1975, 2d v.p., 1977, 1st v.p., 1978, pres., 1979-90, active various coms. and task forces; active on adv. bds. and coms. State Dem. Party; mem. exec. com. Va. Black Elected Ofcls. Orgn., Va. Mcpl. League, 1974, 2d v.p., 1976, 1st v.p., 1977, pres., 1979; chair state adv. com. U.S. Civil Rights Commn.; apptd. trustee Va. Vet. Care Facility. Recipient Cert. of Merit Daus. of Isis, 2d annual Martin Luther King, Jr. Meml. award Old Dominion U., Sojourner Truth award Nat. Assn. of Negro Bus. and Profl. Women's Clubs, Cert. of Appreciation NAACP, Hampton Inst. Presdl. award for Outstanding Citizenship.

RATTMAN, WILLIAM JOHN, electronic and electro-optic engineer, consultant; b. Springfield, Mass., Nov. 16, 1933; s. Frank William and Sylvia Mary (Berry) R.; BSEE, U. Mass., 1955; MSEE, Northeastern U., 1961; m. Jayne Winona Crockett, Aug. 19, 1954; children—Joy Diane, Beth Jayne, Amy Cathryn. Sr. engr. Raytheon Co., Bedford, Mass., 1955-63, prin. engr., 1967-72; engrng. specialist Sylvania Applied Rsch. Lab., Waltham, Mass., 1963-67; mgr. R&D Electro Signal Lab., Inc., Rockland, Mass., 1972-86; cons. electronics, electro-optics to mfg. firms. Co-chmn. Town of Needham United Way Campaign, 1973. Recipient Author's award Raytheon Co., 1970, Inventor's award, 1971. Mem. Soc. Photo-Optical Instrumentation Engrs., S. Yarmouth Hist. Soc. (pres. 1974-75). Patentee optical depth finder, contrast detector, low drive power wideband optical modulator, laser ablative printing system, photoelectric smoke detector, self diagnostic smoke detector. Home and Office: 8047 Bright Ct Orlando FL 32836

RATTNER, JEROME BERNARD, biologist, anatomist, educator; b. Cin., Aug. 12, 1945; m. Eileen; children: John P., Nathalie. BS, Miami U., 1967; MS, U. Tex., 1969; PhD in Biology, Washington U., 1973. Fellow cell biology U. Calif., Irvine, 1973-75, rsch. asst., 1976-81; NATO fellow in biology Nat. Ctr. Sci. Rsch., France, 1975-76; asst. prof. anatomy, molecular biology U. Calgary, Can., 1981-85, assoc. prof. anatomy dept. med. biochemistry, 1985-90, prof. dept. anatomy, med. biochemistry and oncology, 1990—. Office: U CalgaryDept Med Biochemistry, 3330 Hospital Dr NW, Calgary, AB Canada T2N 4N1

RATTNER, STEVEN LAWRENCE, investment banker; b. N.Y.C., July 5, 1952; s. George Seymour and Selma Ann (Silberman) R.; m. P. Maureen White, June 22, 1986; children: Rebecca White, Daniel Irvin, David William, James Brennan. AB in Econ. honors, Brown U., 1974. Asst. to James Reston, corr. N.Y. Times, Washington, N.Y.C., London, 1974-82; assoc., v.p. Lehman Bros. Kuhn Loeb, N.Y.C., 1982-84; assoc., v.p., prin., mng. dir., head communications group Morgan Stanley & Co., N.Y.C., 1984-89; mng. dir., head comms. group Lazard Fréres & Co., LLC, N.Y.C., 1989—; dir. Falcon Cable Holding Group, 1993—. Contbr. articles to various publs. including N.Y. Times, Wall St. Jour., L.A. Times, Newsweek. Trustee Brown U., 1987-93, 94—, Met. Mus. Art, 1996—; trustee Ednl. Broadcasting Corp., 1990—, vice chmn., 1994—; dir. N.Y.C. Outward Bound Ctr., 1990—. Harvey Baker fellow Brown U. 1974, Poynter fellow Yale, 1979. Mem. Coun. Fgn. Rels., Royal Inst. for Internat. Affairs (assoc.). Home: 998 5th Ave New York NY 10028-0126

RATTNER, WILLIAM EDWARD, lawyer; b. Chgo., Sept. 26, 1936; s. Herbert and Ethel (Weiss) R.; m. Gale Golovan, Nov. 27, 1963; 1 child, David Herbert. BS in Econ., U. Pa., 1958; JD, Harvard U., 1961. Bar: Ill. 1962, U.S. Dist. Ct (no. dist.) Ill. 1962, U.S. Ct. Appeals (7th cir.) 1963, U.S. Tax Ct. 1969, U.S. Dist. Ct. (no. dist.) Tex. 1989. Atty. Peterson, Lowry, Rall, Barber & Ross, Chgo., 1962-67, Schwartz & Freeman, Chgo., 1967-72; ptnr. Levy & Erens, Chgo., 1972-86, Hopkins & Sutter, Chgo., 1986—; adj. prof. Northwestern U. Law Sch.; instr. Nat. Inst. for Trial Advocacy. Vice chmn., pres. Chgo. chpt., nat. bd. govs. Am. Jewish Com.; chmn. City of Evanston (Ill.) Bd. Ethics; trustee Evanston Art Ctr. With U.S. Army, 1961-67. Mem. ABA, Chgo. Bar Assn. (vice chmn. urban affairs com. 1970-72), 7th Cir. Bar Assn., Chgo. Coun. Lawyers, Mid-Day Club. Home: 1046 Michigan Ave Evanston IL 60202-1436 Office: Hopkins & Sutter 3 First National Plz Chicago IL 60602

RATZAN, KENNETH ROY, physician; b. Bklyn., May 8, 1940; s. Albert Jerome and Eve Ratzan; m. R. Judith (div.); children: Stuart, Peter, Jacob; m. Martha L. Hyde, Feb. 14, 1989; 1 child, Leah. AB, Amherst Coll., 1961; MD, Harvard Med. Sch., 1965. Chief hepatitis surveill Ctr. Disease Control, Atlanta, 1968-69; chief divsn. infectious diseases Va. Hosp., Miami, 1972-74; chief divsn. infectious diseases Mount Sinai Med. Ctr., Miami Beach, 1975—, vice chmn. medicine, 1977-96, program dir. internal medicine, 1981-96, chmn. dept. medicine, 1996—. Office: Mount Sinai Med Ctr 4300 Alton Rd Miami Beach FL 33140-2800

RATZER, MARY BOYD, secondary education educator, librarian; b. Troy, N.Y., Sept. 6, 1945; d. John Leo and Katherine M. (Van Derpool) Boyd; m. Philip J. Ratzer, July 30, 1972; children: Joseph, David. BA cum laude, Coll. of St. Rose, Albany, N.Y., 1967; MA, SUNY, Albany, 1968, MLS, 1981. Cert. secondary tchr., sch. libr. media specialist, N.Y. Secondary tchr. English, Shenendehowa Cen. Sch., Clifton Park, N.Y., 1968-85; sch. libr. media specialist Shendehowa Cen. Sch., Clifton Park, N.Y., 1985—; coord., mentor tchr. intern program; lectr. SUNY Grad. Sch. Info. Sci. and Policy, Albany; frequent speaker at state-level confs., 1986—. Contbr.: N.Y. State Teacher Resource Guides for Learning Standards; contbr. articles to profl. jours. Recipient grants. Mem. ALA, N.Y. Libr. Assn., Nat. Coun. Tchrs. English, N.Y. Assn. for Supervision and Curriculum Devel., BIRT, LUERT (past pres.). Home: 433 County Route 68 Saratoga Springs NY 12866-6636

RATZLAFF, JUDITH L., secondary school educator; b. Oakland, Calif., May 2, 1937; d. Jack J. Bayard and Billie (Hart) Mills; m. Rulan R. Ratzlaff, Aug. 3, 1957 (dec. May 1991); children: Guy A., Scott A., Elizabeth A. Ratzlaff Perkins. Student, Southwestern Jr. Coll., San Diego, 1964-65, U. Md., Rota, Spain, 1968-70; BA in History, Spanish, U. Jacksonville, 1971-74. Cert. secondary tchr. history, Spanish, social studies, state trainer ethics, Fla. Tchr. social studies Clay County Sch. Bd., Orange Park, Fla., 1974—; dept. head Clay County Sch. Bd., 1974-77, grade level chairperson, 1977-80, sch. improvement com. 1993-94, 96-98; mem. Edn. Practice Commn., State of Fla., 1985-93, chairperson, 1991-93; participant First China-Am. Edn. Conf., 1992; co-originator Ethics Workshops for New Tchrs.; ethics trainer State of Fla., 1993. Regional dir. Tchrs. Adv. Com., Rep. party State of Fla., 1985—; sec. Clay County Rep. Exec. Com., 1986-93; candidate Fla. State Senate, 1986; sponsor Students Against Drunk Driving, 1982-85; active Rep. Exec. Com.; mem. Sch. Accountability Coun., 1997—. Taft fellow Taft Inst. Polit. Studies Cath. U. Am., 1978, 80, 93. Mem. NEA (del. convs. Miami 1991, Washington 1992, San Francisco 1993, Mpls. 1995, chairperson legis. com. on Fla. tchg. profession 1985-86, bd. dirs. 1996-98), Nat. Coun. Edn. Stds. and Practices Commns. (charter), Clay County Edn. Assn. (pres. 1981-83), N.E. Fla. Univserve Coun. (vice chair 1990, sec. 1991, chairperson 1993-94, 94-95). Baptist. Avocations: scuba diving, swimming, running, knitting. Home: 3211 Doctors Lake Dr Orange Park FL 32073-6927 Office: Orange Park High Sch 2300 Kingsley Ave Orange Park FL 32073-5125

RATZLAFF, RUBEN MENNO, religion educator, minister; b. Burrton, Kans., Jan. 8, 1917; s. Henry and Julia (Foth) R.; m. Frances Irene King, Sept. 7, 1941; children: Keith Lowell, Paul Dennis, Mark Henry, Loren Lee; m. Doris Carr Arneson, Aug. 1, 1992. BA, Johnson Bible Coll., 1940; BD, Butler U., 1955, MA, 1959. Ordained to ministry Chs. of Christ, 1938. Min. Pleasant Hill Christian Ch., Hall, Ind., 1948-50; min. Christian Ch., Clermont, Ind., 1950-55, Kennard, Ind., 1955-59; prof. San Jose (Calif.) Christian Coll., 1959—; ann. vis. lectr. Springdale Coll., Selly Oak Colls., Birmingham, Eng., 1985—; vis. lectr. Zimbabwe Christian Coll., Harare, 1995. Author: Ezra Nehemiah, 1982; contbr. articles to profl. jours. Recipient Hebrew award Hebrew Synagogue, 1950. Mem. Theta Phi. Home: 1567 Willowdale Dr San Jose CA 95118-1346 Also: 72 Wellman Croft, Selly Oak, Birmingham B29 6NS, England Office: San Jose Christian Coll 790 S 12th St San Jose CA 95112-2304 *What amazes me most is that God the Almighty sends His Son to knock at our door, and wait with His hat in His hand while we decide whether to follow Him.*

RATZLAFF, VERNON PAUL, elementary education educator, consultant; b. Mt. Lake, Minn., May 16, 1925; s. Peter Benjamin and Helen (Dick) R.; m. Bonnie Lou Sommers, Dec. 17, 1955; children: Paul, Gwen, Jay, Peter. BA in Elem. Edn., German, Goshen Coll., 1954; MA, U. N.D., 1971; student, U. Minn., 1956-57, U. Oreg., 1965, U. No. Ariz., 1968. Cert. tchr. Elem. tchr. Richfield (Minn.) Pub. Schs., 1954-74; tchr. Tuba City (Ariz.) Pub. Sch., 1975—; resource person to tchrs., Grand Forks, N.C., 1970-72, resource person to upper elem. tchrs. and children, Richfield, 1967-70; adminstr. of Christian Sch. Hopi Mission, Oraibi, Ariz., 1971-75; math tchr. Nortland Pioneer Coll.; established "Look Folks-No Fail" classrooms. Author: Side by Side " Up from the Pit to Become a Shining Star" (Where Students Take Responsibility for Learning), 1990; contbr. articles to numerous jours. Mem. NEA, Ariz. Edn. Assn., Am. Assn. Retired People. Republican. Avocations: cooking, painting, writing, gardening, preaching. Home: 5743 Smoke Rise Dr Flagstaff AZ 86004-2746 *Personal philosophy: Tell me, I forget, Show me, I remember, Involve me, I understand.*

RAU, DAVID EDWARD, real estate company executive; b. Lincoln, Nebr., Sept. 27, 1956; s. Leo George and Anne Marie (Pavel) R.; m. Kathy Georgette Wilcox, May 17, 1980; children: Andrew David, Peter Nicholas, Victoria Anne. BBA, U. Ariz., 1978. CPA, Ariz., N.Mex. Sr. Peat Marwick Main, Albuquerque, 1978-82; supervising sr. Peat Marwick Main, Phoenix, 1982-83; asst. treas. Kroy Inc., Scottsdale, Ariz., 1983-85; acct. Zolondek & Blumenthal, Phoenix, 1985; v.p., controller Del Webb Corp., Phoenix, 1985—; bd. dirs. Ariz. Tax Rsch. Assn. Chmn. Phoenix chpt. walk Juvenile Diabetes Found., 1990, pres. 1992, 93, 94; mem. Ariz. Town Hall; advisor Phoenix Sky Harbour Ctr. Tech. Adv. Panel, 1987; treas. Drugs Don's Work in Ariz., 1994—. Mem. Ariz. Soc. CPAs, Albuquerque Jaycees (treas. 1981-82), Nat. Assn. Real Estate Cos. (tax com.), Ariz. C. of C. (bd. dirs.), Beta Alpha Psi. Republican. Roman Catholic. Avocations: skiing, fishing, family. Office: Del E Webb Corp 2231 E Camelback Rd Phoenix AZ 85016-3453

RAU, LEE ARTHUR, lawyer; b. Mpls., July 22, 1940; s. Arthur W. and Selma A. (Lund) R.; m. Janice R. Childress, June 27, 1964; children—Brendan D., Patrick C., Brian T. BSB, U. Minn., 1962; JD, UCLA, 1965. Bar: Calif. 1966, D.C. 1972, Va. 1986, U.S. Dist. Ct. D.C. 1973, U.S. Dist. Ct. (ea. dist.) Va. 1988, U.S. Ct. Mil. Appeals 1966, U.S. Ct. Appeals (D.C. cir.) 1972, U.S. Ct. Appeals (3d cir.) 1975, U.S. Ct. Appeals (6th cir.) 1980, U.S. Ct. Appeals (4th cir.) 1988, U.S. Supreme Ct. 1971. Trial atty. evaluation sect. antitrust div. U.S. Dept. Justice, Washington, 1965-66, appellate sect., 1970-72; assoc. Reed Smith Shaw & McClay, Washington, 1972-74, ptnr., 1975—; former mem. contl. and adminstrv. law adv. com. Nat. Chamber Litigation Ctr. Inc.; sec., bd. dirs. Old Dominion Land Co., Inc. Contbr. articles to profl. jours. Sec. bd. dris. Reston Found., 1982-93; bd. dirs. Reston Interfaith Inc., 1973-89, pres, 1984-88; bd. dirs. Greater Reston Arts Ctr., 1988-96, pres., 1989-91, sec., 1991-95; mem. Washington Dulles Task Force, 1982-91; mem. exec. com. and ops. com. Fairfax-Falls Ch. United Way, mem. regional coun., 1988-92. Capt. JAGC, U.S. Army, 1966-70. Named Restonian of Yr., 1990; decorated Commendation with oak leaf cluster; recipient Best of Reston award. Mem. ABA (antitrust, adminstrv. law, corp. banking and bus., sci. and tech. sects.), D.C. Bar Assn. (past chmn. energy study group), Calif. Bar Assn., U.S. C. of C. (antitrust policy com.). Democrat. Lutheran. Home: 1930 Upper Lakes Dr Reston VA 22091-3620 Office: Reed Smith Shaw & McClay 8251 Greensboro Dr Ste 1100 Mc Lean VA 22102-3809

RAU, RALPH RONALD, retired physicist; b. Tacoma, Sept. 1, 1920; s. Ralph Campbell and Ida (Montgall) R.; m. Maryjane Uhrlaub, June 2, 1944; children: Whitney Leslie, Littie Elise. B.S. in Physics, Coll. Puget Sound, 1941; M.S. in Physics, Calif. Inst. Tech., 1943, Ph.D. in Physics, 1948. Asst. prof. physics Princeton U., 1947-56; Fulbright research prof. physics Ecole Polytechnique, Paris, 1954-55; physicist Brookhaven Nat. Lab., Upton, N.Y., 1956-66; chmn. dept. physics Brookhaven Nat. Lab., 1966-70, assoc. dir. for high energy physics, 1970-81; adj. prof. U. Wyo.; vis. prof. MIT, 1984-88; staff scientist Desy Lab., Hamburg, Fed. Republic Germany, 1984-85. Trustee U. Puget Sound, 1978-84. Named Alumnus Cum Laude U. Puget Sound, 1968; recipient Alexander von Humboldt U.S. Sr. Scientist award 1988. Mem. Am. Phys. Soc., N.Y. Acad. Sci. Office: Brookhaven Nat Lab Upton NY 11973

RAUBICHECK, CHARLES JOSEPH, lawyer; b. N.Y.C., Oct. 9, 1946; s. Walter Alan and Catherine Gertrude (Fordrung) R.; A.B., Georgetown U., 1968; J.D., Georgetown U., 1971; m. Ann S. Macdonald, Feb. 18, 1978. Admitted to D.C. bar, 1971, N.Y. State bar, 1976; atty. Office Gen. Counsel FDA, Washington, 1971-75; ptnr. Sidley & Austin, N.Y.C., 1997—; adj. prof. N.Y.U. Sch. Law, N.Y.C., 1976—; trustee Riverside Ch., N.Y.C., 1993-94. Mem. ABA, N.Y. State Bar Assn. (chair food, drug, cosmetic law sect. 1986-88, vice-chair 1996—), Assn. Bar City N.Y., Union League Club (N.Y.C.).

RAUCH, ARTHUR IRVING, management consultant; b. N.Y.C., Sept. 18, 1933; s. David and Miriam (Frankel) R.; m. Roxane M. Spiller, Aug. 19, 1962 (div. 1977); children: David S., Janine B.; m. Lynn R Saidenberg, Oct. 11, 1987. BA magna cum laude Dartmouth Coll., 1954, MS, 1955. Chartered fin. analyst. Security analyst Lionel D. Edie & Co., N.Y.C., 1959-64; group dir. rsch. Eastman Dillon, Union Securities & Co., N.Y.C., 1964-68; v.p., sr. analyst Laird, Inc., N.Y.C., 1968-69, dir. rsch., 1969-71, sr. v.p., 1970-73; ptnr. Oppenheimer & Co., N.Y.C., 1973-77; v.p. corp. devel. Rorer Group Inc., Ft. Washington, Pa., 1977-84; v.p. corp. fin. Arnhold & S. Bleichroeder, Inc., 1984-88; cons. corp. devel. ICN Pharms. Inc., N.Y.C., 1988-89; mem. investment com. Becker Fund, 1969-73; bd. dirs. Sonomed Tech., Inc., 1983—, exec. com. Dartmouth Class of 1954, 1968-79, 94—. Lt. (j.g.) USNR, 1956-59. Rufus Choate scholar Dartmouth Coll. Mem. N.Y. Soc. Security Analysts, Assn. Corp. Growth, Fin. Analysts Fedn. (corp. info. com.), Phi Beta Kappa. Home and Office: Apt 9D 115 Central Park West New York NY 10023

RAUCH, GEORGE WASHINGTON, lawyer; b. Marion, Ind., July 18, 1919; s. George W. and Emma Asenath (Nolen) R.; m. Audrey M. Cranfield, Feb. 28, 1943 (div.); children: George Washington III, Nancy Lynn, Jane Nolen; m. Dorothy D. Farlow, June 26, 1970. B.S., Ind. U., 1941; LL.B., U. Va., 1947. Bar: Ind. 1948, Ill. 1957, Mass. and Fla. 1972. Practice law Batton, Harker and Rauch (and predecessor firms), Marion, Ind., 1948-57; v.p., gen. counsel The Greyhound Corp., Chgo., 1957-61; mem. firm Hubachek & Kelly Ltd. and predecessor firms, Chgo., 1961-82; pres. Hubachek & Kelly Ltd., 1972-80; of counsel firm Chapman and Cutler, Chgo., 1982-95; gen. counsel Household Finance Corp., 1967-78, dir., 1967-92, mem. fin. com., 1969-92, exec. com., 1972-92; dir. Edwards Engring. Corp., Constrn. Materials Co., Indsl. Air & Hydraulics Co., 1976-90; dir. Burch Co., 1972—, pres., 1975—; dir. 1242 Lake Shore Dr. Corp., 1971-83, pres., 1973-74; mem. Nat. Conf. Commrs. on Uniform Laws, 1955-57. Served as aviator USNR, 1941-45; lt. comdr. Mem. Raven Soc., Sankaty Head Golf Club (Nantucket, Mass.), Casino Club (Nantucket), Beach Club (Palm Beach, Fla.), Masons, Shriners, Phi Delta Phi, Delta Tau Delta. Home: 455 Australian Ave Palm Beach FL 33480-4526 also: 83 Baxter Rd PO Box 149 Siasconset MA 02564-0149

RAUCH, IRMENGARD, linguist, educator; b. Dayton, Ohio, Apr. 17, 1933; d. Konrad and Elsa (Knott) R.; m. Gerald F. Carr, June 12, 1965; children: Christopher, Gregory. Student, Nat. U. Mex., summer 1954; B.S. with honors, U. Dayton, 1955; M.A., Ohio State U., 1957; postgrad. (Fulbright fellow), U. Munich, Fed. Republic Germany, 1957-58; Ph.D., U. Mich., 1962. Instr., German and linguistics U. Wis., Madison, 1962-63, asst. prof., 1963-66; assoc. prof. German U. Pitts., 1966-68; assoc. prof. German and linguistics U. Ill., Urbana, 1968-72, prof., 1972-79; prof. U. Calif., Berkeley, 1979—. Author: The Old High German Diphthongization: A Description of a Phonemic Change, 1967, The Old Saxon Language: Grammar, Epic Narrative, Linguistic Interference, 1992; editor: (with others) Approaches in Linguistic Methodology, 1967, Spanish edit., 1974, Der Heliand, 1974, Linguistic Method: Essays in Honor of Herbert Penzl, 1979, The Signifying Animal: The Grammar of Language and Experience, 1980, Language Change, 1983, The Semiotic Bridge: Trends From California, 1989, On Germanic Linguistics: Issues and Methods, 1992, Insights in Germanic Linguistics I: Methodology in Transition, 1995, Insights in Germanic Linguistics II: Classic and Contemporary, 1996, Synthesis in Diversity: Semiotics Around the World; editor of three series: Berkeley Insights in Linguistics and Semiotics, Berkeley Models of Grammars, Studies in Old Germanic Languages and Literatures; contbr. articles to profl. jours. Named outstanding woman on campus U. Ill. Sta. WILL, 1975; recipient Disting. Alumnus award U. Dayton, 1985; research grantee U. Wis., summer 1966, U. Ill., 1975-79, Eastern Ill. U., 1976, Nat. Endowment Humanities, 1978, U. Calif., Berkeley, 1979—; travel grantee NSF, Linguistics Soc. Am., 1972; Guggenheim fellow, 1982-83; IBM Distributed Acad. Computing Environment, 1986; NEH grantee, 1988. Mem. Linguistics Soc. Am., MLA, Am. Assn. Tchrs. German (hon.), Society for Germanic Philogy, Philological Assn. of the West Coast, Phonetics Assn., Semiotic Soc. Am. (pres. 1982-83), Semiotic Circle of Calif. (founder), Internat. Assn. for Semiotic Studies (pres., dir. 5th congress 1994), Alpha Sigma Tau, Delta Phi Alpha. Home: 862 Camden Ct Benicia CA 94510-3633 Office: U Calif Dept German Berkeley CA 94720

RAUCH, JANET MELODIE, elementary school educator; b. Mpls., June 17, 1952; d. James Harlan and Myrna Luverne (Prinsen) R. BA, Wheaton Coll., 1974; MA in Tchg., Rockford Coll., 1980; cert. of advanced study, No. Ill. U., 1985. Cert. elem. tchr., spl. edn. tchr., Ill. Elem. sch. tchr. Christian Life Ctr. Sch., Rockford, Ill., 1974-80; remedial reading tchr. Washington Elem. Sch., Belvidere, Ill., 1980—. Mem. NEA, Ill. Edn. Assn., Belvidere Edn. Assn. (bldg. rep. 1980-82), No. Ill. Reading Coun., Nat. Assn. Christian Schs., Alpha Delta Kappa (sec. 1994-96, v.p. 1996—). Avocations: church choral singing, flute, violin, guitar, travel. Home: 1112 Fox Chase Ln Rockford IL 61107-6214

RAUCH, JOHN KEISER, JR., architect; b. Phila., Oct. 23, 1930; s. John Keiser and Marjorie (Gretz) R.; m. Carol Pfaff, Mar. 11, 1953 (div. June 1978); children: John David, Charles Daniel, Kathryn Mari, Peter, Carol Anne; m. Carol A. McConochie, Jan. 10, 1981. Student, Wesleyan U., Middletown, Conn., 1948-51; B.Arch., U. Pa., 1957. Draftsman Cope & Lippincott, Phila., 1957-60; architect Venturi and Short, Phila., 1960-64; partner Venturi and Rauch (Architects and Planners), Phila., 1964-79; partner Venturi, Rauch and Scott Brown, 1980-82, v.p., mng. prin., 1982-87, mgmt. cons., mediator, arbitrator, 1988—; instr. U. Pa. Grad. Sch. Fine Arts, 1969-70, 89; lectr. dept. architecture Princeton (N.J.) U., 1990-94.

Trustee Found. for Architecture, 1977-84, mem. adv. com., 1994—; treas. Phila. Rehab., Inc., 1984-94; pres. Reading Terminal Market Pres. Fund, 1988-93, bd. dirs., 1994—; bd. dirs. United Cerebral Palsy Assn., 1988-91. Recipient Good Neighbor award Mellon/PSFS Bank, 1992. Fellow AIA (Firm award 1983, John Harbeson Disting Svc. Phila. Chpt. award 1992); mem. Pa. Soc. Architects. Democrat. Home and Office: 620 Gate House Ln Philadelphia PA 19118-4303

RAUCH, KATHLEEN, computer executive; b. Franklin Square, N.Y., Oct. 30, 1951; d. William C. and Marian (Shull) R.; B.A., U. Rochester, 1973; M.A. in L.S., U. Mich., 1974; postgrad. N.Y. U., 1981-82. Media specialist Sutton (Mass.) Sch., 1974-76; program cons. Advanced Mgmt. Rsch. Internat., N.Y.C., 1976-79; pub. rels. cons., N.Y.C., 1979; pres. N.Y. chpt. NOW, N.Y.C., 1979-80; computer programmer Blue Cross/Blue Shield of Greater N.Y., N.Y.C., 1981-82; computer programmer analyst Fed. Res. Bank of N.Y., 1983-84; systems officer Citibank, N.A., 1984-85; systems analyst Fed. Res. Bank of N.Y., 1986-89; computer and children's libr. East Meadow (N.Y.) Pub. Libr., 1989-91; pres. Panorama Children's Videos, Inc., 1988-93; microcomputer specialist N.C. State U., 1992-93; prin., v.p. The Computer Lab., Inc., 1993—; v.p., The Computer Lab of Atlanta, Inc., 1994—. Mem. ALA, NOW (dir. pub. rels. N.Y.C. chpt. 1978, v.p. programs 1978, pres. 1979-80, chmn. bd. 1981, founding mem., sec. Svc. Fund NOW, N.Y.C. chpt. 1981), Assn. for Women in Computing (v.p. membership 1984, exec. v.p. 1985, treas. 1986, mem.-at-large 1987, pres. 1988), N.C. Libr. Assn., Triangle Bus. and Profl. Guild. Home and Office: The Computer Lab Inc PO Box 97682 Raleigh NC 27624-7682

RAUCH, LAWRENCE LEE, aerospace and electrical engineer, educator; b. L.A., May 1, 1919; s. James Lee and Mabel (Thompson) R.; m. Norma Ruth Cable, Dec. 15, 1961; children: Lauren, Maury Rauch. AB, U. So. Calif., 1941; postgrad., Cornell U., 1941; AM, Princeton U., 1948, PhD, 1949. Instr. math. Princeton U., 1943- 49; faculty U. Mich., 1949—, prof. aerospace engring., 1953-79, emeritus, 1979, chmn. instrumentation engring. program, 1952-63, chmn. computer, info. and control engring. program, 1971-76, asso. chmn. dept. elec. and computer engring., 1972-75; chief technologist telecommunication sci. and engring. div. NASA/Calif. Inst. Tech. Jet Propulsion Lab., 1979-85; vis. prof. Ecole Nationale Supérieure de L'Aéronautique et de l'Espace, Toulouse, France, 1970, Calif. Inst. Tech., Pasadena, 1977-85, U. Tokyo, 1978; cons. govt. and industry, 1946—; chmn. telemetering working group, panel test range instrumentation Research and Devel. Bd. Dept. Def., 1952-53; mem. exec. com. (Nat. Telemetering Conf.), 1959-64; Western Hemisphere program chmn. (1st Internat. Telemetering Conf.), London, 1963, program chmn., U.S.A., 1967; supr. air blast telemetering, Bikini, 1946; mem. project non-linear differential equations Office Naval Research, 1947-49; mem. research adv. com. on communications, instrumentation and data processing NASA, 1963-68. Author: Radio Telemetry, 1956; also numerous sci. articles and papers on radio telemetry. Recipient award for outstanding contbn. to WWII Army and Navy, 1947, award for outstanding contbn. to telemetering field Nat. Telemetering Conf., 1960; Donald P. Eckman award for disting. achievement in edn. Instrument Soc. Am., 1966; Pioneer award Internat. Telemetering Conf./USA, 1985. Fellow IEEE (spl. award contbns. radio telemetry 1957, adminstrv. com. profl. group space electronics and telemetry 1958-64), AAAS, Explorers Club; mem. Am. Math. Soc., AIAA, U. Mich. Research Club, Phi Beta Kappa, Sigma Xi, Phi Eta Sigma, Phi Kappa Phi. Achievements include patent in field; development of first electronic time-division multiplex radio telemetering system, of pre-detection recording; radio telemetry of first U.S. jet aircraft, of air blast over pressure for Operation Crossroads at Bikini Atoll; analysis of optimum demodulation of frequency-modulated signals. Address: 759 N Citrus Ave Los Angeles CA 90038-3401

RAUCH, PAUL DAVID, television producer; b. Jersey City, N.J.; s. Harry and Ruth (Reyman) R.; children—Stacie Jennifer, Tyler Meade. Classical music corr. Yomiuri Shimbun, 1956-58; corr. Voice of Am., 1958; Supr. prodn. TV programs CBS-TV, 1958-59; supr. prodn. TV programs Procter & Gamble Co., 1960-70; v.p. in charge daytime, east coast programming CBS-TV, 1970-72; exec. producer Another World, others NBC-TV, 1972-82; exec. TV producer Twentieth Century Fox, 1982-83; executive producer One Life To Live ABC-TV, 1983-91; exec. producer Santa Barbara NBC-TV, 1991-93; exec. producer 919 Fifth Ave CBS, 1994-95; producer Lover's Knot, 1995-96; developer Columbia-Tristar TV, FOX TV, USA cable TV, 1994-96; exec. producer Guiding Light CBS, 1996—. Served with AUS, 1956-58. Recipient Emmy award Nat. Acad. TV Arts and Scis., 1975, 76, Emmy award nomination for Another World, NBC-TV, 1976-77, NBC Bicentennial Special, Rachel Jackson, 1976, Top 50 Producers citation Millimeter mag., 1989, others. Office: NBC 300 W Alameda Ave Burbank CA 91506-3314

RAUCH, RUDOLPH STEWART, III, periodical editor, arts education executive; b. Bryn Mawr, Pa., July 5, 1943; s. Rudolph Stewart and Frances (Brewster) R.; m. Sheila Prentice, Oct. 31, 1972; children: Edward Prentice, Michael Brewster. BA, Princeton U., 1965. Corr. Time mag., N.Y.C., 1969-70, Bonn, W. Ger., 1970-71, Saigon, Vietnam, 1971-72, Rio De Janeiro, Brazil, 1972-74, Buenos Aires, Argentina, 1974-76, Atlanta, 1976-79; dep. chief of corrs. Time mag., N.Y.C., 1979-80; asst. to chmn. bd. Time Inc., N.Y.C., 1981-84; internat. dir. mag. devel. Time Inc., 1984-85; exec. editor N.Y. NJ. Conn. Real Estate, 1986-87; mng. editor Constitution, 1989-94; mng. dir. Met. Opera Guild, Inc., N.Y.C., 1994—. Edward R. Murrow Press fellow Council on Fgn. Relations, 1980-81. Mem. Coun. Fgn. Rels., Knickerbocker Club, Century Assn. Office: Met Opera Guild 70 Lincoln Center Plz New York NY 10023-6548

RAUCHER, HERMAN, novelist, screenwriter; b. Bklyn., Apr. 13, 1928; s. Benjamin Brooks and Sophie (Weinshank) R.; m. Mary Kathryn Martinet, Apr. 20, 1960; children: Jacqueline Leigh, Jennifer Brooke. BS, NYU, 1949. Asst. trade ad mgr. 20th Century Fox Films, N.Y.C. and Los Angeles, 1950-54; copy dir. Walt Disney Studios, N.Y.C., 1954-55; copy supr. Calkins & Holden Advt., N.Y.C., 1955-57; copy dir., v.p., dir. Reach McClinton Advt., N.Y.C., 1957-63; v.p., creative dir. Maxon Advt., N.Y.C., 1963-64; creative supr. Gardner Advt., N.Y.C., 1964-65; v.p. advt., cons. Benton & Bowles Advt., N.Y.C., 1965-67; freelance novelist, screenwriter, 1967—; pres. Bearfilm Prodns., 1971-96. Author: (novels and screenplays) Watermelon Man, 1970, Summer of '42 (nominated Acad. award for best original screenplay 1971, Writers Guild award nomination, Photoplay award), Ode to Billy Joe, 1975, A Glimpse of Tiger, 1972, (novels) Sweet November, 1968, Maynard's House, 1979, (screenplays) The Other Side of Midnight, 1977, Class of 44, 1972, Hieronymus Merkin (Best Original Screenplay award Writers Guild of Great Britain 1969), There Should Have Been Castles, 1978, also various dramas appearing on TV in Alcoa Hour, Studio One, Matinee Theatre, Goodyear Playhouse, (TV mini-series under pseudonym) Master of the Game, 1984, (TV pilot) Remember When, 1974; playwright: Harold, 1962, Two Weeks Somewhere Else, 1967, Red Lights and Dragons, 1996; contbg. editor: Greenwich Time; contbr. to book revs. to N.Y. Times. Served with U.S. Army, 1950-52. Mem. Writers Guild Am., Authors League Am., Am. Film Inst., Dramatists Guild, Acad. of Motion Picture Arts and Scis.

RAUE, JORG EMIL, electrical engineer; b. Stettin, Germany, June 13, 1936; came to U.S., 1952; s. Ludwig and Liselotte (Barth) R.; m. Anke Volkmann, June 29, 1957; children: Monika Kay, Jennifer Faye. BSEE, Milw. Sch. Engring., 1961; MSEE, Marquette U., 1965, PhDEE, 1968. Mem. faculty Milw. Sch. Engring., 1961-68, chmn. dept., 1968-69; research engr. TRW Systems, Redondo Beach, Calif., 1969-76; mgr. dept. TRW Systems, Redondo Beach, 1976-79; sr. research scientist TRW Electronic Systems, Rendondo Beach, Calif., advanced systems mgr., 1980-93; tech. cons. Calif., 1993—; chmn. dept. elec. engring. Calif. Polytech State U., San Luis Opispo, 1979-80; mem. faculty Marquette U., Milw., 1966-69, Loyola U., Los Angeles, 1970-72, U. So. Calif., Los Angeles, 1983—. Contbr. articles to profl. jours. Served with U.S. Army, 1955-58. Recipient Disting. Tchr. award Milw. Sch. Engring., 1968; named Outstanding Alumnus Milw. Sch. Engring., 1985. Fellow IEEE; mem. Microwave Soc. of IEEE (sec. adminstrn. com. 1985—), Sigma Xi. Avocations: tennis, bicycling, flying. Home and Office: 28813 Rothrock Dr Palos Verdes Peninsula CA 90275-3060

RAUENHORST, GERALD, architectural, construction and development executive; b. Mpls., Dec. 8, 1927; s6 Henry and Margaret (Keltgen) R.; m. Henrietta Schmoll, Sept. 2, 1950; children: Judith, Mark, Neil, Joseph, Michael, Susan, Amy. BA, U. St. Thomas, 1948, Dr. Laws (hon.), 1971; B.S.C.E., Marquette U., 1951. Instr. in civil engring. Marquette U., 1950-51; engr. Peter Rasmussen & Son, Oshkosh, Wis., 1951-52, Viking Constrn., Mpls., 1952-53; pres., founder Rauenhorst Corp. (named changed to Opus Corp.), Mpls., 1953—, chmn. bd., CEO, 1982-96, chmn. bd. Opus U.S. Corp. and Opus U.S. L.L.C.; chmn. and CEO Opus Nat., L.L.C., 1997—; dep. chmn. 1991-93, chmn. bd. dirs. Fed. Res. Bank, Mpls., 94-95, dir., chmn. human resources com. ConAgra, Omaha; bd. dirs. Cornerstone Properties, Inc., N.Y. Treas., trustee, devel. com. Papal Found.; dir., trustee U. St. Thomas, Marquette U.; chmn. bd. trustees Marquette U., 1985-87. Recipient Disting. engring. award Marquette U., 1974; named Alumnus of Yr., Marquette U., 1969, Coll. St. Thomas, 1978, Minn. Exec. of Yr., Corp. Report Mag., 1983, Devel. of Yr., NAIOP, 1992, # 1 Developer in Country Nat. Real Estate Investor Mag., 1995; named to Minn. Bus. Hall of Fame, 1980. Mem. ASCE, Am. Soc. Profl. Engrs., World Press Orgn., Minn. Soc. Profl. Engrs, Mpls. Club, Interlachen Club. Roman Catholic. Avocations: fishing, golf, pottery. Office: Opus Corp PO Box 150 Minneapolis MN 55440-0150

RAUH, CARL STEPHEN, lawyer; b. Washington, Dec. 14, 1940; s. Joseph L. and Olie (Westheimer) R. A.B., Columbia U., 1962; LL.B., U. Pa., 1965; LL.M., Georgetown U., 1968. Bar: D.C. 1966, U.S. Supreme Ct. 1969. Asst. U.S. atty. for D.C., 1966-69; atty. Dep. Atty Gen.'s Office Dept. Justice, Washington, 1969-71; 1st asst. atty. gen. U.S. V.I., 1971-73; prin. asst. U.S. atty. for D.C., 1974-79, U.S. atty. for D.C., 1979; ptnr. Dunnells, Duvall, Bennett & Porter, Washington, 1980-90, Skadden, Arps, Slate, Meagher & Flom, Washington, 1990—. Mem. D.C. Jud. Nomination Commn., 1985-90. Recipient Dir.'s award Dept. Justice, 1976; Atty. Gen.'s Disting. Service award, 1980. Fellow Am. Coll. Trial Lawyers; mem. ABA, D.C. Bar Assn., Nat. Assn. Former U.S. Attys., Asst. U.S. Attys. Assn. (Harold J. Sullivan award 1980). Office: 1440 New York Ave NW Washington DC 20005-2111

RAUH, JOHN DAVID, manufacturing company executive; b. Cin., May 28, 1932; s. Carl J. and Grace (Stix) R.; m. Elizabeth Gibbons, June 19, 1954; children: Carol Miller, Daniel Gibbons.; m. Mary Stoner, Dec. 23, 1984; children: Brooks Tomb, Howard Tomb. AB, Harvard U., 1954, MBA, 1956. Gen. mgr. Rauh Shirt Co., Cin., 1959-61, Clopay Corp., Cin., 1961-85; pres. Clopay Corp., 1972-75, chmn., chief exec. officer, 1975-85, also chmn.; adj. faculty mktg. Colby-Sawyer Coll., New London, N.H., 1989—; fellow Kennedy Sch., Harvard, 1989. Pres. Charter Com. Greater Cin., 1969-76; canidate U.S. Senate, N.H., 1990, 92, 96. 1st lt. Finance Corps. AUS, 1956-59. Home: 11 Clearwater Dr # 729 Sunapee NH 03782-2608

RAUH, RICHARD PAUL, architect; b. Covington, Ky., Mar. 27, 1948; s. Robert Paul and Pauline (Farmer) R.; m. Mary Darlene Bailey, Oct. 6, 1975. AB in History of Art, Columbia U., 1970; BArch, MArch., Harvard U., 1974; DMD, U. Ky., 1980. Registered arch., 30 states; lic. dentist, Ky., Va. Asst. prof. U. Ky. Coll. Arch., Lexington, 1976-80, adj. asst. prof., 1980-81; prin. Carpenter/Rauh, Lexington, 1978-80; prin. Rabun Hatch Portman McWhorter Hatch & Rauh Architects, Atlanta, 1981-85; prin. Richard Rauh & Assocs., Archs., Atlanta, 1984—; cons. Macon (Ga.) Heritage Found., City of Cin., Tampa Preservation Bd., Battle House Found., Mobile, Ala., City of Norwood, Ohio, St. Petersburg (Fla.) Preservation, Inc., City of West Palm Beach, Booker Creek Preservation Inc. Works published in numerous books and mags.; works include: Norfolk Hilton Hotel, Va., 1985, Omni Netherland Plaza Hotel restoration, Cin., 1982-83, Bridgeport Plaza Hilton Hotel, Conn., 1985, Carew Tower Block restoration, Cin., 1983-91, master plan Gaines Ctr. for Humanities U. Ky. Lexington, 1984, La Concha Hotel, Key West, Fla., 1986, Carolina Head Injury Ctr., Durham, N.C., 1987, Albany (Ga.) Holiday Inn Hotel, 1989, Shenandoah Head Injury Ctr., Manassas, Va., 1989, Kenner Toy Products Gen. Offices, Cin., 1990, Cin. Club, 1991, Tower Pl.-Emery Arcade Restoration, Cinn., 1991, Urban Design Masterplan, Mobile, Ala., 1993, O'Neil Cinemas, Duluth, Ga., 1994; author (with David G. Wright) Design Courses at Schools of Architecture in Western Europe: A Documentary Study, 1975. Pres., Hist. South Hill Assn., Lexington, 1978-80; bd. dirs. Margaret Mitchell House, Inc., 1987-92, pres. 1989, Preservation Action, Washington, 1988—, City of Atlanta Neighborhood Planning unit (Buckhead) bd., 1996, Planning adv. bd. 1996. Sheldon fellow, Harvard U., 1974-75, Appleton fellow, 1974-75; recipient LUMEN excellence award Illuminating Engring. Soc. N.Am., 1985; Harvard Book award Harvard Club Cin., 1965; U.S. Dept. Interior grantee Ky. Heritage Commn., 1978, U.S. Dept. of HUD Urban Devel. Action grantee, 1988; recipient honor awards Nat. Trust Historic Preservation U.S., 1985, AIA South Atlantic Regional council, 1984, Ga. Assn. AIA, 1984, 88, 89, 94, Ga. Young Arch. award 1988, Ky. Soc. Archs. AIA, 1986, Nat. award Soc. Am. Reg. Archs., 1986, 89, 90, 94, Build Am. award AGC/Motorola, 1992, Greater Cin. Beautiful award City of Cin., 1984, Ohio Hist. Soc., 1987, Fla. Keys Preservation Bd., 1987, City of Miami Beach, 1990, Nat. Hist. Landmark Designation U.S. Dept. Interior, 1995. Mem. Art Deco Soc. Am., Harvard Club of Ga., Harvard Club of Ky., Filson Club (Ky.), Order Ky. Cols. Democrat. Presbyterian. Home: Box 18560 Atlanta GA 31126 Office: Richard Rauh & Assocs 3400 Peachtree Rd NE Atlanta GA 30326-1107

RAUHALA, ANN ELAINE, reporter; b. Sudbury, Ont., Can., Dec. 7, 1954; d. Esko Alexander and Iona Anna (Tormala) R.; m. Lorne Franklin Slotnick, Feb. 27, 1990; 1 child, Sam Aleksander Nathan. BA in Arts, U. Toronto, 1977; B in Applied Arts, Ryerson U., 1979. Copy editor Globe and Mail, Toronto, Ont., 1979-83, asst. fgn. editor, 1983-86, reporter, 1986-89, fgn. editor, 1989-95, columnist, 1993-95; TV reporter Can. Broadcasting Corp., Toronto, 1995-97; panelist, organizer Can. Assn. Journalists of Toronto, 1990, Ottawa, Ont., 1992, Winnipeg, Man., 1993. Bd. dirs. YMCA, Toronto, 1989-92, Montrose Child Care, Inc., Toronto, 1992—. Recipient Robertine Berry award Can. Rsch. Inst. for Advancement of Women, Ottawa, 1987. Avocations: film, travel, literature. Office: Can Broadcasting Corp, PO Box 500 Sta A, Toronto, ON Canada M5W 1E6

RAUHUT, HORST WILFRIED, research scientist; b. Duesseldorf, Germany, May 4, 1930; came to U.S., 1964; s. Gustav Adolf and Johanna (Klose) R.; m. Magdalena Winkel, July 16, 1957; children: Birgit, Monika, Michael Winfred. BSc, U. Bonn., Germany, 1954, MSc, 1956; D in Natural Scis., U. Munich, 1958. Lab. supr. Henkel of CIE, Duesseldorf, 1959-64; chemist Harry Diamond Lab., U.S. Army, Washington, 1964-68, Morton Internat., Woodstock, Ill., 1968-71, Acme Resin, Forest Park, Ill., 1971-73; rsch. scientist Dexter Electronic Materials, Olean, N.Y., 1973—; dir., program coord. Plastics Engrs., Chgo., 1971-73; instr. Jamestown C.C., Olean, 1977; author, presenter tech. seminars, 1976-88. Author: Ueber Bicyclische Ketale mit Spiran-Struktur, 1958, Microelectronics Packaging and Processing Engrs. Tutorial on Epoxies, 1994; contbr. articles to sci. jours. Treas. Haskell Cmty., Cuba, N.Y., 1977-94, local historian, 1991. Named Outstanding New Citizen, Citizenship Coun. Met. Chgo., 1970. Mem. Am. Chem. Soc., Soc. Plastics Engrs. (dir. thermoset divsn. 1973-81, chmn. divsn. 1981-82, mem. internat. rels. com. 1973-84, thermoset divsn. award 1978, chmn.'s award 1982, award for significant contbn. to plastics industry 1988). Democrat. Achievements include Belgian, French and German patents for epoxy compositions, U.S. patents for foam sandwich structure, for flammable striker; research in areas of synthetic organic chemistry, adhesives/adhesion, ordnance, epoxy encapsulation compounds, low-stress technology and dielectric analysis. Avocations: photography, hiking, history. Home: 3551 Willow Rd Cuba NY 14727-9425 Office: Dexter Electronic Materials 211 Franklin St Olean NY 14760-1211

RAUL, ALAN CHARLES, lawyer; b. Bronx, N.Y., Sept. 9, 1954; s. Eugene and Eduarda (Müller-Mañas) R.; m. Mary Tinsley, Jan. 30, 1988; children: Caroline Tinsley, William Eduardo Tinsley. AB magna cum laude, Harvard U., 1975, MPA, 1977; JD, Yale U., 1980. Bar: N.Y. 1982, D.C. 1982, U.S. Ct. Appeals (D.C. cir.) 1982, U.S. Dist. Ct. D.C. 1986, U.S. Ct. Internat. Trade 1988, U.S. Claims Ct. 1988, U.S. Ct. Appeals (fed. cir.) 1988, U.S. Supreme Ct. 1988, U.S. Ct. Appeals (9th cir.) 1991, U.S. Ct. Appeals (4th cir.) 1994, U.S. Ct. Appeals (11th cir.) 1996. Law clk. to judge U.S. Ct. Appeals (D.C. cir.), Washington, 1980-81; assoc. Debevoise & Plimpton, N.Y.C., 1981-86; White House assoc. counsel Pres. Reagan, Washington, 1986-88; gen. counsel Office Mgmt. and Budget, Washington, 1988-89, USDA, Washington, 1989-93; prin. Beveridge & Diamond P.C., Washington, 1993-97; ptnr. Sidley & Austin, Washington, 1997—; cons. Reagan-Bush campaign, N.Y.C., 1984; com. mem. Food and Drug Law Inst. Co-chairperson, co-founder Lawyers Have Heart; chmn. bd. USDA Grad. Sch., 1991-93; bd. dirs. Am. Heart Assn., Nations Capital Affiliate, 1993—; treas., dir. Citizens Assn. Georgetown; mem. Nat. Policy Forum's Environ. Policy Coun. Recipient Disting. Achievement award Am. Heart Assn., 1991, Vol. of Yr. award, 1993. Mem. ABA (coun. sect. internat. law and practice 1992—, chmn. com. on nat. security and internat. law 1990-92, standing com. on election law 1995—, sect. internat. law and practice govt. affairs officer 1996—), Assn. of Bar of City of N.Y. (chmn. subcom. on Cen. Am. issues 1985, mem. com. on inter-Am. affairs 1983), Federalist Soc. (mem. nat. practitioners adv. coun., chair environ. and property rights practice group), Coun. on Fgn. Rels. Office: Sidley & Austin 1722 Eye St NW Washington DC 20006-3705

RAULERSON, PHOEBE HODGES, school superintendent; b. Cin., Mar. 16, 1939; d. LeRoy Allen and Thelma A. (Stewart) Hodges; m. David Earl Raulerson, Dec. 26, 1959; children: Julie, Lynn, David Earl, Jr., Roy Allen. BA in Edn., U. Fla., 1963, MEd, 1964. Tchr. several schs., Okeechobee, Fla., 1964-79; asst. prin. Okeechobee Jr. H.S., 1979-81, prin., 1983-84; asst. prin. South Elem. Sch., Okeechobee, 1981-82; asst. prin. Okeechobee H.S., 1982-83, prin., 1984-96, asst. supt. for curriculum and instrn., 1996—; mem. Dept. Edn. Commr.'s Task Force on H.S. Preparation, 1993-94, chair Task Force Tchr. Preparation & Certification, 1995-96. Mem. Okeechobee Exchange Club. Recipient Outstanding Citizen award Okeechobee Rotary Club, 1986; week named in her honor, Okeechobee County Commrs., 1990. Mem. Am. Bus. Women's Assn., Fla. Assn. Secondary Sch. Prins. (pres. 1993-94, Fla. Prin. of Yr. award 1990), Fla. Assn. Sch. Adminstrs. (bd. dirs. 1992-95), Okeechobee Cattlewomen's Assn. Democrat. Episcopalian. Home: 3898 NW 144th Dr Okeechobee FL 34972-0930 Office: Okeechobee County Sch Dist 700 SW 2nd Ave Okeechobee FL 34974-5117

RAULINAITIS, PRANAS ALGIS, electronics executive; b. Kaunas, Lithuania, May 13, 1927; came to U.S., 1954, naturalized, 1960; s. Pranas Viktoras and Paulina (Gervaite) R.; m. Angele Staugaityte, Oct. 4, 1952; 1 son, Pranas Darius. With Commonwealth Rys. of Australia, Melbourne, 1949-53; asst. to fin. acct. Kitchen & Sons, Pty. Ltd., Melbourne, 1953-54; v.p. Photo div. Interphoto Corp., Los Angeles, 1954-71; sr. v.p., sec. Craig Corp., Los Angeles, 1971-87; pres. PAR Enterprises, Burbank, Calif., 1987—; adviser Ministry Fgn. Affairs Republic of Lithuania, 1992. Former pres. Lithuanian Am. Coun., Inc. of Calif.; bd. dirs. Lithuanian-Am. assns.; founder, treas. Baltic Am. Freedom League; former mem. Am. Soc. Internat. Law. Home and Office: Par Enterprises 1501 W Riverside Dr Burbank CA 91506-3027

RAULLERSON, CALVIN HENRY, political scientist, consultant; b. Utica, N.Y., Dec. 18, 1920; s. Calvin Thomas and Cora (White) R.; m. Olive Lewis, Dec. 1, 1956; children: Kevin Greer, Cheryl Harp, Earl Henry. A.B., Lincoln (Pa.) U., 1943; M.P.A., NYU, 1949; postgrad., Harvard, 1947, Harvard Bus. Sch., 1979. Instr. polit. sci. Lincoln U., 1946, 49; editor, dir. research Christian E. Burckell Assocs., Yonkers, N.Y., 1950-52; asst. to exec. dir. United Negro College Fund, 1952-57, dir. ednl. services, 1957-61; dir. African programs Am. Soc. African Culture, Lagos, Nigeria, 1961-64; exec. dir. Am. Soc. African Culture, N.Y.C., 1964-66; chief Peace Corps, East and So. Africa, 1966-69; dir. Kenya, 1969-71, Africa regional dir., 1971-73; exec. asst. to dean Sch. Medicine, spl. asst. to pres. for internat. programs, spl. cons. research and devel., exec. dir. Internat. Ctr. for Arid and Semi-Arid Lands, Tex. Tech U., 1973-78; asst. prof. health orgn. mgmt., Health Svcs. Ctr. Tex. Tech U., 1973-78; asst. adminstr. Bur. Pvt. Devel. Cooperation, AID, 1978-81; v.p. African Am. Inst., 1981-84; assoc. Keene, Monk Assocs., Middleburg, Va., 1985-86; dir. internat. programs One Am., Inc., 1987-88; pres. internat. group LABAT Anderson, 1988-94; v.p. internat. group Gardner Kamya Inc., Washington, 1994-95; sr. project mgr. Labat-Anderson Inc., McLean, Va., 1995—; mgmt. cons. Mgmt. Devel. Consortium, Phelps Stokes Fund, 1973-75; Mem. information resources com. group on bus. affairs Assn. Am. Med. Colls.; mem. adv. com. on desertification AAAS, 1976-78; mem. Career Ministers Selection Bd., Dept. State, 1980; U.S. del. U.N. Conf. Desertification Nairobi, 1977; chmn. U.S. del. Com. on Food Aid and Policy, World Food Program, Rome, 1980; research analyst Pres.'s Com. on Fair Employment Practices, 1944; treas. U.S. planning com. 1st World Festival Negro Art, Dakar, 1965-66; del. Internat. Conf. on African History, U. Ibadan (Nigeria), 1962, Internat. Conf. on African Affairs, U. Ghana, 1963. Assoc. editor: Who's Who in the United Nations, 1952; Contbr. to: Negro Yearbook, 1952. Mem. nat. adv. com. Peace Corps, 1986-89; trustee African Wildlife Found., 1992—, chmn. strategic planning com., 1993-95. Rockefeller travel grantee East and Central Africa, 1960; Woodrow Wilson scholar, 1978-79. Mem. Harvard Club (Washington), Nat. Press Club. Home: 5823 Bradley Blvd Bethesda MD 20814-1104

RAUM, ARNOLD, federal judge; b. Lynn, Mass., Oct. 27, 1908; s. Isaac and Ida (Ross) R.; m. Muriel Leidner Slaff, Jan. 26, 1944 (div.); m. Violet Gang Kopp, Apr. 26, 1957; stepchildren—Robert E., Elizabeth A., Katherine F. AB summa cum laude, Harvard, 1929, LLB magna cum laude, 1932. Bar: Mass. 1932, U.S. Supreme Ct. 1935, D.C. 1935, bars of various other fed. cts 1935. Sheldon fellow Cambridge U., Eng., 1932; atty. for RFC, 1932-34; spl. asst. to atty. gen. U.S., 1934-50; spl. prosecutor in connection with fed. grand jury investigation of corruption La., 1939; 1st dep. solicitor gen. U.S., also occasional acting, 1939-1950; directed litigation of all Fed. tax cases as well as other types of cases in U.S. Supreme Court, 1939-1950; made arguments in numerous Supreme Ct. cases, including Calif. Tidelands case; judge U.S. Tax Ct., Washington, 1950—; lectr. on taxation Yale Law Sch., 1937-38; mem. faculty Harvard Law Sch., 1947. Editor Harvard Law Rev. 1930-32. Served as lt. comdr. USCGR, World War II. Hon. mem. D.C. Bar Assn., Fed. Bar Assn.; mem. Am. Law Inst., Phi Beta Kappa. Club: Cosmos (Washington). Home: 2622 31st St NW Washington DC 20008-3519 also: 1211 Crandon Blvd Apt F1106 Key Biscayne FL 33149 Office: US Tax Ct 400 2nd St NW Washington DC 20217-0001

RAUP, DAVID MALCOLM, paleontology educator; b. Boston, Apr. 24, 1933; s. Hugh Miller and Lucy (Gibson) R.; m. Susan Creer Shepard, Aug. 25, 1956; 1 son, Mitchell D.; m. Judith T. Yamamoto, May 30, 1987. B.S., U. Chgo., 1953; M.A., Harvard U., 1955, Ph.D., 1957. Instr. Calif. Inst. Tech., 1956-57; mem. faculty Johns Hopkins U., 1957-65, assoc. prof., 1963-65; mem. faculty U. Rochester, 1965-78, prof. geology, 1966-78, chmn. dept. geol. scis., 1968-71, dir. Center for Evolution and Paleobiology, 1977-78; curator geology, chmn. dept. geology Field Mus. Natural History, Chgo., 1978-80; dean of sci. Field Mus. Natural History, 1980-82; prof. geophys. sci. U. Chgo., 1980-95, chmn. dept., 1982-85, Sewell L. Avery disting. service prof., 1984-95; prof. emeritus, Sewell L. Avery disting. svc. prof. emeritus, 1995—; geologist U.S. Geol. Survey, part-time, 1959-77; vis. prof. U. Tubingen, Germany, 1965, 72. Author: (with S. Stanley) Principles of Paleontology, 1971, 78, The Nemesis Affair, 1986, Extinction: Bad Genes of Bad Luck?, 1991; editor: (with B. Kummel) Handbook of Paleontological Techniques, 1965; contbr. articles to profl. jours. Recipient Best Paper award Jour. Paleontology, 1966; Schuchert award Paleontol. Soc., 1973; grantee Calif. Rsch. Corp., 1955-56, Am. Assn. Petroleum Geologists, 1957, Am. Philos. Soc., 1957, NSF, 1960-66, 75-81, Chem. Soc., 1965-71, NASA, 1983-95. Mem. Am. Acad. Arts and Scis., Nat. Acad. Sci., Paleontol. Soc. (pres. 1976-77), Am. Soc. Naturalists (v.p. 1983), AAAS. Home: RR 1 Box 168-y Washington Island WI 54246-9753

RAUSCH, HOWARD, information service executive; b. N.Y.C., June 29, 1928; s. Sol and Helen (Kartiganer) R.; m. Sidra Cohn, Apr. 22, 1979. A.B., Syracuse U., 1950. Reporter Phila. Bull., 1961; copy editor Wall St. Jour., 1961-63, N.Y. Times, 1963-64; editor, fgn. corr. McGraw-Hill, N.Y.C. and Moscow, 1964-68; pres. Advanced Tech. Publs., Inc., Newton, Mass., 1968-80; editor, pub. Laser Focus mag., 1968-80; editor, founder Energy Research, 1975-80; editor Electronic Business, 1980-82; founder, pub. Lightwave Jour., 1983-90; tech. dir. Optical Soc. Am., Washington, 1991-93; pres. Capitol Gains, Info. and Cons. Svcs., Washington, 1993—. Home and Office: 2541 Waterside Dr NW Washington DC 20008-2820

RAUSCH, JEFFREY LYNN, psychiatrist, psychopharmacologist; b. Butler, Pa., Jan. 10, 1953; s. John Kenneth and June Alice (Morrow) R.; m. Catherine Rebecca Montgomery, Aug. 24, 1974; children: Jeffrey David, Caroline Rebecca, Lauren Elizabeth. BS in Biology summa cum laude,

Mercer U., Macon, Ga., 1974; MD, Med. Coll. Ga., 1978. Resident in psychiatry U. S.C., 1978-80; clin. psychopharmacology rsch. fellow U. Calif., San Diego, 1980-82; staff psychiatrist San Diego VA Med. Ctr., La Jolla, 1980-91; asst. prof. U. Calif., San Diego, 1982-89; assoc. prof. U. Calif., 1989-91, dir. psychoneuroendocrinology lab., 1990-91; acting assoc. chief psychiatry San Diego VA Med. Ctr., 1989-90; prof., vice chmn. dept. psychiatry Med. Coll. Ga., Augusta, 1991—; dir. lab. clin. neurosci. Augusta VA Med. ctr., 1991—; sci. cons. NIMH Study Sect.; pres. Med. Assn. Ga. Psychiatry Sci. Assembly, 1996. Contbr. articles to profl. jours. Recipient NIMH First award, 1987, NIMH ROI award, 1996. Mem. AAAS, Am. Assn. Chairs Depts. Psychiatry, Nat. Alliance Mentally Ill, N.Y. Acad. Sci., Soc. Biol. Psychiatry, Psychiat. Rsch. Soc. Presbyterian. Avocations: surfing, skiing, biking, fishing, windsurfing. Office: Med Coll Ga Dept Psychiatry Health Behavior 1515 Pope Ave Augusta GA 30904-5843

RAUSCH, JOAN MARY, art historian; b. Calmar, Iowa, Dec. 25, 1937; d. Bernard Joseph and Irene Sophia (Wieling) Menne; m. Gerald William Rausch, Sept. 3, 1960; children: John Thomas, Jennifer Nicole Rausch Goodhart. BS, Coll. St. Teresa, Winona, Minn., 1959; postgrad., U. Wis., LaCrosse, 1974-79; MA, U. Wis., Milw., 1982. Instr. nursing Mercy Hosp., Iowa City, Iowa, 1960-63, St. Francis Hosp./Viterbo Coll., LaCrosse, 1966-71; rsch. asst. dept. art U. Wis., LaCrosse, 1977-79; asst. dept. art history U. Wis., Milw., 1979-81; historic planner Southwest Regional Planning Commn., Platteville, Wis., 1982-83; pres. Archtl. Researches, Inc., LaCrosse, 1983—; cons. historic preservation divsn. State Hist. Soc. Wis., 1983—, Wis. Dept. of Transp., Dist. 5, 1991—. Author: A Catalog of the Oyen Collection, 1979, Historic LaCrosse Architectural and Historic Record, 1984, Chippewa Falls, 1985, Watertown, A Guide to Its Historic Architecture, 1987; (with Joyce Mckay) Richland Center Wisconsin, Architectural and Historical Survey Report, 1988; (with Carol Cartwright) City of Mineral Point, Architectural and Historic Survey Report, 1992, LaCrosse Wisconsin: Architectural and Historical Survey Report, 1996. Pres. Women's Polit. Caucus, 1972-78, coord., 1974-75. Recipienc Scholarship award Victorian Soc. in Am., 1981, Workshop award Ctr. for Art Criticism, Mpls., 1986. Mem. Soc. Archtl. Historians (pres. Wis. chpt. 1982-84), Nat. Trust Hist. Preservation (Preservation Forum(, Wis. Trust Hist. Preservation (charter, task force mem. 1986), Preservation Alliance of LaCrosse (bd. dirs. 1982-88, Heritage award 1989), LaCrosse County Hist. Soc. (hist. preservation com. 1992—, bd. dirs. 1994—). Avocations: painting, ceramics, landscape gardening, travel, swimming. Home and Office: Archtl Researches Inc W5722 Sherwood Dr La Crosse WI 54601-8442

RAUSCH, PAUL MATTHEW, financial executive; b. Lafayette, Ind., Dec. 14, 1953; s. Richard Leo and Vernice Ruth (Rhoades) R. Student, Purdue U., 1976. County supr. Farmers Home Adminstrn., Richmond and Falmouth, Ky., 1979-87; loan officer spl. accounts team Farm Credit Svcs., LaPorte, Ind., 1987; br. mgr. Nat. Mortgage Corp., Merrillville, Ind., 1987-89; collection mgr. Greentree Acceptance, Lexington, Ky., 1989; county supr. Farmers Home Adminstrn., Springfield and Alamosa, Colo., 1990-96; v.p. Hershey (Nebr.) State Bank, 1996—; bd. dirs. Internat. Children's Soc., Hooper, Colo., 1993-96. Pres. rural devel. Madison County, Richmond, 1980-85; bd. dirs. Mosca-Hooper Soil Conservation Dist., 1993-94, San Luis Valley Rural Devel. Coun., Alamosa, 1993-94. Recipient Dedication to Cmty. award Madison County, Richmond, 1983; named Ky. Col., Richmond, 1985. Mem. Nat. Parks and Conservation Assn., Am. Soc. Farm Mgrs. and Rural Appraisers, Nature Conservancy, Wilderness Soc., Sierra Club (agr. com. 1987-94), Kiwanis (bd. dirs. 1980-85). Avocations: music collecting, antiques and art collecting, Studebaker vehicle restoration, hunting, farming. Home: 9531 Ln 9N Mosca CO 81146 Office: Hershey State Bank 100 S Lincoln Hershey NE 69143

RAUSCHENBERG, BRADFORD LEE, museum research director; b. Atlanta, Sept. 11, 1940. BS in Archaeology and Biology, Ga. State Coll., 1963; MA in History, Wake Forest U., 1995. Archaeologist Ga. Hist. Commn., 1963-64; site supr., asst. Stanley South, State Archaeologist of N.C., 1964-66; antiquarian, asst. Dir. Restoration Old Salem, Inc., Winston-Salem, N.C., 1966-73; asst. to dir. Mus. Early So. Decorative Arts, Winston-Salem, 1973-76, rsch. fellow, 1976-87, dir. rsch., 1987-93; dir. rsch. Mus. Early So. Decorative Arts and Old Salem, Inc., Winston-Salem, 1993—; cons., lectr. in field. Author: British Regional Carving (1600-1640), and Furniture (1600-1800), 1984, Wachovia Historical Society: 1895-1995, 1995. With USCG, 1964-72. Recipient Halifax Resolves award, 1986; grantee NEH, 1972-81, Kaufman Americana Found., 1981-82. Mem. Am. Ceramic Circle (grantee), Orgn. Am. Historians, No. Ceramic Soc., So. Hist. Assn., Friends of Swiss Ceramic Circle, Regioanl Furniture Soc., Furniture History Soc., Soc. Hist. Archaeology, Soc. Post-Medieval Archaeology, Soc. Historians Early Am. Republic. Address: 221 Harmon Ct Winston Salem NC 27106-4613 Office: Mus Early So Decorative Arts PO Box 10310 Winston Salem NC 27108-0310

RAUSCHENBERG, ROBERT, artist; b. Port Arthur, Tex., Oct. 22, 1925; m. Sue Weil, 1950 (div. 1952); 1 child, Christopher. Student, U. Tex., Kansas City Art Inst., Academie Julian, Paris, Black Mountain Coll., N.C., Art Students League, N.Y.C.; LHD (hon.), Grinnell Coll., 1967; DFA (hon.), U. So. Fla., 1976. One man shows include Parsons Gallery, N.Y.C., 1951, Stable Gallery, N.Y.C., 1953, White Chapel Art Gallery, London, 1964, Leo Castelli Gallery, 1972, 73, Galerie Ileana Sonnabend, Paris, 1971, 72, 73, Ace Gallery, Los Angeles, 1973, Vancouver Art Gallery, 1978, Tate Gallery, London, 1981, Phoenix Art Mus., 1982, G.H. Dalsheimer Gallery, Balt., 1983, Castelli Graphics, 1984, others; exhbn. art constructions Rome and Florence Italy, 1953, Leo Castelli Gallery, N.Y.C., 1957—; rep. internat. art festivals, Carnegie Inst. Internat. exhbns., Sao Paulo Biennial, 1959, Exposition Internat. du Surrealisme, Paris, 1959-60, Amsterdam, others; group shows include Mus. Modern Art, 1959, Guggenheim Mus., 1961, 92, N.Y. Collection in Stockholm, 1972, Whitney Mus., N.Y.C., 1972, 73, Garage Show, Rome, 1973, Automme Festival d'Artes, Paris, 1973, Mus. South Tex., Corpus Christi, 1974, N.Y. Cultural Center, 1973, retrospective exhbn., Nat. Collection Fine Arts, Smithsonian Inst., Washington, 1976, Mus. Modern Art, N.Y.C., 1977, Albright Knox Gallery, 1977, San Francisco Mus. Modern Art, 1977, Art Inst. Chgo., 1977, Staatliche Kunsthalle, Berlin, 1980, Kunsthalle, Düsseldorf, 1980, Louisiana Mus., Copenhagen, 1980, Stadelsches Kunstinstitut, Frankfurt, 1981, Städtische Galerie im Lembachhaus, Munich, 1981, Tate Gallery, London, 1981, Galerie Beyeler, Basle, 1984, Juan March, Madrid, 1985, Inst. Contemporary Art, London, 1987, L.A. County Mus. Art, 1987, Galerie Alfred Kren, Cologne, Germany, 1988-89, Tretyakov Gallery, Moscow, 1989, Nat. Art Gallery, Kuala Lampur, Malaysia, 1990; permanent collections include Albright-Knox Art Gallery, Whitney Mus. Am. Art, Wadsworth Atheneum, Tate Gallery, Mus. Modern Art, Neue Galerie Aachen, Fed. Republic Germany, Hirshhorn Mus., Moderna Museet, Stockholm, others; reprodn. photographs by silk screen stenciling technique to allow change in scale; set and costume designer, lighting expert, stage mgr. Merce Cunningham Dance Co., 1964; choreographer: dance Pelican; others; works include electronic sculpture Soundings; paintings Tut-Scape; originator Overseas Culture Interchange traveling exhbn., 1985—. Served with USNR, World War II; neuropsychiat. tech. Calif. Naval Hosps. Recipient 1st prize Internat. Exbn. Prints Gallery Modern Art, Ljubljana, Yugoslavia, 1963, 1st prize Venice Biennale, 1964, 1st prize Corcoran Biennial Contemporary Am. Painters, 1965, Skowhegan Sch. Painting and Sculpture medal, 1982, NAD assoc., 1983, Grammy award, 1984. Mem. Am. Acad. and Inst. Arts and Letters. Gallery: Avanti Editions 22 E 72nd St New York NY 10021-4907*

RAUSCHER, TOMLINSON GENE, electronics company executive; b. Oneida, N.Y., May 27, 1946; s. Grant Koster and Rosalind Rebecca (Smith) R.; B.S., Yale U., 1968; M.S., U. N.C., Chapel Hill, 1971; Ph.D., U. Md., 1975; M.B.A., U. Rochester, 1984; children—David Grant, Tasha Candice, April Abigail, Nathan Tomlinson. Computer specialist Naval Research Lab., Washington, 1972-75; mgr. software tech. applications NCR Corp., Cambridge, Ohio, 1975-76; sr. computer architect Amdahl Corp., Sunnyvale, Calif., 1976-77; mgr. software systems GTE Labs., Waltham, Mass., 1977-78; mgr. product devel. and software systems design Xerox Corp., Rochester, N.Y., 1978-95, mgr. sys. products family group, 1995-97; pres., CEO Digi-Data Corp., Jessup, Md., 1997—; vis. asst. prof. Ohio U., 1976; adj. prof. Rochester Inst. Tech., 1991. Cert. computer programmer, data processor. Winner Masters Pole Vault—Empire State Games Championship, Eastern Region Masters Championship, Can. Nat. Masters Championship, U.S. Nat. Championship, N.Am. Masters Championship; named All-Am. champion. Mem. IEEE (sr.), Assn. Computing Machinery, Greater Rochester Track Club. Author: (with A. Agrawala) Foundations of Microprogramming—Architecture, Software and Applications, 1976, Software Development and Management for Microprocessor-Based Systems, 1987; contbr. articles on time to market, orgn., mgmt., software engring., computer architecture, microprogramming to profl. jours.; patentee computer systems design. Home: 9517 Valleymede Ct Ellicott City MD 21042 Office: 8580 Dorsey Run Rd Jessup MD 20794-9487 *You can accomplish more with others than by yourself. Delegate decision making responsiblity to those who have the knowledge to make those decisions.*

RAUSHENBUSH, WALTER BRANDEIS, law educator; b. Madison, Wis., June 13, 1928; s. Paul A. and Elizabeth (Brandeis) R.; m. Marylu de Watteville, May 3, 1956; children: Lorraine Elizabeth, Richard Walter, Carla de Watteville, Paul Brandeis. AB magna cum laude in Govt., Harvard U., 1950; JD with high honors, U. Wis., 1953. Bar: Wis. 1953. Ptnr. LaFollette, Sinykin & Doyle, Madison, 1956-58; mem. faculty U. Wis.-Madison, 1958—, prof. law, 1966-95; prof. emeritus, 1995—; vis. prof. law U. San Diego, 1992-94, 96, 97; project dir. real estate transfer study Am. Bar Found., 1967-72; trustee nat. Law Sch. Admission Coun., 1968-70, 72-95, chmn. pre-law com., 1970-74, chmn. svcs. com., 1976-78, pres., 1980-82; legal advisor Madison Citizens Fair Housing, 1961-63, Wis. Citizens Family Planning, 1965-73; mem. real property drafting com. Multistate Bar Exam., 1986—. Author: Wisconsin Construction Lien Law, 1974, (with others) Wisconsin Real Estate Law, 1984, 4th edit., 1994, Brown on Personal Property, 3d edit., 1975, Real Estate Transactions Cases and Materials, 1994. Served with USAF, 1953-56, col. Res. ret. Mem. ABA, State Bar Wis., Dane County Bar Assn., AAUP, Order of Coif, Phi Beta Kappa, Phi Delta Phi (province pres. 1963-75). Presbyterian (elder). Club: Stage Harbor Yacht (Chatham, Mass.). Home: 3942 Plymouth Cir Madison WI 53705-5212 Office: U Wis Law Sch Madison WI 53706-1399

RAUSHER, DAVID BENJAMIN, internist, gastroenterologist; b. Bklyn., Sept. 15, 1952; s. Herbert and Shirley Ruth R.; m. Judy A. Steinlaufs, Aug. 8, 1976; children: Scott, Michael, Steven. BA, Hamilton Coll., 1973; MD, SUNY, Bklyn., 1977. Diplomate Am. Bd. Internal Medicine, Am. Bd. Gastroenterology. Resident Emory U. Hosp., Atlanta, 1977-80, fellow in gastroenterology, 1980-82; pres. Atlanta Ctr. for Gastroenterology, Decatur, Ga., 1982—; med. dir. Atlanta Endoscopy Ctr., Decatur, 1994—; chmn. diagnostic treatment ctr. De Kalb Med. Ctr., Decatur, Ga., 1985—, co-chief gastroenterology, 1995—. Office: Atlanta Ctr Gastro 2665 N Decatur Rd Decatur GA 30033-6125

RAUTENBERG, ROBERT FRANK, consulting research statistician; b. Milw., Sept. 14, 1943; s. Raymond Clarence and Anna Josephine (Winter) R.; m. Meredith Taylor, June 2, 1965 (div. Feb. 1975); 1 child, Matthew Carl. PhD in Bus. Adminstrn., Pacific Western U., 1983; postgrad., Sorbonne U., Paris. Pvt. practice Kansas City, Mo., 1975-76; pres. Seven Diamond Enterprises, San Francisco, 1976-78; CEO Assurance Sys., San Francisco, 1984-96, Honolulu, 1997—. Author: The Analytical Management Handbook, 1985, Supplement to the Analytical Management Handbook, 1991, London edit., 1996, A Bayesian Approach to Management, 1996; contbr. articles to profl. jours. and conf. proceedings. Fellow Royal Statis. Soc.; mem. Internat. Soc. Bayesian Analysis (charter). Episcopalian. Avocations: swimming, skiing, traveling. Office: Ste 124 Box 210 1164 Bishop St Honolulu HI 96813-2810 *Personal philosophy: I am always surprised at the willingness of the human spirit to face new challenges.*

RAVAL, DILIP N., retired pharmaceutical executive; b. 1933. BS in Physics and Chemistry, U. Bombay, India, 1953, MS in Clin. Biochemistry, 1955; PhD in Physics and Chemistry, U. Oregon, 1962. Mgr. Varian Aerowgraph, Calif., 1955-68; dir. U. Calif. Med. Ctr., San Francisco, 1968-70; dir. rsch. Alcon Labs., Inc., Fort Worth, 1970-72, gen. mgr. science and tech., 1972-75, v.p. rsch. and devel., 1975-88, sr. v.p. rsch. and devel., 1988-96; now exec. v.p. rsch. and devel.

RAVE, JAMES A., bishop. Bishop of Northwestern Ohio, Evang. Luth. Ch. in Am., Toledo. Office: Evang Luth Ch Am 621 Bright Rd Findlay OH 45840-6940*

RAVECH, KARL, sports anchor, reporter; b. Jan. 19, 1965. BS in Comms., Ithaca Coll., 1987; M in Mgmt. & Leadership, SUNY, Binghampton, 1990. Sports dir. NewsCenter 7, Ithaca, N.Y., 1986-87; sports anchor, reporter WBNG-TV, Binghampton, 1987-90; weekend sports anchor, reporter WHTM-TV, Harrisburg, Pa., 1990-93; anchor, reporter SportsCenter ESPN, 1993—. Office: ESPN ESPN Plaza Bristol CT 06010

RAVEN, BERTRAM H(ERBERT), psychology educator; b. Youngstown, Ohio, Sept. 26, 1926; s. Morris and Lillian (Greenfeld) R.; m. Celia Cutler, Jan. 21, 1961; children: Michelle G., Jonathan H. BA, Ohio State U., 1948, MA, 1949; PhD, U. Mich., 1953. Rsch. assoc. Rsch. Ctr. for Group Dynamics, Ann Arbor, Mich., 1952-54; lectr. psychology U. Mich., Ann Arbor, 1953-54; vis. prof. U. Nijmegen, U. Utrecht, The Netherlands, 1954-55; psychologist RAND Corp., Santa Monica, Calif., 1955-56; prof. UCLA, 1956—, chair dept. psychology, 1983-88; vis. prof. Hebrew U., Jerusalem, 1962-63, U. Wash., Seattle, U. Hawaii, Honolulu, 1968, London Sch. Econs. and Polit. Sci., London, 1969-70; external examiner U. of the W.I., Trinidad and Jamaica, 1980—, rsch. assoc. Psychol. Rsch. Ctr., 1993—; participant Internat. Expert Conf. on Health Psychology, Tilburg, The Netherlands, 1986; cons., expert witness in field, 1979—. co-dir. Tng. Program in Health Psychology, UCLA, 1979-88; cons. World Health Orgn., Manila, 1985-86; cons., expert witness various Calif. cts., 1978—. Author: (with others) People in Groups, 1976, Discovering Psychology, 1977, Social Psychology, 1983, Social Psychology: People in Groups (Chinese edition), 1994; editor: (with others) Contemporary Health Services, 1982, Policy Studies Rev. Ann., 1980; editor: Jour. Social Issues, 1969-74; contbr. articles to profl. jours. Guggenheim fellow, Israel, 1962-63; Fulbright scholar The Netherlands, 1954-55, Israel, 1962-63, Britain, 1969-70; Citation from Los Angeles City Council, 1966, Rsch. on Soc. power by Calif. Sch. of profl. psychology, L.A., 1991; NATO sr. fellow, Italy, 1989. Fellow APA (chair bd. social and ethical responsibility 1978-82), Am. Psychol. Soc., Soc. for Psychol. Study of Social Issues (pres. 1973-74, coun. 1995—); mem. AAAS, Am. Sociol. Assn., Internat. Assn. Applied Psychology, Soc. Exptl. Social Psychology, Assn. Advancement of Psychology (founding, bd. dirs. 1974-81), Internat. Soc. Polit. Psychology (governing coun. 1996—), Interam. Psychol. Soc., Am. Psychology-Law Soc. Avocations: guitar, travel, international studies. Home: 2212 Camden Ave Los Angeles CA 90064-1906 Office: UCLA Dept Psychology Los Angeles CA 90095-1563

RAVEN, GREGORY KURT, retail executive; b. Elmhurst, Ill., Sept. 14, 1949; s. Eugene Alexander and Eloise Irene (McGhee) R.; m. Margot Clesta Theis, Feb. 2, 1974; children: Scott, Bryan, Ashley, Michael. B.B.A., Bucknell U., 1971. Second v.p. Chase Manhattan Bank, N.Y.C., 1973-76; corp. fin. specialist, dir. corp. fin. Gt. Atlantic and Pacific Tea Co., Inc., Montvale, N.J., 1977-80, asst. treas., 1980-82, treas., asst. chief fin. officer, 1982-87; v.p., treas. Revco Drug Stores, Twinsburg, Ohio, 1987-88, exec. v.p. fin. and chief fin. officer, 1988-95; pres., CEO Hills Stores Co., Canton, Mass., 1996—. Republican. Office: Hills Stores Co 15 Dan Rd Canton MA 02021-2847

RAVEN, ROBERT DUNBAR, lawyer; b. Cadillac, Mich., Sept. 26, 1923; s. Christian and Gladys L. (Dunbar) R.; m. Leslie Kay Erickson, June 21, 1947; children: Marta Ellen, Matt Robert, Brett Lincoln. AB with honors, Mich. State U., 1949; LLB, U. Calif., Berkeley, 1952. Bar: Calif. 1953. Assoc. Morrison & Foerster and predecessor, San Francisco, 1952-56, ptnr., 1956-94, sr. of counsel, 1994—; chmn. Morrison & Foerster (and predecessor), San Francisco, 1974-82; mem. Jud. Coun. of Calif., 1983-87. Bd. dirs. Bay Area USO, 1964-73, pres., 1968-70; mem. San Francisco Mayor's Criminal Justice Coun., 1971-72; co-chmn. San Francisco Lawyer's Com. for Urban Affairs, 1976-78; bd. dirs. Lawyers Com. for Civil Rights Under Law, 1976-96. With USAAF, 1942-45. Decorated Air medal with oak leaf cluster. Mem. ABA (pres. 1989, mem. standing com. fed. judiciary 1975-80, chmn. 1978-80, chmn. standing com. on legal aid and indigent defendants 1981-83, chair standing com. dispute resolution 1991-93, chair sect. dispute resolution 1993-94), FBA, Am. Arbitration Assn. (bd. dirs. 1988-96), CPR Inst. for Dispute Resolution (mem. exec. com.), Internat. Acad. Trial Lawyers, State Bar Calif. (gov. 1978-81, pres. 1981), Bar Assn. San Francisco (pres. 1971), Am. Law Inst., Am. Bar Found., Am. Judicature Soc., Boalt Hall Alumni Assn. (pres. 1972-73), World Trade Club (San Francisco), Order of Coif. Democrat. Home: 1064 Via Alta Lafayette CA 94549-2916 Office: Morrison & Foerster 425 Market St San Francisco CA 94105

RAVENAL, EARL CEDRIC, international relations educator, author; b. N.Y.C., Mar. 29, 1931; s. Alan M. and Mildred S. (Sherman) R.; m. Carol Bird Myers, May 26, 1956; children: Cornelia Jane, John Brodhead, Rebecca Eliza. B.A., Harvard U., 1952; postgrad., U. Cambridge, Eng., 1952-53; M.M.P. diploma, Harvard Bus. Sch., 1958; M.A., Johns Hopkins U., 1971; Ph.D., John Hopkins U., 1975. Treas. Elbe File & Binder Co., Inc., Fall River, Mass., 1955-64, pres., 1965-67; dir. Asian div. systems analysis Office Sec. Def., Washington, 1967-69; prof. internat. relations Johns Hopkins U. Sch. Advanced Internat. Studies, Washington, 1973-78, Georgetown U. Sch. Fgn. Service, Washington, 1976—; mem. bd. advisors Ctr. for Def. Info., Washington, 1971—, Ctr. for Study of Conflict, 1983—. Author: (with others) Peace with China?, 1971, (with James Chace) Atlantis Lost, 1976, Never Again, 1979, Toward World Security, 1978, Strategic Disengagement and World Peace, 1979, NATO's Unremarked Demise, 1979, Defining Def., 1984, NATO: The Tides of Discontent, 1985, Large-Scale Foreign Policy Change, 1989, Designing Defense, 1991, Defending America in an Uncontrollable World, 1997; contbg. editor Inquiry Mag., 1976-85, Critical Rev., 1987—; contbr. articles in field to profl. jours. Advisor Democratic Presdl. Campaign, 1972; advisor Jerry Brown Presdl. Campaign, 1976, Libertarian Presdl. Campaign, 1980. Served with JAGC U.S. Army, 1953-55. Henry fellow U. Cambridge, 1952-53; mem. faculty Salzburg Seminar in Am. Studies, 1977; fellow Bellagio Ctr. Rockefeller Found., 1975, Woodrow Wilson Internat. Ctr. for Scholars, 1973, Washington Ctr. for Fgn. Policy Research, 1974, Inst. Policy Studies, 1977-80; sr. fellow Cato Inst., 1985-91, 97—. Mem. Council Fgn. Relations, Am. Polit. Sci. Assn., Internat. Inst. Strategic Studies, Fed. Am. Scientists, Internat. Studies Assn. Libertarian. Clubs: Cosmos (Washington); Fed. City (Washington); Harvard (N.Y.C.); Signet (Cambridge, Mass.); Tred Avon Yacht (Oxford, Md.). Home: 4439 Cathedral Ave NW Washington DC 20016-3562

RAVENHOLT, REIMERT THOROLF, epidemiologist; b. Milltown, Wis., Mar. 9, 1925; s. Ansgar Benedikt and Kristine Henriette (Petersen) R.; divorced; children: Janna, Mark, Lisa, Dane; m. Betty Butler Howell, Sept. 26, 1981. B.S., U. Minn., 1948, M.B., 1951, M.D., 1952; M.P.H., U. Calif.-Berkeley, 1956. Intern USPHS Hosp., San Francisco, 1951-52; epidemic intelligence service officer USPHS Communicable Disease Ctr., Atlanta, 1952-54; dir. epidemiology and communicable disease div. Seattle-King County Health Dept., 1954-61; epidemiology cons. European area USPHS, Paris, 1961-63; assoc. prof. preventive medicine U. Wash. Med. Sch., Seattle, 1963-66; dir. Office of Population, AID, Washington, 1966-79, World Health Surveys, Ctrs. for Disease Control, 1980-82; asst. dir. epidemiology and research Nat. Inst. Drug Abuse, Rockville, Md., 1982-84; chief epidemiology br. FDA, Rockville, Md., 1984-87; dir. World Health Surveys, Inc., Seattle, 1987-93; pres. Population Health Imperatives, Seattle, 1993—. Contbr. articles to profl. publs. Served with USPHS, 1951-54, 61-63. Recipient Disting Honor award AID, 1973, Hugh Moore Meml. award IPPF and Population Crisis Com., 1974. Fellow Am. Coll. Epidemiology, APHA (Carl Schultz award 1978); mem. Am. Coun. on Sci. and Health (bd. dirs.), N.W. Danish Found. (bd. dirs.), Cosmos Club (Washington). Independent. Home: 3156 E Laurelhurst Dr NE Seattle WA 98105-5333

RAVENTOS, ANTOLIN, radiology educator; b. Wilmette, Ill., June 3, 1925; s. Enrique Antolin and Juanita (Gillespie) R.; m. Anne Patricia Gray, 1976. Student, Northwestern U., 1941-44; S.B., U. Chgo., 1945, M.D., 1947; M.Sc., U. Pa., 1954. From instr. to prof. radiology Sch. Medicine U. Pa., Phila., 1950-70; prof. radiology Sch. Medicine, U. Calif.-Davis, 1970-91, chmn. dept., 1970-77, prof. emeritus, 1991—. Assoc. editor: Cancer, 1964-91. Served with AUS, 1944-46, 52-54. Fellow Am. Coll. Radiology (chancellor 1964-70), Am. Radium Soc. (pres. 1972-73). Home: PO Box 3136 El Macero CA 95618-0736 Office: 44434 Country Club Dr El Macero CA 95618-1043

RAVETCH, IRVING, screenwriter; b. Newark, Nov. 14, 1920; s. I. Shalom and Sylvia (Shapiro) R.; m. Harriet Frank Jr., Nov. 24, 1946. BA, UCLA, 1941. Screenwriter: (films) (with La Cava) Living in a Big Way, 1947, The Outriders, 1950, Vengeance Valley, 1951; (with Harriet Frank, Jr.) The Long, Hot Summer, 1958, The Sound and the Fury, 1959, Home from the Hill, 1959, The Dark at the Top of the Stairs, 1960, House of Cards, 1969, The Cowboys, 1972, Conrak, 1974, The Spikes Gang, 1974, Norma Rae, 1979 (Academy award nomination best adapted screenplay 1979), Murphy's Romance, 1985, Stanley and Iris, 1990; writer, prodr.: (with Frank) Hud, 1963 (Academy award nomination best adapted screenplay 1963, N.Y. Film Critics Circle award best screenplay 1963), Hombre, 1967, The Reivers, 1969; story: (with Frank) Ten Wanted Men, 1955. Recipient N.Y. Film Critics award, 1963, Writers' Guild Am. award, 1988; Oscar nomination for Hud, Acad. Motion Picture Arts and Scis., 1963, Norma Rae, 1979.

RAVIS, HOWARD SHEPARD, conference planner and publishing consultant; b. Waterbury, Conn., Mar. 3, 1934; s. Paul Morton and Ida Ruth (Levin) R.; m. Sophie G. Simons, Nov. 1, 1959; 1 dau., Heidi. B.S. in Journalism, Boston U., 1959. Sports editor Milford (Conn.) Citizen, 1959-60; editor Stratford (Conn.) News, 1960-61; news editor Wallingford (Conn.) Post, 1961-62; editor Needham (Mass.) Chronicle, 1962-66; reunion coordinator Boston U. Alumni Assn., 1966; copy desk man, writer Boston Globe, 1966; news editor Scholastic Tchr. mag., 1966-67; mgmt. and careers editor Electronic Design mag., 1967-68; mng. editor Teacher mag., 1968-74; editor, assoc. pub. Folio: The Magazine for Mag. Mgmt., New Canaan, Conn., 1974-77; v.p. seminar programming, also creative dir. Conf. Mgmt. Corp., Stamford, Conn., 1978-80; speaker; bd. dirs. Ossining (N.Y.) Open Door Med. Assocs., 1973-77; chmn. United Ossining Party, 1973, Ossining Citizens Com. Edn., 1972-73; treas., bd. dirs. Ossining Interfaith Council for Action, 1970-73. Editor: Magazine Publishing Management, 1976, the Handbook of Magazine Publishing, 2d edit., 1983. Rep. Town Meeting, Needham, 1966; mem. nat. alumni coun. Boston U., 1977-91; trustee Ossining Pub. Libr., 1986-96, v.p., 1988-89, pres., 1989-91, 95-96. With AUS, 1956-58. Recipient Jesse H. Neal Editorial Achievement award Am. Bus. Press, 1976; Top News Writing award New Eng. Press Assn., 1962. Mem. Boston U. Alumni Assn. (chmn. Westchester County 1972-83). Democrat. Home: 5 Amawalk Ct Ossining NY 10562-4509

RAVITCH, DIANE SILVERS, historian, educator, author, government official; b. Houston, July 1, 1938; d. Walter Cracker and Ann Celia (Katz) Silvers; m. Richard Ravitch, June 26, 1960 (div. 1986); children: Joseph, Steven (dec.), Michael. BA, Wellesley Coll., 1960; PhD, Columbia U., 1975; LHD (hon.), Williams Coll., 1984, Reed Coll., 1985, Amherst Coll., 1986, SUNY, 1988, Ramapo Coll., 1990, St. Joseph's Coll., N.Y., 1991, Middlebury Coll., 1997. Adj. asst. prof. Tchrs. Coll., Columbia U., N.Y.C., 1975-78, assoc. prof., 1978-83, adj. prof., 1983-91; asst. sec. office ednl. rsch. and improvement U.S. Dept. Edn., Washington, 1991-93, counselor to the sec. edn., 1991-93; vis. fellow Brookings Instn., Washington, 1993-94, nonresident sr. fellow, 1994—, editor papers on edn. policy, 1997—, Brown chair in edn. policy, 1997—; sr. rsch. scholar NYU, 1994—; adj. fellow Manhattan Inst., 1996—. Author: The Great School Wars, 1974, The Revisionists Revised, 1977, The Troubled Crusade, 1983, The Schools We Deserve, 1985, National Standards in American Education, A Citizens Guide, 1995, (with others) Educating an Urban People, 1981, The School and the City, 1983, Against Mediocrity, 1984, Challenges to the Humanities, 1985, What Do Our 17 Year Olds Know?, 1987, The American Reader, 1990; editor: New Schools for a New Century, 1997; co-editor: The Democracy Reader, 1992; editor: Learning from the Past, 1995, Debating the Future of American Education, 1995. Chair Ednl. Excellence Network, 1988-91, 94-96; trustee N.Y. Pub. Libr., N.Y.C., 1981-87, hon. life trustee, 1988—; trustee N.Y. Coun. on Humanities, 1996—; bd. dirs. Woodrow Wilson Nat. Fellowship Found., 1987-91, Coun. Basic Edn., 1989-91. Recipient Award for Disting. Svc., N.Y. Acad. Pub. Edn., 1994; Guggenheim fellow, 1977-78; Phi Beta Kappa vis. scholar. Mem. Nat. Acad. Edn., Am. Acad. Arts and Scis., Soc. Am. Historians, N.Y. Hist. Soc. (trustee 1995—). Office: NYU 82 Washington Sqare E New York NY 10003-6644

RAVITZ, LEONARD, JR., physician, scientist, consultant; b. Cuyahoga County, Ohio, Apr. 17; s. Leonard Robert and Esther Evelyn (Skerball) R. BS, Case Western Res. U., 1944; MD, Wayne State U., 1946; MS, Yale U., 1950. Diplomate Am. Bd. Psychiatry and Neurology, 1952, Am. Bd. Forensic Examiners, 1996, Am. Bd. Forensic Medicine, 1996. Rsch. asst. EEG to A.J. Derbyshire, PhD Harper Hosp., Detroit, 1943-46; spl. trainee in hypnosis to Milton H. Erickson, MD Wayne County Gen. Hosp., Eloise, Mich., 1945-46, 46-80; rotating intern St. Elizabeth's Hosp., Washington, 1946-47; jr./sr. asst. resident in psychiatry Yale-New Haven Hosp.; asst. in psychiatry and mental hygiene Yale Med. Sch., 1947-48, assoc. in psychiatry and mental hygiene, 1948-49, rsch. fellow to Harold S. Burr, PhD, sect. neuro-anatomy, 1949-50, sr. resident in neuropsychiatry Richard S. Lyman svc., 1950-51; instr. Duke U. Med. Sch., Durham, 1950-51; assoc. to R. Burke Suitt, MD, Pvt. Diagnostic Clinic, Duke Hosp., Durham, 1951-53; assoc. Duke U. Med. Sch., 1951-53; vis. asst. prof. neuropsychiatry and asst. to vis. prof. Richard S. Lyman, MD, Meharry Med. Ctr., Nashville, 1953; asst. dir. profl. edn. in charge tng. U. Wyo. Nursing Sch. Affiliates; chief rsch. rehab. bldg. Downey VA Hosp. (now called VA Hosp.), N. Chicago, Ill., 1953-54; assoc. psychiatry Sch. Medicine and Hosp., U. Pa., Phila., 1955-58; electromagnetic field measurement project office dep. asst. sec. def. in charge health & med. E.H. Cushing M.D. Dept. Def., Pentagon, 1958; dir. tng. and rsch. Ea. State Hosp., Williamsburg, Va., 1958-60; pvt. practice neuropsychiatry specializing in hypnosis Norfolk, Va., 1961—; psychiatrist, cons. Divsn. Alcohol Studies and Rehab. Va. Dept. Health (later Va. Dept. Mental Health and Mental Retardation), 1961-81; psychiatrist Greenpoint Clinic, Bklyn., 1983-87, 17th St. Clinic, N.Y.C., 1987-92, Downstate Mental Hygiene Assocs., Bklyn., 1983—; sec.-treas. Euclid-97th St. Clinic, Inc., Cleve., 1957-63, pres., 1963-69; spl. tng. in epistemology and methodologic foundations of sci. knowledge F.S.C. Northrop, PhD, 1973-92; electrodynamic field rschr. with Harold S. Burr, PhD, sect. neuro-anatomy Yale Med. Sch., 1948-73; cons. hypnosis with Milton H. Erickson, MD, 1945-80; clin. asst. prof. psychiatry SUNY Health Sci. Ctr. Med. Sch., 1983—; pvt. cons., Cleve., 1961-69, Upper Montclair, N.J., 1982—; lectr. sociology Old Dominion U., Norfolk, 1961-62, cons. nutrition rsch. project Old Dominion U. Rsch. Found., 1978-90; spl. med. cons. Frederick Mil. Acad., Portsmouth, Va., 1963-71; cons. Tidewater Epilepsy Found., Chesapeake, Va., 1962-68, USPH Hosp. Alcohol Unit, Norfolk, 1980-81, Nat. Inst. Rehab. Therapy, Butler, N.J., 1982-83; participant 5th Internat. Congress for Hypnosis and Psychosomatic Medicine, Gutenburg U., Mainz, Germany, 1970; organizer symposia on hypnosis in psychiatry and medicine, field theory as an integrationof knowledge, hypnosis in gen. practice, history of certain forensic and psychotherapeutic aspects of the study of man, Eastern State Hosp., Coll. William and Mary, James City County Med. Soc., Va. Soc. Clin. Hypnosis, Williamsburg, Va., 1959-60; founding pres. Found. for Study Electrodynamic Theory of Life, Inc., 1989—. Asst. editor Jour. Am. Soc. Psychosomatic Dentistry and Medicine, 1980-83; mem. editorial bd. Internat. Jour. Psychosomatics, 1984—; contbr. sects. to books, articles, book revs., abstracts to profl. publs. Sr. v.p. Willoughby Civic League, 1971-75. 1st lt. AUS, 1943-46. Lyman Rsch. Fund grantee, 1950-53. Fellow AAAS, Am. Psychiat. Assn. (life), N.Y. Acad. Scis., Am. Soc. Clin. Hypnosis (charter, cons. cert. program), Royal Soc. Health (London); mem. Va. Soc. Clin. Hypnosis (founding pres. 1959-60), Norfolk Acad. Medicine, Soc. for Investigation of Recurring Events, Va. Med. Soc., Sigma Xi, Nu Sigma Nu. Achievements include discovery of electromagetic field correlates of hypnosis, emotions, psychiatric/medical disorders, aging, and electrocyclic phenomena in humans which parallel those of other life forms, earth and atmosphere underwriting beginning short- and long-range predictions, such seemingly disparate phenomena united under a single regulating principle defined in terms of measurable field intensity and polarity. Office: SUNY Health Sci Ctr Dept Psyc 450 Clarkson Ave # 1203 Brooklyn NY 11203-2012 also: PO Box 9409 Norfolk VA 23505-0409

RAVNIKAR, VERONIKA A., medical educator; b. Bklyn., Jan. 16, 1950; m. Dr. Leonard Sicilian; 3 children. AB in premedicine magna cum laude, Immaculata (Pa.) Coll., 1971; MD, SUNY Upstate, 1975. Diplomate Am. Bd. Ob-gyn. Resident in ob-gyn Prentice Women's Hosp. of Northwestern Med. Ctr., Chgo., 1975-79; fellow in reproductive endocrinology and infertility Brigham and Women's Hosp.-Harvard Med. Sch., Boston, 1979-81, obstetrician-gynecologist, 1981-89; asst. prof. ob-gyn, and reproductive biology Harvard Med. Sch., 1987-92, part-time lectr., 1992—; prof. U. Mass. Med. Ctr., 1992—, obstetrician-gynecologist, 1993—, dir. divsn. reproductive endocrine and infertility and menopause, 1992—; cons. in field. Mem. editl. bd. Women's Health Digest Med., 1994, Prevention Mag., 1994. Recipient rsch. paper award Dist. VI meeting, Milw., 1979, rsch. paper award Boston Obstetrical Soc., 1981; Bristol Myers grantee, NIH grantee; Grace La Gendre fellow Com. of Nat. Bus. and Profl. Women's Club in N.Y., 1973. Fellow Am. Coll. Obstetricians and Gynecologists; mem. Am. Fertility Soc., Soc. Reproductive Endocrinologists, The Endocrine Soc., Assn. Gynecologic Laparoscopists, Am. Heart Assn., North Am. Menopause Soc. (founding mem.), others. Home: 423 Commonwealth Ave Newton MA 02159-1301*

RAWDIN, GRANT, lawyer, financial planning company executive; b. N.Y.C., Nov. 17, 1959; s. Eugene and Nona (Neubauer) R.; m. Laura S. Schecter; children: Alexander, Jacob, Jesse, Aaron. BA, Temple U., 1981, JD, 1987. Bar: Pa. 1987, N.J. 1987; CFP, Colo. Tax acct. Hepburn Willcox Hamilton & Putnam, Phila., 1978-81; mgr. tax acctg. dept. Duane Morris & Heckscher, Phila., 1981-86, dir. personal fin. planning, 1986-87; pres. Wescott Fin. Planning Group Inc. subs. Duane Morris & Heckscher, Phila., 1987—, also bd. dirs.; mem. adj. faculty Coll. for Fin. Planning, Denver, 1987-95; lectr. Inst. Tax and Fiduciary Mgmt., 1988-95. bd. dirs. Phila. Child Guidance Ctr., 1991-94, Am. Poetry Ctr., 1989—, People's Emergency Ctr., 1995—; pres. PEC Found., 1996—. Mem. ABA, Phila. Bar Assn., Internat. Assn. Fin. Planners (chmn.), Inst. CFP (bd. dirs. 1987-93). Home: 7615 Seminole Ave Melrose Park PA 19027 Office: Wescott Fin Planning Group Inc 1 Liberty Pl Philadelphia PA 19103-7396

RAWDON, CHERYL ANN, elementary school educator; b. Dallas, June 13, 1957; d. Billy Wayne and Carol Ann (Murdock) R.; 1 child, Meagan. BS, East Tex. State U., 1979. Cert. kindergarten, elem., jr. high sch. reading and English tchr., Tex. Tchr. reading and spelling Canton (Tex.) Ind. Sch. Dist. Jr. High Sch.; tchr. pre 1st grade Midlothian (Tex.) Ind. Sch. Dist., tchr. kindergarten. Mem. First Bapt. Ch., Midlothian, tchr. Sunday sch., mem. choir, mission friends tchr., Awana leader; active numerous cmty. orgns. Recipient Golden Poet award, 1989, 90. Mem. Canton Tchrs. Assn. (pres.), Tex. State Tchrs. Assn., Canton Classroom Tchrs. Assn.

RAWITCH, ROBERT JOE, journalist, educator; b. L.A., Oct. 11, 1945; s. Sam and Jean (Reifman) R.; m. Cynthia Z. Knee, Oct. 27, 1968; children—Dana Leigh, Jeremy Aaron, Joshua Eric. BA in Journalism, Calif. State U.-Northridge, 1967; MS in Journalism, Northwestern U., 1968. Reporter L.A. Times, 1968-80, asst. met. editor, 1980-82, editor Valley sect., 1982-83, suburban editor, 1983-89, exec. editor Valley and Ventura County edits., 1989-93; dir. editorial ops. Valley and Ventura County edits., 1993-95; v.p. Winner/Wagner and Assocs., 1996—; lectr. Calif. State U.-Norridge, 1971-83, 95-96. Co-author: Adat Ari El, The First Fifty Years, 1988. Chmn. Calif. Freedom of Info. Com., 1978-79; pres. Calif. First Amendment coalition, 1991-93; bd. dirs. Temple Adat Ari El, 1987-92; pres. Calif. Soc. Newspaper Editors, 1995-96. Recipient Greater L.A. Press Club award, 1973, 75, 79, L.A. Jewish Youth of Yr. award United Jewish Fund, 1963, Clarence Darrow Found. award, 1979. Mem. Soc. Profl. Journalists (nat. bd. dirs. 1979-82). Avocation: tennis. Office: Winner/Wagner & Assocs 16501 Ventura Blvd Encino CA 91436

RAWL, ARTHUR JULIAN (LORD OF CURSONS), retail executive, accountant, consultant, author; b. Boston, July 6, 1942; s. Philip and Evelyn (Rosoff) R.; m. Karen Lee Werby, June 4, 1967; 1 child, Kristen Alexandra. BBA, Boston U., 1967, postgrad, 1972-74. CPA, Mass., N.Y., La. Audit mgr. Touche Ross & Co., Boston, 1967-77; audit mgr. Touche Ross & Co., N.Y.C., 1977-79, ptnr., 1979; ptnr. Touche Ross & Co., Newark, 1980-88, N.Y.C., 1988-89; ptnr. Deloite & Touche, N.Y.C., 1989-90; ptnr. Deloitte & Touche, N.Y.C., N.J., 1990; exec. v.p., chief fin. officer Hanlin Group, Inc., Linden, N.J., 1990-94, United Auto Group, Inc., N.Y.C., 1994-97; bd. dirs. BiakalInterPlast (USSR), Kuperwood Enterprises, Hanlin Group, Inc.; mem. adj. faculty Boston U., 1971-75. Contbr. articles to profl. journals, mags. and trade publs. Mem. Newton Upper Falls (Mass.) Hist. Commn., 1977; bd. dirs. Sherburne Scholarship Fund Boston U., 1977-80; mem. Englewood (N.J.) Planning Bd., 1981-83; trustee Englewood Bd. Edn., 1983-85, 89-93, pres., 1991-92; trustee, treas. exec. com. Englewood Econ. Devel. Corp., 1986-89; fin. and compensation com. Dwight Englewood Sch., 1985-90; mem. parent devel. com. Mt. Holyoke Coll., 1991-94. Served to 2d class petty officer USN, 1960-63. Fellow AICPA, Mass. Soc. CPAs, N.Y. Soc. CPAs; mem. VFW, Am. Legion, Navy League U.S., N.J. Hist. Soc. (bd. govs., exec. com., nominating com., treas. 1987—), St. George's Soc. N.Y., Univ. Club, Essex Club, Sloane Club (London). Home: 72 Booth Ave Englewood NJ 07631-1907

RAWLES, EDWARD HUGH, lawyer; b. Chgo., May 7, 1945; s. Fred Wilson and Nancy (Hughes) R.; m. Margaret Mary O'Donoghue, Oct. 20, 1979; children: Lee Kathryn, Jacklyn Ann. BA, U. Ill., 1967; JD summa cum laude, Ill. Inst. Tech., 1970. Bar: Ill., 1970, Colo. 1984, U.S. Dist. Ct. (cen. dist.) Ill. 1970, U.S. Ct. Appeals (7th cir.) 1983, U.S. Supreme Ct. 1973. Assoc. Reno, O'Byrne & Kepley, Champaign, Ill., 1970-73, ptnr., 1973-84; pres. Rawles, O'Byrne, Stanko & Kepley P.C., Champaign, 1984—, pres., 1990—; mem. student legal svc. adv. bd. U. Ill., Urbana, 1982—; hearing officer Ill. Fair Employment Practice Commn., Springfield, 1972-74. Diplomate Nat. Bd. Trial Advocacy. Fellow Ill. State Bar Found., 1984. Mem. Ill. Bar Assn., Bar Assn. 7th Fed. Cir., Assn. Trial Lawyers Am., Ill. Trial Lawyers Assn., Colo. Trial Lawyers Assn., Kent Soc. Honor Men, Phi Delta Theta. Roman Catholic. Home: 6 Alice Dr White Heath IL 61884-9747 Office: Rawles O'Byrne Stanko & Kepley PC 501 W Church St Champaign IL 61820-3412

RAWLEY, ANN KEYSER, small business owner, picture framer; b. N.Y.C., July 11, 1923; d. Ernest Wise and Beatrice (Oberndorf) Keyser; m. James Albert Rawley, Apr. 7, 1945; children: John Franklin, James Albert. BA, Smith Coll., 1944. Owner Ann Rawley Custom Framing, Lincoln, Nebr., 1969—. Pres. Friends of Fairview, Lincoln, 1976, Lincoln City Ballet Co., 1983-84; bd. dirs. Lincoln Community Playhouse; mem. adv. bd. Nebr. Repertory Theatre. Mem. Nebr. Art Assn. (sec. 1976-77, life trustee). Republican. Episcopalian. Avocations: foreign travel, tennis, needle work. Home and Office: 2300 Bretigne Dr Lincoln NE 68512-1910

RAWLEY, JAMES ALBERT, history educator; b. Terre Haute, Ind., Nov. 9, 1916; s. Frank S. and Annie B. (Vanes) R.; m. Ann F. Keyser, Apr. 7, 1945; children: John Franklin, James Albert. A.B., U. Mich., 1938, A.M., 1939; Ph.D., Columbia U., 1949. Instr., Columbia U., 1946-48; Instr. N.Y. U., 1946-51, Hunter Coll., 1951-53; asso. prof. to prof. Sweet Briar Coll., 1953-64, chmn. history dept., 1953-57, chmn. div. social studies, 1962-64; prof. U. Nebr., 1964-87, prof. emeritus, 1987—, chmn. history dept., 1966-67, 73-82, acting dean univ. libraries, 1984-85, honors MASUA lectr., 1984-85, Carl Happold Disting. prof., 1986-87; resident scholar Rockefeller Study and Conf. Center, Italy, 1977; vis. prof. U. Hanover, 1990; mem. adv. bd. Salmon P. Chase Papers and Abraham Lincoln Prize. Author: Edwin D. Morgan: Merchant in Politics, 1811-1883, 1955, Turning Points of the Civil War, 1966, Race and Politics, 1969, The Politics of Union, 1974, The Transatlantic Slave Trade, 1981, Secession: The Disruption of the American Republic, 1844-1861, 1989, Abraham Lincoln and a Nation Worth Fighting For, 1996; editor: The American Civil War: An English View, 1964; editor: Lincoln and Civil War Politics, 1969; contbr.: Essays in American Historiography, 1960. Served to 1st lt. AUS, 1942-46. Recipient Outstanding Research and Creativity award U. Nebr., 1983, George Howard-Louise Pound Disting. Career award U. Nebr., 1991; NEH fellow Huntington Library, 1979. Fellow Royal Hist. Soc.; mem. Am. Hist. Assn., So. Hist. Assn., Nebr. State Hist. Soc. (past pres.), Orgn. Am. Historians, Soc. Am. Historians, Civil War Round Table Nebr. (charter pres. 1989-90), Lincoln U. Club, Lincoln Country Club, Phi Beta Kappa. Home: 2300 Bretigne Dr Lincoln NE 68512-1910

RAWLINGS, HUNTER RIPLEY, III, university president; b. Norfolk, Va., Dec. 14, 1944; married; 4 children. BA, Haverford Coll., 1966; PhD in Classics, Princeton U., 1970. Asst. prof. U. Colo., Boulder, 1970-75, assoc. prof., 1975-80, prof. classics, 1980-88, v.p. acad. affairs, rsch., dean System Grad. Sch., 1984-88; pres. U. Iowa, 1988-95; pres., prof. classics Cornell U., Ithaca, N.Y., 1995—; chair Iowa Commn. on Fgn. Lang. Studies and Internat. Edn., 1988-91; bd. dirs. Tompkins County Trust Co. Author: The Structure of Thucydides' History, 1981; editor-in-chief: Classical Jour., 1977-83; contbr. articles to jours. Bd. dirs. Norwest Bank Iowa, N.A., 1988-95, Tompkins County Trust Co., 1996—. Jr. fellow Ctr. Hellenic Studies, 1975-76. Fellow Am. Acad. Arts and Scis.; mem. Assn. Am. Univs. (exec. com. 1990-92), Am. Coun. on Edn. (bd. dirs. 1994—), Nat. Fgn. Lang. Ctr. (mem. nat. adv. bd. 1995—). Office: Cornell U Office of Pres Ithaca NY 14853*

RAWLINGS, JOHN OREN, statistician, researcher; b. Archer, Nebr., July 26, 1932; s. Cecil Curtis and Mildred Louise (Suck) R.; m. Mary Jane Reichardt, Aug. 17, 1952; children: Gweneth Marie, Bradley John, Kalen Louise. BSc, U. Nebr., 1953, MSc, 1957; PhD, N.C. State U., 1960. Geneticist USDA/Agrl. Rsch. Svc., Raleigh, N.C., 1959-60; asst. statis. N.C. State U., Raleigh, 1960-61, asst. prof., 1961-63, assoc. prof., 1963-68, prof., 1968-94; prof. emeritus, 1994—. Author: Applied Regression Analysis: A Research Tool, 1988; contbr. over 75 articles to profl. jours. Lt. U.S. Army, 1953-55. U. Reading (Eng.) fellow, 1967-68. Fellow Am. Soc. Agronomy, Am. Stats. Assn.; mem. Crop Sci. Soc. Am., Biometrics Soc., Gamma Sigma Delta (Cert. merit 1979), Sigma Xi (Rsch. award 1964), Phi Kappa Phi. Home: 6216 Splitrock Trl Apex NC 27502-9778

RAWLINGS, PAUL C., retired government official; b. Cave City, Ark., June 21, 1928; s. Otha A. and Leona (King) R.; m. Catherine Terral, 1951 (div. 1970); children: William A., Rebecca, Neal; m. Erma Martin, June 20, 1971 (div. Jan. 1997). Grad., Little Rock Jr. Coll.; LL.B., Ark. Law Sch., 1950. Bar: Ark. 1950. Practiced in Little Rock, 1950, 52-73; adminstrv. law judge Office Hearings and Appeals, Social Security Adminstrn., HEW, Hattiesburg, Miss., 1973-92; ret. adminstrv. law judge sr. status, 1992; partner firm Terral, Rawlings, Matthews & Purtle, until 1973; asst. atty. gen., Ark., 1955-56. Bd. dirs. Ark. Enterprises for Blind, 1964-67. Served with AUS, 1950-52. Mem. Ark. Bar Assn., Law Sci. Acad. Methodist (past chmn. bd. adminstrn., trustee). Club: Lion (past pres.). Home: 107 Swinging Bridge Dr Heber Springs AR 72543

RAWLINGS, ROBERT HOAG, newspaper publisher; b. Pueblo, Colo., Aug. 3, 1924; s. John W. and Dorothy (Hoag) R. Student Colo. U., 1943-44; BA, Colo. Coll., 1947; m. Mary Alexandra Graham, Oct. 18, 1947; children: Jane Louise, John Graham, Carolyn Anne, Robert Hoag II. Reporter Pueblo Chieftain and Pueblo Star-Jour., 1947-51, advt. rep. 1951-62, gen. mgr., 1962-79, pub. and editor, 1980—; sec. Star-Jour. Pub. Corp., 1962-84, pres., 1984—; Past chmn. bd. dir. Colo. Nat. Bank-Pueblo; bd. dir. U.S. Air Force Acad. Found., U. So. Colo. Found., Colo. Water Edn. Found.; pres. Robert Hoag Rawlings Found. Served with USNR, 1942-46. Named Colo. Newspaper Person of the Year, 1989, Disting. Univ. Fellow Pres. Club U. So. Colo., 1993, Outstanding Citizen of Yr. Pueblo C. of C., 1994, Colo. Bus. Leader of the Yr. Colo. Assn. of Commerce and Industry, 1994; recipient Outstanding Svc. to Univ. award U. So. Colo. Alumni Assn., 1993, Colo. Corp. Philanthropy award Nat. Philanthropy Assoc., 1993, Louis T. Benezet award Colo. Coll. Alumni Assn., 1996, Outstanding Am. Achievement award U. So. Colo., 1997; named Donor of Yr. Nat. Assn. Univ. Athletic Devel. Dirs., 1995. Mem. Colo. Press Assn., (dir. 1963-66, 76-78, pres. 1985, chmn. bd. dirs. 1986), Rocky Mountain Ad Mgrs. (past pres.), Colo. AP (past pres.), Elks, Rotary. Presbyterian. Home: 27 Calle del Sol Pueblo CO 81008 Office: Star-Jour Pub Corp PO Box 4040 Pueblo CO 81003-0040

RAWLINSON, DENNIS PATRICK, lawyer; b. Portland, Oreg., Mar. 1, 1947; s. Thomas F. and Betty (Price) R.; m. M. Diane Schatz, Apr. 26, 1980. BA, U. Notre Dame, 1969; MBA, Cornell U., 1976, JD, 1976. Bar: Oreg. 1976, U.S. Dist. Ct. Oreg. 1976; cert. civil trial lawyer Nat. Inst. Trial Advocacy. Assoc. Miller, Nash, Wiener, Hager & Carlsen, Portland, Oreg., 1976-82, ptnr., 1982—. Contbr. articles to profl. jours. Pres., bd. dirs. Portland Opera Assn., 1990-96. 1st lt. Army Med. Svc. Corps, 1970-72, Korea. Mem. ABA (chair creditor's rights subsection and task force on discovery guidelines litigation sect.), Oreg. State Bar Assn. (mem. exec. com. debtor/creditor sect. 1988-91, chair-elect and mem. exec. com. litigation sect. 1992—, mng. editor litigation jour. 1992—, mng. editor Oreg. Comml. Practice manual 1988—), Owen Panner Inn of Ct. (master), Arlington Club Toastmasters (pres.), Rotary Club Portland (pres., bd. dirs.), Multnomah Athletic Club (pres., trustee). Avocations: running, backpacking, white water rafting, wine collecting. Office: Miller Nash Wiener Hager & Carlsen 111 SW 5th Ave Ste 3500 Portland OR 97204-3638

RAWLINSON, HELEN ANN, librarian; b. Columbia, S.C., Mar. 30, 1948; d. Alfred Harris and Mary Taylor (Moon) R. BA, U. S.C., 1970; MLS, Emory U., 1972. Asst. children's librarian Greenville (S.C.) County Library, 1972-74, br. supr., 1974-76, asst. head extension div., 1976-78; children's room librarian Richland County Pub. Library, Columbia, 1978-81; sr. adult services librarian Richland County Pub. Library, 1981-82, chief adult services, 1982-85, dep. dir., 1985—; mem. adv. com. S.C. Pre-White House Conf. on Libr. and Info. Svcs., chmn. program com.; mem. tech. com. Columbia World Affairs Coun. Mem. ALA, S.E. Libr. Assn., S.C. Libr. Assn. (2d v.p. 1987-89, editl. com. 1993, chmn. pub. libr. sect. 1995), U. S.C. Thomas Cooper Soc. (bd. dirs., v.p., pres.-elect). Baptist. Home: 1316 Guignard Ave West Columbia SC 29169-6137 Office: Richland County Pub Libr 1431 Assembly St Columbia SC 29201-3101

RAWLS, EUGENIA, actress; b. Macon, Ga.; d. Hubert Fields and Louise (Roberts) R.; m. Donald Ray Seawell, Apr. 5, 1941; children: Brook Ashley, Donald Brockman. Grad., Wesleyan Conservatory, Macon, 1932; student, U. N.C., 1933; L.H.D., U. No. Colo., Greeley, 1978; D.F.A., Wesleyan Coll., Macon, Ga., 1982. Participant 25th Anniversary of Lillian Smith Book Awards, Atlanta, 1993. Author: Tallulah—A Memory, 1979; Broadway appearances include The Children's Hour, 1934, Pride and Prejudice, 1936, The Little Foxes, 1939, 41, Guest in the House, 1942, Rebecca, 1945, The Second Mrs. Tanqueray, 1940, The Shrike, 1952, Private Lives, 1949, The Great Sebastians, 1956, First Love, 1961, The Glass Menagerie, 1964, 67, Our Town, 1967, Tallulah: A Memory; appeared at Lincoln Ctr., 1971, London, 1974, U.S. tour, 1979, Denver Ctr. Performing Arts, 1980, Theatre of Mus., N.Y.C., 1980, Four Arts Soc., Palm Beach, Fla., 1981, Herbst Theater, San Francisco, 1981, Kennedy Ctr. (cable TV), 1981, Nat. Theatre Great Britain, 1984, Queen Elizabeth II, 1984-86; one-woman show Affectionately Yours Fanny Kemble, London, 1974, U.S. tour, 1979, Nat. Portrait Gallery, Washington, 1983, Grolier Club Exhbn., N.Y.C., 1988; appeared in The Enchanted, 1973, Sweet Bird of Youth, 1975, 76, Daughter of the Regiment, 1978, Just the Immediate Family, 1978, Women of the West, U.S. tour, 1979, Am. Mus. in Britain, Bath, Eng., 1981, Kennedy Ctr. and Denver Ctr. Performing Arts, 1980; one-woman show Fanny Kemble, Arts Theatre, London, 1969, Queen's Hall, Edinburgh, 1980, St. Peter's Ch., N.Y.C., 1980, Internat. Theater Festival, Denver, 1982, also Kennedy Center; appeared as Emily, Denver, 1976; with Abbey Theatre, Dublin, Ireland, 1972; one-woman show tour of Europe, 1972; appeared as: Fanny Kemble, Shakespeare World Congress, Washington, 1976; TV appearances, U.S. Steel Hour, Love of Life, Women of the West; (for ednl. TV) Tallulah: A Memory (performed for presdl. inauguration), 1977; Memory of a Large Christmas, Folger Shakespeare Library, 1977, Memory of a Large Christmas, 1996; mem., Sarah Caldwell Opera Co., Boston, 1978; rec. talking books for blind; mem. com.: Plays for Living, 1964-67; Rockefeller Found. artist-in-residence, Denver U., 1967, 68, U. Tampa, Fla., 1970, artist-in-residence, U. No. Colo., 1971, 72, 73; artist Annenberg Theatre, Desert Art Mus., Palm Springs, Calif., 1988, 89, "Our Town" Pitts. Pub. Theatre, 1990; author: (poems) A Moment Ago, 1984; participant Edwin Forrest Day Celebrating Shakespeare's 427th Birthday The Actors' Fund of Am.'s Nursing and Retirement Home Lucille Lortel Theatre, 1991; appeared in Our Town, Pitts. Pub. Theater, 1990-91, Three Sisters, 1991—. Mem. Internat. Women's Forum, Vail, Colo., 1989. Recipient Alumna award U. N.C., 1969; Disting. Achievement award Wesleyan Coll., 1969; Gold Chair award Central City (Colo.) Opera House Assn., 1973; (with husband) Frederick H. Koch Drama award U. N.C., 1974; citation Smithsonian Instn., 1977. Address: care Donald Seawell 1050 13th St Denver CO 80204-2157

RAWN, WILLIAM LEETE, III, architect; b. Berkeley, Calif., Aug. 8, 1943; s. William Leete Jr. and Betsy (Blanckenburg) R. BA, Yale U., 1965; JD, Harvard U., 1969; MArch, MIT, 1979. Bar: D.C., 1969. Assoc. Arent, Fox, Kintner, Plotkin & Kahn, Washington, 1969-71; asst. to pres. U. Mass., Boston, 1971-73, asst. chancellor phys. planning, 1973-75; architect Davis Brody & Assocs., N.Y.C., 1979-83, William Rawn Assocs., Boston, 1983—. Designer serigraphs, 1971-79; contbr. articles to profl. jours., newspapers. Mem. Boston Civic Design Com., 1990; trustee 1000 Friends of Mass., Boston, 1990, Bennington Coll., Inst. Contemporary Art, Boston, 1994. Recipient Urban Design citation Progressive Architecture, U. Va./City of Charlottesville Urban Plan, 1995. Fellow AIA (hon., Nat. AIA Award of Excellence, 1993, AIA Award in Urban Design, 1996, Nat. AIA Honor Award in Arch. 1994, 95, Louis Sullivan award 1995); mem. Boston Soc. Architects (20 regional and local AIA design awards 1985-96), D.C. Bar Assn., Yale Club of N.Y.C., Harvard Club (Boston). Office: William Rawn Assocs Archs Inc 101 Tremont St Ste 204 Boston MA 02108-5004*

RAWNSLEY, HOWARD MELODY, physician, educator; b. Long Branch, N.J., Nov. 20, 1925; s. Walter A. and Elizabeth (Melody) R.; m. B. Eileen Fiddes, Sept. 5, 1967; children—Virgilia Ingram, Elizabeth Sue. A.B., Haverford Coll., 1949; M.D., U. Pa., 1952. Diplomate Am. Bd. Pathology (trustee 1988-96). Intern Hosp. U. Pa., 1952-53, resident, 1953-57; practice medicine, specializing in pathology Phila., 1957-75; mem. Wm. Pepper Lab., U. Pa., 1957-75, asst. dir., 1960-68, dir., 1968-75; assoc. dir. Clin. Research Ctr., 1962-67, acting dir., 1969—70, asst. prof. pathology and medicine, 1960-65, assoc. prof., 1965-69, prof., 1969-75; prof. pathology Dartmouth Hitchcock Med. Ctr., Hanover, N.H., 1975-95, chmn. dept., 1980-87, sr. v.p. med. affairs, 1987-94, emeritus, 1995—; cons. VA Hosp. Served with AUS, 1944-46. Woodward fellow in chemistry, 1953-55. Mem. AMA, ARC (biomed. svcs. com. 1990-92), Pathology Soc. Phila. (pres.), Coll. Am. Pathologists (bd. govs. 1985-93), Am. Soc. Clin. Pathologists (Disting. Svc. award 1995). Home: 7 Haskins Rd Hanover NH 03755-2204

RAWSKI, CONRAD H(ENRY), humanities educator, medievalist; b. Vienna, Austria, May 25, 1914; came to U.S., 1939, naturalized, 1944; s. Stanislaus and Johanna (Buberl-Maffei) R.; m. Helen Orr, July 5, 1957; children: Thomas George, Judith Ellen Rawski Kleen. M.A., U. Vienna, 1936, Ph.D., 1937; postgrad., Péter Pázmány Egyetem, Budapest, 1938-39, Harvard U., 1939-40; M.S. in L.S, Western Res. U., 1957. Lectr. in music U. Louisville, 1940; asst. prof., assoc. prof., prof. music Ithaca (N.Y.) Coll., 1940-56; dir. grad. studies, dean Ithaca (N.Y.) Coll. (Sch. Music), 1951-56; head fine arts dept. Cleve. Public Library, 1957-62; assoc. prof., prof. library sci., coordinator Ph.D. program in info. sci. M.A. Baxter Sch. Info. and Libr. Sci., Case Western Res. U., Cleve., 1957-80; prof., sr. research scholar M.A. Baxter Sch. Info. and Libr. Sci., Case Western Res. U., 1980-85, prof. emeritus for life, dean emeritus, 1985; music columnist Boston Evening Transcript, 1939-40, Ithaca Jour., 1943-50; lectr. in musicology, medieval studies, info. sci. Fellow Fund for the Advancement of Edn., Ford Found., 1952-53, Nat. Endowment for Humanities, 1979. Author: Petrarch: Four Dialogues for Scholars, 1967, Toward a Theory of Librarianship, 1973, Petrarch's Latin Prose Works and the Modern Translator, 1977, Introduction to Research in Information Sciane, 1982; translator, editor: Petrarch's Remedies for Fortune Fair and Foul, 5 vols., 1991, Petrarch to Boccaccio: The Griseldis Letters, 1994, Francisci Petrarchae lectoris Adminiculum: Late Antique and Medieval Latin Words in the Works of Petrarch, 1996; contbr. papers on Petrarch's Latin prose works, Petrarch's Latinity, medieval music, info. sci. and theory to profl. jours. and encys. Mem. Renaissance Soc. Am., Medieval Acad. Am., Soc. for Medieval Latin, ALA (nat. Beta Phi Mu award 1979), Am. Musicol. Soc., Wembley Club. Club: Rowfant of Cleve. Address: 17877 Lost Trl Chagrin Falls OH 44023-5835

RAWSKI, EVELYN SAKAKIDA, history educator; b. Honolulu, Feb. 2, 1939; d. Evan T. and Teruko (Watase) Sakakida; m. Thomas G. Rawski, Dec. 16, 1967. B.A., Cornell U., 1961; M.A., Radcliffe Coll., 1962; Ph.D., Harvard U., 1968. Asst. prof. history U. Pitts., 1967-72, assoc. prof., 1973-79, prof. history, 1980—; univ. prof., 1996—. Author: Agricultural Change and the Peasant Economy of South China, 1972, Education and Popular Literacy in Ch'ing China, 1979; co-author: Chinese Society in the Eighteenth Century, 1987; co-editor: Popular Culture in Late Imperial and Modern China, 1988, Harmony and Counterpoint: Chinese Music in Ritual Context, 1996. Am. Coun. Learned Soc. grantee, 1973-74; NEH fellow, 1979-80, Chinese Studies fellow Am. Coun. Learned Soc./Sci. Rsch. Coun., 1989, Guggenheim Meml. Found. fellow, 1990, Woodrow Wilson Internat. Ctr. fellow 1992-93. Mem. Assn. Asian Studies (China-Inner Asia coun., bd.

dirs. 1976-79, v.p. 1994-95, pres. 1995-96). Home: 5317 Westminster Pl Pittsburgh PA 15232-2120 Office: U Pitts Dept History Pittsburgh PA 15260

RAWSON, CLAUDE JULIEN, English educator; b. Shanghai, Feb. 8, 1935; came to U.S., 1985; m. Judith Ann Hammond, July 14, 1959; children: Hugh, Tim, Mark, Harriet, Annabel. BA, Oxford (Eng.) U., 1955, MA, BLitt, 1959. English lectr. U. Newcastle, Eng., 1957-65; from lectr. to prof., chmn. dept. U. Warwick, Coventry, Eng., 1965-85, hon. prof., 1986—; George Sherburn prof. English U. Ill., Urbana, 1985-86; George M. Bodman prof. English Yale U., New Haven, Conn., 1986-96, Maynard Mack prof. English, 1996—; vis. prof. U. Pa., Phila., 1973, U. Calif., Berkeley, 1980. Author: Henry Fielding and the Augustan Ideal, 1972, 2d edit., 1991, Gulliver and the Gentle Reader, 1973, 2d edit., 1991, Order from Confusion Sprung, 1985, 2d edit., 1992, Satire and Sentiment 1660-1830, 1994; editor: Modern Lang. Rev. and Yearbook of English Studies, London, 1974-78; gen. editor: Cambridge (Eng.) History of Literary Criticism, 1983—, Unwin Critical Libr., London, 1974—, Blackwell Critical Biographies, 1985—; chmn., gen. editor: Yale Boswell Papers, 1990—. Recipient Cert. of Merit for Disting. Svc. Conf. of Editors of Learned Jours., 1988; Andrew Mellon fellow Clark and Huntington Libr., 1980, 90, Guggenheim fellow, 1991-92, Sr. Faculty fellow Yale U., 1991-92; NEH grantee, 1991. Mem. Modern Humanities Rsch. Assn. (life mem., com. mem. 1974-88), Internat. Soc. 18th Century Studies, Am. Soc. for 18th Century Studies, Brit. Soc. for 18th Century Studies (pres. 1973-74). Office: Yale U Dept English PO Box 208302 New Haven CT 06520-8302

RAWSON, ELEANOR S., publishing company executive; m. Kennett Longley Rawson (dec.); children: Kennett Longley, Linda. V.p., exec. editor David McKay Co.; exec. v.p., editor-in-chief Rawson, Wade Publishers, Inc.; v.p. Scribner Book Cos.; pub. Rawson Assocs. (divsn. Macmillan Pub. Co.), v.p., chmn.; teaching staff Columbia U.; now pub. Rawson Assocs./Simon & Schuster; lectr. NYU, New Sch., N.Y.; organizer, panelist various writers' confs.; mem. exec. coun., nominating chair Am. Assn. Pubs., 1970-74. Former editorial staff writer Am. mag.; free-lance writer radio and mags., newspaper syndicates; fiction editor Collier's mag., Today's Woman. Trustee, past v.p. Museums at Stony Brook. Mem. Assn. Women's Nat. Book Assn., P.E.N., Am. Assn. Museums, Yale Club, Cosmopolitan Club, Old Field Club, Women's Forum, Women In Media, Women in Comms. Office: 1230 Avenue Of The Americas New York NY 10020-1513

RAWSON, ERIC GORDON, optical engineer; b. Saskatoon, Sask., Can., Mar. 4, 1937; s. Donald Strathern and Hildred Iantha (Patton) R.; m. Zivile Anne Nalivaika, May 5, 1966; children: Carol, Dalia, Cliff. BA, U. Saskatchewan, 1959, MA, 1960; PhD, U. Toronto, Ont., 1966. Mem. tech. staff Bell Telephone Labs., Murray Hill, N.J., 1966-73; mem. rsch. staff Xerox PARC, Palo Alto, Calif., 1973-78, area mgr., 1978-94; pres. Rawson Optics, Saratoga, Calif., 1994—; bd. dirs., sec. Alamed. Corp., Palo Alto, 1991—. Editor: Book of Milestones Fiber Optics Local Area Networks, 1994; contbr. over 60 articles to profl. jours. Fellow Optical Soc. Am. (mem. engring. coun. 1995—, Engring. Excellence award 1 990), Soc. Photo-Instrumentation Engrs.; mem. IEEE (sr.). Achievements include over 25 patents for optics and biomedical monitoring. Home and Office: 20887 Maureen Way Saratoga CA 95070-3014

RAWSON, WILLIAM ROBERT, lawyer, retired manufacturing company executive; b. Montclair, N.J., Mar. 14, 1925; s. William Howard and Maude Elizabeth (Wheeler) R.; m. Elizabeth S. Crandall, Sept. 30, 1949; children—Shirley, Jean, Elizabeth. A.B., Brown U., 1947; LL.B., N.Y. U., 1950. Bar: N.J. 1950, Ill. 1974. Practice of law Bloomfield, N.J., 1950-52; legal asst. Thomas A. Edison Industries, West Orange, N.J., 1952-57; asst. counsel T.A. Edison div. McGraw-Edison Co., Elgin, Ill., 1957-67; v.p. adminstrn., div. T.A. Edison div. McGraw-Edison Co., 1967-72, asst. gen. counsel, 1972-77, corp. v.p. adminstrn., 1977-80, v.p. law, adminstrn. also corporate sec., 1980-85; corp. counsel L. Kaiser/Estech div. Vigoro Industries, Inc., Savannah, Ga., 1985-89; dir. Chgo. Econ. Devel. Corp. Chmn. Millburn (N.J.) Planning Bd. and Bd. Adjustment, 1962-70, Millburn Red Cross, 1969-70; mem. twp. coun., dep. mayor Twp. of Millburn, 1970-72; v.p. Elgin (Ill.) United Way, 1978-79; bd. dirs. United Way Suburban Chgo., 1981-85; pres. Regional Adult Literacy Partnership, Savannah, 1990-91; pres., bd. dirs. The Landings Homeowners Assn., 1992-94, pres., 1992-93. Lt. (j.g.) USN, 1943-46. Mem. ABA, Ill. State Bar Assn., Am. Arbitration Assn. (arbitrator constrn. industry panel 1985—), Elgin C. of C. (v.p. 1978-79). Republican. Episcopalian. Home: 4 Sandsfield Way Savannah GA 31411-2511

RAY, ALBERT, family physician; b. N.Y.C., Aug. 8, 1948; s. Herman and Stella (Meritz) R.; m. Cheryl Antecol, Oct. 8, 1977; children: Heather, Erin, Samantha. BA, Bklyn. Coll., 1969; MD, Catholic U. of Louvain, Belgium, 1976. Diplomate Am. Bd. Family Practice, Canadian Coll. Family Physicians. Intern Meml. U. of NFLD, Saint John's, Canada, 1976; resident McGill U., Montreal, Canada, 1978; family physician SCPMG, San Diego, 1978—; assoc. clin. prof. U. Calif., San Diego, 1978—; mem. cmty. faculty UCLA, USD, U. Calif., Davis, USC; mem. clerkship cmty. adv. bd. U. Calif., San Diego, 1995—; pres. profl. staff Kaiser Found. Hosp.; bd. dirs. So. Calif. Perm. Med Group. Author: Lecons d'Histologie, 1973. Program chair adult edn. Cong. Beth Israel, 1995; mem. bd. dirs. Temple Emanuel, San Diego, 1990; expert reviewer Med. Bd. Calif., 1995; bd. dirs. Agy. for Jewish Edn.; spl. med. cons. Calif. Dept. of Corrections, 1996. Fellow Am. Acad. Family Physicians; mem. Calif. Med. Assn., San Diego County Med. Soc. (mem. profl. conduct com. 1994), San Diego Acad. Family Physicians (pres.), Calif. Acad. Physicians (trustee found.), Calif. Acad. of Family Physicians (chair scientific program com. 1997). Avocations: golf, tennis, travel, antiques. Office: Kaiser Permanente 4405 Vandever Ave San Diego CA 92120-3315

RAY, ANNETTE D., business executive; b. Decatur, Ind., Mar. 24, 1950; d. Gilbert O. and Florence L. Hoffman; m. Richard M. Ray, Nov. 28, 1975; children: Michelle Ann, Ellen Marie, Laura Leigh, David Richard, Ruth Anne. AA, Concordia Jr. Coll., Ann Arbor, Mich., 1970; BS, Concordia Tchrs. Coll., Seward, Nebr., 1972; attended, Ctrl. Fla. C.C., Ocala, 1974. Lic. real estate, Ind.; lic. tchr., Ind., Fla. Elem. tchr. St. John's Luth., Ocala, 1972-74; mgr. apt. complex Victoria Sq. Apts., Ft. Wayne, Ind., 1974-75; substitute tchr. East Allen County Schs., Allen County, Ind., 1976-79, Circut A Luth. Schs., Adams and Allen County, Ind., 1977-81; corp. sec., treas., office mgr. Heritage Wire Die, Monroeville, Ind., 1987—. Co-author, co-editor: 1928-1988 A Rememberance, 1988, Coming to America--32 Families 1597-1997. Vol. Monroeville C. of C., 1987—, Concerned Area Residents Quality Edn., Allen County, 1990—, Am. Cancer Soc., Allen County, 1991—, chairperson Celebrity Bagger Day, 1995, 96; bd. dirs. Hoagland (Ind.) Hist. Soc., 1985—. Lutheran. Avocations: remodeling old homes, reading, genealogy, gardening, floral arranging. Home: 16901 Berning Rd Hoagland IN 46745-9753 Office: Heritage Wire Die Inc 19819 Monroeville Rd Monroeville IN 46773-9113

RAY, BETTY JEAN G., lawyer; b. New Orleans, June 7, 1943; d. William E. George and Iris U. (Berthold) Grizzell; m. Gerald L. Ray, June 9, 1962; children: Gerald L. Ray, Jr., Brian P. BS Psychology, La. State U., 1976, JD, 1980. Bar: La., 1980; U.S. Dist. Ct. (ea., mid. and we. dists.) La. 1981; U.S. Ct. Appeal (5th cir.) 1981. Jud. law clk. 19th Jud. Dist. Ct., Baton Rouge, 1980-81; atty. Jean G. Ray, Baton Rouge, 1981-83; counsel Gulf Stream, Inc., Baton Rouge, 1982-83; staff atty. La. Dept. Justice, Baton Rouge, 1983-84, asst. atty. gen., 1984-87; staff atty. FDIC, Shreveport, La., 1987-88, mng. atty., 1988-94; spl. dep. receiver Receivership Office, La. Dept. Ins., Baton Rouge, 1994-95; spl. counsel Brook, Pizza & van Loon, L.L.P., Baton Rouge, 1995—. Mem. La. Bar Assn., Baton Rouge Bar Assn., Baton Rouge Assn. Women Attys., Order of Coif, Phi Beta Kappa, Phi Delta Phi (scholar 1980). Episcopalian. Home: 1143 Oakley Dr Baton Rouge LA 70806 Office: Brook Pizza & van Loon Ste 402 9100 Bluebonnet Centre Blvd Baton Rouge LA 70809-2985

RAY, CHARLES AARON, foreign service officer; b. Center, Tex., July 5, 1945; m. Myung Wook Soe, Nov. 3, 1973; children: David Edward, Denise Ellen. BSBA, Benedictine Coll., 1972; MS in Sys. Mgmt., U. So. Calif., 1981; MS in Nat. Security Strategy, Nat. War Coll., 1997. Commd. 2d lt. U.S. Army, 1965, advanced through grades to maj., 1982; consular officer U.S. Consulate Gen., Guangzhou, China, 1983-84; chief consular sect. U.S. Consulate Gen., Shenyang, China, 1985-87; chief adminstrv. sect. U.S. Consulate Gen., Chiangmai, Thailand, 1988-91; spl. asst. to dir. Office Def. Trade Controls, Washington, 1991-93; dep. chief of mission Am. Embassy, Freetown, Sierra Leone, 1993-96; detailed to Nat. War Coll., Washington, 1996-97, Nat. Fgn. Tng. Ctr., Arlington, Va., 1997—. Editl. cartoonist Spring Lake News, 1975-79; contbr. articles to Asia Mag., 1974-79; editor mag. Psyop Digest, 1976-78; exec. editor Def. Trade News, 1992-93. Mem. Heritage Found., Washington, 1991. Avocations: taekwondo, softball, tennis, painting, poetry. Office: Nat Fgn Tng Ctr, Dept of State, Washington Sierra Leone

RAY, CHARLES JACKSON, retired surgeon; b. Greenville, Ala., Dec. 20, 1920; s. Winston J. Ray and Frances G. McMallan; m. Betty Shelton, Mar. 21, 1947; 3 children. MD, Tulane U., 1945. Diplomate Am. Bd. Surgeons, Am. Bd. Colon Rectal Surgeons. Intern Charity Hosp., New Orleans, 1945-46; resident in gen. surgery Tulane U., New Orleans, 1948-49; fellow in gen. surgery Ochsner Clin., New Orleans, 1949-52; pvt. practice Meml. Hosp., Chattanooga; assoc. prof. surgery U. Tenn.; ret., 1995. Fellow ACS; mem. AMA. Address: 324 Marina Blvd Mandeville LA 70471-1532

RAY, CHARLES KENDALL, retired university dean; b. Boise City, Okla., Mar. 15, 1928; s. Volney Holt and Mamie (Burton) R.; m. Doris Derby, Aug. 26, 1951. B.A., U. Colo., 1951; M.A., Columbia, 1955, Ed.D., 1959. Teaching prin. Bur. Indian Affairs, Savoonga, Alaska, 1951-54; mem. faculty U. Alaska, 1957-93, prof. edn., 1960-93, dean Sch. Edn., 1961-80, dir. summer sessions, 1980-93. Author: A Program of Education for Alaska Natives, 1959, Alaskan Native Secondary School Dropouts, 1961. Mem. N.E.A., Am. Assn. Sch. Adminstrs., Am. Assn. U. Profs., Am. Assn. Colls. Tchr. Edn. (state liaison officer), Phi Delta Kappa. Home: 2000 1st Ave Apt 2204 Seattle WA 98121-2171

RAY, CREAD L., JR., retired state supreme court justice; b. Waskom, Tex., Mar. 10, 1931; s. Cread L. and Antonia (Hardesty) R.; m. Janet Watson Keller, Aug. 12, 1977; children: Sue Ann (dec.), Robert E., Glenn L., David B., Marcie Lynn, Anne Marie. B.B.A., Tex. A&M U., 1952; J.D., U. Tex., 1957; L.H.D. (hon.), Wiley Coll., Marshall, Tex., 1980. Bar: Tex. 1957. Practiced in Marshall, 1957-59; judge Harrison County, 1959-61; justice 6th dist. Ct. Civil Appeals, Texarkana, 1970-80, Supreme Ct. Tex., 1980-90; ret. Supreme Ct. Tex., Austin, 1990; prin. C.L Ray, Austin, 1991—. Past pres. Marshall Jaycees, Marshall C. of C.; mem. Tex. Ho. of Reps., 1966-70; active local, regional, nat. Boy Scouts Am.; trustee Wiley Coll. Lt. col. USAF, 1952-54, Korea; ret. Recipient various Boy Scouts awards. Mem. State Bar Tex., N.E. Tex. Bar Assn. (past pres.), VFW, Am. Legion, Rotary, Tex. Aggies. Democrat. Methodist. Home: 604 Beardsley Ln Austin TX 78746 Office: 400 W 15th St Ste 600 Austin TX 78701-1647

RAY, DENNIS JAY, utilities and business educator, researcher; b. Hobbs, N.Mex., Jan. 29, 1950; s. J.W. and Beatrice Doris (Smith) R.; m. Mary Barnard, June 7, 1973; children: Mark Wilson, Kathryn Barnard, William Eric. BSEE, U. N.Mex., 1972; MBA in Finance, U. Wis., 1983, PhD in Bus., 1987. Rsch. analyst Pub. Svcs. Commn. Wis., Madison, 1977-79; rsch. asst. U. Wis., Madison, 1979-82; program mgr. Wis. Pub. Utility Inst., Madison, 1982-87, dir, 1987—; asst. prof. sch. bus. U. Wis., Madison, 1992—; mem. rsch. adv. com. Wis. Ctr. for Demand-Side Rsch., Madison, 1992-95; mem. Power Sys. Engring. Rsch. Consortium. Contbr. articles to profl. jours. Chmn. pastoral rels. com. First Bapt. Ch., Madison, 1988-89, chmn. budget com., 1993-94; bd. dirs. Capital City United Youth Soccer, Madison, 1990-91, Wayland Found., Madison, 1992—. Mem. IEEE, Am. Econ. Assn., Transp. and Pub. Utilities Group (vice chmn. 1994, chmn. 1995). Avocations: travel, camping, computers, softball. Office: Wis Pub Utility Inst U Wis Madison Sch Bus 975 University Ave Madison WI 53706-1324

RAY, DONALD HENSLEY, biologist; b. Hamilton AFB, Calif., Sept. 23, 1952; s. Cecil C. and Harriet Ellen (Graham) R.; m. Joni Lynn Rogers, June 26, 1976. AA, Okaloosa Walton Jr. Coll., 1972; BS in Biology, U. West Fla., 1974. Range technician Vitro Services, Eglin AFB, Fla., 1972; survey asst. Lowe Engrs., Fort Walton Beach, Fla., 1972; research asst. Hennison, Durham, Richardson Engrs., Pensacola, Fla., 1973-74, U. West Fla., Pensacola, 1974; v.p. Theta Analysis, Inc., Pensacola, 1974-75, pres., 1975; biologist Fla. Dept. Environ. Regulation, Gulf Breeze, Fla., 1976—, biol. scientist supr., 1989—, environ. specialist, 1990, environ. supr., 1992; charter affiliate Jour. Freshwater Invertebrate Biology, Port Washington, Wis., 1982; staff mem. Gov.'s Fla. Rivers Study com., Tallahassee, Fla., 1985; research subcom. Bayou Area Foresight com., Pensacola, 1987—; mem. Fla. Dept. Environ. Regulations Biocriteria Com., Tallahassee, 1991; mem. environ. adv. com. Pensacola Jr. Coll., Milton, Fla., 1991. Contbr. articles to profl. jours. Mem. N.Am. Benthological Soc., Southeastern Pollution Biologists Assn. (exec. com., moderator 1985—), Fla. Benthological Assn., Sigma Xi. Discovered hydroperla phormidia species U.S. Nat. Mus. Natural History at Smithsonian Inst., Washington, 1981. Avocations: sports, natural history. Office: Fla Dept Environ Protection 160 Governmental Ctr Pensacola FL 32501

RAY, DOUGLAS, newspaper executive. Sr. v.p. Daily Herald/Sunday Herald, Arlington Heights, Ill. Office: Daily Herald/Sunday Herald Paddock Publs PO Box 280 Arlington Heights IL 60006-0280

RAY, EDWARD JOHN, economics educator, administrator; b. Jackson Heights, N.Y., Sept. 10, 1944; s. Thomas Paul and Cecelia Francis (Hiney) R.; m. Virginia Beth Phelps, June 14, 1969; children: Stephanie Elizabeth, Katherine Rebecca, Michael Edward. B.A., Queens Coll., CUNY, 1966; M.A., Stanford U., 1969, Ph.D., 1971. Asst. prof. econs. Ohio State U., Columbus, 1970-74, assoc. prof., 1974-77, prof., 1977—, chmn. dept. econs., 1976-92, assoc. provost acad. affairs Office Acad. Affairs, 1992-93; sr. vice provost, chief info. officer Office Acad. Affairs, 1993—; cons. Dept. Labor, 1974-76, Dept. Commerce, 1977; cons. AID, Office Tech. Assessment, winter 1982. Contbr. numerous articles on econs. to profl. jours. Active Upper Arlington Civic Assn., Columbus, 1983—. Mem. Am. Econs. Assn., Western Econ. Assn., Econ. History Assn., Phi Beta Kappa. Home: 1977 Rosebery Dr Columbus OH 43220-3044 Office: Ohio State U Acad Affairs 203 Bricker Hall 190 N Oval Mall Columbus OH 43210-1321

RAY, FRANK ALLEN, lawyer; b. Lafayette, Ind., Jan. 30, 1949; s. Dale Allen and Merry Ann (Fleming) R.; m. Carol Ann Olmutz, Oct. 1, 1982; children: Erica Fleming, Robert Allen. BA, Ohio State U., 1970, JD, 1973. Bar: Ohio 1973, U.S. Dist. Ct. (so. dist.) Ohio 1975, U.S. Supreme Ct. 1976, U.S. Tax Ct. 1977, U.S. Ct. Appeals (6th cir.) 1977, U.S. Dist Ct. (no. dist.) Ohio 1980, Pa. 1983, U.S. Dist. Ct. (ea. dist.) Mich. 1983, U.S. Ct. Appeals (1st cir.) 1986; cert. civil trial adv. Nat. Bd. Trial Advocacy. Asst. pros. atty. Franklin County, Ohio, 1973-75, chief civil counsel, 1976-78; dir. econ. crime project Nat. Dist. Attys. Assn., Washington, 1975-76; assoc. Brownfield, Kosydar, Bowen, Bally & Sturtz, Columbus, Ohio, 1978, Michael F. Colley Co., L.P.A., Columbus, 1979-83; pres. Frank A. Ray Co., L.P.A., Columbus, 1983-93, Ray & Todaro Co., LPA, Columbus, 1993-94, Ray, Todaro & Alton Co., L.P.A., Columbus, 1994-96, Ray, Todaro, Alton & Kirstein Co., L.P.A., Columbus, 1996, Columbus, Ray, Alton & Kirstein Co., L.P.A., 1996-; mem. seminar faculty Nat. Coll. Dist. Attys., Houston, 1975-77; mem. nat. conf. faculty Fed. Jud. Ctr., Washington, 1976-77; bd. mem. bar examiners Ohio Supreme Ct., 1992-95, Rules Adv. Com., 1995—. Editor: Economic Crime Digest, 1975-76; co-author: Personal Injury Litigation Practice in Ohio, 1988, 91. Mem. fin. com. Franklin County Rep. Orgn., Columbus, 1979-84; trustee Ohio State U. Coll. Humanities Alumni Soc., 1991-93. 1st lt. inf. U.S. Army, 1973. Named to Ten Outstanding Young Citizens of Columbus, Columbus Jaycees, 1976; recipient Nat. award of Distinctive Svc., Nat. Dist. Attys. Assn., 1977. Fellow Am. Coll. Trial Lawyers, Internat. Soc. Barristers, Columbus Bar Found., Roscoe Pound Found., Ohio Acad. Trial Lawyers; mem. ABA, Am. Bd. Trial Advocates (trustee Ohio chpt. 1996—), Columbus Bar Assn. (com. profl. ethics and grievances 1990-93, chmn. professionalism com. 1994-96, bd. govs. 1996—), Ohio State Bar Assn. (com. negligence law 1990—), Assn. Trial Lawyers Am. (state del. 1990-92), Ohio Acad. Trial Lawyers (trustee 1984-87, sec. 1987-88, pres.-elect 1988-89, pres. 1989-90, legis. coord. 1986-88, Pres.' award 1986), Franklin County Trial Lawyers Assn. (trustee 1982-83, treas. 1984-85, chmn. com. negligence law 1983-87, sec. 1985-86, v.p. 1986-87, pres. 1987-88, Pres.'s award 1990), Inns of Ct. (sec. Judge Robert M. Duncan chpt. 1991-93, pres. 1993-94). Presbyterian. Home: 2030 Tremont Rd Columbus OH 43221-4330 Office: 175 S 3rd St Ste 350 Columbus OH 43215-5134

RAY, FRANK DAVID, government agency official; b. Mt. Vernon, Ohio, Dec. 1, 1940; s. John Paul and Lola Mae (Miller) R.; children: Susan M., Frank D. II; BS in Edn., Ohio State U., 1964, JD, 1967. Bar: Ohio 1967, U.S. Dist. Ct. 1969, U.S. Cir. Ct. Appeals (6th cir.) 1970, U.S. Supreme Ct. 1971. Legal aide to atty. gen. Ohio, 1965-66; bailiff probate ct., Franklin County, Ohio, 1966-67, gen. referee, 1967-68; with firm Stouffer, Wait and Ashbrook, Columbus, Ohio, 1967-71; jour. clk. Ohio Ho. of Reps., 1969-71; dist. dir. SBA, 1971—; mem. Ohio Pub. Defender Commn., 1983-91; mem. U.S. Dept. Commerce So. Ohio Dist. Export Council, 1988—; mem. Ohio Export Promotion and Trade Coun., 1992-96, Ohio Rural Devel. Coun., 1993—; mem. vocat. edn. adv. com. Columbus Pub. Schs., 1993-95; mem. Columbus Mayor's Econ. Devel. Council, 1983-84; mem. Small Bus. and High Tech. adv. com. Ohio Div. Securities, 1983-84; mem. tech. alliance Central Ohio Adv. Bd., 1983-89; mem. Ohio Small Bus. and Entrepreneurship Coun., 1994-95. Editl. adv. bd. Columbus CEO Mag., 1995-96. Mem. Upper Arlington (Ohio) Bd. Health, 1970-75; pres. Buckeye Republican Club, 1970, Franklin County Forum, 1970; chmn. Central Ohio chpt. Nat. Found.-March of Dimes, 1974-77; trustee Columbus Acad. Contemporary Art, 1976. Recipient Service award Nat. Found.-March of Dimes, 1974, 75, 76, 77; Am. Jurisprudence award for Excellence, 1967, In Search of Excellence award SBA, 1985; named Ohio Commodore, 1973. Mem. Leadership Columbus (grad. 1976), Delta Upsilon, Alpha Epsilon Delta. Clubs: Ohio Press, Ohio State U. Pres. Home: 4200 Dublin Rd Columbus OH 43221-5005

RAY, GAYLE ELROD, sheriff; b. Murfreesboro, Tenn., Oct. 22, 1945; d. Jesse Smith and Jennie Hare (McElroy) Elrod; m. Roy Norman Ray, Dec. 27, 1970; children: Molly Elizabeth, Austin Elrod. BA, Mid. Tenn. State U., 1967; MA, U. Ark., 1969; MBA, Belmont U., 1989. Instr. English La. State U., Baton Rouge, 1969-72, Tenn. State U., Nashville, 1972-76; program coord. Vanderbilt U., Nashville, 1992-94; sheriff Davidson County, Nashville, 1994—. Pres. LWV, Nashville, 1987-89; mem. Women's Polit. Caucus, Nashville, 1987—; mem. alumni bd. Leadership Nashville, 1993. Recipient Polit. Star award Davidson County Dem. Women, 1993, Athena award, 1997. Avocations: reading, hiking.

RAY, GENE WELLS, industrial executive; b. Murray, Ky., Apr. 23, 1938; s. Terry Lee and Loreen (Lovett) R.; m. Becky Huie, Mar. 5, 1956 (dec. 1976); m. Taffin Ray; children: Don Dickerson, Kathy Pratt, Nancy Solomon. BS in Math., Physics and Chemistry, Murray State U., 1956; MS in Physics, U. Tenn., 1962, PhD in Theoretical Physics, 1965. With tech. staff Aerospace Corp., San Bernardino, Calif., 1965-68; mgr. strategic div. USAF (OA), Washington, 1968-70; scientist, sr. v.p., systems group mgr. Sci. Applications Inc., La Jolla, Calif., 1970-81, also bd. dirs.; pres., chief exec. officer Titan Systems Inc., San Diego, 1981-85, ceo, 1985—; assoc. prof. Carson Newman Coll., Tenn., 1964-65. Inventor mass flow meter. 1st lt. USAR, 1963-68. Republican. Avocations: tennis, wine collecting. Home: PO Box 2464 Rancho Santa Fe CA 92067-2464 Office: Titan Corp 3033 Science Park Rd San Diego CA 92121-1101

RAY, GEORGE EINAR, lawyer; b. Gloucester, Mass., Apr. 23, 1910; s. Matti and Sandra Sofia (Kujala) R.; m. Mary Lee Osborne, Sept. 7, 1940 (dec.); children: Mary Danforth White, Priscilla Ray Sartwelle, Elizabeth Ray Haenchen, George Einar Jr., Clifford Osborne, Michael Gritton (dec.). AB, Harvard U., 1932, JD, 1935; postgrad. Sch. Mil. Govt., Columbia U., 1944. Bar: Mass. 1935. Practiced in N.Y.C., 1936-38, Boston, 1942-44; lawyer Ray, Trotti, Hemphill, Finfrock & Needham, P.C., Dallas, 1946-94, pvt. practice, Dallas, 1995—; faculty assoc. Sch. Law Columbia U., 1935-36; atty. U.S. Bd. Tax Appeals, Washington, 1938-41; spl. asst. to atty. gen. U.S., tax divsn. U.S. Dept. Justice, 1941; prin. atty. Office Tax Legis. Counsel, U.S. Dept. Treasury, 1941-42; adj. prof. So. Meth. U. Law Sch., NYU Tax Inst., Practicing Law Inst.; head dept. internat. law Naval Sch. Mil. Govt., Princeton, 1944-45; chief counsel Office Army-Navy Liquidation Commr., M.T.O., 1945; dep. exec. dir. Office Fgn. Liquidation Commr., State Dept., 1946. Author: Incorporating the Professional Practice, 1972, 3d edit., 1984; also articles in legal publs. Deacon Bapt. Ch. Lt. comdr. USNR, WWII. Mem. Am., Tex., Dallas County bar assns., Tex. Bar, Tex. Bar Found., Southwestern Legal Found., Harvard Law Sch. Assn. Tex. (ex-pres.), Dallas Estate Coun. (pres. 1949-50), Northwood Club, Harvard Club (pres. 1950-51), Salesmanship Club, Dallas Knife and Fork Club (pres. 1967-68). Home: 12615 Breckenridge Dr Dallas TX 75230-2001

RAY, GEORGE WASHINGTON, III, English language educator; b. Binghamton, N.Y., Dec. 4, 1932; s. George Washington and Margaret (Nicholson) R.; m. Elizabeth DuPree Osborn, Dec. 29, 1956; children—Virginia, George, Melissa, Grace Elizabeth. A.B., Wesleyan U., 1954; postgrad., Colgate U., 1957-59; Ph.D., U. Rochester, 1966. Instr. English U. Rochester, N.Y., 1961-62, U. Va., Charlottesville, 1962-64; instr. English Washington and Lee U., Lexington, Va., 1964-66; asst. prof. Washington and Lee U., 1966-69, assoc. prof., 1969-74, prof., 1974—, acting chmn. dept., 1985, 91-92; vis. fellow Univ. Coll., Oxford (Eng.) U., 1980. Editor: Duke of Byron, 1979, The Chi Psi Story, 1995. Bd. dirs. Rockbridge Concert-Theater Series, 1966-83, Lime Kiln Arts Inc., 1983-86, Rockbridge Area Mental Health Assn., 1975-78, English Speaking Union, 1993—. Served as 1st lt. USMC, 1954-57. Recipient various fellowships. Mem. Southeastern Renaissance Conf., Renaissance Soc. Am., Chi Psi (nat. Disting. Svc. award 1985, trustee ednl. trust 1989-95, nat. pres. 1995—), Am. Soc. Theatre Rsch. Democrat. Presbyterian (elder 1979-85, 89-91). Home: 13 Sellers Ave Lexington VA 24450-1930 Office: Dept English Washington and Lee U Lexington VA 24450

RAY, GILBERT T., lawyer; b. Mansfield, Ohio, Sept. 18, 1944; s. Robert Lee Ray and Renatha (Goldie) Washington; m. Valerie J. Reynolds, June 14, 1969; children: Tanika, Tarlin. BA, Ashland Coll., 1966; MBA, U. Toledo, 1968; JD, Howard U., 1972. Assoc. O'Melveny & Myers, Los Angeles, 1972-79, ptnr., 1980—. Bd. dirs. Host Marriott Svcs. Corp., L.A. Area C. of C., NAACP Legal Def. Fund, Haynes Found., Ashland U., UCLA/Hammer Mus. Mem. Riviera Club (L.A.), The Calif. Club, L.A. Country Club. Democrat. Office: O'Melveny & Myers 400 S Hope St Los Angeles CA 90071-2801

RAY, H. M., lawyer; b. Rienzi, Miss., Aug. 9, 1924; s. Thomas Henry and Isabelle (Dunlap) R.; m. Merle Burt, Nov. 28, 1953 (dec. Dec. 1993); children: Howard Manfred, Mark Andrew. J.D., U. Miss., 1949. Bar: Miss. 1949. U.S. atty. No. Dist. Miss. Oxford, 1961-81; pvt. practice law Corinth, Miss., 1949-61, Jackson, Miss., 1981-85, 90—; asst. atty. gen. State of Miss., Jackson, 1986-90; mem. Atty. Gen.'s Adv. Com. U.S. Attys., 1973-78, chmn., 1976; vis. lectr. UN, Asia and Far East, UN (Inst. for Prevention Crime and Treatment of Offenders), Tokyo, 1977; pros. atty. Alcorn County, Miss., 1956-57, 68-61; mem. Miss. Ho. of RReps., 1948-51; mem. Miss. Gov.'s Com. to Study Laws Regarding Use of Deadly Force on Fleeing Felons, 1982-83, Miss. Gov.'s Constl. Study Commn., 1985-86. Co-author: Miss. Workmens' Compensation Act, 1948. Chmn. Corinth-Alcorn County Airport Bd., 1959-61; trustee Alcorn County Public Library, 1959-62. Served with USAAC, 1943-45, ETO; with USAF, 1951-53. Recipient Corinth's Young Man of Yr. award, 1958. Presbyterian (elder). Clubs: Kiwanis (lt. gov. 1955-56, dist. chmn. 1956-57, pres. Corinth 1943-53). Home: 12 Windy Ridge Cv Jackson MS 39211-2904 Office: PO Box 13415 Jackson MS 39236-3415

RAY, HUGH MASSEY, JR., lawyer; b. Vicksburg, Miss., Feb. 1, 1943; s. Hugh Massey and Lollie Landon (Powell) R.; m. Florence Hargrove, Sept. 3, 1966; children—Hugh, Hallie. B.A., Vanderbilt U., 1965, J.D., 1967. Bar: Tex. 1967, U.S. Dist. Ct. (so. dist.) Tex. 1967, U.S. Dist.Ct. (we. dist.) La. 1979, U.S. Dist. Ct. (we. dist.) Tex. 1979, U.S. Dist. Ct. (no. dist.) Tex. 1980, U.S. Ct. Appeals (11th cir.) 1982, U.S. Dist. Ct. (no. dist.) Calif. 1989, D.C. 1991, N.Y. 1992. Asst. U.S. atty. So. Dist. Tex., 1967-68; assoc. Andrews & Kurth, Houston, 1968-77, ptnr., 1977—; lectr. Ctrl. and Ea. European Law Initiative, Vilnius, Lithuania, 1996. Co-author: Bankruptcy Investing, 1992; editor-in-chief Creditor's Rights in Texas, 1975; contbr. articles to law revs. Mem. ABA (chmn. real property practice com. 1975-77, chmn. continuing legal edn. com. young lawyers divsn. 1976-78, vice chmn. 1979, chmn. oil and gas subcom. bus. bankruptcy com. 1985-89, chmn. executory contracts subcom. 1989-93, chmn. bus. bankruptcy com. 1993-96, chair com. on trust indentures and indenture trustees 1995—, mem. standing com. on jud. selection, tenure and compensation 1996—), Fed. Bar Assn., Houston Bar Assn., Tex. Bar Assn. (chmn. bankruptcy com. 1985-88), Am. Law Inst., Tex. Bd. Legal Specialization (cert.), Pro Bono Coll. State Bar Tex., Houston Country Club, Tex. Club, Houston Club. Episcopalian. Home: 5785 Indian Cir Houston TX 77057-1302 Office: Andrews & Kurth 4200 Tex Commerce Tower Houston TX 77002

RAY, JAMES ALLEN, research consultant; b. Lexington, Ky., Feb. 21, 1931; s. Allen Brice and Elizabeth Logan (Simpson) R.; m. Mary Ruth Johnston, June 8, 1958; children: James Edward, Allen Bruce, John David. BS in Geology, U. N.C., 1958; MS, N.C. State Coll., 1962. Chief petrographic rsch. Master Builders divsn. Martin Marietta Corp., Cleve., 1959-73, asst. dir. rsch., 1973-77, dir. rsch., 1977-78, dir. rsch. and engring, 1978-79, v.p. rsch., 1979-80, v.p. creative rsch., 1980-82; cons., 1982—; pres. James A. Ray Corp. 1986—. Patentee in field. With USAF, 1951-55. Recipient Jefferson cup Martin Marietta Corp., 1977. Fellow Am. Inst. Chemists, Inc.; mem. ASTM, Res. Officers Assn. (life), NRA (life), Ret. Officers Assn. (life). Republican. Home: 9891 Stamm Rd PO Box 1072 Mantua OH 44255

RAY, JEANNE CULLINAN, lawyer, insurance company executive; b. N.Y.C., May 5, 1943; d. Thomas Patrick and Agnes Joan (Buckley) C.; m. John Joseph Ray, Jan. 20, 1968 (dec. Mar. 1993); children: Christopher Lawrence, Douglas James. Student, Univ. Coll., Dublin, Ireland, 1963; AB, Coll. Mt. St. Vincent, Riverdale, N.Y., 1964; LLB, Fordham U., 1967. Bar: N.Y. 1967. Atty. Mut. Life Ins. Co. N.Y. (MONY), N.Y.C., 1967-68, asst. counsel, 1969-72, assoc. counsel, 1972-73, counsel, 1974-75, asst. gen. counsel, 1976-80, assoc. gen counsel, 1981-83, v.p. pension counsel, 1984-85, v.p. area counsel group and pension ops., 1985-87; v.p. sector counsel group and pension ops., 1988, v.p., chief counsel exec. and corp. affairs, 1988-89; v.p. law, sec. MONY Securities Corp., N.Y.C., 1980-85; v.p. law, sec. MONY Advisers, Inc., N.Y.C., 1980-88; sec. MONYCO, Inc., N.Y.C., 1980-85; v.p., counsel MONY Series Fund, Inc., Balt., 1984-87; v.p., assoc. gen. counsel Tchrs. Ins. and Annuity Assoc. Coll. Ret. Equities Fund (TIAA-CREF), N.Y.C., 1989-91, v.p., chief counsel ins., 1991—. Contbr. articles to legal jours. Cubmaster, den mother Greater N.Y. coun. Boy Scouts Am., N.Y.C., 1978-84, mem. bd. rev. and scouting com., 1985—. Mem. ABA (chmn employee benefits com. Tort and Ins. Practice sect. 1981-82, vice-chmn. 1983-96), Assn. Life Ins. Counsel (chmn. policyholders tax com. tax sect. 1982-91, vice chmn. tax sect. 1991-93, chmn. 1993—), Assn. Bar City N.Y. (chmn. employee benefits com. 1992-95), Investment Co. Inst. (mem. pension com. 1993—, Am. Coun. Life Ins. (chmn. fiduciary task force of pension com. 1990—), Am. Coun. Life Ins. Democrat. Roman Catholic.

RAY, JENNY, artist; b. Ontario, Oreg.; d. Thompson and Othela Jean Towell Carper; m. Gary Wayne Limbaugh, Apr. 14, 1971; children: Cindy Sue, Tina Marie, Kay Jean, Tamara Rae, Cody Wayne. Cosmetologist, Pendleton (Oreg.) Coll. Beauty, 1972; student, Blue Mountain C.C., 1979-80, Ea. Oreg. State Coll., 1991-92. Owner Butter Creek Beauty Salon, Hermiston, Oreg., 1977-80, Pretty Quick Constrn. Co., Hermiston, Oreg., 1978-93, McCord's Corner Art Gallery, Baker City, Oreg., 1986-88, Creations, Inc., Baker City, 1984-85, Western Mountain Art, Inc., Joseph, Oreg., 1982-95, Age of Bronze Art Foundry, Joseph, 1992-95, Moriah Foundry, Inc., Wallowa, Oreg., 1995—. Author: Self Esteem Repair in Recovery, 1992; artist oil portraits of famous native Americans, 1985—; one woman shows at McCords Corner Art Gallery, 1986, Klondikes of Baker City, 1987, Baker County Chamber Office, 1988, Sumpter Valley R.R. Baker, 1988. Asst. dir. Ch. of Christ Christian Sch., Hermiston, 1980, Wallowa Valley Players, Joseph, 1990-92; econ. devel. com. Wallowa Valley Arts Coun., Enterprise, Oreg., 1993—; exec. dir. Wallowa Valley Mktg. Assn., Joseph, 1994; chair Jane Jefferson Club, Pendleton, Oreg., 1975; del. Umatilla County Dem. Com., Pendleton, 1976; campaign chair Jimmy Carter Campaign, Umatilla County, 1976; mem. Dakota Sioux Tribe. Recipient Cert. of Merit Pendleton Coll. Beauty, 1980; Western Art Prodns. scholar, 1988; Ea. Oreg. Regional Arts Commn. grantee, 1996; recycle project grantee Sustainable N.W., 1996. Mem. Lakota Sioux Tribe, Nat. Mus. of the Am. Indian (charter), Nat. Mus. of Women in the Arts, Smithsonian Assocs., Grant County Art Assn., Union County Art Guild, Cross Roads Art Ctr. Avocations: fishing, hiking, raising and training Egyptian Arabian horses, camping, writing. Home: PO Box 516 Wallowa OR 97885-0516 Office: Moriah Foundry Inc 101 S Storie Wallowa OR 97885

RAY, JOHN WALKER, otolaryngologist, educator, broadcast commentator; b. Columbus, Ohio, Jan. 12, 1936; s. Kenneth Clark and Hope (Walker) Ray; m. Susanne Gettings, July 15, 1961; children: Nancy Ann, Susan Christy. AB magna cum laude, Marietta Coll., 1956; MD cum laude, Ohio State U., 1960; postgrad. Temple U., 1964, Mt. Sinai Hosp. and Columbia U., 1964, 66, Northwestern U., 1967, 71, U. Ill., 1968, U. Ind., 1969, Tulane U., 1969. Intern, Ohio State U. Hosps., Columbus, 1960-61, clin. rsch. trainee NIH, 1963-65, resident dept. otolaryngology, 1963-65, 1966-67, resident dept. surgery 1965-66, instr. dept. otolaryngology, 1966-67, 70-75, clin. asst. prof., 1975-82, clin. assoc. prof., 1982-92, clin. prof., 1992—; active staff, past chief of staff Bethesda Hosp.; active staff, past chief of staff Good Samaritan Hosp., Zanesville, Ohio, 1967—; courtesy staff Ohio State U. Hosps., Columbus, 1970—; hon. active staff Meml. Hosp., Marietta, Ohio, 1992—; radio-TV health commentator, 1982—. Past pres. Muskingum chpt. Am. Cancer Soc.; bd. dirs. Zanesville Art Ctr. Capt. USAF, 1961-63. Recipient Barraquer Meml. award, 1965; named to Order of Ky. Col., 1966, Muskingum County Country Music Hall of Fame. Diplomate Am. Bd. Otolaryngology. Fellow ACS, Am. Soc. Otolaryn. Allergy, Am. Acad. Otolaryngology-Head and Neck Surgery (gov.), Am. Acad. Facial Plastic and Reconstructive Surgery; mem. Nat. Assn. Physician Broadcasters, Muskingum County Acad. Medicine (past pres.), AMA (del. hosp. med. Staff sect.), Ohio Med. Assn. (del.), Columbus Ophthalmol. and Otolaryngol. Soc. (past pres.), Ohio Soc. Otolaryngology (past pres.), Pan-Am. Assn. Otolaryngology and Bronchoesophagology, Pan-Am. Allergy Soc., Am. Acad. Invitro Allergy, Am. Soc. Contemporary Medicine and Surgery, Acad. Radio and TV Health Communicators, Fraternal Order Police Assocs., Phi Beta Kappa, Alpha Tau Omega, Alpha Kappa Kappa, Alpha Omega Alpha, Beta Beta Beta. Presbyterian. Contbr. articles to sci., med. jours; collaborator with surg. motion picture: Laryngectomy and Neck Dissection, 1964. Office: 2945 Maple Ave Zanesville OH 43701-1753

RAY, LEO ELDON, fish breeding and marketing company executive; b. Logan County, Okla., Dec. 9, 1937; s. Wilbur Houston and Florence Ivy (Doggett) R.; B.S. in Zoology, U. Okla., 1963; m. Judith Kay Croddy, Aug. 29, 1959; children—Tana Kim, Tod Kent, Kacy Kay. Research asst. U. Okla., 1961-63; tchr. public schs., Dumas, Tex., 1963-64, Grants, N.Mex., 1964-65, Anaheim, Calif., 1965-69; co-owner Fish Breeders, Niland, Calif., 1969-87; owner, pres. Fish Breeders of Idaho, Inc., Buhl, 1971—, Fish Processors, Inc., 1971—. Served with U.S. Army, 1957-60. Mem. Calif. Catfish Farmers Am. (past pres.), Catfish Farmers Am. (past pres., dir.), U.S. Trout Farmers Assn. (past pres., dir.). Address: 4647 River Rd # D Buhl ID 83316-5104

RAY, MICHAEL EDWIN, lawyer; b. Charlotte, N.C., Dec. 13, 1949; s. Daniel Shaw Ray and Jane (Horne) Keziah; m. Janet Langston Jones, July 14, 1973; children: John Daniel, Jennifer Marjory. BA, Furman U., 1972; JD, U. S.C., 1978. Bar: N.C. 1978, S.C. 1978, U.S. Dist. Ct. (ea., mid. and we. dists.) N.C. 1978, U.S. Ct. Appeals (4th cir.) 1981, U.S. Ct. Appeals (Fed. cir.) 1989. Legal adminstr. Wyche Burgess Freeman & Parham, Greenville, S.C., 1973-75; assoc. Womble Carlyle Sandridge & Rice, PLLC, Winston-Salem, N.C., 1978-85, mgr., 1985—. Editor-in-chief S.C. Law Rev., 1977-78. Bd. dirs. Piedmont Opera Theatre, Inc., 1997—; active S.C. Manpower Planning Coun., Columbia, 1971-72. T.B. Clarkson scholar Furman U., 1971-72. Mem. ABA, N.C. Bar Assn., S.C. Bar Assn., Fed. Cir. Bar Assn. (bd. govs. 1994-97), Am. Intellectual Property Law Assn., N.C. Assn. Def. Attys., Forsyth County Bar Assn., Furman U. Alumni Assn. (bd. govs. 1995—), Lex Mundi, Ltd. (dir., 1995—, sec. 1996-97). Democrat. Presbyterian. Avocations: sailing, woodworking, music. Home: 4269 Stonehenge Ln Winston Salem NC 27106-3535 Office: Womble Carlyle Sandridge & Rice PLLC PO Drawer 84 Winston Salem NC 27102-0084

RAY, NORMAN WILSON, career officer; b. Hillsboro, Ill., June 26, 1942; s. Glen B. and Courtenay (Sandifer) R.; m. Priscilla Songer, Dec. 27, 1964; children: Melinda Caron, Molly Ellen. BS, U.S. Naval Acad., 1964. Commd. ensign USN, 1964, advanced through grades to vice adm., 1992, pilot Patrol Squadron 50, 1965; with Test Pilot Sch., 1969; project test pilot Naval Air Test Ctr. USN, 1970-72; advanced VP systems project officer Naval Air Systems USN, Washington, 1972-75; pilot Patrol Squadron 16 USN, Jacksonville, Fla., 1975-78; comdr. Patrol Squadron 56 USN, 1978-81; air readiness officer ASW Systems Project Office USN, Washington, 1981-82; naval armaments officer, dep. nat. armaments rep. U.S. Mission to NATO, Brussels, 1982-84; air ASW br. head, dep. div. dir. for force level plans and warfare appraisal Dir. Naval Warfare, Washington, 1984-87; exec. asst., naval aide Under Sec. Navy, Washington, 1987-88; comdr. Naval Air Sta., Jacksonville, 1988-89; exec. asst. Sec. Navy, Washington, 1989-90; dir. Office of Program Appraisal USN, 1990-92; dep. chmn. NATO Mil. Com., Brussels, 1992-95; ret., 1995; asst. sec. gen. for def. support NATO, 1995—. Decorated D.S.M., Legion of Merit with 2 gold stars. Mem. Army and Navy Club (Washington and Arlington, Va.). Avocation: golf. Office: USNATO/USM PSC 81 Box 151 APO AE 09724

RAY, PAUL DUBOSE, lawyer; b. Barnwell, S.C., July 1, 1966; s. Albert DuBose and Harriet Jane (LaMaster) R. BA, Furman U., 1988; JD, U. S.C., 1991. Bar: S.C. Asst. contracts atty. County of Charleston, S.C., 1992-94; projects officer County of Charleston, 1994; pres. Palmetto Practice Systems, Charleston, 1994—. Mem. Phi Beta Kappa. Office: Palmetto Practice Systems 21 Broad St Charleston SC 29401-3001

RAY, PAUL RICHARD, JR., executive search consultant; b. Columbus, Ga., Nov. 6, 1943; s. Paul Richard and Sarah (Campbell) R.; m. Elizabeth Richards, June 29, 1968; children: Paul Richard III, John Ray, Alice Ray. BSBA, U. Ark., 1966; JD, U. Tex., 1969. Bar: Tex. 1970. Dir. mktg., various mktg. positions tobacco divsn. R.J. Reynolds Tobacco Co., Winston-Salem, N.C., 1969-78; cons. Paul R. Ray & Co., Ft. Worth, 1978, v.p., 1978-79, sr. v.p., 1979-83, exec. v.p., 1983-84, pres., 1984—, COO, 1984-86; CEO Ray & Berndtson, Ft. Worth, 1986—. Bd. dirs. Cook-Ft. Worth Children's Med. Ctr., United Way Met. Tarrant County; mem. liberal arts adv. bd. U. Tex.; mem. dean's exec. adv. bd. U. Ark. Mem. ABA, Assn. Exec. Search Cons. (chmn. 1995-99), Tex. Bar Assn., Young Pres.' Orgn., River Crest Country Club, City Club. Office: Ray & Berndtson Inc 301 Commerce St Ste 2300 Fort Worth TX 76102-4123

RAY, ROGER BUCHANAN, retired communications executive, lawyer; b. Tampa, Fla., Aug. 12, 1935; s. Ralph Jackson and Virginia Marie (Stewart) R.; m. Mary Frye Gaillard, Dec. 27, 1957; children: Mary Katherine, Roger Buchanan Jr. BA in Acctg., U. South Fla., 1967; MBA with honors, U. Notre Dame, 1984; JD, Stetson U., 1991. Bar: Fla. 1992. Acct. Gen. Telephone Co. Fla., Tampa, 1959-67; internal audit mgr. GTE Service Co., N.Y.C., 1967-69; budget dir. Gen. Telephone Co. of S.E., Durham, N.C., 1969-74; v.p., controller Gen. Telephone Co. Mich., Muskegon, 1974-78; regional v.p. fin. GTE Service Corp., Westfield, Ind., 1978-82; v.p. fin. Gen. Telephone Co. Wis., 1982-84, Gen. Telephone Co. Ohio, 1982-84, Gen. Telephone Co. Pa., 1982-84, Gen. Telephone Co. Ill., 1982-84; v.p. fin., bd. dirs. Gen. Telephone Co. Mich., 1982-84, Gen. Telephone Co. Ind., 1982-84; v.p. fin., mem. exec. com., bd. dirs. GTE Communications Systems, Phoenix, 1985-87; asst. state's atty. 13th jud. cir. Tampa, Fla. bar, 1992; asst. state atty. 6th Jud. Cir., Pinellas County, Fla., 1992-96; ret., 1996. Lay eucharistic min., former vestry mem., sr. warden Ch. of Ascension, Clearwater, Fla. Mem. Fin. Execs. Inst., Clearwater Bar Assn., Triad of Pinellas County (pres.), Notre Dame Alumni Assn., Kappa Alpha. Republican. Episcopalian. Avocations: jogging, golf, reading, church work. Home: 2337 Kings Point Dr Largo FL 33774-1010

RAY, THOMAS KREIDER, clergyman. Bishop No. Mich. region Episcopal Ch., 1982—. Office: Diocese of No Mich 131 E Ridge St Marquette MI 49855-4208*

RAY, TUHIN, computer engineer; b. London, Aug. 28, 1963; came to U.S., 1987; s. Natabar and Rekha (Bhattacharya) R. B of Engring., Delhi (India) U., 1985; MSEE, Mich. State U., 1989; MBA, Ind. U., 1995. Project engr. Allen Bradley Ltd., Sahibabad, India, 1985-87; grad. rsch. asst. elec. engring. dept. Mich. State U., East Lansing, 1987-89; mgr. applied engring. Total Control Products Inc., Melrose Park, Ill., 1989-92; advanced software engr. Delco Electronics, Kokomo, Ind., 1992-95, software project mgr., 1995—; cons. Motorola Inc., Northbrook, Ill., 1988; teaching asst. De Paul U., Chgo., 1990-92. Capt. sch. and coll. field hockey, Delhi, 1981-84. Recipient Merit cert. Math. Olympiad, New Delhi, 1981, Appreciation award Monsanto Chemical, Sauget, Ill., 1990. Mem. IEEE, Engring. Soc. Detroit. Avocations: windows programming, music, tennis, reading autobiographies. Home: 3010 Courthouse Dr E Apt 2C West Lafayette IN 47906-1006 Office: Delco Electronics MS CT-60-I One Corporate Ctr Kokomo IN 46904-9005

RAY, WAYNE ALLEN, epidemiologist; b. Yakima, Wash., July 2, 1949; s. Allen and Patsy (McKay) R.; m. Janine Elise Thorson, June 11, 1972; children: Lily Amelia, Lea Camille. BS, U. Washington, 1971; MS, Vanderbilt U., 1974, PhD, 1981. Research assoc. Vanderbilt U. Sch. Medicine, Nashville, 1974-75, research instr., 1975-78, research asst. prof., 1979-83, asst. prof., 1984-85, dir. div. pharmacoepidemiology, 1984—, assoc. prof., 1985-90, prof., 1991—. Contbr. articles to profl. jours. Recipient Burroughs Wellcome scholar in Pharmacoepidemiology Am. Coll. Preventive Medicine, 1984. Mem. Am. Statis. Assn., Assn. Computing Machinery, Computer Soc. of IEEE, Soc. Epidemiologic Research, Am. Pub. Health Assn., Phi Beta Kappa. Avocations: gardening. Office: Vanderbilt Univ A-1124 Medical Ctr N Sch Medicine Nashville TN 37232-2637*

RAY, WILLIAM F., banker; b. Cin., Sept. 17, 1915; s. William F. and Adele (Daller) R.; m. Helen Payne, 1939; children: Katharine Ray Sturgis, Barbara Ray Stevens, Mary Ray Struthers, Margaret Ray Gilbert, Whitney Ray Dawson, William F. III, Susan. A.B., U. Cin., 1935; M.B.A., Harvard, 1937. With Brown Bros. Harriman & Co., 1937—, asst. mgr., 1944-49; mgr. Brown Bros. Harriman & Co., Boston, 1950-67; ptnr. Brown Bros. Harriman & Co., N.Y.C., 1968-94; ptnr. Brown Bros. Harriman & Co., Boston, 1994-95, ltd. ptnr., 1996—; trustee emeritus Altantic Mut. Ins. Co., N.Y.C.; mem. internat. bd. advisors Australia and new Zealand Banking Group, Ltd., 1987-91; bd. dirs. U.S.-New Zealand Bus. Coun., 1990-95. Bd. dirs. Robert Brunner Found., 1957-94, Downtown-Lower Manhattan Assn., Inc., 1978-89; bd. dirs., trustee Am. Friends of the Australian Nat. Gallery; mem. Am. adv. bd. John Curtin Ctr., Perth, Australia. Mem. Bankers Assn. for Fgn. Trade (pres. 1966-67), Harvard Bus. Sch. Assn. (pres. 1963-64, exec. coun.), Robert Morris Assocs. (pres. N.E. 1962-63), Pilgrims U.S., Am. Australian Assn. (patron), U.S.-New Zealand Bus. Coun., S.R. (life), Asia Soc. (Ann. award 1988), Skating Club Boston (pres. 1956-58), Brookline (Mass.) Country Club, Union Club N.Y.C., India House N.Y.C., Fishers Island (N.Y.) Club, Mountain Lake Club (Lake Wales, Fla.), Order of Australia (hon., officer), Order of Malta, Somerset Club Boston, Phi Beta Kappa Assocs. (hon. bd. dirs.). Republican. Office: Brown Bros Harriman & Co 40 Water St Boston MA 02109-3604

RAY, WILLIAM JACKSON, psychologist; b. Birmingham, Ala., Sept. 3, 1945; s. Norman M. and Mary K. Agnew; m. Judith Mebane, Aug. 22, 1987; children from previous marriage: Adam, Lauren. BA, Eckerd Coll., 1967; MA, Vanderbilt U., 1969, PhD, 1971; Fellow in med. psychology, Langley Porter Neuropsychiat. Inst., U. Calif. Med. Center, San Francisco, 1971-72. Prof., dir. clin. psychology tng. program Pa. State U., 1972—, dir. clin. trng., 1991—. Author: (with R.M. Stern) Biofeedback, 1977, (with others) Evaluation of Clinical Biofeedback, 1979, (with R.M. Stern and C.M. Davis) Psychophysiological Recording, 1980, Methods Toward a Science of Behavior and Experience, 1981, 5th edit., 1997, (with E. Susman & L. Feajous) Emotion, Cognition, Health and Development in Children and Adolescents, 1992, (with L. Michelson) Handbook of Dissociation, 1996; series editor: Plenum Series in Behavioral Psychophysiology and Medicine. Recipient Nat. Media award Am. Psychol. Found., 1976, 78. Mem. AAAS, APA, APS, Soc. Psychophysiol. Rsch. Office: Dept Psychology Pa State U University Park PA 16802

RAY, WILLIAM MELVIN, newsletter publishing executive; b. Dutchmills, Ark., Mar. 13, 1935; s. William Estes and Verda Lou (Robbins) R.; m. Janet Drachman, June 6, 1969; children: Matthew Stephen, Susannah Brett. BA, U. Redlands, 1959. Reporter Sun-Telegram, San Bernardino, Calif., 1959-60; sports editor Times-Delta, Visalia, Calif., 1961-62; reporter Progress-Bull., Pomona, Calif., 1962-63; copy editor, reporter Newsday, Garden City, N.Y., 1963-65; news editor Nat. Petroleum News, McGraw-Hill, N.Y.C., 1966-71; Washington editor/chief editor Energy Newsletters, McGraw-Hill, 1972-80; v.p., gen.mgr. Energy Newsletters, McGraw-Hill, N.Y.C., 1980—; new product champion McGraw-Hill, N.Y.C., 1989-92, chmn. newsletter editl. bd., 1985-88, seminar spkr., 1985—. Author: Newsletter Publishing, 1990, Business Newsletter Promotion, 1991. Office: The McGraw-Hill Companies 1221 Avenue Of The Americas New York NY 10020-1001

RAYBECK, MICHAEL JOSEPH, surgeon; b. Danbury, Conn., Oct. 5, 1945; s. Michael Thomas and Edythe Caroline (Tomaino) R. BS, Mt. St. Mary's Coll., Emmitsburg, Md., 1967; MD, Tulane U., 1971. Diplomate Am. Bd. Surgery, Am. Bd. Quality Assurance Utilization Rev. Physicians. Intern in surgery St. Vincent's Hosp. and Med. Ctr., N.Y.C., 1971-72; resident in gen. and vascular surgery Ochsner Found. Hosp., New Orleans, 1974-78; ptnr. Burshan, Raybeck, MD, P.A., Pompano Beach, Fla., 1978-82, Lauderdale Surg. Group, P.A., Ft. Lauderdale, 1982—; med. adv. com. Dept. Profl. Regulation, State of Fla.; pres. med. staff Holy Cross Hosp., 1995, vice chmn. PHO, assoc. v.p. med. affairs, 1997—. Bd. dirs. Am. Heart Assn., Ft. Lauderdale, 1988-91. Fellow ACS, Internat. Coll. Surgeons, Soc. Am. Gastrointestinal Endoscopic Surgeons; mem. Am. Soc. Colon-Rectal Surgeons. Republican. Roman Catholic. Avocations: swimming, travel, fgn. lang. Office: Lauderdale Surg Group 4701 N Federal Hwy Fort Lauderdale FL 33308-4608

RAYBURN, BILLY J., Church administrator. Dir. of cross cultural ministries Ch. of God. Office: Ch of God PO Box 2430 Cleveland TN 37320-2430

RAYBURN, CAROLE (MARY AIDA) ANN, psychologist, researcher, writer; b. Washington, Feb. 14, 1938; d. Carl Frederick and Mary Helen (Milkie) Miller; m. Ronald Allen Rayburn (dec. Apr. 1970). BA in Psychology, Am. U., 1961; MA in Clin. Psychology, George Washington U., 1965; PhD in Ednl. Psychology, Cath. U. Am., 1969; MDiv in Ministry, Andrews U., 1980. Lic. psychologist, Md., Mich. Psychometrician Columbian Prep. Sch., Washington, 1963; clin. psychologist Spring Grove State Hosp., Catonsville, Md., 1966-68; pvt. practice, 1969, 71—; staff clin. psychologist Instl. Care Svcs. Div. D.C. Children's Ctr., Laurel, Md., 1970-78; psychologist Md. Dept. Vocat. Rehab., 1973-74; psychometrician Montgomery County Pub. Schs., 1981-85; lectr. Strayer Coll., Washington, 1969-70; forensic psychology expert witness, 1973—; guest lectr. Andrews U., Berrien Springs, Mich., 1979, Hood Coll,, Frederick, Md., 1986-88; instr. Johns Hopkins U., 1986, 88-89; adj. faculty Profl. Sch. Psychology Studies, San Diego, 1987; adj. asst. prof. Loyola Coll., Columbia, Md., 1987; cons. Julia Brown Montessori Schs., 1972, 78, 82—, VA Ctr., 1978, 91-93. Editor: (with M.J. Meadow) A Time to Weep and a Time to Sing, 1985; contbg. author: Montessori: Her Method and the Movement (What You Need to Know), 1973, Drugs, Alcohol and Women: A National Forum Source Book, 1975, The Other Side of the Couch: Faith of thge Psychotherapist, 1981, Clinical Handbook of Pastoral Counseling, 1985, An Encyclopedic Dictionary of Pastoral Care and Counseling, 1990, Religion Personality and Mental Health, 1993; author copyrighted inventories Religious Occupationl and Stress Questionnaire, 1986, Religion and Stress Questionnaire, 1986, Organizational Relationships Survey, 1987, Attitudes Toward Children Inventory, 1987, State-Trait Morality Inventory, 1987, Body Awareness and Sexual Intimacy Comfort Scale (Basics), 1993; cons. editor Profl. Psychology, 1980-83; assoc. editor Jour. Pastoral Counseling, 1985-90, guest editor, 1988; contbr. numerous articles to profl. jours. Recipient Svc. award Coun. for Advancement Psychol. Professions and Scis., 1975, cert. D.C. Dept. Human Resources, 1975, 76, cert. recognition D.C. Psychol. Assn., 1976, 1985; AAUW rsch. grantee, 1983. Fellow APA (pres. divsn. psychology of religion 1995-96, psychology of women, clin. psychology, cons. psychology, psychotherapy, state assn. affairs, chair equal opportunity affirmative action divsn. clin. psychology 1980-82, mem. editl. bd. Jour. Child Clin. Psychology 1978-82, pres. clin psychology women's sect. 1984-86, program chair 1991-94, divsn. psychology women chair task force on women and religion 1980-81, divsn. psychology issues in grad. edn. and clin. tng. 1988—, pres. 1995-96), Am. Orthopsychiat. Assn., Md. Psychol. Assn. (editor newsletter 1975-76, chpt. recognition 1978, chair ins. com. 1981-83, pres. 1984-85, exec. adv. com. 1985—), Am. Assn. Applied & Preventive Psychology (sec. 1992-93, chair fellows com. 1992-93); mem. Assn. Practicing Psychologists Montgomery-Prince George's Counties (pres. 1986-88, editor newsletter 1990—), Balt Assn. Cons. Psychologists (pres. D.C. chpt. 1991-92), Psi Chi (hon.). Achievements include research on stress in religious professionals, women and stress, women and religion, pastoral counseling, state-trait morality inventory, leadership, psychotherapy, children. Address: 1200 Morningside Dr Silver Spring MD 20904-3149

RAYBURN, GEORGE MARVIN, business executive, investment executive; b. Cape Girardeau, Mo., Jan. 30, 1920; s. Walter Marvin and Alma Fay (McBride) R.; m. Louise Tinder, Feb. 6, 1990; 1 child from previous marriage, George Marvin. Student, Central Coll., Fayette, Mo., 1937-39; B.S. in Bus. Adminstrn, Washington U., St. Louis, 1941, M.S. in Bus. Adminstrn, 1947. Auditor Internat. Harvester Co., 1941-45; accountant Tallman Co., 1946-47; asst. prof. U. Omaha, 1947-49; assoc. prof. Millikin U., 1949-52; pvt. practice as George M. Rayburn (C.P.A.), 1948-52; regional internal auditor Olin-Mathieson Chem. Corp., 1952-55; comptroller Orchard Paper Co., 1955-56; asst. controller St. L.S.F. Ry., St. Louis, 1956-62; sec., treas. St. L.S.F. Ry., 1963-69, v.p., 1969-72; pres., dir. N.M. & Ariz. Land Co., 1966-81; chmn., dir. G.M. Resources, Inc., 1982—. Author: Standard Costs Applied to Distribution Costs, 1947, Budgets Bewitched or Bewildered, 1960. Served to capt. AUS, 1942-45, 51-52. Mem. AICPA, Am. Accounting Assn., Financial Execs. Inst., Planning Forum Inc., Delta Sigma Pi, Phi Sigma Phi, Phi Kappa Delta. Methodist. Home and Office: 12410 W 82nd Pl Lenexa KS 66215-2738

RAYBURN, S. T., lawyer; b. Brookhaven, Miss., Aug. 26, 1947; s. Harry Newton and Margaret Elaine (Zeigler) R.; m. Elizabeth Hooker, June 6, 1970 (div. Nov. 1990); children: Andrew Newton, Thomas McCarver, Shelby Hooker; m. Paige Bruce, Feb. 1, 1992; 1 child, Samuel Taylor. BA, Miss. State U., 1970; JD cum laude, U. Miss., 1972. Bar: Miss. 1972, U.S. Dist. Ct. (no. dist.) Miss. 1972, U.S. Ct. Appeals (5th cir.) 1973, U.S. Supreme Ct. 1976, U.S. Ct. Appeals (11th cir.) 1981, U.S. Dist. Ct. (so. dist.) Miss. 1984. Assoc. Sumners & Hickman, Oxford, Miss., 1972-75; ptnr. Sumners, Hickman & Rayburn, Oxford, Miss., 1975-89, Hickman, Rayburn & Goza, Oxford, Miss., 1989-92; shareholder Mitchell, McNutt, Threadgill, Smith & Sams, Oxford, Miss., 1992-97; ptnr. Rayburn & Pierie, Oxford, 1997—; mem. character & fitness com. Miss. State Bd. Bar Examiners, 1990—. sec. Lafayette County Dem. Exec. Com., Oxford, 1976-80, chmn., 1980-88; chmn. Miss. Commn. Wildlife Conservation, Jackson, Miss., 1984-89. Mem. Miss. Bar Assn. (commr.), Miss. Def. Lawyers Assn., 3rd Cir. Bar Assn. (pres.), Intern Assn. of Def. Counsel, Def. Rsch. Inst., Oxford-Lafayette County C. of C. (pres.). Presbyterian. Avocations: boating, scuba diving. Home: PO Box 430 Oxford MS 38655-0430 Office: Raymond & Pierie PO Box 430 Oxford MS 38655-0430

RAYBURN, TED RYE, newspaper editor; b. Manchester, Tenn., Dec. 16, 1956; s. Ted and Thelma (Taylor) R.; m. Kimberly Ann Pearce, June 4, 1983. BS in Mass Comm., Mid. Tenn. State U., 1986. State corr. Nashville Banner, Murfreesboro, Tenn., 1978-79; reporter, photographer, sports editor Murfeesboro Press, 1978-80; state corr. The Tennessean, Murfreesboro, 1979-80; copy editor Jackson (Tenn.) Sun, 1980-82, asst. copy desk chief, 1982-85; copy editor Tennessean, Nashville, 1985-90, page one editor, 1990—, asst. copy desk chief, 1994—. Avocations: film, literature, jazz music. Office: The Tennessean 1100 Broadway Nashville TN 37203-3116

RAYBURN, WILLIAM FRAZIER, obstetrician, gynecologist, educator; b. Lexington, Ky., Aug. 19, 1950; s. Charles Calvin and Charlotte Elizabeth (Ballard) R.; m. Pamela Rae Gilleland, Nov. 27, 1976; children: Lindsay Ann, Britany Beth, Drake Tanner. BS, Hampden Sydney Coll., 1971; MD, U. Ky., 1975. Diplomate Nat. Bd. Med. Examiners, Am. Bd. Ob.-Gyn. (examiner), Divsn. Maternal-Fetal Medicine. Intern family medicine U. Iowa Hosps. and Clinics, Iowa City, Iowa, 1975-76; resident ob.-gyn. U. Ky. Med. Ctr., Lexington, 1976-79; fellow in maternal-fetal medicine dept. ob.-gyn.

Ohio State U. Hosps., Columbus, 1979-81; asst. prof. ob.-gyn. U. Mich. Med. Sch., Ann Arbor, 1981-83, assoc. prof. ob.-gyn., 1983-86; assoc. prof. dept. ob.-gyn. and pharmacology U. Nebr. Coll. of Medicine, Omaha, 1985-88, prof. dept. ob-gyn. and pharmacology, 1988-92; prof. dept. ob-gyn. and pharmacology U. Okla. Coll. Medicine, Oklahoma City, 1992—, John W. Records endowed chair, 1992—; chief of obstetrics U. Okla. Coll. of Medicine, Okla. City, 1992—; dir. maternal fetal medicine dept. ob-gyn U. Mich. Med. Ctr., 1981-85, med. edn.; reviewer for Ob and Gyn., Am. Jour. Ob-Gyn., Jour. Reproductive Medicine, Internat. Jour. Gyn. and Ob., New Eng. Jour. Medicine, Jour. Maternal-Fetal Medicine, Jour. Maternal-Fetal Investigation; U. Nebr. Med. Ctr., 1985-92, U. Okla. Health Sci. Ctr., 1992—, Presbyn. Hosp., Okla. City, 1992—. Author: (books) Obstetrics/Gynecology: Pre Test Self Assessment and Review, 1982; (with others), Every Woman's Pharmacy: A Guide to Safe Drug Use, 1983, Obstetrics for the House Officer, 1984, 2d rev. edition, 1988, Every Woman's Pharmacy, 1984, The Women's Health and Drug Reference, 1993, Oklahoma Notes: Obstetrics and Gynecology, 1994, 2d. rev. edit., 1996, Obstetrics and Gynecology for the House Officer, 1996; editor: (with F.P. Zuspan) Drug Therapy in Obstetrics and Gynecology, 1982, 3d rev. edit., 1992; symposia editor Diagnosis and Management of the Malformed Fetus, Jour. Reprod. Medicine, 1982, Operative Obstetrics, Clinics in Perinatology, 1983, Controversies in Fetal Drug Therapy, Clin. Obstetrics and Gynecology, 1991; contbr. 50 chpts. to books, articles to over 180 profl. jours. including Am. Jour. Obstetric Gynecology, Obstetrics Gynecology, Jour. Reproductive Medicine, Am. Jour. Perinatology and many others; also speaker and lectr. at sci. confs. and seminars and author of audio visual ednl. material for universities and in continuing med. edn.; contbr. over 110 abstracts at sci. meetings; reviewer for Ob. and Gyn., Am. Jour. Ob.-Gyn., Jour. Reproductive Medicine, Internat. Jour. Gyn. and Ob., New Eng. Jour. Medicine, Jour. Maternal-Fetal Medicine, Jour. Maternal-Fetal Investigation. Dir. maternal and infant care programs U. Nebr. Med. Ctr., Omaha, 1986-92; U.S. Pharmacopeia Conv. field reviewer, 1983—. Recipient Residents' prize paper award Ky. Ob.-Gyn. Soc., 1978, 79, Faculty Teaching award for Excellence, 1993, 94.car. Fellow Am. Coll. Obstetricians and Gynecologists (Ephraim McDowell) prize paper award 2d pl. 1978, 1st pl. 1979, Searle-Donald F. Richardson Prize Paper award 1980, Best Doctors in Am., 1996); mem. Soc. Perinatal Obstetricians, Assn. of Profs. in Gyn.-Ob., Soc. for Gynecol. Investigation, Teratology Soc., N.Y. Acad. Sci., Neurobehavioral Teratology Soc., Okla. State Med. Soc. Achievements include contributions to the knowledge of drug effcts on developing fetus and of principals of induction of labor and to the influence he has had on peers not only through teaching and patient care but through his extensive writing. Office: U Okla Health Sci Ctr PO Box 6901 WP2410 Oklahoma City OK 73190

RAYFIEL, DAVID, screenwriter; b. N.Y.C., Sept. 9, 1923; s. Leo F. and Flora (Marks) R.; m. Lila Paris, 1950 (div. 1953); 1 child, Eliza; m. Maureen Stapleton, 1963 (div. 1969); m. Lynne Schwarzenbek, 1988. AB, Bklyn. Coll., 1947; MFA, Yale U., 1950. Scripts include (with Daniel Taradash) Castle Keep, 1968, (with Roland Kibbee) Valdez Is Coming, 1970, (with Lorenzo Semple, Jr.) Three Days of the Condor, 1975 (Edgar Allan Poe award best screenplay Mystery Writers of Am. 1975), Lipstick, 1976, (with Bertrand Tavernier) Death Watch, 1982, (with Tavernier) Round Midnight, 1986, (with Judith Rascoe) Havana, 1990, The Firm, 1993, (with Marshall Brickman) Intersection, 1994, (with Barbara Benedek) Sabrina, 1995; plays include P.S. 193, 1962, Nathan Weinstein, Mystic, Connecticut, 1966.

RAYFIELD, GORDON ELLIOTT, playwright, political risk consultant; b. Newark, Sept. 1, 1950; s. Bernard George and Rhoda Gertrude (Glucklisch) R.; m. Jean Metzger, July 12, 1981; children—Michael Evan, Jillian Amy. B.A., The American U., 1972; Ph.D., CUNY, 1980. Adj. lectr. Hunter Coll., CUNY, 1977-79, Bklyn Coll., Bklyn., 1977-79; research assoc. Ralph Bunche Inst., UN, N.Y.C., 1978-79; dir. Assn. Polit. Risk Analysts, N.Y.C., 1980-84, 87-90; polit. risk analyst Gen. Motors Corp., N.Y.C., 1979-86; prin. Rayfield Assocs., N.Y.C., 1986—; writing instr. Rutgers U., 1993. Editor newsletter Polit. Risk Rev., 1983-87; columnist World Wide Projects, 1985-87; staff writer One Life to Live, 1996—; author: (plays) Fever of Unknown Origin, 1988, Bitter Friends, 1989, Living Proof, 1995, ABC-TV aftersch. spl. It's Only Rock and Roll, 1991 (nominated Writer's Guild award, nominated Emmy award 1996), PBS dramatic spl. In the Shadow of Love, 1991 (nominated Emmy award), Fox TV Pilot Skin-to-Skin, 1992, HBO life stories: Portrait of a Bulimic (nominated Cable Ace award); episodes of Law and Order, One Life to Live, CBS Schoolbreak Spl. Stand Up, 1995 (Writers' Guild award 1996, Emmy award 1996). Mem. Dramatists Guild, Writers Guild of Am. East, Assn. Polit. Risk Analysts (co-founder 1980, pres. 1981-83). Home and Office: 47 Nance Rd West Orange NJ 07052-1630

RAYLESBERG, ALAN IRA, lawyer; b. N.Y.C., Dec. 6, 1950; s. Daniel David and Sally Doris (Mantell) R.; m. Caren Thea Coven, Nov. 20, 1983; children: Lisa Maris, Jason Todd. BA, NYU, 1972; JD cum laude, Boston U., 1975. Bar: N.Y. 1976, U.S. Dist. Ct. (so. dist.) N.Y. 1976, U.S. Dist. Ct. (ea. dist.) N.Y. 1978, U.S. Tax Ct. 1981, U.S. Ct. Appeals (2d and 5th cirs.) 1982, U.S. Ct. Appeals (1st cir.) 1986, U.S. Ct. Appeals (9th cir.) 1996. Assoc. Orans, Elsen & Polstein, N.Y.C., 1975-77; assoc. Guggenheimer & Untermyer, N.Y.C., 1977-83, ptnr., 1983-85; ptnr. Rosenman & Colin, N.Y.C., 1985—; adj. instr. N.Y. Law Sch., 1980-83; instr. Nat. Inst. of Trial Advocacy; mem. adv. group comml. divsn., mem. mediation panel N.Y. State Supreme Ct. Bd. dirs. Fund for Modern Cts., 1994—. Mem. ABA, Fed. Bar Coun., Assn. Bar City N.Y., N.Y. County Lawyers Assn. (bd. dirs. 1995—, fed. ct. com. 1988—, co-chmn. appellate ct. com. 1992-93, chair appellate ct. com. 1993-96), N.Y. State Bar Assn. (ho. delegates 1996—), Securities Industry Assn. (legal and compliance divsn N.Y. Coun. Def. Lawyers. Democrat. Jewish. Office: Rosenman & Colin 575 Madison Ave New York NY 10022-2511

RAYMER, WARREN JOSEPH, retired allergist; b. Seguin, Tex., Aug. 23, 1920; s. Milam R. and O'TTilie H. (Fischer) R.; m. Viola M. Glover, July 16, 1945. BA in Zoology, U. Tex., 1942; MD, Baylor Coll. of Medicine, 1947. Diplomate Am. Bd. Allergy and Immunology. Intern Methodist Hosp., Houston, 1947-48, resident, 1948-49; resident in internal medicine So. Pacific Hosp., Houston, 1949-50; fellow in allergy U. Va. Hosp., Charlottesville, 1952-53; pvt. practice Houston, 1950-84; ret., 1984; clin. asst. prof. medicine U. Tex., Houston; mem. staff Hermann Hosp., Houston; hon. mem. Park Plaza Hosp., Houston, Diagnostic Hosp., Houston. Contbr. articles to profl. jours. Capt. USMC, Korean War. Fellow Am. Acad. Allergy, Am. Coll. Allergists (pres. 1981-82), Am. Assn. Cert. Allergists; mem. AMA (life), World Med. Assn., Am. Assn. Physicians and Surgeons, Southwest Allergy Forum, Tex. Med. Assn. (life), Tex. Allergy Immunology Soc. (sec./treas.), Harris County Med. Soc., Greater Houston Allergy Soc., N.Y. Acad. Sci., Masons. Office: Houston Allergy Clinic 1213 Hermann Dr # 444 Park Plz Profl Bldg Houston TX 77004

RAYMOND, ARTHUR EMMONS, aerospace engineer; b. Boston, Mar. 24, 1899. BS, Harvard U., 1920; MS, MIT, 1921; DSc (hon.), Poly. Inst. Bklyn., 1947. Engr. Douglass Aircraft Co., 1925-34, v.p. engring., 1934-60; cons. Rand Corp., 1960-85; ret., 1985; mem. Nat. Adv. Com. Aero., 1946-56; cons. NASA, 1962-68. Trustee Aerospace Corp., 1960-71, Rsch. Analysis Corp., 1965-71. Recipient Nat. Air and Space Mus. Trophy/Lifetime Achievement award Smithsonian Instn., 1991. Fellow AIAA (hon.); mem. NAS, Nat. Acad. Engring. Achievements include research in aeronautics and astronautics. Home: 65 Oakmont St Los Angeles CA 90049-1901

RAYMOND, DAVID WALKER, lawyer; b. Chelsea, Mass., Aug. 23, 1945; s. John Walker and Jane (Beck) R.; m. Sandra Sue Broadwater, Aug. 12, 1967 (div.); m. Margaret Byrd Payne, May 25, 1974; children: Pamela Payne, Russell Wyatt. BA, Gettysburg Coll., 1967; JD, Temple U., 1970. Bar: Pa. 1970, D.C. 1971, U.S. Supreme Ct. 1974, Ill. 1975, U.S. Dist. Ct. (no. dist.) Ill. 1981. Govtl. affairs atty. Sears, Roebuck and Co., Washington, 1970-74, atty. Sears hdqrs. law dept., Chgo., 1974-80, asst. gen. counsel advt., trademarks and customs, 1981-84, asst. gen. counsel adminstrn., 1984-86, mgr. planning and analysis corp. planning dept., 1986-89, sr. corp. counsel pub. policy corp. law dept., 1989-90; assoc. gen. counsel litigation and adminstrn. law dept. Sears Mdse. Group, 1990-92, dep. gen. counsel, 1992-93, v.p. and gen. counsel, 1993-95, v.p. law, Sears Roebuck and Co., 1996; of counsel Winston & Strawn, Washington, 1996—. Staff Temple Law Quar., 1968-69, editor, 1969-70; mem. bd. trustees No. Ill. U., 1996—. Mem. ABA, Ill. Bar Assn., Chgo. Bar Assn., Phi Alpha Delta. Presbyterian. Office: Winston & Strawn 1400 L St NW Washington DC 20005-3509

RAYMOND, DENNIS KENNETH, army officer; b. Witherbee, N.Y., Feb. 21, 1947; s. Kenneth Andrew and Theresa Lillian (Barnes) R.; m. Vivian Velsini, Aug. 23, 1969 (div. June 1982); 1 child, Dennis Kenneth Jr. (dec.); m. Sondra Lynne Mayhew, Apr. 24, 1987; 1 child, Aaron Paul. BSEE, Norwich U., 1969; MA in Internat. Rels., Salve Regina Coll., Newport, R.I., 1983; MS in Sys. Mgmt., U. So. Calif., 1986; postgrad., Indsl. Coll. Armed Forces, Ft. McNair, Washington, 1991-92. Indsl. engr. N.Y. State Electric & Gas Co., Binghamton, 1969-70; commd. 2nd lt. U.S. Army, 1970, advanced through grades to col., 1993; comdg. officer TUSLOG Detachment 169, Sinop, Turkey, 1977-79; brigade C-E officer air def. arty., then ops. officer 9th Inf. Divsn., Ft. Lewis, Wash., 1979-82; comm. sys. engr. Command Sys. Integration Office, Washington, 1983-86; chief current sys. divsn. Command Sys. Integration Agy., Arlington Hall Station, Va., 1986-89; product mgr. western hemisphere transmission sys. Project Mgmt. Office, Def. Comm. and Army Transmission Sys., Ft. Monmouth, N.J., 1989-91, spl. asst. to program exec. officer, 1992-93; project mgr. satellite comms. Program Exec. Office for Comm. Sys., Ft. Monmouth, 1993-96; ret. U.S. Army, 1996; program mgr. pub. safety wireless network VGS, Inc., McLean, Va., 1996—. Recipient Order of Silver Mercury, Signal Corps Regtl. Assn., 1995. Mem. IEEE, Armed Forces Comm. and Electronics Assn. (v.p., bd. dirs. 1994—, pres. Ft. Monmouth chpt. 1994-95), Assn. U.S. Army (bd. dirs. 1995—). Roman Catholic. Avocations: golf, hunting, woodworking, collectibles. Office: VGS Inc 8301 Greensboro Dr Mc Lean VA 22103

RAYMOND, DOROTHY GILL, lawyer; b. Greeley, Colo., June 2, 1954; d. Robert Marshall and Roberta (McClure) Gill; m. Peter J. Raymond, June 8, 1974. BA summa cum laude, U. Denver, 1975; JD, U. Colo., 1978. Bar: Conn. 1978, Colo. 1981. Assoc. Dworkin, Minogue & Bucci, Bridgeport, Conn., 1978-80; counsel Tele-Communications, Inc., Englewood, Colo., 1981-88; v.p., gen. counsel WestMarc Communications, Inc., Denver, 1988-91; v.p., gen. counsel Cable Television Labs., Inc., Boulder, Colo., 1991-96, sr. v.p., gen. counsel, 1996—. Mem. Am. Corp. Counsel Assn. (pres. 1990-91, Colo. chpt. dir. 1988-94), Colo. Assn. Corp. Counsel (pres. 1987), Sports Car Club Am. (nat. champion ladies stock competition 1981, 85, 86, 88). Avocations: sewing, reading, outdoor activities. Office: Cable Television Labs Inc 400 Centennial Pkwy Louisville CO 80027-1266

RAYMOND, GEORGE MARC, city planner, educator; b. Odessa, Russia, Jan. 1, 1919; came to U.S., 1937, naturalized, 1942; s. Mark J. and Rachelle (Schneiderman) R.; m. Kathleen E. Waid, Oct. 3, 1942 (div. Mar. 1978); 1 dau., Valerie M.; m. Lois Jean Gainsboro, Mar. 26, 1979. BArch, Columbia, 1946. Planning dir. Harrison, Ballard & Allen, Inc., N.Y.C., 1952-54; founder, pres. Raymond, Parish, Pine & Weiner, Inc., 1954-83; pres. George M. Raymond Assocs., 1983—; prof. planning, chmn. dept. city and regional planning Pratt Inst., Bklyn., 1959-75; founder, dir. Pratt Ctr. for Community Improvement, Bklyn., 1963-70; lectr. planning Columbia U., 1955-58; lectr. planning and urban renewal New Sch. Social Rsch., 1967-72; pres. Assn. Collegiate Sch. Planning, 1968-69; chmn. Westchester County Housing Implementation Commn., 1992-93. Editor: Pratt Planning Papers, 1963-73, (with Astrid Monson) Pratt Guide to Housing, Planning and Urban Renewal for New Yorkers, 1965. V.p. Citizens Housing and Planning Coun. N.Y.C., 1967-86, N.Y. Assn. Environ. Profls., 1977-79; pres. Westchester Citizens Housing Coun., 1964-66, Met. Com. on Planning, 1950-51; founder, pres. Friends of Music Concerts, 1954-57, Spoken Arts Soc., 1966-67; bd. dirs. Nat. Housing Conf.; past 1st v.p. Federated Conservationists Westchester County; past dir. Phipps Houses, Wave Hill, Settlement Housing Fund; chmn. Westchester County Housing Opportunity Commn., 1994—; land use adv. com. N.Y. State Legis. Commn. on Rural Resources, 1992—. Mem. Am. Soc. Cons. Planners (pres. 1968-70), Am. Inst. Cert. Planners, Am. Planning Assn. (pres. N.Y. met. chpt. 1983-95). Home: 192 Locust Ln Irvington NY 10533-2315 Office: 560 White Plains Rd Tarrytown NY 10591-5112

RAYMOND, JACK, journalist, public relations executive, foundation executive; b. Sulejow, Poland, Oct. 6, 1918; s. Harry and Anna (Lange) R.; m. Gertrude Silverman, Oct. 6, 1946; children: David Alan, Judith. Student, CCNY, 1939. Sports writer N.Y. World-Telegram, 1934-38; ct. reporter, city editor, columnist N.Y. Daily North Side News, 1938-40; Corr. N.Y. Times, 1940-66, Berlin, 1946-47, Frankfurt, 1947-49, Bonn, 1949-52, Balkans, Belgrade, 1952-56, Moscow, 1956; Pentagon corr. N.Y. Times, Washington, 1956-66; pub. relations exec., pres. Thomas J. Deegan Co., Washington and N.Y.C., 1966-70; v.p. Bryan Publs., N.Y.C., 1970-74; founding pres. Internat. Inst. for Environ. Devel., 1970; pres. Dialog div. J. Walter Thompson Co., 1973-75; pres. Jack Raymond & Co., Inc., N.Y.C., 1975-87; chmn. Jack Raymond & Co., Inc., 1987-92; pres. JR Cons. Svc., Inc., 1987—; acting communications dir. Commonwealth Fund, 1987; book reviewer The Villager, N.Y.C., 1970-74; cons. UN Conf. on Human Environment, 1972, Aspen Inst. Humanistic Studies, HABITAT, UN Conf. Human Settlements; adv. com. Ctr. for Environ. Info. UN Assn. U.S., 1975-78; mem. Rumanian-U.S. econ. coun. U.S. C. of C., 1973-75; project dir. 1987 Workshop Internat. Environ. Bur. Internat. C. of C.; cons. INFORM, 1989, The Rene Dubos Ctr. for Human Environments, 1989—; mem. adv. bd. Volvo Journalists Retreat Duke U., 1992; internat. adv. bd. Ctr. for Social Policy in Mid-East, 1983-91; mem. exec. bd. Ency. of Environment. Author: Power at Pentagon, 1964, Your Military Obligations and Opportunities, 1963, Robert O. Anderson: Oil Man/Environmentalist, 1988; co-author: This is Germany, 1950; editor Upton Nooz, 1942-43; combat correspondant Stars and Stripes, news editor Naples and Rome edits., mng. editor Marseilles edit.; combat correspondant, war editor, editor Stars and Stripes mag. Paris edit., combat correspondant, news editor Frankfurt edit., 1943-45; also author articles. Trustee N.Y. Urban League, 1969-72; bd. dirs. Internat. Inst. Environ. Affairs, N.Y.C., 1970-74, pres., 1970-73; bd. dirs. Internat. Inst. Environment and Devel., London, 1974-89, mem. adv. coun., 1978-82, mem. exec. com., 1982-89; bd. dirs. Epoch B. Found., La Jolla, Calif., acting pres., 1977-85; trustee Moroccan-Am. Found., 1982-88; bd. overseers Heller Grad. Sch., Brandeis U., 1981-88; founding assoc. John J. McCloy Internat. Ctr., N.Y.C.,1986, bd. dirs., 1987—; mem. adv. bd. Ctr. for East-West Dynamics, 1992-95, Volvo JNLSTS Retreat, Williamsburg, Va., 1992. Decorated 5 Battle Stars, Bronze Star, Purple Heart. Mem. Council on Fgn. Relations. Clubs: Overseas Press Am. (N.Y.C.) (pres. 1972-76), Century Assn. (N.Y.C.), Nat. Press (Washington). Home: 340 E 57th St New York NY 10022-2951 Office: J R Cons Svcs 6 Flintlock Ridge Rd Katonah NY 10536-2508

RAYMOND, KAY E(NGELMANN), Spanish language educator, consultant; b. Cin., Feb. 1, 1939; d. Gerson Silas and Pauline Coleman (Early) Engelmann; m. O. Ralph Raymond II, Feb. 1, 1964 (div. Nov. 1977); 1 child, Jenifer Kay Raymond-Judy. AB magna cum laude, Radcliffe Coll., 1961; MA, Brown U., 1964; PhD, Ind. U., 1983. Lectr. Boston U., 1965-68; lectr. Assumption Coll., Worcester, Mass., 1965-67; instr. Regis Coll., Weston, Mass., 1967-71; assoc. instr. Ind. U., Bloomington, 1972-83; lectr. Emporia (Kans.) State U., 1983-84; asst. prof. U. Ala. at Huntsville, 1984-89, Sam Houston State U., Huntsville, Tex., 1989-94; assoc. prof. Sam Houston State U., 1994—, coord. fgn. langs., 1995—. Advisor Internat. Hispanic Assn., Sam Houston State U., 1990—, Sigma Delta Pi, 1990—; vol. translator City of Huntsville, 1993—. Named Top Prof Bapt. Student Ministry Sam Houston State U., 1996, Outstanding Advisor Internat. Hispanic Assn., 1996, 97. Mem. MLA, Asociación de Literatura Femenina, Phi Sigma Iota (life), Pi Delta Phi (hon.), Sigma Delta Pi (hon.). Democrat. Home: 3644 Youpon St Huntsville TX 77340-8920 Office: Sam Houston State U Fgn Langs Box 2147 Huntsville TX 77341

RAYMOND, KENNETH NORMAN, chemistry educator, research chemist; b. Astoria, Oreg., Jan. 7, 1942; s. George Norman and Helen May (Dunn) R.; m. Jane Galbraith Shell, June 19, 1965 (div. 1976); children: Mary Katherine, Alan Norman; m. Barbara Gabriele Sternitzke, June 17, 1977; children: Gabriella Petra, Christopher Norman. B.A., Reed Coll., 1964; Ph.D., Northwestern U., 1968. Asst. prof. chemistry U. Calif.-Berkeley, 1967-74, assoc. prof., 1974-78, prof., 1978—; vice chmn. dept. U. Calif. Berkeley, 1982-84, chmn., 1993-96; mem. study sect. NIH, 1983; mem. chemistry adv. com. NSF, 1985-87. Editor: Biorganic Chemistry II, 1977; assoc. editor Biology of Metals, 1987-91; editl. bd. Inorganic Chemistry, 1976-86, Accounts Chem. Rsch., 1982-90, Inorganica Chemica Acta f-Block Elements, 1984-90, Jour. Coordination Chemistry, 1981—, Jour. Inorganic and Nuclear Chemistry, 1974-81, Jour. Am. Chem. Soc., 1983-95, Topics in Current Chemistry, 1981—, Metals in Biology, 1993—, Jour. Supramolecular Chemistry, 1992, Jour. Biol. Inorganic Chemistry, 1996—; U.S. editl. advisor Springer-Verlag in Chemistry, 1972-91; contbr. articles to profl. jours.; author more than 275 papers, 8 patents in field. Alfred P. Sloan rsch. fellow, 1971-73; Miller rsch. prof., 1977-78, 96; Guggenheim fellow, 1980-81; recipient E.O. Lawrence award, Dept. Energy, 1984, Humboldt Rsch. award for U.S. Scientists, 1982, Alfred R. Bader award Am. Chem. Soc., 1994. Mem. Am. Chem. Soc. (chair divsn. inorganic chemistry 1996), Am. Crystallographic Soc., Sigma Xi. Democrat. Office: U Calif Berkeley Dept Chemistry Berkeley CA 94720

RAYMOND, LEE R., oil company executive; b. Watertown, S.D., Aug. 13, 1938; m. Charlene Raymond. BSChemE, U. Wis., 1960; PhDChemE, U. Minn., 1963. Various engring. positions Exxon Corp., Tulsa, Houston, N.Y.C. and Caracas, Venezuela, 1963-72; mgr. planning Internat. Co. divsn. Exxon Corp., N.Y.C., 1972-75, pres. Exxon Nuc. Co. divsn., 1979-81, exec. v.p. Exxon Enterprises Inc. divsn., 1981-83, sr. v.p., dir., 1984-86, pres., dir., 1987-93, chmn., CEO, 1993—; v.p. Lago Oil, Netherlands Antilles, 1975-76, pres., dir., 1976-79; pres., dir. Esso Inter-Am. Inc., Coral Gables, Fla., 1983-84, sr. v.p., dir., 1984—; bd. dirs. J.P. Morgan & Co., Inc., N.Y.C., Morgan Guaranty Trust Co. of N.Y., N.Y.C.; chmn. Am. Petroleum Inst. Bd. dirs. United Negro Coll. Fund, New Am. Schs. Devel. Corp., 1991—, Project Shelter PRO-AM, 1991—, Dallas Citizens Coun.; trustee Wis. Alumni Rsch. Found., 1987—, Bus. Coun. Internat. Understanding, Inc., 1988—; trustee So. Meth. U.; mem. Tri Lateral Commn., U. Wis. Found., Nat. Rep. Senatorial Com.; mem. emergency com. Am. trade; ptnr. emeritus N.Y.C. Partnership; mem. bd. govs. United Way Am.; active Am. Coun. on Germany, Dallas Com. Fgn. Rels., Dallas Wildcat Com., 1993. Mem. Am. Soc. Engring. (nat. adv. coun.), Am. Soc. Royal Bot. Garden (founder), Bus. coun., Bus. Roundtable (policy taxation task force 1993), Nat. Petroleum Coun., Coun. Fgn. Rels., Singapore-U.S. Bus. Coun., Nat. Senatorial Com.

RAYMONDA, JAMES EARL, retired banker; b. Piseco, N.Y., Feb. 20, 1933; s. Floyd E. and Bertha (Kramer) R.; m. Marie A. Countryman, Aug. 18, 1956; children—David J., Diane J., Daniel J. B.S. magna cum laude, Syracuse U., 1955. With Fleet Bank (formerly Oneida Nat. Bank & Trust Co. Cen. N.Y.), Utica, 1957—; v.p., comptroller Norstar Bank (formerly Oneida Nat. Bank & Trust Co. Central N.Y.), 1968—, adminstrv. v.p., until 1973, exec. v.p., 1973—, regional pres., 1987-90; chmn. reg. bd. Fleet Bank, 1990-94. Treas. Oneida County chpt. Nat. Found.; pres. Whitestown Jaycees, 1964; adv. com., sec. Whitestown Sr. Ctr., 1965-87; trustee St. Elizabeth Hosp., Utica, N.Y.; gen. chmn. campaign Greater Utica United Way, 1977, pres., 1979-80, 95; mem. Utica Found. bd., Oneida County Hist. Soc. bd. Recipient Len Wilbur award Utica Kiwanis, 1980, Indsl. Man Yr. award, 1981, Humanitarian of Yr. award St. Elizabeth Hosp., 1989, Business Man of Year award Utica Observer Dispatch, 1990. Mem. KC (Utica), Nat. Assn. Accts., C. of C. Greater Utica Area (v.p. adminstrn., Person of Yr. 1991), Rotary (pres. 1985-86, dist. gov. 1993-94). Home: 35 Chateau Dr Whitesboro NY 13492-2528

RAYMUND, STEVEN A., computer company executive; b. 1955. BS, U. Oreg.; Georgetown U. Sch. Fgn. Svc. Pres., CEO, chmn. bd., dir. Tech Data Corp., 1981—. Office: Tech Data Corp 5350 Tech Data Dr Clearwater FL 33760-3122*

RAYNAULD, ANDRE, economist, educator; b. Quebec, Que., Can., Oct. 20, 1927; s. Léopold and Blanche (Gauthier) R.; m. Michelle Nolin, Oct. 15, 1951; children: Francoy, Olivier, Dominique, Isabelle. BA cum laude, U. Montreal, 1948, MA in Indsl. Rels. magna cum laude, 1951; D. in Econs., U. Paris, 1954; D. in Econs. (hon.), U. Ottawa, 1976, U. Sherbrooke, 1976. Mem. faculty U. Montreal, 1954-71, founder, dir. Ctr. Econ. Research and Devel., 1970-72; vis. prof. U. Toronto, 1962-63; chmn. Economic Council Can., Ottawa, 1971-76; mem. Que. Nat. Assembly, Montreal, 1976-80; prof. U. Montreal, 1980-93, prof. emeritus, 1993—; exec. com. Can. Social Sci. Rsch. Coun., 1961-63, 64-65; pres. Inst. Canadien Affaires Publiques, 1961-62; bd. govs. Can. Labour Coll., 1962-66; dir., exec. com. CBC, 1964-67; trustee CBC Pension Fund, 1967-70; pres. Soc. Canadienne de Sci. Economique, 1967-69; mem. Royal Commn. Bilingualism and Biculturalism, 1969-70, Can. Coun. Urban and Regional Rsch., 1971, Quebec Coun. Planning and Devel., 1971; chmn. com. inquiry French-lang. tchr.-tng. Western provinces Dept. Sec. State, 1971; mem. interfutures study group OECD, Paris, 1976-78; mem. bd. Inst. Rsch. Pub. Policy, 1980—; rsch. fellow Devel. Ctr. OECD, Paris, 1986—; invited prof. College de France, Paris, 1987. Author: Economic Growth in Quebec, 1961, The Canadian Economic System, 1967, La propriete des entreprises au Quebec, 1974, Institutions Economiques Canadiennes, 2d edition, 1977, Le financement des exportations, 1979, Government Assistance to Export Financing, 1984, The External Financing of Tunisia's Imports, OECD, 1988, Financing Exports to Developing Countries, OECD, 1992; co-editor: Economic Integration in Europe and North America, 1992; editor Can. Jour. Econs., 1965-70. Recipient ann. award des Diplomes de l'U. de Montreal, 1974; apptd. Officer of Order of Can., 1986; fellow Walter Levy Coun. on Fgn. Rels., Boston, 1977. Fellow Royal Soc. Can.; mem. Can. Econs. Assn. (pres. 1983-84), Am. Econs. Assn., Atlantic Econ. Soc. (disting. assoc.). Liberal. Roman Catholic. Home: 4820 Roslyn St, Montreal, PQ Canada H3W 2L2

RAYNER, ROBERT MARTIN, financial executive; b. London, Sept. 21, 1946; s. Henry John and Kathleen Mary (Edwards) R.; m. Mindy S. Miller, May 28, 1979. BSc with honors in Eng., Bristol (Eng.) U., 1968; MBA, London Bus. Sch., 1976. Sr. engr. Halcrow and Ptnrs., London, 1968-74; fin. dir. Pepsico Inc., Purchase, N.Y., 1976-88; pres. constrn. materials group, sr. v.p., CFO ESSROC Corp., Nazareth, Pa., 1988-94, pres., COO, 1994—; bd. dirs. Essroc Cement Corp., Nazareth, San Juan Cement Co., P.R., Ciment Quebec Inc., St. Basile. Mem. Inst. Civil Engrs. Avocations: running, golf, theatre, music. Office: Essroc Italcementi Group 3251 Bath Pike Nazareth PA 18064-8928

RAYNER, WILLIAM ALEXANDER, retired newspaper editor; b. Winnipeg, Man., Can., Nov. 7, 1929; s. William and Annie Mitchell (McDonald) R.; divorced; 1 child, Robert William. Student Can. schs. Sports editor Trail Times, B.C., 1954-55; sportswriter Victoria (B.C.) Times, 1955-57, Vancouver (B.C.) Herald, 1957; copy editor, reporter Montreal (Que.) Star, 1957-58; asst. sports editor Vancouver Sun, 1958-62, copy editor, then slotman, 1962-74, news editor, 1974-83, systems mgr., 1983-88, ret., 1988; copy editor Toronto Globe & Mail, 1962. Author: Vancouver Sun Style Guide, 1976. Dir. B.C. Newspaper Found. Mem. Vancouver Press Club.

RAYNOLDS, DAVID ROBERT, buffalo breeder, author; b. N.Y., Feb. 15, 1928; s. Robert Frederick and Marguerite Evelyn (Gerdau) R.; m. May (Kean) Raynolds, May 12, 1951; children: Robert, Linda, Martha, Laura, David A.F. AB, Dartmouth Coll., 1949; MA, Wesleyan U., Middletown, Conn., 1955; predoctoral, Johns Hopkins Sch. Advanced Internat. Studies, Washington, 1956; grad., Nat. War Coll., Washington, 1973. Account exec. R.H. Morris Assoc., Newtown, Conn., 1949-50; fgn. svc. officer Dept. of State, Washington, 1956-76; pres. Ranch Rangers, Inc., Lander, Wyo., 1976—; pres. Nat. Buffalo Assn., Ft. Pierre, S.D., 1987-88. Author: Rapid Development in Small Economies (Praeger); contbr. articles to profl. jours. Mem. mgmt. com. Wyo. Heritage Soc.; bd. dirs. Liberty Hall Found., Wyo. Community Found. With U.S. Army, 1950-53. Recipient Meritorious Svc. Award, Dept. of State, Washington, 1966. Mem. The Explorers Club, Fremont County Farm Bur., Fgn. Svc. Assn., Am. Legion, Rotary, Elks. Republican. Episcopalian. Avocation: travel. Office: Table Mountain Group PO Box 1310 Lander WY 82520-1310

RAYNOLDS, HAROLD, JR., retired state education commissioner; b. Chgo., Feb. 7, 1925; s. Harold and Dorothy (Smith) R.; m. Ann Richards Ellis, June 1950 (div. 1968); children—Christopher, Timothy, Madeline, Dorothy, m. Patricia Adele Miller, Jan. 20, 1973. BS, Cornell U., 1948, MA, 1953; postgrad., NYU, 1968-69. Cert. supt. schs., N.Y., Maine, Alaska. Supt. schs. Cape Elizabeth Sch. Dist., Maine, 1969-74; supt. schs. Portland Sch. Dist., Maine, 1974-79; commr. edn. State of Maine, Augusta, 1979-83, State of Alaska, Juneau, 1983-86, Commonwealth of Mass., 1986-91; interim supt. Windsor Ctrl. Supervisory Union Sch. Dist., Woodstock, Vt., 1991-92; vice chair Windsor Ctrl. Supervisory Union Sch. Dist., Woodstock, 1993—; supt. Springfield (Vt.) Sch. Dist., 1994—. Contbr. articles to ednl. jours. Mem. sch. com., Pomfret, Vt., 1993—; vice chair Windsor Ctrl. Supervisory Union Bd., 1993—; mem. Vt. Senate, 1965-66; chmn. Vt. Bd. Edn., Montpelier, 1963-68; trustee U. Maine, Orono, 1979-83; Dem. candidate for U.S. Congress, Vt., 1962. Staff sgt. U.S. Army, 1943-45, ETO. Mem. Am. Assn. Sch. Adminstrs., Chief State Sch. Officers, Phi Delta Kappa. Unitarian-Universalist. Avocations: reading; gardening; cross-country skiing; theater; music.

RAYNOR, JOHN PATRICK, university administrator; b. Omaha, Oct. 1, 1923; s. Walter V. and Mary Clare (May) R. AB, St. Louis U., 1947, MA, 1948, Licentiate in Philosophy, 1949, Licentiate in Theology, 1956; PhD, U. Chgo., 1959. Ordained priest Roman Cath. Ch., 1954. Joined Soc. of Jesus, 1941; instr. St. Louis U. High Sch., 1948-51, asst. prin., 1951; asst. to dean Coll. Liberal Arts, Marquette U., 1960, asst. to v.p. acad. affairs, 1961-62, v.p. acad. affairs, 1962-65, pres., 1965-90, ret., 1990; now, chancellor Marquette Univ., Milwaukee, Wis.; dir. Kimberly-Clark Corp. Mem. Greater Milw. Com.; Pub. Policy Forum; corp. mem. United Community Services Greater Milw.; hon. bd. dirs. Goethe House; mem. Froedtert Meml. Luth. Hosp. Corp.; hon. com. mem. Endowment Fund Metro Milw. Luth. Campus Ministry; trustee Milw. Heart Research Found., Inc.; bd. dirs. Greater Milw. Edn. Trust, Mus. Sci., Econs. & Tech., Inc. Discovery World. Recipient Disting. Service award Edn. Commn. of States, 1977. Mem. Nat. Cath. Edn. Assn., North Central Assn. (examiner, cons.), Am. Council Edn., Wis. Assn. Ind. Colls. and Univs. (past pres., exec. com.), Wis. Found. Ind. Colls. (past pres.), Assn. Jesuit Colls. and Univs. (past chmn., dir., mem. exec. com.), Internat. Fedn. Cath. Colls. and Univs., Met. Milw. Assn. Commerce, Phi Beta Kappa, Phi Delta Kappa, Alpha Sigma Nu. Office: Marquette U 615 N 11th St Milwaukee WI 53233-2305

RAYNOR, RICHARD BENJAMIN, neurosurgeon, educator; b. N.Y.C., Aug. 16, 1928; s. Murray and Mildred (Pitt) R.; m. Barbara Golob; children: Geoffrey, Michele. BSME, U. Mich., 1950; MD, U. Vt., 1955. Diplomate Am. Bd. Neurol. Surgery. Intern Mt. Sinai, N.Y.C., 1955-56; residency Neurol. Inst. Presbyn. Hosp., N.Y.C., 1956-57, Nat. Hosp., London, 1957; residency neurosurgery Neurol. Inst. Presbyn. Hosp., 1958-62; assoc. in neurosurgery Coll. Physicians and Surgeons Columbia U., N.Y.C., 1965-77; clin. assoc. prof. NYU, N.Y.C., 1977-84, clin. prof., 1984—; pvt. practice neurosurgery, N.Y.C., 1965—. Consulting editor Spine; contbr. more than 40 articles to profl. jours., chpts. to books. Served as capt. U.S. Army, 1962-64. Fellow Am. Coll. Surgeons; mem. Cervical Spine Research Soc. (pres. 1986-87), Am. Assn. Neurol. Surgeons, Congress Neurol. Surgeons. Club: University (N.Y.C.). Avocations: skiing, squash. Office: 112 E 74th St New York NY 10021-3503

RAYNOR, WANDRA ADAMS, middle school educator; b. Angier, N.C., Oct. 29, 1942; d. Lacoma Eldridge and Edna (Mangum) Adams; m. Donald David Stewart, June 16, 1964 (dec. Dec. 1965); 1 child, Dona Jean Stewart Raynor; m. Ira Kent Raynor, June 28, 1969; children: Richard Kent, Ira Adam. BS in Edn., Campbell Coll., 1971; MA in Early Childhood Edn., Campbell U., 1979; EdS in Adminstrn. Supervision, East Carolina U., 1983. Cert. tchr., advanced adminstr., supr., N.C. Clk. Am. Guaranty Ins. Co., Fayetteville, N.C., 1960-62; sec. Am. Defender Life, Fayetteville, 1962-64; tchr. Gentry Primary Sch., Erwin, N.C., 1971-73; tchr., asst. prin. North Harnett Primary Sch., Angier, 1973-85; tchr. Angier Mid. Sch., 1986—, Harnett Cen. Middle Sch., 1993—, Inst. Children's Lit., 1994—. Mem. Internat. Reading Assn. (pres. Lillington, N.C. 1983-84, treas. Harnett coun. 1992-93, participant state conf. seminars 1992—), N.C. Assn. Educators, Math. Tchrs. Assn., Environ. Educators, N.C. Writers Network, Crepe Myrtle Investors (pres. 1997), Angier C. of C. (Disting. Educator award 1983), Order Ea. Star (worthy matron 1973-75, dist. dep. grand matron 1976-77), Delta Kappa Gamma, Epsilon Phi Beta. Democrat. Baptist. Avocations: golf, reading, snow skiing, writing. Home: 203 Pleasant St Angier NC 27501-9257 Office: Harnett Cen Middle RR 4 Box 293-b Angier NC 27501-9804

RAYNOVICH, GEORGE, JR., lawyer; b. Pitts., Dec. 30, 1931; s. George Sr. and Zora (Mamula) R.; m. Mary Ann Senay, July 11, 1953; children: George III, Andrew. BS, U. Pitts., 1957; JD, Duquesne U., 1961. Bar: Pa. 1962, U.S. Dist. Ct. (we. dist.) Pa. 1962, U.S. Patent and Trademark Office 1962, U.S. Supreme Ct. 1966, U.S. Ct. Appeals (fed. cir.) 1986. Patent agt. Consolidation Coal Co., Library, Pa., 1959-62; ptnr. Stone & Raynovich, Pitts., 1962-75; atty. Wheeling-Pitts. Steel Corp., Pitts., 1975-77, gen. counsel, sec., 1978-85, v.p., 1980-85, bd. dirs., 1983-85; sr. atty. Buchanan Ingersol P.C., Pitts., 1986-88, 89-96; ptnr. Price & Raynovich, Pitts., 1988-89; of counsel Gorr Moser Dell and Loughney, 1997—. Councilman Borough of Baldwin, Allegheny County, Pa., 1972-75, govt. study commr., 1973. 1st lt. USAF, 1952-56. Mem. ABA, Pa. Bar Assn., Allegheny County Bar Assn., Pitts. Intellectual Property Law Assn., Fed. Cir. Bar Assn., Acad. Trial Lawyers Allegheny County. Democrat. Mem. Serbian Orthodox Ch. Home: 335 Jean Dr Pittsburgh PA 15236 Office: Buchanan & Ingersoll PC One Oxford Ctr 301 Grant St Ste 20 Pittsburgh PA 15219-1408

RAYSON, EDWIN HOPE, lawyer; b. Earlville, Ill., Jan. 13, 1923; s. Edwin H. and Lillian (Astley) R.; m. Evelyn Sherry Kirkland, Oct. 1, 1983; children: Jane Rayson Young, Edwin Hope III, G. Scott. A.B., U. Tenn., 1944, LL.B., 1948. Bar: Tenn. 1948. Pvt. practice Knoxville, 1948—; ptnr. Kramer, Rayson, Leake, Rodgers & Morgan, 1949—; lectr. labor law U. Tenn. Coll. Law, 1951-71. Served to lt. (j.g.) USNR, 1944-46. Mem. Order of Coif, Sigma Chi, Omicron Delta Kappa. Home: 501 River Rd Loudon TN 37774-5555 Office: 25th Flr 1st Tennessee Plaza Knoxville TN 37901

RAYSON, GLENDON ENNES, internist, preventive medicine specialist, writer; b. Oak Park, Ill., Dec. 2, 1915; s. Ennes Charles and Beatrice Margaret (Rowland) R. AB, U. Rochester, 1939; MD, U. Ill., Chgo., 1948; MPH, Johns Hopkins U., 1965; MA, Northwestern U., 1965. Diplomate Am. Bd. Internal Medicine, Am. Bd. Preventive Medicine, Am. Bd. Forensic Medicine. Resident in internal medicine Presbyn.-St. Luke's Hosp., Chgo., 1953-56; physician-in-charge Contagious Disease Hosp., Chgo., 1956-58, asst. med. supt., 1958-64; rsch. assoc. Sch. Hygiene and Pub. Health Johns Hopkins U., Balt., 1966-71; internist Johns Hopkins Hosp., 1971-82, Columbia Free State Health Plan, Balt., 1984-91; pvt. practice Balt., 1984—; with Neurodiagnostics Assocs., 1990—; attending internist emergency rm. South Balt. Gen. Hosp., 1982-84; asst. prof. health sci. U. Ill., Chgo., 1958-64; fellow in gastroenterology and endocrinology Presbyn.-St. Luke's Hosp., 1956-58. Contbr. articles to med. jours., chpt. to book. Vol. physician, Vietnam, 1968, 71, 72, 73; mem. Citizens Amb. Program Delegation to Vietnam, 1993. Capt. M.C., USAF, 1951-53. Fellow Am. Coll. Preventive Medicine, Am Geriatrics Soc.; mem. AMA, Am. Pub. Health Assn. Avocations: writing poetry, short stories, composing songs. Home: 337 Poplar Point Rd Perryville MD 21903-1803 Office: 218 N Charles St Apt 1407 Baltimore MD 21201-4027

RAYWARD, WARDEN BOYD, librarian, educator; b. Inverell, New South Wales, Australia, June 24, 1939; s. Warden and Ellie Rayward. B.A., U. Sydney, 1960; diploma in libr., U. NSW, 1964; M.S. in L.S, U. Ill., 1965; Ph.D., U. Chgo., 1973. Asst. state library NSW, 1961-64, research librarian planning and devel., 1970; lectr. Sch. Librarianship U. NSW, 1971-72, head sch. Info., Libr. and Archive Studies, 1986-92, prof., 1986—, dean Faculty of Profl. Studies, 1993-96; asst. prof. U. Western Ont., 1973-74; asst. prof. Grad. Library Sch. U. Chgo., 1975-77, assoc. prof., 1978-80, prof., 1980-86; dean U. Chgo. Grad. Library Sch., 1980-86; cons. NEH, 1976-79, U.S. Dept. Edn., 1981; bd. govs. Charles Stuart U., 1994-96; bd. dirs. Internat. House-U. N.S.W., 1992-97; George A. Miller vis. prof. U. Ill., 1997—. Author: The Universe of Information: The Work of Paul Otlet for Documentation and International Organization, 1975 (also transl. Russian and Spanish); editor: The Variety of Librarianship: Essays in Honour of John Wallace Metcalfe, 1976, The Public Library: Circumstances and Prospects, 1978, Library Quar., 1975-79, Library History in Context, 1988, Libraries and Life in a Changing World: the Metcalfe Years 1920-1970, 1993; editor, translator: International Organization and the Dissemination of Knowledge: Selected Papers of Paul Otlet, 1990; editor Confronting the Future, University Libraries in the Next Decade, 1992, Developing a Profession in Librarianship in Australia: Travel Diaries and Other Papers, 1996; mem. internat. editorial adv. bd. World Book of Encyclopedia, 1990-97; contbr. articles to profl. jours. Coun. on Library Resources fellow, 1978; vis. fellow U. Coll. London, 1986, 90, Mortenson fellow U. Ill., 1992-93. Mem. ALA, Australian Library and Info. Assn., Bibliog. Soc. Australia and New Zealand, Am. Soc. for Info. Sci. Office: U New South Wales, PO Box 1, Kensington NSW 2033, Australia

RAZ, HILDA, editor-in-chief periodical, educator; b. Rochester, N.Y., May 4, 1938; d. Franklyn Emmanuel and Dolly (Horwich) R.; m. Frederick M. Link, June 9, 1957 (div. 1969); children: John Franklin Link, Aaron Link; m. Dale Nordyke, Oct. 4, 1980. BA, Boston U., 1960. Asst. dir. Planned Parenthood League of Mass., Boston, 1960-62; edit. asst. Prairie Schooner, Lincoln, Nebr., 1970-74; contbg. editor Prairie Schooner, 1974-77, assoc. editor, 1977-87, acting editor, 1981-83, 85, poetry editor, 1980-87, editor-in-chief, 1987—; assoc. prof. dept Eng. U. Nebr., Lincoln, 1990—; lectr., reader, panelist in field; participant many workshops, symposia, confs.; panelist arts com. NEA, 1994; judge Kenyon Rev., 1990, Soc. Midland Authors Best Book of 1987 award, 198, Ill. Art Coun./NEA fellowships, 1987; bd. govs. Ctr. for Great Plains Studies, U. Nebr., 1989-95. Author numerous poems, essays; editor Nebr. Humanist, 1990. Pres. Assoc. Writing Programs, bd. dirs., 1988-89, ex-officio pres., 1989-90, v.p., 1987-88; mem. program com. Friends of Librs. U. Nebr., 1989-90; bd. dirs. Nebr. Libr. Heritage Assn., 1988-91; mem. Mayor's Blue Ribbon Com. on Arts, 1985-88; bd. dirs. Planned Parenthood League Nebr., 1978-83, sec. bd. dirs., 1979-80, chairperson long-term planning com., 1980-81, 81-82. Recipient Literary Heritage award Mayor's Art Awards, Lincoln, 1988; Bread Loaf scholar editors, 1974, poetry, 1985; Robert Frost fellow, 1988, 89, Mag. Panel fellow, 1993, 94. Avocations: gardening. Home: 960 S Cotner Blvd Lincoln NE 68510-4926 Office: Univ of Nebraska Lincoln Prairie Schooner 201 Andrews Hall Lincoln NE 68588-0334

RAZZANO, FRANK CHARLES, lawyer; b. Bklyn., Feb. 25, 1948; s. Pasquale Anthony and Agnes Mary (Borgia) R.; m. Stephanie Anne Lucas, Jan. 10, 1970; children: Joseph, Francis, Catherine. BA, St. Louis U., 1969; JD, Georgetown U., 1972. Bar: N.Y. 1973, U.S. Dist. Ct. (so. dist.) N.Y. 1973, U.S. Dist. Ct. (es. dist.) N.Y. 1973, N.J. 1976, D.C. 1981, Va. 1984, U.S. Dist. Ct. N.J. 1976, U.S. Dist. Ct. Md. 1977, U.S. Dist. Ct. (no. dist.) Calif. 1981, U.S. Dist. Ct. D.C. 1982, U.S. Dist. Ct. (ea. dist.) Va. 1989, U.S. Dist. Ct. (we. dist.) Va. 1990, U.S. Ct. Appeals (2d cir.) 1973, U.S. Ct. Appeals (3d cir.) 1975, U.S. Ct. Appeals (D.C. and 5th cirs.) 1983, U.S. Ct. Appeals (4th cir.) 1984, U.S. Ct. Appeals (6th cir.) 1990, U.S. Supreme Ct. 1976. Assoc. Shea & Gould, N.Y.C., 1972-75; asst. U.S. atty. Dist. of N.J., Newark, 1975-78; asst. chief trial atty. SEC, Washington, 1978-82; ptnr. Shea & Gould, Washington, 1982-94, mng. ptnr., 1991-92; ptnr. Camhy Karlinsky Stein Razzano & Rubin, Washington, 1994-96, Dickstein, Shapiro, Morin & Oshinsky, Washington, 1996—; lectr. in field. Civil law editor Rico Law Reporter; mem. adv. bd. Corp. Confidentiality and Disclosure Letter; hon. adv. com. Jour. Internat. Law and Practice, Detroit Coll. Law; contbr. articles to legal jours. Scoutmaster Vienna coun. Boy Scouts Am., 1984. Recipient spl. achievement award Justice Dept., 1977, spl. commendation, 1978, Outstanding Achievement award Detroit Coll. of Law, 1993. Mem. ABA (chmn. criminal law com., sect. bus. law 1996—), Va. Bar, D.C. Bar (chmn. litigation sect. 1987-89, vice-chmn. coun. sects. 1988-89), Assn. Securities & Exch. Commn. Alumni (pres. 1993-95), Phi Beta Kappa, Eta Sigma Phi. Roman Catholic. Home: 1713 Paisley Blue Ct Vienna VA 22182-2326

RAZZANO, PASQUALE ANGELO, lawyer; b. Bklyn., Apr. 3, 1943; s. Pasquale Anthony and Agnes Mary (Borgia) R.; m. Maryann Walker, Jan. 29, 1966; children: Elizabeth, Pasquale, Susan, ChristyAnn. BSCE, Poly. Inst. Bklyn., 1964; student law, NYU, 1964-66; JD, Georgetown U., 1969. Bar: Va. 1969, N.Y. 1970, U.S. Ct. Appeals (2d, 3d, 7th, 9th and fed. cirs.), U.S. Supreme Ct., U.S. Dist. Ct. (so., ea. and western dists.) N.Y., U.S. Dist. Ct. (we. dist.) Tex., U.S. Dist. Ct. Hawaii, U.S. Dist. Ct. Conn. Examiner U.S. Patent Office, 1966-69; assoc. Curtis, Morris & Safford, P.C., 1969-71, ptnr., 1971-91; ptnr. Fitzpatrick, Cella, Harper & Scinto, 1991—; guest lectr. U.S. Trademark Assn., Am. Intellectual Property Law Assn., Practicing Law Inst., NYU Law Ctr., ABA, N.Y. Intellectual Property Law Assn. Mem. bd. editors Licensing Jour., 1986—; mem. bd. editors Trademark Reporter, 1987—, book rev. editor, 1989-91, pub. articles editor, 1991-94, domestic articles editor, 1992-93, 95, editor-in-chief 1996—. Rep. committeeman Rockland County. Recipient Robert Ridgeway award, 1964. Mem. ABA (guest lectr.), Fed. Bar Assn. (chmn. trademark law com. 1997—), N.Y. Intellectual Property Law Assn. (bd. dirs. 1985—, sec. 1988-91, pres. 1994-95), Licensing Exec. Soc. (chmn. N.Y. chpt. 1996—), Internat. Trademark Assn. (bd. dirs. 1996—), Am. Intellectual Property Law Assn., N.Y. Bar Assn., N.Y. Coun. Bar Leaders (exec. coun. 1993-94), Va. Bar Assn., Italian Am. Bar Assn., Bar Assn. City N.Y., Columban Laws Assn., N.Y. Athletic Club, Minute Man Yacht Club, Shorehaven Golf Club. Republican. Roman Catholic. Address: 15 White Woods Ln Westport CT 06880-1837 also: 14 Deerwood Trl Lake Placid NY 12946-1834

RE, EDWARD DOMENIC, law educator, retired federal judge; b. Santa Marina, Italy, Oct. 14, 1920; s. Anthony and Marina (Maetta) R.; m. Margaret A. Corcoran, June 3, 1950; children: Mary Ann, Anthony John, Marina, Edward, Victor, Margaret, Matthew, Joseph, Mary Elizabeth, Mary Joan, Mary Ellen, Nancy Madeleine. BS cum laude, St. John's U., 1941, LLB summa cum laude, 1943, LLD (hon.), 1968; JSD, NYU, 1950; DPed, Aquila, Italy, 1960; LL.D. (hon.), St. Mary's Coll., Notre Dame, Ind., 1968, Maryville Coll., St. Louis, 1969, N.Y. Law Sch., 1976, Bklyn. Coll., CUNY, 1978, Nova U., 1980, Roger Williams Coll., 1982, Dickinson Sch. Law, Carlisle, Pa., 1983, Seton Hall U., 1984, Stetson U., 1990, William Mitchell Coll. Law, 1992, St. Francis Coll., Bklyn., 1993; L.H.D. (hon.), DePaul U., 1980, Coll. S.I., CUNY, 1981, Pace U., 1985, Am. U. of Rome, 1995; D.C.S. (hon.), U. Verona, Italy, 1987; J.D. (hon.), U. Bologna, Italy, 1988, U. Urbino, Italy, 1994. Bar: N.Y. 1943. Appointed faculty St. John's U., N.Y., 1947, prof. law, 1951-69, adj. prof. law, 1969-80, Disting. prof., from 1980; vis. prof. Georgetown U. Sch. Law, 1962-67; adj. prof. law N.Y. Law Sch., 1972-82, Martin disting. vis. prof., 1982-90; spl. hearing officer U.S. Dept. Justice, 1956-61; chmn. Fgn. Claims Settlement Commn. of U.S., 1961-68; asst. sec. ednl. and cultural affairs U.S. Dept. State, 1968-69; judge U.S. Customs Ct. (now U.S. Ct. Internat. Trade), N.Y.C., 1969-91, chief judge, 1977-91, chief judge emeritus, 1991—; mem. Jud. Conf. U.S., 1986-91, adv. com. on appellate rules, 1976-88, com. on internat. jud. rels., 1994—; chmn. adv. com. on experimentation in the law Fed. Jud. Ctr., 1978-81; mem. bd. higher edn. City of N.Y., 1958-69, emeritus, 1969—; Jackson lectr. Nat. Coll. State Trial Judges, U. Nev., 1970. Author: Foreign Confiscations in Anglo-American Law, 1951, (with Lester D. Orfield) Cases and Materials on International Law, rev. edit., 1965, Selected Essays on Equity, 1955, Brief Writing and Oral Argument, 6th edit., 1987, (with Joseph R. Re) 7th edit., 1993, (with Zechariah Chafee Jr.) Cases and Materials on Equity, 1967, Cases and Materials on Equitable Remedies, 1975; (with Joseph R. Re) Law Students' Manual on Legal Writing and Oral Argument, 1991; chpt., freedom in internat. soc. Concept of Freedom (editor Rev. Carl W. Grindel), 1955; Cases and Materials on Remedies, 1982, (with Joseph R. Re) 4th edit., 1996; contbr. articles to legal jours. Served with USAAF, 1943-47; col. JAGC, ret. Decorated Grand Cross Order of Merit Italy; recipient Am. Bill of Rights citation; Morgenstern Found. Interfaith award; USAF commendation medal; Distinguished service award Bklyn. Jr. C. of C., 1956. Mem. ABA (ho. of dels. 1976-78, chmn. sect. internat. and comparative law 1965-67), Am. Fgn. Law Assn. (pres. 1971-73), Am. Law Inst., Fed. Bar Coun. (pres. 1973-74), Am. Soc. Comparative Law (pres. 1969-91), Am. Justinian Soc. Jurists (pres. 1974-76), Internat. Assn. Jurists: Italy-USA (pres. 1991—), Internat. Assn. Judges (prin. rep. to UN 1993—), Scribes Am. Soc. Writers on Legal Subjects (pres. 1978). Office: 305 B 147th St Neponsit NY 11694

RE, EDWARD DOMENIC, JR., construction executive; b. Bklyn., Aug. 11, 1955; s. Edward Domenic Sr. and Margaret (Corcoran) R.; m. Eileen Frances McMahon, Jan. 14, 1989; children: Edward, Joseph. AAS, N.Y.C. Tech. Coll., 1978; BS, Pratt Inst., 1981, MS, 1997; postgrad., Inst. Design and Constrn., 1992. Cert. environ. inspector; cert. real estate appraiser; cert. profl. constructor. V.p. Con-Solid Contracting, Inc., 1986—; founder, pres. Rockaway Park Realty Corp., Belle Harbor Devel. Corp.; prof. constrn. mgmt. Pratt Inst., 1992—, prof. facility mgmt., 1993—; cons. in field. Mem. N.Y.C. Cmty. Bd. 14 Zoning Com., 1985-87. Mem. Constrn. Mgmt. Assn. Am. (founder), Am. Inst. Constructors (trustee, question formulator for examination), Am. Arbitration Assn., N.Y.C. Tech. Coll. Alumni Assn. (hon. life), Pratt Inst. Constrn. Mgmt. Alumni Assn. (founder constrn. mgmt. scholarship fund, Golden Hammer award). Home: 186 Beach 137th St Belle Harbor NY 11694 Office: 410 Beach 129th St Far Rockaway NY 11694-1517

RE, RICHARD NOEL, endocrinologist; b. Palisade, N.J., Sept. 4, 1944; m. Martha Jean Macdonald, 1979; children: Richard Macdonald, Christopher Moran, Gregory Noël. AB summa cum laude, Harvard U., 1965, MD cum laude, 1969. Diplomate Am. Bd. Internal Medicine, Am. Bd. Endocrinology and Metabolism. Med. intern Mass. Gen. Hosp., Boston, 1969-70, med. resident, 1970-71, clin. and rsch. fellow in endocrinology, 1971-74, clin. asst. in medicine, 1974-76, chief Hypertension Clinic, 1975-79, asst. in medicine, 1976-79; rsch. fellow Harvard Med. Sch., Boston, 1971-74, instr. in medicine, 1975-76, asst. prof. medicine, 1977-79; mem. staff Ochsner Med. Instns., New Orleans, 1979—; assoc. clin. prof. medicine Tulane U. Sch. Medicine, New Orleans, 1980—; head sect. on hypertensive diseases Ochsner Clinic, New Orleans, 1981—; v.p., dir. rsch. Alton Ochsner Med. Found., New Orleans, 1985—; adj. prof. biology U. New Orleans, 1984—; chmn. clin. investigations com. Alton Ochsner Med. Found., 1980-86; mem. sci. rev. panel VA, 1988—; chmn. sci. resources com. Blood Rsch. Ctr., New Orleans, 1989-91, trustee, 1989-91; mem. adv. bd. Internat. Consortium for the Study of Tissue Renin Angiotensin Systems, 1990-92; mem. rsch. com. Am. Heart Assn.-La., Inc., 1990, mem. sci. peer rev. com., 1990-91; mem. rsch. adv. com. Medicare Clinics Pilot Project, 1990-92. Author: Bioburst: The Impact of Modern Biology on the Affairs of Man, 1986; author: (with others) Clinical Pharmacy and Clinical Pharmacology, 1976, Biological Handbook II, 1977, Methods in Immunodiagnosis, 1981, Prostaglandins, Platelets, and Salicylates: Basic and Clinical Aspects, 1982, Systemic Disease in Dental Treatment, 1982, Kidney in Essential Hypertension, 1984, Current Clinical Practice, 1987, Current Advances in ACE Inhibition, 1989, Advances in Vascular Pathology, 1990; contbr. numerous articles to profl. jours. including Am. Jour. Hypertension, New Eng. Jour. Medicine, Jour. Inorganic Biochemistry, Current Opinion in Cardiology, Contemporary Internal Medicine, Lancet, Modern Medicine, Am. Jour. Cardiology. Fellow coun. on high blood pressure rsch. Am. Heart Assn. Grantee Nat. Heart and Lung Inst. NIH, 1981-85, La. Heart Assn., 1981-83, Indsl. Support, 1981-91. Fellow Am. Coll. Physicians; mem. AAAS, Am. Fedn. for Clin. Rsch., Assn. Am. Med. Colls. Group on Med. Edn., N.Y. Acad. Scis., Cen. Soc. for Clin. Investigation, So. Soc. for Clin. Investigation (Tinsley Harrison award 1996), So. Med. Assn., Internat. Soc. Hypertension, Endocrine Soc., Soc. for Exptl. Biology and Medicine, Phi Beta Kappa. Achievements include research on growth factors and cardiovascular structure, on angiotensin and regulation of cellular growth, and on hypertension. Office: Alton Ochsner Med Found 1516 Jefferson Hwy New Orleans LA 70121-2429

REA, AMADEO MICHAEL, ethnobiologist, ornithologist; b. Oakland, Calif., Oct. 15, 1939. BA, San Luis Rey Coll., 1963; MS, Ariz. State U., 1969; PhD, U. Ariz., 1977. Curator birds and mammals San Diego Natural History Mus., 1977-91, rsch. assoc., 1991—. Author: Once a River, Bird Life and Habitat Changes on the Middle Gila, 1983. Mem. Soc. Ethnobiology (pres. 1987-89). Democrat. Roman Catholic. Home: 1455 49th St San Diego CA 92102-2625

REA, ANN W., librarian; b. Jefferson City, Mo., Aug. 3, 1944; d. William H. and Ruby (Fogleman) Webb; m. Glen N. Rea, Sept. 28, 1974; children: Sarah, Rebecca. BA, U. Mo., 1966; MLS, U. So. Calif., 1968. Libr. St. Charles (Mo.) County Libr., 1967-71; libr. adult svcs. Paterson (N.J.) Free Pub. Libr., 1971-74; libr. Beal Coll. Libr., Bangor, Maine, 1983—. Mem. Am. Libr. Assn., Maine Libr. Assn. Office: Beal Coll Libr 629 Main St Bangor ME 04401-6848

REA, DAVID K., geology and oceanography educator; b. Pitts., June 2, 1942; m. Donna M. Harshbarger, Feb. 11, 1967; children: Gregory, Margaret. AB, Princeton U., 1964; MS, U. Ariz., 1967; PhD, Oreg. State U., 1974. Prof. geology & oceanography U. Mich., Ann Arbor, 1975—; assoc. dir. NSF Climate Dynamics Program, Washington, 1986-87; interim dir. Ctr. for Great Lakes and Aquatic Scis., 1988-89, chmn. dept. geol. scis., 1995—. Contbr. more than 300 articles, reports to profl. publs. Recipient numerous NSF rsch. grants, 1976—. Office: U Mich Dept Geological Sci Ann Arbor MI 48109-1063

REA, STEPHEN, actor; b. Belfast, Ireland, 1949; m. Dolours Price, 1983; children: Oscar, Danny. Student, Queens Univ., Belfast. Formed (with Brian Friel) Field Day Theatre Co., 1980. Stage appearances include (London) The Shadow of a Gunman, The Cherry Orchard, Miss Julie, High Society; (Royal Court Theatre) Endgame, The Freedom of the City; (Field Day Theatre Co.) Translations, Communication Card, St. Oscar, Boesman and Lena, Hightime and Riot Act, Double Cross, Pentecost, Making History, Three Sisters (dir. only), The Cure at Troy (dir. only); (Broadway) Someone Who'll Watch Over Me, 1992 (Tony award nominee 1993), Uncle Vanya, 1995; (Double Tap Theatre) Ashes to Ashes, 1996; films include Angel, 1982, Danny Boy, 1984, Company of Wolves, 1985, The Doctor and the Devils, 1985, Loose Connections, 1988, Life Is Sweet, 1991, The Crying Game, 1992 (Acad. award nominee best actor 1993), Bad Behavior, 1993, Princess Caraboo, 1993, Angie, 1994, Interview with the Vampire, 1994, Ready to Wear (Prêt-à-Porter), 1994, All Men Are Mortal, 1994, Citizen X, 1994, The Devil and the Deep Blue Sea, 1994, Michael Collins, 1995, 96 Trojah Eddzie, 1995, Butcher Boy, 1995, 97, Crime of The Century, 1995, Troja Eddie, 1996, ; TV appearances include Four Days in July, Lost Belongings, Scout, St. Oscar, Not with a Bang, Hedda Gabler. Office: Peters Fraser & Dunlop Ltd, 503 The Chambers Lots Rd, Chelsea Harbor London SW10 0XF, England

REA, WILLIAM J., district judge; b. 1950; BA, Loyola U., 1942, LLB, U. Colo., 1949. With U.S. Census Bur., Denver, 1949-50; adjuster Farmers Ins. Group, L.A., 1950; pvt. practice law, L.A., 1950-64, Santa Ana, Calif., 1964-68; judge Superior Ct., L.A., 1968-84; judge U.S. Dist. Ct. (cen. dist.) Calif., L.A., 1984—. Past pres. L.A. chpt. Nat. Exec. Com.; chmn. Constn. and By-Laws Com. With USN, WWII. Mem. L.A. County Bar Assn. (Outstanding Jurist award 1985), So. Calif. Def. Counsel Assn. Disting. Svc. award 1982), Internat. Acad. Trial Lawyers (Trial Judge of Yr. 1982), L.A. Trial Lawyers Assn., Am. Bd. Trial Advs. (nat. pres.). Office: US Dist Ct 312 N Spring St Ste 128 Los Angeles CA 90012-4703*

REABOLD, ANTHONY MAURICE, school system administrator; b. Cornelia, Ga., June 25, 1962; s. Maurice Johnny and Anna Ruth (Free) R.; m. Martha Elizabeth Lewis, Aug. 25, 1984; children: Geoffrey Lewis, Gregory Maurice. BS, U. Ga., 1985, EdS, 1994; MEd, Ga. State U., 1991; grad., Gov.'s Sch. Leadership Inst. Elem. specialist Fulton County Sch. Sys., Alpharetta, Ga., 1985-87; tchr. Gwinnett County Schs., Lawrenceville, Ga., 1988-93; asst. prin. Cornelia (Ga.) Elem. Sch., 1993—; mem. League of Profl. Schs., Athens, Ga., 1992-93. Deacon Atkinson Rd. Bapt. Ch., Lawrenceville, 1991, Bethlehem Bapt. Ch., Clarkesville, Ga., 1997, sec. to body of deacons; mem. youth adv. coun. Bethlehem Bapt. Ch., Clarksville, Ga., 1995—, Sunday sch. tchr., 1994—; bd. dirs. Safe Haven Ministries, Mt. Airy, Ga., 1994—, editor The Navigator newsletter; vol. Am. Cancer Soc., Cornelia, 1995—, World Changers, Nashville, 1995—; vol. coach Habersham County Recreation Dept., Clarksville, 1996. Instrnl. grantee Lawrenceville Elem., 1991. Mem. Golden Key, Kappa Delta Pi, Phi Delta Kappa. Avocations: jogging, camping, hiking, reading. Home: PO Box 1524 Clarkesville GA 30523 Office: Cornelia Elem Sch 24 Cash St Cornelia GA 30531

READ, ALLAN ALEXANDER, minister; b. Toronto, Ont., Can., Sept. 19, 1923; s. Alec P. and Lillice (Matthews) R.; m. Mary Beverly Roberts, Sept. 28, 1949; children—John Allan, Elizabeth Anne, Peter Michael, Martha Ruth. B.A., U. Toronto, Can., 1946; Licentiate in Theology, Trinity Coll., Toronto, 1947, D.D., 1972; D.D., Wycliffe Coll., Toronto, 1972; D.S.T. (hon.), Thornloe Coll., Sudbury, Ont., 1982. Ordained diaconate, 1948, priest, 1949, Anglican Ch. of Can.; lic. Diocese of Albany, N.Y., 1996—. Rector 7 chs. Diocese Toronto-Anglican Ch., Parish of East and West Mono, Ont., Can., 1947-54; rector Diocese of Toronto-Trinity Anglican Ch., Christ Ch. Vespra, Barrie, Ont., Can., 1954-72; founder Barrie East End Mission, Parish of St. Giles, 1954; chaplain Simcoe County Gaol, 1954-72; Suffragan bishop Diocese of Toronto-Anglican Ch., Toronto, Ont., Can., 1972-81; bishop Diocese of Ont., Kingston, Ont., Can., 1981-92; canon St. James Cathedral, Toronto, 1957-61; mem., chmn. provincial synod rural chmn. com., 1953-63, Diocese of Toronto Exec. Com., 1959-71, Diocesan Com. Prayer and Evang., 1950-70, Ont. Guelph Agr. Coll. Planning Com. on

Courses for Clergy in Rural Areas, 1950-54, Anglican Gen. Synod Com. on Ministry in Rural Areas, 1952-65; Diocesan Com. Corrections, 1950-72, Gen. Synod Com. Music and Hymn Book, 1965-71, chmn. and chaplin, Boy Scout Com., Barrie #1, 1954-71, Govt. of Ont. Dept. Lands and Forests adv. com. on reforestation, 1950-54, provincial synod, 1955-91, rural ch. unit gen. synod Anglican Ch. Can., 1959-89; archdeacon of Simcoe, 1961-72, Can. churchmn. bd. trustees; participant World Anglican Congress, Toronto, 1963; mem. Anglican World Wide Lambeth Conf., 1978, 88; dir. Anglican Found., Toronto; priest-in-charge St. Patrick's Cathedral, Trim, Ireland, 1992, Parish of Dunster Diocese of Bath and Wells, Eng., 1993, Parish of St. Ippolyts, Diocese St. Alban's, Eng., 1994, Parish of St. Mary the Virgin Westerham, Diocese of Rochester Eng., 1995, Cathedral of St. John and St. Patrick, Ch. of Ireland, Eire, 1956; hon. asst. St. George's Cath., Kingston, ONt., 1992—. Author: Unto The Hills, 1951; Shepherds in Green Pastures, 1953. Patron Grenville Christian Coll., Brockville, Ont., 1981—; mem., hon. pres. Can. Coll. Organists, Simcoe Br., 1954-71; hon. Reeve, Black Creek Pioneer Village, 1981-82; mem. Barrie and Dist. High Sch. Bd., 1961-70; exec. com. Alcohol and Drug Concerns, 1971-83. Recipient Rural Workers Fellowship award Episcopal Ch. U.S., 1952, Citizenship awards Gov. of Ont., 1980, 85, 90; named Citizen of Yr. City of Barrie, 1967. Mem. Rural Workers Fellowship (hon. pres. 1967—), Barrie Ministerial Assn. (sec. 1954-81). Home: 39 Riverside Dr, RR 1, Kingston, ON Canada K7L 4V1

READ, DAVID HAXTON CARSWELL, clergyman; b. Cupar, Fife, Scotland, Jan. 2, 1910; came to U.S., 1956; s. John Alexander and Catherine Haxton (Carswell) R.; m. Dorothy Florence Patricia Gilbert, 1936; 1 son, Rory David Gilbert. Grad., Daniel Stewart's Coll., Edinburgh, 1927; M.A. summa cum laude, U. Edinburgh, 1932, D.D., 1957; student, Montpelier, Strasbourg, Paris, 1932-33, Marburg, 1934; B.D., New Coll., Edinburgh, Scotland, 1936; D.D., Yale U., 1959, Lafayette Coll., 1965, Hope Coll., 1969; Litt.D., Coll. Wooster, 1966; L.H.D., Trinity U., 1972, Hobart Coll., 1972, Knox Coll., 1979; D.H.L., Japan Internat. Christian U., 1979, Rockford Coll., 1982. Ordained to ministry Ch. Scotland, 1936; min. Coldstream West, 1936-39; minister Greenbank Ch., Edinburgh, 1939-49; chaplain U. Edinburgh, 1949-55; chaplain to Her Majesty the Queen, Scotland, 1952-56; minister Madison Ave. Presbyn. Ch., 1956-89, minister emeritus, 1989—. Author: The Spirit of Life, 1939, Prisoners' Quest, 1944, The Communication of the Gospel, 1952, The Christian Faith, 1956, I Am Persuaded, 1962, Sons of Anak, 1964, God's Mobile Family, 1966, Whose God is Dead?, 1966, The Pattern of Christ, 1967, Holy Common Sense, 1966, The Presence of Christ, 1968, Christian Ethics, 1968, Virginia Woolf Meets Charlie Brown, 1968, Religion without Wrappings, 1970, Overheard, 1971, Curious Christians, 1972, An Expanding Faith, 1973, Sent from God, 1974, Good News in the Letters of Paul, 1976, Go . . . And Make Disciples, 1978, Unfinished Easter, 1978, The Faith is Still There, 1980, This Grace Given, 1984, Grace Thus Far, 1986, Preaching About the Needs of Real People, 1988, Christmas Tales for All Ages, 1989; translator (from German): The Church to Come, 1939; editor-in-chief: The Living Pulpit, 1992; contbr. articles religious jours. Chaplain Brit. Army, 1939-45. Mem. Century Assn. (N.Y.C.), Pilgrims Club. Prisoner of war, 1940-45. Home: 258 Riverside Dr Apt 9A New York NY 10025-6161

READ, ELEANOR MAY, financial analyst; b. Arcadia, N.Y., July 4, 1940; d. Henry and Lena May (Fagner) Van Koevering; 1 child, Robin Jo. Typist, clk., sec., credit corr. Sarah Coventry, Inc., Newark, N.Y., 1957-61; exec. sec. Mobil Chem. Co., Macedon, N.Y., 1961-68; bus. mgr. Henry's Hardware, Newark, 1968-72; with Xerox Corp., Fremont, Calif., 1973—, internat. clk. analyst, personnel adminstrv. asst., employment coordinator, exec. sec., cycle count analyst., acctg. specialist, tax preparer H&R Block, 1985-92. Mem. Xerox/Diablo Mgmt. Assn., Am. Mgmt. Assn., Profl. Businesswomen's Assn., NAFE. Office: Xerox AMTX 5450 Campus Dr Canandaigua NY 14424-8200

READ, FREDERICK WILSON, JR., lawyer, educator; b. Providence, July 30, 1908; s. Frederick Wilson and Araminta Rowena (Briggs) R.; m. Evelyn Elaine Avery, Feb. 21, 1942; children: Frederick Wilson III, Cynthia Avery. Student, Trinity Coll., 1925-26; AB, Columbia U., 1930, LLB, 1932. Bar: N.Y. 1933, Mass. 1939, U.S. Supreme Ct. 1955. Assoc. Hervey, Barber & McKee, N.Y.C., 1932-35, Menken, Ferguson & Idler, N.Y.C., 1937-39; atty. legal dept. Nat. Realty Mgmt. Co., N.Y.C., 1935-37, French Air Commn., N.Y.C., 1939-40; mem. legal and contracts depts. Brit. Purchasing Commn., Brit. Air Commn., N.Y.C. and Washington, 1940-41; atty. Glenn L. Martin Co., Middle River, Md., 1941-42; with Home Life Ins. Co., N.Y.C., 1945-73; atty. Home Life Ins. Co., 1945-47, asst. counsel, 1947-54, counsel, 1954-64, gen. counsel, 1964-71, v.p., gen. counsel, 1971-73; counsel Daiker, D'Elia, Turtletaub & Cantino, Port Washington, N.Y., 1973-77, D'Elia, Turtletaub & Cantino, 1977-80, Capobianco, D'Elia, Turtletaub, Cantino & Aitken (P.C.), 1980-83, D'Elia & Turtletaub, 1983—; prof. Coll. Ins., 1974-84, N.Y. Law Sch., 1974-76; counsel N.Y.C. Life Underwriters Assn., 1974-83, hon. mem., 1984—. Mem. Bd. Edn., Port Washington, 1949-52, 59-66, pres., 1950-52, v.p., 1962-66; trustee McAuley Water St. Mission, 1970-81, trustee emeritus, 1981—; dir. John Philip Sousa Meml. Band Shell, Inc., 1990—; mem. sr. adv. coun. Port Washington Pub. Libr., 1991—. Capt. USNR, 1942-45; mem. Res. (ret.). Recipient Bishops Cross, 1988. Fellow Am. Bar Found. (life); mem. ABA (rep. ho. dels. 1969-77, sr. lawyer div. com. liaison with state and local bar sr. lawyers 1986—), N.Y. State Bar Assn. (assn. ins. program com. 1973-84, vice-chmn. 1974-77, chmn. 1977-84), Nassau County Bar Assn. (chmn. assn. ins. plans com. 1973-83, dir. 1977-80), Assn. of Bar of City of N.Y. (ins. law com. 1946-49, 61-64, mil. justice and mil. affairs com. 1951-68, chmn. 1965-68), Assn. Life Ins. Counsel (sec.-treas. 1960-63, v.p. 1965-66, pres. 1967-68), Judge Advs. Assn. (life), Am. Council Life Ins., Health Ins. Assn. Am., Am. Soc. CLUs, Ins. Soc. of N.Y. (1974-84), Cow Neck Peninsula Hist. Soc. (trustee, 3d v.p.-legal 1974-83, trustee emeritus 1983—), U.S. Naval Inst. (life), Naval Res. Assn. (life), Ret. Officers Assn., Nat. Maritime Hist. Soc., Acad. Political Sci., Alpha Delta Phi. Episcopalian. Clubs: Lions (Port Washington) (bd. dirs. 1980-82, 87—); Masons. Home: 2 Lynn Rd Port Washington NY 11050-4447 Office: 927 Port Washington Blvd Port Washington NY 11050-2910

READ, GREGORY CHARLES, lawyer; b. St. Louis, Jan. 21, 1942; s. Charles Hadley and Margaret Olive (Kumlien) R.; m. Mary Beth Bartulis, Aug. 28, 1965; children: Laura Elizabeth, Andrew Nathan. BA, U. Ill., 1964, JD, 1967. Bar: Ill. 1967, Calif. 1971, U.S. Dist. Ct. (no., ea. and cen. dists.) Calif., U.S. Ct. Claims, U.S. Ct. Appeals (9th cir.), U.S. Ct. Appeals (fed. cir.), U.S. Supreme Ct. Law clk. to Hon. Henry Wise U.S. Dist. Ct. Ill., Danville, 1967; assoc. Sedgwick, Detert, Moran & Arnold, San Francisco, 1971-76, ptnr., 1976—. Contbr. articles to profl. jours. Lt. JAGC, USN, 1968-70. Mem. ABA, Am. Bd. Trial Advocates, Ill. Bar Assn., Calif. Bar Assn., Internat. Assn. Def. Counsel, Def. Rsch. Inst. Home: 66 La Cuesta Orinda CA 94563-2326 Office: Sedgwick Detert Moran & Arnold 1 Embarcadero Ctr Fl 16 San Francisco CA 94111-3628

READ, SISTER JOEL, academic administrator. BS in Edn., Alverno Coll., 1948; MA in History, Fordham U., 1951; hon. degrees, Lakeland Coll., 1972, Wittenburg U., 1976, Marymount Manhattan Coll., 1978, DePaul U., 1985, Northland Coll., 1986, SUNY, 1986. Former prof., dept. chmn. history dept. Alverno Coll., Milw., pres., 1968—; pres. Am. Assn. for Higher Edn., 1976-77; mem. coun. NEH, 1977-83; bd. dirs. Ednl. Testing Svc., 1987-93, Neylan Commn., 1985-90; past pres. Wis. Assn. Ind. Colls. and Univs.; mem. Commn. on Status of Edn. for Women, 1971-76, Am. Assn. Colls., 1971-77; sec. Found. for Ind. Higher Edn., 1994—; mem. exec. com. Greater Milw. com. GMC Edn. Trust. Mem. exec. bd. Milw. YMCA. First recipient Anne Roe award Harvard U. Grad. Sch. Edn., 1980. Fellow Am. Acad. Arts and Scis.; mem. Found. for Higher Edn. Office: Alverno Coll Office of Pres PO Box 343922 Milwaukee WI 53234-3922

READ, JOHN CONYERS, industrial management; b. N.Y.C., May 21, 1947; s. Edward Cameron Kirk and Louise (Geary) R.; m. Alexandra Gould, Mar. 30, 1968; children: Cameron Kirk, Trevor Conyers, Alexandra. AB, Harvard, 1969, MBA, 1971. Ops. rsch. analyst HEW, Washington, 1971-72; exec. asst. to dir. Cost of Living Council, Washington, 1973; chief econ. adviser to Gov. Mass., 1974; exec. asst., counselor to sec. labor Washington, 1975; asst. sec. labor for employment standards, 1976-77; dir. corp. employee rels., pers. Cummins Engine Co., Columbus, Ind., 1977-80, plant mgr., 1980-85; v.p. Midrange Engines, 1986-90; v.p., gen. mgr. engine group Donaldson Co., Inc., Mpls., 1990-92; exec. v.p., 1992-94; ptnr. Hidden Creek Industries, Mpls., 1996—; cons. nat. productivity and energy policies; chmn. NAM Task Force on Wage and Price Policies, 1978-80. Author Ford Found. monograph on occupational disease and workers' compensation; contbr. articles to newspapers and mags. Trustee Nat. Ctr. Occupl. Readjustment, 1984-87; trustee N.C. Outward Bound Sch., dir., 1995—, chmn., 1997; chmn. Charleston Pvt. Industry Coun., 1985; mem. plant closing task force U. S. Dept. Labor, 1986, mfg. task force NRC, 1989, critical industries task force Def. Dept., 1989. Mem. Nat. Assn. Mfrs. (bd. dirs., chair employee rels. com. 1993-95). Home: 2697 E Lake Of The Isles Pky Minneapolis MN 55408-1051

READ, MICHAEL OSCAR, editor, consultant; b. Amarillo, Tex., July 11, 1942; s. Harold Eugene and Madeline (Welch) R.; m. Jill Kay Vanderby, July 6, 1963 (div. Apr. 1967); 1 child, Rebecca Anne; m. Fawn Dale Barby, Apr. 10, 1977; 1 child, Nathan Michael. AA in Chemistry, Amarillo Coll., 1962; BA in Journalism, Tex. Tech. U., 1965. News editor Olton (Tex.) Enterprise, 1963-64; reporter, photographer Lubbock (Tex.) Avalanche-Jour., 1964-67, copy editor, 1967-70, city editor, 1970-72; copy editor Houston Post, 1972-74, systems editor, 1974-89, dir. news tech., 1989-95; electronic media content coord. Houston Chronicle, 1995—; supervisory com. Shell Employees Fed. Credit Union, Houston; bd. dirs. Meadows (Tex.) Econ. Devel. Corp.; tchr. Let's Compute!, Stafford, Tex., 1985—; cons. Newspaper Pub. Sys., Stafford, 1989—; mem. joint Newspaper Assn. Am.-Internat. Press. Telecomm. Coun. Com. Wire Svc. Standards; mem. adv. bd. Found. for Am. Comms. FACSNET. Author weekly newspaper column, 1977—. Vol. United Way, Houston, 1973—; bd. dirs. Meadows Community Improvement Assn., 1985-95, Meadows Utility Dist., 1988-93. Eldon Durrett scholar, 1961-65. Mem. Am. MENSA, Am. Philatelic Soc., Am. 1st Day Cov. Soc. (life), U.S. Chess Fedn. (life), Soc. Profl. Journalists (conv. com. 1989-90), Press Club of Houston. Avocations: philately, photography, gardening. Home: 12023 Alston Dr Stafford TX 77477-1505 Office: Houston Chronicle 801 Texas St Houston TX 77002-2906

READ, PIERS PAUL, author; b. Beaconsfield, Eng., Mar. 7, 1941; s. Herbert Edward and Margaret (Ludwig) R.; m. Emily Albertine Boothby, July 29, 1967; children: Albert Nathaniel, Martha Marianna, William Edward, Beatrice Mary. B.A., St. John's Coll., Cambridge U., 1962, M.A., 1963. Sub-editor Times Lit. Supplement, 1963-64; adj. prof. writing Columbia U., 1980; lit. panel mem. Arts Coun. Gt. Britain, 1974-76; gov. Cardinal Manning Boys Sch., 1985; chmn. Cath. Writers Guild, 1993-97. Author: (novels) Game in Heaven with Tussy Marx, 1966, The Junkers, 1968 (Sir Geoffrey Faber Meml. prize 1969), Monk Dawson, 1970 (Somerset Maugham award, Hawthornden prize 1970), The Professor's Daughter, 1971, The Upstart, 1973, Polonaise, 1976, A Married Man, 1980, The Villa Golitsyn, 1982, The Free Frenchman, 1986, A Season in the West, 1988 (James Tait Black Meml. prize), On the Third Day, 1990, (non-fiction) Alive: The Story of the Andes Survivors, 1974 (Thomas More medal), The Train Robbers, 1978, Ablaze: The Heros and Victims of Chernobyl, 1993, The Patriot, 1996, Knights of the Cross, 1997, (TV plays) Coincidence, The Family Firm, The House of Highbury Hill. Mem. Brit. bd. of Aid to Church in Need, 1988. Ford Found. fellow, 1963-64; Harkness fellow, 1967-68. Fellow Royal Soc. Lit.; mem. Soc. Authors (com. mgmt. 1972-74), Inst. Contemporary Arts (com. mgmt. 1972-74). Roman Catholic. Address: 50 Portland Rd, W11 4LG London England

READ, VIRGINIA HALL, biochemistry educator; b. Louisville, Miss., Oct. 15, 1937; d. Angus R. and Hassie (Bowie) Hall; m. Dale Gilbert Read Sr., Mar. 5, 1960; children: Laura Read Sprabery, Dale Gilbert Jr., Eva Read Warden. BS, U. Miss., 1959; MS, U. Miss., Jackson, 1962, PhD, 1964. Instr. biochemistry U. Miss., Jackson, 1965-66, asst. prof. biochemistry, 1966-68, 70-74, assoc. prof. biochemistry, 1974—, assoc prof. pathology, 1979—; asst. prof. medicine U. Ala., Birmingham, 1968-70. Contbr. articles to Jour. Clin. Investigation, Jour. Clin. Endocrinology and Metabolism, Nature, Biochem. Pharmacology. Grantee U.S. Pub. Health Svc., 1960-62, fellow, 1968-70. Mem. Am. Assn. Clin. Chmeistry, Acad. Clin. Biochemistry, Endocrine Soc., Sigma Xi. United Methodist. Home: 311 Hand Dr Brandon MS 39042-8309

READ, WILLIAM MCCLAIN, retired oil company executive; b. Phila., July 30, 1918; s. William Tucker and Grace (McNeal) R.; m. Esther Donahoo, Sept. 15, 1945; children: Deborah Read Yoder, Suzanne Read DiFulvio, William W. B.A., Washington and Lee U., 1940; postgrad., U. Pa., 1941-42. Personal asst. Atlantic Refining Co., Phila., 1943-50, dir. tng., 1950-72; v.p. employee relations Atlantic Richfield Co., Los Angeles, 1972-78, sr. v.p. employee relations, 1978-83; now ret. Author: Now You Are a Supervisor, 1962; contbr. articles to profl. jours. Chmn. Verdugo Hills Hosp., Glendale, Calif., 1980-81, 85-86; dir. Hosp. Coun. So. Calif., L.A., 1982-84, chmn. trustees com., 1983-84; chmn. bd. dirs. Pacific Clinics, 1993. Recipient Algernon Sydney Sullivan award Washington and Lee U., 1940. Mem. Phi Beta Kappa, Omicron Delta Kappa. Home: 4141 Cambridge Rd Flintridge CA 91011-4003

READE, CLAIRE ELIZABETH, lawyer; b. Waltham, Mass., June 2, 1952; d. Kemp Brownell and Suzanne Helen (Dorntge) R.; m. Earl Phillip Steinberg, Nov. 22, 1980; children: Evan Samuel, Emma Miriam. BA, Conn. Wesleyan U., 1973; JD, Harvard U., 1979; MA in Law and Diplomacy, Tufts U., 1979. Bar: Mass. 1980, D.C. 1983. Sheldon fellow Harvard U., Cambridge, Mass. and, Republic of China, 1979-80; assoc. Ropes & Gray, Boston, 1980-82; assoc. Arnold & Porter, Washington, 1982-86, ptnr., 1987—. Exec. editor: International Trade Policy: The Lawyer's Perspective, 1985; contbr. articles to profl. jours. Mem. ABA (co-chair internat. trade com.), D.C. Bar Assn., Fed. Bar Assn., Am. Soc. Internat. Law, Washington Coun. Lawyers, Women in Internat. Trade. Office: Arnold & Porter 555 12th St NW Washington DC 20004-1200

READE, KATHLEEN MARGARET, paralegal; b. Ft. Worth, Tex., Sept. 6, 1947; d. Ralph S. and Margaret Catherine (Stark) R.; m. John Mason Smith; 1 child, Kathryn Michelle Carter. BA in English and Polit. Sci., Tex. Christian U., postgrad.; postgrad., Tex. Tech, El Centro Coll., Dallas. Asst. land and legal dept. Am. Quasar Petroleum, Ft. Worth, 1971-74; paralegal and office mgr. Law Offices of George Sims, Ft. Worth, 1974-81; asst. Criminal Cts. #2 and #3 Tarrant County Dist. Atty., Ft. Worth, 1981; ind. paralegal Ft. Worth, 1982-84; paralegal Law Offices of Brent Burford, Ft. Worth, 1982-85; sr. paralegal/litigation Law Offices of Windle Turley, Dallas, 1985-90; major case supr. The Dent Law Firm, Ft. Worth, 1990-96, Michener, Larimore, Swindle, Whitaker, Flowers, Sawyer, Reynolds & Chalk, L.L.P., 1996—; instr. paralegal program, U. Tex., Arlington, 1996—; active Tex. Christian U. Writer's Continuous Workshop. Author: Plaintiff's Personal Injury Handbook, 1994; contbg. author: Legal Assistant's Letter Book, 1995; editl. com. Tex. Paralegal Jour.; contbr. articles to profl. jours. Recipient scholarship Tex. Christian U., Ft. Worth. Mem. AAUW, Am. Assn. Paralegal Edn., Assn. Trial Lawyers, State Bar of Tex. (Legal Asst. Divsn.), Nat. Assn. Legal Assts., Nat. Paralegal Assn., Ft. Worth Paralegal Assn., Freelance Writers' Network, Austin Writer's League, Okla. Writers' Fedn. Home: PO Box 101641 Fort Worth TX 76185

READE, LEWIS POLLOCK, retired diplomat, engineer; b. N.Y.C., Nov. 1, 1932; s. Herman Ross and Dorothy Stella (Pollock) R.; m. Anne Carol Kulka, July 3, 1953 (div. Feb. 1968); children: Steven Gordon, Nicholas Edward; m. Margaret Ann Kilpatrick, Mar. 30, 1968; 1 child, Jonathan Collins. BS in Mech. Engrin., U. Miami, 1953; postgrad., Hofstra U., 1953-54, U. Balt., 1957-59. Product engr. Sperry Gyroscope, Lake Success, N.Y., 1953-54; project engr. ARMA, Garden City, N.Y., 1954-55; field engr. Westinghouse Electric Corp., Balt. & Rome, 1957-66; v.p. Westinghouse Learning Corp., Washington & Pitts., 1966-70; v.p. corp. planning & devel. Tyco Labs., Waltham, Mass., 1970-71; chmn., chief exec. officer, treas. Kellett Corp., Willow Grove, Pa., 1971-72; exec. v.p. Big Bros./Big Sisters of Am., Phila., 1973-80; mission dir. U.S. Agency Internat. Devel., Kingston, Jamaica, Amman, Jordan, & Jakarta, Indonesia, 1980-92; dir. gen. U.S.-Asia Environ. Ptnrship., Washington, 1992-97; ret., 1997. Sgt. US Army, 1955-57. Mem. Athenaeum of Phila., Soc. Internat. Devel., Am. Fgn. Svc. Assn., Vesper (Phila.), Soc. Hill (Phila.), Internat. (Washington), Jamaica Club (Kingston), Royal Jordanian Automobile Club, Am. Club (Jakarta, Indonesia). Home: 42 Vista de la Montana Loop Placitas NM 87043

READER, GEORGE GORDON, physician, educator; b. Bklyn., Feb. 8, 1919; s. Houston Parker and Marion J. (Payne) R.; m. Helen C. Brown, May 23, 1942; children: Jonathan, David, Mark, Peter. BA, Cornell U., 1940, MD, 1943; DSc (hon.), Drew U., 1988. Diplomate Am. Bd. Internal Medicine. Intern N.Y. Hosp., N.Y.C., 1944; resident N.Y. Hosp., 1947-49, attending physician, 1962-92; hon. staff, 1992—; dir. comprehensive care and teaching program N.Y. Hosp., 1952-66, chief med. clinic, 1952-72; practice medicine specializing in internal medicine N.Y.C., 1949-93; chief div. ambulatory and community medicine N.Y. Hosp.-Cornell Med. Center, N.Y.C., 1969-72; prof. medicine Cornell U. Med. Coll., 1957-89, Livingston Farrand prof. pub. health, 1972-89, prof. emeritus pub. health and medicine, 1989—, chmn. dept. pub. health, 1972-92; chmn. human ecology study sect. NIH, 1961-65; chmn. med. adv. com. Vis. Nurse Svc., N.Y., 1963—; mem. med. control bd. Health Ins. Plan Greater N.Y., 1964—; mem. Gov.'s Health Adv. Coun., N.Y., 1974-79. Author: (with R. Merton, P. Kendall) The Student Physician, 1957, (with Goss) Comprehensive Medical Care and Teaching, 1967, (with Goodrich and Olendzki) Welfare Medical Care: An Experiment, 1969; mem. editorial bd. Medical Care, 1969-70, Jour. Med. Edn, 1975-79; editor-in-chief Milbank Meml. Fund Quar.: Health and Society, 1972-76. Bd. dirs. N.Y.C. Vis. Nurse Svc., The Osborn Retirement Community, Health Ins. Plan Greater N.Y., 1983-93, Helen Keller Internat.; trustee Cornell U., 1982-87; bd. visitors Columbia U. Sch. Nursing. Lt. USNR, 1944-46, PTO. Fellow ACP, APHA (governing coun. 1968-69), AAAS, Am. Coll. Preventive Medicine; mem. AMA, N.Y. Acad. Medicine (chmn. com. med. edn. 1968-71, v.p. 1978-80), Am. Sociol. Assn., Harvey Soc., Internat. Sociol. Assn., Internat. Epidemiol. Assn., N.Y.C. Pub. Health Assn. (pres. 1956), Inst. Medicine Nat. Acad. Scis. (sr. mem.), Sigma Xi, Alpha Omega Alpha. Home: 155 Stuyvesant Ave Rye NY 10580-3112

READER, JOSEPH, physicist; b. Chgo., Dec. 1, 1934. BS, Purdue U., 1956, MS, 1957; PhD in Physics, U. Calif., 1962. Rsch. assoc. physics Argonne Nat. Lab., 1962-63; staff physicist Nat. Inst. Standards and Tech., Gaithersburg, Md., 1963—. Recipient Gold medal Dept. Commerce, 1989. Fellow Am. Phys. Soc., Optical Soc. Am. (William F. Meggers award 1992). Achievements include research in experimental atomic physics, optical spectroscopy, hyperfine structure, electronic structure of highly ionized atoms, wave length standards, and ionization energies of atoms and ions. Office: Natl Inst Of Standards & Tech Gaithersburg MD 20899

READING, ANTHONY JOHN, physician; b. Sydney, Australia, Sept. 10, 1933; s. Abe Stanley and Esma Daisy R.; m. Elisabeth Ann Hoffman, July 27, 1975; children—Wendy Virginia Elisabeth, Sarah Alexandra Jane. M.B., B.S., U. Sydney, 1956; M.P.H., Johns Hopkins U., 1961, Sc.D., 1964. Intern Sydney Hosp., 1957-58; resident in psychiatry Johns Hopkins Hosp., Balt., 1965-68; asst. prof. psychiatry and medicine Johns Hopkins U. Sch. Medicine, Balt., 1968-73, assoc. prof. psychiatry, 1973-75, dir. psychiat. liaison service, 1974-75; dir. comprehensive alcoholism program Johns Hopkins Hosp., 1972-75; prof., chmn. dept. psychiatry and behavioral medicine U. South Fla. Coll. Medicine, 1975—, assoc. dean, 1993-96. Mem. AMA, AAAS, Am. Psychosomatic Soc., Am. Psychiat. Assn. Home: 1171 Shipwatch Cir Tampa FL 33602-5787 Office: 3515 E Fletcher Ave Tampa FL 33613-4706

READING, ANTHONY JOHN, business executive, accountant; b. London, Aug. 8, 1943; came to U.S., 1993; m. Myra Elizabeth Steer, Aug. 27, 1966; 1 child, Jason. Chartered acct. Mng. dir., dir. mfg., dir. fin. Donaldson Co. Inc., Brussels, 1970-80; group exec. Thomas Tilling Plc, London, 1980-83; divisional group chief exec. BTR Plc, London, 1983-87; group mng. dir. Polly Peck Internat., London, 1987-89, Pepe Group Plc, London, 1989-90; divisional dir. Tomkins Plc, London, 1990-92, also bd. dirs.; chmn., CEO Tomkins Corp., Dayton, Ohio, 1992—. Named Mem. of Most Excellent Order of Brit. Empire, Her Majesty Queen Elizabeth II, 1978. Fellow Inst. Chartered Accts. Eng. and Wales, Inst. Mgmt. Eng.; mem. Naval Club, Mil. Club London. Avocations: music, golf, water sports. Office: Tomkins Corp 4801 Springfield St Dayton OH 45431-1084

READING, JAMES EDWARD, transportation executive; b. Milw., June 26, 1924; s. James Edwards and Helen Marie (Boehm) R.; m. Ada Irene Kelly, May 24, 1944; children—Wendy Irene, James David, Christopher Kelly, Mary Katherine, Kevin Sinclair. Student, San Diego State U., 1942, Ga. Inst. Tech., 1944. With Union-Tribune Pub. Co., San Diego, 1942-59, dist. mgr., 1953-58; circulation promotion mgr. Union-Tribune Pub. Co., 1958-59; adminstrv. asst. to v.p. Copley Newspapers, La Jolla, Calif., 1959-60; dir. advt. and public relations San Diego Transit System, 1960-67; dir. mktg. Calif. Motor Express, 1967-68; asst. to exec. v.p. Am. Transit Assn., Washington, 1968; v.p. Nat. City Mgmt. Co.; resident mgr. Regional Transit Service, Rochester, N.Y., 1968-74; asst. gen. mgr. ops. Regional Transit Dist., Denver, 1974-77; gen. mgr. Central Ohio Transit Authority, Columbus, 1977-85; dir. Santa Clara County Transp. Agy., San Jose, Calif., 1985-90; ind. cons. San Diego, 1990—; guest lectr. numerous univs. Served with U.S. Army, 1943-46, ETO. Named Public Relations Man of Yr. Public Relations Club, San Diego, 1962; recipient Urban Mass Transp. Adminstrs. award for outstanding pub. service, 1980, 82. Mem. Pub. Rels. Soc. Am. (past pres. 4 chpts.), Am. Pub. Transit Assn. (bd. dirs., past v.p., elected Hall of Fame 1995), Transp. Rsch. Bd., Am. Soc. Pub. Adminstrs., Am. Pub. Works Assn., Am. Legion, Rotary Club Rancho Bernardo (pres.-elect), Press Club of Rancho Bernardo (pres.), Tau Kappa Epsilon. Republican. Roman Catholic. Home: 11728 Caminito Corriente San Diego CA 92128-4548

READING, SADIE ETHEL, retired public health nurse; b. Louisiana, Mo., Dec. 16, 1915; d. William M. Reading and Sadie E. Vasconcellos. RN, St. Luke's Hosp. Sch. Nursing, St. Louis, 1937; BSN, Vanderbilt U., 1948; MA, Columbia U., 1956. RN, Mo., Tenn., Fla. Asst. supr. Children's Hosp., Chattanooga, Tenn., 1937-42; sr. staff nurse Chattanooga-Hamilton County Health Dept., Chattanooga, 1948-52; supr. pub. health nursing Gibson County Health Dept., Trenton, Tenn., 1952-55; asst. supr., ednl. dir. Chattanooga-Hamilton County Health Dept., Chattanooga, 1956-59; cons. pub. health nursing Fla. State Bd. Health, Jacksonville, 1959-64, asst. dir. pub. health nursing, 1964-75; pub. health nursing supr. health program office Dept. of Health, Tallahassee, 1975-80; adj. prof. U. Mich. Sch. Pub. Health, Ann Arbor, 1960-74; dist. pres. Tenn. Nurses Assn., 1953; v.p. Fla. Nurses Assn., 1971-72, pres., 1972-73. Author: Blue and Gray: Nursing Outlook, 1962. 1st female lobbyist Fla. State Bd. Health, Jacksonville and Tallahassee, 1974; mem. Common Cause, Hunter Mus., Friends of Chattanooga Pub. Libr., Friends of Signal Mountain Libr., Tenn. Aquarium, Chattanooga. Capt. USAF and Army Nurse Corps, 1942-46, ETO. Mem. AAUW, ANA (vice chair pub. health nursing sect. 1952), LWV, DAR, Fla. Pub. Health Assn. (life, Meritorious Svc. award 1975), Women in Mil. Svc. for Am. (charter), U.S. Golf Assn., Am. Assn. Ret. People, Fla. Sheriff's Assn., Signal Mountain Golf and Country Club, Vanderbilt Alumni Assn., Sigma Theta Tau. Democrat. Avocations: golf, bowling, volunteer activities. Home: 100 James Blvd Apt S-313 Signal Mountain TN 37377-1860

READY, ROBERT JAMES, financial company executive; b. Bridgeport, Conn., June 26, 1952; s. John Edward and Anne (Salata) R.; m. Margaret S. Neale, Aug. 23, 1975; children: Carolyn, Christopher and Steven (twins). AS, Housatonic Community Coll., 1972; BS, Babson Coll., 1974. CLU; chartered fin. cons.; cert. ins. cons. Agt. John Hancock Mut. Life Ins. Co., Hamden, Conn., 1975-77; broker Beardsley, Brown & Bassett Inc., Bridgeport, Conn., 1977-80; agt. Aetna Life and Casualty Ins. Co., Trumbull, Conn., 1980-83; v.p. Crestview Fin. Services Inc., Westport, Conn., 1983—, Crestview Securities Inc., Westport, Conn., 1983—, Crestview Investment Advisors Inc., Westport, Conn., 1983—. Mem. Nat. Assn. Life Underwriters, Conn. Assn. Life Underwriters, Bridgeport Life Underwriters (bd. dirs. 1977), Nat. Assn. Health Underwriters, Conn. Assn. Health Underwriters, Am. Soc. CLU and Chartered Fin. Cons., New Haven County CLU and Chartered Fin. Cons., Bridgeport Jaycees. Roman Catholic. Avocations: golf, tennis. Office: The Crestview Fin Group 431 Post Rd E Ste 1 Westport CT 06880-4403

REAGAN, BARBARA BENTON, economics educator. B.S. with honors, U. Tex., 1941; M.A. in Stats., Am. U., 1947; M.A. in Econs., Harvard U., 1949, Ph.D. in Econs., 1952. Econ. researcher Dept. Agr., 1942-47; sr. project leader Agrl. Research Service, Washington, 1949-55; prof. econs. Tex. Woman's U., Denton, 1959-67; prof. econs. So. Meth. U., Dallas, 1967-90, prof. emeritus, 1990—, chmn. dept., 1984-90; dir. interdisciplinary research project So. Meth. U., 1969-70, dir. undergrad. studies econs. dept., 1972-75, assoc. dean Univ. Coll., 1975, asst. to pres. for student acad. services, 1975-76, pres. faculty senate, 1981-82, mem. exec. com., 1981-84; dir. Region IX Fed. Home Loan Bank, 1981-85; mem. Dallas Morning News Bd. Economists, 1982-88; dir. Agrl. Rsch. Svc. Project, Dallas, 1970-71; mem. adv. bd. econs. USA Wharton Econometric Forecasting Assocs., 1983-85; reviewer NSF; disting. vis. prof. econs. Kenyon Coll., spring, 1979; bd. dirs. 1st Am. Savs. Bank, 1990-95, North Tex. Mesbic, 1991-93, Tex. Guaranteed Student Loan Corp., 1991-97, sec., exec. com., chmn. policy com., 1992-93, chmn. bd., 1993-95. Author: Economic Foundations of Labor Supply of Women, 1981; co-editor, contbg. author: Women in the Workplace: Implications of Occupational Segregation, 1976; editor, contbg. author: Issues in Federal Statistical Needs Relating to Women, 1979; bd. editors: Jour. Econ. Lit., 1977-79, Jour. Econ. Edn., 1984-92; referee profl. jours. contbr. articles to profl. publs. Mem. Nat. Adv. Food and Drug Coun., 1968-71; mem. adv. com. Nat. Rsch. Inst. on Family, 1973-76; nat. coord. on issues in fed. statis. needs for women Census Bur. Conf., 1978; mem. Tex. adv. bd. Tex Coastal Mgmt. Program, 1977-78; mem. adv. com. White House Conf. on Balance Nat. Growth and Econ. Devel., 1977-78; bd. dirs. League for Ednl. Advancement in Dallas, 1972-75; trustee, mem. instrnl. TV com. Pub. Comm. Found. North Tex., 1973-76; mem. North Tex. Coun. Govts.' Manpower Coun., 1972-74; mem. adv. bd. Women's Ctr. Dallas, 1975-79, 82-85, 95—, pres. 1981, bd. dirs. 1990-92; bd. dirs. Dallas Urban League, 1975-79, co-chmn. com. on skills bank, 1977-79; Leadership Am., 1989-90. Ferguson fellow Harvard U., 1947-49; named Outstanding Tchr., So. Meth. U. 1972; recipient Women's Ctr. Dallas award as one of Dallas Outstanding Women, 1980,So. Meth. U. M award 1972, Willis M. Tate award as outstanding faculty mem., 1982, Laurel award AAUW, 1983, Headliner award Dallas Press Club, 1985, 86, Disting. Alumna award Mary Baldwin Coll., 1986. Mem. Am. Econ. Assn. (chmn. sessions 1977, 80, chmn. com. on status of women in econs. profession 1974-78), Southwestern Social Sci. Assn. (exec. com. 1977-80, pres. 1978-79), Assn. Am. Colls. (faculty rep. 1984), Dallas Economists Club, Dallas C. of C. (com. on urban affairs 1975), Phi Beta Kappa (pres. So. Meth. U. chpt. 1975-76), Town and Gown Club (pres. 1986-87), The Dallas Summit (exec. com. 1990-92). Home: 10 Duncannon Ct Dallas TX 75225-1809 Office: So Meth U Dept Econs Dallas TX 75275 *America's productivity can be improved greatly by making better use of its human resources. Equality of opportunity needs to become a reality.*

REAGAN, GARY DON, state legislator, lawyer; b. Amarillo, Tex., Aug. 23, 1941; s. Hester and Lois Irene (Marcum) R.; m. Nedra Ann Nash, Sept. 12, 1964; children: Marc, Kristi, Kari, Brent. AB, Stanford U., 1963, JD, 1965. Bar: N.Mex. 1965, U.S. Dist. Ct. N.Mex., 1965, U.S. Supreme Ct. 1986. Assoc. Smith & Ransom, Albuquerque, 1965-67; ptnr. Smith, Ransom, Deaton & Reagan, Albuquerque, 1967-68, Williams, Johnson, Houston, Reagan & Porter, Hobbs, N.Mex., 1968-77, Williams, Johnson, Reagan, Porter & Love, Hobbs, 1977-82; sole practice, Hobbs, 1982—; city atty. City of Hobbs, 1978-80, City of Eunice, N.M., 1980—; mem. N.Mex. State Senate, 1993-96; instr. N.Mex. Jr. Coll. and Coll. of S.W., Hobbs, 1978-84; N.Mex. commr. Nat. Conf. Commrs. Uniform State Laws, 1993-96; mem. adv. mem. N.Mex. Constl. Revision Commn., 1993-95. Mayor, City of Hobbs, 1972-73, 76-77, city commr., 1970-78; pres., dir. Jr. Achievement of Hobbs, 1974-85; pres., trustee Landsun Homes, Inc., Carlsbad, N.Mex., 1972-84; trustee Lydia Patterson Inst., El Paso, Tex., 1972-84, N.Mex. Conf. United Meth. Ch., 1988—, Coll. of S.W., Hobbs, 1989—; chmn. County Democratic Com., 1983-85. Mem. ABA, State Bar N.Mex. (coms. 1989-96, v.p. 1992-93, pres. 1994-95), Lea County Bar Assn. (pres. 1976-77), Hobbs C. of C. (pres. 1989-90), Rotary (pres. Hobbs 1985-86), Hobbs Tennis (pres. 1974-75). Home: 200 E Eagle Dr Hobbs NM 88240-5323 Office: 501 N Linam St Hobbs NM 88240-5715

REAGAN, HARRY EDWIN, III, lawyer; b. Wichita, Kans., Sept. 9, 1940; s. Harry E. II and Mary Elizabeth (O'Steen) R.; m. Marvene R. Rogers, June 17, 1965; children: Kathleen, Leigh, Mairen. BS, U. Pa., 1962, JD, 1965. Bar: Pa. 1965, U.S. Dist. Ct. (ea. dist.) Pa. 1965, U.S. Ct. Appeals (3d cir.) 1965. From assoc. to ptnr. Morgan, Lewis & Bockius, Phila., 1965—. Chmn. Northhampton Twp. Planning Commn., Bucks County, Pa., 1974-79; mem. Warwick Twp. Planning Commn., 1980-95, chmn., 1994; supr. Warwick Twp., 1996—, chmn., 1997. Mem. ABA (labor sect.), Pa. Bar Assn. (labor sect.), Phila. Bar Assn. (labor sect.), Indsl. Rels. Assn. (pres. Phila. chpt. 1990-91). Republican. Presbyterian. Avocations: coaching rugby, skiing, raising horses, bicycling, Pa. Relays official. Home: 2930 Wilkinson Rd Rushland PA 18956 Office: Morgan Lewis & Bockius 2000 One Logan Sq Philadelphia PA 19103

REAGAN, JANET THOMPSON, psychologist, educator; b. Monticello, Ken., Sept. 15, 1945; d. Virgil Joe and Carrie Mae (Alexander) Thompson; m. Robert Barry Reagan, Jr., Aug. 7, 1977; children: Natalia Alexandria, Robert Barry. B.A. in Psychology, Berea Coll., 1967; Ph.D. in Psychology, Vanderbilt U., 1972. Mgr. research and eval. Nashville Mental Health Center, 1971-72; mgr. eval. Family Health Found., New Orleans, 1973-74; asst. prof. dept. health systems mgmt. Tulane U., New Orleans, 1974-77; dir. eval. Project Heavy West, Los Angeles, 1977-78; asst. prof. health adminstrn. Calif. State U.-Northridge, 1978-83, assoc. prof., director health adminstrn., 1983-87, prof., dir. health adminstrn., 1987—; cons. in field. Mem. Am. Pub. Health Assn., Am. Coll. Health Care Adminstrn., Assn. Health Svcs. Rsch., Am. Coll. Health Care Execs. (com. on higher edn. 1987, chmn. 1991), Assn. Univ. Programs in Health Adminstrn. (task force on undergrad. edn. 1985-90, chmn. 1988-90, mem. bd. dirs. 1995), Psi Chi, Phi Kappa Phi. Mem. editorial adv. bd. Jour. of Long Term Care Adminstrn.; contbr. to books, articles to profl. jours., papers to profl. assns. Home: 9354 Encino Ave Northridge CA 91325-2414 Office: Calif State U Dept Health Sci Northridge CA 91330

REAGAN, JOSEPH BERNARD, retired aerospace executive, management consultant; b. Somerville, Mass., Nov. 26, 1934; s. Joseph B. and Helen Lowry R.; m. Dorothy Hughes; children: Patrick, Michael, Kevin, Kathleen, Brian, John, Maureen. BS in Physics, Boston Coll., 1956, MS in Physics, 1959; PhD in Space Sci., Stanford U., 1975; postgrad. exec. mgmt., Pa. State U., State College, 1981. Staff scientist, rsch. scientist, sr. scientist, scientist Lockheed Rsch. & Devel. Div., Palo Alto, Calif., 1959-75, mgr., 1975-84, dir., 1984-86, dep. gen. mgr., 1986-88, v.p., asst. gen. mgr., 1988-90; v.p. gen. mgr., 1991-96; bd. dirs. Southwall Technologies Inc., Palo Alto. Contbr. articles to profl. jours. Bd. dirs. Tech. Mus., San Jose. Capt. U.S. Army, 1956-64. Recipient Career Achievement in Sci. award Boston Coll. Alumni Assn., 1993. Fellow AIAA (outstanding engr. San Francisco chpt. 1988); mem. Am. Geophys. Union. Republican. Roman Catholic. Avocations: computer and woodworking hobbies. Home and Office: 13554 Mandarin Way Saratoga CA 95070-4847

REAGAN, LARRY GAY, dean; b. Jackson, Tenn., Mar. 30, 1938; d. Larry Alfred and Ann Mabel (Welker) Lane. BA, Union U., 1959; MA, Tulane U., 1961; MS, Ea. Ky. U., 1971; EdD, Vanderbilt U., 1975. Instr. Ill. Coll., Jacksonville, 1961-63, Union Univ., Jackson, Tenn., 1963-64, Chipola Jr. Coll., Marianna, Fla., 1964-67; asst. prof. Campbellsville (Ky.) Coll., 1967-70; divsn. dir. arts and letters, dean acad. affairs Manatee C.C., Bradenton, Fla., 1972—; health educator Tenn. Dept. Pub. Health, Nashville, 1974-75; chair dept. Volunteer State C.C., Gallatin, Tenn., 1975-90, divsn. chair, prof., 1990-92; v.p. Shelby State C.C., Memphis, 1991-92; v.p. Nat. Inst. Leadership Devel., New Coll. Libr. Assn.; lectr. in China, England, and Mexico. Contbr. poems to profl. publs. Bd. dirs. Fla./Colombia Alliance, Marianna, 1964-67; trustee Christian Sr. Housing, Atlanta, 1990—; pres. Tenn. Assn. of Women in C.C.'s, Nashville, 1991-92; mem. Manatee Cultural Alliance, Bradenton, 1993—. Recipient citation award Mex. Sec. of Edn., 1983, award Nat. Inst. Leadership, 1989. Mem. AAUW, AAHPERD, LWV, Am. Assn. Women in C.C.'s (keynote speaker, regional dir., v.p.), Fla. Assn. Women in C.C.'s (bd. dirs. 1993—), Nat. Coun. Instrnl. Adminstrn., Rotary Club, Phi Kappa Iota. Home: 6605 Gulfside Rd Longboat Key FL 34228-1416 Office: Manatee CC 5840 26th St W Bradenton FL 34207-3522

REAGAN, LAWRENCE PAUL, JR., systems engineer; b. Honolulu, Nov. 5, 1957; s. Lawrence Paul Sr. and Laura Louise (Sears) R.; m. Ann Marie Decker, Apr. 15, 1989; children: Lawrence P. III, Andrew Scott, Kelly Rene. BS in Mech. & Aerospace Engring., Ill. Inst. Tech., 1979; MS in Acquisition & Contract Mgmt., West Coast U., Santa Barbara, Calif., 1986. Product engr. R.G. Ray Corp., Schaumburg, Ill., 1978-80; launch integration mgr. USAF Hqrs. Space Divsn., L.A. AFB, 1980-84; chief Titan program mgmt. USAF Aerospace Test Group, Vandenberg AFB, Calif., 1984-89; chief joint communication br. USAF Pentagon, Washington, 1989-91; sr. sys. engr. Dynamics Rsch. Corp., Arlington, Va., 1992-96; dir. Md. ops. Dynamics Rsch. Corp., California, Md., 1996—; CEO Jacob's Well, Inc., Lexington Park, Md., 1993—. Contbr. papers to profl. publs. Named Outstanding Young Engr., Air Force Assn. Mem. AIAA, Soc. Logistics Engring., Air Force Assn. Home: PO Box 22 Lusby MD 20657-0022 Office: Dynamics Rsch Corp 45370 Alton Ln Ste 1 California MD 20619-3136

REAGAN, NANCY DAVIS (ANNE FRANCIS ROBBINS), volunteer, wife of former President of United States; b. N.Y.C., July 6, 1923; d. Kenneth and Edith (Luckett) Robbins; step dau. Loyal Davis; m. Ronald Reagan, Mar. 4, 1952; children: Patricia Ann, Ronald Prescott; stepchildren: Maureen, Michael. BA, Smith Coll.; LLD (hon.), Pepperdine U., 1983; LHD (hon.), Georgetown U., 1987. Contract actress, MGM, 1949-56; films include The Next Voice You Hear, 1950, Donovan's Brain, 1953, Hellcats of the Navy, 1957; Author: Nancy, 1980; formerly author syndicated column on prisoner-of-war and missing-in-action soldiers and their families; author: (with Jane Wilkie) To Love a Child, (with William Novak) My Turn: The Memoirs of Nancy Reagan, 1989. Civic worker, visited wounded Viet Nam vets., sr. citizens, hosps. and schs. for physically and emotionally handicapped children, active in furthering foster grandparents for handicapped children program; hon. nat. chmn. Aid to Adoption of Spl. Kids, 1977; spl. interest in fighting alcohol and drug abuse among youth: hosted first ladies from around the world for 2d Internat. Drug Conf., 1985; hon. chmn. Just Say No Found., Nat. Fedn. of Parents for Drug-Free Youth, Nat. Child Watch Campaign, President's Com. on the Arts and Humanities, Wolf Trap Found. bd. of trustees, Nat. Trust for Historic Preservation, Cystic Fibrosis Found., Nat. Republican Women's Club; hon. pres. Girl Scouts of Am. Named one of Ten Most Admired Am. Women, Good Housekeeping mag., ranking #1 in poll, 1984, 85, 86; Woman of Yr. Los Angeles Times, 1977; permanent mem. Hall of Fame of Ten Best Dressed Women in U.S.; recipient humanitarian awards from Am. Camping Assn., Nat. Council on Alcoholism, United Cerebral Palsy Assn., Internat. Ctr. for Disabled; Boys Town Father Flanagan award; 1986 Kiwanis World Service medal; Variety Clubs Internat. Lifeline award; numerous awards for her role in fight against drug abuse. Address: Century City Fox Plaza 11000 Wilshire Blvd Los Angeles CA 90022-5010*

REAGAN, RONALD WILSON, former President of United States; b. Tampico, Ill., Feb. 6, 1911; s. John Edward and Nelle (Wilson) R.; m. Jane Wyman, Jan. 25, 1940 (div. 1948); children: Maureen E., Michael E.; m. Nancy Davis, Mar. 4, 1952; children: Patricia, Ronald. AB, Eureka Coll., 1932, MA (hon.), 1957. Actor GE Theatre, 1954-62; host TV series Death Valley Days, 1962-66; gov. State of Calif., 1967-74; businessman, rancher, commentator on public policy, 1975-80, Pres. of U.S., 1981-89. Sports announcer, motion picture and TV actor, 1932-66. Author: Where's The Rest of Me?, Speaking My Mind: Selected Speeches, 1989, An American Life: The Autobiography, 1990. Mem. Calif. State Rep. Ctrl. Com., 1964-66; del. Rep. Nat. Conv., 1968, 72; chmn. Rep. Gov. Assn., 1968-73; mem. presdl. Commn. CIA Activities Within U.S., 1975; bd. dirs. Com. Present Danger, Washington, 1977—; cand. for Rep. nomination for Pres., 1976. Served as capt. USAAF, 1942-45. Recipient Great Am. of Decade award, Va. Young Am. for Freedom, Man of Yr. Free Enterprise award, San Fernando Valley Bus. & Profl. award, 1964, Am. Legion award, 1965, Horation Alger award, 1969, George Washington Honor medal, Freedoms Found. Valley Forge award, 1971, Disting. Am. award; inducted into Nat. Football Found. Hall of Fame, Am. Patriots Hall of Fame. Mem. SAG (pres. 1947-52, 59), Am. Fedn. Radio & TV Artists, Lions, Friars, Tau Kappa Epsilon. Republican. Address: Century City Fox Plaza 11000 Wilshire Blvd Los Angeles CA 90022*

REAL, MANUEL LAWRENCE, federal judge; b. San Pedro, Calif., Jan. 27, 1924; s. Francisco Jose and Maria (Mansano) R.; m. Stella Emilia Michalik, Oct. 15, 1955; children: Michael, Melanie Marie, Timothy, John Robert. B.S., U. So. Calif., 1944, student fgn. trade, 1946-48; LL.B., Loyola Sch. Law, Los Angeles, 1951. Bar: Calif. 1952. Asst. U.S. Atty.'s Office, Los Angeles, 1952-55; pvt. practice law San Pedro, Calif., 1955-64; U.S. atty. So. Dist. Calif., 1964-66; judge U.S. Dist. Ct. (cen. dist.) Calif., L.A., 1966—. Served to ensign USNR, 1943-46. Mem. Am., Fed., Los Angeles County bar assns., State Bar Calif., Am. Judicature Soc., Chief Spl. Agts. Assn., Phi Delta Phi, Sigma Chi. Roman Catholic. Club: Anchor (Los Angeles). Office: US Dist Ct 312 N Spring St Ste 217P Los Angeles CA 90012-4704*

REALS, WILLIAM JOSEPH, pathologist, academic administrator, educator; b. Hot Springs, S.D., June 22, 1920; s. Reuben Joseph and Gertrude Cecilia (Harrigan) R.;m. Norma Rosalie Monahan, May 6, 1944; children: William J. Jr., John F., Elaine A., Mary C., Thomas C. BS, Creighton U., 1944, MD, MS in Medicine, 1945. Diplomate Am. Bd. Pathology (trustee 1973-80). Intern Creighton Meml./St. Joseph Hosp., Omaha, 1945-46; resident Creighton Meml./St. Joseph Hosp.; resident Creighton U. Sch. Medicine, Omaha, 1946-49, instr. in pathology, 1949-50; dir. labs. St. Joseph Med. Ctr., Wichita, Kans., 1953-80; prof. pathology, dean U. Kans. Med. Ctr., Wichita, 1980-91, vice chancellor, 1988—; cons. Office Pathology, VA, Washington, 1963-79, Under-sec. Def., Rsch. and Engring., Washington, 1975-79, Office Surgeon Gen., USAF, Washington, 1980—. Author: Aerospace Pathology, 1973; editor: Poems of Alice Henry Boone, 1980; contbr. numerous articles to profl. jours. Trustee Inst. Logopedics, Wichita, 1986, Kans. Newman Coll., Wichita, 1988, Kans. region NCCJ, 1988—. Brig. gen. USAF, 1950-80. Recipient Alumni Achievement citation Creighton U., 1986. Fellow ACP, Coll. Am. Pathologists (pres. 1970-73), Royal Coll. Pathologists Australia, Aerospace Med. Assn.; mem. Can. Assn. Pathologists (hon.), Most Venerable Order Hosp. of St. John of Jerusalem, Cosmos Club (Washington), Army-Navy Club (Washington), Alpha Omega Alpha. Home: 706 N Stratford St Wichita KS 67206-1455 Office: U Kans Sch Medicine 1010 N Kansas St Wichita KS 67214-3124

REAM, JAMES TERRILL, architect, sculptor; b. Summit, N.J., Sept. 8, 1929; s. Merrill Jay and Catherine Ada (Terrill) R.; m. Joyce Kimball Johnson, June 9, 1953 (div. Dec. 1976); children—Claudia, Sarah, Benjamin, m. Nancy Ann Buford, Jan. 1, 1980; stepchildren—Kathleen, Ann Maguire. BArch, Cornell U., 1953; postgrad., Pratt Inst., 1953-54, U. Rome, 1956-57. Registered architect. Assoc. W. C. Muchow Assocs., Denver, 1959-62; prin. Ream, Quinn & Assocs., Denver, 1962-66; v.p. design John Carl Warnecke & Assocs., San Francisco, 1966-69; prin., pres. James Ream & Assocs., Inc., San Francisco, 1969-78, Robbins and Ream Inc., San Francisco, 1978-83; prin. James Ream Architect, San Francisco, 1983—. Prin. archtl. works include Denver Convention Ctr., Currigan Hall, Pasadena Conf. Ctr., Stapleton Plaza Hotel, Vail Transp. Ctr. Bd. dirs. San Francisco Planning and Urban Rsch. Assn., 1977—; chmn. bd. dirs. San Francisco Heritage, 1984-91, pres., 1983-84. Served to 1st lt. USAF, 1954-56. Recipient citation for design in steel Am. Iron and Steel Inst., 1975; Honor award Am. Concrete Inst., 1975; Nat. Design award Prestressed Concrete Inst., 1983; Honor award for design in steel Am. Inst. Steel Constrn., 1970. Fellow AIA (honor award western region 1969, fellowship in design 1979, honor award for design excellence 1983, design cons. San Jose Arena). Democrat. Avocations: opera, theater, hiking, tennis. Office: 3385 Clay St San Francisco CA 94118-2006*

REAMAN, GREGORY HAROLD, pediatric hematologist, oncologist; b. Akron, Ohio, Sept. 9, 1947; s. Harold J. and Margaret U. (D'Alfonso) R.; m. Susan J. Pristo, Sept. 7, 1974; children: Emily Margaret, Sarah Elizabeth. BS in Biology, U. Detroit, 1969; MD, Loyola U., Chgo., 1973. Diplomate Nat. Bd. Med. Examiners, Am. Bd. Pediatrics. Pediatric intern Loyola U. Med. Ctr., 1973-74; resident in pediatrics Montreal Children's Hosp., McGill U., 1974-76; clin. assoc. pediatric oncology br. Nat. Cancer Inst., NIH, Bethesda, Md., 1976-78, investigator pediatric oncology br., 1978-79; assoc. dept. hematology/oncology, attending physician Children's Nat. Med. Ctr., Washington, 1979-87, chmn. dept. hematology/oncology, 1987—; asst. prof. pediatrics Sch. Medicine and Health Scis., George Washington U., 1979-82, assoc. prof. pediatrics, 1982-87, prof. pediatrics, 1987—; mem. immunology devices panel FDA; assoc. chmn. Children's Cancer Group; bd. dirs., mem. med. affairs com., chmn., strategic planning com. Children's Oncology Scs. of Met. Washington. Mem. editorial bd. Cancer Physicians Data Query, Nat. Cancer Inst.; reviewer Cancer Treatment Resports, Blood, Jour. Clin. Oncology; contbr. articles to profl. publs. Trustee Nat. Childhood Cancer Found., Arcadia, Calif.; bd. dirs. Am. Cancer Soc., Atlanta; trustee, chmn. patient care and profl. edn. coms. Leukemia Soc. Am. Lt. comdr. USPHS, 1976-79, Res., 1979—. Folger Summer scholar Am. Cancer Soc.; recipient Spl. Fellowship Rsch. award Leukemia Soc. Am., 1980-82; grantee DHHS, Nat. Cancer Inst., 1987—. Mem. Soc. Pediatric Rsch., Am. Fedn. Clin. Rsch., Am. Soc. Clin. Oncology, Am. Assn. Cancer Rsch., Am. Soc. Pediatric Hematology/Oncology, Children's Cancer Group, Washington Blood Club, Alpha Omega Alpha. Democrat. Roman Catholic. Home: 7306 Brennon Ln Chevy Chase MD 20815-4064 Office: Children's Nat Med Ctr 111 Michigan Ave NW Washington DC 20010-2916*

REAMS, BERNARD DINSMORE, JR., lawyer, educator; b. Lynchburg, Va., Aug. 17, 1943; s. Bernard Dinsmore and Martha Eloise (Hickman) R.; m. Rosemarie Bridget Boyle, Oct. 26, 1968 (dec. Oct. 1996); children: Andrew Dennet, Adriane Bevin. BA, Lynchburg Coll., 1965; MS, Drexel U., 1966; JD, U. Kans., 1972; PhD, St. Louis U., 1983. Bar: Kans. 1973, Mo. 1986, N.Y. 1996. Instr., asst. librarian Rutgers U., 1966-69; asst. prof. law, librarian U. Kans., Lawrence, 1969-74; mem. faculty law sch. Washington U., St. Louis, 1974-95, prof. law, 1976-95, prof. tech. mgmt., 1990-95, librarian, 1974-76, acting dean univ. libraries, 1987-88; prof. law, assoc. dean, dir. Law Libr. St. John's U. Sch. Law, Jamaica, N.Y., 1995—; rsch. scientist Max-Planck Inst., Hamburg, 1995, 97. Author: Law For The Businessman, 1974, Reader in Law Librarianship, 1976, Federal Price and Wage Control Programs 1917-1979: Legis. Histories and Laws, 1980, Education of the Handicapped: Laws, Legislative Histories, and Administrative Documents, 1982, Housing and Transportation of the Handicapped: Laws and Legislative Histories, 1983, Internal Revenue Acts of the United States: The Revenue Act of 1954 with Legislative Histories and Congressional Documents, 1983 Congress and the Courts: A Legislative History 1978-1984, 1984, University-Industry Research Partnerships: The Major Issues in Research and Development Agreements, 1986, Deficit Control and the Gramm-Rudman-Hollings Act, 1986, The Semiconductor Chip and the Law: A Legislative History of the Semiconductor Chip Protection Act of 1984, 1986, American International Law Cases, 2d series, 1986, Technology Transfer Law: The Export Administration Acts of the U.S., 1987, Insider Trading and the Law: A Legislative History of the Insider Trading Sanctions Act, 1989, Insider Trading and Securities Fraud, 1989, The Health Care Quality Improvement Act of 1989: A Legislative History of P.L. No. 99-660, 1990; The National Organ Transplant Act of 1984: A Legislative History of P.L. No. 98-507, 1990, A Legislative History of Individuals with Disabilities Education Act, 1994, Federal Legislative Histories: An Annotated Bibliography and Index to Officially Published Sources, 1994, Electronic Contracting Law, 1996; co-author: Segregation and the Fourteenth Amendment in the States, 1975, Historic Preservation Law: An Annotated Bibliography, 1976, Congress and the Courts: A Legislative History 1787-1977, 1978, Federal Consumer Protection Laws, Rules and Regulations, 1979, A Guide and Analytical Index to the Internal Revenue Acts of the U.S., 1909-1950, 1979, The Numerical Lists and Schedule of Volumes of the U.S. Congressional Serial Set: 73d Congress through the 96th Congress, 1984, Human Experimentation: Federal Laws, Legislative Histories, Regulations and Related Documents, 1985, American Legal Literature: A Guide to Selected Legal Resources, 1985, The Constitution of the United States: A Guide and Bibliography, 1987, The Congressional Impeachment Process and the Judiciary, 1987, Tax Reform 1986: A Legislative History of the Tax Refrom Act of 1986, 1988, The Constitutions of the States: A State by State Guide and Bibliography, 1988, Executive and Professional Employment Contracts, 1988, The Legislative History of the Export Trading Company Act of 1982 Including the Foreign Trade Antitrust Improvements Act, 1989, Federal Deficit Control, 1989, The Legislative History of the Export Trading Company Act of 1982 Including the Foreign Trade Antitrust Improvements Act, 1989, United States-Canada Free Trade Act: A Legislative History, 1990, Trade Reform Legislation 1988: A Legislative History of the Omnibus Trade and Competitiveness Act of 1988, 1992, Disability Law in the United States, 1992, Bankruptcy Reform Amendments, 1992, The Law of Hospital and Health Care Administration: Case and Materials, 1993, The Civil Rights Act of 1991: A Legislative History, 1994, The North American Free Trade Agreement, 1994, Catalonia, Spain, Europe, and Latin America: Regional Legal Systems and their Literature, 1995. Bd. trustees Quincy Found. for Med. Rsch. Charitable Trust, San Francisco. Fellow Am. Bar Foun.; recipient Thornton award for excellence Lynchburg Coll., 1986, Joseph L. Andrews Bibliog. award, 1995; named to Hon. Order Ky. Cols., 1992. Mem. ABA, Am. Law Inst., ALA, Am. Soc. Law and Medicine, Nat. Health Lawyers Assn., Am. Assn. Higher Edn., Spl. Librs. Assn., Internat. Assn. Law Libr. Coll. and Univ. Attys., Order of Coif, Phi Beta Kappa, Sigma Xi, Beta Phi Mu, Phi Delta Phi, Phi Delta Epsilon, Kappa Delta Pi, Pi Lambda Theta. Office: St Johns U Sch Law 8000 Utopia Pkwy Jamaica NY 11432-1335

REANEY, GILBERT, musician, educator; b. Sheffield, Eng., Jan. 11, 1924; came to U.S., 1960; s. Lawrence and Mabel (Crookes) R. BA with honors, Sheffield U., 1948, BMus, 1950, MA, 1951; postgrad., U. Paris, 1950-52. Researcher, tchr. Reading (Eng.) U., 1953-56, Birmingham (Eng.) U., 1956-59; vis. prof. musicology U. Hamburg, Fed. Republic Germany, 1960; assoc. prof. music dept. UCLA, 1960-62, prof., 1963—; founder, dir. London Medieval Group, 1958—; cons. panel BBC, 1958-60; guest lectr. Eng., Germany, U.S. Author: Early 15th Century Music, 7 vols., 1955-83, (with A. Gilles and J. Maillard) Philippe de Vitry, Ars Nova, 1964, International Inventory of Musical Sources, 2 vols., 1966-69, Machaut, 1971, (with Gilles) Franconis de Colonia Ars Cantus mensurabilis, 1974; gen. editor: Corpus Scriptorum de Musica, 1966—, Johannes Hothby, Opera Omnia de Musica Mensurabili, 1983, (with H. Ristory) Johannes dictus Balloce, Abreviatio Magistri Franconis, etc., 1987, Avon, De Musica Libellus and Discant Treatises, 1996; asst. editor: Musica Disciplina, 1956-76, co-editor: (with F. D'Accone), 1989—. With Brit. Army, 1943-46. Guggenheim fellow, 1964-65, Nat. Humanities Found. sr. fellow, 1967-68. Mem. European Acad., Am. Musicol. Soc., Internat. Musicol. Soc., Royal Mus. Assn. (Dent medal 1961), Plainsong & Medieval Music Soc. Home: 1001 3rd St Santa Monica CA 90403 Office: UCLA Musicology Dept Los Angeles CA 90025-1623

REANEY, JAMES CRERAR, dramatist, poet, educator; b. South Easthope, Ont., Can., Sept. 1, 1926; s. James Nesbitt and Elizabeth Henrietta (Crerar) R.; m. Colleen Thibaudeau, Dec. 29, 1951; children: James Stewart, Susan Alice. B.A., U. Toronto, 1948, M.A., 1949, Ph.D., 1957; D.Litt., Carleton U., 1975. Asst. prof. English U. Man., 1949-60; prof. English U. Western Ont., London, 1960—. (Recipient Massey award for the Killdeer 1960, Chalmers award for best Can. play The St. Nicholas Hotel 1975); Author: Killdeer, 1960 (Massey award), Poems, 1972, Colours in the Dark, 1969, Masks of Childhood, 1972, Listen to the Wind, 1972, Apple Butter and Other Plays for Children, 1973; plays include The St. Nicholas Hotel, 1975 (Chalmers award for best Can. play), Sticks and Stones: The Donnellys Part I, 1975, The Donnellys Part II, 1976, Handcuffs: The Donnellys Part III, 1977, 14 Barrels from Sea to Sea, 1977, The Dismissal, 1978, Wacousta, 1978, 1980, King Whistle, 1982, I the Parade, 1983, The House by the Churchyard, 1985, Alice Through the Looking-Glass, 1994, Serinette (opera libretto), 1986, Crazy to Kill (opera libretto), Performance Poems, 1991; novels for children include: The Boy with an R on his Hand, 1963, Take the Big Picture, 1986, Box Social & Other Stories, 1996; editor, pub.: Alphabet, 1960-70; contbr. articles to profl. jours. Decorated Order of Can. Fellow Royal Soc. Can.; mem. Playwrights Union Can., Can. Poetry League. Mem. New Democratic Party. Home: 276 Huron St, London, ON Canada N6A 2J9 Office: U We Ont, Dept English, London, ON Canada N6A 3K7 also: John Miller Lit Agt, 14 Earl St, Toronto, ON Canada M4Y 1M3

REAP, JAMES B., judge; b. Oct. 17, 1930; s. James S. and Jessie Burnett R.; m. Nancy Leigh Jenkins, Sept. 21, 1957; children: James J., Michael H., Jessica Leigh. BA cum laude, Weslyan U., 1952; JD, Harvard U., 1957; diploma, U.S. Naval War Coll., Armed Forces Staff Coll., Nat. War Coll., Armed Forces Pub. Info. Sch., U.S. Naval Sch. of Justice. Bar: N.Y. 1957, U.S. Dist. Ct. (ea. and so. dists.) N.Y. 1957, U.S. Ct. Mil. Appeals 1957, U.S. Ct. Internat. Trade 1957, U.S. Supreme Ct., U.S. Ct. of Claims. Commd. USN, 1951, advanced through grades to rear admiral, 1990; ptnr. Kent Hazzard et al, 1957-77, Campbell, Hyman and Reap, 1977-79; chief judge White Plains City Ct., 1980-92; U.S. adminstrn. law judge, 1993—. Merit badge counselor Boy Scouts of Am. Recipient N.Y. State Conspicuous Svc. medal, Disting. Svc. award Jaycees, Presdl. Meritorious Svc.

medal, 1978, Presdl. Legions of Merit, 1984, 85. Mem. ABA, N.Y. Bar Assn., N.Y. Assn. City Ct. Judges, Nat. Trial Ct. Judges Assn., Am. Judges Found., Assn. of Adminstrv. Law Judges, Westchester County Bar Assn., Univ. Club, Legal Aid Soc., Am. Legion, USN Inst., Smithsonian Inst., Am. Acad. Polit. and Social Sci., Naval Res. Assn., Militia Assn. of N.Y., N.Y. Commandery Navy Order U.S.A., Naval Acad. Found., Havillands Manor Assn., Chi Psi. Office: 399 Knollwood Rd White Plains NY 10603-1931

REAP, SISTER MARY MARGARET, college administrator; b. Carbondale, Pa., Sept. 8, 1941; d. Charles Vincent and Anna Rose (Ahern) R. BA, Marywood Coll., Scranton, Pa., 1965; MA, Assumption Coll., Worcester, Mass., 1972; PhD, Pa. State U., 1979. Elem. tchr. St. Ephrem's, Bklyn., 1966-67; secondary tchr. South Catholic High, Scranton, Pa., 1967-69, Maria Regina High Sch., Uniondale, N.Y., 1969-72; mem. faculty Marywood Coll., Scranton, Pa., 1972-86, dean, 1986-88, pres., 1988—; tchr. Mainland China, Wuhan, 1982, Marygrove Coll., Detroit, 1979; bd. dirs. Moses Taylor Hops., Scranton Prep. Sch.; bd. dirs., exec. com. Lourdesmont Sch., Neylan Commn. Contbr. articles to profl. jours. Recipient bilingual fellowship Pa. State U., 1976-79, Local Chpt. Svc. award UN, 1984, Woman of Yr. awrd Boy Scouts Am., 1993; named Outstanding Alumna, Pa. State Coll. Edn., 1989. Mem. Pa. Assn. for Colls. and Univs. (exec. com., program com.), Coun. for Ind. Colls. and Univs., Am. Assn. Cath. Colls., Phi Delta Kappa (Northeast Woman 1986, 96, Educator of Yr. award 1990). Office: Marywood Coll Office of the President Scranton PA 18509-1598

REARDEN, CAROLE ANN, clinical pathologist, educator; b. Belleville, Ont., Can., June 11, 1946; d. Joseph Brady and Honora Patricia (O'Halloran) R. BSc, McGill U., 1969, MSc, MDCM, 1971. Diplomate Am. Bd. Pathology, Am. Bd. Immunohematology and Blood Banking, Am. Bd. Histocompatibility and Immunogenetics. Resident and fellow Children's Meml. Hosp., Chgo., 1971-73; resident in pediatrics U. Calif., San Diego, 1974, resident then fellow, 1975-79, asst. prof. pathology, 1979-86, dir. histocompatability and immunogenetics lab., 1979-94, assoc. prof., 1986-92, prof., 1992—, head divsn. lab. medicine, 1989-94; dir. med. ctr. U. Calif. Thornton Hosp. Clin. Labs., San Diego, 1993—; prin. investigator devel. monoclonal antibodies to erythroid antigens, recombinant autoantigens; dir. lab. exam. com. Am. Bd. Histocompatibility and Immunogenetics. Contbr. articles to profl. jours.; patentee autoantigen pinch. Mem. Mayor's Task Force on AIDS, San Diego, 1983. Recipient Young Investigator Rsch. award NIH, 1979; grantee U. Calif. Cancer Rsch. Coordinating Com., 1982, NIH, 1983; scholar Nat. Blood Found. Mem. Am. Soc. Investigative Pathology, Am. Soc. Hematology, Am. Assn. Blood Banks (com. organ transplantation and tissue typing 1982-87, tech. com. 13 edit. tech. manual 1996—), Am. Soc. Histocompatibility and Immunogenetics. Office: U Calif San Diego Dept Pathology 0612 9500 Gilman Dr La Jolla CA 92093-5003

REARDON, FRANK EMOND, lawyer; b. Providence, May 22, 1953; s. J. Clarke and Dorothy (Emond) R.; m. Deborah Walsh, Sept. 30, 1978; children: Kathleen Elizabeth, Brendan Francis, William James, Sean Patrick. BA, Holy Cross Coll., Worcester, Mass., 1975; JD, Suffolk U., 1978; MS, Harvard U., 1981. Bar: Mass. 1978, R.I. 1978, U.S. Dist. Ct. Mass. 1980, U.S. Dist. Ct. R.I. 1980, U.S. Supreme Ct. 1986. Counsel Nat. Assn. Govtl. Employment and Internat. Brotherhood Police Officers, Cranston, R.I., 1978-81; asst. gen. counsel Brigham and Women's Hosp., Boston, 1981-84; litigation counsel Risk Mgmt. Found. Harvard Med. Instns., Cambridge, Mass., 1984-87; ptnr. Hassan and Reardon, Boston, 1987—; chmn. bd. dirs. St. Monica's Nursing Home, 1984-89, Med. Area Fed. Credit Unon, 1984-89; clk., trustee Deaconness Glover Hosp., Needham, Mass.; ethics com. Boston Children's Hosp., 1993-96. Contbr. articles to profl. jours. Chmn. fin. com. Town of Needham, Mass.; mem. pres.'s council Coll. Holy Cross, 1985—. Beuilacqua scholar, 1978. Mem. ABA, Mass. Bar Assn. (chmn. health law sect. 1987—), Assn. Trial Lawyers Am., Am. Soc. Law and Medicine (cmty. rep. children's hosp. ethics com.). Democrat. Roman Catholic. Avocations: tennis, sailing, golf, writing. Home: 44 Sargent St Needham MA 02192-3434 Office: Hassan & Reardon 535 Boylston St Boston MA 02116-3720

REARDON, JAMES LOUIS, education educator, consultant; b. Vinton, Iowa, June 29, 1943; s. James Harold and Hazel Alice (Pieper) R.; m. Antonia Anita Boni, July 3, 1971. BSBA, U. Iowa, 1964, MA in Edn., 1966; EdD, U. LaVerne, 1985. Cert. tchr., Calif. Supr. tchr. edn. U. Calif., Riverside, 1971—, coord. intern credential program, 1994; co-dir. Inland Area History-Social Sci. Project, Riverside, 1990-94; cons. We. Assn. Schs. and Colls., State Dept. Edn. Expanded Accreditation, Sacramento, 1990-92; reviewer Charles Merrill Pubs., Columbus, Ohio, 1988-91; convenor Tech. Edn. Program Area Com., Riverside, 1990; edn. specialist Nat. Assn. Trade and Tech. Schs., Washington, 1983—. Recipient People Who Make a Difference award, Riverside Press, 1989. Mem. Inland Empire Coun. for the Social Studies (treas. 1986—, Leadership in Social Studies Edn. award 1993), Calif. Coun. for the Social Studies (mem. editl. bd. 1985—), Nat. Coun. for the Social Studies, Network for Secondary Edn. Profs. (pres. 1985-86). Home: 1513 Lynne Ct Redlands CA 92373-7143 Office: U Calif 2105 Sproul Hall Riverside CA 92521

REASONER, BARRETT HODGES, lawyer; b. Houston, Apr. 16, 1964; s. Harry Max and Macey (Hodges) R.; m. Susan Hardig; children: Matthew Joseph, Caroline Macey. BA cum laude, Duke U., 1986; Grad. Dipl., London Sch. Econs., 1987; JD with honors, U. Tex., 1990. Bar: Tex. 1990, U.S. Dist. Ct. (so., we., and no. dists.) Tex. 1993, U.S. Ct. Appeals (5th cir.) 1993. Asst. dist. atty. Harris County Dist. Atty.'s Office, Houston, 1990-92; ptnr. Gibbs & Bruns, L.L.P., Houston, 1992—. Fellow Houston Bar Found.; mem. Am. Judicature Soc. (bd. dirs. 1994—), State Bar Tex., Houston Bar Assn. (legal lines com. 1994-96), Houston Young Lawyers Assn. (pub. schs. and pub. edn. com. 1994—), Order of Barristers. Episcopalian. Home: 6139 Cedar Creek Dr Houston TX 77057-1801

REASONER, HARRY MAX, lawyer; b. San Marcos, Tex., July 15, 1939; s. Harry Edward and Joyce Majorie (Barrett) R.; m. Elizabeth Macey Hodges, Apr. 15, 1963; children: Barrett Hodges, Elizabeth Macey Reasoner Stokes. BA in Philosophy summa cum laude, Rice U., 1960; JD with highest honors, U. Tex., 1962; postgrad., U. London, 1962-63. Bar: Tex., D.C., N.Y. Law clk. U.S. Ct. Appeals (2d cir.), 1963-64; assoc. Vinson & Elkins, Houston, 1964-69, ptnr., 1970—, mng.ptnr., 1992—; vis. prof. U. Tex. Sch. Law, 1971, Rice U., 1976, U. Houston Sch. Law, 1977; chair adv. group U.S. Dist Ct. (so. dist.) Tex.; mem. adv. com. Supreme Ct. Tex. Author: (with Charles Alan Wright) Procedure: The Handmaid of Justice, 1965; author: (with others) American Economic Policy in the 1980s, 1994. Life trustee U. Tex. Law Sch. Found.; trustee Southwestern Legal Found., 1990—, Baylor Coll. Medicine, 1992—; chair Tex. Higher Edn. Coordinating Bd., 1991; bd. govs. Rice U., 1994—; bd. dirs. Greater Houston Partnership, 1992—; mem. exec. coun. Ex-Student's Assn. U. Tex., 1992—; gov. Houston Forum, 1992—; bd. dirs. Central Houston, Inc., 1993—, Houston Music Hall Found. Bd., 1996—, Houston Annenberg Challenge Child Centered Schs. Initiative Bd., 1997—. Rotary Found. fellow 1962-63; recipient Disting. Alumnus award for cmty. svc. U. Tex. Law Alumni Assn., 1995; named Disting. Alumnus, U. Tex., 1997. Fellow Am. Coll. Trial Lawyers, Internat. Acad. Trial Lawyers, Internat. Soc. Barristers, ABA Found., Tex. Bar Found.; mem. ABA (chmn. antitrust sect. 1989-90), Houston Bar Assn., Assn. Bar City N.Y., Am. Law Inst., Chancellors, Houston Com. Fgn. Rels., Houston Philos. Soc., Philos. Soc. Tex., Am. Bd. Trial Advocates, Century Assn. N.Y.C., Houston Country Club, Rotary Club, Ramada Tex. Club, Eldorado Country Club (Calif.), Castle Pines Golf Club (Castle Rock, Colo.), Cosmos Club of Washington, Galveston Artillery Club, Phi Beta Kappa, Phi Delta Phi. Democrat. Baptist. Office: Vinson & Elkins 2800 First City Tower 1001 Fannin St Houston TX 77002-6706

REASONER, STEPHEN M., federal judge; b. 1944. BA in Econs., U. Ark., 1966, JD, 1969. Mem. firm Barret, Wheatley, Smith & Deacon, Jonesboro, Ark., 1969-88; from judge to chief judge U.S. Dist. Ct. (ea. dist.) Ark., Little Rock, 1988—; bd. dirs. U. Ark. Law Rev.; mem. judicial coun. 8th cir., 1990-93. Trustee Craighead-Jonesboro Pub. Libr., 1972—, chmn. 1984-88; bd. dirs. Jonesboro C. of C., 1981-84, Ark. IOLTA, 1987—, Abilities Unltd., 1974-81; mem. St. Marks Episcopal Ch. Vestry, 1976-79, sr. warden, 1979. With USAR, 1969-73. Mem. ABA, Am. Counsel Assn., Am. Judicature Soc., Ark. Bar Assn. (exec. com., ho. of dels. 1984-87), Craighead County Bar Assn. (pres. 1983-84). Avocation: flying. Office: Courthouse 600 W Capitol Ave Rm 60 Little Rock AR 72201-3329*

REASONER, WILLIS IRL, III, lawyer; b. Hamilton, Ohio, Dec. 24, 1951; s. W. Irl Jr. and Nancy Jane (Mitchell) R.; m. Lana Jean Mayes, Apr. 19, 1975 (div. Sept. 1985); 1 child, Erick; m. Joan Marie Mogil, Dec. 30, 1986; children: Scott, Sally. BA in History, Ind. U., 1974; JD cum laude, U. S.C., 1978. Bar: Ohio 1978, U.S. Dist. Ct. (so. dist.) Ohio 1978, U.S. Dist. Ct. (no. dist.) Ohio 1979, U.S. Ct. Appeals (6th cir.) 1988, U.S. Ct. Appeals (1st cir.) 1991. Assoc. Porter, Wright, Morris & Arthur, Columbus, Ohio, 1978-83; ptnr. Baker & Hostetler, Columbus, 1983-94, Habash, Reasoner & Frazier, 1994—. Mem. ABA, Ohio Bar Assn., Columbus Bar Assn. Home: 1101 Riva Ridge Blvd Columbus OH 43230-3808 Office: Habash, Reasoner & Frazier 471 E Broad St Ste 1600 Columbus OH 43215-3842

REASOR, RODERICK JACKSON, industrial engineer; b. Hampton, Va., Apr. 8, 1953; s. Emmett Jackson and Cora (Keller) R.; m. Anita Marie Knibb, June 29, 1974; children: Rebecca Eileen, Matthew Ryan, Christopher James, Laura Kathleen. BS, Va. Poly. Inst. & State U., 1976, MS, 1981, PhD in Indsl. Engring. and Ops. Rsch., 1990. Registered profl. engr., Va. Indsl. engr. Tenn. Eastman Co., Kingsport, Tenn., 1977-83; program mgr. Mgmt. Systems Labs., Blacksburg, Va., 1983-86; instr. IEOR Va. Poly. Inst. & State U., Blacksburg, 1986-89, asst. prof. indsl. and systems engring., dir. lab., 1989-95; prin. indsl. engr. Eastman Chem. Co., Kingsport, Tenn., 1995—; mem. Indsl. Engring. Fundamentals of Engring./Profl. Engr. Exam com. Nat. Coun. Examiners for Engring. and Surveying, 1996; cons. in field. Author: (with others) Occupational Ergonomics, 1995; referee jours.; contbr. articles to proceedings. Deacon, elder 1st Christian Ch., Kingsport, Tenn., 1979-83, 96—, vice chmn. bd., 1982, sec. bd., 1981, bible sch. supt., 1982-83, chmn. coms., 1979-83, 97—; vol. econ. discussion series for high sch. srs. Kingsport (Tenn.) C. of C., 1983; judge annual product fair Jr. Achievement Kingsport, 1983; vice chmn. bd. Blacksburg Christian Ch., 1985-88, elder, 1988-95, treas., 1989-90, chmn. bd., 1991-92; bd. dirs. Woodbine Homes Assn., Blacksburg, 1990-91, v.p., 1991-92, pres., 1992-93; bd. dirs. Kingsport Youth Soccer Assn., 1997—. Grantee ITT Teves, 1991-92, NSF, 1991-93, Computer Aided Mfg. Internat., 1991-92, Barden corp., 1989-90, Aluminum Co. Am., 1984-85. Mem. Am. Soc. Engring. Edn. (sec.-treas. 1991-92, editor newsletter 1992-93, program chmn. 1993-94, chmn. indsl. engring. divsn. 1994-95), Inst. Indsl. Engrs. (sr., pres. Tri-Cities Tenn. chpt. 1979-83, Award of Excellence 1983, adv. bd. chmn., dir., program chmn. 1985-89, Pride award 1988, bd. dirs. 1988-89, chpt. devel. chmn. 1990-93, asst. dir. dist. III 1990-92, Excellence award 1990, 91), Coll. Industry Coun. Material Handling Edn. (chmn. acad. programs and activities com. 1994-95, adv. bd. 1994-95), Inst. Ops. Rsch. and Mgmt. Scis. (session chmn. fall ann. meeting 1989), East Tenn. Engring. Assn. Coun., Kiwanis (pub. affairs com. 1982-83), Alpha Pi Mu. Home: 1104 Hillsboro Cir Kingsport TN 37660-8478 Office: Eastman Chem Co PO Box 1973 Kingsport TN 37662

REAST, DEBORAH STANEK, ophthalmology center administrator; b. Phila., Feb. 25, 1955; d. Chester Joseph and Thelma Sylvia (Hop) S. AA, Gwynedd Mercy Coll., 1975; Cert. Mgmt., Villanova U., 1987. Cert. med. mgr. Billing clk. Ophthalmic Assocs., Lansdale, Pa., 1971-75, exec. sec., 1975-80, ops. mgr., 1980—; treas., bd. dirs. Montgomery County Chpt. Profl. Secs. Internat. Ch. organist Corpus Christi Parish, Gwynedd, 1970-86, Saint Marie Goretti Parish, Hatfield, 1986—, ch. organist, 1986-96. Mem. Am. Soc. Ophthalmic Adminstrs., Profl. Assn. Health Care Office Mgrs., Pa. Assn. Notaries, The Wine Connection Bucks. Democrat. Roman Catholic. Avocations: writing, traveling, collecting. Office: Ophthalmic Assocs 1000 N Broad St Lansdale PA 19446-1138 also: 478 Main St Collegeville PA 19426

REATH, GEORGE, JR., lawyer; b. Phila., Mar. 14, 1939; s. George and Isabel Duer (West) R.; children from a previous marriage: Eric (dec. 1995), Amanda; m. Ann B. Rowland, 1990. BA, Williams Coll., 1961; LLB, Harvard U., 1964. Bar: Pa. 1965, U.S. Dist. Ct. (ea. dist.) Pa. 1966, U.S. Ct. Appeals (3d cir.) 1996. Assoc. Dechert Price & Rhoads, Phila., 1964-70, Brussels, 1971-74; atty. Pennwalt Corp., Phila., 1974-78, mgr. legal dept., asst. sec., 1978-87, sr. v.p.-law, sec., 1987-89; sr. v.p., gen. counsel, sec. Elf Atochem N.Am., Inc. (formerly Pennwalt Corp.), Phila., 1990-92; sr. v.p., gen counsel, sec. Legal Triage Svcs., Inc., Phila., 1993—; bd. dirs. Internat. Bus. Forum, Inc., 1978-91; arbitrator Am. Arbitration Assn. Trustee Children's Hosp., Phila., 1974—, sec., 1980-81, vice chmn., 1984—; bd. mgrs. Phila. City Inst. Libr., 1974—, treas., 1981-88, pres., 1989—; bd. dirs. Phila. Festival Theatre for New Plays, 1983-94, Ctrl. Phila. Devel. Corp., 1987-93; bd. dirs. Bach Festival Phila., 1990—, v.p., 1992-93; bd. dirs. Crime Commn. Delaware Valley, 1st vice chmn., 1992-94, chmn., 1994-96; exec. com., 1996—. Mem. ABA, Pa. Bar Assn., Am. Soc. Corp. Secs., Phila. Bar Assn., Penllyn Club, Winter Harbor Yacht Club, Am. Corp. Counsel Assn., Phi Beta Kappa.

REAVES, JOHN DANIEL, lawyer, playwright, actor; b. Camp Hill, Ala., Mar. 14, 1939; s. William Newell and Katherine (Rawlinson) R.; m. Wendy Wick; children: Paul Newell, Caroline Rawlinson. BS, Auburn U., 1961; LLB, U. Va., 1964. Bar: Ala. 1965, D.C. 1972, U.S. Supreme Ct. 1977. Law clk. to Hon. Richard T. Rives U.S. Ct. Appeals (5th cir.), 1964-65; asst. prof. law U. Ga., 1965-71; fellow Fed. Jud. Ctr., Washington, 1971-72; atty. Bur. Competition, FTC, Washington, 1972-73; legal advisor to Hon. Elizabeth Dole, commr. FTC, Washington, 1973-77; ptnr. Baker & Hostetler, Washington, Montedomico, Hamilton & Altar, Washington; vis. prof. law George Washington U., Washington, 1975. mem. editorial bd. Va. Law Rev.; founder Ga. Law Rev., 1966; writer, performer H.L. Mencken: Reveries of an Iconoclast, 1981; appeared in The Kingfish, 1979. Bd. dirs. Woolly Mammoth Theatre Co., 1992—. Mem. D.C. Bar, Ala. State Bar Assn., Cosmos Club (Washington). Office: Montedomico, Hamilton & Altman 5301 Wisconsin Ave NW Ste 400 Washington DC 20015-2015

REAVES, RAY DONALD, civil engineer; b. Jacksonville, Ala., Aug. 6, 1935; s. William Ozzie and Josephine (Jackson) R.; m. Annette Baird, Dec. 18, 1959; children: Tanya Ann Walker, Ronald Ray. BS in Civil Engring., Auburn (Ala.) U., 1960; MBA, U. Utah, 1976; postgrad., U. Mo., Kansas City. Registered profl. engr., Okla.; diplomate Am. Acad. Environ. Engrs. Commd. 2d lt. USAF, 1961, advanced through grades to col., 1981; comdt. Airlift Ops. Sch., Scott AFB, Ill., 1980-82; dep. base comdr. Little Rock AFB, 1982-83; base comdr. Kunsan Air Base, Korea, 1983-84, Tinker AFB, Oklahoma City, 1984-85; dir. environ. mgr. Oklahoma City Air Logistics Ctr., Tinker AFB, 1985-89; ret. USAF, 1989; mgr. environ. engring. Oklahoma County, Oklahoma City, 1989-95, Okla. county engr., 1995—; Bus. Tech. Delegation Citizen to Citizen ambassador to Russia and Ukraine, 1992. Mem. ASCE, NSPE, Okla. Soc. Profl. Engrs. (citizen ambassador to Russia and Ukraine 1992), Midwest City C. of C., Rotary, Masons, Shriners. Avocations: golf, boating, tinkering.

REAVIS, HUBERT GRAY, JR., metal products executive; b. Winston-Salem, N.C., May 4, 1945; s. Hubert Gray and Marie (Long) R.; m. Brenda Todd, Oct. 19, 1969; children: Anna Caroline, Jennifer Rebecca. BS in Engring., N.C. State U., 1967. Metall. engr. Alumninun Co. Am., Alcoa, Tenn., 1967-73; divisional metall. engr. Aluminum Co. Am., Newburgh, Ind., 1973-79; product metall. engr. Aluminum Co. Am., Pitts., 1979-86; quality assurance mgr. Alumninun Co. Am., Newburgh, Ind., 1986-88; tech. mgr. Aluminum Co. Am., Newburgh, Ind., 1988-96, mgr. materials devel. group, 1997—. Patentee in field. Mem. Alumninum Co. Am. Polit. Action, Pitts., 1979-86, Newburgh, 1986—. Recipient (2) Arthur Vining Davis awards. Mem. Am. Soc. for Metals, N.C. State Alumni Loyalty Fund, Phi Kappa Phi, Theta Tau, Alpha Sigma Mu, Tau Beta Pi. Office: Aluminum Co Am PO Box 10 Newburgh IN 47629-0010

REAVIS, LIZA ANNE, semiconductor executive; b. N.Y.C., July 27, 1959; d. William Ralph and Juliette (Bustillo y Zelaya) Bartlett; m. Paul H. Reavis, May 25, 1985. BA in Internat. Rels., Rice U., 1981; MBA, Georgetown U., 1988. Project asst. Latham, Watkins & Hills, Washington, 1982-83; assoc. mgr. countertrade Sears World Trade, Washington, 1983-85; export asst. Weadon, Dibble & Rehm, Washington, 1985-86; assoc. cons. Vanguard Comm. Corp., Palo Alto, Calif., 1988-90; bus. mgr. Teleport Comm. Corp., San Francisco, 1990-94; sr. fin. analyst, contr. Nat. Semicondr. Corp., 1995—. Contbr. Project Open Hand, San Francisco, Calif. Wheelchair Vets. Assn., Am. Assn. for AIDS Rsch., San Francisco, 1990—; mem. Golden Gate Nat. Recreation Area, San Francisco, 1990—. Recipient Teleport Comms. Group Ann. Hero award, 1994; Presdl. scholar Dept. HEW. Mem. Women in Tech., Acad. Polit. Sci., Club des Hiboux (sec. 1979-80), Commonwealth Club, Sierra Club, Cousteau Soc., Phi Beta Kappa, Beta Gamma Sigma, Pi Delta Phi. Avocations: international cultures and politics, classical ballet, poetry, piano. Home: 6931 Geary Blvd San Francisco CA 94121-1620 Office: Nat Semicondr Corp 2900 Semiconductor Dr Mail Stop D2710 Santa Clara CA 95052-8090

REAVLEY, THOMAS MORROW, federal judge; b. Quitman, Tex., June 21, 1921; s. Thomas Mark and Mattie (Morrow) R.; m. Florence Montgomery Wilson, July 24, 1943; children—Thomas Wilson, Marian, Paul Stuart, Margaret. B.A., U. Tex., 1942; J.D., Harvard, 1948; LL.D., Austin Coll., 1974, Southwestern U., 1977, Tex. Wesleyan, 1982; LL.M., U. Va., 1983; LLD, Pepperdine U., 1993. Bar: Tex. 1948. Asst. dist. atty. Dallas, 1948-49; mem. firm Bell & Reavley, Nacogdoches, Tex., 1949-51; county atty. Nacogdoches, 1951; with Collins, Garrison, Renfro & Zeleskey, 1951-52; mem. firm Fisher, Tonahill & Reavley, Jasper, Tex., 1952-55; sec. state Tex., 1955-57; mem. firm Powell, Rauhut, McGinnis & Reavley, Austin, Tex., 1957-64; dist. judge Austin, 1964-68; justice Supreme Ct., Tex., 1968-77; counsel Scott & Douglass, 1977-79; judge U.S. Ct. Appeals (5th cir.), Austin, 1979-90; now sr. judge U.S. Ct. Appeals (5th cir.), Austin, TX, 1990—; lectr. Baylor U. Law Sch., 1976-94; adj. prof. U. Tex. Law Sch., 1958-59, 78-79, 88-95. Chancellor S.W. Tex. conf. United Meth. Ch., 1972-93, chancellor emeritus, 1993—. Lt. USNR, 1943-45. Club: Mason (33 deg.). Home: 24 Woodstone Sq Austin TX 78703-1159 Office: US Ct Appeals 903 San Jacinto Blvd # 434 Austin TX 78701-2450

REBACK, JOYCE ELLEN, lawyer; b. Phila., July 11, 1948; d. William and Sue (Goldstein) R.; m. Itzhak Brook, Aug. 2, 1981; children: Jonathan Zev, Sara Jennie. BA magna cum laude, Brown U., 1970; JD with honors, George Washington U., 1976. Bar: D.C. 1976, U.S. Dist. Ct. D.C. 1976, U.S. Ct. Appeals (D.C. cir.) 1976, U.S. Ct. Appeals (3d cir.) 1983, U.S. Ct. Appeals (Fed. cir.) 1985. Assoc. Fulbright & Jaworski, Washington, 1976-84, ptnr., 1984-87; legal cons. IMF, Washington, 1987—. Contbr. articles to profl. jours. Mem. ABA, D.C. Bar Assn., Phi Beta Kappa. Jewish. Office: Internat Monetary Fund 700 19th St NW Washington DC 20431-0001

REBANE, JOHN T., lawyer; b. Bamberg, Germany, Oct. 29, 1946; s. Henn and Anna (Inna) R.; m. Linda Kay Morgan, Sept. 22, 1972; children: Alexis Morgan, Morgan James. BA, U. Minn., 1970, JD, 1973. Bar: Minn. 1973. Atty. Land O'Lakes, Inc., Arden Hills, Minn., 1973-80, assoc. gen counsel, 1983, v.p., gen. counsel, 1984—; sec. Cenex Land O'Lakes Agronomy Co.; sec., dir. Land O' Lakes Internat. Devel. Corp. Mem. ABA, Minn. Bar Assn., Hennepin County Bar Assn., Nat. Coun. Farm Coop. (exec. com. chmn.). Office: Land O'Lakes Inc PO Box 116 Minneapolis MN 55440-0116

REBAY, LUCIANO, Italian literature educator, literary critic; b. Milan, Italy, Apr. 23, 1928; came to U.S., 1955; s. Angelo and Pierina (Doniselli) R.; m. Martha Virginia Krauss, Aug. 2, 1952; children: Alexandra, Ilaria. Maturita classica Liceo Manzoni, Milan, 1946; Licence es lettres, U. Aix-en-Provence, France, 1951; Ph.D., Columbia U., 1960. Instr. Italian Columbia U., N.Y.C., 1957-60, asst. prof., 1960-63, assoc. prof., 1963-65, prof., 1965-73, Giuseppe Ungaretti prof. Italian lit., 1973—; chmn. Italian Dept. Columbia U., 1970-73; dir. Ctr. Italian Studies, 1985-88; cons. to scholarly jours.; mem. Nat. Bd. Translators, Columbia U. Transl. Ctr. Author: Le origini della poesia di Giuseppe Ungaretti, 1962, Invitation to Italian Poetry, 1969, Alberto Moravia, 1970, Giuseppe Ungaretti, Gli scritti egiziani, 1909-1912, 1980, Montale, Clizia e l'America, 1982; editor: Giuseppe Ungaretti, Saggi e interventi, 1974, Jean Paulhan-Giuseppe Ungaretti, Correspondance, 1921-68, 1989, Montale per amico, 1994. Guggenheim fellow, 1966-67; Am. Council Learned Socs. fellow, 1970-71; NEH fellow, 1980-81; Am. Philos. Soc. research grantee, 1970, 75. Mem. MLA, Am. Assn. Tchrs. of Italian, Associazione Internazionale per gli Studi di Lingua e Letteratura Italiana. Office: Columbia U Dept Italian New York NY 10027

REBEC, GEORGE VINCENT, neuroscience researcher, educator, administrator; b. Harrisburg, Pa. Apr. 6, 1949; s. George Martin and Nadine (Bosko) R. AB, Villanova U., 1971; MA, U. Colo., 1974, PhD, 1975. Postdoctoral fellow U. Calif., San Diego, 1975-77; asst. prof. Ind. U., Bloomington, 1977-81, assoc. prof., 1981-85, prof. psychology, 1985—, dir. program in neural sci., 1985—; mem. rsch. rev. com. NIMH. Author: (with P.M. Groves) Introduction to Biological Psychology, 1988, 92; contbr. articles to profl. jours. Recipient Eli Lilly Teaching award, 1978, Pres.' award Ind. U., 1990; grantee NIDA, 1979—, NSF, 1985-96, NINDS, 1996—. Fellow AAAS; mem. Soc. for Neurosci. (chmn. Ind. U. chpt.), Internat. Brain Rsch. Orgn., Am. Psychol. Soc., Assn. Neurosci. Depts. and Programs (treas.). Roman Catholic. Avocation: sports. Office: Ind U Program in Neural Sci Dept Psychology Bloomington IN 47405

REBEIZ, CONSTANTIN A., plant physiology educator; b. Beirut, July 11, 1936; came to U.S., 1969, naturalized, 1975; s. Anis C. and Valentine A. (Choueyri) R.; m. Carole Louise Conness, Aug. 18, 1962; children: Paul A., Natalie, Mark J. B.S., Am. U., Beirut, 1959; M.S., U. Calif. - Davis, 1960, Ph.D., 1965. Dir. dept. biol. scis. Agrl. Research Inst., Beirut, 1965-69; research assoc. biology U. Calif. - Davis, 1969-71; assoc. prof. plant physiology U. Ill., Urbana-Champaign, 1972-76, prof., 1976—. Contbr. articles to sci. publs. plant physiology and biochemistry. Recipient Beckman research awards, 1982, 85, Funk award, 1985, John P. Trebellas Research Endowment, 1986, Sr. Rsch. award Univ. Ill., 1994; named One of 100 Outstanding Innovators, Sci. Digest, 1984-85. Mem. Am. Soc. Plant Physiologists, Comite Internat. de Photobiologie, Am. Soc. Photobiology, AAAS, Lebanese Assn. Advancement Scis. (exec. com. 1967-69), Sigma Xi. Achievements include research on pathway of chlorophyll biosynthesis, chloroplast devel., bioengring. of photosynthetic reactors; pioneered biosynthesis of chlorophyll in vitro; duplication of greening process of plants in test tube, demonstration of operation of multibranched chlorophyll biosynthetic pathway in nature; formulation and design of laser herbicides, insecticides and cancer chemotherapeutic agents. Home: 2503 W Springfield Ave Apt D2 Champaign IL 61821-2840 Office: U Ill 240A Pabl Urbana IL 61801 *Meaningful scientific discoveries are those that help humans achieve a better understanding of themselves, of their environment or of the universe at large, as well as those that contribute to the betterment of the human spiritual, psychological and physical condition.*

REBENACK, JOHN HENRY, retired librarian; b. Wilkinsburg, Pa., Feb. 10, 1918; s. Charles Lewis and Carrie (Fielding) R.; m. Dorothy Merle Treat, Oct. 31, 1942 (dec. Apr. 1971); children: Charles Edwin, Christine (Mrs. Clair N. Hayes III); m. Frances Strabley Krieger, May 6, 1972. A.B., U. Pitts., 1942; B.S. in L.S, Carnegie Library Sch., 1947. Reference asst. Carnegie Library, Pitts., 1947-50; librarian Salem (Ohio) Pub. Library, 1950-53, Elyria (Ohio) Library, 1953-57; asst. librarian Akron (Ohio) Public Library, 1957-65, assoc. librarian, 1965-67, librarian-dir., 1967-80; dir. U.S. Book Exchange, Inc., 1972. Mem. United Community Council, Citizens' Com. Pub. Welfare, 1965-66, chmn. group work and recreation div., 1963-66, v.p., 1967-68, pres. conf. of execs., 1975-76; mem. steering com., planning div. United Way; mem. Akron Mayor's Task Force on Human Relations, 1962; mem. library com. President's Com. on Employment of Handicapped, 1967-80, chmn., 1973-80, mem. sch. library manpower adv. com., 1967-73; mem. coll. adv. com. U. Akron, 1972-85; mem. adv. council on fed. programs State Library of Ohio, 1975-79; Bd. visitors Grad. Sch. Library and Info. Sci., U. Pitts., 1968-74; mem. exec. bd. Gt. Trail council Boy Scouts Am., 1977-80; bd. dirs. Summit County unit Am. Cancer Soc., 1976—, pres., 1979-81; bd. dirs. Ohio div., 1981-91, chmn. pub. info. com., 1989-90, exec. com. 1988-91. With AUS, 1942-45. Recipient Newton D. Baker citation, 1968. Mem. ALA (chmn. personnel adminstrv. sect. 1966-67, chmn. bldgs. and equipment sect. 1971-73, chmn. legislation assembly 1976-77), Ohio Library Assn. (exec. bd. 1957-60, chmn. adult edn. round table 1963, chmn. legis. com. 1965-66, 70-72, 76-80, pres. 1966-67, Librarian of Year 1979, named to Hall of Fame 1989), Ohio Library Found. (privileged mem. 1980, privileged dir. 1988—), Carnegie Library Sch. Assn. (pres. 1961-63), U. Pitts. Grad. Sch. Library and Info. Sci. Alumni Assn. (exec. com. 1978-79, Disting. Alumnus award 1980), Am. Assn. UN (v.p. Akron chpt. 1960), Beta Phi Mu. Congregationalist. Clubs: Torch (pres. 1968-69), Kiwanis (pres. Akron 1978-79). Home: 2095 Brookshire Rd Akron OH 44313-5323

REBENFELD, LUDWIG, chemist, educator; b. Prague, Czechoslovakia, July 10, 1928; came to U.S., 1939, naturalized, 1946; s. Carl and Martha (Scheib) R.; m. Ellen Vogel, July 27, 1956. BS, Lowell Tech. Inst., 1951; MA, Princeton, 1954, PhD, 1955; D Textile Sci. (hon.), Phila. Coll. Textiles and Sci., 1980, Liberec Tech U., Czech Republic, 1993. Rsch. fellow, sr. scientist Textile Rsch. Inst., Princeton, N.J., 1951-59, assoc. rsch. dir., also edn. program dir., 1960-66, v.p. edn. and rsch., 1966-70, pres., 1971-92, pres. emeritus and rsch. assoc., 1993—; vis. lectr., assoc. prof., prof. chem. engring. Princeton U., 1964—; life trustee Phila. Coll. Textiles and Sci. Editor Textile Rsch. Jour., 1992—. Recipient Distinguished Achievement award Fiber Soc., Harold DeWitt Smith Meml. medal ASTM. Fellow Am. Inst. Chemists, Brit. Textile Inst. (hon., Inst. medal), Inst. Textile Sci. Can.; mem. AAAS, Am. Chem. Soc., Am. Assn. Textile Chemists and Colorists (Olney medal 1987), Fiber Soc. (governing coun., sec.-treas. 1962-84), Nat. Coun. Textile Edn., Sigma Xi, Phi Psi. Home: 49 Pardoe Rd Princeton NJ 08540-2617 Office: Textile Rsch Inst PO Box 625 601 Prospect Ave Princeton NJ 08540-4034

REBER, DAVID JAMES, lawyer; b. Las Vegas, Nev., Mar. 1, 1944; s. James Rice and Helen Ruth (Cusick) R.; m. Jacqueline Yee, Aug. 31, 1968; children: Emily, Brad, Cecily. BA, Occidental Coll., L.A., 1965; JD, Harvard U., 1968. Bar: Calif. 1969, Hawaii 1975, U.S. Dist. Ct. Hawaii, U.S. Ct. Appeals (9th cir.), U.S. Supreme Ct. Asst. prof. law U. Iowa, Iowa City, 1968-70; assoc. Sheppard Mullin Richter & Hampton, L.A., 1970-75, Goodsill Anderson Quinn & Stifel, Honolulu, 1975-76; ptnr. Goodsill Anderson Quinn & Stifel, 1976—. Dir. Oahu Econ. Devel. Bd., Honolulu. Mem. ABA (bus., antitrust and pub. utilities sects.), Hawaii Bar Assn. Avocations: golf, tennis, softball, travel. Office: Goodsill Anderson Quinn & Stifel 1099 Alakea St Honolulu HI 96813-4500

REBER, RAYMOND ANDREW, chemical engineer; b. Bklyn., Apr. 16, 1942; s. Herbert and Dorothy Agnes (Schmidt) R.; m. Anita Jean Roe, June 22, 1963; children: Laura Jean Bucci, Paul Raymond, Jill Anita. BChemE, NYU, 1963, MChemE, 1966. Engr. M.W. Kellogg, N.Y.C., 1964-69; devel. engr., supr. Union Carbide, Tarrytown, N.Y., 1970-74, lic. bus. mgr., 1975-81; new bus. devel. mgr. Union Carbide, Danbury, Conn., 1982-84; tech. mgr. Union Carbide, Tarrytown, 1985-87; dir. of tech. UOP, Tarrytown, 1988-93; exec. v.p., COO Balchem Corp., Slate Hill, N.Y., 1994-96, pres., CEO, 1997—. Patentee in field. Commr. Montrose (N.Y.) Improvement Dist. 1970—; soccer referee, 1977-93. Recipient Kirkpatrick award McGraw-Hill, 1967, 87. Mem. AIChE, NSPE, Comml. Devel. Assn. Episcopalian. Avocations: soccer, boating, table games, philatelist. Home: 10 Bonnie Hollow Ln Montrose NY 10548-1314 Office: PO Box 175 Slate Hill NY 10973-0175

REBERG, ROSALIE, vice principal; m. Larry Alan Reberg, Aug. 16, 1975; children: Camden Ashleigh, Jacob Alan. BA, Holy Names Coll., 1971; MA with distinction, Calif. State U., Stanislaus, 1994. Elem. edn. tchr. Stanislaus Union Sch. Dist., Modesto, Calif., 1974-96; vice prin. Chrysler Elem. Sch., Modesto, Calif., 1996—; classroom mgmt. mentor tchr., Stanislaus Union Sch. Dist., 1988-89. Mem. Tchrs. English to Spkrs. of Other Langs., Assn. Calif. Sch. Adminstrs. Avocations: reading, computers. Office: Chrysler Elem Sch 2818 Conant Ave Modesto CA 95350-1752

REBIK, JAMES MICHAEL, otolaryngologist; b. Marshalltown, Iowa, July 10, 1953; s. Hubert James and Donna Jean (Grandgeorge) R.; m. Sue Ellyn Primmer, Dec. 22, 1979; children: Christopher James, Kristin Leigh, Robert James, Jonathan Michael. BA summa cum laude, U. No. Iowa, 1981; DO, Kirksville Coll. Osteo. Med., 1985. Diplomate in otorhinolaryngology and facial plastic surgery Am. Osteo. Bd. Ophthalmology and Otorhinolaryngology; diplomate Nat. Bd. Med. Examiners for Osteo. Physicians and Surgeons; lic. physician, Mo., Iowa, Minn., Tex. Intern Kirksville (Mo.) Osteo Med. Ctr., 1985-86, resident otorhinolaryngology/oro-facial plastic surgery, 1986-90; otolaryngologist Landstuhl (Germany) Army Regional Med. Ctr., 1990-92; chief otolaryngology-head and neck surgery svc. Reynolds Army Community Hosp., Ft. Sill, Okla., 1992-94; with Primary Med. Clinic, Midland, Tex., 1996—; cons. otolaryngology VA Med Ctr., Big Spring, Tex., 1996—. Maj. M.C. U.S. Army, 1990-94. Recipient 1st degree brown belt Gup U.S. Tang Soo Do Moo Duk Kwan Fedn., 1979. Fellow Soc. Mil. Otolaryngologists, Am. Osteo. Coll. Otolaryngology-Head and Neck Surgery; mem. AMA, Am. Osteo. Assn., Assn. Mil. Surgeons U.S., Am. Coll. Osteopathic Family Physicians, Am. Acad. Otolaryngic Allergy, Am. Acad. Otolaryngology-Head and Neck Surgery, Christian Soc. Otolaryngology-Head and Neck Surgery, Freeborn County Med Soc., Minn. Med. Assn., Pan-Am. Assn. Otorhinolaryngology-Head and Neck Surgery, Tex. Osteo. Med. Assn., Tex. Med. Found., Mensa. Baptist. Avocations: jogging, medieval and World War II history, baroque and classical music. Home: 7005 Chadwick Ct Midland TX 79707 Office: 4214 Andrews Hwy Ste 100 Midland TX 79703-4861

RECABO, JAIME MIGUEL, lawyer; b. Manila, Philippines, Oct. 6, 1950; came to U.S., 1969; s. Matthew M. and Luisa (De Leon) R.; children: James M., Danielle M.; m. Maureen Susan Ward, Dec. 1980; children: Matthew J., Maura E., Joseph A., Olivia M. BA, Fordham U., 1973, JD, 1988; MBA in Fin., St. John's U., 1977. Bar: N.Y. 1989, N.J. 1989, Conn. 1989. Bus. office mgr. Eger Nursing Home Inc., S.I., N.Y., 1974-77; sr. acct. Kingsbrook Jewish Med. Ctr., Bklyn., 1977-78; asst. compt. Jewish Home & Hosp. for the Aged, Bronx, N.Y., 1978-79; dir. fiscal svcs. Frances Schervier Home & Hosp., Bronx, 1979-86; exec. v.p. finance & legal affairs Franciscan Health System N.Y., Bronx, 1986-89; mgmt. cons., health and immigration atty. N.Y.C., 1989—. Bd. dirs. Frances Schervier Home & Hosp., Bronx, 1987-90, Bklyn. United Meth. Ch. Home, 1991—; vice-chmn. NYAHSA Contrs. Com., N.Y.C., 1985-86, N.Y. Archdiocese Contrs. Coun., N.Y.C., 1980-83. Mem. ABA, Am. Immigration Lawyers Assn., N.J. Bar Assn., N.Y. Bar Assn., Conn. Bar Assn., Healthcare Fin. Mgmt. Assn., Nat. Health Lawyers Assn. Roman Catholic. Office: 34 Palmer Ave Bronxville NY 10708-3404

RECCHIA, CHRISTOPHER, state agency environmental administrator; b. Wantagh, N.Y., Nov. 29, 1958; s. Michael Anthony and Adele Alma (Gluck) R. BA in Zoology, U. Vt., 1980; M Studies in Environ. Law cum laude, Vt. Law Sch., 1982; M of Environ. Studies, Yale U., 1984. Rsch. technician dept. physiology and biophysics U. Vt. Coll. Medicine, Burlington, 1980-81; environ. intern The Conservation Found., Washington, 1983; environ. analyst Coastal Resource Mgmt. div. Conn. Dept. Environ. Protection, Hartford, 1984-85, sr. environ. analyst, 1985-89; mgr. environ. programs Conn. Resources Recovery Authority, Hartford, 1989-91, dir. environ. programs, 1991—; tech. expert Solar Energy Rsch. Inst. and U.S. Dept. Energy, Washington, 1991-92; speaker Inst. Clean Air Cos. Conf., 1996; founder, pres. Advanced Environmental Alternatives, 1996. Mem. spkrs. bur. Union Concerned Scientists; commr. New Haven City Plan Commn., 1995—; bd. dirs. New Haven Land Trust, 1985—, v.p., 1989-90, 93-94, pres., 1995—; mem. New Haven Environ. Adv. Coun., 1988-90, Vt. Natural Resources Coun., 1979—; mem. intermodal concept devel. com. Conn. Dept. Transp., 1993—; field guide, naturalist New Haven Land Trust Coastal Areas, 1984—. Mem. New Haven Preservation Trust (Merit award for home restoration 1992). Avocations: music, skating, theatre, bicycling, home renovation. Home: 98 Clinton Ave New Haven CT 06513-3101 Office: Conn Resources Recovery Authority 179 Allyn St Hartford CT 06103-1424

RECH, SUSAN ANITA, obstetrician, gynecologist; b. Summit, N.J., Nov. 5, 1957; d. William F. and Mary Jane (Crooks) R. BA in Biology, Swarthmore Coll., 1979; MD, U. Medicine Dentistry N.J., Newark, 1984. Diplomate Am. Bd. Ob-Gyn. Resident in ob-gyn. Temple U. Hosp., Phila., 1984-88; pvt. practice, Plattsburgh, N.Y., 1988—; asst. clin. prof. dept. ob-gyn. U. Vt. Sch. Medicine, 1991—; mem. med. adv. bd. Planned Parenthood No. N.Y., Plattsburgh, 1989—, Clinton County Health Dept., Plattsburgh, 1989—; bd. dirs. Cmty. Providers, Inc., Plattsburgh, 1994—. Active Newman Ctr., John XXIII Cath. Parish, Plattsburgh, 1990—; mem. alumni coun. Swarthmore (Pa.) Coll., 1994-96; mem. Seton Cath. H.S. Sch. Bd., Plattsburgh, 1995—. Rsch. grantee U. Medicine and Dentistry N.J., summer 1980. Fellow ACOG; mem. AMA, Am. Med. Women's Assn. (founding pres. Champlain Valley chpt. 1991), No. N.Y. Ind. Practice Assn. (bd. dirs. 1994—), Champlain Valley Oratorio Soc. (soloist 1989—), Nat. Honor Soc. Avocations: choral singing, skiing, running, gardening, reading. Home: 244 Smith Dr Plattsburgh NY 12901 Office: Assocs in Ob-Gyn PC 210 Cornelia St Ste 201 Plattsburgh NY 12901-2330

RECHARD, OTTIS WILLIAM, mathematics and computer science educator; b. Laramie, Wyo., Nov. 13, 1924; s. Ottis H. and Mary (Bird) R.; m. Dorothy Lee Duble, Nov. 19, 1943; children—Katherine L. (Mrs. Larry V. Baxter), Carol G. (Mrs. David P. Reiter), Nancy L. (Mrs. William Moore), Elizabeth A. B.A., U. Wyo., 1943; postgrad., U. Calif., Los Angeles, 1943; M.A., U. Wis., 1946, Ph.D., 1948. Instr. U. Wis., 1948; instr., asst. prof. Ohio State U., 1948-51; staff mem. Los Alamos (N.Mex.) Nat. Lab., 1951-56; prof., dir. computing ctr. Wash. State U., Pullman, 1956-68; prof., chmn. dept. computer sci. Wash. State U., 1963-76, prof., dir. systems and computing, 1968-70; prof. math. and computer scis. U. Denver, 1976-95, prof. emeritus, 1995—, dir. computing services, 1976-79; vis. prof., chmn. dept. computer sci. U. Wyo., 1986-87; cons. NSF, Idaho Nuclear Corp., Los Alamos Nat. Lab.; program dir. computer sci. program NSF, 1964-65, chmn. adv. panel on instl. computing facilities, 1969-70. Mem. Los Alamos Sch. Bd., 1954-56; mem. Pullman Sch. Bd., 1967-74; Trustee, past pres. Westminster Found., Synod Wash.-Alaska. Served to 1st lt. USAAF, 1943-45. Decorated Order of Leopold II Belgium). Fellow AAAS; mem. Assn. for Computing Machinery, Am. Math. Soc., Math. Assn. Am., IEEE Computer Soc., Soc. Indsl. and Applied Math., AAUP, Phi Beta Kappa, Sigma Xi, Phi Kappa Phi. Presbyn. (elder). Club: Rotarian. Home: RR 3 Box 369 Calder ID 83808 also: 6980 E Girard Ave Apt 405 Denver CO 80224-2915

RECHARD, PAUL ALBERT, consulting civil engineering company executive; b. Laramie, Wyo., June 4, 1927; s. Ottis H. and Mary R. (Bird) R.; m. Mary Lou Roper, June 26, 1949; children: Robert Paul, Karen Ann. BS, U. Wyo., 1948, MS, 1949, CE, 1955. Registered land surveyor, Wyo.; registered profl. engr., Wyo., Utah, Mont., Colo., Calif., Nebr., S.D., N.Mex.; cert. profl. hydrologist Am. Inst. Hydrology; diplomate Am. Acad. Environ. Engrs. Hydraulic engr. U.S. Bur. Reclamation, Cody, Wyo. and Billings, Mont., 1949-54; dir. water resources Natural Resource Bd., Cheyenne, Wyo., 1954-58; prin. hydraulic engr. Upper Colorado River Commn., Salt Lake City, 1958-64; dir. Water Resources Research Inst., U. Wyo., Laramie, 1964-81, mem. faculty dept. civil engring., 1964-82, prof., 1964-82; pres. Western Water Cons., Laramie, 1980—, Hydrology Assocs., Laramie, 1978-80; owner Paul A. Rechard, P.E., Laramie, 1964-78. Editor: Compacts, Treaties and Court Decrees Affecting Wyoming Water, 1956. Contbr. articles to tech. publs. Pres., Thayer Sch. PTA, Laramie, 1965; mem. Laramie City Planning Commn., 1974-80. Served with USNR, 1945-46. Recipient Wyo. Eminent Engr. award Tau Beta Pi, 1993. Fellow ASCE (life mem., pres. Wyo. sect. 1968); mem. Am. Soc. Testing Materials, NSPE, Am. Geophys. Union, Nat. Water Well Assn., Wyo. Engring. Soc. (pres. 1976, hon.), Am. Water Works Assn., Am. Water Resources Assn., U.S. Com. on Irrigation and Drainage, U.S. Com. on Large Dams, Sigma Xi (pres. Wyo. chpt. 1973), Phi Kappa Phi (pres. Wyo. chpt. 1969), Gamma Sigma Delta, Sigma Tau (pres. Wyo. chpt. 1948, selected Wyo. Eminent Engr. 1993). Republican. Presbyterian. Lodges: Lions (pres. Laramie 1968), Masons. Home: 316 Stuart St Laramie WY 82070-4866 Office: Western Water Cons Inc 611 Skyline Rd Laramie WY 82070-8909

RECHCIGL, JACK EDWARD, soil and environmental sciences educator; b. Washington, Feb. 27, 1960; s. Miloslav and Eva (Edwards) R.; m. Nancy Ann Palko, Sept. 30, 1983; children: Gregory John, Kevin Thomas, Lindsey Nicole. BS, U. Del., 1982; MS, Va. Poly. Inst. and State U., 1983, PhD, 1986. Asst. prof. soil sci. U. Fla. Agrl. Rsch. and Edn. Ctr., Ona, 1986-91, assoc. prof. soil and environ. scis., 1991-96; prof. soil and environ. scis., 1996—. Editor: Soil Amendments and Environmental Quality, 1995, Soil Amendments: Impact on Biotic Systems, 1995, Use of By-Products and Wastes in Agriculture, 1997, Environmentally Safe Approaches to Crop Disease Control, 1997; assoc. editor: Jour. Environ. Quality, 1994—; editor-in-chief: (book series) Agriculture and Environment; contbr. chpts. to books, articles to Environ. Quality, Soil Sci., Soil Fertility, Water Quality. Recipient rsch. achievement award U. Fla., 1991; rsch grantee TVA, 1984-86, Allied Signal, 1987—, So. Fla. Water Mgmt. Dist., 1987-90, Fla. Inst. Phosphate Rsch., 1990—, USDA, 1992—. Mem. Am. Soc. Agronomy, Soil Sci. Soc. Am., Sigma Xi, Gamma Beta Phi, Gamma Sigma Delta, Phi Sigma. Achievements include research leading to the reduction of fertilizer recommendations in Florida, thereby helping to improve water quality; utilization of industrial organic and inorganic wastes (ex. phosphogypsum and granular biosolids) as potential fertilizers in agriculture. Home: 13511 4th Plz E Bradenton FL 34202-9682 Office: Fla Agrl Rsch and Edn Ctr RR 1 Box 62 Ona FL 33865-9706

RECHCIGL, MILOSLAV, JR., government official; b. Mlada Boleslav, Czechoslovakia, July 30, 1930; s. Miloslav and Marie (Rajtrova) R.; came to U.S., 1950, naturalized, 1955; m. Eva Marie Edwards, Aug. 29, 1953; children: John Edward, Karen Marie. BS, Cornell U., 1954, M of Nutrition Sci., 1955, PhD, 1958. Teaching asst. Cornell U., Ithaca, N.Y., 1953-57, grad. rsch. asst., 1957-58, rsch. assoc., 1958; USPHS rsch. fellow Nat. Cancer Inst., 1958-60, chemist enzymes and metabolism sect., 1960-61, rsch. biochemist, tumor host rels. sect., 1962-64, sr. investigator, 1964-68; grants assoc. program NIH, 1968-69; spl. asst. for nutrition and health to dir. Regional Med. Programs Svc., Health Svcs. and Mental Health Adminstrn., HEW, 1969-70, exec. sec. nutrition program adv. com. Health Svcs. and Mental Health Adminstrn., 1969-70; nutrition adviser AID, Dept. State, Washington, 1970—, chief Rsch. and Instl. Grants div., 1970-73, exec. sec. rsch. and instl. grants coun., 1970-74, exec. sec. AID rsch. adv. com., 1971-83, AID rep. USC/FAR com., 1972-82, asst. dir. Office Rsch. and Instl. Grants, 1973-74, acting dir., 1974-75, dir. interregional rsch. staff, 1975-78, devel. studies program, 1978, chief rsch. and methodology div., 1979-82, rsch. mgmt. and rev. dir. Office of the Sci. Advisor, 1982-91, Office of Rsch., 1992-94, rsch. and methodology specialist, Bur. for Program and Policy Coordination, 1994—; del. White House Conf. on Food, Nutrition and Health, 1969, Agrl. Rsch. Policy Adv. Com. Conf. on Rsch. to Meet U.S. and World Food Needs, 1975; cons. Office Sec. Agr., 1969-70, Dept. Treasury, 1973, Office Technol. Assessment, 1977, FDA, 1979, NAS, NRC, 1985-93. Author: The Czechoslovak Contribution to World Culture, 1964, Czechoslovakia Past and Present, 1968, (with Z. Hruban) Microbodies and Related Particles: Morphology, Biochemistry and Physiology, 1969, Russian edit., 1972, Enzyme Synthesis and Degradation in Mammalian Systems, 1971, (with Eva Rechcigl) Biographical Directory of the Members of the Czechoslovak Society of Arts and Sciences in America, 3d edit., 1972, 4th edit., 1978, 5th edit., 1983, 6th edit., 1988, 7th edit., 1992, Food, Nutrition and Health: A Multidisciplinary Treatise Addressed to the Major Nutrition Problems from a World Wide Perspective, 1973, Man, Food and Nutrition: Strategies and Technological Measures for Alleviating the World Food Problem, 1973, World Food Problem: A Selective Bibliography of Reviews, 1975, Carbohydrates, Lipids and Accessory Growth Factors, 1976, Nutrient Elements and Toxicants, 1977, Nitrogen, Electrolytes, Water and Energy Metabolism, 1979, Nutrition and the World Food Problem, 1979, Educators with Czechoslovak Roots: A U.S. and Canadian Faculty Roster, 1980, Physiology of Growth and Nutrition, 1981, Nutritional Requirements, 1977, Diet, Culture Media and Food Supplements, 4 vols., 1977, Nutritional Disorders, 3 vols., 1978, Handbook of Nutritional Requirements in a Functional Context, 2 vols., 1981, Handbook of Agricultural Productivity, 2 vols., 1981, Handbook of Nutritive Value of Processed Food, 2 vols., 1982, Handbook of Foodborne Diseases of Biological Origin, 1983, Handbook of Naturally Occurring Food Toxicants, 1983, Handbook of Nutritional Supplements, 2 vols, 1983, U.S. Legislators with Czechoslovak Roots from Colonial Times to Present, 1987, others; co-editor: Internat. Jour. of Cycle Research, 1969-74, Jour. Applied Nutrition, 1970-82; series editor: Comparative Animal Nutrition, 1976-81; editor-in-chief: (series) Nutrition and Food, 1977—; mem. editorial bd.: Nutrition Reports Internat., 1977-80; translator: Chemical Abstracts, 1959-61; contbr. articles to sci. jours. Organizer, mem. council Montrose Civic Assn., Rockville, Md.; mem. ethnic affairs com., Montgomery County, Md., 1990-92, vice chair, 1991-92. Recipient Josef Hlavka Commemorative medal Czechoslovak Acad. Scis., 1991, Superior Unit citation Agy. Internat. Devel., 1996; NAS grantee, 1962. Fellow AAAS, Am. Inst. Chemists (councilor 1972-74, program chmn. 1974 ann. meeting, mem. program com. 1980 meeting), Internat. Coll. Applied Nutrition, Intercontinental Biog. Assn.. Washington Acad. Scis. (del. 1972—); mem. Am. Inst. Nutrition (com. Western Hemisphere Nutrition Congress 1971, 74, program com. 1979-82), Am. Soc. Biol. Chemists, Am. Chem. Soc. (joint bd.-council com. on internat. activities 1975-76), D.C. Inst. Chemists (pres. 1972-74, councilor 1974-80), Am. Inst. Biol. Scis., Soc. for Exptl. Biology and Medicine, Am. Soc. Animal Sci., Internat., Am. socs. cell biology, Soc. for Developmental Biology, Am. Assn. for Cancer Research, Soc. for Biol. Rhythm, Am. Pub. Health Assn., N.Y. Acad. Scis., Chem. Soc. Washington (symposium com. 1970, 71), Internat. Coll. Applied Nutrition, Internat. Soc. for Research on Civilization Diseases and Vital Substances, Soc. for Geochemistry and Health, Soc. for Internat. Devel., Internat. Platform Assn., Am. Assn. for Advancement Slavic Studies, Czechoslovak Soc. Arts and Scis. in Am. (hon., dir.-at-large 1962—, dir. publs. 1962-68, 70-74, v.p. 1968-74, pres. 1974-78, 94—, pres. collegium 1978—), History of Sci. Soc., Soc. Research Adminstrs., Sigma Xi, Phi Kappa Phi, Delta Tau Kappa (hon.). Clubs: Cosmos, Cornell (Washington). Home: 1703 Mark Ln Rockville MD 20852-4106

RECHT, ARTHUR, judge; b. Feb. 4, 1938; m. Karen Markham, June 10, 1962; children: Jason Markham, Judd Samuel. BA in Polit. Sci., U. Pitts., 1959; JD, W.Va. U., 1962. Ptnr. Schrader, Miller, Stamp & Recht, Wheeling, W.Va., 1962-81; judge 1st Jud. Cir., Hancock, Brooke and Ohio Counties, W.Va., 1981-83; ptnr. Recht & Johnson, Wheeling, 1984-87, Volk, Frankovich, Anetakis, Recht, Robertson & Hellerstedt, Wheeling, 1987-93, Schrader, Recht, Byrd, Companion & Gurley, Wheeling, 1993-95; justice W.Va. Supreme Ct. Appeals, Charleston, 1995—; asst. solicitor City of Wheeling, 1963-64; chair com. legal ethics West Va. State Bar, 1985-91; mem. Gov.'s Com. Selection of Jud. Candidates for Circuit Ct., 1990-95. Active Wheeling Human Rights Commn., 1974-79; pres. Police Civil Svc. Commn., Wheeling, 1984-91. Named West Virginian of Yr., Sunday Gazette Mail, 1982, Woodland Scholar Inst., 1986; recipient cert. of merit W.Va. State Bar, 1991. Home: 30 Forest Hills Wheeling WV 26003 Office: WVa Supreme Ct 1900 Kanawha Blvd E Rm E-306 Charleston WV 25305-0009

RECHTIN, EBERHARDT, retired aerospace executive, retired educator; b. East Orange, N.J., Jan. 16, 1926; s. Eberhardt Carl and Ida H. (Pfarrer) R.; m. Dorothy Diane Denebrink, June 10, 1951; children: Andrea C., Nina, Julie Anne, Erica, Mark. B.S., Calif. Inst. Tech., 1946, Ph.D. cum laude, 1950. Dir. Deep Space Network, 1958-67; asst. dir. Calif. Inst. Tech. Jet Propulsion Lab., 1960-67; dir. Advanced Rsch. Projects Agy., Dept. Def., 1967-70, prin. dep. dir. def. rsch. and engring., 1970-71, asst. sec. def. for telecom., 1972-73; chief engr. Hewlett-Packard Co., Palo Alto, Calif., 1973-77; pres., CEO Aerospace Corp., El Segundo, Calif., 1977-87; pres.-emeritus Aerospace Corp., El Segundo, 1988; prof. U. So. Calif., 1988-94, emeritus prof., 1994—. Author: Systems Architecting. Creating and Building Complex Systems, 1991, The Art of Systems Architecture, 1997. Served to lt. USNR, 1943-56. Recipient maj. awards NASA, Dept. Def., USN, Disting. Alumni award Calif. Inst. Tech., 1984, NEC C&C prize, Japan, 1992. Fellow AAAS, AIAA (Robert H. Goddard Astronautics award 1991), IEEE (Alexander Graham Bell award 1977); mem. NAE, Tau Beta Pi. Home: 1665 Cataluna Pl Palos Verdes Peninsula CA 90274-2162

RECHTZIGEL, SUE MARIE (SUZANNE RECHTZIGEL), child care center executive; b. St. Paul, May 27, 1947; d. Carl Stinson and Muriel Agnes (Oestrich) Miller; m. Gary Elmer Rechtzigel, Aug. 20, 1968 (div. Feb. 1982); children: Brian Carl, Lori Ann. BA in Psychology, Sociology, Mankato (Minn.) State U., 1969. Lic. in child care, Minn. Rep. ins. State Farm Ins. Co., Albert Lea, Minn., 1969-73; free-lance child caretaker Albert Lea, Minn., 1973-78; owner, dir. Lakeside Day Care, Albert Lea, Minn., 1983—; asst. Hawthorne Sch. Learning Ctr., Albert Lea, 1978-83. Mem. New Residents and Newcomers Orgn., Albert Lea, 1970—, past. pres.; asst. pre-sch. United Meth. Ch., Albert Lea, 1975-78, tchr. Sunday sch., 1976-80, tchr. Bible sch., 1980-85; active Ascension Luth. Ch., 1976-80. Mem. Freeborn Lic. Day Care Assn. (v.p. 1986, pres. 1987), AAUW (home tour 1977, treas. 1980-81), Bus. and Profl. Women, YMCA, Albert Lea Art Ctr. Republican. Club: 3M Families. Avocations: ceramics, calligraphy, painting, art, sewing. Home and Office: 1919 Brookside Dr Albert Lea MN 56007-2142

RECHY, JOHN FRANCISCO, author; b. El Paso, Tex.; s. Roberto Sixto and Guadalupe (Flores) R. B.A., U. Tex., El Paso; student, New Sch. Social Research. Instr. creative writing UCLA, Occidental Coll., U. So. Calif. Author: City of Night, 1963, Numbers, 1967, this Day's Death, 1969, The Vampires, 1971, The Fourth Angel, 1973, The Sexual Outlaw, 1977, Rushes, 1979, Bodies and Souls, 1983, Marilyn's Daughter, 1988, The Miraculous Day of Amalia Gõmez, 1991, Our Lady of Babylon, 1996; (plays) Momma As She Became-Not As She Was, 1968, Rushes, 1978, Tigers Wild, 1986; contbr.: short stories and articles to Tex. Observer, The Nation, Village Voice, London mag., Saturday Rev., N.Y. Times Book Rev., L.A. Times, Washington Post Book World, Phila. Inquirer, Contemporary Fiction, Big Table, others; also anthologies Chicano Voices, Black Humor, Urban Reader, Evergreen Rev. Reader, New Am. Story, The Moderns, Rediscoveries, Men on Men, others; trans.: stories and articles for Tex. Quar., Evergreen Rev. Served with AUS. Recipient Longview Found. award for short story The Fabulous Wedding of Miss Destiny; Nat. Endowment for Arts grantee, 1976. Mem. Authors Guild, Tex. Inst. Letters, PEN, Nat. Writers Union.

RECINE, JUDY ANN, surgical nurse; b. Trenton, N.J., Oct. 13, 1963; d. Donald Vito and Gail Patricia (Walsh) R. BSN, West Chester U., 1986. Cert. in intravenous therapy, CPR. Surg. staff nurse, mentor, charge nurse Grad. Hosp., Phila., 1986—. Mem. Med.-Surg. Nursing Soc. Phila. (pres.), Sigma Theta Tau Xi Delta (West Chester U. chpt.).

RECK, ANDREW JOSEPH, philosophy educator; b. New Orleans, Oct. 29, 1927; s. Andrew Gervais and Katie (Mangiaracina) R.; m. Elizabeth Lassiter Torre, June 17, 1987. B.A., Tulane U., 1947, M.A., 1949; Ph.D., Yale U., 1954; student, U. St. Andrews, Scotland, 1952-53, U. Paris, summers 1962, 64. Instr. English U. Conn., 1949-50; instr. philosophy Yale, 1951-52, 55-58; mem. faculty Tulane U., 1958—, prof. philosophy, 1964—, chmn. dept., 1969-89, dir. Master Liberal Arts program, 1984—; Thomasfest lectr. Xavier U., Cin., 1970; Suarez Lectr. Spring Hill Coll., 1971; Niebuhr lectr. Elmhurst (Ill.) Coll., 1976; vis. prof. Fordham U., 1979; vis. scholar Hastings Ctr. (N.Y.), 1981; Woodruff lectr. Emory U., 1982; Fairchild lectr. U. So. Miss., 1982, 87: Matchette Found. lectr. Cath. U. Am., 1991, 95; Sr. Scholar Inst. Humane Studies, Menlo Park, Calif., 1982; vis. scholar Poynter Ctr., Ind. U., Bloomington, 1983; Tulane U. faculty rep. to bd. adminstrs. Tulane Ednl. Fund., 1988-91. Author: Recent American Philosophy, 1964, Introduction to William James, 1967, New American Philosophers, 1968, Speculative Philosophy, 1972; editor: George Herbert Mead Selected Writings, 1964, 2d edit., 1981, Knowledge and Value, 1972, (with T. Horvath, T. Krittek and S. Grean) American Philosophers' Ideas of Ultimate Reality and Meaning, 1993; co-editor Ultimate Reality and Meaning, Interdisciplinary Studies in the Philosophy of Understanding, 1990—; mem. adv. editl. bd. Internat. Jour. World Peace, Trans. Charles Peirce Soc., Santayana edit. So. Jour. Philosophy; editor History of Philosophy Quar., 1993—. Served with AUS, 1953-55. Howard fellow, 1962-63, Liberty Fund grantee, 1982, Newcomb fellow, 1991-93; Fulbright scholar, 1952-53; Am. Coun. Lerned Socs. grantee, 1961-62, Am. Philos. Soc. grantee, 1972, Huntington Libr. grantee, 1973, La. Ednl. Quality State Found. grantee, 1994-96, U.S. Info. Agy. grantee, Brazil, 1993. Mem. Am. Philos. Assn. (program com. eastern divsn. 1969, adv. com. to program com. eastern divsn., 1994—, nominating com. western divsn. 1975-76, 81-82, mem., chair ad hoc com. on history 1992, 96—), Southwestern Philos. Soc. (exec. com. 1965-69, v.p. 1971-72, pres. 1972-73), So. Soc. Philosophy and Psychology (treas. 1968-71, pres. 1976-77), Am. Coun. Learned Socs. (Am. studies adv. com. 1972-76), Coun. for Internat. Rsch. Scholars (philosophy screening com. 1974-77), Metaphys. Soc. Am. (councillor 1971-75, pres. 1977-78, program com. 1989-90, chair program com. 1995-96), Soc. Advancement Am. Philosophy (exec. com. 1980-82), Charles S. Peirce Soc. (sec.-treas. 1985-86, v.p. 1986-87, pres. 1987-88), Internat. SOc. for Study of Human Ideas of Ultimate Reality and Meaning (bd. dirs. 1989—), La. Endowment for Humanities (bd. dirs. 1990-96), Phi Beta Kappa (pres. Alpha of La. 1966-67), Alpha Sigma Lambda (hon. Theta chpt. of La.). Home: 6125 Patton St New Orleans LA 70118-5832 Office: Tulane U Dept Philosophy New Orleans LA 70118

RECKER, THOMAS EDWARD, fraternal organization executive; b. Livonia, Mich., Feb. 28, 1960; s. Peter Edward and Patricia Ann (Heidenwolf) R. BA in Ednl. Psychology, U. Mich., 1982; MA in Coll. Student Personnel, Bowling Green State U., 1985. Asst. exec. dir. Grand Chpt. of Phi Sigma Kappa, Indpls., 1985-87, exec. dir., 1987-90; exec. v.p.

Grand Chpt. of Phi Sigma Kappa and Phi Sigma Kappa Found., Indpls., 1990—. Mem. Am. Soc. Assn. Execs., Assn. Frat. Advisers, Frat. Execs. Assn. Office: Phi Sigma Kappa Frat 2925 E 96th St Indianapolis IN 46240-1368*

RECORD, PHILLIP JULIUS, newspaper executive; b. Fort Worth, Jan. 12, 1929; s. Phillip Cross and Frances Virginia (McElwee) R.; m. Patricia Ann Edwards, Sept. 29, 1954; children: Christopher Phillip, Gregory Edwards, Timothy James. B.A. in Journalism, U. Notre Dame, 1950. Gen. reporter Lubbock Avalanche-Jour., Tex., 1950-54; copy editor, reporter Fort Worth Star-Telegram, 1954-67, asst. city editor, 1967-68, city editor evening edit., 1968-76, mng. editor, 1976-80, assoc. exec. editor, 1980-91, spl. asst. to pub., ombudsman, 1991—; dir. Freedom Info. Found. Tex., 1987-93; mem. mass comms. com. Tex. Tech. U., chmn., 1990-92. Mem. conciliation/arbitration bd. Cath. Diocese of Ft. Worth, 1994—, chair, 1996—, publs. adv. com., 1982—; founding mem. Ft. Worth Theatre; mem. Friends of Ft. Worth Pub. Libr.; bd. dirs. Tarrant County Mental Health Assn., 1990-95. With U.S. Army, 1950-52. Recipient 3d ann. Ethics award Tex. Christian U., 1991, numerous other awards for reporting, photography and headline writing; named to Tex. Tech U. Mass Comms. Hall of Fame. Mem. ABA (nat. commn. on pub. understanding about law 1984-90, commn. on partnership programs 1990-93), Investigative Reporters and Editors Inc., Soc. Profl. Journalists (pres. 1983-84, bd. dirs. Found. 1980—, v.p. Found., 1991-94, bd. chair 1994—, Wells Key 1991), Creative Thinking Assn., Orgn. News Ombudsmen (dir. 1994—, v.p. 1995-96, pres. 1996—), Petroleum Club. Avocation: tennis. Home: 6144 Walla Ave Fort Worth TX 76133-3557 Office: Fort Worth Star-Telegram 400 W 7th St Fort Worth TX 76102-4701 *As a journalist, I strive to be a servant of the truth and a servant of the people. As a follower of Jesus, I try to live my life as he would. But, being human, I fail frequently. But I try and I care. I think that makes me OK in God's eyes.*

RECORDS, RAYMOND EDWIN, ophthalmologist, medical educator; b. Ft. Morgan, Colo., May 30, 1930; s. George Harvey and Sara Barbara (Louden) R.; 1 child, Lisa Rae. BS in Chemistry, U. Denver, 1956; MD, St. Louis U., 1961. Diplomate Am. Bd. Ophthalmology. Intern St. Louis U. Hosp. Group, 1961-62; resident in ophthalmology U. Colo. Med. Ctr., Denver, 1962-65; instr. ophthalmology, 1965-67, asst. prof., 1967-70; prof. ophthalmology U. Nebr. Coll. Medicine, Omaha, 1970-93, prof. emeritus, 1993, dept. chmn., 1970-89. Author: Physiology of Human Eye (Med. Writers award 1980), 1979. Author, editor: Biomedical Foundations of Ophthalmology, 1982. Med. dir. Nebr. Lions Eye Bank, 1970-81. Fellow Am. Acad. of Ophthalmology (outstanding contbn. award 1978, lifelong edn. award 1995); mem. AMA, Nev. Med. Assn., Clark County Med. Soc., Omaha Ophthal. Soc. (pres. 1981-82), Assn. Rsch. in Vision and Ophthalmology. Home: 21919 Riverside Cir Elkhorn NE 68022-1708 Office: 1640 Alta Dr Ste 1 Las Vegas NV 89106-4165

RECTOR, FLOYD CLINTON, JR., physiologist, physician; b. Slaton, Tex., Jan. 28, 1929; s. Floyd Clinton and Faye Elizabeth (Tucker) R.; m. Marjory L. Bullen, May 27, 1950; children—Lynn, Ruth, Janet. BS, Tex. Tech. Coll., 1950; MD, U. Tex. Southwestern Med. Sch., 954. Instr. U. Tex. Southwestern Med. Sch., Dallas, 1958-59; asst. prof. medicine U. Tex. Southwestern Med. Sch., 1959-63, assoc. prof., 1963-66, prof., 1966-73; prof. medicine and physiology, sr. scientist Cardiovascular Research Inst.; dir. div. nephrology U. Calif., San Francisco, 1973-89, chmn. dept. medicine, 1989-95, prof. medicine emeritus, 1995—. Editor: (with B.M. Brenner) The Kidney, 1976, 81, 85, 90-91, 94. Served with USPHS, 1956-58. NIH grantee, 1973—. Mem. Am. Soc. Nephrology, Am. Soc. Clin. Investigation, Am. Assn. Physicians, Am. Physiol. Soc. Office: U Calif PO Box 0120 San Francisco CA 94143

RECTOR, JOHN MICHAEL, association executive, lawyer; b. Seattle, Aug. 15, 1943; s. Michael Robert and Bernice Jane (Allison) R.; m. Mary Kaaren Sueta Jolly, Feb. 8, 1977 (div. 1994); children: Chriatian Phillip, Gloria Rose. BA, U. Calif., Berkeley, 1966; JD, U. Calif., Hastings, 1969; PharmD (hon.), Ark. State Bd. Pharmacy, 1991. Bar: Calif. 1970, U.S. Supreme Ct. 1974. Trial atty. civil rights div. Dept. Justice, 1969-71; dep. chief counsel judiciary com. U.S. Senate, 1971-73, counsel to Sen. Birch Bayh, 1971-77, chief counsel, staff dir., 1973-77; confirmed by U.S. Senate as assoc. adminstr. to Law Enforcement Assistance Adminstn. and adminstr. of Office Juvenile Justice Dept. Justice, 1977-79; spl. counsel to U.S. Atty. Gen., 1979-80; dir. govt. affairs Nat. Assn. Retail Druggists, Washington, 1980-85; sr. v.p. govt. affairs, gen. counsel Nat. Assn. Retail Druggists, 1986—; chmn. adv. bd. Nat. Juvenile Law Center, 1973-77; mem. Hew panel Drug Use and Criminal Behavior, 1974-77; mem. cons. panel Nat. Commn. Protection Human Subjects of Biomed. and Behavioral Research, 1975-76; mem. bd. Nat. Inst. Corrections, 1977-79; chmn. U.S. Interdepartmental Council Juvenile Justice, 1977-79; mem. bd. com. civil rights and liberties Am. Democratic Action, 1976-80, Pres.'s Com. Mental Health-Justice Group, 1978; com. youth citizenship ABA, 1978-84; mem. Pharm. Industry Adv. Com.; exec. dir., treas. polit. action com. Nat. Pharmacists Assn., 1981—; exec. dir. Retail Druggist Legal Legis. Def. Fund, 1985—, founder, chmn. Washington Pharmacy Industry Forum; mem. numerous fed. narcotic and crime panels and coms.; owner Second Genesis, an antique and furniture restoration co. Mem. editorial bd. Managed Care Law; contbr. articles to profl. jours. Exec. com. small bus. and fin. couns. Dem. Nat. Com.; dir. Dem. Leadership Coun.'s Network, 1989—, bd. advisers, 1992—, Clinton-Gore Washington Bus. adv. com.; bd. dirs. Small Bus. Legis. Coun., 1987—; bd. dirs. Nat. Bus. Coalition for Fair Competition, 1984—. Perry E. Towne scholar, 1966-67, mem. U.S. Atty. Gen.'s Honors Program, 1968-71; recipient Children's Express Juvenile Justice award, 1981. Mem. Calif. Bar Assn., Nat. Health Lawyers Assn., Am. Soc. Assn. Execs. (govt. affirs sect.), Washington Coun. Lawyers, Assn. of Former Senior Senate Aides, Vinifera Wine Growers Assn. Va. (life), Health R Us, Am. League of Lobbyists, Theta Chi. Democrat. Avocation: collecting antique furniture, books and documents. Office: Nat Assn Retail Druggists 205 Daingerfield Rd Alexandria VA 22314-2833

RECTOR, MILTON GAGE, social work educator, former association executive; b. Fallon, Nev., Jan. 3, 1918; s. William L. and Virginia E. (Renfro) R.; m. Harriet Louise Phibbs, Aug. 1, 1940; children: Brian Eugene (dec.), Barbara Elaine (dec.), Dianne Eileen, Bruce Alan. B.A., U. So. Calif., 1940; postgrad., U. Calif.-Berkeley, Columbia U. With Los Angeles County Probation Dept., 1940-46, probation officer charge forestry camp for delinquent boys, 1943-46; with Nat. Council Crime and Delinquency, 1946-82, cons. Western region, 1946-52, dir. parole services, 1952-55, asst. exec. dir., 1955-59, exec. dir., 1959-82, pres., 1972-82; vis. prof. Grad. Sch. Social Work U. Utah, 1982-84; Mem. President's Adv. Com. on Delinquency and Youth Crime, 1960-66; Cons. to U.S. Senate subcom. investigation delinquency, 1953; organized Nat. Conf. Parole, 1956; bd. dirs. Am. Correctional Assn., 1959-73, Osborne Assn., 1960-75, Nat. Study Service, 1960-76, U. Md. Inst. Criminal Justice, 1972-78, Center for Correctional Justice, 1972-78, SUNY-Albany Criminal Justice Inst., Acad. Jud. Edn., 1970-75, Law in Am. Society Found.; chmn. bd. dirs. Joint Commn. Correctional Manpower and Tng., 1965-70; cons. Pres.'s Crime Commn., 1965-68; U.S. rep. UN Social Def. Sect., 1965-75; U.S. del. UN World Congress on Crime and Delinquency, Stockholm, 1965, Kyoto, Japan, 1970; mem. Nat. Commn. on Reform Fed. Criminal Laws, 1969-70, N.Y.C. Criminal Justice Coordinating Council, 1967-73, Nat. Commn. on Criminal Justice Standards and Goals, 1971-73, Inst. on Jud. Adminstrn.-Am. Bar Assn. Commn. on Juvenile Justice Standards, 1973-76; mem. adv. com. on correctional edn. Edn. Commn. of States, 1975-77. Contbr. numerous articles profl. jours., procs., Nat. Council Crime and Delinquency; syndicated columnist: Of Crime and Punishment. Served to lt. (j.g.) USNR, 1944-46; commdr. Res. Recipient August Volmer award Am. Criminological Soc., 1971; Meritorious Service award Nat. Council Juvenile and Family Ct. Judges, 1962; John Howard award John Howard Assn., 1974; award John Jay Coll. Criminal Justice, 1979; Karl Menninger award Fortune Soc., 1979; Harold DeWolf award Offender Aid and Restoration U.S.A. Inc., 1980; award Nat. Forum on Criminal Justice, 1981; Margaret Mead award Internat. Halfway House Assn., 1982; award for enhancement profl. edn. U. Utah Grad. Sch. Social Work, 1983. Home: 27 James Buchanan Dr Cranbury NJ 08512-4847 *My life work in the field of juvenile and criminal justice and its insights into the depths of man's inhumanity to man have enabled me to serve in a ministry for the reform of a system which at times seems impervious to reform, and thus continues to deny the attainment of social justice in my country.*

RECTOR, ROBERT WAYMAN, mathematics and engineering educator, former association executive; b. San Jose, Calif., Jan. 28, 1916; s. Joseph Jones and Eva (Hembree) R.; m. Margaret Eileen Hayden, Aug. 25, 1940; children: Cleone Rector Black, Robin Rector Krupp, Bruce Hayden. B.A., San Jose State U., 1937; M.A., Stanford U., 1939; Ph.D., U. Md., 1956. Instr. Compton (Calif.) Coll., 1939-42; asso. prof. math. U.S. Naval Acad., 1946-56; staff mathematician Space Tech. Labs., Los Angeles, 1956-61; asso. dir. computation center Aerospace Corp., El Segundo, Calif., 1961-65; v.p. Informatics, Inc., Van Nuys, Calif., 1965-70, Cognitive Systems, Inc., Beverly Hills, Calif., 1970-71; asso. dir. continuing edn. engring. and math. UCLA, 1971-73, 81-92; dean Coll. Engring. and Computer Sci. West Cost U., L.A., 1992—; Exec. dir. Am. Fedn. Info. Processing Socs., Montvale, N.J., 1973-79; spl. asst. White House Conf. Library and Info. Services, 1979; v.p. Conf. and Meeting Assistance Corp., East Greenwich, R.I., 1980—. Bd. govs.: Pacific Jour. Math, 1957-92. Mem. Los Angeles Mayor's Space Adv. Com., 1964-73, Calif. Mus. Found. (aviation and space hist. research com. 1984—). Served with USNR, 1942-46. Mem. Math. Assn. Am., Assn. Computing Machinery, Naval Res. Assn., Res. Officers Assn., Ret. Officers Assn. Home: 10700 Stradella Ct Los Angeles CA 90077-2604

REDA, JAMES FRANCIS, business consultant; b. Bklyn., Aug. 27, 1953; s. Ralph Charles and Evelyn Susan (Buchan) R.; m. Susan Rosemary Hisnay, June 10, 1982 (div. Oct. 1993); 1 child, Jennifer Beryl; m. Deborah Linda Grannis, July 4, 1994; children: Jennifer Rose, James Francis Jr., Linda Victoria. BS in Indsl. Engring., Columbia U., 1981; MS in Mgmt., MIT, 1983. 1st class FCC lic. Indsl. engr. IBM Corp., Bklyn., 1980, East Fishkill, N.Y., 1981; process engr. Hewlett-Packard Co., Andover, Mass., 1982; bus. mgr. Wang Labs., Inc., Lowell, Mass., 1983-85; sr. product mgr. Honeywell Fed. Systems, Inc., McLean, Va., 1985-87; assoc. cons. Touche Ross & Co., N.Y.C., 1987; v.p., cons. The Bachelder Group, N.Y.C., 1987-96; cons. Buck Cons., N.Y.C., 1996—. Campaign advisor Friends of Vincent Gentile, Bklyn., 1994. With USN, 1971-77; lt. comdr. USCGR. Mem. Internat. Inst. Indsl. Engrs. (sr. mem., chpt. pres. 1979-81, Walter Rautenstrauch award 1981), Res. Officers Assn. (Top Grad. award 1983), Internat. Assn. Fin. Engring., U.S. Naval Inst., Armed Forces Comms. Assn., Ret. Officers Assn., Am. Legion, The Wings Club, Tau Beta Pi, Alpha Pi Mu. Republican. Methodist. Avocations: spectator sports, exercise, travel, history, current events. Home: 60 Marion Ave Staten Island NY 10304-2134 Office: Buck Cons Inc 2 Pennsylvania Plz 23d Fl New York NY 10121

REDA, ROBERT SALVATORE, lawyer; b. Chgo., Feb. 23, 1962; s. Robert Charles and Elizabeth (Barrett) R.; m. Joyce Karen Bettinger, May 19, 1990. BA, Drake U., 1984; JD, John Marshall Law Sch., Chgo., 1988. Bar: Ill. 1989, U.S. Dist. Ct. (no. dist.) Ill. 1989, U.S. Dist. Ct. (no. dist. trial bar) Ill. 1991, U.S. Supreme Ct. 1993. Pvt. practice Chgo., 1989-91; pres. Robert S. Reda & Assocs., P.C., Chgo., 1991—. Mem. ATLA, Nat Inst. for Trial Advocacy, Ill. Bar Assn., Ill. Trial Lawyers Assn., Chgo. Bar Assn., 1st 100 Group, Ltd. (pres. 1993—), Union League Club. Office: Robert S Reda & Assocs PC 53 W Jackson Blvd Ste 715 Chicago IL 60604-3607

REDBONE, LEON, singer, musician. Albums include: On the Track, 1975, Double Time, 1976, Champagne Charlie, 1977, From Branch to Branch, 1981, Red to Blue, 1985, Christmas Island, 1988, No Regrets, 1988, Sugar, 1990, Up a Lazy River, 1992, Whistling in the Wind, 1994, (with others) Red to Blue, 1995. also: Sugar Hill PO Box 55300 Durham NC 27717-5300*

REDDA, KINFE KEN, chemist, educator; b. Senafe, Eritrea (Africa), Mar. 21, 1948; arrived in Can., 1973; came to U.S., 1979; s. Guangul and Demekech (Zewde) R.; m. Abeda Hindeya, 1978 (div. 1983); 1 child, Fre; m. Lul Haile, 1989; children: Aman, Aaron, Semhal. BS in Pharmacy, Haile Selassie U., Addis Ababa, Ethiopia, 1970; PhD in Medicinal Chemistry, U. Alberta, Edmonton, Can., 1978. Lic. pharmacist, Ethiopia. Postdoctoral fellow U. Alberta, Edmonton, Can., 1977-78, Dalhousie U., Halifax, Can., 1978-79; asst. prof. U. Puerto Rico, San Juan, 1980-85; assoc. prof. Fla. A&M U., Tallahassee, 1985-89, prof., 1989—; nat. grant reviewer Nat. Inst. Drug Abuse, Rockville, Md., 1985-88; dir. space life scis. tng. program NASA, Kennedy Space Ctr., Tallahassee, 1987-95; dir. NIH minority biomed. rsch. support program, Fla. A&M U., Tallahassee, 1988—. Chief editor: Cocaine, Marijuana and Designer Drugs Chemistry, Pharamacology and Behavior, 1989; contbr. articles to profl. jours; patentee synthesis of new biologically active compounds Tetrahydropyridines, 1979—. Mem. NAACP (Tallahassee chpt.), Tallahassee Urban League, Harambe Festival, Tallahassee. Recipient Inventor's medal, Canadian Patents & Developments, Ottawa, Can., 1978, grant Nat. Inst. Health, Bethesda, Md., 1985—, NASA. Washington, 1987—. Mem. numerous nat. and internat. profl. orgns. Democrat. Mem. Coptic Christian Ch. Avocations: jogging, swimming, reading, travel, spectator sports. *Sincere and voluntary service to others is the deepest form of human kindness.*

REDDAN, HAROLD JEROME, sociologist, educator; b. N.Y.C., Dec. 4, 1926; s. Harold B. and Catherine G. (Kelly) R.; m. Margaret M. Byrne, Oct. 11, 1952; children: Harold James, Patricia Anne, James Joseph, Kathleen Mary. B.A., St. Francis Coll., 1950; M.S., St. Johns U., 1957, Ph.D., 1961. Social investigator N.Y.C. Dept. Welfare, 1950-58; assoc. prof. sociology St. Johns U., 1958-69; lectr. sociology Kings County Hosp. Center Sch. of Nursing, N.Y.C., 1961-66; family counselor, 1961—; adj. assoc. prof. Manhattan Coll., 1968-69, prof. sociology, head dept. managerial scis., 1969-73; adj. sociology faculty Nassau Community Coll., 1971—, Mercy Coll.; adj. prof. L.I. corr. facility, 1980-84; adminstrv. cons. Molloy Coll., 1973-74; adj. prof. sociology and bus. adminstrn. C.W. Post Coll., 1974-80; mem. behavioral scis. faculty, police sci. program N.Y. Inst. Tech., 1974-75; adj. prof. sociology SUNY, Farmingdale; provost Molloy Coll., 1975-78, v.p. for planning and spl. programs, 1978-79; ednl. cons., 1979—. Author: Sociology, 1971, Arco GRE Tests, 1985. Dir. Jamaica VI Peace Corps Tng. Program, 1965; Coordinator New Hyde Park Citizens for Kennedy, 1960, campaign mgr. 1st Assembly Dist., 1962-64. Served with AUS, 1945-46. Mem. Am. Sociol. Assn., Am. Acad. Polit. and Social Sci., Am. Acad. Mgmt., Assn. Psychiat. Treatment Offenders, VFW, Garden City Park Hist. Soc. (pres. 1960-63), Delta Mu Delta, Delta Sigma Pi, Alpha Sigma Pi, Alpha Kappa Delta. Democrat. Home: 96 5th St New Hyde Park NY 11040-4108

REDDEL, CARL WALTER, education adminstration; b. Gurley, Neb., May 31, 1937; s. Walter Julius and Friedora Regina (Sorge) R.; m. Colette Marie Antoinette Mansuy, Oct. 26, 1963; children: Eric, Damien. BSED, Drake U., 1959; MA in Russian studies, Syracuse U., 1962; PhD in Russian history, Ind. U., 1973, cert. Russian studies, 1973. Lectr. U. Md., Toul-Rosieres, France, 1963-66; instr. U.S.A.F. Acad., Colo. Springs, Colo., 1967-68, 71-72, asst. prof., 1972-73, assoc. prof., 1973-80; prof., head dept. history, post-doctoral fellow U. Edinburgh, Edinburgh, Scotland, 1981-82; prof., head dept. history U.S. Air Force Acad., 1982—; nat. coord., regional World History Assn., Phila., 1990-95; bd. editors, mem. Joun. Slavic Military, London, 1988—; series editor Military Hist. Symposium Series, Colo. Springs, 1993—. Editor: Transformation in Russian and Soviet Military History, 1990; contbr. articles to profl. jours. Mem. Rotary Internat., 1994—. With U.S. Air Force, 1962—. Recipient Young Faculty exchange Internat. Rsch. Exchanges Bd., Moscoe, 1975; Woodrow Wilson fellow, 1959-60, Danforth fellowship Danforth Found., 1959-61. Mem. Am. Historical Assn., Am. Assn. Advancement of Slavic Studies, World History Assn., Rocky Mountain World History Assn., Cen. Slavic Assn. Lutheran. Home: 4504 Bell Flower Dr Colorado Springs CO 80917 Office: U S A F Acad Dept History Colorado Springs CO 80840

REDDELL, DONALD LEE, agricultural engineer; b. Tulia, Tex., Sept. 28, 1937; s. Kimball Tuscola and Winonah (Claiborne) R.; m. Minnie Ellen Cox, Jan. 27, 1957; children: Revis Diane, Cheryl Reneé, Stephen Patrick. BS, Tex. Tech U., 1960; MS, Colo. State U., 1967, PhD, 1969. Registered profl. engr., Tex. Jr. engr. High Plains Underground Water Conservation Dist. No. 1, Lubbock, Tex., 1960-61, agrl. engr., 1961-63, engr., 1963-65; NSF trainee civil and agrl. engring. dept. Colo. State U., Ft. Collins, 1965-69; asst. prof. agrl. engring. dept. Tex. A&M U., College Station, 1969-72, assoc. prof. agrl. engring. dept., 1972-77, prof. agrl. engring. dept., 1977-89, prof. and head agrl. engring. dept., 1989-93, prof., 1993—. Author: Numerical Simulation of Dispersion in Groundwater Aquifers, 1970; assoc. editor: Jour. Environ. Quality, 1979-85, Energy in Agr. (The Netherlands), 1981-85; contbr. articles to profl. jours. Recipient Outstanding Jour. Paper award ASCE Jour. Irrigation and Drainage, 1989. Fellow Am. Soc. Agrl. Engrs. (pres. Tex. sect. 1979-80, ASAE Paper award 1977, 82, Agrl. Engr. of Yr. award Tex. sect. 1975, Disting. Young Agrl. Engr. of Yr. award SW region chpt. 1977); mem. Am. Geophys. Union, NSPE. Achievements include co-development of the Laplace Transform Finite Difference, Laplace Transform Finite Element, Laplace Transform Boundary Element, Laplace Transform Solute Transport techniques for modeling groundwater flow, eliminating the need for discretizing time in numerical simulations; development of Method of Characteristics used to describe solute transport in ground water, of automatic advance rate feedback furrow irrigation system. Home: 3808 Courtney Cir Bryan TX 77802-3407 Office: Tex A&M U Agrl Engring Dept College Station TX 77843

REDDEN, JAMES ANTHONY, federal judge; b. Springfield, Mass., Mar. 13, 1929; s. James A. and Alma (Cheek) R.; m. Joan Ida Johnson, July 13, 1950; children: James A., William F. Student, Boston U., 1951; LL.B., Boston Coll., 1954. Bar: Mass., 1954, Oreg., 1955. Pvt. practice Mass., 1954-55; title examiner Title & Trust Ins. Co., Oreg., 1955; claims adjuster Allstate Ins. Co., 1956; mem. firm Collins, Redden, Ferris & Velure, Medford, Oreg., 1957-73; treas. State of Oreg., 1973-77; atty. gen., 1977-80; U.S. dist. judge, now sr. judge U.S. Dist. Ct. Oreg., Portland, 1980—. Chmn. Oreg. Pub. Employee Relations Bd.; mem. Oreg. Ho. of Reps., 1963-69, minority leader, 1967-69. With AUS, 1946-48. Mem. ABA, Mass. Bar Assn., Oreg. State Bar. Office: US Dist Ct 612 US Courthouse 620 SW Main St Portland OR 97205-3037

REDDEN, LAWRENCE DREW, lawyer; b. Tallassee, Ala., Dec. 16, 1922; s. A. Drew and Berta (Baker) R.; m. Christine U. Cunningham, Dec. 20, 1943. A.B., U. Ala., 1943, LL.B., 1949. Bar: Ala. bar 1949. Since practiced in Birmingham; asst. U.S. atty. No. Dist. Ala., 1949-52; partner firm Rogers, Howard, Redden & Mills, 1952-79, Redden, Mills & Clark, 1979—; Civilian aide for Ala. to sec. army, 1965-69; mem. Ala. Democratic Exec. Com., 1966-74. Editor-in-chief: Ala. Law Rev, 1948. Trustee Ala. Law Sch. Found.; adv. council Cumberland Law Sch. Served with AUS, 1943-46; maj. gen. Res. ret. Decorated D.S.M.; recipient Outstanding Civilian Service medal Dept. Army, 1970. Fellow Am. Coll. Trial Lawyers, Internat. Soc. Barristers; mem. ABA, Am. Judicature Soc., Ala. Bar Assn. (pres. 1972-73), Birmingham Bar Assn. (past pres.), Ala. Law Inst. (mem. coun.), U. Ala. Law Sch. Alumni Assn. (past pres.), Phi Beta Kappa, Alpha Tau Omega, Omicron Delta Kappa. Baptist. Home: 2513 Beaumont Cir Birmingham AL 35216-1301

REDDEN, NIGEL A., performing company executive; b. Nicosia, Cyprus, Nov. 12, 1950; s. Normand William and Annabel (Austin) R.; m. Arlene Shuler; children: William Austin, Julia Austin. B.A. in Art History, Yale U., 1972. Asst. dir. Italo-American Med. Edn. Found., Rome, 1975-76; press rep. Am. Dance Festival, New London, Conn., 1976; dir. performing arts Walker Art Ctr., Mpls., 1976-82; dir. dance programs Nat. Endowment for the Arts, Washington, 1982-86; gen. mgr. Spoleto Festival USA, Charleston, S.C., 1986-91; exec. dir. Santa Fe (N.Mex.) Opera, 1992-95; exec. prodr. Lincoln Ctr. Festival, N.Y.C., 1995; gen. mgr. Spoleto Festival USA, Charleston, S.C., 1995-96, gen. dir., 1996—; cons., panelist Visual Arts program Nat. Endowment for Arts, 1978, Inter-Arts program, 1979-82, N.W. Area Found., Mpls., 1981-82, MacArthur Found., Chgo., 1983-84; pres. New Music Alliance, Mpls., 1979-80, Am. Music Theater Festival, 1992-94; cons. Tenn. Bicentennial Commn., 1991-96, Lincoln Ctr. for Performing Arts, 1994-95. Office: Spoleto Festival USA PO Box 157 Charleston SC 29402

REDDEN, ROGER DUFFEY, lawyer; b. Washington, Dec. 19, 1932; s. Layman J. and Elizabeth (Duffey) R.; m. Gretchen Sause, July 14, 1962. A.B., Yale Coll., 1954; LL.B., U. Md., 1957. Bar: Md. 1958, U.S. Dist. Ct. Md. 1958, U.S. Ct. Appeals (4th cir.) 1958, U.S. Supreme Ct. 1965. Law clk. to judge U.S. Ct. Appeals (4th cir.), 1957-58; assoc. Smith, Somerville & Case, Balt., 1959-63, ptnr., 1965-68; asst. atty. gen. State of Md., 1964-65; ptnr. Piper & Marbury, Balt., 1969—; bd. dirs. Peoples Water Svc. Co.; draftsman Md. State Dept. Legis. Reference, 1958; counsel Md. Savs. and Loan Study Commn., 1960-61; mem. Gov.'s Commn. to revise testamentary laws of Md., 1965-70; mem. standing com. on rules of practice and procedure Md. Ct. Appeals, 1969-73, 88-91, Md. code revision com., 1970—, Appellate Jud. Nominating Commn., 1975-79, Commn. to study Md. Tax Ct., 1978-79, Gov.'s Task Force on Energy, 1991-95; chmn. Task Force on Permits Simplification, 1979-81. Editor in chief Md. Law Rev., 1956-57; contbr. articles to legal jours. Served with U.S. Army, 1958-59, 61-62. Fellow Am. Bar Found., Md. Bar Found.; mem. Md. State Bar Assn. (chmn. probate and estate law sect. 1966-68, chmn. long range planning com. 1972-73, chmn. com. on laws 1988-89, council sect. adminstrv. law 1980-82, council sect. bus. law 1978-81), Balt. City Bar Assn. (chmn. com. on continuing legal edn. 1976-77, chmn. com. on judiciary 1978-79, chmn. com. on by-laws 1981-82), ABA, Jud. Conf. U.S. Ct. Appeals for 4th Cir. (conf. study com. 1982-83). Democrat. Episcopalian. Office: Piper & Marbury 36 S Charles St Baltimore MD 21201-3020

REDDICLIFFE, STEVEN, editor-in-chief periodical. Office: TV Guide News Amer Pub Inc 1211 Avenue Of The Americas New York NY 10036-8701*

REDDIN, GEORGE, religious organization administrator. Dir. Lifeword Broadcast Ministries, Conway, Ark. Office: Lifeword Broadcast Ministries PO Box 6 Conway AR 72033-0006*

REDDING, BARBARA J., nursing administrator, occupational health nurse; b. Youngstown, Ohio, Jan. 5, 1938; d. Richard Howard and Helen N. (Price) Sterling; m. Philip L. Redding, Nov. 7, 1957; children: Cheryl L., Jeffrey A., Scott P. Diploma in nursing, Miami Valley Hosp., Dayton, Ohio, 1959; AA in Sociology, Miami U., Oxford, Ohio, 1984; postgrad., U. Cin. RN, Ohio; cert. EMT, CPR, BLS. Office nurse Dr. Stewart Adam, Dayton; primary nurse Miami Valley Hosp; adminstr. employee health Armco Steel Co., L.P., Middletown, Ohio; v.p. Redding Ins. Agy., Inc., Middletown, Ohio, 1993—. Instr. CPR, ARC. Mem. NAFE, Am. Assn. Occupational Health Nurses, Ind. Ins. Agts. Am., Inc. Home: 4501 Riverview Ave Middletown OH 45042-2938

REDDING, EVELYN A., dean, nursing educator; b. Gulfport, Miss., Mar. 13, 1945; d. Arthur Edward and Rebecca (Morris) R. BSN, U. Ala., 1967; MS, Fla. State U., 1971; EdD, Okla. State U., 1974; cert. PNP, Tex. Women's U., 1974; MSN, Wichita State U., 1980. Psychiat. nurse Camp Ponderosa, Mentone, Ala., 1967; dir. health svcs. Community Action Agy., Head Start, Dadeville, Ala., 1967-68; pediatric nurse All Children's Hosp., St. Petersburg, Fla., 1968-69; instr. Sch. Nursing A&M U., Tallahassee, 1969-71; coord. mater and child health Western Ky. U., Bowling Green, 1971-72; dir. grad. program U. Tex. Health Sci. Ctr., Houston, 1974-78; prof., assoc. dean Coll. Nursing U. Tulsa, 1978-81; dean, prof. Coll. Nursing U. Southwestern La., Lafayette, 1981—; presenter in field. Contbr. articles to profl. jours. Mem. policy adv. bd. Northwest Fla. Family Planning Project, 1969-71, Nurses Coalition for Action in Politics; mem. exec. com. Hospice of Acadiana, 1982-85, pres., bd. dirs., 1984; cons. big Bend Comprehensive Svcs. Clinic, Tallahassee, 1970-71; cons. family planning nurse practitioner program Planned Parenthood Ctr., Houston, 1975-78; cons. grad. edn., nurse clinician program Madigan Army Med. Ctr., Washington, 1975; pres. Dirs. Nursing Edn. and Nursing Svc. Acadiana, 1982-83; docent intern Gilcrease Mus.; chairperson Tulsa Area Dirs. Nursing Svc. and Nursing Edn. Mem. AAUW (cultural affairs and community com.), ANA, Nat. League for Nursing, ANA Coun. Nurse Researchers, Soc. for Rsch. Nursing Edn., La. State Nurses Assn. (program com. dist. IV 1986), Okla. Nurses Assn. (nurse edn. com. dist. 2 1978-79, by-laws com. 1978-80), Tex. Nurses Assn. (chairperson task force for profl. self-determination 1976-78), Coun. Adminstrs. Nursing Edn. La. (presenter 1987-88), Sigma Theta Tau, Omicron Nu. Avocations: bike riding, reading, fishing, yard work. Home: 125 Alyene Dr Lafayette LA 70506-6811 Office: U Southwestern La Coll Nursing PO Box 42490 Lafayette LA 70504-2490*

REDDING, ROGERS WALKER, physics educator; b. Louisville, July 15, 1942; s. George Walker and Carolyn Lorraine (Rogers) R.; m. Jennie Ruth Fincher, Sept. 6, 1966 (div.); children: Jeffrey Walker, Jonathan Hull; m. Shirley Rubrecht, Aug. 24, 1991. BS, Georgia Tech., 1965; PhD, Vanderbilt U., 1969. Research assoc. Nat. Bur. Standards, Washington, 1969-70; from asst. prof. to assoc. prof. North Tex. State U. (name now U. North Tex.), Denton, 1970-78, prof. physics, 1978-94, dept. chmn., 1980-87, dir. Tex. Acad. Math. and Sci., 1987-89, assoc. dean arts and scis., 1990-94; prof. physics, dean Coll. Arts and Scis. No. Ky. U., Highland Heights; disting. vis. prof. USAF Acad., 1989-90. Author: Exploring Physics, 1984; contbr. articles to profl. jours. Mem. Am. Phys. Soc., Am. Assn. Physics Tchrs., AAAS, Optical Soc. Am. Democrat. Lodge: Kiwanis. Avocations: handball, jogging, referee college football, little league coach. Home: 10501 Cheshire Ridge Dr Florence KY 41042-3197 Office: No Ky U Coll Arts & Scis Highland Heights KY 41099

REDDY, GERARD ANTHONY, corporate training executive; b. N.Y.C., Sept. 25, 1958; s. Warren and Julia (O'Reilly) R.; m. Lorraine Bush, Feb. 20, 1994. BA in English Writing and Comms. Media, Queens Coll., 1981. Rsch. analyst John Blair and Co., N.Y.C., 1981-82, Katz Ind. TV Sales, N.Y.C., 1982-83; sr. rsch. analyst Seltel, N.Y.C., 1983-84; sales presentation writer Capital Cities/ABC TV Sales, N.Y.C., 1984-86; client svc. exec. A.C. Nielsen Co., N.Y.C., 1986-87; rsch. mgr. off network programming MCA-TV, N.Y.C., 1987-88; mgr. corp. tng. and instrn. Dale Carnegie Tng., N.Y.C., 1989-96, major accounts bus. mgr., 1996—. Mgr. Little League Our Lady Miraculous Medal, Ridgewood, N.Y., 1993, 94; campaigner Rudolph Guliani for Mayor, N.Y.C., Ridgewood, 1994. Mem. ASTD, Am. Soc. Quality Control, Am. Mgmt. Assn., Soc. Human Resource Mgmt. Avocations: script writing, motorcycle touring, meditation, jogging. Home: 3 Smith St East Rockaway NY 11518 Office: Dale Carnegie Tng NY 125 Park Ave New York NY 10017-5529

REDDY, JANARDAN K., medical educator; b. Moolasaal, India, Oct. 7, 1938. MB, BS, Osmania U., Hyderabad, India, 1961; MD in Pathology, All India Inst. Med. Scis., 1965. Lic. physicain, Mo., Kans., Ill.; diplomate Am. Bd. Pathology. Rotating house officer Osmania Gen. Hosp., 1961-62; instr. pathology Kakatiya Med. Coll., Warangal, India, 1962-63, asst. prof., 1965-66; resident fellow pathology U. Kans. Med. Ctr., 1966-68, rsch. fellow pathology, 1968-70, asst. prof., 1970-73, assoc. prof., 1973-76, prof., 1976; prof. pathology Northwestern U. Med. Sch., Chgo., 1976—; dir. med. scientist tng. program Northwestern U. Med. Sch., 1990-93, chmn. pathology, 1993—; dir. anatomic pathology Northwestern Meml. Hosp., 1978-81, mem. med. staff, 1976—; mem. Northwestern U. Cancer Ctr., 1976—; mem. med. staff VA Lakeside Hosp., 1990—; group leader Chem.Carcinogenesis Rsch. Group, Northwestern U. Cancer Ctr., 1990—, assoc. dir. cancer edn., 1991—; mem. Task Force on an Environ. Sci./Policy Initiative, Northwestern U., 1991—; chmn. NIH clin. scis. study sect., 1990-91; mem. NIH spl. study sect., 1992; mem. com. on comparative toxicity of naturally occurring carcinogens, 1993—; mem. Nat. Toxicology Program Rev. Com., 1992—; mem. monograph com. WHO, Internat. Agy. on Cancer Rsch., Lyon, France, 1994. Mem. editl. bds. Jour. Histochemistry and Cytochemistry, 1973-76, Exptl. Pathology, 1982—, Toxicologic Pathology, 1983—, Internat. Jour. Pancreatology, 1986—, Lab. Investigation, 1988—, Carcinogenesis, 1989—, The Jour. Northwestern U. Cancer Ctr., 1990—, Gene Expression, 1990—, Internat. Jour. Toxicology, Occupational and Environ. Health, 1992—, Life Sci. Advanced, Oncology, 1991—; assoc. editor Jour. Toxicology and Environ. Health, 1984—, Cancer Rsch., 1985-90. Grantee Joseph Mayberry Endowment Fund, Cancer Rsch. Found., 1991-93, NIEHS, 1995—, NIGMS, 1992-97, NIDDK, 1995—, NIGMS, 1992-97; merit scholar Osmania U., 1954-61, Govt. of Andhra Pradesh merit scholar, 1963-65; WHO Yamagiwa-Yoshida Internat. Cancer fellow in Japan, 1985; recipient NIH merit award, 1987, UN Devel. Programme-Tokten award, 1988, Fletscher scholar award, 1991; named George H. Joost Outstanding Basic Sci. Tchr., 1995. Mem. AAAS, Assn. Scientists of Indian Origin in Am. (pres. 1983-84, sr. scientist award 1991), Soc. Toxicology (v.p. molecular toxicology speciality sect. 1990-91, pres. 1991-92, pres. carcinogenesis specialty sect. 1990-91, Kenneth P. Dubois award 1990), Am. Pancreatic Assn., Am. Assn. Pathologists (mem. program com. 1989-93), Am. Assn. Cancer Rsch. (mem. program com. 1990-91), Internat. Acad. Pathology, Am. Soc. Cell Biology, Histochem. Soc., Soc. Exptl. Biology and Medicine, Biochem. Soc. London, Soc. Toxicology Pathologists, Internat. Assn. Pancreatology, N.Y. Acad. Scis. Home: 1212 Asbury Ave Evanston IL 60202-1102 Office: Northwestern U Med Sch Dept Pathology Ward 6-204 303 E Chicago Ave Chicago IL 60611-3008*

REDDY, KAMBHAM RAJA, plant physiology educator; b. Ambuvari Palli, India, July 1, 1953; came to U.S., 1988; s. Kambi Kambham and Ammannamma (Reddy) R.; m. Anasuya Kambham, Feb. 9, 1982; 1 child, Sasank. BSc, S.V. U., Tirupati, India, 1975, MSc in Botany, 1977, PhD in Botany, 1984. Curator in botany S.V. U., 1977-88; asst. prof. plant physiology Miss. State U., 1988—; vis. scientist Govt. of India, 1988. Contbg. author: Climate Change and Agriculture: Analysis of Potential International Impacts, 1995; contbr. articles to profl. jours., chpts. to books. Mem. Agronomy Soc. Am., Crop Sci. Soc. Am., Biol. Sys. Simulation Work Group, Gamma Sigma Delta (Rsch. award of merit 1995). Achievements include development of new theories and concepts in plant growth regulation and incorporated into a cotton simulation model GOSSYM/COMAX, used by cotton producers, consultants and researchers across the cotton belt; extensive contributions to and studies of how crops respond to changes in global climate. Home: PO Box 3648 Mississippi State MS 39762-3648 Office: Mississippi State U PO Box 5367 Mississippi State MS 39762-5367

REDDY, KRISHNA NARAYANA, artist, educator; b. Chittoor, India, July 15, 1925; s. Narayana B. and Laksmamma R.; m. Judith Blum, June 30, 1967; 1 child, Aparna. Diploma in Fine Arts, Internat. U. Santiniketan, India, 1947; cert. in Fine Arts, Slade Sch. Fine Arts, U. London, 1952; student of Zadkine in sculpture, Academie Grande Chaumière, Paris, 1952-55; student of Marino Marini in sculpture, Academia di Belle Arti di Brera, Milan, 1956-57; specialist in Gravure, Internat. Ctr. for Graphics, Atelier 17, Paris, 1953-55; D.Litt. (hon.), S.V. Univ., India, 1984. Asst. dir. Internat. Ctr. for Graphics, Atelier 17, Paris, 1957-64, prof., co-dir., 1964-76; prof. art, dir. graphics and printmaking program, dept. art and art edn. N.Y. U., N.Y.C., 1977—; lectr. art Arundale Montessori Tchrs. Tng. Center, 1948-49; dir. art dept. Coll. Fine Arts, Kalakshetra, Madras, India, 1947-49; vis. prof. Yale U. Summer Sch. Music and Art, 1978, Am. U., 1964, Kala Inst. Graphics, Berkeley, Calif., 1979, U. Calif., Santa Cruz, 1979; Andrew Mellon vis. prof. Cooper Union Sch. Art and Architecture, 1977; prof. U. Wis., Madison, 1973, U. Calif., Davis, 1970-71; guest prof. Yale U. Summer Sch. Music and Art, 1973. Retrospective exhbns., Bronx Mus. Arts, 1981-82, Indian Council for Cultual Relations, Ministry of Culture and India Nat. Acad. Fine Arts, 1984-85, Museo del Palacio de Bellas Artes, Mexico City, 1988-89. Recipient Gagan-Abani Puraskar Nat. award Viswa-Bharati, 1983; named Featured Guest Artist Printmaker of Yr., Northwest Print Council Ann. Meeting, 1985. Title of Padma Shree awarded by Pres. of India, 1972. Home: 80 Wooster St New York NY 10012-4347 Office: NYU Dept Art and Art Edn New York NY 10003

REDDY, PRATAP CHANDUPATLA, cardiologist, educator, researcher; b. Laxmipur, Andhra Pradesh, India, Apr. 12, 1944; came to U.S., 1969; s. Chandra C. and Butchamma (Kota) R.; m. Shobha Katangur, May 15, 1971; children: Ashutosh, Kirthi. MBBS, Osmania U., Hyderabad, India, 1968. Diplomate Am. Bd. Internal Medicine, Am. Bd. Cardiovascular Diseases. Resident in internal medicine St. Vincent Med. Ctr., S.I., N.Y., 1969-73; fellow in cardiology Maimonide Med. Ctr., Bklyn., 1973-74; rsch. assoc. USPHS Hosp., S.I., 1974-76; asst. prof. medicine U. Ky., Lexington, 1976-81, dir. cardiac electrophysiology, 1976-84, assoc. prof., 1981-84; prof. medicine La. State U. Med. Ctr., Shreveport, 1984—, assoc. dir. cardiology, 1984—, dir. cardiac electrophysiology program, 1984—; attending cardiologist VA Med. Ctr., Shreveport, La. Editor: Tachycardia, 1984; contbr. articles to profl. jours. Named Kentucky Colonel Gov. Ky., 1983. Fellow ACP, Am. Coll. Cardiology; mem. AMA, Am. Heart Assn. (v.p. La. affiliate 1988-89, pres. 1991-92, mem. coun. clin. cardiology), Cen. Soc. for Clin. Rsch., N.Am. Soc. Pacing and Electrophysiology. Office: La State U Med Sch 1530 Kings Hwy Shreveport LA 71103-4229

REDDY, THIKKAVARAPU RAMACHANDRA, electrical engineer; b. Nellore, India, June 4, 1944; came to the U.S., 1979; s. Thikkavarapu Kota and Saraswathi T. (Sivareddy) R.; m. Padmavathi Reddy Kakuturu Thikkavarapu, Aug. 17, 1973; children: Lavanya T., Samatha T. BSEE, Osmania U., 1968; diploma in computer sci., Coll. Engring., Madras, India, 1978. Cert. profl. engr., chartered engr. Supervising engr. APSE Bd., Hyderabad, India, 1969-79; elec. design engr. Sargent & Lundy, Chgo., 1979-80; engr. Bechtel Corp., San Francisco, 1980-82; supr. Bechtel Corp., Athens, Ala., 1989-92; sr. project engr. EGS, Inc., Huntsville, Ala., 1983-84; sr. start-up engr. Gilbert Commonwealth Co., Reading, Pa., 1984-86; cons. Quantum Resources, Decatur, Ala., 1986-87; prin. engr. Ebasco Svcs. Inc., N.Y.C., 1987-89; pres. LSP Internat. Inc., Huntsville, 1992—, LASA Internat., Huntsville, 1992—; guest lectr. gen. interest and wide range of engring. issues; pres. Lasa Internat. Inc., Huntsville, 1992—. Author: Qualification of Electrical Distribution Components, 1984, Thermal Aging Techniques of Organic Materials, 1984, and others; contbr. articles to profl. jours.; guest lectr. on wide range of engring. issues. Mem. NSPE (Outstanding Profl. award 1991, Profl. Engr. of Yr. award 1996), IEEE (Meritorious Svc. award 1985), Commonwealth Engrs. Coun., Project Mgmt. Inst., Am. Telugu Assn. (life), Telugu Assn. N.Am. (life), Internat. Platform Assn., C. of C. Avocations: journalism, table tennis, anthropology, archaeology, classic and modern art, literature. Home: 1213 Willowbrook Dr SE Apt 7 Huntsville AL 35802-3800

REDDY, VENKAT NARSIMHA, ophthalmalogist, researcher; b. Hyderabad, India, Nov. 4, 1922; came to U.S., 1947; s. Malla and Manik (Devi) R.; m. Alvira M. DeMello, Dec. 10, 1955; children: Vinay Neville, Marlita Alvira. BSc, U. Madras, 1945; MS, PhD, Fordham U., 1952. Rsch. assoc. Coll. of Physicians and Surgeons Columbia U., N.Y.C., 1952-56, Banting and Best Inst., Toronto, Can., 1956; ass. and assoc. prof. ophthalmology Kresge Eye Inst. Wayne State U., Detroit, 1957-68; prof., biomed. scis., asst. dir. Eye Rsch. Inst. Oakland U., Rochester, Mich., 1968-75, prof., dir., 1975—; Disting. prof. biomed. scis., dir. Oakland U., Rochester, 1996; mem. study sect. NIH, Bethesda, 1966-70, nat. adv. eye coun., 1982-87, mem. bd. sci. counselors Nat. Eye Inst., 1977-81. Mem. editorial bd. Investigative Ophthalmology and Visual Scis., 1969-72, 78-88, Ophthalmic Research, 1978-90, Experimental Eye Research, 1985—; contbr. articles to profl. jours. Recipient Friendenwald award Assn. Rsch. in Ophthalmology, 1979, Rsch. award Cataract Rsch. Found., 1987, Merit award Nat. Eye Inst., 1989; named Scientist of Yr. State of Mich., 1991, Disting. Faculty Mem. Mich. Assn. Governing Bds. State Univs., 1994. Mem. AAAS, Internat. Soc. Eye Rsch., The Biochem. Soc., Assn. Rsch. in Vision and Ophthalmology (pres. 1985), Am. Soc. for Biochemistry and Molecular Biology, Soc. Free Radicals, Oxygen Soc. Sigma Xi. Achievements include research on cataract etiology, intraocular fluids dynamics relating to glaucoma, cell biology of lens, ciliary body and retinal pigment epithelium, cell differentiation. Office: Oakland U Eye Rsch Inst 422 Dodge Hall Rochester MI 48309

REDDY, YENAMALA RAMACHANDRA, metal processing executive; b. Polavaram, Andhra, India, Feb. 12, 1939; came to U.S., 1974; s. Y. Venkata and Y. Lakshamamma Reddy; m. Y. Uma Reddy, May 30, 1965; children: Y. Sharath, Y. Jay. BME, S.V. U., Andhra, 1961; M in Tech., IIT, Bombay, 1966, PhD, 1970. Lic. profl. engr., Wis. Asst. prof. IIT, Bombay, 1966-69; research and devel. mgr. Jyoti Pumps, Baroda, 1973-74; chief engr. Patterson Pumps, Toccoa, Ga., 1974-80; pres. R.B. Pump Co., Baxley, 1980—, U.B. Cons., Ga., 1980—; pres. Falcon Castings, Inc., 1996, Eagle Motors, Inc., 1996. Contbr. articles to tech. jours. Postdoctoral fellow U. of Tech., Loughborough, Eng., 1970-73. Mem. ASME, IEEE, Am. Foundryman's Soc., Nat. Fire Protection Assn. Office: R B Pump Co 1 Dixie Dr # 557 Baxley GA 31513-2671

REDDY, YENEMALA JAYSIMHA, mechanical engineer; b. Andrha Pradesh, India, May 17, 1968; came to U.S., 1975; s. Yenemala Ramachandra and Yenemala (Uma) R. B in Mech. Engring., Ga. Inst. Tech., 1991. Cert. engr.-in-tng., Ga. Machinist R-B Pump Inc., Baxley, Ga., 1984-85, draftsman, 1985-88, product devel. engr., 1988—, adminstr. govt. contracts, 1988—, test engr., 1988—, v.p., 1992—. Mem. ASME, NSPE, Lions Club (Rookie of Yr. 1992). Republican. Mem. Christian Ch. Avocations: tennis, water skiing, coin collecting, flying. Office: R-B Pump Inc PO Box 557 # 1 Dixie Dr Baxley GA 31513

REDEKER, ALLAN GRANT, physician, medical educator; b. Lincoln, Nebr., Sept. 10, 1924; s. Fred Julius and Fern Frances (Grant) R.; m. Andrea K. Siedschlag, June 16, 1979; children by previous marriage—Martha, James, Thomas. B.S., Northwestern U., Chgo., 1949, M.D., 1952. Intern Hollywood Presbyn. Hosp., Los Angeles, 1952-53; resident in internal medicine Hollywood Presbyn. Hosp., 1953-54; asst. prof. medicine U. So. Calif., 1959-62, assoc. prof., 1962-69, prof., 1969—; mem. Nat. Digestive Diseases Adv. Bd., 1985-88; mem. U.S.-Japan Med. Sci. Program, U.S. Dept. State, 1978—; bd. dirs. Am. Liver Found. Contbr. numerous articles to research jours. Served with AUS, 1943-46. Recipient Research Career Devel. award NIH, 1962-69; research fellow Giannini Found., 1956-58. Mem. Assn. Am. Physicians, Am. Soc. Clin. Investigation, Am. Gastroent. Assn. Home: 9323 Samoline Ave Downey CA 90240-2716 Office: 7601 Imperial Hwy Downey CA 90242-3456

REDENBACH, SANDRA IRENE, educational consultant; b. Boston, Nov. 18, 1940; d. David and Celia (Wish) Goldstein; m. Gunter L. Redenbach, Mar. 16, 1963 (div. 1980); 1 child, Cori-Lin; m. Kenneth L. Gelatt, June 25, 1989. BA, U. Calif., Davis, 1972; MEd in Ednl. Leadership, St. Mary's Coll., Moraga, Calif., 1995. Cert. tchr., Calif. Tchr. Solano County Juvenile Hall, Fairfield, Calif., 1968-70, St. Basil's Sch., Vallejo, Calif., 1970-73, St. Philomenes Sch., Sacramento, 1973; tchr., assoc. dean Vet.'s Spl. Edn. Program, U. Calif., Davis, 1973-75, Woodland (Calif.) Jr. High Sch., 1973-76, Lee Jr. High Sch., Woodland, 1976-79, Woodland High Sch., 1979-87; founder, coord., tchr. Ind. Learning Ctr., Woodland, 1987-94; dir. curriculum and instrn. Dixon (Calif.) Unified Sch. Dist., 1994—; teaching asst., lectr. U. Calif., Davis, 1985-86; pres., cons. Esteem Seminar Programs and Pubs., Davis, 1983—; cons., leader workshop. Author: Self-Esteem: The Necessary Ingredient for Success, 1991; author tng. manual: Self-Esteem: A Training Manual, 1990-91, Innovative Discipline: Managing Your Own Flight Plan, 1994, Autobiography of a Dropout: Dear Diary, 1996. Active Dem. Club of Davis, 1976-79; human rights chair Capitol Svc. Ctr., Sacramento, 1987-92. Martin Luther King scholar, 1986; Nat. Found. for Improvement of Edn. grantee, 1987-88. Mem. Assn. Calif. Sch. Adminstrs., Woodland Edn. Assn. (pres. 1980-83, Outstanding Educator 1992, 93), Phi Delta Kappa (pres. 1992-93). Jewish. Avocations: singing, acting, dancing, travel, theatre. Home: 313 Del Oro Ave Davis CA 95616-0416 Office: Esteem Seminar Programs & Publs 313 Del Oro Ave Davis CA 95616-0416

REDER, ROBERT FRANK, physician; b. Verwyn, Ill., Mar. 31, 1947; s. Robert and Bernice Reder; divorced; 1 child, Robert S. BA, U. Wis., 1969; MD, Mt. Sinai Sch. Medicine, 1973. Asst. prof. pediatrics Columbia-Presbyn. Hosp., N.Y.C., 1979-80, Mt. Sinai Hosp., N.Y.C., 1980-83; assoc. dir. cardiovascular & clin. rsch. Bristol Myers, Evansville, Ind., 1983-84; v.p. med. affairs Knoll Pharm. Co., Whippany, N.J., 1984-90; v.p. clin. rsch. Sanofi Pharm. Co., N.Y.C., 1990-91; v.p., med. dir. Purdue Frederick Co., Norwalk, Conn., 1992—. Fellow Am. Acad. Pediatrics, N.Y. Acad. Medicine; mem. Am. Acad. Pharm. Physicians. Office: Purdue Frederick Co 100 Connecticut Ave Norwalk CT 06850-3541

REDFERN, JOHN D., manufacturing company executive; b. 1935. Grad. Queen's U., Kingston, Ont., 1958, DEng (honoris causa), Carleton U., 1992. With Lafarge Can. Inc. (formerly Can. Cement Lafarge Ltd.), Montreal, 1977—, pres., chief exec. officer, 1977-84, chmn., 1985—; chmn. bd. parent co. Lafarge Corp., Reston, Va., 1985-88, vice-chmn., 1989-96. Office: Lafarge Can Inc, 606 Cathcart Ste 800, Montreal, PQ Canada H3B 1L7

REDFORD, DONALD BRUCE, historian, archaeologist; b. Toronto, Ont., Can., Sept. 2, 1934; s. Cyril Fitzjames and Kathleen Beryl (Coe) R.; m. Susan Pirritano, Jan. 30, 1982; children: Alexander, Aksel; children by previous marriage: Christopher, Philip. B.A., U. Toronto, 1957, M.A., 1958; Ph.D., Brown U., 1965. Lectr. Brown U., 1960-61; lectr. U. Toronto, 1961-64, asst. prof. Egyptian history and language, 1965-67, asso. prof., 1967-69, prof., 1969—; site supr. Brit. Sch. Archaeol. Excavations, Jerusalem, 1964-67; dir. Soc. Study Egyptian Antiquities Expdn. to, Karnak, Egypt, 1970-72, Akhenaten Temple Project, Luxor, Egypt, 1972—; research asso. Univ. Museum, U. Pa., Royal Ont. Mus.; vis. prof. Ben Gurion U., Beersheva, Israel, 1986, U. Pa., 1995-96. Author: History and Chronology of the Egyptian 18th Dynasty, 1967, A Study of the Biblical Joseph Story, 1970, Papyrus and Tablet, 1973, The Akhenaten Temple Project, vol. I, 1977, Akhenaten, the Heretic King, 1984; Annals, King-Lists and Daybooks, 1986, The Akhenaten Temple Project, vol. II, 1988, Egypt, Canaan and Israel in Ancient Times, 1992. Killam grantee, 1975-79; Smithsonian Fgn. Currency grantee, 1973-76, 1979, Social Scis. Humanities Research Council Can. grantee, 1980—. Fellow Royal Soc. Can. Discovered Temple of Akhenaten at Luxor, 1976. Office: U Toronto, 4 Bancroft Ave, Toronto, ON Canada M5S 1A1 Office: U Toronto, Near & Mid Eastern Civs, Toronto, ON Canada M5S 1A1

REDFORD, ROBERT (CHARLES ROBERT REDFORD), actor, director; b. Santa Monica, Calif., Aug. 18, 1937; m. Lola Van Wegenen (div.); children: Shauna, Jamie, Amy. Student, U. Colo., Pratt Inst. Design, Am. Acad. Dramatic Arts; LHD (hon.), U. Colo., 1987; D (hon.), U. Mass., 1990. Owner ski resort Sundance, Provo, Utah. Stage appearances include: Tall Story, The Highest Tree, Sunday in New York, Barefoot in the Park; Films include: (actor) War Hunt, 1961, Situation Hopeless But Not Serious, 1965, Inside Daisy Clover, 1965, The Chase, 1966, This Property Is Condemned, 1966, Barefoot in the Park, 1967, Butch Cassidy and the Sundance Kid, 1969, Tell Them Willie Boy is Here, 1969, Little Fauss and Big Halsey, 1970, The Hot Rock, 1972, Jeremiah Johnson, 1972, The Way We Were, 1973, The Sting, 1973 (Academy award nominee), The Great Gatsby, 1974, The Great Waldo Pepper, 1975, Three Days of the Condor, 1975, A Bridge Too Far, 1977, The Electric Horseman, 1979, Brubaker, 1980, The Natural, 1984, Out of Africa, 1985, Legal Eagles, 1986, Havana, 1990, Sneakers, 1992, Indecent Proposal, 1993, Up Close and Personal, 1996; (actor, exec. prodr.) Downhill Racer, 1969, The Candidate, 1972, All The President's Men, 1976; (exec. prodr.) Promised Land, 1988, Some Girls, 1988, The Dark Wind; (exec. prodr., narrator) Yosemite: The Fate of Heaven, 1989, Incident at Ogala, 1992; (dir.) Ordinary People, 1980 (Academy and Golden Globe Awards, Best Director); (dir., prodr.) The Milagro Beanfield War, 1988, Quiz Show, 1994; (dir., prodr., narrator) A River Runs Through It, 1993. Recipient Audubon medal, 1989, Dartmouth Film Soc. award, 1990; Cecil B. Demille Golden Globe Award for Lifetime Achievement, 1994. Office: 1223 Wilshire Blvd # 412 Santa Monica CA 90403-5400 also: Wildwood Prod 1101 Montava Ave Ste E Santa Monica CA 90403*

REDGRAVE, LYNN, actress; b. London, Mar. 8, 1943; d. Michael Scudemore and Rachel (Kempson) R.; m. John Clark, Apr. 2, 1967; children: Benjamin, Kelly, Annabel. Ed., Queensgate Sch., London, Central Sch. Speech and Drama, London. Stage debut as Helena in Midsummer Night's Dream, 1962; theatrical appearances include The Tulip Tree, Andorra, Hayfever, Much Ado About Nothing, Mother Courage, Love for Love, Zoo, Zoo, Widdershins Zoo, Edinburgh Festival, 1969, The Two of Us, London, 1970, Slag, London, 1971, A Better Place, Dublin, 1972, Born Yesterday, Greenwich, 1973, Hellzapoppin, N.Y., 1976, California Suite, 1977, Twelfth Night, Stratford Conn. Shakespeare Festival, 1978, The King and I, St. Louis, 1983, Les Liaisons Dangereuses, L.A., 1989, The Cherry Orchard, L.A., 1990, Three Sisters, London, 1990, Notebook of Trigorin, U.S., 1996; Broadway appearances include Black Comedy, 1967, My Fat Friend, 1974, Mrs. Warren's Profession (Tony award nomination), 1975, Knock, Knock, 1976, St. Joan, 1977, Sister Mary Ignatius Explains It All, 1985, Aren't We All?, 1985, Sweet Sue, 1987, A Little Hotel on the Side, 1992, The Masterbuilder, 1992, Shakespeare For My Father (Tony and Drama Desk nominations, Elliot Norton award 1993)), 1993, also nat. tour, 1993, Moon over Buffalo, 1996; film appearances include Tom Jones, Girl With Green Eyes, Georgy Girl (Recipient N.Y. Film Critics award, Golden Globe award, Oscar nomination for best actress 1967), The Deadly Affair, Smashing Time, The Virgin Soldiers, Last of the Mobile Hotshots, Don't Turn the Other Cheek, Every Little Crook and Nanny, Everything You Always Wanted to Know About Sex, The National Health, The Happy Hooker, The Big Bus, Sunday Lovers, Morgan Stuart's Coming Home, Getting It Right, Shine, 1996; TV appearances include: The Turn of the Screw, Centennial, 1978, The Muppets, Gauguin the Savage, Beggarman Thief, The Seduction of Miss Leona, Rehearsal for Murder, 1982, Walking On Air, The Fainthearted Feminist (BBC-TV), 1984, My Two Loves, 1986, The Old Reliable, 1988, Jury Duty 1989, Whatever Happened to Baby Jane, 1990, Fighting Back (BBC-TV), 1992, Calling the Shots (Masterpiece Theatre), 1993; guest appearances include Carol Burnett Show, Evening at the Improv and Steve Martin's Best show Ever, Circus of the Stars; co-host nat. TV syndication Not for Women Only, 1977—; nat., TV spokesperson Weightwatchers, 1984-92; TV series include House Calls, 1981, Teachers Only, 1982, Chicken Soup, 1989; albums: Make Mine Manhattan, 1978, Cole Porter Revisited, 1979; video: (for children) Meet Your Animal Friends, Off We Go, Off We Go Again: audio book readings include, Pride and Prejudice, The Shell Seekers, The Blue Bedroom, The Anastasia Syndrome, The Women in His Life, Snow In April, Gone With The Wind, 1994, The World of Philosophy, 1996; author: This is Living, 1990, Shakespare For My Father, 1993. Named Runner-up Actress, All Am. Favorites, Box Office Barometer 1975; recipient Sarah Siddons award as Chgo.'s best stage actress of 1976, 94. Mem. The Players (pres. 1994). Office: care John Clark PO Box 1207 Topanga CA 90290-1207

REDGRAVE, VANESSA, actress; b. London, Jan. 30, 1937; d. Michael and Rachel (Kempson) R.; m. Tony Richardson, Apr. 28, 1962 (div.); children: Natasha Jane, Joely Kim, Carlo. Student, Central Sch. Speech and Drama, London, 1955-57. First stage appearances include: Reluctant Debutante, Frincton Summer Theater, 1957, Come On Jeeves, Arts Theater, Cambridge, 1957, A Touch of the Sun, Saville Theater, London, 1958, Major Barbara, Royal Court, 1958, Mother Goose, Leatherhead, 1958,; Prin. theatrical roles include Helena in Midsummer Night's Dream, 1959, Stella in Tiger and the Horse, 1960, Katerina in The Taming of the Shrew, 1961, Rosalind in As You Like It, 1962, Imogene in Cymbeline, 1962, Nina in The Seagull, 1969, Miss Brodie in The Prime of Miss Jean Brodie, 1966; other plays include Cato Street, 1971, Threepenny Opera, 1972, Twelfth Night, 1972, Antony and Cleopatra, 1973, Design for Living, 1973, Macbeth, 1975, Lady from the Sea, 1976, 78, 79, (Best Actress award Evening Standard, 1979), The Aspern Papers, 1984, The Seagull, 1969, 85 (London Standard Drama award for Best Actress), Chekhov's Women, 1985, The Taming of the Shrew, Ghosts, 1986, Touch of the Poet, 1988, Orpheus Descending, 1989, A Madhouse in Goa, 1989, Chekov's Women, 1989, Three Sisters, 1990, When She Danced, 1991, Heartbreak House, 1991, Maybe, 1993, Brecht in Hollywood, 1994, Vita and Virginia, 1994—; film roles include Behind The Mask, 1958, Leonie in Morgan-A Suitable Case for Treatment, 1965 (Best Actress award Cannes Film Festival 1966), Sheila in Sailor from Gibraltar, 1965, Anne-Marie in La Musica, 1965, A Man For All Seasons, 1966, Red And Blue, 1966, Jane in Blow-Up, 1967, Guinevere in Camelot, 1967, Isadora in Isadora Duncan, 1968 (Best Actress award Cannes Film Festival); other films include The Charge of the Light Brigade, 1968, The Seagull, 1968, A Quiet Place in the Country, 1968, Daniel Deronda, 1969, Dropout, 1969, The Trojan Women, 1970, The Devils, 1970, The Holiday, 1971, Mary, Queen of Scots, 1971, Murder on the Orient Express, 1974, Winter Rates, 1974, 7 per cent solution, 1975, Julia, 1977 (Academy award Best Supporting Actress, Golden Globe award), Agatha, 1978, Yanks, 1978, Bear Island, 1979, Playing for Time, 1980, My Body My Child, 1981, Wagner, 1981, The Bostonians, 1983 (Oscar nomination Best Actress, Golden Globe nomination, Best Actress Nat. Film Critics, Best Actress New Delhi Internat. Film Festival), Wetherby, 1985, Steaming, 1985, Prick Up Your Ears, 1987, Comrades, 1987, Consuming Passions, 1988, Diceria dell'Untore, 1989, The Ballad of the Sad Café, 1990, Young Catherine, 1990, Howard's End, 1992 (Oscar nomination Best Supporting Actress), Crime and Punishment, 1993, The House of the Spirits, 1994, Mother's Boys, 1994, A Month by the Lake, 1995 (Golden Globe nomination for Best Actress 1996), Little Odessa, 1995, Mission Impossible, 1996, For The Love Of Tyler, 1996, Smilla's Sense of Snow, 1996; TV film and miniseries appearances include Snow White and the Seven Dwarfs, 1985, Three Sovereigns for Sarah, 1985, Peter the Great, 1986, Second Serve, 1986 (Emmy award, Golden Globe award), A Man for All Seasons, 1988, Young Catherine, 1990, Whatever Happened to Baby Jane, 1990, The Three Sisters, 1990, When She Danced, 1991, Playing for Time (Emmy award, TV Times award), The Wall, 1992, Heartbreak House, 1992, Great Moments In Aviation, 1993, Down Came A Blackbird, 1994; Author: Pussies and Tigers, 1964, (autobiography) Vanessa, 1991, Vanessa Redgrave: An Autobiography, 1994. Bd. govs. Central Sch. Speech and Drama, 1963—. Decorated comdr. Order Brit. Empire; recipient 4 times Drama award Evening Standard, 1961-91, Best Actress award Variety Club Gt. Brit., 1961, 66, Best Actress award Brit. Guild TV Producers and Dirs., 1966, Laurence Olivier award Best Actress for The Aspern Papers, 1984, London Standard Drama award Best Actress for The Seagull, 1985, New York Film Critics Circle award Best Supporting Actress for Prick Up Your Ears, 1988, Evening Standard award

Best Actress for When She Danced, 1991, Ace award Best Supporting Actress movie/mini-series for Young Catherine, 1992, Variety Club of Great Britain award, 1992, Best Actress Nat. Film Critics (USA) New Delhi Internat. Film Festival for The Bostonians, Laurence Olivier award Actress of the Yr. in a Revival for A Touch of the Poet; fellow Brit. Film Inst., 1988.

RED HAWK, VIRGINIA A. See LYNCH, VIRGINIA ANNE

REDHEAD, PAUL AVELING, physicist; b. Brighton, Eng., May 25, 1924; m. Doris Packman, 1948; children: Janet, Patricia. BA with honors in Physics, Cambridge (Eng.) U., 1944, MA, 1948, PhD, 1969. Sci. officer dept. naval ordnance Brit. Admiralty, 1944-45, svcs. electronics rsch. lab., 1945-47; rsch. officer NRC Can., Ottawa, Ont., 1947-69; dir. planning group NRC Can., 1970-72, dir.-gen. planning, 1972-73, dir. div. physics, 1973-86, chmn. com. of lab. dirs., 1981-86, sec. sci. and tech. policy com., 1986-89, researcher emeritus, 1989—. Author: Physical Basis of Ultrahigh Vacuum, 1968, 2d edit., 1993; editor: Jour. Vacuum Scis. and Tech., 1969-74; contbr. numerous articles to profl. jours. Fellow IEEE, Royal Soc. Can., Am. Phys. Soc., Am. Vacuum Soc. (past pres., Medard W. Welch award 1975); mem. Can. Assn. Physicists (medal for achievement in physics 1989). Patentee in field. Home: 1958 Norway Crescent, Ottawa, ON Canada K1H 5N7 Office: Nat Rsch Coun Can, Inst Microstructural Scis, Ottawa, ON Canada K1A OR6

REDIKER, ROBERT HARMON, physicist; b. Bklyn., June 7, 1924; s. Moe J. and Estelle (Rosenwasser) R.; m. Barbara June Zenn, May 26, 1980; children by previous marriage: Richard J., Donald E. SB, MIT, 1947, PhD, 1950. Research asso. physics MIT, 1950-51; rsch. assoc. physics Ind. U., 1952-53; staff Lincoln Lab., Lexington, Mass., 1951-52, 53-57; asst. group leader semi-conductor physics Lincoln Lab., 1957-59, group leader applied physics, 1959-66; prof. dept. elec. engring. MIT, 1966-76, adj. prof., 1976-82, sr. rsch. scientist, 1982-96, rsch. affiliate, 1996—, assoc. head optics divsn. Lincoln Lab., 1970-72, head optics divsn. Lincoln Lab., 1972-80, sr. staff Lincoln Lab., 1980-91; sr. v.p. advanced R&D Cynosure Inc., 1992-96, cons., 1996—; Vice pres. Newton Lower Falls Improvement Assn., 1968-71; Mem. spl. group optical masers Def. Dept., 1966-73, working group D (lasers), 1973-76, working group C (electro-optics), 1979-92, mem. adv. group on electron devices, high energy laser rev. group, 1973-75; mem. ad hoc com. on materials and processes for electron devices Nat. Acad. Scis., 1970-72; mem. evaluation panel Nat. Bur. Standards, 1975-78; mem. panel on Office of Naval Research Opportunities in Physics, 1988, 91. Author. Served with Signal Corps AUS, 1943-46. Fellow IEEE (chmn. com. solid state devices 1961-63, sec. treas. group electron devices 1965-66, vice chmn. 1967, awards bd. 1976-79, chmn. Liebmann awards com. 1977-78, David Sarnoff award 1969), Am. Phys. Soc., Optical Soc. Am.; mem. Nat. Acad. Engring., Sigma Xi, Alpha Epsilon Pi. Jewish. Patentee in field. Home: 151 Coolidge Ave Watertown MA 02172-2863 Office: MIT Rm 36-233 Cambridge MA 02139

REDING, JOHN A., lawyer; b. Orange, Calif., May 26, 1944. AB, U. Calif., Berkeley, 1966, JD, 1969. Bar: Calif. 1970, U.S. Dist. Ct. (no., ctrl. ea. and so. dists.) Calif., U.S. Claims Ct., U.S. Supreme Ct. Formerly mem. Crosby, Heafey, Roach & May P.C., Oakland, Calif.; now ptnr. Paul, Hastings, Janofsky & Walter LLP, San Francisco. Mem. ABA (sects. on litigation, intellectual property, and natural resources, energy and eviron. law, coms. on bus. torts, internat. law, trial practice and torts and insurance), Am. Intellectual Property Law Assn., State Bar Calif. (sect. on litigation), Alameda County Bar Assn., Bar Assn. San Francisco, Assn. Bus. Trial Lawyers. Office: Paul Hastings et al 345 California St San Francisco CA 94104-2606

REDISH, EDWARD FREDERICK, physicist, educator; b. N.Y.C., Apr. 1, 1942; s. Jules and Sylvia (Coslow) R.; m. Janice Copen, June 18, 1967; children: A. David, Deborah. AB, Princeton U., 1963; PhD, MIT, 1968. CTP fellow U. Md., College Park, 1968-70, from asst. prof. to assoc. prof., 1970-79, prof., 1979—, chmn. dept. phys. astronomy, 1982-85; vis. prof. Ind. U., Bloomington, 1985-86, U. washington, Seattle, 1992-93; vis. fgn. collaborator CEN, Saclay, France, 1973-74; co-dir. U. Md. Project in Physics and Ednl. Tech., 1983-93, Comprehensive Unified Physics Learning Environment, 1989-96; mem. Nuclear Sci. Adv. Com., Dept. of Energy/NSF, 1987-90; mem. program adv. com. Ind. U. Cyclotron Facility, 1985-89, chmn., 1986-89; mem. Internat. Commn. on Physics Edn., 1993—. Author: (software) Orbits, 1989, The M.U.P.P.E.T. Utilities, 1994, The Comprehensive Unified Physics Learning Environment, 1994; editor: (conf. procs.) Computers in Physics Instrn., 1990, Internat. Conf. Undergrad. Physics Edn., 1997; contbr. over 60 articles to profl. jours. Named Sr. Resident Rsch. Assoc., NAS-NRC, 1977-78; recipient Inst. medal Ctrl. Rsch. Inst. for Physics, 1979, Leo Schubert award Wash. Acad. Sci., 1988, Educator award Md. Assn. Higher Edn., 1989, Glover award Dickinson Coll., 1991, Forman award Vanderbilt U., 1996. Fellow AAAS, Am. Phys. Soc., Wash. Acad. Sci.; mem. Am. Assn. Physics Tchrs. Office: U Md Dept Physics College Park MD 20742-4111

REDLICH, NORMAN, lawyer, educator; b. N.Y.C., Nov. 12, 1925; s. Milton and Pauline (Durst) R.; m. Evelyn Jane Grobow, June 3, 1951; children: Margaret Bonny-Claire, Carrie Ann, Edward Grobow. AB, Williams Coll., 1947, LLD (hon.), 1976; LLB, Yale U., 1950; LLM, NYU, 1955; LLD (hon.), John Marshall Law Sch., 1990. Bar: N.Y. 1951. Practiced in N.Y.C., 1951-59; assoc. prof. law NYU, 1960-62, prof. law, 1962-74, assoc. dean Sch. Law, 1974-75, dean Sch. Law, 1975-88, dean emeritus, 1992—, Judge Edward Weinfeld prof. law, 1982—; counsel Wachtell, Lipton, Rosen & Katz, N.Y.C., 1988—; editor-in-chief Tax Law Rev., 1960-66; mem. adv. com. Inst. Fed. Taxation, 1963-68; exec. asst. corp. counsel, N.Y.C., 1966-68, 1st asst. corp. counsel, 1970-72, corp. counsel, 1972-74; asst. counsel Pres. Commn. on Assassination Pres. Kennedy, 1963-64; mem. com. on admissions and grievances U.S. 2d Circuit Ct. Appeals, 1978—, chmn., 1978-87. Author: Professional Responsibility: A Problem Approach, 1976, Constitutional Law, Cases and Materials, 1983, rev. edit., 1996, Understanding Constitutional Law, 1995; contbr. articles in field. Chmn. commn. on law and social action Am. Jewish Congress, 1978—, chmn. governing coun., 1996; mem. Borough Pres.'s Planning Bd. Number 2, 1959-70, counsel N.Y. Com. to Abolish Capital Punishment, 1958-77; mem. N.Y.C. Bd. Edn., 1969; mem. bd. overseers Jewish Theol. Sem., 1973—; trustee Law Ctr. Found. of NYU, 1975—, Freedom House, 1976-86, Vt. Law Sch., 1977—, Practicing Law Inst., 1980—; trustee Lawyers Com. for Civil Rights Under Law, 1976—, co-chmn., 1979-81; bd. dirs. Legal Aid Soc., 1983-88, NAACP Legal Def. Fund, 1985—, Greenwich House, 1987—. Decorated Combat Infantryman's Badge. Mem. ABA (coun. legal edn. and admissions to bar 1981—, vice chmn. 1987-88, chmn. 1989-90, equal opportunities in legal profession 1986-92, ho. of dels. 1991—), Assn. of Bar of City of N.Y. (exec. com. 1975-79, professionalism com. 1988-92). Office: 51 W 52nd St Fl 30 New York NY 10019-6119

REDMAN, BARBARA KLUG, nursing educator; b. Mitchell, S.D.; d. Harlan Lyle and Darlien Grace (Bock) Klug; m. Robert S. Redman, Sept. 14, 1958; 1 child, Melissa Darlien. BS, S.D. State U., 1958; MEd, U. Minn., 1959, PhD, 1964; LHD (hon.), Georgetown U., 1988; DSc (hon.), U. Colo., 1991. RN. Asst. prof. U. Wash., Seattle, 1964-69; assoc. dean U. Minn., Mpls., 1969-75; dean Sch. Nursing U. Colo., Denver, 1975-78; VA scholar VA Cen. Office, Washington, 1978-81; postdoctoral fellow Johns Hopkins U., Balt., 1982-83; exec. dir. Am. Assn. Colls. Nursing, Washington, 1983-89, ANA, Washington, 1989-93; prof. nursing Johns Hopkins U., Balt., 1993-95; dean, prof. Sch. Nursing U. Conn., Storrs, 1995—; vis. fellow Kennedy Inst. Ethics, Georgetown U., 1993-94; fellow in med. ethics Harvard Med. Sch., 1994-95. Author: Practice of Patient Education, 1968—; contbr. articles to profl. jours. Bd. dirs. Friends of Nat. Libr. of Medicine, Washington, 1987—. Recipient Disting. Alumnus award S.D. State U., 1975, Outstanding Achievement award U. Minn., 1989. Fellow Am. Acad. Nursing. Home: 12425 Bobbink Ct Potomac MD 20854-3005 Office: U Conn 231 Glenbrook Rd Storrs CT 06269-2026

REDMAN, CLARENCE OWEN, lawyer; b. Joliet, Ill., Nov. 23, 1942; s. Harold F. and Edith L. (Read) R.; m. Barbara Ann Pawlan, Jan. 26, 1964 (div.); children: Scott, Steven; m. 2d, Carla J. Rozycki, Sept. 24, 1983. B.S., U. Ill., 1964, J.D., 1966, M.A., 1967. Bar: Ill. 1966, U.S. Dist. Ct. (ea. dist.) Ill. 1966, U.S. Dist. Ct. (no. dist.) Ill. 1970, U.S. Ct. Appeals (7th cir.), 1973, U.S. Ct. Appeals (4th cir.) 1982, U.S. Supreme Ct. 1975. Assoc., Keck, Mahin & Cate, Chgo., 1969-73, ptnr., 1973—, CEO, 1986—; spl. asst. atty. gen. Ill., 1975-8; bd. dirs. AMCOL Internat. Corp. Mem. bd. visitors U. Ill. Coll. of Law, 1991-95. Served to capt. U.S. Army, 1967-69. Decorated Bronze Star. Mem. ABA, Ill. State Bar Assn. (chmn. young lawyers sect. 1977-78, del. assembly 1978-81, 84-87), Chgo. Bar Assn., Seventh Cir. Bar Assn., Am. Legion (Roselle, Ill.). Office: Keck Mahin & Cate 77 W Wacker Dr Ste 4400 Chicago IL 60601

REDMAN, DALE E., diversified financial services company executive; b. 1947. B in Acctg., La. State U., 1968, M in Acctg., 1972. CPA. With Ernst & Whinney CPA's, Baton Rouge, La., 1968-80; exec. v.p., cfo United Co. Fin. Corp., Baton Rouge, La., 1980—; v. chmn. United Co. Lending corp. Office: United Companies Financial Corp 4041 Essen Ln Baton Rouge LA 70809-2129

REDMAN, ERIC, lawyer; b. Palo Alto, Calif., June 3, 1948; s. M. Chandler and Marjorie Jane (Sachs) R.; children: Ian Michael, Graham James; m. Heather Bell, 1996. AB, Harvard U., 1970, JD, 1975; BA, Oxford U., 1972, MA, 1980. Bar: Wash. 1975, U.S. Dist. Ct. (we. dist.) Wash. 1975, D.C. 1979, U.S. Ct. Appeals (9th cir.) 1981, U.S. Supreme Ct. 1983. Asst. U.S. senator W.G. Magnuson, Washington and Seattle, 1968-71, 74-75; assoc. Preston, Thorgrimson et al, Seattle, 1975-78, ptnr., 1979-82; ptnr. Heller, Ehrman, White & McAuliffe, Seattle, 1983—. Author: Dance of Legislation, 1973; also book revs., articles. Office: Heller Ehrman White & McAuliffe 6100 Columbia Ctr 701 5th Ave Seattle WA 98104-7016

REDMAN, TIMOTHY PAUL, English language educator, author, chess federation administrator; b. Elmhurst, Ill., June 26, 1950; s. William Charles and Eileen Marie (Keenan) R. B.A., Loyola U., Chgo., 1973; M.A., U. Chgo., 1974, Ph.D., 1987. Instr. Loyola U., Rome, 1977, Ill. Inst. Tech., Chgo., 1980-84; lectr. English dept. Loyola U., Chgo., 1982-84; lectr. U. Wis., Parkside, 1984-85; instr. Ohio State U., Lima, 1985-87, asst. prof., 1987-89; asst. prof. U. Tex., Dallas, 1989-91, assoc. dean, coll. master, 1991-92, assoc. prof., 1991—. Author: Ezra Pound and Italian Fascism, 1991; editor: Official Rules of Chess, 3d edit., 1987. Whiting fellow, 1981-82, NEH fellow, 1992-93. Mem. MLA, U.S. Chess Fedn. (past pres.), Nat. Coun. Tchrs. English, PEN U.S.A. West. Roman Catholic. Home: 3034 Brookshire Dr Plano TX 75075-7644 Office: U Tex at Dallas Sch Arts & Humanities JO31 PO Box 830688 Richardson TX 75083-0688 also: US Chess Fedn 186 US Highway 9W New Windsor NY 12553-7624

REDMAN, WILLIAM WALTER, JR., realtor; b. Statesville, N.C., Oct. 15, 1933; s. William Walter and Mildred Huie R.; Student U. So. Calif., 1966; BS, Embry-Riddle Aeronaut. U., 1972; postgrad. Jud. Coll., 1987; m. Elizabeth Ann Wilhelm, Dec. 28, 1956; children—Lisa Dawn, Kathryn Marlene, Adrienne Ann. Enlisted U.S. Army, 1954, advanced through grades to lt. col., 1974, ret., 1974; dir. public relations Northwestern Bank, Statesville, N.C., 1974-76; pres. Redman Realty, Statesville, N.C., 1976-92 ; mem. N.C. State Senate, 26th dist., 1978-87; Senate minority leader, 1986-87; commr. pub. utilities State of N.C., Raleigh, 1987-95; chmn. N.C. Utilities Commn.; apptd. to exec. com., vice chmn. com. on adminstrn., comm. com. Nat. Assn. Regulatory Utility Commrs., apptd. chmn., bd. dirs. Natl. Regulatory Rsch. Inst., Ohio State U., 1993; apptd. mem. exec. com. Southeastern Assn. Regulatory Utilities Commrs. Bd. trustees Gardner-Webb Coll.; bd. advisors Sch. Bus. Pub. Utility Regulatory Bd. N.Mex. State U.; dir. N.C. Solar Ctr.; mem. N.C. Enrgy Policy Coun., N.C. Tax Rev. Bd. Recipient Valand award N.C. Mental Assns.; named to Inf. Officers' Sch. Hall of Fame, Ft. Benning, Ga., 1981, Disting. Mem. of Regiment U.S. Transp. Corps, 1990; decorated DFC with oak leaf cluster, Bronze Star medal with two oak leaf clusters, Air medal with sixteen oak leaf clusters, Meritorious Service medal. Mem. VFW (life mem.), Ret. Officers Assn. (life mem.), Nat. Assn. Adminstrv. Law Judges, Am. Legion (life mem.), Raleigh Exec. Club, N.C. State U. Faculty Club, Kiwanis . Republican. Baptist. Address: 2329 Airline Dr Raleigh NC 27607-3109

REDMON, AGILE HUGH, JR., allergist; b. Galveston, Tex., Dec. 17, 1924; s. Agile H. and Natalie Mary (Collins) R.; m. Dora Mary Bastiani, May 18, 1957 (dec. Apr. 1996); children—James Joseph, John Gerard. Student Tex. A&M U., 1942-43, U. Southwestern La., 1943-44; M.D., Baylor U., 1948. Diplomate Am. Bd. Allergy and Immunology. Intern U.S. Naval Hosp., San Diego, 1948-49; resident in allergy, 1955-56; resident in internal medicine Baylor/VA Hosp., Houston, 1950-53; assoc. prof. medicine Baylor U., Houston, 1957—; sr. ptnr. Allergy Asthma Assocs., Houston, 1970—. Served with M.C., USN, 1943-48, 53-57. Fellow Am. Acad. Allergy and Immunology (chmn. council local soc. pres.'s); mem. AMA, Tex. Med. Assn., Harris County Med. Soc. (v.p. 1984), Tex. Allergy Soc. (pres. 1984-88), Houston Allergy Soc. (past pres.). Republican. Roman Catholic. Home: 5223 Contour Pl Houston TX 77096-4117 Office: 7505 Fannin St Ste 515 Houston TX 77054-1913

REDMOND, DONALD EUGENE, JR., neuroscientist, educator; b. San Antonio, June 17, 1939; s. Donald Eugene and Viola (Kellum) R.; m. Patricia Welder Robinson, Dec. 22, 1972; 1 child, Andy J. BA, So. Meth. U., 1961; MD, Baylor U., 1968; MAH, Yale U., 1987. Diplomate Am. Bd. Psychiatry and Neurology. With Lab. of Clin. Sci., NIMH, Bethesda, Md., 1973-74; assoc. chief clin. neurosci. unit Conn. Mental Health Ctr., New Haven, 1974-87; asst. prof. psychiatry Yale U., New Haven, 1974-77; assoc. prof. psychiatry Yale U., 1978-87, prof. psychiatry, dir. neurobehavior lab., 1987—, dir. neural transplant program for neurol. diseases, 1987—; pres. St. Kitts Biomed. Rsch. Found., St. Kitts, W.I., 1983—, Axion Rsch. Found., Hamden, Conn., 1985—; prof. neurosurgery, 1993—. Contbr. articles to profl. jours.; patentee in field. With USPHS, 1972-74. Recipient Rsch. Scientist award NIMH, 1980— Founds. Fund prize, 1981; grantee NIMH, 1974-91, Nat. Inst. Neurol. Diseases and Stroke, 1986—, others. Mem. Am. Psychiat. Assn., Am. Coll. Neuropsychopharmacology, Am. Soc. Neural Transplantation (coun. mem. 1994—), Internat. Med. Soc. Motor Disturbances. Office: Neurobehavior Lab PO Box 3333 New Haven CT 06510-0333

REDMOND, DOUGLAS MICHAEL, diversified company executive; b. Central Islip, N.Y., May 13, 1954; s. Ronald George and Josephine Bernadette (Donelon) R.; m. Millie Vidal, Oct. 13, 1985; children: Douglas Michael Jr., Brandon Richard, Chelsea Lynn. BA in Bus., SUNY, Oneonta, 1976; MS, SUNY, Stony Brook, 1984. Ops. mgr. Whitman Labs Ltd., Petersfield, Eng., 1981-82; line supr. Estee Lauder Inc., Melville, N.Y., 1976-78; materials supr. Estee Lauder Inc., Melville, 1978-79, prodn. control mgr., 1979-81, materials mgr., 1980-81; cons. Estee Lauder Internat., N.Y.C., 1982-83; dir. materials Estee Lauder Internat., Melville, 1983-86, dir. mfg. svcs., 1986-88, exec. dir., 1988-92, v.p. supply, 1992-94; prin. Redmond Enterprises, Inc., East Islip, N.Y., 1987—, Global Decisions, Inc., 1991—, Oxygene Internat., Ltd., 1994—. Active in Bush campaign Rep. Com., Babylon, N.Y., 1988. Mem. Am. Prodn. and Inventory Control Soc. Roman Catholic.

REDMOND, JOHN, oncologist; b. Tampa, Fla., July 21, 1944; s. John and Sara (Lee) R.; divorced; 1 child, Geoff. BS, West Point Acad., 1965; MD, Emory U., 1974. Diplomate Nat. Bd. Med. Examiners, Am. Bd. Internal Medicine. Chief hematology and oncology Walter Reed Meml. Hosp., Washington, 1987-90; chief oncology Abington (Pa.) Meml. Hosp., 1990—. Fellow Am. Coll. Physicians; mem. Am. Soc. Hematology, Am. Soc. Clin. Oncology, Am. Assn. Cancer Rsch., Phila. Coll. Physicians, Am. Assn. Cancer Edn., AMA, Pa. Med. Soc., Am. Cancer Soc. Avocation: cycling. Office: Abington Meml Hosp 1200 Old York Rd Abington PA 19001-3720

REDMOND, ROBERT FRANCIS, nuclear engineering educator; b. Indpls., July 15, 1927; s. John Felix and Marguerite Catherine (Breinig) R.; m. Mary Catherine Cangany, Oct. 18, 1952 (dec. May 1988); children: Catherine, Robert, Kevin, Thomas, John; m. Carole Moon Jacobs, Apr. 9, 1994. B.S. in Chem. Engring, Purdue U., 1950; M.S. in Math, U. Tenn., 1955; Ph.D. in Physics, Ohio State U., 1961. Engr. Oak Ridge Nat. Lab., 1950-53; scientist, adviser-cons. Battelle Meml. Inst., Columbus, Ohio, 1953-70; prof. nuclear engring. Ohio State U., Columbus, 1970-92; assoc. dean Coll. Engring. Ohio State U., dir. Engring. Experiment Sta., 1977-92, acting dean, 1990-92, prof. emeritus mech. engring., assoc. dean emeritus, 1992—. Contbr. articles to profl. jours. V.p. Argonne Univs. Assn., 1976-77, trustee, 1972-80; mem. Ohio Power Siting Commn., 1978-82; trustee Edison Welding Inst., 1988-92. With AUS, 1945-46. Mem. Am. Nuclear Soc. (chmn. Southwestern Ohio sect.), AAAS, Nat. Regulatory Rsch. Inst. (bd. dirs. 1988-92), Trans. Rsch. Ctr., Am. Soc. Engring. Edn., Sigma Xi, Tau Beta Pi. Home: 4621 Nugent Dr Columbus OH 43220-3047 Office: Ohio State U Coll Engring Columbus OH

REDMONT, BERNARD SIDNEY, university dean, journalism educator; b. N.Y.C., Nov. 8, 1918; s. Morris Abraham and Bessie (Kamerman) R.; m. Joan Rothenberg, Mar. 12, 1940; children: Dennis Foster, Jane Carol. B.A., CCNY, 1938; M.J., Columbia U., 1939; D.H.L., Fla. Internat. U., 1980. Reporter, book reviewer Bklyn. Daily Eagle, 1936-38; free lance corr. Europe, 1939, Mexico City, 1939-40; telegraph editor, editorial writer Herkimer (N.Y.) Evening Telegram, 1941-42; newswriter U.S. Office of Inter-Am. Affairs (Washington shortwave radio newscasts to Latin Am.), 1942-43, dir. News div., 1944-46; staff corr., bur. chief U.S. News & World Report, Buenos Aires and Paris, 1946-51; columnist Continental Daily Mail, Paris, 1951-53; chief corr. English Lang. World News Service Agence France-Presse, Paris, 1953-65; European corr. Paris news bur. chief Westinghouse Broadcasting Co., Paris, 1961-76; corr., bur. chief CBS News, Moscow, 1976-79; corr. CBS News, Paris, 1979-81; prof. journalism, dir. broadcast journalism program, dean Boston U. Coll. Communication, 1982-86, dean emeritus, prof. journalism, 1986—, mem. adv. bd. Latin Am. journalism program, 1989—; cons. Exec. Svc. Corps. of New Eng., 1991—, Internat. Exec. Svc. Corps, 1992—. Author: Risks Worth Taking: The Odyssey of a Foreign Correspondent, Univ. Press of Am., 1992, Friendly Moderation, 1997. Served with USMCR, 1943-44. Decorated Purple Heart, chevalier Legion of Honor (France); recipient award for advancement of journalism Columbia U., 1986, Townsend Harris medal for life achievement, 1991, Yankee Quill award for disting. contbns. to betterment of journalism, 1995; Pulitzer travel fellow. Mem. Overseas Press Club (award best radio reporting from abroad 1968, 73), Soc. Profl. Journalists, Nat. Press Club, Anglo-American Press Assn. of Paris (pres. 1961, treas. 1970-73, sec. 1974-76). Unitarian. *Life has more meaning when it affirms, with grace, the Yang and the Yin, reconciling opposites--independence, yet cooperative effort and community caring; courage and hard work, yet moderation and generosity; hatred of injustice, yet kindness,fairness and compassion.*

REDO, DAVID LUCIEN, investment company executive; b. Lakewood, Ohio, Sept. 1, 1937; s. Joseph L. and Florence M. (Morse) R.; m. Judy L. Ijams, Aug. 4, 1962; children: Jenny, Mark. BSEE, U. Calif., Berkeley, 1961; MBA, U. Santa Clara, 1967. Registered investment advisor. Asst. engring. mgr. AT&T, N.Y.C., 1968-71; pension fund mgr. Pacific Telephone, San Francisco, 1971-77; mng. dir. The Fremont Group (formerly Bechtel Investments Inc.), San Francisco, 1977—; pres., CEO Fremont Investment Advisors, Inc., San Francisco, 1986—; chmn., CEO Fremont Mutual Funds, 1986—; bd. dirs. The Fremont Group (formerly Bechtel Investments, Inc.) San Francisco, Fremont Investors, Inc., J.P. Morgan Securities Asia, Singapore, Sequoia Ventures Inc., San Francisco, Fremont Investment Advisors, Sit/Kim Internat. Investments; chmn., CEO Fremont Mutual Funds. Bd. trustees U. Calif., Berkeley, 1988—; chmn. investment com. U. Calif. Found., 1988—. Mem. Sentinel Pension Inst. (bd. advisors), Treas. Club of San Francisco, Internat. Assn. of Fin. Planners. Avocations: golf, traveling, reading, walking. Office: Fremont Investment Advisors 333 Market St Ste 2600 San Francisco CA 94105-2127

REDO, S(AVERIO) FRANK, surgeon; b. Bklyn., Dec. 28, 1920; s. Frank and Maria (Guida) R.; m. Maria Lappano, June 27, 1948; children—Philip, Martha. B.S., Queens Coll., 1942; M.D., Cornell U., 1950. Diplomate: Am. Bd. Thoracic Surgery, Am. Bd. Surgery (pediatric surgery). Intern in surgery N.Y. Hosp., N.Y.C., 1950-51; asst. resident surgeon N.Y. Hosp., 1951-56, resident surgeon, 1956-57, asst. attending surgeon, 1958-60, assoc. attending surgeon, 1960-66, surgeon in charge pediatric surgery, 1960, attending surgeon, 1966—; practice medicine specializing in surgery; clin. asso. prof. surgery Cornell U. Med. Coll., 1963-72, prof., 1972—. Author: Surgery in the Ambulatory Child, 1961, Principles of Surgery in the First Six Months of Life, 1976, Atlas of Surgery in the First Six Months of Life, 1977; contbr. articles to profl. jours. Served to capt. USAAF, 1942-46. Fellow A.C.S., Am. Coll. Chest Physicians; mem. Harvey Soc., Pan Am. Med. Assn., Soc. Univ. Surgeons, Am. Acad. Pediatrics, Am. Fedn. for Clin. Research, Internat. Cardiovascular Soc., Am. Surg. Assn., Am. Assn. Thoracic Surgery, Soc. for Surgery Alimentary Tract, Am. Soc. Artificial Internat. Organs, Am. Acad. Pediatrics, Assn. Advancement Med. Instrumentation, Soc. Thoracic Surgeons, Internat. Soc. Surgery, N.Y. Gastroent. Soc., N.Y. Acad. Sci., N.Y. Cardiovascular Soc., N.Y. Acad. Medicine, N.Y. Soc. Thoracic Surgery, N.Y. Pediatric Soc., Med. Soc. County N.Y., Queens Coll. Alumni Assn. (gov. 1962—), Sigma Xi. Patentee in field. Home: 435 E 70th St New York NY 10021-5342 Office: 525 E 68th St New York NY 10021-4873 *My life is based on the principles of doing as much for others as possible and doing no harm; to offer advice only when asked; to apply myself unstintingly, but not selfishly, to my work; to learn from my mistakes; to strive for perfection; and to always have a project and a dream.*

REDRUELLO, ROSA INCHAUSTEGUI, municipal official; b. Havana, Cuba, Dec. 6, 1951; came to U.S., 1961, naturalized, 1971; d. Julio Lorenzo and Laudelina (Vazquez) Inchaustegui; m. John Robert Redruello, Dec. 14, 1972; 1 child, Michelle. AA, Miami-Dade Community Coll., 1972; BS, Fla. Internat. U., 1974. Cert. systems profl. With Fla. Power & Light Co., Miami, 1975-81, records analyst, 1981-84, sr. records analyst, 1984-87, office mgr. Miami Beach Sanitation Dept., 1987—; exec. Mcpl. Dept., 1986-89; police officer patrol divsn. Miami Police Dept., 1989-91, narcotics divsn., 1991—; mem. spl. task force Drug Enforcement Adminstrn. HDTA Group 1, 1994-97; cons. United Bus. Records, Miami, 1985—. Editor South Fla. Record newsletter, 1983-86; editor, producer Files Mgmt. video tape, 1984-85. Rotary Club scholar, 1970. Mem. Assn. Records Mgrs. and Adminstrs. (chpt. chmn. bd. 1985—, chpt. mem. of yr. 1985), Assn. for Info. and Image Mgmt., Exec. Female, Nuclear Info. and Records Mgmt. Assn. (Appreciation award 1985). Republican. Roman Catholic. Avocations: swimming, jazzercise, reading. Office: Miami Beach Police Dept 1100 Washington Ave Miami FL 33139-4612

REDSTONE, DANIEL AARON, architect; b. Detroit, Apr. 24, 1942; s. Louis Gordon and Ruth Roslyn (Rosenbaum) R.; m. Barbara Osten, June 29, 1980; children—Adam, Carly. BArch, U. Mich., 1965, M.B.A., 1967. Registered architect, Mich. Architect., Chair Redstone Tiseo Architects, 1996—; mem. bd. dirs. AIA-Mich., 1988-94, Nat. Coun. Archtl. Reg. Bds., Mich. Bd. Architects, 1992—, Mich. Bd. Engrs., 1994-97, NCCJ Interfaith Roundtable (Detroit chpt.). Jewish. Avocations: raquet sports. Home: 3347 Bloomfield Shore West Bloomfield MI 48323-3303 Office: 29201 Telegraph Rd Ste 400 Southfield MI 48034-7647

REDSTONE, LOUIS GORDON, architect; b. Poland, Mar. 16, 1903; came to U.S., 1923; s. Abraham Aaron and Anna (Gordon) Routenstein; m. Ruth R. Rosenbaum, June 25, 1939; children: Daniel Aaron, Eliel Gordon. BS in Architecture, U. Mich., 1929; MArch, Cranbrook Acad. Arts, 1948. Pvt. practice architecture Israel, 1933-37; founder Louis G. Redstone Assocs. Inc. (architects/engrs./planners), Detroit, 1937-85; pres., chmn. Redstone Assocs. Inc. (architects/engrs./planners), 1985-96; cons. Redstone and Tiseo Architects, 1996—; Del. internat. congresses, Caracas, Tokyo, Moscow and, Buenos Aires; exec. com. Pan Am. Fedn. Architects, 1955-70; juror archtl. and artists exhbns., profl. adviser archtl. competitions sponsored by Dow Chem. Co.; mem. Mich. Commn. on Art in State Bldgs., 1975-82; moderator Internat. Sculpture Conf., Washington, 1990. Author: Art in Architecture, 1968, New Dimensions in Shopping Centers and Stores, 1973, The New Downtown-Rebuilding Business Districts, 1976, Hospitals and Health Care Facilities, 1978, Institutional Buildings, 1980, Public Art-New Directions, 1981, Masonry in Architecture, 1984, From Israeli Pioneer to American Architect, 1989; contbr. articles to profl. mags. and newspapers; one-man shows include Macomb County Art Ctr., Mt. Clemens, Mich., 1992, T'Marra Gallery, Ann Arbor, 1991-93, Livonia (Mich.) Art Ctr., 1993, Detroit Inst. Art, 1993, Cranbrook Acad. Art, 1994; represented in permanent collections Long Beach (Calif.) Mus. Art, Detroit Inst. Art, Cranbrook Acad. Art. Trustee Mich. Found. for Arts; co-chmn. Bus. Consortium for Arts Sculpture Exhbns., Southfield, Mich. Recipient Patron award Mich. Found. for Arts, 1977, Detroit's Disting. Recognition award City Coun., 1993, Disting. Vol. Svc. award City of Southfield, 1993, Mich. Gov.'s Civic Leader award, 1993, Arts Advocate award Wayne State Univ., 1997. Fellow

AIA (pres. Detroit 1965, Gold medal outstanding contbn. to profession, Significant Lifetime Achievement award Detroit chpt. 1993), Mich. Soc. Architects (Robert F. Hastings award for outstanding achievement 1983), Engring. Soc. Detroit, Royal Acad. Fine Arts Netherlands (hon.); mem. Royal Acad. Fine Arts, San Fernando, Spain (corr. academician). Home: 19303 Appoline St Detroit MI 48235-1216 Office: Redstone and Tiseo Architects 29201 Telegraph Rd Ste 400 Southfield MI 48034-7647 *The architect must be a positive force in creating surroundings that enhance and fulfill all human needs, in which the arts become an integral part of man's daily environment. He must implement this approach by studying the specific needs and requirements of those who will use the building. These needs must then be satisfied within an aesthetically designed and functional enclosure that is in harmony with its surroundings. This basic concept must not be limited in application to individual buildings; it must be extended to the wider horizon of the total urban environment.*

REDSTONE, SUMNER MURRAY, entertainment company executive; b. Boston, May 27, 1923; s. Michael and Belle (Ostrovsky) R.; m. Phyllis Gloria Raphael, July 6, 1947; children: Brent Dale, Shari Ellin. B.A., Harvard U., 1944, LL.B., 1947; LLD (hon.), Boston U., 1994; LHD (hon.), N.Y. Inst. Tech., 1996. Bar: Mass. 1947, U.S. Ct. Appeals (1st cir.) 1948, U.S. Ct. Appeals (8th cir.) 1950, U.S. Ct. Appeals (9th cir.) 1948, D.C. 1951, U.S. Supreme Ct. 1952. Law sec. U.S. Ct. Appeals for 9th Circuit, San Francisco, 1947-48; instr. law and labor mgmt. U. San Francisco, 1947; spl. asst. to U.S. Atty. Gen., Washington, 1948-51; ptnr. Ford, Bergson, Adams, Borkland & Redstone, Washington, 1951-54; pres., CEO Nat. Amusements Inc., Dedham, Mass., 1967—, chmn. bd., 1986—; chmn. bd. Viacom, Inc., N.Y.C., 1987—; prof. Boston U. Law Sch., 1982, 85-86; bd. dirs. TV Acad. Arts and Scis. Found.; vis. prof. Brandeis U., Waltham, Mass.; lectr. Harvard Law Sch., Cambridge, Mass.; Judge on Kennedy Libr. Found., (sel. comm. John F. Kennedy Profile in Courage award). Chmn. met. divsn. NE Combined Jewish Philanthropies, Boston, 1963; mem. exec. bd. Combined Jewish Philanthropies of Greater Boston; mem. corp. New Eng. Med. Ctr., 1967—, Mass. Gen. Hosp. Corp.; trustee Children's Cancer Rsch. Found.; founding trustee Am. Cancer Soc.; chmn. Am. Cancer Crusade, State of Mass., 1984-86; Art Lending Libr.; sponsor Boston Mus. Sci.; chmn. Jimmy Fund Found., 1960; v.p., mem. exec. com. Will Rogers Meml. Fund; bd. dirs. Boston Arts Festival; bd. overseers Dana Farber Cancer Ctr., Boston Mus. Fine Arts; mem. presdl. adv. com. on arts John F. Kennedy Libr. Found., also judge ann. John F. Kennedy Profile in Courage Award com. 1st lt. AUS, 1943-45. Decorated Army Commendation medal; named 1 of 10 Outstanding Young Men in New Eng., Boston Jr. C. of C., 1958; recipient William J. German Human Rels. award Am. Jewish Com. Entertainment/Comm. Divsn., 1977, Silver Shingle award Boston U. Law Sch., 1985, Variety New Eng. Humanitarian award, 1989, Golden Plate award Am. Acad. Achievement, 1993, 32d Ann. Salute to Excellence Program, 1993, Bus. Excellence award U. So. Calif. Sch. Bus. Adminstrn., 1994, The Stephen S. Wise award The Am. Jewish Congress, 1994, Man of Yr. award MIPCOM, the Internat. Film and Programme Market for TV, Video, Cable and Satellite, 1994, The Legends in Leadership award Emory U., 1995, Allan K. Jonas Lifetime Achievement award Am. Cancer Soc., 1995, Humanitarian award Variety Club Internat., 1995, Expeditioner's award N.Y.C. Outward Bound Ctr., 1996, Patron Arts award Songwriter's Hall Fame, 1996, Vision 21 award N.Y. Inst. Tech., 1996; named Communicator of Yr., B'nai B'rith Comm./Cinema Lodge, 1980, Man of Yr., Entertainment Industries Divsn. of UJA Fedn., 1988, Pioneer of Yr., Motion Picture Pioneers, 1991, Grad. of Yr., Boston Latin Sch., 1989, Honoree 7th ann. fundraiser Montefiore Med. Ctr., 1995, Hall of Fame award Broadcasting and Cable mag., 1995. Mem. ABA, Nat. Assn. Theatre Owners (chmn. bd. dirs. 1965-66, exec. comm. 1995—), Theatre Owners Am. (asst. pres. 1960-63, pres. 1964-65), Motion Picture Pioneers (bd. dirs.), Boston Bar Assn., Mass. Bar Assn., Harvard Law Sch. Assn., Am. Judicature Soc., Masons, Univ. Club, Harvard Club. Home: 98 Baldpate Hill Rd Newton MA 02159-2825 Office: Nat Amusements Inc PO Box 9126 Dedham MA 02027-9126

REDWAY, ALAN ARTHUR SYDNEY, Canadian legislator, lawyer; b. Toronto, Ont., Can., Mar. 11, 1935; s. Alan Edwin Sydney and Phyllis May (Turner) R.; m. Mary Louise Harvey, Apr. 21, 1962; children: Kimberley Ann, Andrea Elizabeth. B. Commerce, U. Toronto, 1958; LLB, Osgoode Hall, Toronto, 1961; Diploma of Applied Arts and Scis. (hon.), Centennial Coll., Toronto, 1985. Bar: Ont. 1963; apptd. Queen's Counsel, 1977. Ptnr. Frost & Redway, Toronto, 1966-84, Redway Cooney & Roherty, Toronto, 1984-87, Redway & Butler, Toronto, 1987-89, 92—; M.P. Ho. of Commons, Ottawa, Ont., 1984-93, min. state for housing, 1989-91, chmn. spl. rev. com. on Employment Equity Act, 1991-92; vice chmn. Aboriginal affairs com., 1992-93. Recipient Hon. Diploma of Applied Arts and Tech., Centennial Coll., Toronto, 1985. Mem. Leaside Lions Club (pres. 1971-72). Progressive Conservative. Avocations: cross country skiing, gardening. Office: Ste 4086, 3080 Yonge St, Toronto, ON Canada M4N 3N1*

REDWINE, JOHN NEWLAND, physician; b. Pratt, Kans., Oct. 28, 1950; s. Albert Herold and Joyce Nadean (Durall R.; m. Barbara Ann Bomgaars, Dec. 27, 1975; children: John Newland II, William Merritt, Adam Boone. BA with honors, U. Kans., 1972; cert. med. technology, U. Tex. at Houston, 1974; DO, U. Health Scis., Kansas City, Mo., 1978. Diplomate Am. Bd. of Family Practice. Intern U. Hosp., Ctr. for Health Scis., Kansas City, Mo., 1978-79; family practice resident Siouxland Med. Edn. Found., Sioux City, Iowa, 1979-81; med. dir. Morningside Family Practice, Sioux City, Iowa, 1981-95; sr. v.p. med. affairs St. Luke's Health Sys., Inc., Sioux City, Iowa, 1995—; sr. aviation med. examiner FAA, 1979-95; clin. lectr. Iowa U. Coll. Medicine, Iowa City, 1983-95; past pres. Siouxland Med. Edn. Found., 1982—; past chmn. family practice St. Luke's Regional Med. Ctr., Sioux City, Iowa, pres. elect, 1993-95. Contbr. articles to profl. jours. V.p. dist. activities Prairie Gold Area coun. Boy Scouts Am. (Silver Beaver award, 1997), Sioux City; bd. dirs. Sioux City Cmty. Sch. Dist., 1994-97; elected 2d dist. Iowa Senate, 1996-2001. Recipient achievement award, Upjohn Pharm. Co., Kansas City, 1978, Silver Beaver award Praire Gold Area Coun., Boy Scouts Am., 1997. Fellow Am. Acad. Family Physicians; mem. AMA, Iowa Med. Soc., Woodbury Med. Soc. (past pres.), Flying Physicians Assn. Republican. Methodist. Avocations: flying, politics. Office: St Luke's Health Sys Inc 2720 Stone Park Blvd Sioux City IA 51104-3734

REDWINE, ROBERT PAGE, physicist, educator; b. Raleigh, N.C., Dec. 3, 1947; s. Robert Word and Hazel Virginia (Green) R.; m. Jacqueline Nina Hewitt, Nov. 22, 1986; children: Keith Hewitt, Jonathan Hewitt. AB, Cornell U., 1969; PhD, Northwestern U., 1973. Rsch. assoc. Los Alamos (N.Mex.) Nat. Lab, 1973-77, staff sci., 1977-79; rsch. assoc. U. Berne, Switzerland, 1974-75; asst. prof. physics MIT, Cambridge, Mass., 1979-82, assoc. prof., 1982-89, prof., 1989—, dir. lab. nuclear sci., 1992—; cons. Los Alamos Nat. Lab., 1980—. Contbr. articles to profl. jours. Fellow AAAS, Am. Phys. Soc. Office: MIT Lab Nuclear Sci Bldg 26-505 Cambridge MA 02139

REEB, PATRICIA A., nursing educator, administrator; b. Springfield, Ohio. BSN, Edgecliff Coll., 1958; MSN, Case Western Res. U., 1971; EdD, U. Cin., 1981. RN/BSN coord. Coll. Mt. St. Joseph (Ohio); cons. Sacred Heart Coll., Belmont, N.C.; asst. prof. U. Cin.; chairperson dept. nursing Coll. Mt. St. Joseph; dir. edn., aging svcs. Mercy Health System, Cin.; dir. mission svcs. Mercy St. Theresa Ctr., Cin. Mem. Ohio League Nursing (pres. 1982-84), SWONA (program chair 1988-89), OCLN (bd. dirs. southwestern Ohio action group). Home: 3107 Epworth Ave Cincinnati OH 45211-7008 Office: Mercy St Theresa Ctr 7010 Rowan Hill Dr Cincinnati OH 45227-3380

REECE, E. ALBERT, obstetrician, gynecologist, perinatologist; b. Spanishtown, Jamaica, Jan. 3, 1950; came to U.S., 1969; s. Wilfred Anderson Reece and Daisy Lucinda (Price) Reece Batten; m. Sharon Andrea Blake, July 28, 1974; children: Kelie, Brynne, Sharon-Andrea II. BS with honors, L.I. U., 1973; MD, NYU, 1978; ob/gyn specialty diploma, Columbia U., 1982; maternal-fetal subspecialty diploma, Yale U., 1984. Diplomate Am. Bd. Ob-Gyn.; bd. cert. maternal-fetal medicine. Intern, resident Columbia U., Presbyn. Med. Ctr., N.Y.C., 1978-82; materal-fetal medicine fellow Yale U. Sch. Medicine, 1982-84; asst. prof. ob-gyn Yale U. Sch. Medicine, New Haven, 1984-87, assoc. prof. ob-gyn, 1987-90; prof., chmn. ob-gyn Temple U. Sch. Medicine, Phila., 1991—. Co-editor Diabetes Mellitus in Pregnancy: Principles and Practice, 1st edit., 1988, 2nd edit., 1995, Medicine of the Fetus and Mother, 1992, A Study Guide for Medicine of the Fetus and Mother, 1992, A Handbook of Medicine of the Fetus and Mother, 1995; co-author: Fundamentals in Obstetric and Gynecologic Ultrasonography, 1993; contbr. articles, abstract to profl. jours. in excess of 250. Mem. sci. adv. com. March of Dimes, 1993—; mem. sci. adv. bd. NIH-DC Infant Mortality Initiative, 1993—; mem. adv. com. Nat. Inst. Child Health and Human Diseases, NIH, 1994—; trustee Reading Rehab. Hosp., 1992—; mem. bioeffects com. AIUM, 1992-95. Grantee March of Dimes, 1985-87, Friedman Found., 1990-92, William Penn Found., 1989-93, Am. Diabetes Assn., 1991-93, NIH, 1992—. Fellow Am. Coll. Ob-Gyn., Coll. Physicians Phila.; mem. Am. Diabetes Assn. (coun. on diabetes in pregnancy), Am. Inst. Ultrasound in Medicine, Hellenic Perinatal Soc. Greece (hon.), Nat. Med. Assn. (exec. com. 1987-88, chmn. ob-gyn sect. 1991-93), New Haven Obstet. Soc., Soc. for Gynecol. Investigation, Soc. Perinatal Obstetricians (leader diabetes spl. interest 1992-94, bd. mem. 1995—), Phila. Perinatal Soc. (program chair 1993—), Phila. Obstet. Soc. (mem. coun. 1992-94). Seventh-Day Adventist. Office: Temple U Sch Medicine 3401 N Broad St # 70pd Philadelphia PA 19140-5103

REECE, GERALDINE MAXINE, elementary education educator; b. L.A., May 13, 1917; d. Charles Kenneth and Bertha (Austin) Ballou; m. Thomas Charles Bauman, Aug. 16, 1942 (div. Oct. 1971); children: Thomas Charles Bauman, Jr., Kathleen Marie Bauman Messenger, Stephen Kenneth Bauman; m. Wilbert Wallingford Reece, Nov. 3, 1973 (dec. 1988). AA, L.A. City Coll., 1942; BA, U. So. Calif., L.A., 1966. Specialist tchr. in reading, elem. edn. Tchr. Archdiocese of L.A., Altadena, Calif., 1962-66; master tchr. Alhambra (Calif.) City and H.S., 1966-79, writer multicultural component early childhood edn. program. Author poetry. Mem. San Gabriel Child Care Task Force, 1984-86; mem. steering com. West San Gabriel Valley Cmty. Awareness Forum, 1985-87; past pres. women's divsn., bd. dirs. San Gabriel C. of C., 1989-90, publicity chair, 1994-95, 96-97 (Woman of the Chair, 1996, 97, 98); mem. sch. site and facilities com. Sch. Dist. Unification, San Gabriel, 1992-93; mem. task force Episcopal Parish/Healing Our Cities, San Gabriel, 1992-93; docent San Gabriel Mus., 1989, 92-93. Recipient Exceptional Svc. awards Am. Heart Assn., West San Gabriel Valley, 1990, 91, 93, 94, 95, Dedicated Svc. award San Gabriel C. of C., 1989, Outstanding and Dedicated Cmty. Svc. award Fedn. Cmty. Coord. Couns., San Gabriel, 1986, 87, others, Woman of Yr. award City of San Gabriel, 1994, Diamond Homer trophy Famous Poet Soc., 1995, 96. Mem. AAUW (Money Talks sect. chairperson 1981, 82, corr. sec./treas. Alhambra-San Gabriel 1982-83, 83-85), Calif. Ret. Tchrs. Assn. (past pres. 1989-91, Outstanding Svc. plaque 1994), Nat. Soc. DAR (3rd vice regent 1994, 95, 96-97, 97—), Pasadena Women's City Club, St. Francis Guild, San Gabriel Ret. Tchrs. (pres. 1985-89, cmty. rep. 1990, 91, 92, 93, 94, 95, 96, 97), San Gabriel Hist. Assn., San Gabriel Cmty. Coord. Coun. (pres. 1986, 1st v.p. 1997—). Democrat. Episcopalian. Avocations: reading, Bridge, writing poetry, stitchery.

REECE, JOE WILSON, engineering company executive; b. Elkin, N.C., Mar. 1, 1935; s. Thad Marshall and Anita (Hobson) R.; m. Nancy Lee Fletcher, Aug. 25, 1955; children: James Thad, Joel Wade; m. Ellen Frances West, Nov. 21, 1992; 1 child, Joe Wilson Jr. B in Nuclear Engring., N.C. State U., 1957, MS, 1961; PhD, U. Fla., 1963. Registered profl. engr., Ala. Instr. engring. mechanics N.C. State U., Raleigh, 1958-61; asst. prof. mech. engring. Auburn (Ala.) U., 1963-67, assoc. prof., 1967-76, prof., 1976-85; dep. dir. operating reactors div. U.S. Nuclear Regulatory Commn., 1976-78; pres. Reece Engring. Assocs., 1985—; cons. U.S. Army Missile Command, Combustion Engring. Co., Westinghouse, others. Campus drive chmn. Auburn United Fund, 1969, chmn. bd., 1971. Named Disting. Classroom Tchr. N.C. State U. Sch. Engring., 1961, Outstanding Faculty mem. Auburn U. Sch. Engring., 1965, 73. Mem. Am. Soc. Engring. Edn. (pres. SE sect. 1977), ASME, Ala. Acad. Sci., Scabbard and Blade, Sigma Xi, Phi Kappa Phi, Tau Beta Pi, Phi Eta Sigma, Sigma Pi Sigma, Theta Tau, Pi Tau Sigma. Methodist (lay leader 1967, chmn. trustees 1972). Club: Civitan (Auburn) (pres. 1968). Home: 402 N Carolina Ave Boonville NC 27011-9701

REECE, MARILYN KING, college dean; b. Cullman, Ala., July 7, 1949; d. John McCarley and Florence Augusta (Freeman) King; m. John Robert Williamson, Aug. 23, 1970 (div. 1987); children: Joan King, Rachel King; m. David Ronald Reece, Apr. 15, 1995. BA, U. Ala., Tuscaloosa, 1971, MA, 1972. Instr. English, N.E. Ala. C.C., Rainsville, 1973-89, dean extended day, 1989—. Mem. AAUW, MLA, NEA, Nat. Coun. Tchrs. English, Conf. on Coll. Composition and Comm., Ala. Assn. for Women in Edn. Democrat. Office: NE Ala CC PO Box 159 Rainsville AL 35986-0159

REECE, MAYNARD FRED, artist, author; b. Arnolds Park, Iowa, Apr. 26, 1920; s. Waldo H. and Inez V. (Latson) R.; m. June Carman, Apr. 7, 1946; children: Mark A., Brad D. Privately educated. Artist Meredith Pub. Co., Des Moines, 1938-40; artist, asst., mus. dir. Iowa Dept. History and Archives, Des Moines, 1940-50. Artist: Fish and Fishing, 1963, Waterfowl of Iowa, 1943; watercolor Trout, Saturday Evening Post (award of Distinctive Merit 1962); watercolors 73 Fish, Life mag. (cert. of merit 1955); print of Water's Edge Canada Geese for Am. Artist Collection, Am. Artist Mag., 1985; author, artist: The Waterfowl Art of Maynard Reece, 1985, The Upland Bird Art of Maynard Reece, 1997. Chmn. Gov.'s Com. Conservation of Outdoor Resource, 1963-64; trustee Iowa Natural Heritage Found., Des Moines, 1979—; hon. trustee Ducks Unltd., Inc., 1983—; trustee J.N. "Ding" Darling Conservation Found., Inc., Des Moines, 1962—. Served with AUS, 1943-45. Recipient awards for duck stamps and others Dept. Interior, 1948, 51, 59, 69, 71; recipient award Govt. Bermuda, 1963, award Iowa Conservation Commn., 1972, 77, 80, 81, award Fish and Game Commn., Little Rock, 1982, 88, award Tex. Parks and Wild Life Dept., 1983, award Nat. Fish & Wildlife Found., 1988, award Wash. State Dept. Wildlife, 1989; named Artist of Yr. Ducks Unltd. Inc., 1973; chosen Master Artist 1989, Leigh Yawkey Woodson Art Mus., Wausau, Wis., 1989. Mem. Nat. Audubon Soc., Nat. Wildlife Fedn., Izaak Walton League Am. (hon. pres. 1974-75). Home and Office: 5315 Robertson Dr Des Moines IA 50312-2133

REECE, ROBERT WILLIAM, zoological park administrator; b. Saginaw, Mich., Jan. 21, 1942; s. William Andrews and Mary Barbara (Murphy) R.; m. Jill Whetstone, Aug. 21, 1965; children: William Clayton, Gregory Scott, Mark Andrews. B.S., Mich. State U., 1964; postgrad., U. West Fla., 1969-71, U. South Fla., 1974-76. Dir. Northwest Fla. Zool. Gardens, Pensacola, Fla., 1970-72; zool. dir. Lion Country Ga., Stockbridge, 1972-73; asst. dir. Salisbury Zoo, Md., 1976-77; dir. zoology Wild Animal Habitat, Kings Island, Ohio, 1977-92; exec. dir. The Wilds Internat. Ctr. for Preservation of Wild Animals, Columbus, Ohio, 1992—. Assoc. editor: Sci. Jour. Zoo Biology, 1982—. Lt. USN, 1964-69, Korea. Profl. fellow Am. Assn. Zool. Parks and Aqariums; mem. Cin. Wildlife Rsch. Fedn., Am. Soc. Mammalogists, Animal Behavior Soc., Captive Breeding Specialist Group, Species Survival Commn., Internat. Union for Conservation of Nature and Natural Resources. Republican. Episcopalian. Home: 11784 Canterbury Ave Pickerington OH 43147-8490 Office: The Wilds 1400 International Rd Cumberland OH 43732

REECE, THOMAS L., manufacturing executive. Pres., CEO Dover Corp., N.Y.C. Office: Dover Corp 280 Park Ave New York NY 10017-1216*

REECE-PORTER, SHARON ANN, global education educator; b. Cin., Nov. 28, 1953; d. Edward and Claudia (Ownes) Reece; divorced, 1981; children: Erika Lynn, Melanie Joyce. BS in Textiles & Clothing, Edgecliff Coll., 1975; cert. clerical computer, So. Ohio Coll., 1984; MEd in Gen. Edn., SUNY, Buffalo, 1994; postgrad. in Adult Edn. Global Studies, Nova U., 1994—; EdD in Global Edn. (hon.), Australian Inst. Coordinated Rsch., Victoria, 1995. Cert. tchr., Ohio. Dept. supr., asst. buyer Mabley & Carew, Cin., 1975-76; claims adjuster Allstate Ins. Co., Cin., 1976-78; sales merchandiser Ekco Houseware, Cin., 1979-80; sales rep. Met. Life Inc., Cin., 1981-83; info. processing specialist GPA/Robert Half/Word Source, Cin., Dallas, 1985-87; tchr. adult edn. Princeton City Schs., Cin., 1984-90; with Rainbow Internat. Non-Profit Adult Ednl. Rsch. Ctr., Honolulu, 1990—; edn. specialist rsch. found. SUNY, Buffalo, 1993; prof. computer sci. So. Ohio Tech. and Bus. Coll., Cin., 1986-90; computer software tng. cons., 1987-89; part-time tchr. adult GED classes Adult Learning Ctr. Buffalo Bd. Edn., 1994-95; participant Am. Forum for Global Edn., Honolulu. Tutor U.S. div. Internat. Laubach Literacy, Clermont County, Ohio, 1984. Fellow Australian Inst. for Coordinated Rsch. (life); mem. NAFE, ASTD, Internat. DOS Users Group, Am. Ednl. Rsch. Assn., Nat. Assn. Women Bus. Owners, World Assn. Women Entrepreneurs, Assn. Baha'i Studies in Australia, Boston Computer Soc., Cin. Orgn. Data Processing Educators and Trainers, Internat. Platform Assn., Cin. C. of C. (cert. minority supplier devel. coun.). Baha'i. Home: 173 Palmdale Dr Buffalo NY 14221-4006 Office: Rainbow Internat A Global Edn Inst 7954 Transit Rd Ste 253 Buffalo NY 14221-4117

REED, ADAM VICTOR, psychologist, engineer; b. Torun, Poland, Jan. 11, 1946; came to U.S., 1959, naturalized, 1965; s. Henry Kenneth and Eva (Tenenbaum) R.; B.S. in E.E., M.I.T., 1967, M.S. in Biology and M.S. in E.E., 1970; Ph.D., U. Oreg., 1974; m. Barbara Irene Birnbaum, Dec. 26, 1982; 1 child, Halina Brooke. Research programmer Artificial Intelligence Lab., M.I.T., Cambridge, 1965; research engr. Hewlett Packard Co., Palo Alto, Calif., 1966-67; mem. research staff Riverside Research Inst., N.Y.C., 1970-71; postdoctoral fellow, adj. asst. prof. Rockefeller U., N.Y.C., 1974-78; asst. prof., vis. lectr. psychology Grad. Faculty Social and Polit. Sci., New Sch. Social Research, N.Y.C., 1977-82; mem. tech. staff Bell Labs., 1981—; peer rev. referee NSF, others. Sci. and tech. adv. Libertarian Party v.p. candidate Tonie Nathan, 1972; mem. Marlboro Twp. Bd. Edn., N.J., 1994-97. NDEA Title IV fellow, 1967-70; NSF fellow, 1970-73; NIMH Research Service fellow, 1974-77. Mem. N.Y. Acad. Sci., IEEE, Am. Psychol. Assn., Soc. Engring. Psychologists, Assn. Computing Machinery, Am. Soc. Cybernetics, AAAS, Sigma Xi, Tau Beta Pi, Eta Kappa Nu. Libertarian. Achievements include patents in field; first implementation of steepest descent, first statistically adaptive user interface, first switch-based facsimile server; research on experimental psychology-response signals method; contbr. articles to profl. jours.

REED, ALFRED, composer, conductor; b. N.Y.C., Jan. 25, 1921; s. Carl Mark and Elizabeth (Strasser) Friedman; m. Marjorie Beth Deley, June 20, 1941; children: Michael Carlson, Richard Judson. Student, Juilliard Sch. Music, 1946-48; MusB, Baylor U., 1955, MusM, 1956; MusD, Internat. Conservatory of Music, Lima, Peru, 1968. Exec. editor Hansen Publs., N.Y.C., 1955-66; prof. music U. Miami (Fla.) Sch. Music, 1966-93. Composer, arranger, N.Y.C., 1941-60; condr. Tri-State Music Festival, Okla., 1956-57, 60-66, 70, 73, Midwest Nat. Band Clinic, 1960-91, Bemidji (Minn.) Summer Music Camp, 1970-71, 75, Mid-East Instrumental Music Conf., Pitts., 1957-60, Can. Music Educators Assn., Edmonton, Alta., 1975; composer: Russian Christmas Music, 1944, Symphony for Brass and Percussion, 1952, Rhapsody for Viola and Orch, 1956, Choric Song, 1966, Titania's Nocturne, 1967, A Festival Prelude, 1962, Passacaglia, 1968, Music for Hamlet, 1973, Armenian Dances, 1974-75, Punchinello, Overture to a Romantic Comedy, 1974, Testament of an American, 1974, First Suite for Band, 1975, Othello, A Symphonic Portrait in Five Scenes, 1976, Prelude and Capriccio, 1977, Second Symphony, 1978, Siciliana Notturno, 1978, Second Suite for Band, 1978, The Enchanted Island, 1979, The Hounds of Spring, 1980, Third Suite for Band, 1981, Queenston Overture, 1982, Viva Musica!, 1983, A Little Concert Suite, 1983, El Camino Real, 1985, Centennial!, 1985, Three Revelations from the Lotus Sutra, 1985, Golden Jubilee, 1986, A Christmas Celebration, 1986, Praise Jerusalem!, 1987, Third Symphony, 1988, Eventide, 1988, Golden Eagle, 1989, Curtain Up!, 1990, A Springtime Celebration, Hymn Variants, 1991, With Trumpets and Drums, 1991, Concertino for Marimba and Winds, 1991, 4th Symphony, 1992, Fourth Suite for Band, 1993, Evolutions, A Concert Overture, 1993, 5th Symphony, 1994, Fifth Suite for Band, 1995, also others. Served with AUS, 1942-46. Mem. ASCAP, Am. Bandmasters Assn., Am. Fedn. Musicians, Nat. Band Assn., Music Educators Nat. Conv. Home: 1405 Ancona Ave Miami FL 33146-1903 *As a composer, my desire has always been to achieve both a depth and intensity of communication between myself, my music and my audiences that would enable me to express something of value as regards myself and my time that, hopefully, would give rise to a deeply felt response on the part of my fellow human beings. I suppose this is true of the arts in general, and all artists, regardless of their medium of expression, but music, for me at least, has been the supreme expression of all time, for all men.*

REED, A(LFRED) BYRON, retired apparel and textile manufacturing company; b. Indpls., June 30, 1916; s. Alfred Lumpkin and Myrtle (Wood) R.; m. Mary Ellen Myers, Sept. 1, 1950; 1 child, Charles W. B.S., Butler U., 1939; postgrad., U. Chgo., 1946-47. Asst. brokerage mgr. Conn. Gen. Life Ins. Co., Chgo., 1939-41; sales mgr., mktg. mgr., asst. gen. mgr. Vassar Co., Chgo., 1946-57; gen. mgr. women's div. Munsingwear, Inc., Mpls., 1958-66; pres., chief exec. officer Munsingwear, Inc., 1966-79, chmn., 1979-81, also dir.; dir., trust com., exec. com. 1st Nat. Bank Mpls., Hoerner Waldorf Co., St. Paul, 1973-77, Murphy Motor Freight; mem. mgmt.-labor textile adv. com. U.S. Dept. Commerce. Chmn. Nat. Alliance Businessmen, Mpls., l41972; mem. Adv. Council U.S.-Japan Econ. Relations, Washington, also exec. com.; adviser Council Fin. Aid to Edn.; chmn. U.S. Savs. Bond Drive, 1975-76; bd. dirs. Better Bus. Bur. Mpls., 1973-74, Minn. Pvt. Coll. Fund, Mpls. YMCA; trustee Butler U. Served to lt. USNR, 1942-46. Mem. Am. Apparel Mfrs. Assn. (chmn. bd. dirs., exec. com.), U.S. C. of C. (internat. policy com., internat. trade subcom.), Mpls. C. of C. (dir.), Minneapolis Club, Minikahda Club, Mission Viejo Country Club, Indian Wells Country Club, Phi Delta Theta. Republican. Episcopalian. Home: 76-750 Iroquois Dr Indian Wells CA 92210-9019

REED, ALFRED DOUGLAS, university director; b. Bristol, Tenn., July 18, 1928; s. Roy Theodore and Elizabeth Brown (Tuft) R.; m. Emily Joyce Freeman, Mar. 18, 1950; children: Roy Frederick, Robert Douglas, David Clark, Timothy Wayne, Joseph William. AB, Erskine Coll., Due West, S.C., 1949. Reporter Citizen-Times, Asheville, N.C., 1949-51, city editor, 1953-60, mng. editor, 1962-63, assoc. editor, 1963-66, capital corr., 1959-66; asst. editor The Presbyn. Jour., Weaverville, N.C., 1951-52; assoc. editor Shelby (N.C.) Daily Star, 1961-62; dir. pub. info. Western Carolina U., Cullowhee, N.C., 1966-96, asst. to the chancellor, 1996—; cons. Devel. Office, East Carolina U., Greenville, 1980; bd. dirs. Wachovia Bank and Trust Co., Sylva, N.C., 1969—. Author: Prologue, 1968, Decade of Development, 1984, Our Second Century, 1992; exec. editor: Western, The Mag. of Western Carolina University, 1991-96. Mem. Asheville City Bd. Edn., 1958-62; vice chmn. bd. dirs. Sta. WCQS FM, Western N.C. Pub. Radio Inc., Asheville, 1978-88; bd. dirs. Cherokee Hist. Assn., 1985—, Western N.C. Assn. Comtys., 1985—, Jackson County Fund of N.C. Comty. Found., 1991-93; mem. Hunter Libr. Adv. Bd., 1991—, Pack Place Adv. Coun., Asheville, 1991—. Recipient Paul A. Reid Disting. Svc. award Western Carolina U., 1980, Disting. Svc. award, 1996. Mem. Pub. Rels. Assn. Western N.C. (bd. dirs., treas.), Coll. News Assn. Carolinas (bd. dirs. 1968-71, 80-82), Smoky Mountain Host Assn. (bd. dirs., 1st v.p. 1988-96, pres. 1996—). Democrat. Presbyterian. Avocations: travel, stamps, gardening. Home: 310 University Hts Cullowhee NC 28723-9691 Office: Western Carolina U Asst to Chancellor 528 Robinson Cullowhee NC 28723

REED, ANDRE DARNELL, professional football player; b. Allentown, Pa., Jan. 29, 1964. Grad., Kutztown State. Wide receiver Buffalo Bills, N.Y., 1985—. Pro Bowl Selection, 1988-93, Played in Super Bowl XXV, 1990, XXVI, 1991, XXVII, 1992, XXVIII, 1993. Office: Buffalo Bills 1 Bills Dr Orchard Park NY 14127-2237*

REED, BERENICE ANNE, art historian, artist, government official; b. Memphis, Jan. 1, 1934; d. Glenn Andrew and Berenice Marie (Kallaher) R. BFA, St. Mary-of-the-Woods Coll., Ind., 1955; MFA in Painting and Art History, Istituto Pio XII, Villa Schifanoia, Florence, Italy, 1964. Cert. art tchr., Tenn. Comml. artist Memphis Pub. Co., 1955-56; arts adminstr., educator pub. and pvt. instns., Washington, Memphis, 1957-70; arts adminstr. Nat. Park Svc., 1970-73; mem. staff U.S. Dept. of Energy, Washington, 1973-81, U.S. Dept. Commerce, Washington, 1983-84, Exec. Office of the Pres., Office of Mgmt. and Budget, Washington, 1985; with fin. mgmt. svc. U.S. Treasury Dept., Washington, 1985—; cons. on art and architecture in recreation AIA, 1972-73; artist-in-residence St. Mary-of-the-Woods Coll., Ind., 1965; guest lectr. instr. Nat. Sch. Fine Arts, Tegucigalpa, Honduras, 1968; mem. exec. com. Parks, Arts and Leisure Project, Washington, 1972-73; researcher art projects, Washington, 1981-83. Developer (video) In Your Intere$t, 1992; TV interviewer Am. Fin. Skylink satellite programs, 1996, 97. Bd. dirs. Am. Irish Bicentennial Com., 1974-76; advisor Royal Oak Found. Recipient various awards for painting; installed as Dame of Merit, Sacred Mil. Constantinian Order of St. George, 1997. Mem. Soc. Woman Geographers, Nat. Soc. Arts and Letters, Ctr. for Advanced Study in Visual Arts, Art Barn Assn. (bd. dirs. 1973-83), Patrons of the Arts in the Vatican

Mus., Irish Georgian Soc. Roman Catholic. Avocations: photography, performing arts. Home: PO Box 34253 Bethesda MD 20827-0253 Office: Dept Treasury Fin Mgmt Svc 401 14th St SW Washington DC 20227-0001

REED, CATHY LORRAINE, elementary education educator; b. Beckley, W.Va., Sept. 23, 1956; d. Clarence and Beulah mae (Perdue) R. AA, Beckley Coll., 1977; BS in Edn., Concord Coll., Athens, W.Va., 1979; MA, Marshall U., 1989. Cert. tchr. elem. edn. 1-6, reading specialist K-12, W.Va. Tchr. Raleigh County Bd. Edn., Beckley, 1979—. Avocations: sewing, reading, travel. Office: Shady Spring Elem Drawer K Shady Spring WV 25918

REED, CHARLES ALLEN, anthropologist; b. Portland, Oreg., June 6, 1912; s. C. Allen and Gladys (Donohoe) R.; m. Lois Wells, Aug. 18, 1951; children: C. Allen, Robin M., Brian W. Student, Whitman Coll., 1929-30; B.S., U. Oreg., 1937; Ph.D., U. Calif. at Berkeley, 1943. Instr. biology U. Oreg., 1936-37; lectr. anatomy U. Calif. Med. Sch. at Berkeley, 1943; instr. biology Reed Coll., 1943-46; asst. prof. zoology U. Ariz., 1946-49; asst. prof., assoc. prof. zoology U. Ill. Sch. Pharmacy, 1949-54, 55-61; research assoc. anthropology U. Chgo., 1954-55; assoc. prof. biology Yale U., 1961-66; prof. biology and anthropology U. Ill., Chgo., 1966-67; prof. anthropology U. Ill., 1967—, acting head dept., 1967-70; Mem. Catlow Caves archeol. expdn. U. Oreg., 1937; Iraq-Jarmo archeol. expdn. Oriental Inst. U. Chgo., 1954-55; Iranian prehistoric project Oriental Inst., 1960; U. Istanbul-Chgo. Prehistoric project, Turkey, 1970, U. Ill. archeol. expedition to Sinai, 1986; curator mammals and reptiles Peabody Mus., Yale, 1961-66; dir. Yale prehistoric expdn. to Nubia, 1962-65; research asso. vertebrate anatomy Field Mus. Natural History, Chgo., 1966—; mem. U.S. com. Nat. Acad. Scis. for Internat. Union for Quaternary Research, 1967-74. Editor: Origins of Agriculture, 1977; Contbr. articles to profl. jours. Recipient Pomerance award for sci. excellence in archaeology Archaeol. Inst. Am. Fellow Am. Assn. Anthropologists (life), Asso. Current Anthropology, AAAS (life); mem. Am. Soc. Mammalogists (life), Am. Soc. Ichthyologists and Herpetologists (life), Am. Assn. Phys. Anthropology, Am. Soc. Zoologists, Am. Soc. Anatomists, Soc. Study Evolution, Soc. Vertebrate Paleontology, Am. Assn. Quaternary Research, Explorers Club, Chgo. Acad. Scis. (bd. sci. govs.), Chgo. Anthrop. Soc. (pres. 1979-81), Phi Beta Kappa, Sigma Xi (life). Home: 151 N Kenilworth Ave Oak Park IL 60301 Office: U Ill Chgo Dept Anthropology Chicago IL 60607

REED, CHARLES BASS, academic administrator; b. Harrisburg, Pa., Sept. 29, 1941; s. Samuel Ross and Elizabeth (Johnson) R.; m. Catherine A. Sayers, Aug. 22, 1964; children: Charles B. Jr., Susan Allison. BS, George Washington U., 1963, MA, 1964, EdD, 1970; postgrad. Summer Inst. for Chief State Sch. Officers,, Harvard U. Grad Sch. Edn., 1977; D of Pub. Svc. (hon.), George Washington U., 1987; LLD (hon.), Stetson U., 1987; LittD (hon.), Waynesburg Coll., 1988; LHD (hon.), St. Thomas U., 1988. From asst. prof. to assoc. prof. George Washington U., Washington, 1963-70; asst. dir. Nat. Performance-Based Tchr. Edn. Project, Am. Assn. Colls. for Tchr. Edn., Washington, 1970-71; assoc. for planning and coordination Fla. Dept. Edn., Tallahassee, 1971-75, dir. Office Ednl. Planning, Budgeting, and Evaluation, 1975-79; edn. policy coord. Exec. Office of Gov., Tallahassee, 1979-80, dir. legis. affairs, 1980-81, dep. chief of staff, 1981-84, chief of staff, 1984-85; chancellor State Univ. System Fla., Tallahassee, 1985—; Fulbright 50th Anniversary Disting. fellow Peru, 1996; bd. dirs. Fla. Progress Corp., Capital Health Plan; chmn. bd. dirs. Regional Tech. Strategies, Inc.; disting. fellow Fulbright Commn. 50th Anniversary, Peru, 1996. Mem. Coun. for Advancement and Support of Edn., Coun. on Fgn. Rels., Bus.-Higher Edn. Forum, Coun. of 100. Recipient Disting. Alumni award George Washington U., 1987. Mem. Am. Assn. State Colls. and Univs., Am. Assn. for Higher Edn., Am. Coun. on Edn., Fla. Assn. Colls. and Univs., Edn. Commn. of States (exec. com. 1984-87, exec. com. for campus compact project, Disting. Svc. award 1982), So. Regional Ednl. Bd. (vice-chmn. 1988-90, exec. com.), Assn. Governing Bds. of Univs. and Colls., Nat. Assn. State Univs. and Land-Grant Colls., Nat. Assn. Sys. Heads, Golden Key. Democrat. Roman Catholic. Office: State U System Fla Office of Chancellor 325 W Gaines St Tallahassee FL 32399-6557

REED, CHARLES ELI, retired chemist, chemical engineer; b. Findlay, Ohio, Aug. 11, 1913. BS, Case Inst. Tech., 1934; ScD in Chem. Engring., MIT, 1937. Asst. prof. chem. engring. MIT, Cambridge, Mass., 1937-42; rsch. assoc. rsch. lab. GE, 1942-45, engring. mgr. chem. divsn., 1945-52, gen. mgr. silicone products dept., 1952-59, gen. mgr. metall. products dept., 1959-62, v.p., gen. mgr. chem. and metall. divsn., 1962-68, v.p., group exec. components and materials group, 1968-71, sr. v.p. corp. tech., 1971-79; ret., 1979. Recipient Nat. Medal of Technology, U.S. Dept. of Commerce Technology Admin., 191. Fellow AICE, Am. Inst. Chemistst; mem. AAAS, Mat. Acad. Engring., Am. Chem. Soc. Achievements include research in colloid chemistry, high polymers, distillation. Home: 3030 Park Ave Bridgeport CT 06604-1142

REED, CLARENCE RAYMOND, retired association executive; b. Shamokin, Pa., Sept. 23, 1932; s. Benton Howard and Gerda Maude (Hoover) R.; m. Joan Ann Engle, June 25, 1955; children: Ann Elizabeth, Susan Engle. B.A., U. Pa., 1954, M.B.A. with distinction, 1958; grad., Stonier Grad. Sch. Banking, 1969. With Prudential Ins. Co. Am., 1954; with Robert Morris Assos., Phila., 1958-95; asst. sec. Robert Morris Assos., 1959-60, sec.-treas., 1960-74, exec. mgr., 1961-74, exec. v.p., 1974-95, mem. exec. com., 1980-95, pres., 1995—, also dir., 1995; mem. faculty loan mgmt. seminar Ind. U., 1971-72; Chmn. Shares in Edn., 1968. Pres. Council Springfield (Pa.) Twp. Home and Sch. Assns., 1969-70. Served with AUS, 1954-56. Mem. Credit Assn. Delaware Valley, Am. Soc. Assn. Execs., Am. Mgmt. Assn., Cen. Home and Sch. Assn. (pres. 1966-67), Wharton M.B.A. Alumni Assn., Exchequer Club (chancellor 1984-85/Washington). Presbyterian (fin. sec. 1970, 79, ruling elder 1972-74, 83-85, 96—, chmn. 50th anniversary com. 1974, trustee 1977-79). Home: 15 Long Rd Berwyn PA 19312-1211

REED, CONSTANCE LOUISE, materials management and purchasing consultant; b. Point Pleasant, W.Va.; d. John Melvin Supple and Garnet L. Tooley; m. James Wesley Reed Jr., Sept. 20, 1985. Student, Ohio State U., 1974-76, Capital U., 1984-85. Buyer Abex Corp., Columbus, Ohio, 1971-79; maj. component buyer Grumman Corp., Delaware, Ohio, 1979-81; purchasing mgr. Atlantic Richfield (ANATEC), Dublin, Ohio, 1981-85; purchasing agt. Columbus Lodging, Inc., 1986-87, Monitronix Corp., Westerville, Ohio, 1988-89; contracts adminstr. Cellular Communications Inc., Worthington, Ohio, 1989-90; dir. materials mgmt. Fibrebond Corp., Minden, La., 1991-92; v.p. C&P Mgmt. Cons., Powell, Ohio, 1985—. Mem. NAFE, Am. Mgmt. Assn., Nat. Assn. Purchasing Mgmt., Bus. and Profl. Women's Club. Republican. Roman Catholic. Avocations: writing, photography, bear collection. Home: 1166 Highland Dr Columbus OH 43220-4940 Office: C&P Mgmt PO Box 158 Powell OH 43065-0158

REED, CYNTHIA KAY, minister; b. Amarillo, Tex., July 10, 1952; d. Carlos Eugene and Marjorie Marie (Daughetee) R. B of Music Edn., McMurry Coll., Abilene, Tex., 1976; MDiv, Perkins Sch. Theol., Dallas, 1991. Ordained to ministry Meth. Ch., 1989; cert. dir. music. Dir. music and Christian edn. Oakwood United Meth. Ch., Lubbock, Tex., 1978-84; dir. music and Christian edn. 1st United Meth. Ch., Childress, Tex., 1976-78, Littlefield, Tex., 1984-86; intern min. 1st United Meth. Ch., Lubbock, 1989-90, assoc. min., 1990-91; min. Meadow and Ropesville United Meth. Chs., 1991-93, Earth (Tex.) United Meth. Ch., 1993-97, First United Meth. Ch., Colorado City, Tex., 1997—; extern chaplain Meth. Hosp., Lubbock, 1989—, Walk to Emmaus Renewal Movement, Lubbock, 1990—. Com. mem. Life Gift-Organ Donation, Lubbock, 1991; mem. Arthritis Found., Lubbock, 1991. Georgia Harkness scholar Div. Ordained Ministry, 1989. Mem. Christian Educators & Musicians Fellowship, Am. Guild Organists.

REED, D. GARY, lawyer; b. Covington, Ky., June 4, 1949; m. Mary Elizabeth Goetz, May 20, 1972; children: Mark, Stacey. BA, Xavier U., 1971; JD, Catholic U. Am., 1974. Bar: Ohio 1974, Ky. 1975, U.S. Ct. Appeals (6th cir.) 1975, U.S. Dist. Ct. (so. dist.) Ohio 1974, U.S. Dist. Ct. (ea. dist.) Ky. 1977, U.S. Dist. Ct. (we. dist.) Ky. 1980. Law clk. to judge U.S. Dist. Ct. (so. dist.) Ohio, Cin., 1974-75; assoc. Dinsmore & Shohl, Cin., 1976-82, ptnr., 1982-90; dir. legal svcs. Choice Care Health Plans, Inc., Cin., 1991-96; asst. gen. coun., 1996—; asst. sec. Choice Care Found., 1996—. Contbg. author: Woodside, Drug Product Liability, vol. 3, 1987. Mem. ABA, Ky. Bar Assn., Ohio Bar Assn., Nat. Health Lawyers Assn., No. Ky. C. of C. (Leadership award 1988), Greater Cin. Coun. for Epilepsy (bd. dirs. 1990—), Leadership No. Ky. Alumni Assn., The Choice Care Found. (asst. sec. 1996—). Office: Choice Care 655 Eden Park Dr Cincinnati OH 45202-6000

REED, DARWIN CRAMER, health care consultant; b. Artesia, N.Mex., July 24, 1915; s. Darwin W. and Candace (Cramer) R.; m. Martha Gene Thalmann, Aug. 15, 1940; children—Geney Catherine Reed Fuller, Darwin Kim. A.B., Wichita U., 1937; M.D., Washington U., St. Louis, 1941; M.S., U. Pa., 1954. Diplomate: Am. Bd. Urology. Intern St. Francis Hosp., Wichita, Kans., 1941-42; resident St. Francis Hosp., 1946-48, U. Pa. Hosp., Phila., 1952-54, Med. Coll. Va. Hosp., 1954-55; practice medicine Wichita, 1948-52; partner Wichita Urology Group, Kans., 1955-70; dean Coll. Health Related Professions, Wichita State U., 1970-73, v.p. for health edn., 1973-77; prof. surgery, vice chancellor U. Kans. Sch. Medicine, Wichita, 1975-78; sr. v.p. Wesley Med. Center, Wichita, 1978-86; pres. Health Strategies, Inc., 1980-86; exec. dir. Greater Wichita Community Found., 1986-88; program cons. Kans. Health Found., 1989-93; pres. Cramer Reed & Assocs., 1993-95; v.p. sr. initiatives, Columbia-Wesley Med. Ctr., 1995—; mem. Kans. Bd. Healing Arts, 1964-67; chmn. dean's com. Wichita VA Hosp., 1975-78. Chmn. bd. trustees Wichita State U., 1966-68. Lt. col. M.C., USAAF, 1942-46. Fellow A.C.S.; mem. AMA, Pan Am. Med. Assn., Am. Urologic Assn., Am. Cancer Soc. (pres. Kans. div. 1960-61, 65-66). Methodist. Home: 7520 E 21st St N Apt 22 Wichita KS 67206-1086

REED, DAVID ANDREW, foundation executive; b. Butler, Pa., Feb. 24, 1933; s. Sherman W. and Caroline (Janner) R.; m. Virginia Rogers, Dec. 1, 1956; children: Kristine Lynn, Katherine Louise, Elizabeth Anne, Amy Janner. A.B., Allegheny Coll., 1955; M.S., U. Pitts., 1961. Diplomate: Sch. Pub. Health, Columbia U. Adminstrv. resident Titusville (Pa.) Hosp., 1959, Cin. Gen. Hosp., 1960-61; asst. adminstr. Warren (Pa.) Gen. Hosp., 1961-62, Western Pa. Gen. Hosp., Pitts., 1962-63; with Cin. Gen. Hosp., 1963-69, adminstr., 1964-69; asso. prof. hosp. adminstrn. U. Cin. Coll. Medicine, 1966-69; preceptor program med. and hosp. adminstrn. U. Pitts. Grad. Sch. Pub. Health, 1966-69; pres. Lenox Hill Hosp., N.Y.C., 1969-78; v.p., chief exec. officer Good Samaritan Hosp., Phoenix, 1978-82; pres. SamCor/Samaritan Health Service, Phoenix, 1982-89; pres., chief exec. officer The Samaritan Found., Phoenix, 1989, St. Joseph Health System, Orange, Calif., 1990-95; pres. DAR Consulting Group, Dana Point, 1995—; instr.; past pres. Greater Cin. Hosp. Council, Phoenix Regional Hosp. Council; bd. govs. Greater N.Y. Hosp. Assn.; chmn. Am. Hosp. Assn., also trustee; cons. Hosp. Devel. and Research Inst. Contbr. articles to profl. jours. Bd. dirs. Urban League Cin. Served with AUS, 1955-57. Fellow Am. Coll. Hosp. Adminstrs.; mem. Catalina Island Yacht Club, Dana West Yacht Club, Phi Gamma Delta. Presbyterian. Club: Marbella Country. Office: DAR Cons Grp 24681 La Plz Ste 240 Dana Point CA 92629-2563

REED, DAVID BENSON, bishop; b. Tulsa, Feb. 16, 1927; s. Paul Spencer and Bonnie Frances (Taylor) R.; m. Susan Henry Riggs, Oct. 30, 1954 (div.); children: Mary, Jennifer, David, Sarah, Catherine; m. Catherine Camp Luckett, Apr. 15, 1984. A.B., Harvard U., 1948; M.Div., Va. Theol. Sem., 1951, D.D., 1964; D.D., U. of South, 1972, Episc. Theol. Sem., Ky., 1985. Ordained priest Episcopal Ch., 1952; missionary priest in Panama and Colombia, 1951-58; with Nat. Ch. Exec. Office, 1958-61; mission priest S.D., 1961-63; bishop of Colombia, 1964-72, Ecuador, 1964-70; bishop coadjutor Diocese of Ky., Louisville, 1972-74; bishop of Ky. Diocese of Ky., 1974-94; asst. bishop of Conn. Episcopal Diocese of Conn., Hartford, 1994-95; 1st pres. Anglican Council Latin Am., 1969-72; chmn. standing commn. on ecumenical relations Episcopal Ch., 1979-82; pres. Ky. Coun. Chs., 1988-91; mem. governing bd. Nat. Coun. of Chs. of Christ in U.S.A., 1982-91, mem. exec. com., 1985-91, sec., 1988-91; Anglican co-chmn. Anglican Orthodox Theol. Cons., 1984-94. Bd. dirs. Alliant Health Systems (formerly Norton Kosair Children's Hosp.), Louisville, 1979-94; trustee U. of the South, 1972—, regent, 1979-82; chmn. Louisville United Against Hunger, 1980-84, 86-87; chmn. Presiding Bishop's Com. on Interfaith Rels., 1991—. Mem. Harvard Club of Western Ky. (pres. 1992-94). Democrat. Home: 5226 Moccasin Trl Louisville KY 40207-1634

REED, DAVID FREDRICK, artist; b. San Diego, Jan. 20, 1946; s. David Fredrick II and Beverly (Behl) R.; m. Lillian Ball, June 28, 1986; 1 child previous marriage, John. Student, Skowhegan (Maine) Sch. Painting and Sculpture, 1966, N.Y. Studio Sch., 1966-67; BA, Reed Coll., 1968. One-man shows include Max Protetch Gallery, N.Y.C., 1977, 79, 83, 85, 86, 88, 89, 91, 92, 95, Asher/Faure Gallery, L.A., 1988, 97, Galerie Rolf Ricke, Cologne, Germany, 1991, 93, 97, San Francisco Art Inst., 1992, Kölnischer Kunstverein, Cologne, 1995. Rockefeller Found. fellow, 1966, John Simon Guggenheim Meml. Found. fellow, 1988, Nat. Endowment Arts Visual Arts fellow, 1991; grantee Roswell (N.Mex.) Mus. and Art Ctr., 1969.

REED, DAVID GEORGE, entrepreneur; b. Alameda, Calif., July 19, 1945; s. David Francis and Anna Amelia Vangeline (Paulson) R.; m. Marianne Louise Watson, Apr. 7, 1971 (div. June 1975); m. Michele Ann Hock, June 28, 1989; 1 child, Casey Christine Michele. AA in Bus. Adminstrn., Diablo Valley Coll., Pleasant Hill, Calif., 1965; BA in Design and Industry, San Francisco State U., 1967, MBA in Mktg., 1969; cert. res. police officer, Los Medanos Coll., Pittsburg, Calif., 1977. Owner Western Furs, Ltd., Walnut Creek, Calif., 1963-72; mgmt. cons. Controlled Interval Scheduling, Rolling Hills Estates, Calif., 1972-73; owner Dave Reed's Texaco, Concord, Calif., 1973-76; mgmt. cons. Scheduling Systems, Houston, 1974-76, Thomas-Ross Assocs., Mercer Island, Wash., 1972-82; plant mgr. Bonner Packing, Morgan Hill, Calif., 1981; mfg. engr. Systron Donner, Concord, 1982-84, Beckman Instruments, San Ramon, Calif., 1984-90; owner Dave Reed & Co. Water Ski Sch., White Water Rafting, Chiloquin, Oreg., 1987—, Dave Reed & Co., design, market, mfg. Contender boats, Chiloquin, Oreg., 1976—; lectr. wildlife mgmt. Dave Reed & Co., Chiloquin, 1965—, lectr. mgmt. seminars, 1982—; coach Japanese Water Ski Team, Bluff Water Ski Club, Tokyo, 1984; fin. mgr. Japanese investors Dave Reed & Co., Chiloquin, 1986—, design and supply solar electric power sys., 1994—. Res. dep. sheriff Contra Costa County Sheriff's Dept., Martinez, Calif., 1977-80. With U.S. Army, 1969-71, Vietnam. Recipient Gold medal internat. freestyle wrestling Sr. Olympics, Fullerton, Calif., 1983. Mem. Am. Water Ski Assn. (Calif. state water ski champion 1977, 86, western region water ski champion 1977, silver medal nat. water ski championships 1977), Bay Area Tournament Assn. (chmn. 1968—), Diablo Water Ski Club (bd. dirs. 1968—). Republican. Avocations: water skiing, snow skiing, surfing, camping, fly fishing. Home: PO Box 336 Chiloquin OR 97624-0336

REED, DAVID PATRICK, infosystems specialist; b. Portsmouth, Va., Jan. 31, 1952; s. Sherman Clark and Bernice Lois (Maul) R.; m. Lynn Susan Schwartz, June 10, 1973 (div. Mar. 1979); 1 child, Colin Alexander; m. Jessica Amy Kenn, Sept. 4, 1983; children: Katherine Anne, Carly Diana. BS, MIT, 1973, SM, 1975, degree in elec. engring., 1976, PhD, 1978. Asst. prof. computer sci. and engring. MIT, Cambridge, 1978-84, lectr., 1984-86; chief scientist Software Arts, Wellesley, Mass., 1983-84, v.p. research and devel., 1984-85; v.p. rsch. and devel., chief scientist Lotus Devel., Cambridge, 1985-92; sr. scientist Interval Rsch. Corp., 1992-96; pvt. practice, 1996—; mem. adv. bd. CSC Index Vanguard Rsch. and Adv. Program, 1991—; Contbr. articles to profl. jours. Recipient Teaching award MIT Elec. Engring. Dept., 1975; fellow Diamond Exchange Program Diamond Tech. Ptnrs., 1996—. Mem. IEEE, Assn. Computing Machinery, Computer Soc., Sigma Xi. Democrat.

REED, DIANE MARIE, psychologist; b. Joplin, Mo., Jan. 11, 1934; d. William Marion and Olive Francis (Smith) Kinney; m. William J. Shotten; children: Wendy Robison, Douglas Funkhouser. Student, Art Ctr. Col., L.A., 1951-54; BS, U. Oreg., 1976, MS, 1977, PhD, 1981. Lic. psychologist. Illustrator J.L. Hudson Co., Detroit, 1954-56; designer, stylist N.Y.C., 1960-70; designer, owner Decor To You, Inc., Stamford, Conn., 1970-76; founder, exec. dir. Alcohol Counseling and Edn. Svcs., Inc., Eugene, Oreg., 1981-86, clin. supr., 1986; clin. supr. Christian Family Svcs., Eugene, 1986-87; pvt. practice Eugene, 1985-94; co-founder Reed Consulting, Bend, Oreg., 1995—. Evaluator Vocat. Rehab. Div., Eugene, 1982—; alcohol and drug evaluator and commitment examiner Oreg. Mental Health Div., 1981-86; life mem. Rep. Presdl. Task Force. Mem. APA, Oreg. Psychol. Assn., Lane County Psychol. Assn. (pres. 1989-90, Psychologist Yr. 1991), Network of Entrepreneurial Women, Bend C. of C., Sunriver Area C. of C., mem. bd., (1997—). Rotary Internat.club (Rotarian Yr. 1996, pres., 1997—). Avocations: photography, skiing, running, hiking, llama packing.

REED, DONALD ANTHONY, executive; b. New Orleans, Nov. 22, 1935; s. Roscoe and Mildred (Fauria) R. BS, Loyola U., 1957; MSLS, U. So. Calif., 1958, JD, 1968. Instr. U. Beverly Hills, L.A.; libr. Woodburg U., L.A.; instr. L.A. Valley Coll., Calif. Inst. of Arts, L.A.; founder, pres. Coun. Film Orgns., L.A., 1980—, Acad. of Family Films, L.A., 1980—, The Count Dracula Soc., L.A., 1962—, Acad. Sci. Fiction Fantacy & Horror Films, L.A., 1972—; cons. in field. Author: The Vampire on the Screen, 1964, The Outlawry of War in Outer Space, 1966, Admiral Leahy at Vichy France, 1968, Robert Redford, 1975, Science Fiction Film Awards, 1981. Recipient The Saturn award, 1978, Count Dracula Soc. award, 1964. Mem. Acad. Magical Arts, Sons of the Desert, Beta Phi Mu (pres. 1958-60), Phi Alpha Theta, Phi Kappa Alpha. Democrat. Roman Catholic. Avocations: comic operas of Gilbert and Sullivan, Count Dracula books and films, Calvin Coolidge, Abbott and Costello, dir. Bryan Singer. Office: Acad Sci Fiction Fantasy & Horror 334 W 54th St Los Angeles CA 90037-3806

REED, DWAYNE MILTON, medical epidemiologist, educator; b. Kinsley, Kans., Dec. 10, 1933; s. John Milton and Margaret (Reger) R.; m. Leslie Smith, June 28, 1962 (div. 1968); children: Colin, Heather. BA, U. Calif., Berkeley, 1956; MD, U. Calif., San Francisco, 1960; MPH, U. Calif., 1962, PhD in Epidemiology, 1968. Dep. chief epidemiology Nat. Inst. Neurol. Disease NIH, Bethesda, Md., 1962-64; chief epidemiology Arctic Health Ctr. USPHS, 1964-66; assoc. prof. Sch. Pub. Health R. Tex., Houston, 1968-70; chief epidemiology NIH Neurology Field Ctr., Agana, Guam, 1970-72; epidemiologist South Pacific Commn., New Caledonia, 1972-75; chief epidemiology br. Nat. Inst. Child Health, NIH, Bethesda, 1975-78; dir. environ. epidemiology Calif. Dept. Health, Berkeley, 1978-79; dir. Honolulu health program Nat. Heart Lung Blood Inst. NIH, 1980-93; sr. epidemiologist Buck Ctr. for Rsch. in Aging, Novato, Calif., 1993—; adj. prof. epidemiology Sch. Pub. Health U. Calif., Berkeley, 1978-78, Sch. Pub. Health U. Honolulu, 1980—; cons. WHO-Pacific, Manila, 1983, 86-87, 89, Hawaii State Dept. Health, Honolulu, 1988-93. Editor: The Epidemiology of Premature, 1977; contbr.. chpts. to books and over 120 sci. articles on med. epidemiology to profl. jours. Recipient Commendation medal USPHS, 1987. Fellow Am. Heart Assn.; mem. Am. Pub. Health Assn., Am. Coll. Epidemiology, Am. Epidemiology Soc., Soc. Epidemiologic Rsch., Delta Omega. Achievements include research in public health, epidemiology. Office: Buck Ctr for Rsch in Aging 505 San Marin Dr Novato CA 94945-1309

REED, EDWARD CORNELIUS, JR., federal judge; b. Mason, Nev., July 8, 1924; s. Edward Cornelius Sr. and Evelyn (Walker) R.; m. Sally Torrance, June 14, 1952; children: Edward T., William W., John A., Mary E. BA, U. Nev., 1949; JD, Harvard U., 1952. Bar: Nev. 1952, U.S. Dist Ct. Nev. 1957, U.S. Supreme Ct. 1974. Atty. Arthur Andersen & Co., 1952-53; spl. dep. atty. gen. State of Nev., 1967-79; judge U.S. Dist. Ct. Nev., Reno, 1979—, chief judge, now sr. judge. Former vol. atty. Girl Scouts Am., Sierra Nevada Council, U. Nev., Nev. Agrl. Found., Nev. State Sch. Adminstrs. Assn., Nev. Congress of Parents and Teachers; mem. Washoe County Sch. Bd., 1956-72, pres. 1959, 63, 69; chmn. Gov.'s Sch. Survey Com., 1958-61; mem. Washoe County Bd. Tax Equalization, 1957-58, Washoe County Annexation Commn., 1968-72, Washoe County Personnel Com., 1973-77, chmn. 1973; mem. citizens adv. com. Washoe County Sch. Bond Issue, 1977-78, Sun Valley, Nev., Swimming Pool Com., 1978, Washoe County Blue Ribbon Task Force Com. on Growth, Nev. PTA (life); chmn. profl. div. United Way, 1978; bd. dirs. Reno Siver Sox, 1962-65. Served as staff sgt. U.S. Army, 1943-46, ETO, PTO. Mem. ABA (jud. adminstrn. sect.), Nev. State Bar Assn. (adminstrv. com. dist. 5, 1967-79, lien law com. 1965-78, chmn. 1965-72, probate law com. 1963-66, tax law com. 1962-65), Am. Judicature Soc. Democrat. Baptist. Office: US Dist Ct 400 S Virginia St Ste 606 Reno NV 89501-2182

REED, EVA SILVER STAR, chieftain; b. Vinita, Okla., Nov. 29, 1929; d. Robert Elbert Jones and Anna Mae (Campfield) Reed; m. Johnnie Silver Eagle Reed, June 10, 1946 (dec. Sept. 1982); children: Patty Deeanne, Lorrie Ann, Billy John. Sec. United Lumbee Nation of N.C. and Am., Fall River Mills, Calif., 1979-82; nat. head chieftain United Lumbee Nation of N.C. and Am., Fall River Mills, 1982—, also bd. dirs.; bd. dirs., sec. Chapel of Our Lord Jesus, Exeter, Calif., 1974—, Native Am. Wolf Clan, Calif., 1977—; tchr. Indian beading and crafts, Calif., 1977—. Author, compiler: Over the Cooking Fires, 1982, Lumbee Indian Ceremonies, 1982, United Lumbee Deer Clan Cook Book, 1988; editor: (newspaper) United Lumbee Nation Times, 1981—. Mem. parent com. Title IV & Johnson O'Malley Indian Edn. Program, Tulare/Kings County, 1976-80, Shasta County, Calif., 1982-84. Recipient United Lumbee Nation of N.C. and Am.'s Silver Eagle award, 1991, also various awards for beadwork Intermountain Fair, Shasta County, 1982-96. Avocations: writing, Indian beadwork, basket making, Indian crafts. Office: United Lumbee Nation of NC & Am PO Box 512 Fall River Mills CA 96028

REED, FRANK FREMONT, II, retired lawyer; b. Chgo., June 15, 1928; s. Allen Martin and Frances (Faurot) R.; m. Jaquelin Silverthorne Cox, Apr. 27, 1963; children: Elizabeth Matthiessen Mason, Laurie Matthiessen Stern, Mark Matthiessen, Jeffrey, Nancy, Sarah. Student Chgo. Latin Sch.; grad. St. Paul's Sch., 1946; A.B., U. Mich., 1952, J.D., 1957. Bar: Ill., 1958. Assoc. Byron, Hume, Groen & Clement, 1958-61, Marks & Clerk, 1961-63; pvt. practice law, Chgo., 1963-78; dir. Western Acadia (Western Felt Works), 1960-75, chmn. exec. com., 1969-71. Rep. precinct capt. 1972-78; candidate for 43d ward alderman, 1975; bd. dirs., sec. Chgo. Found. Theater Arts, 1959-64; vestryman St. Chrysostom's Ch., 1975-79, mem. ushers guild, 1964-79, chmn., 1976-78; bd. dirs. North State, Astor, Lake Shore Dr. Assn., 1975-78, pres. 1977-78; bd. dirs. Community Arts Music Assn. of Santa Barbara, 1984-93, treas. 1988-93; bd. dirs. Santa Barbara Arts Coun., 1987-89. Cpl. AUS, 1952-54. Mem. ABA, Ill. Bar Assn., Phi Alpha Delta, Racquet Club, Wausaukee Club (sec., dir. 1968-71, 92-94) (Chgo.); Birnam Wood Golf Club (Santa Barbara, Calif.). Episcopalian. Author: History of the Silverthorn Family, 4 vols., 1982, Allen Family of Allen's Grove, 1983, Goddard and Ware Ancestors, 1987, Faurot Family, 1988. Contbr. articles to The Am. Genealogist, 1972-73, 76-77. Home: 1944 E Valley Rd Santa Barbara CA 93108-1428

REED, FRANK METCALF, bank executive; b. Seattle, Dec. 22, 1912; s. Frank Ivan and Pauline B. (Hovey) R.; student U. Alaska, 1931-32; BA, U. Wash., 1937; m. Maxine Vivian McGary, June 11, 1937; children: Pauline Reed Mackay, Frank Metcalf. V.p. Anchorage Light & Power Co., 1937-42; pres. Alaska Electric & Equipment Co., Anchorage, 1946-50; sec., mgr. Turnagain, Inc., Anchorage, 1950-56; mgr. Gen. Credit Corp., Anchorage, 1957; br. mgr. Alaska SBA, Anchorage, 1958-60; sr. v.p. First Interstate Bank of Alaska, Anchorage, 1960-87, also dir., corp. sec.; dir. First Interstate Corp. of Alaska, First Nat. Bank of Fairbanks; pres., dir. Anchorage Broadcasters, Inc.; past pres., chmn. Microfast Software Corp.; dir., treas. R.M.R. Inc.; dir. Anchorage Light & Power Co., Turnagain, Inc., Alaska Fish and Farm, Inc., Life Ins. Co. Alaska. Pres., Anchorage Federated Charities, Inc., 1953-54; mem. advisory bd. Salvation Army, 1948-58; mem. Alaska adv. bd. Hugh O'Brian Youth Found., 1987-91; trustee Anchor Age Endowment Fund, 1988-96, chmn., 1991; mem. City of Anchorage Planning Commn., 1956; mem. City of Anchorage Coun., 1956-57; police commr. Ter. of Alaska, 1957-58; chmn. City Charter Commn., 1958; mem. exec. com. Greater Anchorage, Inc., 1955-65; pres. Sch. Bd., 1961-64; mem. Gov.'s Investment adv. com., 1970-72; mem. Alaska State Bd. Edn.; mem. citizens adv. com. Alaska Meth. U.; chmn. Anchorage Charter Commn., 1975; chmn. bldg. fund dr. Cmty. YMCA, 1976-97; sec.-treas. Breakthrough, 1976-78; bd. dirs Alaska Treatment Ctr., 1980-87, pres. 1985-86; trustee Marston Found., Inc., 1978, exec. dir. 1988. Served as lt. USNR, 1942-46. Elected to Hall Fame, Alaska Press Club, 1969; named Outstanding Alaskan of Year Alaska C. of C., 1976, Alaskan of Yr., 1990, Outstanding Vol. in Philanthropy Alaska chpt. Nat. Soc. Fundraising Execs, 1991. Mem. Am. Inst. Banking, Am. (exec. council 1971-72) Alaska (pres. 1970-71) bankers assns., Nat. Assn. State Bds. Edn. (sec.-treas. 1969-70), Anchorage C. of C. (pres. 1966-67, dir.), Pioneers of Alaska, Navy League (pres. Anchorage council 1961-62). Clubs: Tower (life), San Francisco Tennis. Lodges: Lions (sec.

Anchorage, 1953-54, dir. 1988, pres., 1962-63, life), Elks (life). Home: 1361 W 12th Ave Anchorage AK 99501-4252

REED, GEORGE ELLIOTT, surgery educator; b. N.Y.C., Aug. 4, 1923; s. Morris and Mary R.; children: Elizabeth E., George E. Jr.; m. Anne Miller Moore, 1995. DVM, Cornell U., 1944; MD, NYU, 1951. Diplomate Am. Bd. Surgery, Am. Bd. Thoracic Surgery. Successively intern, resident, chief resident NYU Bellevue Med. Ctr., N.Y.C., 1951-56, Berg fellow in cardiovascular surgery, 1956-58; from asst. prof. to assoc. prof. surgery NYU, N.Y.C., 1959-69, prof., 1969-77; prof. N.Y. Med. Coll., Valhalla, 1977—; pres. med. staff Westchester County Med. Ctr., Valhalla, N.Y., 1989-92; med. dir. acting Westchester County Med. Ctr., Valhalla, 1992-95, med. dir., 1995—, dir. George E. Reed Heart Ctr., 1994—; pres. Med. Coll. Health Alliance, Valhalla, 1994—; vice dean N.Y. Med. Coll., 1995—; cons. surgery N.Y. State Dept. Health, Albany, 1963-90, VA, N.Y.C., 1969-77, Lennox Hill Hosp., N.Y.C., 1971-91, Kingston (N.Y.) Hosp., 1971-90; pres. Federated Faculty Practise Plan, 1996—; presenter in field. Contbr. articles to profl. jours., chpts. to books. Capt. U.S. Army, 1944-47. Fellow ACS, Am. Coll. Cardiology; mem. Am. Assn. Thoracic Surgery, Soc. Thoracic Surgeons, Alpha Omega Alpha (faculty). Avocations: woodworking. Office: Westchester County Med Ctr Macy 203 Valhalla NY 10595

REED, GEORGE FORD, JR., investment executive; b. Hollywood, Calif., Dec. 26, 1946; s. George Ford and Mary Anita Reed; B.A. in Econs. with honors, U. So. Calif., 1969, M.A., 1971; m. Kathryn Nixon, 1981. Analyst planning and research Larwin Group, Beverly Hills, Calif., 1971-72; with Automobile Club So. Calif., Los Angeles, 1972-76, supr. mgmt. info., research and devel., 1973-74, mgr. fin. and market analysis, 1975-81, group mgr. fin. analysis and forecasting, 1981-86; pres. Reed Asset Mgmt. Co., Inc., Los Angeles, 1986—; instr. bus. and econs. Los Angeles Community Coll. Mem. population task force Los Angeles C. of C., 1974; mem. Gov. Calif. Statewide Econ. Summit Conf., 1974. Served with U.S. Army, 1969. Mem. Assn. Corp. Real Estate Execs., Fin. Execs. Inst., Nat. Assn. Bus. Economists, Western Regional Sci. Assn., Am. Mgmt. Assn., Am. Fin. Assn., So. Calif. Planners Assn., Rotary Internat., Omicron Delta Epsilon. Home: 1001 S Westgate Ave Los Angeles CA 90049-5905 Office: 10940 Wilshire Blvd Ste 1600 Los Angeles CA 90024-3943

REED, GLEN ALFRED, lawyer; b. Memphis, Sept. 24, 1951; s. Thomas Henry and Evelyn Merle (Roddy) R.; m. Edith Jean Renick, June 17, 1972; children: Adam Christopher, Alec Benjamin. BA, U. Tenn., 1972; JD, Yale U., 1976. Bar: Ga. 1976. Project dir. Tenn. Research Coordinating Unit, Knoxville, 1972-73; assoc. Alston Miller & Gaines, Atlanta, 1976-77; assoc. Bordurant Miller Hishon & Stephenson, Atlanta, 1978-81, ptnr., 1981-85; ptnr., King & Spalding, Atlanta, 1985—. Author: Practical Hospital Law, 1979. legal adv. Ga. Gov.'s Commn. on Healthcare, 1994; Gen. counsel Assn. Retarded Citizens-Atlanta, 1979—, pres., 1992-96; vice-chmn. CARE Atlanta adv. bd., 1992-94, chmn., 1994—; v.p. Ga. Network for People with Developmental Disabilities, 1991-92; bd. dirs. Ctrl. Health Ctr., 1989-95, Vis. Nurse Health System, 1991—, chair, 1995—, Sch. Pub. Health Emory U., Atlanta, 1993—. Mem. ABA, Ga. Bar Assn., Acad. Hosp. Attys. (bd. dirs. 1991—, pres.- elect 1996—), Ga. Acad. Hosp. Attys. (pres. 1991-92), Nat. Health Lawyers Assn., Phi Beta Kappa. Methodist. Office: King & Spalding 191 Peachtree St NE Atlanta GA 30303-1740

REED, GRANT, phamaceutical executive. CEO LaRoche Holdings. Office: 1100 Johnson Ferry Rd NE Atlanta GA 30342-1709*

REED, GREGORY, lawyer; b. Washington, 1945. AB, Duke U., 1967; JD, U. Md., 1971. Bar: Md. 1972. Law clk. U.S. Dist. Ct. Md., 1971-72; mem. Ballard Spahr Andrews & Ingersoll, Balt.; lectr. Md. Inst. Continuing Profl. Edn. Lawyers, Inc., 1976—; instr. sch. law U. Md., 1986—. Co-author: Residential Real Estate Transactions, 1996; editor-in-chief Md. Law Rev., 1970-71. Mem. Am. Coll. Real Estate Lawyers. Office: Ballard Spahr Andrews & Ingersoll 19th Flr 300 E Lombard St Lowr 19 Baltimore MD 21202-3219

REED, HELEN I., medical, surgical nurse; b. Radford, Va., Aug. 3, 1967; d. Billy Wayne and Beverly Gayle (Sparks) R. Cert. Practical Nursing, Radford City Sch. Nursing, 1986; BSN, Radford U., 1990, postgrad. RN, Va.; cert. med.-surg. nurse ANCC; cert. ACLS provider, CPR instr. Student nurse intern Radford Cmty. Hosp., 1989-90, staff nurse, 1990—; substitute instr. Radford City Sch. Practical Nursing, preceptor to new staff. Jr. vol. Radford Cmty. Hosp., 1981-85; Sunday sch. tchr., children's sermon leader Meth. Ch. Nette Whitehead nursing scholar, John Nye scholar, jr. vol. scholar. Mem. ANA, NSNA. Methodist. Office: Carilion Radford Cmty Hosp Med Care Unit 700 Randolph St Radford VA 24141-2430

REED, HOWARD ALEXANDER, historian, educator; b. Izmir, Turkey, Feb. 26, 1920; s. Cass Arthur and Rosalind Christine (MacLachlan) R.; m. Shafiga Daulet, May 25, 1985; children from previous marriage: Seth Olcott, Heather MacLachlan, Deborah Lamont; stepchildren: Aylin, Sibel. Ed., Phillips Acad., Andover, Mass., 1935-37, Wellington Coll., Berkshire, Eng., 1937-38; B.A. with high orations, Yale, 1942; M.A., Princeton, 1949, Ph.D., 1951. Instr. history Princeton U., 1949-50; Instr. history Yale U., also dir. Internat. Student Ctr., 1950-52; co-founder, asst. dir., prof. Inst. Islamic Studies, McGill U., 1952-55; dir. Inst. Internat. and Intercultural Studies, U. Conn., 1967-71, prof. history, 1967-89, prof. emeritus, cons., 1989—; del. UNRRA and World Student Svc., Greece, 1946-47; program specialist internat. tng. and rsch. Ford Found., 1955-57; dir. coll. and youth programs Am. Friends Svc. Com., 1958-60; assoc. dir. Danforth Found., St. Louis, 1960-64; exec. assoc. Edn. World Affairs, N.Y.C., 1964-67; dir. Nat. Survey Non-Western Studies in Liberal Arts Colls. Dept. Edn., Assn. Am. Colls., 1963-64; participant internat. confs.; cons. Dept. State, U.S. A.I.D., World Bank, India, Oman, Turkey, various unvis., lectr. Author: Non-Western Studies in the Liberal Arts College, 1964; contbr. author: Ency. Islam, 2d edit., 1954—, Foreign Affairs Bibliography, 1942-52, 55, Islam and the West, 1957, A Guide to Historical Literature, 1961, Ency. Americana, 1964-, General Education, Current Ideas and Concerns, 1964, The Emergence of the Modern Middle East, 1970, Expanding Dimensions of World Education, 1976, Internat. Ency. Higher Edn., 1977, Social and Economic History of Turkey (1071-1920), 1980, Islam in the Contemporary World, 1981, 2d edit. 1986, Contributions à l'histoire économique et sociale de l'empire ottoman, 1980, 83, Issues and Opportunities in Turkish Education, 1991, The Oxford Encyclopedia of the Modern Islamic World, 1995; adv. editor: Muslim World, 1970-95; bd. adv. editors: The Middle East Jour, 1977—; contbr. articles to profl. jours. Bd. dirs. Assn. Princeton Grad. Alumni, 1961-63, Lisle Fellowship, 1948-52, 58-60, 65-70, Pendle Hill, Wallingford, Pa., 1958-73, 75-86, Campus Christian Found., 1969-73, Univ. Senate, 1969-72, Am. Research Inst. Turkey, 1969-74, 77-79, Middle East Studies Assn., 1977-80; trustee Friends World Coll., 1976-87; bd. overseers Moses Brown Sch., 1975-77; mem. exec. council Conf. Peace Research in History, 1972-75. Served to lt. (s.g.) USNR, 1942-46. Decorated Legion of Merit; D.S.C. (Gt. Britain); fellow Internat. Scholboy, 1937-38, Mid. East Inst., 1948-49, Rockefeller Found., 1949-50, 52, Ford Found., 1954, Fulbright fellow, 1970, 81, fellow Am. Coun. Learned Socs.-Social Sci. Rsch. Coun., 1977. Fellow Mid. East Studies Assn. (charter), Soc. Values in Higher Edn., Turkish Studies Assn. (co-founder, sec.), Inst. Turkish Studies (hon.), AHEPA (hon.); mem. Am. Hist. Assn., Conf. on Peace Rsch. in History, Mid. East Inst., Internat. Soc. Oriental Rsch., Brit.-Am. Alumni, Turkish Hist. Soc. (hon.), Am.-Turkish Friendship Coun. (nat. adv. bd., Chmn.'s award in edn. 1991), Am.-Turkish Coun., Atatürk Soc. Am., Phi Beta Kappa, Phi Kappa Phi. Mem. Soc. of Friends. Office: U Conn Dept History U-103 241 Glenbrook Rd Storrs Mansfield CT 06268

REED, ISHMAEL SCOTT (EMMETT COLEMAN), writer; b. Chattanooga, Feb. 22, 1938; s. Bennie Stephen (stepfather) and Thelma (Coleman) R.; m. Priscilla Rose, 1960 (div. 1970); children: Timothy, Brett; m. Carla Blank; 1 child, Tennessee Maria. Co-founder Yardbird Pub. Co. Inc., Berkeley, 1971, editorial dir., 1971-75; editor Yardbird Reader, 1972-76; co-founder Reed, Cannon & Johnson Comm. Co., Berkeley, 1973—, Before Columbus Found., Berkeley, 1976—; editor-in-chief Y'Bird mag., 1978-80; co-founder Ishmael Reed and Al Young's Quilt, Berkeley, 1980—; co-editor Quilt mag., 1981—; co-founder East Village Other, 1965, Advance, 1965; tchr. St. Mark's in the Bowery prose workshop, 1966; guest lectr. U. Calif., Berkeley, 1968—, U. Wash., 1969-70, SUNY, Buffalo, 1975, 79, Yale U., 1979, Dartmouth Coll., 1980-81, Sitka Cmty. Assn., 1982, U. Ark., Fayetteville, 1982, Columbia U., 1983, Harvard U., 1987; assoc. fellow Calhoun Coll., Yale U., 1982—, Harvard Signet Soc., 1987—; regents lectr. U. Calif., Santa Barbara, 1988; mem. usage panel Am. Heritage Dictionary. Author: (novels) The Free-Lance Pallbearers, 1967, Yellow Back Radio Broke-Down, 1969, Mumbo Jumbo, 1972 (Nat. Book award nomination 1973), The Last Days of Louisiana Red, 1974 (Richard and Hinda Rosenthal Found. award Nat. Inst. Arts and Letters 1975), Flight to Canada, 1976, The Terrible Twos, 1982, Reckless Eyeballing, 1986, Cab Calloway Stands In for The Moon, 1986, The Terrible Threes, 1989, Japanese By Spring, 1993; (poetry) Catechism of d neoamerican hoodoo church, 1970, Conjure: Selected Poems 1963-70, 1972 (Nat. Book award nomination 1973, Pulitzer prize nomination 1973), Chattanooga, 1973, A Secretary to the Spirits, 1978, Ishmael Reed: New and Collected Poems, 1989; (essays) Shrovetide in Old New Orleans, 1978, God Made Alaska for the Indians, 1981, Airing Dirty Laundry, 1993, Multi-America, 1996; (play) (with Carla Blank and Suzushi Hanayagi) The Lost State of Franklin, 1976; editor: The Rise, Fall, and...? of Adam Clayton Powell, 1967, 19 Necromancers from Now, 1970 (Calif. Assn. Eng. Tchrs. certificate of merit 1972), Yardbird Lives!, 1978, Calafia: The California Poetry, 1979, Writin' Is Fightin': Thirty-seven Years of Boxing on Paper, 1988; exec. prodr.: (TV pilot) Personal Problems. Chmn. Berkeley Arts Commn., 1980, 81; bd. dirs. chmn. Coordinating Council Lit. Mags., 1975-79, adv. bd. chmn., 1977-79. Recipient John Simon Guggenheim Meml. Found. award for fiction, 1974, Lewis Michaux award, 1978, ACLU award, 1978, Pushcart prize, 1979; Wis. Arts Bd. fellow, 1982; Nat. Endowment for Arts writing fellow, 1974; Guggenheim fellow, 1975. Mem. Author's Guild Am., PEN, Celtic Found. Office: Penguin USA 375 Hudson St New York NY 10014*

REED, JACQUELINE K(EMP), educational researcher; b. Newark, June 12, 1947; d. Thomas and Jessie (Bullock) R.; 1 child, Cecil Bernard Brown Jr. BA, U. Ill., Chgo., 1970; MA, Northeastern Ill. U., 1976; PhD, U. Wis., 1978. Rsch. asst. U. Ill., Chgo., 1970-72; zonal coord. Model Cities-Chgo. Com. on Urban Opportunities, Chgo., 1972-73; vocat. specialist Model Cities-CCUO, Chgo., 1973-74, child care tng. coord., 1974-76; program coord. U. Wis., Madison, 1977-79; post-doctoral rsch. fellow Mich. State U., East Lansing, 1979-80; acting asst. dean U. Md., College Park, 1980-81; rsch. assoc. D.C. Pub. Schs., Washington, 1983-85; spl. asst. U. Md., College Park, 1985-89; instructional rsch. coord. Prince George's County Pub. Schs., Upper Marlboro, Md., 1989—; resource colleague Human Rels. Commn., Evanston, Ill., 1971; reviewer U.S. Dept. Edn., Washington, 1979-81; cons. NEA, Washington, 1982; adv. com. P.G. County Correctional Ctr., Upper Marlboro, 1990—; presenter in field. Contbr. chpt. to book and articles to profl. jours. Exec. bd. Eleanor Roosevelt High Sch. PTSA, Greenbelt, Md., 1980-84; vol. United Communities Against Poverty, Capitol Heights, Md., 1987-89, Md. Higher Edn. Commn., Prince George's County Commn. Women, 1990; bd. dirs. Towns of Kettering, Upper Marlboro, 1992; rep. to NGO Forum on Women, UN 4th World Conf. on Women, Beijing, mem. Prince George's County Commn. for Women, 1997—. Recipient Vol. award United Communities Against Poverty, Capitol Heights, 1989. Mem. AAUW (membership chari Bowie br. 1997), Nat. Assn. Multi-Cultural Edn. (exec. bd. mem. 1990—, editorial bd. mem. 1990—), Am. Ednl. Rsch. Assn., Nat. Coun. Negro Women, Inc., U. Ill. Alumni Assn., U. Wis. Alumni Assn., Md. Choral Soc., Phi Delta Kappa, Pi Lambda Theta (eligibility co-chair 1977-78). Democrat. Office: Prince Georges Pub Sch Divsn Instrn Rm 201F 14201 School Ln Upper Marlboro MD 20772-2866

REED, JAMES ALEXANDER, JR., lawyer; b. Rochester, N.Y., Feb. 7, 1930; s. James Alexander and Rose Winifred (Nellist) R.; m. Dora Anne DeVries, Feb. 17, 1972 (div. Mar. 1983); children: Geoffrey M., Diane E. BA cum laude, Amherst Coll., 1952; JD, Harvard U., 1955. Bar: N.Y. 1958, U.S. Dist. Ct. (we. dist.) N.Y. 1959, U.S. Dist. Ct. (no. dist.) N.Y. 1960. Assoc. Osborn, Reed, Burke & Tobin and predecessor firms, Rochester, 1958-63, ptnr., 1964-96, of counsel, 1997—; dep. atty. Town of Pittsford, N.Y., 1976-77, atty., 1977-95. Served to lt. USNR, 1955-58. Mem. ABA, N.Y. State Bar Assn., Monroe County Bar Assn., Am. Judicature Assn. Republican. Episcopalian. Home: 8 Greenwood Park Pittsford NY 14534-2912 Office: Osborn Reed Burke & Tobin 1 Exchange St Rochester NY 14614-1403

REED, JAMES DONALD, journalist, author; b. Jackson, Mich., Oct. 7, 1940; s. Clair and Esther (Bryden) R.; m. Christine Flowers, June 14, 1969; children: Phoebe C., Alicia M., Gabrielle A. Student, Albion Coll., 1958-60; BA, Mich. State U., 1962; postgrad., SUNY-Stony Brook, 1967-69; MFA, U. Mont., 1970. Mem. faculty dept. creative writing U. Mass., 1970-75; dir. M.F.A. program, 1974; staff writer Sports Illustrated, N.Y.C., 1975-80; assoc. editor Time mag., 1980-90; sr. writer People mag., N.Y.C., 1990-91, sr. editor, 1991-93; sr. assoc. editor spl. tissues, 1993—. Author: (poetry) Expressways, 1970, Fatback Odes, 1973; (fiction) Free Fall, 1980; (with Christine Reed) Exposure, 1987. Guggenheim fellow, 1971. Office: People Mag Time Life Bldg Rockefeller Ctr New York NY 10020

REED, JAMES EARL, fire department commander; b. San Francisco, Mar. 21, 1957; s. Arlen Earl and Louise (Gibbs) R.; m. Jody Lynn Bales, Feb. 14, 1976 (div. Aug. 1978); 1 child, Darci Lynn; m. Donna Kaye Lewis, June 25, 1994. A in fire sci., Casper Coll., 1995. State cert. fire fighter I, II, III, state cert. fire svc. instr. I, state cert. fire prevention officer I. Shop worker, shop foreman, salesman Becker Fire Equipment, Casper, Wyo., 1975-78; safety equipment maintance Bell H2S Safety and Oilind Safety Engring., Casper, 1978-80; tchr. outreach program Casper Coll., 1988-90; owner operator J.R.'s Custom Hand Planted Signs, 1980-93; capt. Casper (Wyo.) Fire Dept., 1978-93, comdr., 1993—; artist Images Studio, Casper, 1991—; instr. CPR courses Am. Heart Soc., ARC, 1980—; instr. SCBA courses, 1983-85. Active fund raisers City/County Fire Fighters Burn Fund, 1982, 84—, fund raisers Muscular Dystrophy Assn., 1981, 82, 85-89, fund raisers March of Dimes, 1984, 85, 87, fund raisers Casper Mountain Racers Youth Olympics, 1985-87, Casper Event Ctr.'s "Spl. Christmas for Spl. Kids," 1984-87. Named Firefighter of Yr. Casper Fire Dept., Casper Ladies Auxiliary, Am. Legion Regional and Post 2, 1984, Man in Blue, Casper Fire Dept., 1994. Mem. Casper Fire Fighters Assn. (entertainment com. 1980—, exec. com. 1988-90), City County Fire Fighters Burn Fund (trustee 1985-86, treas. 1986-89, sec. 1989-91, pres. 1992—). Republican. Seventh-day Adventist. Avocations: painting, alpine and water skiing, weight lifting, racquetball. Home: 1847 Jim Bridger Ave Casper WY 82604-3118

REED, JAMES ELDIN, historian, educator; b. Walla Walla, Wash., Mar. 13, 1945; s. Eldin Wallace and Mary Ellen (White) R.; m. Deborah Jane Addis, Apr. 14, 1983. AB, Ripon Coll., 1967; AM, Harvard U., 1968, MTS, 1971, PhD, 1976. Tchg. fellow Harvard U., Cambridge, Mass., 1972-77; founder, pres., chmn. Addis & Reed Cons., Inc., Boston, 1977—; chmn. ARC Publs., Boston, 1995—; vis. scholar Harvard U., 1992-94, 96—; rsch. assoc. North Pacific program Fletcher Sch. Law and Diplomacy, Medford, Mass., 1994-96; v.p., pres. Assn. Mgmt. Cons., Boston, 1985-89; founder, bd. dirs. Nat. Coun. Pub. History, Washington, 1980-83. Author: The Missionary Mind, 1983; editor: (newsletter) American Canada Watch, 1995—; contbr. numerous articles, papers, and revs. to profl. publs. including Christian Sci. Monitor, and newspapers. Cons. House Agr. Com. Washington, 1978; invited witness Senate Judiciary Com., Washington, 1990; legis. dir. Asbestos Victims Campaign, Boston, 1987-90. Woodrow Wilson fellow, 1967-68. Mem. Am. Hist. Assn., Can. Inst. Internat. Affairs, Boston Athenaeum, Harvard Club of Boston, Phi Beta Kappa. Independent. Unitarian. Achievements include study of traditional Far East policy of U.S. Avocation: Language - French. Home: 25 Holly Ln Chestnut Hill MA 02167-2156 Office: Addis & Reed Cons PO Box 85 Chestnut Hill MA 02167

REED, JAMES WESLEY, social historian, educator; b. New Orleans, Oct. 17, 1944; married. BA, U. New Orleans, 1967; AM, Harvard U., 1968, PhD, 1974. Research fellow in history Schlesinger Library, 1973-75; prof. history Rutgers U., New Brunswick, N.J., 1975—; dean Rutgers Coll., Rutgers U., New Brunswick, 1985-94. Author: From Private Vice to Public Virtue: The Birth Control Movement and American Society Since 1830, 1978. Office: Rutgers U Dept of History Van Dyke Hall New Brunswick NJ 08903-5059

REED, JAMES WHITFIELD, physician, educator; b. Pahokee, Fla., Nov. 1, 1935; s. Thomas Reed and Chineater (Grey) Whitfield; married; children: David M., Robert A., Mary I., Katherine E. BS, W.Va. State Coll., 1954; MD, Howard U., 1963. Diplomate Am. Bd. Internal Medicine, Am. Bd. Endocrinology and Metabolism. Commd. U.S. Army, 1963; advanced through grades to col., 1981; resident in internal medicine Madigan Army Med. Ctr., Tacoma, Wash., 1966-69, chief endocrinology and metabolism, 1971-76, chief dept. clin. rsch., 1976-78; chief dept. medicine Eisenhower Army Med. Ctr., Augusta, Ga., 1978-81; assoc. prof. internal medicine edn. for FP program U. Tex. at Dallas, 1981-84; prof. medicine Morehouse Sch. Medicine, Atlanta, 1985—, chmn. dept., 1985-92, chmn. grad. med. edn., 1992—, activity chmn., 1986-88; postdoctoral fellow in endocrinology and metabolism U. Calif. Med. Ctr., San Francisco, 1969-71; dir. endocrinology, fellow Madigan Army Med. Ctr., 1976-78; dir. internal medicine residency program Eisenhower Army Med. Ctr., 1978-81, chmn. directorate of clin. investigation, 1978-81, dir. endocrinology fellowship program; med. cons. Tuskgee (Ala.) VA Hosp., 1985—; mem. nat. high blood pressure edn. com. NHLBI/NIH, Nat. Diabetes Mellitus Adv. Coun., Nat. Diabetes Adv. Bd., NHLBI working Com. on Hypertension and Diabetes; chmn. Sub Com. Special Population and Situations, chmn. subcom., mem. exec. com. Joint Nat. Commn. for Detection Evaluation and Treatment of High Blood Pressure. Author: Black Man's Guide to Good Health, 1994; contbr. articles to profl. publs. Med. advisor, chmn. March of Dimes, Pierce County, Tacoma, 1976-78; pres. Charles Drew Sickle Cell and Health Bd., Tacoma, 1976-78; mem. task force on cardiovascular risk reduction Am. Heart Assn. Decorated Legion of Merit; recipient Disting. Alumni award Nat. Assn. for Equal Opportunity in Higher Edn., 1988, Nat. Alumnus of Yr. award W.Va. State Coll., 1987; inducted into ROTC Hall of Fame, W.Va. State Coll., 1987. Fellow ACP, Am. Coll. Clin. Endocrinologist; mem. Assn. Profs. Medicine, Endocrine Soc., Internat. Soc. Hypertension in Blacks (v.p. 1986, pres. 1992—), Assn. of Program Dirs. in Internal Medicine, Am. Heart Assn. Task Force on Cardiovascular Risk, Alpha Phi Alpha. Democrat. Avocations: bowling, skiing. Home: 380 Mcgill Pl NE Atlanta GA 30312-1069 Office: Morehouse Sch Medicine 720 Westview Dr SW Atlanta GA 30310-1458 *One cannot control the circumstance of one's birth, but with keen alertness and honest hard work there are no limits to what one can achieve. So hitch your wagon to a star and never lose sight of it.*

REED, JESSE FRANCIS, entrepreneur, artist, inventor, theologian, business consultant; b. Federalsburg, Md., June 6, 1925; s. Homer F. and Lola Irene (Stevens) R.; BFA, Montclair Coll., 1950; DD, Gnostic Sem., 1968; m. Mary Grace Mayo, July 9, 1944; 1 son, Gary. Owner, Reed's Frozen Foods, Paterson, N.J., 1950-59; pres. A.E. Inc., N.Y.C., 1959-72, Intercontinental Bus. Rsch. & Devel. Inc., San Francisco, 1959-72, chmn. bd., pres. Dallas and Washington, 1972—, Intercontinental Oil & Ore Inc., Carson City, Nev. and Dallas, 1972—; chmn. bd., pres. COSMO U.S.A., Inc., Dallas and Washington, 1974—, Internat. Art Exchange Ltd., Dallas and Los Angeles, 1980—; chmn. bd. Gnosis (Self Discovery and Identification Sys.), 1980—. Chmn. bd. Internat. Arts Soc., Inc., Dallas, 1981—; dir. XTR Corp. Bd. dirs. Am. Art Alliance, Inc., Internat. Fine Art, Inc., Worldwide Art Exchange, Inc., IBR&D, Inc. Gnostic Ch. Served with USN, 1942-46. Recipient various Art Show awards in Tex., Calif., N.J., N.Y., Ga., Fla., Wash., Ill., Hawaii, Minn., Nev., N.Mex., Oreg., Mo., Can., Eng., France, Belgium, Norway, Sweden, Denmark, Switzerland, Australia, N.Z. Mem. Screen Writers Guild, Cattlemen's Assn. Inventor protein converter (controlled environ. food prodn. chain), visual edn. system to translate all ednl. disciplines into their pictorial presentations, modular prefabricate bldg. systems, BIO-HAB (a self energizing life-support system employing; bio chemical, wind, solar, voltaic-cell, energy to powerheat-cool and feed humans and animals), solar energy systems, hydroponic systems, plasma energy systems, electric vehicle systems, subliminal learning systems, precious metal recovery/assaying systems, currency system based upon precious metal art creations, estate protection systems, health systems. Office: PO Box 12488 Dallas TX 75225-0488

REED, JOAN-MARIE, special education educator; b. St. Paul, Sept. 8, 1960; d. William Martin Reed and Diana-Marie (Miller) Reed Moss. BA, U. Minn., 1982, BS, 1983; MEd, Tex. Woman's U., 1986. Cert. tchr., Tex. Tchr. emotionally disturbed Birdville Ind. Sch. Dist., Ft. Worth, 1984-86; tchr. emotionally disturbed Goose Creek Ind. Sch. Dist., Baytown, Tex., 1986-92, ctr. leader, 1992-93, dept. chairperson, 1987-91; tchr. emotionally disturbed Conroe (Tex.) Ind. Sch. Dist., 1993-94, Willis (Tex.) Ind. Sch. Dist., 1994-95, Jefferson County Pub. Schs., 1995—; Co-editor: New Teacher Handbook, 1986-87, Behavior Improvement Program Handbook, 1987-88. Mem. NEA, Coun. for Exceptional Children. Congregationalist. Avocations: reading, classical literature, traveling, walking, biking. Office: Ctrl Lakewood Adolescent Day Treatment Program 1005 Wadsworth Blvd Lakewood CO 80215-5101

REED, JODY ERIC, professional baseball player; b. Tampa, Fla., June 26, 1962. Student, Manatee Jr. Coll.; BA, Fla. State U., 1985. With Milw. Brewers, Boston Red Sox, 1987-92, L.A. Dodgers, 1993; 2d baseman San Diego Padres, 1995—. Achievements include mem. Am. League East Divsn. Champions, 1988, 90. Office: San Diego Padres PO Box 2000 San Diego CA 92112*

REED, JOHN ALTON, lawyer; b. Washington, June 29, 1931; s. John Alton and Emma Powers (Ball) R.; m. Louisa Wardman, June 6, 1953; children: Donna, Joanne, Deborah. AB, Duke U., 1954, LLB, 1956. Bar: Fla. 1956. Assoc. firm Fowler-White, Tampa, Fla., 1956-57; partner firm Rush, Reed & Marshall, Orlando, Fla., 1957-67; judge Fla. 4th Dist. Ct. Appeal, 1967-73, chief judge, 1971-73; judge U.S. Dist. Ct. for Middle Dist. Fla., Orlando, 1973-84; ptnr., chmn. dept. litigation Lowndes, Drosdick, Doster, Kantor & Reed, Orlando, 1985—; mem. com. on standard civil jury instructions Fla. Supreme Ct. Bd. visitors Duke U. Law Sch., 1983—. Mem. Am., Orange County, Fla. bar assns., Am. Judicature Soc. Republican. Episcopalian. Home: 1146 Washington Ave Winter Park FL 32789-2613 Office: PO Box 2809 215 N Eola Dr Orlando FL 32802

REED, JOHN FRANCIS (JACK REED), senator; b. Providence, Nov. 12, 1949; s. Joseph Anthony and Mary Louise (Monahan) R. BS, U.S. Mil. Acad., 1971; M in Pub. Policy, Harvard U., 1973, JD cum laude, 1982. Bar: D.C. 1982, R.I. 1983. Commd. 2d. lt. U.S. Army, 1971, served with 82d Airborne Div., 1973-77; asst. prof. U.S. Mil. Acad., West Point, N.Y., 1977-79; resigned U.S. Army, 1979; assoc. Sutherland, Asbill & Brennan, Washington, 1982-83, Edwards & Angell, Providence, 1983-89; mem. R.I. Senate, 1984-90, 102nd-104th Congresses from 2d R.I. dist., 1990-96; mem. judiciary com., mem. econ. and ednl. opportunity com., regional whip for New Eng. Dem. del.; senator U.S. Senate, 1996—; vice chair N.E.-Midwest Congl. Coalition. Author: (with others) American National Security, 1981. Recipient Disting. Svc. award AARP, 1989, John Fogarty award, 1990, Disting. Legislator award United Way Southeastern New Eng., 1988. Mem. ABA, R.I. Bar Assn., D.C. Bar Assn., Environ. and Energy Study Inst., Phi Kappa Phi. Democrat. Roman Catholic. Avocations: reading, hiking. Office: US Senate 339 Russell Senate Bldg Washington DC 20510 also: Dist Office 100 Midway Rd Ste 5 Cranston RI 02920-5742*

REED, JOHN FRANKLIN, instrument manufacturing company executive; b. Winfield, Mo., Aug. 10, 1917; s. Claude F. and Inez (Crenshaw) R.; m. Ann M. Walter, Aug. 31, 1940; children: John Franklin, James D., Thomas W., William C., Robert D. B.S. in Mining Engring, Mo. Sch. Mines and Metallurgy, 1940. Indsl. engr. Tenn. Coal Iron R.R. Co., 1940-42; time study methods engr. McDonnell Aircraft Corp., 1943; prodn. planner, chief estimator Fairchild Aircraft Co., 1944; joined Manning, Maxwell & Moore, Inc., Stratford, Conn., 1944; works mgr. Manning, Maxwell & Moore Inc., Tulsa, Shaw Box, Crane and Hoist div., Muskegon, Mich., 1951-57; gen. mgr. Instrument and Gauge div., 1957-59, v.p., gen. mgr., 1959, exec. v.p., 1959-62, pres., chief exec. officer, dir., 1962-65; pres., dir. Manning, Maxwell and Moore of Can., Ltd., Galt, Ont., 1962-65; pres., chief oper. officer Hupp Corp., Cleve., 1965-67, pres., dir., 1967-68; pres., chief exec. officer, dir. Hercules Galion Products, Inc., Ohio, 1968-69; pres., chief exec., dir. Canrad Inc., Newark, 1969—; chmn. Canrad Inc., 1976-86; mem. exec. com. Canrad-Hanovia Inc., 1984-89, also bd. dirs., 1984-89; bd. dirs. Rhein Med., Tampa, Fla.; Am. Health Capital, Irving, Tex. Mem. Royal Poinciana Golf. Presbyterian. Home: 745 Willowhead Dr Naples FL 34103-3543

REED, JOHN HATHAWAY, former ambassador; b. Fort Fairfield, Maine, Jan. 5, 1921; s. Walter and Eva Ruth (Seeley) R.; m. Cora Mitchell Davison,

Mar. 24, 1944; children—Cheryl, Ruth. B.S., U. Maine, 1942, LL.D. (hon.), 1960; LL.D. (hon.), Ricker Coll.; grad., Harvard Naval Supply Sch., 1944. Officer Reed Farms, Inc., Fort Fairfield, Maine, 1948—; pres. Aroostook Raceway, Inc., 1958-59; adv. com. Fort Fairfield br. No. Nat. Bank of Presque Isle; mem. Nat. Transp. Safety Bd., Washington, 1967-75, chmn., 1969-75; ambassador to Sri Lanka Colombo, 1975-77; dir. govt. rels. Assoc. Builders & Contractors, Inc., Washington, 1978-81; ambassador to Sri Lanka and Republic of Maldives, 1982-85; cons. Dept. State, 1985-90; pvt. practice cons. Washington, 1990—; chmn. Nat. Govs. Conf. Rep., 1966; rep. Fort Fairfield to Maine Legislature, 1954-56; mem. Senate, 1957-59, pres., 1959-60; gov. State of Maine, 1960-67. Pres. bd. Community Gen. Hosp., Fort Fairfield, 1952-54, No. Maine Fair, 1953-59; trustee Ricker Coll., 1953-60, Oak Grove Sch., Vassalboro, Maine; bd. advisors Coll. of Democracy, 1986—, chmn., 1991—. Served to lt. (j.g.) USNR, 1942-46. Mem. Am. Fgn. Svc. Assn., Coun. Am. Abassadors, Soc. Sr. Aerospace Execs. Inc. (bd. dirs. 1987—, pres. 1988-91), Nat. Inst. Former Govs. (bd. dirs. 1992—), Am. Legion, VFW, Grange, Maine Assn. Agrl. Fairs (pres. 1956), Mil. Order of Carabao, Capitol Hill Club, Driving Club (Ft. Fairfield) (pres. 1950-53), Rotary, Masons, KP. Republican. Congregationalist. Office: 410 O St SW Washington DC 20024-2239

REED, JOHN HOWARD, school administrator; b. Bloomfield, Mo., July 14, 1934; s. Floyd John and Lena Joyce (Howard) R.; m. Weymuth Heuiser; children: Cathy, David. BS cum laude, SE Mo. State U., 1956; M., U. Mo., 1959; edn. specialist, SE Mo. State U., 1977; PhD, So. Ill. U., 1983. Cert. supt., prin., tchr. Tchr., coach Scott County R-6 Schs., Sikeston, Mo., 1956-63; supr. student tchr. SE Mo. State U., Cape Girardeau, 1963-75; prin. Scott County R-3 Schs., Oran, Mo., 1975-76; supt. schs. Scott County R-2 Schs., Chaffee, Mo., 1976-79; bus. mgr. SE Mo. State U., Cape Girardeau, 1980-83; dean, pres. Sikeston C.C., 1983-86; supt. Marion County Sch. Dist. 1, Centralia, Ill., 1986-88; head New Life Montessori Sch., Shreveport, La., 1989-90, Belleview Schs., Westminster, Colo., 1990—. Editor: History of Missouri National Guard, 1963. Bd. dirs., sec. Scott County Bd. Edn., Benton, Mo., 1970-79. Lt. col. U.S. Army, 1960-63. Mem. Rotary (sec. 1976-78), Phi Alpha Theta (pres. 1976-78). Baptist. Avocation: history. Home: 8175 Green Ct Westminster CO 80030-4101 Office: Belleview Schs 3455 W 83rd Ave Westminster CO 80030-4005

REED, JOHN SHEDD, former railway executive; b. Chgo., June 9, 1917; s. Kersey Coates and Helen May (Shedd) R.; m. Marjorie Lindsay, May 4, 1946; children: Ginevra, Keith, Helen, Peter, John Shedd Jr. Student, Chgo. Latin Sch., Hotchkiss Sch.; BS in Indsl. Adminstrn., Yale U., 1939; grad., Advanced Mgmt. Program, Harvard U., 1955. With A.T. & S.F. Ry., 1939-83; test dept. asst., successively spl. rep. to gen. supt. transp. Chgo.; transp. insp. Amarillo, Tex.; trainmaster Slaton, Tex., Pueblo, Colo.; supt. Mo. div., Marceline, Mo.; asst. to v.p. Chgo., 1957-59, exec. asst. to pres., 1957-59, v.p. finance, 1959-64, v.p. exec. dept., 1964-67, pres., 1967-78, chief exec. officer, 1968-82, chmn. bd., 1973-83; pres. Santa Fe Industries, Inc., 1968-78, chmn. bd. dirs., CEO Santa Fe So. Pacific Corp., 1987, chmn., 1987-88. Dir. Nat. Merit Scholarship Corp., 1996, past chmn.; trustee Shedd Aquarium, Chgo., 1996, past pres. With USNR, 1940-45. Mem. Chgo. Club, Old Elm Club, Shoreacres Club, Onwentsia Club (Lake Forest). Home: 301 W Laurel Ave # 112 Lake Forest IL 60045-1180 Office: 224 S Michigan Ave Ste 200 Chicago IL 60604-2500

REED, JOHN SHEPARD, bank executive; b. Chgo., Feb. 7, 1939; divorced; 4 children; m. Cindy McCarthy, 1994. BA and BS, Washington and Jefferson Coll., MIT, 1961; MS, Sloan Sch. MIT, 1965. With Citicorp/Citibank, 1965—, chmn., CEO, 1984—; bd. dirs. Philip Morris Inc., Monsanto Co.; mem. Bus. Coun.; mem. policy com., Bus. Roundtable; chmn. Coalition of Svc. Inds., svcs. policy adv. com. to the U.S. Trade Rep. Mem. bd. MIT, Meml. Sloan-Kettering Cancer Ctr., Rand Corp., Spencer Found., Am. Mus. Nat. History. Served with C.E. U.S. Army, Korea, 1962-64. Office: Citibank NA/Citicorp 153 E 53rd St New York NY 10022-4611*

REED, JOHN SQUIRES, II, lawyer; b. Lexington, Ky., Mar. 20, 1949; s. John Squires and Mary Alexander (O'Hara) R.; m. Nancy Claire Battles, Dec. 29, 1973; children: Alexandra Simmons, John Squires III. AB in Polit. Sci., U. Ky., 1971; JD, U. Va., 1974. Bar: Ky. 1974, U.S. Dist. Ct. (we. dist.) Ky. 1975, U.S. Ct. Appeals (6th cir.) 1975, U.S. Dist. Ct. (ea. dist.) Ky. 1979, U.S. Supreme Ct. 1980, U.S. Ct. Appeals (fed. cir.) 1985. Assoc. Greenebaum Doll & McDonald, Louisville, 1974-79, ptnr., 1979-87; ptnr. Hirn, Doheny, Reed & Harper, Louisville, 1987-96, Reed Weitkamp Schell Cox & Vice, Louisville, 1996—. Mem. Leadership Louisville, 1982, treas., mem. exec. com. Leadership Louisville Alumni Assn., 1984, pres., 1985; bd. dirs. Ky. Coun. Econ. Edn., 1985—, Nat. Assn. Community Leadership, 1986-91, treas. 1987-88, v.p. 1988-89, pres., 1989-90, Leadership Louisville Found., Inc., 1986-92, Greater Louisville Econ. Devel. Partnership, 1987—; chair. Leadership USA, Inc., 1997. 1st lt. U.S. Army, 1974. Mem. ABA (antitrust, patent, trademark, copyright, litigation, torts, and ins. practice sects.), Ky. Bar Assn., Louisville Bar Assn. (bd. dirs. 1985-86, treas. 1988, sec. 1989, v.p. 1990, pres. 1992), Phi Beta Kappa. Democrat. Mem. Disciples of Christ. Club: Louisville Boat, Valhalla Golf. Office: Reed Weitkamp Schell Cox & Vice 2400 Citizens Plz Louisville KY 40202

REED, JOHN THEODORE, publisher, writer; b. Camden, N.J., July 5, 1946; s. Theodore and Marion Theresa (Simonsick) R.; m. Margaret Ogden Tunnell, May 31, 1975; children: Daniel Tunnell, Steven Tunnell, Michael Tunnell. BS in Mil. Sci., U.S. Mil. Acad., West Point, N.Y., 1968; MBA, Harvard U., 1977. Salesman Pritchett & Co., Pine Hill and Collingswood, N.J., 1972-74; property mgr. Fox & Lazo Inc., Cherry Hill, N.J., 1974-75; writer Harcourt Brace Jovanovich, Boston, 1976-86; bank exec. Crocker Nat. Bank, San Francisco, 1977-78; writer, pub. Danville, Calif., 1977—. Author, pub.: Apartment Investing Check Lists, 1978, Aggressive Tax Avoidance for Real Estate Investors, 1981, 15th edit., 1996, How to Manage Residential Property for Maximum Cash Flow and Resale Value, 1995, 4th edit., 1991, How to Use Leverage to Maximize Your Real Estate Investment Return, 1984, 86, How to Increase the Value of Real Estate, 1986, Office Building Acquisition Handbook, 1982, 85, 87, Residential Property Acquisition Handbook, 1991, How To Buy Real Estate for at Least 20% Below Market Value, 1993, 2d edit., 1996; Coaching Youth Football Defense, 1994, 2d edit., 1996; John T. Reed's Real Estate Investor's Monthly Newsletter, 1986—, Coaching Youth Football, 1995, 2d edit., 1997, Football Clock Management, 1997. Served to 1st lt. U.S. Army, 1968-72, Vietnam. Mem. Nat. Assn. Real Estate Editors, Am. Baseball Coaches Assn., Am. Football Coaches Assn., Nat. Youth Sports Coaches Assn., Nat. Fedn. Interscholastic Coaches Assn., Calif. Coaches Assn. Avocations: reading, youth and high sch. coaching, activities with family. Home: 342 Bryan Dr Danville CA 94526-1258 Office: John T. Reed Pub 342 Bryan Dr Danville CA 94526-1258

REED, JOHN WESLEY, lawyer, educator; b. Independence, Mo., Dec. 11, 1918; s. Novus H. and Lilian (Houchens) R.; m. Imogene Fay Vonada, Oct. 5, 1946 (div. 1958); m. Dorothy Elaine Floyd, Mar. 5, 1961; children: Alison A., John M. (dec.), Mary V., Randolph F., Suzanne M. AB, William Jewell Coll., 1939, LLD, 1995; LLB, Cornell U., 1942; LLM, Columbia U., 1949, JSD, 1957. Bar: Mo. 1942, Mich. 1953. Assoc. Stinson, Mag, Thomson, McEvers & Fizzell, Kansas City, Mo., 1942-46; assoc. prof. law U. Okla., 1946-49; assoc. prof. U. Mich., 1949-53, prof., 1953-64, 68-85, Thomas M. Cooley prof., 1985-87, Thomas M. Cooley prof. emeritus, 1987—; dean, prof. U. Colo., 1964-68; dean, prof. Wayne State U., Detroit, 1987-92, prof. emeritus, 1992—; vis. prof. NYU, 1949, U. Chgo., 1960, Yale U., 1963-64, Harvard U., 1982, U. San Diego, 1993; dir. Inst. Continuing Legal Edn., 1968-73; reporter Mich. Rules of Evidence Com., 1975-78, 83-84. Author: (with W.W. Blume) Pleading and Joinder, 1952; (with others) Introduction to Law and Equity, 1953, Advocacy Course Handbook series, 1963-81; editor in chief Cornell Law Quar., 1941-42; contbr. articles to profl. jours. Pres. bd. mgrs. of mins. and missionaries benefit bd. Am. Bapt. Chs. U.S.A., 1967-74, 82-85, 88-94; mem. com. visitors JAG Sch., 1971-76; trustee Kalamazoo Coll., 1954-64, 68-70. Recipient Harrison Tweed award Assn. Continuing Legal Edn. Adminstrs., 1983, Samuel E. Gates award Am. Coll. Trial Lawyers, 1985, Roberts P. Hudson award State Bar Mich., 1989. Fellow Internat. Soc. Barristers (editor jour. 1980—); mem. ABA (mem. coun. litigation sect.), Assn. Am. Law Schs. (mem. exec. com. 1965-67), Am. Acad. Jud. Edn. (v.p. 1978-80), Colo. Bar Assn. (mem. bd. govs. 1964-68), Mich. Supreme Ct. Hist. Soc. (bd. dirs. 1991—), Sci. Club Mich., Order of Coif. Office: U Mich Sch Law Ann Arbor MI 48109-1215

REED, JOSEPH RAYMOND, civil engineering educator, academic administrator; b. Pitts., Aug. 15, 1930; s. David Raymond and Mary (O'Neil) R.; m. Mary Morris Leggett, Mar. 19, 1960; children: Michelle Edwards, Stephanie Anne Reed Wilkinson, David Shepard Reed. BS in Civil Engring., Pa. State U., 1952, MS in Civil Engring., 1955; PhD in Civil Engring., Cornell U., 1971. Registered profl. engr., Tex. Asst. engr. George H. McGinness Assocs., Pitts., 1953-55; constrn. liaison officer USAF, Dallas, 1956-59; civil engring. faculty Pa. State U., University Park, 1959-64; rsch. asst. Cornell U., Ithaca, N.Y., 1964-67; prof. civil engring. Pa. State U., 1967-95, prof. emeritus, 1996; cons. Westvaco, Tyrone, Pa., 1981, Ketron, Inc., Phila., 1982-83, McGraw-Hill Book Co., N.Y.C., 1984-91, MacMillan Pub. Co., N.Y.C., 1987, others; acad. officer dept. civil engring. Pa. State U., 1989-95. Chmn. Stormwater Authority, State College, Pa., 1974-78; coach State Little League, Teener League (All-Star team state championship 1986) and Am. Legion Baseball, State College, 1978-89. Capt. USAF, 1956-59, USAFR, 1959-71. Sci.-Faculty fellow NSF, 1966-67; recipient Adviser Leadership award Tau Beta Pi Assn., 1986. Mem. ASCE, Internat. Assn. Hydraulic Rsch., Elks, Scottish Rite, Sigma Xi, Tau Beta Pi, Chi Epsilon, Phi Sigma Kappa (v.p. 1952). Presbyterian. Avocations: golf, bowling, youth baseball. Home: 1394 Penfield Rd State College PA 16801-6419 Office: Pa State U Dept Civil Engring 212 Sackett Bldg University Park PA 16802-1408 *Everyone will probably be a teacher at some point in their lives, be it as a professional, a parent, a coach, a supervisor, etc. An effective philosophy to follow is to teach the way you would like to be taught.*

REED, JOSEPH VERNER, JR., diplomat; b. N.Y.C., Dec. 17, 1937; s. Joseph V. and Permelia (Pryor) R; m. Marie Maude Byers, Dec. 19, 1959; children: Serena, Electra. BA, Yale U., 1961. With office of pres. The World Bank, Washington, 1959-62; asst. to pres. IBRD, 1961-63; asst. to dir. Chase Manhattan Bank, 1963-68, v.p., exec. asst. to chmn., 1969-81; U.S. amb. to Morocco, 1981-85; amb. to ECOSOC of UN, N.Y.C., 1985-87; undersec. gen. UN, 1987-89; U.S. chief of protocol, The White Ho., Washington, 1989-91; U.S. rep. to UN Gen. Assembly, 1992—; under-sec. gen. UN spl. rep. pub. affairs, 1992—. Mem. Coun. on Fgn. Rels., Met. Club, Links club, River Club. Republican. Episcopalian. Home: 73 Sterling Rd Greenwich CT 06831-2627 Office: Under-Sec-Gen UN Rm S-3161A New York NY 10017

REED, JOSEPH WAYNE, American studies educator, artist; b. St. Petersburg, Fla., May 31, 1932; s. Joseph Wayne and Gertrude (Cain) R.; m. Kit Craig, Dec. 10, 1955; children: Joseph McKean, John Craig, Katherine Hyde Maruyama. BA, Yale U., 1954, MA, 1958, PhD, 1961. Rsch. asst. Yale Libr., 1956-57; instr. English Wesleyan U., Middletown, Conn., 1960-61, asst. prof., 1961-67, assoc. prof., 1967-71, prof., 1971—, chmn. dept., 1971-73, 75-76, 85-86, prof. English and Am. studies, 1987; vis. lectr. Yale U., New Haven, 1974; lectr. U.S. dept. State and USIS, Can., India, Nepal, 1974; coord. cultural exch., New Delhi, Bombay, 1992; coord. music and writing workshop U. Va., Georgetown U., others. Author: English Biography in the Early Nineteenth Century, 1801-38, 1966, Faulkner's Narrative, 1973, Three American Originals: John Ford, William Faulkner, Charles Ives, 1984, American Scenarios, 1989, rev. edit., 1990; editor: Barbara Bodichon's American Diary, 1972, (with W.S. Lewis) Horace Walpole's Family Correspondence, 1975, (with F.A. Pottle) Boswell, Laird of Auchinleck, 1977, 2d edit., 1994; one-man shows include Portal Gallery, London, 1971, USIS Libr., New Delhi, 1974, 92, Addison/Ripley Gallery, Washington, 1987, 92, 95. Chmn. Wesleyan Sesquicentennial, 1982; chmn. bd. trustees Yale Libr. Assocs., 1984—. Lt. (j.g.) USNR, 1954-56. Mem. Elizabethan Club, The Johnsonians (chmn. 1988). Democrat. Episcopalian. Home: 45 Lawn Ave Middletown CT 06457-3135

REED, KATHLYN LOUISE, occupational therapist, educator; b. Detroit, June 2, 1940; d. Herbert C. and Jessie R. (Krehbiel) R. BS in Occupational Therapy, U. Kans., 1964; MA, Western Mich. U., 1966; PhD, U. Wash., 1973; MLS, U. Okla., 1987. Occupational therapist in psychiatry Kans. U. Med. Center, Kansas City, 1964-65; instr. occupational therapy U. Wash., Seattle, 1967-70; assoc. prof. dept. occupational therapy U. Okla. Health Scis. Ctr., Oklahoma City, 1973-77, prof., 1978-85; chmn. dept. occupational therapy U. Okla. Health Scis. Ctr., 1973-85; libr. edn. info. svcs. Houston Acad. Medicine Tex. Med. Ctr. Libr., 1988-97; cons. to Okla. State Dept. Health, 1976-77, Children's Convalescent Ctr., Oklahoma City, 1977-80, Oklahoma City pub. schs., 1980-81; vis. scholars program Tex. Woman's U., 1991-94, adj. prof. Sch. Occupational Therapy, Tex. Woman's U., 1992—. Author: (with Sharon Sanderson) Concepts of Occupational Therapy, 1980, 2d edit., 1983, 3rd edit., 1992, Models of Practice in Occupational Therapy, 1983, Quick Reference to Occupational Therapy, 1991, (with Julie Pauls) Quick Reference to Physical Therapy, 1996, (with S. Cunningham) Internet Guide for Rehabilitation Professionals, 1997. Vol. crisis counselor Open Door Clinic, Seattle, 1968-72; mem. exec. bd. Seattle Mental Health Inst., 1971-72; Mem. Citizen Participation Liaison Council, Seattle, 1970-72. Recipient Award of Merit, Can. Assn. Occupational Therapists, 1988. Fellow Am. Occupational Therapy Assn. (Merit award 1983, Slagle lecture award 1985, Svc. award 1985); mem. ALA, World Fedn. Occupational Therapists, Coun. Exceptional Children, Okla. Occupational Therapy Assn. (pres. 1974-76), Tex. Occupational Therapy Assn., Med. Libr. Assn. (Rittenhouse award 1987, Acad. Health Info. Professions), Nat. Rehab. Assn., Am. Occupational Therapy Found., Assn. Advancement Rehab. Tech., Sensory Integration Internat., Sigma Kappa (Colby award 1994). Democrat. Home: 6699 De Moss Dr Houston TX 77074-5003

REED, KEITH ALLEN, lawyer; b. Anamosa, Iowa, Mar. 5, 1939; s. John Ivan and Florence Lorine (Larson) R.; m. Beth Illana Kesterson, June 22, 1963; children: Melissa Beth, Matthew Keith. BBA, U. Iowa, 1960, JD, 1963. Bar: Ill. and Iowa 1963. Ptnr. Seyfarth, Shaw, Fairweather & Geraldson, Chgo., 1963—. Co-author: Labor Arbitration in Healthcare, 1981; co-editor: Chicagoland Employment Law Manual, 1994, Employment and Discrimination, 1996, Federal Employment Law and Regulations, 1997; co-contbr. articles to Am. Hosp. Assn. publs., 1986-89. Trustee Meth. Hosp. Chgo., 1985—, Trinity Ch. North Shore, Wilmette, Ill., 1983—; mem. ad hoc labor adv. com. Am. Hosp. Assn., Chgo., 1980—; bd. dirs. Lyric Opera Chgo. Ctr. for Am. Artists, pres., 1983-86. Mem. ABA (dir. health law forum 1979-82), Chgo. Bar Assn. (labor and employment law com. 1978—), Union League Club Chgo. (bd. dirs. 1985-88), Sunset Ridge Country Club (Northbrook, Ill.). Republican. Methodist. Avocations: music, community theater, tennis, golf. Office: Seyfarth Shaw Fairweather & Geraldson 55 E Monroe St Ste 4200 Chicago IL 60603-5803

REED, KENNETH G., petroleum company executive; b. 1917; married. Ed., U. Tex. With Amerada Petroleum Corp., Tulsa, 1948-70; sr. v.p. Amerada Petroleum Corp., 1967-70; exec. v.p. internat. operations Amerada Hess Corp., N.Y.C., 1970; pres., chief exec. officer APEXCO, Inc., Tulsa, 1971-77; pres., chief exec. officer Natomas Internat. Corp., 1977, also dir.; exec. v.p. energy, dir. Natomas Co., San Francisco, 1977-83, vice chmn., pres., 1983—; pres., dir. Natomas Energy Co., 1979—; chmn., chief exec. officer Overseas Petroleum Ltd., San Francisco, 1984—; dir. Natomas N.Am. Inc., 1st Nat. Bank & Trust Co., Tulsa, Oneok Inc., Tulsa. Home: 7 BC Rocky Pl Condominium 1400 Poly Dr Billings MT 59102-1737 Office: 100 N 27th St Ste 440 Billings MT 59101-2054

REED, KENNETH PAUL, industrial hygienist, consultant; b. Covington, Ky., Aug. 30, 1937; s. George Anderson and Alice Martha (Spritzky) R.; m. Carol Irene Luken, May 21, 1966; children: Ann E., Susan L., Pamela N. AB, Thomas More Coll., 1957; MS, Xavier U., 1959; PhD, La. State U., 1968. Cert. indsl. hygienist Am. Bd. Indsl. Hygiene. Prof. chemistry Thomas More Coll., Ft. Mitchell, Ky., 1959-78, dir. devel., 1975-78, chmn. dept., 1969-75, asst. dean freshman & gen. studies, 1972-75; gen. mgr. Actus Environ. Service, Florence, Ky., 1978-80; pres., founder Kenneth P. Reed and Assocs., Covington, 1980—; cons. Nat. Inst. Occupational Safety and Health, Cin., 1975—, U.S. Geol. Survey, Doraville, Ga., 1980-82, No. Ky. Bd. Health, Covington, 1980—, Hamilton County Bd. Health, 1996—. Author: Venture, 1975, (with others) Quantitative Chemistry, 1965; contbr. articles to profl. jours. NSF fellow, 1966-67. Mem. ASHRAE, AOAC, NRA (life), Am. Chem. Soc., Am. Indsl. Hygiene Assn., Am. Conf. Govtl. Indsl. Hygienists, Greater Cin. Area Safety Coun. (founder), Kenton (Ky.) Fish and Game Club, Rotary (bd. dirs. Covnnington 1982-87, pres. 1986-87). Republican. Roman Catholic. Home: 609 Oak Ridge Dr Edgewood KY 41017-3231 Office: 3027 Dixie Hwy Ste 117 Covington KY 41017-2361

REED, LEON SAMUEL, policy analyst; b. Warren, Ohio, July 6, 1949; s. Walter Charles and Lois Avalene (Botroff) R. BA in Econs. and Journalism, Antioch Coll., 1971; m. Margaret Smith, Dec. 27, 1975 (div.); m. Lois S. Lembo; children: Samuel Currier, Stephen Walter, Catherine Lois. Project dir. Coun. on Econ. Priorities, N.Y.C. and Washington, 1970-75; sr. mem. profl. staff Joint Com. on Def. Prodn., U.S. Congress, Washington, 1975-77; mem. profl. staff Com. on Banking, Housing and Urban Affairs, U.S. Senate, Washington, 1977-81; analyst TASC, 1981-82, mgr. contingency planning, 1982-85, mgr. indsl. resources dept., 1985-91, dir. indsl. and mfg. scis. div., 1991-197; dir. strategic planning Mgmt. Sys. Group, 1997—; staff writer, photographer Md. Soccer News; bd. dirs. Council on Econ. Priorities, 1971-73; del. White House Conf. on Youth, 1971. Mem. exec. com., Randolph Civic Assn., 1977-83, pres., 1978-80; v.p. North Bethesda Congress of Citizens Assns., 1983-84, pres., 1984-86, sec., 1986-88; mem. Montgomery County Council of Pres., 1982-88, chmn. 1986-87; soccer coach Montgomery Soccer, Inc., 1986—, bd. dir., 1994—, dir. player devel., 1996—. Inducted into Warren H.S. Alumni Hall of Fame, 1997; named MSI Coach of Yr., 1996. Mem. Disciples of Christ Ch. Co-author: Guide to Corporations, 1973, Report of the National Critical Technologies Panel, 1991; author: Military Maneuvers, 1975, Resource Management: A Historical Perspective, 1988; contbr. Strategic Survey, 1981-82, The American Defense Mobilization Intrastructure, 1983; author numerous congressional and exec. br. reports, mag. and jour. articles.

REED, LEONARD NEWTON, secondary school educator; b. Alva, Okla., Feb. 27, 1952; s. Leonard S. and Vevian M. (Chew) R. BA, Northwestern Okla. State U., 1970, MA, 1980; postgrad., No. Ariz. U., 1982-89; cert. ESL, U. Phoenix, 1992. Cert. social sci. tchr., Ariz., Okla., ESL, Ariz. Social sci. tchr. Chinle (Ariz.) Unified Sch. Dist., 1974—; night staff Navajo C.C., 1988—; student coun. advisor Chinle Unified Sch. Dist., 1975-76, 78-83, 84-93. Mem. com. Apache County (Ariz.) Dem. Party, 1980-88, 93-96; state del. Ariz. Dem. Party, 1980; mem. Nat. Gay and Lesbian Task Force, 1976—. 20868551 (gay and lesbian caucus 1988—, rural and small caucus, 1986—, Ariz. Edn. Assn. (bd. dirs. 1984-88, 89-90, human rels. com. 1987-94, 95—, chair, human rels. com. 1992-94, treas. N.E. adv. coun., Bill Hodge award 1989, first male co-chair gay, lesbian caucus 1995-97, founder 1995—), Ariz. Student Coun. Advisors Assn., Chinle Edn. Assn. (past pres. 1979, 81, treas.), CHS (social sci. dept. chair 1981-84, 85-93). Home: PO Box 1678 Chinle AZ 86503-1678 Office: Chinle Unified Sch Dist # 24 PO Box 587 Chinle AZ 86503-0587

REED, LESTER JAMES, biochemist, educator; b. New Orleans, Jan. 3, 1925; s. John T. and Sophie (Pastor) R.; m. Janet Louise Gruschow, Aug. 7, 1948; children—Pamela, Sharon, Richard, Robert. B.S., Tulane U., 1943; D.Sc. (hon.), 1977; Ph.D., U. Ill., 1946. Rsch. asst. NDRC, Urbana, Ill., 1944-46; rsch. assoc. biochemistry Cornell U. Med. Coll., 1946-48; faculty U. Tex., Austin, 1948—; prof. chemistry U. Tex., 1958—, Ashbel Smith prof., 1984—; rsch. sci. Clayton Found. Biochem. Inst., 1949—, assoc. dir., 1962-63, dir., 1963-96. Contbr. articles profl. jours. Recipient ASBMB-Merk award Am. Soc. for Biochemistry, 1994. Mem. NAS, Am. Acad. Arts and Scis., Am. Soc. for Biochemistry and Molecular Biology (Merck award 1994), Am. Chem. Soc. (Eli Lilly & Co. award in biol. chemistry 1958), Phi Beta Kappa, Sigma Xi. Home: 3502 Balcones Dr Austin TX 78731-5802 Office: U Tex Biochem Inst Experimental Sci Bldg 442 Austin TX 78712

REED, LOU, musician; b. Bklyn., Mar. 2, 1942; s. Sidney Joseph and Toby (Futterman) R.; m. Sylvia Morales, Feb. 14, 1980. B.A., Syracuse U., 1964. Songwriter Pickwick Records, N.Y.C., 1965; rec. artist Verve, MGM, Atlantic, Arista, RCA, Sire Record Cos., N.Y.C., 1965—. Solo albums include Lou Reed, 1972, Berlin, 1973, Rock 'N' Roll Animal, 1974, Sally Can't Dance, 1974, Metal Machine Music, 1975, Lou Reed Live, 1975, Coney Island Baby, 1976, Walk on the Wild Side, 1977, Street Hassle, 1978, Live, Take No Prisoners, 1978, Vicious, 1979, The Bells, 1979, Growing Up in Public, 1980, Rock 'n' Roll Diary, 1967-80, 1980, Blue Mask, Legendary Hearts, 1983, New Sensations, 1984, Mistrial, 1986, New York, 1987, Songs for Drella, 1990, Magic and Loss, 1992, Between Thought and Expression: The Lou Reed Anthology, 1992, Different Times: Lou Reed In The 70's, 1996, Set The Twilight Reeling, 1996; founding mem. (band) The Velvet Underground, 1966-70, touring with Andy Warhol's The Exploding Plastic Inevitable; albums include The Velvet Underground and Nico, 1967, White Light White Heat, The Velvet Underground, Loaded, 1970; albums after Velvet Underground include Andy Warhol's Velvet Underground, 1971, Live at Max's Kansas City, 1972, Velvet Underground, Lou Reed, 1973, Velvet Underground Live, 1974, VU, 1985, Another VU; writer of poetry pub. in Fusion mag.; actor in some film roles. Recipient Best New Poet award Council on Small Lit. Mags., 1977. Mem. Musician's Union Local 802, Screen Actors Guild. Jewish. Address: RCA Records 1133 6th Ave New York NY 10036*

REED, LOWELL A., JR., federal judge; b. Westchester, Pa., 1930; s. Lowell A. Sr. and Catherine Elizabeth (Pauly) R.; m. Diane Benson; children: Jeffrey Barton, Lowell Andrew, Diane Reed Marsh, Christopher Benson. BBA, U. Wis., 1952; JD, Temple U., 1958. Bar: Pa. 1959, U.S. Dist. Ct. (ea. dist.) Pa. 1961, U.S. Ct. Appeals (3d cir.) 1962, U.S. Supreme Ct. 1970. Corp. trial counsel PMA Group, Phila., 1958-63; assoc. Rawle & Henderson, Phila., 1963-65, gen. ptnr., 1966-88; judge U.S. Dist Ct., Phila., 1988—; lectr. law Temple U., 1965-81, faculty Acad. Advocacy, 1988—, Pa. Bar Inst., 1972—. Contbr. articles to profl. jours. Elder Abington (Pa.) Presbyn. Ch.; past. mem. Pa. Senate Select Com. Med. Malpractice; past pres., bd. dirs. Rydal Meadowbrook Civic Assn.; bd. dirs. Abington Sch. Bd., 1971, World Affairs Coun. Phila., 1983-88; trustee Abington Health Care Corp., 1983-88, 90-93. Lt. comdr. USNR, 1952-57. Recipient Alumni Achievement award Temple U. 1988. Mem. ABA, Pa. Bar Assn., Phila. Bar Assn. (chmn. medico legal com. 1975, constl. bicentennial com. 1986-87, commn. on jud. selection and retention 1983-87), Temple Am. Inn of Ct. (pres. 1990-93, master of bench 1990—), Am. Judicature Soc., Temple U. Law Alumni Assn. (exec. com. 1987-90), Hist. Soc. U.S. Supreme Ct., Hist. Soc. U.S. Dist. Ct. Ea. Dist. Pa. Republican. Office: US Dist Ct 11614 US Courthouse Independence Mall W Philadelphia PA 19106

REED, LOY WAYNE, minister, ministry director; b. Springfield, Mo., June 19, 1948; s. George Wayne and Stella Gertrude (Miller); m. Glenda Ann Shores, Aug. 24, 1968; children: Danna, Dania, Dawn, Diedra. BA in Philosphy, William Jewell Coll., Liberty, Mo., 1970; MDiv, Midwestern Bapt. Theol. Sem., 1978, D of Ministry, 1984. Campus min. Mo. Western Coll., St. Joseph, 1976-77; campus min., adminstr. U. Mo., 1977-80; pastor Harmony Bapt. Ch., Rogersville, Mo., 1980-85; v.p. Mo. Bapt. Convention, Jefferson City, 1986-87; pastor Calvary Bapt. Ch., Columbia, Mo., 1985-91; dir. student ministries Fla. Bapt. Convention, Jacksonville, Fla., 1991—; cons. Reality Enterprises, Jacksonville, 1995—. Contbr. articles to mags. in field. Named Outstanding Young Man Jaycees, 1976, 79, 80. Mem. Nat. Assn. State Student Dirs. Avocations: writing, hunting, golf, fishing, reading. Home: 321 Edinburgh Lane Orange Park FL 32073 Office: Fla Bapt Convention 1230 Hendricks Ave Jacksonville FL 32207-8619

REED, MICHAEL A., agricultural products supplier; b. 1947. Grad., U. Mo., 1969, JD, 1976. With Poole, Reed and Croessmann, Springfield, Mo., 1977-80, Tindle Mills, Springfield, 1980-83, Vigortone Ag Products, Inc., Cedar Rapids, Iowa, 1983-85; with PM AG Products Inc., Homewood, Ill., 1985—, now pres. With USAF, 1970-74. Office: PM AG Products Inc 17475 Jovanna Dr Homewood IL 60430-4623*

REED, MICHAEL HAYWOOD, lawyer; b. Phila., Jan. 17, 1949; s. Soloman Taylor and Vivian (Haywood) Reed; m. Yalta Gilmore, Aug. 12, 1978; children: Alexandra Haywood, Michael Haywood Jr. BA in Polit. Sci., Temple U., 1969; JD, Yale U., 1972. Bar: Pa. 1972, U.S. Dist. Ct. (ea. dist.) Pa. 1972, U.S. Dist. Ct. (ea. dist.) Mich. 1982, U.S. Supreme Ct. 1982, U.S. Ct. Appeals (3d cir.) 1985. Assoc. Pepper, Hamilton & Scheetz, Phila., 1972-80, ptnr., 1980—; co-adj. prof. law Rutgers U., Camden, N.J., 1983, 85; adj. prof. sch. law Temple U., Phila., 1989; mem. Pa. Judicial Inquiry and Rev. Bd., 1990-93; mem. steering com. Ea. Dist. Pa. Bankruptcy Conf., 1992—. Contbr. articles to profl. jours. Advisor Post 913 Law Explorers, Phila., 1974-84; trustee Acad. Natural Scis., Phila., 1988—, Episcopal Hosp., Phila., 1986—; mem. bd. advisors Pub. Interest Law Ctr., Phila., 1992—; mem. exec. bd. Com. of Seventy, Phila., 1985—. Recipient cert. of honor Alumnus of Yr. Coll. of Arts and Scis. Temple U., 1995. Fellow Am. Coll.

Bankruptcy; mem. ABA (chmn. subcom. labor and employment law, bus bankruptcy com. sect. bus. law 1991-97, chmn. subcom. on labor and employment law 1997—), Nat. Bar Assn., Pa. Bar Assn. (mem. ho. of dels. 1985—, chmn. minority bar com. 1988-90, mem. bd. govs. 1993-96, cochairperson 1994 ann. meeting, Spl. Achievement award 1989, Cert. of Honor award 1995), Barristers Assn. Phila. (1st v.p. 1974-76), Alpha Phi Alpha, Yale Club (Phila.). Democrat. Baptist. Avocations: racquetball, film, theatre, biking, piano. Home: 225 N 23rd St Philadelphia PA 19103-1005 Office: Pepper Hamilton & Scheetz 3000 Two Logan Sq 18th Arch St Philadelphia PA 19103

REED, MICHAEL ROBERT, agricultural economist; b. Lawrence, Kans., July 11, 1953; s. Robert Stanley and Marian Lucille (Karr) R.; m. Patricia Gail Gurtler, Mar. 16, 1973; children: Laura Gail, Brian Michael. BS, Kans. State U., 1974; MS, Iowa State U., 1976, PhD, 1979. Asst. prof. U. Ky., Lexington, 1978-83, assoc. prof., 1983-89; prof., 1989—, exec. dir. Ctr. for Export Devel., 1988-95; dir. office of internat. affairs U. Ky., Lexington, 1994—; cons. USDA, 1994, 96, U.S. AID, Washington, 1983-86. Editorial council So. Jour. of Agrl. Econs., 1983-86; contbr. articles to profl. jours. Recipient Outstanding Jour. Article award Soc. Farm Mgrs. and Rural Appraisers, 1986; grantee Farmer Coop. Svcs., 1982-84, 87-88, TVA, 1982-85, Fed. Crop Ins. Corp., 1985-87, USDA, 1986—. Mem. Am. Agrl. Econs. Assn., So. Agrl. Econs. Assn., Gamma Sigma Delta, Omicron Delta Epsilon. Home: 2216 Bonhaven Rd Lexington KY 40515-1150 Office: U Ky Dept Agrl Econs 300 Bradley Hall Lexington KY 40546-0215

REED, MILLARD C., academic administrator; b. Hannibal, Mo., Nov. 19, 1933; s. Harlow and Mary Agnes R.; m. Barbara Jean Cunningham, Nov. 26, 1953; children: Stephen, Deborah, Paul, John. AB, Olivet Nazarene Coll., 1955; MDiv, Eden Theol. Sem., 1961; postgrad., U. Chgo., 1961-63; D of Ministry, Vanderbilt U., 1979. Pres. Trevecca Nazarene U., Nashville. Author: Let Your Church Grow: Proclaiming the Spirit, Take Care Man: Family Love in All Dimensions, Biblical PReaching for Contemporary Man, How to Live the Holy Life. Chaplain Nashville Optimist Club, Rotary Club, Billy Graham exec. com. Nashville Crusade; bd. dirs. Nashville Coop. Ministry, Tenn. Preparatory Sch., Czar Palaver Club. Office: Trevecca Nazarene U 333 Murfreesboro Rd Nashville TN 37210-2834

REED, NANCY BINNS, composer, poet, artist; b. Palo Alto, Calif., Dec. 11, 1924; d. Clyde Arthur and Mary Ella (Loder) Binns; m. Ogden Cartwright Reed, Jan. 17, 1948 (dec. Feb. 1980); children: Hayward C., Cartwright, Chris B., Amy Reed Geiger. BA, U. Calif., Davis and Berkeley, 1945; postgrad. in social work, U. Calif., Berkeley, 1946-47; AA in Fine Arts, No. Va. C.C., 1990. Composer, poet, artist, 1941—; social worker in Calif., Washington, 1947-50; tchr. art, music and poetry at Mildred Green Elem. Sch., Anacostia, Washington, 1981-96. Composer: (songs) Oh Happy Day, 1952 (Nat. hit, three different recordings simultaneously on Hit Parade), Our Lions (march), 1971, Civilian March, 1974 (performed ann. at Pentagon Civilian award ceremonies), Tocqueville! (musical), 1976, Ali Baba (musical), 1977, The Halloween Suite, 1978, The Duckling (full symphony), 1981, Royalty Revisited (string quartet), 1986, Frank Rowley's Rally, 1991, American Patchwork: The Star, The Eagle, The Parade, The Ring and The Rose, 1987, Vive Leche! (musical), 1992, Dragon Divertimento, 1992, Concert Christmas Music, 1992, (opera) David, David Jesse's Son, 1993, others; author, illustrator: The Magic Gourds, 1969, The Sun and the Moon, 1969, A Tale of the Heidelberg Lion, 1974, Le Conte Du Lion De Heidelberg, 1983; music recorded by London Philharmonia Winds, 1984. Mem. ASCAP (recipient 18 awards for compositions, 1977-96). Avocation: home-based studio equipped with Kurzweil 250 keyboard and Macintosh computer on which to create music.

REED, NANCY BOYD, English language and elementary education educator; b. Lodi, Calif., Oct. 10, 1946; d. Leo H. and Anna Gwen (Coombes) Boyd; m. Maurice Allen Reed, Dec. 22, 1966; 1 child, Scot Alastair. AA Recreational Adminstrn. with honors, Delta Coll., 1974; BA Recreational Adminstrn. with honors, Calif. State U., Sacramento, 1976, MA in Edn., English Lang. Devel., 1988; cert. computers in edn., U. Calif., Davis, 1984. Cert. multiple subject, phys. edn., computers in edn. teaching. Tchr. 4th grade Hagginwood Sch., Sacramento, 1980-81; tchr. 4th/5th grade impacted lang. Noralto Sch., Sacramento, 1981-88, bilingual resource tchr., 1988-91, tchr. English lang. devel., 1991-96, bilingual resource tchr., 1996—; mentor tchr. North Sacramento Sch. Dist., Sacramento, 1992-95, bilingual resource tchr., 1996—; fellow, tchr./cons. No. Calif. Math. Project, U. Calif., Davis, 1985—. Dir. Jasmine Flower Dancers, Sacramento, 1984-96; comty. rep. Am. Host Found., Sacramento, 1976—. Named Outstanding Educator Capitol Svc. Ctr., 1992, Tchr. of Yr., Noralto Sch., North Sacramento Sch., 1996; scholar Fridtjof-Nansen-Akademie, Ingleheim, Germany, 1993, Adenauer Found., Berlin, 1982, 93. Mem. NEA, Nat. Vis. Tchrs. Assn. (bd. dirs. 1994—), Nat. Assn. Bilingual Edn., Nat. Coun. Tchrs. Math., Calif. Tchrs. Assn. (state coun. rep. 1995-96), North Sacramento Edn. Assn. (sec. 1986-88, v.p. 1988-90, pres. 1990-92, outstanding educator 1992). Avocations: travel, photography, camping. Home: 3665 Halter Ct Sacramento CA 95821-3266 Office: Noralto Sch North Sacramento Sch Dist 477 Las Palmas Ave Sacramento CA 95815-1605

REED, NANCY ELLEN, computer science educator; b. Mpls., Aug. 11, 1955; d. Jacob Alen and Mary Emeline (Howser) Lundgren; m. Todd Randall Reed, June 18, 1977. BS in Biology, U. Minn., 1977, MS in Computer Sci., 1988, PhD in Computer Sci., 1995. Rsch. lab. technician gastroenterology rsch. unit Mayo Clinic, Rochester, Minn., 1978-81; phys. sci. technician U.S. Environ. Hygiene Agy., Fitzsimmons Army Med. Ctr., Aurora, Colo., 1982-83; profl. rsch. asst. molecular, cellular, devel. biology dept. U. Colo., Boulder, 1983-84; tchg. asst. U. Minn., 1985-86, rsch. asst., 1985-88; computer programmer Control Data Corp., Arden Hills, Minn., 1986; asst. Artificial Intelligence Lab. Swiss Fed. Inst. Tech., Lausanne, 1989-91; lectr. computer and info. sci. dept. Sonoma State U., Rohnert Park, Calif., 1993-94; lectr. U. Calif., Davis, 1994-95, 96, rschr., 1995, asst. adj. prof. computer sci. dept., 1996—. Contbr. articles to profl. jours.; spkr. in field; reviewer for Artificial Intelligence in Medicine, Internat. Jour. of Man-Machine Studies, Integrated Computer-Aided Engring. Microelectronic and Info. Scis. Fellowship, 1984-85, Am. Electronics Assn. Fellowship, 1985-89. Mem. IEEE, Am. Assn. for Artificial Intelligence (scholarship for travel nat. conf. on artificial intelligence 1992, 94, session chair for spring syposium 1994), Assn. for Computing Machinery. Office: U Calif Computer Sci Dept Davis CA 95616-8562

REED, PATSY BOSTICK, university administrator, nutrition educator; b. Holland, Tex., Jan. 5, 1936; d. William T. and Evelyn R. (Smith) Bostick; m. F. Dewitt Reed, Sept. 6, 1958. BS, U. Tex., 1959, MS, 1967, PhD, 1969. Tchr. pub. schs., Austin and Port Arthur, Tex., 1959-65; postdoctoral fellow U. Va., Charlottesville, 1969-70; research chemist U. Heidelberg, W.Ger., 1970-72; assoc. prof. nutrition Idaho State U., Pocatello, 1973-79; prof. nutrition, adminstr. No. Ariz. U., Flagstaff, 1979-94, dean Coll. Design and Tech., 1981-85; asst. v.p. acad. affairs U. N.C., Asheville, 1985-87, v.p. acad. affairs, 1987-93, interim pres., 1994, chancellor, 1994—. Author: Nutrition: An Applied Science, 1980. Mem. AAAS, Am. Chem. Soc., Am. Dietetic Assn., Phi Kappa Phi, Sigma Xi. Office: U NC 1 University Hts Asheville NC 28804-3251

REED, PAUL ALLEN, artist; b. Washington, Mar. 28, 1919; s. Charles Miler and Lula Rachael (Annadale) R.; m. Esther Kishter, July 10, 1939; children—Jean Reed Roberts, Thomas, Robert. Student, San Diego State Coll., 1936, Corcoran Sch. Art, 1937. Asst. art dir. USAF mag., N.Y.C., 1942-44; artist B.D. Adams Advt. Agy., Montclair, N.J., 1944-48; asst. art dir. M.F. Dreher Advt. Agy., N.Y.C., 1948-50; free lance graphics designer Washington, 1950-62; graphics dir. U.S. Peace Corps, Washington, 1962-71; asst. prof. Corcoran Sch. Art, Washington, 1971-81. Exhibited in one man shows at, Corcoran Gallery Art, 1966, Washington U., 1967, Ariz. State U., 1971, Phoenix Art Mus., 1977; represented in more than 50 permanent collections at Hirshhorn Mus., Nat. Mus. Am. Art, N.C. Mus. Art, Corcoran Gallery, San Francisco Mus. Art, Detroit Inst. Art, others; artist in residence, Phoenix Art Mus., 1976, Am. U., 1997; vis. artist Ariz. State U., Tempe, 1980. Home: 3541 N Utah St Arlington VA 22207-4444

REED, RALPH EUGENE, JR., association executive, writer; b. Portsmouth, Va., June 24, 1961; s. Ralph Sr. and Marcy R.; m. Jo Anne Young, 1987; children: Brittany, Ralph III, Christopher. BA in History, U. Ga., 1985; D in Am. History, Emory U., 1991. Exec. dir. Christian Coalition, Chesapeake, Va., 1989-97; pres. Century Strategies, Strategies Consulting Co., 1997—; founder Students for Am., Raleigh, N.C., 1984; lobbyist; spkr. in field. Office: Christian Coalition 1801 Sara Dr Ste L Chesapeake VA 23320-2647

REED, RAYMOND DERYL, architect; b. Alturas, Calif., Mar. 29, 1930; s. Russell Jacob and Nita Ferne (Wilcox) R.; m. Patricia Reinerth, Apr. 30, 1954; children—Kathryn, Russell, Ann, Andrea. B.Arch., Tulane U., 1953; M.Arch., Harvard U., 1958. Chmn. architecture and interior design dept. U. Southwestern La., 1958-64; head dept. architecture Iowa State U., 1964-70, dir. grad. research in architecture, 1970-73; mem. faculty Tex. A&M U., 1973—, prof. architecture, 1973—; dean Tex. A&M U. (Coll. Architecture and Environ. Design), 1973-80; dir. Internat. Ctr. for Cybernetics and Informatics, 1990. Author: Sustainable Architecture, 1988, rev. edit, 1990; contbr. numerous articles on energy conservation and post petroleum architecture to research publs. Served with USNR, 1953-58. Mem. AIA, Nat. Council Archtl. Registration Bds., Am. Collegiate Schs. Architecture, Tex. Soc. Architects, La. Architects Soc. Home: 1601 Wolf Pen Ct College Station TX 77840-3169 Office: Tex A&M U Dept Architecture College Station TX 77843

REED, REX, author, critic; b. Ft. Worth, Oct. 2, 1938; s. Jimmy M. and Jewell (Smith) R. BA, La. State U., 1960. Film critic Holiday mag., Women's Wear Daily, 1968-71; music critic Stereo Rev., 1968-75; syndicated columnist Chgo. Tribune-N.Y. Daily News Syndicate, 1971—; film critic N.Y. Daily News, 1971-75; now columnist N.Y. Observer, N.Y.C.; critic At the Movies, public TV series, 1986. Appeared in film Myra Breckenridge, 1970, Superman, 1978; author: Do You Sleep in the Nude?, 1968, Conversations in the Raw, 1969, Big Screen, Little Screen, 1971, People Are Crazy Here, 1974, Valentines and Vitriol, 1977, Travolta to Keaton, 1979; author: (novel) Personal Effects, 1986. Office: NY Observer 54 E 64th St New York NY 10021-7306

REED, REX RAYMOND, retired telephone company executive; b. Peterson, Iowa, Mar. 19, 1922; s. Charles Bernard and Dagmar Helen (Heick) R.; m. Rita Compton, Dec. 3, 1944; children: Julie, Nancy, Linda; m. Mary Connors, June 13, 1992. Student, Morningside Coll., 1940-41, Iowa State U., 1941-43, 46-47, U. Notre Dame, 1943-44; B.S. in Gen. Engring, Iowa State U., 1947. With Northwestern Bell Telephone Co. (various locations), 1947-60, 61-66; employee info. mgr., pub. relations dept. Northwestern Bell Telephone Co. (various locations), Omaha, 1957-58; gen. comml. mgr., comml. dept. Northwestern Bell Telephone Co. (various locations), Fargo, N.D., 1958-60; asst. v.p. personnel and employment Northwestern Bell Telephone Co. (various locations), 1961-62; asst. v.p. personnel Northwestern Bell Telephone Co. (various locations), Nebr. area, 1962-64; asst. v.p. personnel and labor relations Northwestern Bell Telephone Co. (various locations), 1964-66; with AT&T Corp., N.Y.C., 1960-61, 66-84; dir. labor relations, personnel dept. AT&T Corp., 1966-71, v.p. labor relations, 1971-83, sr. v.p. labor relations, 1984; ret., 1984; dir. Ind. Bell Telephone Co., Ill. Bell Telephone Co., First Investors Corp N.Y.C. Mem. Madison (N.J.) Bd. Edn., 1969-70, pres., 1971-75; Trustee Menninger Found., Topeka, 1979—, Morristown (N.J.) Meml. Hosp., 1977—; bd. dirs. Nat. Urban Coalition, 1981-84. Served with USMC, 1943-46; to capt. 1951-53. Mem. Bus. Roundtable (chmn. labor-mgmt. com. 1976-77), Labor Policy Assn. (chmn. 1979-83), Inst. Collective Bargaining (bd. dirs. 1976-84), Orgn. Resources Counselors, Morris County Golf Club (Morristown, N.J., pres. bd. govs. 1991-92). Home: 259 Governors Dr Kiawah Island SC 29455

REED, RICHARD JOHN, retired meteorology educator; b. Braintree, Mass., June 18, 1922; s. William Amber and Gertrude Helen (Volk) R.; m. Joan Murray, June 10, 1950; children: Ralph Murray, Richard Cobden, Elizabeth Ann. Student, Boston Coll., 1940-41, Dartmouth Coll., 1943-44; BS, Calif. Inst. Tech., 1945; ScD, MIT, 1949. Research staff mem. MIT, Cambridge, 1950-54; asst. prof. dept. atmospheric scis. U. Wash., Seattle, 1954-58, assoc. prof., 1958-63, prof., 1963-91, prof. emeritus, 1991—; cons. U.S. Weather Service, Suitland, Md., 1961-62, European Ctr. for Medium Range Weather Forecasts, Reading, Eng., 1985-86; exec. scientist NRC, Washington, 1968-69; trustee Univ. Corp. for Atmospheric Research, Boulder, Colo., 1987-92. Served to lt. (j.g.) USN, 1942-46. Fellow AAAS, Am. Meteorol. Soc. (pres. 1972, Meisinger award 1964, Second Half Century award 1972, Charles Franklin Brooks award 1983, Carl-Gustaf Rossby Rsch. medal 1989), Am. Geophys. Union; mem. NAS. Democrat. Unitarian. Office: U Wash Box 351640 Dept Atmospheric Scis Seattle WA 98195-1640

REED, ROBERT DANIEL, publisher; b. Pottsville, Pa., May 24, 1941; s. Robert Daniel R.; children: Robert Duane, Alan Andrija, Tanya. Purchasing mgr. Ogden Tech. Labs., Sunnyvale, Calif., 1962-69; mktg. mgr. Plaza Press, Sunnyvale, 1969-94; pub. R & E Pubs., Saratoga, Calif., 1966-94; founder Bob Reed Studios; ptnr. Reed's Mktg. Svcs.; co-founder Ceasefire USA; founder, pres. Green PR Internat. Mktg. Cons.; pres. Robert D. Reed Pubs. Author: We Care Cookbook, 1974; pub. over 1150 books on human rights, ethnic history edn., criminology, AIDS, Alzheimers disease, teen suicide, also how-to, trade, and humor books; co-author 50 books on poverty, hunger, homelessness, abuse, sexual assault. With U.S. Army, 1959-61. Mem. Ctr. for Dem. Instns., Nat. Fedn. Ind. Bus., Calif. Inventors Coun., Smithsonian Instn., Soc. for Scholarly Pub., World Future Soc. Inventor electro mech.-electronics devices, creative humor products. Home: 750 La Playa St # 647 San Francisco CA 94121-3262 *Spend your life doing what you like to do, by putting all your efforts into it. Don't be afraid to take a chance. Remember, if life gets dull-Risk it a bit.*

REED, ROBERT MONROE, publishing executive b. Sheldon, Iowa, Feb. 18, 1932; s. Carl A. and Hazel A. (Dockendorf) R.; m. Maxine Kathryn Gordon, June 7, 1954; children—Robert G., Richard K., Deri L. B.A., U. Iowa, 1956; M.A., U. Mich., 1958. Prodn. mgr. Sta. WETV, Atlanta, 1958-60; program mgr. Sta. WHA-TV, Madison, Wis., 1960-62; founder, gen. mgr. Sta. KHET-TV, Honolulu, 1962-69; exec. dir. PBS Video, Washington, 1969-76; gen. mgr. Sta. KUED-TV, Salt Lake City, 1976-78; exec. v.p. Nat. Video Clearinghouse, Inc., Syosset, N.Y., 1978-88; pres. Reed-Gordon Books Inc., 1988—; asst. prof. U. Wis.-Madison, 1960-62; assoc. prof. U. Hawaii, 1962-69; cons HEW, Dept. Army, Toronto Bd. Edn., NSF, others. Author: American Telecommunications Market, 1982; Career Opportunities: TV/Video, 1982, 86, 90, Ency. of TV, Cable and Video, 1992, Dictionary of TV, Cable and Video, 1994, The Potluck Dinner That Went Astray, 1996; pub.: The Video Source Book, ann. 1978-89; Video Tape/Disc Guides, ann. 1978-88; contbr. articles to profl. jours. Chmn., Honolulu Council Chs., 1965; troop leader Boy Scouts Am., Honolulu, 1966. With USN, 1949-52; Korea. Mem. Nat. Assn. Ednl. Broadcasters, Assn. Ednl. Communications Tech., Rocky Mountain Corp. Pub. Broadcasting (dir. 1977-79), Pacific Mountain Network (dir. 1976-79), Pub. Broadcasting Service (dir. 1978-79). Presbyterian. Lodge: Masons. Home: 285 Burr Rd East Northport NY 11731-5201

REED, ROBERT PHILLIP, lawyer; b. Springfield, Ill., June 14, 1952; s. Robert Edward and Rita Anne (Kane) R.; m. Janice Leigh Kloppenburg, Oct. 8, 1976; children: Kevin Michael, Matthew Carl, Jennifer Leigh, Rebecca Ann. AB, St. Louis U., 1974; JD, U. Ill., 1977. Bar: Ill. 1977, U.S. Dist. Ct. (ctrl. dist.) Ill. 1979, U.S.Ct. Appeals (7th cir.) 1983, U.S. Dist. Ct. (so. dist.) Ill. 1992, Colo. 1993. Intern Ill. Legislature, Springfield, 1977-78; assoc. Traynor & Hendricks, Springfield, 1979-80; ptnr. Traynor, Hendricks & Reed, Springfield, 1981-88; pvt. practice Springfield, 1988—; pub. defender Sangamon County, Ill., Springfield, 1979-81; hearing examiner Ill. State Bd. Elections, Springfield, 1981-88; spl. asst. atty. gen. State of Ill., Springfield, 1983—; instr. Lincoln Land Community Coll., Springfield, 1988. Trustee Springfield Pk. Dist., 1985-89. Mem. Nat. Assn. Securities Dealers, Inc. (arbitrator 1996—), Comml. Law League Am., Christian Legal Soc., Ill. State Bar Assn., Colo. Bar Assn., Attys. Title Guaranty Fund, Inc., Phi Beta Kappa. Roman Catholic. Office: 1129 S 7th St Springfield IL 62703-2418

REED, SHERMAN KENNEDY, chemical consultant; b. Chgo., Apr. 11, 1919; s. Frank Hynes and Helen Louise (Kennedy) R.; m. Octavia Bailey, Oct. 11, 1943; children: Martin Bailey, Holly Anne, Julie Marie Reed. B.S. with honors, U. Ill., 1940; Ph.D., Cornell U., 1949. Asst. instr. chemistry Cornell U., 1940-43; asst. research scientist Manhattan Project, N.Y.C., 1942-46; asst. prof. Bucknell U., Lewisburg, Pa., 1946-50; with FMC Corp., 1950—, mgr., asst. dir. research, 1950-60, divisional dir. research and devel., central research dir., 1960-76, v.p., 1976-82; cons. FMC Corp., Chgo., 1983—; dir. Avicon, Inc., 1970-82; pres., dir. FMC Gold Corp.; mng. dir. COGAS Devel. Co., 1975—; dir. Indsl. Research Inst., N.Y.C., Franklin Inst., Phila., 1976-83; chmn. bd. Franklin Research Ctr., Phila., 1976-83. Fellow Am. Inst. Chemists; mem. Am. Chem. Soc., AAAS, Assn. Research Dirs. (pres. 1973). Republican. Clubs: Union League (Phila.); Nassau (Princeton, N.J.). Home and Office: 14 Sailfish Rd Vero Beach FL 32960-5279

REED, STANLEY FOSTER, editor, writer, publisher, lecturer; b. Bogota, N.J., Sept. 28, 1917; s. Morton H. and Beryl (Turner) R.; m. Stella Swingle, Sept. 28, 1940 (div. 1978); children: Nancie, Beryl Ann, Alexandra; m. Shirley Weihman, Sept. 28, 1985 (dec. Feb. 1988); m. Catherine Case Commander, Dec. 16, 1989 (div. 1991). Student, George Washington U., 1939-40, Johns Hopkins, 1940-41; MBA, Loyola U., Md., 1981. Registered profl. engr., D.C. With Bethlehem Steel Corp., Balt., 1940-41; cons. engr., 1942-44; founder, pres. Reed Research, Inc., Washington, 1945-62; pres. Reed Research Inst. Creative Studies, Washington, from 1951; founder, chmn. LogEtronics, Inc., 1955; founder, pres., chmn. Tech. Audit Corp., 1962; assoc. Mgmt. Analysis Corp., 1978-81; sr. cons. Hay Assocs., Phila., 1980-83; entrepreneur in residence Coll. Charleston; co-chmn. semi-ann. Merger Week Northwestern U.; lectr. numerous U.S. and fgn. groups and instns. including Union Theol. Sem., U. Pa., Pa. State U., U. Colo., Georgetown U., Rensselaer Poly. Inst., Am. U., Claremont Coll., So. Meth. U., Pace U., Wayne State U., U. Oreg., U. Conn., St. John's U., Pepperdine U., Loyola Coll. of Md., San Francisco State U., U. Pitts., U. R.I., Marquette U., Vanderbilt U., Boston U., U. Cin., Gustavus Adolphus Coll., U. Mo., Mich. State U., Lehigh U., Calif. Inst. Tech., Denver U., George Washington U., Elmhurst Coll.; vis. fellow Wilton Pk. Conf., Eng., 1968. Author: The Art of M&A: A Merger/Aquisition/Buyout Guide, 1989, 2d edit., 1995, The Toxic Executive, 1993; founder, editor, pub.: Mergers and Acqusitions mag., 1965—, Dirs. and Bds. mag., 1976—; founder, editor, pub.: Campaigns and Elections mag., 1980; founder, pub. Export Today mag., 1985; contbr. articles to leading jours., chpts. to books; patentee. Bd. dirs. Nat. Patent Coun., 1970—; founder, chmn. ann Merger Week, Washington, 1973-77, Northwestern U., 1977-87. Mem. Soc. Naval Architects and Marine Engrs. (life), Am. Econ. Assn., Dictionary Soc. of N.Am., N.Y. Yacht Club. Home: 330 Concord St Charleston SC 29401-1549 Office: 9 Liberty St Charleston SC 29401-1400

REED, SUELLEN KINDER, state education administrator. BA in History, Polit. Sci.and Secondary Edn., Hanover Coll.; MA in Elem. Edn. and History, Ball State U., PhD in Adminstrn. and Supervision; postgrad., Fla. Atlantic U., U. Scranton, Purdue U., Earlham Coll., Ind. U.; Ind. State U. Cert. secondary tchr., elem. tchr., gifted and talented tchr., administr., supr., Fla., Ind., supt., Ind. Tchr. 5th and 6th grades Rushville (Ind.) Consol. Sch. Corp., 1967-70, asst. supt., 1987-91, supt., 1991-93; tchr. Shelbyville (Ind.) High Sch., 1970-71; tchr. 6th, 7th and 8th grade social studies, curriculum Broward County (Fla.) Sch. Corp., 1971-76; tchr. Rushville Jr. High Sch., 1976-77; asst. prin. Rushville Elem. Sch., 1977-79; prin. Frazee Elem. Sch., Connersville, Ind., 1979-87; asst. supt. Rushville Consolidated Schs., 1987-90, supt., 1991-93; supt. pub. instrn., chairperson bd. edn., CEO dept. edn. State of Indiana, Indpls., 1993—. Mem. ASCD (nat. and Ind. chpts.), Internat. Reading Assn., Nat. Assn. Elem. Sch. Prins. (assoc.), Ind. Assn. Pub. Sch. Supts., Ind. Assn. Elem. and Mid. Sch. Prins. (assoc.), Ind. Assn., Network Woman Adminstrs., Indpls. Zoo, Indpls. Art Mus., Bus. and Profl. Women of Rushville, Altrusa Club Connersville (chmn. internat. rels. 1979-87), Connersville Area Reading Coun., Smithsonian, Rushville County Players, Rotary (Rushville chpt.), Monday Cir., Delta Kappa Gamma (past pres., Phi Lambda Theta, Phi Delta Kappa (Conner Prairie). Office: Superintendent Edn Dept 229 State House Indianapolis IN 46204-2798

REED, THOMAS LEE, II, minister, elementary education educator; b. Kansas City, Jan. 9, 1964; s. Thomas Lee and Kathleen E. (Green) R. BA in Preaching, Okla. Christian, 1986; BS in Edn., Mo. Southern State Coll., Joplin, 1994. Cert. elem. edn. Assoc. min Ch. of Christ, Nevada, Mo., 1986-89; music min. Plymouth, Ind., 1989; assoc. min. Nevada, Mo., 1990—; clin. tchr. 3rd grade Mo. Sch. Dist., Joplin, 1992; practicum tchr. Early Childhood Devel. Ctr. MSSC, Joplin, Mo., 1993; student tchr. 4th grade Web City (Mo.) Sch. Dist., 1994; music dir., 1981-89, 90—, youth min., 1984, religious edn., 1986—, Ch. of Christ, Nev., Mo. Recipient Key Charitable Fund scholarship, 1993, Selected for Acad. fellowship Mo. So. State Coll., Oxford U., Eng., 1994. Mem. Assn. Childhood Edn. Internat., Phi Eta Sigma. Mem. Churches of Christ. Avocations: music composition, writing, vocal performance, drawing, painting.

REED, TONY NORMAN, aviation company executive; b. Odessa, Tex., Apr. 12, 1951; s. Norman W. and Naoma N. (Johnson) R.; m. Gwen Stanphill, Mar. 29, 1973; 3 children. Pres. Trinity Aviation, Trinity Communication, Tyler, Tex., 1986-90; v.p. internat. mktg. Cardinal Aerospace, Inc., Independence, Mo., 1990-92; v.p. comml. programs Multinat. Enterprises, Inc., N.Y.C., 1992—; internat. sales profl. Puritan-Bennett Aero Systems, Inc., Lenexa, Kans., 1993—; bd. dirs. Missionary Aviation Svcs., Tyler. Mem. Aircraft Owners and Pilots Assn. Home: PO Box 1085 Blue Springs MO 64013-1085

REED, TRAVIS DEAN, public relations executive; b. Trinity, Tex., Sept. 27, 1930; s. Travis and Alma (Rains) R.; m. Caroline M. McDonald, June 15, 1957; children: Anne Reed Adams, Lisa Reed Lettau. Student, Tex. A&M U., 1948-51, U. Houston, 1951-53. Reporter Houston Post, 1951-53; Washington Bur. corr. McGraw-Hill Pub. Co., 1955-61, Boston Herald-Traveler, 1961-62; with Newhouse News Svc., Washington, 1962-79, chief corr., 1964-67, editor, 1967-79; pub. rels. cons. Washington, 1979—. 1st lt. U.S. Army, 1953-55. Mem. Nat. Press Club, Federal City Club, Gridiron Club. Home: 37277 Branchriver Rd Purcellville VA 20132 Office: T Dean Reed Co Madison Office Bldg 1155 15th St NW Ste 1003 Washington DC 20005-2706

REED, VANESSA REGINA, secondary education educator; b. Grenada, Miss., Oct. 4, 1965; d. Willie Mann and Elma Lee (Finley) R. BS in Social Sci. Edn., Miss. Valley State U., 1987; MA in History, Jackson State U., 1988; postgrad., Miss. State U., Meridian, 1991, 92. Cert. tchr. social sci. History tchr. Jackson (Miss.) State U., 1987-88; social studies tchr. Magnolia Mid. Sch., Meridian, 1988-93; U.S. history tchr. Kate Griffin Jr. H.S., Meridian, 1993—. Sunday sch. tchr., dir. children's ch. Mt. Olive Bapt. Ch.; mem. Heroines of Jericho. Mem. Am. Fedn. Tchrs., Sigma Gamma Rho. Democrat. Avocations: traveling, geneology, reading. Office: Kate Griffin Jr HS 2814 Davis St Meridian MS 39301-5655

REED, VASTINA KATHRYN (TINA REED), child psychotherapist; b. Chgo., Mar. 5, 1960; d. Alvin Hillard and Ruth Gwendolyn (Thomas) R.; 1 child, Alvin J. BA in Human Svcs. magna cum laude, Nat.-Louis U., Chgo., 1988; MA, Ill. Sch. Profl. Psychology, 1991. Tchr. early childhood edn. Kendall Coll. Lab. Sch., Evanston, Ill., 1983-85, Rogers Park Children's Learning Ctr., Chgo., 1983-85; child life therapist Mt. Sinai Hosp., Chgo., 1988; child psychotherapist Nicholas Barnes Therapeutic Day Sch., Chgo., 1989-90. Den leader Boy Scouts Am., Chgo., 1989-92, scoutmaster troop 267, 1992—. Recipient Cub Scouter award Boy Scouts Am., 1990, Scoutmaster award of merit, 1993, 94, Scouters Vet. award, 1994, Scouters Tng. award, 1995, Scoutmasters Key award, 1996, Okpik Cold Weather Camping cert., 1994-95. Mem. APA, Nat. Orgn. for Human Svc. Edn., Order of the Arrow, Ea. Stars, Phi Theta Kappa, Kappa Delta Pi. Democrat. Roman Catholic. Avocations: camping, cruising, music, archery, air rifle shooting. Home: 1872 S Millard Ave Chicago IL 60623-2542

REED, VINCENT EMORY, federal education official; b. St. Louis, Mar. 1, 1928; s. Artie David and Velma Veander (Body) R.; m. Frances Bullitt, Sept. 20, 1952. B.S. in Edn., W.Va. State Coll., 1952, H.L.D., 1977; M.A., Howard U., Washington, 1965; D.P.A. (hon.), Southeastern U., Washington, 1976; postgrad., Wharton Sch., U. Pa., 1969; Ph.D. (hon.), Georgetown U., 1977; L.H.D. (hon.), Strayer Coll., Harris-Stowe U., 1983, Slippery Rock U., 1990; LLD (hon.), U. D.C., 1984. Football coach W.Va. State Coll., 1955; mem. staff D.C. Pub. Schs., 1962—, asst. supt. secondary schs., 1971-74, assoc. supt. state office, 1974-75, supt. schs., 1975-80; asst. sec. for elem. and secondary edn. U.S. Dept. Edn., 1981—. Author articles, book revs. Dir.

Home Fed. Savs. and Loan Assn.; bd. dirs. D.C. Goodwill Industries, Washington YMCA, 12 Neediest Kids; vol. worker S.E. Boys' Club, S.E. Youth Football Assn. Served as 1st lt. AUS, 1953-55, Korea. Named All-Am. Football Player Pitts. Courier, 1951, to W.Va. ROTC Hall of Fame, 1981; recipient Superior Service award D.C. Bicentennial Assembly, 1976; Outstanding Achievement award W.Va. State Coll., 1976; Alumnus of Yr., 1976; named to Athletic Hall of Fame, 1983; Outstanding Community Service award NAACP, 1977; Scouter of Yr. award Washington, 1981; Human Relations award NCCJ, 1981; Man of Yr. award YMCA, 1984; Excellent Role Models for Edn. award Colgate-Palmolive; Martin Luther King, Jr. Civil Rights for Edn. award Com. Civil Rights and Urban Affairs; many others. Mem. Nat. Assn. Secondary Sch. Prins., Am. Assn. Sch. Personnel Adminstrs., Nat. Assn. Sch. Security Officers, Am. Soc. Bus. Ofcls., NAACP, NEA., D.C. PTA, Washington Sch., Club, Phi Delta Kappa, Kappa Alpha Psi. Baptist. Clubs: Pigskin, Kiwanis. Home: 7115 16th St NW Washington DC 20012-1537 Office: Washington Post Company 1150 15th St NW Washington DC 20071-0001

REED, W. FRANKLIN, lawyer; b. Louisville, Dec. 30, 1946; s. William Ferguson and Stella Elizabeth (Richardson) R.; m. Sharon Ann Coss, June 16, 1973; children: Jonathan Franklin, William Brian, Carrie Ann. BA, Williams Coll., 1968; JD, Columbia U., 1971. Bar: N.Y. 1972, U.S. Dist. Ct. (so. dist.) N.Y. 1975, U.S. Ct. Appeals (2d cir.) 1975, Pa. 1982, U.S. Dist. Ct. (we. dist.) 1983. Assoc. Milbank, Tweed, Hadley & McCloy, N.Y.C., 1971-82, Reed Smith Shaw & McClay, Pitts., 1982-83; ptnr. Reed, Smith, Shaw & McClay, Pitts., 1984—; with Instnl. Devel. Com., The Pitts. Cultural Trust. Mem. ABA, Pa. Bar Assn., Allegheny Bar Assn., Carnegie 100, Williams Coll. Alumni Soc. W. Pa. (sec. 1983—), Rivers Club (Pitts.), St. Clair Country Club (Upper St. Clair, Pa.), Duquesne Club (Pitts.), Phi Beta Kappa. Democrat. Presbyterian. Avocations: fishing, golf. Home: 525 Miranda Dr Pittsburgh PA 15241-2039 Office: Reed Smith Shaw & McClay 435 6th Ave Pittsburgh PA 15219-1809

REED, WALLACE ALLISON, physician; b. Covina, Calif., May 19, 1916; s. Wallace Allison and Mary Julia (Birdsall) R.; m. Maria Eva Wiemers, Jan. 20, 1938; children: Ellen E., Barbara R. (Mrs. David Maurice Knize), Wallace J., Michael E., Kathryn L., Vikki T. (Mrs. Michael Swanson). A.B., UCLA, Los Angeles, 1937; postgrad., U. Cologne, 1937-38; U. Freiburg, Breisgau, 1938-39; M.D., U. So. Calif., 1944. Diplomate: Am. Bd. Anesthesiology. Intern Santa Fe Coast Lines Hosp., Los Angeles, 1943-44; resident Los Angeles County Gen. Hosp., 1946-47, asst. to head dept. anesthesiology, 1946-47; clin. instr. surgery U. So. Calif. Sch. Medicine, 1946-47; practice medicine, specializing in anesthesiology Phoenix, 1948-89; hon. staff mem. Good Samaritan Hosp., St. Joseph Hosp., Maricopa County Gen. Hosp.; mem. hon. staff Children's Hosp.; co-founder John L. Ford, M.D., Surgicenter, 1970; vice pres. Maricopa Found. for Med. Care, 1970-74, pres., 1975-76; mem. House Ways and Means Adv. Com.; adv. coun. Nat. Health Inst., 1975-76; mem. accreditation coun. for ambulatory health care Joint Commn. on Accreditation of Hosps., 1975-79; vice-chmn. Accreditation Assn. for Ambulatory Health Care, 1979-81, pres., 1981-83; mem. panel for study Nat. Health Ins., Congl. GAO; chmn. bd. Alterna Care Corp., 1984-87, now chmn. bd. emeritus; mem. adv. bd. Kino Inst., 1994-95. Bd. dirs. South Phoenix Montessori Sch., pres. bd., 1971-75; bd. dirs. Ctrl. Ariz. Health Sys. Agy., 1975-78; exec. dir. Surgictr. of Phoenix, 1987-97. Capt. M.C., AUS, 1944-46. Recipient Pinal award Ariz. Psychiat. Soc., 1967-68, Gerard B. Lambert Merit award for innovative ideas that improve patient care; John L. Ford M.D., 1972. Fellow Am. Coll. Anesthesiologists; mem. Am. Soc. Anesthesiologists, Ariz., Maricopa County socs. anesthesiologists, AMA, Acad. Anesthesiology (pres. 1969, dir. 1966-72), Federated Amb. Surgery Assn. (pres. 1974-75, dir.), Soc. for Ambulatory Anesthesia (bd. dirs. 1985-87), Ariz. Med. Assn. (dir. 1972-78), Maricopa County Med. Soc. (pres. 1964, dir., Salsbury medal 1967, 71, Thomas Dooley medal 1970), Central Ariz. Physicians Service Assn. (pres. 1982-83), Am. Assn. Founds. for Med. Care (dir. 1970-74), Guedel Assn. (pres. 1972), Seed Money for Growth Found. (pres. 1984—), Internat. Assn. for Amb. Surgery (hon.). Methodist. Home: 4716 N Dromedary Rd Phoenix AZ 85018-2939 Office: 1040 E Mcdowell Rd Phoenix AZ 85006-2622

REED, WILLIAM EDWARD, government official, educator; b. Columbia, La., July 15, 1914; s. William Reed and Virginia (Barnes) R.; m. Mattye Marie Scott, Aug. 27, 1942; children: Edwarda Marie (Mrs. Lucien L. Johnson), Carol Ann, Beverlyn Bernetiae. B.S., So. U., 1937; M.S., Iowa State U., 1941; Ph.D., Cornell U., 1946. County agrl. agt. Agr. and Home Econs. Extension Service, La. State U., 1937-41; lectr. soil sci. and chemistry So. U., 1942-47; agrl. research specialist U.S. Econ. Mission to Liberia, 1947-49; dean agr. Agrl. and Tech. Coll. N.C., 1949-61; mem. U.S. del. Russia; rep. ICA in Togo, 1961; asst. dir. AID Mission to Nigeria, 1961-68; mem. U.S. del. to UN Conf. on Application Sci. and Tech., 1963; dep. dir. AID Mission to Ethiopia, 1968-72; fgn. service officer in residence N.C. A. & T. State U., Greensboro, 1972-74; spl. asst. to chancellor for internat. programs N.C. A. & T. State U., 1974-76, asso. dean research and spl. projects, 1976-78, dir. internat. programs, 1978-84; cons. in field, 1984—. State rep. Sisters Cities Internat. Mem. Nat. Planning Assn., Am. Fgn. Svc. Assn., Sigma Xi, Phi Kappa Phi, Beta Kappa Chi, Sigma Pi Phi, Gamma Sigma Delta, Beta Epsilon (trustee Boulé Found. 1964—). Episcopalian. Home: 2711 Mcconnell Rd Greensboro NC 27401-4534

REED, WILLIAM H., federal agency administrator. Dir. Def. Contract Audit Agy. Dept. Def., Washington, 1986—. Office: Dept of Defense Defense Contract Audit Agency 8725 John J Kingman Rd Fort Belvoir VA 22060-6217*

REED, WILLIS, professional basketball team executive, former head coach; b. Hico, La., June 25, 1942; s. Willis and Inell R.; m. Geraldine Oliver (div.); children: Carl, Veronica. Student, Grambling Coll., 1960-64. Center, forward N.Y. Knickerbockers, NBA, 1964-74; coach N.Y. Knickerbockers, NBA, 1977-79, Creighton U., Omaha, 1981-85; asst. coach Atlanta Hawks, N.B.A., 1985-88, Sacramento Kings, NBA, 1988; head coach New Jersey Nets, NBA, 1988-89, v.p. basketball and bus. dev., 1989-90, sr. v.p., player personnel, 1990—, exec. v.p. basketball, gen mgr. Author: (with Phil Pepe) The View from the Rim, 1971. Mem. Nat. Basketball Assn. All-Star team, 1965-71, 73; mem. World Championship team, 1970, 73; recipient Most Valuable Player awards for playoffs and all-star games, 1970; named Nat. Basketball Assn. Rookie of Yr., 1965, NBA Playoffs Most Valuable Player, 1970, 73; named to Naismith Meml. Hall of Fame, 1981. Office: NJ Nets 405 Murray Hill Pky East Rutherford NJ 07073-2136

REEDER, CECELIA PAINTER, English educator; b. Tampa, Fla., Oct. 9, 1936; d. William Painter and Cecelia (Bachman) Hendry; children: Susan Reeder Shipp, William J. BEd, U. Miami, 1958; MA in Gifted Edn., U. South Fla., 1983. Cert. elem./gifted-talented tchr., K-12, English 7-9, Fla. Elem. tchr. Dade County Bd. Pub. Inst., Miami, Fla., 1958-70, 83-86, tchr., English, 1986-89; tchr. gifted English and Social Studies 7th and 8th grades Richmond Heights Mid. Sch., Miami, Fla., 1989-94; tchr. 5th grade St. John's Episcopal Day Sch., 1996—; part-time tchr. gifted English and geography grades 6-7 Homestead Mid. Sch. Recipient Assoc. Master Tchr. award State of Fla., 1986. Home: 1520 NW 10th St Homestead FL 33030-3872

REEDER, CHARLES BENTON, economic consultant; b. Columbus, Ohio, Oct. 31, 1922; s. Charles Wells and Lydia (Morrow) R.; m. Carol Lincoln, June 25, 1949 (div. June 1972); 1 son, Charles; m. Beverly Lawrence, Nov. 11, 1972; adopted children: Keith, Sue. BS, Ohio State U., 1945, PhD, 1951; MBA, Harvard U., 1947. Econ. analyst Cleve. Elec. Illuminating Co., 1947-48; instr. Ohio State U., Columbus, 1948-51; econ. analyst, asst. economist Armstrong Cork. Co., Lancaster, Pa., 1951-55; assoc. economist E. I. Du-Pont de Nemours & Co., Inc., Wilmington, Del., 1955-70; chief economist E.I. DuPont de Nemours & Co., Inc., Wilmington, Del., 1970-85; pres. Charles Reeder Assocs., 1986—; bd. dirs. OP Am. Growth Fund, Amsterdam, The Netherlands. Author: The Sobering Seventies, 1981. Bd. dirs. Greater Wilmington Devel. Coun., 1963-84; treas. Del. Coun. on Econ. Edn., 1958-85, Bank of Del., Wilmington, 1975-92. 1st lt. Q.M.C., AUS, 1943-46. Recipient Silbert award Sterling Nat. Bank of N.Y., 1982. Fellow Nat. Assn. Bus. Economists (pres. 1966-67); mem. Nat. Bur. Econ. Research (past bd. dirs.). Methodist. Clubs: Wilmington, Greenville Country. Home: 16 Brendle Ln Wilmington DE 19807-1300 Office: 16 Brendle Ln Ste 4 Wilmington DE 19807-1300

REEDER, ELLEN DRYDEN, museum curator; b. Balt., Apr. 11, 1947; d. Oliver Howard and Nancy Hardcastle (Fisher) R. BA, Wellesley U., 1969; MA, Princeton U., 1972, PhD, 1974. Curator archaeological collection John Hopkins U., Balt., 1974-78; asst. prof. art George Washington U., Washington, 1978-84; assoc. curator ancient art Walters Art Gallery, Balt., 1984-86, curator ancient art, 1986—; mem. at large mng. com. Am. Sch. Classical Studies, Athens, Greece, 1987—, adv. bd. U.S. Ctr. Lexicon Iconographicum Mythologiae Classicae, New Brunswick, N.J., 1986—. Author: The Archaeological Collection of the Johns Hopkins University, 1984; author, editor: Hellenistic Art in the Walters Art Gallery, 1988, mem. editl. bd., 1985—; author, editor: Pandora: Women in Classical Greece, 1995, Pandora: Frauen im Klassischen Griechenland, 1996; contbr. articles to profl. jours. Trustee Calvert Sch., Balt., 1990—. Woodrow Wilson fellow, 1969, Princeton Nat. U. fellow, 1969-74. Mem. Archaeol. Inst. Am., Coll. Art Assn., Phi Beta Kappa Assocs. (bd. dirs. 1993—, sec.-treas. 1994—), Phi Beta Kappa. Office: Walters Art Gallery 600 N Charles St Baltimore MD 21201-5118

REEDER, F. ROBERT, lawyer; b. Brigham City, Utah, Jan. 23, 1943; s. Frank O. and Helen H. (Heninger) R.; m. Joannie Anderson, May 4, 1974; children: David, Kristina, Adam. JD, U. Utah, 1967. Bar: Utah 1967, U.S. Ct. Appeals (10th cir.) 1967, U.S. Ct. Mil. Appeals 1968, U.S. Supreme Ct. 1972, U.S. Ct. Appeals (D.C. and 5th cirs.) 1979. Shareholder Parsons, Behle & Latimer, Salt Lake City, 1968—, bd. dirs., 1974-92. Bd. dirs. Holy Cross Found., 1981-90, chmn., 1987-90; bd. dirs. Holy Cross Hosp., 1990-93, treas., 1986-87, vice chmn., 1987-93; bd. dirs. Holy Cross Health Svcs. Utah, 1993-94, treas., 1993-94; bd. dirs., vice chmn. Salt Lake Regional Med. Ctr., 1995—; trustee Univ. Hosp. Found., 1995; hon. col. Salt Lake City Police, Salt Lake County Sheriff. Served with USAR, 1967-73. Mem. ABA, Utah State Bar, Salt Lake County Bar (ethic adv. com. 1989-94), Cottonwood Country Club (bd. dirs. 1978-82, 83-86, pres. 1981-82), Rotary. Office: Parsons Behle & Latimer PO Box 45898 Salt Lake City UT 84145-0898

REEDER, FRANKLIN S., retired federal agency administrator. BA in Internat. Rels., U. Pa.; student, George Washington U. Various positions Treasury and Defense Depts., Washington, 1961-70; dep. dir. house info. sys. U.S. Ho. of Reps., Washington, 1977-80; dir. info. policy staff Office of Mgmt. and Budget, Washington, dep. asst. dir. gen. mgmt., asst. dir. gen. mgmt., dep. assoc. dir. vet. affairs and personnel; dir. office of adminstrn. Exec. Office of Pres., Washington, 1995-97; mem. career Sr. Exec. Svc., 1984-95; adj. faculty U. Md., George Washington U.; mem. Nat. Adv. Bd. Ctr. Informatics Law John Marshall Law Sch., Chgo.; U.S. del., chair pub. mgmt. com. Orgn. Econ. Coop. and Devel. Office: The Reeder Group 3200 N Nottingham St Arlington VA 22207-1362

REEDER, JAMES ARTHUR, lawyer; b. Baton Rouge, June 29, 1933; s. James Brown and Grace (Britt) R.; m. Mary Leone Guthrie, Dec. 30, 1958; children: Mary Virginia, James Jr., Elizabeth Colby. BA, Washington and Lee U., Lexington, Va., 1955; LLB, U. Tex., 1960; JD, La. State U., 1961. Ptnr. Booth, Lockard, Jack et al, Shreveport, La., 1961-72; pres. and mgng. ptnr. Shreveport Broadcasting Co., 1972-86; Chief exec. officer and mgng. gen. ptnr. Radio USA Limited, Houston, 1986-89; pres. SW subsidiaries Sun Group, Inc., Houston, 1990-92; atty. Patton & Boggs, LLP, Washington, 1991-94; ptnr. Patton, Boggs & Blow, Washington, 1994—; dir. ABC Radio Sta. Affiliates adv. bd., N.Y.C., 1978-84. Dir. Boys Country, Houston, 1986-90; pres. Holiday in Dixie, Shreveport, 1968; chmn. Ambassadors Club, Shreveport, 1979. 1st Lt. U.S. Army, 1955-57. Named La. Outstanding Young Man, La. Jaycees, 1969. Mem. ABA (bd. dirs. young lawyers sect. 1967-68, Gavel awards com. 1980), La. Bar Assn. (pres. young lawyers sect. 1966, La. Outstanding Young Lawyer award 1968), D.C. Bar Assn., Tex. Bar Assn., Nat. Assn. Broadcasters, Houston Country Club, Demoiselle Club (Shreveport), Allegro Club (Houston). Roman Catholic.

REEDER, JOE ROBERT, federal official; b. Tacoma, Nov. 28, 1947; s. William Thomas and Marilyn Ruth (Parker) R.; m. Katharine Randolph Boyce, Jan 1, 1983; children: Rachael Anne, Aubrilyn, Julia, Kelsey. BS, U.S. Mil. Acad., West Point, N.Y., 1970; JD, U. Tex., 1975; LLM, Georgetown U., 1981. Bar: Tex. 1975, D.C. 1979, U.S. Dist. Ct. (so. dist.) Tex 1975, U.S. Ct. Appeals (5th cir.) 1989, U.S. Ct. Claims 1979, U.S. Dist. Ct. D.C. 1982, U.S. Ct. Appeals (Fed. cir.) 1984, U.S. Supreme Ct. 1988, U.S. Ct. Appeals (4th cir.) 1988, Md. 1989, U.S. Dist. Ct. (Md. dist) 1989, U.S. Dist. Ct. (no. dist.) Tex. 1991, U.S. Dist. Ct. (so. dist.) Tex. 1991. Commd. 2d lt. U.S. Army, 1970, advanced through grades to maj., 1985; law clk. to presiding justice U.S. Dist. Ct. (so. dist.) Tex., 1976; trial atty. litigation div. U.S. Army, Pentagon, D.C., 1976-78; trial atty. contract appeals div. U.S. Army, Pentagon, 1978-79; assoc. Patton, Boggs & Blow, Washington, 1979-82, ptnr., 1983-93; under sec. of U.S. Army U.S. Dept. Def., Washington, 1993—; chmn. bd. Panama Canal Commn., 1994—. Mem. ABA (assoc. editor pub. contract law jour. 1985-93), ATLA, Am. Law Inst., Fed. Bar Assn., D.C. Bar Assn., Tex. Bar Assn., Bar Assn. 5th Fed. Circuit, Bd. Contract Appeals Bar Assn., Rotary. Episcopalian. Home: 106 W Rosemont Ave Alexandria VA 22301 Office: Under Sec of Army 102 Army Pentagon Washington DC 20310-0102

REEDER, OLIVER HOWARD, paint products manufacturing executive; b. Balt., Sept. 19, 1916; s. Charles Howard and Nannie Dryden (Kensett) R.; m. Nancy Hardcastle Fisher, Apr. 18, 1942; children: Nancy Fisher, Ellen Dryden. A.B., Princeton U., 1939. With Balt. Copper Paint Co., Balt., 1939—; tech. dir., treas. Balt. Copper Paint Co., 1939-47, pres., 1947—, chmn., 1959—; v.p. Balt. Copper Paint div. Glidden-Durkee Div. SCM Corp., 1969—; pres. Jotun-Balt. Copper Paint Co., Inc., 1974-76, v.p., 1976-81. Pres. Hosp. for Consumptives of Md., 1968-84, trustee, 1951-95, trustee emeritus, 1995—; trustee Gilman Sch., Balt., 1948-65, Walters Art Gallery, 1978-83, U.S. Frigate Constellation Found., 1976-89; trustee Johns Hopkins Hosp., 1957-87, trustee emeritus, 1987—, vice chmn. bd., 1986-87; trustee Md. Hosp. Laundry, 1970-89, pres., 1975-84. Fellow Am. Inst. Chemists; mem. Am. Chem. Soc., Soc. Naval Architects and Marine Engrs., Phi Beta Kappa, Sigma Xi. Home: 1300 Dulaney Valley Rd Baltimore MD 21286-1308

REEDER, ROBERT HARRY, retired lawyer; b. Topeka, Dec. 3, 1930; s. William Harry and Florence Mae (Cochran) R. AB Washburn U., 1952, JD, 1960. Bar: U.S. Dist. Ct. Kans. 1960, Kans. 1960, U.S. Supreme Ct. 1968. Rsch. asst. Kans. Legis. Council Rsch. Dept., Topeka, 1955-60; asst. counsel Traffic Inst., Northwestern U., Evanston, Ill., 1960-67, gen. counsel, 1967-92; exec. dir. Nat. Com. on Uniform Traffic Laws and Ordinances, Evanston, 1982-90. Co-author: Vehicle Traffic Law, 1974; The Evidence Handbook, 1980. Author: Interpretation of Implied Consent by the Courts, 1972. Served with U.S. Army, 1952-54. Mem. Com. Alcohol and Other Drugs (chmn. 1973-75). Republican. Methodist.

REEDY, CATHERINE IRENE, science and health educator, library/media specialist; b. Suffolk County, N.Y., Dec. 27, 1953; d. Edward and Catherine (Spindler) Grafenstein. AA, Suffolk C.C., Selden, N.Y., 1980; BA in Social Sci., summa cum laude, Dowling Coll., Oakdale, N.Y., 1983, MS in Edn., 1986. Media specialist, tchr. coord. for sci. and health St. Ignatius Sch., Hicksville, N.Y., 1983—, dir. sci. lab. and media ctr. Contbr. poetry to Beyond the Stars, 1996, Walk Through Paradise, 1995, Best Poems of 1996. Recipient Editor's Choice award Nat. Soc. Poetry, 1995, Nat. Lib. Poetry, 1995. Mem. ASCD, AAUW, N.Y. Acad. Scis., N.Y. Sci. Tchrs. Assn., Nat. Assn. Univ. Women, Nat. Poet Soc., Internat. Soc. Poets, Alpha Zeta Nu (1st sec.), Phi Theta Kappa, Phi Alpha Sigma, Kappa Delta Pi (pres. Xi Chi chpt. 1985-87). Home: 15 Nikia Dr Islip NY 11751-2630 Office: St Ignatius Sch 30 E Cherry St Hicksville NY 11801-4302

REEDY, EDWARD K., research operations administrator. Assoc. dir. Georgia Tech. Rsch. Inst., Atlanta, Ga.; dir. rsch. ops. Georgia Tech. Rsch. Inst., Atlanta; v.p. Ga. Inst. of Tech.; dir. Ga. Tech. Rsch. Inst. Office: Ga Tech Rsch Inst Centennial Rsch Bldg #212 Atlanta GA 30332

REEDY, GEORGE EDWARD, educator, author, lecturer; b. East Chicago, Ind., Aug. 5, 1917; s. George Edward and Mary (Mulvaney) R.; m. Lillian Greenwald, Mar. 22, 1948 (dec.); children: Michael Andrew, William James; m. Ruth Brial Wissman, May 7, 1988. BA in Sociology, U. Chgo., 1938; D. of Canon Law, Nashota Sem., 1981; LHD, Lycoming Coll., 1991. Reporter Phila. Inquirer, summer 1937; congl. corr. U.P., 1938-41, 46-51; staff cons. armed svcs. preparedness subcom. U.S. Senate, 1951-52, staff dir. minority policy com., 1953-54, staff dir. majority policy com., 1955-60; spl. asst. to V.P. Lyndon B. Johnson, 1961-63; press sec. to Pres. Lyndon B. Johnson, 1964-65; pres. Struthers R & D Corp., Washington, 1966-68; v.p. planning Struthers Wells Corp., N.Y.C., 1966-68; spl. cons. to Pres. Lyndon B. Johnson, 1968-69; writer, lectr., cons., 1969—; dean, Nieman prof. Coll. Journalism, Marquette U., Milw., 1972-77, Nieman prof., 1977-90, prof. emeritus, 1991—; mem. Pres.'s Commn. on White House Fellowships, 1993; former fellow Woodrow Wilson Internat. Ctr. for Scholars, Smithsonian Instn., Washington; fellow in communication Duke U., 1973-74; lectr. S.Am., Cen. Am., Asia, India, 1975-84. Author: Who Will Do Our Fighting for Us?, 1969, The Twilight of the Presidency, 1970, The Presidency in Flux, 1973, Lyndon B. Johnson, A Memoir, 1982; The U.S. Senate: Paralysis or Search for Consensus, 1986, The Twilight of the Presidency, Johnson to Reagan, 1987, From the Ward to the White House, The Irish in American Politics, 1991; numerous articles on govt. and politics in mags. and newspapers. Mem. Pres.'s Nat. Adv. Commn. Selective Svc., 1966-67, Marine Sci., Engring. Resources, 1967-68, Pres.'s Commn. on White House Fellowships, 1993; mem. diocesan coun. Washington Diocese, Episcopal Ch. With USAAF, 1942-45. Mem. Alpha Sigma Nu. Office: Marquette U Coll Communications Milwaukee WI 53233

REEDY, JERRY EDWARD, editor, writer; b. Aberdeen, S.D., Feb. 4, 1936; s. Robert Emmett and Helen Mary (Issenhuth) R.; m. Susan Mary Rogers, June 22, 1968; children: Megan Marie, Erin Elizabeth, Matthew Robert-Emmett, Thomas Walter. AB, U. Notre Dame, 1958; MA, U. S.D., 1961. Area editor Red Wing (Minn.) Daily Republican Eagle, 1959-60; with Better Homes & Gardens mag. Meredith Pub. Co., Des Moines, 1961-69; assoc. editor Better Homes & Gardens mag. Meredith Pub. Co., 1966-67, spl. assignments editor, 1967-69; editor in chief, contbg. author Odyssey Mag., Chgo., 1969-78; free-lance editor, writer and photographer for nat. mags. and maj. met. daily newspapers, 1978—; travel editor Better Homes and Gardens Brides Book, 1983-84; instr. English, U. S.D., 1960-61; instr. mag. writing Drake U., 1966-68, Barat Coll., 1976-77. Author: Great American Indian Leaders, Notable Quotables, Family Adventure Guide and Road Atlas, God, Country, Notre Dame: The Autobiography of Theodore M. Hesburgh, 1990, (with Rev. Theodore Hesbough); editor: Travels with Ted and Ned, 1992; contbr. to Ency. Brit., 1980, World Book, 1984, Family Vacation Atlas, 1986 and various nat. mags. Pres. Com. on Cmty. Life, Chgo., 1976-78; chmn. bd. dirs. The Shelter, 1980-85. Recipient certs. of excellence Chgo. Comm. Collaborative, 1976, Addy Gold 1st pl. award for mags. Am. Advt. Fedn., 1976, 1st pl. awards of excellence for overall quality and for photojournalism Chgo. Assn. Bus. Communicators, 1977. Mem. Am. Soc. Journalists and Authors (pres. Chgo. chpt. 1995—), Midwest Writers. Roman Catholic. Home and Office: 3542 N Pine Grove Ave Chicago IL 60657-1877

REEF, ARTHUR, industry business consultant; b. N.Y.C., Sept. 21, 1916; s. Herman and Eva (Van Panich) R.; m. Betty Olsen, Aug. 1995; children from previous marriage: Jennifer, Nancy. B.A., CCNY, 1937; postgrad., U. Pa., 1937-38, Am. U., 1941-42, Sorbonne, U. Paris, 1949. With Ruder & Finn. Internat., N.Y.C., 1955-57, Barnet & Reef, N.Y.C., 1957-64; with AMAX, Inc., Greenwich, Conn., 1964-81, sr. v.p. and dir. office communications and pub. affairs; sr. cons. to exec. office AMAX, Inc., Greenwich and N.Y.C., 1981-87; dir. AMAX Australia Ltd.; trustee, chmn. U.S. com. Internat. Inst. Communications, 1979-81; bd. mem. World Environ. Ctr. N.Y., 1974-79, Ctr. for the Study of the Presidency; trustee Am. Coun. of Young Polit. Leaders; councillor Am.-Australian Bi-Centennial Commn. Fellow Inst. Mining and Metallurgy London, Acad. Internat. Bus.; mem. French Am. C. of C. (former councillor), Chaine des Rotisseurs (chevalier), Am. Food and Wine Inst., Fgn. Policy Assn. (assoc.), Overseas Press Club Am. (chmn. fgn. journalism com. 1958-63). Home: 2000 S Ocean Blvd Apt 608 Delray Beach FL 33483-6413

REEHER, JAMES IRWIN, minister; b. Sharon, Pa., Dec. 6, 1948; s. James William and Lillian (Irwin) R.; m. Marian Powell, Oct. 25, 1969; children: Elizabeth Margret, James Michael. BA, U. Tampa, 1975; MDiv, Emory U., 1978; DD, Boston U., 1989. Ordained to ministry United Ch. Ch., 1978. Min. Christ United Meth. Ch., Tampa, Fla., 1972-75, Lamar United Meth. Ch., Barnesville, Ga., 1975-78, 1st United Meth. Ch., Seffner, Fla., 1986-90; asst. min. Grace United Meth. Ch., Venice, Fla., 1978-79; founding min. 1st United Meth. Ch., Sarasota, Fla., 1980-86; min. Forest Hills United Meth. Ch., Tampa, 1990—; del. bd. ordained ministry Tampa Dist., 1987—; del. stewardship com. Fla. United Meth. Ch., Tampa, 1988—; bd. dirs. Jim Russo Prison Ministries, Bradenton, Fla., 1990—; chmn. anti-gambling campaign Fla. United Meth. Conf., 1986. Founding chmn. East Hillsborough Orgn., Seffner, 1988; bd. dirs. Life Enrichment Sr. Ctr., Tampa, 1990—. Recipient Outstanding Religious Leader award Sarasota Jaycees, 1985. Mem. Assn. for Clin. Pastoral Edn., Alban Inst., North Tampa Ministerial Assn. Democrat. Home: 3020 Saint Charles Dr Tampa FL 33618-3238 Office: Forest Hills United Meth Ch 904 W Linebaugh Ave Tampa FL 33612-7858

REEL, SHAUN DELANE, institutional consultant, business executive; b. N.Y.C., Oct. 14, 1964; s. Gregory Lane and Pearlie (Mays) R. BBA in Fin., Baruch Coll., 1992; postgrad., NYU, 1992—. Asst. computer analyst Prudential Bache, N.Y.C., 1982-84; regional sales asst. Saks Fifth Ave., N.Y.C., 1984-85; fin. analyst Merrill Lynch, N.Y.C., 1986-87; rsch. analyst The Carter Orgn., N.Y.C., 1988-90; account exec. D.F. King & Co., N.Y.C., 1991—. Vol. marshall Walk Am., March of Dimes, 1988—; co-v.p. Archbishop Leadership Program, 1982-92. Mem. Nat. Assn. Black Accts., Phi Beta Sigma (v.p. 1990-91). Baptist. Avocations: weightlifting, basketball, boxing, reading, running. Home: 1527 Metropolitan Ave Bronx NY 10462-6171 Office: DF King & Co 77 Water St Fl 20 New York NY 10005-4401

REELING, PATRICIA GLUECK, library educator, educational consultant; b. Cin., June 6, 1939; d. Arthur William and Bertha Louise Glueck; m. Glenn Eugene Reeling, Aug. 18, 1962; children: Craig Patrick, Aimee Reeling Berger. BA, Edgecliff Coll., Cin., 1960; MA, Ind. U., 1961; DLS, Columbia U., 1969. Reference libr. Ohio State U., Columbus, 1961-62; asst. to dir. Boston Coll. Librs., 1962-63; assoc. prof. Sch. Comm., Info. and Libr. Studies Rutgers U., New Brunswick, N.J., 1970—, chmn. dept. libr. and info. studies, 1984-89; ednl. cons. Reeling Assocs., Somerset, N.J., 1969—; evaluator Mid. States Assn. Commn. on Higher Edn., Phila., 1975—; vis. prof. Emporia State U., Denver, 1991—. Editor: Education for the Library/Information Profession: Strategies for the Mid-90s, 1993; editor column Govt. Info., RQ, 1983-85; contbr. articles to profl. jours. Mem. depository libr. coun. to pub. printer U.S. Govt. Printing Office, Washington, 1982-85; mem. network rev. bd. N.J. State Libr., Trenton, 1989-90. Recipient 1st Leadership award N.J. State Libr., 1987; grantee Rutgers U., 1983. Mem. ALA (life, mem. or chmn. numerous coms. 1961—, James Bennett Childs award 1988, Libr. Edn. Centennial Honor Role award 1988), AAUP (officer Rutgers coun. chpts. 1967—), Assn. for Libr. and Info. Sci. Edn. (mem. or chmn. various coms. 1964—), Documents Assn. N.J. (pres. 1981-82, archivist 1983—), N.J. Libr. Assn. (various coms. 1964—, Disting. Svc. award coll. and univ. sect. 1984), Beta Phi Mu (officer Omicron chpt. 1961—). Home: 131 Drake Rd Somerset NJ 08873-2317 Office: Rutgers U Sch Comm Info Libr Studies Alexander Library College Ave New Brunswick NJ 08901-1071

REEMTSMA, KEITH, surgeon, educator; b. Madera, Calif., Dec. 5, 1925; children: Lance Brewster, Dirk Van Horn. BS, Idaho State Coll., 1948; MD, U. Pa., 1949; D in Med.Sc., Columbia U., 1958. Diplomate Am. Bd. Med. Examiners, Am. Bd. Surgery (planning com. 1968-70, nominating com. 1970, com. on certification for spl. competence 1971), Am. Bd. Thoracic Surgery. Intern Presbyn. Hosp., N.Y.C., 1950-51, asst. resident in surgery, 1951-55, resident in surgery, 1956, chief resident in surgery, 1957; asst. surgery Columbia Coll. Physicians and Surgeons, N.Y.C., 1957; mem. faculty Tulane U. Sch. Medicine, New Orleans, 1957-66, prof. surgery, 1966—; head dept. surgery U. Utah Coll. Medicine, Salt Lake City, 1966-71; chmn. dept. surgery, Valentine Mott prof. surgery, Johnson and Johnson disting. prof. surgery Columbia U., N.Y.C., 1971-94; dir. surg. svc. U. Utah, 1966-71,

Presbyn. Hosp., 1971-94. Contbr. articles to profl. jours. Lt. (j.g.) USNR, 1951-53; lt. MC USN, 1953. Mem. AMA, ACS, Soc. Clin. Surgery, Am. Surg. Assn., Soc. U. Surgeons (treas. 1962-75), So. Soc. for Clin. Rsch., Am. Fedn. for Clin. Rsch., Am. Assn. for Thoracic Surgery, Soc. for Vascular Surgery, Internat. Cardiovascular Soc., So. Thoracic Surg. Assn., New Orleans Surg. Soc., Surg. Assn. La., La. Med. Soc., Orleans Parish Med. Soc., Surg. Biology Club II, Western Surg. Assn., Alpha Omega Alpha. Office: Columbia University Dept Surgery 630 W 168th St New York NY 10032-3702

REEP, EDWARD ARNOLD, artist; b. Bklyn., May 10, 1918; s. Joseph and Elsie (Abramson) R.; m. Karen Patricia Stevens, Dec. 9, 1942; children—Susan Kay, Cristine Elyse, Janine J., Mitchell Jules. Student, Art Center Coll. Design, 1936-41. Instr. painting and drawing Art Center Coll. Design, Los Angeles, 1946-50, Chouinard Art Inst., Los Angeles, 1950-69; prof. painting, chmn. dept., artist in residence E. Carolina U., 1970-85, prof. emeritus, 1985—; cons. editor Van Nostrand Reinhold Pub. Co.; ofcl. war artist-corr. WWII, Africa and Italy. Author: The Content of Watercolor, 1968, A Combat Artist in World War II, 1987; shows include Whitney Mus. Am. Art Ann., N.Y.C., 1946-48, Los Angeles County Mus. Ann., 1946-60, Corcoran Gallery Art Biennial, Washington, 1949, Nat. Gallery Art, Washington, 1945, Mus. Modern Art, N.Y.C.; represented in permanent collections Los Angeles County Mus., U.S. War Dept., Grunwald Graphic Arts Collection, UCLA, Nat. Mus. Am. Art, Washington, Lytton Collection, Los Angeles, State of Calif. Collection, Sacramento. Guggenheim fellow, 1945-46; Nat. Endowment for Arts grantee, 1975. Mem. AAUP, Nat. Watercolor Soc. (past pres.), Watercolor USA Honor Soc. Democrat. Home: 9021 Crowningshield Dr Bakersfield CA 93311-1901 *I once was consumed by the desire to become an artist. I feel no differently today. There is work ahead. If I had set goals for myself I no longer can recall what they may have been; I go along painting as well or as inventively as I can. Never have I sacrificed living life as I feel I must for my art. My work is a reflection of my life—experiences real and imagined.*

REES, CHARLES H. G., retired financial officer, investor, consultant; b. Trenton, N.J., Mar. 6, 1922; s. Albert H. and Helen (Gallagher) R.; m. Nancy Thomas, Oct. 30, 1954; children: Liberty, Camilla, Nancy, Hilleary. BA, Princeton U., 1948. Salesman John A. Roebling's Sons Co., Trenton, 1948-50; staff officer CIA, Washington, 1951-54; assoc. J.H. Whitney & Co., N.Y.C., 1954-59; gen. ptnr. Whitcom Investment Co., N.Y.C., 1967-85; with Whitney Comm. Corp., N.Y.C., 1960-85, pres., 1982-85. Trustee Riverside Rsch. Inst., N.Y.C. Capt. U.S. Army, 1942-46, 50-51. Decorated Bronze Star. Mem. Brook Club, Pilgrims of N.Y.C., Ivy Club, Misquamicut Club, Watch Hill (R.I.) Yacht Club, Stonington Country Club, Wadawanuck Club (Stonington). Republican. Home: 215 Farmholme Rd Stonington CT 06378-2205

REES, CLIFFORD HARCOURT, JR. (TED REES), association executive, retired air force officer; b. Newport News, Va., Dec. 11, 1936; s. Clifford Harcourt Sr. and Mary Evelyn (Brooks) R.; m. Joan Elizabeth Mittong, July 26, 1958; children—Clifford Harcourt III, Steven M., Daniel B., William B. BS in Fgn. Svc., Georgetown U., 1958; MS in Polit. Sci., Auburn U., 1969; grad., Air War Coll., Montgomery, Ala., 1978. Commd. 2d lt. U.S. Air Force, 1958; advanced through grades to lt. gen., 1988; later comdr. 421st Tactical Fighter Squadron, Udorn Royal Thai AFB, 1974-75; chief, house liaison office U.S. Ho. Reps., Washington, 1978-80; asst. col. assignments Randolph AFB, 1980-82; vice-comdr. Air Force Manpower and Personnel Ctr., 1982; dep. dir. legis. liaison Office Sec. Air Force, 1982-84, dir. legis. liaison, 1984-86; comdr. USAF Air Defense Weapons Ctr., Tyndall AFB, Fla., 1986-88; vice comdr. in chief USAF in Europe, Ramstein AB, Federal Republic of Germany, 1988-92; ret. USAF in Europe, 1992; founder, pres. Rees Group Cons.; pres. Air Conditioning and Refrigeration Inst., Arlington, Va., 1993—; U.S. rep. to v.p. Internat. Coun. Mil. Sports, Brussels, 1982-94. Decorated D.S.M. with one oak leaf cluster, DFC with one oak leaf cluster, Legion of Merit with one oak leaf cluster, Meritorious Svc. medal with one oak leaf cluster, Air medal with 11 oak leaf clusters USAF, Das Grosse Verdienstkreuz Mit Stern, Pres. Fed. Republic Germany, 1993; named Commander Order of Meritorious Svc. Mil. Sports Coun., 1993. Mem. Delta Phi Epsilon (v.p. membership 1957-58, nat. pres. 1984-86). Methodist. Home: 2487 Oakton Hills Dr Oakton VA 22124-1530 Office: Air Conditioning & Refrigeration Inst 4301 Fairfax Dr Ste 425 Arlington VA 22203-1627

REES, FRANK WILLIAM, JR., architect; b. Rochester, N.Y., June 5, 1943; s. Frank William and Elizabeth R. (Miller) R.; m. Joan Mary Keevers, Apr. 1, 1967; children: Michelle, Christopher. BS in Architecture, U. Okla., 1970; postgrad., Harvard U., Boston, 1979, 90; OPM, Harvard U., 1990. Registered architect, 32 states; cert. Nat. Coun. Archtl. Registration Bds. Sales mgr. Sta. KFOM, Oklahoma City, 1967-70; project architect Benham-Blair & Affiliates, Oklahoma City, 1970-75; pres., CEO, founder Rees Assocs., Inc., Oklahoma City, 1975—; pres., chmn. bd. Weatherscan Radio Network, Oklahoma City, 1973-78; chmn. bd. Weatherscan Internat., Oklahoma City, 1972-78; pres. Frontier Communications, Oklahoma City, 1980-84; chmn. architecture bd. U. Okla., Norman, 1988-91; bd. dirs. Century, Inc., Oklahoma City. Past pres. Lake Hefner Trails, Oklahoma City, Hosp. Hospitality House, Oklahoma City, Oklahoma City Beautiful; mem. Leadership Oklahoma City. Mem. AIA, Am. Assn. Hosp. Architects, Am. Healthcare Assn., Tex. Hosp. Assn., World Pres. Orgn. (chmn. 1997-98), Nat. Assn. Sr. Living Industries, Assisted Living Fedn. of Am., Am. Assn. Homes and Svcs. for the Agig. Home: 1104 Stone Gate Dr Irving TX 75063-4676 Office: 3102 Oak Lawn Ave Ste 200 Dallas TX 75219-4241

REES, JAMES CONWAY, IV, historic site administrator; b. Richmond, Va., May 5, 1952. BA, Coll. William & Mary, 1974; MPA, George Washington U., 1978. Reporter, photographer Newport News Daily-Press, 1974; coord. radio and television programming The Coll. William & Mary, 1974-78; mng. editor The William & Mary Mag., 1978-82; promotions dir. Va. Shakespeare Festival, 1980; dir. annual giving and pub. info. The Coll. William & Mary, 1978-80, dir. annual support and corp. rels., 1980-81, dir. capital support, 1981-82; asst. dir. devel. Nat. Trust Historic Preservation, 1982-83, assoc. dir. devel., 1983; dir. devel. and comms. Historic Mount Vernon, 1983-85, assoc. dir., 1985-94, resident dir., 1994—; exec. v.p. Mount Vernon Inn, Inc., 1994—; Mem. bd. dirs. Va. Shakespeare Festival, Washington Area Chpt. WIlliam and Mary Alumni Soc. Mem. Nat. Trust for Historic Preservation, Friends of the Nat. Symphony, WETA Pub. Television. Mem. Am. Film Inst., Va. Assn. Mus. (pres. 1991-94). Methodist. Home: 710 A St NE Washington DC 20002 Office: Mount Vernon Ladies Assn Mount Vernon VA 22121

REES, MORGAN ROWLANDS, engineer, educator; b. Kingston, Pa., Jan. 17, 1940; s. William Arthur and Anna Fae (Mericle) R.; m. Janet Marsello, May 15, 1965; 1 child, Bradley Alan. BS in Civil Engring., Worcester Poly. Inst., 1961, MS in Civil Engring., 1969; M Pub. Adminstrn., U. So. Calif., Washington, 1988, D Pub. Adminstrn., 1993. Registered profl. engr., Mass. Mgmt. trainee Bell Telephone of Pa., Scranton, 1961-62; appraisal engr. Am. Appraisal Co., N.Y.C., 1964-67; hydraulic rsch. engr. Worcester (Mass.) Poly. Inst., 1967-69; coastal engr. New Eng. Corps Engrs., Waltham, Mass., 1969-73, chief regulatory br., 1973-81; chief regulatory policy sect. Hqrs. Army C.E., Washington, 1981-82; asst. regulatory affairs U.S. Army Civil Works, Washington, 1982-86, dep. asst. sec., 1986-95; prin. Rees Engring. and Environ. Svcs., Alexandria, Va., 1995—; civil engring. dept. adv. com. Worcester Poly. Inst., 1988—. Jr. warden St. Luke's Ch., Worcester, 1974-79; v.p. Collingwood Citizen's Assn., Alexandria, Va., 1983-84. 1st lt. U.S. Army, 1962-64. Named to Athletic Hall of Fame Worcester Poly. Inst., 1984. Mem. ASCE, Soc. Am. Mil. Engrs., Sr. Exec. Assn., Am. Assn. Port Authorities. Avocations: jogging, reading, home remodeling.

REES, NORMA S., academic administrator; b. N.Y.C., Dec. 27, 1929; d. Benjamin and Lottie (Schwartz) D.; m. Raymond R. Rees, Mar. 19, 1960; children—Evan Lloyd, Raymond Arthur. B.A., Queens Coll., 1952; M.A., Bklyn. Coll., 1954; Ph.D., NYU, 1959. Cert. speech-language pathology, audiology. Prof. communicative disorders Hunter Coll., N.Y.C., 1967-72; exec. officer, speech and hearing scis. grad. sch. CUNY, N.Y.C., 1972-74, assoc. dean for grad. studies, 1974-76, dean grad. studies, 1976-82; vice chancellor for acad. affairs U. Wis., Milw., 1982-85, from 1986, acting chancellor, 1985-86; vice chancellor for acad. policy and planning Mass. Bd. Regents for Higher Edn., Boston, 1987-90; pres. Calif. State U., Hayward, 1990—; bd. dirs. Am. Assn. State Colls. and Univs., 1995—, Coun. of Postsecondary Accreditation, Washington, 1985-94; chmn. Commn. Recognition of Postsecondary Accreditation, 1994-96. Contbr. articles to profl. jours. Trustee Citizens Govtl. Rsch. Bur., Milw., 1985-87; active Task Force on Wis. World Trade Ctr., 1985-87; bd. dirs. Greater Boston YWCA, 1987-90; mem. Mayor's Cabinet Ednl. Excellence, Oakland, Calif.; mem. steering com. Econ. Devel. Adv. Bd Alameda County, 1995—. Fellow Am. Speech-Lang-Hearing Assn. (honors); mem. Am. Coun. Edn. (com. internat. edn. 1991-93), Am. Assn. Colls. and Univs. (chair task force on quality assessment 1991-92, mem. steering com. of coun. of urban met. colls. & univs. 1992—), Nat. Assn. State Univs. and Land Grant Colls. (exec. com. divsn. urban affairs 1985-87, com. accreditation 1987-90), Oakland C. of C. (bd. dirs. 1997—). Office: Calif State Univ-Hayward 25800 Carlos Bee Blvd Hayward CA 94542-3001

REES, PATRICIA GLINES, occupational health nurse, consultant, educator; b. Santa Maria, Calif., Aug. 28, 1945; d. Jack Holloway and Frances Ruth (Baril) Glines; m. Nov. 28, 1970 (div. July 1989); children: Eric Michael, Jennifer Lynne. BSN with honors, U. Calif., San Francisco, 1968; MSN, Clarkson Coll., Omaha, 1994. RN, Nebr., Calif.; cert. occupational health nurse-specialist; cert. BLS, CPR, first aid instr., hearing conservationist. Staff nurse Marin Gen. Hosp., Marin County, Calif., 1968-70; sch. health nurse Novato (Calif.) Unified Sch. Dist., 1968-70; obstetrics office nurse Oxon Hill, Md., 1971-72; vol. sch. health svcs. Sullivan Sch., Yokosuka, Japan, 1976-80; sch. health nurse, client svcs. rep. Vis. Nurse Assn., Omaha, 1987-89; occupational health nurse Armour Swift-Eckrich, Omaha, 1989-91; program dir. Advantage Health Sys., Inc., Kansas City, Mo., 1991—; preceptor U. Nebr. Med. Ctr., Omaha, 1994-95; vol./instr. ARC, Omaha, 1989-96; presenter in field. Co-author: Cumulative Trauma Disorders, 1991, Case Management, 1994, Work Injury Management, 1996; contbr. articles to profl. jours. Mem. Nebr. Safety Coun., Omaha, 1989-91, U.S. Swimming, Omaha, 1981-89. Pres.'s scholar U. Calif., San Francisco, 1967-68. Mem. APHA, Am. Assn. Occupational Health Nurses, Nebr. Assn. Occupational Health Nurses (edn. com. 1995—), Clarkson Honor Soc. (pres. 1994-96), Sigma Theta Tau, Alpha Xi Delta. Avocations: travel, miniatures, stitchery. Home: 1311 Beechwood Ave Papillion NE 68133-2509

REESE, ALFERD GEORGE, retired army civilian logistics specialist; b. Granville, N.D., Apr. 5, 1934; s. Ferdinand Emil and lola May (Boulds) R.; m. Donna Mae Berger, 1955 (div. 1972); children: Rick, Denise, Roxanna; m. Nelda Cecilia Pena, May 31, 1985; children: Nancy, Joyce, Alfred, Jeffrey, Jessica, James, Alicia. AS, Humphreys Coll., 1963; BS, U. State of N.Y., Albany, 1983; MPA, U. Colo., Colorado Springs, 1985; postgrad., Ga. State U., 1987-88; PhD, Columbia Pacific U., 1994. Inspector, mechanic Sharp Army Depot, Lathrop, Calif., 1958-66; equipment specialist various stations U.S. Army Aviation Systems Command, 1966-84; supervisory equipment specialist U.S. Army Aviation Systems Command, Atlanta, 1984-88; supervisory logistics specialist U.S. Army Aviation Systems Command, St. Louis, 1988-93; ret. Civil Svc., 1993. Mem. com. Boy Scouts Am., Fed. Republic Germany, 1979-81. With USAF, 1953-57. Mem. Army Aviation Assn. Assn. (USAEUR Dept. Army Civilian of Yr. 1980, 81), Ctr. for the Study of the Presidency, Acad. Polit. Sci., Am. Soc. for Pub. Adminstrn., Nat. Rifle Assn. Avocations: golf, skiing, photography, painting. Home: 1590 Fairmount Dr Florissant MO 63033-2645

REESE, CHARLES EDGAR, columnist; b. Washington, Ga., Jan. 29, 1937; s. Edgar Ernest and Neoma (Moody) R.; m. Gretchen Elise Krughoff, May 16, 1965 (div. July 1984); children: Benjamin, Alice, Theodore. PhD (hon.), Webber Coll., 1989. Caption writer Planet Newspictures Ltd., London, 1956-57; reporter Pensacola (Fla.) News-Jour., 1957-67; account exec. Dodson, Craddock & Born, Pensacola, 1967-69, Fry, Hammond & Born, Pensacola, 1971-72; chief bur. media svcs. State of Fla. Dept. of Commerce, Tallahassee, 1969-71; asst. metro editor Orlando Sentinel, 1972-75, asst. to pub., 1975-78, columnist, mem. editorial bd., 1978—. Author: Great Gods of the Potomac, Common Sense for the 80s. Active Hist. Commn., Pensacola, 1968; bd. dirs. Holocaust Meml., Orlando, 1985-90. With USAR, 1959-65. Named Best Columnist, Fla. Press Club, 1984, Fla. Soc. Newspaper Editors. Mem. SCV. Democrat. Avocations: pistol shooting, hunting, sketching. Office: Orlando Sentinel 633 N Orange Ave Orlando FL 32801-1300*

REESE, DOUGLAS WAYNE, geologist; b. Omaha, June 27, 1963; s. Larry Wayne and Sandra Kay (Bullerdick) R. BA in Geology, Case Western Res. U., 1987. Geologist, technician Mason de Verteuil Geotech. Svcs., Columbus, Ohio, 1987—, lab. supr., 1990—; owner D.R. Info. Sys., Reynoldsburg, Ohio. Mem. ASTM, ACLU, Am. Assn. Petroleum Geologists, Amnesty Internat., Electronic Frontier Found. Avocations: computers, investing, golf. Home: 1650 Hallworth Ct Columbus OH 43232-7400 also: DR Info Sys 6326 E Livingston Ave # 199 Reynoldsburg OH 43068-2754

REESE, FLOYD, professional sports team executive. Exec. v.p., gen. mgr. Houston Oilers. Office: Houston Oilers 8030 El Rio St Houston TX 77054-4184

REESE, FRANCIS EDWARD, retired chemical company executive, consultant; b. Monaca, Pa., Nov. 3, 1919; s. Francis Edward and Vivian Iris (Hancuff) R.; m. Katherine Mary McBrien, June 29, 1946; 1 son, Francis Edward III. B.S. in Chem. Engring, Purdue U., 1941. Registered profl. engr., Pa. With Monsanto Co., St. Louis, 1941; research engr. plastics div. Monsanto Co., 1941-48, chief devel. engring. plastics div., 1948-53, asst. engr. plastics div., 1953-56, dir. engring. plastics div., 1956-59, asst. gen. mgr. plastics div., 1959-61, asst. gen. mgr. hydrocarbons div., 1961-65, asst. gen. mgr., hydrocarbons and polymers div., 1965-66, gen. mgr. internat. div., 1966-68, corp. v.p., 1968-74, gen. mgr., hydrocarbons and polymers div., 1968-71, gen. mgr. polymers and petrochems. div., 1971-73, gen. mgr. internat. div., 1973-74, dir., 1973-84, group v.p., 1974-79, sr. v.p., 1979-84; pres. FTR Assocs., Inc.; mem. engring. found. adv. coun. U. Tex. Fellow AAAS, Am. Inst. Chem. Engrs.; mem. Am. Chem. Soc., Nat. Soc. Profl. Engrs., Soc. Chem. Industry, Tau Beta Pi, Phi Lambda Upsilon. Home: Rydal Park 271W 1515 The Fairway Rydal PA 19046-1628 Office: 801 Old York Rd Ste 316 Jenkintown PA 19046-1611

REESE, HAROLD HENRY, retired baseball player; b. Ekron, N.Y., July 23, 1918. Baseball player Bklyn. Dodgers, 194-42, 46-57; baseball player L.A. Dodgers, 1958, coach, 1959; TV broadcaster. Named to Baseball Hall of Fame, 1984; selected All-Star Team, 1942, 46-54; mem. World Series Champions, 1954. Office: care Nat Baseball Hall Fame PO Box 590 Cooperstown NY 13326

REESE, HARRY EDWIN, JR., electronics executive; b. Balt., Oct. 27, 1928; s. Harry Edwin and Margery Lee (Stroud) R.; m. Elizabeth Syra Pfeiffer, Oct. 15, 1955; children: Clifford Owen, Susan Syra, Peter Eyre. BSEE, Tufts U., 1950; MS in Stats., Villanova U., 1960. Engr. Philco Corp., Phila., 1950-54; project engr. Burroughs Corp., Paoli, Pa., 1956-59, dept. mgr., 1959-65; dept. mgr. GE Co., King of Prussia, Pa., 1965-69; group staff mgr. Burroughs Corp., Paoli, Pa., 1969-75; gen. mgr. Burroughs Corp., Plainfield, N.J., 1975-82; corp. staff dir. Burroughs Corp., Detroit, 1982-83; v.p. quality assurance Am. Electronic Labs., Inc., Lansdale, Pa., 1984-90, ret., 1990. Chmn. Charlestown Twp. Planning Commn., Pa., 1973-75. With U.S. Army, 1954-56. Fellow IEEE (life, pres. Reliability Soc. 1969-70, gen. chmn. Rams symposium 1968, chmn. bd. 1969, Centennial medal 1984); mem. Nat. Mgmt. Assn. (life, chmn. formation com. Am. Electronics Labs. chpt. 1985, Leadership award 1973, 86), Lake Hopatcong Yacht Club (treas., rear commodore), Masons, Rotary (Paul Harris fellow, treas.). Republican. Episcopalian. Avocations: carpentry, architecture, boating, antiques, travel. Home: 17 Bass Rock Rd Hopatcong NJ 07843-1901

REESE, HAYNE WARING, psychologist; b. Comanche, Tex., Jan. 14, 1931; s. Tom F. and Marion (Waring) R.; m. Patsy Atwood, Aug. 24, 1957 (div. Apr. 1967); children: Anne, William, Margaret; m. Nancy Mann, Dec. 16, 1967; 1 child, Bradley. Student, So. Meth. U., 1949-50; B.A., U. Tex., 1953, M.A., 1955; Ph.D., U. Iowa, 1958. Asst. prof. U. Buffalo, 1958-62; assoc. prof. SUNY-Buffalo, 1962-66, prof., 1966-67; prof. U. Kans., Lawrence, 1967-70; Centennial prof. psychology W.Va. U., Morgantown, 1970—, dir. grad. tng. in life-span devel. psychology, 1973—; mem. initial rev. groups div. research grants NIH, Washington, 1974-78, 79-84. Author: Perception of Stimulus Relations, 1968; co-author: Life-Span Developmental Psychology, 1977, Child Development, 1979; editor: Advances in Child Development and Behavior, 23 vols., 1969-96; co-editor: Life-Span Developmental Psychology, 8 vols., 1973-97; assoc. editor: Jour. Exptl. Child Psychology, 1975-83, editor, 1983-97. Served with U.S. Army, 1954. Fellow AAAS, Am. Psychol. Soc.; mem. AAUP, Soc. for Rsch. in Child Devel., Psychonomic Soc., Assn. for Behavior Analysis, Ea. Psychol. Assn., Internat. Soc. for Study Behavioral Devel. Office: W Va U Dept Psychology PO Box 6040 Morgantown WV 26506-6040

REESE, JAMES W., orthodontist; b. Detroit, July 2, 1928; s. Ralph W. and Clarice M. (Turner) R.; m. Antonia L. Frazer, June 26, 1964; children: Matthew W., Gregory F., Elizabeth G. DDS, U. Mich., 1953, MS, 1959. Diplomate Am. Bd. Orthodontics. Dentist USNR, Calif., Korea, Japan, 1953-55; instr. U. Mich., Ann Arbor, 1955-59, asst. prof. grad. orthodontics Sch. Dentistry, 1964-85; pvt. practice San Francisco, 1959-64, Ann Arbor, Mich., 1964—; prof. emeritus, bd. regents, U. Mich., 1985; chmn. State Peer Review Panel, 1989—. Dental chmn. United Way, Ann Arbor, Mich., 1984-86. Lt. USNR, 1953-55. Fellow Internat. Coll. Dentists; mem. Am. Dental Assn., Am. Assn. Orthodontists, Mich. Dental Assn. (trustee 1976-81), Washtenaw Dist. Dental Soc. (pres. 1987), Mich. Assn. Orthodontists (pres. 1980). Avocations: tennis, skiing. Home: 2009 Vinewood Blvd Ann Arbor MI 48104-3613 Office: James W Reese DDS MS 3250 Plymouth Rd Ste 102 Ann Arbor MI 48105-2555

REESE, JOHN ROBERT, lawyer; b. Salt Lake City, Nov. 3, 1939; s. Robert McCann and Glade (Stauffer) R.; m. Francesca Marroquin Gardner, Sept. 5, 1964 (div.); children—Jennifer Marie, Justine Francesca; m. Robin Ann Gunsul, June 18, 1988. AB cum laude, Harvard U., 1962; LLB, Stanford U., 1965. Bar: Calif. 1966, U.S. Dist. Ct. (no. dist.) Calif. 1966, U.S. Ct. Appeals (9th cir.) 1966, U.S. Dist. Ct. (cen. dist.) Calif. 1974, U.S. Supreme Ct. 1976, U.S. Dist. Ct. (ea. dist.) Calif. 1977, U.S. Ct. Appeals (6th cir.) 1982, U.S. Ct. Appeals (8th cir.) 1985, U.S. Ct. Appeals (10th cir.) 1992, U.S. Ct. Appeals (Fed. cir.) 1994. Assoc. McCutchen, Doyle, Brown & Enersen, San Francisco, 1965-74, ptnr., 1974—; adj. asst. prof. law Hastings Coll. of Law, 1991; lectr. U. Calif., Berkeley, 1987, 92. Mem. editorial, adv. bds. Antitrust Bull., Jour. Reprints for Antitrust Law and Econs. Bd. dirs. Friends of San Francisco Pub. Libr., 1981-87; bd. vis. Stanford U., 1983-86. Capt. U.S. Army, 1966-68. Decorated Bronze Star. Mem. ABA, State Bar Calif., San Francisco Bar Assn., U.S. Supreme Ct. Hist. Soc., Ninth Jud. Cir. Hist. Soc., Calif. Acad. Appellate Lawyers, Order of the Coif. Avocations: aviculture, gardening. Home: 9 Morning Sun Dr Petaluma CA 94952-4780 Office: McCutchen Doyle Brown & Enersen 3 Embarcadero Ctr San Francisco CA 94111-4003

REESE, MONTE NELSON, agricultural association executive; b. Mooreland, Okla., Mar. 31, 1947; s. James Nelson and Ruby Edith (Bond) R.; m. Treisa Lou Bartow, May 25, 1968; children: Bartow Allan, Monica Lynnelle. BS in Agrl. Econs., Okla. State U., 1969. Staff asst. Wilson Cert. Foods, Oklahoma City, 1969-71; assoc. farm dir. Sta. WKY Radio and TV, Oklahoma City, 1971-73; radio-TV specialist Tex. A&M U., College Station, 1973; dir. agrl. devel. Oklahoma City C. of C., 1973-76; asst. exec. dir. Am. Morgan Horse Assn., Westmoreland, N.Y., 1976-77; v.p. pub. affairs Farm Credit Banks of Wichita, Kans., 1977-87; exec. dir. Coffey County Econ. Devel., Burlington, Kans., 1987-88; farm dir. Mid-Am. Ag Network, Wichita, 1988-89; CEO Cattlemen's Beef Promotion and Rsch. Bd., Englewood, Colo., 1989-96; exec. dir. Cattlemen's Beef Promotion & Rsch. Bd., Englewood, CO, 1996—. Lt. col. USAR, 1969—. Home: 982 S Dearborn Way Apt 2 Aurora CO 80012-3878 Office: Cattlemen's Beef Promotion and Rsch Bd 5420 S Quebec St Englewood CO 80111-1905*

REESE, WILLIAM ALBERT, III, psychologist; b. Tabor, Iowa, Nov. 23, 1932; s. William Albert and Mary-Evelyn Hope (Lundeen) R.; B.A., U. Washington Reed Coll., 1955; M.Ed., U. Ariz., 1964, Ph.D., 1981; m. Barbara Diane Windermere, Dec. 22, 1954 (dec. Jan. 1995); children: Judy, Diane, William IV, Sandra-Siobhan, Debra-Anne, Robert-Gregory, Barbara-Joanne; m. Ruth Alice Moller, Sept. 12, 1996. Diplomate Am. Bd. Christian Psychology. Clin. Psychology cons. Nogales Pub. Schs., Nogales-Tucson, Ariz., 1971-79; clin. psychologist Astra Found., N.Y.C., 1979-86, chief psychology svc., neuropsychiatry, 1980-89; chief psychologist Family Support Ctr. Community-Family Exceptional Mem. Svcs., Sonoita, Ariz., 1986-89, Psychol. Svc. Ctr., Mount Tabor, Iowa, 1989-95, Calif. Ctr., 1995—; dir. religious Marriage and Family Life Wilderness Ctr., Berchtesgaden, W.Ger., summer 1981-82; exec. sec. Astra Ednl. Found., 1975-79, bd. dirs., 1979—, EEO officer, 1978—. Served with USAF, 1967-71: Vietnam. Decorated Bronze Star. Fellow in cons. psychology and holistic medicine Clin. Services Found., Ariz., 1979—. Fellow Am. Psychol. Soc.; mem. APA, Calif. Psychol. Assn., Am. Counseling Assn., Iowa Psychol. Assn. Clubs: Los Padres Wilderness Center, Outdoor, Sierra, Skyline Estates Golf and Country (Tucson), K.C. Author: Developing a Scale of Human Values for Adults of Diverse Cultural Backgrounds, 1981, rev. edit., 1988. Office: Psychol Service Ctr Integrated Med Ctr-Wellness Clin 225 Crossroads Blvd Ste 274 Carmel CA 93923-8649 also: PO Box 1089 Bellevue NE 68005-1089

REESE, WILLIAM LEWIS, philosophy educator; b. Jefferson City, Mo., Feb. 15, 1921; s. William Lewis and Lillian Amelia (Fisher) R.; m. Louise Weeks, June 11, 1945; children: Claudia, Patricia, William Lewis III. A.B., Drury Coll., 1942; B.D., U. Chgo., 1945, Ph.D., 1947; postdoctoral, Yale U., 1955-56. Asst. prof. philosophy Drake U., 1947-49, asso. prof. philosophy, 1949-57, head dept., 1954-57; asso. prof. philosophy Grinnell Coll., 1957-60; vis. prof. philosophy Iowa State U., 1958; prof. philosophy, chmn. dept. U. Del., Newark, 1960-67, dir. seminar in philosophy of sci., 1960-66; H. Rodney Sharp prof. philosophy U. Del., 1965-67; prof. philosophy SUNY-Albany, 1967—, chmn. dept., 1968-74, 84; Tully Cleon Knoles lectr. U. Pacific, 1962; Del. U.S. Nat. Commn. for UNESCO, 1963; gen. mem. 4th East-West Philosophers Conf., 1964. Author, contbr.: Studies in C.S. Peirce, 1952, (with Charles Hartshorne) Philosophers Speak of God, 1953, The Ascent from Below, 1959, 2d edit., 1987, (with Eugene Freeman) Process and Divinity, 1964, Dictionary of Philosophy and Religion: Eastern and Western Thought, 1980, 2d edit., 1996; gen. editor: Philosophy of Science, The Delaware Seminar, vols. 1, 2, 1963, vol. 3, 1967; editor: Philosophy and World Religions: The Reader's Adviser, vol. 4, 1988; contbg. editor: Philosophical Interrogations, 1964; co-editor: Metaphilosophy, 1967-75; editl. bd.: State of N.Y. Press, 1968-78; contbr. articles to profl. jours. Recipient Ford Found. Study award Argentina, 1967; Fulbright lectr. Argentina, summer 1971; Inst. Humanistic Studies fellow, 1977—. Mem. AAUP, Am. Philos. Assn., Metaphysical Soc. Am. (sec.-treas. 1962-65). Mem. Christian Ch. (Disciples of Christ). Home: Font Grove Rd Slingerlands NY 12159 Office: SUNY Dept Philosophy Albany NY 12222 *To have before one always the realistic sense that if one has been successful in one way one has failed in others, and that one's failures surely outnumber one's successes.*

REESE, WILLIAM WILLIS, banker; b. N.Y.C., July 8, 1940; s. Willis Livingston Meiser and Frances Galletin (Stevens) R.; BA, Trinity Coll., 1963; MBA, JD, Columbia U., 1970. Admitted to N.Y. bar, 1972; rsch. analyst Morgan Guaranty Trust Co., N.Y.C., 1971-73, investment rsch. officer, 1973-77, asst. v.p., 1977-86, v.p., 1986— . Bd. dirs. N.Y.C. Ballet, 1975-87, Counseling and Human Devel. Ctr., 1977-89, 3d St. Music Sch. Settlement, 1976—; trustee Millbrook Sch., 1972-91. Served with USAF, 1963-67. Mem. Am., Inter-Am., N.Y. State (sec. com. on internat. law 1973-76), Dutchess County bar assns., N.Y. Soc. Security Analysts, Certified Fin. Analysts, Assn. Bar City N.Y., Union, Club, Racquet and Tennis Club, Rockaway Hunt Club, Soldiers', Sailors' & Airmen's Club (bd. dirs. 1991—), Mt. Holyoke Lodge. Republican. Episcopalian. Home: 910 Park Ave New York NY 10021-0255 Office: Morgan Guaranty Trust Co 522 5th Ave New York NY 10036-7601

REESE, WINA HARNER, speech pathologist, consultant; b. Greensburg, Pa., Jan. 27, 1940; d. Clarence N. Harner and Gladys (Kell) Jaros; m. Richard F. Reese, Aug. 3, 1989; 1 child, Brian Olmsted. BS in Edn., Bowling Green (Ohio) State U., 1961. Speech pathologist La Grange (Ill.) Highlands, 1961-69, Richland Co., Mansfield, Ohio, 1970, Rehab. Svcs. N.C. Ohio, Mansfield, 1970-77; pvt. practice Lexington, Ohio, 1977-89; speech pathologist Mansfield City Schs., 1977—; cons., tutor Bur. Vocat. Rehab., Mansfield, 1980—; adj. prof. North Ctrl. Tech. Coll., 1995-96. Mem.

Learning Disabilities Assn., Ohio Speech-Lang.-Hearing Assn. (dist. rep. 1975-76), N.C. Ohio Speech-Hearing Assn. (pres. 1975-76), Orton Dyslexia Soc. Avocations: reading, needlework, music, gardening. Home: 95 Otterbein Dr Mansfield OH 44904-9341 Office: Mansfield City/St Peters 67 Mulberry St S Mansfield OH 44902-1909

REESE-BROWN, BRENDA, primary education educator, mathematics specialist; b. Tampa, Fla., Mar. 22, 1948; d. James T. and Mary Reese; m. Willie L. Brown. AA, Hillsborough C.C., Tampa, 1976; BA, U. South Fla., 1979; M in Early Childhood, Nova U., 1993. Cert. elem. and early childhood tchr., Fla. Tchr. kindergarten Town n County Elem. Sch., Tampa, 1979-80; primary tchr. Temple Terrace Elem. Sch., Tampa, 1980-91, tchr. kindergarten, 1991—, mem. sch. improvement team, 1992-95, math. specialist, 1992—. Mem. Zeta Phi Beta, Inc. (grammateus Nu Upsilon Zeta chpt. 1990-92). Avocations: sewing, cooking, reading, listening to gospel music, arts and crafts. Office: Temple Terrace Elem Sch 124 Flotto Ave Tampa FL 33617-5524

REESER, RACHEL ANNE EVERSON, graphic designer, artist; b. Shreveport, La., Nov. 16, 1964; d. Robert Higgins and Marian Louise (Wimberly) Everson; m. Kirk Allen "Korky" Reeser, Feb. 1, 1994. BS, Okla. State U., 1986. Mgr. Fabric, Floors & Such, Oklahoma City, Okla., 1986-87; advt. dir. Pipkin Cameras & Video, Oklahoma City, 1987-88; asst. nat. advt. mgr. Morgan Bldgs. & Spas, Dallas, 1988-89; sr. art dir. Avrea/Pugliese, Coconut Grove, Dallas, 1989-91; prin. Freestyle Studio, Dallas, 1991—. Vol. SPCA, Literacy Vols. Am. Mem. Dallas Soc. Illustrators (bd. dirs. 1992—, v.p. membership 1997—, Merit award 1993), Dallas Soc. Visual Comms., Graphic Artists Guild, Tex. Visual Arts Assn. Avocations: painting, tennis. Office: Freestyle Studio PO Box 823554 Dallas TX 75382-3554

REETZ, HAROLD FRANK, JR., industrial agronomist; b. Wat., Ill.; s. Harold Frank and Evelyn Evedeen (Russell) R.; m. Christine Lee Kaiser, Aug. 25, 1973; children: Carrie, Wesley, Anthony. BS in Agrl. Sci., U. Ill., 1970; MS in Agronomy, Purdue U., 1972, PhD in Agronomy, 1976. Rsch. specialist Purdue U., West Lafayette, Ind., 1974-82; regional dir. Potash & Phosphate Inst., Monticello, Ill, 1982—; v.p. Found. for Agronomic Rsch., 1996—; cons. Control Data Corp., Mpls., 1978-82, Internat. Harvester Co., Chgo., 1979-82, Monsanto Agrl. Chem. Co., St. Louis, 1981-82. Author: Crop Simulation Model, CORNCROPS, 1976, several crops mgmt. computer programs; contbr. articles to profl. jours. Chmn. Ill. Com. for Agrl. Edn., 1987-89; mem. Ill. Groundwater Adv. Coun., 1988—; mem. Ill. Fertilizer Rsch. and Edn. Coun., Ill. Dept. Agr., 1989—; chmn. Ill. Cert. Crop Adviser State Bd., 1992-94; mem. Monticello Unit 25 Bd. Edn., 1989-93; bd. dirs. Conservation Tech. Info. Ctr., 1995—. Recipient Hon. mem. Hon. State Farmer Ill. Assn. FFA, Urbana, 1987; IFCA Spl. Recognition award Ill. Fertilizer and Chem. Assn., 1988. Fellow Crop Sci. Soc. Am., Am. Soc. Agronomy; mem. Soil Sci. Soc. Am. (divsn. chmn. editl. bd., chmn. internat. cert. crop adviser exec. com. 1996—), Ill. Assn. Vocat. Agrl. Tchrs. (hon. life 1989—). Methodist. Avocations: photography, travel, computers.

REEVE, JOHN NEWTON, molecular biology and microbiology educator; b. Wakefield, W. Yorkshire, Eng., June 21, 1947; came to U.S., 1979; s. Arthur Newton and Lilian Elsworth (Tallant) R.; m. Patricia Margaret Watson, Sept. 21, 1967; children: Simon Arthur, Daniel John. BS with 1st class honors, U. Birmingham, Eng., 1968; PhD, U. B.C., Vancouver, Can., 1971. Rsch. scientist U. Ariz., Tucson, 1971-73, Nat. Inst. Med. Rsch., Mill Hill, London, 1973-74; rsch. dir. Max-Planck Inst., Berlin, 1974-79; prof. Ohio State U., Columbus, 1979—, chair dept. microbiology, 1985—; cons. Battelle Rsch. Lab., Columbus, 1982-87, Govt. of Bulgaria, Sofia, 1987, Promega Corp., Madison, Wis., 1990, Procter and Gamble Co., Cin., 1990; mem. sci. adv. bd. BioTrol. Inc., Chaska, Minn., 1986-90; Disting. vis. prof. U. Adelaide, Australia, 1984, U. Wyo., Laramie, 1988, U. Calcutta, India, 1989, Frei U., Berlin, 1991, U. Karachi, Pakistan, 1995, U. Concepcion, Chile, 1995. Named Disting. Rsch. Scholar Ohio State U., 1989. Mem. Am. Soc. for Microbiology (lectr. Found. for Microbiology 1987-88, 94-96). Office: Ohio State U Dept of Microbiology 484 W 12th Ave Columbus OH 43210-1214

REEVE, RONALD CROPPER, JR., manufacturing executive; b. Logan, Utah, Jan. 29, 1943; s. Ronald Cropper and Aldus (Moser) R.; m. Susan Leticia Gardner, July 4, 1966 (div. June 1975); children: Heather Renee, Michael Scott; m. Deborah Lynn Crooks, Dec. 31, 1976 (div. Apr. 1986); 1 child, Thomas Adam; m. Barbara Ruttan Avery, June 20, 1992; 2 stepchildren: Bryan Keith Avery, Allison Kathleen Avery. BS in Physics, Ohio State U., 1967; MBA in Mktg., Xavier U., 1972. Successively devel. engr., research engr., product planner Specialty Materials dept. Gen. Electric Co., Worthington, Ohio, 1969-73; successively product mgr., mktg. mgr., gen. mgr. Air Products & Chems., Inc., Lancaster, Ohio, 1974-79; founder, pres., chmn. Advanced Robotics Corp., Columbus, Ohio, 1979-84; founder, pres. R.C. Reeve, Inc., Westerville, Ohio, 1983—; founder, chief exec. officer Edison Welding Inst., Columbus, 1984-87; chief exec. officer Control Systems and Equipment Co., Inc., Columbus, 1987-90, CYBO Robots, Inc., 1988—, Check Guarantee Inc., Columbus, 1989-92, Indpls., 1991-92, Robot One Inc., Indpls. Tech. adv. bd. Franklin U., Civil Engring. Rsch. Found., dir. Internat. Assn. of Automation and Robotics in Constrn. Served with USAF, 1968-69. Named Small Businessman of Year, SBA, 1981. Mem. Am. Welding Soc., Am. Soc. Metals, Soc. Mfg. Engrs., Robot Inst. Am., Internat. Inst. Welding, Welding Inst., Robotics Internat., Hoover Yacht Club, Worthington Hill Country Club. Patentee diamond crystal structure. Home: 1460 Briarcliffe Dr Powell OH 43065-9060 Office: CYBO Robots Inc Indianapolis IN 46241

REEVE, THOMAS GILMOUR, physical education educator; b. Memphis, Sept. 23, 1946; s. Paul Goodwin and Dorothy (Bourke) R.; m. Sandra Weidner, Mar. 26, 1992; children: Bourke, Spencer. BS in Phys. Edn., Tex. Tech. U., 1969, MEd, 1972; PhD, Tex. A&M U., 1976. Asst. prof. Auburn (Ala.) U., 1977-82, assoc. prof., 1982-87, prof., 1987-91, asst. v.p. for acad. affairs, 1992-93, alumni prof., 1991-95, prof. phys. edn., 1995—; vis. asst. prof. Tex. A&M U., College Station, 1976-77. Co-editor: Stimulus-Response Compatibility, 1990; sect. editor Rsch. Quar. for Exercise and Sport, 1990-92; assoc. editor Jour. Sport Behavior, 1983—. Fellow AAHPERD, Rsch. Consortium, Am. Acad. Kinesiology and Phys. Edn.; mem. N.Am. Soc. Psychology of Sport and Phys. Activity (publ. dir. 1985-87, pres. 1991-92). Avocation: masters swimming. Office: Auburn U Dept Health and Human Performance Auburn AL 36849-5323

REEVES, A. SUE WINDSOR, healthcare administrator; b. Oxford, Miss., Mar. 1, 1947; d. Alton Eugene and Mary Emma (Haney) Windsor; m. Johnny Lafayette Reeves Jr., Nov. 1, 1969; children: Ashley Renee, Lesley Windsor, Douglas Stephens. BA in Edn., U. Miss., 1969; MEd, La. State U., 1972. Cert. tchr., La. Tchr. Jackson (Miss.) Pub. Schs., 1969-71; profl. vol. Nat. Assn. Jr. Aux., Slidell, La., 1979-87; tchr. St. Tammany Parish Schs., Slidell, 1981-83; dir. infant youth services Slidell Meml. Hosp., 1984, dir. community relations, 1984-85, dir. women's ctr., 1985-87, dir. physician recruitment, 1985-87, dir. physician services, 1987-90; exec. dir. Women's Health Found. Am. Med. Internat., New Orleans, 1986-88; asst. chair for adminstrn. dept. ob/gyn. U. N.C. Sch. Medicine, Chapel Hill, 1990-91; asst. adminstr. Highland Med. Ctr., Lubbock, Tex., 1991-94; physician recruitment dir. Tex. Tech. U. Health Sci. Ctr. and Univ. Med. Ctr., 1994-95; adminstr. Lubbock Ind. Physician Assn., 1995—; exec. dir. Open Air MRI of Lubbock, 1997—; mem. com. Women's Health Found. Lit.; healthcare cons., 1989-96; cons. Pro-Active Mgmt., 1995—; ind. rep. Excel Telecomms. Project designer Vol. Coord. Ctr., 1983, bd. dirs., 1983-88; exec. dir. Women's Health Found., 1987-88; mem. gala com. Leukemia Soc. Am., 1989; founding bd., v.p. Women's Health Care Exec. Network, New Orleans, 1988-90, West Tex. Speakers, 1992; sec. Lubbock Mentor Coun., 1993-96, Exec. Forum, 1994—, Women's Fin. Forum, 1995—; speaker Ann. Women's Wellness Conf., Lubbock, 1992—, 94, Teen Health Conf., Lubbock, 1994. State La. grantee, 1982; recipient Tex. Vol. award Tex. Dept. of Human Svcs., 1994, Commendation award Lubbock Mentoring Coun., 1995. Mem. NAFE, Am. Assn. Med. Colls., Nat. Assn. Jr. Aux. (Martha Wise award 1984, nat. com. woman 1982-87), Am. Coll. Healthcare Execs., Assn. for Mgrs., Ob-Gyn. Med. Group Mgmt. Assn., Assn. for Profl. Women Medicine, Slidell Panhellenic, Univ. Women's Club, Nat. Assn. Women's Health Profls., Lubbock C. of C. (healthcare com.), Phi Kappa Phi, Phi Mu. Republican. Avocations: reading, developing community progs., pub. speaking. Home: 3504 84th Lubbock TX 79423-2025 Office: PO Box 53104 Lubbock TX 79453-3104

REEVES, BARBARA ANN, lawyer; b. Buffalo, Mar. 29, 1949; d. Prentice W. and Doris Reeves; m. Richard C. Neal; children: Timothy R. Neal, Stephen S. Neal (dec.), Robert S. Neal, Richard R. Neal. Student, Wellesley Coll., 1967-68; B.A. (NSF fellow, Lehman fellow), New Coll., Sarasota, Fla., 1970; J.D. cum laude, Harvard U., 1973. Bar: Calif. 1973, D.C. 1977. Law clk. U.S. Ct. Appeals, 9th Circuit, Portland, Oreg., 1973-74; assoc. firm Munger, Tolles and Rickershauser, L.A., 1977-78; trial atty. spl. trial sect. Dept. Justice (Antitrust div.), 1974-75; spl. asst. to asst. atty. gen. Antitrust div. Dept. Justice, Washington, 1976-77; chief antitrust div. L.A. field office, 1978-81; ptnr. Morrison & Foerster, L.A., 1981-94, Fried, Frank, Harris, Shriver & Jacobson, L.A., 1995—; mem. exec. com. state bar conf. of dels. L.A. Delegation, 1982-91; del. 9th Cir. Jud. Conf., 1984-88; mem. Fed. Ct. Magistrate Selection Com., 1989; bd. dirs. Pub. Counsel, 1988-92, Western Ctr. Law and Poverty, 1992—; lectr. in field. Editor: Federal Criminal Litigation, 1994; contbg. author: International Antitrust, 1995; contbr. articles to profl. jours. Mem. ABA (litigation sect., antitrust sect.), Am. Arbitration Assn. (arbitrator, mediator, mem. adv. panel large complex case program), L.A. County Bar Assn. (antitrust sect. officer 1980-81, litigation sect. officer 1988-93 trustee 1990-92, chair alternative dispute resolution sec. 1992-95, L.A. County Ct. ADR com.). Home: 1410 Hillcrest Ave Pasadena CA 91106-4503 Office: Fried Frank Harris Shriver & Jacobson 350 S Grand Ave Ste 32 Los Angeles CA 90071-3459

REEVES, BRUCE, social worker; b. Centerville, Utah, Jan. 8, 1955; s. Leon W. and Maxine (Hodson) R. BA, U. Utah, 1979, MSW, 1983. Mental health caseworker Traveler's Aid Soc. Salt Lake City, 1983-86; socialwork cons. Home Health of Utah, Bountiful, 1985-86; victim svcs. counselor Salt Lake County Atty's. Office, Salt Lake City, 1986-87; mgr., cons. AIDS and employee assistance program Aetna and Human Affairs Internat., Salt Lake City, 1987-96; dir. social work and therapies Paracelsus Home Care & Hospice, Salt Lake City, 1996—; health educator Health Horizons, L.C., 1996—; presenter in field. Bd. dirs. Walk-ons, Inc., Salt Lake City, 1989—; mem. appropriations com. United Way Greater Salt Lake, Salt Lake City, 1990—, bd. assocs. Ririe-Woodbury Dance Co., Salt Lake City, 1991-95, human svcs. com. Utah Stonewall Ctr., Salt Lake City, 1992-95. Mem. NASW, APHA, NLGHA. Democrat. Avocations: dance, theatre, music, literature. Office: Paracelsus Home Care 1002 E South Temple Ste 101 Salt Lake City UT 84102-1525

REEVES, DANIEL EDWARD, professional football coach; b. Rome, Ga., Jan. 19, 1944; m. Pam Reeves; children: Dana, Laura, Lee. Grad., U. S.C. Running back Dallas Cowboys, NFL, 1965-72, player-coach, 1970-71, asst. coach, 1972, 74-80; head coach Denver Broncos, NFL, 1981-92, also v.p.; head coach N.Y. Giants, 1993-96, Atlanta Falcons, 1997—. Player NFL Championship Game, 1966, 67, 70, 71; recipient NFL Coach of the Year award, 1993; named to S.C. Hall Fame. Office: Atlanta Falcons One Falcon Pl Suwanee GA 30174 also: Denver Broncos 13665 E Davies Pl Englewood CO 80112-4004*

REEVES, DANIEL MCDONOUGH, video artist; b. Washington, Aug. 1, 1948; s. Suzanne Sticha Reeves; m. Debra Schweitzer, 1979 (div. 1986); m. Linda Garwood, Apr. 20, 1987; 1 child, Adele Grace. AS, Ithaca Coll., 1976, BA, 1979. Exec. prodr. Shakti Prodns., N.Y.C., 1980—. Artist Eingang/The Way In, 1990-94, Smothering Dreams, 1982 (Three Emmy awards), Crazy Wisdom, 1997; exec. prodr., creator Obsessive Becoming, 1995; creator, prodr. One With Everything, 1996—. With USMC, 1965-69, Vietnam. Decorated Silver Star medal for gallantry in action USMC; recipient Blue ribbon Am. Film Inst., 1983; Guggenheim fellow, 1983, Rockefeller fellow, 1995. Buddhist. Avocations: computer graphics programs, poetry, writing, music, hiking. Home and Office: Carrick House West Loch, Tarbert Argyll PA 296YX, Scotland

REEVES, DIANNE L., artist; b. Milw., Apr. 8, 1948; d. John J. and Bernice M. (Hendricksen) Kleczka; m. Robert A. McCoy, Oct. 15, 1983 (div. June 1988). BFA, U. Wis., Milw., 1968; student, Mus. Fine Arts, Houston, 1974-77, 83, Glassell Sch. Art, Houston, 1980-83. Instr. papermaking Glassell Sch. Art, 1984-85. Exhibited in solo shows at Women and Their Work Gallery, Austin, Tex., 1988, Moreau Galleries/Hamms Gallery, Notre Dame, Ind., 1991, The Martin Mus. of Art, Waco, Tex., 1996; internat. exhibns. include Leopold-Hoesch Mus., Duren, Germany, 1991, 92, 93, galleries in Netherlands, Copenhagen, Denmark, Kungalvs and Bollebygds, Sweden, and Basel, Switzerland; exhibited in numerous group exhbns.; author: (ltd. edit.) From Fiber to Paper, 1991. Bd. dirs., sec. Friends of Dard Hunter, Inc., 1993-94. NEA/Tex. fellow Mid-Am. Arts Alliance/NEA, 1986; recipient awards for art work. Mem. Internat. Assn. Hand Papermakers and Paper Artists (co-chair nominating com. 1993-94), Women and Their Work, Inc., Sierra Club, Tex. Fine Arts Assn., Austin Visual Arts Assn. Avocations: archaeology/anthropology, camping, reading, travel, environmental issues. Home and Studio: 1103 S 3rd St Austin TX 78704

REEVES, DONNA ANDREWS, golfer; b. Boston, Apr. 12, 1967; d. James Barclay and Helen Louise (Munsey) Andrews; m. John A. Reeves, Nov. 13, 1993. BBA, U. N.C., 1989. Qualified golfer LPGA Tour, Fla., 1990; winner Ping-Cellular One Golf Tounament, Portland, Oreg., 1993, Ping-Welch's Golf Tournament, Tucson, Ariz., 1994, Dinah Shore Major Golf Tournament, Palm Springs, Calif., 1994. Office: LPGA 100 International Golf Dr Daytona Beach FL 32124-1082*

REEVES, GEORGE MCMILLAN, JR., comparative literature educator, educational administrator; b. Spartanburg, S.C., Oct. 18, 1921; s. George McMillan and Bina Fay (Garvey) R.; m. Francine Helene Wickman, Jan. 27, 1950 (div. 1962); m. 2d Mary Carolyn Honeycutt, Apr. 14, 1964; children: George McMillan III, Marianne Elizabeth, Miriam Katherine, Alison Adams. B.S., Wofford Coll., 1942; M.A., U. Ala., 1948; Doctorat D'Universite, Sorbonne U. Paris, 1953; cert. in meteorology, NYU, 1943; DLitt (hon.), Wofford Coll., 1992. Asst. prof. English Presbyn. Coll., Clinton, S.C., 1948-50; from instr. to prof. English and comparative lit. U. S.C., Columbia, 1953-68, chmn. comparative lit. program, 1966-72, assoc. dean Grad. Sch., 1968-72, head dept. fgn. langs., 1972-74, dean Grad. Sch., 1974-94, interim provost, 1990-92, asst. to pres., 1992-93, dep. provost, 1993-94, dean emeritus, cons. to office of provost, 1994—; cons. lit. The Explicator, Columbia, 1957-65; mem. vis. teams So. Assn. Colls. and Schs., Atlanta, 1970—, SREB Small Grants program, Atlanta, 1980—; mem. exec. bd. Conf. So. Grad. Schs., 1983-86; mem. awards com. Drug Sci. Found., 1985-88; chmn. bd. Greenville, S.C. Higher Edn. Ctr., 1990-92; mem. bd. S.C. Humanities Coun., 1994—. Author: Thomas Wolfe et L'Europe, 1955; editor: Gustave Flaubert: Poesies de Jeunesse Inedites, 1968; editor and translator: The Time of William Faulkner, 1971 (MLA Scholars Libarary award 1971). Mem. Columbia Mus. Art and Sci., 1957—. Served to capt. USAAF, 1946-42, ETO. Fulbright scholar Sorbonne, Paris, 1951-52. Mem. MLA, S. Atlantic MLA (chmn. comparative lit. sect. 1970-71), AAUP, Phi Beta Kappa. Democrat. Club: Quail Hollow Swim and Racquet (pres.) (1979-80). Home: 1436 Mohawk Dr West Columbia SC 29169-6201 Office: U SC Office of Provost Columbia SC 29208-0001

REEVES, JOHN DRUMMOND, English language professional, writer; b. Troy, N.Y., Dec. 8, 1914; s. Robert Brockway and Emma Caroline (Mausert) R.; m. Mary Markwick Moore, Sept. 1, 1951. AB, Williams Coll., Williamstown, Mass., 1937; AM, Columbia U., 1941. Instr. in Eng. Irving Sch., Tarrytown, N.Y., 1937-40, Horace Mann Sch., N.Y.C., 1940-41, 46-47; asst. prof. of classics and Eng. Whitman Coll., Walla Walla, Wash., 1956-62; assoc. prof. English Millikin U., Decatur, Ill., 1962-65; lectr. in Eng. Hofstra U., Hempstead, N.Y., 1965-73, ret., 1973. Contbr. articles to profl. jours. Lt. USNR, 1941-45, PTO. Mem. AAUP, Coll. Eng. Assn., Am. Coun. Learned Soc. (reg. assoc. 1957-59), Walla Walla Archaeol. Assn. (pres. 1959-62), SR (N.Y. state chpt.), Masons. Home: Newey Ln Brookhaven NY 11719

REEVES, KEANU, actor; b. Beirut, Sept. 2, 1964. Stage appearances: Wolf Boy (debut), For Adults Only, Romeo and Juliet; films: Flying, 1986, Youngblood, 1986, River's Edge, 1987, Permanent Record, 1988, The Night Before, 1988, The Prince of Pennsylvania, 1988, Dangerous Liaisons, 1988, Bill and Ted's Excellent Adventure, 1989, Parenthood, 1989, I Love You to Death, 1990, Tune in Tomorrow, 1990, Bill and Ted's Bogus Journey, 1991, Point Break, 1991, My Own Private Idaho, 1991, Bram Stoker's Dracula, 1992, Much Ado About Nothing, 1993, Little Buddha, 1994, Even Cowgirls Get the Blues, 1994, Speed, 1994, Johnny Mnemonic, 1995, A Walk in the Clouds, 1995, Feeling Minnesota, 1996, Chain Reaction, 1996, Devil's Advocate, 1997, The Last Time I Committed Suicide, 1997; TV films: Letting Go, 1985, Act of Vengeance, 1986, Young Again, 1986, Babes in Toyland, 1986, Under the Influence, 1986, Brotherhood of Justice, 1986, Children Remember the Holocaust, 1995; TV special: Save the Planet, 1990. Office: Jake Bloom Agy care Erwin Stoff 7920 W Sunset Blvd Ste 350 Los Angeles CA 90064-3300*

REEVES, LUCY MARY, retired secondary school educator; b. Pewamo, Mich., July 2, 1932; d. Lavaldin Edgar and Marian S. (Lee) Hull; m. Walter Emery Reeves, Jan. 21, 1922. BS, Western Mich. U., Kalamazoo, 1965; postgrad., Western Mich. U., 1965-75. Tchr. Country Sch. One Room, Matherton, Mich., 1956-57, Ionia, Mich., 1957-58, Belding, Mich., 1958-62, Saranac, Mich., Belding, Mich., 1965; tchr. Belding (Mich.) Area Schs., 1965-89; ret. Mem. NEA, Mich. Edn. Assn., Belding Area Edn., Profl. Businesswomen's Assn. Avocations: computers, reading, travelling, sewing.

REEVES, MARYLOU, financial planner; b. Summit, N.J., Dec. 19, 1959; d. Richard Otto and Helen Elizabeth (Drennan) Wellbrock; m. Richard Harold Reeves, Jan. 13, 1985; children: Rachael Elizabeth, Thomas Mack. BS in Commerce, Rider Coll., 1981. Cert. Fin. Planner; Registry of Fin. Planning Practitioners. Asst. v.p. E.F. Hutton, N.Y.C., 1981-86, Summit Bancorp., Summit, N.J., 1986-89; owner Thomas Mack Assocs., Rockaway, N.J., 1989—. Contbr. newspaper column. Councilwoman Rockaway Twp., N.J., 1988-95; mem. Civic Affairs Com., White Meadow, N.J., 1987—, coun. pres. 1994-95; vice chmn. Rockaway Twp. Rep. Com., 1987. Mem. Internat. Assn. Fin. Planners. Republican. Roman Catholic. Office: Thomas Mack Assocs 31 Valley View Dr Rockaway NJ 07866-1506

REEVES, MICHAEL STANLEY, public utility executive; b. Memphis, Oct. 2, 1935; m. Patricia Ann Board, June 27, 1959; children: Michael, Michelle. Student Iowa State U., 1954-56; B.A., Roosevelt U., 1964; M.B.A., Northwestern U., 1972. With People Gas Light and Coke Co., Chgo., 1956—, supr., 1967-69, asst. supt., 1969-72, supt., 1972-75, gen. supt., 1975-77, v.p. mktg. and customer relations, 1977-87, exec. v.p., 1987—. Bd. dirs. Better Bus. Bur., Chgo., No. Ill.; mem. Local Initiatives Support Corp. Chgo. Adv. Com.; trustee Shedd Aquarium, Abraham Lincoln Centre; bd. dirs. Peoples Energy Corp., 1991, Children's Meml. Hosp. Served with U.S. Army. Mem. Chgo. Assn. Commerce and Industry, Am. Gas Assn., Am. Assn. Blacks in Energy, Am. Heart Assn. (Met. Chgo. bd. govs.), Chgo. Econ. Club. Club: University (Chgo., mem. bd. dirs.). Office: Peoples Energy Corp 122 S Michigan Ave Lbby 2 Chicago IL 60603-6107

REEVES, NANCY ALICE, critical care nurse; b. Manhasset, N.Y., Aug. 19, 1965; d. Kenneth George and Jean Adele (Reineke) Leib. BSN, Hartwick Coll., 1988. RN, N.Y. Staff nurse intermediate care unit Mercy Med. Ctr., Rockville Center, N.Y., 1988-92, staff nurse CCU, 1992—; office nurse Gary Friedman, MD, Rockville Center, 1993—. Mem. AACN, N.Y. State Nurses Assn., Alpha Omicron Pi. Avocations: needlework, collecting.

REEVES, PATRICIA RUTH, heavy machinery manufacturing company executive; b. Bklyn., Mar. 26, 1931; d. Maurice G. and Ethel Helen (Kessler) Der Brucke m. Cedric E. Reeves, June 22, 1952. BA, Adelphi U., 1952. Chief of records sect. Hydrocarbon Rsch., Inc., N.Y.C., 1952-65; lead sec. C.F. Braun & Co., Murray Hill, N.J., 1965-69; exec. sec. Wilputte Corp., Murray Hill, N.J., 1969-75, adminstrv. asst., 1975-79, sales coord., 1979-81, pers. adminstr., 1981-82; sales coord. Krupp Wilputte Corp., Murray Hill, N.J., 1982-84; pers. adminstr. Somerset Techs., Inc., N.J., 1984-85, pers. mgr., 1985-95; pres. Human Resources Svcs., Watchung, N.J., 1995—. Pres. Mountain Jewish Community Ctr., Warren, N.J., 1976-77, bd. dirs., 1972-81. Mem. NAFE, AAUW, Women's Network Ctrl. N.J. (v.p., editor newsletter 1981-83, coord. career assistance 1984-85, membership chair 1986-89), Am. Soc. Pers. Adminstrs. (membership chair 1986-88, sec. 1986-88), Soc. Human Resources Mgmt. (sec. Ctrl. N.J. chpt. 1986-88, v.p. 1988-89, pres. 1989-90, sec.-treas. N.J. State Coun. 1990-92, sec.-treas. Area I bd. 1993-95, dir. mem. at large 1996, co-chair N.J. conf., 1994-95, chair chpt. awards 1996, sr. advisor 1996, N.J. State Coun. dir. 1997—). Home and Office: Human Resources Svcs 89 Knollwood Dr Watchung NJ 07060-6245

REEVES, PEGGY LOIS ZEIGLER, accountant; b. Orangeburg, S.C., May 12, 1940; d. Joseph Harold and Lois Vivian (Stroman) Zeigler; m. Donald Preston Reeves, Sept. 9, 1961. Degree in Secretarial Sci., Coker Coll., 1960. Sec. Ladson Beach, CPA, Orangeburg, 1960-61; acctg. clk. Milliken & Co., Laurens, S.C., 1962-67, sec., 1967-73, mgmt. trainee, 1973, plant contr., 1973-74, 76-81; cost acctg. supr. Milliken & Co., Spartanburg, S.C., 1974-76, 81—. Chair bd. dirs. Enoree (S.C.)-Lanford Fire dist., 1982—, treas., 1988—; mem. alumni exec. bd. Coker Coll., 1996—. H.L. Jones scholar Coker Coll., 1959-60. Mem. Inst. Mgmt. Accts. (sec. 1991-94, v.p. membership 1994-95, v.p. adminstrn. and fin. 1995-96, pres.-elect 1996-97, pres. 1997—), Profl. Secs. Internat. (v.p., rec. sec., Sec. of Yr. 1973). Baptist. Avocations: reading, collecting plates and antiques.

REEVES, RALPH B., III, publisher, editor; b. Raleigh, N.C., Apr. 2, 1947; s. Ralph Bernard Reeves Jr. and Frances Rhoda (Campbell) M.; m. Caroline Holton Green, Apr. 24, 1971 (div. 1986); children: Ralph B. IV, Daniel MacQuarrie. AB in History, U. N.C., 1970. Field coord. FMI Mgmt. Group, Raleigh, N.C., 1972-76; gen. mgr., v.p. The Leader Newspaper, Rsch. Triangle Pk., N.C., 1976-78; pres., pub., founder Spectator Pubs. Inc., Raleigh, N.C., 1978—, Triad Bus., Greensboro, N.C., 1986-88, Triangle Bus., Raleigh, 1985-91, Spectator Pub., N.C. Architect, 1981-84. Editor: Mr. Spectator, 1978—. 1st v.p. Mordecai Square Hist. Soc., Raleigh, 1980-83; pres. Hilltop Home, 1982-84; chmn. Downtown Adv. Com., 1983-85; mem. Bus. Adv. Com. for N.C. Sec. of State, Raleigh, 1992—; bd. dirs. N.C. State U. Friends of Libr., Nike Carolina Classic Golf Tournament. Gov's. Bus. award in the Arts and Humanities, 1986, Benjamin Fine award, 1991, AABP award Triangle Bus., 1st place award Feature Writing, 1991. Mem. Fifty Group, U. N.C. Dean's Club, English Speaking Union (past pres. RTP br. 1988—), Carolina Co. Club, Sphinx Club. Democrat. Episcopalian. Avocations: golf, history, travel. Home: 1707 Mcdonald Ln Raleigh NC 27608-2111 Office: Spectator Pubs Inc 1318 Dale St Ste 200 Raleigh NC 27605-1275

REEVES, RICHARD, writer, historian; b. N.Y.C., Nov. 28, 1936; s. Furman W. and Dorothy (Forshay) R.; m. Carol A. Wiegand, June 1, 1959 (div. 1971); m. Catherine E. O'Neill, July 28, 1979; children: Cynthia Ann, Jeffrey Richard, Colin O'Neill, Cono O'Neill, Fiona O'Neill. ME, Stevens Inst. Tech., 1960. Engr. Ingersoll-Rand Co., Phillipsburg, N.J., 1960-61; editor Phillipsburg Free Press, 1961-63; reporter Newark News, 1963-65, N.Y. Herald Tribune, 1965-66; chief polit. corr. N.Y. Times, 1966-71; editor N.Y., 1971-77; lectr. Hunter Coll., 1969-70, Columbia U., 1971-72; nat. editor Esquire, 1977-79; syndicated columnist, 1979—; chief corr. Frontline, 1984—; Regents prof. polit. sci. UCLA, 1992-93; host "Sunday" NBC-TV, 1972-75, "American Journey" PBS-TV, 1983. Author: A Ford, Not a Lincoln, 1975, Old Faces of 1976, 1976, Convention, 1977, Jet Lag: The Running Commentary of a Bi-coastal Reporter, 1981, American Journey: Travelling with Tocqueville in Search of Democracy in America, 1982, The Reagan Detour: Conservative Revolution, 1985, A Passage to Peshawar: Pakistan Between the Hindu Kush and the Arabian Sea, 1985, President Kennedy: Profile of Power, 1993 (Book of Yr., Time 1993), Family Travels, 1997; columnist; article writer. Recipient Emmy award, 1980, Christopher Book award, 1983, PEN Non-Fiction Book of Yr. award, 1993. Home: 300 E 57th St New York NY 10022 Office: Reeves-O'Neill Inc 286 Main St Sag Harbor NY 11963-2668

REEVES, ROSSER SCOTT, III, retired investment company executive; b. N.Y.C., Aug. 20, 1936; s. Rosser and Elizabeth (Street) R.; m. Colin McRae Squibb, Dec. 14, 1963; 1 dau., Elizabeth Robinson. Acad. degree with honors, Westminster Sch., 1954; postgrad., Yale, 1954-55; BS with honors in architecture, U. Va., 1961. Assoc. real estate firm Douglas L. Elliman & Co., N.Y.C., 1961-62; investment banker Lazard Freres & Co., N.Y.C., 1962-67; founder, mng. partner R.S. Reeves & Co., N.Y.C., 1967-68; sr.

mng. partner Bacon, Stevenson & Reeves, N.Y.C., 1968-70; chmn. bd. Quantum Corp., N.Y.C., 1970-75; pres. Rosser Reeves Holdings, Ltd., N.Y.C., 1975—; pres., chief exec. officer dir. Rosser Reeves, Inc., N.Y.C., 1976—; pres. Charlie O Co., 1980-82; pres., chief exec. officer Tiderock Corp., Little Rock, Ark., 1990—; founder, CEO The Recovery Found., 1992—; mem. N.Y. Stock Exch., 1967-69; mng. ptnr. Wall St. Leasing Assn., 1968-70; chmn. bd. Internat. Subsea Devel. Corp., N.Y.C., 1969-75, Mil. Armament Corp., N.Y.C., 1969-75. Trustee Youth Consultation Service, N.Y.C., 1968-72; bd. dirs. Ark. Symphony Orch., 1982-85. Mem. Scarab. Clubs: Union League (N.Y.C.), Racquet and Tennis (N.Y.C.), N.Y. Stock Exchange Lunch (N.Y.C.); Little Rock (Ark.). Home: 14201 Orleans Dr Little Rock AR 72211

REEVES, VAN KIRK, lawyer; b. N.Y.C., May 14, 1939; arrived in France, 1967; s. William Harvey and Caroline (Buck) R.; m. Ann Murchison, June 24, 1967; children: Daisy Fiona, Evander James. BA, Harvard U., 1961, JD, 1964. Ptnr. Coudert Frères, Paris, 1973-95, Coudert Bros., N.Y.C., 1973-95, Porter & Reeves, Paris, 1995—. Author: Confessions of an Art Lawyer, 1997, The Structure and Financing of Art Transactions, 1994; co-author: (with Dr. J. Boll) Auction Sales and Conditions, 1991. Bd. mem., v.p. Internat. Coun. Muss. Found., Paris, 1972-95; bd. suprs. Am. Tax Inst., London, 1978; bd. mem. Fabergé Arts Found., Washington, 1992. Mem. Inst. Internat. Bus. Law and Practice (corr. mem.). Avocations: projects for the preservation of cultural heritage, hiking. Home: 8 Cité Nicolas Poussin, 240 Blvd Raspail, 75014 Paris France Office: Porter & Reeves, 5 Rue Cambon, 75001 Paris France

REEVES, WILLIAM BOYD, lawyer; b. Easley, S.C., Mar. 24, 1932; s. William C. and Elise B. (Brooks) R.; m. Rose Mary Weil, Sept. 7, 1957 (dec. Nov. 1977); 1 dau., Gabrielle; m. Gladys Frances Brown, Nov. 24, 1978; children: Stephanie, William. B.A., Furman U., 1954; LL.B., Tulane U., 1959. Bar: La. 1959, Ala. 1960, U.S. Supreme Ct 1971. Law clk. to U.S. Dist. Judge, So. Dist. Ala., 1959-61; assoc. firm Armbrecht, Jackson & DeMouy, 1961-65; ptnr. Armbrecht, Jackson, DeMouy, Crowe, Holmes & Reeves, Mobile, 1965—. Chancellor St. Lukes Episcopal Ch. and Sch., 1973—. Served to capt. U.S. Army, 1954-56. Fellow Am. Coll. Trial Lawyers, Am. Coll. Legal Medicine, Internat. Soc. Barristers; mem. ABA., Ala. State Bar, La. State Bar, Mobile Bar Assn. (pres. 1981), Internat. Assn. Ins. Counsel, Fedn. Ins. and Corp. Counsel, Maritime Law Assn. U.S. (exec. coun. 1988-90), Ala. Defense Lawyers Assn. (past pres.), Southeastern Admiralty Law Inst. (past pres.), Nat. Bd. Trial Advocates, Am. Bd. Trial Advocates (pres. Ala. chpt. 1986-87), Am. Bd. Profl. Liability Attys., Nat. Health Law Assn., Athelstan Club, Mobile Country Club, Internat. Trade Club, Bienville Club, Propeller Club, Masons. Home: 3755 Rhonda Dr S Mobile AL 36608-1733

REFINETTI, ROBERTO, physiological psychologist; b. Sao Paulo, Brazil, Nov. 19, 1957; came to U.S., 1988; s. Renato and Maria Stella (Barroso) R.; m. Kathleen Diane Zylan, Mar. 5, 1988 (div. Aug. 1991); 1 child, Lauren Lynne. BA in Philosophy, Pontifical Cath. U., Sao Paulo, 1981; BS in Psychology, U. Sao Paulo, 1981, MA in Psychology, 1983; PhD in Psychology, U. Calif., Santa Barbara, 1987. Asst. prof. U. Sao Paulo, 1986-88; postdoctoral fellow U. Calif., Santa Barbara, 1988-89, U. Ill., Champaign, 1989-90, U. Va., Charlottesville, 1990-92; asst. prof. Coll. William and Mary, Williamsburg, Va., 1992—. Contbr. over 100 articles to profl. jours. Area grantee NIH, 1996; recipient Nat. Rsch. Svc. Individual award NIMH, 1991, Career award NSF, 1995. Mem. Am. Physiol. Soc., Am. Psychol. Soc., Soc. Neuroscience, Soc. Rsch. on Biol. Rhythms. Office: Coll of William and Mary Dept Psychology Williamsburg VA 23187

REFIOR, EVERETT LEE, labor economist, educator; b. Donnellson, Iowa, Jan. 23, 1919; s. Fred C. and Daisy E. (Gardner) R.; m. Marie Emma Culp, Sept. 12, 1943; children: Gene A., Wendell F., Paul D., Donna M.; m. Betty Pottenger Phelps, Nov. 27, 1993. BA, Iowa Wesleyan Coll., 1942; postgrad., U. Glasgow, 1945; MA, U. Chgo., 1955; PhD, U. Iowa, 1962. Instr. econs. and bus. Iowa Wesleyan Coll., 1947-50; teaching asst. U. Iowa, 1950-51; research asst. Bur. of Labor and Mgmt., 1951-52, instr. mgmt. and social sci., 1954-55; assoc. prof. econs. Simpson Coll., 1952-54; asst. prof. econs. U. Wis. at Whitewater, 1955-62, assoc. prof., 1962-64, prof., 1964-83, prof. emeritus, 1983—, chmn., 1966-75. Lyricist (hymns) Eternal Love, 1980, Divine Order, 1980, If We But Dare, 1984, Humanity, 1989, others. Found. pres. Whitewater chpt. World Federalists Assn., 1960-68, 76-78, 86-92, midwest regional pres., 1969-71, 75-87, nat. bd., 1968-89, 92—; del. World Congress, Ottawa, 1970, Brussels, 1972, Paris, 1977, Tokyo, 1980, Phila., 1987, San Francisco, 1995; exec. com. Assn. World Citizens, 1980-96; sec. World Govt. Orgns. Coalition, 1987-96; mem. Gov.'s Commn. on UN, 1971-89, state coord. Campaign for UN Reform, 1984-96, nat. pres., 1996—; mem. Wis. Conf. bd. Social Concerns, Meth. Ch., 1961-68, 70-76; Dem. precinct com. Whitewater, 1966-96; chmn. Walworth County Dem. Party, 1975-78, Wis. Dem. Platform Com., 1978—; bd. dirs. Alcohol Problems Coun. Wis., 1976—. Mem. Indsl. Rels. Rsch. Assn. (adv. bd. Wis. chpt. 1964-78, acad. v.p. 1978-83), Peace Action, Population Inst., Fedn. Am. Scientists, South Ctrl. Wis. UN Assn. (pres. 1979-80, v.p. 1995-97), Kiwanis (pres. local club 1987-88). Methodist (lay speaker). Home: 205 N Fremont St Whitewater WI 53190-1322 *Life is too precious to be spent on ourselves. We show love for our Creator by what we do for others. Happiness is a by-product.*

REFO, PATRICIA LEE, lawyer; b. Alexandria, Va., Dec. 31, 1958. BA with high honors and high distinction, U. Mich., 1980, JD cum laude, 1983. Bar: Ill. 1983, Ariz. 1996, U.S. Dist. Ct. (no. dist.) Ill. 1988, U.S. Ct. Appeals (7th cir.) 1989, U.S. Ct. Appeals (11th cir.) 1990, U.S. Ct. Appeals (5th cir.) 1992, Fed. Trial Bar (no. dist.) Ill. 1993, U.S. Dist. Ct. Ariz. 1996. Ptnr. Jenner & Block, Chgo., 1991-96, Snell & Wilmer L.L.P., Phoenix, 1996—; mem. faculty Nat. Inst. Trial Advocacy, 1989—; bd. advisors Lender Liability News; lectr. ALI/ABA and Practicing Law Inst. on Various subjects including trial advocacy and lender liability. Co-author: Class Action Controversies, 1989, Notice to Members of the Class, IICLE Class Actions Handbook, 1986. Dir. Legal Clinic for the Disabled, 1994-96, Chgo. Lawyers' Com. Civil Rights Under Law, 1987-91, Cabrini Green Legal Aid Clinic, 1987-91. Mem. ABA (chair sect. litigation 1990 annual meeting, co-chair sect. litigation Pro Bono com. 1990-93, dir. divsns. sect. litigation 1993-94, sec. sect. litigation 1994—). Office: Snell & Wilmer LLP One Arizona Ctr Phoenix AZ 85004-0001

REGALADO, RAUL L., airport parking executive; b. L.A., Jan. 31, 1945; s. Raul and Antonia (Estavillo) R.; m. Helen Sutcliffe; children: Stephanie, Jennifer. BS, Embry-Riddle Aero. U., 1972. Mgr. airport City of Klamath Falls, Oreg., 1972-74, City of Fresno, Calif., 1974-79, Orange County, Santa Ana, Calif., 1979-80; dir. aviation San Jose (Calif.) Airport, 1980-89; aviation cons. Raul Regalado & Assocs., Huntington Beach, Calif., 1989-91; dep. dir. aviation Houston Dept. Aviation, 1991-95; market pres. airport properties APCOA, Inc., Vancouver, Wash., 1995—. Capt. U.S. Army, 1966-71, col. USAR (retired). Decorated Legion of Merit, Bronze Star, DFC, Air medal with 49 oak leaf clusters, Meritorious Svc. medal, Army Commendation medal with 3 oak leaf clusters. Mem. Am. Assn. Airport Execs., Calif. Assn. Airport Execs. (pres. 1980-81), Airport Operators Coun. Internat. (bd. dirs. 1986-88), Vietnam Helicopter Pilots Assn., Nat. Parking Assn., Assn. of U.S. Army, Aero. Club No. Calif. (bd. dirs. 1982-91, pres. 1987-89), Quiet Birdmen.

REGALMUTO, NANCY MARIE, small business owner, psychic consultant, therapist; b. Bay Shore, N.Y., Aug. 24, 1956; d. Antonio J. Jr. and Agnes C. (Dietz) R. Student, SUNY, Stony Brook. Sales mgr. Fire, Inc., Hempstead, N.Y., 1976-78; sports handicapper Red Hot Sport, J. Dime Sports, Diamond Sports, Hicksville, N.Y., 1978—; small bus. owner, pres. Synergy (vitamin/nutritional product mfr. and distributor), Bellport, N.Y., 1981—; cons. on medicine, fin., past life, bus. readings, hypnosis, substance abuse, archeology, law enforcement investigations, family, counseling, inter-species comm., animal therapy, psychic surgery, healing, 1989—; lectr. in field, specializing in holistic remedies and therapies, 1989-91. Columnist Daily Racing Form, 1989-91; appeared on numerous TV programs, worldwide radio, mags., newspapers. Lectr., seminar leader, written about in several books. Min. Universal Life Ch., 1996, 97, Ch. of Inner Wisdom, 1996, 97. Mem. NAFE, Horse Protection Assn., Am. Biog. Inst. (named Woman of Yr. 1994). Office: 44 E 32nd St New York NY 10016-5508 also: 18 Woodland Park Rd Bellport NY 11713

REGAN, DAVID, brain researcher, educator; b. Scarborough, Eng., May 5, 1935; arrived in Can., 1976; s. Randolph and Muriel Frances (Varley) R.; m. Marian Pauline Marsh, Aug. 15, 1959; children: Douglas Lawrence, Howard Michael. BSc, London U., 1957, MSc, 1958, PhD, 1964, DSc, 1974. Lectr. physics London U., 1960-65; reader neurosci. Keele U., Eng., 1965-75; prof. psychology Dalhousie U., Can., 1976-80, prof. physiology, 1980-84, assoc. prof. medicine, 1978-84, prof. medicine, 1984-87, prof. ophthalmology, 1980-87, prof. otolaryngology, 1980-84, Killam rsch. prof., 1978-82; prof. engring. Rutgers U., 1985-86; prof. psychology York U., Can., 1987—, prof. biology; prof. ophthalmology U. Toronto, Ont., Can., 1987—; retained inventor Wilkinson-Graviner Group, Eng., 1970-75; cons. Westinghouse, Pitts., 1980-86; co-dir. human performance in space lab. Inst. for Space and Terrestrial Sci., York U., 1989—, disting. rsch. prof., 1991—; indsl. rsch. chair aviation vision Natural Sci. and Engring. Rsch. Coun. Can./Can. Aviation Electronics, 1993. Author: Human Evoked Potentials, 1972, Human Brain Electrophysiology, 1989; editor: Spatial Vision, 1989, Binocular Vision, 1989, Vision Research, 1992; contbr. more than 250 articles to profl. jours.; holder 8 patents. Recipient Forman prize for med. rsch., 1983, Prentice medal, 1990; rsch. grantee NIH, NRC, Air Force Office Sci. Rsch., Nat. Scis. and Engring. Rsch. Coun. Can., Med. Rsch. Coun.; Killam fellow, 1990. Fellow Royal Soc. Can., Optical Soc. Am.; mem. Exptl. Psychology Soc., Soc. Clin. Electroretinography, Assn. Rsch. in Vision and Ophthalmology, Royal Coll. Sci. (London, assoc.), Am. Acad. Optometry. Avocations: cricket, walking, modern European history. Office: York U Dept Psychology, 4700 Keele St, North York, ON Canada M3J 1P3

REGAN, DAVID MICHAEL, health care administrator; b. Phila., Oct. 3, 1955; s. James Rodman and Dorothy Marie (Jones) R.; m. Cathy Jean Aspril, June 13, 1981; children: Bethany Ann, Sarah Kathleen. BA, Franklin and Marshall Coll., 1977; MS in Health Planning and Adminstrn., Pa. State U., 1984. Cert. med. practice exec. Adminstrv. asst. York (Pa.) Hosp., 1983; asst. dir. office emergency med. services Pa. State U., University Park, 1983-84; adminstrv. asst., research analyst L.I. Jewish Med. Ctr., New Hyde Park, N.Y., 1984-85; asst. adminstr. Geisinger Clinic, Lewistown, Pa., 1985-88, mgr. of revenue, reimbursement, 1987-90, adminstrv. dir. primary care svcs., 1990-93; dir. HealthAm., 1993-96; COO Lexington Clinic, Ky., 1996—; bd. dirs. Geisinger Fed. Credit Union. Mem. Pa. Med. Group Mgmt. Assn. (pres. 1995-96), Pa. Med. Soc., Med. Group Mgmt. Assn., Juniata Area C. of C. (bd. dirs. 1987-88), Nat. Health Lawyers Assn., Rotary Club. Avocations: stained glass window/lamp design and constrn., golf, skiing, aviation. Office: Lexington Clinic 1221 S Broadway St Lexington KY 40504-2701

REGAN, DONALD THOMAS, financier, writer, lecturer; b. Cambridge, Mass., Dec. 21, 1918; m. Ann G. Buchanan, July 11, 1942. BA, Harvard U., 1940; LLD (hon.), Hahnemann Med. Coll. Hosp., 1968, U. Pa., 1972, Pace U., 1973; DHL (hon.), Colgate U. With Merrill Lynch, Pierce, Fenner & Smith Inc. (and predecessor), 1946-81, sec., dir. adminstrv. div., 1960-64, exec. v.p., 1964-68, pres., 1968-70, chmn., chief exec. officer, 1971-80; chmn. bd., chief exec. officer Merrill Lynch & Co. Inc., 1973-81; sec. Dept. of Treasury, Washington, 1981-85; White House chief of staff Washington, 1985-87; vice chmn., dir. N.Y. Stock Exchange, 1972-75. Author: A View from the Street, 1972, For the Record, 1988. Trustee Charles E. Merrill Trust, 1961-80; chmn. bd. trustees U. Pa., 1974-78, life trustee, 1978-80; mem. policy com. Bus. Roundtable, 1978-80; trustee Com. for Econ. Devel., 1978-80. Served to lt. col. USMCR, World War II. Laureat Bus. Hall of Fame, 1981. Clubs: Army-Navy. Office: 240 Mclaws Cir Williamsburg VA 23185-5650

REGAN, ELLEN FRANCES (MRS. WALSTON SHEPARD BROWN), ophthalmologist; b. Boston, Feb. 1, 1919; d. Edward Francis and Margaret (Moynihan) R.; AB, Wellesley Coll., 1940; MD, Yale U., 1943; m. Walston Shepard Brown, Aug. 13, 1955. Intern, Boston City Hosp., 1944; asst. resident, resident Inst. Ophthalmology, Presbyn. Hosp., N.Y.C., 1944-47, asst. ophthalmologist, 1947-56, asst. attending ophthalmologist, 1956-84; instr. ophthalmology Columbia Coll. Physicians and Surgeons, 1947-55, asso. ophthalmology, 1955-67, asst. clin. prof., 1967-84. Mem. Am. Ophthal. Soc., AMA, Am. Acad. Ophthalmology, N.Y. Acad. Medicine, N.Y. State Med. Soc., Mass. Med. Soc., River Club. Office: PO Box 632 Tuxedo Park NY 10987-0632

REGAN, JOHN BERNARD (JACK REGAN), community relations executive, senator; b. Chgo., Feb. 2, 1934; s. Andrew J. and Frances (O'Born) R.; m. Rosemary E. Seger, Aug. 17, 1980. BA, So. Ill. U., 1960. V.p. Collins Bros., Las Vegas, Nev., 1971-76; pres. Terra, Inc., Las Vegas, 1973-80; owner Jack's Place, Las Vegas, 1980-95; govt. and mil. affairs liaison C.C. So. Nev., North Las Vegas, 1984-95; dist. dir. Nat. Coun. for Community Rels., 1984-86; nat. treas. Nat. Coun. Mktg. and Pub. Rels., 1986-88; state dir. Internat. Coun. of Shopping Ctrs., Nev., 1976. State assemblyman Nev. State Legis., Carson City, 1988-90, 92-93, state senator 1994-96; past chmn. Am. Legis. Exch. Coun., 1990-93; trade, travel and tourism com. mem. Nat. Conf. of State Legis., 1990-93, com. on devel. disabilities, mem. exec. com., 1996; active Las Vegas Habitat for Humanity. With USN, 1951-55. Recipient Lion of Yr. award Las Vegas Lions Club, 1978, Paragon award Nat. Coun. for Cmty. Rels., 1985, Legislator of Yr. award Am. Legis. Exch. Coun., 1996. Mem. Thunderbird Chpt. Air Force Assn. (pres. 1989-90, named hon. Thunderbird, Nighthawk, stealth fighter), North Las Vegas C. of C. (v.p. 1986). Democrat. Jewish. Avocations: reading, community service, coin collecting. Home: 1650 Cookson Ct Las Vegas NV 89115-6948

REGAN, JUDITH THERESA, publishing executive; b. Leominster, Mass., Aug. 17, 1953; d. Leo James and Rita Ann (Imprescia) R.; children: Patrick, Lara. BA, Vassar Coll., 1975. Sr. editor, v.p. Simon & Schuster, N.Y.C., 1989-94; pres., pub. Regan Books, N.Y.C., 1994—; TV prodr. Entertainment Tonight, N.Y.C., Geraldo, N.Y.C.; prodr. 20th Century Fox Films, Fox TV; corr. Full Disclosure, Fox TV; pub. Regan Books, Harper Collins. Author: The Art of War for Women; editor numerous books including And the Beat Goes On (Sonny Bono), 1991, The Way Things Ought to Be (Rush Limbaugh), 1992, Shampoo Planet and Life After God (Douglas Coupland), 1992, She's Come Undone (Wally Lamb), 1992, Rogue Warrior (Richard Marcinko), 1992, Feminine Force: Release the Power Within You to Create the Life You Deserve (Georgette Mosbacher), 1993, Private Parts (Howard Stern), 1993, I Can't Believe I Said That (Kathie Lee Gifford), 1994. Office: Regan Books 10 E 53rd St New York NY 10022-5244*

REGAN, MURIEL, librarian; b. N.Y.C., July 15, 1930; d. William and Matilda (Riebel) Blome; m. Robert Regan, 1966 (div. 1976); 1 child, Jeanne Booth. BA, Hunter Coll., N.Y.C., 1950; MLS, Columbia U., 1952; MBA, Pace U., N.Y.C., 1982. Post libr. US Army, Okinawa, 1952-53; researcher P.F. Collier, N.Y.C., 1953-57; asst. libr. to libr. Rockefeller Found., N.Y.C., 1957-67; dep. chief libr. Manhattan Community Coll., N.Y.C., 1967-68; libr. Booz Allen & Hamilton, N.Y.C., 1968-69, Rockefeller Found., N.Y.C., 1969-82; prin. Gossage Regan Assocs., Inc., N.Y.C., 1980-95; pub. svcs. libr. Carlsbad (N.Mex.) Pub. Libr., 1995—; dir. N.Y. Met. Reference and Rsch. Libr. Agy., 1988-95, Coun. Nat. Libr. and Info. Assns., 1991-95; cons. Librs. Info. Ctrs. Elder First Presbyn. Ch. of Carlsbad, 1997—. Mem. ALA, Spl. Librs. Assn. pres. 1989-90), N.Mex. Libr. Assn., Archons of Colophon. Avocations: cats, reading, playing piano, traveling. Home: 604 N Lake St Carlsbad NM 88220 Office: Carlsbad Pub Libr 101 S Halagueno St Carlsbad NM 88220-5726

REGAN, PAUL JEROME, JR., manufacturing company executive, consultant; b. Ithaca, N.Y., Mar. 13, 1940; s. Paul Jerome and Mildred (Dempsey) R.; m. Barbara Ann Easton, Feb. 4, 1962 (dec. Nov. 1996); children: Paul J. III, Timothy Andrew, Allison Ann. BS, Cornell U., 1962, MBA, 1965. Pers. asst. Corning (N.Y.) Glass Works, 1963; pers. mgr. Corning (N.Y.) Glass Works, Corning and State College, 1964-68; dept. mgr. mfg. Corning (N.Y.) Glass Works, State College, 1968-70; personnel devel. cons. Corning (N.Y.) Glass Works, Corning, 1970-72; prodn. supt. Corning (N.Y.) Glass Works, Wilmington, N.C., 1972-74; devel. mgr. Corning (N.Y.) Glass Works, Corning, 1974-77, corp. dir., 1977-83, v.p. human resources, 1983-86; sr. v.p. Corning Inc., Corning, 1986-93; ret.; mem. adv. bd. Cornell U., Ithaca, N.Y., 1970-82, lectr., 1977—; founding mem. Human Resource Planning Soc., 1974—; dir. Corning Can. Inc., Toronto, 1983-93. Contbr. articles to books and profl. jours. including Human Resource Planning Soc. jour.; expert comment on exec. compensation and succession including Wall St. Jour., N.Y. Times, Bus. Week, Forbes. Mem. exec. bd. Thousand Islands Assn., Gananoque, Ont., Can., 1988—; chmn. Blue Ribbon Fund, Corning Hosp., 1989-93; mem. Rep. Nat. Com., Washington, 1984—; dir. State College C. of C., 1967-93, Half Moon Bay Found. Johnson Soc. fellow Cornell U., 1991; named Ky. Col., State of Ky., 1984. Mem. Am. Compensation Assn. (regional chair 1978-81), Am. Acad. Polit. and Social Sci., Heron Soc. (life.), Cornell Club, Nat. Mus. Am. Indian (charter, membership com. 1991—), Antique Boat Mus., Save the River Com. (adv. 1982—), Menninger Found. (patron), Trust for Historic Preservation, Delta Phi (past pres.). Avocations: antique wooden boats, decoys, photographs, Inuit art, poetry.

REGAN, PAUL MICHAEL, lawyer; b. Detroit, May 8, 1953; s. Timothy J. and Adele (Anthony) R. BA, Duke U., 1975; JD, Cath. U., 1979. Bar: N.Y. 1983. Clearance officer, counsel Ticor Title Guarantee Co., Syracuse, N.Y., 1980-84; assoc. Van Epps & Shulman, Syracuse, 1984-87, Shulman Law Firm, Syracuse, 1987-91; ptnr. Shulman Curtin Grundner Regan & Snyder, P.C., Syracuse, 1992—; speaker Nat. Bus. Inst., 1991, N.Y. State Bar Seminars, 1990-94. Vestry Christ Ch., Malius, N.Y., 1991-96; bd. dirs. Cazenovia (N.Y.) Childrens House, 1990-94; counsel Save Our Cmty., Inc., Cazenovia, 1989-93. Mem. N.Y. State Bar Assn., Onondaga County Bar Assn. (chmn. real estate contract com. 1990-96, com. on title standards 1990-96). Office: Shulman Curtin Grundner Regan & Snyder 250 S Clinton St Syracuse NY 13202-1263

REGAN, PETER FRANCIS, III, physician, psychiatry educator; b. Bklyn., Nov. 11, 1924; s. Peter Francis Jr. and Veronica (Tierney) R.; m. Laurette Patricia O'Connor, June 18, 1949; children: Peter, Stephen, William, Elizabeth, John, Carol. MD, Cornell U., Ithaca, N.Y., 1949. Diplomate Am. Bd. Psychiatry and Neurology, Nat. Bd. Med. Examiners. Intern in medicine N.Y. Hosp., 1949-50; asst. resident psychiatry Payne Whitney Psychiat. Clinic, 1950, 53-54, resident, 1954-56; asst. prof. psychiatry Cornell U. Med. Coll., 1956-58; prof., head dept. psychiatry U. Fla. Coll. Medicine, chief psychiat. svc. Univ. Teaching Hosp., 1958-64; prof. psychiatry SUNY, Buffalo, 1964-84, v.p. health affairs, 1964-67, exec. v.p. univ., 1967-69, exec. v.p., acting pres. univ., 1969-70, vice chancellor acad. programs, 1970-71; assoc. chief staff for edn. Buffalo VA Med. Ctr., 1979-84; prof. psychiatry U. Tex. Health Sci. Ctr., San Antonio, 1984-87, assoc. dean Sch. Medicine, 1986-87; assoc. chief staff for edn. San Antonio VA Med. Ctr., 1984-86, chief staff, 1986-87; dep. assoc. chief med. dir. for acad. affairs VA Cen. Office, Washington, 1987-88, assoc. chief med. dir. for acad. affairs, 1988-92; prof. emeritus / sen. cons. dept. psychiatry SUNY, Buffalo, N.Y., 1992—; project dir. Ctr. for Ednl. Rsch. and Innovation, OECD, 1972-74. Author: (with F. Flach) Chemotherapy in Emotional Disorders, 1960, (With E. Pattishall) Behavioral Science Contributions to Psychiatry; contbr. articles to profl. jours. Capt. M.C. AUS, 1951-52. Fellow Am. Psychiat. Assn., Am. Coll. Psychiatrists (bd. regents 1986-95, 2d v.p. 1988, 1st v.p. 1989, pres.-elect 1990, pres. 1991); mem. AMA, Alpha Omega Alpha. Home: 900 Delaware Ave # 504 Buffalo NY 14209-2012 Office: SUNY Dept Psychiatry 462 Grider St Buffalo NY 14215-3021

REGAN, ROBERT CHARLES, English language educator; b. Indpls., Mar. 13, 1930; s. Francis Bernard and Alma Ophelia (McBride) R.; m. Katherine Jeanclos, Aug. 11, 1989; children by previous marriage: Christopher, Alison, Amelia. B.A., Centenary Coll., 1951; M.A., Harvard U., 1952; Ph.D., U. Calif., Berkeley, 1965. Instr. English, Centenary Coll., 1956-57; asst. prof. English, U. Va., 1963-67; Fulbright-Hays lectr. Am. civilization U. Montpellier, France, 1967-68; assoc. prof. English, U. Pa., Phila., 1968-82, prof., 1982—, undergrad. chmn. dept. English, 1978-80, 81-83, 89-90, dir. Penn-in-London program; lectr. Internat. Communications Agy., Morocco, Algeria, Jordan, 1980; vis. prof. King's Coll., London, 1983-84. Author: Unpromising Heroes; Mark Twain and His Characters, 1966, Poe: A Collection of Critical Essays, 1967; mng. editor: Am. Quar., 1969-72; contbr. articles to lit. jours. Served with USNR, 1952-56, 61-62. Woodrow Wilson fellow, 1962-63; Am. Philos. Soc. research grantee, 1970. Democrat. Episcopalian. Office: U Pa Dept English Philadelphia PA 19104

REGAN, SYLVIA, playwright; b. N.Y.C., Apr. 15, 1908; d. Louis and Esther (Albert) Hoffenberg; m. James J. Regan, Feb. 11, 1931 (div. June 1936); m. 2d Abraham Ellstein, Nov. 7, 1940 (dec. Mar. 1963). Student pub. schs. Broadway actress N.Y.C., 1927-31; with pub. relations and promotion dept. Theatre Union and Orson Welles Mercury Theatre, N.Y.C., 1932-39; playwright, 1940—. Author: Morning Star, 1940, The Golden Door, 1951; musical Great to be Alive, 1951; The Fifth Season, 1953; libretto for grand opera The Golem, N.Y.C., 1962; Zelda, 1969. Sec. Sydney Epstein Meml. Fund for Strang Cancer Clinic, N.Y.C., 1948-68. Recipient citition Fedn. Women Zionists of Gt. Britain and Ireland, 1953. Mem. Dramatists Guild, Authors League of Am., Am. Jewish Hist. Soc., Nat. Council Jewish Women (citation of merit 1953). Democrat. Home: 55 E 9th St New York NY 10003-6311

REGAN, TIMOTHY JAMES, grain company executive; b. Atchison, Kans., July 31, 1956; s. Vincent James and Phyllis (Brull) R.; m. Veronica Sue Kasten, June 25, 1977; children: Katrina Sue, Brian James. BS, Kans. State U., 1978. Corp. acct. Lincoln Grain Co., Atchison, 1978-80; acctg. supr. Pillsbury Co., St. Joseph, Mo., 1980; br. account mgr. Pillsbury Co., St. Joseph, 1980-82, Omaha, 1982; internal auditor Pillsbury Co., Mpls., 1983; regional account mgr. Pillsbury Co., Huron, Ohio, 1983-84; regional account mgr. Scoular Grain Co., Omaha, 1984-87, controller, 1987-91, v.p., mem. exec. com., 1990—, CFO, 1991—; Fin. advisor Grace Abbott Sch. PTO, Omaha, 1987, treas., 1990-91. Fin. adviser Grace Abbott Sch. PTO, Omaha, 1987, treas., 1990-91; dir. Cath. Charities, 1994—; coach Little League Baseball and Soccer. Mem. KC, Elks. Republican. Roman Catholic. Avocations: jogging, basketball, coaching little league baseball and soccer. Home: 2009 S 182nd Cir Omaha NE 68130-2748 Office: Scoular Co 2027 Dodge St Omaha NE 68102-1227

REGAN, WILLIAM JOSEPH, JR., energy company executive; b. Bronx, N.Y., Mar. 7, 1946; s. William Joseph and Eleanor F. (Malone) R.; m. Mary Lee Wynn; children—Katrina Lee, Thomas Wynn, James William. B.S., U.S. Air Force Acad., 1967; M.B.A., U. Wis.-Madison, 1969, Ph.D., 1972. Asst. prof. Wayne State U., Detroit, 1971-75; with Nat. Bank Detroit, 1975-77; sr. bus. planner Am. Natural Resources Co., Detroit, 1977-78, dir. fin. planning, 1978-82, v.p., treas., 1982-85; v.p. corp. fin. United Svcs. Automobile Assn., San Antonio, 1986-88, sr. v.p., treas., 1988-95; v.p., treas. Entergy Corp., New Orleans, 1995—. Mem. English Turn Golf Club, The City Energy Club. Republican. Roman Catholic. Home: 104 English Turn Dr New Orleans LA 70131

REGAN-GERACI, THERESA ELIZABETH, learning disability educator, consultant; b. Jersey City, Jan. 17, 1947; d. Thomas Edward and Elizabeth Marie (Waleck) Regan; m. Baldassero (Bob) Charles Geraci, June 12, 1987; 1 child, Matthew Regan Geraci. BA, Caldwell Coll., 1968; MA, William Paterson Coll., 1977; postgrad., Boston Coll., 1981. Cert. tchr., prin., N.J. Tchr. art, spl. edn., elem., prin./supr., LDT-C Our Lady of Good Counsel Sch., Pompton Plains, N.J., 1968-75, Little Falls (N.J.) Sch. # 2, 1975-77, Little Falls Schs. # 1 and # 2, 1977-85, Little Falls Sch. # 1, 1985—; mem. bd. edn. Our Lady of Good Counsel Sch., 1976-77, St. Mary's Sch., Pompton Lakes, 1981-83; instr. Devel. Ctr. Tutoring, Pompton Lakes, 1979-85, cons.; dir. Learning Disability Summer Sch., Bloomingdale, N.J., 1979-80. Tchr. C.C.D. program St. Mary's Sch., 1985—, Project SMART, NJIT 1996—. Mem. Little Falls Edn. Assn. (sec. 1980-83, v.p. 1983-84, pres. 1985-88), Pi Lambda Theta. Democrat. Avocations: reading, painting, ceramics, biking, museums, gardening. Home: 8 Berry Pl Pompton Plains NJ 07444 Office: Little Falls Sch # 1 Stevens Ave Little Falls NJ 07424

REGAZZI, JOHN HENRY, retired corporate executive; b. N.Y.C., Jan. 4, 1921; s. Caesar B. and Jennie (Moruzzi) R.; m. Doris Mary Litzau, Feb. 16, 1946; children: Mark, Dale. B.B.A., Pace Coll., 1951. C.P.A., N.Y. Mgr. Price Waterhouse, N.Y.C., 1946-62; comptroller ABC, N.Y.C., 1962-70; sr. v.p., CFO Avnet, Inc., N.Y.C., 1970-93; retired, 1993. Contbr. articles to profl. jours. Pres. bd. River Dell Regional High Sch., Oradell, N.J., 1962-65; trustee, treas. Oradell Pub. Library, 1970-79; councilman Borough of Oradell, 1979-88. Served as staff sgt. USAF, 1942-45. Mem. Fin. Execs.

Inst., Am. Inst. CPA's, Inst. Mgmt. Accts., Nat. Assn. Corp. Treas. Republican. Roman Catholic. Lodge: Lions. Home: 8980 King John Ct Las Vegas NV 89129

REGAZZI, JOHN JAMES, III, publishing executive; b. Bklyn., June 8, 1948; s. John James Jr. and Theresa Cecil (Fiore) R.; m. Marie Louise Ford, May 30, 1971; children: John James IV, Thomas Paul, Michael Rees. BS, St. John's U., Queens, N.Y., 1970; MA, U. Iowa, 1972; MS, Columbia U., 1974; PhD, Rutgers U., 1983. Systems mgr. No. Ill. U., De Kalb, Ill., 1974-76; dir. pub. Found. Ctr., N.Y.C., 1976-79; assoc. prof. Rutgers U., New Brunswick, N.J., 1979-81; v.p. The H.W. Wilson Co., N.Y.C., 1981-88; pres., chief exec. officer Engring. Info., Inc., N.Y.C., 1988—; chmn. Article Express Internat., 1992-94; bd. dirs. ICSTI; adj. prof. SUNY, Albany, Columbia U., Rutgers U. Author: Guide to Periodicals in Religion, 1974. Mem. AAAS, IEEE, ALA, Am. Assn. Pubs. (bd. dirs. N.Y.C. chpt. 1987-88), Nat. Info. Standards Orgn. (vice chmn. 1989-90), Nat. Fedn. of Abstracting and Info. Svcs. (bd. dirs. 1980-81, 88), Assn. Computing Machinery, N.Y. Acad. Sci. Avocation: tennis. Office: Engring Info Inc 1 Castle Point Ter Hoboken NJ 07030-5906

REGEIMBAL, NEIL ROBERT, SR., retired journalist; b. Mpls., Mar. 16, 1929; s. Louis Odlin and Marie Elizabeth (O'Neill) R.; m. Mary Elizabeth Sutton, Aug. 18, 1950; children—Neil Robert, James Michael, Claire Marie, Stephen Louis, Mary Suzanne, Elizabeth Anne. B.S. in Journalism, U. Md., 1951. With AP, Washington, 1949-50; asso. editor Takoma (Md.) Jour., 1950-51; reporter Washington Times-Herald, 1951-54, Washington Post, 1954; Washington corr. Chilton Publs., 1954-71, Wash. bur. chief, v.p., 1975-91; dir. publ. relations Motor Vehicle Mfrs. Assn., Detroit, 1971-74; Washington editor Oil and Gas Jour., Washington; ret., 1991. Recipient Tom Campbell Editorial Achievement award, 1968, 69, 71, 78, Jesse H. Neal Editorial Achievement award, 1982, 84. Mem. White House Corrs. Assn., Sigma Delta Chi. Republican. Roman Catholic. Club: Nat. Press. Home and Office: 13811 Marianna Dr Rockville MD 20853-2737

REGELBRUGGE, ROGER RAFAEL, steel company executive; b. Eeklo, Belgium, May 22, 1930; came to U.S., 1953, naturalized, 1961; s. Victor and Rachel (Roesbeke) R.; m. Dorcas Merchant; children: Anita, Marc, Laurie, Jon, Craig, Kurt, Christiane, Lauren, Roger Rafael Jr. B.Sc. in Mech. Engring, State Tech. Coll., Ghent, 1951; B.Sc. in Indsl. Engring, Gen. Motors Inst., Flint, Mich., 1955; M.Sc. in Mech. Engring, Mich. State U., 1964. Supr. product engring. dept. Gen. Motors Corp., Antwerp, 1955-58; chief devel. engr., then gen. mgr. Airmaster div. Hayes Industries Inc., Jackson, Mich., 1958-66; with Koehring Co., 1966-74; group v.p. internat. ops. Koehring Co., Milw., 1969-74; exec. v.p. Korf Industries, Inc., Charlotte, N.C., 1974-77; chmn., pres., CEO, Georgetown Industries, Inc. (formerly Korf Industries, Inc.), 1977-95; chmn., CEO GS Industries, Inc., 1995—; chmn. bd. Georgetown Steel Corp.; chmn. GS Technologies, GST Operating Co.; bd. dirs. Steel Mfrs. Assn., Am. Iron and Steel Inst.; chmn., CEO Fla. Wire and Cable, Inc. N.C. adv. bd. Fuqua Sch. Bus. Duke U.; mem. Charlotte Chamber Bd. Advisors; mem. adv. coun. Coll. Engring. U. Notre Dame; trustee Belmont (N.C.) Abbey Coll.; bd. trustees Charlotte County Day Sch. Mem. ASME, Am. Soc. Automotive Engrs., Carmel Country Club, Tower Club (Charlotte), Georgetown Club (Washington). Roman Catholic. Office: GS Industries Inc Ste 200 1901 Roxborough Rd Charlotte NC 28211-3482

REGENBOGEN, ADAM, lawyer; b. Steyer, Austria, June 12, 1947; s. William and Pauline (Feuerstein) R.; m. Paula Ruth Rothenberg, June 27, 1970 (div. Oct. 1993); children: Stacy, Candice; m. Helen Busuttil Drwal, Apr. 20, 1996; 1 stepchild, Jason A. Drwal. BA, Temple U., 1969; MSW, U. Pa., 1972; JD, Temple U., 1980. Bar: N.Y. 1983. Social worker VA, Coatesville, Pa., 1974-78; supr. VA, Northport, N.Y., 1978-80, quality assurance dir., 1980-87; dir. quality assurance N.Y. State Office Mental Health, Willard, 1987-91; atty. N.Y. State Workers Compensation Bd., Binghamton, 1992—; pvt. practice N.Y., 1983—. Organizer/incorporator Ithaca (N.Y.) Reform Temple, 1992; organizer Parents Without Partners, Ithaca, 1992. Recipient Pro Bono Svc. award Suffolk County Bar Assn., 1986. Home: 9 Oak Brook Dr Ithaca NY 14850 Office: Workers Compensation Bd 44 Hawley St Binghamton NY 13901-4400

REGENSTEIN, LEWIS GRAHAM, conservationist, author, lecturer, speech writer; b. Washington, Feb. 21, 1943; s. Louis and Helen Lucile (Moses) R.; divorced; children: Anna Lucile, Daniel Louis. Cert. of European studies, Inst. Am. Univs., Aix-en-Provence, France, 1964; B.A. in Polit. Sci., U. Pa., 1965; M.A. in Polit. Sci., Emory U., 1975. Intelligence officer, analyst C.I.A., Washington, 1966-71; wildlife editor Environ. Quality mag., 1973; real estate agt., 1984—; v.p. Help Our Planet Earth; bd. dirs. The Monitor Consortium, 1977—, pres., 1979-81; bd. dirs. Washington Humane Soc., 1978-84, Interfaith Coun. for Protection Animals and Nature, 1982-88, Atlanta Outdoor Activities Coun., Ctr. for Respect of Life and Environment, 1989—, Earth Save Found., 1989—. Author: The Politics of Extinction: The Story of the World's Endangered Wildlife, 1975, America the Poisoned: How Deadly Chemicals are Destroying Our Environment, Our Wildlife— And Ourselves, 1982, paperback edit., 1983, How to Survive in America the Poisoned, 1987, Replenish the Earth: The Teachings of Religion on Protecting Animals and Nature, 1991, Cleaning Up America the Poisoned: How to Survive Our Polluted Society, 1993; co-author: (jokebook) Sex, Wealth, and Power: How to Live Without Them, 1990; contbr. Environmental Encyclopedia, 1993; mem. editorial bd. the Westminster Schs., 1991—; contbr. numerous articles and book revs. on environ. and nat. security to maj. newspapers; author text of comml. record album; writes speeches and humor for corp. execs. and polit. leaders. Alumni exec. bd. The Lovett Sch., 1986—; co-chmn. Mayor's Environ. Task Force City of Atlanta, 1994—; dir. Piedmont Park Conservancy, Atlanta; steering com. Global Forum Ga., 1991. Home and Office: 3691 Tuxedo Rd NW Atlanta GA 30305-1061

REGENSTEINER, ELSE FRIEDSAM (MRS. BERTOLD REGENSTEINER), textile designer, educator; b. Munich, Apr. 21, 1906; came to U.S., 1936, naturalized, 1942; d. Ludwig and Hilda (Nelson-Bachhofer) Friedsam; m. Bertold Regensteiner, Oct. 3, 1926; 1 dau., Helga Regensteiner Sinaiko-Botts. Tchrs. degree, Deutsche Frauenschule, Munich, 1925; student, U. Munich, Inst. Design, Chgo. Instr. Hull House, Chgo., 1941-45, Inst. Design, Chgo., 1942-46; asst. prof. Sch. Art Inst. Chgo., 1945-57, prof., 1957-71, prof. emeritus, 1971—; textile designer for industry; partner Reg/Wick Studios, 1945-80; also lectr.; Cons. Am. Farm Sch., Thessaloniki, Greece, 1972-78. Exhibited one man shows throughout U.S., 1946—; represented in permanent collection, Art Inst. Chgo., Cooper-Hewitt Mus., N.Y.C.; Author: The Art of Weaving, 2d edit. 1981, 3d edit., 1986, German edit., 1987, Program for a Weaving Study Group, 1974, Weaver's Study Course- Sourcebook for Ideas and Techniques, 1982, 2d edit., 1987, Geometric Design in Weaving, 1986; contbr. articles to profl. mags. Recipient 1st prize for drapery and upholstery Internat. Textile Exhbn., 1946; five citations merit Am. Inst. Decorators, 1947, 48, 50; Regensteiner award Midwest Weavers Assn., 1980; Award of Merit in Textiles, The Textile Arts Ctr., Chgo., 1994. Fellow Collegium Craftsmen of Am. Crafts Coun.; mem. Am. Crafts Coun., Handweavers Guild Am. (bd. dirs. 1970-78). Address: 1416 E 55th St Chicago IL 60615-5409

REGENSTREIF, HERBERT, lawyer; b. N.Y.C., May 13, 1935; s. Max and Jeannette (Hacker) R.; m. Patricia Friedman, Dec. 20, 1967 (div. July 1968); m. Charlotte Lois Levy, Dec. 11, 1980; 1 child, Cara Rachael. BA, Hobart Coll., 1957; JD, N.Y. Law Sch., 1960; MS, Pratt Inst., 1985. Bar: N.Y. 1961, Ky. 1985, U.S. Dist. Ct. (ea. and so. dists.) N.Y. 1962, U.S. Tax Ct. 1967, U.S. Ct. Appeals (2d cir.) 1962, U.S. Supreme Ct. 1967. Ptnr. Fried & Regenstreif, P.C., Mineola, N.Y., 1963—; cons. in field; arbitrator Dist. Ct., Nassau County, N.Y., 1989—, N.Y.C. Civil Ct., 1984-86. Contbr. articles to profl. jours. County committeeman Dem. Com., Queens County, N.Y., 1978-79. Mem. Bar Assn. Nassau County, Ky. Bar Assn., Phi Delta Phi, Beta Phi Mu, Hobart Club of N.Y. (gov. 1968-69).

REGENSTREIF, S(AMUEL) PETER, political scientist, educator; b. Montreal, Que., Can., Sept. 9, 1936; s. Albert Benjamin and Miriam Lillian (Issenman) R.; children: Anne Erica, Mitchell Chester, Jeffrey Gershon, Gail Aviva. BA, McGill U., 1957; PhD, Cornell U., 1963. Mem. faculty U. Rochester, 1961—, prof. polit. sci., 1971—; coordinator Can. studies program, 1967—; editl. cons. Toronto Star, 1968-82, Chgo. Sun-Times, 1988-89; polit. cons. Bunting Warburg, Toronto, 1973-90, Coopers & Lybrand, Ltd., 1981-89, Loewen, Ondaatje, McCutcheon, 1991-94; prin. Policy Concepts Inc., Toronto; broadcaster CKO Radio Network, 1983-89; pvt. polit. cons. Author: The Diefenbaker Interlude: Parties and Voting in Canada, 1965; syndicated columnist: Toronto Star, 1963-82; contbr. articles to profl. jours. Served to lt. Canadian Army, 1957. Ford. Found. fellow, 1960; Can. Council fellow, 1960, 65; Canadian Royal Commn. on Bilingualism and Biculturalism grantee, 1964-66; recipient Edward Peck Curtis award U. Rochester, 1979. Mem. AAAS, Am. Polit. Sci. Assn., Can. Polit. Sci. Assn., Assn. Can. Studies in U.S., Phi Beta Kappa. Jewish. Clubs: Faculty, Tennis. Home: 30 Glen Ellyn Way Rochester NY 14618-1502 Office: Univ Rochester Dept Polit Sci Rochester NY 14627

REGENTHAL, JEANINE A., immunologist, researcher; b. Elizabeth, N.J., Sept. 2, 1964; d. Joseph M. and Frances M. (Sullivan) Todaro; m. Mark A. Regenthal, June 27, 1992. BS in Biology, Cook Coll., Rutgers U., New Brunswick, N.J., 1986; MS in Cell Devel. Biology, U. Medicine and Dentistry of N.J. and Rutgers Grad. Sch. of Biomed. Scis., New Brunswick, 1995. Rsch. assoc. Human Immunology Found., Red Bank, N.J., 1987-89, Dept. Toxicology, Coll. Pharmacy, Rutgers U., New Brunswick, 1989-93; assoc. scientist Immunobiology Rsch. Inst. Johnson & Johnson, Annandale, N.J., 1993-94; assoc. immunologist Ortho Diagnostic Systems, Inc. Johnson & Johnson, Raritan, N.J., 1994-95, assoc. scientist Robert Wood Johnson Pharm. Rsch. Inst., 1995-97; assoc. scientist Merck Rsch. Labs., Rahway, N.J., 1997—. Contbr. numerous articles to sci. jours. including Jour. of Leukocyte Biology, Hepatology, chpts. to books. Vol. League of Women Voters, Ocean County, 1991, AIDS Resource Found. for Children, Neptune, 1995, Coalition for Peace Action, N.J., 1995. Mem. AAAS, NOW. Democrat. Roman Catholic. Avocations: pilot ultra lights (recreational aircraft), fishing, cycling, motorcycles. Home: 1310 Eisenhower St Lakewood NJ 08701-6005 Office: Merck Rsch Labs Merck & Co Inc PO Box 2000 Rahway NJ 07065

REGER, LAWRENCE LEE, trade association administrator; b. Lincoln, Nebr., June 23, 1939; s. Lawrence John and Bertha (Hergenrader) R. Student, U. Nebr., 1961; LL.B., Vanderbilt U., 1964. Bar: Nebr 1964. Asso. firm Crosby, Guenzel & Binning, Lincoln, 1964-70; gen. counsel Nat. Endowment Arts, 1970-72, dir. program devel. and coordination, 1972-78; dir. Am. Assn. Mus., Washington, 1978-86; pres. Nat. Instn. for Conservation of Cultural Property, Washington, 1988—; mem. visual arts vis. com. U. Del., 1995—; mem. cultural property adv. com. USIA, 1996—; mem. bd. trustees St. Petersburg Internat. Preservation Ctr., 1996—; mem. adv. com. Nat. Red Cross History and Learning Ctr. Chmn. Nat. Humanities Alliance, 1982-86; bd. dirs. Nat. Musical Arts, 1990—. Home: 5101 44th St NW Washington DC 20016 Office: Inst Conserv Cultural Prop Ste 602 3299 K St NW Apt 602 Washington DC 20007-4449

REGES, MARIANNA ALICE, marketing executive; b. Budapest, Hungary, Mar. 23, 1947; came to U.S., 1956, naturalized, 1963; d. Otto H. and Alice M. R.; children: Rebecca, Charles III. AAS with honors, Fashion Inst. Tech., N.Y.C., 1967; BBA magna cum laude, Baruch Coll., 1971, MBA in Stats., 1978. Media rsch. analyst Doyle, Dane, Bernbach Advt., N.Y.C., 1967-70; rsch. supr. Sta. WCBS-TV, N.Y.C., 1970-71; rsch. mgr. Woman's Day mag., N.Y.C., 1971-72; asst. media dir. Benton & Bowles Advt., N.Y.C., 1972-75; mgr. rsch. and sales devel. NBC Radio, N.Y.C., 1975-77; sr. rsch. mgr. Ziff-Davis Pub. Co., N.Y.C., 1977-84; media mgr. Bristol-Myers Squibb Co., 1984—; mem. Spanish Radio Adv. Coun., N.Y.C., 1986-88; mem. Pan-European TV Audience Rsch. Mgmt. Com., 1988—. Mem. Vt. Natural Resources Council, 1977—; advisor Baruch Coll. Advt. Soc., 1975—. Mem. Am. Mktg. Assn., Am. Advt. Fedn., Media Rsch. Dirs. Assn., Radio and TV Rsch. Coun., Advt. Rsch. Found., Nature Conservancy, Vt. Natural Resources Coun., Anthroposophical Soc., Beta Gamma Sigma. Home: 626 E 20th St New York NY 10009-1509 Office: Bristol-Myers Squibb Co 345 Park Ave New York NY 10154-0004

REGGIO, GODFREY, film director; b. New Orleans, 1940. Dir. (films) Koyaanisqatsi, 1983, Powaqqatsi, 1988 (Best Film, Sao Paolo Film festival), Anima Mundi, 1992, Evidence, 1995. Mem. Christian Bros., 1954-68; founder Inst. for Regional Edn., Santa Fe, N.Mex., 1972. Home: care Inst for Regional Edn PO Box 2404 Santa Fe NM 87504*

REGGIO, VITO ANTHONY, management consultant; b. Rochester, N.Y., Dec. 17, 1929; s. Salvatore and Carrie Angela (LoRe) R.; m. Mary Ann Dolores Pippie, Sept. 28, 1957; children: Salvatore, Angela. BS, Purdue U., 1952; postgrad. sch. modern langs., Middlebury Coll., 1948; postgrad. fellowship, U. Ky., U. Tenn. and U. Ala., 1952-53. Jr. engr. Rochester (N.Y.) Gas and Electric Co., 1950; designer/drafter Globe Constrn. Co., Rochester, 1951; rsch. analyst Commonwealth of Ky., Frankfort, 1952; orgn. & methods analyst, then wage adminstrn. specialist USN Dept. Indsl. Rels., Indpls., 1955-56; cons. mgmt. engr. to project mgr. to account exec. Bus. Rsch. Corp., Chgo., 1956-60; sr. cons. econ. feasibilities Ebasco Svcs., Inc., Chgo., 1960-63, dir. pers. mgmt. cons. dept., 1970-77; regional mgr., orgn. and pers. mgmt. svcs. EBS Mgmt. Cons., Chgo., 1963-65, nat. dir. orgn. and pers. mgmt. svcs., 1965-70; pres., bd. dirs. Reggio and Assocs., Inc., Chgo., 1977—; mng. dir. Pay Data Svc., 1977—; bd. dirs. Pay Data Svcs., Chgo. Contbr. papers to profl. publs. With U.S. Army, 1953-55. Named Solco Cultural Soc. fellow, Rochester, N.Y., 1948. Mem. Am. Compensation Assn., Am. Mgmt. Assn., Chgo. Compensation Assn., Soc. Human Resources Profls., Soc. Human Resources Mgmt., Human Resources Mgmt. Assn. Chgo., Western Soc. Engrs. Office: Reggio and Assocs Inc 550 W Jackson Blvd Chicago IL 60661-5716

REGINATO, ROBERT JOSEPH, soil scientist; b. Palo Alto, Calif., Apr. 13, 1935; s. Guiseppe Primo and Carolina Theresa (Boccignone) R.; m. Donna Marie LeStum, Aug. 26, 1956; children: Richard Lynn, David Lewis, Christopher Michael, Michael Jeffrey. B.S., U. Calif., Davis, 1957; M.S., U. Ill., 1959; Ph.D., U. Calif., Riverside, 1973. Rsch. asst. U. Calif., Davis, 1956-57, U. Ill., Urbana, 1957-59; soil scientist U.S. Water Conservation Lab., USDA-Agrl. Rsch. Svc., Phoenix, 1959-89 , rsch. leader, 1980-89; assoc. dir. Pacific W. Area USDA Agrl. Rsch. Svc., Albany, Calif., 1989-91, dir., 1991-96; assoc. adminstr. ARS, Washington, 1996—; vis. scientist U. Calif., Davis, 1977-78; USDA collaborator U. Ariz., Tucson, 1959-89. Contbr. over 180 articles to tech. jours. Active Roosevelt coun. Boy Scouts Am., 1960-76. Fellow Am. Soc. Agronomy, Soil Sci. Soc. Am.; mem. Am. Geophys. Union, Internat. Soil Sci. Soc., Western Soil Sci. Soc., Sigma Xi, Alpha Zeta, Kappa Sigma. Roman Catholic. Office: USDA Agrl Rsch Svc Jamie Whitten Bldg Rm 302-A 14th & Independence Ave SW Washington DC 20250

REGIS, NINA, librarian, educator; b. Corinth, Miss., Oct. 19, 1928; d. W.C. and Mary Isabelle (Rushing) Hanner; m. George Regis, Sept. 5, 1949 (dec. Jan. 6, 1990); 1 child, Simonne Marie. BA, Bridgewater (Mass.) State U., 1971, MEd, 1975; MALS, U. South Fla., 1981. Cert. libr., tchr., Fla., Mass. Geneal. libr., asst. rschr. to curator New Bedford (Mass.) Pub. Libr., 1963-71; assoc. libr. New England Hist. Geneal. Soc., Boston, 1972-73; media specialist, libr. Brevard County Schs., Port Malabar Elem. Sch., Palm Bay, Fla., 1978-90; libr., faculty Brevard C.C., Palm Bay, 1990—. Developer and organizer libraries, 1968, 80, 91—. Mem. ALA, Fla. Assn. C.C.s, Libr. Assn. of Brevard County, Internat. Platform Assn., Phi Kappa Phi, Beta Phi Mu. Avocations: creative writing, genealogical research. Office: Brevard Community Coll Melbourne Campus Libr 3865 N Wickham Rd Melbourne FL 32935-2310

REGN FRAHER, BONNIE, special education educator. BA, U. Calif., Santa Cruz, 1978; EdS, Rutgers U., 1982, MA, 1983. Cert. tchr. of the handicapped, cert. elem. tchr. Tchr. Search Day Program, Wanamassa, N.J., 1978-87; v.p. Fin-Addict Charters, Wall, N.J., 1987-93, Archtl. Woodworking, Bradley Beach, N.J., 1994-95; v.p., dir. fin. William Cook Custom Homes, Wall, 1987-95; v.p. Archtl. Woodworking, 1993-95; tchr. Palm Beach County Sch. Dist., 1995-96; preschool tchr., daycare provider, 1996—. Mem. sisterhood Temple Beth Torah. Mem. Autism Soc. Am., Long Branch Ski Club. Avocation: writing (short story pub.).

RÉGNIER, MARC CHARLES, lawyer, corporate executive; b. Rockland, Ont., Can., Apr. 24, 1939; s. Lucien and Joséphine (Mattar) R.; m. Claudette Picard, July 29, 1989; 1 child, Mathieu. BA, U. Ottawa, Ont., 1960, LLB, 1964. Bar: Que. 1969. Spl. asst. combines br. Dept. Justice, Ottawa, 1960-66; sollicitor, sec. Celanese Can. Ltd., Montréal, Que., Can., 1966-72; sec., legal counsel Microsystems Internat., Montréal, 1972-75; sr. group counsel No. Telecom Ltd., Montréal, 1974-75; sr. v.p., gen. counsel Avenor Inc. (formerly Can. Pacific Forest Products Ltd.), Montréal, 1976—; bd. dirs. Avenor Maritimes Inc., Dalhousie, N.B., Can., Pacific Forest Products Ltd., Vancouver, B.C., Can. Bd. dirs. CARE Can., Montréal Internat. Music Competition, Montréal Symphony Orch., Festival de Theatre des Ameriques, Fondation Hôpital St.-Luc, Montréal. Mem. Can. Bar Assn., Que. Bar Assn., Law Soc. Upper Can., Assn. Can. Gen. Counsel (pres. 1987-88), Club St.-Denis. Avocations: music, travel, fishing. Office: Avenor Inc, 1250 René-Lévesque Blvd West, Montreal, PQ Canada H3B 4Y3

REGULA, RALPH, congressman, lawyer; b. Beach City, Ohio, Dec. 3, 1924; s. O.F. and Orpha (Walter) R.; m. Mary Rogusky, Aug. 5, 1950; children: Martha, David, Richard. B.A., Mt. Union Coll., 1948, LL.D., 1981; LL.B., William McKinley Sch. Law, 1952; LL.D., Malone Coll., 1976. Bar: Ohio 1952. Sch. adminstr. Stark County Bd. Edn., 1948-55; practiced law Navarre, from 1952; mem. Ohio Ho. of Reps., 1965-66, Ohio Senate, 1967-72, 93rd-105th Congresses from 16th Ohio dist., 1973—; chmn. appropriations subcom. on the interior; ptnr. Regula Bros.; Mem. Pres.'s Commn. on Fin. Structures and Regulation, 1970-71. Mem. Ohio Bd. Edn., 1960-64; hon. mem. adv. bd. Walsh Coll., Canton, Ohio; Trustee Mt. Union Coll., Alliance, Ohio, Stark County Hist. Soc., Stark County Wilderness Soc. Served with USNR, 1944-46. Recipient Community Service award Navarre Kiwanis Club, 1963; Meritorious Service in Conservation award Canton Audubon Soc., 1965; Ohio Conservation award Gov. James Rhodes, 1969; named Outstanding Young Man of Yr. Canton Jr. C. of C., 1957, Legis. Conservationist of Yr. Ohio League Sportsmen, 1969. Republican. Episcopalian. Office: US Ho of Reps 2309 Rayburn HOB Washington DC 20515*

REH, JOHN W., engineer, consultant; b. Saline County, Kans., July 2, 1935; s. Leslie W. and Vera M. (Snyder) R.; m. Judith A. Kirkland, June 1, 1957; children: Elaine M. Edwards, Jeffrey K., Kirk W. BS in Agrl. Engring., Kans. State U., 1958; postgrad., U. Kans., 1964, Utah State U., 1973. Registered profl. engr., Kans., Mo. Hydraulic engr. USDA Soil Conservation Svc., Salina, Kans., 1958-61, 63-70; constrn. engr. USDA Soil Conservation Svc., Cheney, Kans., 1961-63; leader water resource planning staff USDA Soil Conservation Svc., Salina, 1970-84, asst. state conservationist, 1984-91; pres., owner REH & Assocs., Salina, 1992—; conservation and watershed advisor Kans. water plan Kans. Water Authority, Topeka, 1980-91. Recipient Disting. Svc. award State Assn. Kans. Watersheds, 1992, NSPE Award, 1992, Nat. Soc. Profl. Engr. Mem. NSPE (v.p. 1966-93, engrs. in govt., chmn. various coms., rep. to First Nat. Water Symposium 1982, Leadership award 1985, award 1992), Soil and Water Conservation Soc., Kans. Engring. Soc. Republican. Roman Catholic. Achievements include development of hydrologic procedures. Office: Reh & Assocs Inc 909 E Wayne Ave # 8 Salina KS 67401-2201

REHART, BURTON SCHYLER, journalism educator, freelance writer; b. Pacific Grove, Calif., July 24, 1934; s. Burton Schyler Sr. and Ruth Evelyn (Whitaker) R.; m. Catherine Loverne Morison, Apr. 14, 1962 (div. Aug. 1983); children: William, Anne Marie, Catherine Evelyn; m. Felicia Rose Cousart, June 30, 1984 (div. Aug. 1995); m. Shirlee Jan Mynatt, July 20, 1996. BA in Journalism, Fresno (Calif.) State Coll., 1957; MA in History, Calif. State U., Fresno, 1966; cert., Coro found., 1961, Stanford U., summer 1975. Cert. adult edn. tchr., Calif. Reporter Bakersfield Californian, 1955; reporter, photographer Fresno Bee, 1957, Madera (Calif.) Daily Tribune, 1960-61, Ventura (Calif.) Free Press, 1961-62; from instr. to prof. journalism Calif. State U., Fresno, 1963—, prof. journalism, 1979—, chmn. dept. journalism, 1992-94. Author: M. Theo. Kearney-Prince of Fresno, 1988, (with others) Fresno in the 20th Century, 1986; editor, chmn. editorial bd. Fresno City, County Hist. Soc. Jour.; contbr. articles to profl. jours. Asst. foreman Fresno County Grand Jury, 1969. With U.S. Army, 1958-60. Mem. Soc. Profl. Journalists (pres. 1987-89), World Future Soc. (writer), Phi Kappa Phi (pres. 1977-78, Calif. State U. Fresno chpt.), Kappa Tau Alpha. Democrat. Episcopalian. Avocations: model ship building, photography, writing local history, historical romances. Home: 1557 E Roberts Ave Fresno CA 93710-6433 Office: Calif State U Dept Journalism Shaw and Cedar Avenues Fresno CA 93740-0010

REHART, MARGARET LEE, controller; b. Van Nuys, Calif., Apr. 11, 1961; d. Ross Leo and Carolyn Lee (Stewart) R.; m. Robert Leslie Putnam, June 13, 1981 (div. July 1988); 1 child, Sabrina Nicole. Degree in bus. mgmt., LaSalle U., 1996. Gen. acct. Whittaker, ERI, Inc., Simi Valley, Calif., 1988-89; acct. ASNA, Big Bear Lake, Calif., 1990; asst. controller Splendor Tile Co., Calabasas, Calif., 1990-95; controller Wesco Sales Corp., Chatsworth, Calif., 1995—; cons. Earth & Art Landscape, Van Nuys, 1993—. Author: Accounting Procedures for the Small Construction Company, 1994. Mem. Am. Mgmt. Assn. Republican. Mem. Reorganized Ch. Latter Day Saints. Avocations: music, counted cross stitch, floral arrangements. Home: 2006 Cheam Ave Simi Valley CA 93063-3814

REHM, JOHN BARTRAM, lawyer; b. Paris, Nov. 23, 1930; s. George and Mary (Torr) R.; m. Diana Mary Aed, Dec. 19, 1959; children: David Bartram, Jennifer Aed. AB, Harvard U., 1952; LLB, Columbia U., 1955; M.T.S., Wesley Sem., 1990. Bar: N.Y. 1955, D.C. 1969, U.S. Dist. Ct. D.C. 1971, U.S. Ct. Internat. Trade 1980, U.S. Supreme Ct. 1988. Assoc. Willkie, Owen, Farr, Gallagher & Walton, N.Y.C., 1955-56; atty.-advisor U.S. Dept. State, Washington, 1956-62, asst. legal advisor for econ. affairs, 1962-63; gen. counsel Office of Spl. Trade Rep., Washington, 1963-69; ptnr. Busby, Rivkin, Sherman, Levy & Rehm, Washington, 1969-77, Busby, Rehm and Leonard, Washington, 1977-87, Dorsey & Whitney, Washington, 1988—. Democrat. Episcopalian. Home: 5005 Worthington Dr Bethesda MD 20816-2748 Office: Dorsey & Whitney 1330 Connecticut Ave NW Washington DC 20036-1704

REHM, LEO FRANK, civil engineer; b. Milw., Jan. 8, 1916; s. Joseph V. and Theresa (Binder) R.; m. Irene R. Kegel, Aug. 24, 1940; children: Judith Ann LeDoux, Cecelia C. Nelson. B.C.E., Marquette U., 1938. Civil engr. Consoer, Townsend & Quinlan, Chgo., 1938-43; asso. Consoer Townsend & Assocs. (Cons. Engrs.), Chgo., 1946-53; gen. partner Consoer Townsend & Assocs. (Cons. Engrs.), 1953-74, mng. partner, 1974-76; pres. PRC Consoer Townsend, Chgo., 1976-83, pres. emeritus, 1983-85; v.p. PRC Engring., Inc., Chgo., 1976-85; chmn. bd. Environ. Engring., Inc., 1976-83, Consoer Townsend Harris Internat., Inc., 1976-83; dir., v.p. Planning Research Corp., 1976-80; Mem. planning and adv. bd. Village of River Forest (Ill.), 1964-76; mem. exec. senate Marquette U., Milw., 1978—; mem., chmn. adv. council Marquette U. (Coll. Engring.), 1976-89. Mem. bldg. bd. appeals Village of River Forest, Ill., 1977-87, pres.'s adv. council Rosary Coll., River Forest, 1986-91, Exec. Svc. Corps Chgo. With U.S. Army, 1943-46. Recipient Disting. Engring. Alumnus award Marquette U. Coll. Engring., 1975; Alumnus of Yr. award Marquette U., 1983. Mem. Am. Public Works Assn., Am. Water Resources Assn., Am. Water Works Assn., Water Environ. Fedn., Inter-Am. Assn. San. Engring., NSPE, Western Soc. Engrs., Ill. State C. of C. (bd. dirs. 1981-85), VFW, KC, Country Club of Naples. Roman Catholic.

REHME, ROBERT G., film company executive; b. Cin., May 5, 1935; s. Gordon W. and Helen H. (Henkel) R.; m. Kay Yazell, Jan. 9, 1964; children: Robin, Tracy. Ed., U. Cin. Theatre mgr. RKO Theatres, Cin.; asst. mgr. Cin. Theatre Co., 1961; publicist United Artists Pictures, 1965-67; dir. advt. and publicity United Artists Pictures and Paramount Pictures, 1967-69; pres., CEO Avco Embassy Pictures Corp., Los Angeles, 1978-81; pres. distbn. and mktg. Universal Pictures Corp., 1981-82; pres. motion picture group MCA Universal, 1982-83; chief exec. officer New World Pictures, Los Angeles, 1983-89; prin. Neufeld/Rehme Prodns., 1989—; pres. Acad. Motion Picture Arts and Scis., 1992-93. Mem. Am. Film Inst. (trustee), Acad. Motion Picture Arts and Scis. Democrat. Presbyterian. Club: Variety. Office: Paramount Pictures 5555 Melrose Ave Los Angeles CA 90038-3112

REHMUS, CHARLES MARTIN, law educator, arbitrator; b. Ann Arbor, Mich., June 27, 1926; s. Paul A. and Amy D. (Martin) R.; m. Carolyn Brown, Dec. 21, 1948 (div. July 1982); children—Paul, James, Jon, David;

m. Laura Carlson, Sept. 4, 1982. A.B., Kenyon Coll., 1947; M.A., Stanford U., 1951, Ph.D., 1955. Commr. Fed. Mediation and Conciliation Service, San Francisco, 1952-58; staff dir. Presdl. R.R. Commn., Washington, 1959-61; prof. polit. sci. U. Mich., Ann Arbor, 1962-80, dir. Inst. Labor and Indsl. Relations, 1962-76; chmn. Mich. Employment Relations Commn., Detroit, 1976-80; dean N.Y. State Sch. Indsl. and Labor Relations, Cornell U., Ithaca, 1980-86; prof. law U. San Diego, 1988—. Author: Final-Offer Arbitration, 1975, The Railway Labor Act at Fifty, 1977, Labor and American Politics, 1967, rev. edit., 1978, The National Mediation Board, 1984, Emergency Strikes Revisited, 1990. Chmn. 4 Presdl. emergency bds. at various times. Served to lt. USNR, 1943-45; PTO. Mem. Internat. Inst. Labor Studies (bd. govs. 1984-92), Indsl. Rels. Rsch. Assn. (exec. bd. 1984-88), Nat. Acad. Arbitrators (bd. govs. 1979-82, v.p. 1993-95).

REHNQUIST, WILLIAM HUBBS, United States supreme court chief justice; b. Milw., Oct. 1, 1924; s. William Benjamin and Margery (Peck) R.; m. Natalie Cornell, Aug. 29, 1953; children: James, Janet, Nancy. BA, MA, Stanford U., 1948; MA, Harvard U., 1949; LLB, Stanford U., 1952. Bar: Ariz. Law clk. to former justice Robert H. Jackson, U.S. Supreme Ct., 1952-53; with Evans, Kitchel & Jenckes, Phoenix, 1953-55; mem. Ragan & Rehnquist, Phoenix, 1956-57; ptnr. Cunningham, Carson & Messenger, Phoenix, 1957-60, Powers & Rehnquist, Phoenix, 1960-69; asst. atty.-gen. office of legal counsel Dept. of Justice, Washington, 1969-71; assoc. justice U.S. Supreme Ct., 1971-1986, chief justice, 1986—; mem. Nat. Conf. Commrs. Uniform State Laws, 1963-69. Author: Grand Inquests: The Historic Impeachments of Justice Samuel Chase and President Andrew Johnson, 1992; contbr. articles to law jours., nat. mags. Served with USAAF, 1943-46, NATOUSA. Mem. Fed., Am. Maricopa (Ariz.) County bar assns., State Bar Ariz., Nat. Conf. Lawyers and Realtors, Phi Beta Kappa, Order of Coif, Phi Delta Phi. Lutheran. Office: Supreme Ct US Supreme Ct Bldg 1 1st St NE Washington DC 20543*

REHORN, LOIS M(ARIE), nursing administrator; b. Larned, Kans., Apr. 15, 1919; d. Charles and Ethel L. (Canaday) Williamson; m. C. Howard Smith, Feb. 15, 1946 (dec. Aug. 1980); 1 child, Cynthia A. Huddleston; m. Harlan W. Rehorn, Aug. 25, 1981. RN, Bethany Hosp. Sch. Nursing, Kansas City, Kans., 1943; BS, Ft. Hays Kans. State U., Hays, 1968, MS, 1970. RN, N.Mex. Office nurse, surg. asst. Dr. John H. Luke, Kansas City, Kans., 1943-47; supr. nursing unit Larned (Kans.) State Hosp., 1949-68, dir. nursing edn., 1968-71, dir. nursing, 1972-81, ret., 1981. Named Nurse of Yr. DNA-4, 1986. Mem. Am. Nurses Assn., Kans. Nurses Assn. (dist. treas.), N.Mex. Nurses Assn. (dist. pres. 1982-86, dist. bd. dirs. 1992-94). Home: 1436 Brentwood Dr Clovis NM 88101-4602 *Keep within you a place where dreams may grow. The fountain of understanding is the willingness to listen.*

REIBEL, KURT, physicist, educator; b. Vienna, Austria, May 23, 1926; came to U.S., 1938; s. Michael and Regina (Pak) R.; m. Eleanor Elvira Mannino, June 10, 1954; children—Leah, Michael, David. B.A., Temple U., Phila., 1954; M.S., U. Pa., Phila., 1956, Ph.D., 1959. Jr. research assoc. in physics Brookhaven Nat. Lab., 1957-59; research assoc. U. Pa., Phila., 1959-61; asst. prof. Ohio State U., Columbus, 1961-64, assoc. prof., 1964-70, prof. physics, 1970-92, prof. emeritus, 1992—; vis. scientist CERN, Geneva, Switzerland, 1968-69, 75-76. Author research papers on nuclear and elementary particle physics. NSF fellow, 1954-56. Mem. Am. Phys. Soc., AAUP, Fedn. Am. Scientists, Union Concerned Scientists, Sigma Xi. Jewish. Office: Ohio State U Dept Physics 174 W 18th Ave Columbus OH 43210-1106

REIBMAN, JEANETTE FICHMAN, retired state senator; b. Ft. Wayne, Ind., Aug. 18, 1915; d. Meir and Pearl (Schwartz) Fichman; m. Nathan L. Reibman, June 20, 1943; children: Joseph M. Edward D., James E. AB, Hunter Coll., 1937; LLB, U. Ind., 1940; LLD, Lafayette Coll., 1969; hon. degree, Lehigh U., 1986, Wilson Coll., 1974, Cedar Crest Coll., 1977, Moravian Coll., 1990. Bar: Ind., 1940, U.S. Supreme Ct. 1944. Pvt. practice law Ft. Wayne, 1940; atty. U.S. War Dept., Washington, 1940-42, U.S. War Prodn. Bd., Washington, 1942-44; mem. Pa. Ho. of Reps., 1956-66, Pa. State Senate, Harrisburg, 1966-94; chmn. com. on edn. Pa. State Senate, 1971-81, minority chmn., 1981-90, majority caucus adminstr., 1992-94; mem. Edn. Commn. of the States. Trustee emeritus Lafayette Coll.; bd. mem. Pa. Higher Edn. Assistance Agy., Pa. Coun. on Arts, Camphill Schs. Recipient Disting. Dau. of Pa. award and medal Gov. Pa., 1968, citation on naming of Jeanette F. Reibman Adminstrn. Bldg., East Stroudsburg State Coll., 1972, Early Childhood Learning Ctr. Northampton Community Coll., 1992, Pub. Svc. award Pa. Psychol. Assn., 1977, Jerusalem City of Peace award Govt. Israel, 1977; named to Hunter Coll. Alumni Hall of Fame, 1974; U. Ind. Law Alumni fellow, 1993. Mem. Hadassah (Myrtle Wreath award 1976), Sigma Delta Tau, Delta Kappa Gamma, Phi Delta Kappa, Order Ea. Star. Democrat. Jewish. Office: 711 Lehigh St Easton PA 18042-4325

REIBSTEIN, RICHARD JAY, lawyer; b. Phila., Mar. 12, 1951; s. Albert Simon and Alma (Wilf) R.; m. Susan Barbara Fisch, May 18, 1975. BA with distinction, U. Rochester, 1973; JD with honors, George Washington U., 1976. Bar: Pa. 1976 (nonresident inactive), N.Y. 1979, N.J. 1979, U.S. Dist. Ct. (so. dist.) N.Y. 1979, U.S. Dist. Ct. (ea. dist.) N.Y. 1979, N.J. 1979, U.S. Ct. Appeals (3d cir.) 1980, U.S. Ct. Appeals (2d cir.) 1982, U.S. Supreme Ct. 1983. Staff atty. Dept. Labor, Washington, 1976; counsel NLRB, Washington, 1976-78; assoc. Seham, Klein & Zelman (formerly Surrey, Karasik, Morse & Seham), N.Y.C., 1978-81; assoc. Epstein Becker & Green, P.C., N.Y.C., 1981-86, ptnr., 1986-91; ptnr. McDermott, Will & Emery, N.Y.C., 1992—. Co-author: Negligent Hiring, Fraud, Defamation, and Other Emerging Areas of Employer Liability, 1988, Employer's Guide to Workplace Torts, 1992; contbr. articles to legal jours. Mem. ABA (devel. of law under NLRA com., sect. labor and employment law 1976—), N.Y. State Bar Assn. Democrat. Office: McDermott Will & Emery 1211 Avenue Of The Americas New York NY 10036-8701

REICH, ABRAHAM CHARLES, lawyer; b. Waterbury, Conn., Apr. 17, 1949; s. Samuel and Esther (Gurvitz) R.; m. Sherri Engelman, Aug. 15, 1971; children: Spencer, Alexander. BA, U. Conn., 1971; JD, Temple U., 1974. Bar: Pa. 1974, U.S. Supreme Ct. 1979. Assoc. Fox, Rothschild, O'Brien & Frankel, Phila., 1974-81, ptnr., 1981—. Mem. ABA (Ho. of Dels. 1997), Phila. Bar Assn. (chairperson profl. responsibility com. 1983-84, chairperson bench-bar com. 1985, chairperson profl. guidance com. 1987-88, bd. govs. 1987-89, chair bd. govs. 1989, vice chancellor 1993, chancellor-elect 1994, chancellor 1995). Home: 2224 Mt Vernon St Philadelphia PA 19130-3115 Office: Fox Rothschild O'Brien Frankel 2000 Market St Ste 10 Philadelphia PA 19103-3201

REICH, ALAN ANDERSON, foundation administrator; b. Pearl River, N.Y., Jan. 1, 1930; s. Oswald David and Alma Carolyn (Anderson) R.; m. Gay Ann Forsythe, Dec. 19, 1954; children: James, Jeffrey, Andrew, Elizabeth. B.A., Dartmouth Coll., 1952; diploma in Slavic Studies, Oxford U., 1953; M.A., Russian Inst., Middlebury Coll., 1953; M.B.A., Harvard U., 1959; LLD (hon.), Gallaudet Coll., 1981, Dartmouth Coll., 1992. Exec. Polaroid Corp., Cambridge, Mass., 1960-70; dep. asst. sec. ednl. and cultural affairs Dept. State, Washington, 1970-75; spl. asst. to sec. HEW, 1976-77; dep. asst. sec. commerce, dir. Bur. East-West Trade, Dept. Commerce, 1977-78; pres. U.S. Council for Internat. Yr. of Disabled Persons, Washington, 1978-81, Nat. Orgn. Disability, Washington, 1982—, Bimillennium Found., 1982—, Disability 2000 CEO coun., 1991—. Chmn. Sudbury (Mass.) Community United Fund, 1962, 66; mem. U.S. del. WHO Gen. Assembly, 1970; pres. Nat. Paraplegia Found.; chmn. bd. dirs. Paralysis Cure Research Found., bd. dirs. of the Healing Community, chmn. People-to-people Com. for Handicapped; Impact Found., 1986—; chmn. World Com. on Disability, 1985—. Served to 1st lt. inf. AUS, 1953-57. Named to U.S. Army Inf. OCS Hall of Fame, 1994; recipient Sevier award for svc. to handicapped, 1994. Mem. Paralyzed Vets. Am., Cosmos Club, Achilles Club (London), Beta Theta Pi. Republican. Methodist. Home: 6017 Copely Ln Mc Lean VA 22101-2507 Office: Nat Orgn on Disability 910 16th St NW Ste 600 Washington DC 20006-2903

REICH, ALLAN J., lawyer; b. Chgo., July 9, 1948; s. H. Robert and Sonya (Minsky) R.; m. Lynne Susan Roth, May 23, 1971; children: Allison, Marissa, Scott. BA, Cornell U., 1970; JD cum laude, U. Mich., 1973. Bar: Ill. 1973, U.S. Dist. Ct. (no. dist.) Ill. 1973. Ptnr. McDermott, Will & Emery, Chgo., 1973-93; ptnr., chairperson corp./securities group D'Ancona & Pflaum, Chgo., 1993—, trustee Oakmar Family of Mutual Funds, 1994—. Bd. dirs., pres. Young Men's Jewish Council, Chgo., 1974-84, Coun. for Jewish Elderly, 1986—, v.p., mem. exec. com., 1989—; mem. men's council Mus. Contemporary Art, Chgo., 1983-90, pres. 1988-89; trustee Mus. of Contemporary Art, Chgo., 1988-89; v.p., mem. Chgo. exec. bd. Am. Jewish Com., 1989—; mem. adv. bd. Columbia Dance Ctr., 1992—. Mem. ABA, Chgo. Bar Assn. Clubs: Standard (Chgo.); Northmoor Country (Highland Park, Ill.). Home: 936 Skokie Ridge Dr Glencoe IL 60022-1434 Office: D'Ancona & Pflaum 30 N La Salle St Chicago IL 60602-2502

REICH, BERNARD, telecommunications engineer; b. N.Y.C., Jan. 7, 1926; s. Adolph and Rose (Gluck) R.; m. Sylvia Greenberg, June 15, 1947; children: Robin Reich Murphy, Richard. BS in Physics, CCNY, 1948; postgrad., Rutgers U., 1954. Electronic engr., supervisory electronic engr. U.S. Army Electronics R & D Command, Ft. Monmouth, N.J., 1948-81; unit mgr. Semcor, Farmingdale, N.J., 1981-88; telecommunications engr. Telos Corp., Shrewsbury, N.J., 1988—; chmn. spl. working group on semicondrs. and microelectronics NATO, Brussels, 1959-80, chmn. group experts on electronic parts, 1972-80; adv. editor Microelectronics and Reliability, 1970—. Contbr. over 100 articles to tech. jours.; patentee in field. Mem. Juvenile Conf. Com., Ocean Twp., N.J., 1964—; pres. Manor at Wayside Condominium Assn., Ocean Twp., 1990-91. Sgt. U.S. Army, 1945-46, ETO. Recipient decoration for meritorious civilian svc. U.S. Army Electronics R & D Command, 1981. Fellow IEEE (chartered,), IEE (Eng.). Avocations: walking, grandparenting. Home: 45 Gimbel Pl Ocean NJ 07712-2565 Office: Telos Corp 656 Shrewsbury Ave Shrewsbury NJ 07701-4915

REICH, BERNARD, political science educator; b. Bklyn., Dec. 5, 1941; s. Moe and Rosalyn (Hartglass) R.; m. Madelyn Sue Ingber, June 16, 1963; children—Barry, Norman, Michael, Jennifer. BA cum laude with spl. honors, CCNY, 1961; MA, U. Va., 1963, PhD, 1964. Asst. prof. polit. sci. and internat. affairs George Washington U., Washington, 1964-70, assoc. prof., 1970-76, prof., 1976—, chmn. dept. polit. sci., 1976-82, 88-91; vis. prof. U. Va., 1969, 94, Sch. Advanced Internat. Studies Johns Hopkins U., 1978-80; vis. rsch. assoc. Tel Aviv U., 1971-72. Author: Quest for Peace: United States-Israel Relations and the Arab-Israel Conflict, 1977, The U.S. and Israel: Influence in the Special Relationship, 1984, Israel: Land of Tradition and Conflict, 1985, 93, Historical Dictionary of Israel, 1992, Securing the Covenant: United States-Israel Relations After the Cold War, 1995; editor, co-author: Government and Politics of the Middle East and North Africa, 1980, 86, 95; editor, co-author: Israel Faces the Future, 1986, The Powers in the Middle East, 1987, Israeli National Security Policy: Political Actors and Perspectives, 1988, Political Leaders of the Contemporary Middle East and North Africa: A Biographical Dictionary, 1990, Israeli Politics in the 1990's Key Domestic and Foreign Policy Factors, 1991, Arab-Israeli Conflict and Conciliation: A Documentary History, 1995, An Historical Encyclopedia of the Arab-Israeli Conflict, 1996; co-author: United States Foreign Policy and the Middle East/North Africa: A Bibliography of Twentieth-Century Research, 1990, Asian States' Relations with the Middle East and North Africa: A Bibliography, 1950-93, 94, U.S. Foreign Relations with the Middle East and North Africa: A Bibliography, 1994; mem. adv. bd. editors Middle East Jour., 1977—, Jour. Israel Affairs, 1994—, Terrorism, 1987-93, Fgn. Svc. Jour., 1987-90; contbr. articles to profl. jours. Bd. govs. Middle East Inst. Fulbright research scholar, UAR, 1965; NSF postdoctoral fellow, 1971-72. Mem. Internat. Inst. Strategic Studies, Middle East Studies Assn., Phi Beta Kappa. Home: 13800 Turnmore Rd Silver Spring MD 20906-2134 Office: George Washington U Dept Polit Sci Washington DC 20052

REICH, CHARLES WILLIAM, nuclear physicist; b. Oklahoma City, Sept. 12, 1930; s. Fred William And Gertrude Evelyn (Veal) R.; m. Juana Sue Woods, June 8, 1952; children: Paul William, Jane Kristen, Donna Karen. BS in Physics, U. Okla., 1952; MA in Physics, Rice U., 1954, PhD in Physics, 1956. Physicist, group leader Atomic Energy Div. Phillips Petroleum Co., Idaho Falls, Idaho, 1956-66; group leader, sect. chief Idaho Nuclear Corp., Idaho Falls, 1966-71; sect. chief Aerojet Nuclear Corp., Idaho Falls, 1971-76; prin. scientist, sect. chief EG&G Idaho, Inc., Idaho Falls, 1976-82, sci., engring. fellow, 1982-92, fellow emeritus, 1992—; guest scientist Niels Bohr Inst., Copenhagen, 1964-65; U.S. rep., coord. coordinated rsch. program IAEA, 1977-86; mem. transplutonium program com. U.S. Dept. Energy, 1978-90; chmn. decay data subcom. Cross Sects. Evaluation Working Group, 1974-86; mem. task force on decay heat predictions nuclear data com. Nuclear Energy Agy., 1988-90; mem. sci. framework writing com. State of Idaho Dept. Edn., 1994. Contbr. articles to profl. jours. Recipient H.A. Wilson rsch. award Rice Inst., 1956; predoctoral fellow NSF, 1954-55. Fellow Am. Phys. Soc. (editl. bd. Phys. Rev. C 1978, 82-84); mem. N.Y. Acad. Scis., Sigma Xi, Phi Beta Kappa. Mem. Ch. Nazarene. Office: Idaho Nat Engring Lab PO Box 1625 Idaho Falls ID 83415-2114

REICH, DAVID LEE, library director; b. Orlando, Fla., Nov. 25, 1930; s. P.F. and Opal Katherine (Wood) Reichelderfer; m. Kathleen Johanna Weichel, Aug. 2, 1954 (div. Sept. 1964); 1 son, Robert Weichel. Ph.B. magna cum laude, U. Detroit, 1961; A.M. in L.S. (Carnegie Library Sci. Endowment scholar), U. Mich., 1963. Tchr. English Jefferson Davis Jr. Sch., San Antonio, 1961-62; dir. engring. library Radiation Inc., Melbourne, Fla., 1963-64; asst. to dir. libraries Miami-Dade Jr. Coll., Miami, Fla., 1964-65; dir. learning resources Monroe County Community Coll., Monroe, Mich., 1965-68; dep. dir. Dallas Pub. Library, 1968-73; dep. chief librarian The Chgo. Pub. Library, 1973-74, commr., 1975-78; dir. Bd. Library Commrs., Commonwealth of Mass., Boston, 1978-80; exec. sec. New Eng. Library Bd., Augusta, Maine, 1980-82; dir. Lakeland Pub. Library, Lakeland, Fla., 1983—; vice chmn. New Eng. Library Bd., 1979-80; libr. cons. Macomb County C.C., Warren, Mich., 1967; chmn. adv. com. to libr. tech. asst. program El Centro Coll., Dallas, 1969-71; mem. inter-task working group Goals for Dallas, 1968-70, mem. Dallas Area Libr. planning coun., 1970-73; mem. adv. coun. dept. libr. sci. No. Ill. U., 1975-78; v.p., pres.-elect Tampa Bay Libr. Consortium, 1985-86, pres., 1986-87. Co-author: The Public Library in Non-traditional Education, 1974; Contbr. articles to library jours. Bd. dirs. The Villas II Homeowners Assn., 1994-96. Sgt. U.S. Army, 1952-55. Recipient Disting. Alumnus award U. Mich., 1978; William B. Calkins Found. scholar Orlando, 1963. Mem. ALA (coun.-at-large 1968-72, 75-79), S.E. Libr. Assn., Fla. Libr. Assn. (sec.-treas. coll. and spl. librs. divsn. 1965, steering com. mcpl. librs. caucus 1983-84, chmn. 1984-85, exec. bd. 1984-87), Soc. Fla. Archivists (exec. bd. 1994-96, sec. 1996-97), Fla. Pub. Libr. Assn. (pres. 1987-88, exec. bd. 1988-89, 94-95, pres. emeritus 1996—, editor newsletter 1992-93, 96-97, chmn. libr. adminstrn. divsn. 1992, friends and trustees divsn. 1993, 95), Alumni Assn. U. Mich. (pres. Libr. Sch. alumni 1973). Home: 3929 Old Road 37 Villa 134 Lakeland FL 33813-1058 Office: Lakeland Pub Libr 100 Lake Morton Dr Lakeland FL 33801-5347

REICH, HERB, editor; b. N.Y.C.; s. Herman S. and Hattie (Davis) R.; m. Gerri Toog, Aug. 7, 1960; children: Amanda Suri, Elizabeth Jo. B.A., Bklyn. Coll., 1950; M.A., Bklyn. Coll. and Kings County Hosp., 1951; postgrad., Columbia U., 1951-54. Author sketches and lyrics Tamiment Revues (Pa.), 1951; staff writer NBC-TV, N.Y.C. and Los Angeles, 1955-57; research coordinator Inst. for Motivational Research, Croton-on-Hudson, N.Y., 1958-59; research dir. Scientist and Engr. Technol. Inst., N.Y.C., 1960-64; mng. editor SETI Pubs. Inc., N.Y.C., 1961-64; sr. editor Odyssey Press, N.Y.C., 1964-65; editorial dir. Profl. and Tech. Programs Inc., N.Y.C., 1966-72; dir. Behavioral Sci. Book Service, N.Y.C., 1966-72; dir. behavioral scis. program Basic Books Inc., N.Y.C., 1973-79; editor intersci. div. John Wiley & Sons. Inc., N.Y.C., 1979-87, sr. editor profl. and trade divsn., 1987-95; pres. H&G Reich, Publ., Hastings Hdsn., N.Y., 1980—; publ., rsch., advt. and polit. cons.; rschr., statistician, rsch. cons. Am. Found. for Blind, Pepsi Cola Co., Nowland and Co., Comms. and Media Rsch. Svcs.; freelance TV writer. Mng. editor: Odyssey Science Library Ency. of Engring., Signs and Symbols, 1965, Dictionary of Physics and Mathematics Abbreviations, Signs and Symbols, 1965, Dictionary of Electronics Abbreviations, Signs and Symbols, 1965, Dictionary of Computers and Control Systems Abbreviations, Signs and Symbols, 1965; contbr. Random House Dictionary of the English Language, 1967, rev. edit., 1987, The Greatest Revue Sketches, 1982, Ency. of Psychology, 2d edit., 1994; TV writer: Broadway Open House, 1951, Milton Berle Texaco Star Theatre, 1952, All-Star Revue, 1952, Mel Torme Show, 1952, Red Buttons Show, 1954, Jerry Lester Show, 1954, Jan Murray Time, 1955, Wayne and Schuster Hour, 1957. Co-founder, vice chmn. Mt. Vernon United for Better Edn., N.Y., 1970-73; mem. Westchester County Democratic Com., 1972-76; exec. com. Mt. Vernon Dem. City Com., 1973-76; mem. supt.'s adv. com. Hastings Schs., Hastings-on-Hudson, N.Y., 1981-82. Recipient Gold award of excellence for radio advt. Advt. Club of Westchester, 1980; recipient Gold and Bronze awards of excellence for radio advt. Advt. Club of Westchester, 1981. Mem. AAAS, APA, N.Y. Acad. Scis., Alpha Phi Omega. Office: PO Box 38 Hastings On Hudson NY 10706

REICH, KENNETH IRVIN, journalist; b. Los Angeles, Mar. 7, 1938; s. Herman and Ruth Alberta (Nussbaum) R.; children: Kathleen, David. B.A., Dartmouth Coll., 1960; M.A. (Woodrow Wilson fellow), U. Calif., Berkeley, 1962. With UPI, Sacramento, 1962-63, Life mag., 1963-65; with Los Angeles Times, 1965—, polit. writer, 1972-77, 1984 Olympics writer, 1977-84, investigative reporter ins. law, ins. politics & fin. sports, 1985-92; lectr. in field. Author: Making it Happen, Peter Ueberroth and the 1984 Olympics, 1985, Covering Earthquakes, Volcanos and Other Issues Relating to Geology, 1992—; contbr. articles to mags. Daniel Webster Nat. Honor scholar Dartmouth Coll., 1956-60. Mem. Dartmouth Alumni Club (chpt. officer 1991—, dist. enrollment dir. 1992-95, meml. chmn. Dartmouth Class of 1960 1993-95, class sec. 1995—). Office: Times-Mirror Sq Los Angeles CA 90053

REICH, MERRILL DRURY, intelligence consultant, writer; b. Washington, Aug. 28, 1930; s. Merrill Dale Reich and Evelyn Merle Wright; m. Georgia Ann Ewing, Aug. 28, 1953; 1 child, Alexandra Therese. BA in History, Govt., Rollins Coll., 1954; postgrad., U. Vienna, 1954-55, Naval War Coll., 1973-74; MA in Mgmt., Cen. Mich. U., 1981. Commd. ensign USN, 1956, advanced through grades to capt., ret., 1982; dir. systems mgmt. BDM Corp., Columbia, Md., 1982-92; cons. Crytec, Inc., 1992-95. Fulbright scholar, 1954-55. Mem. Nat. Trust for Hist. Preservation, U.S. Naval Inst., Naval War Coll. Found., Assn. Former Intelligence Officers, Navy Cryptologic Vets. Assn., Fulbright Assn., New Eng. Hist. Geneal. Soc., Omicron Delta Kappa, Pi Gamma Mu, Phi Kappa Tau. Republican. Avocations: genealogy, lapidary, antiques, swimming, sailing. Home: 514 Kirkwood Ln Camden SC 29020

REICH, MICHAEL, economics educator; b. Poland, Oct. 18, 1945; came to U.S., 1949; s. Melvin and Betty (Mandelbaum) R.; children: Rachel, Gabriel. BA, Swarthmore Coll., 1966; PhD, Harvard U., 1974. Asst. prof. Boston U., 1971-74; asst. prof. U. Calif., Berkeley, 1974-81, acting assoc. prof., 1981-82, assoc. prof., 1982-89, prof., 1989—; rsch. dir. Nat. Ctr. for the Workplace, 1993—. Author: Segmented Work, Divided Workers, 1982, Racial Inequality, 1981, The Capitalist System, 1986, Social Structures of Accumulation, 1994, Work and Pay in the U.S. and Japan, 1997; editor: Indsl. Rels. Jour., 1986-94; contbr. articles to profl. jours. Mem. Am. Econ. Assn., Indsl. Rels. Rsch. Assn., Phi Beta Kappa, Sigma Xi. Office: Dept of Econs U Calif 611 Evans Hall Berkeley CA 94720

REICH, NATHANIEL EDWIN, physician, poet, author, artist, educator; b. N.Y.C., May 19, 1907; s. Alexander and Betty (Feigenbaum) R.; m. Joan Finkel, May 22, 1943; children: Andrew, Matthew. B.S., NYU, 1927; student, Marquette U. Coll. Medicine, 1927-29; M.D., Rush Med. Coll., U. Chgo., 1932. Diplomate Am. Bd. Internal Medicine. Intern, resident pathologist City Hosp., N.Y.C., 1931-33; emeritus attending physician Kingsbrook Jewish Med. Center Hosp.; vis. physician Kings County Hosp., Bklyn.; attending physician State U. Hosp.; faculty SUNY Downstate Med. Center, 1938—, asso. clin. prof. medicine, 1952-74, clin. prof., 1974-77, emeritus prof., 1977—; vis. prof. San Marcos U. Coll. Medicine, Lima, Peru, 1968, U. Afghanistan, 1970, U. Indonesia, 1972, U. Sri Lanka, 1975; asst. attending physician N.Y. Postgrad. Hosp., Columbia U., 1940; cons. Dept. H and HS; cardiac cons. U.S. R.R. Retirement Bd., 1965—; program cons. Acad. Family Physicians, 1973, N.Y. State Disability Determinations; lectr. univs., Rome, Moscow, Rijeka, Haiti, Jerusalem, Cairo, Athens, Bangkok, Bucharest, Manila, Lisbon, Beijing, Shanghai, Romania, Taiwan, Cairo, Athens, Tunis, Triente, Madras, Dakar, Senegal, Durban, Witwatersrand, Capetown, Natal, Lima, Buenos Aires, Rio de Janeiro, Quito; 1st Am. physician invited to lecture in USSR, 1956; lectr. univs. U. Madras (India), 1969, Spain, 1971, Auckland, N.Z., Sydney, Australia, Senegal, Portugal; lectr. Japan Med. Assn., Philippine Heart Assn., Royal Thai Air Force Med. Svc., China Med. Assn., Shanghai, 1978, Nat. Taiwan U., Taipei, 1978, Beijing Cardiac Inst., 1986; chmn. internat. cardiology sect. Congress Chest Diseases, Cologne, Germany, 1956; impartial specialist U.S. Fed. Employees; cons. N.Y. State Bur. Disability Determinations, N.Y.C., Office Vocat. Rehab., Dept. Health and Human Svcs., 1965—; chief med. examiner SSS, 1942-44 (Presdl. commendation). One-man shows include L.I. U., 1961, NYU Loeb Ctr., 1962, 72, 74, Greer Gallery, 1962, 64, St. Charles, La., 1964, Nyack, N.Y., 1986, Prospect Park Ctrl. Art Show, 1966, Art Inst. Boston, 1970, 76, George Wiener Gallery, 1972; exhibited in group shows at Little Studio, 1952, Mus. Modern Art, Paris, 1970, Bodley Gallery, 1965, 69, Nyack, N.Y., 1987, others; represented in permanent collections at Huntington Hartford collection N.Y. Cultural Ctr., 1969, Washington County Mus. of Fine Arts, Hagerstown, md.; author 3 textbooks on cardiology; author chpts. in 3 encys.; author: A Renaissance Man at Large; author: (collected poems) Reflections, 1993. Served from 1st lt. to maj. M.C., AUS, 1944-47. Recipient St. Gaudens award, 1923, 1st prize Art Assn. AMA, 1948, 1st prize Art Assn. Literary Soc., 1949, Disting. Achievement award Boys' H.S. Alumni Assn., 1988, Am. Poetry Assn. Hon. mention World of Poetry, 1990; named Best New Poets of 1989, 94, 95. Fellow ACP, Royal Soc. Medicine (London), Am. Coll. Cardiology, Am. Coll. Angiology (med. honor award 1956, 59), Am. Coll. Legal Medicine (founder), Am. Coll. Chest Physicians (chmn. exhibits com. 1961, cardiovascular rehab. com. 1965, coronary disease com. 1968, pres. N.Y. state chpt. 1970); mem. N.Y. State Med. Soc. (vice chmn. space med. sect. 1967, 75, chmn. chest sect. 1972), Internat. Soc. Internal Medicine, World Med. Assn., Am. Heart Assn. (coun. on thrombosis), N.Y. Heart Assn., N.Y. Cardiol. Soc. (exec. bd., pres.), Explorers Club (5 explorations described in jour. 1966—), Temple Club (v.p.), Doctors Club Bklyn. (vice chmn. bd. govs.), Circumnavigators. Home: 1620 Avenue I Brooklyn NY 11230-3050

REICH, PAULA JUDY, nursing educator; b. Troy, N.Y., Jan. 27, 1942; d. Samuel and Dora (Luskin) Bendick; m. Lawrence W. Reich, Nov. 1, 1964; children: Ronna, Heather, Sheara. AAS in Nursing, Queens Coll., 1961; BSN, St. John's U., Queens, N.Y., 1964; MS in Curriculum and Instrn., SUNY, Albany, 1975; MS in Nursing, Adelphi U., 1982. RN, N.Y. Staff nurse obstetrics Flushing Hosp., Queens, 1962-63; staff nurse ob/gyn. Queens Gen. Hosp., 1963-64; sr. staff nurse pediatrics Mt. Sinai Hosp., N.Y.C., 1964-65; supr. ob-gyn. Nassau Hosp., Mineola, N.Y., 1965-67; staff nurse obstetrics St. Peters Hosp., Albany, 1968-73; dir. Tri Cities Childbirth Instrn., Albany, 1973-78; mem. faculty dept. nursing Adelphi U., Garden City, N.Y., 1978-79, SUNY, Farmingdale, 1978—; clin. instr. Albany Jr. Coll., 1977-78; cons. maternal/child continuing edn. Adelphi U., 1984; dir. nursing continuing edn. SUNY, Farmingdale, 1985-91, dir. LPN/ADN nursing ract, 1990-94. V.p. bd. dirs. Suffolk Network Adolescent Pregnancy, Suffolk County, N.Y., 1985-90. Mem. Suffolk Perinatal Coalition. Avocations: sailing, travel, reading. Office: SUNY Farmingdale Dept Nursing Rt 110 Melville NY 11735

REICH, PAULINE CAROLE, international business consultant, educator, author; b. Kew Gardens, N.Y., Nov. 13, 1946; d. Stanley Garfield and Elsa Olga (Doctor) R. Cert. in critical langs. program, Princeton U., 1967; BA, CCNY, 1968; MA, CUNY, 1972; JD, N.Y. Law Sch., 1985; grad., Coro Found. Pub. Affairs Leadership Program, 1981. Bar: N.J., U.S. Ct. Internat. Trade, U.S. Ct. Appeals (Fed. cir.). Cons. Pan Pacific, Inc., Bayside, N.Y., 1988-90, Japan Pacific Group, N.Y.C., 1990-93, Asia Pacific Group, N.Y.C., 1994—; prof. Waseda U. Sch. Law, Tokyo, 1995—. Contbr. book chpts. and articles to profl. jours. Japan Found. fellow, 1973, Princeton Found. fellow, 1966-67, Carnegie Found. fellow, 1966-67, Nat. Def. Edn. Act. fellow, 1966; elected East Coast Dir. Ind. Scholars Asia, 1981-86. Mem. ABA (vice chmn. legal edn. com. sect. internat. law and practice 1996—, co-chmn. Pacific Rim com. sect. dispute resolution 1995—), Am. C. of C. in Japan (legal svcs. com.), Am. Arbitration Assn. (arbitration panel), U.S. Coun. for Internat. Bus. (arbitration panel), Assn. for Asian Studies (com. on Asian law), Law Soc. Asia and Pacific. Avocations: international travel, underwater photography, genealogy. Office: Waseda U Sch Law, 1-6-1 Nishi-Waseda, Shinjuku-ku Tokyo Japan

REICH, ROBERT BERNARD, federal official, political economics educator; b. Scranton, Pa., June 24, 1946; s. Edwin Saul and Mildred Dorf (Freshman) R.; m. Clare Dalton, July 7, 1973. BA, Dartmouth Coll., 1968, MA (hon.), 1988; MA, Oxford (Eng.) U., 1970; JD, Yale U., 1973. Asst. solicitor gen. U.S. Dept. Justice, Washington, 1974-76; dir. policy planning FTC, Washington, 1976-81; mem. faculty John F. Kennedy Sch. Govt. Harvard U., Cambridge, Mass., 1981—; sec. Dept. of Labor, Washington, 1993—; chmn. biotech. sect. U.S. Office Tech. Assessment, Washington, 1990-91. Author: The Next American Frontier, 1983, Tales of a New America, 1987, The Work of Nations, 1991; co-author: The Power of Public Ideas, 1987; contbg. editor The New Republic, Washington, 1982-93; chmn. editorial bd. The Am. Prospect, 1990-93. Mem. governing bd. Common Cause, Washington, 1981-85; bd. dirs. Bus. Enterprise Trust, Palo Alto, Calif., 1989-93; trustee Dartmouth Coll., Hanover, N.H., 1989-93. Rhodes scholar, 1968; recipient Louis Brownlow award ASPA, 1983.

REICH, ROBERT SIGMUND, landscape architect; b. N.Y.C., Mar. 22, 1913; s. Ulysses S. and Adele G. R.; m. Helen Elizabeth Adams, May, 1945; children—Barbara, Betsy, Bob, Bill. B.S., Cornell U., 1934, Ph.D., 1941; postgrad., U. So. Calif., 1951. Instr. landscape design Cornell U., 1936-39, 40-41; instr. landscape design U. Conn., 1939-40; Inst. Land Design La. State U., 1941-46, asst. prof. landscape architecture, 1946-49, asso. prof., 1949-60, prof., 1960—, Alumni prof., 1967—, head dept. landscape architecture, 1964-79, dir. Sch.Landscape Architecture, 1979-83; prof. Landscape Architecture, 1992—; instr. Shrivenham (Eng.) Am. U., 1946, Biarritz (France) Am. U., 1947; vis. lectr. Tulane U., 1958-67; judge, instr. Nat. Council Garden Clubs, 1956—; mem. task force on parks, recreation and tourism Goals for La. Program; mem. com. to establish Chicot State Park Arboretum, Ville Plate, La., 1964, mem. steering com., 1964-75; examiner La. Bd. Examination for Landscape Architects, 1957-77. Co-author: Landscape and You, 1953. Mem. com. to establish City/Parish Beautification Commn., 1961-82; mem. area and facilities com. Baton Rouge Recreation and Parks Commn., 1957-83; bd. dirs. Hubbard Edn. Trust, Weston, Mass., 1967—; adv. com. Friends of Frederick Law Olmsted Papers, 1983—. With U.S. Army, 1942-45; in charge alter arrangements U. United Meth. Ch., 1945—. Recipient Teaching award of merit Gamma Sigma Delta, 1963, Baton Rouge Green Individual Honor award, 1996. Fellow Am. Soc. Landscape Architects (trustee 1968-71, 83-86, 3d v.p. 1971-73, Medal 1992); mem. S.W. Park and Recreation Tng. Inst. (dir. 1975-77, award of merit 1968), Phi Kappa Phi, Pi Alpha xi, Omicron Delta Kappa, Sigma Lambda Alpha. Home: 333 E Boyd Dr Baton Rouge LA 70808-4507 Office: La State U Sch Landscape Architecture Coll Design Bldg Baton Rouge LA 70803

REICH, ROSE MARIE, retired art educator; b. Milw., Dec. 24, 1937; d. Valentine John and Mary Jane (Grochowski) Kosmatka; m. Kenneth Pierce Reich, July 13, 1968; 1 stepson, Lance Pierce. BA, Milw. Downer Coll., 1959; MA, U. Wyo., 1967. Art tchr. Oconomowoc (Wis.) Area Schs., 1959-93, ret., 1993. Mem. Oconomowoc Edn. Assn., NEA (life), Wis. Edn. Assn., AAUW (v.p. membership 1989—), Delta Kappa Gamma (past pres.), Oconomowoc Woman's Club. Roman Catholic. Avocations: Newfoundland dogs, needlework, designing stationery, Polish paper cutting, restoring old church statues and mannequins. Home: 3717 N Golden Lake Rd Oconomowoc WI 53066-4104

REICH, STEVE, composer; b. N.Y.C., Oct. 3, 1936; m. Beryl Korot; children: Ezra, Michael. Studies in percussion with Roland Kohloff, 1950-53; BA in Philosophy with honors, Cornell U., 1957; studies in composition with Hall Overton, 1957-58; studies with Bergsma and Persichetti, Julliard Sch. Music, 1958-61; MA in Music, Mills Coll., 1963; studies in composition with Darius Milhaud and Luciano Berio; studies in drumming, Inst. for African Studies, U. Ghana, 1971; student, Am. Soc. for Ea. Arts, Seattle and Berkeley, 1973, 74, Cantillation of Hebrew Scriptures, N.Y.C. and Jerusalem, 1976-77. Organized ensemble Steve Reich and Musicians, 1966; performed throughout the world, 1971—; recs. with various cos. including Columbia Records, Disques Shandar, Hungaraton, Argel, ECM, Deutsche Grammophon, Nonesuch, Phillips, Virgin Classics, Argo. Composer, performer: (albums) Come Out, 1967, It's Gonna Rain, 1969, Violin Phase, 1969, Four Organs, 1970, Phase Patterns, 1970, Drumming, 1971, Four Organs, 1973, Six Pianos, 1973, Music for Mallet Instruments, Voices, and Organ, 1973, Music for Eighteen Musicians, 1978, Octet, 1980, Music for a Large Ensemble, 1980,Tehillim, 1982, The Desert Music, 1984, Sextet, 1986, Six Marimbas, 1986, Electric Counterpoint, 1987, Different Trains, 1988 (Grammy award 1989), The Four Sections, 1987, The Cave, 1994, City Life, 1995, Proverb, 1996, others; composer: Vermont Counterpoint, Variations for Winds, Strings and Keyboards, Eight Lines for Chamber Orchestra, Piano Phase, Clapping Music, Pendulum Music, Music for Pieces of Wood, Nagoya Marimbas, other works performed by major orchs. and ensembles; commd. to compose for Holland Festival, 1978, Radio Frankfurt, 1979, San Francisco Symphony, 1980, Rothko Chapel, 1981, West German Radio, Cologne, 1984, Fromm Music Found., 1985, Richard Stoltzman, 1985, Bklyn. Acad. Music, 1987, Kronos Quartet, 1988, St. Louis Sympnony, 1987, The Cave commd. by Vienna Festival, Holland Festival, Festival d'Automne à Paris, Theatre de la Monnaie, Brussels, Hebbel Theatre, Berlin, South Bank Centre/Serious Speakout, London and the Brooklyn Acad. Music, Next Wave Festival, 1993. Recipient Koussevitzky Found. award, 1981; Rockefeller Found. grantee 1975, 78, 81, 90, Nat. Endowment for the Arts grantee, 1974, 76, 91, N.Y. State Council on the Arts grantee, 1974; Guggenheim fellow, 1978; elected to Am. Acad. Arts and Letters, 1994, Bagerische Akademie der Schönen Künst, 1995. Office: care IMG Artists 22 E 71st St New York NY 10021-4911

REICH, WILLIAM MICHAEL, advertising executive; b. N.Y.C., July 28, 1943; s. William Adolph and Mildred Joan (Chestaro) R.; m. Carmela Louise Ezzone; children: Concetta M., John M., Russell D. Student, N.Y.C. Community Coll., 1961-62, Sch. Visual Arts, N.Y.C., 1962-65. Tech. illustrator Grumman Aerospace Corp., Bethpage, N.Y., 1965-67; tech. illustrator Dayton T. Brown, Inc., Bohemia, N.Y., 1967-68, art dir., 1968-69, art dir., prodn. mgr., 1969-71, sales and estimating mgr., 1971-74; art dir. Volt Info. Scis., Garden City, N.Y., 1974-75, salesman, 1975-78, directories mgr., 1978-80; corp. publs. mgr. Loral Microwave Group, Hauppauge, N.Y., 1980-93, mgr. sales adminstrn., 1993—. Recipient Bronze award Gold Book, 1980, Cert. of Merit award, Printing Industries of Metro N.Y., 1983. Mem. Bus. Mktg. Assn. (Bus. to Bus. Best award for product brochure 1993, Cert. Merit full line catalogs 1994), L.I. Advt. Club (Cert. of Merit award 1980-82, 85). Republican. Clubs: L.I. Studebaker (editor, Massapequa, N.Y.). Office: Narda AN L3 Comms Co 435 Moreland Rd Hauppauge NY 11788-3926

REICHARD, HUGO MANLEY, English literature educator; b. South Plainfield, N.J., Jan. 21, 1918; s. Bernard and Emma (Klein) R.; m. Virginia Evelyn Kougias, Aug. 28, 1943; children—Enid Evelyn Reichard Satariano, Claude Manley, Eric George. B.A., U. Mich., 1939; M.A., Harvard U., 1948, Ph.D., 1951. Instr. English lit. Duke U., 1951-56; mem. faculty Purdue U., 1956-88, prof. English lit., 1970-88, prof. emeritus, 1988—. Author articles in field. Served with AUS, 1941-46. Decorated Bronze Star. Mem. MLA, Johnson Soc. Central Region (pres. 1979-80). Office: Purdue U Heavilon Hall English Dept West Lafayette IN 47907

REICHARD, JOHN FRANCIS, education consultant; b. Abington, Pa., June 2, 1924; s. Francis Radcliffe and Katharine (Butler) R.; m. Ruth Naomi Nachod, Aug. 5, 1950; children: Scot, John Nicholas. BA, Wesleyan U., 1949, postgrad., 1949-50; postgrad., Glasgow U., Scotland, 1950-51. Instr. English/humanities Wesleyan U., Middletown, Conn., 1951-52, Ohio Wesleyan U., Delaware, 1952-54; internat. campus adminstr. U.S. Nat. Student Assn., Cambridge, Mass., 1954; exec. dir. Internat. Student Assn. Greater Boston, 1955-60; pres. Phila. Coun. for Internat. Visitors, 1960-73; internat. coord. Phila. 76, 1973-75; exec. dir. Global Interdependence Ctr., 1975-79; exec. v.p. NAFSA: Assn. of Internat. Educators, Washington, 1980-92; internat. edn. cons., Bethesda, Md., 1992—. Bd. Internat. Devel. Conf.; mem. internat. program com. USDA Grad. Sch. Counselor Meridian House Internat.; travel adv. com. U.S. Travel Svc., 1963-64; pres. Nat. Coun. Internat. Visitors, 1963-65; organizer, co-chmn. Internat. Yr. of Child, UNICEF, Phila., 1977-78; internat. adv. bd. Bryn Mawr Coll., 1975-79; chmn. schools com. Phila. steering com. on alumni affairs Wesleyan U., 1968-76; adv. bd. Hariri Found.; mem. Nat. Liaison Com. on Fgn. Student Admissions. Contbr. articles to profl. jours. Served with USAAF, 1943-46. Winchester fellow Wesleyan U., 1949; Fulbright scholar Glasgow U., 1950-51; recipient Tribute of Appreciation, U.S. Dept. State, 1973, 92, Svc. award Coun. on Internat. Ednl. Exch., 1991. Mem. Am. Coun. on Edn. (secretariat, commn. on internat. edn. 1980-92), Alliance for Internat. Edn. (chmn. 1982-84), Test of English as a Fgn. Lang. (policy coun.), Fulbright Alumni Assn. (v.p. 1978-80), Cosmos Club, Phi Beta Kappa. Democrat. Home: 4974 Sentinel Dr Apt 301 Bethesda MD 20816-3571

REICHARDT, PAUL BERNARD, dean, chemistry educator; b. St. Louis, Aug. 15, 1943; s. Bernard George and Elaine Charlotte (Schmudde) R.; m. Cordelia Morris Hufnagel, Apr. 27, 1968; children: Laura, Rebecca, Daniel. BS, Davidson Coll., 1965; PhD in Organic Chemistry, U. Wis., 1969. Post-doctoral rsch. assoc. Yale U., New Haven, 1969-71, instr., 1971; asst. prof. Ohio State U., Columbus, 1971-72; asst. prof. chemistry U. Alaska, Fairbanks, 1972-75, assoc. prof. chemistry, 1975-81, prof. chemistry, 1981—, dean coll. natural scis., 1991-96, dean coll. sci., engring. & math., 1996—; head dept. chemistry U. Alaska, Fairbanks, 1978-82, 88-90, interim dean coll. natural scis., 1990-91, interim provost, 1993-94; interim dir. U. Alaska Mus., 1992-93; mem. Gov.'s Sci. & Engring. Adv. Com., 1986-90, Alaska 2000 Sci. Standards Com., 1992-93. Contbr. articles to profl. jours., chpts. to books and monographs. Named one of Outstanding Young Men of Am., Jaycees, 1980; recipient Inspirational Tchr. award U. Alaska at Fairbanks Alumni Assn., 1982. Mem. AAAS, Am. Chem. Soc., Internat. Soc. Chem. Ecology, Phi Beta Kappa, Sigma Xi (pres. local chpt. 1994-95), Phi Kappa Phi. Presbyterian. Avocations: fishing, camping, hiking. Office: University of Alaska Coll Sci Engring & Math 358 Natural Scis Bldg Fairbanks AK 99775-5940

REICHART, STUART RICHARD, lawyer; b. N.Y.C., Nov. 18, 1924; s. Stanley and Rae (Wein) R.; m. Joan Feirtag, Mar. 28, 1981. LLB, Bklyn. Law Sch., 1948; LLM, NYU, 1951. Bar: N.Y. 1949, D.C. 1971, U.S. Supreme Ct. Adminstrv. judge Armed Services Bd. Contract Appeals, Washington, 1966-72; asst. gen. counsel for procurement USAF, Washington, 1972-75, dep. gen. counsel, 1975-78, gen. counsel, 1978-81; of counsel Fried, Frank, Harris, Shriver & Jacobson, Washington, 1982-90; ind. cons., 1991—; instr. govt. procurement Ohio State U., U. Dayton, U. Md., 1960-70. Contbr. legal articles on govt. procurement to profl. jours. Served with AUS, 1942-45; served to col. USAF, 1951-71. Decorated Legion of Merit, D.F.C., Air medal with silver oak leaf cluster, Purple Heart; recipient Disting. Civilian Service medals Dept. Air Force, 1979, Dept. Def., 1982, Stuart R. Reichart award USAF, 1982. Mem. ABA, Fed. Bar Assn. Lodge: Masons. Avocations: bridge, tennis, golf. Home and Office: 8000 Grand Teton Dr Potomac MD 20854-4074 also: 16873C Isle of Palm Dr Delray Beach FL 33484-6941

REICHBLUM, AUDREY ROSENTHAL, public relations executive; b. Pitts., June 28, 1935; d. Emanuel Nathan and Willa (Handmacher) Rosenthal; m. M. Charles Reichblum, Jan. 25, 1956; children: Robert Nathan, William Mark. Student, Bennington Coll., 1952-53; BS, Carnegie Mellon U., 1956. Accredited Pub. Rels. Soc. Pitts. Founder, creator, chmn. Pitts. Children's Mus., 1970-73; mag. writer Pitts. Mag., 1978; dir. pub. rels. Pitts. Pub. Theater, 1978-79; pres. arPR audrey reichblum PUB. RELS. inc., Pitts., 1980—; pub. rels. cons., bd. mem. Pitts. Planned Parenthood, 1980—, United Jewish Fedn., Bus. and Profl. Women, Pitts., 1980-85, Pitts. City Theater, 1985-94, Pa. Coun. on Aging, 1996—; chmn. Villa de Marillac Nursing. Recipient Gold Cindy award Info. Film Producers Am., 1982, award of excellence Internat. Assn. Bus. Communicators, Pitts., 1986, Matrix award Three Rivers Arts Festival, Lifetime Achievement award NAWBD-YWCA. Mem. Publ. Rels. Soc. Am. (award of merit 1983, G. Victor Barkman award for excellence 1984, 1st place award Race For The Cure), Women in Comm. (Matrix-sales promotion award 1987), Nat. Assn. Women Bus. Owners (Life Time Achievement award 1995), Exec. Women's Coun., Am. Women in Radio and TV, Am. Mktg. Assn., Rotary. Office: 1420 Centre Ave Ste 2216 Pittsburgh PA 15219-3528

REICHE, FRANK PERLEY, lawyer, former federal commissioner; b. Hartford, Conn., May 8, 1929; s. Karl Augustus and LaFetra (Perley) R.; m. Janet Taylor, Sept. 26, 1953; children: Cynthia Reiche Schumacker, Dean S. AB, Williams Coll., 1951; LLB, Columbia U., 1959; MA, George Washington U., 1959; LLM in Taxation, NYU, 1966. Bar: N.J. 1960, D.C. 1981. Assoc. Stryker, Tams & Dill, Newark, 1959-61; assoc. Smith, Stratton, Wise & Heher, Princeton, N.J., 1962-64, ptnr., 1964-79; commr. Fed. Election Commn., Washington, 1979-85; chmn. Fed. Election Commn., 1982; ptnr. Katzenbach, Gildea & Rudner, Lawrenceville, N.J., 1986-93; pvt. practice law Princeton, N.J., 1993-97; of counsel Schragger, Lorral & Nagy, West Trenton, N.J., 1997—. Trustee Westminster Choir Coll., Princeton, 1974-86, Ctr. Theol. Inquiry, Princeton, 1991-97, Wells Coll., Aurora, N.Y., 1994—; mem. planned giving com. Williams Coll., Williamstown, Mass., 1973-87, nat. chmn. planned giving, 1983-87. Lt. USN, 1952-56. Mem. ABA, D.C. Bar Assn., N.J. Bar Assn., Am. Coll. Trust and Estate Counsel (N.J. state chair 1995—). Republican. Presbyterian. Clubs: Washington Golf and Country, Capitol Hill.

REICHEK, JESSE, artist; b. Bklyn., Aug. 16, 1916; s. Morris and Celia (Bernstein) R.; m. Laure Guyot, May 16, 1950; children—Jonathan, Joshua. Student, Inst. Design, Chgo., 1941-42; diploma, Academie Julian, Paris, 1951. Instr. dept. architecture U. Mich., Ann Arbor, 1946-47; prof. Inst. Design Ill. Inst. Tech., Chgo., 1951-53; prof. dept. architecture U. Calif., Berkeley, 1953-87, prof. emeritus, 1987—; cons. Nat. Design Inst. Ford Found. project, Ahmedabad, India, 1963, San Francisco Redevel. Agy. Embarcadero Center, 1966—; lectr. Nat. Inst. Architects, Rome, 1960, U. Florence, 1960, U. Naples, 1960, Israel Inst. Tech., 1960, Greek Architects Soc., Athens, 1960, U. Belgrade, 1960, MIT, 1965, U. N.Mex., 1964, Am. Cultural Center, Paris, 1960, 64, Gujarat Inst. Engrs. and Architects, 1963, U. Colo., 1961, Harvard, 1962, U. Minn., 1962, U. Coll. London, 1967, Inst. Contemporary Arts, London, 1967, Ecole Nationale des Beaux-Arts, 1967; artist in residence Tamarind Lithography Workshop, 1966, Am. Acad. in Rome, 1971-72; research prof. Creative Arts Inst. U. Calif., 1966-67; artist in residence IBM Los Angeles Sci. Center, 1970-71. Exhibited one man shows at, Galerie Cahiers d'Art Paris, 1951, 59, 68, U. Calif. at Berkeley, 1954, Betty Parsons Gallery, N.Y.C., 1958, 59, 63, 65, 67, 69, 70, Molton Gallery, London, 1962, Am. Culture Center, Florence, Italy, 1962, Bennington Coll., 1963, U. N.Mex., 1966, U. So. Calif., 1967, Axiom Gallery, London, 1968, Yoseido Gallery, Tokyo, 1968, Los Angeles County Mus. Art, 1971; exhibited in group shows, Bklyn. Mus., 1959, Mus. Modern Art, N.Y.C., 1962, 65, 69, Knox-Albright Art Gallery, 1962, Art Inst. Chgo., 1963, Cin. Art Mus., 1966, Balt. Art Mus., 1966, Yale Art Gallery, 1967, Grand Palais, Paris, 1970, Nat. Mus. Art, Santiago, Chile, 1970, art and tech. exhibit, Los Angeles County Mus. Art, 1971, Maeght Found., St. Paul de Vence, France, 1971, Mus. Modern Art, Paris, 1971; represented in permanent collections, Mus. Modern Art, Art Inst. Chgo., Bibliotheque Nationale, Paris, Victoria & Albert Mus., London, Los Angeles County Art Mus., Grunwald Graphic Arts Found., U. Calif. at Los Angeles, San Diego Mus. Art, Amon Carter Mus., Fort Worth; Author: Jesse Reichek-Dessins, 1960, La Monte de la Nuit, 1961, Fontis, 1961, Etcetera, 1965, Le Bulletin Des Baux, 1972; e.g., 1976. Served to capt. C.E. AUS, 1942-46. Home: 5925 Red Hill Rd Petaluma CA 94952-9437

REICHEK, MORTON ARTHUR, retired magazine editor, writer; b. N.Y.C., Nov. 2, 1924; s. Meyer and Katherine (Rabinowitz) R.; m. Sybil Green, June 13, 1953; children: Amy, Marjorie (dec.), James. BS, NYU, 1948; postgrad., Am. U., 1948-50. Press officer, editor U.S. Fish & Wildlife Svc., Washington, 1948-49, U.S. Br. Labor Statistics, Washington, 1949-51, U.S. Nat. Prodn. Authority, Washington, 1951-52; Washington corr. McGraw-Hill Mags., 1952-63, Newhouse Newspapers, 1963-65; assoc. editor Forbes, N.Y.C., 1965-66; assoc. editor Bus. WeeK, N.Y.C., 1966-76, sr. editor, writer, 1978-88; dir. editorial svcs. Gulf & Western. Industries, Inc., N.Y.C., 1976-78; U.S. rep. NATO journalist program U.S. Dept. State, France, 1957; adj. lectr. Columbia U. Graduate Sch. Journalism, N.Y.C., 1981. Contbr. articles to N.Y. Times Mag., New Republic, others. Staff sgt. U.S. Army, 1943-46, China-Burma-India. Journalist fellow Carnegie-Mellon U. Grad. Sch. Indsl. Adminstrn., 1979; grantee NEH, 1980. Avocations: tennis, computers, music. Home: 1 Worchester Dr Cranbury NJ 08512-4723 Home (winter): 14388 Emerald Lake Dr Apt 1 Delray Beach FL 33446-3382

REICHEL, WALTER EMIL, advertising executive; b. Irvington, N.J., Dec. 12, 1935; s. Walter Edwin and Flora Maria (Pfister) R.; m. Priscilla Tedesco, Feb. 1, 1969; 1 son, Bradley Joseph. B.A., Columbia, 1959; M.A., N.Y. U., 1971, M. Philosophy, 1989, postgrad., 1989—. With Benton & Bowles, N.Y.C., 1959-67; v.p. Benton & Bowles, 1965-67, assoc. media dir., 1965-67; with Ted Bates & Co., Inc. N.Y.C., 1967-87; sr. v.p. Ted Bates & Co., Inc., N.Y.C., 1973-82; exec. dir. media and programs Ted Bates & Co., Inc., 1974-82, exec. v.p., 1982-87, dir.; cons., 1987-91; mng. ptnr. A.S. Link Inc., N.Y.C., 1991—. Mem. Advt. Rsch. Found. Home: 449 1/2 Henry St Brooklyn NY 11231-3011 Office: 100 Avenue Of The Americas New York NY 10013-1689

REICHENTHAL, JAY JEFFREY, health facility administrator; b. N.Y.C., Feb. 12, 1943; s. Abraham and Frieda (Hirshberg) R.; m. Marilyn Solodky; 1 child, David. Student, Calif. State U., Northridge. Dir. gen. med. and surg. svcs. Cedars-Sinai Med. Ctr., L.A., 1975—. Campaign cabinet United Way, L.A., 1986—. Sgt. U.S. Army, 1963-68. Mem. Am. Coll. Healthcare Execs. Avocation: auto racing. Office: Cedars Sinai Med Ctr 8700 Beverly Blvd Los Angeles CA 90048-1804

REICHERT, DAVID, lawyer; b. Cin., Nov. 23, 1929; s. Victor E. and Louise F. (Feibel) R.; m. Marilyn Frankel, May 31, 1959; children—James G., Steven F., William M. B.A., Bowling Green State U., 1951; J.D., U. Cin., 1954. Bar: Ohio 1954, U.S. Supreme Ct. 1963. Ptnr. firm Porter, Wright, Morris & Arthur, formerly sr. ptnr. Reichert, Strauss & Reed and predecessors, Cin.; dir. numerous corps. Monthly columnist: Scrap Age mag, 1966-74; bd. editors: U. Cin. Law Rev, 1953-54. Pres. brotherhood Rockdale Temple, Cin., 1960-61, temple treas., 1973-75, v.p., 1975-79, pres., 1979-81; mem. Amberley Village Planning Comm. & Zoning Bd. Appeals, 1972-79, Ohio Solid Waste Adv. Group, 1974; treas. Contemporary Arts Ctr., Cin., 1973-75, pres., 1976-77, trustee, 1982-88; trustee Cin. Art Mus., 1978-93, v.p., 1992-93, chmn. vis. com. for contemporary art, 1990-92; trustee Jewish Publ. Soc., 1980-86, Cin. Sculpture Coun., 1984-87; mem. acquisitions com. Miami U. Art Mus., 1982-85. Mem. Cin. Print and Drawing Cir. (pres. 1974-76), The Literary Club (sec. 1988-91, v.p. 1991-92, pres. 1992-93), Losantiville Country Club (bd. govs. 1985-92, sec. 1986-90, pres. 1990-92), Omicron Delta Kappa, Sigma Tau Delta, Phi Delta Phi, Zeta Beta Tau. Office: Porter Wright Morris & Arthur 250 E 5th St Ste 2200 Cincinnati OH 45202-5117

REICHERT, JACK FRANK, manufacturing company executive; b. West Allis, Wis., Sept. 27, 1930; s. Arthur Andrew and Emily Bertha (Wallinger) R.; m. Corrine Violet Helf, Apr. 5, 1952; children: Susan Marie, John Arthur. Cert. mktg., U. Wis., Milw., 1957; AMP, Harvard U., 1970; LLD (hon.), Marian Coll., 1994. Various mktg. positions GE, 1948-57; with Brunswick Corp., Lake Forest, Ill., 1957-95; pres. Mercury Marine div. Brunswick Corp., 1972-77; corp. v.p. Brunswick Corp., Lake Forest, 1974-77, group v.p. Marine Power Group, 1974-77, pres., COO, 1977-93; CEO Brunswick Corp., 1982-95; chmn. bd. dirs. Brunswick Corp., Lake Forest, Ill., 1983-95; dir. Brunswick Corp., 1977—; bd. dirs. The Viad Corp., Phoenix; dir. Strike Ten Entertainment, Inc. Trustee Carroll Coll., Waukesha, Wis., 1972; indsl. chmn. Fond du Lac United Fund, 1977. With C.E. U.S. Army, 1951-53. Named Disting. Alumnus of the Yr., U. Wis., Milw. 1979, Top Chief Exec. Officer in Multi-Industry Group, Fin. World Mag., 1984; recipient Gold award in leisure industry Wall St. Transcript, 1983, 86, Bronze award in multi-industry category Wall St. Transcript, 1985, Leisure Industry Silver award, 1988. Mem. Am. Mgmt. Assn., U. Wis.-Milw. Alumni Assn., Knollwood Club, Harvard Club, Mid-Am. Club, Profl. Bowlers Assn. (dir.), Beta Gamma Sigma (hon.). Presbyterian. Avocations: golf, reading. Home: 580 Douglas Dr Lake Forest IL 60045-3342 Office: Brunswick Corp 1 N Field Ct Lake Forest IL 60045-4810 *To meet with any success, one must have a sense of urgency to get things done.*

REICHERT, LEO EDMUND, JR., biochemist, endocrinologist; b. N.Y.C., Jan. 9, 1932; s. Leo and Anne (Holsten) R.; m. Gerda Sihler, July 20, 1957; children: Leo, Christine, Linda, Andrew. B.S., Manhattan Coll., N.Y.C., 1955; Ph.D., Loyola U., Chgo., 1960. Asst. prof. biochemistry Emory U. Med. Sch., Atlanta, 1960-66; assoc. prof. Emory U. Med. Sch., 1966-72, prof., 1972-79; prof., chmn. dept. biochemistry Albany (N.Y.) Med. Coll., 1979-88, prof. biochemistry and molecular biology, 1988—; dir. human and animal hormone isolation and distbn. program (NIH), Emory U. Med. Sch., 1960-85; mem. med. adv. bd. Nat. Pituitary Agy., 1971-74; com. on glycoprotein hormones Nat. Hormone and Pituitary Program, 1968-86; mem. reproductive biology study sect. NIH, 1971-75; mem. adv. panel on cellular physiology NSF, 1983-86, div. of integrative and neuro biology, 1992; mem. WHO Expert Adv. Panel on Biol. Standardization, 1984—, Nat. Bd. Med. Examiners, Part I, 1989-91. Mem. editl. bd. Endocrinology, 1967-75, Molecular and Cellular Endocrinology, 1977-83, 90-94, Biology of Reproduction, 1968-70, 86-90, Andrology, 1983-86, Molecular Andrology, 1989—; contbr. more than 275 articles to profl. jours.; patentee in field. Served with USMC, 1950-52. List among 75 endocrinologists, 1000 scientists most cited, 1965-78. Mem. AAAS, Am. Soc. Biol. Chemists, Endocrine Soc. (Ayerst award 1970), Andrology Soc. (coun. 1983-87), Soc. for Study of Reprodn. Home: 10 Laurel Dr Albany NY 12211-1618 Office: Albany Med Coll Dept Biochemistry Albany NY 12208

REICHERT, MARLENE JOY, secondary school educator; b. Davao City, Philippines, Nov. 29, 1957; d. Jacob and Lois Marie Bouw; m. David Julius Reichert, June 13, 1981 (June 23, 1991). BA in English, Nyack Coll., 1980; postgrad., St. Thomas Aquinas, 1987-88. Cert. tchr., N.Y., N.J. Tchr. St. Anne's Sch., Yonkers, N.Y., 1988-89; substitute tchr. Rockland County Pub. Schs., 1989-91; tchr. BOCES Night High Schs., West Nyack, N.Y., 1989-92, John Peter Tetard Mid. Sch. 143, Bronx, N.Y., 1991—; instr. after sch. program Achieving Success, 1992-94. Contbr. short story to profl. publ. Democrat. Episcopalian. Avocations: writing, gardening. Home: 114 Depot Pl Nyack NY 10960-4426 Office: John Peter Tetard Int Sch 120 W 231st St Bronx NY 10463-5905

REICHERT, NORMAN VERNON, financial services consultant; b. Berwyn, Ill., Apr. 17, 1921; s. John G. and Valeria (Hoffman) R.; m. Wilma Eleanor Catey, Feb. 5, 1944; children: Susan, Norman Vernon. BS, Northwestern U., 1943; MBA, Harvard Bus. Sch., 1944. CPA, Ill. Acct. Arthur Young & Co., Chgo., 1946-50; central fin. staff, controller styling div. Ford Motor Co., Dearborn, Mich., 1950-61; treas. Philco Ford Corp., Phila., 1961-69; asst. treas. United Air Lines, Inc., Chgo., 1969-72; v.p. fin. Trailer Train Co., Railbox Co., Railgon Co., Chgo., 1972-83; v.p. fin., treas. U.S. Windpower, Inc., San Francisco, 1983-86; pres. Blackhawk Fin., 1986—. Served to lt. USNR, 1943-46. Mem. AICPA, Fin. Execs. Inst., Navy League U.S., Exptl. Aircraft Assn., Union League Chgo., Knollwood Club (Lake Forest), Olympic Club San Francisco, Beta Alpha Psi, Sigma Alpha Epsilon. Home and Office: 921 Grandview Ln Lake Forest IL 60045-3913 *Each day we must start over. One cannot live on yesterday's accomplishments, but instead, must establish new goals. Last year's champion is soon forgotten as we focus on the current achiever. This is the way I try to approach each new day. And, at the end of each day, I evaluate my performance against my goals for that day.*

REICHGOTT JUNGE, EMBER D., state legislator, lawyer; b. Detroit, Aug. 22, 1953; d. Norbert Arnold and Diane (Pincich) R.; m. Michael Junge. BA summa cum laude, St. Olaf Coll., Minn., 1974; JD, Duke U., 1977; MBA, U. of St. Thomas, 1991. Bar: Minn. 1977, D.C. 1978. Assoc., Larkin, Hoffman, Daly & Lindgren, Bloomington, Minn., 1977-84; counsel Control Data Corp., Bloomington, Minn., 1984-86; atty. The Gen. Counsel, Ltd., 1987—; mem. Minn. State Senate, 1983—, chmn. legis. com. on econ. status of women, 1984-86, vice chmn. senate edn. com., 1987-88, senate majority whip, 1990-94, chmn. property tax div. senate tax com., 1991-92, chmn. senate judiciary com., 1993-94; senate asst. majority leader, 1995—, chmn. spl. subcom. on Ethical Conduct; instr. polit. sci. St. Olaf. Coll., Northfield, Minn., 1993; dir. Citizens Ind. Bank, St. Louis Park, Minn., 1993—. Host (cable TV monthly series) Legis. Report, 1985-92. Trustee, bd. dirs. N.W. YMCA, New Hope, Minn., 1983-88; Greater Mpls. Red Cross, 1988—, United Way Mpls., 1989—. Youngest woman ever elected to Minn. State Senate, 1983; recipient Woman of Yr. award North Hennepin Bus. and Prof. Women, 1983, Award for Contbn. to Human Svcs., Minn. Social Svcs. Assn., 1983, Clean Air award Minn. Lung Assn., 1988, Disting. Svc. award Mpls. Jaycees, 1984, Minn. Dept. Human Rights award, 1989,

Myra Bradwell award Minn. Women Lawyers, 1993, Disting. Alumnae award Lake Conf. Schs., 1993; named One of Ten Outstanding Young Minnesotans, Minn. Jaycees, 1984, Policy Advocate of Yr. NAWBO, 1988, Woman of Achievement Twin West C. of C., 1989, Marvelous Minn. Woman, 1993. Mem. Minn. Bar Assn. (bd. govs. 1992-96, Pro Bono Publico Atty. award 1990), Hennepin County Bar Assn., Corporate Counsel Assn. (v.p. 1989-96), Minn. Dem. Farmer-Labor Party (state co-chair Clinton/Gore Presdl. Campaign 1992, 96, del. nat. Dem. conv. 1984, 92, 96). Home: 7701 48th Ave N Minneapolis MN 55428-4515

REICHL, RUTH MOLLY, restaurant critic; b. N.Y.C., Jan. 16, 1948; d. Ernst and Miriam and (Brudno) R.; m. Douglas Wilder Hollis, Sept. 5, 1970 (div. 1985); married. BA, U. Mich., 1968, MA in History of Art, 1970. Chef, owner The Swallow Restaurant, Berkeley, Calif., 1973-77; food writer, editor New West mag., San Francisco, 1978-84; editor restaurant column L.A. Times, 1984-93, food editor, 1990-93; restaurant critic N.Y. Times, 1993—. Author: Mmmm: A Feastiary, 1972, The Contest Book, 1977; contbr. articles to profl. jours. Office: NY Times 229 W 43rd St New York NY 10036-3913

REICHLIN, SEYMOUR, physician, educator; b. N.Y.C., May 31, 1924; s. Henry and Celia (Rosen) R.; m. Elinor Thurman Dameshek, June 24, 1951; children: Seth David, Douglas James, Ann Elise. Student, CCNY, 1940-41; AB, Antioch Coll., 1945; MD, Washington U., St. Louis, 1948; PhD, U. London, 1954. Intern N.Y. Hosp., 1948-49; asst. resident Barnes Hosp., St. Louis, 1949-50, N.Y. Hosp., 1950-51; chief resident Barnes Hosp., 1951-52; research fellow physiology dept. Maudsley Hosp., London, Eng., 1952-54; instr. psychiatry Washington U., 1954-55, asst. prof. psychiatry and medicine, 1955-60; pvt. practice clin. endocrinology, St. Louis, 1955-60, Rochester, 1961-69, Hartford, Conn., 1969-71, Boston, 1972—; asso. prof. medicine U. Rochester, 1960-66, prof., 1966-69; prof., head dept. med. and pediatric spltys. Sch. Medicine U. Conn., 1969-71, prof., head dept. physiology, 1971-72; prof. medicine Tufts U., 1972-96; rsch. prof. U. Ariz., 1994—; sr. physician New Eng. Med. Ctr., 1972-93, sr. endocrinologist, 1993-96; cons. Genesee and Rochester Gen. Hosp., 1960-69, Hartford Hosp., 1970—, New Britain (Conn.) Gen. Hosp., 1970-72; mem. endocrinology study sect. HIH, 1966-70; mem. adv. panel FDA, 1977-79; mem. coun. Nat. Inst. Kidney, Diabetes, Digestive Diseases, 1987-90. Mem. editl. bd. Endocrinology, 1969-74, New Eng. Jour. Medicine, 1976-79, Jour. Psychoneuroendocrinology, 1979—, Brain, Brhavior and Immunity, 1990—; contbr. articles to profl. jours., also monographs. Bd. dirs. Founds. Fund, New Haven, 1968-70; med. adv. bd. Med. Found., Boston, adv. bd. MacArthur Found., 1988. Served with AUS, 1943-44. Commonwealth Fund fellow, 1952-54, Lowell M. Palmer fellow, 1954-56. Master ACP; fellow AAAS, Am. Acad. Arts and Scis.; mem. Ctrl. Soc. Clin. Rsch., Am. Soc. Clin. Investigation, Assn. Am. Physicians, Am. Physiol. Soc., Endocrine Soc. (Eli Lilly award 1972, pres. 1975-76), Brit. Soc. Endocrinology, Am. Psychosomatic Soc., Am. Thyroid Assn., Internat. Brain Orgn., Assn. for Rsch. in Nervous and Mental Disease (pres. 1976), Pituitary Soc. (pres. 1994-95), Alpha Omega Alpha. Home: X-9 Ranch Vail AZ 85641 also: U Ariz Coll Medicine Tucson AZ 85724

REICHMAN, FREDRICK THOMAS, artist; b. Bellingham, Wash., Jan. 28, 1925; s. Frederick and Ilma Lucia (Yearing) R.; m. Michela Madelene Robbins, Sept. 24, 1955; children: Alexandra Ilma, Matthew Nathaniel. BA cum laude, U. Calif., Berkeley, 1950, MA in Art, 1952; postgrad., San Francisco Art Inst., 1946-47. Instr. art San Francisco Art Inst., 1952, U. Calif., Davis, 1963-66, Dominican Coll., San Rafael, Calif., summer 1974, Calif. Coll. Arts and Crafts, Oakland, 1976, U. Calif. extension, San Francisco, 1966—; lectr. U. Calif., Berkeley, 1953; dir. children's art classes Jr. Center Art and Sci., Oakland, 1953-64, 66-77. One-man exhbns. include Rose Rabow Galleries, San Francisco, 1958, 61, 63, 65, 69, 73, 75, San Francisco Mus. Modern Art, 1969, Benson Gallery, Bridgehampton, N.Y., 1966-72, Silvan Simone Gallery, L.A., 1971-73, Santa Barbara (Calif.) Mus. Art, 1974, Rose Rabow Galleries-James Willis Gallery, San Francisco, 1976, Gallery Paule Anglim, San Francisco, 1979-81, Chikyudo Gallery, Tokyo, 1980, Espace Doyoo, Tokyo, 1982, Ki-Do-Ai-Raku, Tokyo, 1982, Maeitetsu-Marukoshi, Kanazawa, Japan, 1982, The New Gallery, Taos, N.Mex., 1982, Charles Campbell Gallery, San Francisco, 1984, 86, David Barnett Gallery, Milw., 1985, 89, Artform Gallery, 1985, The New Gallery, Houston, 1985, Mekler Gallery Inc., L.A., 1988, Ruth Siegel Gallery, N.Y., 1991, U. Calif., Santa Cruz, Ann Porter Sesnon Art Gallery, 1991, Galerie B. Haasner, Germany, 1990, 92, 94, 96, Harcourts Contemporary, San Francisco, 1992, 95, Louis Newman Galleries, Beverly Hills, Calif., 1992, 93, 94, Horwitch Newman Gallery, Scottsdale, 1995; 2-man show, Iannetti-Lanzone Gallery, San Francisco, 1989, Miyagi Mus. Art, Sendai, Japan, 1982, R.B. Stevenson Gallery, La Jolla, 1995; 3-man show, Milw. Art Mus., 1982, group exhbns. include, Esther Robles Gallery, L.A., 1961, Whitney Mus. Am. Art traveling exhbn., 1962-63, Expo '70, Osaka, Japan, 1970, Oakland Mus., 1971, Joslyn Art Mus. traveling exhbn., 1973-74, San Francisco Mus. Modern Art, 1974, Martha Jackson Gallery, N.Y.C., 1978, New Gallery, 1981, Forum Gallery, N.Y.C., 1984, Smith Andersen Gallery, Palo Alto, 1986, Ruth Siegel Gallery, N.Y.C., 1986, Kultorvert Galerie, Copenhagen, 1986, Richmond (Calif.) Art Ctr., 1987, Nat. Mus. Am. Art, Washington, 1989, Arte 7, San Francisco, 1990, Harcourts Contemporary, San Francisco, 1991, Kouros Gallery, N.Y.C., 1993, Berkeley Art Ctr., 1993, Estudio Moyo Coyatzin, San Jose, Costa Rica; represented in permanent collections throughout U.S., including Nat. Mus. Am. Art, San Francisco Mus. Modern Art, Oakland Mus., Univ. Art Mus., Berkeley, Santa Barbara Mus. Art, Milw. Art Mus., Ulrich Mus. Art, Stanford U. Mus., Wichita, Fine Arts Museums San Francisco, Okla. Art Center, Oklahoma City, Bank Am. World Hdqrs., San Francisco, Achenbach Found., San Francisco, Mills Coll. Art Gallery, Oakland, U. Calif., San Francisco; works rep. art publs.; commns. include stage set for, San Francisco Mime Troupe, The Exception to the Rule, 1965; mural, Boche Pediatrics Outpatient Clinic, Stanford U. Med. Sch., 1961, San Francisco Civic Center, 1968. Served with USNR, 1943-45. Recipient Purchase prize San Francisco Art Festival, 1964, One-Man Show award, 1968; Irving prize Am. Wit and Humor U. Calif., Berkeley, 1951; Taussig traveling fellow U. Calif., Berkeley, 1952; profiled in 50 West Coast Artists by Henry Hopkins, 1981, Art in the San Francisco Bay Area 1945-80 by Thomas Albright, 1985. *There is a unique energy that exists on the Pacific Coast. It is different from our eastern seaboard, different from Europe and the Orient—yet it comes out of all these sources to create inspiration and fresh insights. The light and the land, the atmosphere that exist here, have their own particular ambience. I feel a part of this energy.*

REICHMAN, JOEL H., retail executive. With The GAP, San Francisco, 1971-76, Slak Shak Inc., Boston, 1971-76; with Designs, Inc., 1976—, exec. v.p., 1985-93, dir., 1987; pres., COO Designs, Inc., Chestnut Hill, Mass., 1993-94; pres., CEO, 1994—. Office: Designs Inc 66 B St Needham MA 02194-2702

REICHMAN, LEE BRODERSOHN, physician; b. N.Y.C., June 25, 1938; s. Theodore and Elinore (Brodersohn) R.; m. Rose Ehrinpreis, Oct. 9, 1965; children: Daniel Mark, Deborah Gar. AB, Oberlin Coll., 1960; MD, NYU, 1964; MPH, Johns Hopkins U., 1971. Intern Bellevue Hosp., I Med. Divsn., N.Y.C., 1964-65, resident, 1967-68; resident Harlem Hosp. Ctr., N.Y.C., 1968-69; fellow in pulmonary medicine Harlem Hosp. Ctr., 1969-70; dir. Bur. Tb, Bur. Chronic Disease, N.Y.C. Health Dept., 1971-73, asst. commr. health, 1973-74; assoc. prof. medicine N.J. Med. Sch., Newark, 1974-78, prof. medicine, 1978—, prof. medicine cmty. health, 1993—; dir. pulmonary div. U. Medicine and Dentistry N.J.-N.J. Med. Sch. Univ. Hosp., 1974-92; exec. dir. N.J. Med. Sch. Nat. Tuberculosis Ctr., 1993—; cons. CDC, Atlanta, 1970—; prin. investigator pulmonary complications of HIV Infection, Nat. Heart Lung Blood Inst., 1987-95, Model TB Ctr. for Disease Control and Prevention, 1993—, Nat. Rsch. Consortium (CDC), 1994—. Contbr. articles to profl. jours. Bd. dirs. Art Ctr. No. N.J., 1979-86; chmn. N.J. Commn. on Smoking of Health, 1986-87; mem. N.J. TB Adv. Coun., 1976—, chmn. 1991-93; chair Nat. Coalition for Elemination of Tuberculosis, 1992—; mem. N.J. Clean Air Coun., 1987. With USPHS, 1965-67. Recipient Nat. Heart Lung and Blood Inst., Pulmonary Acad. career award, 1975-80, Preventive Pulmonary Acad. career award, 1987-92, Tb Acad. career award, 1993—. Fellow ACP, Am. Coll. Chest Physicians (gov. 1984-90, pres. N.J. chpt. 1982-84), Acad. Medicine of N.J.; mem. Am. Thoracic Soc., Internat. Union Against Tb and Lung Disease (exec. com. 1982-92, vice chair exec. com. 1989-91), Am. Lung Assn. (nat. bd. dirs. 1980-94, pres.-elect 1991-92, pres. 1992-93, past pres. 1993-94), N.J. Thoracic Soc. (pres. 1982-84), Am. Lung Assn. N.J. (bd. dirs. 1976—, pres. 1984-86). Office: 65 Bergen St Ste Gbl Newark NJ 07107-3001

REICHMAN, NANCI SATIN, oil company owner; b. Tulsa, July 7, 1939; d. Jack Harold and Tybie Mary (Davis) Satin; m. Louis Reichman, Dec. 25, 1960 (dec. Feb. 1972); children: David Michael, Jill Satin; life ptnr. Phillip M. Citrin. Student, Sarah Lawrence Coll., Bronxville, N.Y., 1957-59; cert. Jungian psychology, C.G. Jung Inst., Evanston, Ill., 1988. Fashion model Miss Jackson's, Tulsa, 1969-70; pres. LIR Investments, Tulsa, 1972-78; pres., dir. devel. Tymar Oil Co., Tulsa and Santa Fe, N.Mex., 1990—; owner ind. oil prodn. Chgo., 1972—; audio tape lectr for various workshops. Pres. C.G. Jung Inst., Evanston, Ill., 1980-81, 81-82, 84-85, also mem. adv. bd.; v.p. Tulsa Jr. Philharm., 1968; sec. Tulsa Ballet, 1968; mem. Women's Forum N.Mex., 1996—; bd. dirs. Found. Santa Fe Cmty. Coll., 1995—. Avocations: poetry writing, travel, reading, philanthropy. Home: 653 Canyon Rd # 4 Santa Fe NM 87501

REICHMANIS, ELSA, chemist; b. Melbourne, Victoria, Australia, Dec. 9, 1953; came to U.S., 1962; d. Peteris and Nina (Meiers) R.; m. Francis Joseph Purcell, June 2, 1979; children: Patrick William, Elizabeth Anne, Edward Andrew, Thomas Alexander. BS in Chemistry, Syracuse U., 1972, PhD in Chemistry, 1975. Postdoctoral intern Syracuse (N.Y.) U., 1975-76, Chaim Weizmann rsch. fellow, 1976-78; mem. tech. staff AT&T Bell Labs., Murray Hill, N.J., 1978-84, supr. radiation sensitive materials and applications, 1984-94, head organic and polymer materials, 1994-95; head polymer and organic materials Lucent Techs., Bell Labs., New Providence, N.J., 1996—; mem. panel on advanced materials. Japanese Tech. Evaluation Prog., NSF, Washington, 1986, mem. com. to survey materials. rsch. opportunities and needs for electronic industry, Nat. Rsch. Coun., 1986, Nat. Materials Adv. Bd., 1993—. Editor: The Effects of Radiation on High Tech Polymers, 1989, Polymers in Microlithography, 1989, Irradiation of Polymer Materials, 1993, Microelectronics Technology: Polymers for Advanced Imaging and Packaging, 1995; patentee in field; assoc. editor Chemistry of Materials, 1996—; contbr. numerous articles to profl. jours. Recipient Soc. of Women Engrs. Achievement award, 1993, Engring. Materials award ASM, 1996. Mem. AAAS, Nat. Acad. Engring. (elected mem.), Am. Chem. Soc. (mem.-at-large 1986-90, sec. 1991-92, vice chair 1993, chair-elect 1994, chair 1995, polymer materials sci. and engring divsn. 1991—), Soc. for Photo-optical Engrs. Avocations: music, reading, needlepoint.

REICIN, RONALD IAN, lawyer; b. Chgo., Dec. 11, 1942; s. Frank Edward and Abranita (Rome) R.; m. Alyta Friedland, May 23, 1965; children—Eric, Kael. B.B.A., U. Mich., 1964, M.B.A., 1967, J.D. cum laude, 1967. Bar: Ill. 1967, U.S. Tax Ct. 1967; CPA, Ill. Mem. staff Price Waterhouse & Co., Chgo., 1966; ptnr. Jenner & Block, Chgo., 1967—. Bd. dirs. Nat. Kidney Found., Ill., 1978—, v.p., 1992-95, pres., 1995—; bd. dirs. Ruth Page Found., 1985—, v.p., 1990—; bd. dirs. Scoliosis Assn. Chgo., 1981-90, Kohl Children's Mus., 1991-95. Mem. Chgo. Bar Assn., Internat. Conf. Shopping Ctrs., ABA, Ill. Bar Assn., Chgo. Mortgage Attys. Assn., Phi Kappa Phi, Beta Gamma Sigma, Beta Alpha Psi. Clubs: Executive, Legal (Chgo.). Office: Jenner & Block 1 E Ibm Plz Fl 41 Chicago IL 60611-3586

REID, ANTONIO (L. A. REID), musician, songwriter. With musical group The Deele; songwriter with Kenny Edmonds, also occasionally with Darryl Simmons. Songs include Girlfriend, 1987, Rock Steady, 1987, Two Occasions, 1987, Don't Be Cruel, 1988, Love Saw It, 1988, Lover In Me, 1988, Every Little Step, 1988 (Grammy award nomination for R&B Song of Yr. 1989), Dial My Heart, 1988, Way You Love Me, 1988, Secret Rendezvous, 1988, Superwoman, 1988, Roses Are Red, 1988, Can't Stop, 1989, My Kinda Girl, 1989, It's No Crime, 1989, On Our Own, 1989, Ready or Not, 1989, Tender Lover, 1989, Giving You the Benefit, 1990, I'm Your Baby Tonight, 1990, Shock Dat Monkey, 1992, End of the Road, 1996. Office: Sony Music Entertainment Inc Epic Records 550 Madison Ave New York NY 10022-3211*

REID, BELMONT MERVYN, brokerage house executive; b. San Jose, Calif., May 17, 1927; s. C. Belmont and Mary Irene (Kilfoyl) R. BS in Engring., San Jose State U., 1950, postgrad.; m. Evangeline Joan Rogers, June 1, 1952. Pres., Lifetime Realty Corp., San Jose, 1969-77, Lifetime Fin. Planning Corp., San Jose, 1967-77; founder, chmn. bd. Belmont Reid & Co., Inc., San Jose, 1960-77; pres., registered investment advisor JOBEL Fin. Inc., Carson City, Nev., 1980—; pres., chmn. bd. Data-West Systems, Inc., 1984-85. County chmn. 1982-85, Carson City Rep. Cen. Com., treas., 1979-81; chmn. Carson City Gen. Obligation Bond Commn., 1986—; rural county chmn. Nev. Rep. Cen. Com., 1984-88; mem. Carson City Charter Rev. Com., 1986-91, chmn., 1988-91. With USN, 1945-46, 51-55. Decorated Air medals. Mem. Nat. Assn. Securities Dealers, Mcpl. Securities Rulemaking Bd., Carson City C. of C. (pres. 1986-87, bd. dir. 1982-88), Capital Club of Carson City, Rotary (rsch. sec. 1983-84, 86-87, pres. 1988-89, Paul Harris fellow). Home: 610 Bonanza Dr Carson City NV 89706-0201 Office: 711 E Washington St Carson City NV 89701-4063

REID, CHARLES ADAMS, III, lawyer; b. Plainfield, N.J., Apr. 21, 1947; s. Charles Adams Jr. and Gertrude C. (Egan) R.; m. Teresa Keenan, May 11, 1974. BA, Colgate U., 1969; JD, Columbia U., 1974. Bar: N.Y. 1974, U.S. Dist. Ct. (ea. and so. dists.) N.Y. 1975, U.S. Dist. Ct. N.J. 1976, U.S. Ct. Appeals (3d cir.) 1983, U.S. Ct. Appeals (fed. cir.) 1989, U.S. Ct. Appeals (2d cir.) 1991. Law clk. to hon. John R. Bartels U.S. Dist. Ct. (ea. dist.) N.Y., Bklyn., 1974-75; assoc. Coudert Bros., N.Y.C., 1975-77, Shanley & Fisher, Newark, 1977-82; ptnr. Shanley & Fisher, Newark and Morristown, N.J., 1983—. Mem. planning bd. Peapack-Gladstone, N.J., 1984-88, chmn., 1987-88; bd. dirs. Morris Ctr. YMCA, Cedar Knolls, N.J., 1986-93. Served with U.S. Army, 1970-72, Vietnam. Mem. ABA (litigation sect.), N.J. Bar Assn., Morris County Bar Assn., Essex County Bar Assn., Morristown Club, Park Avenue Club (Florham Park). Home: PO Box 398 Gladstone NJ 07934-0398 Office: Shanley & Fisher PC 131 Madison Ave Morristown NJ 07960-6086

REID, CHARLES MURRY, insurance company executive. CEO, pres. United Guaranty Corp., Greensboro, N.C., 1987—. Office: United Guaranty Corp 230 N Elm St Greensboro NC 27401-2436

REID, CHARLES PHILLIP PATRICK, academic administrator, researcher, educator; b. Columbia, Mo., Jan. 8, 1940; s. Charles Henry and Fern Elnora (Chorlton) R.; m. Miriam Davis, July 17, 1961; children: Clayton Patrick, Miriam. BSF, U. Mo., 1961; MF, Duke U., 1966, PhD, 1968. Asst. prof. dept. forest and wood scis. Colo. State U., Ft. Collins, 1969-73, assoc. prof. dept. forest and wood scis., 1973-77, prof. dept. forest and wood scis., 1977-86; prof., chmn. dept. forestry U. Fla., Gainesville, 1986-92, interim dir. Sch. Forest Resources and Conservation, 1991-92; prof., dir. Sch. Renewable Natural Resources U. Ariz., Tucson, 1992—; vis. faculty mem. dept. botany Sheffield (Eng.) U., fall 1973; vis. scientist div. of soils Commonwealth Sci. and Indsl. Rsch. Orgn., Glen Osmond, South Australia, 1976-77; sr. Fulbright fellow dept. microbiology U. Innsbruck, Austria, 1985-86; chmn. working group on root physiology and symbiosis Internat. Union Forestry Rsch. Orgns., 1984-88. Contbr. articles to profl. jours. Copres. Barton Elem. Parent Tchr. Orgn., Ft. Collins, 1979-80; bd. dirs. Vol. Clearing House, Ft. Collins, 1974-76, Fla. 4-H Found., Gainesville, 1988-89. Lt. (j.g.) USNR, 1961-64, comdr. USNR, ret. Mem. AAAS, Ecol. Soc. Am., Soc. Am. Foresters, Nat. Assn. Profl. Forestry Schs. and Colls. (exec. com. 1994—), Sertoma (treas., bd. dirs. Ft. Collins chpt. 1972-75), Rotary. Republican. Episcopalian. Office: U Ariz Sch Renewable Natural Resources Bioscience East Tucson AZ 85721

REID, CLARICE DELORES, physician; b. Birmingham, Ala., Nov. 21, 1931; d. Noah Edgar, Sr., and Willie Mae (Brown) Wills; m. Arthur Joseph Reid, Jr., June 11, 1955; children: Kevin, Sheila, Jill, Clarice A. BS, Talladega Coll., 1952; cert. and Degree Med. Tech., Meharry Med. Coll., 1954; MD, U. Cin., 1959. Med. technologist Jewish Hosp., Cin., 1954-55, 57-59; intern, Jewish Hosp., Cin., 1959-60; resident, Jewish Hosp. and Children's Hosp., Cin., 1960-62; practice medicine specializing in pediatrice, Cin., 1962-68; dir. pediatric edn. Jewish Hosp., Cin., 1968-69, chmn. dept. pediatrics, 1969-70; dep. dir. sickle cell disease, USPHS, Rockville, Md., 1973-76; chief sickle cell disease NIH, Bethesda, Md., 1976-94, dir. divsn. blood disease and resources; nat. coordinator sickle cell disease program, 1994—; med. cons. USPHS, Rockville, 1971-73. Contbr. chpts. to books; editor proceedings, 1977. Named Outstanding Student, Meharry Med. Coll., 1954, Pres.' award, 1980; recipient NIH Dir.'s award, 1979, Pres. Meritorious Exec. award, 1991; charter mem. sr. Exec. Service, 1979. Mem. Acad. Pediatrics, Nat. Med. Assn., Am. Soc. Hematology. Roman Catholic. Club: Links. Home: 9715 Fernwood Rd Bethesda MD 20817-1554 Office: DHHS Nat Heart Lung & Blood Inst Blood Diseases and Resources 6701 Rockledge Dr Bethesda MD 20817-1813

REID, DANIEL JAMES, public relations executive; b. Grand Rapids, Mich., Sept. 7, 1960; s. Robert Alexander and Janette Helen (Hickey) R.; m. Meredith Christine Ryan, Apr. 30, 1994; 1 child, Ryan Paul. BA, Mich. State U., 1983. Sr. account exec. Burson-Marsteller, Chgo., 1983-88; group dir. Ogilvy & Mather, Chgo., 1988-90; sr. ptnr., nat. dir. Fin. Rels. Bd., Inc., Chgo., 1990—; prodr. Stas. WLAV-WTWN, Grand Rapids, 1980-81. Contbr. articles to profl. publs. and newspapers. Recipient Bronze Anvil award Pub. Rels. Soc. Am., 1984, creative excellence award U.S. Film Festival, 1984, 87, gold award Fin. World mag., 1990-94, numerous others. Mem. Nat. Investor Rels. Inst., Union League Club Chgo. Republican. Roman Catholic. Office: Fin Rels Bd Inc 875 N Michigan Ave Chicago IL 60611-1803

REID, DAVID, Olympic athlete; b. Phila., Sept. 17, 1973. Winner U.S. Jr. Championships, 1991, U.S. Olympic Festival, 1993, U.S. Championships, 1994, 96, U.S. Olympic Festival, 1995, Pan Am. Trials, 1995; recipient Gold medal 156 pound boxing divsn. Atlanta Olympics, 1996. Office: USA Boxing One Olympic Plz Colorado Springs CO 80909

REID, DAVID EVANS, pipeline company executive; b. St. Thomas, Ont., Can., Jan. 10, 1943; s. Murray Reid and Betty Evans; m. Nancy Blake, Dec. 6, 1969; children: Lindsay, Graeme. BSc with honors, Queen's U., Kingston, Ont., 1965; MASc, Toronto (Ont.) U., 1967. Registered profl. engr., Ont., Alta. Various positions in head and field offices TransCanada PipeLines, Toronto and Winnipeg, Man., 1967-89; v.p. ops. TransCanada PipeLines, Toronto, 1989-90; v.p. for engring. TransCanada PipeLines, Calgary, Alta., 1990—. Mem. Assn. Profl. Engrs. in Province Ont., Assn. Profl. Engrs., Geologists and Geophysicists Alta., Glencoe Golf and Country Club, Glencoe Club. Office: TransCanada PipeLines Ltd, 111 5th Ave SW, Calgary, AB Canada T2P 4K5

REID, DONNA JOYCE, small business owner; b. Springfield, Tenn., June 25, 1954; d. Leonard Earl Reid and Joyce (Robertson) Kirby; m. Kenneth Bruce Sadler, June 26, 1976 (div. Apr. 1980); m. John Christopher Moulton, Oct. 18, 1987 (div. Dec. 1992); m. Peter Leatherland, Apr. 3, 1993. Student, Austin Peay State U., Clarksville, Tenn., 1972-75. Show writer, producer WTVF-TV (CBS affiliate), Nashville, 1977-83, promotion producer, 1983-85, on-air promotion mgr., 1985-86; gen. mgr. Steadi-Film Corp., Nashville, 1986-90; co-owner Options Internat., Nashville, 1990—. Big sister Buddies of Nashville, 1981-87. Named to Honorable Order of Ky. Cols. John Y. Brown, Gov., 1980; recipient Significant Svc. award ARC, 1982, Clara Barton Communications award, 1983. Mem. NAFE, Nat. Assn. TV Arts and Scis., Nat. Film Inst., Nat. Assn. Broadcasters, Internat. Platform Assn. Methodist. Avocations: reading, outdoor sports, travel. Office: Options Internat Inc 913 18th Ave S Nashville TN 37212-2102

REID, EDWARD SNOVER, III, lawyer; b. Detroit, Mar. 24, 1930; s. Edward S. Jr. and Margaret (Overington) R.; m. Carroll Grylls, Dec. 30, 1953; children: Carroll Reid Highet, Richard Gerveys, Jane Reid McTique, Margaret Reid Boyer. B.A., Yale U., 1951; LL.B. magna cum laude (Sheldon fellow), Harvard U., 1956. Bar: Mich. 1957, N.Y. 1958, D.C. 1982, Gaikokuho jimu-bengoshi, Tokyo 1991-96. Asso. Davis, Polk & Wardwell, N.Y.C., 1957-64; partner Davis, Polk & Wardwell, 1964-95, sr. counsel, 1996—; dir. Gen. Mills, Inc., 1974-89. Mem. N.Y.C. Bd. Higher Edn., 1971-73; trustee Bklyn. Inst. Arts and Scis., 1966-93, chmn., 1974-79; trustee Bklyn. Mus., 1973-93, 94—; bd. dirs. Bklyn. Bot. Garden Corp., 1977-92, 96—, Bargemusic Ltd., 1990-93. Lt. USMCR, 1951-53. Mem. ABA, N.Y. State Bar Assn., Assn. of Bar of City of N.Y., Am. Law Inst., Internat. Bar Assn., Inter-Pacific Bar Assn., Heights Casino Club, Rembrandt Club, Century Assn. Club, Yale Club, L.I. Wyandanch Club, Quoque Beach Club, Shinnecock Yacht Club. Home: 1 Pierrepont St Apt 5-a Brooklyn NY 11201-3361 Office: Davis Polk & Wardwell 450 Lexington Ave New York NY 10017-3911

REID, GEORGE KELL, biology educator, researcher, author; b. Fitzgerald, Ga., Mar. 23, 1918; s. George Kell and Pauline (Bowles) R.; m. Eugénie Louise Chazal, July 23, 1949 (div. Dec. 1978); children: George Philip (dec.), Deborah Louise. BS, Presbyn. Coll., Clinton, S.C., 1940; MS, U. Fla., 1949, PhD, 1952. Instr. U. Fla., Gainesville, 1949-52; asst. prof. Coll. William and Mary, Williamsburg, Va., 1952-53, Tex. A&M U., College Station, 1953-56, Rutgers U., New Brunswick, N.J., 1956-60; prof. Eckerd Coll., St. Petersburg, Fla., 1960-83, prof. emeritus, 1983—; pvt. practice cons., writer Boca Raton, Fla., 1988—; rsch. scientist Va. Inst. Marine Sci., Gloucester, 1953; rsch. biologist Tex. Game and Fish. Commn., Rockport, 1954-56; cons. in field, 1955—. Author: Ecology of Cedar Key Fishes, 1954, Ecology of Inland Waters and Estuaries, 1961, (co-author) rev. edit., 1976, Pond Life, 1967, rev. edit., 1992, Ecology of Intertidal Zones, 1967; co-author: Bioscience, 1967; contbr. articles to profl. jours. and popular periodicals. Mem. City Environ. Com., St. Petersburg, 1975. 1st lt. U.S. Army, 1942-46. Recipient numerous grants NIH, NSF, Explorers Club, others, 1953—. Fellow AAAS; mem. Am. Soc. Limnology and Oceanography, Am. Inst. Biol. Scis., Fla. Acad. Sci. (pres. 1963-64), Ecol. Soc. Am. (chmn. aquatic ecology sec. 1964-66), Sigma Xi, Phi Sigma, Chi Beta Phi, Sigma Chi. Presbyterian. Achievements include pioneering in fish community ecology research in Gulf of Mexico localities; research in population dynamics in mangrove ecosystems, Wetland utilization, early literature on natural history of Florida. Home: 6079 Town Colony Dr Apt 1022 Boca Raton FL 33433-1911

REID, GINGER MEREDITH, school counselor, educator; b. Atlanta, Dec. 5, 1969; d. Ronald Davis Balser and Temme Barkin-Leeds; m. Wayne Dale Reid, II, Aug. 12, 1995. BA in Psychology, Emory U., 1993; MEd in Sch. Counseling, Ga. State U., 1995. Cert. sch. counselor, Ga. Summer day camp counselor Frog Hollow Day Camp, Atlanta, 1988-91; tchr., counselor Haverty Hollow Pre-Sch. Enrichment Program, Atlanta, 1991-92, 93-96; rsch. asst. Emory Univ., Atlanta, 1992-93; sch. counselor Dacula (Ga.) Mid. Sch., 1996—. Mem. Ga. Sch. Counselors Assn., Ga. Assn. Play Therapy, Ga. Sch. Age Care Assn., Phi Bet Kappa, Psi Chi. Jewish. Avocations: jogging, weight lifting, aerobics, hiking, scuba diving. Home: 1702 Defoors Mill Ct Atlanta GA 30318 Office: Dacula Mid Sch 6th Grade Counselor Office Dacula GA 30211

REID, HARRY, senator; b. Searchlight, Nev., Dec. 2, 1939; s. Harry and Inez Reid; m. Landra Joy Gould; children—Lana, Rory, Leif, Josh, Key. AS, Southern Utah State U., 1959; LLD (hon.), U. So. Utah, 1984; BA, Utah State U., 1961; JD, George Washington U., 1964. Senator, chmn. dem. policy com. 104th Congress U.S. Senate, Washington; mem. appropriations, ethics/environment & pub. works, Indian affairs coms.*

REID, HOCH, lawyer; b. Chanute, Kans., Dec. 27, 1909; s. James W. and Anna (Hoch) R.; m. Mona McMillan, July 3, 1937; children: Wallis H., Luanna Reid. A.B., Amherst Coll., 1931; LL.B., Columbia U., 1934. Bar: N.Y. 1935. Practiced in N.Y.C., 1935-86; ptnr. Valicenti, Leighton, Reid & Pine, 1942-75, Burke & Burke, Daniels, Leighton & Reid, 1976-78; ptnr. Townley & Updike, 1978-86, retired ptnr., 1986-95; with staff Navy Price Adjustment Bd., 1944-46. Author: How to Use Investment Company Shares in Estate Planning, 1972, Paying Up for Services, 1976. Trustee Village of Pleasantville, N.Y., 1961-63; chmn. Pleasantville Library Bd., 1955-61; mem. Mt. Pleasant Pub. libr. bd., 1982-86; mem. social policy com., planning com. on aging Fedn. Protestant Welfare Agys., N.Y.C., 1970-86; mem. com. agrl. missions Nat. Council Chs., 1962-91, chmn., 1962-76; bd. dirs. Bethel Methodist Homes, Ossining, N.Y., 1948-82, pres., 1962-75, hon. dir., 1982—; bd. dirs. Agrl. Missions, Inc., 1950-91, pres., 1962-76; bd. dirs., mem. exec. com. Japan Internat. Christian U. Found., 1965-91; pres., trustee Open Space Inst., 1969-72; trustee Natural Area Council, 1975-85. Mem. ABA, Assn. Bar City N.Y., Sawmill River Audubon Soc. (pres. 1984-86), Nature Conservancy, World Affairs Coun. (Hartford) Mark Twain Meml. Congregationalist. Home: Duncaster 60 Loeffler Rd Bloomfield CT 06002-2279

REID, INEZ SMITH, lawyer, educator; b. New Orleans, Apr. 7, 1937; d. Sidney Randall Dickerson and Beatrice Virginia (Bundy) Smith. BA, Tufts U., 1959; LLB, Yale U., 1962; MA, UCLA, 1963; PhD, Columbia U., 1968. Bar: Calif. 1963, N.Y. 1972, D.C. 1980. Assoc. prof. Barnard Coll. Columbia U., N.Y.C., 1972-76; gen. counsel youth div. State of N.Y., 1976-77; dep. gen. counsel HEW, Washington, 1977-79; inspector gen. EPA, Washington, 1979-81; chief legis. and opinions, dep. corp. counsel Office of Corp. Counsel, Washington, 1981-83; corp. counsel D.C., 1983-85; counsel Laxalt, Washington, Perito & Dubuc, Washington, 1986-90, ptnr., 1990-91; counsel Graham & James, 1991-93, Lewis, White & Clay, P.C., 1994-95; assoc. judge D.C. Ct. Appeals, 1995—. William J. Maier, Jr. vis. prof. law W.Va. U. Coll. Law, Morgantown, 1985-86. Author: Together Black Women, 1972; contbr. articles to profl. jours. and publs. Bd. dirs. Homeland Ministries Bd. United Ch. of Christ, N.Y.C., 1978-83, vice chmn., 1981-83; chmn. bd. govs. Antioch Law Sch., Washington, 1979-81; chmn. bd. trustees Antioch U., Yellow Springs, Ohio, 1981-82; bd. trustees Tufts U., Medford, Mass., 1988—, Lancaster (Pa.) Sem., 1988—; bd. govs. D.C. Sch. Law, 1990-96, chmn., 1991-95. Recipient Emily Gregory award Barnard Coll., 1976, Arthur Morgan award Antioch U., 1982, Service award United Ch. of Christ, 1983, Disting. Service (Profl. Life) award Tufts U. Alumni Assn., 1988. Office: DC Ct Appeals 500 Indiana Ave NW Ste 6 Washington DC 20001-2131

REID, JACKSON BROCK, psychologist, educator; b. Honea Path, S.C., Sept. 18, 1921; s. Alexander Mack and Ann Orr (Brock) R.; m. Avis Boykin Long, Jan. 12, 1947; step-children: Jules Heywood Long, Barbara Banning Long. B.S., The Citadel, 1942; postgrad., Ariz. State Coll., Flagstaff, 1948; Ph.D., UCLA, 1951, postgrad., summer 1951. Cert., lic. psychologist, Tex. Asst. prof. ednl. psychology U. Tex., Austin, 1951-55; assoc. prof. U. Tex., 1955-59, prof., 1959-93, prof. emeritus, 1993—, assoc. dean for grad. studies in edn., 1965-73; coordinator ESEA programs U.S. Office Edn., 1969—, chmn. dept. ednl. psychology, 1972-84; cons. in field. Served to capt. U.S. Army, 1942-47. Office Edn. grantee, 1966-73. Fellow Am. Psychol. Assn. (exptl. and ednl. divs.); mem. AAAS, Am. Ednl. Research Assn., Interam. Soc. Psychology, AAUP, Southwestern Psychol. Assn. (sec.-treas. 1965-66, pres. 1967-68), Tex. Psychol. Assn., Ret. Officers Assn., Nat. Psoriasis Found., ACLU, Common Cause, Fund for Peace, Planned Parenthood of Am., Sigma Xi. Clubs: U. Tex. Faculty Center; Lighthouse Resort and Club (Sanibel Island, Fla.). Research, publs. in learning theory, behavioral effects of radiation and drugs, child and adolescent behavior, programmed instn., computer-assisted instrn., 1951. Office: U Tex Dept Ednl Psychology Austin TX 78712 *The principal goal in my career has been to preserve psychology as an academic discipline devoted to objective inquiry into the etiology of behavior on the basis of logically directed empirical investigation as opposed to rationalistic - mystical - doctrinaire approaches.*

REID, JAMES DOLAN, mathematics educator, researcher; b. Augusta, Ga., June 24, 1930; s. Richard and Katherine (O'Leary) R.; m. Anne Carmody Donohue, Jan. 7, 1959; children: James Jr., Margaret, Gerald. BS, Fordham Coll., 1952, MA, 1954; PhD, U. Wash., 1960; MA (hon.), Wesleyan U., 1972. Asst. prof. Syracuse (N.Y.) U., 1960-61, 1963-65, assoc. prof., 1965-69; research assoc. Yale U., New Haven, 1961-62; asst. prof. Amherst (Mass.) Coll., 1962-63; assoc. prof. math. Wesleyan U., Middletown, Conn., 1969-70, prof., 1970—, chmn. math. dept., 1970-73, 85-88, cons. ednl. studies program, 1980—; vis. prof. U. Würzburg, Fed. Republic Germany, 1989. Contbr. numerous articles on algebra (Abelian groups) to profl. jours. Mem. Bd. Edn., Regional Sch. Dist. #17, 1983-87. With USN, 1954-56. Mem. Am. Math. Soc., Irish Math. Soc., Math. Assn. of Am. Home: PO Box 444 New Harbor ME 04554-0444 Office: Wesleyan U Dept Math Middletown CT 06459

REID, JAMES SIMS, JR., automobile parts manufacturer; b. Cleve., Jan. 15, 1926; s. James Sims and Felice (Crowl) R.; m. Donna Smith, Sept. 2, 1950; children: Sally, Susan, Anne (dec.), Jeanne. AB cum laude, Harvard U., 1948, JD, 1951. Bar: Mich., Ohio 1951. Pvt. practice law Detroit, 1951-52, Cleve., 1953-56; with Standard Products Co., Cleve., 1956—, dir., 1959, pres., 1962-89, chmn., chief exec. officer, 1989—. Trustee John Carroll U., 1967—, chmn., 1987-91, Musical Arts Assn. of Cleve. Orch., 1973—. Office: Standard Products Co 2130 W 110th St Cleveland OH 44102-3510

REID, JOHN MITCHELL, biomedical engineer, researcher; b. Mpls., June 8, 1926; s. Robert Sherman and Meryl (Mitchell) R.; m. Virginia Montgomery, Dec. 31, 1949 (div.); children: Donald, Kathryn, Richard; m. Shadi Wang, June 30, 1983. BS, U. Minn., 1950, MS, 1957; PhD, U. Pa., 1965. Engring. assoc. U. Minn., Mpls., 1950-54; rsch. engr. St. Barnabas Hosp., Mpls., 1954-57; assoc. U. Pa., Phila., 1957-66; rsch. asst. prof. U. Wash., Seattle, 1966-72; rsch. engr. Providence Hosp., 1972-74; dir. bioengring. Inst. of Applied Physiology & Medicine, 1973-81; Calhoun prof. Drexel U., Phila., 1981-94, prof. emeritus, rsch. prof., 1994; adj. prof. radiology Thomas Jefferson Med. Sch., Phila., 1982—; affiliate prof. U. Washington, 1995—; cons. Inst. Applied Physiology and Medicine, Seattle. Contbr. over 100 articles to profl. jours.; 5 U.S. patents on devel. of ultrasonic med. imaging. Scoutmaster Boy Scouts Am., Mpls., 1955-57, Phila., 1960-65, cub and scoutmaster, Seattle, 1965-70. With USN, 1950-52, World War II. Recipient Pioneer award Soc. of Vascular Technologists, 1994; grantee NIH. Fellow IEEE, Am. Inst. Ultrasound in Medicine (bd. govs., Pioneer award), Acoustical Soc. Am., Engring. in Medicine and Biology Soc. (Lifetime Achievement award 1993), Am. Inst. Med. and Biol. Engrs. Home: 16711 254th Ave SE Issaquah WA 98027-6973 also: Inst Applied Physiology and Medicine 701 16th Ave Seattle WA 98122-4525

REID, JOHN PHILLIP, law educator; b. Weehawken, N.J., May 17, 1930; s. Thomas Francis and Teresa Elizabeth (Murphy) R. B.S.S., Georgetown U., 1952; LL.B., Harvard U., 1955; M.A., U. N.H., 1957; J.S.D., NYU, 1962. Bar: N.H. 1955. Law clk. U.S. Dist. Ct. N.H., 1956; instr. NYU, N.Y.C., 1960-62, asst. prof. law, 1962-64, assoc. prof., 1964-65, prof. Sch. Law, 1966—. Author: Chief Justice: The Judicial World of Charles Doe, 1967, A Law of Blood: The Primitive Law of the Cherokee Nation, 1970, In a Defiant Stance, 1977, Ina Rebellious Spirit, 1979, Law for the Elephant: Property and Social Behavior on the Overland Trail, 1980, In Defiance of the Law, 1981, Constitutional History of the American Revolution: The Authority of Rights, 1986, Constitutional History of the American Revolution: The Authority to Tax, 1987, The Concept of Liberty in the Age of the American Revolution, 1988, The Concept of Representation in the Age of the American Revolution, 1989, Constitutional History of the American Revolution: The Authority to Legislate, 1991, Constitutional History of the American Revolution: The Authority of Law, 1993, Policing the Elephant: Crime, Punishment, and Social Behavior on the Overland Trail, 1997. Fellow Guggenheim Found., 1980, Huntington Library-NEH, 1980, 84; hon. fellow Am. Soc. Legal History, 1986. Republican. Roman Catholic. Office: NYU Law Sch 40 Washington Sq S New York NY 10012-1005

REID, JOSEPH BROWNING, architect; b. Flint Hill, Va., June 24, 1924; s. Charles Garrison and Grace Pearl (Bradley) R.; m. Maria Aida Amadounian, July 5, 1957; children: Charles, Avedis, Robert. Student, U. Va., 1948; BS in Forestry with highest honors, N.C. State U., 1952; postgrad., Columbia U., 1955; cert. in architecture, Cooper Union, 1960. Registered architect, N.Y., Va., Md., Pa., D.C.; cert. Nat. Coun. Archtl. Registration Bds.; lic. interior designer, D.C. Staff architect Charles Luckman & Assocs., N.Y.C., 1956-63; sr. architect Clive Entwistle & Assocs., N.Y.C., 1963-64; sr. assoc. Perkins & Will, Washington, 1964-74; v.p. John Carl Warnecke FAIA, Washington, 1974-82; founding ptnr. Kemnitzer Reid & Haffler, Washington, 1982-89; prin. Einhorn Yaffee Prescott, Washington, 1989—; advis0r interior design program Marymount Coll., 1982-85; profl. coord. off-campus work program for architecture students Va. Poly. Inst., 1975-81; lectr. No. Va. C.C.; a juror for residential awards Washingtonian mag., 1986; advisor, organizer archtl. awards program Washington Mayor's Award Program. With Mcht. Marine, 1942-47. Recipient Disting. Svc. cert. USO, Washington, 1976, Presdl. Design award Nat. Endowment for Arts, 1987, Hist. Preservation Honor award, 1988, Design award Washington Metro chpt. Am. Soc. Interior Designers, 1989, 2 awards GSA, 1992; Hilda Johnson Cox scholar N.C. State U., 1950. Mem. AIA (sr. dir. Washington Met. chpt. 1979-80, treas. 1981-82, sec. 1982-83, v.p. 1983-84, pres. 1984-85, cert. of deep appreciation 1984, cert. of appreciation 1984), Constrn. Specifications Inst. (bd. dirs. 1979-81, 91-92, citation for disting. svc. 1982, nat. honor awards 1992), Soc. Archtl. Adminstrs. (co-founder Washington chpt.), Phi Eta Sigma, Alpha Zeta, Xi Sigma Pi, Alpha Sigma Pi. Democrat. Methodist. Avocations: surf fishing, Greek history, travel in Greece. Home: 6926 Tyndale St Mc Lean VA 22101-5070 Office: Einhorn Yaffee Prescott Arch 1000 Potomac St NW # 1 Washington DC 20007-3501

REID, LANGHORNE, III, merchant banker; b. Dallas, Apr. 3, 1950; s. Langhorne Jr. and Mary Anne (Beasley) R.; m. Sally Wolf, Dec. 26, 1972 (div. Aug. 1977); m. Eve Catherine Murphy, Sept. 6, 1986; 1 child, Claire Hart Reid. BA in Psychology, U. Tex., 1972, JD, 1975; MBA, U. Pa., 1977. Bar: Tex. 1975. V.p. Dillon, Read & Co., Inc., N.Y.C., 1977-82; mng. dir. Drexel Burnham Lambert Inc., N.Y.C., 1982-87; co-dir. mergers and acquisitions Paine Webber Group, N.Y.C., 1987-89; ptnr. Gordon Investment Inc., N.Y.C., 1989-93; pres. Beacon Advisors, Inc., Dallas, 1993—; bd. dirs. Windmill Holdings; pres. Partnership Svcs., 1992-93; chmn. Amtex Holdings, Inc., 1996—. Trustee, treas. Animal Med. Ctr., N.Y.C., 1981—. Mem. Tex. Bar Assn. Home: 4307 University Blvd Dallas TX 75205 Office: Beacon Advisors Inc Box 285 25 Highland Park Village Ste 100 Dallas TX 75205

REID, LOREN DUDLEY, speech educator; b. Gilman City, Mo., Aug. 26, 1905; s. Dudley Alver and Josephine (Tarwater) R.; m. Mary Augusta Towner, Aug. 28, 1930; children: Jane Ellen, John Christopher, Stephen Dudley Towner, Don Anthony. A.B., Grinnell Coll., 1927; A.M., State U. Iowa, 1930, Ph.D., 1932. Tchr. Vermillion (S.D.) High Sch., 1927-29; instr. State U. Iowa, 1931-33; tchr. Westport High Sch., Kansas City, Mo., 1933-35; English instr. U. Mo., 1935-37, asst. prof., 1937-39; asst. prof. and later assoc. prof. of speech Syracuse U., 1939-44; prof. of speech U. Mo., 1944—, sesquicentennial prof., 1990, chmn. dept. speech, 1947-52; vis. prof. speech U. So. Calif., summer, 1947; summer lectr. La. State U., 1949, Mich., 1950, 56; summer lectr. State U. Iowa, 1952, Denver, 1960, Oklahoma, 1962; vis. prof. U. Utah, summer 1952, San Diego State Coll., summer 1954, U. So. Calif., summer 1954; European staff U. Md., 1952-53, summer, 1955, 1961-62, London; European staff U. Mich., summer 1957, State U. Iowa, summer 1958; Carnegie vis. prof. U. Hawaii, 1957, La. State U., 1985; vis. lectr. Kyoto (Japan) Sangyo U., 1987. Author: Charles James Fox: An Eighteenth Century Parliamentary Speaker, 1932, Course Book in Public Speaking, (with Gilman and Aly) Speech Preparation, 1946, Fundamentals of Speaking, 1951, Teaching Speech in High School, 1952, Teaching Speech, rev. edit., 1960, 4th edit., 1971, First Principles of Public Speaking, 1960, rev. edit., published in 1962, Studies in American Public Address, 1961, Speaking Well, 4th edit., 1982, Hurry Home Wednesday (Mo. Writers Guild award), Finally It's Friday, 1981, Professor on the Loose, 1992, Reflections, 1995. Recipient Alumni Achievement award Grinnell Coll., 1962. Fellow Royal Hist. Soc.; mem. Speech Comm. Assn. (exec. sec. 1945-51, pres. Disting. Svc. award 1981, Pres.'s Citation 1996), N.Y. State Speech Assn. (pres. 1942-44, Spl. award for outstanding svc. 1967), Cen. States Speech Assn. (exec. sec. 1937-39, Disting. Svc. award 1979), Speech and Theatre Assn. Mo. (Disting. Svc. award 1982), AAUP, Conf. on Brit. Studies. U. Mo. Club (pres. 1947). Democrat. Episcopalian. Home: 200 E Brandon Rd Columbia MO 65203-3566

REID, LORENE FRANCES, middle school educator; b. St. Louis, May 28, 1946; d. Frank Bernard and Marcella Marie (Froechtenigt) Niemeyer; m. Patrick Joseph Reid, Aug. 11, 1967; 1 child, Christina Marie. BA in Spanish, Maryville U., 1968; MED in Secondary Edn., U. Mo., St. Louis, 1990; PhD in Edn., St. Louis U., 1995; MA in English, Southeast Mo. State U., 1996. Cert. Spanish, social studies, ESL tchr., Mo. Spanish tchr. Rosary H.S., Spanish Lake, Mo., 1968-69, Taylor Sch., Clayton, Mo., 1969-70, Roosevelt H.S., St. Louis, 1988-89, Cleve. Jr. Naval Acad., St. Louis, 1989-90, Thomas Dunn Meml. Adult Edn., St. Louis, 1992—; social studies tchr. St. Luke's Sch., Richmond Heights, Mo., 1981-88; ESL tchr. Grant Mid. Sch., St. Louis, 1990-92, Fanning Mid. Sch., St. Louis, 1992—; tutor Sylvan Learning Ctr., Crestwood, Mo., 1990-92; mem. St. Louis Ednl. Leadership Inst., 1994—. Mem. Cmty. Leadership Program for Tchrs., St. Louis, 1993-94. Recipient Emerson Electric Excellence in Teaching award, 1994; named Tchr. of Yr., St. Louis Pub. Schs., 1994-95; named as one of 60 tchrs. recognized by Disney Channel Salutes the Am. Tchr., 1995-96. Mem. ASCD, Am. Ednl. Rsch. Assn., Tchrs. English to Spkrs. of Other Langs., Nat. Coun. Tchrs. English, Midam. Tchs. English to Spkrs. of Other Langs., Phi Delta Kappa.

REID, LYLE, judge; b. Brownsville, Tenn., June 17, 1930; m. Elizabeth W.; children: Betsy, Martha Lyle. BSBA, U. Tenn., JD, 1956. Asst. state atty. gen. State of Tenn., Nashville, 1961-63; county atty. Haywood County, Brownsville, Tenn., 1964-86; atty. Reid & Banks, Brownsville, Tenn., 1963-66; assoc. judge Tenn. Ct. Criminal Appeals, Tenn., 1987-90; chief justice Tenn. Supreme Ct., Nashville, 1990-94; deputy commr. Dept. Commerce & Ins., Tenn. With USAF, Korea. Mem. ABA, Am. Bar Found., Tenn. Bar Assn. Democrat. Methodist. Office: Tenn Supreme Ct 321 Supreme Ct Bldg 401 7th Ave N Nashville TN 37219-1406

REID, LYNNE MCARTHUR, pathologist; b. Melbourne, Australia, Nov. 12, 1923; d. Robert Muir and Violet Annie (McArthur) R. M.D., U. Melbourne, 1946; M.D. (hon.), Harvard U., 1976. Reader in exptl. pathology London U., 1964-67, prof. exptl. pathology, 1967-76; dean Cardiothoracic Inst., 1973-76; pathologist-in-chief Children's Hosp., Boston, 1976-89, pathologist-in-chief emeritus, 1990—; S. Burt Wolbach prof. pathology Harvard Med. Sch., Boston, 1976—. Fellow Royal Coll. Physicians (U.K.), Royal Australian Coll. Physicians, Royal Coll. Pathologists, Royal Coll. Radiologists (hon.), Royal Soc. Medicine, Royal Inst. Gt. Britain, Pathol. Soc. Gt. Britain and Ireland, Thoracic Soc., Assn. Clin. Pathologists, Brit. Thoracic Soc., Fleischner Soc., Can. Thoracic Soc., Neonatal Soc., Am. Thoracic Soc., Am. Soc. Pathologists, Fedn. Am. Socs. Exptl. Biology. Office: 300 Longwood Ave Boston MA 02115-5724

REID, MARILYN JOANNE, state legislator, lawyer; b. Chgo., Aug. 14, 1941; d. Kermit and Newell Azile (Hahn) N.; m. M. David Reid, Nov. 26, 1966 (div. Mar. 1983); children: David, Nelson. Student, Miami U., 1959-61; BA, U. Ill, 1963; JD, Ohio No. U., 1966. Bar: Ohio 1966, Ark. 1967, U.S. Dist. Ct. 1967. Trust adminstr. First Nat. Bank, Dayton, Ohio, 1966-67; assoc. Sloan & Ragsdale, Little Rock, Ohio, 1967-69; ptnr. Reid and Reid, Dayton, 1969-76, Reid & Buckwalter, Dayton, 1975—; mem. Ohio Ho. of Reps., 1993—; mem. Judiciary and Criminal Justice com., vice chmn. ins. com., Vets. com., Pub. utilities com. Mem. Ohio adv. bd. U.S. Commn. Civil Rights; chmn., treas. various polit. campaigns, 1975—; trustee Friends Libr. Beavercreek (Ohio); bd. dirs. Beavercreek YMCA, 1985-88; active Mt. Zion United Ch. of Christ. Mem. ABA, Ohio Bar Assn., Greene County Bar Assn., Beavercreek C. of C. (pres. 1986-87), Dayton Panhellenic Assn. (pres. 1982), Altrusa (v.p. Greene County 1978-79, pres. 1979-80), Lioness (pres. Beavercreek 1975), Rotary, Kappa Beta Pi, Gamma Phi Beta (v.p. 1974-75). Republican. Mem. Ch. Christ. Avocations: tennis, skiing, boating, bridge. Office: Reid & Buckwalter 3866 Indian Ripple Rd Dayton OH 45440-3448

REID, RALPH WALDO EMERSON, management consultant; b. Phila., July 5, 1915; s. Ralph Waldo Emerson and Alice Myrtle (Stuart) R.; m. Ruth Bull, Dec. 7, 1946; 1 child, Robert. Student, Temple U., 1932-34. BS, Northwestern U., 1936; MA, U. Hawaii, 1938; PhD, Harvard U., 1948. Cert. mgmt. cons. Asst. to v.p. Northwestern U., Evanston, Ill., 1938-40; chief mcpl. govt. br., spl. asst. govt. sect. Supreme Comdr. Allied Powers, 1946-47; spl. asst. Under Sec. of Army, 1948-49; chief Far Eastern affairs div. Office Occupied Areas, chief econs. div. Office Civil Affairs and Mil. Govt., Dept. of Army, 1950-53; asst. to dir. U.S. Bur. of Budget, Washington, 1953-55, asst. dir., 1955-61; resident mgr. A.T. Kearney Inc., Washington, 1961-72, mng. dir., Tokyo, 1972-81, cons., Alexandria, Va., 1981—; former dir. Nihon Regulator Co., Tokyo, Yuasa-Ionics Ltd., Tokyo, Japan DME, Tokyo. Served to comdr. USNR, 1941-46, PTO. Decorated Commendation Ribbon, USN; Order of Rising Sun 3d class (Japan); recipient Exceptional Civilian Service award U.S. Army, 1954. Mem. Inst. Mgmt. Consultants, Am. Polit. Sci. Assn. Republican. Am. Baptist. Clubs: Cosmos, Capitol Hill (Washington); Union League (Chgo.). Home: 412 Monticello Blvd Alexandria VA 22305-1616 Office: A T Kearney Inc PO Box 1405 Alexandria VA 22313-1405

REID, ROBERT CLARK, chemical engineering educator; b. Denver, June 11, 1924; s. Frank B. and Florence (Seerley) R.; m. Anna Marie Murphy, Aug. 26, 1950; children: Donald M., Ann Christine. BS, Colo. Sch. Mines, 1946-48; MS, Purdue U., 1950; ScD, MIT, 1954. Prof. chem. engring. MIT, Cambridge, from 1954; now prof. emeritus chem. engring. MIT; Olaf A. Hougen prof. chem. engring. U. Wis., 1980-81. Author: (with J.M. Prausnitz and B.E. Poling) Properties of Gases and Liquids, 1966, 4th edit., 1987, (with M. Ohara) Modeling Crystal Growth Rates from Solution, 1973, (with M. Modell) Thermodynamics and Its Applications, 1974, 2d edit., 1983; Contbr. articles to profl. jours. Recipient Warren K. Lewis award, 1976; Chem. Engring. award Am. Soc. Engring. Edn., 1977; research fellow Harvard U., 1963-64. Mem. Am. Inst. Chem. Engrs. (Ann. lectr. 1967, council 1969-71, editor jour. 1970-76, Founders award 1986), Nat. Acad. Engring., Blue Key, Sigma Alpha Epsilon, Tau Beta Pi. Home: 22 Burroughs Rd Lexington MA 02173-1908 Office: MIT 66-468 Cambridge MA 02139

REID, ROBERT LELON, college dean, mechanical engineer; b. Detroit, May 20, 1942; s. Lelon Reid and Verna Beulah (Custer) Cook; m. Judy Elaine Nestell, July 21, 1962; children: Robert James, Bonnie Kay, Matthew Lelon. ASE, Mott C.C., Flint, Mich., 1961; BChemE, U. Mich., 1963; MME, So. Meth. U., 1966, PhDME, 1969. Registered profl. engr., Tenn., Tex., Wis. Asst. rsch. engr. Atlantic Richfield Co., Dallas, 1964-65; assoc. staff engr. Linde Div., Union Carbide Corp., Tonawanda, N.Y., 1966-68; from asst. to assoc. prof. U. Tenn., Knoxville, 1969-75; assoc. prof. Cleve. State U., 1975-77; from assoc. to full prof. U. Tenn., Knoxville, 1977-82; prof., chmn. U. Tex., El Paso, 1982-87; dean Coll. Engring. Marquette U., Milw., 1987—; summer prof. NASA Marshall Space Ctr., Huntsville, Ala., 1970, EXXON Prodn. Rsch., Houston, 1972, 73, NASA Lewis Space Ctr., Cleve., 1986; cons. Oak Ridge Nat. Lab., 1974-75, TVA, 1978, 79, State of Calif., Sacramento, 1985, Tex. Higher Edn. Coordinating Bd., Austin, 1987. Contbr. 80 articles on heat transfer and solar energy to books, jours. and procs. Grantee NSF, DOE, TVA, NASA, DOI, 1976-87; named Engr. of Yr. Engring. Socs. El Paso, 1986. Fellow ASME (Centennial medallion 1980, chmn. cryogenics com. 1977-81, chmn. solar energy divsn. 1983-84, chmn. Rio Grande sect. 1985-87, John Yellott award, 1997); mem. ASHRAE, Engrs. and Scientists Milw. (bd. dirs. 1988-93, v.p. 1989-90, pres. 1991-92), Wis. Assn. Rsch. Mgmt. (pres. 1996-97). Lutheran. Avocations: travel, classic car restoration. Office: Marquette U Coll Engring PO Box 1881 Milwaukee WI 53201-1881

REID, ROBERT NEWTON, retired lawyer, mortgage and financial consultant; b. Ottawa, Ill., Mar. 28, 1908; s. Robert Joseph and Mae (Newton) R. Ph.B., U. Chgo., 1929, J.D., 1930. Bar: Ill. 1930, U.S. Supreme Ct. 1949, Md. 1961, D.C. 1961. Practiced in Chgo., 1930-39; with Follansbee, Shorey & Schupp, 1933-39; govt. atty. FCA, Washington, 1939-42; atty., counsel RFC, Fed. Nat. Mortgage Assn., 1942-49; asst. gen. counsel Fed. Nat. Mortgage Assn., 1949-50, gen. counsel, 1950-70, spl. counsel, 1970-73, v.p., 1950-59, 68-73, dir., 1954-59, cons., 1973-95; retired, 1995. Mem. bd. advisors Washington Studio Sch., 1985-95. Served from 2d lt. to lt. col. Judge Adv. Gen. Corps USAR, 1942-46. Decorated Legion of Merit. Mem. ABA (life), Fed. Bar Assn. D.C. Bar Assn. (life), Am. Judicature Soc., Supreme Ct. Hist. Soc., Res. Officers Assn. (life), Am. Legion (life), SAR (life), Ret. Officers Assn. (life), Mil. Order of World Wars (life), Nat. Assn., Uniformed Svcs., English Speaking Union, Delta Sigma Phi (life), Phi Alpha Delta. Clubs: Nat. Lawyers (life), University (life) (Washington). Lodge: Masons (life). Home: University Club 1135 16th St NW Washington DC 20036-4801

REID, RUFUS LAMAR, jazz bassist, educator; b. Atlanta, Feb. 10, 1944; s. Alvin and Sylvia (Lindsey) R.; m. Doris Audrey Bangs; 1 child, Michel Matthew. Assoc. in Music, Olympic Coll., 1967-69; MusB, Northwestern U., 1969-71. Instr. No. Ill. U., Dekalb, 1973-76; prof. William Paterson Coll., Wayne, N.J., 1980—; dir. jazz studies and performance William Paterson Coll., Wayne, N.J., 1980—; dir. jazz residency Carter G. Woodson Found., Paterson, N.J.; panelist, Nat. Found. for Advancement in the Arts, Miami, 1982-85. Author: The Evolving Bassist, 1974 (internat. trilingual edition), Evolving Upward, 1977; rec. and touring artist with Stan Getz, Dexter Gordon, Thad Jones and Mel Lewis Orch., J.J. Johnson, Nancy Wilson, Freddie Hubbard, Jack DeJohnette, Eddie Harris, Kenny Burrell, others; recorder over 200 recs.; co-leader performing ensemble Tanareid with drummer Akira Tana. Served to E-4 USAF, 1961-66. Recipient Humanitarian award Internat. Assn. Jazz Educators, 1977. Avocation: model trains. Office: Myriad Ltd PO Box 757 Teaneck NJ 07666-0757

REID, SARAH LAYFIELD, lawyer; b. Kansas City, Mo., Sept. 22, 1952; d. Jim Tom and Sarah Pauline (Clark) R.; m. David Harris Gikow, June 12, 1983; children: Stephen Nathaniel, Emily Pauline. AB, Bryn Mawr Coll., 1974; JD, Harvard U., 1977. Bar: N.Y. 1978, U.S. Dist. Ct. (so. and ea. dists.) N.Y. 1978, U.S. Ct. Appeals (11th cir.) 1981, U.S. Ct. Appeals (2d cir.) 1982, U.S. Supreme Ct. 1988, U.S. Ct. Appeals (3d cir.) 1990. Assoc. Kelley Drye & Warren, N.Y.C., 1977-85, ptnr., 1986—, co-head securities litigation practice group, 1995—. Mem. ABA, N.Y. State Bar Assn., Fed. Bar Coun., Assn. of Bar of City of N.Y. (mem. task force on women in the profession). Office: Kelley Drye & Warren 101 Park Ave New York NY 10178

REID, SHARON LEA, educational facilitator; b. Wheeler, Tex., Apr. 24, 1949; d. George S. and Arvazine (Deering) Robinson; m. Thomas Michael Reid, July 9, 1989. BS, McMurry Coll., 1970; MEd, Tarleton State U., 1979. Cert. tchr., edn. adminstr., supr., Tex. Tchr. Fleming Elem., San Antonio, Tex., 1971-72, Peebles Elem., Killeen, Tex., 1972-84; tchr. Sugar Loaf Elem., Killeen, 1984-85, facilitator, 1985—; trainer/dir. Marilyn Burns Problem Solving, Killeen, 1982-85, trainer/campus 4 MAT Lesson Design/Excel, Inc., Killeen, 1994—. Mem. Heights Concert Band, Harker Heights, Tex. Recipient music scholarship McMurry Coll., Abilene, Tex., 1968. Mem. ASCD, Tex. State Tchrs. Assn., Phi Delta Kappa. Avocations: instrumental music, bowling, sewing, cross-stitch. Office: Sugar Loaf Elem Sch 1517 Barbara Ln Killeen TX 76542-1423

REID, SIDNEY WEBB, English educator; b. Neptune, N.J., Nov. 24, 1943; s. Sidney Webb and Mary Cook (Bennett) R.; m. Judith Wright, Aug. 22, 1969; 1 child, Laura. BA, Duke U., 1965; MA, U. Va., 1966, PhD, 1972. Grad. tchg. fellow U. Va., Charlottesville, 1968-70; asst. prof. English, Kent (Ohio) State U., 1970-75, assoc. prof., 1975-84, prof., 1984—, dir. Inst. Bibliography and Editing, 1985—; vis. fellow Clare Hall, Cambridge (Eng.) U., 1992-93, life mem., 1993—. Textual editor Bicentennial Edition of Charles Brockden Brown, 6 vols., 1977-87; editor-in-chief: (Cambridge edits. of Joseph Conrad) The Secret Agent, 1990, Almayer's Folly, 1994. NDEA fellow U. Va., 1965-68; Rsch. grantee NEH, 1977-84. Office: Kent State University Inst Bibliography-Editing 1118 Library Kent OH 44242

REID, SUE TITUS, law educator; b. Bryan, Tex., Nov. 13, 1939; d. Andrew Jackson Jr. and Loraine (Wylie) Titus. BS with honors, Tex. Woman's U., 1960; MA, U. Mo., 1962, PhD, 1965; JD, U. Iowa, 1972. Bar: Iowa 1972, U.S. Ct. Appeals (D.C. cir.) 1978, U.S. Supreme Ct. 1978. From instr. to assoc. prof. sociology Cornell Coll., Mt. Vernon, Iowa, 1963-72; assoc. prof., chmn. dept. sociology Coe Coll., Cedar Rapids, Iowa, 1972-74; assoc. prof. law. U. Wash., Seattle, 1974-76; exec. assoc. Am. Sociol. Assn., Washington, 1976-77; prof. law U. Tulsa, 1978-88; dean, prof. Sch. Criminology, Fla. State U., Tallahassee, 1988-90; prof. pub. adminstrn. and policy Fla. State U., 1990—; acting chmn. dept. sociology Cornell Coll., 1965-66; vis. assoc. prof. sociology U. Nebr., Lincoln, 1970; vis. disting. prof. law and sociology U. Tulsa, 1977-78, assoc. dean 1979-81; vis. prof. law U. San Diego, 1981-82; mem. People-to-People Crime Prevention Del. to People's Republic of China, 1982; George Beto Vis. Prof. criminal justice Sam Houston U., Huntsville, Tex., 1984-85; lecture/study tour of Criminal Justice systems of 10 European countries, 1985; cons. Evaluation Policy Rsch. Assocs., Inc., Milw., 1976-77, Nat. Inst. Corrections, Idaho Dept. Corrections, 1984, Am. Correctional Inst., Price-Waterhouse. Author: (with others) Bibliographies on Role Methodology and Propositions Volume D - Studies in the Role of the Public School Teacher, 1962, The Correctional System: An Introduction, 1981, Crime and Criminology, 7th edit., 1994, 8th edit., 1997, Criminal Justice, 1987, 3d edit., 1993, 4th edit. Brown and Benchmark, 1996, Criminal Law, 1989, 3d edit., 1995; editor: (with David Lyon) Population Crisis: An Interdisciplinary Perspective, 1972; contbr. articles to profl. jours. Recipient Disting. Alumni award Tex. Woman's U., 1979; named One of Okla. Young Leaders of 80's Oklahoma Monthly, 1980. Mem. Am. Soc. Criminology, Acad. Criminal Justice Scis., Soc. Criminal Jus. Assn. Avocations: walking, swimming, reading, cooking. Office: Fla State Univ Dept Pub Adminstrn Tallahassee FL 32306

REID, TERENCE C. W., corporation executive; b. Johannesburg, Republic of South Africa, Oct. 28, 1941; arrived in Canada, 1964; s. Edward Harold and Constance Mary (Jenner) R.; m. Carole Julie Davies; children: Alison, Michael, Christopher. Diploma in law, Witwatersrand U., Johannesburg, 1962; MBA, Toronto U., 1966. Articled clk. Bowen's Co., Johannesburg, 1959-64; various positions to vice chmn. CIBC Wood Gundy Securities, Inc., Toronto and Montreal, 1966—; Dir. Kinross Gold Corp. Office: CIBC Wood Gundy Securities Inc, BCE Pl, PO Box 500, Toronto, ON Canada M5J 2S8

REID, THOMAS FENTON, minister; b. Buffalo, Sept. 9, 1932; s. Albert E. and Helen Gertrude (Rice) R.; m. Wanda Darlene Bousum, July 7, 1968; 1 child, Aimee Linette. Diploma, Cen. Bible Coll., Springfield, Mo., 1953; DD (hon.), Calif. Grad. Sch. Theology, 1981; LHD (hon.), Oral Roberts U., 1987. Ordained to ministry Assemblies of God, 1956. Missionary, evangelist Assemblies of God, Springfield, 1953-63; pastor Bethel Temple, Manila, 1959-60; st. pastor Full Gospel Tabernacle, Orchard Park, N.Y., 1963—; pres. Buffalo Sch. Bible, 1976—; pres. Nat. Ch. Growth Conf., Washington, 1984; sec., bd. dirs. Ch. Growth Inc., Seoul, Republic of Korea, 1979—. Author: The Exploding Church, 1979, Kingdom Now But Not Yet, 1988, Ethics, Excellence and Economics, 1989. Mem. Nat. Assn. Evangelicals (bd. dirs. 1979—), Nat. Religious Broadcasters, Friends of Anwar Sadat, Christians for Friends in Middle East. Republican. Home: 701 Willardshire Rd Orchard Park NY 14127-2038 Office: Full Gospel Tabernacle 3210 Southwestern Blvd Orchard Park NY 14127-1229 *The very center of my belief system is that God made man in His own image. Man has great value, dignity and purpose. It is my responsibility to lead men to God, and help them find their true purpose and potential through Jesus Christ.*

REID, WILLIAM HILL, mathematics educator; b. Oakland, Calif., Sept. 10, 1926; s. William Macdonald and Edna Caroline (Hill) R.; m. Elizabeth Mary Kidner, May 26, 1962; 1 child, Margaret Frances. BS, U. Calif., Berkeley, 1949, MS, 1951; PhD, Cambridge U., Eng., 1955, ScD (hon.), 1968; AM (hon.), Brown U., 1961. Lectr. Johns Hopkins U., Balt., 1955-56; NSF fellow Yerkes Observatory, Williams Bay, Wis., 1957-58; asst. prof. Brown U., Providence, 1958-61, assoc. prof., 1961-63; assoc. prof. U. Chgo., 1963-65, prof., 1965-89, prof. emeritus, 1989—; prof. Ind. U.-Purdue U., Indianapolis, 1989—; cons. research labs. Gen. Motors Corp., Warren, Mich., 1960-73. Author: (with P.G. Drazin) Hydrodynamic Stability, 1981; contbr. articles to profl. jours. Served with U.S. Mcht. Marine, 1945-47, with AUS, 1954-56. Fulbright research scholar Australian Nat. U., 1964-65. Fellow Am. Phys. Soc., Cambridge Philos. Soc.; mem. Am. Math. Soc., Am. Meteorol. Soc., Sigma Xi. Home: 7554 Ballinshire N Indianapolis IN 46254-9772 Office: Ind U-Purdue U Dept Math Scis 402 N Blackford St Indianapolis IN 46202-3272

REID, WILLIAM JAMES, social work educator; b. Detroit, Nov. 14, 1928; s. James Macknight and Sophie Amelia (Schneider) R.; m. Anne E. Fortune, May 22, 1988; children by previous marriage—Valerie, Steven. B.A., U. Mich., 1950, M.S.W., 1952; D.S.W., Columbia U., 1963. Caseworker-in-charge Family Service of Westchester, Mt. Kisco, N.Y., 1956-59; asst. prof. social work U. Chgo., 1962-65, prof., 1968-75, George Herbert Jones prof., 1975-80; prof. Sch. Social Welfare, SUNY, Albany, 1980—; dir. Center for Social Casework Research, Community Service Soc., N.Y.C., 1965-68. Author: Brief and Extended Casework, 1969, Task-Centered Casework, 1972, Task-Centered Practice, 1977, The Task-Centered System, 1978, Models of Family Treatment, 1981, Research in Social Work, 1981, 2d edit., 1989, Family Problem Solving, 1985, The Role-Sharing Marriage, 1986, Advances in Clinical Social Work Research, 1990, Task Strategies, 1992, Qualitative Research in Social Work, 1994, Generalist Practice: A Task-Centered Approach, 1994. Served with U.S. Army, 1952-56. Recipient excellence in rsch. award Nat. Assn. Social Workers, 1990. Mem. Phi Beta Kappa. Office: 135 Western Ave Albany NY 12203-1011

REID, WILLIAM JAMES, retired physicist, educator; b. Abbeville, S.C., Nov. 2, 1927; s. William James and Mary Lelia (Shelley) R.; m. Nancy Louise Edwards, Nov. 25, 1964; children: Laura Louise, William James III, Sandra Shelley. AB in Chemistry, Erskine Coll., 1949; MS in Chemistry, Duke U., 1958; PhD in Physics, Clemson U., 1967. Instr. Erskine Coll., Due West, S.C., 1949-51, field rep., 1951-52; svc. mgr. Reid Motor Co., Abbeville, S.C., 1954-57; asst. prof. Erskine Coll., Due West, 1957-62, assoc. prof., 1966-68; prof., head physics dept. Jacksonville (Ala.) State U., 1968-91, head dept. phys. scis. and engring., 1991-94, ret., 1994; pres. faculty senate Jacksonville State U., 1971-72, 76-77, 88-89. Contbr. various articles to profl. jours. With U.S. Army, 1945-46,, 1st lt. S.C. NG, 1948-56. Recipient Disting. Svc. award Jr. C. of C. Abbeville, S.C., 1960; named Kiwanian of Yr., Jacksonville, 1975. Mem. Am. Phys. Soc., Am. Assn. Physics Tchrs., Ala. Acad. Sci., Rotary Club Clemson, Sigma Xi, Phi Lambda Upsilon, Sigma Pi Sigma, Omicron Delta Kappa, Alpha Mu Gamma, Pi Kappa Phi. Methodist. Home: 3240 Six Mile Hwy Central SC 29630-9021

REID-BILLS, MAE, editor, historian; b. Shreveport, La.; d. Dayton Taylor and Bessie Oline (Boles) Reid; m. Frederick Gurdon Bills (div.); children: Marjorie Reid, Nancy Hawkins, Frederick Taylor, Virginia Thomas, Elizabeth Sharples. AB, Stanford U., 1942, MA, 1965; PhD, U. Denver, 1977. Mng. editor Am. West mag., Tucson, Ariz., 1979-89; cons. editor, 1989—. Gen. Electric fellow, 1963, William Robertson Coe fellow, 1964. Mem. Orgn. Am. Historians, Am. Hist. Assn., Phi Beta Kappa, Phi Alpha Theta.

REIDE, JEROME L., humanities educator, lawyer; b. Bklyn., Apr. 23, 1954; s. St. Clair E. and Leonora E. R. BA, SUNY, New Paltz, 1977; JD, Hofstra U., 1981; MS in Journalism, Columbia U., 1982; PhD, Mich. State U., 1991. Bar: Mich. 1996. Lectr. labor ctr. Empire State Coll., N.Y.C., 1984-86; lectr. African Am. Studies Ea. Mich. U., Ypsilanti, 1987-88; rsch. asst., dean urban affairs Mich. State U., East Lansing, Mich., 1988-90; exec. producer urban affairs Mich. State U., East Lansing, 1989-93; guest curator Mus. African Am. History, Detroit, 1990-91; lectr. Sch. Edn. Wayne State U., Detroit, 1990-92; dir. devel. NAACP Spl. Contribution Fund, Detroit, 1990-93; legis. aide Wayne County Ways and Means Commn., Detroit, 1993-94; asst. prof. interdisciplinary studies Wayne State U., Detroit, 1994—; pres. Global Econ. Devel. Conf., Detroit, 1993—; mem. exec. com. Ctr. for Peace and Conflict Studies, Wayne State U., Detroit, 1994—; mem. Exec. Leadership Devel., Lansing, 1994—; mem. Mich. Educators Network for Dispute Resolution. Author: (book) Justice: Evicted, 1987; editor: (book) Multicultural Curriculum Resource Guide, 1990; contbr. articles to profl. jours. Bd. dirs. Dispute Rsolution Coun. Ctr., Detroit, 1990-95, Bonifact Cmty. Svcs., 1992-95; mem. Voter Edn. Com., NAACP, Detroit, 1990—, Nat. Urban League, Detroit, 1991—. Recipient Spl. Recognition Jackson (Mich.) Fair Housing Ctr., 1992, Spl. Tribute, Mich. Legislature, Lansing, 1994; named Most Inspirational Tchr. U. Mich. Flint Coll. Bond, 1992, Man of Yr. New Grace Missionary Bapt. Ch., Detroit, 1993. Fellow Com. on Instl. Coop., (Eagle award 1993); mem. ABA, State Bar of Mich., Nat. Bar Assn., Nat. Conf. of Black Lawyers (press sec.), Nat. Assn. Black Journalists, Soc. Profl. Journalists. Democrat. Baptist. Home: Brightmoor Sta PO Box 23384 Detroit MI 48223 Office: Wayne State U Coll Lifelong Lrng Interdiscpl Study Prog 5700 Cass Ave Detroit MI 48202-3629

REIDENBAUGH, LOWELL HENRY, retired sports editor; b. Lititz, Pa., Sept. 7, 1919; s. Harry Martin and Marian Marie (Nies) R.; m. Ruth Elizabeth Cameron, Nov. 23, 1944; children: Karen Lee (Mrs. William Rogers), Kathy Jean (Mrs. William J. Schuchman). A.B., Elizabethtown (Pa.) Coll., 1941. Gen. reporter Lancaster (Pa.) Intelligencer Jour., 1941-42; sports writer Phila. Inquirer, 1944-47; mem. staff The Sporting News, St. Louis, 1947-89; mng. editor The Sporting News, 1962-79, sr. editor, 1980-83, corp. editor, 1983-89. Author: National League History, 1976, The Super Bowl Book, 1981, Cooperstown, Where Baseball's Legends Live, 1983, Take Me Out to the Ballpark, 1983, The Sporting News, First 100 Years, 1985, The 50 Greatest Games, 1986, History 33d Va. Infantry Regiment, CSA, 1987, 25 Greatest Pennant Races, 1987, 25 Greatest Teams, 1988, History 27th Va. Infantry Regiment, CSA, 1993, The Battle of Kernstown, 1997. Served with AUS, 1942-43.

REIDENBERG, MARCUS MILTON, physician, educator; b. Phila., Jan. 3, 1934; s. Leon and Adeline Reidenberg; m. June Wilson, July 14, 1957; children: Bruce, Joel, Julie. Student, Cornell U., 1951-54; MD, Temple U., 1958. Diplomate Am. Bd. Internal Medicine. Intern Community Gen. Hosp., Reading, Pa., 1958-59; resident Temple U. Hosp., Phila., 1962-65; from instr. to assoc. prof. Temple U. Med. Sch., Phila., 1962-75; assoc. prof. Cornell U. Med. Coll., N.Y.C., 1975-76, prof. pharmacology, head div. clin. pharmacology, 1976—, prof. medicine, 1980—, acting assoc. dean, 1981-82, asst. dean, 1988—; attending physician N.Y. Hosp., 1980—; vis. physician Rockefeller U. Hosp., N.Y.C., 1980—; mem. project adv. group FDA, Rockville, Md., 1977-82; vice chmn. Joint Commn. on Prescription Drug Use, Washington, 1977-80; mem. study sect. NIH, Bethesda, Md., 1980-86; del. U.S. Pharmacopeal Conv., 1975-80. Author: Renal Function and Drug Action, 1971; editor various books; editor Clin. Pharmacology and Therapeutics, 1985—; contbr. articles to profl. jours. Served to lt. M.C., USNR, 1960-62. Recipient Research Career Devel. award NIH, 1970, Julius Sturmer award Phila. Coll. Pharmacy and Sci., 1982. Fellow ACP; mem. Am. Soc. Clin. Investigations, Assn. Am. Physicians, Am. Soc. Clin. Pharmacology and Therapeutics (pres. 1984-85, Rawls Palmer award 1981), Am. Soc. Pharmacology and Exptl. Therapeutics (award 1983), Internat. Union Pharmacology (vice chmn. sect. clin. pharmacology 1984-87, chmn. 1987-89). Office: Cornell U Med Coll Dept Clin Pharmacology 1300 York Ave New York NY 10021-4805

REIDER, MARTHA CRAWFORD, industrial immunologist; b. Red Bank, N.J., Apr. 29, 1954; d. Harry Edward and Ernestine (Bird) Crawford; m. Michael John Reider, Sept. 22, 1979. BA in Biol. Scis., Ohio No. U., 1976; postgrad., Kennedy-Western U., 1993—. Product devel. scientist E.I. Du-Pont de Nemours and Co., Newark, Del., 1976-82, supr. animal facility, 1982-84, rsch. immunologist, 1984-87, mfg. process scientist, 1987-89, quality assurance supr. testing and release, 1989-90; co-founder, v.p. mfg. Strategic Diagnostics Inc., Newark, 1990—; co-founder, dir. quality assurance TSD Biosvcs., Newark, 1991—; mem. product quality com., mem. customer focus group, human resources com.; facilitator for multiple pers. tng. programs. Contbr. articles to profl. conf. procs. Water safety and CPR/first aid trainer/instr. ARC, 1977—, bd. dirs. Del. br., Wilmington; instr. aquatics YMCA Del., Newark, 1988—. Mem. ASTD, NAFE, Am. Soc. Quality Control (cert. quality auditor), Soc. Human Resources Mgmt., Am. Mgmt. Assn., Beta Beta Beta. Methodist. Avocations: American sign language, teaching swimming. Office: Strategic Diagnostics Inc 128 Sandy Dr Newark DE 19713-1147

REIDINGER, RUSSELL FREDERICK, JR., fish and wildlife scientist; b. Reading, Pa., June 19, 1945. BS, Albright Coll., 1967; PhD in Zoology, U. Ariz., 1972. Asst. prof. biology Augustana Coll., 1971-74; rsch. physiologist The Philippines, 1974-78; asst. mem., wildlife biologist Monell Chem. Senses Ctr., 1978-86; dir. Denver Wildlife Rsch. Ctr. U.S. Dept. Agr., Denver, 1987-93; dir. Ctr. Excellence Nat. Resources Mgmt. Lincoln U., Jefferson City, Mo., 1993—; vis. prof. dept. zoology U. Philippines, 1975-78; cons. Bangladesh Agr. Rsch. Coun., USAID, 1977, Ministry Agrl. Devel. & Agrarian Reform, Nicaragua, 1981, CID, Uganda, 1996. Mem. Am. Soc. Mammalogists, Wildlife Soc., Nat. Animal Damage Control Assn. Office: Lincoln U Dept Ag Nat & Home Econ Jefferson City MO 65102-0029

REID-ROBERTS, DAYL HELEN, mental health counselor; b. Rochester, N.Y., Oct. 15, 1941; d. Russell Harrison and Elizabeth Spencer (Page) Ferrey; m. David Alan Reid, July 16, 1960 (div. 1982); children: Deborah Elizabeth, Patricia Anne, David Alan Jr. (dec.), Matthew Stephen; m. David Gillies Roberts, Aug. 9, 1985. BA, Salisbury (Md.) State U., 1988, MEd, 1990. Lic. profl. counselor; cert. group psychotherapist. Clinician Community Svcs. Bd., Eastern Shore, Nassawadox, Va., 1990—; clinician substance abuse svc. Community Svcs. Bd., Eastern Shore, Onancock, Va., 1990—; clinican, mental social worker, psychiat. Northampton Accomack Meml. Hosp., Nassawadox, 1992-93; v.p. Humanitec, Inc., Accomac, Va., 1993—; instr. philosophy, psychology Ea. Shore Cmty. Coll., 1995—; asst. dir. Literacy Coun. of No. Va., Annandale, 1980-85; adj. clin. instr. Old Dominion U. Contbr. articles to profl. jours. Treas., co-founder Ea. Shore Literacy Coun., 1986. Mem. Am. Counseling Assn., Am. Psychologists Assn. (student), Phi Sigma Tau, Kappa Delta Phi. Republican. Presbyterian. Avocations: reading, needlepoint, house renovation, antiques, bridge. Home: The Oliver House Onancock VA 23417 Office: Humanitec Inc Front St PO Box 580 Accomac VA 23301-0580

REIDY, CAROLYN KROLL, publisher; b. Washington, May 2, 1949; d. Henry August and Mildred Josephine (Mencke) Kroll; m. Stephen Kroll Reidy, Dec. 28, 1974. BA, Middlebury Coll., 1971; MA, Ind. U., 1974, PhD, 1982. Various positions to mgr. subs. rights Random House, Inc., N.Y.C., 1975-83, assoc. pub., 1987-88; dir. subs. rights William Morrow & Co., N.Y.C., 1983-85; v.p., assoc. pub. Vintage Books, N.Y.C., 1985-87, pub., 1987-88; pub. Anchor Books, Doubleday & Co., N.Y.C., 1988; pres., pub. Avon Books, N.Y.C., 1988-92; pres., pub. trade div. Simon & Schuster, N.Y.C., 1992—. Bd. dis. NAMES Project, 1994—. Mem. Women's Media Group, Pubs. Lunch Club. Office: Simon & Schuster 1230 Avenue Of The Americas New York NY 10020-1513

REIDY, GERALD PATRICK, federal organization executive, arbitrator, mediator, fact-finder; b. N.Y.C., Apr. 25, 1929; s. Patrick Joseph and Kathleen Theresa (Holohan) R.; m. Patricia Hope Johnston, Nov. 28, 1953; children: Anne Marie Reidy Borenstein, James M., Susan P., Patricia Reidy Conrad, Daniel E., Thomas J., John G. BS, Fordham Coll., 1949, JD, 1952; LLM in Labor Law, Georgetown U., NYU, 1958; MBA, Iona Coll., 1969. Spl. agent FBI, Phila., Washington, N.Y.C., 1954-65; mgr. indsl. rels., asst. dir. pers. Canada Dry Corp., N.Y.C., 1965-68; dir., adminstr. pers. Bunker Ramo Corp., Trumbull, Conn., 1968-71; dir. pers. The Roosevelt Hosp., N.Y.C., 1971-73; regional dir. U.S. Dept. Labor, Boston, 1973-77, fact-finder, mediator, arbitrator, 1977-78; asst. dir. labor rels. Boston Pub. Libr., 1978-83; regional adminstr. OSHA U.S. Dept. Labor, N.Y.C., 1983-87; dir. Office of Constrn. and Maritime Compliance Assistance OSHA U.S. Dept. Labor, Washington, 1987-91, dir. Office of Constrn. and Civil Engring. Safety Standards OSHA, 1991-95; dir. Office of Constrn. Stds. and Compliance Assistance OSHA, 1995-96, Office of Constrn. Svcs., 1996-97; spl. asst. to gen. counsel Office of Compliance U.S. Congress, Washington, 1997—. Lt. USAF, 1952-54. Mem. Internat. Soc. for Fall Protection, Soc. of Former Spl. Agents FBI, Design Loads on Structures During Constrn. Standards Com. Republican. Roman Catholic. Avocations: fishing, walking seashore, reading, gourmet cooking. Office: US Congress Office of Gen Counsel Office of Compliance 110 2nd St SE Rm LA-200 Washington DC 20540-1999

REIDY, RICHARD ROBERT, publishing company executive; b. Patchogue, N.Y., May 9, 1947; s. Joseph Robert and Irene (Jennings) R.; m. Carolyn Alyce Armstrong, Mar. 21, 1970; children: Dawn Patricia, Shawn Patrick, Christopher Keith. Student, Suffolk County Community Coll., 1966-68, L.I. Tech. Sch., 1969-70, Scottsdale Community Coll., 1983-84, 85-86. Lic. real estate agt., Ariz. Restaurant owner Reidy's, Patchogue, 1973-77; design draftsman Sverdrop & Parcel, Tempe, Ariz., 1978-79, Sullivan & Masson, Phoenix, 1979-81; pres. Success Pub. Co., Scottsdale, Ariz., 1983—; with U.S. Postal Dept., 1980—. Editor, owner, pub.: Who's Who in Arizona, 1984-85, 89-90. Chief Scottsdale YMCA, 1983-84; eucharistic minister St. Daniel the Prophet Cath. Ch., Scottsdale, 1985—; mem. World Wide Marriage Encounter, 1986—; pres. Coronado High Sch. Band Boosters, 1988-89. Mem. Scottsdale C. of C., Phoenix Better Bus. Bur. Office: Success Pub Co PO Box 3431 Scottsdale AZ 85271-3431

REIDY, THOMAS ANTHONY, lawyer; b. Bronx, N.Y., Sept. 30, 1952; s. John Alexander and Elinor Ann (Tracey) R.; m. Victoria Mary Moxham, Mar. 12, 1977; children: J. Benjamin, Jacob T., Thomas A. II. BA with honors, Lehigh U., 1974; JD, U. Va., 1978. Bar: Ohio 1978, U.S. Dist. Ct. (so. dist.) Ohio 1980. Assoc. Moritz, McClure, Hughes, Kerscher & Price, Columbus, Ohio, 1978-80; assoc. Porter, Wright, Morris & Arthur, Columbus, 1980-87, ptnr., 1987-92; v.p. human resources and employment counsel The Longaberger Co., Dresden, Ohio, 1993-94, gen. counsel, 1994—; First v.p. Easter Seals Soc. Ctrl. Ohio, Columbus, 1990-92. Office: Longaberger Co PO Box 73 Dresden OH 43821-0073

REIF, (FRANK) DAVID, artist, educator; b. Cin., Dec. 14, 1941; s. Carl A. and Rachel L. (Clifton) R.; m. Ilona Jekabsons, July 30, 1966; 1 child, Megan Elizabeth. BFA, Art Inst. Chgo., 1968; MFA, Yale U., 1970. Asst. prof. art U. Wyo., Laramie, 1970-74, assoc. prof., 1974-81, prof., 1981—; assoc. prof. U. Mich., Ann Arbor, 1980-81; acting head dept. art U. Wyo., Laramie, 1986-87; selection cons. Ucross Found. Residency Program, Wyo., 1983—; exhibit juror Artwest Nat., Jackson, Wyo., 1986; panelist Colo. State U., Ft. Collins, 1981; lectr. U. Mich., 1980; apptd. Wyo. Arts Coun., 1993—; vis. artist lectr. Colo. State U., 1996; vis. artist Colo. State U., Ft. Collins, 1996. One-man shows include U. Wyo. Art Mus., 1993, Dorsky Galleries, N.Y.C., 1980, No. Ariz. U., 1977, 87, U. Mich., 1980, 81, One West Ctr. Contemporary Art, Ft. Collins, 1991; exhibited in group shows at First, Second and Third Who. Biennial Tour, 1984-88, U.S. Olympics Art Exhbn., L.A., 1984, Miss. Mus. Art and NEA Tour, 1981-83, L.A. Invitational Sculpture Tour Exhbn., 1991-92, Nicolaysen Art Mus., Casper, Wyo., 1994. Apptd. chair Wyo. Arts Coun., 1995-96. With USAR, 1963-69. Recipient F.D. Pardee award Yale U., 1970; Best Sculpture award Joslyn Art Mus. Omaha, 1978; Nat. Endowment Arts grantee, 1978-79, Wyo. Basic Rsch. grantee, 1983-84, 86-87. Mem. Coll. Art Assn., Internat. Sculpture Ctr. Democrat. Home: 3340 Aspen Ln Laramie WY 82070-5702 Office: U Wyo Dept Art PO Box 3138 Laramie WY 82071-3138

REIF, LOUIS RAYMOND, lawyer, utilities executive; b. Buffalo, July 4, 1923; s. John Dennis and Sadie (Wilkenson) R.; m. Nancy C. Heuer, Apr. 12, 1958; children: Tracey Lynn, Christopher Louis. Student, Mich. State U., 1941-42, The Citadel, 1943; AB, U. Buffalo, 1948; JD, U. Mich., 1951. Bar: N.Y. 1953. Pvt. practice Chgo., 1951-52, Buffalo, 1953—; atty. Continental Ill. Nat. Bank, Chgo., 1951-52; from atty. to sr. v.p. Iroquois Gas Corp., Buffalo, 1952-71; pres. Iroquois Gas Corp., 1971—, also bd. dirs.; from v.p. to pres., CEO Nat. Fuel Gas Co., N.Y.C., 1960-87, chmn., CEO, 1988—; asst. to chmn. Del. North Cos., Buffalo, 1988, COO, 1989—, also bd. dirs., 1989; chmn. Bio-Quest Inc., Houston, 1996; bd. dirs. Goldome Bank; chmn. N.Y. Gas Group, 1973—; chmn. 17th World Gas Conf., Internat. Gas Union, 1986-88. Pres., dir. Buffalo Better Bus. Bur., 1970; trustee SUNY-Buffalo Found. Served with C.E. AUS, 1943-46, ETO. Mem. ABA, N.Y. Bar Assn., Fed. Power Bar Assn., Erie County Bar Assn., Barrister Soc., Am. Gas Assn. (chmn. dir. 1984-85, Disting. Svc. award 1986), Nat. Alliance Businessmen (dir., chmn. 1967-68), Buffalo C. of C. (dir. 1973—), chmn. nat. affairs com. 1969—), Buffalo Club (bd. dirs. 1988, pres. 1991-92), Phi Alpha Delta. Office: Bioquest 333 N Sam Houston Pkwy E Houston TX 77060-2414

REIFF, PATRICIA HOFER, space physicist, educator; b. Oklahoma City, Mar. 14, 1950; d. William Henry and Maxine Ruth (Hoffer) R.; m. Thomas Westfall Hill, July 4, 1976; children: Andrea Hofer Hill, Adam Reiff Hill, Amelia Reiff Hill. Student, Wellesley Coll., 1967-68; BS, Okla. State U., 1971; MS, Rice U., 1974, PhD, 1975. Cert. secondary tchr., Okla., Tex. Rsch. assoc. space physics and astronomy dept. Rice U., Houston, 1975, asst. prof. space physics and astronomy dept., 1978-81, asst. chmn. space physics and astronomy dept., 1979-85, assoc. rsch. sci., 1981-87, sr. rsch. scientist, 1987-90; resident rsch. assoc. Marshall Space Flight Ctr., Huntsville, Ala., 1975-76; adj. asst. prof. Rice U., 1976-78, disting. faculty fellow, 1990-92, prof. 1992—, chmn. dept. space physics and astronomy, 1996—; mem. sci. team Atmosphere Explorer Mission, Dynamics Explorer Mission, Global Geospace Sci. Mission, ESA/Cluster Mission; prin. investigator The Public Connection NASA; cons. Houston Mus. Natural Sci., 1986—; adv. com. on atmospheric scis. NSF, Washington, 1988-92; mem. stategic implementation study panel NASA, Washington, 1989-91; mem. space sci. adv. com. NASA, 1993—, mem. space sta. utilization subcom., 1995—; univ. rep. U. Space Rsch. Assn., Washington, 1993— (mem. nom. com.); exec. com. George Observatory, Houston, 1989-92, others. Designer Cockrell Sundial/Solar Telescope, 1989; editor EOS (sci. newspaper), 1986-89; contbr. articles to profl. jours. Trustee, Citizens' Environ. Coalition, Houston, 1978—, pres. 1980-85; mem. air quality com. Houston/Galveston Area Coun., 1980-83, Green Ribbon Com., City of Houston, 1981-83; active coms. Macedonia United Meth. Ch., 1988—. Named rsch. fellow NAS/NRC., 1975, an Outstanding Young Woman Am., 1977, '80, to Houston's Women on the Move, 1990; recipient grant NSF, Houston, 1990-92, NASA, 1993, 94. Fellow Am. Geophys. Union (fin. com. 1980-82, editor search com. 1992, pub. edn. com.); mem. Am. Meteorol. Soc. (coun. 1985-88), Cosmos Club, Wellesley Club, Internat. Union of Geodesy and Geophysics (del. 1975, 81, 83, 89, 91, 93, 95, chair working group 2F, 1991-95). Avocations: organic gardening, beef ranching. Office: Rice U Dept Space Physics 6100 S Main St Houston TX 77251-1892

REIFFEL, LEONARD, physicist, scientific consultant; b. Chgo., Sept. 30, 1927; s. Carl and Sophie (Miller) R.; m. Judith Eve Blumenthal, 1952 (div. 1962); children—Evan Carl, David Lee; m. Nancy L. Jeffers, 1971. B.Sc., Ill. Inst. Tech., 1947, M.Sc., 1948, Ph.D., 1953. Physicist Perkin-Elmer Corp., Conn., 1948; engring. physicist U. Chgo. Inst. Nuclear Studies, 1948-49; with Ill. Inst. Tech. Research Inst., Chgo., 1949-65, dir. physics research, 1956-63, v.p., 1963-65; cons. to Apollo program NASA Hdqrs., 1965-70, pvt. practice cons., 1970—; tech. dir. manned space flight expts. bd. NASA, 1966-68; chmn. bd. Instructional Dynamics, Inc., 1966-81, Interand Corp., 1969-91, Telestrator Industries, Inc., 1970-73; sci. editor Sta. WBBM-CBS radio, Chgo.; sci. cons./commentator WBBM-TV, 1971-72; host Backyard Safari, 1971-73; sci. feature broadcaster WEEI-CBS radio, Boston, 1965-75; syndicated newspaper columnist World Book Ency. Sci. Service, Inc. (later Universal Sci. News, Inc.), 1966-72, Los Angeles Times Syndicate, 1972-76; sci. cons. CBS Network, 1967-71; chmn., CEO Exelar Corp., Chgo., 1991—; chmn. bd., pres., CEO Ameraine Corp., Chgo., 1992-95; mem. bd of overseers Armour Coll. Ill. Inst. Tech., 1995—; cons. Korean Govt. on establishment atomic energy rsch. program; mem. adv. com. isotope and radiation devel. AEC; com. rsch. reactors NAS, 1958-64; cons. U.S. Army, 1976—. Author: (book) The Contaminant, 1979; author numerous sci. papers. Bd. dirs. Student Competitions on Relevant Engring. Named Outstanding Young Man of Year Chgo. Jr. C. of C., 1954, 61; recipient Merit award Chgo. Tech. Socs., 1968; Peabody award for radio edn., 1968; IR-100 award for inventing Telestrator CBS Chalkboard, 1970; award for coverage space events Aviation Writers Assn., 1971; IR-100 award for invention underwater diver communications system, 1972, IR-100 award for DISCON video teleconferencing systems, 1985, Third Annual High Tech Entrepreneur award, 1986; also for invention Audiografix, 1973; Disting. Alumni Achievement award Ill. Inst. Tech., 1974, named to Hall of Fame IIT, 1984. Fellow Am. Phys. Soc.; mem. AAAS, Chgo. Literary Club, Sigma Xi, Tau Beta Pi, Eta Kappa Nu. Patentee in field; responsible for world's 1st indsl. nuclear reactor, 1956. Home: 602 W Deming Pl Chicago IL 60614-2618

REIFLER, CLIFFORD BRUCE, psychiatrist, educator; b. Chgo., Dec. 28, 1931; s. Eugene Alan and Harriet (Offer) R.; m. Barbara Karnuth, Sept. 11, 1954; children: Margery Sue, Cynthia Jean, Angela Harriet. AB, U. Chgo., 1951; BS, Northwestern U., 1953; MD, Yale U., 1957; MPH, U. N.C., 1967. Intern Univ. Hosps., Ann Arbor, Mich., 1957-58; resident in psychiatry Strong Meml. Hosp., Rochester, N.Y., 1958-61; mem. faculty U. N.C. Med. Sch., 1963-70, assoc. prof. psychiatry, 1969-70, assoc. prof. mental health Sch. Pub. Health, 1969-70, sr. psychiatrist, chief mental health sect., student health svc., 1963-70; prof. health svcs., psychiatry and community and preventive medicine U. Rochester Med. Sch., 1970-94, dir. univ. health svc., 1970-80, 81-94, prof. emeritus of psychiatry and health svcs., dir. emeritus, 1994—, interim v.p. student affairs, 1980-81, sr. assoc. dean for clin. affairs Sch. Medicine and Dentistry, acting chmn. dept. health svcs., 1983-85; med. dir. Strong Meml. Hosp., 1983-85; bd. dirs. Genesee Valley Group Health Assn., 1972-82; cons. in field; vis. prof. of psychiatry, Harvard U. Med. Sch., 1987; Dana L. Farnsworth hon. cons. Harvard U. Health Service, 1987. Co-author: Mental Health on the Campus-A Field Study, 1973; co-author: The Alternative Services: Their Role in Mental Health, 1975, Old Folks at Home-A Field Study of Nursing and Board-and-Care Homes, 1976; exec. editor Jour. Am. Coll. Health, 1983-97; mem. editl. bd. Jour. of Coll. Student Psychotherapy, 1986—; contbr. profl. jours. Bd. dirs. Am. Coll. Health Found., 1994—, chair 1995—; bd. dirs. Rochester Meml. Soc., 1971-74; mem. med. adv. com., bd. dirs. Planned Parenthood Rochester and Monroe County, 1973-74; mem. devel. com. Seneca Zool. Soc., 1990-95, trustee, 1991—, chair, 1993-95, mem. pers. com. 1995—, chair, 1997—; mem. mem. com. Rochester Philharm. Orch. Inc., 1981-83. With M.C., USAF, 1961-63. Fellow Am. Coll. Health Assn. (pres. 1976-77, Edward Hitchcock award 1981, Ruth C. Boynton award 1988), Am. Psychiat. Assn. (life), Am. Coll. Physician Execs. (disting.); mem. N.Y. State Coll. Health Assn. Home: 143

Palmerston Rd Rochester NY 14618-1247 Office: U Health Svc 250 Crittenden Blvd Box 617 Rochester NY 14642-8617

REIFSNIDER, KENNETH LEONARD, metallurgist, educator; b. Balt., Feb. 19, 1940; s. David Leonard and Daisy Pearl (Hess) R.; m. Loretta Lieb, June 15, 1963; children—Eric Scott, Jason Miles. BA, Western Md. Coll., 1963; BS in Engring., Johns Hopkins U., 1963, MS in Engring., 1965, PhD, 1968. Jr. instr. John Hopkins U., Balt., 1966-67; asst. prof. Va. Poly. Inst. and State U., Blacksburg, 1968-72, assoc. prof., 1972-75, prof., 1975-83, Reynolds Metals prof. engring. sci. and mechanics, 1983-90, Alexander Giacco prof., 1990—, also chmn. materials engring. sci. Ph.D. program, 1974-92, chmn. adminstrn. bd. Ctr. Composite Materials and Structures, 1984, 1994—; dir. Va. Inst. for Material Systems, 1988—, assoc. provost for interdisciplinary programs, 1996—; engr. Lawrence Livermore Nat. Lab., 1981; cons. in materials sci. NATO, 1969, 75. Mem. troop 44 com. Boy Scouts Am., Blacksburg, Va. Recipient Va. Acad. Sci. J. Shelton Horsley award, 1978, Va. Poly. Inst. Alumni award, 1982, Disting. Rsch. award Am. Soc. Composites, 1992. Fellow ASTM (founder Jour. of Composites Tech. and Rsch., vice chmn. standing com. on publs., award of merit 1982); mem. ASME, Council on Engring. Editor, co-editor, author books, book chpts., articles for profl. publs.

REIFSNYDER, WILLIAM EDWARD, meteorologist; b. Ridgway, Pa., Mar. 29, 1924; s. Howard William and Madolin (Boyer) R.; m. Marylou Bishop, Dec. 19, 1954 (dec. July 1990); children: Rita, Cheryl, Gawain. B.S. in Meteorology, NYU, 1944; M.F., U. Calif., Berkeley, 1949; Ph.D., Yale U., 1954. Cert. cons. meteorologist. Meteorologist Pacific S.W. Forest and Range Expt. Sta., 1952-55; mem. faculty Yale U., 1955-90, prof. emeritus, 1990—, prof. forest meteorology and biometeorology, 1967-90; vis. scientist Max Planck Inst. for Meteorology, Hamburg, U. Munich, Environ. Rsch. Labs., Nat. Oceanic and Atmospheric Adminstrn.; cons. World Meteorol. Orgn., UN Univ., Internat. Coun. Rsch. in Agroforestry. Author: Hut Hopping in the Austrian Alps, Footloose in the Swiss Alps, The High Huts of the White Mountains, Radiant Energy in Relation to Forests, Weathering the Wilderness, Adventuring in the Alps; editor-in-chief Agrl. and Forest Meteorology; editor: Meteorology and Agroforestry. Bd. dirs. Am. Youth Hostels. Service with USAAF, 1943-47. Fellow AAAS; mem. Conn. Acad. Sci. and Engring. (corr.), Am. Meteorol. Soc. (Outstanding Achievement in Biometeorology award), Soc. Am. Foresters, Internat. Soc. Biometeorology (v.p.). Home: HC81 (Lama) Box 3 Questa NM 87556 Office: Sch Forestry and Environ Studies Yale U New Haven CT 06511

REIG, JUNE WILSON, writer, director, producer; b. Schenectady, N.Y., June 1, 1933; d. Wallace John and Lillian Lucy (Gay) Wilson; m. Robert Maxwell, Nov. 26, 1969. BA summa cum laude, N.Y. State U., 1954; MA in Dramatic Arts, NYU, 1962. Instr. NYU, 1962-67; producer, dir. NYU Theater, 1963-67; dir.-prodr., writer news and pub. affairs NBC TV Network, N.Y.C., 1963-67; dir., writer, prodr. program dept. NBC-TV Network, N.Y.C., 1967-73; pres. Bunny/Chord Prodns., N.Y.C., 1972—. Author: Diary of the Boy King Tut-Ankh-Amen, 1978; writer, dir. (TV film spl.) Stuart Little, 1966 (Peabody award Prix Jeunesse); writer (TV spl.) The Reluctant Dragon, 1968 (Brotherhood award), (music spls.) The Heart of Christmas, 1965, An Afternoon at Tanglewood (Peabody award); writer, dir., producer (TV spls.) Rabbit Hill, 1966 (ALA award) Bill Cosby As I See It, 1970 (Ohio State award) A Day With Bill Cosby, 1971, Jennifer & Me, 1972; (TV daily series) Watch Your Child - The Me Too Show, 1973 (Action for Children's TV Achievement award); prodr., writer (TV spl.) Little Women, the ballet, 1976, Tut, the Boy King, 1978 (Peabody award); films in permanent collection of Mus. Broadcasting, N.Y.C. Recipient Prix Jeunesse, 1966, Christopher award, 1970, Emmy award nomination, 1966, 76. Mem. Writers Guild Am., Dirs. Guild Am., Nat. Acad. TV Arts and Scis., NYU Alumni Assn., Internat. Soc. Animal Rights, Friends of Animals, Audubon Soc. Club: Alan Devoe Bird (Old Chatham, N.Y.). Avocations: photography, music, animals. Office: Bunny/Chord Prodns Inc Ste 1405 119 W 57th St New York NY 10019-2401 *Whether I am working on a teleplay or book, I write about things I believe children are interested in: feelings, aspirations, caring, animals, loving. As I see it, too much of the fare for young people gives them a distorted view of how much violence there is in the world, and I want to counteract that impression. I want to write about things that create a sense of worth, warm security, and an absence of unnecessary anxiety. When I do write about the darker things that happen in life, it is to help the young person understand himself and the world a little better.*

REIGHARD, HOMER LEROY, physician; b. Martinsburg, Pa., Dec. 1, 1924; s. David F. and Cora E. (Steel) R.; m. Barbara Jane Suttell, Dec. 14, 1951; children: Carol, Janet, Paul. B.S., Franklin and Marshall Coll., 1945; M.D., Temple U., 1948; M.P.H., Harvard U., 1961. Intern Temple U. Hosp., Phila., 1948-49; physician-in charge accidents dispensary Temple U. Hosp., 1949-50; med. officer CAA, Washington, 1953-59; practice medicine Bethesda, Md., 1953-60; chief med. standards div. FAA, 1959-61, spl. asst. to civil air surgeon, 1962-63, dep. fed. air surgeon, 1963-75, fed. air surgeon, 1975-84; cons. in aviation medicine, 1984—, workplace anti-drug programs, 1987—. Bd.dirs. Aviation Rsch. & Edn. Found., 1985-92. Served with M.C, USAF, 1950-53. Recipient Meritorious Service award FAA, 1970, Disting. Career Service award, FAA, 1984. Fellow Aerospace Med. Assn. (Harry G. Moseley flight safety award 1977); mem. Phi Beta Kappa. Developer passenger screening system to identify potential hijackers. Home: 10215 Hatherleigh Dr Bethesda MD 20814-2223

REIGROD, ROBERT HULL, manufacturing executive; b. N.Y.C., Mar. 26, 1941; s. David and Beatrice (Simon) R.; divorced; children: Sandra, Donald. BA in Anthropology, Calif. State U., Long Beach, 1973. Account exec. Ira Haupt & Co., N.Y.C., 1961-64; regional adminstrv. mgr. Brother Internat. Corp., Los Angeles, 1964-70; regional sales mgr. Brother Internat. Corp., Irvine, Calif., 1970-77, gen. mgr. west region, 1977-82; v.p. Brother Internat. Corp., 1982-86; dir., sr. v.p. Brother Internat. Corp., Somerset, N.J., 1986—; pres. Brother Internat. de Mexico, S.A. de C.V., 1992—. Trustee Leukemia Soc. Am., 1982-84; bd. dirs. Irvine Children's Fund, 1988-90. Mem. Japan Soc. South Fla. (dir. 1994—, trustee). Office: Brother Internat Corp 3333 W Commercial Blvd Fort Lauderdale FL 33309-3441

REIK, RITA ANN FITZPATRICK, pathologist; b. Cleve., Mar. 9, 1951; d. Charles Robert Sr. and Rita Mae (Wilke) Fitzpatrick; m. Curtis A. Reik, Oct. 19, 1974. BA in Chemistry, Fla. Internat. U., 1985; MD, U. Miami, 1989. Diplomate Am. Bd. Anatomic and Clinical Pathology. Resident in pathology Jackson Meml. Hosp., Miami, Fla., 1989-95; mem. faculty dept. pathology U. Miami Sch. Medicine, 1995—; attending physician transfusion med. svcs. U. Miami/Jackson Meml. Hosp., 1996—; dir. stem cell processing and graft engring. lab. U. Miami Sch. Medicine/Jackson Meml. Hosp.; dir. lab. svcs. Jackson U. Maternity Ctr., Miami; dir. lab. svcs. North Dade Amb. Care Ctr. Fellow Coll. Am. Pathologists; mem. AMA, NOW, U. Miami Med. Women (pres. 1988-89), Am. Soc. Clin. Pathologists, Alpha Omega Alpha, Phi Kappa Phi. Achievements include research in bone marrow and stem cell transplantation. Avocations: painting, raising Japanese Koi, gardening. Office: U Miami Jackson Meml Hosp Dept Pathology 1611 NW 12th Ave Miami FL 33136-1005

REILAND, LOWELL KEITH, sculptor; b. Wahpeton, N.D., May 11, 1948; s. Peter Paul And Evelyn Ruth (Huss) R. Student, N.D. State U., 1966-68; BA, BS, Moorhead State U., 1971; MFA, Cornell U., 1974. Intern teaching Anglo-Am. Sch., Stockholm, 1971; artist-in-residence Pulpit Rock Artist's Community, Woodstock, Conn., 1974-76; asst. to Richard Lippold, Archtl. Sculptor, N.Y.C., 1970, 75, 77; artist-in-residence Moorhead (Minn.) State U., 1978; artist N.Y.C., 1976-92; lectr.-at-large N.D. State U., Fargo, 1988; lectr. art Conn. Assn. Psychiatrists Ann. Meeting, New Haven, 1985, New Sch., N.Y.C., 1986, Plains Art Mus., Moorhead, 1988, philosophy N.D. State U., Fargo, 1988, Westchester C.C., Westerly Pub. Libr., 1992, Lyman Allyn Art Mus., 1993; participant bronze casting invitational U. Conn., Storrs, 1982. Exhibited at Sarah Y. Rentschler Gallery, N.Y.C., 1979-83, Soho Ctr. for Visual Artists, N.Y.C., 1978, 87, DiLaurenti Gallery, N.Y.C., 1987, Aldrich Mus., Contemporary Art, Ridgefield, Conn., 1988, Plains Art Mus., Moorhead, 1988, Bayly Art Mus. of U. Va., Charlottesville, Travel: Studio Sch., N.Y.C., 1990, Wichita (Kans.) Art Mus., 1990, Lyman Allyn Art Mus., 1993-94, Virginia Lynch Gallery, R.I., 1994, 96; prin. works include City of Fargo, 1978, Moorhead State U., 1978, collection Clara M. Eagle Mus., Murray, Ky., 1984, collection Palace of the Sultan of Brunei, 1985; contbr. articles to profl. jours. Recipient Art award/prize Am. Acad. and Inst. Arts and Letters, N.Y.C., 1986; artist's grantee Pollock/Krasner Found., N.Y.C., 1987-88, Change, Inc., 1989, exhbn. grantee Artist's Space, N.Y.C., 1985; grantee, resident Art League Schleswig-Holsteinisches Kunstlerhaus, Selk, Fed. Republic Germany, 1990. Avocations: studies Cen., S.Am. and Asian primative arts, studies Italian Renaissance art. Home and Studio: Lowell Reiland Sculpture Indsl Trust Co Bldg 14 High St Westerly RI 02891-1854

REILEY, T. PHILLIP, systems analyst, consultant; b. Ft. Lewis, Wash., May 5, 1950; s. Thomas Phillip and Anne Marie (Russick) R. BSc in Biophysics, Pa. State U., 1973; postgrad. in Bus. Adminstrn., Rutgers U.; MBA, NYU, 1991. Cert. prodn. and inventory mgmt., cert. integrated resource mgmt. Inventory supr. Leland Tube Co., South Plainfield, N.J., 1973-76; prodn. inventory control supr. Bomar Crystal Co., Middlesex, N.J., 1976-79; prodn. control mgr. Codi Semicondr. Inc., Linden, N.J., 1979-81; mfg. systems analyst Western Union Info. Systems, Mahwah, N.J., 1981-85; bus. analyst Nabisco Brands Biscuit Div., Parsippany, N.J., 1985-91, sr. systems analyst, 1991-94, tech. advisor, cons., 1994—. Mem. Am. Prodn. and Inventory Control Soc. (past chmn. edn. com. Raritan Valley chpt.), N.Y. Acad. Scis., Mensa, Coun. Logistics Mgmt., Am. Inst. Mgmt. Accts. Republican. Home: 56 Carlton Club Dr Piscataway NJ 08854-3114 Office: Nabisco Brands 100 Deforest Ave East Hanover NJ 07936-2813

REILING, HENRY BERNARD, business educator; b. Richmond, Ky., Feb. 5, 1938; s. Henry Bernard and Lucille Frances (Fowler) R.; m. Carol-Lina Maria Schuetz, June 4, 1962; children: Christina Lucille, Maria Hays, Carol-Lena Alexis. B.A., Northwestern U., 1960; M.B.A., Harvard U., 1962; J.D., Columbia U., 1965. Bar: N.Y. 1965. Mem. faculty Columbia U. Bus. Sch., 1965-76, prof., 1974-76; vis. prof. Stanford U. Bus. Sch., 1974-75; vis. asso. prof. Harvard U. Bus. Sch., 1972-73, prof., 1976—, Eli Goldston prof. bus. adminstrn., 1978—; bd. dirs. Levitz Furniture Inc. Contbr. bus. and law jours. Trustee Riverside Ch., N.Y.C., 1976-77; mem. vis. com. Northwestern U. Coll. Arts and Scis., 1989—. Recipient Alumnus Merit award Northwestern U., 1996. Mem. ABA, N.Y. Bar Assn., Bar Assn. City N.Y., Am. Fin. Assn., Fin. Mgmt. Assn., Nat. Tax Assn., Tax Inst. Am., Union Club (N.Y.C.), Beta Gamma Sigma (hon.). Home: 28 Meriam St Lexington MA 02173-3618 Office: Harvard U Bus Sch Boston MA 02163

REILLEY, JAMES CLARK, artist, cartoonist, small business owner; b. Detroit, Nov. 4, 1919; s. James Aloyisus and Lillian May (Cole) R.; m. Beatrice C. Clemente, May 10, 1952; children: James A. (dec.), Anthony Francis, Beatrice Anita. Grad., Art Inst. of Pitts., 1948. Artist Banner Advt., Phila., 1948-49; layout artist Lit Bros. Dept. Store, Phila., 1949; comic book illustrator John Prentice, Long Island, N.Y., 1950; artist DuPont Co., Wilmington, Del., 1950-59; artist/owner Jim Reilley Studio, Wilmington, 1959-94; ret. Sgt. USAAF, 1942-45. Inducted to Penns Grove H.S. Personal Achievement Hall of Fame, 1996. Roman Catholic. Avocations: fishing, music, sports. Home: 110 N Broad St Penns Grove NJ 08069-1269

REILLY, ANNE CAULFIELD (NANCY REILLY), painter; b. Bryn Mawr, Pa., Mar. 29, 1927; d. Ralph Caulfield and Claire Helena (Roesch) Goodman; m. Donald Elliott Reilly, May 14, 1949; children: Kevin Caulfield, William Stockbridge, Peter Elliott. Studies with Samuel E. Brown, Westport, Conn., 1955-63; studies with Mimi Jennewein, Larchmont, N.Y., 1964-65. demonstrator, lectr. in portrait painting Bridgeport (Conn.) Art League, Milford (Conn.) Art League, Pen and Brush Club, New Haven, Conn., Conn. Classic Arts Assn., Allied Artists Am., Kent (Conn.) Art Assn., SCAN, Newtown, Conn. Exhibited in group shows at Nat. Acad. Design, N.Y.C., 1964, 65, 69, 70, Nat. Acad. Arts and Letters, N.Y.C., 1971, Wadsworth Antheum, Hartford, Conn., 1966, 72, Stamford (Conn.) Mus., 1965, Mus. Sci. and Industry, Bridgeport, 1972, Salmagundi Club, N.Y.C., Nat. Arts Club, N.Y.C. Vol. artist rehab. unit Norwalk Hosp., 1984-95. Recipient Gold medal for oil painting Catherine Lorillard Wolfe Art Club, 1965, Silver medal for oil painting Nat. Arts Club, 1969, Bronze medal for oil painting Hudson Valley Art Assn., 1981, George Height award for portrait, 1969, Blanche Farr award 1971, Best in Show Kent Art Assn., 1991, J.D. Altobello Meml. award Conn. Pastel Soc., 1995. Mem. Allied Artists Am. (bd. dirs. 1991—, Jane Peterson award for portrait 1971), Am. Artists Profl. League, Nat. Arts Club (Bruce Stevenson award for portrait 1971, 88, 91), Pastel Soc. Am., Hudson Valley Art Assn. (Thora M. Jensen award 1989), Kent Art Assn. (Gordon C. Aymar award for oil 1993, Mabel Rowe Aiken award for oil 1995), New Haven Paint and Clay Club (Merit award 1992), Acad. Artists Assn. Springfield. Home and Studio: 9 Marilane Westport CT 06880-1008

REILLY, CONOR DESMOND, lawyer; b. Kansas City, Mo., Feb. 12, 1952; s. Desmond M. and Patricia (Carton) R.; m. Margaret M. Cannella, June 8, 1975; children: Katherine C., Michael C. BS, MIT, 1972; JD cum laude, Harvard U., 1975. Bar: N.Y. 1976, U.S. Dist. Ct. (ea. and so. dists.) N.Y. 1976, U.S. Ct. Appeals (2d. cir.) 1977, U.S. Dist. Ct. (D.C. cir.) 1979, U.S. Dist. Ct. (no. dist.) Calif. 1981, U.S. Dist. Ct. (cen. dist.) Calif. 1982. Law clk. to judge U.S. Dist. Ct. (ea. dist.), Bklyn., 1975-76; assoc. Cravath, Swaine & Moore, N.Y.C., 1976-77, Coudert Bros., N.Y.C., 1977-83; assoc. LeBoeuf, Lamb, Leiby & MacRae, N.Y.C., 1983-84, ptnr., 1985-88; ptnr. Gibson, Dunn & Crutcher, N.Y.C., 1988—. Editor Harvard U. Law Rev., 1973-74. Hearing officer N.Y.C. Bd. Edn., 1977-79; elected mem. Millburn Twp. Bd. Edn., 1987-92. Mem. ABA, Am. Arbitration Assn. (arbitrator). Democrat. Avocation: tennis. Home: 62 Joanna Way Short Hills NJ 07078-3241 Office: Gibson Dunn & Crutcher 200 Park Ave New York NY 10166-0005

REILLY, DANIEL PATRICK, bishop; b. Providence, May 12, 1928; s. Francis E. and Mary (Burns) R. Student, Our Lady of Providence Sem., 1943-48, Grand Seminaire, St. Brieuc, France, 1948-53, Harvard U., 1954-55, Boston Coll., 1955-56; D (hon.), Providence Coll.; D. (hon.), St. Michael's Coll.; D (hon.), Holy Apostles Coll. and Sem., Salve Regina Coll., Our Lady of Providence Coll., Sacred Heart U., Assumption Coll., 1995, Anna Maria Coll., 1995, Holy Cross Coll., 1996. Ordained priest Roman Catholic Ch., 1953; asst. pastor Cathedral Saints Peter and Paul, Providence, 1953-54; asst. chancellor Diocese of Providence, 1954-56, sec. to bishop, 1956-64, chancellor, 1964-72, adminstr., 1971-72, vicar gen., 1972-75; became monsignor, 1964, consecrated bishop, 1975; bishop of Norwich, Conn., 1975-94; installed bishop of Worcester, Mass., 1994—; Conn. state chaplain K.C., 1976-94; Episcopal moderator Nat. Cath. Cemetery Corp., 1977-87; ad hoc mem. to aid ch. in Ea. Europe NCCB/U.S. Cath. Conf., adminstrv. com. mem., 1976-86, 92—; pro-life com. mem. NCCB, 1989-92, chmn. 10th anniversary peace pastoral com., 1992-93, chmn. internat. policy com., 1993; mem. Priestly Life and Ministry Commn., 1991-94; past pres. New Eng. Consultation Ch. Leaders; drafting com. mem. U.S. Cath. Conf. Pastoral Letter on Peace, 1983, mem. com. on coms.; active Holy See Pontifical Coun.-Cor Unum, 1984-89. Trustee Cath. Mut. Relief Soc., Omaha, 1979—, St. John's Sem., Brighton, Mass., 1987—, Am. Coll., Louvain, Belgium, St. Mary's Sem., Balt.; bd. dirs. United Way Southeastern Conn., 1976-94, Conn. Drug and Adv. Coun., 1978-80; chmn. bd. Cath. Relief Svcs., 1978-86; mem. fin. and budget com. U.S. Cath. Conf., 1985-87; chancellor Holy Apostles Coll. and Sem., Cromwell, Conn., 1982-94; pres. Conn. Interfaith Housing, 1975-94; cons. Pontifical Coun. Justice and Peace, 1995. Mem. Rotary. Home: 2 High Ridge Rd Worcester MA 01602-1432 *If you would make a true success of your life for time and for eternity, never forget that it will be achieved by your willingness to make countless efforts that will be known only to God.*

REILLY, DAVID HENRY, university dean; b. Paterson, N.J., Nov. 7, 1936; s. David Henry and Ethel Taylor (Alt) R.; m. Jean Lockwood, July 2, 1960; children—David Scott, Chris Robert, Sandra Jean, Reilly Kennon Bozeman. B.A., U. Vt., 1959; Ed.M., Rutgers U., 1962, Ed.D., 1965. Diplomate: Am. Bd. Profl. Psychology. Remedial reading instr. Drake Sch. of N.J. Neuro-Psychiat. Inst., Princeton, 1959-62; jr. fellow psychol. services at inst. Drake Sch. of N.J. Neuro-Psychiat. Inst., summer 1962-63; research asst. N.J. Bur. Research Neurology and Psychiatry; also sch. psychologist Woodbridge (N.J.) sch. system, 1962-63; clin. psychologist, then research asso. N.J. Bur. Research Neurology and Psychiatry, 1963-64, 65; sch. and research psychologist Woodbridge sch. system, 1964-65; post doctoral fellow clin. child psychology Devereux Found., Devon, Pa., 1965-66; mem. faculty U. N.C., Chapel Hill, 1966-74; prof. psychology U. N.C., 1974—, chmn. dept. sch. psychology program, 1966-74; dean U. N.C. (Sch. Edn.), Greensboro, 1974-86; dean Coll. of Grad. and Profl. Studies The Citadel, Charleston, 1992—; Mem. N.C. Bd. Examiners Practicing Psychologists, 1973—, treas., 1975, chmn., 1976. Contbr. articles to profl. jours. Research grantee NIMH, 1963; Fulbright Vis. scholar Republic of Cyprus, 1986-87, USSR, 1990. Fellow Am. Psychol. Assn.; mem. Am. Acad. Sch. Psychology (pres.-elect 1996-97), Southeastern Psychol. Assn., N.C. Psychol. Assn. (pres. 1980-81), N.C. Assn. Coll. Tchr. Edn. (pres. 1981), N.C. Sch. Psychology Assn. (pres. 1976-77). Home: 306 Mimms Ave Charleston SC 29409

REILLY, EDWARD ARTHUR, lawyer; b. N.Y.C., Dec. 17, 1943; s. Edward Arthur and Anna Marguerite (Sautter) R.; children: M. Teresa, Edward A. A.B., Princeton U., 1965; J.D., Duke U., 1968. Bar: N.Y. 1969, N.C. 1971, Fla. 1979, Conn. 1983. Asst. dean law sch. Duke U., 1970-72; assoc. Shearman & Sterling, N.Y.C., 1972-80, ptnr., 1980-87; ptnr. Harlow, Reilly, Derr & Stark, Research Triangle Park, N.C., 1988-90; counsel Morris & McVeigh, N.Y.C., 1991-93, ptnr., 1993—. Lt. USNR, 1968-80. Decorated Chevalier de l'Ordre des Arts et des Lettres, French Govt.-Ministry of Culture and Comm., 1992. Fellow Am. Coll. Trust & Estate Counsel; mem. N.Y. State Bar Assn., Fla. Bar Assn., Conn. Bar Assn. Episcopalian. Office: Morris & McVeigh 767 3rd Ave New York NY 10017-2023

REILLY, EDWARD FRANCIS, JR., former state senator, federal agency administrator; b. Leavenworth, Kans., Mar. 24, 1937; s. Edward F. and Marian C. (Sullivan) R.; BA, U. Kans., 1961. V.p. Reilly & Sons, Inc., Leavenworth, 1967-92; pres. Yllier Lake Estates, Inc., Easton, Kans., 1965-89; mem. Kans. Ho. of Reps., 1963-64; mem. Kans. State Senate, 1964-92, asst. majority leader, 1977-80, vice-chmn. govtl. orgn., chmn. ins. subcom., chmn. fed. and state affairs com. Mem. Nat. Commn. on Accreditation of Law Enforcement Agys.; chmn. U.S. Parole Commission Dept. of Justice, Md., 1992—; commr. ex officio U.S. Sentencing Commn., Washington; del. to Republican Nat. Conv., Miami Beach, Fla., 1968; chmn. Leavenworth County Radio Free Europe Fund, 1972; bd. dirs. St. John's Hosp., Leavenworth, 1970-79, sec.; bd. dirs. Leavenworth Assn. for Handicapped, 1968-69, ARC, Leavenworth chpt., Kans. Blue Cross/Blue Shield, 1969-72; apptd. by Pres. Reagan Nat. Hwy. Safety Adv. Com.; active Trinity Nat. Leadership Roundtable, Cath. Campaign Am., Kans. Adv. Bd. Juvenile Offenders, Nat. Com. Cmty. Corrections. Recipient Community Leaders of Am., 1971, 85, 86, Hallpac Pub. Svc. award, 1988, Am. Police Hall of Fame award, 1990, Good Samaritan award Order of Michael the Arch Angel Police Legion, 1990, Commendation award mayor and city commn. of Leavenworth, Kans., 1990, Carnegie Hero Fund Commn. award and medallion, 1991, Silver Angel award Kans. Cath. Conf., 1992; named Outstanding Young Men Am., 1965-76. Mem. Nat. Inst. Corrections (adv. bd.), Am. Paroling Authorities Internat., Am. Correctional Assn., Am. Probation and Paroling Assn., Leavenworth C. of C. (hon. dir. 1970-73), No. Assn. Chiefs Police, Assn. U.S. Army (Henry Leavenworth award 1960), Kansas City (Kans.) C. of C., Leavenworth Hist. Soc. (dir. 1968-73), John Carroll Soc., Native Sons of Kansas City, Ancient Order of Hibernians, U.S. Supreme Ct. Hist. Soc., Kiwanis (dir. 1969-70, Connelly award 1991, Legion of Honor award 1996), K.C., Elks, Eagles, Order of Malta, Equestrian Order Holy Sepulchre Jerusalem. Republican. Roman Catholic.

REILLY, FRANK KELLY, business educator; b. Chgo., Dec. 30, 1935; s. Clarence Raymond and Mary Josephine (Ruckrigel) R.; m. Therese Adele Bourke, Aug. 2, 1958; children: Frank Kelly III, Clarence Raymond II, Therese B., Edgar B. BBA, U. Notre Dame, 1957; MBA, Northwestern U., 1961, U. Chgo., 1964; PhD, U. Chgo., 1968; LLD (hon.), St. Michael's Coll., 1991. CFA. Trader Goldman Sachs & Co., Chgo., 1958-59; security analyst Tech. Fund, Chgo., 1959-62; asst. prof. U. Kans., Lawrence, 1965-68, assoc. prof., 1968-72; prof. bus., assoc. dir. divsn. bus. and econ. rsch. U. Wyo., Laramie, 1972-75; prof. fin. U. Ill., Champaign-Urbana, 1975-81; Bernard J. Hank prof. U. Notre Dame, Ind., 1981—, dean Coll. Bus. Adminstrn., 1981-87; bd. dirs. Brinson Global Fund Inc. (also chmn.), Assn. Investment Mgmt. and Rsch., Inst. Chartered Fin. Analysts (also chmn.), NIBCO Corp., Internat. Bd. CFPs, Greenwood Trust Corp., Ft. Dearborn Income Securities, Battery Park High Yield Fund., Dean Witter Trust FSB. Author: Investment Analysis and Portfolio Management, 1979, 5th edit., 1997, Investments, 1982, 4th edit., 1995; co-editor: Ethics and the Investment Industry, 1989; editor: Readings and Issues in Investments, 1975, High Yield Bonds: Analysis and Risk Assessment, 1990; assoc. editor Fin. Mgmt., 1977-82, Quar. Rev. Econs. and Bus, 1979-87, Fin. Rev., 1979-87, 92—, Jour. Fin. Edn., 1981—, Jour. Applied Bus. Rsch., 1986—, Fin. Svcs. Rev., 1989-96, Internat. Rev. Econs. and Fin., 1992—, European Jour. Fin., 1994—. Arthur J. Schmidt Found. fellow, 1962-65; U. Chgo. fellow, 1963-65. Mem. Midwest Bus. Adminstrn. Assn. (pres. 1974-75), Am. Fin. Assn., Western Fin. Assn. (exec. com. 1973-75), Ea. Fin. Assn. (exec. com. 1979-84, pres. 1982-83), Midwest Fin. Assn. (pres. 1993-94), Fin. Analysts Fedn., Fin. Mgmt. Assn. (pres. 1983-84, chmn. 1985-91, bd. dirs.), Acad. Fin. Svcs. (pres. 1990-91), Inst. Chartered Fin. Analysts (coun. of examiners, rsch. and edn. com., edn. steering com., C. Stewart Sheppard award 1991), Internat. Assoc. Fin. Planners (ednl. resource com., bd. dirs.), Assn. of Investment Mgmt. and Rsch., Investments Analysts Soc. Chgo. (bd. dirs. 1988-89), Beta Gamma Sigma. Roman Catholic. Office: U Notre Dame Coll Bus Adminstrn Notre Dame IN 46556 *Any success I have enjoyed is due to the talents God has given me and my belief that I have an obligation to maximize the output from those talents by hard work, while never forgetting that my family comes first because they have always provided me with the love and support necessary for success and happiness.*

REILLY, JEANETTE P., clinical psychologist; b. Denver, Oct. 19, 1908; d. George L. and Marie (Bloedorn) Parker; A.B., U. Colo., 1929; M.A., Columbia U., 1951, Ed.D., 1959; m. Peter C. Reilly, Sept. 15, 1932; children: Marie Reilly Heed, Sara Jean Reilly Wilhelm, Patricia Reilly Davis. Lectr. psychology Butler U., Indpls., 1957-58, 60-65; cons. child psychologist Mental Hygiene Clinic, Episcopal Community Services, Indpls., 1959-65; cons. clin. psychologist VA Hosp., Indpls., 1965-66; Christian Theol. Sem., 1968-70; pvt. practice clin. psychology, Indpls., 1967-89; cons. clin. psychologist St. Vincent's Hosp., 1973-86; adv. cons. middle mgmt. group Indpls. City Council, 1980-81. Mem. women's aux. council U. Notre Dame, 1953-65; trustee Hanover (Ind.) Coll., 1975-91; bd. dirs. Community Hosp. Found., Indpls., 1978-92, Regional Cancer Hosp. Bd., 1988-90, Indpls. Mus. Art, 1987-93; mem. Ind. Bd. Examiners in Psychology, 1969-73; mem. Com. for Future of Butler U., 1985-86. Mem. Am. Psychol. Assn., Am. Personnel and Guidance Assn., Am. Vocat. Assn., Ind. Psychol. Assn., Central Ind. Psychol. Assn., Ind. Personnel and Guidance Assn., Nat. Registry Psychologists in U.S.A. Office: 3777 Bay Road N Dr Indianapolis IN 46240-2973

REILLY, JOHN B., lawyer; b. Bangor, Maine, Sept. 12, 1947; s. Louis J. and Evelyn I. (Lindsay) R.; m. Susan P. Viselli, May 13, 1978; children: Carolyn, Bridget. BA, U. R.I., 1970; JD cum laude, Suffolk U., 1976. Bar: R.I. 1976, U.S. Dist. Ct. R.I. 1976, U.S. Claims Ct. 1980, U.S. Supreme Ct. 1983, U.S. Ct. Appeals (1st and 2d cirs.) 1984, Mass. 1985, U.S. Dist. Ct. Mass. 1985, U.S. Ct. Appeals (3rd cir.) 1985, U.S. Dist. Ct. Conn. 1995; cert. fraud examiner. Sole practice, Providence, 1976-81, Warwick, R.I., 1981-83; sr. ptnr. John Reilly & Assocs. predecessor firms, Warwick, 1984-89. Mem. Def. Rsch. Inst., Gov's Automobile Ins. Reform Task Force, 1992-93. Mem. troop council Narragansett coun. Boy Scouts Am., Warwick, 1982-88. Mem. ABA, R.I. Bar Assn., Trucking Ind. Def. Assn., Pi Sigma Alpha, Phi Kappa Psi. Home: 80 Paterson Ave Warwick RI 02886-9110 Office: John Reilly & Assoc 300 Centerville Rd Warwick RI 02886-0200

REILLY, MICHAEL JAMES, law librarian; b. Wilkes-Barre, Pa., May 6, 1958; s. Neil Aloysius and Rita Margaret (Hoffman) R. BA in Criminal Justice, Govt., Politics, King's Coll., Wilkes-Barre, 1980, cert. Legal Asst., 1986; cert. Computer Skills, Wilkes Coll., Wilkes-Barre, 1988. Law libr. Hourigan, Kluger, Spohrer and Quinn, Wilkes-Barre, 1986—. Contb. articles to profl. jours. Mem. Friends of the Osterhout Free Libr., Wilkes-Barre. Democrat. Roman Catholic. Home: 260 Blackman St Wilkes Barre PA 18702-4577 Office: Hourigan Kluger et al 700 Mellon Bank Ctr 8 W Market St Wilkes Barre PA 18701-1801

REILLY, MICHAEL THOMAS, chemical engineer; b. Pitts., June 3, 1955; s. Thomas Paul and Doris Jane (Stoehr) R.; m. Laura Ann Bruening, May 13, 1989; 1 child, Kevin Jae. BS in Biology, Muskingum Coll., 1977; MSChemE, Carnegie-Mellon U., 1980; PhD in Chem. Engring., Lehigh U., 1987. Sr. engr. Westvaco Corp., Laurel, Md., 1980-82; rsch. engr. Pfizer, Inc., Easton, Pa., 1982-83, DuPont Co., Wilmington, Del., 1986-92; rsch. scientist Upjohn Co., Kalamazoo, Mich., 1992-95; rsch. assoc. Nat. Starch & Chem. Co., Salisbury, N.C., 1995-96; dir. process devel. Nat. Starch & Chem. Co., Salisbury, 1996—; cons. Assoc. Bioengrs. and Cons., Bethlehem, Pa., 1984-86. Contbr. article to profl. publ., chpt. to book. Fellow Carnegie-Mellon U., 1978, Benedum Found., 1979, Air Products and Chems., 1983. Mem. AAAS, Am. Inst. Chem. Engrs., Am. Chem. Soc., Inst. Food Technologists. Democrat. Roman Catholic. Home: 250 Kimberly Rd Davidson NC 28036 Office: Nat Starch & Chemical Co PO Box 399 Salisbury NC 28145-0399

REILLY, PHILIP RAYMOND, medical research administrator; b. Albany, N.Y., Oct. 3, 1947. MD, Yale U., New Haven, 1981. Diplomate Am. Bd. Clin. Genetics. Intern Boston City Hosp., 1983-85, resident, 1983-85; staff Mass. Gen. Hosp., Boston; dir. Eunice Kennedy Shriver Ctr. for Mental Retardation, Waltham, Mass. Mem. Am. Assn. for the Advancement of Sci., Am. Soc. of Human Genetics. Office: Eunice Kennedy Shriver Ctn 200 Trapelo Rd Waltham MA 02154-6332

REILLY, ROBERT FREDERICK, valuation consultant; b. N.Y.C., Oct. 3, 1952; s. James J. and Marie (Griebel) R.; m. Janet H. Steiner, Apr. 16, 1975; children: Ashley Lauren, Brandon Christopher, Cameron Courtney. BA in Econs., Columbia U., 1974, MBA in Fin., 1975. CPA, Ohio, Ill.; cert. mgmt. acct., CFA; cert. real estate appraiser; cert. review appraiser; cert. gen. appraiser Ill., Va., Utah, Oreg. Sr. cons. Booz, Allen & Hamilton, Cin., 1975-76; dir. corp. planning Huffy Corp., Dayton, Ohio, 1976-81; v.p. Arthur D. Little Valuation, Inc., Chgo., 1981-85; ptnr., nat. dir. of valuation svcs. Deloitte & Touche, Chgo., 1985-91; mng. dir. Willamette Mgmt. Assocs., Chgo., 1991—; adj. prof. accounting U. Dayton Grad. Sch. Bus., 1977-81; adj. prof. fin. econs., Elmhurst (Ill.) Coll., 1982-87; adj. prof. fin. Ill. Inst. Tech. Grad. Sch. Bus., Chgo., 1985—; adj. prof. taxation U. Chgo. Grad. Sch. Bus., 1985-87. Co-author: Valuing Small Businesses and Professional Practices, 1993, Business Valuation Video Course, 1993, Valuing a Business, 1995, Valuing Accounting Practices, 1997, Valuing Professional Practices—A Practicioners Approach, 1997; editor, columnist Small Bus. Taxation, 1989-90, Bus. Valuation Rev., 1989-90, Jour. of Real Estate Acctg. and Taxation, 1991-93, Ohio CPA Jour., 1984-86, 91—, Jour. Property Taxation Mgmt., 1993—, Jour. Am. Bankruptcy Inst., 1993—; co-editor: Financial Valuation-Valuation of Businesses and Business Interests, 1997; contbr. more than 200 articles to profl. jours.; editor: Financial Valuation: Businesses and Business Interests, 1997. Mem. AICPA, Am. Soc. Appraisers (mem. bd. examiners 1985-89), Nat. Assn. Real Estate Appraisers, Nat. Assn. Accts. (chpt. dir. 1976—), Inst. Property Taxation, Soc. Mfg. Engrs., Ill. Soc. CPAs, Ohio Soc. CPAs (chpt. dir. 1978-81), Accreditation Coun. Accountancy (accredited in fed. income taxation), Bus. Valuation Assn., Chgo. Soc. Investment Analysts, Inst. CFAs, Am. Bamkruptcy Inst., Am. Econ. Assn., Nat. Assn. Bus. Economists, Appraisal Inst. Home: 310 Algonquin Rd Barrington IL 60010-6109 Office: 8600 W Bryn Mawr Ave Chicago IL 60631-3579

REILLY, ROBERT JOSEPH, counselor; b. Spokane, Wash., Mar. 7, 1936; s. John Francis and Vivian Helen (White) R.; m. Joan Steiner, June 20, 1960; children: Sean Michael, Patrick Joseph, Bridget Colleen. BA in Psychology, Seattle U., 1985; postgrad., Infantry Officer Candidate Sch, Ft. Benning, 1960, EOAC, Ft. Belvoir, 1968, Leadership Inst. Seattle/City U., 1991-92. Ordained Congl. Ch. Practical Theology, 1992. Enlisted U.S. Army, 1953, advanced through grades to maj., 1981, ret., 1981; with U.S. Army, Korea, 1961-62, Vietnam, 1966-69; counseling supr. Schick Shadel Hosp., Seattle, 1984-89; dir. Canyon Counseling, Puyallup, Wash., 1987-92, 95—; social worker Wash. State Employee Adv. Svc., Olympia, 1992—; v.p. Nat. Bd. for Hypnotherapy and Hypnotic Anaesthesiology, 1991-97, pres. Wash. chpt. 1991-94; exec. v.p. Coll. Therapeutic Hypnosis, Puyallup, 1989-94; mem. adj. faculty Pierce Coll., Tacoma, 1991-92. Pres. Irish Cultural Club, Tacoma, 1983-85, 93-94; sec. Tacoma chpt. Ret. Officers Assn., 1983-87, pres., 1993-96, bd. dirs., 1992-97. Decorated Vietnamese Cross of Gallantry with silver star, Bronze Star with oak leaf cluster, Army Commendation medal with 2 oak leaf clusters; named Profl. of Yr. Chem. Dependency Profls. Wash., 1994. Mem. Nat. Bd. Hypnotherapy and Hypnotic Anesthesiology (v.p. 1991-97, Mem of Yr. 1994, pres. Wash. chpt. 1991-94), Nat. Guild Hypnotists, Nat. Assn. Alcohol and Drug Abuse Counselors (mem. del. Russia & Czech Rep. 1996), Am. Congress Hypnotist Examiners, Army Engr. Assn., Nat. 4th Inf. Divsn. Assn. (sec.-treas. N.W. chpt. 1993—), Employee Assistance Profls. Assn. Avocations: volksmarching, symphony music, theater. Office: Wash State Employee Adv Svc PO Box 47540 Olympia WA 98504-7540

REILLY, THOMAS, humanities educator; b. Hollymount, Mayo, Ireland, Dec. 16, 1941; arrived in Eng., 1967; s. Patrick and Josephine (Sheridan) R.; m. Feb. 22, 1977; children: Anna, Siobhān. BA, U. Coll. Dublin, Ireland, 1967; MSc, Royal Free Hosp., London, 1971; PhD, Liverpool (Eng.) Poly., 1975; M.I. Biology, Inst. Biology, London, 1977. Clerical officer Dublin Corp., 1960-65; tchr., athletic coach Govt. of Cameroun, 1968-70; technician Med. Rsch. Coun., London, 1971; rsch. asst. Liverpool Poly., 1972-75, lectr., then prin. lectr., reader, 1975-88, prof. sports sci., 1988—; dir. sch. Liverpool John Moores U., 1991-95, head grad. sch., 1995—; vis. prof. Tsukuba (Japan) U., 1977; vis. coach Nigerian Sports Coun., 1976; vis. rsch. assoc. U. Calif. Berkeley, 1980; invited spkr. 2d World Congress on Sci. and Football, The Netherlands, 1991, 3d World Congress on Sci. and Football, Cardiff, 1995; contbd. consensus statement on nutrition for soccer F.I.F.A., Zürich, 1994. Editor: Sports Fitness and Sports Issues, 1981, Physiology of Sports, 1990, Science and Football, 1988, Science and Football II, 1993, Science and Soccer, 1996, Science and Football III, 1997; editor Jour. Sports Sci., 1983-96. Organizer Hollymount Internat. Rd. Race, Mayo, Ireland, 1976—; coord. acclimation strategy Brit. Olympic Assn., London, 1993—, chair exercise physiology steering group, 1992—. Mem. Brit. Assn. Sport and Exercise Sci. (chmn. 1994-96), Internat. Steering Group on Sci. and Football (chmn. 1987—), European Coll. Sport Sci. (founder). Roman Catholic. Avocations: soccer, Gaelic football, running, squash, orienteering. Office: Liverpool John Moores U, 2 Rodney St/Grad Sch, Liverpool England

REILLY, WILLIAM FRANCIS, media company executive; b. N.Y.C., June 8, 1938; s. William F. and Genevieve Reilly; m. Ellen Chapman, Nov. 19, 1966; children: Anthony Chapman and Jane Wasey (twins). AB cum laude, U. Notre Dame, 1959; MBA, Harvard U., 1964. Mgr. fin. analysis W.R. Grace & Co., N.Y.C., 1964-67, asst. to pres., 1969-71, CEO Bekaert Textile Divsn., 1971-74; pres., CEO Herman's World of Sporting Goods, Carteret, N.J., 1974-77; v.p., pres. W.R. Grace and Co., 1978; pres., CEO Home Ctr. Div., 1979-80; pres. Macmillan, Inc., N.Y.C., 1980-90; chmn., CEO K-III Comm. Corp., N.Y.C., 1990—. 1st lt. U.S. Army, 1959-61. Home: 7 Sutton Sq New York NY 10022 Office: K-III Comm Corp 745 5th Ave New York NY 10151

REILLY, WILLIAM THOMAS, lawyer; b. Passaic, N.J., Feb. 25, 1949; s. Thomas Edwin and Edna May (Dorritie) R.; m. Sheila Mary Brogan, Aug. 1, 1981; children: Kathleen Anne, Brendan Thomas, Timothy John. BS, Boston Coll., 1971; JD, Harvard U., 1974. Bar: N.J. 1974, U.S. Dist. Ct. N.J. 1974, U.S. Supreme Ct. 1979, U.S. Ct. Appeals (3rd cir.) 1984, U.S. Ct. Claims, 1996. Assoc. McCarter & English, Newark, 1974-81, ptnr., 1982--. Trustee United Hosps. Med. Ctr., Newark, 1983-89, One-to-One/N.J., Inc., 1990—, chmn., 1993—. Mem. ABA, N.J. State Bar Assn., Harvard Law Sch. Assn., Eastward Ho Country Club. Avocation: golf. Home: 302 Kensington Dr Ridgewood NJ 07450-1822 Office: McCarter & English Four Gateway Ctr 100 Mulberry St Newark NJ 07102-4004

REIMAN, DONALD HENRY, English language educator; b. Erie, Pa., May 17, 1934; s. Henry Ward and Mildred Abbie (Pearce) R.; m. Mary Warner, 1958 (div. 1974); 1 child, Laurel Elizabeth Reiman Henneman; m. Hélène Liberman Dworzan, Oct. 3, 1975. A.B., Coll. of Wooster, 1956, Litt.D., 1981; M.A., U. Ill., 1957, Ph.D., 1960. Instr. English, Duke U., Durham, N.C., 1960-62, asst. prof., 1962-64; assoc. prof. U. Wis., Milw., 1964-65; adj. assoc. prof. grad. program in English CUNY, 1967-68; adj. prof. Columbia U., N.Y.C., 1969-70, sr. rsch. assoc. in English, 1970-73; vis. prof. St. John's U., Jamaica, N.Y., 1974-75; editor Shelley and His Circle, Carl H. Pforzheimer Library, N.Y.C., 1965-86, N.Y. Pub. Libr., 1986-92; with Carl & Lily Pforzheimer Found., 1992—; vis. lectr. U. Ill., 1963; vis. prof. U. Wash., Seattle, 1981, NYU, 1992; Lyell reader in bibliography Oxford U., 1988-89; adj. prof. English U. Del., 1992—; cons. Harvard U. Press, Yale U. Press, Princeton U. Press, Johns Hopkins U. Press, Garland Pub. Inc., W.W. Norton, Oxford U. Press, others. Author: Shelley's The Triumph of Life, A Critical Study, 1965, 2d edit., 1979, Percy Bysshe Shelley, 1969, 2d edit., 1990, (with D.D. Fischer) Byron on the Continent, 1974, English Romantic Poetry, 1800-1835, 1979, Romantic Texts and Contexts, 1987, Intervals of Inspiration: The Skeptical Tradition and the Psychology of Romanticism, 1988, The Study of Modern Manuscripts, 1993; editor: Shelley and His Circle, Vols. V-VI, 1973, Vols. VII-VIII, 1986, The Romantics Reviewed: Contemporary Reviews of English Romantic Writers, 9 vols., 1972, (with S.B. Powers) Shelley's Poetry and Prose: A Norton Critical Edition, 1977, The Romantic Context: Poetry, 128 vols., 1976-79, (with M.C. Jaye and B.T. Bennett) The Evidence of the Imagination, 1978; gen. editor: Manuscripts of the Younger Romantics; I The Esdaile Notebook: A Facsimile, 1985, II The Mask of Anarchy: Facsimiles, 1985, III Hellas, 1985, V The Harvard Shelley Poetic Manuscripts, 1991; (with M. O'Neill) VIII Fair-Copy Manuscripts of Shelley's Poems, 1997; editor-in-chief: The Bodleian Shelley Manuscripts, 1984—, I Peter Bell The Third and the Triumph of Life, 1986, VII Shelley's Last Notebook and Other MSS, 1990, (with M.J. Neth) XVI The Hellas Notebook, 1994; mem. editl. com. adv. bd. Keats-Shelley Jour., 1968-73, Milton and the Romantics, 1975-80, Studies in Romanticism, 1977—, Romanticism Past and Present, 1980-86, Text, 1981—, Nineteenth-Century Literature, 1986—, Nineteenth-Century Contexts, 1987-90; co-founder, editor (with others) Romantic Cirs. Website; contbr. articles to encyclopedias, books and profl. jours. Active Common Cause. Am. Coun. Learned Socs. fellow, 1963-64, Wesleyan Ctr. Advanced Studies fellow, 1963-64, NEH fellow, 1978; grantee Am. Coun. Learned Socs., 1961, NEH, 1983—. Mem. AAUP, MLA (life), Modern Humanities Rsch. Assn. (life), Wordsworth-Coleridge Assn. Am. (founder), Byron Soc. (Am. com. 1973—), Keats-Shelley Assn. Am. (bd. dirs., treas. 1973-91, v.p. 1991—, Disting. Scholar award 1987), Bibliog. Soc. Am., Soc. Textual Scholarship (exec. com. 1981-93), Coleridge in Somerset Assn., Charles Lamb Soc., Assn. Documentary Editing, N.Am. Soc. Study of Romanticism, Assn. Literary Scholars and Critics. Democrat. Presbyterian. Office: NY Pub Libr Fifth Ave at 42nd St Rm 226 New York NY 10018

REIMANN, WILLIAM PAGE, artist, educator; b. Mpls., Nov. 29, 1935; s. Hobart and Dorothy (Sampson) R.; m. Helen Vera Sadowy, June 3, 1961; children: Christopher, Katherine. BA, Yale U., 1957, BFA, 1959, MFA in Sculpture, 1961. Instr. Old Dominion U., Norfolk, Va., 1961-62; asst. prof. Old Dominion U., 1962-64; asst. prof. design Harvard U., 1964-67, lectr., 1969-75, sr. preceptor in visual studies, 1975—, head tutor dept. visual studies, 1986-94. Recent major commns. include Tropicana Corp., Bradenton, Fla., Mass. Port Authority, Boston, Mass. Turnpike Authority, Boston, Shell Oil Co., Houston, 1st Ch. of Christ, Scientist, Boston; designated artist Radnor (Pa.) Twp. Gateway Enhancement Project, Boston Redsox Baseball Club; represented in permanent collections, Mus. Modern Art, N.Y.C., Nat. Gallery Art, Washington, Whitney Mus. Am. Art, Boston Mus. Fine Art, Rockefeller U., Yale U., Harvard U., also numerous pvt. collections. Recipient 2 Gold medals U.S. Master's Rowing Nat. Championships, 1996, 4 Gold medals F.I.S.A. world Vets.' Rowing Competitions, Budapest. Mem. Cambridge Boat Club (bd. dirs.). Home: 1 Gerrys Landing Cambridge MA 02138-5511 Office: Carpenter Ctr Visual Arts 24 Quincy St Cambridge MA 02138-3804

REIMER, BENNETT, music educator, writer; b. N.Y.C., June 19, 1932; s. George and Sarah (Talkofsky) R.; children: Jan Ellen, Terry. BM, State Tchr.'s Coll. (now SUNY-Fredonia), 1954; MM, U. Ill., 1955, EdD, 1963. Asst. prof. music edn. U. Ill., Urbana, 1960-65; Kulas prof., chmn. dept. music edn. Case Western Res. U., Cleve., 1965-78; John W. Beattie prof., chmn. dept. Northwestern U., Evanston, Ill., 1978—. Author: A Philosophy of Music Education, 1970, 2d edit., 1989, Developing the Experience of Music, 1985; editor: Toward an Aesthetic Education, 1971, The Arts, Education and Aesthetic Knowing, 1992, On the Nature of Musical Experience, 1992; co-author: The Experience of Music, 1972, Silver Burdett Music Grades 1-8, 1974, 4th edit., 1985; contbr. over 100 articles on music and arts edn. to profl. jours. Mem. Music Educators Nat. Conf., Music Edn. Research Council, Edn. Aesthetic Awareness (bd. dirs.). Office: Northwestern U Sch Music Evanston IL 60208

REIMER, DENNIS J., career military officer. Gen. U.S. Army, Ft. McPherson, Ga.; chief of staff U.S. Army, Washington. Office: Pentagon Chief of Staff 200 Army Pentagon Washington DC 20310-0200*

REIMER, JAN RHEA, former mayor; b. Edmonton, Alta., Can., May 23, 1952; married; 2 children. BA, U. Alta., 1973. Councillor for Ward 2 City Coun. of Edmonton, 1980-89, chair various standing coms.; mayor City of Edmonton, 1989-95; former chair City of Edmonton Task Force Econ. Devel., Inter-Mcpl. Task Force Out-of-Sch. Care, River Valley Steering Com., Mayor's Task Force Safer Cities; chair Safer Cities Initiatives Com., No. Alta. Mayors' Caucus; mem. Bd. Edmonton Power; Edmonton rep. Big City Mayors' Caucus, Can.; mem. Winter Cities Secretariat; organizer Edmonton Region Mayors and Reeves Caucus. Co-author: N.U.T.S. & B.O.L.T.S.: A Self-Help Guide for Community Groups. Pres. Mcpl. Non-Profit Housing Corp.; organizer Toxic Round-Up, Blue Box, various other environ. programs; mem. Bd. Edmonton Pub. Libr., Edmonton Met. Regional Planning Commn., Mayor's Task Force Citizen Participation, Inter-Mcpl. Task Force Waste Mgmt.; citizen coord. Calder Action Com., Edmonton; mem. bd. govs. Royal Alexandra Hosp.; bd. dirs. Edmonton Social Planning Coun., Econ. Devel. Edmonton; chair Red Shield Appeal, Salvation Army, 1996. Recipient Spl. award as Woman of Distinction, YWCA, 1996. Address: 10114 87th St, Edmonton, AB Canada T5H 1N4

REIN, BERT WALTER, lawyer; b. Bklyn., Feb. 7, 1941; s. Moe and Florence (Fishman) R.; m. Jennifer Christine Bulson, July 11, 1966 (dec. Mar. 1989); children: Joanna, Benjamin, Samantha; m. Barbara Jean Kahn, Oct. 18, 1992. BA, Amherst Coll., 1961; LLB, Harvard U., 1964. Bar: D.C. 1965, U.S. Dist. Ct. D.C. 1965, U.S. Ct. Appeals (D.C. cir.) 1968, U.S. Ct. Appeals (2d cir.) 1973, U.S. Ct. Appeals (8th cir.) 1974, U.S. Ct. Appeals (4th cir.) 1976, U.S. Ct. Appeals (11th cir.) 1982, U.S. Supreme Ct. 1982. Law ck. to Justice John M. Harlan U.S. Supreme Ct., Washington, 1966-67; assoc. Kirkland & Ellis, Washington, 1967-69, ptnr., 1973-83; spl. asst. U.S. Dept. State, Washington, 1969-70, dep. asst. sec., 1970-73; ptnr. Wiley, Rein & Fielding, Washington, 1983—; bd. dirs., chmn. govt. and regulation affairs com. U.S. C. of C., 1986-90; bd. dirs. Nat. Chamber Litigation Ctr.; advisor Reagan Dept. Justice Transition, Washington, 1980; mem. adv. com. U.S. Sentencing Commn., 1988-89; edn. gen. counsel Comty. Learning and Info. Network, 1992—. Contbr. articles to profl. publs. Capt. USAR, 1964-68. Mem. ABA, Am. Law Inst., Internat. Trade Commn. Trial Lawyers Assn. (pres. 1990-91), Internat. Aviation Club. Republican. Jewish. Home: 6423 Shadow Rd Chevy Chase MD 20815-6613 Office: Wiley Rein & Fielding 1776 K St NW Washington DC 20006-2304

REIN, CATHERINE AMELIA, financial services executive, lawyer; b. Lebanon, Pa., Feb. 7, 1943; d. John and Esther (Scott) Shultz. BA summa cum laude, Pa. State U., 1965; JD magna cum laude, NYU ., 1968. Bar: N.Y. 1968, U.S. Supreme Ct. 1971. Assoc. Dewey, Ballantine, Bushby, Palmer & Wood, N.Y.C., 1968-74; with Continental Group, Stamford, Conn., 1974-85, sec., sr. atty., 1976-77, v.p., gen. counsel, 1980-85; sec., asst. gen. counsel Continental Diversified Ops., 1978-80; v.p. human resources Met. Life Ins. Co., N.Y.C., 1985-88, sr. v.p. human resources, 1988-89, exec. v.p. corp. and profl. svcs. dept., 1989—; bd. dirs Bank of NY., Gen. Pub. Utilities, Corning Inc., Inroads, N.Y.C. Trustee emeritus Nat. Urban League, NYU Sch. Law Found. Mem. ABA, Assn. of Bar of City of N.Y. Episcopalian. Avocations: decorating, restoration, cooking. Home: 21 E 22nd St Apt 8B New York NY 10010-5335 Office: Met Life Ins Co 1 Madison Ave New York NY 10010-3603

REIN, STANLEY MICHAEL, lawyer; b. St. Paul, Apr. 15, 1946; s. Clayton George Rein and Rose Gertrude (Mintz) Brown; m. Linda. R. Arnold; children: Gabriel Todd, Leah Suzanne. BA, U. Minn., 1968; JD cum laude, Harvard U., 1973. Bar: Minn. 1973, U.S. Tax Ct. 1973. Assoc. Dorsey & Whitney, LLP, Mpls., 1973-78; ptnr. Dorsey & Whitney PLLP, Mpls., 1979—. Mem. planned giving adv. coun. ARC Mpls. chpt., 1986, 88, planned giving adv. com. Minn. Pub. Radio, 1988-89; bd. dirs. South Metro Airport Action Council, Mpls., 1986, 87. With U.S. Army, 1966-70, Vietnam. Fellow Am. Coll. of Trust and Estate Counsel; mem. Minn. Bar Assn. (probate and trust law sect.), Hennepin County Bar Assn. (probate and trust law sect.), Phi Beta Kappa. Jewish. Avocations: reading, travel. Office: Dorsey & Whitney LLP 220 S 6th St Minneapolis MN 55402-4502

REINBOLD, DARREL WILLIAM, energy engineering specialist; b. Louisville, Nov. 13, 1960; s. Paul William and Betty Lou (Buechler) R.; m. Theresa Marie Morris, June 17, 1989; children: Jessica Marie, Elizabeth Ashley. Cert. heating, air condit., refrig., Pleasure Ridge Pk. Vocat. Sch., Louisville, 1978; AAS, U. Louisville, 1987, BS in Occupational Edn., 1987; cert. universal technician, Esco Inst., 1994. Lic. journeyman HVAC mechanic, Ky. Apprentice pipe fitter A & A Mech., Louisville, 1978-80; heating, ventilation, air conditioning technician Prudential Heating and Air Conditioning, Louisville, 1980-87; heating, ventilation, air conditioning mechanic U. Louisville, 1988-89; svc. sys. specialist Honeywell Inc., Louisville, 1989-93; air conditioning estimator Ware Energy, Louisville, 1993—. Mem. baseball team U. Louisville, 1980-81. Mem. Assn. of Energy Engrs., Honorable Order Ky. Cols. Avocations: fishing, skiing. Home: 3219 La Vel Ln Louisville KY 40216-1217 Office: Ware Energy 4005 Produce Rd Louisville KY 40218-3007

REINCKE, RHONDA, nursing educator; b. Waterloo, Iowa, Dec. 23, 1958; d. Donald L. and Phyllis A. (Spiegler) R. BS cum laude, Mt. Mercy Coll., Cedar Rapids, Iowa, 1981; MS, U. Minn., 1988, postgrad. Cert ACLS. Staff nurse, respiratory/surg. ICU St. Marys Hosp., Rochester, Minn., 1981-86; instr. Red Wing (Minn.) Tech. Coll., 1986-88, Coll. St. Benedict, St. Joseph, Minn., 1988-91; assoc. dir. nursing, outpatient RN Fed. Med. Ctr., Rochester, Minn., 1991-93; asst. prof. nursing Luther Coll., Decorah, Iowa, 1993-96; pub. health nurse Olmsted County, Rochester, 1996—. Mem. Am. Heart Assn. (coun. cardiovascular nursing), Sigma Theta Tau, Kappa Gamma Pi. Home: RR 1 Box 163 Plainview MN 55964-9552

REINECKE, MANFRED G., chemistry educator; b. Milw., May 19, 1935; s. Fritz Wilhelm and Erna (Rittmeyer) R.; m. Marlene Zwisler, June 15, 1957; children: Kurt, Kryn, Claire. BS in Chemistry, U. Wis., 1956; PhD in Organic Chemistry, U. Calif., 1960. Asst. prof. U. Calif., Riverside, 1959-64; asst. prof. Tex. Christian U., Ft. Worth, 1964-68, assoc. prof., 1968-73; vis. prof. U. Tubingen, Fed. Republic of Germany, 1971-72; prof. Tex. Christian U., Ft. Worth, 1973—; vis. prof. U. British Columbia, Vancouver, Can., 1987; chmn. health professions adv. com. Tex. Christian U., 1974-91; mem. sci. adv. bd. Univera Phytoceuticals, Inc., 1996—; cons. in field. Contbr. more than 70 articles on natural product, organic chemistry and chem. edn. to profl. jours. Recipient W.T. Doherty award Ft. Worth, Dallas sect. Am. Chem. Soc., 1984; Nat. Sci. Found. Teaching fellow, 1971-72, NAS fellow, 1979, 90. Mem. Am. Chem. Soc. (chmn. Ft. Worth, Dallas sect. 1976), So. Assn. Advisors Health Professions (bd. dirs. 1986-89), Alpha Epsilon Delta (dir. SW region 1985—). Office: Tex Christian Univ Dept Of Chemistry Fort Worth TX 76129

REINECKE, ROBERT DALE, ophthalmologist; b. Ft. Scott, Kans., Mar. 26, 1929; s. George Alfred and Bessie Irene (Newell) R.; m. Mary Jeannetta Portwood, Oct. 5, 1952; 1 child, Karen Denise. O.D., Ill. Coll. Optometry, 1951; A.B., U. Kans., 1955, M.D., 1959. Diplomate: Am. Bd. Ophthalmology. Research fellow ophthalmology Harvard U. Med. Sch., 1957, 58; intern U. Kans. Med. Center, 1959-60; resident in ophthalmology Mass. Eye and Ear Infirmary, Boston, 1961-63; asst. in ophthalmology Mass. Eye and Ear Infirmary, 1963-69; asst. prof. ophthalmology Harvard U. Med. Sch., 1967-69; mem. faculty Albany (N.Y.) Med. Sch., 1970-81, prof. ophthalmology, 1970-81, chmn. dept., 1970-81; prof. ophthalmology Jefferson Med. Coll., Phila., 1981—; chmn. dept. Jefferson Med. Coll., 1981-85; ophthalmologist-in-chief Wills Eye Hosp., 1981-85, dir. Foerderer Eye Movement Ctr., 1985—; bd. dirs. Conrad Berens Internat. Eye Film Library, 1970-80; exec. com. N.Y. State Bd. Medicine, 1978-80, chmn., 1980-81; com. vision NRC, 1976-81, chmn., 1979-80; Alumni lectr. Georgetown U. Med. Sch., 1970; Proctor lectr. U. Calif. Med. Sch., San Francisco, 1977; Schoenberg lectr. N.Y. Acad. Medicine, 1979; Spaeth lectr. Coll. Physicians, 1982; Bajandas lectr., 1989. Contbr. numerous articles to med. jours. USPHS summer fellow, 1956, 58; Fight for Sight fellow, summers 1957, 60; recipient Senior Honor award Am. Acad. Ophthalmology, 1986. Fellow Am. Acad. Ophthalmology (sec. govt. rels. 1980-86, pres. 1989); mem. ACS, AMA, Am. Bd. Ophthalmology (bd. dirs. 1984-87), Assn. Rsch. Vision and Ophthalmology (trustee sect. on eye movements, strabismus and amblyopia 1986-91), Am. Acad. Ophthalmology (sec. for program 1986-87), Pa. Med. Soc., N.Y. State Ophthal. Assn., Am. Assn. Pediatric Ophthalmology (pres. 1975-76), Phila. County Med. Soc. (chmn. med. econ. com. 1994-95), Pa. Acad. Ophthalmology (pres. 1991), Pa. Med. Soc., Coll. of POhysicians, Ophthalmic Club of Phila. Office: Wills Eye Hosp 9th And Walnut St Philadelphia PA 19107-5599

REINER, ROB, actor, writer, director; b. N.Y.C., Mar. 6, 1947; s. Carl and Estelle (Lebost) R.; m. Penny Marshall, 1971 (div.), m. Michele Singer, May 19, 1989. Student, UCLA. Co-founder Castle Rock Entertainment, Beverly Hills, Calif. Actor: (TV series) All In the Family, 1971-78 (Emmy award 1974, 78), (TV movie) Thursday's Game, 1974 (films) Throw Momma From the Train, 1987, Postcards From the Edge, 1990, The Spirit of '76, 1990, Sleepless in Seattle, 1993, Bullets Over Broadway, 1994, Mixed Nuts, 1994, Bye Bye, Love, 1995, First Wives Club, 1996, (theatre) The Roast, 1980; actor, writer: (films) Halls of Anger, 1970, Where's Pappa?, 1970, Summertree, 1971, Fire Sale, 1971; actor (film) Enter Laughing, 1967; actor, co-writer, prodr. (TV) More Than Friends, 1978, Million Dollar Infield, 1982; actor, co-writer, dir. (film) This Is Spinal Tap, 1984; dir. (films) The Sure Thing, 1985, Stand By Me, 1986; dir. prodr. (films) The Princess Bride, 1987, When Harry Met Sally, 1989, Misery, 1990, A Few Good Men, 1992, North, 1994, The American President, 1995, Ghosts of Mississippi, 1996; co-creator (TV series) The Super, 1972; co-creator, actor (TV series) Free Country, 1977-78. Mem. SAG, AFTRA, Dir. Guild Am., Writers Guild Am. Office: Castle Rock Entertainment 335 N Maple Dr Ste 135 Beverly Hills CA 90210-3858

REINER, THOMAS KARL, manufacturing company executive; b. Budapest, Hungary, Dec. 29, 1931; came to U.S., 1959; s. Pál and Jozefa (Keller) R.; m. Joyce Reiner; children: Paul A., Reneé K. Hedsand; m. Eleanor Ruth Aldridge (div.). Diploma optics trade sch., Budapest, 1952; MSME, Tech. U., Budapest, 1955; postgrad., London Coll., 1958, U. Pitts., Carnegie Inst. Tech. Engr. Cen. Power Generating Sta., Hungary, 1954-56; cons. engr., test engr. Blaw-Knox Co., London, 1956-57; sr. engr. Eubank & Ptnrs., London, 1957-59; rsch. engr. Pitts. Plate Glass Co., 1959-60, product mgr. Copes-Vulcan divsn., 1960-62; chief engr. J.W. Fecker divsn. Am. Optical Co., 1962-66; product mgr. Carco Electronics, Menlo Park, Calif., 1966-68; chief engr. Fairchild Camera, El Segundo, Calif., 1968-70; dir. engring. Templeton, Kenly & Co., L.A. and Chgo., 1970-72; gen. mgr. Foremark Corp., Gardena, 1972-74; pres. Kinetron, Inc., Long Beach, Calif., 1974-76; pres., prin. owner GRW, Inc., Hawthorne, Calif., 1977—; adj. prof. Tech. U., Budapest, 1951-54. Patentee in post tension device for concrete, spherical air bearing and gimballed slave connector, synchronization of hydraulic jacking sys., bending of automotive side windows; inventor tug/barge latching sys., membrane type loadcell, ultra low profile platform and truck-scales. Bd. pres. Peacock Ridge Homeowners Assn., Palos Verdes, Calif. Lt. Hungarian Army, 1951-57. Mem. Internat. Soc. Weighing and Measurements. Home: 14110 Valley Vista Blvd Sherman Oaks CA 91423-4657

REINERT, JAMES A., entomologist, educator; b. Enid, Okla., Jan. 26, 1944; s. Andrew J. and Emma Reinert; m. Anita Irwin; children: Travis J., Gina N., Mindy K., Melanie B., Gregory W., Teresa J. BS, Okla. State U., 1966; MS, Clemson U., 1968, PhD, 1970. Asst. state entomologist U. Md., College Park, 1970; asst. prof. entomology to prof. entomology Ft. Lauderdale Rsch. and Edn. Ctr., U. Fla., 1970-84; resident dir., prof. entomology Rsch. and Ext. Ctr., Tex. A&M U. Sys., Dallas, 1984-94; prof. entomology Tex. A&M Univ. System, Dallas, 1994—. Contbr. over 275 articles to profl. jours. NDEA fellow, 1968; recipient Porter Henegar Meml. award., So. Nurserymen's Assn., 1982. Mem. Inter-Turfgrass Soc., Entomol.

Soc. Am., Fla. Entomol. Soc. (v.p. 1983, pres. 1984, Entomologist of Yr. 1985), Fla. State Hort. Soc. (v.p. 1982), S.C. Entomol. Soc., Rsch. Ctr. Adminstrs. Soc. (v.p. 1994, state rep. 1991-92, sec. 1993), Dallas Agr. Club (bd. dirs. 1989, v.p. 1990, pres. 1991). Roman Catholic. Home: 3805 Covinton Ln Plano TX 75023-7731 Office: Tex A&M Univ Rsch and Ext Ctr 17360 Coit Rd Dallas TX 75252-6502

REINERT, NORBERT FREDERICK, patent lawyer, retired chemical company executive; b. Hamilton, Ohio, Apr. 12, 1928; s. Fred F. and Jennie A. R.; m. Ida Elizabeth Barickman, Jan. 26, 1956; children: Matthew W., Paul H. B.Ch.E., Ohio State U., 1951; LL.B., Cleve.-Marshall Law Sch., 1959. Bar: Ohio 1959, D.C. 1961. Patent agt. Standard of Ohio, Cleve., 1957-59; patent lawyer Standard of Ohio, 1959-60, E.I. duPont de Nemours & Co., Wilmington, Del., 1960-91; dir. investor relations E.I. duPont de Nemours & Co., 1981-84, mng. counsel, 1985-91; v.p., gen. counsel Endo Labs, Inc. subs. DuPont, Garden City, N.Y., 1971-73; exec. v.p. Endo Labs, Inc. subs. DuPont, 1973-77, pres., 1977-81; pvt. practice patent law, 1991—. Served with Chem. Corps AUS, 1955-56. Mem. Am. Patent Law Assn., Tau Beta Pi. Republican. Roman Catholic. Home: PO Box 311 Mendenhall PA 19357-0311

REINERT, PAUL CLARE, university chancellor emeritus; b. Boulder, Colo., Aug. 12, 1910; s. Francis John and Emma (Voegtle) R. A.B., St. Louis U., 1933, A.M., 1934; Ph.D., U. Chgo., 1944; LL.D. (hon.), St. Ambrose Coll., 1951, Xavier U., 1954, Washington U., 1955, Colo. Coll., 1956, Loyola U., 1957, U. Mo., 1957, John Carroll U., 1961, U. Notre Dame, 1964, St. Joseph's Coll., 1964; Ped.D. (hon.), Bradley U., 1956; L.H.D. (hon.), Manhattan Coll., 1963; Litt.D. (hon.), McKendree Coll., 1966, St. Norbert Coll., 1975; LL.D. (hon.), St. Anselm's Coll., 1967, Coll. Mt. St. Joseph of Ohio, 1970, Loyola U., New Orleans, 1973, So. Ill. U., 1973, Creighton U., 1976; L.H.D. (hon.), Lindenwood Colls., 1972, DePaul U., 1973, Carroll Coll., 1974, St. Francis Coll., 1974, Canisius Coll., 1975, Brandeis U., 1975, Wittenberg U., 1976, Ursuline Coll., 1976, U. Portland, 1977, Tarkio Coll., 1977; P.C.S. (hon.), Regis Coll., 1977; Ed.Adm.D. (hon.), Drury Coll., 1973, numerous others. Entered Soc. of Jesus, 1927, ordained priest, 1940; instr. classical langs. and English Creighton U. High Sch., Omaha, Neb., 1934-37; instr. edn. and registrar St. Mary's Coll., St. Marys, Kan., 1938-41; prof. edn. St. Louis U., 1950—; dean St. Louis U. (Coll. Arts and Scis.), 1944-48, dir. summer sessions, 1945-48, v.p., 1948, pres., 1949-74, chancellor, 1974-90, chancellor emeritus, 1990—; chmn. St. Louis Edn. TV Commn., 1955-57; Mem. President's Com. Edn. Beyond High Sch., 1956-57; co-chmn. Mayor's Commn. Equal Employment Opportunities, 1963-65; mem. Pres. Nixon's Task Force on Edn., 1968-69; bd. dirs. St. Louis Civic Alliance for Housing, 1969-71. Author: The Urban Catholic University, 1970, To Turn the Tide, 1972. Bd. dirs. Assn. Am. Colls., 1970—, chmn., 1972; trustee Ednl. Testing Service, 1969—; bd. dirs. Midwest Research Inst., 1962—; pres. Midtown, Inc., 1972—; mem. Mo. Commn. for Humanities, 1975—; trustee Regis Coll.; bd. overseers St. Meinrad Coll. Mem. N. Central Assn. Colls. and Secondary Schs. (pres. 1956-57), Nat. Cath. Ednl. Assn. (pres. coll. and univ. dept. 1956-58, v.p. 1964-65, pres. 1968-70, exec. bd. 1956-65), Am. Council Edn. (dir. 1965-68), Assn. Urban Univs. (pres. 1950-51), Nat. Council Ind. Colls. and Univs. (pres. 1973), Cath. Commn. on Intellectual and Cultural Affairs, NEA, Assn. for Higher Edn., Ind. Colls. and Univs. Mo. (pres. 1974), Jesuit Edn. Assn. (pres. 1966-70), Phi Beta Kappa, Phi Delta Kappa. Address: Saint Louis U 221 N Grand Blvd Saint Louis MO 63103-2006

REINERTSEN, NORMAN, retired aircraft systems company executive; b. Bklyn., Mar. 27, 1934; s. Berthin and Malene Katherine (Dahl) R.; m. Elizabeth T. O'Shea, Aug. 30, 1958; children: Michael, Christopher, Katherine. BEE, CCNY, 1960; postgrad., Harvard U., 1982. Registered profl. engr., Calif. Various positions Grumman Aerospace Corp., 1960-75; gen. mgr. Grumman Aerospace Corp. (Great River ops.), 1975-77; v.p. automotive Grumman Allied Industries, Melville, N.Y., 1977-83; sr. v.p. vehicle div. Grumman Allied Industries, 1983-94; sr. v.p. Olson Bodies, Inc., 1977-79; exec. v.p. Grumman Flexible, Delaware, Ohio, 1979-82; pres. Grumman Olson, Mellville, 1983-85; sr. v.p. Vehicle div. Grumman Allied, 1985-87; v.p. quality ops. Grumman Aircraft Sys. div. Northrop Grumman, 1987-94; ret., 1994. With U.S. Army, 1955-57. Mem. Air Force Assn., Northport Yacht Club. Home: 7 Oleander Dr Northport NY 11768-3438

REINERTSON, JAMES WAYNE, pediatrician; b. Des Moines, Jan. 25, 1927; s. A. Jennings and Bonnie V. (Wald) R.; m. Beverly E. Sampson, June 6, 1958; children: Mark W., Merilee Reinertson Torres. BA, Luther Coll., 1948; MS in Pub. Health, U. N.C., 1949; MD, U. Iowa, 1959. Diplomate Am. Bd. Pediatrics. Rsch. asst. in parasitology U. Iowa Med. Coll., Iowa City, 1954-59; intern Mercy Hosp., Cedar Rapids, Iowa, 1959-60; resident pediatrics Raymond Blank Hosp., Des Moines, 1960-62; assoc. rsch. parasitologist Parke Davis & Co., Detroit; pvt. practice, Cedar Rapids, Iowa, 1962—; pres. med. staff St. Lukes Hosp., Cedar Rapids, 1979, mem. staff Mercy Hosp.; instr. Cedar Rapids Med. Edn. Program; bd. Luther Coll. Alumni Coun., 1988-97. Bd. dirs. Linn County Assn. Retarded Citizens, 1972-78; commr. Iowa Substance Abuse Commn., Des Moines, 1984, chmn., 1988-90. Wyeth Pediatric fellow, 1960-62. Mem. AMA, Am. Acad. Pediatrics, Iowa Med. Soc. Lutheran. Office: 855 A Ave NE Cedar Rapids IA 52402-5064

REINES, FREDERICK, physicist, educator; b. Paterson, N.J., Mar. 16, 1918; s. Israel and Gussie (Cohen) R.; m. Sylvia Samuels, Aug. 30, 1940; children: Robert G., Alisa K. ME in Mech. Engring., Stevens Inst. Tech., 1939, MA in Sci., 1941; PhD in Physics, NYU, 1944, D. Engring. (hon.), 1984; DSc (hon.), U. Witwatersrand, Johannesburg, South Africa, 1966. Mem. staff, group leader Theoretical divsn. Los Alamos Sci. Lab., 1944-59; dir. Los Alamos Experiments Op. Greenhouse, Eniwetok, 1951; prof. physics, head dept. physics dept. Case Inst. Tech., 1959-66; prof. physics U. Calif., Irvine, 1966-88, founding dean phys. scis., 1966-74, prof. radiol. scis. Med. Sch., 1970—, Disting. prof. physics, 1987-88, prof. emeritus, 1988—; Centennial lectr. U. Md., 1956; Disting. Faculty lectr. U. Calif., Irvine, 1979; L.I. Schiff Meml. lectr. Stanford U., 1988; Albert Einstein Meml. lectr. Israel Acad. Scis. and Humanities, Jerusalem, 1988; Goudschmidt Meml. lectr., 1990; co-discoverer elementary nuclear particles, free antineutrino, 1956; cons. Los Alamos Sci. Lab., Inst. for Def. analysis, 1965-69. Contbr. numerous articles to profl. jours.; contbg. author: Effects of Atomic Weapons, 1950. Mem. Cleve. Symphony Chorus, 1959-62. Recipient Stevens Honor award, 1971, J. Robert Oppenheimer Meml. prize, 1981, Nat. Medal Sci., 1985, Michelson-Morley award, 1990, Disting. Alumnus award NYU, 1990, Franklin medal Benjamin Franklin inst. Com. on Sci. and the Arts, 1992; co-recipient Rossi prize Am. Astron. Soc., 1989; Guggenheim fellow, 1958-59, Alfred P. Sloan fellow, 1959-63, Franklin medal Franklin Inst., 1992, Nobel Prize in physics, 1995. Fellow Am. Phys. Soc. (W.K.H. Panofsky prize 1992), AAAS (mem. nominating com. 1988-89), Am. Acad. Arts and Scis.; mem. NAS, Am. Assn. Physics Tchrs., Argonne U. Assn. (trustee 1965-66), Russian Acad. Sci. (fgn. mem.), Phi Beta Kappa, Sigma Xi, Tau Beta Pi. Office: U Calif Dept Physics and Astronomy Campus Dr Irvine CA 92697-4575

REINFELDS, JURIS, computer science educator; b. Riga, Latvia, Apr. 1, 1936; came to U.S., 1989; s. Nikolais Janis and Irma (Kaulins) R.; m. Lauma Petersons, Sept. 15, 1962; children: Peteris Maris, Ivars Valdis, Martins Nikolais. BSc, U. Adelaide, Australia, 1959; PhD, U. Adelaide, 1963; postdoctoral work, ICI. Postdoctoral fellow U. Edinburgh, Scotland, 1961-64; postdoctoral rsch. fellow U. Adelaide, Australia, 1964-65; NSF postdoctoral rsch. assoc. NASA, Huntsville, Ala., 1965-66; asst. prof. computer sci. U. Ga., Athens, 1966-72; vis. scientist CERN, Geneva, 1972-75; found. prof. computer sci. U. Wollongong NSW, Australia, 1975-89; prof. computer sci. N.Mex. State U., Las Cruces, 1989—; cons. Australian Internat. Devel. Program, Hat Yai, Thailand, 1983-91, Los Banos, Philippines, 1983-90. Mem. IEEE Computer Soc., Assn. for Computer Machinery, Australian Computer Soc., Las Cruces Rotary Club. Avocations: skiing, hiking. Office: NMex State U Klipsch Sch Elec & Computer Engring Dept 3-0 Las Cruces NM 88003-8001 also: 445 E Cheyenne Mtn Blvd # C-368 Colorado Springs CO 80906-4570

REINGLASS, MICHELLE ANNETTE, lawyer; b. L.A., Dec. 9, 1954; d. Darwin and Shirley (Steiner) R. Student, U. Calif., Irvine, 1972-75; BSL, Western State U., 1977, JD, 1978. Bar: Calif. 1979, U.S. Dist. Ct. (ctrl. dist.) Calif. 1979, U.S. Ct. Appeals (9th cir.) 1981, U.S. Dist. Ct. (so. dist.) Calif. 1989. Pvt. practice Laguna Hills, Calif., 1979—; instr. Calif. Continuing Edn. of Bar, 1990—, We. State Coll., 1991, Rutter Group, 1994—; chmn. magistrate selection com. U.S. Dist. Ct. (ctrl. dist.) Calif., L.A., 1991, 93, 94, 95; lectr. in field. Contbr. articles to profl. jours. Pres. Child or Parental Emergency Svcs., Santa Ana, Calif., 1990-92; bd. dirs. Pub. Law Ctr., Santa Ana. Recipient award for evidence Am. Jurisprudence; named to Hall of Fame Western State U., 1993, Jurisprudence award Anti-defamation League, 1997. Mem. State Bar Calif., Orange County Bar Assn. (del. to state conv. 1980—, bd. dirs. 1983-94, chmn. bus. litigation sect. 1989, sec. 1990, treas. 1991, pres.-elect 1992, pres. 1993), Orange County Trial Lawyers Assn. (bd. dirs. 1987-89, Bus. Trial Lawyer of Yr. award 1995), Orange County Women Lawyers (Lawyer of Yr. award 1996), Vols. in Parole (chmn. adv. com. 1990-91), Peter Elliot Inns Ct. (master). Avocations: distance running, skiing. Office: 23161 Mill Creek Dr Ste 170 Laguna Beach CA 92653-1649

REINGOLD, HAIM, mathematics educator; b. Lodz, Poland, Mar. 16, 1910; came to U.S., 1930, naturalized, 1942; s. Shmaryahu and Esther (Rudnianski) R.; m. Leah Jacobson, Apr. 16, 1942 (dec. Mar. 1964); children—Edward M., Arthur L.; m. Badonna Levinson, Nov. 16, 1966; 1 son, David A. Student, NYU, 1931; AB, U. Cin., 1933, MA, 1934, PhD in Math, 1938. Tchg. asst. U. Cin., 1936-38; head dept. math. Our Lady of Cin. Coll., 1938-42; supr. math. Ill. Inst. Tech., 1942-43, asst. prof., 1943-47, assoc. prof., 1947-56, prof., 1956-75, prof. emeritus, 1975—, chmn. dept. math., 1951-75; adj. prof. math. Ind. U. Northwest, 1975-82; vis. prof. Purdue U.-Calumet (Ind.), 1982-84; prof., chmn. dept. math. Mundelein Coll., 1984-91; sr. prof. Loyola U., Chgo., 1991. Author: (with Andres, Miser) Basic Mathematics for Engineers, 1944, Basic Mathematics for Science and Engineering, 1955. Mem. Am. Math. Soc., Math. Assn. Am., Am. Soc. Engring. Edn. (chmn. math. div. 1955-56, mem. council 1957-59), AAAS, Soc. Engring. Sci., Sigma Xi (chpt. pres. 1966-67). Jewish. Home: 1329 E 55th St Chicago IL 60615-5301

REINGOLD, NATHAN, historian; b. N.Y.C., Mar. 23, 1927; s. Benjamin and Fanny R.; m. Ida Hornstein, Jan. 1, 1955 (dec. 1988); children: Matthew H., Nicholas F.; m. Ellen Miles, Nov. 28, 1992. B.A., NYU, 1947, M.A., 1948; Ph.D., U. Pa., 1951. Staff mem. Nat. Archives, Washington, 1951-59; history of sci. specialist Library of Congress, Washington, 1959-66; editor Papers of Joseph Henry, Smithsonian Instn., Washington, 1966-85; sr. historian Nat. Mus. Am. History, 1985—, historian emeritus, 1993; vis. prof. Johns Hopkins U., 1993-95; adj. fellow Woodrow Wilson Internat. Ctr. for Scholars, 1975; planning com. program on knowledge in Am. soc. Am. Acad. Arts and Scis., 1970-83; com. on history applied math. in World War II, Math. Assn. Am., 1979; adv. bd. archives History Am. Psychology, 1970; mem. oversight com. for history and philosophy sci. program NSF, 1981; Allen lectr. history of math. Rensselaer Poly. Inst., 1981. Contbr. sects. to books, numerous articles to profl. jours. Editorial bd. Hist. Studies of Phys. Scis., 1968-79, N.Y. History, 1973-77; editorial adv. bd. Social Studies of Sci., 1974-80, Isis, 1971-75. Council mem. Rockefeller Archive Ctr., Rockefeller U., 1973-82, 85-91, spl. con. governing council, 1983-84; pres. commn. on documentation Internat. Union History and Philosophy of Sci., 1981; panel for history and philosophy sci. NSF, 1976-78. Recipient Centennial medal Nat. Acad. Scis., 1963. Sesquicentennial medal Coast and Geodetic Survey, 1956; scholar: N.Y. State Regents, 1945-47, NYU, 1945-48; sr. fellow Yale, 1960-61; research grantee Am. Philos. Soc., 1962-63, NSF, 1965-66, 67-72, NEH, 1973-78, Lounsbery Found., 1982-83. Mem. Assn. for Documentary Editing (dir. publs. 1980-81), Soc. for History Tech. (adv. council 1962-65), History Sci. Soc. (council 1964-67), Phi Beta Kappa (selection com. sci. book award 1966-69). Jewish. Club: Cosmos (Washington). Office: Nat Mus Am History Smithsonian Instn Washington DC 20560

REINHARD, CHRISTOPHER JOHN, merchant banking, venture capital executive; b. Bridgeport, Conn., Nov. 11, 1953; s. Warren John and Marian Louise (Dutter) R.; m. Maureen Francis, Sept. 24, 1977; 1 child, Griffin John. BS, Babson Coll., 1976, MBA, 1977. Sr. fin. analyst Gen. Motors Corp., Detroit and N.Y.C., 1977-81; asst. sec. Wheelabrator-Frye Inc., N.H., 1981-83; asst. sec., asst. treas. The Signal Cos., Inc., La Jolla, Calif., 1983-86; mng. dir., v.p. The Henley Group, Inc., La Jolla, 1986-90; mng. dir. Fisher Sci. Group, Inc., La Jolla, 1986-90; mng. dir., v.p. Wheelabrator Tech. Inc., Henley Mfg. Corp., 1987-90; founder, pres. Colony Group Inc., Rancho Santa Fe, 1990—, Reinhard Assocs., Rancho Santa Fe, 1990-95; founder, v.p., CFO Advanced Access, Inc., San Diego, 1995—; pres. Direct Feedback, Inc., 1990, Dairy Queen Ventures, 1990—, Winsor Sport Fencing, 1993—; v.p., founder, CFO, COO Collateral Therapeutics Inc., 1995—; gen. ptnr. Cabrillo Ventures, 1995—. Mem. Boston Athenaeum, N.Y. Athletic Club, San Diego Polo Club, Rancho Santa Fe Polo Club, Duquesne Club. Office: 9395 Cabot Dr San Diego CA 92126-4310

REINHARD, JAMES RICHARD, judge; b. Pollock, Mo., July 7, 1929; s. Virgil and Meltha (Anspach) R.; m. Shari L. Horton, Dec. 30, 1958; 1 child, James K. Student, N.E. Mo. State U., 1947-50; AB, U. Mo., 1951, JD, 1953. Bar: Mo. 1953. Prosecuting atty. Sullivan County (Mo.), 1955-57; prosecuting atty. Monroe County (Mo.), 1959-65; spl. asst. atty. gen. State of Mo., 1967-68; judge 10th Jud. Circuit, 1973-77; judge Mo. Ct. Appeals (ea. dist.), St. Louis, 1977—, chief judge, 1984-85; pvt. practice Milan, Mo., 1955-57, Paris, Mo., 1957-73. Bd. regents N.E. Mo. State U., Kirksville, 1965-73, pres., 1967-73. Sgt. U.S. Army, 1953-55. Mem. ABA, 10th Jud. Bar Assn. (pres. 1972), Mo. Bar Assn. (bd. govs. 1965-69), Met. Bar Assn. St. Louis, Lawyers Assn. St. Louis, Mo. Bd. Cert. Ct. Reporter Examiner (vice chmn. 1988-90), Mo. Press-Bar Commn., Judicial Fin. Commn. (chmn. 1990-94). Home: 5 Hamlin Heights Dr Hannibal MO 63401-1903 Office: Mo Ct Appeals Ea Dist 111N N 7th St Saint Louis MO 63101-2133

REINHARD, KEITH LEON, advertising executive; b. Berne, Ind., Jan. 20, 1935; s. Herman L. and Agnes V. R.; m. Rose-Lee Simons, Nov. 7, 1976; children: Rachel, Elizabeth; children by previous marriage: Christopher, Timothy, Matthew, Geoffrey, Jacqueline. Student public schs., Berne. Comml. artist Kling Studios, Chgo., 1954-56; mgr. tech. communications dept. Magnavox Co., Ft. Wayne, Ind., 1957-60; creative/account exec. Biddle Co., Bloomington, Ill., 1961-63; exec. v.p., dir. creative services, pres. Needham, Harper & Steers, Inc., Chgo., from 1964; then chmn., chief exec. officer Needham, Harper & Steers/USA, Chgo.; also dir. Needham, Harper & Steers, Inc.; chmn., chief exec. officer DDB Needham Worldwide Inc., N.Y.C., 1986—, chmn. exec. com., 1989—. Episcopalian. Office: DDB Needham Worldwide Inc 437 Madison Ave New York NY 10022-7001*

REINHARD, SISTER MARY MARTHE, educational organization administrator; b. McKeesport, Pa., Aug. 29, 1929; d. Regis C. and Leona (Reese) R. AB, Notre Dame Coll.; MA, U. Notre Dame. Asst. prin. Regina High Sch., Cleve., 1960-62, prin., 1963-64; prin. Notre Dame Acad., Chardon, Ohio, 1965-72; pres. Notre Dame Coll. of Ohio, Cleve., 1973-88; dir. devel. Sisters of Notre Dame Ednl. Ctr., Chardon, 1989—. Trustee, mem. exec. com. NCCJ, Cleve., 1987; bd. dirs. Centerior Energy, 1986—; mem. coun. Geagua United Way Svcs., 1990-97, vice-chair fund raising, 1991-94, vice-chair planning, 1995-97; mem. adv. bd. Kent State U., Geauga campus, 1991-94; trustee Leadership Geauga, 1995-96. Recipient Humanitarian award Cleve. chpt. NCCJ, 1990; named one of 100 most influential women in Cleve., Women's City Club, 1982, one of 79 most interesting people in Cleve., The Cleve. Mag., 1979, Cleve. United Way Vol. of Yr., 1997; elected to Hall of Excellence, Ohio Found. of Ind. Colls., 1996. Roman Catholic. Home and Office: 13000 Auburn Rd Chardon OH 44024-9330

REINHARD, PHILIP G., federal judge; b. LaSalle, Ill., Jan. 12, 1941; s. Godfrey and Ruth R.; married Virginia Reinhard; children: Bruce, Brian, David, Philip. BA, U. Ill., Champaign, 1962, JD, 1964. Asst. state atty. Winnebago County, 1964-67; atty. Hyer, Gill & Brown, 1967-68; state atty. Winnebago County, 1968-76; judge 17th Jud. Cir., 1976-80, Appellate Ct., 1980-92, U.S. Dist. Ct. (no. dist.) Ill., 1992—; mem. security, space and facilities com. U.S. Jud. Conf. Mem. Am. Jud. Edn., Winnebago County Bar Assn. Office: US Courthouse 211 S Court St Ste 215 Rockford IL 61101-1219

REINHARDT, BENJAMIN MAX, lawyer, arbitrator, mediator; b. N.Y.C., Dec. 29, 1917; s. Meyer and Miriam (Fischer) R.; mn. Marlaena M. Chubey, May 23, 1971; children: Dennis, Dixie. BA, Harvard U., 1940; JD magna cum laude, Southwestern U., L.A., 1956. Bar: Calif. 1956, U.S. Supreme Ct. 1960. Pvt. practice Van Nuys, Calif., 1957-87, Palm Desert, Calif., 1987—; chief legal counsel Northridge (Calif.) Hosp. Found., 1965-75; atty. Calif. Psychol. Assn., San Francisco, 1965-70; tchr. law Los Angeles County Bd. Edn., L.A., 1965-73; instr. law U. So. Calif., L.A., 1963-69, Coll. of Desert, Palm Desert, Calif., 1992-94; arbitrator Superior Ct. Calif., Palm Springs, 1994—; atty. Sr. T.V., Indian Wells, Calif., 1992—. Mem. Palm Desert Police Adv. Com., 1993—; mem. adv. bd. Ret. Sr. Vol. Program, Palm Desert, 1994—; instr. law Elderhostel, Indian Wells, Calif., 1993—. Capt. U.S. Army, 1941-46. Mem. State Bar Calif., Desert Bar Assn. Republican. Avocations: golf, reading. Office: 73880 Grapevine St Palm Desert CA 92260-5561

REINHARDT, JOHN EDWARD, former international affairs specialist; b. Glade Spring, Va., Mar. 8, 1920; s. Edward Vinton and Alice (Miller) R.; m. Carolyn Lillian Daves, Sept. 2, 1947; children: Sharman W. Reinhardt Lancefield, Alice N. Reinhardt Jeffers, Carolyn C. Reinhardt Fenstermaker. A.B., Knoxville Coll., 1939; M.S., U. Wis., 1947, Ph.D., 1950. Prof. English Va. State Coll., Petersburg, 1950-56; cultural affairs officer USIS, Manila, 1956-58; dir. Am. Cultural Ctr., Kyoto, Japan, 1958-63; cultural attache USIS, Tehran, Iran, 1963-66; dep. asst. dir. Office East Asia and Pacific, USIA, Washington, 1966-68, 70-71, asst. dir. Office for Africa, 1968-70; ambassador to Nigeria, 1971-75, asst. sec. state for pub. affairs, 1975-77; dir. USIA, Washington, 1977-78, U.S. Internat. Communication Agy., Washington, 1978-81; acting dir. Smithsonian Mus. African Art, Washington, 1981-83; asst. sec. for history and art Smithsonian Instn., Washington, 1983-84; dir. directorate internat. activities Smithsonian Instn., 1984-87; prof. polit. sci. U. Vt., Burlington, 1987-90, prof. emeritus, 1990—. Served as officer AUS, 1942-46. Mem. MLA, Am. Fgn. Svc. Assn. (v.p. 1969-71). Methodist. Clubs: Cosmos.

REINHARDT, STEPHEN ROY, federal judge; b. N.Y.C., Mar. 27, 1931; s. Gottfried and Silvia (Hanlon) R.; children: Mark, Justin, Dana. B.A. cum laude, Pomona Coll., 1951; LL.B., Yale, 1954. Bar: Calif. 1958. Law clk. to U.S. Dist. Judge Luther W. Youngdahl, Washington, 1956-57; atty. O'Melveny & Myers, L.A., 1957-59; partner Fogel Julber Reinhardt Rothschild & Feldman (L.C.), L.A., 1959-80; judge U.S. Ct. Appeals (9th cir.), L.A., 1980—; Mem. exec. com. Dem. Nat. Com., 1969-72, nat. Dem. committeeman for Calif., 1976-80; pres. L.A. Recreation an dParks Commn., 1974-75; mem. Coliseum Commn., 1974-75; mem. L.A. Police Commn., 1974-78, pres., 1978-80; sec., mem. exec. com. L.A. Olympic Organizing com., 1980-84; bd. dirs. Amateur Athletic Found. of L.A., 1984-92; adj. prof. Loyola Law Sch., L.A., 1988-90. Served to 1st lt. USAF, 1954-56. Mem. ABA (labor law coun. 1975-77). *

REINHARDT, WILLIAM PARKER, chemical physicist, educator; b. San Francisco, May 22, 1942; s. William Oscar and Elizabeth Ellen (Parker) R.; m. Katrina Hawley Currens, Mar. 14, 1979; children: James William, Alexander Hawley. BS in Basic Chemistry, U. Calif., Berkeley, 1964; AM in Chemistry, Harvard U., 1966, PhD in Chem. Physics, 1968; MA (hon.), U. Pa., 1985. Instr. chemistry Harvard U., 1967-69, asst. prof. chemistry, 1969-72, assoc. prof., 1972-74; prof. U. Colo., Boulder, 1974-84, chmn. dept. chemistry, 1977-80; prof. chemistry U. Pa., Phila., 1984-91, chmn. dept., 1985-88, D. Michael Crow prof., 1987-91; prof. chemistry U.Wash., Seattle, 1991—, assoc. chmn. undergrad. program, 1993-96; vis. fellow Joint Inst. for Lab. Astrophysics of Nat. Bur. Stds. and U. Colo., 1972, 74, fellow, 1974-84; dir. Telluride Summer Rsch. Ctr., 1986-89, treas., 1989-93; com. on atomic, molecular and optical scis. NRC, 1988-90; vis. scientist Nat. Inst. Stds. and Tech., summers 1993, 94, 96, 97; vis. prof. chemistry U. Melbourne, Australia, 1997, Harvard U., 1998. Mem. editl. bd. Phys. Rev. A., 1979-81, Chem. Physics, 1985-94, Jour. Chem. Physics, 1987-89, Jour. Physics B. (U.K.), 1992—, Internat. Jour. Quantum Chemistry, 1994—; rschr. theoretical chem. physics, theoretical atomic and molecular physics for numerous publs. Recipient Camille and Henry Dreyfus Tchr. Scholar award, 1972; Alfred P. Sloan fellow, 1972; J.S. Guggenheim Meml. fellow, 1978; Coun. on Rsch. and Creative Work faculty fellow, 1978; Wilsmore fellow U. Melbourne (Australia), 1997; J.W. Fulbright sr. scholar, Australia, 1997. Fellow AAAS, Am. Phys. Soc.; mem. Am. Chem. Soc., Phi Beta Kappa, Sigma Xi (nat. lectr. 1980-82), Phi Lambda Upsilon (Fresenius award 1977). Office: U Wash Dept Chemistry Box 351700 Seattle WA 98195-1700

REINHART, DIETRICH THOMAS, university president, history educator; b. Mpls., May 17, 1949; s. Donald Irving and Eleanor Therese (Noonan) R. BA in History, St. John's U., Collegeville, Minn., 1971; AM in History, Brown U., 1976, PhD in History, 1984. Benedictine monk St. John's Abbey, 1971—; assoc. prof. history St. John's U., 1981—, dean of the coll., 1988-91, pres., 1991—; dir. liturgy St. John's Abbey, 1983-88. Bd. dirs. Minn. Pvt. Coll. Coun., 1991—, George A. MacPherson Fund, 1991—, Hill Monastic Manuscript Library, 1991—, Inst. for Ecumenical and Cultural Rsch., 1991—, First Am. Nat. Bank St. Cloud., 1992—; bd. overseers St. John's Prep. Sch., 1990—. Home: St John's Abbey Collegeville MN 56321 Office: St John's U Office of Pres Collegeville MN 56321*

REINHART, JOHN BELVIN, child and adolescent psychiatrist, educator; b. Merrill, Wis., Dec. 22, 1917; s. Dabney Belvin and Ann (Toomey) R.; m. Helen Elsen Reinhart, Jan. 3, 1994; children: Peter, Catherine, Ann, John, Frederick, Andrew. BA, Duke U., 1939; MD, Bowman Gray Sch. Medicine, Winston-Salem, N.C., 1943. Diplomate Am. Bd. Pediatrics, Am. Bd. Psychiatry in child and adolescent psychiatry. Instr. pediatrics Bowman Gray Sch. Medicine, Winston-Salem, 1950-52; asst. prof., assoc. prof., prof. pediatrics and psychiatry U. Pitts. Sch. Medicine, 1956-83, emeritus prof. pediatrics, 1983—; clin. prof. psychiatry Bowman Gray Sch. Medicine, Winston-Salem, 1986—. Co-Author: A Baby's First Year, 1956. Capt. M.C. AUS, 1946-48. Roman Catholic. Avocations: reading, golf, tennis, travel. Home: 34 Hunter's Ln Hendersonville NC 28791 Office: Trend MHS Cons Hendersonville NC 28791

REINHART, KELLEE CONNELY, journalist; b. Kearney, Nebr., Dec. 15, 1951; d. Vaughn Eugene and Mary Jo (Mullen) Connely; m. Stephen Wayne Reinhart, June 15, 1974; children: Keegan Connely, Channing Mullen. B.A., U. Ala., 1972, M.S., 1974. Advt. copywriter Stas. WTBC-AM, WUOA-FM, 1970-72; asst. mgr. Ala. Press Assn., 1972-74; asst. to the editor Antique Monthly mag., 1974-75, mng. editor, 1975-77; editorial dir. Antique Monthly and Horizons mags., 1977-89; dir. univ. rels. U. Ala. System, Tuscaloosa, 1989—. Editor: Wild Birds of America: The Art of Basil Ede, 1991. Bd. dirs. Ala. Humanities Found., Ala. Writers Forum. Recipient Druids Arts award, 1995. Mem. Soc. Profl. Journalists, Am. Soc. Mag. Editors, Newcomen Soc. U.S., Art Table. Office: 401 Queen City Ave Tuscaloosa AL 35401-1551

REINHART, MARY ANN, medical board executive; b. Jackson, Mich., Aug. 14, 1942; d. Herbert Martin and Josephine Marie (Keyes) Conway; m. David Lee Reinhart, Dec. 28, 1963; children: Stephen Paul, Michael David. MA, Mich. State U., 1983, PhD, 1985. Rsch. asst. Mich. State U., East Lansing, 1979-82, 85, teaching asst. dept psychology, 1982-84, asst. prof. Office Med. Edn. R&D, Coll. Human Medicine, 1985-88; assoc. exec. dir. Am. Bd. Emergency Medicine, East Lansing, 1988-95, dep. exec. dir., 1995—; cons. Am. Bd. Emergency Medicine, 1985-88; chairperson collegewide evaluation com. Coll. Human Medicine, Mich. State U., East Lansing, 1985-88; adj. asst. prof. Office Med. Edn. Rsch. and Devel., Coll. Human Medicine, 1988—. Reviewer Annals of Emergency Medicine, 1987-95, Acad. Emergency Medicine, 1995—. Bd. dirs. Neahtawanta Rsch. and Edn. Ctr., Traverse City, Mich., 1991—. Mem. APA (divsn. indsl./orgnl. psychology, health psychology), Phi Kappa Phi. Achievements include application of chart stimulated recall method of assessment in a national medical recertification examination; development and implementation of national longitudinal study of emergency medicine residents and emergency physicians. Office: Am Bd Emergency Medicine 3000 Coolidge Rd East Lansing MI 48823-6319

REINHART, PETER SARGENT, corporate executive, lawyer; b. Mineola, N.Y., May 17, 1950; s. Charles Woodham and Martha Way (Sargent) R.; m. Susan Stockwell, Aug. 29, 1970 (div. Jan. 1976); 1 child, Amy Lynn; m. Gale McElroy, Oct. 16, 1976 (div. May 1985); 1 child, James Gharrett; m. Carol O. Gaffney, Jan. 4, 1992. BA, Franklin and Marshall Coll., 1971; JD, Rutgers U., 1975. Bar: N.J. 1975. Atty. Pillsbury and Russell, Atlantic

Highlands, N.J., 1975-78; corp. counsel K. Hovnanian Enterprises, Inc., Red Bank, N.J., 1978-81, sr. v.p., gen. counsel, 1981—; also bd. dirs.; pres. Inst. Multi-Family Housing, Plainsboro, N.J., 1989-90. Trustee, mem. editorial bd. Housing N.J. mag., 1991—. Trustee Community Assns. Inst., Arlington, Va., pres. N.J. chpt., 1988; trustee Assn. for Children of N.J., Newark, 1988-93, Keep Middlesex Moving, New Brunswick, 1990-93, Bayshore Cmty. Hosp., Holmdel, N.J., 1992—, v.p., 1995, chmn., 1997; pres. Greater Red Bank Jaycees, 1978-79, Atlantic Highlands Rep. Club, 1978; v.p. Monmouth coun. Boy Scouts Am., Oakhurst, N.J., 1987-94, pres., 1994-95; v.p. Garden State Games, Edison, N.J., 1991-94; mem. Coun. Affordable Housing, Trenton, N.J., 1993—. Named to Community Assns. Inst. Hall of Fame, 1988; named Jaycee of Yr. Greater Red Bank Jaycees, 1977. Mem. N.J. State Bar Assn., N.J. Shore Builders Assn. (pres. 1989-90, Builder of Yr. 1987, Hall of Fame 1991), Ea. Monmouth C. of C. (trustee 1992—), Nat. Assn. Indsl. and Office Parks (bd. dirs. 1990-92), N.J. Builders Assn. (v.p. 1992-94, pres. 1995-96, Builder of Yr. award 1995, Shore Athletic Club (Oakhurst). Avocations: road racing, marathon running. Home: 2 Bayhill Rd Leonardo NJ 07737-1801 Office: Hovnanian Enterprises Inc 10 Hwy 35 PO Box 500 Red Bank NJ 07701

REINHART, ROBERT ROUNTREE, JR., lawyer; b. Chgo., Oct. 21, 1947; s. Robert Rountree and Ruth (Duncan) R.; m. Elizabeth Aileen Plews, July 26, 1969; children: Andrea Jean, Jessica Elizabeth, Rebecca Jill. BA, Northwestern U., 1968; JD, U. Mich., 1971. Bar: Ill. 1971, Mich. 1972, Minn. 1973, U.S. Supreme Ct. 1976. Law clk. to judge U.S. Dist. Ct. (we. dist.) Mich., Grand Rapids, 1971-73; assoc. Oppenheimer Wolff & Donnelly, Mpls., 1973-77, ptnr., 1978-96, chair labor and employment bus. group, 1985-92; ptnr. Dorsey & Whitney, Mpls., 1996—; co-chair Upper Midwest Employment Law Inst., Mpls., 1984—. Mem. ABA (labor and employment, civil litigation sects.), Minn. Bar Assn. Office: Dorsey & Whitney 1400 Pillsbury Ctr S 220 S 6th St Minneapolis MN 55402-4502

REINHARZ, JEHUDA, academic administrator, history educator; b. Haifa, Israel, Aug. 1, 1944; came to U.S., 1961; s. Fred and Anita (Weigler) R.; m. Shulamit Rothschild, Nov. 26, 1967; children—Yael, Naomi. B.S., Columbia U., 1967; B.R.E., Jewish Theol. Sem., 1967; M.A., Harvard U., 1968; Ph.D., Brandeis U., 1972; LHD, Hebrew Union Coll., 1995; DHL, The Jewish Theol. Sem. of Am., 1996. Prof. modern Jewish history U. Mich., Ann Arbor, 1972-82; Richard Koret prof. modern Jewish history Brandeis U., Waltham, Mass., 1982—, dir. Tauber Inst. Study of European Jewry, 1984-94; provost, sr. v.p. for acad. affairs Brandels U., Waltham, Mass., 1992-94; pres. Brandeis U., Waltham, Mass., 1994—; mem. internat. acad. bd. Annenberg Rsch. Inst., 1986-90; bd. dirs. Yad Chaim Weizmann, 1990—, Internat. Editl. Bd. Pardès, 1996—; pres. Israel Prize, 1990, Akiba award, Am.-Jewish Com., 1996. Author: Fatherland or Promised Land: The Dilemma of the German Jew 1893-1914, 1975, Chaim Weizmann: The Making of a Zionist Leader, 1985 (Present Tense Literary award 1985, Kenneth B. Smilen Literary award 1985, Nat. Jewish Book award 1986, Shazar prize in history Israel, 1988), (in Hebrew) Hashomer Hazair in Germany, 1931-39, 1989, Chaim Weizmann: The Making of a Statesman, 1993 (Nat. Jewish Book award 1994); also numerous articles in French, German, Hebrew and English; gen. editor: Studies in Jewish History, 1984, European Jewish History, 1985; co-editor: The Jew in the Modern World, 1980, 2d edit. 1995, Mystics, Philosophers and Politicians, 1982, Israel in the Middle East 1948-83, 1984, The Jewish Response to German Culture, 1985, The Jews of Poland Between Two World Wars, 1989, The Impact of Western Nationalisms, 1992, Zionism and Religion, Hebrew edit., 1994, Essential Papers on Zionism, 1996; editor: The Letters and Papers of Chaim Weizmann, 1918-20, 1977, Dokumente zur Geschichte des deutschen Zionismus, 1882-1933, 1981, Living with Antisemitism, 1987. Bd. govs. United Israel Appeal/Jewish Agy., 1994; mem. bd. dir., exec. com. Am. Joint Distbn. Com., 1994; mem. acad. com. U.S. Holocaust Mus., 1990—. Fellow Leo Baeck Inst., Royal Hist. Soc., Am. Acad. Jewish Rsch., Am. Acad. Arts and Scis.; mem. Yad Vashem Soc. (adv. bd. 1983), Nat. Coun. Shazar Ctr., Assn. for Jewish Studies (sec. 1986-88, treas./sec., 1988-94), Commn. on Israel-Diaspora Rels., 1996—; com. on conscience nat. adv. forum U.S. Holocaust Mus., 1996—. Home: 66 Beaumont Ave Newton MA 02160-2331 Office: Brandeis U Office of Pres Waltham MA 02254-9110*

REINHERZ, HELEN ZARSKY, social services educator; b. Boston, Aug. 4, 1923; d. Zachary and Anna (Cohen) Zarsky; m. Samuel E. Reinherz, Aug. 29, 1943; 1 son, Ellis. A.B. magna cum laude, Wheaton Coll., 1944; M.S., Simmons Coll., 1946; S.M., Harvard U., 1962, Sc.D., 1965. Social worker Newton Family Service, Mass., 1946-49, Mass. Gen. Hosp., Boston, 1949-51; supr. psychiat. social work State Hosp., Waltham, Mass., 1958-61; faculty mem. Simmons Coll., Boston, 1965—, prof. methods rsch., 1972—, dir. research Sch. Social Work, 1968-93, dir. PhD program, 1993-96; prin. investigator Identifying Children at Risk, 1976-84, Adaption in Adolescence, 1987-93, Early Adulthood Rsch. Project, 1993—; rsch. cons. Dept. Mental Health, 1970-80; prin. investigator Study Adolescent Drug Abuse, 1971-73; chmn. Gov.'s Adv. Coun. on Mental Health and Retardation, 1972; mem. adv. com. Mental Health Manpower to Fed. Govt., 1980-82. Author: (with H. Wechler, D. Dobbins) Social Work Research in the Human Services, 1976, (with M. Heywood, J. Camp) A Community Response to Drug Abuse, 1976; cons., assoc. editor: Jour. Prevention, 1980-91; mem. fed. adv. com. Rsch. in Prevention Rev., 1984-87; editorial bd. Jour. Early Adolescence; assoc. editor NASW Jour.; contbr. 55 articles to profl. jours. Recipient Maida H. Solomon award Simmons Coll. Alumni, 1961; NIH tng. fellow, 1961-65; Grant Found. grantee, 1963; Med. Found. grantee, 1967-69; NIMH grantee, 1975-84, 87—. Fellow Am. Orthopyschiat. Assn.; mem. Acad. Cert. Social Workers, Am. Pub. Health Assn., Council Social Work Edn., Harvard Sch. Pub. Health Alumni Assn. (sec.-treas. 1965-68), Phi Beta Kappa, Delta Omega. Home: 17 Corey Rd Malden MA 02148-1116 Office: Simmons Sch Social Work 51 Commonwealth Ave Boston MA 02116-2348 *As a teacher and researcher my efforts have been directed towards encouraging students to formulate the right questions about human problems as a first step to understanding and change.*

REINHOLD, RICHARD LAWRENCE, lawyer; b. Buffalo, Feb. 24, 1951; s. Richard J. and Ann J. R.; m. Beth Stacey Grossman, May 11, 1991; 1 child: Elizabeth Jane. AB, Cornell U., 1973; JD, SUNY, Buffalo, 1976. Bar: N.Y. 1977, Fla. 1977. Assoc. Hodgson, Russ, Andrews, Woods & Goodyear, Buffalo, 1976-81; with office of tax legis. counsel U.S. Dept. Treasury, Washington, 1982-84; ptnr. Cahill Gordon & Reindel, N.Y.C., 1985—. Contbr. articles to profl. jours. Trustee The Healthcare Chaplaincy. Fellow Am. Coll. of Tax Counsel; mem. N.Y. State Bar Assn. (chair tax sect. 1996-97), Internat. Fiscal Assn., Tax Club. Office: Cahill Gordon & Reindel 80 Pine St New York NY 10005-1702

REINHORN, ANDREI M., civil engineering educator, consultant; b. Bucharest, Romania, Oct. 23, 1945; s. Moritz A. and Dina (Rosenfeld) R.; m. Tova A. Waldman, Oct. 15, 1968; children: Michael, Gad. BSc, Technion - Israel Inst. Tech., Haifa, 1968, DSc, 1978. Registered profl. engr., N.Y., Israel. Structural engr. Milstein & Singer, Cons. Engrs., Tel Aviv, 1972-73; structural engr. Haifa, 1973-79, Buffalo, 1980-85; structural engr. Reinhorn Consulting Engrs., 1990—; vis. asst. prof. U. Buffalo, 1979-81, asst. prof., 1981-86, assoc. prof., 1986-90, prof., 1990—; chmn. dept. civil engring. SUNY, Buffalo, 1996—; cons. Niagara Machine & Tools, Buffalo, 1982—, WSF Industries, Buffalo, 1983—, Walt Disney World, Lake Buenavista, Fla., 1986, Westinghouse, 1987-89, West Valley Nuclear Site, 1989, Princeton U., 1992, LeMessurier Cons., 1992, Dames & Moore, 1990-92, County of L.A., 1993; investigator Nat. Ctr. Earthquake Engring. Rsch., 1986—. Inventor, patentee press brake deflection compensation structure, automatic diagnostic sys. for elec. cir. breakers; contbr. over 250 articles to profl. jours., chpts. to books and conf. procs. Pres. W.E.S.T. Age Group Swim Club, Buffalo, 1985. Served to capt. Israel Def. Force, 1968-72. Rsch. grantee NSF, 1983-84, 86-95, 94—, Nalge/Snyder Industries, 1987. Fellow ASCE (faculty advisor 1981-83, bd. dirs. 1986-96, pres. Buffalo sect. 1993-94, Outstanding Svc. award 1982, 83); mem. N.Y. State Profl. Engring. Assn. (Engring. Educator of Yr. award 1991, Hist. Achievement award 1995), Am. Concrete Inst., Earthquake Engring. Rsch. Inst., Nat. Ctr. for Earthquake Engring. Rsch. Avocations: photography, skiing, bicycling. Home: 12 Troy View Ln Buffalo NY 14221-3522 Office: SUNY Buffalo Dept Civil Engring 231 Ketter Hall Amherst NY 14260

REINIGER, DOUGLAS HAIGH, lawyer; b. Mt. Kisco, N.Y., Nov. 8, 1948; s. Haigh McDiarmid and Virginia (Munson) R.; m. Margaret Vrablic, Aug. 31, 1968 (div. Jan. 1983); 1 child, Brian Christopher; m. Anne Fanning, Aug. 5, 1984. BA, Iona Coll., 1970; MSW, Fordham U., 1974, JD, 1980. Bar: N.Y. 1981, U.S. Dist. Ct. (so. dist.) N.Y. 1982, U.S. Dist. Ct. (ea. dist.) N.Y., 1991, U.S. Cir. Ct. Appeals (2d cir.) 1997, U.S. Supreme Ct 1986. Psychiat. aide St. Vincent's Psychiat. Hosp., Harrison, N.Y., 1968-69; child care worker Cardinal McCloskey Home for Children, White Plains, N.Y., 1969-71, social worker, 1971-75, dir. legal affairs, 1975-81; sole practice N.Y.C., 1981-83; ptnr. Rosin & Reiniger, N.Y.C., 1983—; assoc. prof. Sch. Social Work Columbia U., N.Y.C., 1991—, coord. law minor program, Sch. Social Work, 1994—; lectr. appellate divsn. N.Y. Supreme Ct., N.Y.C., 1985, Fedn. Protestant Welfare, N.Y.C., 1987-91, Ct. Apptd. Spl. Advs., N.Y.C., 1987-94, Practicing Law Inst., N.Y.C., 1988. Mem. ABA (family law sect., com. on adoption, com. on custody 1992—), N.Y. State Bar Assn. (lectr. 1988, 91, family law sect., com. on family ct., com. on adoption), Assn. Bar City N.Y. (lectr. 1995, com. on family law and family ct. 1985-88, com. on juvenile justice 1989-91, com. on children and the law 1993-97—), Am. Acad. Adoptive Attys. (lectr. 1995-96), N.Y. State Foster and Adoptive Parents Assn. (bd. dirs. 1992—, lectr. 1992-96), N.Y. County Lawyers' Assn. (lectr. 1994-97). Roman Catholic. Office: Rosin & Reiniger 630 3rd Ave New York NY 10017-6705

REININGHAUS, RUTH, artist; b. N.Y.C., Oct. 4, 1922; d. Emil William and Pauline Rosa (Lazarik) R.; m. George H. Morales, Feb. 20, 1944; children: George James, Robert Charles; m. Allan Joseph Smith, May 28, 1960. Student, Hunter Coll., NYU, Nat. Acad. Sch. of Design, 1960-61, Frank Reilly Sch. of Art, 1963, Art Students League, 1968. Instr. art Banker's Trust, N.Y.C., 1971-77, 79—, Kittredge Club for Women, N.Y.C., 1967-77. Exhibited in group shows at Berkshire Art Mus., 1970s, Hammer Galleries, Inc., N.Y.C., 1974, Far Gallery, N.Y.C., 1974, Mufalli Gallery, N.Y. and Fla., 1983-90, Pen and Brush Club, 1985—, Petrucci Gallery, Saugerties, N.Y., 1988-94, Pastel Soc. Am., 1988—, John Lane Gallery, Rhinebeck, N.Y., 1992—, Regianni Gallery, N.Y.C., 1994, Catherine Lorillard Wolfe Club, Salmagundi Club, Allied Arts Am., Heidi Newhoff Gallery, N.Y.C., Hudson Valley Art Assn., Knickerbocker Artists, N.Y.C., Pastel Soc. Am., others. Recipient Robert Lehman award, 1960s, 3d prize in oils Murray Hill Art Show, 1968; scholar Nat. Acad., 1962, Frank Reilly Sch. Art, 1963, NYU, 1968; subject NBC TV show You Are an Artist, 1950s. Fellow Am. Artists Profl. League (Claude Parsons Meml. award 1974, 2d prize oils 1992, 3d prize oils 1993, Pres. award 1994), Hudson Valley Art Assn.; mem. Pastel Soc. Am. (bd. dirs. 1988-90, J. Giffuni purchase award 1988, Flora B. Giffuni pres.' award 1990), Allied Artists Am. (assoc.), Soc. Illustrators (hon. 1983-87), Nat. Arts Club, Reciprocal, Artists Fellowship, Washington Sq. Outdoor Art Assn. (bd. dirs. 1983-90, Talens award 1963, Richtone Artists award 1968), Salmagundi Club N.Y. (pres. 1983-87, curator 1989—, Baker Brush award 1969, scholar 1969, Philip Isenberg award 1974, 89, 90, 92, 95, hon. mention 1983, 84, 91, 96, Salmagundi Club prize 1985, Franklin B. Williams Fund prize 1987, Tom Picard award 1987, Mortimer E. Freehof award 1988, John N. Lewis award 1988, 89, Salmagundi Club medal of honor 1989, Samuel T. Shaw award 1990, Thomas Moran award 1990, Helen S. Coes award 1990, Alice B. McReynolds award 1991, Salmagundi award 1991, Alphaeus Cole Meml. award 1991), Catharine Lorillard Wolfe Art Club (bd. dirs. 1987—, Anna Hyatt Huntington award 1978), Coun. Am. Artists (award 1985, hon. mention 1991, Catharine Lorillard Wolfe award for pastel 1992, cash award 1993), Pen and Brush Club (Helen Slotman award 1986, Gene Alden Walker award 1988, Pen and Brush Solo award 1992, hon. mention 1991, Margaret Sussman award 1996), Knickerbocker Artists (Flora B. Giffuni PSA Pres.' award 1990), Oil Pastel Assn. (Pen and Brush award 1987, Strathmore award 1989), Alpha Delta Pi. Lutheran. Avocations: travel, tech. illustration, oil and pastel painting, collecting antique music boxes and watches. Home: 222 E 93rd St Apt 26A New York NY 10128-3758

REINISCH, BODO WALTER, atmospheric science educator; b. Beuthen, Germany, Nov. 26, 1936; came to U.S., 1965; s. Kurt and Alice Ada (Walleiser) R.; m. Gerda Seidenschwand, June 1, 1963; children: Karin, Ulrike. MS, U. Freiburg, Germany, 1963; PhD, Lowell Tech. Inst., 1970. Rsch. asst. Ionosphären Inst., Breisach, Germany, 1961-63, physicist, 1963-65; physicist Lowell (Mass.) Tech. Inst., 1965-75; dir. Ctr. for Atmospheric Rsch. U. Mass., Lowell, 1975—, assoc. prof. elec. engring., 1980-83, prof., 1983-96, dept. head, 1988-94, prof. atmospheric scis., 1996—; cons. Royal Meteorol. Inst., Brussels, 1970-71; guest prof. physics U. Linz, Austria, 1978-79. Contbr. over 100 articles to Radio Sci., Jour. Geophys. Rsch., Advances of Space Rsch., others. Mem. sch. com. German Saturday Sch., Boston, 1979—. Grantee USAF, NASA, NSF, others; awarded Bundesverdienstkreuz by Pres. of Germany, 1987; Univ. Prof. U. Mass., Lowell, 1987-90; recipient Outstanding Achievement award U. Mass., Lowell, 1986, 87, 88. Sr. mem. IEEE; mem. Am. Geophys. Union, Internat. Union Radio Sci. (vice chair COSPAR/URSI Task Force on Internat. Reference Ionosphere, internat. chmn. com. G 1996—), Sigma Pi Sigma, Sigma Ksi. Achievements include development of global network of "digisonde" sounders; established HF Doppler observations for ionospheric drift studies; 2 patents. Office: U Mass Lowell Ctr Atmospheric Rsch 600 Suffolk St Lowell MA 01854-3629

REINISCH, JUNE MACHOVER, psychologist, educator; b. N.Y.C., Feb. 2, 1943; d. Mann Barnett and Lillian (Machover) R. BS cum laude, NYU, 1966; MA, Columbia U., 1970, PhD with distinction, 1976. Asst. prof. psychology Rutgers U., New Brunswich, N.J., 1975-80; assoc. prof. psychology Rutgers U., New Brunswick, N.J., 1980-82, adj. assoc. prof. psychiatry, 1981-82; prof. psychology Ind. U., Bloomington, 1982-93, dir. Kinsey Inst. Rsch. in Sex, Gender, and Reprodn., 1982-93; prof. clin. psychology Sch. Medicine, Indpls., 1983-93; dir. emeritus Kinsey Inst., 1993—; dir., prin. investigator Prenatal Devel. Projects, Copenhagen, 1976—, sr. rsch. fellow, trustee The Kinsey Inst., 1993—; pres. R2 Sci. Comms., Inc., Ind., N.Y., 1985—; vis. sr. rschr. Inst. for Preventive Medicine, Copenhagen Health Svcs., Kommunehospitalet, Copenhagen, 1994—; cons. SUNY. Author: The Kinsey Institute New Report on Sex, 1990, 94, pub. 8 fgn. edits.; editor books Kinsey Inst. series; syndicated newspaper columnist: The Kinsey Report; contbr. rsch. reports, revs., articles to profl. jours.; appeared on TV shows including PBS, Discovery, Oprah Winfrey, Sally Jessy Rafael, Good Morning Am., Today Show, CBS This Morning; guest host TV shows including CNBC Real Personal, TalkLive, also fgn. appearances. Founders day scholar NYU, 1966; NIMH trainee, 1971-74; NIMH grantee, 1978-80, Ford Found. grantee, 1973-75, Nat. Inst. Edn. grantee, 1973-74, Erikson Ednl. Found. grantee, 1973-74, grantee Nat. Inst. Child Health and Human Devel., 1981-88, Nat. Inst. on Drug Abuse, 1989-95; recipient Morton Prince award Am. Psychopath. Assn., 1976, medal for 9th Dr. S.T. Huang-Chan Meml. Lectr. in anatomy Hong Kong U., 1988, Dr. Richard J. Cross award Robert Wood Johnson Med. Sch., 1991, Award First Internat. Conf. on Orgasm, New Delhi, 1991, Disting. Alumnae award Tchrs. Coll. Columbia U., 1992. Fellow AAAS, APA, Am. Psychol. Soc., Soc. for Sci. Study Sex; mem. Internat. Acad. Sex Rsch. (charter), Internat. Women's Forum, Women's Forum. Inc., Internat. Soc. Psychoneuroendocrinology, Internat. Soc. Rsch. Aggression, Internat. Soc. Devel. Psychobiology, Am. Assn. Sex. Educators, Counselors and Therapists, Sigma Xi. Office: SUNY HSCB PBL Box 120 450 Clarkson Ave Brooklyn NY 11203-2012 also: The Kinsey Inst Prenatal Devel Project Ind U Bloomington IN 47405

REINKE, DORIS MARIE, retired elementary education educator; b. Racine, Wis., Jan. 12, 1922; d. Otto William Reinke and Louise Amelia Goehring. BS, U. Wis., Milw., 1943; MS, U. Wis., Whitewater, 1967. Tchr. kindergarten Elkhorn (Wis.) Area Sch. Sys., 1943-69, bldg. prin., 1968-70, summer sch. dir., 1974-75, grade 2 tchr., 1970-84, primary dept. chmn., 1971-84, administrv. asst., supervising tchr., 1957-83, student tchr., 1984, ret., 1984; oriented experience tchr. Program Area Sch. Sys., Elkhorn, 1966; pres. Elkhorn Edn. Assn., 1949-50; rep. dist. State Kindergarten Conf., Oshkosh, Wis., 1966; participant early edn. conf. State Early Edn. Conf., Eagle River, Wis., 1968. Columnist Mature Life Styles newspaper; monthly columnist Beacon, 1994-97; contbr. weekly newspaper column Webster Notes, 1989; Walworth County Diary Monthly column in The Week, 1991—; author Doris' Corner newsletter Walworth County Geneal. Soc., 1992—. Bd. dirs. Food Pantry, Elkhorn, 1985-88, 95—, RSVP Vol. Food Pantry, Elkhorn, 1985-95; del. dist. constn. conv. Evang. Luth. Ch. Am., Beloit, Wis., 1987; com. mem. Luth. Ch., Elkhorn, 1987; chmn. sch. centennial, Elkhorn, 1987; mem. Elkhorn Hist. Preservation Com., 1991—: archivist Sugar Creek Luth. Ch., 1992—, choir mem., 1995—; dir. Webster House Mus., 1991—. Recipient Wis. Edn. Research, West Bend, Wis., 1966, Outstanding Elem. Tchrs., Wash., 1973, Wis. Dept. Edn., Madison, 1980, Local History award State Hist. Soc. Wis., 1993. Mem. Nat. Ret. Tchrs. Assn., Walworth County Ret. Tchrs. Assn. (v.p. 1988, pres . 1991), Walworth County Hist. Soc. (treas. 1985-89, v.p. 1990-91, pres. 1991-96), Walworth County Geneal. Soc. (bd. dirs. 1991-92), Alpha Delta Kappa (state pres. 1968-70, 76-78). Avocations: reading, baseball, bird watching, traveling. Home: 516 N Wisconsin St Elkhorn WI 53121-1119

REINKE, JOHN HENRY, educational administrator, clergyman; b. Covington, Ky., Sept. 14, 1915; s. Henry Tilden and Helena (Ungeheuer) R. B.A., Loyola U., 1937, M.A., 1942, postgrad., 1947-54; postgrad., UCLA, 1948-49. Ordained priest Roman Cath. Ch., 1945; instr. psychology Loyola U., Chgo., 1947-54, vice chancellor, 1975-76, chancellor, 1976—; instr. psychology Xavier U., Cin., 1954-56, asst. prof., 1956-59; dir. guidance Loyola Acad., Wilmette, Ill., 1959-60, headmaster, 1960-65, pres., 1965-75; instr. music therapy Ind. U., Bloomington, summers 1958-60; trustee Regis Coll., Denver, 1973—, Xavier U., 1973—, Hadley Sch. for Blind, Winnetka, 1971—; chancellor emeritus Loyola U. of Chgo., Chgo., 1993—. Mem. Nat. Cath. Ednl. Assn., Nat. Sch. Public Relations Assn., Conf. Religious Dirs. Edn., Chgo. Art Inst., Field Mus., Nat. Assn. Ind. Schs., Jesuit Adminstrs. Assn., Nat. Cath. Guidance Conf. Clubs: Mid-Am, Internat, Plaza. Lodge: K.C. 1st U.S. priest to appear as soloist with maj. symphony orch., Cin., 1956, 57, 60. Office: Loyola U 6525 N Sheridan Rd Chicago IL 60626-5311*

REINKE, RALPH LOUIS, retired academic administrator; b. Elmhurst, Ill., June 22, 1927; s. Louis Fred and Malinda Marie (Beckmann) R.; m. Lois Hermine Borneman, Aug. 28, 1948 (dec. Mar. 1984); children: Janice Reinke Eisenloeffell, Stephan, Sharon Reinke Holaway; m. Carole Louise Rediehs, June 14, 1986. Student, U. Ill., 1945-46; BS, Concordia Tchrs. Coll., River Forest, Ill., 1949; MA, Northwestern U., 1952; postgrad., U. Chgo., 1956-63; LittD, Concordia Sem., 1972. Prin. St. John Elem. Sch., Houston, 1949-56; assoc. prof. psychology and edn. Concordia U., River Forest, 1956-68; pres., chief exec. officer Concordia Pub. House, St. Louis, 1968-86; pres. Concordia Coll., Seward, Nebr., 1986-90; ret., 1990. Author: Christian Spelling Series, 2d edit, 1971. Mem. sch. bd. selecting com., Oak Park, Ill., 1965-67, chmn. lit. commn. Mo. Synod Luth. Ch., 1967-69. with USNR, 1944-46. Mem. Am. Assn. Ednl. Rschrs., Am. Mgmt. Assn., Protestant Ch. Owned Pubs. Assn. (dir. 1969-84, pres. 1982-84), St. Louis Printing Assn. (bd. dirs. 1975-77), Am. Assn. Indsl. Mgmt. (bd. dirs. 1981-85), Assn. Ind. Colls. and Univs. of Nebr. (pres. 1988-89), Concordia Univ. (bd. dirs. 1992—), Luth. Edn. Assn. (pres. 1967-69), Rotary, Phi Delta Kappa. Lutheran. *Life is a most precious and finite gift of God to man. Those who would lead must make a commitment to devote their full energies and intellects to the improvement of the quality of life of their fellowmen. In the highest sense, leadership is the integrity to heed the quiet voice of conscience from within in the quest of that quality.*

REINKE, WILLIAM JOHN, lawyer; b. South Bend, Ind., Aug. 7, 1930; s. William August and Eva Marie (Hein) R.; m. Sue Carol Colvin, 1951 (div. 1988); children: Sally Sue Taelman, William A., Andrew J.; m. Elizabeth Beck Lockwood, 1991. A.B. cum laude, Wabash Coll., 1952; J.D., U. Chgo., 1955. Bar: Ind. 1955. Assoc. Barnes & Thornburg and predecessors, South Bend, Ind., 1957-61, ptnr., 1961—, former chmn. compensation com., former mem. mgmt. com.; trustee Stanley Clark Sch., 1969-80, pres. 1977-80; mem. adv. bd. Salvation Army, 1973-96, pres., 1990-92; bd. dirs. NABE Mich. chpt., 1990-94, pres. 1993-94, Isaac Walton League, 1970-81, United Way 1978-81; pres. South Bend Round Table, 1963-65; trustee First Meth. Ch., 1967-70. Served with U.S. Army, 1955-57. Recipient Outstanding Local Pres. award Ind. Jaycees, 1960-61, Boss of Yr. award, 1969, South Bend Outstanding Young Man award, 1961. Mem. ABA, Ind. State Bar Assn., St. Joseph County Bar Assn., Ind. Bar Found. (patron fellow), Am. Judicature Soc., Def. Rsch. Inst., Ind. Soc. Chgo., Summit Club (past gov., founders com.), Rotary (bd. dirs. 1970-73, 94-97). Home: 51795 Waterton Square Cir Granger IN 46530-8317 Office: Barnes & Thornburg 600 1st Source Bank Ctr 100 N Michigan St South Bend IN 46601-1610

REINKER, NANCY CLAYTON COOKE, artist; b. Owensboro, Ky., July 6, 1936; d. Billie Clayton and Barbara Jane (Mitchell) Cooke; m. Dale Bruce Reinker, Sept. 29, 1956; children: Shahn Elizabeth, Laura Beth, Karen Christian. Student, Kent State U., 1954-55, Cleve. Art Inst., 1956-57; studied sculpture with, Stanley Bleifeld, 1979-80; student, Silvermine Sch. of Art, 1988-89. Owner Nettle Creek Shops of Westport and Cos Cob, Conn., 1974-86, Cross River Design Studio, 1986-89. One woman shows at Hayes Gallery, 1992 Silvermine Guild Arts Ctr., 1992, Art Place, 1993, 95, Westport Art Ctr., 1994, also in numerous nat. and internat. exhbns. Chmn. Commn. for The Arts, Weston, Conn., 1993-94; pres. Inst. for Visual Artists, New Canaan, Conn., 1992-93; v.p., pres. Art Place Gallery, Southprot, Conn., 1991-92. Named to 1992 Cir. of Excellence, Soc. Nat. Art Patrons, 1992; recipient 1st prize Spectrum, 1992, 93, 94. Mem. ASID, Silvermine Guild of Artists (trustee 1994—), New Haven Paint and Clay (Merit award 1993), Nat. Assn. Women Artists, Conn. Women Artists (Painting award 1991), Greenwich Art Soc. (Randolph Chitwood award 1994), Women's Caucus for Art, Chi Omega. Home and Studio: 87 Valley Forge Rd Weston CT 06883-1913

REINKING, ANN H., actress, dancer; b. Seattle, Nov. 10, 1950; d. Walter Floyd and Francis Holmes (Harrison) R.; m. Larry Small, 1970; m. Herbert A. Allen; Aug. 25, 1982; (stepchildren): Leslie, Christie, Herbert, Charlie. Student public schs. Guest tchr. NYU, Duke U., Durham, N.C., Rutgers, N.J., Harvard, Cambridge, Mass.; choreographer Pal Joey, Goodman Theater, Chgo., 1988. Broadway appearances include Coco, 1970, Wild and Wonderful, 1972, Pippin, 1973, Over Here, 1974, Goodtime Charlie, 1975, Chicago, 1977, A Chorus Line, 1976, Dancin', 1978, Sweet Charity, 1986-87; TV appearances include Ellery Queen, Doug Henning: Magic on Broadway, 1982, Parade of Stars, 1983, American Treasury, 1985, Salute to Jules Styne, Broadway Salutes Washington, An Introduction to the Dance Gala of the Stars; film appearances include Movie, Movie, 1978, All That Jazz, 1979-80, Annie, 1982, Micki and Maude, 1984; play Ann Reinking ... Music Moves Me, 1984; choreography: Chicago, 1996 (Tony award 1997). Recipient Clarence Derwent award, 1974, Outer Critics Circle award, 1974, Theatre World award, 1974, Dance Educators Am. award, 1979, Harkness Dance award, 1979, two Tony award nominations, Tony award for Choregraphy, 1997; Ford Found. scholar, 1964-66; Robert Joffery scholar, 1967; Harkness scholar; Nat. Dance Educators award. Mem. Actors Equity, AFTRA, Stage Actors Guild. Avocations: horseback riding, skiing, swimming, hiking. also: Steps Contemporary & Classical Dance 2121 Broadway Fl 3 New York NY 10023-1786*

REINMUTH, OSCAR MACNAUGHTON, physician, educator; b. Lincoln, Nebr., Oct. 23, 1927; s. Oscar William and Catharine Anne (MacNaughton) R.; m. Patricia Dixon, June 19, 1951 (div. Jan. 1977); children—David Dixon, Diane MacNaughton, Douglas Stewart; m. Audrey Longridge Holland, June 26, 1980. B.S., U. Tex., Austin, 1948; M.D. (F.B. Hanes research fellow 1950-51), Duke U., 1952. Intern Duke Hosp., 1952-53; asst. resident in medicine Yale U. Med. Ctr., 1953-54, NIH research trainee, 1954-55; asst. resident in neurology Boston City Hosp., 1955-56, chief resident, teaching fellow in neurology Harvard U. Neurol. unit, 1956-57; NIH spl. trainee, clin. asst. Nat. Hosp., London, 1957-58; from asst. prof. to prof. neurology U. Miami (Fla.) Med. Sch., 1958-77; prof. neurology and behavioral neuroscience, chmn. dept. U. Pitts. Med. Sch., 1977-93, prof. emeritus, 1994—; prof. neurology U. Ariz. Med. Sch., Tucson, 1993—; mem. research tng. com. A and C NIH, 1966-73. Served with AUS, 1946-47. Recipient Mosby award, 1952. Fellow ACP, Am. Acad. Neurology (1st v.p. 1973-76), Am. Neurol. Assn. (1st v.p. 1977-78, 2d v.p. 1976-77), Am. Heart Assn. (fellow stroke coun., vice chmn. 1978-79, chmn. 1980-82, editor publs. 1975-78, editor-in-chief Stroke jour. 1987-91, Award of Merit 1992). Home: 5545 N Entrada Quince Tucson AZ 85718-4709 Office: U Med Ctr Dept Neurology 1501 N Campbell Ave Tucson AZ 85724-0001

REINOEHL, RICHARD LOUIS, artist, scholar, martial artist; b. Omaha, Oct. 11, 1944; s. Louis Lawrence and Frances Margaret (Robinson) R.; m. Linda Dale Iroff, Feb. 28, 1982; 1 child, Joy Margaret Iroff-Reinoehl. BS in Sociology, Portland State U., 1970; MSW, U. Minn., Duluth, 1977; postgrad., Cornell U., 1984-88. Acting dir. Vanguard Group Homes, Virginia, Minn., 1976-77; dir. Minn. Chippewa Tribe Group Home, Duluth, 1978, Human Devel. Consortium, Minn., N.Y., Ohio, 1978—; faculty Social Work Program U. Wis., Superior, 1981-84; adv. bd. Computers in Social Svcs. Network, 1982-85; mem. Com. on Internat. Social Welfare Edn., 1982-86, Am. Evaluation Assn., 1986-89; affiliate scholar Oberlin Coll., 1991—. Editor: Computer Literacy in Human Services Education, 1990, Computer Literacy in Human Services, 1990, Men of Achievement, 16th edit., 1993; mem. editorial bd. Computers in Human Svcs., 1983-96, assoc. editor book rev., 1996; contbr. numerous articles to profl. jours. Mem. Legis. Task Force Regional Alcoholism Bd., 1972-73, Assn. Drug Abuse, Prevention and Treatment, 1973-74, Minn. Pub. Health Assn., 1976-78, Minn. Social Svc. Assn., 1976-83, Wis. Coun. Social Work Edn., 1983-84, N.Y. State Coun. Family Rels., 1986-89, Nat. Coun. Family Rels., 1986-89; exec. bd. Duluth Community Action Program, 1982-83; Dem. precinct chair, Portland, Oreg., 1972-74; precinct vice-chair Dem. Farmer-Labor Party, Duluth, 1979-81, chair, 1981-83, 2d vice-chair exec. bd., 1981-83; mem. Zoning Appeals Bd., New Russia Twp., Ohio, 1996—; mem. art edn. com. Fireland Assn. Visual Arts, 1996—. Mem. NASW (exec. com., chair program com. Arrowhead Region Minn. chpt., 1980-81, co-chair task force on computers in social work, 1981-82), Acad. Cert. Social Workers, Cornell U. Sailing Club (pres. 1990). Avocations: canoeing, sailing, wilderness hiking. Office: Human Devel Consortium Inc 46180 Butternut Ridge Rd Oberlin OH 44074-9778 *It's noteworthy that the most sought-after items in a society cannot be bought or sold. Included are wisdom, respect, generosity, truthfulness, and the love of family and friends.*

REINS, RALPH ERICH, automotive components supply company executive; b. Detroit, Sept. 18, 1940; s. Erich John and Florence (Franz) R.; m. Victoria Louise Kolts, Sept. 14, 1963; children—Ann Marie, Christine Louise. B.S.I.E., U. Mich., 1963. Asst. supt. Chevrolet Motor div., Gen. Motors Corp., Detroit, 1963-72; v.p., pres. hwy. product ops. Rockwell Internat., Troy, Mich., 1972-85; sr. v.p. ITT Corp., Bloomfield Hills, Mich., 1985-89; chmn. of the bd., pres., chief exec. officer Mack Trucks, Inc., Allentown, Pa., 1989-90; pres. United Tech. Automotive, Dearborn, Mich., 1990-91; exec. v.p., pres. automotive sector Allied Signal Corp., 1991-94; pres., CEO Envirotest Sys. Corp., Phoenix, 1995-96, A.P. Parts Internat., Toledo, 1996—; bd. dirs. Rofin-Sinar Corp. Mem. nat. adv. com. U. Mich. Mem. Soc. Automotive Engrs., Bloomfield Hills Country Club. Republican. Avocations: golf; hunting; fishing. Home: 29612 Durham Dr Perrysburg OH 43551-3409 Office: A P Parts Internat PO Box 64010 315 Matzinger Rd Toledo OH 43612-0010

REINSCH, WILLIAM ALAN, government executive, educator; b. Evanston, Ill., Jan. 15, 1946; s. Bert and Kathleen (Penn) R.; m. Susan Polley Reinsch, Jan. 3, 1970; children: Andrew, Christian. BA, Johns Hopkins U., 1968; MA in Internat. Rels., Johns Hopkins U.-Sch. Advanced Internat. Studies, 1969. Legis. asst. Congressman Gilbert Gude, Washington, 1973-76, Congressman Richard Ottinger, Washington, 1976; chief legis. asst. Senator John Heinz, Washington, 1977-91; legis. asst. Senator John D. Rockefeller IV, Washington, 1991-93; cons., under sec. for export administrn. Dept. Commerce, Washington, 1994—; tchr. Landon Sch., Bethesda, Md., 1968-73; adj. assoc. prof. U. Md. U. Coll. Grad. Sch. Mgmt. and Tech., College Park, Md., 1990—; acting staff dir. Environmental Study Conf. U.S. Ho. Reps., 1976. Contbr. articles to profl. jours. Pres. St. Mark Elderly Housing Corp., Rockville, Md. Mem. Phi Beta Kappa, Omicron Delta Kappa, Alpha Delta Phi. Democrat. Presbyterian. Office: Dept Commerce Office of the Secretary 14th & Constitution NW Washington DC 20230

REINSCHMIDT, KENNETH FRANK, engineering and construction executive; b. Cin., Mar. 26, 1938; s. Christian Edward and Martha Marie (Kellerman) R.; m. Marlene Faye Taub, Dec. 16, 1967. BSCE, MIT, 1960, MSCE, 1962, PhD in Engring., 1965. Assoc. prof. civil engring. MIT, Cambridge, 1965-75; sr. v.p. Stone & Webster Engring. Corp., Boston, 1975-93, also bd. dirs.; pres. Stone & Webster Advanced Systems Devel. Svcs., Boston, 1988-96; bd. dirs. Stone & Webster Advanced Tech. Applications Inc., N.Y.C., 1990-94; sr. v.p. Stone & Webster, Inc., 1993-96; ind. cons., 1996—; chmn. com. on oversight of Ctr. for Bldg. Tech., Nat. Inst. Standards and Tech., Gaithersburg, Md., 1986-89. Author: Stress: A User's Manual, 1963; editor: Systems Building, 1974; contbr. numerous articles to profl. jours. Capt. U.S. Army, 1966-67. Decorated Legion of Merit; NSF fellow, 1962. Fellow AAAS; mem. NAE, ASCE, INFORMS. Office: Stone & Webster Inc 20 Tahattawan Rd Littleton MA 01460-1605

REINSDORF, JERRY MICHAEL, professional sports teams executive, real estate executive, lawyer, accountant; b. Bklyn., Feb. 25, 1936; s. Max and Marion (Smith) R.; m. Martyl F. Rifkin, Dec. 29, 1956; children: David Jason, Susan Janeen, Michael Andrew, Jonathan Milton. BA, George Washington U., 1957; JD, Northwestern U., 1960. Bar: D.C., Ill. 1960; CPA, Ill.; cert. specialist real estate securities, rev. appraiser; registered mortgage underwriter. Atty. staff regional counsel IRS, Chgo., 1960-64; assoc. law firm Chapman & Cutler, 1964-68; ptnr. Altman, Kurlander & Weiss, 1968-74; of counsel firm Katten, Muchin, Gitles, Zavis, Pearl & Galler, 1974-79; gen. ptnr. Carlyle Real Estate Ltd. Partnerships, 1971, 72; chmn. bd. Balcor Co., 1973-87; mng. ptnr. TBC Films, 1975-83; chmn. Chgo. White Sox, 1981—, Chgo. Bulls Basketball Team, 1985—; ptnr. Bojer Fin., 1987—; lectr. John Marshall Law Sch., 1966-68; former bd. dirs. Shearson Lehman Bros., Inc., Project Academus of DePaul U., Chgo., Sports Immortals Mus., 1987-89, Com. Commemorate U.S. Constn., 1987; bd. dirs. La Salle Nat. Bank, La Salle Nat. Corp.; bd. overseers Inst. for Civil Justice, 1996—; lectr. in real estate, sports and taxation. Author: (with L. Herbert Schneider) Uses of Life Insurance in Qualified Employee Benefit Plans, 1970. Co-chmn. Ill. Profls. for Senator Ralph Smith, 1970; mem. Chgo. region bd. Anti-Defamation League, 1986—; mem., trustee Ill. Inst. Tech., 1991-96; mem. Ill. Commn. on African-Am. Males, 1992—; bd. dirs. Chgo. Youth Success Found., 1992—, Corp. for Supportive Housing, 1995—; nat. trustee Northwestern U., 1993—; bd. govs. Hugh O'Brian Youth Found.; mem. internat. adv. bd. Barrow Neurol. Found., 1996-97; trustee Ill. Inst. Technology, 1991-96. Recipient Hallmark award Chgo. Baseball Cancer Charities, 1986, Corp. Superstar award Ill. chpt. Cystic Fibrosis Found., 1988, Sportsman of Yr. award, 1994, Chicagoan of Yr. award Chgo. Park Dist., 1990, Kellogg Excellence award, 1991, Cmty. Hero award Interfaith Organizing Project, 1991, Operation Push Bridgebuilder award, 1992, Alumni Merit award Northwestern U., 1992, Ellis Island Medal of Honor award Nat. Ethnic Coalition of Orgns., 1993, Lifetime Achievement award March of Dimes, 1994, Hallmark Hall of Fame Civic award Ind. Sports Charities, 1994, Am. Spirit award USAF, 1995, Alpha Epsilon Pi Arthur and Simiteich Outstanding Alumnus award, 1995, Order of Lincoln, 1997; inductee B'nai B'rith Nat. Jewish Am. Sports Hall of Fame, 1994. Mem. ABA, FBA, Ill. Bar Assn., Chgo. Bar Assn., Nat. Sports Lawyers Assn., Nat. Assn. Rev. Appraisers and Mortgage Underwriters, Northwestern U. Law Sch. Alumni Assn. (bd. dirs.), Comml. Club Chgo., Order of Coif, Omega Tau Rho. Office: Chgo White Sox 333 W 35th St Chicago IL 60616-3621

REINSTEIN, JOEL, lawyer; b. N.Y.C., July 23, 1946; s. Louis and Ruth Shukovsky; children: Lesli, Louis, Mindy. B.S.E., U. Pa., 1968; J.D. cum laude, U. Fla., 1971; LL.M. in Taxation, NYU, 1974. Bar: Fla. 1971, U.S. Tax Ct. 1973, U.S. Dist. Ct. (so. dist.) Fla. 1976. Atty., office of chief counsel IRS, 1971-74; ptnr. Capp, Reinstein, Kopelowitz and Atlas, P.A., Ft. Lauderdale, Fla., 1975-85; dir., ptnr. Greenberg, Traurig, Hoffman, Lipoff, Rosen & Quentel, P.A., Ft. Lauderdale, 1985-92; gen. counsel Internat. Magnetic Imaging, Inc., Boca Raton, Fla., 1992-94; prin. Law Offices of Joel Reinstein, Boca Raton, 1993—; lectr. Advanced Pension Planning, Am. Soc. C.L.U.s; lectr. in field. Mem. Fla. Bar Assn. (tax sect.), ABA (tax sect, adj. mem. com. employee benefits), Order of Coif, Phi Kappa Phi, Phi Delta Phi. Mem. editorial bd. U. Fla. Law Rev., 1970-71; contbr. articles to profl. jours. Office: The Plaza 5355 Town Center Rd Ste 801 Boca Raton FL 33486-1069

REINTHALER, RICHARD WALTER, lawyer; b. N.Y.C., Feb. 27, 1949; s. Walter F. and Maureen C. (Tully) R.; m. Mary E. Maloney, Aug. 8, 1970; children: Brian, Scott, Amy. BA in Govt. magna cum laude, U. Notre Dame, 1970, JD summa cum laude, 1973. Bar: N.Y. 1974, U.S. Dist. Ct. (so. and ea. dists.) N.Y. 1974, U.S. Ct. Appeals (2d cir.) 1974, U.S. Ct. Appeals (9th cir.) 1976, U.S. Ct. Appeals (5th cir.) 1978, U.S. Ct. Appeals (11th cir.) 1981, U.S. Supreme Ct. 1977. Assoc. White & Case, N.Y.C., 1973-81, ptnr., 1981-95; ptnr. Dewey Ballantine, N.Y.C., 1995—; mem. adv. group U.S. Dist. Ct. (ea. dist.) N.Y., 1992—, chairperson subgroup on ethics, 1993—. Contbr. articles to profl. jours. Served to 1st lt. U.S. Army, 1974. Fellow Am. Bar Found.; mem. ABA (2d cir. chmn. discovery com. 1982-87, program coord. 1986, ann. meeting litigation sect., vice chmn. com. on fed. procedure 1988-89, co-chmn. com. on profl. responsibility 1989-92, vice chmn. securities litigation com. 1993-94, vice chair Hong Kong meeting 1995, co-chair energy litigation com. 1996—), N.Y. State Bar Assn., Assn. of Bar of City of N.Y. (mem. com. to enhance diversity in the profession 1990—, mem. Orison S. Marden Meml. Lectrs. com. 1994—, chair 1997—, spl. com. on mergers, acquisitions and corp. control contests 1995—), Scarsdale Golf Club (Hartsdale, N.Y., bd. govs. 1994—), Capital Hill Club (Washington). Republican. Roman Catholic. Avocations: golf, tennis. Office: Dewey & Ballantine 1301 Avenue Of The Americas New York NY 10019-6022

REIS, ARTHUR ROBERT, JR., men's furnishings manufacturer; b. N.Y.C., Dec. 8, 1916; s. Arthur M. and Claire (Raphael) R.; m. Muriel Henle, Sept. 25, 1953; children: Arthur, Diane, Pamela. B.A., Princeton U., 1939. Joined Pan. Am. Airways, 1940, asst. to v.p., 1943; joined Robert Reis & Co., N.Y.C., 1946, pres., 1947-79; ptnr. Energy Applications Assocs., 1980-82; mem. departmental disciplinary com. Appellate Ct. N.Y., 1994; supr. cons. Nat. Exec. Svcs. Corps. Mem. N.Y. State Com. on Refugee Relief Act of 1953; trustee, mem. exec. com. Storm King Sch., Cornwall-on-Hudson, N.Y. Served from pvt. to capt. Air Transport Command USAAF, 1943-46; asst. chief of staff Central Pacific Wing. Decorated B.S.M. Mem. Young Pres.' Orgn. (co-founder), N.Y.C. of C. (exec. com.), Princeton Club of N.Y. (bd. govs.). Home: 1136 5th Ave New York NY 10128-0122

REIS, DON, publishing executive; b. N.Y.C., Nov. 19, 1927; m. Barbara Weinberg, 1947; children: Robert, Richard. AB, Princeton U., 1947; MA, NYU, 1955. Rsch. editor Bantam Books, 1952-55, edn. editor, 1955-66; editor-in-chief Washington Square Press Divsn. Simon & Schuster, 1966-68; v.p., editorial dir. Ednl. Directions Inc., Westport, Conn., 1968-85; mng. editor Barron's Ednl. Series, 1985-87; gen. and ednl. editor Barron's, 1987-93, sr. cons. editor, 1993—; editorial dir. Reis Assocs., Forest Hills, N.Y., 1993—. Author (with A. Butman and D. Sohn) Paperback Books in the Schools, 1962; editor The Collected Essays of Aldous Huxley, 1958. Home: 57 Summer St Forest Hills NY 11375-6035 Office: Barron's Edn Series Inc 250 Wireless Blvd Hauppauge NY 11788-3924

REIS, DONALD JEFFERY, neurologist, neurobiologist, educator; b. N.Y.C., Sept. 9, 1931; s. Samuel H. and Alice (Kiesler) R.; m. Cornelia Langer Noland, Apr. 13, 1985. A.B., Cornell U., 1953, M.D., 1956. Intern N.Y. Hosp., N.Y.C., 1956; resident in neurology Boston City Hosp.-Harvard Med. Sch., 1957-59; Fulbright fellow, United Cerebral Palsy Found. fellow London and Stockholm, 1959-60; rsch. assoc. NIMH, Bethesda, Md., 1960-62; spl. fellow NIH, Nobel Neurophysiology Inst., Stockholm, 1962-63; asst. prof. neurology Cornell U. Med. Sch., N.Y.C., 1963-67; assoc. prof. neurology and psychiatry Cornell U. Med. Sch., 1967-71, prof., 1971—, First George C. Cotzias Disting. prof. neurology, 1982—; mem. U.S.-Soviet Exch. Program; mem. adv. coun. NIH; bd. sci. advisers Merck, Sharpe & Dohm, Sterling Rsch. Group; cons. Eli Lilly, Servier Pharms.; bd. dirs. China Seas, Inc., Charles masterson Burke Rsch. Found. Contbr. articles to profl. jours.; mem. editorial bd. various profl. jours. Recipient CIBA Prize award Am. Heart Assn. Fellow AAAS, ACP; mem. Am. Physiol. Soc., Am. Neurol. Assn., Am. Pharmacol. Soc., Am. Assn. Physicians, Telluride Assn., Am. Soc. Clin. Investigation, Century Assn., Ellis Island Yacht Club (commadore), Phi Beta Kappa, Sigma Xi, Alpha Omega Alpha. Home: 190 E 72nd St New York NY 10021-4370 also: 73 Water St Stonington CT 06378-1433 Office: 1300 York Ave New York NY 10021-4805

REIS, EDWARD THOMAS, JR., insurance executive, educator; b. Fresno, Calif., Aug. 27, 1948; s. Edward Thomas and Eleanor Virginia (Read) R.; m. Deborah Gerace; 1 child, Edward Thomas III. Cert., Ins. Inst. of Am., 1983; chartered, Am. Inst. for Property and Casualty Underwriters, 1986; CLU/Chartered Fin. Cons., Am. Coll., 1988. Agt. Farmers Ins., Simi Valley, Calif., 1975-82; dist. mgr. Farmers Ins., Santa Barbara, Calif., 1982-97; founder Money Seminars, 1995—; with Reis Fin. Svcs., 1996—. Active Farmers Pres. Coun. Mem. Nat. Assn. Life Underwriters (pres. local chpt.), Profl. Ins. Agts. Assn., Nat. Spkrs. Assn., Am. Seminar Leaders Assn., Internat. Assn. for Fin. Planning, Santa Barbara C. of C., Elks. Republican. Methodist. Avocations: golf, scuba diving. Office: Edward Reis Inc 519 W Pueblo St Santa Barbara CA 93105-4229

REIS, JEAN STEVENSON, administrative secretary; b. Wilburton, Okla., Nov. 30, 1914; d. Robert Emory and Ada (Ross) Stevenson; m. George William Reis, June 24, 1939 (dec. 1980). BA, U. Tex., El Paso, 1934; MA, So. Meth. U., 1935; postgrad., U. Chgo., summers 1937-38, U. Wash., 1948-49. Tchr. El Paso High Sch., 1935-39; safety engr., trainer Safety and Security Div., Office of Chief Ordnance, Chgo., 1942-45; tchr. Lovenberg Jr. High Sch., Galveston, Tex., 1946; parish sec. Trinity Parish Episcopal Ch., Seattle, 1950-65; adminstrv. sec., asst. Office Resident Bishop, United Meth. Ch., Seattle, 1965-94; observer Africa U. installation, Mutare, Zimbabwe, 1994; mem. com. on legislation for the 1996 gen. conf. Hist. Soc. of United Meth. Ch. Recip. Bishop's award, 1980. Mem. AAUW, Beta Beta Beta. Home: 9310 42nd Ave NE Seattle WA 98115-3814

REIS, JUDSON PATTERSON, investment manager; b. Bryn Mawr, Pa., July 31, 1942; s. Maurice J. and Wiley W. (Patterson) R.; m. Judith Morse (div.); children: Judson P. Jr., C. Parker; m. Kathryn Ann Fortuin, June 16, 1972; children: Mark B., Nicholas D., A. Curtis. BA cum laude, Washington and Lee U., 1964; MBA with distinction, Harvard U., 1966. Assoc. Morgan Stanley & Co., Inc., N.Y.C., 1966-72, v.p., 1973, prin., 1974, mng. dir., 1975-88; exec. v.p., mng. dir. Kleinwort Benson N.A., N.Y.C., 1988-91; pres. Sire Mgmt. Corp., N.Y.C., 1991—; mng. gen. ptnr. Sire Ptnrs., L.P., 1991—; bd. dirs. Kleinwort Benson Ltd., London; Morris vis. prof. bus. adminstrn. Colgate Darden Grad. Sch. Bus. U. Va., 1987-88, 1989—. Treas. Caputo for Congress com., N.Y.C., 1977; treas. Caputo for Lt. Gov. com., 1978; bd. dirs. Pilobolus Dance Co.; pres. bd. trustees Showhegan Sch. Painting and Sculpture. Republican. Clubs: University (N.Y.C.), Farmington Country, Charlottesville, Va., Bond, Links (N.Y.C.); Bridgehampton (N.Y.). Office: Sire Ptnrs LP 630 5th Ave New York NY 10111-0100

REIS, MURIEL HENLE, lawyer, broadcast executive/television commentator; b. N.Y.C.; d. Frederick S. and Mary (Meyers) Henle; m. Arthur Reis Jr., Sept. 25, 1953; children: Arthur Henle, Diane Mary, Pamela Robin. BA, Vassar Coll., 1946; LLB, Columbia U., 1949. Bar: N.Y. 1950, U.S. Ct. Appeals (2d cir.) 1964, U.S. Dist. Ct. (so. dist.) N.Y. 1992, U.S. Dist. Ct. (ea. dist.) N.Y. 1992. Assoc. MS-I Isaacs, N.Y.C., 1950-52; asst. gen. counsel ABC, N.Y.C., 1952-54; from asst. gen. counsel to assoc. gen. counsel Metromedia Inc., N.Y.C., 1956-86; v.p. WNEW, N.Y.C., 1974-86; v.p., legal affairs Fox TV Sta. Inc., N.Y.C., 1986—, on-air legal commentator, 1995—. Mem. Assn. of Bar of City of N.Y., Internat. Soc. Radio and TV Execs. Home: 1136 Fifth Ave New York NY 10128-0122 Office: Fox TV Sta Inc 205 E 67th St New York NY 10021-6002

REIS, VICTOR H., mechanical engineer, government official. PhD in Mech. Engring., Princeton U. Formerly sr. v.p. for strategic planning Sci. Applications Internat. Corp.; security adviser Office Sci. and Tech. Policy, Washington; spl. asst. to dir. Lincoln Labs MIT; dep. dir. Def. Advanced Rsch. Projects Agy., Arlington, Va., 1989-90, dir., 1990-93; asst. sec. Dept. Energy Def. Programs, Washington, 1993—. Office: Dept Energy Def Programs 1000 Independence Ave SW Washington DC 20585-0001

REISBERG, BARRY, geropsychiatrist, neuropsychopharmacologist; b. Bklyn., Dec. 3, 1947; s. Harry and Claire (Cohen) R.; m. Rosalie DePaola, Feb. 23, 1974 (dec. Oct. 1975); m. Nancy A. Minich, May 7, 1988. BA, CUNY, Bklyn., 1968; MD, N.Y. Med. Coll., 1972. Diplomate Am. Bd. Psychiatry and Neurology, Am. Bd. Geriatric Psychiatry. Intern N.Y. Med. Coll./Met. Hosp., N.Y.C., 1972-75, resident in psychiatry, 1972-75; fellow dept. psychiatry Middlesex Hosp. Med. Sch. U. London, 1975; staff psychiatrist Franklin D. Roosevelt VA Hosp., Montrose, N.Y., 1975-78; staff psychiatrist Neuropsychopharmacology Rsch. Unit NYU Med. Ctr., N.Y.C., 1978-80, clin. dir. Aging and Dementia Rsch. Ctr., 1978—; adj. prof. Ctr. for Studies in Aging McGill U., Montreal, Que., Can., 1993—; clin. instr. dept. psychiatry N.Y. Med. Coll., Valhalla, 1975-78; asst. prof. NYU Sch. Medicine, N.Y.C., 1978-84, assoc. prof., 1984-90, prof., 1990—; rsch. collaborator, vis. clinician Brookhaven Nat. Labs., Upton, N.Y., 1979-80; dir. clin. core NIMH Clin. Rsch. Ctr., 1989-93, Nat. Inst. Aging Alzheimer's Disease Ctr., 1990—; dir. Zachary and Elizabeth M. Fisher Alzheimer's Disease Edn. and Resources Program NYU Med. Ctr., 1995—; med. and sci. adv. bd. Alzheimer's Assn., Chgo., 1993—; cons. psychiatrist N.Y. VA Hosp., 1980-89; chmn. work group WHO, Copenhagen, 1984; mem. aging sect. NIH, 1986-90; vis. prof. Palmerston North Postgrad. Med. Soc., New Zealand, 1991. Author: Brain Failure, 1981; editor: Alzheimer's Disease, 1983; (with others) Diagnosis and Treatment of Senile Dementia, 1989; mem. editl. bd. Jour. Am. Aging Assn., 1985—, Alzheimer's Disease and Associated Disorders, 1985—, Jour. Geriat. Psychiatry and Neurology, 1986—, Am. Jour. Alzheimer's Care, 1986—, Internat. Psychogeriat., 1989-96, Am. Jour. Geriat. Psychiatry, 1992—, Integrative Psychiatry, 1994—; contbr. over 175 articles to med. and sci. jours. Fellow NSF, 1963, Coun. on Internat. Ednl. Exch.-Japan Soc., Tokyo, 1968; grantee NIH, 1979-81, 82-85, 87, 90, 92—, NIMH, 1983-85. Mem. Internat. Psychogeriat. Assn. (bd. dirs. 1985-93, treas. 1993-95, pres.-elect 1995—), Am. Aging Assn. (bd. dirs. 1990-92), Alzheimer's and Related Disorders Soc. India (hon.), Am. Assn. Geriat. Psychiatry (sec. 1991-92, bd. dirs. 1992-96), Am. Coll. Neuropsychopharmacology. Office: NYU Med Ctr Aging and Dementia Rsch Ctr 550 1st Ave New York NY 10016-6481 *Our studies have demonstrated that Alzheimer's disease (AD) recapitulates normal human development inversely in terms of cognition, functioning and in other ways. These findings have profound implications, e.g. a better understanding of AD can improve understanding of normal human development and behavior and vice versa.*

REISBERG, LEON ELTON, education educator; b. Dallas, Sept. 1, 1949; s. Morris Abraham and Gertrude (Turner) R.; m. Iris Fudell, July 3, 1973 (div. 1986); children: Joshua Fudell, Leah Fudell; m. Donna Brodigan, July 11, 1993. BS in Edn., U. Tex., Austin, 1971; MEd, U. Ark., Fayetteville, 1972; EdD, U. Kans., Lawrence, 1981. Tchr. Oklahoma City Sch. Dist., 1972-75, Putnam City Sch. Dist., Oklahoma City, 1975-78, U. Kans. Med. Ctr., Kansas City, 1978-79; asst. prof. Pacific Luth. U., Tacoma, 1981-88; tchr. Tacoma (Wash.) Sch. Dist., 1989-90; assoc. prof. edn. Pacific Luth. U., 1988-94; chmn. dept. spl. edn. Pacific Luth. U., Tacoma, 1986-93, chmn. profl. edn. adv. bd., 1992-94, assoc. dean sch. edn., 1993—, prof., 1995—; project dir., Consulting Spl. Edn. Personnel Tng. Project, Tacoma, 1983-86; chmn. Profl. Edn. Adv. Bd. Cons. editor Learning Disability Quar., 1981-89, Acad. Therapy, 1988-90, Intervention, 1990—; contbr. articles to profl. publs. Mem. Coun. Exceptional Children, Coun. Learning Disabilities (Pacific Rim region rep. 1993-96), Assn. Trainer Spl. Edn. Pers. (chmn. 1991), Phi Kappa Phi. Democrat. Jewish. Office: Pacific Luth U Sch Edn Tacoma WA 98447 *Personal philosophy: Research and professional interests in promoting the inclusion of students with disabilities in regular classrooms.*

REISCH, MICHAEL STEWART, social work educator; b. N.Y.C., Mar. 4, 1948; s. Joseph and Charlotte (Rosenberg) R.; m. Amy Jane Lewis, May 21, 1972; children: Jennifer, Nikki. BA in History with highest honors, NYU, 1968; PhD in History with distinction, SUNY, Binghamton, 1975; MSW with honors, CUNY, 1979. Youth worker Washington-Heights-Inwood YM-YWHA, N.Y.C., 1965-66; editor, columnist Heights Daily News, Bronx, N.Y., 1966-68; rsch./teaching asst. SUNY, Binghamton, 1970-72; unit dir., program cons. Child Study Assn.-Wel Met, Inc., N.Y.C., 1970-72; asst. dir. youth div. Mosholu-Montefiore Community Ctr., Bronx, 1972-73; project dir. Silberman Found./N.Y. Assn. Deans, N.Y.C., 1973-74; asst. dean Sch. Social Welfare, asst. prof. SUNY, Stony Brook, 1974-79; asst. prof., then assoc. prof. Sch. Social Work U. Md., Balt., 1979-86; dir. Sch. Social Work, prof. social work/pub. adminstrn. San Francisco State U., 1986-95; prof. social work U. Pa., Phila., 1995—; cons. and spkr. in field. Co-author: From Charity to Enterprise, 1989 (Social Sci. Book of Month), Social Work in the 21st Century, 1997; editor, author various books in field; contbr. articles to profl. publs., chpts. to books. Cons. to numerous local, state, and fed. polit. campaigns, 1971—; mem. Gov.'s Adv. Coun. Human Resources, Md., 1983-86; pres. Welfare Advs., Md., 1983-86; campaign mgr. Rep. Barbara Mikulski, Balt., 1982; bd. dirs. Coleman Advs. for Children and Youth, 1987-95, San Francisco Internat. Program, 1987-95, Calif. Social Work Edn. Ctr., 1991-95, Ctr. for S.E. Asian Refugee Resettlement, 1992-95, Am. Jewish Congress, N. Calif., 1994-95, Coun. Internat. Programs, 1995; chair Children's Budget Task Force City of San Francisco, 1989-92; mem. Mayor's Adv. Coun. on Drug Abuse, San Francisco, 1988-91; mem. steering com. Poverty Action Alliance, 1993-95. Woodrow Wilson Found. fellow, 1972-73. Mem. NASW (del. 1990-92, 94-96, chair peace and justice com. 1992—), Coun. on Social Work Edn. (com. on status of women 1989-92, bd. dirs. 1993—, chair commn. on ednl. policy 1994—), Am. Hist. Assn., Bertha Capen Reynolds Soc., Soc. for Social Work Rsch., Assn. for Advancement of Social Work with Groups, Assn. Cmty. Orgns. and Social Adminstrn. Avocations: travel, hiking, cooking, swimming, creative writing.

REISER, MORTON FRANCIS, psychiatrist, educator; b. Cin., Aug. 22, 1919; s. Sigmund and Mary (Roth) R.; m. Lynn B. Whisnant, Dec. 19, 1976; children: David E., Barbara, Linda. B.S., U. Cin., 1940, M.D., 1943; grad., N.Y. Psychoanalytic Inst., 1960. Diplomate Am. Bd. Psychiatry and Neurology. Intern King's County Hosp., Bklyn., 1944; resident Cin. Gen. Hosp., 1944-49; practice medicine, specializing in psychiatry Cin., 1947-52, Washington, 1954-55, N.Y.C., 1955-69; mem. faculty Cin. Gen. Hosp., also U. Cin. Coll. Medicine, 1949-52, Washington Sch. Psychiatry, 1953-55; faculty Albert Einstein Coll. Medicine, Yeshiva U., N.Y.C., 1955-69; prof. psychiatry Albert Einstein Coll. Medicine, Yeshiva U., 1958-69, dir. research dept. psychiatry, 1958-65; chief div. psychiatry Montefiore Hosp. and Med. Center, N.Y.C., 1965-69; chmn. dept. psychiatry Yale Med. Sch., 1969—, prof., 1969-78, chmn. dept., 1969-86, Charles B.G. Murphy prof., 1978-86, Albert E. Kent prof., 1986-90, Albert E. Kent prof. emeritus, 1990—; cons. Walter Reed Army Inst. Research, 1957-58, High Point Hosp., Port Chester, N.Y., 1957-69; com. WHO, 1963; mem. profl. adv. com. Jerusalem Mental Health Center, 1972—; mem. clin. program projects rev. com. NIMH, 1970—, chmn., 1973-74. Author: (with H. Leigh) The Patient: Biological, Psychological, and Social Dimensions of Medical Practice, 1980, Mind, Brain, Body: Toward a Convergence of Psychoanalysis and Neurobiology, 1984; (with H. Leigh) The Patient, 3d edit., 1992; Memory in Mind and Brain: What Dream Imagery Reveals, 1990; editor: American Handbook of Psychiatry, vol. IV, 1975; editor in chief Psychosomatic Medicine, 1962-72; mem. editorial bd. AMA Archives of Gen. Psychiatry, 1961-71, (with H. Leigh) Psychiatry Medicine and Primary Care, 1978; contbr. articles to profl. jours. and books. Fellow Am. Coll. Psychiatrists, Am. Psychiat. Assn. (Seymour Vestermark award 1986); mem. Am. Soc. Clin. Investigation, Am. Psychosomatic Soc. (pres. 1960-61), Am. Fedn. Clin. Research, Am. Assn. Chairmen Depts. Psychiatry (exec. com. 1971—, pres. 1975-76), Acad. Behavioral Medicine Research (exec. council 1978), Am. Psychoanalytic Assn. (pres.-elect 1980-82, pres. 1982-84), Internat. Psycho-Analytical Assn., Assn. Psychophysiol. Study of Sleep, Internat. Coll. Psychosomatic Medicine (pres. 1975), Psychiat. Research Soc., A. Graeme Mitchell Undergrad. Pediatric Soc., Benjamin Rush Soc., Rapaport-Klein Study Group, World Psychiat. Assn. (organizing com. sect. psychosomatic medicine 1967), Sigma Xi, Phi Eta Sigma, Pi Kappa Epsilon, Alpha Omega Alpha. Home: 200 Todd St Hamden CT 06518-1511 Office: 255 Bradley St New Haven CT 06510-1105

REISER, PAUL, actor, comedian; b. N.Y.C., Mar. 30, 1957; m. Paula Reiser. BFA in Music, SUNY, Binghampton, 1977. comedian various nightclubs and venues including Catch a Rising Star, N.Y.C., The Comic Strip, N.Y.C., The Improv, N.Y.C., 1979—. Performances include (feature films) Diner, 1982, Beverly Hills Cop, 1984, Aliens, 1986, Beverly Hills Cop II, 1987, Cross My Heart, 1987, Crazy People, 1990, The Marrying Man, 1991, Bye Bye, Love, 1995, (TV series) The Investigator, HBO, The Comedy Zone, (TV spls.) Paul Reiser: Out on a Whim, HBO, 1987, (TV pilots) Diner, CBS, Just Married, ABC, (TV movies) Sunset Limousine, 1987, You Ruined My Life, 1987, The Tower, 1993; regular (TV series) My Two Dads, NBC, 1987-1991, Mad About You, NBC, 1992— (Emmy nomination, Lead Actor - Comedy Series, 1994); guest star various talk shows including The Tonight Show, Late Night with David Letterman; author: Couplehood, 1994. *

REISERT, CHARLES EDWARD, JR., real estate executive; b. New Albany, Ind., Apr. 5, 1941; s. Charles Edward Sr. and Jane. W. (Willcox) R.; m. Mary Lynn Nunemacher, Nov. 9, 1963; children: Perry G., Heidi L. BS in Edn., Ind. U., 1963, MA, 1968. Cert. residential specialist, residential broker. Tchr. Ind. Pub. Schs., 1963-67; mgr. Ind. Bell Tel. Co., Indpls., 1967-70; trust officer Ind. Nat. Bank, Indpls., 1970-72; ptnr. R.F.R. Prodns. Inc., Zionsville; dir. Wichita (Kans.) Art Assn., 1972-73; realtor Century 21 Reisert, Baker, Walker & Assocs., Jeffersonville, Ind., 1973—. Mem. Ind. Real Estate Commn., 1982-90, chmn., 1990; pres. bd. dirs. Clark County Youth Shelter, 1987—; bd. dirs., past pres. United Way Clark County; bd. dirs. New Hope, Inc., Sagamore of Wabash; mem. Leadership So. Ind., Leadership Louisville; trustee Jeffersonville Twp. Pub. Libr. Mem. So. Ind. Realtors Assn., (past pres. Realtor of Yr.) Nat. Assn. Realtors, Ind. Assn. Realtor (bd. dirs.), Realtors Nat. Mktg. Inst., So. Ind. C. of C. (past bd. dirs., Profl. of Yr.), Rotary (past pres., Paul Harris fellow). Roman Catholic. Home: 2005 Utica Pike Jeffersonville IN 47130-5003 Office: Century 21 Reisert Baker Walker & Assocs 1302 E 10th St Jeffersonville IN 47130-4231

REISIN, EFRAIN, nephrologist, researcher, educator; b. Cordoba, Argentina, Feb. 25, 1943; came to U.S., 1979; s. Maximo and Elisa Reisin; m. Ilana Hershkovitz, Sept. 6, 1971; children: Eyal, Thalia Alexis. MD, Nat. U., Cordoba, 1966. Intern internal medicine Nat. U. Cordoba-Clinicas Hosp., 1966; resident Jimenes Diaz Found., Madrid, 1966-68; resident Chaim Sheba Med. Ctr., Tel Hashomer, Israel, 1968-71, fellow in nephrology, 1971-74, staff physician nephrology, 1974-77; rsch. fellow in hypertension Health Sci. Ctr., Winnipeg, Man., Can., 1977-78; vis. scientist in hypertension Nat. Health Welfare Can., Winnipeg, Man., 1978-79; Ochsner vis. scientist in hypertension Ochsner Found. Hosp., New Orleans, 1979-82; from asst. prof. to assoc. prof. medicine La. State U., New Orleans, 1982-89, prof. medicine, 1989—; dir. dept. nephrology Med. Ctr. Charity Hosp., New Orleans, 1985—; panelist Consensus Conf., NIH, Bethesda, Md., 1991. Author numerous articles and book chpts. on hypertension and nephrology; conducted 1st research study documenting positive effects of weight reduction in treatment of hypertension, 1978 (citation classic Inst. Sci. Info. 1988). 1st lt. Israel Army, 1971-72. Grantee Nat. Health and Welfare Can., 1978-79, Am. Heart Assn., 1980-81, also several pharm. cos., 1984—. Fellow ACP, Am. Coun. High Blood Pressure Rsch., Am. Heart Fund, Am. Coll. Clin. Pharmacology (counselor south ctrl. regional chpt. 1991-92), Am. Fedn. Clin. Rsch., So. Soc. for Clin. Investigation; mem. Internat. Soc. Nephrology, Internat. Soc. Hypertension, Am. Soc. Nephrology, Am. Soc. Hypertension, Coun. Nephrology, Am. Heart Assn., Inter-Am. Soc. Hypertension, Orleans Parish Med. Soc. Avocations: tennis, reading, movies. Office: La State U Sch Medicine 1542 Tulane Ave New Orleans LA 70112-2825

REISINGER, GEORGE LAMBERT, management consultant; b. Pitts., Aug. 28, 1930; s. Eugene Merle and Pauline Jane (Lambert) R.; m. Judith Ann Brush, Nov. 24, 1967; children—Douglas Lambert, Christine Elizabeth. B.S. in Bus. Adminstrn., Central Coll., 1953; postgrad., Cleveland-Marshall Law Sch., 1962-67. Asst. personnel mgr. Continental Can Co., Houston, 1958-60; mgr. labor relations The Glidden Co., Cleve., 1960-67; dir. employee relations Mobil Oil Corp., N.Y.C., Caracas, Dallas, Denver, 1967-78; sr. v.p. Minton & Assocs., Denver, 1978-82; v.p., ptnr. Korn-Ferry Internat., Denver, 1982-86; pres. The Sigma Group, Inc., Denver, 1986—. Bd. dirs. Ponderosa Hills Civic Assn., 1977-80, Arapahoe County Youth League, Parker Action Team for Drug Free Colo.; pres. Douglas County Youth League; bd. dirs., steering com. Rocky Mountain Lions Eye Inst. With USAF, 1953-58. Mem. Am. Soc. Pers. Adminstrs., N.Y. Pers. Mgmt. Soc., Colo. Soc. Pers. Adminstrn., Am. Soc. Profl. Cons., Rocky Mountain Inst. Fgn. Trade and Fin., Employment Mgmt. Assn. Republican. Methodist. Clubs: Denver Petroleum, Pinery Country, Republican 1200. Home: 7924 Deertrail Dr Parker CO 80134-8262 Office: Sigma Group Internat 6551 S Revere Pkwy Ste 125 Englewood CO 80111-6410

REISINGER, SANDRA SUE, journalist, lawyer; b. Washington Court House, Ohio, Feb. 27, 1946; d. Dale E. and Elinor Jean (McMurray) R. BS, Ohio State U., 1968, MA, 1969; JD, U. Dayton (Ohio), 1980. Bar: Ohio 1980. Teaching asst. Ohio State U., 1968-69; with Dayton Daily News, 1969-81, asst. mng. editor, 1976-81; mng. editor The Miami (Fla.) News, 1981-89, Broward Miami (Fla.) Herald, 1989-93, dep. mng. editor, 1994—; adj. prof. Sinclair (Ohio) C.C., 1971-74, U. Dayton, Ohio, 1980-81. Mem. ABA, AP Mng. Editors Assn. (bd. dirs. 1982-87, exec. com. 1987-94, pres. 1992). Office: The Miami Herald Pub Co One Herald Plz Miami FL 33132-1693*

REISMAN, ARNOLD, retired management science educator; b. Lodz, Poland, Aug. 2, 1934; came to U.S., 1946, naturalized, 1955; s. Isadore and Rose (Joskowitz) R.; m. Mar. 12, 1955 (div. 1978); children—Miriam Jennie, Ada Jo, Deborah Fawn, Nina Michelle; m. Ellen Kronheim, Aug. 3, 1980. B.S., UCLA, 1955, M.S., 1957, Ph.D., 1963. Registered profl. engr., Calif., Wis., Ohio. Design engr. Los Angeles Dept. Water and Power, 1955-57; assoc. prof. Calif. State U.-, Los Angeles, 1957-66; prof. U. Wis., Milw., 1966-68; prof. ops. research Case-Western Res. U., Cleve., 1968-95; chmn. dept., 1982-87, ret., 1995; vis. prof. Hebrew U., Jerusalem, 1975; affiliate faculty Japan-Am. Inst. Mgmt. Sci., Honolulu, 1975—; vis. prof. U. Hawaii, Honolulu, 1971; asso. research engr. Western Mgmt. Sci. Inst., UCLA, 1964-65; coordinator programs between Inst. Mgmt. Scis. and AAAS, 1971—; examiner N. Central Assn. Colls., Univs. and Secondary Schs., 1971; v.p. Univ. Assos., Inc., Cleve., 1968-75; expert witness solicitor gen. Dept. Labor, 1969-70, U.S. Equal Opportunities Commn., 1976-79, Office of Atty. Gen., State of Ohio, 1981; cons. to asst. sec. HEW, 1971-72, Office Program Planning and Evaln., U.S. Office Edn., 1972-73; cons. Project Hope, 1981-82, Pan Am. Health Orgn., 1981—, Minister of Health, Barbados, 1989—, IRS Div. Research, 1985, UN Devel. Programme, 1988; cons. in gen. field systems analysis to numerous corps. and instns.; invited lectr. USSR Acad. Scis., 1989, Hungarian Acad. Sci.s, 1989. Author: Managerial and Engineering Economics, 1971, Systems Approach and The City, 1972, Industrial Inventory Control, 1972, Health Care Delivery Planning, 1973, Systems Analysis in Health Care Delivery, 1979, Materials Management for Health Services, 1980, Computer System Selection, 1981, Management Science Knowledge: Its Creation, Generalization and Consolidation, 1992; co-author: Welcome Tomorrow, 1982; series editor: Operations Management; assoc. editor: Socio Economic Planning Sciences; contbr. numerous articles to profl. jours. U.S. del. to Internat. Fedn. Ops. Research Socs., Conv., Dublin, Ireland, 1972; Review Bd. mem. Lake Erie Regional Transp. Authority, 1974-75; mem. del. assembly Jewish Community Fedn. Cleve., 1974-76; mem. Shaker Heights (Ohio) Citizens adv. com., 1972-84; bd. dirs., founder Greater Cleve. Coalition on Health Care Cost Effectiveness.; Trustee Hillel Found. Named Cleve. Engr. of Yr., 1973; NSF fellow, 1963. Fellow AAAS (council), Soc. Advanced Med. Systems; mem. Ops. Rsch. Soc. Am., Inst. Mgmt. Scis., ASME, Pan Am. Health Orgn., Am. Soc. Engring. Edn., AAUP, Am. Inst. Indsl. Engrs., N.Y. Acad. Scis., Nat. Soc. Profl. Engrs., Sigma Xi, Phi Delta Kappa. Home: 18428 Parkland Dr Cleveland OH 44122-3451

REISMAN, BERNARD, theology educator; b. N.Y.C., July 15, 1926; s. Herman and Esther Sarah (Kavesh) R.; m. Elaine Betty Sokol, Aug. 26, 1951; children: Joel Ira, Sharon Fay, Eric K., Robin Sue. B in Social Sci, CCNY, 1949; M in Social Sci. and Adminstrn., Western Res. U., 1951; LHD, Hebrew Coll., Boston, 1995; DHL (hon.), Gratz Coll., Phila., 1995. Agy. dir. Jewish Community Ctr., Chgo., 1951-67; prof. Brandeis U., Waltham, Mass., 1969—, dir. Hornstein program in Jewish communal svc., 1971-93, Klutznick prof. Contemporary Jewish Studies, 1993—; lectr. in field; vis. prof. Baerwald Sch. Social Work, Hebrew U., Jerusalem, 1978, Ctr. Jewish Edn. in Diaspora, 1978; sr. cons. Josephtal Found., Jerusalem, 1978; cons. European coun. Am. Joint Distbn. Com., 1978, Inst. for Jewish Life, N.Y.C., 1972-76; rsch. assoc. on future of religion Nat. Coun. Chs., 1972-73; Arnulf Pins meml. lectr. Hebrew U., Jerusalem, 1983, 84. Author: Reform Is a Verb, 1972, The Jewish Experimental Book: Quest for Jewish Identity, 1978, The Chavurah: A Contemporary Jewish Experience, 1977. Mem. Conf. Jewish Communal Svc. (chmn. publs. com. 1980—), Nat. Jewish Family Ctr., Am. Jewish Com. (1st chmn. acad. adv. com. 1979-82, 75th Anniversary award 1981), Am. Jewish Hist. Soc. (acad. coun. 1979—), Assn. for Jewish Studies. Home: 28 Fairway Dr Newton MA 02165-1713 Office: Brandeis Univ Hornstein Prog in Jewish Communal Svc Waltham MA 02254

REISMAN, FREDRICKA KAUFFMAN, education educator; b. Rochester, N.Y., Sept. 22, 1930; d. Samuel Hopkins and Rosalind (Lessen) Kauffman; 1 dau., Lisa Reisman Halterman. Student, Barnard Coll., 1951; B.A., Syracuse U., 1952, M.S., 1963, Ph.D., 1968. Lectr. Syracuse U., 1967-69; adj. assoc. prof. ednl. psychology Maria Regina Coll., Syracuse, N.Y., 1968; asst. prof. elem. edn. U. Ga., Athens, 1969-74; assoc. prof. U. Ga., 1974-79, prof. and chair early childhood middle sch. and elem. edn., prof. math. edn. and spl. edn., 1979-83; vis. prof., dept. human behavior and devel.; coordinator tchr.-scholar program Drexel U., Phila., 1984-85, dir. divsn. instrn. and program, head tchr. preparation, 1991—, prof., dir. tchr. preparation, cert. officer, 1986—; vis. prof. U. Calif., Riverside, Marianne Frostig Center Ednl. Therapy, Los Angeles; cons. diagnostic teaching math.; mem. program approval com. Pa. State Dept. Edn., 1984—, tchr. cert. com., 1984—; dir. Drexel U. Sch. of Edn. of the Coll. of Arts and Scis., 1997—. Author: Guide to the Diagnostic Teaching of Arithmetic, 1972, 3d edit., 1982, Diagnostic Teaching of Elementary School Mathematics: Methods and Content, 1977, 2d edit., 1981, (with S. H. Kaufman) Teaching Mathematics to Children with Special Needs, 1980, Sequential Assessment in Mathematics, 1985, Elementary Education: A Basic Text, 1987; contbr. articles to profl. jours. Recipient outstanding faculty citizen recognition Am. Assn. Higher Edn., 1994. Mem. Nat. Coun. Tchrs. Math., Am. Psychol. Assn., Internat. Assn. Applied Psychology, Soc. for Rsch. in Child Devel., Sch. Sci. and Math. Assn., ASCD, Assn. for Tchr. Educators, Am. Edn. Rsch. Assn., Sigma Xi, Pi Lambda Theta, Phi Delta Kappa. Office: Drexel U 109 Disque Philadelphia PA 19106

REISMAN, ROBERT E., physician, educator; b. Buffalo, Nov. 1, 1932; s. Harry S. and Jessie (Goldberg) R.; m. Rena Estry, Sept. 5, 1954; children: Jeanne, Linda, Nancy, David. M.D., SUNY-Buffalo, 1956; Dr.h.c., U. Montpellier (France), 1982. Diplomate Am. Bd. Internal Medicine (bd. dirs. 1984-86), Am. Bd. Allergy and Clin. Immunology (bd. dirs. 1981-86, chmn. 1985, mem. residency rev. com. for allergy and immunology, 1988-93, chmn. 1990-91). Intern Buffalo Gen. Hosp., 1956-57, resident in medicine, 1957-59; practice medicine specializing in allergy and clin. immunology Buffalo, 1961—; clin. prof. pediatrics and medicine SUNY, Buffalo, 1978—; co-dir. Allergy Research Lab., Buffalo Gen. Hosp., 1970-90 ; mem. panel on allergenic extracts Bur. Biologics, FDA. Served with U.S. Army, 1968-69. Master ACP; fellow Am. Acad. Allergy (pres. 1980-81). Home: 113 Carriage Cir Buffalo NY 14221-2163 Office: 295 Essjay Rd Williamsville NY 14221-8216 also: 85 High St Buffalo NY 14203-1149

REISMAN, ROSEMARY MOODY CANFIELD, writer, humanities educator; b. Des Moines, Iowa, Nov. 18, 1927; d. V. Alton and Lois Gloria (Slee) Moody; m. Michael Ellison Canfield, Sept. 6, 1952 (div. May 1961); children: Michael, John Charles, Celia Catherine, Christopher James; m. Maurice Reisman, May 10, 1986 (dec. 1990). BA in English, U. Minn., 1949, MA in English, 1952; PhD in English, La. State U., 1971. Reporter Ames Tribune, summer 1944; writer, actor Sta. WOI Pub. Radio, Ames, Iowa, 1944-48; dir., writer children's plays Sta. KASI, Ames, 1949; tchg. asst. U. Minn., 1949-52; writer Sta. WOI-TV, Ames, summer 1952; writer, show host Sta. WDGY, Mpls., 1952-54; instr. La. State U., 1961-69, NDEA fellow, 1969-71; asst. prof. English Troy (Ala.) State U., 1971-80, assoc. prof., 1980-90, chairperson dept. English, 1985-90, prof., 1990-94; mem. honors coun. Troy State U., 1985-94, mem. honors faculty, 1986-94, mem. acad. coun., 1989-92, mem. faculty adv. coun., 1990-92, Rhodes scholar instnl. rep., 1987-91; adj. prof. Charleston So. U., 1996—; coord. sr. honors seminar Coll. of Charleston, 1996—; writer, cons. Baton Rouge State Times—Morning Adv., 1963-70; prodr., writer Perspectives project films Ala. ETV, 1977-80; chairperson conf. sessions South Ctrl. Soc. for 18th-Century Studies, 1988, Southeastern Am. Soc. for 18th Century Studies, 1991, 93; chairperson workshop Ala. Coun. Tchrs. of English, fall 1987; grant writer, project dir. Ala. Humanities Found., 1980, 89, asst. project dir. summer grad. course, 1990, presenter various instns., 1985-94; NEH grant writer, project dir. Ala. Pub. Libr. Sys., 1977-80; past presenter, lectr. Read Ala.! program, most recently NEH conf., 1989, various pub. librs. for Auburn Ctr. for Arts and Humanities, 1989-90; presenter numerous lectures and lectr. series, various instns., 1970—. Author: Perspectives: The Alabama Heritage, 1978; co-author: Contemporary Southern Women Fiction Writers, 1994; chairperson editl. adv. bd. Ala. Lit. Rev., 1986-94; mem. editl. bd. Biog. Guide to Ala. Lit., 1985—; guest editor spl. issue Ala. English 7, spring 1995; contbr. essays, articles and revs. to lit. publs. Baldwin County Humanities scholar Ala. Humanities Found., 1983, 84; finalist Ingalls award for Outstanding Tchg., 1991. Mem. NEA, AAUW (past pres.), AAUP, MLA, South Atlantic MLA, Assn. Depts. of English (mem. exec. com. 1991-94), Assn. Coll. English Tchrs. of Ala. (state pres. 1986-88, mem. steering com.), Ala. Edn. Assn., Fitzgerald Soc., Troy State U. Edn. Assn. (pres. 1990-93), Low Country Assn. (pres. 1996—), Phi Beta Kappa (past pres. S.E. Ala. assn., del. to nat. triennial coun. 1991, alt. 1994), Gamma Beta Phi (nat. pres. 1978-79, cert. of merit 1979). Democrat. Episcopalian. Home and Office: 121 Innisbrook Bend Summerville SC 29483-5084

REISMAN, WILLIAM M., lawyer, educator; b. 1939. LL.B., Hebrew U., 1963; LL.M., Yale U., 1964, J.S.D., 1965. Bar: Conn. 1964. Assoc. prof. Yale U. Law Sch., New Haven, 1969-72, prof., 1972-82, Hohfeld prof. jurisprudence, 1982—; mem. Inter-Am. Commn. on Human Rights, 1990-95, chmn., 1994-95; vice-chmn. Policy Scis. Ctr., Inc., 1992—. Author: Nullity and Revision, 1971, Art of the Possible: Diplomatic Alternatives in Middle East, 1970, Puerto Rico and the International Process, 1974, Folded Lies: Bribery, Crusades and Reforms, 1979, (with Weston) Toward World Order and Human Dignity, 1976, (with McDougal) International Law in Contemporary Perspective, 1981, (with McDougal) Internaitonal Law Essays, 1981, (with McDougal) Power and Policy in Quest of Law: Essays in Honor of Eugene V. Rostow, 1985, (with Schreiber) Jurisprudence: Understanding and Shaping Law, 1986, (with Willard) International Incidents: The Law that Counts in World Politics, 1988, (with James E. Baker) Regulating Covert Action: Practices, Contexts and Policies of Covert Coercion Abroad in International and American Laqw, 1991, Systems of Control in International Adjudication and Arbitration: Breakdown and Repair, 1992, (with Westerman) Straight Baselines in International Maritime Boundary Delimitation, 1992, (with C. Antoniou) The Laws of War, 1994. Fulbright grantee, 1966-67. Office: Yale U Law Sch PO Box 208215 New Haven CT 06520-8215

REISMANN, HERBERT, engineer, educator; b. Vienna, Austria, Jan. 26, 1926; s. Henrik and Olga (Pokorny) R.; m. Edith Falber, Aug. 14, 1952; children—Sandra Jean, Barbara Anne. BS in Aero. Engring., Ill. Inst. Tech., 1947, MS, 1949; PhD in Engring., U. Colo., 1962. Project engr. Convair, Ft. Worth, 1951-53; prin. structures engr. Republic Aviation Corp., Hicksville, N.Y., 1954-56; chief engr. systems analysis, chief solid mechanics Martin Marietta Corp., 1957-64; prof., dir. aerospace engring. SUNY, Buffalo, 1964—; Cons. NASA, Bell Aero Systems Corp. Co-author: Elastokinetics, 1974, Elasticity, 1980; author: Elastic Plates, 1988; contbr. articles to profl. jours. Assoc. fellow AIAA (award best tech. paper 1962, oustanding aerospace achievement award 1987); mem. ASME, Internat. Assn. Bridge and Structural Engring., AAUP, Sigma Xi, Tau Beta Pi. Home: 71 Chaumont Dr Buffalo NY 14221-3511 Office: SUNY-Buffalo 605 Furnas Hall Buffalo NY 14260

REISNER, MILTON, psychiatrist, psychoanalyst; b. N.Y.C., Jan. 30, 1934; s. Maximillian and Dora Reisner; m. Linda Ellis, Mar. 3, 1959 (div. 1975); children: Margaret Ann, Amanda Lee. BA, NYU, 1954; MD, Downstate Med. Ctr., 1958. Diplomate Am. Bd. Forensic Examiners, Nat. Bd. Med. Examiners, Am. Bd. Forensic Medicine, N.Y. State Bd. Psychiat. Examiners. Resident in psychiatry Kings County Hosp., Bklyn., 1959-62; sr. psychiatrist Manhattan VA Hosp., N.Y.C., 1962-66; assoc. dir. psychiatry Westchester Community Mental Health Bd., White Plains, N.Y., 1966-69; dir. psychiatry Westchester Mental Health Bd., White Plains, 1969-74; pvt. practice N.Y.C., 1976—; cons. Cath. Charities, N.Y.C., 1965-66, H.I.P., N.Y.C., 1973-74, NYU Med. Ctr., 1963-68. Contbr. articles to profl. jours. Lt. j.g. USPHS, 1958-59. Fellow Am. Soc. Psychoanalytic Physicians; mem. Am. Assn. Psychoanalytic Physicians (pres. 1985-86, 87-88, Plaque 1988), Nat. Arts Club, Phi Beta Kappa. Achievements include research in mirroring as a technique for treating delusions. Office: 200 E 84th St New York NY 10028-2906

REISS, ALBERT JOHN, JR., sociology educator; b. Cascade, Wis., Dec. 9, 1922; s. Albert John and Erma Amanda (Schueler) R.; children: Peter C., Paul Wetherington, Amy. Student, Mission House Coll., 1939-42; Ph.B., Marquette U., 1944; M.A., U. Chgo., 1948, Ph.D., 1949; LL.D. (hon.), CUNY, 1980; Docteur (honoris causa), U. Montreal, 1985. Instr. sociology U. Chgo., 1947-49, asst. prof., 1949-52; asso. dir. Chgo. Community Inventory (U. Chgo.), 1948-51, acting dir., 1951-52; asso. prof. sociology Vanderbilt U., 1952-58, prof., 1954-58, chmn. dept., 1952-58; prof. sociology and dir. Iowa Urban Community Research Center, State U. Iowa, 1958-60; prof. sociology, dir. survey research labs. U. Wis., 1960-61; prof. sociology, dir. U. Mich. Center for Research on Social Orgn., Ann Arbor, 1961-70, chmn. dept., 1970; prof. sociology Yale U., 1970—, prof. social sci. Inst. Social and Polit. Sci., 1970-87, William Graham Sumner prof., 1977—, chmn. dept., 1972-80, 85-89; chmn. Census Com. on Enumeration Areas, Chgo., 1950-52, Nashville, 1952-58; mem. tech. adv. com. Chgo. Plan Commn., 1951-52; cons. USAF Human Resources Research Inst., 1952-54. Author: A Survey of Probation Needs and Services in Illinois, 1947, (with Paul K. Hatt) Reader in Urban Sociology, 1951, (with Evelyn R. Kitagawa) Mobility of Chicago Workers, 1951, Social Characteristics of Rural and Urban Communities, 1950 (with Otis Dudley Duncan), 1956, Cities and Society, 1958, Occupational and Social Status, 1960, The Police and the Public, 1971, (with J. Roth) Understanding and Preventing Violence, 1993. Served as pvt., meteorology program A.C., AUS, 1943-44. Recipient Disting. Alumnus award Lakeland Coll., 1990, Beccaria Gold medal, 1990. Fellow Am. Sociol. Assn. (chmn. methodology sect. 1960, coun. and exec. com. 1962-65), Sociol. Rsch. Assn. (pres. 1969), Am. Statis. Assn.; mem. NAS (chmn.), Ohio Valley Sociol. Soc. (pres. 1966), Am. Soc. Criminology (pres. 1983-84), Soc. for Study Social Problems (pres. 1968), Social Rsch. (pres. 1949), Internat. Soc. Criminology (sci. commn. 1982-89, pres. sci. commn. 1985-89, pres. 1990-95). Home: 600 Prospect St Apt 7A New Haven CT 06511-2116 Office: Yale U Dept Sociology PO Box 208265 New Haven CT 06520-8265

REISS, ALVIN, writer; b. Ft. Sill, Okla., Oct. 31, 1932; s. Clarence Gustav Alvin and Mabel Alma (Craig) R.; m. Audrey Spencer, Sept. 1, 1951 (div. 1974); children—Belinda, Karen. Student, U. Oreg., 1950-51, So. Oreg. Coll., 1969. With Union Pacific and Denver & Rio Grande, 1951-61, chief clk., 1955-61; with KBOY-FM, Medford, Oreg., 1961-68; FM program dir. KBOY-FM, 1966-68; news dir. KYJC, Medford, 1969-73; staff writer Medford Mail Tribune, 1969—; dir. Rogue Valley Writers Conf. So. Oreg. State Coll., 1992, 93, 94, 95, 96. Screenwriter, Larry Lansburgh Films, Inc., 1972 (recipient John Masefield Meml. award Poetry Soc. Am. 1970, regional award for playwriting, Oreg. 1965, Ala. 1963); author: (plays) The Smallest Giant, 1963, River Children, 1983, Nines and Lunch, 1986, The Last Beach Ball, 1995, The Times, 1997, also stories and poetry; contbg. writer: Matinee at the Bijou, 1984-85, This Month on Stage, 1995—. Recipient Fiction prize West Wind Review, 1986, 2d prize Oreg. State Poetry Assn., 1987, 1st prize Oreg. State Poetry Assn., 1988. Mem. Am. Theater Critics Assn. (exec. com. 1983-86, adv. council 1986), Internat. Assn. Theatre Critics, Poetry Soc. Am., Jacksonville Art Alliance (poetry instr., dir. 1983), Mensa, Dramatists Guild, Authors League Am., Sigma Delta Chi (pres. So. Oreg. chpt. 1977-78). Home: PO Box 597 115 F St Jacksonville OR 97530 Office: care Archer King Ltd 10 Columbus Cir New York NY 10019-1203

REISS, DALE ANNE, accounting executive, investment company executive; b. Chgo., Sept. 3, 1947; d. Max and Nan (Hart) R.; m. Jerome L. King, Mar. 5, 1978; 3 children: Matthew Reiss, Mitchell, Stacey King. BS, Ill. Inst. Tech., 1967; MBA, U. Chgo., 1970. CPA, Ill., Mich., Mo. Cost acct. First Nat. Bank, Chgo., 1967; asst. controller City Colls. of Chgo., 1967-71; dir. fin. Chgo. Dept. Pub. Works, 1971-73; prin. Arthur Young & Co., Chgo., 1973-80; sr. v.p., controller Urban Investment & Devel. Co., Chgo., 1980-85, mng. ptnr. E & Y Kenneth Leventhal Ernst & Young LLP, Chgo., 1985—; bd. dirs. Ill. Inst. Tech., Urban Land Inst., The Chgo. Network; adv. bd. Kellogg Real Estate, Northwestern U. Mem. Fin. Execs. Inst., AICPA, Chgo. Network. Clubs: Econ. of Chgo., Metropolitan, Chgo. Yacht. Office: E & Y Kenneth Leventhal 1 N Franklin St Ste 2100 Chicago IL 60606-3421

REISS, GEORGE RUSSELL, JR., physician; b. Phila., Dec. 25, 1928; s. G. Russell Sr. and Mary Ellen (Brogan) R.; m. Rosemarie Theresa Curcillo, Sept. 19, 1959; children: Mary Elizabeth, Stephanie, G. Russell III, Charlene. BA, LaSalle U., 1953; MD, Temple U., 1957. Diplomate Am. Bd. Pediatrics. Intern Misericordia Hosp., Phila., 1957-58; resident pediatrics St. Christopher Hosp. for Children, Phila., 1958-60; pvt. practice Glenside, Pa., 1960—. With USCG, 1946-49. Mem. Montgomery County Med. Soc., Pa. Med. Soc., Am. Acad. Pediatrics, AMA, Am. Assn. Pro-Life Pediatricians. Roman Catholic. Office: 2220 Mount Carmel Ave Glenside PA 19038-4610

REISS, HOWARD, chemistry educator; b. N.Y.C., Apr. 5, 1922; s. Isidor and Jean (Goldstein) R.; m. Phyllis Kohn, July 25, 1945; children: Gloria, Steven. A.B. in Chemistry, NYU, 1943; Ph.D. in Chemistry, Columbia U., 1949. With Manhattan Project, 1944-46; instr., then asst. prof. chemistry Boston U., 1949-51; with Central Research Lab., Celanese Corp. Am., 1951-52, Edgar C. Bain Lab. Fundamental Research, U.S. Steel Corp., 1957, Bell Telephone Labs., 1952-60; asso. dir., then dir. research div. Atomics Internat., div. N.Am. Aviation, Inc., 1960-62; dir. N.Am. Aviation Sci. Center, 1962-67, v.p. co., 1963-67; v.p. research aerospace systems group N.Am. Rockwell Corp., 1967-68; vis. lectr. chemistry U. Calif. at Berkeley, summer 1957; vis. prof. chemistry UCLA, 1961, 62, 64, 67, prof., 1968-91, prof. emeritus, 1991—; vis. prof. U. Louis Pasteur, Strasbourg, France, 1986, U. Pa., 1989; vis. fellow Victoria U., Wellington, New Zealand, 1989; vis. fellow Princeton (N.J.) Materials Inst., 1996; cons. to chem.-physics program USAF Cambridge Rsch. Labs., 1950-52; chmn. editor Procs. Internat. Conf. Nucleation and Interfacial Phenomena, Boston; mem. USAF Office Sci. Rsch. Physics and Chemistry Rsch. Evaluation Groups, 1966—, Oak Ridge Nat. Lab. Reactor Chemistry Adv. Com., 1966-68; adv. com. math. and phys. scis. NSF, 1970-72, ARPA Materials Rsch. Coun., 1968—; chmn. site rev. com. NRC Associateships Program, Naval Rsch. Lab., 1989. Author: The Methods of Thermodynamics, 1965; author articles; editor in field.; editor: Progress in Solid State Chemistry, 1962-71, Jour. Statis. Physics, 1968-75, Jour. Colloid Interface Sci; mem. editorial adv. bd. Internat. Jour. Physics and Chemistry of Solids, 1955, Progress in Solid State Chemistry, 1962-73, Jour. Solid State Chemistry, 1969, Jour. Phys. Chemistry, 1970-73, Ency. of Solid State, 1970, Jour. Nonmetals, 1971—, Jour. Colloid and Interface Sci., 1976-79, Langmuir, 1985—. Guggenheim Meml. fellow, 1978. Fellow AAAS, Am. Phys. Soc. (exec. com. div. chem. physics 1966-69); mem. NAS, Am. Chem. Soc. (chmn. phys. chemistry sect. N.J. sect. 1957, Richard C. Tolman medal 1973, Kendall award in colloid and surface chemistry 1980, J.H. Hildebrand award in theoretical and exptl. phys. chemistry of liquids 1991, Van Arkel hon. chair in chemistry U. Leiden, The Netherlands, 1994), Phi Beta Kappa, Sigma Xi, Phi Lambda Upsilon. Office: U Calif Dept Chemistry and Biochemistry Los Angeles CA 90024

REISS, IRA LEONARD, retired sociology educator, writer; b. N.Y.C., Dec. 8, 1925; s. Philip and Dorothy (Jacobs) R.; m. Harriet Marilyn Eisman, Sept. 4, 1955; children: David, Pamela, Joel. BS cum laude, Syracuse U., 1949; MA, Pa. State U., 1951, PhD, 1953. Instr. in sociology Bowdoin Coll., Brunswick, Maine, 1953-55; asst. prof. sociology Coll. William and Mary, Williamsburg, Va., 1955-59; asst. prof. Bard Coll., Annandale-0n-Hudson, N.Y., 1959-61; assoc. to full prof. U. Iowa, Iowa City, 1961-69; prof. U. Minn., Mpls., 1969-96; rsch. evaluator U.S. Dept. Edn. and Nat. Inst. Child Health and Human Devel., Washington, 1966-78; rsch. dir. Family Study Ctr., U. Minn., 1969-74; ednl. advisor Kimberly-Clark Corp., Neenah, Wis., 1971-75; chair planning com. and bd. dirs. Inst. for Child, Adolescent Sexual Health, 1992-93; lectr. at 200 univs., 150 profl. mtgs., 100 civic groups, 1953-96; vis. prof. Uppsala Univ., Sweden, 1975-76. Author: Premarital Sexual Standards in America, 1960, The Social Context of Premarital Sexual Permissiveness, 1967, Family Systems in America (4 edits.), 1971, 76, 80, 88, Journey into Sexuality: An Exploratory Voyage, 1986, An End to Shame: Shaping Our Next Sexual Revolution, 1990; editor 3 textbooks; contbr. over 100 articles to jours. and chpts. to textbooks in field. Mem. ACLU, 1948—, Planned Parenthood, 1960—, Nat. Abortion Rights Action League 1975—, Amnesty Internat., 1984—.With U.S. Army, 1944-46, ETO. Mem. Midwest Sociol. Soc. (pres. 1971-72), Am. Sociol. Assn. (chair family sect. 1975-76), Nat. Coun. on Family Rels. (pres. 1979-80, Reuben Hill award 1980, E.W. Burgess award 1984), Polish Acad. Sexual Sci. (hon., Internat. Sexual Sci. award 1989), Soc. for Sci. Study Sex (pres. 1980-81, Disting. Sci. Achievement award 1982, Alfred Kinsey award 1990), Internat. Acad. Sex Rsch. (pres. 1984-85), Am. Assn. Sex Educators, Counselors and Therapists (leadership award 1993). Democrat. Jewish. Avocations: good conversations with family and friends. Home: 5932 Medicine Lake Rd Minneapolis MN 55422-3328

REISS, JOHN BARLOW, lawyer; b. London, Aug. 29, 1939; came to U.S., 1963; s. James Martin and Margaret Joan (Ping) R.; m. Mary Jean Maudsley, Aug. 6, 1967 (div. 1978); m. Kathleen Strouse, Aug. 2, 1979; 1 child, Juliette Blanche. BA with honors, Exeter U., Devon, Eng., 1961; AM, Washington U., St. Louis, 1966, PhD, 1971; JD, Temple U., 1977. Bar: Pa. 1977, N.J. 1977, U.S. Dist. Ct. N.J. 1977, D.C. 1980, U.S. Supreme Ct. 1981, U.S. Dist. Ct. D.C. 1982. Economist Commonwealth Econ. Com., London, 1962-63; asst. prof. Allegheny Coll., Meadville, Pa., 1967-71; assoc. prof. Stockton State Coll., Pomona, N.J., 1971-75; asst. health commr. State of N.J., Trenton, 1975-79; dir. office of health regulation U.S. Dept. HHS, Washington, 1979-81; assoc. Baker & Hostetler, Washington, 1981-82; assoc. Dechert Price & Rhoads, Phila., 1982-86, ptnr., 1986-93, asst. chair health law group, 1984-91, chmn. health law group, 1991-93; ptnr. Saul, Ewing, Remick & Saul, Phila., 1993—, chmn. health law dept., 1995—. Mem. editl. bd. Topics in Hosp. Law, 1985-86, Hosp. Legal Forms Manual, 1985—, Jour. Health Care Tech., 1984-86; contbr. Hosp. Contracts Manual, 1983—; contbr. articles to profl. jours., chpts. to books. Bd. dirs. Gateway Sch. Little Children, Phila., 1986—, ECRI, Plymouth Meeting, Pa., 1994—, stewardship chmn., 1992-93, 96—; mem. vestry All Saints Ch., Wynnewood, Pa., 1993, 96—; mem. The Union League of Phila., 1995—. Pub. Health Svc. fellow, 1979-81, English Speaking Union fellow, 1963-66, Econ. Devel. Adminstr. fellow Washington U., 1966-67. Mem. Nat. Health Lawyers Assn., N.J. Soc. Hosp. Attys., Phila. Bar Assn., Am. Hosp. Assn., Union League of Phila., N.J. Hosp. Assn., Brit. Am. C. of C. of Greater Phila. (bd. dirs. 1991), Univ. Barge Club. Avocations: gardening, house restoring, reading, philately. Home: 415 Wister Rd Wynnewood PA 19096-1808 Office: Saul Ewing Remick & Saul 3800 Centre Sq W Philadelphia PA 19102

REISS, JOHN C., bishop; b. Red Bank, N.J., May 13, 1922; s. Alfred and Sophia (Telljohan) R. Student, Immaculate Conception Sem., 1941-46; B.A., Steon Hall U., 1947; S.T.L., Catholic U., 1947, J.C.D., 1953. Ordained Priest Roman Catholic Ch., 1947. Asst. chancellor Diocese of Trenton, 1954, sec., master ceremonies, 1953-62, vice chancellor, 1956-62, officialis, 1962-80, aux. bishop, 1967-80, bishop, 1982—. Mem. Trenton Mayor's Adv. Commn. on Civil Rights, 1962-68. Home: 901 W State St Trenton NJ 08618-5327 Office: 701 Lawrenceville Rd Trenton NJ 08648-4209*

REISS, MARTIN HAROLD, engineering executive; b. Long Beach, N.Y., Aug. 16, 1935; s. Arthur and Mary (Schreckinger) R.; m. Rhea Cohen, June 24, 1956; children—Mitchell, Randi, Robyn. B.S., MIT, 1956; M.S., Ohio State U., 1959; M.S., MIT, 1961. Staff member MIT Inst. Lab., Cambridge, 1959-61; tech. dir. Raytheon Co., Sudbury, Mass., 1961-65; pres. Alarmtronics Engring., Newton, Mass., 1965-73, Gamewell Corp., Medway, Mass., 1973-83, chmn. bd., 1983-90; dir. Cerberus Techs., Inc., Waltham, Mass., 1990-93, pres., Rolf, Jensen & Assoc., 1993—, pres., CEO, 1996—, pres. CEO The RJA Group, Inc. 1996—; sustaining fellow MIT, 1981—; bd. overseers WPI Fire Scis., Worcester, Mass., 1985—, chmn., 1989—; dir. Practicorp, Newton, 1984-88; dir., treas. Nat. Fire Protection Research Found., Quincy, Mass., 1982—; dir. Nat. Fire Protection Assn., Quincy, 1991—, vice chair, 1996—. Patentee in field. Trustee Mass. Bay Community Coll., Wellesley, 1980-90, chmn. bd., 1985-86. Served to capt. USAF, 1956-59. Fellow Soc. Fire Protection Engrs. (bd. dirs. 1988-94); mem. Nat. Elec. Mfg. Assn. (sect. chmn. 1983-85, Man of Yr. award 1985), Automatic Fire Alarm Assn. (pres. 1978-80, Man of Yr. award 1985, bd. dirs. 1980-93). Office: Rolf Jensen & Assoc 1661 Worcester Rd Framingham MA 01701-5401

REISS, PAUL JACOB, college president; b. Lake Placid, N.Y., Aug. 10, 1930; s. Julian J. and Daisy M. (Smith) R.; m. Rosemary A. Donohue, June 25, 1955; children: Catherine, Paul, Gregory, Mark, Julia, David, Steven, Martha, John. B.S., Holy Cross Coll., 1952; M.A., Fordham U., 1954; Ph.D., Harvard U., 1960. Tutor Harvard U., 1954-57; instr., asst. prof. Marquette U., 1957-63, chmn. dept. sociology, 1961-63; asso. prof. sociology Fordham U., Bronx, N.Y., 1963-75, prof., 1976-85, chmn. dept. sociology and anthropology, 1964-68; dean Fordham U. (Liberal Arts Coll.), 1968-69, v.p. acad. affairs, 1969-75, exec. v.p., 1975-85; pres. St. Michael's Coll., Colchester, Vt., 1985-96; pres. emeritus St. Michael's Coll., Colchester, 1996—. Editor: Sociological Analysis: A Journal in the Sociology of Religion, 1961-68; contbr. articles to profl. jours. Exec. dir. Julian Reiss Found., Lake Placid, N.Y.; trustee Wadhams Hall Sem. Coll.; bd. dirs. Lake Placid Sinfonietta, Greater Burlington Indsl. Commn., Nat. Assn. Ind. Colls. and Univs., Assn. Cath. Colls. and Univs.; chmn. Vt. World Trade Office. Fellow Am. Sociol. Assn.; mem. Assn. for Sociology of Religion (pres.), Assn. Vt. Ind. Colls. (pres.), Vt. Higher Edn. Coun. (pres.), Vt. Bus. Roundtable, Vt. World Trade Office (pres.). Democrat. Roman Catholic. Home: 140 Saranac Ave Lake Placid NY 12946

REISS, ROBERT FRANCIS, physician; b. Watertown, N.Y., Dec. 11, 1938; s. Ernest Paul and Elizabeth Munk (Clark) R.; m. Giovanna Dora Bassi, Apr. 18, 1964; children: Carroll, Christian, Mark, Dylan. AB, Syracuse U., 1959; MD, U. Bologna, Italy, 1965. Diplomate Am. Bd. Pathology (hematology, transfusion medicine). Dir. lab. hematology and blood bank State U. Hosp., Bklyn., 1975-77; asst. prof. pathology SUNY Downstate Med. Ctr., Bklyn., 1975-77; dir. Hudson Valley Blood Svc., Valhalla, N.Y., 1978-85; assoc. prof. pathology and medicine N.Y. Med. Coll., Valhalla, 1978-88; med. dir. N.Y. Blood Ctr., N.Y.C., 1985-88; dir. lab. hematology and transfusion medicine Columbia-Presbyn. Med. Ctr., N.Y.C., 1988—; prof. clin. pathology and clin. medicine Columbia U. Coll. Physicians and Surgeons, N.Y.C., 1988—; chmn. steering com. Hudson Valley Blood Resources Assn., Valhalla, 1981-85; chief examiner blood banking N.Y.C. Dept. Health, 1980-86, mem. adv. com. on blood banking, 1988-90; mem. instnl. rev. bd. N.Y. Blood Ctr., N.Y.C., 1991—. Bd. mgrs. camping plus N.Y.C. Mission Soc., 1975-78; scout leader Boy Scouts Am., N.Y.C., 1975-80. Lt. Col. U.S. army, 1966-69, res., 1988—. Editor, author: Clinical Laboratory Medicine, 1992; contbr. over 30 articles ot med. jours., chpts. to books. Fellow Assn. Clin. Scientists; mem. Am. Assn. Blood Banks (dist. advisor 1982-88), Coun. Hosp. Blook Bank Dirs. Greater N.Y. (bd. dirs. 1989—), Am. Soc. Hematology. Avocations: travel, running, stamps. Office: Columbia-Presbyn Med Ctr 622 W 168th St New York NY 10032

REISS, STEVEN ALAN, lawyer, law educator; b. N.Y.C., Dec. 18, 1951; s. Louis and Ruth (Harrow) R.; m. Mary A. Mattingly; children: Alexandra Mattingly Reiss, Tyler Brennan Reiss. BA, Vassar Coll., 1973; JD, Stanford (Calif.) U., 1976. Bar: N.Y., D.C., Calif. Law clk. to John Minor Wisdom U.S. Ct. Appeals for 5th Cir., New Orleans, 1976-77; law clk. to justice William J. Brennan U.S Supreme Ct., Washington, 1977-78; assoc. Miller, Cassidy, Larroca & Lewin, Washington, 1978-80; vis. prof. Georgetown U. Law Ctr., Washington, 1981; asst. prof. Law Sch., NYU, 1981-83, assoc. prof., 1984-87, prof., 1987-91; ptnr. Weil, Gotshal & Manges, N.Y.C., 1990—. Editor-in-chief White Collar Crime Reporter, 1987-91, contbg. editor, 1991—. Trustee Vassar Coll. Poughkeepsie, N.Y., 1978-82; bd. dirs. NYU Cmty. Fund, 1984-87, Concert Artists Guild, 1991-94; gen. counsel Brennan Ctr. for Justice, 1996—. Mem. N.Y. State Bar Assn., D.C. Bar Assn., Calif. Bar Assn., Assn. of Bar of City of N.Y. (fed. legis. com. 1981-87), 2d Jud. Conf. (reporter 1984—). Home: 25 E 86th St New York NY 10028-0553 Office: Weil Gotshal & Manges 767 Fifth Ave New York NY 10153

REISS, SUSAN MARIE, editor, writer; b. Washington, Sept. 14, 1963; m. Paul L. Roney Jr., May 25, 1991. BA in English Lit., U. Va., 1985; MA in English, George Mason U., 1989. Editorial asst. Water Pollution Control Fedn., Alexandria, Va., 1985-87; freelance writer, editor Arlington, Va., 1987-90; staff writer George Mason U., Fairfax, Va., 1988-90; staff writer Optical Soc. Am., Washington, 1990-91, news editor, 1991-93, mng. editor, 1993-96; freelance writer, editor Arlington, 1996—. Newsletter editor: Arlington County Tennis Assn., 1990-91; contbr. articles to profl. jours. and mags. Mem. Nat. Press Club, Washington Ind. Writers, D.C. Sci. Writers Assn., N.Y. Acad. Scis., Sigma Tau Delta (founding mem. U. Va. chpt.). Avocations: tennis, piano, cross-country skiing. Home and Office: 6814 30th Rd N Arlington VA 22213-1602

REISS, TIMOTHY JAMES, comparative literature educator, writer; b. Stanmore, Eng., May 14, 1942; came to U.S., 1964, 84; s. James Martin and Margaret Joan (Ping) R.; m. Patricia J. Penn Hilden, 1988; children from previous marriage: Matthew James, Suzanna Jean, Justin Timothy. B.A. hons., Manchester U., Eng., 1964; M.A., U. Ill., 1965, Ph.D., 1968. Instr. French U. Ill., Urbana, 1967-68; instr., then asst. prof. Yale U., New Haven, 1968-73; assoc. prof., then prof. comparative lit. U. Montreal, Can., 1973-84, dir. comparative lit., 1976-81; prof. comparative lit., French and philosophy Emory U., Atlanta, 1983-86, Samuel Candler Dobbs prof. French and comparative lit., 1986-87; prof. comparative lit. NYU, 1987—, chmn., 1987-94; vis. prof. U. Toronto, 1976-77, U. B.C., Vancouver, 1979, NYU, N.Y.C., 1982, U. Montreal, 1984-87, Grad. Ctr. CUNY, 1985, SUNY, Binghamton, 1988-89, U. Calif., Berkeley, 1996-97. Author: Toward Dramatic Illusion, 1971, Tragedy and Truth, 1980, Discourse of Modernism, 1982, The Uncertainty of Analysis, 1988, The Meaning of Literature, 1992 (Morris D. Forkosch Intellectual History prize), Knowledge, Discovery and Imagination in Early Modern Europe, 1997; editor: Science, Language and the Perspective Mind, 1973; (with others) Opening Up the Disciplines, 1982, Tragedy and the Tragic, 1983, Sisyphus and Eldorado: Magical and Other Realisms in Caribbean Literature, 1996. Morse fellow, 1971-72; Am. Counc. Learned Socs. travel grantee, 1976, fellow, 1986-87; Can. Council fellow Oxford, Eng., 1977-78; rsch. fellow U. Montreal, 1979-80; Social Scis. and Humanities Rsch. Coun. of Can.; sr. fellow Oxford, Eng., 1983-84; Emory U. faculty fellow, 1986-87; Guggenheim fellow, 1990-91. Fellow Royal Soc. Can., Acad. Literary Studies; mem. MLA, Am. Comparative Lit. Assn., Renaissance Soc. Am., C. S. Peirce Soc., Can. Assn. Comparative Lit. (v.p. 1981-83), Internat. Comparative Lit. Assn., Can. Soc. Research in Semiotics. Office: NYU Dept Comparative Lit 19 University Pl New York NY 10003-4556

REISSMAN, ROSE CHERIE, elementary education educator; b. N.Y.C., Nov. 4, 1951; d. Seymour Frank and Sidonia (Blank) R.; m. Steven Feld. Cert. tchr., N.Y. Classroom tchr. various schs., N.Y.C., from 1972; now tchr. specialist for curriculum design Sch. Dist. 25, N.Y.C.; founder, mgr. Writing Inst. Peer Teaching, Forum, and Oral History, 1983—; grant writer, curriculum writer N.Y.C. Bd. Edn.; adj. prof. edn. Manhattanville (N.Y.) Coll., Fordham U., N.Y.C.; mem. tchr. network Cradle Ctr. for Law-Related Edn., Writing Notebook; mem. adv. bd. Giraffe Educator, N.Y. Newsday; v.p. edn. Wedgewood Brandeis Community Group; mem. tchr. adv. coun. Impact II; presenter workshops on grant writing. Author: Newday's 1988 Elections, 1989, Mayoral Curriculum, 1990, Gubernatorial Presidentes Curriculum, 1987, N.Y. Board of Education Infusing Critical Thinking in the Middle Schools with World Processing Software and Picture Disc, 1994, Entrepreneurial Empowerment 6-12 Curriculum Workbook, Rights and Responsibilities, 1992, Mayoral Campaign, 1993, The Evolving Multicultural Classroom, 1995, The Sun's On - It's Your Turn, 1997, Rhythm & Dues, 1997; field editor Learning Mag., 1991—. Christa McAuliffe fellow, 1988; grantee Dupont Found., Am. Cancer Heart Assn., 1992; recipient Judy Blume Ctr. award, 1988, Valley Forge Bill of Rights medal, 1992, Newspaper in Edn. Curriculum award, 1996, Md. English Coun. Multicultural award, 1996; named NYSEC Tchr. of Excellence, 1993; recipient numerous other awards and grants. Mem. Nat. Coun. Tchrs. English (dir. funding), N.Y.C. Assn. Tchrs. English (v.p. 1993, pres. 1994), Nat. Found. Teaching Entrepreneurships (cons., bd. dirs.), Assn. Computers in Edn. (pres.). Office: Writing Inst 110 Seaman Ave Apt 5C New York NY 10034-2808

REISSNER, ERIC (MAX ERICH REISSNER), applied mechanics researcher; b. Aachen, Germany, Jan. 5, 1913; came to U.S., 1936, naturalized, 1945; s. Hans and Josephine (Reichenberger) R.; m. Johanna Siegel, Apr. 19, 1938; children: John E., Eva M. Dipl. Ing., Technische Hochschule, Berlin, 1935, Dr. Ing., 1936; Ph.D., MIT, 1938; Dr. Ing. (hon.), U. Hannover, Germany, 1964. Mem. faculty MIT, Cambridge, 1939-69, prof. math., 1949-66; prof. applied math. MIT, 1966-69; prof. applied mechanics U. Calif., San Diego, 1970-78, prof. emeritus, 1978—; aero. rsch. scientist NACA, Langley Field, 1948, 51, Ramo, Wooldridge, 1954, 55, Lockheed, Palo Alto, 1956, 57; vis. prof. U. Mich., Ann Arbor, 1949, U. Calif., San Diego, 1967. Cons. editor Addison-Wesley Pub. Co., 1949-60; mng. editor Jour. Math. and Physics, 1945-67; assoc. editor Quar. Applied Math., 1946-95, Studies Applied Math., 1970—, Internat. Jour. Solids and Structures, 1983-95; contbr. chpts. to books, articles to profl. jours. Recipient Clemens Herschel award Boston Soc. Civil Engrs., 1956, Theodore von Karman medal ASCE, 1964; Guggenheim fellow, 1962. Fellow ASME (hon. mem. 1991; Timoshenko medal 1973, ASME medal 1988), AIAA (Structures and Materials award 1984), Am. Acad. Arts and Scis., Am. Acad. Mechanics; mem. NAE, Internat. Acad. Astronautics, Am. Math. Soc., Gesellschaft für Angewandte Mathematik und Mechanik (hon.). Office: U Calif San Diego Dept Applied Mechs Eng S La Jolla CA 92093-0411

REISTER, RAYMOND ALEX, retired lawyer; b. Sioux City, Iowa, Dec. 22, 1929; s. Harold William and Anne (Eberhardt) R.; m. Ruth Elizabeth Alkema, Oct. 7, 1967. AB, Harvard U., 1952, LLB, 1955. Bar: N.Y. 1956, Minn. 1960. Assoc. Paul, Weiss, Rifkind, Wharton & Garrison, N.Y.C., 1955-56; ptnr. Dorsey & Whitney, Mpls., 1959-92; ret., 1993; instr. U. Minn. Extension Divsn., 1964-66. Editor (with Larry W. Johnson): Minnesota Probate Administration, 1968. Trustee Mpls. Soc. Fine Arts, 1981-87; v.p. Minn. Hist. Soc., 1994—. 1st lt. U.S. Army, 1956-59. Mem. Am. Coll. Trust and Estate Counsel (regent 1980-86), ABA, Minn. Bar Assn., Hennepin County Bar Assn., Mpls. Athenaeum (bd. dirs. 1992—),. Home: 93 Groveland Ter Minneapolis MN 55403-1142 Office: Dorsey & Whitney 220 S 6th St Minneapolis MN 55402-4502

REISTER, RUTH ALKEMA, lawyer, business executive; b. Grand Rapids, Mich., May 30, 1936; d. Henry and Lena (Land) Alkema; m. Raymond A. Reister, Oct. 7, 1967. B.A., U. Mich., 1958, J.D., 1964; grad. Program in Bus. Administrn., Harvard U., 1959, postgrad. Program in Mgmt. Devel., 1976. Bar: Minn., Mich. 1964, U.S. Supreme Ct. 1976. Trust officer Northwestern Nat. Bank, Mpls., 1964-70; asst. counsel, asst. v.p., sec. Fed. Res. Bank, Mpls., 1970-81; asst. sec., bd. govs. Fed. Res. System, 1977; dep. under sec. U.S. Dept. Agr., Washington, 1981-83; pres. First Bank Systems Agrl. Credit Corp., Mpls., 1983-84; pres. Groveland Corp., Mpls., 1986—; dir. Herman Miller, Inc., Zealand, Mich., 1984—. Bd. dirs. United Way, ARC, Jones Harrison Home, Mpls., Gustavus Adolfus Coll., 1995—; chmn. Jones-Harrison Found. Mem. Harvard Bus. Sch. Club Minn., Minn. Women's Econ. Round Table (pres. 1980-81). Republican.

REISZ, HOWARD FREDERICK, JR., seminary president, theology educator; b. Balt., May 13, 1939; s. Howard Frederick and Katheryn M. (Gwynn) R.; m. Mabel (May) Martha Martin, June 6, 1965; children: Lisa Katherine, Heather Lyn. AB magna cum laude in English lit., Gettysburg (Pa.) Coll., 1961; BD, Luth. Theol. Sem., Gettysburg, 1965; AM in Systematic Theology, U. Chgo., 1967, PhD in Systematic Theology, 1977. Ordained to ministry Luth. Ch., 1969. Co-resident head undergrad. women's resident halls U. Chgo., 1965-69, 72-73, lectr. new collegiate divsn., 1969; assoc. Luth. campus pastor Pa. State U., State College, 1969-72; asst. pastor Trinity Luth Ch., 1969-72; pastor to univ. Wittenberg U., Springfield, Ohio, 1973-78; Luth. denominational counselor Harvard Div. Sch., 1980-92; sr. pastor Univ. Luth. Ch., Cambridge, Mass., 1978-92; pres., prof. theology Luth. Theol. So. Sem., Columbia, S.C., 1992—; instr. grad. student seminars Div. Sch., U. Chgo., summer 1968; lectr. new collegiate divsn. U. Chgo., 1969; tchr. dept. religion Wittenberg U., Springfield, Ohio, 1974-78; Luth. counselor Harvard Div. Sch., 1980-92; tchr. ann. theology Seminars So. Sem., 1993—; leader monthly theology discussion group for area Luth. mins., 1983-92; tchr. ann. non-credit seminars MIT, 1979-92; tchr. courses Diakonia, Lay Theology Sch., Boston, 1987-88; lectr.-spkr. nat. and regional events., 1992—; exec. bd. divsn. edn. and schs. Evang. Luth. Ch. Am., 1991—; bd. mem. Mass. Coun. Chs., Boston, 1985-92; mem. adv. bd. Word & World Jour., Mpls., 1982—; chair Luth. Orientation Com., Boston, 1980-92; mem. Coun. for Theol. Edn. in N.E., Com. on Svcs. to Students in Non-Luth. Sems., 1980-92; mem. staff associated with Campus Min. Com. New Eng. Synod, 1978-87, 91-92; mem. Luth. Roman Cath. Dialogue New Eng., 1984-92, Luth.-Episcopal Dialogue New Eng., 1989-92; chair New Eng. Synod Continuing Edn., 1989-92; ecumenical officer for Mass., 1988-92; sec. bd. Nat. Luth. Campus Ministry, Inc., 1991-97; mem. exec. com. bd. Divsn. Higher Edn. and Schs., Evang. Luth. Ch. Am., 1991-97; bd. mem. Mass. Coun. Chs., 1985-92; bishop's staff person Boston Ch. Leader's Covenant Group, 1988-92; ecumenical officer Evang. Luth. Ch. Am. Synod Bishop, 1988-92; mem. bd. ministry Harvard U., 1981-84, 86-90, 90-93, chair, 1989-91; founding mem. adv. com. Harvard Weekly Meal Program for Hungry, 1982-93, chair adv. bd., 1985-92; sec. Harvard Square Clergy, 1984-92; v.p. United Ministry at Harvard/Radcliffe, 1991-92. Contbr. articles to profl. jours. Mem. Mayor's Adv. Com. on Homelessness, Cambridge, Mass., 1987-89; vol. magician Children's Hosp., Columbia, S.C., 1993—; mem. Spl. Task Force for Cambridge Emergency Sheltering, 1987, Mayor's Adv. Com. on Homelessness, Cambridge, 1987-89, Cambridge/Somerville Com. on Homelessness, 1986-91, Cambridge Clergy for Affordable Housing, 1990-92; chair Harvard Square Affordable Housing, 1989-90; lectr. Cambridge Hospice, 1985-88, pastor resource, 1991-92; advisor, host pastor Emergency Winter Shelter Univ. Luth. Ch., 1983-92; mem. Liferaft network Harvard U., 1984-92; mem. Greater Columbia Cmty. Rels. Coun., 1994—; performer monthly charity magic shows Boston area hosps. and in Columbia, S.C. Recipient Fellowship Luth. Theol. Sem., Gettysburg, Underwood grad. fellowship Danforth Found., 1972-73, Leadership award Shelter, Inc., Cambridge, Mass., 1986, Nat. Disting. Svc. award Luth. Campus Ministry, 1990, Joseph Sittler award, 1992. Mem. Am. Acad. Religion, Ctr. for Process Studies, Bread for the World, Luth. Peace Fellowship, N.Am. Paul Tillich Soc. (bd. dirs. 1982-87, 89-92, pres. 1990-92, v.p. 1989-90, sec.-treas., editor newsletter 1984-87), Internat. Brotherhood of Magicians, Soc. Am. Magicians (local hosp. show chair 1978-92), Am. Acad. Religion, Boston Mins. Club, Rotary, Phi Beta Kappa, Eta Sigma Phi. Avocations: professional magic, poetry, art. Home: 4202 N Main St Columbia SC 29203 Office: Luth Theol So Sem 4201 Main St Columbia SC 29203-5863

REITAN, DANIEL KINSETH, electrical and computer engineering educator; b. Duluth, Minn., Aug. 13, 1921; s. Conrad Ulfred and Joy Elizabeth R.; m. Marian Anne Stemme, July 18, 1946; children: Debra Leah, Danielle Karen. BSEE, N.D. State U., 1946; MSEE, U. Wis., 1949, PhD, 1952. Registered profl. engr., Wis. Control engr. Gen. Electric Co., Schenectady, N.Y., 1946-48; transmission line engr. Gen. Telephone Co., Madison, Wis., 1949-50; mem. faculty Coll. Engring. U. Wis., Madison, 1952-85; prof. elec. and computer engring. Coll. Engring. U. Wis., 1962-85; cons. Energy Industries, 1985-95; dir. power systems simulation lab. Coll. Engring. U. Wis., 1968-84, also dir. wind power research Energy Ctr.; cons. Nat. Inst. Sci. and Tech. (formerly U.S. Nat. Bur. Standards). Contbr. articles to profl. jours.; patentee in field. Served with U.S. Army, World War II. Recipient Outstanding Tchr. award Polygon Engring. Council., Gov.'s citation for service to State of Wis. Fellow IEEE (Centennial medal and cert. for outstanding achievement 1984, Centennial medal and cert. dept. ECE U. Wis., 1991, IEE power Engring., Computer Control Indsl. Applications and Edn. Soc.), Conf. Internat. des Grand Reseaux Electriques a Haute Tension, Am. Soc. Engring. Edn., Wis. Acad. Scis., Am. Wind Energy Assn., Sigma Xi, Tau Delta Pi, Tau Beta Pi, Eta Kappa Nu, Kappa Eta Kappa. Lutheran. *I believe that in one's career professionalism and perseverance are key factors in success. In one's personal life, the family should be the center, but not the circumference, about which all activities revolve.*

REITAN, PAUL HARTMAN, geologist, educator; b. Kanawha, Iowa, Aug. 18, 1928; s. John Olsen and Anna (Meldahl) R.; m. Reidun Engebretsen, Sept. 28, 1962; children: Kirsten Berit, Eric Hartmann. A.B. (Salisbury fellow), U. Chgo., 1953; Ph.D. (Fulbright fellow), U. Oslo, Norway, 1959. Instr. U. Ill., Chgo., 1955; geologist U.S. Geol. Survey, 1953-56; state geologist Geol. Survey of Norway, 1956-60; asst. prof. mineralogy Stanford U., 1960-66; mem. faculty SUNY, Buffalo, 1966—; now prof. dept. geology SUNY, dean, 1975-79; cons. U. Calif.-Davis, Am. Geol. Inst.; guest scientist Centre for Geol. Sci., Acad. Sci., Warsaw, Poland, Geol. Survey Prague, Czechoslovakia., Geol. Survey, Norway, Nat. Geophys. Rsch. Inst. and Geol. Survey, India. Author: (with Davis and Pestrong) Geology, 1976; contbr. articles to profl. jours. Served with U.S. Army, 1946-49. NATO sr. fellow in sci., 1972; G. Unger Vetlesen fellow, 1973; Fulbright sr. lectr., India, 1986; Norwegian Marshall Fund grantee, 1986, 93. Fellow Geol. Soc. Am., Mineral. Soc. Am., Soc. Econ. Geology, Geol. Soc. India; mem. AAAS, Internat. Assn. Geochemistry and Cosmochemistry, Royal Norwegian Soc. Scis. and Letters (fgn.), Norsk Geologisk Forening (life), Sigma Xi. Home: 120 Walton Dr Buffalo NY 14226-4556 Office: SUNY Buffalo NY 14260-3050

REITEMEIER, RICHARD JOSEPH, physician; b. Pueblo, Colo., Jan. 2, 1923; s. Paul John and Ethel Regina (McCarthy) R.; m. Patricia Claire Mulligan, July 21, 1951; children: Mary Louise, Paul, Joseph, Susan, Robert, Patrick, Daniel. A.B., U. Denver, 1944; M.D., U. Colo., 1946; M.S. in Internal Medicine, U. Minn., 1954. Diplomate: Am. Bd. Internal Medicine (gov. 1971-79, chmn. 1978-79, rep. to Federated Council Internal Medicine 1977-80, 83-84, accreditation council grad. med. edn. 1979-85, chmn. 1982-83). Intern Corwin Hosp., Pueblo, 1946-47; resident Henry Ford Hosp., Detroit, 1949-50, Mayo Found., Rochester, Minn., 1950-53; cons. internal medicine and gastroenterology Mayo Clinic, Rochester, 1954-87; chmn. dept. internal medicine Mayo Clinic (Mayo Clinic and Mayo Med. Sch.), 1967-74, prof., 1971—; bd. govs. Mayo Clinic, 1970-74; bd. dirs. Sisters of Mercy Health System, St. Louis, 1986-92; mem. governing bd. Am. Bd. Med. Specialties, 1983-86; sci. and med. dir. Ludwig Inst. Cancer Rsch., 1987-88; cons. Kaiser Family Med. Found., 1989-90; med. dir. Phoenix Alliance Inc., 1990-93. Author: (with C. G. Moertel) Advanced Gastrointestinal Cancer, Clinical Management and Chemotherapy, 1969; contbr. numerous articles to med. jours. Trustee Mayo Found., 1970-74; trustee St. Mary's Hosp., Rochester, 1976-82. Served with U.S. Army, 1947-49. Recipient Alumni award U. Colo. Sch. Medicine; Irving Cutter award Phi Rho Sigma, 1986, Disting. Alumnus award Mayo Found., 1997. Master ACP (regent 1979-82, gov. for Minn. 1975-79, pres. 1983-84, Alfred Stengel Meml. award 1990); fellow Am. Gastroenterol. Assn., AMA, Am. Clin. and Climatol. Assn., Am. Fedn. Clin. Rsch., Am. Soc. Clin. Oncology, Coun. Med. Splty. Socs., Inst. Medicine, Am. Assn. Cancer Rsch., Am. Assn. Study Liver Disease, Nat. Bd. Med. Examiners (treas. 1987-89), Alpha Omega Alpha. Republican. Roman Catholic. Home: 707 12th Ave SW Rochester MN 55902-2027 Office: 200 1st Ave SW Rochester MN 55902-3129

REITEN, RICHARD G., natural gas industry executive; b. 1939. BA, U. Wash., 1962. With Simpson Timber Co., Seattle, 1962-64, St. Regis Paper Co., Tacoma, 1964-66, Hearin Products, Inc., Portland, Oreg., 1966-71; with Di Giorgio Corp., San Francisco, 1971-79, pres. bldg. material group; with Nicoli Co., Portland, 1979-87; dir. Oreg. Econ. Devel. Dept., Salem, 1987-89; pres. Portland Gen. Corp., 1989-92; pres. Portland Gen. Electric Co., 1992-95, pres., COO, 1996—. Office: Northwest Natural Gas Co One Pacific Square 13th Fl 220 NW 2nd Ave Portland OR 97209-3943

REITER, DAISY K., elementary education educator, retired; b. Lewisburg, Pa., Aug. 25, 1936; d. Clark B. and Maude E. (Bensinger) Zimmerman; m. Edward P. Reiter, June 3, 1978; children: Edward, Amy, Russ, Elizabeth Sieber White, Katheryn Sieber Ellis, Ann Sieber Myers. BS in Elem. Edn., Pa. State U., 1957; postgrad., U. No. Colo., Greeley, Pa. State U. Lic. real estate agt. Tchr. grade 4 Hershey (Pa.) Sch. Dist., 1957-58; tchr. grades 4 and 5 Red Land Sch. Dist., New Cumberland, Pa., 1959-61; kindergarten tchr. Topeka City Schs., 1958-59; tchr. grade 5 Wallaceton-Boggs Elem. Sch. Philipsburg (Pa.)-Osceola Area Sch. Dist., 1975-97, ret., 1997—; inservice leader transactional analysis and arts in edn.; researcher Civil War, newspapers, animals and habitats, body systems. Mem. choir lst Luth Ch. Recipient Arts in Edn. grants (4 yrs.). Mem. NEA, Pa. State Edn. Assn., Philipsburg-Osceola Edn. Assn, Toughlove Chpt. (founder). Home: PO Box 704 Philipsburg PA 16866-0704

REITER, GLENN MITCHELL, lawyer; b. N.Y.C., Feb. 1, 1951; s. Bernard Leon and Helene (Edson) R.; m. Marilyn Beckhorn, Sept. 5, 1976; children: Benjamin, Diana, Julie. BA, Yale U., 1973, JD, 1976. Bar: N.J. 1976, Pa. 1977, D.C. 1978, N.Y. 1979. Law clk. to judge U.S. Ct. Appeals, Phila., 1976-77; assoc. Schnader, Harrison, Segal & Lewis, Phila., 1977-78; assoc. Simpson Thacher & Bartlett, N.Y.C., 1978-84, ptnr., 1984—; resident ptnr. Simpson Thacher & Bartlett, London, 1986-90. Mem. Phi Beta Kappa.

REITER, JOSEPH HENRY, lawyer, retired judge; b. Phila., Mar. 21, 1929; s. Nicholas and Barbara (Hellmann) R.; m. Beverlee A. Bearman, Nov. 8, 1993. AB, Temple U., 1950, LLB, 1953. Bar: D.C. 1953, Pa. 1954. Atty. advisor U.S. Army, 1955-61; asst. U.S. atty. Ea. Dist. Pa., 1961-63, asst. U.S. atty. in charge of civil div., 1963-69; chief organized crime and racketeering strike force Western N.Y. State, U.S. Dept. Justice, 1969-70, sr. trial atty. tax div. 1970-72, regional dir. office of drug abuse law enforcement, 1972-73; dep. atty. gen., dir. Drug Law Enforcement Office of Pa., 1973-77; ptnr. Stassen, Kostos and Mason, Phila. 1978-85, Kostos Reiter & Lamer, 1985-89; judge Armed Svcs. Bd. of Contract Appeals, Falls Church, Va., 1989-95;

of counsel Kostos & Lamer, Phila., 1995—; mem. adv. com. Joint State Commn. on Procurement; lectr. in field. Contbr. articles to profl. jours. Mem. Citizens Crime Commn. Pa. With U.S. Army, 1953-55. Recipient Meritorious Svc. award U.S. Atty. Gen. Clark, 1967, Spl. Commendation Asst. U.S. Atty. Gen. Tax Div., 1969, Outstanding Performance award U.S. Atty. Gen. Richardson, 1973. Mem. ABA, Fed. Bar Assn., D.C. Bar Assn., Pa. Bar Assn., Phila. Bar Assn., Am. Legion, Vesper Club, Downtown Club. Office: Kostos & Lamer 1608 Walnut St Ste 1300 Philadelphia PA 19103-5407

REITER, MICHAEL A., lawyer, educator; b. Pitts., Nov. 15, 1941. BS, U. Wis., 1963, MS, 1964, JD, 1967, PhD, 1969. Bar: Wis. 1967, Ill. 1975, U.S. Supreme Ct. 1975. Ptnr. Holleb & Coff, Chgo., 1987—; adj. prof. law Northwestern U., Chgo., 1977—; mem. faculty Nat. Inst. Trial Advocacy, 1980—. Office: Holleb & Coff 55 E Monroe St Ste 4100 Chicago IL 60603-5803

REITER, ROBERT EDWARD, banker; b. Kansas City, Mo., Dec. 27, 1943; s. Robert Vincent and Helen Margaret (Petrus) R.; m. Mary J. Darby, June 20, 1964; children: Mollie K., Jennifer M., Ellen R., Robert E. Jr. BA, Rockhurst Coll., 1964; JD, St. Louis U., 1967; LLM, U. Mo., Kansas City, 1969. Bar: Mo. 1967. Assoc. atty. Burke, Jackson & Millin, Kansas City, 1967-69; personal trust adminstr. City Nat. Bank and Trust Co., Kansas City, 1969-71; estate planning officer United Mo. Bank of Kansas City, 1971-73, v.p., 1973-80, sr. v.p., 1980-85, exec. v.p., 1985—; pres., corp. bd. Seton Ctr., Kansas City, 1992-95. Contbr. articles to profl. jours. Bd. of Counselors St. Joseph Health Ctr., Kansas City, 1977-85; pres. St. Joseph Health Ctr. Adv. Coun., Kansas City, 1985-86; sec. United Mo. Polit. Action Com., Kansas City, 1987-88. Grantee St. Louis U. Sch. of Law, 1964-67. Mem. Mo. Bar Assn., Kansas City Bar Assn. (chmn. employee benefits com. 1989-90), Employee Benefit Inst. (adv. bd. 1986—, chmn. 1989), Estate Planning Soc. Kansas City (pres. 1985-86), Serra Club of Kansas City (v.p. 1987-89). Avocation: coaching youth soccer. Home: 1024 W 70th St Kansas City MO 64113-2004 Office: UMB Bank NA 1010 Grand Blvd PO Box 419692 Kansas City MO 64141-6692

REITER, STANLEY, economist, educator; b. N.Y.C., Apr. 26, 1925; s. Frank and Fanny (Rosenberg) R.; m. Nina Sarah Breger, June 13, 1944; children: Carla Frances, Frank Joseph. A.B., Queens Coll., 1947; M.A., U. Chgo., 1950, Ph.D., 1955. Rsch. assoc. Cowles Commn., U. Chgo., 1949-50; mem. faculty Stanford U., 1950-54, Purdue U., 1954-67; prof. econs. and math. Northwestern U., 1967—, now Morrison prof. econs. and math. Coll. Arts and Scis., Morrison prof. managerial econs. and decision scis. Kellogg Grad. Sch. Mgmt.; dir. Ctr. for Math. Studies in Econs. and Mgmt. Sci.; cons. in field. Trustee Roycemore Sch., Evanston, Ill., 1969-71, treas., 1970-71. Served with inf. AUS, 1943-45. Decorated Purple Heart. Fellow Econometric Soc., AAAS; mem. Soc. Indsl. and Applied Math., Inst. Mgmt. Scis., Ops. Rsch. Soc. Am., Am. Math. Soc., Math. Assn. Am., Am. Acad. of Arts and Scis. Home: 2138 Orrington Ave Evanston IL 60201-2914 Office: Northwestern U Ctr for Math Studies 2001 Sheridan Rd Evanston IL 60201-2925

REITH, CARL JOSEPH, apparel industry executive; b. Peoria, Ill., Jan. 11, 1914; s. Joseph and May (Kolb) R.; m. Jennie S. Habbinga, Apr. 3, 1936; 1 child, Joyce Elaine. Grad. high sch. Office staff sales Peoria Creamery Co., Ill., 1932; with Kroger Co., 1934-60; successively asst. br. acct., office mgr., acct. Kroger Co., Terre Haute, Ind., Atlanta; adminstr., coord. tng. and mgmt. devel. programing Kroger Co. (Gen. Offices), Cin.; gen. merchandising mgr. Kroger Co. (St. Louis br.), 1946-50; br. mgr. Kroger Co., Indpls., 1950-55; div. v.p. Kroger Co., Cin., 1955-57; regional v.p. Kroger Co., 1957-60; pres., chief exec. officer Colonial Stores, Inc., 1960-67; bd. dir., pres. Oxford Industries, 1967-78, now dir. Adv. bd. Salvation Army, Atlanta.; bd. dirs. Atlanta Coll. Art; trustee Robert Woodruff Art Ctr. Mem. Indiana Chain Store Council (pres., v.p. 1951-55), Ind. C. of C. (bd. 1954-55), Indpls. C. of C. (bd. 1950), Ga. C. of C. (indsl. devel. council), Atlanta C. of C. (v.p., bd. dir. 1964-67), Augusta (Ga.) Nat. Golf Club, Piedmont Driving Club, Capital City Club, Peachtree Golf Club, Masons, Shriners, Rotary. Home: 3747 Peachtree Rd NE Apt 1708 Atlanta GA 30319-1366 Office: Oxford Industries Inc 222 Piedmont Ave NE Atlanta GA 30308-3306

REITMAN, IVAN, film director, producer; b. Komarmo, Czechoslovakia, Oct. 27, 1946; came to Can., 1951; s. Leslie and Clara R.; m. Genevieve Robert, Sept. 12, 1976; children: Jason, Catherine, Caroline. MusB, McMaster U., 1969. Judge FOCUS Nissan-Datsun, N.Y.C., 1981-83. Theatrical prodr.: The Magic show, 1974, The National Lampoon Show, 1975, Merlin, 1983 (also dir.); Films include: (dir., exec. prodr.) Cannibal Girls, 1973; (prodr.) They Came From Within (aka Shivers), 1975, Death Weekend (aka The House by the Lake), 1977, Blackout, 1978, National Lampoon's Animal House, 1978, Heavy Metal, 1981, Stop! Or My Mom Will Shoot, 1992, Space Jam, 1996, Private Parts, 1996; (prodr., dir.) Foxy Lady, 1971, Meatballs, 1979, Stripes, 1981, Ghostbusters, 1984, Legal Eagles, 1986, Twins, 1988, Ghostbusters II, 1989, Kindergarten Cop, 1990, Dave, 1993, Junior, 1994; (exec. prodr.) Rabid, 1976, Spacehunter: Adventures in the Forbidden Zone, 1983, Big Shots, 1987, Casual Sex?, 1988, Feds, 1988, Beethoven, 1992, Beethoven's 2nd, 1993, Commandments, 1996; TV Series: (prodr., dir.) Delta House, 1978; TV film exec. prodr. The Late Shift, 1996, Fathers Day, 1997. Mem. Dirs. Guild Am. Office: CAA 9830 Wilshire Blvd Beverly Hills CA 90212-1804 also: Northern Lights Entertainment Bldg 489 100 Universal City Plz Universal City CA 91608*

REITMAN, JERRY IRVING, advertising agency executive; b. Phila., Jan. 9, 1938; s. Benjamin and Ruth (Eisenberg) R.; m. Monica Birgitta Hall, Oct. 27, 1968; children—Jennifer Sharon, Sarah Beth. B.S. in Fin., Pa. State U., 1961. Exec. v.p., chief exec. officer Brit. Pubs., N.Y.C. and London, 1965-69; pres., pub. Acad. Media, Sherman Oaks, Calif., 1969-73; v.p. Pubs. Clearing House, Port Washington, N.Y., 1973-78; exec. v.p. Ogilvy & Mather, N.Y.C., 1978-81; with Scali, McCabe, Sloves, Inc., N.Y.C., 1981-86; pres. Scali, McCabe, Sloves Direct, N.Y.C.; chmn. bd. The Reitman Group, 1986-87; exec. v.p. The Leo Burnett Co., Chgo., 1986-96; pres., CEO, vice chair Internat. Data Response Corp., Chgo., 1996&; dir. Scandinavian Airlines System Pub./Distbn. Svcs.; mem. adv. bd. Ill. Dept. Trade and Tourism, 1988—; internat. awards chmn., bd. dirs. John Caples Internat., 1989—; mem. Internat. Direct Mktg. Symposium, Zurich, Switzerland. Author: A Common Sense Approach to Small Business, 1968, Beyond 2000: The Future of Direct Marketing, 1994; contbr. articles to profl. jours. Trustee Locust Valley Libr. Assn., N.Y., 1982—; exec. com. mem. Pub. Hall of Fame, 1987—; bd. govs. Children's Miracle Network, 1992—, vice chmn.; bd. dirs. Children's Meml. Found. Telethon, The Direct Mktg. Ednl. Found., exec, dir., 1996—. Anderson scholar, 1960; recipient Key to City, New Orleans, 1959, Silver Apple award N.Y. Direct Mktg. Club, 1989, Ed Mayer award Ednl. Found., 1996, Charles S. Downs award, 1997. Fellow Psychiat. Re-Edn. Assn.; mem. Direct Mktg. Assn. (bd. mem. ethics com. 1984), Creative Guild (dir. 1984), Internat. Direct Mktg. Assn. (bd. dirs. 1981-82), Publ. Hall of Fame (exec. com. 1988—), Direct Mktg. Club N.Y. (pres. 1983-84), Beta Gamma Sigma, Delta Sigma Pi. Avocations: tennis; old car restoration; classical woodworking. Home: 2204 N Leavitt St Chicago IL 60647-3204 Office: Internat Data Response Corp 1735 N Paulina St Chicago IL 60622-1461

REITMAN, ROBERT STANLEY, manufacturing and marketing executive; b. Fairmont, W.Va., Nov. 18, 1933; s. Isadore and Freda A. (Layman) R.; m. Sylvia K. Golden, Dec. 24, 1955; children: Scott Alan, Alayne Louise. BS in Acctg., W.Va. U., 1955; JD, Case Western Res. U., 1958. Bar: Ohio 1958. Mem. firm Burke, Haber & Berick, Cleve., 1958-60; ptnr. Burke, Haber & Berick, 1960-68; exec. v.p., vice chmn. Tranzonic Cos. (formerly AAV Cos.), Pepper Pike, Ohio, 1968-70; pres., vice-chmn. Tranzonic Cos. (formerly AAV Cos.), 1970-73, chief exec. officer, pres., vice chmn., 1973-82, pres., chmn., chief exec. officer, 1982—; bd. dirs. Key Bank, N.A., Weirton Steel Corp., mem. Bus. adv.Com. Mandel Ctr. for non-profit Organ. Case Western Reserve U., 1995, vis. com. Weatherhead Sch. of Bus. Case Western Reserve U., 1995; chmn. Dean's Nat. Adv. Com., Sch. of Law, Case Western Res. U., 1997. Mem. Republican fin. com., Cuyahoga County, 1968-78; mem. Com. for Econ. Growth for Israel, Cleve., 1977-80, pres., 1978-80; mem. adv. coun. Cleve. Mus. Nat. History, 1982-85, Cleve. Opera, 1977—; del. Coun. of Jewish Fedns., N.Y.C., 1981—; gen. co-chmn. Jewish Welfare Fund, Cleve., 1975-78, 81-85, gen. vice chmn., 1985-89, gen. chmn., 1989-91; sect. and div. chmn., team capt. United Way Svcs., 1974—, mem. del. assembly, 1976-85, trustee, 1977-83, 84-90, 91—, v.p., 1985-88, chmn. nominating. com., 1988-90, campaign chmn., 1993, chair fund raising planning com., 1994-97, chair bd. trustees 1997; mem. employment com. Jewish Vocat. Svc., Cleve., 1974-83; bd. dirs. Capital for Israel, Inc., N.Y.C., 1986-87; nat. vice chmn. United Jewish Appeal, 1987-92, nat. allocations chmn., 1987-90, trustee, 1988-94, chair retirement fund com., 1994—; trustee B'nai B'rith Hillel Found., 1975-81, Cleve. Jewish News, 1976-79, Ednl. TV Sta. WVIZ, Cleve., 1976—, vice chmn. 1986-90, chmn. bd., 1990-97; trustee, pres. Bus. Volunteerism Coun., 1994-96, chmn. 1996-97; trustee Jewish Community Fedn. Cleve., 1983—, treas., 1991-94, v.p., 1995—, Jewish Edn. Ctr. of Cleve., 1993-96, Cleve. Zool. Soc., 1972—, pres., 1979-87, chmn., 1987-92, chmn. emeritus, 1992—, chmn. JDC-Brookdale Inst. of Gerontology and Human Devel., 1995; trustee Am. Jewish Joint Distbn. Com., 1988-96, United Israel Appeal, 1987-94, Mt. Sinai Med. Ctr., Cleve., 1976-96, chmn., 1982-85; trustee Cleve. State U. Devel. Found., 1986-89, Greater Cleve. Roundtable, 1991—; pres., trustee The Wilds, 1995—. Mem. ABA, Cleve. Growth Assn., The 50 Club Cleve., Case Western Res. Univ. Sch. of Law Soc. Benchers, Am. Kennel Club (regional del. 1960-75), Western Res. Kennel Club (officer, trustee 1959-75), Beechmont Club (fin. com. 1972-80, house com. 1974), Pepper Pike Club, Union Club, Masons, B'nai Brith, Zeta Beta Tau, Tau Epsilon Rho. Avocations: golf, swimming, pure-bred dogs. Office: Tranzonic Cos 30195 Chagrin Blvd # 224E Cleveland OH 44124-5703

REITSEMA, HAROLD JAMES, aerospace engineer; b. Kalamazoo, Jan. 19, 1948; s. Robert Harold and Bernice Jean (Hoogsteen) R.; m. Mary Jo Gunnink, Aug. 6, 1970; children: Ellen Celeste, Laurie Jean. BA, Calvin Coll., 1972; PhD, N.Mex. State U., 1977. Rsch. assoc. U. Ariz., Tucson, 1977-79, sr. rsch. assoc., 1979-82, vis. scientist, 1987—; sr. mem. tech. staff Ball Aerospace, Boulder, Colo., 1982-85, prin. systems engr., 1985-88, program mgr., 1988-89, staff cons., 1989-96, dir., 1996—; cons. Aerospace Tech., 1987—. Contbr. articles to Astrophys. Jour., Aston. Jour., Nature, Sci., Icarus. Bd. dirs. EE Barnard Obs., Golden, Colo., 1984-91. Fellow AIAA (assoc., tech. com. chair 1991, Engr. of Yr. Colo. region 1990); mem. Am. Astron. Soc. (planetary sci. com. 1991-94), Internat. Astron. Union. Achievements include discovery of Larissa, fifth satellite of Neptune; codiscovery of Telesto, seventeenth satellite of Saturn; patents for Optically-coupled Shaft Angle Encoder. Home: 4795 Hancock Driver Boulder CO 80303 Office: Ball Aerospace 1600 Commerce St Boulder CO 80301-2734

REITTER, CHARLES ANDREW, management consultant; b. Chgo., Oct. 28, 1956; s. LeRoy Maurice and Carolyn Ruth (Nelson) R.; m. Kimberly Ann Uthoff, June 2, 1979; children: April Suzanne, Andrew Christopher. BJ, U. Mo., Columbia, 1978; MA in Mgmt., Webster U., Webster Groves, Mo., 1989. Sports editor Jefferson County Newspapers, Festus, Mo., 1978-79, Cleburne (Tex.) Times Rev., 1979-80; sports editor Jefferson County Newspapers, Festus, 1980, reporter, editor, 1980-81; asst. editor Am. Paint Jour. Co., St. Louis, 1981, editor, 1981-87, editor, v.p., 1987-91, pres., chief operating officer, 1991-94; personal fin. planner IDS/Am. Express, 1994-95; bus. process analyst Comml. Letter Inc, St. Louis; group pub. Douglas Pubs., Inc., 1996; mgmt. cons. Reitter Mgmt. Solutions Co., 1997—. Contbr. articles to profl. jours. Mem. Webster U. Presdl. Search Com., 1989-90; mem. pastorial search com. St. Lucas United Ch. of Christ, 1993. Recipient Outstanding Grad. award Webster U. Alumni Assn., 1989. Mem. Fedn. Socs. for Coatings Tech., St. Louis Soc. Coatings Tech. Mem. United Ch. of Christ. Avocations: old cars, music, bus., family. Office: Reitter Mgmt Solutions Cos 3590 Round Bottom Rd # 16251 Cincinnati OH 45244-3026

REITZ, ALLEN BERNARD, organic chemist; b. Alameda, Calif., Apr. 7, 1956; s. Arnold Benno and Ruth Hazel (Stillings) R.; m. Evelyn June McCullough, Nov. 24, 1978; children: Darryl, Meredith. BA in Biochemistry and Molecular Biology, U. Calif., Santa Barbara, 1977; MS in Chemistry, U. Calif., San Diego, 1979, PhD in Chemistry, 1982. Postdoctoral rsch. fellow McNeil Pharm., Spring House, Pa., 1982-83, rsch. scientist, 1983-84, sr. scientist, 1984-87; prin. scientist Janssen Rsch. Found., Spring House, 1987-89; rsch. fellow R.W. Johnson Pharm. Rsch. Inst., Spring House, 1990—; reviewer Jour. Organic Chemistry, Tetrahedron Letters, Jour. Am. Chem. Soc. Editor symposium series Inositol Phosphates and Derivatives, 1991; contbr. articles to profl. jours., chpt. to books; expert analyst Chemtracts-Organic Chemistry. Recipient Johnson & Johnson Achievement awards, 1990, 97, Philip B. Hofmann Rsch. award, 1994. Mem. N.Y. Acad. Sci., Am. Chem. Soc., Phila. Organic Chemists Club (sec. 1986-88, chmn. 1996), Sigma Xi. Achievements include patents and patents pending; research on mechanistic synthetic organic chemistry, medicinal chemistry, stereocontrol, carbohydrate chemistry, and conformational analysis. Home: 109 Greenbriar Rd Lansdale PA 19446-1519 Office: RW Johnson Pharm Rsch Inst Welsh And Mckean Rd Spring House PA 19477

REITZ, BRUCE ARNOLD, cardiac surgeon, educator; b. Seattle, Sept. 14, 1944; s. Arnold B. and Ruth (Stillings) R.; m. Nan Norton, Oct. 3, 1970; children: Megan, Jay. BS, Stanford U., 1966; MD, Yale U., 1970. Diplomate: Am. Bd. Surgery, Am. Bd. Thoracic Surgery. Intern Johns Hopkins Hosp., Balt., 1970-71, cardiac surgeon-in-charge, 1982-92; resident Stanford U. Hosp., (Calif.), 1971-72, 74-78; clin. assoc. Nat. Heart Lung Blood Inst., NIH, Bethesda, Md., 1972-74; asst. prof. Stanford U. Sch. Medicine, 1977-81, assoc. prof., 1981-82; prof. surgery Johns Hopkins U. Sch. Medicine, Balt., 1982-92; prof., chmn. Sch Medicine Stanford (Calif.) U., 1992—. Developer heart-lung transplant technique, 1981. Office: Stanford U Sch Medicine Dept Cardiothoracic Surgery Stanford CA 94305

REITZ, CURTIS RANDALL, lawyer, educator; b. Reading, Pa.; s. Lester S. and Magdalene A. (Crouse) R.; m. Virginia R. Patterson, Dec. 19, 1953 (div.); children—Kevin R., Joanne E., Whitney A.; m. Judith N. Renzulli, Sept. 18, 1983. B.A., U. Pa., 1951, LL.B., 1956. Bar: Pa. 1957, U.S. Supreme Ct. 1959. Law clk. to Chief Justice Earl Warren U.S. Supreme Ct., 1956-57; mem. faculty law U. Pa., Phila., 1957—; asst. prof. law U. Pa., 1957-60, assoc. prof., 1960-63, prof., 1963—, provost, v.p., 1970-71, Algernon Sydney Biddle prof. law, 1985—. Trustee Internat. House Phila.; bd. mgrs. Glen Mills Schs., Pa. Served to 1st lt. U.S. Army, 1951-53. Mem. Am. Law Inst., Nat. Conf. Commrs. on Uniform State Laws, Order of Coif. Office: U Pa Law Sch 3400 Chestnut St Philadelphia PA 19104-6204

REJAI, MOSTAFA, political science educator; b. Tehran, Iran, Mar. 11, 1931; came to U.S., 1954; s. Taghi and Forough (Lashgari) R. AA, Pasadena City Coll., 1957; BA, Calif. State U., L.A., 1959, MS, 1961; PhD, UCLA, 1964. Teaching fellow UCLA, 1963-64; asst. prof. polit. sci. Miami U., Oxford, Ohio, 1964-67, assoc. prof., 1967-70, prof., 1970-83, Disting. prof., 1983—; vis. scholar Ctr. for Internat. Affairs, Harvard U., 1972, Hoover Instn. on War, Revolution and Peace, Stanford U., 1973, Inst. Internat. Studies, Iran, 1974-75; vis. prof. Western Coll., Oxford, 1971, 72. Author: World Military Leaders: A Collective and Comparative Analysis, 1966, The Strategy of Political Revolution, 1973, The Comparative Study of Revolutionary Strategy, 1977, Comparative Political Ideologies, 1984; (with Kay Phillips) Leaders of Revolution, 1979, World Revolutionary Leaders, 1983, Loyalists and Revolutionaries: Political Leaders Compared, 1988, Demythogizing an Elite: American Presidents in Empirical, Comparative, and Historical Perspectives, 1993, World Military Leaders: A Collective and Comparative Analysis, 1996, Leaders and Leadership: An Appraisal of Theory and Research, 1997, Political Ideologies: A Comparative Approach, 1991, 2d edit., 1995; editor, contbr.: Democracy: The Contemporary Theories, 1967, Decline of Ideology?, 1971; editor: Mao Tse-Tung on Revolution and War, 1969, rev. edit., 1970; assoc. editor Jour. Polit. and Mil. Sociology, 1973—; contbr. articles to profl. jours., book chpts. Recipient Outstanding Teaching award Miami U., 1970. Mem. Am. Polit. Sci. Assn. (polit. psychology sect.), Am. Sociol. Assn. (polit. soc. sect.), Internat. Polit. Sci. Assn., Internat. Soc. Polit. Psychology, Internat. Studies Assn., Inter-Univ. Seminar on Armed Forces and Soc., Conf. for Study Polit. Thought, Midwest Polit. Sci. Assn., So. Polit. Sci. Assn., Western Polit. Sci. Assn., Pi Gamma Mu, Pi Sigma Alpha. Office: Miami U Dept of Political Science Oxford OH 45056

REJENT, MARIAN MAGDALEN, pediatrician; b. Toledo, Aug. 12, 1920; d. Casimir Stanley and Magdalen (Szymanowski) R. BS, Mary Manse Coll., 1943; MD, Marquette U., 1946; MPH, U. Mich., 1960. Diplomate Am. Bd. Pediatrics. Intern St. Vincent Med. Ctr., Toledo, 1946-47; resident communicable diseases City Hosp., Cleve., 1947-48; resident pediatrics Childrens Hosp., Akron, Ohio, 1948-50; pvt. practice Toledo, 1950-54; chief div. maternal child health Toledo Bd. Health, 1953-64; dir. pediatrics Maumee Valley Hosp., Toledo, 1964-69; assoc. prof. pediatrics Med. Coll. Ohio, Toledo, 1969-76; med. dir. State Crippled Childrens Program, Columbus, Ohio, 1976-78; attendant pediatrician St. Vincent Med. Ctr., Toledo, 1978-80, 87—; chief pediatric svcs. Wake County Health Dept., Raleigh, N.C., 1980-87; clin. prof. pediatrics Med. Coll. Ohio, 1981—. Exec. com. March of Dimes, 1988-92. Mem. AMA, APHA, Am. Acad. Pediatrics, Am. Med. Women's Assn., Ohio PHA, Ohio State Med. Assn., NW Ohio Pediatric Assn., Acad. Medicine Toledo, Alpha Omega Alpha. Republican. Roman Catholic. Avocations: travel, photography, painting. Home: 2902 Evergreen Rd Toledo OH 43606-2724

REKATE, ALBERT C., physician; b. Buffalo, June 12, 1916; s. Gustave E. and Fannie (Hummell) R.; m. Elizabeth Foster, June 12 1943 (dec. 1985); 1 child, Suzanne (Mrs. R. Willis Post); m. Linda Ann Holt, Aug. 1, 1992. M.D., U. Buffalo, 1940. Diplomate Am. Bd. Internal Medicine. Intern E.J. Meyer Meml. Hosp., Buffalo, 1940-41, med. resident, 1941-44; asst. prof. medicine SUNY-Buffalo, 1954-61, assoc. prof., 1961-65, prof., 1965-86, prof. emeritus, 1986—; dir. rehab. medicine SUNY, Buffalo, 1965-72, acting dean Sch. Health Related Professions, 1965-66, assoc. dean, 1966-74, acting chmn. dept. rehab. medicine, 1972-75; assoc. dir. medicine E.J. Meyer Meml. Hosp., Buffalo, 1957-63, head dept. rehab. medicine, 1964-69, dir. primary rehab. center, 1965-69, acting head cardiology, 1966-69, dir., 1970-72; bd. dirs. Buffalo Hearing and Speech Ctr., 1973—; mem. adv. bd. Coastal Empire Mental Health Ctr., S.C., 1980-81, bd. dirs., 1981-93; mem. dean's adv. coun. SUNY-Buffalo Sch. Medicine and Biomed. Scis., 1995—. Contbr. articles to profl. jours. Served with M.C. AUS, World War II. Mem. Am. Heart Assn., Western N.Y. Heart Assn. (pres. 1954-55), Assn. Am. Med. Colls., N.Y. State Heart Assembly, N.Y. Acad. Scis., Med. Union (pres. 1974-75), Buffalo Acad. Medicine (pres. 1969-70), Erie County Med. Soc., Med. Alumni Assn. U. Buffalo (pres. 1960-61), Beaufort-Jasper Mental Health Assn. (dir. 1980-86). Home: PO Box 3164 Hilton Head Island SC 29928-0164 Office: 462 Grider St Buffalo NY 14215-3021

REKSTIS, WALTER J., III, lawyer; b. San Diego, 1945. BBA, U. Cin., 1968, JD, 1972. Bar: Ohio 1972. Ptnr. Squire, Sanders & Dempsey, Cleve. Office: Squire Sanders & Dempsey 4900 Society Ct 127 Public Sq Cleveland OH 44114-1216

REKTORIK-SPRINKLE, PATRICIA JEAN, Latin language educator; b. Robstown, Tex., Feb. 19, 1941; d. Julius and Elizabeth Lollie (Ermis) Rektorik; m. Edgar Eugene Sprinkle, June 22, 1963; children: Julie Anne, Mark. BA in English and Latin, Our Lady of the Lake Coll., San Antonio, 1963, MA, 1967; doctoral student, Tex. A&M U., 1968-74, U. North Tex., 1987—. Cert. secondary tchr., Tex. Latin and English tchr. Ysleta Independent Sch. Dist., El Paso, Tex., 1963-64, El Paso Independent Sch. Dist., 1964-65; instr. Our Lady of the Lake Coll., 1965-66; rhetoric and composition instr. Tex. A&M U., College Station, 1968-69, 72-74, Harford Community Coll., Bel Aire, Md., 1970-71; Latin tchr. Denton (Tex.) Pub. Schs., 1974—; mem. residents adv. com. Tex. Acad. Math. and Sci., Denton, 1987-88; chmn. Latin reading competition Nat. Jr. Classical League, Miami, Ohio, 1988-93; mem. methodology com. Am. Classical League, 1993-95; dir. Tex. State Jr. Classical League Conv., 1996; presenter workshops in field; mem. Tex. State Textbook Adv. Com., 1989-90. Costume designer Denton Cmty. Theater, 1984; choir dir. Immaculate Conception Ch., Denton, 1985-87; chmn. costume competition Tex. State Jr. Classical League, 1987—, exec. bd. sponsor, 1981—. Arthur Patch McKinlay scholar, 1986, 91. Mem. Am. Classical Assn., Classical Assn. of the Mid-West and South, Metroplex Classics Assn. (constl. adv. com. 1988), Classics Assn. Southwestern U.S. (pres. 1987-88), Tex. Classics Assn., Tex. Fgn. Lang. Assn. (chmn. hon. mem. 1988-89, chmn. local arrangements 1977). Roman Catholic. Office: Billy Ryan High Sch 5101 E Mckinney St Denton TX 76208-4630

RELIAS, JOHN ALEXIS, lawyer; b. Chgo., Apr. 2, 1946; s. Alexis John and Marie Helen (Metos) R.; m. Linda Ann Pontious, Nov. 27, 1971; children: Anne, Alexandra. BA, Northwestern U., Evanston, 1968; LLB, Northwestern U., Chgo., 1972. Bar: Ill., 1972, U.S. Dist. Ct. (no. dist.) Ill. 1972, U.S. Ct. Appeals (9th cir.) 1981, U.S. Ct. Appeals (7th cir.) 1983. Assoc. Vedder, Price, Kaufman & Kammholz, Chgo., 1972-78; ptnr. Vedder, Price, Kaufman & Kammholz, 1979-94, Franczek, Sullivan, Mann, Crement, Hein & Relias, Chgo., 1994—. Mem. bd. edn. Wilmette (Ill.) Sch. Dist. 39, 1989—, pres., 1992-93, 1995-96. Mem. Nat. Assn. Sch. Attys., Ill. Assn. Sch. Attys., Chgo. Bar Assn., Order of the Coif, Phi Beta Kappa. Greek Orthodox. Home: 2500 Kenilworth Ave Wilmette IL 60091-1337 Office: Franczek Sulian Mann Crement Hein & Relias 300 S Wacker Dr Chicago IL 60606-6628

RELIGA, JAMES PAUL, software engineer; b. Berwyn, Ill., Sept. 11, 1953; s. John James and Stella Gertrude (Pavlis) R.; m. Peggy Lee Partlow, Mar. 15, 1982. BA in Physics, U. Calif., Irvine, 1975. Sci. programming specialist Lockheed Missiles and Space Co., Sunnyvale, Calif., 1983, sr. rsch. engr., 1983-85, rsch. specialist, 1985-94; software cons., 1994—. Avocation: ballroom dancing.

RELL, M. JODI, state official; b. Norfolk, Va.. Student, Old Dominion U., Western Conn. State U. Mem., dep. minority leader Conn. Ho. Reps., 1984-94; lt. gov. State of Conn., 1995—. Past vice chmn. Brookfield Rep. Town Com.; trustee YMCA Western Conn. Mem. Nat. Order Women Legislators (past nat. pres., former v.p., treas., corr. sec.), Brookfield Rep. Women's Club (past pres.), Brookfield Bus. and Profl. Women's Club. Address: 125 Long Meadow Hill Rd Brookfield CT 06804-1339 Office: Office Lt Governor State Capitol Rm 304 Hartford CT 06106

RELLE, FERENC MATYAS, chemist; b. Gyor, Hungary, June 13, 1922; came to U.S., 1951, naturalized, 1956; s. Ferenc and Elizabeth (Netratics) R.; m. Gertrud B. Tubach, Oct. 9, 1946; children: Ferenc, Ava, Attila. B-SChemE, Jozsef Nador Poly. U., Budapest, 1944, MS, 1944. Lab. mgr. Karl Kohn Ltd. Co., Landshut, W.Ger., 1947-48; resettlement officer IRO, Munich, 1948-51; chemist Farm Bur. Coop. Assn., Columbus, Ohio, 1951-56; indsl. engr. N.Am. Aviation, Inc., Columbus, 1956-57; rsch. chemist Keever Starch Co., Columbus, 1957-65; rsch. chemist Ross Labs. div. Abbott Labs., Columbus, 1965-70, rsch. scientist, 1970-89; cons. in field. Chmn. Columbus and Central Ohio UN Week, 1963; pres. Berwick Manor Civic Assn., 1968; trustee Stelios Stelson Found., 1968-69; deacon Brookwood Presbyn. Ch., 1963-65, 92-93, trustee, 1990-91. Mem. Am. Chem. Soc. (alt. councilor 1973, chmn. long range planning com. Columbus sect. 1972-76, 78-80), Am. Assn. Cereal Chemists (chmn. Cin. sect. 1974-75), Ohio Acad. Sci., Arpad Acad., Internat. Tech. Inst. (adv. dir. 1977-82), Nat. Intercollegiate Soccer Ofcls. Assn., Am. Hungarian Assn., Hungarian Cultural Assn. (pres. 1978-81), Ohio Soccer Ofcls. Assn., Columbus Männerchor, Germania Singing and Sport Soc., Civitan (gov. Ohio dist. 1970-71, dist. treas. 1982-83, pres. Eastern Columbus 1963-64, 72-73, gen. sec. for Hungary 1991-92, Eastern European Growth Mgr., 1993-94, amb. at large, 1994—, established 1st Civitan club in Hungary 1991, Ukraine 1992, Slovakia 1994, Internat. Gov. of Yr. award 1971, Internat. Honor Key 1992, master club builder award 1992, various other awards), World Fedn. of Hungarian Engrs. Home and Office: 3487 Roswell Dr Columbus OH 43227-3560

RELMAN, ARNOLD SEYMOUR, physician, educator, editor; b. N.Y.C., June 17, 1923; s. Simon and Rose (Mallach) R.; m. Harriet Morse Vitkin, June 26, 1953; children: David Arnold, John Peter, Margaret Rose. A.B., Cornell U., 1943; M.D., Columbia U., 1946; LLD (hon.), U. Pa.; ScD (hon.), Med. Coll. Wis., Union U., Med. Coll. Ohio, CUNY; DMSc (hon.), Brown U.; DLH (hon.), SUNY; LittD (hon.), Temple U. Diplomate Am. Bd. Internal Medicine. House officer New Haven Hosp., Yale, 1946-49; NRC fellow Evans Meml., Mass. Meml. hosps., 1949-50; practice medicine, specializing in internal medicine Boston, 1950-68, Phila., 1968-77; asst. prof., prof. medicine Boston U. Sch. Medicine, 1950-68; dir. Boston U. Med. Services, Boston City Hosp., 1967-68; prof. medicine, chmn. dept. medicine U. Pa.; chief med. services Hosp. of U. Pa., 1968-77; editor New Eng. Jour. Medicine, Boston, 1977-91, editor emeritus, 1991—; sr. physician Brigham and Women's Hosp., Boston, 1977—; prof. medicine and social medicine Harvard Med. Sch., 1977-93, prof. medicine and social medicine emeritus, 1993—; cons. NIH, USPHS.; mem. bd. registration in medicine Commonwealth of Mass., 1995—. Editor: Jour. Clin. Investigation, 1962-67, (with F.J. Ingelfinger and M. Finland) Controversy in Internal Medicine, Vol. 1, 1966, Vol. 2, 1974; contbr. articles to profl. jours. Trustee Columbia U., 1990—; bd. dirs. Hastings Ctr., 1981-83. Recipient Columbia Alumni Gold medal, 1980, Disting. Svc. award Am. Coll. Cardiology, 1987, McGovern award Cosmos Club Washington, 1991, John Peters award Am. Soc. Nephrology, 1992. Fellow ACP (master, John Phillips medal 1985), Am. Acad. Arts and Scis.; mem. AMA, Assn. Am. Physicians (coun., pres. 1983-84, Kober medal 1993), Am. Physiol. Soc., Mass. Med. Soc., Inst. Medicine of NAS (coun. 1979-82), Am. Soc. Clin. Investigation (past pres.), Am. Fedn. Clin. Rsch. (past pres.), Phi Beta Kappa (senator 1991—), Alpha Omega Alpha. Office: Brigham and Women's Hosp Dept of Medicine 181 Longwood Ave Fl 5 Boston MA 02115-5804

RELWANI, NIRMALKUMAR MURLIDHAR (NICK RELWANI), mechanical engineer; b. Aug. 9, 1954; married. BS in Mech. Engring., U. Baroda, 1976; student, U. Nebr., 1977-78; MS in Mech. Engring., U. Wis., Milw., 1980. Registered profl engr., Wis., Ill. Rsch. asst. dept. mech. engring. U. Nebr., Lincoln, 1978; design engr. Allis Chalmers Corp., Milw., 1978-80; engring. cons. Bombay, 1980-86; assoc. engr. IIT Rsch. Inst., Chgo., 1986; mech. engr. Gen. Energy Corp., Oak Park, Ill., 1987-89, Arrowhead Environ. Control, Chgo., 1989-90; environ. engr. Ill. Dept. Pub. Health, Bellwood, 1990-92; environ. protection engr. field ops. sect. bur. air Ill. EPA, Maywood, 1992—. Recipient Cert. of appreciation Ill. EPA, 1993. Mem. ASME, ASHRAE (energy conservation award 1991), Assn. Energy Engrs. (sr.). Home: 413 Home Ave Apt 2B Oak Park IL 60302-3720

REMBAR, CHARLES (ISAIAH), lawyer, writer; b. Oceanport, N.J., Mar. 12, 1915; s. Louis S. and Rebecca (Schneider) Zaremba; m. Billie Ann Olsson, Feb. 23, 1944; children: Lance Richard, James Carlson. A.B., Harvard U., 1935; LL.B., Columbia U., 1938. Bar: N.Y. 1938. Atty. govt. agencies, 1938-42, 45; law sec. N.Y. Supreme Ct., 1946; practice law N.Y.C., 1947—. Author: The End of Obscenity, 1968, Perspective, 1975, The Law of the Land, 1980; Editor: Columbia Law Rev, 1936-38; Contbr. articles to various periodicals. With USAAF, 1942-45. Recipient George Polk Meml. award for outstanding book of 1968, 1969. Mem. Assn. Bar City N.Y. (chmn. spl. com. on communications 1972-78), Authors League, P.E.N. Clubs: Century Assn. (N.Y.C.), Harvard (N.Y.C.). Office: Rembar & Curtis 19 W 44th St New York NY 10036-5902

REMBE, TONI, lawyer; b. Seattle, Apr. 23, 1936; d. Armin and Doris (McVay) R.; m. Arthur Rock, July 19, 1975. Cert. in French Studies, U. Geneva, 1956; LL.B., U. Wash., 1960; LLM in Taxation, NYU, 1961. Bar: N.Y., Wash., Calif. Assoc. Chadbourne, Parke, Whiteside & Wolff, N.Y.C., 1961-63; assoc. Pillsbury, Madison & Sutro, San Francisco, 1964-71, ptnr., 1971—; bd dirs. Potlatch Corp., San Francisco, Pacific Telesis, San Francisco, APL, Ltd., Oakland, Calif., Transamerica Corp., San Francisco. Pres. Van Loben Sels Charitable Found., San Francisco; trustee Am. Conservatory Theatre, San Francisco. Fellow Am. Bar Found.; mem. ABA, Am. Judicature Soc., State Bar Calif., Bar Assn. San Francisco, Commonwealth Club of Calif. (govs. of the club). Office: Pillsbury Madison & Sutro 235 Montgomery St San Francisco CA 94104-2902

REMENICK, SEYMOUR, artist, educator; b. Detroit, Apr. 3, 1923; s. Oscar and Luba (Shackman) R.; m. Diane Kathryn Thommen, Aug. 30, 1950; children: Richard Vincent, Catherine Ann. Student, Tyles Sch. Fine Arts, Phila., 1940-42, 46, Hans Hofmann Sch., N.Y.C., 1946-48, Pa. Acad. Fine Arts, 1948. Instr. Pa. Acad. Fine Arts, Phila., 1977—; 1977-96. Exhibited one-man shows: Davis Gallery, N.Y.C., annually, 1954-62, Peridot Gallery, N.Y.C., annually, 1967-71, Pearl Fox Gallery, Pa., 1969, 73, 76, Gross McCleaf Gallery, Phila., 1981, Gallery K, Washington, 1983, (retrospective) Rosemont Coll., Pa., 1983; group shows: 3d Biennial Exhbn., Italy, 1955, Am. Painting, Rome, 1955, Paris exhbn., 1956, 57, Pa. Acad. Fine Arts, 1957, 59, 64, 68, Festival of Arts, Spoleto, 1959, Nat. Acad., 1960, 63, 66, Phila. Mus. Art. Served with U.S. Army, 1942-45, ETO. Recipient Tiffany Found. award NAD, N.Y.C., 1955; recipient Altman Landscape Prize, 1960, Hallmark Purchase award Hallmark Co., 1960. Mem. NAD (academician 1983). Home: 812 Catharine St Philadelphia PA 19147-3902

REMER, DONALD SHERWOOD, engineering economist, cost estimator, educator; b. Detroit, Mich., Feb. 16, 1943; s. Nathan and Harriet R.; m. Louise Collen, Dec. 21, 1969; children: Tanya, Candace, Miles. BS, U. Mich., 1965; MS, Calif. Inst. Tech., 1966, PhD, 1970. Registered profl. engr., Calif., Mich., La. Tech. service engr., chem. raw materials div. coordinator, sr. running plan coordinator, task team mgr. Exxon, Baton Rouge, 1970-75; assoc. prof. engring. Harvey Mudd Coll., Claremont, Calif., 1975-79, prof., 1980—, Oliver C. Field prof. engring., dir. Energy Inst., 1981-83; cons., mem. tech. staff, mgr. planning analysis Jet Propulsion Lab., Calif. Inst. Tech., 1976—; co-founder, ptnr. Claremont Cons. Group, 1979—; mem. adv. council Nat. Energy Found., N.Y.C., 1981-85; mem. Inst. Mgmt. Cons., 1988-89; presenter short courses Caltech's Indsl. Rels. Ctr. and UCLA's Engring. and Mgmt. Program, 1994—, also to industry and vogt. on cost estimation of projects, econ. evaluation of projects, software devel., schedule estimation. Case study editor Am. Soc. Engring. Edn., Inst. Indsl. Engrs., Engring. Economist, 1977-89; mem. editorial bd. Jour. Engring. Costs and Prodn. Econs., 1985-91, Internat. Jour. Prodn. Econs., 1992—; contbr. articles to profl. jours. Shelter mgr. ARC, Baton Rouge, 1965-70. Recipient Outstanding Chem. Engr. award U. Mich., 1965, First Place Pub. Relations award Am. Inst. Chem. Engring., 1975, Outstanding Alumni Fund Achievement award Calif. Inst. Tech., 1976, Outstanding Young Man of Am. award, 1976, NASA award, 1983, Best Paper of the Year in Jour. Parametrics, Internat. Soc. Parametric Analysts, 1991-92, Centennial award certificate Am. Soc. Engring. Edn., 1993; named Outstanding Research Seminar Speaker Occidental Research Corp., 1976. Mem. Am. Soc. Engring. Mgmt. (bd. dirs. 1981-83), Toastmasters Club (pres. Claremont-Pomona chpt. 1978).

REMER, VERNON RALPH, travel consultant; b. Urbana, Iowa, July 14, 1918; s. Ralph William and Kittie (Weisbard) R.; m. Jane V. Bush, Sept. 19, 1941; children—Richard Charles, Linda Jane (Mrs. A.D. Bleiberg). B.S., U. Iowa, 1939. With Central Life Assurance Co., Des Moines, Iowa, 1939-78; sr. v.p. Central Life Assurance Co., 1972-77; travel cons., 1977—; pres. Urbana Savs. Bank, 1944-64, dir., 1944-67. Precinct committeeman Republican party, 1952-60; mem. Polk County Rep. Central Com., 1953-56. Fellow Life Office Mgmt. Assn.; mem. Life Ins. Mktg. and Research Assn. (dir. 1971-74, chmn. agy. mgmt. conf. com. 1971—), Am. Soc. Travel Agts. (diploma), Sigma Nu. Congregationalist. Clubs: Masons, Des Moines. Home: 13018 Pomard Way Poway CA 92064-1108

REMICK, FORREST JEROME, JR., former university official; b. Lock Haven, Pa., Mar. 16, 1931; s. Forrest Jerome Sr. and Ruth Betsy (Saiers) R.; m. Grace Louise Grove, June 7, 1953; children: Beth Ann Remick Gillio, Eric Forrest. BSME, Pa. State U., 1955, MSME, 1958, PhD in ME, 1963; diploma, Oak Ridge (Tenn.) Sch. Reactor Tech., 1956. Engr. Bell Telephone Labs., Whippany, N.J., 1955-56; dir. nuclear reactor facility Pa. State U., University Park, 1959-65, dir. Inst. Sci. Engring., 1967-79, acting dir. Ctr. Air Environ. Studies, 1976-78, dir. intercoll. research programs, 1979-85, asst. v.p. research, grad. studies, 1979-84, assoc. v.p. research, 1985-89; dir. Curtiss Wright Nuclear Research Lab., Quehanna, Pa., 1960-65; chief tng. sect. dept. tech. assistance IAEA, Vienna, Austria, 1965-67; mem. Nat. Nuclear Accrediting Bd., Inst. Nuclear Power Ops., Atlanta, mem. adv. coun., 1995—; mem. Sci. Adv. Com. Idaho Nat. Engring. Lab., Idaho Falls, 1984-89, Reactor Safety Adv. Com., Savannah River Lab., Aiken, S.C., 1986-89, chmn., 1989; mem. Adv. Com. on Reactor Safeguards, Washington, 1982, vice chmn., 1987-88, chmn., 1989; commr. U.S. Nuclear Regulatory Commn., 1989-94, cons., 1994—; bd. dirs. Pub. Svc. Enterprise Group, Pub. Svc. Electric and Gas; mem. adv. bd. Applied Rsch. Lab., Pa. State U., 1994—. Served to sgt. U.S. Army, 1951-52. Named Outstanding Engring. Alumnus, Pa. State U., 1993; recipient Thomas P. Hamrick award for contbns. to tng. of nuclear facility pers., 1995. Fellow Am. Nuclear Soc. (bd. dirs. 1995—, meml. lectr. award 1971, disting. speaker award 1983); mem. ASME, Am. Soc. Engring. Edn., Nuclear Accrediting Bd. Republican. Lutheran. Home and Office: 305 E Hamilton Ave State College PA 16801-5413

REMICK, OSCAR EUGENE, academic administrator; b. Ellsworth, Maine, Aug. 24, 1932; s. Horace and Blanche (Rich) R.; m. Emma L. Lorance, Dec. 18, 1959; children: Mark Stephen, John Andrew, Paul Thomas. A.B., Ea. Coll., 1954; B.D. magna cum laude, Ea. Bapt. Theol. Sem., 1957; M.A., U.Pa., 1957; Ph.D., Boston U., 1966; student, Columbia U., 1959-61, Andover Newton Theol. Sem., 1957-58, Heidelberg (Germany) U., 1958-59; postdoctoral study, India, 1967; D.D., Assumption Coll., 1971, Allegheny Coll., 1974, Ea. Bapt. Theol. Sem., 1993; LL.D. (hon.), Alma Coll., 1987, Davis and Elkins Coll., 1991; HHD (hon.), Carroll Coll., 1991. Ordained to ministry Presbyn. Ch. (U.S.A.), 1957. Ordained minister United Presbyn. Ch. U.S.A.; minister United Baptist Ch., Topsham, Maine, 1961-63; part-time instr. philosophy Bates Coll., 1962-63; minister First Congregational Ch., Paxton, Mass., 1963-66; asst. prof. philosophy and theology Assumption Coll., 1966-67, assoc. prof., 1967-71, prof. religious studies, 1969-71, v.p., acad. dean, coordinator acad. affairs, 1968-71; co-dir. ecumenical Inst. Religious Studies, 1967-71; Minister theol. studies First Baptist Ch., Worcester, Mass., 1966-71; pres. Chautauqua (N.Y.) Instn., 1971-77; lectr. State U. N.Y., 1972-77, prof. philosophy, dean for arts and humanities, dir. internat. edn., 1977-80; theologian-in-residence First Presbyn. Ch., Jamestown, N.Y., 1974-80; pres. Alma (Mich.) Coll., 1980-87, prof. philosophy and religion, 1980-87; pres., prof. philosophy Westminster Coll., New Wilmington, Pa., 1987-95, chancellor, 1995—; bd. dirs. Integra North Bank, Titusville, Pa. Author: Value in the Thought of Paul Tillich; Christianity and Other Major Religions, 1968, India and Hinduism, 1968, Responding to God's Call, 1970, The Hidden Crisis in Education, 1971. Pres. Worcester Area Coun. Chs., 1970-71; mem., chmn. Mich. Coun. for the Arts, 1981-87; mem. N.Y. State Coun. on the Arts, 1983-87; mem., chmn. Pa. Coun. on Arts, 1990—; mem. Hoyt Inst. for Arts; bd. dirs. Found. for Ind. Colls. Inc., Jameson Hosp.; bd. dirs., chmn. Pa. Assn. Colls. and Univs.; mem. exec. com., chmn. Pa. Commn. for Ind. Colls. and Univs.; mem. exec. com., chmn. Assn. Presbyn. Colls. and Univs., 1992—. Mem. Am. Philos. Assn., Soc. Advancement Continuing Edn. for Ministry, Am. Assn. for Advancement of Humanities, Paul Tillich Soc. N.Am., Deutsche Paul-Tillich-Gesellschaft, Am. Assn. Higher Edn., Soc. Sci. Study Religion, Am. Acad. Religion, N.Am. Acad. Ecumenists, Soc. for Arts, Religion and Contemporary Culture, Assn. Presbyn. Colls. and Univs. (exec. com., vice chmn.), Nat. Assn. Ind. Colls. and Univs. (commn. on fins., higher edn.), Lawrence County C. of C. (past pres.). Home: 521 S New Castle St New Wilmington PA 16142-1426 Office: Westminster Coll South Market St New Wilmington PA 16172-0001 *The striving for excellence cannot be limited to a single discipline, task, or job. It involves a commitment of such intensity that the quest for excellence must be regarded as a way of life. I have taken a great deal of inspiration from both great artists and athletes whose achievements tell us that even if excellence cannot be readily defined, there is no way it can be approximated or achieved without self-discipline, dedication and commitment.*

REMINE, WILLIAM HERVEY, JR., surgeon; b. Richmond, Va., Oct. 11, 1918; s. William Hervey and Mabel Inez (Walthall) ReM.; m. Doris Irene Grumbacher, June 9, 1943; children: William H., Stephen Gordon, Walter James, Gary Craig. B.S. in Biology, U. Richmond, 1940, D.Sc. (hon.), 1965; M.D., Med. Coll. Va., Richmond, 1943; M.S. in Surgery, U. Minn., Mpls., 1952. Diplomate Am. Bd. Surgery. Intern Doctor's Hosp., Washington, 1944; fellow in surgery Mayo Clinic, Rochester, Minn., 1944-45, 47-52; instr. surgery Mayo Grad. Sch. Medicine, Rochester, Minn., 1954-59, asst. prof. surgery, 1959-65, assoc. prof. surgery, 1965-70, prof. surgery, 1970-83, prof. surgery emeritus, 1983—; surg. cons. to surgeon gen. U.S. Army, 1965-75; surg. lectr., USSR, 1987, 89, Japan, 1988, 90, Egypt, 1990; lectr. Soviet-Am. seminars, USSR, 1987, 89. Sr. author: Cancer of the Stomach, 1964, Manual of Upper Gastro-intestinal Surgery, 1985; editor: Problems in General Surgery, Surgery of the Biliary Tract, 1986; mem. editorial bd. Rev. Surgery, 1965-75, Jour. Lancet, 1968-77; contbr. 200 articles to profl. jours. Served to capt. U.S. Army, 1945-47. Recipient St. Francis surg. award St. Francis Hosp., Pitts., 1976, disting. service award Alumni Council, U. Richmond, 1976. Mem. ACS, AAAS, Am. Assn. History of Medicine, AMA, Am. Med. Writers Assn., Am. Soc. Colon and Rectal Surgeons, Soc. Surgery Alimentary Tract (v.p. 1983-84), Am. Surg. Assn., Assn. Mil. Surgeons U.S., Internat. Soc. Surgery, Digestive Disease Found., Priestley Soc. (pres. 1968-69), Central Assn. Physicians and Dentists (pres. 1972-73), Central Surg. Assn., Soc. Med. Cons. Armed Forces, Mayo Clinic Surg. Soc. (chmn. 1964-66), Soc. Head and Neck Surgeons, Soc. Surg. Oncology, So. Surg. Assn., Western Surg. Assn. (pres. 1979-80), Minn. State Med. Assn., Minn. Surg. Soc. (pres. 1966-67), Zumbro Valley Med. Soc., Sigma Xi; hon. mem. Colombian Coll. Surgeons, St. Paul Surg. Soc., Flint Surg. Soc., Venezuelan Surg. Soc., Colombian Soc. Gastroenterology, Dallas So. Clin. Soc., Ga. Surg. Soc., Soc. Postgrad. Surgeons Los Angeles County, Japanese Surg. Soc., Argentine Surg. Digestive Soc., Bassanese Surg. Assn. (Italy), Tex. Surg. Soc., Omicron Delta Kappa, Alpha Omega Alpha, Beta Beta Beta, Kappa Sigma. Methodist. Avocations: hunting, fishing, golf, photography, boating, music. Home: Sawgrass Players Club 8212 Seven Mile Dr Ponte Vedra Beach FL 32082-3129

REMINGER, RICHARD THOMAS, lawyer; b. Cleve., Apr. 3, 1931; s. Edwin Carl and Theresa Henrietta (Bookmyer) R.; m. Billie Carmen Greer, June 26, 1954; children: Susan Greer, Patricia Allison, Richard Thomas. A.B., Case-Western Res. U., 1953; J.D., Cleve.-Marshall Law Sch., 1957. Bar: Ohio 1957, Pa. 1978, U.S. Supreme Ct. 1961. Personnel and safety dir. Motor Express, Inc., Cleve., 1954-58; mng. ptnr. Reminger & Reminger Co., L.P.A., Cleve., 1958-90; mem. nat. claims couns. adv. bd. Comml. Union Assurance Co., 1980-90; lectr. transp. law Fenn Coll., 1960-62; lectr. bus. law Case Western Res. U., 1962-64; lectr. products liability U. Wirtschaft at Schloss Gracht, Erfstadt-Liblar, Germany, 1990-91, Bar Assn. City of Hamburg, Germany, 1990; mem. faculty Nat. Inst. for Trial Advocacy, 1992. Mem. joint com. Cleve. Acad. Medicine-Greater Cleve. Bar Assn.; trustee Cleve. Zool. Soc., mem. exec. com., 1984-89, v.p., 1987-89; trustee Andrew Sch., 1984-96; Meridia Huron Hosp., Cleve., Cleve. Sch. for Blind, 1987-88, Cerebral Palsy Assn., 1984-87; trustee Intracoastal Health Sys., Palm Beach, Fla., 1992—. With AC, USNR, 1950-58. Named Man of Yr. Cleve.-Marshall Law Sch., 1989. Mem. ABA (com. on law and medicine, profl. responsibility com. 1977-90), FBA, ATLA, Fedn. Ins. and Corp. Counsel, Internat. Bar Assn., Ohio Bar Assn. (coun. dels. 1987-90, internat. law com. 1990-91), Pa. Bar Assn., Cleve. Bar Assn. (chmn. med.-legal com. 1978-79, profl. liability com. 1977-90), Transp. Lawyers Assn., Cleve. Assn. Civil Trial Attys., Am. Soc. Hosp. Attys., Soc. Ohio Hosp. Attys., Ohio Assn. Civil Trial Attys., Am. Judicature Soc., Def. Rsch. Inst., Maritime Law Assn. U.S., Am. Coll. Law and Medicine, 8th Jud. Bar Assn. (life Ohio dist.), Internat. Ins. Law Soc., Oil Painters Am., Internat. Soc. Marine Painters (profl. mem., v.p.), Lost Tree Property Owners Assn., Mayfield Country Club (pres. 1980-82), Union Club, Hermit Club (pres. 1973-75), Lost Tree Club (bd. govs. 1991-94), Everglades Club (Fla.), Kirtland Counry Club, Rolling Rock Club (Pa.), The Bohemian Club (Calif.), Salmagundi Club (N.Y.C.).

REMINGTON, DEBORAH WILLIAMS, artist; b. Haddonfield, N.J., June 25, 1935; d. Malcolm Van Dyke and Hazel Irwin (Stewart) R. BFA, San Francisco Art Inst., 1957. Adj. prof. art Cooper Union, N.Y.C., 1973-97, NYU, 1994—. One-woman shows include Dilexi Gallery, San Francisco, 1962, 63, 65, San Francisco Mus. Art, 1964, Bykert Gallery, N.Y.C., 1967, 69, 72, 74, Galerie Darthea Speyer, Paris, 1968, 71, 73, 92, Pyramid Gallery, Washington DC, 1973, 76, zola-Leiberman Gallery, Chgo., 1976, Hamilton Gallery, N.Y.C., 1977, Portland (Oreg.) Ctr. for Visual Arts, 1977, Michael Berger Gallery, Pitts., 1979, Mary Ryan Gallery, N.Y.C., 1982, Ramon Osuna Gallery, Washington D.C., 1983, Newport Harbor Art Mus., 1983, Oakland (Calif.) Mus., 1984, Jack Shainman Gallery, N.Y.C., 1987, Shoshana Wayne Gallery, Los Angeles, 1988; group shows include Whitney Mus. Am. Art, N.Y.C., 1965, 67, 72, San Francisco Mus. Art, 1956, 60, 61, 63, 64, 65, Lausanne Mus., Switz., 1966, Fondation Maeght, St. Paul de Vence, France, 1968, Smithsonial Inst., Washington, D.C., 1968, Art. Inst., Chgo., 1974, Inst. Contemporary Art, Boston, 1975, Nat. Gallery Modern Art, Lisbon, Portugal, 1981, Toledo Mus. Art, 1975, The 6 Gallery, 1954-57, Natsoulas Gallery, Davis, Calif., 1990, 1st Trienalle des Ameriques Maubeuge, France, 1993, and numerous others; "Surveying the Century, American Drawings", curated by Paul Cummings for the American Federation of the Arts, travels to 4 museums in 1998; represented in permanent collections of Whitney Mus. Am. Art, Nat. Mus. Am. Art, Washington, Art Inst., Chgo., Centre d'Art et de Culture Georges Pompidou, Paris,Carnegie Mus., Pitts. Recipient Hassam and Speicher Purchase award Am. Acad. and Inst. Arts and Letters, 1988; NEA fellow, 1979-80; Tamarind Inst. fellow, 1973; Guggenheim fellow, 1984. Home and Studio: 309 W Broadway New York NY 10013-2226 *Be aware of yourself, aware of what makes you distinctive from others, and make those individual characteristics part of your work, whatever that may be. Read philosophy. Develop your own. This gives you ballast when the pendulum swings too far in one direction.*

REMINGTON, PAUL JAMES, mechanical engineer, educator; b. Plainfield, N.J., Mar. 19, 1943; s. Elmer Joseph and Genevieve Leona (Kehoe) R.; m. Lynne Louise Harris, Aug. 21, 1965; children: Christopher, Alexander. BSME, MSME, MIT, 1966, PhD, 1970. Prin. engr. Bolt Beranek & Newman Inc., Cambridge, Mass., 1969—; adj. prof. mech. engring. Boston U., 1995; vis. lectr. Tufts U., Medford, Mass., 1979; vis. scientist Tech. U. Berlin, 1990; organizer 3rd Internat. Workshop on Rlwy. and Tracked Transit System Noise, 1981. Contbr. chpts. to: Handbook of Machine Design, 1986, Transportation Noise Reference Book, 1987, Handbook of Acoustics, 1995, also articles to profl. publs. Recipient Cert. of Recognition, NASA, 1976, Excellence in Presentation award Soc. Automotive Engrs., 1984. Fellow Acoustical Soc. Am. (assoc. editor jour. 1982—, nominee Biennial award 1977); mem. ASME, Tau Beta Pi, Pi Tau Sigma (pres. 1964-65). Achievements include development of basic understanding of rolling noise generation, development of approaches for controlling wheel/rail noise from trains. Avocations: hiking, downhill and cross-country skiing, tennis, cabinet making. Office: BBN Sys and Technologies 10 Moulton St Cambridge MA 02138-1119

REMIS, SHEPARD M., lawyer; b. Boston, Apr. 20, 1943. AB, Bowdoin Coll., 1964; LLB, Columbia U., 1967. Bar: Mass. 1967, U.S. Dist. Ct. Mass. 1969, U.S. Ct. Appeals (1st cir.) 1973, U.S. Supreme Ct. 1977, U.S. Ct. Appeals (5th cir.) 1984, U.S. Ct. Appeals (3d cir.) 1985, U.S. Ct. Appeals (4th and 11th cirs.) 1986. Atty. Goodwin, Procter & Hoar, Boston. City councillor Peabody, Mass., 1972-75. Mem. ABA (mem. litigation sect.), Mass. Bar Assn., Boston Bar Assn., Def. Rsch. Inst. Office: Goodwin Proctor & Hoar Exchange Pl Boston MA 02109

REMKE, RICHARD EDWIN, lumber company executive; b. Cin., Mar. 26, 1943; s. Howard A. and Elizabeth I. (Rothert) R.; m. Kathryn France, May 26, 1973. BS in Indsl. Mgmt., U. CIn., 1966; MBA, Ohio State U., 1969. V.p. Weidemann Industries, Pinellas Park, Fla., 1983-85, Weiss-Hamilton, Largo, Fla., 1985-91, Deck & Docks Lumber Co., Saint Petersburg, Fla., 1991—; instr. U. South Fla., Saint Petersburg, 1986-94. Tampa Coll., Saint Petersburg, 1992-93. Home: 2011 Michigan Ave NE Saint Petersburg FL 33703-3407 Office: Decks & Docks 4801 95th St N Saint Petersburg FL 33708-3725

REMLEY, AUDREY WRIGHT, retired educational administrator, psychologist; b. Warrenton, Mo., Dec. 26, 1931; d. Leslie Frank and Irene Lesetta (Graue) Wright; m. Alvin Remley, Mar. 25, 1951 (dec. Mar. 1986); children: Steven Leslie, David Mark. AA, Hannibal-LaGrange Coll., 1951; BS in Edn. cum laude, U. Mo., 1963, MA, 1969, PhD, 1974; LHD (hon.) Westminster Coll., 1996. Lic. psychologist, Mo; cert. health svc. provider, Mo. Asst. prof. psychology Westminster Coll., Fulton, Mo., 1969-74, assoc. prof., 1975-88, prof., 1988-95, prof., assoc. dean faculty, 1989-95, chmn. dept. psychology, 1975-78, dir. counseling svcs., 1975-79, dir. student devel., 1979-80, dir. acad. advising and counseling svcs., 1980-88; owner It's A Crock Antiques; cons. OVID Bell Press, 1988-89; mem. adv. bd. Callaway Cmty. Hosp., 1988-95, pres. 1992-95; bd. dirs. Serve, Inc., Fulton, 1989-95, pres. 1991-93; mem. adv. bd. social learning program Fulton State Hosp., chair, 1992-94, mng. county govt. task force fin. mgmt. chair; bd. dirs. Ctrl. Mo. Food Bank. Recipient Outstanding Young Woman of Am. award Jaycettes, 1965, Athena award, 1991; NDEA fellow, 1968. Mem. APA, AACD, Am. Coll. Pers. Assn. (exec. coun. 1982-85, co-editor ACPA Developments, 1984-87, v.p. state divs., 1987-89, treas.-elect 1990-91, treas., 1991-93, treas. ednl. found. bd., 1994—, Outstanding State Div. Leader 1982, profl. svc. award 1991, Annuit Coeptis awrd 1994), Mo. Coll. Pers. Assn. (pres. 1981-82, profl. svc. award 1987), Mo. Psychol. Assn. (lic.), Kiwanis (exec. bd. 1989-92, v.p. 1992, pres.-elect 1992-93, pres. 1993-94, disting. 1995). Presbyterian. Avocations: singing; antique collecting; knitting.

REMLEY, THEODORE PHANT, JR., counseling educator, lawyer; b. Eustis, Fla., Feb. 7, 1947; s. Theodore Phant Sr. and Era Annie (Forehand) R. BA, U. Fla., 1969, EdS, 1971, PhD, 1980; JD, Catholic U., 1980. Bar: Va. 1981, Fla. 1982; lic. profl. counselor, Va., Miss., La. Exec. dir. Am. Counseling Assn., Alexandria, Va., 1990-94; prof. counseling U. New Orleans, 1994—. Contbr. articles to profl. jours., chpts. to books. Mem. Am. Counseling Assn., Am. Assn. State Counseling Bds. Democrat. Roman Catholic. Home: 3800 Camp St New Orleans LA 70115-2629 Office: Dept Edn Leadership Counseling & Founds U New Orleans New Orleans LA 70148

REMNICK, DAVID J., journalist; b. Hackensack, N.J., Oct. 29, 1958; s. Edward C. and Barbara (Seigel) R.; m. Esther B. Fein; children: Alexander, Noah. AB, Princeton U., 1981. Reporter The Washington Post, 1982-91; staff writer The New Yorker, N.Y.C., 1992—; vis. fellow Coun. Fgn. Rels., N.Y.C., 1992-94. Author: Lenin's Tomb: The Last Days of the Soviet Empire, 1993 (Pulitzer Prize for gen. non-fiction 1994, George Polk award 1994). Recipient Livingston award, 1991, Helen Bernstein award N.Y. Pub. Libr., 1994. Home: 322 W 72nd St New York NY 10023-2676 Office: The New Yorker 20 W 43rd St New York NY 10036-7400*

REMPEL, GARRY LLEWELLYN, chemical engineering educator, consultant; b. Regina, Sask., Can., Aug. 20, 1944; s. Henry Jacob and Grace Violet (Pullman) R.; m. Flora Tak Tak Ng, Sept. 20, 1975. BSc with 1st class honours, U. B.C., Vancouver, Can., 1965, PhD in Catalysis, 1968. Nat. Rsch. Coun. Can. postdoctoral fellow Imperial Coll. Sci. and Tech., London, 1968-69; asst. prof. chem. engring. U. Waterloo, 1969-73, assoc. prof., 1973-80, prof., 1980—, chmn. dept., 1988-96, mem. faculty dept. chemistry, 1976—, cons. Inst. for Polymer Rsch., 1984—, bd. dirs. Waterloo Ctr. for Process Devel., 1988-90; vis. scientist Inst. for Catalysis Rsch., Nat. Ctr. Sci. Rsch., Lyon, France, 1978; vis. rsch. fellow dept. chemistry U. Chgo., 1978-79; dir. applied scis. divsn. Royal Soc. Can.; mem. grant selection com. in chem. and metall. engring. Natural Scis. and Engring. Rsch. Coun., 1992-95; mem. sci. program com. Ont. Ctr. for Materials Rsch., 1991-95, acad. leader polymers and plastic program mgmt. com., 1992-95; cons. Polysar Rubber Corp., Sarnia, Ont., 1981-95, Rempel Rsch. Inc., Waterloo, 1981, Ortho McNeil Inc., Toronto, 1992—, Bayer Rubber Inc., Sarnia, 1995—. Contbr. over 140 articles to profl. jours.; patentee for novel catalyst sys. and methods of preparation, polymer hydrogenation processes, oxidation of polythionates, gas consumption measuring sys., amine modified hydrogeneration of nitrile rubber, nitrile rubber hydrogenation, hydrogenation of nitrile rubber, catalytic hydrogenation of nitrile rubber, catalytic solution hydrogenation of nitrile rubber. Grantee Nat. Scis. and Engring. Rsch. Coun., 1987-88, 90, 92-95, Polysar Ltd., 1987-88, Province of Ont. URIF, 1987-88, 90-92, 93, Nova Husky, 1989-91, Polysar Rubber Corp., 1989-92, 95, Ortho McNeil Inc., 1992-93; recipient Best Rsch. Paper award U. Waterloo Dept. Chem. Engring., 1988, 93, Univ.-Industry Rsch. Partnership award Conf. Bd. Can., 1995, Macromolecular Sci. and Engineering Lectr. award The Chemical Inst. of Can., 1997. Fellow Royal Soc. Can. (Thomas W. Eadie medal 1993), Chem. Inst. Can.; mem. AIChE, Can. Soc. for Chem. Engring. (award in indsl. practice 1994), Am. Chem. Soc., Soc. Chem. Industry. Office: U Waterloo, Dept Chem Engring, Waterloo, ON Canada N2L 3G1

REMSEN, CHARLES CORNELL, III, microbiologist, educator, research administrator; b. Newark, N.J., May 16, 1937; s. Charles Cornell Jr. and Elizabeth Havens (Atwood) Remsen; children: David Pratt, Linda Remsen Brandenburg, Stephen Dwyer, Andrew Walker; m. Margaret Ellis Fairchild, June 19, 1976; stepchildren: Elizabeth Hoffman Herzog, Jennifer Hoffman Jonas. BS in Food Chemistry and Microbiology, Delaware Valley Coll. Sci. and Agr., 1960; MS in Microbiology, Syracuse U., 1963, PhD in Microbiology, 1965. Rsch. asst. Schering Pharm., Bloomfield, N.J., 1959-60; rsch. asst. dept. preventive medicine Upstate Med. Ctr., Syracuse, N.Y., 1961-63; grad. teaching asst. Syracuse U., 1962-63, grad. rsch. asst., 1963-65; NIH post-doctoral fellow dept. gen. biology Swiss Fed. Inst. Tech., Zurich,

Switzerland, 1965-67; asst. scientist Woods Hole (Mass.) Oceanographic Inst., 1967-71, assoc. scientist, 1971-75; rsch. assoc. in microbial ecology Marine Biol. Labs., Woods Hole, 1973-74; assoc. prof. dept. zoology/microbiology, assoc. scientist Ctr. Great Lakes Studies U. Wis., Milw., 1975-83, prof., sr. scientist, 1983—, coord. zoology/microbiology, 1976-84, acting dir. Ctr. Great Lakes Studies, Great Lakes Rsch. Facility, 1987-89, interim dir., 1987-89, dir., 1989—; mem. editorial bd. Jour. of Bacteriology, 1969-77; external examiner McGill U. Grad. Sch., 1971-73; chmn. joint com. for biol. oceanography MIT-WHOI PhD Program, 1971-74; mem. internat. adv. bd. ScienceQuest. Author: (with others) The Encyclopedia of Microscopy and Microtechnique, 1973, Effect of the Ocean Environment on Microbial Activities, 1974, The Phytosynthetic Bacteria, 1978, Responses of Marine Organisms to Pollutants, 1984, Structure of Photosynthetic Prokaryotes, 1991; contbr. articles to profl. jours. Del. Coun. on Ocean Affairs. Recipient NIH Foreign Postdoctoral fellowship, 1965-67, Disting. Svc. award Jour. of Bacteriology, 1977. Mem. Nat. Assn. Marine Labs. (exec. com.), Am. Geophys. Union, Am. Soc. for Microbiology, Internat. Assn. for Great Lakes Rsch., Coun. Great Lakes Rsch. Mgrs. (internat. joint commn.), N.E. Assn. Marine Labs. (co-v.p.), N.E. Assn. Marine and Great Lakes Labs., Nature Conservancy (bd. trustees Wis. chpt. 1987, exec. com. 1989—, sec. 1989—), Sigma Xi. Achievements include research in relating the structure of chemolithotrophs to their ecological niche, and to their response to the environment, methane-oxidizing bacteria and how these microorganisms fit into the overall carbon cycle in the Great Lakes, the study of sediment samples from Lakes Superior, Michigan and Huron in order to determine the extent and rate of organic matter diagenesis in sediments, the exchange of gases (CO_2, CH_4, O_2) with overlying waters and ultimately the atmosphere, the ecological role and significance of chemosynthesis and photosynthesis in sublacustrine hydrothermal vents and gas fumaroles. Office: University of Wisconsin Mil Ctr for Great Lakes Studies Milwaukee WI 53201

RENARD, KENNETH GEORGE, civil engineer; b. Sturgeon Bay, Wis., May 5, 1934; s. Harry Henry and Margaret (Buechner) R.; m. Virginia Rae Heibel, Sept 8, 1956; children: Kenlynn T., Craig G., Andrew T. BCE, U. Wis., 1957, MCE, 1959; PhD in Civil Engring., U. Ariz., 1972. Registered profl. civil engr., Ariz. Hydraulic engr. Agrl. Rsch. Svc., USDA, Madison, Wis., 1957-59; resident engr. Agrl. Rsch. Svc., USDA, Tombstone, Ariz., 1959-64; rsch. hydraulic engr. Agrl. Rsch. Svc., USDA, Tucson, 1964-72, rsch. leader, 1972-87, rsch. hydraulic engr., 1987-95, collaborator, 1995—; adj. prof. agrl. and biosys. engring. U. Ariz., Tucson, 1990—. Contbr. articles to profl. jours. Fellow ASCE (pres. Ariz. sect. 1981, exec. com. irrigation and drainage divsn. 1987—, chair 1990, mgmt. group D 1991—, editor Jour. Irrigation and Drainage Engring. 1983-85, John C. Park award 1987, Arid Lands Hydraulic Engr. award 1992), Soil Conservation Soc. Am. (pres. Ariz. sect. 1975, Conservationist of Yr. 1983), Am. Geophys. Union; mem. Lions (pres. Tombstone chpt. 1963). Roman Catholic. Home: 4822 E Paseo Del Bac Tucson AZ 85718-6708 Office: USDA Agrl Rsch Svc 2000 E Allen Rd Tucson AZ 85719-1520

RENAUD, BERNADETTE MARIE ELISE, author; b. Ascot Corner, Que., Can., Apr. 18, 1945; d. Albert and Aline (Audet) R. Diploma, Présentation de Marie, Granby, Que., 1962-64. Librarian asst. Schs. of Waterloo, Que., 1964-67; tchr. primary schs. Schs. of Waterloo, 1967-70; adminstrv. sec. Assn. Medi-Tech-Sci., Montreal, Que., 1972-76. Author: Emilie La Baignoire A Pattes, 1976 (Can. Coun. Children's Lit. prize 1976, Assn. Advancement of Scis. and Technics of Documentation award 1976); adaptations of 8 children's classics, 1977; 20 Short Stories for Young Children, 1978, 79, 80, Le Chat de l'Oratoire, 1978, Emilie la baignoire à pattes album, 1978, La maison tête de pioche, 1979, La révolte de la courte pointe, 1979; mem. adminstrv. bd.: Communication-Jeunesse, 1977-82, Consil culturel de la Montérègie, 1987-90; author: La dèpression de l'ordinateur, 1981, Une boîte Magique Très Embêtante, 1981, The Cat in the Cathedral, 1983, La grande question de Tomatelle, 1982, The Computer Revolts, 1984, Comment on fait un livre?, 1983; author (book and movie) Bach et Bottine, 1986 (awards for movie, 19 awards across the world, transl. into 8 langs., and subtitled into 18 langs.); (novel) Un Homme Comme Tant d'Autres, tome I 1992, tome II, 1993, tome III, 1994; (short movie for Nat. Film Bd. of Can.) Quand l'accent devient grave, 1989; dir., coord. Écrire pour la jeunesse project, 1990, La quete de Kurweena, 1997, Le petit violon muet, 1997.

RENCIS, JOSEPH JOHN, engineering educator, mechanical/civil engineer; b. Denville, N.J., May 19, 1958; s. Joseph John and Leila Jean (Colin) R.; m. Minerva Vasquez, Sept. 14, 1991; 1 child, Christina. AAS in Archtl. & Bldg. Constrn. Engring., Milw. (Wis.) Sch. Engring., 1978, BS in Archtl. & Bldg. Constrn. Engring., 1980; MS in Theoretical & Applied Mechanics, Northwestern U., 1982; PhD in Engring. Mechanics, Case Western Res. U., 1985. Registered profl. engr., Mass. Engring. technician U.S. Army Armament Rsch., Devel. and Engring. Ctr., Picatinny Arsenal, N.J., summer 1979; instr., grader dept. archtl. & bldg. constrn. engring. tech. Milw. (Wis.) Sch. Engring., 1979-80; rsch. asst. dept. civil engring. Northwestern U., Evanston, Ill., 1980-81; rsch. and tchg. asst. dept. civil engring. Case Western Res. U., Cleve., 1982-85; grad. student rschr. Flight Dynamics Lab. Wright-Patterson AFB, Dayton, Ohio, summer 1984; instr. engring. tech. dept. Cuyahoga C.C., Cleve., 1984; asst. prof. mech. engring. dept. Worcester (Mass.) Poly. Inst., 1985-90, assoc. prof. mech. engring. dept., 1990-95, assoc. prof., Russel M. Searle disting. instr. mech. engring., 1994—; engring. cons. Brooks Sci., Inc., Cambridge, Mass., 1986-89; ASEE-NASA faculty fellow NASA-Lewis Rsch. Ctr., Cleve., summers 1989, 90; rsch. assoc. Phillips Lab., Geophysics Directorate, Space Sys. Tech. br., Hanscom AFB, Mass., summer 1991; mem. adv. bd. for engring. tech. Sussex County Vocat. Tech. H.S., Sparta, N.J., 1994—. Mem. editl. bd. Boundary Elements Commn., 1989—, Engring. Analysis with Boundary Elements, 1993—; asssoc. editor Advances in Boundary Elements, 1996—; contbr. articles to profl. jours. Recipient Class of 1980 Outstanding Alumni award Milw. (Wis.) Sch. Engring., 1990, Citizen of the Yr. award West Boylston (Mass.) Sch. Sys., 1992; Walter P. Murphy fellow Northwestern U., Evanston, 1980-81. Mem. ASME (sec. Ctrl. Mass. sect. 1988-89, vice-chair 1989-90, chair 1990-92), ASCE (structural divsn. com. on electronic computation, subcom. on personal computers and work stas. 1986-91), Internat. Soc. for Boundary Elements (sci. steering com. 1989—), Am. Soc. Engring. Edn., Am. Acad. Mechanics, Internat. Assn. for Boundary Element Methods, Pi Tau Sigma, Tau Omega Mu. Roman Catholic. Achievements include pioneering work on error estimation and self-adaptive mesh refinement technique for Boundary Element Method; research on iterative/direct equation solving strategies for Boundary Element Method. Home: 2 Keep Ave Paxton MA 01612-1038 Office: Worcester Poly Inst Mech Engring Dept 100 Institute Rd Worcester MA 01609-2247

RENDA, DOMINIC PHILLIP, airline executive; b. Steubenville, Ohio, Dec. 25, 1913; s. Joseph J. and Catherine (Roberta) R.; m. Delores E. Noland, July 12, 1980; children: Dominique Patricia, Dominic Phillip, Patrick Blake. B.S. in Bus. Adminstrn; J.D., Ohio State U., 1938. Bar: Ohio 1938. Practice law Steubenville, 1938-41; adminstrv. asst. to mem. Congress, 1941-42; with Western Air Lines, Inc., Los Angeles, 1946-68; asst. sec. Western Air Lines, Inc., 1947, v.p. legal, 1954-65, sr. v.p. legal, corp. sec., 1958-68; pres. Air Micronesia, Inc., Los Angeles, 1968-73; sr. v.p. internat. and pub. affairs Continental Air Lines, Inc., 1968-73; exec. v.p., dir., mem. exec. com. Western Air Lines, 1973-76, pres., mem. exec. and nominating coms., 1976-81, chief exec. officer, mem. mgmt. resources and compensation com., 1979-81, chmn. bd., 1981, emeritus chmn., 1982-85; dir. Bank of Montreal, Calif.; Mem. bus. adminstrn. adv. council Coll. Adminstrv. Sci., Ohio State U., 1974-82; bd. councilors Sch. Internat. Relations, U. So. Calif., 1967-82. Trustee Peace Found., Ponape, Caroline Islands, 1976-84; chmn. devel. com. Marymount High Sch., 1977-82. Served to lt. comdr. USNR, 1942-46. Mem. Calif., Ohio state bars, ABA, Los Angeles County Bar Assn. (past trustee), Calif. C. of C. (dir.), Phi Alpha Delta (pres. Los Angeles 1965-66). Clubs: Los Angeles Chancery (pres. 1966-67), Bel-Air Country, Calif.

RENDA, ROSA A., special education educator; b. Jamaica, N.Y., Nov. 3; d. Liborio and Josephine (Finamore) Lombardo; m. Philip F. Renda, Mar. 30, 1980; children: Felicia-Anne, Philip Jr. BA, Molloy Coll., 1971; MEd, St. John's U., Jamaica, N.Y., 1973; postgrad., L.I. U., 1977. Tchr., asst. prin. St. Rose of Lima, Massapequa, N.Y., 1967-73, Acad. of St. Joseph, Brentwood, N.Y., 1973-79; tchr. Sewanhaka H.S., Floral Park, N.Y., 1979-81, Queen of the Rosary Acad., Amityville, N.Y., 1981-86; tchr. Blessed Trinity, Ocala, Fla., 1987-93, math. coord., 1993-94; S.E.D. tchr. Emerald Ctr., Ocala, Fla., 1994; tchr./children's supr. for the emotionally/mentally disturbed Marion Citrus Mental Health, Ocala, 1994-96; tchr. for autistic children Maplewood Sch., Ocala, 1996—. Author: Teaching Metrics, 1975. Vol. Nassau County Rep. Club, Hempstead, N.Y., 1974-76. Mem. ASCD, NEA, Nat. Coun. Tchrs. Math., Nat. Cath. Edn. Assn., Marion Edn. Assn., Nassau/Suffolk Math. Tchrs., Women of the Moose, Columbiettes, K.C. Aux. Roman Catholic. Avocations: reading, swimming, gourmet cooking.

RENDALL, STEVEN FINLAY, language educator, editor, translator, critic; b. Geneva, Ill., May 2, 1939; s. Harvard John and Jessie Evangeline (Galbraith) R.; children from previous marriage: Matthew, Ruby Larisch; m. Lisa Dow Neal, May, 1992; 1 child, Josephine Dow Neal. BA summa cum laude in Philosophy, U. Colo., 1961; postgrad., Univ. de Lille, 1961-62, Johns Hopkins U., 1962-67; PhD, Johns Hopkins U., 1967. From asst. prof. romance langs. to assoc. prof. romance langs. U. Oreg., Eugene, 1967-79, prof. romance langs., 1979—; guest prof. Universität Konstanz, 1981; leader NEH summer seminar, 1987. Author: Distinguo: Reading Montaigne Differently, 1992; editor: Montaigne, 1984, Of History, 1994; translator: de Cesteau,The Practice of Everyday Life, 1984, History and Memory, 1992, Astrea, 1995, Hitler, 1996, Torments of Love, 1996, Shipwreck with Spectator, 1996; translator: Black Fire on White Fire: An Essay on Jewish Hermeneutics (Betty Rojtman), 1997, Pius XI's Hidden Encyclical: A Missed Opportunity to Confront Anti-Semitism (Georges Passelecq and Bernard Suchecky), 1997, Political Writings on the New Germany (Jurgen Habermas), 1997; co-editor: Comparative Literature, 1990—, assoc. editor 1978—, asst. editor, 1972-78, acting editor, 1980, 85-86; mem. editl. bd., adv. com. Montaigne Studies, 1989—; contbr. 40 articles to profl. jours., 37 book revs. Rsch. on Translation SUNY, Binghamton, 1993, Camargo Found. fellow, 1988, Alexander von Humboldt-Stiftung Rsch. fellow, 1980-82, 95, NEH fellow, 1977, Danforth fellow, 1962-67, Gilman fellow, 1964-67, Woodrow Wilson fellow, 1962-63; Fulbright scholar, 1961-62. Mem. Modern Lang. Assn., Phi Beta Kappa. Home: 3217 N 25th St Tacoma WA 98406-6115 Office: U Oregon 223 Friendly Hall Eugene OR 97403

RENDELL, EDWARD GENE, mayor, lawyer; b. N.Y.C., Jan. 5, 1944; s. Jesse T. and Emma (Sloat) R.; B.A. in Polit. Sci., U. Pa., 1965; J.D., Villanova (Pa.) U., 1968; m. Marjorie Osterlund, July 10, 1971; 1 son, Jesse Thompson. Admitted to Pa. bar, 1968, U.S. Supreme Ct., 1981; asst. dist. atty., chief homicide unit Office Dist. Atty. Phila., 1968-74; dep. spl. prosecutor Phila., 1976; dist. atty. Phila., 1978-86; mayor City of Phila., 1992—. Served as 2d lt. USAR, 1968-74. Recipient Man of Year award VFW, 1980, Am. Cancer League, 1981; Disting. Public Service award Pa. County Detectives Assn., 1981. Mem. Am. Bar Assn., Pa. Dist. Attys. Assn. (legis. chmn. 1979—), Phila. Bar Assn., United Jewish Orgns., Jewish War Vets, Democrat. Club: B'nai B'rith. Office: Office of the Mayor 215 City Hall Philadelphia PA 19107-3201*

RENDELL, KENNETH WILLIAM, rare and historical documents dealer, consultant; b. Boston, May 12, 1943; s. Harry H. and Pauline (Walsh) R.; m. Diana J. Angelo, June 3, 1967 (div. 1985); children: Jeffrey H., Jason J.; m. Shirley L. McNerney, July 14, 1985; 1 child, Julia Louise. Student, Boston U., 1961-63. Pres. Kingston Galleries, Inc., Somerville, Mass., 1960-67, Kenneth W. Rendell, Inc., Newton, Mass., 1967—, Kenneth W. Rendell, Ltd., London, 1970—, Kenneth W. Rendell Gallery, Inc., N.Y.C., Tokyo, 1985—; bd. dirs. John Wilson Autographs Ltd., London, 1961-75, Charles Ede Gallery Ltd., London, 1976-92; chmn. New England Antiquarian Booksellers Assn., 1975-77; pres. Internat. League Autograph and Manuscript Dealers, 1975-77; cons. numerous univ. librs., govtl. and media orgns. Author: The Fundamentals of Autograph Collecting, 1976, Tax Appraisals of Manuscript Collections, 1983, Changing Concepts of Value and Rarity, 1985, The Hitler Diaries: Bad Forgeries But a Great Hoax, 1986, The Mormon Conman, Forger and Killer, 1987, Other People's Mail: 30 Years As a Dealer in Historical Documents, 1988, The One Hundred Americans Who Have Made America What it is Today, 1989, The Detection of Forged Historical Letters and Documents, 1990, With Weapons and Wits: Propaganda and Psychological Warfare in World War II, 1991, Forging History: The Detection of Fake Historical Letters and Documents, 1994, History Comes to Life, 1995; co-editor: Autographs and Manuscripts: A Collector's Manual, 1978 (Outstanding Reference Book award ALA); contbr. numerous articles in field to mags. and profl. jours. Recipient Dept. Justice award, 1991. Fellow Manuscript Soc. (bd. dirs. 1968-74, pres. 1972-74); mem. Assn. Internat. de Bibliophilie Paris, Art and Antique Dealers League Am., Inc., Grolier Club, Union League Club, Army and Navy Club, India House, Am. Antiquarian Soc. Avocation: ski racing. Office: Kenneth W Rendell Inc 46 Eliot St Natick MA 01760-6042 also: 989 Madison Ave New York NY 10021-1825 also: PO Box 9001 Wellesley MA 02181-9001

RENDELL, MARJORIE O., federal judge; m. Edward G. Rendell. BA, U. Pa., 1969; postgrad., Georgetown U., 1970-71; JD, Villanova U., 1973; LLD (hon.), Phila. Coll. Textile and Sci., 1992. Ptnr. Duane, Morris & Heckscher, Phila., 1972-93; judge U.S. Dist. Ct. (ea. dist.) Pa., 1994—; asst. to dir. annual giving Dept. Devel., U. Pa., 1973-78; mem. adv. bd. Chestnut Hill Nat. Bank/East Falls Adv. Bd.; mem. alternative dispute resolution com. mediation divsn. Ea. Dist. Pa. Bankruptcy Conf. Active Acad. Vocal Arts, Market St. East Improvement Assn., Pa.'s Campaign for Choice, Phila. Friends Outward Bound; vice chair Ave. of Arts, Inc.; vice chair bd. trustees Vis. Nurse Assn. Greater Phila. Mem. ABA, Am. Bankruptcy Inst., Pa. Bar Assn., Phila. Bar Assn. (bd. dirs. young lawyers sect. 1973-78), Phila. Bar Found. (bd. dirs.), Forum Exec. Women, Internat. Women's Forum, Phi Beta Kappa. Office: US Courthouse 601 Market St Rm 3114 Philadelphia PA 19106-1713*

RENDELL-BAKER, LESLIE, anesthesiologist, educator; b. St. Helens, Eng., Mar. 27, 1917; came to U.S., 1957, naturalized, 1963; s. Frank Nelder and Ada (Gill) Rendell-B.; m. Rosemary Carr Hogg, Aug. 17, 1946; children: Sheila Diane, Helen Rosemary, Frances Nelda. BS, MB, Guy's Hosp. Med. Sch., London, 1941. Diplomate: Am. Bd. Anesthesiology. Resident anesthesia Brit. Army of Rhine Hosps., 1945-46, Guy's Hosp., London, 1946-48; sr. asst. (assoc. prof.) anesthesiology Welsh Nat. Sch. Medicine, Cardiff, 1948-57; Fulbright asst. prof. anesthesiology U. Pitts., 1955-56; from asst. prof. to assoc. prof. Sch. Medicine Case Western Res. U., Cleve., 1957-62; dir. dept. anesthesiology Mt. Sinai Hosp., N.Y.C., 1962-79; prof., chmn. dept. anesthesiology Mt. Sinai Sch. Medicine, CUNY, 1966-79; prof. dept. anesthesiology Sch. Medicine Loma Linda (Calif.) U., 1979—; Chmn. sect. com. Z79 standards for anesthesia and respiratory equipment Am. Nat. Standards Instn., 1962-68, vice chmn., 1969-81, mem. exec. com. med. devices standards mgmt. bd., 1973-79, bd. dirs., 1976-79; chmn. classification panel on anesthesiology devices FDA, 1972-76. Author: (with W.W. Mushin) Principles of Thoracic Anesthesia, 1953, (with W.W. Mushin and Thompson) Automatic Ventilation of the Lungs, 3d edit., 1980, The Origins of Thoracic Anesthesia, 1991; editor: Problems with Anesthetic and Respiratory Therapy Equipment, 1982, Maintenance, Cleaning and Sterilization of Anesthetic Equipment, 1997, Future Directions in Anesthesia Apparatus, 1997, The History and Evolution of Pediatric Anesthesia Equipment, 1992; author (with others) The Care of Anesthesia Equipment, 1992. Served to capt. Royal Army Med. Corps, 1942-46. Fellow Royal Coll. Anaesthetists; fellow Royal Soc. Medicine, Assn. Anaesthetists Gt. Britain and Ireland; mem. Am. Soc. Anesthesiologists (chmn. com. equipment and standardization 1962-68), Am. Soc. for Testing and Materials (chmn. subcom. D10-34 1981-91), Assn. Advancement Med. Instrumentation , AAAS. Inventor baby endotracheal connector, pediatric face masks and equipment. Home: 630 Beauregard Cres Redlands CA 92373-5602 Office: Loma Linda U Sch Medicine Dept Anesthesiology 11234 Anderson St Loma Linda CA 92354-2804

RENDER, ARLENE, ambassador. Joined Fgn. Svc., Dept. State, 1970; consular officer Fgn. Svc., Dept. State, Abidjan, Cote D'Ivoire, 1971-73, Tehran, Iran, 1973-76, Genoa, Italy, 1976-78; polit. officer Fgn. Svc., Dept. State, 1978-79, internat. rels. officer AF/C, 1979-81; dep. chief of mission Fgn. Svc., Dept. State, Brazzaville, Republic of the Congo, 1981-84; consulgen. Fgn. Svc., Dept. State, Kingston, Jamaica, 1984-86; dep. chief of mission Fgn. Svc., Dept. State, Accra, Ghana, 1986-89; mem. sr. seminar Fgn. Svc., Dept. State, 1989-90, amb. to The Gambia, 1990-93; dir. Office of Ctrl. African Affairs Fgn. Svc., Dept State, Washington, 1993—; amb. to Zambia, 1996—. Office: State Dept Office Ctrl African Affairs Washington DC 20520

RENDL-MARCUS, MILDRED, artist, economist; b. N.Y.C., May 30, 1928; d. Julius and Agnes (Hokr) Rendl. BS, NYU, 1948, MBA, 1950; PhD, Radcliffe Coll., 1954; m. Edward Marcus, Aug. 10, 1956. Economist, GE, 1953-56, Bigelow-Sanford Carpet Co., Inc., 1956-58; lectr. econs. evening sessions CCNY, 1953-58; rsch. investment problems in tropical Africa, 1958-59; instr. econs. Hunter Coll. CUNY, 1959-60; lectr. econs. Columbia U., 1960-61; rsch. econ. devel. Nigeria, West Africa, 1961-63; sr. economist Internat. div. Nat. Indsl. Conf. Bd., 1963-66; asst. prof. Grad. Sch. Bus. Adminstrn., Pace Coll., 1964-66; assoc. prof. Borough of Manhattan C.C., CUNY, 1966-71, prof., 1972-85; vis. prof. Fla. Internat. U., 1986; prin. MRM Assocs., Rendl Fine Art; corp. art econ. and contemporary art cons.; fine arts appraiser; artist Allied Social Sci. Assn. Conf., Boston, 1994; participant Internat. Econ. Meeting, Amsterdam, 1968, Prague, Czech Republic, 1993, Brussels, 1994, Econs. of Fine Arts in Age of Tech., 1984, Internat. Economic Assn. N.Am., Laredo, Tex., 1987-88, London, 1994, Soc. Southwestern Economists, San Antonio, 1988, New Orleans, 1989, Dallas, 1989, Houston, 1991, Dallas, 1994, S.W. Soc. Economists, San Antonio, 1992, Dallas, 1994, San Diego, 1990, 92, Reno, 1991, Western Econ. Assn. Internat., 1990, Ind. U. Pa., 1990, London, 1992-93, Ariz. Sr. Acad., Tucson, 1995. Exhibited New Canaan Art Show, 1982-85, Am. Soc. of Bus. and Behavioral Scis, Las Vegas, 1996, New Canaan Soc. for Arts Ann., 1983, 85, New Canaan Arts, 1985, Silvermine Galleries, 1986, Stamford Art Assn., 1987, Women in the Arts at Phoenix Gallery, Group Show, N.Y.C., 1988, Parkview Point Gallery, Miami Beach, Fla., 1982-89, Art Complex, New Canaan, Miami Beach, 1985—; group shows include Lever House, N.Y.C., 1990, Cork Gallery, Lincoln Ctr., N.Y.C., 1990, Women's Caucus for Art, San Antonio, 1990, Artist's Equity, Broome St. Gallery, N.Y.C., 1991, Greater Hartford Architecture Conservancy, 1991; symposium participant Sienna, Italy, 1988, South Fla. Art Ctr., Miami Beach, 1990, 92-93, Wadsworth Atheneum, Hartford, Conn., 1994-95, Annual Barnum Festival, 1995-96, Discovery Mus., Bridgeport, Conn., 1995, 96, Art Comm. Internet, Phila., 1996-97. Bd. dirs. N.Y.C. Coun. on Econ. Edn., 1970—; mem. program planning com. Women's Econ. Roundtable, N.Y.C.; participant Eastern Econ. Assn., Boston, 1988, Art and Personal Property Appraisal, NYU, 1986-88. Recipient Disting. Svc. award CUNY, 1985; Dean Bernice Brown Cronkhite fellow Radcliffe Coll., 1950-51, Anne Radcliffe Econ. Rsch. Sub-Sahara Africa fellow, 1958-59. Fellow Gerontol. Assn.; mem. Internat. Schumpeter Econs. Soc. (founding), Comm. Internat. Internat., Am. (vice chmn. ann. meeting 1973), Met. (sec. 1954-56) econ. assns., Indsl. Rels. Rsch. Assn., Audubon Artists and Nat. Soc. Painters in Casein (assoc. 1987-88) Allied Social Sci. Assn. (vice chmn. conv. 1973, artist Boston nat. conv. 1994), AAUW, N.Y.C. Women in Arts, Allied Social Sci. Assn. (artist 1994), Women's Econ. Roundtable, Art Comm. Internat. (Phila.), Greater Hartford Architecture Conservancy, NYU Grad. Sch. Bus. Adminstrn. Alumni (sec. 1956-58), Radcliffe Club, Women's City Club (art and landmarks com.). Author: (with husband) Investment and Development of Tropical Africa, 1959, International Trade and Finance, 1965, Monetary and Banking Theory, 1965; Economics, 1969; (with husband) Principles of Economics, 1969; Economic Progress and the Developing World, 1970; Economics, 1978, Fine Art with Many Equilibrium Prices, 1995; also monographs and articles in field. Econ. and internat. rsch. on industrialization less developed areas, internat. debtor nations and workability of buffer stock schemes, pricing fine art; columnist economics of art, Art As An Investment, Money Substitute, or Consumer Durable Good Art Valuation; When Is A Price of Fine Art The Price?, Prices and Varied Appraisals, Fine Art with Many Equilibrium Prices: Price Distortion-A Segmented Market in Fine Art, Am. Soc. of Bus. and Behavioral Sci. (Las Vegas Ann. Meeting 1996); editor Women in the Arts Found. Newsletter, 1986-92; contbr. Coalition Womens Art Orgs., 1986-92, other profl. publs. Home: PO Box 814 New Canaan CT 06840-0814 Office: Art Complex PO Box 814 New Canaan CT 06840-0814 also: 7441 Wayne Ave Miami Beach FL 33141

RENDON-PELLERANO, MARTA INES, dermatologist; b. Sept. 19, 1957; d. Uriel and Rosa Rendon. BA and Scis., U. P.R., Mayaquez, 1977; postgrad., Autonoma U., Santo Domingo, Dominican Republic, 1977-79; MD, U. P.R., San Juan, 1982. Diplomate Am. Bd. Internal Medicine, Am. Bd. Dermatology; lic. physician, Fla., Tex., Pa., ACLS, Drug Enforcement Adminstrn. Intern and resident in internal medicine Albert Einstein Med. Ctr., Phila., 1982-85; resident in dermatology Parkland Meml. Hosp., Southwestern Med. Sch., Dallas, 1985-88; emergency rm. physician Pottsborough (Tex.) Med. Clinic, 1985-86; coord. dermatology clinic Kayser Permanente Med. Assn. Tex., Dallas, 1986-88; dermatology assoc. Dermatology Ctr., Dallas, 1988-89; staff physician Southwestern Med. Sch., Vets. Hosp., Dallas, 1988-89; clin. asst. prof. dept. deramtology U. Miami (Fla.) Sch. Medicine, 1989—; chief dept. dermatology Cleveland Clinic Fla., Ft. Lauderdale, 1989—; mem. adv. bd. South Fla. Vis. Lectureship Series, 1991-92; mem. rsch. bd. advisors Medecis Corp. Featured on TV shows and in popular mags.; contbr. articles to profl. jours., chpts. to books. Recipient Radio Klaridad award for best sci. work, Miami, 1990. Fellow Am. Acad. Dermatology; mem. ACP (assoc.), AAUW, Womens Med. Assn., Womens Dermatol. Soc., Cuban-Interam. Dermatol. Soc., Women of Spanish Origin, Tex. Med. Assn., Miami Dermatology Soc., Fla. Med. Assn., Broward Dermatology Soc., Broward County Med. Assn., Etta Gamma Delta. Roman Catholic. Avocations: swimming, music, writing, tennis. Office: Cleveland Clinic Fla 3000 W Cypress Creek Rd Fort Lauderdale FL 33309-1710

RENDU, JEAN-MICHEL MARIE, mining executive; b. Tunis, Tunisia, Feb. 25, 1944; s. Paul C. and Solange M. (Krebs) R.; m. Karla M. Meyer, Aug. 18, 1973; children: Yannick P., Mikaël P. Ingénieur des Mines, Ecole des Mines St. Etienne, France, 1966; MS, Columbia U., 1968, D. Engring. Sci., 1971. Mgr. ops. rsch. Anglovaal, Johannesburg, Republic of South Africa, 1972-76; assoc. prof. U. Wis., Madison, 1976-79; assoc. Golder Assocs., Denver, 1979-84; dir. tech. and sci. systems Newmont Mining Corp., Danbury, Conn., 1984-88; v.p. Newmont Gold Co., Denver, 1988—. Author: An Introduction to Geostatistical Methods of Mineral Evaluation, 1978, 81; contbr. tech. papers to profl. jours. Recipient Jackling award medal SMME, 1994, Pres.'s citation, 1993. Fellow South African Inst. of Mining and Metallurgy (corr. mem. of coun.); mem. NAE, N.Y. Acad. Sci., Internat. Assn. for Math. Geology, Soc. Mining Engrs., Sigma Xi. Roman Catholic. Office: Newmont Gold Co 1700 Lincoln St Denver CO 80203-4500

RENEAU, DANIEL D., university administrator. Prof., head dept. biomed. engring. La. Tech. U., Ruston, 1973-80, v.p. acad. affairs, 1980-87, pres., 1987—. Office: La Tech U Tech Station PO Box 3168 Ruston LA 71272

RENEBERG, RICHARD (RICHEY RENEBERG), professional tennis player; b. Phoenix, Oct. 5, 1965; m. Marget Reneberg, Nov. 16, 1991. Student, SMU, 1985-87. Ranked 10th U.S. Tennis Assn., 1991, ranked 8th U.S. Tennis Assn., 1993. Named All-American NCAA, 1985, 86, 87; winner of U.S. Open Men's Double Title (with Jim Grabb), 1992; mem. U.S. Davis Cup Team, 1993, (with Jared Palmer) Australian Open Men's Doubles Title, 1995, 8 U.S. Junior Titles, 2 Profl. Singles Titles. Office: US Tennis Assn 70 W Red Oak Ln White Plains NY 10604*

RENEE, LISABETH MARY, art educator, artist, galley director; b. Bklyn., July 28, 1952; d. Lino P. and Elizabeth M. (Dines) Rivano; m. John S. Witanowski, May 15, 1982. Student, U. Puget Sound, 1972-74; BA in Art, SUNY, Buffalo, 1977; MFA, L.I. U., 1982; EdD, U. Ctrl. Fla., 1996. Cert. art tchr., Fla. Adj. faculty L.I. U., Greenvale, N.Y., 1980-82, Rollins Coll., Winter Park, Fla., 1982; art tchr. Phyllis Wheatley Elem. Sch., Apopka, Fla., 1983-85, McCoy Elem. Sch., Orlando, Fla., 1985-86, Lake Howell H.S., Winter Park, Fla., 1986-93; adj. faculty U. Ctrl. Fla., 1994-95, vis. instr., coord. art edn., 1995-96; gallery dir., prof. West Campus Valencia (Fla.) C.C., 1996—; adj. faculty Valencia C.C., 1995-96; dir. So. Artists Registry, Winter Park, 1984-87; cons. Fla. Dept. Edn., 1989-90, mem. curriculum writing team for arts edn. program; mem. com. Fla. Bd. Edn. Task Force for Subject Area Subtest of Fla. Tech. Cert. Exam.; visual arts dir. Very Spl. Arts Ctr. Fla. Fest, 1996; presenter at profl. confs. Author: The Phenomenological Significance of Aesthetic Communion, 1996, Co-operative Art, 1991; editor: Children and the Arts in Florida, 1990. Visual arts dir. Very Spl. Arts Ctrl. Fla. Festival, 1995; mem. local Sch. Adv. Coun., Winter Park, 1992. Grantee Found. for Advancement of Cmty. Through Schs., 1991, Divsn. Blind Svcs. Invision, 1995, Tangelo Park Project, 1995; ACE scholar Arts Leadership Inst., 1993-96; recipient Tchr. Merit award Walt Disney World Co., 1990. Mem. NEA, ASCD, Nat. Art Edn. Assn., Fla. Art Edn.

Assn. (regional rep. 1989-94), Seminole County Art Edn. Assn., Coll. Art Assn., Caucus on Social Theory and Art Edn., Women's Caucus for Art, Phi Kappa Phi, Kappa Delta Pi. Home: 20 Cobblestone Ct Casselberry FL 32707-5410 Office: Valencia CC West Campus Humanities Dept MC 4-11 Orlando FL 32802

RENEHAN, ROBERT FRANCIS XAVIER, Greek and Latin educator; b. Boston, Apr. 25, 1935; s. Francis Xavier and Ethel Mary (Sullivan) R.; m. Joan Lee Axtell-Damerow, Sept. 9, 1966; children—Martin, Sharon, Stephen, Judith, John. A.B., Boston Coll., Chestnut Hill, Mass., 1956; A.M., Harvard, 1958, Ph.D., 1963. Instr. Greek and Latin U. Calif. at Berkeley, 1963-64; instr. Harvard U., 1964-65; asst. prof. Boston Coll., 1966-69, assoc. prof., 1969-71, prof., 1971-77, chmn. dept. classical studies, 1969-77; prof. Greek and Latin U. Calif. at Santa Barbara, 1976—, chmn. dept., 1984-88, 93—. Author: Greek Textual Criticism, 1969, Leo Medicus, 1969, Greek Lexicographical Notes, 1975, 2d series, 1982, Studies in Greek Texts, 1975; assoc. editor Classical Philology, 1976—, Am. Jour. Philology, 1987-95; sr. mem. editl. bd. Classical Antiquity, 1980-87, Revised Supplement to Liddell-Scott-Jones Greek-English Lexicon, 1987-96; contbr. articles to profl. jours. Nat. Endowment for Humanities Sr. fellow, 1972-73. Mem. Am. Philol. Assn., Soc. for Ancient Medicine. Office: Dept of Classics Univ of Calif Santa Barbara CA 93106

RENEKER, MAXINE HOHMAN, librarian; b. Chgo., Dec. 2, 1942; d. Roy Max and Helen Anna Christina (Anacker) Hohman; m. David Lee Reneker, June 20, 1964 (dec. Dec. 1979); children: Sarah Roeder, Amy Johannah, Benjamin Congdon. BA, Carleton Coll., 1964; MA, U. Chgo., 1970; DLS, Columbia U., 1992. Asst. reference libr. U. Chgo. Libraries, 1965-66; classics libr. U. Chgo. Libr., 1967-70, asst. head acquisitions, 1970-71, personnel libr., 1971-73; personnel/bus. libr. U. Colo. Libr., Boulder, 1978-80; asst. dir. sci. and engring. div. Columbia U., N.Y.C., 1981-85; assoc. dean of univ. librs. for pub. svcs. Ariz. State U. Libr., Tempe, 1985-89; dir. instrnl. and rsch. svcs. Stanford (Calif.) Univ. Librs., 1989-90; dir. info. svcs., dir. Dudley Knox Libr. Naval Postgrad. Sch., Monterey, Calif., 1993—; acad. libr. mgmt. intern Coun. on Libr. Resources, 1980-81; chmn. univ. librs. sect. Assn. Coll. and Rsch. Librs., 1989-90. Contbr. articles to profl. jours. Rsch. grantee Coun. on Library Resources, Columbia U., 1970-71, fellow, 1990-92. Mem. ALA, Am. Soc. Info. Sci., Sherlockian Scion Soc., Phi Beta Kappa, Beta Phi Mu. Home: 740 Dry Creek Rd Monterey CA 93940-4208 Office: Naval Postgrad Sch Dudley Knox Libr 411 Dyer Rd Monterey CA 93943-5198

RENFREW, CHARLES BYRON, oil company executive, lawyer; b. Detroit, Oct. 31, 1928; s. Charles Warren and Louise (McGuire) R.; m. Susan Wheelock, June 28, 1952 (div. June 1984); children: Taylor Allison Ingham, Charles Robin, Todd Wheelock, James Bartlett; m. Barbara Jones Orser, Oct. 6, 1984; 5 stepchildren. AB, Princeton U., 1952; JD, U. Mich., 1956. Bar: Calif. 1956. Assoc. Pillsbury, Madison & Sutro, San Francisco, 1956-65, ptnr., 1965-72, 81-82; U.S. dist. judge No. Dist. Calif., San Francisco, 1972-80; dep. atty. gen. U.S. Washington, 1980-81; instr. U. Calif. Boalt Hall Sch. Law, 1977-80; v.p. law Chevron Corp. (formerly Standard Oil Co. Calif.), San Francisco, 1983-93, also bd. dirs.; ptnr. LeBoeuf, Lamb, Greene & McRae, San Francisco, 1994—; mem. exec. com. 9th Cir. Jud. Conf., 1976-78, congl. liaison com. 9th Cir. Jud. Council, 1976-79, spl. com. to propose standards for admission to practice in fed. cts. U.S. Jud. Conf., 1976-79; chmn. spl. com. to study problems of discovery Fed. Jud. Ctr., 1978-79; mem. council on role of cts. U.S. Dept. Justice, 1978-83; mem. jud. panel Ctr. for Pub. Resources, 1981—; head U.S. del. to 6th UN Congress on Prevention of Crime and Treatment of Offenders, 1980; co-chmn. San Francisco Lawyers Com. for Urban Affairs, 1971-72, mem., 1983—; bd. dirs. Internat. Hospitality Ctr., 1961-74, pres., 1967-70; mem. adv. bd. Internat. Comparative Law Ctr., Southwestern Legal Found., 1983-93; trustee World Affairs Council No. Calif., 1984-87, 94—, Nat. Jud. Coll., 1985-91, Grace Cathedral, 1986-89. Contbr. articles to profl. jours. Bd. fellow Claremont U., 1986-94; bd. dirs. San Francisco Symphony Found., 1964-80, pres., 1971-72; bd. dirs. Coun. Civic Unity, 1962-73, pres., 1971-72; bd. dirs. Opportunity Through Ownership, 1969-72, Marin County Day Sch., 1972-74, No. Calif. Svc. League, 1975-76, Am. Petroleum Inst., 1984—, Nat. Crime Prevention Coun., 1982—; alumni trustee Princeton U., 1976-80; mem. vis. com. u. chgo. Law Sch., 1977-79, u.Mich. Law Sch., 1977-81; bd. visitors J. Reuben Clark Law Sch., Brigham Young U., 1981-83, Stanford Law Sch., 1983-86; trustee Town Sch. for Boys, 1972-80,pres. 1975-80; gov. San Fransciso Symphony Assn., 1974—; mem. nat. adv. bd. Ctr. for Nat. Policy, 1982—; bd. dirs. Nat. Coun. Crime and Deliquency, 1981-82,NAACP Legal Def. and Edn. Fund, 1982—; parish chancellor St. Luke's Episcopal Ch., 1968-71, sr. warden, 1974-76; mem. exec. coun. San Francisco Deanery, 1969-70; mem. diocesan coun. Episcopal Diocese of Calif., 1970; chmn. Diocesan Conv., 1977, 78, 79. Served with USN, 1946-48, 1st lt. U.S. Army, 1952-53. Fellow Am. Bar Found.; mem. ABA (coun. mem. sect. antitrust law 19778-82, vice c hmn. sect. antitrust law 1982-83), San Francisco Bar Assn. (past bd. dirs.), Assn. Gen. Counsel, State Bar Calif., Am. Judicature Soc., Am. Coll. Trial Lawyers (pres. 1995-96), Am. Law Inst., Coun. Fgn. Rels., Order of Coif, Phi Beta Kappa, Phi Delta Phi. Office: LeBoeuf Lamb Greene & MacRae 4th fl One Embarcadero Ctr San Francisco CA 94111

RENFREW, JOSEPH, communications technologist; b. Bogota, NJ, 1955; s. Paul Herbert and Josephine (Singleton) R.; m. Anna P. Adams, Nov., 1980; children: Paul, Ashley. BFA, Bergen C.C., NJ, 1976; MBA, Fairleigh Dickenson U, Teaneck, NJ, 1979. From designer to mgr. Sir Speedy Printers, Hackensack, NJ, 1976-86; mgr. Instant Printers Inc., Bismark, ND, 1986-94; mgmt. exec. Werik Printing and Design, Bismark, 1994—. Troop leader Boy Scouts of Am., 1988—. Mem. Designers Ink, Bismark art assn., Bismark C.of C. Avocations include: fine art, cycling, cooking. Office: Werik Printing and Design 2910 E Broadway Ave Bismarck ND 58501-5186

RENFREW, MALCOLM MACKENZIE, chemist, educator; b. Spokane, Wash., Oct. 12, 1910; s. Earl Edgar and Elsie Pauline (MacKenzie) R.; m. Carol Joy Campbell, June 26, 1938. B.S., U. Idaho, 1932, M.S., 1934, D.Sc., 1976; Ph.D., U. Minn., 1938. Asst. physics U. Idaho, 1932-33, Asst. chemistry, 1933-35; Asst. chemistry U. Minn., 1935-37, duPont fellow, 1937-38; research chemist plastics dept. duPont Co., 1938-44, supr. process devel., 1944-46, supr. product devel., 1946-49; head chem. research dept., research labs. Gen. Mills, Inc., 1949-52, dir. chem. research, 1952-53, dir. chem. research and devel., 1953-54; dir. research and devel. Spencer Kellogg & Sons, Inc., 1954-58; phys. sci. div. head, prof. chemistry U. Idaho, 1959-73, prof., 1973-76, emeritus, 1976—; dir. U. Idaho (Coll. Chem. Cons. Service), 1969-76; on leave as sr. staff asso. Adv. Council Coll. Chemistry, Stanford, 1967-68; mem. materials adv. bd. Nat. Acad. Scis.; exec. v.p. Idaho Research Found., 1977-78, patent dir., 1978-88. Editor: Safety in the Chemical Laboratory, Vol. IV, 1981, (with Peter Ashbrook), Safe Laboratories: Principles and Practices for Design and Remodeling, 1991; safety editor: Jour. Chem. Edn, 1977-91; Contbr. to tech. and trade publs. on plastics, coatings, safety, chem. edn. Recipient Excellence in Teaching award Chem. Mfrs. Assn., 1977, Outstanding Achievement award U. Minn., 1977; named to U. Idaho Hall of Fame, 1977, 96, Idaho Hall of Fame, 1996. Fellow AAAS, Am. Inst. Chemists; mem. Am. Chem. Soc. (councilor 1948, 59, 67-89 , chmn. paint varnish and plastics div. 1949, chmn. chem. mktg. and econs. div. 1958-59, chmn. chem. health and safety div. 1982, James Flack Norris award 1976, Chem. Health and Safety award 1985, Mosher award 1986), Am. Inst. Chem. Engrs., Soc. Chem. Industry, Phi Beta Kappa, Sigma Xi, Phi Kappa Phi, Sigma Pi Sigma, Phi Gamma Delta (disting. Fiji 1986). Presbyterian. Home: 1271 Walenta Dr Moscow ID 83843-2426

RENFRO, MEL, retired football player; b. Houston, Dec. 30, 1941. Student, U. Oreg. Defensive back Dallas Cowboys, 1964-77. Recipient All-Pro honors NFL, 1971, 73, All-NFC honors. Achievements include 52 pass interceptions, 109 punt returns, 85 kickoff returns, 6 touchdowns, player in 8 NFL/NFC championship games and 4 Super Bowls. Office: care Football Hall of Fame 2121 George Halas Dr NW Canton OH 44708

RENGARAJAN, SEMBIAM RAJAGOPAL, electrical engineering educator, researcher, consultant; b. Mannargudi, Tamil Nadu, India, Dec. 12, 1948; came to U.S., 1980; s. Srinivasan and Rajalakshmi (Renganathan) Rajagopalan; m. Kalyani Srinivasan, June 24, 1982; children: Michelle, Sophie. BE with honors, U. Madras, India, 1971; MTech, Indian Inst. Tech., Kharagpur, 1974; PhD in Elec. Engring., U. N.B., Fredericton, Can., 1980. Mem. tech. staff Jet Propulsion Lab., Pasadena, Calif., 1983-84; asst. prof. elec. engring. Calif. State U., Northridge, 1980-83, assoc. prof., 1984-87, prof., 1987—; vis. rschr. UCLA, 1984-93, vis. prof., 1987-88; vis. prof. U. de Santiago de Compastela, Spain, 1996; cons. Hughes Aircraft Co., Canoga Park, Calif., 1982-87, NASA-Jet Propulsion Lab., Pasadena, 1987-90, 92-94, 96—, Ericsson Radar Electronics, Sweden, 1990-92, Martin Mariette, 1995; guest rschr. Chalmers U., Sweden, 1990, UN Devel. Program, 1993, Rome Lab., USAF, summer 1995. Contbr. sci. papers to profl. publs. recipient Outstanding Faculty award Calif. State U., Northridge, 1985, Disting. Engring. Educator or Yr. award Engrs. Coun., L.A., 1995, Meritorious Performance and profl. Promise award, 1986, 88, Merit award San Fernando Valley Engrs., Coun., 1989, cert. of recognition NASA, 1991, 92; Nat. Merit scholar Govt. India, 1965-71. Fellow Inst. Advancement Engrs., IEEE (L.A. chpt. sec., treas. antennas and propagation soc. 1981-82, vice chmn. 1982-83, chmn. 1983-84), Internat. Union Radio Sci. (U.S. nat. com.), The Electromagnetics Acad. Avocations: swimming, camping, jogging, tennis. Office: Calif State U 18111 Nordhoff St Northridge CA 91330-0001 *Personal philosophy: I wish to contribute to the society through my work in science and technology.*

RENICK, KYLE, artistic director; b. St. Louis, Apr. 24, 1948; s. Mark Allen and Annabelle (Myers) R. B.A. magna cum laude, Tufts U., 1970. Sr. fund acct. New Eng. Mchts. Nat. Bank, Boston, 1970-73; fund acct. Fidelity Mgmt. and Research Corp., Boston, 1973; bus. mgr. American Place Theatre, N.Y.C., 1973-78; producing dir. WPA Theatre, N.Y.C., 1977-82, artistic dir., 1982—; pres. WPA Prodns., Inc., N.Y.C., 1987—; trustee Alliance of Resident Theatres-N.Y., 1982-92; cons. N.Y. State Council on Arts, 1982-85, Nat. Endowment for Arts, 1986. Producer Steel Magnolias, 1987, The Lady In Question, 1989; contbr. articles to profl. publs. Recipient spl. award for outstanding achievement Drama Desk Assn., 1983. Mem. N.Y. Zool. Soc., Soc. Preservation Film Music, Nev. Hist. Soc., Phi Beta Kappa. Club: The Players (N.Y.C.), The Packard Club. Avocations: early music; record collecting. Home: 2 Bethune St Apt 4B New York NY 10014-1860 Office: WPA Theatre 519 W 23rd St New York NY 10011-1102

RENK, CAROL ANN, secondary education educator; b. Elizabeth, Pa., May 19, 1937; d. Benjamin Franklin and Anna Jeannette (Carnahan) Smart; m. Ralph Charles Renk, Oct. 5, 1961 (dec. May 1965); 1 child, Tracy Renk Caldwell. BS in Biol. Scis., U. Pitts., 1959, MEd, 1970. Cert. secondary edn. biol. and social scis. Tchr. Quaker Valley Schs., Leetsdale, Pa., 1959-60, Pitts. City Schs., 1960-94; liaison tchr. South Hills H.S., Pitts., 1984-86. Coach Pleasant Hills (Pa.) Area Recreation Assn., 1970-73. NSF grantee, 1965. Mem. Pitts. Fedn. Tchrs., Am. Legion, Allegheny Club, Alpha Delta Kappa (state, local office 1969-73), Beta Beta Beta, Alpha Psi Omega, Delta Zeta (sec. 1958-59). Republican. Methodist. Home: 349 Tara Dr Pittsburgh PA 15236-4318

RENKAR-JANDA, JARRI J., paint manufacturing executive; b. Chicago Heights, Ill., Feb. 26, 1951; d. Eugene N. and RoseMarie (Morgenson) Zar; m. Leonard F. Renkar (div.); 1 child, Sandra R.; m. James E. Janda. Student, Northeastern Ill. U., 1978, Harper Jr. Coll., 1978, Mundelein Coll., 1979-80. Acctg. clk. Wittek Mfg., Chgo., 1970-73; credit clk. McKesson Chem., Chgo., 1973, purchasing agt., 1973-75; product supply mgr. Gen. Paint and Chem., Cary, Ill., 1975-78; purchasing mgr. Glidden Coatings and Resins, Chgo., 1978-80, Columbus and Oakwood, Ga., 1980-84; purchasing mgr. paint div. Ace Hardware Corp., Matteson, Ill., 1984-87, materials mgr. paint div., 1987-96; software cons. Sys. Software Assocs., Inc., Chgo., 1996—; software cons. Sys. Software Assocs., Inc., Chgo., 1996. Counselor Shelter for Battered Women, Gainesville, Ga., 1982; chairperson Ill. Paint Coun., 1996—. Mem. Chgo. Paint and Coatings Assn. (buyers com. 1985-87, bd. dirs. 1990—, chmn. com. Chgo. legis. affairs, mem. legis. and reg. com. 1991—, pres. 1994-95, chmn. bd. dirs. 1995-96), Chgo. Soc. Coatings (mfg. com. 1986-87). Office: System Software Assn Inc 500 W Madison St Chicago IL 60661-2511

RENNE, LOUISE HORNBECK, lawyer; b. Pitts., Aug. 26, 1937; d. Lewis Alvin and Anne (Bartrem) Hornbeck; m. Paul A. Renne, July 11, 1959; Christine, Anne. BA, Mich. State U., 1958; postgrad. law, Harvard U., 1958-59, U. Pa., 1959-60; JD, Columbia U., 1961. Bar: Calif. 1964, D.C. 1961, U.S. Supreme Ct. 1969. With broadcast bur., office gen. counsel FCC, 1961-64; assoc. Peterson & Barr, San Francisco, 1964-66; dep. atty. gen. State of Calif., San Francisco, 1966-77; pres. Calif. Women Lawyers, San Francisco, 1977-78; mem. Bd. Suprs., San Francisco, 1978-86; city atty. San Francisco, 1986—. Office: Office of City Atty 1390 Market St Fl 5 San Francisco CA 94102-5402

RENNELS, MARSHALL LEIGH, neuroanatomist, biomedical scientist, educator; b. Marshall, Mo., Sept. 2, 1939; s. Ivory P. and Alfrieda S. Rennels; m. Margaret Ann Baker, Dec. 28, 1971. B.S., Eastern Ill. U., 1961; M.A., U. Tex.-Galveston, 1964, Ph.D., 1966. Asst. prof. anatomy U. Md., Balt., 1966-71; assoc. prof., 1971-79, prof., 1979—, dir. MD/PhD Program, 1989—. Contbr. articles to sci. jours. Mem. AAAS, Am. Assn. Anatomists, Soc. Neurosci., Soc. Cerebral Blood Flow and Metabolism. Office: Dept Anatomy & Neurobiology Sch Medicine Univ Md Sch Medicine Baltimore MD 21201

RENNER, ANDREW IHOR, surgeon; b. Buenos Aires, Aug. 1, 1951; came to U.S., 1956; s. Vladimir and Emelia (Dzyga) R.; m. Cristina Sasyk, Apr. 17, 1982. MD, Albert Einstein Coll. Medicine, 1975. Diplomate Am. Bd. Surgery. Pvt. practice gen. surgery Burbank, Calif.; chmn. dept. surgery St. Joseph Hosp., Burbank, 1995-97. Fellow ACS, Internat. Coll. Surgeons, Am. Soc. Gen. Surgeons. Office: 2701 W Alameda Ave Ste 300 Burbank CA 91505-4402

RENNER, GERALD ANTHONY, journalist; b. Phila., June 5, 1932; s. Walter C. and Marie (Watson) R.; m. Jacquelyn Breen, Sept. 7, 1957; children: Margaret, Anne Victoria, Mary X., Andrea, John. BS, Georgetown U., 1959. Reporter UPI, Washington, 1956, Reading (Pa.) Eagle, 1959-65; assoc. info. dir. Nat. Conf. Cath. Bishops, Washington, 1965-67; dir. pub. rels. NCCJ, N.Y.C., 1967-69; exec. dir. regional NCCJ, Ill., Md., 1969-76; mng. editor Religious News Svc., N.Y.C., 1976-79, editor, dir., 1979-84; religion writer Hartford (Conn.) Courant, 1985—. With USN, 1951-55. Office: Hartford Courant Co 285 Broad St Hartford CT 06155-2510

RENNER, RICHARD HENRY, industrial engineer; b. Burlington, Iowa, Aug. 28, 1962; s. William Charles and Florence Helen (Derga) R.; m. Kelly Colleen Farris, June 14, 1986; children: Jennifer Rene, Nathaniel James. BS in Indsl. Tech., Iowa State U., 1985; MS in Prod. Ops. Mgmt., U. Wis., Milw., 1993. Coop engr. Rockwell Internat., Cedar Rapids, Iowa, 1985-86; mfg. engr. Allen-Bradley Co., Milw., 1986-87, dept. supr., 1987-90, sr. industrialization engr., 1990—. Mem. Employee Polit. Action Com., Milw., 1986-92; liaison Jr. Achievement, Milw., 1989-91; amb., mem. Midwest indsl. engring. delegation to visit Soviet Union and China, People to People, 1989; bd. trustees Christ United Methodist Ch., Greenfield, Wis., 1994—. Recipient Citizenship award Kiwanis Club, 1981. Mem. Soc. Mfg. Engrs. Roman Catholic. Avocations: bicycling, camping, jogging, reading. Home: 6023 W Allwood Dr Franklin WI 53132-9260 Office: Allen Bradley Co 1201 S 2nd St Milwaukee WI 53204-2410

RENNER, SIMON EDWARD, steel company executive; b. Florence, S.C., Feb. 5, 1934; s. Simon Samson and Ruby (Pickett) R.; m. Katherine May Schneider, May 10, 1958; children: Katherine Leah, J. Eric, Philip E., S. Todd. BS, Yale U., 1956; diploma, Carnegie Mellon U., 1972. Gen. mgr. specialty steel Jones & Laughlin Steel Corp., Pitts, 1973-74; gen. mgr. basic steel Jones & Laughlin Steel Corp., Pitts., 1974-75, v.p. prodn., 1975-77, pres. eastern div., 1977-79, corp. v.p., 1979-86; pres. LTV R.R.'s, 1986-94; v.p. LTV Steel, 1994—; pres. LTV R.R.s, 1994—. Vice pres. Allegheny Trails council, Boy Scouts Am.; pres. Quigley High Sch. Bd. End., Baden. Pa., 1982. Capt. USMC, 1956-59. Mem. Am. Iron and Steel Inst. (chmn. mfg. com. 1980-82), Assn. Iron and Steel Engrs., Am. Short Line RR Assn. (bd. dirs.). Republican. Clubs: Duquesne (Pitts.); Allegheny Country (Sewickley, Pa.); Harvard-Yale-Princeton. Home: 104 Willow Rd Sewickley PA 15143 Office: LTV RRs 200 Public Sq Cleveland OH 44114-2301

RENNERFELDT, EARL RONALD, state legislator, farmer, rancher; b. Epping, N.D., July 10, 1938; s. Carl John and Margaret E. (Long) R.; m. Lois Ann Thune, Sept. 12, 1959; children: Charysse Renee, Carter Ryan. Student, NDSSS, Wahpeton, N.D., 1958. Farmer/rancher, Williston, N.D.; mem. N.D. Ho. of Reps., Bismarck, 1991—; bd. dirs. Am. State Bank. Mem. Lake Sacajawea Planning Bd., Williston, 1992; mem. Am. Legis. Exch. Coun., 1991-92; mem. adv. bd. N.D. State U. Exptl.. Sta.; bd. dirs. Mercy Med. Found., 1990-96. With U.S. Army, 1962-64. Recipient Harvest Bowl award N.D. State U., 1988; named Outstanding Young Farmer C. of C., 1972. Mem. Am. Legion, N.D. Grain growers, N.D. Durum Growers, Williston C. of C., N.D. Stockmen's Assn., Elks. Republican. Mem. Evangelical Free Ch. Avocations: antiques, golf. Home and Office: 1704 Rose Ln Williston ND 58801-4362

RENNERT, IRA LEON, heavy manufacturing executive; b. 1934. BA, Bklyn. Coll., 1954; MBA, NYU, 1956. Credit analyst M. Lowenstein Corp., N.Y.C., 1956-57; salesman Underwood Corp., N.Y.C., 1957-58; registered rep. Francis I. Dupont & Co., N.Y.C., 1958-60; established I.L. Rennert & Co., Inc. (formerly Rubin, Rennert & Co., Inc.), N.Y.C., 1960-64; cons. N.Y.C., 1964-75; pres. Consolidated Sewing Machine Corp., N.Y.C., 1975—; pres., ceo Renco Group, Inc., N.Y.C., 1980—; ceo WCI Steel Inc., Warren, Ohio, 1988—; chmn. bd. Am. Gen. Corp., South Bend, Ind., 1992. Office: Renco Group 30 Rockefeller Plz New York NY 10112*

RENNERT, OWEN MURRAY, physician, educator; b. N.Y.C., Aug. 8, 1938; s. David Rennert and Frieda (Weinsteiner) Sommer; m. Sandra Serota, Mar. 22, 1964; children: Laura, Rachel, Ian. BS, BA, U. Chgo., 1957, MD, 1961, MS in Biochemistry, 1963. Diplomate Am. Bd. Pediatrics, Am. Bd. Genetics, Am. Bd. Med. Genetics. Assoc. prof. pediatrics U. Fla., Gainesville, 1968-71, prof. pediatrics and biochemistry, 1971-78; prof. biochemistry, prof. and head dept. pediatrics U. Okla., Oklahoma City, 1977-88; chief pediatrics service and head genetics, endocrinology and metabolics Okla. Children's Mem. Hosp., Oklahoma City, 1977-88; prof., chmn. dept. pediatrics Georgetown U. Sch. Medicine, Washington, 1988—. Co-author: Metabolism of Trace Metals in Man: Developmental Biology and Genetic Implications (2 vols.), 1983; contbr. articles to profl. jours. Bd. dirs. Children's Med. Research, Oklahoma City, 1984-88. Served to sr. surgeon USPHS, 1964-66. Named Clin. Scientist of Yr., Am. Assn. Clin. Scientists, 1978. Mem. Am. Pediatric Soc., Am. Acad. Pediatrics, Soc. Pediatric Research, Am. Coll. Clin. Nutrition, Biochem. Soc., Am. Soc. Molecular Biology and Biochemistry. Office: Georgetown U Childrens Med Ctr Dept Pediatrics 3800 Reservoir Rd NW Washington DC 20007-2113

RENNIE, PAUL STEVEN, research scientist; b. Toronto, Ont., Can., Feb. 9, 1946; m. Carol Andrews, 1968; 1 child, Jan. BSc, U. Western Ont., 1969; PhD in Biochemistry, U. Alta., 1973. Rsch. assoc. U. Alta., 1975-76, asst. prof. medicine, 1976-79, assoc. prof., 1979; rsch. scientist B.C. Cancer Agy., 1979-92, dir. rsch., 1992—; prof. surgery U. B.C., 1986—. Med. Rsch. Coun. rsch. fellow Imperial Cancer Rsch. Fund, 1973-75; rsch. scholar Nat. Cancer Inst. Can., 1976-79. Mem. Can. Soc. Clin. Investigation, Biochem. Soc., Endocrine Soc. Achievements include research on biochemical control of growth in androgen responsive organs and neoplasms; genetic markers in prostate cancer. Office: B C Cancer Agy, 600 W 10th Ave, Vancouver, BC Canada V5Z 4E6

RENNINGER, MARY KAREN, librarian; b. Pitts., Apr. 30, 1945; d. Jack Burnell and Jane (Hammerly) Gunderman; m. Norman Christian Renninger, Sept. 3, 1965 (div. 1980); 1 child, David Christian. B.A., U. Md., 1969, M.A., 1972, M.L.S., 1975. Tchr. English West Carteret High Sch., Morehead City, N.C., 1969-70; instr. in English U. Md., College Park, 1970-72; head network services Nat. Libr. Svc., Libr. of Congress, Washington, 1974-78, asst. for network support, 1978-80; mem. fed. women's program com. Libr. of Congress, Washington, 1978-80; chief libr. divsn. Dept. Vets. Affairs, Washington, 1980-90; chief serial and govt. publs. divsn. Libr. of Congress, Washington, 1991—, mem. fed. libr. com., 1980-90, mem. exec. adv. bd., 1985-90; mem. USBE pers. subcom., 1982-84; bd. regents Nat. Libr. of Medicine, 1986-90, mem. outreach panel, 1988-89; fed. libr. task force for 1990 White House Conf. on Librs., 1986-90; liaison to The White House Conf. Med. Libr. Assn., 1989-90. Recipient Meritorious Svc. award Libr. of Congress, 1974, Spl. Achievement award, 1976, Performance award VA, ann. 1982-89, Adminstr.'s Commendation, 1985, Spl. Contbn. award, 1986. Mem. ALA (Govt. Documents Roundtable), Libr. Tech. Assn., Med. Libr. Assn. (govt. rels. com. 1985—), D.C. Libr. Assn., Soc. Applied Learning Tech., Med. Interactive Videodisc Consortium, Govt. Documents Roundtable, Knowledge Utilization Soc., Nat. Multimedia Assn. Am., U.S. Tennis Assn., Phi Beta Kappa, Alpha Lambda Delta, Beta Phi Mu. Home: 840 College Pky Rockville MD 20850-1931 Office: Libr of Congress Ser and Govt Pub Divsn LM 133 Washington DC 20540

RENO, JANET, federal official, lawyer; b. Miami, Fla., July 21, 1938; d. Henry and Jane (Wood) R. A.B. in Chemistry, Cornell U., 1960; LL.B., Harvard U., 1963. Bar: Fla. 1963. Assoc. Brigham & Brigham, 1963-67; ptnr. Lewis & Reno, 1967-71; staff dir. judiciary com. Fla. Ho. of Reps., Tallahassee, 1971-72; cons. Fla. Senate Criminal Justice Com. for Revision Fla.'s Criminal Code, spring 1973; adminstrv. asst. state atty. 11th Jud. Circuit Fla., Miami, 1973-76, state atty., 1978-93; ptnr. Steel Hector and Davis, Miami, 1976-78; atty. gen. Dept. Justice, Washington, 1993—; mem. jud. nominating commn. 11th Jud. Circuit Fla., 1976-78; chmn. Fla. Gov.'s Council for Prosecution Organized Crime, 1979-80. Recipient Women First award YWCA, 1993. Mem. ABA (Inst. Jud. Adminstrn. Juvenile Justice Standards Commn. 1973-76), Am. Law Inst., Am. Judicature Soc. (Herbert Harley award 1981), Dade County Bar Assn., Fla. Pros. Atty.'s Assn. (pres. 1984-86). Democrat. Office: Dept Justice 10th & Constitution Ave NW Washington DC 20530

RENO, JOHN F., communications equipment company executive; b. Peoria, Ill., June 15, 1939; s. John Henkle and Alice Hanna (Findley) R.; m. Suzanne McKnight, Apr. 18, 1964; children: David, Anne. AB, Dartmouth Coll., 1961; MBA, Northwestern U., 1963. Ptnr. G.H. Walker & Co., Boston, 1968-74; divsn. pres. Dynatech Cryomedical Co., Burlington, Mass., 1974-79; corp. v.p. Dynatech Corp., Burlington, 1979-82, group v.p., 1982-87, pres., COO, 1987-93, pres., CEO, 1993—, chmn., 1996—; bd. dirs. Millipre Corp., Bedford, Mass. Trustee Boston Mus. of Sci., 1992—; bd. dirs. CEOs for Fundamental Change in Edn., Cambridge, Mass. Named Entrepreneur of Yr., Inc. mag., 1995. Avocation: oil painting. Office: Dynatech Corp 3 NE Executive Park Burlington MA 01803

RENO, JOSEPH HARRY, retired orthopedic surgeon; b. Allentown, Pa., Mar. 5, 1915; s. Harvey Luther and Olive May (Wilson) R.; m. Maude Olivia Mutchler, June 27, 1942; children: Joseph David, Sally Jo, Diana Jane, Deborah Marion. Student, Temple U., 1934-37, MD, 1941. Intern. Chester (Pa.) Hosp., 1941-42; residency Tex. Scottish Rite Hosp. for Crippled Children, Dallas, 1942-43, 44-45, Robert Packer Hosp., Sayre, Pa., 1943-44; assoc. Homer Stryker, M.D., Kalamazoo, 1945-46; pvt. practice Bethlehem, Pa., 1946-71, Flagstaff, Ariz., 1971-93; team physician Lehigh U., Bethlehem, 1946-70, No. Ariz. U., Flagstaff, 1971-77, Ariz. State U., Tempe, 1977-84; chief surg. staff Flagstaff Hosp., 1975. Contbr. articles to profl. jours.; prodr. surg. films for Am. Acad. Ortho. Surgeons and others, 1952-70. Pres. Coconino County Easter Seal Soc., 1973; bd. dirs., med. advisor Ariz. Easter Seal Soc., 1974-84. Recipient Pioneer award Ariz. Med. Assn., 1981, Cert. of Appreciation, Pa. Dept. Health Crippled Children's Div., 1971; Dr. Joseph Reno Sports Medicine award named in honor, No. Ariz. State U. and Blue Cross Blue Shield, 1986. Fellow Am. Acad. Ortho. Surgeons, Am. Assn. for Surgery of Trauma, Am. Coll. Sports Med., Am. Coll. Surgeons (chmn. Lehigh Valley subcom. on trauma 1954-66, Ea. Pa. chpt. pres. 1969); mem. NRA, Am. Bd. Ortho. Surgery (cert., diplomate 1948), Coconino County Med. Soc. (pres. 1976), Western Ortho. Assn., Babcock Surg. Soc., Mason, Phi Chi, Alpha Tau Omega. Home: 621 Beal Rd Flagstaff AZ 86001-3008

RENO, OTTIE WAYNE, former judge; b. Pike County, Ohio, Apr. 7, 1929; s. Eli Enos and Arbannah Belle (Jones) R.; A in Bus. Adminstrn., Franklin U., 1949; LLB, Franklin Law Sch., 1953; JD, Capital U., 1966; grad. Coll. Juvenile Justice, U. Nev., 1973; m. Janet Gay McCann, May 22, 1947; children: Ottie Wayne II, Jennifer Lynn, Lorna Victoria. Admitted to Ohio bar, 1953; practiced in Pike County; recorder Pike County, 1957-73; common pleas judge Probate and Juvenile divs. Pike County, 1973-79. Mem. adv. bd.

Ohio Youth Services, 1972-74. Mem. Dem. Central Com. Camp Creek precinct, 1956-72, 83-90; sec. Pike County Central Com., 1960-70, 83-87; chmn. Pike County Dem. Exec. Com., 1971-72, 1988-90; del. Dem. Nat. Conv., 1972, 96; mem. Ohio Dem. Central Com., 1969-70; Dem. candidate 6th Ohio dist. U.S. Ho. of Reps., 1966, 88th Dist. Ohio Ho. of Reps., 1992; pres. Scioto Valley Local Sch. Dist., 1962-66. Recipient Distinguished Service award Ohio Youth Commn., 1974; 6 Outstanding Jud. Service awards Ohio Supreme Ct.; 15 times Ala. horseshoe pitching champion; named to Nat. Horseshoe Pitchers Hall of Fame, 1978; mem. internat. sports exchange, U.S. and Republic South Africa, 1972, 80, 82. Mem. Ohio, Pike County (pres. 1964) Bar Assns., Nat. Council Juvenile Ct. Judges, Am. Legion. Mem. Ch. of Christ in Christian Union. Author: Story of Horseshoes, 1963; Pitching Championship Horseshoes, 1971, 2d rev. edit., 1975; The American Directory of Horseshoe Pitching, 1983, Ohio vs. Smith, Murder, 1990, Reno and Apsaalooka Survive Custer, 1996. Home: 148 Reno Rd Lucasville OH 45648-9580

RENO, ROGER, lawyer; b. Rockford, Ill., May 16, 1924; s. Guy B. and Hazel (Kinnear) R.; m. Janice Marie Odelius, May 17, 1952; children: Susan Marie, Sheri Jan Reno-Rudolph, Michael Guy. Student, Kenyon Coll., 1943-44, Yale U., 1944, U. Wis., 1946; A.B., Carleton Coll., 1947; LL.B., Yale U., 1950. Bar: Ill. 1950. Practiced in Rockford, 1950; assoc. firm Reno, Zahm, Folgate, Lindberg & Powell, 1950-56, partner, 1956-84, of counsel, 1984—; chmn. Amcore Fin. Inc., 1982-95; atty. Rockford Bd. Edn., 1955-64. Past pres., bd. dirs. Childrens Home Rockford; trustee Swedish-Am. Hosp. Assn., 1967-77, Keith Country Day Sch. Served to 1st lt. USAAF, 1943-46. Mem. ABA, Ill. Bar Assn., Winnebago County Bar Assn. (pres. 1979-80). Republican. Methodist. Club: Forest Hills Country (Rockford). Home: 2515 Chickadee Trl Rockford IL 61107 Office: Reno Zahm Folgate Lindberg & Powell Amcore Fin Plaza Rockford IL 61104

RENO, RUSSELL RONALD, JR., lawyer; b. Gary, Ind., Nov. 28, 1933; s. Russell Ronald Sr. and Katherine Narcissus (White) R.; m. Mary Ellen Klock, Jan. 30, 1956; children: Mary Hall, Russell III, William, Elizabeth. AB, Haverford Coll., 1954; JD, U. Pa., 1957. Bar: Md. 1957, D.C. 1983. Assoc. Venable, Baetjer & Howard, Balt., 1958-66, ptnr., 1966—; asst. atty. gen. State of Md., Balt., 1962-64. Author: Maryland Real Estate Law-Practice, 1983. Bd. dirs. Balt. Choral Arts Soc., 1966—; trustee Goucher Coll., Balt., 1978—; chancellor Episcopal Diocese of Md., Balt., 1985—; bd. mgrs. Haverford Coll., 1990—. Fellow Am. Bar Found., Md. Bar Found.; mem. ABA, Md. State Bar Assn., Am. Coll. Real Estate Lawyers, Hamilton St. Club, Wednesday Law Club. Home: 706 W Joppa Rd Baltimore MD 21204-3810 Office: Venable Baetjer & Howard 2 Hopkins Plz Baltimore MD 21201-2930

RENOUF, EDDA, artist; b. Mexico City, June 17, 1943; d. Edward and Catharine (Smith) R.; m. Alain Middleton, Sept. 20, 1977; 1 child, Mélisande. B.A., Sarah Lawrence Coll., 1965; M.F.A., Columbia U., 1971. One-woman exhbns. include Yvon Lambert Gallery, Paris, 1972, 74, 76, 78, 80, 82, 84, 93, Konrad Fischer Gallery, Düsseldorf, Fed. Republic Germany, 1974, 79, Blum-Helman Gallery, N.Y.C., 1978, 80, 82, 85, 87, 89, U. Mich. Mus. Art, 1995, Elizabeth Kaufmann Gallery, Basel Switzerland, 1994, 96, Staatliche Kunsthalle Karlsruhe, Germany, 1997; group exhbns. include 8th Paris Biennale, 1973, Mus. Modern Art, N.Y.C., 1973, 90, Stedelijk Mus., Amsterdam, 1974, Whitney Mus. Am. Art, N.Y.C., 1979, 85, Centre Georges Pompidou, Paris, 1979, Met. Mus. Art, N.Y.C., 1982, 87, Serpentine Gallery, 1984, Galerie Denise René, Paris, 1985, The Tel Aviv Mus., 1986, Mus. Fridericianum, Kassel, Fed. Republic of Germany, 1988, Mus. d'Art Moderne de Lille, France, 1992, Bibliothèque Nationale, Paris, 1992, Nat. Gallery Art, Washington, 1993, 94, Harvard U. Straus Gallery, 1996; represented in permanent collections, Mus. Modern Art, Whitney Mus. Am. Art, Met. Mus. Art, Centre Georges Pompidou, Chgo. Art Inst., Phila. Art Mus., Yale U. Art Gallery, Met. Mus. Art, Neuberger Mus., Australian Nat. Gallery, Cin. Mus. Art, St. Louis Art Mus., Tel Aviv Mus., La. Mus., Denmark, Walker Art Ctr., Nat. Gallery Art, Washington, Biblioteque Nationale Paris; subject of articles in art publs. Nat. Endowment Arts grantee, 1976-77, Pollock-Krasner Found. Inc. grantee, 1990-91. Address: 37 Rue Volta, 75003 Paris France

RENOUF, HAROLD AUGUSTUS, business consultant; b. Sandy Point, Nfld., Can., June 15, 1917; s. John Robert and Louisa Maud (LeRoux) R.; m. Janet Dorothy Munro, June 16, 1942; children: Janet Dorothy, Ann Louise Petley-Jones, John Robert, Susan Elizabeth Thompson. B.Commerce, Dalhousie U., 1938, LL.D. (hon.), 1981. N.S.C.A., Halifax, 1942 C.M.A., 1950. With H.R. Doane and Co., Halifax, N.S., Can., 1938-75, ptnr., 1942-75; ptnr. in charge H.R. Doane and Co., New Glasgow, N.S., Can., 1947-62; ptnr. in charge mgmt. svcs. H.R. Doane and Co., Halifax, 1963-67, chmn., 1967-75; bd. dirs. Associated Acctg. Firms Internat., N.Y.C., 1967-75; commr. Anti-Inflation Bd., Ottawa, Ont., 1975-77, chmn., 1977-79; chmn. Petroleum Monitoring Agy., Ottawa, 1980-82, VIA Rail Can. Inc., Montreal, Que., 1982-85; pres. Fundy Industries Ltd., Halifax, 1990-94; ret., 1996; cons. to N.S. Provincial Mcpl. Fact-Finding Com., 1967-70; pres. Can. Inst. Chartered Accts., 1974-75. Contbr. articles to profl. publs. Chmn. adv. commn. Dalhousie U. Grad. Sch. Bus. Adminstrn., 1978-86; trustee St. Andrew's United Ch., Halifax; past dir. Can. Inst. Child Health. Decorated Queen's medal, 1977, officer Order of Can., 1979; recipient Commemorative medal for 125th anniversary of Can. Confederation, 1992; named to Acctg. Hall of Fame St. Mary's Univ., N.S., 1993. Fellow Inst. Chartered Accts. N.S. (pres. 1948); mem. Soc. Can. Inst. Chartered Accts. (pres. 1974-75), Can. Tax Found. (gov. 1969-71), Soc. Mgmt. Accts. N.S., Dalhousie U. Alumni Assn. (hon. chmn. 1987-89), Halifax Club, Saraguay Club (treas. 1972-75), Waegwaltic Club. Liberal. Mem. United Ch. Can. Avocations: boating, fishing. Home: 6369 Coburg Rd Apt 1605, Halifax, NS Canada B3H 4J7

RENOUX, ANDRÉ, physician educator; b. Courbevoie, France, Oct. 27, 1937; s. Robert and Jeanne (Noël) R.; divorced; children: Vincent, Nathalie. Lic. Sci., Faculty Scis. Paris, 1958, Dr 3rd cycle, 1961, Drs, 1965. Asst. Faculty Scis., Paris, 1959-61, master asst., 1961-66; prof. sci. Faculty Scis., Tunis, 1966-79; prof. Faculty Scis., Brest, France, 1969-80; prof. U. Paris, 1980—, dir. lab. physique des aérosols et transfert des comta, omatopms, 1980—, dir. DESS (3d cycle) sci. des aerosols-génie de l'Aérocontamination, 1983—; gen. conf. chmn. European Aerosol Conf., Blois, France, 1994. Editl. bd. Idojaras, 1979—, Pollution Atmospherique, 1979—, Aerosol Sci. & Tech., 1992—; contbr. over 250 articles to sci. publs. Gen. sec. Syndicat d'initiative, Brest, 1973-77; mem. Cons. Com. Univs., France, 1973-80. Mem. AAAS, N.Y. Acad. Scis., Com. Regional Anti-Pollution Brest (pres. 1973-80), Soc. France for Nuclear Energy (pres. 1987-91), Am. Assn. Aerosol Rsch., Gesellschaft Aerosolforschung, Hungarian Meteorol. soc. (hon.), French Aerosol. Rsch. Assn. (pres. 1983—), European Aerosol Assembly (co-founder), Entreprises de l'Ultrapropreté (pres. profl. qualification 1995—), N.Y. Acad. Sci. Avocations: tennis, opera. Home: 11 Sq de L'eau Vive, 94000 Creteil France Office: U Paris XII, Lab Phys Aerosols, 94000 Créteil France

RENSE, PAIGE, editor, publishing company executive; b. Iowa, May 4, 1929; m. Kenneth Noland, Apr. 10, 1994. Student, Calif. State U., L.A. Editor-in-chief Architectural Digest, L.A., 1970—. Recipient Nat. Headliner award Women in Communications, 1983, pacifica award So. Calif. Resources Coun., 1978, editl. award Dallas Market Ctr., 1978, golden award Chgo. Design Resources Svc., 12982, Agora award, 1982, outstanding profl. in comms. award, 1982, trailblazers award, 1983, disting. svcs. award Resources Coun., Inc., 1988; named woman of yr. L.A. Times, 1986, Muses, 1986, woman of internat. accomplisment, 1991; named to Interior Design Hall of Fame. Office: Architectural Digest 6300 Wilshire Blvd Fl 11 Los Angeles CA 90048-5204*

RENSHAW, AMANDA FRANCES, retired physicist, nuclear engineer; b. Wheelwright, Ky., Dec. 10, 1934; d. Taft and Mamie Nell (Russell) Wilson; divorced; children: Linda, Michael, Billy. BS in Physics, Antioch Coll., 1972; MS in Physics, U. Tenn., 1982, MS in Nuclear Engring., 1991. Rsch. asst. U. Mich., Ann Arbor, 1970-71; teaching asst. Antioch Coll., Yellow Springs, Ohio, 1971-72; physicist GE, Schenectady, N.Y., 1972-74, Union Carbide Corp., Oak Ridge, Tenn., 1974-79; rsch. assoc. Oak Ridge Nat. Lab., 1979-91, mgr. strategic planning, 1991-92, liaison for environ. scis., 1993-96; ret., 1996; asst. to counselor for sci. and tech. Am. Embassy, Moscow, 1990; asst. to dir. nat. acid precipitation assessment program Office of Pres. U.S., 1993-94. Contbr. articles to profl. jours. Mem. AAUW, Am. Women in Sci., Am. Nuclear Soc. (Oak Ridge chpt.), Soc. Black Physicists. Avocations: reading, travelling. Home: 1850 Cherokee Bluff Dr Knoxville TN 37920-2215

RENSHAW, JOHN HUBERT, retired secondary education educator; b. Hazleton, Pa., July 9, 1936; s. Charles William and Mary (Drobeck) R.; m. Dorothy Sharon Montgomery, June 20, 1964; children: John Michael, Rebecca Lynn. BS in Edn., East Stroudsburg State U., 1961; MA in History, U. Del., 1965. Cert. tchr., Del. 10th and 12th grade social studies tchr. Pocomoke City (Md.) High Sch., 1961-64; 7th and 8th grade social studies tchr. Forwood Jr. High Sch., Wilmington, Del., 1965-78; 8th grade U.S. govt. and U.S. history tchr. Springer Jr. High Sch., Wilmington, 1978-81; 8th grade U.S. history tchr. Hanby Middle Sch., Wilmington, 1981-96, ret., 1996; audiovisual dir., equipment maintenenace Hanby Jr. High Sch. and Brandywine Sch. Dist., 1981-94; curriculum leader social studies dept. Hanby Jr. High Sch., 1988—, chmn. social studies dept., 1994—; coach baseball, girl's softball teams Forwood Jr. High Sch., 1973-78, Springer Jr. High Sch., 1979-81, Hanby High Sch., 1982-86. Cpl. USMC, 1954-57. Mem. Nat. Coun. Social Studies, Del. Edn. Assn., Brandywine and New Castle County Edn. Assn. (rep. 1978-81). Republican. Methodist. Avocations: jogging, reading, mind-body readings and projects, baseball card collecting, sports watching and participation. Home: 2506 Bona Rd Wilmington DE 19810-2220

RENSI, EDWARD HENRY, restaurant chain executive; b. Hopedale, Ohio, Aug. 15, 1944; s. Ernest Henry and Virginia Marie (Gill) R.; m. F. Anne Bossick, Oct. 9, 1965. Student, Ohio State U., 1962-66. Ind. paint contractor, 1963; salesman Hillcrest Dairy, Steubenville, Ohio, 1964, Borden's Dairy, Columbus, Ohio, 1965, Shoe Corp. Am., Columbus, 1966; with McDonald's Corp., Oak Brook, Ill., 1966—; v.p. McDonald's Corp., 1976-78, sr. v.p. ops., tng. and product devel., 1978-80, sr. exec. v.p., chief operating officer, 1980-84; pres. McDonald's U.S.A., 1984—. Mem. nat. adv. bd. dirs. Children's Oncology Svcs., Oak Brook. Office: McDonald's Corp 1 Kroc Dr Oak Brook IL 60523-2275

RENSINK, JACQUELINE B., secondary school educator; b. Spruce Pine, N.C., May 17, 1954; d. Joe and Virginia Dare (Glenn) Biddix; m. Michael Lynn Rensink, Apr. 2, 1988; 1 child, Sarah Jane Buchanan. MusB, Appalachian State U., 1976, MA, 1983, specialist in mid. grades edn., 1990. Cert. level A music, N.C., level G middle grades edn., N.C. Band dir. Mitchell County Sch. System, Bakersville, N.C., 1977, tchr., 1981—; mem. supt. adv. coun. Mitchell County Sch. System, 1986-88, site-based mgmt. team Harris Mid. Sch., Spruce Pine, 1992-93; student-tchr. supr. Harris Mid. Sch., 1988, 89, 90; coord. World Day Festival Harris Mid. Sch, 1988—. Organist Cen. Bapt. Ch., Spruce Pine, 1990—; bd. dirs. Winterstar-Fairway Assn., Burnsville, N.C., 1992-93. Named Tchr. of Yr., Harris Mid. Sch., 1992, 94. Mem. NEA, Nat. Coun. Social Studies, N.C. Assn. Educators (treas. 1987-88, 91-92, assn. rep. 1992-93), N.C./Nat. Geographic Alliance, N.C. Coun. Social Studies, Delta Kappa Gamma. Republican. Baptist. Avocations: reading, hiking, piano. Home: 1175 Hwy 80 S Burnsville NC 28714-9536 Office: Harris Middle Sch 231 Harris St Spruce Pine NC 28777-3119

RENSON, JEAN FELIX, psychiatry educator; b. Liège, Belgium, Nov. 9, 1930; came to U.S., 1960; s. Louis and Laurence (Crahai) R.; m. Gisèle Bouillenne, Sept. 8, 1956; children: Marc, Dominique, Jean-Luc. MD, U. Liege, 1959; PhD in Biochemistry, George Washington U., 1971. Diplomate Am. Bd. Psychiatry. Asst. prof. U. Liège, 1957-60; rsch. fellow U. Liege, 1966-72; clin. assoc. prof. dept. psychiatry U. Calif., San Francisco, 1978—; vis. asst. prof. Stanford U., Palo Alto, Calif., 1972-77. Assoc. editor: Fundamentals of Biochemical Pharmacology, 1971. NIH fellow, 1960-66. Democrat. Avocations: neurosciences, music.

RENT, CLYDA STOKES, academic administrator; b. Jacksonville, Fla., Mar. 1, 1942; d. Clyde Parker Stokes Sr. and Edna Mae (Edwards) Shuemake; m. George Seymour Rent, Aug. 12, 1966; 1 child, Cason Rent Lynley. BA, Fla. State U., 1964, MA, 1966, PhD, 1968; LHD (hon.), Judson Coll., 1993. Asst. prof. Western Carolina U., Cullowhee, N.C., 1968-70; asst. prof. Queens Coll., Charlotte, N.C., 1972-74, dept. chair, 1974-78, dean Grad. Sch. and New Coll., 1979-84, v.p. for Grad. Sch. and New Coll., 1984-85, v.p. acad. affairs, 1985-87, v.p. community affairs, 1987-89; pres. Miss. U. for Women, Columbus, 1989—; bd. dirs. Trustmark Nat. Bank, Trustmark Corp.; mem. bd. advisors Entergy/Miss., The Freedom Forum First Amendment Ctr. at Vanderbilt U., Nat. Women's Hall of Fame; cons. Coll. Eb. N.Y.C., 1983-89; sci. cons. N.C. Alcohol Rsch. Authority, Chapel Hill, 1976-89; bd. mem. So. Growth Policies Bd., 1992-94; mem. adv. bd. Nat. Women's Hall of Fame; rotating chair Miss. Instns. Higher Learning Pres. Coun., 1990-91; commn. govtl. rels. Am. Coun. Edn., 1990-93; adv. bd. Energy/Miss., 1994—; adv. bd. Freedom Forum First Amendment Ctr., 1996—; Rhodes Scholar selection com. of Miss., 1996—. Mem. editl. rev. bd. Planning for Higher Education, 1995; author rsch. articles in acad. jours.; speeches pub. in Vital Speeches; mem. editl. bds. acad. jours. Trustee N.C. Performing Arts Ctr., Charlotte, 1988-89, Charlotte County Day Sch., 1987-89; bd. visitors Johnson C. Smith U., Charlotte, 1985-89; exec. com. bd. dirs. United Way Allocations and Rev., Charlotte, 1982-88; bd. advisors Charlotte Mecklenburg Hosp. Authority, 1985-89; bd. dirs. Jr. Achievement, Charlotte, 1983-89, Miss. Humanities Coun., Miss. Inst. Arts and Letters, Miss. Symphony, Miss. Econ. Coun.; chair Leadership Miss. and Collegiate Miss.; chmn. bd. dirs. Charlotte/Mecklenburg Arts and Sci. Coun., 1987-88; Danforth assoc. Danforth Found., St. Louis, 1976-88, Leadership Am., 1989; golden triangle adv. bd. Bapt. Meml. Hosp.; pres. So. Univs. Conf., 1994-95; mem. commn. govt. rels. Am. Coun. Edn., 1990-93. Recipient Grad. Made Good award Fla. State U., 1990, medal of excellence Miss. U. for Women, 1995; named Prof. of Yr., Queens Coll., 1979, One of 10 Most Admired Women Mgrs. in Am., Working Women mag., 1993, One of 1000 Women of the 90's, Mirabella mag., 1994; Ford Found. grantee, 1981; Paul Harris fellow, 1992. Mem. Am. Assn. State Colls. and Univs. (bd. dirs. 1994-96), Sociol. Soc., So. Assn. Colls. and Schs. (mem. commn. on colls. 1996), N.C. Assn. Colls. and Univs. (exec. com. 1988-89), N.C. Assn. Acad. Officers (sec.-treas. 1987-88), Soc. Internat. Bus. Fellows, Miss. Assn. Colls. (pres. 1992), Newcomen Soc. U.S., Internat. Women's Forum, Univ. Club, Rotary. 1st female pres. of Miss. U. for Women (1st pub. coll. for women in Am.). Office: Miss U Women Pres Office Box W 1600 Columbus MS 39701-9998

RENTOUMIS, ANN MASTROIANNI, psychotherapist; b. New Haven, Apr. 27, 1928; d. Luigi Mastroianni and Marion Dallas; m. George Rentoumis, June 27, 1959; children: Michael, Mary, Anne. BA in Psychology, Vassar Coll., 1949; postgrad., Boston U., 1949-50; MS in Social Work, Columbia U., 1952. Diplomate Am. Bd. Social Work; lic. cert. social worker; lic. marriage and family therapist. Child and adolescent therapist Bklyn. Psychiat., 1952-55; family therapist Community Svc. Soc., N.Y.C., 1955-58; psychotherapist Bleuler Psychotherapy Ctr., L.I., N.Y., 1958-60, Adolescent Psychiat. Clinic, Tex. Children's Hosp., Houston, 1975-76; pvt. practice, Houston, 1976-77; pvt. practice Lauderdale Psychiat. Group, Ft. Lauderdale, Fla., 1978-90; pvt. practice, Pompano Beach, Fla., 1990-93; psychotherapist New River Group, Ft. Lauderdale, 1993—. Pres. Pine Crest Sch. Mothers Club, 1985-86; v.p. Opera Soc., 1987-88; bd. govs., v.p. exec. bd. Fla. Philharm Orch., 1988-91, bd. dirs., 1990—; pres. Ft. Lauderdale Philharm. Soc., 1988-90. Named Woman of Yr., Am. Cancer Soc., 1989, Golden Rule award J.C. Penney, 1990. Fellow Am. Orthopsychiat. Assn.; mem. Am. Assn. Marriage and Family Therapists, Am. Group Therapy Assn., Fla. Assn. Psychotherapists, Harbor Beach Surf Club (v.p. 1986-90). Avocations: piano, tennis, swimming. Home: 1535 E Lake Dr Fort Lauderdale FL 33316-3205 Office: New River Group 901 S Federal Hwy Ph L Fort Lauderdale FL 33316-1266

RENTSCHLER, WILLIAM HENRY, publisher, editor, columnist, writer, corporate executive; b. Hamilton, Ohio, May 11, 1925; s. Peter Earl and Barbara (Schlosser) R.; AB, Princeton U., 1949; m. Sylvia Gale Angevin, Dec. 20, 1948; children: Sarah Yorke, Peter Ferris, Mary Rentschler Alley, Phoebe Rentschler Cole; m. Martha Guthrie Snowdon, Jan. 20, 1967; 1 child, Hope Snowdon. Reporter, Cin. Times-Star, 1946; chmn. The Daily Princetonian, 1948; reporter, asst. to exec. editor Mpls. Star & Tribune, 1949-53; 2d v.p. No. Trust Co., Chgo., 1953-56; pres. Martha Washington Kitchens, Inc., and Stevens Candy Kitchens, Inc., 1957-68; investor closely-held cos.; bus. and mktg. cons., 1970—; chmn., CEO Medart, Inc., Greenwood, Miss., 1981-87, Roper Whitney Corp., Rockford, Ill., 1985-87; editor, pub. News/Voice Newspapers, Inc., Highland Park, Lake Bluff, Ill., 1983-91. editor/pub. San Francisco Progress, 1986-88; editor, pres. and founder VOICE Pub. USA, Ltd., 1995—; columnist Chgo. Life Mag., 1994—, Chgo. Sun-Times, 1995; commentator WBEZ-FM, Nat. Pub. Radio, Chgo., 1995. Spl. adviser Pres.'s Nat. Program for Vol. Action, 1969; chmn. Ill. Low Tech./High Return Adv. Bd., 1986, bd. dirs.; exec. com. Nat. Council Crime and Delinquency, 1980—; with Better Boys Found. Family Svcs., 1970—, Citizens Info. Svc.; pres. John Howard Assn., 1985-87; Rep. candidate U.S. Senate, 1960, 70; chmn. Ill. Citizens for Nixon, 1968; pres. Young Reps. Ill., 1957-59; exec. com. United Rep. Fund Ill., 1963-69; former trustee Rockford Coll., Goodwill Industries, Chgo., Coun. on Fgn. Rels.; mem. San Francisco mayor's Fiscal Adv. Com., Blue Ribbon Com. on Bus., 1987-88, Com. of 100, Voices for Ill. Children, Chgo. Mayor Daley's Task Force on Youth Devel., 1993-95; chair adv. bd. Citizens for a Safe America, 1995—. Recipient 1st Ann. Buddy Hackett award for svc. to young men, 1968, Voice for Children award Coleman Advs., San Francisco, 1987, Nat. Media award Arbor Day Found., 1989, Peter Lisagor award for Exemplary journalism, 1989, 90, 92, John Howard Assn. Media award, 1990, Nat. Media award Nat. Coun. Crime and Delinquency, 1990, Mackey award BBF Family Svcs., 1996, Ethics in Journalism award Chgo. Headline Club, 1996, 1st Place award Nat. Soc. Newspaper Columnists, 1996; Pulitzer prize nominee, 1985, 87, 88, 89, 90, 95. Mem. Nat. Press Club, Economic Club, Sky-Line Club (Chgo.). Home: 1088 Griffith Rd Lake Forest IL 60045-1319

RENTZ, TAMARA HOLMES, software consultant; b. Austin, Tex., Nov. 23, 1964; d. Thomas Michael and Elizabeth Dianne (Ames) Holmes; m. Christopher Michael Rentz, Sept. 21, 1991. BS in Speech/Orgnl. Comm., U. Tex., 1987. Cert. meeting facilitator; notary public State of Tex. Mgr. PC Sta., Inc., Austin, 1985-86; telecom. advisor Internat. Talent Network, Austin, 1986-87; mktg. rep. Wm. Ross & Co., Austin, 1987; life ins. rep. A.L. Williams, Austin, 1987-88; exec. sec. Adia Temporaries/SEMATECH, Austin, 1988; tng. adminstr. SEMATECH, Austin, 1988-89, data coord. equipment improvement program, 1989-90, user group program mgr., 1992-93; pres. Innovative Bus. Solutions, Austin, 1994—. Mem. Austin Software Coun. Avocations: weight lifting, golf. Home and Office: 4004 Love Bird Ln Austin TX 78730-3522

RENTZEPIS, PETER M., chemistry educator; b. Kalamata, Greece, Dec. 11, 1934; m. Alma Elizabeth Keenan; children—Michael, John. B.S., Denison U., 1957, D.Sc. (hon.), 1981; M.S., Syracuse U., 1959, Ph.D. (hon.), 1980; Ph.D., Cambridge U., 1963; DSc (hon.), Carnegie-Mellon U., 1983, Tech. U. Greece, Athens, Greece, 1995. Mem. tech. staff, rsch. labs. Gen. Electric Co., Schenectady, 1960-62; mem. tech. staff AT&T Bell Labs., Murray Hill, N.J., 1963-73, head phys. and inorganic chemistry rsch. dept., 1973-85; Presdl. prof. chemistry U. Calif., Irvine, 1986—, Presdl. chair, 1985—, regent lectr., 1984; vis. prof. Rockefeller U., N.Y.C., 1971, MIT, Cambridge, to 1975; vis. prof. chemistry U. Tel Aviv; adj. prof. U. Pa., Phila.; with Ctr. Biol. Studies, SUNY-Albany, 1979—; adj. prof. chemistry and biophysics Yale U., New Haven, 1980—; mem. numerous adv. bodies; lectr. Robert A. Welch Found., 1975; faculty lectr. Rensselaer Poly. Inst., Troy, N.Y., 1978; IBM lectr. Williams Coll., 1979; lectr. disting. lecture series U. Utah, 1980; Xerox lectr. N.C. State U., 1980; Frank C. Whitmore lectr. in chemistry Pa. State U., 1981; Dreyfus disting. scholar lectr., 1982; regent lectr. U. Calif., 1982, UCLA, 1985; Harry S. Ganning disting. lectr. U. Alta., Can., 1984; mem. IUPAC Commn. on Molecular Structure and Spectroscopy; chmn. 1981 Internat. Conf. on Photochemistry and Photobiology; bd. dirs. KRIKOS Sci. and Tech. Resources for Greece; mem. com. on kinetics Nat. Acad. Scis., NRC; chmn. fast reaction chemistry U.S. Fgn. Applied Sci. Assessment Ctr.; with NATO Advanced Study Insts., 1984—; dir. Quanex Corp. Assoc. editor Chem. Physics, Jour. Lasers and Chemistry, Jour. Biochem. and Biophys. Methods; editorial bd. Biophys. Jour., Jour. Chem. Intermediates; contbr. articles, papers to profl. publs.; patentee in field. Recipient Scientist of Yr. award, 1977, award for significant contbns. to field of biochem. instrumentation ISCO, 1979, award for leadership in sci. and edn. AHEPA, Disting. Alumni award SUNY, 1982, H.S. Ganning award U. Alta., 1984; Camille and Henry Dreyfus disting. scholar Williams Coll., 1982; AAAS fellow, 1985; alumni scholar Denison U., 1978. Fellow N.Y. Acad. Scis. (A Cressy Morrison award 1978), Am. Phys. Soc. (chmn. chem. physics divsn. 1979-80, exec. com. 1980-82, chmn. nominating com. 1981, Irving Langmuir award 1973); mem. NAS, Nat. Acad. Greece, Am. Chem. Soc. (exec. com. divsn. phys. chemistry to 1978, Peter Debye award phys. chemistry 1982), Inter-Am. Photochem. Soc. (nominating coun., chmn. phys. divsn. Laser Conf. prize 1989), Sigma Xi. Office: U Calif Dept Chemistry Irvine CA 92717

RENWICK, EDWARD S., lawyer; b. L.A., May 10, 1934. AB, Stanford U., 1956, LLB, 1958. Bar: Calif. 1959, U.S. Dist. Ct. (cen. dist.) Calif. 1959, U.S. Ct. Appeals (9th cir.) 1963, U.S. Dist. Ct. (so. dist.) Calif. 1973, U.S. Dist. Ct. (no. dist.) Calif. 1977, U.S. Dist. Ct. (ea. dist.) Calif. 1981, U.S. Supreme Ct. 1985. Ptnr. Hanna and Morton, L.A.; mem., bd. vis. Stanford Law Sch., 1967-69; mem. environ. and natural resources adv. bd. Stanford Law Sch. Bd. dirs. Calif. Supreme Ct. Hist. Soc. Fellow Am. Coll. Trial Lawyers, Am. Bar Found.; mem. ABA (mem. sect. on litigation, antitrust law, bus. law, chmn. sect. of nat. resources, energy and environ. law 1987-88, mem. at large coord. group energy law 1989-92, sect. rep. coord. group energy law 1995-97, Calif. del. legal com., interstate oil compact com.), Calif. Arboretum Assn. (trustee 1986-92), L.A. County Bar Assn. (chmn. natural resources law sect. 1974-75), The State Bar of Calif., Assn. Atty.- Mediators, Chancery Club (pres. 1992-93), Phi Delta Phi. Office: Hanna & Morton 600 Wilshire Blvd Fl 17 Los Angeles CA 90017-3212

RENWICK, KEN, retail executive. CEO, pres All-Phase Electric Supply, Benton Harbor, Mich. Office: All Phase Electric Supply 3401 S Lakeshore Dr Saint Joseph MI 49085*

RENZETTI, ATTILIO DAVID, physician; b. N.Y.C., Nov. 11, 1920; s. Attilio and Anna (Accardi) R.; m. Mabel Lucille Woodruff, May 24, 1947; children: Patricia Ann, Laurence, Pamela Sorensen, David. AB, Columbia Coll., 1941, MD, 1944. Diplomate: Am. Bd. Internal Medicine (chmn. subsplty. bd. pulmonary disease 1970-72). Intern, resident Bellevue Hosp., N.Y.C., 1944-45, 47-49, 51-52; fellow cardiopulmonary physiology Bellevue Hosp., 1949-51; asst. prof. medicine U. Utah, 1952-53, State U. N.Y., Syracuse, 1953-57; assoc. prof. SUNY, 1957-60; asst. prof. Johns Hopkins U., 1960-61; assoc. prof. U. Md., 1960-61, U. Utah, Salt Lake City, 1961-67; prof. U. Utah, 1967-90, emeritus, 1990—. Editorial bd.: Am. Rev. Respiratory Disease, 1964-67; Contbr. articles to med. jours. Pres. Utah TB and Health Assn., 1965-66; bd. dirs. Am. Lung Assn., 1965-74, 78-81. With M.C. AUS, 1945-47. Mem. Am. Thoracic Soc. (pres. 1975-76). Home and Office: 1801 London Plane Rd Salt Lake City UT 84124-3531

REOCK, ERNEST C., JR., retired government services educator, academic director; b. Belleville, N.J., Oct. 13, 1924; s. Ernest C. and Helen Rutan (Evans) R.; m. Jeanne Elizabeth Thomason, Jan. 25, 1953; children: Michael, Thomas, Kathleen. BS, Swarthmore Coll., 1945; AB, Rutgers U., 1948, MA, 1950, PhD, 1959. Rsch. assoc. bur. govt. rsch. Rutgers U., New Brunswick, N.J., 1950-59, asst. prof., dir., 1960-63, assoc. prof., dir., 1963-68, prof., dir., 1968-92; cons. N.J. Constnl. Conv., New Brunswick, 1966, N.J. State and Local Revenue and Expenditure Commns., 1986-88. Author: Handbook for New Jersey Assessors, 1962, School Budget Caps in New Jersey, 1981 (Govtl. Rsch. Assn. award 1983); editor: New Jersey Legislative District Data Book, 1972-92. Chmn. Middlesex County Charter Study Commn., New Brunswick, 1973-74; cons. various mcpl. charter commns., 1965-93. Lt. USN, 1943-46, 51-53. Mem. Am. Soc. Pub. Adminstrn. (Pub. Adminstr. of Yr. 1982), Am. Ednl. Fin. Assn. Avocations: sailing, swimming. Home: 7 Kendall Rd Kendall Park NJ 08824-1010 Office: Rutgers U Ctr Govt Svcs 33 Livingston Ave New Brunswick NJ 08901-1900

REPHAN, JACK, lawyer; b. Little Rock, Mar. 16, 1932; s. Henry and Mildred (Frank) R.; m. Arlene Clark, June 23, 1957; children: Amy Carol, James Clark. BS in Commerce, 1954; LLB, U. Va., 1959. Bar: Va. 1959, D.C. 1961. Assoc. Kanter & Kanter, Norfolk, Va., 1959-60; law clk. to Judge Sam E. Whitaker, U.S. Ct. Claims, Washington, 1960-62; assoc. Pierson, Ball & Dowd, Washington, 1962-64; ptnr. Danzansky, Dickey,

Tydings, Quint & Gordon, Washington, 1964-77; mem. Braude, Margulies, Sacks & Rephan, Washington, 1977-87; ptnr. Porter, Wright, Morris & Arthur, Washington, 1987-88, Sadur, Pelland & Rubinstein, Washington, 1988-93; counsel Hofheimer, Nusbaum, McPhaul & Samuels, Norfolk, Va., 1993—; mem. nat. panel arbitrators Am. Arbitration Assn.; lectr. joint com. continuing legal edn. State Bar Va. Contbr. articles to legal jours. Pres. Patrick Henry PTA, Alexandria, Va., 1968-69; treas. John Adams Mid. Sch. PTA, Alexandria, 1970-71; pres. Seminary Ridge Citizens Assn., 1976-77; Dem. candidate for Alexandria City Com., 1969. 1st lt. AUS, 1955-57. Mem. ABA (chmn. subcom. on procurement of jud. remedies pub. contract sect. 1973-74), Va. Bar Assn. (govt. sect. constrn. law 1979—, vice chmn. 1980-81, chmn. 1981-82), D.C. Bar Assn., Kiwanis (pres. Landmark Club 1969), Westwood Country Club (v.p. 1977-78), Belle Haven Country Club, Cavalier Golf and Yacht Club. Jewish. Home: 3978 Ocean Hills Ct Virginia Beach VA 23451-2631 Office: 1700 Dominion Towers PO Box 3460 Norfolk VA 23514-3460

REPINE, JOHN E., internist, educator; b. Rock Island, Ill., Dec. 26, 1944; married, 1969, 88; 6 children. BS, U. Wis., 1967; MD, U. Minn., 1971. Instr., then assoc. prof. internal medicine U. Minn., Mpls., 1974-79; asst. dir divsn. exptl. medicine Webb-Waring for Bromedical Rsch., Denver, 1979-89, prof. medicine, pres. and dir., 1989—; prof. medicine U. Colo., Denver, 1979—, prof. pediatrics, 1981-96; James J. Waring prof. Webb-Waring for Bromedical Rsch., 1996—; mem. rsch. com., co-chmn. steering com. Aspen Lung Conf., 1980, chmn., 1981; assoc. dean for student advocacy Nat. Heart and Lung Inst., 1990—. Young Pulmonary Investigator grantee Nat. Heart & Lung Inst., 1974-75; recipient Basil O'Connor Starter Rsch. award Nat. Found. March of Dimes, 1975-77. Mem. AAAS, Am. Assn. Immunologists, Am. Fedn. Clin. Rsch., Am. Heart Assn. (established investigator award 1976-81), Am. Thoracic Soc., Am. Soc. Clin. Investigators, Assn. Am. Physicians. Achievements include research in role of phagocytes and oxygen radicals in lung injury and host defense (ARDS). Office: Webb-Waring Lung Inst 4200 E 9th Ave Denver CO 80220-3706

REPLINGER, JOHN GORDON, architect, retired educator; b. Chgo., Nov. 9, 1923; s. Roy Lodawick and Dorothy Caroline (Thornstrom) R.; m. Dorothy Thiele, June 26, 1945; children: John Gordon Jr., Robert Louis, James Alan. B.S. in Architecture with highest honors, U. Ill., Urbana, 1949, M.S. in Architecture, 1952. Registered architect, Ill. Designer-draftsman L. Morgan Yost (Architect), Kenilworth, Ill., 1949-50; instr. U. Ill., 1951-53, asst. prof. architecture, 1953-57, assoc. prof. architecture, 1957-61, prof. architecture, 1961-85, prof. housing research and devel., 1972-85, prof. emeritus, 1985—, assoc. head dept. for acad. affairs, 1970-71; practice architecture Urbana, 1951—. Served as combat pilot USAAF, 1943-45. Decorated Air medal with oak leaf clusters; recipient Sch. medal AIA, 1949, List of Tchrs. Ranked as Excellent by Their Students award U. Ill., 1976, 77, 78, 82, 83; Allerton Am. travelling scholar, 1948. Mem. Nat. Trust Hist. Preservation. Home and Office: 403 Yankee Ridge Ln Urbana IL 61802-7113

REPLOGLE, DAVID ROBERT, publishing company executive; b. Chgo., Feb. 24, 1931; s. Homer Mock and Helen (Fluke) R.; m. Jeanne Lonnquist, Nov. 4, 1954; children: William T., Bruce R., Stewart D., James M., John B. A.B., Dartmouth Coll., 1953; postgrad., Princeton U., 1957-58. V.p., gen. mgr. Doubleday & Co., Inc., N.Y.C., 1958-70; pres., chmn. bd. G. & C. Merriam Co., Springfield, Mass., 1970-75; pres. Praeger Publishers, N.Y.C., 1970-75; exec. v.p., dir. Houghton Mifflin Co., Boston, 1975-91; chmn. DR&A Inc., Hingham, Mass., 1992—. Trustee L.I. Replogle Found., Chgo., 1982—. Served to lt. USNR, 1953-57. Mem. Cohasset Golf Club, Plantation Golf and Country Club. Home: 84 Gammons Rd Cohasset MA 02025-1406 Office: David Replogle & Assocs 75 Terry Dr Hingham MA 02043-1518

REPLOGLE, ROBERT L., cardiovascular and thoracic surgeon; b. Ottumwa, Iowa, Sept. 30, 1931; s. Ralph Ruby and Edith Dorothy (Swartz) R.; m. Carol A. Heeschen, Aug. 24, 1958; children: Robert E., Jennifer Bremer, Edith. MD cum laude, Cornell Coll., 1956, DSc (hon.), 1972; postgrad., Harvard U., 1956-60. Diplomate Am. Bd. Surgery, Am. Bd. Thoracic Surgery, Am. Bd. Pediat. Surgery. Intern in surgery U. Minn. Hosp., 1960-61; asst. resident in surgery Peter Bent Brigham Hosp., Boston, 1961-63, Mass. Gen. Hosp., Boston, 1965-66; sr. resident in surgery Children's Hosp. Med. Ctr., Boston, 1966; asst. in surgery Children's Hosp. Med. Ctr. and Harvard Med. Sch., Boston, 1966-67; asst. prof. surgery Pritzker Sch. Medicine U. Chgo., 1967-70, assoc. prof. surgery and head, sect. pediat. surgery, 1970-73, prof. surgery and head, sect. pediat. surgery, 1973-74, prof. surgery and head, sect. cardiac surgery, 1973-80, prof. surgery, sect. cardiac surgery, 1973—; mem. med. staff, divsn. cardiac surgery Humana Michael Reese Hosp. and Med. Ctr., Chgo., 1977—; med. dir. cardiac surgery unit Ingalls Meml. Hosp., 1989—; chief divsn. cardiac surgery Columbus Hosp., Chgo., 1987—; vis. prof. Albany Med. Coll., 1974, Dalhousie Sch. of Medicine, Halifax, 1975, Walter Reed Army Med. Ctr., 1978, U. Miami Med. Sch., 1992, Philippine Heart Ctr. for Asia March, 1979, Health Inst. Japan, Tokyo, 1982, Creighton Med. Sch., 1988, Brooke Army Med. Ctr., 1993, U. Heidelberg, 1995, Kerkoff Clinic/Max Planct Inst., Bad Nanheim, Germany, 1995, German Heart Ctr., Munich, 1995, Peter Bent Brigham Hosp. Harvard Med. Sch., 1996; mem. surgery and bioengring. study sect. HHS, NIH, 1979-83; mem. ad hoc adv. com. bypass angioplasty revascularization investigation, NIH, 1993-94; mem. subcom. on quality N.Y. State Dept. Health, 1989-93, mem. subcom. on resources and facilities, 1993—, mem. cardiac adv. com., 1989—. Author: (with others) Microcirculation, Perfusion, and Transplantation of Organs, 1970, The Critically Ill Child, 1972, Surgical Clinics in North America, 1976, Biprosthetic Vardiac Valves, 1979, Year Book of Nuclear Medicine, 1981, among others; mem. editl. bd. Jour. Cardiac Surgery, 1982—; contbr. more than 125 articles to profl. jours. With USN, 1951-54. Recipient Merit award Philippine Heart ctr. for Asia, Manila, 1985, Friendship award Shanghai Chest Hosp., 1987. Mem. AMA (diagnostic and therapeutic tech. assessment panel 1995—, ho. of dels. 1992—, joint rev. com. on ednl. programs for physicians assts. 1979-84), ACS (com. on allied health pers. 1979-84, chmn. 1983-84, com. on med. motion pictures 1979-85, com. on membership 1988—, residency rev. com. for thoracic surgery of the accreditation com. for grad. med. edn. 1992-95, 96—), Ill. State Med. Soc., Chgo. Med. Soc., Am. Surg. Assn., European Assn. for Cardiothoracic Surgery, Soc. for Acad. Surgery, Am. Heart Assn. (adv. coun. cardiovasc. surgery 1968-71), Soc. Univ. Surgeons, Internat. Cardiovasc. Soc., Societe Internationale de Chirurgie (N.Am. chpt.), Am. Assn. for Thoracic Surgery (del. AMA 1992—, com. on soc. responsibility 1991—), Soc. Thoracic Surgeons (program com. 1978-81, chmn. 1981, com. on medico-legal affairs, chmn. 1985-88, ad hoc fin. adv. com. 1987-89, ad hoc exhibitors adv. com. 1988-89, ad hoc com. on social responsibility 1992-95, ad hoc database liaison com. 1993-94, database liaison com. 1994—, ad hoc com. on physician-specific mortality for cardiac surgery 1993-96, stds. and ethics com. 1984-88, treas. 1986-92, exec. com. 1986—, pres.-elect. 1995-96, pres. 1996-97, rep. to the coun. of med. specialty socs. 1990—, annals of thoracic surgery liaision com. 1992—, com. on grad. edn. in thoracic surgery 1992—, com. on major issues in thoracic surgery 1993, chmn. 1994, 95). Avocations: wine collecting, photography, travel. Home: 1160 E 56th St Chicago IL 60637-1541 Office: Ingalls Meml Hosp One Ingalls Dr West 536 Harvey IL 60426

REPP, RONALD STEWART, insurance company executive; b. Phila., Dec. 12, 1944; s. Carl George Jr. and Pauline Francis (Hunley) R.; m. Nancy Elaine Hannigan, Sept. 16, 1967; children: Christopher Robert, Justin Ronald. Grad. high sch., Pitts.; cert., Am. Coll., Bryn Mawr, Pa., 1973, Am. Inst., Malvern, Pa., 1977. CLU, CPCU, assoc. in risk mgmt. Admistr. Liberty Mut. Ins. Group, Pitts., 1963-65, sales rep., 1967-70, sales supr., 1970-72, sales mgr., 1972-78; spl. agt. The Prudential, Pitts., 1966-67; account exec. Ind. Ins. Svc. Corp., Canton, Ohio, 1978-83, v.p., 1983-90, sr.v.p., 1990—; mem. adv. bd. dirs. Silver Lake Estates. Contbr. articles to profl. jours. Staff sgt. U.S. Army, 1964-65. Mem. Soc. CPCUs, Soc. CLUs, Ind. Ins. Agts. Assn., Akron City Club (chmn. mem. com. 1992-94), Bay Point Yacht Club, Akron Cruising Club (bd. trustees), Silver Lake Country Club. Lutheran. Avocation: sailing. Home: 3103 Silver Lake Blvd Silver Lake OH 44224-3130 Office: Ind Ins Svc Corp 236 3rd St SW Canton OH 44702-1622

REPPEN, NORBJORN DAG, electrical engineer, consultant; b. Hadsel, Norway, May 10, 1940; came to U.S., 1966; s. Harald and Bergit (Bakke) R.; m. Grete Elisabeth Holm, July 25, 1964; children: Dag, Anne, Erik Harald. Degree in elec. engring., Norwegian Inst. Tech., 1965. Registered profl. engr., N.Y. Application engr. GE, Schenectady, N.Y., 1966-69; application engr. Power Techs., Inc., Schenectady, 1969-73, sr. engr., 1973-84, sr. cons., 1984-91, unit mgr., 1991-97, sr. cons., 1997—; bd. dirs. Hydro Techs., Inc., Schenectady, Power Techs., Inc., Schenectady. Bd. dirs. 1st Unitarian Soc. Schenectady, 1984-87, 93. Fellow IEEE. Avocations: sailing, cross country skiing.

REPPERT, RICHARD LEVI, lawyer; b. Phila., Nov. 6, 1948; s. William Downing and Angela R. (Schmid) R.; m. Faith Simpson, Dec. 30, 1972 (div. Aug. 1992); 1 child, Richard Jacob; m. Jeanette T. deHaven, Apr. 10, 1994. BA, Lehigh U., 1970; JD, Villanova U., 1974. Bar: Ohio 1974, U.S. Dist. Ct. (no. dist.) Ohio 1974, Pa. 1993. Assoc. Thompson, Hine and Flory, Cleve., 1974-82, ptnr., 1982-89; ptnr. Jones, Day, Reavis & Pogue, Cleve., 1989—. Mem. ABA, Am. Coll. Real Estate Lawyers, Nat. Assn. Office and Indsl. Pks., Ohio State Bar Assn., Cleve. Bar Assn., Mortgage Bankers Assn. Greater Cleve. Office: Jones Day Reavis & Pogue 901 Lakeside Ave E Cleveland OH 44114-1116

REPPERT, STEVEN MARION, pediatrician, scientist, educator; b. Sioux City, Iowa, Sept. 4, 1946; s. Ray Fred and Norma Grace (Coppock) R.; m. Mary Alice Herman, Dec. 28, 1968; children—Jason Steven, Katherine Mary, Christina Marie. BS, U. Nebr., Lincoln, 1973; MD with distinction, U. Nebr.-Omaha, 1973, MA (hon.), Harvard U., 1993. Diplomate Nat. Bd. Med. Examiners. Intern, Mass. Gen. Hosp., Boston, 1973-74, resident in pediatrics, 1974-76, asst. in pediatrics, 1979-80, asst. pediatrician, 1980-85, dir. lab. devel. chronobiology, 1983—, assoc. pediatrician, 1985—; pvt. practice medicine specializing in pediatrics, Boston, 1973-88; clin. assoc. NIH, Bethesda, Md., 1976-79; instr. pediatrics Harvard Med. Sch., Boston, 1979-81, asst. prof., 1981-85, assoc. prof., 1985-93, prof. 1993—; vis. scientist Lab. Molecular Neurobiology Mass. Gen. Hosp., 1989-90. Mem. adv. com. Charles H. Hood Found., 1993—. Editor: Development of Circadian Rhythmicity and Photoperiodism in Mammals, 1989; co-editor: Suprachiasmatic Nucleus: The Mind's Clock, 1991; mem. edtl. bd. Neuron, 1997—; contbr. articles to sci. jours, chpts. to books. Regents scholar U. Nebr., 1971; Pfizer Labs. Med. scholar, 1971; Charles King Trust research fellow, 1981-83; Grantee NIH, 1981—, Nat. Found/March of Dimes, 1981-88; recipient E. Mead Johnson award, 1989, NIH Merit award, 1992. Mem. Am. Physiol. Soc., Am. Soc. for Clin. Investigation, Endocrine Soc., Soc. for Pediatric Research, Soc. for Neurosci., Soc. for Research on Biol. Rhythms (adv. com.), Am. Heart Assn. (established investigator 1985-90), Lepidopterists Soc., Cambridge Entomol. Club, Alpha Omega Alpha. Democrat. Avocation: natural history of saturniid moths. Office: Mass Gen Hosp 32 Fruit St Boston MA 02114-2620

REPPUCCI, NICHOLAS DICKON, psychologist, educator; b. Boston, May 1, 1941; s. Nicholas Ralph and Bertha Elizabeth (Williams) R.; m. Christine Marlow Onufrock, Sept. 10, 1967; children: Nicholas Jason, Jonathan Dickon, Anna Jin Marlow. BA with honors, U. N.C., 1962; MA, Harvard U., 1964, PhD, 1968. Lectr., rsch. assoc. Harvard U., Cambridge, Mass., 1967-68; asst. prof. Yale U., New Haven, 1968-73, assoc. prof., 1973-76; prof. psychology U. Va., Charlottesville, 1976—, dir. grad. studies in psychology, 1984-95; originator biennial conf. on community rsch. and action, 1986. Assoc. editor Law and Human Behavior, 1986-96; mem. editl. bd. Am. Jour. Cmty. Psychology, 1974-83, 88-91; author: (with J. Haugaard) Sexual Abuse of Children, 1988, (with P. Britner and J. Wooland) Preventing Child Abuse and Neglect Through Parent Education, 1997; editor: (with J. Haugaard) Prevention in Community Mental Health Practice, (with E. Mulvey, L. Weithorn and J. Monahan) Mental Health, Law and Children, 1984; contbr. over 100 articles to profl. publs., chpts. in books. Adv. bd. on prevention Va. Dept. Mental Health, Mental Retardation and Substance Abuse Svcs., Richmond, 1986-92. Disting. scholar in psychology Va. Assn. Social Sci., 1991. Fellow APA (chair task force on pub. policy 1980-84), Am. Psychol. Soc., Soc. for Community Rsch. and Action (pres. 1986), Phi Beta Kappa. Office: U Va Dept Psychology Charlottesville VA 22903

REPS, DAVID NATHAN, finance educator; b. N.Y.C., July 30, 1926; s. Samuel and Fannie (Ginsberg) R.; m. Helene Shifrin, Aug. 10, 1958; children: Tamara, Aaron, Steven, Jennifer. BSEE, Columbia U., 1948; MSEE, U. Pitts., 1953, PhD, 1966. Elec. utility systems engr. Westinghouse Elec. Corp., Pitts., 1950-63, corp. planner, 1963-67; prin. mgmt. svcs. Ernst & Young, N.Y.C., 1967-75; prof., chmn. bus. econs., fin., pub. policy L.I. Univ., N.Y.C., 1975-78; prof. fin. Pace U., Pleasantville, N.Y., 1978—; v.p. Video Frame Store, Inc., N.Y.C., 1983—, The Photoboard Group, N.Y.C., 1989-92; v.p. and treas. Digital Video Photo Imaging, Inc., N.Y.C., 1992—; bd. dirs. The Storyboard Group, Inc., N.Y.C.; exec. v.p. Video Frame Imaging, Inc., N.Y.C., 1994—. Contbr. articles to profl. jours. With USN, 1944-46. Home: 98 Soundview Ave White Plains NY 10606-3617 Office: Pace U Bedford Rd Pleasantville NY 10570

REQUARTH, WILLIAM HENRY, surgeon; b. Charlotte, N.C., Jan. 23, 1913; s. Charles William and Amelia (George) R.; m. Nancy Charlton, 1948 (div. 1966); children—Kurt, Betsy, Jeff, Jan, Tim, Suzanna; m. Connie Harper, 1977. AB, Millikin U., 1934, LLD, 1996; MD, U. Ill., 1938, MS, 1939. Diplomate: Am. Bd. Surgery. Intern St. Luke's Hosp., Chgo., 1938-39; resident Cook County Hosp., Chgo., 1940-42, 46-48; pvt. practice medicine, specializing in surgery Decatur, Ill., 1950—; clin. prof. surgery U. Ill. Med. Sch., from 1962, now emeritus; Mem. Chgo. Bd. Trade. Author: Diagnosis of Abdominal Pain, 1953, The Acute Abdomen, 1958; also contbg. author chpts. books. Chmn. trustees Millikin U.; chmn. James Millikin Found.; bd. dirs. Decatur Meml. Hosp. Served to comdr. USNR, 1941-46. Mem. ACS, Cen. Surg. Assn., Western Surg. Assn., Chgo. Surg. Soc., Ill. Surg. Soc. (pres. 1970-71), Am. Soc. Surgery Hand (founder), Am. Soc. Surgery Trauma, Soc. Surgery Alimentary Tract, Warren Cole Soc., Societe Internationale Chirurgie, Nat. Pilots Assn. (pres. 1960-61), Soaring Soc. Am., Sportsman Pilot Assn. (pres. 1966-67), Aerobatic Club Am., Internat. Aerobatic Club. Home: 1860 S Spitler Dr Decatur IL 62521-4417 Office: 158 W Prairie Ave Decatur IL 62523-1230

RESCH, JOSEPH ANTHONY, neurologist; b. Milw., Apr. 29, 1914; s. Frank and Elizabeth (Zetsch) R.; m. Rose Catherine Ritz, May 25, 1939; children—Rose, Frank, Catherine. Student, Milw. State Tchrs. Coll., 1931-34; B.S., U. Wis., Madison, 1936, M.D., 1938. Intern St. Francis Hosp., LaCrosse, Wis., 1938-39; gen. practice medicine Holmen, Wis., 1939-40; med. fellow in neurology U. Minn., 1946-48, clin. instr. neurology, 1948-51, clin. asst. prof., 1951-55, clin. assoc. prof., 1955-62, assoc. prof., 1962-65, prof., 1965-84, prof. emeritus, 1984—, head dept. neurology, 1976-82, asst. v.p. health sci., 1970-79, prof. lab. medicine and pathology, 1979-84; practice medicine specializing in neurology Mpls., 1948-62. Contbr. articles and abstracts to profl. jours., chpts. in books. Served to lt. col. M.C. U.S. Army, 1940-46; col. Med. Res. 1946-53. Mem. Hennepin County Med. Soc., Minn. Med. Assn., AMA, Minn. Soc. Neurol. Scis., Central Assn. Electroencephalographers, Am. Acad. Neurology, Am. Neurol. Assn., Am. Assn. Neuropathologists, Am. EEG Soc., Sonoma County Med. Assn., Am. Epilepsy Soc. Home: 301 White Oak Dr Santa Rosa CA 95409

RESCH, MARY LOUISE, social services administrator; b. David City, Nebr., Oct. 26, 1956; d. Ernest John and Mary Jean (Roelandts) Cermak; m. Eugene Joseph Resch, Apr. 28, 1979. BS in Psychology, SUNY, Albany, 1984; MS in Counseling and Edn. with high honors, U. Wis., Platteville, 1986. Enlisted U.S. Army, 1974, advance through ranks to sgt., 1982; bomb disposal tech. U.S. Army, Ft. Riley, Kans., 1977-79; bomb disposal instr. U.S. Army, Indian Head, Md., 1979-80; resigned U.S. Army, 1985; instr., intern family advocacy Army Community Svc., U.S. Army, Ft. Belvoir, 1986; sr. counselor, child therapist Community Crisis and Referral Ctr., Inc., Waldorf, Md., 1986-87; adminstr. Walter Reed Army Med. Ctr. USDA Grad. Sch., Washington, 1987-88; contract mgr. USDA Grad. Sch., Ft. Jackson, S.C., 1988-91; pres. Athena Cons., Columbia, S.C., 1991-93; dir. spl. programs Newberry (S.C.) Commn. on Alcohol and Drug Abuse, 1993-95; resource devel. coord. Cities in Schs.-SC, Inc., Columbia, 1995—; human svcs. cons., Washington, 1986-87; adj. instr. Coker Coll., Ft. Jackson, 1989-95. Mem. NAFE, ACA, Nat. Contract Mgmt. Assn. (fellow, former pres., mentor), Mil. Educators and Counselors Assn., Com. Mil. Edn. S.C. Republican. Lutheran. Avocations: needlepoint, racquetball, reading, bowling. Home: 1016 Harvey Killian Rd Chapin SC 29036-7807 Office: Cities in Schs SC Inc PO Box 773 1200 Catawba St Columbia SC 29202

RESCHER, NICHOLAS, philosophy educator; b. Hagen, Westphalia, Germany, July 15, 1928; came to U.S. 1938, naturalized 1944; s. Erwin Hans and Meta Anna (Landau) R.; m. Dorothy Henle, Feb. 10, 1968; children: Mark, Owen, Catherine; 1 child from a previous marriage, Elizabeth. BS in Math., Queens Coll., 1949; PhD, Princeton U., 1951; LHD (hon.), Loyola U.-Chgo., 1970, Lehigh U., 1993; Dr. honoris causa U. Córdoba, Argentina, 1992, U. Konstanz, Germany, 1995. Instr. philosophy Princeton U., N.J., 1951-52; mathematician RAND Corp., 1954-56; assoc. prof. philosophy Lehigh U., Bethlehem, Pa., 1957-61; Univ. prof. philosophy U. Pitts., 1961—, vice chmn. Ctr. for Philosophy of Sci., 1988—; trustee St. Edmunds Acad., Pitts., 1980-85; nonresident mem. Corpus Christi Coll., Oxford; disting. vis. lectr. Oxford, Salamanca, Munich, Konstanz. Author: The Coherence Theory of Truth, 1973, Scientific Progress, 1978, The Limits of Science, 1985, Luck, 1995, Predicting the Future, 1997; others; exec. editor: Am. Philos. Quar., 1961—; mem. editl. bd. 15 jours.; contbr. over 250 articles to profl. jours. Sec. gen. Internat. Union of History and Philosophy of Sci. (UNESCO), 1969-75. Served with USMC, 1952-54. Recipient Alexander von Humboldt Humanities prize 1983. Mem. Am. Philos. Assn. (past pres.), Royal Asiatic Soc., G.W. Leibniz Soc. Am. (past pres.), C.S. Peirce Soc. (past pres.), Inst. Internat. de Philosophie, Academie Internationale de Philosophie des Sciences. Roman Catholic. Avocation: reading history and biography. Home: 5818 Aylesboro Ave Pittsburgh PA 15217-1446 Office: Univ of Pitts Dept Philosophy 1012 Cathedral Pittsburgh PA 15260

RESCHKE, MICHAEL W., real estate executive; b. Chgo., Nov. 29, 1955; s. Don J. and Vera R. (Helmer) R.; m. Kim P. Shaw, July 17, 1977; children: Michael W. Jr., Tiffanie G. BS summa cum laude with univ. honors, No. Ill. U., 1977; JD summa cum laude, U. Ill., 1980. Bar: Ill. 1980; CPA, Ill. Assoc. Winston & Strawn, Chgo., 1980-82; pres., CEO The Prime Group, Inc., Chgo., 1982—, also chmn. bd. dirs.; chmn. bd. dirs. Prime Retail, Inc., NASDAQ: PRME and PRMEP, NASD: BLCI; bd. dirs. Amb. Apts., Inc., NYSE: AAH. Mem. Chgo. Devel. Coun., 1987; chmn. bd. Brookdale Living Comtys., Inc. Mem. ABA, Ill. Bar Assn., Urban Land Inst., Chgo. Club, Econ. Club Chgo., Nat. Realty Com. (mem. chmn.'s roundtable 1992—), Nat. Assn. Real Estate Investment Trusts, Order of Coif, Phi Delta Phi, Beta Alpha Psi. Office: The Prime Group 77 W Wacker Dr Ste 3900 Chicago IL 60601-1629

RESCIGNO, RICHARD JOSEPH, editor; b. N.Y.C., Apr. 13, 1946; s. Vincent James and Rose (Sofia) R.; m. Carol Sue Conyne, Apr. 22, 1978; children: Timothy, Daniel. BA in English Lit., Fairleigh Dickinson U., 1967; MS in Journalism, Columbia U., 1968. Reporter The Hudson Dispatch, Union City, N.J., 1967; reporter, copy editor The Bergen Record, Hackensack, N.J., 1971-75; reporter, copy editor, asst. city editor Newsday, Melville, N.Y., 1975-81; sr. editor, news editor, asst. mng. editor, mng. editor Barron's, The Dow Jones Bus. and Fin. Weekly, N.Y.C., 1981—. With U.S. Army, 1968-70. Avocations: foreign languages, travel, sports. Office: Barron's 200 Liberty St New York NY 10281-1003

RESCORLA, ROBERT ARTHUR, psychology educator; b. Pitts, May 9, 1940; s. Arthur R. and Mildred J. (Jenkins) R.; m. Shirley Steele; children: Eric, Michael. BA, Swarthmore Coll., 1962; PhD, U. Pa., 1966; MA, Yale U., 1974. Successively asst. prof., assoc. prof., prof. Yale U., New Haven, 1966-80; prof. psychology U. Pa., Phila., 1981—, James Skinner prof. sci., 1986—, dean of coll. Sch. of Arts and Scis., 1994—. Author: Pavlovian Second-Order Conditioning, 1980; editor: Animal Learning and Behavior, 1995—; contbr. articles to profl. jours. Mem. APA (pres. div. 3 1985, Disting. Sci. Contbn. award 1986), Am. Psychol. Soc. (William James fellow 1988), NAS, AAAS (pres. sect. J., psychology 1988-89), Soc. Exptl. Psychologists (Warren medal 1991), Psychonomic Soc. (mem. governing bd. 1979-85, chmn. publ. bd. 1985-86), Ea. Psychol. Assn. (bd. dirs. 1983-86, pres. 1986-87). Office: U Pa Dept Psychology 3815 Walnut St Philadelphia PA 19104-3604

RESDEN, RONALD EVERETT, medical devices product development engineer; b. Littleton, N.H., Oct. 27, 1944; s. Lawrence A. and Rita Mae (Bowen) R.; m. Dee Kronenburg, Apr. 20, 1974 (div.); children: Philip, Alison; m. Louise Simons, June 18, 1994. Cons. Franklin Mfg. Co., Norwood, Mass., 1984—, Boston Sci. Co., Watertown, Mass., 1985—, Via Med, Easton, Mass., 1986—, White Marsh Labs., Balt., 1989—, Spectraphos Malmo Sweden, 1991—, Vision Scis. Inc., Natick, Mass., 1991—, Cordis Corp., Miami, Fla., 1993—; cons. Cardiology Catheter Lab. Mass. Hosp. Cardiology, Boston, 1993—; Active MIT Enterprise Forum. Author: Hologram Control Transfer, 1984; inventor, patentee in field; mem. rev. bd. Medica Plastics and Biomaterials mag. Mem. NRA (life), Soc. Plastics Engrs. (mem. med. plastics and biomaterials mag. rev. bd.), Soc. Mfg. Engrs., Nat. Geog. Soc., Mass. Chiefs of Police Assn., Citizens for Ltd. Taxation. Home and Office: Arrowhead Rsch Inc 44 Arrowhead Rd Weston MA 02193-1707

RESEK, ROBERT WILLIAM, economist; b. Berwyn, Ill., July 2, 1935; s. Ephraim Frederick and Ruth Elizabeth (Rummele) R.; m. Lois Doll, July 9, 1960; 1 child, Richard Alden. BA, U. Ill., 1957; AM, Harvard U., 1960, PhD, 1961. Vis. scholar MIT, Cambridge, 1967-68; asst. prof. econs. U. Ill., Urbana, 1961-65, assoc. prof., 1965-70, prof., 1970—; dir. Bur. Econ. and Bus. Rsch., 1977-89, acting v.p. for acad. affairs, 1987-89, v.p. for acad. affairs, 1989-94; prof. Inst. Govt. and Pub. Affairs, 1994—; tchg. fellow Harvard U., 1959-61; vis. prof. U. Colo., 1967, 74, 75, 76, 82, Kyoto (Japan) U., 1976; cons. GM, 1964-66, U.S. Congress Joint Econ. Com., 1978-80, ABA, 1980-82; vis. scholar UCLA, 1994-95; co-dir. Midwest Economy: Issues and Policy, Midwest Govs. Conf., 1981; bd. dirs. Midwest U. Consortium Internat. Activities, v.p., 1991-94. Co-author: Environmental Contamination by Lead and Other Heavy Metals—Synthesis and Modeling, 1978, Special Topics in Mathematics for Economists, 1976, A Comparative Cost Study of Staff Panel and Participating Attorney Panel Prepaid Legal Service Plans, 1981; editor: Illinois Economic Outlook, 1982-87, Illinois Economic Statistics, 1981; co-editor: The Midwest Economy: Issues and Policy, 1982, Frontiers of Business and Economic Research Management, 1983, Illinois Statistical Abstract, 1987. Woodrow Wilson fellow, 1957; Social Sci. Rsch. Coun. grantee, 1964; NSF fellow, 1967-69, grantee, 1974-77; U.S. Dept. State scholar, Japan, 1976. Mem. Assn. Univ. Bus. and Econ. Rsch. (mem. exec. com. 1977-89, v.p. 1978-82, pres. 1982-83), Econometric Soc., Beta Gamma Sigma, Phi Kappa Phi. Home: 201 E Holmes St Urbana IL 61801-6612 Office: Univ Ill 211 IGPA 1007 W Nevada St Urbana IL 61801-3812

RESHOTKO, ELI, aerospace engineer, educator; b. N.Y.C., Nov. 18, 1930; s. Max and Sarah (Kalisky) R.; m. Adina Venit, June 7, 1953; children: Deborah, Naomi, Miriam Ruth. B.S., Cooper Union, 1950; M.S., Cornell U., 1951; Ph.D., Calif. Inst. Tech., 1960. Aero. research engr. NASA-Lewis Flight Propulsion Lab., Cleve., 1951-56; head fluid mechanics sect. NASA-Lewis Flight Propulsion Lab., 1956-57; head high temperature plasma sect. NASA-Lewis Research Center, 1960-61, chief plasma physics br., 1961-64; asso. prof. engring. Case Inst. Tech., Cleve., 1964-66, dean, 1986-87; prof. engring. Case Western Res. U., 1966-88, chmn. dept. fluid thermal and aerospace scis., 1970-76, chmn. dept. mech. and aerospace engring., 1976-79, Kent H. Smith prof. engring., 1989—; Susman vis. prof. dept. aero. engring. Technion-Israel Inst. Tech., Haifa, Israel, 1969-70; cons. United Technologies Research Ctr., United Research Corp., Dynamics Tech. Inc., Micro Craft Tech., Martin-Marietta Corp., Rockwell Internat.; mem. adv. com. fluid dynamics NASA, 1961-64; mem. aero. adv. com. NASA, 1980-87, chmn. adv. subcom. on aerodynamics, 1983-85; chmn. U.S. Boundary Layer Transition Study Group, NASA/USAF, 1970—; U.S. mem. fluid dynamics panel AGARD-NATO, 1981-88; chmn. steering com. Symposium on Engring. Aspects Magneto-hydro-dynamics, 1966, Case-NASA Inst. for Computational Mechanics in Propulsion, 1985-92, USRA/NASA ICASE Sci. Coun., 1992; Joseph Wunsch lectr. Technion-Israel Inst. Tech., 1990. Contbr. articles to tech. jours. Chmn. bd. govs. Cleve. Coll. Jewish Studies, 1981-84. Guggenheim fellow Calif. Inst. Tech., 1957-59. Fellow ASME, AAAS, AIAA (Fluid and Plasma Dynamics award 1980, Dryden lectr. in rsch. 1994), Am. Phys. Soc., Am. Acad. Mechanics (pres. 1986-87); mem. NAE, AAUP, Ohio Sci. and Engring. Roundtable, Sigma Xi, Tau Beta Pi, Pi Tau Sigma. Office: Case Western Reserve Univ University Cir Cleveland OH 44106

RESIKA, PAUL, artist; b. N.Y.C., Aug. 15, 1928. Student, Sol Wilson, N.Y.C., 1940-44, Hans Hofmann Sch., 1945-47, Venice, Italy, 1950-53. adj. prof. art Cooper Union, 1966-78; instr. Art Students League, 1968-69; faculty Skowhagen Sch. Painting and Sculpture, 1973, 76; chmn. M.F.A. program Parsons Sch. Design, 1978-89. Artist-in-residence, Dartmouth Coll., 1972; one-man shows include George Dix Gallery, N.Y.C., 1948, Peridot Gallery, N.Y.C., 1965, 67, 68, 69, 70, Washburn Gallery, N.Y.C., 1971, 73, Hopkins Ctr. Dartmouth Coll., 1972, Graham Gallery, N.Y.C., 1976, 79, 81, 83, 85, Longpoint Gelelry, Provincetown, Mass., 1979, 81, 95, 89, 92, 25-yr. survey Artists Choice Mus., 1985, Merideth Long Gallery, Houston, 1986, 97, Kornbluth Gallery, Fairlawn, N.J., 1986, Crane Kalman Gallery, London, 1986, Graham/Modern Gallery, 1987-88, 90, Salander-O'Reilly Galleries, N.Y.C., 1993, 94, 95 Am. Acad. Arts and Letters, 1994, Walker-Kornbluth Gallery, Fairlawn, 1995, 97, Vered Gallery, East Hampton, N.Y., 1995, Longpoint Gallery, Provincetown, 1995, Gerald Peters Gallery, Santa Fe, 1996; represented in permanent collections U. Nebr. Art Gallery, Indpls. Mus. Art, Chase Manhattan Bank, N.Y.C., Neuberger Mus., SUNY, Pruchase, U. Wyo., Laramie, Met. Mus. Art N.Y., Colby Coll., NAD, Owensboro (Ky.) Mus. Art, U. Ariz., William Benton Mus. Art, Hood Museum, Darthmouth Coll., Hanover, N.H., Tucson Mus. Art, U. Conn., Crackow Mus. Art, Poland, Parish Art Mus., Southampton, N.Y., Heckscher Mus., Huntington, N.Y., Mills Coll. Mus., Oakland, Calif., pvt. collections. Recipient award Am. Acad. Arts and Letters, 1977, Altman prize NAD, 1982, 91; Louis Comfort Tiffany grantee, 1959; Ingram Merrill grantee, 1969; John Simon Guggenheim Meml. fellow, 1984. Mem. NAD, Am. Acad. Arts and Letters. Office: care Salander-O'Reilly Galleries 20 E 79th St New York NY 10021-0106

RESKE, STEVEN DAVID, lawyer, writer; b. Mpls., May 31, 1962; s. Albert Edgar Reske and Florence Mae Altland. BA with distinction, St. Olaf Coll., Northfield, Minn., 1985; JD cum laude, Boston U., 1988. Bar: Ill. 1988, Minn. 1989, D.C. 1997, U.S. Dist. Ct. Minn. 1991, U.S. Ct. Appeals (5th cir.) 1989, (7th and 8th cir.) 1992, (D.C. circuit) 1997, U.S. Supreme Ct. 1993. Intern U.S. Senator Durenberger, Washington, 1981-82, Citizens for Ednl. Freedom, Washington, D.C., 1981-82, Abbott-Northwestern Hosp., Mpls., 1984, U.S. Dist. Ct. Judge Magnuson, St. Paul, 1986; summer assoc. Faegre & Benson, Mpls., 1987; assoc. Sidley & Austin, Chgo., 1988; law clk. U.S. Ct. Appeals 5th cir. Judge Politz, Shreveport, La., 1988-89. Contbr. CD Rev., 1993-95, JAZZIZ, 1996—; contbr. articles to profl. jours.; mem. Am. Jour. Law and Medicine, 1986-87, editor, 1987-88. Recipient Am. Jurisprudence award Boston U. Sch. Law, 1987, Edward F. Hennessey scholar, 1987, G. Joseph Tauro scholar, 1986. Mem. ABA (anti-trust divsn.), Minn. State Bar Assn., Hennepin County Bar Assn., Am. Econ. Assn., Am. Philos. Assn., Jazz Journalist Assn. Office: 110 W Grant St # 20-c Minneapolis MN 55403

RESMINI, RONALD JOSEPH, lawyer; b. Providence, June 16, 1942; s. Joseph Andrew and Corrine Marie (Barrette) R.; m. Paula Oliver, July 1, 1979; children: R. Jason, Adam Joseph, Andrew Oliver. BA, Providence Coll., 1965; JD, Suffolk U., 1968. Bar: R.I. 1969, U.S. Dist. Ct. R.I. 1972, U.S. Supreme Ct. 1972, U.S. Ct. Mil. Appeals 1981, Mass. 1984. Substitute tchr. pub. schs., Cranston, Providence, R.I., 1968-69; law clk. to justice R.I. Supreme Ct., Providence, 1971; pvt. practice Providence, 1981—; mem. faculty R.I. Trial Inst., 1988-89; instr. bus. law Roger Williams U., Providence, 1969-73; asst. town solicitor Town of Coventry (R.I.), 1970-72; lectr. continuing legal edn. program R.I. Bar Assn., 1978—; lectr. Roger William Sch. Law, 1996; instr. R.I. Law Inst.; mem. R.I. Continuing Legal Edn. Com., 1992; lectr. personal injury Nat. Bus. Inst., 1988. Author: Handbook on Uninsured-Underinsured Motorist Coverage, 1984, Bad Faith Litigation, 1985, Soft Tissue Injury Handbook, 1986, R.I. Tort Series, 1988, Tort Law and Personal Injury Practice, 2 vols., 1988, R.I. Action and Remedies, 1992, Domestic Relations Encyclopedia, 1996. Bd. dirs. Providence chpt. ARC, 1974-78; campaign fin. chmn. for R.I. atty. gen., 1986; coach Barrington (R.I.) Little League, 1988, 93, 94, 95; coach Sr. League and All Stars, 1990, 91, 92, 93, 94; soccer coach McDonald's All Stars, 1995; pres. Parent-Child Indian Guide Orgn., Barrington YMCA, 1988; Eucharistic min. St. Lukes, Orchard View Nursing Home. Served to capt. U.S. Army, 1969-71; USAR, 1971-77, ret. Decorated Meritorious Svc. medal; recipient Arbitration award, Am. Arbitration Assn., 1987. Fellow R.I. Bar Found.; mem. Interest Lawyer's Trust Accounts (founder, chmn. 1984), R.I. Trial Lawyers Assn. (treas. 1975-85, bd. govs. 1986—), Nat. Bd. Trial Advocacy (bd. examiner 1990), Univ. Club, R.I. Country Club, Turks Head Club, Crestwood Country Club. Roman Catholic. Home: 43 Riverside Dr Barrington RI 02806-3615 Office: 155 S Main St Ste 400 Providence RI 02903-2963 also: 41 Mink St Seekonk MA 02771-5914

RESNICK, ALAN HOWARD, eye care executive; b. Boston, Nov. 1, 1943; s. Max Lawrence and Natalie (Levine) R.; m. Janice M. Mark, Jan. 26, 1948; children: Stephen Seth, Helaine Elise, Eileen, Michelle. BS, Tufts U., 1965; MBA, Columbia U., 1967. Fin. analyst E.I. DuPont de Nemours & Co., Wilmington, Del., 1967-73; various positions Bausch & Lomb Inc., Rochester, N.Y., 1973—, treas., 1986—; mem. adv. bd. Allendale Ins. Co., Johnston, R.I., 1987. Bd. dirs. Rochester Monroe County chpt. ARC, 1988—, Park Ridge Hosp., 1990—. Jewish. Avocation: stamp collecting. Office: Bausch & Lomb Inc 1 Bausch And Lomb Pl Rochester NY 14604-2701

RESNICK, ALICE ROBIE, state supreme court justice; b. Erie, Pa., Aug. 21, 1939; d. Adam Joseph and Alice Suzanne (Spizarny) Robie; m. Melvin L. Resnick, Mar. 20, 1970. PhB, Siena Heights Coll., 1961; JD, U. Detroit, 1964. Bar: Ohio 1964, Mich. 1965, U.S. Supreme Ct. 1970. Asst. county prosecutor Lucas County Prosecutor's Office, Toledo, 1964-75, trial atty., 1965-75; judge Toledo Mcpl. Ct., 1976-83, 6th Dist. Ct. Appeals, State of Ohio, Toledo, 1983-88; instr. U. Toledo, 1968-69; justice Ohio Supreme Ct., 1989—; co-chairperson Ohio State Gender Fairness Task Force. Trustee Siena Heights Coll., Adrian, Mich., 1982—; organizer Crime Stopper Inc., Toledo, 1981—; mem. Mayor's Drug Coun.; bd. dirs. Guest House Inc. Mem. ABA, Toledo Bar Assn., Lucas County Bar Assn., Nat. Assn. Women Judges, Am. Judicature Soc., Toledo Women's Bar Assn., Ohio State Women's Bar Assn. (organizer), Toledo Mus. Art, Internat. Inst. Toledo. Roman Catholic. Home: 2407 Edgehill Rd Toledo OH 43615-2321 Office: Supreme Ct Office 30 E Broad St Fl 3 Columbus OH 43215-3414

RESNICK, DONALD IRA, lawyer; b. Chgo., July 19, 1950; s. Roland S. and Marilyn B. (Weiss) R.; m. Jill Allison White, July 3, 1977; children: Daniel, Allison. BS with high honors, U. Ill., 1972; JD, Harvard U., 1975. Bar: Ill. 1975, U.S. Dist. Ct. (no. dist.) Ill. 1975. Assoc. Arvey, Hodes, Costello & Burman, Chgo., 1975-80, ptnr., 1981-83; sr. ptnr. Nagelberg & Resnick, Chgo., 1983-89, Levenstein & Resnick, Chgo., 1989-91; chmn. real estate dept. Jenner & Block, Chgo., 1992—. Bd. dirs. Ill. chpt. Real Estate/Investment Assn., Chgo., 1986—. Mem. ABA, Birchwood (Highland Park, Ill.) Club. Office: Jenner & Block 1 E Ibm Plz Chicago IL 60611-3586

RESNICK, IDRIAN NAVARRE, foundation administrator; b. Wichita, Kans., Apr. 24, 1936; s. Herbert and Virginiae Miriam (Goldsmith) Speer; m. Jane Letham Riley (div. 1980); children: Michael Mosi, David Shaka; m. Kathleen Margaret Pelich (div. 1993); stepchildren: Robert Andrew, Kathleen Mary, Janice Margaret; m. Louise LaMontagne, 1996. BA, Clark U., 1958; MA, Boston U., 1961, PhD, 1966. Lectr. dept. econs. Boston U., 1962-63; asst. prof. econs. Howard U., Washington, 1963-64; lectr. econs. U. Dar es Salaam, Tanzania, 1964-67; vis. prof. econs. Princeton (N.J.) U., 1967-68; asst. prof. econs. Columbia U., N.Y.C., 1968-70; sr. economist Ministry Econ. Planning, Dar es Salaam, 1970-72; exec. dir. Econ. Devel. Bur., New Haven, 1974-81; pres. Resnick Devel. Services, New Haven, 1982—; exec. dir. Assn. Am. Indian Affairs, N.Y.C., 1985-89, Action for Corp. Accountability, New Haven, 1991-94; prof. Cornell U., Ithaca, N.Y., 1982-84; cons. Govt. of Nicaragua, Managua, 1979-81, Govt. of the Netherlands, The Hague, 1977, Govt. of Somalia, Mogodishu, 1985. Author: The Long Transition: Building Socialism in Tanzania, 1981, Controlling Consulting, 1989; editor: Tanzania: Revolution by Education, 1968; video producer (in the Lakota lang.) AIDS, 1989; contbr. articles to profl. jours. Organizer Namibia Com., New Haven, 1977-79, Conn. Task Force on Cen. Am., 1985; mem. Pledge of Resistance, U.S., 1985—; vol. adviser AIDS Interfaith Network, New Haven, 1990. Nat. Edn. scholar U.S. Govt., 1959-62; Albert Schweitzer Resh fellow Columbia U., 1969-70. Avocations: chess, theatre, travel, tennis, golf, photography, woodworking, classical music. Home: 16 Old Pawson Rd Branford CT 06405-5117

RESNICK, JEFFREY LANCE, federal magistrate judge; b. Bklyn., Mar. 5, 1943; s. Bernard and Selma (Monheit) R.; m. Margery O'Connor, May 27, 1990. BA, U. Conn., 1964; LLB, U. Conn., West Hartford, 1967. Bar: Conn. 1967, N.Y. 1968, U.S.V.I. 1968, D.C. 1979, U.S. Ct. Appeals (3d cir.) 1979. Assoc. Office of J.D. Marsh, Christiansted, St. Croix, V.I., 1967-69; asst. atty. gen. Dept. Law, Christiansted, 1969-73; ptnr. James & Resnick, Christiansted, 1973-89; magistrate judge U.S. Dist. Ct. V.I., Christiansted, 1989—. Active V.I. Bridge Team, 1971—. Jewish. Avocations: writing poetry and palindromes. Office: US District Court 3013 Est Golden Rock Christiansted VI 00820-4256

RESNICK, MYRON J., retired insurance company executive, lawyer; b. Louisville, July 13, 1931; s. Harry C. and Sybil G. (Glick) R.; m. Alicia M. Ward, Dec. 16, 1967; children—Hugh, Clay, David. B.S. in Econs., U. Pa., 1953; J.D., U. Mich., 1956. Various positions Allstate Ins. Co., Northbrook, Ill., 1959-88, sr. v.p., treas. bd. dirs., 1959-95; chmn. bd. Federated Ins. Co. Ltd. (U.K.), Sale, Cheshire, Eng., 1979-81; dir. Allstate Ins. Co. Ltd. (U.K.), Sale; pres. Allstate Investment Mgmt. Co.; mem. adj. faculty John Marshall Law Sch., Chgo., 1996—. Mem. Chgo. exec. com. Anti-Defamation League, 1975—; bd. dirs. Chgo. Urban League, 1987—, St. Scholastica High Sch., Chgo., 1977-79; trustee George Williams Coll., Downers Grove, Ill., 1981-93, chmn. bd. trustees, 1991-93; trustee Aurora U., 1993—; bd. advisors Inst. Law and Econs. U. Pa., 1994—. With U.S. Army, 1956-58. Mem. ABA, Chgo. Bar Assn., Ill. Bar Assn., Assn. Life Ins. Counsel, Chgo. Mortgage Attys. Assn. (bd. dirs. 1965-75), Reform Club (London).

RESNICK, OSCAR, neuroscientist; b. Bayonne, N.J., Apr. 27, 1924; s. Samuel and Rebecca (Rubinstein) R.; m. Janice Zelda Ravitz, July 13, 1949; children—Sandra, Scott. A.B., Clark U., Worcester, Mass., 1944; M.A., Harvard U., 1945; Ph.D., Boston U., 1955. Research fellow U. Iowa Med. Sch., 1945-46; instr. St. Petersburg Jr. Coll., 1946-47; research fellow U. Kans., 1947-49; instr. U. Minn., 1949-50; editorial asst. Biol. Abstracts, U. Pa., 1950-51; scientist Nat. Drug Co., Phila., 1951-53, Worcester Found. Exptl. Biology, Shrewsbury, Mass., 1953—; now sr. scientist, lectr. Boston U., 1961—, Clark U., 1965—; dir. research Worcester County Rehab. and Detention Ctr., West Boylston, Mass., 1965-76; cons. Medfield State Hosp., Mass., Norwich State Hosp., Conn. Contbr. articles to profl. jours. Mem. mental retardation research com. NIH, 1975-78. NIH grantee, 1957—. Fellow Am. Coll. Neuopsychopharmacology; mem. AAAS, Soc. Biol. Psychiatry, Am. Psychopath. Soc., N.Y. Acad. Sci., Soc. Neurosci., Sigma Xi. Home: 270 E Douglas Ave El Cajon CA 92020-4534 Office: Boston U Sch Medicine Ctr Behavioral Dev Mental Retardation 85 E Newton St Roxbury MA 02118-2340 Address: 270 E Douglas Ave El Cajon CA 92020-4534

RESNICK, PAUL R., research chemist; b. N.Y.C., Apr. 7, 1934; married, 1966; 1 child. BA, Swarthmore Coll., 1955; PhD in Organic Chemistry, Cornell U., 1961. Fellow U. Calif., Berkeley, 1960-62; from chemist to sr. rsch. chemist E.I. DuPont De Nemours & Co., Inc., 1962-74, rsch. assoc., 1974-85, rsch. fellow, 1985-88, sr. rsch. fellow, 1988-91, DuPont fellow, 1991—. Mem. Am. Chem. Soc. (Award for Creative Work in Fluorine Chemistry 1995). Office: DuPont Fluoroproducts PO Drawer Z Fayetteville NC 28302-1770

RESNICK, ROBERT, physicist, educator; b. Balt., Jan. 11, 1923; s. Abraham and Anna (Dubin) R.; m. Mildred Saltzman, Oct. 14, 1945; children—Trudy, Abby, Regina. A.B., Johns Hopkins U., 1943, Ph.D. (Pres.'s Fund scholar 1946-49), 1949. Physicist NACA, Cleve., 1944-46; asst. prof., assoc. prof. physics U. Pitts., 1949-56; assoc. prof., prof. physics Rensselaer Poly. Inst., Troy, N.Y., 1956-93; prof. emeritus, 1993—; chmn. interdisciplinary sci. curriculum Rensselaer Poly. Inst., Troy, N.Y., 1973-88, Edward P. Hamilton Disting. prof. sci., 1975-93; hon. research fellow Harvard U., 1964-65; Fulbright prof. Peru, 1971; hon. vis. prof. Peoples Republic of China, 1981, 85; mem. Commn. on Coll. Physics, 1960-68; commencement speaker Rensselaer Poly. Inst., 1993. Author: A Manual for Laboratory Physics, 1954, (with D. Halliday) Physics, 1960, 3d edit., 1978, 4th edit., 1991, extended version, 1986, 2d edit. extended version, 1991, Introduction to Special Relativity, 1968, (with R. Eisberg) Notes on Quantum Theory, 1968, Notes on Modern Physics, 1969, Quantum Physics of Atoms, Molecules, Solids, Nuclei and Particles, 1974, 2d edit., 1985, (with D. Halliday) Fundamentals of Physics, 1970, 4th edit., 1996, extended version, 1988, 2d edit., 1993, 3rd edit., 1996, (with others) Student Study Guide for Physics, 1970, 5th edit., 1993, Basic Concepts in Relativity and Early Quantum Theory, 1972, 2d edit., 1985, Basic Concepts in Relativity, 1991; author: (with others) Sourcebook for Programmable Calculators, 1978, (with E. Derringh) Solutions to Physics Problems, 1980, 4th edit., 1992, (with K. Brownstein) Tests for Physics, 1987; books translated into numerous fgn. langs; mem. adv. bd., project staff: Physical Science for Non-Scientists, 1964-1968, pub., 1968; co-dir.: Project Physics Demonstration Experiments, 1962-70; pub. project, 1970, Workshop on Apparatus for College Physics, 1964-65, 66, Videotapes in Physics Instruction, 1975-78, 1978; dir. project Physics Demonstration and Laboratory Apparatus Workshop, 1960-61; pub. project, 1961; adv editor: John Wiley & Sons, Inc., 1967-89, Macmillan Pubs., 1990-94; mem. U.S. adv. bd. Quantum joint USSR/USA sci. mag., 1989-93. Recipient Disting. Svc. citation Am. Assn. Physics Tchrs., 1967, Hans Christian Oersted medal, 1974, Esso award for outstanding teaching, 1953, Disting. Faculty award Rensselaer Poly. Inst., 1971; named to Hall of Fame, Balt. City Coll., 1989; Robert Resnick Ctr. for Physics established at Rensselaer Poly. Inst., 1993, Robert Resnick Ann. Sci. Lectr. series endowed, 1993. Fellow AAAS, Am. Phys. Soc.; mem. AAUP, Am. Assn. Physics Tchrs. (v.p. 1986, pres.-elect 1987, pres. 1988), Am. Soc. Engring. Edn., Am. Inst. Physics (governing bd. 1987-90), Textbook Author Assn. (coun. 1990-93), Phi Beta Kappa, Sigma Xi. Rsch. publs. in aerodynamics, nuclear physics, atomic physics, upper atmosphere physics, history of physics, physics edn. Home: 23221 L'Ermitage Cir Boca Raton FL 33433-7144

RESNICK, STEWART ALLEN, diversified company executive; b. Jersey City, Dec. 24, 1936; s. David and Yetta (Goldmaker) R.; children from previous marriage: Jeffrey Brian, Ilene Sue, William Jay; m. Lynda Rae Harris, Nov. 26, 1972; children: Jonathon Charles Sinay, Jason Daniel Sinay. BS, UCLA, 1959, LLB, 1962. Chmn., owner Roll Internat. Corp., L.A., 1958—; chmn. The Franklin Mint, Franklin Center, Pa., 1985—; chmn., owner Teleflora, L.A., Paramount Citrus Co., L.A., Paramount Farming Co., L.A. Bd. trustees Bard Coll., N.Y.C.; acquistions com. Nat. Gallery, Washington; co-chmn. mktg. dept., adv. bd., mem. Mgmt. Edn. Coun., The Wharton Sch., U. Pa. Avocations: health and fitness related activities. Office: The Franklin Mint US Rt 1 Franklin Center PA 19091

RESNIK, HARVEY LEWIS PAUL, psychiatrist; b. Buffalo, Apr. 6, 1930; s. Samuel andCelia (Greenberg) R.; m. Audrey Ruth Frey, Aug. 30, 1964 (dec. 1993); children: Rebecca Gabrielle, Henry Seth Maccabee, Jessica Ruth. B.A. magna cum laude, U. Buffalo, 1951; M.D., Columbia, 1955; grad., Phila. Psychoanalytic Inst., 1967. Diplomate: Am. Bd. Psychiatry and Neurology. Intern Phila. Gen. Hosp., 1955-56, resident in surgery, 1956-57; resident in psychiatry Jackson Meml. Hosp., Miami, Fla., 1959-61; fellow U. Pa. Hosp., 1961-62, mem. staff, 1962-67; instr; Sch. Medicine, U. Pa., 1962-66; instr. med. hypnosis Sch. Medicine, U. Pa. (Grad. Sch. Medicine), 1963-65; clin. dir. psychiatry E. J. Meyer Meml. Hosp., Buffalo, 1967; dir. psychiatry E. J. Meyer Meml. Hosp., 1968; assoc. prof. psychiatry Sch. Medicine, SUNY at Buffalo, 1967, prof., 1968-70, dep. chmn. dept. psychiatry, 1968-69; chief Nat. Center for Studies of Suicide Prevention, NIMH, 1969-74, chief mental health emergencies sect., 1974-76; with Reproductive Biology Research Found., St. Louis, 1971; clin. prof. psychiatry Sch. Medicine, George Washington U., 1969—; dir. Human Behavior Found., 1975—; lectr. Sch. Medicine, Johns Hopkins, 1969-74; adj. prof. Johns Hopkins U. Sch. Pub. Health, 1981-82; prof. cmty. health Fed. City Coll., 1971-75; med. dir. Human Behavior Found., 1975—, Johns Hopkins U. Compulsive Gambling Ctr. (now Washington Ctr. for Pathol. Gambling); mem. dir. Univ. Alcohol and Substance Abuse Program, 1986—; CEO Assoc. Mental Helath Profls.; instr. Delaware Valley Group Therapy Inst.; vis. prof. Katholieke U., Leuven, Belgium, 1986—; cons. to Sec.-Gen. Ministry of Health, Belgium, 1986-95, NATO, 1986-87, also fellow Ten Kerselaere Psycho-Geriatric Hosp.; bd. dirs. Internat. Helath Ctr., Belgium, Human Behavior Found.; cons. various hosps. and orgns. Author: Suicidal Behaviors: Diagnosis and Management, 1968, 2d edit., 1994, (with M. E. Wolfgang) Treatment of the Sexual Offender, 1971, Sexual Behaviors: Social, Clinical and Legal Aspects, 1972, (with B. Hathorne) Suicide Prevention in the Seventies, 1973, (with H.L. Ruben) Emergency Psychiatric Care, 1974, (with others) The Prediction of Suicide, 1974, Emergency and Disaster Management, 1976; (with J.T. Mitchell) Emergency Response to Crisis, 1981; Editor: Bull. Suicidology, 1969-74; Contbr. (with others) articles on hypnosis, sexual offenders, marriage and sexual dysfunction treatment, suicide, death and dying, emergency psychiatric care. Mem. Addictions Adv. Bd. Prince Georges County, 1980-85. Served to capt. USAF, 1957-59, ETO-Middle East; capt. USNR; ret. Decorated officer in the Order King Leopold, Belgium, 1990. Fellow Am. Coll. Mental Health Adminstrs., Am. Coll. Psychiatrists (life), Am. Psychiat. Assn. (life); mem. Med-Chi of Md., Prince Georges County Med. Assn., Phila. Psychoanalytic Soc., NIH Alumni Assn., Columbia Med. Alumni Assn. (bd. dirs. 1993-95), Phi Beta Kappa, Beta Sigma Rho (grand vice warden 1963), Cosmos Club (Washington). Jewish. Office: Air Rights Ctr # 1300W 7315 Wisconsin Ave Bethesda MD 20814-3202 also: Univ Profl Ctr 4700 Berwyn House Rd # 201 College Park MD 20740-2474

RESNIK, LINDA ILENE, marketing and information executive, consultant; b. Dallas, Oct. 26, 1950; d. Harold and Reatha (Gordon) R. BJ in Broadcast Journalism, U. Mo., 1971; MA in Journalism, U. North Tex., 1977, MBA in Mktg., 1980. News and documentary producer Sta. KDFW-TV, Dallas, 1971-73; mktg.-info. officer Dallas County Community Coll. Dist., 1973-79; dir. mktg. The Learning Channel, Washington, 1980-82; dir. Nat. Narrowcast Service, Pub. Broadcasting Service, Washington, 1982-85; exec. dir. Am. Soc. Info. Sci., Washington, 1985-89, White House Conf. on Libr. and Info. Svcs., Washington, 1990—; mem. adv. com. ALA Library/Book Fellows Project; fellow Ctr. for Info. and Communication Scis., Ball State U.; mem. U.S. exec. com. U. of the World; mktg., tng. and telecommunications cons. to ednl. assns., others. Writer and editor college-level study guides; scriptwriter college credit TV courses. Youth activities coordinator YMCA, Dallas, 1975-78; spl. event organizer Am. Cancer Soc., Dallas, 1976-77; com. leader Goals for Dallas, 1978-80. Recipient Best TV Feature Story award AP, Tex., 1973. Mem. Am. Soc. Assn. Execs., Am. Soc. Info. Sci. (pub. bull. 1985-89), Women in Cable, Info. Inst., Am. Mktg. Assn., Washington Met. Cable Club. Avocations: travel, racquet sports, reading, theater. Office: 1708 Wendover Pl Tyler TX 75703

RESNIK, REGINA, operatic singer; b. N.Y.C., Aug. 30, 1924; d. Sam and Ruth R.; m. Harry W. Davis, July 18, 1946; 1 son, Michael Philip; m. Arbit Blatas, 1975. B.A., Hunter Coll., 1942. condr. seminars on opera New Sch. for Social Research. Debut as Lady Macbeth, 1942; soprano debut Met. Opera Co., N.Y.C., 1944; mezzo-soprano debut, Met. Opera Co., N.Y.C., 1946; regular guest, Vienna Staatsoper, La Scala, Milan, Covent Garden, Salzburg, Deutsche Opera, Berlin, Teatro Colon, Buenos Aires, Bayreuth Festival, Germany, Munich Staatsoper, Chgo., Phila., San Francisco, others; co-dir., starred in: Carmen, Hamburg Opera, 1971, Electra, 1971, Falstaff at Nat. Opera Poland, 1975; starred in broadway prodn. Cabaret, 1987-88 (nominated for Tony award), prize-winning documentary Ghetto of Venice, PBS, 1983-87; has recorded extensively. Decorated comdr. French Acad. Arts, Scis. and Letters; recipient awards including U.S. Pres.'s medal, 40th Anniversary medal San Francisco Opera, 1982; named Kammersänger in Austria.

RESNIK, ROBERT, medical educator; b. New Haven, Dec. 7, 1938; s. Nathan Alfred and Elsie (Hershman) R.; m. Lauren Brahms, Oct. 29, 1966; children: Andrew Scott, Jamie Layne. BA, Yale U., 1960; MD, Case Western Res. U., 1965. Intern in internal medicine Mt. Sinai Hosp., Cleve., 1965-66; resident in ob-gyn. Yale U. Sch. Medicine, 1966-70; asst. prof. Sch. Medicine U. Calif., San Diego, 1974-78, assoc. prof., 1978-82, prof. reproductive medicine, 1982—, chmn. dept., 1982-95, dean clin. affairs, 1988-90, dean admissions, 1995—; cons. Nat. Heart, Lung and Blood Inst. NIH, Washington, 1987; mem. exec. com. Coun. Residency Edn. Ob-Gyn, Washington, 1988-94, residency rev. com., 1988-94. Editor: (textbook) Maternal-Fetal Medicine: Principles and Practice, 1984, 3d edit., 1994; contbr. numerous articles to profl. jours. Major U.S. Army, 1970-72. Rsch. grantee Nat. Found., NIH. Fellow Am. Coll. Obstetrics and Gynecology, Pacific Coast Obstet. and Gynecol. Soc.; mem. Soc. Gynecologic Investigation (coun. 1983-88), Perinatal Rsch. Soc. (pres. 1985), Am. Gynecologic and Obstet. Soc., San Diego Gynecol. Soc. (pres. 1982), Yale Club. Office: U Calif Sch Medicine Dept 0621 9500 Gilman Dr Dept 0621 La Jolla CA 92093-5003

RESO, ANTHONY, geologist, earth resources economist; b. London, Eng., Aug. 10, 1934; s. Harry and Marion (Gerth) R.; came to U.S., 1940, naturalized, 1952. AB, Columbia Coll., N.Y.C., 1954; MA, Columbia U., 1955; postgrad. U. Cin., 1956-57; PhD (fellow) Rice U., 1960; postgrad. Grad. Sch. Bus. U. Houston, 1964-68. Instr. geology Queens Coll., Flushing, N.Y., 1954; geologist Atlantic Richfield Corp., Midland, Tex., 1955-56; asst. prof. geology and curator invertebrate paleontology Pratt Mus., Amherst (Mass.) Coll., 1959-62; staff rsch. geologist Tenneco Oil Co., Houston, 1962-86; geol. mgr. Peak Prodn. Co., Houston, 1986—, v.p., 1988—. Cons. in geol. rsch. Tenn. Gas and Oil Co., 1960-61; lectr. U. Houston, 1962-65; vis. prof. Rice U., 1980; mem. bd. advisers Gulf Univs. Rsch. Corp., Galveston, Tex., 1967-75, chmn., 1968-69; dir. Stewardship Properties, Houston, 1968—. Recipient rsch. grants Am. Assn. Petroleum Geologists, 1958, 59, Geol. Soc. Am., 1958, Eastman Fund, 1962; NSF fellow, 1959. Fellow Geol. Soc. Am. (com. investments 1984-95, chmn. 1985-92, budget com. 1993-95, Disting. Svc. award 1996), AAAS; mem. Am. Assn. Petroleum Geologists (life, com. convs. 1977-83, chmn. 1980-83, gen. chmn. nat. conv. 1979, com. on investments 1982-88, chmn. com. group ins. 1986-88, treas. 1986-88; Disting. svc. award 1985, found. trustee assoc. 1991), Paleontol. Soc., SEPM Soc. for Sedimentary Geology (com. on investments 1990—, chmn. 1992-95), Paleontol. Rsch. Instn., Tex. Acad. Sci., Houston Geol. Soc. (v.p. 1973-75, pres. 1975-76, chmn. constn. revision com. 1981, Disting. svc. award 1985), English-Speaking Union U.S. (dir. Houston chpt. 1978—, v.p. 1982-88, 94—, mem. scholarship com. 1988—, chmn. 1991—), Varsity C Club, Sigma Xi, Sigma Gamma Epsilon, Beta Theta Pi. Episcopalian. Contbr. profl. jours. Home: 1801 Huldy St Houston TX 77019-5767 Office: care Peak Prodn Co PO Box 130785 Houston TX 77219-0785

RESOR, STANLEY ROGERS, lawyer; b. N.Y.C., Dec. 5, 1917; s. Stanley Burnet and Helen (Lansdowne) R.; m. Jane Lawler Pillsbury, Apr. 4, 1942 (dec.); children: Stanley R., Charles P., John L., Edmund L., William B., Thomas S., James P. BA, Yale U., 1939, LLB, 1946. Bar: N.Y. 1947. Assoc., then ptnr. firm Debevoise & Plimpton, N.Y.C., 1946-65, 71-73, 79-87, of counsel, 1988-90; undersec. Dept. Army, 1965, sec., 1965-71, ambassador negotiations for Mut. and Balanced Force Reductions in Central Europe, 1973-78; undersec. for policy Dept. Def., 1978-79. Fellow Yale Corp., 1979-86. Served to maj. AUS, 1942-45. Decorated Silver Star, Bronze Star, Purple Heart; recipient George C. Marshall award Assn. U.S. Army, 1974, Sylvanus Thayer award Assn. Graduates of U.S. Mil. Acad., 1984. Mem. ABA, Assn. of Bar of City of N.Y. (chmn. com. internat. arms control and security affairs 1983-86), Atlantic Coun. (bd. dirs.), Arms Control Assn. (chmn. bd.), UN Assn. U.S.A. (nat. coun.), Coun. Fgn. Rels., Lawyers Alliance for World Security (bd. dirs.), Internat. Inst. Strategic Studies. Republican. Episcopalian. Home: 809 Weed St New Canaan CT 06840-4023 Office: Debevoise & Plimpton 875 3rd Ave New York NY 10022-6225

RESTANI, JANE A., federal judge; b. San Francisco, Feb. 27, 1948; d. Roy J. and Emilia C. Restani. BA, U. Calif., Berkeley, 1969; JD, U. Calif., Davis, 1973. Bar: Calif., 1973. Trial atty. U.S. Dept. Justice, Washington, 1973-76, asst. chief comml. litigation sect., 1976-80, dir. comml. litigation sect., 1980-83; judge U.S. Ct. Internat. Trade, N.Y.C., 1983—. Mem. Order of Coif. Office: US Ct Internat Trade 1 Federal Plz New York NY 10278-0001*

RESTIVO, JAMES JOHN, JR., lawyer; b. Pitts., Aug. 15, 1946; s. James J. and Dorothy (Ardolino) R.; m. Gail Sharon Hackenburg, July 11, 1970; 4 children. BA in History, U. Pa., 1968; JD, Georgetown U., 1971. Bar: Pa. 1971, U.S. Dist. Ct. (we. and ea. dists.) Pa. 1971, U.S. Ct. Appeals (3d cir.) 1971, U.S. Supreme Ct. 1979. Ptnr. Reed, Smith, Shaw & McClay, Pitts., 1979—, head litigation dept., 1986—. Mem. editl. staff Georgetown Law

Rev., 1970-71. Bd. dirs. Greater Pitts. C. of C. Mem. ABA, Acad. Trial Lawyers Allegheny County, Allegheny County Bar Assn., Pa. Economy League (Western divsn.), Def. Rsch. Inst. Home: 209 Deer Meadow Dr Pittsburgh PA 15241-2253 Office: Reed Smith Shaw & McClay 435 6th Ave Pittsburgh PA 15219-1809

RESWICK, JAMES BIGELOW, former government official, rehabilitation engineer, educator; b. Ellwood City, Pa., Apr. 16, 1922; s. Maurice and Katherine (Parker) R.; children: James Bigelow, David Parker (dec.), Pamela Reswick; m. Irmtraud Orthlies Hoelzerkopf, Dec., 27, 1973. SBME, MIT, 1943; SM, Mass. Inst. Tech., 1948, ScD, 1952; DEng (hon.), Rose Poly. Inst., 1968. Asst. prof., then assoc. prof., head machine design and graphics div. MIT, 1948-59; Leonard Case prof. engring., dir. Engring. Design Ctr., Case Western Res. U., 1959-70; prof. biomed. engring. and orthopaedics U. So. Calif., also dir. of rsch. dept. orthopaedics, 1970-80; assoc. dir. tech. Nat. Inst. Handicapped Rsch., U.S. Dept. Edn.; dir. VA Rehab. R & D Evaluation Unit VA Med. Ctr., Washington, 1984-88; dir. rsch. scis. Nat. Inst. on Disability and Rehab. Rsch. U.S. Dept. Edn., Washington, 1989-94; ret.; engring. cons. on automatic control, product devel., automation and biomed. engring. Mem. com. prosthetics R & D Nat. Acad. Scis., 1962—; chmn. design and devel. com.; mem. bd. rev. Army R & D Office, 1965—; mem. applied physiology and biomed. engring. study sect. NIH, 1972—. Author: (with C.K. Taft) Introduction to Dynamic Systems, 1967; also articles.; Editor: (with F.T. Hambrecht) Functional Electrical Stimulation, 1977; series on engring. design, 1963—. Chmn. Mayor's Commn. for Urban Transp., Cleve., 1969. Served to lt. (j.g.) USNR, 1943-46, PTO. Decorated officer Yugoslav Flag with golden wreath medal (Yugoslavia), 1990; recipient Product Engring. Master Designer award, 1969, Isabelle and Leonard H. Goldenson award United Cerebral Palsy Assn., 1973; NSR sr. postdoctoral fellow Imperial Coll., London, 1957. Fellow IEEE, Am. Inst. Med. and Biological Engring. (founder); mem. ASME (honor award for best paper 1956, sr. mem.), Am. Soc. Engring. Edn., Instrument Soc. Am., Biomed. Engring. Soc. (sr. mem., pres. 1973, dir.), Am. Acad. Orthopedic Surgeons (asso.), Inst. Medicine of Nat. Acad. Scis., Nat. Acad. Engring., Internat. Soc. Orthotics and Prosthetics, Orthopaedics Research Soc., Rehab. Engring. Soc. N.Am. (founding pres.), Sigma XI. Patentee in field. Home: 1003 Dead Run Dr Mc Lean VA 22101-2120

RESZKA, ALFONS, computer systems architect; b. Imielin, Poland, Dec. 17, 1924; s. Alfons and Maria (Galazka) R.; m. Betty Reszka; children: Ann, Elizabeth, Alfred, Catherine. B.S., U. London, 1954; M.S.E.E., Northwestern U., 1960, Ph.D., 1976. Engr. Brit. Jeffrey Diamond, Wakefield, Eng., 1954-55; lectr. Bradford Tech. Coll., Eng., 1955-56; engr. A.C. Nielson, Chgo., 1956-59; with Teletype Corp., Skokie, Ill., 1959-80, project dir., 1969-75, sr. staff engr., 1975-80; cons. computer architecture, computer networks and data base mgmt. systems Bell Labbs., Naperville, Ill., 1980-85; prof. info. sci. North Central Coll., Naperville, 1983-86; computer systems cons. ARC, Wheaton, Ill., 1986—. Patentee in electronics. Mem. IEEE, Computer Soc., Tech. Com. of Computer Architecture. Home: 1090 Creekside Dr Wheaton IL 60187-6173 Office: ARC 1090 Creekside Dr Wheaton IL 60187-6173

RETALLACK, GREGORY JOHN, geologist, educator; b. Hobart, Australia, Nov. 8, 1951; came to U.S., 1977; s. Kenneth John Retallack and Moira Wynn (Dean) Gollan; m. Diane Alice Johnson, May 21, 1981; children: Nicholas John, Jeremy Douglas. B.A., Macquarie U., Sydney, 1973; B.Sc. with honors, U. New Eng., 1974, Ph.D., 1978. Vis. asst. prof. Northern Ill. U., Dekalb, 1977-78; vis. scholar Ind. U., Bloomington, 1978-81; asst. prof. U. Oreg., Eugene, 1981-86, assoc. prof., 1986-92, prof., 1992—. Author: Geological Excursion Guide to the Sea Cliffs North of Sydney, 1978, Late Eocene and Oligocene Paleosols from Badlands National Park, South Dakota, 1983, Soils of the Past, 1990, Miocene Paleosols and Ape Habitats in Pakistan and Kenya, 1991; contbr. numerous articles in field to profl. jours. Grantee NSF, 1979—, Wenner-Gren Found., 1983. Mem. Geol. Soc. Am., Geol. Soc. Australia, Bot. Soc. Am., Paleontol. Soc. (pres. Pacific sect. 1986), Oreg. Acad. Sci. (pres. 1986), Soc. Econ. Paleontologists and Mineralogists, Sigma Xi (pres. U. Oreg. chpt. 1983-84). Home: 2715 Elinor St Eugene OR 97403-2513

RETHEMEYER, ROBERT JOHN, social studies educator; b. St. Louis, Jan. 20, 1948; s. John Henry and Olivia Antonia (Fallbeck) R.; m. Kay Lynn Jones, Aug. 22, 1971; children: Robin Lynn, Rustin John. BS in Edn., Cen. Mo. State Coll., 1970; M in Sch. Adminstrn., Cen. Mo. State U., 1973, EdS in Supt., 1985. Tchr. 7th grade social studies Smith-Hale Jr. H.S., Kansas City, Mo., 1970-78, asst. prin., 1978-80, tchr. 7th and 8th grade social studies, 1980—, summer sch. prin., 1981—; chmn. bldg. dept. Cons. Sch. Dist. 1, Kansas City, 1982—, alt. sch. com., 1993—. Mem. NEA, Nat. Coun. for Social Studies, Phi Delta Kappa. Home: 1026 SE Timbercreek Ln Lees Summit MO 64081-3003 Office: Smith-Hale Jr H S 8925 Longview Rd Kansas City MO 64134-4110

RETHORE, BERNARD GABRIEL, diversified company executive; b. Bklyn., May 22, 1941; s. Francis Joseph and Katharine Eunice (MacDwyer) R.; BA, Yale U., 1962; MBA, U. Pa., 1967; m. Marilyn Irene Watt, Dec. 1, 1962; children: Bernard Michael, Tara Jean, Kevin Watt, Alexandra Marie, Rebecca Ann, Christopher Philip, Abigail Lyn. Assoc., McKinsey & Co., Inc., Washington, 1967, then sr. assoc., 1973; v.p./gen. mgr. Greer div. Microdot, Inc., Darien, Conn., 1973-77, v.p. ops. connector group, 1977-78, pres. bus. devel. group, 1978-82, pres. fastening systems and sealing devices groups, 1982-84, pres. Microdot Industries, 1984-87, pres., chief exec. officer, 1988; pres. Microdot Europe Ltd., 1984-88; sr. v.p. Phelps Dodge Corp., Phoenix, 1989-95; group exec. Phelps Dodge Industries, 1989-90, pres., 1990-95; pres., CEO, bd. dirs. BW/IP Internat. Inc., 1995—, chmn., 1997—; bd. dirs. Maytag Corp., Belden, Inc.; cons. U.S. Govt., UN; mem. Global Adv. Coun., Am. Grad. Sch. Internat. Mgmt., 1990—, chmn., 1991-94. Mem. dean's adv. bd. Wharton Sch. Bus., U. Pa., 1972-80; chmn. Emmaus adv. bd. Fairfield Prep. Sch.-Lauralton Hall Acad., 1981-85; elected mem. bd. fin. Town of Westport, Conn., 1986-90; trustee Ballet Arizona, 1989-95, vice chmn. 1991-95; bd. dirs. Boys Hope of Phoenix, 1989-95; trustee Phoenix Country Day Sch., 1992—; trustee Am. Grad. Sch. Internat. Mgmt., 1994—. Served to capt., inf., AUS, 1962-65. Decorated Bronze Star. Mem. Nat. Assn. Mfrs. (bd. dirs. 1994-95,96—), Yale Club (N.Y.C.), Union League (Chgo.). Home: 6533 E Maverick Rd Paradise Valley AZ 85253-2632 Office: BW/IP Internat Inc 200 Oceangate Ste 900 Long Beach CA 90802

RETSINAS, NICOLAS P., federal official. BA in Economics, NYU; M in City Planning, Harvard U. Exec. dir. Housing and Mortgage Corp., R.I., 1987-93; asst. sec. for Housing-Fed. Housing Commr., Washington, 1993—; dir. OTS FDIC, Washington; dir. policy for Gov. R.I., 1991; adj. asst. prof. urban studies Brown U. Mem. Nat. Coun. State Housing Authorities (past sec.), Nat. Community Devel. Assn. (past pres.). Office: Fed Housing Finance Bd 451 7th St SW Washington DC 20410-0001*

RETTERER, BERNARD LEE, electronic engineering consultant; b. Waldo, Ohio, Sept. 23, 1930; s. Calvin C. and Gertrude S. (Kries) R.; m. Mary Susan Gaster, Dec. 22, 1951; children: John, Jeffrey, Laura. BSEE, Ohio No. U., 1952; MS in System Mgmt., George Washington U., 1972. Registered profl. engr., Ohio. Program mgr. RCA, Cherry Hill, N.J., 1953-65; v.p. engring. ARINC Rsch., Annapolis, Md., 1965-90; Del. to Internat. Electrotechnical Commn., 1975-85; cons. Inst. for Def. Analyses, Alexandria, Va., 1990—. Contbr. 39 tech. articles on maintainability to profl. jours. Mem. adv. bd. Embry-Riddle U., Daytona Beach, Fla., 1988-90, Anne Arundel Coll., Arnold, Md., 1987-90. Mem. IEEE (v.p. tech-ops. 1982), Operation Rsch. Soc., Armed Forces Prep. Assn., Armed Forces Comms. Assn. Achievements include development (with others) of maintainability prediction technique for electronic equipment; research into the use of information content of failure symptoms as a predictor of diagnostic time. Home: 37 Whittier Pky Severna Park MD 21146-3049

RETTIG, TERRY, veterinarian, wildlife consultant; b. Houston, Jan. 30, 1947; s. William E. and Rose (Munves) R.; m. Helen Rettig, Mar. 12, 1996; 1 child, Bill; children from previous marriage: Michael Thomas, Jennifer Suzanne, Bill Rettig. BS in Zoology, Duke U., 1969, MAT in Sci., 1970; DVM, U. Ga., 1975. Resident veterinarian, mgr. animal health The Wildlife Preserve, Largo, Md., 1975-76; wildlife veterinarian dept. environ. conservation State of N.Y., Delmar, 1976-77; owner Atlanta Animal Hosp., 1976—; sec., dir. Atlanta Pet Supply, Inc., 1983-89; cons. Six Flags Over Ga., Yellow River Game Ranch, Stone Mountain Park Animal Forest, Atlanta Zoo. Author: (with Murray Fowler) Zoo and Wild Animal Medicine (Aardvark award 1978), 1978, 2d edit., 1986 (Order of Kukukifuku award 1986); contbr. articles to profl. jours. Del. Dekalb County Republican Conv., 1983; mem. Roswell United Meth. Ch., Boy Scouts Am., 1954—, mem. troop coun., asst. scoutmaster, scout master, Philmont expedition leader, 1988, 89. Spl. scholar Cambridge U. Coll. Vet. Medicine, 1973-74. Mem. AVMA, Ga. Vet. Med. Assn., Greater Atlanta Vet. Med. Assn., Dekalb Vet. Soc., Acad. Vet. Medicine, Am. Assn. Zoo Veterinarians, Am. Assn. Zool. Parks and Aquaria, Nat. Wildlife Health Found., Nat. Wildlife Assn., Atlanta Zool. Soc., Am. Fedn. Aviculturists, Cousteau Soc., Am. Assn. Avian Veterinarians, Am. Animal Hosp. Assn., Internat. Wildlife Assn., Soc. Aquatic Veterinary Medicine, Am. Buffalo Assn. Methodist. Home: 5005 Kimball Bridge Rd Alpharetta GA 30202-5649 Office: Atlanta Animal Hosp 5005 Kimball Bridge Rd Alpharetta GA 30005-5649

RETZ, WILLIAM ANDREW, retired naval officer; b. Blauvelt, N.Y., June 3, 1940; s. Andrew Macmillan and Katherine (Deyoe) R.; m. Julia Irene Patterson, Sept. 23, 1989; children: Andrew, Gregory, Mark, Alyse Reavis, Mark Rogers. Student, Tex. A&M U., 1957; BS in Mech. Engring., U. N.Mex., 1963; MS, George Washington U., 1970; grad., Naval War Coll., 1972. Commd. ensign USN, 1963, advanced through grades to rear adm., 1991; patrol officer river div. 511 USN, Vietnam, 1968-69; flag sec. to comdr. Amphibious Group Two USN, Norfolk, Va., 1972-74, exec. officer USS Ainsworth, 1974-76, commanding officer USS Stump, 1980-82, commodore Destroyer Squadron 22, 1985-87; dep. for ops. U.S. Cen. Command USN, Tampa, Fla., 1987-90; comdr. Naval Base Pearl Harbor, 1992-94, Naval Surface Group Mid. Pacific, 1992-94; commanded and closed Naval Base Phila., 1994-95; ret. USN, 1995; v.p. govt. svcs. Aramark Corp., Phila., 1996—. Active Episcopal Ch., Media, Pa. Decorated Navy Dist. Svc. medal, Legion of Merit, Def. Disting. Svc. medal, Meritorious Svc. medal, Bronze star. Mem. U.S. Naval Inst., BOD Surf Warfare Assn., BOD Leadership Inc., BOD Ind. Seaport Mus. Avocations: running, sailing.

RETZER, MARY ELIZABETH HELM, retired librarian; b. Balt.; d. Francis Leslie C. and Edna (Smith) Helm; m. William Raymond Retzer, June 28, 1945; children: Lesley Elizabeth, April Christine. BA, Western Md. Coll., 1940; MA, Columbia U., 1946; postgrad., George Washington U., 1941, Ind. U., 1952, U. Ill., 1958-59, Ill. State U., 1964-66, Bradley U.; PhD, Western Colo. U., 1972. Mem. faculty Rockville (Md.) Bd. Edn., 1940-47, elem. supr., 1945-47; mem. staff Peoria Pub. Libr., 1957-63, homebound libr., 1961-63; cons., organizer libr. Bergan High Sch., 1964-67; condr. libr. sci. course in reference Bradley U., 1966—; libr. Hines Elem. Sch., 1963-66, Roosevelt Jr. High Sch., 1966-69; head media ctr. Manual High Sch., Peoria, Ill., 1969-83. Instr. water safety courses ARC, 1938—; pres. women's bd. Salvation Army, 1952-54; pres. Peoria Nursery Sch. Assn., 1953-54; mem. legis. action com. Ill. Congress PTA, 1955-56; mem. Crippled Children's Adv. Com., Peoria, 1957-60; active various community drives; mem. women's adv. bd. Peoria Jr. Star, 1970-73. Mem. AAUW, NEA, ALA, Ill. Edn. Assn., Peoria Edn. Assn., Ill. Libr. Assn., Ill. Valley Librs. Assn. (pres. 1971-72), Ill. Assn. Media in Edn. (cert. com. 1973—), Ill. Audiovisual Assn., Internat. Platform Assn., Order Ea. Star, Ill. State U. Adminstrs. Club, Willowknolls Country Club, Sarasota Yacht Club. Republican. Presbyterian. Home: Unit 308 435 S Gulfstream Ave Sarasota FL 34236

RETZLER, KURT EGON, diversified management company executive, hospitality, travel and marketing company executive; b. Bechkerek, Mar. 31, 1927; came to U.S., 1950, naturalized, 1954; s. Joseph J. and Melinda (Beno) R.; m. Rali Tjotis, Aug. 3, 1957; children: Jo Elaine, Kurt Steven. B.B.A. with distinction, U. Mich., 1955, M.B.A. with distinction, 1956. C.P.A., Mich., Minn. C.P.A. Arthur Andersen & Co., Detroit, 1956-63; asst. controller Carlson Cos., Inc., Mpls., 1963-65; v.p., controller Carlson Cos., Inc., 1965-74, v.p., 1974—, v.p. corp. acquisitions and devel., 1974—, mem. fin. com., 1974—; ret., 1996; bd. dirs. TGI Fridays, Inc., Dallas, Carlson Travel Network, Radisson Hotel Corp., Carlson Properties, Inc., Country Kitchen Internat., Inc. Treas. PTA, Golden Valley, Minn., 1967. Served with AUS, 1951-53. Mem. Financial Execs. Inst. (dir. Twin Cities chpt. 1969-70, treas. 1971-72), Nat. Assn. Accountants, Am. Inst. C.P.A.'s, Minn. Assn. C.P.A.'s, Am. Accounting Assn., Assn. for Corp. Growth, Beta Gamma Sigma, Phi Kappa Phi, Beta Alpha Psi. Home: 1100 Heritage Ln Wayzata MN 55391-9133 Office: Carlson Cos Inc Carlson Pkwy PO Box 59159 Minneapolis MN 55459-8214

REUBEN, ALVIN BERNARD, entertainment executive; b. Harrisburg, Pa., Aug. 11, 1940; s. Maurice and Lillian (Katzef) R.; m. Barbara Ann Harrison, Mar. 18, 1967; 1 dau., Mindee Jill. B.S. in Commerce, Rider U., 1962. Buyer Pomeroy's div. Allied Stores Corp., Harrisburg, 1962-67; sales rep. Random House, Inc., N.Y.C., 1967-74; dir. mktg. Ballantine Books, Inc. (div. Random House), N.Y.C., 1974-76; v.p. sales Simon & Schuster, N.Y.C., 1976-79, sr. v.p. sales Pocket Books div., 1979-81, sr. v.p. mktg., 1981-82, pres. promotional pub. group, 1982-83, exec. v.p. electronic pub. div., 1983-85; exec. v.p. Prentice Hall div. Simon & Schuster, 1985-86; sr. v.p. mktg., sales and distbn. Vestron, Inc., 1986-89; sr. v.p. St. Martin's Press, N.Y.C., 1989-91; sr. v.p. sales, mktg. Sony Music Video, N.Y.C., 1991-92; sr. v.p. spl. markets Sony Music, N.Y.C., 1992-95; sr.v.p. video and interactive sales and distbn. BMG Entertainment, 1995-97; pres. BMG Video, 1997—; instr. edn. in pub. program, grad. program SUNY; active problem solving seminar Pubs. Weekly, N.Y.C., 1980. With USAFR, 1963-69. Mem. Tau Kappa Epsilon. Home: 54 High Point Rd Westport CT 06880-3911 Office: 1540 Broadway New York NY 10036-4039

REUBEN, DON HAROLD, lawyer; b. Chgo., Sept. 1, 1928; s. Michael B. and Sally (Chapman) R.; m. Evelyn Long, Aug. 27, 1948 (div.); children: Hope Reuben Paul, Michael Barrett, Timothy Don, Jeffrey Long, Howard Ellis; m. Jeannette Hurley Haywood, Dec. 13, 1971; stepchildren: Harris Hurley Haywood, Edward Gregory Haywood. BS, Northwestern U., 1949, JD, 1952. Bar: Ill. 1952, Calif. 1996. With firm Kirkland & Ellis, Chgo., 1952-78, sr. ptnr., until 1978; sr. ptnr. Reuben & Proctor, Chgo., 1978-86, Isham, Lincoln & Beale, Chgo., 1986-88; sr. counsel Winston & Strawn, 1988-94; of counsel Altheimer & Gray, Chgo., 1994—; spl. asst. atty. gen. State of Ill., 1963-64, 69, 84; gen. coun. Tribune Co., 1965-88, Chgo. Bears Football Club, 1965-88, Cath. Archdiocese of Chgo., 1975-88; coun. spl. session Ill. Ho. of Reps., 1964, for Ill. treas. for congl., state legis. and jud. reapportionment, 1963; spl. fed. ct. master, 1968-70; dir. Lake Shore Nat. Bank, 1973-93; dir. Heitman Fin., 1993—; mem. citizens adv. bd. to sheriff County of Cook, 1962-66, mem. jury instrn. com., 1963-68; rules com. Ill. Supreme Ct., 1963-73; mem. pub. rels. com. Nat. Conf. State Trial Judges; mem. com. study caseflow mgmt. in law div. Cook County Cir. Ct., 1979-88; mem. adv. implementation com. U.S. Dist. Ct. for No. Dist. Ill., 1981-82; mem. Chgo. Better Schs. Com., 1968-69, Chgo. Crime Commn., 1970-80; mem. supervisory panel Fed. Defender Program; lectr. on libel, slander, privacy and freedom of press. Bd. dirs. Lincoln Park Zool. Soc., 1972-84 ; trustee Northwestern U., 1977—; mem. vis. com. U. Chgo. Law Sch., 1976-79. Mem. Ill. Bar Assn., Chgo. Bar Assn. (chmn. subcom. on propriety and regulation of contingent fees com. devel. law 1966-69, subcom. on media liaison 1980-82, mem. com. on profl. info. 1980-82), ABA (standing com. on fed. judiciary 1973-79, standing com. on jud. selection, tenure and compensation 1982-85), Am. Law Inst., Am. Judicature Soc., Fellows Am. Bar Found., Am. Coll. Trial Lawyers (Rule 23 com. 1975-82, judiciary com. 1987-91), Am. Arbitration Assn. (nat. panel arbitrators), Calif. Bar Assn., Desert Bar Assn., Internat. Acad. Trial Lawyers, Union League Club (Chgo.), Tavern Club, Mid-Am. Club, Law Club, Casino Club, The Springs Club, Desert Riders of Palm Springs, The Chgo. Club, Phi Eta Sigma, Beta Alpha Psi, Beta Gamma Sigma, Order of Coif. Home: 20 Jill Ter Rancho Mirage CA 92270-2635

REUBER, GRANT LOUIS, banking insurance company executive; b. Mildmay, Ont., Can., Nov. 23, 1927; s. Jacob Daniel and Gertrude Catherine (Wahl) R.; m. Margaret Louise Julia Summerhayes, Oct. 21, 1951; children: Rebecca, Barbara, Mary. BA, U. Western Ont., 1950; AM, Harvard U., 1954, PhD, 1957; LLD (hon.), Wilfred Laurier U., 1983, Simon Fraser U., 1985; U. Western Ont., 1985, McMaster U., 1994; postgrad., Cambridge U., 1954-55. Mem. research dept. Bank Can., Ottawa, 1950-52; mem. Can. Dept. Finance, Ottawa, 1955-57; asst. prof. econ. U. Western Ont., London, 1957-59, assoc. prof., 1959-62, prof., head dept., 1963-69; prof., head dept., 1963-69; mem. bd. govs. U. Western Ont., London, 1974-78, acad. v.p., provost, 1975-78, chancellor, 1988-92; sr. v.p., chief economist Bank of Montreal, Que., Can., 1978-79; exec. v.p. Bank of Montreal, 1980-81, dep. chmn., dep. chief exec. officer, 1981-83, dir., mem. exec. com., 1981-89, pres., chief operating officer, 1983-87, dep. chmn., 1987-89; dep. minister fin. Can., 1979-80; chmn. Can. Deposit Ins. Corp., 1993—; mem. Royal Commn. Banking and Fin., Toronto, 1962-63; chmn. Ont. Econ. Coun., 1973-78; cons. Can. Internat. Devel. Agy., 1968-69; hon. rsch. assoc. in econs. Harvard U., 1968-69; cons. devel. ctr. OECD, 1969-73; bd. dirs. Can. Niagara Power; mem. adv. com. U. Western Ont. Sch. Bus.; lectr. U. Chgo. Sch. Bus., 1992-93; econ. advisor to prime min. of Lithuania, 1991-92. Author: Private Foreign Investment in Development, 1973, Canada's Political Economy, 1980; contbr. articles to profl. jours. Pres. Can. Ditchley Found., 1991—; chmn. Can. Merit Scholarship Found., 1994—. Decorated officer Order of Can. Fellow Royal Soc. Can.

REUM, JAMES MICHAEL, lawyer; b. Oak Park, Ill., Nov. 1, 1946; s. Walter John and Lucy (Bellegay) R. BA cum laude, Harvard U., 1968, JD cum laude, 1972. Bar: N.Y. 1973, D.C. 1974, U.S. Dist. Ct. (so. dist.) N.Y. 1974, Ill. 1979, U.S. Dist. Ct. (no. dist.) Ill. 1982. Assoc. Davis Polk & Wardwell, N.Y.C., 1973-78; assoc. Minority Counsel Com. on Judiciary U.S. Ho. of Reps., Washington, 1974; ptnr. Hopkins & Sutter, Chgo., 1979-93, Winston & Strawn, Chgo., 1994—. Midwest advance rep. Nat. Reagan Bush Com., 1980; nominee commr. Securities and Exchange Comm., Pres. Bush, 1992. Served to SP4 USAR, 1969-75. Recipient Harvard U. Honorary Nat. Scholarship, 1964-72. Mem. ABA, Monte Carlo Country Club (Monaco), Chgo. Club, Univ. Club (N.Y.C.). Republican. Home: 12 E Scott St Chicago IL 60610-2320 Office: Winston & Strawn 35 W Wacker Dr Chicago IL 60601-1614

REUM, W. ROBERT, manufacturing executive; b. Oak Park, Ill., July 22, 1942; m. Sharon Milliken. BA, Yale U., 1964; JD, U. Mich., 1967; MBA, Harvard U., 1969. Dir. investment analysis City Investing Co., N.Y.C., 1969-72; v.p. corp fin. Mich. Nat. Corp., Bloomfield Hills, Mich., 1972-78; v.p., treas. White Motor Corp., Cleve., 1978-79; v.p. fin., chief fin. officer Lamson & Sessions, Cleve., 1980-82; v.p. fin., chief fin. officer The Interlake Corp., Oak Brook, Ill., 1982-88, exec. v.p., 1988-90, chmn., pres., chief exec. officer, 1991—; bd. dirs. Amsted Industries, Inc., Chgo., Morton Arboretum, Lisle, Ill.; pres. bd. trustees Elgin (Ill.) Acad. Contbr. articles to Harvard Bus. Rev. Bd. trustee Mfrs. Alliance, Washington. Mem. Chgo. Golf Club, Chgo. Club, Dunham Woods Riding Club (Wayne, Ill.), Rolling Rock Club (Ligonier, Pa.). Office: Interlake Corp 550 Warrenville Rd Lisle IL 60532-4308

REUMAN, ROBERT EVERETT, philosophy educator; b. Foochow, China, Feb. 16, 1923; s. Otto G. and Martha Lydia (Bourne) R.; m. Dorothy Ann Swan, Sept. 2, 1949; children: Martha Claire, David Alan, Jonathan Robert, Ann Evalyn, Elizabeth Linda. A.B., Middlebury Coll., 1945; M.A., U. Pa., 1946, Ph.D., 1949. Asst. instr. U. Pa., 1946-48; instr. Temple U., 1947-49; mem. Friends' Ambulance Service Unit, China, 1949-51, chmn., 1950-51; dir. Quaker Student House, Freiburg im Breisgau, Fed. Republic Germany, 1951-53; instr. Lafayette Coll., 1953-54, asst. prof., 1954-56; mem. faculty Colby Coll., Waterville, Maine, 1956—, prof. philosophy, 1969—, chmn. social sci. div., 1975-78, chmn. dept. philosophy and religion, 1975-78; Dana prof. philosophy Colby Coll., 1986-91, ret., 1991. Author: Mauern, 1965, (with others) Anatomy of Anti-Communism, 1969; pamphlet Walls, 1966; contbr. articles to profl. jours. New Eng. regional chmn. Danforth Assocs., 1963-64; Quaker internat. affairs rep., Germany, 1964-66; bd. dirs. Am. Friends of Le College Cevenol, 1975-85; mem. Maine Humanities Coun., 1980-85, mem. exec. com., 1981-84. With Civilian Pub. Svc., 1943-46. Harrison fellow, 1945-46; Colby Coll. grantee, 1972, 79, 82. Mem. Am. Philos. Assn., AAUP, Soc. for Values in Higher Edn. Democrat. Unitarian-Quaker.

REUSCHLEIN, HAROLD GILL, university dean; b. Burlington, Wis., Dec. 2, 1904; s. Joseph Felix and Frances (Gill) R.; m. Marcella Christien, Apr. 24, 1930; 1 dau., Mary Frances. A.B., U. Iowa, 1927; LL.B., Yale, 1933; J.S.D., Cornell, 1934; LL.D., Dominican Coll., 1955, Dickinson Sch. Law, 1970, LaSalle Coll., 1971, Creighton U., 1975, St. Mary's U., 1984; L.H.D., Villanova U., 1972. Bar: Wis. 1936, U.S. Supreme Ct. 1944, Pa. 1955. Instr. history N.Y. U., 1930-32; asst. gen. counsel Fidelity Mut. Life Ins. Co., 1934; prof. law Georgetown U., 1934-46, U. Notre Dame, 1946-47, Syracuse U., 1947-48, U. Pitts., 1948-53; dean Sch. Law, Villanova U., 1953-72, dean emeritus, 1984; Ryan Distinguished prof. law St. Mary's U., 1972-84; vis. prof. Case Western Res. U., 1967-68. Author: The Schools of Corporate Reform, 1950, Jurisprudence-Its American Prophets, 1951, Cases on Unincorporated Business, 1952, Cases on Agency and Partnership, 1962, Handbook of Law of Agency and Partnership, 1990. Choirmaster, organist First Meth. Episcopal Ch., New Haven, 1927-33, Ch. St. Bernard of Clarivaux, Pitts., 1948-53; dir. Pub. Health Law Project, U. Pittsburgh. Served as col. Judge Adv. Gen. Dept., World War II; chief Office Legislative Service Hdqrs. AAF. Awarded Legion of Merit; Decorated Papal Knight of the Holy Sepulchre, Knight St. Gregory the Great. Mem. ABA, Wis. Bar Assn., Pa. Bar Assn., Cosmos Club (Washington), Order of Coif, Pi Kappa Alpha, Pi Gamma Mu. Roman Catholic. Home: Riddle Village Williamsburgh Bldg # 106 Media PA 19063

REUSCHLEIN, ROBERT WILLIAM, accountant, researcher; b. Madison, Wis., Jan. 8, 1950; s. Earl Vincent and Rosemary Markham R. BSEE, U. Wis., 1972; MBA, Oregon State U., 1977. Surveyor and draftsman Ctrl. Wis. Builders, Madison, 1971-72; estimator Dyson Constrn., Madison, 1972; pub. acct. Earl V. Reuschlein & Assocs., Madison, 1973-74; mgmt. intern Portland (Oreg.) Gen. Elec., 1976; contr. Doorcraft, Inc., Harrisburg, Oreg., 1977-79; pub. acct. C.F. Rogers CPA, Eugene, Oreg., 1980; lobbyist Dem. Party of Oregon, Salem, 1981-85; rschr. Earlwal, Ltd., Eugene, 1986-93; acct., pres. Earlwal, Ltd., Madison, Wis., 1993—; mem. Citizen Involvement Com., City of Springfield, Oreg., 1979; founding dir. Neighborhood Econ. Devel. Corp., Eugene, 1979-81; dir. Eugene Peace Works, 1991-93; gen. mgr. Jomblee, Inc., Madison, 1995-96, controller, 1997—; instr. peace econs. U. Oreg., 1987, 89; prof. U. of the Air, Radio for Peace Internat., Costa Rica, 1996—; lectr. Econ. Conversion Conf., Miami, Fla., 1990. Author: Peace Economics, 1986, Strength Through Peace, 1989; columnist Peace Economics in Oreg. Peace Worker, 1989— (columns also played on Radio for Peace Internat., Costa Rica, 1993); developer Natural Global Warming Theory, 1991. Mem. Dem. Exec. Com., Oreg., 1981-87; del. Dem. Nat. Conv., San Francisco, 1984; chmn. 4th Congl. Dist. Dems., Oreg., 1982-87; program dir. Prairie Soc. Unitarian Ch., 1995-97. Mem. AICPA, Wis. Inst. CPAs, Madison Progressive Inst., World Federalists (bd. dirs. local chpt.). Avocations: hiking, politics, lecturing, dancing. Office: Earlwal Ltd 6515 Grand Teton Plz Ste 120 Madison WI 53719-1048

REUSS, ROBERT PERSHING, telecommunications executive, consultant; b. Aurora, Ill., Mar. 23, 1918; s. George John and Mary Belle (Gorrie) R.; m. Mildred Louise Daly, Dec. 22, 1940 (dec. May 1985); children: Lynn Ann (Mrs. David Bohmer), Robert Cameron; m. Grace K. Brady, Aug. 28, 1986. BS, U. Ill., 1939; postgrad., Harvard U., 1943; MBA, U. Chgo., 1950; D Bus. Adminstrn., Blackburn Coll., 1976. Staff AT&T, 1955-58, asst. compt., 1958-59; v.p. Ill. Bell Tel. Co., 1959-72, dir., 1970-72; pres., chief exec. officer, dir. Centel Corp., Chgo., 1972-76, chmn., 1977-88; cons. Chgo., 1988-93, Sprint Corp., 1993—; bd. govs. Midwest Stock Exch., 1978-82; bd. dirs. Tellabs, Inc. Trustee Rush-Presbyn.-St. Luke's Med. Ctr., Chgo., Blackburn Coll., 1953-83, Aurora U., 1986—, Lyric Opera, 1987—; bd. dirs. U. Ill. Found., 1979—. Lt. (s.g.) USNR, 1943-46, PTO. Mem. Chgo. Assn. Commerce & Industry (bd. dirs. 1971-78), Comml. Club, Chgo. Club, Chgo. Golf Club, Ocean Club, Country Club of Fla., Phi Kappa Phi. Presbyterian (deacon, trustee). Office: 40 Shuman Blvd Ste 240 Naperville IL 60563-8465

REUTER, CAROL JOAN, insurance company executive; b. Bklyn., June 1, 1941; d. Michael John and Elizabeth Lucille (Garmer) R. BA, St. John's U., 1962. Pres., CEO N.Y. Life Found., N.Y.C., 1979-89, sec., 1989-90, pres., 1990-96, CEO, 1996—; also bd. dirs.; asst. v.p. N.Y. Life Ins. Co., N.Y.C., 1984-89, corp. v.p., 1990-95, v.p., 1995—. Mem., former chmn. contbns. coun. Conf. Bd., N.Y. Contbns. Adv. Group; corp. adv. coun. ARC; chmn. corp. assocs. United Way of Am. Named Acad. of Women's Achievers, YWCA, 1987. Republican. Roman Catholic. Office: NY Life Ins Co 51 Madison Ave New York NY 10010-1603

REUTER, FRANK THEODORE, history educator; b. Kankakee, Ill., Mar. 18, 1926; s. Frank Theodore and Evelyn Marie (Scott) R.; m. Kathleen Ann Pester, June 16, 1951; children: Mark, Stephen, Christopher, Ann, Katherine. B.S., U. Ill., 1950, M.A., 1959, Ph.D., 1960. Instr. West Liberty (W. Va.) State Coll., 1960-62; asst. prof. Texas Christian U., Fort Worth, 1962-66; assoc. prof. Texas Christian U., 1966-71; prof. history Tex. Christian U., 1971-92; dean Texas Christian U. (Grad. Sch.), 1970-75, chmn. dept. history, 1980-83; prof. emeritus Tex. Christian U., 1992—. Author: West Liberty State College: The First 125 Years, 1963, Catholic Influence on American Colonial Policies, 1898-1904, 1967, Trials and Triumphs: George Washington's Foreign Policy, 1983; co-author: Injured Honor: The Chesapeake-Leopard Affair, 1996. Served with USNR, 1944-46. U. Durham Rsch. fellow, 1991. Mem. Orgn. Am. Historians, Am. Hist. Assn., Soc. Historians Early Republic, Soc. Historians Am. Fgn. Relations, Phi Beta Kappa, Phi Alpha Theta. Roman Catholic. Home: 3617 Winifred Dr Fort Worth TX 76133-2126 Office: Tex Christian U History Dept Fort Worth TX 76129

REUTER, JAMES WILLIAM, lawyer; b. Bemidji, Minn., Sept. 30, 1948; s. John Renee and Monica (Dugas) R.; m. Patricia Carol Creelman, Mar. 30, 1968; children: Kristine, Suzanne, Natalee. B.A., St. John's U., 1970; J.D., William Mitchell Coll. of Law, 1974. Bar: Minn. 1974, U.S. Dist. Ct. Minn. 1975, U.S. Ct. Appeals (8th cir.) 1985; cert. civil trial specialist. Editor, West Pub. Co., St. Paul, 1970-73; assoc. Terpstra & Merrill, Mpls., 1974-77; ptnr. Barna, Guzy, Merrill, Hynes & Giancola, Ltd., Mpls., 1977-89, ptnr. Lindquist & Vennum, Mpls., 1989—. Recipient Cert. award Nat. Inst. Trial Advocacy, 1978. Mem. ABA (intellectual property, torts and insur practice, and civil litigation sects.), Assn. Trial Lawyers Am., Minn. Bar Assn. (civil litigation and computer sects.), Hennepin County Bar Assn. (ins. com.), Anoka County Bar Assn. (pres. 1981-82). Avocations: skiing; golf; camping; reading. Office: Lindquist & Vennum 4200 IDS Ctr 80 S 8th St Minneapolis MN 55402-2100

REUTER, STEWART RALSTON, radiologist, lawyer, educator; b. Detroit, Feb. 14, 1934; s. Carl H. and Grace M. R.; m. Marianne Ahfeldt, June 6, 1966. B.A., Ohio Wesleyan U., 1955; M.D., Case Western Res. U., 1959; J.D., U. San Francisco, 1980. Diplomate: Am. Bd. Radiology. Bar: Tex. 1981. Intern U. Calif., San Francisco, 1959-60, resident in radiology, 1960-63; instr. radiology Stanford (Calif.) U., 1963-64; asst. prof. U. Mich., Ann Arbor, 1966-69, prof., 1972-76; assoc. prof. U. Calif., San Diego, 1969-72; prof. U. Calif., San Francisco and Davis, 1976-80; prof., chmn. dept. radiology Health Scis. Ctr., U. Tex., San Antonio, 1980—. Co-author: Gastrointestinal Radiology, 3d edit., 1986; mem. editorial bd. Am. Jour. Roentgenology, 1975-91, Iatrogenics, 1990-93; contbr. articles to profl. jours. Picker fellow, 1964-66. Fellow Am. Coll. Radiology (councillor 1996—), Am. Heart Assn., Am. Coll. Legal Medicine (bd. govs. 1985-91, 92-94, sec. 1994, pres.-elect 1995, pres. 1996); mem. ABA, Assn. Univ. Radiologists, Am. Roentgen Ray Soc., Tex. Radiol. Assn. (trustee 1989-92, pres. 1994), Soc. Cardiovascular and Interventional Radiologists (pres. 1979), Soc. Gastrointestinal Radiologists, Tex. Bar Assn. Home: 3923 Morgans Crk San Antonio TX 78230-1945 Office: U Tex Health Sci Ctr Dept Radiology 7703 Floyd Curl Dr San Antonio TX 78284-6200

REUTHER, DAVID LOUIS, children's book publisher, writer; b. Detroit, Nov. 2, 1946; s. Roy Louis and Fania (Sonkin) R.; m. Margaret Alexander Miller, July 21, 1973; children: Katherine Anna, Jacob Alexander. BA with honors, U. Mich., 1968. Tchr. Lewis-Wadhams Sch., Westport, N.Y., 1969-71; asst. dir. Children's Book Council, N.Y.C., 1971-73; editor children's books Macmillan Publishing Co., N.Y.C., 1973-76; sr. editor Four Winds Press-Scholastic Inc., N.Y.C., 1976-82; sr. v.p., editor-in-chief Morrow Jr. Books, N.Y.C., 1982—; co-founder Baseball Ink, Inc., 1986-90; mem. Nat. Sci. Tchrs. Assn.-Children's Book Coun. Joint Com., 1982-85; joint com. mem. Am. Bookseller Assn., 1990-93; treas. Childrens Book Coun., 1986, chmn., 1993-94. Author: with Roy Doty) Fun To Go, A Take-Along Activity Book, 1982, Save-the-Animals Activity Book, 1982, (with John Thorn and Pete Palmer) The Hidden Game of Baseball, 1984, Total Baseball, 1989, The Whole Baseball Catalog, 1990, Total Baseball II, 1991; editor: (with John Thorn) The Armchair Quarterback, 1982, The Armchair Aviator, 1983, The Armchair Mountaineer, 1984, The Armchair Book of Baseball, 1985, The Armchair Angler, 1986, The Armchair Book of Basesball II, 1987, The Armchair Traveler, 1988. Mem. ALA, Authors Guild, Soc. Children's Book Writers. Home: 271 Central Park W New York NY 10024-3020 Office: William Morrow & Co 1350 Avenue Of The Americas New York NY 10019-4702

REUTHER, WALTER, horticulture educator; b. Manganoui County, North Is., New Zealand, Sept. 21, 1911; came to U.S., 1919; s. Arthur W.G. and Martha (Krüger) R.; m. Flora Astbury Nelson, Aug. 4, 1935; children: David Walter, Charles Arthur. BS in Chemistry, U. Fla., 1933; PhD in Plant Physiology, Cornell U., 1940. Asst. horticulturist Agrl. Experiment Sta., U. Fla., Gainesville, 1933-37; rsch. asst. in pomology Cornell U., Ithaca, N.Y., 1937-40; asst. prof. pomology Cornell U., Ithaca, 1940; assoc. horticulturist, then prin. horticulturist USDA, Orlando, Fla., 1941-55; head dept. horticulture U. Fla., Gainesville, 1955-56; prof., chmn. dept. horticulture, researcher Citrus Ctr., U. Calif., Riverside, 1956-66, prof., horticulturist, 1966-72, 74-79; coord. regional rsch. Inst. Nat. Investigations in Agriculture, Valencia, Spain, 1972-74; prof. emeritus U. Calif., Riverside, 1979—; cons. Del Monte Corp., 1962-72, Govt. of Greece, 1963, 64, Rockefeller Found., 1965, 66-67, 69, UN, 1970, 75, 77, Govt. of Spain, 1972-74, Govt. of Brazil, 1975, 81, Govt. of Indonesia, 1977-78, 84, Govt. of Republic of China, 1979, Govt. of Honduras, 1980, Govt. of Mex., 1982, Govt. of Colombia, 1982. Editor: The Citrus Industry, 1967-90; contbr. 130 articles to profl. jours. Fellow Am. Soc. Hort. Sci. (pres. 1962-63, chmn. bd. dirs. 1963-64). Democrat. Avocations: reading, gradening, walking. Home: 12751 Gateway Park Rd Ste 322 Poway CA 92064-2064 Office: U Calif Dept Botany and Plant Sci Riverside CA 92521

REUTIMAN, ROBERT WILLIAM, JR., lawyer; b. Mpls., June 4, 1944; s. Robert William and Elsbeth Bertha (Doering) R.; m. Virginia Lee Traxler, June 25, 1983; children: Robert James, Joseph Lee. BA magna cum laude, U. Minn., 1966, JD, 1969. Bar: Minn. 1969, U.S. Ct. Mil. Appeals 1969, U.S. Dist. Ct. Minn. 1973, U.S. Ct. Appeals (8th cir.) 1976, U.S. Tax. Ct. 1979. Mem. Armstrong, Phleger, Reutiman & Vinokour, Ltd., Wayzata, Minn., 1973-76; ptnr. Phleger & Reutiman, Wayzata, 1976-81; pvt. practice Wayzata, 1981—. Chmn. Spring Pk. Planning Commn., 1978. Capt. U.S. Army, 1969-73. Decorated Army Commendation medal. Mem. ABA, Minn. Bar Assn., Hennepin County Bar Assn., Am. Arbitration Assn. (panel of arbitrators), Phi Beta Kappa. Lutheran. Avocations: fishing, rose growing. Home: 11610 3rd Ave N Plymouth MN 55441-5919 Office: 305 Rice St E Wayzata MN 55391-1615

REUTTER, EBERHARD EDMUND, JR., education and law educator; b. Balt., May 28, 1924; s. Eberhard Edmund and Irene Louise (Loewer) R.; m. Bettie Marie Lytle, Aug. 16, 1947; 1 son, Mark Douglas. B.A., Johns Hopkins U., 1944; M.A., Columbia U., 1948, Ph.D., 1950. Dir., Tokyo Army Edn. Program Sch., 1945-47; head math. dept. Barnard Sch., N.Y.C., 1947-49; mem. faculty Tchrs. Coll., Columbia U., 1950—, prof., 1957—; vis. prof. U. Alaska, 1960, 66, U. P.R., 1954, U. So. Calif., 1960; speaker, cons. Coordinator spl. edn. projects NAACP Legal Def. Fund, 1965-68. Author: The School Administrator and Subversive Activities, 1951, Schools and the Law, 5th edit., 1981, (with W.S. Elsbree) Staff Personnel in the Public Schools, 1954, (with R.R. Hamilton) Legal Aspects of School Board Operation, 1958, (with W.S. Elsbree) Principles of Staff Personnel Administration in Public Schools, 1959, (with L.O. Garber) The Yearbook of School Law, 1967, 68, 69, 70, Legal Aspects of Control of Student Activities by Public School Authorities, 1970, The Law of Public Education, 4th edit., 1994, The Courts and Student Conduct, 1975, The Supreme Court's Impact on Public Education, 1982; also articles, chpts. in books. Chmn. citizens adv. com. Emerson (N.J.) Bd. Edn., 1954-57. Served from pvt. to 1st lt. inf. AUS, 1943-46. Recipient Marion A. McGhehey award for outstanding service in field edn. law, 1986. Mem. Nat. Orgn. Legal Problems of Edn. (pres. 1967), AAUP, Am. Assn. Sch. Adminstrs., NEA, Am. Assn. Sch. Personnel Adminstrs., Internat. Personnel Mgmt. Assn., Phi Beta Kappa, Kappa Delta Pi, Phi Delta Kappa. Home: 316 Grand Blvd Emerson NJ 07630-1157 Office: Columbia Univ Tchrs Coll New York NY 10027

REVEAL, ARLENE HADFIELD, librarian, consultant; b. Riverside, Utah, May 21, 1916; d. Job Oliver and Mabel Olive (Smith) Hadfield; children: James L., Jon A. BS with hons., Utah State U., 1938; grad. in librarianship San Diego State U., 1968; M in Libr. and Info. Sci., Brigham Young U., 1976. Social case worker Boxelder County Welfare, Brigham City, Utah, 1938-40; office mgr. Dodge Ridge Ski Corp., Long Barn, Calif., 1948-65, Strawberry (Calif.) Inn, 1950-65, Pinecrest Permittees Assn., 1955-66; adminstrv. asst. Mono County Office of Edn., Bridgeport, Calif., 1961-67; catalog libr. La Mesa (Calif.)-Spring Valley Sch. Dist., 1968-71; libr. Mono County Libr., Bridgeport, Calif., 1971-96; chair Mountain Valley Library System, 1987-89. Author: Mono County Courthouse, 1980. Active Devel. Disabilities Area Bd. # 12, 1974-96, chair, 1990-92. Recipient John Cotton Dana award H.W. Wilson Co., 1974; named Bridgeport Citizen of Yr., 1993, Wild Iris Woman of Yr., Mono County, 1996. Mem. Rebekah (treas. 1973-90), Delta Kappa Gamma (pres. Epsilon Alpha chpt. 1984-88), Beta Sigma Phi (treas. Xi Omicron Epsilon chpt. 1981, 83-85, 91-96, pres. 1982, 85, 89), Beta Phi Mu. Home: 15425 N 5250 W Riverside UT 84334-0156

REVEAL, ERNEST IRA, III, lawyer; b. Chgo., Oct. 19, 1948; s. Ernest Ira Jr. and Hazel (Holt) R.; m. Katherine Trennerry, Nov. 24, 1979; children: Genevieve, Adrienne, Danielle. BA, Cornell U., 1970; JD, U. Mich., 1973. Bar: Minn. 1973, U.S. Dist. Ct. Minn. 1973, U.S. Ct. Appeals (8th cir.) 1974, U.S. Dist. Ct. S.D. 1976, U.S. Ct. Claims 1976, U.S. Ct. Appeals (7th cir.) 1984, U.S. Dist. Ct. (so. dist.) Calif. 1991, U.S. Ct. Appeals (9th cir.) 1991, U.S. Supreme Ct., 1991. Assoc. Robins, Kaplan, Miller & Ciresi, Mpls., 1973-79, ptnr., 1979—. Author: Public Sector Labor Law, 1983. Mem. Civil Svc. Commn., St. Paul, Minn., 1976. Mem. ABA, Minn. Bar Assn. (past chair labor law and employment law sect.), Cornell Club of Minn. (past pres.), Assn. Trial Lawyers Am. Democrat. Presbyterian. Avocations: sports, reading. Office: Robins Kaplan Miller & Ciresi 600 Anton Blvd Ste 1600 Costa Mesa CA 92626-7147

REVEIZ, FUAD, professional football player; b. Bogota, Colombia, Feb. 24, 1963. Student, U. Tenn. Placekicker Minn. Vikings. Named to NFL Pro Bowl Team, 1994; tied record for most field goals made in NFL, 1994. Office: Minn Vikings 9520 Viking Dr Eden Prairie MN 55344-3825*

REVEL, JEAN-PAUL, biology educator; b. Strasbourg, France, Dec. 7, 1930; came to U.S., 1953; s. Gaston Benjamin and Suzanne (Neher) R.; m. Helen Ruth Bowser, July 27, 1957 (div. 1986); children: David, Daniel Neher, Steven Robert; m. Galina Avdeeva Moller, Dec. 24, 1986; 1 stepchild, Karen. BS, U. Strasbourg, 1949; PhD, Harvard U., 1957. Rsch. fellow Cornell U. Med. Sch., N.Y.C., 1958-59; from instr. to prof. Harvard Med. Sch., Boston, 1959-71; prof. Calif. Inst. Tech., Pasadena, 1971—; AB Ruddock chair in biology Calif. Inst. Tech., 1978—, dean of students, 1996—; mem. sch. advisors bd. Nat. Insts. Aging, Balt., 1977-80; mem. ad hoc adv. biology NSF, Washington, 1982-83; mem. Nat. High Voltage Microscopy Adv. Group, Bethesda, Md., 1983, Nat. Rsch. Resources Adv. Coun., 1986-90. Author: (with E.D. Hay) Fine Structure of Developing Avian Cornea, 1969; editor: Cell Shape and Surface Architecture, 1977, Science of Biological Specimen Preparation, 1986; mem. editl. bd. Jour. Cell Biology, 1969-72, Internat. Rev. Cytology, 1970, Cell and Tissue Rsch., 1979—, Molecular and Cell Biology, 1983-91; editor in chief Jour. Microscopy Soc. Am., 1994-96. Fellow AAAS (leader biol. scis. sect. 1991-92, Gordon conf. cell adhesion); mem. Am. Soc. Cell Biology (pres. 1972-73), Electron Micros. Soc. Am. (pres. 1988, Disting. Scientist award 1993), Soc. Devel. Biology. Avocations: watercolors, photography. Office: Calif Inst Tech # 156-29 Pasadena CA 91125

REVELEY, WALTER TAYLOR, III, lawyer; b. Churchville, Va., Jan. 6, 1943; s. Walter Taylor and Marie (Eason) R.; m. Helen Bond, Dec. 18, 1971; children: Walter Taylor, George Everett Bond, Nelson Martin Eason, Helen Lanier. AB, Princeton U., 1965; JD, U. Va., 1968. Bar: Va. 1970, D.C. 1976. Asst. prof. law U. Ala., 1968-69; law clk. to Justice Brennan U.S. Supreme Ct., Washington, 1969-70; fellow Woodrow Wilson Internat. Ctr. for Scholars, 1972-73; internat. affairs fellow Coun. on Fgn. Rels., N.Y.C., 1972-73; assoc. Hunton & Williams, Richmond, Va., 1970-76, ptnr., 1976—, mng. ptnr., 1982-91; lectr. Coll. William and Mary Law Sch., 1978-80. Author: War Powers of the President and Congress: Who Holds the Arrows and Olive Branch, 1981; mem. editorial & mng. bds. Va. Law Rev., 1966-68; contbr. articles to profl. jours. Trustee Princeton U., 1986—, Presbyn. Ch. (U.S.A.) Found., 1991—, Va. Hist. Soc., 1991-96, Union Theol. Sem., 1992—, Andrew W. Mellon Found., 1994—, Va. Mus. Fine Arts, 1995—, pres. 1996—; bd. dirs. Fan Dist. Assn., Richmond, Inc., 1976-80, pres., 1979-80; bd. dirs. Richmond Symphony, 1980-92, pres., 1988-90, pres. symphony coun., 1994—; bd. dirs. Presbyn. Outlook Found. and Book Svc., 1985—, pres., 1992-95; bd. dirs. Va. Mus. Found., 1990—; elder Grace Covenant Presbyn. Ch. Mem. ABA, Va. Bar Assn., D.C. Bar Assn., Richmond Bar Assn., Am. Soc. Internat. Law, Am. Judicature Soc., Am. Bar Found., Princeton Assn. Va. (bd. dirs. 1981—, pres. 1983-85), Edn. Lawyers (chmn. Va. State Bar sect. 1992-95), Raven Soc., Knickerbocker Club (N.Y.C.), Country Club Va., Downtown Club, Order of Coif, Phi Beta Kappa, Omicron Delta Kappa. Home: 2314 Monument Ave Richmond VA 23220-2604 Office: Hunton & Williams Riverfront Pla East Tower 951 E Byrd St Richmond VA 23219-4040

REVELL, DOROTHY EVANGELINE TOMPKINS, dietitian; b. Rugby, N.D., Dec. 22, 1911; d. Clarence Herbert and Regina Andrea (Bergh) Tompkins; m. Eugene Allen Revell, Sept 17, 1935; children: Eugene Allen II, Dorothy Ann. BS in Food and Nutrition, U. N.D., Grand Forks, 1933. Lic. registered dietitian, N.D. Dietetic intern Harper Hosp., Detroit, 1933-34, staff dietitian, 1934-35; nutrition instr. student nurses Mercy Hosp., Valley City, N.D., 1958; dietitian Dakota Clinic, Fargo, N.D., 1958-76; pvt. practice Revell's Diet Svc., Fargo, 1977—; home nursing chmn. ARC, Fargo, 1952-54; participant at internat. dietetic meetings. Author 8 books; contbr. articles to profl. jours. Invitee Dietetic Assn. South Africa, Cape Town, 1974, Nutrition and Health Care Study, China, 1984; del. People to People, China, 1987; mem. nutrition study to former USSR, 1974. Recipient Sioux Award to Alumni U. of N.D., named Outstanding Alumni of U. N.D. Mem. Am. Dietetic Assn. (registered dietitian), N.D. Affiliate of Am. Dietetic Assn. (pres. 1950-59), United Empire Loyalists of Can., Daughters Am. Colonists, Pi Beta Phi. Republican. Episcopalian. Home: 2407 E Country Club Dr Fargo ND 58103-5730 Office: Revell's Diet Svc 2407 E Country Club Dr Fargo ND 58103-5730

REVELL, GRAEME, composer. Film scores include Dead Calm, 1989, Spontaneous Combustion, 1990, Child's Play 2, 1990, Until the End of the World, 1991, The Hand That Rocks the Cradle, 1991, Love Crimes, 1992, Traces of Red, 1992, Body of Evidence, 1993, Hear No Evil, 1993, The Crush, 1993, Hard Target, 1993, Boxing Helena, 1993, The Crow, 1994, Ghost in the Machine, 1994, The Basketball Diaries, 1995. Office: 5093 N Pkwy Calabasas CA 91302*

REVELLE, CHARLES S., environmental engineer, geophysicist, systems analysis and economics educator; b. Mar. 26, 1938; m. Penelope ReVelle; 2 children. BChemE, Cornell U., 1961, PhD, 1967. Chemist Nat. Starch and Chem. Co., Plainfield, N.J., 1961; rsch. engr., instr. dept. sanitary engring. Cornell U., 1962, environ. systems engring. fellow, 1963-67, asst. prof. dept. environ. systems engring., 1967-71; on leave to Johns Hopkins U. 1968-69; asst. prof. Johns Hopkins U., Balt., 1971, assoc. prof., 1971-75, prof. program in systems analysis and econs. for pub. decision making, dept. geography and environ. engring., 1975—; part-time vis. scholar Inst. Water Resources, U.S. Army Corps of Engrs., Ft. Belvoir, Va., 1993—; vis. prof. dept. geography U. Iowa, 1976; invited lectr. Oxford U., Eng., 1974, U. Genoa, 1975, 82, U. Bristol, U.K., 1975, U. Stirling, Scotland, 1975, Internat. Inst. for Applied Systems Analysis, Vienna, Austria, 1980, U. N.C., Chapel Hill, 1984, Ohio State U., 1987, others; del. Univ. Coun. on Water Resources, 1984—; mem. com. on water resources of water scis. and tech. bd. NAE/NAS, 1985-87, subcom. on instl. rsch., 1986; advisor water resources rsch. com. ASCE, 1989; cons. in field; presenter papers at numerous profl. meetings. Co-author: (with Penelope ReVelle) Sourcebook on the Environment: The Scientific Perspective, 1974, The Environment: Issues and Choices for Society, 1981, 3d edit., 1988; (with Penelope ReVelle) The Global Environment: Securing a Sustainable Future, 1992; (with Whitlatch and Wright) Civil and Environmental Systems Engineering, 1997; mem. edtl. bd. Geog. Analysis, 1987-91, European Jour. Ops. Rsch., 1991—, Envrion. Modeling and Assesment, Socio-Econ. Planning Scis.; assoc. editor Mgmt. Sci.; contbr. over 130 articles to profl. jours. Recipient Robert B. Pond Sr. Excellence in Teaching award Johns Hopkins U., 1990; Fulbright-Hays fellow Erasmus U., The Netherlands, 1975; rsch. grantee City of Balt., 1975-76, 81-82, Nat. Bur. Standards, 1977, Office of Water Rsch. and Tech., 1977-81, U.S. Dept. Energy, 1980-82, N.J. Dept. Energy, 1980-81, Dept. Navy, 1985-87. Mem. Am. Geophys. Union, Arms Control Assn., Inst. Ops. Rsch. and Mgmt. Sci., Internat. Regional Sci. Assn., Phi Kappa Phi, Sigma Xi. Research in: (1) siting of emergency and other public sector facilities; (2) water quality and water resources systems; (3) forestry and natural area preservation models. Office: Johns Hopkins U Dept Geography & Environ Engring Ames Hall Baltimore MD 21218 *"Our challenge is to begin to erect the structure that preserves the earth we inherited."*

REVELLE, DONALD GENE, manufacturing and health care company executive, consultant; b. Cape Girardeau, Mo., July 16, 1930; s. Lewis W. and Dorothy R.; m. Jo M. Revelle, Aug. 1, 1954; children—Douglas, David, Daniel, Dianne. BA, U. Mo., 1952; JD, U. Colo., 1957; grad., Harvard U. Bus. Sch., 1971. Dir. employee relations Westinghouse Corp., Pitts., 1957-65; asst. to v.p. Diebold Corp., 1966; v.p. human resources TRW Corp., Cleve., 1967-84; sr. v.p. human resources Black and Decker Co., Towson, Md., 1984-86; exec. v.p. corp. rels. Montefiore Acad. Med. Ctr., Bronx, 1987—; univ. lectr.; cons. Duerba Ship, Blue Cross N.Y., Windsor Hosp., Salvation Army. Contbr. articles to profl. jours. Mem. sch. bd. State of N.Y. Lt. USNR, 1952-54. Mem. ABA (labor law com.), Colo. Bar Assn., Fed. Bar Assn., Human Resource Planning Soc., MBA Assn. Methodist. Home: 1004 Chestnut Ridge Dr Lutherville Timonium MD 21093-1725 Office: Montefiore Acad Med Ctr 111 E 210th St Bronx NY 10467-2401

RE VELLE, JACK B(OYER), statistician, consultant; b. Rochester, N.Y., Aug. 2, 1935; s. Mark A. and Myril (Bubes) Re V.; m. Brenda Lorraine Newcombe, Aug. 2, 1968; 1 child, Karen Alyssa. BS in Chem. Engring., Purdue U., 1957; MS in Indsl. Engring. and Mgmt., Okla. State U., 1965, PhD in Indsl. Engring. and Mgmt., 1970. Commd. 2d lt. USAF, 1957, advanced through grades to major, 1968, resigned, 1968; adminstrv. asst. Gen. Dynamics, Ft. Worth, 1970-71; cons. engr. Denver, 1971-72; chmn. decision scis. U. Nebr., Omaha, 1972-77; dean Sch. Bus. and Mgmt. Chapman U., Orange, Calif., 1977-79; sr. staff engr. McDonnell Douglas Space Systems, Huntington Beach, Calif., 1979-81; head mfg. tng. and devel. Hughes Aircraft Co., Fullerton, Calif., 1981-82, sr. statistician, 1982-86; corp. mgr. R & D Hughes Aircraft Co., L.A., 1986-88, corp. chief statistician, 1988-93; leader continuous improvement Hughes Missile Systems Co., Tucson, Ariz., 1994—; mem. bd. examiners Malcolm Baldridge nat. quality award Nat. Inst. Stds. and Tech., U.S. Dept. Commerce, Washington, 1990, 93; judge Ariz. Quality Alliance, Phoenix, 1994-96, Rochester Inst. Tech.-USA Today Quality Cup Competition, 1994—, Def. Contract Mgmt. Command-Commdrs. Cup, 1995—; cons. to various pub. and pvt. orgns.; presenter, lectr. in field. Author: Safety Training Methods, 1980, The Two-Day Statistician, 1986, The New Quality Technology, 1988, Policy Deployment, 1993, (with others) Quest for Quality, 1986, Mechanical Engineers Handbook, 1986, Production Handbook, 1987, Handbook of Occupational Safety and Health, 1987, A Quality Revolution in Manufacturing, 1989, Quality Engineering Handbook, 1991; co-author: Quantitative Methods for Managerial Decisions, 1978, The Executive's Handbook on Quality Function Deployment, 1994, From Concept to Customer, 1995, The Quality Function Deployment Handbook, 1997, (software packages) TQM ToolSchool, 1995, QFD/Pathway, 1997. Bd. dirs. Assn. for Quality and Participation, Cin., 1985-86. Fellow Inst. for the Advancement Engring., 1986; recipient Disting. Econs. Devel. award Soc. Mfg. Engrs., 1990. Fellow Am. Soc. for Quality Control (co-chair total quality mgmt. com. 1990-92), Am. Soc. Safety Engrs. (nat. accreditation project dir. 1978-80), Inst. Indsl. Engrs. (regional v.p. 1982-84, treas. 1992-93, sr. v.p. 1993-94), Aerospace and Defense Soc. (pres. 1997—). Office: Hughes Missile Systems Co Old Nogales Hwy Tucson AZ 85734

REVELS, RICHARD W., JR., lawyer; b. Bastrop, La., June 27, 1950. BA, La. State U., 1972, JD, 1980; BA, La. Tech U., 1975, MA, 1975. Bar: La. 1980. Law clk. to Hon. James L. Dennis La. State Supreme Ct., 1980-81; atty. Liskow & Lewis, Lafayette, La. Assoc. editor: La. Law Rev., 1979-80. Mem. ABA, La. State Bar Assn., Lafayette Parish Bar Assn., Order of Coif, Phi Kappa Phi. Office: Liskow & Lewis 822 Harding St PO Box 52008 Lafayette LA 70503

REVENS, JOHN COSGROVE, JR., state senator, lawyer; b. Providence, Jan. 29, 1947; s. John C. and Rita M. (Williams) R.; AA, C.C. of R.I., 1966; BA, Providence Coll., 1969; JD, Suffolk U., 1973; m. Susan L. Shaw, Aug. 31, 1974; children: Leigh Elizabeth, Marcie Greene, Emily May. Mem. R.I. Ho. of Reps., 1968-74, sec. house steering com., 1971-74, mem. edn. and welfare com., 1968-70; admitted to R.I. bar, 1973; pres. firm Revens, Lanni, Revens & St. Pierre, Warwick, R.I., 1977—; mem. R.I. Senate, 1974-89, 1991—, mem. jud. and labor coms., 1974, chmn. jud. com., 1980-83, majority whip, 1977-80, Senate majority leader, 1983-89; Senate pres., pro tempore, 1993-95; dir. New Eng. Bd. Higher Edn., 1975-83, chmn., 1977-81; chmn. R.I. Children's Code Commn., 1979-83; bd. dirs. C.C. of R.I. Found., Vols. of Warwick Schs., R.I. Acad. Decathlon Assn.; mem. Commn. on Jud. Tenure and Discipline, 1982-84, Family Ct. Bench Bar Com., 1980-82, Women and Infants Hosp. Corp., 1983—; commr. Uniform State Laws, 1982-84. Mem. R.I. Bar Assn., Kent County Bar Assn., Am. Arbitration Assn. (panel of arbitrators 1980—), KC. Democrat. Roman Catholic. Office: 946 Centerville Rd Warwick RI 02886-4398

REVER, GEORGE WRIGHT, psychiatrist, health facility administrator; b. Balt., May 18, 1928; s. William Benjamin and Amy Blanche (Wright) R.; m. Bridget Valerie Hanley, 1961 (dec. 1988); children: Kurt, Maeve Rever Raedle; m. Ann Roe, Feb. 4, 1994. BS, U. Md., 1950; MD, U. Md., Balt., 1957. Rotating intern Mercy Hosp., Balt., 1957-58; resident psychiatry and neurology VA Hosp., Boston, 1958-60; fellow Harvard Med. Sch., Cambridge, Mass., 1960-64, clin. instr. psychiatry, 1964—; psychiatrist divsn. legal medicine Cambridge Ct., 1960-71; psychiatrist Cambridge Ct. Clinic Divsn. of Legal Medicine, Mass., 1960-71; pvt. practice Cohasset, Mass., 1963-90, Easton, Md., 1990-93; psychiatric cons. Travelers Aid Soc., Boston, 1966-74; psychiatrist Eunice Kennedy Shriver Ctr., Waltham, Mass., 1967-90; fellow child psychiatry Mass. Gen. Hosp., Boston, 1960-61, 62-63, fellow community mental health, 1963-64, staff psychiatrist, 1964-90, dir. child psychiatry tng. program neuropsychiatry devel. disabilities sect., 1967-90, asst. pediatrician, 1969-71, psychiat. cons. social svc. dept., 1970-74, psychiatrist Chelsea Health Ctr., 1974-77, hon. psychiatrist, 1991—; med. dir. Brockton (Mass.) Family and Community Rsch., 1979-90; child and adolescent psychiatrist Wicomico County Health Dept., Salisbury, Md., 1990-91, Queen Anne County Mental Health, Centreville, Md., 1990-92; child and adolescent psychiatrist Talbot County Mental Health, Easton, 1990-92, med. dir., 1992—; psychiatric cons. Benedictine Sch., Ridgely, Md., 1990—; part-time fellow child psychiatry Mass. Gen. Hosp., Boston, 1961-62, James Jackson Putnam Children's Ctr., Roxbury, Mass., 1961-62; cons. Am. Heritage Dictionaries, 1992. Editl. cons. The Am. Jour. of Child and Adolescent Psychiatry, 1994—. Sgt. U.S. Army, 1950-52, Korea. Decorated Bronze Star medal; Recipient Talbot County Assn. Retarded Citizens award, 1993. Mem. AMA, Am. Acad. Child and Adolescent Psychiatry, Am. Psychiatric Assn., Md. Psychiatric Soc., Med. and Chirurg. Faculty Md., Talbot County Med. Soc. Home: 8627 N Bend Cir Easton MD 21601

REVERDIN, BERNARD J., lawyer; b. Baden, Switzerland, June 21, 1919; came to U.S., 1948, naturalized, 1954; s. Jean and Germaine Reverdin; children: Caroline Reverdin Flanagan, Brigitte Reverdin Sarasin, Nathalie. LLB, U. Geneva, 1942; postgrad., Harvard Law Sch., 1949. Bar: Switzerland 1945, N.Y. 1955. Atty., legal asst. Geneva Govt., 1945-48; assoc. Sullivan & Cromwell, N.Y.C., 1949-51; assoc., ptnr. Lovejoy, Wasson & Ashton, N.Y.C., 1951-84; ptnr., counsel Hunton & Williams, N.Y.C., 1984-88; ptnr. Eaton & Van Winkle, N.Y.C., 1988—; dir. subs. of European corps. Contbr. articles to profl. jours.; lectr. in field. V. p., treas., bd. dirs. Friends of Cuttington Coll., Liberia; v.p. LCM Found. on European Affairs Inc. Mem. N.Y. State Bar Assn. (chair com. internat. trust and estate 1988-90), Am. Fgn. Law Assn. (past pres.), Consular Law Soc. (past pres.), Internat. Law Assn., Union Internat. des Avocats, Swiss Soc. N.Y., German Am. Law Assn. Home: 4 Drohan St Huntington NY 11743 Office: Eaton & Van Winkle 600 3rd Ave Fl 39 New York NY 10016-2001

REVERE, VIRGINIA LEHR, clinical psychologist; b. Long Branch, N.J.; d. Joseph and Essie Lehr; m. Robert B. Revere; children: Elspeth, Andrew, Lisa, Robert Jr. PhB, U. Chgo., 1949, MA, 1959, PhD, 1971. Lic. cons. clin. psychologist, Va. Intern, staff psychologist Ea. Mental Health Reception Ctr., Phila., 1959-61; instr. Trenton (N.J.) State Coll., 1962-63; staff psychologist Trenton State Hosp., 1964-65, Bucks County Psychiat. Ctr., Phila., 1965-67; assoc. prof. Mansfield (Pa.) State U., 1967-77; clin. rsch. psychologist St. Elizabeth Hosp., Washington, 1977-81, tng. psychology coord., 1981-83, staff psychologist, 1985-91; child psychologist Community Mental Health Ctr., Washington, 1983-85; pvt. practice Alexandria, Va., 1980—; cons., lectr. in field. Author: Applied Psychology for Criminal Justice Professionals, 1982; contbr. articles to profl. jours. Recipient Group Merit award St. Elizabeth's Hosp., 1983, Community Svc. award D.C. Psychol. Assn., 1978, Outstanding Educator award, 1972; traineeship NIH, USPHS, Chgo., 1963-65; fellow Family Svcs. Assn., 1958-59. Mem. APA, No. Va. Soc. Clin. Psychologists, Va. Acad. Clin. Psychologists. Home: 9012 Linton Ln Alexandria VA 22308-2733 Office: 5021 Seminary Rd Ste 110 Alexandria VA 22311-1923

REVES, JOSEPH GERALD, anesthesiology educator; b. Charleston, S.C., Aug. 14, 1943; s. George Everett and Frances (Masterson) R.; m. Virginia Cathcart, Jan. 05, 1945; children: Virginia Masterson, Christine Frances, Elizabeth Cathcart. BA, Vanderbilt U., 1965; MD, Medical Coll. S.C., 1969; MS, U. Ala., Birmingham, 1973. Lic. anesthesiologist S.C., Ala., Md., N.C.; Diplomate Am. Coll. Anesthesiology, Am. Bd. Anesthesiology. Rsch. asst., dept. pharmacology Med. Coll. S.C., 1965, 66 (summers); intern U. Ala. Hosp. and Clinics, Birmingham, Ala., 1969-70, resident in anesthesiology, 1970-72; post-doctoral, dept. anesthesia and physiology U. Ala. Med. Sch., 1972; instr., dept anesthesiology U. Ala. Hosp. and Clinics, 1973; dept. tng. staff, anesthesiology Nat. Naval Med. Ctr., Bethesda, Md., 1973-75; clin. instr., dept. anesthesiology George Washington U. Sch. Med., Washington, 1973-75; assoc. prof., dept. anesthesiology U. Ala. Hosp. and Clinics, 1975-78; dir., div. anesthesiology rsch. U. Ala., 1977-84, prof. anesthesiology, 1978-84; clin. anesthesia coord. UAB Cardiac Transplant Program, Birmingham, 1982-84; prof. anesthesiology, dir. cardiothoracic anesthesia Duke U. Med. Ctr., Durham, N.C., 1984-1991; dir., Duke Heart Ctr., Duke Med. Ctr., Durham, N.C., 1987—; interim chmn., dept. anesthesiology Duke U. Med. Ctr., 1990-91, prof. and chmn., dept. anesthesiology, 1991—; cons. Hoffman-LaRoche, Somatogen, Abbott/Oximetric. Contbr. to numerous profl. jours., refereed jours., chpts. in books, published scientific reviews, selected abstracts, editorials, films, audio visual presentations, letters, positions and background papers; author: Acute Revascularization of the Infracted Heart, 1987, Common Problems in Cardiac Anesthesia, 1987, Intravenous Anesthesia and Analgesia, 1988, Anesthesiology Clinics of North America, 1988, Anesthesia, 1990, International Anesthesiology Clinics, 1991; Cardiac Anesthesia, Privileges and Practice, 1994; editor: Anesthesia and Analgesia, 1984—, cardiovascular sect. editor 1991—; editorial bd. Society Cardiovascular Anesthesia Monograph Series (chmn. 1986-89), Current Opinion in Anaesthesia 1987—, American Antec Newsletter 1989—; co-editor in chief: Current Opinion in Anaesthesiology 1990—. Dir. Clairmont Ave Hist. Preservation Com. 1976-78; Am. Heart Assn. (Durham chpt. pres. 1988-90, com. mem. anesthesiology, radiology and surgery rsch. study com. 1988-91). Grantee NIH 1991—, Janssen Pharmaceutica 1991-93, Anaquest 1989-92, Diprivan Ednl. grant ICI Pharmaceuticals Group 1991-92. Fellow Am. Coll. Cardiology; mem. AMA, Durham County Medical Soc., Internat. Soc. on Oxygen Transport to Tissue, N.C. Soc. Anesthesiologist (edn. com. 1992—), N.C. State Medical Soc., Birmingham Vanderbilt Club (bd. dirs. 1975-80, 1st v.p. 1979, pres. 1980), Southern Med. Assn. (chmn. elect. anesthesiology sect. 1976-77, chmn. 1977-78, chmn. 1988-89), Southern Soc. Anesthesiologists (v.p. 1978-79, pres. elect 1979-80, pres. 1980-81), Soc. Cardiovascular Anesthesiologists (pres. 1979-80), Assn. Univ. Anesthetists (elected to mem. 1980), Assn. Cardiac Anesthesiologists (elected to mem. 1982, pres. 1990), Soc. for Neuroleptanalgesia (bd. dirs. 1988), U. Ala. Birmingham Nat. Alumni Soc. (dist. dir., bd. dirs. 1991-93), Internat. Anesthesia Rsch. Soc. (bd. Trustees 1992—), Am. Soc. Anesthesiologists (com. sub-specialty representation 1980—, subcommittee on clin. circulation 1992—, com. geriatric anesthesia 1992—), Sigma Xi, Alpha Omega Alpha. Achievements include research on effects of age on neurologic response to cardiopulmonary bypass; cerebral blood flow and metabolism during cardiac surgery; automated delivery system of intravenous anesthetic drugs; pathophysiology of cardiopulmonary bypass. Office: Duke U Med Ctr Dept Anesthesiology PO Box 3094 Durham NC 27710*

REVOILE, CHARLES PATRICK, lawyer; b. Newark, Jan. 15, 1934; s. Charles Patrick and Olga Lydia (Zecca) R.; m. Sally Cole Gates, Nov. 8, 1963. B.A., U. Md., 1957, LL.B., 1960. Bar: Md. 1962, U.S. Dist. Ct. Md. 1962, U.S. Supreme Ct. 1970, U.S. Ct. Claims 1976, U.S. Ct. Appeals (fed. cir.) 1982. Legis. counsel Nat. Canners Assn., Washington, 1960-64; asst. counsel Deco Electronics Inc., Washington, 1964-67; div. counsel Westinghouse Electric, Leesburg, Va., 1967-71; v.p., gen. counsel Stanwick Corp., Arlington, Va., 1971-85, sr. v.p., gen. counsel, sec. CACI Internat. Inc., 1985-92, bd. dirs., 1992—, chmn. compensation com., 1996—; ret. lawyer and cons., 1993—; mem. regional adv. coun. NASD, 1989-92; lectr., panelist, advisor. Active in Md. Ednl. Found., College Park, 1974—; assoc. Nat. Symphony Orchestra, Washington, 1972-93, Smithsonian Instn., 1980-93, M Club Found., 1985—; lawyer, lobbyist various non profit orgns., Washington, 1984—; mem. exec. com. ann. bus. campaign Gallaudet U., 1989-91; chmh. various coms. Kemper Open Championships, 1980-86; exec. com. 1995 USGA Sr. Open, 1997 USGA Open Championships; gen. counsel, mem. exec. com. 1995 and 1996 Kemper Open Championship. Mem. Md. Bar Assn., Wash. Corp. Counsels Assn., Am. Corp. Counsels Assn., U.S. Golf Assn., Mid. Atlantic Golf Assn. (exec. com. 1989—, v.p.), Roger Howell Soc. U. Md. Sch. Law (charter). Republican. Roman Catholic. Club: Congl. Country (com. chmn. 1966-92, bd. govs. 1987-93, Bethesda, Md.), Avondale Golf (Pymble, Australia). Home: 4112 Culver St Kensington MD 20895-3624

REVOR, BARBARA KAY, secondary school educator; b. Mt. Vernon, Ill., June 16, 1948; d. Russell Harold and Mary Alice (Byars) Page; m. Bryan J. Revor, Dec. 19, 1981; children: Rachel, Joshua, Jacob. BA, Okla. Bapt. U., 1971; MS in Edn., Nat. Louis U., 1991. Tchr., chair English dept. North Palos Sch. Dist. 117, Hickory Hills, Ill., 1971—. Mem. Nat. Coun. Tchrs. of English, Ill. Assn. Tchrs. of English, Romance Writers Am., Windy City Romance Writers.

REVSINE, LAWRENCE, accounting educator, consultant; b. Chgo., May 29, 1942; s. Victor and Pauline (Berger) R.; m. Barbara Sue Epstein, 1963; children: Pamela, David. B.S., Northwestern U., 1963, M.B.A., 1965, Ph.D., 1968. C.P.A., Ill. Staff acct. Peat, Marwick, Mitchell & Co., Chgo., 1963-64; asst. prof. U. Ill., Urbana, 1968-70, assoc. prof., 1970-71; assoc. prof. acctg. Northwestern U., 1971-74, prof., 1975-79, Eric L. Kohler prof. acctg., 1979-86, John and Norma Darling disting. prof. fin. acctg., 1986—, chmn. dept. acctg. and info. systems, 1985-93; vis. prof. U. Wis., Madison, 1974-75; cons. in field. Author: Replacement Cost Accounting, 1973, Accounting in An Inflationary Enviroment, 1977, (with others) Statement on Accounting Theory and Theory Acceptance, 1977; contbr. articles to profl. jours.; editorial cons.: Acctg. Rev., 1977-80, mem. editorial bd., 1971-74, Jour. Acctg. and Pub. Policy, 1982—, Jour. Acctg. and Bus., 1986—. Recipient commendation for teaching excellence Northwestern U. Grad. Mgmt. Assn., 1981, 82, 86, 91; recipient Tchr. of Yr. award Northwestern U. Grad. Mgmt. Assn., 1983; Ford Found. doctoral fellow, 1966-68; Peat, Marwick, Mitchell Found. grantee, 1978, Kellogg Alumni Choice Faculty award, 1995. Mem. AICPAs, Am. Acctg. Assn. (chmn. com. on concepts and standards-external fin. reports 1974-76, disting. overseas lectr. 1991, outstanding educator 1992, chmn. fin. reporting issues conf. com. 1994), Ill. Soc. CPAs (outstanding educator 1993, fin. acctg. standards adv. coun. 1992-95), Beta Alpha Psi, Beta Gamma Sigma. Office: Northwestern U Kellogg Grad Sch Mgmt Evanston IL 60208

REVUELTA, RENÉ SERGIO, marine scientist, educator; b. La Habana, Cuba, Sept. 9, 1956; s. René Juan and Yolanda Paula (López) R.; m. Maria Soledad Tosteson, June 17, 1984 (div. 1993); children: Zinfandel, Luna. BA, U. Miami, 1978; PhD in Marine Scis., U. P.R., 1986. Grad. rsch. assoc. dept. marine scis. U. P.R., Mayaguez, 1978-86; postdoctoral fellow dept. biology and McCollum-Pratt Inst. Johns Hopkins U., Balt., 1986-88; postdoctoral assoc. divsn. marine and atmospheric chemistry U. Miami, Fla., 1988-89; asst. prof. dept. natural scis. Miami-Dade C.C., 1989-92, assoc. prof., 1992—. Editor: Physical Geography, 5th edit., 1993; contbr. articles to profl. jours. Mem. AAAS, Nat. Geog. Soc., Am. Mus. Nat. History (assoc.), Geol. Soc. Am. Avocations: reading, anthropology, history, fiction, music. Home: P O Box 902020 Homestead FL 33090 Office: Miami-Dade CC Dept Natural Scis 500 College Ter Homestead FL 33030-6009

REVZEN, JOEL, conductor. BS, MS, The Juilliard Sch. Music; studies with Jorge Mester, Jean Martinon,Margaret Hills, Abraham Kaplan. Music dir., condr. Prince William Symphony Orch., Lake Ridge, Va.; mem. Fargo-Moorhead Symphony, Fargo, N.D., Berkshire Opera Co.; former dean St. Louis Conservatory Music. Recipient Grammy award for recording with Soprano Arleen Anger, 1993; named guest conductor of Kirov Opera, St. Petersburg, Russia, 1994, 95. Office: Fargo Moorhead Symphony 810 4th Ave S Moorhead MN 56560-2844*

REWCASTLE, NEILL BARRY, neuropathology educator; b. Sunderland, Eng., Dec. 12, 1931; arrived in Can., 1955; s. William Alexander and Eva (Coapes) R.; m. Eleanor Elizabeth Barton Boyd, Sept. 27, 1958; 4 children. MB, ChB in Medicine cum laude, U. St. Andrews, Scotland, 1955; M.A., U. Toronto, 1962, FRCPC in gen. pathology, 1962, FRCPC in neuropathology, 1968. Rotating intern U. Vancouver, 1955-56; resident in pathology Shaughnessy Hosp., Vancouver, 1956-57, U. Toronto, Ont., Can., 1957-60; fellow Med. Rsch. Coun. Can., 1960-64; demonstrator dept. pathology U. Toronto, Ont., Can., 1964-65, lectr., acting head neuropathology, 1965-69, assoc. prof., 1969-70, prof. div. neuropathology, 1970-81, head div. neuropathology, 1969-81; prof., head dept. pathology U. Calgary, Alta., Can., 1981-91, prof., 1981—; dir. dept. histopathology Foothills Hosp., Calgary, 1981-91, pathologist, 1981—, cons. neuropathology, 1981—; spl. acad. adv. to dean faculty medicine U. Calgary. Recipient Queen Elizabeth Silver Jubilee medal, 1977. Fellow: Royal Coll. Physicians (cert.); mem. Can. Assn. Neuropathologists (sec. 1965-69, pres. 1976-79). Office: Foothills Hosp Dept Histopathology, 1403 29th St NW, Calgary, AB Canada T2N 2T9

REX, CHRISTOPHER DAVIS, classical musician; b. Orlando, Fla., Feb. 1, 1951; s. Charles Gordon Rex and Betty Helen (MacCauslin) Soubricas; m. Martha Anne Wilkins, Nov. 30, 1985; 1 child, Caroline Bethea. MusB, Curtis Inst. of Music, Phila., 1972; postgrad., The Juilliard Sch., 1972-73. Cellist Lyric Opera and Grand Opera, Phila., 1970-75, Phila. Orchestra, 1972-79, Georgian Chamber Players, Atlanta, 1984—; cello tchr. Gettsburg (Pa.) Coll., 1972-73, New Sch. of Music, Phila., 1969-74, Ga. State U., 1980-83; cellist, tchr. Eastern Music Festival, Greensboro, N.C., 1969-74; prin. cello Atlanta Symphony Orchestra, 1979—; concert soloist Hillyer Internat. Inc., N.Y.C., 1984—; bd. dirs. Ga. Cello Soc., Inc., Atlanta, Georgian Chamber Players, Atlanta; acting prin. during Europe Tour Cello of N.Y. Philharm., 1988; premiered Double Concerto for Violin, Cello, and Orch. N.Y. Philharm., 1994. Editor: (mus. transcription) Pictures at an Exhibition (Moussorgsky), 1987. Recipient First prize Young Artist Competition Am. Fedn. of Music Clubs, 1979. Mem. Phila. Musical Soc., Atlanta Fedn. of Music. Presbyterian. Avocations: art, watercolor painting. Home: 1237 Woods Cir NE Atlanta GA 30324-2725 Office: Atlanta Symphony Orch Woodruff Arts Ctr Atlanta GA 30309

REX, DAVID LAWRENCE, project manager; b. Elizabeth, N.J., Oct. 26, 1935; s. Harland Earl and Kathryn Elizabeth (Murphy) R.; m. Ann Ivy Dipple, Sept. 26, 1964 (div. Dec. 1995); children: Harland Edward, Bradley David. BS in Mech. Engring., U. Wis., Madison, 1958. Registered profl. engr., Tex. Project engr. Bechtel Corp., San Francisco, 1961-67; sr. project engr. Arabian Am. Oil Co., Dhahran, Saudi Arabia, 1967-83; project mgr. Creole Prodn. Svcs. Inc., Houston, 1983-85, Frederic R. Harris, Suez, Egypt, 1986-88; constrn. mgr. Morton Thiokol Inc., Karnack, Tex., 1988; project mgr. Bechtel Corp., Houston, 1988-92, Morrison Knudsen, Cleve., 1992-94; sales engr. McCracken & Assocs., Bristol, Tenn., 1994-95; sales rep. Touch Controls, Inc., Oceanside, Calif., 1996—. Life mem. Rep. Nat. Com. Capt. USAFR, 1958-61. Mem. VFW, U.S. Cycling Fedn., Nat. W Club, Kingsport Bicycle Assn., Res. Officers Assn., Am. Legion, U. Wis. Alumni (life), USCG Alumni Assn., Airport Christian Ch., Disciples of Christ, U. Wis. Alumni Assn. (life), Beta Theta Pi. Home: 777 Lebanon Rd Kingsport TN 37663

REX, LONNIE ROYCE, religious organization administrator; b. Caddo, Okla., May 11, 1928; s. Robert Lavern and Lennie Cordy (Gilcrease) R.; m. Betty Louise Sorrells, Apr. 8, 1949; children: Royce DeWayne, Patricia Louise, Debra Kaye. MusB, Oklahoma City U., 1950; DD (hon.), Am. Bible Inst., 1970. Advt. mgr. Oral Roberts Evang. Assn., Tulsa, 1955-57; bus. mgr. T.L. Osborn Found., Tulsa, 1957-69; gen. mgr. Christian Crusade, Tulsa, 1969-80; sec.-treas. David Livingstone Missionary Found., Tulsa, 1970-80, pres., 1980—; dep. dir. gen. Internat. Biog. Assn.; bd. dirs. Intra-Ch. Pension Fund, Bethany, Okla.; speaker internat. confs. Eng., Hungary, Korea, Singapore, Spain, N.Y.C. Author: Never a Child, 1989. Mem. Internat. PHC Loan Fund; bd. dirs. Armand Hammer United World Coll. of Am. West, 1993—. Recipient Merit award Korea, 1975, Moran medal Republic of Korea, Humanitarian award Senator Hugh Scott, 1983, Svc. to Mankind award Internat. Biog. Congress, Spain, 1987, Internat. Lions Club award, UN award; named Outstanding Humanitarian of Yr., Am. Biog. Inst., 1987, Man of Yr., 1990, 1993; knighted in Moscow, 1993. Mem. Knights of Malta (Sword of Svc. 1996), Phi Beta Kappa. Home: 6919 S Columbia Ave Tulsa OK 74136-4328 Office: David Livingstone Missionary Found 6555 S Lewis Ave Tulsa OK 74136-1010 *In my work among the starving in Ethiopia, I walked into a tent of over 100 mothers, lying on mats, who had given birth during the last three days. It was silent! Morbid silence! That haunting silence lives with me since that moment. I asked why? I was informed the babies did not have the strength to cry. I have given my life to "cry out" for those in need that did not have the strength to "cry".*

REXROTH, NANCY LOUISE, photographer; b. Washington, June 27, 1946; d. John Augustus and Florence Bertha (Young) R. B.F.A., Am. U., 1969; M.F.A. in Photography, Ohio U., Athens, 1971. Asst. prof. photography Antioch Coll., Yellow Springs, Ohio, 1977-79, Wright State U., Dayton, Ohio, 1979-82; dealer Light Gallery, 1995—. Author: Iowa, 1976, The Platinotype, 1977, 1976. Nat. Endowment Arts grantee, 1973; Ohio Arts Council, 1981. Mem. Am. Massage Therapy Assn. Democrat. Home and Office: 2631 Cleinview Ave Cincinnati OH 45206-1810

REY, NICHOLAS ANDREW, ambassador; b. Warsaw, Poland, Jan. 23, 1938; m. Louisa Machado; 3 children. BA, Princeton U.; MA, Johns Hopkins U. From economist to dir. exec. secretariat, staff asst. to sec. Dept. Treasury, 1963-66; v.p. Drexel, Harriman, Ripley, Inc., 1968-70; staff mem. Pres.'s Commn. Internat. Trade and Investment Policy, 1970-71; mng. dir. Merrill Lynch Capital Markets, 1971-87, Bear, Stearns & Co., Inc., 1987-92; vice chair Polish-Am. Fund, 1990-92; with Productivity Consulting Firm, 1992-93; U.S. amb. to Poland, 1993—; Bd. dirs. Resource Found.; mem. Coun. Fgn. Rels., 1972—, N.Y. Stock Exchange; chmn. adv. com. Internat. Capital Markets; mem. internat. com. Security Industry Assn., 1987-92; participant sem. on fin. markets Soviet-N.Y. Stock Exchange, Moscow, 1990; mem. econ. devel. com., transitional corp. and Third World devel. subcom., 1980; mem. internat. Montary Fund study on access to capital markets Internat. Bank for Reconstrn. and Devel., 1978-79; mem. dept. treasury Clinton-Gore Transition Team; mem. fgn. portfolio investment adv. com. Dept. Treasury, 1979-80. Mem. Human Rights Commn., Larchmont, N.Y., 1984-92. With USAR, 1962-68. Office: Am Embassy Warsaw Unit 1340 APO AE 09213-1340*

REYDMAN, MELVIN MAXWELL, thoracic surgeon; b. Milw., Nov. 30, 1920; s. Saul and Rose Rebecca (Grossman) R.; m. Gladys Berger; children: Sally, Laurie. BA, U. Wis., 1941, MD, 1944. Diplomate Am. Bd. Surgery, am. Bd. Thoracic Surgery. Resident tng. surgeon Mt. Sinai Med. Ctr., Cleve., 1945-50; resident tng. thoracic surgery Met. Gen. Hosp., Cleve., 1950-52, traveling fellowship, 1952-53; fellow in cardiac surgery Univ. Hosp./Mt. Sinai Med. Ctr., Cleve., 1955-56; instr. surgery Case Western Res. Sch. Medicine, Cleve., 1953, sr. instr. surgery, 1954-60, asst. clin. prof., 1960—; pro tem chief dept. surgery Mt. Sinai Med. Ctr., 1980-81; surgeon-in-charge outpatient dept. surgery, 1993—; organized pulmonary function lab. USMC, 1950, organized non-invasive vascular lab., 1980. Achievements include patent for instruments for closed aortic valve surgery, movie-open heart surgery, mitral valve replacement. Mem. Shaker Heights Indoor Theatre, Cleve. Recipient Disting. Svc. award 50 Yrs. Svc. Ohio State Med. Assn., 1994. Mem. Cleve. Surg. Soc., Cleve. Vascular Soc. Democrat. Jewish. Home: 2950 Weybridge Rd Cleveland OH 44120-1874 Office: Mount Sinai Med Ctr Dept Surgery One Mount Sinai Dr Cleveland OH 44120

REYES, EDWARD, pharmacology educator; b. Albuquerque, May 5, 1944; s. Salvador and Faustina (Gabaldon) R.; m. Shirley Ann Trott, Aug. 15, 1970; children: David Joshua, Elizabeth Ann, Steven Mark. BS in Pharmacy, U. N.Mex., 1968; MS in Pharmacology, U. Colo., 1970, PhD in Pharmacology, 1974. Asst. prof. pharmacy U. Wyo. Sch. of Pharmacy, Laramie, 1974-75; asst. prof. pharmacology Dept. Pharmacology, U. N.Mex., Albuquerque, 1976-85, assoc. prof. pharmacology, 1985—; dir. minority biomed. rsch. support program U. N.Mex. Sch. of Medicine, Albuquerque, 1994—; referee Pharmacology Biochemistry Behavior, San Antonio, 1986—; adv. com. mem. NIMH Minority Neuro Sci. Fellowship, Washington, 1991—. Author: (with others) Alcohol and Drug Abuse Review, 1991; contbr. articles to profl. jours. Scoutmaster Boy Scouts Am., Albuquerque, 1986-94, dist. camping com. chair, 1994—, Silver Beaver, 1996; vis. scientist N.Mex. Acad. Sci., Las Vegas, 1988—; youth preacher Rio Grande Bapt. Ch., Albuquerque, 1980—. Grantee Nat. Inst. of Alcohol Abuse and Alcoholism, NSF. Mem. Rsch. Soc. on Alcoholism, Western Pharmacology Soc., Soc. for Neurosci. (chair minority edn. tng. and profl. adv. 1987-94), Soc. for Advancement of Chicanos and Native Ams. in Sci. Achievements include rsch. that the in utero adminstration of alcohol produces an increase in liver and brain Y-glutamyl transpeptidase activity; isolated GTP from brain of rats, in utero adminstration of alcohol lowers GSH in liver and brain. Office: Univ NMex Sch Medicine 915 Camino de Salud NE Albuquerque NM 87131

REYES, JOSE ANTONIO, SR., minister; b. Canovanas, P.R., May 24, 1940; s. Dionisio Reyes and Antonia (Rodriguez) R.; m. Olfa R. Martinez, May 30, 1964; 1 child, Jose A. BA in Edn., U. P.R., 1962; MA, Sch. Theology, Cleveland, Tenn., 1984; D Ministry, Logos Sch., 1985. Ordained to ministry Ch. of God of Prophecy, 1969. Youth dir. Ch. of God of Prophecy, Rio Piedras, P.R., 1956-58, pastor, 1963-68; mission rep. for Latin Am. Ch. of God of Prophecy, Cleveland, Tenn., 1969-75, internat. radio speaker, 1969—, internat. asst. gen. overseer, 1981—; pres. Hispanic Nat. Religious Broadcasting, Parsippany, 1985-88; v.p. Nat. Orgn. Advancement of Hispanic, 1983-86; com. mem. Hispanic Task Force of Am. Bible Soc., 1985-87; mem. Hispanic Commn., Nat. Assn. Evangelicals, Carol Stream, Ill., 1988—; exec. com. Nat. Religious Broadcasters, 1990-93, bd. dirs., 1990—; founding mem. Alliance Nat. Evang. Ministries, 1993—; pres. ref. com. Latin Am. Christian Comm., 1992—; mem. exec. com. Washington for Jesus, 199—; founding mem. Israel Christian adv. coun., 1996. Author: The Hispanics in USA - A Challenge, An Opportunity for the Church, 1984; author 10 Bible Study Guides on books of the Bible, 1985-90. Recipient Excellence in Hispanic Program Producer award Nat. Religious Broadcasters, 1988, Excellence in Ministry award Internat. Ministry Com., 1990. Mem. Spanish Voice of Salvation Sponsorship Club (pres.). Republican. Home: 218 Bartlett Cir NE Cleveland TN 37312-4779 *Equalling our Lord is an impossible task, but imitating Him is our supreme duty.*

REYES, LILLIAN JENNY, lawyer; b. Covington, Ky., June 23, 1955; d. Luis and Lillian Ann (Barroso) R.; m. Robert Timothy Joyce, May 16, 1986. BA magnum cum laude, U. Miami, Fla., 1977; JD with honors, U. Fla., 1980. Bar: Fla. 1980, U.S. Dist. Ct. (mid. dist.) Fla. 1981, U.S. Ct. Appeals (11th cir.) 1981. Assoc. Carlton, Fields, Ward, Emmanual, Smith & Cutler, Tampa, Fla., 1980-87; ptnr. Joyce & Reyes, Tampa, 1987—. Bd. dirs. Suncoast counsel Girl Scouts Am., 1981-83; bd. dirs., past chmn. aging rsch. unit, chmn. ombudsman counsel project, community rsch. devel. bd., pub. affairs com., legis. breakfast com. Jr. League Tampa. Recipient George W. Milan award U. Fla. Law Rev.; named Ms. Clearwater, Fla., Miss Am. Pageant, 1973, princess Orange Bowl Com., 1977. Mem. Fla. Bar Assn., Hillsborough County Bar Assn. (probate and guardianship rules com. 1981-87, asst. chmn. law week 1984-85, bd. dirs. young lawyers sect. 1985-87, law week chmn. 1987-88, bd. dirs. 1987—), Assn. Trial Lawyers Am., Fla. Trial Lawyers Assn., Bay Area Legal Svcs. Vol. Lawyers Program, U. Fla. Law Rev. Alumni Assn. Democrat. Roman Catholic. Avocations: acting, travel. Office: Joyce & Reyes 101 E Kennedy Blvd Ste 3875 Tampa FL 33602-5152

REYES, ROSE MARIE, nursing educator; b. San Antonio, Sept. 27, 1940; d. Rudolfo Davila and Maria de la Luz (Acosta) Lagunas; m. Maximilian Ortegon Reyes, Nov. 23, 1961; children: Cheryl Yvette, Karen Renee Reyes Vieira, Max Eric. Student, San Antonio C.C., 1958-59, AA, 1980; diploma, Bapt. Meml. Hosp. Sch. Nursing, San Antonio, 1961; grad. in Instrn. Health Occupations, Tex. A&M U., 1982; BS in Health Professions, S.W. Tex. State U., 1987, postgrad. RN, cert. instr. vocat. nursing, Tex.; cert. neonatal care. Charge nurse dept. pediatrics Bexar County Hosp., San Antonio, 1961-62; charge nurse depts. pediatrics and med.-surg. Bapt. Meml. Hosp., San Antonio, 1962-65; clin. nurse specialist dept. pediatrics Brooke Army Med. Ctr., San Antonio, 1965-66; charge nurse newborn nursery S.W. Tex. Meth. Hosp., San Antonio, 1967-70, from charge nurse to head nurse and relief supr. newborn nursery and neonatal ICU, 1970-80; instr. vocat. nursing San Antonio Sch. Dist., 1980-88, migrant health nurse, 1988-90; instr. vocat. nursing, program team leader, chair curriculum com. Bapt. Meml. Hosp. Sch. Vocat. Nursing, San Antonio, 1990—; tchr. nurse aide course, unit sec. course; edn. coun. chair Bapt. Meml. Hosp. Sch., 1996, mem. nursing audit com., assoc. mem. curriculum com. Sch. Profl. Nursing. Mem. adoption com. Luth. Social Svcs., San Antonio, 1993-96; active King of Kings Luth. Ch. Recipient Nurses Assn. Ob-Gyn. award. Mem. Tex. Assn. Vocat. Nursing Educators (membership com. 1990-95, mem. panel to rev. Nclex.PN), Luth. Women's Missionary League (treas.). Avocations: reading, travel, history, music. Office: Bapt Meml Hosp Sch Vocat Nursing 730 N Main Ave Ste 212 San Antonio TX 78205-1115

REYES, SILVESTRE, congressman; m. Carolina Gaytan; children: Monica, Rebecca, Silvestre Jr. AA, El Paso C. C.; student, U. Tex. Mem. 105th Congress from 16th Tex. Dist., 1996—; asst. regional commr. U.S. Immigration and Naturalization Svc., chief, 1984-95.

REYNA, CLAUDIO, soccer player; b. Springfield, N.J., July 20, 1973. Student, U. Va. Midfielder Bayer Leverkusen (German Bundesliga), 1994—, U.S. Nat. Soccer Team, Chgo.; mem. 1994 World Cup Team. Named Freshman of Yr., Soccer Am., 1991, Player of Yr., 1992, 93, 3-time first-team All-Am., Nat. Soccer Coaches Assn. of Am.; recipient Player of Yr. award Mo. Athletic Club, 1992, 93. Office: US Soccer Fedn US Soccer House 1801 S Prairie Ave Chicago IL 60616-1319*

REYNIK, ROBERT J., materials scientist, research and education administrator; b. Bayonne, N.J., Dec. 25, 1932; s. Mary Reynik; m. Georgiana M. Walker, Apr. 12, 1959; children: Michael, Christopher, Jonathan, Katherine, Steven, Kevin. BS in Math. and Physics, U. Detroit, 1956; MSEE, U. Cin., 1960, PhD in Phys. Chemistry, 1963. Rsch. assoc. Sch. Metall. Engring. U. Pa., Phila., 1963-64, asst. prof., 1964-67; assoc. prof. Drexel U., Phila., 1967-70; assoc. dir. engring. materials program NSF, Washington, 1970-71, dir. engring. materials program, 1971-74, dir. metallurgy program, 1974-82, head metallurgy, polymers, ceramics and electronics material, 1983-90, head office spl. programs in materials, 1990-94; sr. staff scientist divsn. materials rsch. NSF, Arlington, Va., 1994-96; exec. sec. and cognizant program dir. US-USSR Internat. Agreement in Sci. and Tech., Washington, 1974-79; NSF liaison rep. Nat. Materials Adv. Bd., Washington, 1985-94; sr. scientist Office of Asst. Dir., Math. and Phys. Scis. Directorate, 1997—; dir. electrometallurgy and materials, corrosion, program US-USSR internat. agreement sci. and tech., 1974-80; mem. First U.S. Metall. Del. People's Republic China, 1978; vis. prof. materials sci. and engring. U. Pa., 1982-83; tech. coord. Sci. & Tech. Ctrs. in Material Sci. & Engring., 1990-94; co-chair Fed. Coord. Coun. for Sci., Engring. and Tech. joint com. edn. and tng. Office of Sci. and Tech. Policy, 1992-93; co-chair task group edn. and tng. Aeronautics Materials and mfg. Techs. Working Groups Nat. Sci. and Tech. coun., Office of Vice Pres. of U.S., 1994; tech. mgr. rsch. grants mfg. devel. and mfg. Tech. Reinvestment Project, Fed. Govt., 1994-96. Fellow Am. Soc. Materials Internat. (fellow 1993, mem.-at-large materials sci. coun. 1990—, mem. govt. and pub. affairs com. 1996—, mem. golf medal selection com.); mem. AAAS, AIME (chairperson govt. pub. affairs com. 1994-96), Am. Chem. Soc., Am.

Phys. Soc., Am. Assn. Engring. Socs. (mem. honors and awards com.), The Metals, Minerals and Materials Soc. (mem. and chmn. various coms.), Materials Rsch. Soc., Sr. Exec. Assn., Sigma Xi (past chpt. pres., exec. com.), Tau Beta Pi. Office: Nat Sci Found Office Sci Tech Infrastrctr 4201 Wilson Blvd Rm 1270 Arlington VA 22203-1859

REYNOLDS, ALAN ANTHONY, economist, speaker, consultant; b. Abilene, Tex., Apr. 11, 1942; s. Alan DeForrest and Rosine (McDougall) R.; m. Karen Kane, Feb. 27, 1965; children: John Alan, Melissa Maurine. BA, UCLA, 1965; postgrad., Sacramento State Coll., 1967-71. Dept. mgr. J.C. Penny Co., Sacramento, 1965-71; assoc. editor Nat. Review, N.Y.C., 1972-75; sr. economist Argus Rsch. Corp., N.Y.C., 1976; v.p., economist First Nat. Bank, Chgo., 1977-80; v.p., chief economist Polyconomics Inc., Morristown, N.J., 1981-89; dir. econ. rsch. Hudson Inst., Indpls., 1990—; sr. v.p. H.C. Wainright & Co. Econs., Boston; cons. Leading Authorities, Washington; rsch. dir. Kemp Tax Reform Commn., 1995. Contbr. Wall St. Jour., Washington Times, Forbes, Nat. Rev., Internat. Economy. Mem. Mont Pelerin Soc., Nat. Tax Assn. (mem. fed. tax com.). Office: Hudson Inst 1015 18th St NW Ste 300 Washington DC 20036-5215

REYNOLDS, ALBERT BARNETT, nuclear engineer, educator; b. Lebanon, Tenn., Feb. 1, 1931; s. George Lazenby and Marion (Barnett) R.; m. Helen Buck, Sept. 6, 1954; children—Albert Jr., Charlotte, Marion. Student, U. of South, 1948-51; S.B. in Physics, MIT, 1953, S.M. in Nuclear Engring., 1955, Sc.D. in Chem. Engring., 1959. Physicist-mgr. Gen. Electric Co., San Jose, Calif., 1959-68; prof. nuclear engring. U. Va., Charlottesville, 1968-96, chmn. dept. nuclear engring. and engring. physics, 1991-92, prof. emeritus, 1996—; cons. NRC, Washington, 1970-84, U.S. Dept. Energy, 1987-89; fields of rsch. include liquid metal reactor safety, electric cable aging, boron neutron capture therapy, radiation detection for nuclear test ban treaty. Author: Bluebells and Nuclear Energy, 1996; co-author: Fast Breeder Reactors, 1981; contbr. numerous articles to profl. jours. Fellow Am. Nuclear Soc. (exec. com. div. nuclear reactor safety 1980-83, chair Va. sect. 1986-87); mem. ASME, IEEE, Am. Soc. Engring. Edn., Sigma Xi, Tau Beta Pi. Home: 1502 Holly Rd Charlottesville VA 22901-3132 Office: U Va Dept Mech Aerospace & Nuclear Engring Charlottesville VA 22903

REYNOLDS, BENEDICT MICHAEL, surgeon; b. N.Y.C., Sept. 12, 1925; s. Benedict and Delia (Coan) R.; m. Alice Marie Hodnett, May 3, 1952; children: Benedict, John, Ann Marie, Mary Alice, Daniel. Student, Columbia U., 1942-43, U. Rochester, 1943-44; MD, NYU, 1948. Diplomate: Am. Bd. Surgery, Pan Am. Med. Assn. Intern Bellevue Med. Center, N.Y.C., 1948-49; surg. resident Bellevue Med. Center, 1951-55; asst. in surgery N.Y. U., N.Y.C., 1953-55; instr. surgery Albert Einstein Coll. Medicine, Bronx, N.Y., 1955-56; asst. prof. surgery Albert Einstein Coll. Medicine, 1956-58, clin. asst. prof., 1958-71, vis. prof. surgery, 1977; prof. surgery N.Y. Med. Coll., N.Y.C., 1971—; practice medicine specializing in surgery Bronx, 1955—; dir. surgery Misericordia Hosp. Med. Center, Bronx, 1962-83, Fordham Hosp., 1964-76; chmn. dept. surgery Lincoln Hosp., Bronx, 1976-82; attending surgeon Met. Hosp., N.Y.C., 1972—; cons. Community Gen. Hosp. of Sullivan County, 1972—. Contbr. articles in field to med. jours. Served with USN, 1943-45, 49-51. Fellow N.Y. Acad. Medicine, A.C.S.; mem. AMA, N.Y. State Med. Soc., N.Y. Acad. Sci., Soc. Surgery Alimentary Tract, N.Y. and Bklyn. Regional Chpt. on Trauma, Internat. Soc. Lymphology, N.Y. Surg. Soc., Am. Gastroent. Assn. Roman Catholic. Home: 55 Roundtop Rd Yonkers NY 10710 Office: 1578 Williamsbridge Rd Bronx NY 10461-6265

REYNOLDS, BILL See ARCHER, WILLIAM REYNOLDS, JR.

REYNOLDS, BILLIE ILES, financial representative and counselor, former association executive; b. Oakland, Calif., Mar. 26, 1929; d. Walter F. and Frances Olive (Blakesley) Iles; m. William V. Reynolds, June 23, 1950; children: Gilbert, Wendy Lee Bryant, Cynthia Lea Waple, Christy Dirren. Registered fin. rep.; registered fin. counselor; registered pension and retirement specialist. Ptnr. Reynolds Advt. Agy., 1963-70; asst. to exec. dir. Nat. Sch. Transp. Assn., Springfield, Va., 1964-76; exec. dir. Nat. Sch. Transp. Assn., 1976-83, Ariz. Landscape Contractors Assn., 1984-86; Registered life and health ins. agt. Freelance writer scripts for radio, TV, newspapers, nat. mags., 1953-70; author: Planning is the Key: Basics of Financial Understanding for Beginners, 1984. Methodist. *You can accomplish anything, if you don't care who gets the credit. Freedom must also be balanced with responsibility...and truth.*

REYNOLDS, BURT, actor, director; b. Waycross, Ga., Feb. 11, 1936; s. Burt R.; m. Judy Carne (div. 1965); m. Loni Anderson, Apr. 29, 1988 (div. 1994). Ed., Fla. State U., Palm Beach Jr. Coll. Owner ranch, Jupiter, Fla. Actor numerous stage prodns. including The Rainmaker; movie appearances include: Angel Baby, 1961, Armored Command, 1961, Operation CIA, 1965, Navajo Joe, 1967, Impasse, 1969, 100 Rifles, 1969, Sam Whiskey, 1969, Skullduggery, 1970, Shark, 1970, Deliverance, 1972, Fuzz, 1972, Everything You've Always Wanted to Know about Sex But Were Afraid to Ask, 1972, Shamus, 1973, The Man Who Loved Cat Dancing, 1973, White Lightning, 1973, The Longest Yard, 1974, At Long Last Love, 1975, W.W. and the Dixie Dance Kings, 1975, Hustle, 1975, Lucky Lady, 1975, Silent Movie, 1976, Nickelodeon, 1976, Smokey and the Bandit, 1977, Semi-Tough, 1977, Hooper, 1978, Starting Over, 1979, Rough Cut, 1980, Smokey and the Bandit II, 1980, Cannonball Run, 1981, Paternity, 1981, The Best Little Whorehouse in Texas, 1982, Best Friends, 1982, Stroker Ace, 1983, The Man Who Loved Women, 1983, City Heat, 1984, Cannonball Run II, 1984, Stick, 1985, Uphill All The Way, 1986, Rent A Cop, 1987, Heat, 1987, Malone, 1987, Switching Channels, 1988, Physical Evidence, 1989, Breaking In, 1989, Modern Love, 1990, Cop and a Half, 1993, also voice in All Dogs Go To Heaven, 1989, The Maddening, 1996, Striptease, 1996, Ravin, 1996, Mad Dog Time, 1996, Frankenstein and Me, 1996, Citizen Ruth, 1996, Meet Wally Sparks, 1997, Crazy Six, 1997, Boogie Nights, 1997; dir., actor: Gator, 1976, The End, 1978, Sharkey's Machine, 1981; TV appearances include: Branded, 1964; regular appearances on Gunsmoke, 1962-65; star series Hawk, 1966, Dan August, 1970-71, B.L. Stryker, 1989, ABC Saturday Mystery Movie, 1988, Evening Shade, 1990-94, (TV movie) The Cherokee Kid, 1996. Recipient Emmy award as Outstanding Lead Actor in a Comedy Series ("Evening Shade") Nat. Acad. TV Arts and Scis., 1991. Mem. Dirs. Guild Am. Office: Sutton & Assocs 145 S Fairfax Ave Ste 310 Los Angeles CA 90036*

REYNOLDS, CALVIN, management consultant, business educator; b. N.Y.C., Oct. 2, 1928; s. Charles Edward and Edna (Klockgeter) R.; m. E. Juana Jaynes, Aug. 22, 1955 (div. 1984); m. Mary Virginia Gregg, May 4, 1985; children: Dwight, Neal J. BS in Bus., Columbia U., 1952, MS in Bus., 1959. Dir. ops. Europe Uniroyal Internat., Geneva, 1956-67; v.p. Nat. Fgn. Trade Coun., N.Y.C., 1967-74; sr. v.p. Orgn. Resources Counselors, N.Y.C., 1975-92; sr. counselor Orgn. Resources Counselors, Ossining, N.Y., 1993—; pres. Calvin Reynolds and Assocs., Inc., Ossining, N.Y., 1993—; dir. Yokogawa-ORC, Tokyo, Am. Compensation Assn. Contbr. articles to profl. jours. Wharton Sch. U. Pa. sr. fellow, 1993-94. Mem. Inst. for Internat. Human Resource Mgmt., Acad. Mgmt. Republican. Congregationalist. Avocations: golf, music, reading. Home and Office: Calvin Reynolds & Assocs Inc 52 Underhill Rd Ossining NY 10562-5118

REYNOLDS, CARL CHRISTIANSEN, government official; b. Wellsville, Utah, Sept. 8, 1934; s. Joseph William and Theresa (Christiansen) R.; m. Sharon Zollinger, Feb. 15, 1963; children: Rose Marie, Jeffrey Wayne. BS, Utah State U., 1957. Lab. technician Thiokol Chem. Corp., Brigham City, Utah, 1960-62; investigator FDA, Denver, 1962-66; resident investigator FDA, Albuquerque, 1966-72; supervisory investigator FDA, Dallas, 1972-77; dir. investigations FDA, Orlando, Fla., 1977-89; dist. dir. FDA, Detroit, 1989-95; dir. office field programs FDA, Washington, 1995—. Mem. council exec. bd. Boy Scouts Am., Albuquerque, 1967-72, mem. nat. com. Dallas, 1982-86, dist. com., Orlando and Dallas, 1972-87. Served with U.S. Army, 1957-59. Recipient Award of Merit Boy Scouts Am., 1975, Silver Beaver award, 1986. Mem. Assn. Food and Drug Officials. Republican. Mormons. Avocations: camping, computer programming, electronics.

REYNOLDS, CAROLYN MARY, elementary education educator; b. Bklyn., May 17, 1936; d. Wesley and Christine (Cardieri) Russo; m. Richard Martin Reynolds, Apr. 12, 1958; children: Donna Marie Reynolds Dewey, Richard Edward. BS, Adelphi U., 1968; MA, SUNY, Stony Brook, 1971. Cert. tchr., N.Y. Tchr. Rocky Point (N.Y.) Sch., 1956-57, Little Flower Sch., Wading River, N.Y., 1957-59, Shoreham (N.Y.)-Wading River Sch. Dist., 1969—; mem. sch. consolidation task force Shoreham-Wading River Sch. Dist., 1992-93, mem. supt. search com., 1995, mem. dist. shared decision making team, 1995-96; supervising tchr. St. Joseph Coll., 1991, 95, 96, Dowling Coll., Oakdale, N.Y., 1992, C.W. Post Coll., Southampton, N.Y., SUNY, Stonybrook; coord. constructivist course Briarcliff Sch., Shoreham, N.Y., 1990-93. Editor tchr. union publ. VOX, 1989-90 (award 1990). Leader Girl Scouts U.S., Rocky Point, N.Y., 1956. Noyes Found. fellow; NSF grantee. Mem. ASCD, Nat. Coun. Tchrs. English, N.Y. State United Tchrs., Shoreham-Wading River Tchrs. Assn. (co-pres., sec., negotiator tchrs. contract 1996-97), United Fedn. Tchrs. (10 Yr. pin for leadership), Internat. Reading Assn. (coun. pres. 1980—). Home: 50 Highland Down Shoreham NY 11786-1122

REYNOLDS, CLARK WINTON, economist, educator; b. Chgo., Mar. 13, 1934; m. Nydia O'Connor Viales; children: Rebecca, C. Winton III, Matthew, Camila. AB, Claremont (Calif.) Men's Coll., 1956; student, MIT, 1956-57, 58; student divinity sch., Harvard U., 1957-58; MA, U. Calif., Berkeley, 1961, PhD in Econs., 1962. Asst. prof. Occidental Coll., L.A., 1961-62; from asst. to assoc. prof. dept. edn. and econ. growth Yale U., New Haven, 1962-67; sr. fellow The Brookings Inst., Washington, 1975-76; prof. econs., prin. investigator, founding dir. Ams. program Stanford (Calif.) U., 1967-96, sr. fellow Inst. Internat. Studies, 1996—, prof. emeritus econs., 1996—; vis. prof. Nat. U. Mex., Chapingo, 1966, El Colegio de Mex., Mexico City, 1964, 65, 79; vis. lectr. in econs. Stockholm U. Econs., 1968; vis. rsch. scholar Internat. Inst. for Applied Systems Analysis, Laxenburg, Austria, 1978. Author: The Mexican Economy, 1970; co-editor: Essays on the Chilean Economy, 1965, (with C. Tello) U.s.-Mexican Relations: Economic and Social Aspects, Las Relaciones Mexico Estados Unidos, 1983, Dynamics of North American Trade, 1991, North American Labor Market Interdependence, 1992, Open Regionalism in the Andes, 1996. Dir. Monticello West Found., 1980—. Woodrow Wilson Found. fellow, 1956-57, Rockefeller Found. fellow, 1957-58, Doherty Found. fellow, 1960-61, Inst. Internat. Studies fellow Stanford U., 1990—; grantee Social Sci. Rsch. Coun., Ford Found., Hewlett Found., Rockefeller Found., Mellon Found., MacArthur Found., Tinker Found. Mem. Am. Econ. Assn., Cosmos Club (Washington). Office: Stanford U Inst Internat Studies Encina Hall W Rm 305/306 Stanford CA 94305-6084

REYNOLDS, COLLINS JAMES, III, foundation administrator; b. N.Y.C., Feb. 28, 1937; s. Collins James and Alta Roberta (Carr) R.; m. Harriet Virginia Blackburn (div. 1965); children: Collins James IV, Quentin Scott; m. Carol Ann Miller, June 24, 1967; children: Justin Blake, Carson Jonathan. Student govt. and econs., Harvard U., George Washington U. Data processing supr. missile and space vehicle div. Gen. Electric, Phila., 1961; contract adminstr. Allison div. Gen. Motors, Indpls., 1962-65; country dir. Peace Corps, Mauritania, 1966-67; dir. Peace Corps, Sierra Leone, 1971-74; dir. div. ops. Gen. Learning Corp., Time Inc., Washington, 1968-71; trustee, sec., treas., exec. dir. Center for Research and Edn., Denver, 1974-79; Carter Presdl. appointee, assoc. dir. Internat. Devel. Coop. Agy., AID, 1980; dir. mktg. Am. TV & Communications Corp., Time Inc., Denver, 1980-81; founder, chmn. bd., pres. Omnicom, Inc., Denver, 1981-87; Bush Presdl. appointee, sr. exec. svc., assoc. dir. mgmt. Peace Corps, 1989-92; dir. comms. divsn. Am. Water Works Assn., 1994—; cons., UN Secretariat, Econ. Devel. Adminstrn., OECD, USAID, USDA; project dir. Model Cities Edn. Plan, HUD, Gen. Learning, Balt., Dept. Labor/HEW Remedial Edn. and Job Placement Program, Transcentury Corp., Washington; program mgr. Ft. Lincoln New Town Sch. System, Washington; supervising dir. VISTA, Boston, N.Y.C., Atlanta; dir. adminstrn. Job Corps, Kansas City; bd. dirs. The Groundwater Found. Founder, editor, pub.: The Bridge; patentee in field. Served as aviator USMCR, 1956-60. Home: 1615 Krameria St Denver CO 80220-1552

REYNOLDS, DAVID G(EORGE), physiologist, educator; b. South Chicago Heights, Ill., Nov. 25, 1933; s. Gilbert J. and Louise C. (Roescheisen) R.; m. Carol J. Adams, Nov. 8, 1958 (div. 1981); children: Stephen D., Douglas S.; m. Julia M. Davis, Aug. 26, 1987. BA, Knox Coll., 1955; MS, U. Ill., 1957; PhD, U. Iowa, 1963. Commd. 2d lt. M.C., U.S. Army, 1957, advanced through grades to lt. col., 1971; chief basic scis. Med. Field Sci. Sch., Fort Sam Houston, Tex., 1957-60, 1963-65; chief gastroenterology Walter Reed Army Inst. Research, Washington, 1965-72, dir. surgery, 1972-77; ret., 1977; prof. surgery, dir. surg. research U. Iowa Hosp., Iowa City, 1977-87, U. South Fla., Tampa, 1987-90; prof. surgery, dir. exptl. surgery, dir. divsn. surg. scis. U. Minn., Mpls., 1991—. Co-editor: Advances in Shock Research, 1983; others; contbr. numerous articles, chpts., abstracts to profl. publs. Active youth athletics, Iowa City. Mem. AAAS, Am. Physiol. Soc., Assn. Acad. Surgery, Shock Soc. (pres. 1986-87), Soc. Exptl. Biology and Medicine. Home: 110 Bank St SE Apt 504 Minneapolis MN 55414-3902 Office: U Minn Dept Surgery Minneapolis MN 55455

REYNOLDS, DAVID PARHAM, metals company executive; b. Bristol, Tenn., June 16, 1915; s. Richard S. and Julia L. (Parham) R.; m. Margaret Harrison, Mar. 25, 1944 (dec. 1992); children: Margaret A., Julia P., Dorothy H. Student, Princeton U. With Reynolds Metals Co., Louisville, 1937—, salesman, 1937-41, asst. mgr. aircraft parts div., 1941-44, asst. v.p., 1944-46, v.p., 1946-58, exec. v.p., 1958-69, exec. v.p., gen. mgr., 1969-75, vice chmn., chmn. exec. com., 1975-76, chief exec. officer, 1976-86, chmn. bd., 1986-88, chmn. emeritus, 1988—; former chmn. bd. dirs. Eskimo Pie Corp. Trustee emeritus Lawrenceville (N.J.) Sch., U. Richmond. Mem. AIA (hon.), Primary Aluminum Inst., Aluminum Assn. (past chmn.). Office: Reynolds Metals Co 6601 W Broad St Richmond VA 23230-1701

REYNOLDS, DEBBIE (MARY FRANCES REYNOLDS), actress; b. El Paso, Tex., Apr. 1, 1932; m. Eddie Fisher, Sept. 26, 1955 (div. 1959); children—Carrie, Todd; m. Harry Karl, Nov., 1960 (div. 1973); m. Richard Hamlett (div. May 1996). Active high sch. plays; screen debut Daughter of Rosie O'Grady; motion pictures include: June Bride, 1948, The Daughter of Rosie O'Grady, 1950, Three Little Words, 1950, Two Weeks With Love, 1950, Mr. Imperium, 1951, Singin' in the Rain, 1952, Skirts Ahoy!, 1952, I Love Melvin, 1953, The Affairs of Dobie Gillis, 1953, Give a Girl a Break, 1953, Susan Slept Here, 1954, Athena, 1954, Hit the Deck, 1955, The Tender Trap, 1955, The Catered Affair, 1956, Bundle of Joy, 1956, Tammy and the Bachelor, 1957, This Happy Feeling, 1958, The Mating Game, 1959, Say One for Me, 1959, It Started With a Kiss, 1959, The Gazebo, 1959, The Rat Race, 1960, Pepe, 1960, The Pleasure of His Company, 1961, The Second Time Around, 1961, How the West Was Won, 1962, My Six Loves, 1963, Mary, Mary, 1963, The Unsinkable Molly Brown, 1964, Goodbye Charlie, 1964, The Singing Nun, 1966, Divorce American Style, 1967, How Sweet It Is!, 1968, What's the Matter with Helen?, 1971, Charlotte's Web, (voice only) 1973, That's Entertainment!, 1974, The Bodyguard, 1992, Heaven and Earth, 1993, (with Albert Brooks) Mother, 1996; star TV program The Debbie Reynolds Show, 1969; star Broadway show Irene, 1973-74, Annie Get Your Gun, Los Angeles, San Francisco, 1977, Woman of the Year, 1984, The Unsinkable Molly Brown, 1989-90 (nat. tour); author: If I Knew Then, 1963, Debbie-My Life, 1988; creator exercise video Do It Debbie's Way, 1984. Prin. Debbie Reynolds's Hotel/Casino and Hollywood Motion Picture Mus., Las Vegas, 1993—. Named Miss Burbank, 1948. Office: Debbie Reynolds Studios care Margie Duncan 6514 Lankershim Blvd North Hollywood CA 91606-2409

REYNOLDS, DONALD MARTIN, art historian, foundation administrator, educator; b. Kansas City, Mo., Jan. 11, 1931; s. James Martin and Mary Helen (Hughes) R.; m. Nancy Zlobik, June 5, 1970. Student, Amarillo Coll., 1949-51; BA, Assumption Sem., San Antonio, 1955, Columbia U., 1968; MA, Columbia U., 1970, PhD, 1975. Announcer KGNC Radio/TV, Amarillo, Tex., 1949-51; account exec. Monte Rosenwald & Assocs., Amarillo, Tex., 1957-59; copy writer, account rep., account supr. J. Walter Thompson, N.Y.C., C.Am., 1959-61; mgr. Ctrl. Am., Young & Rubicam Advt., N.Y.C., Panama, 1961-62; advt. mgr., mktg. dir. Colgate-Palmolive Co. Western Hemisphere Divsn., 1962-64; founder, dir. Image, Internat. Mktg. Agy., N.Y.C., 1964-66; mus. educator in charge Dept. Pub. Edn. Met. Mus. of Art, 1977-79; curator of parks Dept. Parks and Recreation, N.Y.C., 1986-88; founder, coord. Ann. Symposium on Pub. Monuments, N.Y.C., 1991—; founder, dir. The Monuments Conservancy, Inc., N.Y.C., 1992—; adj. prof. art history Columbia U., N.Y.C., 1973—; adj. prof. art history Fairfield (Conn.) U., 1981—; adj. asst. prof. art history Hunter Coll., 1972-81; asst. prof. art history Coll. Mt. St. Vincent and Manhattan Coll., 1973-77. Author: The Ideal Sculpture of Hiram Powers, 1977, Manhattan Architecture, 1988, Eng., French edits., The Architecture of New York City: Histories and Views of Important Structures, Sites, and Symbols, 1984, paper, 1988, rev. edit., 1994, Monuments and Masterpieces: Histories and Views of Public Sculpture in New York City, 1988, Nineteenth-Century Art, 1985, also fgn. langs. edits., Nineteenth Century Architecture, 1992, Masters of American Scultpure, the Figurative Tradition from the American Renaissance to the Millennium, 1993; editor, compiler: The Impact of Non-European Civilizations on the Art of the West: Selected Lectures of Rudolf Wittkower, 1989; contbg. author The Macmillan Ency. of Architects, 1982. Trustee Brookgreen Gardens, S.C., Brookgreen Gardens Mus., S.C. With U.S. Army, 1955-61. Mem. Nat. Sculpture Soc., Coll. Art Assn., Authors Guild. Office: PO Box 608 Cooper Sta New York NY 10003

REYNOLDS, EDWARD, book publisher; b. N.Y.C., Apr. 25, 1926; s. Edward and Dorothea Curtis (Jordan) R.; m. Joan Gale, Sept. 13, 1953; children—Edward, Peter Winsor, James Lyman, Joseph Warren. A.B., Harvard U., 1950, M.B.A., 1953. With United Aircraft Can. Ltd., Montreal, 1953-60; v.p. fin. and adminstn. Mitre Corp., Bedford, Mass., 1960-66; sr. v.p. fin. and adminstrn. Houghton Mifflin Co., Boston, 1967-76; dir. fin. New England Med. Ctr. Hosp., Boston, 1978-79; v.p. fin. and adminstrn. John Wiley & Sons, Inc., N.Y.C., 1980-83, sr. v.p. fin. and adminstrn., 1983-86; pres., chief exec. officer Innovative Scis., Inc., Stamford, Conn., 1987-90, treas., 1991—, also bd. dirs. With USNR, 1944-46. Clubs: Union League., Cruising of Am. Office: Innovative Scis Inc 975 Walnut St Cary NC 27511-4216

REYNOLDS, EDWIN WILFRED, JR., retired secondary education educator; b. Englewood, N.J., Mar. 23, 1937; s. Edwin W. and Ellen H. (Hueber) R.; m. Sharon Policastro, Feb. 12, 1983. BA cum laude, Fairleigh Dickinson U, 1961, MAT magna cum laude, 1966; postgrad., NYU, 1964-65, Seton Hall U., 1970-71, Montclair State Coll., 1972-73. Cert. social studies tchr., supr., tchr. psychology, N.J. Supr. installation Western Electric Co., N.Y.C., 1961-65; tchr. social studies Teaneck (N.J.) High Sch., 1965-92, chmn. dept. social studies, 1968-71; supr. social studies Teaneck Secondary Schs., 1971-80, supr. grades K-12, 1980-92, supr. bus. edn. grades 7-12, 1984-92, ret., 1992; pres. bd. dirs. Global Learning, Inc.; sr. state cons. in Holocaust Edn., N.J.; curriculum coord. Ctr. for Holocaust/Genocide Studies, Ramapo Coll.; guest lectr. Kean Coll.; coord. M.A.T. program Fairleigh Dickinson U., 1969-71; mem. planning com. N.E. Regional Social Studies Conf., mem. steering com. Mid-Atlantic Conf.; mem. N.J. Dept. Edn. Social Studies Adv. Com., N.J. Gov.'s Adv. Coun. for Holocaust Edn. in the Pub. Schs.; cons. world history Scott Foresman Pub. Co. Author curriculum devel. and learning guides, 1973-92; co-editor: Holocaust and Genocide: A Search for Conscience. Elder Presbyn. Ch., U.S; v.p., newsletter editor Pike County Hist. Soc. With USN, 1955-57. Recipient Human Rights Award Temple Beth Tikvah, 1985, Brotherhood Award B'nai B'rith No. and Pascack Valleys, 1986, Daniel Roselle Lectr. award Mid. States Coun. for Social Studies, 1988. Mem. ASCD, Nat. Coun. for Social Studies (former bd. dirs.), N.J. Coun. for Social Studies (bd. dirs., past pres.), Greater Bergen County (N.J.) Coun. for Social Studies (bd. dirs., past pres.), Nat. Social Studies Suprs. Assn. (bd. dirs., past pres.), Assn. Ednl. Suprs. (bd. dirs., past pres.), Am. Hist. Assn., Phi Delta Kappa, Phi Omega Epsilon. Home: PO Box 626 Milford PA 18337-0626

REYNOLDS, ERNEST WEST, physician, educator; b. Bristow, Okla., May 11, 1920; s. Ernest West and Florence (Brown) R. B.S., U. Okla., 1942, M.D., 1946, M.S., 1952. Diplomate: Am. Bd. Internal Medicine. Intern Boston City Hosp., 1946-47; resident Grady Meml. Hosp., Atlanta, 1949-50; practice medicine Tulsa, Okla., 1953-54; prof. medicine U Mich., 1965-72; prof. medicine, dir. cardiology U. Wis., 1972—; dir. Kellogg Found. Comprehensive Coronary Care Project, 1967-72; chmn. NIH Cardiovascular Study Sect. A, 1972-73. Mem. editorial bd.: Am. Heart Jour; Contbr. articles to profl. jours. Served to capt. AUS, 1947-49. Mem. Am. Heart Assn. (fellow council clin. cardiology); mem. Central Soc. Clin. Research. Home: 17 Red Maple Trl Madison WI 53717-1515 Office: U Wis 600 Highland Ave Madison WI 53792-0001 *In the academic environment, research oriented toward the solution of human problems is more productive in career advancement than the pursuit of applications of new technology. In the private sector applied research which solves real problems rather than copies or improves existing technology is met with surprising sales success and few failures.*

REYNOLDS, FRANK EVERETT, religious studies educator; b. Hartford, Conn., Nov. 13, 1930; s. Howard Wesley and Caroline Mills Roys R.; m. Mani Bloch, Mar. 28, 1959 (dec. 1993); children: Roy Howard, Andrew Everett, Roger Frank. Student, Princeton U., 1948-51; B.A., Oberlin U., 1952; B.D., Yale Div. Sch., 1955; M.A., U. Chgo., 1963, Ph.D., 1971. Ordained to ministry Am. Baptist Ch., 1955. Program dir. Student Christian Ctr., Bangkok, Thailand, 1956-59; minister to fgn. students U. Chgo. Ecumenical Ministries, 1961-64; instr. U. Chgo., 1967-69, asst. prof. then assoc. prof., 1969-79, prof. history of religions and Buddhist studies, 1979—; program dir. Inst. for the Advanced Study of Religions, 1992—; co-dir. Liberal Arts and Study of Religions Project, 1985-90, NEH Sangitiyavasama Transl. Porject, 1991-93. Author: Guide to Buddhist Religion, 1981, (with others) Two Wheels of Dhamma, 1971, Religions of the World, 3d edit., 1993; editor, co-translator: 3 Worlds According to King Ruang, 1981; co-editor: Anthropology and the Study of Religion, 1984, Cosmology and Ethical Order, 1985, Myth and Philosophy, 1990, Beyond the Classics: Religious Studies and Liberal Education, 1990, Discourse and Practice, 1992, Religion and Practical Reason, 1994, History of Religion Jour., 1977—, Towards a Comparative Philosophy of Religious Series, 1990-95; assoc. editor Jour. Religion, 1976—, Jour. Religious Ethics, 1981—. Chair organizing com. Sawyer Seminar on Religious Law and Constrn. of Identities, 1996-97. Jacob Fox Found. fellow, 1952, Danforth Found. fellow, 1960, 64; sr. rsch. grantee Fulbright Commn., 1973-74, NEH, 1978-79. Mem. Am. Coun. Learned Socs. (com. on history of religions 1985-94), Am. Soc. Study Religion, Am. Acad. Religion (chmn. com. on history of religions 1993-96), Assn. Asian Studies (co-editor monograph series 1978-86, mem. Benda prize com. 1993-96), Internat. History of Religions, Internat. Assn. Buddhist Studies, Law and Soc. Home: 5433 S Blackstone Ave Chicago IL 60615-5406 Office: U Chgo Swift Hall 1025 E 58th St Chicago IL 60637-1509

REYNOLDS, FRANK MILLER, retired government administrator; b. Tulsa, Jan. 8, 1917; s. Frank Miller and Grace (Shields) R.; m. Barbara G. MacWilliams, Dec. 7, 1946; children: Susan G., Ellen M., Frank M. A.B., LL.B., U. Okla., 1939; LL.M., George Washington U., 1942; B.S., Georgetown Sch. Fgn. Service, 1946. Bar: Okla. 1940. Mem. firm Flippo & Reynolds, Tulsa, 1940; elec. engr. Bur. Ships, Dept. of Navy, 1942-43; with Office Gen. Counsel, Dept. of Navy, 1946; chief negotiator, dep. dir. contract div. Office Naval Research, 1947-54; dep. dir., dir. resources div. Office Asst. Sec. Def., 1954-57; asst. sec. Inst. for Defense Analyses, 1957-61; sec., treas. Logistics Management Inst., Washington, 1961-65; v.p. Logistics Management Inst., 1966-76; dir. adminstrv. affairs Uniformed Services U. Health Scis., Bethesda, Md., 1976-78; dir. resource mgmt. Uniformed Services U. Health Scis., 1978-82, exec. sec. bd. regents, 1978-83; dir. patient relations Sibley Meml. Hosp., 1983-84, cons., 1984-87; professorial lectr. mgmt. research George Washington U. Sch. Engring., 1956—; cons. Nat. Exec. Service Corps., United Srs. Health Coop., 1984—. Served with radio div. Naval Research Lab., 1944-46. Mem. Okla. Bar Assn., Congl. Country Club, Delta Upsilon. Home: 9107 River Rd Potomac MD 20854-4627

REYNOLDS, GARY KEMP, librarian; b. Phila., June 2, 1944; s. Thomas Clifford and Lillian Olive (Thompson) R.; m. Regina Romano, May 16, 1970; 1 child, Elizabeth Alexandra Marie. BA in History with honors, Pa. State U., 1973, BA in East Asian Studies magna cum laude, 1973; MA in E.Asian Studies, U. Mich., 1975, MLS, 1976. Reference libr. George Washington U., Washington, 1977-80; info. rsch. specialist congl. rsch. svc. Libr. of Congress, Washington, 1980—. Reviewer manuscripts for profl. jours.; contbr. articles to profl. publs. Sgt. USAF, 1962-66. Mem. Phi Beta Kappa, Phi Kappa Phi, Phi Alpha Theta, Mensa. Republican. Episcopalian. Avocations: painting, Oriental arts and antiques, science fiction. Home: 7472

Covent Wood Ct Annandale VA 22003 Office: Libr of Congress Washington DC 20540

REYNOLDS, GENEVA B., special education educator; b. Saginaw, Mich., Nov. 2, 1953; d. Roger and Alrine (Braddock) Rucker; m. Montie Reynolds, Aug. 1, 1981; children: Monte, Marcus. BS, Chgo. State U., 1992. Cert. educable mental handicap and learning disability, social/emotional disturbed. Adminstrv. specialist USAF, 1973-77, command and control specialist, 1977-81; info. supt. USAFR, Chgo., 1981—; head tchr. South Ctrl. Cmty. Svcs., Chgo., 1986—. SM sgt. USAF, 1973-81, USAFR, 1981—. Mem. Coun. for Exceptional Children, Kappa Delta Pi. Democrat. Baptist. Avocations: reading, computers, going to plays.

REYNOLDS, GEORGE ANTHONY, JR., engineering executive; b. Columbia, S.C., May 5, 1961; s., George Anthony and Flora Mae (La Coste) R.; m. Katherine Alison Albea, Apr. 14, 1984; children: Amanda Kate, William Anthony. BSME, Clemson U., 1983; postgrad., U. Ala., Huntsville, 1985. Design engr. Motorola, Plantation, Fla., 1983-85; sr. engr. Chrysler, Huntsville, Ala., 1985-88; prin. engr. NCR, Liberty, S.C., 1988-91, project leader, 1991-94; mgr. mech. engring. Sensormatic Electronics, Boca Raton, Fla., 1994-96, dir. product engring., 1996—. Mem. editl. quality audit panel Electronic Packaging & Prodn. Mag., N.Y.C., 1992. Advisor Clemson U. Mech. Engring. Endowment Fund; mem. edn. dir. search com., mem. Christian edn. com., Christian Edn. Ctr. 1st Presbyn. Ch., Delray Beach, Fla. Mem. ASME (assoc.), NRA (Legion of Honor), S.E. Pro/Engr. User Group (pres. 1992-93), Nature Conservancy, Nat. Wildlife Fedn., Ducks Unltd., Fla. Sheriff's Assn. (life), Men of Achievement 1996, Fla. Wildlife Fedn., N.Am. Hunting Club, Billfish Found., Tau Beta Pi, Phi Kappa Phi, Alpha Tau Omega (mem. alumni adv. bd. Eta Pi chpt. 1993-94). Republican. Presbyterian. Avocations: genealogy, hunting, fishing. Home: 927 Seagate Dr Delray Beach FL 33483-6617 Office: Sensormatic Electronic Corp 951 Yamato Rd Boca Raton FL 33431-0700

REYNOLDS, GEORGE THOMAS, physics educator, researcher, consultant; b. Trenton, May 27, 1917. B.Sc. in Physics and Math., Rutgers U., 1939; M.A. in Physics, Princeton U., 1942, Ph.D. in Physics, 1943. Research physicist Princeton (N.J.) U., 1943-44, asst. prof., 1946-51, assoc. prof., 1951-59, prof., 1959-78, Class of 1909 prof. physics, 1978-87, emeritus, 1987—, dir. high energy physics program, 1948-70, dir. sci. in human affairs program, 1963-67, dir. Ctr. Environ. Studies, 1970-73, mem. council on environ. studies, 1970-73, 80-87, prin. investigator biophysics program, 1964-87; mem. univ. research bd. Princeton (N.J.), 1980-86; assoc. faculty Princeton Environ. Inst., 1996—; physicist Manhattan Project, 1944-46; mem. NSF Adv. Com. for Planning and Instl. Relations, 1971-74; mem. vis. adv. com. dept. applied sci. Brookhaven Nat. Lab., 1971-74; mem. corp. Marine Biol. Lab., Woods Hole, Mass., 1968—, chmn. radiation com., 1973-77; mem. ad hoc adv. panel for environ. problems Dept. Energy Div. Biomed. and Environ Research; vis. prof. Imperial Coll.-U. London, 1955-56, Open U. (U.K.), 1981-82; cons. in field; mem. adv. panel for radiation physics Nat. Bur. Standards, 1962-64; seminar assoc. Columbia U. Sem. on Tech. and Social Change, 1966-85; mem. study panel on physics edn. Nat. Acad. Scis., 1970-72; cons. NSF div. Policy Research and Analysis, 1985-88. Bd. editors: Rev. Sci. Instruments, 1955-58; contbr. chpts. to books, numerous jour. articles. Chmn. adv. council for research and grad. edn. Rutgers U., New Brunswick, N.J., 1969-72, trustee, 1974-86, 89—. Served to lt. (j.g.) USNR, 1944-46. Recipient cert. appreciation Army-Navy, 1948; Guggenheim fellow U. London, 1955-56; Churchill fellow Cambridge (Eng.) U., 1973-74; vis. sr. research fellow Oxford (Eng.), 1981-82; Royal Soc. guest research fellow, 1985. Fellow AAAS, Am. Phys. Soc.; mem. Biophys. Soc., Am. Geophys. Union, IEEE, Am. Soc. Photobiology, Phi Beta Kappa, Sigma Xi (local pres. 1962-63). Office: Princeton U Dept Physics Joseph Henry Labs Jadwin Hall PO Box 708 Princeton NJ 08544

REYNOLDS, GLENN FRANKLIN, medicinal research scientist; b. Rahway, N.J., July 16, 1944; s. Frank Vanderbilt and Estelle (Ohlott) R.; m. Marianne DelliSanti, Nov. 25, 1967; children William Matthew, David Glenn, Wendy Joy. Student, Rutgers U., 1962-63, Union Coll., 1963-65; BS in Chemistry, Phila. Coll. Pharmacy and Sci., 1967. Rsch. scientist Merck & Co., Rahway, 1967-70, staff chemist, 1970-77, rsch. chemist, 1977-86, sr. rsch. assoc., 1991—; Merck recruiter Fairleigh Dickinson U., 1980, Howard U., 1980, U. N.C., 1981, Rutgers U., 1985. Inventor Proscar; contbr. articles to profl. jours.; patentee in field. Named Inventor of Yr. Intellectual Property Owners, 1993. Mem. Am. Chem. Soc., Masons (Lafayette lodge #27). Presbyterian. Avocations: computer science, biking, skiing, reading. Home: 252 Edgewood Ave Westfield NJ 07090-3918 Office: Merck & Co Inc PO Box 2000 126 E Lincoln Ave 121/267C Rahway NJ 07065

REYNOLDS, GLENN HARLAN, law educator; b. Birmingham, Ala., Aug. 27, 1960; s. Charles Harlan Reynolds and Glenda Lorraine (Teal) Childress. BA, U. Tenn., 1982; JD, Yale U., 1985. Bar: Tenn. 1985, D.C. 1986. Law clk. U.S. Ct. Appeals, Nashville, 1985-86; assoc. Dewey, Ballantine, Bushby, Palmer & Wood, Washington, 1986-89; assoc. prof. law U. Tenn., Knoxville, 1989—. Author: Outer Space: Problems of Law and Policy, 1989, 97, The Appearance of Propriety, 1997. Recipient Outstanding Svc. award Space Cause, Washington, 1990. Mem. AAAS, Nat. Space Soc. (chair legis. com. 1989-93, CEO 1994-95, Space Pioneer award 1991). Office: U Tenn 1505 Cumberland Ave Knoxville TN 37916-3199

REYNOLDS, HAROLD CRAIG, professional baseball player; b. Eugene, Oreg., Nov. 26, 1960. Student, San Diego State U., Canada Coll., Redwood City, Calif., Calif. State U., Long Beach. Infielder Seattle Mariners, 1983-92; with Balt. Orioles, 1993, Calif. Angels, 1994; broadcaster, analyst ESPN, Bristol, Conn., 1996—. Mem. Am. League All-Star Team, 1987-88. Office: care ESPN Baseball Tonight ESPN Plaza Bristol CT 06010*

REYNOLDS, HARRY LINCOLN, physicist; b. Port Chester, N.Y., Mar. 31, 1925; s. Harry Benson and Lydia (Wilde) R.; m. Katherine Haile, 1950; children: Patricia Reynolds Cabral, Margaret Benson Neufeld. B.S., Rensselaer Poly. Inst., 1947; Ph.D., U. Rochester, 1951. Sr. scientist Oak Ridge Nat. Lab., 1951-55; physicist Lawrence Livermore Nat. Lab., 1955-65; asst. program mgr. NASA Manned Spacecraft Center, Houston, 1965; asso. dir. nuclear test, nuclear design and nuclear explosives programs Lawrence Livermore Nat. Lab., Calif., 1965-80, spl. asst. to dir., 1980-81; dep. asso. dir. advanced concepts Los Alamos Nat. Lab., 1981-85; dir. advanced concepts Rockwell Internat. Corp., Seal Beach, Calif., 1985-94; cons. in field. Contbr. articles to profl. jours. Trustee Valley Meml. Hosp., Livermore, 1980-81; mem. Army Sci. Bd., 1982-88. Served with U.S. Navy, 1944-46. AEC fellow, 1947-49. Fellow Am. Phys. Soc. Home: 801 Via Somonte Palos Verdes Peninsula CA 90274-1631

REYNOLDS, HELEN ELIZABETH, management services consultant; b. Minerva, N.Y., Aug. 30, 1925; d. Henry James and Margurite Catherine (Gallagher) McNally; m. Theodore Laurence Reynolds, Feb. 27, 1948; children: Laurence McBride, David Scott, William Herbert. BA, SUNY, Albany, 1967; MA, Union Coll., Schenectady, N.Y., 1971. Grad. Realtors Inst., N.Y. Owner, mgr. Schafer Studio, Schenectady, 1970-73; co-owner, v.p. Reynolds Chalmers Inc., Schenectady, 1971—; pres. HR Mgmt. Cons., Schenectady, 1994—; program coord. Schenectady County, 1980-81; adminstr. Wellspring House of Albany, N.Y., 1981-94; cons., examiner N.Y. State Civil Service, Albany, 1971-81; mem. adv. council SBA, Washington, 1978-80. Mem. planning bd. Town of Niskayuna, N.Y., 1977-81, town councilwoman, 1986-94; co-chair Great N.E. Festival on the Mohawk River, 1989, 90; bd. dir. HAVEN, Schenectady YWCA; mem. Schenectady Indsl. Devel. Agy., N.Y. State Commn. on The Capital Region, 1994—, Acad. of Women of Achievement, Schenectady, 1994, Libr. of Congress, Vis. Nurse Svc. Assn. Coun. Schenectady; dir. Photo Arts Group of Charlotte City. Named Woman Vision, 1986, 87, Today's Woman, 1987, Schenectady YWCA. Mem. Antique and Classic Boat Soc. (bd. dirs. 1974-89, Disting. Svc. award 1979, Founders award 1989), Assn. Adminstrs. Ind. Housing (pres. 1986-88, 92-94), Zonta (pres. 1981-82), Nat. Trust for Historic Preservation, Adirondack Mus., Antique Boat Mus., Schenectady Mus., League of Schenectady Symphony Orch., Union Coll. Alumni Assn., Charlotte Harbor Yacht Club, Charlotte County Art Guild. Avocations: photography, reading, writing, skiing, canoeing. Home: 1365 Van Antwerp Rd Apt J104 Niskayuna NY 12309-4441 Office: 104 Leland St SW Pt Charlotte FL 33952-9131

REYNOLDS, HERBERT HAL, academic administrator; b. Frankston, Tex., Mar. 20, 1930; s. Herbert Joseph and Ava Nell (Taylor) R.; m. Joy Myrla Copeland, June 17, 1950; children: Kevin Hal, Kent Andrew, Rhonda Sheryl. BS, Trinity U., 1952; MS, Baylor U., 1958, PhD, 1961; ScD (hon.), Baylor Coll. Dentistry, Seinan Gakuin U., Japan. Entered USAF, 1948, advanced through grades to col., 1966; service in Japan, Europe; dir. research (Aeromed. Lab.), Alamogordo, N. Mex., 1961-67; comdr. (Air Force Human Resources Lab.), San Antonio, Tex., 1968; ret., 1968; exec. v.p. Baylor U., Waco, Tex., 1969-81, pres., 1981-95, chancellor, 1995—; vis. fellow, scholar Cambridge U., 1994-97. Contbr. articles to profl. jours. Mem. Sigma Xi, Alpha Chi, Omicron Delta Kappa, Mortar Bd., Kappa Kappa Psi, Beta Theta Pi. Office: Baylor U Office of Chancellor Waco TX 76798

REYNOLDS, HERBERT YOUNG, physician, internist; b. Richmond, Va., Aug. 20, 1939; s. George Audney and Pearle Maupin (Young) R.; m. Anne Browning Leavell, July 11, 1964; children: Nancy, George, William Stuart. BA in English, U. Va., 1961, MD, 1965; MA (hon.), Yale U., 1979. Diplomate Am. Bd. Internal Medicine, Am. Bd. Allergy and Immunology. Intern in medicine The N.Y. Hosp., Cornell Med. Ctr., N.Y.C., 1965-66, asst. physician, fellow in medicine, 1966-67; clin. assoc., lab. clin. investigation Nat. Inst. Allergy and Infectious Diseases, NIH, Bethesda, Md., 1967-70, chief clin. assoc. lab. clin. investigation, 1968-69; sr. investigator lab. of clin. investigation Nat. Inst. Allergy and Infectious Diseases, NIH, 1971-76; chief resident, instr. medicine U. Hosp. U. Wash., Seattle, 1970-71; assoc. prof. internal medicine, head pulmonary div. Sch. Medicine Yale U., New Haven, 1976-79, prof., 1979-88; J. Lloyd Huck prof. medicine, chmn. dept. Pa. State U.-Milton S. Hershey Med. Ctr., 1988—; mem. exec. com. Coll. Medicine Pa. State U.-Hershey Med. Ctr., 1988—, mem. exec. bd. U. Hosp., 1988—, mem. fin. bd. acad. enrichment fun, 1988-95, mem. dean's adv. com., 1988-96, mem. diversity task force, 1995—, Univ. Physicians Faculty Practice Plan Exec. Com. 1996—, others; cons. in infectious diseases Nat. Naval Med. Ctr. NIH, Bethesda, 1971-76, mem. clin. rsch. com., 1971-76, chmn., 1974-76, med. bd., 1974-76, pulmonary disease adv. com. divsn. of lung diseases Nat. Heart, Lung and Blood Inst., 1978-82, mem. sci. counselors bd., 1984-88, mem. data and safety monitoring bd. registry of patientss with deficiency of Alpha-1 Antitrypsin, 1989-96. Assoc. editor, mem. editl. bd. Lung, 1978-97, Am. Jour. Medicine, 1979-89, Jour. Clin. Investigation, 1980-86, Am. Rev. Respiratory Disease, 1980-87, Jour. Applied Physiology, 1981-89, Resident Physician, 1981-95; contbr. over 265 articles and revs. to profl. jours. Mem. parent com. Troop 1 Boy Scouts Am., Madison, 1979-82; bd. dirs. Neighborhood Music Sch., Guilford, Conn., 1978-87, Music at Gretna, 1994—; bd. dirs. Harrisburg Symphony, 1996—; active All Saints Episc. Ch., Hershey; mem. pulmonary infections com. Cystic Fibrosis Found., Bethesda, 1980-86; mem. coun. sci. advisors Parker B. Francis Found., Kansas City, Kans., 1983-87; mem. internat. com. World Orgn. for Sarcoidosis and other Granulomatous Disorders, 1987-95; bd. dirs., mem. coun. Am. Lung Assn., 1989-93, bd. govs. 1990-93, various com. positions, 1990—; coach Guilford Soccer League, 1985-88. Surgeon USPHS, 1967-70. John Edward Nobel fellow, 1961-65; named Outstanding Med. Specialist in USA, Town and Country Mag., 1989, The Best Med. Specialists, Town & Country mag., 1995, One of 400 Best Doctors in U.S. Good Housekeeping Mag., 1991, named in The Best Doctors in Am., 1st edit. 1992-93, 2d edit. 1994-95, The Best Doctors in Am., N.E., 1st edit., 1996-97. Fellow ACP (coun. subsplty. socs. 1989—), Am. Coll. Chest Physicians (program com. 1978-84), Infectious Disease Soc. Am., Coll. Physicians Phila.; mem. Am. Thoracic Soc. (sec.-treas. 1987-88, bd. dirs. 1989-93, v.p. 1988-89, pres. 1992-93), Am. Soc. Clin. Investigation, Assn. Am. Physicians, Am. Assn. Immunologists, Am. Fedn. Clin. Rsch., Am. Clin. and Climatological Soc., Interurban Clin. Club (emeritus 1989), Assn. Profs. Medicine, Country Club of Hershey, Farmington Country Club, Raven Soc., Phi Beta Kappa, Alpha Omega Alpha, Omicron Delta Kappa. Republican. Avocations: tennis, violin. Home: 226 E Caracas Ave Hershey PA 17033-1309 Office: Pa State U Milton S Hershey Med Ctr 850 University Dr Hershey PA 17033

REYNOLDS, JACK MASON, manufacturing company executive; b. East Orange, N.J., Jan. 27, 1927; s. Frederick Lynn and Bernice (Mason) R.; m. Rhea Evans, June 14, 1949; children: Jeff, Jennifer Reynolds Brickley, Mark. B.S., U.S. Mcht. Marine Acad., 1948. With Bendix Corp., Southfield, Mich., 1948-83, exec. v.p. automotive group, 1979-80, pres. automotive group, 1980-83; pres. automotive sector, exec. v.p. Allied-Signal Inc., Morristown, N.J., 1983-89; dir. NBD Bancorp Inc. Bd. dirs. Detroit Renaissance, 1983-89, Citizens Rsch. Coun. of Mich., 1983-89, Detroit Econ. Growth Corp., 1983-89, Detroit Symphony Orch., 1983-89. With USNR, 1944-48. Mem. Soc. Automotive Engrs., Renaissance (Detroit) Club. Home: PO Box 744 Cooperstown NY 13326-0744

REYNOLDS, JACK W., retired utility company executive; b. Magazine, Ark., Feb. 28, 1923; s. Robert H. and Effie (Files) R.; m. Alberta Barkett, Nov. 13, 1949; children: John, David, Steven, Thomas, Laurie. B.S. in Phys. Sci., Okla. State U., 1943, B.S. in Indsl. Engring., 1947. With B.F. Goodrich Co., Akron, Ohio, 1947-75, dir. union relations, 1969-70, dir. indsl. rels., 1970-75; v.p. pers. Consumers Power Co., Jackson, Mich., 1975-78, sr. v.p. pers. and pub. affairs, 1978-81, exec. v.p. energy supply, 1981-88; pres. Mich. Gas Storage Co., Jackson, 1981-88, Plateau Resources, Ltd., Jackson, 1988; now ret. Served to 1st lt. C.E. U.S. Army, 1943-46, CBI. Republican. Methodist. Clubs: Jackson Country.

REYNOLDS, JAMES, management consultant; b. Detroit, Mar. 22, 1941; s. Richard James and Esther (Nikander) R.; m. Joanne M.J. B.A. in Econs., NYU, 1965, postgrad., 1965-66. Cons. to pres. Rothrock, Reynolds & Reynolds Inc., N.Y.C., 1966-70; sr. v.p. health, med. div. Booz, Allen & Hamilton, N.Y.C., 1970-80; pres. Reynolds & Co. (mgmt. cons.), San Francisco, N.Y.C., Washington, 1981—; developer 1978, orgn. concepts for multihosp. systems, 1983, managed care contracting strategies, 1988, value chain analysis in the health field, 1994, leading the transition to Integrated Healthcare Sys.; bd. dirs. Booz, Allen & Hamilton, 1977-79; chmn. bd. J.X. Reynolds Fine Arts, Ltd., 1979—; bd. dirs. Health Center Mgmt. Inst.; lectr. Harvard Sch. Pub. Health; faculty mem. Am. Coll. of Healthcare Execs.; bd. dirs. Health Center Mgmt. Inst., Richmond, Va., 1977; mem. health adv. bd. Hunter Coll., 1980—. Editorial bd. Physicians Fin. News. Recipient NYU Founders award, 1965. Mem. Am. Pub. Health Assn., Am. Mgmt. Assn., Assn. Am. Med. Colls., Am. Hosp. Assn., Hosp. Mgmt. Systems Soc., Hosp. Fin. Mgmt. Assn., Asia Soc., Phi Beta Kappa, Mus. Modern Art, Met. Mus. Art, Met. Opera Guild (N.Y.C.). Episcopalian. Home and Office: Reynolds Co 333 E 51st St New York NY 10022-6702 also: 2500 3 Mile Run Rd Perkasie PA 18944-2020

REYNOLDS, JEAN EDWARDS, publishing executive; b. Saginaw, Mich., Dec. 11, 1941; d. F. Perry and Kathrine (Edwards) R.; m. Cary Wellington, Sept. 10, 1975 (div. 1982); children, Bradley, Abigail, Benjamin. BA, Wells Coll., 1963; postgrad., CCNY, 1965-67. Asst. editor, sr. editor trade book div. Prentice-Hall, Englewood Cliffs, N.J., 1963-66; dir. children's books Prentice-Hall, Englewood Cliffs, 1966-69, McCall Pub. Co., N.Y.C., 1969-71; sr. v.p., editorial dir. Franklin Watts Inc., N.Y.C., 1971-75; pres. Pet Projects Inc., Ridgefield, Conn., 1975-81; editor in chief young people's publs. Grolier Inc., Danbury, Conn., 1981-89; pub., sr. v.p. The Millbrook Press, Brookfield, Conn., 1989—; bd. dirs. Wellington Leisure Products, Atlanta, Kiper Enterprises, Oswego, N.Y.; chairperson Conn. Ctr. for the Book, 1991-94. Bd. dirs. Jewish Home for the Elderly, Fairfield, Conn., 1989-90, Book Industry Study Group, 1991—, The Wooster Sch., Danbury, Conn., 1992—, Temple Shearith Israel, Ridgefield, Conn., 1994—, The Children's Book Coun., 1996—, The Ridgefield Symphony, 1997—; pres. Jewish Fedn. Greater Danbury, 1991-93. Mem. ALA, Children's Book Coun., Mensa, Assn. for Sch. Librs. Internat. (bd. dirs. 1993-94). Jewish. Avocations: skiing, tennis, sailing, needlework, SCUBA. Home: 33 Corntassle Rd Danbury CT 06811-3208 Office: The Millbrook Press Inc 2 Old New Milford Rd Brookfield CT 06804-2426

REYNOLDS, JOHN FRANCIS, insurance company executive; b. Escanaba, Mich., Mar. 29, 1921; s. Edward Peter and Lillian (Harris) R.; m. Dorothy Gustafson, May 1, 1946; children—Lois, Margaret, Michael. B.S., Mich. State U., 1942. Claims and assoc. surety mgr. Hartford Ins. Co., Escanaba, Mich. and Chgo., 1946-55; asst. v.p., bond mgr. Wolverine Ins. Co., Battle Creek, Mich., 1955-64, v.p. underwriting, 1964-69; Midwest zone underwriting mgr. Transamerica Ins. Co. (Wolverine Ins. Co.), Battle Creek, Mich., 1969-74; pres., gen. mgr. Can. Surety Co. subs. Transamerica Ins. Co., Toronto, Ont., Canada, 1974-75; v.p. midwestern zone mgr. Transamerica Ins. Group, Battle Creek, Mich., 1975-83; pres., chief operating officer Transamerica Ins. Group, Los Angeles, 1983-84, chmn., chief exec. officer, 1984-85; apptd. spl. dep. ins. commr., dep. conservator Cadillac Inc. Co., 1989; pres. Underwriting Exec. Council Midwest, 1967; dir. Underwriters Adjustment Bur., Toronto, 1974, Underwriters Labs. of Canada, Montreal, 1974; chmn. Mich. Assn. Ins. Cos., Lansing, 1976, Mich. Basic Property Ins. Assn., Detroit, 1973. Commr. City of Battle Creek, 1967-69; dir. Urban League, Battle Creek, 1969, 70, dir. Mich. Ins. Fedn., Lansing, 1975-83. Served to sgt. U.S. Army, 1942-45; New Guinea. Roman Catholic. Avocations: golf; fishing.

REYNOLDS, JOHN HAMILTON, physicist, educator; b. Cambridge, Mass., Apr. 3, 1923; s. Horace Mason and Catharine (Coffeen) R.; m. Ann Burchard Arnold, July 19, 1975; children from previous marriages: Amy, Horace Marshall, Brian Marshall, Karen Leigh, Petra Catharine. AB, Harvard U., 1943; MS, U. Chgo., 1948, PhD, 1950; D. honoris causa, U. Coimbra, Portugal, 1987. Rsch. asst. Electroacoustic Lab., Harvard U., 1941-43; assoc. physicist Argonne Nat. Lab., 1950; physicist U. Calif. at Berkeley, 1950—, prof. physics, 1961-88; chmn. dept. physics U. Calif., Berkeley, 1984-86, faculty rsch. lectr., 1974; prof. emeritus U. Calif.-Berkeley, Berkeley, 1989—. Contbr. articles to profl. jours. Lt. USNR, 1943-46. Recipient Wetherill medal Franklin Inst., 1965, Golden Plate award Am. Acad. Achievement, 1968, Exceptional Sci. Achievement award NASA, 1973; Guggenheim fellow U. Bristol, Eng., 1956-57, Los Alamos Nat. Lab., 1987, NSF fellow U. São Paulo, Brazil, 1963-64; Fulbright-Hays rsch. grantee U. Coimbra, Portugal, 1971-72; U.S.-Australia Coop. Sci. Program awardee U. Western Australia, 1978-79, Berkeley citation, 1988. Fellow AAAS, Am. Acad. Arts and Scis., Am. Phys. Soc., Am. Geophys. Union, Geochem. Soc., European Assn. Geochemistry, Calif. Acad. Scis. (hon.), Meteoritical Soc. (Leonard medal 1973); mem. NAS (J. Lawrence Smith medal 1967), Faculty Club (Berkeley), Phi Beta Kappa. Democrat. Office: U Calif Dept Physics Berkeley CA 94720

REYNOLDS, JOHN TERRENCE, oil industry executive; b. Madison, Wis., Oct. 2, 1944; s. John Francis and Evelyn Ruth (Straus) R.; m. Diane Marie Princl-Reynolds, Sept. 3, 1966; 1 child, Channing. BSME, U. Wis., 1967, MS in Metallurgical Engring., 1968. Engr. Shell Chem. Co., Denver, 1968-70, Royal Dutch/Shell, The Hague, The Netherlands, 1970-72; sr. engr. Shell Devel. Co., Houston, 1972-75, Shell Oil Co., Houston, 1975-78; staff engr. Shell Oil Co., Deer Park, Tex., 1978-81; engring. mgr. Shell Oil Co., Anacortes, Wash., 1981-87; engring. advisor Shell Oil Co., Houston, 1987—; chmn. inspection codes com., 1989—, inspection subcommittee, 1993—, Am. Petroleum Inst., Washington. Author: Mechanical Integrity of Refinery Equipment, 1993, The New In-Service Piping Inspection Code, 1993. Recipient of numerous certificates of appreciation. Mem. ASME, Am. Soc. for Metals, Nat. Assn. Corrosion Engrs., Am. Petroleum Inst., Nat. Petroleum Refiners Assn. Avocations: mountain climbing, backpacking, kayaking, rafting, fishing. Office: Shell Oil Co 3333 Highway 6 S Houston TX 77082-3101

REYNOLDS, JOHN W., federal judge; b. Green Bay, Wis., Apr. 4, 1921; s. John W. and Madge (Flatley) R.; m. Patricia Ann Brody, May 26, 1947 (dec. Dec. 1967); children: Kate M. Reynolds Lindquist, Molly A., James B.; m. Jane Conway, July 31, 1971; children: Jacob F., Thomas J., Frances P., John W. III. PhB, U. Wis., 1946, LLB, 1949. Bar: Wis. 1949. Since practiced in Green Bay, dist. dir. price stblzn., 1951-53, U.S. commr., 1953-58, atty. gen. of Wis., 1958-62; gov. State of Wis., 1963-65; U.S. dist. judge Ea. Dist. Wis., Milwa., 1965-71, chief judge, 1971-86, sr. judge, 1986—. Served with U.S. Army, 1942-46. Mem. State Bar Wis., Am. Law Inst., Fed. Judges Assn., Former Govs. Assn. Office: US Dist Ct 296 US Courthouse 517 E Wisconsin Ave Milwaukee WI 53202-4504

REYNOLDS, KATHLEEN DIANE FOY (K.D.F. REYNOLDS), transportation executive; b. Chgo., Dec. 9, 1946; d. David Chancy Foy and Vivian Anne (Schwartz) R. Student, San Francisco State U., 1964-68. Taxicab medallion permit holder, City and County of San Francisco, 1995—. Studio coord. KTVU-TV, Oakland, Calif., 1968-70; assoc. prodr. KPIX-TV, San Francisco, 1970-72; music publicist Oakland, 1966-78; writer PLEXUS, West Coast Women's Press, Oakland, 1974-82, gen. mgr., 1984-86; screen writer Oakland, 1970—; gen. ptnr. Designated Driver Group, Oakland, 1990-97; assoc. owner DeSoto Cab, San Francisco, 1995—; mng. ptnr. Foy Scribes, divsn. The Tallahassee Group, Oakland, Calif., 1997—; coun. mem. West Coast Women's Press, Oakland, 1975-86; founding assoc. Women's Inst. for Freedom of the Press, Washington, 1977—; assoc. owner DeSoto Cab, San Francisco, 1995—; medallion permit owner City & County San Francisco, 1995—. Author of periodical news, reviews, features, 1974-82; author of six documentaries for comml. and PBS-TV, 1968-73. Mem. Soc. Mayflower Descendants, Casper, Wyo., 1967—. Mem. San Francisco Film Soc. Avocations: archery, reading, film festival attendance. Home: PO Box 2742 Oakland CA 94602-0042

REYNOLDS, LEWIS DAYTON, administrator, pastor; b. Charleston, W.Va., July 26, 1937; s. James Shelby and Sybil Catherine (Lanham) R.; m. Ann Kathryn Combs, Aug. 25, 1962; children: John Mark, Daniel Adam. BBA, Marshall U., 1959; BTh, Aurora U., 1961; MDiv, Evang. Theol. Sem., Naperville, Ill., 1962. Ordained to ministry Advent Christian Ch., 1962. Pastor Mendota (Ill.) Advent Christian Ch., Mendota, Ill., 1961-64, Clendenin (W.Va.) Advent Christian Ch., Clendenin, W.Va., 1964-72, New Covenant Fellowship, Penfield, N.Y., 1972-89; gen. overseer Elim Fellowship, Lima, N.Y., 1989-97; mem. bd. adminstrn. Nat. Assn. Evangelists, Wheaton, Ill., 1989—, Pentecostal Fellowship N.Am. (now Pentecostal/Charismatic Chs. N.Am.), 1989—; bd. dirs. Elim Bible Inst., Lima; mem. steering com. N.Am. Renewal Svcs., Virginia Beach, 1990—. Editor Elim Herald mag. Mem. Phi Eta Sigma. Republican. Home: 1701 Dalton Rd Apt 503 Lima NY 14485-9542

REYNOLDS, LLOYD GEORGE, economist, educator; b. Wainwright, Alberta, Can., Dec. 22, 1910; came to U.S., 1934, naturalized, 1940; s. George F. and Dorothy (Carl) R.; m. Mary F. Trackett, June 12, 1937; children: Anne Reynolds Skinner, Priscilla Reynolds Roosevelt, Bruce Lloyd. A.B., U. Alberta, 1931, LL.D., 1958; A.M., McGill U., 1933; Ph.D., Harvard, 1936. Instr. econs. Harvard, 1936-39; asso. polit. economy Johns Hopkins, 1939-41, asso. prof., 1941-45; asso. prof. econs. Yale, 1945-47, prof. econs., 1947-52, Sterling prof. econs., 1952-81, chmn. dept. econs., 1951-59, prof. emeritus, 1981—; dir Econ. Growth Center, 1961-67; vis. fellow All Souls Coll., Oxford, 1967-68; Mem. adv. bd. Pakistan Inst. Devel. Econs., 1965-73; cons. to Social Sci. Research Center, U. P.R., 1951-65; dir. Nat. Bureau Econ. Research, 1958-81; Research dir. labor studies 20th Century Fund, 1940-43; research sec., com. on employment Social Sci. Research Council, 1941-42; co-chmn. appeals com. N.W.L.B., 1943-45; cons. Bur. of Budget, 1945-47; Guggenheim fellow, 1954-55, 1966-67; dir. program in econs. and bus. adminstrn. Ford Found., 1955-57. Author: The British Immigrant in Canada, 1935, Control of Competition in Canada, 1940, Labor and National Defense, 1941, An Index to Trade Union Publications, 1945, Labor Economics and Labor Relations, 1949, The Structure of Labor Markets, 1951, The Evolution of Wage Structure, 1956, Economics: A General Introduction, 1963, Wages, Productivity and Industrialization in Puerto Rico, 1965, The Three Worlds of Economics, 1971, Agriculture in Development Theory, 1975, Image and Reality in Economic Development, 1977, The American Economy in Perspective, 1981, Economic Growth in the Third World, 1850-1980, 1985; contbr. articles to profl. jours. Fellow Am. Acad. Arts and Scis.; mem. Indsl. Rls. Rsch. Assn. (pres. 1955), Am. Econ. Assn. (v.p. 1959, exec. com. 1952-54), Am. Acad. Polit. Sci., Am. Statis. Assn., Phi Beta Kappa. Clubs: Graduates (New Haven) (pres. 1961-64); Harvard (Boston); Century (N.Y.C.); Cosmos (Washington). Home: 4000 Cathedral Ave NW Washington DC 20016-5249 Office: Yale University Economics Dept New Haven CT 06520

REYNOLDS, LOUISE MAXINE KRUSE, retired school nurse; b. Waynesboro, Va., May 28, 1935; d. Emil Herman and Cora Lee (Hammer) Kruse; m. Elbert B. Reynolds Jr., June 13, 1964; children: David Emil, Jane Marie. Diploma, Rockingham Meml. Hosp., 1956; student, Madison Coll., Tex. Tech U. RN, Tex., Va, cert. sch. nurse. Head nurse orthopedic, opthalmology dept. surgery Duke U., Durham, N.C., 1961-62; head nurse surg. fl. Waynesboro (Va.) Hosp., 1962-64; sch. nurse Lubbock (Tex.) Ind.

Sch. Dist., 1974-94, ret., 1994. Mem. Va. Nurses Assn. (dist. sec., chair), Tex. Assn. Sch. Nurses (sec., treas. dist. 17, program chair 1989 state conv.).

REYNOLDS, MARJORIE LAVERS, nutrition educator; b. Collingwood, Ont., Can., Jan. 10, 1931; d. Henry James and Laura (Wilson) Lavers; m. John Horace Reynolds, Aug. 17, 1963; children: Steven, Mark. BA, U. Toronto, 1953; MS, U. Minn., 1957; PhD, U. Wis., 1964; AS, State Tech. Inst. Knoxville, 1982. Registered dietitian. Rsch. dietitian Mayo Clinic, Rochester, Minn., 1957-59; rsch. dietitian Cleve. Met. Gen. Hosp., 1959-60; rsch. assoc. U. Tenn., Knoxville, 1963-66; instr. Ft. Sanders Sch. Nursing, Knoxville, 1967-76, State Tech. Inst., Knoxville, 1982-88; substitute secondary sch. tchr. Knox County Schs., Knoxville, 1989-93. Contbr. articles to biochem. and nutrition jours.; newsletter editor Juvenile Diabetes Found., Knoxville, 1985-93. Sec. Midway Rehab. Ctr., Knoxville, 1987—; mem. LWV, Knoxville, 1965—. Mem. Knoxville Dist. Dietetic Assn. (pres. 1971-72, Outstanding Dietitian 1973-1974), Tenn. Dietetic Assn. (pres. 1973-74, Outstanding Dietitian 1973-74), Omicron Nu. Democrat. Presbyterian. Avocations: reading, sports. Home: 7112 Stockton Dr Knoxville TN 37909-2534

REYNOLDS, MARSHALL TRUMAN, printing company executive; b. Logan, W.Va., Feb. 21, 1937; s. Douglas Vernon and Dorothy Lee (Dingess) R.; m. Shirley Ann Earwood, Mar. 24, 1968; children: Jack Marine, Douglas Vernon. Student, Marshall U., 1956-58. Sales mgr. Chapman Printing Co., Huntington, W.Va., 1960-61, gen. mgr., 1961-64; pres., gen. mgr. Chapman Printing Co., Huntington, Parkersburg and Charleston, W.Va., Lexington, Ky., 1964—; chmn. bd. McCorkle Machine & Engring., Huntington, KY-OWVA Corrugated Container, Huntington, Stationers, Inc., Huntington, Charleston, Radisson Hotel, Huntington, Huntington Indsl. Corp., Champion Industries Inc., Am. Babbit Bearing Inc.; bd. dirs. Guyan Machinery, Huntington, United Huntington Industries, Persinger Supply Co., Prichard, W.Va., First Guaranty Bank, Hammond, La., Banc One WV Corp., Charleston, W.Va. Bd. dirs. W.Va. Roundtable, Huntington, 1989—, W. Va. Bus. Found., Huntington, 1989—, Boys and Girls Club, Huntington, 1989—, Huntington United Way, 1989—; mem. Gov.'s Task Force on Children, Youth and Families, 1989—; guest lectr. various high schs. on free enterprise. Named Outstanding Small Businessman of Yr., Huntington Jaycees, 1983, Business Man of Yr. Jaycess, 1988. Mem. Huntington C. of C., Western Star Lodge (Guyandotte, W.Va.). Republican. Baptist. Avocation: raising cattle. Home: 1130 13th St Huntington WV 25701-3632 Office: Chapman Printing Co 2450 1st Ave Huntington WV 25703-1218

REYNOLDS, MARY TRACKETT, political scientist; b. Milw., Jan. 11, 1913; d. James P. and Mary (Nachtwey) Trackett; m. Lloyd G. Reynolds, June 12, 1937; children: Anne Reynolds Skinner, Priscilla Reynolds Roosevelt, Bruce; m. Yoke San Lee. BA, U. Wis., 1935, MA, 1935; postgrad. (Rebecca Green fellow), Radcliffe Coll., 1935-36; PhD (U. fellow, Barnard fellow), Columbia U., 1939. Rsch. asst. Littauer Sch. Harvard U., 1938-39; instr. Queens Coll., 1939-40; instr. Hunter Coll., 1941-42, lectr., 1945-47; assoc. in polit. sci. Johns Hopkins U., 1942-43; lectr. Conn. Coll., 1947-48, asst. prof., 1948-50; rsch. assoc. in econs. Yale U., 1961-67, vis. lectr. in English, 1973-82; meml. lectr. Joyce Centennial, 1982; assoc. fellow Berkeley Coll., 1982—. Author: Interdepartmental Committees in the National Administration, 1940, Joyce and Nora, 1964, Source Documents in Economic Development, 1966, Joyce and D'Annunzio, 1976, Joyce and Dante: The Shaping Imagination, 1982, Mr. Bloom and the Lost Vermeer, 1989, James Joyce: New Century Views, 1993; bd. editors James Joyce Quar., 1985—, James Joyce Studies Ann., 1990—. Rsch. asst. Pres.'s Com. Adminstrn. Mgmt., 1936; sr. economist Nat. Econ. Com., 1940; adminstrn. asst. Glenn L. Martin Aircraft Co., Balt., 1942-43; editorial asst. pub. adminstrn. com. Social Sci. Rsch. Coun., 1944-45; cons. Nat. Def. Adv. Commn., 1949, Nat. Mcpl. Assn., 1956, Orgn. Econ. Cooperation and Devel., Paris, 1964, U.S. State Dept.-AID 1965. Mem. MLA, AAUP, LWV, Am. Polit. Sci. Assn., Dante Soc. Am., Internat. James Joyce Found. (bd. trustees 1995—), Conn. Acad. Arts and Scis. (coun. 1988-89), Elizabethan Club (sec.-treas. 1984-89, bd. incorporators 1986-89), Sulgrave Club (Washington), Grolier Club, Appalachian Mountain Club, Phi Beta Kappa. Home: 4000 Cathedral Ave NW Apt 147B Washington DC 20016-5249

REYNOLDS, NANCY BRADFORD DUPONT (MRS. WILLIAM GLASGOW REYNOLDS), sculptor; b. Greenville, Del., Dec. 28, 1919; d. Eugene Eleuthere and Catherine Dulcinea (Moxham) duPont; m. William Glasgow Reynolds, May 18, 1940; children: Kathrine Glasgow Reynolds, William Bradford, Mary Parminter Reynolds Savage, Cynthia duPont Reynolds Farris. Student, Goldey-Beacom Coll., Wilmington, Del., 1938. One-woman show includes Caldwell Inc., 1975; exhibited group shows Corcoran Gallery, Washington, 1943, Soc. Fine Arts, Wilmington, 1937, 38, 40, 41, 48, 50, 62, 65, Rehoboth (Del.) Art League, 1963, NAD, N.Y.C., 1964, Pa. Mil. Coll., Chester, 1966, Del. Art Ctr., 1967, Del. Art Mus., Wilmington, Wilmington Art Mus., 1976, Corcoran Gallery, Met. Mus. Art, N.Y.C., 1977, Lever House, N.Y.C., 1979; sculpture work Brookgreen Gardens, S.C.; represented in permanent collections Wilmington Trust Co., E.I. duPont de Nemours & Co., Children's Home, Inc., Claymont, Del., Children's Bur., Wilmington, Stephenson Sci. Ctr., Vanderbilt U., Nashville, Lutheran Towers Bldg., Travelers Aid and Family Soc. Bldg., Wilmington, bronze fountain head Longwood Gardens, Kennett Square, Pa., bronze statue Brookgreen Gardens, Murrells Inlet, S.C.; contbr. articles to profl. jours. Organizer vol. svc. Del. chpt. ARC, 1938-39; chmn. Com. for Revision Del. Child Adoption Law, 1950-52; pres., bd. dirs. Children Bur. Del.; pres., trustee Children's Home, Inc.; del., past regent Gunston Hall Plantation, Lorton, Va.; mem. adv. com. Longwood Gardens, Kennett Sq., Pa.; garden and grounds com. Winterthur (Del.) Mus.; mem. rsch. staff Henry Francis DuPont Winterthur Mus., 1955-63; mem. archtl. com. U. Del., Newark. Recipient Confrerie des Chevaliers du Tastevin Clos de Vougeot-Bourgogne France, 1960; Hort. award Garden Club Am., 1964, medal of Merit, 1976; Dorothy Platt award Garden Club of Phila., 1980; Alumni medal of merit Westover Sch., Middlebury, Conn. Mem. Pa. Hort. Soc., Wilmington Soc. Fine Arts, Mayflower Descs., Del. Hist. Soc., Colonial Dames, League Am. Pen Women, Nat. Trust Hist. Preservation. Garden Club of Wilmington (past pres.), Garden Club of Am. (past asst. zone 4 chmn.), Vicmead Hunt Club, Greenville Country Club, Chevy Chase Club (Washington), Colony Club (N.Y.C.). Episcopalian. Address: PO Box 3919 Greenville DE 19807-0919

REYNOLDS, NANCY REMICK, editor, writer; b. San Antonio, July 15, 1938; d. Donald Worthington and Edith (Remick) R.; m. Brian Rushton, June 25, 1983; 1 child, Ehren T. Park. Student, Sch. Am. Ballet, 1951, 53-61, Juilliard Sch. Music, 1957, Martha Graham Sch. Contemporary Dance, N.Y.C., 1959, U. Sorbonne, Paris, 1962; BA in Art History, Columbia U., 1965; postgrad., Goethe Inst., Prien, 1972, U. Chgo. and Sarah Lawrence Coll., 1974-77. Dancer N.Y.C. Ballet, 1956-61; editor Praeger Pubs., N.Y.C., 1965-71; dir. rsch. book Choreography by George Balanchine: A Catalogue of Works, N.Y., 1979-82 (pub. 1983); dir. rsch. pub. TV spl. Balanchine, N.Y., 1983-84; assoc. editor Internat. Ency. of Dance, 1982—; dir. rsch. The George Balanchine Found., N.Y.C., 1994—; co-pub. Twentieth-Century Dance in Slides, 1978-93. Author: Repertory in Review: Forty Years of the New York City Ballet, 1977 (De la Torre Bueno prize 1977), The Dance Catalog: A Complete Guide to Today's World of Dance, 1979, co-author: In Performance,1980, Dance Classics, 1991 (rec. for teen age N.Y. Pub Libr.); editor: Movement and Metaphor: Four Centuries of Ballet (Lincoln Kirstein), 1970, Dance as a Theatre Art: Source Readings in Dance History from 1581 to the Present (Selma Jeanne Cohen), 1974, School of Classical Dance (V. Kostrovitskaya and A. Pisarev), 1978; contbr. (book) Ballet: Bias and Belief, "Three Pamphlets Collected" and Other Dance Writings of Lincoln Kirstein, 1983, also numerous articles and revs. to Dancing Times, Ballet News, Playbill, ArtsLine, Dancemag., Town & Country, Connoisseur, N.Y. Times, Ency. Britannica., Ency. of N.Y.C., others. Ford Found. Travel and Study grantee, 1974; Mary Duke Biddle Found. grantee, 1990. Mem. Dance Critics Assn. (pres. 1986-87), Soc. Dance History Scholars, Soc. for Dance Rsch., Am. Soc. for Theatre Rsch., European Assn. Dance Historians, Internat. Fedn. for Theatre Rsch. in affiliation with Societe Internat. des Bibliotheques et Musees des Arts du Spectacle, Phi Beta Kappa. Home: 9 Prospect Park W Brooklyn NY 11215-1758

REYNOLDS, NORMAN, production designer, art director. Prodn. designer: (films) The Little Prince, 1974, Mr. Quilp, 1975, (with Leslie Dilley and John Barry) Star Wars, 1977 (Academy award best art direction 1977), (with Dilley, Harry Lange, and Alan Tomkins) The Empire Strikes Back, 1980 (Academy award nomination best art direction 1980), (with Dilley) Raiders of the Lost Ark, 1981 (Academy award best art direction 1981), (with Fred Hole and James Schoppe) Return of the Jedi, 1983 (Academy award nomination best art direction 1983), Return to Oz, 1985, Young Sherlock Holmes, 1985, Empire of the Sun, 1987 (Academy award nomination best art direction 1987), Avalon, 1990, Mountains of the Moon, 1990, Alien 3, 1992, Alive, 1993; art dir.: (films) The Incredible Sarah, 1976 (Academy award nomination best art direction 1976). Office: care Spyros Skouras Skouras Agency 725 Arizona Ave Santa Monica CA 90401-1733*

REYNOLDS, NORMAN EBEN, lawyer; b. Muskogee, Okla., Dec. 1, 1919; s. Norman Eben and Elizabeth (Boyd) R.; m. Margaret Maxey Cooper, Nov. 21, 1953; children: Norman Eben III, Margaret Boyd, Nancy Elizabeth, Robert Cooper. A.B., U. Okla., 1941, LL.B., 1947. Bar: Okla. 1942, U.S. Supreme Ct. 1961. Ptnr. Reynolds, Ridings, Vogt & Morgan, Oklahoma City, 1947-89, of counsel, 1989—; dir. Oharco Corp.; mem. Okla. Ho. of Reps., 1949-55; spl. legal cons. Gov. Okla., 1959-63; spl. justice Okla. Supreme Ct., 1961. Pres. trustees Heritage Hall, 1970. Served to capt. AUS, 1942-46. Named Outstanding Young Man in Oklahoma City, 1951. Mem. Comml. Law League Am. (past nat. sec., Pres.'s Cup for disting. svc. 1980), ABA (co-chmn. nat. conf. lawyers and collection agys. 1979), Okla. Bar Assn., Okla. County Bar Assn. (most Outstanding Voluntary Pub. Svc. ann. award 1989), Am. Judicature Soc., Mil. Order World Wars, Phi Beta Kappa (past pres. alumni assn., Phi Beta Kappa of Yr. 1993), Sigma Alpha Epsilon (past pres. alumni assn.), Sooner Dinner Club (Oklahoma City) (pres. 1969), Kiwanis (Oklahoma City), Men's Dinner Club. Episcopalian (sr. warden 1971, chmn. com. to build Canterbury Living Ctr., pres. Episc. Retirement Community, Inc. 1981-94). Club: Sooner Dinner (Oklahoma City) (pres. 1969). Lodge: Kiwanis (Oklahoma City) (pres. 1968). Home: 2212 NW 56th St Oklahoma City OK 73112-7702 Office: Reynolds Ridings Vogt & Morgan 2200 First Nat Ctr Oklahoma City OK 73102

REYNOLDS, PAMELA PRESTON, historian, physician; b. Corpus Christi, Tex., Nov. 9, 1956; d. Charles Wesley and Joyce Carol (Frame) R.; m. John Robert Ball, Jan. 9, 1988; children: Kristen Ann Ball, John Robert Ball. AB, Duke U., 1979, MA, 1981, PhD, 1986, MD, 1987. Diplomat Am. Bd. Internal Medicine, Nat. Bd. Med. Examiners. Intern internal medicine The John Hopkins Hosp., Balt., 1989-90, sr. resident internal medicine, 1990-92; asst. prof. medicine U. Pa., Phila., 1994-96; assoc. prof. medicine Eastern Va. U., Norfolk, 1996—, vice chair dept. medicine, chief divsn. gen. internal medicine, 1996—; cons. Josiah Macy Jr. Found., N.Y., 1994-95, vis. scientist Hopkins U., 1995—. Author: Watts Hospital of Durham, N.C., 1991, contbr. articles to profl. jours. Postdoctoral fellow U. Pa., Phila., 1988-89, fellow, 1992-94, sr. rsch. fellow Leonard Davis Inst. Health Econs., 1993—. Mem ACP (chair coun. of assocs. 1991-92), Am. Med. Student Assoc. (pres. 1987-88), Am. Assoc. History of Medicine, Physicians for Human Rights (bd. dir. 1987—), Soc. of Gen. Internal Med., Alpha Omega Alpha. Demcrat. Presbyterian. Avocations: sailing, tennis, reading, hiking. Home: 6 Concord Pl Havre De Grace MD 21078

REYNOLDS, PETER JAMES, physicist; b. N.Y.C., Nov. 19, 1949; s. Rudolph and Lydia Mary (Schanzer) R.; m. Louise Perini, Aug. 7, 1982. AB in Physics, U. Calif., Berkeley, 1971; PhD, MIT, 1979. Rsch. assoc. and lectr. Boston U., 1979, asst. rsch. prof., 1979-83; mem. sci. staff Nat. Resource for Computation in Chemistry, Lawrence Berkeley Lab., U. Calif., 1980-81, mem. rsch. staff materials and chem. scis. div., 1982-88; vis. scientist NEC Fundamental Rsch. Lab., Kawasaki, Japan, 1986; vis. rsch. chemist, U. Calif., Berkeley, 1988; adj. assoc. prof. dept. chemistry San Francisco State U., 1988-91; program mgr. Office Naval Rsch., 1988—; rsch. prof. Georgetown U., Washington, 1996—; lectr. and rschr. in field of statis., chem. and computational physics and Monte Carlo Methods; program mgr. atomic physics, atom lasers, quantum computing, laser cooling. Editor: On Clusters and Clustering: From Atoms to Fractals, 1993; co-author: Monte Carlo Methods in Ab Initio Quantum Chemistry, 1994; contbr. articles to profl. jours., also rev. articles, book chpts. NSF fellow, 1971-74, IBM fellow, 1975; Lawrence Berkeley Lab. grantee, 1982-83. Fellow Am. Phys. Soc. (membership com., nominating com. Divsn. of Computational Physics and Forum on Physics and Soc., formerly exec. com. Divsn. Computational Physics); mem. Materials Rsch. Soc., Optical Soc. Am., N.Y. Acad. Scis., Phi Beta Kappa, Sigma Xi. Lutheran. Office: ONR Phys Scis Divsn 800 N Quincy St Arlington VA 22203-1906

REYNOLDS, R. JOHN, university administrator; b. Milw., Dec. 3, 1936; s. Edward R. and Elizabeth (Wickenhauser) R.; m. Carol G. Lucas, Dec. 15, 1956; children: John D., Katherine A. BEd, U. Wis., Whitewater, 1961; MA, No. Mich. U., 1967; PhD, So. Ill. U., 1971. Bus. instr. Green Bay (Wis.) Tech. Inst., 1964-65; dir. vocat. tng. No. Mich. U., Marquette, 1965-68; v.p. Tech. Edn. Corp., St. Louis, 1968-69, prof., 1969-71; acting dean, chmn dept. So. Ill. U., Carbondale, 1969-71, 74-80, 81-82; assoc. acad. dean N.H. Coll., Manchester, 1971-74; head. bus. and econs. dept. Lake Superior State U., Sault Ste. Marie, Mich., 1981-82; pres. Nat. Coll., Rapid City, S.D., 1982-84, Huron (S.D.) U., 1984-93, Tri-State U., Angola, Ind., 1993—; cons. various colls. and schs. Contbr. articles to profl. jours. Pres. Dakotaland Mus., Huron, 1986-91. Named Researcher of Yr. Ill. Bus. Edn. Assn., 1971.

REYNOLDS, RICHARD CLYDE, physician, educator; b. Saugerties, N.Y., Sept. 2, 1929; s. Thomas Watson and Myrtle Edith (Myer) R.; m. Mary Jane Beck, July 7, 1954; children—Karen Sue, Stephanie Ann, Wayne Thomas. B.Sc., Rutgers U., 1949; M.D., Johns Hopkins U., 1953; D.Sc. (hon.), Hahnemann U., 1988, N.Y. Med. Coll., 1992; DSc, Uniformed Svcs. U. Health Sci., 1995. Diplomate Am. Bd. Internal Medicine. Intern Johns Hopkins Hosp., Balt., 1953-54; asst. resident Johns Hopkins Hosp., 1954-55, 57-58, fellow in infectious disease, 1958-59; practice medicine specializing in internal medicine Frederick, Md., 1959-68; mem. faculty U. Fla. Coll. Medicine, 1968-78, prof. medicine, prof., chmn. dept. community health and family medicine, 1970-78; prof. medicine, prof. environ. and community medicine, dean U. Medicine and Dentistry N.J., Robert Wood Johnson Med. Sch., 1978-87; sr. v.p. acad. affairs U. Medicine and Dentistry N.J., 1984-87; exec. v.p. Robert Wood Johnson Found., 1987-96; mem. faculty U. Fla. Coll. Medicine, Gainesville, 1997—; mem. Liaison Com. on Med. Edn., 1982-87. Co-author: The Health of a Rural County: Perspectives and Problems, 1976, Patient Wishes and Physician Obligations, 1978; co-editor: On Doctoring: Stories, Poems, Essays, 1991, 2d edit., 1995; contbr. articles to med. publs. Sr. asst. surgeon USPHS, 1955-57. Mem. ACP, AMA. Office: U Fla Coll Medicine PO Box 100277 Gainesville FL 32610-0277

REYNOLDS, ROBERT EDGAR, academic administrator, physician; b. Pontiac, Mich., June 3, 1938; s. Arthur James and Jean Lucille (Thompson) R.; m. Barbara Fisher, June 11, 1961 (div. May 1980); children: Jennifer Robin, Lisa Anne; m. Erika Renate Forte, July 25, 1981; children: Timothy Williams, Julia Renate. BA, Yale U., 1960; MD, Harvard U., 1964; MPH, Johns Hopkins U., 1967, DrPH, 1970. Med. dir. Chonic Disease Hosp., Balt. City Hosps., 1968-70; assoc. prof. medicine and community medicine, assoc. dean Med. Coll. Ga., Augusta, 1970-73; med. dir. br. hosps. Rush Presbyn. St. Lukes Med. Ctr., Chgo., 1973-81, assoc. prof. internal medicine, prof. preventive medicine, 1973-81, med. dir., 1975-81; assoc. dean, assoc. prof. medicine Johns Hopkins U. Sch. Medicine, Balt., 1981-88; sr. assoc. v.p. for health scis., prof. medicine U. Va. Health Sci. Ctr., Charlottesville, 1988-96; prof. health evaluation scis. U. Va., Charlottesville, 1995—, dir. divsn. clin. info., 1997—, vice provost for health scis., 1997—; sec.-treas. Med. Adminstrs. Conf., 1979-80, pres., 1981. Served to capt. USAR, 1965-73. Fellow ACP, Am. Coll. Preventive Medicine; mem. AMA, Assn. Am. Med. Colls. (assoc., chmn. group on instnl. planning 1988-89), Found. for Health Svcs. Rsch. (nat. adv. com.), Assn. for Health Svc. Rsch., Nat. Libr. Medicine (biomed. rev. com. 1992-95), Computer-based Patient Record Inst. (bd. dirs. 1992—). Office: U Va Med Ctr Charlottesville VA 22908

REYNOLDS, ROBERT GREGORY, toxicologist, management consultant; b. Chgo., July 29, 1952; s. Robert G. and Loys Delle (Kever) R.; m. Phyllis Thurrell, May 1983. BS in Nutrition and Food Sci., MIT, 1973, postgrad. in toxicology, 1973-78; postgrad. in mgmt. Sloan Sch. Mgmt., 1977-78. Mng. editor The Graduate Mag., MIT, 1975-78; v.p. Internat. Contact Bur., Ft. Lauderdale, Fla., 1977—; staff toxicologist, asst. to v.p. mktg. Enviro Control, Inc., Rockville, Md., 1978-79; dir. tech. resources Borriston Rsch. Labs., Inc., Temple Hills, Md., 1979-80; dir. mktg. Northrop Svcs., Inc., Rsch. Triangle Park, N.C., 1980-88, mgr. bus. devel., NSI Tech. Svcs.Corp., 1988-89; mgr. proposal mgmt. Roy F. Weston, Inc., West Chester, Pa., 1989-90; project dir. Human Health Scis., 1990-91; pres. Spectrum Assocs., Uwchland, Pa., 1991—; mgmt. cons., 1981—; dir. bus. devel. Groundwater Tech., Inc., Chadds Ford, Pa., 1992-93; v.p. fed. programs ETG Environ. Inc., Blue Bell, Pa., 1993-94; dir. govt. bus. devel. OHM Corp., Findlay, Ohio, 1994—; toxicol. cons. Energy Resources Co., Inc., Cambridge, 1976-77. NSF fellow, 1973. Mem. Am. Def. Preparedness Assn., Soc. Am. Mil. Engrs. Episcopalian. Contbr. chpts. to textbook, lab. manual, sci. jours. and govt. publs. Home: 455 Fox Run Rd Findlay OH 45840-7454 Office: OHM Corp PO Box 551 Findlay OH 45839-0551

REYNOLDS, ROBERT HARRISON, retired export company executive; b. Mpls., Sept. 6, 1913; s. Clarence H. and Helen (Doyle) R.; m. Gladys Marie Gaster, Apr. 7, 1934; 1 child, Shirley Anne Reynolds Potestio (dec.); m. Viola E. Shimel, June 26, 1982. Export sales mgr., rolled products sales mgr. Colo. Fuel & Iron Corp., Denver, 1938-46; pres. Rocky Mountain Export Co., Inc., Denver, 1941-93. Mem. Denver Club (life). Home: 13850 E Marina Dr Aurora CO 80014-5509 Office: 12331 E Cornell Ave Aurora CO 80014-3323

REYNOLDS, ROBERT HUGH, lawyer; b. St. Louis, Jan. 3, 1937; s. Leslie A. and Rebecca (McWaters) R.; m. Carol Jemison, Apr. 8, 1961; children: Stephen H., Cynthia C., Laura M. BA, Yale U., 1958; JD, Harvard U., 1964. Assoc. Barnes & Thornburg, Indpls., 1964-70, ptnr., 1970—, chmn. bus. dept., 1983-91; chmn. internat. practice group, 1992—. Co-chmn., editor Comml. Real Estate Financing for Ind. Attys., 1968; vice-chmn., co-editor Advising Ind. Businesses, 1974; chmn., editor Counseling Ind. Businesses, 1981, The Purchase and Sale of a Business, 1987. Bd. dirs. Crossroads Am. Coun. Boy Scouts Am., 1970—, v.p., 1971-75, pres., 1987-89; v.p. Area 4 Ctrl. Region Boy Scouts Am., 1989-92, pres., 1992-93, pres. Ctrl. Region, 1993-96, Nat. Exec. Bd., 1993— (Silver Buffalo award); bd. dirs. Family Svc. Assn. Indpls., 1974-81, pres., 1978-80; bd. dirs. Family Svc. Am., 1979-88, Greater Indpls. Fgn. Trade Zone, 1987—, Indpls. Conv. and Visitors Assn., 1989—, Indpls. Econ. Devel. Corp., 1983—; bd. dirs. Greater Indpls. Progress Com., 1986—, exec. com., vice chmn. (Charles L. Whistler award); disting. adviser Children's Mus. Indpls., trustee, 1988-96, chmn., 1992-94; bd. dirs. Indpls. Downtown Inc., chmn., 1993—; bd. gov. Legacy Fund, 1992—; bd. dirs. Noyes Mem. Found., 1986—, Japan-Am. Soc. Ind., 1988—, pres., 1994—, Terralex, co-chmn. N.Am., 1996—. Fellow Ind. Bar Found., Indpls. Bar Found.; mem. ABA, Ind. Bar Assn. (chmn. corp., banking and bus. law sect. 1981-82, chmn. internat. sect. 1994-96), Internat. Bar Assn., Indpls. Bar Assn., Greater Indpls. C. of C. (bd. dirs. 1987—), Econ. Club Indpls. (bd. dirs. 1995—). Republican. Clubs: Univ., Skyline (Indpls.). Lodge: Kiwanis. Office: Barnes & Thornburg 11 S Meridian St Ste 1313 Indianapolis IN 46204-3506

REYNOLDS, ROBERT JOEL, economist, consultant; b. Indpls., May 13, 1944; s. Joel Burr and Betty (Schimpf) R.; m. Lucinda Margaret Lewis, May 27, 1979; children: Joel, Sarah. BSBA in Fin., Northwestern U., 1965, PhD in Econs., 1970. Asst. prof. econs. U. Idaho, Moscow, 1969-73, assoc. prof., 1973-75; asst. dir, sr. economist econ. policy office Dept. Justice, Washington, 1973-81; sr. economist, v.p. ICF Inc., Washington, 1981-87, sr. v.p., 1987-91; exec. v.p., prin. Econsult Corp., Washington, 1991-96; chmn. Econsult of D.C., Inc., Washington, 1997—; vis. assoc. prof. U. Calif., Berkeley, 1976-77, Cornell U., Ithaca, N.Y., 1981. Reviewer: NSF, Rand Jour. of Econs., Internat. Econ. Rev., Internat. Jour. Indsl. Orgn., Jour. Indsl. Econs., Am. Econ. Rev.; mem. editorial bd. Managerial and Decision Econs.; contbr. numerous papers to profl. jours. Recipient Dow Jones award Wall St. Jour., 1965; AT&T grantee, 1971-72, Brookings Instl. grantee, 1968-69, NDEA fellow, 1965-69. Mem. AAAS, IEEE (computer sect.), SIAM, Am. Math. Assn., Am. Econ. Assn., Econometric Soc., Royal Econ. Soc., Am. Statis. Assn., European Assn. for Rsch. in Indsl. Econs., Soc. for the Promotion of Econ. Theory, Math. Assn. Am. Congregationalist. Home: PO Box 59712 Potomac MD 20859-9712 Office: Econsult Corp 901 15th St NW Ste 370 Washington DC 20005-2327

REYNOLDS, ROGER LEE, composer; b. Detroit, July 18, 1934; s. George Arthur and Katherine Adelaide (Butler) R.; m. Karen Jeanne Hill, Apr. 11, 1964; children: Erika Lynn, Wendy Claire. BSE in Physics, U. Mich., 1957, MusB in Music Lit., 1960, MusM in Composition, 1961. Assoc. prof. U. Calif. San Diego, La Jolla, 1969-73, founding dir. Ctr. Music Expt. and Related Rsch., 1972-77, prof., 1973—; George Miller prof. U. Ill., 1971—; George Miller prof. U. Ill., 1971; vis. prof. Yale U., New Haven, 1981; sr. rsch. fellow ISAM, Bklyn. Coll., 1985; Valentine prof. Amherst (Mass.) Coll., 1988; Valentine prof. Amherst (Mass.) Coll., 1988; Rothschild composer in residence Peabody Conservatory of Music, 1992-93. Author: MIND MODELS: New Forms of Musical Experience, 1975, A Searcher's Path: A Composer's Ways, 1987, A Jostled Silence: Contemporary Japanese Musical Thought, 1992-93; contbr. numerous articles and revs. to profl. jours. Bd. dirs. Am. Music. Ctr., Meet the Composer, Fromm Found. Harvard U.; mem. bd. govs. Inst. Current World Affairs. Recipient Koussevitzky Internat. Rec. award, 1970, citation Nat. Inst. Arts and Letters, 1971, Koussevitzky Internat. Rec. award 1971, NEA awards, 1975, 78, 79, 86, Pulitzer prize for music, 1989; sr. fellow Inst. Studies in Am. Music, 1985, fellow Inst. Current World Affairs, Rockefeller Found., Guggenheim Found.; Fulbright scholar. Office: U Calif San Diego Dept Music 0326 La Jolla CA 92093

REYNOLDS, RONALD DAVISON, family physician; b. Boston, July 31, 1958; s. Orland Bruce and Moira (Davison) R.; m. Diana May Prieur; children: Brittany, Andrew, Avery. BS in Biochemistry, No. Mich. U., 1980; MD, U. Mich., 1984. Bd. cert. family practice. Resident family practice Flower Meml. Hosp., Sylvania, Ohio, 1984-87; family physician, ctr. dir. So. Ohio Health Svcs. Network, New Richmond (Ohio) Family Practice, 1987—; instr. family medicine U. Cin. Coll. Medicine, 1988-96, asst. prof., 1996—; mem. quality assurance com. So. Ohio Health Svcs. Network, Cin., 1993—; mem. Tri Health steering com. for computerized med. records, 1996—; presenter in field. Reviewer Am. Family Physician, Jour. Family Practice, Mosby-Year Book Publishers; contbr. chpts. to books and articles to profl. jours. Fellow Am. Acad. Family Physicians; mem. Ohio Acad. Family Physicians, Southwestern Ohio Soc. Family Physicians, Assn. for Voluntary Surg. Contraception. Achievements include; development of modified U. technique of Norplant removal; trainer in no-scalpel vasectomy. Office: New Richmond Family Practice 1050 Old US 52 New Richmond OH 45157-9773

REYNOLDS, RUTH CARMEN, school administrator, secondary school educator; b. Dec. 30; d. Jim and Beulah Eliza (Woods) R. BS in Math., Chgo. State U., 1973, BS in Acctg., 1983, MS in Edn., 1986; MA in Math. Edn., DePaul U., 1991. Cert. tchr., high sch. math., gen. adminstrv. Tchr. Chgo. Pub. Schs., 1973—; adminstrv. asst. South Shore Cmty. Acad., Chgo., 1995-96, registrar, 1995-96, dir. scheduling, grade coord., 1995-96; dir. scheduling, registrar Phillips H.S. Acad., Chgo., 1996—; adj. prof. Columbia Coll., Chgo., 1988-89; program officer Lindblom Tech. H.S., Chgo., 1985-95; chmn. pub. com. Chgo. Pub. Schs. Student Sci. Fair, Inc. Contbr. articles to profl. jours. Treas. Chgo. Chpt. NAAF, 1988, nat. phone contact. Frye Found. Math. fellow U. Chgo., 1991. Mem. ASCD, Nat. Coun. Tchrs. Math., Internat. Study Group Ethnomath., Ill. Coun. Tchrs. Math. (del. to Japan 1988), Nat. Coun. Suprs. Math., Notaries Assn. Ill., Benjamin Banneker Assn., Andover-Dartmouth Urban Tchr. Inst., Exeter Math. Inst., Nat. Afro-Am. Hist. and Geneal. Soc., Patricia Liddell Rschrs., Afro-Am. Geneal. and Hist. Soc. Chgo., Afro-Am. Hist. & Geneal. Soc. Washington, Nat. Coun. Negro Women, Math. Club Chgo., Phi Delta Kappa. Avocations: reading mystery novels, travel, genealogy. Home: 2901 S King Dr Apt 1802 Chicago IL 60616-3315 Office: Phillips HS Acad 244 E Pershing Rd Chicago IL 60653-2222

REYNOLDS, SCOTT WALTON, academic administrator; b. Summit, N.J., July 15, 1941; s. Clark Leonard and Shirley (Hill) R.; m. Margaret Ann Johnson, July 5, 1969; children: Jane, Amy, David. B.A., Trinity Coll., Hartford, Conn., 1963; M.B.A., Harvard U., 1965. Mng. dir. corp. staff Bankers Trust Co., N.Y.C., 1967-94; asst. to the pres. St. Peter's Coll., Jersey City, 1994-96, Trinity Coll., Hartford, Conn., 1996—. Chmn. fund campaign Montclair (N.J.) ARC, 1974; chmn. bus. and fraternal group Montclair Bicentennial Com., 1976; bd. fellows Trinity Coll., 1982-88, trustee, 1992—, sec., exec. com., 1993—. 1st lt. U.S. Army, 1965-67. Recipient 150th Anniversary award Trinity Coll., 1978, Alumni medal for Excellence, 1988, Pres.' Leadership medal, 1993. Mem. Montclair Jaycees (treas. 1973), Trinity Coll. Alumni Assn. N.Y. (pres. 1972-73). Episcopalian. Club: Harvard (N.Y.C.). Office: Trinity Coll 300 Summit St Hartford CT 06106-3100

REYNOLDS, VALRAE, museum curator; b. San Francisco, Dec. 18, 1944; d. Ralph Stanley and Valberta May (Eversole) R.; m. Richard Lee Huffman, Sept. 14, 1974; children: Elizabeth Anne, Margaret Lee. BA in Fine Arts with honors, U. Calif., Davis, 1966; MA, NYU, 1969. Asst. curator Asian collections Newark Mus., 1969-70, curator Asian collections, 1970—; cons. SITES Exhbn., 1988; adj. prof. art history Columbia U., 1996; lectr., presenter in field. Editor: Newark Mus. Quar., 1976, Tibetan Jour., 1976, Asia Soc., 1977, Arts of Asia, 1989, Explore Tibet, 1992; contbr. over 36 articles and revs. to profl. jours.; prodr. multimedia prodns. in field. Grantee NEA, NEH, 1972-74, 82-83, 85-86, 88-91, 89-92, J. Paul Getty grantee, 1986, 89-91, Travel grantee Asian Cultural Coun., 1989. Mem. Japan Soc. (art com.). Home: 229 Baltic St Brooklyn NY 11201-6403 Office: Newark Mus PO Box 540 49 Washington St Newark NJ 07102-3109

REYNOLDS, WARREN JAY, retired publisher; b. Chgo., Mar. 10, 1918; s. Bradford Jay and Bessie Pearl (Bon Durant) R.; m. Mary Ellen Seaman, June 29, 1940 (dec. Sept. 1995); children: William, Nancy, David, Linda. BA, DePauw U., 1939. Retail salesman Gen. Foods Corp., Chgo., 1939-41; advt. salesman Capper Publs., Chgo., 1941-42, 45-47; with Parade Publs., Inc., N.Y.C., 1947—; pub., dir. Parade Publs., Inc. (Parade Mag.), 1967-83; pub. emeritus Parade Publs., Inc., 1983—. Served to lt. comdr. USN, 1942-45. Recipient Alumnus of Yr. award DePauw U., 1968. Republican. Club: Venice Yacht (Fla.). Home: 312 Yacht Harbor Dr Osprey FL 34229-9151 Office: 711 3rd Ave New York NY 10017-4014

REYNOLDS, WILLIAM BRADFORD, lawyer; b. Bridgeport, Conn., June 21, 1942; s. William Glasgow and Nancy Bradford (DuPont) R.; m. Marguerite Lynn Morgan, June 27, 1964 (div. Feb. 1987); children: William Bradford Jr., Melissa Morgan, Kristina DuPont, Wendy Riker; m. Clare Alice Conroy, Aug. 29, 1987; 1 child, Linda Matisan. BA, Yale U., 1964; LLB, Vanderbilt U., 1967. Bar: N.Y. 1968, D.C. 1973, U.S. Supreme Ct. 1971. Assoc. Sullivan and Cromwell, N.Y.C., 1967-70; asst. to Solicitor Gen. U.S. Dept. Justice, Washington, 1970-73; ptnr. Shaw, Pittman, Potts & Trowbridge, Washington, 1973-81; asst. atty. gen. Civil Rights div. U.S. Dept. Justice, Washington, 1981-88, counselor to Atty. Gen., 1987-88; ptnr. Ross & Hardies, 1989-91, Dickstein, Shapiro & Morin, 1991-94, Collier, Shannon, Rill & Scott, 1994—; chmn. Archtl. Transp. Barriers Compliance Bd., 1982-84. Editor-in-chief Vanderbilt Law Rev., 1966. Disting. scholar Free Congress Found., 1989-93, Disting. fellow Nat. Legal Ctr. for Pub. Interest, Washington, 1989-90. Mem. ABA, Fed. Bar Assn., D.C. Bar Assn., Order of Coif. Republican. Epsicopalian.

REYNOLDS, WILLIAM CRAIG, mechanical engineer, educator; b. Berkeley, Calif., Mar. 16, 1933; s. Merrill and Patricia Pope (Galt) R.; m. Janice Erma, Sept. 18, 1953; children—Russell, Peter, Margery. B.S. in Mech. Engring., Stanford U., 1954, M.S. in Mech. Engring., 1955, Ph.D. in Mech. Engring., 1957. Faculty mech. engring. Stanford U., 1957—, chmn. dept. mech. engring., 1972-82, 89-93, Donald Whittier prof. mech. engring., 1986—, chmn. Inst. for Energy Studies, 1974-81; staff scientist NASA/Ames Rsch. Ctr., 1987—. Author: books, including Energy Thermodynamics, 2d edit, 1976; contbr. numerous articles to profl. jours. NSF sr. scientist fellow Eng., 1964, Otto Laporte awd., Am. Physical Soc., 1992. Fellow ASME, Am. Phys. Soc. Am. Acad. Arts Sci.; mem. AAUP, AIAA, Nat. Acad. Engring, Stanford Integrated Mfg. Assn. (co-chmn. 1990-94), Sigma Xi, Tau Beta Pi. Achievements include research in fluid mechanics and applied thermodynamics. Office: Stanford U Dept Mechanical Engineering Stanford CA 94305*

REYNOLDS, WILLIAM FRANCIS, mathematics educator; b. Boston, Jan. 31, 1930; s. William Leo and Grace Regina (Devlin) R.; m. Pauline Jane Fitzgerald, Aug. 5, 1962; children—Nancy, Jane. A.B. summa cum laude, Holy Cross Coll., 1950; A.M., Harvard, 1951, Ph.D., 1954. Instr. Holy Cross Coll., Worcester, Mass., 1954-55; instr. Mass. Inst. Tech., Cambridge, 1955-57; asst. prof. math. Tufts U., Medford, Mass., 1957-60, assoc. prof., 1960-67, prof., 1967—, Walker prof. math., 1970—. Contbr. articles to math. jours. Mem. Am. Math. Soc., Math. Assn. Am., Sigma Xi. Achievements include research on modular and projective representations of finite groups. Home: 3 Preble Gardens Rd Belmont MA 02178-3460 Office: Dept Math Tufts U Medford MA 02155

REYNOLDS, WILLIAM HENRY, film editor; b. Elmira, N.Y., June 14, 1910. Grad., Princeton Univ. Swing gang laborer Fox Film Corp., 1934; asst. editor Paramount, 1936-37, editor, 1937-42; editor Twentieth Century-Fox, 1947-62; free-lance editor, 1962—. Asst. editor: (films) The Farmer Takes a Wife, 1935, The Gay Deception, 1935, Big Brown Eyes, 1936, Her Master's Voice, 1936, Palm Springs, 1936, Spendthrift, 1936, John Meade's Woman, 1937, Honeymoon in Bali, 1939, A Night at Earl Carroll's, 1940, Typhoon, 1940; editor: (films) (with Otto Lovering) 52nd Street, 1937, (with Lovering) Algiers, 1938, So Ends Our Night, 1941, Moontide, 1942, Carnival in Costa Rica, 1947, Give My Regards to Broadway, 1948, The Street with No Name, 1948, You Were Meant for Me, 1948, Come to the Stable, 1949, Mother Is a Freshman, 1949, Halls of Montezuma, 1951, The Day the Earth Stood Still, 1951, The Frogmen, 1951, Take Care of My Little Girl, 1951, The Outcasts of Poker Flat, 1952, Red Skies of Montana, 1952, Beneath the 12-Mile Reef, 1953, Dangerous Crossing, 1953, The Kid from Left Field, 1953, Desiree, 1954, Three Coins in the Fountain, 1954, Daddy Long Legs, 1955, Good Morning, Miss Dove, 1955, Love Is a Many-Splendored Thing, 1955, Bus Stop, 1956, Carousel, 1956, In Love and War, 1958, Beloved Infidel, 1959, Blue Denim, 1959, Compulsion, 1959, Wild River, 1960, Tender Is the Night, 1961, Fanny, 1961 (Academy award nomination best film editing 1961), (with Gene Milford, Eda Warren, and Folmar Blangsted) Taras Bulba, 1962, Kings of the Sun, 1963, Ensign Pulver, 1964, The Sound of Music, 1965 (Academy award best film editing 1965), Our Man Flint, 1966, The Sand Pebbles, 1966 (Academy award nomination best film editing 1966), Star!, 1968, Hello, Dolly!, 1969 (Academy award nomination best film editing 1969), The Great White Hope, 1970, What's the Matter with Helen?, 1971, (with Peter Zinner) The Godfather, 1972 (Academy award nomination best film editing 1972), Two People, 1973, The Sting, 1973 (Academy award best film editing 1973), The Great Waldo Pepper, 1975, (with Danford Greene) The Master Gunfighter, 1975, The Seven-Percent Solution, 1977, The Turning Point, 1977 (Academy award nomination best film editing 1977), Old Boyfriends, 1979, A Little Romance, 1979, (with Lisa Fruchtman, Gerald Greenberg, and Tom Rolf) Heaven's Gate, 1980, Nijinsky, 1980, Making Love, 1982, Author! Author!, 1982, Yellowbeard, 1983, (with Raja Gosnell) The Lonely Guy, 1984, The Little Drummer Girl, 1984, (with Herve De Luze) Pirates, 1986, Dancers, 1987, (with Richard A. Cirincione and Stephen A. Rotter) Ishtar, 1987, A New Life, 1988, Rooftops, 1989, Taking Care of Business, 1990, Newsies, 1992; prodr.: (films) (with Richard Widmark) Time Limit, 1957. Office: The Gersh Agency 232 N Canon Dr Beverly Hills CA 90210-5302*

REYNOLDS, WILLIAM LEROY, lawyer, educator; b. Balt., July 26, 1945; s. Austin Leroy and Doris (Hill) R.; m. Theodora Hoe, Sept. 3, 1966; children: William, Megan, Sarah. A.B., Dartmouth Coll., 1967; J.D., Harvard U., 1970. Bar: Md. 1972, U.S. Supreme Ct. 1975. Clk. to judge U.S. Dist. Ct. Md., 1970-71; asst. prof. law U. Md., 1971-74, assoc. prof., 1974-77, prof., 1977—; of counsel Piper & Marbury, Balt., 1992—; bd. dirs. Md. Jud. Inst. Author: Judicial Process in a Nutshell, 1980, 2d edit., 1991, Understanding the Conflict of Laws, 1984, 2d edit., 1993, Cases and Materials on Conflict of Laws, 1990. Mem. Am. Law Inst., Md. State Bar Assn., Am. Judicature Soc. Clubs: Serjeants' Inn, Wranglers (Balt.); St. Regis Yacht (Paul Smiths, N.Y.), Hamilton St. Office: U Md Sch Law 500 W Baltimore St Baltimore MD 21201-1701

REYNOLDS, W(YNETKA) ANN, academic administrator, educator; b. Coffeyville, Kans., Nov. 3, 1937; d. John Ethelbert and Glennie (Beanland) King; m. Thomas H. Kirschbaum; children—Rachel Rebecca, Rex King. BS in Biology-Chemistry, Kans. State Tchrs. Coll., Emporia, 1958; MS in Zoology, U. Iowa, Iowa City, 1960, PhD, 1962; DSc (hon.), Ind. State U., Evansville, 1980; LHD (hon.), McKendree Coll., 1984, U. N.C., Charlotte, 1988, U. Judaism, L.A., 1989, U. Nebr., Kearney, 1992; DSc (hon.), Ball State U., Muncie, Ind., 1985, Emporia (Kans.) State U., 1987; PhD (hon.), Fu Jen Cath. U., Republic of China, 1987; LHD (hon.), U. Nebr., Kearney, 1992, Colgate U., 1993; LHD, No. Mich. U., 1995. Asst. prof. biology Ball State U., Muncie, Ind., 1962-65; asst. prof. anatomy U. Ill. Coll. Medicine, Chgo., 1965-68, assoc. prof. anatomy, 1968-73, research prof. ob-gyn, from 1973, prof. anatomy, from 1973, acting assoc. dean acad. affairs Coll. Medicine, 1977, assoc. vice chancellor, dean grad. coll., 1977-79; provost, v.p. for acad. affairs, prof. ob-gyn. and anatomy Ohio State U., Columbus, 1979-82; chancellor Calif. State Univ. system, Long Beach, 1982-90, prof. biology, 1982-90; bd. dirs. Abbott Labs., Maytag, Owens-Corning, Humana, Inc.; clin. prof. ob/gyn. UCLA, 1985-90; chancellor CUNY, 1990—; mem. Nat. Rsch. Coun. Com. Undergrad. Sci. Edn., 1993—; co-chair Fed. Task Force on Women, Minorities and Handicapped in Sci. and Tech., 1987-90, Pacesetter Program Reform for Secondary Sch. Coll. Bd., 1992—; adv. bd. Congl. Black Caucus Inst. Sci., Space and Tech., 1987-91; Calif. Labor Employment and Tng. Corp., 1993—;. Contbr. chpts. to books, articles to profl. jours; assoc. editor Am. Biology Tchr., 1964-67. Active numerous civic activities involving edn. and the arts; mem. nat. adv. bd. Inst. Am. Indian Arts, 1992—; bd. dirs. Lincoln Ctr. Inst., 1993—, UAW Calif., Calif. Econ. Devel. Corp., 1984-90; trustee Internat. Life Scis. Inst.-Nutrition Found., 1987—, Southwest Mus., L.A. County High Sch. for Arts Found., 1985-90. Recipient Disting. Alumni award Kans. State Tchrs. Coll., 1972, Calif. Gov.'s Award for the Arts for an Outstanding Individual in Arts in Edn., 1989, Prize award Cen. Assn. Obstetricians and Gynecologists, 1968; NSF Predoctoral fellow, 1958-62, Woodrow Wilson Hon. fellow, 1958. Fellow ACOG; mem. AAAS, Perinatal Rsch. Soc., Soc. Gynecol. Investigation (sec./treas. 1980-83, pres. 1992-93), Nat. Assn. Systems Heads (pres. 1987-88), Sigma Xi. Office: CUNY Office of the Chancellor 535 E 80th St New York NY 10021-0767

REYNOLDSON, WALTER WARD, state supreme court chief justice; b. St. Edward, Nebr., May 17, 1920; s. Walter Scorer and Mabel Matilda (Sallach) R.; m. Janet Aline Mills, Dec. 24, 1942 (dec. 1986); children: Vicki (Mrs. Gary Kimes), Robert; m. Patricia A. Frey, June 3, 1989. BA, State Tchrs. Coll., 1942; JD, U. Iowa, 1948; LLD (hon.), Simpson Coll., 1983, Drake U., 1987. Bar: Iowa 1948. Justice Iowa Supreme Ct., 1971-78, chief justice, 1978-87, sr. judge, 1989-93; of counsel Reynoldson Law Firm, Osceola, Iowa, 1993—; adj. prof. law Drake U., 1989-93; county atty., Clarke County, Iowa, 1953-57. Contbg. author: Trial Handbook, 1969. Pres. Nat. Ctr. for State Cts., 1984-85. Served with USNR, 1942-46. Recipient Osceola Community Svc. award, 1968. Mem. Iowa Bar Assn. (chmn. com. on legal edn. and admission to bar 1964-71), ABA, Am. Judicature Soc. (bd. dirs. 1983-87, Herbert Harley award 1990), Iowa Acad. Trial Lawyers, Conf. Chief Justices (pres. 1984-85), Am. Coll. Trial Lawyers. Office: Reynoldson Law Firm 200 W Jefferson St Osceola IA 50213-1206

REYNOLDS-SAKOWSKI, DANA RENEE, science educator; b. Centralia, Ill., June 28, 1968; d. David Lavern and Betty Lou (Shelton) Reynolds; m. Jason Bielas Sakowski, Oct. 8, 1994. BS in Edn., U. No. Colo., 1991, MEd in Middle Sch. Edn., 1996. Tchr. life sci. and math. Ken Caryl Mid. Sch., Littleton, Colo., 1991-92; tchr. sci. Moore Mid. Sch., Arvada, Colo., 1992-93; tchr. life sci. Moore Mid. Sch., Arvada, 1993—. Mem. Nat. Wildlife Fedn., Colo. Assn. Sci. Tchrs., Colo. Biology Tchrs. Assn., Sierra Club, World Wildlife Fund, Nat. Parks and Conservation Assn., Natural Resources Def. Coun., Audubon Soc., Nature Conservancy. Avocations: camping, writing poetry, hiking, singing. Office: Moore Mid Sch 8455 W 88th Ave Arvada CO 80005-1620

REZAK, RICHARD, geology and oceanography educator; b. Syracuse, N.Y., Apr. 26, 1920; s. Habib and Radia (Khouri) R.; m. Hifa Hider, July 1, 1944 (div. Mar. 1965); 1 child, Christine Sara; m. Anna Lucile Nesselrode, Mar. 18, 1965. MA, Washington U., St. Louis, 1949; PhD, Syracuse U., 1957. Geologist U.S. Geol. Survey, Denver, 1952-58; rsch. assoc. Shell Devel. Co., Houston, 1958-67; assoc. prof. oceanography Tex. A&M U., College Station, Tex., 1967-71; prof. Tex. A&M U., College Station, 1971-91, prof. emeritus, 1991—; mem. edit. bd. Geo-MArine Letters, N.Y.C., 1981—; coun. SEPM, Tulsa, Okla., 1968-69; mem. govs. adv. panel Offshore Oil & Chem. Spill Response, Austin, Tex., 1984-85. Co-author: Reefs and Banks of the Northwest Gulf of Mexico, 1985; co-editor: Contributions on the Geological Oceanography of the Gulf of Mexico, 1972, Carbonate Microfabrics, 1993; contbr. articles to profl. jours. Comdr. USNR, 1942-64. Rsch. grantee various fed. agys., 1968-90. Mem. Lions (Melvin Jones fellow). Episcopalian. Home: 3600 Stillmeadow Dr Bryan TX 77802-3324 Office: Tex A&M U Dept Oceanography College Station TX 77843

REZIN, JOYCE JUNE, pediatric nurse practitioner; b. Kalamazoo, Apr. 29, 1936; d. Stephen Palc and Alexandra Kwiatkowski Salerno; m. Joseph Gerald Rezin, Feb. 15, 1958; children: Michael, William, Valerie. BSN, San Diego State U., 1971; MS, U. LaVerne, 1991. Cert. pediatric nurse practitioner; RN, Calif. Staff nurse med./surg. St. Vincent's Hosp., L.A., 1957-58; staff nurse surgery City of Hope Med. Ctr., Duarte, Calif., 1958-59; sch. nurse Sweetwater Union H.S. Dist., Chula Vista, Calif., 1973-84, San Diego Unified Sch. Dist., 1984—; guest lectr. San Diego State U. Sch. Pub. Health, 1994, 95, 96, 97. Vol. nurse Otay Cmty. Clinic, Chula Vista, 1978-79; CPR instr., ARC, Chula Vista, 1977-81, 95, 96, 97; sch. nurse governance team mem. San Diego Unified Sch. Dist., 1991-94; bd. dirs. Adult Protective Svcs., Inc., San Diego, 1995-96, 97. Named Woman of Achievement, Southland Bus. and Profl. Woman's Club, 1987. Fellow Nat. Assn. Pediatric Nurse Assocs. and Practitioners (bd. dirs. San Diego chpt. 1984-85, 95—, vol. liaison to Healthy Child Care Am. Campaign 1996-97, vol. adv. task force Healthy Child Care Calif. 1997); mem. Calif. Sch. Nurse Orgn. (bd. dirs. San Diego/Imperial counties chpt. 1981-86), Nat. Assn. Sch. Nurses. Roman Catholic. Avocations: travel, reading. Home: 10747 Viacha Dr San Diego CA 92124-3418 Office: San Diego City Schs Child Devel Program 4100 Normal St San Diego CA 92103-2653

REZNECK, DANIEL ALBERT, lawyer; b. Troy, N.Y., Apr. 26, 1935; s. Samuel and Elizabeth (Fishburne) R.; m. Beverly Ann Macht, Mar. 7, 1971; children: Jonathan Noah, Abigail Rebecca. BA, Harvard U., 1956, JD, 1959. Bar: N.Y. 1959, D.C. 1961. Rsch. asst. Harvard U. Law Sch., Cambridge, Mass., 1959-60; law clk. to Justice William J. Brennan U.S. Supreme Ct., Washington, 1960-61; asst. U.S. atty. Dept. Justice, Washington, 1961-64; assoc. Arnold & Porter, Washington, 1964-68, ptnr., 1969-95; gen. counsel D.C. Fin. Responsibility and Mgmt. Assistance Authority, Washington, 1995—; adj. prof. law Georgetown U., Washington, 1963—; mem. D.C. Commn. on Jud. Disabilities and Tenure, 1979-86, D.C. Bd. Profl. Responsibility, 1994—; trustee D.C. Pub. Defender Svc., 1981-87. Contbr. articles to profl. jours. Named Young Lawyer of Yr. for D.C., 1971. Fellow Am. Coll. Trial Lawyers, Am. Bar Found.; mem. ABA, D.C. Bar (pres. 1975-76, pres. Bar Found. 1994—), Bar Assn. D.C., Asst. U.S. Attys. Assn., D.C. B'nai Brith. Jewish. Avocations: American history; reading; writing. Home: 2852 Albemarle St NW Washington DC 20008-1036 Office: DC Fin Respons/Mgmt Asst Au 1 Thomas Cir NW Ste 900 Washington DC 20005-5802

REZNICK, RICHARD HOWARD, pediatrician; b. Chgo., Oct. 31, 1939; s. Louis and Mae Reznick; m. Barbara Ann Glantz, June 20, 1965; children: Steven L., Alicia T., Scott M., Stacey R. BS, U. Ill., 1961; MD, Loyola U., Chgo., 1965. Diplomate Am. Bd. Pediatrics. Intern Michael Reese Hosp., Chgo., 1965-66; pediatrician USAF, Homestead AFB, Fla., 1968-70; resident in pediatrics USAF, Homestead AFB, 1966-68; pediatrician pvt. practice Winnetka, Ill., 1970-71, Scottsdale, Ariz., 1971—; pres. med. staff Phoenix Children's Hosp., 1990-93, bd. dirs. 1990-94. Capt. USAF, 1968-70. Fellow Am. Acad. Pediatrics (treas. Ariz. chpt. 1982-84); mem. AMA, Ariz. Med. Assn., Phoenix Pediatric Soc. (treas. 1976-77), Maricopa County Med. Soc. Avocations: aerobics, bicycling, gardening, classical music, collecting stamps. Office: Papago Buttes Pediatric Ctr 6390-3 E Thomas Rd Ste 130 Scottsdale AZ 85251

REZNIK, ALAN A., petroleum engineering educator; b. Pitts., Sept. 25, 1939; s. Lawrence S. and Rose (Fairman) R.; m. Marion Bergstein, Sept. 8, 1963; children—Amy Jean, Robert I.S. B.S., U. Pitts., 1963, M.S., 1964, Ph.D., 1971. Research scientist Continental Oil Co., Ponca City, Okla., 1964-66; instr. chem. and petroleum engring. dept. U. Pitts., 1966-67; instr. dept. civil engring. Technion-Israel Inst. Tech., Haifa, 1967-68; sr. research assoc. Calgon Corp., Pitts., 1969; engring. supr. U.S. Bur. Mines, Pitts., 1973-75; assoc. prof. chem. and petroleum engring. U. Pitts., 1975—, dir. petroleum engring. program, 1981-92 ; cons. and lectr. in field. Assoc. editor Jour. Petroleum Sci. and Engring., 1986-93 . Contbr. articles to profl. jours. Recipient Continental Oil Co. fellowship, 1961, Socony Mobil Internat. fellowship, 1962, U. Pitts. Outstanding Sr. award, 1963; U.S. Dept. Energy grantee, 1976-78, Gulf Oil Found. grantee, 1979, U.S. Dept. Energy grantee, 1978-79, 80-82, 85-86. Mem. Soc. Petroleum Engrs. of AIME, Am. Chem. Soc. (sec.-treas. 1975-76), Sigma Xi, Sigma Tau, Sigma Gamma Epsilon. Democrat. Jewish. Clubs: Train Collectors Assn. (Strassburg, Pa.), Israel Numesmatic Soc. (Pitts., founder, dir. 1969-78), Antique Toy Collectors Am. Achievements include research in flow in porous media enhanced petroleum recovery and metane production from coals, tensor analysis. Office: U Pitts Chem & Petroleum Engring Dept 1249 Benedum Hall Pittsburgh PA 15261-2212

REZNOR, TRENT, musician; b. Mercer, Pa., May 17, 1965. Albums include Broken, 1992, The Downward Spiral, 1994; composer, writer, actor video Broken, 1992, film Lost Highway, 1996; composer film Natural Born Killers, 1994; performer Woodstock '94. Named Most Vital Artist in Music, Spin Mag., 1997, One of Most Influential Americans, Time Mag., 1997. Office: Nothing Records Interscope Records 540 Madison Ave New York NY 10022

RHAME, THOMAS GENE, army officer; b. Winnfield, La., Jan. 27, 1941; s. Thomas Elton and Mary Sue (Blair) R.; m. Linda Ann Saunders, Jan. 21, 1961; children: Rebecca Jean Rhame Barton, Thomas Gregory. BS, La. State U., 1963; MBA, Syracuse U., 1970. Commd. 2d lt. U.S. Army, 1963, advanced through grades to lt. gen., 1993; co. comdr., advisor 1st Cavalry Div., Republic of Vietnam, 1967-71; student Armed Forces Staff Coll., Norfolk, Va., 1975; bn. comdr. 2d Armored Div., Ft. Hood, Tex., 1976-78; advisor Calif. N.G. 40th Inf. Div., L.A., 1979-80; student Army War Coll., Carlisle, Pa., 1981; brigade comdr. 3d Inf., Kitzingen, Fed. Republic Germany, 1981-83; chief of staff 3d Armored Div., Frankfurt, Fed. Republic Germany, 1983; community comdr., asst. div. comdr. U.S. Army Europe, Hanau, Fed. Republic Germany, 1985-86; dep. chief of staff for pers. U.S. Army Staff, Washington, 1986-89; comdr. 1st Inf. Divsn., Ft. Riley, Kans., 1989-91; chief U.S. Mil. Tng. Mission, Operation Desert Storm U.S. Ctrl. Command, Riyadh, Saudi Arabia, 1991-93; dir. Def. Security Assistance Agy., Washington, 1993—. Mem. Transatlantic coun. Boy Scouts Am., Fed. Republic Germany, 1985-86; bd. dirs. Soc. Big Red One, 1989-91. Decorated Legion of Merit, Bronze Star (3), Silver Star (2), M.S.M. (3), Army D.S.M. (2), Def. D.S.M., Air Medal, Army Commendation Medal; named to La. State Hall of Disting. Grads., 1991. Mem. Assn. U.S. Army. Republican. Baptist. Avocations: golf, hunting, fishing.

RHAMES, VING, actor. Appeared in films Stop! Or My Mom Will SHoot, 1992, The People Under the Stairs, 1992, Dave, 1993, The Saint of Fort Washington, 1993, Bound By Honor Blood In Blood Out, 1993, Pulp Fiction, 1994, Drop Squad, 1994, Kiss of Death, 1995, Ed McBain's 87th Precinct, 1995, Deadly Whispers, 1995, Mission: Impossible, 1996, Striptease, 1996, Con Air, 1997, Rosewood, 1997, others. Office: William Morris Agy 151 El Camino Beverly Hills CA 90212*

RHEAMS, ANNIE ELIZABETH, education educator; b. Lake Providence, La.; d. Curtis Kleinpeter Sr. and Annie Augusta (Webb) Kleinpeter; 1 child, Darryl Jemall Rheams. BA, Grambling (La.) U., 1971; MS, Ala. A&M U., 1975; PhD, U. Wis., Milw., 1989. Cert. tchr. in exceptional edn., adminstrn. Tchr. Ala. A&M U., Normal, 1971-79, adminstr., 1977-79; acad. specialist U. Wis., Milw., 1979-82, Parkside, 1982-84; tchr. diagnostician, adminstr. Milw. Schs., 1984-89; asst. prof. dept. edn. Marquette U., Milw., 1989-96; asst. prin. North Division H.S., Milw., 1996—; career counselor Madison County Career Counseling Svcs., Huntsville, 1975; adj. prof. Oakwood (Ala.) SDA Coll., 1975-78; tchr. Gateway to Engring. Program, Milw., 1984-88; cons. pub. schs./Wee Care Day Care, Milw., 1992-96; condr. workshops in field. Author: P.A.C.E.: A Thematic Approach to Developing Essential Experiences, 1996. Voter registrar/poll watcher NAACP, Lake Providence, 1966; v.p. Work for Wis., Inc., Milw., 1993-94, Messmer H.S. Bd., Milw., 1990-94; com. chmn. Citizen's Rev. Bd., Milw., 1980-82, Met. Milw. Alliance Black Sch. Educators, 1994-95. Assoc. fellow Ctr. for Great Plains Studies, U. Nebr.-Lincoln, 1995; named Outstanding Tchr. Educator, Am. Assn. for Coll. Tchr. Educators Directory, 1995. Mem. Zonta Internat., Alpha Kappa Alpha, Phi Delta Kappa. Avocations: tennis, sewing, ceramics, horseback riding, biking. Home: PO Box 09681 Milwaukee WI 53209-0681

RHEE, SUE-GOO, biochemist, researcher; b. Seoul, Republic of Korea, July 6, 1943; s. Man-Hoon Rhee and Yong-Hee Lee; m. Young-Kyu Park, Sept. 29, 1971; children: Ina, Eugene. BS in Chemistry, Seoul Nat. U., 1965; PhD in Chemistry, Cath. U. Am., 1972. Postdoctoral fellow NIH, Bethesda, Md., 1973-75, staff fellow, 1975-79, sr. biochemist, 1979-88, sect. chief, 1988-94; lab. chief Lab. Cell Signaling Nat. Heart, Lung and Blood Inst., NIH, Bethesda, 1994—. Author chpts. to books; contbr. articles to profl. jours. Recipient Ho Am award Sam Sung Corp., 1995. Mem. Am. Soc. Biochemistry and Molecular Biology (editor jour. 1991-96), Brit. Biochem. Soc. (mem. adv. bd. 1992-97), Korean Molecular Biology (mem. adv. bd. 1994—). Office: Lab Cell Signaling 9000 Rockville Pike Rm 120 Bethesda MD 20814-1436

RHEIN, MURRAY HAROLD, management consultant; b. N.Y.C., June 7, 1912; s. Aaron and Celia (Hagler) R.; m. Miriam Eisenstadt, Dec. 22, 1940; children: Alan A., Barbara (Mrs. Allan D. Kramer). B.A., U. Ark., 1932, postgrad., 1932-33. Jr. exec. R.H. Macy & Co., N.Y.C., 1934-39; with Platt & Munk Co., N.Y.C., 1940-78, sales mgr., 1958-64, exec. v.p., 1964-67, pres., 1967-77; v.p. Questor Edn. Products Co., 1969-78; with M & M Rhein (mgmt. consultants to pub. industry), 1978-97. Pub.: The Little Engine that Could. Served with USCGR, 1943-46. Jewish (trustee, v.p. temple).

RHEINBOLDT, WERNER CARL, mathematics educator, researcher; b. Berlin, Sept. 18, 1927; came to U.S., 1956; s. Karl L. and Gertrud (Hartwig) R. Dipl Math, U. Heidelberg, Fed. Republic Germany, 1952; Dr rer nat, U. Freiburg, Fed. Republic Germany, 1955. Mathematician Computer Lab., Nat. Bur. Standards, Washington, 1957-59; asst. prof. math., dir. Computer Ctr., Syracuse (N.Y.) U., 1959-62; dir. Computer Sci. Ctr., U. Md., College Park, 1962-65, prof. math. and computer sci., 1965-78, dir. applied math. program, 1974-78; A.W. Mellon prof. math. U. Pitts., 1978—; cons. various orgns., 1965—; cons. editor Acad. Press, Inc., N.Y.C., 1987—; mem. adv. panel NSF, Army Rsch. Office, Office Naval Rsch., NASA. Author: (with J. Ortega) Iterative Solution of Nonlinear Equations in Several Variable, 1970; Methods of Solving Systems on Nonlinear Equations, 1974, Numerical Analysis of Parametrized Equations, 1985; also over 130 articles. With German Army, 1943-45. Recipient Av. Humboldt Disting. Scientist award, Alexander von Humboldt Found., Germany; grantee NSF, 1965—, Office Naval Rsch., 1972—. Fellow AAAS; mem. Am. Math. Soc., Soc. for Indsl. and Applied Math. (editor 1964—, v.p. publs. 1976, pres. 1977-78, coun. 1979-80, trustee, 1982, chmn. bd. trustees 1985-90). Office: U Pitts Dept Math and Stats 612 Thackeray Building Pittsburgh PA 15260-4146

RHEINSTEIN, PETER HOWARD, government official, physician, lawyer; b. Cleve., Sept. 7, 1943; s. Franz Joseph Rheinstein and Hede Henrietta (Neheimer) Rheinstein Lerner; m. Miriam Ruth Weissman, Feb. 22, 1969; 1 child, Jason Edward. BA with high honors, Mich. State U., 1963, MS, 1964; MD, Johns Hopkins U., 1967; JD, U. Md., 1973. Bar: Md., D.C.; diplomate Am. Bd. Family Practice; cert. added qualifications in geriatric medicine. Intern USPHS Hosp., San Francisco, 1967-68; resident in internal medicine USPHS Hosp., Balt., 1968-70; practice medicine specializing in internal medicine Balt., 1970—; instr. medicine U. Md., Balt., 1970-73; med. dir. extended care facilities CHC Corp., Balt., 1972-74; dir. drug advt. and labeling div. FDA, Rockville, Md., 1974-82, acting dep. dir. Office Drugs, 1982-83, acting dir. Office Drugs, 1983-84, dir. Office Drug Standards, 1984-90; dir. medicine staff, Office Health Affairs FDA, 1990—; chmn. Com. on Advanced Sci. Edn., 1978-86, Rsch. in Human Subjects Com., 1990-92; adj. prof. forensic medicine George Washington U., 1974-76; WHO cons. on drug regulation Nat. Inst. for Control Pharm. and Biol. Products, People's Republic of China, 1981—; advisor on essential drugs WHO, 1985—; FDA del. to U.S. Pharmacopeial Conv., 1985-90. Co-author: (with others) Human

Organ Transplantation, 1987; spl. editorial advisor Good Housekeeping Guide to Medicine and Drugs, 1977—; mem. editorial bd. Legal Aspects Med. Practice, 1981-89, Drug Info. Jour., 1982-86, 91-95; contbr. articles to profl. jours. Recipient Commendable Svc. award FDA, 1981, Group award of merit, 1983, 88, Group Commendable Svc. award 1989, 92, 93, 95, Commr.'s Spl. citation, 1993. Fellow Am. Coll. Legal Medicine (bd. govs. 1983-93, treas., chmn. fin. com. 1985-88, 90-91, chmn. publs. com. 1988-93, jud. coun. 1993-95; Pres.'s awards 1985, 86, 89, 90, 91, 93), Am. Acad. Family Physicians; mem. Am. Acad. Pharm. Phys., AMA, ABA, Drug Info. Assn. (bd. dirs. 1982-90, pres. 1984-85, 88-89, v.p. 1986-87, chmn. ann. meeting 1991, 94, steering com. Ams. 1991—, Outstanding Svc. award 1990), Fed. Bar Assn. (chmn. food and drug com. 1976-79, Disting. Svc. award 1977), Med. and Chirurgical Faculty Md., Balt. City Med. Soc., Johns Hopkins Med. and Surg. Assn., Am. Pub Health Assn., Md. Bar Assn., Math. Assn. Am., Soc. Indsl. and Applied Math., Mensa (life), U. Md. Alumni Assn. (life), Fed. Exec. Inst. Alumni Assn. (life), Johns Hopkins U. Alumni Assn. (life), Chartwell Golf and Country Club, Annapolis Yacht Club, Johns Hopkins Club, Delta Theta Phi. Avocations: boating, electronics, physical fitness, real estate investments. Home: 621 Holly Ridge Rd Severna Park MD 21146-3520 Office: FDA Office of Health Affairs Dir Medicine Staff 5600 Fishers Ln Rockville MD 20857-0001

RHEINTGEN, LAURA DALE, research center official; b. Takoma Park, Md., July 13, 1962; d. Robert William and Ethel Frances (Snyder) Schiedel. BA in Internat. Studies and German, W.Va. U., 1984; MA in Internat. Affairs, Am. U., 1988. Rsch. asst. Brookings Instn., Washington, 1986; staff cons. Birch & Davis Assocs., Inc., Silver Spring, Md., 1988-89; devel. analyst Ctr. for Strategic and Internat. Studies, Washington, 1989-92, mgr. devel. rsch. and records, 1992-93; asst. dir. devel. Ctr. for Strategic and Internat. Studies, 1994-95, dir. found. rels., 1995-97; assoc. dir. devel. Aspen Inst., Washington, 1997—. Mem. Women in Internat. Security Studies, German Lang. Soc. Office: Ste 1070 1333 New Hampshire Ave NW Washington DC 20036-1528

RHETT, HASKELL EMERY SMITH, educator; b. Evanston, Ill., Aug. 29, 1936; s. Haskell Smith and Eunice Campbell (Emery) R.; m. Roberta Teel Oliver, Sept. 9, 1961 (div. 1973); children: Kathryn Emery, Cecily Coffin; m. Anita Leone, May 30, 1983 (div. 1993). AB, Hamilton Coll., 1958; MA, Cornell U., 1967, PhD, 1968. Asst. to the pres. Hamilton Coll., Clinton, N.Y., 1961-64; rsch. asst. Cornell U., Ithaca, N.Y., 1964-66; rsch. assoc. U. London, 1966-67; dir. program devel. Ednl. Testing Svc., Princeton, N.J., 1967-73; asst. chancellor N.J. Dept. Higher Edn., Trenton, 1973-85; v.p. The Coll. Bd., N.Y.C., 1985-90; pres. The Woodrow Wilson Nat. Fellowship Found., Princeton, 1990-97. Author: Going to College in New Jersey, 1978; contbg. author: Government's Role in Supporting College Savings, 1990. Commr. N.J. Pub. Broadcasting Authority, Trenton, 1983-85; mem. Nat. Task Force on Student Aid Problems, Washington, 1974-75; mem. Gov.'s Adv. Panel on Higher Edn. Restructuring, State of N.J., 1994; trustee Dominican Coll., San Rafael, Calif., 1990—; del. Dem. Nat. Conv., Miami, 1972; sr. warden Trinity Episcopal Ch., Princeton, 1988-92, vestryman, 1979-82, dep. Gen. Conv., Detroit, 1988, Phoenix, 1991; mem. standing com. Episcopal Diocese of N.J., 1992-97; trustee The Coll. of N.J., 1992—, vice-chmn., 1995—, Gov. Dummer Acad., Mass., 1993—, Heartland Edn. Comty., Ohio, 1992-97. Nat. Def. fellow U.S. Govt., 1966-67, Eliot-Winant fellow Brit.-Am. Assocs., 1982, Harvard U. fellow, 1985, faculty fellow Wilson Coll., Princeton U., 1993—. Mem. Am. Assn. for Higher Edn., Nat. Assn. State Scholarship and Grant Programs (pres. 1976-78), Nassau Club, Cornell Club (N.Y.), Springdale Golf Club. Avocations: tennis, golf, sailing, classic automobiles. Home: 80 Province Line Rd Skillman NJ 08558

RHETT, JOHN TAYLOR, JR., government official, civil engineer; b. Fort Benning, Ga., Feb. 20, 1925; s. John Taylor and Bessie (Grier) R.; m. Helen Watson, Nov. 5, 1949; children—Elizabeth, John Taylor III. B.S. in Mil. Engring., U.S. Mil. Acad., 1945; M.E. in Civil Engring., U. Calif.-Berkeley, 1952; M.S. in Internat. Relations, George Washington U., 1965. Registered civil engr., Fla., D.C. Commd. 2d lt. U.S. Army, 1942, advanced through grades to col., 1967; chief engring. U.S. Army Constrn. Agy., Vietnam, 1968-69; dist. engr. C.E., U.S. Army, Louisville, Ky., 1969-72; resident mem. Rivers and Harbors Bd., C.E., U.S. Army, 1972-73; ret. U.S. Army, 1973; dep. asst. adminstr. water program ops. EPA, Washington, 1973-79; fed. insp. Alaska Natural Gas Transp. System, Washington, 1979-86; self-employed cons. Arlington, Va., 1986—. Decorated Legion of Merit; recipient Gold medal EPA, 1976, Disting. Career award EPA, 1979. Fellow ASCE, Soc. Mil. Engrs.; mem. Am. Acad. Environ. Engrs. (diplomate). Presbyterian.

RHI, SANG-KYU, lawyer, educator; b. Namwon, Cheon-buk, Republic Korea, July 1, 1933; s. Byong-Choon and Pil-Soon (Huh) R.; m. Hyo-Sook Kim, June 4, 1956; children: Eun-Sook, Jihn-u, Eun-Yong, Jihn-Soo. LLB, Chongchy Coll., 1955; LLM, So. Meth. U., 1961; postgrad., Nottingham (Eng.) U., 1966-67; LLD (hon.), Harding U., 1992. Legislating officer Office Legislation, Republic Korea, 1961-67; pres. Korea Environ. Law Assn., Seoul, 1977-83; vice min. Ministry Edn., Republic Korea, 1980; lawyer Rhi Law Offices, Seoul, 1981—; prof. Coll. Law Korea U., Seoul, 1982-94; rep. Korea Legal Ctr., Seoul, 1989-93. Author: American Administrative Law, 1962, Administrative Law, 1965, Law of Administrative Remedy, 1985, State Liability and Compensation, 1995. 1st Lt. Republic Korea army, 1957-58. Recipient Presdl. commendation Govt. Korea, 1963, Red-Stripe Keunjeong medal, 1971. Mem. Seoul Bar Assn. (chmn. legis. com. 1989-91, Commendation Merit 1990), Korea Bar Assn. (exec. dir. 1991-93, bd. dirs. 1994—, pres. Tng. Inst. for Lawyers 1997—), Inter-Pacific Bar Assn. (coun. mem. 1995—), Internat. Bar Assn., Lawasia (coun. mem. 1995—). Avocations: golf, classical music. Home: 2-201 Asia Athletes Apt, 86 Jamshil 7-dong, Songpa-ku, Seoul 138-227, Republic of Korea Office: Rhi Law Offices Ste 1153, KCCI BLDG 45 Namdaemunro 4ka, Seoul 100-743, Republic of Korea

RHIEW, FRANCIS CHANGNAM, physician; b. Korea, Dec. 3, 1938; came to U.S., 1967, naturalized, 1977; s. Byung Kyun and In Sil (Lee) R.; m. Kay Kyungja Chang, June 11, 1967; children: Richard C., Elizabeth. BS, Seoul Nat. U., 1960, MD, 1964. Intern, St. Mary's Hosp., Waterbury, Conn., 1967-68; resident in radiology and nuclear medicine L.I.U.-Queens Hosp. Ctr., N.Y., 1968-71; instr. radiology W. Va. U. Sch. Medicine, Morgantown, 1971-73; mem. staff Mercy Hosp. and Moses Taylor Hosp., Scranton, Pa., 1973—, also dir. nuclear medicine; clin. instr., Temple U., 1987—; pres. Radiol. Consultants, Inc., 1984—. Served with M.C., Korean Army, 1964-67. Recipient Minister of Health and Welfare award, 1963; certified Am. Bd. Nuclear Medicine. Mem. AMA, Soc. Nuclear Medicine, Radiol. Soc. N.Am., Am. Coll. Nuclear Medicine, Am. Coll. Radiology, Am. Inst. Ultra Sound, Country Club Scranton, Pres.'s Club U. Scranton, Elks. Home: 14 Lakeside Dr Clarks Summit PA 18411-9419 Office: 746 Jefferson Ave Scranton PA 18510-1624

RHIND, JAMES THOMAS, lawyer; b. Chgo., July 21, 1922; s. John Gray and Eleanor (Bradley) R.; m. Laura Haney Campbell, Apr. 19, 1958; children: Anne Constance, James Campbell, David Scott. Student, Hamilton Coll., 1940-42; A.B. cum laude, Ohio State U., 1944; LL.B. cum laude, Harvard U., 1950. Bar: Ill. bar 1950. Japanese translator U.S. War Dept., Tokyo, Japan, 1946-47; congl. liaison Fgn. Operations Adminstrn., Washington, 1954; atty. Bell, Boyd & Lloyd, Chgo., 1950-53, 55—, ptnr., 1958-92, of counsel, 1993—; Bd. dirs. Kewaunee Scientific Corp., Statesville, N.C., Lindberg Corp., Rosemont, Ill., Microseal Corp., Zion, Ill., Griffith Labs., Inc., Alsip, Ill. Commr. Gen. Assembly United Presbyn. Ch., 1963; life trustee Ravinia Festival Assn., Hamilton Coll., Clinton, N.Y., U. Chgo.; Northwestern Univ. Assocs.; chmn. Cook County Young Republican Orgn., 1957; Ill. Young Rep. nat. committeeman, 1957-58; v.p., mem. bd. govs. United Rep. Fund Ill., 1965-84; pres. Ill. Childrens Home and Aid Soc., 1971-73, life trustee; bd. dirs. E.J. Dalton Youth Center, 1966- 69; governing mem. Orchestral Assn., Chgo.; mem. Ill. Arts Council, 1971-75; mem. exec. com. div. Met. Mission and Ch. Extension Bd., Chgo. Presbytery, 1966-68; trustee Presbyn. Home, W. Clement and Jessie V. Stone Found., U. Chgo. Hosps. Served with M.I. AUS, 1943-46. Mem. ABA, Ill. Bar Assn., Chgo. Bar Assn. (bd. mgrs. 1967-69), Fed. Bar Assns., Chgo. Council on Fgn. Relations, Japan Am. Soc. Chgo., Legal Club Chgo., Law Club Chgo., Phi Beta Kappa, Sigma Phi. Clubs: Chicago, Glen View (Ill.), Commercial (Chgo.), Mid-Day Club (Chgo.), Economic (Chgo.). Home: 830 Normandy Ln Glenview IL 60025-3210 Office: Bell Boyd & Lloyd 3 First National Pla 70 W Madison St Ste 3200 Chicago IL 60602-4244

RHINE, JOHN E., lawyer; b. Eldorado, Ill., Nov. 12, 1952; s. R.L. and Iris Faye (Harlow) R.; m. Susan L. Edwards, Dec. 28, 1974; children: Oliver Sampson, Tison Hausser, Julia Eva. BA, So. Ill. U., 1974; JD magna cum laude, U. Ill., 1977. Bar: Ill. 1977, U.S. Dist. Ct. (so. dist.) Ill. 1979, U.S. Ct. Appeals (7th cir.) 1985. Law clk. to justice Ill. Supreme Ct., Springfield, 1977-78; pvt. practice law Mt. Carmel, Ill., 1978-79; ptnr. Rhine, Ernest & Vargo, Mt. Carmel, 1979—; bd. dirs. Nat. Land & Mineral Co., Inc., Starlight TV Corp., chmn., 1989-94; vis. prof. law Moscow State Inst. Internat. Rels., 1993, 95. Adv. coun. mineral lands mgmt. U. Evansville (Ind.), 1984-88; active Mr. Carmel Planning Commn., 1986-88; del. Moscow Conf. on Law and Econs., 1990; bd. dirs. Voices Ill. Children, chmn. bd. dirs., 1993-96. Mem. Ill. Bar Assn. (mineral law subcom. 1984, law office econs. sect. coun. 1986-93, chmn. 1991-92 4, mineral law sect. coun. 1993—). Presbyterian. Office: Rhine Ernest & Vargo 631 N Market St Mount Carmel IL 62863-1458

RHINELANDER, ESTHER RICHARD, secondary school educator; b. Honolulu, Aug. 31, 1940; d. William Wise and Elizabeth (Chilton) Richard; m. Harvey James Rhinelander, July 24, 1965; 1 child, Lori. BEd, U. Hawaii, 1963, profl. cert., 1964. Tchr. music Kamehameha Sch., Honolulu, 1965—, Kamehameha Sch. for Girls, Honolulu, 1964, Waianae High and Intermediate Sch., Honolulu, 1965; dir. Waiokeola Ch. Choir, Honolulu, 1964-67, Kawaiahao Ch. Choir, Honolulu, 1980-87; judge song contest Kamehameha Schs., 1972, 88; judge choral composition contest Hawaii Found. on Culture and Arts, Honolulu, 1984, 85; pianist Kahikuonalani Ch., Honolulu, 1987—, Ch. Choral Ensemble, 1987—; tchr. Sunday Sch., 1988—. Mem., asst. accompanist Honolulu Opera Guild, 1955-59. Mem. Am. Choral Dirs. Assn., Soc. Gen. Music Tchrs. (sec. 1989-90), Music Educators Nat. Conf., Hawaii Music Educators Assn. Democrat. Mem. United Ch. of Christ. Avocations: reading, gardening, baking. Office: Highlands Child Care Ctr 757 Hoomalu St Pearl City HI 96782-2711

RHINES, PETER BROOMELL, oceanographer, atmospheric scientist; b. Hartford, Conn., July 23, 1942; s. Thomas B. and Olive (Symonds) R.; m. Marie Louise Lenos, Oct. 12, 1968; (div. 1983); m. Linda Jean Mattson; 1 child, Andrew Nelson. B.S., M.S., M.I.T., Cambridge U., 1964; Ph.D., Trinity Coll., Cambridge U., Eng., 1967. Asst. prof. oceanography M.I.T., Cambridge, 1968-71; rsch. asst. dept. applied math. and theoretical physics Cambridge U., Eng., 1971-72; scientist Woods Hole Oceanographic Inst., Woods Hole, Mass., 1972-84; prof. oceanography and atmospheric scis. U. Wash., Seattle, 1984—; vis. fellow Christ's Coll., Cambridge, Eng., 1979-80, 1983. Recipient de Florez research award MIT, 1963; NSF fellow, 1963-64; Guggenheim fellow, 1979-80; Queen's fellow in marine scis., Australia, 1988; A.E. Sloan Research scholar MIT, 1960-63; Marshall scholar Cambridge, 1964-67; Green scholar U. Calif., San Diego, 1981. Fellow Am. Geophys. Union, Am. Meterol. Soc.; mem. Nat. Acad. Scis. Avocations: guitar, walking, studying the global environment. Home: 5753 61st Ave NE Seattle WA 98105-2037 Office: Sch Oceanography U Wash WB-10 Seattle WA 98195

RHINESMITH, STEPHEN HEADLEY, international management consultant; b. Mineola, N.Y., Dec. 13, 1942; s. Homer Kern and Winifred Headley (Long) R.; m. Kathleen Alys Law, Aug. 28, 1965; children: Chrisopher Law, Colin Headley. BA (Baker scholar), Wesleyan U., 1965; M in Pub. and Internat. Affairs, (Heinz fellow), U. Pitts., 1966, PhD (NDEA fellow), 1972. Dir. internat. svcs. McBer and Co., Cambridge, Mass., 1969-71; pres. AFS Intercultural Programs, N.Y.C., 1972-80, 87-89, Holland Am. Cruises, N.Y.C., 1980-82, Moran, Stahl, Boyer, N.Y.C., 1982-84, Rhinesmith & Assocs. Inc., N.Y.C., 1984—; named amb., coord. Pres.'s U.S.-Soviet Exch. Initiative, 1986-87; chmn. dept. orgnl. sociology Moscow State U., 1991-96. Author: Bring Home the World: A Management Guide for Community Leaders of International Programs, 1975, 85; A Manager's Guide to Globalization: Six Skills for Success in a Changing World, 1993, 2d edit., 1996. Mem. ASTD (chair 1994), Met. Club (Washington). Office: 1 Devonshire Pl Apt 3513 Boston MA 02109-3517

RHO, EDWARD, information systems professional; b. Naples, Italy, Nov. 10, 1941; s. Pasquale and Rosa (Esposito) Rho; m. Lorraine Therese Craveira. BS equivalency, U. Naples, Taranto, Italy, 1964; postgrad., various schs., 1986-90. Programmer, analyst Cross & Brown, N.Y.C., 1967-69; project leader, sr. programmer, analyst Honfed Bank, 1970-81; d.p. cons., project mgr., sr. programmer, analyst Fin. Banking, Ins. and other orgns., Honolulu, 1981-83; cons., project mgr. MTL, Inc., Honolulu, 1983-84; data base analyst, chief analyst, project mgr. Universo Assicurazioni, Bologna, Italy, 1984-86; sr. programmer, analyst, project leader Allied Forces So. Europe/NATO, Naples, Italy, 1986-88; data base analyst, sr. systems analyst, acting task mgr. Planning Rsch. Corp./Hickam AFB, Aiea, Hawaii, 1989; sr. systems analyst, project leader, quality assurance rep. U.S. Dept. Def., Am. Express Bank, Ltd., Merchants Nat. Bank, Honolulu, 1989-90; data processing systems analyst V, project mgr. State of Hawaii/Exec. Br. Budget and Fin. Dept., 1990-91, data processing systems analyst VI, project mgr./sect. chief, 1991—. Designer, developer computer software. Mem. Hist. Hawaii Found., Friends of Italy Soc. of Hawaii, Sacred Heart League. Home: 47-409 Lulani St Kaneohe HI 96744-4718 Office: State of Hawaii Dept Acctg & Gen Svcs 1151 Punchbowl St Honolulu HI 96813-3007

RHOADES, DENNIS KEITH, legal foundation administrator; b. Burbank, Calif., Aug. 1, 1944; s. Charles Bernis Rhoades and Madeline Fern (Miller) Regan; m. Julie Rae Zukovsky, Nov. 10, 1970 (div. Sept. 1984). BA, UCLA, 1966; postgrad., U. Wyoming, 1970-71. Spl. asst. to gen. counsel VA, Washington, 1978-79; field ops. dir. VA, L.A., 1983-84; exec. dir. White House Vets. Com., Washington, 1980-81, Vietnam Vets. Am., Washington, 1984-85; nat. econs. dir. Am. Legion, Washington, 1985-88; exec. dir. Agt. Orange Class Assistance Program, Washington, 1989—; bd. dirs. Inst. for Vets. Studies Purdue U., 1979-81; mem. vets. com. Office of Sec. Labor, Washington, 1984-88, readjustment adv. com. VA, Washington, 1985-88; exec. com. Pres.'s Com. on Employment of People with Disabilities, Washington, 1987-89. Author: (with others) Viet Vet Survival Guide, 1985; prin. editor: Legacy of Vietnam Veterans, 1995. With U.S. Army, 1967-70, S.E. Asia. Recipient Outstanding Young Man in Am. award U.S. Jaycees, 1978, Outstanding Svc. award Nat. Assn. Concerned Vets., 1980, Profl. Svc. award Fed. Exec. Bd., 1985, Leadership award Pres.'s Com. on Employment of People with Disabilities, 1988. Mem. VFW, Vietnam Vets. Am., Am. Legion. Democrat. Avocations: fiction writing, oil painting, American history, amateur astronomy. Office: Agt Orange Class Assistance Program PO Box 27413 Washington DC 20038-7413

RHOADES, JOHN SKYLSTEAD, SR., federal judge; b. 1925; m. Carmel Rhoades; children: Mark, John, Matthew, Peter, Christopher. AB, Stanford U., 1948; JD, U. Calif., San Francisco, 1951. Prosecuting atty. City of San Diego, 1955-56, dep. city atty., 1956-57; pvt. practice San Diego, 1957-60; ptnr. Rhoades, Hollywood & Neil, San Diego, 1960-85; judge U.S. Dist. Ct. (so. dist.) Calif., San Diego, 1985—. With USN, 1943-46. Office: US Dist Ct 940 Front St San Diego CA 92101-8994

RHOADES, MARYE FRANCES, paralegal; b. Ft. Defiance, Va., Jan. 29, 1937; d. Silas Caswell Sr. and Mary Ann Frances (James) Rhodes; m. Minter James Rowe, May 1964 (div. 1968); children: Margaret Frances Omar, James Robert; m. Robert Charles Rhoades Jr., July 25, 1980. Student, Coll. W.Va., 1956-58, 68, U. Charleston, 1962-63, 74, 89, Antioch U., 1972-73; grad., Mike Tyree Sch. Real Estate, 1984, Evans Coll. Legal Studies, 1990. Educator Nicholas County Sch. Sys., Summersville, W.Va., 1958-61; edit. staff, columnist, staff writer, reporter, photographer Beckley Newspapers Corp., 1962-76; educator Raleigh County Bd. Edn., Beckley, W.Va., 1967-68; exec. editor, columnist Local News Jour., Whitesville, W.Va., 1976-77; libr. bookmobile, asst. ref. libr., outreach coord. Raleigh County Pub. Libr., Beckley, 1977-78; agt. Combined Ins. Co., Chgo., 1978-79; legal sec., paralegal W.Va. Legal Svcs. Inc., Beckley, 1979-82; paralegal Applachian Rsch and Defense Fund Inc., Beckley, 1982-83; exec. dir., owner Rhoades and Rowe, Beckley, 1983-85; paralegal patinet advocate Comty. Health Sys. Inc., Beckley, 1986-96; pvt. practice Beckley, 1996—. Contbr. articles to mags. State bd. dirs., pub. resl. LWV, Beckley; pub. rels., various coms. Raleigh County Dem. Women, Beckley; sec., pub. rels. Orchard Valley Women's Club, Crab Orchard, W.Va.; trustee Fraternal Order Eagles; pub. rels., various coms. Loyal Order Moose, Beckley, Beckley Profl. Bus. Women; com. mem. Nat. Coalition to Save the New River; sales rep. So. U.S. Rep. to U.S. Mil. Acad., West Point, N.Y.; active Am. Legion Aux., Mullens, W.Va. Mem. NEA, Classroom Tchrs. Assn., Nat. Paralegal Assn., Nat. Fedn. Paralegals Assn., Nat. Ind. Paralegals Assn., Nat. Com. Save Soc., Sec. Medicare, Nat. Legal Aid and Def. Assn., Nat. Orgn. Social Security Claimants Reps., State Soc. Sec. Task Force, Nat. Vets. Legal Svcs. Project Inc., W.Va. U. Alumni Assn., Community AIDS Edn. Com., W.Va. Edn. Assn. Democrat. Pentacostal Holiness. Avocations: creative arts and music, walking, NASCAR, doll collecting. Home: PO Box 416 Mac Arthur WV 25873-0416 Office: Benefit Services PO Box 7265 Sprague WV 25926

RHOADES, RODNEY ALLEN, physiologist, educator; b. Greenville, Ohio, Jan. 5, 1939; s. John H. and Floris L. Rhoades; m. Judith Ann Brown, Aug. 6, 1961; children: Annelisa, Kirsten. BS, Miami U., 1961, MS, 1963; PhD, Ohio State U., 1966. Asst. prof. Pa. State U., State College, 1966-72, assoc. prof., 1972-75; rsch. scientist NIH, Bethesda, Md., 1975-76; prof. Ind. U. Sch. Medicine, Indpls., 1976-81, prof., chmn., 1981—; dir. Indpls. Ctr. for Advanced Rsch. Author: Physiology, 1984; contbr. articles to profl. jours. Recipient NASA fellow, 1964-66, Rsch. Career Devel. award NIH, 1975-80. Mem. Am. Physiol. Soc., Am. Heart Assn., Am. Thoracic Soc., Biophysics Soc., Sigma Xi. Home: 1768 Spruce Dr Carmel IN 46033-9025 Office: Ind U Sch Medicine 635 Barnhill Dr Indianapolis IN 46202-5126

RHOADS, GEORGE GRANT, medical epidemiologist; b. Phila., Feb. 11, 1940; s. Jonathan Evans and Teresa (Folin) R.; m. Frances Ann Secker, June 5, 1965; children: Thomas C., James E. MD, Harvard U., 1965; MPH, U. Hawaii, 1970. Intern Hosp. of U. Pa., Phila., 1965-66, resident in internal medicine, 1966-68; resident in preventive medicine U. Hawaii Sch. Pub. Health, 1968-71; epidemiologist Japan-Hawaii Cancer Study, Honolulu, 1974-75; assoc. prof. U. Hawaii, Honolulu, 1974-79, chair dept. pub. health sci., 1978-81, dir. gen. preventive medicine, 1978-81, prof. pub. health, 1979-82; chief epidemiology br. Nat. Inst. Child Health and Human Devel./NIH, Bethesda, Md., 1982-89; prof., dir. grad program in pub. health U. Medicine and Dentistry N.J.-Robert Wood Johnson Med. Sch., Piscataway, 1989—. Contbr. more than 130 articles on the epidemiology of non-infectious diseases to profl. jours. Recipient Dirs. award NIH, 1987, EEO award NICHD, 1984. Fellow Am. Coll. Physicians; mem. Am. Epidemiol. Soc. Mem. Soc. of Friends. Achievements include research on the protective effect of high density Lipoprotein in the blood against development of heart attacks. Office: Environ and Occupl Health Scis Inst PO Box 1179 681 Frelinghuysen Rd Piscataway NJ 08855-1179

RHOADS, GERALDINE EMELINE, editor; b. Phila., Jan. 29, 1914; d. Lawrence Dry and Alice Fegley (Rice) R. A.B., Bryn Mawr Coll., 1935. Publicity asst. Bryn Mawr (Pa.) Coll., 1935-37; asst. Internat. Students House, Phila., 1937-39; mng. editor The Woman mag., N.Y.C., 1939-42; editor Life Story mag., 1942-45, Today's Woman mag., N.Y.C., 1945-52, Today's Family Mag., N.Y.C., 1952-53; lectr. Columbia U., 1954-56; assoc. editor Readers Digest, 1954-55; producer NBC, 1955-56; assoc. editor Ladies Home Jour., 1956-62, mng. editor, 1962-63; exec. editor McCall's mag., 1963-66; editor Woman's Day mag., 1966-82, editorial dir., 1982-84; editorial dir. Woman's Day Resource Center, 1984-89; v.p. Woman's Day mag., 1972-77, 78-84, CBS Consumer Publs., 1977-84; cons. Woman's Day, N.Y.C., 1989-91; editorial cons., dir. Nat. Mag. Awards, 1991-94. Author: (with others) Woman's Day Help Book, 1988. Recipient award for profl. achievement Diet Workshop Internat., 1977; Elizabeth Cutter Morrow award YWCA Salute to Women in Bus., 1977; Recipient Econ. Equity award Women's Equity Action League, 1982; March of Dimes Women Editor's citation, 1982. Mem. Nat. Press Club (dir.), Fashion Group (bd. govs. 1977-79, 87-88, chmn. bd. govs. 1978-80, treas. bd. govs. 1983-85, bd. dirs. Found. 1980-81), Am. Soc. Mag. Editors (chmn. exec. com. 1971-73), N.Y. Women in Comms. (Matrix award 1975), Advt. Women in N.Y. (bd. govs. 1983-85, 2d v.p. 1985-87, 1st v.p. 1987-89, bd. dirs. 1989-90, Pres.'s award 1987), Women's Forum (bd. dirs. 1985-87), YWCA Acad. Women Achievers, Women's City Club of N.Y. (bd. dirs. 1996—), Literacy Vols. of N.Y.C. (bd. dirs. 1986-93), Turtle Bay Assn. (bd. dirs. 1989-92), Bryn Mawr Coll. Alumni Assn. (bd. dirs. 1989-94), Bryn Mawr Club of N.Y.C. (bd. dirs. 1994—). Home: # 21M 185 W End Ave Apt 21M New York NY 10023-5549

RHOADS, JAMES BERTON, archivist, former government official, consultant, educator; b. Sioux City, Iowa, Sept. 17, 1928; s. James Harrison and Mary (Keenan) R.; m. S. Angela Handy, Aug. 12, 1947; children: Cynthia Patrice Neven, James Berton, Marcia Marie MacKellar. Student, Southwestern Jr. Coll., 1946-47, Union Coll., Lincoln, Neb., 1947-48; BA, U. Calif.-Berkeley, 1950, MA, 1952; PhD, Am. U., 1965. With GSA-Nat. Archives and Records Service, Washington, 1952-79; asst. archivist for civil archives GSA-Nat. Archives and Records Service, 1965, dept. archivist U.S., 1966-68, archivist U.S., 1968-79; chmn. Nat. Archives Trust Fund Bd., 1968-79; chmn. adminstrv. com. Fed. Register, 1968-79; chmn. Nat. Hist. Publs. and Records Commn., 1968-79; mem. Fed. Council on Arts and Humanities, 1970-79; pres. Rhoads Assos. Internat., 1980-84; dir. grad. program in archives and records mgmt. Western Wash. U., Bellingham, 1984-94, prof. history, 1987—, dir. Ctr. for Pacific N.W. studies, 1994—; prof. emeritus, 1994—. Trustee Woodrow Wilson Internat. Center for Scholars, 1969-79; v.p. Intergovtl. Coun. UNESCO Info. Program, 1977-79; mem. adv. bd. Wash. State Hist. Records, 1990—. Recipient Meritorious and Disting. Service awards GSA, 1966, 68, 79. Fellow Soc. Am. Archivists (pres. 1974-75); mem. Internat. Coun. Archives (pres. 1976-79), Am. Antiquarian Soc., Am. Coun. Learned Socs. (com. Soviet-Am. archival coop. 1986-91), Mass. Hist. Soc. (corr.), Wash. State Hist. Soc. (trustee 1986-95), Acad. Cert. Archivists (pres. 1992-94).

RHOADS, JONATHAN EVANS, surgeon; b. Phila., May 9, 1907; s. Edward G. and Margaret (Ely Paxson) R.; m. Teresa Folin, July 4, 1936 (dec. 1987); children: Margaret Rhoads Kendon, Jonathan Evans Jr., George Grant, Edward Otto Folin, Philip Garrett, Charles James; m. Katharine Evans Goddard, Oct. 13, 1990. BA, Haverford Coll., 1928, DSc (hon.), 1962; MD, Johns Hopkins U., 1932; D. Med. Sci., U. Pa., 1940, LLD (hon.), 1960; DSc (hon.), Swarthmore Coll., 1969, Hahnemann Med. Coll., 1978, Duke U., 1979, Med. Coll. Ohio, 1985; DSc (Med.) (hon.), Med. Coll. Pa., 1974, Georgetown U., 1981, Yale U., 1990; LittD (hon.), Thomas Jefferson U., 1979. Intern Hosp. of U. Pa., 1932-34, fellow, instr. surgery, 1934-39; assoc. surgery, surg. research U. Pa. Med. Sch., Grad. Sch. Medicine, 1939-47, asst. prof. surg. research, 1944-47, asst. prof. surgery, 1946-47, assoc. prof., 1947-49; J. William White prof. surg. research U. Pa., 1949-51; prof. surgery Grad. Sch. Medicine, U. Pa., 1950—; prof. surgery and surg. research U. Pa. Sch. Med., 1951-57, prof. surgery, 1957-59; provost U. Pa., 1956-59, provost emeritus, 1977—, John Rhea Barton prof. surgery, chmn. dept. surgery, 1959-72, prof. surgery, 1972—, acting dir. Harrison dept. surg. research, 1944-46, asst. dir., 1946-59, dir., 1959-72; chief surgery Hosp. U. Pa., 1959-72, chmn. med. bd., 1959-61; dir. surgery Pa. Hosp., 1972-74; surg. cons. Pa. Hosp., Germantown (Pa.); mem. staff Hosp. of U. Pa.; mem. bd. pub. edn., City of Phila., 1965-69; co-chmn. Phila. Mayor's Commn. on Health Aspects of Trash to Steam Plant, 1986, chief justice Pa. Com. on Phila. Traffic Ct.; former mem. bd. mgrs. Haverford Coll., chmn., 1963-72, pres. corp., 1963-78, emeritus bd. mgrs. 1989—; bd. mgrs. Friends Hosp. of Phila., 1952—; trustee Coriell Inst. Med. Rsch., 1957-90, v.p. sci. affairs, 1964-76, life trustee, 1990—; trustee GM Cancer Rsch. Found.; chmn. bd. trustees Measey Found.; trustee emeritus Bryn Mawr Coll.; mem. com. in charge Westtown Sch., 1962-94, emeritus, 1994; treas. Germantown Friends Sch.; cons. Bur. State Services, VA, 1963; cons. to divsn. med. scis. NIH, 1962-63; nat. adv. gen. medical scis. council USPHS, 1963; adv. council Life Ins. Med. Research Fund., 1961-66; Pres. Phila. div., 1955-56; chmn. adv. commn. on research on pathogenesis of cancer Am. Cancer Soc., 1956-57, del., 1956-61, dir. at large, 1965—, pres., 1969-70, past officer dir., 1970-77, hon. life mem., 1977—; chmn. surgery adv. com. Food and Drug Adminstrn., 1972-74; chmn. Nat. Cancer Adv. Bd., 1972-79; Mem. Am. Bd. Surgery, 1963-69, sr. mem., 1969—. Author, co-editor: Surgery: Principles and Practice, 1957, 61, 65, 70; author: (with J.M. Howard) The Chemistry of Trauma; mem. editl. bd. Jour. Surg. Rsch., 1960-71, Oncology Times, 1979—; co-editor: Accomplishments in Cancer research, 1979-94; editor Jour. Cancer, 1972-91, editor emeritus, 1991—, Festschrift Dedicated in Cancer, 1997; editl. bd. Annals of Surgery, 1947-77, emeritus, 1977-95, sr. 1995—, chmn. 1971-73; editl. adv. bd. Guthrie Bull., 1986—; contbr. articles to med. jours., chpts. to books. Trustee John Rhea Barton Surg. Found. Recipient Roswell Park medal, 1973, Papanicolaou award, 1977, Phila. award, 1976, Swanberg award, 1987, Benjamin Franklin medal Am. Philos. Soc., Medal of the Surgeon Gen. of U.S., Disting. Alumnus award U. Pa., 1993, Russell W. Richie award Friends Hosp. Phila., 1994, Presdl. award Nat. Assn. Psychiat. Health Systems, 1994; hon. Benjamin Franklin fellow Royal Soc. Arts; Patient Care Pavilion at Hosp. U. Pa. named in honor of Jonathan Evans Rhoads, 1994, Clarence E. Shaffrey S.J. medal 1996, Cosmos Club award, 1997. Fellow Am. Med. Writers Assn., Am. Surg. Assn., Am. Philos. Soc. (sec. 1963-66, pres. 1976-84), ACS (regent, chmn. bd. regents 1967-69, pres. 1971-72), Royal Coll. Surgeons (Eng.) (hon.), Royal Coll. Surgeons Edinburgh (hon.), Deutsches Gesellschaft für Chirurgie (corr.), Assn. Surgeons India (hon.), Royal Coll. Physicians and Surgeons Can. (hon.), Coll. Medicine South Africa (hon.), Polish Assn. Surgeons (hon.), Royal Coll. Surgeons in Ireland (hon.), AAAS (sec. med. sci. sect. 1980-86); mem. Hollandsche Maatschappij der Wetenschappen (fgn.), Am. Public Health Assn., Assn. Am. Med. Colls. (chmn. council acad. socs. 1968-69, disting. service mem. 1974—), Fedn. Am. Socs. Exptl. Biology, Am. Assn. Surgery Trauma (Fitts lectr., 1995), Am. Soc. Clin. Nutrition, Am. Trauma Soc. (founding mem., chmn. bd. dirs. 1986-94, Curtis Artz award 1996), AMA (co-recipient Goldberger award 1970, Dr. Rodman and Thomas G. Sheen award 1980), Pa. Med. Soc. (mem. jud. coun. 1991-94, vice chmn. 1994-96, chmn. 1996, Disting. Svc. award 1975), Phila. County Med. Soc. (pres. 1970, Strittmater award 1968), Coll. Physicians Phila. (v.p. 1954-57, pres. 1958-60, Disting. Svc. award 1987), Phila. Acad. Surgery (pres. 1964-66. Ann. Oration named for Jonathan E. Rhoads 1985), Phila. Physiol. Soc. (v.p. 1945-46), Am. Surg. Assn. (pres. 1972-73, Disting. Service medal, trustee found., vice chmn. 1992-96, Flance/Karl award 1997), Pan Pacific Surg. Assn. (v.p. 1975-77), So. Surg. Assn., The Internat. Surg. Group (pres. 1958), Internat. Fedn. Surg. Colls. (v.p. 1972-78, pres. 1978-81, hon. pres. 1987—), Fellows of Am. Studies, Soc. of U. Surgeons, Soc. Clin. Surgery (pres. 1966-68), Am. Assn. for Cancer Research, Am. Chem. Soc., Am. Physiol. Soc., Coun. Biology Editors, Internat. Soc. Surgery (hon.) N.Y. Acad. Scis., Surg. Infection Soc. (pres. 1984-85), Surgeons Travel Club (pres. 1976, hon. mem.), Am. Inst. Nutrition, World Med. Assn., Am. Acad. Arts and Scis. (mem. coun. 1977-81), Inst. of Medicine (sr.), Soc. for Surgery Alimentary Tract (pres. 1967-68), Southeastern Surg. Congress, Soc. Surg. Chmn. (pres. 1966-68), Buckingham Mountain Found. (sec., treas., pres., 1996—), James IV Soc. (hon.), Phi Beta Kappa, Alpha Omega Alpha, Sigma Xi. Clubs: Rittenhouse, Union League, Philadelphia; Cosmos (D.C.). Achievements include demonstration that protein malnutrition could retard callus formation in experimental fractures and that positive nitrogen balance could be induced in protein deficient patients who could not take things by mouth. Office: 3400 Spruce St Philadelphia PA 19104

RHOADS, NANCY GLENN, lawyer; b. Washington, Oct. 15, 1957; d. Donald L. and Gerry R. R.; m. Robert A. Koons, June 23, 1984. BA, Gettysburg Coll., 1980; JD, Temple U., 1983. Bar: Pa., U.S. Dist. Ct. (ea. dist.) Pa. 1983. Rsch. asst. Prof. Mikochick, Phila., 1982-83; law clk. Phila. Ct. of Common Pleas, 1983-85; assoc. Post and Schell P.C., Phila., 1985-90, Sheller, Ludwig and Badey, Phila., 1990—. Co-author: Aging and the Aged: Problems, Opportunities, Challenges, 1980. Vol. Spl. Olympics. Mem. Phila. Bar Assn. (med. legal com.), Phi Beta Kappa, Phi Alpha Theta, Pi Delta Epsilon, Eta Sigma Phi. Avocations: classical piano, horticulture, swimming. Home: Gwynedd Knoll 1374 Tanglewood Dr North Wales PA 19454-3671 Office: Sheller Ludwig and Badey 1528 Walnut St Philadelphia PA 19102-3604

RHOADS, PAUL KELLY, lawyer; b. La Grange, Ill., Sept. 4, 1940; s. Herbert Graves and Mary Margaret (Gurrie) R.; m. Katheryn Virginia Reissaus, Sept. 14, 1963; children: Elizabeth R. Saline, Katheryn R. Meek, Julia S. BA, Washington & Lee U., 1962; JD, Loyola U., Chgo., 1967. Bar: Ill. 1967, U.S. Dist. Ct. (no. dist.) Ill. 1967, U.S. Tax Ct. 1980. Trust officer 1st Nat. Bank Chgo., 1963-69; with Schiff Hardin & Waite, Chgo., 1969—, ptnr., 1973—; bd. dirs. McKay Enterprises, Chgo., Haymarsh Corp., Glen Ellyn, Ill., Philanthrophy Roundtable, Washington. Author: Starting a Private Foundation, 1993; contbr. articles to profl. jours. and chpts. to books. Trustee Ill. Inst. Tech., 1985-95, Western Springs (Ill.) Hist. Soc., 1983-92; bd. dirs. Cyrus Tang Scholarship Found., 1984-91; bd. overseers Ill. Inst. Tech. Chgo.-Kent Coll. Law, 1985-95; pres., bd. dirs. Grover Hermann Found., Chgo., 1984—; sec., bd. dirs. Western Springs Svc. Club, 1976-86; sec. Vandivort Properties, Inc., Cape Girardeau, Mo.; mem. adv. com. estate, tax and fin. planning Loyola U., 1986-92; adv. com. Thomas A. Roe Inst. for Econ. Policy Studies, Heritage Found., 1989—. Mem. Ill. State Bar Assn., Chgo. Bar Assn., Union League, Salt Creek Club (Hinsdale, Ill.) (pres. 1982, bd. dirs. 1981-83), Portage Lake Yacht Club (Onekama, Mich.) (commodore 1988, bd. dirs. 1985-89), Manistee (Mich.) Golf and Country Club. Republican. Avocations: sailing, golf, tennis. Office: Schiff Hardin & Waite 233 S Wacker Dr Chicago IL 60606-6306

RHOADS, STEVEN ERIC, political science educator; b. Abington, Pa., May 12, 1939; s. John Reginald and Barbara Ann (Dugan) R.; m. Diana Cabanis Akers, May 17, 1944; children—Christopher, Nicholas, John. B.A., Princeton U., 1961; M.P.A., Cornell U., 1965, Ph.D., 1972. Mem. staff Office Mgmt. and Budget, Washington, 1965-66; asst. prof. dept. govt. and fgn. affairs U. Va., Charlottesville, 1970-76, assoc. prof., 1977-86, prof. 1986—. Served to lt. (j.g.) USN, 1961-63. Fellow NEH, Inst. Ednl. Affairs, Earhart Found., Bradley Found., Olin Found. Mem. Am. Polit. Sci. Assn., Assn. Pub. Policy and Mgmt. Author: Policy Analysis in the Federal Aviation Administration, 1974; Valuing Life: Public Policy Dilemmas, 1980; The Economist's View of the World: Government, Markets and Public Policy, 1985, Incomparable Worth: Pay Equity Meets the Market, 1993; contbr. articles to profl. publs. Home: 3190 Dundee Rd Earlysville VA 22936-9621 Office: U Va Dept Govt and Fgn Affairs Cabell Hall 232 Charlottesville VA 22903

RHODE, ALFRED SHIMON, business consultant, educator; b. Vienna, Austria, July 31, 1928; s. Aron and Olga (Schwarz) Rothkirch; came to U.S., 1940, naturalized, 1949; m. Phyllis Mazur, Dec. 28, 1959; children: Yael, Tamar, Yvette, Liane. BCE, CUNY, 1950; MEA, George Washington U., 1959; PhD, Am. U., 1973. Engr., Bur. of Reclamation, Sacramento, 1950-52; various engring. positions U.S. Govt., 1954-63; head logistics rsch. Navy Supply Systems Command, Washington, 1963-68; head support forces, manpower and logistics br. Navy Program Planning Office, Washington, 1968-75; sr. v.p. nat. security analysis and warfare support group Info. Spectrum, Inc., Arlington, Va., 1976-89, cons., 1989-92; professorial lectr. George Washington U., Washington, 1969-75; adj. faculty Sch. Bus. Adminstrn. George Mason U., Fairfax, Va., 1990—; exec. dir. Montgomery County Retail Security and Loss Prevention Assn. Contbr. articles to profl. jours. Served to capt. USAF, 1952-54. Congl. fellow, 1962. Registered profl. engr., Md. Fellow Mil. Ops. Rsch. Soc. (1st v.p., dir.); mem. Inst. Ops. Rsch. and Mgmt. Scis. (chmn. mil. applications sect.), Washington Ops. Rsch. Sci. Coun., Internat. Inst. Strategic Studies. Home: 8305 Fox Run Potomac MD 20854-2576

RHODE, DEBORAH LYNN, law educator; b. Jan. 29, 1952. BA, Yale U., 1974, JD, 1977. Bar: D.C. 1977, Calif. 1981. Law clk. to judge U.S. Ct. Appeals (2d cir.), N.Y.C., 1977-78; law clk. to Hon. Justice Thurgood Marshall U.S. Supreme Ct., D.C., 1978-79; asst. prof. law Stanford (Calif.) U., 1979-82, assoc. prof., 1982-85, prof., 1985—; dir. Inst. for Rsch. on Women and Gender, 1986-90, Keck Ctr. of Legal Ethics and The Legal Profession, 1994—; trustee Yale U., 1983-89; chmn. profl. responsibility sect. Assn. Am. Law Schs., co-chmn. ABA com. profl. responsibility, pres.-elect., 1997. Author several books; contbr. articles to profl. jours. Office: Stanford U Law Sch Crown Quadrangle Stanford CA 94305

RHODE, EDWARD ALBERT, veterinary medicine educator, veterinary cardiologist; b. Amsterdam, N.Y., July 25, 1926; s. Edward A. and Katherine (Webb) R.; m. Dolores Bangert, 1955; children: David E., Peter R., Paul W., Robert M., Catherine E. DVM, Cornell U., 1947. Diplomate Am. Coll. Veterinary Internal Medicine. Prof. emeritus vet. medicine U. Calif., Davis, 1964—, chmn. dept. vet. medicine, 1968-71, assoc. dean instrn. Sch. Vet. Medicine, 1971-77, 78-81, dean sch. Vet. Medicine, 1982-91. Mem. AAAS, Nat. Acad. Practices, Am. Coll. Vet. Internal Medicine, Am. Vet. Medicine Assn., Basic Sci. Coun., Am. Heart Assn., Am. Acad. Vet. Cardiology, Am. Physiol. Soc., Calif. Vet. Medicine Assn. Office: U Calif Sch Vet Medicine Davis CA 95616

RHODES, ALFRED WILLIAM, former insurance company executive; b. Manchester, Eng., Dec. 20, 1922; came to U.S., 1930, naturalized, 1943; s. William Henry and Agnes Anna (King) R.; m. Joan Helen LaVine, Oct. 12, 1947; children: Alfred William, Ellen Jeanne, Thomas John, Phyllis Irene, Kenneth James. BS, Hofstra U., 1947; AMP, Harvard U., 1967. With John Hancock Mut. Life Ins. Co., Boston, 1942-85; regional supr. John Hancock Mut. Life Ins. Co., 1953-54, field v.p., 1954-69, 2d v.p., 1969-71, v.p., 1971-74, sr. v.p., 1974-85; ret., 1985. Past pres. Needham (Mass.) Youth Soccer Program; host family Mass. chpt. Am. Field Service, 1971-72, pres., 1972-75; mem. Town of Needham Finance Com., 1973-80. Served with AUS, 1943-46. Decorated Bronze Star. Mem. AARP (instr. and counselor tax counseling for the elderly), Nat. Assn. Life Underwriters, Gen. Agts. and Mgrs. Conf., Life Underwriter Tng. Coun. (past trustee), Life Ins. Mktg. and Rsch. Assn. (past bd. dirs.), CLUs, Club Med, Sandpiper Golf Club. Episcopalian. Home: 1761 SE Adair Rd Port Saint Lucie FL 34952-5739

RHODES, ALICE GRAHAM, lawyer; b. Phila., June 15, 1941; d. Peter Graham III and Fannie Isadora (Bennett) Graham; m. Charles Milton Rhodes, Oct. 14, 1971 (div. Apr. 21, 1997); children: Helen, Carla, Shauna. BS, East Stroudsburg U. Pa., 1962; MS, U. Pa., 1966, LLB, 1969, JD, 1970. Bar: N.Y. 1970, U.S. Dist. Ct. (so. and ea. dists.) N.Y. 1971, U.S. Ct. Appeals (2d cir.) 1971, Ky. 1983, U.S. Dist. Ct. (ea. dist.) Ky. 1985, 69-72. Staff atty. Harlem Assertion Rights, Mobilization of Youth Office Econ. Opportunity, N.Y.C., 1969-70, coord. Cmty. Action Legal Svcs., 1970-72; assoc. dir. in charge of civil representation HUD Model Cities Cmty. Law Offices, N.Y.C., 1972-73; resource assoc. Commn. on Women, N.C. Dept. Adminstrn., Raleigh, 1975-76; mgr. policies and procedures Div. for Youth, N.C. Dept. Human Resources, Raleigh, 1976; petroleum atty. Ashland (Ky.), Inc. (formerly Ashland Oil, Inc.), 1980-82; corp. atty. Ashland (Ky.), Inc., 1985-87, 88-91; Ashland City Commn. Human Rights, 1993—; bd. regents Ea. Ky. U., 1994—; mem. task force on sex discrimination ins. N.C. Dept. Ins., 1976; mem. disciplinary appeals com. bd. regents Ea. Ky. U., 1994—; mem. Property Valuation Appeals Commn., 1994; pub. mem. selection and performance stds. review bd. Fgn. Svc., U.S. Dept. State, 1995. Mem. Usher bd. New Hope Bapt. Ch., Ashland, 1980-94; bd. dirs. YWCA Ashland, 1983-84; bd. dirs. Ashland Heritage Pk. Commn., 1983-85; bd. dirs., budget com. United Way, Greenup County, Ashland, 1988-92; driver Meals on Wheels, Ashland, 1983-91; vol. Am. Heart Assn., 1982-91; bd. dirs. Our Lady of Bellefonte Hosp. Found. (Franciscan Sisters of the Poor), 1996—, County Dem. Women, 1996, Carter G. Woodson Found. Study Afro-Am. Life and History; mem. adv. com. task force post secondary edn. Gov. of Ky. Recipient Cmty. Svc. award Queens Community Corp., N.Y.C., 1972, Ashland C.C., 1986, Cmty. Svc. award NAACP, Ky.; NSF fellow, 1964, 65, Reginald Heber Smith fellow 1969; faculty friends of Pa. scholar U. Pa., 1966-69, postgrad. fellow cmty. law, 1969-71; named to Hon. Order of Ky. Cols., 1989. Fellow Ky. Bar Found.; mem. AAUW (bd. dirs. Phila. chpt. 1963-65), Nat. Bar Assn., N.Y. Bar, Ky. Bar Assn., Boyd County Bar Assn., Ky. Assn. Black Pub. Adminstrs., Nat. Forum Black Pub. Adminstrs., Pilot Club (exec. bd. Ashland 1983), Links, Inc., Paramount Women's Assn., Penn Club Alliance, Aux. Our Lady of Bellefonte Hosp., Pub. Mems. Assn. of Fgn. Svc. Democrat. Avocations: interior decorating, sports, dancing, gourmet cooking, travel. Home: 507 Country Club Dr Ashland KY 41101-2143

RHODES, ANN L., theatrical producer, invester; b. Ft. Worth, Oct. 17, 1941; d. Jon Knox and Carol Jane (Greene) R.; student Tex. Christian U., 1960-63. V.p. Rhodes Enterprises Inc., Ft. Worth, 1963-77; owner-mgr. Lucky R Ranch, Ft. Worth, 1969—, Ann L. Rhodes Investments, Ft. Worth, 1976—; pres., chmn. bd. ALR Enterprises, Inc., Ft. Worth, 1977-93; pres. ALR Prodns., Inc., 1993—. Bd. dirs. Tarrant Coun. Alcoholism, 1973-78, hon. bd. dirs., 1978—; bd. dirs. N.W. Tex. coun. Arthritis Found., 1977-84; adv. bd. Stage West, 1987—, Hip Pocket Theatre, 1994—; bd. dirs. Circle Theater, 1987-94, Arts Coun. of Ft. Worth and Tarrant County, 1991-94; bd. govs. Ft. Worth Theatre, 1989-93; mem. pro-arts bd. TCU Coll. Fine Arts & Communications, 1994; exec. com. Tarrant County Rep. Party, 1964-69; bd. dirs. Live Theatre League Tarrant County, 1993—, Casa Mañana Theatre, 1993—, exec. com., 1995—. Recipient various svc. awards, including Patron of Yr. award Live Theatre League Tarrant County, 1992-93. Mem. Jr. League Ft. Worth, Addison and Randolph Clark Soc. Tex. Christian U., Alpha Psi Omega, Kappa Kappa Gamma. Episcopalian. Office: Ste 908 Ridglea Bank Bldg Fort Worth TX 76116

RHODES, BETTY FLEMING, rehabilitation services professional, nurse; b. Franklin, Pa., Nov. 28, 1920; d. John and Twyla Odella (Callen) Fleming; m. Donald Muir Cain, Dec. 31, 1952 (div.); m. Lee Chester Rhodes, June 23, 1962. RN, Allegheny Gen. Hosp., Pitts., 1942. Lic. phys. therapist, Pa. Phys. therapist Ky. Soc. for Crippled Children, Louisville, 1947-51, St. Anthony Hosp., Louisville, 1953-78. Nurse U.S. Army, 1943-45; capt. Army Nurse Corps, 1951-52. Decorated Bronze Star. Mem. Am. Phys Therapy Assn. (pres. Ky. chpt.). Roman Catholic. Home: 5 Woodland Road Oak Pk Jeffersonville IN 47130

RHODES, CHARLES HARKER, JR., lawyer; b. Chgo., May 24, 1930; s. Charles Harker and Claire (Hepner) R.; m. Mae Ellen Svoboda, Apr. 19, 1952; children: Charles Harker, James Albert, Edward Joseph. BA, U. Chgo., 1948, JD, 1951. Bar: Ill. 1951. Assoc. Schatz & Busch, Chgo., 1951-53; assoc. Sonnenschein Nath & Rosenthal, Chgo., 1953-60, ptnr., 1961—; dir. Ill. Inst. for Continuing Legal Edn., Springfield, 1977-84, 86-88; pres. Ill. Bar Automated Rsch., 1975-85. Trustee Nat. Ctr. for Automated Info. Rsch., N.Y.C., 1976-94; pres. B.R. Ryall YMCA, Glen Ellyn, Ill., 1967. Fellow Am. Bar Found. (devel. com. 1988—), Chgo. Bar Found. (pres. 1977-80), Ill. Bar Found. (fellows chmn. 1990-91); mem. ABA (mem. tort and ins. practice sect., long range planning com. 1991-92, mem. pub. editorial bd. com. 1993—), Ill. State Bar Assn. (bd. govs. 1975-79, chmn. liaison com. Atty. Registration and Disciplinary Commn. 1992-93), Chgo. Bar Assn. (libr., bd. mgrs. 1969-72), Am. Arbitration Assn. (arbitrator), Nat. Conf. Bar Founds. (trustee, pres. 1987-88), Met. Club Chgo. Republican. Presbyterian. Avocations: world travel, photography. Home: 267 N Montclair Ave Glen Ellyn IL 60137-5508 Office: Sonnenschein Nath & Rosenthal 233 S Wacker Dr Ste 8000 Chicago IL 60606-6342

RHODES, DONALD ROBERT, musicologist, retired electrical engineer; b. Detroit, Dec. 31, 1923; s. Donald Eber and Edna Mae (Fulmer) R.; children: Joyce R. Bridges, Jane E., Roger C., Diane R. Herran. BEE, Ohio State U., 1945, MEE, 1948, PhD, 1953. Research assoc. Ohio State U., Columbus, 1945-54; research engr. Cornell Aero. Lab., Buffalo, 1954-57; head basic research dept. Radiation, Inc., Orlando, Fla., 1957-61; sr. scientist Radiation, Inc., Melbourne, Fla., 1961-66; Univ. prof. N.C. State U., Raleigh, 1966-94, univ. prof. emeritus, 1994—. Author: Introduction to Monopulse, 1959, 2d edit., 1980, Synthesis of Planar Antenna Sources, 1974, A Reactance Theorem, 1977. Co-founder Central Fla. Community Orch., Winter Park, 1961, pres., 1961-62. Recipient Benjamin G. Lamme medal Ohio State U., 1975; Eminent Engr. award Tau Beta Pi, 1976; named to N.C. State U. Acad. Outstanding Tchrs., 1980. Fellow AAAS, IEEE (John T. Bolljahn award 1963, pres. Antennas and Propagation Soc. 1969); mem. Am. Musicological Soc. Home: 625 Cardinal Gibbons Dr Apt 101 Raleigh NC 27606-3255 Office: PO Box 7911 Raleigh NC 27695

RHODES, EDDIE, JR., medical technologist, phlebotomy technician, educator; b. Memphis, Apr. 14, 1955; s. Eddie Sr. and Mabel (Payne) R. AS, Shelby State C.C., Memphis, 1979; BS, Memphis State U., 1981. Cert. med. technologist. Rsch. technologist St. Jude's Children Rsch. Hosp., Memphis, Ga., 1980-81; med. lab. asst. Roche Biomedical Lab., Tucker, Ga., 1991-92; med. technologist Damon / MetPath Clin. Lab., Smyrna, Ga., 1992-93, ARC, Norcross, Ga., 1993-95, Ga. Bapt. Med. Ctr., Atlanta, 1994—; instr. microbiology Atlanta Area Tech., 1995-96; adv. bd. mem. Atlanta Area Tech., Atlanta, 1995—; blood donor specialist Civitan Regl. Blood Sys., Atlanta, 1996—; med. lab./phlebotomy program coord. W. Ga. Tech., LaGrange, 1996—. Named one of the Outstanding Young Men of Am., Atlanta, 1989. Mem. Am. Soc. Microbiology, Am. Soc. of Phlebotomy Technicians. Avocations: cycling, basketball, chess. Home: 410 Park Pl La Grange GA 30240 Office: West Ga Technical 303 Fort Dr La Grange GA 30240

RHODES, ERIC FOSTER, arbitrator, employee relations consultant, insurance executive; b. Luray, Va., Feb. 5, 1927; s. Wallace Keith and Bertha (Foster) R.; m. Barbara Ellen Henson, Oct. 19, 1946; children: Roxanne Jane, Laurel Lee; m. Lorraine Endresen, July 29, 1972; m. Daisy Chun, May 31, 1980. AA, George Washington U., 1949, AB, 1950, MA, 1952, EdD, 1967. Tchr. high sch. Arlington, Va., 1950-52; counselor Washington Lee High Sch., Arlington, Va., 1952-53, dir. publs., 1953-54, chmn. dept. English, 1954-55; exec. sec. Arlington Edn. Assn., Arlington, Va., 1952-53, Montgomery County (Md.) Edn. Assn., Rockville, Md., 1955-57; lectr. edn. George Washington U., Washington, 1955-60, 65-70; salary cons. NEA, Washington, 1957-58, asst. dir. membership div., 1958-60; dir. N.Y. regional office, N.Y.C., 1960-64; ednl. cons. Ednl. Rsch. Svcs., White Plains, N.Y., 1964-65; pres. Ednl. Svc. Bur., Inc., Arlington, Va., 1965-72, chmn. bd., 1972-80; pres. Negotiations Consultation Svcs., Inc., Arlington, 1969-80, Eastern States Advt. Inc., Arlington, 1970-79, EFR Corp., Arlington, 1972-90; exec. dir. Assn. Negotiators and Contract Adminstrs., Arlington, 1981-89; area coord. U.S. Legal Protection Co., 1989—; pres. Employee Futures Rsch., Colorado Springs, Colo., 1980—, Waterfront Only Real Estate, New Port Richey, Fla., 1988-92, Inst. for Negotiations Tng., New Port Richey, 1989-95, Asset Protection Co., 1991—; asst. supt. for adminstrn. Brighton Schs., Rochester, N.Y., 1983-88; owner Frederick Foster Galleries, Arlington, 1974-80; cons. Va. Dept. Community Colls., Richmond, 1965-77; vice chancellor Va. Community Coll. System, 1970-71; employee rels. ofcl. City of Orlando, 1980-83; lectr. edn. Frostburg (Md.) State Coll., 1967. Author: Negotiating Salaries, 41 Ways to Cut Budget Costs, Making Good Things Happen Through Negotiation; editor: Inside Negotiations, Wages and Benefits, Employers' Negotiating Service. Mem. Civil Rights Commn., Franklin Twp., N.J., 1962-64; mem. Franklin Twp. Bd. Edn., 1964-65; mem. adv. bd. Keep Am. Beautiful, 1964-75, nat. chmn., 1968; bd. dirs., v.p. Unitarian-Universalist Ch., Tarpon Springs, Fla., 1990-95, pres., 1994-95. With U.S. Army, 1945-47. Mem. Am. Assn. Sch. Adminstrs., Internat. Assn. Sch. Bus. Officials, NEA, Edn. Press Assn., Nat. Assn. Ednl. Negotiators (exec. dir. 1971-81), Am. Arbitration Assn. (labor arbitrator), Indsl. Rels. Rsch. Assn., United C. of C. of Pasco County (sec., treas. 1989-90, exec. dir. 1990-91), Am. Legion, Fed. Schoolmen's Club, N.Y. Schoolmen's Club, Lions (v.p. N.Y.C. club 1964-65), Kiwanis (pres. West Pasco club 1991-93), Order of St. John of Jerusalem, Phi Delta Kappa (chpt. pres. 1959-60). Home: 1994 Copper Creek Dr Colorado Springs CO 80910 Office: PO Box 15236 Colorado Springs CO 80935-5236

RHODES, FRANK HAROLD TREVOR, university president emeritus, geologist; b. Warwickshire, Eng., Oct. 29, 1926; came to U.S., 1968, naturalized, 1976; s. Harold Cecil and Gladys (Ford) R.; m. Rosa Carlson, Aug. 16, 1952; children: Jennifer, Catherine, Penelope, Deborah. BSc, U. Birmingham, 1948, PhD, 1950, DSc (hon.), 1963; LLD (hon.), Wooster Coll., 1976, Nazareth Coll. Rochester, 1979, Skidmore Coll., 1989, U. Mich., 1990, Clemson U., 1991, Dartmouth Coll., 1993; LHD (hon.), Colgate U., 1980, Johns Hopkins U., 1982, Wagner Coll., 1982, Hope Coll., 1982, Rensselaer Poly Inst., 1982, LeMoyne Coll., 1984, Pace U., 1986, Alaska Pacific U., 1987, Hamilton Coll., 1987, SUNY, 1992, Canisius Coll., 1994, Ithaca Coll., 1995; DSc (hon.), U. Wales, Eng., 1981, Fla. Atlantic U., 1996, Bucknell U., 1985, U. Ill., 1986, Reed Coll., 1988, Elmira Coll., 1989, U. Southampton, U.K., 1989, U. Sydney, Australia, 1995, U. Durham, Eng., 1995, Millsaps Coll., Eng., 1996; DLitt (hon.), U. Nev., 1982; EdD (hon.), Ohio State U., 1992; D. Univ. (hon.), U. Stirling, Eng., 1994. Post-doctoral fellow, Fulbright scholar U. Ill., 1950-51, vis. lectr. geology, summers 1951, 52; lectr. geology U. Durham, 1951-54; asst. prof. U. Ill., 1954-55, assoc. prof., 1955-56; dir. U. Ill. Field Sta., Wyo., 1956; prof. geology, head geology dept. U. Wales, Swansea, 1956-68, dean faculty of sci., 1967-68; prof. geology and mineralogy Coll. Lit., Sci. and Arts, U. Mich., 1968-77, dean, 1971-74, v.p. for acad. affairs, 1974-77; pres., prof. geology Cornell U., Ithaca, N.Y., 1977-95; Gurley lectr. Cornell U., 1960; Bownocker lectr. Ohio State U., 1966; Case lectr. U. Mich., 1976; dir. NSF, Am. Geol. Inst., summer field inst., 1963; Australian vice-chancellors' visitor to Australian univs., 1964; vis. fellow Clare Hall, Cambridge, Summer 1982; Bye fellow Robinson Coll., Cambridge, Summers, 1986, 87; Am. Fulbright Disting. fellow, Kuwait, 1987, scholar in residence, Bellagio study and conf. ctr., 1995. Author: The Evolution of Life, 1962, 2d edit., 1976, Fossils, 1963, Geology, 1972, Evolution, 1974, Language of the Earth, 1981; author numerous articles and monographs on sci. and edn. Trustee Carnegie Found. for Advancement Teaching, 1978-86, vice chmn., 1983-85, chmn. 1985-86; trustee The Freedom Forum, 1983-93; trustee Com. for Econ. Devel., 1984-93; bd. trustees Andrew W. Mellon Found., 1984—; prin. Washington Adv. Group, 1997—; bd. dirs. KMI Continental, Inc., 1979-86, Tompkins County Trust Co., 1984—, Gen. Electric Co., 1984—, NBC, 1986—, H. John Heinz III Ctr. Sci., Econs. & Environ., 1996—; Am. Council on Edn., 1983-88, vice chair, 1985-86, chair, 1986-88; bd. overseers Meml. Sloan-Kettering Cancer Ctr., 1979-91; chmn. adv. bd. Freedom Forum Media Studies Ctr., 1984-93; mem. Nat. Sci. Bd., 1987—, chair, 1994-96, Internat. Exec. Svc. Corps Coun., 1984-95; v.p. Dyson Charitable Trust, 1996—. Recipient Clark Kerr medal U. Calif., Berkeley, 1995; NSF sr. vis. rsch. fellow, 1965-66; scholar U. Calif., Berkeley, 1995. Fellow Geol. Soc. London (council 1963-66, Bigsby medal 1967); mem. Palaeontol. Assn. (v.p. 1963-68), Brit. Assn. Advancement Sci., Geol. Soc. Am., Am. Assn. Petroleum Geologists, Soc. Econ. Paleontologists and Mineralogists, Phi Beta Kappa (hon.). Office: Cornell U Office of President Emeritus 3104 Snee Hall Ithaca NY 14853-1504

RHODES, GERALDINE BRYAN, secondary school administrator; b. Asheville, N.C., Dec. 7, 1941; d. Robert Gerald and Myrtle (Bartlett) B.; m. Gayle Dean Rhodes, May 27, 1967; children: Jennifer Ellen, Leah Rebecca. BM, So. Meth. U., 1967; MA, Columbia U., 1987, MEd, 1988, postgrad., 1988—. Permanent tchr. cert., N.Y. Music tchr. Dallas Ind. Sch. Dist., 1967-69, Yamaha Music Sch., Poughkeepsie, N.Y., 1971-75, Hudson Valley Philharmonic Music Sch., Poughkeepsie, 1986-88; music tchr. Poughkeepsie Day Sch., 1987-90, dir. music edn., 1990-92; tchr. fine arts Ctrl. Tex. Coll., Youngsan U.S. Army Base, Seoul, 1992-94; music tchr. Arlington Ctrl Schs, Poughkeepsie, NY, 95—; tchr., cons. Dutchess Arts Camp, Poughkeepsie, 1986-92, Hollingworth Pre-sch., Columbia U., N.Y.C., 1987-88; tchr., dir. Inter-generation Chorus N.Y. State Coun. Arts, Poughkeepsie, 1988-92. Mem. Music Educators Nat. Congress, N.Y. State Sch. Music Assn., Am. Orff Schulwerk Assn. Republican. Episcopalian. Office: Arlington Ctrl Schs 120 Dutchess Tpke Poughkeepsie NY 12603-6426

RHODES, JAMES DEVERS, psychotherapist; b. Midland, Tex., Apr. 28, 1955; s. James Ireland and Loys Ruth (McElrath) R.; m. Moira Sheelagh Josephine Fox Elmore, June 21, 1986. BS, Tex. Christian U., 1978; MEd, U. North Tex., 1991. Lic. profl. counselor, Tex.; lic. chem. dependency counselor, Tex.; nat. cert. addictions counselor II.; nat. cert. clin. hypnotherapist. Substance abuse technician Tarrant Coun. Mental Health-Mental Retardation, Ft. Worth, 1986; substance abuse counselor CPC Millwood Hosp., Arlington, Tex., 1986-89; family therapist Parkside Lodge-Westgate, Denton, Tex., 1989-90; co-dependence therapist, dir. Parkside Outpatient Svcs., Ft. Worth, 1990-91; psychotherapist Behavioral Health Unit La Hacienda Treatment Ctr., Hunt, Tex.; pvt. practice Kerrville, Tex., 1991—; peer evaluator Tex. Bd. Alcoholism and Drug Counselors, Austin, 1988-96; allied staff La Hacienda, Charter Hosp., Hill Country Crisis Coun., Hill Country Ind. House, Sid Peterson Regional Hosp.; ct. cons. 216th Dist. Ct., Kerrville, Tex.; clin. supr. Youth Habitat Tex., 1995-97; chief clin. svcs. Healthcare 2000, San Antonio, 1996—; adj. psychology faculty San Antonio Jr. Coll. Author: Adult Recovery Handbook, 1988. Comty. liaison Mid-South Redevel. Assn., Ft. Worth, 1979-83; mem. Fairmount Assn., Ft. Worth, 1979-84; bd. dirs. Mid-South Housing Coop. Study, Ft. Worth, 1983, Ctr. Point Alliance for Progress, 1995—, Hill County Rehab House, 1993-96. Mem. ACA, Am. Acad. Forensic Counselors (assoc.), Tex. Counseling Assn., Tex. Mental Health Counselors Assn. (treas. 1994-97), Matt Talbot Retreat Movement (sec. 1989-91), Nat. Assn. Eagle Scouts, Assn. of Ambulatory Behavioral Healthcare, Rotary. Episcopalian. Avocations: reading, investing, acting, Beatlemania, traveling. Office: The Comfort Zone 180 Guadalupe Plz Kerrville TX 78028-4545

RHODES, JOHN BOWER, management consultant; b. Pitts., July 8, 1925; s. John Bower and Mary Lucile (Lewis) R.; m. Joan Ann Black, June 11, 1955; children: John Bower, III, Mark Lewis, Lydia Black. B.S. in Mech. Engring, Princeton U., 1946; postgrad., N.Y. U. Law Sch., 1953-55. With internat. ops. California Texas Oil Co., N.Y.C., 1946-59; mgr. ops. in California Texas Oil Co., Arabia, 1947-50, Calif. Tex. Oil Co., India, 1955-59; mng. officer Europe Booz, Allen & Hamilton Internat. NV, Zurich,

Switzerland, 1959-63, Dusseldorf, Fed. Republic of Germany, 1963-68; v.p. internat. affairs Booz, Allen & Hamilton Inc., N.Y.C., 1968-70, vice chmn., 1970-90, of counsel, 1990—. Mgr. N.Y. Inst. for Edn. of Blind, 1976—. Served with USMC, 1943-45, 51-52. Mem. Internat. C. of C. (U.S. council), Council Fgn. Relations, Orgn. Econ. Coop. and Devel. Clubs: Princeton, N.Y. Yacht, Colonial, Nantucket (Mass.) Yacht. Office: Booz Allen Hamilton Inc 101 Park Ave New York NY 10178

RHODES, JOHN JACOB, lawyer, former congressman; b. Council Grove, Kans., Sept. 18, 1916; s. John Jacob and Gladys Anne (Thomas) R.; m. Mary Elizabeth Harvey, May 24, 1942; children: John Jacob 3d, Thomas H., Elizabeth C. Rhodes Reich, James Scott. BS, Kans. State U., 1938; LLB, Harvard U., 1942. Bar: Kans. 1942, Ariz. 1945, D.C. 1965. Mem. 83d-97th congresses from 1st Dist. Ariz., chmn. Republican policy com. 89th-93d congresses, house minority leader, 1973-81; of counsel Hunton & Williams, Washington, 1985-97; mem. bd. overseers Hoover Instn., 1984-92; chmn. platform com. Nat. Rep. Conv., 1972, permanent chmn., 1976, 80. Mem. Ariz. Bd. Pub. Welfare, 1951-52. Served with AUS, World War II; Col., ret. Mem. Mesa C. of C. (pres. 1950), SAR, Am. Legion, Ariz. Club, Mesa Golf and Country Club, Capitol Hill Club, Met. Club, Burning Tree Club (Bethesda, Md.), Pinetop Country Club, Masons (33 deg., Grand Cross), KP, Elks, Moose, Rotary, Beta Theta Pi (internat. pres. 1984-87). Republican. Methodist.

RHODES, LAWRENCE, artistic director; b. Mt. Hope, W.Va., Nov. 24, 1939. Studied with Violette Armand. Joined Ballet Russe de Monte Carlo, 1958-60; from dancer to prin. dancer Joffrey Ballet, N.Y.C., 1960-64; prin. dancer Harkness Ballet, 1964-68, dir., prin. dancer, 1968-70; tchr. dance dept. NYU, 1978—, prin. ballet tchr., 1981—, chmn. dance dept., 1981-91; prin. dancer, ballet master, choreographer, tchr., artistic dir. Les Grands Ballets Canadiens, Montreal, 1989—; guest artist Het Nationale Ballet, Amsterdam, 1970-71, Pa. Ballet, 1971-76, Feld Ballet, N.Y.C., 1973-75. Danced with Makarova, Hayden and Fracci; danced for Butler, Joffrey, Ailey, Lubovitch, Harkarvy, Nault, Van Dantzig and Mac Donald; featured dancer in film A Dancer's Vocabulary, PBS's Dance Am. series, CBS's Camera Three. Office: Les Grands Ballets Canadiens, 4816, rue Rivard, Montreal, PQ Canada H2J 2N6*

RHODES, LINDA JANE, psychiatrist; b. San Antonio, May 23, 1950; d. George Vernon and Lucy Agnes (O'Dowd) R. BA, Trinity U., 1972; MD, U. Tex. Med. Br., 1975. Diplomate Am. Bd. Pediat. Resident in pediat. U. Tex. Med. Br., Galveston, 1975-78; fellow in ambulatory pediat. U. Tex. Health Sci. Ctr., Houston, 1978-80; asst. prof. psychiatry U. Tex. Health Sci. Ctr., San Antonio, 1995—, resident in psychiatry, 1990-92, child and adolescent psychiatrist, fellow in biol. psychiatry, 1992-95; pediatrician Kelsey Seybold Clinic, P.A., Houston, 1980-95; pediat. rep. Tex. Lay Midwifery Bd. Tex. Dept. Health, Austin, 1994—. Active San Antonio Conservation Soc., San Antonio Zool. Soc., San Antonio Mus. Assn., Trinity U. Assocs., 1992—, Witte Mus. Assn.; patron McNay Art Inst.; bd. dirs. Tex. Found. for Psychiatric Edn. & Rsch., 1997—; bd. trustees U. Tex. Health Sci. Ctr., San Antonio to Sci. Found., 1997—. Fellow Am. Acad. Pediat.; mem. Am. Psychiat. Assn., Ambulatory Pediat. Assn., Tex. Pediat. Soc., Tex. Soc. Psychiat. Physicians, Tex. Acad. Child and Adolescent Psychiatry, Am. Med. Women's Assn., Am. Soc. Clin. Psychopharmacology, Tex. Med. Assn., AMA, Bexar County Psychait. Soc. Office: U Tex Health Sci Ctr-SA Dept Psychiatry/Divsn Biol 7703 Floyd Curl Dr San Antonio TX 78284-6200

RHODES, MARLENE RUTHERFORD, counseling educator, educational consultant; b. St. Louis; d. Odie Douglas and Helen (Ward) Rutherford; m. David L. Rhodes, Nob. 18, 1961; children: Jay David, Michael Stanford, John David, Mark Stanford. BS in Psychology cum laude, Washington U., St. Louis, 1973, MA in Counseling Edn., 1975; postgrad., St. Louis U., 1987—. Registered med. record libr. Caseworker I and II, Mo. Div. Family Svcs., St. Louis, 1961-65, supr. caseworker II's, 1965-70; personal effectiveness trainer women's program U. Mo., St. Louis, 1974-77; assoc. prof. counseling, chair counseling St. Louis C.C. at Forest Park, 1975—, chmn. dept., 1993—, dir. step up coll. program, 1990-93; developer, coord. crisis intervention facilitation tng. St. Louis Pub. Schs., 1987-88; ednl. project cons. Project Achievement, Ralston Purina Co., 1993-94; developer, presenter over 80 ednl. project consultations for area colls., profl. orgns. and bus. groups, 1975—. Author: Crisis Intervention Facilitation Training Manual, 1988. Chmn. Ft. Louis Friends of Arts, 1984—; coord. for coun. of elders for Better Family Life Orgn., 1995—; com. co-chmn. for black dance and unity ball Better Family Inc., St. Louis, 1990—; panelist for counseling support svcs. for families United Way Greater St. Louis, 1993—; mem. fin. com. St. Thomas Archdiocese, 1995—; bd. dirs. Bishop Hearly Cath. Sch. Recipient Disting. Svc. as Am. Educator award Alpha Zeta chpt. Iota Phi Lambda, 1990, role model award St. Louis Pub. Schs., 1993, cert. of achievement Nat. Orgn. for Victim Assistance, 1993. Mem. NEA (co-coord. polit. action com. St. Louis 1985-90, bargaining negotiator 1987—), ACA (nat. chair orgn., adminstrn. and mgmt. com. 1994-95), Assn. Multicultural Counseling and Devel. (nat. pres. 1994-95), Nat. Assn. for Multicultural Counseling and Devel. (rep. for 13 states 1990-92, Exemplary Svc. award 1992, 94), Mo. Assn. Multicultural Counseling and Devel. (chpt. pres. 1977-78). Democrat. Roman Catholic. Avocations: reading, scrabble, chess, African dance, ping pong. Home: 5935 Pershing Ave Saint Louis MO 63112-1513 Office: St Louis CC at Forest Park 5600 Oakland Ave Saint Louis MO 63110-1316

RHODES, MARY, mayor; m. Donald A. Rhodes; children: Bryan, Randy. Grad., Youngstown Hosp. Assn. Mem. council. City of Corpus Christi, Tex., mayor, 1991—. Mem. LWV, Bus. and Profl. Womens Assn. Presbyterian. Office: Office of the Mayor PO Box 9277 1201 Leopard St Corpus Christi TX 78401-2162*

RHODES, PETER EDWARD, label company executive; b. Rochester, N.Y., Sept. 25, 1942; s. Robert A. and Anne (Ward) R.; m. Cassandra Durkee, May 26, 1962 (div. Sept. 1991); children: Tamara, Amy, Brian. B.S., Rochester Inst. Tech., 1964, M.B.A., 1970. With Touche Ross & Co., Rochester, 1962-69; sr. auditor Touche Ross & Co., to 1969; with Xerox Co., Rochester, 1969, Fay's Drug Co., Inc., Liverpool, N.Y., 1970-87; exec. v.p. Fay's Drug Co., Inc., 1974-87, also dir.; exec. v.p. Syracuse Label Co., Inc., Liverpool, 1987—, also bd. dirs.; dir. Byrne Dairy Inc. Mem. N.Y. State Soc. C.P.A.s, Am. Inst. C.P.A.s, Fin. Execs. Inst. Club: Belevue Country.

RHODES, RAYMOND EARL, professional sports team executive; b. Mexia, Tex., Oct. 20, 1950. Student, Tex. Christian. Asst. def. backs coach San Francisco 49ers/NFL, 1981-82, def. backs coach, 1982-91; def. coord. Green Bay Packers NFL, 1992-93, San Francisco 49ers/NFL, 1994; head coach Phila. Eagles, 1995—. Named NFL Coach of the Yr., The Sporting News, 1995. Office: Philadelphia Eagles 3501 S Broad St Philadelphia PA 19148-5249

RHODES, RICHARD LEE, writer; b. Kansas City, Kans., July 4, 1937; s. Arthur and Georgia Saphronia (Collier) R.; children: Timothy James, Katherine Hampton; m. Ginger Kay Untrif, Oct. 3, 1993. BA cum laude, Yale U., 1959; LHD (hon.), Westminster Coll., Fulton, Mo., 1988. Author: The Inland Ground, 1970, The Last Safari, 1970, The Ungodly, 1973, The Ozarks, 1974, Holy Secrets, 1978, Looking for America, 1979, Sons of the Earth, 1981, The Making of the Atomic Bomb, 1987, Farm, 1989, A Hole in the World, 1990, Making Love, 1992, Nuclear Renewal, 1993, How to Write, 1995, Dark Sun, 1995, (with Ginger Rhodes) Trying to Get Some Dignity, 1996, Deadly Feasts, 1997. Trustee Andrew Drumm Inst., Independence, Mo., 1991—, Menninger Found., Topeka, 1993—. Recipient Nat. Book Critics Cir. award for nonfiction, Nat. Book award for nonfiction, 1987, Pulitzer prize, 1988; Guggenheim fellow, 1974-75, fellow Nat. Endowment for Arts, 1978-79, Ford Found., 1981-83, Sloan Found., 1985, 89, 91, 92, MacArthur Found., 1990-91. Office: Janklow & Nesbit Assoc 598 Madison Ave New York NY 10022-1614

RHODES, ROBERTA ANN, dietitian; b. Red Bank, N.J., Apr. 11; d. Franklin Galloway and Frances (Kieswetter) DuBuy; m. Albert Lewis Rhodes, Feb. 10, 1978; 1 child, Juliet. BS, Fla. State U., 1977, MS, 1988. Lic. dietitian, Fla., Ga. Clin. dietitian Archbold Hosp., Thomasville, Ga., 1988-90; nutritionist Women, Infant and Children program, Tallahassee, 1990-91; sr. mgmt. clin. and adminstrv. dietitian Sunrise Community, Inc., Tallahassee, 1991-93; clin. svcs. specialist Heritage Health Care Ctr., Tallahassee, 1993-94; clin. dietitian Arbors, Tallahassee, 1994-95; clin. dietitian cons. Southwestern State Hosp., Thomasville, Ga.; clin. dietitian Fla. State Hosp., Chattahoochie, 1995—, Southwestern State Hosp., Thomasville, Ga., 1995—. Mem. Am. Dietetic Assn., Fla. Dietetic Assn., Sigma Xi, Omicron Nu. Home: 4112 Alpine Way Tallahassee FL 32303-2244

RHODES, SAMUEL, violist, educator; b. Long Beach, N.Y., Feb. 13, 1941; s. Bernard and Martha (Ephraim) R.; m. Hiroko Yajima, Dec. 30, 1968; children—Amy, Harumi. B.A., Queen's Coll., CUNY, 1963; M.F.A., Princeton U., 1967; D.F.A. (hon.), Mich. State U., 1984; MusD (hon.), Jacksonville U., 1986, San Francisco Conservatory, 1996. Mem. faculty Juilliard Sch., N.Y.C., 1969—, Mich. State U., East Lansing, 1977-85, SUNY-Purchase, 1982-86; violist Marlboro Festival, 1960-68, 78-81, 91—, Galimir String Quartet, 1961-68, Juilliard String Quartet, 1969—; mem. faculty Tanglewood Music Ctr., 1988—. Office: Juilliard Sch Music Lincoln Ctr New York NY 10023

RHODES, THOMAS WILLARD, lawyer; b. Lynchburg, Va., Mar. 9, 1946; s. Howard W. and Ruth (Diehl) R.; m. Ann Bloodworth, May 31, 1975; children: Mildred, Andrew. AB, Davidson (N.C.) Coll., 1968; JD, U. Va., 1971. Bar: Ga. 1971. Assoc. Smith, Gambrell & Russell and predecessor firms, Atlanta, 1971-76, ptnr., 1976—; dir., pres. Atlanta Vol. Lawyers Found., 1984-89, Fed. Defender Program, Atlanta, 1989-94. Contbr. articles to profl. jours. Capt. USAR, 1971-72. Recipient Heiner award, Atlanta Vol. Lawyers Found., 1989. Fellow Am. Law Inst.; mem. Ga. Bar Assn. (past chmn. antitrust law sect.), ABA. Office: Smith Gambrell & Russell Promenade II 1230 Peachtree St NE Ste 3100 Atlanta GA 30309-3575

RHODES, WILLIAM REGINALD, banker; b. N.Y.C., Aug. 15, 1935; s. Edward R. and Elsie R.; divorced; 1 child, Elizabeth. BA in History, Brown U., 1957. Sr. officer internat. banking group-Latin Am. and Caribbean Citibank, N.A., N.Y.C., 1977-80, sr. corp. officer Latin Am. and Caribbean, 1980-84, chmn. restructuring com., 1984-90, group exec., 1986-90, also chmn. bank adv. coms. for Brazil, Argentina, Peru, and Uruguay, 1982-90, co-chmn. bank adv. com. for Mexico, 1982-90, sr. exec.-internat., 1990-91; vice chmn. Citicorp, N.Y.C., 1991—; vice chmn. Inst. Internat. Fin., Met. Mus. Bus. Com.; mem. exec. com. Bretton Woods Com., U.S.-Russia Bus. Coun.; past chmn. adv. com. Export-Import Bank of U.S.; past chmn. U.S. Sect., Venezuela-U.S. Bus. Coun., External Adv. bd. for Columbia U. Program in Econ. Policy Mgmt.; founding mem. U.S. Nat. Adv. Coun. to the Internat. Mgmt. Ctr., Budapest; active U.S.-Egyptian Pres. Coun.; bd. dirs. Citicorp/Citibank, Pvt. Export Funding Corp., Coun. Econ. Devel. Trustee Brown U.; chmn. Northfield-Mt. Hermon Sch.; bd. dirs. N.Y. Hosp., N.Y.C. Partnership; bd. overseers of Watson Inst. for Internat. Studies; active Lincoln Ctr. Corporate Leadership Com.; bd. dirs. African-Am. Inst. Decorated comdr. Nat. Order of the Southern Cross, Brazil, chevalier Legion of Honor, France, Orden de Mayo, Argentina, officer Order Francisco Miranda 1st and 3rd classes, Order Merito en el Trabajo 1st class, Venezuela. Mem. Americas Soc. (bd. dirs.), Coun. of Ams. (trustee), Inst. for EastWest Studies (bd. dirs.), Bankers Assn. for Fgn. Trade (past pres.), Coun. Fgn. Rels., Venezuelan-Am. C. of C. (past pres.), Bankers Roundtable. Avocations: reading history, jogging, swimming, archeology. Office: Citibank, NA 399 Park Ave New York NY 10022

RHODES, YORKE E(DWARD), organic chemistry educator; b. Elizabeth, N.J., Mar. 25, 1936; s. Yorke Edward and Helen (Pyper) R.; m. Mechthilde Weggenmann, May 24, 1975; children: Yorke Edward III, Christopher A., Matthias Raabe, Timothy A. B.S., U. Del., 1957, M.S., 1959; Ph.D., U. Ill., 1963. Chemist, Thiokol Chem. Corp., Elkton, Md., 1959; lectr. Yale U., New Haven, 1964-65; asst. prof. chemistry NYU, N.Y.C., 1965-71, assoc. prof., 1971—, asst. dean Coll. Arts and Sci., 1987-89, dir. NYU-Stevens Dual Degree Program in Sci. and Engring., 1988—; vis. prof. Universitat Freiburg, Fed. Republic Germany, 1972-73, Technische Universitat Munich, Fed. Republic Germany, 1977; vis. prof. artsophysics Univ. Grenoble, France, 1987; named Humboldt vis. prof. tech. U. Munich, 1978; Dept. State sci. exchange visitor Zagreb, Yugoslavia, and Prague, Czechoslovakia, 1977. Contbr. articles to profl. publs. Englewood Democratic committeeman, N.J., 1968-72. NIH fellow Yale U., 1964-65; NASA summer faculty fellow Jet Propulsion Labs., Pasadena, Calif., 1980, 81. Mem. Am. Chem. Soc. (vice chmn. N.Y. sect. 1997), Royal Chem. Soc., Planetary Soc., N.Y. Acad Scis., Sigma Xi. Avocations: opera; photography; travel; gardening; railroads. Office: NYU Dept Chemistry 100 Washington Sq E New York NY 10003-6688

RHODIN, THOR NATHANIEL, educational administrator; b. Dec. 9, 1920; m. Elspeth Lindsay, Sept. 21, 1949; children: Robert, Ann, Lindsay, Jeffrey. BS in Chemistry, Haverford Coll., 1942; AM in Chem. Physics, Princeton U., 1945, PhD in Chem. Physics, 1946. Rsch. asst. Manhattan Project, Princeton U., 1944-46; rsch. assoc. James Franck Inst., Chgo., 1946-51; jr. faculty dept. chemistry U. Chgo., 1946-51; rsch. assoc. E.I. duPont de Nemours & Co., Inc., Wilmington, Del., 1951-58; assoc. prof. applied engring. physics Cornell U., Ithaca, N.Y., 1958-65, prof. applied engring. physics, 1965-91, acting assoc. dean grad. rsch. and edn. Coll. Engring., 1988-89, assoc. dean and dir. continuing edn. Coll. Engring., 1989-90, dir. master of engring. program, chmn. grad. profl. program, 1988-90, assoc. dir. Mario Einaudi Ctr. for Internat. Studies, 1991-94, rsch. prof., 1994—; prof. emeritus applied and engring. physics Cornell U., 1991—; vis. prof. materials sci. and solid State physics MIT, 1973, Japan Soc. for Promotion of Sci., U. Tokyo, 1976, U. Osaka, 1992; cons. Kodak, IBM, duPont; referee reviewer of proposals and pubs. Am. Chem. Soc., Am. Phys. Soc., NSF, Surface Sci. Surface Sci. Letters; co-prin. investigator synchrotron radiation beamline (U16-B), Nat. Synchrotron Light Source, Brookhaven Nat. Lab., 1985—. Editor: Stress-Corrosion Fracture, 1959; co-editor: Nature of the Surface Chemical Bond, 1979, Proceedings Microphysics of Beams, Adsorbates and Surfaces, 1989; author: Chemistry and Physics of Surfaces and Interfaces, 1992; adv. editor Surface Sci., Physics Status Solidi(a), Progress in Surface Sci., Langmuir Surface Chemistry Jour.; contbr. over 150 articles to profl. jours. NSF sr. fellow, 1964-65, NATO sr. fellow, 1975; named Disting. Vis. Faculty, NATO Adv. Study Inst. on Electron Structure and Reactivity of Metal Surfaces, Namur, Belgium, 1971-75; Humboldt Sr. Scientist Inst. of Phys. Chemistry, Maximillian U., Munich, 1985; others. Fellow Am. Phys. Soc., Am. Vacuum Soc.; mem. Am. Chem. Soc., Am. Soc. for Materials Rsch. Office: Cornell Univ 217 Clark Hall Ithaca NY 14853-2501

RHODY, RONALD EDWARD, banker, communications executive; b. Frankfort, Ky., Jan. 27, 1932; s. James B. and Mary M. (Clark) R.; m. Patricia Schupp, Apr. 23, 1955; children: Leslie K., Mary M., Virginia K., Ronald C. Student, Georgetown Coll., Ky., 1950-52, U. Ky., 1953-55. Accredited pub. relations Pub. Relations Soc. Am. Pub. relations dir. Kaiser Aluminum & Chem. Corp., Ravenswood, W.Va., 1959-62, N.Y.C., 1962-67; corporate v.p. Kaiser Aluminum & Chem. Corp., Oakland, Calif., 1967-83; sr. v.p. corp comm. Bank of Am. NT&SA, San Francisco, 1983—, exec. v.p., 1992-94; CEO Rhody, Inc., 1994—. Contbr. articles to profl. jours. Mem. exec. steering com. St. Mary's Coll., Moraga, Calif.; mem. adv. bd. U. Tex. Sch. Journalism and Mass Communications; chmn. media adv. coun., Media Inst., Washington. Named Pub. Relations Profl. of Yr. Pub. Relations News, 1981. Mem. Pub. Relations Soc. Am. (pres.'s adv. council Rex Harlow award), Internat. Assn. Bus. Communicators (Gold Quill award 1980), Pub. Relations Roundtable San Francisco (bd. govs., awards 1980, 85). Clubs: San Francisco Press; International (Washington); Nat. Press (Washington). Office: 712 Bancroft Rd Walnut Creek CA 94598-1531

RHONE, DOUGLAS PIERCE, pathologist, educator; b. Bloomsburg, Pa., Mar. 27, 1940; s. Wilbur Clayton and Marian Faye (Shaffer) R.; m. Leta Daiva Budelskis, Sept. 27, 1969; children: Jennifer Ann, Todd Brader. BS, Ill. Benedictine U., 1965; MD, MS in Pathology, U. Ill., 1969. Diplomate Am. Bd. Pathology. Attending pathologist Ill. Masonic Med. Ctr., Chgo., 1976, chmn. dept. pathology, 1976—; asst. prof. pathology U. Ill. Coll. Medicine, Chgo., 1976-80, assoc. prof. pathology, 1980—; dir. residency pathology Ill. Masonic Med. Ctr., Chgo., 1976-90; dir. residency pathology U. Ill. Met. Hosps., Chgo., 1990—, assoc. dir. med. affairs, 1992-95; assoc. dir. med. affairs Ill. Masonic Med. Ctr. Pathologists, S.C., Chgo., 1977—, Lab. Cons., Ltd., Chgo., 1977—. Contbr. articles to profl. jours. Maj. U.S. Army, 1974-76. Recipient Raymond B. Allen award U. Ill. Coll. Medicine, 1979, 80, 95, 97, C. Thomas Bombeck award, 1991. Fellow Am. Soc. Clin. Pathologists (Sheard-Sanford Rsch. award 1969), Coll. Am. Pathologists; mem. Chgo. Pathology Soc., Ill. Soc. Pathologists. Roman Catholic. Avocations: antiquities, gardening, oil painting, classical music and opera, Russian history and culture. Home: 222 S Spring Ave La Grange IL 60525-2243 Office: Ill Masonic Med Ctr Dept Pathology 836 W Wellington Ave Chicago IL 60657-5147

RHONE, SYLVIA, recording industry executive; b. Philadelphia, PA, Mar. 11, 1952; d. James and Marie (Christmas) R.; 1 daughter, Quinn. M.A., Wharton Sch. Bus. U. Pa., 1974. Dir. nat. black music promotion Atlantic Records, New York, N.Y., 1985-88; Sr. V.P. Atlantic Records, New York, N.Y., 1988-91; chair/CEO EastWest Records America, New York, N.Y., 1991—; chair Elektra Entertainment, N.Y.C., N.Y., 1994—. Mem., bd. dirs. Alvin Ailey Am. Dance Theatre, The RIAA, Rock n' Roll Hall of Fame, Jazz at Lincoln Ctr., R&B Found. Became 1st African American and first women chmn. and CEO of a major record company, 1994. Office: Elektra Entertainment 75 Rockefeller Plz New York NY 10019-6908

RHOTON, ALBERT LOREN, JR., neurological surgery educator; b. Parvin, Ky., Nov. 18, 1932; s. Albert Loren and Hazel Arnette (Van Cleve) R.; m. Joyce L. Moldenhauer, June 23, 1957; children: Eric L., Albert J., Alice S., Laural A. BS, Ohio State U., 1954; MD cum laude, Washington U., St. Louis, 1959. Diplomate Am. Bd. Neurol. Surgery (bd. dirs. 1985-91, vice chmn. 1991). Intern, Columbia Presbyn. Med. Ctr., N.Y.C., 1959; resident in neurol. surgery Barnes Hosp., St. Louis, 1961-65; cons. neurol. surgery Mayo Clinic, Rochester, Minn., 1965-72; chief div. neurol. surgery U. Fla., Gainesville, 1972-80, R.D. Keene prof. and chmn. dept. neurol. surgery, 1980—; developer microsurg. tng. ctr.; guest lectr. Neurol. Socs. Switzerland, Japan, Venezuela, France, Columbia, Middle East, Brazil, Japan, Mex., Can., Costa Rica, Uruguay, Korea, Australia, Egypt, Argentina, Hong Kong, UK, Turkey, Latin Am.; invited faculty and guest lectr. Harvard U., Washington U., Emory, U., UCLA, U. Calif., San Francisco, U. Miami, U. Okla., U. So. Calif., U. Mich., Northwestern U., U. Chgo., U. Pa., Johns Hopkins U., Ohio State U., Temple U., Duke U., Cornell U., NYU, U. Cin., Tulane U., Vanderbilt, U. Minnesota, U. Md., U. Pa., Albany Med. Coll., Cleve. Clin. Found., St. Louis U., Henry Ford Med. Found., Med. Coll. N.Y., Jefferson Med. Coll., Hahnamann Med. Coll., U. P.R., U. Calif., Irvine, U. Hong Kong, La. State U., U. Ky., U. Louisville, Singapore Nat. U. Author: The Orbit and Sellar Region: Microsurgical Anatomy and Operative Approaches, 1996. Recipient Disting. Faculty award U. Fla., 1981, Alumni Achievement award Washington U. Sch. Medicine, 1985, Jones award for outstanding spl. med. exhibit of yr. Am. Assn. Med. Illustrators, 1969; grantee NIH, VA, Am. Heart Assn.; awarded hon. memberships neurosurg. socs. of Brazil, Japan, Mex., Can., Uruguay, Venezuela, Turkey, Tex., Okla., Wis., Ga., Rocky Mountain. Mem. ACS (bd. govs. 1978-84), Congress Neurol. Surgeons (pres. 1978, honored guest 1993), Nat. Found. Brain Rsch. (bd. dirs. 1990-94), Nat. Coalition for Rsch. in Neurol. Disorders (bd. dirs. 1990-94), Fla. Neurosurgical Soc. (pres. 1978), Am. Assn. Neurol. Surgeons (chmn. vascular sect., treas. 1983-86, v.p. 1987-88, pres. 1989-90, exec. com. 1993), Soc. Neurol. Surgeons (treas. 1975-81, pres. 1993), So. Neurol. Soc. (v.p. 1976), Alachua County Med. Soc. (exec. com. 1978), AMA (Billings Bronze medal for sci. exhibit 1969), Fla. Med. Assn., Am. Surg. Assn., Soc. Univ. Neurosurgeons, Am. Heart Assn. (stroke coun., Outstanding Achievement award 1971), North Am. Skull Base Soc. (pres. 1993-94), Am. Acad. Neurol. Surgery, Neurol. Soc. Am., Acoustic Neuroma Assn. (med. adv. bd. 1983—, chmn. 1992—), Trigeminal Neurol. Assn. (med. advisor bd. 1992—), Internat. Interdisciplinary Congress on Craniofacial and Skull Base Surgery (pres. 1996—). Designed over 200 microsurgery instruments. Author: Orbit and Sellar Region, 1996; contbr. numerous articles to profl. jours.; mem. editorial bd. Neurosurgery, Jour. Microsurgery, Surgical Neurology, Jour. Fla. Med. Assn., Am. Jour. Otology, Skull Base Surgery. Home: 2505 NW 22nd Ave Gainesville FL 32605-3819 Office: U Fla Shands Hosp Gainesville FL 32610

RHYNE, CHARLES SYLVANUS, lawyer; b. Charlotte, N.C., June 23, 1912; s. Sydneyham S. and Mary (Wilson) R.; m. Sue Cotton, Sept. 16, 1932 (dec. Mar. 1974); children: Mary Margaret, William Sylvanus; m. Sarah P. Hendon, Oct. 2, 1976; children: Sarah Wilson, Elizabeth Parkhill. BA, Duke U., 1934, LLD, 1958; JD, George Washington U., 1937, DCL, 1958; LLD, Loyola U., Calif., 1958, Dickinson Law Sch., 1959, Ohio No. U., 1966, De Paul U., 1968, Centre, 1969, U. Richmond, 1970, Howard U., 1975, Belmont Abbey, 1981. Bar: D.C. 1937. Pvt. practice Washington; sr. ptnr. Rhyne & Rhyne; gen. counsel Nat. Inst. Mcpl. Law Officers, 1937-88, of counsel; prof. govt. and aviation law George Washington U., 1948-53; prof. govt. Am. U., 1939-44; gen. counsel Fed. Commn. Jud. and Congl. Salaries, 1953-54; spl. cons. Pres. Eisenhower, 1957-60; Dir. Nat. Savs. & Trust Co., 1941-76, ACCIA Life Ins. Co., 1966-84; Mem. Internat Commn. Rules Judicial Procedures, 1959-61, Pres.'s Commn. on UN, 1969-71; spl. ambassador, personal rep. of Pres. U.S. to UN High Commr. for Refugees, 1971-73. Author: Civil Aeronautics Act, Annotated, 1939, Airports and the Courts, 1944, Aviation Accident Law, 1947, Airport Lease and Concession Agreements, 1948, Cases on Aviation Law, 1950, The Law of Municipal Contracts, 1952, Municipal Law, 1957, International Law, 1971, Renowned Law Givers and Great Law Documents of Humankind, 1975, International Refugee Law, 1976, Law and Judicial Systems of Nations, 1978, Law of Local Government Operations, 1980, Working for Justice in America and Justice in the World, 1996; editor Mcpl. Atty., 1937-88; contbr. articles to profl. jours. Trustee George Washington U., 1957-67, Duke U., 1961-85, now trustee emeritus. Recipient Freedoms Found. award for creation Law Day-U.S.A., 1959; Alumni Achievement award George Washington U., 1960; Nat. Bar Assn. Stradford award, 1962; 1st Whitney M. Young award, 1972; Harris award Rotary, 1974; U.S. Dept. State appreciation award, 1976; Nansen Ring for refugee work, 1976, 1st Peacemaker award Rotary Internat., 1988. Mem. ABA (pres. 1957-58, chmn. ho. dels. 1956-58, chmn. commn. world peace through law 1958-66, chmn. com. aero. law 1946-48, 51-54, chmn. internat. and comparative law sect. 1948-49, chmn. UN com., chmn. commn. on nat. inst. justice 1972-76, nat. chmn. Jr. Bar Conf. 1944-45, ABA Gold Medal 1966), D.C. Bar Assn. (pres. 1955-56, Disting. Svc. award, Grotius Peace award 1958), Inter-Am. Bar Assn. (v.p. 1957-59), Am. Bar Found. (pres. 1957-58, chmn. fellows 1958-59), Internat. Bar (founder patron 1947, v.p. 1957-58), Am. Judicature Soc. (dir. life), Am. Law Inst. (life), Am. Soc. Internat. Law (life), World Peace Through Law Ctr. (pres. 1963-89), World Jurist Assn. (life, pres. 1989-91, hon. pres. for life), Nat. Aero. Assn. (bd. dirs. 1945-47), Washington Bd. Trade, Duke U. Alumni Assn. (chmn. nat. coun. 1955-56, pres. 1959-60), Barristers, Met. Club (life), Nat. Press Club, Congl. Country Club (life), Nat. Lawyers Club (life), Univ. Club, Order of Coif (life), ABA House Del.f (life), Scribes, Delta Theta Phi (life), Omicron Delta Kappa. Home and Office: 1404 Langley Pl Mc Lean VA 22101-3010

RHYNE, JAMES JENNINGS, condensed matter physicist; b. Oklahoma City, Nov. 14, 1938; s. Jennings Jefferson and Clyde Margaret (Russell) R.; m. Susan Margaret Watson, May 26, 1990; children: Nancy Marie, Edward Paxton. BS in Physics, U. Okla., 1959; MS in Physics, U. Ill., 1961; PhD in Physics, Iowa State U., 1965. Rsch. scientist Naval Ordnance Lab., White Oak, Md., 1965-75; rsch. physicist Nat. Inst. of Stds. and Tech., Gaithersburg, Md., 1975-90; prof. physics U. Mo., Columbia, 1991—, dir. Rsch. Reactor Ctr., 1991-96. Adv. editor Jour. of Magnetism and Mag. Materials, 1990—; editl. bd. Jour. Applied Physics, 1986-89; co-editor procs. Fellow Am. Phys. Soc. Home: 2704 Westbrook Way Columbia MO 65203-5221 Office: U Mo Dept Physics and Astronomy Columbia MO 65211

RHYNE, VERNON THOMAS, III, electrical engineer, consultant; b. Gulfport, Miss., Feb. 18, 1942; s. Vernon T. and Elizabeth (Brame) R.; m. Glenda Pevey, June 5, 1961; children: Amber Ruth, Tommy. BSEE, Miss. State U., 1962; MEE, U. Va., 1964; PhD, Ga. Inst. Tech., 1967. Registered profl. engr., Tex. Mem. tech. staff NASA Langley Rsch. Ctr., Hampton, Va., 1962-65; prof. elec. engring. Tex. A&M U., College Station, 1967-83; v.p. R&D MCC, Austin, Tex., 1983-94; mgr. strategic programs, semiconductor products sector Motorola, Austin; patent cons., expert witness, N.Y.C., Houston, L.A., 1975—. Author: Fundamentals of Digital Systems Design, 1973 (Terman award Am. Soc. Engring. Edn. 1980). Pres. bd. trustees Eanes Ind. Sch. Dist., Austin, 1987-90, trustee, 1990-95, pres., 1995—. Fellow IEEE (bd. dirs. 1990-95, treas. 1995), Accreditation Bd. for Engring. and Tech. Baptist. Home: 3410 Day Star Cv Austin TX 78746-1433 Office: Motorola MD: TX30/OE14 6501 W William Cannon Dr Austin TX 78735-8523

RHYNEDANCE, HAROLD DEXTER, JR., lawyer, consultant; b. New Haven, Conn., Feb. 13, 1922; s. Harold Dexter and Gladys (Evans) R.; 1 son by previous marriage: Harold Dexter III; m. Ruth Cosline Hakanson. BA, Cornell U., 1943, JD, 1949; grad., U.S. Army Command and Gen. Staff Coll., 1961, U.S. Army War Coll., 1970. Bar: N.Y. 1949, D.C. 1956, U.S. Tax Ct. 1950, U.S. Ct. Mil. Appeals 1954, U.S. Supreme Ct. 1954, U.S. Ct. Appeals (D.C. cir.) 1956, (2d cir.) 1963, (3rd cir.) 1965, (4th cir.) 1973, (5th cir.) 1968, (7th cir.) 1973, (9th cir.) 1964, U.S. Temporary Emergency Ct. Appeals 1975, U.S. Dist. Ct. D.C. 1956, U.S. Dist. Ct. (so. and ea. dist.) N.Y. 1963. Pvt. practice Buffalo, Eggertsville, N.Y., 1949-50; examiner/gen. atty. ICC, Washington, 1950-51; atty.-advisor Subversive Activities Control Bd., Washington, 1951-52; trial atty., spl. asst. to atty. gen., asst. U.S. atty. U.S. Dept. Justice, Washington, 1953-62; sr. trial atty., asst. gen. counsel, gen. counsel FTC, Washington, 1962-73; counsel Howrey & Simon, Washington, 1973-76; mng. atty., asst. gen. counsel, corp. counsel Washington Gas Light Co., 1977-87; counsel Conner & Wetterhahn, 1987-90; cons. Fairview, N.C., 1990—; exec. sec. adv. coun. on rules of practice and procedures FTC; mem. Jud. Conf. (D.C. Cir.), 1967—; chmn. legal and regulatory subcom. Solar Energy Com., Am. Gas Assn., Washington, 1978-84; lectr. George Washington U. Law Ctr., 1974; faculty moderator Def. Strategy Seminar Nat. War Coll., 1973; participant spl. programs Indsl. Coll. of Armed Forces, 1962, 69, Armed Forces Staff Coll., 1964. V.p. bd. dirs. Peninsula Symphony Assn., Palos Verdes Peninsula, Calif., 1989-94; bd. dirs. Help-The-Homeless-Help-Themselves, Inc., Palos Verdes Peninsula, 1991-93. 1st lt. U.S. Army, 1943-46, PTO; col. AUS, 1982—. Mem. ABA, Fed. Bar Assn., D.C. Bar Assn., Bar Assn. of D.C., Washington Met. Area Corp. Counsel Assn. (bd. dirs. 1981-84), Cornell Lawyers Club D.C. (pres. 1959-61), The Selden Soc. (London), Biltmore Forest Country Club (Asheville, N.C.), Montreat (N.C.) Scottish Soc., Res. Officers Assn. (life), Mil. Order Carabao, U.S. Army War Coll. Alumni Assn. (life), Leadership Asheville Forum, Downtown Club Asheville, Cornell Alumni Assn., Sigma Chi, Phi Delta Phi. Republican. Episcopalian. Home and Office: Eagles View 286 Sugar Hollow Rd Fairview NC 28730-9559

RIACH, DOUGLAS ALEXANDER, marketing and sales executive, retired military officer; b. Victoria, B.C., Can., Oct. 8, 1919; s. Alex and Gladys (Provis) R.; came to U.S., 1925, naturalized, 1942; BA, UCLA, 1948; postgrad. in mktg. Fenn Coll., 1959, Grad. Sch. Sales Mgmt. and Mktg., 1960, U.S. Army Command and Gen. Staff Coll., 1966, Armed Forces Staff Coll., 1968, Indsl. Coll. of the Armed Forces, 1970-71; m. Eleanor Montague, Mar. 28, 1942; 1 child, Sandra Jean. With Gen. Foods Corp., 1948-80, terr. sales mgr., San Francisco, 1962-80; with Food Brokers, San Francisco Bay area, 1980-90; exec. v.p. Visual Market Plans Inc., Novato, Calif., 1984-87; ter. mgr. Ibbotson, Berri, DeNola Brokerage, Inc., Emeryville, Calif., 1990-96; account exec. Sales Max Inc., Richmond, Calif., 1996—. Served to capt. inf. AUS, 1941-46, ETO; to col. inf. USAR, 1946-79, from comdr. 2d inf. brigade Calif. State mil. res., 1984-87 to brigadier gen. (ret.) 1990. Decorated Legion of Merit, Bronze Star with V device and oak leaf cluster, Purple Heart, Combat Infantry Badge, Croix de Guerre avec Palme (France and Belgium), Fouragerre (Belgium), Combattant Cross-Voluntaire (France), Combattant Cross-Soldier (France), Medaille-Commemorative de la Liberee (France), Medaille-Commemorative Francais (France), Medaille-War Wounded (France), Medaille-Commemorative Belgique (Belgium), Medaille-de la Reconnaissance (Belgium), Medaille du Voluntaire (Belgium), Cross of Freedom (Poland), Virtuti Militari-Silver Cross (Poland), Royal Commemorative War Cross (Yugoslavia); named knight Order of the Compassionate Heart (internat.), knight Magnus Officialis (GOTJ), Sovereign Mil. Order, Temple of Jerusalem (knights templar), CDR Commandery of Calif. (knights templar 1992-94), comdr. Commandery of St. Francis (knights templar); knight commdr. sovereign Order of St. John of Jerusalem (knights hospitaller), knight commdr. Cross with Star Polonia Restituta, knight comdr. Cross with Star Order of St. Stanislaus; named to U.S. Army Inf. Hall of Fame, 1982; recipient Calif. Medal of Merit and cluster, Commendation medal. Mem. Long Beach Food Sales Assn. (pres. 1950), Assn. Grocers Mfrs. Reps. (dir. 1955), Am. Security Coun. (nat. adv. bd. 1975—), Res. Officers Assn. (San Francisco Presidio pres. 1974-76, v.p. 1977-82, v.p. dept. Calif. 1979, exec. v.p. 1980, pres. 1981, nat. councilman 1981-82), Nat. Assn. Uniformed Svcs., Exchange Club (v.p. Long Beach 1955), St. Andrews Soc. Queens Club San Francisco, Combat Infantry Assn., Assn. U.S. Army, Am. Legion, Assn. Former Intelligence Officers, Presidio Soc., Navy League, Ret. Officers Assn., Mil. Order Purple Heart, DAV, Psychol. Ops. Assn., Nat. Guard Assn. Calif., State Def. Force Assn. Calif., Internat. Diplomacy Coun. San Francisco, Nat. Assn. Uniformed Svcs., Merchandising Execs. San Francisco (dir. 1970-75, sec. 1976-77, v.p. 1978-79, pres. 1980, bd. dirs. 1981-89), Commonwealth of Club Calif. (nat. def. sect. vice chmn. 1964-66, chmn. 1967-72), Elks, Masons (master, lodge 400, Shrine, Islam Temple, 32d degree Scottish Rite, sojouner chpt. #277). Republican. Episcopalian. Home: 2609 Trousdale Dr Burlingame CA 94010-5706

RIASANOVSKY, NICHOLAS VALENTINE, historian, educator; b. Harbin, China, Dec. 21, 1923; came to U.S., 1938, naturalized, 1943; m. Arlene Ruth Schlegel, Feb. 15, 1955; children—John, Nicholas, Maria. B.A., U. Oreg., 1942; A.M., Harvard U., 1947; D.Phil., Oxford (Eng.) U., 1949. Mem. faculty U. Iowa, 1949-57; mem. faculty U. Calif., Berkeley, 1957—, prof. history, 1961—, Sidney Hellman Ehrman prof. European history, 1969—; trustee Nat. Council Soviet and E. European Research, 1978-82; mem. Kennan Inst. Acad. Council, 1986-89; vis. research prof. USSR Acad. Scis., Moscow, 1969, Moscow and Leningrad, 1974, 79. Author: Russia and the West in Teaching of the Slavophiles: A Study of Romantic Ideology, 1952, Nicholas I and Official Nationality in Russia, 1825-1855, 1959, A History of Russia, 1963, 5th edit., 1993, The Teaching of Charles Fourier, 1969, A Parting of Ways: Government and the Educated Public in Russia, 1801-1855, 1976, The Image of Peter the Great in Russian History and Thought, 1985, The Emergence of Romanticism, 1992, Collected Writings 1947-94, 1993; co-editor: California Slavic Studies, 1960—; editl. bd. Russian rev., Zarubezhnaia Periodicheskaia Pechat' Na Russkom Iazyke, Simvol; contbr. articles to profl. jours. Served to 2d lt. AUS, 1943-46. Decorated Bronze Star; recipient Silver medal Commonwealth Club Calif., 1964; Rhodes scholar, 1947-49; Fulbright grantee, 1954-55, 74, 79; Guggenheim fellow, 1969; sr. fellow Nat. Endowment Humanities, 1975; Fulbright sr. scholar, sr. fellow Ctr. Advanced Studies in Behavioral Scis., 1984-85; sr. fellow Woodrow Wilson Internat. Ctr. for Scholars, 1989-90. Mem. AAAS, Am. Assn. Advancement Slavic Studies (pres. 1973-76, Disting. Contbr. award 1993), Am. Hist. Assn. (award for Scholarly Distinction 1995).

RIBA, NETTA EILEEN, secondary school educator; b. Bronx, N.Y., Apr. 6, 1944; d. Jack and Anne (Parnes) Browner; m. Benjamin Riba, July 22, 1975; children: Rebecca, Joseph. BS, Queens Coll., 1965, MS, 1968. Cert. tchr., N.Y. Math. tchr. Bayside (N.Y.) H.S., 1965-68, Flushing (N.Y.) H.S., 1968-75, Harry S Truman H.S., Bronx, 1975-95, Christopher Columbus H.S., Bronx, 1996—. Vol. guide N.Y. Zool. Soc., Bronx, 1973-75; leader Rockland County Coun. Girl Scouts USA, 1985-88. Mem. Nat. Coun. Tchrs. Math. Jewish. Avocations: animal behavior, sewing. Office: Christopher Columbus HS 925 Astor Ave Bronx NY 10469-4901

RIBBANS, GEOFFREY WILFRID, Spanish educator; b. London, Apr. 15, 1927; came to U.S. 1978; s. Wilfrid Henry and Rose Matilda (Burton)R.; m. Magdalena Willmann, Apr. 21, 1956; children: Madeleine Elizabeth, Helen Margaret, Peter John. BA with 1st class hons., Kings Coll., U. London, 1948, MA, 1953. Asst. lectr. U. Sheffield, Eng., 1954-56; lectr. U. Sheffield, 1956-61, sr. lectr. Spanish, 1961-63; Gilmour prof. Spanish U. Liverpool, Eng., 1963-78; vis. Mellon prof. Spanish U. Pitts., 1970-71; Wm. R. Kenan Jr. U. prof. Spanish Brown U., Providence, 1978—, chmn. dept., 1981-84; editor Bull. Hispanic Studies, 1964-78; vis. prof. U. Salamanca, Spain, 1995. Author: Catalunya i Valencia al Segle XVIII, 1955, 2d edit., 1993, Niebla y Soledad: Aspectos de Unamuno y Machado, 1971, Galdós: Fortunata y Jacinta, 1977 (Spanish transl. 1988); editor: Antonio Machado, Soledades, Galerias, Otros Poemas, 1984, 13th edit., 1996, Campos de Castilla, 1989, 6th edit., 1995, History and Fiction in Galdós's Narratives, 1993, 2d edit., 1995, Conflicts and Conciliations: The Evolution of Galdós's "Fortunata y Jacinta", 1997. Hispanic studies in his honour, Liverpool, 1992. Mem. MLA, Internat. Assn. Hispanists (v.p. 1974-80), Internat. Assn. Galdós Scholars (pres. 1988-89). Office: Brown U Dept Hispanic Studies PO Box 1961 Providence RI 02912-1961

RIBBLE, ANNE HOERNER, communications representative; b. Balt., Oct. 30, 1932; B.A., Smith Coll., 1954; M.A., Harvard U., 1955; m. John C. Ribble, July 26, 1974; tech. asst. IBM, N.Y.C., 1958-63, editor, Armonk and White Plains, N.Y., 1969-75, mgr. editorial services data processing div., White Plains, 1976-77, program adminstr. systems communications div., N.Y.C., 1977-78, staff tech. edn., fed. systems div., Houston, 1978-80, info. rep., 1980-87, staff info. IBM Federal Systems Co., 1988-93; prin. Creative Commn., 1993—. Bd. dirs. Stanley Isaacs Community Center, N.Y.C., 1968-72; mem. United Way allocations com., Houston, 1989-94. Mem. Pub. Rels. Soc. Am. (accredited), Internat. Assn. Bus. Communicators (pres. Houston chpt. 1982, community rels. dir. 1989-92), Women In Communications Inc. (program v.p. 1994-95). Home: 6200 Willers Way Houston TX 77057-2808 Office: Creative Commn 6355 Westheimer Rd # 171 Houston TX 77057-5103

RIBBLE, JOHN CHARLES, medical educator; b. Paris, Tex., July 26, 1931; s. Elbert Alfred and Dorothy (Pyeatt) R.; m. Anne Blythe Hoerner; 1 stepchild Helen Blythe Strate Kielty. MD, U. Tex., 1955. Diplomate Am. Bd. Internal Medicine. Asst. prof. medicine Cornell U., N.Y.C., 1962-66, assoc. prof. pediatrics, 1966-78, assoc. dean, 1974-78; assoc. dean Med. Sch., U. Tex., Houston, 1978-86, dean, 1986-95; vis. scholar The Health Inst. New Eng. Med. Ctr., Boston, 1995-96; prof. medicine, pub. health U. Tex., Houston, 1996—; mem. Nat. Adv. Coun. Gen. Med. Scis. NIH, Bethesda, Md., 1988-91. Episcopalian. Home: 6200 Willers Way Houston TX 77057-2808 Office: U Tex Med Sch 6431 Fannin St Houston TX 77030-1501

RIBBLE, RONALD GEORGE, psychologist, educator, writer; b. West Reading, Pa., May 7, 1937; s. Jeremiah George and Mildred Sarah (Folk) R.; m. Catalina Valenzuela (Torres), Sept. 30, 1961; children: Christina, Timothy, Kenneth. BSEE cum laude, U. Mo., 1968, MSEE, 1969, MA, 1985, PhD, 1986. Diplomate Am. Bd. Forensic Examiners, Am. Bd. Psychol. Specialties. Enlisted man USAF, 1956-60, advance through grades to lt. col., 1976; rsch. dir. Coping Resources, Inc., Columbia, Mo., 1986; pres., co-owner Towers and Rushing Ltd., San Antonio, 1986—; referral devel. Laughlin Pavilion Psychiat. Hosp., Kirksville, Mo., 1987; program dir. Psychiat. Insts. of Am., Iowa Falls, Iowa, 1987-88; lead psychotherapist Gasconade County Counseling Ctr., Hermann, Mo., 1988; lectr. U. Tex., San Antonio, 1989—, Trinity U., San Antonio, 1995-96; assessment clinician Afton Oaks Psychiat. Hosp., San Antonio, 1989-91; faculty cons. ETS, 1997; psychologist Olmos Psychol. Svcs., Inc., San Antonio, 1991-93; vol. assessor Holmgreen Children's Shelter, San Antonio, 1992-93; founder Ruth Bohn Weissman Scholarship in Creative Writing, U. Tex., San Antonio, 1994; condr. seminars, revs. for maj. publs. Author: Apples, Weeds, and Doggie Poo, 1995; contbr. essays to psychol. reference books and poetry to anthologies periodicals, lyrics to popular music; columnist Feelings, 1993—; public access TV appearances, 1991—. Del. Boone County (Mo.) Dem. Conv., 1984; vol. announcer pub. radio sta., Columbia, 1993; contbg. mem. Dem. Nat. Com., 1983—, Presdl. Congl. Task Force, 1994; vol. counselor Cath. Family and Children's Svc., San Antonio, 1989-91; chpt. advisor Rational Recovery Program for Alcoholics, San Antonio, 1991-92; mem. Pres. Leadership Cir., 1994-95. Recipient Roberts Meml. Prize in Poetry, 1995. Mem. APA, AAUP, NEA, ACLU, Am. Coll. Forensic Examiners, Internat. Soc. for Study of Individual Differences, Internat. Platform Assn. (Poetry award 1995), Bexar County Psychol. Assn., Air Force Assn., Ret. Officers Assn., People for the Am. Way, Nat. Writers Assn., Soc. Profl. Journalists, Poetry Soc. Am., Acad. Am. Poets. Roman Catholic. Avocations: running and fitness, poetry, singing, pub. speaking. Home: 14023 N Hills Village Dr San Antonio TX 78249-2531 Office: U Tex Divsn Cultural and Sci San Antonio TX 78249 also: Towers and Rushing Ltd San Antonio TX 78249

RIBBY, ALICE MARIE, nurse; b. Lowell, Mich., Oct. 16, 1943; d. Merle Levi and Merleen Maude (Gooden) Bickford; children: Bobette Morgan, Mylie Wasylewski, Joseph R. Ribby, Barbara A. Cupp. AD in Gen. Edn. cum laude, Lansing (Mich.) Community Coll., 1975, AS in Nursing cum laude, 1976; BA in Family Life Edn., Spring Arbor Coll., 1992. Nurse ICU Ingham Med. Ctr., Lansing, Mich., 1976-81; nurse acute and chronic hemo and peritoneal dialysis Sparrow Hosp., Lansing, Mich., 1983-84; head nurse, alternate CEO Community Dialysis Ctr., Jackson, Mich., 1984-87, dir. Continuous Ambulatory Peritoneal Dialysis Program; dialysis cons. Cmty. Dialysis Ctr.; nursing supr. Doctor's Hosp., Jackson, Mich., 1987-90; co-founder, co-owner, nurse therapist St. Lawrence Hosp., Diamondale and Lansing, Mich., 1990-95, Ptnrs. Psychol. Svcs., Lansing, 1994—; nurse cons., mental health therapist OBRA program Cmty. Mental Health-Older Adults Svcs., Lansing, 1996—; lectr. in field, presenter workshops and seminars on childhood sexual abuse; founder One Another's Support Group. Mem. Am. Assn. Christian Counselors, Profl. Staff Devel. Orgn. Republican. Avocations: religious study, travel, theater. Address: PO Box 158 Holt MI 48842-0158

RIBICOFF, ABRAHAM A., lawyer, former senator; b. New Britain, Conn., Apr. 9, 1910; s. Samuel and Rose (Sable) R.; m. Ruth Siegel, June 28, 1931 (dec.); children: Peter, Jane; m. Lois Mathes, 1972. Student, NYU; LL.B. cum laude, U. Chgo., 1933. Bar: Conn. 1933, N.Y. 1981, U.S. Ct. Appeals (D.C. cir.) 1982, U.S. Supreme Ct. 1981. Mem. Conn. Ho. of Reps., 1939-42; mcpl. judge Hartford, Conn., 1942-43, 45-47; chmn. Conn. Assembly Mcpl. Ct. Judges, 1942; mem. 81st—82d congresses from 1st Conn. Dist., mem. com. fgn. affairs; gov. Conn., 1955-61; sec. HEW, 1961-62; mem. U.S. Senate from Conn., 1963-81, mem. fin., joint econ. coms., chmn. govt. affairs com.; spl. counsel firm Kaye, Scholer, Fierman, Hays & Handler, N.Y.C. and Washington, 1981—; dir. Hartford Ins. Group, United Television, Inc. Author: Politics: The American Way, 1967, America Can Make It, 1972, The American Medical Machine, 1972. Democrat. Office: 425 Park Ave New York NY 10022-3506

RIBLE, MORTON, financial services and manufacturing executive; b. Los Angeles, July 30, 1938; s. Ulysses Floyd and Ruth (Morton) R.; m. Ann Martin, June 22, 1963; children: Kimberly, Kristen. AB cum laude, Princeton U., 1961; JD, Stanford U., 1964; MBA, U. So. Calif., 1973. Bar: Calif. 1964. Ptnr. Darling, Mack, Hall & Call, Los Angeles, 1965-69; v.p., gen. counsel, sec. The Leisure Group Inc., Los Angeles, 1969-76; sr. v.p., gen. counsel, dir. Calif. Life Corp., Los Angeles, 1976-78; v.p., gen. counsel, sec. Pacific S.W. Airlines, San Diego, 1978-85, v.p. human resources and adminstrn., 1985-87; v.p., gen. counsel, sec. PS Group Inc., San Diego, 1978-87; sr. v.p., gen. counsel, chief adminstrv. officer AM Internat., Inc., Chgo., 1988-94; chmn. San Diego Travel Group, Inc., 1994—, Simpact Inc., San Diego, 1995—; pres., CEO Bus. Backers' Mgmt. Corp., San Diego and San Jose, 1996—. Bd. dirs. San Diego C. of C., 1983-86, Rancho Santa Fe (Calif.) Community Found., 1981-89; pres. Palos Verdes (Calif.) Community Arts Assn., 1976-77; trustee Rancho Santa Fe Youth Inc., 1980-82. Mem. ABA, Calif. Bar Assn. Avocations: running, skiing. Address: PO Box 945 Rancho Santa Fe CA 92067-0945

RIBMAN, RONALD BURT, playwright; b. N.Y.C., May 28, 1932; s. Samuel M. and Rosa (Lerner) R.; m. Alice S. Rosen, Aug. 27, 1967; 2 children. BBA, U. Pitts., 1954, MLitt, 1958, PhD, 1962. Asst. prof. English lit. Otterbein Coll., 1962-63. Author plays including: Harry, Noon and Night, 1965, The Journey of the Fifth Horse, 1966 (Obie award Best Play, 1965-66), The Ceremony of Innocence, 1967, Passing Through From Exotic Places (includes The Son Who Hunted Tigers in Jakarta, Sunstroke, The Burial of Esposito), 1969, Fingernails Blue as Flowers, 1971, A Break in the Skin, 1972, The Poison Tree, 1976 (Straw Hat award Best New Play, 1973), Cold Storage, 1977 (Elizabeth Hull-Kate Warriner award Dramatists Guild 1977), Buck, 1983 (Playwrights USA award 1984), The Cannibal Masque, 1987, A Serpent's Egg, 1987, Sweet Table at the Richelieu, 1987, The Rug Merchants Of Chaos, 1991, Dream of the Red Spider, 1993, (screenplays) The Final War of Olly Winter, 1967 (Emmy award nomination 1967), The Angel Levine, 1969, Seize The Day, 1986; (miniseries) The Sunset Gang, 1991. With AUS, 1954-56. Rockefeller Found grantee, 1966, 68; Guggenheim fellow, 1970; Nat. Endowment Arts fellow, 1974, 86-87; Rockefeller Found. awardee for contbn. to Am. Theatre, 1975. Address: 152 Stone Meadow South Salem NY 10590 Address: BDP 11532 Chiquita St Studio City CA 91604-2914*

RIBNER, HERBERT SPENCER, physicist, educator; b. Seattle, Apr. 9, 1913; s. Joseph Herman and Rose Esther (Goldberg) R.; m. Lelia Carolyn Byrd, Oct. 29, 1949; children—Carol Anne, David Byrd. B.S., Calif. Inst. Tech., 1935; M.S., Washington U., St. Louis, 1937; Ph.D., Washington U., 1939. From physicist to dir. lab. Brown Geophys. Co., Tex., 1939-40; from physicist to head stability sect. Langley Lab., NACA, Va., 1940-49; cons. to head boundary layer sects. Lewis Lab. NACA, Cleve., 1949-54; research assoc. Inst. aerospace studies U. Toronto, Ont., Can., 1955-56; asst. prof. U. Toronto, 1956-57, assoc. prof., 1957-59, prof., 1959-78, prof. emeritus, 1978—; vis. prof. U. Southampton, 1960-61; staff scientist NASA Langley Research Ctr., 1975-76, disting. rsch. assoc., 1979—; chmn. sonic boom panel Internat. Civil Aviation Orgn., 1969-70; adviser com. on hearing, bioacoustics and mechanics Nat. Acad. Scis., 1972-74. Contbr. over 100 articles to profl. jours. Recipient Can. 125th Commemorative medal, 1993, Pub. Svc. medal NASA, 1994. Fellow AIAA (Aero-Acoustics award 1976, Dryden lectr. 1981), Royal Soc. Can., Am. Phys. Soc., Acoustical Soc. Am., Can. Aero. and Space Inst. (Turnbull lectr. 1968); mem. Can. Acoustical Assn. (chmn. 1966-68). Office: U Toronto Inst Aerospace Studies, 4925 Dufferin St, Downsview, ON Canada M3H 5T6

RICARD, JOHN H., bishop, educator; b. Baton Rouge, Feb. 29, 1940; s. Maceo and Albanie (St. Amant) R. BA, St. Joseph Sem., 1962, MA, 1968; MS, Tulane U., 1970. Ordained priest Roman Cath. Ch., 1968. Pastor Holy Redeemer Ch., Washington, 1972-75, Holy Comforter Ch., Washington, 1975-84; ordained titular bishop of Rucuma, 1984; aux. bishop Balt., 1984; assoc. prof. Cath. U. Am., Washington, 1973—; mem. priest's senate Archdiocese of Washington, 1974—, mem. shc. bd., 1976—. Chmn. Com. on Social Devel. and World Peace, Domestic Social Devel., 1992-95; pres. Catholic. Relief Svcs. USCC, 1995—; mem. Pontifical Coun., COR UNUM, 1996—. Mem. Secretariat of Black Caths. Office: St Francis Xavier Rectory 1501 E Oliver St Baltimore MD 21213-2910*

RICARD, THOMAS ARMAND, electrical engineer; b. Waterbury, Conn., Sept. 10, 1954; s. Armand Andrew and Mary Jean (Clark) R.; m. Gina Marie Harris, Sept. 10, 1983; children: Bernadette Allison, Amanda Valentine. BSEE, U. Hartford, 1988; MSEE, Syracuse U., 1991. Engr. in tng., Conn. Edison engr. GE, Syracuse, N.Y., 1988-92; radio frequency/microwave engr. EZ Form Cable Corp., New Haven, Conn., 1992—; mem. Electronic Industry Assn. Working Group on Cable and Connectors, New Haven, 1995—. Mem. Am. Radio Relay League, Tau Beta Pi, Eta Kappa Nu. Avocations: amateur radio. Home: 186 Peck Ln Cheshire CT 06410-2000 Office: EZ Form Cable Corporation 315 Peck St Ste 24 New Haven CT 06513-2951

RICARDI, LEON JOSEPH, electrical engineer; b. Brockton, Mass., Mar. 21, 1924; s. Philip Julius and Eva Isabel (DuBois) R.; m. Angelena Marie Giorgio, Jan. 19, 1947; children: Eva Marie, John Philip, Richard Christopher. B.S. in Elec. Engring, Northeastern U., 1949, M.S., 1952, Ph.D., 1969. Engr. Andrew Alford Cons. Engrs., Boston, 1950-51; project engr. Gabirel Labs., Needham, Mass., 1951-54; group leader, head Tech. Adv. Office, MIT-Lincoln Lab., Lexington, Mass., 1954-84; pres. L.J. Ricardi, Inc., El Segundo, Calif., 1984-95, Creative Engring., Manhattan Beach, Calif., 1996—; part-time tchr. Northeastern U., Boston, 1969-80; cons. U.S. Air Force, 1965-85. Served with USAF, 1943-45. Fellow IEEE. Roman Catholic. Office: Creative Engring 865 Manhattan Beach Blvd Manhattan Beach CA 90266-4900 *Listen as much as possible but never fail to speak when you feel that you are right and what you have to say is more than of average importance.*

RICARDO-CAMPBELL, RITA, economist, educator; b. Boston, Mar. 16, 1920; d. David and Elizabeth (Jones) Ricardo; m. Wesley Glenn Campbell, Sept. 15, 1946; children: Barbara Lee, Diane Rita, Nancy Elizabeth. BS, Simmons Coll., 1941; MA, Harvard U., 1945, PhD, 1946. Instr. Harvard U., Cambridge, Mass., 1946-48; asst. prof. Tufts U., Medford, Mass., 1948-51; labor economist U.S. Wage Stabilization Bd., 1951-53; economist Ways and Means Com. U.S. Ho. of Reps., 1953; cons. economist, 1957-60; vis. prof. San Jose State Coll., 1960-61; sr. fellow Hoover Instn. on War, Revolution, and Peace, Stanford, Calif., 1968-95, sr. fellow emerita, 1995—; lectr. health svc. adminstrn. Stanford U. Med. Sch., 1973-78; bd. dirs. Watkins-Johnson Co., Palo Alto, Calif., Gillette Co., Boston; mgmt. bd. Samaritan Med. Ctr., San Jose, Calif. Author: Voluntary Health Insurance in the U.S., 1960, Economics of Health and Public Policy, 1971, Food Safety Regulation: Use and Limitations of Cost-Benefit Analysis, 1974, Drug Lag: Federal Government Decision Making, 1976, Social Security: Promise and Reality, 1977, The Economics and Politics of Health, 1982, 2d edit., 1985; co-editor: Below-Replacement Fertility in Industrial Societies, 1987, Issues in Contemporary Retirement, 1988, Resisting Hostile Takeovers: The Gillette Company, 1997; contbr. articles to profl. jours. Commr. Western Interstate Commn. for Higher Edn. Calif., 1967-75, chmn., 1970-71; mem. Pres. Nixon's Adv. Coun. on Status Women, 1969-76; mem. task force on taxation Pres.'s Coun. on Environ. Quality, 1970-72; mem. Pres.'s Com. Health Services Industry, 1971-73, FDA Nat. Adv. Drug Com., 1972-75; mem. Econ. Policy Adv. Bd., 1981-90, Pres. Reagan's Nat. Coun. on Humanities, 1982-89, Pres. Nat. Medal of Sci. com., 1988-94; bd. dirs. Ind. Colls. No. Calif., 1971-87; mem. com. assessment of safety, benefits, risks Citizens Commn. Sci., Law and Food Supply, Rockefeller U., 1973-75; mem. adv. com. Ctr. Health Policy Rsch., Am. Enterprise Inst. Pub. Policy Rsch., Washington, 1974-80; mem. adv. coun. on social security Social Security Adminstrn., 1974-75; bd. dirs. Simmons Coll. Corp., Boston, 1975-80; mem. adv. coun. bd. assocs. Stanford Librs., 1975-78; mem. coun. SRI Internat., Menlo Park, Calif., 1977-90. Mem. Am. Econ. Assn., Mont Pelerin Soc. (bd. dirs. 1988-92, v.p. 1992-94), Harvard Grad. Soc. (coun. 1991), Phi Beta Kappa. Home: 26915 Alejandro Dr Los Altos Hills CA 94022-1932 Office: Stanford U Hoover Instn Stanford CA 94305-6010

RICARDS, JUNE ELAINE, nursing consultant, administrator; b. Nebr., June 3, 1939; d. Carl F. and Merle E. (Block) Middendorf; children: Elaine R. Hertz, Kristine K. Hineline. Diploma, Lincoln Gen. Hosp., 1960; BSN, Calif. State U., Bakersfield, 1980. Cert. nurse operating room, nurse adminstrn. Asst. dir. nursing svc. Kern Med. Ctr., Bakersfield, 1976-80; mgr. surg. svcs. St. Vincent Hosp., Billings, Mont., 1980-84; sr. coord. consultation Assn. Operating Room Nurses, Denver, 1984-87; dir. surg. svcs. Boone Hosp. Ctr., Columbia, Mo., 1989-92; nurse cons. Higman Healthcare, St. Petersburg, Fla., 1992-94, Allegiance Healthcare, Chgo., 1994—. Mem. ANA, Am. Coll. Healthcare Execs., Assn. Operating Room Nurses, Sigma Theta Tau.

RICART, FRED, automotive company executive. CEO Ricart Automotive, Groveport, Ohio. Office: Ricart Automotive 4255 S Hamilton Rd Groveport OH 43125-9332*

RICCA, JOSEPH JOHN, internist, gastroenterologist; b. Bklyn., Nov. 26, 1925; s. John F. and Josephine C. (Ingegno) R.; m. Heather Moira Dorman, Dec. 11, 1965; children: Gerald, Laurie Ellen, Joseph Patrick. BS, Fordham U., 1949; MD, SUNY, Bklyn., 1953. Diplomate Am. Bd. Internal Medicine, Am. Bd. Gastroenterology. Intern L.I. Coll. Hosp., Bklyn., 1953-54, resident, 1954-56; chief resident Bklyn. VA Hosp., 1956-57; gastroenterology fellow L.I. Coll. Hosp., 1972-73, chief gastroenterology, 1979-84; chief gastroenterology Victory Meml. Hosp., Bklyn., 1984-94; attending staff Victory Meml. Hosp., 1984—; pvt. practice Bklyn., 1957—; cons. medicine, L.I. Coll. Hosp., 1991—; clin. asst. prof. SUNY, Bklyn., 1972-89. Contbg. author: Prevention of Kidney Disease and Long Term Survival, 1982; contbr. articles to profl. jours. Recipient Physicians Recognition award AMA, 1969-73, 73-77, 77-83. Fellow ACP, Am. Coll. Gastroenterology. Avocations: landscape photography; professional actor. Office: 235 Bay Ridge Pkwy Brooklyn NY 11209-2403

RICCARDI, ROBERT, advertising executive. Ptnr., gen. mgr. Goodby, Silverstein & Ptnrs., San Francisco. Office: Goodby Silverstein & Ptnrs 921 Front St San Francisco CA 94111-1426

RICCARDS, MICHAEL PATRICK, academic administrator; b. Hillside, N.J., Oct. 2, 1944; s. Patrick and Margaret (Finelli) R.; m. Barbara Dunlop, June 6, 1970; children: Patrick, Catherine, Abigail. BA, Rutgers U., 1966, MA, 1967, MPhil, 1969, PhD, 1970. Spl. asst. to chancellor Dept. Higher Edn., Trenton, N.J., 1969-70; from asst. prof. to assoc. prof. SUNY, Buffalo, 1970-77; dean U. Mass., Boston, 1977-82; provost, prof. Hunter Coll.-CUNY, 1982-86; pres. St. John's Coll., Santa Fe, 1986-89, Shepherd Coll., Shepherdstown, W.Va., 1989-95, Fitchburg (Mass.) State Coll., 1995—.

Author: The Making of the American Citizenry, 1973, A Republic If You Can Keep It, 1987, The Ferocious Engine of Democracy, 2 vols., 1995; co-editor: Reflections on American Political Thought, 1973. Chmn. N.Mex. Endowment for Humanities, 1989; mem. nat. adv. com. Ctr. for Study of Presidency, 1987—; mem. bd. trustees Albuquerque Acad.; mem. Coun. Humanities W.Va. Fulbright fellow 1973, Huntington Libr. fellow 1974, NEH fellow Princeton U. 1976-77. Home: 123 Apple Tree Hl Fitchburg MA 01420-2471 Office: Fitchburg State Coll Office of the Pres Fitchburg MA 01420

RICCELLI, RICHARD JOSEPH, advertising agency executive; b. Winchester, Mass., Dec. 7, 1954; s. Carmen Joseph and Arline Muriel (Young) R.; m. Constance Elizabeth McCabe, May 17, 1980 (div. Oct. 1987). BS, Kent State U., 1977. Copywriter Ogilvy & Mather, Inc., N.Y.C., 1978-80; creative supr. Bozell & Jacobs, Inc., Mpls., 1980-81; v.p. Quinn & Johnson, BBDO, Boston, 1982-85; pres. Smith & Jones Inc., Newburyport, Mass., 1985-86; v.p. Mullen, Inc., Prides Crossing, Mass., 1986-87; pres. Riccelli Direct, Inc., Boston, 1987—. Recipient Echo award Direct Mktg. Assn., N.Y.C., 1979, 91, Caples award, N.Y.C., 1991, Circulation Direct Mktg. award, 1991, 92, 93, 94, Mag. Pubs. Assn. and Folio Mag., N.Y.C. Home: 32 Claremont Park Boston MA 02118 Office: Riccelli Direct Inc 32 Claremont Park Boston MA 02118-3002

RICCI, CHRISTINA, actress. Appeared in films Mermaids, 1990, The Hard Way, 1991, The Addams Family, 1991, The Cemetery Club, 1993, Addams Family Values, 1993, Casper, 1995, Now and Then, 1995, Gold Diggers: The Secret of Bear Mountain, 1995, That Darn Cat, 1996, Ice Storm, 1997. Office: ICM 8942 Wilshire Blvd Beverly Hills CA 90211*

RICCI, DANIEL MICHAEL, protective services official; b. Troy, N.Y., Sept. 23, 1955; s. Anthony Joseph and Dolores Margaret (Poland) R.; m. Joan Frances Fleming, May 14, 1977; children: Brian Matthew, Scott Michael. AA in Criminal Justice, L.A. City Coll., 1978; grad., FBI Nat. Acad. Cert. police instr. N.Y. State Divsn. of Criminal Justice Svcs. Police officer Various Cities, 1979-89; sgt. Stony Point (N.Y.) Police Dept., 1989, adminstrv. sgt., 1989-96, lt., exec. officer, 1996—; accreditation project mgr. Stony Point Police Dept., 1991—. Dep. mayor Village of Highland Falls, 1993—, trustee, 1993—, vol. counselor Birch Summer Project, Springfield Gardens, N.Y., 1995. Recipient Cert. of Merit N.Y. Sen., 1991, Cert. of Achievement N.Y. State Divsn. Criminal Justice Svcs., 1992. Mem. FBI Nat. Acad. Assn., Mensa, Rockland County Police Benevolent Assn., Stony Point Police Benevolent Assn. Home: 26 South St Highland Falls NY 10928 Office: Stony Point Police Dept 79 Route 210 Stony Point NY 10980-1750

RICCI, GIOVANNI MARIO, finance company executive, government consultant; b. Barga, Lucca, Italy, Aug. 7, 1929; s. Ettore and Jolanda (Bardoni) R.; m. Lia Cheli, Feb. 14, 1949 (div. 1970); children: Ettore, Franco, Cristiana; m. Angela Carbognin, Oct. 21, 1973; children: Mariangela, Rebecca. Ed. Italian schs.; D. honoris causa in Theology, 1983. Fin. advisor Seychelles Republic, 1974—; journalist, corr. ANSA (Italian News Agy.), 1980—; chmn., CEO sales, restructuring, mergers and indsl. mgmt. GMR Group A.G.; founder, hon. chmn. Fondazione Ricci, Lucca, Italy, 1990—. Office: Arbobyl Ltd, GMR Group AG, Via Canonica 14, CH-6900 Lugano Switzerland

RICCI, ROBERT RONALD, manufacturing company executive; b. N.Y.C., Jan. 11, 1945; s. George and Mary Pauline (Barbieri) R.; m. Sandra Piccione, Jan. 18, 1948; children: Jason, Sean. AAS, S.I. Community Coll., 1972; BBA, Bernard Baruch Coll., 1974, MBA, 1976. Sales mgr. G.A.F. Photo, Elizabeth, N.J., 1974-76; v.p. Photo Drive Thru, Pennsauken, N.J., 1976-80; head nat. accounts Berkey Photo, Phila., 1980-85; dir. nat. account sales Qualex, Inc., Durham, N.C., 1988-92, v.p. sales east, 1993-95; v.p. new acct. devel. sales National, 1995—; pres. Sanjasean, Inc., Marlton, N.J., 1978-86. Served with USN, 1966-70. Mem. Photo Mktg. Assn. Republican. Roman Catholic. Avocations: photography, carpentry, computers. Home: 1001 Clingmans Pl Raleigh NC 27614-8199 Office: Qualex Inc 3404 N Duke St Durham NC 27704-2108

RICCI, RUGGIERO, violinist, educator; b. San Francisco, July 24, 1918; s. Pietro Ricci and Emma Bacigalupi; m. Ruth Rink, 1942; m. Valma Rodriguez, 1957; m. Julia Whitehurst Clemenceau, 1978; 5 children. Pupil, Louis Persinger, Mischel Piastro, Paul Stassevitch, Georg Kulenkampff. Began career as child prodigy; N.Y. debut Manhattan Symphony, 1929; performed concert engagements throughout world including unaccompanied violin recitals, 1st European tour, 1932, specializes in violin solo, introduced Ginastera, von Einem and Veerhoff violin concerti, U.S. premiere Paganini, 6th violin concerto; prof. music Ind. U., 1971-74, Juilliard Sch., 1974-79, U. Mich., Ann Arbor, 1982-87; prof. Mozarteum, Salzburg, Austria, 1989—. Recordings include The GreatViolinist Series, The Making of a Legend, Vols. 3, 4, Portrait of an Artist, Vol. 4, Vol. 6, Ruggiero Ricci, Virtuoso Recital. Served with USAAF, 1942-45. Decorated Knight Order of Merit Italy. Mem. Royal Acad. Music (hon.). Made first complete recording of Paganini's Caprices. Office: Intermusica Stephen Lumsden, 16 Duncan Terr, London N1 8B2, England also: One-Eleven Ltd c/o Albany Music Distrs Inc P O Box 5011 Albany NY 12205 also: c/o John Gingrich Mgmt Inc P O Box 1515 New York NY 10023*

RICCIARDI, ANTONIO, prosthodontist, implantologist, educator; b. Jersey City, June 5, 1922; s. Frank and Eugenia (Izzo) R.; m. Lucy DePalma, June 21, 1945; children: Eugenia, Lynda. BA in Chemistry, Upsala Coll., 1951; DDS, Temple U., 1958. Diplomate Am. Bd. Oral Implantology, Am. Bd. Implant Dentistry. Purchasing agt. Dade Bros., Newark, Airport, 1951-52; asst. work mgr. Cooper Alloy Steel Co., Hillside, N.J., 1954; chemist White's Pharm. Co., Union, N.J., 1954; practice gen. dentistry, Westfield, N.J., 1958—; dentist Westfield Public Schs., 1958-60; mem. staff Mountainside Hosp., Montclair, N.J., St. Elizabeth's Hosp., Elizabeth, N.J.; implant staff John F. Kennedy Hosp., Edison, N.J., chief of prosthetics, 1980—; clin. chmn. implant study Columbia U. Sch. Oral Surgery and Dentistry; implant cons. Columbia Presbyn. Sch. Oral Surgery and Dentistry, N.Y.C.; cons. Implants Internat., N.Y.C., 1971—; pres. Universal Dental Implements, Inc., 1979—. Pres. Nat. Gymnastics Clinic, Sarasota, Fla., 1968—; v.p. rebound tumbling center Welmarick Inc.,Plainfield, 1958—. Gymnastics ofcl. Eastern Coll. Conf., 1954—. Served to lt. col. USMCR, fighter pilot, 1942-48, jet fighter pilot, 52-54, Korea. Fellow Acad. Gen. Dentistry, Royal Soc. Health (Eng.), Internat. Coll. Oral Implantology (founding mem.), Am. Acad. Gen. Dentistry, Am. Acad. Implant Dentistry (program chmn. nat. conv. 1974, sec. 1976, pres. N.E. sect. 1978, chmn. ethics com. 1980, ethics chmn. 1981, credentialling mem. 1985—), Acad. Dentistry Internat., Am. Acad. Implant Dentistry, Fedn. Dentistry Internat.; hon fellow Italian and German implant socs.; mem. Inst. Endosseous Implants, Inst. for Advance Dental Research, ADA, Middlesex County Dental Assn., Union County and Plainfield Dental Soc. Fedn. Prosthodontics Orgns., Internat. Research Com. on Oral Implantology (pres. U.S. chpt.), Am. Acad. Oral Implantology, Nat. Gymnastics Judges Assn. (pres. Eastern div.; named to Gymnastic Hall of Fame 1978), Delta Sigma Delta. Writer, tchr. on implantology. Achievements include the introduction first instrument for intraligamentary anesthesia in the U.S.; introduction of the first removable head on endosseous blade implants in the U.S. Address: 1450 Fernwood Rd Mountainside NJ 07092-2503 *Living a life not just for oneself contributes not only to the elevation of humankind but also to the ennoblement and enrichment of one's own life.*

RICCIARDI, LOUIS MICHAEL, brokerage house executive; b. Worcester, Mass., Oct. 15, 1959; s. Michael Joseph and Mary Theresa (Searles) R.; m. Cynthia Anne Booth, Mar. 20, 1982. BA, Bridgewater State Coll., 1981. Account exec. Shearson/Am. Express, Brockton, Mass., 1981-83; v.p. Thomson McKinnon, Taunton, Mass., 1983-87; sr. v.p. Dean Witter-Reynolds, Taunton, Mass., 1988—; bd. corporators Bristol County Savs. Bank, Taunton, Mass., 1985—, bd. trustees, 1992—; trustee Taunton Devel. Corp., 1994—, treas. 1995—; mem. Nuveen Adv. Coun., Chgo., 1986—. Weekly investment columnist, 1983—. Bd. corporators Morton Hosp., Taunton, 1987—, trustee, 1994—; pres. Heart of Taunton (Mass.) Revitalization Corp., 1988-89; trustee Bridgewater (Mass.) State Coll., 1989—, chmn. 1990-94; trustee Bridgewater Found., 1989—, chmn. 1996—. Mem. Taunton Area C. of C. (dir. 1988-94, treas. 1993-94), Taunton Rotary Club (pres. 1991-92), Bridgewater Coll. Alumni Assn. (treas. 1988-95). Avocations: guitar, coin collecting, baseball, community svc., Coca Cola memorabilia. Home: PO Box 228 Taunton MA 02780

RICCIARELLI, KATIA, soprano; b. Rovigo, Italy, Jan. 18, 1946; m. Pippo Baudo, 1986. Grad. summa cum laude, Benedetto Marcello Conservatory, Venice, Italy. Operatic debut as Mimi in La Boheme, Mantua, Italy, 1969, also Covent Garden, London, 1974, I Due Foscari, Lyric Opera, Chgo., 1972; appeared in Suor Angelica, La Scala, Milan, 1976, La Boheme, Met. Opera Co., N.Y.C., 1975; other roles include Donizetti's Caterina Cornaro, Maria de Rohan and Lucrezia Borgia, and Bellini's Imogene, Elisabeth de Valois in Don Carlos, Covent Garden, 1989; numerous appearances in maj. opera houses throughout U.S. and Europe including San Francisco Opera, Paris Opera, Verona Festival; leading roles in Anna Bolena; recs. include I Due Foscari, Turandot, Carmen, Aida, Un Ballo in Maschera, Falstaff, Il Trovatore, La Boheme, Tosca, Pavarotti and Ricciarelli Live, Duetti d'Amore with Jose Carreras; also appears as Desdemona in Franco Zeffirelli's video Otello. Office: Harold Hoyt Ltd, 31 Sinclair Rd, London England WI4 0NS Office: Via Magellana 2, I-20097 Corsica Italy*

RICCIO-SAUER, JOYCE, art educator; b. Jersey City, Nov. 19, 1950; d. Frank and Jennie (Giuliano) Riccio; children: Jessica, Joshua; m. Peter Edmund Sauer, Aug. 8, 1992. BA, William Paterson Coll., 1972, MA, 1981. Cert. elem. tchr., art tchr., N.J., supr. cert., 1997. Elem. art tchr. West Milford (N.J.) Bd. Edn., 1972-74; art tchr. Bridgewater Raritan Bd. of Edn., Raritan, N.J., 1974-81, tchr. 4th grade, 1975-76, tchr. 6th grade, 1981-82; tchr. reading, social studies 7th and 8th grade Wood-Ridge (N.J.) Bd. Edn., 1985-86; secondary tchr. visual arts Ridgewood (N.J.) High Sch., 1986—; Cons. Grove Pubs., Teaneck, N.J., 1992. Mem. NEA, N.J. Edn. Assn., Nat. Art Edn. Assn., Art Educators of N.J. (conf. speaker), Ridgewood Edn. Assn. (rep. 1991—), Internat. Platform Assn. Avocations: ceramics, canoeing, travel, silver smith. Office: Ridgewood High Sch 627 E Ridgewood Ave Ridgewood NJ 07450-3394

RICE, (ETHEL) ANN, publishing executive, editor; b. South Bend, Ind., July 3, 1933; d. Walter A. and Ethylan Maude (Worden) R. A.B., Nazareth Coll., Kalamazoo, 1955. Editorial asst. Ave Maria mag., Notre Dame, Ind., 1955-63, asst. editor, 1963-64; asst. editor Today mag., Notre Dame, 1963-64, Scott, Foresman & Co., Chgo., 1964-67; editor U. Notre Dame Press, 1967-74, exec. editor, 1974—. Democrat. Roman Catholic. Office: U Notre Dame Press Notre Dame IN 46556

RICE, ANNE, author; b. New Orleans, Oct. 14, 1941; d. Howard and Katherine (Allen) O'Brien; m. Stan Rice, Oct. 14, 1961; children: Michele (dec.), Christopher. Student, Tex. Woman's U., 1959-60; BA, San Francisco State Coll., 1964, MA, 1971. Author: Interview with the Vampire, 1976, The Feast of all Saints, 1980, Cry to Heaven, 1982, The Vampire Lestat, 1985, The Queen of the Damned, 1988, The Mummy or Ramses the Damned, 1989, The Witching Hour, 1990, Tale of the Body Thief, 1992, Lasher, 1993, Taltos, 1994, Memnoch the Devil, 1995, Violin, 1997; (as A.N. Roquelaure) The Claiming of Sleeping Beauty, 1983, Beauty's Punishment, 1984, Beauty's Release: The Continued Erotic Adventures of Sleeping Beauty, 1985, Memnoch the Devil, Servant of the Bone, 1996; (as Anne Rampling) Exit to Eden, 1985, Belinda, 1986; screenwriter: Interview with a Vampire, 1994. Office: care Alfred A Knopf Inc 201 E 50th St New York NY 10022-7703*

RICE, ANNIE L. KEMPTON, medical, surgical and rehabilitation nurse; b. West Fairlee, Vt., Oct. 26, 1932; d. James Warren and Lena May (Bower) R.; m. Abbott Eames Rice, Aug. 29, 1959; children: James W., Beverly A., Abbott Jr., David K. Diploma, Mary Hitchcock Sch. Nursing, Hanover, N.H., 1955; student, U. R.I., 1956-57; BSN, Boston U., 1959; postgrad., St. Anthlems Coll., Manchester, N.H. RN. Staff nurse spl. care unit R.I. Hosp., 1955; staff nurse New England Deaconess Hosp., Boston, 1957; head nurse Jordan Hosp, Plymouth, Mass., 1960; staff nurse ICU/emergency Lakes Region Hosp., Laconia, N.H., 1968; staff nurse Pine Hill Nurses Registry, Nashua, N.H., 1976; charge nurse Greenbriar Terr., Nashua, 1985—. Past mem. Arthritis Found. Mem. Mary Hitchcock Sch. Nursing Alumnae, Boston U. Alumnae, Order Ea. Star, Grange. Home: 28 Sunland Dr Hudson NH 03051-3209

RICE, ARGYLL PRYOR, Hispanic studies and Spanish language educator; b. Va.; d. Theodorick Pryor and Argyll (Campbell) R. BA, Smith Coll., 1952; MA, Yale U., 1956, PhD, 1961. Spanish instr. Yale U., New Haven, 1959-60, 61-63; asst. prof. Spanish, Conn. Coll., New London, 1964-67, assoc. prof., 1967-72, prof., 1972—, chair dept. Hispanic Studies, 1971-74, 77-84. Author: Emilio Ballagas: poeta o poesia, 1967, Emilio Ballagas, Latin American Writers III; editor in chief Carlos A. Sole, Charles Scribner's Sons, 1989. Mem. MLA, Am. Assn. Tchrs. of Spanish and Portuguese, New Eng. Coun. Latin Am. Studies, U.S. Tennis Assn. (New England hall of fame), Phi Beta Kappa. Avocations: music, tennis. Home: 292 Pequot Ave New London CT 06320-4451 Office: Conn Coll Dept of Hispanic Studies New London CT 06320

RICE, CHARLES DUNCAN, university official; b. Aberdeen, Scotland, Oct. 20, 1942; came to U.S., 1969; s. James Inglis and Jane Meauras (Scroggie) R.; m. Susan Ilene Wunsch, July 5, 1967; children: James Duncan, Samuel Duncan, Jane Emma. MA with 1st class honors, U. Aberdeen, 1966; PhD, U. Edinburgh, Scotland, 1969. Lectr. history U. Aberdeen, 1966-69; asst. prof. history Yale U., New Haven, 1970-76, assoc. prof., 1976-79; prof. history Hamilton Coll., Clinton, N.Y., 1979-85, dean, 1979-85; prof. history, dean faculty of arts and sci. NYU, 1985-95, vice chancellor, 1991-96; prin., vice chancellor U. Aberdeen, Scotland, 1996—. Author: Rise and Fall of Black Slavery, 1975, The Scots Abolitionists, 1982; assoc. editor: Slavery and Abolition, 1979-86; contbr. articles and revs. in field. Trustee The Peddie Sch., Hightstown, N.J., 1973-82, 86—. C. & J. Henry Fund fellow, 1965-66, Am. Coun. Learned Socs. fellow, 1969-70, Morse fellow, 1976-75. Office: U Aberdeen, Office of Vice Chancellor, Aberdeen Scotland

RICE, CHARLES EDWARD, bank executive; b. Chattanooga, Tenn., Aug. 4, 1936; s. Charles Edward and Louise (Goodson) R.; m. Dianne Tauscher; children: Danny, Celeste, Michelle. B.B.A., U. Miami, 1958; M.B.A., Rollins Coll., Winter Park, Fla., 1964; grad., Advanced Mgmt. Program, Harvard U., 1975. Vice pres., then pres. Barnett Bank, Winter Park, 1965-71; exec. v.p. Barnett Banks Fla., Inc., Jacksonville, 1971-73, pres., from 1973, chief exec. officer, 1979—, now also chmn., bd. dirs.; bd. dirs. Sprint Corp., CSX Corp. Trustee Univ. of Miami, Rollins Coll. Office: Barnett Banks Inc 50 N Laura St Jacksonville FL 32202-3664*

RICE, CHARLES LANE, surgical educator; b. Atlanta, May 22, 1945; s. Marion Jennings and Molly Black (Moore) R.; m. Lynn Carol Inscoe, Dec. 27, 1968 (div. 1976); m. Judith Josephine Bousha, July 9, 1977; children: Aaron Nicholas, Patrick Marion. AB, U. Ga., 1964; MD, Med. Coll. Ga., 1968. Commd. ensign USN, 1966, advanced through grades to comdr., 1976, ret., 1977; intern Bowman Gray Sch. Medicine, Winston-Salem, N.C., 1968-69; resident Nat. Naval Med. Ctr., Bethesda, Md., 1969-73; asst. prof. surgery U. Chgo., 1977-80, assoc. prof. surgery, 1980-84; dir. intensive care unit Michael Reese Hosp., Chgo., 1977-84; prof., vice chmn. dept. surgery U. Wash., Seattle, 1985-92; surgeon-in-chief Harborview Med. Ctr., Seattle, 1985-92; Dr. Lee Hudson- Robert R. Penn prof., chmn., divsn. gen. surgery U. Tex. Southwestern Med. Ctr., Dallas, 1992-93; prof. surgery U. Ill., Chgo., 1993—; vice dean Coll. Medicine, 1994—; Robert Wood Johnson Health Policy fellow, 1991-92; legis. asst. to U.S. senator Tom Daschle, 1991-92; ann. lectr. U. Wash. Assoc. editor Jour. of Surg. Rsch., 1983-90; contbr. articles to profl. jours. Capt. U.S. Naval Res., 1989—. Fellow ACS (gov. 1992— vice chmn. com. on trauma 1992-93), Am. Surg. Assn., Am. Assn. for Surgery of Trauma (com. chair 1989-91); mem. Soc. Univ. Surgeons, Am. Physiol. Soc., Shock Soc. (pres. 1991-92). Democrat. Episcopalian. Office: U of IL Com Office of the Dean 1819 W Polk St # C 784 Chicago IL 60612-7331

RICE, CLARE I., electronics company executive; b. Rice Lake, Wis., Nov. 3, 1918; s. Chris Nilson and Ingeborg (Haug) R.; m. Virginia M. Bateman; children: Karen Bateman, Carol Rice Brannon, David Alan; m. Theda Baker. B.S. in Elec. Engring, U. Wis., 1943; B.S. in Law, St. Paul Coll. Law, 1950; D.Engring., Rose-Hulman Inst. Tech., 1979. Registered profl. engr., Minn., D.C. Supr. aircraft radio engring. Northwest Airlines, Inc., Mpls., 1946-51; staff engr. Aero. Radio, Inc., Washington, 1951-53; aviation sales mgr., gen. mgr. Bendix Avionics Div., Balt., 1953-62; pres. Sunbeam Electronics, Inc., Ft. Lauderdale, Fla., 1962-66; v.p. Nova U., Ft. Lauderdale, 1966-68; asst. v.p., v.p., sr. v.p. Collins Radio Co., pres. Collins Avionics group Rockwell Internat. Corp., Cedar Rapids, Iowa, 1968-83; dir. Rockwell-Collins Internat., Inc., Dallas. Chmn. United Way, Cedar Rapids, 1973-74; trustee Coe Coll., 1979-83, Hoover Presdl. Libr.; bd. dirs. St. Luke's Hosp., 1976-82, Mchts. Nat. Bank, 1977-83; chmn. Mcpl. Airport Commn., Cedar Rapids, 1980-84; charter mem. Aviation Hall of Fame; capt. Hon. Dep. Sheriffs Assn., 1987—; pres. Cmty. Assn. Rancho Bernardo Heights, 1988-91; dir. Rancho Bernardo Cmty. Found. Lt. comdr. USNR, 1943-46. Recipient Disting. Svc. citation U. Wis., 1979, 84; Pioneer award Milw. Sch. Engring., 1981. Sr. mem. IEEE; mem. Iowa Mfrs. Assn. (bd. dirs. 1975-81), Gen. Aviation Mfrs. Assn. (dir. 1970-81, chmn. 1979), U. Wis. Alumni Assn. (chmn. 1981-82, pres. 1980-81, Disting. Service award 1984), Hon. Dep. Sheriff's Assn. (capt.). Republican. Presbyn. Clubs: Wings (N.Y.C.); Nat. Aviation (Washington); Rancho Bernardo Heights Country. Lodge: Royal Order of Jesters (dir. 1979). Home: 12201 Fairway Pointe San Diego CA 92128-3230

RICE, DARREL ALAN, lawyer; b. Denver, Jan. 8, 1947; s. Dale Harvey and Dorothy (Enewold) F.; m. Jeffrey Lynn Taylor, May 31, 1970; children: Ashley, Justin, Chandler. BSIE, U. Ark., 1969; JD, So. Meth. U., 1972. Bar: Tex. 1972. Assoc. Butler & Binion, Houston, 1972-75, Winstead, McGuire, Sechrest & Minick, P.C., Dallas, 1975-78; shareholder Winstead Sechrest & Minick, P.C., Dallas, 1978—. Trustee 1st Presbyn. Ch. Found., Dallas, 1982-94; adv. dir. Spl. Camps for Spl. Kids, Dallas, 1987-90, bd. dirs., mem. exec. com., 1990—; bd. dirs. Tex. Bus. Law Found., 1989—; bd. dirs., mem. exec. com. Dallas CASA, 1989—, Dallas Opera, 1997—; mem. exec. bd. So. Meth. U. Law Sch., 1991—. Mem. ABA, Tex. Bar Assn., State Bar Tex. (chmn. legal opinions com. 1989-92, mem. coun. bus. law sect. 1992-94), Dallas Bar Assn., Tex. Assn. Bank Counsel, Tower Club. Office: Winstead Sechrest & Minick PC 5400 Renaissance Tower 1201 Elm St Dallas TX 75270-2102

RICE, DENIS TIMLIN, lawyer; b. Milw., July 11, 1932; s. Cyrus Francis and Kathleen (Timlin) R.; children: James Connelly, Tracy Ellen. A.B., Princeton U., 1954; J.D., U. Mich., 1959. Bar: Calif. 1960. Practiced in San Francisco, 1959—; assoc. firm Pillsbury, Madison & Sutro, 1959-61, Howard & Prim, 1961-63; prin. firm Howard, Rice, Nemerovski, Canady, Falk & Rabkin, 1964—; bd. dirs. Gensler & Assocs., Inc., San Francisco, Vanguard Airlines; chmn., mng. com. San Francisco Inst. Fin. Svcs., 1983-92. Councilman, City of Tiburon, Calif., 1968-72, mayor, 1970-72; dir. Marin County Transit Dist., 1970-72, 77-81, chmn., 1979-81; supr. Marin County, 1977-81, chmn., 1979-80; commr. Marin Housing Authority, 1977-81; mem. San Francisco Bay Conservation and Devel. Commn., 1977-83; bd. dirs. Planning and Conservation League, 1981, Marin Symphony, 1984-92, Marin Theatre Co., 1987—, Marin Conservation League, 1995—, Digital Village Found., 1995—; mem. Met. Transp. Commn., 1980-83; mem. bd. visitors U. Mich. Law Sch. 1st lt. AUS, 1955-57. Recipient Freedom Found. medal, 1956. Fellow Am. Bar Found.; mem. ABA (fed. regulation of securities com., chair Asia-Pacific Bus. Law Com.), State Bar Calif., San Francisco Bar Assn., Am. Judicature Soc., Bankers Club, Tiburon Peninsula Club, Nassau Club, Olympic Club, Order of Coif, Phi Beta Kappa, Phi Delta Phi. Home: 98 Main St # 609 Belvedere Tiburon CA 94920-2566 Office: 3 Embarcadero Ctr Ste 700 San Francisco CA 94111-4065

RICE, DONALD BLESSING, business executive, former secretary of air force; b. Frederick, Md., June 4, 1939; s. Donald Blessing and Mary Celia (Santangelo) R.; m. Susan Fitzgerald, Aug. 25, 1962; children: Donald Blessing III, Joseph John, Matthew Fitzgerald. BSChemE, U. Notre Dame, 1961, DEng (hon.), 1975; MS in Indsl. Adminstrn., Purdue U., 1962, PhD in Mgmt. and Econs., 1965, D. Mgmt. (hon.), 1985; LLD (hon.), Pepperdine U., 1989; LHD (hon.), West Coast U., 1993; D in Pub. Policy (hon.), Rand Grad. Sch., 1995. Dir. cost analysis Office Sec. Def., Washington, 1967-69, dep. asst. sec. def. resource analysis, 1969-70; asst. dir. Office Mgmt. and Budget, Exec. Office Pres., 1970-72; pres., CEO The Rand Corp., Calif., 1972-89; sec. USAF, 1989-93; pres., COO Teledyne, Inc., L.A., 1993-96; pres., CEO Urogenesys., Santa Monica, Calif., 1996—; bd. dirs. Vulcan Materials Co., Wells Fargo Bank, Wells Fargo & Co.; mem. Nat. Sci. Bd., 1974-86; chmn. Nat. Commn. Supplies and Shortages, 1975-77; mem. Nat. Commn. on U.S.-China Relations; mem. nat. adv. com. oceans and atmosphere Dept. Commerce, 1972-75; mem. adv. panel Office Tech. Assessment, 1976-79; adv. council Coll. Engring., U. Notre Dame, 1974-88; mem. Def. Sci. Bd., 1977-83, sr. cons., 1984-88; U.S. mem. Trilateral Commn.; dir. for sec. def. and Pres. Def. Resource Mgmt. Study, 1977-79. Author articles. Served to capt. AUS, 1965-67. Recipient Sec. Def. Meritorious Civilian Service medal, 1970, Def. Exceptional Civilian Svc. medal, 1993, Forrestal award, 1992; Ford Found. fellow, 1962-65. Fellow AAAS; mem. Council Fgn. Relations, Inst. Mgmt. Scis. (past pres.), Tau Beta Pi. Office: Urogenesys 1701 Colorado Ave Santa Monica CA 90404-3436*

RICE, DONALD SANDS, lawyer, entrepreneur; b. Bronxville, N.Y., Mar. 25, 1940; s. Anton Henry and Lydia Phipps (Sands) R.; m. Edgenie Higgins, Aug. 27, 1966; children: Alice Higgins, Edgenie Reynolds. AB magna cum laude, Harvard U., 1961, LLB cum laude, 1964; LLM in Taxation, NYU, 1965. Bar: N.Y. 1964, U.S. Ct. Claims 1965, U.S. Supreme Ct. 1981. Law clk. to judge U.S. Ct. Claims, 1965-67; assoc. Barrett, Smith, Schapiro & Simon, N.Y.C., 1967-71; ptnr. Barrett, Smith, Schapiro, Simon & Armstrong, N.Y.C., 1971-86; vice chmn. bd. The Bowery Savs. Bank, N.Y.C., 1986-88; also bd. dirs. The Bowery Savs. Bank; ptnr. Chadbourne & Parke, N.Y.C., 1988-96; mng. dir. and prin. Ravitch Rice & Co. LLC, N.Y.C., 1996—; lectr. Nat. Assn. Real Estate Investment Trusts, Bank Adminstrs. Inst., Bank Tax Inst., 1971-86; chmn., bd. dirs. Corp. of Yaddo, 1986—; co-chmn. Soviet-Am. Banking Law Working Group, 1991—; v.p., treas., bd. dirs. Soviet Bus. and Comml. Law Edn. Found., 1991-96; vol. lectr. Fin. Svcs. Vol. Corps Mongolian Bank Tng. Program, 1993, Georgetown Internat. Law Inst., NYU Sch. Continuing Edn., Russian Trade Fair-U.S. Dept. Commerce, 1994; mem. nat. com. Am. fgn. policy study group delegation to China, Taiwan, 1996; mem. real estate adv. bd. to N.Y. State Comptr., 1987-93. Bd. dirs. African Med. Rsch. Found., 1978—; trustee Marimed Found., 1984—, Chapin Sch., 1980-91, The Hackley Sch., 1974-81, St. Philip's Episcopal Ch., Mattapoisett, Mass., 1987—; trustee Nat. Com. Am. Fgn. Policy, 1994—, sr. v.p. 1996—. Mem. ABA, Internat. Bar Assn., Coun. Fgn. Rels., N.Y. State Bar Assn. (chmn. fin. instns. com. tax sect. 1984-86), Bar Assn. of City of N.Y., Century Assn., Harvard Club, N.Y. Yacht Club, River Club. Home: 1120 Fifth Ave New York NY 10128-0144 Office: Ravitch Rice & Co LLC 156 W 56th St Ste 902 New York NY 10019-3800

RICE, DOROTHY PECHMAN (MRS. JOHN DONALD RICE), medical economist; b. Bklyn., June 11, 1922; d. Gershon and Lena (Schiff) Pechman; m. John Donald Rice, Apr. 3, 1943; children: Kenneth D., Donald B., Thomas H. Student, Bklyn. Coll., 1938-39; BA, U. Wis., 1941; DSc (hon.), Coll. Medicine and Dentistry N.J., 1979. With hosp., and med. facilities USPHS, Washington, 1960-61; med. econs. studies Social Security Adminstrn., 1962-63; health econs. br. Community Health Svc., USPHS, 1964-65; chief health ins. rsch. br. Social Security Adminstrn., 1966-72, dep. asst. commr. for rsch. and statistics, 1972-75; dir. Nat. Ctr. for Health Stats., Rockville, Md., 1976-82; prof. Inst. Health & Aging U. Calif., San Francisco, 1982-94, prof. emeritus, 1994—; developer, mgr. nationwide health info. svcs.; expert on aging, health care costs, disability, and cost-of-illness. Contbr. articles to profl. jours. Recipient Social Security Adminstrn. citation, 1968, Disting. Service medal HEW, 1974, Jack C. Massey Found. award, 1978. Fellow Am. Public Health Assn. (domestic award for excellence 1978, Sedgwick Meml. medal, 1988), Am. Statis. Assn.; mem. Inst. Medicine, Assn. Health Scvs. Rsch. (President's award 1988), Am. Econ. Assn., Population Assn. Am., LWV. Home: 13895 Campus Dr Oakland CA 94605-3831 Office: U Calif Sch Nursing Calif San Francisco CA 94143-0646

RICE, EDWARD EARL, former government official, author; b. Saginaw, Mich., Feb. 6, 1909; s. William Edward and Katherine Marie (Meyer) R.; m. Mary June Kellogg, Oct. 26, 1942. Student, U. Wis., 1926-28; BS, U. Ill., 1930, postgrad., 1934-35; postgrad., U. Mex., 1931, Coll. Chinese Studies, also pvt. tutors, Beijing, 1935-37. Joined Fgn. Svc., Dept. State, 1935; lang. attache Beijing, 1935-37; vice consul Canton, China, 1938-40; consul

Foochow, China, 1940-42; 2d sec. Am. Embassy, Chungking, China, 1942-45; asst. chief div. Chinese affairs Dept. State, 1946-48, asst. chief div. Philippine affairs, 1948-49; 1st sec., consul Am. Embassy, Manila, 1949-51; consul gen. Stuttgart, Fed. Republic Germany, 1952-56; fgn. svc. insp. Dept. State, 1956-58, dep. dir. pers., 1959, mem. plicy planning coun., 1959-61, dep. asst. sec. of state for Far Ea. affairs, 1962-63; consul gen., min. Hong Kong, 1964-67; diplomat in residence with rank of prof. U. Calif., Berkeley, 1968-69, rsch. assoc. Ctr. for Chinese Studies, 1969—; vis. prof. Marquette U., 1973; advisor U.S. del. 3d, 4th and 5th sessions Econ. Commn. for Asia Far East, 1948-49. Author: Mao's Way, 1972, Wars of the Third Kind, 1988. Recipient Gold medal for non-fiction Commonwealth Club, 1973. Mem. Beta Gamma Sigma. Home: 1819 Lagoon View Dr Belvedere Tiburon CA 94920-1807 Office: U Calif Ctr for Chinese Studies Berkeley CA 94720

RICE, EMILY JOY, retired secondary school and adult educator; b. Terrell, Tex., Aug. 30, 1928; d. Martin Alexander Joy Jr. and Susan Martha (Helen) Ruth Joy; m. LeRoy Noonon Rice Jr., May 30, 1951; children: Edna Anne Rice-Padhi, Margaret Elizabeth (dec.). BS, Tex. Woman's U.; postgrad., U. Tex., Tex. A&I U. Tchr. adult Bible studies First United Meth. Ch., Harlingen and Austin, Tex., Bellaire United Meth. Ch., Houston; instr. Austin C.C., 1982-90; tchr. Austin Ind. Sch. Dist., 1982-92; writer, lectr. Vol. Meth. Hosp., Houston; mem. scholarship com. U. Tex. Mem. Delta Kappa Gamma. Home: 5220 Weslayan St # 201 Houston TX 77005-1095

RICE, EUGENE FRANKLIN, JR., history educator; b. Lexington, Ky., Aug. 20, 1924; s. Eugene Franklin and Lula (Piper) R.; m. Charlotte Bloch, Aug. 26, 1952 (dec. Oct. 1982); children: Eugene, John, Louise. BA, Harvard U., 1947, MA, 1948, PhD, 1953; postgrad., Ecole Normale Superieure, 1951-52. Instr. Harvard U., Cambridge, Mass., 1953-55; asst. prof. Cornell U., Ithaca, N.Y., 1955-59, assoc. prof., 1959-63; prof. Cornell U., Ithaca, 1963-64; prof. Columbia U., N.Y.C., 1964-74, William R. Shepperd prof., 1974—; chmn. dept. history Columbia U., 1970-73; advisor in history Random House, Knopf, N.Y.C., 1964-90; chmn., founder seminar Columbia U. Seminar Homosexualities. Author: The Renaissance Idea of Wisdom, 1958, The Foundations of Early Modern Europe, 1970, The Epistles of Lefevre d'Etaples, 1972, St. Jerome in the Renaissance, 1985; contbr. articles to profl. jours. Staff sgt. U.S. Army, 1943-45, ETO. Guggenheim Found. fellow Inst. for Advanced Study, 1959-60, 62-63, NEH fellow, 1974-75. Mem. Am. Hist. Assn. (v.p. rsch. 1979-81), Renaissance Soc. Am. (exec. dir. 1966-88), Soc. for Reformation Rsch. Democrat. Home: 560 Riverside Dr Apt 12J New York NY 10027-3214 Office: Columbia U Dept Of History New York NY 10027

RICE, FERILL JEANE, writer, civic worker; b. Hemingford, Nebr., July 4, 1926; d. Derrick and Helen Agnes (Moffatt) Dalton; m. Otis LaVerne Rice, Mar. 7, 1946; children: LaVeria June McMichael, Larry L. Student, U. Omaha, 1961. Dir. jr. and sr. choir Congl. Ch., Tabor, Iowa, 1952-66; tchr. Fox Valley Tech. Inst., Appleton, Wis., 1970-77; activity dir. Family Heritage Nursing Home, Appleton, Wis., 1972-75; dir. activity Peabody Manor, Appleton, Wis., 1975-76. Editor: Moffatt and Related Families, 1981; asst. editor (mag.) Yester-Year, 1975-76; contbr. articles to profl jours. Chmn. edn. Am. Cancer Soc., Fremont County, 1962, 63, 64; founder, 1st pres. Mothers Club Nishna Valley chpt. Demolay for Boys. Mem. DAR, Internat. Carnival Glass Assn., Heart Am. Carnival Glass Assn., Nat. Cambridge Collectors, Heisey Collectors Am., Iowa Fedn. Women's Clubs (Fremont county chmn. 1964, 65, 66, 67, 7th dist. chmn. libr. svcs. 1966-67), Tabor Women's Club (pres. 1962, 63, 64), Jr. Legion Aux. (founder, 1st dir. 1951-52), Fenton Art Glass Collectors Am. (co-founder 1977, sec., editor newsletter 1976-86, editor/sec. 1988-93, pres./editor 1993-95, treas. 1995-96), Mayflower Soc., John Howland Soc., Ross County Ohio Geneal. Soc., Iowa Geneal. Soc., Dallas County Mo. Geneal. Soc., Imperial Collectors Am., Clay County (Ind.) Geneal. Soc., Owen County (Ind.) Geneal. Soc., Fenton Finders of Wis. (chpt. #1 pres. 1988-90). Republican. Methodist: Lodges: Order Ea. Star (worthy matron 1956, 64), Rainbow for Girls (bd. dirs. 1964), Internat. Order Job's Daus. (honored queen 1945). Home: 302 Pheasant Run Kaukauna WI 54130-1802 Office: Rice Enterprises & Rice & Rice 1665 Lamers Dr # 305 Little Chute WI 54140-2519

RICE, FRANCES MAE, pediatrician; b. Oakland, Calif., Apr. 19, 1931; d. George Henry and Clare Evelyn (Youngman) Rice. AB cum laude, U. Calif., Berkeley, 1953, MPH in Epidemiology, 1964; MD, U. Calif., San Francisco, 1957. Intern U. Calif. Hosp., San Francisco, 1957-58; pediatric resident U. Calif., San Francisco, 1959-61; pediatric and family physician HMO, Hanford, Calif., 1974-75; clin. pediatrician Kern County Health Dept., Bakersfield, Calif., 1975-76; physician Kern Med. Group, Inc., Bakersfield, 1976-83; pvt. practice Shafter, Calif., 1983-89; physician Kern County Health Dept., Bakersfield, 1989, Mercy Medicenter, Bakersfield, 1990-91, K.C.E.O.C. Family Clinic, Bakersfield, 1993—. USPHS fellow, 1963-64. Fellow Royal Soc. Medicine; mem. AMA, N.Y. Acad. Sci., Calif. Med. Assn., Kern County Med. Soc. Avocation: hiking and music. Home: 5909 Lindbrook Way Bakersfield CA 93309 Office: KCEOC Family Health Clinic 1611 1st St Bakersfield CA 93304-2901

RICE, FREDERICK COLTON, environmental management consultant; b. Exeter, N.H., Aug. 8, 1938; s. Frederick Nott and Mary (Colton) R.; m. Joan Alis Lambrecht, June 25, 1962; children: Frederick Lambrecht, Janelle Alis. BS, U.S. Mil. Acad., 1960. Registered environ. assessor. Commd. 2d lt. U.S. Army, 1960, advanced through grades to maj., 1967, resigned, 1970; supr. Pacific Bell, San Bruno, Calif., 1970-71; area mgr. Sta-Power Industries, San Francisco, Phoenix and Balt., 1971-73; v.p. Getty Synthetic Fuels, Signal Hill, Calif., 1974-83; dir. land resources The Irvine Co., Newport Beach, Calif., 1983-84; pres. F. C. Rice & Co., Inc., Orange, Calif., 1984-88; nat. tech. dir. HDR Engring., Inc., Irvine, 1988-89; So. Calif. mgr. R. W. Beck and Assocs., Irvine, 1990-91; pres. F.C. Rice & Co., Laguna Hills, Calif., 1991-92; project dir. Roy F. Weston, Inc., Wilmington, Mass., 1993-95; pres. F.C. Rice & Co. Inc., Hampton, N.H., 1995—. Contbr. articles to profl. jours. Mem. nat. referee com. Am. Youth Soccer Orgn., Tustin, Calif., 1978-79; admissions rep., U.S. Mil. Acad. Admissions Office, 1975-87, area coord., Orange County, Calif., 1987-92, So. Calif. coord., 1992-93, N.H. coord., 1996—; chmn. Hampton Heritage Commn., 1996—; mem. bd. of selectmen, Hampton, N.H., 1997—; mem. Hampton Planning Bd., 1997—. Mem. Solid Waste Assn. N.Am. (so. Calif. chpt. bd. dirs. 1989-91, chmn. landfill gas com. 1979-80, resource recovery com. 1981-83, control tech. com. 1988-89, landfill gas divsn. 1991-93, Profl. Achievement award 1994), West Point Soc. Orange County (pres. 1975-76, bd. govs. 1975-93, Duty, Honor, Country award 1987), West Point Soc. New Eng. (sec., bd. govs. 1996—, bd. govs. 1996—), U.S. Mil. Acad. Assn. Grads. (trustee-at-large 1992-95, societies com. 1991—, chmn. mem. subcom. 1994-95, alumni support com. 1996—), Am. Legion, Rotary, Spl. Forces Assn. Republican. Roman Catholic. Avocations: skiing, golf, backpacking. Home: 15 Heather Ln Hampton NH 03842-1118 Office: FC Rice & Co Inc 15 Heather Ln Hampton NH 03842-1118

RICE, GARY RUSSELL, special education educator; b. Franklin, Pa., Oct. 11, 1951; s. Robert Russell and Della Elizabeth Rice. Grad. cum laude, Cleve. State U., 1973. Cert. polit. sci. tchr., learning disabilities, behavioral disorders, Ohio. Substitute tchr. Lakewood, Rocky River, Westlake (Ohio) Schs., 1973-77; instr. West Side Inst. Tech., Cleve., 1977-78; spl. edn. tchr. Parma (Ohio) City Sch. Dist., 1978—; learning disabilities tutor, Lakewood, 1974-75; guitar conservator Rock and Roll Hall of Fame and Mus., Cleve. Asst. scoutmaster, leader Boy Scouts Am., Cleve.; Sunday sch. tchr. local ch., Cleve.; spkr. to various groups on Exceptional Children, the Holocaust and Native Americans; charter mem. U.S. Holocaust Meml. Mus. Recipient Outstanding Spl. Educator award Parma PTA Spl. Edn. com., 1985, Thanks to Tchrs. award Sta. TV-8 WJW, Cleve., 1994. Mem. Parma Edn. Assn., Cleve. Fedn. Musicians, DeMolay (active Legion of Honor 1996), Masons, Shriners. Avocations: music, photography.

RICE, GEORGE LAWRENCE, III (LARRY RICE), lawyer; b. Jackson, Tenn., Sept. 24, 1951; s. George Lawrence Jr. and Judith W. (Pierce) R.; m. Joy Gaia, Sept. 14, 1974; children: George Lawrence IV, Amy Colleen. Student, Oxford U., 1972-73; BA with honors, Rhodes Coll., 1974; JD, Memphis State U., 1976; Nat. Coll. Advocacy, ATLA, 1978. Bar: Tenn. 1977, U.S. Supreme Ct. 1980. Assoc. Rice, Rice, Smith, Bursi, Veazey, 1976-81, ptnr., 1981—, acting sr. ptnr., 1995. Author: Divorce Practice in Tennessee, 1987, Divorce Lawyer's Handbook, 1989, (video) Divorce: What You Need to Know When it Happens to You, 1990, The Complete Guide to Divorce Practice, 1993, 2d edit., 1997, Visual Persuasion, AIDS and Clients, Prenuptial Agreements, 1996, The Ethical Effective Lawyer: Divorce and Personal Injury, 1996, In Pursuit of the Perfect Personal Injury Practice, 1997, Wiley Family Law Update Discovery Supplement, 1997; mem. bd. editors Matrimonial Strategist, 1994-96, Hunt, Hide Shoot--a Guide to Paintball, 1996, Wiley Family Law Update, 1997; mem. editl. bd. Active Supreme Ct. Child Support Guidelines Commn., 1989, Family Law Revision Commn., 1990-91. Mem. Timberwolves Paintball Team. Named One of Best Lawyers in Am., 1993, 94. Mem. ABA (conv. lectr. 1993, 94), ATLA, Tenn. Bar Assn. (chmn. family law sect. 1987-88), Memphis Bar Assn. (founding chmn. family law sect.), Tenn. Trial Lawyers Assn. Office: Rice Rice Smith Bursi Veazey Amundsen & Jewell 44 N 2nd St Fl 10 Memphis TN 38103-2251

RICE, JAMES ROBERT, engineering scientist, geophysicist; b. Frederick, Md., Dec. 3, 1940; s. Donald Blessing and Mary Celia (Santangelo) R.; m. Renata Dmowska, Feb. 28, 1981; children by previous marriage: Douglas, Jonathan. B.S., Lehigh U., 1962, Sc.M., 1963, Ph.D., 1964; DSc (hon.), Northwestern U., Evanston, Ill., 1996. Postdoctoral fellow Brown U., Providence, 1964-65, asst. prof. engring., 1965-68, assoc. prof., 1968-70, prof., 1970-81, Ballou prof. theoretical and applied mechanics, 1973-81; McKay prof. engring. sci. and geophysics Harvard U., Cambridge, Mass., 1981—. Recipient awards for sci. publs. ASME, awards for sci. publs. ASTM, awards for sci. publs. U.S. Nat. Com. Rock Mechanics, Timoshenko medal Am. Soc of Mechanical Engineers, 1994, Francis J. Clamer medal Franklin Institute, 1995. Fellow ASME, AAAS; mem. NAS, NAE, ASCE, Am. Geophys. Union, Fgn. Mem. Royal Soc. Research contbns. to solid mechanics, materials sci. and geophysics. Office: Harvard U Div Applied Sci Cambridge MA 02138

RICE, JERRY LEE, professional football player; b. Starkville, Miss., Oct. 13, 1962; m. Jackie Rice; children, Jaqui, Jerry Jr. Student, Miss. State Valley U. Football player San Francisco 49ers, 1985—; Sports Illustrated Player of the Year, 1986, 90, NFL MVP, 1987, AP/NFL/Sports Illustrated Offensive Player of the Year, 1993; MVP in Blue-Gray Game. Named MVP, Super Bowl XXIII, 1989, Sporting News NFL Player of Yr., 1987, 90; named to Sporting News Coll. All-Am. team, 1984, Sporting News All-Pro team, 1986-92, Pro Bowl team, 1986-96, 95, Pro Bowl MVP, 1995. Holder NFL career records for most touchdown receptions (131), most touchdowns (139); most consecutive games with one or more touchdowns (13), 1987; NFL single-season record for most touchdown receptions (22), 1987; shares NFL single-game record for most touchdown receptions (5), 1990. Office: care San Francisco 49ers 4949 Centennial Blvd Santa Clara CA 95054-1229*

RICE, JERRY MERCER, biochemist; b. Washington, Oct. 3, 1940; s. John Earle Rice and Leona (Mercer) Greiner; m. Mary Jane Janocha, Jan. 10, 1978; children: Stacey Lynn, Stephen Mark. BA, Wesleyan U., 1962; PhD, Harvard U., 1966. Commd. officer USPHS, 1966; rsch. scientist Nat. Cancer Inst., Bethesda, Md., 1966-81, chief Lab. of Comparative Carcinogenesis, Frederick, Md., 1981-94, 96; assoc. dir. Frederick Cancer Rsch. and Devel. Ctr., Nat. Cancer Inst., Frederick, Md., 1994-95, acting dir. divsn. cancer etiology, 1994-95; sr. scientist WHO, 1996—; chief Unit of Carcinogen Identification and Evaluation Internat. Agy. for Rsch. on Cancer, Lyons, France, 1996—; lectr. univs., profl. groups, med. socs. Editor: Perinatal Carcinogenesis, 1979. Co-editor: Organ and Species Specificity in Chemical Carcinogenesis, 1983, Perinatal and Multigeneration Carcinogenesis, 1989; contbr. rsch. articles and revs. in mechanisms of chem. carcinogenesis to profl. jours. Mem. Am. Soc. Microbiology, Am. Assn. Cancer Research, Internat. Soc. of Differentiation, Teratology Soc., Phi Beta Kappa, Sigma Xi. Avocation: viticulture. Home: 3213 Coquelin Ter Bethesda MD 20815-4840 Office: Internat Agy Rsch Cancer, 150 Cours Albert Thomas, 69372 Cedex 08 Lyon France

RICE, JOHN RISCHARD, computer scientist, researcher, educator; b. Tulsa, June 6, 1934; s. John Coykendal Kirk and Margaret Lucille (Rischard) R.; m. Nancy Ann Bradfield, Dec. 19, 1954; children: Amy Lynn, Jenna Margaret. BS, Okla. State U., 1954, MS, 1956; PhD, Calif. Inst. Tech., 1959. Postdoctoral fellow Nat. Bur. Standards, Washington, 1959-60; rsch. mathematician GM Rsch. Labs., Warren, Mich., 1960-64; prof. Purdue U., West Lafayette, Ind., 1964-89; head dept. computer sci. Purdue U., West Lafayette, 1983-96, disting. prof., 1989—; editor-in-chief ACM Trans. Math. Software, N.Y.C., 1975-93; chmn. ACM-Signum, N.Y.C., 1977-79; dir. Computing Rsch. Bd., Washington, 1987-94; chair Computing Rsch. Assn., Washington, 1991-93. Author: The Approximation of Functions, 1964, Vol. 2, 1969, Numerical Methods, Software and Analysis, 1983; author and editor: Mathematical Software, 1971; editor: Intelligent Scientific Software Systems, 1991. Fellow AAAS, ACM (George Forsythe Meml. lectr. 1975); mem. IFIP (working group 2.5, vice chmn. 1977-91), Soc. Indsl. and Applied Math., Nat. Acad. Engring., Phi Kappa Phi. Home: 112 E Navajo St West Lafayette IN 47906-2153 Office: Purdue U Computer Sci Dept West Lafayette IN 47907

RICE, JOHN THOMAS, architecture educator; b. New London, Conn., Feb. 4, 1931; s. Clarence Benjamin and Emily (Gudal) R. BS in Engring., U. Conn., 1952; MSME, Newark Coll. Engring., 1954; D.Sc. in Engring., Columbia U., 1962. Registered profl. engr., N.Y. Test equipment designer propeller div. Curitss-Wright Corp., Caldwell, N.J., 1952-54; stress analyst Wright Aeronautical div. Curtiss-Wright Corp., Woodridge, N.J., 1954-59; chief structural mechanics Gen. Dynamics/Electric Boat, Groton, Conn., 1962-64; asst. prof. mech. engring. Pratt Inst., Bklyn., 1964-66, assoc. prof., 1966-74, prof., 1974—, chmn. dept. mech. engring., 1981-90. Mem. ASME (chmn. mech. engring. dept. heads com. region II 1987-89, chmn. profl. devel. region II 1989-93, mem. exec. com. met. sect. 1990—, vice chmn. 1991-92, chmn. 1992-93, sec. region II 1993-96), Pi Tau Sigma, Tau Beta Pi. Office: Pratt Inst Dept of Architecture 200 Willoughby Ave Brooklyn NY 11205-3817

RICE, JON RICHARD, state health officer, physician; b. Grand Forks, N.D., July 10, 1946; s. Harry Frazer and Marian (Lund) R.; m. Roberta Jane Lindbergh, June 7, 1969; children: Kristen, Jennifer. BA, U. N.D., 1969, BS, 1970; MD, U. Tex., San Antonio, 1972; MS in Health Adminstrn., U. Colo., 1991. Intern U.S. Naval Hosp., San Diego, 1972-73; resident U. N.D. Sch. Medicine, Minot, 1975-77; physician Valley Med., Grand Forks, 1977-93; state health officer N.D. Dept. Health, Bismarck, 1993—. Contbg. author: Pilots, Personality and Performance. Lt. USN, 1972-75. Recipient Outstanding Vol. award Dakota Heart Assn., 1989, YMCA, 1992, Outstanding Health Care Provider Grand Forks C. of C., 1992, Award of Excellence N.D. Hosp. Assn., 1995. Mem. AMA, Am. Acad. Family Physicians, Am. Coll. Physician Execs., Rotary, Alpha Omega Alpha. Office: ND Dept Health 600 E Boulevard Ave Bismarck ND 58505-0660

RICE, JONATHAN C., retired educational television executive; b. St. Louis, Feb. 19, 1916; s. Charles M. and May R. (Goldman) R.; m. Kathleen Feibleman, Aug. 6, 1946 (dec. June 1964); children: Jefferson Charles, Kit (dec.), May Nanette. AB, Stanford U., 1938. War photographer, reporter Acme Newspix/NEA Svc., PTO of WWII, 1941-43; picture book editor Look Mag., N.Y.C., 1947-48; news/spl. events dir. Sta. KTLA-TV, L.A., 1948-53; program mgr. Sta. KQED-TV, San Francisco, 1953-67, dir. program ops., 1967-78, asst. to pres., 1978-90, bd. dirs., 1990-96, spl. advisor to the bd., 1997—, bd. dirs., 1990-96; cons. NET, PBS, Corp. for Pub. Broadcasting, Ford Found., TV Lima Peru, Sta. WGBH-TV, Boston, Sta. WNET-TV, N.Y.C., French TV, Europe Eastern Edn. TV, Dept. Justice, 1955-90; lectr. Stanford U., 1958-77. Editor: Look at America, The South, Official Picture Story of the FBI, 1947. Bd. dirs. NATAS, San Francisco, Planned Parenthood, San Francisco and Marin County, Calif. Maj. USMC, 1943-47, PTO. Recipient George Foster Peabody award, 1956, Thomas Alva Edison award for best station, N.Y.C., 1960, Gov.'s award NATAS, 1972-73, Ralph Lowell award Corp. for Pub. Broadcasting, 1972; Jonathan Rice Studio named in his honor, 1986. Avocations: rowing, bicycling, cooking, photography, travel. Home: 1 Russian Hill Pl San Francisco CA 94133-3605

RICE, JOSEPH ALBERT, banker; b. Cranford, N.J., Oct. 11, 1924; s. Louis A. and Elizabeth J. (Michael) R.; m. Katharine Wolfe, Sept. 11, 1948; children: Walter, Carol, Philip, Alan. B in Aero. Engring., Rensselear Poly. Inst., 1948; M in Indsl. Engring., NYU, 1952, MA, 1968. With Grumman Aircraft Engring. Corp., 1948-53; with IBM, N.Y.C., 1953-65, mgr. ops., real estate, constrn. divsns., 1963-65; dep. group exec. N.Am. comml. telecommunications group, pres. telecommunications div. ITT, N.Y.C., 1965-67; sr. v.p. Irving Trust Co., N.Y.C., 1967-69, exec. v.p., 1969-72, sr. exec. v.p., 1972-73, vice chmn., 1973-74, pres., 1974—, chmn., 1984-88; exec. v.p. Irving Bank Corp., 1971-74, vice chmn., 1974-75, pres., 1975-83, chmn. bd., CEO, 1984-88; bd. dirs. Avon Products, Inc., Apache Corp. Trustee John Simon Guggenheim Meml. Found., Hist. Hudson Valley, Insts. Religion and Health. Mem. Coun. Fgn. Rels., N.Y. Acad. Scis., Univ. Club, Links, Sky Club.

RICE, JOSEPH LEE, III, lawyer; b. Bklyn., Feb. 24, 1932; s. Joseph Lee Jr. and Frances (Plunkett) R.; m. Franci Blassberg, Jan. 4, 1992; children: Kimberley, Daniel, Lee Ann. BA, Williams Coll., Williamstown, Mass., 1954; LLB, Harvard U., 1960. Assoc. Sullivan & Cromwell, N.Y.C., 1960-66; v.p. Laird Inc., N.Y.C., 1966-68, McDonnell & Co., N.Y.C., 1968-69; founding ptnr. Gibbons, Green & Rice, N.Y.C., 1969-78; founder, chmn., CEO Clayton, Dubilier & Rice, Inc., N.Y.C., 1978—. Trustee, Williams Coll., 1988—. Lt. USMC, 1954-57. Mem. Maidstone Club, The Links Club, River Club, Univ. Club. Office: Clayton Dubilier & Rice Inc 375 Park Ave New York NY 10152-0002

RICE, JOY KATHARINE, psychologist, educational policy studies and women's studies educator; b. Oak Park, Ill., Mar. 26, 1939; d. Joseph Theodore and Margaret Sophia (Bednarik) Straka; m. David Gordon Rice, Sept. 1, 1962; children: Scott Alan, Andrew David. B.F.A. with high honors, U. Ill., Urbana, 1960; M.S., U. Wis., Madison, 1962, U. Wis., Madison, 1964; Ph.D., U. Wis., Madison, 1967. Lic. clin. psychologist. USPHS predoctoral fellow dept. psychiatry Med. Sch. U. Wis., Madison, 1964-65, asst. dir. Counseling Ctr., 1966-74, dir. Office Continuing Edn. Svcs., 1972-78, prof. ednl. policy studies and women's studies, 1974-95, clin. prof. psychiatry, 1995—; pvt. practice psychology Psychiat. Svcs., S.C., Madison, 1967—; mem. State Wis. Ednl. Approval Bd., Madison, 1972-73; mem. Adult Edn. Commn., U.S. Office Career Edn., Washington, 1978. Author: Living Through Divorce, A Developmental Approach to Divorce Therapy, 1985, 2d edit., 1989; edit. bd. Lifelong Learning, 1979-86; cons. editor Psychology of Women Quar., 1986-88, assoc. editor, 1989-94; cons. editor Handbook of Adult and Continuing Education, 1989; contbr. articles to profl. jours. Knapp fellow U. Wis.-Madison, 1960-62, teaching fellow, 1962-63; recipient Disting. Achievement award Ednl. Press Assn. Am., 1992. Fellow APA (exec. bd. Psychology of Women divsn. 1994—); mem. Nat. Assn. Women in Edn. (editl. bd. jour. 1984-88, cons. editor Initiatives 1988-91), Internat. Coun. Psychologists, Am. Assn. Continuing and Adult Edn. (meritorious svc. award 1978-80, 82), Wis. Psychol. Assn., Phi Delta Kappa. Avocations: interior design, collecting art, gardening, travel. Home: 4230 Waban Hl Madison WI 53711-3711 Office: 2727 Marshall Ct Madison WI 53705-2255

RICE, JULIAN CASAVANT, lawyer; b. Miami, Fla., Dec. 31, 1923; s. Sylvan J. and Maybelle (Casavant) R.; m. Dorothy Mae Haynes, Feb. 14, 1958; children—Scott B., Craig M. (dec.), Julianne C., Linda D., Janette M. Student, U. San Francisco, 1941-43; JD cum laude, Gonzaga U., 1950. Bar: Wash. 1950, Alaska 1959, U.S. Tax Ct. 1988. Pvt. practice law Spokane, 1950-56, Fairbanks, Alaska, 1959—; prin. Law Office Julian C. Rice (and predecessor firms), Fairbanks, 1959; bd. dirs. Key Bank of Alaska, Anchorage; founder, gen. counsel Mt. McKinley Mut. Savs. Bank, Fairbanks, 1965—, chmn. bd., 1979-80; v.p., bd. dirs., gen. counsel Skimmers, Inc., Anchorage, 1966-67; gen. counsel Alaska Carriers Assn., Anchorage, 1960-71, Alaska Transp. Conf., 1960-67. Mayor City of Fairbanks, 1970-72. Served to maj. USNG and USAR, 1943-58. Decorated Bronze Star, Combat Infantryman's Badge. Fellow Am. Bar Found. (life); mem. ABA, Wash. Bar Assn., Alaska Bar Assn., Transp. Lawyers Assn., Spokane Exchange Club (pres. 1956). Office: 1008 16th Ave Ste 102 Fairbanks AK 99701-6078 Office: PO Box 70516 Fairbanks AK 99707-0516

RICE, KAY DIANE, elementary education educator, consultant; b. Redding, Calif., Mar. 21, 1952; d. Ray H. and Patricia Barton (Stabler) Quibell; m. 1976 (div. 1982); 1 child, Brooke Elise; m. F. Scott Rice. AA in Gen. Edn., Shasta Coll., Redding, 1972; BA in Liberal Studies, Calif. State U., Chico, 1975; EdM in Policy and Govt., U. Wash., 1991. Cert. tchr., Calif., Wash., cert. prin., Wash. Tchr. grade 3 Anderson (Calif.) Schs., 1976-79; tchr. grades 1, 2, and 3 Redding (Calif.) Elem. Schs., 1979-81, tchr. grade 1, 1981-83, tchr. grade 5, 1986-87; tchr. grade 2 Bellevue (Wash.) Pub. Schs., 1987-88; tchr. grade 4 Lake Wash. Sch. Dist., Kirkland, Wash., 1988-89; tchr. grades 3-4 Bellevue (Wash.) Pub. Schs., 1989-90; prin. intern Bellevue (Wash.) and Mercer Island (Wash.) Schs., 1990-91; tchr. grades K-1 Bellevue (Wash.) Pub. Schs., 1991-93, tchr. grades 1-2, 1993—; mem. adv. com. Ednl. Program Com., Bellevue Pub. Schs., 1992-94, mem. Early Childhood Assessment Project, 1993—; presenter in field. Vol. ZEST Sch. Dist. Vol. Program, Bellevue, 1991-93. Recipient Pres.'s Merit award Parent Student Tchr. Assn., 1988, U.S. Presdl. EPA award, 1987; Bellevue Schs. Found. grantee, 1987, 95-96, 96-97, Danforth Edn. Leadership grantee Bellevue Pub. Schs., 1990-91, Ednl. Travel Study grantee Shunju Club, Japanese Bus. People Wash., 1994. Mem. ASCD, NEA, AAUW (hospitality com. 1982), PTSA, Wash. Orgn. for Reading Devel., PEO. Avocations: cooking, outdoor sports, reading, writing, religious studies. Home: 6818 205th Ave NE Redmond WA 98053-4721 Office: Somerset Elem Sch 14100 SE Somerset Blvd Bellevue WA 98006-2329

RICE, KENNER CRALLE, medicinal chemist; b. Rocky Mount, Va., May 14, 1940; s. Kenner Cralle Jr. and Annie Grace (Early) R. BS, Va. Mil. Inst., 1961; PhD, Ga. Inst. Tech., 1966. Sr. scientist Ciba-Geigy Corp., Summit, N.J., 1969-72; sr. staff fellow NIH, Bethesda, Md., 1972-76, rsch. chemist, 1977-86; chief sect. drug design and synthesis Nat. Inst. Diabetes, Digestive and Kidney Diseases, Bethesda, Md., 1987-88; chief lab. medicinal chemistry NIDDK, NIH, Bethesda, Md., 1989—; adj. prof. pharmacology U. Md., Balt., 1985—; mem. fed. sr. exec. svc. U.S. Govt., Bethesda, 1989—; affiliate prof. Va. Commonwealth U., Richmond, 1995—; vis. prof. pharmacology, U. Ill., Peoria, 1995—; adj. prof. medicinal chemistry Comprehensive Drug Rsch. Ctr., U. Miami, 1995—. Author: (with others) Pharmalogical Reviews, 1987; editor: NIDA Research Monograph, 1990; contbr. articles to Jour. Medicinal Chemistry. Capt. U.S. Army, 1966-68. Recipient Internat. Sato Meml. award Japanese Pharm. Soc., 1983, Rsch. Achievement award Am. Pharm. Assn., 1987, Hillebrand prize Chem. Soc. Washington, 1986, Divsn. Medicinal Chemistry award Am. Chem. Soc., 1996. Fellow Coll. on Problems of Drug Dependence (bd. dirs. 1988-92); mem. Am. Coll. Neuropsychopharmacology, Cosmos Club. Achievements include 17 patents for organic chemical synthesis and pharmacology of drugs of abuse; development of NIH opiate total synthesis as first practical synthesis of opium alkaloids as narcotics and narcotic antagonists. Office: NIH NIDDK Lab Medicinal Chemist Bldg 8 Rm B1 23 Bethesda MD 20892

RICE, KENNETH LLOYD, environmental services executive, educator; b. St. Paul, June 17, 1937; m. Elizabeth Lyman VanKat, May 11, 1963 (dec. 1992); children: Anne Louise, Ken neth L. Jr., Elizabeth Ellen, Stephen James. BBA, U. Wis., 1959; postgrad., N.Y. Inst. Finance, 1960-64; completed 71st Advanced Mgmt. Program, Harvard U., 1975. Trainee, asst. br. mgr. JW Sparks & Co., St. Paul, 1959-64, mgr. corp. fin., 1964-70; mgr. corp. finance The Milw. Co., St. Paul, 1969-70; dir. finance Cedar Riverside Assocs. Inc., Mpls., 1970-71; prin. Kenneth L. Rice & Assocs., St. Paul, 1971-88; chmn., CEO investment banking Allegro Tech. Corp., St. Paul, 1988-92; prof. mgmt. and environ. econs. Budapest (Hungary) U. Econs. Scis., 1992—; chmn., edtl. bd. New Horizons Magazine, Hungary, 1995—; Minn. del. World Trade Ctrs. Assn., Budapest, Hungary, 1987; dir. Hungarian U.S. Fulbright Commn., 1995—. Founder Chimera Theatre, St. Paul, 1969; pres. Liberty Pla. Non-Profit Housing Project, St. Paul, 1975-77; judge Leadership Fellows Bush Found., St. Paul, 1985-90; co-chmn. Parents Fund, Macalester Coll., St. Paul, 1985-87; Hungary hon. rep. State of Minn. Trade Office, 1992—. Bush Leadership fellow, 1974. Mem. Environ. Mgmt. and Law Assn. Hungary, Harvard Bus. Club (local bd. dirs. 1978-83), Harvard Club of Hungary (v.p. 1994—), Am. C. of C. in Hungary (dir. 1995—, v.p. 1997—), Masons, KT, Shriners. Home: Kuny Domokos 13, III Em 311, H 1012 Budapest Hungary

RICE, LACY I., JR., lawyer; b. Martinsburg, W.Va., Dec. 29, 1931; s. Lacy Isaac and Anna (Thorn) R.; m. Linda Watkins, Mar. 2, 1957; children: Anne

W., Lacy I. III, William T. BA, Princeton U., 1953; LLB, U. Va., 1956. Bar: W.Va. 1956, U.S. Dist. Ct. (no. Dist.) W.Va. 1956, U.S. Cir. Ct. Appeals (3d and 4th cirs.) 1968. Ptnr. Lacy I. Rice Sr. law firm & Rice, Hannis & Rice & successors, Martinsburg, 1956-89; sr. ptnr. Bowles, Rice, McDavid, Graff & Love, Martinsburg, 1989—; pres. Old Nat. Bank of Martinsburg, 1978, chmn. bd.; chmn., CEO One Valley Bank-East N.A.; vice chmn. One Valley Bancorp, Inc.; bd. dirs. Continental Brick Co., C&P Telephone Co., W.Va. Mem. W.Va. Bar Assn. (pres. 1984-85). Home: 600 N Tennessee Ave Martinsburg WV 25401-9281 Office: PO Drawer 1419 105 W Burke St Martinsburg WV 25401

RICE, LESTER, electronics company executive; b. Detroit, Feb. 23, 1927; s. Carvel Lester and Irene R.; m. Barbara Helen Winston, June 27, 1957; children—Scott W., Jody I., Jeffrey C., Judy A., Timohty D. B.S.E.E., U. Mich., 1951. Gen. sales mgr. Westinghouse Semicondr. Div., Youngwood, Pa., 1951-68; pres. Airco Speer Elec. div. Airco Inc., Bradford, Pa., 1968-80; vice chmn., dir. KOA Speer Electronics, Inc., Bradford, 1980—; bd. dirs. DeFond No. Am. Inc.; chmn. bd. Lester Rice, Inc., Bradford, 1980—. Adv. bd. U. Pitts. With USN, 1945-46. Mem. IEEE, Electronics Industries Assn. (bd. govs.), Am. Legion, Masons. Republican. Home: 2 Vista Avenue Ext Bradford PA 16701-2759 Office: PO Box 547 Bradford PA 16701-0547

RICE, LINDA JOHNSON, publishing executive; b. Chgo., Mar. 22, 1958; d. John J. and Eunice Johnson; m. Andre Rice, 1984. BA Journalism, Univ. Southern California, Los angeles, 1980; MBA, Northwestern Univ., Evanston, 1988. With Johnson Pub. Co., 1980—, past v.p. and asst. to pub., pres., 1987—, also chief oper. officer. Office: Johnson Pub Co Inc 820 S Michigan Ave Chicago IL 60605-2103*

RICE, LOIS DICKSON, former computer company executive; b. Portland, Maine, Feb. 28, 1933; d. David A. and Mary D. Dickson; m. Alfred B. Fitt, Jan. 7, 1978 (dec. 1992); children: Susan, John Rice. A.B. magna cum laude, Radcliffe Coll., 1954; postgrad. (Woodrow Wilson fellow), Columbia U., 1954-55; LL.D.s (hon.), Brown U., 1981; LL.D. (hon.), Bowdoin Coll., 1984. Dir. counseling services Nat. Scholarship Service and Fund for Negro Students, N.Y.C., 1955-59; with The Coll. Bd., N.Y.C. and Washington, 1959-81; v.p. The Coll. Bd., Washington, 1973-81; sr. v.p. govt. affairs, bd. dirs. Control Data Corp., 1981-91; guest scholar The Brookings Inst., Washington, 1991—; bd. dirs. McGraw Hill Inc., Hartford Steam Boiler Inspection and Ins. Co., Internat. Multifoods, Fleet Fin. Group, UNUM Corp.; overseer Tuck Sch. Mgmt. Dartmouth Coll., 1990-94; mem. Pres. Fgn. Intelligence adv. bd., 1993—; trustee George Washington U., 1992-94; trustee CNA Corp. Pub. Agenda Found., Harry Frank Guggenheim Found. Contbr. articles on edn. to profl. publs.; editor: Student Loans: Problems and Policy Alternatives, 1977. Mem. Gov.'s Commn. on Future of Postsecondary Edn. in N.Y. State, 1976-77; mem. Carnegie Coun. on Higher Edn., 1975-80; bd. dirs. Potomac Inst., 1977-92, German Marshall Fund, 1984-94, Joint Ctr. Polit. and Econ. Studies, 1991-94, Harry Frank Guggenheim Found., 1990—, Reading is Fundamental, 1991—; trustee Radcliffe Coll., 1969-75, Stephens Coll., Mo., 1976-78, Beauvoir Sch., Washington, 1970-76, Children's TV Workshop, 1970-73; chmn. adv. bd. to dir. NSF, 1981-89, chair 1986-89. Recipient Disting. Service award HEW, 1977. Mem. Cosmos Club, Phi Beta Kappa. Episcopalian. Home: 2332 Massachusetts Ave NW Washington DC 20008-2801 Office: The Brookings Instn 1775 Massachusetts Ave NW Washington DC 20036-2188

RICE, MARGARET LUCILLE, computer technology educator; b. Saginaw, Mich., May 18, 1958; d. Richard Joseph Glowacki and Carolyn Ann (Roberts) Hajos. BS in Edn., Ctrl. Mich. U., 1980; MA, U. Ala., 1986, PhD, 1991. Instr. U. Ala., Tuscaloosa, 1990-92, asst. rsch. ednl. psychologist, 1988-91, assoc. rsch. ednl. psychologist, 1991-93, assoc. rsch. computer technologist, 1993-94, asst. prof. ednl. computer tech., 1994—; cons. Tuscaloosa City Schs., 1993-94. Prodn. editor Rsch. in the Schs., 1993-94. Mem. Internat. Reading Assn., Am. Ednl. Rsch. Assn., Mid-South Ednl. Rsch. Assn. (mem. program com. 1993-94, Disting. Dissertation award 1991), Phi Delta Kappa, Mu Sigma Rho. Avocations: reading, creative writing. Home: 2308 Lane Cir Birmingham AL 35223-1714 Office: U Ala Box 870302 204 Wilson Hall Tuscaloosa AL 35487

RICE, MARY ESTHER, biologist; b. Washington, Aug. 3, 1926; d. Daniel Gibbons and Florence Catharine (Pyles) R. AB, Drew U., 1947; MA, Oberlin Coll., 1949; PhD, U. Wash., 1966. Instr. biology Drew U., Madison, N.J., 1949-50; rsch. assoc. Columbia U., N.Y.C., 1950-53; rsch. asst. NIH, Bethesda, Md., 1953-61; curator invertebrate zoology and dir. Smithsonian Marine Sta., Smithsonian Instn., Washington, 1966—; mem. adv. panel on systematic biology NSF, Washington, 1977-78; mem. com. on marine invertebrates Nat. Acad. Sci., 1976-81; mem. overseers com. on biology Harvard U., Cambridge, Mass., 1982-88. Assoc. editor Jour. Morphology, Ann Arbor, Mich., 1985-91, Invertebrate Biology, 1995—; editor: (with M. Todorovic) Biology of Sipuncula and Echiura, 1975, 2nd vol., 1976, (with F.S. Chia) Settlement and Metamorphosis of Marine Invertebrate Larvae, 1978, (with F.W. Harrison) Microscopic Anatomy of Invertebrates, Vol. 12, 1993; contbr. articles to profl. jours. Recipient Drew U. Alumni Achievement award in sci., 1980. Fellow AAAS; mem. Am. Soc. Zoologists (pres. 1979), Phi Beta Kappa. Office: Smithsonian Marine Sta 5612 Old Dixie Hwy Fort Pierce FL 34946-7303

RICE, NANCY MARIE, nursing consultant; b. Murphy, N.C., Aug. 3, 1940; d. Berlon and Elizabeth Beryl (Ammons) Lovingood; m. Lewis T. Rice, Jan. 23, 1976; 1 child, Elizabeth Robertson Flowers. Diploma, Grady Meml. Hosp., Atlanta, 1961; BA, U. West Fla., Pensacola, 1973; MS, Fla. State U., Tallahassee, 1979. Cert. cmty. health nurse, nursing administr.; diplomate Am. Bd. Quality Assurance and Utilization Review Physicians. Staff nurse Riegel Community Hosp., Trion, Ga., 1961; pub. health nurse Escambia County Health Unit, Pensacola, 1962-63, Santa Rosa County Health Unit, Milton, Fla., 1963-73; pub. health nursing supr. I Leon County Health Unit, Tallahassee, Fla., 1973-77; pub. health nurse Broward County Health Unit, Ft. Lauderdale, Fla., 1977-78; nursing cons. social and econ. svcs. Tallahassee, 1978-79; HMO program specialist social and econ. scvs. program office DHRS Dist. X, Ft. Lauderdale, 1979; pub. health nurse, supr. II Sarasota (Fla.) County Health Unit, 1979-81; health program specialist health program office DHRS Dist X, Ft. Lauderdale, Fla., 1981-83; nursing cons. Dept. Labor, Div. Workers' Compensation, Tallahassee, 1983—. Recipient Cert. of Svc. State of Fla., 10 yr., 20 yr., 25 yrs., 30 yrs., Cert. of Appreciation, 1976, Leon County-Tallahassee Community Action Program. Mem. Am. Nurses Assn., Fla. Nurses Assn., Eta Sigma Gamma. Home: PO Box 13731 Tallahassee FL 32317-3731

RICE, NORMAN B., mayor; b. Denver, May 4, 1943; m. Constance Rice; 1 child, Mian. BA in Comm., U. Wash., MPA. Past mgr. corp. contbns. and soc. policy Seafirst Bank; past dir. govt. svcs. Puget Sound Coun. Govts.; past asst. dir. Seattle Urban League; past reporter KIXI Radio; past editor, writer KOMO TV; with govt. City of Seattle, 1978—, city councilman, 1978-89, mayor, 1990—; pres. U.S. Conf. of Mayors, 1995, chmn. super task force welfare reform. Office: Office of the Mayor Municipal Bldg 12th Fl 600 4th Ave Seattle WA 98104-1826

RICE, PATRICIA OPPENHEIM LEVIN, special education educator, consultant; b. Detroit, Apr. 5, 1932; d. Royal A. and Elsa (Freeman) Oppenheim; m. Charles L. Levin, Feb. 21, 1956 (div. Dec. 1981); children: Arthur David, Amy Ragen, Fredrick Stuart; m. Howard T. Rice, Dec. 16, 1990 (div. Apr. 1994). AB in History, U. Mich., 1954, PhD, 1981; MEd, Marygrove Coll., 1973. Tchr. reading and learning disabled, cons., Detroit, 1967-76, Marygrove Coll.; coord. spl. edn., Marygrove Coll., 1976-86; adj. prof. Oakland U., 1987-90, U. Miami, 1989-95; edn., curriculum cons. Lady Elizabeth Sch., Jávea (Alicante) Spain, 1988-91; dir. Oppenheim Tchr. Tng. Inst., Detroit; v.p. Machpelah Cemetary Bd., Ferndale, Mich., 1978—; mem. adv. bd. Eton Acad., Birmingham, Mich., 1991-93; internat. conf. presenter; workshop presenter Dade City Schs., 1992—. Mem. Mich. regional bd. ORT, 1965-68, 86—; mem. youth svcs. adv. com. S.E. Mich. chpt. ARC Bd., 1973-79; mem. Met. Mus., N.Y.C., Seattle Art Mus., Detroit Art Mus., Smithsonian Instn., Mus. Contemporary Art, Miami; v.p. women's aux. Children's Hosp. Mich.; bd. dirs. women's com. United Cmty. Svcs., 1968-73; judge Dade County Schs. for Tchr. Grants, 1996; women's com. Detroit Grand Opera Assn., 1970-75; mem. coms. Detroit Symphony Orch., Detroit Inst. Arts; torch drive area chmn. United Found., 1967-70; benefactor Fla. Grand Opera Dade Guild, 1990—, bd. dirs., 1992, Artist Circle, 1990—, Miami City Ballet, Men's Opera Guild, 1996-97, Opera Ball com., 1992, Lincoln Rd. Walk, chair, 1996, Diabetes Rsch. Inst. & Found. Love & Hope Com., Fla. Concert Assn. Cresendo Soc., 1993—, Villa Maria Angel, 1996—. Mem. NAACP (life), Navy League (mem. Miami Coun., greater Miami social register 1996—), Internat. Reading Assn., Nat. Coun. Tchrs. of English, Assn. Supervision and Curriculum Devel., Nat. Assn. Edn. of Young Children, Mich. Assn. Children with Learning Disabilities (edn. v.p., exec. bd. 1976-80), Coun. Exceptional Children, Williams Island Club, Westview Country Club, Turnberry Isle Clubs (signiture), Phi Delta Kappa, Pi Lambda Theta.

RICE, PAUL JACKSON, lawyer, educator; b. East St. Louis, Ill., July 15, 1938; s. Ray Jackson and Mary Margaret (Campbell) R.; m. Carole Jeanne Valentine, June 6, 1959; children: Rebecca Jeanne Ross, Melissa Ann Hansen, Paul Jackson Jr. BA, U. Mo., 1960, JD, 1962; LLM, Northwestern U., 1970; student, Command and Gen. Staff Coll., 1974-75, Army War Coll., 1982-83. Bar: Mo. 1962, Ill. 1969, U.S. Dist. Ct. (no. dist.) Ill. 1970, U.S. Supreme Ct. 1972, U.S. Ct. Appeals (D.C. cir.) 1991, D.C. 1993. Commd. 1st lt. U.S. Army, 1962, advanced through grades to col., 1980; asst. judge advocate 4th Armored Div., Goeppingen, Fed. Republc Germany, 1966-69; dep. staff judge advocate 1st Cavalry Div., Republic Vietnam, 1970-71; inst., prof. The Judge Adv. Gen. Sch., Charlottesville, Va., 1971-74, commdt., dean, 1985-88; br. chief Gen. Law Br., Pentagon, 1975-78; chief adminstrv. law div. Office Judge Adv. Gen., Pentagon, Washington, 1978-79; staff judge adv. 1st Inf. Div., Ft. Riley, Kans., 1979-82, V Corps U.S. Army, Frankfurt, Fed. Republic Germany, 1983-85, USACAC, Ft. Leavenworth, Kans., 1989-90; faculty Indsl. Coll. Armed Forces, 1988-89; chief counsel Nat. Hwy. Traffic Safety Adminstrn., Washington, 1990-93; ptnr. Arent Fox Kintner Plotkin & Kahn, Washington, 1993—. Contbr. articles to profl. jours. Granted Legal Svc. award State of Hessen, Weisbaden, Fed. Republic Germany, 1985, Cert. Merit U. Mo. Alumni Assn., 1987. Mem. ABA, Fed. Bar Assn. (pres. local chpt. 1986-88), Mo. Bar Assn., Ctr. For Law and Nat. Security, U. Va. Sch. Law (1985-89), Lion Tamers, Phi Delta Phi. Methodist. Avocations: writing, reading, sports. Home: 7835 Vervain Ct Springfield VA 22152-3107 Office: Arent Fox Kintner Plotkin & Kahn 1050 Connecticut Ave NW Washington DC 20036

RICE, REGINA KELLY, marketing executive; b. Yonkers, N.Y., July 11, 1955; d. Howard Adrian and Lucy Virginia (Butler) Kelly; m. Mark Christopher Rice, Sept. 11, 1981; children: Amanda Kelly, Jaime Brannen. BS in Community Nutrition, Cornell U., 1948. Account exec. J. Walter Thompson Co., N.Y.C., 1978-79; sr. account exec. Ketchum, MacLeod & Grove, N.Y.C., 1979-80; supr. Burson Marstellar, Hong Kong, 1981-83; v.p., dep. dir. food and beverage unit, creative dir. N.Y. office Hill and Knowlton, N.Y.C., 1983-91; mktg. cons. Rice & Rohr, N.Y.C., 1991-93; sr. v.p., dir. consumer mktg. practice Manning, Selvage & Lee, N.Y.C., 1993—. Writer Fast and Healthy Mag., 1991. Mem. Pub. Rels. Soc. Am., Women Execs. in Pub. Rels. Roman Catholic. Avocations: aerobics, baking. Home: 18 Westminster Dr Croton On Hudson NY 10520-1008 Office: Manning Selvage & Lee 79 Madison Ave New York NY 10016-7802

RICE, RICHARD CAMPBELL, retired state official, retired army officer; b. Atchison, Kans., Dec. 11, 1933; s. Olive Campbell and Ruby Thelma (Rose) R.; m. Donna Marie Lincoln, Aug. 4, 1956; children: Robert Alden, Holly Elizabeth. BS in History, Kans. State U., 1955; MA in Social Studies, Eastern Mich. U., 1965; grad. U.S. Army Command and Gen. Staff Coll., 1968, U.S. Army War Coll., 1977, FBI Nat. Exec. Inst., 1990, grad. program for sr. execs. in state and local govt., Harvard U., 1985. Commd. 2d lt. U.S. Army, 1955; advanced through grades to col., 1976; with Joint Chiefs of Staff, Washington, 1975-76; faculty U.S. Army War Coll., Carlisle Barracks, Pa., 1977-79; chief of staff Hdqrs. 3d ROTC Region, Ft. Riley, Kans., 1982-83; ret. 1983; dir. Mo. State Emergency Mgmt. Agy., Jefferson City, 1983-85, dir. Mo. Dept. Pub. Safety, Jefferson City, 1985-93; trustee Mo. State Employees Retirement System, 1990-93; bd. visitors Nat. Emergency Mgmt. Inst., 1991-92. Grad. Leadership, Mo., 1991; mem. Coordinating Coun. Health Edn., Mo.'s Children and Adolescents., Mo. Jail and Prison Overcrowding Task Force, Gov.'s Domestic Violence Task Force, Gov.'s Conf. Health Needs Children, Gov.'s Commn. on Crime, Gov.'s Adv. Coun. on Driving While Intoxicated, Mo. Children's Svcs. Commn., Blue Ribbon Commn. on Svcs. to Youth, Campaign to Protect Our Children; mem. policy com. Mo. Youth Initiative; chmn. Gov.'s Cabinet Coun. for Justice Administrn., Mo. Statistical Analysis Ctr. adv. bd., adv. bd. Mo. Criminal Hist. Records; bd. dirs. Mo. Law Enforcement Meml. Found, Gt. Rivers coun. Boy Scouts Am., 1993—; peer rev. cons. Nat. Inst. of Justice; chmn. Alliance for Uniform Hazmat Transp. Procedures, 1991-93. Decorated Legion of Merit, Bronze Star (3), Meritorious Service medal (4), Air medal (2), Joint Service Commendation medal, Army Commendation medal (2); Republic of Vietnam Cross of Gallantry with Silver Star; recipient Conspicuous Svc. medal State of Mo. Mem. Nat. Eagle Scout Assn., Assn. U.S. Army, Soc. First Div., Am. Legion, VFW, Disabled Am. Vets., AMVETS, Mil. Order of World Wars, Nat. Soc., Sons Am. Revolution, The Retired Officers Assn., Nat. Criminal Justice Assn. (bd. dirs. 1987-93), Rotary (Paul Harris fellow), St. Andrews Soc., Theta Xi. Republican. Avocation: sailing.

RICE, RICHARD CHARLES, academic administrator, educator, consultant; b. N.Y.C., June 22, 1940; s. George Washington Rice and Louise Eleanor (Clarius) Russell; m. Barbara Elizabeth Freiberg, Aug. 28, 1965; children: Jon Everett, Andrew Christopher, Karen Leigh. BS, Wagner Coll., N.Y.C., 1962; MS, Hofstra U., Hempstead, N.Y., 1969; MEd, Columbia U., 1985, EdD, 1986. Cert. tchr., prin., N.J., N.Y., sch. adminstr., N.J. Tchr., coach, dir. Sch. Dist. 12, L.I., N.Y., 1965-68; prin. Cresskill (N.J.) Pub. Schs., 1968-72, Hillsdale (N.J.) Pub. Schs., 1972-74; instr. Fairleigh Dickinson U., Teaneck, N.J., 1970-71; supt. schs. Montvale (N.J.) Pub. Schs., 1974-95; acting dir. evening programs Bergen C.C., Paramus, N.J., 1996—; interim supt. schs. Oradell Pub. Sch. Dist., 1996—; Chmn. Ridgewood (N.J.) Reorgn. Study, Tchrs. Coll., Columbia U., N.Y.C., 1983. Author: Journey to the Golden Door, 1995; co-author: How to Organize an Administrators Bargaining Unit, 1974, Human Rights and Prejudice, 1988 (Aaron Flanzbaum 21st Century Dem. Heritage award B'nai Brith Anti-Defamation League 1988); editor Montvale Schs. in Action, 1975-95. Trustee Montvale Free Pub. Libr., 1974-95, Wagner Coll., N.Y.C., 1979-84; bd. mem. Girl Scout coun. of Bergen County, N.J., 1976-81; pres. Gifted Child Soc., Bergen County, 1979-80; mem. Mercedes Benz of N.Am. Scholarship Coms., Montvale, 1984—; mem. Nat. Rep. Senatorial Com., 1988—; sec.-treas. Sammartino Inst. for Arts in Edn., F.D.U., Teaneck, N.J., 1989-95; exec. bd. mem. Met. Sch. Study Coun., Horace Mann Lincoln Inst., Tchrs. Coll., Columbia U., 1987-95, pres., 1988-89; mem Am. Educators Delegation to Moscow and St. Petersburg, 1993; student exch. facilitator with Russia, England, France, Germany and Spain. Capt. USMC, 1961-65. Recipient Disting. Svc. award Berger County Supts. Assn., 1984, Outstanding Leadership and Svc. award Acad. Decathlon N.J., Summit, 1994; named one of Outstanding 100 U.S. Supts. The Exec. Educator/IBM, Alexandria, Va., 1986. Mem. N.J. Assn. Elem. Sch. Adminstrs. (Northeastern N.J. field rep. 1973-74), IDEA Acad. Fellows, Middle States Assn. Colls. and Schs., N.J. Schoolmasters Club, Am. Assn. Sch. Adminstrs., N.J. Coun. Edn., Phi Delta Kappa. Lutheran. Avocations: reading, model building, travel, golf, flying. Home: 508 Franklin Ter Wyckoff NJ 07481

RICE, RICHARD LEE, retired architect; b. Raleigh, N.C., May 4, 1919; s. Robert Edward Lee and Grace Lucille (Betts) R.; m. Cora Belle Stegall, Apr. 12, 1946; children—Richard Lee, Westwood Carter, David Sinclair. BS in Archtl. Engring., N.C. State U., 1941; grad., U.S. Army Command and Gen. Staff Coll., 1961. Assoc. Cooper-Shumaker, Architects, Raleigh, 1946-47; prin. Richard L. Rice, Architects, Raleigh, 1947-48; assoc. Cooper, Haskins & Rice and predecessor firm, Raleigh, 1948-52, ptnr., 1953-54; ptnr. Haskins & Rice, Architects, Raleigh, 1954-85; prin. Haskins, Rice, Savage & Pearce, Architects, 1985-91, pres., 1985-91; v.p. N.C. Design Found., 1973; pres. N.C. Archtl. Found., 1975; mem. Raleigh Arts Commn., 1978-82, Raleigh Hist. Properties Commn., 1990-92, Raleigh Hist. Dists. Commn., 1991-92. Archtl. works include renovations, Raleigh Meml. Auditorium, 1964, 78, 91 (SE Regional AIA award of merit 1964), Auditorium, 4 high schs. and 13 elem. schs., Raleigh Civic Ctr., stack addition Wilson Libr. U. N.C., Chapel Hill, 1977, Reidsville, N.C. Jr. High Sch.; assoc. architect Raleigh Radisson Hotel, 1980, One Hanover Sq. Office Bldg., 1985, Two Hannover Sq. Office Bldg., 1990, additions and renovations to Raleigh Meml. Auditorium, 1989, 3 indsl. plants, 7 bldgs., Wake Tech. C.C., 50 chs. Pre.s Wake County (N.C.) Hist. Soc., 1973-74; mem. N.C. Gov.'s Com. for Facilities for Physically Handicapped, 1970-73; arbitrator Am. Arbitration Assn. With inf. and C.E. U.S. Army, 1941-46, ETO; col. USAR; ret. Decorated Silver Star.; Legion of Merit; Bronze Star; Purple Heart. Fellow AIA (pres. N.C. chpt. 1970, Disting. Svc. award N.C. chpt. 1975); mem. Raleigh Council Architects (pres. 1950), Nat. Trust for Hist. Preservation, N.C. State Art Soc., Res. Officers Assn. U.S., Ret. Officers Assn. U.S. (pres. Triangle chpt. 1983), N.C. State U. Gen. Alumni Assn. (pres., chmn. bd. 1960-61, pres. Class 1941, 1986-91), Carolina Country Club, Lions, Torch Club (pres. 1982-83), Phi Eta Sigma, Phi Kappa Phi. Democrat. Baptist.

RICE, RICHARD LEE, JR., architect; b. Raleigh, N.C., Aug. 8, 1949; s. Richard Lee and Cora (Stegall) R. BArch, N.C. State U., 1972, BA in Econs., 1979; MArch, Harvard U., 1973, MBA, 1982. Registered architect, N.Y., N.J., Md., N.C., Conn., Mass. Designer Kahn & Jacobs/HOK Architects, N.Y.C., 1973-75; prin. designer, assoc. The Gruzen Partnership, N.Y.C., 1975-80; prin., founder Richard Rice Architects, N.Y.C., 1982—. Prin. archtl. works include renovations Morgans Hotel, N.Y.C., 1984, First Presbyn. ch., Phila., 1985, 1790 Broadway lobby and fls., N.Y.C., 1988, Fordham Law Sch. Computer Ctr., N.Y.C., 1992, The Heights Casino Squash Cts., Bklyn., 1993, Fordham Bus. Sch., N.Y.C., 1995, Fordham Law Sch. Reading Rm., 1995. Deacon The Brick Presbyn. Ch. Mem. AIA, Archtl. League N.Y., N.C. Soc. N.Y. (trustee). Home: 27 W 71st St Apt 4A New York NY 10023-4143 Office: Richard Rice Architect 121 W 27th St Ste 1101 New York NY 10001-6207

RICE, ROBERT ARNOT, school administrator; b. San Francisco, Apr. 4, 1911; s. Abraham Lincoln and Mary Eugenia (Arnot) R.; m. Frances Von Dorsten, Aug. 15, 1936 (dec. sept. 1986); m. Esther Pauline Railton, July 11, 1989. BA, U. Calif., Berkeley, 1934, MA, 1947; postgrad., Columbia U., 1948. Various ednl. positions, 1935-61; supr. sci. and math. Berkeley Unified Sch. Dist., 1961-64; adminstr. NSF Summer Insts. for Sci. Tchr., U. Calif., Berkeley, 1957-65; dir. On Target Sch., Berkeley Unified Sch. Dist., 1971-73; coord. pub. programs Lawrence Hall of Sci., 1964-70; work experience edn. coord. Berkeley Unified Sch. Dist., 1973-75; exec. dir. Calif. Sci. Tchr. Assn., 1964-90; dir. No. Calif.-Western Nev. Jr. Sci. and Humanities Symposium, 1962-93; cons. Berkley Unified Sch. Dist., 1964-70; bd. dirs. San Francisco Bay Area Sci. Fair, 1960—; mem. steering com. Chem. Study, 1960-75; coord. Industry Initiatives for Sci. and Math. Edn. Program, 1985-86; dir. Industry Initiatives for Sci. and Math. Edn. Acad., 1987; mem. Internat. Sci. and Engring. Fair Coun., Sci. Svc., Inc., 1959-68; dir. 18th Internat. Sci. and Engring. Fair, San Francisco, 1967; exec. dir. San Francisco Bay Area Sci. Fair, 1954-59; resource cons. Calif. Farm Bur. Fedn.-Youth Power Conf., Asilomar, 1966; judging chair Nat. Jr. Sci. and Humanities Symposium, 1993—. Contbr. articles to profl. publs. Bd. dirs. Calif. Heart Assn., 1966-71, Alameda County Heart Assn., 1966-71; mem. Cen. Calif. Sci. Com., 1965-70; mem. rsch. com. Alameda County TB and Health Assn., 1965-69, mem. adv. com., 1965-69. Recipient Benjamin Ide Wheeler medal, 1985, San Francisco Bay Area Sci. Fair award of honor Calif. Acad. Sci., 1970, Armed Forces Chem. Assn. award for outstanding chemistry tchr. in San Francisco Bay Area, 1965; named to Berkeley H.S. Hall of Fame, 1994. Mem. NEA, Nat. Sci. Tchrs. Assn. (region VIII dir. 1955-57, Calif. state dir. 1949-56, mem. chemistry com. 1956-60, pres. 1960-61, Disting. Svc. to Sci. Edn. award 1986), No. Calif. Com. on Problem Solving in Sci., Calif. Sci. Tchrs. Assn. (pres. no. sect. 1949-50, Disting. Svc. to Sci. Teaching award 1981), Calif. Tchrs. Assn., Bay Area Curriculum Coords. (N.C. Sci. Specialists), Berkeley Kiwanis Club, Phi Delta Kappa (pres. Lambda chpt. 1942-43). Office: U Calif Berkeley Lawrence Hall of Sci Berkeley CA 94720-5200

RICE, ROGER DOUGLAS, television executive, artist; b. Spokane, Wash., Feb. 20, 1921; s. Leland L. and Bernice B. (Metcalf) R.; m. Molly Herron, Feb. 22, 1946; children: Stephannie Lee, Roger Douglas. B.S., U. Wash., 1944. With KING Radio, Seattle, 1947-51, 53-54; sta. mgr. KTVW-TV, Seattle, Tacoma, 1954-55; gen. sales mgr. WIIC-TV, Pitts., 1955-66; gen. mgr. WIIC-TV, 1966-68; v.p., gen. mgr. Cox Broadcasting Corp. KTVU, San Francisco, Oakland, Calif., 1968-74; pres., chief exec. officer TV Bur. Advt., N.Y.C., 1974-88; also abstract artist; bd. dirs. Palm Springs Air Mus. Chmn. U.S./Japan Cultural Exchange, 1974; mem. Japan-U.S. Friendship Commn.; bd. dirs. Advt. Council. Mem. Nat. Assn. Broadcasters (bd. dirs. TV code rev. bd. 1971-74). Clubs: Pres. Com. of 25 (v.p.), Thunderbird Country (bd. dirs., Rancho Mirage, Calif.).

RICE, RONALD JAMES, hospital administrator; b. Springfield, Mo., Feb. 5, 1944; s. Glen Elwood and Alice Jeanett (Robinson) R. BSBA, Cen. Mo. State U., 1966, MABA, 1969, Specialist, 1972. Lic. nursing home adminstr.; lic. risk mgr. Unit mgr. Bapt. Med. Ctr., Kansas City, Mo., 1970-71; dir. unit mgmt. Ind. Health Ctr., Independence, Mo., 1971-72; adminstrv. officer Meth. Hosp., Jacksonville, Fla., 1972-73, dir. personnel, 1973-74; assoc. adminstr. Humana Hosp. Orange Park (Fla.), 1974-77; adminstr. Cathedral Rehab. Hosp., Jacksonville, 1977-79, Marion County Gen. Hosp., Hamilton, Ala., 1979-80, Nassau Gen. Hosp., Fernandina Beach, Fla., 1980-85, Reception Med. Ctr., Lake Butler, Fla., 1985-91; regional adminstr. health svcs. Dept. Corrections, Gainesville, Fla., 1991—; cons. Clay Meml. Hosp., Green Cove Springs, Fla., 1976-77, Allied Health Care, Jacksonville, 1989. Mem. Polit. Action Com., Fla. Hosp. Assn., 1990, Coun. on Crime and Delinquency, Gainesville, 1990, Human Resources Com., Orlando, 1991. With U.S. Army, 1967-69. Decorated Army Commendation medal. Fellow Am. Coll. Health Care Execs.; mem. Am. acad. Med. Adminstrs., Am. Coll. Health Care Adminstrs., Am. Soc. Personnel Adminstrs., Fla. Hosp. Assn., Rotary (pres. 1984-86). Democrat. Unity Sch. Christianity. Avocations: boating, auto collecting model, antique juke box collecting, reading. Home: 1744 Horton Dr Orange Park FL 32073-2757

RICE, ROSS R(ICHARD), political science educator; b. Shenandoah, Iowa, Jan. 13, 1922; s. Bird O. and Della (Goodner) R.; m. Marie Puzach, Mar. 20, 1948; children: Marilyn, Roxanne, Valerie, Laurie. Student, Creighton U., 1939-41, U. No. Iowa, 1941-42; MA, U. Chgo., 1949, PhD, 1956. Elem. sch. tchr., 1941-42; Instr. Ariz. State U., Tempe, 1950-53; asst. prof. Ariz. State U., 1953-57, assoc. prof., 1957-60, prof. polit. sci., 1960-89, prof. emeritus, 1989—. Author: Extremist Politics, 1964, An Annotated Bibliography of Arizona Politics and Government, 1976, Carl Hayden: Builder of the American West, 1994; contbr. numerous articles to scholarly publs. Mem. council, mayor City of Tempe, 1958-62. With Air Corps U.S. Army, 1942-45. NEH grantee, 1972. Mem. Tempe Hist. Soc. (pres. 1971-73), Am. Polit. Sci. Assn., Western Polit. Sci. Assn. Democrat. Home: 108 W Palmcroft Dr Tempe AZ 85282-2120

RICE, SHARON MARGARET, clinical psychologist; b. Detroit, Sept. 4, 1943; d. William Christopher and Sylvia Lucille (Lawecki) R.; m. John Robert Speer, Aug. 14, 1977 (dec. Mar. 1994). AB, Oberlin Coll., 1965; MA, Boston U., 1968, PhD, 1977. Clin. psychologist Los Angeles County Juvenile Probation, L.A., 1969-75, Las Vegas (Nev.) Mental Health Ctr., 1976-81, Foothills Psychol. Assn., Upland, Calif., 1981—; pvt. cons., Claremont, Calif., 1984—. NIMH grantee, 1967-69; recipient Good Apple award Las Vegas Tchrs. Ctr., 1978-80. Mem. APA, Calif. Psychol. Assn., Internat. Soc. for Study of Dissociation, Inst. Noetic Scis., Sigma Xi. Avocations: dog breeding and showing, sailing. Office: Foothills Psychol Assn 715 N Mountain Ave # G Upland CA 91786-4364

RICE, STANLEY ARTHUR, biology educator; b. Cushing, Okla., May 30, 1957; s. Arthur John and Nina Irene (Hicks) R.; m. Althea Lisette Clarkston, June 9, 1984; 1 child, Anita. BA, U. Calif., Santa Barbara, 1979; PhD, U. Ill., 1987. Vis. teaching specialist Univ. Ill., Urbana, 1986-87; asst. prof. The King's Coll., Briarcliff Manor, N.Y., 1987-90; vis. faculty Sarah Lawrence Coll., Bronxville, N.Y., 1989-90; asst. prof. Huntington (Ind.) Coll., 1990-93, S.W. State U., Marshall, Minn., 1993—; vis. faculty mem. Wheaton (Ill.) Coll. Sci. Sta., 1993—, Taylor U., Upland, Ind., 1993. Contbr. articles to Oecologia, Perspectives on Sci. and Christian Faith, Creation/Evolution. Predoctoral fellowship NSF, Univ. Ill., 1980. Mem. Ecol. Soc. Am., British Ecol. Soc., Bot. Soc. Am., Am. Sci. Affiliation. Office: SW State Univ Dept Biology Marshall MN 56258

RICE, STANLEY TRAVIS, JR., poet, painter, English language educator; b. Dallas, Nov. 7, 1942; s. Stanley Travis and Margaret Nolia (Cruse) R.; m. Anne O'Brien, Oct. 14, 1961; children: Michele (dec.), Christopher. BA, San Francisco State U., 1963, MA, 1965. Asst. prof. San Francisco State U.,

1965-71, assoc. prof., 1971-76, prof. English and creative writing, 1977-88, asst. dir. Poetry Ctr., 1964-72, chmn. dept. creative writing, 1980-88, ret. Author: Some Lamb, 1975, Whiteboy, 1976 (Edgar Allen Poe award Acad. Am. Poets 1977), Body of Work, 1983, Singing Yet: New and Selected Poems, 1992, Fear Itself, 1995, Paintings—Stan Rice, 1997; one-man show of paintings Gallerie Simone Stern, New Orleans, La., 1992. Nat. Endowment Arts grantee, 1966, writing fellow, 1972; recipient Joseph Henry Jackson award San Francisco Found., 1968.

RICE, STEPHEN GARY, medical educator; b. Bklyn., Dec. 21, 1945; s. Abraham S. and Anne (Shelling) R.; m. Hilary Jo Turett, May 10, 1987; children: Adam, Bryan. AB, Columbia Coll., 1967; MD, PhD, NYU, 1974; MPH, U. Wash., 1983. Intern, resident Children's Hosp. & U. Wash., Seattle, 1974-77; faculty mem. sports medicine U. Wash., Seattle, 1977-96; dir. primary care sports medicine fellowship program Jersey Shore Med. Ctr., Neptune, N.J., 1996—; sec. Am. Bd. Sports Medicine, Inc., 1991; developer, dir. Athletic Health Care Sys., 1978—; cons. in field. Author: Athletic Health Care System, 1988. Team physician U. Wash., 1977-81, Garfield H.S., Seattle, 1975-96. Fellow Am. Acad. Pediatrics, Am. Coll. Sports Medicine; mem. Am. Alliance Health, Phys. Edn., Recreation and Dance, Nat. Strength & Conditioning Assn., Am. Med. Soc. Sports Medicine, Columbia Coll. Alumni Assn. (mem. nat. coun.). Avocations: sports, cooking, gardening, Gilbert & Sullivan, chess. Home: 6 Wildflower Ct Manalapan NJ 07726 Office: Jersey Shore Med Ctr Dept Pediatrics PO Box 397 Neptune NJ 07754-0397

RICE, STEPHEN LANDON, university official; b. Oakland, Calif., Nov. 23, 1941; s. Landon Frederick and E. Genevieve (Hunt) R.; m. Penny Louise Baum, Dec. 29, 1965; children: Andrew Landon, Katherine Grace. BS, U. Calif., Berkeley, 1964, MEngring., 1969, PhD, 1972. Registered profl. engr., Fla. Design engr. Lawrence Berkeley Lab., 1964-69; asst. prof. U. Conn., Storrs, 1972-77, assoc. prof., 1977-82, prof., 1982-83; prof., chmn. U. Ctrl. Fla., Orlando, 1983-88, assoc. dean, rsch. dir., 1988-96, interim asst. v.p. acad. affairs, 1995-96; assoc. provost for rsch. U. Nev., Las Vegas, 1996—; program evaluator ASME/ABET, N.Y.C., 1988-93; NASA predoctoral fellow, 1969-72; U.S. del. to Internat. Rsch. Group, Orgn. for Econ. Cmty. Devel., 1993—. Inventor impact wear apparatus, 1975. Named Outstanding Young Faculty Dow/ASEE, 1975, Eminent Engr., Tau Beta Pi, 1988; Fulbright rsch. scholar U. South Pacific, 1978-79; participant Fulbright exch. program for adminstrs. in internat. edn., Germany, 1995. Fellow ASME; mem. Am. Soc. Engring. Edn., Orlando C. of C. (mem. Goals 2000 1988-92), Theta Delta Chi. Avocations: sailing, tennis. Office: U Nev Box 451046 4505 Maryland Pky Las Vegas NV 89154-1046

RICE, STUART ALAN, chemist, educator; b. N.Y.C., Jan. 6, 1932; s. Harry L. and Helen (Rayfield) R.; m. Marian Ruth Coopersmith, June 1, 1952; children—Barbara, Janet. BS, Bklyn. Coll., 1952; MA, Harvard, 1954, PhD, 1955. Jr. fellow Harvard, 1955-57; faculty U. Chgo., 1957—, prof. chemistry, 1960-69, Louis Block prof. phys. scis., 1969-77, chmn. dept. chemistry, 1971-76, Frank P. Hixon disting. service prof., 1977—, dean phys. scis. div., 1981-95, dir. Inst. Study Metals, 1981-95; mem. Nat. Sci. Bd., 1980-86; nat. Phi Beta Kappa lectr., 1994-95. Author: Polyelectrolyte Solutions, 1961, Statistical Mechanics of Simple Liquids, 1965, Physical Chemistry, 1980; bd. dirs.: also numerous articles. Bull. Atomic Scientists. Guggenheim fellow, 1960-61; Falk-Plautt lectr. Columbia U., 1964; Riley lectr. Notre Dame U., 1964; NSF sr. postdoctoral fellow, 1965-66; USPHS spl. postdoctoral fellow U. Copenhagen, 1970-71; Univ. lectr. chemistry U. Western Ont., 1970; Seaver lectr. U. Soc. Calif., 1972; Noyes lectr. U. Tex., Austin, 1975; Foster lectr. SUNY, Buffalo, 1976; Frank T. Gucker lectr. Ind. U., 1976; Fairchild lectr. Calif. Inst. Tech., 1979; Baker lectr. Cornell U. 1985-86; Centenary lectr. Royal Soc. Chemistry, 1986-87, Nat. Phi Beta Kappa lectr., 1994-95. Fellow Am. Philos. Soc.; mem. Am. Chem. Soc. (award Pure Chemistry 1963, Leo Hendrik Baekland award 1971, Peter Debye award 1985, Hildebrand award 1987), Nat. Acad. Sci., Am. Acad. Sci., Am. Phys. Soc., AAAS, Faraday Soc. (Marlowe medal 1963), N.Y. Acad. Scis. (A. Cressy Morrison prize 1955), Danish Acad. Sci. and Letters (fgn.).

RICE, SUSAN ELIZABETH, federal agency official; m. Ian Cameron. BA in History, Stanford U., 1986; MPhil, Oxford U., 1988, DPhil, 1990. Mgmt. cons. McKinsey and Co., Toronto, Ontario, Can., 1991-93; dir. internat. orgns. and peacekeeping NSC, Washington, 1993-95, spl. asst. to pres., sr. dir. African affairs, 1995—. Fgn. policy aide Dem. Pres. Campaign, Boston, 1988;. Harry S. Truman scholar, 1984, Rhodes scholar, 1986; recipient Walter Frewen Lord prize, Royal Commonwealth Soc., 1990, Assn. prize, Chatham House-British Internat. Studies, 1992. Mem. Phi Beta Kappa. Office: African Affairs Directorate Nat Security Coun 1600 Pennsylvania Ave NW Washington DC 20500-0005

RICE, SUSAN F., fundraising counsel executive; b. Chgo., Dec. 10, 1939. BA, St. Mary's Coll., 1961; MPA, UCLA, 1976; EdD, Pepperdine U., 1986. Pres. YWCA, Santa Monica, Calif., 1978, League of Women Voters Calif., San Francisco, 1979-81; sr. fundraising profl. adminstr., instr. Santa Monica (Calif.) Coll., 1978-81; dir. govtl. rels. UCLA Alumni Assn., 1981-82; dir. devel. UCLA Grad. Sch. Mgmt., 1982-89; dep. dir. mktg. and devel., dir. major gifts Spl. Olympics Internat., Washington, 1989-90; v.p. devel. Bus. Exec. Nat. Security, Washington, 1991-92; pres., CEO Greater L.A. Zoo Assn., 1992-96. Co-author: Women, Money and Political Clout in Women as Donors, Woman as Philanthropists, 1994. Bd. dirs. St. Mary's Coll. Alumnae Assn., Notre Dame, Ind., 1982-84, Santa Monica Coll. Associs., 1984-94, Internat. Human Rights Law Group, 1990-92; trustee, chair pers. compensation com. L.A. Mus. Nat. History Found., 1982-89; treas. Women's Commn. Refugee Women, 1990-96; vice chmn. pers. commn. Santa Monica Coll. Dist., 1985-89. Recipient Disting. Alumna award St. Mary's Coll., 1986, Humanitarian award, NCCJ-L.A., 1995. Mem. Nat. Soc. Fundraising Execs. (bd. dirs. 1995—, v.p. Greater L.A. chpt.). Office: The Wachtell Group 611 W 6th St Ste 3250 Los Angeles CA 90017-3133

RICE, VICTOR ALBERT, manufacturing executive, heavy; b. Hitchin, Hertfordshire, Eng., Mar. 7, 1941. With Ford Motor Co., U.K., 1957-64, Cummins Engines, U.K., 1964-67, Chrysler Corp., U.K., 1968-70; comptroller N. European ops. Perkins Engines Group Ltd., Peterborough, U.K., subsequently Group's dir. fin., Group dir. sales, and dep. mng. dir. ops., 1970-75; comptroller world-wide Varity Corp. (formerly Massey-Ferguson Ltd.), Toronto, Ont., Can., 1975-77; v.p. staff ops. Varity Corp., Toronto, Ont., Can., 1977-78, pres., chief operating officer, 1978-80; chmn., chief exec. officer Lucas Varity Corp., Buffalo, N.Y., 1980—, also bd. dirs. Mem. Chief Execs. Orgns., World Pres. Orgns., Toronto Club, Toronto Golf Club, Country Club of Buffalo, Buffalo Club. Office: Varity Corp 672 Delaware Ave Buffalo NY 14209-2202*

RICE, WALTER HERBERT, federal judge; b. Pitts., May 27, 1937; s. Harry D. and Elizabeth L. (Braemer) R.; m. Bonnie Rice; children: Michael, Hilary, Harry, Courtney Elizabeth. BA, Northwestern U., 1958; JD, MBA, Columbia U., 1962; LLD (hon.), U. Dayton, 1991. Bar: Ohio 1963. Asst. county prosecutor Montgomery County, Ohio, 1964-66; assoc. Gallon & Miller, Dayton, Ohio, 1966-69; 1st asst. Montgomery County Prosecutor's Office, 1969; judge Dayton Mcpl. Ct., 1970-71, Montgomery County Ct. Common Pleas, 1971-80, U.S. Dist. Ct. (so. dist.) Ohio, 1980—; adj. prof. U. Dayton Law Sch., 1976—, bd. visitors, 1976—; chmn. Montgomery County Supervisory Council on Crime and Deliquency, 1972-74; vice chmn. bd. dirs. Pretrial Release, Inc., 1975-79. Author papers in field. Pres. Dayton Area Coun. on Alcoholism and Drug Abuse, 1971-73; chmn. bd. trustees Stillwater Health Ctr., Dayton, 1976-79, Family Svc. Assn. Dayton, 1978-80; chmn. RTA in 2000 Com., 2003 Com. Designed To Bring Nat. Park to Dayton To Honor Wright Bros. and Birth of Aviation; chmn. Martin Luther King Jr. Meml. Com.; trustee Montgomery County Vol. Lawyers Project, Miami Valley Cultural Alliance, Sinclair Community Coll. Found., U.S. Air & Trade Show, Barbara Jordan Com. Racial Justice. Recipient Excellent Jud. Service award Ohio Supreme Ct., 1976, 77, Outstanding Jud. Service award, 1973, 74, 76, Man of Yr. award Disting. Service Awards Council, Dayton, 1977, Outstanding Jurist in Ohio award Ohio Acad. Trial Lawyers, 1986, Pub. Ofcl. of Yr. award Ohio region of Nat. Assn. Social Workers, 1992, Humanitarian award NCCJ, 1993, Paul Laurence Dunbar Humanitarian award, 1996, Pres.' award NAACP, 1996. Mem. Dayton Bar Assn., Carl D. Kessler Inn of Ct. (founder, former chmn.).

RICE, WILLIAM EDWARD, newspaper columnist; b. Albany, N.Y., July 26, 1938; s. Harry Edward, Jr. and Elizabeth (Lally) R.; m. Carol Timmon, June 3, 1978 (div.); m. Jill Van Cleave, Aug. 20, 1983. BA in History, U. Va., 1960; MS with honors, Columbia U., 1963. Reporter, editorial writer, critic Washington Post, 1963-69; student LeCordon Bleu, Paris, 1969-70; dir. L'Ecole de Cuisine, Bethesda, Md., 1971-72; freelance writer, restaurant critic Washingtonian Mag., 1971-72; exec. food editor Washington Post, 1972-80; editor-in-chief Food and Wine Mag., N.Y.C., 1980-85; food and wine columnist Chgo. Tribune, 1986—; Dining In columnist Gentlemen's Quarterly, 1987-89; chmn. restaurant awards com.James Beard Found., 1993-. Author: Feasts of Wine and Food, 1986; editor: (with others) Where to Eat in America, 1978, 2d edit., 1980, 3d edit., 1987. Served with USN, 1960-62. Recipient Vesta award as outstanding newspaper food editor, 1979, Ordre du Merite Agricole (France), 1983. Home: 3000 N Sheridan Rd Chicago IL 60657-5553 Office: Chgo Tribune Co Po Box 25340 435 N Michigan Ave Chicago IL 60611-4001

RICE, WILLIAM PHIPPS, investment counselor; b. Bronxville, N.Y., Mar. 27, 1944; s. Anton Henry Jr. and Lydia Phipps (Sands) R.; m. Lynn Lucas Rice, May 21, 1972; children: William Phipps Jr., Paige Sands Rice. BA cum laude, Kenyon Coll., 1966. Analyst Spencer Trask & Co., N.Y.C., 1960-67; v.p., portfolio mgr. Endowment Mgmt. and Rsch. Corp., Boston, 1969-77, Ft. Hill Investors Mgmt. Corp., Boston, 1977-83; pres., founder Anchor Capital Advisors Inc., Boston, 1983—, Anchor/Russell Capital Advisors, Boston, 1989—; bd. dirs. Claw Island Foods. Pres., trustee Mass. Bible Soc., Boston, 1985-89; trustee of donations Episcopal Ch. Diocese of Mass., Boston, 1989—. With U.S. Army, 1967-69. Mem. Assn. for Investment Mgmt. and Rsch., Assn. Investment Mgmt. Sales Execs., Boston Security Analysts Soc., Boston C. of C., N.Y. Yacht Club, Duxbury Yacht Club. Avocations: skiing, boating, woodworking. Home: PO Box 1599 Duxbury MA 02331-1599 Office: Anchor Capital Advisors Inc 1 Post Office Sq Boston MA 02109

RICE, WINSTON EDWARD, lawyer; b. Shreveport, La., Feb. 22, 1946; s. Winston Churchill and Margaret (Coughlin) R.; m. Barbara Reily Gay, Apr. 16, 1977; 1 child, Andrew Hynes; children by previous marriage: Winston Hobson, Christian MacTaggart. Student Centenary Coll. La., 1967; JD, La. State U., 1971. Bar: La. 1971, Colo. 1990, Tex. 1992. Cons. geologist Gulfport, Miss., 1968-70; ptnr. Phelps, Dunbar, New Orleans, 1971-88; sr. ptnr. Rice, Fowler, New Orleans, San Francisco, San Diego, Houston, Miami, Fla., London, Bogata and Beijing, 1988—; instr. law La. State U., Baton Rouge, 1970-71. Assoc. editor La. Law Rev., 1970-71. Mem. La. Bar Assn., Colo. State Bar Assn., Tex. State Bar, New Orleans Bar Assn., New Orleans Assn. Def. Counsel, La. Assn. Def. Counsel, Fedn. Ins. and Corporate Counsel, Maritime Law Assn. U.S. (chmn. subcom. on offshore exploration and devel. 1985-88, vice chmn. com. internat. law of the sea 1988-91, chmn. 1991-95, mem. exec. com. 1992-94), Assn. Average Adjusters U.S., Assn. Average Adjusters (U.K.), Mariners Club (treas. 1974-75, 78-79, sec. 1975-76, v.p. 1976-77, pres. 1977-78), Boston Club, Stratford Club, New Orleans Country Club, Coral Beach and Tennis Club, Order of Coif, Phi Delta Phi, Phi Kappa Phi, Kappa Alpha. Republican. Episcopalian. Office: 201 St Charles Ave Ste 3600 New Orleans LA 70170-1000

RICH, ADRIENNE, writer; b. Balt., May 16, 1929; d. Arnold Rice and Helen Elizabeth (Jones) R.; m. Alfred H. Conrad (dec. 1970); children: David, Paul, Jacob. AB, Radcliffe Coll., 1951; LittD (hon.), Wheaton Coll., 1967, Smith Coll., 1979, Brandeis U., 1987, Coll. Wooster, Ohio, 1988, CCNY, Harvard U., 1990, Swarthmore Coll., 1992. Tchr. workshop YM-WHA Poetry Ctr., N.Y.C., 1966-67; vis. lectr. Swarthmore Coll., 1967-69; adj. prof. writing divsn. Columbia U., 1967-69; lectr. CCNY, 1968-70, instr., 1970-71, asst. prof. English, 1971-72, 74-75; Fannie Hurst vis. prof. creative lit. Brandeis U., 1972-73; prof. English Douglass Coll., Rutgers U., 1976-79; Clark lectr., disting. vis. prof. Scripps Coll., 1983-84; A.D. White prof.-at-large Cornell U., 1981-87; disting. vis. prof. San Jose State U., 1984-85; prof. English and feminist studies Stanford U., 1986-93; Marjorie Kovler vis. lectr. U. Chgo., 1989. Author: (poetry) Collected Early Poems, 1950-1970, 1993, Diving into the Wreck, 1973, The Dream of a Common Language, 1978, A Wild Patience Has Taken Me This Far, 1981, Your Native Land, Your Life, 1986, Time's Power, 1989, An Atlas of the Difficult World, 1991, Dark Fields of the Republic, 1995; (prose) Of Woman Born: Motherhood as Experience and Institution, 1976, 10th anniversary edit., 1986, On Lies, Secrets and Silence, 1979, Blood, Bread and Poetry, 1986, What Is Found There: Notebooks on Poetry and Politics, 1993. Mem. nat. adv. bd. Bridges, Boston Women's Fund, Sisterhood in Support of Sisters in South Africa, Nat. Writers Union. Recipient Yale Series of Younger Poets award, 1951, Nat. Inst. Arts and letters award in poetry, 1961, Eunice Tietjens Meml. prize, 1968, Shelley Meml. award, 1971, Nat. Book award, 1974, Fund for Human Dignity award Nat. Gay Task Force, 1981, Ruth Lilly Poetry prize, 1986, Brandeis U. Creative Arts medal for Poetry, 1987, Nat. Poetry Assn. award, 1989, Elmer Holmes Bobst award arts and letters NYU, 1989, MacArthur fellowship, 1994—, Dorothea Tanning award Acad. Am. Poets, 1996, others. Mem. PEN, Am. Acad. Arts and Letters, Nat. Writers Union, Am. Acad. Arts and Scis. Office: care W W Norton Co 500 5th Ave New York NY 10110

RICH, ALAN, music critic, editor, author; b. Boston, June 17, 1924; s. Edward and Helen (Hirshberg) R. A.B., Harvard, 1945; M.A., U. Calif.-Berkeley, 1952. Alfred Hertz Meml. Traveling fellow in music Vienna, Austria, 1952-53; Asst. music critic Boston Herald, 1944-45, N.Y. Sun, 1947-48; contbr. Am. Record Guide, 1947-61, Saturday Rev., 1952-53, Mus. Am., 1955-61, Mus. Quar., 1957-58; tchr. music U. Calif. at Berkeley, 1950-58; program and music dir. Pacifica Found., FM radio, 1953-61; asst. music critic N.Y. Times, 1961-63; chief music critic, editor N.Y. Herald Tribune, 1963-66; music critic, editor N.Y. World Jour. Tribune, 1966-67; contbg. editor Time mag., 1967-68; music and drama critic, arts editor N.Y. mag., 1968-81, contbg. editor, 1981-83; music critic, arts editor Calif. (formerly New West mag.), 1979-83, contbg. editor, 1983-85; gen. editor Newsweek mag., N.Y.C., 1983-87; music critic L.A. Herald Examiner, 1987-89, L.A. Daily News, 1989-92, L.A. Weekly, 1992—; tchr. New Sch. for Social Rsch., 1972-75, 77-79, U. So. Calif. Sch. Journalism, 1980-82, Calif. Inst. Art, 1982-94, UCLA, 1990-91; artist-in-residence Davis Ctr. for Performing Arts CUNY, 1975-76. Author: Careers and Opportunities in Music, 1964, Music: Mirror of the Arts, 1969, Listeners Guides to Classical Music, Opera, Jazz, 3 vols., 1980, The Lincoln Center Story, 1984, Play-by-Play: Bach, Mozart, Beethoven, Tchaikovsky, 4 vols., 1995, American Pioneers, 1995, Play-by-Play: Handel, The Romantics, 2 vols., 1997; author: (interactive CD-ROM computer programs): Schubert's Trout Quintet, 1991, So I've Heard: Bach and Before, 1992, So I've Heard: The Classical Ideal, 1993, So I've Heard: Beethoven and Beyond, 1993; contbr. articles to entertainment mags. Recipient Deems Taylor award ASCAP, 1970, 73, 74. Mem. Music Critics Circle N.Y. (sec. 1961-63, chmn. 1963-64), N.Y. Drama Critics Circle, Am. Theatre Critics Assn., Music Critics Assn., PEN. Home: 2925 Greenfield Ave Los Angeles CA 90064-4019

RICH, ALEXANDER, molecular biologist, educator; b. Hartford, Conn., Nov. 15, 1924; s. Max and Bella (Shub) R.; m. Jane Erving King, July 5, 1952; children: Benjamin, Josiah, Rebecca, Jessica. A.B. magna cum laude in Biochem. Scis, Harvard U., 1947, M.D. cum laude, 1949; Dr. (hon.), Fed. U. Rio de Janeiro, 1981; PhD honoris causa, Weizmann Inst. Sci., Rehovot, Israel, 1992; DSc (hon.), Eidgenössische Technische Hochschule, Zurich, Switzerland, 1993. Research fellow Gates and Crellin Labs., Calif. Inst. Tech., Pasadena, 1949-54; chief sect. phys. chemistry NIMH, Bethesda, Md., 1954-58; vis. scientist Cavendish Lab., Cambridge (Eng.) U., 1955-56; asso. prof. biophysics MIT, Cambridge, 1958-61; prof. biohpysics MIT, 1961—, William Thompson Sedgwick prof. biophysics, 1974—; Fairchild disting. scholar Calif. Inst. Tech., Pasadena, 1976; mem. AAAS (coun. mem. 1967-71), Biophysical Soc (coun. mem. 1960-69), com. career devel. awards NIH, 1964-67, mem. postdoctoral fellowship bd., 1955-58; mem. com. exobiology space sci. bd. NAS, 1964-65; mem. U.S. nat. com. Internat. Orgn. Pure Applied Biophysics, 1965-67; mem. vis. com. dept. biology Weizmann Inst. Sci., 1965-66, co-chmn. sci. and adv. com. 1987-91; mem. vis. com. biology dept. Yale U.1963; mem. life scis. com. NASA, 1970-75, mem. lunar planetary missions bd., 1968-70; mem. biology team Viking Mars Mission, 1969-80; mem. corp. Marine Biol. Lab., Woods Hole, Mass., 1965-77, 87—; mem. sci. rev. com. Howard Hughes Med. Inst., Miami, Fla., 1978-90; mem. vis. com. biology div. Oak Ridge Nat. Lab., 1972-76; chmn. com. on USSR and Ea. Europe Exch. Bd. NAS, 1973-76; mem. Internat. Rsch. and Exchs. Bd. Am. Coun. Learned Socs., N.Y.C., 1973-76, mem. panel judges N.Y. Acad. Sci. ann. book award for children's sci. books, N.Y.C.,1973-90; chmn. nominating com. Am. Acad. Arts and Scis., 1974-77, adv. bd., acad. forum NAS, 1975-82; mem. sci. adv. bd. Stanford Synchrotron Radiation Project, 1976-80, Mass. Gen. Hosp., Boston, 1978-83; mem. U.S. Nat. Sci. Bd., 1976-82; mem. bd. govs. Weizmann Inst. Sci., 1976—; mem. research com. Med. Found., Boston, 1976-80; mem. U.S.-USSR Joint Commn. on Sci. and Tech., Dept. State, Washington, 1977-82; sr. cons. Office of Sci. and Tech. Policy, Exec. Office of Pres., Washington, 1977-81; mem. council Pugwash Confs. on Sci. and World Affairs, Geneva, 1977-82; chmn. basic research com. Nat. Sci. Bd., Washington, 1978-82; mem. U.S. Nat. Com. for Internat. Union for Pure and Applied Biophysics, NAS, 1979-83; mem. nominating com. NAS, 1980; bd. dirs. Med. Found., Boston, 1981-90; mem. vis. com. for Div. Med. Sci., Harvard U., 1981-87; mem. exec. com. of council, 1985-88, mem. govt.-univ.-industry research round table, 1984-87; chmn. sci. adv. com. dept. molecular biology Mass. Gen. Hosp., Boston, 1983-87; mem. governing bd. NRC, 1985-88; mem. nat. adv. com. Pew Scholars program Pew Meml. Trust, 1986-88; mem. com. on USSR and Eastern Europe Nat. Research Council, Washington, 1986—; mem. external adv. com. Ctr. for Human Genome Studies, Los Alamos Nat. Lab., N.Mex., 1989—, Nat. Critical Techs. Panel, Office of Sci. & Tech. Policy, Exec. Office of Pres., Washington, 1990-91; mem. vis. com. NASA Ctr. Exobiology, La Jolla, Calif., 1992—; fgn. mem. Russian Acad. Scis., Moscow, 1994—; vis. prof. Collège de France, Paris, 1987. Editor: (with Norman Davidson) Structural Chemistry and Molecular Biology, 1968;mem. editorial bd. Biophys. Jour, 1961-63, Currents Modern Biology, 1966-72, Science, 1963-69, Analytical Biochemistry, 1969-81, Bio-Systems, 1973-86, Molecular Biology Reports, 1974-85, Procs. NAS, 1973-78, Jour. Molecular and Applied Genetics, 1980-84, DNA, 1981-89, EMBO Jour., 1988-90, Jour. Biotech., 1987—, Genomics, 1987—, Proteins, Structure, Function and Genetics, 1986-91, Jour. Molecular Evolution, 1983—; Springer Series on Molecular Biology, 1980-88; editorial advisory bd. Jour. Molecular Biology, 1959-66, Accounts of Chemical Research, 1980-82, Jour. Biomolecular Structure and Dynamics, 1983—, PAABS Revista, 1972-77, Biopolymers, 1963-74; contbr. articles to profl. jours. Served with USN, 1943-46. Recipient Skylab Achievement award NASA, 1974, Theodore von Karmin award Viking Mars Mission, 1976, Presdl. award N.Y. Acad. Scis., 1977, Jabotinsky medal Jabotinsky Found., 1980, James R. Killian Faculty Achievement award MIT, 1980, Lewis S. Rosenstiel Basic Biomed. Rsch. award Brandeis U., 1983, Nat. Sci. medal, 1995; NRC fellow, 1949-51; Guggenheim Found. fellow, 1963; mem. Pontifical Acad. Scis. The Vatican, 1978. Fellow AAAS; mem. NAS (chmn. biotech., program, com. on scholarly comm. with China 1986—, exec. com. 1985—, com. on sci. comm. and nat. security 1982—), Am. Chem. Soc. (exec. com. div. biol. chemistry 1962, Linus Pauling award 1995), Biophys. Soc. (coun. 1960-69), Am. Soc. Biol. Chemists, Am. Crystallographic Soc., Internat. Soc. for Study of Origin of Life, French Acad. Scis. (fgn.), European Molecular Biology Orgn. (assoc.), Japanese Biochem. Soc. (hon.), Physicians for Social Responsibility (nat. adv. bd. 1983—), Am. Philos. Soc., Inst. of Medicine (sr. mem. 1990), Phi Beta Kappa, Alpha Omega Alpha. Office: MIT Dept Biology 77 Massachusetts Ave Rm 68-233 Cambridge MA 02139-4301

RICH, ARTHUR LOWNDES, music educator; b. Woodcliff, N.J., May 7, 1905; s. Frank Joseph and Ruth (Lowndes) R.; m. Helen Wall, July 26, 1934; children: Arthur Lowndes, Ruth Anne. A.B., Rutgers U., 1926; A.M., Columbia U., 1928; Ph.D., NYU, 1940; diploma, Julliard Sch. Music, 1928; licentiate, Royal Schs. Music (Royal Acad. Music, Royal Coll. of Music), London, 1939; spl. study, Harvard, 1943, Christiansen Choral Sch., 1948; 52. Prof. music Catawba Coll., Salisbury, N.C., 1928-43; dir. music Belhaven Coll., Jackson, Miss., 1943-44, Mercer U., Macon, Ga., 1944—; Roberts prof. music Mercer U., 1945-74, prof. emeritus, dir. concert series and cultural affairs, 1974—; Choral condr., adjudicator, Ga. and S.E.; music critic Macon News; corr. Mus. Am.; pres. Tudor Apts., Biscayne Apts., Inc. Author: Lowell Mason, the Father of Singing Among the Children, 1945; Contbr. articles to ednl., music jours., reference books. Bd. dirs. Macon Arts Council, Middle Ga. Symphony Orch. Life hon. mem. Community Concert Assn. (dir.); mem. Mark Twain Soc. (hon.), Am. Assn. Coll. and Univ. Concert Mgrs., Nat. Assn. Schs. Music, Phi Mu Alpha Sinfonia Soc., Macon Morning Music Club (hon.), Macon Federated Music Club (hon.). Lodge: Rotary. Home: 369 Candler Dr Macon GA 31204-2450

RICH, BEN ARTHUR, lawyer, educator; b. Springfield, Ill., Mar. 27, 1947; s. Ben Morris and Betty Lorraine (Ingalls) R.; m. Caroline Rose Castle, Oct. 4, 1984 (div. Nov. 1988); m. Kathleen Mills, Aug. 17, 1991. Student, U. St. Andrews, Scotland, 1967-68; BA, DePauw U., 1969; JD, Washington U., 1973; postgrad., U. Colo. Bar: Ill. 1973, N.C. 1975, Colo. 1984. Rsch. assoc. U. Ill. Coll. Law, Urbana, 1973-74; staff atty. Nat. Assn. Attys. Gen., Raleigh, N.C., 1974-76; prin. Hollowell, Silverstein, Rich & Brady, Raleigh, 1976-80; dep. commr. N.C. Indsl. Commn., Raleigh, 1980-81; counsel N.C. Meml. Hosp., Chapel Hill, 1981-84; assoc. univ. counsel U. Colo. Health Scis. Ctr., Denver, 1984-86; gen. counsel U. Colo., Boulder, 1986-89, spl. counsel to the regents, 1989-90; asst. clin. prof. U. Colo. Sch. Medicine, 1992-94; asst. prof. U. Colo. Health Scis. Ctr., 1995—, asst. dir. program in healthcare ethics, humanities and law, 1995—; asst. prof. attendent U. Colo. Sch. Medicine, 1986-91, adj. instr. Sch. Law, 1988-95, adj. prof., 1996—; vis. assoc. prof., 1990-91; lectr. U. Denver Coll. Law. Contbr. articles to jours., chpt. to book. Mem. Am. Coll. Legal Medicine (assoc.-in-law 1987), Am. Philos. Assn., Soc. for Health and Human Values, Am. Soc. Medicine and Ethics (health law tchrs. sect.), Toastmasters Internat. (pres. Raleigh chpt. 1978). Unitarian. Avocations: sailing, jogging, tennis. Home: 222 S Elm St Denver CO 80222-1133 Office: Univ Colo Health Scis Ctr Box B137 4200 E 9th Ave Denver CO 80262

RICH, DANIEL HULBERT, chemistry educator; b. Fairmont, Minn., Dec. 12, 1942; married, 1964; 2 children. BS, U. Minn., 1964; PhD in Organic Chemistry, Cornell U., 1968. Rsch. assoc. organic chemist Cornell U., 1968; rsch. chemist Dow Chem. Co., 1968-69; rsch. assoc., organic chemist Stanford U., 1969-70; asst. prof. pharm. chemistry U. Wis., Madison, 1970-75, assoc. prof., 1975-81, prof. dept. medical chemistry, 1981—, prof. dept. organic chemistry, 1988—, Ralph F. Hirschmann prof. medicinal and organic chemistry, 1994—; cons. biorganic natural product study sect., NIH, 1980—, mem., 1981—. Recipient H.I. Romnes award, 1980, Vincent du Vigneaud award, 1990, Hitchings award for innovative methods in drug design, 1992, Alexander von Humboldt award, 1993, E. Volwiler award Am. Assn. Colls. Pharmacy, 1995; fellow NIH, 1968. Fellow AAAS, Am. Chem. Soc. (Ralph F. Hirschmann award in peptide chemistry 1993, divsn. medicinal chemistry award 1991), Am. Assn. Pharm. Sci. (rsch. achievement award 1992), Am. Assn. Coll. Pharmacy (Volwiler award 1995). Achievements include research in synthesis in peptides and hormones, inhibition of peptide receptors and proteases, characterization, synthesis and mechanisms of action of peptide natural products. Office: U Wis Dept Med Chemistry 425 N Charter St Madison WI 53706-1508

RICH, DAVID BARRY, city official, auditor, accountant, entertainer; b. Bronx, N.Y., July 3, 1952; s. Steven and Gizella (Kornfeld) R.; m. Biverly Hayag, Dec. 6, 1995; 1 child, Suzanne Stephanie. BS in Health Adminstrn., Ithaca Coll., 1976; postgrad. in acctg., Bryant and Stratton Coll., Buffalo, 1977. Office mgr. Rubin Gorewitz, CPA, N.Y.C., 1977-78; auditor State of Ariz., Phoenix, 1979-83; internal auditor City of Phoenix, 1983-84; sales use tax auditor City of Mesa (Ariz.), 1984—; pres. Clovis Acctg. Inc., Mesa, 1980-94; rep. H.D. Vest Investment Inc., Irving, Tex., 1984-94; owner D.B. Rich Enterprises Import/Export, Mesa, 1992—; stage name Barry Rich, Stand-up Comedy, 1994—. Treas., bd. dirs. Missing Mutts Inc., Tempe, Ariz., 1986-88. With USAF, 1971-76. Fellow Nat. Assn. Tax Preparers; mem. Toastmasters (treas. Mesa 1986-87), Phi Beta Kappa. *The world is one big neighborhood and we are all neighbors. If we will survive as a planet we must work together as friends. We must treat all people as our equals.*

RICH, DOROTHY KOVITZ, educational administrator, author. BA in Journalism and Psychology, Wayne U.; MA, Columbia U.; EdD, Catholic U. Founder, pres. The Home and Sch. Inst., Inc., Washington, 1964—; adv. coun. Nat. Health Edn. Consortium; adv. com. Ctr. for Workplace Prep. and Quality Edn., U.S. C. of C.; mem. readiness to learn task force U.S. Dept. Edn., urban edn. team Coun. Gt. City Schs.; legislative nat. initiatives including work on Family/Sch. Partnership Act, 1989; formulator New Partnerships for Student Achievement program, 1987; creator MegaSkills Edn. Ctr. The Home and Sch. Inst. Inc., 1990; designer MegaSkills Leader

Tng. for Parent Workshops, 1988, MegaSkills Essentials for the Classroom, 1991, learning and working program for sch.-to-work initiatives, 1996, New MegaSkills Bond Tchr./Parent Partnership, 1994. Author: MegaSkills in School in Life: The Best Gift You Can Give Your Child, 1988, rev. edit., 1992, What Do We Say? What Do We Do? Vital Solutions for Children's Educationsl Success, 1997, MegaSkills, 3d edit., 1997, 12 tng. books; TV appearances include The Learning Channel, NBC Today Show, Good Morning Am.; subject of videos: Families and Schools: Teaming for Success, Survival Guide for Today's Parents. Recipient Am. Woman Leader award, Citation U.S. Dept. Edn., Nat. Gov.'s Assn., Alumni Achievement award in edn. Cath. U., 1992, Golden Apple award for MegaSkills Tchrs. Coll., Columbia U., 1996; grantee John D. and Catherine T. MacArthur Found.; named Washingtonian of Yr. Mem. Cosmos Club. Office: MegaSkills Edn Ctr Home and Sch Inst Inc 1500 Massachusetts Ave NW Washington DC 20005-1821

RICH, ELIZABETH MARIE, nursing educator; b. Bklyn., Nov. 20, 1949; d. Oren Edward and Catherine (Raffaele) R. ADN, Grossmont Coll., El Cajon, Calif., 1983; BSN, U. Phoenix, 1988; MS, Nat. U., San Diego, 1991. Cert. pub. health nurse, gerontol. nurse. ICU-CCU staff nurse Villa View, San Diego, 1983-85, AMI Valley Hosp., El Cajon, 1985-86; nurse Nursing Registries, 1986-87; charge nurse, supr. nights Beverly Manor Convalescent Home, Escondido, Calif., 1987-88; dir. staff devel. Beverly Manor Convalescent Home, Escondido, 1988-90; DON, nurse educator cons. Vista Del Mar Care Ctr., San Diego, 1990; instr. vocat. nursing Maric Coll. Med. Careers, Vista, Calif., 1991—, curriculum coord., placement coord., 1992-94; faculty St. John's U., Springfield, La., 1995—. Mem. Calif. Vocat. Nurse Educators. Home: 872 Venice Gln Escondido CA 92026-3165

RICH, FRANK HART, critic; b. Washington, June 2, 1949; s. Frank Hart Rich and Helene Bernice (Aaronson) Fisher; m. Alexandra Rachelle Witchel, 1991; children from previous marriage: Nathaniel Howard, Simon Hart. B.A. in Am. History and Lit. magna cum laude, Harvard U., 1971. Co-editor Richmond (Va.) Mercury, 1972-73; sr. editor, film critic New Times mag., N.Y.C., 1973-75; film critic N.Y. Post, N.Y.C., 1975-77; film and TV critic Time mag., N.Y.C., 1977-80; chief drama critic N.Y. Times, N.Y.C., 1980-93; columnist N.Y. Times Sunday Mag., N.Y.C., 1993; Op-Ed columnist N.Y. Times, N.Y.C., 1994—. Author: (with others) The Theatre Art of Boris Aronson, 1987. Office: The NY Times 229 W 43rd St New York NY 10036-3913

RICH, GILES SUTHERLAND, federal judge; b. Rochester, N.Y., May 30, 1904; s. Giles Willard and Sarah Thompson (Sutherland) R.; m. Gertrude Verity Braun, Jan. 10, 1931 (dec.); 1 child, Verity Sutherland Grinnell (Mrs. John M. Hallinan); m. Helen Gill Field, Oct. 10, 1953. SB, Harvard, 1926; LLB, Columbia, 1929; LLD (hon.), John Marshall Law Sch., Chgo., 1981, George Washington U., 1989, Franklin Pierce Law Ctr., 1993. Bar: N.Y. 1929, U.S. Patent Office 1934. Pvt. practice N.Y.C., 1929-56; ptnr. specializing patent and trademark law Williams, Rich & Morse, 1937-52, Churchill, Rich, Weymouth & Engel, 1952-56; assoc. judge U.S. Ct. Customs and Patent Appeals, 1956-82; cir. judge U.S. Ct. Appeals (Fed. cir.), 1982—; lectr. patent law Columbia, 1942-56, N.Y. Law Sch., 1952; adj. prof. Georgetown U. Law Sch., 1963-69. Contbr. articles to profl. jours. Recipient Jefferson medal N.J. Patent Law Assn., 1955, Kettering award Patent Trademark and Copyright Inst. George Washington U., 1963, Founder's Day award for disting. govt. svcs., 1970, Freedom Found. award Am. Inst. Chemists, 1967, Eli Whitney award Conn. Patent Law Assn., 1972, Columbia U. Sch. Law medal for Excellence, 1994, Licensing Execs. Soc. of U.S.A. and Can. award, 1994. Mem. ABA, Assn. of Bar of City of N.Y., Am. Intellectual Property Law Assn., N.Y. Patent Law Assn. (pres. 1950-51), Rochester Patent Law Assn. (hon. life), L.A. Patent Law Assn. (hon.), San Francisco Patent Law Assn. (hon. life). Clubs: Harvard (Washington), Cosmos. Office: US Ct Appeals Fed Cir 717 Madison Pl NW Washington DC 20439-0002

RICH, HARRY E., financial executive; b. Wichita, Kans., Mar. 5, 1940; s. Hubert E. and Lorene (Sadler) R.; m. Elfreda Elizabeth Babcock, Aug. 8, 1964; children: Lisa G., Carey E., Ashley H. BA, Harvard U., 1962, MBA, 1968. Pres. instrumentation divsn. Baxter Travenol, Deerfield, Ill., 1977-78; group v.p. Mallinckrodt, Inc., St. Louis, 1978-83; sr. v.p., chief fin. officer Brown Group, Inc., St. Louis, 1983-88, exec. v.p., chief fin. officer, 1988—, also bd. dirs.; bd. dirs. Gen. Am. Capital Co. divsn. Gen. Am. Life Ins. Co. Bd. dirs. Repertory Theatre, 1984-90, pres. bd. dirs.,1988-90; treas., v.p. Fair Found., 1985-88; bd. trustees Mary Inst., 1986-90, Mary Inst./St. Louis Country Day Sch., 1990-97. Lt. USN, 1962-66. Avocations: tennis, jogging, sailing. Home: 101 Fair Oaks Saint Louis MO 63124-1579 Office: Brown Group Inc 8300 Maryland Ave Saint Louis MO 63105-3645

RICH, JOHN, film and television producer, director; b. Rockaway Beach, N.Y., July 6, 1925; s. Louis and Jennie R.; m. Patricia Dodds Benton; children: Catherine Lee, Anthony Joseph, Robert Lawrence, Kimberly Beres, Megan Lewis, Dana Benton. AB, U. Mich., 1948, MA, 1949. Exec. prodr. TV series MacGyver, 1984-93; dir. (films) Wives and Lovers, 1963, The New Interns, 1964, Roustabout, 1964, Boeing-Boeing, 1965, Easy Come, Easy Go, 1967, (TV) Academy Awards, The Dick Van Dyke Show, All in the Family, other series include Bob Newhart, Barney Miller, Benson, Dear John, Murphy Brown, Hudson Street. Served to capt. USAAF, 1943-46. Recipient Outstanding Comedy Direction awards Acad. TV Arts and Scis. for The Dick Van Dyke Show, 1963, All in the Family, 1972, 73; Sesquicentennial award U. Mich., 1967; Dirs. Guild Am. award for most outstanding directorial achievement, 1972, Robert B. Aldrich award, 1992; Golden Globe awards for All in the Family, 1972, 73, Emmy award as prodr., 1973, Christopher award for Henry Fonda as Clarence Darrow, 1974. Mem. Dirs. Guild Am. (bd. dirs., founding trustee DGA-Prodrs. Pension Plan, chmn. 1964-65, 68-69, 92-93, 95-96), Phi Beta Kappa, Phi Kappa Phi.

RICH, JOHN MARTIN, humanities educator, researcher; b. Tuscaloosa, Ala., Dec. 14, 1931; s. Emanuel Morris and Bertha (Rose) R.; m. Martha Elaine Schur, June 6, 1955 (div. June 1966); children—Jeffrey Brian, Suzanne Elon; m. Joyce Ann Stegemoller, Aug. 28, 1967 (div. Mar. 1985); m. Audrey Faye Arnold, Aug. 1, 1987. B.A., U. Ala., 1954, M.A., 1955; Ph.D., Ohio State U., 1958. Grad. asst. Ohio State U., Columbus, 1955; asst. instr. edn. Ohio State U., 1956-58; asst. prof. edn. U. Tenn.-Martin, 1958-60; assoc. prof. edn. Coll. SUNY-Oneonta, 1960-61; from asst. prof. to assoc. prof. Iowa State U., Ames, 1961-66; assoc. prof. social and philos. studies U. Ky., Lexington, 1966-69; prof. cultural founds. edn. U. Tex., Austin, 1969-96, prof. emeritus, 1996—, chmn. dept. cultural founds. edn., 1969-75; vis. lectr. Nat. Kaohsiung (Taiwan) Normal U., 1993. Author: (books) Education and Human Values, 1968, Humanistic Foundations of Education, 1971, Portuguese translation, 1975, Korean translation, 1985, Challenge and Response, 1974, New Directions in Educational Policy, 1974, Discipline and Authority in School and Family, 1982, Professional Ethics in Education, 1984, Innovative School Discipline, 1985, Foundations of Education, 1992; co-author: Theories of Moral Development, 1985 (named an Outstanding Book of 1985-86 Choice mag.), 2d edit., 1994, Helping and Intervention, 1988, Competition in Education, 1992, The Success Ethic, Education, and the American Dream, 1996; editor: Readings in the Philosophy of Education, 1966, 2d edit., 1972, Conflict and Decision, 1972, Innovations in Education, 6th edit., 1992; co-editor, editl. adv. bd. Ednl. Studies, 1970-74, 77-80, 89-91; bd. contbg. editors Rev. Edn., 1977-85; editl. bd. Focus on Learning, 1980-84, Educational Foundations, 1985-91; bd. cons. Jour. Rsch. and Devel. in Edn., 1982-96, Ednl. Theory, 1991-95; contbr. articles to profl. jours., U.S., Can., Eng., Australia. Recipient Faculty Research Assignment award Univ. Research Inst., Austin, Tex., 1983-84; vis. scholar U. London, 1977; Univ. Research Inst. grantee, 1981-82, 84-85. Mem. North Central Philosophy of Edn. Soc. (pres. 1966-67), Ohio Valley Philosophy of Edn. Soc. (pres. 1967-68), Philosophy of Edn. Soc. (exec. bd. 1967-68, 80-82, Cert. Significant Svc.), Am. Ednl. Studies Assn. (exec. council 1972-74, pres. 1975-76). Home: 1801 Lavaca St Apt 8M Austin TX 78701-1307 Office: U Tex Edn Bldg 406 Austin TX 78712

RICH, JOHN TOWNSEND, lawyer; b. Lansing, Mich., Mar. 10, 1943; s. Townsend and Jean (Trembley) R.; m. Charlotte Pia Mahon, Nov. 25, 1978; children: Anna-Sophie, Lucia Danforth. B.A., Harvard U., 1965, postgrad., 1965-66; LL.B., Yale U., 1969; postgrad. Univ. Coll., Oxford, Eng., 1969-70. Bar: N.Y. 1970, D.C. 1972. Law clk. to chief judge David L. Bazelon, U.S. Ct. Appeals D.C. Cir., 1970-71; law clk. to Assoc. Justice Harry A. Blackmun, U.S. Supreme Ct., Washington, 1971-72; assoc. firm Shea & Gardner, Washington, 1972-76, ptnr., 1976—; adj. prof. law Georgetown U. Law Ctr., 1972-75; spl. master U.S. Dist. Ct. for No. Dist. Tex., 1985-88. Home: 6309 Kenhowe Dr Bethesda MD 20817-5419 Office: Shea & Gardner 1800 Massachusetts Ave NW Washington DC 20036-1806

RICH, KENNETH MALCOLM, executive search and management consultant; b. Newark, N.J., Aug. 17, 1946; s. Lucien Ludwell and Grace (Hardy) R.; m. Sandra Ann Arrington; children: Stephen Montgomery, Khristine Nicole. AB in Chemistry, Lafayette Coll., 1967; MBA in Fin., Mktg., U. Chgo., 1969; cert. in acctg., NYU, 1979. Assoc., corp. fin. Kuhn, Loeb & Co., N.Y.C., 1969-73; special asst. to the asst. sec. policy, devel. and rsch. HUD, Washington, 1973-74; mng. dir. fgn. investments The Dornbush Co., Atlanta, 1974; resident v.p. Citibank, N.A., N.Y.C., Athens and Dubai, U.A.E., 1975-78; mng., cons. div. Peat, Marwick, Mitchell & Co., N.Y.C., 1978-80; mng., strategic planning Gen. Elec. Credit Corp., Stamford, Conn., 1981-83; ptnr. Paul Ray Berndtson Inc., N.Y.C., 1983—; mem. mktg. com. Paul R. Ray & Co., Inc., N.Y.C., 1985-88, chmn. fin. svcs. practice com., 1989-92, mem. fin. svcs. practice com., 1989—, chmn. investment com., 1995-96; mem. stk. com., bd. dirs. practice group; also bd. dirs. Paul Ray Berndtson Inc., N.Y.C., 1989-96; trustee Lafayette Coll., Easton, Pa., 1970-75. Chief umpire Ridgefield (Conn.) Little League, 1980-89; mem. Lafayette Leadership Coun., 1993—; bd. dirs. Juvenile Diabetes Found. Internat., 1993—, exec. com., 1995—, chair nominating com., 1995-97, mem. long range planning com., 1995, 1997—. Standard Oil of N.J. fellow U. Chgo., 1967-69; named one of N.Am.'s top exec. recruiters The New Career Makers (by John Sibbald), 1994. Mem. Assn. Exec. Search Cons. (bd. dirs. 1994-97, chair regional affairs com. 1995-97). Presbyterian. Avocations: reading, music, cross training. Home: 67 St Johns Rd Ridgefield CT 06877-5524 Office: Ray & Berndtson Inc 245 Park Ave New York NY 10167-0002 *At the end of the day, all anyone really has is his integrity. That is why I place such a high value on honesty, sincerity, empathy, and generosity. But unless you have a sense of humor, no one will ever notice your other virtues.*

RICH, LAWRENCE VINCENT, manufacturing and engineering company executive; b. Ambridge, Pa., May 23, 1951; s. Frank Joseph and Letizia Mary (Giammatteo) R.; m. Frances Ann Banks, July 8, 1977; children: Alison, Amy. BS in Chemistry, Pa. State U., 1974; postgrad., U. Pitts., 1975-76. Cert. in combustion tech.; pres. ALFA Industries, Inc., bd. dirs., exec. bd. dirs.; cons. Hal Roach Cos., Birmingham, Ala. Project engr. Bricmont and Assocs., McMurray, Pa., 1977-81; corp. combustion engr. Wheeling-Pitts. Steel Corp., Wheeling, W.Va., 1981-85; mgr. steel sales and furnace tech. N.Am. Mfg. Co., Cleve., 1985—; exec. bd. dirs. A-PAC Sys., Pitts.; cons. Weirton (W.Va.) Steel Co., 1992. Mem., coach Soccer Assn., Moon Twp., Pa., 1997; mem. fin. and planning bd. and cluster reorgn. bd. St. Catherine's Ch., Wireton, Pa., 1997; mem. Crimewatch Orgn., Moon Twp., 1997; mem. adv. com. Internat. Airport, Pitts., 1992. Mem. Am. Iron and Steel Engrs. (Recognition award 1987, 89, 92, 93, 96), Iron and Steel Soc. of AIME (Recognition award 1990), Steel Mfrs. Assn. (co. rep.), Materials Engring. Soc., KC (3d degree), Chanticlear Swimming Club (bd. dirs.). Republican. Roman Catholic. Avocations: racquetball, squash, swimming, working with computers. Home: 2006 Broad Hill Farms Rd Coraopolis PA 15108-9008 Office: NAm Mfg Co 4455 E 71st St Cleveland OH 44105-5601

RICH, LEE, entertainment industry executive; b. Cleve.; children by previous marriage: Jessica, Miranda. B.A., Ohio U., hon. degree in communications, 1982; LL.D. (hon.), Southwestern U., 1983. Advt. exec., resigned as sr. TV v.p. Benton & Bowles to become pres. Mirisch Rich TV, 1965-67; with Leo Burnett Agy., 1967-69; pres., co-owner Lorimar Prodns., Culver City, Calif., 1969—; chmn., chief exec. officer MGM/UA Communications Co., Beverly Hills, Calif., 1986-89; chmn. bd. Lee Rich Prodns., Burbank; co-chmn. Eagle Point Prodn., Culver City, Calif., 1995—. Prodr: (TV movie) Sybil, (films) Helter Skelter, Green Eyes, Eric, The Homecoming, The Blue Knight, Skag, Two of a Kind, (TV series) Dallas, The Waltons (Emmy awards), Eight is Enough, Knots Landing, Falcon Crest; film prodr.: Being There, The Big Red One, The Postman Always Rings Twice, Who Is Killing the Great Chefs of Europe, Victory, S.O.B., Hard to Kill, 1990, Passenger 57, 1992, Innocent Blood, 1992, Little Panda, 1994, Just Cause, 1994. Recipient Disting. Citizenship award Southwestern U. Sch. Law, 1983. Office: Eagle Point Prodn 10202 Washington Blvd Culver City CA 90232-3119

RICH, MICHAEL DAVID, research corporation executive, lawyer; b. Los Angeles, Jan. 23, 1953; s. Ben Robert and Faye (Mayer) R.; m. Debra Paige Granfield, Jan. 12, 1980; children: Matthew, William. AB, U. Calif., Berkeley, 1973; JD, UCLA, 1976. Bar: Calif., 1976. Law clk. to judge U.S. Dist. Ct., Boston, 1976; staff mem. RAND, Santa Monica, Calif., 1976-85, dir. resource mgmt. program, 1980-85, dep. v.p., 1986, v.p. nat. security rsch. and dir. Nat. Def. Rsch. Inst., 1986-93; sr. v.p. RAND, 1993-95, exec. v.p., 1995—; chmn. bd. dirs. Coun. for Aid to Edn., 1996—. Author numerous classified and unclassified reports and articles. Sec., bd. dirs. WISE Sr. Svcs.; chmn. bd. dirs. Coun. Aid Edn. Mem. Council Fgn. Relations. Office: RAND PO Box 2138 1700 Main St Santa Monica CA 90407-2138

RICH, MICHAEL JOSEPH, lawyer; b. N.Y.C., June 19, 1945; s. Jesse and Phyllis (Sternfeld) R.; m. Linda Christine Kubis, July 19, 1969; children: David Lawrence, Lisa Diane. BA, Gettysburg Coll., 1967; JD, Am. U., 1972. Bar: Del. 1973, U.S. Dist. Ct. Del. 1973, U.S. Supreme Ct. 1976, Pa. 1981. Law clk. Del. Supreme Ct., Georgetown, 1972-73; assoc. Tunnell & Raysor, Georgetown, 1973-76; ptnr. Dunlap, Holland & Rich, P.A., Georgetown, 1976-80; gen. counsel Pearlette Fashions, Inc., Lebanon, Pa., 1981-83; assoc. Morris, Nichols, Arsht & Tunnell, Georgetown, 1983-86, ptnr., 1987-91; ptnr. Twilley, Street, Rich, Braverman & Hindman, P.A., Dover, Del., 1991-95; state solicitor, 1995—; mem. Bd. Bar Examiners, Del., 1986—, chair, 1996—; minority counsel Del. Ho. of Reps., Dover, 1977-79; mem. Del. Gov's Magistrate Commn., 1980, 83-86; sec. Del. Gov's. Jud. Nominating Commn., 1986-89. Bd. dirs. People's Place II, Inc., Milford, Del., 1973-77; pres. Bi-County United Way, Inc., Milford, 1977-78; mem. Partnership Greater Milford Commn., 1987-89, Friends Milford Library. Served to 1st lt. U.S. Army, 1967-69, Vietnam. Dean's fellow Am. U., 1971-72. Mem. ABA, Am. Judicature Soc., Del. Bar Assn. (pres. 1990-91), Sussex County Bar Assn. (pres. 1987-89). Republican. Office: Dept Justice 820 N French St Wilmington DE 19801-3509

RICH, PHILIP DEWEY, publishing executive; b. Nashua, N.H., Feb. 1, 1940; s. John Parker and Olive Frances (Hussey) R.; m. Leslie Ann Burke, June 14, 1974 (div. 1982). AB magna cum laude, Harvard U., 1961; MA, NYU, 1962; postgrad., Princeton U., 1962. Editor Houghton Mifflin Co., Boston, 1964-73; asst. mng. editor UpCountry Mag. Berkshire Eagle, Pittsfield, Mass., 1976-77; editor Book Creations Inc., Canaan, N.Y., 1977-80, editor-in-chief, 1980-91, v.p., exec. editor, 1991-92; cons. editor Berkshire Ho. Publs., Lee, Mass., 1992-93, mng. editor, 1993-96, mng. editor and prodn. editor, 1996—. Office: Berkshire House Pubs Ste 5 480 Pleasant St Lee MA 01238

RICH, R(OBERT) BRUCE, lawyer; b. N.Y.C., Oct. 28, 1949; s. John J. and Sylvia (Berkenblit) R.; m. Melissa Jo Saxe; children—Megan, Alexander. A.B., Dartmouth Coll., 1970; J.D., U. Pa., 1973. Bar: N.Y. 1974, U.S. Dist. Ct. (so. and ea. dists.) N.Y. 1974, U.S. Ct. Appeals (2d cir.) 1980, U.S. Supreme Ct. 1980, U.S. Ct. Appeals (D.C. cir.) 1985. Assoc. firm Weil, Gotshal & Manges, N.Y.C., 1973-81, ptnr., 1981—. Contbg. author: Cultivating the Wasteland: Can Cable Put the Vision Back in TV?, 1983, The International Libel Handbook, 1995. Contbr. articles to profl. jours.; co-editor: Legal Issues Involved in Online/Internet Law, 1997. Mem. ABA (antitrust law sect., forum com. on communications law), Assn. Bar City N.Y. (com. on trade regulation 1982-85, communications law com. 1985-88), Phi Beta Kappa. Office: Weil Gotshal & Manges 767 5th Ave New York NY 10153-0001

RICH, ROBERT C., manufacturing executive; b. 1944. BA, Brigham Young U., 1969; MBA, Northwestern U., 1971. Fin. analyst, supr. Ford Motor Co., Dearborn, Mich., 1971-75; divsn. contr. Pullman, Inc., Chgo., 1975-81; v.p. fin. men's apparel group Hartmarx Corp., Chgo., 1981-87; v.p. fin. Tonka Corp., Minnetonka, Minn., 1987-88; sr. v.p. Masterbrand Industries, 1988-92; exec. v.p. ops. Master Lock Co., Milw., 1993—. Office: Master Lock Co 2600 N 32nd St Milwaukee WI 53210-2506

RICH, ROBERT E., JR., food products company executive; b. 1941. Student, Williams Coll.; MBA, U. Rochester. Pres., bd. dirs. Rich Products Corp., Buffalo; also vice-chmn. bd. dirs. Buffalo Sabres Hockey Club. Office: Rich Products Corp 1150 Niagara St Buffalo NY 14213-1714 also: Buffalo Sabres Meml Auditorium 140 Main St Buffalo NY 14202-4110*

RICH, ROBERT EDWARD, lawyer; b. Corbin, Ky., Feb. 4, 1944; s. Edward Bluch and Marjorie Brooks (Wentworth) R.; m. Janet Sue Shearer, May 14, 1966; children: Susan M., Christopher R., David E., Sarah M. AB, U. Ky., 1966; JD, Harvard U., 1969. Bar: Ohio 1970. Jud. clk. U.S. Ct. Appeals for 6th Cir., Louisville, 1969-70; assoc. Taft, Stettinius & Hollister, Cin., 1970, ptnr., 1978—. V.p. Lighthouse Youth Svcs., Inc., Cin., 1985; trustee Ky. Youth Assn., State YMCA, Frankfort, Ky., 1990; pres. Ctr. for Hope, Inc., Mt. Health, Ohio, 1991, Cin. Bar Found., 1991. Mem. ABA, Cin. Bar Assn. Republican. Presbyterian. Home: 215 Hilltop Ln Wyoming OH 45215-4121 Office: 1800 Star Bank Ctr 425 Walnut St Cincinnati OH 45202

RICH, ROBERT F., political sciences educator, academic administrator; married; 3 children. BA in Govt. with high honors, Oberlin Coll., 1971; student, Free U. of Berlin, 1971-72; MA in Polit. Scis., U. Chgo., 1973, PhD in Polit. Scis., 1975. Project dir., asst. rsch. scientist Ctr. for Rsch. on Utilization Sci. Knowledge, Inst. Social Rsch., U. Mich., lectr. dept. polit. sci., 1975-76; asst. prof. politics and pub. affairs Princeton U., 1976-82, coord. domestic and urban policy field Woodrow Wilson Sch., 1979-81; assoc. prof. polit. sci., pub. policy and mgmt. Sch. Urban and Pub. Affairs, Carnegie-Mellon U., 1982-86; prof. polit. sci. law, health resources mgmt., medical humanities and social svcs., community health, prof. Inst. Environ. Studies U. Ill., Urbana, 1986—, dir. Inst. Govt. and Publ. Affairs; acting head med. humanities and social scis. program U. Ill., Urbana-Champaign, 1988-90, prof. Inst. for Environ. Studies; fellow Johns Hopkins U. Ctr. for Study of Am. Govt., Washington, 1993-95; cons. Carnegie-Mellon U., 1986—, MacArthur Found., NIMH, 1988-89, Food, Drug and Law Inst., HHS, 1989, Am. Career Soc., 1996-97. Author: Social Science Information and Public Policy Making: The Interaction Between Bureaucratic Politics and the Use of Survey Data, 1981; co-author: Government Information Management: A Counter-Report of the Commission on Federal Paperwork, 1980; editor: Translating Evaluation into Policy, 1979, The Knowledge Cycle, 1981, Knowledge, Creation, Diffusion, Utilization, 1979-88, 88-91; co-editor: Competitive Approaches to Health Policy Reform, 1993, Health Policy, Health Federalism and the Role of the American States, 1996; assoc. editor Society, 1984-88, Evaluation Rev., 1985-89; mem. editorial adv. rev. bd. Policy Studies Rev. Series, 1980-83; mem. editl. bd. Evaluation and Change, 1979-82; mem. editorial adv. bd. Law and Human Behavior, 1983-87; contbr. numerous articles to profl. jours., book chpts. Recipient Emil Limbach Teaching award Carnegie-Mellon U., Sch. Urban and Pub. Affairs, 1985; fellow German Acad. Exch. Program, Fed. Republic Germany, 1971-72, Nat. Opinion Rsch. Ctr. fellow, 1972-73, German Govt. fellow, 1974, Russel Sage Found. Rsch. fellow, 1974-75; vis. scholar Hastings Ctr. for Society, Ethics and Life Scis., 1982. Mem. APA (task force on victims of crime and violence 1982-84), Soc. for Traumatic Stress Studies (bd. dirs. 1980—), World Fedn. for Mental Health (chmn. com. on mental health needs of victims 1985—, vice chmn. 1981-83, Robert F. Rich rsch. ann. award established in his honor, sci. com. on mental health needs of victims 1983), Howard R. Davis Soc. for Knowledge Utilization and Planned Change (pres. 1986-89), Polit. Sci. 400, Policy Studies Assn. (Aaron Wildausky award 1994), Phi Beta Kappa, Sigma Xi, Phi Kappa Phi. Office: U Ill Inst Govt & Pub Affairs 1007 W Nevada St # 204 Urbana IL 61801-3812 also: 921 W Van Buren St # C 191 Chicago IL 60607-3542

RICH, ROBERT REGIER, immunology educator, physician; b. Newton, Kans., Mar. 7, 1941; s. Eldon Stahly and Margaret Joy (Regier) R.; m. Susan Jepson Solliday, Mar. 22, 1974; children from previous marriage: Kenneth Eldon, Cathryn Louise. A.B., Oberlin Coll., 1962; M.D., U. Kans., 1966. Diplomate Am. Bd. Internal Medicine (bd. dirs. 1990-93), Am. Bd. Allergy and Immunology (bd. dirs. 1987-93, chmn. 1991); cert. spl. qualification Diagnostic Lab. Immunology. Intern, resident in internal medicine U. Wash., Seattle, 1966-68; clin. asso., chief clin. asso., sr. staff fellow NIH, Bethesda, Md., 1968-71; research asso. Harvard Med. Sch., Boston, 1971-73; asst. in medicine Peter Bent Brigham Hosp., 1972-73; asst. prof., assoc. prof. microbiology, immunology and internal medicine Baylor Coll. Medicine, Houston, 1973-78, prof., 1978-95, Disting. Svc. prof., 1995—, head immunology sect., 1978—, chief clin. immunology, 1979-91, v.p., dean rsch., 1990—; investigator Howard Hughes Med. Inst., Bethesda, Md., 1977-91; mem. immunobiology study sect. NIH, 1977-81; mem. med. staff Harris County Hosp. Dist., Meth. Hosp., Houston; mem. transplantation biology and immunology com. Nat. Inst. Allergy and Infectious Disease, 1982-86, chmn., 1984-86; mem. nat. ctr. grants com. Arthritis Found., 1983-86, chmn., 1984-86, nat. rsch. com., 1984-89, chmn., 1986-89, ho. of dels., 1985-91; mem. rsch. adv. com. Nat. Multiple Sclerosis Soc., 1989-94, chmn., 1993-94; adv. panel on biomedical rsch. Assn. Am. Medical Coll., 1990—, shared responsibility advocacy com., 1997—; chmn. ctrs. working group Nat. Inst. ARthritis Musculoskeletal Skin Diseases, 1996-97. Assoc. editor: Jour. Immunology, 1978-82, sect. editor, 1991-96, deputy editor, 1997—; assoc. editor: Jour. Infectious Diseases, 1984-88; adv. editor: Jour. Exptl. Medicine, 1980-84; mem. editl. bd. Jour. Clin. Immunology, 1989-96, Clin. and Exptl. Immunology, 1995—; editor-in-chief Clin. Immunology: Principles and Practice; contbr. articles to profl. jours. Served with USPHS, 1968-70. Recipient Research Career Devel. award NIH, 1975-77, Merit award NIH, 1987. Fellow ACP, Am. Acad. Allergy, Asthma, and Immunology (chmn. basic and clin. immunology interest sect. 1992-93, chmn. profl. edn. coun. 1996—), Infectious Diseases Soc. Am., Molecular Medicine Soc.; mem. AMA, AAAS, Am. Bd. Internal Medicine (diplomate, bd. dirs. 1990-93), Am. Bd. Allergy and Immunology (diplomate, bd. dirs. 1987-93), Assn. Am. Physicians, Am. Soc. Clin. Investigation, Am. Soc. Histocompatibility and Immunogenetics, Am. Assn. Immunologists (chmn. pub. affairs com. 1994—), Am. Assn. Investigative Pathology, Transplantation Soc., Am. Soc. Microbiologists, So. Soc. Clin. Investigation, Am. Fedn. Med. Rsch., Am. Clin. Climatological Assn., Harris County Med. Soc., Tex. Med. Assn., Clin. Immunology Soc. (coun. 1990-96, pres. 1995), Alpha Omega Alpha, Sigma Xi. Office: Baylor Coll Medicine One Baylor Pla Houston TX 77030

RICH, ROBERT STEPHEN, lawyer; b. N.Y.C., Apr. 30, 1938; s. Maurice H. and Natalie (Priess) R.; m. Myra N. Lakoff, May 31, 1964; children: David, Rebecca, Sarah. AB, Cornell U., 1959; JD, Yale U., 1963. Bar: N.Y. 1964, Colo. 1973, U.S. Tax Ct. 1966, U.S. Supreme Ct. 1967, U.S. Ct. Claims 1968, U.S. Dist. Ct. (so. dist.) N.Y. 1965, U.S. Dist. Ct. (ea. dist.) N.Y. 1965, U.S. Dist. Ct. Colo. 1980, U.S. Ct. Appeals (2d cir.) 1964, U.S. Ct. Appeals (10th cir.) 1978; conseil juridique, Paris, 1968. Assoc. Shearman & Sterling, N.Y.C., Paris, London, 1963-72; ptnr. Davis, Graham & Stubbs, Denver, 1973—; adj. faculty U. Denver Law Sch., 1977—; adv. bd. U. Denver Ann. Tax Inst., 1985—; adv. bd. global bus. and culture divsn. U. Denver, 1992—, Denver World Affairs Coun., 1993—; bd. dirs. Clos du Val Wine Co. Ltd., Anschutz Family Found., Danskin Cattle Co., Areti Wines, Ltd., Taltarni Vineyards, Christy Sports, Copper Valley Assn., pres.; bd. dirs. several other corps.; mem. Colo. Internat. Trade Adv. Coun., 1985—, tax adv. com. U.S. Senator Hank Brown; mem. Rocky Mountain Dist. Export Coun. U.S. Dept. Commerce, 1993—. Author treatises on internat. taxation; contbr. articles to profl. jours. Bd. dirs. Denver Internat. Film Festival, 1978-79, Alliance Française, 1977—; actor, musician N.Y. Shakespeare Festival, 1960; sponsor Am. Tax Policy inst., 1991—; trustee, sec. Denver Art Mus., 1982—; mem. adv. bd. Denver World Affairs Coun., 1993—. Capt., AUS, 1959-60. Fellow Am. Coll. Tax Counsel (bd. regents 10th cir. 1992—); mem. ABA, Internat. Bar Assn., Colo. Bar Assn., N.Y. State Bar Assn., Assn. of Bar of City of N.Y., Asia-Pacific Lawyers Assn., Union Internationale des Avocats, Internat. Fiscal Assn. (pres. Rocky Mt. br. 1992—, U.S. regional v.p. 1988—), Japan-Am. Soc. Colo. (bd. dirs., 1989—, pres. 1991-93), Confrerie des Chevaliers du Tastevin, Meadowood Club, Denver Club, Mile High Club, Cactus Club Denver, Yale Club, Denver Tennis Club. Office: Cherry Creek Sta PO Box 61429 Denver CO 80206-8429 also: Antelope Co 555 Seventeenth St Ste 2400 Denver CO 80202

RICH, S. JUDITH, public relations executive; b. Chgo., Apr. 14; d. Irwin M. and Sarah I. (Sandock) R. BA, U. Ill., 1960. Staff writer, reporter Economist Newspapers, Chgo., 1960-61; asst. dir. pub. rels. and communications Coun. Profit Sharing Industries, Chgo., 1961-62; dir. advt. and pub. rels. Chgo. Indsl. Dist., 1962-63; account exec., account supr., v.p., sr. v.p., exec. v.p. and nat. creative dir. Edelman Pub. Rels. Worldwide, Chgo., 1963-85; exec. v.p., dir. Ketchum Pub. Rels. Worldwide, Chgo., 1985-89, exec. v.p., exec. creative dir. USA, 1990—; frequent spkr. on creativity and brainstorming. workshop facilitator, spkr. in field. Mem. pub. rels. adv. bd. U. Chgo. Grad Sch. Bus., Roosevelt U., Chgo., DePaul U., Chgo., Gov.'s State U. Mem. Pub. Rels. Soc. Am. (Silver Anvil award, judge Silver Anvil awards), Counselors Acad. of Pub. Rels. Soc. Am. (exec. bd.), Chgo. Publicity Club (8 Golden Trumpet awards). Avocations: theatre, swimming, cycling, racquetball. Home: 2500 N Lakeview Ave Chicago IL 60614 Office: Ketchum Pub Rels # 3400 205 N Michigan Ave Chicago IL 60601-5925

RICH, SHARON LEE, financial planner; b. Houston, Sept. 7, 1956; d. Hershel Maurice and Hilda R.; children: Mariah, Sophie. BA, Cornell U., 1977; MAT, U. Chgo., 1978; diploma in fin. planning, Boston U., 1985; EdD, Harvard U., 1986. High sch. tchr. Clear Lake High Sch., Houston, 1978-80; rschr. Harvard U., Cambridge, Mass., 1981-86; fin. planner, pres. Womoney, Belmont, Mass., 1984—; instr. Cambridge Ctr. for Adult Edn. Co-author: The Challenges of Wealth, 1988; co-editor: Women's Experience and Education, 1985. Conf. organizer Haymarket People's Fund, Jamaica Plain, Mass., 1988—; bd. dirs. Boston Women's Fund, 1988-90; speaker Pub. Edn. Svcs., Boston, 1984—; organizer, mem. The Consortium, Boston, 1991—; referral for battered women B'nai Brith Women's Connection Card, Boston, 1991—. Named One of Ams. Top Fin. Advisors, Worth Mag., 1994, 96. Mem. Internat. Assn. Fin. Planners, U.S. Security and Exch. Commn. (registered investment advisor), Nat. Assn. Personal Fin. Advisors, Social Investment Forum, Coop. Am. (bus. mem.). Avocations: parenting. Office: Womoney 76 Townsend Rd Belmont MA 02178-3435

RICH, THOMAS PAUL, engineering educator, administrator; b. Pitts., Nov. 18, 1943; s. Paul Felix and Jean M. (Ritter) R.; m. Mary Lou Colver, Aug. 5, 1967; children: Wendy Jean Rich Stetson, Thomas Wesley Rich. BSME, Carnegie Mellon U., Pitts., 1965; MSME, Lehigh U., Bethlehem, Pa., 1967, PhD in Mech. Engring., 1969. Engr. Peoples Natural Gas Co., Gibsonia, Pa., 1963, Blaw Knox Co., Pitts., 1964; rsch. mech. engr. Army Materials & Mechanics Rsch. Ctr., Watertown, Mass., 1970-73, 75-78; vis. prof. U. Southampton, 1974; assoc. prof. Mech. Engring. Dept. Tex. A&M U., College Station, 1978-81; assoc. prof. Mech. Engring. Dept. Bucknell U., Lewisburg, Pa., 1982-86, prof. and dean engring., 1986—; mem. adv. bd. Ben Franklin Partnership, Pa., 1985—, Pa. Small Bus. Devel. Ctrs., 1989—; mem. Assn. Engring. Colls. Pa., 1986—, pres., 1989-90; presenter in field. Editor: (book) Case Histories in Fatigue and Fracture Mechanics, 1986. sponsor pre-coll. engring. activities for high sch. students Jr. Engring. Tech. Soc., 1989—. Capt. U.S. Army, 1970-71. Recipient Wm. Spraragen award Am. Welding Soc., 1971; 12 external rsch. grants from fed., state and pvt. sources. Mem. ASME, Am. Soc. Engring. Edn., Am. Acad. Mechanics, Sigma Xi, Tau Beta Pi. Presbyn. Avocations: hiking, camping, sports memorabilia, history of technology. Office: Coll Engring Bucknell U Lewisburg PA 17837

RICH, WILLIS FRANK, JR., banker; b. Ft. Dodge, Iowa, July 26, 1919; s. Willis Frank and Agnes Reed (Paterson) R.; m. Jo Ann Rockwell, Apr. 12, 1947; children: Ronald Rockwell, Roxanne, Andrew Paterson. B.A., Princeton U., 1941. Credit analyst Northwestern Nat. Bank, Mpls., 1947-52; asst. cashier Northwestern Nat. Bank, 1952-55, asst. v.p., 1955, v.p., 1955-57; pres. N.W. Nat. Bank, Bloomington-Richfield, Minn., 1952-58; v.p., cashier N.W. Nat. Bank, 1957-60, v.p. div. A, 1960-68, sr. v.p. nat. and internat. divs., 1968-73; exec. v.p. N.W. Nat. Bank, Mpls., 1973-81, vice chmn. bd. dirs., chief credit officer, 1981-84; fin. cons., 1984—; dir. Advance Acceptance Corp. Pres. Viking coun. Boy Scouts Am., 1970-71, trustee found., 1971-86; mem. exec. bd. Minn. Cmty. Rsch. Coun., 1969-77; dir. Minn. Zoo, 1987-95; trustee St. Martin's Found., 1986-90; vestry mem. St. Martin's-By-The-Lake Ch. With AUS, 1941-46. Decorated Bronze Star. Mem. Robert Morris Assocs. (nat. pres. 1977-78). Episcopalian. Clubs: Woodhill, Swan Lake Country. Home: 4770 Manitou Rd Excelsior MN 55331-9400

RICHARD, ALISON FETTES, anthropology educator; b. Great Britain, Mar. 1, 1948. BA, Cambridge U., 1969; PhD, London U., 1973. Asst. prof. anthropology Yale U., New Haven, 1972-76, assoc.prof. anthropology, 1976-85, prof. anthropology, 1985—, provost prof., 1994—; dir. Yale Peabody Mus. Natural History, 1990-94. Bd. dirs. Yale-New Haven Health Svcs., 1994—, World Wildlife Fund, 1995—. Mem. Am. Primatological Soc., Am. Assn. Phys. Anthropologists, Am. Anthrop. Assn., Brit. Ecol. Soc., Primate Soc. Gt. Britain, Zool. Soc. London, Cambridge Philosophical Soc. Office: Office of the Provost Yale U New Haven CT 06520-8118

RICHARD, ANN BERTHA, nursing administrator; b. Hartford, Conn., Mar. 21, 1944; d. Victor Charles and Theresa (Gasper) R.; children: Elena Skrinak, Judith Dunn. Diploma, Capital City Sch. Nursing, Washington, 1965; BSN summa cum laude, U. Hartford, Bloomfield, Conn., 1982; MS, U. Conn., 1986. RN, Conn.; cert. nurse adminstr., med.-surg. nurse. Staff nurse D.C. Gen. Hosp., Washington, 1965-66; staff nurse Hartford Hosp., 1972-73, asst. head nurse, 1973-74, head nurse, 1974-83, nutritional support clinician, 1983-85; total nursing care project cons. Hosp. of St. Raphael, New Haven, 1986-88, assoc. dir. gen. surg. nursing and spltys., 1986-88; v.p. for patient svcs. Manchester (Conn.) Meml. Hosp., 1988—. Contbr. chpt. to book. Passini scholar, 1985. Mem. ANA (nuring adminstrn. coun. 1986—), Conn. Nurses Assn. (govt. rels. com. 1984-88, bd. dirs. 1990-94), Conn. Orgn. Nurse Execs. (nominating com. 1986-88), Am. Coll. Healthcare Execs., Conn. Hosp. Assoc. (chairperson nurse exec. conf. 1993-95, bd. dirs. 1995—), Sigma Theta Tau (program com. 1986-88, nominating com. 1988-89), Alpha Chi, Conn. League Nursing (bd. dirs. 1990-92), Nat. League Nursing. Office: Meml Hosp 71 Haynes St Manchester CT 06040-4112

RICHARD, EDWARD H., manufaturing company executive, former municipal government official; b. N.Y.C., Mar. 15, 1937; s. Henry and Ida Richard; B.A., Antioch Coll., 1959. Pres., chmn. bd. dirs. Magnetics Internat. Inc., Maple Heights, Ohio, 1967-86, exec. v.p. Stearns Magnetics S.A., Brussels, Belgium, 1974-77; prin. Edward H. Richard & Assocs., Cleve., 1967-96; pres., treas. David Round & Son, Inc., Cleve; exec. adminstrv. asst. to mayor City of Cleve., 1979-87, dir. dept. pub. utilities, 1981-89, dep. to mayor, chief adminstrv. officer, 1986-89; dir. airports and port control City of Cleve., 1988-90; pres., CEO David Round & Son, Inc., Solon, Ohio, 1967-96; chmn. Cleve. dist. adv. council Small Bus. Adminstrn., 1975-79; former mem. nat. adv. council Dept. Treasury; cons. and advisor in field; del. world trade fairs. Former trustee Regional Econ. Devel. Council, Met. Cleve. Jobs Council, Cleve. Devel. Found., Cleve. Better Bus. Bur.; former trustee Hiram House, Antioch U., former treas., 1972-77; N.E. Ohio Regional Sewer Dist., Greater Cleve. Domed Stadium Corp., Greater Cleve. Conv. and Vis. Bur.; former trustee, vice-chmn. Cleve. Center Econ. Edn.; former pres. Bratenahl Condominium Assn.; mem., chmn. fin. com. Bratenahl Bd. Edn., 1971-75, mem., bd. trustees La Jolla Playhouse.

RICHARD, ELLEN, theater executive; b. Bridgeport, Conn., Dec. 12, 1957; d. Laurent and Anne (Markham) R. Bus. mgr. Atlas Scenic Studio, Bridgeport, 1977-82; theater mgr. Stamford (Conn.) Ctr. for Arts, 1980-83; bus. mgr. Westport (Conn.) Country Playhouse, 1982-84; gen. mgr. Roundabout Theatre Co. Inc., N.Y.C., 1983—. Mem. N.Y. Cycling Club. Republican. Avocations: cycling, skiing. Office: Roundabout Theatre Co 1530 Broadway New York NY 10036-4002*

RICHARD, GERALD LAWRENCE, soil scientist; b. Brush, Colo., Oct. 26, 1931; s. Donald Lehman and Gladys Lucile (Eikenbary) R.; m. Phyllis Darlene Hansen, Dec. 28, 1952; children: Donald Lawrence, Dale Kendall, Lori Ann Fosmire, Julie Lynn Young. BS in Agronomy, Colo. State U., 1956. Soil scientist Soil Conservation Svc., Wheatland, Wyo., 1957, Torrington and Cheyenne, Wyo., 1959-65; work unit conservationist Soil Conservation Svc., Laramie, Wyo., 1965; area soil scientist Soil Conservation Svc., Bellefonte, Pa., 1965-71; asst. state soil scientist Soil Conservation Svc., Spokane, Wash., 1971-78; sr. soil scientist Soil Conservation Svc./U.S. Agy. for Internat. Devel., Lashkar Gah, Afghanistan, 1978-79; soil scientist/land use interpreter Soil Conservation Svc./U.S. Agy. for Internat. Devel., Kathmandu, Nepal, 1979-80; dep. co-mgr./soil scientist Soil Conservation Svc./Western Carolina U., Kathmandu, 1980-82, team leader resource conservation project, 1982-85; state soil scientist Soil Conservation Svc., Boise, Idaho, 1985-89; cons. soil scientist Spokane, 1989—; Contbr. articles to profl. publs. 1st lt. U.S. Army, 1957-59. Mem. Am. Soc. of Agronomy, Soil Sci. Soc. Am., Soil and Water Conservation Soc. (pres. keystone chpt. Pa. 1971), Washington Soc. of Profl. Soil Scientists. Methodist. Avocations: woodworking, fishing, travel. Home: 2709 S Post St Spokane WA 99203-1877

RICHARD, LYLE ELMORE, retired school social worker, consultant; b. Lansing, Mich., Aug. 15, 1939; s. Lloyd M. and Ruth (Rider) R.; m. Karen Ann Gustafson, June 1963 (div. 1980); children: Deborah Ann, David Lyle; m. Julia Ann Quake, Sept. 19, 1981. BA, Albion (Mich.) Coll., 1961; MSW, U. Mich., 1963. cert. social worker, Mich. Psychiat. soc. worker Wayne County Gen. Hosp., Eloise, Mich., 1963-64; sr. social worker Los Guilocos Sch. for Girls Calif. Youth Authority, Santa Rosa, 1964-65; social worker Family Resource Ctr. Marin County Probation Dept., San Rafael, Calif., 1965-67, Sunny Hills Children Svcs., San Anselmo, Calif., 1967-68; sch. social worker Jackson (Mich.) Pub. Schs., 1968-92, ret., 1992; pres. Acad. Behavior Cons.; behavior mgmt. cons. Cline/Fay Inst., Golden, Colo., 1985—. Mem. ASCD, Coun. Exceptional Children (v.p. 1990-91, pres. 1991-92), Clowns Am.-Internat., Midwest Sch. Social Work Coun. (bd. dirs. 1971-84), Mich. Assn. Sch. Social Workers (state offices, Sch. Social Worker of Yr. 1989), Elks. Avocations: boating, camping, hunting. Home: 3106 Faith Dr Spring Arbor MI 49283-9739

RICHARD, MARK M., government official, lawyer; b. N.Y.C., Nov. 16, 1939; s. Louis and Rae (Karnefsky) R.; m. Sheila Levitan, Aug. 6, 1960; children: Cara, Alisa, Daniel. B.A., Bklyn. Law Sch., 1961, J.D., 1967. Bar: N.Y. 1968, D.C. Trial atty. fraud sect., criminal div. Dept. Justice, Washington, 1967-75; exec. sec. Atty. Gen.'s White Collar Crime Com., Washington, 1975-76; chief fraud sect., criminal div. Dept. Justice, Washington, 1976-79, dept. asst. atty. gen. criminal div., 1979—; mem. econ. crime com. ABA, Washington, 1977-79. Recipient Legal award Assn. Fed. Investigators, 1981, Meritorious Exec. award Pres. of U.S., 1980, Legal award Assn. Fed. Prosecutors, 1981; fellow Harvard U., 1989. Mem. N.Y. State Bar Assn., D.C. Bar. Home: 912 Burnt Crest Ln Silver Spring MD 20903-1340 Office: Dept Justice Criminal Divsn 10th Constitution Ave NW Washington DC 20570

RICHARD, OLIVER, III (RICK RICHARD), gas company executive; b. Lake Charles, La., Oct. 11, 1952; s. Oliver Gonzard and Mary Jean (Turvey) R.; m. Donna Margaret Guzman, July 6, 1974; 1 child, David Turvey. B.A., La. State U., 1974, J.D., 1977; M.L.T., Georgetown U., 1981. Bar: La. 1977, U.S. Dist. Ct. (ea. dist.) La. 1977, U.S. Dist. Ct. (we. dist.) La. 1977, U.S. Dist. Ct. (mid. dist.) La. 1977, U.S. Supreme Ct. 1981. Assoc., Sanders, Downing, Kean & Cazedessus, Baton Rouge, 1977; legis. asst. to U.S. Senator J. Bennett Johnston, Washington, 1977-81; ptnr. Hayes Durio & Richard, Lafayette, La., 1981-82; mem. FERC, Washington, 1982-85; v.p., gen. counsel Tenngasco Corp. div. Tenneco, 1985-87, v.p. regulatory and competitive analysis Enron Corp., 1987-88; pres., CEO No. Natural Gas Co., 1989-91; chmn. CEO, pres. N.J. Resources Corp., 1995, Columbia Gas Sys., Inc., Wilmington, Del., 1995—. Mem. Pres.'s Commn. Critical Infrastructure Protection. Mem. Interstate Pipeline Assn. (dir. exec. com.), Nat. Petroleum Coun. (congressional award svc.), Am. Gas Assn. (v.p.), Omicron Delta Kappa. Democrat. Roman Catholic. Office: 12355 Sunrise Valley Dr Reston VA 20191-3458

RICHARD, PATRICIA ANTOINETTE, physician, dentist; b. Bridgeport, Conn., June 15, 1950; d. Mr. and Mrs. Richard. DMD, U. Conn., 1976; MD, Hahnemann U., 1980. Cert. sr. FAA med. examiner. Intern in internal medicine St. Vincents Med. Ctr., Bridgeport, Conn., 1980-81; resident in surgery U. Med. and Dentistry, Rutgers U., Camden, N.J., 1983-84; resident in internal medicine U. Hosp., Jacksonville, Fla., 1984-85; sr. resident in internal medicine Hartford (Conn.) Hosp., 1985-86; emergency medicine physician St. Francis Hosp., Hartford, 1985-87, U. Conn.-John Dempsey Hosp., Farmington, 1986-88, Bristol (Conn.) Hosp., 1986-87; pvt. practice in medicine and dentistry, biotech. R&D cons. Fairfield, Conn., 1987—; mem. medico-legal com. Fairfield County Med. Assn., 1994—, Fairfield County Ctr. for Trauma and Internal Medicine, Temporomandibular Joint Disorders, Aviation Medicine and Biotech., R&D, 1993—. Mem. Rep. Senatorial Inner Cir., Washington, 1992; perpetual mem. Franciscan Benefactors Assn., Mt. Vernon, N.Y., 1994; mem. Lourdes Prayer League, Shrine of Our Lady of Snows, Belleville, Ill., 1995. Recipient Rep. Presidential award Bd. of Govs.-Rep. Presidential Task Force, 1994. Mem. AIAA, AMA, ADA, Aerospace Med. Assn., Am. Bd. Forensic Examiners. Achievements include 3 patents in fields of hematology, metabolism, endocrinology, pharmacology and orthopedics. Office: 1735 Post Rd PO Box 702 Fairfield CT 06430

RICHARD, PATRICK, science research administrator, nuclear scientist; b. Crowley, La., Apr. 28, 1938; married; two children. BS, U. Southwestern La., 1961; PhD, Fla. State U., 1964. Rsch. assoc. prof. nuclear physics U. Wash., 1965-68; from asst. prof. to prof. physics U. Tex., Austin, 1968-72; dir. J.R. MacDonald Lab. physics dept., prof. physics Kansas State U., 1972—; cons. Columbia Sci. Rsch. Inst., 1969-71. Mem. Am. Phys. Soc. Office: Kans State U J R MacDonald Lab Physic Dept Cardwell Hall Manhattan KS 66506 Office: Kans State U Physics Dept Cardwell Hall Manhattan KS 66506*

RICHARD, PAUL, art critic; b. Chgo., Nov. 22, 1939. BA, Harvard U., 1961; student, U. Pa. Art critic Washington Post, 1967—. Office: Washington Post Co 1150 15th St NW Washington DC 20071-0001*

RICHARD, SCOTT F., portfolio manager; b. Chgo., Dec. 13, 1946; s. Jerome and Sue (Selig) Richard; m. Susan L. Diamond, June 15, 1969 (div. May 1983); children: Rebecca, Michael; m. Roberta C. Meyerson, Oct. 1, 1983. BS, MIT, 1968; D Bus. Adminstrn., Harvard U., 1972. Prof. fin. Carnegie-Mellon U., Pitts., 1972-87; v.p. fixed income rsch., co-dir. rsch. and model devel. Goldman, Sachs & Co., N.Y.C., 1987-92; portfolio mgr. Miller, Anderson & Sherrerd, West Conshohocken, Pa., 1992—, ptnr., 1993—; mng. dir. Mongan Stanley & Co., 1996—; vis. prof. fin. MIT, Cambridge, Mass., 1986-87; advt. bd. Jour. of Portfolio Mgmt., 1989—, Jour. of Fixed Income, 1991—. Author: (with A.H. Meltzer and A. Cukierman) Political Economy, 1991; assoc. editor: Jour. of Fin., 1983-88, Jour. Fin. Econs., 1976-83, Mgmt. Sci., 1977-78; contbr. articles to profl. jours. Mem. Am. Econs. Assn., Am. Fin. Assn., The Econometric Soc., Inst. Mgmt. Sci. Office: Miller Anderson & Sherrerd One Tower Bridge West Conshohocken PA 19428

RICHARD, SUSAN MATHIS, communications executive; b. Detroit, June 21, 1949; d. Robert Louis and Maybelle Ann (Kromm) Engel; m. Paul Carl Mathis, May 12, 1973 (div. 1982); m. Robert Stephen Richard, Oct. 26, 1985. BA, U. Mich., 1971. Cert. tchr., Mich. Tchr. Carl Brablec High Sch., Roseville, Mich., 1971-73; anchorperson, producer Sta. WNCC-Cable TV, East Lansing, Mich., 1973-76; press asst. Ford-Dole Presdl. Campaign, Washington, 1976; TV and radio reporter Cox Communications, Washington, 1977-81; dep. dir. media rels. White House, Washington, 1981-84, spl. asst. to Pres., dir. media rels., 1985-87; mgr. pub. rels. Walt Disney World, Lake Buena Vista, Fla., 1987-88; v.p. industry communications Nat. Cable TV Assn., Washington, 1989; dep. assoc. adminstr. for pub. affairs Nat. Aeros. and Space Adminstrn., 1990-93; v.p. comm. ETC w/tci, 1996—; mem. exec. com. Radio-TV Corrs. Galleries, Washington, 1978-81. Dir. promotions Action for Children's TV, East Lansing, 1975; mem. Strategic Planning Adv. Coun. of the Orange County (Fla.) Pub. Schs., 1988; communications dir. Bush-Quayle Fla. Campaign, 1988. Named Outstanding Young Working Woman, Lansing C. of C., 1975, Outstanding Working Woman, Washington Woman mag., 1985. Mem. AAUW (bd. dirs. Lansing chpt. 1974), Am. Soc. Assn. Execs. (Pub. Rels. trophy 1994), Radio-TV News Dirs. Assn., Fla. Youth and Family Svcs. Network (bd. dirs. 1988), Acad. TV Arts and Scis. (pub. rels. com. 1989), Women in Aerospace, Women in Wireless, U. Mich. Alumni Assn. (bd. dirs. 1983-85), Gamma Phi Beta Alumnae Assn. Episcopalian.

RICHARDS, ANN WILLIS, former governor; b. Lakeview, Tex., Sept. 1, 1933; d. Cecil and Ona Willis; children: Cecile, Daniel, Clark, Ellen. B.A., Baylor U., 1954; postgrad., U. Tex., 1954-55. Cert. tchr. Tex. Tchr. Austin Ind. Sch. Dist., Tex.; mgr. Sarah Weddington Campaign, Austin, Tex., 1972, adminstrv. asst., 1973-74; county commr. Travis County, Austin, 1976-82; treas. State of Tex., Austin, 1983-91; gov. State of Tex., 1991-95; sr. advisor Verner, Liipfert, Bernhard, McPherson & Hand, Austin, 1995—; chair Dem. Nat. Conv. 1992; Austin Transp. Study, Tex., 1977-82, Capital Indsl. Devel. Corp., Austin, Tex., 1980-81, Spl. Commn. Delivery Human Services in Tex., 1979-81; Dem. com. Southern Governor's Assn. Travis County Dem. com. Author (with Peter Knobler): Straight From the Heart, 1989. Mem. com. strategic planning Dem. Nat. Com., 1983; keynote speaker Dem. Nat. Conv., 1988. Named Woman of Yr. Tex. Women's Polit. Caucus, 1981, 83. Mem. Nat. Govs. Assn. Office: Verner, Liipfert, Bernhard, McPherson & Hand PO Box 684746 Austin TX 78768

RICHARDS, BERNARD, investment company executive; b. N.Y.C., July 12, 1927; s. Charles and Sadie (Rubin) R.; m. Arlene Kaye, Dec. 23, 1948; children: Carol Leslie, Patricia Ellen, Lori Gale. BBA, Baruch Coll., 1949. CPA, N.Y. Acct. Eisner & Lubin, N.Y.C., 1949-53, S.D. Leidesdorf, N.Y.C., 1953-56; from controller to treas. to v.p. fin. to pres. Slattery Group Inc., N.Y.C., 1956-87; pres. Slattery Investors Corp., N.Y.C., 1988—; chmn. bd. dirs. Slattery Assocs., Inc., N.Y.C., 1968-87. Trustee Temple Sinai, Roslyn, N.Y., 1987-89; bd. dirs. Variety Boys Club, Queens, N.Y., 1972-96; bd. dirs. N.Y.C. Indsl. Devel. Bd., 1973-76; bd. dirs. Baruch Coll. Fund, N.Y.C., 1975—, pres., 1996—, Man Yr., 1972. Recipient Heavy Constrn. award United Jewish Appeal, 1980, Pres.'s medal Baruch Coll., 1989; named Oustanding Alumnus of Yr. Baruch Coll., 1979, Man of Yr. United Jewish Appeal, 1980, March of Dimes, 1983; Wood fellow Baruch Coll., 1979. Mem. AICPA, N.Y. State Soc. CPAs, Moles, Beavers (bd. dirs. 1982-96), Shelter Rock Tennis Club. Republican. Jewish. Avocations: tennis, travel, cycling, swimming, hiking. Home: 18 Applegreen Dr Old Westbury NY 11568-1203 Office: Slattery Investors Corp 1 Hollow Ln Ste 311 New Hyde Park NY 11042-1215

RICHARDS, CAROL ANN RUBRIGHT, editor, columnist; b. Buffalo, Sept. 24, 1944; d. Jesse Bailey and Emma Amanda (Fisher) Rubright; m. Clay F. Richards, Aug. 12, 1967; children: Elizabeth Amanda, Rebecca Diana. BA, Syracuse U., 1966. Reporter Rochester (N.Y.) Times-Union, 1966; legis. corr. Gannett News Svc., Albany, N.Y., 1967-73; White House corr. Gannett News Svc., Washington, 1974-76, regional/nat. editor, 1979-84; founding editor USA Today, Arlington, Va., 1982, mem. editl. bd., 1985-87; dep. editor editl. page Newsday, Melville, N.Y., 1987—. Pres. Washington Press Club, 1981-82. Mem. Nat. Press Club. Episcopalian. Home: 352 Scudder Ave Northport NY 11768 Office: Newsday 235 Pinelawn Rd Melville NY 11747-4226

RICHARDS, CHARLENE ANNA, computer manufacturing company executive; b. Muncie, Ind., May 10, 1963; d. Delmar Gene and Mary Catherine (O'Bryant) Coffman; m. Bruce Richards, Aug. 26, 1983; children: Shaun Michael, Shannon Michelle, Shayna Marie. Grad. high sch., Albuquerque. Dispatcher asst. Morgan Drive Agy., Albuquerque, 1979-80; account asst. Sta. KOB-TV, Albuquerque, 1980-81, TV copywriter, 1982-83; display advt. cons. Albuquerque Jour.-Tribune, 1981-82; mgr. TLC Svcs., Albuquerque, 1983-87; owner, mgr. The Computer Man, Beaufort, S.C., 1988-91; pres. Computer Techs. Systems, Inc., Beaufort, 1991—, East Coast Holdings, Ltd., Beaufort, 1994-95; mgr. Computer Outlet, Beaufort, 1995—; instr. Tech. Coll. Low Country, Beaufort, 1989. Designer mfg. computer systems. Mem. NAFE, Nat. Fedn. Ind. Bus., U.S. C. of C., Nat. Platform Assn. Republican. Baptist. Avocations: fishing, gardening, decorating, boating. Home: 10 Wiggins Rd Beaufort SC 29902-2630 Office: 422C Parris Island Gateway Beaufort SC 29902

RICHARDS, CHARLES FRANKLIN, JR., lawyer; b. Evergreen Park, Ill., Jan. 30, 1949; s. Charles Franklin and Mary Corinne (Joyce) R.; m. Maureen Patricia Duffy, June 17, 1972 (div. Mar. 1989); m. Deborah Ann Murphy, May 20, 1991; children: Patrick, Corrine, Meghan, Shannon. BA, St. Mary's of Minn., 1971; JD, U. Ill., 1974. Bar: Minn. 1974, U.S. Dist. Ct. Minn. 1974, Ariz. 1985, U.S. Dist. Ct. Ariz. 1985, U.S. Ct. Appeals (9th cir.) 1985; cert. civil trial adv. Nat. Bd. Trial Advocacy. Asst. city atty. City of Rochester, Minn., 1974-76; assoc., then ptnr. O'Brien, Ehrick, Wolf, Deaner & Downing, Rochester, 1976-85; assoc., shareholder Gallagher & Kennedy, PA, Phoenix, 1985-94; pvt. practice, Phoenix, 1994—; judge pro tem Ariz. Ct. Appeals, 1994. Contbr. articles to legal publs. Bd. dirs. St. Mary's Hosp., Rochester, 1983-85; del. Dem. Nat. Conv., San Francisco, 1984. Mem. ABA, ATLA, State Bar Ariz. (mem. trial practice sect. exec. coun. 1994—, mem. civil jury instrns. com. 1994—, co-editor Trial Practice Newsletter 1990—), Ariz. Assn. Def. Counsel, Ariz. Trial Lawyers Assn., Maricopa County Bar Assn. (mem. CLE com. 1988-91), Minn. Bar Assn. Roman Catholic. Avocations: golf, bicycling, hiking, reading, astronomy. Office: 5308 N 12th St Ste 401 Phoenix AZ 85014-2903

RICHARDS, CRAIG M., wholesale distribution executive; b. 1950. BA, Brigham Young Univ., 1975. Audit staff Arthur Andersen & Co., 1975-77; dir. fin. reporting Marriott Corp., 1978-86; dir. fin. analysis, v.p. project finance Bear Stearns, N.Y., 1986-92; CEO Baker & Taylor, 1992—. Office: 2709 Water Ridge Pkwy Ste 500 Charlotte NC 28217-4538*

RICHARDS, DANIEL WELLS, company executive; b. Taylor, Pa., Dec. 16, 1928; s. Daniel Wells and Bernice (Robling) R.; m. Helen Reilly, Feb. 10, 1979; children: Kenneth, Deborah, Thomas. BA, Dickinson Coll., 1950; postgrad., U. Pitts., 1953-54. Mgr. advt. prodn. Miller Machine Co., Pitts., 1954-55; mgr. sales promotion Gen. Paper Co., Pitts., 1955-57; advt. and product mgr. Harris Seybold Co., Cleve., 1957-67; v.p. mktg. Colwell Systems Inc., Champaign, Ill., 1967-86, pres., 1986-91; Disting. lectr., exec. in residence Ill. State U., 1991-93; pres. D.W. Richards & Assocs., Champaign, 1994—. Mem. Urbana (Ill.) City Council, 1975-77; budget dir. Ill. Humanities Council, 1980-84; bd. dirs. United Way Champaign County, 1987—, Sinfonia da Camert, 1987—. Served to lt. U.S. Army, 1950-53. Unitarian. Home and Office: 1704 Coventry Dr Champaign IL 61821-5242

RICHARDS, DARRIE HEWITT, investment company executive; b. Washington, May 31, 1921; s. George Jacob and Esmee (MacMahon) R.; m. Patricia Louise Moses, Jan. 1, 1947; children: Hilary Wade, Craig Hewitt, Lynn Cotter. Student, Brown U., 1937-39; B.S., U.S. Mil. Acad., 1943; M.S., Princeton U., 1949. Commd. 2d lt. U.S. Army, 1943, advanced through grades to maj. gen., 1970; mem. Army Gen. Staff Logistics, 1962-66; brigade comdr., logistics staff officer Europe, 1966-68; comdr. Qui Nhon (Vietnam) Support Command, 1968-69, Western Area Mil. Traffic Mgmt. and Terminal Service, 1969-70; asst. dep. chief staff for logistics Dept. Army, 1970-73; dep. dir. Def. Logistics Agy., 1973-74, ret., 1974; v.p. Capital Resources Inc., Washington, 1974-75; asso. Devel. Resources, Inc., Alexandria, Va., 1975-79; pres. the Montgomery Corp., Alexandria, 1976-84; gen. partner Craighill Co., Alexandria, 1980—; pres., chmn. Montgomery Group, Inc., 1987—. Author publs. on devel allied strategy in World War II, also nat. transp. policy. Decorated D.S.M. with oak leaf cluster, Legion of Merit with 3 oak leaf clusters, Bronze Star, Air medal with 3 oak leaf clusters; Order Chung Mu Republic Korea; Disting. Service Order; Honor medal 1st class Vietnam. Mem. Def. Mgmt. Assn. (v.p. 1973-74), Am. Def. Preparedness Assn. (nat. council 1974-76), Assn. U.S. Army (pres. Heidelburg chpt. 1967-68), alumni assns. U.S. Mil Acad., Princeton U., Brown U. Episcopalian. Home: 1250 S Washington St Apt 709 Alexandria VA 22314-4454 Office: 300 Montgomery St # 200 Alexandria VA 22314-1516

RICHARDS, DAVID ALAN, lawyer; b. Dayton, Ohio, Sept. 21, 1945; s. Charles Vernon and Betty Ann (Macher) R.; m. Marianne Catherine Del Monaco, June 26, 1971; children: Christopher, Courtney. BA summa cum laude, Yale U., 1967, JD, 1972; MA, Cambridge U., 1969. Bar: N.Y., 1973. Assoc. Paul, Weiss, Rifkind, Wharton & Garrison, N.Y.C., 1972-77, Coudert Bros., N.Y.C., 1977-80, ptnr., 1981-82; ptnr., head real estate group Sidley & Austin, N.Y.C., 1983—; gov. Anglo-Am. Real Property Inst. U.S./U.K., 1983-88, chair, 1993; mem. Chgo. Title N.Y. Realty Adv. Bd., 1992—. Contbr. articles to profl. jours. Trustee Scarsdale Pub. Libr., 1984-89, pres., 1988-89; co-chair N.Y. Lawyers for Clinton/Gore, 1996. Fellow Am. Bar Found.; mem. ABA (real property, probate and trust sect., coun. 1982-88, chair 1991-92), Am. Coll. Real Estate Lawyers (gov. 1987-93), Internat. Bar Assn., Assn. of Bar of City of N.Y. (real property com. 1978-80, 84-87), Shenorock Shore Club (Rye, N.Y.), The Grolier Club (N.Y.C.). Democrat.

United Ch. of Christ. Home: 18 Forest Ln Scarsdale NY 10583-6464 Office: Sidley & Austin 875 3rd Ave New York NY 10022-6225

RICHARDS, DAVID GLEYRE, German educator; b. Salt Lake City, July 27, 1935; s. Oliver L. and Lilian Marie (Powell) R.; m. Annegret Horn, Sept. 3, 1959 (div. 1992); 1 child, Stephanie Suzanne. BA, U. Utah, 1960, MA, 1961; PhD, U. Calif.-Berkeley, 1968. Asst. prof. German SUNY, Buffalo, 1968-74, assoc. prof., 1974-84, prof., 1984—. Author: Georg Buchners Woyzeck, 1975, George Buchner and the Birth of the Modern Drama, 1976, The Hero's Quest for the Self: An Archetypal Approach to Hesse's Demian and other Novels, 1987; editor: (with H. Schulte) Crisis and Culture in Post-Enlightenment Germany: Essays in Honor of Peter Heller, 1993, Exploring the Divided Self: Hermann Hesse's Steppenwolf and its Critics, 1996. SUNY grantee, 1973; NEH grantee, 1977-78, Fulbright Commn. grantee, 1980; Rsch. Found. of SUNY fellow, 1982. Mem. Am. Assn. Tchrs. German. Democrat. Avocation: photography. Office: SUNY Buffalo Dept Modern Langs & Lits 910 Clemens Hall Buffalo NY 14260

RICHARDS, DAVID KIMBALL, investor; b. Portland, Maine, May 14, 1939; s. Robert Ladd and Janice (Kimball) R.; m. Carol Ann Liebich, May 27, 1967; children: Adam, Peter. A.B. cum laude, Harvard U., 1961, M.B.A., 1965; B.A., Wadham Coll., Oxford, Eng., 1963. Research analyst H.C. Wainwright & Co., N.Y.C., 1965-71, ptnr., 1971-73; sr. v.p., dir. Capital Research & Mgmt. Co., Los Angeles, 1973-85; v.p. Income Fund of Am., Los Angeles, 1976-85; pres. Fundamental Investors Co., Los Angeles, 1982-85; vice chmn. Primecap Mgmt., Pasadena, Calif., 1985-91; pvt. investor, 1991—. Republican. Home: 109 Esparta Way Santa Monica CA 90402-2137

RICHARDS, EDGAR LESTER, psychologist, educator; b. Albany, N.Y., Apr. 20, 1942; s. Edgar Lester and Gertrude Veronica (Halpin) R.; B.S. in Biology, Siena Coll., 1966, M.S. in Edn., 1968; M.A., U. Pa., 1975; C.A.S., Wesleyan U., 1976; M.Phil., Columbia U., 1977, Ph.D., 1981; m. Ruth Anne Farrar, Dec. 21, 1968; children—Edgar Lester, Christopher Hartington, James Gerald, Ruth Anne. Tchr. secondary sch. biology Stillwater Central Sch. Dist. (N.Y.), 1966-71; NSF grantee, 1969, 70; adminstrv. asst. to supt. City Sch. Dist., Watervliet, N.Y., 1971-72, supt. schs., 1972-74; research and devel. assoc. Ctr. for Sch. Study Councils Grad. Sch. Edn., U. Pa., Phila., 1974-75; research scientist N.Y. State Psychiat. Inst., 1975-77; asst. dir. for research and devel. Nat. Bd. Med. Examiners, Phila., 1977-78; research and evaluation coordinator Research for Better Schs., Inc., Phila., 1979-80, coordinator field support services, 1980-81, specialist in evaluation and devel., 1981-82; adj. asst. prof. Grad. Sch. Edn., Fordham U., N.Y.C., 1985-86, 88, adj. assoc. prof., 1990—; asst. supt. schs. Mahopac Central Sch. Dist. (N.Y.), 1982—; cons. Nat. Tng. and Evaluation Center, N.Y.C., 1977-79, N.Y.C. Bd. Edn., 1977-79, Research for Better Schs., Inc., 1974-75, 84. Cert. secondary sch. biology and gen. sci. tchr., sch. dist. adminstr., secondary prin., N.Y. State; cert. secondary sch. biology, chemistry, and gen. sci. tchr., prin., Mass. Mem. Am. Assn. Sch. Adminstrs., Am. Assn. Sch. Pers. Adminstrs., Am. Ednl. Research Assn., Am. Psychol. Assn., Assn. for Supervision and Curriculum Devel., Nat. Council on Measurement in Edn., Phi Delta Kappa. Democrat. Roman Catholic. Author: Career Education Linking Agents: Perspectives and Roles, 1981, Career Education Program Design, 1981, Perceptions of the Preparation of Youth for Work: Report of a Three State Survey, 1980, Sharing Career Education Resources with Schools: An Exploratory Study of Employer Willingness, 1980; contbr. articles to profl. jours. Home: 26 Nevins Rd Mahopac NY 10541-3034 Office: Mahopac Pub Schs Dist Cen Office Mahopac NY 10541

RICHARDS, FREDERIC MIDDLEBROOK, biochemist, educator; b. N.Y.C., Aug. 19, 1925; s. George and Marianna Richards; m. Heidi Clarke, 1948 (div. 1955); children: Sarah, Ruth Gray; m. Sarah Wheatland, 1959; 1 child, George Huntington. BS, MIT, 1948; PhD, Harvard U., 1952; DSc (hon.), U. New Haven, 1982. Rsch. fellow in phys. chemistry Harvard Med. Sch., Cambridge, Mass., 1952-53; NRC postdoctoral fellow Carlsberg Lab., Denmark, 1954; NSF fellow Cambridge U., Eng., 1955; asst. prof. biochemistry Yale U., New Haven, Conn., 1955-59, assoc. prof., 1959-62, prof., 1963-89, Henry Ford II prof. molecular biophysics, 1967-89, Sterling prof. molecular biophysics, 1989-91, Sterling prof. emeritus, 1991—, chmn. dept. molecular biology and biophysics, 1963-67, chmn. dept. molecular biophysics and biochemistry, 1969-73; dir. Jane Coffin Childs Meml. Fund Med. Rsch., 1976-91, bd. dirs., 1997—; mem. Nat. Adv. Rsch. & Resources Coun., 1983-87; mem. corp. Woods Hole Oceanographic Inst., 1977-83, 84-90; mem. bd. advisors Whitney Marine Lab., 1979-84, Purdue U. Magnetic Resonance Lab., 1980-84, Biology divsn. Argonne Nat. Lab., 1982-84, Brookhaven Nat. Lab., Nat. Synchrotron Light Source; mem. sci. adv. bd. structural biology Howard Hughes Med. Inst., 1988-89, adv. bd., 1989-92; mem. sci. adv. bd. Donaghue Found. Med. Rsch., 1991-92. Mem. editorial bd. Jour. Biol. Chemistry, 1963-69, 82-84, Jour. Molecular Biology, 1973-75, Advances in Protein Chemistry, 1963—; contbr. articles on protein and enzyme chemistry to profl. jours. Sgt. U.S. Army, 1944-46. Recipient Pfizer-Paul Lewis award in enzyme chemistry, 1965, Kai Linderstrom-Lang prize in protein chemistry, 1978, Sci. medal State of Conn., 1995; Guggenheim fellow, 1967-68. Fellow AAAS, Am. Acad. Arts and Scis.; mem. NAS, Am. Philos. Soc., Am. Soc. Biochemistry and Molecular Biology (Merck award 1988), Protein Soc. (Stein and Moore award 1988), Internat. Union Pure and Applied Biophysics (mem. coun. 1975-81), Am. Soc. Biol. Chemists (pres. 1979-80), Biophys. Soc. (pres. 1972-73), Am. Chem. Soc., Am. Crystallographic Assn., Conn. Acad. Sci. and Engring. Avocation: sailing. Home: 69 Andrews Rd Guilford CT 06437-3715 Office: Yale U Dept Molecular Biophysics 260 Whitney Ave PO Box 208114 New Haven CT 06520-8114

RICHARDS, HERBERT EAST, minister emeritus, commentator; b. Hazleton, Pa., Dec. 30, 1919; s. Herbert E. and Mabel (Vannaucker) R.; m. Lois Marcey, Jan. 1, 1942; children: Herbert Charles, Marcey Lynn, Robyn Lois, Fredrick East, Mark Allen. AB, Dickinson Coll., 1941; BD, Drew U., 1944; MA, Columbia, 1944; DD, Coll. of Idaho, 1953; postgrad., Union Theol. Sem., 1941-48, Bucknell U., 1943-44. Accredited news reporter Nat. Assn. Broadcasters. Ordained to ministry Methodist Ch., 1944; pastor in Boiling Springs, Pa., 1937-40, West Chester, Pa., 1940-41, Basking Ridge, N.J., 1941-47; mem. faculty Drew U. and Theol. Sem., 1944-51, assoc. prof. homiletics and Christian criticism, chmn. dept., asst. dean, 1947-51; spl. lectr. religion Howard U., 1947; minister 1st Meth. Cathedral, Boise, Idaho, 1951-69, 1st United Meth. Ch., Eugene, Oreg., 1969-78; minister Tabor Heights United Meth. Ch., Portland, Oreg., 1978-86, minister emeritus, 1986—; weekly radio broadcaster Sta. KBOI, Sta. KIDO, 1941—; weekly TV broadcaster CBS, 1945—, ABC, 1969—, NBC, 1973; pres. Inspiration, Inc., TV Found., 1965—, TV Ecology, 1973; producer Life TV series ABC, 1974-85, PBS TV, 1968-85, also BBC, Eng., Suise Romande, Geneva; chmn. Idaho bd. ministerial tng. Meth. Conf., 1954-60, TV, Radio and Film Commn., 1954-62, Oreg. Coun. Public Broadcasting, 1973; del. Idaho Conf. Meth. Gen. Conf., 1956, Jurisdictional Conf., 1956, World Meth. Coun., 1957, 81, World Meth. Conf., 1981, mem. Gen. Conf., 1956-60, Jurisdictional Conf., 1956, 60; meml. chaplain Idaho Supreme Ct., 1960; chaplain Idaho Senate, 1960-68; mem. Task Force on TV and Ch., 1983. Author: In Time of Need, 1986, Faith and the Pursuit of Healing, 1996; contbr. articles to religious publs.; composer: oratorios Prophet Unwilling, 1966, Meet Martin Luther, 1968, Dear Jesus Boy, 1973. Mem. Commn. on Centennial Celebration for Idaho, 1962-63; committeeman Boy Scouts Am.; bd. dirs. Eugene chpt. ARC, 1954-73; trustee Willamette U., Cascade Manor Homes; adv. bd. Medic-Alert Found. Recipient Alumni citation in religious edn. Dickinson Coll., 1948, Golden Plate award Am. Acad. Achievement, 1965, Jason Lee Mass Media TV award, 1983, Disting. Citizen award Idaho Statesman Newspaper, 1964, Disting. Alumnus award Drew U., 1965 ; named Clergyman of Yr., Religious Heritage Am., 1964. Mem. AAUP, CAP (chaplain Idaho wing, lt. col.), Am. Acad. Achievement (bd. govs. 1967—), Am. Found. Religion and Psychiatry (charter gov.), Idaho Found. Medicine and Biology (charter), Greater Boise Ministerial Assn. (pres.), Eugene Ministerial Assn. (pres. 1978), Masons (33 degree, editor Pike's Peak Albert That Is), Shriners, Elks, Rotary (editor Key and Cog, pres. dist. 510 Pioneer Club), Kappa Sigma (Grand Master of Beta Pi). Home: 10172 SE 99th Dr Portland OR 97266-7227 Office: Tabor Heights United Meth Ch 6161 SE Stark St Portland OR 97215-1935 *When a person presses his face against the window pane of life, he becomes as a child waiting for his father's return; simple, trusting and infinitely wiser. In our present time of growth/conflict, such a face-pressing is essential to get us safely from where we are to where we ought to be.*

RICHARDS, HILDA, academic administrator; b. St. Joseph, Mo., Feb. 7, 1936; d. Togar and Rose Avalynne (Williams) Young-Ballard. Diploma nursing St. John's Sch. Nursing, St. Louis, 1956; BS cum laude, CUNY, 1961; MEd, Columbia U., 1965, EdD, 1976; MPA, NYU, 1971. Dep. chief dept. psychiatry Harlem Rehab. Ctr., N.Y.C., 1969-71; prof., dir. nursing Medgar Evers Coll., CUNY, N.Y.C., 1971-76, prof., assoc. dean, 1976-79; dean Coll. Health and Human Service, Ohio U., Athens, 1979-86; provost, v.p. for acad. affairs Indiana U., Pa., 1986-93; chancellor Ind. U. N.W., Gary, 1993—; bd. dirs. Sta. 56-TV; active N.W. Satir Inst., Execs. Coun. N.W. Ind., ACE Commn. on Minorities in Higher Edn., AASCU Com. on Diversity and Social Change. Author: (with others) Curriculum Development and People of Color: Strategies and Change, 1983; editor Black Conf. on Higher Edn. Jour., 1989-93. Bd. dirs. Avanta Network, 1984—, Urban League N.W. Ind., 1993, N.W. Ind. Forum, 1993, Bank One Regional Bd., Merrillville, Ind., 1994, The Meth. Hosps., Inc., Gary.Merrillville, 1994, Lake Area United Way, 1994, Boys and Girls Clubs N.W. Ind.; life mem. Gary chpt. NAACP; exec. com. Pa. Black Conf. on Higher Edn., 1988-93. Recipient Rockefeller Found. award Am. Council Edn., Washington, 1976-77, Black Achiever award Black Opinion Mag., 1989, Athena award Bus. and Profl. Women's Club Ind., 1991; Martin Luther King grantee NYU, N.Y.C., 1969-70, Gunt Found. grantee Harvard Inst. Ednl. Mgmt., Cambridge, Mass., 1981. Fellow Am. Acad. Nursing; mem. ANA (Outstanding Woman of Color award 1990), AAHE, AAUW, APHA, Am. Assn. State Colls. and Univs., Nat. Assn. Allied Health Profls., Am. Assn. Univ. Adminstrs., Assn. Black Nursing Faculty in Higher Edn. (bd. dirs. 1989—), Pa. Nurses Assn., Assn. Black Women in Higher Edn., Inc., Nat. Black Nurses Assn. (bd. dirs., 1st v.p. 1984—, editor jour. 1985—, Spl. Recognition award 1991, Disting. African-Am. Nurse Educator award Queens County chpt., 1991), Nat. Assn. Women in Edn., Am. Coun. Edn. (exec. com. coun. fellows), Internat. Assn. Univ. Pres., N.W. Rotary, N.W. Kiwanis, Phi Delta Kappa, Sigma Theta Tau, Zonta Club of Ind. County. Democrat. Avocations: needlepoint, travel. Home: 7807 Hemlock Ave Gary IN 46403-2164 Office: Ind U NW Office of Chancellor 3400 Broadway Gary IN 46408-1101

RICHARDS, HUGH TAYLOR, physics educator; b. Baca County, Colo., Nov. 7, 1918; s. Dean Willard and Kate Bell (Taylor) R.; m. Mildred Elizabeth Paddock, Feb. 11, 1944; children: David Taylor, Thomas Martin, John Willard, Margaret Paddock, Elizabeth Nicholls, Robert Dean. BA, Park Coll., 1939; MA, Rice U., 1940, PhD, 1942. Research assoc. Rice U., Houston, 1942; scientist U. Minn., Mpls., 1942-43, U. Calif. Sci. Labs., Los Alamos, N.Mex., 1943-46; research assoc. U. Wis., Madison, 1946-47, mem. faculty, 1947-52, prof., 1952-88, prof. emeritus, 1988—, physics dept. chairperson, 1960-63, 66-69, 85-88; assoc. dean Coll. Letters and Sci., U. Wis, 1963-66. Author: Through Los Alamos 1945: Memoirs of a Nuclear Physicist, 1993; contbr. articles to profl. jours. Fellow Am. Phys. Soc.; mem. Am. Assn. Physics Tchrs. Unitarian-Universalist. Achievements include neutron measurements first A-Bomb test; fission neutron (and other) spectra by new photo-emulsion techniques; mock fission neutron source; spherical electrostatic analyzer for precise reaction energy measurements; negative ion sources for accelerators (He ALPHATROSS, SNICS); accurate proton, deuteron, and alpha particle scattering and reaction cross sections; systematics mirror nuclei; isospin violations in nuclear reactions. Home: 1902 Arlington Pl Madison WI 53705-4002 Office: Univ of Wis Dept Of Physics Madison WI 53706

RICHARDS, J. SCOTT, rehabilitation medicine professional. BA in Psychology cum laude, Oberlin Coll., 1968; Cert. in Elem. Edn., Wayne State U., 1969; MS in Resource Ecology, U. Mich., 1973; PhD in Psychology, Kent State U., 1977. Elem. tchr. Detroit Pub. Schs., 1968-71; rsch. asst. Inst. Fisheries Rsch., 1971-73; teaching asst. Kent State U., 1973-74; psychology intern, 1973-77; dir. psychology and instr. dept. rehab. medicine, co-dir. pain control program SRC, with depts. psychiatry and psychology U. Ala., Birmingham, 1977—, from asst. to assoc. prof. dept. rehab. medicine, 1980-90, prof., 1990—, dir. tng. med. rehab. rsch. tng. ctr., 1985-87, dir. rsch. and dir. of Psychology, Dept. of Physical Med. & Rehab., 1987—, co-dir. UAB Spinal Cord Injury Care System, 1989—; cons. Ctrs. Disease Control, Nat. Inst. Disability & Rehab. Rsch. Contbr. articles to profl. jours. Fellow APA. Office: U Ala Sch Medicine Dept Phys Med & Rehab 1717 6th Ave S Rm 530 Birmingham AL 35233-1801*

RICHARDS, JAMES CARLTON, microbiologist, business executive; b. Storm Lake, Iowa, Aug. 19, 1947; s. Jack M. and June G. Richards; m. Lois Ruth Rebbe, July 22, 1974 (div. Sept. 1986); 1 child, Kimberly Ann; m. Susan M. Wos, Aug. 27, 1988; children: Derek Anthony, Kristin Marie. BS in Microbiology, U. Ill., 1970; PhD in Microbiology, So. Ill. U., 1977. Postdoctoral fellow Pa. State U. Med. Ctr., Hershey, Pa., 1977-79; sr. scientist E.I. duPont de Nemours, Wilmington, Del., 1979-85; program mgr. Amoco, Naperville, Ill., 1985-86; dir. bus. Gene-Trak Systems, Framingham, Mass., 1986-90; mng. dir. Carlton BioVenture Ptnrs., Sudbury, Mass., 1990—; pres., CEO, bd. dirs. Symbollon Corp., Sudbury, Mass., 1991-95; pres., CEO, bd. dirs. IntelliGene, Ltd., Sudbury, Mass., 1995—, Jerusalem, Israel, 1995—; invited lectr. on genetic analysis and advances in gene amplification and detection 4th ann. Advances in Gene Amplification and Selection Conf. Cambridge Healthtech Inst., McLean, Va., 1996. Contbr. chpt. to books, articles to sci. jours.; patentee in field. Deacon United Ch. of Christ, Framingham, 1988—. Mem. AAAS, Am. Soc. for Microbiology, Am. Chem. Soc., Inst. Food Technologists, N.Y. Acad. Scis., Clin. Ligand Soc., Ill. Alumni Assn., Sigma Xi, Theta Xi. Avocations: golf, travel, jogging, gardening, skiing. Home and office: 44 Codman Dr Sudbury MA 01776-1745

RICHARDS, JAY CLAUDE, commercial photographer, news service executive, historian; b. Glen Ridge, N.J., Apr. 6, 1954; s. Jacob Tilghman and Joan Louise (Walsh) R. Student, Tenn. Wesleyan Coll., Athens, 1972-73. Various positions armed security work, 1973-75; reporter, photographer Press Publs.: The News, Belvidere, N.J., 1977—; pres. J.C. Richards Assocs., Harmony Twp., N.J., 1980—; owner Poor Richards' Brit. Gun Shop, Harmony Twp., 1976—; photography judge Warren County 4-H, Belvidere, 1990—; press officer Warren County Office Emergency Mgmt., Belvidere, 1989—. Author: Penn, Patriots and the Pequest: The History of Pre-Victorian Belvidere, 1716-1845, 1995, Flames Along the Delaware, 1996 (N.J. Frontier Guard's Book award 1997); photographer (video) From Flax to Linen, 1993, Belvidere: N.J.'s Best Kept Secret, 1994, Heritage Festival TV commls.; contbr. photographs to mags., calendars, coll. catalogs. Mem. Hazardous Materials Adv. Coun., Warren County, N.J.; mem. Joint Emergency Mgmt. Coun., Belvidere/White Twp., N.J.; mem. Warren County Arts Adv. Coun. Named Hon. Mem. Boy Scout Troop 141, Belvidere, 1993; recipient Outstanding Cmty. Svc. award Am. Legion Post 131, 1994. Mem. Nat. Press Photographers Assn., Soc. Profl. Journalists, Res. Officers Assn. U.S., Sr. Army Res. Comdrs. Assn., U.S. Naval Inst. Episcopalian. Avocations: militaria collecting, gourmet cooking, gardening, herbal medicine. Home and Office: 3110 Belvidere Rd Phillipsburg NJ 08865-9515

RICHARDS, JEANNE HERRON, artist; b. Aurora, Ill., Apr. 8, 1923; d. Robert Watt and Ida (Herron) R. B.F.A., U. Iowa, 1952, M.F.A., 1954. instr. art State U. Iowa, 1955-56; instr. U. Nebr., 1957-59, asst. prof., 1959-63; instr. Ascension Acad., Alexandria, Va., 1967-68. One-woman shows include U. Nebr. Art Galleries, Lincoln, 1959, U. Ill., Champaign-Urbana, 1969, group shows include Library of Congress, 1947-61, Corcoran Gallery, Washington, 1974; represented in permanent collections Lessing J. Rosenwald Collection, Library of Congress, Nat. Mus. Am. Art, Smithsonian Instn. Served with USNR, 1943-46. Fulbright grantee, 1954-55. Mem. Soc. Am. Graphic Artists, Soc. Washington Printmakers, Gamma Phi Beta. Address: 9526 Liptonshire Dr Dallas TX 75238-2727

RICHARDS, JERRY LEE, academic administrator, religious educator; b. Lawrenceville, Ill., Nov. 4, 1939; s. Russell O. and Elvessa A. (Goodman) R.; m. Lee Ann, Apr. 25, 1986; children: Mark, Renee, Teresa, Angela. BA, Lycoming Coll., 1965; BD, Evang. Congregational Sch. Theology, 1967; MDiv, Garrett Theol. Sem., 1968; D in Ministry, St. Paul Sch. Theology, 1975. Ordained to ministry Meth. Ch., 1968. Pastor chs. Pa., 1960-65, Williamsport, Iowa, 1965-70; mem. faculty Iowa Wesleyan U., Mt Pleasant, 1970-85; prof. religion, dir. responsible social involvement Iowa Wesleyan U., Mt. Pleasant, 1975-85, v.p. for acad. affairs, 1975-82, pres., 1982-85; dir. gift planning U. Wis., Eau Claire, 1985—. Pres. Mental Health Inst. Aux., Mt. Pleasant, 1976. Mem. Phi Alpha Theta. Office: U Wis Office of Devel 215 Schofield Hall Eau Claire WI 54701

RICHARDS, JOHN DALE, sociology and philosophy educator, counselor; b. South Charleston, W.Va., July 31, 1958; s. Guy Edward and Margaret Jane (Gray) R.; m. Susan Lynn McCallister, June 23, 1990. BA, W.Va. State Coll., 1978; MA, Ohio U., 1982, 88. Lic. profl. counselor, W.Va. Bd. Examiners in Counseling; lic. cert. social worker, W.Va. Bd. Social Work Examiners. Family counselor Family Svc. Kanawha Valley, Charleston, W.Va., 1988-93; pvt. practice family counselor South Charleston, 1991-93; asst. prof. W.Va. State Coll., Institute, 1993—; cons. Gov.'s Cabinet on Families and Children, Charleston, 1995, Human Resource Mgmt. Co., Charleston, 1995. Author: Coping with Grief, 1995, (poetry) Uncreated Light, 1995; co-author; The Family Education Experience, 1995. Pres. bd. dirs. Dreikurs Family Edn. Ctr., Charleston, 1995—; mem. adv. bd. Glenwood Family Resource Ctr., Charleston, 1995—. Recipient Dr. W.E.B. Dubois award Alpha Kappa Delta, 1995. Mem. Am. Sociol. Assn., W.Va. Soc. Adlerian Psychology (pres. 1995-96, Dr. Manford A. Sonstegard award 1995), W.Va. Sociol. Assn. (v.p. 1995-96), Masons. Democrat. Avocations: writing music, writing poetry, collecting rocks, woodworking, archaeology. Home: 1211 Strawberry Rd Saint Albans WV 25177

RICHARDS, JON FREDERICK, physician; b. Hays, Kans., May 1, 1950; s. Robert Clare and Jean G. (Fuller) R.; m. Kate Haines, July 31, 1973; children: Robert C. II, Travis Walker, Frederick Dinsmore, Jon Charles. BA in Psychology, U. Kans., 1972, MD, 1975. Intern internal medicine Brown U.-Miriam Hosp., Providence, 1976; resident internal medicine U. Kans. Sch. Medicine, Kansas City, 1981; physician pvt. practice, Phillipsburg, Kans., 1976-79, 81-85; attending physician Salina (Kans.) Regional Health Ctr., 1985—; ptnr. Salina Clinic, 1985—; bd. trustees Kans. Found. Med. Care, Topeka, 1983—, chmn., 1984—; clin. asst. prof. Smoky Hill Family Practice Residency, Wichita, 1989—; pres. Smoky Hill Ednl. Found., 1992—. Cubmaster Boy Scouts Am., Salina, 1987-91; asst. scoutmaster, 1990—. Summerfield scholar U. Kans., Lawrence, 1968-72. Mem. AMA, Am. Coll. Physicians, Kans. Med. Soc., Salina County Med. Soc. (pres. 1994), Phi Beta Kappa. Avocations: jogging, camping, backpacking. Home: 2404 N Halstead Rd Salina KS 67401-9244 Office: Salina Clinic 501 S Santa Fe Ave Salina KS 67401-4189

RICHARDS, JOSEPH EDWARD, artist; b. Des Moines, Oct. 10, 1921; s. Earl L. and Ivanore M. (Shelledy) R.; m. Elizabeth Anne Morrow, Mar. 23, 1943. Student Am. Acad. Art, Chgo., 1946-49, Art Inst. Chgo., 1949-50, Pa. Acad. Fine Arts, 1950-52. Exhbns. include: Butler Inst. Am. Art, Youngstown, Ohio, 1976, 77, 78, 81, Tex. Fine Arts Assn./Laguna Gloria Art Mus., Austin, Tex., 1977, NAD, N.Y.C., 1978, Silvermine Guild Artists, New Cannan, Conn., 1978, 79, Pa. Acad. Fine Arts, Phila., 1978, 80, 94, Va. Mus., Richmond, 1979, O.K. Harris Gallery, N.Y.C., 1982, 89, 92, 94, O.K. Harris West Gallery, Scottsdale, Ariz., 1981, 82, Robert Kidd Galleries, Birmingham, Mich., 1984, Soghor, Leonard & Assocs. Gallery, N.Y.C., 1985, O.K. Harris South, Miami, Fla., 1986, Butler Inst. Am. Art, Youngstown, Ohio, 1987, Tortue Gallery, Santa Monica, Calif., 1988, Art Expo, Tokyo, 1990, Art Now Gallery, Gothenburg, Sweden, 1990, Louis Stern Gallery, Beverly Hills, Calif., 1991, Bobbitt Visual Arts Ctr. Albion (Mich.) Coll., 1991, Survey of Am. Realism, Seoul, Korea, 1996. Represented in private and corp. collections in U.S., Can., Europe. Recipient Disting. Artists award Va. Mus. Fine Art, 1979. Fellow Pa. Acad. Fine Arts. Home: PO Box 374 Hillsdale NY 12529-0374

RICHARDS, KEITH, musician; b. Dartford, Kent, Eng., Dec. 18, 1943; s. Bert and Doris Richards; m. Anita Pallenberg; children: Marlon, Angela; m. Patti Hansen, Dec. 18, 1983; children: Theodora, Alexandra. Student, Sidcup Art Sch. Lead & rhythm guitarist, vocalist, Rolling Stones, 1962—; films include: Sympathy for the Devil, 1970, Gimme Shelter, 1970, Ladies and Gentlemen, the Rolling Stones, 1974, Let's Spend the Night Together, 1983, film mus. dir. (with Chuck Berry, Eric Clapton and friends) Hail! Hail! Rock & Roll, 1987; composer (with Mick Jagger) numerous songs and ablums, 1964—, including (albums) The Rolling Stones, Now!, 1964, Aftermath, 1966, Flowers, 1967, Beggars Banquet, 1968, Let It Bleed, 1969, Sticky Fingers, 1971, Hot Rocks, 1972, Exile on Main Street, 1972, Goat's Head Soup, 1973, It's Only Rock and Roll, 1974, Metamorphosis, 1975, Black and Blue, 1976, Some Girls, Emotional Rescue, 1980, Tatoo You, 1981, Still Life, 1982, Under Cover, 1983, Dirty Work, 1986, Steel Wheels, 1989, Flashpoint, 1991, Voodoo Lounge, 1994 (Grammy award Best Rock Album), Stripped, 1995; (songs) Wild Horses, Angie, Start Me Up, Honky Tonk Woman, Jumpin' Jack Flash, (I Can't Get No) Satisfaction, Before They Make Me Run, Miss You, Happy, Shattered, Paint It Black, Waiting On a Friend, Ruby Tuesday, You Can't Always Get What You Want, Brown Sugar, Tumbling Dice, Faraway Eyes, Mixed Emotions, Rock and a Hard Place, Highwire, Love is Strong; producer (soundtrack album) Hail! Hail! Rock 'N Roll, 1987; solo albums: Talk Is Cheap, 1988, Keith Richards & The X-Pensive Winos Live At The Hollywood Palladium, Dec. 15, 1988, 1991, Main Offender, 1992. Recipient Living Legend award Internat. Rock; inducted into Rock and Roll Hall of Fame, 1989. Address: care Raindrop Svcs 1776 Broadway New York NY 10019-2002

RICHARDS, KENNETH EDWIN, management consultant; b. N.J., Oct. 9, 1917; s. Kenneth G. and Laura (Benson) R.; m. Evelyn Henderson, Dec. 12, 1942 (div. June 1963); children: Kenneth A., Grant B., Kyle E. Umansky, Diane L. Parmley, Kathleen E. Hilton, Kim E. Richards-Davis, Cynthia G. Burger, Cheri O. Greer, Steven E. Benedict; m. Sylvia Marie Benedict, Nov. 1979. BA, Wesleyan U., 1939. Asst. buyer J.C. Penney Co., 1945-48, buyer, 1948-55, dept. head women's & girl's sportswear apparel, 1955-58; from v.p., mdse. mgr. to dir. S.H. Kress Co., 1958-60; v.p. mdse. and sales Firth Carpet Co., 1960-62, dir., 1961-62; spl. cons. to pres. Mohasco Industries Inc., 1962-63; v.p., dir. Yorkshire Terrace Motel Corp., 1963-66; ptnr. Roxbury Hollow Farm, Claverack, N.Y., 1955-66; sr. ptnr. Mgmt. Assocs., 1963-95; pres. Western Dept. Stores, L.A., 1968-70; v.p. merchandising Rapid Merchandising, Costa Mesa, Calif., 1970-72; exec. v.p., gen. mgr. Skor-Mor Products, Santa Barbara, Calif., 1972-75; pres., CEO Resort to Life, Inc., Calabasas, Calif., 1980-84; exec. dir. Retirement Jobs of Idaho, Boise, 1985-87; pres. Seniors, Inc., Boise, 1987-94; CEO Compunet, Boise, 1995—. Mem. adv. editorial bd. Surgeon Gen. U.S. Army, 1948-55; co-developer no-iron cotton; developer women's wear "skort"; pioneer use of mix and match sportswear. Lt. col. AUS, 1940-45. Decorated for action against enemy in Normandy, France, 1944. Mem. Chi Psi. Methodist.

RICHARDS, LACLAIRE LISSETTA JONES (MRS. GEORGE A. RICHARDS), social worker; b. Pine Bluff, Ark.; d. Artie William and Geraldine (Adams) Jones; m. George Alvarez Richards, July 26, 1958; children: Leslie Rosario, Lia Mercedes, Jorge Ferguson. BA, Nat. Coll. Christian Workers, 1953; MSW, U. Kans., 1956; postgrad. Columbia U., 1960. Diplomate Clin. Social Work, Am. Bd. of Examiners in Clin. Social Work, Nat. Assn. Social Workers; cert. gerontologist. Psychiat. supervisory, teaching, community orgn., adminstrv. and consultative duties Hastings Regional Ctr., Ingleside, Nebr., 1956-60; supervisory, consultative and adminstrv. responsibilities for psychiat. and geriatric patients VA Hosp., Knoxville, Iowa, 1960-74, field instr. for grad. students from U. Mo., EEO counselor, 1969-74, 78-90, com. chmn., 1969-70, Fed. women's program coordinator, 1972-74; sr. social worker Mental Health Inst., Cherokee, Iowa, 1974-77; adj. asst. prof. dept. social behavior U. S.D.; instr. Dept. of Psychiatry U. S.D Sch. of Medicine, 1988-96, Augustana Coll., 1981-86; outpatient social worker VA Med. and Regional Office Center, Sioux Falls, S.D., 1978-96; med., surg. & intensive care social worker, 1990-92, surg. & intermediate care social worker, 1992-96; EEO counselor. Mem. Knoxville Juvenile Adv. Com., 1963-65, 68-70, sec., 1965-66, chmn., 1966-68; sec. Urban Renewal Citizens' Adv. Com., Knoxville, 1966-68; mem. United Methodist Ch. Task Force Exptl. Styles Ministry and Leadership, 1973-74, mem. adult choir, mem. ch. and society com.; counselor Knoxville Youth Line program; sec. exec. com. Vis. Nurse Assn., 1979-80; canvasser community fund drs., Knoxville; mem. Cherokee Civil Rights Commn.; bd. dirs., pub. relations, membership devel. and program devel. cons. YWCA, 1983-85; bd. dirs. Family Svc. Agy., 1989-90, Food Svcs. Ctr. Inc., 1992-96; mem. S.D. Symphonic Choir, 1991—; mem. Youth-At-Risk Task Force and Multicultural Ctr. Advocate. Named S.D. Social Worker of Yr., 1983. Mem. NAACP (chmn. edn. com. 1983-85), AAUW (sec. Hastings chpt. 1958-60), Nat. Assn. Social Workers (co-chmn. Nebr. chpt. profl. standards com. 1958-59), Acad. Cert. Social Workers, S.D. Assn. Social Workers (chmn. minority affairs com., v.p. S.E. region 1980, pres. 1980-82 exec. com. 1982-84, mem. social policy and action com.), Nebr. Assn. Social Workers (chmn. 1958-59), Seventh Dist. S.D. Med. Soc. Aux., Coalition on Aging., Nat. Assn. Social Workers (qualified clin. social worker 1991—), Methodist (Sunday sch. tchr. adult div.; mem. commn. on edn.; mem. Core com. for adult edn.; mem. Adult Choir; mem. Social Concerns Work Area); mem. 1st Evangelical Free Ch., 1995—. Home: 1701 E Ponderosa Dr Sioux Falls SD 57103-5019

RICHARDS, LISLE FREDERICK, architect; b. Merrick, N.Y., Dec. 28, 1909. B.Arch., U. So. Calif., 1934. Draftsman H.C. Nickerson, 1935, Lawrence Test, 1936-40, Raimond Johnson, 1937; with Richards & Logue (architects); practice as L.F. Richards Santa Clara, Calif., 1947-78. Prin. works include Labor Temple, San Jose, Calif., 1948, Swimming Center, Santa Clara, 1949, C.W. Haman Sch, Santa Clara, 1952, Scott Lane Sch, Santa Clara, 1953, W.A. Wilson Sch, Santa Clara, 1954, Westwood Sch, Santa Clara, 1955, Civic Center, Santa Clara, 1962, Santa Clara Internat. Swim Center, 1970. Mem. Santa Clara County Appeals Bd., 1952; mem. Santa Clara Code Com., 1954. Fellow AIA (pres. Coast Valleys chpt. 1956, pres. Calif. Council 1958, Disting. Service award 1959, Disting. Service citation Santa Clara Valley chpt. 1982, Testimonial Appreciation 1990). Home: 1660 Gaton Dr ACI San Jose CA 95125-5751 *As I look back on the past seventy years—what a wonderful and terrible time it has been to live.*

RICHARDS, LLOYD GEORGE, theatrical director, university administrator; b. Toronto, Ont., Can.; came to U.S., 1923; s. Albert George and Rose Isabella (Coote) R.; m. Barbara Davenport, Oct. 11, 1957; children: Scott, Thomas. Grad., Wayne U., 1944. Head actor tng. NYU Sch. Arts, N.Y.C., 1966-72; artistic dir. Nat. Playwrights Conf., Eugene O'Neill Meml. Theatre Ctr., Waterford, Conn., 1969—; prof. theatre and cinema Hunter Coll., N.Y.C., 1972-79; dean Yale U. Sch. Drama, New Haven, 1979-91; artistic dir Yale Repertory Theatre, New Haven, 1979-91; prof. emeritus Sch. Drama, 1991—; artistic dir. Yale Repertory Theater, 1979-91; pres. Theater Devel. Fund; head actor tng. Sch. Arts NYU, 1966-72; lectr., cons. in field; bd. dirs. Theatre Comm. Group, U.S. Bicentennial World Theatre Festival; mem. various profl. adv. groups, task forces; mem. playwrights selection com. Rockefeller Found.; mem. new Am. plays program com. Ford Found.; mem. com. on profl. theater tng. Nat. Endowment Arts. Actor on radio, TV and theater, 1943—; including Broadway plays The Egghead, 1957, Freight, 1956; disc jockey, Detroit; dir. for: radio, TV, film and theater, including Broadway plays A Raisin in the Sun, 1958, The Long Dream, 1960, The Moon Besieged, 1962, I Had a Ball, 1964, The Yearling, 1966, Paul Robeson, 1977-78, Ma Rainey's Black Bottom, 1984, Fences, 1987 (Tony award 1987), Joe Turner's Come and Gone, 1986, The Piano Lesson, 1990, Two Trains Running, 1992, 7 Guitars, 1996; and TV prodns. include: segment of Roots: The Next Generation, 1979, Bill Moyers' Jour, 1979, Robeson, 1979, Hallmark Piano Lesson 95. Served with USAAF, 1943-44. Recipient Pioneer award AUDELCO, 1986-87, Frederick Douglas award, 1986-87, Golden Plate award, 1987, Nat. Medal of Arts, 1993, Mr. Abbott award, 1996; Hoffman Eminent scholar Fla. State U., 1997. Mem. Soc. Stage Dirs. and Choreographers (pres.), Actors Equity Assn., AFTRA, Dirs. Guild Am. Office: 18 W 95th St New York NY 10025-6708

RICHARDS, MARTA ALISON, lawyer; b. Memphis, Mar. 15, 1952; d. Howard Jay and Mary Dean (Nix) Richards; m. Jon Michael Hobson, May 5, 1973 (div. Jan. 1976); m. 2d, Richard Peter Massony, June 16, 1979 (div. Apr. 1988); 1 child, Richard Peter Massony, Jr. Student Vassar Coll., 1969-70; AB cum laude, Princeton U., 1973; JD, George Washington U., 1976. Bar: La. 1976, U.S. Dist. Ct. (ea. dist.) La. 1976, U.S. Ct. of Appeals (5th cir.) 1981, U.S. Supreme Ct. 1988, U.S. Dist. Ct. (mid. dist.) La., 1991. Assoc. Phelps, Dunbar, Marks, Claverie & Sims, New Orleans, 1976-77; assoc. counsel Hibernia Nat. Bank, New Orleans, 1978; assoc. Singer, Hutner, Levine, Seeman & Stuart, New Orleans, 1978-80, Jones, Walker, Waechter, Poitevent, Carrere & Denegre, New Orleans, 1980-84; ptnr. Mmahat, Duffy, & Richards, 1984, Montgomery, Barnett, Brown, Read, Hammond & Mintz, 1984-86, Montgomery, Richards & Ballin, 1986-89, Gelpi, Sullivan, Carroll and Laborde, 1989; gen. counsel Maison Blanche Inc., Baton Rouge, 1990-92; gen. counsel La. State Bond Commn., 1992—; lectr. paralegal inst. U. New Orleans, 1984-89, adj. prof., 1989. Contbr. articles to legal jours. Treas. alumni coun. Princeton U., 1979-81. Mem. ABA, La. State Bar Assn., New Orleans Bar Assn., Baton Rouge Bar Assn., Nat. Assn. Bond Lawyers, Princeton Alumni Assn. New Orleans (pres. 1982-86). Episcopalian. Home: 4075 S Ramsey Dr Baton Rouge LA 70808 Office: La State Bond Commn State Capitol Bldg 21st Fl PO Box 44154 Baton Rouge LA 70804

RICHARDS, MAX DE VOE, management educator, consultant, researcher, author; b. Nova, Ohio, May 23, 1923; s. Paul Leroy and Dorothy Charlotte (Daniels) Richards; m. Winona Marie Petersen, Mar. 3, 1950 (div. Dec. 1974); children: Cassandra, Elizabeth; m. Ruth Sara Nixon, Nov. 12, 1977. M.B.A., Harvard U., 1947; Ph.D., U. Ill., 1955. Indsl. engr. Nat. Tube div. U.S. Steel Co., 1948-49; instr. mgmt. U. Ill., Urbana, 1949-54; assoc. prof., head dept. mgmt. U. Wichita, Kans., 1954-56; assoc. prof., head div. mgmt. Pa. State U., University Park, 1956-64, prof., head dept. mgmt., 1964-67, 78-81, prof., asst. dean, dir. grad. programs Coll. Bus. Adminstrn., 1966-77; disting. prof. mgmt. Rollins Coll., Winter Park, Fla., 1981-85; organizational and strategic mgmt. cons., program speaker, U.S., internationally, 1954—; bd. dirs. Inst. for Adminstrv. Research, 1967-69; evaluator Middle States Accrediting Assn., Newark, 1973—. Author: Organizational Goal Structures, 1978, Intermediate and Long Term Credit Small Corporations, 1980, Setting Strategic Goals and Objectives, rev. edit., 1986; co-author: Management Decisions and Behavior, 2d edit. 1973; editor: Readings in Management, 7th edit. 1986. Ford Found. faculty fellow, 1965-66; Social Sci. Research Council fellow, 1966. Fellow Acad. Mgmt. (dir. 1961-68, v.p., program chmn. 1965-66, pres. 1966-67, chmn. policy and planning div. 1975, dir. div. 1974-78); mem. Strategic Mgmt. Soc. (editorial bd. 1983—), Order of Artus, Sigma Iota Epsilon (trustee 1968), Beta Gamma Sigma, Beech Mountain Club (N.C.), Tuscawilla Country Club (Winter Springs, Fla.), Elks. Home: 1117 Winged Foot Cir W Winter Spgs FL 32708-4201 Office: Crummer Grad Sch Bus Rollins Coll Winter Park FL 32789

RICHARDS, MERLON FOSS, retired diversified technical services company executive; b. Farmington, Utah, May 18, 1920; s. Ezra Foss and Mertie Malinda (Hunt) R.; m. Caryle Jane Vandenberg, July 18, 1945 (dec. 1994); children: Craig M., Cathy Jean, Cynthia Jane, Julie Ann. BS, U. Utah, 1942; MBA, Harvard U., 1947. CPA, Ill. Pub. acct. Arthur Andersen & Co., Chgo., 1947-52; asst. treas. to exec. v.p. Land-Air, Inc., Chgo., 1952-59; from v.p. to vice chmn., chief exec. officer DynCorp (formerly Dynalectron Corp.), Washington, 1959-85, bd. dirs., mem. exec. com., 1971-88; consulting fin. officer Indsl. Tng. Corp., Herndon, Va., 1988-89; former dir. over 20 DynCorp subs.; mem. adv. bd. Sycom Inc., 1986-88; dir. Riggs Nat. Bank, 1979-81. Chmn., vice chmn. membership, vice chmn.-at-large Potomac dist. Nat. Capital Area coun. Boy Scouts Am., 1989—; pub. affairs dir. Washington region LDS Ch., 1984-94; mem. fin. com. Interfaith Conf. of Met. Washington, 1992—. Maj. F.A., U.S. Army, 1941-54, ETO. Decorated Bronze Star, Silver Star. Mem. Pi Kappa Alpha. Republican. Home and Office: 4701 Willard Ave Apt 436 Chevy Chase MD 20815-4613

RICHARDS, MICHAEL, actor, comedian; b. 1949; 1 child. TV appearences include Fridays, 1980-82, Marblehead Manor, 1987, Seinfeld, 1990— (Emmy award, Outstanding Supporting Actor in a Comedy Series, 1993, 94); films include Young Doctors in Love, 1982, Transylvania 6-5000, 1985, UHF, 1989, Problem Child, 1990, Coneheads, 1993, Unstrung Heroes, 1995. Office: APA 9000 W Sunset Blvd Ste 1200 Los Angeles CA 90069-5812

RICHARDS, NORMAN BLANCHARD, lawyer; b. Melrose, Mass., May 27, 1924; s. Henry Edward and Annie Jane (Blanchard) R.; m. Diane Maionchi, July 9, 1977; children—Terri, Jeffrey. B.S., Bowdoin Coll., 1945; J.D., Stanford U., 1951. Bar: Calif. bar 1951. Mem. firm McCutchen Doyle Brown & Enersen, San Francisco, 1951—; partner McCutchen Doyle Brown & Enersen, 1960—; mem. faculty Tulane Admiralty Law Inst., Hastings Coll. Advocacy. Bd. visitors Stanford Law Sch. With USN, 1943-46. Fellow Am. Coll. Trial Lawyers; mem. ABA, Calif. State Bar, San Francisco Bar ASsn., Maritime Law Assn. U.S. Home: 85 Platt Ave Sausalito CA 94965-1897 Office: McCutchen Doyle Brown & Enerson 3 Embarcadero Ctr San Francisco CA 94111-4003

RICHARDS, PAUL A., lawyer; b. Oakland, Calif., May 27, 1927; s. Donnell C. and Theresa (Pasquale) R.; m. Ann Morgans, May 20, 1948 (dec. 1984); 1 child, Paul M. Office: 248 S Sierra St Reno NV 89501-1908

RICHARDS, PAUL GRANSTON, geophysics educator, seismologist; b. Cirencester, Eng., Mar. 31, 1943; came to U.S., 1965; s. Albert George and Kathleen Margaret (Harding) R.; m. Jody Margaret Porterfield, June 1, 1968; children: Mark, Jessica, Gillian. BA, Cambridge (Eng.) U., 1965; MS, Calif. Inst. Tech., Pasadena, 1966, PhD, 1970. Prof. geol. scis. Columbia U., N.Y.C., 1971—, chmn. dept. geol. scis., 1980-83. Co-author: Quantitative Seismology, 2 vols., 1980. Guggenheim Found. fellow, 1977-78, MacArthur Found. fellow, 1981-86. Fellow Royal Astron. Soc.; mem. Am. Geophys. Union (Macelwane award 1976), Coun. Fgn. Rels. Episcopalian. Office: Lamont-Doherty Earth OBS Palisades NY 10964

RICHARDS, PAUL LINFORD, physics educator, researcher; b. Ithaca, N.Y., June 4, 1934; s. Lorenzo Adolph and Zilla (Linford) R.; m. Audrey Jarratt, Aug. 24, 1965; children: Elizabeth Anne, Mary-Ann. AB, Harvard U., 1956; PhD, U. Calif., Berkeley, 1960. Postdoctoral fellow U. Cambridge (Eng.), 1959-60; mem. tech. staff Bell Telephone Labs., Murray Hill, N.J., 1960-66; prof. physics U. Calif., Berkeley, 1966—; faculty sr. scientist Lawrence Berkeley Lab., 1966—; advisor NASA, 1975-92, Conductus Inc., Mountain View, Calif., 1988—; hon. prof. Miller Inst. Rsch. in Phys. Scis., Berkeley, 1969-70, 87-88; vis. prof. Ecole Normale Superieure, Paris, 1984, 92; vis. astronomer Paris Obs., 1984. Contbr. over 300 articles to profl. jours. Guggenheim Meml. Found. fellow, Cambridge, Eng., 1973-74; named Calif. Scientist of Yr. Mus. Sci., L.A., 1981; recipient sr. scientist award Alexander von Humboldt Found., Stuttgart, Fed. Republic Germany, 1982, Button medal, 1997; Berkeley Faculty Rsch. lectr. 1991. Fellow NAS, Am. Phys. Soc., Am. Acad. Arts and Scis. Avocations: vineyardist, wine making.

RICHARDS, REUBEN FRANCIS, natural resource company executive; b. Aug. 15, 1929; s. Junius A. and Marie R. (Thayer) R.; m. Elizabeth Brady, Nov. 28, 1953; children: Reuben Francis, Timothy T., Andrew H. AB, Harvard U., 1952. With Citibank, N.A., N.Y.C., 1953-82, exec. v.p., 1970-82; chmn. Terra Industries Inc., N.Y.C., 1982-96; bd. dirs. Ecolab, Inc., St. Paul, Potlatch Corp., San Francisco, Minorco, Luxembourg, Santa Fe Energy Resources, Inc., Houston, Engelhard Corp., Iselin, N.J.; chmn., pres., CEO Minorco (U.S.A.) Inc., 1990-96. With USNR, 1948-50. Office: 250 Park Ave Ste 1900 New York NY 10177-1999

RICHARDS, RILEY HARRY, insurance company executive; b. North Judson, Ind., Oct. 6, 1912; s. Harry J. and Chestie (Johnson) R.; m. Eloise Quinn Smith, May 4, 1940; children: Roy, Lynne. AB, U. Calif., Berkeley, 1934; MBA, Harvard U., 1937. Chartered fin. analyst. Fin. analyst Savs. Bank Trust Co. N.Y.C., 1937-40, SEC, Washington, Phila., 1940-45; accountant U.S. Steel Co., Pitts., 1945-47; with Equitable Life Ins. Co. Iowa, Des Moines, 1947-77; v.p. finance Equitable Life Ins. Co. Iowa, 1961-73, v.p., sec., treas., 1973-76, sr. v.p., sec.-treas., 1976-77; dir., mem. exec. com. Equitable of Iowa Cos., 1977-84; pres. Westminster House, Inc., 1989-96; dir. F.M. Hubbell Sons & Co., 1977-85. Mem. Des Moines Plan and Zoning Commn., 1959-70, chmn., 1968-69; mem. bd. pensions U.P. Ch. in U.S.A., 1960-72, chmn. finance com., 1963-72; trustee United Presbyn. Found., 1979-87, vice chmn., 1981-83, chmn., 1983-87; bd. regents Life Officers Investment Seminar, 1969-70; trustee Thompson Trust, 1976—, Frederick M. Hubbell Estate, 1977-85. Mem. Am. Coun. Life Ins. (chmn. fin. sect. 1970), Iowa Soc. Fin. Analysts (pres. 1965-67), Sigma Alpha Epsilon. Republican. Club: Des Moines. Lodges: Masons, Rotary. Home: 2909 Woodland Ave Apt 310 Des Moines IA 50312-3863

RICHARDS, ROBERT WADSWORTH, civil engineer, consultant; b. Beacon, N.Y., Jan. 26, 1921; s. Parke and Lois Richmond (Tracy) R.; m. Cynthia Elizabeth Pigot, May 31, 1952; children: Sarah Palmer Richards Graves III, Robert Wadsworth, Tracy Leigh Richards Purdy. BS, Princeton U., 1943, MCE, 1944. Registered profl. engr., Ga. Instr. civil engring. Swarthmore (Pa.) Coll., 1944-45; rsch. engr. The Budd Co., Phila., 1945-50; assoc. charge Atlanta office Howard, Needles, Tammen & Bergendoff, 1950-88; cons. engr. Tech. & Creative Writing, 1988—. Contbr. articles to tech. and bus. jours. Named Eminent Engr., Tau Beta Pi. Fellow ASCE; mem. Am. Soc. Engring. Edn. (life), Princeton Campus Club. Home and Office: 1051 Winding Branch Ln Atlanta GA 30338-3947

RICHARDS, ROY, JR., wire and cable manufacturing company executive. Chmn., CEO, dir. Southwire Co., Carrollton, Ga. Office: Southwire Co Inc PO Box 1000 Carrollton GA 30119*

RICHARDS, STEPHEN HAROLD, engineering educator; b. Austin, Tex., July 19, 1952; s. Harold Richards Jr. and Janice Valerie (Mahone) Jackson; m. Mary Kathryn King Coleman, Aug. 15, 1974 (div. July 1981); 1 child, Adam King. BSCE, U. Tex., 1976; MCE, Tex. A&M U., 1977; PhDCE, U. Tenn., 1989. Registered profl. engr., Tenn., Tex. Rsch. asst. Tex. Transp. Inst., Tex. A&M U., 1976-77, engrng. rsch. assoc., 1977-81, asst. rsch. engr., 1982-84; asst. dir. transp. ctr. U. Tenn., Knoxville, 1984-87, acting dir. transp. ctr., 1987-89, dir. transp., 1989—, assoc. prof. civil engring., 1989—; traffic engring. cons., 1976—; engr., mgr. Walton & Assocs./Cons. Engrs., Inc., Houston, 1981-82; lectr. in civl engring. U. Houston, 1982, Tex. A&M U., 1978-81, 83-84; instr. Tex. Engring. Extension Svc., Tex. A&M U., 1978-84; Dwight D. Eisenhower Fellowship Rev. Com., Tenn. State U., 1993, N.C. A&T Univ., 1992; Bicentennial planning Com. U. Tenn., 1993, dir. program for minority student recruitment into transp. careers, 1992—, coll. engring. awards com., 1991—, chmn. spl. events traffic planning com., 1985—. Contbr. numerous articles to profl. jours. Mem. Cumberland Gateway Com., 1993—; edn. com. Southeastern Transp. Ctr., 1992—; exec. dir. Southeastern Consortium of U. Transp. Ctrs., 1992—; chmn. Knoxville Transp. Authority, 1992-94, vice-chmn., 1990-92, commr., 1989-93; rep. Coun. of Univ. Transp. Ctrs. U. Tenn., 1987—, bd. dirs. 1992—, sec., 1994-95, v.p., 1995-96, pres., 1996—; adv. com. Ga. State u. Transp. Ctr., 1989—; traffic control device subcom. Transp. Rsch. Bd., 1989-91, traffic control devices, 1991—, many other coms. Hwy. Safety fellowship Fed. Hwy. Adminstrn., U.S. Dept. Transp., 1976-77. Mem. ASCE, Inst. of Transp. Engrs. (chmn. tech. com. Tenn. sect. 1988—, area coord. Tex. sect. 1982-84, guidelines for driveway design and location), Transp. Rsch. Bd., Soc. Profl. Engrs., Am. Road and Transp. Builders Assn. (edn. com. 1988—), Phi Kappa Phi, Chi Epsilon. Office: U Tenn Knoxville Transt Ctr 600 Henley St Ste 309 Knoxville TN 37902

RICHARDS, SUZANNE V., lawyer; b. Columbia, S.C., Sept. 7, 1927; d. Raymond E. and Elise C. (Gray) R. AB, George Washington U., 1948, JD with distinction, 1957, LLM, 1959. Bar: D.C., 1958. Sole practice, Washington, 1974—; lectr. in family and probate law. Recipient John Bell Larner award George Washington U., 1958; named Woman Lawyer of the Yr., Women's Bar Assn. D.C., 1977. Mem. Bar Assn. D.C. (pres. 1989-90), Women's Bar Assn. (pres. 1977-78), Trial Lawyers Assn. of D.C. (bd. govs. 1978-82, 85—, treas. 1982-85), D.C. Bar, Fed. Bar Assn., Nat. Assn. Women Lawyers, ABA (mem. ho. dels. 1988-90), D.C. Jud. Conf. Office: 1701 K St NW Washington DC 20006

RICHARDS, THOMAS H., lawyer, arbitrator; b. Exeter, N.H., May 29, 1942; s. Frank F. and Ella (Higgins) R.; m. Barbara M. Blackmer, Mar. 23, 1975; children: Daniel, Matthew. BA cum laude, U. N.H., 1964; JD, NYU, 1967. Bar: N.H. 1967, U.S. Dist. Ct. N.H., U.S. Ct. Appeals (1st cir., D.C. cir.) 1987. Assoc. to v.p. Sheehan Phinney Bass & Green, Manchester, N.H., 1967-68, 70—. Mem. N.H. Jud. Coun., Concord, 1988-90; mem. long range planning com. N.H. Supreme Ct., 1989-90, mem. profl. conduct com., 1989-90. With U.S. Army, 1968-69. Root-Tilden fellow. Fellow Am. Bar Found., Am. Coll. Trial Lawyers, Internat. Soc. Barristers, N.H. Bar Found. (chmn. 1991-92); mem. Manchester Bar Assn. (bd. govs. 1975-80), New Eng. Bar Assn. (bd. govs. 1989-92), N.H. Bar Assn. (bd. govs. 1985-87, pres. 1989-90), Nat. Conf. Bar Pres., Phi Beta Kappa. Avocations: carpentry, collecting and restoring antique tools. Home: 377 Briar Hill Rd Hopkinton NH 03229-2869 Office: Sheehan Phinney Bass & Green 1000 Elm St Manchester NH 03101-1730

RICHARDS, THOMAS SAVIDGE, utility company executive; b. Dansville, Pa., July 8, 1943; s. Thomas Beddoe and Mary (Savidge) R.; m. Betty Stalter Richards, Aug. 4, 1969; children: Ted, Matthew. BS, Bucknell U., 1965; JD, Cornell U., 1972. Bar: N.Y. 1973. Assoc. Nixon, Hargrave, Devans & Doyle, Rochester, N.Y., 1972-79; ptnr. Nixon, Hargrave, Devans & Doyle, Rochester, 1979-91; gen. counsel Rochester (N.Y.) Gas & Electric Corp., 1991-93, sr. v.p. fin., gen. counsel 1993-95, sr. v.p. energy svcs., 1995-96, pres., 1996—; also bd. dirs.; bd. dirs. Eltrex Industries, Inc., Rochester, Rochester Econ. Devel. Corp. Mem. exec. bd. Boy Scout Am., Otetiana Coun., Rochester; mem. governing bd. Colgate Rochester Divinity Sch.; chmn. bd. dirs. Greater Rochester Housing Partnership; dir. Highland Hosp., Rochester, Rochester Pub. Libr., Vis. Nurse Found., Rochester; dir. Strong Ptnrs. Health Sys. Lt. USN, 1965-69. Mem. ABA, N.Y. State Bar Assn., Monroe County Bar Assn. Office: Rochester Gas & Elec Corp 89 East Ave Rochester NY 14649-0001

RICHARDS, VINCENT PHILIP HASLEWOOD, librarian; b. Sutton Bonington, Nottinghamshire, Eng., Aug. 1, 1933; emigrated to Can., 1956, naturalized, 1961; s. Philip Haslewood and Alice Hilda (Moore) R.; m. Ann Beardshall, Apr. 3, 1961; children: Mark, Christopher, Erika. A.L.A., Ealing Coll., London, 1954; B.L.S. with distinction, U. Okla., 1966. Cert. profl. librarian, B.C. Joined Third Order Mt. Carmel, Roman Catholic Ch., 1976; with Brentford and Chiswick Pub. Libraries, London, 1949-56; asst. librarian B.C. (Can.) Pub. Library Commn., Dawson Creek, 1956-57; asst. dir. Fraser Valley Regional Library, Abbotsford, B.C., 1957-67; chief librarian Red Deer (Alta., Can.) Coll., 1967-77; dir. libraries Edmonton (Alta.) Pub. Library, 1977-89; libr. and book industry cons. Ganges, Can., 1990—; pres. Faculty Assn. Red Deer Coll., 1971-72, bd. govs., 1972-73. Contbr. articles to profl. jours., 1954—. Vice pres. Jeunesses Musicales, Red Deer, 1969-70; bd. dirs. Red Deer TV Authority, 1975-76, Alta. Found. Lit. Arts, 1984-86; mem. Reform Party Can. Served with Royal Army Ednl. Corps, 1951-53. Office: 105 1049 Costin Ave, Victoria, BC Canada V9B 2T4 *Dedication to public service, in spite of its frustrating aspects, diversity of experience, people and places, and the avoidance of overspecialization are great contributors to an enjoyable working life.*

RICHARDS, WALTER DUBOIS, artist, illustrator; b. Penfield, Ohio, Sept. 18, 1907; s. Ralph DuBois and Ruby Mildred (Smith) R.; m. Glenora Case, June 20, 1931; children: Timothy, Henry Tracy. Grad., Cleve. Sch. Art, 1930. With Sundblom Studios, Chgo., 1930-31, Tranquillini Studios, Cleve., 1931-36, Charles E. Cooper Studios, N.Y.C., 1936-50. Freelance artist, 1950—; executed paintings and illustrations for leading indsl. corps., nat. mags.; designed: U.S. postage stamps including Frederick Douglas 25 cent stamp; block of 4 stamps on beautification of Am.; Am. bald eagle-Mus. Natural History with commemorative; Cape Hatteras Nat. Parks Centennial block of four stamps; Paul Lawrence Dunbar Am. Poets commemorative; block of 4 stamps on Am. trees, 1978, blocks of 4 stamps on Am. architecture, 1979, 80, 81, 82; co-designer anti-pollution block of four stamps; James Hoban stamp, 1981, Timberline Lodge 50th Anniversary U.S. commerorative stamp, 1987; exhibited, Cleve. Mus. Art, Art Inst., Chgo., Met. Mus., N.Y.C., Pa. Acad. Fine Arts, Bklyn. Mus., N.A.D., Whitney Mus., 200 Years Watercolor Painting, Met. Mus., 1966, 200 Years Am. Illustration, N.Y. Hist. Soc., 1976; represented in permanent collection, Whitney Mus., New Britain Mus. Am. Art, Cleve. Mus. Art, William A. Farnsworth Library and Art Mus., West Point Mus., Worcester (Mass.) Art Mus., Yale U. Art Gallery-New Haven, Conn. Bd. dirs. Rowayton Art Center, Historic New Orleans Collection, 1989. Recipient highest award in lithography Cleve. Mus. Art, ann. 1935-38; Spl. Honor USAF, 1964; ann. Environ. Improvement award, 1983; named to Rocky River (Ohio) High Sch. Hall of Fame, 1991. Mem. Am. Watercolor Soc. (2d v.p. 1965-67), Conn. Watercolor Soc., NAD, Soc. of Illustrators, Fairfield Watercolor Group (pres., founder), Westport Artists. Address: 87 Oak St New Canaan CT 06840

RICHARDS, WANDA JAMIE, education educator; b. Brownwood, Tex., Jan. 11, 1930; d. William Steven and Mary (Effie) Rodgers; m. Kenneth E. Graham, Mar. 29, 1949 (div. Jan. 3, 1963); 1 child, Kenneth Jr.; m. Neill Richards, Mar. 15, 1972 (dec. Dec. 2, 1982). BA, Eastern N.Mex. U., 1962; MA, Colo. State Coll., 1964; EdD, U. No. Colo., 1966. Tchr. spl. edn. Pub. Sch., Roswell, N.Mex., 1961-63; dept. head spl. edn. Eastern N.Mex. U., Portales, 1965-69; curriculum researcher N.Mex. State U., Las Cruces, 1969-71; dir. edn. Inst. of Logopedics, Wichita, Kans., 1971-72; owner W. J. Enterprises, Kans., 1973-89; pres., treas. W.J.G. Enterprise Corp., Sedona, Ariz., 1990—; pres.'s coun. on spl. edn. Fed. Govt., Washington, 1967-69; planning cons. in field. Contbr. articles to profl. jours. Mem. Citizens for Quality Edn., Sedona, 1991, C. of C., Sedona, 1990-91, Humane Soc., Sedona, 1991. Recipient Fellowship in Spl. Edn., Fed. Govt. Pub. Law 85962, 1963-65; named Faculty Woman of Yr., Eastern New Mex. U., 1967. Republican. Home: 30 Sedona St Sedona AZ 86351-7752

RICHARDS-KORTUM, REBECCA RAE, biomedical engineering educator; b. Grand Island, Nebr., Apr. 14, 1964; d. Larry Alan and Linda Mae (Hohnstein) Richards; m. Philip Ted Kortum, May 12, 1985; children: Alexander Scott, Maxwell James, Zachary Alan. BS, U. Nebr., 1985; MS, MIT, 1987, PhD, 1990. Assoc. U. Tex., Austin, 1990—. Named Presdl. Young Investigator NSF, Washington, 1991; NSF presdl. faculty fellow, Washington, 1992; recipient Career Achievement award Assn. Advancement Med. Instrumentation, 1992, Dow Outstanding Young Faculty awd., Am. Soc. for Engineering Education, 1992. Mem. AAAS, Am. Soc. Engring. Edn. (Outstanding Young Faculty award 1992), Optical Soc. Am., Am. Soc. Photobiology. Achievements include research in photochemistry, photobiology, applied optics and bioengring. Office: U Tex Dept Elec & Computer Engring Austin TX 78712

RICHARDSON, ANN BISHOP, foundation executive, lawyer; b. New Rochelle, N.Y., Dec. 15, 1940; d. Erwin Julius and Mary Frances (Stuart) Heilemann; children: Timothy William, Lynn Patricia, Melanie Elizabeth. BA summa cum laude, Georgetown U., 1977; JD, George Washington U., 1984; cert. Oxford U., Eng., 1986. Bar: Md. 1988, DC 1989. Student counselor Amideast, Beirut, 1967-68, program specialist 1970-73; adminstrv. asst. UN Devel. Program, Yaounde, Cameroon, 1968-70; adminstrv. mgr. Antioch Sch. Law, Washington, 1977-79; chief adminstrv. officer for internat. ops. Peace Corps, Washington, 1980-84; dir. adminstrn. and fin. African Devel. Found., Washington, 1984-87; atty. Karr and McLain, Washington, 1987-92; v.p., gen. counsel Time Dollar, Inc., Washington, 1992—; adj. prof. law D.C. Sch. Law, Washington, 1994—. Mem. Neighbors, Inc., Washington, 1976—. Recipient spl. achievement award Peace Corps, 1981, 82, African Devel. Found., 1986. Mem. ABA, ACLU, D.C. Bar Assn., Assn. Am. Women Univ. Grads., Soc. for Internat. Devel. Phi Beta Kappa. Office: Time Dollar Inc 5500 39th St NW Washington DC 20015-2904

RICHARDSON, ARLINE ANNETTE, accountant, comptroller; b. N.Y.C., Aug. 20, 1939; d. Charles Sidney and Kathleen Gertrude (Sinclair) Hunt; m. David Edward Richardson, Sept. 13, 1958; children: Valerie-Jayne, LaVerne. AA, Bronx (N.Y.) C.C., 1976; BBA, CUNY, 1979, MPA, 1984. Mgr. patient accounts Jewish Home and Hosp. for Aged, N.Y.C., 1960-80; chief bookkeeper Edwin Gould Svcs. for Children, N.Y.C., 1980-81; staff acct. N.Y. Hosp., N.Y.C., 1981-84; mgr. Met. Transp. Authority, N.Y.C., 1984-92; compt. The Computer Lab., Morrisville, N.C., 1993—. Vol. cmty. tax aide, N.Y.C., 1979-83; tutor Henderson (N.C.) Mid. Sch., 1993-95; vol. Maria Parham Hosp., 1993—, mem. ethics com., 1996—; mem. Henderson-Vance County Human Rels. Commn., 1996—; active Leadership Vance, 1996. Recipient Mitchell-Titus award, 1979. Mem. Am. Assn. Ret. Persons (assoc. dist. coord., instr. tax-aide program North Ctrl. N.C. 1993—, dist. coord.), Henderson Bus. and Profl. Women's Club, Beta Gamma Sigma, Phi Theta Kappa (Mitchell-Titus award 1979). Home: 1614 Peace St Henderson NC 27536-3549 Office: The Computer Lab 2700 Gateway Centre Blvd Morrisville NC 27560-9137

RICHARDSON, ARTEMAS P(ARTRIDGE), landscape architect; b. Phila., May 24, 1918; s. Eugene Stanley and Jessica (Ripple) R.; m. Frederica

McAfee, Sept. 2, 1945; children: Steven, David, Ann, Vida, Stanley. BA in Fine Arts, Williams Coll., 1940; student, Pa. State U., 1940-42; BS in Landscape Architecture, Iowa State U., 1947. Registered landscape architect, Conn., Fla., Md., Mass., Miss., N.Y., Ohio, R.I., Tenn. Asst. landscape architect McCloud & Scatchard, Lilitz, Pa., 1947-48; asst. landscape architect Olmsted Bros., Brookline, Mass., 1949-50, ptnr., 1950-61; ptnr. Olmsted Assocs., Brookline, 1961-64, pres, treas., 1964-80; owner The Olmsted Office, Fremont, N.H., 1980—; lectr. Harvard U., Cambridge, 1961; mem., chair Bd. Registration Landscape Architects, Mass., 1968-77. Illustrator: Trees for Every Purpose, 1980. Mem., chair Planning Bd., Needham, Mass., 1956-62, Conservation Commn., Fremont, 1982—, chair, 1984—; mem. N.H. Gov.'s Task Force on Community Trees, Concord, 1989-91; mem., chair Exeter River Local Adv. Com., 1995—. Lt. USNR, 1942-46, ETO. Fellow Am. Soc. Landscape Architects, Boston Soc. Landscape Architects (pres. 1952-56); mem. N.H. Landscape Assn. (bd. dirs. 1984-87), Granite State Landscape Architects (vice chair 1990-91), Herb Soc. Am. (life), Scarab, Rotary (pres. local club 1965-66, dist. trustee 1968-69, dist. gov. 1970-71, bd. dirs. R.I. 1978-80), Delta Phi, Tau Sigma Delta, Pi Gamma Alpha. Avocations: photography, woodworking, gardening. Home: 106 North Rd Fremont NH 03044-3100 Office: The Olmsted Office 106 North Rd Fremont NH 03044-3100

RICHARDSON, A(RTHUR) LESLIE, former medical group consultant; b. Ramsgate, Kent, Eng., Feb. 21, 1910; s. John William and Emily Lilian (Wilkins) R.; came to U.S., 1930, naturalized, 1937; student spl. courses U. So. Calif., 1933-35; m. B. Kathleen Sargent, Oct. 15, 1937. Mgr., Tower Theater, Los Angeles, 1931-33; accountant Felix-Krueper Co., Los Angeles, 1933-35; indsl. engr. Pettengill, Inc., Los Angeles, 1935-37; purchasing agt. Gen. Petroleum Corp. Los Angeles, 1937-46; adminstr. Beaver Med. Clinic, Redlands, Calif., 1946-72, exec. cons. 1972-75, 95; sec.-treas. Fern Properties, Inc., Redlands, 1955-75, Redelco, Inc., Redlands, 1960-67; pres. Buinco, Inc., Redlands, 1956-65; vice chmn. Redlands adv. bd. Bank of Am., 1973-80; exec. cons. Med. Adminstrs. Calif., 1975-83. Pres., Redlands Area Community Chest, 1953; volunteer exec. Internat. Exec. Service Corps; mem. San Bernardino County (Calif.) Grand Jury, 1952-53. Bd. dirs. Beaver Med. Clinic Found., Redlands, 1961—, sec.-treas., 1961-74, pres., 1974-75, chmn. bd. dirs. 1992—. Served to lt. Med. Adminstrv. Corps., AUS, 1942-45. Recipient Redlands Civic award Elks, 1953. Fellow Am. Coll. Med. Practice Execs. (life, disting. fellow 1980, pres. 1965-66, dir.); mem. Med. Group Mgmt. Assn. (hon. life; mem. nat. long range planning com. 1963-68, pres. western sect. 1960), Kiwanis (pres. 1951), Masons. Episcopalian. Home: 1 Verlie Dr Redlands CA 92373-6943 *Personal philosophy: Do unto others as you would have them do unto you.*

RICHARDSON, ARTHUR WILHELM, lawyer; b. Glendale, Calif., Apr. 3, 1963; s. Douglas Fielding and Leni (Tempelaar-Lietz) R. AB, Occidental Coll., 1985; student, London Sch. Econs., 1983; JD, Harvard U., 1988. Bar: Calif. 1989. Assoc. Morgan, Lewis and Bockius, L.A., 1988-90; staff lawyer U.S. SEC, L.A., 1990-92, br. chief, 1992-96, sr. counsel, 1996—. Mem. ABA, Calif. Bar Assn., L.A. County Bar Assn., Harvard/Radcliffe Club So. Calif., Town Hall Calif., L.A. World Affairs Coun., Sierra Club, Phi Beta Kappa. Presbyterian. Home: 2615 Canada Blvd Apt 208 Glendale CA 91208-2077 Office: US SEC 11th Fl 5670 Wilshire Blvd Fl 11 Los Angeles CA 90036-5679

RICHARDSON, BARBARA HULL, state legislator, social worker; b. Danville, Pa., Sept. 30, 1922; d. Robert Alonzo and Clara Lucille (Woodruff) H.; widowed; children: Barbara Follansbee, Lawrence, Christine, Lovel Pratt. BA, Bryn Mawr Coll., 1944; MSW, Smith Coll., 1973. Social worker child and family svcs. divsn. children and youth svcs. HHS, Keene, N.H., 1969-71; administr. child and family svcs. HHS, Concord, N.H., 1975-88, supr., policy writer, 1988-91; mem. N.H. Ho. Reps., Concord, 1992—. Trustee Meeting Sch., 1980—; bd. dirs. Cheshire Housing Trust, 1986-93, pres., 1993—; adv. bd. Casey Family Svcs. N.H., 1990—; vol. Hospice Monadnock Region, 1991—; mem. community coun. Luth. Social Svcs. New England, 1993—. Democrat. Home: 101 Morgan Rd Richmond NH 03470-4909 Office: NH Ho of Reps State Capitol Concord NH 03301

RICHARDSON, BETTY H., prosecutor; b. Oct. 3, 1953. BA, U. Idaho, 1976; JD, Hastings Coll. Law, 1982. Jud. law clk. Chamber of Idaho Supreme Ct. Justice Robert C. Huntley, Jr., 1984-86; legal rsch. asst. Criminal divsn. San Francisco Superior Ct., 1982-84; teaching asst. Hastings Coll. Law, 1980-82; atty. U.S. Dept. Justice, Boise, Idaho, 1993—; instr. Boise State U., 1987, 89; mem. U.S. Atty. Gen.'s Adv. Com. subcoms. on environ. juvenile justice issues; mem. hon. adv. bd. fro Crime Victims Amendment in Idaho, 1994; mem. Dist. of Idaho Judges and Lawyer Reps. com. and gender fairness com. Mem. Idaho Indsl. Commn., 1991-93, chmn., 1993—; bd. dirs. Parents and Youth Against Drug Abuse; adv. bd. of the Family and Workplace Consortium. Tony Patino fellow Hastings Coll. Law, 1982. Mem. Idaho State Bar Assn. (Pro Bono Svc. award 1988—), Idaho State Prosecuting Attys. Assn. Office: US Attys Office PO Box 32 Boise ID 83707-0032

RICHARDSON, BRUCE LEVOYLE, dentist; b. Corvallis, Oreg., Jan. 28, 1950; s. Richard LeVoyle Richardson and Bonney Willard (Blair) Williams; m. Rhonda Kay Stratton, Sept. ll, 1976; children: Zachary LeVoyle, Nicklis Emery Christopher, Jessica Christine. BS, U. Oreg., 1972; DDS, U. Oreg., Portland, 1977. Pvt. practice Newport, Oreg., 1977—. Chmn. Lincoln County Extension Citizens Adv. Com., 1980-82; trustee Pacific Communities Hosp. Found., 1991; bd. dirs. Lincoln County YMCA, 1983—, chmn. advance gifts campaign, 1984, active current support campaign, 1985, mem. bldg. com., 1985—. Fellow Nat. Acad. Gen. Dentistry (mem. long-range planning coun. 1986-88, mem. ann. meeting coun. 1991—, Mastership award 1987); mem. Oreg. Dental Assn. (mem. ho. dels. 1983-87, trustee 1984-87, v.p. 1987-88, pres. 1989—, Oreg. Young Dentist award 1990), Advanced Periodontic Study Club, Lincoln County Study Club, Newport C. of C., Rotary. Republican. Methodist. Avocations: whitewater rafting, camping, fishing, biking, raising cattle. Home: 333 NW Beaver Valley Dr Seal Rock OR 97376-9523 Office: 123 SE Douglas St Newport OR 97365

RICHARDSON, CAMPBELL, lawyer; b. Woodland, Calif., June 18, 1930; s. George Arthur and Mary (Hall) R.; m. Patricia Packwood, Sept. 3, 1958 (dec. Oct. 1971); children: Catherine, Sarah, Thomas; m. Carol Tamblyn, June 1975 (div. Dec. 1977); m. Susan J. Lienhart, May 3, 1980; 1 child, Laura. AB, Dartmouth Coll., 1952; JD, NYU, 1955. Bar: Oreg. 1955, U.S. Dist. Ct. Oreg. 1957. Ptnr. Stoel Rives LLP, Portland, 1964—. Co-author: Contemporary Trust and Will Forms for Oregon Attorneys; contbr. articles to profl. jours. Mem. Portland/Metro Govt. Boundary Commn., 1976; mem. Oreg. Adv. Com. to U.S. Commn. on Civil Rights, 1976-84; bd. dirs. Ctr. for Urban Edn., Portland, 1980-84, Dorchester Conf., Inc., Bend, Oreg., 1982, Friends of the Zoo, 1993—; chmn. planned giving com. St. Vincent Med. Found., 1988—; planned giving com. Oregon Health Scis. Found., 1994—; trustee Met. Family Svc. Found., 1990—. Served with U.S. Army, 1955-57. Mem. ABA, Oreg. Bar Assn., Multnomah County Bar Assn., Estate Planning Coun. Portland (pres. 1978), Am. Coll. Trust and Estate Counsel, City Club, Multnomah Athletic Club (Portland). Republican. Home: 1500 SW 5th Ave Unit 1701 Portland OR 97201-5430 Office: Stoel Rives LLP 900 SW 5th Ave Ste 2300 Portland OR 97204-1232

RICHARDSON, CHARLES CLIFTON, biochemist, educator; b. Wilson, N.C., May 7, 1935; s. Barney Clifton and Florence Elizabeth (Barefoot) R.; m. Ute Ingrid Hanssum, July 29, 1961; children—Thomas Clifton, Matthew Wilfrid. B.S.M., Duke U., 1959, M.D., 1960; A.M. (hon.), Harvard U., 1967. Intern dept. medicine Duke U., Durham, N.C., 1960-61; postdoctoral fellow dept. biochemistry Stanford U. Med. Sch., Calif., 1961-63; asst. prof. biol. chemistry Harvard Med. Sch., Boston, 1964-67, assoc. prof., 1967-69, prof. biol. chemistry, 1969—, chmn. dept. biol. chemistry, 1978-87, Edward S. Wood prof., 1979—; mem. physiol. chemistry study sect. NIH, 1970-74; mem. Fachbeirat of Max-Planck Inst. für Moleculare Genetik, Berlin, Fed. Republic Germany, 1980-89; mem. sci. adv. com. Genetics Inst., Cambridge, Mass., 1986—; mem. Nat. Bd. Med. Examiners, 1973-76; mem. nucleic acids and protein adv. com., Am. Cancer Soc. Inst., 1975-78; mem. vis. com. Boston Biomed. Rsch. Found., 1985—; assoc. Helicon Found., San Diego, 1983—. Editor: Ann. Rev. Biochemistry, 1983—(assoc. editor 1973-82) ; mem. editorial bd. Jour. Biol. Chemistry, 1968-73, 84-88, Jour. Molecular Biology, 1976-79. Recipient Career Devel. award NIH, 1967-76, Merit award, 1986. Fellow Am. Acad. Arts and Scis., Inst. of Medicine; mem. Nat. Acad. Scis., Am. Chem. Soc. (Eli Lilly Co. biol. chem. award 1968), Am. Soc. Biol. Chemsits (mem. nominating com. 1974-75, 1983-84), Am. Cancer Soc. (coun. for rsch. and clin. investigation 1989-92), Am. Soc. Biochemistry and Molecular Biology (Merck award in biochemistry and molecular biology 1996).

RICHARDSON, CURTIS JOHN, ecology educator; b. Gouverneur, N.Y., July 27, 1944; s. Nilie John and Rose Marie (LaPierre) R.; m. Carol Bartlett, Aug. 22, 1972; children: John, Suzanne. BS in Biology, SUNY, Cortland, 1966; PhD in Ecology, U. Tenn., 1972. Asst. prof. resource ecology Sch. Natural Resources U. Mich., Ann Arbor, 1972-77; asst. prof. plant ecology U. Mich., Biologican Station, Mich., summer 1973; assoc. prof. resource ecology Sch. Forestry and Environ. Studies Duke U., Durham, N.C., 1977-87, prof. resource ecology, 1988—, dir. Wetland Ctr., 1990—; sr. rsch. fellow in applied ecology and forestry U. Edinburgh, Scotland, 1982; mem. sci. adv. bd. Nat. Wetland Rsch. Plan, U.S. EPA, Washington, 1991, chmn. Nat. Wetland EMAP rev. panel, 1992; panel mgr. competitive grants program water quality USDA, Washington, 1990-91. Mem. AAAS, Am. Inst. Biol. Scis., Am. Soc. Agronomy, Ecol. Soc. Am., Soc. Wetland Scientists (v.p. 1986-87, prs. 1987-88, assoc. editor 1987-93). Avocations: jogging, hiking, fishing. Office: Duke U Wetland Ctr Nichols Sch Environ LSRC Research Dr Durham NC 27708-0333 Home: 717 Anderson St Durham NC 27706

RICHARDSON, DANA ROLAND, video producer; b. Mason City, Iowa, Jan. 11, 1945; s. Dana Roland Richardson and Louise Marion (Duke) Sarles; m. Sandra Anderson, June 12, 1966; children: Patricia Nan, Dana Roland, Jr. BS, UCLA, 1966, MBA, 1967. CPA, Calif., N.Y. Staff acct. Arthur Young, L.A., 1967-72, mgr., 1972-76; prin. Arthur Young, N.Y.C., 1976-78; ptnr. Ernst & Young, N.Y.C., 1978-94, Dream Street Prodns., New Canaan, Conn., 1994—. Author: A Manager's Guide to Computer Timesharing, 1975, Audit and Control of Information Systems, 1987. Staff sgt. Reserves USANG, 1967-73. Named one of Techology 100 Top 100 Achievers in Technology in Am., Technology Mag., 1982. Mem. AICPA, Calif. Soc. CPA's. Republican. Episcopalian. Avocations: boating, fishing, music, videography, multimedia. Office: Dream St Prodns PO Box 73 New Canaan CT 06840

RICHARDSON, DANIEL PUTNAM, headmaster, history, economics and criminal law educator; b. Boston, Sept. 17, 1941; s. Frederick Leopold William Jr. and Helen (Warren) R.; m. Patricia Randle, Apr. 6, 1962; children: Daniel P. Jr., Randle Bayard, Mary Elizabeth. BA in Econs. and History, U. Denver, 1965; MEd, Harvard U., 1982. Tchr., dir. ops. Woodstock (Vt.) Country Sch., 1970-73; tchr., asst. headmaster Barlow Sch., Amenia, N.Y., 1975-76; tchr., head of sch. Wykham Rise Sch., Washington, Conn., 1976-80; interim head of sch. St. Michael's Sch., Newport, R.I., 1980-81; tchr., head of upper sch. Tatnall Sch., Wilmington, Del., 1982-87, dir. athletics, 1985-86; tchr., head of sch. Cape Henry Collegiate Sch., Virginia Beach, Va., 1987—; mgr. Gillette Co., 1965-70; pres. Real Estate and Contrn. Co., 1973-75. Treas., bd. dirs. Urban League, Hampton Road, Va., 1990—; treas. Chesapeake Bay Acad.; active NCCJ. Mem. Nat. Assn. Prins. Schs. for Girls, Va. Assn. Ind. Schs. (treas.), Two Dans Discussion Group (co-founder 1991—). Office: Cape Henry Collegiate Sch 1320 Mill Dam Rd Virginia Beach VA 23454-2306

RICHARDSON, DANIEL RALPH, lawyer; b. Pasadena, Calif., Jan. 18, 1945; s. Ralph Claude and Rosemary Clare (Lowery) R.; m. Virginia Ann Lorton, Sept. 4, 1965; children: Brian Daniel, Neil Ryan. BS, Colo. State U., 1969; MBA, St. Mary's Coll. of Calif., 1977; JD, JFK U., 1992. Bar: Calif. Systems engr. Electronic Data Systems, San Francisco, 1972-73; programmer/analyst Wells Fargo Bank, San Francisco, 1973-74; systems analyst Crown-Zellerbach Corp., San Francisco, 1974; programming mgr. Calif. Dental Svc., San Francisco, 1974-75, Fairchild Camera and Inst., Mountain View, Calif., 1975-77; sr. systems analyst Bechtel Corp., San Francisco, 1977; pres. Richardson Software Cons., Inc., San Francisco, 1977—; pvt. practice San Francisco, 1993—; instr. data processing Diablo Valley Coll., Concord, Calif., 1979-80. Author: (book) System Development Life Cycle, 1976, (computer software) The Richardson Automated Agent, 1985. Asst. scoutmaster Boy Scouts Am., Clayton, Calif., 1983-91; soccer coach Am. Youth Soccer League, Clayton, 1978-83. 1st lt. USAF, 1966-72. Mem. ABA, State Bar Calif., Computer Law Assn., Acad. Profl. Cons. and Advisers (cert. profl. cons.), Assn. Systems Mgrs. Avocations: travel, reading, writing, computer repair. Office: 870 Market St Ste 400 San Francisco CA 94102-3010

RICHARDSON, DAVID BACON, writer, journalist; b. Maplewood, N.J., July 13, 1916; s. Percy Bacon and Elizabeth (Jones) R.; m. Ruth Cummings (dec.); children: Hilary C., Julia R. Neilson, Francesca Richardson-Allen; m. Anne Phelan Werner, Oct. 8, 1994. BA, Ind. U., 1940; postgrad. press fellow, Princeton U., 1953-54. Sports reporter Daily Courier, Orange, N.J., 1934-36; mng. editor, editor-in-chief Ind. Daily Student, 1939-40; editorial staff N.Y. Herald Tribune, N.Y.C., 1940-41; combat corres. Yank, The Army Weekly, PTO, CBI, 1942-45; corr. Time Mag., India, 1945-46, Fed. Republic Germany, 1947-50, U.K., 1950-52, Mideast, 1952-53, Mex., 1954-56; bur. chief S.Am. U.S. News & World Report, Buenos Aires, 1959-64; chief domestic news burs. U.S. News & World Report, Washington, 1964-73; chief European corr. U.S. News & World Report, Rome, 1974-81; chief nat. corr. U.S. News & World Report, Washington, 1981-82; freelance writer Washington, 1983—; lectr. in field, 1986—; Ernie Pyle lectr. Ind. U., 1958. Contbr. to books The Best From Yank, 1945, Yank, the GI Story of the War, 1947. V.p., bd. dirs. Iona Sr. Svcs., 1993-96, steering com. Citizens Adv. Coun. Sr. Svcs., 1996—; pres., bd. dirs. Greenbriar Condo., Washington, 1984-87; comms. adviser Samaritan Ministry, 1989-96. Sgn. U.S. Army, 1942-45, CBI. Decorated Legion of Merit, Bronze Star; recipient Valor medal Nat. Headliners Club, Disting. Alumni Svc. award Ind. U.; Cmty. Hero torchbearer Olympic Torch Relay, 1996. Mem. Coun. Fgn. Rels., Washington Inst. Fgn. Affairs, Overseas Writers Assn., Soc. Profl. Journalists, Merrill's Marauders Assn. (mil. liaison officer 1995—), Internat. Combat Camera Assn., Cosmos Club. Episcopalian. Home and Office: #1014 E 4201 Cathedral Ave NW Washington DC 20016-4901

RICHARDSON, DAVID WALTHALL, cardiologic educator, consultant; b. Nanking, China, Mar. 22, 1925; s. Donald William and Virginia (McIlwaine) R.; m. Frances Lee Wingfield, June 12, 1948; children—Donald, Sarah, David. B.S., Davidson Coll., 1947; M.D., Harvard U., 1951. Diplomate Am. Bd. Internal Medicine, Am. Bd. Cardiology. Intern, resident Yale New Haven Hosp., Conn., 1951-53; resident, fellow Med. Coll. Va., Richmond, 1953-56, assoc. prof. to prof. medicine, 1962-95, prof. emeritus, 1995—, chmn. div. cardiology, 1972-87; interim chmn. dept. medicine, 1973-74; chief cardiology, assoc. chief staff for rsch. VA Hosp., Richmond, 1956-61, dir. cardiology tng. program, 1990-95; vis. scientist Oxford U., Eng., 1961-62; vis. prof. U. Milan, Italy, 1972-73. Contbr. articles to profl. jours. Moderator Hanover Presbytery, Presbyterian Ch. U.S., Richmond, 1970; chmn. events com. NHLBI Cardiac Arrhythmia Suppression Trial, 1983-92, NHLBI Anti-Arrhythmics Versus Implantable Defibrillators Trial, 1993-97. Served with USN, 1944-46. Fellow. Am. Coll. Cardiology (gov. VA. 1970-72), Am. Heart Assn. (coun. clin. cardiology and high blood pressure rsch.); mem. Am. Soc. Clin. Investigation, Am. Clin. and Climatol. Assn. Home: 5501 Queensbury Rd Richmond VA 23226-2121

RICHARDSON, DEAN EUGENE, retired banker; b. West Branch, Mich., Dec. 27, 1927; s. Robert F. and Helen (Husted) R.; m. Barbara Trytten, June 14, 1952; children: Ann Elizabeth, John Matthew. AB, Mich. State U., 1950; JD, U. Mich., 1953; postgrad., Stonier Grad. Sch. Banking, 1965. With Indsl. Nat. Bank, Detroit, 1953-55; with Mfrs. Nat. Bank, Detroit, 1955-90; v.p. adminstrn. Mfrs. Nat. Bank, 1964-66, sr. v.p., 1966-67, exec. v.p., 1967-69, pres., 1969-73, chmn. bd. dirs., 1973-89, chmn. exec. com., 1989-90; chmn. bd. Mfrs.-Detroit Internat. Corp., 1973-90; chmn. exec. com. Mfrs. Nat. Bank, 1989-90; bd. dirs. Detroit Edison Co., Tecumseh Products Co., AAA of Mich. Served with USNR, 1945-46. Mem. Mich. Bar Assn., Detroit Bar Assn., Masons, KT, Detroit Athletic Club Country Club Detroit. Episcopalian. Office: Comerica Bank Bldg 20180 Mack Ave Grosse Pointe MI 48236-1836

RICHARDSON, DON ORLAND, agricultural educator; b. Auglaize County, Ohio, May 12, 1934; s. Dana Orland and Mary Isabell (Bowersock) R.; m. Shirley Ann Richardson (div. 1982); children: Daniel, Bradley, Eric, Laura. BS, Ohio State U., 1956, MS, 1957, PhD, 1961. Asst. prof. to prof. U. Tenn., Knoxville, 1963—, head Animal Sci. Dept., 1982-88, dean Agrl. Exptl. Sta., 1988—. Mem. Am. Dairy Sci. Assn., Am. Soc. Animal Sci., Coun. Agrl. Sci. and Tech., Holstein Assn. Am., Rotary Club Knoxville. Office: Tenn Agrl Exptl Sta 103 Morgan Hall PO Box 1071 Knoxville TN 37901-1071

RICHARDSON, DONN CHARLES, business and marketing educator; b. Indpls., Mar. 3, 1940; s. George Covey and Edythe Francis (Chesterfield) R.; m. Carolyn Jean Hassan, Nov. 8, 1969; children: Bradley George, Jason Arthur, Christopher Charles. BA in Journalism and Polit. Sci., Butler U., 1962; MA in Mass Comm., Ohio State U., 1969. Staff editor Cin. Bell Mag. Cin. (Ohio) Bell, 1969-73; mgmt. newsletter editor, spl. projects mgr. US West Comms., Denver, 1973-76; Colo. pub. rels. and outreach dir. US West Comms., Boulder, 1976-84, Colo. employee comm. mgr., 1984-85, market mgr. market planning, 1986-88; fed. govt. market mgr. US West Comms., Englewood, Colo., 1989-94; pres. Richardson Info. Resources, Boulder, Colo., 1994—; cons. Northglenn (Colo.) Recreation Ctr., 1982; presenter in field. Author, pub.: The Quick Consultant's Guide to Public Speaking; contbr. articles to profl. jours. Pres. Shannon Estates Homeowners Assn., Boulder, 1978-80; pub. rels. dir. Boulder (Colo.) Mental Health Ctr. Benefit, 1980; publicity dir. FC Boulder (Colo.) Soccer Club, 1991-94. Capt. USAF, 1963-69. Mem. Internat. Assn. Bus. Communicators (dist. profl. devel. chair 1982-84, chpt. v.p. 1985, internat. pub. rels. chair 1985-86, regional conf. program chair 1996, accredited bus. communicator), Pub. Rels. Soc. Am. (dist. conf. program chair 1996, accreditation judge 1989, accredited pub. rels. profl.). Avocations: youth recreation coaching, traveling. Home: 1212 Cavan St Boulder CO 80303-1602

RICHARDSON, DOT, softball player; b. Sept. 22, 1961. Student, Western Ill. U., UCLA. Ortho. surgeon. Recipient Gold medal Pan. Am. Games, 1979, 87, 95, ISF Women's World Championship, 1986, 94, South Pacific Classic, 1994, Superball Classic, 1995, Atlanta Olympics, 1996, Rev Linda award; named All-Am. Am. Softball Assn., MVP Am. Softball Assn. Major Fast Pitch Nat. Championship, Player of 1980s NCAA. Office: Amateur Softball Assn 2801 NE 50th St Oklahoma City OK 73111-7203

RICHARDSON, DOUGLAS FIELDING, lawyer; b. Glendale, Calif., Mar. 17, 1929; s. James D. and Dorothy (Huskins) R.; m. Leni Tempelaar-Lietz, June 26, 1959; children—Arthur Wilhelm, John Douglas. A.B., UCLA, 1950; J.D., Harvard U., 1953. Bar: Calif. 1953. Assoc. O'Melveny & Myers, Los Angeles, 1953-68, ptnr., 1968-86, of counsel, 1986—. Author: (with others) Drafting Agreements for the Sale of Businesses, 1971, Term Loan Handbook, 1983. Bd. govs. Town Hall of Calif., L.A., 1974-87, sec., 1977, v.p., 1978-79, pres., 1984, mem. adv. coun., 1987—, chmn. sect. on legis. and adminstrn. of justice, 1968-70, pres. Town Hall West, 1975, mem. exec. bd., 1973-93; bd. dirs. Hist. Soc. Calif., 1976-82, pres., 1980-81; bd. dirs. Alliance Francaise de Pasadena, treas., 1993-95. Mem. ABA (com. on devels. in bus. financing, com. state regulation of securities, com. corp. law and acctg., com. employee benefits and exec. compensation of sect corp. banking and bus. law.), Calif. Bar Assn., Los Angeles County Bar Assn. (chmn. com. Law Day 1968, exec. com. comml. law sect. 1974-78, exec. com. corp. law sect. 1975-86), Kiwanis, Phi Beta Kappa. Republican. Presbyterian (elder). Clubs: California, Harvard So. Calif. Home: 1637 Valley View Rd Glendale CA 91202-1340 Office: O'Melveny & Myers 400 S Hope St Los Angeles CA 90071-2801

RICHARDSON, EDWARD R., state agency administrator; b. Pensacola, Fla., Jan. 24, 1939; s. Edward H. and Doria (Parker) R.; m. Nell C.; children: Merit Lynn Richardson Smith, Laura Leigh. BS, Auburn U., 1962, MEd, 1967, EdD, 1972. Sci. tchr. Montgomery Pub. Schs., Montgomery, Ala., 1962-64; prin. Montgomery Pub. Schs., 1967-70, Andalusia High Sch., Andalusia, Ala., 1972-80; asst. prof. Auburn U., Montgomery, 1980-82; supt. Auburn City Schs., Auburn, Ala., 1982-95, state of Ala., Montgomery, 1995—; bd. mem. So. Regional Edn. Bd., Atlanta, 1989—; co-dir. Ala. Mgmt. Inst. Sch. Leaders, Montgomery, 1980-82. Ednl. advisor Gov. Guy Hunt, Montgomery, 1987—; active Landmarks Found., Montgomery, 1968-69. Named Supt. of Yr., State PTA, Montgomery, 1986-87, Educator of Yr., Andalusia Jaycees, 1973-74. Mem. Ala. Assn. Secondary Sch. Adminstrs. (pres. 1978-79), Ala. Assn. Sch. Adminstrs. (pres. 1986-87), Rotary (Auburn chpt. pres. 1987-88), Capitol Lions Club (pres. 1968-69), Phi Delta Kappa (Auburn U. chpt. pres. 1971-72). Republican. Methodist. Avocations: tennis, reading, gardening. Home: 8106 Lichfield Ct Montgomery AL 36117-5124 Office: Ala Dept of Edn 5303 Gordon Persons Bldg PO Box 302101 Montgomery AL 36130-2101*

RICHARDSON, ELLIOT LEE, lawyer; b. Boston, July 20, 1920; s. Edward P. and Clara (Shattuck) R.; m. Anne F. Hazard, Aug. 2, 1952; children: Henry, Nancy, Michael. AB cum laude, Harvard U., 1941, LLB cum laude, 1947, LLD (hon.), 1971; other hon. degrees. Bar: Mass. 1949, D.C. 1980. Law clk. Judge Learned Hand, U.S. Ct. Appeals (2d cir.), N.Y., 1947-48, Supreme Ct. Justice Felix Frankfurter, 1948-49; assoc. Ropes, Gray, Best, Coolidge & Rugg, Boston, 1949-53, 55-56; asst. to Mass. Senator Leverett Saltonstall, 1953-54; acting counsel to Mass. Gov. Christian A. Herter, 1956; asst. sec. legis. HEW, 1957-59; U.S. atty. for Mass., 1959-61, spl. asst. to atty. gen. U.S., 1961; ptnr. Ropes & Gray, Boston, 1961-64; lt. gov. Mass., 1965-67, atty. gen. Mass., 1967-69, under sec. state, 1969-70; sec. HEW, 1970-73; sec. def., 1973, atty. gen. U.S., 1973; fellow Woodrow Wilson Internat. Ctr. for Scholars, Washington, 1974-75; ambassador Ct. St. James's, London, 1975-76; sec. commerce, 1976-77; ambassador-at-large, spl. rep. of pres. Law of Sea Conf., Washington, 1977-80; sr. ptnr. Milbank, Tweed, Hadley & McCloy, Washington, 1980-92; personal rep. SG of UN for Nicaraguan Elections, 1989-90; spl. rep. of Pres. of U.S. for multilateral assistance in The Philippines, 1989-94; bd. dirs. Oak Industries, BNFL Inc.; mem. adv. bd. Am. Flywheel Systems; former dir. John Hancock Life Ins. Co. Author: The Creative Balance, 1976, Reflections of a Radical Moderate, 1996; contbr. numerous articles to profl. jours. and others. Former trustee Radcliffe Coll., Mass. Gen. Hosp.; hon. trustee Roger Tory Peterson Inst.; pres. World Affairs Coun., Boston; dir. Mass. Bay United Fund, past chmn. Greater Boston United Fund Campaign; mem. bd. overseers Harvard Coll.; chmn. overseers com. to visit John F. Kennedy Sch. Govt., Harvard U.; mem. overseers com. to visit Harvard U. Law Sch.; bd. dirs. U.S. Coun. Internat. Bus., Urban Inst.; chmn. Coun. on Ocean Law, Hitachi Found., Japan-Am. Soc. Washington; co-chmn. Nat. Coun., UN Assn. U.S.; chmn. overseers com. to visit Harvard Med. Sch. and Sch. Dental Medicine; vice chmn. Citizens Network Fgn. Affairs; mem. Compt. Gen.'s cons. panel; chmn. quality rev. bd. GAO; mem. adv. com. for commemoration World War II, Dept. Def.; bd. dirs. Am. Acad. Diplomacy. Served to 1st lt. inf. U.S. Army, 1942-45. Decorated Bronze Star, Purple Heart with oak leaf cluster, Lègion d'Honneur; recipient Jefferson award Am. Inst. Pub. Svc., Thomas Hart Benton award Kansas City Art Inst., Emory R. Buckner medal Fed. Bar Coun., Penn Club award, Albert Lasker Spl. Pub. Svc. award, Neptune award, Meritorious Pub. Svc. award USCG, Harry Truman Good Neighbor award, Spkr. Thomas P. O'Neill Jr. award for pub. svc., Sam Rayburn award, F.D. Roosevelt Freedom medal, and other awards. Fellow AAAS, Am. Bar Found., Mass. Bar Found.; mem. ABA, ASPA, D.C. Bar Assn., Mass. Bar Assn., Harvard U. Alumni Assn. (former elected dir.), Coun. on Fgn. Rels., Am. Law Inst., Am. Soc. Internat. Law, Bretton Woods Com., Am. Acad. Diplomacy, Am. Acad. Social Ins., Internat. Law Assn., Nat. Acad. Pub. Adminstrn., Coun. on Excellence in Govt., DAV, VFW, Am. Legion, Alfalfa Club, F Street Club. Office: Milbank Tweed Hadley McCloy 1825 I St NW Ste 1100 Washington DC 20006-5417

RICHARDSON, ELSIE HELEN, retired elementary education educator; b. Vancouver, Wash., Feb. 1, 1918; d. Anthony William and Marie Julia (Dušek) Podhora-Clark; m. Clyde Stanley Richardson, Oct. 16, 1944 (dec. 1989). BA, Cen. Washington Coll. Edn., 1939. Cert. jr. high sch. prin.; cert. life elem. tchr., Calif., life spl. secondary to teach mentally retarded; cert. psychometrist, Calif. Tchr. 2d and 3d grades Randle (Wash.) Sch. Dist., 1939-40; remedial tchr. Randle, 1940-41; 2d grade tchr. Seattle Sch. Dist., 1941-44; remedial tchr., mental testing specialist Vancouver, Wash., 1944-45; tchr. 3rd grade Lancaster (Calif.) Sch. Dist., 1946-48; tchr. spl. edn. Bakersfield (Calif.) Sch. Dist., 1948-49; tchr. 2d grade Norco (Calif.) Sch. Dist., 1950-51; tchr. 4th grade Chino (Calif.) Sch. Dist., 1951-55, tchr. spl. edn., 1955-79, ret., 1979. Leader Girl Res., Camp Rimrock, Wash., summer

1939; leader Bluebird Club, 1939. Recipient Cert. of Appreciaiton, State Assembly of Calif., 1979. Mem. NEA, AAUW, Am. Assn. Ret. Persons, Calif. Tchrs. Assn. (rep.), Calif. Ret. Tchrs. Assn., Vancouver Edn. Assn., Chino Tchrs. Assn. (past v.p., sec.), Wash. State Tchrs. Assn. (rep.), PTA (life), Fun After Fifty Club, Delta Kappa Gamma.

RICHARDSON, EMILIE WHITE, manufacturing company executive, investment company executive, lecturer; b. Chattanooga, July 8; d. Emmett and Mildred Evelyn (Harbin) White; B.A., Wheaton Coll., 1951; 1 dau., Julie Richardson Morphis. With Christy Mfg. Co., Inc., Fayetteville, N.C., 1952—, sec. 1956-66, v.p., 1967-74, exec. v.p., 1975-79, pres., chief exec. officer, 1980—; v.p. E. White Investment Co., 1968-83, pres., 1983—; cons. Aerostatic Industries, 1979—; v.p. Gannon Corp., 1981—; cons. govt. contacts and offshore mfg., 1981—; lectr., speaker in field. Vice pres. public relations Ft. Lauderdale Symphony Soc., 1974-76, v.p. membership, 1976-77, adv. bd., 1978—; active Atlantic Found., Ft. Lauderdale Mus. Art, Beaux Arts, Freedoms Found.; mem. East Broward Women's Republican Club, 1968—, Americanism chmn., 1971-72. Mem. Internat. Platform Assn., Nat. Speakers Assn., Fla. Speakers Assn. Presbyterian. Clubs: Toastmasters, Coral Ridge Yacht Club. Home: 1531 NE 51st St Fort Lauderdale FL 33334-5709 Office: 3311 Fort Bragg Rd Fayetteville NC 28303-4763

RICHARDSON, ERNEST RAY (ROCKY RICHARDSON), housing program supervisor; b. Dermott, Ark., Sept. 5, 1932; s. Louis Jr. and Leila Mae (Purdom) R.; m. Deloris Cobb, Mar. 25, 1955 (div. Apr. 1964); children: Victor Ray, Rodney Lynn, Regenia Ann; stepchildren, Denise Nelson, Darrin Hicks; m. Doretha Tolbert, Apr. 1964 (div. June 1978); m. Shirley Ann Johnson, June 8, 1978; 1 child, Kimberly Ann; stepchildren: Janet, Kay, and Jerome Pate. BA in Bus. Adminstrn., Franklin U., 1975; AA in Real Estate, Parkland Coll., 1980; postgrad., Lewis U., 1980-83; grad., Intergovtl. Mgmt. Tng., 1993, Leadership Modesto, 1996. Cert. real estate broker, Ill. Dir. edn. & tng. Champaign County Opportunities Industrialization Ctr., Champaign, Ill., 1968-70, exec. dir., pers. dir., 1970-73; fin. specialist City of Urbana, Ill., 1975-79; fin. specialist City of Joliet, Ill., 1979-82, dir. neighborhood svcs. divsn., 1982-87; exec. pers. dir. Aurora (Ill.) Housing Authority, 1987-89; housing program supr. City of Modesto, Calif., 1989—; mem. adv. bd. Ctrl. Valley Opportunities Ctr., Inc. Modesto, 1992-96; vice chmn. mgmt. devel. com., City of Modesto, 1993-94, mem. mgmts. continuous improvement com., 1995, 96; alt. Stanislaus County Civil Grand Jury, 1996-97; mem. nat. funds allocation rev. com. Opportunities Industrialization Ctr., 1971-72. Sgt. USAF, 1951-67. Mem. nat. Assn. Real Estate Appraisers (pres.-elect Ill. chpt. 1984-85, pres. Ill. chpt. 1985-86, Ill. chpt. Mem. of the Yr., 1988), Am. Legion, Modesto Kiwanis Club. Avocations: income tax business and real estate appraisal, walking, reading, travel. Home: 309 Yuba Ridge Ln Modesto CA 95354-3369 Office: City of Modesto Ofc Housing/Neighborhoods 940 11th St Modesto CA 95354-2319

RICHARDSON, EVERETT VERN, hydraulic engineer, educator, administrator, consultant; b. Scottsbluff, Nebr., Jan. 5, 1924; s. Thomas Otis and Jean Marie (Everett) R.; m. Billie Ann Kleckner, June 23, 1948; children—Gail Lee, Thomas Everett, Jerry Ray. B.S., Colo. State U., 1949, M.S., 1960, Ph.D., 1965. Registered profl. engr., Colo. Hydraulic engr. U.S. Geol. Survey, Wyo., 1949-52; hydraulic engr. U.S. Geol. Survey, Iowa, 1953-56; rsch. hydraulic engr. U.S. Geol. Survey, Ft. Collins, Colo., 1956-63, project chief, 1963-68; prof. civil engring., adminstr. engring. rsch. ctr. Colo. State U., Ft. Collins, 1968-82, prof. in charge of hydraulic program, 1982-88, prof. civil engring., 1988-94, prof. emeritus, 1994—, dir. hydraulic lab. engring. rsch. ctr., 1982-88, dir. Egypt water use project, 1977-84, dir. Egypt irrigation improvement project, 1985-90; dir. Egypt Water Rsch. Ctr. Egypt Water Rsch. Ctr. Project, Ft. Collins, 1988-89; sr. assoc. Ayers Assocs. Inc. (formerly Resource Cons./Engrs., Inc.), Ft. Collins, Colo., 1989-93, Ayres Assocs., Ft. Collins, Colo., 1994—; dir. Consortium for Internat. Devel., Tucson, Ariz., 1972-87; developer, instr. stream stability and scour at hwy. bridges course for State Dept. Transps. for NHI, FHWA; cons. in field. Sr. author: Highways in the River Environment, Fed. Hwy. Adminstrn., 1975, 90, Evaluating Scour at Bridges, Fed. Hwy. Adminstrn., 1991, 93, 95; contbr. articles to profl. jours., chpts. in books. Mem. Ft. Collins Water Bd., 1969-84; mem. N.Y. State Bridge Safety Assurance Task Force, 1988-91. Decorated Bronze Star, Purple Heart; Combat Infantry Badge, U.S. Govt. fellow MIT, 1962-63. Fellow ASCE (J.S. Stevens award 1961, chair task com., bridge scour rsch. 1990-96, hydraulics divsn. task com. excellence award, 1993, Hans Albert Einstein award 1996); mem. Internat. Congress for Irrigation and Drainage (bd. dirs.), Sigma Xi, Chi Epsilon, Sigma Tau. Home: 824 Gregory Rd Fort Collins CO 80524-1504 Office: Ayres Assocs PO Box 270460 Fort Collins CO 80527-0460

RICHARDSON, FRANK H., retired oil industry executive; b. Mar. 15, 1933. BS, South Dakota Sch. Mines, 1955. With Shell Oil Co., Houston, 1955-93, exec. v.p., 1983-88, pres., CEO, 1988-93. Address: 2001 Kirby Dr Ste 504 Houston TX 77019-6033

RICHARDSON, GRACE ELIZABETH, consumer products company executive; b. Salem, Mass., Nov. 22, 1938; d. George and Julia (Sheridan) R.; m. Ralph B. Henderson, Mar. 3, 1979. B.S., Simmons Coll., 1960; M.S., Cornell U., 1962; M.B.A., NYU, 1981. Textile technologist Harris Research Lab., Washington, 1962-65; instr. Simmons Coll., Boston, 1965-66; dir. consumer edn. materials J.C. Penney, N.Y.C., 1966-73; dir. residential conservation Con Edison, N.Y.C., 1974-81; dir. consumer affairs Chesebrough-Ponds, Greenwich, Conn., 1981-85; v.p. global consumer affairs Colgate Palmolive, N.Y.C., 1985—. Bd. dirs. Cornell Club, N.Y.C., 1989—, chair Simmons Coll. Leadership Coun., 1993-97; com. mem. Julliard Sch., 1996—; bd. dirs. City Vols. Corps, 1996—, SOCAP, 1996—. Named Nat. Bus. Home Economist of Yr., Home Economists in Bus., 1979. Mem. Cornell U. Coun. (chair pub. rels. com. 1988—), Nat. Coalition Consumer Edn. (bd. dirs. 1983-93), Women's Forum. Home: 180 E 79th St New York NY 10021 Office: Colgate Palmolive Co 300 Park Ave New York NY 10022-7402

RICHARDSON, HERBERT HEATH, mechanical engineer, educator, institute director; b. Lynn, Mass., Sept. 24, 1930; s. Walter Blake and Isabel Emily (Heath) R.; m. Barbara Ellsworth, Oct. 6, 1973. SB, SM with honors, MIT, 1955, ScD, 1958. Registered profl. engr., Mass., Tex. Research asst., research engr. Dynamic Analysis and Control Lab. MIT, 1953-57, instr. Dept. Mech. Engring., 1957-58, mem. faculty, 1958-84, prof. mech. engring., 1968-85, head dept., 1974-82, assoc. dean engring., 1982-84; Disting. prof. engring. Tex. A&M U., 1984—; Regents prof. Tex. A&M U. System, College Station, 1993—; dean, vice chancellor engring. Tex. A&M U. Sys., 1984-85; dep. chancellor, dean, dir. Tex. Engring. Expt. Sta. Tex. A&M U., 1985-91; chancellor Tex. A&M U. System, College Station, 1991-93, assoc. vice chancellor engring., 1993—, assoc. dean engring., 1993—; dir. Tex. Trans. Inst., Tex. A&M Univ. Sys., 1993—; with Ballistics Rsch. Lab. Abderdeen Proving Ground, Md., 1958; chief scientist U.S. Dept. Transp., 1970-72; bd. dirs. Foster-Miller Inc., Mass., Ten X Inc., Tex. Utilities Co.; chmn. adv. com. for engring. NSF, 1987-89, adv. com. basic energy scis. U.S. Dept. Energy, 1987-91. Author: Introduction to System Dynamics, 1971; contbr. articles to profl. publs. Trustee S.W. Rsch. Inst. Officer U.S. Army, 1968. Recipient medal Am. Ordnance Assn., 1953, Gold medal Pi Tau Sigma, 1963, Meritorious Service award and medal Dept. Transp., 1972. Fellow AAAS, ASME (Moody award fluid engring. divsn. 1970, Centennial medallion 1983, Rufus Oldenberger medal 1984, Meritorious Svc. medal 1986, Disting. Svc. award 1986, hon. mem. 1987); mem. NAE (coun. 1986-92, com. on engring. edn.), Am. Soc. Engring. Edn. (Disting. Svc. medal 1993, Lamme award 1997), N.Y. Acad. Sci., Inst. Transp. Engrs., Nat. Rsch. Coun. (gov. bd. 1986-92, chmn. transp. rsch. bd. 1988-89), Sigma Xi, Tau Beta Pi. Office: Tex A&M U Sys CE TTI Bldg MS 3135 College Station TX 77843-3135

RICHARDSON, IRENE M., health facility administrator; b. Columbia, Tenn., Oct. 22, 1938; d. John Frank and Beatrice (Hill) Murphy; m. Joseph Richardson, Dec. 27, 1960; children: Pamela, Joseph, John, Karen. BS, Ramapo Coll., Mahwah, N.J., 1981; MBA, Farleigh Dickinson U., 1987; nursing diploma summa cum laude, St. Thomas Sch. of Nursing, Nashville, 1959. RN, N.J.; cert. sr. profl. in human resources. Clin. instr. St. Thomas Hosp., Nashville; coord. edn., staff nurse St. Clare's Hosp., Denville, N.J.; pres. Cygnus Assocs., Inc., Kinnelon, N.J., 1986-95; dir. edn. and tng. Northwest Covenant Med. Ctr. (formerly St. Clares Riverside), Denville, N.J., 1995—. Author: RN Job Satisfaction. Recipient U.S. Pub. Health Svc. scholarship. Mem. Am. Soc. for Health Care Edn. and Tng., Soc. for Health Care Edn. and Tng. N.J. (bd. dirs.), Women's Svc. Orgn. (pres. 1995-96). Home: 65 Fayson Lake Rd Kinnelon NJ 07405-3129

RICHARDSON, JANE, librarian; b. Sept. 16, 1946; d. Robert Clark and Evagene (Davis) Richardson; m. Frank Velasques Martinez Jr., May 28, 1966 (div. July 1970); 1 child, Robert Louis Martinez; m. William John Lorance, Feb. 14, 1983 (div. 1996). BA in History, U. Wyo., 1971; MLibr, U. Wash., 1972. Reference and fine arts libr. Clark County Libr., 1973; dept. head Clark County Libr. Dist., 1974-77; br. supr./adminstr. Newport Beach (Calif.) Pub. Libr., 1978-82; on-call libr. Santa Ana and Newport Beach Pub. Librs., Calif. State U., Fullerton, 1984; br. adminstr. Las Vegas-Clark County Libr. Dist., 1985—. Mem. Freedom to Read Found. Mem. ALA, Popular Culture Assn., Nev. Libr. Assn., Mountain Plains Libr. Assn., So. Calif. On-Line Users Group, Newport Beach Profl. and Tech. Employees Assn. Office: Las Vegas-Clark County Libr 833 Las Vegas Blvd N Las Vegas NV 89101-2030

RICHARDSON, JOHN, retired international relations executive; b. Boston, Feb. 4, 1921; s. John and Hope (Hemenway) R.; m. Thelma Ingram, Jan. 19, 1945; children: Eva Selek Teleki, Teren de Cossy, Hope Gravelly, Catherine Munch, Hetty L. A.B., Harvard U., 1943, J.D., 1949. Bar: N.Y. 1949. Assoc. Sullivan & Cromwell, N.Y.C., 1949-55; with Paine, Webber, Jackson & Curtis, N.Y.C., 1955-69, gen. ptnr., 1958-61, ltd. ptnr., 1961-69; pres., chief exec. officer Free Europe, Inc. (Radio Free Europe), 1961-68; asst. sec. for edn1. and cultural affairs Dept. State, 1969-77, also acting asst. sec. state for pub. affairs, 1971-73; exec. dir. for social policy Ctr. for Strategic and Internat. Studies; research prof. internat. communication Sch. Fgn. Service, Georgetown U., Washington, 1977-78; pres., chief exec. officer Youth for Understanding, Inc., 1978-86, bd. dirs., 1986—, vice chmn., 1989—; counselor U.S. Inst. of Peace, 1987-90; spl. advisor Aspen Inst. Humanistic Studies, 1977-80. Mem. Coun. Fgn. Rels., 1957—, Citizens Commn. on S.E. Asian Refugees, 1978—; founder Polish Med. Aid Project, 1957-61; cofounder, chmn. bd. Am. Com. to Aid Poland, 1989-95; pres. Internat. Rescue Com., 1960-61, bd. dirs., 1958-61, 78—; chmn. N.Y.C. Met. Mission United Ch. of Christ, 1966-69, Am. Coun. for UN U., 1977-87, Consortium for Internat. Citizens Exch., 1980-84; bd. dirs. Coun. for Advancement of Citizenship, 1991—, Delphi Internat., 1991—, chmn., 1995—, Freedom House, 1963-69, pres., 1977-84; chmn. Nat. Endowment for Democracy, 1984-88, 91-92, bd. dirs., 1984-92, chmn. emeritus, 1992—; bd. dirs. Kennedy Ctr. for Performing Arts, 1970-77, Inter-Am. Found., 1970-77, East-West Ctr., 1975-77, Fgn. Policy Assn., 1958-68, 77-86, Japan-U.S. Friendship Commn., 1976-77, Am. Forum, 1977—, Social Sci. Found., U. Denver, 1992—, Meridian House Internat., 1978-83, Atlantic Coun. U.S., 1982-84, Fgn. Student Svc. Coun., 1978-82. With U.S. Army, World War II. Decorated Bronze Star with v device, Order of the Sacred Treasure, Gold and Silver Star, Japan; Commdr.'s. Cross, Order of Merit Fed. Republic Germany. Home: # 1104 9707 Old George Town Rd Bethesda MD 20814-1727

RICHARDSON, JOHN CARROLL, lawyer, tax legislative consultant; b. Mobile, Ala., May 3, 1932; s. Robert Felder and Louise (Simmons) R.; m. Cicely Tomlinson, July 27, 1961; children: Nancy Louise, Robert Felder III, Leslie. BA, Tulane U., 1954; LLB cum laude, Harvard U., 1960. Bar: Colo. 1960, N.Y. 1965, D.C. 1972. Assoc. Holland & Hart, Denver, 1960-64; legal v.p. Hoover Worldwide Corp., N.Y.C., 1964-69; v.p., gen. counsel Continental Investment Corp., Boston, 1969; dep. tax legis. counsel U.S. Dept. Treasury, Washington, 1970-71, tax legis. counsel, 1972-73; ptnr. Brown, Wood, Ivey, Mitchell & Petty, N.Y.C., 1973-79, LeBoeuf, Lamb, Leiby & MacRae, N.Y.C., 1979-88, Morgan, Lewis & Bockius, N.Y.C., 1988-93; ret., 1993; tax legis. cons., Orford, N.H., 1993—; adj. prof. Law Sch. Fordham U., 1990-94. Served to lt. comdr. USN, 1954-57. Mem. ABA (chmn. com. adminstrv. practice tax sect. 1984-86), N.Y. State Bar Assn. (exec. com. tax sect. 1975-84), D.C. Bar Assn., Am. Coll. Tax Counsel, N.Y. Athletic Club, Royal Automobile Club.

RICHARDSON, JOHN EDMON, marketing educator; b. Whittier, Calif., Oct. 22, 1942; s. John Edmon and Mildred Alice (Miller) R.; m. Dianne Elaine Ewald, July 15, 1967; 1 child, Sara Beth. BS, Calif. State U., Long Beach, 1964; MBA, U. So. Calif., 1966; MDiv, Fuller Theol. Sem., 1969, D of Ministry, 1981. Assoc. prof. mgmt. Sch. Bus. and Mgmt. Pepperdine U., Malibu, Calif., 1969—. Author: (leader's guides) Caring Enough to Confront, 1984, The Measure of a Man, 1985; editor: Ann. Editions: Marketing, 1987—, Bus. Ethics, 1990—. Lay counselor La Canada (Calif.) Presbyn. Ch., 1978-84, mem. lay counseling task force, 1982-84. Mem. Am. Mgmt. Assn., Soc. Bus. Ethics, Christian Writers Guild, Fuller Sem. Alumni Cabinet (pres. 1982-85), Am. Mktg. Assn., Beta Gamma Sigma. Avocations: fishing, woodworking, tennis, photography. Office: Pepperdine U Sch Bus and Mgmt 400 Corporate Pt Culver City CA 90230-7615

RICHARDSON, JOHN MACLAREN, JR., school superintendent; b. Plainfield, N.J., Nov. 6, 1942; s. John MacLaren and Lucy Lenox (Baker) R.; m. Sharon Rae Kellogg, June 20, 1964; children: Elizabeth R. Updike, John M. III, James Kellogg. AA, George Washington U., 1965, BA, 1969; MA, Grace Theol. Sem., 1993. Bus. mgr. ComMission, Inc., Harrisonburg, Va., 1983-84; cons. in human resources/edn., 1980-88; prin. The Norman A. Whitesel Christian Sch., Mt. Crawford, Va., 1988-90; supt., founding mem. Blue Ridge Christian Sch., Bridgewater, Va., 1990—; bd. dirs. Trinity Christian Sch., Mt. Crawford, Va., 1985-88. Elder Grace Covenant Ch., Harrisonburg, 1988-92, 97—. With USN, 1962-66, lt. comdr. USNR, 1966-80. Decorated Nat. Def. medal, USN, 1964, Navy Good Conduct medal, USN, 1966, Armed Forces Reserve medal, USN, 1976. Mem. Internat. Fellowship Christian Sch. Adminstrs., Naval Res. Assn., Res. Officers Assn., Am. Legion, Rotary Internat. Republican. Home: 310 Broad St Bridgewater VA 22812-1718 Office: Blue Ridge Christian Sch PO Box 207 100 Dinkel Ave Bridgewater VA 22812-0207 *I am convinced that an education which is not based upon the unchanging truth of the Holy Bible is, at best, irrelevant and, at worst, entirely misleading and without legitimate foundation.*

RICHARDSON, JOHN THOMAS, academic administrator, clergyman; b. Dallas, Dec. 20, 1923; s. Patrick and Mary (Walsh) R. B.A., St. Mary's Sem., Perryville, Mo., 1946; S.T.D., Angelicum U., Rome, Italy, 1951; M.A., St. Louis U., 1954. Prof. theology, dean studies Kenrick Sem., St. Louis, 1951-54; lectr. Webster Coll., 1954; dean Grad. Sch. DePaul U., Chgo., 1954-60, exec. v.p., dean faculties, 1960-81, pres., 1981-93; prof. DePaul U. Coll. Law, Chgo., 1955; chancellor DePaul U., Chgo., 1993—. Trustee DePaul U., Chgo., 1954—. Home: 2233 N Kenmore Ave Chicago IL 60614-3504 Office: De Paul U 1 E Jackson Blvd Chicago IL 60604-2201

RICHARDSON, JOHN VINSON, JR., library science educator; b. Columbus, Ohio, Dec. 27, 1949; s. John Vinson Sr. and Hope Irene (Smith) R.; m. Nancy Lee Brown, Aug. 22, 1971. BA, Ohio State U., 1971; MLS, Vanderbilt U., 1972; PhD, Ind. U., 1978. Asst. prof. UCLA, 1978-83, assoc. prof., 1983—, editor The Libr. Quar., 1994—; faculty coord. UCLA-St. Petersburg State Acad. of Culture Exch. Program, 1996—; fellow advanced rsch. Inst. U. Ill., 1991; pres. Info. Transfer, Inglewood, Calif., 1988—; mem. editl. bd. Ref. Svcs. Rev., Ann Arbor, Mich., 1991—, Jour. Govt. Info., Oxford, Eng., 1975—, Index to Current Urban Documents, Westport, Conn., 1987—, U. Calif. Press Catalogues and Bibliographies series, 1993—; vis. fellow Charles Stuart U. NSW Australia, 1990; vis. scholar ALISE Russia Project, St. Petersburg and Moscow, 1996; vis. disting. scholar OCLC Inc., Dublin, Ohio, 1996-97; chmn. Calif. Pacific Ann. Conf. Com. on Archives and History, 1992-96; Henderson lectr. U. N.C., Chapel Hill, 1997. Author: Spirit of Inquiry, 1982, Gospel of Scholarship, 1992, Knowledge-based Systems for General Reference Work, 1995; editor elect The Libr. Quar., 1994-95, editor, 1995—. Mem. UCLA Grad. Coun., 1992-96, chair, 1995-96; mem. U. Calif. systemwide coord. com. on grad. affairs, 1993-96; pres. Wesley Found., L.A., 1981-87; lay del. Cal-Pac Conf. United Meth. Ch., 1985, 86, 92-96, chair conf. commn. on archives and history, 1992—96. Rsch. grantee Coun. on Libr. Resources, 1985, 90, Assn. Libr. and Info. Sci. Educators rsch. grantee, 1984, 87; Harold Lancour scholar Beta Phi Mu, 1986; recipient Louise Maxwell award Ind. U. Alumni Assn., 1995. Mem. ALA (Justin Winsor prize 1990, Ref. and Adult Svcs. divsn. Outstanding Paper award 1992), AAAS, Assn. Libr. and Info. Sci. Educators (rsch. paper prize 1986, 91), Am. Soc. for Info. Sci. (Best Info. Sci. book 1995), Am. Statis. Assn., Sigma Xi. Democrat. Avocations: wine tasting,reading, fgn. travel, lilac point Siamese. Office: UCLA GSE&IS/DLIS PO Box 951520 300 Circle Dr N Ste 204 Los Angeles CA 90095-1520 *By our common action, we can bend the flow of history.*

RICHARDSON, JOSEPH BLANCET, former biology educator, educational facilities planning consultant; b. Louisville, Nov. 12, 1936; s. Orla Coburn and Alma (Mason) R. m. Mary Irene Murphy, Dec. 27, 1960; children: Pamela, Joseph Blancet Jr., John, Karen. BSCE, The Citadel, 1958; BA with high honors in Zoology, Rutgers U., 1973, PhD in Zoology, 1979; MS in Anatomy, N.Y. Med. Coll., 1975. Design engr. Ky. Hwy. Dept., 1958-59; tech. rep. Shell Oil Co., Balt., 1968-72; asst. prof. biology Ramapo Coll., Mahwah, N.J., 1976-80, program coord. for biology, 1979-80, asst. dir. campus planning, 1980-82, dir. campus planning, 1982-86; pres. Richardson Recreational Svcs., Inc., Kinnelon, N.J., 1981-88, Whitehall Assocs., Inc., Kinnelon, 1986—. Dir. recreational water testing programs Kinnelon Environ. Commn., 1977-82; trustee Kinnelon (N.J.) Bd. Edn., 1989-94; pres. Morris County Ednl. Svcs. Commn., 1991-92; deacon Our Lady of the Magnificat Roman Cath. Ch., Kinnnelon, N.J. Capt. U.S. Army, 1959-68, Vietnam. Mem. N.J. Sch. Bds. Assn., N.J. Assn. Sch. Bus. Adminstrs., N.J. Assn. Sch. Bus. Ofcls., Soc. Am. Mil. Engrs. (treas. N.J. post 1988-90), The Citadel Alumni Assn., Rutgers U. Alumni Assn., N.Y. Med. Coll. Alumni Assn., N.Y. Acad. Sci., Coun. Ednl. Facility Planners, Sigma Xi. Republican. Home and Office: 65 Fayson Lake Rd Kinnelon NJ 07405-3129

RICHARDSON, JOSEPH HILL, physician, medical educator; b. Rensselaer, Ind., June 16, 1928; s. William Clark and Vera (Hill) R.; m. Joan Grace Meininger, July 8, 1950; children: Lois N., Ellen M., James K. MS in Medicine Northwestern U., 1950, MD, 1953. Intern, U.S. Naval Hosp., Great Lakes, Ill., 1953-54; fellow in medicine Cleve. Clinic, 1956-59; individual practice medicine specializing in internal medicine and hematology, Marion, Ind., 1959-67, Ft. Wayne, Ind., 1967—; assoc. clin. prof. medicine, Ind. U. Sch. Medicine, 1993—; med. dir. emeritus The Med. Protective Co., Ft. Wayne, 1995—. Served to lt. MC USNR, 1953-56. Diplomate Am. Bd. Internal Medicine. Fellow ACP, AAAS; mem. AMA, Masons. Contbr. articles to med. jours. Home and Office: 8726 Fortuna Way Fort Wayne IN 46815-5725

RICHARDSON, KENNETH T., JR., psychotherapist, consultant, educator, author; b. Santa Monica, Calif., Sept. 16, 1948; s. Kenneth T. Richardson and Florence (Wheeler) Neal; m. Mary L. Nutter, Dec. 31, 1983; children: Kenneth T. III, Russell A., Shad Martin, Cheralyn Martin. BA, Prescott (Ariz.) Coll., 1985; postgrad., Antioch (Ohio) Coll., 1987-88. Cert. addictions counselor, Ariz.; nat. cert. NCRC/ADOA. Program dir. Calvary Rehab. Ctr., Phoenix, 1979-82; clin. dir. Friendship House Comprehensive Recovery Ctr., San Francisco, 1982-84; dir. treatment The Meadows, Wickenburg, Ariz., 1984-87; co-founder, dir. The Orion Found., Phoenix, 1989—; owner, dir. Phoenix Cons. and Counseling Assocs., 1987—; cons. Addictions Svcs., The Hopi Tribe, Kykotsmoni, Ariz., 1989—, Baywood Hosp., Houston, 1988-89; advisor Nat. Coun. on Co-Dependence, Phoenix, 1990—, Recourse Found., Phoenix, 1989-93; faculty instr. Rio Salado C.C., Phoenix, 1987-90, The Recovery Source, Houston, 1989-90; co-chair Nat. Conv. of Men., Relationships and Recovery, Phoenix, 1990, 91. Creator, presenter audiotape series: Codependence and the Development of Addictions, 1991, Your Spiritual Self: The Child Within, 1991, Relationship Recovery, 1992, Men's Sexuality and Relationships, 1993-96, Body Mind and Spirit, 1994-96; creator edn. and support materials related to addictions, relationships and family sys., 1987—. Mem. Nat. Assn. Alcoholism and Drug Counselors, Am. Counseling Assn., Internat. Certification Reciprocity Consortium.

RICHARDSON, LAUREL WALUM, sociology educator; b. Chgo., July 15, 1938; d. Tyrrell Alexander and Rose (Foreman) R.; m. Herb Walum, Dec. 27, 1959 (div. 1972); children: Benjamin, Joshua; m. Ernest Lockridge, Dec. 12, 1981. AB, U. Chgo., 1955, BA, 1956; PhD, U. Colo., 1963. Asst. prof. Calif. State U., Los Angeles, 1962-64; postdoctoral fellow Sch. Medicine Ohio State U., Columbus, 1964-65, asst. prof. sociology, 1970-75, assoc. prof., 1975-79; prof. sociology Sch. Medicine Ohio State U., Columbus, 1979—; prof. cultural studies, edn. policy and leadership Sch. Medicine Ohio State U.; asst. prof. sociology Denison U., Granville, Ohio, 1965-69; mem. editorial bd. Jour. Contemporary Ethnography, Symbolic Interaction, Gender & Soc., Qualitative Sociology, The Sociol. Quar. Author: Dynamics of Sex and Gender, 1977, 3d edit. 1988, The New Other Woman, 1985, Die Neve Andere, 1987, A Nova Outra Mulher, 1987, Writing Strategies: Reaching Diverse Audiences, 1990, Gender and University Teaching: A Negotiated Difference, 1995; editor: Feminist Frontiers, 1983, 4th edit., 1997, Fields of Play Constructing and Academic Life, 1997; author more that 100 rsch. articles and papers. Ford Found. fellow, 1954-56; NSF dissertation fellow, 1960-62; post doctoral fellow Vocat. Rehab., Columbus, 1964; grantee Ohio Dept. Health, 1986-87, Nat. Inst. Edn., 1981-82, NIMH, 1972-74, NSF, 1963-64, NEH, 1992; recipient Disting. Affirmative Action award Ohio State U., 1983. Mem. Am. Sociol. Assn. (com. on coms. 1980-81, com. on pub. info. 1987—), North Ctrl. Sociol. Assn. (pres. 1986-87), Sociologists for Women in Soc. (coun. mem. 1978-80), Ctrl. Ohio Sociologists for Women in Soc. (past pres.), Women's Poetry Workshop, Soc. for Study of Symbolic Interaction (publs. com.). Democrat. Avocations: hiking, poetry, reading, antiques. Office: Ohio State Univ Dept of Sociology 190 N Oval Mall Columbus OH 43210-1321

RICHARDSON, LAWRENCE, JR., Latin language educator, archeologist; b. Altoona, Pa., Dec. 2, 1920; married. B.A., Yale U., 1942, Ph.D. in Classics, 1952. Instr. classics Yale U., New Haven, 1946-47, instr. to assoc. prof., 1955-66; prof. Duke U., Durham, N.C., 1966-78, James B. Duke prof. Latin, 1978-91, prof. emeritus, 1991—; field archeologist Am. Acad. Rome, 1952-55, Mellon prof., 1980-81; mem. Inst. Advanced Study, 1967-68. Author: Pompeii: An Architectural History, 1988, A New Topographical Dictionary of Ancient Rome, 1992; contbr. articles to profl. jours. Guggenheim fellow, 1958-59; Am. Council Learned Socs. fellow, 1967-68, 72-73; NEH fellow, 1979-80. Mem. German Archeol. Inst. (corr.), Am. Philol. Assn., Archeol. Inst. Am. Office: Duke U West Campus Dept Classical Studies Durham NC 27708

RICHARDSON, MARGARET MILNER, federal agency administrator, lawyer; b. Waco, Tex., May 14, 1943; d. James W. and Margaret Wiebusch Milner; m. John L. Richardson, July 22, 1967; 1 child, Margaret Lawrence. AB in Polit. Sci., Vassar Coll., 1965; JD with honors, George Washington U., 1968. Bar: Va. 1968, D.C. 1968, U.S. Dist. Ct. D.C. 1968, U.S. Ct. Appeals (4th, 5th, D.C. and Fed. cirs.) 1968, U.S. Claims Ct. 1969, U.S. Tax Ct. 1970, U.S. Supreme Ct. 1971. Clk. U.S. Ct. Claims, Washington; with Office Chief Counsel IRS, Washington, 1969-77; with Sutherland, Asbill and Brennan, Washington, 1977-80, ptnr., 1980-93; commr. IRS, Washington, 1993—; mem. commr.'s adv. group IRS, 1988-90, chair, 1990; mem. fed. tax adv. group Prentice Hall. Contbr. articles to profl. jours. Assisted Clinton 1992 gen. election campaign; served as team leader Justice Dept./Civil Rights Cluster during Presdl. Transition. Mem. ABA, D.C. Bar Assn. (tax sect.), Va. State Bar Assn., Fed. Bar Assn. (coun. taxation), Fin. Women's Assn. N.Y. Avocations: foreign travel, collecting antiques, needlepoint, gardening. Office: IRS 1111 Constitution Ave NW Washington DC 20224-0001

RICHARDSON, MARK, state legislator; b. Poplar Bluff, Mar. 19, 1952; married; children: Todd, Chris, Megan. BA in Polit. Sci. and History, S.E. Mo. State U., MA in Psychology; JD, Memphis State U., 1980. City atty. City of Poplar Bluff, 1984-86; asst. prosecuting atty. City of Butler County, 1980-86; sr. ptnr. Richardson and Duncan; rep. Mo. Ho. of Reps., 1990—; minority fl. leader Mo. Ho. of Reps., 1994; mem. follow ho. coms. accounts, ops. and fin., join com. on wetlands, judiciary and ethics, rules, join rules, bill perfected and printed, workers compensation; mem. govs. standing com. on job tng. and work force readiness, 1993—, mem. Rep. caucus com. for higher edn., policy devel. com. Rep. campaign com., mem. statewide bldg. code com., 1994—; bd. dirs. Mo. First Vote Program; del. Am. Coun. of Young Polit. Leaders to Austria and Hungary, 1992; ACYPL task force to the Pacific Mantle Countries of Sinapore, Thailand and South Korea. Scoutmaster Boy Scout Troop #166; elder, bd. dirs. First Christian Ch., Poplar Bluff; former pres. bd. Local Shelter Workshop, March of Dimes, Poplar Bluff H.S. task force on drug abuse. Recipient Award of Merit Boy

Scouts Am., 1990; named Outstanding Young Men, 1981. Office: Minority Fl Leader House of Reps Rm 204 Jefferson MO 65101

RICHARDSON, MARY LOU, psychotherapist; b. Topeka, Oct. 4, 1953; d. Darrell and Beverly Nutter; m. Kenneth T Richardson Jr. children: Shad Martin, Cheralyn Pasbrig, Kenneth T Richardson III, Russ Richardson. Cert. behavioral health examiner, addictions counselor, Ariz.; cert. Nat. Assn. of Alcolism and Drug Abuse Counselors. Counselor Compcare Alcoholism Ctr. The Meadows Treatment Ctr., Phoenix, 1986-88; co-dir. Phoenix Cons. & Counseling Assocs., Ariz., 1989—; founder and adminstr. The Orion Found., Ariz.; project mem. The Hutoomkhum Com. and Support Program, Hopi Reservation, Ariz.; cons. Baywood Hosp., 1988-89; faculty instr. The Recovery Source, 1989-90; chair Nat. Conv. Women, 1992. Author: Women's Acts of Power, 1991-93, Relationship Recover, 1992—, Women's Empowerment, 1992—, Body, Mind & Spirit, 1994—. Mem. Am. Mental Health Counselors, Am. Counseling Assn., Nat. Assn. Alcoholism & Drug Abuse Counselors, Nat. Reciprocity Consortium. Avocations: writing, sculpting, dancing. Office: Phoenix Cons & Counseling Assocs 5333 N 7th St Ste A202 Phoenix AZ 85014-2821

RICHARDSON, MAURICE M., manufacturing executive; b. 1933. Pres., CEO Engraph Inc. (now Sonoco Engraph), Atlanta, 1983—; now pres., ceo. Office: Sonoco Engraph 2635 Century Pkwy NE Atlanta GA 30345-3112

RICHARDSON, NATASHA JANE, actress; b. May 11, 1963; d. Tony Richardson and Vanessa Redgrave; m. Liam Neeson, July 3, 1994; children: Micheal Richard Antonio, Daniel Jack. Acting debut on stage at Leeds (England) Playhouse, 1983; appearances include (plays) A Midsummer's Night Dream, Hamlet, 1985, The Seagull, 1985, High Society, 1987, Anna Christie, 1993, (Tony award nominee 1993, Drama Desk award), (TV) In a Secret State, 1984, The Copper Beaches, 1984, Ghosts, 1986, Suddenly Last Summer, 1992, Hostages, 1993, Zelda, 1993, (Cable Ace nomination), (films) Every Picture Tells a Story, 1984, Gothic, 1987, A Month in the Country, 1987, Patty Hearst, 1988, Fat Man and Little Boy, 1989, The Handmaid's Tale, 1990, The Comfort of Strangers, 1991, The Favor, The Watch and the Very Big Fish, 1992, Past Midnight, Widow's Peak, 1994, (Best Actress Karlovy Vary), Nell, 1995, The Parent Trap, 1997. Recipient Most Promising Newcomer award Plays & Players, 1986; named Best Actress by London Theatre Critics, Plays & Players, 1990, Evening Standard Best Actress, 1990.

RICHARDSON, NOLAN, university athletic coach. Head coach U. Arkansas Razorbacks, 1985—. Coach NCAA championship team 1994, NCAA 2nd place team, 1995; recipient Naismith award for Best NCAA Divsn. IA coach, 1994. Office: Univ Arkansas Broyles Athletic Ctr Fayetteville AR 72701*

RICHARDSON, PETER DAMIAN, mechanical engineering educator; b. West Wickham, Eng., Aug. 22, 1935; came to U.S., 1958; s. Reginald W. and Marie S. (Ouseley) R. B.Sc. in Engring, Imperial Coll., U. London, 1955, A.C.G.I., 1955, Ph.D. (Unwin scholar), 1958, D.I.C., 1958; D.Sc. in Engring, U. London, 1974, D.Sc. in Physiology, 1983. Demonstrator dept. mech. engring. Imperial Coll., U. London, 1955-58; vis. lectr. Brown U., Providence, 1958-59; research asso. Brown U., 1959-60, asst. prof. engring., 1960-65, asso. prof., 1965-68, prof., 1968-84, prof. engring. and physiology, 1984—, chmn. faculty, 1987-88; chmn. exec. com. Center Biomed. Engring., 1972—; cons. to industry, U.S. govt. agys; on leave at U. London, 1967, U. Paris, 1968, Orta Dogu Teknik Universitesi, Ankara, Turkey, 1969, Medizinischen Fakultat, RWTH, Aachen, Germany, 1976, U. Paris XIII, 1991. Co-author: Principles of Cell Adhesion, 1995; contbr. articles to profl. pubs. Recipient Sr. Scientist award Alexander Von Humboldt Found., 1976; named Laureate in Medicine, Jung Found., 1987. Fellow ASME, Royal Soc., Am. Inst. Med. Biol. Engring.; mem. Am. Soc. Engring. Edn., Am. Soc. Artificial Internal Organs (past assoc. editor jour.), European Soc. Artificial Organs., Biomed. Engring. Soc. Office: Brown U Box D 79 Waterman St Providence RI 02912-9104

RICHARDSON, RALPH HERMAN, lawyer; b. Detroit, Oct. 12, 1935; s. Ralph Onazime and Lucinda Ollie (Fluence) R.; m. Arvie Y., June 1, 1956 (div. 1961); children: Cassandra, Tanya, Arvie Lynn; m. Julia A., Sept. 16, 1962 (div. 1982); children: Traci, Theron. BA, Wayne State U., 1964, JD, 1970. Bar: Mich., U.S. Ct. Appeals (6th cir.), Supreme Ct. U.S., 1970. Postal transp. clk. U.S. P. O., Detroit, 1954-56; clk. pub. aid worker City Detroit, 1956-65; sr. labor relations rep. Ford Motor Co., Ypsilanti, Mich., 1965-70, wage admins., 1966, labor relations rep., 1967; atty. Brown Grier, Richardson P.C., Detroit, 1970-71; atty Richardson, Grier P.C., Detroit, 1971-73; ptnr. Stone, Richardson P.C., Detroit, 1973—; bd. dirs. Legal Aid, Defender Assn. Detroit, 1985-86; apptd. hon. spl. agt. Office of Investigations, Office Inspector gen., U.S. Printing Office, 1997. Mem. bd. dirs. YMCA Fisher Branch; Boy Scouts Am.; apptd. to Bd. Appeals for Hosp. Bed Reduction by Gov. State of Mich., 1982, apptd. Spl. Asst. Atty. Gen., by Frank J. Kelley, Atty Gen. for the State Mich., May 23, 1984, apptd. to Task Oriented Com. to review the issue in-home child care by Detroit City Council Mem., Maryann Mahaffey. With U.S. Army, 1964. Mem. NAACP (life), Am. Arbitration Assn., Legal Aid Defender Assn., Mich. State Bar Fellows, Optimists, Masons, Shriners (imperial legal advisor, gen. counsel 1994-97, Right Eminent Grand Comdr. of the Knights Templar, State of Mich. 1997—), Phi Alpha Delta, Kappa Alpha Psi. Democrat. Office: Stone Richardson PC 2910 E Jefferson Ave Detroit MI 48207-4208

RICHARDSON, RICHARD COLBY, JR., leadership and policy studies educator, researcher; b. Burlington, Vt., Sept. 10, 1933; s. Richard Colby and Florence May (Barlow) R.; m. Patricia Ann Barnhart, Dec. 21, 1954; children—Richard Colby III, Michael Donald, Christopher Robin. BS, Castleton State Coll., 1954; MA, Mich. State U., 1958; PhD, U. Tex., 1963; Litt.D. (hon.), Lafayette Coll., 1973. Instr., counselor Vt. Coll., Montpelier, 1958-61; dean instrn. Forest Park Community Coll., St. Louis, 1963-67; pres. Northampton County Area Community Coll., Bethelehem, Pa., 1967-77; chmn. dept. higher edn. and adult edn. Ariz. State U., Tempe, 1977-84, prof. edn. leadership and policy studies, 1984—. Jr. author: The Two Year College: A Social Synthesis, 1965; sr. author: Governance for the Two-Year College, 1972, Functional Literacy in the College Setting, 1981, Literacy in the Open Access College, 1983, Fostering Minority Acess and Achievement in Higher Education, 1987, Achieving Quality and Diversity, 1991. Bd. dirs. Easton Hosp., 1973-77, v.p., 1975-77; exec. council Minsi Trails council Boy Scouts Am., Bethelehem, 1973-77. Named Disting. Grad., Coll. Edn., U. Tex., Austin, 1982; recipient Outstanding Research Publ. award Council Univ. and Colls.-Am. Assn. Community and Jr. Colls., 1983, Disting. Service award, 1984. Mem. Am. Assn. Higher Edn. (charter life, dir. 1970-73), AAUP, Assn. for Study of Higher Edn. (bd. dirs. 1984), Am. Assn. Community and Jr. Colls. (dir. 1980-83). Democrat. Home: 5654 E Wilshire Dr Scottsdale AZ 85257-1950 Office: Ariz State U Dept Higher Edn Tempe AZ 85287

RICHARDSON, RICHARD JUDSON, political science educator; b. Poplar Bluff, Mo., Feb. 16, 1935; s. Jewell Judson and Naomi Fern (Watson) R.; m. Sammie Sue Cullum, Dec. 29, 1961; children: Jon Mark, Anna Cecile, Ellen Elizabeth, Megan Leigh. BS, Harding Coll., 1957; cert., U. Dublin, 1958; MA, Tulane U., 1961, PhD, 1967. Instr. Tulane U., 1962-65; asst. prof. polit. sci. Western Mich. U., Kalamazoo, 1965-67; assoc. prof. Western Mich. U., 1967-69; vis. assoc. prof. U. Hawaii, 1967-68; asso. prof. U. N.C., Chapel Hill, 1969-72, prof., 1972-77, Burton Craige prof., 1977—, assoc. chmn. dept., 1972-73, chmn. dept., 1975-80, 85-90, chmn. curriculum in justice, 1990-95, assoc. v.p. acad. affairs univ. gen. adminstrn., 1991-92; adj. prof. Duke U., Durham, 1972-74; provost, vice chancellor acad. affairs U. N.C., 1995—; cons. in field. Author: (with Kenneth Vines) The Politics of Federal Courts, 1971, (with Darlene Walker) People and the Police, 1973, (with Marian Irish, James Prothro) The Politics of American Democracy, 1981. Del. County Dem. Conv., 1972, 83; vice chmn. Dem. Party Precinct, 1983-85; chmn. bldg. fund YMCA, 1976; chmn. Carolina Challenge for endowment U. N.C., Chapel Hill, 1979-80; chmn. U. N.C. Bicentennial Observance, 1991-94; chmn. United Way, 1983, pres., 1985; pres. PTA County Coun., 1984. Recipient Edward S. Corwin award Am. Polit. Sci. Assn., 1967, Tanner Disting. Teaching award U. N.C., 1972, Univ. award for Outstanding Teaching, 1981, Thomas Jefferson award, 1987, Alumni Faculty Disting. Svc. award, 1994, James Johnston Disting. Teaching award, 1993; Edgar Stern fellow, 1959-61; NEH grantee, 1970. Mem. N.C. Polit. Sci. Assn. (pres. 1978-79), Am. Polit. Sci. Assn., So. Polit. Sci. Assn., ACLU (bd. dirs. local chpt. 1985-88, state bd. dirs. 1988-89), Order of Janus, Order of the Long Leaf Pine, Order of Golden Fleece, Order of the Grail. Home: 1135 River Rd Pittsboro NC 27312-8108 Office: U NC Dept Polit Sci Chapel Hill NC 27514

RICHARDSON, RICHARD LEWIS, lawyer; b. Balt., Aug. 27, 1952; s. terry Cole and marion cecilia (Kubin) R. AA, U. South Fla., 1973, BA with honors, 1974, MA in Philosophy summa cum laude, 1975; JD, Stetson U., 1979. Bar: Fla. 1979, Fed,. 1980; cert. expert in marital law, Fla., U.S. Dist. Ct. Fla. 1980. Mng. atty. Family Legal Ctrs., Port Richey, Fla., 1980-86; pvt. practice Port Richey, 1986—. Author: Lenin's Materialsm and Empirio-Criticism, 1976. Vol. legal rep. for incompetent juveniles 6th Jud. Cir., Pasco and Pinellas Counties, Fla., 1983—; mem. Pub. Defender's Clinic, St. Petersburg, Fla., 1979. Recipient Award of Participation as Pub. Defender, Pub. Defender's Office, 1979. Mem. ABA (family law sect.), Acad. Am. Trial Lawyers, Fla. Bar Assn. (marital and family law sect.), Themis Acad. Fraternity (v.p. 1971). Avocations: miniature modeling, piano, guitar, medieval history, toy collecting. Home: 10227 Turkey Oak Dr New Port Richey FL 34654-5838

RICHARDSON, RICHARD THOMAS, retired banker; b. Hackensack, N.J., Dec. 16, 1933; s. Rolande Herbert and Rose Hortense (Collina) R.; m. Melinda Davis Murphy; children: Lisa Richardson Charles, Heidi Davis, Peter Thomas. B.S., Yale U., 1955. With Chem. Bank, N.Y.C., 1960-92, v.p., 1969-74; v.p., gen. mgr. Chem. Bank, London, 1974-77; sr. v.p., head audit div. Chem. Bank, N.Y.C., 1977-80, sr. v.p., head Middle East, Africa, 1980-87, mng. dir., head instl. banking-internat., 1987-92; dir. Wiremold Co., West Hartford, Conn., 1980—; dir. Fosterlane Holdings Corp., Wilmington, Del., 1992—, Mitsui Trust Bank (U.S.A.), N.Y.C., 1994—. Trustee Internat. Coll., Beirut, Lebanon, 1986-93, N.J. Ctr. for Visual Arts, Summit, 1993-94. Mem. Yale Club (N.Y.C.), Beacon Hill Club (Summit, N.J.).

RICHARDSON, ROBERT ALLEN, lawyer, educator; b. Cleve., Feb. 15, 1939; s. Allen B. and Margaret C. (Thomas) R.; m. Carolyn Eck Richardson, Dec. 9, 1968. BA, Ohio Wesleyan U., 1961; LLB, Harvard U., 1964. Bar: Ohio 1964, Hawaii 1990. Ptnr. Caffee, Halter & Griswold, Cleve., 1968-89; counsel Mancini, Rowland & Welch (formerly Case & Lynch), Maui, Hawaii, 1990—; lectr., affirmative action officer, atty. Maui (Hawaii) C.C., 1989—; chmn. gov. fin. dept., chmn. cmty. svc. com., mem. oper. com. Caffee, Halter & Griswold; past lectr. Sch. Law Cleve. State U.; counsel Maui C. of C., Kahului, 1994—. Pres. trustee Big Bros., Big Sisters of Maui, 1990-94; v.p., trustee, pres. Ka Hole A Ke Ole Homeless Resource Ctr., 1990—; trustee Maui Acad. Performing Arts, Maui Symphony, Maul Counseling Svc., Kapalua Music Festival, Hawaii Legal Aid Found.; v.p., trustee, chmn. devel. com. Cleve. Playhouse, 1984-89; trustee, mem. exec. com., program chmn. Cleve. Coun. World Affairs, 1970-89; past model UN chmn. Cleve. Com. on Fgn. Rels.; trustee, mem. exec. com., budget chmn. Neighborhood Ctrs. Assn., 1980-89. Mem. Rotary Club of Maui, Maui Country Club, Roufant Club (adv.), Cleve. Skating Club. Home: 106 Poohina Rd Kula HI 96790 Office: Mancini Rowland & Welch 33 Lono Ave Kahului HI 96732-1608

RICHARDSON, ROBERT CARLETON, engineering consultant; b. Grand Junction, Colo., Mar. 17, 1925; s. Carleton O. and Mabel Grace (Davy) R.; m. Ruby Lucille Morrison, Jan. 11, 1947 (dec.); children: Robert James, Lori Dianne Richardson Dismont. Student, U. Colo., Boulder, 1943-44, U. Calif., Berkeley, 1946-47, I.C.S., Scranton, Pa., 1947-50, Calif. State U., Long Beach, 1983, John F. Kennedy U., Martinez, Calif., 1967. Chief engr., gen. mgr. Gilmore Fabricators, Oakland, Calif., 1948-56; nat. sales mgr. Gilmore Steel Contrs., Oakland, 1957-72; v.p. engring. R&D Davis Walker Corp., L.A., 1972-86; tech. dir. Ivy Steel divsn. MMI, Houston, 1986-93; engring. cons. R.C. Richardson & Assocs., Sun Lakes, Ariz., 1993—; engring. instr. Calif. State U., Long Beach, 1983-85; pres. Nat. Concrete Industry Bd., San Francisco, 1984; chmn. bd. Wire Reinforcement Inst., Findlay, Ohio, 1978, 82; bd. dirs. ASCC, 1982-84. Chpt. author: Manual of Standard Practice, 1988-90, Structural Detailing Manual, 1990-94. With USMC, 1943-45. Recipient Outstanding Achievement award Wire Reinforcement Inst., 1993; named Boss of the Yr., Women in Constrn., Oakland, 1964, 65. Fellow Am. Concrete Inst. Internat. (chair 439-A 1991—); mem. ASTM, ASCE/Fed. Emergency Mgmt. Agy., Structural Engrs. Assn. of Calif., Marines Meml. Assn., Earthquake Engring. Rsch. Inst. Republican. Achievements include research on high strength steel reinforcement under seismic loadings; research on fatigue of wire reinforcement under dynamic loads; research on crack behavior of shear reinforcement in concrete beams and girders. Avocations: swimming, walking, golf, fishing, hunting. Home and Office: 10930 E San Tan Blvd Sun Lakes AZ 85248

RICHARDSON, ROBERT CHARLWOOD, III, management consultant, retired air force officer; b. Rockford, Ill., Jan. 5, 1918; s. Robert Charlwood, Jr. and Lois (Farman) R.; m. Anne Waln Taylor, Sept. 13, 1952; children: Anne Newbold, Robert Charlwood, Lydia Farman. B.S., U.S. Mil. Acad., 1939; grad., Nat. War Coll., 1956. Commd. 2d lt. U.S. Army, 1939; advanced through grades to brig. gen. USAF, 1960; squadron comdg. officer Ascension Island, 1942-43; (Army Air Force Bd.), Orlando, Fla., 1943- 44; assigned U.K. and France, 1944-45; comdg. officer 365th Fighter Group, 9th Air Force, 1945-46; assigned joint war plans com. Joint Chiefs Staff, NATO, 1946-49, Washington and Paris, 1949-54; U.S. mil. rep. European Def. Community, 1954-55, comdg. officer 83d and 4th Fighter Wing, Tactical Air Command, 1956-58, assigned plans div. Hdqrs. USAF, 1958-61, mil. rep. NATO Council Paris, 1962-64, dep. chief staff for sci. and tech. Air Force Systems Command, 1964-66; dep. comdr., field command Def. Atomic Support Agy. Sandia Base, 1966-67, ret., 1967; sr. assoc. Schriever & McKee Assos., Inc., 1967-70; policy cons., pres. Encabulator Corp., 1970-80; pres. Global Activities Ltd.; v.p. Cons.'s Internat. Inc., 1973-77; dep. dir. High Frontier Inc., 1981—; pres. Exim Corp., 1977-82. Contbr. numerous articles on atomic warfare, NATO, strategy and concepts. Bd. dirs., sec./treas. Am. Cause, 1975-80, Security and Intelligence Fund, 1977-90; exec. dir. Am. Fgn. Policy Inst., 1976-86; bd. dirs., sec.-treas. Space Transp. Assn., 1991—. Decorated Legion of Merit with oak leaf cluster, Air medal, Army Commendation medal; Croix de Guerre with silver star France). Home: 212 S St Asaph St Alexandria VA 22314-3744

RICHARDSON, ROBERT COLEMAN, physics educator, researcher; b. Washington, June 26, 1937; s. Robert Franklin and Lois (Price) R.; m. Betty Marilyn McCarthy, Sept. 2, 1962; children: Jennifer, Pamela. BS in Physics, Va. Poly. Inst. and State U., 1958, MS, 1960; PhD in Physics, Duke U., 1966. Research assoc. Cornell U., Ithaca, N.Y., 1966-67, asst. prof., 1968-71, assoc. prof., 1972-74, prof., 1975—; chmn. Internat. Union Pure and Applied Physics Commn. (C-5), 1981-84; mem. bd. assessment Nat. Bur. Standards, 1983—. Mem. editorial bd. Jour. of Low Temperature Physics, 1984—. Served to 2d lt. U.S. Army, 1959-60. Guggenheim fellow 1975, 83; recipient Simon Meml. prize Brit. Phys. Soc., 1976; co-recipient Nobel prize in physics, 1996. Fellow AAAS, Am. Phys. Soc. (Oliver E. Buckley prize 1981); mem. Nat. Acad. Scis. Avocations: photography, gardening. Office: Cornell Univ Dept Physics Clark Hall Ithaca NY 14853

RICHARDSON, ROBERT DALE, JR., English language educator; b. Milw., June 14, 1934; s. Robert Dale and Lucy Baldwin (Marsh) R.; m. Elizabeth Hall, Nov. 7, 1959 (div. 1987); m. Annie Dillard, Dec. 10, 1988; children: Elisabeth, Anne, Rosy. AB magna cum laude in English, Harvard U., 1956, PhD in English Lit., 1961. Instr. English Harvard U., Cambridge, Mass., 1961-63; asst. prof. English U. Denver, 1963-68, assoc. prof., 1968-72, prof., 1972-87, Lawrence C. Phipps prof. humanities, 1979-82, chmn. dept., 1968-73, pres. Univ. senate, 1972-73, assoc. dean grad. studies, 1975-76; prof. English, U. Colo., Boulder, 1987; vis. prof. letters Wesleyan U., Middletown, Conn., 1989-94; vis. prof. Harvard U., summer 1976, CUNY, 1978, Sichuan U., 1983; vis. fellow Huntington Libr., 1973-74; vis. instr. Yale U., 1988; bd. dirs. David R. Godine Pub. Author: Literature and Film, 1969, Henry Thoreau: A Life of the Mind, 1986 (Melcher award 1986), Emerson: The Mind on Fire, 1995 (Parkman prize 1995, Melcher award 1995, Washington Irving award 1995), Myth and Literature in the American Renaissance, 1978; (with Burton Feldman) The Rise of Modern Mythology 1680-1860, 1972. Trustee Meadville-Lombard Theol. Sch., 1981-87. Guggenheim fellow, 1990. Mem. Soc. Am. Hist., Soc. Eighteenth Century Studies, Melville Soc., Author's Guild, Thoreau Soc., Emerson Soc., Assn. Lit. Scholars and Critics. Democrat. Unitarian.

RICHARDSON, R(OSS) FRED(ERICK), insurance executive; b. Renfrew, Ont., Can., Feb. 4, 1928; came to U.S., 1980; s. Garfield Newton and Grace Mary (MacLean) R.; m. Betty Blanche Betts, Feb. 4, 1972; children by previous marriage—Sheri Joan, Robert John, Paul Frederick. BA in Math. and Physics with honors, Queens U., 1950. CLU. Actuarial asst. Empire Life Ins. Co., Kingston, Ont., Can., 1950-55; sec. Maritime Life Ins. Co., Halifax, N.S., Can., 1955-59, dir. sales, 1959-65, chief exec. officer, 1967-72; mng. dir., chief exec. officer Abbey Life Ins. Co., U.K., 1972-80; group gen. mgr. Hartford Europe Group, 1975-80; sr. v.p., dir. worldwide life ins. ops. Hartford Ins. Group, Conn., 1980-83, dir. worldwide life ins. ops., 1983-88; pres., chief operating officer Hartford Life Cos., 1983-88; pvt. ins. cons. Boca Raton, Fla., 1988; pres., chief exec. officer Crown Life Ins. Co., 1988-93; cons. INSCE, Boca Raton, 1993—. Fellow Soc. Actuaries; mem. Inst. Actuaries Gt. Britain. Home and Office: 17047 Boca Club Blvd Apt 165B Boca Raton FL 33487-1253

RICHARDSON, ROY, management consultant; b. Chgo., Mar. 22, 1931; s. John George and Margaret Beattie (Henderson) R.; BA in Psychology, Macalester Coll., 1952; MA in Labor and Indsl. Relations, U. Ill., 1953; PhD in Indsl. Relations, U. Minn., 1969; m. Mary C. Westphal, May 16, 1970; children: Beth Barnett, Jessica, Adam, Roman, Alexis. With Honeywell, Inc., Mpls., 1956-70, corp. manpower mgr., 1967-70; mgr. manpower devel. and tng. Internat. Harvester, Chgo., 1970-73; dir. personnel U. Minn., 1973-75; v.p. human resources Onan Corp., Mpls., 1975-82; v.p. human resources Graco Corp., Mpls., 1982-84, v.p. human resources and corp. devel., 1985-91; v.p. Human Resources and Quality Mgmt. Systems, 1992-94; pres. Intergrated Mgmt. Systems, 1994—; pres. Pers.l Surveys, Inc., Mpls., 1978-80; dir., chmn. exec. com. Kotz Grad. Sch. Mgmt., St. Paul, 1984-90. V.p. Mpls. Urban League, 1962-64. Recipient Disting. Citizens award City of Mpls., 1964; adj. prof., exec. fellow U. St. Thomas, Mpls. Mem. Soc. for Human Resource Mgmt., U. Minn. Indsl. Rels. Alumni Soc. (dir. 1979-85, pres. 1981), Am. Soc. Quality Ctrl. Republican. Episcopalian. Club: Ford's Colony Country. Author: Fair Pay and Work, 1971.

RICHARDSON, RUDY JAMES, toxicology and neurosciences educator; b. May 13, 1945. B.S. magna cum laude, Wichita State U., 1967; Sc.M., Harvard U., 1973, Sc.D., 1974. Diplomate Am. Bd. Toxicology. Research geochemist Columbia U., N.Y.C., summer 1966; NASA trainee SUNY, Stony Brook, 1967-70; research biochemist Med. Research Council, Carshalton, Eng., 1974-75; asst. prof. U. Mich., Ann Arbor, 1975-79, assoc. prof., 1979-84, prof. toxicology, 1984—, assoc. prof. neurotoxicology neurology dept., 1987—, acting dir. dept. Toxicology, 1993; dir., 1994—; vis. scientist Warner-Lambert Co., Ann Arbor, 1982-83; vis. prof. U. Padua, Italy, 1991; cons. NAS, Washington, 1978-79, 84, Office Tech. Assessment U.S. Congress, 1988-90, Nat. Toxic Substance Disease Registry, 1990—; mem. sci. adv. panel on neurotoxicology EPA, 1987-89; chmn. work group on neurotoxicity guidelines Orgn. for Econ. Coop. and Devel., 1990, Nat. Inst. Orgnl. Safety and Health, 1990, 94; mem. acute cholinesterase rsik assessement expert panel Internat. Life Scis. Inst., 1996; mem. steering com., working group Risk Sci. Inst., 1997—. Contbr. articles to profl. jours., chpts. to books; mem. editorial bd. Neurotoxicology, 1980—, Toxicology and Indsl. Health, 1986—, Toxicology and Applied Pharmacology, 1989—, Jour. Toxicology and Environ. Health. Mem. Mich. Lupus Found., Ann Arbor, 1979—. Grantee NIH, 1977-86, 95—, EPA, 1977-86; invited speaker Gordon Conf., Meriden, N.H., 1984, Cholinesterase Congress, Bled, Yugoslavia, 1983. Mem. AAAS, Soc. Toxicology (pres. neurotoxicology sect. 1987-88, councillor 1988-89), Soc. for Neurosci., Am. Diabetes Assn., Am. Chem. Soc., Internat. Soc. Neurochemistry, Internat. Brain Rsch. Orgn. Achievements include co-discoverer (with B.R. Dudek) of lymphocyte neurotoxic esterase (NTE); development of lymphocyte NTE as biomarker of exposure to neuropathic organophosphates; refinement of NTE assay for use in neurotoxicity testing. Office: U Mich Toxicology Program M 7525 Sph # 2 Ann Arbor MI 48109

RICHARDSON, SHARON YOUNG, marketing professional; b. Washington, Mar. 13, 1961; d. James Thomas and Evelyn Pollard (Branche) Young; m. Claiborne Turner Richardson II, Nov. 5, 1988; children: Lauren Evelyn, Olivia Jeanette. BS in Mass Comm., Va. Commonwealth U., 1983. Reporter Virginian-Pilot, Norfolk, Va., 1983-85; assoc. editor Times News Svc., Springfield, Va., 1985-87; state reporter Times-Dispatch, Richmond, Va., 1987-88; publs. dir. Nat. Assn. Black Journalists, Reston, Va., 1989-90; assoc. editor Assn. Governing Bds. Univ. and Colls., Washington, 1991-93; publs. writer George Mason U., Fairfax, Va., 1993-96; owner Richardson Comm., Woodbridge, Va., 1996—; writing cons. Dynamic Tech. Sys., Alexandria, Va., 1993-97. Editor: Economic Prospects for American Higher Education, 1992, Alcohol and Drug Abuse: Policy Guidelines for Boards, 1992. Chairperson publicity com. St. Margaret's Episcopal, Woodbridge, 1994—. Mem. Nat. Assn. Black Journalists, Soc. Profl. Journalists (Sigma Delta Chi Mark of Excellence 1983), Washington Ind. Writers (sec. bd. dirs. 1996—), Washington Assn. Black Journalists. Episcopalian. Home: 11954 Cotton Mill Dr Woodbridge VA 22192-1508

RICHARDSON, STEPHEN GILES, biotechnology company executive; b. Mpls., Sept. 17, 1951; s. Richard Giles and Constance Bernice (Krieg) R.; m. Maureane Hoffman, Mar. 21, 1981. BA cum laude, Wartburg Coll., 1972; MS, U. Iowa, 1974, PhD, 1981; postdoctoral, Duke U., 1982-84. Territory mgr. Wyeth Labs., Phila., 1974-76; research asst. U. Iowa, Iowa City, 1976-82; research assoc. Duke, Durham, N.C., 1982-84; scientist Becton Dickinson Rsch. Ctr., Research Triangle Park, N.C., 1984-86; devel. group leader divsn. Dade Diagnostics Baxter Healthcare, Miami, Fla., 1986; research group leader Organon Teknika Corp., Durham, N.C., 1987-89; R&D sect. head, internat. R&D area mgr., 1989-90; program mgr. divsn. Akzo Nobel, N.V. Organon Teknika Corp., Durham, N.C., 1990-94, assoc. dir., head product devel., 1994—. Contbr. articles to profl. jours.; patentee in field. Cofounder Libertarian Party Minn., Mpls., 1972; exec. sec. Iowa Council to Repeal Conscription, Waterloo, 1971. Mem. Am. Chem. Soc., Am. Assn. Blood Banks, Am. Assn. for Clin. Chemistry, Royal Soc. Chemistry (U.K.), N.Y. Acad. Sci., Electronic Frontier Found., Citizens Internet Empowerment Coalition, Sigma Xi. Achievements include discovery of transient neutral heteroaryl radicals as viable organic synthetic intermediates, such as, to halopurine nucleosides; MDA-180 Hemostasis Analyzer System. Home: 5408 Sunny Ridge Dr Durham NC 27705-8552 Office: Organon Teknika Corp Divsn Akzo Nobel NV 100 Akzo Ave Durham NC 27712-9402

RICHARDSON, SYLVIA ONESTI, physician; b. San Francisco, Sept. 12, 1920; d. Silvio J. and Johanna (Kristoffy) Onesti; m. William R. Richardson, Sept. 8, 1951 (dec. 1994); children: William Charles, Christopher Lee. B.A., Stanford, 1940; postgrad., U. Wash., 1940-41; M.A., Columbia U., 1942; M.D., McGill U., 1948; D.Litt. (hon.), Emerson Coll. Intern Children's Meml. Hosp., Montreal, 1948-49; resident Children's Med. Center, Boston, 1949-50; instr. spl. edn. Columbia, 1942-43; supr. hearing handicapped New Rochelle (N.Y.) Pub. Schs., 1942-43; clin. fellow in medicine Boston Children's Med. Center, 1949-51, dir. speech clinic, 1950-52, asso. physician, 1951-52, research fellow in surgery, 1954-55; instr. speech dept. Boston U., 1950-52, San Diego State Coll., 1952-54; teaching fellow in medicine Harvard U., 1951-52; cons. dept. child health and maternal welfare State of Mass., 1951-52; asst. clin. prof. pediatrics State U. N.Y., Downstate Med. Center, Bklyn., 1957-58; asso. prof. pediatrics and psychiatry, dir. child study center U. Okla. Sch. Medicine, 1958-65; asst. clin. prof. pediatrics U. Cin. Sch. Medicine, 1965-67, asso. prof., 1967-80; dir. learning disabilities program Center for Developmental Disorders, 1966-80; disting. prof. communication scis. and disorders, clin. prof. pediatrics U. South Fla., 1980—; cons. dept. child health and maternal welfare State of Okla., 1957-65; spl. cons. Nat. Inst. Nervous Diseases and Blindness, 1960-62; spl. cons. on mental retardation Okla. State Dept. Pub. Welfare, 1963-65; cons. Bur. State Services, USPHS, Bur. Edn. Handicapped, U.S. Office Edn. Editor: Children's House mag, 1966-67; mem. editorial bd. Jour. Learning Disbailities, Topics in Lang. Disorders. Mem. Okla. gov.'s com. White House Conf., 1960, White House Conf. on Children, 1970; Okla. citizen's com. Adequate Higher Edn., 1958-62. Recipient award for mental health planning Gov. of Okla., 1966; Distinguished Service award Internat. Assn. Children with Learning Disabilities, 1969; Old Master award Purdue U., 1972; named Okla. Woman of the Year, 1964; Talisman Service award Ohio Assn. Children with Learning Disabilities, 1974; Newell Kephart award for services to exceptional children, 1976. Fellow Am. Speech and Hearing Assn. (mem. exec. council 1957-59, chmn. elect ho. of dels. 1965, pres. 1973, honor award 1988), Royal Soc. Health, Internat. Assn. Rsch. in Learning Disabilities, Multidisciplinary Acad. for Clin. Edn., Internat. Assn. for Logopedics and Phoniatrics; mem. AMA, Mass. Speech and Hearing Assn. (co-founder, pres. 1950-52), Okla. Speech and Hearing Assn. (exec. council), Orton Dyslexia Soc. (bd. dirs. 1978-84, pres. 1984-88, Samuel T. Orton award 1992), Ohio Speech and Hearing Assn. (nat. joint com. on learning disabilities 1976—, chmn. 1997), Oklahoma County Council Mentally Retarded Children (bd. dirs. 1960-65), Oklahoma County Mental Health Assn. (profl. adv. bd. 1961-65), Okla. Hearing Soc. (v.p., bd. dirs. 1959-61), Soc. Research in Child Devel., Assn. Children with Learning Disabilities (chmn. profl. adv. bd.), Council Exceptional Children, Cin. Pediatric Soc. Home: 4141 Bayshore Blvd Apt 1701 Tampa FL 33611-1802

RICHARDSON, THOMAS HAMPTON, design consulting engineer; b. St. Louis, Nov. 25, 1941; s. Claude Hampton and Pearl Lily (Burks) R.; m. Lois Louise Atteberry June 8, 1963; children: Shelley Ann, David Hampton, Stephanie Lynn. BTEE, Wash. U., St. Louis, 1974. Registered profl. engr., Mo., Ill., Ind., Kans., Iowa, Fla., Ky., Miss. Elec. project designer Fruco Engrs. Inc., St. Louis, 1967-68; mgr., mech./elec. engr. MBA Engrs. Inc., St. Louis, 1968-74, Kenneth Balk and Assoc., St. Louis, 1974-76; instr. elec. engring. Wash. U., St. Louis, 1976; v.p., chief engr. John F. Steffen Assoc., St. Louis, 1976-79; prin. ptnr. Keeler, Webb and Richardson, St. Louis, 1979-94; pres./owner The Richardson Engring. Group, St. Louis, 1979—. Contbr. articles to profl. jours. Recipient Internat. Lgt. Des. award Illuminating Engr. Soc. St. Louis 1985, Edwin F. Guth award of Merit Illuminating Engr. Soc. N.Am. 1986. Mem. NSPE, ASHRAE, Am. Cons. Engr. Coun., Illuminating Engring. Soc. Past pres.), Soc. for Mkt. Profl. Svcs. (v.p.), Profl. Svcs. Mgmt. Assn. (bd. dirs.), Mo. Soc. Profl. Engrs. (govt. rels. com.), Nat. Fire Protection Assn., Green Turtle Bay Yacht Club, Grand Lake Yacht Club, Ky. Lake Club. Avocations: sailing, flying, horses, photography. Office: The Richardson Engring 7227 Devonshire Ave Saint Louis MO 63119-3419

RICHARDSON, W. FRANKLYN, minister. Gen. sec. Nat. Bapt. Conv. USA, Mt. Vernon, N.Y., 1994; pastor Grace Bapt. Ch., Mt. Vernon, 1994—. Address: 52 S 6th Ave Mount Vernon NY 10550-3005*

RICHARDSON, WALTER JOHN, architect; b. Long Beach, Calif., Nov. 14, 1926; s. Walter Francis and Ava Elizabeth (Brown) R.; m. Marilyn Joyce Brown, June 26, 1949 (div. 1982); children: Mark Steven, Glenn Stewart; m. Mary Sue Sutton, Dec. 4, 1982. Student, UCLA, 1944-45, Long Beach City Coll., 1946; BA, U. Calif., Berkeley, 1950. Registered architect, Ala., Ariz., Calif., Colo., Fla., Hawaii, Ill., Kans., Md., Mass., Nev., N.J., N.Y., Okla., Oreg., Tex., Utah, Vt., Va., Wash. Draftsman Wurster, Bernardi, Emmons, San Francisco, 1950-51, Skidmore, Owings & Merrill, San Francisco, 1951; designer Hugh Gibbs Architect, Long Beach, 1952-58; ptnr. Thomas & Richardson Architects, Long Beach, Costa Mesa, 1958-70; pres. Walter Richardson Assocs. Architects, Newport Beach, Calif., 1970-74; chmn. bd. Richardson, Nagy, Martin Architects and Planners, Newport Beach, 1974—. Co-author: The Architect and the Shelter Industry, 1975. Chmn. Planning Commn., City of Orange, Calif., 1967-68. With USAF, 1945. Recipient over 200 Gold Nugget Design awards Pacific Coast Builders Conf., San Francisco, 1969-96, 12 Builders Choice Design awards Builder Mag.; named Architect of Yr. Profl. Builder mag., 1986. Fellow AIA (pres. Orange County chpt. 1970, chmn. nat. housing com. 1976, 7 design awards); mem. Nat. Assn. Home Builders, Nat. Coun. Archtl. Registration Bds., Urban Land Inst., Alpha Tau Omega. Republican. Avocations: photography, downhill skiing, travel, tennis. Office: Richardson Nagy Martin 4611 Teller Ave Ste 100 Newport Beach CA 92660-2104

RICHARDSON, WANDA LOUISE GIBSON, family practice nurse; b. Dallas; d. Ralph Harrison Gibson and Letha Lee Thompson; children: James L. (dec.), Bruce S., Judith Richardson Holt, Janai Richardson Buentello. Lic. vocat. nurse, Dallas Vocat. Sch., 1960; ADN, Dallas/El Centro Coll., 1981; student, U. Dallas, Irving, 1978. RN, Tex. Staff nurse RHD Hosp., Dallas, 1981; head nurse physicians office, Irving, 1960-80; sr. nurse family practice residency program St. Paul Hosp./U. Tex. Southwestern Med. Sch., Dallas, 1984—. Contbg. columnist Lake Cities Sun News; contbr. poems to anthologies. Vol. tutor Literacy Program, Denton, Tex.; founding mem., mem. choir Cornerstone Bapt. Ch., Plano, 1990; mem. Friends of Libr. of Denton; vol. Big Sisters/Big Bros., Denton. Named one of Notable Women Tex., 1984; recipient Golden Poet award World Poetry, 1991, 92. Mem. Cercle Internat. le Recherches Culturelles et Spirituelles Inc. (charter, officer local chpt.), Nurse Healers Profl. Assn., Dallas Archeol. Soc., Denton J.S. Bach Soc., Dallas Inst. Culture and Humanities, Isthmus Inst.

RICHARDSON, WILLIAM BLAINE, former congressman, ambassador; b. Pasadena, Calif., Nov. 15, 1947; m. Barbara Flavin, 1972. BA, Tufts U., Medford, Mass., 1970; MA, Fletcher Sch. Law and Diplomacy, 1971. Mem. staff U.S. Ho. of Reps., 1971-72, Dept. State, 1973-75; mem. staff fgn. relations com. U.S. Senate, 1975-78; exec. dir. N. Mex. State Democratic Com., 1978, Bernalillo County Democratic Com., 1978; businessman Santa Fe, N. Mex., 1978-82; mem. 98th-103rd Congresses from 3rd N.Mex. dist., Washington, 1982-96; democratic chief dep. majority whip 103d Congress; U.S. amb. U.S. Mission to UN, 1997—; ranking minority mem. Resources Com. on Nat. Pks., Forests and Lands; mem. Select Com. on intelligence, Helsinki Commn. Vice chair Dem. Nat. Com.; active Big Bros.-Big Sisters, Santa Fe. Mem. Santa Fe Hispanic C. of C., Santa Fe C. of C., Council Fgn. Relations, NATO 2000 Bd., Congl. Hispanic Caucus, Am. G.I. Forum. Office: US Mission to UN 799 UN Plz New York NY 10017*

RICHARDSON, WILLIAM CHASE, foundation executive; b. Passaic, N.J., May 11, 1940; s. Henry Burtt and Frances (Chase) R.; m. Nancy Freeland, June 18, 1966; children: Elizabeth, Jennifer. BA, Trinity Coll., 1962; MBA, U. Chgo., 1964, PhD, 1971. Rsch. assoc., instr. U. Chgo., 1967-70; asst. prof. health services U. Wash., 1971-73, assoc. prof., 1973-76, prof., 1976-84, chmn. dept. health services, 1973-76, assoc. dean Sch. Pub. Health, 1976-81, acting dean, 1977, 78, dean Grad. Sch., vice provost, 1981-84; exec. v.p., provost, prof. dept. family and community medicine Pa. State U., 1984-90; pres. Johns Hopkins U., Balt., 1990-95, pres., prof. emeritus, 1995, prof. dept. health policy, mgmt., 1990-95, prof. emeritus, 1995—; pres., CEO W.K. Kellogg Found, Battle Creek, Mich., 1995—; cons. in field; bd. dirs. Kellogg Co., CSX Corp., Mercantile Bankshares Corp., Mercantile-Safe Deposit & Trust Co. Author: books, including Ambulatory Use of Physicians Services, 1971, Health Program Evaluation, 1978; contbr. articles to profl. jours. Mem. external adv. com. Fred Hutchinson Cancer Rsch. Ctr. Kellogg fellow, 1965-67. Fellow Am. Public Health Assn.; mem. Inst. Medicine, Nat. Acad. Scis. Office: WK Kellogg Found One Michigan Ave E Battle Creek MI 49017*

RICHARDSON, WILLIAM F., lawyer; b. Harvey, Ill., Apr. 20, 1948; s. Donald and Dorothy (Warren) R. BS, U. Ill., 1970, JD, 1973. Bar: Ill. 1973. Ptnr. Peterson and Ross, Chgo., 1973-94, Blatt, Hammesfahr & Eaton, Chgo., 1994—. Mem. ABA. Office: Blatt Hammesfahr & Eaton 333 W Wacker Dr Ste 1900 Chicago IL 60606-1226

RICHARDSON-MELECH, JOYCE SUZANNE, secondary school educator, singer; b. Perth Amboy, N.J., Nov. 15, 1957; d. Herbert Nathaniel and Fannie Elaine (Franklin) Richardson; m. Gerald Melech, July 28, 1990. MusB, Westminster Choir Coll., 1979, MusM, 1981. Cert. music tchr., N.J. Musical play dir. Perth Amboy H.S., 1989-92, asst. band dir., 1984-94; music tchr. Perth Amboy Bd. Edn., 1981—, gifted and talented music tchr., 1992-96; vocal soloist N.Y.C.; vocal soloist N.Y. Philharm. and Westminster Symphonic Choir, 1977, United Moravian Ch., N.Y.C., 1980-81, Ctrl. Jersey Concert Orch., Perth Amboy, 1994-96. Participant Perth Amboy Adult Cmty. Theatre, 1983. Mem. Am. Fedn. Tchrs., Am. Fedn. Musicians (local 373), Music Educators Nat. Conf., Ctrl. Jersey Music Educators, Alpha Phi Omega. Democrat. Mem. African Meth. Episcopal Zion Ch. Avocations: needlepoint, cross-stitch, knitting, sewing, crocheting. Home: 148 Carson Ct Somerset NJ 08873-4790 Office: Samuel Shull Sch 380 Hall Ave Perth Amboy NJ 08861-3205

RICHART, JOHN DOUGLAS, investment banker; b. Urbana, Ill., Jan. 16, 1947; s. Frank Edwin and Elizabeth Norma (Goldthorp) R.; m. Nan Jackson, June 27, 1970. BS in Engring., U. Mich., 1967, MS in Engring., 1968; MBA, Harvard U., 1973. V.p. Donaldson, Lufkin and Jenrette Securities Corp., N.Y.C., 1973-82; mng. dir. Chase Investment Bank div. Chase Manhattan Bank, N.A., N.Y.C., 1982-89; 1st v.p. mgr. mergers and acquisitions Australia and New Zealand Banking Group, N.Y.C., 1989-91; pres. Richart & Co., Upper Montclair, N.J., 1991-95; v.p. corp. devel. Heritage Network Inc., Southgate, Mich., 1996—. Lt. (j.g.) USCG, 1968-71. Mem. PGA West, Travis Point Country Club. Republican. Avocations: golf, platform tennis. Home: 3332 Alpine St Ann Arbor MI 48108 also: 54-981 Southern Hls La Quinta CA 92253-5634 Office: Heritage Network Inc Ste 400 One Heritage Pl Southgate MI 48195

RICHBART, CAROLYN MAE, mathematics educator; b. Catskill, N.Y., Aug. 12, 1945; d. George R. and Frances (Reynolds) Eden; m. Lynn A. Richbart, Aug. 15, 1987. BS, SUNY, Geneseo, 1967, MEd, 1982; PhD, U. Albany, 1992. Cert. math. tchr., elem. tchr., N.Y. Tchr. Wolcott St. Sch., Le Roy, N.Y., 1967-69; math. tchr. Le Roy Cen. High Sch., 1969-72, Attica (N.Y.) Mid. Sch., 1978-84; assoc. prof. Genesee C.C., Batavia, N.Y., 1984-87; grad. asst. U. Albany, 1987-90; asst. prof. Russell Sage Coll., Troy, N.Y., 1990-92, SUNY, New Paltz, 1992—; project dir. grades kindergarten through 6, N.Y. State Math Mentor Network. Contbr. articles to profl. jours. Mem. Nat. Coun. Tchrs. Math. (speaker), Assn. Math. Tchrs. N.Y. State (rec. sec. 1988-89, corr. sec. 1991-92, pres. 1995-96, chair workshop 1992, chair program 1989, chair Wyoming County sect. 1985-88), N.Y. State Assn. Two-Yr. Colls. (exec. bd. 1986-90, legis. chair 1986-89, curriculum chair 1989-90). Home: 25 Marthas Ct Saugerties NY 12477-4235 Office: SUNY at New Paltz Old Main New Paltz NY 12561-2499

RICHBOURG, DONNA S., federal agency adminstrator; m. Bill Richbourg; 1 child, Billy. BA in Bus., Am. U.; cert., Fed. Exec. Inst., Naval Air Sys. Command Sr. Exec. Mgmt. Devel. Program, Def. Sys. Mgmt. Coll. Exec. Program Mgr.'s Course. Mgr. F-14 production, indsl. specialist, 1975-83; dep. program mgr. F-14 Tomcat Aircraft Program Mgmt. Office Naval Air Sys. Command, 1983-90; dep. program exec. officer acquisition Office Program Exec. Officer Air Anti-Submarine Warefare, Assault and Spl. Mission Programs, 1990-94; asst. dep. under sec., prin. advisor to dep. under sec. Def. Acquisition Reform, 1994-97, acting dep. under sec., 1997—. V.P. U.S. Heroes of Reinvention award. Mem. Fed. Sr. Exec. Svc., Dept. Def. Acquisition Corps. Office: Acquisition 8725 John J Kingman Rd Fort Belvoir VA 22060-6219*

RICHBURG, KEITH BERNARD, journalist, foreign correspondent; b. Detroit, May 19, 1958; s. Walter Arthur and Katie Lee (Clemons) R. BA in Polit. Sci., U. Mich., 1980; MSc in Internat. Rels., London Sch. Econs., 1984. Met. staff reporter Washington Post, 1980-83, nat. staff corr., 1984-86; S.E. Asia bur. chief Washington Post, Manila, 1986-90; Africa bur. chief Washington Post, Nairobi, Keyna, 1991-94; Hong Kong bur. chief Washington Post, 1995—. Recipient fgn. reporting award Nat. Assn. Black Journalists, 1993, UN reporting award Korn-Ferry, 1993, George Polk award for fgn. reporting L.I. U., 1994; Harry S Truman scholar Truman Found., 1978. Mem. Am. Friends London Sch. Econs., U. Mich. Alumni Assn., Phi Beta Kappa. Home and Office: Washington Post (Fgn Desk) 1150 15th St NW Washington DC 20071-0001*

RICHBURG, W. EDWARD, nurse educator; b. New Orleans, Jan. 18, 1948; m. Kathryn S. Richburg, June 24, 1972; children: Bill, Kate. BA, U. Miss., 1970; BSN, U. Miss., Jackson, 1973; MEd, Memphis State U., 1977; MSN, Med. U. of S.C., 1991. RN, Fla., S.C.; cert. nursing adminstrn. advance, continuing edn. and staff devel. Commd. ensign USN, 1971, advanced through grades to comdr.; instr. hosp. corps Naval Sch. of Health Sci., San Diego, 1978-81; head nurse U.S. Naval Hosp.; dir. nursing svcs. Branch Med. Clinic, Mayport, Fla., 1983-87; head staff edn. and tng. U.S. Naval Hosp., Charleston, S.C., 1987-92; asst. dir. nursing U.S. Naval Hosp., Yokosuka, Japan, 1992-95; head Command Edn. Dept., 1995—; head command edn. dept. U.S. Naval Hosp., Yokosuka, Japan, 1995-96; performance improvement coord. U.S. Naval Hosp., Charleston, S.C., 1996—. Recipient Excellence in Nursing Education award Trident Nurses' Assn., 1991, S. C. Nurses' Assn., 1992. Mem. ANA (cert.), S.C. Nurses Assn. (chair continuing edn. com., treas. dist. chpt.), Continuing Edn. Coun., Sigma Theta Tau. Office: US Naval Hosp Code 09PI 3600 Rivers Ave Charleston SC 29405-7747

RICHELSON, HARVEY, lawyer, educator; b. N.Y.C., Sept. 5, 1951; s. Nathan Eli and Rose (Michalofsky) R. BS in Bus., U. Ariz., 1973; JD, Southwestern U., L.A., 1977; Diploma in Postgrad. Studies Taxation, U. San Diego, 1986, LLM in Taxation cum laude, 1988. Bar: Calif. 1978, Ariz. 1978, U.S. Dist. Ct. (ctrl. dist.) Calif. 1978, U.S. Tax Ct. 1978, U.S. Dist. Ct. (so. dist.) Calif. 1988, U.S. Ct. Appeals (9th cir.) 1986. Pvt. practice Ventura, Calif., 1978-79; ptnr. Hughes & Richelson, Thousand Oaks, Calif., 1979-84; corp. counsel Consolidated Energy Sys., Inc., Thousand Oaks, 1986-91; pvt. practice Thousand Oaks, 1984—; prof. bus. law Moorpark (Calif.) C.C., 1981-93, Calif. C.C., 1981; pres. Consul-Tax Corp., Inc., 1979-81. Screenwriter (theatrical movie) Punk Vacation, 1986. Exec. dir. Scrub Oaks Self-Help Housing, 1984-86, trustee, 1983-88; mem. citizens adv. com. City of Thousand Oaks, 1984-85. Recipient Am. Jurisprudence Book award, West Pub. Co., 1976. Mem. Calif. State Bar Assn., Ariz. State Bar Assn. Office: 223 E Thousand Oaks Blvd Thousand Oaks CA 91360-5803

RICHELSON, PAUL WILLIAM, curator; b. Montpelier, Idaho, Sept. 27, 1939; s. Paul Newton and June (Quayle) R. BA, Yale U., 1961; MFA, Princeton U., 1967, PhD, 1974. Asst. prof. Lawrence U., Appleton, Wis., 1970-77, U. Denver, 1977-84; asst. dir., curator Trisolini Gallery of Ohio U., Athens, 1984-87; chief curator Grand Rapids (Mich.) Mus., 1987-91; curator of Am. art Mobile Mus. Art, Mobile, Ala., 1991—. Author: (book) Studies in the Personal Imagery Collection of 20th Prints Ohio University, 1985, (catalogue) The Golden Age 19th Century Prints by David Roberts, 1988, Lee Loring: A Southern Sophisticate, 1992, Modernism and American Painting of the 1930s, 1993, ThirtySomething, 1994, Alabama Impact: Contemporary Artists with Alabama Ties, 1995, Louise Lyons Heistis (1965-1951): A Retrospective, 1995, The French Connection: Jean Simon Chaudron Returns To Mobile, 1996. Lt. (j.g.) USN, 1961-63. Fulbright-Hays fellow to Italy, 1967-69; Mus. Purchase Plan grantee Nat. Endowment for the Arts, 1991. Mem. Southeastern Museums Conf. Home: 6427 Grelot Rd Apt 405 Mobile AL 36695-2630 Office: Mobile Museum of Art PO Box 8426 Mobile AL 36689-0426

RICHENBACHER, WAYNE EDWARD, cardiothoracic surgeon; b. Akron, May 2, 1954. BS with high honors, Case Western Res. U., 1976; MD, U. Cin., 1980. Resident Pa. State U., Hershey, 1980-88, instr., 1988-89; asst. prof. U. Utah, Salt Lake City, 1989-93; assoc. prof. U. Iowa, Iowa City, 1993—. Rsch. fellow Pa. State U., 1982-83, 85-86. Fellow ACS; mem. Am. Soc. Artificial Internal Organs (travel fellow 1986, Graphic Forum award 1986), Internat. Soc. Heart and Lung Transplant, Internat. Soc. Artificial Organs, Assn. Acad. Surgery, Soc. Thoracic Surgeons, Am. Assn. Thoracic Surgery. Office: U Iowa Hosps & Clinics 1613-B JCP 200 Hawkins Dr Iowa City IA 52242-1009

RICHENBURG, ROBERT BARTLETT, artist, retired art educator; b. Boston, July 14, 1917; s. Frederick Henry and Spray (Bartlett) R.; m. Libby Chic Peltyn, Nov. 11, 1942 (dec. 1977); 1 child, Ronald P.; m. Margaret Kerr, Feb. 9, 1980; stepchildren: William Blakeley Kerr, David Garrett Kerr, Margaret Frances Kerr. Student, Boston U., George Washington U., Corcoran Sch. Art, Art Students League N.Y., Ozenfant Sch. Fine Arts, Hans Hofmann Sch. Art. Tchr. painting Schrivenham Am. U., Eng., 1945; instr. Coll. City N.Y., 1947-52, Cooper Union, 1954-55; instr., dir. Bklyn.-Queens Central YMCA, 1947-51; instr. NYU, 1960-61, Pratt Inst., Bklyn., 1951-64; assoc. prof. art Cornell U., Ithaca, N.Y., 1964-67; prof. art Hunter Coll., N.Y.C., 1967-70, Aruba (Netherlands Antiles) Research Center, 1970; prof. art Ithaca Coll., 1970-83, mem. council on arts; panelist various orgns. One-man shows Hendler Gallery, Phila., N.Y. Artists Gallery, Tibor DeNagy Gallery, Hansa Gallery, N.Y., Dwan Gallery, Los Angeles, Santa Barbara Mus. (Calif.), Dayton Art Inst., Dana Arts Center Colgate U., Ithaca Coll. Mus. Art, Grad. Sch. Bus. Cornell U., others; exhibited in group shows Mus. Modern Art, Solomon Guggenheim Mus., N.Y.C., Chrysler Art Mus., Yale Art Gallery, Whitney Mus., N.Y.C., Univ. Art Mus., Austin, Tex., Balt. Mus., Cocoran Mus. Art, Washington, Bklyn. Mus., Knox Albright Mus., Buffalo, Larry Aldrich Mus., Seattle Art Mus., Boston Mus. Fine Arts, numerous others; represented in permanent collections Chrysler Mus. Art, Norfolk Mus. Art, Coll. of William and Mary, Whitney Mus., Phila. Mus. Art, Pasadena Mus. Fine Art, Mus. Modern Art, Univ. Art Mus., U. Calif.-Berkeley, U. Tex. Art Mus., Austin, Ithaca Coll. Mus., Hirschorn Mus., Smithsonian Instn., Washington, many others. Served with AUS, 1942-45. Mem. Am. Assn. U. Profs., Coll. Art Assn., Internat. Platform Assn., Art Students League N.Y. (life). Club: (N.Y.C.). Home: 1006 Springs Fireplace Rd East Hampton NY 11937-1432

RICHENS, MURIEL WHITTAKER, AIDS therapist, counselor and educator; b. Prineville, Oreg.; d. John Reginald and Victoria Cecilia (Pascale) Whittaker; children: Karen, John, Candice, Stephanie, Rebecca. BS, Oreg. State U.; MA, San Francisco State U., 1962; postgrad., U. Calif., Berkeley, 1967-69, U. Birmingham, Eng., 1973, U. Soria, Spain, 1981. Lic. sch. adminstr., tchr. 7-12, pupil personnel specialist, Calif., marriage, child and family counselor, Calif. Instr. Springfield (Oreg.) High Sch., San Francisco State U.; instr., counselor Coll. San Mateo, Calif., San Mateo High Sch. Dist., 1963-86; therapist AIDS Health Project U. Calif., San Francisco, 1988—; pvt. practice MFCC San Mateo; guest West German-European Acad. seminar, Berlin, 1975. Lifeguard, ARC. postgrad. student Ctr. for Human Communications, Los Gatos, Calif., 1974, U. P.R., 1977, U. Guadalajara (Mex.), 1978, U. Durango (Mex.), 1980, U. Guanajuato (Mex.) 1982. Mem. U. Calif. Berkeley Alumni Assn., Am. Contract Bridge League (Diamond Life Master, cert. instr., tournament dir.), Women in Comm., Computer-Using Educators, Commonwealth Club, Pi Lambda Theta, Delta Pi Epsilon. Republican. Roman Catholic. Home and Office: 847 N Humboldt St Apt 309 San Mateo CA 94401-1451

RICHERSON, HAL BATES, physician, internist, allergist, immunologist, educator; b. Phoenix, Feb. 16, 1929; s. George Edward and Eva Louise (Steere) R.; m. Julia Suzanne Bradley, Sept. 5, 1953; children: Anne, George, Miriam, Julia, Susan. BS with distinction, U. Ariz., 1950; MD, Northwestern U., 1954. Diplomate Am. Bd. Internal Medicine, Am. Bd. Allergy and Immunology, Bd. Diagnostic Lab. Immunology; lic. physician, Ariz., Iowa. Intern Kansas City (Mo.) Gen. Hosp., 1954-55; resident in pathology St. Luke's Hosp., Kansas City, 1955-56; trainee in neuropsychiatry Brooke Army Hosp., San Antonio, 1956; resident in medicine U. Iowa Hosps., Iowa City, 1961-64, fellow in allergy and immunology, 1964-66; fellow in immunology Mass. Gen. Hosp., Boston, 1968-69, instr. internal medicine, 1964-66, asst. prof., 1966-70, assoc. prof., 1970-74, prof., 1974—, acting dir. divsn. allergy/applied immunology, 1970-72, dir. allergy and clin. immunology sect., 1972-78, dir. divsn. allergy and immunology, 1978-91; gen. practice, asst. to Gen. Surgeon Ukiah, Calif., 1958; gen. practice medicine Holbrook, Ariz., 1958-61; vis. lectr. medicine Harvard U. Sch. Medicine, Boston, 1968-69; vis. prof., rsch. scientist U. London and Brompton Hosp., 1984; prin. investigator Nat. Heart, Lung and Blood Inst., 1971—, mem. pulmonary diseases adv. com., 1983-87; prin. investigator Nat. Inst. Allergy and Infectious Diseases, 1983-94; dir. Nat. Inst. Allergy and Infectious Diseases' Asthma and Allergic Diseases Ctr., U. Iowa, 1983-94; mem. VA Merit Rev. Bd. in Respiration, 1981-84; mem. com. NIH Gen. Clin. Rsch. Ctrs., 1989-93; mem. rev. reserve NIH, 1993—; mem. bd. sci. advisors Merck Inst., 1990-94; presenter lectures, seminars, continuing edn. courses; mem. numerous univ., coll. and hosp. coms., 1970—; cons. Merck Manual, 1982, 87, 92, 96-97. Contbr. numerous articles and revs. to profl. jours., chpts. to books; reviewer Sci., Jour. Immunology, Jour. Allergy and Clin. Immunology, Am. Rev. Respiratory Disease, New Eng. Jour. Medicine, Ann. Internal Medicine. Served to capt. U.S. Army, 1956-58. NIH fellow 1968-69. Fellow ACP, Am. Acad. Allergy; mem. AMA (mem. residency and rev. com. for allergy and immunology; mem. accreditation coun. for grad. med. edn. 1980-85, vice-chmn. 1984-85), AAAS, Iowa Med. Soc., Iowa Thoracic Soc. (chmn. program com. 1964-65, 69-71, pres. 1972-73, mem. exec. com. 1972-74), Am. Thoracic Soc. (bd. dirs. 1981-82, councilor assembly on allergy and immunology 1980-81, mem. nominating com. 1988-90), Iowa Clin. Med. Soc., Am. Fedn. Clin. Rsch., Am. Assn. Immunologists, Ctrl. Soc. Clin. Rsch. (chmn. sect. on allergy-immunology 1980-81, mem. coun. 1981-84), Alpha Omega Alpha. Avocations: reading, swimming, handball, scuba diving. Home: 331 Lucon Dr Iowa City IA 52246-3300 Office: U Iowa Hosps and Clinics Dept Internal Medicine SE 630 Gen Hosp Iowa City IA 52242

RICHERSON, STEPHEN WAYNE, minister; b. Jackson, Tenn., Sept. 15, 1951; s. Claude Burnette and Mary Cathryn (Greathouse) R.; m. Rebecca Sue Darnell, Sept. 19, 1970; children: Mary Rebecca, Susan Virginia, James Stephen. BSBA, U. Richmond, 1973; MDiv, Southeastern Bapt. Theol. Sem., Wake Forest, N.C., 1979, DMin, 1984. Ordained to ministry Bapt. Ch., 1978. Minister music Hampton (Va.) Roads Bapt. Ch., 1974-76; assoc. minister music and youth Rolesville (N.C.) Bapt. Ch., 1976-78; minister Lea Bethel Bapt. Ch., Prospect Hill, N.C., 1978-80, Menchville Bapt. Ch., Newport News, Va., 1980-87, Westover Bapt. Ch., Richmond, Va., 1987—; br. mgr. Old Point Nat. Bank, Hampton, Va., 1973-76; trustee Va. Bapt. Children's Home, Salem, 1984-85, 878-96, v.p., 1990-91, pres. 1991-96; bd. dirs. Va. Bapt. Gen. Bd., Richmond, 1986-87; faculty Boyce Bible Sch. So. Bapt. Sem., Louisville, 1984-89. Author: Developing a Ministry Dream, 1984. Bd. dirs., swim and dive dir. Shenandoah Cmty. Assn., Richmond, 1990-92, pres., 1990-95; soccer coach Reams Rd. Athletic Assn., Richmond, 1988-89; mem. Choral Boosters, PTA, Monacan H.S., Richmond, 1992—; vis. prof. Christian Ministry, 1996—, Bapt. Theol. Sem., Richmond, 1996-97. Mem. Am. Acad. Ministry, Richmond Bapt. Mins. Conf., Peninsula Bapt. Mins. Conf. (v.p. 1980-87, moderator 1985-86, Pastor of Yr. 1986), Ministerial Support Group Richmond, Chaplain Assn. Chippenham Med. Ctr. Richmond. Office: Westover Bapt Ch PO Box 13048 Richmond VA 23225-0048 *Of all the opportunities and experiences of life that demand our attention and involvement, I have discovered that time spent for oneself and one's family is the best investment I can make towards a fulfilling life in the ministry.*

RICHERT, HARVEY MILLER, II, ophthalmologist; b. Weatherford, Okla., Aug. 25, 1948; s. Harvey Miller and Catherine Cornelia (Ryan) R.; m. Diana Dee Sisney, Nov. 23, 1966; children: Ronald Lance, Rachelle Lea. BS, Southwestern Okla. State U., 1970; MD, U. Okla., Oklahoma City, 1974. Intern St. Anthony Hosp., Oklahoma City, 1974-75; resident in ophthalmology Tulane U., New Orleans, 1975-78; physician Tucker & Walker Ophthalmology Assocs., Abilene, Tex., 1978-80; ptnr. Tucker, Walker & Richert, Abilene, 1980-86; pvt. practice Abilene, 1986—; med. dir. Lions Eye Bank, Abilene, 1979—; head opthalmology sect. Humana Hosp., 1984-90, Hendrick Med. Ctr., 1984-92. V.p. Chisholm Trail coun. Boy Scouts Am., 1984-89, 92—, dist. chmn., 1990-92, asst. scoutmaster, 1982-85, scoutmaster, 1985-88. Recipient Scoutmaster of Merit award, Silver Beaver award, Dist. award of Merit, Boy Scouts Am., 1988. Fellow Am. Acad. Ophthalmology, Castroviejo Soc. (assoc.); mem. AMA, Tex. Ophthal. Assn., Tex. Med. Assn., Lions (founders club), Abilene C. of C. Republican. Baptist. Avocations: backpacking, snow skiing, tennis, camping. Home: 15 Glen Abbey St Abilene TX 79606-5023 Office: 950 N 19th St Ste 200 Abilene TX 79601-2420

RICHERT, PAUL, law educator; b. Elwood, Ind., Aug. 31, 1948; s. Clarendon George and Margaret Ann (Cummins) R.; m. Catherine George Stanton, June 24, 1972; children: John Cummins, William Stanton. AB, U. Ill.-Urbana, 1970, MS, 1971; JD, Tulane U., 1977. Bar: Ohio 1977. Asst. law librarian U. Akron, 1977-78, law librarian, asst. prof. law, 1978-83, assoc. prof., 1983-87, prof. law, 1987—; cons. to cts. Served with U.S. Army, 1971-74. Mem. Am. Assn. Law Libraries, Akron Bar Assn., ABA. Mem. United Churches of Christ. Editor: Ohio Appellate Decision on Fiche, 1981; indexer Publs. Clearing House Bull., vols. 1-4. Home: 2030 Ganyard Rd Akron OH 44313-6050 Office: U Akron Sch of Law Libr 150 University Ave Akron OH 44304-1502

RICHES, KENNETH WILLIAM, nuclear regulatory engineer; b. Long Beach, Calif., Oct. 23, 1962; s. William Murray Riches and Carlene Katherine (Simmons) Anderson; m. Susan Ruth Flagg, Aug. 11, 1990; children: Benjamin William Bancroft Riches, Jennifer Ella Noel Riches. BSEE, U. Ill., 1984; MS in Engring. Mgmt., Santa Clara U., 1989. Registered profl. engr., Calif. Engr. Detroit Edison Co., Monroe, Mich.; engr. Pacific Gas &

Electric Co., San Luis Obispo, Calif., 1984-95, elec. engr., 1988—; prin. K.W. Riches & Assocs., Arroyo Grande, Calif., 1988—; owner The Peaberry Coffee Pub, Arroyo Grande, Calif., 1991-92, Riches to Rags, Clown Alley, 1995—. Mem. Rep. Nat. Com., 1986—; active Corp. Action in Pub. Schs., San Francisco, 1987, 88, World Wildlife Fund. Univs. Rsch. Assn. scholar, 1980. Mem. NSPE, IEEE (chpt. chmn. 1986-87, sect. dir. 1988-90), Am. Nuclear Soc., Power Engring. Soc. of IEEE (mem. nat. chpts. coun. 1988-92), Pacific Coast Engring. Assn., Nature Conservancy, Order of DeMolay (master counselor Paul Revere chpt. 1979), Eagle Alliance. Methodist. Avocations: golf, skiing, reading, travel. Home: 236 Bates Ln Monroe MI 48162 Office: Detroit Edison Fermi 2 Power Plant 6400 N Dixie Hwy Newport MI 48166-9726

RICHES, WENDY, advertising executive. Dir. pub. rels. Save the Children Fund, dir. mktg. and fundraising; exec. creative dir. Ogilvy & Mather Direct, London, mng. dir. Office: Ogilvy & Mather Direct 309 W 49th St New York NY 10019-7316

RICHEY, CLARENCE BENTLEY, agricultural engineering educator; b. Winnipeg, Manitoba, Can., Dec. 28, 1910; s. Raus Spears and Emily Cornelia (Bentley) R.; m. Marguerite Anne Jannusch, Dec. 27, 1936; children: David Volkman, Stephen Bentley. BS in Agrl. Engring., Iowa State U., 1933; BS in Mech. Engring., Purdue U., 1939. Registered agrl. engr., Calif. Instr. agrl. engring. Purdue U., West Lafayette, Ind., 1936-41; asst. prof. dept. agrl. engring. Ohio State U., Columbus, 1941-43; head devel., engr. Electric Wheel Co., Quincy, Ill., 1943-46; project engr. Harry Ferguson, Inc., Detroit, 1946-47; sr. project engr. Dearborn Motors Corp., Detroit, 1947-54; supt., chief rsch. engr. Ford Tractor Divsn., Birmingham, Mich., 1954-62; chief engr. Fowler (Calif.) divsn. Massey-Ferguson Ltd., 1964-69; product mgmt. engr. Massey-Ferguson Ltd., Toronto, Ont., Can., 1970-71; assoc. prof. agrl. engring. Purdue U., West Lafayette, 1971-76, prof. emeritus, 1976—; farm equipment cons. Ford Found., Allahabad, India, 1963. Author: (autobiography) Fifty Years of Engineering Farm Equipment, 1989; editor-in-chief: Agricultural Engineer's Handbook, 1961; contbr. bulls. and articles to profl. jours. Fellow Am. Soc. Agrl. Engrs. (Cyrus Hall McCormick Gold medal 1977); mem. Lafayette Kiwanis. Achievements include patent for farm equipment; holder or co-holder of 79 patents. Home: 2217 Delaware Dr West Lafayette IN 47906-1917

RICHEY, EVERETT ELDON, religion educator; b. Claremont, Ill., Nov. 1, 1923; s. Hugh Arthur and Elosia Emma (Longnecker) R.; m. Mary Elizabeth Reynolds, Apr. 9, 1944; children: Eldon Arthur, Clive Everett, Loretta Arlene, Charles Estel. ThB, Anderson U., 1946; MDiv, Sch. Theology, Anderson, Ind., 1956; ThD, Iliff Sch. of Theology, Denver, 1960. Pastor Ch. of God, Bremen, Ind., 1946-47, Laurel, Miss., 1947-48; pastor First Ch. of God, Fordyce, Ark., 1948-52; prof. Arlington Coll., Long Beach, Calif., 1961-68; pastor Cherry Ave. Ch. of God, Long Beach, 1964-68; prof. Azusa (Calif.) Pacific U., 1968-93; mem. Christian Ministries Tng. Assn., 1968; mem., chmn. Commn. on Christian Higher Edn./Ch. of God, 1982-93; pres. Ch. Growth Investors, Inc., 1981—. Author: ednl. manual Church Periodical--Curriculum, 1971-83. Mem. Assn. Profs. and Rschrs. Religious Edn., Christian Ministries Tng. Assn. Republican. Avocation: gardening. Home and Office: 413 N Valencia St Glendora CA 91741-2418

RICHEY, PHIL HORACE, former manufacturing executive, consultant; b. Detroit, July 30, 1923; s. Lawrence Kennedy and Hazel Annsonia (Stuckey) R.; children: Karen L. Richey Forrester, Ann C. Richey Zepke; stepchildren: Gregory F. Lloyd, Charles E. Lloyd III.; m. Mary Elizabeth McCulloch, June 30, 1984; stepchildren: Julie Ann McCulloch Beal, Mary Elizabeth McCulloch, Claire May Thompson. B.A. with distinction, U. Mich., 1948. With Detrex Chem. Industries Inc., Detroit, 1948-56; group v.p. Detrex Chem. Industries Inc., 1962-71; with Allied Research Products Co., 1956-59, v.p. fin., 1958-59; with U.S. Chem. Milling Co., Manhattan Beach, Calif., 1959-61; v.p. U.S. Chem. Milling Co., 1960-61; with Olin Corp., Stamford, Conn., 1971-81; corp. v.p., pres. Winchester group, 1977-81; mgmt. cons., 1981—; bd. dirs. Assn. Chems. and Svcs., Inc. 1st lt. AUS, 1942-46. Mem. Phi Kappa Phi, Beta Gamma Sigma. Home and Office: 342 Winamar Ave La Jolla CA 92037-6549

RICHEY, THOMAS ADAM, advertising executive; b. Cleve., Feb. 3, 1934; s. Clyde Frank and Elsie (Long) R.; divorced; children: Thomas John, Robert Joseph; m. LaVerle C. Aughdahl, May 1, 1977; children: Kelly Rae, Michael Adam. BS, Kent State U., 1960. Field rep. GMAC, CLeve., 1960-65; account exec. Nationwide Advt. Service, Inc., Cleve., 1966-68, mgr., 1969-71, regional mgr., 1971-73, v.p., 1974-75, exec. v.p., 1975-83, pres., chief operating officer, 1983—.

RICHEY, THOMAS S., lawyer; b. Asheville, N.C., Aug. 27, 1944. BA cum laude, Wesleyan U., 1966; JD with distinction, Duke U., 1975. Bar: Ga. 1975. Mem. Powell, Goldstein, Frazer & Murphy, Atlanta. Editorial bd. Duke Law Jour., 1974-75. Fulbright grantee U. Marburg, Ger., 1966-67. Mem. ABA, State Bar Ga., Atlanta Bar Assn., Phi Beta Kappa, Order of Coif. Address: Powell Goldstein Frazer & Murphy 16th flr 191 Peachtree St NE Fl 16 Atlanta GA 30303-1741

RICHIE, JEROME PAUL, surgeon, educator; b. San Antonio, 1944. MD, U. Tex., 1969. Surg. intern UCLA, 1969-70, resident in gen. surgery, 1970-71, resident in urology, 1971-75, lectr. surg. urology, 1974-75; asst. clin. prof. U. Calif., San Diego, 1975-77; asst. prof. urology Harvard U., 1977-80, assoc. prof., 1980-86, prof., 1986—, Elliott C. Cutler prof. surgery, 1987—, chmn. program in urology, 1987—; chief urol. Brigham and Women's Hosp., Boston, 1977—; cons. Dana Farber Cancer Ctr., Boston, 1977—. Lt. comdr. M.C., USN, 1975-77. Mem. ACS, Am. Assn. Gerito-Urinary Surgeons, Am. Urol. Assn., Assn. Acad. Surgery, Am. Soc. (Clin.) Oncology, Am. Surg. Assn. Office: Brigham & Womens Hosp 45 Francis St # 3 Boston MA 02115-6105

RICHIE, LIONEL B., JR., singer, songwriter, producer; b. Tuskegee, Ala., June 20, 1949; s. Lyonel B. Sr. and Alberta (Foster) R.; m. Brenda Harvey, 1975. BS in Econs., Tuskegee U., 1971, MusD (hon.), 1985; MusD (hon.), Boston Coll., 1986. Pres. Brockman Music, L.A. Mem. group The Mystics (name changed to The Commodores), 1969-81; writer, producer songs for Commodores including: Easy, Three Times a Lady (Am. Music award 1979, People's Choice award for best song 1979), Still (People's Choice award for best song 1980), Sail On, Lady (Nat. Music Pubs. award 1980, 81, People's Choice award for best composer 1981); songwriter, producer album for Kenny Rogers; albums (with The Commodores) include Midnight Magic, Machine Gun, Movin' On, Commodores, Caught in the Act, Hot on the Tracks, Natural High, Heroes, (solo albums) Lionel Richie, Can't Slow Down, 1984 (Grammy award Album of Yr. 1985), Dancing on the Ceiling, 1986, Back to Front, 1992, Louder Than Words, 1996; producer, composer: (songs) Truly (Grammy award 1982, 2 Am. Music awards 1983, People's Choice award Best Song, 1983), All Night Long (Nat. Music Pubs. award 1984, 3 Black Gold awards 1984, Am. Music award 1984, Hello (2 Am. Music awards 1985), Say You, Say Me (ASCAP Pop award 1987, Am. Music award 1987, Oscar award Best Song 1986, Golden Globe award Best Song 1986), Dancing on the Ceiling (3 Am. Music awards 1987), (duet with Diana Ross) Endless Love (Grammy award 1982, 2 Am. Music awards 1982, Am. Movie award 1982, Rojo award Gold Status in Hong Kong 1982, People's Choice award Best Song 1982), (sung by Kenny Rogers) Lady, (with Michael Jackson) We Are The World, 1985 (Grammy awards Best Song, Record of Yr. 1986, People's Choice award Best Song 1986). Recipient Best Young Artist in Film award, 1980, 2 NAACP image awards, 1983, Favorite Male Vocalist Pop/Rock award Am. Music Acad., 1987, Favorite Male Vocalist Soul/R&B award Am. Music Acad., 1987; named Man of Yr. Children's Diabetes Found., 1984, Alumnus of Yr. United Negro Coll. Fund, 1984, Favorite Male Singer People mag. Readers Poll, 1985, Entertainer of Yr., NAACP, 1987. Mem. ASCAP (Writer of Yr. 1984, 85, 86, Pub. of Yr. 1985). also: Motown Records 5750 Wilshire Blvd Ste 300 Los Angeles CA 90036*

RICHIE, RODNEY CHARLES, critical care and pulmonary medicine physician; b. Big Springs, Tex., Aug. 17, 1946; s. Howard Mouzon and Gloria (Hollingshead) R.; m. Sara Lee Dilley, July 13, 1968; children: Megan Kathryn, Paul Nathan. BA in Chemistry, So. Meth. U., 1968; MD cum laude, Baylor Coll., 1972. Diplomate in Internal Medicine, Pulmonary, Crit. Care and Ins. Medicine. Resident in medicine Baylor Affiliated Hosps., Houston, 1973-75, chief med. resident, 1975, fellow in pulmonary medicine, 1976-77; pvt. practice, pres. Waco (Tex.) Lung Assocs., 1977—; v.p. IMS, Houston, 1995—; med. dir. Tex. Life Ins., Waco, 1985—, Cmty. Hospice of Waco, 1996—, PMSI, Waco, Tex., 1997—. Chmn. med. staff Hillcrest Bapt. Med. Ctr., Waco, 1993; chmn. bd. dirs. GH Pape Found., Waco, 1993. Fellow Am. Coll. Chest Physicians; mem. ACP, AMA, Am. Thoracic Soc., Tex. Club Internists. Episcopalian. Avocations: snow skiing, writing, reading. Home: 3509 Lake Heights Dr Waco TX 76708-1005 Office: Waco Med Group 2911 Herring Ave Ste 212 Waco TX 76708-3244

RICHIE, SHARON I., retired army nursing officer; b. Phila., Dec. 14, 1949; d. William Joseph and Helen Lucille (Oglesby) R.; m. Paul Henri, Jan. 1, 1986. BS, Wagner Coll., 1971; MS, U. Tex. Grad. Sch. Nursing, San Antonio, 1976; postgrad. George Washington U., 1987—;student Army War Coll., 1987-88. Commd. 2d lt. U.S. Army, advanced through grades to col., 1988; clin. staff nurse Walter Reed Army Med. Ctr., Washington 1971-74; hosp. pschiat. nurse cons., head nurse 5th Gen. Hosp., Landstuhl, Germany, 1976-77; psychiat. clin. nurse specialist Alcholism Treatment Facility, Stuttgart, Germany, 1977-79; cons. alcohol and drug abuse nursing U.S. Army Surg. Gen., The Pentagon, Washington, 1980, also clin. liaison officer; asst. dir. edn. and rehab. Office Drug and Alcohol Abuse Prevention, Dept. Def., Pentagon, 1980-82; White House fellow, 1982-83; asst. chief nurse evenings/nights Letterman Army Med. ctr., San Francisco, 1983-84, chief ambulatory nursing service, 1984-85, dir. quality assurance, dept. nursing, 1985-86; PROFIS chief nurse, 8th Evacuation Hosp., Fort Ord, Calif., 1984-86; asst. chief nurse Kimbrough Army Hosp., Ft. Meade, Md., 1986, chief dept. nursing, 1986-87; chief clin. nursing svc. Walter Reed Army Med. Ctr., Washington, 1988-90; chief dept. nursing Letterman Army Med. Ctr., San Francisco, 1990-91; dir. med. directorate U.S. Army Recruiting Command, Ft. Sheridan, Ill., 1991; dir Health Svcs. Directorate U.S. Army Recruiting Command, Ft. Knox, Ky., 1991-93; chief nurse S.E. Regional Health Svcs. Support Area and dir. Nursing Eisenhower Army Med. Ctr., Fort Gordon, Ga., 1993-96; cons. Regional Commrs. Pres's Commn. on White House Fellow, 1985-86, sec. White House Fellow Assn. and Found.; healthcare orgnl. cons. Bd. Named Alumni of Yr., Wagner Coll., S.I., 1983; White House fellow, 1982; recipient Meritorious medal sec. Def., 1982, A Prefix U.S. Army Surgeon Gen., 1992, 2 Legion of Merit 1993, 96, Presdl. Svc. Badge (white house) 1993. Mem. Nat. Black Nurses Assn., Am. Nurses Assn., Am. Nurses Found., Assn. U.S. Army, Assn. U.S. Mil. Surgeons, Sigma Theta Tau. Clubs: Presidio Officers (co chmn. council 1985-86), Army and Navy Club, Rocks (Washington) (former v.p.). Avocations: weight lifting, collecting angels, indoor gardening. Home: 3019 Bransford Rd Augusta GA 30909-3090 Office: Marshall Qualtec Inc 8757 E Via de Commercio Scottsdale AZ 85258

RICHKIN, BARRY ELLIOTT, financial services executive; b. N.Y.C., Apr. 14, 1944; s. Harry and Celia (Goldberg) R. BA, Bklyn. Coll., 1964. CLU, cert. in personal fin. planning, NASD. Auditor First Nat. Bank of N.Y., N.Y.C., 1968-70; sr. supr. ABC, N.Y.C., 1970-73; account rep. Met. Life Ins. co., Atlanta, 1973-74; rep. Mixon-Baker Fin. Svcs., Atlanta, 1974-78; owner Barry Richkin Fin. Svcs., Roswell, Ga., 1978—; owner Barry Richkin Philatelics, Roswell, 1991—; cons., owner Benefit Cons. Group, Roswell, 1989—; cons., pres., bd. dirs. Am. Health Network, Roswell, 1982—. Author: Guide to Preferred Provider Organizations, 1986. Mem. Am. Soc. CLU and ChFC, Am. Philatelic Soc., Manuscript Soc., U.S. Postal Hist. Soc., Conn. Hist. Soc. Avocations: manuscripts, philatelics, jogging. Office: Barry Richkin Fin Svcs PO Box 2071 600 Houze Way Bldg C-6 Roswell GA 30076-1435 also: PO Box 2071 Roswell GA 30076

RICHLEN, SCOTT LANE, federal government program administrator; b. Ames, Iowa, July 23, 1949; s. Ellsworth Mark and Betty Jane (Wegner) R.; m. Deborah Lou Dick, Feb. 6, 1971; children: Mindy Lou, Gwendolyn Anne. BSME, Mont. State U., 1972; M.Engring. in Mech. Engring., U. Idaho, 1982; grad. exec. potential program, Office Pers. Mgmt., 1995. Assoc. engr. Thiokol Chem. Corp., Brigham City, Utah, 1973-75; rsch. engr. EG&G Idaho, Inc., Idaho Falls, 1975-79, sr. program specialist, 1979-84; program mgr. indsl. heat pumps U.S. Dept. Energy, Washington, 1984-87, program mgr. advanced heat exchangers, 1984-94, program mgr. continuous fiber ceramic composites, 1990-95; team leader steel industry R&D U.S. Dept. Energy, 1995—; lectr. profl. extension U. Wis., Madison, 1982-83. Author: (reference text) ASM, Engineered Materials, 1992, Ceramics Information Analysis Center/American Ceramic Society Handbook on Continuous Fiber Reinforced Ceramic Matrix Composites, 1993; editor (conf. procs.) Industrial Heat Exchangers, 1985; inventor, patentee corrosive resistant heat exchanger. Vol. Martha's Table, Washington, 1986—; v.p. Aid Assn for Lutherans, Br. 2792, Annandale, Va., 1988-92. Mem. Precision Aerobatics Model Pilots Assn., No. Va. Control-line Assn. (pres. 1987-89, 91-92), Mont. State Soc. Mont. State U. Alumni Assn. (life). Avocations: woodworking, martial arts, control-line model airplanes, gardening, readings in psychology, history and law. Office: US Dept Energy 1000 Independence Ave SW Washington DC 20585-0001

RICHLER, MORDECAI, writer; b. Montreal, Que., Can., Jan. 27, 1931; s. Moses Isaac and Lily (Rosenberg) R.; m. Florence Wood, July 27, 1959; children: Daniel, Noah, Emma, Martha, Jacob. Student, Sir George Williams U., 1948-50. vis. prof. Carleton U., Ottawa, Ont., 1972-74; assoc. judge for Can., Book-of-the-Month Club, 1974-88, also mem. editorial bd., N.Y. Author: (novels) The Acrobats, 1954, Son of a Smaller Hero, 1955, A Choice of Enemies, 1957, The Apprenticeship of Duddy Kravitz, 1959, Stick Your Neck Out, 1963, Cocksure, 1967, St. Urbain's Horseman, 1971, Joshua Then and Now, 1980, Solomon Gursky Was Here, 1990, (essays) Notes on an Endangered Species, 1974, Home Sweet Home, 1984, Oh Canada!, Oh Quebec! A Lament for a Divided Nation, 1992, (stories) The Street, 1975, (nonfiction) Oh Canada! Oh Quebec! Requiem for a Divided Country, 1992, This Year in Jerusalem, a memoir, 1994; children books Jacob Two-Two Meets The Hooded Fang, 1975, Jacob Two-Two and the Dinosaur, 1987; film The Apprenticeship of Duddy Kravitz, 1974 (Acad. award nomination 1974, Writers Guild of Am. award 1974), Joshua, Then and Now, 1985, Jacob Two-Two's First Spy Case, 1995; editor: The Best of Modern Humor, 1983, Writers on World War II, 1991; contbr. articles to profl. jours. Recipient Gov.-Gen.'s award for lit., 1968, 71, Paris Rev. Humour prize, 1968, Commonwealth Writer's prize, 1990; Guggenheim fellow, 1961; various Can. Coun. fellowships. Mem. Montreal Press Club. Home: Apt 80 C, 1321 Sherbrooke St W, Montreal, PQ Canada H3G 1J4

RICHMAN, ALAN, magazine editor; b. Bronx, N.Y., Nov. 12, 1939; s. Louis and Sonia (Carity) R.; m. Kelli Shor, June 21, 1964; children: Lincoln Seth Shor, Matthew Mackenzie Shor. B.A., Hunter Coll., 1960. Reporter Leader-Observer (weekly newspaper), N.Y.C., 1960-61; asst. editor Modern Tire Dealer (publ.), N.Y.C., 1962-64; assoc. editor ASTA Travel News, N.Y.C., 1964-65; pub. relations rep. M.J. Jacobs, Inc. (advt. agy.), N.Y.C., 1965-66; mng. editor Modern Floor Coverings, N.Y.C., 1966-68; editor Bank Systems & Equipment, N.Y.C., 1968-79, Health Care Product News, N.Y.C., 1976; asso. pub. Bank Systems & Equipment, 1969-71, co-pub., 1971-73, pub., 1973-79; editorial dir. Nat. Jeweler, N.Y.C., 1979-81; editor Health Foods Bus.; editorial dir. Army/Navy Store and Outdoor Merchandiser, 1981-88, The Pet Dealer, 1983-88; editor Cabinet Mfg. and Fabricating KBC Publs., 1988-94; program dir. Cabinet Mfg. Fair, 1989-94; adj. faculty NYU, 1989—, Brookdale Community Coll., 1992—, Bergen County Community Coll., 1994—. Exec. editor: Kitchen and Beth Design News, 1992-93; editor-in-chief Wood Digest, PTN Pub. Co., 1992-94; editor: Whole Foods, 1994—; author: Czechoslovakia in Pictures, 1969, A Book on the Chair, 1968. Served with AUS, 1961-62. Recipient Jesse H. Neal certificate merit Am. Bus. Press, 1973. Mem. Internat. Platform Assn.

RICHMAN, ARTHUR SHERMAN, sports association executive; b. N.Y.C., Mar. 21, 1926; s. Samuel Abraham and Clara (Ganbarg) R.; m. Martha Landgrebe, Nov. 9, 1979. Student, Bklyn. Coll., 1942-44. Baseball writer, columnist N.Y. Mirror, N.Y.C., 1943-63; acct. exec. Grey Pub. Rels., N.Y.C., 1963-65; dir. promotions, pub. rels., traveling sec., spl. asst. to gen. mgr. N.Y. Mets, Flushing, 1965-89; sr. v.p. N.Y. Yankees, Bronx, 1989—. Contbr. articles to profl. and popular jours. Leader baseball groups USO/U.S. Dept. Def., Vietnam, Thailand, Japan, Korea, Philippines, Guam, Hawaii and Greenland, 1965-74;. Recipient Ben Epstein Good Guy award N.Y. Baseball Writers, 1983, Long and Meritorious Svc. award Major League Baseball Scouts, 1984, Good Guy award N.Y. Press Photographers, 1988, Geroge Sisler Long and Meritorious Svc. award St. Louis Browns Hist. Soc., 1996; electo to Bklyn. Coll. Atletic Hall of Fame, 1984, St. Louis Browns Baseball Media Hall of Fame, 1986; inducted into Nat. Jewish Am. Sports Hall of Fame, 1996. Mem. Assn. Profl. Baseball Players Am. (v.p. 1986—). Jewish. Office: NY Yankees Yankee Stadium E 161st St & River Ave Bronx NY 10451

RICHMAN, DAVID PAUL, neurologist, researcher; b. Boston, June 9, 1943; s. Harry S. and Anne (Goodkin) R.; m. Carol Mae von Bastian, Aug. 31, 1969; children—Sarah Ann, Jacob Charles. A.B., Princeton U., 1965; M.D., Johns Hopkins U., 1969. Diplomate Am. Bd. Psychiatry and Neurology. Intern, asst. resident in medicine Albert Einstein Coll. Medicine, N.Y.C., 1969-71; resident in neurology Mass. Gen. Hosp., Boston, 1971-73, chief resident in neurology, 1973-74; instr. neurology Harvard Med. Sch., Boston, 1975-76; asst. prof. neurology U. Chgo., 1976-80, assoc. prof. dept. neurology, mem. immunology and neurobiology coms., 1981-85, prof. dept. neurology and com. on immunology, 1985-91, Straus prof. neurol. scis., 1988-91; prof., chair dept. neurology U. Calif., Davis, 1991—; mem. com. Nat. Inst. Aging, NIH, 1984-85, mem. immunogical scis. study sect., 1986-90. Mem. AAAS, Am. Assn. Immunologists, Am. Acad. Neurology, Am. Neurol. Assn., Phi Beta Kappa, Sigma Xi. Office: U Calif Davis Neurology Dept Davis CA 95616-8603

RICHMAN, GERTRUDE GROSS (MRS. BERNARD RICHMAN), civic worker; b. N.Y.C., May 16, 1908; d. Samuel and Sarah Yetta (Seltzer) Gross; B.S., Tchrs. Coll. Columbia U., 1948, M.A., 1949; m. Bernard Richman, Apr. 5, 1930; children—Doris Ann, Susan. Vol. worker Hackensack Hosp., 1948-70; mem. bd. dirs. YM-YWHA, Bergen County, N.J., 1950-75, bd. mem. emeritus, 1975—; chmn. Leonia Friends of Bergen County Mental Health Consultation Center, 1959; founder, hon. pres. Bergen County Serv-A-Com., affiliated with women orgns. Div. Nat. Jewish Welfare Bd.; v.p. N.J. sect. Nat. Jewish Welfare Bd., 1964-71; hon. trustee women's div. Bergen County United Jewish Community; mem. adv. council Bergen County Office on Aging, 1968-83, reappointed, 1984—; mem. Hackensack Bd. Edn., 1946-51; mem. pub. relations com. Leonia Pub. Schs., 1957-58; N.J. del. White House Conf. on Aging, 1971; trustee Mary McLeod Bethune Scholarship Fund; v.p. Bergen County nat. women's com. Brandeis U., 1966-67. Recipient citation Nat. Council Jewish Women and YWCA in Bergen County, 1962; citation Nat. Jewish Welfare Bd., 1964, Harry S. Feller award N.J. Region, 1965; 14th Ann. Good Scout award Bergen council Boy Scouts Am., 1977; Woman Vol. of Distinction, Bergen County council Girl Scouts, 1979; Human Relations award Bergen County sect. Nat. Council Negro Women, 1982; recipient Gov.'s award, 1988, Cert. of Commendation County Exec. and the Bergen County Bd. of Chosen Freeholders, 1989; honored at testimonial United Jewish Community Bergen County, 1987; Senior Advocate award Divsn. on Aging, 1993; honoree Temple Beth El, 1997. Mem. Kappa Delta Pi.

RICHMAN, HAROLD ALAN, social welfare policy educator; b. Chgo., May 15, 1937; s. Leon H. and Rebecca (Klieman) R.; m. Marlene M. Forland, Apr. 25, 1965; children: Andrew, Robert. AB, Harvard U., 1959; MA, U. Chgo., 1961, PhD, 1969. Asst. prof., dir. Ctr. for Study Welfare Policy, Sch. Social Svc., U. Chgo., 1967-69, dean, prof. social welfare policy, 1969-78, Hermon Dunlap Smith prof., 1978—, dir. of ctr., 1978-81, dir. Children's Policy Rsch. Project, 1978-84, dir. Chapin Hall Ctr. for Children, 1985—, chmn. univ. com. on pub. policy studies, 1974-77; chmn. Univ. Lab. Schs., 1985-88; cons. to gov. State of Ill., Edna McConnell Clark Found., 1984-95, Lilly Endowment, 1987-90, Ford Found., 1987-89; co-chair roundtable on comprehensive cmty. initiatives, 1993—. Chmn. editorial bd. Social Svcs. Rev., 1970-79; contbr. articles to profl. jours. Bd. dirs. Chgo. Com. Fgn. and Domestic Policy, 1969-78, S.E. Chgo. Commn., 1970—, Jewish Fedn. Met. Chgo., 1970-75, Ill. Facilities Fund, 1989-94, Welfare Coun. Met. Chgo., 1970-72, Erikson Inst. Early Childhood Edn., 1972-79, Nat. Urban Coalition, 1975-86, Family Focus, 1980-89, Jewish Coun. Urban Affairs, 1982-87, Ctr. for Study Social Policy, 1983-92, Nat. Family Resource Coalition, 1990-93, Pub./Pvt. Ventures, 1992—, Benton Found., 1994—; bd. dirs. Israel Ctr. on Children, chmn., 1995—. Capt. USPHS, 1961-63. White House fellow, Washington, 1965-66; recipient Disting. Svc. citation U.S. Dept. Health, Edn. & Welfare, 1970, Quantrell award U. Chgo., 1990. Mem. White House Fellows Assn. (v.p. 1976-77), Am. Pub. Welfare Assn. (bd. dirs. 1989-92). Home: 5715 S Dorchester Ave Chicago IL 60637-1726 Office: U Chgo Chapin Hall Ctr for Children 1313 E 60th St Chicago IL 60637-2830

RICHMAN, JOAN F., television consultant; b. St. Louis, Apr. 10, 1939; d. Stanley M. and Barbara (Friedman) R. B.A., Wellesley (Mass.) Coll., 1961. Asst. producer Sta. WNDT, N.Y.C., 1964-65; researcher CBS News, N.Y.C., 1961-64, researcher spl. events unit, 1965-67; mgr. rsch. CBS News (Rep. and Dem. nat. convs.), N.Y.C., 1968; assoc. producer CBS News, N.Y.C., 1968, producer spl. events, 1969-72; sr. producer The Reasoner Report, ABC News, N.Y.C., 1972-75; exec. producer Sports Spectacular CBS, N.Y.C., 1975-76; exec. producer CBS Evening News weekend broadcasts CBS News, N.Y.C., 1976-81, v.p., dir. spl. events, 1982-87, v.p. news coverage, 1987-89; fellow Inst. Politics, John F. Kennedy Sch. Govt., Harvard U., 1990. Chair nat. patrons com. Opera Theatre St. Louis. Recipient Emmy award for CBS News space coverage Nat. TV Acad. Arts and Scis., 1970-71; Alumnae Achievement award Wellesley Coll., 1973. Mem. Coun. on Fgn. Rels., Wellesley Coll. Alumnae Assn. (pres. class of 1961, 1966-70). Home: 14 Tinicum Creek Rd Erwinna PA 18920-9246

RICHMAN, JOEL ESER, lawyer, mediator, arbitrator; b. Brockton, Mass., Feb. 17, 1947; s. Nathan and Ruth Miriam (Bick) R.; m. Elaine R. Thompson, Aug. 21, 1987; children: Shawn Jonah, Jesse Ray, Eva Rose. BA in Psychology, Grinnell Coll., 1969; JD, Boston U., 1975. Bar: Mass. 1975, U.S. Dist. Ct. MAss. 1977, U.S. Supreme Ct. 1980, U.S. Ct. Appeals (1st cir.) 1982, Hawaii 1985, U.S. Dist. Ct. Hawaii 1987. Law clk. Richman & Perenyi, Brockton, Mass., 1973-75, atty., 1975-77; atty. pvt. practice, Provincetown, Mass., 1977-82, Paia, Hawaii, 1985—; arbitrator Am. Arbitration Assn., Paia, 1992—, mediator, 1994—. Pres. Jewish Congregation Maui (Hawaii), 1989-97, bd. dirs., 1984-89; bd. dirs. Pacific Primate Ctr., 1991—, pres., 1994—. Avocations: windsurfing, softball, T'ai Chi. Office: PO Box 46 Paia HI 96779-0046

RICHMAN, JOHN MARSHALL, lawyer, business executive; b. N.Y.C., Nov. 9, 1927; s. Arthur and Madeleine (Marshall) R.; m. Priscilla Frary, Sept. 3, 1951; children: Catherine Richman Wallace, Diana H. BA, Yale U., 1949; LLB, Harvard U., 1952. Bar: N.Y. 1953, Ill. 1973. Assoc. Leve, Hecht, Hadfield & McAlpin, N.Y.C., 1952-54; mem. law dept. Kraft, Inc., Glenview, Ill., 1954-63; gen. counsel Sealtest Foods div. Kraft, Inc., Glenview, 1963-67, asst. gen. counsel, 1967-70, v.p., gen. counsel, 1970-73, sr. v.p., gen. counsel, 1973-75, sr. v.p. adminstrn., gen. counsel, 1975-79, chmn. bd., chief exec. officer, 1979; chmn. bd., chief exec. officer Dart & Kraft, Inc. (name changed to Kraft, Inc. 1986), Glenview, 1980; chmn. Kraft Gen. Foods, Glenview, Ill., 1988-89; counsel Wachtell, Lipton, Rosen & Katz, Chgo., 1990—; bd. dirs. BankAm. Corp. and Bank of Am. Nat. Trust and Savs. Assn., R.R. Donnelley & Sons Co., USX Corp., Security Capital Atlantic Inc.; mem. Bus. Coun. Trustee Chgo. Symphony Orch.; trustee Northwestern U.; trustee Johnson Found.; bd. dirs. Evanston Hosp. Corp., Chgo. Coun. on Fgn. Rels., Lyric Opera Chgo. Mem. Comml. Club, Econ. Club, Chgo. Club, Casino Club (Chgo.); Union League Club (N.Y.C.); Westmoreland Country Club (Wilmette, Ill.); Old Elm Club (Ft. Sheridan, Ill.); Lost Tree Club (N. Palm Beach, Fla.), Shoreacres, Lake Bluff, Ill. Congregationalist. Office: Wachtell Lipton et al 227 W Monroe St Ste 4825 Chicago IL 60606-5018

RICHMAN, JOSEPH HERBERT, public health services official; b. Balt., Aug. 13, 1941; s. Samuel and Beatrice R. BS, Howard U., 1962, MD, 1966; MPH, Johns Hopkins U., 1974. Intern Maimonides Med. Ctr., Bklyn., 1966-67; rotating resident pediats. Sinai Hosp. of Balt., 1967-69; chief sch. health P.G. Health Dept. of Md., Cheverly, Md., 1972-75; dir. area health svcs. Montgomery County Health Dept., Bethesda, Md., 1975-82; county chief pub. health physician State of Del., Dover, 1982—. Maj. USAF, 1969-71. Fellow Am. Acad. Pediatrics, Am. Coll. Preventive Medicine; mem. Masons, Rotary, Phi Beta Kappa. Democrat. Jewish. Avocations: golf, photography. Home: PO Box 386 Dover DE 19903-0386 Office: Divsn Pub Health of Del 805 River Rd Dover DE 19901-3753

RICHMAN, MARC HERBERT, forensic engineer, educator; b. Boston, Oct. 14, 1936; s. Samuel and Janet (Gordon) R.; m. Ann Raeshel Yoffa, Aug. 31, 1963. BS, MIT, 1957, ScD, 1963; MA, Brown U., 1967. Registered profl. engr., Conn., Mass., R.I.; cert. forensic examiner. Cons. engr., 1957—; engr. shipbldg. div. Bethlehem Steel Corp., Quincy, Mass., 1957; instr. metallurgy MIT, Cambridge, 1957-60, research asst. dept. metallurgy, 1960-63; instr. metallurgy div. univ. extension Commonwealth of Mass., 1958-62; asst. prof. engring. Brown U., Providence, 1963-67, assoc. prof., 1967-70, prof., 1970—, dir. central electron microscopy facility Materials Research program, 1971-86, dir. undergrad. program in engring., 1991—; pres. Ednl. Aids of Newton Inc., Providence, 1968-71, Marc H. Richman Inc., Providence, 1981—; guest scientist Franklin Inst., Phila., 1959; vis. prof. U. R.I., Kingston, 1970-71; biophysicist dept. medicine Miriam Hosp., Providence, 1974-87; biogengr. dept. orthopaedics R.I. Hosp., 1979-93. Author: Introduction to Science of Metals, 1967; also articles; editor Soviet Physics: Crystallography, 1970-94; mem. editorial adv. bd. Metallography, 1970—; mem. editorial adv. bd. Jour. Forensic Engring., 1985-88. Maj. Ordnance Corps, U.S. Army, 1963. Served to maj. Ordnance Corps, U.S. Army, 1963. Recipient Engr. of Yr. award R.I. Soc. Profl. Engrs., 1993. Fellow Nat. Acad. Forensic Engrs. (cert.), Am. Coll. Forensic Examiners (cert.), Am. Inst. Chemists, Inst. Materials (U.K.); mem. ASCE, AIME, NSPE, ASEE (Outstanding Young Faculty award 1969), NAFE (bd. cert. diplomate in forensic engring.), Am. Acad. Forensic Scis., Am. Soc. Metals (sec.-treas. 1965-68, chmn. R.I. chpt. 1968-69, Albert Sauveur Meml. award 1968, 69), Providence Engring. Soc. (pres. 1991-92, Freeman award for engring. achievement 1989), B'nai B'rith, Sigma Xi, Tau Beta Pi. Home: 291 Cole Ave Providence RI 02906-3452 Office: Brown U Divsn Engring Box D Providence RI 02912 also: One Richmond Sq Providence RI 02906

RICHMAN, MARTIN FRANKLIN, lawyer; b. Newark, Feb. 23, 1930; s. Samuel L. and Betty E. (Goldstein) R.; stepson Doris (Bloom) R.; m. Florence E. Reif, May 6, 1962; children—Judith, Andrew. B.A. magna cum laude, St. Lawrence U., 1950; LL.B. magna cum laude, Harvard U., 1953. Bar: N.Y. 1953. Law clk. to Judge Calvert Magruder and Chief Justice Earl Warren, 1955-57; assoc., mem. firm Lord Day & Lord, Barrett Smith (and predecessors), N.Y.C., 1957-66, 69-94; of counsel Kirkpatrick & Lockhart, LLP, N.Y.C., 1994—; dep. asst. atty. gen. Office Legal Counsel, Dept. Justice, Washington, 1966-69; Public mem. Adminstrv. Conf. U.S., 1970-76; bd. dirs. Community Action for Legal Services, 1977-80. Trustee St. Lawrence U., 1979-95, trustee emeritus, 1995—, vice chmn. bd., 1988-95; bd. dirs. Friends of Law Libr. of Congress, 1992—. Recipient Alumni citation St. Lawrence U., 1972. Fellow Am. Bar Found., N.Y. Bar Found.; mem. ABA (chmn. sect. adminstrv. law 1983-84), N.Y. State Bar Assn. (ho. of dels. 1981-84), Assn. of Bar of City of N.Y. (sec. and mem. exec. com. 1976-79, chmn. com. fed. legislation 1972-75, com. lawyer's pro bono obligations 1977-81), Am. Law Inst. Office: Kirkpatrick & Lockhart LLP 1251 Avenue of the Americas New York NY 10020-1104

RICHMAN, MARVIN JORDAN, real estate developer, investor, educator; b. N.Y.C., July 13, 1939; s. Morris and Minnie (Graubart) R.; m. Amy Paula Rubin, July 31, 1966; children: Mark Jason, Keith Hayden, Susanne Elizabeth, Jessica Paige. BArch, MIT, 1962; M Urban Planning, NYU, 1966, postgrad., 1967-69; MBA, U. Chgo., 1977; U.S. Dept. State fellow U. Chile, 1960. Architect, planner Skidmore, Owings & Merrill, N.Y.C., 1964, Conklin & Rossant, N.Y.C., 1965-67; ptnr. Vizbaras & Ptnrs., N.Y.C., 1968-69; v.p. Urban Investment & Devel. Co., Chgo., 1969-79, sr. v.p., 1979; pres. bd. dirs. First City Devels. Corp., Beverly Hills, Calif., 1979-80; pres. Olympia & York (U.S.) Devel. (West), 1987-89, Olympia & York Calif. Equities Corp., L.A., 1981-87, Olympia & York Calif. Devel. Corp., 1981-87, Olympia & York Hope St. Mgmt. Corp., 1982-87, Olympia & York Homes Corp., 1983-89, Olympia & York Calif. Constrn. Corp., 1986-89, The Richman Co., L.A., 1989-96, pres. Richman Real Estate Group, Salt Lake City, 1995—; dean Sch. Bus. and Mgmt. Woodbury U., Burbank, Calif., 1993—; pres. Millennium Holdings, Beverly Hills, Calif., 1996—; lectr. NYU, 1967-69, UCLA, 1989-90, Nat. Humanities Inst., other univs. Adv. NEA. Bd. advisors UCLA Ctr. Fin. and Real Estate. With USAF, 1963-64. Registered architect; lic. real estate broker. Mem. AIA, Am Planning Assn., Internat. Coun. Shopping Ctrs., L.A. World Affairs Coun., Urban Land Inst., Nat. Assn. Office and Indsl. Parks, Chief Exec.'s Round Table, Air Force Assn., Lambda Alpha.

RICHMAN, PAUL, semiconductor industry executive, educator; b. N.Y.C., Nov. 17, 1942; s. Harry and Molly (Armel) R.; m. Ellen Margaret Kleiman, July 3, 1966; children: Lee Stuart, Alyson Michelle, Daniel Noah. BSEE, MIT, 1963; MSEE, Columbia U., 1964. V.p. R & D Standard Microsystems Corp., Hauppauge, N.Y., 1971-76, pres., 1976-81, pres., chief exec. officer, 1981-83, pres., chmn. bd., chief exec. officer, 1983—; co-founder Toyo Microsystems Corp., Tokyo, 1987—; pres. The Consortium for Tech. Licensing, Ltd., Nissequogue, N.Y., 1994—; vis. prof. elec. engring. SUNY, Stony Brook, 1976-85; mem. vis. com. for elec. engring. and computer sci. dept. MIT, 1996—. Author: Characteristics and Operation of MOS Field Effect Devices, 1967, MOS Field Effect Transistors and Integrated Circuits, 1974; inventor: COPLAMOS tech. Recipient ann. award for achievement in electronics, Electronics Mag., 1978; named one of 30 most Important Contbrs. in the world to devel. integrated cir. tech., Elec. Engring. Times/Elec. Buyers' News/V.L.S.I. Systems Design, 1988. Fellow IEEE (award for outstanding tech. achievement 1980).

RICHMAN, PETER, electronics executive; b. N.Y.C., Nov. 7, 1927; s. Emil H. and Janet (Seidler) R.; m. Vivian Hoffman, July 29, 1951; children: Meredith, Jeremy. BS, MIT, 1946; MS, NYU, 1953. Asst. chief engr. Reeves Instrument Corp., Garden City, N.Y., 1948-58; chief engr. Epsco, Inc., Cambridge, Mass., 1959-60; v.p., co-founder Rotek Instrument Corp., Watertown, Mass., 1960-64; v.p. Weston-Rotek, Lexington, Mass., 1964-67; cons. electronics engr. Lexington, 1967—; bd. dirs. Thermo Voltek Corp; founder, pres. KeyTek Instrument Corp., 1975-93; mem. NRC/NAS/Nat. Acad. Engring. Evaluation Panel for electricity divsn. Nat. Bur. Standards; mem. sci. adv. groups for several indsl. and sci. orgns. Patentee in precision electronic instrumentation; pioneer in precision dc and audio-frequency measurements, surge electrostatic discharge generation and electrostatic discharge measurements; author: The Insider's Guide to Growing a Small Business, 1996; contbr. articles to profl. jours. Mem. bd. overseers Boston Mus. Sci. Fellow IEEE; mem. Electromagnetics Acad., Instrument Soc. Am. (sr.), Sigma Xi, Tau Beta Pi.

RICHMAN, PETER MARK, actor, painter, writer; b. Phila., Apr. 16, 1927; s. Benjamin and Yetta Dora (Peck) R.; m. Theodora Helen Landess, May 10, 1953; children: Howard Bennett, Kelly Allyn, Lucas Dion, Orien, Roger Lloyd. BS in Pharmacy, Phila. Coll. Pharmacy and Sci., 1951; student of Lee Strasberg, N.Y.C., 1952-54; mem., Actors' Studio, N.Y.C., 1954—. Registered pharmacist, Pa., N.Y. Appeared in little theater, Phila., 1946-51, on stage radio and in live TV, Phila., N.Y.C., and Los Angeles, 1948-65, including Have I Got a Girl for You (pre-Broadway tryout), Biltmore Theater, L.A., 1962, The Deputy, Ctr. Theater Group, L.A., 1965; appeared at Grove Theater, Nuangola, Pa., 1952, Westchester Playhouse, 1953, Drury Lane, Chicago, 1957, Strand, N.J., 1957, Capri, 1959, Ogonquit (Maine) Playhouse, 1955-62, Matunuck, R.I., 1955, Falmouth, Mass., 1953-55, Westport, Conn., 1955, Harrison, Maine, 1962, Dennis, Mass., 1955-62, Phila. Playhouse in the Park, 1962-63; Broadway plays include End as a Man, 1953, Hatful of Rain,Broadway and Nat. Tour, 1956-57, Masquerade, 1959; off-Broadway plays include End as a Man, 1953, The Dybbuk, 1954, The Zoo Story (400 performances), 1960-61; Rainmaker, Private Lives, Angel Street, Arms and the Man, Funny Girl, Owl and the Pussycat, Hold Me, Equus, Night of the Iguana, Blithe Spirit, Twelve Angry Men, Henry Fonda Theatre, L.A., 1985, Babes in Toyland, Calif. Mus. Theater, 1988, Ray Bradbury's Next in Line, L.A., 1992, and numerous others; writer, performer (one man show) 4 Faces, L.A., 1995, N.Y.C., 1996, and others; motion pictures include Friendly Persuasion, 1956, The Strange One, 1956, Black Orchid, 1958, The Dark Intruder, 1965, Agent for HARM, 1965, For Singles Only, 1967, Judgement Day (formerly The Third Hand), 1988, Friday the 13th, Part 8 (Jason Takes Manhattan), 1989, Naked Gun 2 1/2 (The Smell of Fear), 1991; appeared on TV series as Nick Cain in Cain's Hundred, 1961-62, as David in David Chapter III for CBC, 1966, as Duke Page in series Longstreet, 1971-72, as Andrew Laird in series Dynasty, 1981-84, as Channing Capwell in series Santa Barbara, 1984, voice of God series Heroes of the Bible, 1979, voice of the Phantom in animated series Defenders of the Earth, 1986, as Madros in Berlin series My Secret Summer (formerly Mystery of the Keys), 1991; guest star over 500 TV shows, including Hotel, Dallas, Hart to Hart, Fantasy Island, Murder She Wrote, T.J. Hooker, Three's Company, Knight Rider, Star Trek: The Next Generation, Matlock, Beverly Hills 90210, others; starred in TV movies House on Greenapple Road, 1968, McCloud, 1969, Yuma, 1970, Nightmare at 43 Hillcrest (Wide World of Entertainment), 1974, Mallory, 1975, The Islander, 1978, Greatest Heroes of the Bible, 1979, Blind Ambition, 1979, The PSI Factor, 1981, Dynasty, 1981, Dempsey, 1983, City Killer, 1984, Bonanza, The Next Generation, 1988; one-man shows (paintings) Am. Masters Gallery, L.A., 1967, Orlando Gallery, L.A., 1966, McKenzie Gallery, L.A., 1969, 73, Hopkins Gallery, L.A., 1971, Goldfield Gallery, L.A., 1979, Galerie des Stars, L.A., 1988, Crocker Mus., Sacramento, Calif., 1967, others; group shows include Bednarz Gallery, L.A., 1968, Dohan Gallery, L.A., 1966, Celebrity Art Exhibits, 55-city tour, 1964-65, Parkhurst Gallery, Seal Beach, Calif., 1991; 1996; March Thru July, inaugural exhibition of the Henley Gallery Chapman U., Orange, Calif., (a 30-yr retrospective, A life in Art), represented in permanent collections U.S. and abroad; playwright: Heavy, Heavy What Hangs Over? , 1971, a Medal for Murray, 1991 4 Faces, 1995; dir. plays Apple of His Eye, 1954, Glass Menagerie, 1954; featured in book Actor as Artists, 1992, Guide to Artists in Southern California, 1994. Trustee Motion Picture and TV Fund. Served with USN, 1945-46. Recipient silver medallion Motion Picture TV Fund, 1990, Sybil Brand Humanitarian award Jeffrey Found., 1990, Spl. award, 1997, Drama-Logue critics performance award for 4 Faces, 1996, Golden Halo Eagle award, So. Calif. Motion Picture Coun., 1997. Mem. SAG, AFTRA, Actors Equity Assn., Assn. Can. TV and Radio Artists, Acad. Motion Picture Arts and Scis., Acad. TV Arts and Scis. Office: c/o Dale Olson 6310 San Vicente Blvd #340 Los Angeles CA 90048 *I have always been grateful to be able to work in more than one medium. In a way they are all related, each solidifying and nurturing the other. I have a strong belief in God...and spiritual values. This, along with my marriage, children, and family life, has helped me enormously to express my own individuality as an artist.*

RICHMAN, PHYLLIS CHASANOW, newspaper critic; b. Washington, Mar. 21, 1939; d. Abraham and Helen (Lieberman) C.; m. Alvin Richman, June 5, 1960 (div. 1984); children—Joseph, Matthew, Libby. B.A., Brandeis U., 1961; postgrad., U. Pa., 1961-63, Purdue U., 1966-70. Restaurant critic Washington Post, 1976—, exec. food editor, 1980-88, food critic, 1988—. Author: Barter, 1976, Best Restaurants, 1980, 82, 85, 89, The Washington Post Dining Guide, 1996, The Butter Did It, 1997. Mem. Washington Ind. Writers (adv. bd.), James Beard Restaurant Awards (exec. com.). Home: 2118 O St NW Washington DC 20037-1007 Office: Washington Post 1150 15th St NW Washington DC 20071-0001

RICHMAN, STEPHEN ERIK, lawyer; b. Austin, Tex., Mar. 10, 1945; s. Allen A. and Erika (Zimmerman) R.; m. Frances Ellen Sharpe, Aug. 29, 1971; children: Joshua Eric, Wendy Michelle. BA magna cum laude, Amherst Coll., 1967; JD cum laude, Harvard U., 1970. Bar: Wis. 1972. Assoc. Webster Sheffield, N.Y.C., 1970-72; assoc. Quarles & Brady, Milw., 1972-78, ptnr., 1978—. Pres. Milw. Youth Symphony Orch., 1985-87; mem. exec. com. Milw. Jewish Fedn., 1990—, pres., 1996—; mem. exec. com. Milw. Symphony Orch., 1992—; bd. dirs. Jewish Cmty. Found., Milw., 1992—. Mem. ABA, Nat. Assn. Bond Lawyers, State Bar Wis., Phi Beta Kappa. Home: 709 E Carlisle Ave Milwaukee WI 53217-4835 Office: Quarles & Brady 411 E Wisconsin Ave Milwaukee WI 53202-4409

RICHMAN, STEPHEN I., lawyer; b. Washington, Pa., Mar. 26, 1933; m. Audrey May Gefsky. BS, Northwestern U., 1954; JD, U. Pa., 1957. Bar: Pa. 1958, U.S. Dist. Ct. (we. dist.) Pa. With McCune Greenlee & Richman, 1960-63, Greenlee Richman Derrico & Posa, 1963-84, ptnr. Richman, Smith Law Firm, P.A., Washington, 1985—; bd. dirs. Three Rivers Bank; lectr. U. South Fla. Sch. Medicine, Mine Safe Internat. Chamber of Mines of Western Australia, W.Va. U. Med. Ctr. Grand Rounds, Am. Coll. Chest Physicians, Pa. Thoracic Soc., Am. Thoracic Soc., The Energy Bur., Coll. of Am. Pathologists, Allegheny County Health Dept., APHA, Internat. Assn. Ind. Accident Bds. and Commns., Indsl. Health Found., Nat. Coun. Self-Insurers Assn., Am. Iron and Steel Inst., Can. Thoracic Soc., I.L.O./N.I.O.S.H., Univs. Associated for Rsch. and Edn. in Pathology, Am. Ceramics Soc., Nat. Sand Assn.; mem. adv. com. U.S. Dist. Ct. Western Dist. Pa., 1994—; lectr. in field. Author: Meaning of Impairment and Disability, Chest, 1980, Legal Aspects for the Pathologist, in Pathology of Occupational and Environmental Lung Disease, 1988, A Review of the Medical and Legal Definitions of Related Impairment and Disability, Report to the Department of Labor and the Congress, 1986, Medicolegal Aspects of Asbestos for Pathologists, Arch. Pathology and Laboratory Medicine, 1983, Legal Aspects of Occupational and Environmental Disease, Human Pathology, 1993, Impairment and Disability in Pneunoconiosis, State of the Art Reviews in Occupational Medicine-The Mining Industry, 1993, other publs. and articles; author House Bills 2103 and 885 co-author Act 44 and 57 amending Pa. Workmen's Compensation Act. Mem. legal com. Indsl. Health Found., Pitts.; bd. dirs. Pitts. Opera Soc., 1994—, Pitts. Jewish Fedn., 1994—; dir. Jewish Family and Children's Svc., Pitts., 1995—. Mem. ABA (former vice chair workers compensation and employers liability law com., toxic and hazardous substance and environ. law com., lectr.), ATLA, Pa. Bar Assn. (former mem. coun. of worker's compensation sect., lectr., contbg. author bar assn. quarterly 1992, 93), Pa. Chamber Bus. and Industry (workers' compensation com., chmn. subcom. on legis. drafting, lectr.). Home: 820 E Beau St Washington PA 15301 Office: Washington Trust Bldg Ste 200 Washington PA 15301

RICHMOND, ALICE ELENOR, lawyer; b. N.Y.C.; d. Louis A. and Estelle (Muraskin) R.; m. David L. Rosenbloom, July 26, 1981; 1 child, Elizabeth Lara. BA magna cum laude, Cornell U., 1968; JD, Harvard U., 1972; DLH (hon.), North Adams State U., 1987. Bar: Mass. 1973, U.S. Dist. Ct. Mass. 1975, U.S. Ct. Appeals (1st cir.) 1982, U.S. Supreme Ct. 1985. Law clk. to justices Superior Ct., Boston, 1972-73; asst. dist. atty. Office of Dist. Atty., Boston, 1973-76; spl. asst. atty. gen. Office of Atty. Gen., Boston, 1975-77; asst. prof. New Eng. Sch. of Law, Boston, 1976-78; assoc. Lappin, Rosen, Boston, 1978-81; ptnr. Hemenway & Barnes, Boston, 1982-92, Deutsch, Williams, Boston, 1993-95, Richmond, Pauly & Ault, Boston, 1996—; asst. team leader, faculty Trial Advocacy Course, Boston, 1978-82; examiner Mass. Bd. Bar Examiners, Boston, 1983—; trustee Mass. Continuing Legal Edn., Inc., Boston, 1985-96, Nat. Conf. Bar Examiners, 1995—; bd. dirs. Am. Bar Ins., Inc., 1996—. Author (2 chpts.) Rape Crisis Intervention Handbook, 1976; contbr. articles to profl. jours. Bd. of overseers Handel & Haydn Soc., Boston, 1985-94, mem. bd. govs. Handel & Haydn Soc., 1994— (v.p. bd. govs. 1996—); mem. Pres. Adv. Com. on the Arts, 1995—. Named one of Outstanding Young Leaders Boston Jaycees, 1982; Sloan Found. Urban fellow, N.Y.C., 1969. Fellow Am. Coll. Trial Lawyers; mem. ABA (ho. of dels. 1980—, vice chmn. com. on rules and calendar 1986-88), Am. Law Inst., Mass. Bar Assn. (pres. 1986-87), Mass. Bar Found. (pres. 1988-91), Pres. Coun. of Cornell Women; (Trustee, legal def. and edn. fund 1995—), Harvard Club. Office: Richmond Pauly & Ault One Beacon St Boston MA 02108

RICHMOND, ALLEN MARTIN, speech pathologist, educator; b. N.Y.C., July 24, 1936; m. Deborah Moll. BS, SUNY, Geneseo, 1958; MEd, Pa. State U., 1961; PhD, Ohio U., 1965. Instr. N.Y.S. Public Schools, 1958-60, Penn. Rehab. Ctr., 1960-62, Buffalo Hearing and Speech Ctr., 1969-88; clin. instr. dept. otolaryngology SUNY Med. Sch., 1980—; speech pathologist dept. otolaryngology SUNY, Buffalo, 1989—; vis. prof. U. Md., 1968; adj. asst. prof. comm. disorders dept., 1989—; staff Sisters of Charity Hosp.; advisor New Voice Club of Niagara Frontier, Buffalo, 1980-90; cons. Bry-Lin Hosp., Buffalo, 1989—, W.B. Saunders Co., 1988. Contbg. author: An Atlas of Head and Neck Surgery. Participant Very Spl. Arts, Niagara, 1990—. Mem. Am. Speech-Lang.-Hearing Assn. Avocations: running, baseball, reading, travel. Home: 423 Walton Dr Buffalo NY 14225-1005 Office: Sisters Hosp Head and Neck Ctr 2157 Main St Buffalo NY 14214-2648

RICHMOND, ANTHONY HENRY, sociologist, emeritus educator; b. Ilford, Essex, Eng., June 8, 1925; s. Henry James and Ellen Bertha (Hankin) R.; m. Freda Williams, Mar. 29, 1952; 1 dau., Glenys Cathleen Richmond Troth. BSc in Econs., London Sch. Econs., 1949; MA, U. Liverpool (Eng.), 1951; PhD, U. London, 1965. Rsch. officer U. Liverpool, 1949-51; lectr. dept. social study U. Edinburgh, Scotland, 1952-63; reader in sociology Bristol (Eng.) Coll. Sci. and Tech., 1963-65; prof. sociology York U., Toronto, Ont., Can., 1965-89; prof. emeritus, sr. scholar York U., Toronto, 1989—; dir. York U. (Inst. Behavioral Rsch.), 1979-82; social rsch. cons.; vis. prof. Australian Nat. U., Canberra, 1971, 77, St. Antony's Coll., Oxford, Eng., 1984-85. Author: Colour Prejudice in Britain, 1954, 2d edit., 1971, The Colour Problem: A Study of Racial Relations in Britain, Africa and the West Indies, 1955, rev. edit., 1961, Post-War Immigrants in Canada, 1967, (with others) Immigrant Integration and Urban Renewal in Toronto, 1973, Migration and Race Relations in an English City, 1973, (with W. E. Kalbach) Factors in the Adjustment of Immigrants and Their Descendants, 1980, Immigration and Ethnic Conflict, 1988, Caribbean Immigrants: A Demoeconomic Analysis, 1989, Global Apartheid: Refugees, Racism and the New World Order, 1994; editor: Readings in Race and Ethnic Relations, 1972, (with D. Kubat) Internal Migration: The New World and the Third World, 1976; contbr. chpts. to books, articles to profl. jours. Recipient research grants and scholarships. Fellow Royal Soc. Can.; mem. Can. Sociology and Anthropology Assn., Can. Population Soc. Mem. Soc. of Friends. Avocations: classical music, photography. Office: York U, Dept Sociology, 4700 Keele St, North York, ON Canada M3J 1P3

RICHMOND, DAVID WALKER, lawyer; b. Silver Hill, W.Va., Apr. 20, 1914; s. David Walker and Louise (Finlaw) R.; m. Gladys Evelyn Mallard, Dec. 19, 1936; children: David Walker, Nancy L. LL.B., George Washington U., 1937. Bar: D.C. 1936, Ill. 1946, Md. 1950. Partner firm Miller & Chevalier, Washington; lectr. fed. taxation. Contbr. to profl. jours. Served from ensign to lt. comdr. USNR, 1942-46. Decorated Bronze Star; recipient Disting. Alumni Achievement award George Washington U., 1976. Fellow Am. Bar Found., Am. Coll. Trial Lawyers, Am. Coll. Tax Counsel; mem. ABA (chmn. taxation sect. 1955-57, ho. of dels. 1958-60), Am. Law Inst., Lawyers' Club of Washington, Union League (Chgo.), Bird Key Yacht Club (Sarasota), Masons. Republican. Methodist. Home: 988 Boulevard Of The Arts Sarasota FL 34236-4872 Office: 655 15th St NW Washington DC 20005-5701

RICHMOND, ERNEST LEON, research engineer, consultant; b. Catskill, N.Y., Sept. 11, 1914; s. Leon J. and Beulah B. (Garling) R.; m. Constance R. Vroom, Oct. 9, 1943. B of Mech. Engring. cum laude, Clarkson U., 1942; postgrad., N.J. Inst. Tech., 1950-60, Rutgers U., 1950-60. Registered profl. engr., N.J. Test engr. Mack Trucks, Inc., Plainfield, N.J., 1936-45; from asst chief to chief engr. Worthington Corp., Plainfield Works, 1945-58; rsch. engr. Ethicon, Inc. (div. Johnson & Johnson), Somerville, N.J., 1958-75, ret., 1975; consulting engr. Dunellen, N.J., 1975—; seminar speaker Worthington Corp. Speakers' Bur., Plainfield, 1950-58. Author design papers; patentee in field. Vol. United Fund, Plainfield, 1940-50, Cancer Fund, Plainfield, 1940-50, Heart Fund, Plainfield, 1940-50; coach YMCA Ch. Basketball League, Plainfield, 1960-65, chmn. exec. com., 1964-65. Mem. ASME, NSPE, Am. Electroplaters and Surface Finishers Soc. Republican. Presbyterian. Avocations: civil war history, golf, working with young people. Office: PO Box 314 Dunellen NJ 08812-0314

RICHMOND, GAIL LEVIN, law educator; b. Gary, Ind., Jan. 9, 1946; d. Herbert Irving and Sylvia Esther (Given) Levin; children: Henry, Amy. AB, U. Mich., 1966, MBA, 1967; JD, Duke U., 1971. Bar: Ohio 1971, U.S. Claims Ct. 1986, U.S. Ct. Mil. Appeals, 1994; CPA, Ill. Acct. Arthur Andersen & Co., Chgo., 1967-68; assoc. Jones, Day, Cleve., 1971-72; asst. prof. Capital U. Law Sch., Columbus, Ohio, 1972-73, U. N.C. Law Sch., Chapel Hill, 1973-78; vis. asst. prof. U. Tex. Law Sch., Austin, 1977-78, Nova U. Law Ctr., Ft. Lauderdale, Fla., 1979-80; assoc. prof. Nova U. Law Ctr., Ft. Lauderdale, 1980-81, assoc. prof., assoc. dean, 1981-85, prof., assoc. dean., 1985-93, 95—, prof., acting dean, 1993-95. Author: Federal Tax Research, 5th edit., 1997; contbr. articles to profl. jours. Pres. Greater Ft. Lauderdale Tax Coun., 1987-88; chair Law Sch. Admission Coun. Audit Com., 1991-93; chair Assn. Am. Law Schs. Audit Com., 1992, svcs. & programs com., 1997—; trustee Law Sch. Admission Coun., 1994—. Mem. ABA, Am. Assn. Atty.-CPAs (dir. Fla. chpt. 1992—), Assn. Am. Law Schs. (mem. audit com. 1990-92, chair sect. adminstrn. of law schs. 1996, pres. S.E. chpt. 1993-94, sec. S.E. chpt. 1995—), Broward County Women Lawyers Assn. Democrat. Jewish. Avocation: reading. Office: Nova Southeastern U Shepard Broad Law Ctr 3305 College Ave Fort Lauderdale FL 33314-7721

RICHMOND, HAROLD NICHOLAS, lawyer; b. Elizabeth, N.J., Apr. 5, 1935; s. Benjamin I. and Eleanor (Turbowitz) R.; m. Elaine Zemel, June 16, 1957 (div. Nov. 1972); children: Bonnie J. Ross, Michele Weinfeld; m. Marilyn A. Wenrich, Aug. 26, 1973; children: Eric L., Kacy L. BA, Tulane U., 1957; LLB, NYU, 1961, LLM in Taxation, 1965. Estate tax examiner IRS, Newark, 1963-65; tax mgr. Puder & Puder/Touche Ross & Co., CPAs, Newark, 1965-73; ptnr. Sodowick Richmond & Crecca, Newark, 1973-84; prin. Harold N. Richmond, West Orange, N.J., 1984-86; ptnr. Wallerstein Hauptman & Richmond, West Orange, 1986-91, Hauptman & Richmond, West Orange, 1992—. With U.S. Army, 1959-60. Mem. ABA (tax sect. closely held bus. com., real property and probate sect.), N.J. Bar Assn. (tax, real property and probate sects.), Essex County Bar Assn. (chmn. tax com. 1989, real property and probate sect.). Avocations: running, tennis. Office: Hauptman & Richmond 200 Executive Dr West Orange NJ 07052-3303

RICHMOND, JAMES ELLIS, restaurant company executive; b. Chgo., Feb. 16, 1938; s. Kenneth E. and Irene M. (Anderson) R.; m. Karen Ann Ryder, Oct. 6, 1956; children: Scott, Brian, Ann, Susan. BBA, Case Western Res. U., 1960. CPA, Ohio. Sr. auditor Ernst & Ernst, Cleve., 1960-64; treas. Cook United, Inc., Cleve., 1964-75; treas. Fairmont Foods Co., Houston, 1975-80, v.p. ops., 1980-82; v.p., treas. U-tote-M, Inc., 1982-84; mktg. exec. Circle K Convenience Stores, 1984-86; v.p. Consol. Products, Inc., Indpls., 1986—. Lutheran. Home: 13088 Tarkington Common Carmel IN 46033-9352 Office: Consol Products Inc 36 S Pennsylvania St Indianapolis IN 46204-3634

RICHMOND, JAMES G., lawyer; b. Sacramento, Feb. 20, 1944; s. James Gibbs and Martha Ellen (Glidden) R.; m. Lois Marie Bennett, Oct. 22, 1988; 1 child, Mark R. BS in Mgmt., Ind. U., 1966, postgrad., 1966-69, JD, 1969. Bar: Ind. 1969, Ill. 1991, U.S. Dist. Ct. (no. dist.) Ind. 1971, U.S. Dist. Ct. (so. dist.) Ind., 1969, U.S. Ct. Appeals (7th cir.) 1975, U.S. Tax Ct. 1980. Spl. agent FBI, 1970-74; spl. agent Criminal Investigation Divsn. IRS, 1974-76; asst. U.S. atty. no. dist. U.S. Atty. Office, Ind., 1976-80; assoc. Galvin, Stalmack & Kirschner, Hammond, Ind., 1980-81; pvt. practice Highland, Ind., 1981-83; ptnr. Goodman, Ball & Van Bokkelen, Highland, Ind., 1983-85; U.S. atty. no. dist. State of Ind., Hammond, 1985-91; spl. counsel to dep. atty. gen. of the U.S. U.S. Dept. Justice, Washington, 1990-91; mng. ptnr. Ungaretti and Harris, Chgo., 1991-92, ptnr., 1995—; exec. v.p., gen. counsel Nat. Health Labs., 1992-95; practitioner in residence Ind. U. Sch. Law, Bloomington, 1989. Fellow Am. Coll. Trial Lawyers. Republican. Avocation: fishing. Office: Ungaretti & Harris 3500 Three First National Plz Chicago IL 60602-4283

RICHMOND, JULIUS BENJAMIN, retired physician, health policy educator emeritus; b. Chgo., Sept. 26, 1916; s. Jacob and Anna (Dayno) R.; m. Rhee Chidekel, June 3, 1937 (dec. Oct. 9, 1985); children: Barry J., Charles Allen, Dale Keith (dec.); m. Jean Rabow, Jan. 11, 1987. BS, U. Ill., 1937, MS, MD, 1939; DSc (hon.), Ind. U., 1978, Rush-Presbyn.-St. Luke Med. Ctr., 1978, U. Ill., 1979, Georgetown U., 1980, SUNY, Syracuse, 1986, U. Ariz., 1991; DMS (hon.), Med. Coll. Pa., 1980; D in Pub. Svc. (hon.), Nat. Coll. Edn., Evanston, Ill., 1980; LHD (hon.), Tufts U., 1986. Intern Cook County Hosp., Chgo., 1939-41, resident, 1941-42, 46; resident Mcpl. Contagious Disease Hosp., Chgo., 1941; mem. faculty U. Ill. Med. Sch., Chgo., 1946-53, prof. pediatrics, 1950-53; dir. Inst. Juvenile Research Inst. Juvenile Rsch., Chgo., 1952-53; prof., chmn. dept. pediatrics Coll. Medicine, SUNY at Syracuse, 1953-65, dean med. faculty, chmn. dept. pediatrics, 1965-70; prof. child psychiatry and human devel., prof., chmn. dept. preventive and social medicine Harvard Med. Sch., 1971-77, prof. health policy, 1981-88, dir. divsn. health policy rsch. and edn., 1983-88, prof. health policy emeritus, 1988—; also faculty Harvard Sch. Pub. Health; psychiatrist-in-chief Children's Hosp. Med. Center, Boston, 1971-77, adv. on child health policy, 1981—; dir. Judge Baker Guidance Center, Boston, 1971-77; asst. sec. health and surgeon gen. HHS, 1977-81; mem. Pres.'s Commn. on Mental Health, 1977. Author: Pediatric Diagnosis, 1962, Currents in American Medicine, 1969. Nat. dir. Project Head Start; dir. Office Health Affairs OEO, 1965-66. Served as flight surgeon USAAF, 1942-46. Recipient Agnes Bruce Greig

Sch. award, 1966, Parents Mag. award, 1966, Disting. Service award Office Econ. Opportunity, 1967, Family Health Mag. award, 1977, Myrdal award Assn. For Evaluation Rsch., 1977, award for disting. sci. contbn. Soc. for Research in Child Devel., 1979, Dolly Madison award Inst. on Clin. Infants Programs, 1979, Public Health Disting. Service award HEW, 1980, Illini Achievement award U. Ill. Alumni Assn., 1982, Community Service award Health Planning Council Greater Boston, 1985, Lemuel Shattuck award Mass. Pub. Health Assn., 1985, 1st Ann. Ronald McDonald Children's Charities award for Outstanding Contbns. to Child Health and Welfare, 1986, Sedgwick award APHA, 1992. Fellow Am. Orthopsychiat. Assn. (Ittleson award 1994), Am. Psychiat. Assn. (disting.); mem. Am. Acad. Child Psychiatry (hon.), New Eng. Coun. Child Psychiatry (assoc.), Inst. Medicine of NAS (1st Ann. Gustav O. Lienhard award 1986), AMA (AMA-ERF award in health edn. 1988), Am. Pediatric Soc. (John Howland award 1990), Am. Acad. Pediatrics (C. Anderson Aldrich award 1966, ann. award sect. on community pediatrics 1977, Outstanding Contbn. award sect. community pediatrics 1978), Soc. Pediatric Rsch., Am. Psychosomatic Soc., APHA (Martha May Eliot award 1970, Sedgwick Medal 1992), Sigma Xi, Alpha Omega Alpha, Phi Eta Sigma.

RICHMOND, MARILYN SUSAN, lawyer; b. Bethesda, Md., Oct. 19, 1949; d. Carl Hutchins Jr. and Elizabeth Adeline (Saeger) R. BA with honors, U. Fla., 1971; JD, Georgetown U., 1974. Bar: Md. 1974, D.C. 1975. Atty. Office of Gen. Counsel, FTC, Washington, 1974-77, antitrust atty. Bur. of Competition, 1977-81; counsel, consumer subcom. of com. on commerce, sci. and transp. U.S. Senate, Washington, 1981-85; assoc. Heron, Burchette, Ruckert & Rothwell, Washington, 1985-87, ptnr., 1987-90; dep. asst. sec. for govtl. affairs U.S. Dept. Transp., Washington, 1990-91, acting asst. sec. for govtl. affairs, 1991-92; cons. Raffaelli, Spees, Springer & Smith, Washington, 1993-94; asst. exec. dir. govt. rels. APA Practice Directorate, 1995—; lectr. Brookings Instn. Ctr. for Pub. Policy Edn., Washington, 1985-88. Active Lawyers for Bush-Quayle, Washington, 1988. Mem. ABA (antitrust, adminstrv. law sect., vice chair transp. industry com. antitrust sect. 1992-95), Trade Assn. (vice chair com. antitrust sect. 1995). Republican. Methodist. Avocations: horseback riding, tennis. Home: Apt 601 2725 Connecticut Ave NW Washington DC 20008-5305

RICHMOND, MITCHELL JAMES, professional basketball player; b. Ft. Lauderdale, Fla., June 30, 1965; M. Juli Richmond; children: Phillip Mitchell, Jerin Mikell. Bachelor in Social Sci., Kansas State U., 1988. Guard Golden State Warriors, 1988-91, Sacramento Kings, 1991—. Hon. bd. dirs. NCPCA (Spl. Friend award); established Solid As A Rock Scholarship Found., Ft. Lauderdale, 1992. Selected Rookie of the Yr., 1989, Rookie of the Month 3 times, Dec., Jan., March; named NBA Player of the Week, Mar. 25, 1991; selected to NBA All-Star Team, 1993, 94, 95. Avocations: bowling, video games. Office: Sacramento Kings One Sports Parkway Sacramento CA 95834*

RICHMOND, RICHARD THOMAS, journalist; b. Parma, Ohio, May 16, 1933; s. Arthur James and Frances Marie (Visosky) R.; m. Charlotte Jean Schwoebel, Dec. 19, 1933; children: Kris Elaine, Leigh Alison, Paul Evan. AB, Washington U., St. Louis, 1961. Bur. mgr. UPI News Pictures, St. Louis, 1957-62; from asst. picture editor to editor color sect. Post-Dispatch, St. Louis, 1962-80; columnist Post-Dispatch, Clayton, Mo., 1971—; editor calendar sect. Post-Dispatch, St. Louis, 1983-94, asst. entertainment editor, 1995-96, prodn. coord. Get Out Mag., 1996; v.p. Golden Royal Enterprises, St. Louis, 1976-78; pres. Oroquest Press, St. Louis, 1977-80; dir. U.S. Mortgage & Investment Corp., Hilton Head Island, N.C., 1977-81; pres. Magalar Mining, Texarkana, Ark., 1979-83; prodn. coord. Get Out Mag., 1996—. Co-author: Treasure Under Your Feet, 1974, In the Wake of the Golden Galleons, 1976, Diabetes: The Facts That Will Let You Regain Control of Your Life, 1986; editor: You Can Be Rich By Thursday, 1997, Male Homemaker's Handbook, 1997. Avocation: undersea treasure hunting. Home: 307 Lebanon Ave Belleville IL 62220-4126 Office: St Louis Post-Dispatch 200 S Bemiston Ave Clayton MO 63105-1915

RICHMOND, RONALD LEROY, aerospace engineer; b. L.A., Aug. 16, 1931; s. William Paul and Martha Emelia (Anderson) R.; m. Mary Louise Gates, Jan. 2, 1955; children: Pandora Deanne Richmond Perry, Steven Lee. BSME, U. Calif., Berkeley, 1952; MS in Aero. Engring., Calif. Inst. Tech., 1953, PhD in Aero. Engring., 1957. Aerodynamicist Lockheed Aircraft Co., Burbank, Calif., 1952-54; teaching/rsch. asst. Calif. Inst. Tech., Pasadena, 1952-57; asst. group leader aero. performance Douglas Aircraft Co., Long Beach, Calif., 1957-59; chief engr. adv. devel. Ford Aerospace, Newport Beach, Calif., 1959-87; adj. assoc. prof. Sch. Engring., U. Calif., Irvine, 1987-88; dir. engring. Brunswick Def., Costa Mesa, Calif., 1988-94; aerodynamics cons. Douglas Aircraft, 1956-57, Shelby-Am. (Ford) Auto., L.A., 1960-62; subgroup leader NATO Indsl. Adv. Group #16, Brussels, Belgium, 1984-86. Res. dep. Orange County Sheriff's Dept., 1976—. Calif. Inst. Tech. Rsch. assistantship, 1953, 54, 55, 56, 57, teaching asst., 1955, 56, 57, grantee, 1955, 56, 57. Assoc. fellow AIAA (Orange County sect. chmn. 1989-90); mem. Western States Assn. Sheriff's Air squadrons (comdr. 1987-88), Skylarks of So. Calif. (pres., chmn. bd. 1987-88). Republican. Achievements include experimentally proved that skin friction forces on long, slender cylinders was several times that on flat plates, at Mach 5.8 for both laminar and turbulent boundary layers. Home: 1307 Seacrest Dr Corona Del Mar CA 92625-1227

RICHMOND, SAMUEL BERNARD, management educator; b. Boston, Oct. 14, 1919; s. David E. and Freda (Braman) R.; m. Evelyn Ruth Kravitz, Nov. 26, 1944; children: Phyllis Gail, Douglas Emerson, Clifford Owen. AB cum laude, Harvard U., 1940; MBA, Columbia U., 1948, PhD, 1951. Mem. faculty Columbia U., 1946-76, assoc. prof., 1957-60, prof. econ. and statistics, 1960-76; assoc. dean Grad. Sch. Bus. Columbia U., 1971-72, acting dean, 1972-73; dean prof. mgmt. Owen Grad. Sch. Mgmt. Vanderbilt U., Nashville, 1976-86, Ralph Owen prof. mgmt., 1984-88, Ralph Owen prof. mgmt. emeritus, dean emeritus, 1988—, adj. prof., 1988-96; vis. prof. U. Sherbrooke, Que., 1967, U. Buenos Aires, Argentina, 1964, 65, Case Inst. Tech., Cleve., 1958-59, Fordham U., N.Y.C., 1952-53; dir. IMS Internat. Inc., N.Y.C., 1978-88, 1st Am. Corp., Nashville, 1981-86, Winners Corp., Nashville, 1983-89, Corbin Ltd., N.Y.C., 1970-85, Ingram Industries Inc., Nashville, 1981-92; cons. to maj. comml., ednl., profl. and govtl. orgns. Author: Operations Research for Management Decisions, 1968, Statistical Analysis, 1957, 2d. edit., 1964, Regulation and Competition in Air Transportation, 1961; talk show host Nashville Bus. Edit., WDCN-TV, 1984-86. Trustee Ramapo Coll., N.J., 1975-76; bd. dirs. Jewish Fedn. Nashville and Middle Tenn., Temple Ohabai Shalom, Nashville; trustee Endowment Fund Jewish Fedn. Nashville and Middle Tenn. 1st lt. USAAF, 1943-45. Recipient Honor award CAB, 1971, Alumni award for outstanding svc. Grad. Sch. Bus., Columbia U., 1973. Mem. Am. Statis. Assn. (chmn. adv. com. rsch. to CAB 1966-74, dir. 1965-67), Am. Econ. Assn., Inst. Mgmt. Sci., Ops. Rsch. Soc. Am., Beta Gamma Sigma. Home: 5404 Camelot Rd Brentwood TN 37027-4113 Office: Vanderbilt U Owen Grad Sch Mgmt Nashville TN 37203

RICHMOND, WILLIAM PATRICK, lawyer; b. Cicero, Ill., Apr. 5, 1932; s. Edwin and Mary (Allgier) R.; m. Elizabeth A., Jan. 9, 1954 (div.); children: Stephen, Janet, Timothy; m. Magda, June 8, 1992. AB, Albion Coll., 1954; JD, U. Chgo., 1959. Bar: Ill. 1959, N.Y. 1985. Assoc. Sidley & Austin, Chgo., 1960-67, ptnr., 1967—. Served with U.S. Army, 1954-56. Fellow Am. Coll. Trial Lawyers; mem. ABA, Soc. Trial Lawyers, Chgo. Bar Assn. Republican. Methodist. Clubs: Mid-Day; Legal; Ruth Lake Country (Hinsdale, Ill.). Home: 4 Tartan Ridge Burr Ridge IL 60521-8904 Office: Sidley & Austin 1 First Natl Plz Chicago IL 60603-2003

RICHSTEIN, ABRAHAM RICHARD, lawyer; b. N.Y.C., Apr. 18, 1919; s. Morris and Ida (Stupp) R.; m. Rosalind Bauman; children: Eric, Jonathan. B.S., CCNY, 1939; J.D., Fordham U., 1942; LL.M. in Internat. Law, NYU, 1956; M.S. in Internat. Affairs, George Washington U., 1966; diploma, Command and Gen. Staff Coll., 1958, Nat. War Coll., 1966. Bar: N.Y. 1942, U.S. Supreme Ct 1956, U.S. Ct. of Mil. Appeals, 1956, U.S. Dist. Ct. S.D., N.Y., 1957, D.C. 1977. Enlisted as pvt. U.S. Army, 1942, advanced through grades to col., 1966; served with Mil. Intelligence, U.S. 9th Army U.S. Army, Europe, 1944; legal staff U.S. War Crimes Commn. U.S. Army, Ger., 1946; staff officer UN Command (U.S. Army), Far East, 1951-53; mil. law judge (Hdqrs. First Army), 1954-57; chief internat. affairs Office Judge Adv., Hdqrs. US Army Europe U.S. Army, 1960-63; chief plans office Office Judge Adv. Gen., Washington, 1963-64; Judge Adv. Hdqtrs. U.S. Army Combat Devels. Command, 1964-66; ret., 1969; asst. gen. counsel AID, State Dept., 1969-81; gen. counsel ACDA, Washington, 1981-83; mem. faculty Nat. War Coll., 1966-68; adj. prof. Def. Intelligence Coll., Washington, 1989-91; joint staff planner, policy and planning directorate Joint Chiefs Staff, Washington, 1968-69. Mem. editorial bd. Mil. Law and Law of War Rev., 1960-63, Fed. Bar News Jour., 1988-89; book rev. editor: Fordham U. Law Rev., 1941-42. Decorated Bronze Star.; recipient AID Superior Honor award, 1980, ACDA Meritorious Honor award, 1983. Mem. Am. Soc. Internat. Law. Home: 8713 Mary Lee Ln Annandale VA 22003-3659

RICHSTONE, BEVERLY JUNE, psychologist; b. N.Y.C., June 8, 1952; d. Max and Rosalyn Richstone. BA summa cum laude, Queens Coll., 1975; MEd, U. Miami, 1978; PsyD, Nova U., 1982. Lic. clin. psychologist. Clin. fellow Harvard Med. Sch., 1982-83; staff psychologist Met. State Hosp., Waltham, Mass., 1983-85; asst. attending psychologist McLean Hosp., Belmont, Mass., 1983-84; asst. psychologist Cambridge Hosp./N. Charles Mental Health Rsch./Tng. Found., Cambridge, Mass., 1984-85; assoc. dir. Coastal Geriatric Svcs., Hingham, Mass., 1985-86, Alpha Geriatric Svcs., Hingham, 1986-87; rsch. assoc. Harvard Sch. Pub. Health, Boston, 1992-94; instr. psychology Harvard Med. Sch., Boston, 1983-84; consulting psychologist Coastal Geriatric Svcs., Hingham, 1985. Contbg. author: The New Our Bodies, Ourselves, 1992. Cmty. advisor Mass. Office Disability, Boston, 1992—. Mem. APA, Phi Beta Kappa.

RICHTER, BURTON, physicist, educator; b. N.Y.C., Mar. 22, 1931; s. Abraham and Fanny (Pollack) R.; m. Laurose Becker, July 1, 1960; children: Elizabeth, Matthew. B.S., MIT, 1952, Ph.D., 1956. Research assoc. Stanford U., 1956-60, asst. prof. physics, 1960-63, assoc. prof., 1963-67, prof., 1967—, Paul Pigott prof. phys. sci., 1980—, tech. dir. Linear Accelerator Ctr., 1982-84, dir. Linear Accelerator Ctr., 1984—; cons. NSF, Dept. Energy; bd. dirs. Varian Corp., Litel Instruments; Loeb lectr. Harvard U., 1974; DeShalit lectr. Weizmann Inst., 1975; pres. Internat. Union of Pure and Applied Physics. Contbr. over 300 articles to profl. publs. Recipient E.O. Lawrence medal Dept. Energy, 1975; Nobel prize in physics, 1976. Fellow Am. Phys. Soc. (pres. 1994), AAAS; mem. NAS, Am. Acad. Arts and Scis. Achievements include research in elementary particle physics. Office: Stanford Linear Accel Ctr PO Box 4349 Stanford CA 94309-4349

RICHTER, DONALD PAUL, lawyer; b. New Britain, Conn., Feb. 15, 1924; s. Paul John and Helen (Racoske) R.; m. Jane Frances Gumpright, Aug. 10, 1946; children: Christopher Dean, Cynthia Louise. A.B., Bates Coll., 1947; LL.B., Yale U., 1950. Bar: N.Y. 1951, Conn. 1953. Assoc. Winthrop, Stimson, Putnam & Roberts, N.Y.C., 1950-52; ptnr. Murtha, Cullina, Richter and Pinney, Hartford, Conn., 1954-94, counsel, 1994—. Trustee Bates Coll., 1962-94, Manchester (Conn.) Meml. Hosp., 1963-94, Hartford Sem., 1973-85; trustee Suffield Acad., 1974—, pres., 1982-89; bd. dirs. Met. YMCA Greater Hartford, 1970-94, pres., 1976-81, trustee, 1994—; mem. nat. coun. YMCA, 1978-82; bd. dirs. Church Homes, 1967-81; trustee, v.p., Silver Bay Assn., 1971—. With USNR, 1943-46. Fellow Am. Coll. Trust and Estate Counsel; mem. ABA, Conn. Bar Assn., Univ. Club, Hartford Club, Rotary (Paul Harris fellow 1996), Phi Beta Kappa, Delta Sigma Rho. Congregationalist. Home: 140 Boulder Rd Manchester CT 06040-4508 Office: Murtha Cullina Richter & Pinney City Place I 185 Asylum St Hartford CT 06103-3402

RICHTER, JUDITH ANNE, pharmacology educator; b. Wilmington, Del., Mar. 4, 1942; d. Henry John and Dorothy Madelyn (Schroeder) R. BA, U. Colo., 1964; PhD, Stanford U., 1969. Postdoctoral fellow Cambridge (Eng.) U., 1969-70, U. London, 1970-71; asst. prof. pharmacology Sch. Medicine Ind. U., Indpls., 1971-78, assoc. prof. pharmacology and neurobiology, 1978-84, prof., 1984—; vis. assoc. prof. U. Ariz. Health Sci. Ctr., Tucson, 1983; mem. biomed. rsch. rev. com. Nat. Inst. on Drug Abuse, 1983-87. Mem. editorial bd. Jour. Neurochemistry, 1982-87; contbr. numerous articles to sci. jours. Scholar Boettcher Found., 1960-64; fellow Wellcome Trust, 1969-71. Mem. AAAS, Am. Soc. for Pharmacology and Exptl. Therapeutics (exec. com. neuropharmacology div. 1989-91), Am. Soc. for Neurochemistry, Internat. Soc. for Neurochemistry, Soc. for Neurosci., Women in Neurosci., Assn. Women in Sci., Phi Beta Kappa, Sigma Xi. Achievements include research in neuropharmacology, especially barbiturates and neurobiology of mutant mice and dopaminergic systems. Office: Ind U Sch Medicine 791 Union Dr Indianapolis IN 46202-2873

RICHTER, MICHAEL THOMAS, professional hockey player; b. Phila., Sept. 22, 1966. Student, U. Wisconsin. With N.Y. Rangers, 1985—; goalie U.S. Nat. Team, 1987-88, U.S. Olympic Team, 1987-88. Recipient WCHA Rookie of the Yr. award, 1985-86; named MVP, All-Star Game, 1994. Played in NHL All-Star Game, 1992-93, Stanley Cup Championship, 1994. Office: NY Rangers 4 Pennsylvania Plz New York NY 10001*

RICHTER, PETER CHRISTIAN, lawyer; b. Opava, Czechoslovakia, June 13, 1944; came to U.S., 1951; s. Hanus and Alzbeta (Kindlarova) R.; m. Leslie Diane Rousseau, Nov. 25, 1967; children: Timothy Jason, Lindsey Berta. BS, U. Oreg., 1967, JD, 1971. Bar: Oreg. 1971, U.S. Dist. Ct. 1972, U.S. Ct. Appeals (9th cir.) 1972, U.S. Supreme Ct. 1983. Assoc. Veatch, Lovett & Stiner, Portland, Oreg., 1971-73; ptnr. Miller, Nash, Wiener, Hager & Carlsen, Portland, 1973—; adj. prof. law trial advocacy Northwestern Sch. of Law, Lewis and Clark Coll., Portland, 1986—; pro tempore judge Multnomah County Cir. Ct., Portland, 1985—, Oreg. State Bar Trial Advocacy Seminars, 1988—. Author: (handbook) Oregon State Bar, 1987, 88, 89; co-author: (chpt. in book) Oregon State Bar Damage Manual, 1985, 90; editor, program planner Sales: The Oregon Experience, 1989. Trustee, bd. dirs. Parry Ctr. for Children, Portland, 1990; former bd. dir. Boy Scouts of Am., Columbia Pacific Coun., Portland, Nat. Conf. Christians and Jews, Portland, 1983. With Oreg. Army N.G., 1967-75. Recipient Cert. of Appreciation Northwestern Sch. of Law, 1990. Fellow Am. Bar Found.; mem. ABA (trial techniques com.), Fed. Bar Assn. (Oreg. chpt.), Am. Bd. Trial Advocates (advocate), Oreg. Bar Assn. (lectr. trial advocacy seminars 1988—, mem. jud. adminstn. com, bus. lit. sec. exec. comm.), Multnomah Bar Assn. (bd dirs.), Oreg. Assn. Def. Counsel (cert. of appreciation 1987, 89) Inns of Ct., Multnomah Athletic Club, Arlington Club. Avocations: squash, tennis, skiing, golf, reading. Office: Miller Nash Wiener Hager & Carlsen 111 SW 5th Ave Portland OR 97204-3604

RICHTER, RICHARD PAUL, academic administrator; b. Bryn Mawr, Pa., Mar. 6, 1931; s. Manuel DeWitt and Emma Margaret (Theilacker) R.; m. Margot Denithorne, Sept. 5, 1953; children: Karen Lee, Kurt Richard. BA, Ursinus Coll., 1953, LLD (hon.), 1976; MA, U. Pa., 1957; cert., Inst. Ednl. Mgmt., Harvard U., 1974; DHL (hon.), Tohoku Gakuin U., Sendai, Japan, 1986, Muhlenberg Coll., 1989. Editor Provident Mut. Life Ins. Co., Phila., 1956-58; supr. employee communications Phila. Gas Works divsn. UGI Corp., 1958-65; alumni dir. Ursinus Coll., Collegeville, Pa., 1965-67, asst. to pres., 1967-69, v.p. adminstrv. affairs, 1969-76, pres., 1976-94; pres. emeritus, 1995—; instr. in English Ursinus Coll., Collegeville, Pa., 1965-73, asst. prof. English, 1973-86; prof. of coll. Ursinus Coll., Collegville, Pa., 1986-94; chmn. Commn. for Ind. Colls. and Univs. Pa., 1984, Found. for Ind. Colls. of Pa., Harrisburg, 1985; past chmn. Coun. for Higher Edn. United Ch. of Christ; bd. dirs. Core Technologies, Inc. Contbtr. articles, poems to various publs. Chmn. CMMC, Inc. Montgomery Hosp., Norristown, Pa. Recipient Gold Quill award Am. Assn. Indsl. Editors, 1964, Lindback award for excellence in tchg. Ursinus Coll., 1973, Silver Beaver award Boy Scouts Am., 1985, Muhlenberg Leadership award Hist. Soc. Trappe, Pa., 1994, Francis J. Michelini award for outstanding svc. Assn. Ind. Colls. and Univs. of Pa., 1996, Arthur V. Ciervo award Coll. and Univ. Pub. Rels. Assn. of Pa., 1996. Mem. Pa. Assn. Colls. and Univs. (bd. dirs.), Del. Valley Assn. Communicators (past treas.), Pa. Folklife Soc., Montgomery County Hist. Soc. Home: 236 6th Ave Collegeville PA 19426-2510 Office: Ursinus Coll PO Box 1000 Collegeville PA 19426-1000

RICHTER, SUSAN MARY, medical and surgical nurse; b. Breese, Ill., Aug. 17, 1959; d. Jerome J. and Emilia C. (Robke) Albers; m. Michael Richter, Nov. 14, 1980; children: David, Timothy, Alicia. ADN, Kaskaskia Coll., 1979. Nurse aide St. Joseph's Hosp., Breese, Ill., 1977-79; staff nurse ICU/telemetry unit St. Joseph's Hosp., Breese, 1979—; instr. BCLS, ACLS. Com. chmn. pack 273 Boy Scouts Am., Germantown, 1993. Recipient ARC Nurse Vol. award; named Outstanding Young Women in Am., 1989. Mem. Emergency Nurses Assn. (cert. Trauma Nursing Core Course Provider, Pediatric Advanced Life Support Provider).

RICHTER, W. D., screenwriter, director, producer; b. New Britain, Conn., Dec. 7, 1945; s. Walter Oswald and Hedwig (Duch) R.; m. Susan Booth, June 22, 1968. BA, Dartmouth Coll., 1968; postgrad., U. So. Calif., 1968-70. Freelance writer, producer, director, 1973—. Screenwriter: Slither, 1973, Peeper, 1975, Nickelodeon, 1976, Invasion of the Body Snatchers, 1978, Dracula, 1979, Brubaker, 1980 (Academy award nomination best original screenplay 1980), All Night Long, 1981, Big Trouble in Little China, 1986, Needful Things, 1993, Home for The Holidays, 1995; prodr., dir.: (films) Buckaroo Banzai, 1984, Late for Dinner, 1991. Mem. Writers Guild Am., Dirs. Guild Am. Office: The Shapiro/Lichtman Agency 8827 Beverly Blvd Los Angeles CA 90048-2405

RICHTER, WILLIAM, JR., technical management consulting executive; b. Bklyn., Aug. 20, 1934; s. William and Emma (Zehender) R.; m. Eleanor E. Wharton, Nov. 1956; children; Mike S., John E., Kathryn L. AAS, N.Y. C.C., 1956; BSEE, NYU, 1957; MBA, U. Ala., 1970. Program mgr., group engr. Walleye, GPS, Mil Systems, Titan, Gemini Martin Marietta, Denver, 1960-67; program mgr. Skylab Martin Marietta, Huntsville, Ala., 1967-75; from dir. mil. space systems, program dir. space station, mgr. system integration .MX to program mgr. Manned Manuvering Unit Martin Marietta, Denver, 1975-89; mgr. program devel., space and launch sys. SCI Sys. Inc., Huntsville, 1989-96; pres. Guest Assocs. Inc., 1996—; assoc. prof. Met. State U., Denver, 1964-67. Mem. sch. bd. Cherry Creek, Colo., 1976. Recipient Collier trophy, 1982, Group Achievement award NASA, 1987, Pub. Svc. Group Achievement medal NASA, 1988. Mem. AIAA (sr.), Am. Soc. Quality Control (pres. 1963-65), Am. Def. Preparedness Assn., Armed Forces Comms. and Electronics Assn. Avocations: skiing, flying. Home: 1715 Drake Ave SE Huntsville AL 35802-1042 Office: PO Box 1000 Mail Stop 206 8600 S Meml Pkwy Huntsville AL 35807

RICHTOL, HERBERT HAROLD, science foundation program director; b. Bklyn., Aug. 13, 1932; s. Israel and Pearl (Boshnack) R.; m. Iris Gloria Klar, Aug. 11, 1956; children: Nancy Anne, Susan Gail, Elise Carol, Michael Bruce. BS, St. Lawrence U., 1954; PhD, NYU, 1961. Instr. Queens (N.Y.) Coll., 1960-61; chemistry prof. Rensselaer Poly. Inst., Troy, N.Y., 1961-85, dean undergrad. coll., 1985-94; program dir. Divsn. Undergrad. Edn. NSF, Arlington, Va., 1994—. Contbr. articles to profl. jours. Bd. dirs. Temple Beth El, Troy, 1980-85. Served with U.S. Army, 1954-56. Mem. Am. Chem. Soc., AAAS, Am. Assn. Higher Edn., Woodrow Wilson Soc., Sigma Xi. Democrat. Jewish. Avocations: theater, squash. Home: 850 North Randolph St Arlington VA 22203 Office: NSF Divsn Undergrad Edn 4201 Wilson Blvd Arlington VA 22230-0001

RICK, CHARLES MADEIRA, JR., geneticist, educator; b. Reading, Pa., Apr. 30, 1915; s. Charles Madeira and Miriam Charlotte (Yeager) R.; m. Martha Elizabeth Overholts, Sept. 3, 1938 (dec.); children: Susan Charlotte Rick Baldi, John Winfield. B.S., Pa. State U., 1937; AM, Harvard U., 1938, Ph.D., 1940. Asst. plant breeder W. Atlee Burpee Co., Lompoc, Calif., 1936, 37; instr., jr. geneticist U. Calif., Davis, 1940-44; asst. prof., asst. geneticist U. Calif., 1944-49, asso. prof., asso. geneticist, 1949-55, prof., geneticist, 1955—; chmn. coordinating com. Tomato Genetics Coop., 1950-82; dir. CMR Tomato Genetics Resource Ctr., 1975—; mem. genetics study sect. NIH, 1958-62; mem. Galapagos Internat. Sci. Project, 1964; mem. genetic biology panel NSF, 1971-72; mem. nat. plant genetics resources bd. Dept. Agr., 1975-82; Gen. Edn. Bd. vis. lectr. N.C. State U., 1956; Faculty Research lectr. U. Calif., 1961; Carnegie vis. prof. U. Hawaii, 1963; vis. prof. Universidade São Paulo, Brazil, 1965; vis. scientist U. P.R., 1968; centennial lectr. Ont. Agr. Coll. U. Guelph, Ont., Can., 1974; adj. prof. Univ. de Rosario, Argentina, 1980; univ. lectr. Cornell U., 1987; mem. Plant Breeding Research Forum, 1982-84. Contbr. numerous articles in field to books and sci. jours. Recipient award of distinction Coll. Agr. and Environ. Scis., U. Calif., Davis, 1991, Disting. Svc. award Calif. League Food Processors, 1993, Alexander von Humboldt award Alexander von Humboldt Found., 1993; grantee NSF, USPHS/NIH, Rockefeller Found., 1953-83; Guggenheim fellow, 1948, 50, Pa. State U. Alumni fellow, 1991; C.M. Rick Tomato Genetics Resource Ctr. at U. Calif., Davis named in his honor, 1990. Fellow Calif. Acad. Sci., AAAS (Campbell award 1959), Indian Soc. Genetics and Plant Breeding (hon.), Am. Soc. Horticultural Sci.; mem. Nat. Acad. Scis., Bot. Soc. Am. (Merit award 1976), Am. Soc. Hort. Sci. (M.A. Blake award 1974, Vaughan Research award 1946), Mass. Hort. Soc. (Thomas Roland medal 1983), Soc. Econ. Botany (named Disting. Econ. Botanist 1987), Nat. Council Comml. Plant Breeders (Genetic and Plant Breeding award 1987), Am. Genetics Assn. (Frank N. Meyer medal 1982). Office: U Calif Davis CA 95616-1845

RICKARD, NORMAN EDWARD, office equipment company executive; b. Rochester, N.Y., Apr. 6, 1936; s. Norman E. and Florentine (Jensen) R.; m. Patricia Chester, Jan. 19, 1963 (dec. March 7, 1966); children: Anne, Margaret; m. Carol Miller, Apr. 6, 1968 (div. March 24, 1981); children: Sarah, Catherine, Elizabeth; m. Margaret S., June 6, 1981; stepchildren: Lee Ann, Sarah W. BA, St. John Fisher Coll., 1958; MBA, St. John's U., 1962; postgrad. study, NYU, 1962-64. Instr. St. John's U., N.Y.C., 1962-63; various fin. functions Oxford Paper Co., Rumford, Maine and N.Y.C., 1963-66; various positions planning, fin. Xerox Corp., Rochester, N.Y., 1966-71; controller, N.E. region Xerox Corp. U.S. Mktg., White Plains, N.Y., 1971-73; dir. internat. fin. Xerox Corp., Stamford, Conn., 1974-75; controller Xerox Corp., Rank Xerox, London, 1975-78; v.p. planning & control Xerox Corp., Worldwide Mfg., Stamford, 1978-81; dir. Xerox Corp., Stamford, 1981-87, v.p. quality, 1987-92; pres. Xerox Bus. Svcs., 1992-97, Document Svcs. Group, 1997—; co-chairperson, mem. conf. bd. Total Quality Mgmt. Ctr., bd. dirs.; bd. dirs. Vt. Pure Bottling, Am. Direct; sr. examiner Malcolm Baldridge Nat. Quality Award, 1992-93. Trustee St. John Fisher Coll. With U.S. Army, 1958-60. Mem. Assn. for Quality and Participation (bd. dirs. 1991-94), Whippoorwill Country Club, Stratton Country Club, Manchester Country Club. Republican. Roman Catholic.

RICKARD, RUTH DAVID, retired history and political science educator; b. Fed. Republic Germany, Feb. 20, 1926; came to U.S., 1940; d. Carl and Alice (Koch) David; m. Robert M. Yaffe, Oct. 1949 (dec. 1959); children: David, Steven; m. Norman G. Rickard, June 1968 (dec. 1988); 1 stepson, Douglas. BS cum laude, Northwestern U., 1947, MA, 1948. Law editor Commerce Clearing House, Chgo., 1948; instr. history U. Ill., Chgo., 1949-51; instr. extension program U. Ill., Waukegan, 1960-67; instr. history Waukegan Schs., 1960-69; original faculty, prof. western civilization, polit. sci. Coll. of Lake County, Grayslake, Ill., 1969-92; mem. Inter-Univ. Seminar on Armed Forces and Soc.; mem. Hospitality Info. Svc. for Diplomatic Residents and Families affiliate Meridian Internat. Ctr. Author: History of College of Lake County, 1987 (honored by city of Waukegan 1987), (poem) I Lost My Wings, 1989, Au Revoir from Emeritusdom, 1993, Where are the Safety Zones, 1994; spkr. on various ind. radio and TV programs; contbr. articles to profl. jours. Mem. Econ. Devel. Com., Waukegan, 1992-93. Scholar Freedoms Found. Am. Legion, Valley Forge, Pa., 1967. Mem. AAUW (pres. Waukegan chpt. 1955-57, scholarship named for her 1985, program co-chair McLean chpt. 1997), LWV (charter, v.p. Waukegan chpt.), Nat. Press Club D.C. (co-writer/editor NPC History), Phi Beta Kappa. Avocations: writing, travel, reading, theater.

RICKART, CHARLES EARL, mathematician, educator; b. Osage City, Kans., June 28, 1913; s. Charles Day and Ola May (Brewer) R.; m. Annabel Esther Erickson, Mar. 31, 1942; children: Mark Charles, Eric Alan, Thomas Melvin. B.A., U. Kans., 1937, M.A., 1938; Ph.D., U. Mich., 1941. Peirce instr. math. Harvard U., 1941-43; mem. faculty Yale U., 1943—, prof. math., 1959-83, chmn. dept., 1959-65, Percey F. Smith prof. math., 1963-83, prof. emeritus, 1983—. Author: General Theory of Banach Algebras, 1960, Natural Function Algebras, 1979, Structuralism and Structures, 1995. Mem. AAAS, AAUP, Conn. Acad. Arts and Scis., Am. Math Soc., Math . Assn. of Am. Home: 88 Notch Hill Rd Apt 173 North Branford CT 06471-1848 Office: Yale U Dept Math New Haven CT 06520

RICKE, DAVID LOUIS, agricultural and environmental consultant; b. Greensburg, Ind., Aug. 21, 1942; s. Louis Vincent and Lois (Malone) R.; m.

Susan Jane Spenceman, July 20, 1968; children: Stephanie, Elizabeth, Sarah, Emily. BS in Agrl. Econs., Purdue U., 1964. Cert. to registry of environ. and agrl. profls., Nat. Alliance Profl. Crop Cons. Pres. R & R Farms, Inc., Greensburg, Ind., 1967-81; prin. David L. Ricke Cons. Svcs., Greensburg, Ind., 1981—. 1st lt. U.S. Army, 1965-67. Mem. Am. Soc. Agronomy (cert. crop advisor), Ind. Assn. Profl. Crop Cons. (pres. 1991-92), Am. Soc. Agrl. Cons. (cert. mem.), Nat. Alliance of Ind. Crop Cons., Optimists. Home and Office: 601 E Hendricks St Greensburg IN 47240-1763

RICKEL, ANNETTE URSO, psychology educator; b. Phila.; d. Ralph Francis and Marguerite (Calcaterra) Urso; m. Peter Rupert Fink, July 21, 1989; 1 child, John Ralph. BA, Mich. State U., 1963; MA, U. Mich., 1965, PhD, 1972. Lic. psychologist, Mich. Faculty early childhood edn. Merrill-Palmer Inst., Detroit, 1967-69; adj. faculty U. Mich., Ann Arbor, 1969-75; asst. dir. N.E. Guidance Ctr., Detroit, 1972-75; asst. prof. psychology Wayne State U., Detroit, 1975-81; vis. assoc. prof. Columbia U., N.Y.C., 1982-83; assoc. prof. psychology Wayne State U., 1981-87, asst. provost, 1989-91, prof. psychology, 1987—; Am. Coun. on Edn. fellow Princeton and Rutgers Univs., 1990-91; dir. mental health and devel. Nat. Com. for Quality Assurance, Washington, 1995-96; clin. prof. dept. Psychiatry Georgetown U., Washington, 1995—; AAAS and APA Congl. Sci. fellow on Senate Fin. Subcom. on Health and Pres.'s Nat. Health Care Reform Task Force, 1992-93. Cons. editor Jour. of Cmty. Psychology, Jour. Primary Prevention; co-author: Social and Psychological Problems of Women, 1984, Preventing Maladjustment..., 1987; author: Teenage Pregnancy and Parenting, 1989; contbr. articles to profl. jours. Mem. Pres.'s Task Force on Nat. Health Care Reform, 1993; bd. dirs. Children's Ctr. of Wayne County, Mich., The Epilepsy Ctr. of Mich., Planned Parenthood League, Inc., Nat. Symphony Orch. Grantee NIMH, 1976-86, Eloise and Richard Webber Found., 1977-80, McGregor Fund, 1977-78, 82, David M. Whitney Fund, 1982, Katherine Tuck Fund, 1985-90; recipient Career Devel. Chair award, 1985-86; Congl. Sci. fellow AAAS, 1992-93. Fellow APA (div. pres. 1984-85); mem. Midwestern Psychol. Assn., Mich. Psychol. Assn., Soc. for Rsch. in Child Devel., Soc. for Rsch. in Child and Adolescent Psychopathology, Internat. Assn. of Applied Psychologists, Sigma Xi, Psi Chi. Roman Catholic.

RICKELS, KARL, psychiatrist, physician, educator; b. Wilhelmshaven, Germany, Aug. 17, 1924; came to U.S., 1954, naturalized, 1960; s. Karl E. and Stephanie (Roehrhoff) R.; m. Rosalind Wilson, June 27, 1964; children: Laurence Arthur, Stephen W., Michael R. M.D., U. Muenster, 1951. Intern Dortmund (Germany) Hosp., 1951-52; postgrad. tng. U. Erlangen, U. Frankfurt, City Hosp. Kassel, 1952-54; resident in psychiatry Mental Health Inst., Cherokee, Iowa, 1954-55, Hosp. U. Pa., Phila., 1955-57; from instr. to assoc. prof. U. Pa., Phila., 1957-69; prof. psychiatry U. Pa., 1969—, prof. pharmacology, 1976-96, Stuart and Emily B.H. Mudd prof. human behavior, 1977—, chief mood and anxiety disorders program, 1964—; chmn. com. on studies involving human beings U. Pa., Phila., 1985—; chief psychiatry Phila. Gen. Hosp., 1975-77. Editor, author 7 books; contbr. over 500 articles to profl. publs. Fellow Am. Coll. Neuropsychopharmacology (charter), Am. Coll. Clin. Pharmacology, Am. Psychiat. Assn., Coll. Physicians Phila., Collegium Internat. Neuro-Psychopharmacologicum; mem. Arbeits Gemeinschaft Neuro-Psychopharmacology, Internat. Soc. Investigation of Stress, European Coll. Neuropsychopharmacology (corr.). Home: 1324 Youngsford Rd Gladwyne PA 19035-1231 Office: U Pa Dept Psychiatry 803 Sci Ctr 3600 Market St Philadelphia PA 19104-2641

RICKER, ROBERT S., religious organization administrator. Pres. Bapt. Gen. Conf., Arlington Heights, Ill., 1988—. Office: Bapt Gen Conf 2002 S Arlington Heights Rd Arlington Heights IL 60005-4102*

RICKER, WILLIAM EDWIN, biologist; b. Waterdown, Ont., Can., Aug. 11, 1908; s. Harry Edwin and Rebecca Helena (Rouse) R.; m. Marion Torrance Cardwell, Mar. 30, 1935; children—Karl Edwin, John Fraser, Eric William, Angus Clemens. B.A., U. Toronto, 1930, M.A., 1931, Ph.D., 1936; D.Sc. (hon.), U. Man., 1970; LL.D., Dalhousie U., 1972; DSc (hon.), U. Guelph, 1996. Sci. asst. Fisheries Research Bd. Can., Nanaimo, B.C., 1931-38; editor publs. Fisheries Research Bd. Can., Nanaimo, 1950-62, biol. cons. to chmn. and staff, 1962-63; acting chmn. Fisheries Research Bd. Can., Ottawa, 1963-64; chief scientist Fisheries Research Bd. Can., Nanaimo, 1964-73; jr. scientist Internat. Pacific Salmon Fisheries Commn., New Westminster, B.C., 1938-39; asst. prof., assoc. prof., prof. zoology Ind. U., 1939-50; dir. Ind. Lake and Stream Survey Ind. Dept. Conservation, 1939-50; vol., contract investigator Pacific Biol. Sta., Nanaimo, 1973-96. Contbr. articles to profl. jours. Decorated officer Order of Can., 1986; named Eminent Ecologist Ecol. Soc. Am., 1990; recipient Murray Newman award Vancouver Aquarium, 1995. Fellow Royal Soc. Can. (Flavelle medal 1970), AAAS; mem. Wildlife Soc. (awards 1956, 59), Profl. Inst. Pub. Service Can. (gold medal 1966), Am. Fisheries Soc. (award of excellence 1969), Can. Soc. Zoologists (F.E.J. Fry medal 1983), Am. Soc. Limnology and Oceanography (pres. 1959), Arctic Inst. N.Am., Can. Soc. Wildlife and Fishery Biologists, Entomol. Soc. B.C., Internat. Assn. Limnology, Marine Biol. Assn. India, Ottawa Field-Naturalists Club, Wilson Ornithol. Club, Explorers Club, Sigma Xi. Home: 3052 Hammond Bay Rd, Nanaimo, BC Canada V9T 1E2

RICKERD, DONALD SHERIDAN, foundation executive; b. Smiths Falls, Ont., Can., Nov. 8, 1931; s. Harry M. and Evaline Mildred (Sheridan) R.; m. Julie Rekai, Dec. 14, 1968; 1 child, Christopher. Student, St. Andrews U., Scotland, 1951-52; BA, Queen's U., Can., 1953; LLD, Queen's U., 1985; BA (Rotary Found. fellow), Oxford U., Eng., 1955, MA, 1963; DCL, Mount Allison U., Can., 1985; LLD, Trent U., Can., 1986; LLB, York U., Can., 1991. Bar: Ont. 1959; apptd. Queen's Counsel, 1978. Assoc. Fasken & Calvin, Toronto, 1957-61; registrar, lectr. history, asst. prof. law Faculty of Adminstrv. Studies York U., Toronto, 1961-68; pres. Donner Can. Found., Toronto, 1968-89, W.H. Donner Found., Inc., N.Y.C., 1971-87, Max Bell Found., Toronto, 1989—; chmn. bd. dirs. Draeger Can. Ltd.; bd. dirs. ICWI Found., Kingston, Jamaica. Former chmn. Coun. Ontario Coll. Art, Toronto; past chmn. Ctrl. Hosp., 1993-96; mem. Royal Commn. concerning activities of Royal Canadian Mounted Police, 1977-81; former bd. govs. Upper Can. Coll., Toronto, trustee, vice chmn. bd. trustees, Queen's U.; former mem. bd. regents Mt. Allison U. Decorated Order of Can. Mem. Can. Bar Assn., County of York Law Assn., Toronto Lawyers Club, Bd. Trade Met. Toronto, Univ. Club. Office: Max Bell Found, 79 Wellington St W PO Box 105, Toronto, ON Canada M5K 1G8

RICKERSON, JEAN MARIE, video producer, journalist, photographer; b. Takoma Park, Md., Dec. 29, 1956; d. Charles Marvin and Rita Ann (Smith) Blackburn; m. Ronald Wayne Rickerson, Oct. 18, 1989; children: Drew Elliott, Ella Celine. BS, U. Md., 1978. Pres. Videofax Inc., Bethesda, Md., 1982-90; founder, dir. Found. for Acad. Excellence Inc., Bethesda, 1985-90; video prodr. Applied Measurement Systems Inc., Bremerton, Wash., 1990—; pres. Photo Graphics Inc., Bremerton, 1992—; video coord. 2nd Internat. Submarine Races, Ft. Lauderdale, Fla., 1991. Contbr. articles and photographs to profl. jours; writer, prodr., dir. videotape SEAFAC, 1992, USNS Hayes, 1993, High Gain Array Test Module, 1993, Advanced Mine Detection Sonar, 1995, BQH-9 Signal Data Recording Set, 1996, Submarine Acoustic Maintenance Program, 1996, Intermediate Scale Measurement System, 1996; creator, editor (newsletter) Oceaneer, 1990; editor (newsletter) Crosstalk, 1990—. Avocations: skiing, camping, gardening, scuba diving. Office: Applied Measurement Sys Inc 645 4th St Ste 202 Bremerton WA 98337-1402

RICKERT, EDWIN WEIMER, investment consultant; b. Connersville, Ind., June 17, 1914; s. Edwin and Grace (Weimer) R.; A.B., Columbia U., 1936; m. Ruth Alma Fulcher, July 9, 1942; children—Jean Adelia, Wendy Grace, Allen Edwin. Security analyst, economist Mackubin, Legg & Co., Balt., 1936-40; indsl. analyst Office of Prodn. Mgmt., Washington, 1940-41; supr. commodity econ. research Standard Brnds, Inc., N.Y.C., 1946-53; with Brundage, Story & Rose, N.Y.C., 1953—, partner, 1966-83, sr. investment cons., 1984—. Trustee, Columbia U. Press, 1977-96, trustee emeritus, 1996—; bd. visitors Columbia Coll., N.Y., 1986-92. Served to capt. U.S. Army, 1941-46; ret. lt. col. Res. Mem. Investment Counsel Assn. Am., N.Y. Soc. Security Analysts. Republican. Presbyterian. Clubs: India House (N.Y.C.); Grachur (Balt.). Home: 56 Dogwood Ln Rockville Centre NY 11570-1501 Office: 1 Broadway New York NY 10004-1007

RICKERT, JONATHAN BRADLEY, foreign service officer; b. Washington, July 23, 1937; s. Van Dusen and Margaret Eleanor (Bradley) R.; m. Ulla Gerd Margareta Granstrand, June 20, 1969; children: Ulla Margaret, Jonathan Bernt. AB cum laude, Princeton U, 1959; diploma Russian lang., U.S. Army Lang. Sch., 1962; student, Harvard U., 1976-77; MA, George Washington U., 1982. Rotational jr. officer Exec. Sec. State Dept., 1963-65; consular officer Embassy, London, 1965-66; staff aide to amb., polit. officer Embassy, Moscow, 1966-68; exchanges officer Office Soviet and Eastern European Exchanges State Dept., 1969-70, with Romanian Lang. Tng. FSI, 1971; consular officer Embassy Bucharest, 1971-73, polit. officer, 1973-74; spl. asst. to U.S. Rep. U.S. Delegation MBFR, Vienna, 1974-76; polit./labor officer Embassy Port Spain, 1977-80; desk officer Trinidad, Guyana, Suriname, acting dep. dir. Office Caribbean Affairs State Dept., 1980-82, desk officer Romania, Office Eastern European and Yugoslav Affairs, 1982-84, with Bulgarian Lang. Tng., 1984-85; dep. chief mission Embassy Sofia, 1985-88; chief European Assignments divsn. State Dept., 1988-90; legis. asst. to Sen Bob Packwood, 1990-91; dep. chief mission Embassy Bucharest, 1991-95; dir. Office of N. Cen. European Affairs State Dept., 1995—. With U.S. Army, 1961-62. Mem. Am. Fgn. Svc. Assn. Episcopalian.

RICKERT, ROBERT RICHARD, pathologist, educator; b. Harrisburg, Pa., Oct. 19, 1936; s. Alton G. and Henrietta (Gey) R.; m. Sonja Murray Hansen, Aug. 26, 1961; children: Kristin, Robin, Anne. AB, U. Mich., 1958; MD, John Hopkins U., 1962. Diplomat Am. Bd. of Pathology. Intern Yale-New Haven (Conn.) Med. Ctr., 1962-63, resident, 1963-64, 66-67; rsch. assoc. Atomic Bomb Casulty Commn., Hiroshima, Japan, 1964-66; asst. prof. of Pathology Yale U. Sch. Med., New Haven, 1968-70; attending Pathologist Yale New Haven Med. Ctr., 1968-70; dir. of Surg. Pathology U. Med. and Dentistry N.J.-N.J. Med. Sch., Newark, 1970-73, assoc. prof. Pathology, 1970-73; adj. assoc. prof. of Pathology Columbia U. Coll. of Physicians & Surgs., N.Y.C., 1974-89; clin. prof. of Pathology U. of Med. and Dentistry N.J.-N.J. Med. Sch., Newark, 1985—; co-chmn. Dept. of Pathology St. Barnabas Med. Ctr., Livingston, N.J., 1973—. Author and co-author of more than 60 articles and chpts. Chmn. med. com. Am. Cancer Soc., N.J., 1989-91, v.p. 1991-93, pres. elect 1993-94, pres. 1995-97. Fellow Coll. Am. Pathologists, Am. Soc. Clin. Pathologists, U.S.-Can. Acad. Pathology; mem. AMA, N.J. Soc. Pathologists (pres. 1980-82), Gastrointestinal Pathology Soc. (pres. 1988-89), Med. Soc. N.J., Acad. Medicine N.J. (trustee 1988—, treas. 1994-95, v.p. 1995-97, pres.-elect 1997—), Am. Soc. Cytology, Short Hills Club, Phi Beta Kappa, Alpha Omega Alpha. Republican. Congregational. Avocations: antiques, wine collecting. Office: St Barnabas Med Ctr Dept Pathology Livingston NJ 07039

RICKETTS, GARY EUGENE, animal scientist; b. Willard, Ohio, Aug. 2, 1935; s. Franklin Edward and Berthalda Marie (Albright) R.; m. Audrey May Wheeler, Sept. 14, 1958; children—Dawn, John, Mark. B.S., Ohio State U., 1957, M.S., 1960, Ph.D., 1963. Livestock extension specialist dept. animal sci. U. Ill., Urbana-Champaign, 1964-86, sheep extension specialist and extension program leader, 1986—. Contbr. articles to profl. jours. and livestock publs. Active Little League Baseball, 8 yrs.; leader 4-H Club, 11 yrs. Served with Army N.G., 1958-64. Recipient Beef Bosster award Ill. Red Angus Assn., 1973, G.R. Carlisle Ext. award, 1979, 95, Outstanding Leadership and Recognition award Ill. Sheep Industry, 1984, Sustained Excellence award in ext. Ill. Coop. Ext. Svc., 1984, J.C. Spitler award Epsilon Sigma Phi, 1984, State Disting. Svc. award, 1995, Guy Green award Am. Corriedale Assn., 1992. Mem. Am. Soc. Animal Sci. (Young Scientist award Midwest sect. 1971, Extension award 1984), Am. Registry Profl. Animal Scientists. Republican. Methodist. Home: 2506 S Cottage Grove Ave Urbana IL 61801-6820 Office: 128 ASL 1207 W Gregory Dr Urbana IL 61801-3838

RICKEY, GEORGE WARREN, artist, sculptor, educator; b. South Bend, Ind., June 6, 1907; s. Walter J. and Grace (Landon) R.; m. Edith Leighton, May 24, 1947 (wid. June 1995); children: Stuart Ross, Philip J.L. Ed., Trinity Coll., Glenalmond, Scotland, 1921-26; B.A., Balliol Coll., Oxford U., 1929, MA, 1940; postgrad., Acad. Lhote, Paris, 1929-30, Inst. Fine Arts, NYU, 1945-46, State U. Iowa, 1947, Inst. Design, Chgo., 1948-49; PhD (hon.), Union Coll., Schenectady, 1973, Ind. U., 1974, Kalamazoo Coll., 1977; hon. doctorates, York U., Can., 1978; PhD (hon.), Tulane U., 1983, Rensselaer Polytechnic Inst., Troy, N.Y., 1990. Tchr. Groton Sch., 1930-33; artist-in-residence Olivet Coll., 1937-39, Kalamazoo Coll., 1939-40, Knox Coll., 1940-41; head dept. art Muhlenberg Coll., 1941-42, 46-48; assoc. prof. design Ind. U., Bloomington, 1949-55; prof. Tulane U., New Orleans, 1955-61, head dept., 1955-59; prof. art Sch. Architecture Rensselaer Poly. Inst., Troy, N.Y., 1962-65. Sculptor, DAAD Art Program, Berlin, Germany, 1968-69, 71-72. Exhibited Denver Mus., 1945, 48, Met. Mus. Art, 1951, Pa. Acad. Ann., 1952-54, Whitney Mus., 1952-53, 64, Mus. Modern Art, 1959, Albright-Knox Gallery, 1965, Mus. Modern Art Internat. Council, 1965, Stedelijk Mus., Amsterdam, Holland, 1965, Mus. Tel Aviv, 1965, St. Louis Bicentennial Sculpture Exhbn., 1965, Dag Hammerskjold Plaza, N.Y.C., 1977, Pier and Ocean, Hayward Gallery, London, 1980, Whitney Mus., 1983, Neuer Berliner Kunstverein, 1987, Am. Fedn. Arts, 1991, Found. Maeght, France, 1992, Lumiere et Mouvement, Paris, 1996, other U.S. and fgn. galleries; one man shows: Maxwell Davidson Gallery, N.Y.C., John Herron Art Mus., Indpls., 1953, Delgado Mus., New Orleans, 1955, Kraushaar Gallery, 1955, 1959, Amerika Haus, Hamburg, Germany, 1957, Santa Barbara Mus., 1960, Kunstverein, Düsseldorf, Fed. Republic Germany, 1962, Kunsthalle, Hamburg, 1962, Inst. Contemporary Arts, Boston, 1964, Corcoran Gallery, Washington, 1966, UCLA, 1971, Kestner Gesellschaft, Hannover, 1973, Nationalgalerie, Berlin, 1973-74, Amerika Haus, Berlin, 1979, Guggenheim Mus., 1979, Montreal Musée d'Art Contemporain, 1981, Nat. Sculpture Trust, Glasgow, Scotland, 1982, Sculpture Park, Yorkshire, Eng., 1982, Fairweather Hardin Gallery, 1982, Tulane U. Art Gallery, New Orleans, 1983, Bauhaus Archiv., Berlin, Fed. Republic Germany, 1984, Josef Albers Mus., Bottrop, Fed. Republic Germany, 1984, George Rickey in South Bend, 1985, Neuer Berliner Kunstverein, Berlin, 1986, Neuberger Mus., Purchase, N.Y., 1987, Veranneman Found., Holland, 1988, Mus. Boymans-van Beuningen, Rotterdam, Holland, 1989, Gallery Kasahara, Osaka, Japan, 1989, Artcurial, Paris, 1990, Katonah Mus. Art, 1991, Berlinische Galerie, Berlin, 1992, Foundation Maeght, Vence, France, 1992, UCLA Wright Art Gallery, L.A., 1993, Harenberg Verlag, Dortmund, Germany, 1994, numerous others; represented in permanent collections: Dallas Mus., Kunsthalle, Hamburg, Whitney Mus., Mus. Modern Art, Albright-Knox Gallery, Tate Gallery, London, U. Glasgow, U. Heidelberg, Nationalgalerie, Berlin, Corcoran Gallery of Arts, Washington, Louisiana Mus., Humlebaek, Denmark, Auckland City Art Gallery, New Zealand, Tokyo City Hall, Japan, City of Nurnberg, Germany, Nat. Mus. Fine Art, Osaka, Japan, New Theatre, Rotterdam, Parliament Bldg., Dusseldorf, Fed. Republic Germany, Hara Mus., Tokyo, Berlinische Galerie, Berlin, others, also pvt. collections; executed commns. Ft. Worth City Hall, 1974, Fed. Courthouse, Honolulu, 1976, Tech. U., Ulm, Germany, 1977, Ruhr U., Bochum, Ger., 1978, K.B. Plaza, New Orleans, 1978, Central Trust Center, Cin., 1979, Nat. City Ctr., Cleve., 1980, Pitts. Nat. Steel Ctr., 1982, Gerald Ford Library, Ann Arbor, Mich., 1982, Musée de Grenoble, France, 1991, Nat. Gallery, Washington, 1992, Martin Gropius Bau, Berlin, 1992, Nat. Mus. of Fine Arts, Osaka, 1993, Met. Mus. of Art, N.Y.C., 1994; author: Constructivism: Origins and Evolution, 1967, 95; contbr. to publs. in field. Decorated Order of Merit 1st Class, Germany, 1993; recipient Fine Arts medal AIA, 1972, Skowhegan medal for sculpture Skowhegan Sch. Painting and Sculpture, 1973, Ind. Arts. Commn. award for sculpture, 1975, Creative Arts Award medal Brandeis U., 1979; Guggenheim fellow, 1960-62. Mem. Am. Acad. Arts and Letters (Gold medal for sculpture 1995), Coll. Art Assn., Akademie der Kunste (Berlin). Episcopalian. Club: Century Assn. (N.Y.C.).

RICKLES, DONALD JAY, comedian, actor; b. L.I., N.Y., May 8, 1926; s. Max S. and Etta (Feldman) R.; m. Barbara Sklar, Mar. 14, 1965; children: Mindy Beth, Lawrence Corey. Grad., Am. Acad. Dramatic Arts, N.Y.C. Appeared in TV shows The Don Rickles Show, 1971-72, C.P.O. Sharkey, 1976-77, Foul-Ups, Bleeps and Blunders, 1984, Daddy Dearest, 1993; appeared in movies Run Silent, Run Deep, 1958, The Rabbit Trap, 1959, The Rat Race, 1960, Where It's At, 1969, Innocent Blood, 1992, Kelly's Heroes, 1992, Casino, 1995, Toy Story, 1995, others; appeared as comedian at Desert Inn, Las Vegas, Nev., Harrah's Club, Reno and Lake Tahoe, Nev., Trump Taj Mahal, Atlantic City, numerous other nightclubs; numerous appearances TV variety shows; rec. albums include Don Rickles Speaks. Served with USN, 1943-45. Named Entertainer of Yr., Friars Club, 1974. Jewish. Avocation: golfing. Office: care Shefrin Co PO Box 36066 Los Angeles CA 90036

RICKMAN, TOM, screenwriter, director; b. Sharpe, Ky., Feb. 8, 1940; s. Marshall and Mattie Colleen (Johnston) R. BA, Murray State Coll., 1965; MA, U. Ill., 1969. Fellow Am. Film Inst., Beverly Hills, Calif., 1969-71; founder, dir. Squaw Valley (Calif.) Screenwriters Workshop, 1975—; resource advisor Sundance (Utah) Inst., 1981—, trustee, 1981-88; instr. grad. course in screenwriting U. So. Calif., L.A., 1987. Writer, dir. (short film) What Fixed Me, 1971 (Best Film award Nat. Student Assn. 1971), (feature film) The River Rat, 1984, (TV movie) Shannon's Deal: Wrongful Death, 1991; writer (feature films) The Laughing Policeman, 1973, W.W. and the Dixie Dancekings, 1975, Coal Miner's Daughter, 1980 (Academy award nomination best adapted screenplay 1980), Everybody's All-American, 1988; co-writer (feature films) Kansas City Bomber, 1972, The White Dawn, 1974, Hooper, 1978; author (play) The Collaborators, 1981. Served with USMC, 1958-61. Office: William Morris Agy 151 S El Camino Dr Beverly Hills CA 90212-2704*

RICKS, DONALD JAY, agricultural economist; b. Lansing, Mich., Sept. 14, 1936; s. Glenn L. and Evelyn N. R.; m. Joanne M. Burr, Aug. 24, 1968; children: Mark, Craig. B.S. with highest honors, Mich. State U., 1958, M.S., 1960; Ph.D., Oreg. State U., 1965. Instr. econs. Oreg. State U., 1962-63, asst. in agrl. econs., 1963-64; asst. prof. agrl. econs. Mich. State U., 1964-70, assoc. prof., 1970-76, prof., 1976—, extension mktg. economist, 1973—, project leader, extension mktg., 1976-82; chmn. Fed. Cherry Adminstrv. Bd.; mem. Mich. Apple Com. Contbr. numerous articles to various publs. Recipient State Extension Team award, 1971, Man of Yr. award Nat. Cherry Industry, 1989, Mich. Fruit Industry Man of the Yr. award, 1997. Mem. Am. Agrl. Econs. Assn., Extension Specialists Assn., Mich. Assn. County Agts. (Outstanding Extension Specialist award 1982), Mich. Extension Specialists Assn. (Outstanding Extension Specialist award 1989), Phi Kappa Phi, Epsilon Sigma Phi, Phi Eta Sigma, Alpha Zeta. Home: 953 Barry Rd Haslett MI 48840-9116 Office: Room 23 Agr Hall Mich State U East Lansing MI 48823

RICKS, MARY F(RANCES), academic administrator, anthropologist; b. Portland, Oreg., July 6, 1939; d. Leo and Frances Helen (Corcoran) Samuel; m. Robert Stanley Ricks, Jan. 7, 1961; children: Michael Stanley, Allen Gilbert. BA, Whitman Coll., 1961; MA, Portland State U., 1977, MPA, 1981, PhD, 1995. Asst. to dir. auxiliary services Portland State U., 1975-79, instnl. researcher, 1979-85, dir. instnl. research and planning, 1985—, rsch. assoc. prof., 1994—. Contbr. articles and presentations to profl. socs. Vol. archeologist BLM-USDI, Lakeview, Oreg., 1983—. Fellow Soc. Applied Anthropology; mem. Soc. Am. Archaeology, Soc. Coll. and U. Planning, Pacific N.W. Assn. Instnl. Rsch. and Planning (pres. 1990-91), Assn. Oreg. Archaeologists (v.p. 1988-90), Assn. Instl. Rsch., City Club of Portland, Sigma Xi. Home: 5466 SW Dover Loop Portland OR 97225-1033 Office: Portland State U Office Instnl Rsch/Planning PO Box 751 Portland OR 97207-0751

RICORDI, CAMILLO, surgeon, transplant and diabetes researcher; b. N.Y.C., Apr. 1, 1957; m. Valerie A. Grace, Aug. 8, 1986; children: M. Caterina, Eliana G., Carlo A. MD, U. Milan (Italy) Sch. Medicine, 1982. Trainee in gen. surgery San Raffaele Inst., Milan, 1982-85; NIH trainee Washington U. Sch. Medicine, St. Louis, 1985-88; attending surgeon San Raffaele Inst., Milan, 1988-89; asst. prof. to assoc. prof. surgery U. Pitts., Pa., 1989-93; prof. surgery and medicine, chief divsn. cellular transpl. Diabetes Rsch. Inst., U. Miami, Fla., 1993—, sci. dir., chief acad. officer, 1996—; reviewer of applications for grants Can. and Am. Diabetes Assns., Juvenile Diabetes Found., NIH; chmn. First and Third Internat. Congresses of Cell Transplant Soc., Pitts., 1992, Miami, 1996, 5th Internat. Congress on Pancreas and Islet Transplantation, Miami, 1995, others; mem. editl. bd. Transplantation, Cell Transplantation, Transplantation Procs., Jour. Tissue Engring. Editor: Pancreatic Islet Cell Transplantation, 1992, Methods in Cell Transplantaion, 1995; contbr. numerous chpts. to books and articles to jours. including Immunology Today, Jour. Clin. Investigation, New Eng. Jour. Medicine, Hepatology, Diabetes, Transplantation, Endocrinology, Procs. NAS, USA, Am. Jour. Physiology, Surgery, Nature, Nature Genetics, Lancet. Grantee Juvenile Diabetes Found. Internat., 1988—, NIH, 1993—; recipient NIH traineee award, 1986-88. Mem. AAAS, Cell Transplant Soc. (founder, pres. 1992-94), Am. Soc. Transplant Surgeons, Internat. Pancreas and Islet Transplant Assn. (co-founder), The Transplantation Soc., Am. Diabetes Assn. (Rsch. award 1996), Am. Fedn. Clin. Rsch., Diabetes Rsch. Internat. Network (founder, chmn. 1994—), Nat. Diabetes Coalition (co-founder 1994—, chmn. 1997—). Achievements include patent for Automated Method for Cell Separation. Home: 72 S Hibiscus Dr Hisbiscus Island Miami Beach FL 33139 Office: U Miami Diabetes Rsch Inst 1450 NW 10th Ave Miami FL 33136-1011

RIDDELL, RICHARD ANDERSON, naval officer; b. Cambridge, Md., Nov. 20, 1940; s. Edward Leo and Katherine Francis (Insley) R.; m. Anne Price Fortney, May 10, 1986; children: Joel Anderson, Amy Kirsten. BS, U.S. Naval Acad., 1962. Commd. ensign USN, 1962, advanced through grades to rear adm., 1991; exec. officer USS Spadefish USN, Norfolk, Va., 1973-76; comdg. officer USS Nautilus USN, New London, Conn., 1976-80, dep. comdr. submarine squadron 2, 1980-81; spl. asst to dir. naval nuclear propulsion program Dept. Navy USN, Washington, 1981-84, dep. dir. strategic policy div. Dept. Navy, 1984-86; comdr. submarine squadron 1 USN, Pearl Harbor, Hawaii, 1986-88, chief of staff Pacific submarine force, 1988-90; dir. strategic submarine div. Dept. Navy USN, Washington, 1990-92; comdr. Submarine Group 9/Comdr. Naval Base, Seattle, 1992-94; dir. spl. programs, dir. test evaluation, tech. requiements Dept. Navy, The Pentagon, Washington, 1994—. Mem. U.S. Naval Inst. Office: Dept of Navy Chief of Naval Operations 200 Navy Pentagon Washington DC 20350-2000

RIDDELL, RICHARD HARRY, retired lawyer; b. Seattle, Nov. 29, 1916; s. Charles F. and Kathryn (Wykoff) R.; m. Dolores Gloyd, Feb. 10, 1970; children by previous marriage: Dorothea R. Alleyne, Wendy, Kathryn R. Reeves, Mark W. A.B., Stanford, 1938; LL.B., Harvard, 1941. Bar: Wash. 1941. Ptnr. Riddell, Williams, Bullitt and Walkinshaw and predecessor firms, Seattle, 1941-92; ret., 1992. Chmn. Seattle Transit Commn., 1971. Fellow Am. Coll. Trial Lawyers; mem. ABA, County Bar Assn. (pres. 1963-64), Wash. State Bar Assn. (pres. 1976-77), Seattle Tennis Club, Spanish Trail Golf Club. Home: 7833 Rancho Mirage Dr Las Vegas NV 89113-1239

RIDDER, BERNARD HERMAN, JR., newspaper publisher; b. N.Y.C., Dec. 8, 1916; s. Bernard Herman and Nell (Hickey) R.; m. Jane Delano, Feb. 24, 1939; children: Laura, Paul A., Peter, Robin, Jill. B.A., Princeton U., 1938. Advt. dir. Duluth News-Tribune, 1941-42, gen. mgr., 1947-52, pub., 1952-72; pub. St. Paul Dispatch-Pioneer Press, 1959-73; pres. Ridder Publs., Inc., 1969—; chmn. bd. Knight-Ridder Newspapers, 1979-83; dir. AP, 1954-64, Seattle Times. Served from ensign to lt. USNR, 1942-45. Recipient Journalism award U. Minn., also Regents award. Mem. U.S. Golf Assn. (mem. exec. com. 1958-64), Inland Daily Press Assn. (pres. 1954). Clubs: Royal and Ancient Golf (St. Andrews, Scotland); Somerset Country (St. Paul); Augusta Nat. Golf (Ga.), Gulf Stream Golf (Delray Beach, Fla.). Office: St Paul Pioneer Press NW Publ Inc 345 Cedar St Saint Paul MN 55101-1014

RIDDER, PAUL ANTHONY, newspaper executive; b. Duluth, Minn., Sept. 22, 1940; s. Bernard H. and Jane (Delano) R.; m. Constance Louise Meach, Nov. 6, 1960; children: Katherine Lee Pennoyer, Linda Jane, Susan Delano Cobb, Paul Anthony, Jr. B.A. in Econs., U. Mich., 1962. With Aberdeen (S.D.) Am. News, 1962-63; With Pasadena (Calif.) Star News, 1963-64; with San Jose (Calif.) Mercury News, 1964-86, bus. mgr., 1968-75, gen. mgr., 1975-77, pub., 1977-86, pres., 1979-86; pres. Knight-Ridder Newspaper Div., Miami, Fla., 1986—; pres., chmn., CEO Knight-Ridder, Inc., Miami, 1989—, also bd. dirs.; bd. dirs. Seattle Times, Knight-Ridder, Inc., Newspaper First. Bd. dirs. United Way; mem. adv. bd. Ctr. for Econ. Policy Devel. Stanford U., U. Mich.; mem. pres.' adv. bd. U. Mich. Named Calif. Pub. of Yr., 1983, Newspaper Exec. of Yr., Ad Week, 1991. Mem. Fla. C. of C. (bd. dirs., coun. of 100), Cypress Point Club, Indian Creek Club, Pine Valley Golf Club. *

RIDDICK, DANIEL HOWISON, obstetrics and gynecology educator, priest; b. Lynchburg, Va., Dec. 12, 1941; s. Joseph Henry and Nancy Eloise (Gordon) R.; m. Louisa McIntosh Spruill, June 9, 1963; children: Ellen, Daniel. BA, Duke U., 1963, MD, 1967, PhD in Physiology, 1969. Diplomate Am. Bd. Ob-Gyn, Am. Bd. Reproductive Endocrinology; ordained priest Episc. Ch., 1969. Asst. prof. physiology Duke U., Durham, N.C., 1973-74; asst. prof. ob-gyn U. Conn. Sch. Medicine, Farmington, 1974-76, dir. reproductive endocrinology and infertility, 1974-85, assoc. prof. ob-gyn, 1976-81, prof. ob-gyn, 1981-85; prof., chmn. ob-gyn dept. U. Vt., Burlington, 1985—, assoc. dean grad. med. edn., 1987-88. Editor: Reproductive Endocrinology in Clinical Practice, 1987; editor: (with others) Pathology of Infertility, 1987. Mem. ACOG, Am. Fertility Soc. (pres. 1992-93), Am. Gynecol. and Obstet. Soc. Avocation: sheep-raising. Home: 680 Mayo Rd Huntington VT 05462-9410 Office: Fletcher Allen Health Care Dept of Obstetrics & Gynecology 111 Colchester Ave Burlington VT 05401-1473

RIDDICK, FRANK ADAMS, JR., physician, health care facility administrator; b. Memphis, June 14, 1929; s. Frank Adams and Falba (Crawford) R.; m. Mary Belle Alston, June 15, 1952; children: Laura Elizabeth Dufresne, Frank Adams III, John Alston. BA cum laude, Vanderbilt U., 1951, MD, 1954. Diplomate: Am. Bd. Internal Medicine (bd. govs. 1973-80). Intern Barnes Hosp., St. Louis, 1954-55, resident in medicine, 1957-60; fellow in metabolic diseases Washington U., St. Louis, 1960-61; staff Ochsner Clinic (Ochsner Found. Hosp.), New Orleans, 1961—; head sect. endocrinology and metabolic disease Ochsner Clinic (Ochsner Found. Hosp.), 1976-83, asst. med. dir., 1968-72, assoc. med. dir., 1972-75, med. dir., 1975-92; CEO Alton Ochsner Med. Found., New Orleans, 1992—; clin. prof. Tulane U., New Orleans, 1977—; trustee Alton Ochsner Med. Found., 1973—, CEO, 1991—; chmn. bd. Ochsner Health Plan, 1983-92; pres. Orleans Svc. Corp., 1976-80, South La. Med. Assocs., New Orleans, 1978—; dir. Brent House Corp., New Orleans, 1980—; chmn. Accreditation Coun. on Grad. Med. Edn., 1986-87. v.p. nat. resident matching program, 1986-90, mem. accreditation coun. on med. edn., 1988-90. Trustee St. Martin's Protestant Epis. Sch., Metairie, La., 1970-84; bd. govs. Isidore Newman Sch., New Orleans, 1987-93. Recipient Disting. Alumnus award Castle Heights Mil. Acad., 1979; recipient teaching award Alton Ochsner Med. Found., 1969, Physician Exec. award Am. Coll. Med. Group Adminstrs., 1984, Disting. Alumnus award Vanderbilt U. Sch. Med., 1988. Fellow ACP, Am. Coll. Physician Execs. (pres. 1987-88); mem. AMA (ho. dels. 1971-92, chmn. coun. on med. edn. 1983-85, coun. on jud. and ethical affairs 1995—), NAS Inst. Medicine, Am. Soc. Internal Medicine (trustee 1970-76, disting. internist award), Endocrine Soc., Am. Diabetes Assn., Soc. Med. Adminstrs. (pres. 1995—), Am. Group Practice Assn. (pres. 1992-94), Boston Club, New Orleans Country Club, Cosmos Club. Home: 1923 Octavia St New Orleans LA 70115-5651 Office: Ochsner Clinic 1516 Jefferson Hwy New Orleans LA 70121-2429*

RIDDIFORD, LYNN MOORHEAD, zoologist, educator; b. Knoxville, Tenn., Oct. 18, 1936; d. James Eli and Virginia Amalia (Berry) Moorhead; m. Alan Wistar Riddiford, June 20, 1959 (div. 1966); m. James William Truman, July 28, 1970. AB magna cum laude, Radcliffe Coll., 1958; PhD, Cornell U., 1961. Rsch. fellow in biology Harvard U., Cambridge, Mass., 1961-63, 65-66, asst. prof. biology, 1966-71, assoc. prof., 1971-73; instr. biology Wellesley (Mass.) Coll., 1963-65; assoc. prof. zoology, U. Wash., Seattle, 1973-75, prof., 1975—; mem. study sect. tropical medicine and parasitology NIH, Bethesda, Md., 1974-78; mem. Competitive Grants panel USDA, Arlington, Va., 1979, 89, 95; mem. regulatory biology panel NSF, Washington, 1984-88; mem. governing coun. Internat. Ctr. for Insect Physiology and Ecology, 1985-91, chmn. program com., 1989-91; chmn. adv. com. SeriBiotech, Bangalore, India, 1989; mem. bio. adv. com. NSF, 1992-95. Contbr. articles to profl. jours. Mem. editorial bd. profl. jours. NSF fellow, 1958-60, 61-63; grantee NSF, 1964—, NIH, 1975—, Rockefeller Found., 1970-79, USDA, 1978-82, 89—; fellow John S. Guggenheim, 1979-80, NIH, 1986-87. Fellow AAAS, Am. Acad. Arts and Scis., Royal Entomol. Soc., Entomol. Soc. Am.; mem. Am. Soc. Zoologists (pres. 1991), Am. Soc. Biochem. and Molecular Biology, Entomol. Soc. Am., Am. Soc. Cell Biology, Soc. Devel. Biology. Methodist. Home: 16324 51st Ave SE Bothell WA 98012-6138 Office: U Wash Dept Zoology Box 351800 Seattle WA 98195-1800

RIDDLE, CHARLES ADDISON, III, state legislator, lawyer; b. Marksville, La., June 8, 1955; s. Charles Addison Jr. and Alma Rita (Gremillion) R.; m. Margaret Susan Noone, Mar. 24, 1978; children: Charles Addison IV, John H., Michael J. BA, La. State U., 1976, JD, 1980. Bar: La. 1980, U.S. Dist. Ct. (mid. and we. dists.) La. 1983, U.S. Ct. Appeals (5th cir.) 1988, U.S. Supreme Ct. 1991, U.S. Ct. Vets. Appeals 1994. Assoc. Riddle & Bennett, Marksville, 1980; pvt. practice Marksville, 1981—; mem. La. Ho. of Reps., Baton Rouge, 1992—; reelected La. House of Reps., Baton Rouge, 1995-. Elected La. State Dem. Cen. com., Avoyelles Parish, 1983-87, Parish Exec. Demo. Com. 1987-91. Mem. Avoyelles Bar Assn. (pres. 1987-88), Bunkie Rotary (bd. dirs.), Marksville Lions, Marksville C. of C. (pres. 1988-92). Office: 208 E Mark St Marksville LA 71351-2416

RIDDLE, DONALD HUSTED, former university chancellor; b. Bklyn., Jan. 22, 1921; s. William Ewing and Ruth (Husted) R.; m. Leah Dunlap Gallagher, June 20, 1942; children: Susan Lee and Judith Lee (twins). AB magna cum laude, Princeton U., 1949, MA (Woodrow Wilson fellow), 1951, PhD (Ford Found. fellow), 1956; LLD (hon.), Am. U., 1980, John Jay Coll. Criminal Justice, 1990. Asst. prof. dept. govt. Hamilton Coll., 1952-58; dir. rsch., assoc. prof., prof. politics Eagleton Inst. Politics, Rutgers U., 1958-65; dean faculty John Jay Coll. Criminal Justice, CUNY, 1965-68, pres., 1968-76; chancellor U. Ill. - Chgo., 1976-83, chancellor emeritus, 1983—; staff asst. Conn. Commn. on State Govt. Orgn., 1949; staff mem. Survey Field Services, Dept. Interior, 1950; staff U.S. Senator Paul H. Douglas, 1955-56; cons. N.Y. State Spl. Com. on Constl. Revision and Simplification, 1958. Author: The Truman Committee: A Study in Congressional Responsibility, 1964; Editor, co-author: The Problems and Promise of American Democracy, 1964, Contemporary Issues of American Democracy, 1969; Editor: American Society in Action, 1965. Mem. bd. edn., Princeton, N.J., 1962-64; mem. Mayors Criminal Justice Coordinating Council, N.Y.C., 1968-73; life mem. U. Ill. Pres. Council. Served to lst lt. USAAF, 1942-46. Recipient Presdl. medal John Jay Coll. Criminal Justice, 1979. Mem. Acad. Criminal Justice Scis. (pres. 1970-71; hon. life, Presdl. Disting. award for contbg. to criminal justice edn. 1979), Phi Beta Kappa, Phi Sigma Alpha.

RIDDLE, JAMES DOUGLASS, retired academic administrator; b. Austin, Tex., Oct. 8, 1933; s. Prebble Elmer and Jewel Lee (Nalley) R.; m. Marilyn Brown Moore, Sept. 8, 1956; children: Mary Elizabeth, Margaret Allison, Charles Douglass. BA in History and Govt., Southwestern U., 1958; MDiv in Theology and Social Ethics, Boston U. Sch. Theology, 1962; postgrad., Boston U., 1962-65; D Ministry, San Francisco Theol. Sem., 1991. Ordained to ministry Meth. Ch., 1963, transferred to United Ch. of Christ, 1966. Co-pastor The First Parish Ch., Lincoln, Mass., 1963-67; sr. pastor The Community Ch., Chapel Hill, N.C., 1967-80, Historic First Ch. of Christ Congl. United Ch. of Christ, Springfield, Mass., 1980-89; v.p. devel. Am. Internat. Coll., Springfield, 1989-97; fund devel. prin. The River Group, Springfield; prin., The River Group Consultants; tchg. fellow, lectr. in human rels. Boston U. Sch. Bus., 1960-64; mem. Chapel Hill-Carrboro Bd. Edn., Chapel Hill, 1975-80. Mem. governing bd. Nat. Coun. Chs., 1969-72, commn. on faith and order, 1969-72, com. on future ecumenical study and svc. United Ch. of Christ, 1969-75, del. gen. synod, mem. exec. coun., 1969-75; pres. N.C. Legal Def. Fund, 1969-80, Orange-Chatham Counties Cmty. Action Agy., 1970-76, Chapel Hill-Carrboro Inter-Ch. Coun. Housing Corp., 1969-77; mem. bd. Cmty. Care Mental Health Ctr., 1980-90, chair, 1985-88; chair Downtown Ministry Project, 1981-84; mem. governing bd. Greater Springfield Coun. Chs., 1980-86, Downtown Econ. Devel. Corp., Springfield Ctr., 1981-95, StageWest Regional Theatre Co., 1982-92, Springfield YMCA, 1982-87, City of Springfield 350th Anniversary, 1984-87, Springfield Adult Edn. Coun., 1984—; corporator Zone Arts Ctr., 1986-94; mem., chmn. Hampden Assn. Ch. & Ministry Com. United Ch. of Christ, 1990—. Named Person of Yr. NOW, 1987; recipient 350th Anniversary Medallion, City of Springfield, 1986. Mem. ACLU, Coun. for Advancement and Support of Edn., Nat. Soc. Fund Raising Execs. (Cert. Fund Raising Exec.), Estate Planning Coun. Hampden County, New Eng. Devel. Rsch. Assn., Acad. Religion and Mental Health, Congl. Christian Hist. Soc. (mem. bd. 1987-95), Assn. Humanistic Psychology, Common Cause, The Reality Club of Springfield, Springfield Rotary, The Paul Harris Fellowship. Democrat. Avocations: backpacking, sailing, travel, cooking.

RIDDLE, MARK ALAN, child psychiatrist; b. Huntingburg, Ind., Feb. 18, 1948; s. James G. and Louise (Burgdorf) R.; m. Clarine Carol Nardi, Aug. 15, 1971; children: Carl, Julia. BA, Ind. U., 1970, MS, 1973, MD, 1977. Intern in pediatrics Ind. U. Med. Ctr., Indpls., 1977-78; resident in psychiatry Sch. Medicine Yale U., New Haven, 1978-81; fellow in child psychiatry Yale Child Study Ctr., New Haven, 1981-83; asst. prof. child psychiatry Sch. Medicine Yale U., New Haven, 1983-89, assoc. prof. child psychiatry, 1989-93; dir. divsn. child and adolescent psychiatry Johns Hopkins Med. Inst., 1993—; mem. pediatrics panel U.S. Pharmacopea. Assoc. editor Jour. Child and Adolescent Psychopharmacology; editor Pediatric Psychopharmacology I & II, 1995; contbr. articles to profl. jours. Mem. med. com. Tourette Syndrome Assn., 1989—. Mem. Am. Acad. Child and Adolescent Psychiatry (editorial bd. Jour.). Home: 10607 Millet Seed Hl Columbia MD 21044-4150

RIDDLE, STURGIS LEE, minister; b. Stephenville, Tex., May 26, 1909; s. Lee and Linda (McKinney) R.; m. Elisabeth Pope Sloan, Oct. 14, 1939. B.A. magna cum laude, Stanford U., 1931; student, Gen. Theol. Sem., N.Y.C., 1931-32; B.D. cum laude, Episcopal Theol. Sch., Cambridge, Mass., 1934; D.D., Seabury Western Theol. Sem., Evanston, Ill., 1957. Ordained deacon P.E. Ch., 1934, priest, 1935; Episcopal chaplain U. Calif., 1934-37; instr. church Div. Sch. of Pacific, 1934-37; rector Caroline Ch., Setauket, L.I., 1937-40; asst. minister St. Thomas Ch., N.Y.C., 1940-46; rector St. James Ch., Florence, Italy, 1947-49; dean Am. Cathedral of Holy Trinity, Paris, France, 1949-74; dean emeritus Am. Cathedral of Holy Trinity, 1974—; exchange preacher Trinity Ch., N.Y.C., 1956-57, 62, St. Bartholomew's Ch., N.Y.C., 1958, 63, 73, St. John's Cathedral, Denver, 1959, Grace Cathedral, San Francisco, 1960, Nat. Cathedral, Washington, 1961, Trinity Ch. Boston, 1964, St. Andrew's Cathedral, Honolulu, 1965, St. John's Ch., Washington, 1966, 67, 68, 70, 73, St. Thomas' Ch., N.Y., 1968, 73, St. Paul's Cathedral, Boston, 1969; clerical dep. Europe to Gen. Conv. P.E. Ch., 1949-60, 64, 70. Author: One Hundred Years, 1950; contbg. Author: We Believe in Prayer, 1958, That Day with God, 1965. Hon. gov. Am. Hosp. in Paris; fellow Morgan Library, N.Y.C., trustee bd. fgn. parishes; chmn. Friends of the Am. Cathedral in Paris. Decorated Legion of Honor France; grand cross and grand prelate Sovereign Order St. John of Jerusalem Knights of Malta; grand cross Ordre du Milice de Jesus Christ; Patriarchal Order Mt. Athos. Mem. Nat. Inst. Social Sci., Am. Soc. French Legion of Honor, Phi Beta Kappa. Clubs: Union, University, Pilgrims, Spouting Rock Beach Assn. Home: 870 Fifth Ave New York NY 10021-4953

RIDDLESWORTH, JUDITH HIMES, elementary education educator; b. Hammond, Ind., Feb. 2, 1954; d. James Bernerd and Jane (Hall) Himes; m. Kim A. Riddlesworth, July 30, 1977; children: Sara, Becky. BS, Ill. State U., Normal, 1976; MA, No. Ariz. U., 1981. Cert. elem., spl. edn. tchr., Ariz. With Safford (Ariz.) Sch. Dist., 1976—, tchr. middle sch., 1987—, grade level chmn., 1989-93; mem. bldg. team, dist. lead team mem., tech. team mem., staff devel. mem., inservice facilatator Safford Sch. Dist.; Career Ladder participant. Mem. AAUW, Delta Kappa gamma. Avocations: horse-back riding, cross-country skiing, cooking, aerobics, crafts. Office: Safford Unified Sch Dist 734 W 11th St Safford AZ 85546-2967

RIDENHOUR, JOSEPH CONRAD, textile company executive; b. Rowan County, N.C., Aug. 12, 1920; s. Martin Luther and Mary Virginia (Schaeffer) R.; m. Julia Claire Thorne, Dec. 21, 1943; 1 child; Janis Claire. Student, Duke U., 1938-40; L.H.D., Lenoir Rhyne Coll., 1974. Asst. sec. Cannon Mills Co., Kannapolis, N.C., 1953-63; asst. v.p. Cannon Mills Co., 1959-60, v.p., 1960-71, sr. v.p., dir. mktg., 1971-82, vice chmn. bd., 1981-83, also dir. Mem. Kannapolis Bd. Edn., 1954-65; sec. Home Mission Found., N.C. synod United Lutheran Ch. in Am., 1953-68, dir., 1953—, pres., 1968—; mem. bd. Luth. Theol. So. Sem., 1964-85. Served with arty AUS, World War II, ETO. Home and Office: Oaklynn 420 Idlewood Dr Kannapolis NC 28083-3630

RIDENOUR, JAMES FRANKLIN, fund raising consultant; b. Peoria, Ill., Aug. 2, 1932; s. Arthur S. and Ruth O. (Ohlzen) R.; BS, Ill. Wesleyan U., 1954; MS, Ill. State U., 1970; m. Doris K. Maxeiner, June 21, 1958; children: James Franklin Jr., David Arthur, Eric Carl, Anne Catherine. Mktg. rep. Armstrong Cork Co., 1955-67; assoc. dir. devel. Ill. Wesleyan U., 1967-73; v.p. devel. Western Md. Coll., Westminster, 1973-84; v.p. devel. Berry Coll., Rome, Ga., 1984-88; mgr. Marts and Lundy Inc., Lyndhurst, N.J., 1988, sr. cons., 1989—. Co-author: Handbook of Institutional Advancement, 1986. Chmn., Carroll County Tourism Council, 1976-79; active Boy Scouts Am.; bd. dirs. YMCA, 1976-79; chmn. Families of Evenglow, 1979—, Diocesan devel. com. 1989—; bd. visitors Kanuga Conf. Ctr., 1994—, Ill. Wesleyan U., 1996—. Mem. Council Advancement and Support of Edn. (com. gift standards 1977-84, campaign reporting 1989-94), Crozier Soc. (bd. dirs. 1993—), Six Napoleons, Rotary, Pi Gamma Mu, Gamma Upsilon. Republican. Episcopalian. Home: 648 Regester Ave Baltimore MD 21212-1917 Office: Marts and Lundy Inc 1200 Wall St W Lyndhurst NJ 07071-3517

RIDEOUT, PATRICIA IRENE, operatic, oratorio and concert singer; b. St. John, N.B., Can., Mar. 16, 1931; d. Eric Aubrey and Florence May (Chase) R.; m. Rolf Edmund Dissmann, Sept. 3, 1955 (dec. 1975); m. Leonard R. Rosenberg, May 25, 1987. Ed., U. Toronto Opera Sch., Royal Conservatory Music, 1952-55. Tchr. voice Queen's U., Kingston, Ont., 1980-86, Royal Conservatory Music, Toronto, 1980-91. Singer Can. Opera Co., Toronto, 1954-85; leading roles in operas, Stratford, Ont., Vancouver, B.C., Guelph, Ont., 1956-85, CBC, 1958-90. Mem. Actors Equity Assn., Assn. Radio and TV Artists, Toronto Heliconian Club. Unitarian.

RIDEOUT, WALTER BATES, English educator; b. Lee, Maine, Oct. 21, 1917; s. Walter John and Helen Ruth (Brickett) R.; m. Jeanette Lee Drisko, Aug. 2, 1947; children: Linda Carolyn, Richard Bates, David John. A.B., Colby Coll., 1938; M.A., Harvard U., 1939, Ph.D., 1950. Teaching fellow English Harvard U., 1946-49, asst. prof., summer 1954, prof., summer 1969; from instr. to assoc. prof. English Northwestern U., Evanston, Ill., 1949-63, dir. program Bell System execs., 1957-58, 59-61; prof. English U. Wis., Madison, 1963—, Harry Hayden Clark prof. English, 1972—, chmn. dept., 1965-68, sr. vis. prof. Inst. Research in Humanities, 1968-69; vis. prof. U. Hawaii, summer 1977; Disting. lectr. English Kyoto Am. Studies Summer Seminar, Kyoto, Japan, 1981. Author: The Radical Novel in the United States, 1900-1954, 1956; editor: (with Howard Mumford Jones) Letters of Sherwood Anderson, 1953, (with James K. Robinson) A College Book of Modern Verse, 1958, A College Book of Modern Fiction, 1961, The Experience of Prose, 1960, I. Donnelly-Caesar's Column, 1960, (with G.W. Allen and J.K. Robinson) American Poetry, 1965, Sherwood Anderson: Collection of Critical Essays, 1974. Recipient MidAm. award Soc. for Study of Midwestern Lit., Mich. State U., 1983, Outstanding Educator award, 1993; fellow Newberry Libr., 1951, Guggenheim fellow, 1957; Fulbright grantee to Kyoto, 1981. Mem. ACLU, MLA (mem. nat. exec. council 1970-73), Phi Beta Kappa. Home: 1306 Seminole Hwy Madison WI 53711-3728 Office: Dept English U Wis 600 N Park St Madison WI 53706-1403

RIDER, BRIAN CLAYTON, lawyer; b. San Antonio, Oct. 8, 1948; s. Ralph W. and Emmie (Kott) R.; m. Patsy Anne Ruppert, Dec. 27, 1970; children: Christopher, David, James, Andrew. BA, Rice U., 1969; JD, U. Tex., 1972. Bar: Tex. 1972. Assoc. then ptnr. Dow, Cogburn & Friedman, Houston, 1972-83; ptnr. Brown, McCarroll & Oaks Hartline, Austin, Tex., 1983-96; adj. prof. law U. Tex., 1997—. Contbr. articles to profl. jours.; lectr. in field. Mem. Am. Coll. Real Estate Lawyers, Travis County Bar Assn. (bd. dirs. 1986-88, chmn. Travis County real estate sect. 1986-88), State Bar of Tex. (coun. real estate and probate sect. 1992-96). Home: 2906 Hatley Dr Austin TX 78746-4613 Office: 301 Congress Ave Ste 1 00 Austin TX 78701-4041

RIDER, DIANE ELIZABETH, librarian; b. Kearny, N.J., June 25, 1951; d. Thomas Lindsay and Dorothy Jane (Sommer) R. MusB magna cum laude, Westminster Choir Coll., 1973; MLS, Fla. State U., 1993. Intern preservation dept. U. Fla., Gainesville, 1993; intern free-net libr. Tallahassee (Fla.) Free-Net, 1993; reference libr. Broward County Main Libr., Ft. Lauderdale, Fla., 1994-95; libr., instr. Art Inst. Ft. Lauderdale, 1995-96, dir. Learning Resource Ctr., 1996—; vice chair, assoc. mem. com. S.E. Fla. Libr. Info. Network, Ft. Lauderdale, 1996—; spkr. in field. Soloist St. Paul's Chapel, Columbia U., N.Y.C., 1973, Ch. of St. Mary the Virgin, N.Y.C., 1974. Mem. Co-op Am., Washington, 1990—, Sierra Club, Broward & Leon Counties, Fla., 1988—. Fla. State U. fellow, 1993-94, Coll. Tchg. fellow, 1992-93; Louis Shores scholar, 1992-93. Mem. ALA (intellectual freedom roundtable 1992—), Spl. Librs. Assn. (bd. dirs. Fla. and Caribbean chpt. 1997—), Geneal. Soc. Southwestern Pa., NOW, Sierra Club, Phi Kappa Phi, Beta Phi Mu. Avocations: vegetarian cooking, genealogy, the Internet, reading. Office: Art Inst Ft Lauderdale Learning Resource Ctr 1799 SE 17th St Fort Lauderdale FL 33316-3013

RIDER, JANE LOUISE, artist, educator; b. Brownfield, Tex., Sept. 11, 1919; d. Oscar Thomas and Florence Myrtle (Bliss) Halley; m. Rolla Wilson Rider Jr., Mar. 26, 1944 (dec. July 1992); 1 child, Dorothy Jo Neil. BA, UCLA, Westwood, 1943, tchg. diploma in secondary art; postgrad., Chgo. Art Inst., 1945, Chouinards, L.A., U. Oreg., Scripps, Claremont, Calif. Art supr., elem. and jr. high art tchr. Tulare (Calif.) City Schs. Dist., 1943-44, 44-45; art tchr. Beverly Hills (Calif.) High Sch., 1946-47; art tchr. jr. high gen. art and ceramics Santa Barbara City Schs., Goleta, Calif., 1964-66; head art dept., tchr. Morro Bay (Calif.) Jr.-Sr. High Sch. Dist., 1967-70; pvt. practice studio potter Cambria, Calif., 1961-85; artist, Santa Rosa, Calif., 1985—; founder, dir., tech. La Canada (Calif.) Youth House Art Program, 1953-60; dir. Pinedorado Art Show, Allied Arts Assn., Cambria, 1970-80. Exhibited in group shows Wine Country Artist's Spring Show, 1991, 92, 93, 94, 95, 97, Gualala Art in Redwoods, 1986, 87, 88, 96, Rodney Strong Vineyards Art Guild, 1994; revolving exhibits Berger Ctr. and Chalais-Oakmont, Santa Rosa, 1985-97, Santa Rosa Art Guild, 1986-97; statewide art shows Spring Palettes Mumm Cuvee Winery, Napa, Calif., 1994, Women Creating, Luther Burbank Ctr., 1995, Summer House Gallery, Healdsberg, 1995, Armida Winery Show, 1995, Coddington Mall Show, Watercolor Artists of Sonoma Co., 1995-96, Audubon-Bouverie Preserve Show, Glen Ellen, Calif., 1996, Pedroncelli Winery Show, 1996, Wasco Invitational Show Marin Art Assn., 1996, others. Mem. Nat. League Am. Pen Woman, Inc. (arts 1994-97), Santa Rosa Art Guild (exhibits 1986-95, rec. sec. 1989), Ctrl. Coast Watercolor Soc. (charter 1977), Watercolor Artist Sonoma. Republican. Avocations: photography, gardening, listening to music, traveling, tennis. Home: 7019 Overlook Dr Santa Rosa CA 95409-6376

RIDER, JOHN ALLEN, II, business educator, paralegal; b. Gage, Okla., Mar. 11, 1928; s. George Henry Rider and Laurenna Agnes Meek; m. Audrey Claudine Baker, July 16, 1961; children: Michelle Renee Rider Brown, John Allen III. BS, Northwestern Okla. State U., 1952; MA, U. Wyoming, 1956; EdD, U. Nebr., 1966; postgrad., U. Ky. Cert. profl. tchr., Tenn., Iowa. Court reporter, stenographer USN, 1946-48; dep. ct. clk., ct. reporter Ellis County, Okla., 1948-49; tchr. bus. Rozel (Kans.) Rural High Sch., 1952-53, Norwich (Kans.) High Sch., 1953-54, Bluff City (Kans.) High Sch., 1954-56; instr. Black Hills State Coll., Spearfish, S.D., 1956-58; tchr. bus. Balboa (C.Z.) High Sch., 1958-60; instr. Northwestern Coll., Orange City, Iowa, 1958-60, chair divsn. edn., 1962-64; asst. prof. Northwestern State Coll., Alva, Okla., 1962-63; teaching asst. U. Nebr., Lincoln, 1963-64; head bus. edn. program, assoc. prof. U. N.Mex., Albuquerque, 1966-70; prof. West Tex. State U., Canyon, 1970-74; chair prof. occupational edn. divsn. Coffeyville (Kans.) Community Jr., 1974-75; assoc. prof. East Tenn. State U., Johnson City, 1975-94, coord. bus. edn. program, 1985-94; ret., 1994; cons. various bus.; pres. bd. dirs. Enid Literacy Coun., 1996—, also tutor. Active Johnson City Literacy Coun., v.p./tutor trainer, 1978-80; active Enid Literacy Coun., bd. mem. 1996—; relief worker, registrar Mid-Am.. yearly meeting Friends Ch., Wichita, 1981; cons. yearly meeting N.C. Soc. Friends, 1987. Recipient Meritorious award West Tex. Bus. Tchr., 1970-74, Outstanding Edn. Grad. award Northwestern Okla. State U. Alumni Assn., 1995; named Tchr. of Yr., Dist. 16 Tex. Bus. Edn. Assn., 1973. Mem. NEA (life), Am. Vocat. Assn. (life), Nat. Bus Edn., Nat. Assn. Tchr. Edn. (life, bus. and office edn.), Tex. State Edn. Assn., Tenn. Bus. Edn. Assn. (treas., pres.-elect, pres., past pres., Educator of Yr. 1986), So. Bus. Edn., Kiwanis (Johnson City exec. bd. 1975-80, 92), Am. Legion (King's Mt. post), SAR (former sec., pres. Panhandle-Plains chpt., Tex. soc.), Holt County (Mo.) Hist. Soc. (charter, life), Lion Club (Pioneer-Pleasant Vale 1997—). Republican. Avocations: genealogy, history, photography. Home: 3002 N Grant St Enid OK 73702-1686

RIDER, JOSEPH KUNTZMAN, information systems specialist; b. Sewickley, Pa., Feb. 28, 1939; s. Joseph Weber and Evelyn Margaret (Kuntzman) R.; m. Sharon Pearl Allison, Dec. 26, 1967 (div. Mar. 1993); 1 child, Kendra Allison. BA, Rice U., 1961; postgrad., So. Ill. U., 1961-62; MFA, U. Tex., 1964. Resident designer Ft. Wayne (Ind.) Civic Theatre, 1965-66; guest designer U. Victoria, B.C., Can., 1966; assoc. prof. Sam Houston State Coll., Huntsville, Tex., 1966-67; carpenter, upholsterer Feller Scenery Studios, N.Y.C., 1967-70; design asst. Broadway designers N.Y.C., 1967-74; pres., CEO Theatrical Catalysts, Inc., N.Y.C., 1969-72, Telesette, Inc., N.Y.C., 1972-74; fiscal affairs mgr. N.Y.C. Dept. of Transportation, 1974-80, info. svcs. mgr., 1980-87; v.p. Dreman Value Advisors, Jersey City, N.Y.C., 1987—. Founding v.p. West 71st St. Assn., N.Y.C., 1969-78; pres. Ansonia Dems., N.Y.C., 1975-79; chair, pres. Westside Cmty. Recycling Corp., N.Y.C., 1975-81; jud. del. N.Y.C., 1981-84; pres. 404 West 48th St. Housing Devel. Corp., 1984—; lay reader and vestry St. Clement's Episcopal Ch., Manhattan. Avocations: jazz, writing. Home: 404 W 48th St New York NY 10036 Office: Dreman Value Advisors Inc 280 Park Ave 40th Fl New York NY 10017

RIDGE, MARTIN, historian, educator; b. Chgo., May 7, 1923; s. John and Ann (Lew) R.; m. Marcella Jane VerHoef, Mar. 17, 1948; children: John Andrew, Judith Lee, Curtis Cordell, Wallace Karsten. AB, Chgo. State U., 1943; AM, Northwestern U., 1949, PhD, 1951. Asst. prof. history Westminster Coll., New Wilmington, Pa., 1951-55; from asst. prof. to prof. San Diego State Coll., 1955-66; prof. history Ind. U., Bloomington, 1966-79, Calif. Inst. Tech., 1980-95; prof. emeritus, 1995; vis. prof. UCLA, summer 1963, Northwestern U., summer 1959; editor Jour. Am. History, 1966-77; sr. research assoc. Huntington Library, 1977—; bd. dirs. Calif. Hist. Landmarks Commn., 1954-64; cons. in field; Tanner lectr. Mormon Hist. Assn., 1991; Whitsett Meml. lectr., Calif. State U., 1992. Author: Ignatius Donnelly: Portrait of a Politician, 1962, 91, The New Bilingualism: An American Dilemma, 1981, Frederick Jackson Turner: Wisconsin's Historian of the Frontier, 1986, Atlas of American Frontiers, 1992, My Life East and West, 1994; co-author: California Work and Workers, 1963, The American Adventure, 1964, America's Frontier Story, 1969, Liberty and Union, 1973, American History after 1865, 1981, Westward Expansion, 1982; editor: Children of Ol'Man River, 1988, Westward Journeys, 1989, History, Frontier and Section, 1993. Served with U.S. Maritime Service, 1943-45. William Randolph Hearst fellow, 1950; fellow Social Sci. Research Council, 1952; fellow Guggenheim Found., 1965; fellow Am. Council Learned Socs., 1960; Newberry fellow, 1964; Huntington fellow, 1974; Annenberg scholar U. So. Calif., 1979-80; recipient Best Book award Phi Alpha Theta, 1963, Gilberto Espinos prize N.Mex. Historical Review, 1989, Ray Allan Billington prize Western History Assn., 1991. Mem. Am. Hist. Assn. (v.p. Pacific Coast br. 1994, pres. 1995, Best Book award 1963), Orgn. Am. Historians, Western History Assn. (v.p. 1985-86, pres. 1986-87), So. History Assn., Agrl. History Soc., Social Sci. History Soc., Hist. Soc. So. Calif. (pres. 1994—). Democrat. Address: Huntington Library San Marino CA 91108

RIDGE, THOMAS JOSEPH, governor, former congressman; b. Munhall, Pa., Aug. 26, 1945; m. Michele Moore, 1979. B.A., Harvard U., 1967; J.D., Dickinson Coll. Law, Carlisle, Pa., 1972. Bar: Pa. 1972. Sole practice Erie, Pa., 1972-82; mem. 98th-103rd Congresses from Pa. 21st dist., Washington, D.C., 1983-1995; mem. Banking, Fin., Urban Affairs com., subcoms. Econ. Growth and Credit Formation, Housing and Community Devel., Veteran's Affairs com.; former dist. atty. Erie County; mem. subcom. Hosps. and Healthcare, Oversight and Investigation, Post Office and Civil Svc. com., subcom. Census and Population, Civil Svc.; former legal instructor Erie County; gov. State of Penn., 1995—. Served with inf. U.S. Army, 1968-70, Vietnam. Office: Office of the Gov 245 Main Capitol Building Harrisburg PA 17120-0022*

RIDGEWAY, JAMES FOWLER, journalist; b. Auburn, N.Y., Nov. 1, 1936; s. George L. and Florence (Fowler) R.; m. Patricia Carol Dodge, Nov. 1966; 1 son, David Andrew. A.B., Princeton U., 1959. Assoc. editor New Republic, Washington, 1962-68, contbg. editor, 1968-70; editor Hard Times,

1968-70, Elements, 1974-78; assoc. editor Ramparts, 1970-75; assoc. fellow Inst. for Policy Studies, 1973-77; mem. Pub. Resource Center, 1977—; staff writer Village Voice, 1973—. Author: The Closed Corporation, 1969, Politics of Ecology, 1970, The Last Play, 1973, New Energy, 1975, (with Alexander Cockburn) Smoke, 1978, Political Ecology, 1979, Energy-Efficient Community Planning, 1979, Who Owns the Earth, 1980, Powering Civilization, 1983, Blood in the Face, 1991, The March to War, 1991, (with Jean Casella) To Cast A Cold Eye, 1991, The Haiti Files, 1994, (with Jasmika Udovicki) Yugoslavia's Ethnic Nightmare, 1995, (with Sylvia Plachy) Red Light, 1996. Served with Army N.G., 1959. Home: 3103 Macomb St NW Washington DC 20008-3325

RIDGLEY, THOMAS BRENNAN, lawyer; b. Columbus, Ohio, Apr. 29, 1940; s. Arthur G. and Elizabeth (Tracy) R.; m. Nancy Vaughan, June 27, 1964; children: Elizabeth, Jennifer, Kathryn. BA, Princeton (N.J.) U., 1962; JD with honors, U. Mich., 1965. Bar: Pa. 1965, Ohio 1968, U.S. Dist. Ct. (so. and no. dists.) Ohio, U.S. Dist. Ct. (ea. dist.) Pa., U.S. Ct. Appeals (6th, 3d and 10th cirs.), U.S. Supreme Ct. Assoc. Dechert, Price and Rhoades, Phila., 1965-67; ptnr. Vorys, Sater, Seymour and Pease, Columbus, 1967—. Author: Interstate Conflicts and Cooperation, 1986, (with others) Fending Off Corporate Raiders, 1987. Bd. dirs., mem. exec. com. United Way of Franklin County, Columbus, 1986—, Cmty. Shelter Bd., 1992—. Fellow Am. Coll. Trial Lawyers. Office: Vorys Sater Seymour & Pease 52 E Gay St Columbus OH 43215-3108

RIDGWAY, DAVID WENZEL, educational film producer, director; b. Los Angeles, Dec. 12, 1904; s. David Nelson and Marie (Wenzel) R.; AB UCLA, 1926; MBA, Harvard U., 1928; m. Rochelle Devine, June 22, 1955. With RKO Studios, Hollywood, Calif., 1930-42; motion picture specialist WPB, Washington, 1942-43; prodn. mgr., producer Ency. Brit. Films, Wilmette, Ill., 1946-60; dir. film activities, exec. dir. Chem. Edn. Material Study, U. Calif. at Berkeley, 1960-97, dir., 1990—; producer, on-screen interviewer Am. Chem. Soc. TV series Eminent Chemists, 1981; advisor TV project Mech. Universe, Calif. Inst. Tech., 1985 also Am. Inst. Biol. Scis.; introduced CHEM study films to People's Republic of China, 1983. Lt. comdr. USNR, 1943-46. Recipient Chris award for prodn. CHEM Study Ednl. Films in Chemistry, Film Coun. Greater Columbus, 1962-63; Bronze medal, Padua, Italy, 1963; CINE Golden Eagle awards, 1962-64, 73; Gold Camera award for film Wondering About Things, U.S. Indsl. Film Festival, 1971; diploma of honour Internat. Sci. Film Assn. Festival, Cairo, 1st prize Am. Biol. Photog. Assn. for film MARS: Chemistry Looks for Life, 1978. Mem. Soc. Motion Pictures and TV Engrs. (chmn. San Francisco sect. 1970-72), Am. Chem. Soc., Am. Sci. Film Assn. (trustee 1974-81), Delta Upsilon, Alpha Kappa Psi. Clubs: Faculty (U. Calif.), Bohemian (San Francisco), Harvard (San Francisco). Author: (with Richard J. Merrill) The CHEM Study Story, 1969; also articles in ednl. jours. Home: 1735 Highland Pl Berkeley CA 94709-1074 Office: U Calif Lawrence Hall of Sci Berkeley CA 94720-5200 *Personal philosophy: If someone draws a circle to keep you out, you draw a circle to take him in. Consider your integrity your most valued asset.*

RIDGWAY, MARCELLA DAVIES, veterinarian; b. Sewickley, Pa., Dec. 24, 1957; d. Willis Eugene and Martha Ann (Davies) R. BS, Pa. State U., 1979; VMD, U. Pa., 1983; MS, U. Ill., 1997. Intern Univ. Ill., Urbana, 1983-84, resident in small animal internal medicine, 1984-87; small animal vet. Vet. Cons. Svcs., Savoy, Ill., 1987—. Contbr. articles to profl. jours. Mem. Am. Vet. Med. Assn., Am. Animal Hosp. Assn., Acad. Vet. Clinicians, Ednl. Resources in Environ. Sci. (bd. dirs.), Savoy Prairie Soc. (pres. 1989—), Grand Prairie Friends (bd. dirs. 1993-96), Sangamon Valley Conservancy (bd. dirs. 1995—). Avocations: prairie conservation activities, hiking, horseback riding, long distance running, sketching. Home and Office: Vet Cons Svcs 194 Paddock Dr E Savoy IL 61874-9663

RIDGWAY, ROZANNE LEJEANNE, former diplomat, executive; b. St. Paul, Aug. 22, 1935; d. H. Clay and Ethel Rozanne (Cote) R.; m. Theodore E. Deming. BA, Hamline U., 1957, LLD (hon.), 1978; hon. degrees, U. Helsinki, George Washington U., Elizabethtown Coll.; hon. degree, Coll. of William and Mary, Hood Coll. Career diplomat U.S. Fgn. Svc., 1957-89, amb. at large for oceans and fisheries, 1975-77; amb. to Finland, 1977-80; counselor of the Dept. State, Washington, 1980-81; spl. asst. to sec. state, 1981; amb. to German Dem. Republic, 1982-85; asst. sec. state Europe and Can., 1985-89; pres. The Atlantic Coun. U.S., Washington, 1989-92, co-chair, 1993-96; chair Baltic-Am. Enterprise Fund, 1994—; bd. dirs. 3M Corp., RJR Nabisco, Union Carbide Corp., Bell Atlantic, Citicorp, Citibank, Emerson Electric Co., The Boeing Corp., Sara Lee Corp., Nat. Geog. Soc., Internat. Bd. Advisors, New Perspective Fund. Trustee Hamline U.; bd. dirs. Am. Acad. Diplomacy, Ptnrs. for Democratic Change, Catalyst, Brookings Instn., The Stinson Ctr. Naval Analysis. Recipient Profl. awards Dept. State, Presdl. Disting. Performance award, Joseph C. Wilson internat. rels. achievement award, 1982, Sharansky award Union Couns. Soviet Jewry, 1989, Grand Cross of the Order of the Lion, Finland, 1989; named Person of Yr., Nat. Fisheries Inst., 1977, Knight Comdr. of the Order of Merit, Fed. Republic Germany, 1989, U.S. Presdl. Citizens Achievement medal, 1989. Fellow Nat. Acad. Pub. Adminstrn.; mem. Met. Club, Army-Navy Country Club. Office: Baltic Am Enterprise Fund 1625 K St NW Ste 903 Washington DC 20006

RIDLEN, SAMUEL FRANKLIN, agriculture educator; b. Marion, Ill., Apr. 24, 1916; s. Will and Leoma Josephine (Sneed) R.; m. Helen Louise Camp, Apr. 17, 1946; children: Judith Elaine, Barbara Jo, Mark Ellis. BS, U. Ill., 1940; MS, Mich. State U., 1957. Agr. instr. Westville (Ill.) Twp. High Sch., 1940-43; gen. mgr. Honegger Breeder Hatchery, Forrest, Ill., 1953-56; assoc. prof. poultry sci. U. Conn., Storrs, 1957-58; from asst. prof. to prof. poultry extension U. Ill., Urbana-Champaign, 1946-86, prof. emeritus poultry extension, 1986—, asst. head dept. animal scis., 1978-86. Author: An Idea and An Ideal-Nabor House Fraternity 1939-1989, 1989; poultry editorial cons. Successful Farming, Wonderful World Ency., 1960; poultry editor Am. Farm Youth, 1949-53, Ill. Feed Folks, 1949-53. Founding mem., charter mem. Nabor House Frat. Recipient Superior Svc. award U.S. Dept. Agr., 1982, Paul A. Funk Recognition award Coll. Agr., U. Ill., 1983, numerous others. Fellow Poultry Sci. Assn.; mem. World's Poultry Sci. Assn., Ill. State Turkey Growers Assn., Ill. Poultry Industry Coun., Ill Egg Market Devel. Coun. (adv. mem.), Ill. Animal Industry Coun., Coun. for Agr. Sci. and Tech., Ill. Alumni Assn. (life), DAV (life), Alpha Tau Alpha, Epsilon Sigma Phi, Gamma Sigma Delta (pres. 1982-83). Home: 1901 Lakeside Dr # C Champaign IL 61821-5967

RIDLEY, BETTY ANN, educator, church worker; b. St. Louis, Oct. 19, 1926; d. Rupert Alexis and Virginia Regina (Weikel) Steber; m. Fred A. Ridley, Jr., Sept. 8, 1948; children: Linda Drue, Clay Kent. BA, Scripps Coll., Claremont, Calif., 1948. Christian sci. practitioner, Oklahoma City, 1973—; tchr. Christian sci., 1983—; mem. Christian Sci. Bd. Lectureship, 1980-85. Trustee Daystar Found.; mem. The First Ch. of Christ Scientist, Boston, Fifth Ch. of Christ Scientist, Oklahoma City. Mem. Jr. League Am. Home: 7908 Lakehurst Dr Oklahoma City OK 73120-4324 Office: Suite 100-G 3000 United Founders Blvd Oklahoma City OK 73112 *What makes life a continuing joy and free of all fear is to know that God who is the only Creator is infinitely good. He is our Father and our Mother, our Judge and our best friend. He is our great Physician, caring for us tenderly and uninterruptedly. We have but to know this and live according to His law in order to enjoy His blessings.*

RIDLEY, CAROLYN FLUDD, social studies educator; b. Nashville, Jan. 21, 1942; d. Quitman Daniel and Glennora Elizabeth (Cannon) F.; m. Raymond Bennett, June 23, 1962 (div. 1984); 1 child, Karen Elizabeth Bennett Moore; m. Cornelius Theodore Ridley, July 16, 1988; stepchildren: Constance Maria Ridley Smith, William Keith. BA, CUNY, 1973; MEd, Tenn. State U., 1985. Cert. tchr., prin., Tenn., N.Y. Tchr. N.Y.C. Bd. Edn., 1973-75, Dickson (Tenn.) County Bd. Edn., 1976-77, Hickman County Bd. Edn., Centerville, Tenn., 1977-86, Met. Nashville Bd. Edn., 1986—; dir. Hickman County Career Day, 1982-83; bd. dirs. Assn. Retarded Citizens, Centerville, 1982-86; adv. com. Hickman County Bicentennial Com., Centerville, 1984-86, initiator commemorative quilt; participant NEH lectr. Author: A Black History of Hickman County, 1985. Campaign worker Met. Nashville Bd. Edn., 1991; campaigner Met. Nashville Edn., Assn., 1992; attendant Dem. Socialization Meeting, Nashville, 1992; participant Nat. Endowment for the Humanities Summer Inst. Furman U., Greenville, Tenn., 1995. Grantee Mid. Tenn. State U., Murfreesboro, 1990, Tenn. State U., Nashville, 1992; James R. Stokeley Inst. fellow U. Tenn., 1993; participant NEH Summer Inst. at Furman U., Greenville, Tenn., 1995. Fellow Taft Inst. (cert. 1992); mem. AAUW, NEA, NASA Space Inst. (cert. 1990), Smithsonian Instn., Internat. Platform Assn., Nat. Historic Preservation Soc., Nat. Geographic Soc., Nat. Coun. Social Studies, Internat. Platform Assn. Democrat. Mem. Ch. of Christ. Avocations: travel, reading, music, studying quilting folk art. Home: 4348 Setters Rd Nashville TN 37218-1839 Office: Haynes Mid Sch 510 W Trinity Ln Nashville TN 37207-4944

RIDLOFF, RICHARD, real estate executive, lawyer, consultant; b. N.Y.C., July 18, 1948; s. Sol and Daisey (Metz) R.; m. Caren Sara Berger, Mar. 27, 1977; children: Michael Joshua, Daniel Joseph. BA cum laude, Queens Coll., 1969; JD, Cornell U., 1972. Bar: N.Y. 1973. Assoc. counsel MONY, N.Y.C., 1972-79; sr. v.p., gen. counsel, sec. MONY Real Estate Investors, N.Y.C., 1979-85; v.p. investments MONY Fin. Svcs., N.Y.C., 1985-87; pres. MONY Realty Ptnrs. Inc., Glen Point, N.J., 1985-91; v.p. for investment mgmt. MONY Real Estate Investment Mgmt., N.Y.C., 1988-91; exec. v.p. Tibor Pivko and Co., Clifton, N.J., 1991-94; pres., dir. Growth & Income Inc., 1993-94; spl. projects dir. Kimco Realty Corp., 1995-96; pres. The Richardson Co., 1996—; bd. dirs. Growth & Income Inc.; mem. adv. commn. on real property ins. to Calif. Sen. Com. on Ins. Claims and Corps., 1986-92; adv. com. N.Y. chpt. Nat. Assn. Corp. Real Estate Execs., 1990. Author: A Practical Guide to Construction Lending, 1985; editor Real Estate Financing Newsletter, 1980-85 ; contbr. articles to profl. jours. Mem. secondary sch. interviewing com. Cornell U., Ithaca, N.Y., 1981—; chmn. fed. legis. com. Nat. Assn. Real Estate Investment Trusts, Washington, 1981-82. Mem. ABA (mem. real property com., fin. sect. real property, probate and trustlaw 1979—), N.Y. Bar Assn., Oakwood-Princeton Park Civic Assn., Omicron Delta Epsilon, Pi Sigma Alpha, Alpha Epsilon Pi.

RIDNER, KATHLEEN RADER, elementary education educator; b. Manchester, Ky., Feb. 11, 1949; d. Herman Ralph Sr. and Beatrice (Benge) Rader; m. Daniel Lewis Ridner, Oct. 4, 1969; 1 child, Mark Fredrick. BS, Cumberland Coll., 1980; M in Bus., Ea. Ky. U., 1982. Cert. tchr., Ky. Tchr. Belmont Jr. High Sch., Winchester, Ky., 1982-83; tchr. math. McKee (Ky.) Elem. Sch., 1985-86; tchr. lang. arts North Laurel Mid. Sch., London, Ky., 1986—. Republican. Baptist. Avocations: reading, cross-stitch, travel. Home: 60 Cypress Way London KY 40741-8250 Office: North Laurel Mid Sch 101 Johnson Rd London KY 40741-9500

RIDOUT, DANIEL LYMAN, III, physician, educator; b. Salisbury, Md., June 13, 1953; married. BA in Music, Dartmouth Coll., 1975; MD, U. Cin., 1979. Diplomate Nat. Bd. Med. Examiners, Am. Bd. Internal Medicine, Am. Bd. Gastrointestinal Bd.; lic. physician, Pa., Del; cert. ACLS, Advanced Trauma and Life Support. Intern then resident U. Pa. Hosp., Phila., 1979-82, chief med. resident, clin. instr. internal medicine, 1982-83, clin. instr., 1983-84, attending physician, teaching staff, 1986—; attending physician Crozer-Chester Med. Ctr., Upland, Pa., 1988—; pvt. practice, Upland, 1986—; chief gastrointestinal divsn. VA Hosp., Coatesville, Pa., 1987-89. Contbr. articles to profl. jours. Recipient Achievement and Svc. in Medicine award Afro-Am. Hist. Soc. Del., 1989. Mem. AMA, Am. Profl. Practice Assn., Am. Soc. Gastrointestinal Endoscopy, Pa. Med. Soc., Del. County Med. Soc. (bd. dirs.), Am. Soc. Internal Medicine, Med. Soc. Eastern Pa., Phila. County Med. Soc., Phila. Coll. Physicians, New Castle County Med. Soc. Office: Crozer Chester Med Ctr Profl Office Bldg II 1 Medical Blvd Upland PA 19013

RIECK, JANET RAE, special education educator; b. Atchison, Kans., Oct. 24, 1948; d. Clinton Everett and Bernice Marie (Schreurs) Wendland; m. Arthur Wyman Hand, Mar. 1970 (div. Feb. 1977); m. Doyle Elmer Rieck, Sept. 21, 1986. B in Music Edn., Otterbein Coll., 1970; MA, U. No. Colo., 1980; MS, No. Ill. U., 1989. Cert. tchr. Nebr. Music tchr. Blanchester (Ohio) Schs., 1970-74; tchr. aide N.Mex. Sch. for Visually Handicapped, Alamogordo, 1976-78; tchr. visually impaired Edn. Svc. Unit 7, Columbus, Nebr., 1979—; piano tchr., Cin., 1975-76, Alamogordo, 1976-78. Mem. NEA, Coun. Exceptional Children, Assn. for Edn. and Rehab. of Blind and Visually Impaired (Nebr. pres. elect 1990-92, pres. 1992-94, cert. orientation and mobility specialist). Lutheran. Avocations: piano, sewing, horseback riding, swimming. Home: RR 2 Box 148 Albion NE 68620-9323 Office: Ednl Svc Unit 7 2657 44th Ave Columbus NE 68601-8537

RIECKE, HANS HEINRICH, architect; b. Münster, Westfalia, Germany, Mar. 30, 1929; came to U.S., 1955; s. Hans Joachim and Hildegard (Schwarze) R.; m. Elvira Maria Magdalena Kaatz, Nov. 30, 1954; children: Christine, Annette, Monica, Ralph, Heidi. Student architecture, Technische Hochschule, Hannover, Fed. Republic. Germany, 1953; BA in Architecture, U. Calif., Berkeley, 1957. Registered architect, Calif., Hawaii. Draftsman Orinoco Mining Co., Puerto Ordaz, Venezuela, 1954-55, H.K. Ferguson Co., San Francisco, 1956-57; architect, ptnr. Hammarberg and Herman, Oakland, Calif., 1957-74; prin. Hans Riecke, Architect Inc., Kahului, Maui, Hawaii, 1974-78, Riecke Sunnland Kono Architects Ltd, Kahului, Maui, Hawaii, 1978-96; pres. HR Architect Inc., Maui, 1996—. Bd. dirs. Kihei Community Assn., Maui, Hawaii, 1975-77, Seabury Hall, Makawao, Maui, 1980-82; chmn. Mayor's Com. on Housing, County of Maui, 1984. Recipient Merit award Pacific Coast Builders Con., Kahului, Hawaii, 1990. Fellow AIA (pres. Maui chpt. 1990); mem. Am. Arbitration Assn. (panel of arbitrators 1980). Avocations: biking, gardening. Office: HR Architect Inc 77 Apalapani Ln Haiku HI 96708-5625

RIECKEN, HENRY WILLIAM, psychologist, research director; b. Bklyn., Nov. 11, 1917; s. Henry William and Lilian Antoinette (Nieber) R.; m. Frances Ruth Manson, Aug. 7, 1955; children—Mary Susan, Gilson, Anne. A.B., Harvard U., 1939, Ph.D., 1950; M.A., U. Conn., 1941. Social sci. analyst Dept. Agr., 1941-46; teaching fellow Harvard U., 1947-49, lectr. social psychology, research assoc. clin. psychology, 1949-54; assoc. prof. then prof., sr. mem. lab. research social relations U. Minn., 1954-58; program dir. social sci. research NSF, Washington, 1958-59; head Office Social Sci., Washington, 1959-60, asst. dir. social scis., 1960-64, assoc. dir. sci. edn., 1964-66; v.p. Social Sci. Research Council, N.Y.C., 1966-69; pres. Social Sci. Research Council, 1969-71; prof. behavioral scis. U. Pa., Phila., 1972-85, prof. emeritus, 1985-87; assoc. dir. for planning Nat. Library Medicine, Bethesda, Md., 1985-87; fellow Ctr. Advanced Study Behavioral Scis., Stanford, Calif., 1971-72; Paterson Meml. lectr. U. Minn., 1970; Jensen lectr. Duke U., 1973; mem. adv. com. to dir. NIH, 1966-70, chmn. internat. ctrs. com., 1968-73; pres. Am. Psychol. Found., 1971-73; vice chmn., chmn. com. nat. needs for biomed. and behavioral rsch. pers. NRC, 1975-80; mem. commn. sociotech. systems Nat. Acad. Scis., 1976-79; adj. prof. psychiatry U. Tex. Med. Br., 1988—. Author: The Volunteer Work Camp, 1952, When Prophecy Fails, 1956, Social Experimentation, 1974, Experimental Testing of Public Policy, 1976; contbr. articles to profl. jours. Bd. dirs. Found. Child Devel. (formerly Assn. Aid Crippled Children), N.Y.; trustee W.T. Grant Found., N.Y. Served with USAAC, 1943-45. Fellow Am. Psychol. Assn. (Harold M. Hildreth award 1971), Am. Acad. Arts and Scis.; mem. Am. Assn. Pub. Opinion Research, Sociol. Research Assn. (pres. 1966), Nat. Acad. Scis., Inst. Medicine. Clubs: Harvard (N.Y.C.); Cosmos (Washington).

RIEDEBURG, THEODORE, management consultant; b. Milw., June 7, 1912; s. Theodore and Elva Pauline (Wolf) R.; m. Margaret Anna Louise Oertel, Dec. 24, 1937 (dec.); children: Theodore, Charles Howard; m. Ruth Jones Keith, May 3, 1980. BS, Marquette U., 1934, MS, 1936. Dist. sales mgr. Philip Morris & Co., 1937-42; asst. mgr. fumigants dept. Dow Chem. Co., Midland, Mich., 1942-45; sales mgr. agrichems. Westvaco Chem., N.Y.C., 1945-50; mng. dir. Theodore Riedeburg Assocs., N.Y.C., 1950-80; ind. forensic chemist-pesticides St. Simons Island, Ga., 1980—. Contbr. articles to profl. jours. Pres. Citizens League White Plains, N.Y., 1962; chmn. St. Simone Island Beautification Coun., 1995-97. Fellow Soc. Profl. Mgmt. Cons. (past pres.); mem. Am. Arbitration Assn., Nat. Bur. Profl. Mgmt. Cons. (exec. adv. bd. 198997), Chemists Club (N.Y.C.). Home: 2507 Demere Rd Apt 2 Saint Simons Island GA 31522 Office: PO Box 21158 Saint Simons Island GA 31522-0658

RIEDEL, ALAN ELLIS, manufacturing company executive, lawyer; b. Bellaire, Ohio, June 28, 1930; s. Emil George and Alberta (Shafer) R.; m. Ruby P. Tignor, June 21, 1953; children: Ralph A., Amy L., John T. AB magna cum laude, Ohio U., 1952, LLD (hon.), 1994; JD, Case Western Res. U., 1955; grad., Advanced Mgmt. Program, Harvard, 1971. Bar: Ohio 1955, Tex. 1968. Assoc. Squire, Sanders & Dempsey, Cleve., 1955-60; gen. counsel Cooper Industries Inc. (formerly Cooper Bessemer Co.), Mt. Vernon, Ohio, 1960-63, sec., 1963-68, 1963-68, v.p. indsl. rels., 1968-73; sr. v.p. adminstrn. Cooper Industries, Inc., Houston, 1973-92; dir. Cooper Industries Inc., Houston, 1981-94, vice chmn., 1992-94; bd. dirs. Standard Products Co., Cleve., Arkwright Mut. Ins. Co., Waltham, Mass., Belden Inc., St. Louis, First Knox Nat. Bank Corp., 1994-97; bd. dirs. Gardner Denver Machinery Inc., Quincy, Ill., chmn. bd. dirs., 1994—. Former chmn. bd. dirs. Jr. Achievement of S.E. Tex.; former chmn. bd. trustees Ohio U. Endowment Found. Mem. Order of Coif, Phi Beta Kappa, Omicron Delta Kappa, Delta Tau Delta. Home: 803 Creek Wood Way Houston TX 77024-3023

RIEDEL, BERNARD EDWARD, retired pharmaceutical sciences educator; b. Provost, Alta., Can., Sept. 25, 1919; s. Martin and Naomi E. (Klingaman) R.; m. Julia C. McClurg, Mar. 5, 1944 (dec. Mar. 1992); children: Gail Lynne, Dwain Edward, Barry Robert. BS in Pharmacy, U. Alta., Edmonton, 1943, MS in Pharmacology, 1949; PhD in Biochemistry, U. Western Ont., 1953; DSc (hon.), U. Alta., 1990. Lectr., asst. prof. Faculty of Pharmacy U. Alta., Edmonton, 1946-49, asst. prof. then assoc. prof., 1953-58, prof., 1959-67, exec. asst. to v.p., 1961-67; dean, prof. Faculty Pharm. Scis. U. B.C., Vancouver, 1967-84, coordinator Health Scis. Centre, 1977-84; mem. sci. adv. com. Health Rsch. Found. of B.C., 1991-95. Contbr. numerous articles on pharmacology to profl. jours. Elder Ryerson United Ch.; mem. exec. bd. Boy Scouts Can., Edmonton Region, Alta.; mem. Cancer Control Agy. of B.C., trustee 1979-86, v.p., 1984, pres. 1985-86; bd. dirs. B.C. Lung Assn., 1988—, v.p., 1989, pres., 1990-91; chmn., bd. dirs. B.C. Organ Transplant Soc., 1986-89. Wing comdr. RCAF, 1943-46, 49-67. Recipient Gold medal in Pharmacy, 1943; Centennial medal, 1967, 75th Anniversary medal U. B.C., 1990; Can Forces decoration, 1965; Commemorative medal for 125th Anniversary of the Confedn. of Can., 1992; apptd. mem. Order of Can., 1997. Mem. Alta. Pharm. Assn. (hon. life), Can. Pharm. Assn. (hon. life), Assn. of Faculties of Pharmacy of Can. (hon. life, chmn. 1959, 69), Can. Biochem. Soc., Pharmacol. Soc. Can., Can. Assn. of Univ. Tchrs., Can. Soc. Hosp. Pharmacists, B.C. Coll. Pharmacists (hon. life), U. B.C. Profs. Emeriti Divsn. Alumni Assn. (pres. 1993-95). Home: 8394 Angus Dr, Vancouver, BC Canada V6P 5L2

RIEDL, JOHN JOSEPH, communications executive; b. Rockville Centre, N.Y., May 14, 1943; s. Joseph John and Jane (Mediary) R.; m. Ruth Beiswenger; 1 child, Brandon John. BS, Bowling Green State U., 1965. Media buyer and planner Leo Burnett Advt., Chgo., 1965-68, asst. account exec., 1968; account exec. Sta. WLS-TV, Chgo., 1968-73; account exec. of comml. TV sales ABC, N.Y.C., 1973-74; nat. sales mgr. Sta. KABC-TV, Los Angeles, 1974-84, gen. sales mgr., 1984—; lectr. UCLA and Pepperdine Univ., Los Angeles, 1977—. Mem. TV Advt. Bur. Republican. Roman Catholic. Avocations: golf, basketball, running, sports. Office: Sta KABC-TV 4151 Prospect Ave Los Angeles CA 90027-4524

RIEDL, JOHN ORTH, university dean; b. Milw., Dec. 9, 1937; s. John O. and Clare C. (Quirk) R.; m. Mary Lucille Priestap, Feb. 4, 1961; children: John T., Ann E., James W., Steven E., Daniel J. BS in Math. magna cum laude, Marquette U., Milw., 1958; MS in Math., U. Notre Dame, 1960, PhD in Math., 1963; postgrad., Northwestern U., 1963. Asst. prof. math. Ohio State U., Columbus, 1966-70, assoc. prof., 1970—, asst. dean Coll. Math. and Phys. Sci., 1969-74, assoc. dean, 1974-87, acting dean, 1984-86, spl. asst. to provost, 1987, dean, dir. Mansfield (Ohio) Campus, 1987—, coord. dean regional campus, 1988—; panelist sci. edn. NSF, 1980-91; cons. Ohio Dept. Edn., 1989, Ohio bd. regents subsidy cons., 1991, 95. Pres., v.p. exec. com. Univ. Cmty. Assn., Columbus, 1970-78; mem. edn. commn. St. Peter's Schs., Mansfield, 1989-95; trustee Rehab. Svc. N. Ctrl. Ohio, Mansfield, 1990—, v.p., 1993-94, pres., 1995-97; pres. Ohio Assn. Regional Campuses, 1993-94. NSF grad. fellow, 1960, 61, 62; recipient Faculty Svc. award Nat. U. Continuing Edn. Assn., 1988, Creative Programming award, 1988. Mem. Math. Assn. Am. (chair com. on minicourse 1981-87), Rotary Internat. Democrat. Roman Catholic. Avocations: fishing, woodworking, handball, gardening. Home: 745 Clifton Blvd Mansfield OH 44907-2284 Office: Ohio State U 1680 University Dr Mansfield OH 44906-1547

RIEDLSPERGER, MAX ERNST, history educator; b. San Luis Obispo, Calif., July 7, 1937; s. Helmuth Georg and Jean (Bennett) R.; m. Deanna Beckmann, Feb. 12, 1966; 1 child, Gretchen. AB, Wabash Coll., 1959; MA, U. Mich., 1961; PhD, U. Colo., 1969. Tchr. Eastern High Sch., Detroit, 1961-63, Bay de Noc C.C., Escanaba, Mich., 1963-66; teaching assoc. U. Colo., Denver, 1966-67; instr. Colo. Women's Coll., Denver, 1967-68; asst. prof. Calif. Poly. State U., San Luis Obispo, 1969-72, assoc. prof., 1977-82, prof., 1983—, chmn. history dept., 1985-91; dir. internat. programs Calif. State U., Heidelberg, Fed. Republic Germany, 1983-84. Author: Lingering Shadow of Nazism, 1978; contbr. articles to profl. publs., chpts. to books. Bd. dirs. San Luis Obispo Mozart Festival, 1979-83, 84-85, v.p., 1985-86. Austrian Ministry of Edn. fellow, 1968-69; grantee Am. Coun. Learned Socs., 1972, NEH, 1976, U.S. Dept. Edn., 1986-88. Mem. Am. Hist. Assn., German Studies Assn. Democrat. Avocations: swimming, skiing, tennis, music. Office: Calif Poly State U Dept History San Luis Obispo CA 93407

RIEDTHALER, WILLIAM ALLEN, risk management professional; b. Cleve., May 13, 1948; s. Robert Wilbert and Jean Margaret (Trojanowski) R.; m. Janet Louise Clark, Nov. 10, 1973; children: Jennifer Margaret, Valerie Gretchen. AS in Law Enforcement, Cuyahoga C.C., 1968; BA in Pub. Safety Adminstrn., Kent State, 1974, BA in Criminal Justice Studies, 1974. Cert. instr. and peace officer; cert. tchr., Ohio, Fla., Tex., Mich. Police cadet Cleve. Police Dept., 1967-69, patrolman, 1969-74, detective, 1974-81, sgt. police, 1981-84; assoc. security advisor Cleve. Electric Illuminating Co., 1984-87, investigator, 1987-90; security advisor Centerior Energy Corp., Cleve., 1990-93; supr. claims Centerior Energy Corp., Independence, 1993-96, mgr. risk mgmt., 1996—; instr. gambling and vice Case Western Res. U., Cleve., 1979-90, Cleve. Police Acad., 1974—, Ohio Peace Officers Tng. Acad., 1976—, Cuyahoga County Sheriffs Officers Acad., Cleve., 1981—, Shaker Heights (Ohio) Police Acad., 1990—. Author: An Enforcement Guide to Carnival Games Gambling and Fraud, 1981; contbr. articles to profl. jours. Spl. dep. sheriff Cuyahoga County Sheriff's Office, Cleve., 1985—. Recipient Patrolman of Yr. award Cleve. Exchange Club, 1979. Mem. Am. Soc. Indsl. Security, Met. Crime Bur. (v.p. 1992-93, pres. 1994-95), German Am. Police Assn., Fraternal Order of Police, Cleve. Claims Assn. Republican. Avocations: collecting and writing on gambling, cheating, carnival gambling, coin operated gambling device. Home: 7992 Vesta Ave Northfield OH 44067-2048 Office: Centerior Energy Corp PO Box 5000 6200 Oak Tree Blvd Independence OH 44131

RIEDY, MARK JOSEPH, finance educator; b. Aurora, Ill., July 9, 1942; s. Paul Bernard and Kathryn Veronica R.; m. Erin Jeanne Lynch, Aug. 29, 1964; children: Jennifer Erin, John Mark. BA in Econs. maxima cum laude, Loras Coll., 1964; MBA, Washington U., St. Louis, 1966; PhD, U. Mich., 1971. Asst. prof. bus. adminstrn. U. Colo., Boulder, 1969-71; sr. staff economist Council of Econ. Advisers, Washington, 1971-72; spl. asst. to chmn. Fed. Home Loan Bank Bd., Washington, 1972; v.p., dir. research PMI Investment Corp., San Francisco, 1973; v.p., chief economist Fed. Home Loan Bank of San Francisco, 1973-77; exec. v.p., chief operating officer Mortgage Bankers Assn. of Am., Washington, 1978-84; pres., chief operating officer Fed. Nat. Mortgage Assn., Washington, 1985-86, cons., 1986-87; pres., chief operating officer J.E. Robert Cos., Alexandria, Va., 1987-88; pres., chief exec. officer Nat. Coun. Community Bankers, Washington, 1988-92, also bd. dirs.; Ernest W. Hahn prof. real estate fin. U. San Diego, 1993—; mem. adv. coun. Credit Rsch. Ctr., Purdue U., 1981-82; bd. dirs. Fed. Nat. Mortgage Assn., Am. Residential Mortgage Corp., Continental Savs. Bank, AccuBanc Mortgage Corp., Neighborhood Bancorp, Noble Broadcast Group, Drayton Ins. Cos., Perpetual Savs. Bank, Ctr. for Fin. Studies; mem. San Diego Mayor's Renaissance Commn. Vice chmn. St. Vincent De Paul Village. Woodrow Wilson scholar, 1964; Nat. Def. scholar, 1964-66; U.S. Steel Found. fellow, 1966-68; Robert G. Rodkey Found. fellow, 1966-69; Earhart Found. fellow, 1968-69. Mem. Am. Econ. Assn., Am. Fin. Assn., Nat. Assn. Bus. Economists, Am. Soc. Assn. Execs., Urban Land Economics, Lambda Alpha Internat., Alpha Kappa Psi (hon.). Office: U San Diego Sch Bus Adminstrn 5998 Alcala Park San Diego CA 92110-2429

RIEDY, VIRGINIA KATHLEEN, nursing educator; b. Columbus, Ohio, Apr. 21, 1952; d. Oliver and Barbara A. Sheets; children: Elizabeth, Matthew, Andrew. RN, Ohio; cert. emergency nurse, ACLS provider, instr.; EMT, Ohio; paramedic, Ohio. Staff nurse emergency dept. Children's Hosp., Columbus, Ohio, 1973-74, Good Samaritan Hosp., Sandusky, Ohio, 1974-78, Providence Hosp., Sandusky, Ohio, 1978-86; site evaluator Ohio Bd. Regents, Paramedic Tng. Programs, State of Ohio, 1984—; paramedic coord. ER-DOC Providence Hosp., Sandusky, 1984—; continuing edn. cons. Lucas County/REMSNO, 1990—; program dir. N.W. Paramedic Program Med. Coll. Ohio, Toledo, 1993—; internat. EMS lectr. video game induced seizures; affiliate faculty State of Ohio Basic Trauma Life Support, 1986—; asthma camp nurse supr. Timberlane South Shore Lung Assn., 1984; EMS delegate People to People, Soviet Union and Germany, 1991. Contbr. articles to profl. jours. Trustee Erie County chpt. Am. Heart Assn., 1976—; REMSNO edni. adv. com., 1986—; Erie County EMS Coun. rep., 1986—. Mem. Nat. Assn. EMT, Am. Trauma Soc. (N.W. Ohio unit affiliate), Ohio Instr. Coords. Soc. (charter mem.), Emergency Nurses Assn. (state coun. rep.). Roman Catholic. Home: 358 Portside Cr Apt 3 Perrysburg OH 43551 Office: Paramedic Tng Program 1912 Hayes Ave Sandusky OH 44870-4736

RIEFF, PHILIP, sociologist; b. Chgo., Dec. 15, 1922; s. Gabriel and Ida (Hurwitz) R.; m. Alison Douglas Knox, Dec. 31, 1963; 1 son by previous marriage, David. BA, U. Chgo., 1946, MA, 1947, PhD, 1954. Teaching fellow U. Chgo., 1946, instr., 1947-52; asst. prof. Brandeis U., Waltham, Mass., 1952-57; fellow Ctr. for Advanced Study in Behavior Scis., Palo Alto, Calif., 1957-58; assoc. prof. sociology U. Calif., Berkeley, 1958-61; prof. U. Pa., Phila., 1961—, Univ. prof. sociology, 1965-67, Benjamin Franklin Prof. Sociology, 1967-93, prof. emeritus, 1993—; prof. psychiatry Med. Coll. Pa., Phila., 1993—; chief editorial cons. Beacon Press, Boston, 1952-58; vis. assoc. prof. Harvard U., 1960; vis. fellow Ctr. for Study of Dem. Instns., Santa Barbara, Calif., 1963-64; Gauss lectr. Princeton U., 1975; Terry lectr. Yale U., 1976-77; prof. psychiatry and preventive medicine, Med. Coll. Pa., 1993—; vis. professorial lectr. Naval Acad., 1993. Author: Freud: The Mind of the Moralist, 1959, rev. edit., 1961, The Triumph of the Therapeutic: Uses of Faith After Freud, 1966, Fellow Teachers, 1973, The Feeling Intellect, 1990; editor The Collected Papers of Sigmund Freud (10 vols.), 1961; assoc. editor Am. Sociol. Rev., 1958-61; founding editor Jour. Am. Acad. Arts and Scis., 1956-59, Daedalus. Chief cons. planning dept. Nat. Coun. Chs., 1961-64. Named Fulbright Prof. U. Munich, 1959-60, Guggenheim fellow, 1970, Sometime fellow All Souls Coll., Oxford. Fellow Royal Soc. Arts London; mem. Libr. Co. Phila., Am. Sociol. Assn., Soc. Sci. Study Religion (mem. coun.), Societe Europeene de Culture, Garrick Club of London. Office: Med Coll Pa Dept Psychiatry 3200 Henry Ave Philadelphia PA 19129-1137

RIEFLER, DONALD BROWN, financial consultant; b. Washington, Nov. 10, 1927; s. Winfield W. and Dorothy (Brown) R.; m. Patricia Hawley, Oct. 12, 1957; children: Duncan, Linda, Barbara. BA, Amherst Coll., 1949. With J.P. Morgan & Co. Inc., N.Y.C., 1952-91; v.p. Morgan Guaranty Trust Co. of N.Y., 1962-68, sr. v.p., 1968-77, chmn. market risk com., 1977-91; fin. mkts. cons., 1991—; bd. dirs. Niagara Mohawk Power Corp., Bank of Tokyo Trust Co. With U.S. Army, 1950-52. Mem. John's Island Club, Riomar Country Club, Country Club of the Rockies (Edwards, Colo.), Eagle Springs Club (Wolcott, Colo.). Home: 512 Bay Dr Vero Beach FL 32963-2107

RIEGEL, BYRON WILLIAM, ophthalmologist; b. Evanston, Ill., Jan. 19, 1938; s. Byron and Belle Mae (Huot) R.; BS, Stanford U., 1960; MD, Cornell U., 1964; m. Marilyn Hills, May 18, 1968; children—Marc William, Ryan Marie, Andrea Elizabeth. Intern, King County Hosp., Seattle, 1964-65; asst. resident in surgery U. Wash., Seattle, 1965; resident in ophthalmology U. Fla., 1968-71; pvt. practice medicine specializing in ophthalmology, Sierra Eye Med. Group, Inc., Visalia, Calif., 1972—; mem. staff Kaweah Delta Dist. Hosp., chief of staff, 1978-79. Bd. dirs., asst. sec. Kaweah Delta Dist. Hosp., 1983-90. Served as flight surgeon USN, 1966-68. Co-recipient Fight-for-Sight citation for research in retinal dystrophy, 1970. Diplomate Am. Bd. Ophthalmology, Nat. Bd. Med. Examiners. Fellow ACS, Am. Acad. Ophthalmology; mem. Calif. Med. Assn. (del. 1978-79), Tulare County Med. Assns., Calif. Assn. Ophthalmology (v.p. 3d party liaison 1994-96, dir. 1996—), Am. Soc. Cataract and Refractive Surgery, Internat. Soc. Refractive Surgery, Internat. Phacoemulsification and Cataract Methodology Soc., Rotary (Visalia). Roman Catholic. Home: 3027 W Keogh Ct Visalia CA 93291-4228 Office: 2830 W Main St Visalia CA 93291-4331

RIEGEL, JOHN KENT, corporate lawyer; b. Olean, N.Y., Sept. 24, 1938; s. Forrest M. and Lena (Zilkofsky) R.; m. Betty Ann Eden, Mar. 16, 1968; children: John Kent, Geoffrey. BA, Alfred U., 1961; LLB, Syracuse U., 1963. Bar: N.Y. 1963, Md. 1971. Military lawyer USMC, 1964-68; atty. advisor USN, Washington, 1968-71; asst. atty. gen. State of Md., Annapolis, 1971-72, gen. counsel dept. agriculture, 1972-74; atty. regulatory law ICI Ams. Inc., Wilimington, Del., 1974-76, atty. law dept., 1976-85; gen. counsel ICI Specialty Chems./ICI Ams. Inc., Wilmington, 1985-86; v.p., gen. counsel ICI Ams. Inc., Wilmington, 1986-93, also bd. dirs., exec. com., 1986—, pres., gen counsel, 1993—. Bd. overseers Widener U. Sch. Law, 1987—; bd. trustees Med. Ctr. Del., 1987—; bd. dirs. Child Care Connection, 1991-94. Mem. ABA, N.Y. State Bar Assn., Am. Corp. Counsel Assn. (bd. dirs. Del. Valley chpt. 1987-90, pres. 1989), European-Am. C. of C. (bd. dirs. 1995—), Del. Bus. Rountable (chmn.), Bus./Pub. Edn. Coun. Office: ICI Americas Inc 3411 Silverside Rd Wilmington DE 19810

RIEGEL, KURT WETHERHOLD, environmental protection executive; b. Lexington, Va., Feb. 28, 1939; s. Oscar Wetherhold and Jane Cordelia (Butterworth) R.; children: Tatiana Suzanne, Samuel Brent Oscar, Eden Sonja Jane. BA, Johns Hopkins U., 1961; PhD, U. Md., 1966; PMD, Harvard U., 1977. Asst. prof. astronomy UCLA, 1966-74; prof. astronomy U. Calif. Extension, Los Angeles, 1968-74; mgr. energy conservation program Fed. Energy Adminstrn., Washington, 1974-75; chief tech. and consumer products energy conservation Dept. Energy, Washington, 1975-78, dir. consumer products div., conservation and solar energy, 1978-79; assoc. dir. environ. engring. and tech. EPA, 1979-82; head Astronomy Ctrs. NSF, 1982-89; dir. Environ. Protection Office USN, 1989-94; dir. environ. tech. USN, Washington, 1994—; adj. prof. George Washington U., 1995; vis. prof. Washington & Lee U., 1993; cons. Aerospace Corp., El Segundo, Calif., 1967-70, Rand Corp., Santa Monica, Calif., 1973-74; vis. fellow U. Leiden, Netherlands, 1972-73; Mem. Casualty Council Underwriters Labs., Nat. Radio Astron. Observatory Users Com., 1968-74. Contbr. articles to profl. jours. Mem. AAAS, Am. Phys. Soc., Sierra Club, Audubon Soc., Internat. Radio Sci. Union, Am. Astron. Soc., Internat. Astron. Union, Assn. of Scientists and Engrs. Home: 3019 N Oakland St Arlington VA 22207-5320

RIEGEL, NORMAN, physician; b. N.Y.C., Jan. 22, 1935; children: Bram, Lisa, Karyn, Daniel; m. Joan Ann Gordon, June 17, 1973. AB, Columbia Coll., 1956; MD, Einstein Coll. Med., 1960. Diplomate Am. Bd. Internal Medicine. Intern U. Chgo., 1960-61; resident Kings County Hosp., Bklyn., N.Y., 1961-62; asst. resident Bellevue Hosp., N.Y.C., 1962-63, GI fellow, 1963-64; pvt. practice Hackensack, N.J., 1966—; clin. assoc. prof. medicine Coll. Medicine and Dentistry of N.J., Newark, 1977—; chief dept. gastroeneterol. Bergen Pines County Hosp., Paramus, N.J., 1970—; dir. dept. medicine Bergen Pine County Hosp., Paramus, 1985-87, 89-96. Editor, Jour. of Med. Soc., 1983-87; contbr. numerous articles to profl jours. Served to capt. USAF, 1964-66. Fellow, Am. Coll. Gastroenterol., Am. Soc. Internal Medicine, Am. Coll. Physicians; mem., Am. Soc. Gastrointestinal Endoscopy, Bergen County Med Soc., N.J. Med. Soc. Office: 11 Elm Ave Hackensack NJ 07601-4702

RIEGER, MITCHELL SHERIDAN, lawyer; b. Chgo., Sept. 5, 1922; s. Louis and Evelyn (Sampson) R.; m. Rena White Abelmann, May 17, 1949 (div. 1957); 1 child, Karen Gross Cooper; m. Nancy Horner, May 30, 1961 (div. 1972); stepchildren: Jill Levi, Linda Hanan, Susan Perlstein, James Geoffrey Felsenthal; m. Pearl Handelsman, June 10, 1973; stepchildren: Steven Newman, Mary Ann Malarkey, Nancy Halbeck. A.B., Northwestern U., 1944; J.D., Harvard U., 1949. Bar: Ill. 1950, U.S. Dist. Ct. (no. dist.) Ill. 1950, U.S. Supreme Ct. 1953, U.S. Ct. Mil. Appeals 1953, U.S. Ct. Appeals (7th cir.) 1954. Legal asst. Rieger & Rieger, Chgo., 1949-50, assoc., 1950-54; asst. U.S. atty. No. Dist Ill., Chgo., 1954-60; 1st asst. No. Dist Ill., 1958-60; assoc. gen. counsel SEC, Washington, 1960-61; ptnr. Schiff Hardin & Waite, Chgo., 1961—; instr. John Marshall Law Sch. Chgo., 1952-54. Contbr. articles to profl. jours. Mem. Chgo. Crime Commn., 1964-94, life mem., 1995—; pres. Park View Home for Aged, 1969-71; Rep. precinct committeeman, Highland Park, Ill., 1964-68; bd. dirs. Spertus Mus. Judaica, 1987-91, vis. com., 1991—. Fellow Am. Coll. Trial Lawyers; mem. ABA, FBA (pres. Chgo. chpt. 1959-60, nat. v.p. 1960-61), Chgo. Bar Assn., Ill. Bar Assn., Am. Judicature Soc., 7th Circuit Bar Assn., Standard Club, Law Club Chgo., Vail Racquet Club, Phi Beta Kappa. Jewish. Avocations: photography; skiing; sailing. Home: 4950 S Chicago Beach Dr Chicago IL 60615-3207 Office: Schiff Hardin & Waite 7200 Sears Tower Chicago IL 60606-6327

RIEGER, PHILIP HENRI, chemistry educator; b. Portland, Oreg., June 24, 1935; s. Otto Harry and Carla (Oertli) R.; m. Anne Bioren Lloyd, June 18, 1957; 1 child, Christine Lloyd. B.A., Reed Coll., 1956; Ph.D., Columbia U., 1962. Prof. chemistry Brown U., Providence, 1962—. Contbr. articles to profl. jours. Mem. Am. Chem. Soc. (chmn. R.I. sect. 1978), Royal Soc. Chemistry, New Eng. Assn. Chemistry Tchrs. Epscopalian. Home: 119 Congdon St Providence RI 02906-1462 Office: Brown U Dept Chemistry Box H Providence RI 02912

RIEGER, STEVEN ARTHUR, state legislator, business consultant; b. Pullman, Wash., May 14, 1952; s. Samuel and Olga (Skoblikoff) R.; m. Karen Jean Gibson, July 5, 1992. AB, Harvard U., 1974, MBA, 1976. Asst. to v.p. Crowley Maritime Corp., Seattle, 1976-79; asst. v.p. Seattle-Northwest Securities Corp., Anchorage, 1980-81; spl. asst. Alaska State Legislature, Juneau, 1981-82; v.p. William Kent Co., Anchorage, 1983-84; mem. Alaska Ho. Reps., Juneau, 1985-91; pres. S. Rieger & Co., Anchorage, 1991—; mem. Alaska Senate, Juneau, 1993-97. Bd. dirs. AWAIC women's shelter. Republican. Avocations: running, skiing, outdoor activities. Home: PO Box 110623 Anchorage AK 99511-0623

RIEGERT, ROBERT ADOLF, law educator, consultant; b. Cin., Apr. 21, 1923; s. Adolf and Hulda (Basler) R.; m. Roswitha Victoria Bigalke, Oct. 28, 1966; children: Christine Rose, Douglas Louis. BS, U. Cin., 1948; LLB cum laude, Harvard U., 1953; Doctoris Juris Utriusque magna cum laude, U. Heidelberg, Germany, 1966; postgrad., U. Mich., Harvard U., Yale U., MIT. Bar: D.C. 1953, Cts. Allied High Commn. Germany 1954. Mem. Harvard Legal Aid Bur., 1952-53; sole practice Heidelberg, 1954-63; vis. assoc. prof. So. Meth. U. Law Sch., Dallas, 1967-71; prof. law Cumberland Law Sch., Samford U., Birmingham, Ala., 1971-97; prof. emeritus Cumberland Law Sch., Samford U., Birmingham, 1997—; dir. Cumberland Summer Law Program, Heidelberg, 1981-94; Disting. vis. prof. Salmon P. Chase Coll. Law, 1983-84. Author: (With Robert Braucher) Introduction to Commercial Transactions, 1977, Documents of Title, 1978; contbr. articles to profl. jours. Served to 1st lt. USAAF, 1943-46. Grantee Dana Fund for Internat. and Comparative Law, 1979; grantee Am. Bar Found., 1966-67; German Acad. Exchange, 1953-55, mem. Harvard Legal Aid Bur., Salmon P. Chase Coll. law scholar, 1950; Pres.'s scholar U. Cin., 1941. Mem. ABA (com. on new payment systems), Internat. Acad. Comml. and Consumer Law, Am. Law Inst., Ala. Law Inst. (coun.), Assn. Am. Law Schs. (chmn. exec. com., sect. internat. legal exchs., chmn. subcom. on com. laws), Ala. Pattern Jury Instrns. Com., German Comparative Law Assn., Acad. Soc. German Supreme Cts., Army-Navy Club (Washington). Office: Samford U Cumberland Law Sch Birmingham AL 35229

RIEGSECKER, MARVIN DEAN, pharmacist, state senator; b. Goshen, Ind., July 5, 1937; s. Levi and Mayme (Kauffman) R.; m. Norma Jane Shrock, Aug. 3, 1958; children: Steven Scott, Michael Dean. BA in Pharmacy, U. Colo., 1967. Pharmacist Parkside Pharmacy, Goshen, Ind., 1967-73; pharmacist, mgr. Hooks Drugs, Inc., Goshen, 1973-94; coroner Elkhart County, Goshen, 1977-84; mem. Ind. Senate, Indpls., 1988—; pharmacist Walgreens, Goshen, 1994-96; bus. affairs cons. Goshen Health Sys., 1997—. Rep. commr. Elkhart County, 1985-88; bd. commrs. pres., 1987-88; past adv. bd. dirs. Oaklawn Hosp.; past chmn. Michiana Area Coun. of Govts. Mem. Ind. Pharm. Assn., Elkhart County Pharm. Assn., Exch. Club. Republican. Mennonite. Avocation: jogging. Home: 1814 Kentfield Way Goshen IN 46526-5610 Office: Ind Senate Statehouse 4-D N 200 W Washington St Indianapolis IN 46204-2728

RIEHECKY, JANET ELLEN, writer; b. Waukegan, Ill., Mar. 5, 1953; d. Roland Wayne and Patricia Helen (Anderson) Polsgrove; m. John Jay Riehecky, Aug. 2, 1975; 1 child, Patrick William. BA summa cum laude, Ill. Wesleyan U., 1975; MA in Communication, Ill. State U., 1978; MA in English, Northwestern U., 1983. Tchr. English Blue Mound (Ill.) High Sch., 1977-80, West Chicago (Ill.) High Sch., 1984-86; editor The Child's World Pub. Co., Elgin, Ill., 1987-90; freelance writer Elgin, 1990—. Author: Dinosaur series, 24 vols., 1988, UFOs, 1989, Saving the Forests, 1990, The Mystery of the Missing Money, 1996, The Mystery of the UFO, 1996, Irish Americans, 1995, others. Recipient Summit award for best children's nonfiction Soc. Midland Authors, 1988. Mem. Soc. Am. Magicians, Children's Reading Round Table, Soc. Children's Book Writers and Illustrators, Mystery Writers of Am., Phi Kappa Phi. Democrat. Baptist. Avocations: reading, hiking, dinosaur hunting.

RIEHL, JANE ELLEN, education educator; b. New Albany, Ind., Oct. 17, 1942; d. Henry Gabbart Jr. and Mary Elizabeth (McGraw) Willham; m. Richard Emil Riehl, June 15, 1968; 1 child, Mary Ellen. BA in Elem. Edn., U. Evansville, 1964; MS, Ind. U., Bloomington, 1966; postgrad., Spalding U., 1979, Ind. U. S.E., New Albany, 1991-93. Cert. 1-8 and kindergarten tchr., Ind.; lic. profl. kindergarten tchr., Ind. Elem. tchr. Clarksville (Ind.) Cmty. Sch., 1964-68, 70-75, 81-82, tchr. kindergarten, 1975-81; elem. tchr. Chapelwood Sch. Wayne Twp., Indpls., 1968-70; lectr. edn. Ind. U. S.E., 1988—, dir. tchg. and rsch. project, 1990-91, 92-93; cons. Riehl Assocs., Jeffersonville, Ind., 1995—. Co-author: An Integrated Language Arts Teacher Education Program, 1990, The Reading Professor, 1992, Multimedia: HyperStudio and Language Education, 1996, Technology: Hypermedia and Communications, 1997, others; author procs. Parent vol. Girl Scouts U.S.A., Jeffersonville, 1988-95; mem. adminstrtv. bd. Wall Street United Meth. Ch., Jeffersonville, 1993-95; mem. women's health adv. coun. Clark Meml. Hosp., Jeffersonville, 1995—; bd. dirs. Clark Meml. Hosp. Found.; team mem. People to People Citizen Amb. Program, 1993, 95, 96. Named Young Career Woman of Yr. Bus. and Profl. Women New Albany and Dist. 13 Ind., 1966; tchg. and rsch. grantee Ind. U. S.E., 1990, 94, 95. Mem. Nat. Coun. Tchrs. English, Profs. Reading Tchr. Edn., Altrusa Internat. Inc. (internat. bd. 1993-95, dist. gov.sovss 1993-95, svc. award 1995), Phi Delta Kappa (v.p. 1991-92, pres. 1997—, svc. award 1991), Kappa Kappa Kappa (pres. Jeffersonville 1975-76, 90-91, Outstanding Mem. award 1987). Avocations: travel, reading, crafts, decorating. Home: 1610 Fox Run Trl Jeffersonville IN 47130-8204 Office: Ind U SE 4201 Grant Line Rd New Albany IN 47150-2158

RIEHLE, B. HUDSON, trade association administrator; b. Cin., Sept. 10, 1953; s. Robert Arthur Riehle and Lois W. Hudson; m. Eileen Patricia Betit, Aug. 2, 1986; children: B. Hudson, Jr., Bradley Patrick. BA, Skidmore Coll., 1975; MBA, U. Pa., 1986. Rsch. cons. Avmark, Inc., Washington, 1976-78; rsch. analyst Airline Pilots Assn., Washington, 1978-81, supr. econ. analysis, 1981-84; rsch. mgr. Nat. Restaurant Assn., Washington, 1986-91, sr. rsch. mgr., 1991-95, dir. rsch., 1995—. Editor: Comml. Airline Fleets, 1976-78, Restaurant Industry Ops. Report, 1986—; contbr. to Airline Pilot, 1978-84, Restaurants USA, 1986—. Mem., bd. dirs., 1st v.p. Fairlington Meadows, Arlington, 1990-92. Avocations: geology, cross country skiing, photography. Home: 2431 Davis Ave Alexandria VA 22302 Office: Nat Restaurant Assn 1200 17th St NW Washington DC 20036-3006

RIEHM, SARAH LAWRENCE, writer, arts administrator; b. Iowa City, Sept. 8, 1952; d. Stuart Parker and Elizabeth Jane (Munson) Lawrence; m. Charles Curtis Riehm, May 18, 1974; children: Andrew, Amanda, Jennie Frances. BGS, U. Iowa, 1974; MA in Internat. Fin., U. Tex., 1981. Mgr., adminstr. IBM, Cedar Rapids, Iowa, 1974-75; program mgr. Rockwell Internat., Dallas, 1975-80; mgr. internat. tax Peat, Marwick, Mitchell, Hong Kong, 1981-82; writer, playwright, 1981—; exec. dir. Playwright's Project, Dallas, 1992-94, Tex. Composers Forum, Dallas, 1995-96; faculty mem. U. Tex., Dallas, 1996—; bd. dirs. Dallas Coalition Arts. Playwright: Liberty-A Drama in Two Acts, 1994 (So. Playwrights award 1994), The King & Me, 1994; author: Entrepreneurship: Building the American Dream, 1993, 50 Great Businesses for Teens, 1997. Founder Playwrights Project; chair Dallas 10,000, 1995. Mem. NOW, Handgun Control. Democrat. Presbyterian. Avocations: pipe organ, composer, racquetball, skiing, travel. Office: Tex Composers Forum 7522 Campbell Rd Ste 113-181 Dallas TX 75248-1726

RIEKE, ELIZABETH ANN, legal association administrator; b. Buffalo, July 10, 1943; divorced; children: Frederick Martin, Eowyn Ann. BA in Polit. Sci. summa cum laude, Oberlin Coll., 1965; JD with highest distinction, U. Ariz., 1981. Bar: Ariz., 1981. Rsch. asst. S.W. Environ. Svc., Tuscon, 1976-79; law clk. Snell & Wilmer (formerly Bilby, Shoenhair, Warnock & Dolph), Tuscon, 1979; law clk. Office of Solicitor Divsn. Conservation and Wildlife, Dept. Interior, Washington, 1980; law clk. to Hon. William C. Canby Jr. U.S. Ct. Appeals (9th cir.), 1981-82; dep. legal counsel Ariz. Dept. Water Resources, 1982-85, chief legal counsel, 1985-87, dir., 1991-93; assoc. Jennings, Strouss & Salmon, Phoenix, 1987-89, ptnr., 1989-91; asst. sec. for water and sci. Dept. Interior, Washington, 1993-95; now dir. Natural Resouces Law Ctr Univ. Colorado, Boulder; adj. prof. Ariz. State U., Phoenix, 1989; speaker in field. Recipient Disting. Alumnus award U. Ariz., 1986. Office: Univ Colorado Sch Law Campus 401 Boulder CO 80309-0401

RIEKE, PAUL VICTOR, lawyer; b. Seattle, Apr. 1, 1949; s. Luvern Victor and Anna Jane (Bierstedt) R.; m. Judy Vivian Farr, Jan. 24, 1974; children: Anna Katharina, Peter Johann. BA, Oberlin Coll., 1971; postgrad. U. Wash., 1971, Shoreline C.C., 1972-73; JD, Case Western Res. U., 1976. Bar: Wash. 1976, U.S. Dist. Ct. (we. dist.) Wash. 1976, U.S. Tax Ct. 1978. Assoc. Hatch & Leslie, Seattle, 1976-82, ptnr., 1982-91; ptnr. Foster, Pepper & Shefelman, 1991—. Exec. notes editor Case Western Res. U. Law Rev., 1975-76. Mem. exec. bd. dist. council N. Pacific dist. Am. Luth. Ch., Seattle, 1978-83, council pres. 1983, Am. Luth. Ch. pub. bd., 1984-87; v.p. Northwest Wash. Synod of Evangelical Luth. Ch. Am., Seattle, 1988-90, mem. Synod Coun., 1990-92, del. ELCA Nat. Assembly, 1991, ELCA Northwest Synod Regional Rep., 1992-96, region one coun. pres., 1994-96. Mem. ABA, Wash. State Bar Assn., Seattle-King County Bar Assn., Order of Coif. Democrat. Lodge: Seattle Downtown Central Lions. Home: 321 NE 161st St Seattle WA 98155-5741 Office: Foster Pepper & Shefelman 34th Fl 1111 3rd Ave Seattle WA 98101

RIEKE, WILLIAM OLIVER, foundation director, medical educator, former university president; b. Odessa, Wash., Apr. 26, 1931; s. Henry William and Hutoka S. (Smith) R.; m. Joanne Elynor Schief, Aug. 22, 1954; children: Susan Ruth, Stephen Harold, Marcus Henry. B.A. summa cum laude, Pacific Luth. U., 1953; M.D. with honors, U. Wash., 1958. Instr. anatomy U. Wash. Sch. Medicine, Seattle, 1958; asst. prof. U. Wash. Sch. Medicine, 1961-64, adminstrv. officer, 1963-66, assoc. prof., 1964-66; prof., head dept. anatomy Coll. Medicine U. Iowa, Iowa City, 1966-71; dean protem Coll. Medicine U. Iowa (Coll. Medicine), 1969-70, chmn. exec. com., 1969-70; vice chancellor for health affairs, prof. anatomy U. Kans. Med. Center, Kansas City, 1971-73; exec. vice chancellor, prof. anatomy U. Kans. Med. Center, 1973-75; affiliate prof. biol. structure U. Wash. Sch. Medicine, Seattle, 1975-96; pres. Pacific Lutheran U., Parkland, Wash., 1975-92; pres. emeritus, 1992—; exec. dir. Ben B. Cheney Found., 1992—; Mem. interdisciplinary gen. basic sci. test com. Nat. Bd. Med. Examiners, 1968-72, chmn. anatomy test com., 1972-75, mem. at large, 1975-79; spl. cons. NIH, 1970-72; mem. adv. com. Inst. Medicine, Nat. Acad. Scis., 1974-76; mem. Commn. on Colls., NW Assn. Schs. and Colls., 1979-84. Editor: Procs. 3d Ann. Leucocyte Culture Conf, 1969; editorial bd.: Am. Jour. Anatomy, 1968-71. Bd. dirs. Luth. Edni. Council N. Am., 1980-83, pres., 1982-83; chmn. Wash. Friends Higher Edn., 1983-91. Named one of Most Effective Coll. or Univ. Pres., Bowling Green State U. Rsch. Study, 1986, Disting. Alumnus Pacific Luth. U., 1970, Disting. Alumnus Pi Kappa Delta, 1977, Disting. Alumnus U. of Washington Med. Alumni, 1989; decorated Knight First Class Royal Norwegian Order of Merit, 1989; named to Cashmere H.S. Wall of Fame, 1995. Lutheran (mem. ch. council 1967-70). Home: 13905 18th Ave S Tacoma WA 98444-1006 Office: Ben B Cheney Found 1201 Pacific Ave Ste 1600 Tacoma WA 98402-4322

RIEKEN, DANNY MICHAEL, naval officer, aerospace and systems engineer; b. Hastings, Minn., Aug. 31, 1967; s. Oscar Rieke and Dorothy Ruth (O'Toole) R.; m. Lisa Kae Bruer, June 8, 1991. B Aerospace Engring. and Mechanics, U. Minn., 1991. Enlisted USN, 1984, commd. ensign, 1991; advanced through grades to lt. USN, Ill., 1984; stationed at USN, San Diego and Great Lakes, 1985-86, Pensacola, 1991-93, Great Lakes, 1993-96, Washington, 1996—; stationed at U. Minn./Twin Cities ROTC, 1986-91, USNR, Mpls., 1986-89; co-engr./designer U. Minn./Univ. Space Rsch. Assn./NASA, 1990-91; pub. affairs officer Res. Officers Tng. Corps, U. Minn., Mpls., 1989-90, yearbook editor, 1989-90, adminstrv. asst., staff officer ROTC, 1991-92; Naval ROTC profl. devel. officer Chief of Naval Edn. and Tng., Pensacola, 1992; pvt. pilot single engine land, 1990—; owner, pres. Silver Eagle Investments, Inc., 1992—; lead engr. application software devel. team MIRS, 1993-96; system software engr. for Navy Standard Integrated Pers. System and the Navy's Info. Tech. initiative--Info. Tech. for the 21st century. Co-author: Mars Integrated Transportation System, 1990-91; editor: Winds of Change, 1990. Pres Centennial Hall House 11, U. Minn., 1987-88, mem. Centennial Hall coun., 1986-89; co-chmn. Combined Fed. Campaign, 1993. Decorated Joint Svc. Achievement medal, Nat. Def. Svc. medal, Def. Meritorous Svc. medal; USN scholar, 1988-91. Mem. AIAA, Aircraft Owners and Pilots Assn., U. Minn. ROTC Alumni Assn., U. Minn. Alumni Assn. Democrat. Lutheran. Achievements include design in cooperation with classmates and NASA through USRA of Mars Integrated Transportation System; technical design (to include engring. sys. adminstrn., relational database adminstrn. and TCP/IP network adminstrn.) and program management of new Dept. of Def.-wide computer system MEPCOM Integrated Resource System to process over 1 million applicants annually into all branches of armed forces through 65 offices of U.S. Military Entrance Processing Command, Navy Standard Integrated Pers. Sys. Home: 8579 Enochs Dr Lorton VA 22079-1338 Office: Space and Naval Warfare Systems Command 2451 Crystal Dr Bldg 5 Cpk Arlington VA 22202-4804

RIELLY, JOHN EDWARD, educational association administrator; b. Rapid City, S.D., Dec. 28, 1932; s. Thomas J. and Mary A. (Dowd) R.; m. Elizabeth Downs, Dec. 28, 1957 (marriage annulled 1976); children: Mary Ellen, Catherine Ann, Thomas Patrick, John Downs; m. Irene Diedrich, Aug. 1, 1987. B.A., St. John's U., Collegeville, Minn., 1954; postgrad. (Fulbright scholar), London Sch. Econs. and Polit. Sci., 1955-56; Ph.D., Harvard U., 1961. Faculty dept. govt. Harvard U., 1958-61; with Alliance for Progress programs Dept. State, Washington, 1961-62; fgn. policy asst. to Sen. then Vice Pres. Hubert Humphrey, Washington, 1963-69; cons. office European and internat. affairs Ford Found., N.Y.C., 1969-70; sr. fellow Overseas Devel. Council, Washington, 1970-71; exec. dir. Chgo. Council on Fgn. Relations, 1971-74, pres., 1974—; cons. NSC; mem. adv. bd. Grad. Sch. Arts and Scis., Harvard U.; bd. dirs. Am. Coun. on Germany, Nat. Com. on U.S.-China Rels., China Coun. of Asia Soc., Am. Ditchley Found., Trilateral Commn., commn. on U.S.-Brazilian Rels.; past pres. Nat. Coun. Comty. World Affairs Orgns. Contbr. articles to profl. jours.; editor: American Public Opinion and U.S. Foreign Policy, 1975, 2d edit., 1979, 83, 87, 91, 95; editl. bd. Fgn. Policy Quar., 1974—. Former trustee St. John's U. Mem. Am. Polit. Sci. Assn., Council on Fgn. Relations, N.Y.C. Home: 2021 Kenilworth Ave Wilmette IL 60091-1519 Office: 116 S Michigan Ave Chicago IL 60603-6001

RIELY, CAROLINE ARMISTEAD, physician, medical educator; b. Washington, Feb. 1, 1944; d. John William and Jean Roy (Jones) Riely. AB, Mt. Holyoke Coll., 1966; MD, Columbia U., 1970. Diplomate Am. Bd. Internal Medicine. Med. intern Presbyn. Hosp., N.Y.C., 1970-71, resident in medicine, 1971-73; fellow in liver disease Yale U., New Haven, 1973-75, asst. prof., 1975-80, assoc. prof., 1980-88; prof. medicine U. Tenn., Memphis, 1988—. Fellow ACP, Am. Coll. Gastroenterology; mem. Am. Assn. Study Liver Disease, Internat. Assn. Study Liver, N.Am. Soc. for Pediatric Gastroenterology and Nutrition. Home: 1756 Central Ave Memphis TN 38104-5116 Office: U Tenn 951 Court Ave Rm 555D Memphis TN 38103-2813

RIEMENSCHNEIDER, ALBERT LOUIS, engineering educator; b. Cody, Nebr., May 18, 1936; s. Albert L. and Agnes E. (Schilling) R.; m. Norma Mae Geisler, June 24, 1962 (dec.); children: Richard L., David F., Barbara J. BSEE, S.D. Sch. Mines and Tech., 1959, MSEE, 1962; PhD, U. Wyo., 1969. Registered profl. engr., S.D. Engr. Sperry Utah Corp., Salt Lake City,

1959-60; design engr. Dakota Steel & Supply Co., Rapid City, S.D., 1960-61; instr. U. Wyo., Laramie, 1961-67; chief engr. Dunham Assocs., Rapid City, 1974-80; grad. tchg. asst. S.D. Sch. Mines and Tech., Rapid City, 1961-62, asst. prof., 1967-73, assoc. prof., 1973-74, 80-84, prof., dept. head, 1983-95, prof., 1995—; cons. ALR Engring., RE/SPEC, Inc., Rapid City, 1987—. Mem. IEEE, Am. Soc. Engring. Edn., Nat. Soc. Profl. Engrs. Democrat. Lutheran. Lodge: Elks. Avocations: electronics, computers, hunting, fishing. Home: 4051 Corral Dr Rapid City SD 57702-9128 Office: South Dakota Sch of Mines 501 E Saint Joseph St Rapid City SD 57701-3901

RIEMENSCHNEIDER, DAN LAVERNE, religious organization administrator; b. Pontiac, Mich., July 21, 1952; s. Henry LaVerne and Sarah Lou R.; m. Rebecca Joy Fruth, June 26, 1976; 1 child, Derek Henri. BA in Social Work, Mich. State U., 1974, PhD in Family Ecology, 1985; MA in Religion Edn., Asbury Seminary, Wilmore, Ky., 1976. Min. of Edn. Spring Arbor (Mich.) Free Meth. Ch., 1977-85; asst. prof. social work and family sci. Spring Arbor Coll., 1985-87; exec. dir. dept. edn. Free Meth. Ch. of North Am., Indpls., 1987—; chmn. Samaritan Counseling Ctr., Jackson, Mich., 1985-87. Bd. dirs. Mich. Council on Family Relations, Lansing, Mich., 1985-87. Mem. Nat. Council Family Relations, Nat. Assn. Evangelicals, Nat. Christian Edn. Assn. (bd. dirs.), Nat. Task Force on Family (bd. dirs.). Office: Free Meth World Hdqrs PO Box 535002 770 N High School Rd Indianapolis IN 46214-3756*

RIEMENSCHNEIDER, PAUL ARTHUR, physician, radiologist; b. Cleve., Apr. 17, 1920; s. Albert and Selma (Marting) R.; m. Mildred McCarthy, May 12, 1945; children: Barbara Anne, Nancy Emelia, David Andrew, Paul Albert, Mary Elizabeth, Sarah Bache. BS magna cum laude, Baldwin-Wallace Coll., 1941; MD, Harvard U., 1944. Diplomate Am. Bd. Radiology (trustee 1973-85), Nat. Bd. Med. Examiners. Prof., chmn. dept. radiology SUNY, Syracuse, 1945-64; chief diagnostic radiology Santa Barbara (Calif.) Cottage Hosp., 1964-89, bd. dirs., 1984-90; vis. prof. in residence SUNY, Syracuse, 1983—; Radiology Soc. of No. Am. Internat. vis. prof. of Radiology, Univ. Malaya, 1990-91. Co-editor: N.Y. State Jour. Medicine, 1960-64; mem. editorial adv. bd. Yearbook of Cancer, 1960-64; contbr. articles to profl. jours. Mem. appropriations com. Santa Barbara Found., 1984-93; vestryman All Saints Episc. Ch., 1970-76, sr. warden, 1973; bd. dirs. ARC, Santa Barbara, 1968-72, Am. cancer Soc., Santa Barbara, 1967-70, Casa Dorinda Retirement Residence, 1975-76, 89-96, pres., 1993-96; bd. dirs. Wood Glen Hall Retirement Residence, 1980—, sec., 1987; bd. dirs. Cancer Found. Santa Barbara, 1966-82, 89-95, chmn. equipment com., 1973-82; bd. dirs. Direct Relief Internat., 1997—. Lt. comdr. USNR, 1945-46, 54-56. Recipient Alumni Merit award Baldwin-Wallace Coll., 1985. Fellow Am. Coll. Radiology (cancer com. 1952-54, council 1956-64, bd. chancellors 1967-73, chmn. commn. standards in radiologic practice 1968-71, v.p. 1972, pres. 1974, chmn. com. manpower 1972-86, chmn. com. manpower in armed svcs. 1975-86, Gold medal 1982); mem. AMA, Calif. Med. Assn., Santa Barbara County Med. Soc. (chmn. med. sch. com. 1967-71), Am. Roentgen Ray Soc. (mem. publs. com. 1965-75, chmn. 1970-75, exec. council 1970-75, 77-82, chmn. program com. 1977-79, pres.-elect 1977-79, pres. 1979, Gold medal award 1986), South Coast Radiol. Soc. (pres. 1967), Assn. Univ. Radiologists (sec. 1960, pres. 1961, com. resident tng. 1984-88), Radiol. Soc. N.Am. (Gold medal award 1990), Am. Soc. Neuroradiology, Soc. Pediatric Radiology, Eastern Radiol. Soc. (pres.-elect 1987, pres. 1988-89), Calif. Radiol. Soc., So. Calif. Radiol. Soc., Detroit Roentgen Soc. (hon.), Bluegrass Radiol. Soc. (hon.), Pacific N.W. Radiol. Soc. (hon.), Birnamwood Golf Club (bd. dirs. 1996—), Skaneateles Country Club, Cosmopolitan Club (sec. 1996), Alpha Omega Alpha. Republican. Avocations: tennis, swimming. Home: 112 Olive Mill Rd Santa Barbara CA 93108-2424

RIEMKE, RICHARD ALLAN, mechanical engineer; b. Vallejo, Calif., Oct. 11, 1944; s. Allan Frederick and Frances Jewell (O'Brien) R. BA in Physiology, U. Calif., Berkeley, 1967, MA in Physiology, 1971, PhD in Engring. Sci., 1977. Postdoctoral fellow U. So. Calif., Los Angeles, 1977-78; rsch. engr. Del Mar Avionics, Irvine, Calif., 1979; staff fellow NIH, Bethesda, Md., 1980; adv. engr. Idaho Nat. Engrin. Lab., Idaho Falls, 1980—. Served with U.S. Army, 1969-75. Mem. AAAS, ANS, Am. Soc. Mech. Engrs., Biomed. Engring. Soc., Soc. Computer Simulation, Soc. Math. Biology, Soc. Engring. Sci., Order of Golden Bear, Alpha Sigma Phi. Republican. Roman Catholic. Avocations: swimming, surfing. Home: 1727 Grandview Dr # 4 Idaho Falls ID 83402-5016 Office: Lockheed Martin Ida Techs Inc Idaho Nat Engring Lab Idaho Falls ID 83415-3880

RIENHOFF, JOANNE WINKENWERDER, artist; b. Balt., Nov. 2, 1938; d. Walter L. and Eleanor (Zouck) Winkenwerder; m. George Sloan Oldberg, July 7, 1962 (dec. Mar. 1966); m. MacCallum Rienhoff, Dec. 17, 1966 (dec. May 1994). AB, Radcliffe Coll., 1960; MA in Tchg., Johns Hopkins U., 1963; postgrad., U. Denver, 1984-85. Tchr. Garrison (Md.) Forest Sch., 1961-62, Latin Sch. Chgo., 1963-66, Graland Country Day Sch., Denver, 1972-80; artist, 1984—. Exhibited in group shows at U. Denver, Harvard U., Sigraph Soc., Denver, Mid. Pk. Bank, Granby, Colo., others. Bd. dirs., treas. Denver Sch. Vol. Program, 1969-71; leader Jr. Gt. Books program Denver sch. sys., 1967-69; mem. women's bd. Rush Presbyn. St. Luke's Hosp., Chgo., 1965-94. Mem. Rocky Mountain Harvard U. Club, Grand County Hist. Soc., Friends of Grand County Libr. Home: Ouray Ranch Granby CO 80446

RIENNER, LYNNE CAROL, publisher; b. Pitts., Aug. 3, 1945; d. David and Molly (Rice) R. B.A., U. Pa., 1967. Exec. v.p., assoc. publisher, editorial dir. Westview Press Inc., Boulder, Colo., 1975-84; pres. Lynne Rienner Pub. Inc., Boulder, Colo., 1984—; pub. cons. various orgns.; lectr. U. Denver Pub. Inst., 1981-84, 93—; panelist nat. meetings. Bd. dirs. Boulder Breast Cancer Coalition, 1993-95. Mem. Assn. Am. Pubs. (bd. dirs. 1992-96, exec. coun. of profl. and scholarly pub. divsn. 1996—). Office: Lynne Rienner Pub Inc 1800 30th St Ste 314 Boulder CO 80301-1026

RIENZO, ROBERT JAMES, radiologist; b. Jersey City, N.J., July 27, 1949; s. James Joseph and Marie Nicoletta (Bernardo) R.; m. Janice Meyer, Apr. 8, 1972 (div. Dec. 1991); 1 child, Michael Robert; m. Catherine Elizabeth Rafferty, Jan. 11, 1992; 1 child, Robert Francis. AB, Cornell U., 1971; MD, N.Y. Med. Coll., 1975. Diplomate Am. Bd. Radiology, Am. Bd. Nuclear Medicine. Resident St. Vincent's Hosp., N.Y.C., 1975-80; staff physician Jefferson Hosp., Pitts., 1980-81, Allentown (Pa.) Hosp., Lehigh Valley Hosp., Pa., 1981—. Contbr. articles to profl. jours. Mem. Exch. Club Western LeHigh, Emmaus, Pa., 1983—. Mem. AMA (Physicians Recognition award 1986—), Soc. Nuclear Medicine, Am. Coll. Nuclear Physicians, Am. Coll. Radiology, Soc. Radiologists in Ultrasound. Avocations: skiing, racquetball, golf. Office: Valley Nuclear Med Assoc 5940 Hamilton Blvd Wescosville PA 18106-9648

RIEPE, DALE MAURICE, philosopher, writer, illustrator, educator, Asian art dealer; b. Tacoma, June 22, 1918; s. Rol and Martha (Johnson) R.; m. Charleine Williams, 1948; children: Kathrine Leigh Riepe Herschlag, Dorothy Lorraine. BA, U. Wash., 1944; MA, U. Mich., 1946, PhD, 1954; postgrad. (Rockefeller-Watamull-McInerny fellow), U. Hawaii, Banaras and Madras, India, Tokyo and Waseda, Japan, 1949. Instr. philosophy Carleton Coll., 1948-51; asst. prof. U. S.D., 1952-54; assoc. prof. U. N.D., 1954-59, prof., 1959-62, chmn. dept., 1954-62; prof., chmn. C.W. Post Coll., 1962-63; prof. philosophy SUNY, Buffalo, 1963—; chmn. dept. social scis., assoc. dean SUNY Grad. Sch., 1964—; instr. marine electricity Naval Tng. Program, Seattle, 1943-45; mem. nat. screening bd. South Asia, Fulbright Selection, 1968-70, Asia, 1970-72; chmn. Fulbright Selection Com. for Asia, 1972, 82; vis. Fulbright lectr. Tokyo U., 1957-58; vis. lectr. Western Wash. U., 1961, Delhi U., 1967; exchange lectr. U. Man., 1955, Moscow State U., 1979, Beijing Higher Edn. Inst., 1984; docent Albright-Knox Art Gallery; cons. Ctr. for Sci., Tech. and Devel., Council of Sci. adn Indsl. Rsch., Govt. India, 1978—, Inst. Fang Studies, 1987—; del. Cuban-N.Am. Philosophy Conf., Cuban Inst. Social Sci., 1982, Fang Centennial, Taiwan Nat. U., Taipeh, 1987, Hungarian-Am. Philos. Conf., Budapest, 1988; sports columnist The Town Crier; vis. scholar Andhra U., 1996. Author: The Naturalistic Tradition in Indian Thought, 1961, The Philosophy of India and its Impact on American Thought, 1970, Indian Philosophy Since Independence, 1979, The Owl Flies by Day, 1979, Asian Philosophy Today, 1981, Objectivity and Subjectivism in the Philosophy of Science, 1985, Philosophy and Revolutionary Theory, 1986, also articles in field.; editor: Phenomenology and Natural Existence, 1973, Philosophy and Political Economy; co-editor: The Structure of Philosophy, 1966, Contributions of American Sankritists in the Spread of Indian Philosophy in the United States, 1967, Radical Currents in Contemporary Philosophy, 1970, Reflections on Revolution, 1971, Philosophy at the Barricade, 1971, Contemporary East European Philosophy, 1971, Essays in East-West Dialogue, 1973, Explorations in Philosophy and Society, 1978; illustrator The Quick and the Dead, 1948; editorial com. Chinese Studies in History, 1970—, Chinese Studies in Philosophy, 1970—; publs. bd. Conf. for Asian Affairs; Editor various series.; editl. bd. Philos. Currents and Revolutionary World, 1972-86, Soviet Studies in Philosophy, 1979-87, Marxist Dimensions, 1987—,. Active ACLU; mem. com. overseers Chung-an U., Korea; bd. dirs. Evergreen Coll. Cmty. Orgn., 1988—; bd. dirs. Friends of Evergreen Coll. Libr., 1992—; active Henry Gallery, Frye Gallery, Palm Springs Desert Mus., Seattle Art Mus., Phila. Mus. Art; mem. Capital Mus. and Art Soc., Wash. State Hist. Soc. Fulbright scholar India, 1951-52; Fulbright lectr. U. Tokyo, 1957-58; U. Mich. fellow, 1945-48, Carnegie Corp. fellow Asian Studies, 1960-61, Am. Inst. Indian Studies Rsch. fellow, 1966-67; grantee 4th East-West Philosophers Conf., 1964, Penrose fund Am. Philos. Soc., 1963; SUNY Research Found., 1965-67, 69, 72-73, Bulgarian Acad. Sci., 1975, London Sch. Oriental and African Studies, 1971. Fellow Royal Asiatic Soc., Far Eastern Inst. (Tokyo); mem. AAAS, Internat. Hegel-Vereinigung, Conf. Asian Affairs (sec. 1995), Am. Oriental Soc., Am. Philos. Soc., Indian Inst. Psychology, Philosophy and Psychical Rsch. (hon. adviser), Soc. for Am. Philosophy (chmn. 1960), Am. Inst. Indian Studies (trustee 1965-66), Soc. for Creative Ethics (sec.), Am. Archaeol. Soc., Am. Assn. Asian Studies, Am. Math. Soc., Am. Aesthetics Soc., Internat. Soc. Aesthetics, Am. Soc. Comparative and Asian Philosophy, Asiatic Soc. (Calcutta), Soc. for Philos. Study Dialectical Materialism (founding sec.-treas. 1962—), Soc. for Philos. Study Marxism (publs. sec. 1973-86), Union Am. and Japanese Profls. Against Nuclear Omnicide (treas. U.S. sec. 1978—), Internat. House of Japan, Internat. Philosophers for Prevention Nuclear Omnicide, United Univ. Profs. of SUNY-Buffalo (v.p.), Kokusai Bunka Shinkokai, Union Concerned Scientists, Alpha Pi Zeta. Office: SUNY 605 Baldy Hall Buffalo NY 14261

RIERSON, ROBERT LEAK, retired broadcasting executive, television writer; b. Walnut Cove, N.C., Sept. 5, 1927; s. Sanders C. and Anna (Cox) R.; m. Barbara Eugenia McLeod, Sept. 23, 1950 (dec. Feb. 1988); children: Barbara Elaine, Richard Troy; m. Rosemary L. McCampbell, Apr. 20, 1997. Student, Duke U., 1945-46, Davidson Coll., 1946-47; BS in Speech cum laude, Northwestern U., 1948. Program dir., program ops. mgr. WBT Radio and WBTV, Charlotte, N.C., 1948-66; program mgr. WJBK-TV, Detroit, 1966-69, WTOP-TV, Washington, 1969-71; dir. broadcasting WCBS-TV, N.Y.C., 1971-73; pres. Rierson Broadcast Consultants, N.Y.C., 1973-75; program exec. Grey Advt., N.Y.C., 1975-77; v.p., dir. programming Dancer-Fitzgerald-Sample, N.Y.C., 1977-80; exec. producer Corinthian Prodns., N.Y.C., 1980-82; dir. news programming CNN TV, Atlanta, 1982-96; ret., 1996. Producer-creator TV show ABCs of Democracy, 1965; producer, writer TV show George Washington's Mt. Vernon, 1970; creator, writer TV series 24 Days of Christmas, 1978. Bd. dirs. Mich. Coun. Chs., Detroit, 1968-69, ARC, Charlotte, 1960-62; 1st v.p. Charlotte Oratorio Singers, 1960-66. Lt. USNR, 1952-54. Recipient Edn. award Charlotte Jr. Woman's Club, 1961, George Washington Honor medal Freedoms Found., 1970; named Young Man of Yr., 1960. Mem. Nat. Assn. Radio-TV Program Execs. (charter mem., bd. dirs. 1964—), Radio-TV News Dirs. Assn., Order of Long Leaf Pine. Republican. Mem. Moravian Episcopal Ch. Avocations: reading, travel, movies. Home: 31 S Cherrywood Ln Pisgah Forest NC 28768

RIES, BARBARA ELLEN, alcohol and drug abuse services professional; b. Chgo., Oct. 27, 1952; d. Laurence B. and Genieveve (Wasiek) R. AAS in Human Svcs., Coll. of DuPage, Glen Ellyn, Ill., 1973; BA in Social Work, Sangamon State U., Springfield, Ill., 1978; postgrad., U. Mo., 1987-88, U. Tex., Arlington, 1991—. Cert. social therapist, criminal justice counselor-master addiction counselor; nat., internat. cert. alcohol and drug counselor; qualified chem. dependency counselor. Counselor Ray Graham Assn. for Handicapped, Addison, Ill., 1975-76; child abuse counselor Ill. Dept. Children and Family Svcs., Springfield, 1977-78; alcoholism counselor non-med. detoxification program S.H.A.R.E., Villa Park, Ill., 1978-80; outpatient therapist Ingalls Meml. Hosp., Harvey, Ill., 1980-83; dir. aftercare Lifeline Program, Chgo., 1984-85; case mgr. Lifecenter Program, Kansas City, Mo., 1985-87; counselor, acting clin. coord. Lakeside Hosp., Kansas City, 1988-89; program mgr., dir. chem. recovery programs Two Rivers Psychiat. Hosp., Kansas City, 1989-90; dir. day program and chem. dependency program SW Hosp./Citadel, Dallas, 1990—; dir. Flexcare program Dallas Meml. Hosp., 1990-91; pvt. practice Columbus, Ohio, 1991—; program coord. Advanced Clin. Svcs., Federal Way, 1992-94; recovery svc. adminstr. Orient Correctional Insts., 1996—; spkr. in field. Recipient commendation Ingalls Hosp., 1983. Mem. APA, ACA, nat. Assn. Forensic Counselors (cert. criminal justice specialist), Am. Correctional Assn., Nat. Assn. Drug and Alcohol Counselors (cert., (NCAC II), Nat. Assn. for Relapse Prevention Counselors, Wash. Advs. Mentally Ill, Ohio Assn. Alcoholism and Drug Abuse Counselors, Dual Diagnosis Com. Avocations: exercise, reading, listening to music, writing.

RIES, EDWARD RICHARD, petroleum geologist, consultant; b. Freeman, S.D., Sept. 18, 1918; s. August and Mary F. (Graber) R.; student Freeman Jr. Coll., 1937-39; A.B. magna cum laude, U. S.D., 1941; M.S., U. Okla., 1943, Ph.D. (Warden-Humble fellow), 1951; postgrad. Harvard, 1946-47; m. Amelia D. Capshaw, Jan. 24, 1949 (div. Oct. 16, 1956); children: Rosemary Melinda, Victoria Elise; m. Maria Wipfler, June 12, 1964. Asst. geologist Geol. Survey S.D., White River area, 1941; geophys. interpreter Robert Ray Inc., Western Okla., 1942; jr. geologist Carter Oil Co., Mont., Wyo., 1943-44, geologist Mont., Wyo., Colo., 1944-49; sr. geologist Standard Vacuum Oil Co., Assam, Tripura and Bangladesh, India, 1951-53, sr. regional geologist N.V. Standard Vacuum Petroleum, Maatschappij, Indonesia, 1953-59, geol. adviser for Far East and Africa, White Plains, N.Y., 1959-62; geol. adviser Far East, Africa, Oceania, Mobil Petroleum Co., N.Y.C., N.Y., 1962-65; geol. adviser for Europe, Far East, Mobil Oil Corp., N.Y.C., 1965-71, sr. regional explorationist Far East, Australia, New Zealand, Dallas, 1971-73, Asia-Pacific, Dallas, 1973-76, sr. geol. adviser Rsch. Geology, 1976-79, assoc. geol. advisor Geology-Geophysics, Dallas, 1979-82, sr. geol. cons., 1982-83; ind. internat. petroleum geol. cons. Europe, Africa, Sino-Soviet and S.E. Asia, 1986—. Grad. asst., teaching fellow U. Okla., 1941-43, Harvard, 1946-47. Served with AUS, 1944-46. Mem. AAAS, Am. Assn. Petroleum Geologists (assoc. editor 1978-83, 50 Yr. Mem. Svc. award 1993), Geol. Soc. Am., Am. Geol. Inst., Nat. Wildlife Fedn., Nat. Audubon Soc., N.Y. Acad. Sci., Soc. Exploration Geophysicists, Wilderness Soc., Am. Legion, Phi Beta Kappa, Sigma Xi, Sigma Gamma Epsilon. Republican. Mennonite Am. Inst. Econ. Rsch., Club: Harvard (Dallas). Author numerous domestic and internat. proprietary and pub. hydrocarbon generation and reserve evaluations, reports and profl. papers. Home and Office: 6009 Royal Crest Dr Dallas TX 75230-3434

RIES, MARTIN, artist, educator; b. Washington, Dec. 26, 1926; s. Martin Frank and Kathryn (Stretch) R.; m. Dianys d'Arcy Frobisher, June 8, 1953; children: d'Arcy, Von, Gannett, Nicole. BFA, Am. U., 1950; MA in Art History, Hunter Coll., 1968, postgrad. in mus. adminstrn., 1968. Asst. dir. pub. rels. Nat. Congl. Com., Washington, 1951; asst. dir. Hudson River Mus., 1957-67; advisor Westchester Cultural Ctr., 1965-66; curator instnl. art exhibits, prof. art L.I. U., Bklyn., 1967-94. One-man shows include Atelier Gallery, N.Y.C., 1968, Paul Gallery, Tokyo, 1968, Atelier Terre d'Ocre, France, 1973, Unicorn Gallery, Soho, N.Y., 1976, Gansb Gallery, Lenox, Mass., 1978, Belanthi Gallery, Bklyn., 1984, Stamford Mus., Stamford, Conn., 1987, Raja Idris Gallery, Melbourne, Australia, 1989, Robb St. Gallery, Bairnsdale, Australia, 1989, Salena Gallery, L.I.U., 1996, 2/20 Gallery, N.Y.C.; exhibited in group shows Smithsonian Inst., 1952, Mus. of Modern Art, N.Y.C., 1956, SUNY-Albany, 1967, Casa de la Cultura Ecuatoriana in Cuayaquil, Ecuador, 1979, Hammer Gallery, N.Y.C., 1980, Muestra Internacional de Obra Grafica, Spain, 1982, Aaron Berman Gallery, N.Y.C., 1983, Kenkeleba Gallery, N.Y.C., 1985, Inst. of Contemporary Art, London, 1988; contbr. editor Arts Mag., 1974-75; contbr. articles, revs., catalog introductions, and artists' statements to publs. Art editor Greenwich Village News, 1976-77. With Intelligence and Reconnaissance, U.S. Army, 1945-46. Mem. Artists Representing Environ. Art (bd. dirs.), Assn. Internationale des Critiques d'Art (Am. sect.), Am. Soc. Contemporary Artists, Nat. Writer's Union. Home: 36 Livingston Rd Scarsdale NY 10583-6845

RIES, WILLIAM CAMPBELL, lawyer; b. Pitts., Apr. 8, 1948; s. F. William and Dorothy (Campbell) R.; m. Mallory Burns, Oct. 26, 1968; children: William Sheehan, Sean David. AB, Cath. U. Am., 1970; JD, Duquesne U., 1974; cert. Grad. Sch. Indsl. Adminstrn., Carnegie Mellon U., 1980. Bar: Pa. 1974, U.S. Dist. Ct. (we. dist.) Pa. 1974, U.S. Supreme Ct. 1979. Atty., then mng. counsel trust and investment svc. Mellon Bank, N.A., Pitts., 1974-90; ptnr. Dickie, McCamey and Chilcote, Pitts., 1990—; mem. adv. com. decedents' estates and trust law Pa. Joint State Govt. Commn., 1981—; adj. prof. Duquesne U., 1984—. Pres. McCandless Twp. Civic Assn., Pitts., 1981—, McCandless Town Coun., chair pub. safety com., vice chair fin com.; sec. McCandless Indsl. Devel. Auth.; liaison McCandless zoning hearing bd. Fellow Am. Bar Found.; mem. ABA (chmn. fiduciary svcs. subcom.), Pa. Bar Assn., Allegheny County Bar Assn., Pitts. Estate Planning Coun., Joint State Govt. Commn., Am. Bankers Assn. (co-chmn. nat. conf. lawyers and corp. fiduciaries, chmn. trust counsel com.), Pa. Bankers Assn. (trust com., trust legis. com.), Rivers Club, Treesdale Golf and Country Club. Republican. Avocations: golf, sailing, cross-country skiing, fitness. Home: 9602 Fawn Ln Allison Park PA 15101-1737

RIESENBERGER, JOHN RICHARD, pharmaceutical company executive; b. N.Y.C., Sept. 25, 1948; s. Richard Raymond and Marie Teresa (Long) R.; m. Patricia Ann Casey, Nov. 23, 1974; children: Christine, Jennifer. BS in Econs. and Bus., Hofstra U., 1970, MBA in Mgmt., 1975; cert. internat. sr. mgmt. program, Harvard U., 1989. Customer svc. supr. Chase Manhattan Bank, 1970-72; gen. sales rep. various regions Upjohn Co., 1972-75; sales rep., sales mgr. Upjohn Co., various locations, N.Y., 1976-81; profl. tng. and devel. officer Upjohn Co., Kalamazoo, Mich., 1981-83; dir. Chgo. sales area Upjohn Co., 1983-87; v.p., group mgr. Upjohn Co. of Can., Toronto, Ont., 1987-89; exec. dir., worldwide med. scis. liaison Upjohn Co., Kalamazoo, 1989-92, exec. dir. worldwide strategic mktg., 1992-95; exec. dir. corp. info. tech. Pharmacia & Upjohn, Inc., Kalamazoo, 1995, v.p. bus. info., 1996—; chmn. industry adv. bd. dirs. SEI Ctr. Advanced Studies in Mgmt., Wharton Sch., U. Pa.. Author: (with Robert T. Moran) The Global Challenge: Building the New Worldwide Enterprise, 1994, Global Business Management in the 1990's, 1995. Mem. Am. Mgmt. Assn., Am. Mktg. Assn., Midwest Healthcare Mktg. Assn., World Future Soc., Soc. for Competitive Intelligence Profls., Strategic Mgmt. Soc., Healthcare Mktg. and Comm. Coun., Pharm. Rsch. Mfrs. Am. (chmn. mktg. practices com.), Nat. Pharm. Coun., Am. Med. Informatics Assn., The Planning Forum, Internat. Soc. for Strategic Planning and Mgmt., Harvard Bus. Sch. Club, Pharm. Bus. Intelligence and Rsch. Group. Avocation: golf. Home: 7398 Oak Shore Dr Portage MI 49024

RIESER, JOSEPH A., JR., lawyer; b. Pitts., Aug. 28, 1947; s. Joseph Alexander and Ruth Margaret (Piper) R.; m. Susan Jean Irving, Feb. 28, 1976; 1 child, Alexander H.I. AB, Princeton U., 1969; JD, Harvard U., 1974, MPP, 1974. Bar: Pa. 1974, D.C. 1976, U.S. Supreme Ct. 1979. Assoc. Reed Smith Shaw & McClay, Pitts. and Washington, 1974-82; ptnr. Reed Smith Shaw & McClay, Washington, 1983—. Chmn. nat. alumni assn. Kennedy Sch. Govt., Cambridge, Mass., 1979-82; bd. dirs. Harvard U. Alumni Assn., 1982-84; gen. counsel 1984 Dem. Nat. Conv., Washington, 1983-84; gen. counsel Nat. Dem. Party, Washington, 1985-89; spl. counsel Clinton/Gore '92, Inc.; mem. Clinton-Gore 1992 Presdl. Transition Team. Mem. D.C. Bar (chmn. bus. related taxes com. 1989-92, tax policy steering com., chmn. D.C. Bar Nat. Fed. Tax Inst. 1991, 92, chmn. state and local taxes com. 1994—), Harvard-Yale-Princeton Club, Cosmos Club. Presbyterian. Home: 3517 Davis St NW Washington DC 20007-1426 Office: Reed Smith & McClay 1301 K St NW Washington DC 20005-3317

RIESER, LEONARD MOOS, college administrator, physics educator; b. Chgo., May 18, 1922; s. Leonard Moos and Margaret (Wallerstein) R.; m. Rosemary Littledale, July 16, 1944; children: Leonard, Timothy Savage, Abigail Wild; 1 adopted child, Kenneth Willis. S.B., U. Chgo., 1943; Ph.D., Stanford, 1952; A.M. (hon.), Dartmouth, 1963. Research asst., then research assoc. Stanford, 1949-52; mem. faculty Dartmouth, 1952—, prof. physics, 1960—, dir. grad. study, 1961-66, dean arts and scis., provost, 1967-71, v.p., dean of faculty, 1971-80, provost, 1979-82, dir. Dickey Endowment, 1982—; Pres. New Eng. Conf. Grad. Edn., 1965; mem. com. grants Research Corps, N.Y., 1961-66; chmn. bd. Bull. Atomic Scientists, 1985—; vis. scholar MacArthur Found., 1990. Trustee Hampshire Coll., 1984—, Latin Am. Students in Am. Univs., 1990—. Served with AUS, World War II. Mem. AAAS (chmn. com. sci. edn. 1965, bd. dirs. 1967-75, pres. 1973, chmn. bd. 1974, chmn. com. new directions 1975—, chmn. com. sci. freedom), Interciencia Assn. (v.p. 1976-80, pres. 1980-84), Am. Assn. Physics Tchrs., Am. Phys. Soc., Sigma Xi., Phi Beta Kappa. Home: Elm St Norwich VT 05055 Office: Baker Library Dartmouth Coll Hanover NH 03755

RIESS, GORDON SANDERSON, management consultant; b. Thessaloniki, Greece, Feb. 25, 1928; came to U.S., 1932; s. Lewis William and Dorothy Onward (Sanderson) R.; m. Priscilla Rich, June 2, 1951; children: Mark C., Kimberly A., Blake G. AB with highest honors, Whitman Coll., 1949; MBA cum laude, Harvard U., 1951. Cert. mgmt. cons.; registered profl. cons.; accredited profl. cons. Mgmt. trainee Ford Internat. Div., N.Y.C., 1951-53; asst. fin. mgr. Ford Motor Co., Mid. East, Alexandria, Egypt, 1953-57; gen. sales mgr. Ford Motor Co., Rome, Italy, 1957-60; regional fin. mgr. Ford Motor Co., Scandinavia, Copenhagen, Denmark, 1960-62; gen. mgr. Ford Motor Co., European, Brussels, Belgium, 1962-67; v.p. Internat. Paper Co., Zurich, Switzerland, 1967-71; exec. v.p. Cinema Internat. Corp., London, 1971-75; chmn., pres. Stewart-Riess Labs. Inc., Tarzana, Calif., 1976-83; pres., CEO Intercontinental Enterprises Ltd., Beverly Hills, Calif., 1983—; chmn. Vis. Nurse Found., L.A., 1985-87; bd. dirs., chmn. Vis. Nurse Assn., L.A., 1976-97; bd. dirs. Beverly Found., Pasadena, Calif., 1990-97; vice-chmn. of bd. Witman Coll., Walla Walla, Wash., 1985-96. Inventor/patentee pre-fillable hypodermic syringe. Chmn. Inter-Community Sch. Zurich, 1968-71; trustee Am. Sch. London, 1972-75; vice chmn. Krafterliner Mfgs. Assn., Zurich, 1968-71; bd. dirs. Vols. in Tech. Assistance, Arlington, Va., 1986-93; bd. overseers Muhlenberg Coll., 1993—; internat. bd. Czechoslovak Mgmt. Ctr., 1992—. Sgt. U.S. Army, 1946-47. R.H. Macy scholar, Harvard Bus. Sch., 1949. Mem. Am. Assn. Profl. Cons., Am. Cons. League, L.A. World Affairs Coun., Hollywood Radio & Television Soc., Inst. Mgmt. Cons., Lic. Execs. Soc. Avocations: skiing, scuba diving. Office: Intercontinental Ent Ltd 256 S Robertson Blvd Ste 3194 Beverly Hills CA 90211-2898

RIESSER, GREGOR HANS, arbitrage investment advisor; b. Riga, Latvia, Apr. 13, 1925; came to U.S., 1948; s. Hans Edward and Gilda (Von Scherf) R.; m. Joanna Gray (dec. Aug. 1991); children: Cindy Laughlin, William Riesser; m. Edith Naparst, Dec. 19, 1992; stepchildren: Nicole Naparst, Harold Naparst. MS in Chemistry, U. Geneva, 1949; PhD, U. Calif., Berkeley, 1952. Rsch. chemist Shell Chem. Co., Houston, 1952-70, catalysis bus. ctr., 1970-73; sr. staff chemist Shell Devel. Co., Houston, 1973-84; spkr. on long-term options, scores and primes, arbitrages, dual funds and the stock market; mem. bd. arbitrators NASD. Featured in Forbes, Houston Post, Houston Chronicle. Mem. Am. Assn. Individual Investors, Houston Computer Investment Assn. (dir. 1990—), Guru award). Unitarian. Home and Office: 2309A Nantucket Dr Houston TX 77057-2956

RIESZ, PETER CHARLES, marketing educator, consultant; b. Orange, N.J., Apr. 30, 1937; s. Kolman and Ellen (Wachs) R.; m. Elizabeth Strider Dunkman, Dec. 28, 1968; children—Sarah Kathleen. B.S., Rutgers Coll., 1958; M.B.A., Columbia U., 1963, Ph.D., 1971. Asst. prof. U. Iowa, Iowa City, 1968-73, assoc. prof., 1973-80, prof. mktg., 1980—, chmn. dept. mktg., 1981-84, 85-87, Williams prof. tchg., 1994—; vis. prof. Boston U., 1974-75, Duke U., Durham, N.C., 1984-85; cons. in field. Contbr. articles to profl. jours. Recipient Teaching Excellence award HON Industries, 1989; named MBA Prof. of Yr., 1990; Old Gold fellow U. Iowa, 1972. Mem. Am. Chem. Soc., Am. Mktg. Assn. Democrat. Presbyterian. Avocations: photography. Home: 2411 Tudor Dr Iowa City IA 52245-3638 Office: U Iowa Dept Mktg Coll Bus Adminstrn Iowa City IA 52242

RIETOW, DOTTIE MILLER, government and public relations consultant; b. Mpls., July 11, 1937; d. Wesley Templeton and Sadie Amanda (Tegland) Miller; m. Robert George Rietow, Sept. 12, 1958; children: Cari Lynn, Gregory Thomas, Richard William. BA, U. Minn., 1958, cert. legal asst., 1976. Exec. sec. 1st Nat. Bank, Mpls., 1955-60; exec. sec. to bishop Episcopal Ch., Mpls., 1960-62; legal asst. Popham, Haik, Schobrich, Doty, Mpls.,

1976-82; govt. rels. dir. Rogers Cable Sys., Mpls., 1982-85; pres. Consensus, Mpls., 1985-91, 95—; dir. Office of Waste Mgmt., St. Paul, 1991-92; acting chair Met. Waste Control Commn., St. Paul, 1992; chair Met. Coun., St. Paul, 1992-95; mem. state adv. coun. major transp. projects, Minn. Legis., 1994-95, mem. environ. quality bd., 1991-92, chair aggragate resources com., 1984-85; v.p. Mpls. Synod ELCA, 1995—; mem. policy adv. com. H.H. Humphrey Inst. U. Minn., 1992—. Commr. Miss. River Coord. Commn., St. Paul, 1990-91; mem. task force Mpls. St. Paul Planning Commn., 1991; mem. Met. Coun., St. Paul, 1984-91; bd. dirs. Hamline U. Women Govt., 1993-97. Recipient Outstanding Achievement award Lt. Gov. Jonell Dyrstad, 1995; Dottie Rietow Day in State of Minn., Gov. Arne Carlson, 1995. Mem. Minn. Women's Polit. Caucus, GOP Feminist Caucus (state chair 1980-84), Horizon 100, World Future Soc., St. Louis Park Rotary (bd. mem., Paul Harris fellow 1989). Lutheran. Avocations: reading, travel, golf. Home: 1317 Kilmer Ave Minneapolis MN 55426-1833

RIETSCHEL, ROBERT LOUIS, dermatologist; b. New Orleans, Oct. 9, 1946; s. Frederick Arnt and Estelle Marie (Fleckinger) R.; m. Connie Joanne Dent, Sept. 3, 1966; children: Eric, Penny. BA, North Tex. State U., 1968; MD, U. Tex., Galveston, 1972. Diplomate Am. Bd. Dermatology. Med. intern Letterman Army Med. Ctr., San Francisco, 1972-73, dermatology researcher, 1973-74; resident in dermatology Brooke Army Med. Ctr., San Antonio, 1974-77, staff dermatologist, 1977-79; assoc. prof. dermatology Emory U. Sch. Medicine, Atlanta, 1981-85, acting chmn. dept. dermatology, 1984-85; assoc. chmn. dept. dermatology Ochsner Clinic, New Orleans, 1985-88; chmn. dept. dermatology, 1988—. Contbr. articles to profl jours. Cubmaster, Boy Scouts Am., Decatur, Ga., 1983-84. Served to maj. U.S. Army, 1971-79. NIOSH grantee, 1981-84. Fellow Am. Acad. Dermatology, Soc. for Investigative Dermatology; mem. AMA, N.Am. Contact Dermatitis Group (sec. 1985-93), Am. Contact Dermatitis Soc. (sec. 1989-93, pres. 1993-95). Republican. Lutheran. Avocation: tennis. Office: Ochsner Clinic 1514 Jefferson Hwy New Orleans LA 70121-2429

RIFENBURGH, RICHARD PHILIP, investment company executive; b. Syracuse, N.Y., Mar. 3, 1932; s. Russell D. and Edna (MacKenzie) R.; m. Doris Anita Hohn, June 24, 1950; children: David, Susan, Robert. Student, Wayne State U. With Mohawk Data Scis. Corp., Herkimer, N.Y., 1964-74, pres., 1970-74, chmn., 1974; chmn. Moval Mgmt. Corp., Herkimer, 1968—; CEO, GCA Corp., Andover, Mass., 1986-87; gen. ptnr. Hambrecht and Quist Venture Ptnrs., 1987-90; chmn. Miniscribe Corp., Longmont, Colo., 1988-91, Ironstone Group Inc., 1988-91; dir. Libr. Bur. Inc., Herkimer, 1976-95; chmn. St. G Crystal Ltd., Jeannette, Pa., 1985—; bd. dirs. Concurrent Computer Corp., Cyberguard Corp.; dir. Glasstech Inc., 1995—; chmn. Ross Cosmetics Distbn. Ctrs., Inc. (now named Tristar Corp.), 1992—. With USAF, 1951-55. Address: Moval Mgmt Corp Ste 133 2637 E Atlantic Blvd Pompano Beach FL 33062-4939

RIFKIN, ARNOLD, film company executive; b. Bklyn.; m. Rita George; two children. BA, U. Cin. Founder Rifkin-David, 1974-80; merged to form Rifkin/David/Kimble/Parseghian, 1980-81, DHKPR, 1981-84; head motion picture dept. Triad Artists, Inc., 1984-92, founding ptnr.; exec. v.p., worldwide head motion picture divsn. William Morris Agy., Beverly Hills, Calif., 1992-97; pres. William Morris Talent and Lit. Agy., Beverly Hills, Calif., 1997—; lectr. UCLA. Bd. councillors U. So. Calif. Office: William Morris Agy 151 S El Camino Dr Beverly Hills CA 90212-2704

RIFKIN, HAROLD, physician, educator; b. N.Y.C., Sept. 10, 1916; s. Jack and Rose (Zuckoff) R.; m. Beatrice Weiss, Nov. 25, 1945; children—Janet, Matthew, Phyllis. B.A., U. Mo., 1935; M.D., Dalhousie U., 1940. Diplomate Am. Bd. Internal Medicine. Intern Jewish Hosp., Bklyn, 1940-41; resident in internal medicine Montefiore Hosp., N.Y.C., 1942-43, 46-47; practice medicine specializing in internal medicine and diabetes N.Y.C., 1947—; clin. prof. medicine Albert Einstein Coll. Medicine, N.Y.C., 1974-93, disting. univ. prof. of medicine emeritus, 1993—; prof. clin. medicine NYU Sch. Medicine, 1975—; chief of diabetes svc. emeritus Montefiore Med. Ctr., N.Y.C., 1993—; cons. emeritus Lenox Hill Hosp., N.Y.C., 1992—. With U.S. Army, 1943-46. Fellow ACS, N.Y. Acad. Medicine, N.Y. Acad. Scis.; mem. AMA, Internat. Diabetes Fedn. (chmn. N.Am. region 1985—, assoc. editor-in-chief Bull. 1985-91, v.p. 1988-94, hon. pres. 1994—), Am. Diabetes Assn. (bd. dirs. 1973-79, pres. 1985-86), N.Y. Diabetes Assn. (past pres., bd. dirs. 1970—), N.Y. County Med. Soc., N.Y. State Med. Soc., Am. Soc. Clin. Rsch., Harvey Soc. Home: 885 Park Ave New York NY 10021-0325

RIFKIN, LEONARD, metals company executive; b. N.Y.C., Apr. 10, 1931; s. Irving W. and May (Goldin) R.; m. Norma Jean Smith, Aug. 22, 1954 (dec. Jan. 1983); children: Daniel Mark, Richard Sheldon, Martin Stuart; m. Ariel Kalisky, Jan. 14, 1984. B.S., Ind. U., Bloomington, 1952. Pres., CEO Omni Source Corp., Fort Wayne, Ind., 1960—. Served with U.S. Army, 1956-58. Office: Omni Source Corp 1610 N Calhoun St Fort Wayne IN 46808-2762*

RIFKIN, NED, museum director; b. Florence, Ala., Nov. 10, 1949; s. Arthur Robert and Ina Blanche (Steinberg) R.; m. Diann Carole Kleinman, Mar. 4, 1976; children: Moses Kleinman, Amos Kleinman. BA, Syracuse U., 1972; MA in Art History, U. Mich., 1973, PhD in Art History, 1976. Asst. prof. dept. art U. Tex., Arlington, 1977-80; curator, asst. dir. New Mus. Contemporary Art, N.Y.C., 1980-84; curator contemporary art Corcoran Gallery Art, Washington, 1984-86; chief curator exhbns. Hirshhorn Mus. and Sculpture Garden, Washington, 1986-90, chief curator, 1990-91; dir. High Mus. Art, Atlanta, 1991—. *

RIFKIND, ARLEEN B., physician, researcher; b. N.Y.C., June 29, 1938; d. Michael C. and Regina (Gottlieb) Brenner; m. Robert S. Rifkind, Dec. 24, 1961; children: Amy, Nina. BA, Bryn Mawr Coll., 1960; MD, NYU, 1964. Intern Bellevue Hosp., N.Y.C., 1964-65, resident, 1965; clin. assoc. Endocrine br. Nat. Cancer Inst., 1965-68; research assoc., asst. resident physician Rockefeller U., 1968-71; asst. prof. medicine Cornell U. Med. Coll., N.Y.C., 1971-82, assoc. prof. medicine, 1983—, asst. prof. pharmacology, 1973-78, assoc. prof., 1978-82, prof., 1983—; chmn. Gen. Faculty Council Cornell U. Med. Coll., 1984-86; mem. Nat. Inst. Environ. Health Scis. Rev. Com., 1981-85, chmn., 1985-86; mem. toxicology study sect. Nat. Inst. Health, 1989-91, chmn. 1991-93; bd. sci. counselors USPHS Agy. for Toxic Substances and Disease Registry, 1991-95, adv. com. FDA Ranch Hand., Spl. Studies Relating to the Possible Long-Term Health Effects of Phenoxy Herbicides and Contaminents, 1995—. Mem. editl. bd. Drug Metabolism and Disposition, 1994-96, assoc. editor, 1997—; mem. editl. bd. Toxicology and Applied Pharmacology, 1996—, Biochem. Pharmacology, 1996—; contbr. articles to profl. jours. Chmn. Friends of the Library, Jewish Theol. Sem. Am., 1984-86; trustee Dalton Sch., 1986-92; mem. Environ. Health and Safety Coun. Am. Health Found., 1990—. Recipient Andrew W. Mellon Tchr.-Scientist award, 1976-78; USPHS spl. fellow, 1968-70, 71-72. Mem. Endocrine Soc., Am. Soc. Clin. Investigation, Am. Soc. Pharmacology and Exptl. Therapeutics, AAAS, Internat. Soc. Study Xenobiotics, Soc. Toxicology. Office: Cornell U Med Coll Dept Pharmacology 1300 York Ave New York NY 10021-4805

RIFKIND, ROBERT S(INGER), lawyer; b. N.Y.C., Aug. 31, 1936; s. Simon H. and Adele (Singer) R.; m. Arleen Brenner, Dec. 24, 1961; children: Amy, Nina. BA, Yale U., 1958; JD, Harvard U., 1961. Bar: N.Y. 1961, U.S. Supreme Ct. 1965. Asst. to solicitor gen. Dept. Justice, 1965-68; assoc. firm Cravath, Swaine & Moore, N.Y.C., 1962-65, 68-70; ptnr. Cravath, Swaine & Moore, 1971—. Trustee Dalton Sch., N.Y.C., 1975-83, hon. trustee, 1983—, pres., 1977-79; trustee The Loomis Inst., 1987-95, Citizens Budget Commn.; bd. dirs. Charles H. Revson Found., 1991—, chmn., 1997—; bd. dirs. Jewish Theol. Sem. Am., 1983—, Benjamin N. Cardozo Sch. Law, 1984-89; pres. Am. Jewish Com., 1994—. Recipient Stanley M. Isaacs Human Rels. award Am. Jewish Com., 1983. Fellow Am. Coll. Trial Lawyers, N.Y. Bar Found.; mem. ABA, Coun. Fgn. Rels., Am. Law Inst., Assn. of Bar of City of N.Y., Phi Beta Kappa. Democrat. Office: Cravath Swaine & Moore Worldwide Pla 825 8th Ave New York NY 10019-7416

RIGALI, JUSTIN F., archbishop; b. L.A., Apr. 19, 1935; s. Henry Alphonsus and Frances Irene (White) R. B in Sacred Theology, Cath. U. Am., 1961; Lic. in Canon Law, Gregorian U., Rome, 1963, D in Canon Law, 1964; LHD (hon.), St. Louis U., 1995. Ordained priest Apr. 25, 1961. Titular archbishop of Bolsena, 1985-94; sec. Congregation for Bishops Holy See, Vatican City, 1989-94, sec. Coll. of Cardinals, 1990-94; archbishop Archdiocese of St. Louis, 1994—. Office: Archdiocese of St Louis 4445 Lindell Blvd Saint Louis MO 63108-2403

RIGAS, JOHN, broadcast executive. Chmn., CEO, pres. Adelphia Comm., Coudersport, Pa. Office: Adelphia Comm PO Box 472 5 W Main at Water Sts Coudersport PA 16915*

RIGBY, PAUL CRISPIN, artist, cartoonist; b. Melbourne, Australia, Oct. 25, 1924; came to U.S., 1977; s. James Samuel and Violet Irene (Wood) R.; m. Marlene Anne Cockburn, Nov. 16, 1956; children: Nicole, Pia, Peter, Paul, Danielle. Student, Brighton Tech. Sch., Australia, Art Schs., Victoria, Victoria Nat. Gallery, Australia. Free lance artist, 1940-42; illustrator West Australian News, Ltd., 1948-52; editorial cartoonist Daily News Australia, 1952-69; daily cartoonist London Sun and News of the World, 1969-74; editorial cartoonist New York Post, 1977-84, 93—, New York Daily News, 1984-93. Illustrator numerous books; represented in exhbns. of painting in, Australia, Europe and U.S.A.; Contbr. work to numerous publs., U.S., Europe, Asia. Served with Royal Australian Air Force, 1942-46. Decorated knight comdr. Order of St. John, Knights of Malta; recipient Walkley award Australia, 1960, 61, 63, 66, 69; N.Y. Press Club award for art, 1981, 83, Page One award for excellence in journalism Newspaper Guild, 1982, 83, 84, 85. Mem. Ch. of Eng. Clubs: Rolls Royce Owners, Royal Freshwater Bay Yacht; Friars, Players (N.Y.C.). Home: 72 Kenyon Rd Hampton CT 06247-1123 Office: NY Post 1211 Avenue Of The Americas New York NY 10036-8701*

RIGBY, PAUL HERBERT, management educator, college dean; b. Humboldt, Ariz., Aug. 6, 1924; s. John Herbert and Grace Irene (Dailey) R.; m. Dorothy Ann Sall, Dec. 18, 1954; children—Peter Nathan, Mark Herbert. B.B.A., U. Tex.-Austin, 1945; M.B.A., 1948, Ph.D., 1951. Rsch. assoc., asst. prof. U. Ala., Tuscaloosa, 1952-54; dir., assoc. prof. Ga. State U., Atlanta, 1954-56; dir. rsch., prof. U. Houston, 1956-62; bus. rsch. dir., assoc. prof. U. Mo., Columbia, 1962-64; dir. div. rsch., assoc. dean rsch. and grad. program, prof. mgmt. sci. Pa. State U., University Park, 1964—; treas., bd. dirs. Centre Community Hosp., State College, Pa., 1978-87, pres., chmn. 1987-91; pres. U. Houston Senate, 1961-62. Author: Conceptual Foundations of Business Research, 1965, Models in Business Analysis, 1969; (with others) Corresponding Education in U.S., 1968; contbr. articles to profl. jours. Chmn. Centre Area Transp. Authority, State College, 1975-80; traffic mitigator com., borough planning commn., State College, 1995—; mem. cmty. adv. coun. Ctr. for Performing Arts Pa. State U., 1995—; chair United Way campaign Penn State Retirees, 1997. Served to cpl. U.S. Army, 1945-46. Mem. Inst. Mgmt. Sci. (vice-chmn. Coll. on Mgmt. Policy and Philosophy 1987, chmn. 1988), Am. Statis. Assn., Am. Inst. Decision Scis., Associated Univs. for Bus. and Econ. Research (pres. 1969). Democrat. Unitarian. Home: 131 Legion Ln State College PA 16801-6434 Office: Pa State U Smeal Coll Bus Administrn 801D Bus Adminstrn Bldg University Park PA 16802

RIGBY, PERRY GARDNER, medical center administrator, educator, former university dean, physician; b. East Liverpool, Ohio, July 1, 1932; s. Perry Lawrence and Lucille Ellen (Orin) R.; m. Joan E. Worthington, June 16, 1957; children: Martha, Peter, Thomas, Matthew. B.S. summa cum laude, Mt. Union Coll., 1953, D.Sc. hon., 1976; M.D., Western Res. U., 1957. Diplomate: Am. Bd. Internal Medicine. Intern in medicine U. Va. Hosp., Charlottesville, 1957-58, asst. resident in medicine, 1958-60; research fellow in hematology Mass. Meml. Hosp., Boston, 1960-62; clin. asst. in medicine Boston City Hosp., 1961-62; research assoc. in medicine Mass. Meml. Hosp., Boston U. Med. Ctr., 1961-62; asst. prof. internal medicine and anatomy U. Nebr., Omaha, 1964-66, assoc. prof. internal medicine and anatomy, 1966-69, prof. internal medicine, 1969-78, prof. anatomy, 1969-74, prof. med. edn., 1973-74, head sect. hematology Eugene C. Eppley Inst. for Research in Cancer and Allied Diseases, 1964-68, dir. hematology div., 1968-74, asst. dean for curriculum Coll. Medicine, 1971-72, assoc. dean for acad. affairs, 1972-74, dir. office ednl. services, 1972-74, acting assoc. dean for allied health professions, 1973-74, vice chmn. dept. med. and ednl. adminstrn., 1974, dean, 1974-78, chmn. dept. med. and ednl. adminstrn., 1974; prof. internal medicine La. State U., Shreveport, 1978—, assoc. dean acad. affairs Sch. Medicine, 1978-81, acting dean, 1981-82, dean, 1982-85; chancellor La. State U., 1985-94; dir. Health Care Systems La. State U., New Orleans, 1994—; mem. clin. bd. Univ. Hosp. La. State U., 1978-94, chmn. clin. bd., 1981-85, program dir. biomed. research support grant program, 1980-81; chmn. dean's com. VA Hosp., 1978-85; mem. courtesy staff Immanuel Med. Ctr.; bd. dirs. Health Planning Council of Midlands, Omaha, 1976-78; cons. WHO, Kabul, Afghanistan, 1976. Bd. dirs. Fontenelle Forest, Omaha, 1976-78; bd. dirs. River Cities High Tech. Group, Shreveport, 1982-85. Served as capt. M.C. U.S. Army, 1962-64. Markle scholar, 1965. Fellow ACP; mem. Am. Fedn. Clin. Research (councillor 1971), AMA (del.), Am. Soc. Hematology, N.Y. Acad. Scis., Am. Assn. Med. Colls. (council of deans of Midwest-Gt. Plains 1974-78, chmn. Midwest-Gt. Plains 1976), Am. Assn. Cancer Research, AAAS, Am. Heart Assn., Central Soc. Clin. Research, Internat. Soc. Hematology, Health Edn. Media Assn., Am. Assn. Physicians' Assts., So. Soc. Clin. Investigation, Shreveport C. of C. (dir. 1982-85), Sigma Xi, Alpha Omega Alpha, Phi Rho Sigma. Office: La State U Med Ctr Resource Ctr 433 Bolivar St New Orleans LA 70112-2223

RIGDON, DAVID TEDRICK, air force officer, geneticist, director; b. Laurel, Miss., Jan. 27, 1948; s. James T. and Marie T. (Taylor) R.; m. Elizabeth Sue Jones, June 1, 1973; children: Angela Denise, Michael David. BS in Biology, U. Ala., 1970; MD cum laude, U. Miss., 1975. Diplomate Am. Bd. Pediats., Am. Bd. Med. Genetics. Commd. USAF, 1975, advanced through grades to col., 1991; intern in pediats. USAF Med. Ctr., Keesler AFB, Miss., 1975-76, resident in pediats., 1976-78; fellow in med. genetics U. Ala., Birmingham, 1978-80; med. geneticist USAF Med. Genetics Ctr., Keesler AFB, 1980-85, dir. Air Force Med. Genetics Ctr., 1985—; cons. Surgeon Gen. USAF, Miss. State Dept. Health; clin. asst. prof. pediats. Uniformed Svcs. Univ. of Health Scis., F. Edward Herbert Sch. Medicine, Bethesda, Md. Contbr. articles to profl. jours. Recipient Physician's Recognition award AMA, 1978, 81, 84, 87, 90, 93, 96. Fellow Am. Acad. Pediats.; mem. Am. Soc. Human Genetics, So. Genetics Group, Alpha Omega Alpha. Republican. Methodist. Avocations: boating, fishing. Office: Air Force Med Genetics Ctr 81 MDOS/SGOT Rm 1A 132 301 Fisher St Keesler AFB MS 39534-2508

RIGDON, IMOGENE STEWART, nursing educator, associate dean; b. St. Joseph, Mo., Apr. 2, 1937; d. George Francis and Mary Elizabeth (Byrne) Stewart; m. Michael Allen Rigdon, Nov. 1, 1973; 1 child, Mary Lisa. BSN, Marillac Coll., 1961; MSN, Cath. U. Am., 1973; PhD, U. Utah, 1985. Cert. clin. specialist in adult psychiat.-mental health nursing Am. Nurses Assn. Asst. dir. nursing St. Anthony Hosp., Oklahoma City, 1974-76; regional teaching nurse III Shands Teaching Hosp., Gainsville, Fla., 1977-78; asst. prof. U. Fla., Gainsville, 1978-82; teaching fellow U. Utah Coll. Nursing, Salt Lake City, 1983-85; clin. specialist U. Hosp., Salt Lake City, 1985; asst. prof. U. Utah Coll. Nursing, Salt Lake City, 1985-87, vol. aux. faculty, assoc. prof., 1987-95; dean, assoc. prof. St. Mark's Westminster Sch. Nursing, Salt Lake City, 1987-95; assoc. dean for acad. affairs, assoc. prof. U. Utah Coll. Nursing, Salt Lake City, 1996—; mem. Advanced Practice task force, 1990—, Utah Nursing Resoources task force, 1988-90, Utah Stat Be. Regents' com. on Nursing Edn., 1988-89, Psychiat-Metnal health Nursing Conf. Group; mem. Advanced Psychiat.-Mental Health Nursing Adv. Com. to the State Bd. Nursing, 1986-89; mem. Intermountain Health Care Home Health Av. Com., 1988; group leader grief edn. groups Holy Cross Grief Ctr. and the Sharing Place, 1990-95; others. Contbr. chpts. to books and articles to profl. jours. Bd. mem. Holy Cross Bereavement Program Adv. Coun., 1989-94; mem. Utah Com. for Am.-Soviet Rels., 1988—; bd. trustees Widowed Persons Svc., 1995—; chair Salt Lake County Alcohol & Drug Planning Allocation Coun., 1994—. Capt. USAFR, 1972-82. Mem. AAUW, Am. Assn. Colls. Nursing, Nat. League Nursing, Am. Orthopsychiatric Assn., Soc. for Edn. and Rsch. in Psychiat. Nursing, Coun. Clin. Specialists in Psychiat.-Mental Health Nursing, Utah Nurses' Assn. (Utah health agenda task force 1988-89, gov. bd. 1986-89, dist. 1 treas. 1985-87), Mental Health Assn., Sierra Club, ACLU, Amnesty Internat., Sigma Theta Tau (Kappa chpt., Iota Iota chpt.). Democrat. Roman Catholic. Avocations: guitar playing, cross country skiing, gardening, walking. Home: 3196 Millcreek Canyon Rd Salt Lake City UT 84109-3112 Office: U Utah Coll of Nursing 25 S Medical Dr Salt Lake City UT 84112-8941

RIGERMAN, RUTH UNDERHILL, mathematics educator; b. Batavia, N.Y., Feb. 1, 1944; d. George E. and Caroline E. (Cooper) Underhill; m. David Rigerman, Nov. 17, 1967; children: Cliff, Eileen, Matthew, Glenn, Ardeen. BS, SUNY, Brockport, 1965, MS, 1967. Instr. math. Genesee C.C., Batavia, 1982—, coord. tech. prep. curriculum, 1990—; instr. SUNY, 1990—. Named Master Tchr., U. Tex., 1992, 96. Mem. Math. Assn. Am. Home: 4749 Batavia Elba Townline Rd Batavia NY 14020-1035 Office: Genesee C C 1 College Rd Batavia NY 14020-9703

RIGG, CHARLES ANDREW, pediatrician; b. Hamilton, Vic., Australia, Oct. 18, 1926; came to U.S., 1963; s. Arthur Oscar and Mary Eileen (Wingrove) R. B in Medicine, Surgery with honors, Sydney U., 1951. Staff adolescent medicine Children's Hosp., Boston, 1964-65; chief dept. adolescent medicine Children's Hosp., Washington, 1967-80, Boston City Hosp., 1981-83; med. dir. Outer Cape Health, Provincetown, Mass., 1983-88; pediatrician, med. dir. Medicenter Five, Harwich, Mass., 1988-95, pediatrician, 1995—; from asst. prof. to assoc. prof. child health George Washington U. Med. Sch., 1967-80; cons. Nat. Naval Med. Ctr., Bethesda, Md., 1973-80, Walter Reed Army Med. Ctr., Washington, 1973-80; assoc. prof. pediatrics Boston U. Med. Sch., 1981-83; courtesy staff medicine Children's Hosp., Boston, 1983—. Editor: Adolescent Medicine Present and Future Concepts, 1980; contbr. articles to profl. jours. Mem. Mus. Fine Arts, Boston, Folger Shakespeare Libr., Washington, Nat. Trust for Hist. Preservation. Lt. col. USAR, 1985-91. Decorated Army Commendation medal; model tng. program in adolescent medicine grantee Maternal and Child Health Svcs.-U.S. Govt., 1967-80, Comprehensive Health Svcs. Adolescent Ctr. grantee Mass. Dept. Pub. Health, 1981-83. Fellow Am. Acad. Pediatrics (life), Royal Australasian Coll. Physicians, Soc. Adolescent Medicine (charter, treas., chmn., legis. com.); mem. Royal Sydney Golf Club, City Tavern Club Washington. Episcopalian. Avocations: hist. preservation, gardening, theater, music, walking. Office: Long Pond Medical Ctr 525 Long Pond Dr Harwich MA 02645-1227

RIGGIO, LEONARD, book publishing executive; b. 1941. Merchandise mgr. NYU Bookstore, N.Y.C., 1962-65; pres., CEO, bd. dirs. Barnes & Noble Bookstores, Inc., 1965—; chmn. bd., CEO, pres., treas. Barnes & Noble Inc., N.Y.C., 1986—; chmn. bd., prin. beneficial owner Software Etc. Stores, Inc., Mpls., MBS Textbook Exchange, Inc., Columbia, Mo. Office: Barnes & Noble Inc 122 Fifth Ave New York NY 10011-5605 Address: MBS Textbook Exchange Inc 2711 W Ash St Columbia MO 65203-4613*

RIGGLEMAN, JAMES DAVID, professional baseball team manager; b. Ft. Dix, N.J., Dec. 9, 1952. Degree in Physical Edn., Frostburg State U. Minor league baseball player, 1974-81, minor league baseball mgr., 1982-88, 91-92; dir. player devel., then coach St. Louis Cardinals, 1988-90; mgr. San Diego Padres, 1993-94, Chicago Cubs, 1995—. Office: Wrigley Field 1060 W Addison St Chicago IL 60613-4305*

RIGGS, ARTHUR JORDY, retired lawyer; b. Nyack, N.Y., Apr. 3, 1916; s. Oscar H. and Adele (Jordy) R.; m. Virginia Holloway, Oct. 15, 1942 (dec.); children: Arthur James (dec.), Emily Adele Riggs Freeman, Keith Holloway, George Bennett; m. Priscilla McCormack, Jan. 16, 1993. AB, Princeton U., 1937; LLB, Harvard U., 1940. Bar: Mass. 1940, Tex. 1943; cert. specialist in labor law to 1992. Assoc., Warner, Stackpole, Stetson & Bradlee, Boston, 1940-41; staff mem. Solicitors Office U.S. Dept. Labor, Washington and Dallas, 1941-42; mem. Johnson, Bromberg, Leeds & Riggs, Dallas, 1949-81; of counsel Geary & Spencer, Dallas, 1981-91. Mem. ABA, State Bar Tex., Phi Beta Kappa. Avocations: Maya archeology, photography, scuba diving. Home and Office: 4116 Amherst Ave Dallas TX 75225-6901

RIGGS, BENJAMIN CLAPP, JR., building products manufacturing company executive; b. Boston, Sept. 29, 1945; s. Benjamin Clapp and Norma (Campanaro) R.; m. Cheryl Pusey, July 3, 1970 (div. 1987); children: Sonia Campanaro, Anne Elizabeth; m. Lee Thornton Ainsworth, Feb. 25, 1989. BA, Boston U., 1968. Commd. ens. U.S. Navy, 1969, advanced through grades to capt., 1990, served as pilot and aero. engr., 1969-76, now res.; exec. v.p. Resource Mgmt. Corp., Boston, 1976-78; br. mgr. Reynolds Aluminum Co., Mt. Kisco, N.Y., 1978-80; mktg. dir. Am. Abrasive Metals Co., Irvington, N.J., 1980-83; v.p., gen. mgr. Glen-Gery Corp., River Edge, N.J., 1984-90; dir. Resource Mgmt. Co., Oakland, N.J., 1990—; pres. HAPCO div. Kearney-Nat., Abington, Va., 1992-93; CEO, mng. dir. Resource Mgmt. Co., Bristol, Tenn., 1993—; pres., CEO P&K Pole Products, Inc., Newark, 1996—. Mem. Res. Officers Assn. Republican. Episcopalian. Avocations: sailing, ocean cruising, tennis, skiing, writing. Office: P&K Pole Products 84 Foundry St Newark NJ 07105-4606

RIGGS, DONALD EUGENE, librarian, academic administrator; b. Middlebourne, W.Va., May 11, 1942; m. Jane Vasbinder, Sept. 25, 1964; children: Janna Jennifer, Krista Dyonis. BA, Glenville State Coll., 1964; MA, W.Va. U., 1966; MLS, U. Pitts., 1968; EdD, Va. Poly. Inst. and State U., 1975. Head librarian, tchr. sci. Warwood (W.Va.) High Sch., 1964-65; head librarian, audiovisual dir. Wheeling (W.Va.) High Sch., 1965-67; sci. and econs. librarian California State Coll. of Pa., 1968-70; dir. library and learning center Bluefield State Coll., 1970-72; dir. libraries and media services Bluefield State Coll., Concord Coll., Greenbrier Community Coll., and So. campus W.Va. Coll. of Grad. Studies, 1972-76; dir. libraries U. Colo., Denver, Met. State Coll., and Community Col. of Denver—Auraria Campus, 1976-79; univ. librarian Ariz. State U., 1979-88, dean univ. libraries, 1988-90; prof. info. and libr. sci., dean univ. libr. U. Mich., Ann Arbor, 1991-97; prof., v.p. for info. svcs., univ. libr. Nova Southeastern U., Ft. Lauderdale, Fla., 1997—; adj. prof. Calif. State Coll., 1968-70, W.Va. U., 1970-72, U. Colo., 1977-79, U. Ariz., 1985, Emporia State U., 1996—; fed. rels. coord. Am. and W.Va. Libr. Assns., 1970-75; chmn. bd. dirs. Ctrl. Colo. Libr. Sys., 1976-79; chmn. Colo. Coun. Acad. Librs., 1977-78; mem. exec. bd. Colo. Alliance Rsch. Librs., 1978-79; cons. to librs.; fgn. assignments in Xi'an, People's Republic of China, 1988, Guadalajara, Mex., 1990, Budapest, Hungary, 1991, 95, Hong Kong, 1992, 94, San Juan, P.R., 1993, Melbourne, Australia, 1994, Eupatory, Republic Crimea, Ukraine, 1995, London, 1996, Prague, Czech Republic, 1996, Beijing, China, 1996, Pretoria, South Africa, 1996; del. Users Coun. Online Computer Libr. Ctr., Dublin, Ohio, 1987-91, pres.-elect, 1990-91, chair artificial intelligence and expert systems nat. group, 1987-88; bd. govs. Rsch. Librs. Group, Inc., Mountain View, Calif., 1991-92; vice chmn. mgmt. com. William L. Clements Libr., 1991-97. Editor: W.Va. Librs., 1973-75, Libr. Hi Tech, 1993—, Coll. & Rsch. Librs., 1996—; founding editor: Libr. Adminstrn. and Mgmt., 1987-89; assoc. editor: Southeastern Libr., 1973-75; contbg. editor: Libraries in the Political Process, 1980, Options for the 80's, 1982, Library and Information Technology: At the Crossroads, 1984; contbg. author, editor: Library Leadership: Visualizing the Future, 1982; author: Strategic Planning for Library Managers, 1984, (with Helen Gothberg) Time Management in Academic Libraries, 1986, (with Gordon Sabine) Libraries in the 90's: What the Leaders Expect, 1988, Creativity, Innovation and Entrepreneurship in Libraries, 1989, Library Communication: The Language of Leadership, 1991, (with Rao Aluri) Expert Systems in Libraries, 1990, Cultural Diversity in Libraries, 1994; editl. bd. Am. Librs., 1987-89, Jour. Libr. Adminstrn., 1987-97, Coll. and Rsch. Librs., 1990-96. Trustee Mesa (Ariz.) Pub. Library, 1980-86, chmn., 1985-86; mem. Ariz. State Library Adv. Council, 1981-84; bd. dirs. Documentation Abstracts, Inc., 1986-90. Recipient Alumnus of Yr. award Glenville State Coll., 1992; named Outstanding Young Educator, Ohio County Schs., 1966; Coun. on Libr. Resources grantee, 1985; sr. fellow UCLA, 1989. Mem. ALA (councilor-at-large 1982-86, 89-93, chmn. coun.'s resolutions com. 1985-86, pub. com. 1988-92, Hugh Atkinson award 1991), Ariz. Libr. Assn. (pres. coll. and univ. divsn. 1981-82, pres. 1983-84, Spl. Svc. award 1986, Disting. Svc. award 1990), Colo. Libr. Assn. (pres. 1978-79), W.Va. Libr. Assn. (pres. 1975-76), Assn. Coll. and Rsch. Librs. (pres. Tri-State chpt. 1972-74, pres. Ariz. chpt. 1981-82), So. Libr. Assn. (chmn. coll. and univ. sect. 1982-83), Assn. Rsch. Librs. (100th meeting planning com. 1982, mgmt. of rsch. libr. resources com. 1990-93, rsch. collections com. 1993-96), AMIGOS Bibliograph Coun. (trustee 1986-90, chmn. bd. trustees 1988-89), Libr. Adminstrn. and Mgmt. Assn. (bd. dirs. 1987-89, pres.-elect 1993-94, pres. 1994-95), Libr. Info. and Tech. Assn. (bd. dirs. 1989-93), Ctr. for Rsch. Librs. (councilor 1979-97), Mountain Plains Libr. Assn. (bd. dirs. 1987-90, pres.-elect 1990-91), Beta Phi Mu, Chi Beta Phi, Phi

Delta Kappa, Phi Kappa Phi. Office: Einstein Libr Nova Southeastern U 3301 College Ave Fort Lauderdale FL 33314-7721

RIGGS, FRANK, congressman; b. Louisville, Ky., Sept. 5, 1950; m. Cathy Anne Maillard; three children: Ryan, Matthew, Sarah Anne. BA, Golden Gate U. With Veale Investment Properties, until 1987; co-founder (with wife) Duncan Enterprises; mem. 102nd Congress 1st Calif. Dist., 1991-92, mem. 104th and 105th Congresses, 1995—. With U.S. Army, 1972-75. Republican. Office: US House Reps 1714 Longworth Office Bldg Washington DC 20515-0501

RIGGS, FRANK LEWIS, foundation executive; b. Indpls., Apr. 1, 1937; s. Frank Lloyd Riggs and Marie Loretta (Shaner) Ellis; m. Gail Evelyn Kershner, July 28, 1960 (div. 1987). BS in Bus. Adminstrn., U. Ariz., 1961, EdD, 1976; MBA, George Washington U., 1964. Mktg. adminstr. TRW Systems, L.A., 1964-67; assn. exec. Electric League Ariz., Phoenix, 1967-68; pub. affairs adminstr. Ariz. Regional Med. program Coll. of Medicine, U. Ariz., Tucson, 1968-73; dir. community affairs Tucson Med. Ctr., 1973-82; dir. pub. rels. Good Samaritan Med. Ctr., Phoenix, 1982-85; pres. The Lew Riggs Co., Phoenix, 1985-88; chief exec. officer Tucson Osteo. Med. Found., Tucson, 1988—; adj. prof. U. Ariz. Coll. Edn., Tucson, 1976-79; cons. to hosps. and physicians in group practice nationally; presenter in field. Editor: Public Relations Handbook, 1982; co-author booklets; contbr. articles to profl. jours. Chmn. pub. rels. Nat. Arthritis Found., Atlanta, 1985-87; participant Ariz. Strategic Planning and Econ. Devel., 1991-92. Lt. col. USAFR, 1987. Recipient Silver Anvil award Pub. Rels. Soc. Am., Golden Mike award Am. Legion Aux., MacEachern citation Acad. Hosp. Pub. Rels., Pres.'s citation Pub. Rels. Soc. Mem. Nat. Assn. Osteo. Founds. (pres. 1991—), Student Osteo. Med. Assn. (found. bd. dirs. 1990—), Acad. Hosp. Pub. Rels. (treas. 1980-81), Rotary. Republican. Methodist. Home: 5050 E South Regency Cir Tucson AZ 85711-3040 Office: Tucson Osteo Med Found 4280 N Campbell Ave Ste 200 Tucson AZ 85718-6585

RIGGS, FRED WARREN, political science educator; b. Kuling, China, July 3, 1917; (parents Am. citizens); s. Charles H. and Grace (Frederick) R.; m. Clara-Louise Mather, June 5, 1943; children: Gwendolyn, Ronald (dec.). Student, U. Nanking, China, 1934-35; BA, U. Ill., 1938; MA, Fletcher Sch. Law and Diplomacy, 1941; PhD, Columbia U., 1948. Lectr. CUNY, 1947-48; rsch. assoc. Fgn. Policy Assn., 1948-51; asst. dir. Pub. Adminstrn. Clearing House, N.Y.C., 1951-55; Arthur F. Bentley prof. govt. Ind. U., 1956-67; dir. Social Sci. Rsch. Inst. U. Hawaii, 1970-73, prof. polit. sci., 1967-87, prof. emeritus, 1987—; vis. asst. prof. Yale U., 1955-56; vis. lectr. Nat. Officials Tng. Inst., Korea, 1956; vis. prof. U. Philippines, 1958-59, MIT, 1965-66, CUNY, 1974-75; vis. scholar Inst. Soc. Studies, The Hague, 1972; sr. specialist East-West Ctr. U. Hawaii, 1962-63. Author: Pressures on Congress: A Study of the Repeal of Chinese Exclusion, 1950, reprinted, 1973, Formosa under Chinese Nationalist Rule, 1952, reprinted, 1972, The Ecology of Public Administration, 1961 (pub. in Portuguese, 1964), Administration in Developing Countries: The Theory of Prismatic Society, 1964 (pub. in Korean, 1966, Portuguese, 1968), Thailand: The Modernization of a Bureaucratic Polity, 1966, Organization Theory and International Development, 1969, Administrative Reform and Political Responsiveness: A Theory of Dynamic Balancing, 1971, Prismatic Society Revisited, 1973 (pub. in Korean, 1987), Applied Prismatics, 1978, (with Daya Krishna) Development Debate, 1987; author: (with others) Contemporary Political Systems: Classifications and Typologies, 1990, Handbook of Comparative and Development Public Administration, 1991, Terminology: Applications in Interdisciplinary Communication, 1993, Parliamentary vs. Presidential Government, 1993, Public Administration in the Global Village, 1994, Comparing Nations: Concepts, Strategies, Substance, 1994, Handbook of Bureaucracy, 1994, Standardizing and Harmonizing Terminology, 1995, Korea in the Era of Post-Development and Globalization, 1996, Viable Constitutionalism and Bureaucracy, 1996, Onomantics and Terminology, 1996, Designs for Democratic Stability, 1997; co-author, editor: Frontiers of Development Administration, 1971, Tower of Babel: On the Definition and Analysis of Concepts in the Social Sciences, 1975, Viable Constitutional and Bureaucracy, 1996, Onomantics and Terminology, 1996. Dir. INTERCOCTA project Internat. Social Sci. Coun., 1970-93; chair UNESCO com. INTERCONCEPT project, 1977-79; chair Comm. on Conceptual and Terminological Analysis (COCTA), Internat. Polit. Sci. Assn., Internat. Sociol. Assn. and Internat. Social Sci. Coun., 1973-79; co-chair N.AM. roundtable on cooperation Social Sci. Info. Mpls., 1979; chair lexicographic terminology com. Dictionary Soc. N.Am., 1983-86; co-chair Com. on Viable Constitutionalism (COVICO), 1993—. Decorated Order of White Elephant, King of Thailand, 1986; fellow com. comparative politics Social Sci. Rsch. Coun., 1957-58, Ctr. Advanced Study in Behavioral Scis., 1966-67; honoree Eastern Regional Orgn. Pub. Adminstrn. Conf., 1983. Mem. ASPA (chair comparative adminstrn. group 1960-71, Dwight Waldo award 1991), Am. Polit. Sci. Assn., Internat. Studies Assn. (chair comparative interdisciplinary studies sect. 1970-74, v.p. 1970-71, co-chair ethnicity, nationalism and migration sect. 1994-95), Internat. Polit. Sci. Assn., Internat. Sociol. Assn., Assn. Asian Studies (chair com. rsch. materials S.E. Asia 1969-73). Home: 3920 Lurline Dr Honolulu HI 96816-4006 Office: U Hawaii Political Science Dept 2424 Maile Way Honolulu HI 96822-2223

RIGGS, GINA GINSBERG, educational association administrator; b. Berlin, Germany, Mar. 29, 1921; came to U.S., 1945; d. Hugo Herz and Elisabeth Herrmanns; m. Sidney Ginsberg, Dec. 24, 1954 (dec. (Sept. 1974); children: Matt, Jill; m. Sheldon K. Riggs, June 5, 1976 (dec. Oct. 1985). Sales mgr. Consolidated Bus. Systems, N.Y.C., 1950; exec. dir. Gifted Child Soc., Glen Rock, N.J., 1968-78; project dir. Parent Info. Network for Gifted; con. Nat. Rsch. Ctr. on Gifted and Talented. Contbr. articles to profl. publs. Charter mem. Leadership N.J., 1989—. Recipient cert. of merit U.S. Office Edn., 1980. Avocations: internat. peace, artificial intelligence. Home: 59 Glen Gray Rd Oakland NJ 07436-2301 Office: Gifted Child Soc Inc 190 Rock Rd Glen Rock NJ 07452-1736

RIGGS, GREGORY LYNN, lawyer; b. Columbus, Ohio, Apr. 21, 1948; s. Roy Albert and Edith Myrtle (Riggins) R.; m. Janet Kaye Adams, June 26, 1982; children: Caroline Ashley, Kristen Nicole. BA, U. NC., 1971, Oxford U., 1976; JD, Emory U., 1979. Atty. Delta Air Lines, Atlanta, 1979-84, sr. atty., 1984-92, asst. gen. counsel, 1992-94, assoc. gen. counsel, 1994—. Office: Delta Air Lines Inc Law Dept Hartsfield Internat Airport Atlanta GA 30320

RIGGS, HENRY EARLE, academic administrator, engineering management educator; b. Chgo., Feb. 25, 1935; s. Joseph Agnew and Gretchen (Walser) R.; m. Gayle Carson, May 17, 1958; children: Elizabeth, Peter, Catharine. BS, Stanford U., 1957; MBA, Harvard U., 1960. Indsl. economist SRI Internat., Menlo Park, Calif., 1960-63; v.p. Icore Industries, Sunnyvale, Calif., 1963-67, pres., 1967-70; v.p. fin. Measurex Corp., Cupertino, Calif., 1970-74; prof. engring. mgmt. Stanford U., Calif., 1974-88, Ford prof., 1986-88, Ford prof. emeritus, 1990—, v.p. for devel., 1983-88; pres. Harvey Mudd Coll., Claremont, Calif., 1988-97, pres. emeritus, 1997—; pres. Grad. Inst. Applied Life Scis., Claremont, 1997—; bd. dirs. Mutual Funds of capital Rsch. Group. Author: Accounting: A Survey, 1981, Managing High-Tech Companies, 1983, Financial and Cost Analysis, 1994; contbr. articles to Harvard Bus. Rev. Bd. dirs. Mt. Baldy Coun. Boy Scouts Am., 1993—. Baker scholar Harvard Bus. Sch., Boston, 1959; recipient Gores Teaching award Stanford U., 1980. Mem. Stanford U. Alumni Assn. (bd. dirs. 1990-94, chmn. 1993), Calif. Club, Sunset Club, Phi Beta Kappa, Tau Beta Pi. Congregationalist. Office: Grad Inst Applied Life Scis 1263 N Dartmouth Ave Claremont CA 91711-3941

RIGGS, JACKI PIERACCI, educational consultant; b. San Jose, May 13, 1954; d. Leo A. Pieracci and Laura B. Petersen LaRue; m. Joseph N. Riggs III, Aug. 27, 1978; children: Joseph N. IV, Amanda Marie, Austin Spenser. BS in Child Devel., Brigham Young U., 1981; MA in Spl. Edn., U. N.Mex., 1983, PhD in Spl. Edn., 1992. Treatment liaison ATASC Project, Albuquerque, 1976-79; dir. alcohol edn. program Juvenile Ct., Albuquerque, 1978-79; tchr. Children's Psychiat. Hosp., Albuquerque, 1985-88; div. dir. Juvenile Facilities N.Mex. Corrections Dept., Santa Fe, N.Mex., 1988-89; cabinet sec. N.Mex. Youth Authority, Santa Fe, 1989-90; pvt. practice cons. Albuquerque, 1990—; dir. admissions Bosque Prep. Sch., 1995-96; mem. Gov. Johnson's Transitional Team Children, Youth and Families Dept., 1994; apptd. by Gov. Johnson as commr. Edn. Commn. of States, 1997—. Commr. Youth Authority Commn., Santa Fe, 1988; mem. Gov.'s Substance Abuse Adv. Coun., 1989; mem. Community Corrections Panel, 1988; vol. Bosque Prep. U. N.Mex. fellow, 1986-87, 87-88, 91-92. Mem. NAFE, Coun. for Exceptional Children, Women Execs. in State Govt., Nat. Assn. Juvenile Correctional Adminstrs., Univ. Women. Avocations: writing, photography, travel.

RIGGS, JOHN ALAN, energy institute administrator; b. Chgo., Feb. 19, 1943; s. Joseph Archie and Verna Anne (Christophel) R.; m. Judith Assmus, Mar. 8, 1975; 1 child, Michael Joseph. BA, Swarthmore Coll., 1964; MPA, Princeton U., 1966. Dir. peace corps tng. Princeton (N.J.) U., 1966; program officer Agy. for Internat. Devel., Saigon, Vietnam, 1966-71; capital devel. officer Agy. for Internat. Devel., Rio de Janeiro, Brazil, 1972; legislative asst. U.S. Ho. of Reps., Washington, 1973; campaign mgr. Sharp for Congress, Muncie, Ind., 1974; adminstrv. asst. U.S. Ho. of Reps., Washington, 1975-80; staff dir. House Fossil Fuels Subcom., Washington, 1981-86, House Energy and Power Subcom., Washington, 1987-93; dep. asst. sec. for policy U.S. Dept. Energy, Washington, 1993-95; dir. program energy & environment Aspen Inst., Washington, 1995—; vis. lectr. U. Pa., Phila., 1989-93. Adult leader Boy Scouts Am., Washington, 1986-94; mem adv. com. Johns Hopkins Internat. Energy Program, Washington, 1986-93, alumni coun. Swarthmore (Pa.) Coll., 1993—, pres. 1997—. Recipient Superior Honor award U.S. Agy. for Internat. Devel., Washington, 1971. Home: 5230 Watson St NW Washington DC 20016

RIGGS, LORRIN ANDREWS, psychologist, educator; b. Harput, Turkey, June 11, 1912; parents Am. citizens; s. Ernest Wilson and Alice (Shepard) R.; m. Doris Robinson, 1937 (dec.); children: Douglas Rikert, Dwight Alan; m. Caroline Cressman, 1994. A.B., Dartmouth Coll., 1933; M.A., Clark U., 1934, Ph.D., 1936. NRC fellow biol. scis. U. Pa., 1936-37; instr. U. Vt., 1937-38, 39-41; with Brown U., 1938-39, 41—, from asst. to assoc. prof., 1938-51, prof., 1951—, L. Herbert Ballou prof., 1960-68, E.J. Marston Univ. prof., 1968-77, prof. emeritus, 1977—; Guggenheim fellow U. Cambridge, 1971-72. Author sci. articles on vision, physiol. psychology. Recipient Kenneth Craik award Cambridge U., 1979, Prentice medal Am. Acad. Optometry, 1973. Mem. AAAS (chmn., v.p. sect. 1 1964), APA (div. pres. 1962-63, Disting. Sci. Contn. award 1974), Eastern Psychol. Assn. (pres. 1975-76), Optical Soc. Am. (Tillyer medal 1969, Ives medal 1982), Nat. Acad. Scis., Am. Physiol. Soc., Internat. Brain Rsch. Orgn., Soc. for Neurosci., Soc. Exptl. Psychologists (Howard Crosby Warren medal 1957), Assn. Rsch. in Vision and Ophthalmology (pres. 1977, Friedenwald award 1966), Am. Acad. Arts and Scis., Am. Psychol. Soc. (William James fellow 1989), Sigma Xi (chpt. pres. 1962-64). Home: Kendal at Hanover # 104 80 Lyme Rd Hanover NH 03755-1225

RIGGS, MICHAEL DAVID, magazine editor, writer; b. Frankfort, Ky., Apr. 30, 1951; s. Homer David and Helen Marion (Webber) R.; m. Elizabeth Susan Borman, Apr. 24, 1983; children: David B., William B. AB, Washington U., 1973. Chief trader Thomte & Co., Boston, 1975-77; tech. writer Saddlebrook Corp., Cambridge, Mass., 1977-79; assoc. editor Mini-Micro Systems Mag., Boston, 1979-80; editor High Fidelity Mag., N.Y.C., 1980-89; exec. editor Stereo Review Mag., N.Y.C., 1989-95; editor-in-chief Audio Mag., N.Y.C., 1995—. Author: Understanding Audio and Video, 1989. Mem. Audio Engring. Soc., Boston Audio Soc. Office: Audio Mag 1633 Broadway New York NY 10019-6708

RIGGS, ROBERT DALE, plant pathology/nematology educator, researcher; b. Pocahontas, Ark., June 15, 1932; s. Rosa MacDowell and Grace (Million) R.; m. Jennie Lee Willis, June 6, 1954; children: Rebecca Dawn, Deborah Lee, Robert Dale Jr., James Michael. BS in Agr., U. Ark., 1954, MS, 1956; PhD, N.C. State U., 1958. Grad. asst. U. Ark., Fayetteville, 1954-55, asst. prof., 1958-62, assoc. prof., 1962-68, prof., 1968-92, univ. prof., 1992—; grad. asst. N.C. State U., Raleigh, 1955-58. Editor 2 books, 1980, 92; contbr. articles to profl. jours.; inventor fungal control of nematodes. Recipient John W. White award Coll. Agr. and Home Econs., 1989, Honor award for Rsch. in Environ. Protection USDA, 1994. Fellow Soc. of Nematologists (v.p. 1991-92, pres.-elect 1992-93, pres. 1993-94, editor-in-chief jour. 1987-90); mem. So. Soybean Disease Workers (Disting. Svc. award 1987), U. Ark. Alumni Assn. (Dist. Faculty Achievement award 1993), Am. Phytopathological Soc. (Outstanding plant pathologist in so. region 1994), Wash. Helm. Soc., Sigma Xi, Gamma Sigma Delta. Democrat. Baptist. Home: 1840 Woolsey Ave Fayetteville AR 72703-2557 Office: U Ark 217 Plant Sci Fayetteville AR 72701

RIGGS, SONYA WOICINSKI, elementary school educator; b. Newhall, Calif., Oct. 9, 1935; d. Jack Lewis Woicinski and Mittie Mozelle (Bennett) Gillett; m. Eugene Garland Riggs, Dec. 21, 1956; children: Georgia Ann, Madeline Sue, Dana Eugene. BS in Elem. Edn., U. Tex., 1970; MEd in Reading Edn., S.W. Tex. State U., 1980. Cert. elem. tchr., Tex.; cert. reading specialist K-12. Sec. state govts., Nebr./Tex., 1955-57; piano instr. Elgin, Tex., 1961-66; tchr. 1st grade Elgin Elem. Sch., Elgin, 1967-69, tchr. Music 3rd/4th grades, 1971-72, tchr. 4th grade, 1972-73; pres. El Tesoro internacionale, 1973-74; sec. region office Planned Parenthood/World Population, Austin, 1975-76; tchr. 8th-12th grades Giddings (Tex.) State Sch., 1976-78; tchr. 4th/5th grades Thorndale (Tex.) Ind. Sch. Dist., 1979-80; tchr. remedial reading Brazosport Ind. Sch. Dist., Freeport, Tex., 1980-81; tchr. 6th grade reading and chpt. I Bastrop (Tex.) Mid. Sch., 1981-94, Bastrop Intermediate, 1994—; developer Enrichment Ctr., Bastrop Intermediate, 1995-96; mem. 12th ann. Highlights Found. Writers Workshop at Chautauqua Instn., N.Y., 1996. Contbr. articles to Shih Tzu Reporter, 1993 French Bulldog Ann., French Bullytin, Boston Quar., Golden Retriever World; contbr. poetry to anthologies Garden of Life, 1996, Best Poems of 1996, Of Sunshine and Daydreams, 1996, A View from Afar, 1997. Mem. Elgin Band Boosters, 1970-83, sec., 1976. Mem. Assn. Tex. Profl. Educators (campus rep. 1996-97, state del. 1997), Austin Kennel Club (bd. dirs. 1990-91, 95—, sec. 1996-97), Am. Shih Tzu Club (edn. and rescue com. mem. south ctrl. regional hearing com.), French Bulldog Club Am. (rescue com.), Mission City Ring Stewards Assn., Internat. Soc. Poets, Austin Writers League. Avocations: exhibiting dogs to Am. Kennel Club championships, writing poetry, playing piano, drawing, painting.

RIGGS, TIMOTHY ALLAN, museum curator; b. New Haven, Conn., Feb. 15, 1942; s. Douglas Shepard and Robin (palmer) R.; divorced; 1 child, Emma; m. Carolyn P. Coolidge, June 25, 1995. BA, Swarthmore Coll., 1964; MA, Yale U., 1966, PhD, 1971. Rschr. Print Coun. Am., 1970-73; asst. curator Worcester (Mass.) Art Mus., 1973-76, curator prints and drawings, 1976-84; asst. dir. Ackland Art Mus., Chapel Hill, N.C., 1984—, acting dir., 1986, 94; adj. prof. U. N.C., Chapel Hill, 1984—. Contbr. catalogs. Mem. Print Coun. Am. (bd. dirs. 1981-84), Historians Netherlandish Art. Office: Ackland Art Mus U NC Chapel Hill CB # 3400 S Columbia St near Franklin St Chapel Hill NC 27599-3400

RIGGSBY, DUTCHIE SELLERS, education educator; b. Montgomery, Ala., Oct. 26, 1940; d. Cleveland Malcolm and Marcelia (Bedsole) Sellers; m. Ernest Duward Riggsby, Aug. 25, 1962; 1 child, Lyn. BS, Troy (Ala.) State Coll., 1962, MS, 1965; postgrad., George Peabody Coll., 1963; EdD, Auburn U., 1972. Cert. tchr., Ala., Ga.; cert. libr., Ga. Tchr. Montgomery Pub. Sch.s, 1962-63, Troy City Schs., 1963-67; instr. Auburn (Ala.) U., 1968-69; asst. prof. Columbus (Ga.) Coll., 1972-77, assoc. prof., 1978-83, prof., 1983—; coord. Instrnl. Tech. Sch. Edn., 1996—; vis. prof. U. P.R., Rio Piedras, 1972, 73; cons. schs. Columbus and Ft. Benning, Ga., 1980; leader various workshops, 1989, 93—; software reviewer Nat. Sci. Tchrs. Assn.; chair Ga. Ednl. Tech. Conf., 1994—. Contbr. more than 90 articles on state, regional, nat., and internat. programs to profl. jours., 1968—. Educator internal aerospace CAP, Maxwell AFB, 1980-90; dir. Air and Space Camp for Kids, 1990—. Recipient STAR Tchr. award Nat. Sci. Tchrs. Assn., Washington, 1968. Mem. Assn. for Ednl. Comms. and Tech. (non-periodical publs. com. 1994—, awards com. 1994-96, chair meml. awards com. 1996—), Nat. Congress on Aviation and Space Edn. (dir. spl. promotions 1986-90), World Aerospace Edn. Orgn. (v.p. for the Americas 1996—), Ga. Assn. Instrnl. Tech. (bd. dirs. 1982-84), Phi Delta Kappa (pres. Chattahochee Valley chpt. 1986-87, Svc. award 1989, Svc. Key award 1993). Baptist. Avocations: photography, mining for gemstones. Home: 1709 Ashwood Ct Columbus GA 31904-3009 Office: Columbus State U Sch Edn 4225 University Ave Columbus GA 31907-5679

RIGGSBY, ERNEST DUWARD, science educator, educational development executive; b. Nashville, June 12, 1925; s. James Thomas and Anna Pearl (Turner) R.; m. Dutchie Sellers, Aug. 25, 1964; 1 child, Lyn-Dee. BS, Tenn. Polytech. Inst., 1948; BA, George Peabody Coll. Tchrs., 1952, George Peabody Coll. Tchrs., 1953; MA, George Peabody Coll. Tchrs., 1956, EdS, 1961, EdD, 1964. Vis. grad. prof. U. P.R., Rio Piedras, George Peabody Coll., 1963-64; prof. Auburn (Ala.) U., Troy (Ala.) State U., Columbus (Ga.) Coll.; pres. Ednl. Developers, Inc., Columbus, Ga.; vis. grad. prof. George Peabody Coll., 1963-64; vis. lectr. Fla. Inst. Tech., summers 1967-77. Contbr. articles to profl. jours. Col., USAF, 1944-85. Named to Aerospace Crown Cir., 1984; elected to Aerospace Edn. Hall of Fame, 1982. Fellow AAAS; mem. Nat. Sci. Tchrs. Assn., World Aerospace Edn. Assn. (v.p. for the Ams.). Office: Columbus Coll Columbus GA 31907-5645

RIGHTER, ANNE ROBINSON, clinical social worker, psychotherapist; b. N.Y.C., July 5, 1939; d. Hamilton and Elizabeth Parker (Case) Robinson; m. James Volney Righter, June 22, 1962; children: Eliot Day Righter Ramos, Mark Hamilton Righter. BA in Sociology summa cum laude, U. New Haven, 1974; M of Social Work, U. Conn., 1976; postgrad., Yale U., 1976-77. Lic. ind. clin. social worker, Mass.; cert. Acad. of Cert. Social Workers. Clin. instr. social work Child Psychiatry Unit-Yale U., New Haven, 1977-80; staff social worker Yale Univ. Child Study Ctr., New Haven; clin. instr., field work supr. Simmons Sch. of Social Work, Boston, 1981-82; clin. social worker, chief court clinics Mass. Mental Health Ctr., Boston, 1981-82; clin. social worker Ctr. for Counseling Family Svc. Assn., Boston, 1982-84; chief social worker Ctr. for Therapy, Boston Children's Svc., Boston, 1983-86; pvt. practice Boston, 1982-95; bd. dirs. officer Planned Parenthood Greater New Haven, 1967-75, Affiliated Children's Svcs., Brookline-Lexington, Mass., 1981-85, Island Health Project, Inc., Fishers Island, N.Y., 1991—, Trinity Hospice, Brookline, Mass., 1988—, Rutland Corner House, Inc., Brookline, 1982-96, pres. 1984-91; bd. dirs. Health Care Dimensions, 1996—. Vestry mem. St. Johns Ch., Fishers Island, 1990—; bd. visitors Walnut Hill Sch. Performing Arts, Natick, Mass., 1995—; bd. overseers New Eng. Conservatory, Boston, 1995—. Mem. Nat. Assn. Social Workers, Nat. Registry Health Care Providers in Clin. Social Work, Mass. Acad. Clin. Social Workers, Tuesday Club, Tavern Club. Democrat. Episcopalian. Avocations: musical theatre, singing, creative writing. Home and Office: 72 Pinckney St Boston MA 02114-4304

RIGHTER, WALTER CAMERON, bishop; b. Phila., Oct. 23, 1923; s. Richard and Dorothy Mae (Bottomley) R.; m. Nancy Ruth DeGroot, Aug. 22, 1992; children: Richard, Rebecca. BA, U. Pitts., 1948; MDiv, Berkeley Div. Sch., New Haven, 1951, DD, 1972; DCL, Iowa Wesleyan U., 1982; DD, Seabury Western Sem., 1984. Ordained priest Episcopal Ch., 1951, consecrated bishop, 1972; lay missioner St. Michael's Ch., Rector, Pa., 1947-48; priest-in-charge All Saints Ch., Aliquippa, Pa., 1951-54, St. Luke's, Georgetown, Pa., 1952-54; rector Ch. of Good Shepherd, Nashua, N.H., 1954-71; bishop Diocese of Iowa, Des Moines, 1972-89; asst. bishop Dio. of Newark, 1989-91; interim rector St. Elizabeth's, Ridgewood, N.J., 1991; mem. exec. coun. Protestant Episcopal Ch. U.S.A., 1979-85; spl. adv. NH Cursillo, 1994-96. Mem. N.H. com. White House Conf. on Youth, 1962, Regional Crime Commn., Hillsboro County, N.H., 1969-71; trustee Nashua Libr., 1968-71, Seabury Western Sem., 1986-89; founding trustee The Morris Fund, Des Moines; planning com. Town of Alstead, N.H., 1993-96. Fellow Coll. Preachers, Washington Cathedral. Accused of heresy by Episcopal Church for ordaining gay man--charges dismissed.

RIGHTS, GRAHAM HENRY, minister; b. Winston-Salem, N.C., Jan. 14, 1935; s. Douglas LeTell and Cecil Leona (Burton) R.; m. Sybil Critz Strupe, Sept. 7, 1963; children: Susan Elizabeth, John Graham. BA, U. N.C., 1956; BD, Yale U., 1959; postgrad., Moravian Theol. Sem., 1959-60, DHL (hon.), 1997; postgrad., U. Edinburgh, Scotland, 1965-66; DD (hon.), Wofford Coll., 1989. Ordained to ministry Moravian Ch., 1960. Pastor Union Ch., Managua, Nicaragua, 1960-63, Managua Moravian Ch., 1960-65, Mayodan (N.C.) Moravian Ch., 1966-72, Messiah Moravian Ch., Winston-Salem, 1972-81; exec. dir. Bd. World Mission Moravian Ch., Bethlehem, Pa., 1981-83; pres. exec. bd. so. province Moravian Ch., Winston-Salem, 1983-95; pres. exec. bd. world-wide Moravian Ch., 1991-94; pastor First Moravian Ch., Greensboro, N.C., 1995—. Author: On the Roof of the World, 1961. Bd. dirs. Crisis Control Ministry, Forsyth County, 1976—, Ecumenical Inst., 1995—, Salemtowne Retirement Comty., 1996—, Moravian Ch. Found., 1988—, Moravian Music Found., 1996—. Home: 208 S Elam Ave Greensboro NC 27403 Office: 304 S Elam Ave Greensboro NC 27403-1407

RIGOLO, ARTHUR EMIL, architect; b. Clifton, N.J., May 2, 1909; s. Frank and Mary (Del Favero) R.; m. Elizabeth Olga De Lotto, Sept. 27, 1935; 1 child, Richard. B.S. in Architecture, U. Ill., 1934. Automotive designer Gen. Motors Co., Detroit, 1936-37; exec. designer Norman Bel-Geddes, N.Y.C., 1938-39; ptnr. Rigolo & Leeks, Architects, Clifton, N.J., 1940-42; devel. engr. Curtis-Wright, Bloomfield, N.J., 1943-44; ptnr. Spence-Rigolo, Indsl. Design & Architecture, N.Y.C., 1944-47; prin. Arthur Rigolo, Architect, Clifton, 1948-82; ptnr. Rigolo/Rigolo/Architects, Clifton, 1982-97; vice chmn. N.J. State Sch. Bldg. Guide, 1960-84; chmn. ad hoc com. on architecture Gov.'s Com. to Study Arts in N.J., 1965. Prin. works include St. Philip the Apostle ch. complex, Clifton, high sch. bldg., Clifton, City Hall, Clifton, Master plan and 11 bldgs., Montclair State Coll., N.J., various schs., chs., office bldgs. in N.J. Chmn. Clifton Mcpl. Planning Bd., 1942-56; pres., chmn. bd. Planning Assn. North Jersey, 1967-70. Fellow AIA (bd. dirs. 1972-74); mem. N.J. Soc. Architects (pres. 1964, various awards), Architects' League No. N.J. Home: 56 Woodlawn Ave Clifton NJ 07013-4013 Office: Rigolo/Rigolo/Architects 151 Grove St Ste 46 Clifton NJ 07013-1550

RIGOLOT, FRANÇOIS, French literature educator, literary critic; b. Château-du-Loir, Sarthe, France, May 21, 1939; s. Paul and Madeleine (Overnoy) R.; m. Carol Nolan, Sept. 5, 1970; children—Sophie, Stephanie. Diplôme, Hautes Etudes Commerciales, Paris, 1961; MA in Econs., Northwestern U., 1963; Ph.D. in French, U. Wis.-Madison, 1969. Asst. prof. U. Mich, Ann Arbor, 1969-74; bicentennial preceptor Princeton U., N.J., 1974-77, assoc. prof. dept. romance langs. and lits., 1977-79, prof., 1979-81, Meredith Howland Pyne prof. French lit., chmn. dept., 1984-91, 96—; chair Renaissance studies Princeton U., 1993—; prof. French Middlebury (Vt.) Coll., 1973; dir. NEH seminar for coll. tchrs., Princeton, 1981, 84, 86, 88, 90; vis. prof. Johns Hopkins U., 1981; vis. mem. Inst. for Advanced Study, Princeton, 1982-83; dir. seminar The Folger Inst., Washington, 1987; prof. Inst. d'Etudes Françaises, Avignon, 1989, 95; ofcl. lectr. Alliance Française, 1994-95. Author: Les Langages de Rabelais, 1972, reprint, 1996, Poétique et Onomastique, 1977, Le Texte de la Renaissance, 1982 (Gilbert Chinard Lit. prize 1984), Les Métamorphoses de Montaigne, 1988, La Renaissance au féminin, 1997; editor: Complete Works of Louise Labé, 1986, Journal de Voyage of Montaigne, 1992; co-editor: A New History of French Literature, 1989 (MLA James Russell Lowell prize 1990), De la Littérature Française, 1993; collaborator: Sémantique de La Poésie, 1979. Recipient Médaille de la ville de Bordeaux, Médaille de la ville de Tours, 1992, Officier des Plames Académiques, 1993, Howard T. Behrman award for Disting. Achievement in the Humanities, 1993; NEH fellow, 1979-80, Guggenheim Found. fellow, 1982-83. Mem. Acad. Literary Studies, Am. Assn. Tchrs. French, Renaissance Soc. Am., MLA, Assn. Internat. des Etudes Françaises. Home: 81 Pretty Brook Rd Princeton NJ 08540-7537 Office: Princeton U East Pyne Dept Romance Langs and Lits Princeton NJ 08544-5264

RIGOR, BRADLEY GLENN, bank executive; b. Cheyenne Wells, Colo., Aug. 9, 1955; s. Glenn E. and Lelia (Teed) R.; m. Twyla G. Helweg, Sept. 4, 1983; children: Camille, Brent, Tiffany, Lauren. BS in Mktg., Ft. Hays State U., 1977; JD, Washburn U., 1980. Bar: Kans. 1980, U.S. Dist. Kans., 1980, U.S. Tax Ct. 1981, U.S. Ct. Appeals (10th cir.) 1982, U.S. Supreme Ct. 1986, Colo. 1990, Tex. 1991, U.S. Dist. Ct. Colo. 1991, Mo. 1993; cert. trust and fin. advisor Inst. Cert. Bankers. Ptnr. Zuspann & Rigor, Goodland, Kans., 1980-82; city atty. Goodland, 1981-82; asst. county atty. Wallace County, Sharon Springs, Kans., 1982-84, county atty., 1984; city atty. Sharon Springs, 1983-84; judge Mcpl. Ct., Goodland, 1988-93; ptnr. Fairbanks, Rigor & Irvin, P.A., Goodland, 1982-93; v.p., mgr. personal trusts Merc. Bank, St. Joseph, Mo., 1993-96; sr. v.p., mgr., personal trust adminstr. Sun Trust Bank, Naples, Fla., 1996—. Mem. Estate Planning Coun. of Naples. Mem. Kans. Bar Assn., Tex. Bar Assn., Mo. Bar Assn., Colo. Bar Assn., St.

Joseph Bar Assn., Estate Planning Coun. Naples. Republican. Baptist. Office: Trust and Investment Svcs Group 801 Laurel Oak Dr Naples FL 34108-2748

RIGOUTSOS, ISIDORE, computer scientist; b. Athens, Greece, Feb. 6, 1963; came to U.S., 1985; s. Ioannis and Fragkiska Rigoutsos. BS magna cum laude, Nat. U. Athens, 1984; MS, U. Rochester, 1987, NYU, 1989; PhD, NYU, 1992. Computational biology rschr. IBM Corp., Yorktown Heights, N.Y., 1992—. Fellow Fulbright Found., 1985-90. Mem. IEEE Computer Soc., AAAS. Roman Catholic. Avocation: photography. Office: IBM TJW Rsch Ctr PO Box 704 Yorktown Heights NY 10598

RIGSBEE, STEPHEN REESE, risk management executive; b. Durham, N.C., Mar. 11, 1956; s. William Alton and Shirley (Morgan) R.; m. Lisa Lou Sloan, Dec. 10, 1992; 1 child, Henry Morgan. AB, Duke U., 1978; AM in Econs., U. Chgo., 1982, MBA, 1984. With Allstate Life Ins. Co., Northbrook, Ill., 1978-81; sr. v.p., dir. rsch. GNP Fin., Chgo., 1984-87; pres. Quantitative Risk Mgmt. Group, Chgo., 1987—. Co-author: Handbook of Mortgage Backed Securities, 1988, Asset/Liability Management, 1991, 96; contbr. articles to profl. jours. Mem. Chgo. Coun. on Fgn. Rels. Mem. Am. Fin. Assn., Beta Gamma Sigma. Republican. Home: 2314 N Lincoln Park W Fl 7 Chicago IL 60614-3454 Office: Quantitative Risk Mgmt Group 181 W Madison St Fl 49 Chicago IL 60602-4510

RIGSBY, CAROLYN ERWIN, music educator; b. Franklinton, La., Apr. 11, 1936; d. Sheldon Aubrey and Edna Marie (Fussell) Erwin; m. Michael Hall Rigsby, May 30, 1959; 1 child, Laura Elaine Rigsby Boyd. B in Music Edn., Northwestern State U., La., 1958; MEd, Nicholls State U., 1970. Cert. vocal music tchr. k-12. Music tchr. Terrebonne Parish Sch., Houma, La., 1958-81, 81-83; music coord. Terrebonne Parish Sch., Houma, 1983-84; music tchr. Pasadena (Tex.) Ind. Sch. Dist., 1988—. Mem. Tex. Music Educators Assn., Packard Autombile Classics, Lone Star Packard Club, Delta Kappa Gamma (pres. 1988-90). Republican. Methodist. Avocations: Bay Area chorus, golf, gardening. Home: 16014 Mill Point Dr Houston TX 77059-5216

RIGSBY, LINDA FLORY, lawyer; b. Topeka, Kans., Dec. 16, 1946; d. Alden E. and Lolita M. Flory; m. Michael L. Rigsby, Aug. 14, 1963; children: Michael L. Jr., Elisabeth A. MusB, Va. Commonwealth U., 1969; JD, U. Richmond, 1981. Bar: Va. 1981, D.C. 1988. Assoc. McGuire, Woods, Battle & Boothe, Richmond, Va., 1981-85; dep. gen. counsel and corp. sec. Crestar Fin. Corp., Richmond, 1985—. Recipient Disting. Svc. award U. Richmond, 1987; named Vol. of Yr. U. Richmond, 1986, Woman of Achievement, Met. Richmond Women's Bar, 1995. Mem. Va. Bar Assn. (exec. com. 1993-96), Richmond Bar Assn. (bd. dirs. 1992-95), Va. Bankers Assn. (chair legal affairs 1992-95), U. Richmond Estate Planning Coun. (chmn. 1990-92). Roman Catholic. Avocations: music, gardening. Home: 10005 Ashbridge Pl Richmond VA 23233-5402 Office: Crestar Fin Corp 919 E Main St Richmond VA 23219-4625

RIHA, WILLIAM EDWIN, beverage company executive; b. New Brunswick, N.J., Sept. 15, 1943; s. William Edwin and Grace Blue (McDowell) R.; m. Joan Ann Murphy, June 25, 1967; children: William Edwin III, Jennifer Dawn. BS, Rutgers U., 1965, MS, 1969, PhD, 1972. Mgr. product devel. Hunt-Wesson Foods, Inc., Fullerton, Calif., 1972-76; dir. tech. svcs. Cadbury N.Am., Hazleton, Pa., 1976-78; mgr. food tech. Peter Paul Cadbury, Inc., Naugatuck, Conn., 1978-80; group mgr. U.S. product devel. PepsiCo, Valhalla, N.Y., 1980-84, dir. internat. product devel., 1984-89; v.p. R&D J. E. Seagram & Sons, Ltd., White Plains, N.Y., 1989-93; v.p. rsch. & tech. svc. Tropicana Products Inc., Bradenton, Fla., 1993-96; v.p. rsch. and tech. J.E. Seagram & Sons, Ltd., White Plains, 1996—. Capt. USAR, 1965-73. Mem. Inst. Food Technologists (grad. fellowship Nestle 1968), Indsl. Rsch. Inst. (membership com. 1990-92), Sigma Xi. Avocations: golf, tennis, baseball memorabilia. Home: 71 S Salem Rd Ridgefield CT 06877-4828 Office: Joseph E Seagram & Sons Ltd 103 Corporate Pk Dr White Plains NY 10604

RIKE, SUSAN, public relations executive; b. N.Y.C., Aug. 29, 1952; d. George Carson and Mildred Eleanor (Geehr) R. BA cum laude, Bklyn. Coll., 1975. Editl. asst. Artforum Mag., N.Y.C., 1975-77; co-owner Say Cheese, Bklyn., 1977-80; editl. asst. The Star, N.Y.C., 1980-82; acct. sec. Robert Marston and Assocs., N.Y.C., 1983-84; asst. acct. exec. Marketshare, N.Y.C., 1984; acct. exec. Doremus Pub. Rels. BBDO Internat., N.Y.C., 1984-86; pres. Susan Rike Pub. Rels., Bklyn., 1986—. Democrat. Avocations: travel, music festivals and concerts, literature. Office: Susan Rike Pub Rels 335 State St Apt 3C Brooklyn NY 11217-1719

RIKER, WALTER F., JR., pharmacologist, physician; b. N.Y.C., Mar. 8, 1916; s. Walter F. and Eleanore Louise (Scafard) R.; m. Virginia Helene Jaeger, Nov. 28, 1941; children: Donald K., Walter F., Wayne S. BS, Columbia U., 1939; MD, Cornell U., 1943; D.Sc. (hon.), Med. Coll. Ohio, 1980. Instr. pharmacology Cornell U. Med. Coll., N.Y.C., 1944-47; instr. medicine Cornell U. Med. Coll., 1945-46, asst. prof. pharmacology, 1947-50, assoc. prof., 1950-56, prof., chmn. dept. pharmacology, 1956-83, Revlon chair pharmacology and toxicology, 1980-83, prof. emeritus, 1983—; mem. study sect. NIH, 1956-63, 65-68; mem. Nat. Inst. Gen. Med. Scis. Council., 1963-64, Nat. Inst. Environ. Health Scis. Council, 1971-75, Pres.'s Sci. Adv. Com. on Toxicology, 1964-65; vis. prof. pharmacology U. Kans. Med. Coll., 1953; mem. Unitarian Service Med. Exchange Program, Japan, 1956; mem. sci. adv. com. Pharm. Mfrs.'s Assn. Found., 1966-87; adj. mem. Roche Inst. Molecular Biology, 1972-80; med. advisor on drugs Nat. Football League, 1973-84; adv. com. Irma T. Hirschl Found., N.Y.C., 1973—; bd. sci. advisors Sterling Drug, 1973-76; dir. Richardson-Vicks Inc., 1979-85. Recipient Teaching award Cornell U. Med. Coll., 1968, 78, citation Pharm. Mfrs.'s Assn. Found., 1972, 87, Award of Distinction Cornell U. Med. Coll. Alumni Assn., 1981, Maurice R. Greenberg Svc. award N.Y. Hosp./Cornell U. Med. Ctr., 1990; Sterling Drug vis. professorship established in honor at Cornell U. Med. Coll., 1979; named Hon. Fellow, Am. Coll. Clin. Pharmacology, 1987. Fellow AAAS, N.Y. Acad. Medicine, Harvey Soc.; mem. Am. Soc. Pharmacology and Exptl. Therapeutics (chmn. membership com. 1956-59, councillor 1959-62, bd. publs. trustees 1962-64, chmn. bd. publs. trustees 1964-70, chmn. com. ednl. and profl. affairs 1972-74, John Jacob Abel award 1951, Publs. citation 1970, Torald Sollman award 1986, Oscar B. Hunter award 1990), Japanese Pharmacology Soc., Am. Soc. Clin. Pharmacology and Therapeutics, N.Y. Acad. Scis., Sigma Xi, Alpha Omega Alpha.

RIKER, WILLIAM KAY, pharmacologist, educator; b. N.Y.C., Aug. 31, 1925; s. Walter Franklin and Eleanore Louise (Scafard) R.; m. Carmela Louise DePamphilis, Dec. 21, 1947 (dec. 1981); children: Eleanor Louise, Gainor, Victoria; m. Leena Mela, Aug. 13, 1983. B.A., Columbia U., 1949; M.D., Cornell U., 1953. Intern 2d Cornell med. div., Bellevue Hosp., 1953-54; practice medicine, specializing in pharmacology Phila., 1954-69, Portland, Oreg., 1969—; instr., asst. prof. dept. pharmacology U. Pa. Sch. Medicine, 1954-61; spl. fellow dept. physiology U. Utah Sch. Medicine, 1961-64; assoc. prof., prof., chmn. dept. pharmacology Woman's Med. Coll., Phila., 1964-69; prof., chmn. dept. pharmacology U. Oreg. Sch. Medicine, U. Oreg. Health Scis. Center, 1969-91, prof. emeritus, 1991—, asst. dean. for admissions, 1986-89; mem. neurol. disorders program project com. NIH, 1975-79. Editor: Jour. Pharmacology and Exptl. Therapeutics, 1969-72; contbr. articles to biomed. jours. Served with USNR, 1943-46. Recipient Christian R. and Mary F. Lindback Found. award for disting. teaching, 1968; Pa. Plan scholar, 1957-61; Nat. Inst. Neurol. Diseases and Blindness spl. fellow, 1961-64; USPHS-NIH research grantee, 1958-83. Mem. Am. Soc. Pharmacology and Exptl. Therapeutics (sec.-treas. 1978-81, pres. 1985-86), Western Pharmacol. Soc. (pres. 1976), Japanese Pharmacol. Soc., Assn. Med. Sch. Pharmacologists (sec. 1976-78), Epilepsy Assn. Am., Pharm. Mfrs. Assn. Found. (chmn. pharmacology-morphology adv. com., sci. adv. com. 1976-92), Cosmos Club. Home: 4326 SW Warrens Way Portland OR 97221-3246

RIKLIS, MESHULAM, manufacturing and retail executive; b. Turkey, Dec. 2, 1923; came to U.S., 1947, naturalized, 1955; s. Pinhas and Betty (Guberer) R.; children: Simona Riklis Ackerman, Marcia Riklis Hirschfeld, Ira Doron, Kady Zadora Riklis, Kristofer Riklis. Student, U. Mexico, 1947; BA, Ohio State U., 1950, MBA, 1968. Co-dir. youth activities and mil. tng. Hertzlia High Sch., Tel-Aviv, 1942; tchr. Hebrew Talmud Torah Sch., Mpls., 1951; research dept. Piper, Jaffray & Hopwood, 1951-53, sales rep., 1953-56; vice chmn. McCrory Corp., N.Y.C., 1960-69, vice chmn. exec. com., from 1970, chmn., 1975-85, dir., former pres.; with Rapid-Am. Corp., N.Y.C., 1956—, chmn., 1956—, pres., chief exec. officer, 1957-73, chmn., chief exec. officer, 1973-76, chmn., pres., chief exec. officer, 1976—; E-II Holdins, 1988-90. Served Brit. 8th Army, 1942-46. Mem. Pi Mu Epsilon. Jewish. Office: McCrory Corp 888 7th Ave New York NY 10021 also: Riklis Family Corp 2901 Las Vegas Blvd S Las Vegas NV 89109-1930*

RIKON, MICHAEL, lawyer; b. Bklyn., Feb. 2, 1945; s. Charles and Ruth (Shapiro) R.; m. Leslie Sharon Rein, Feb. 11, 1968; children: Carrie Rachel, Joshua Howard. BS, N.Y. Inst. Tech., 1966; JD, Bklyn. Law Sch., 1969; LLM, NYU, 1974. Bar: N.Y. 1970, U.S. Dist. Ct. (so. and ea. dists.) N.Y. 1971, U.S. Ct. Appeals (2d cir.) 1972, U.S. Supreme Ct. 1973, U.S. Ct. Appeals (5th and 11th cirs.) 1981. Asst. corp. counsel City of N.Y., 1969-73; law clk. N.Y. State Ct. Claims, 1973-80; ptnr. Rudick and Rikon, P.C., N.Y.C., 1980-88; pvt. practice, N.Y.C., 1988-94; ptnr. Goldstein, Goldstein and Rikon, P.C., N.Y.C., 1994—. Contbr. articles to profl. jours. Pres. Village Greens Residents Assn., 1978-79; chmn. bd. Arden Heights Jewish Ctr., Staten Island, N.Y., 1976-77; pres. North Shore Republican Club, 1977; mem. community bd. Staten Island Borough Pres., 1977. Mem. ABA, ATLA, TLPJ Found., N.Y. State Bar Assn. (spl. com. of condemnation law), Suffolk County Bar Assn., N.Y. County Lawyers Assn. Republican. Jewish. Avocations: collecting stamps, photography, collecting miniature soldiers. Home: 133 Avondale Rd Ridgewood NJ 07450-1301 Office: 80 Pine St New York NY 10005-1702

RIKOSKI, RICHARD ANTHONY, engineering executive, electrical engineer; b. Kingston, Pa., Aug. 13, 1941; s. Stanley George and Nellie (Gober) R.; m. Giannina Batchelor Petrullo, Dec. 18, 1971 (div. 1979); children: Richard James, Jennifer Anne. BEE, U. Detroit, 1964; MSEE, Carnegie Inst. Tech., 1965; PhD, Carnegie-Mellon U., 1968; postdoctoral fellow, Case-Western Res. U./NASA, 1971. Registered profl. engr., Ill., Mass., Pa. Engr. 1st communication satellite systems Internat. Tel. & Tel., Nutley, N.J., 1961-64; engr. Titan II ICBM program Gen. Motors, Milw., 1964; trainee NASA, 1964-67; instr. Carnegie-Mellon U., Pitts., 1966-68; asst. prof. U. Pa., Phila., 1968-74; assoc. prof., dir. hybrid microelectronics lab., chmn. ednl. TV com. IIT, Chgo., 1974-80, chmn. ednl. TV com., 1974-80; rsch. engr. nuclear effects ITT Rsch. Inst., Chgo., 1974-75; pres. Tech. Analysis Corp., Chgo., 1980—; engr. color TV colorimetry Hazeltine Rsch., Chgo., 1969; engr. Metroliner rail car/roadbed ride quality dynamics analysis U.S. Dept. Transp., ENSCO, Inc., Springfield, Va., 1970; pres. Tech. Analysis Corp., Chgo., 1978-91; contractor analysis of color TV receiver safety hazards U.S. Consumer Product Safety Commn., 1977, analysis heating effect in aluminum wire Beverly Hills Supper Club Fire, Covington, Ky., 1978; engr. GFCI patent infringement study 3M Corp., St. Paul, 1979-81; elec. systems analyst Coca-Cola Corp., Atlanta, 1983-91; fire investigator McDonald's Corp., Oak Brook, Ill., 1987-90; engring. analyst telephone switching ctrs. ATT, Chgo., 1990-91; expert witness numerous other govtl. and corp. procs. Author: Hybrid Microelectronic Circuits, 1973; editor: Hybrid Microelectronic Technology, 1973; contbr. articles to profl. jours. Officer Planning Commn., Beverly Shores, Ind., 1987-93, trustee town coun., 1992—, police liason 1993-96; mem. Chgo. Coun. Fgn. Rels., USAF SAC Comdrs. Disting.is. Program; adv. coun. Nat. Park Svc. Ind. Dunes Nat. Lake Shore, 1993—. NASA fellow, 1964-67, 70. Mem. IEEE (sr. ednl. activities bd. N.Y.C. 1970-74, USAB career devel. com. 1972-74, editor Soundings 1973-75, Cassette Colloquia 1973-74, del. Popov Soc. Tech. Exch. USSR, mgr. Dial Access Tech. Edn. program 1972), Assn. for Media Based Continuing Engring. Edn. (bd. dirs.), Nat. Fire Protection Assn., Sigma Xi, Tau Beta Pi, Eta Kappa Nu. Republican. Avocations: sailing, travel. Home: One E Lakefront Dr Beverly Shores IN 46301-0444 Office: Tech Analysis Corp 1032 W Diversey Pkwy Chicago IL 60614-1317

RILES, WILSON CAMANZA, educational consultant; b. Alexandria, La., June 27, 1917; m. Mary Louise Phillips, Nov. 13, 1941; children: Michael, Narvia Riles Bostick, Wilson, Phillip. B.A., No. Ariz. U., 1940; M.A., 1947, LL.D., 1976; LL.D., Pepperdine Coll., 1965, Claremont Grad. Sch., 1972, U. So. Calif., 1975, U. Akron, 1976, Golden Gate U., 1981; L.H.D., St. Mary's Coll., 1971, U. Pacific, 1971, U. Judaism, 1972. Tchr. elem. schs., adminstr. pub. schs. Ariz., 1940-54; exec. sec. Pacific Coast region Fellowship of Reconciliation, Los Angeles, 1954-58; with Calif. Dept. Edn., 1958-83, dep. supt. pub. instrn., 1965-70, supt. pub. instruction, 1971-83; pres. Wilson Riles & Assocs., Inc., 1983—; dir. emeritus Wells Fargo Bank, Wells Fargo Co. Past mem. editorial adv. bd.: Early Years mag. Ex-officio mem. bd. regents U. Calif., 1971-82; ex-officio trustee Calif. State Univs. and Colls., 1971-82; nat. adv. council Nat. Schs. Vol. Program; former mem. council Stanford Research Inst.; former mem. adv. council Stanford U. Sch. Bus.; former mem. adv. bd. Calif. Congress Parents and Tchrs.; former trustee Am. Coll. Testing Program; former mem. Edn. Commn. of States; past 2d v.p. Nat. PTA.; former trustee Found. Teaching Econs.; former mem. Joint Council Econ. Edn.; former mem. Nat. Council for Children and TV. With USAF, 1943-46. Recipient Spingarn medal NAACP, 1973. Mem. Assn. Calif. Sch. Adminstrs., Cleve. Conf., NAACP (Spingarn medal 1973), Nat. Acad. Pub. Adminstrn., Phi Beta Kappa. Office: 400 Capitol Mall Ste 1540 Sacramento CA 95814-4408 *Is growing up in rural Louisiana during the depression as an orphan, poor and black, attending a segregated school, a handicap? I have never thought so. Maybe it's because of the superb teachers who never let me feel sorry for myself. As I recall, some did not even have college degrees, but they believed I could learn. Because they did, it never occurred to me that I couldn't. Forrest Paul Augustine, the principal, admonished us to get as much education as we could because, "that is one thing no one can ever take away from you". I chose education as a career because those humble public schools gave me a chance. I want all boys and girls to have a chance, too.*

RILEY, ANN J., former state legislator, technology specialist; b. Memphis, Oct. 27, 1940; m. Ray T. Riley, Apr. 28, 1962. BSBA, U. Albuquerque, 1985; MBA, Webster U., 1988; cert. in pub. policy, Harvard U., 1994. Loan officer Ravenswood Bank, Chgo., 1970-74; mgr. dist. sales Security Lockout, Chgo., 1974-77; owner AR Fasteners, Albuquerque, 1977-82; tech. transfer agt. Sandia Nat. Labs., Albuquerque, 1983—; mem. N.Mex. Senate, Santa Fe, 1993-96; resolutions chair energy com. Nat. Order of Women Legis. Nat. Conf. State Legislators. Bd. dirs. All Faiths Receiving Home. Albuquerque, 1989-92, Law Enforcement Acad., Santa Fe, 1991-92; active Leadership Albuquerque, 1991, state federal task force U.S. Office Sci. & Tech., 1995. Flemming fellow Am. U. Ctr. for Policy Alternatives, 1996. Democrat. Avocations: running, bicycling, politics, reading. Home: 10301 Karen Ave NE Albuquerque NM 87111-3633*

RILEY, ANTHONY WILLIAM, German language and literature educator; b. Radcliffe-on-Trent, Eng., July 23, 1929; s. Cyril Frederick and Winifred Mary (White) R.; m. Maria Theresia Walter, July 16, 1955; children: Christopher, Katherine, Angela. B.A. with honors, U. Manchester, Eng., 1952; Dr. Phil., U. Tübingen, Fed. Republic Germany, 1958. Lectr. U. Tübingen, 1957-59, 60-62; asst. lectr. Queen Mary Coll., U. London, Eng., 1959-60; asst. prof. German lang. and lit. Queen's U., Kingston, Ont., Can., 1962-65; asso. prof. Queen's U., 1965-68, prof., 1968-92; emeritus prof. Queen's U., Kingston, Ont., Can., 1993—; head dept. German lang. and lit. Queen's U., 1967-76, acting head dept., 1979-80, 86-87; vis. prof. U. Munich, 1996. Author: Elisabeth Langgässer Bibliographie mit Nachlassbericht, 1970; also articles on Elisabeth Langgässer, Alfred Döblin, Thomas Mann, Herman Hesse, Frederick Philip Grove, Joseph Wittig; co-editor: The Master Mason's House (F.P. Grove), 1976, Echoes and Influences of German Romanticism, 1987, Muse and Reason, The Relation of Arts and Sciences 1650-1850, 1994; co-translator, co-editor: Fanny Essler, 2 vols. (Grove), 1984; editor: Der Oberst und der Dichter/Die Pilgerin Aetheria (Alfred Döblin), 1978, Der unsterbliche Mensch/Der Kampf mit dem Engel (Alfred Döblin), 1980, Jagende Rosse/Der schwarze Vorhang (Alfred Döblin), 1981, Wadzeks Kampf mit der Dampfturbine (Alfred Döblin), Kleine Schriften I (1902-1921) (Döblin), 1985, Kleine Schriften II (1922-24) (Döblin), 1990, Schicksalsreise (Döblin), 1993. Served with Brit. Army, 1947-49. Summer fellow Weil Inst. for Studies in Religion and the Humanities, Cin., 1965; Can. Council Leave fellow, 1969-70, 76-77, 83-84. Fellow Royal Soc. Can. (sec. acad. humanities and social scis. 1992-95, editor 1995—); mem. Can. Assn. Univ. Tchrs. German (v.p. 1973-75, pres. 1975-76, Hermann Boeschenstein medal 1987, Konrad Adenauer rsch. award Alexander von Humboldt Found. 1989), Deutsche Schillergesellschaft, Internat. Alfred Döblin-Gesellschaft (v.p. 1984-95), Internat. Assn. for German Studies, Elisabeth Langgässer-Gesellschaft (Darmstadt). Home: 108 Queen Mary Rd, Kingston, ON Canada K7M 2A5

RILEY, BOB, congressman; m. Patsy Adams; children: Rob, Jenice, Minda, Krisalyn. BA in Bus. Adminstrn., U. Ala., 1965. Mem. 105th Congress from 3d Ala. dist., 1996—. Sunday sch. tchr. First Bapt. Ch. Ashland, chmn. ch. bd. trustee. Office: 3d Dist Ala 510 Cannon HOB Washington DC 20515

RILEY, CARROLL LAVERN, anthropology educator; b. Summersville, Mo., Apr. 18, 1923; s. Benjamin F. and Minnie B. (Smith) R.; m. Brent Robinson Locke, Mar. 25, 1948; children: Benjamin Locke, Victoria Smith Evans, Cynthia Winningham. A.B., U. N.Mex., 1948, Ph.D., 1952; M.A., UCLA, 1950. Instr. U. Colo., Boulder, 1953-54; asst. prof. U. N.C., Chapel Hill, 1954-55; asst. prof. So. Ill. U., Carbondale, 1955-60, assoc. prof., 1960-67, prof., 1967-86, Disting. prof., 1986-87, Disting. prof. emeritus, 1987—, chmn. dept., 1979-82, dir. mus., 1972-74; rsch. assoc. lab. anthropology Mus. N.Mex., 1987—; rsch. collaborator Smithsonian Instn., 1988—; adj. prof. N.Mex. Highlands U., 1989—. Author: The Origins of Civilization, 1969, The Frontier People, 1982, expanded edit., 1987, Rio del Norte, 1995, Bandelier, 1996; editor: Man Across the Sea, 1971, Southwestern Journals of Adolph F. Bandelier, 4 vols., 1966, 70, 75, 84, Across the Chichimec Sea, 1978, others; contbr. numerous articles to profl. jours. Served in USAAF, 1942-45. Decorated 4 battle stars; grantee Social Sci. Research Council, NIH, Am. Philos. Soc., Am. Council Learned Socs., NEH, others. Home and Office: 1106 6th St Las Vegas NM 87701-4311

RILEY, CATHERINE IRENE, university official, cosultant, former state senator; b. Balt., Mar. 21, 1947; d. Francis Worth and Catherine (Cain) R. BA, Towson State U., 1969. Bacteriologist Balt. City Hosp., 1969-72; legis. aide Md. Ho. of Dels., Annapolis, 1973-74, mem., 1975-82; mem. Md. Senate, Annapolis, 1982-91; ret., 1991; asst. dir. Bur. Govtl. Rsch., U.Md. Sch. Pub. Affairs, College Park, 1992—; cons. Md. State Div. Alcoholism Control, 1973; mem. House Environ. Matters Com., 1975-82; mem. Spl. Joint Com. Energy, 1977-83, chmn., 1978-79, 1980-83; mem. So. Legis. Conf. Energy Com. 1978, Environ. Com., 1983—, vice chmn., 1985—, chair senate fin. com., 1987-91, joint budget & audit com., 1988-91; mem. So. Environ. Resource Coun., 1978, Power Plant Siting Adv. Com., 1977-91, State of Md. Energy Conservation Bd., 1978-83, mem. BiState Cheasapeake Bay Commn., 1981-83, chmn. 1982; chmn. Forest Land Task Force, 1981-84, Budget and Taxation Senate Com., 1983-86, Subcom. Edn., Health, and Human Resources, 1983-86, Nat. Conf. State Legis. Energy Commn., 1983-91; senate chmn. adminstrv. exec. and legis. review com., 1983-86, various state govt. coms. and subcoms. Author: Maryland Profiles, Vol. 2, 1994, vol. 3, 1996; co-author: Maryland Policy Studies, vol. 4, 1991. Contbr. articles to profl. jours. Mem. adv. com. State Edn. Policy Seminars Adv. Com., 1993—, Protective Svcs. to Children and Families, 1983—; exec. bd. Balt. Area Coun. Boy Scouts Am., 1983-88; hon. chmn. Am. Cancer Soc., 1982-83; mem. Harford County Child Protection Coun., 1978-80, vice chmn. 1980; mem. Harford County Coun. Community Svcs., 1976—, Harford County legis. del., 1975-82 , chmn. 1976, 1980-82; mem. Md. Order Women Legislators, 1975—, sec. 1976-79; mem. adv. bd. Susquehanna State Park, 1975-91; mem. Joppatowne Womens Club, 1975—, No. Md. Assn. for Retarded Citizens, Inc., 1975—, Upper Cheasepeake Watershed Assn., Inc., 1975—. Recipient Disting. Svc. award Md. State Troopers, 1980, Community Svc. award, United Way, 1978, Disting. Svc. award Jaycees, 1976, Liberty award Harford Christian High Sch., 1975, Cert. of Appreciation Md. Mcpl. League, 1984, William P. Coliton Outstanding Community Svc. award Johns Hopkins U., 1985, Silver Chalice award Am. Coun. on Alsoholism, 1988, Outstanding Alumni award, Towson State U., 1989, Betty Tyler Pub. Affairs award Planned Parenthood of Md., 1989, Sarah T. Hughes Disting. Pub. Svc. award Goucher Coll., 1990; named Young Dem. of Yr. State of Md., 1975, Women of Yr. Soroptimist Club, 1980; Coun. Guide State Govt. Toll fellow, 1987, other state and civic awards. Mem. Am. Coun. on Alcoholism (bd. dirs.). Avocations: golf, sailing, stamp collecting. Office: 20 Office St Bel Air MD 21014-3704

RILEY, DANIEL EDWARD, air force officer; b. Flint, Mich., Aug. 18, 1915; s. Daniel Edward and Elva (Kirby) R.; m. Margaret E. Marengo, Nov. 28, 1938; children—Dennis M., Patricia A., Daniel R. B. Aero. Engring., U. Detroit, 1940; M.B.A., U. Mich., 1951; postgrad., Indsl. Coll. of Armed Forces, 1959. Commd. 2d lt. USAAF, 1936; advanced through grades to maj. gen. USAF, 1968; chief of plans and ops. (7290th Procurement Squadron at), Rhein/Main Air Base, Germany, 1951-1952; dep., later chief of procurement and prodn. div. (Hdqrs. USAF in), Europe; also comdr. (7290th Procurement Squadron), 1952-54; dep. chief of staff materiel (Directorate of Procurement and Prodn., Hdqrs. USAF), 1954-58; program dir. (MACE missile Air Research and Devel. Command), Wright-Patterson AFB, Ohio, 1959-60; program dir. SAC C&C Systems AFSC, 1961-63; vice comdr. (Electronics Systems div. AFSC), Bedford, Mass., 1965; comdr. (Air Force Contract Mgmt. Div.), Los Angeles, 1965-69; asst. dir. (Def. Supply Agy.), Washington, 1969-70; asst. to pres. Novatronics Inc., Pompano Beach, Fla., 1976-77. Decorated Legion of Merit with 2 oak leaf clusters. Mem. Air Force Assn., Ret. Officer Assn., Embry-Riddle Aero U. Bd. of Visitors, Indsl. Coll. Armed Forces Assn., Mil. Order World Wars, Lindbergh Fund, Halifax River Yacht Club, Beta Gamma Sigma, Phi Kappa Phi. Home: 1566 Poplar Dr Ormond Beach FL 32174-3414

RILEY, DOROTHY COMSTOCK, judge; b. Detroit, Dec. 6, 1924; d. Charles Austin and Josephine (Grima) Comstock; m. Wallace Don Riley, Sept. 13, 1963; 1 child, Peter Comstock. BA with honors in Polit. Sci., Wayne State U., 1946, LLB, 1949; LLD (hon.), Alma Coll., 1988, U. Detroit, 1990. Bar: Mich. 1950, U.S. Dist. Ct. (ea. dist.) Mich. 1950, U.S. Supreme Ct. 1957. Atty. Wayne County Friend of Ct., Detroit, 1956-68; ptnr. Riley & Roumell, Detroit, 1968-72, 73-76; judge Wayne County Cir., Detroit, 1972, Mich. Ct. Appeals, Detroit, 1976-82; assoc. justice Mich. Supreme Ct., Detroit, 1982-83, 85—, chief justice, 1987-91; mem. U.S. Jud. Conf. Commn. on State-Fed. Ct. Rels.; chmn. tort reform com. Conf. of Chief Justices; bd. dirs. Nat. Ctr. for State Cts., Thomas J. Cooley Law Sch. Co-author manuals, articles in field. Mem. steering com. Mich. Children Skillman Found., 1992; mem. multistate profl. responsibility exam. com. Nat. Conf. Bar Examiners, 1992. Recipient Disting. Alumni award Wayne U., 1990; Headliner award Women of Wayne, 1977; Donnelly award, 1946; Law Enforcement Commendation medal Nat. Soc. Sons of Am. Revolution, 1991; inducted in Mich. Women's Hall of Fame, 1991. Mem. ABA (family law sect. 1965—, vice chmn. gen. practice sect. com. on juvenile justice 1975-80, mem. jud. adminstrn. sect. 1973—, standing com. on fed. ct. improvements, mem. judges adv. com. of standing com. on ethics and profl. responsibility 1992), Am. Judicature Soc., Fellows Am. Bar Found., Mich. State Bar Found., State Bar Mich. (civil liberties com. 1954-58), Detroit Bar Assn. (pub. rels. com. 1955-56, author Com. in Action column, Detroit Lawyers 1955, chmn. friend of ct. and family law com. 1974-75), Nat. Women Judges Assn., Nat. Women Lawyers Assn., Women Lawyers Assn. Mich. (pres. 1957-58), Mich. Sup. Ct. Hist. Soc., Karyatides, Pi Sigma Alpha. Republican. Roman Catholic. Avocations: reading, gardening. Office: Mich Supreme Ct 500 Woodward Ave Fl 20 Detroit MI 48226-3423

RILEY, E. MARK, broadcast executive; b. New Rochelle, N.Y., Sept. 22, 1951; s. Elwood Thompson and Janet Louise (Wheeldon) R.; m. Kim Lisa Maria Jack, Nov. 14, 1992; 1 child by previous marriage, Christopher M. Student, NYU, 1969-71. From news editor to pub. affairs reporter WLIB/Inner City Broadcasting, N.Y.C., 1973-1992, program dir., 1992—. Adminstrv. advisor Kips Bay Boys and Girls Club, Bronx, 1994—. Honored by Friends and Family Assn. of Trinidad and Tobago in recognition of promoting Caribbean culture, 1992, by Haitian-Am. Alliance for Progress, 1992; recipient Paul Robeson Contbn. award Coalition of Black Trace Unionists, 1992, Appreciation for Realistic Approach to news award New Rochelle H.S., 1995. Avocation: drum and bugle corps. Office: WLIP/Inner City Broadcasting Corp 3 Park Ave Fl 41 New York NY 10016-5902

RILEY, GEORGIANNE MARIE, lawyer; b. Chgo., Feb. 5, 1953. BA in Psychology, Drake U., 1974, JD, 1978. Bar: Ill., 1978. Chief counsel Ill. Indsl. Commn., Chgo., 1979-83; dep. chief counsel Ill. Dept. Transp., Chgo., 1983-89; counsel Chem. Waste Mgmt., Oakbrook, Ill., 1989-91, sr. counsel, 1991-92; gen. counsel, v.p., sec. Rust Indsl. Svcs., Westchester, Ill., 1993-96;

gen. counsel Underwater Construction Corp., Essex, Conn., 1996—. Office: Waste Mgmt Inc 110 Plains Rd Essex CT 06426-1501

RILEY, HARRIS DEWITT, JR., pediatrician, educator; b. Clarksdale, Miss., Nov. 12, 1924; s. Harris DeWitt and Louise (Allen) R.; m. Margaret Barry, Sept. 16, 1950; children: Steven Allen, Mark Barry, Margaret Ruth. B.A., Vanderbilt U., 1945, M.D., 1948. Intern Balt. City Hosps., Johns Hopkins Hosp., 1948-49; resident in pediatrics Babies and Children's Hosp., Case Western Res. U., Cleve., 1949-50, Vanderbilt U. Hosp., 1950-51; instr., fellow in pediatrics and infectious diseases Vanderbilt U. Med. Sch., 1953-57; prof. pediatrics, chmn. dept. U. Okla. Med. Sch., 1958—; med. dir. Children's Meml. Hosp., 1972—; disting. prof. pediatrics U. Okla., 1976; prof. pediatrics Vanderbilt U. Sch. of Medicine, Nashville, 1991—. Served as capt. M.C. USAF, 1951-53. Office: Vanderbilt Children Hosp Vanderbilt U Med Ctr Nashville TN 37232

RILEY, HELENE MARIA KASTINGER, Germanist; b. Vienna, Austria, Mar. 11, 1939; came to U.S., 1959; d. Josef and Helene (Friedl) Kastinger; m. Edward R. Riley, Nov. 6, 1957 (div. May 1970); children: India Helene, John Edward, Jesse Dale, Michael Rutledge; m. Darius G. Ornston, May 11, 1983. Grad., bus. coll., Vienna, 1955; BA in Music, North Tex. State U., 1970; MA in Germanics, Rice U., 1973, PhD in Germanics, 1975. Teaching asst. Rice U., Houston, 1971-75; asst. prof. German Yale U., New Haven, Conn., 1975-78, head summer lang. inst., 1979-81, assoc. prof., 1979-85; chmn. Dept. Fgn. Langs. Wash. State U., Pullman, 1981-82; head Dept. Langs. Clemson (S.C.) U., 1985-86, prof., 1985-95, Alumni Disting. prof., 1996—; guest prof. Middlebury (Vt.) Coll., 1976; speaker in field. Author: Achim von Arnim, 1979, Virginia Woolf, 1983, Clemens Brentano, 1985, Die Weibliche Muse, 1986, Max Weber, 1991, producer, dir. traveling exhibit Cultural Contbns. of German-speaking Settlers in S.C., 1996—; others; contbr. numerous articles to profl. jours. Recipient German-Am. Friendship award Consul Gen. of the German Fed. Republic, 1989; grantee Griswold Found., 1975-76, 78, S.C. Dept. Edn., 1986, NEH, 1986, Provost's award Clemson U., 1989, 96, Hilles Fund, 1976, 79, 82, S.C. Humanities Coun., 1996; NDEA fellow, 1972, 73, Rice fellow, 1971, 74, Morse fellow, 1977-78, Deutscher Akademischer Austausch-Dienst fellow, 1979, Yale U. sr. faculty fellow, 1981-82, Holland Fund fellow, 1982, Deutsche Forschungsgemeinschaft fellow, 1982, Mesda fellow, 1993. Fellow Davenport Coll., Yale U.; mem. AAUP (v.p. 1987-88, pres. 1988-89), MLA, Am. Assn. Tchrs. German, So. Comparative Lit. Assn., others. Democrat. Avocations: reading, writing, sports, needlecraft, painting. Office: Clemson U Dept Langs 717 Strode Twr Clemson SC 29634-1515

RILEY, HENRY CHARLES, banker; b. Newton, Mass., Mar. 23, 1932; s. Charles Matthew and Marion Anna (Armstrong) R.; m. Patricia Ann Buchanan, Mar. 3, 1962; children: Lauren Elizabeth, Carolyn Ann, Julie Louise. A.B., Yale U., 1954; M.B.A., Boston Coll., 1965. With BayBank Harvard Trust Co., Cambridge, Mass., 1958-89, treas., sec., 1967-70, v.p., treas., 1970-72, sr. v.p., sec., 1972-82; exec. v.p. BayBank Harvard Trust Co., 1982-87; mng. dir. community banking BayBank Systems Inc., Waltham, Mass., 1987-90; exec. v.p., dir. community banking BayBank Boston, 1990-92; exec. v.p. BayBank Systems, Inc., Waltham, 1992-97; bd. dirs. BayBank FSB, Nashua, N.H., BayBank N.H., Derry. Trustee, treas. Longy Sch. Music, 1970-92; bd. dirs. Richard Warren Surg. Rsch. and Ednl. Fund Inc., 1984—; bd. dirs., pres. Cambridge Econ. Devel. Corp., 1982-87; corporator, past asst. treas. Mt. Auburn Hosp.; past mem. exec. bd. Gettysburg Coll. Parents Assn.; past treas. St. John's Episcopal Ch., sr. warden, Westwood, Mass., 1982-85; mem. St. Paul's Cathedral chpt., Boston, 1990-93. With USNR, 1956-57. Mem. Am. Bankers Assn. (chmn. 1991-92, exec. com. br. adminstrv. divsn. 1992, chmn. nat. retail banking conf. 1990), Nat. Br. Adminstrs. Roundtable, Boston Coll. Sch. Mgmt. Alumni Assn. (past dir., pres.), Harvard Sq. Bus. Assn. (past dir.), Cambridge C. of C. (past dir., past treas., v.p. 1975-87), Rotary (club dir. 1976-80, pres. 1979-80), Yale Club (Boston), Harvard Club (Boston), Dennis Yacht Club (mem. bd. govs., treas. 1993-94), The Meadows Country Club (Sarasota, Fla.). Episcopalian. Home: 33 York Way Westwood MA 02090-2633 Office: BayBank Systems Inc One BayBank Technology Pl Waltham MA 02154-7438

RILEY, JACK, actor, writer; b. Cleve., Dec. 30, 1935; s. John A. and Agnes C. (Corrigan) R.; m. Ginger Lawrence, May 18, 1975; children: Jamie, Bryan. BS in English, John Carroll U., 1961. Mem.: Rolling Along of 1960, Dept. Army Travelling Show; co-host: Baxter & Riley, Sta.-WERE, Cleve., 1961-65; numerous TV appearances, including: as Mr. Carlin on Bob Newhart Show, CBS-TV, 1972-78; Occasional Wife, 1966, Mary Tyler Moore, 1972, Barney Miller, 1979, Diff'rent Strokes, 1979, Hart to Hart, 1980, Love Boat, 1984, Night Court, 1985-91, St. Elsewhere, 1986, Babes, 1991, Evening Shade, 1992, Family Matters, 1993, Hangin' with Mr. Cooper, 1993, Dave's World, 1994, Married with Children, 1994, Coach, 1996, The Drew Carey Show, 1996; appeared in feature films including Catch-22, 1969, McCabe and Mrs. Miller, 1970, Long Goodbye, 1972, Calif. Split, 1974, World's Greatest Lover, 1978, High Anxiety, 1978, Butch and Sundance: The Early Years, 1979, History of the World, Part I, 1981, Frances, 1983, To Be or Not To Be, 1983, Finders Keepers, 1984, Spaceballs, 1987, Rented Lips, 1987, Gleaming the Cube, 1988, C.H.U.D. II, 1988, The Player, 1992, T-Rex, 1995, Boogie Nights, 1997; plays West Coast premier of Small Craft Warnings, 1975, Los Angeles revival of 12 Angry Men, 1985, Zeitgeist, 1990, House of Blue Leaves, at Cleve. Playhouse and tour Ea. Europe, 1993; TV writer: Don Rickles Show, 1968, Mort Sahl Show, 1967; writer commls. for, Blore & Richman Inc., Los Angeles, 1966-84; numerous radio commls. and TV voice-overs, Rugrats (cartoon series), 1993. Served with U.S. Army, 1958-61. Mem. Screen Actors Guild, Actor's Equity, AFTRA, Writers Guild Am., Acad. Motion Picture Arts and Scis., Acad. TV Arts and Scis. Office: care Ho of Reps 9911 W Pico Blvd Ste 1060 Los Angeles CA 90035-2712

RILEY, JACK T., JR., lawyer; b. Dayton, Ohio, Feb. 17, 1946. BA, Denison U., 1968; JD cum laude, Georgetown U., 1973. Bar: Ill. 1973, U.S. Dist. Ct. (no. dist.) Ill. 1973. Assoc. Kirkland and Ellis, 1973-75; sr. ptnr. Johnson & Bell Ltd., Chgo., 1975—; lectr. Chgo. Bar Assn., Ill. Assn. Def. Trial Counsel, Fedn. Ins. and Corp. Counsel, The Def. Rsch. Inst. Editor Georgetown Law Jour., 1972-73; founding editor, editor-in-chief IDC Quar., 1989-94; contbr. articles to profl. jours. Mem. ABA, Ill. State Bar Assn., Ill. Assn. Def. Trial Counsel (bd. dirs. 1990—, v.p.), Chgo. Bar Assn., Def. Rsch. Inst., Fed. Trial Bar, Fedn. Ins. and Corp. Counsel (chmn. publs. com., v.p. toxic tort and environ. law sect., regional v.p., bd. dirs.), Soc. Trial Lawyers, Trial Lawyers Club Chgo. Address: Johnson & Bell 222 N La Salle St Ste 2200 Chicago IL 60601-1106

RILEY, JOHN GRAHAM, economics educator; b. Christchurch, New Zealand, Dec. 8, 1945; came to U.S., 1969; s. Charles Graham and Patricia (White) R.; m. Rita Jane Stulin, July 5, 1971 (div. 1981); m. Beverly Fong Lowe, Oct. 16, 1982; 1 child, Alexandra Lowe Riley. BS, U. Canterbury, Christchurch, 1967, M in Commerce, 1969; PhD, MIT, 1972. Instr. Boston Coll., 1971-72, asst. prof., 1972-73; asst. prof. econs. UCLA, 1973-76, assoc. prof., 1976-80, prof., 1980—, chmn. dept., 1987-90, 92-96. Assoc. editor Am. Econs. Rev., 1983-85, co-editor, 1985-87; contbr. numerous articles to profl. jours. Co-chair Ch. and Synagogue Assocs., Inc., 1991-96. Erskine fellow U. Canterbury, 1987; NSF grantee, 1975-89. Fellow Econometrics Soc. Office: UCLA Dept Econs 2263 Bunche Hall Los Angeles CA 90095-1477

RILEY, JOHN WINCHELL, JR., consulting sociologist; b. Brunswick, Maine, June 10, 1908; s. John Winchell and Marjorie Webster (Prince) R.; m. Matilda White, June 19, 1931; children: John Winchell III, Lucy Ellen. AB, Bowdoin Coll., 1930, LLD, 1972; MA, Harvard U., 1933, PhD, 1936. Mem. faculty Marietta Coll., 1933-35, Wellesley Coll., 1935-37, Douglass Coll., 1937-45; mem. faculty Rutgers U., 1945-60, prof. sociology, chmn. dept., 1945-60; v.p., dir. social research Equitable Life Assurance Soc. of U.S., N.Y.C., 1960-68, v.p. corp. relations, 1968—, sr. v.p. corp. relations, 1968-72, sr. v.p. social research, 1972-73, cons., 1973—; mem. faculty Harvard U., 1955; cons. Market Rsch. Co. Am., 1940-45, Columbia Broadcasting Co., 1945-50, Ford Motor Co., 1965, Am. Coun. Life Ins., 1973-90, WHO, 1984—, Internat. Fedn. Aging, 1983—, Scripps Found., 1987—, Max Planck, 1989, numerous others; sr. cons. Matthew Greenwald & Assocs., 1990—, Project Age and Structural Change Nat. Inst. Aging, 1994—; vis. scholar Ctr. for Advanced Study in Behavioral Sci., 1978-79; mem. adv. bd. Carnegie Corp. Aging Soc. project, 1982—, U. Mich. Inst. Gerontology, 1987—, U. So. Calif. Intergenerational Project, 1990; lectr. in field. Author: (with Bryce Ran, Marcia Lifshitz) The Student Looks at His Teacher, 1950 (with Wilbur Schramm) The Reds Take A City, 1951 (with Matilda W. Riley, Jackson Toby) Sociological Studies in Scale Analysis, 1954 (with Matilda W. Riley, Marilyn Johnson) Aging and Society, Vol. II, 1969; editor: The Corporation and Its Public, 1963; contbr. Our Aging Soc., 1986, Nationalization of the Social Sciences, 1987, Ency. of Aging, 1990, The Changing Contract Among Generations, 1993, others. Former trustee Am. Found. Blind, Inst. Edn. Devel., Nat. Urban League, Boethner Rsch. Inst.; trustee Industrywide Network Social Rural and Rural Efforts; mem. capital campaign com. Bowdoin Coll., 1984; rsch. adv. bd. The Am. Coll., 1989—. With OWI, Psychol. Warfare Divsn., AUS, 1944, Far Ea. Rsch. Group, USAF, 1950-51. Recipient Stuart A. Rice Merit award, 1990, Lester F. Ward award for disting. contbns. to applied sociology Soc. for Applied Sociology, 1997. Fellow AAAS; mem. Sociol. Research Assn. (pres. 1964-65), Oliver Wendall Holmes Assn. (former trustee), Am. Sociol. Assn. (sec. 1950-55, Disting. Career award for practice 1983), Eastern Social Soc., Osborne Assn. (former trustee), Am. Assn. Pub. Opinion Research (pres. 1961-62, Disting. Career award 1983), Market Research Council, Am. Assn. Internat. Aging (former trustee), Am. Sociol. Found. (incorporator, mem. adv. com. 1987—), D.C. Sociol. Soc. (co-pres. 1984-85). Home and Office: 4701 Willard Ave Apt 1607 Chevy Chase MD 20815-4630

RILEY, KEVIN M., principal. Prin. Gretna (Nebr.) Jr. Sr. High Sch. Recipient Blue Ribbon award U.S. Dept. Edn., 1990-91. Office: Gretna Sr High Sch 11705 S 216th St Gretna NE 68028-4729*

RILEY, LAWRENCE JOSEPH, bishop; b. Boston, Sept. 6, 1914; s. James and Ellen (Ryan) R. A.B., Boston Coll., 1936, LL.D., 1965; S.T.B., Gregorian U., 1939; S.T.D., Catholic U. Am., 1948; LL.D., Stonehill Coll., 1957. Ordained priest Roman Cath. Ch., 1940. Prof., rector St. John's Sem., Boston, 1941-66; prof. Emmanuel Coll., 1965-66; chaplain Harvard Cath. Club, 1950-54; vice officialis Met. Tribunal, Archdiocese of Boston, 1950-76; sec. to archbishop of Boston, 1951-58; aux. bishop Archdiocese of Boston, 1972-90, aux. bishop emeritus, 1990—; asst. at Pontifical Throne, 1986—; vicar gen. emeritus Archdiocese of Boston; pastor emeritus Most Precious Blood Parish, Hyde Park, Mass. Decorated Knight Comdr. with star Holy Sepulchre of Jerusalem; decorated Knight Order of Star of Italian Solidarity. Mem. Cath. Theol. Soc. Am. (past pres.), Mariological Soc. Am., Canon Law Soc. Am., Dante Alighieri Soc. Mass. (past v.p.), Nat. Cath. Edn Assn., Fellowship of Cath. Scholars, Pope John XXIII Med.-Moral Ctr. Address: 43 Maple St Hyde Park MA 02136-2755

RILEY, MATILDA WHITE (MRS. JOHN W. RILEY, JR.), sociology educator; b. Boston, Apr. 19, 1911; d. Percival and Mary (Cliff) White; m. John Winchell Riley, Jr., June 19, 1931; children: John Winchell III, Lucy Ellen Riley Sallick. BA, Radcliffe Coll., 1931, MA, 1937, DSc (hon.), 1994; DSc, Bowdoin Coll., 1972; LHD (hon.), Rutgers U., 1983, SUNY, Albany, 1997. Rsch. asst. Harvard U., Cambridge, Mass., 1932; v.p. Market Rsch. Co. Am., 1938-49; chief cons. economist WPB, 1941; rsch. specialist Rutgers U., 1950, prof., 1951-73, dir. sociology lab., chmn. dept. sociology and anthropology, 1959-73, emeritus prof., 1973—; Daniel B. Fayerweather prof. polit. econ. and sociology Bowdoin Coll., 1974-78, prof. emeritus, 1978—; assoc. dir. Nat. Inst. on Aging, 1979-91, sr. social scientist, 1991—; mem. faculty Harvard U., summer 1955; staff assoc., dir. aging and society Russell Sage Found., 1964-73, staff sociologist, 1974-77; chmn. com. on life course Social Sci. Rsch. Coun., 1977-80; sr. rsch. assoc. Ctr. for Social Scis., Columbia U., 1978-80; adv. bd. Carnegie Aging Soc. Project, 1985-87; mem. Commn. on Coll. Retirement, 1982-86; vis. prof. NYU, 1954-61; cons. Nat. Coun. on Aging, Acad. Ednl. Devel.; mem. study group NIH, 1971-79, Social Sci. Rsch. Coun. Com. on Middle Years, 1973-77; chmn. NIH Task Force on Health and Behavior, 1986-91; cons. WHO, 1987—; Winkelman lectr. U. Mich., 1984, Selo lectr. U. No. Calif., 1987, Boettner lectr. Am. Coll., 1990, Claude Pepper lectr. Fla. State U., 1993, Disting. lectr. Southwestern Social Scis. Assn., 1990, U. N.C., 1997; Standing lectr. SUNY, 1992, Inaugural lectr. Cornell U., 1992; lectr. Internat. Inst. of Sociology, Plenary, 1993, Inter-Univ. Consortium Pol. and Social Rsch., U. Mich., 1993, Duke U., 1993. Author: (with P. White) Gliding and Soaring, (with Riley and Toby) Sociological Studies in Scale Analysis, 1954, Sociological Research, vols. I, II, 1964, (with others) Aging and Society, vol. I, 1968, vol. II, 1969, vol. III, 1972, (with Nelson) Sociological Observation, 1974, Aging from Birth to Death: Interdisciplinary Perspectives, 1979, (with Merton) Sociological Traditions from Generation to Generation, 1980, (with Abeles and Teitelbaum) Aging from Birth to Death: Sociotemporal Perspectives, 1982, (with Hess and Bond) Aging in Society, 1983; editor: (with M. Ory and D. Zablotsky) AIDS in an Aging Society: What We Need to Know, 1989; (co-editor: Perspectives in Behavioral Medicine: The Aging Dimension, 1987, (with J. W. Riley) The Quality of Aging, 1989, The Annuals, 1989; sr. editor: Structural Lag, 1994; editorial com.: Ann. Rev. Sociology, 1978-81, Social Change and the Life Course, vol. 1, Social Structures and Human Lives, (with B. Huber and B. Hess) Sociological Lives, vol. II, 1988, (with R. Kahn and Anne Foner) Structural Lag, 1994; contbr. chpts. to books, articles to profl. jours. Former trustee The Big Sisters Assn. Recipient Lindback Rsch. award Rutgers U., 1970, Social Sci. award Andrus Gerontology Ctr., U. So. Calif., 1972, Radcliffe Alumnae award, 1982, Commonwealth award 1984, Kesten Lecture award U. So. Calif., 1987, Sci. Achievement award Washington Acad. Scis., 1989, Disting. Sci. award, 1989, Disting. Creative award Gerontol. Soc. Am., 1990, Presdl. Meritorious award, 1990, Stuart Rice award D.C. Columbia Sociol. Soc., 1992, Kent award Gerontol. Soc. Am., 1992; fellow Advanced Study in Behaviorial Scis., 1978-79; Matilda White Riley award in rsch. and methodology established in her honor Rutgers U., 1977; Matilda White Riley prize established Bowdoin Coll., 1987; Matilda White Riley House dedicated Bowdoin Coll., 1996. Fellow AAAS (chmn. sect. on social and econ. scis. 1977-78); mem. NAS, Inst. Medicine of NAS (sr.), Acad. Behavioral Medicine Rsch., Am. Sociol. Assn. (exec. officer 1949-60, v.p. 1973-74, pres. 1986, 91, chmn. sect. on sociology of aging 1989, Disting. Scholar in Aging 1988, Career award 1992), Am. Assn. Public Opinion Rsch (sec.-treas. 1949-51, Disting. Svc. award 1983), Eastern Sociol. Soc. (v.p. 1968-69, pres. 1977-78, Disting. Career award 1986), Soc. for Study Social Biology (bd. dirs. 1986-92), Am. Acad. Arts and Scis., D.C. Sociol. Soc. (co-pres. 1983-84), Sociol. Rsch. Assn., Internat. Orgn. Study Human Devel., Am. Philos. Soc. (membership lectr. 1987), Phi Beta Kappa, Phi Beta Kappa Assocs. Home: 4701 Willard Ave Apt 1607 Chevy Chase MD 20815-4630 Office: NIH Nat Inst on Aging 7201 Wisconsin Ave Bethesda MD 20814-4810

RILEY, MICHAEL JOSEPH, government official; b. Rochester, N.H., Mar. 14, 1943; m. Nancy Sarah, July 25, 1970; children: Shawn, Paul, James, Sarah. B.S., U.S. Naval Acad., 1965; M.B.A., U. So. Calif., Los Angeles, 1972; D. Bus. Adminstrn. in Fin., Harvard U., 1977. Acct. Teradyne, Boston, 1972-73; asst. controller Northeast Utilities, Berlin, Conn., 1976-83; treas. Mich. Bell Telephone Co., Detroit, 1983-85; sr. v.p. fin., chief fin. officer United Airlines, Elk Grove Village, Ill., 1985-86; v.p. fin. Lee Enterprises, Inc., Davenport, Iowa, 1987-93; CFO, sr. v.p. U.S. Postal Svc., Washington, 1993—; lectr. fin. U. Conn., 1977-81, U. Mich., 1985. Author: (with Dwight B. Crane) NOW Accounts: Strategy for Financial Institutions, 1978. Lt. USN, 1965-70, Vietnam. Mem. Fin. Execs. Inst. (pres. Mississippi Valley chpt. 1991, com. on govt. liaison 1993—), Fin. Mgmt. Assn. (dir. 1983-85). Office: US Postal Svc 475 Lenfant Plz SW Washington DC 20260-5000

RILEY, NANCY MAE, retired vocational home economics educator; b. Grand Forks, N.D., May 1, 1939; d. Kenneth Wesley and Jeanne Margaret Olive (Hill) R. BS in Edn., Miami U., 1961; postgrad., Ohio U., 1964-69; MA, Marietta Coll., 1989. Cert. high sch. tchr. Tchr. home econs. Malta-McConnelsville (Ohio) High Sch., 1961-67; tchr. home econs. Waterford (Ohio) High Sch., 1968-92; advisor Malta-McConnelsville Future Homemakers, 1961-66, Waterford Future Homemakers Am., 1968-92; advisor to state officer Ohio Future Homemakers Am., McConnelsville, 1963, Waterford, 1976. Leader Girl Scouts Am., McConnelsville, 1962-66, camp counselor, 1962-76; fair judge Waterford Cmty. Fair, Waterford, 1970-85. Mem. NEA, Am. Vocat. Assn. (life), Ohio Edn. Assn. (life, del. 1979), Ohio Vocat. Assn. (life), DAR, Daus. Union Vets. (del. 1992—, tent pres. 1993-97, dist. pres. 1996), Daus. of War of 1812 (pres. 1991—, state sec. 1995-97), Ohio Geneal. Soc., Order Ea. Star (worthy matron 1967-68, dep. grand matron 1978), White Shrine Jerusalem (worth high priestess 1979-81, 83). Republican. Baptist. Avocations: ceramics, genealogy, camping, reading, handcrafts. Home: PO Box 137 Waterford OH 45786-0137

RILEY, PATRICK JAMES, professional basketball coach; b. Rome, N.Y., Mar. 20, 1945; s. Leon R.; m. Chris Riley; children: James Patrick, Elisabeth. Grad., U. Ky., 1967. Guard San Diego Rockets, 1967-70; guard L.A. Lakers, 1970-75, asst. coach, 1979-81, head coach, 1981-90; head coach N.Y. Knicks, 1991-95; guard Phoenix Suns, 1975-76; broadcaster L.A. Lakers games Sta. KLAC and Sta. KHJ-TV, 1977-79, NBC Sports, 1990-91; player NBA Championship Team, 1972, coach, 1982, 85, 87, 88; head coach Miami (Fla.) Heat, 1995—. Author: The Winner Within: A Life Plan for Team Players, 1993. Named NBA Coach of Yr., 1990, 93. Holder NBA record most playoff wins (137). Office: Miami Heat SunTrust Int'l Ctr One SE 3rd Ave Ste 2300 Miami FL 33131-4102*

RILEY, RICHARD WILSON, federal official; b. Greenville, S.C., Jan. 2, 1933; s. Edward Patterson and Martha Elizabeth (Dixon) R.; m. Ann Osteen Yarborough, Aug. 23, 1957; children: Richard Wilson, Anne Y., Hubert D., Theodore D. B.A., Furman U., 1954; J.D., U. S.C., 1959. Bar: S.C. 1960. Ptnr. Riley & Riley, Greenville, 1959-78, Nelson, Mullins, Riley & Scarborough, Greenville and Columbia, S.C., 1987-93; gov. State of S.C., 1979-87; sec. U.S. Dept. Edn., Washington, 1993—; spl. asst. to subcom. U.S. Senate Jud. Com., 1960; mem. S.C. Ho. of Reps., 1963-66, S.C. Senate senate from Greenville-Laurens Dist., 1966-76. Lt. (j.g.) USNR, 1954-56. Recipient Harold W. McGraw, Jr. Prize in Education, McGraw-Hill, 1989; James Bryant Conant Award, Edn. Comm. of the States, 1995. Mem. S.C., Greenville bar assns., Furman U. Alumni Assn. (pres. 1968-69), Phi Beta Kappa. Rotarian. Office: US Dept Edn Washington DC 20202-0001

RILEY, ROBERT BARTLETT, landscape architect; b. Chgo., Jan. 28, 1931; s. Robert James and Ruth (Collins) R.; m. Nancy Rebecca Mills, Oct. 5, 1956; children: Rebecca Hill, Kimber Bartlett. PhB, U. Chgo., 1949; BArch, MIT, 1954. Chief designer Kea, Shaw, Grimm & Crichton, Hyattsville, Md., 1959-64; prin. partner Robert B. Riley (A.I.A.), Albuquerque, 1964-70; campus planner, asso. prof. architecture, dir. Center Environ. Research and Devel., U. N.Mex., 1966-70; prof. landscape architecture and architecture U. Ill., Urbana-Champaign, 1970—, head dept. landscape architecture, 1970-85; vis. prof. Harvard U., 1996—; sr. fellow landscape architecture studies Dumbarton Oaks/Harvard U., 1992—, chmn. fellows, 1996—; mem. rev. panel landscape architects Fed. Civil Service-Nat. Endowment Arts. Assoc. editor Landscape mag., 1967-70; editor Landscape Jour., 1987—. Served with USAF, 1954-58. Nell Norris fellow U. Melbourne, Australia, 1977; project fellow Nat. Endowment Arts, 1985. Fellow Am. Soc. Landscape Architects (Nat. Honor award 1979); mem. Coun. of Educators in Landscape Architecture, pres. 1984-85, chmn. bd. dirs. 1985-86, Outstanding Educator award 1992, Pres.'s award 1994, chmn. editl. adv. bd. Landscape Architecture 1996—), AIA (Design award Md. 1962, N.Mex. 1968, Environ. Svc. award N.Mex. 1970), Environ. Design Rsch. Assn. (chmn. bd. 1990-91), Phi Beta Epsilon. Unitarian. Home: 407 E Mumford Dr Urbana IL 61801-6231 Office: Univ Ill 101 Temple Buell Hall 611 E Lorado Taft Dr Champaign IL 61820-6921

RILEY, SCOTT C., lawyer; b. Bklyn., Oct. 5, 1959; s. William A. and Kathleen (Howe) R.; m. Kathleen D. O'Connor, Oct. 6, 1984; children: Matthew, Brendan. BA, Seton Hall U., South Orange, N.J., 1981; JD, Seton Hall U., Newark, 1984. Bar: N.J. 1985, U.S. Dist. Ct. N.J. 1985. Assoc. Dwyer, Connell & Lisbona, Montclair, N.J., 1985-87; assoc. gen. counsel, v.p. Consolidated Ins. Group, Wilmington, Del., 1987-91; counsel Cigna Ins. Group, Phila., 1991-94; assoc. gen. counsel KWELM Cos., N.Y.C., 1994—. Mem. ABA (com. on environ. ins. coverage), Fedn. of Ins. and Corp. Counsel, Excess and Surplus Lines Claims Assn., N.J. State Bar Assn. Office: KWELM Companies 599 Lexington Ave New York NY 10022-6030

RILEY, STEPHEN THOMAS, historian, librarian; b. Worcester, Mass., Dec. 28, 1908; s. John and Mary (Ward) R.; m. Alice Amelia Riehle, July 2, 1949. A.B., Clark U., 1931, A.M., 1932, Ph.D. in Am. History, 1953, L.H.D. (hon.), 1981; grad., U. Pa. Army Specialized Tng. Program, 1943-44. Asst. librarian Mass. Hist. Soc., Boston, 1934-47; librarian Mass. Hist. Soc., 1947-62, dir., 1957-76, dir. emeritus, 1977—; mem. Mass. Revolutionary War Bi-Centennial Commn., 1965-91, Mass. Gov.'s Commn. on Need of New Mass. Archives Bldg., 1974, Mass. Archives Adv. Com., 1978-91; mem. adminstrv. bd. Adams Family Papers, 1956-91, George Washington Papers, 1969-91, Daniel Webster Papers, 1966-89; mem. vis. com. Boston Coll. Library, 1964, 67-68, Harvard U. History Dept., 1962-68, Harvard U. Press, 1965-71; cons. N.Y. State Hist. Assn., 1978, Va. Hist. Soc., 1981. Author: The Massachusetts Historical Society, 1791-1959, 1959, Stephen Thomas Riley: The Years of Stewardship, 1976; editor: (with Edward W. Hanson) The Papers of Robert Treat Paine, Vol. I 1746-1756, Vol. II 1757-1774, 1992; contbr. articles and revs. to hist. jours. Bd. dirs. Freedom Trail, Boston, 1965-91; trustee Clark U., 1963-74, hon. trustee, 1974—. Served with U.S. Army, 1942—44; USAAF, 1944-45. Fellow AAAS; mem. Archives Am. Art (adv. com. New Eng. br. 1972-91), Am. Antiquarian Soc., Am. Bostonain Soc., Colonial Soc. Mass. (v.p. 1980-91), Mass. Hist. Soc., New Eng. Hist. Geneal. Soc. (corr. sec. 1973-81), Weston (Mass.) Hist. Soc. (pres. 1977-84), Odd Vols. (Boston, v.p. 1979-83), Grolier Club (N.Y.C.), Odd Vols. Club (v.p. 1979-83), Phi Beta Kappa. Democrat. Roman Catholic. Home: 334 Wellesley St Weston MA 02193-2620 Office: 1154 Boylston St Boston MA 02215-3631

RILEY, THOMAS JOSEPH, anthropologist; b. Portland, Maine, Nov. 2, 1943; s. Joseph Gerard and Virginia C. (Cunningham) R.; m. Karma Jean Ibsen, July 10, 1967 (div. 1985); children: Kirsten, Katherine, Erin; m. Carol Ann, Nov. 21, 1989; 1 child, Julia Wade. BA, Boston Coll., 1965; MA, U. Hawaii, 1970, PhD, 1973. Asst. prof. NYU, 1972-74; from asst. prof. to prof. anthropology U. Ill., Urbana, 1974-96, assoc. dean Grad. Coll., 1983-86, head dept. anthropology, 1986-93, chair univ. senate coun., 1995-96; dean Coll. Humanities and Social Scis., prof. anthropology N.D. State U., Fargo, 1996—; acad. adv. bd. SALT Ctr., Portland, 1980—. Co-author: Prehistoric Agriculture, 1972; mem. editl. bd. Ency. of World Cultures, 1993-96; contbr. over 70 articles to profl. jours. Chair bd. Devel. Svcs. Ctr., Champaign, 1986-89, Human Rels. Area Files at Yale U., 1995-96, v.p. 1996—; sec. bd. C-U Independence, Champaign, 1987—; bd. dirs. Disabled Citizens Found., Champaign, 1988—, Ill. Assn. Retarded Citizens, Chgo., 1988-94, Champaign County Mental Health Bd., 1993—, Ill. State Hist. Sites Adv. Coun., 1986-89. NSF fellow, 1978-79; NSF grantee 1978—. Fellow Am. Anthropology Assn., Ill. Archeol. Survey; mem. Soc. Am. Archaeology, AAAS, Soc. Archeol. Scis. (treas. 1982-83), Sigma Xi (chpt. v.p. 1987-88, chpt. pres. 1988-91). Roman Catholic. Home: 1108 42nd Ave N Fargo ND 58102-5318 Office: ND State U 221 Minard Hall Fargo ND 58105

RILEY, TOM JOSEPH, lawyer; b. Cedar Rapids, Iowa, Jan. 9, 1929; s. Joseph Wendell and Edna (Kyle) R.; m. Nancy Evans, Jan. 21, 1952; children: Pamela Chang, Peter, Lisa Thirnbeck, Martha Brown, Sara Brown, Heather Mescher. BA, U. Iowa, 1950, JD, 1952. Bar: Iowa 1952, U.S. Dist. Ct. (no. dist.) Iowa 1952, U.S. Ct. Appeals (8th cir.) 1960, U.S. Supreme Ct. 1966. Assoc. Simmons, Perrine, Allbright & Ellwood, Cedar Rapids, 1952-60, ptnr., 1960-80; pres. Tom Riley Law Firm, P.C., Cedar Rapids, 1980—; adj. prof. trial advocacy Coll. Law, U. Iowa, Iowa City, 1979. Author: Proving Punitive Damages, 1981, The Price of a Life, 1986, Trial Handbook for Iowa Lawyers (Civil), 1997. Mem. Iowa Ho. of Reps., 1960-64, Iowa Senate, 1965-74. First lt. USAF, 1952-54. Named Outstanding Freshman Legislator, Des Moines Press and Radio Club, 1961. Fellow Iowa Acad. Trial Lawyers (bd. govs. 1982-91); mem. Cedar Rapids Country Club, U. Athletic Club, Iowa City, Des Moines Club, Masons. Republican. Presbyterian. Avocations: tennis, sailing, downhill skiing. Home: 5300 Lakeside Rd Rural Route Marion IA 52302 Office: 4040 1st Ave NE Cedar Rapids IA 52402-3143

RILEY, VICTOR J., JR., financial services company executive; b. Buffalo, Aug. 29, 1931; s. Victor J. and Gwenevieve Riley; m. Marilyn A. Felrath, Aug. 8, 1954; children—Victor J. III, Karen, Patricia, Kevin, Shawn, Mary Katherine. BA in Econs., U. Notre Dame; LLD, Coll. St. Rose, 1983. With trust div. 1st Nat. Bank Miami, Fla., 1955-62; mgr. Miami office Bowles, Andrews & Towne, 1962-64; trust officer Nat. Comml. Bank (now Key Bank N.A.), Albany, N.Y., 1964-73; pres., chief exec. officer KeyCorp (formerly Key Banks Inc.), Albany, 1973-96, chmn. emeritus, 1996—; ret., 1996; also dir.; chmn. bd. Key Bank N.A., Albany, 1984—, Ctr. Econ. Growth; dir. Albany Med. Ctr., Interstate Banking Commn. for State of N.Y., 1986—. Hon. chmn. Capital Dist. Cerebral Palsy Telethon, Albany, 1981-87; bd. dirs. Pop Warner Football League; chmn. various fund raising drives. Served with U.S. Army, 1953-55. Apptd. civilian aide to Sec. Army, 1985—. Decorated Knight of Malta. Mem. N.Y. State Bankers Assn. (long-range planning com.), Interstate Banking Com. State N.Y. Republican. Roman Catholic. Avocations: travel, fishing, cooking. Home: PO Box 2414 Cody WY 82414 Office: KeyCorp 1130 Sheridan Ave Cody WY 82414-3644

RILEY, WILLIAM, corporate executive, writer; b. Indpls., June 30, 1931; s. Leo Michael and Edna (Wilhelm) R.; m. Laura Etz, Apr. 20, 1957. AB, U. Notre Dame, 1952; LLB, Yale U., 1955. V.p., dir., chmn. Ivy Corp., Atlanta, 1960-80; chmn. Moore-Handley, Inc., Birmingham, Ala., 1981—; bd. dirs. Tru-Die, Inc., Franklin Pk., Ill., Fabco-Air, Inc., Gainesville, Fla. Author: (with Laura Riley) Guide to the National Wildlife Refuges, 1979 (Pulitzer prize nominee). Trustee The Raptor Trust, Basking Ridge, N.J., 1980—; bd. dirs. Nat. Wildlife Refuge Assn., Potomac, Md., 1985-94, Hawk Mountain Sanctuary Assn., Kempton, Pa., 1989—, Nat. Audubon Soc., N.Y.C., 1990-94. With U.S. Army, 1957-58. Mem. Met. Club of N.Y.C. Office: 590 Madison Ave New York NY 10022-2524

RILEY, WILLIAM FRANKLIN, mechanical engineering educator; b. Allenport, Pa., Mar. 1, 1925; s. William Andrew and Margaret (James) R.; m. Helen Elizabeth Chilzer, Nov. 5, 1945; children—Carol Ann, William Franklin. B.S. in Mech. Engring., Carnegie Inst. Tech., 1951; M.S. in Mechanics, Ill. Inst. Tech., 1958. Mech. engr. Mesta Machine Co., West Homestead, Pa., 1951-54; research engr. Armour Research Found., Chgo., 1954-61; sect. mgr. IIT Research Inst., Chgo., 1961-64, sci. adviser, 1964-66; prof. Iowa State U., Ames, 1966-78, Disting. prof. engring., 1978-88, prof. emeritus, 1989—; ednl. cons. Bihar Inst. Tech., Sindri, India, 1966, Indian Inst. Tech., Kanpur, summer 1970. Author: (with A.J. Durelli) Introduction to Photmechanics, 1965; (with J. W. Dally) Experimental Stress Analysis, 1991; (with D. Young, K. McConnell and T. Rogge) Essentials of Mechanics, 1974; (with A. Higdon, E. Ohlsen, W. Stiles and J. Weese) mechanics of Materials, 4th edit., 1985; (with J. Dally and K. McConnell) Instrumentation for Engineering Measurements, 1993; (with L.W. Zachary) Introduction to Mechanics of Materials, 1989, (with L.D. Sturges) Engineering Mechanics-Statics and Dynamics, 1993, 2d edit., 1996; also numerous articles and tech. papers. Served to lt. col. USAAF, 1943-46. Fellow Soc. for Exptl. Mechanics (hon. mem.); mem. Soc. for Exptl. Stress Analysis (hon., M.M. Frocht award 1977). Home: 1518 Meadowlane Ave Ames IA 50010-5547

RILEY, WILLIAM JAY, lawyer; b. Lincoln, Nebr., Mar. 11, 1947; s. Don Paul and Marian Frances (Munn) R.; m. Norma Jean Mason, Dec. 27, 1965; children: Brian, Kevin, Erin. BA, U. Nebr., 1969, JD, 1972. Bar: Nebr. 1972, U.S. Dist. Ct. Nebr. 1972, U.S. Ct. Appeals (8th cir.) 1974; cert. civil trial specialist Nat. Bd. Trial Advocacy. Law clk. U.S. Ct. Appeals (8th cir.), Omaha, 1972-73; assoc. Fitzgerald, Schorr Law Firm, Omaha, 1973-79, ptnr., 1979—; adj. prof. trial practice Creighton U. Coll. Law, Omaha, 1991—; chmn. fed. practice com. Fed. Ct., 1992-94. Scoutmaster Boy Scouts Am., Omaha, 1979-89, scout membership chair Mid Am. Coun., 1995—. Recipient Silver Beaver award Boy Scouts Am., 1991. Fellow Am. Coll. Trial Lawyers, Nebr. State Bar Found.; mem. Am. Bd. Trial Advs., Nebr. State Bar Assn. (chmn. ethics com. 1996—), Omaha Bar Assn. (treas. 1997—), Robert M. Spire Inns of Ct. (master 1994—, counselor 1997—). Republican. Methodist. Avocations: reading, hiking, cycling. Office: Fitzgerald Schorr Law Firm 1100 Woodmen Tower Omaha NE 68102

RILEY, WILLIAM JOHN, neurologist; b. Seattle, Oct. 24, 1930; s. William John and Virginia (McCarthy) R.; m. Joan Marie Weismann, 1956 (div. 1976); children: Sean, Kevan, Megan, Janeen, Michael; m. Margit Mary, 1976; children: Britta, Shane, Timothy. MS in Anatomy, U. Chgo., 1958, MD, 1960; PhD, U. Minn., 1965. Intern Mpls. Gen. Hosp., 1961-62; resident U. Minn. Hosps., 1962-65; asst. chief neurology Mpls. Gen. Hosp., 1965-69; chief neurology St. Luke's Episcopal Hosp., Houston, 1970-85; pres., CEO Tex. Neurol. Clinic Assn., Houston, 1969—. Staff sgt. USAF, 1951-55. Recipient Disting. Teaching award Minn. Med. Found., Mpls., 1969. Fellow Am. Acad. Neurology, Am. Coll. Physicians; mem. AMA, Tex. Neurol. Soc. (9th dist.), Tex. Med. Assn. (pres. 1991), Alpha Omega Alpha, Sigma Xi. Roman Catholic. Avocation: ranching. Office: Tex Neurol Clinic Assn 5620 Greenbriar St Ste 203 Houston TX 77005-2659

RILEY-DAVIS, SHIRLEY MERLE, advertising agency executive, marketing consultant, writer; b. Pitts., Feb. 4, 1935; d. William Riley and Beatrice Estelle (Whittaker) Byrd; m. Louis Davis; 1 child, Terri Judith. Student U. Pitts., 1952. Copywriter, Pitts. Mercantile Co., 1954-60; exec. sec. U. Mich., Ann Arbor, 1962-67; copy supr. N.W. Ayer, N.Y.C., 1968-76, assoc. creative dir., Chgo., 1977-81; copy supr. Leo Burnett, Chgo., 1981-86; freelance advt. and mktg. cons., 1986—; advt. and mktg. dir. Child and Family Svc., Ypsilanti, Mich., 1992-96; vis. prof. Urban League Black Exec. Exch. Program; print, radio, and TV commercials; bd. dirs. Sr. Housing Bur., Ann Arbor; mem. adv. bd. Cmty. Diabetes, past bd. dirs. People's Hope for Housing, Ypsilanti, Mich. Recipient Grand and First prize N.Y. Film Festival, 1973, Gold and Silver medal Atlanta Film Festival, 1973, Gold medal V.I. Film Festival, 1974, 50 Best Creatives award Am. Inst. Graphic Arts, 1972, Clio award, 1973, 74, 75, Andy Award of Merit, 1981, Silver medal Internat. Film Festival, 1982, Corp. Mgmt. Assistance Program award, 1986, Good Sam award 1981, Svc. Advt. Creativity of Distinction cert., 1981; Senatorial scholar. Bd. dirs. Housing bur. for Srs. of the U. Mich. Med. Ctr., 1995—. Mem. Women in Film, Facets Multimedia Film Theatre Orgn. (past bd. dirs.), Greater Chgo. Coun. for Prevention of Child Abuse, Internat. Platform Assn., Epilepsy Found. Chgo. (past bd. dirs.). Democrat. Roman Catholic. Avocations: dance, poetry, design, writing, volunteering. Office: 1954 S Industrial Hwy # A Ann Arbor MI 48104-4625

RILEY-SCOTT, BARBARA POLK, retired librarian; b. Roselle, N.J., Nov. 21, 1928; d. Charles Carrington and Olive Bond P.; AB, Howard U., 1950; BS, N.J. Coll. Women, 1951; MS, Columbia U., 1955; m. George Emerson Riley, Feb. 23, 1957 (dec.); children: George E., Glenn C., Karen O.; m. William I. Scott, Oct. 6, 1990. Asst. librarian, Fla. A&M U., 1951-53; with Morgan State Coll., 1955; with Dept. Def., 1955-57, S.C. State Coll., 1957-59, U.Wis., 1958-59; asst. librarian Atlanta U., 1960-68; asst. dir. Union County Anti Poverty Council, 1968; librarian Union County Tech. Inst., Scotch Plains, N.J., 1968-82, Plainfield campus Union County Coll., 1982-95; ret., 1995. Mem. Roselle Bd. Edn., 1976-78; bd. dirs. Union County Anti Poverty Council, 1969-72; mem. Roselle Human Relations Commn., 1971-73, Plainfield Sci. Center, 1974-76, Union County Psychiat. Clinic, 1980-83, Pinewood Sr. Citizens Council, 1981-85; bd. dirs. Project, Women of N.J, 1985-93, Pinewood Sr. Citizen Housing, 1981-85, Black Women's History Conf., 1985-92, pres., 1989-91. Mem. N.J. Library Assn., Council Library Tech., ALA (Black caucas), N.J. Coalition of 100 Black Women, African Am. Women's Polit. Caucus, N.J. Black Librarians Network (bd. dirs.), Links, Inc. (North Jersey chpt.), Black Women's History Conf., Alpha Kappa Alpha. Mem. A.M.E. Ch. Club: Just-A-Mere Lit. Home: 114 E 7th Ave Roselle NJ 07203-2028

RILL, JAMES FRANKLIN, lawyer; b. Evanston, Ill., Mar. 4, 1933; s. John Columbus and Frances Eleanor (Hill) R.; m. Mary Elizabeth Laws, June 14, 1957; children: James Franklin, Roderick M. AB cum laude, Dartmouth Coll., 1954; LLB, Harvard, 1959. Bar: D.C. bar 1959. Legis. asst. Congressman James P. S. Devereux, Washington, 1952; pvt. practice Washington, 1959-89; assoc. Steadman, Collier & Shannon, 1959-63; ptnr. Collier, Shannon & Rill, 1963-69, Collier, Shannon, Rill & Scott, 1969-89; asst. atty. gen., antitrust div. U.S. Dept. Justice, Washington, 1989-92; ptnr. Collier, Shannon, Rill & Scott, Washington, 1992—; pub. mem. Adminstrv. Conf. of U.S., 1992-94; coun. prin. Coun. for Excellence in Govt.; mem., advisor panel Office of Tech. Assessment of Multinat. Firms and U.S. Tech. Base. Contbr. articles to profl. jours. Trustee Bullis Sch., Potomac, Md. Served to 1st lt. arty. AUS, 1954-56. Mem. ABA (founder antitrust law sect. spl. com., mem. coun., past chmn. sect. of antitrust law), D.C. Bar Assn., Phi Delta Theta, Met. Club, Loudon Valley Club. Home: 7305 Masters Dr Potomac MD 20854 Office: Collier Shannon Rill & Scott 3050 K St NW Ste 400 Washington DC 20007-5100

RILLA, DONALD ROBERT, social services administrator; b. Feb. 6, 1941. AS, Berkshire Community Coll., Pittsfield, Mass., 1964; BA, U. Mass., 1967; MSW, U. Conn., 1974. Lic. clin. social worker, Conn.; diplomate Am. Bd. Clin. Social Work. Social worker Children and Youth Svcs., New Haven, Conn., 1967-73, Branford (Conn.) Counseling Ctr., 1973-74; psychiatric social worker Whiting Forensic Inst., Middletown, Conn., 1974-79; psychiatric social worker supr. Cts. Diagnostic Clinic, Hartford, Conn., 1979-87; dir. Bridgeport (Conn.) Ct. Clinic, 1987-97; cons. Bridgeport Mental Health Ctr., 1990-97. Contbr. articles to profl. jours. Chair Town-Bus Safety Commn., North Haven, 1975; mem. Mental Health Assn. Conn., New Haven, 1968-75; chair, mem. New Haven Halfway House, 1969-73. With USN, 1958-62. Mem. NASW, Nat. Orgn. Forensic Social Work (founding mem. 1983—, chair ethics com. 1985—,, treas. 1994-95, pres.- elect 1995, pres. 1996), Acad. Cert. Social Workers, Acad. Forensic Social Workers (diplomate, bd. dirs.), Lion's Club. Avocations: photography, sports, volunteering, Spl. Olympics. Office: 109 Kings Hwy E Fairfield CT 06432-4844 also: Family Resource Assocs Stratford CT 06497

RILLING, DAVID CARL, surgeon; b. Phila., Oct. 10, 1940; s. Carl Adam and Elizabeth Barbara (Young) R.; m. Karina Sturman, Mar. 25, 1972; children: Jonathan David, Alexander Valentine, Claudia Carla. BS with honors in Biology, Dickinson Coll., Carlisle, pa., 1962; MD, Hahnemann U., 1966. Diplomate Am. Bd. Surgery. Intern Hosp. of U. Pa., Phila., 1966-67; resident Abington (Pa.) Meml. Hosp., 1967-68, 70-73; surgeon Pennridge Surg Assocs., Sellersville, Pa., 1973—; active staff Grand View Hosp., Sellersville, Pa., chmn. dept. surgery, 1985-89, pres. med. staff, 1995. Lt. col. U.S. Army, 1968-70, Vietnam, USARMC. Decorated Bronze Star medal, Nat. Def. Svc. medal, Vietnam Svc. medal. Fellow Am. Coll. Surgeons; mem. AMA, Soc. Clin. Vascular Surgery, Pa. Med. Soc., Bucks County Med. Soc., Vietnam Vascular Registry. Avocations: paleontology, tennis, skiing. Office: Pennridge Surg Assocs 670 Lawn Ave Sellersville PA 18960-1571

RILLING, JOHN ROBERT, history educator; b. Wausau, Wis., Apr. 28, 1932; s. John Peter and Esther Laura (Wittig) R.; m. Joanne Marilyn McCrory, Dec. 21, 1953; children—Geoffrey Alan, Andrew Peter. B.A. summa cum laude, U. Minn., 1953; A.M., Harvard U., 1957, Ph.D., 1959. Asst. prof. history U. Richmond, Va., 1959-62, assoc. prof. history, 1962-68, prof. history, 1968—, chmn. dept. history, 1977-83; chmn. Westhampton Coll. dept. history, 1965-71; pres. Faculty Senate of Va., 1975-77. Elder Ginter Park Presbyn. Ch., 1973-83. Served with U.S. Army, 1953-55. Woodrow Wilson fellow, 1955-59; Harvard U. Travelling fellow, 1958; Coolidge fellow, 1955-56; Folger Library fellow, 1960; recipient U. Richmond Disting. Educator award, 1975, 76, 77, 80, 87, Prof. of Yr. finalist Coun. for the Advancement and Support of Edn., 1981 Mem. Am. Hist. Assn., Econ. History Soc., Conf. Brit. Studies, Phi Beta Kappa, Omicron Delta Kappa (prof. of yr. 1995). Contbr. articles to profl. jours. Avocations: hiking, bicycling, enology. Home: 1507 Wilmington Ave Richmond VA 23227-4429 Office: U Richmond Dept History Richmond VA 23173

RIMA, INGRID HAHNE, economics educator; d. Max F. and Hertha G. (Grunsfeld) Hahne; m. Philip W. Rima; children: David, Eric. BA with honors, CUNY, 1945; MA, U. Pa., 1946, PhD, 1951. Prof. econs. Temple U., Phila., 1967—. Author: Development of Economic Analysis, 1967, 5th edit., 1996, Labor Markets Wages and Employment, 1981, The Joan Robinson Legacy, 1991, The Political Economy of Global Restructuring, Vol. I, Production and Organization, Vol. II, Trade and Finance, 1993, Measurement, Quantification and Economic Analysis, 1994, Labor Markets in a Global Economy, 1996. Fellow Ea. Econ. Assn.; mem. Am. Econ. Assn., History of Econs. Soc. (pres. 1993-4), Phi Beta Kappa. Office: Temple U Broad & Montgomery Ave Philadelphia PA 19122

RIMBACH, EVANGELINE LOIS, retired music educator; b. Portland, Oreg., June 28, 1932; d. Raymond Walter and Viola Clara (Gaebler) Rimbach. BA, Valparaiso (Ind.) U., 1954; MMus, Eastman Sch. Music, Rochester, N.Y., 1956; PhD, Eastman Sch. Music, 1967; student, Pacific Luth. U., Parkland, Wash., 1950-52. Vocal music instr. Goodwin Jr. High Sch., Redwood City, Calif., 1956-57; music instr. Calif. Concordia Coll., Oakland, Calif., 1957-62; prof. music Concordia U., River Forest, Ill., 1964-97, chmn. dept., 1989-97; ret., 1997. Contbg. editor: Church Music, 1965-80; editor book: Johann Kuhnau: Magnificat, 1980; editor cantata: Johann Kuhnau: Lobe den Herrn, 1993; contbr. articles to profl. jours. Bd. dirs. Civic Symphony of Oak Park-River Forest, 1974-80, concert com. chmn., 1976-78, prog. annotator, 1976-80; mem. choir Grace Luth. Ch., River Forest, 1964—. AAUW postdoctoral fellow, 1969-70; DAAD grantee, Munich, 1980; recipient Rose of Honor award, Sigma Alpha Iota, 1987. Mem. Am. Musicol. Soc., Am. Recorder Soc., Luth. Edn. Assn., Sigma Alpha Iota (Rose of Dedication award 1997). Republican. Lutheran. Avocations: travel, cooking, needlework. Home: 1115 Bonnie Brae Pl River Forest IL 60305-1515

RIMEL, REBECCA WEBSTER, foundation executive. BS, U. Va., 1973; MBA, James Madison U., 1983. RN, Va. Head nurse, emergency dept. U. Va. Hosp., Charlottesville, 1973-74, coord. med. out-patient dept., 1974-75, nurse practitioner dept. neurosurgery, 1975-77, instr. in neurosurgery, 1975-80, asst. prof., 1981-83; program mgr. health Pew Charitable Trusts, Phila., 1983-84; asst. v.p. Glenmede Trust Co., Pew Charitable Trusts, Phila., 1984-85; v.p. for programs Pew Charitable Trusts, Phila., 1985-88, exec. dir., 1988-94; pres., 1994—; mem. Coun. on Founds., Washington; prin. investigator dept. neurosurgery U. Va., 1981-83; adv. com. for U.S. Olympics on Boxing, 1983-86; adv. coun. Nat. Inst. of Neurol. Disorders and Strokes, 1988-91, also bd. dirs.; bd. dirs. Thomas Jefferson Meml. Found., Alex. Brown Flag Investors Funds, Coun. on Founds. Contbr. articles and abstracts to profl. jours., chpts. in books. Recipient Disting. Nursing Alumni award U. Va., 1988; Kellogg Nat. fellow, 1982. Mem. APHA, ANA, Va. State Nurses Assn. (membership and credentials com. 1982-86), Am. Acad. Nursing, Am. Assn. Neurosurg. Nurses, Emergency Dept. Nurses Assn.

RIMER, JOHN THOMAS, foreign language educator, academic administrator, writer, translator; b. Pitts., Mar. 2, 1933; s. John T. and Naomi (Bowser) R.; m. Laurence E. Mus., Apr. 18, 1964; children: John, Mark. B.A., Princeton U., 1954; M.A., Columbia U., 1969, Ph.D., 1971. Asst. cultural officer USIA, Laos, Japan; then dir. Am. Cultural Ctr. Kobe, Japan, 1958-67; assoc. prof., then prof. Japanese lang. and lit. Washington U., St. Louis, 1973-83, chmn. dept. Chinese and Japanese, 1973-83; chief Asian div. Library of Congress, Washington, 1983-86; chmn. Hebrew and East Asian langs. and lits. U. Maryland, College Park, 1986-91; chmn. East Asian langs. and lits. U. Pitts., 1991—; mem. Am. adv. bd. Japan Found., 1984—. Author: Toward a Modern Japanese Theatre, 1974, Traditions in Modern Japanese Fiction, 1978; translator: stories Mori Ogai, 2 vols., 1977, Mask and Sword: Two Plays for the Contemporary Japanese Theatre, 1980, On the No Drama, 1983, Pilgrimages, 1988, A Reader's Guide to Japanese Literature, 1988; editor: Multiple Meanings, 1987; editor, contbr.: Culture and Identity, Japanese Intellectuals during the Interwar Years, 1990, Shisendo, 1991, Youth and Other Stories by Mori Ogai, 1994, Kyoto Encounters, 1995, A Hidden Fire: Russian and Japanese Cultural Encounters, 1868-1929, 1995. Served with U.S. Army, 1955-58. NEH fellow France, 1976-77; NEH grantee, 1979-81. Mem. Social Sci. Research Council (joint com. on Japan studies 1979-83). Episcopalian. Home: 1400 N Negley Ave Pittsburgh PA 15206-1118 Office: U Pitts Dept East Asian Langs and Lits 1501 CL Pittsburgh PA 15260

RIMERMAN, IRA STEPHEN, banker; b. N.Y.C., Apr. 28, 1938; s. Samuel David and Dorothy (Hoffman) R.; m. Iris Jacqueline, Mar. 10, 1962; children: Traci, Randi-Sue, Judith. BA in Indsl. Engring., Syracuse U., 1960; MBA, U. Pa., 1961; profl. degree indsl. engring., Columbia U., 1968. Tech. data processor ITT, Paramus, N.J., 1962-65, CBS, N.Y.C., 1965-67, Allied Chem., N.Y.C., 1967-69, Computer Usage Corp., N.Y.C., 1969-71; data processing mgr. Citicorp, N.Y.C., 1971; CFO Citicorp subs. Citicorp, Columbus, Ohio, 1971-73; dir., v.p. econ. devel. ctr. Citicorp, N.Y.C., 1974-75, chief of staff, v.p. N.Y. banking group, 1975-76; bus. mgr., v.p. consumer bus. Citicorp, Hong Kong, 1976-81; div. head bank cards Citibank USA div. Citicorp, N.Y.C., 1981-85, group exec. comsumer svc. internat., 1985-87, group exec. card products, 1987-89, sr. v.p. adminstrn., 1989—, sr. v.p., 1992—; sr. account mgr. for Citicorp Wharton Bus. Sch. U. Pa., Phila., 1986—. Trustee The Cmty. Synagogue, 1982-88; bd. dirs. Vis. Nurse Svc., N.Y., treas., 1987—, chmn. fin. com., 1988—; bd. dirs. Beth Israel Med. Ctr., 1989—; mem. Wharton Grad. Exec. Bd., 1989-95; bd. dirs. Wharton Entrepreneurial Ctr., 1990-96. Mem. Am. Inst. Indsl. Engrs., Film Soc. N.Y. (bd. dirs. 1996—), Wharton Alumni Assn. (bd. dirs. 1976-89), Hong Kong Club. Democrat. Jewish. Avocations: swimming, reading. Home: 63 Sands Point Rd Sands Point NY 11050-1645 Office: Citicorp Center 23rd Fl Zone 1 153 E 53rd St New York NY 10022-4611

RIMLAND, LISA PHILLIP, writer, composer, lyricist, artist; b. Stamford, Conn., Mar. 27, 1954; d. Maurice Louis and Eva (Kreiz) R. BA, U. Conn., 1978. Owner Ph Rimland Press, Storrs, Conn., 1991—. Composer numerous songs, including Your Heart or Mine, 1990, Drive Me Crazy, 1991, Send Me an Angel, 1992; contbr. articles, poems, essays to profl. jours. Vol. dairy barn U. Conn., 1992—, vol. photographer Morgan horse facility, 1982-91. Recipient DAR award, 1969, Soc. Women Engrs. award, 1971, Editor's Choice award Nat. Libr. Poetry, 1995, 96; Nat. Merit scholar, 1972. Mem. ASCAP. Avocations: film and drama, art, poetry, athletics, Morgan horses. Home: PO Box 408 Storrs Mansfield CT 06268-0408

RIMMEREIDE, ARNE MAGNAR, engineering executive; b. Fitjar, Norway, Mar. 31, 1963; came to U.S., 1987; s. Torvald and Borghild R. BSME, S.D. Mines and Tech., 1989. Engring. mgr. Vikron Tech., Inc., St. Croix, Wis., 1990-96, DRS Ahead Technology, Inc., St. Croix Falls, Wis., 1996—. With Norwegian Navy, 1984-85. Mem. Am. Soc. Quality Control, Norwegian Am. Tech. Soc. Avocation: soccer. Home: 5037 Drew Ave S Minneapolis MN 55410-2026 Office: Vikron 520 Blanding Woods Rd Saint Croix Falls WI 54024-9001

RIMOIN, DAVID LAWRENCE, physician, geneticist; b. Montreal, Nov. 9, 1936; s. Michael and Fay (Lecker) R.; m. Mary Ann Singleton, 1962 (div. 1979); 1 child, Anne; m. Ann Pilani Garber, July 27, 1980; children: Michael, Lauren. BSc, McGill U., Montreal, 1957, MSc, MD, CM, 1961; PhD, Johns Hopkins U., 1967; LHD (hon.), Finch U., 1997. Asst. prof. medicine, pediatrics Washington U., St. Louis, 1967-70; assoc. prof. medicine, pediatrics UCLA, 1970-73, prof., 1973—, chief med. genetics, Harbor-UCLA Med. Ctr., 1970-86; dir. dept. pediatrics, dir. Med. Genetics and Birth Defects Ctr., 1986—; Steven Spielberg chmn. pediatrics Cedars-Sinai Med. Ctr., L.A., 1989—; chmn. coun. Med. Genetics Orgn., 1993. Coauthor: Principles and Practice of Medical Genetics, 1983, 90, 96; contbr. articles to profl. jours., chpts. to books. Recipient Ross Outstanding Young Investigator award Western Soc. Pediatric Research, 1976, E. Mead Johnson award Am. Acad. Pediatrics, 1976, Col. Harland Saunders award March of Dimes, 1997. Fellow ACP, AAAS, Am. Coll. Med. Genetics (pres. 1991—); mem. Am. Fedn. Clin. Rsch. (sec.-treas. 1972-75), Western Soc. Clin. Rsch. (pres. 1978), Western Soc. Pediatric Rsch. (pres. 1995), Am. Bd. Med. Genetics (pres. 1979-83), Am. Soc. Human Genetics (pres. 1984), Am. Pediatric Soc., Soc. Pediatric Rsch., Am. Soc. Clin. Investigation, Assn. Am. Physicians, Johns Hopkins Soc. Scholars, Inst. Medicine. Office: Cedars-Sinai Med Ctr 8700 Beverly Blvd Los Angeles CA 90048-1804

RIMPEL, AUGUSTE EUGENE, JR., management and technical consulting executive; b. St. Thomas, V.I., Aug. 25, 1939; s. Auguste Eugene and Leah Eudora (Harris) R. B.A. magna cum laude, Inter-Am. U. P.R., 1957; M.S. in Ch.E., M.I.T., 1961; Ph.D., Carnegie Inst. Tech., 1964; M.B.A., Columbia U., 1964-65; m. Maria Czernetski, Sept. 23, 1966; children: Nicole, Christopher. Research chem. engr. Am. Cyanamid Co., Stamford, Conn., 1961-62; with Arthur D. Little, Inc., Cambridge, Mass., 1965-75, sr. staff mem., 1973-75; commr. of commerce, spl. advisor to gov. for econ. affairs Govt. U.S. V.I., St. Thomas, 1975-78; mem. corp. spl. staff Arthur D. Little, Inc., Cambridge, 1978-81, also v.p. Arthur D. Little Internat., Inc.; v.p. Booz-Allen and Hamilton, Inc., 1981-83; v.p., ptnr., Price Waterhouse, 1983—. Bd. dirs. Caribbean/Lat. Am. Action, 1979-94; mem. U.S. del. World Bank Conf. on Caribbean Econ. Devel., 1977-78; mem. subcoms. on internat. econ. devel. U.S. C. of C., 1980-83; V.I. rep. White Ho. Conf. on Balanced Nat. Growth and Econ. Devel., 1978; bd. dirs. travel adv. bd. U.S. Dept. Commerce, 1977-78; pres. Caribbean Tourism Assn., 1977-78; bd. dirs., mem. exec. com. Caribbean Tourism Research Center, 1976-78. Mem. Am. Inst. Chem. Engrs., Am. Chem. Soc., Am. Inst. Chemists, Soc. Internat. Devel., Sigma Xi. Office: 1616 Fort Myer Dr Arlington VA 22209-3100

RIMPILA, CHARLES ROBERT, physician; b. Chgo., June 28, 1945; s. Charles Einar and Verna Catherine (Swanson) R.; m. Ellen D. McSweeney; children: Charles Edward, Erica, Darren, Alison. BA, North Park Coll., 1968; MD, Chgo. Med. Sch., 1972. Emergency physician Riverview Hosp., 1987—; med. dir. Consolidated Papers, Inc., 1994—; instr. Mid. State Tech. Coll., 1992—; co-med. dir. South Wood County (Wis.) EMS, 1992-97. Mem. AMA, Am. Coll. Emergency Medicine, Am. Coll. Occupational Medicine & Environ. Medicine. Avocations: skiing, bicycling, hiking, reading, travel.

RIMROTT, FRIEDRICH PAUL JOHANNES, engineer, educator; b. Halle, Germany, Aug. 4, 1927; emigrated to Can., 1952; s. Hans and Margarete (Hofmeister) R.; m. Doreen McConnell, Apr. 7, 1955; children: Karla, Robert, Kira, Elizabeth-Ann. Dipl. Ing., U. Karlsruhe, Germany, 1951; MASc, U. Toronto, Ont., Can., 1955; PhD, Pa. State U., 1958; Dr Ing., Tech. U., Darmstadt, Germany, 1961; P.Eng., Ontario Prov., 1954; C.Eng., U.K., 1987; D.Eng. (hon.), U. Victoria, 1992; DSc (hon.), St. Petersburg State U., 1996; Dr.Ing. (hon.), Otto-von-Guericke-U., Magdeburg, 1997. Asst. prof. engring. mechanics Pa. State U., 1958-60; mem. faculty dept. mech. engring. U. Toronto, 1960—, assoc. prof., 1962-67, prof., 1967-93, prof. emeritus, 1993—; vis. prof. Tech. U. Vienna, Austria, 1969-70, 86, Tech. U. Hanover, Germany, 1970, U. Bochum, Germany, 1971, U. Wuppertal, Germany, 1987, 89, U. Lanzhou, People's Republic of China, 1989, Otto-von-Guericke-U. Magdeburg, 1992, 93, 94, 95, 96; mng. dir. German Lang. Sch. (Metro Toronto) Inc., 1967-91; pres. 15th Internat. Congress Theoretical and Applied Mechanics, 1980; pres. CSME Mech. Engring. Forum, 1990. Author: Introductory Attitude Dynamics, 1988, Introductory Orbit Dynamics, 1989, (with K.Y. Yeh) Orbital Mechanics Introduction, Chinese edit., 1993, (with B. Tabarrok) Variational Methods and Complementary Formulations in Dynamics, 1994, (with Yongxi Yu) Satellite Gyrodynamics, Chinese edit., 1996; editor: (with J. Schwaighofer) Mechanics of the Solid State, 1968, (with L.E. Jones) Proceedings CANCAM 67, 1968, (with J.T. Pindera, H.H.E. Leipholz, D.E. Grierson) Experimental Mechanics in Research and Development, 1973, (with W. Eichenlaub) Was Du erbst, 1978, (with B. Tabarrok) Theoretical and Applied Mechanics, 1980. Mem. Can. Council on Multiculturalism, 1972-79. NRC postdoctoral fellow, 1959, Alexander von Humboldt sr. fellow, 1962, NRC sr. rsch. fellow, 1969-70; recipient Can. Congress Applied Mechanics award, 1989, Alexander von Humboldt Rsch. prize, 1997. Fellow ASME, Instn. Mech. Engrs., Engring. Inst. Can., Can. Soc. Mech. Engring. (pres. 1974-75), Can. Aero. and Space Inst.; mem. Can. Congress Applied Mechanics (ctrl. com., chmn. congress com. 1967, 69, 71, 77), Can. Metric Assn. (pres. 1971-72), Soc. German Engrs. (Germany), Soc. for Applied Math. and Mechanics (Germany) (dir. 1971-79). Home: 6 Thurgate Cres, Thornhill, ON Canada L3T 4G3 Office: U Toronto, Dept Mech Engring and, Indsl Engring, Toronto, ON Canada M5S 3G8

RIMSZA, SKIP, mayor; b. Chgo.; m. Kim Gill; children: Brian, Jenny, Alexander, Taylor, Nicole. Mem. Phoenix City Coun., 1990-94; vice mayor City of Phoenix, 1993, mayor, 1994—; former pres. Bd. Realtors. Mem. several cmty. bds. Office: Office of the Mayor 11th Fl 200 W Washington St Phoenix AZ 85003-1611

RINALDINI, LUIS EMILIO, investment banker; b. Cambridge, Eng., July 29, 1953; came to U.S., 1964; s. Luis Maria and Fanny Josefina (Lopez) R.; m. Elaine Nash McHugh, June 22, 1974 (div. 1987); m. Julie Sayre Short, Aug. 1, 1987. BSE, Princeton U., 1974; MBA, Harvard U., 1980. Architect Johnson Burgee Architects, N.Y.C., 1974-78; assoc. Lazard Freres & Co. LLC, N.Y.C., 1980-85, mng. dir., 1986—. Mem. Piping Rock Club (Locust Valley, N.Y.), Meadowbrook Club (Jericho, N.Y.), Lyford Cay Club (Bahamas), Raquet and Tennis Club (N.Y.C.). Home: 151 Post Rd Old Westbury NY 11568 Office: Lazard Freres & Co LLC 30 Rockefeller Plz New York NY 10112

RINAMAN, JAMES CURTIS, JR., lawyer; b. Miami, Fla., Feb. 8, 1935; s. James Curtis and Ruth Marie (Rader) R.; m. Gloria Margaret Kaspar; children: James, Mark, Christine, Karen. BA, U. Fla., 1955, JD, 1960. Bar: Fla. 1960, U.S. Dist. Ct. (so. dist.) Fla. 1960, U.S. Ct. Appeals (5th cir.)

1960, U.S. Supreme Ct. 1963, U.S. Dist. Ct. (mid. dist.) Fla. 1967, U.S. Dist. Ct. (no. dist.) Fla. 1981, U.S. Ct. Appeals (11th cir.) 1981, U.S. Ct. Claims 1991, U.S. Ct. Mil. Appeals 1994; cert. civil trial lawyer Fla. Bar. With Marks, Gray, Conroy & Gibbs, P.A., Jacksonville, Fla., 1960—; gen. counsel Fla. Bd. Architecture, 1965-79, City of Jacksonville, 1970-71, Jacksonville C. of C., 1973-76, 90; adj. prof. Coll. Architecture, U. Fla., 1975-90. Pres. Jacksonville Cmty. Coun. Inc., 1985. Leadership Jacksonville, Inc., 1987; mem. Jacksonville Transp. Authority, 1971-80, Jacksonville Base Realignment and Closure Commn., 1993-95. Jacksonville Cecil Field Devel. Commn., 1994-96; chmn. N.E. Fla. chpt. ARC, 1996. With U.S. Army, 1955-57, Fla. NG, 1957-92. ret. brig. gen., 1992. Named to U. Fla. Hall of Fame. Fellow Am. Coll. Trial Lawyers, Am. Bar Found., Fla. Bar Found. (bd. dirs. 1982-87, 88, Disting. Svc. award 1983, 86, Medal of Honor 1988); mem. ABA (ho. of dels. 1982-86), Jacksonville Bar Assn. (pres. 1972-73), The Fla. Bar (pres. 1982-83), Def. Rsch. Inst. (so. regional v.p. 1980-83, bd. dirs. 1976-78, 83-87), Am. Judicature Soc. (Herbert Harley award 1987), Fla. Coun. Bar Pres. (Outstanding Past Pres. award 1989), Lawyers for Civil Justice (pres. 1989-91, chmn. bd. dirs. 1991-94), Vol. Lawyers Resource Ctr. of Fla., (pres. 1984-89, chmn. bd. dirs. 1989-93), So. Conf. of Bar (pres.), Nat. Conf. of Bar (pres.), Assn. Def. Trial Attys. (internat. pres. 1976-77), Internat. Assn. Def. Counsel, Jacksonville Assn. Def. Counsel, Fla. Defense Lawyers Assn. (pres. 1973), Fla. C. of C., Jacksonville C. of C. (chmn. 1994), Meninack Civic Club (pres. 1986), Jacksonville Commodores League, Fla. Blue Key, San. Jose Country Club, River Club, Univ. Club, Phi Gamma Delta (bd. trustees ednl. found. 1995—), Phi Alpha Delta. Republican. Methodist. Office: Marks Gray Conroy & Gibbs 1200 Riverplace Blvd Ste 800 Jacksonville FL 32207-1805 also: PO Box 447 Jacksonville FL 32201-0447

RINDEN, DAVID LEE, editor; b. Lake Mills, Iowa, Aug. 1, 1941; s. Oscar Henry and Iva (Stensrud) R.; m. Gracia Elizabeth Carlson, Sept. 11, 1966; children: Jonathan, Elizabeth, Amy. BA, Moorhead State U., 1964; diploma, Luth. Brethren Sem., 1966; postgrad., Seattle Pacific U., 1973. Ordained to ministry Luth. Ch., 1967. Pastor Bethesda Luth. Ch., Eau Claire, Wis., 1968-72, Maple Pk. Luth. Ch., Lynnwood, Wash., 1972-79; v.p. Ch. of the Luth. Brethren, Fergus Falls, Minn., 1991—; editor Faith & Fellowship, Fergus Falls, Minn., 1979—; exec. dir. ch. svcs. Ch. of the Luth. Brethren, Fergus Falls, 1979—; chmn. com. on commitment Ch. of Luth. Brethren, Fergus Falls, 1981-82, com. on role of women in ch., 1984-86, chmn. com. on 90th anniversary, 1989—, chmn. bd. publs., 1968-78. Editor: Explanation of Luther's Small Catechism, 1988; author: Biblical Foundations, 1981. Founding com. JAIL, Inc., Fergus Falls, 1991; pres. bd. dirs. Fergus Falls Fed. Community Credit Union, 1987—. Mem. Fergus Falls Ministerial Assn. (sec. 1989-90, v.p. 1991-92, pres. 1992-93), Kiwanis (pres. 1994-95, lt. gov. 1996-97). Home: 701 W Channing Ave Fergus Falls MN 56537-3218 Office: Ch of the Luth Brethren # 655 1026 W Alcott Ave # 655 Fergus Falls MN 56537-2641

RINDER, GEORGE GREER, retired retail company executive; b. Chgo., Feb. 3, 1921; s. Carl Otto and Jane (Greer) R.; m. Shirley Laurine Latham, Dec. 21, 1946; children: Robert Latham, Carl Thomas, Susan Jane Sitrick. M.B.A., U. Chgo., 1942. C.P.A., Ill. With Gen. Electric Co., 1941-42; with Marshall Field & Co., Chgo., 1946-86; asst. to gen. mgr. Marshall Field & Co., 1959-62, v.p., comptroller, 1962-67, v.p. finance, 1967-71, exec. v.p. fin., 1971-74, exec. v.p., 1974-78, sr. exec. v.p., 1978-81, vice chmn., 1981-86, dir., 1972-83; ret., 1986; mem. adv. bd. Spectrum Group. Mem. adv. coun. McCormick Theol. Sem.; mem. coun. Grad. Sch. Bus., U. Chgo; mem. assocs. bd. Met. Family Svcs., Chgo. Served to capt. AUS, 1942-46. Recipient Alumni Svc. citation U. Chgo., 1990, Alumni Svc. medal U. Chgo., 1995. Mem. Fin. Execs. Inst., Phi Beta Kappa, Delta Upsilon, Beta Gamma Sigma. Clubs: Chicago (Chgo.), University (Chgo.), Economic (Chgo.); Hinsdale (Ill.) Golf.). Home: 169 Pheasant Hollow Dr Burr Ridge IL 60521-5050

RINDERKNECHT, ROBERT EUGENE, internist; b. Dover, Ohio, Apr. 27, 1921; s. Henry Carl and Mary Dorothy (Walter) R.; m. Janice Marie Rausch, Oct. 14, 1966; children: Mary Ellen, William A., Janis E. BS, Case Western Reserve U., 1943, MD, 1945. Diplomate Am. Bd. Internal Medicine. Intern Grasslands Hosp., Valhalla, N.Y., 1945-46; resident U. Hosps. Cleve., 1948-49, VA Hosp., Cleve., 1949-51; internist pvt. practice, Dover, Ohio, 1951-79; ret., 1979; trustee Physicians Ins. Co. Ohio, Columbus, 1978-79. Pres. Tuscarawas County (Ohio) Heart Br., 1962-64, 75-77, East Ctrl. Ohio Heart Assn., Canton, 1967-69. Fellow ACP; mem. Masons, Shriners, Elks. Republican. Presbyterian. Home: 101 Dewitt Cir Daphne AL 36526-7740

RINDFUSS, RONALD RICHARD, sociology educator; b. Buffalo, Dec. 11, 1946; married Aug. 1968; 2 children. BA, Fordham U., 1968; PhD, Princeton U., 1974. Rsch. asst. Nat. Fertility Study, Office Population Rsch., Princeton U., 1971-73; rsch. assoc. Ctr. Demography and Ecology U. Wis., Madison, 1973-76; asst. prof. sociology U. N.C., Chapel Hill, 1976-79, assoc. prof., 1979-84; prof. sociology U. N.C., 1984—; dir. Carolina Population Ctr., Chapel Hill, 1992—; cons. in field. Contbr. numerous articles to profl. jours.; assoc. editor Social Forces, 1976—; cons. editor Am. Jour. Sociology, 1977-80; contbg. editor Sociol Biology, 1974; referee for numerous jours. NIH traineeship, 1968-71. Mem. Am. Sociol. Assn. (chmn. sociology of population sect. 1989-90, mem. pubs. com. 1983-84), Population Assn. Am. (pres. 1991, mem. Mindel C. Sheps award com. 1990, bd. dirs. 1984-87), Internat. Union for Sci. Study Population, Nat. Coun. on Family Rels., So. Regional Demographic Group, So. Sociol. Soc., Coun. on Family Rsch. Office: Carolina Population Ctr. CB # 8120 University Sq 123 W Franklin St Chapel Hill NC 27516-2524

RINDLAUB, JOHN WADE, advertising agency executive; b. Lancaster, Pa., July 26, 1934; s. Willard Weaner and Jean (Wade) R.; m. Laurette Lukens, June 22, 1956; children: John Wade, Curtis Clay, David Landis. BA, Yale U., 1956. Copywriter, supr. Young & Rubicam, N.Y.C., 1956-68; v.p., creative dir. Toronto, 1968-71; assoc. creative dir. N.Y.C., 1971-73; creative dir. Stockholm and Frankfurt, Fed. Republic Germany, 1973-77; mng. dir. Holter, Young & Rubicam, Oslo, 1977-78; assoc. dir. mktg. Young & Rubicam, N.Y.C., 1978-80, sr. v.p., mgr. creative services, 1980-84, assoc. creative dir., 1984-88, sr. v.p., dir. corp. rels., 1988-90, dir. industry and govt. rels., 1990—. Mem. Yale Club, Riverside Yacht Club. Episcopalian. Home: 8 Hill Lane Ave Riverside CT 06878-2500 Office: Young & Rubicam 285 Madison Ave New York NY 10017-6401

RINEARSON, PETER MARK, journalist, author, software developer; b. Seattle, Aug. 4, 1954; s. Peter Morley and Jeannette Irene (Love) R.; m. Jill Chan, Sept. 15, 1991. Student, U. Wash., 1972-78. Editor Sammamish Valley News, Redmond, Wash., 1975-76; reporter Seattle Times, 1976-78, govt. and polit. reporter, 1979-81, aerospace reporter, 1982-84, Asian corr., 1985-86; pres. Alki Software Corp., Seattle, 1990—, Raster Ranch, Ltd., 1995—; mem. vis. com. Sch. Comm., U. Wash., 1996—. Author: Word Processing Power with Microsoft Word, 4th edit., 1991, Microsoft Word Style Sheets, 1987, Quick Reference Guide to Microsoft Word, 1988, Microsoft Word Companion Disk, 1988, Masterword, 1990, 91, 92, (with Bill Gates and Nathan Myhrvold) The Road Ahead, 1995, rev. edit., 1996. Recipient Spl. Paul Myhre award-series Penney-Mo. Newspaper awards, 1983, Disting. Writing award Am. Soc. Newspaper Editors, 1984, Pulitzer prize for feature writing, 1984, Lowell Thomas Travel Writing award, 1984, John Hancock award,1985, semi-finalist NASA Journalist-in-Space Project, 1986; U.S.-Japan Leadership Program fellow Japan Soc., 1988. Office: 300 Queen Anne Ave N # 410 Seattle WA 98109-4599

RINEHART, CHARLES R., savings and loan association executive; b. San Francisco, Jan. 31, 1947; s. Robert Eugene and Rita Mary Rinehart; married; children: Joseph B., Kimberly D., Michael P., Scott. BS, U. San Francisco, 1968. Exec. v.p. Fireman's Fund Ins. Cos., Novato, Calif., 1969-83; pres., CEO Avco Fin. Services, Irvine, Calif., 1983-89, H.F. Ahmanson & Co., Irwindale, Calif., 1989—; chmn., CEO Home Savs. of Am., Irwindale; mem. Fannie Mae Nat. Adv. Coun., Thrift Instn. Adv. Coun.; bd. dirs. Fed. Home Loan Bank San Francisco, L.A. Bus. Advisors, Kaufman and Broad Home Corp. Mem. adv. com. Drug Use is Life Abuse; mem. Tustin Pub. Sch. Found. Camp com. Served to 2d lt. U.S. Army, 1968-69. Fellow Casualty Actuarial Soc.; mem. Am. Mgmt. Assn., Am. Acad. Actuaries. Republican. Roman Catholic. Avocations: athletics, gourmet cooking, model trains. Office: Ho Savs Am/H F Ahmanson & Co 4900 Rivergrade Rd Irwindale CA 91706-1404

RINEHART, KATHRYN ANN, principal; b. Eaton, Ohio, Nov. 15, 1948; d. Eugene Warner and Alice Kathryn (Eagle) Donson; m. Charles Edward Rinehart, Dec. 26, 1969. BS in Edn., Miami U., 1969, MEd, 1982, postgrad., 1982-85. Cert. local supt., high, middle, and elem. sch. prin., elem. tchr., vocat. home econs. tchr. Vocat. home econs. tchr. Twin Valley Local Schs., West Alexandria, Ohio, 1969-85; community edn. supr. Twin Valley Local Schs., West Alexandria, 1983-90, middle sch. prin., 1985-90; vocat. prin. Ohio Vets. Children's Home, 1991-95; prin. Broadmoor Acad. Trotwood-Madison City Schs., Ohio, 1995—. Author: (manual) Community Education, 1983; (curriculum guide) Career Education, 1985; editor, writer: Entrepreneurship, 1982. Active Preble County Lit. Coun., Eaton, Ohio, 1989. Mem. NAFE, ASCD, Nat. Assn. Elem. Sch. Adminstrs., Nat. Assn. Secondary Sch. Adminstrs., Ohio Assn. Elem. Sch. Adminstrs., Ohio Assn. Secondary Sch. Adminstrs., Ohio Community Edn. Assn. (Gold award 1987, v.p. 1989-92), Ohio Elem. Prins. (county rep. 1987-89). Avocations: sewing, music, crafts. Home: 4496 Sharpsburg Rd Eaton OH 45320-9433

RINES, JOHN RANDOLPH, automotive company executive; b. Balt., Aug. 3, 1947; s. John William and Betty (Singer) R.; m. Peggy J. Daugaard, Sept. 19, 1969 (dec. 1978); m. Katherine M. Duff, Nov. 29, 1980; children: Jacqueline D., Eleanor W. BS in Econs., Colo. State U., 1970; MBA, U. Va., 1977. With GM, 1970-75, 77—; fin. analyst GM, Detroit, 1977-78, dir. product programs, 1978-80, asst. to pres., 1980-81, gen. dir. fin., 1981-82; exec. dir. GM, Sao Paulo, Brazil, 1982-84; dir. fin. Buick/Oldsmobile/Cadillac group GM, Flint, Mich., 1984-85; gen. mgr. motors holding div. and GM auction GM, Detroit, 1985-91, gen. mgr. parts ops., 1991—; pres. GM Acceptance Corp., Detroit, 1992—. Trustee Arts Found. Mich., Detroit. Mem. Grosse Pointe (Mich.) Club, Old Club (Harsen's Island), Birmingham Athletic Club. Office: GM 3044 W Grand Blvd Detroit MI 48202-3037

RINES, S. MELVIN, investment banker; b. Berlin, N.H., Aug. 26, 1924; s. William James and Gladys Olive (Estes) R.; m. Mary Jo Marcy, Feb. 27, 1954; children: Pamela Marcy, Jeffrey William, David Melvin. BA, U. N.H., 1947; OD, No. Ill. Coll., 1950. Asst. v.p. Kidder, Peabody & Co., Inc., N.Y.C., 1970, v.p.,, 1972—, shareholder, 1973—; mng. dir. Kidder, Peabody & Co. Inc., 1986—, sr. v.p., mng. dir., 1986-95; adj. prof. Am. U., Washington, 1986—; chmn Rines Assocs., 1996—. Co-editor: The Supranationals, 1986; contbr. articles to profl. jours. Mem. Bretton Woods Com., Washington, 1987—; trustee U. N.H. Found., 1994—, exec. bd. Whittemore Sch. Bus. and Econs., 1995—. Lt., fighter pilot USN, 1943-46, 50-54, Korea. Mem. Boston Exec. Assn. (pres. 1970-71). Republican. Clubs: Downtown (pres. 1974-81), Bond (Boston) (pres. 1976-77); Met. (Washington); DTA (N.Y.). Avocations: tennis, skiing, sailing, swimming, riding. Home: 21 Sudbury Rd Weston MA 02193-1332 Office: Paine Webber Inc 100 Federal St Boston MA 02110-1802

RINEY, HAL PATRICK, advertising executive; b. Seattle, July 17, 1932; s. Hal Patrick and Inez Marie R.; m. Elizabeth Kennedy; children: Benjamin Kennedy, Samantha Elizabeth. BA, U. Wash., Seattle, 1954. From art dir./writer to v.p., creative dir. BBDO, Inc., San Francisco, 1956-72; exec. v.p., creative dir. Botsford Ketchum, San Francisco, 1972-76; sr. v.p., mng. dir., creative dir. Ogilvy & Mather, San Francisco, 1976-81; exec. v.p. Ogilvy & Mather West, 1981-86; chmn. Hal Riney & Ptnrs., Inc., San Francisco, 1986—. Recipient 5 Lion d'Or du Cannes awards, 17 Clio awards, 15 Addy awards, Grand Prix du Cannes; named to Creative Hall of Fame. Mem. Am. Assn. Advt. Agys., San Francisco Advt. Club, San Francisco Soc. Communicating Arts, Wild Goose Club, Meadow Club, St. Francis Yacht Club. Home: 1 Los Pinos Nicasio CA 94946-9701 Office: Hal Riney & Ptnrs Inc 735 Battery St San Francisco CA 94111-1501

RING, ALICE RUTH BISHOP, physician; b. Ft. Collins, Oct. 11, 1931; d. Ernest Otto and Mary Frances (Drohan) Bishop; m. Wallace Harold Ring, July 26, 1956 (div. 1969); children: Rebecca, Eric, Mark; m. Robert Charles Deifenbach, Sept. 10, 1977. BS, Colo. State U., 1953; MD, U. Colo., 1956; MPH, U. Calif., Berkeley, 1971. Physician cons. Utah State Divsn. Health, Salt Lake City, 1960-65; med. dir., project head start Salt Lake City Cmty. Action Program, 1965-70; resident Utah State Divsn. Health, 1969-71; asst. assoc. reg. health dir. USPHS, San Francisco, 1971-75; med. cons. USPHS, Atlanta, 1975-77, dir. primary care, 1977-84; dir. divsn. diabetes control Ctrs. Disease Control, Atlanta, 1984-88; dir. WHO Collabor Ctr., Atlanta, 1986-91; dir. preventive medicine residency Ctrs. Disease Control, Atlanta, 1988-93; exec. dir. Am. Bd. Preventive Medicine, 1993—; trustee Am. Bd. Preventive Medicine, 1990-92 (diplomate); lectr. Emory U. Sch. Pub. Health, 1988-94. Co-author: Clinical Diabetes, 1991. Bd. dirs. Diabetes Assn. Atlanta, 1985-90, med. adv. com., 1990-94. Fellow Am. Coll. Preventive Medicine (bd. dirs. 1990-94); mem. APHA, AMA (grad. med. edn. adv. com. 1993—), Assn. Tchrs. Preventive Medicine, Am. Acad. Pediatrics, Sigma Xi. Office: Am Bd Preventive Medicine 9950 Lawrence Ave Schiller Park IL 60176-1310

RING, ALVIN MANUEL, pathologist; b. Detroit, Mar. 17, 1933; s. Julius and Helen (Krolik) R.; m. Cynthia Joan Jacobson, Sept. 29, 1963; children—Jeffrey, Melinda, Heather. BS, Wayne State U., 1954; MD, U. Mich., 1958. Intern Mt. Carmel Hosp., Detroit, 1958-59; resident in pathology Michael Reese Hosp., Chgo., 1960-62; asst. pathologist Kings County Hosp., Bklyn., 1962-63; assoc. pathologist El Camino Hosp., Mountain View, Calif., 1963-65; chief pathologist, dir. labs. St. Elizabeth's Hosp., Chgo., 1965-72, Holy Cross Hosp., Chgo., 1972-87, Silver Cross Hosp., Joliet, Ill., 1990—; instr. SUNY, 1962-63, Stanford U., 1963-65; asst. prof. pathology U. Ill., Chgo., 1966-69, assoc. prof., 1969-78, prof., 1978—; adj. clin. prof. No. Ill. U., 1981-87; adj. prof. med. edn. U. Ill. Coll. Medicine, 1988—; chmn. histotech. Nat. Accrediting Agy. for Clin. Lab Scis., 1977-81; mem. spl. adv. com. Health Manpower, 1966-71; pres. Spear Computer Users Group, 1981-82; mem. adv. com. Mid-Am. chpt. ARC, 1979-85; pres. Pathology and Lab Cons., Inc., 1985—; adj. prof., med. dir. Med. Tech., Moraine Valley C.C., 1994—; originator, coord. pathology, med. decision-making courses Nat. Ctr. for Advanced Med. Edn., 1981—, others. Author: Laboratory Correlation Manual, 1968, 82, 86, Laboratory Assistant Examination Review Book, 1971, Review Book in Pathology, Anatomic, 1986, Review Book in Pathology, Clinical, 1986; mem. editorial bd. Lab. Medicine, 1975-87; contbr. articles to med. jours. Fellow Coll. Am. Pathology (insp. 1973—), Am. Soc. Clin. Pathology; mem. AMA, Ill. Med. Soc., Chgo. Med. Soc. (alt. councilor 1980-85, mem. adv. com. on health care delivery), Ill. Pathol. Soc., Chgo. Pathol. Soc. (censor 1980-88, exec. com. 1985-89, program. com. 1987—), Am. Assn. Blood Banks, Assn. Brain Tumor Rsch. (cons.), Exec. Svc. Corps (exec. cons. 1988—), Phi Lambda Kappa. Home: 100 Graymoor Ln Olympia Fields IL 60461-1213 Office: Silver Cross Hosp 1200 Maple Rd Joliet IL 60432-1439

RING, GERALD J., real estate developer, insurance executive; b. Madison, Wis., Oct. 6, 1928; s. John George and Mabel Sarah (Rau) R.; m. Armella Marie Dohm, Aug. 20, 1949; children: Michael J., James J., Joseph W. Student public schs., Madison. With Sub-Zero Freezer Co., Madison, 1948-70; mfr.'s rep. Sub-Zero Freezer Co., 1954-70; founder, pres. Parkwood Hills Corp., Madison, from 1965, Park Towne Devel. Corp., Madison, from 1969, Ring Devel. Co., 1992—; bd. dirs.. CUNA Mut. Ins. Soc., CUNA Mut. Ins. Group, CUNA Mut. Investment Corp., CUDIS Ins. Soc., all Madison, 1968—, exec. com., 1973-83, chmn. bd., 1979-81; bd. dirs. CUMIS Ins. Soc., mem. exec. com., 1973-83, chmn. bd., 1977-79; bd. dirs. CMCI Corp., mem. exec. com., 1974-83, chmn. bd., 1981-83; treas. CUNADATA Corp., 1974-81; bd. dirs. Wis. Credit Union League, 1958-79, pres., 1965-67; mem. Wis. Credit Union Rev. Bd., 1967-83, chmn., 1973-76, 82-83; bd. dirs. CUNA Credit Union Nat. Assn., Inc., 1964-81, League Life Ins. Co., League Gen. Ins. Co., Southfield, Mich., CUNA Mut. Fin. Svcs. Corp., Century Ins. Co. Am., Waverly., Iowa. Chmn. Greater Madison C. of C., 1980, bd. dirs., 1976-89, v.p. econ. devel., 1983-85, v.p. govtl. affairs, 1985-89, mem. capital fund raising com., 1983—, chmn. 1983-86; mem. Mayor's Emergency Housing Com., 1984-85; chmn. fin. com. St. Patrick's Congregation, 1983-89; bd. dirs. Cath. Charities of Madison, 1995—, pres., 1996—; bd. dirs. Future Madison Housing Fund, 1997—. Served with USMC, 1951-53. Mem. Aircraft Owners and Pilots Assn. Roman Catholic. Lodge: Rotary. (bd. dirs. 1981-83). Home: 607 Farwell Dr Madison WI 53704-6029 Office: 402 S Gammon Rd Madison WI 53719-1002

RING, HERBERT EVERETT, management executive; b. Norwich, Conn., Dec. 19, 1925; s. Herbert Everett and Catherine (Riordan) R.; m. Marilyn Elizabeth Dursin, May 21, 1955 (dec. Jan. 1994); children: Nancy Marie, Herbert Everett. BA, Ind. No. U., 1971, MBA, 1973; AMP, Harvard U., 1981. V.p. ops. Ogden Foods, Inc., Toledo, 1963-74; sr. v.p. Ogden Foods, Inc., Boston, 1974-75; v.p. concessions SportSvc. Corp., Buffalo, 1976-78, sr. v.p., 1978-80, pres., 1980-83, bd. dir.; pres. Universal Mgmt. Concept Counseling, Sylvania, Ohio, 1983—; prin. Hysen Group II, Livonia, Mich., 1991-95; counselor L.A. Olympic Concessions Food Svc., 1984, Phila. Meml. Stadium, 1985, Del. North Cos. Internat. London Eng., 1985-86, Chgo. Stadium Corp., 1989-92, Buffalo Sabres N.Y., 1992, Fine Host Inc. Greenwich Ct., 1993, Delaware North of Australia Ltd., 1994, Temp DNC Health Support Ltd., Wellington, New Zealand, 1995, Fanfare Enterprises, 1997, Geneva Lakes Kennel Club, Delavan, Wis., 1997, Geneva Lakes Greyhound Track, Delavan, Wis.; bd. dirs. Greenfield Restaurant Co., Inc., Letheby and Christopher Ltd., Reading, Berkshire, Eng., Air Terminal Svcs., Inc., The Aud Club, Inc., Bluegrass Turf Svc., Inc., Concession Suppliers, Inc., Cosel Drive-In Theatre, Inc., G&H Sports Concessions, Inc., Hazel Park Parking, Inc. Mem. Toledo Mus. Art., 1985-92. Sgt. Air Corps U.S. Army, 1944-46, ETO, USAF, 1950-51. Mem. Internat. Assn. of Auditorium Mgrs., N.W. Ohio Restaurant Assn. (bd. dirs. 1990-93), Am. Culinary Fedn. Inc., Harvard Bus. Club (Detroit). Roman Catholic. Home and Office: 5540 Radcliffe Rd Sylvania OH 43560-3740

RING, JAMES EDWARD PATRICK, mortgage banking consulting executive; b. Washington, Feb. 12, 1940; s. Edward Patrick and Eleanor (Sollers) R.; m. Kathleen Murphy, Aug. 10, 1979; children: Christopher James, Daniel Edward Patrick. Student, Holy Cross Coll., Worcester, Md., 1958-59; BSEE, U.S. Naval Acad., 1963; MBA in Fin., Wharton Sch. Bus., U. Pa., 1972. Lic. securities broker, comml. pilot. Fin. analyst Exec. Office of the President, Washington, 1972-74; sr. budget analyst Bd. Govs. Fed. Res. System, Washington, 1974-77; dir. fin. planning Fed. Home Loan Mortgage Ins., Washington, 1977-83; dir. mktg. Ticor Mortgage Ins., Falls Church, Va., 1983-84, G.E. Mortgage Ins., Mc Lean, Va., 1985-86; sr. v.p. First Chesapeake Mortgage, Beltsville, Md., 1986-88; v.p. G.E. Capital Mortgage Corp., McLean, 1988-94; cons. Mortgage Dynamics, McLean, 1994—. Vol. Big. Bros. Am., Washington, 1973-81; pres. U.S. Naval Acad. Class of 1963 Found., 1983-97. Lt. USN, 1963-69. Mem. Wharton Club (Washington), U.S. Naval Acad. Alumni Assn., Army-Navy Country Club. Republican Roman Catholic. Home: 1716 Stonebridge Rd Alexandria VA 22304-1039 Office: 1355 Beverly Rd Ste 300 Mc Lean VA 22101-3623

RING, JAMES WALTER, physics educator; b. Worcester, N.Y., Feb. 24, 1929; s. Carlyle Conwell and Lois (Tooley) R.; m. Agnes Elizabeth Muir, July 18, 1959; 1 son, Andrew James. AB, Hamilton Coll., 1951; PhD (Root fellow), U. Rochester, 1958. Asst. prof. physics Hamilton Coll., Clinton, N.Y., 1957-62, assoc. prof., 1962-69, prof., 1969—, Winslow prof., 1975—, chmn. dept. physics, 1968-80, 87-88, 91-92, radiation safety Officer, 1964-84, engring. liaison officer, 1969—; attached physicist Atomic Energy Rsch. Establishment, Harwell, Eng., 1965-66; vis. physicist Phys. Chemistry Lab., Oxford (Eng.) U., 1973; vis. fellow Ctr. for Energy and Environ. Studies, Princeton U., 1981; vis. scientist Lab. for Heating and Air Conditioning, Danish Tech. U., Copenhagen, 1987. Contbr. articles to profl. jours. and books in physics, chemistry, solar energy, environ. sci., health physics, archaeology, and engring. Recipient prize Acad. Edn./Devel., 1980; NSF grantee, 1959-66; NSF sci. faculty fellow, 1965-66. Mem. AAUP (chpt. pres. 1987-92), Am. Phys. Soc., Am. Assn. Physics Tchrs., Interant. Solar Energy Soc., Phi Beta Kappa, Sigma Xi. Achievements include solar house design and testing, indoor air studies in radon dangers and thermal comfort, and a study of the use of solar energy by the Romans during the Roman Empire. Office: Hamilton Coll Dept Physics Clinton NY 13323

RING, LUCILE WILEY, lawyer; b. Kearney, Nebr., Jan. 2, 1920; d. Myrtie Mercer and Alice (Cowell) W.; m. John Robert Ring, Mar. 28, 1948; children: John Raymond, James Wiley, Thomas Eric. AB, U. Nebr. at Kearney, 1944; JD, Washington U., 1946. Bar: Mo. 1946, U.S. Dist. Ct. (ea. dist.) Mo. 1947, U.S. Ct. Appeals (8th cir.) 1972. Atty.-adviser, chief legal group adjudications br. Army Fin. Ctr., St. Louis, 1946-52; exec. dir. lawyer referral service St. Louis Bar, 1960-70; pvt. practice, St. Louis, 1960—; staff law clk. U.S. Ct. Appeals (8th cir.), St. Louis, 1970-72; exec. dir. St. Louis Com. on Cts., 1972-85; legal advisor Mo. State Anat. Bd., 1965-95; adj. prof. adminstrv. law Webster Coll., Webster Groves, Mo., 1977-78; mem. Mo. Profl. Liability Rev. Bd., State of Mo., 1977-79. Author, editor: Guide to Community Services - Who Do I Talk To, 1974, 75, 1976-79; St. Louis Court Directories, 1972, 73, 74, 75; Felony Procedures in St. Louis Courts, 1975; author: Breaking Barriers: The St. Louis Legacy of Women in Law 1869-1969, 1996; author (series): Women Lawyers in St. Louis History, 1996; contbr. articles to profl. jours. Mem. Mo. Mental Health Authority, 1964-65; bd. dirs., v.p. Drug and Substance Abuse Council, met. St. Louis, 1976-83; mem. adv. council St. Louis Agy. on Tng. and Employment, 1976-83; mem. Mayor's Jud. Reform Subcom., St. Louis, 1974-76. Washington U. Sch. Law scholar, 1944-46; 1st Mo. woman nominated for St. Louis Ct. Appeals, Mo. Appellate Commn., 1972; 1st woman nominated judgeship Mo. Non-Partisan Ct. Plan, 1972; recipient letter of commendation Office of Chief of Fin., U.S. Army, 1952, Outstanding Alumni award U. Nebr. Kearney, 1994. Mem. Bar Assn. Met. St. Louis (v.p. 1975-76), Legal Services of Eastern Mo., Inc. (v.p. 1978-79, dir.), Legal Aid Soc. of St. Louis City and County (bd. dirs. 1977-78), HUD Women and Housing Commn. (commr. 1975), Women's Bar Assn. (treas. St. Louis chpt. 1949-50), Mo. Assn. Women Lawyers (treas. 1959-60, pres. 1960-61), Pi Kappa Delta, Sigma Tau Delta, Xi Phi, Washington U. Dental Faculty Wives (pres. 1972-74). Methodist. Home: 2041 Reservoir Loop Rd Selah WA 98942 Office: 721 Olive St Ste 1314 Saint Louis MO 63101-2229

RING, MICHAEL WILSON, lawyer; b. Phoenix, Feb. 14, 1943; s. Clifton A. and Leona (Wilson) R. BA, U Wash., 1964; JD, U. Calif., Berkeley, 1968. Bar: Calif. 1969. Assoc. Sheppard, Mullin, Richter & Hampton, L.A., 1968-76, ptnr., 1976-87; ptnr. Mayer, Brown & Platt, L.A., 1987-92, Sonnenschein Nath & Rosenthal, L.A., 1992—. Mem. ABA, L.A. County Bar Assn., Am. Coll. Real Estate Lawyers, Urban Land Inst. (assoc.), Internat. Coun. Shopping Ctrs. (assoc.), L.A. Hdqrs. City Assn. Home: 3658 Mountain View Ave Los Angeles CA 90066-3129 Office: Sonnenschein Nath & Rosenthal 601 S Figueroa St Ste 1500 Los Angeles CA 90017-5720

RING, RENEE E., lawyer; b. Frankfurt, Germany, May 29, 1950; arrived in U.S., 1950; d. Vincent Martin and Etheline Bergetta (Schoolmeesters) R.; m. Paul J. Zofnass, June 24, 1982; Jessica Renee, Rebecca Anne. BA, Catholic U. Am., 1972; JD, U. Va., 1976. Bar: N.Y. 1977. Assoc. Whitman & Ransom, N.Y.C., 1976-83; assoc. Carro, Spanbock, Fass, Geller, Kaster & Cuiffo, N.Y.C., 1983-86, ptnr., 1986; ptnr. Finley Kumble Wagner et. al., N.Y.C., 1987; of counsel Kaye, Scholer, Fierman, Hays & Handler, N.Y.C., 1988; ptnr. Kaye, Scholer, Fierman, Hays & Handler, LLP, N.Y.C., 1989—. Mem. exec. com. Lawyers for Clinton, Washington, 1991-92; team capt. Clinton Transition Team, Washington, 1992-93; mem. Nat. Lawyers Coun. Dem. Nat. Com., 1993—. Mem. ABA, N.Y. Women's Bar Assn. Democrat. Roman Catholic. Office: Kaye Scholer Fierman Hays & Handler LLP 425 Park Ave New York NY 10022-3506

RING, RICHARD G., national park service administrator; b. Paterson, N.J., Oct. 30, 1947; m. Jane rabbit; 1 child, Jennifer. BA in Polit. Sci., Pa. State U., 1969; postgrad., U. R.I., George Washington U. Park aid George Washington Meml. Pkwy. Nat. Park Svc., 1972; various positions in adminstrn. to supervisory park range Nat. Park Svc., various locations, 1972-81; task force detail to Office of Dir. Nat. Park Svc., Washington, 1980; asst. supt. Del. Water Gap Nat. Recreation Area, Pa., 1981-85, supt., 1988-92; supt. Everglades Nat. Park & Dry Tortugas Nat. Park, Fla., 1992—; U.S. coord. and rep. of dir. Nat. Park Svc. for Memorandum of Coop. with Bahamas Nat. Trust, 1995—. Chmn. South Fla. Ecosystem Restoration (Task Force) Working Group, Fla., 1993-94, chmn. infrastructure subgroup, 1994—; Interior Dept. rep. as ex-officio mem. Gov.'s Commn. for a Sustainable South Fla., 1994-95, mem., 1994—. With U.S. Army, 1969-71. Office: Everglades Nation Park Office of Supt 40001 State Road 9336 Homestead FL 33034-6733

RING, VICTORIA A., small business owner; b. Columbus, Ohio, July 5, 1958; d. James H. and Barbara C. (Wise) R. BA, East Tenn. State U., 1984; MA, Columbus Bus. U., 1986. Owner Tri-Angle Supreme Pizza, Sun, Va., 1981-86; typesetter, designer Battelle Meml. Inst., Columbus, Ohio, 1986-88; owner Graphico Pub., Columbus, Ohio, 1988—; instr. Ohio State U., Columbus, 1990-91; creator, designer GrapeVine News, 1992-94, The DynaWEB Link On-Line Newsletter, 1996—; spkr. at seminars and workshops in field. Author: Be "In The Know" With Adsheet Publishing, 1989, Word Perfect Just For Fun. 1991, Something From Nothing, 1993, How To Design Your Own Web Site With Netscape, 1996, My Old Dumb Computer Book, 1997; contbr. articles to profl. publs. Avocations: computer graphic design, web page design and site design, reading, photography.

RINGEL, DEAN, lawyer; b. N.Y.C., Dec. 12, 1947; m. Ronnie Sussman, Aug. 24, 1969; children: Marion, Alicia. BA, Columbia Coll., 1967; JD, Yale U., 1971. Bar: N.Y. 1972, U.S. Ct. Appeals (6th cir.) 1972, U.S. Ct. Appeals (2d and D.C. cirs.) 1974, U.S. Supreme Ct. 1976, U.S. Ct. Appeals (10th cir.) 1982. Law clk. to Judge Anthony J. Celebrezze U.S. Ct. Appeals (6th cir.), 1971-72; assoc. Cahill Gordon & Reindel, N.Y.C., 1972-79; ptnr. Cahill, Gordon & Reindel, N.Y.C., 1979—. Mem. ABA (vice chmn. com. on freedom of speech and press 1978-79), Assn. Bar City N.Y. (commn. com., fed. litigation), N.Y. State Bar (chmn. antitrust com., sect. comml. and fed. litigation 1994-96), Pub. Edn. Assn. (trustee, sec.). Office: Cahill Gordon & Reindel 80 Pine St New York NY 10005-1702

RINGEL, ELEANOR, film critic; b. Atlanta, Nov. 3, 1950; d. Herbert Arthur and Sara (Finklestein) R.; m. John Gillespie, Nov. 18, 1989. BA magna cum laude, Brown U., 1972. With Alliance Theatre, 1974, S.C. Open Road Ensemble, 1974-75, N.Y. Shakespeare Festival, 1975-78, Children's TV Workshop, 1975-77; obituary writer Atlanta Jour., 1978; critic, editor Atlanta Jour.-Constitution Film, 1978—; movie reviewer WXRA-TV, 1983—, WSB Radio, 1996—. Named Best Local Critic Atlanta Mag., 1990, Best of Cox Newspapers Criticisms, 1987, Finalist Citations Criticisms, 1984-85, Best Pop Culture Critic, Atlanta Mag. Mem. Nat. Soc. Film Critics (elected 1994). Home: 235 1/2 E Wesley Rd NE Atlanta GA 30305-3774 Office: Atlanta Journal Constitution Entertainment Desk 72 Marietta St NW Atlanta GA 30303-2804

RINGEL, ROBERT LEWIS, university administrator; b. N.Y.C., Jan. 27, 1937; s. Benjamin Seymour and Beatrice (Salis) R.; m. Estelle Neuman, Jan. 18, 1959; children—Stuart Alan, Mark Joseph. B.A., Bklyn. Coll., 1959; M.S., Purdue U., 1960, Ph.D., 1962. cert. speech pathologist. Rsch. scientist, laryngeal rsch. lab. Ctr. Health Scis., UCLA, 1962-64; asst. prof. communication disorders U. Wis., 1964-66; mem. faculty Purdue U., 1966—, prof., head dept. audiology and speech sci., 1970-73, dean Sch. Humanities, Social Sci. and Edn. (Sch. Liberal Arts), 1973-86, v.p., dean Grad. Sch., 1986-90, exec. v.p. for acad. affairs, 1991—; vis. prof. Inst. Neurology and Nat. Hosps. Coll. Speech Scis., U. London, 1985; cons. NIH, NEH, Bur. Edn. Handicapped of U.S. Office Edn.; bd. dirs. Indpls. Ctr. for Advanced Rsch., 1988-92. Author sci. articles; contbr. to monographs and textbooks; cons. editor Chapman & Hall, London. Bd. dirs. Lafayette Home Hosp., 1978-87, Lafayette Symphony Orch., 1983-85. Recipient Research Career Devel. award Nat. Inst. Dental Research, 1967-70, Award for highest merit for sci. article Jour. Speech and Hearing Research, 1979, Disting. Alumnus award Bklyn. Coll., 1985. Fellow Am. Speech and Hearing Assn. (v.p. Found. 1990—); mem. AAUP, Nat. Assn. State Univs. and Land Grant Colls. (exec. com. 1988-91, rsch. policy and grad. edn., exec. com. coun. on acad. affairs 1991—, com. on instnl. coop., exec. com. provosts instn. coop. com. 1991—), Sigma Xi (v.p. 1986—). Office: Purdue Univ Off Exec VP for Acad Affairs West Lafayette IN 47907-1073

RINGEN, CATHERINE OLESON, linguistics educator; b. Bklyn., June 3, 1943; d. Prince Eric and Geneva Muriel (Leigh) Oleson; m. Jon David Ringen, Nov. 22, 1969; children: Kai Mathias, Whitney Leigh. Student, Cornell U., 1961-63; BA, Indiana U., 1970, MA, 1972, PhD, 1975. Vis. lectr. U. Minn., Mpls., 1973-74; asst. prof. U. Iowa, Iowa City, 1975-79, assoc. prof., 1980-87, prof., 1988—, chair linguistics, 1987-93. Author: Vowel Harmony: Theoretical Implications, 1988; contbr. articles to profl. jours. Sr. Fulbright prof. Trondheim, Norway, 1980, Poznan, Poland, 1994-95. Mem. AAAS, Linguistic Soc. Am., Phi Beta Kappa. Office: U Iowa Dept Linguistics Iowa City IA 52242

RINGER, JAMES MILTON, lawyer; b. Orlando, Fla., July 9, 1943; s. Robert T. and Jessie M. (Rowe) R.; m. Jaquelyn Hope, Apr. 10, 1965; children—Carolyn Hope, James Matthew. A.B., Ohio U., 1965; J.D., Cornell U., 1968. Bar: N.Y. 1968, U.S. Dist. Ct. (no. dist.) N.Y. 1968, U.S. Dist. Ct. (so. and ea. dists.) N.Y. 1972, U.S. Ct. Appeals (2d cir.) 1972, U.S. Ct. Claims 1976, U.S. Dist. Ct. (we. dist.) N.Y. 1978, U.S. Ct. Appeals (4th cir.) 1981, U.S. Ct. Appeals (9th cir.) 1983. Assoc. Rogers & Wells, N.Y.C., 1968-78, ptnr., 1978—; instr. bus. law U. Alaska, 1970-71. Editor Cornell Law Rev., 1967-68. Served to lt. JAGC, USNR, 1969-72. Republican. Episcopalian. Office: Rogers & Wells 200 Park Ave New York NY 10166-0005

RINGGOLD, FAITH, artist; b. N.Y.C., Oct. 8, 1930. B.S., CCNY, 1955; M.A., 1959; DFA (hon.), Moore Coll. Art, Phila., 1986, Coll. Wooster, Ohio, 1987, Mass. Coll. Art, Boston, 1991, CCNY of CUNY, 1991, DSc (hon.), Brockport (N.Y.) State U., 1992, Calif. Coll. Arts. and Crafts, Oakland, Calif., 1993, RISD, 1994. Art tchr. N.Y. Pub. Schs., 1955-73; lectr. Bank St. Coll. Grad. Sch., N.Y.C., 1970-80; prof. art U. Calif., San Diego, 1984—. Solo exhbns. include Spectrum Gallery, N.Y.C., 1967, 70, 10 year retrospective, Voorhees Gallery, Rutgers U., 1973, Summit Gallery, N.Y.C., 1979, 20 year Retrospective, Studio Mus. in Harlem, N.Y.C., 1984, Bernice Steinbaum Gallery, N.Y.C., 1987-88, Balt. Mus., Deland (Fla.) Mus., Faith Ringgold 25 Yr. Survey Fine Arts Museum L.I., Hempstead, 1990-93, Textile Mus., Washington, 1993, Children's Mus. of Manhattan, N.Y.C., 1993-95, Hewlett-Woodmere Pub. Libr., Hewlett, N.Y., 1993-94, St. Louis Art Mus., 1994, Athenaeum, La Jolla, Calif., 1995, A.C.A. Gallery, N.Y.C., 1995, Ind. U. of Pa., 1995, Bowling Green State U., Ind., 1996; exhibited in group shows at Meml. Exhibit for MLK, Mus. Modern Art, N.Y.C., 1968, Chase Manhattan Bank Collection, Martha Jackson Gallery, N.Y.C., 1970, Am. Women Artists, Gedok, Kunstalle, Hamburg, Ger., 1972, Jubilee, Boston Mus. Fine Arts, 1975, Major Contemporary Women Artists, Suzanne Gross Gallery, Phila., 1984, Committed to Print Mus. Modern Art, N.Y.C., 1988, The Art of Black Am. in Japan, Terada Warehouse, Tokyo, Made in the USA, Art in the 50s and 60s U. Calif. Berkeley Art Mus., Craft Today Poetry of the Physical, Am. Craft Mus., N.Y.C., Portraits and Homage to Mothers Hecksher Mus. Huntington, 1987, N.J. State Mus., Trenton, 1992-94, Fukui Fine Art Mus., Fuki, Japan, 1992, Takushima Modern Art Mus., Japan, 1993, Otani Meml. Art Mus., Japan, 1993, Salina Art Ctr., Kans., 1993, Bruce Watkins Ctr. Kansas City, Mo., 1993, Barton county C.C., Great Bend, Kans., 1993, Del. State Coll. Arts Ctr. Gallery, Dover, 1993-94, Roswell Mus. and Art Ctr., N.Mex., 1994, and numerous others; represented in collections at Chase Manhattan Bank, N.Y.C., Philip Morris Collection, N.Y.C., Children's Mus., Bklyn., Newark Mus., The Women's House of Detention, Rikers Island, N.Y., The Studio Mus., N.Y.C., High Mus., Atlanta, Guggenheim Mus., Met. Mus. Art, Boston Mus. Fine Arts, MOMA, AARP, Washington, Am. Craft Mus., N.Y.C., Clark Muys., Williamstown, Mass., Met. Transit Authority, N.Y.C., and numerous others. Author: Tar Beach, 1991, Aunt Harriet's Underground Railroad in the Sky, 1992; contbr. articles to profl. jours. Recipient AAUW travel award to Africa, 1976, Caldecott honor award, Coretta Scott King award best illustrated children's books Tar Beach, 1991; John Simon Guggenheim Meml. Found. Fellowship (painting), 1987, N.Y. Found. for Arts award (painting), 1988, Nat. Endowment Arts award (sculpture) 1978, (painting) 1989, La Napoule Found. award (painting in So. of France) 1990, Arts Internat. award (travel to Morocco) 1992. Office: Marie Brown Assocs 625 Broadway New York NY 10012-2611

RINGLE, BRETT ADELBERT, lawyer; b. Berkeley, Calif., Mar. 17, 1951; Forrest A. and Elizabeth V. (Darnall) R.; m. Sue Kinslow, May 26, 1973. A., U. Tex., 1973, J.D., 1976. Bar: Tex. 1976, U.S. Dist. Ct. (no. dist.) Tex. 76, U.S. Supreme Ct. 1980, U.S. Ct. Appeals (5th cir.) 1984. Ptnr., Shank, Irwin & Conant, Dallas, 1976-86, Jones, Day, Reavis & Pogue, Dallas, 1986-96; v.p. Hunt Petroleum Corp., Dallas, 1996—; adj. prof. law So. Meth. U., Dallas, 1983. Author: (with J. W. Moore and H. I. Bendix) Moore's Federal Practice, 2nd edit., Vol. 12, 1980, Vol. 13, 1981, (with J. W. Moore) Vol. 1A, 1982, Vol. 1A Part 2, 1989. Mem. Dallas Bar Assn. Home: 3514 Gillon Ave Dallas TX 75205-3220 Office: Hunt Petroleum Corp 1601 Elm St 5000 Thanksgiving Tower Dallas TX 75201

RINGLEE, ROBERT JAMES, consulting engineering executive; b. Sacramento, Apr. 23, 1926; s. Francis and Marie N. R.; m. Helen Laura Carleton, Aug. 27, 1949; children—Sarah N., Jane C., Robert K. B.S.E.E., U. Wash., 1946, M.S.E.E., 1948; Ph.D. in Mechanics, Rensselaer Poly. Inst., 1964. Registered profl. engr., N.Y. With advanced engrng. program Gen. Electric Co., 1948-51, advanced devel. engr., power transformer dept., 1951-55, supr. power transformer design, 1955-60, sr. analytical engr., 1960-65, mgr. system and equipment reliability, 1965-69; prin. engr. dir. Power Technologies, Inc., Schenectady, 1969-86; prin cons. Power Technologies, Inc., 1986-93; TAG assoc. Power Techs., Inc., 1993-94; assoc. cons., 1994—. Contbr. articles to profl. publs. Mem. Schalmont Bd. Edn., 1966-70, pres., 1968-69. Served with USNR, 1944-46. Recipient Managerial award Gen. Electric Co., 1953. Fellow IEEE (3 prize paper awards), AAAS; mem. Internat. Conf. on High Voltage Power Systems (expert advisor, Attwood Assoc.), Adirondack Mountain Club (pres. 1990-93, acting exec. dir. 1994). Democrat. Unitarian. Patentee. Home: 315 Juniper Dr Schenectady NY 12306-1705 Office: PO Box 1058 Schenectady NY 12301-1058

RINGLER, JAMES M., cookware company executive; b. 1945. BS, U. Buffalo, 1967, MBA, 1968. Mgr., cons. Arthur Andersen & Co., 1968-76; v.p. appliance group Tappan Co., Mansfield, Ohio, 1976-78, gen. v.p., mgr. appliance div., 1978-87, pres., chief operating officer, 1987—, also bd. dirs.; pres., CEO Premark Internat., Inc., Deerfield, Ill., 1996—. Office: Premark Internat Inc 1717 Deerfield Rd Deerfield IL 60015-3977

RINGLER, JEROME LAWRENCE, lawyer; b. Detroit, Dec. 26, 1948. BA, Mich. State U., 1970; JD, U. San Francisco, 1974. Bar: Calif. 1974, U.S. Ct. Appeals (9th cir.) 1974, U.S. Dist. Ct. (no. dist.) Calif. 1974, U.S. Dist. Ct. (ctrl. dist.) Calif. 1975, U.S. Dist. Ct. (so. dist.) Calif. 1981. Assoc. Parker, Stansbury et al, L.A., 1974-76; assoc. Fogel, Feldman, Ostrov, Ringler & Klevens, Santa Monica, Calif., 1976-80, ptnr., 1980—; arbitrator L.A. Superior Ct. Arbitration Program, 1980-85. Named O'Brien's Evaluator 1996 Trial Lawyer of the Yr., Verdictum Juris Trial Lawyer of Yr., 1996. Mem. ATLA, ABA, State Bar Calif., L.A. County Bar Assn. (litigation sect., exec. com. 1994—), L.A. Trial Lawyers Assn. (bd. govs. 1981—, treas. 1988, sec. 1989, v.p. 1990, pres.-elect 1991, pres. 1992, Trial Lawyer of the Yr. 1987), Calif. Trial Lawyers Assn., Am. Bd. Trial Advs. (assoc. 1988, adv. 1991), Inns of Ct. (master). Avocations: skiing, tennis. Office: Fogel Feldman Ostrov et al 1620 26th St # 100 S Santa Monica CA 90404-4013

RINGLER, LENORE, educational psychologist; d. Albert Haendel and Ida (Brafstein) Haendel; 1 son., Adam. BA, Bklyn. Coll.; MA, Queens Coll., 1954; PhD, NYU, 1965. Tchr., then reading specialist N.Y.C. Bd. Edn.; prof. NYU, 1965—, chair dept. ednl. psychology, 1974-79; ednl. cons. Psychol. Corp., Council on Interracial Books for Children, N.Y.C. Bd. Edn. Author: Skills Monitoring System-Reading, 1977, A Language-Thinking Approach to Reading, 1984; author reading series for Holt Rhinehart & Winston, 1989; contbr. articles to profl. jours. Mem. Citizens Com. for Children; mem. Commn. on Reading Nat. Acad. Edn., 1983-85. Grantee U.S. Office Edn., 1968-69, Newspapers in Edn., 1990. Mem. Am. Psychol. Assn., Am. Ednl. Rsch. Assn., Internat. Reading Assn. (past pres. Manhattan coun.), Nat. Reading Conf. (v.p. 1982-84, pres. 1984-85), Pi Lambda Theta (rsch. fellow 1963-64), Kappa Delta Pi. Office: NYU 239 Greene St Rm 400 New York NY 10003-6674

RINGWALD, LYDIA ELAINE, artist, poet; b. L.A., Oct. 8, 1949; d. Siegfried Carl Ringwald and Eva M. (Macksoud) Mack; m. Hal von Hofe, July 31, 1972 (div. 1978). BA, Scripps Coll., 1970; student, Ruprecht-Karl Univ., Heidelberg, Germany, 1971; MA in Comparative Lit., U. Calif., Irvine, 1972; studied with William Bailey, Yale Art Sch., 1972-74; postgrad., U. Conn., 1976. Instr. English and German Cerritos (Calif.) Coll., 1975-83; instr. German Golden West Coll., Huntington Beach, Calif., 1976-83; instr. English Saddleback Coll., Mission Viejo, Calif., 1976-81, Long Beach (Calif.) City Coll., 1976-83; curator exhbns. Cultural Affairs Satellite Dept., L.A., 1994; cons., lectr. in field. Solo exhbns. include Great Western Bank, 1989, Atlantis Gallery, 1992, L.A. Pub. Libr., Sherman Oaks, Calif., 1993, Sumitomo Bank, 1993, Phoenix Gallery, 1994; group exhbns. include Long Beach (Calif.) Arts, 1988-89, Installations One, 1989, 90, Heidelberger Kunstverein, Heidelberg, Germany, 1990, Barbara Mendes Gallery, L.A., 1991, Folktree Gallery, 1991-92, Armand Hammer Mus., 1992, Jansen-Perez Gallery, L.A., 1993; author: Blessings in Disguise: Life is a Gift; Accept it with Both Hands, 1990, Blau: Kaleidescope einer Farbe, 1992. Mem. Internat. Friends Transformative Arts, Humanistic Arts Alliance, Nat. Mus. Women in Arts, L.A. Mcpl. Art Gallery, Mus. Contemporary Art, L.A. County Mus., U. Calif. Irvine Alumni Assn., Scripps Coll. Alumni Assn., Inst. Noetic Scis., Philosophical Rsch. Soc. Avocations: modern dance, ballet, music, piano. Home and Office: Creative Realities 2801 Coldwater Canyon Dr Beverly Hills CA 90210-1305

RINK, LAWRENCE DONALD, cardiologist; b. Indpls., Oct. 14, 1940; s. Joe Donald and Mary Ellen (Rand) R.; m. Eleanor Jane Zimmerly, Aug. 10, 1963; children: Scott, Virginia. BS, DePauw U., 1962; MD, Ind. U., 1966. Diplomate Am. Bd. Internal Medicine, Am. Bd. Cardiology, Critical Care Medicine. Clin. asst. prof. Ind. U. Med. Sch., Indpls., 1973-79, clin. assoc. prof., 1979-85; clin. prof. med. Ind. Univ. Med. Sch., Indpls., 1985—; cardiologist Internal Medicine Assocs., Bloomington, Ind., 1974-95, pres.; dir. cardiac rehab. Bloomington Hosp., 1976—, dir. cardiology, 1983—; pres., chief med. officer Unity Physician Group, Bloomington, 1995—; physician Ind. U. Basketball Team, 1979—; dir. med. edn. Bloomington Hosp., 1976—; med. dir. Track and Field Pan Am. Games, 1987; U.S. Olympic Physician Olympic Sports Festival, 1989, World Univ. Games, 1990, Olympic Games, Barcelona, 1992, World Univ. Games, Fukuoka, Japan, 1995; N. Am. continent rep. Fed. Internat. Student Univ. Sports. Bd. dirs. J.O. Ritchie Soc., Ind. U. Med. Sch. Bd. dirs., dean's coun. Ind. U. Med. Sch., 1992—. Recipient Quality of Life award Major Bloomington, 1978; named Most Outstanding Flight Surgeon, USN, 1968. Fellow Am. Coll. Cardiology, Am. Heart Assn., Am. Soc. Critical Care, Am. Coll. Sports Medicine; mem. AMA, Ind. U. Med. Alumnae Assn. (pres. 1986-87, exec. alumna coun.). Avocations: reading, writing, golf, tennis. Office: Internal Medicine Assn 719 S Rogers St Bloomington IN 47403-2335

RINK, WESLEY WINFRED, banker; b. Hickory, N.C., June 14, 1922; s. Dewey Lee and Mabel E. (Yount) R.; m. Doreen M. Warman, Sept. 7, 1946; children: Rebecca S., Christopher L. B.S. in Accountancy, U. Ill., 1947, M.S., 1948. Acct., Glidden Co., Chgo., 1948-58; adminstrv. mgr. Central Soya Co., Chgo., 1958-65; v.p., comptroller State Nat. Bank, Evanston, Ill., 1965-71; exec. v.p., dir. Pioneer Trust & Savs. Bank, Chgo., 1971-76; corp. v.p. Exchange Bancorp., Inc., Tampa, 1977-82; sr. v.p. NCNB Nat. Bank Fla., Tampa, 1982-86; fin cons. Temple Terrace, Fla., 1986—; dir. 1st Bank of the Villages, Lady Lake, Fla. Served to capt. USAAF, 1942-46. Home: 523 Garrard Dr Temple Terrace FL 33617-3819 Office: 9400 N 56th St Temple Ter FL 33617-5506

RINKENBERGER, RICHARD KRUG, physical scientist, geologist; b. Gridley, Ill., May 15, 1933; s. Burl E. and Olive J. (Krug) R.; children: Janice L., Ginger R., Rebekah P. BA in Geology, U. Colo., 1959. Dir. prospecting Grubstake Assn., Sask., Can., 1958-59; engr. Martin-Marietta Aerospace Co., Denver, 1960-75; geologist U.S. Geol. Survey, Denver, 1975; geologist remote sensing U.S. Mine Safety and Health Adminstrn., Denver, 1975-79; pres., exploration geologist Banner Set, Ltd., Denver, 1980-84; pres., cons. geologist R.K. Rinkenberger & Assocs., Aurora, Colo., 1979-87; phys. scientist U.S. Dept. Energy, Germantown, Md., 1987—; educator prospecting Denver Sch. Prospecting, 1968-71, U. Colo., Denver, Boulder, 1970-75; rsch. geochemist Heritage Chem. Co., Englewood, 1984-86; prospecting researcher, gold and silver prospector R.K. Rinkenberger & Assocs., 1965—. Contbr. articles to profl. publs. Mem. parent adv. bd, supt. of schs. Westminster, Colo., 1982-83. Recipient High Quality Performance award U.S. Mine Safety and Health Adminstrn., 1977; grantee Saskatchewan (Can.) Dept. Mineral Resources, 1958, 59, U.S. Geol. Survey (remote sensing), 1978. Mem. hon. geol. soc., Sigma Gamma Epsilon. Mem. Ch. of the Nazarene. Avocations: cross country skiing, geological thorist experimentalist, student of animal killing mechanisms leading to dinosaur extinction, writing. Office: PO Box 5523 Rockville MD 20855-0523

RINKER, RUBY STEWART, foundation administrator; b. Dayton, Ohio, June 11, 1936; d. Encle Stewart and Addie (Hamilton) Stewart-Smith; children: William Bertram Klawonn, Elizabeth Lynn Dennis, William Stewart-Bradley Klawonn. Human relations counselor Palm Beach County Sch. System, West Palm Beach, Fla., 1974-84; adminstrv. asst. Bohmfalk Estate, Palm Beach, Fla., N.Y.C, Newport, R.I., 1984—; pres., CEO Ruby S. Rinker Co., Inc.; hon. counselor U.S. Naval Acad., U.S. Air Force Acad. Trustee Bohmfalk Charitable Found.; bd. dirs. Capital Cathedral Ministries Internat. Bd. Mem. Phi Delta Kappa. Home: 561 Island Dr Palm Beach FL 33480-4746

RINKEVICH, CHARLES FRANCIS, federal official; b. Grand Rapids, Mich., June 28, 1940; s. Peter Paul and Mabel (Knauf) R.; m. Sara Frances Rees, Aug. 2, 1969; children: Charles Francis, Monica. AA, Grand Rapids Jr. Coll., 1960; BS in Police Adminstrn., Mich. State U., 1962; MPA, Ga. State U., 1985. Patrolman Mich. State U. Police Dept., East Lansing, 1963-65; lt. Savannah (Ga.) Police Dept., 1965-67; law enforcement cons. U. Ga., 1967-68; police mgmt. cons. Internat. Assn. Chiefs Police, Washington, 1968-69; exec. dir. Pa. Crime Commn., Harrisburg, 1969-71; regional adminstr. Law Enforcement Assistance Adminstrn., Justice Dept., Phila., 1971-74, regional adminstr., Atlanta, 1974-83; dir. Fed. Law Enforcement Tng. Ctr., Glynco, Ga., 1983—. Mem. law enforcement exploring com. Boy Scouts Am. Recipient Presdl. Meritorious and Disting. Rank awards. Mem. Nat. Sheriff's Assn., Internat. Assn. Chiefs Police. Office: Dept Treasury Fed Law Enforcement Tr Ctr Glynco GA 31524

RINNE, AUSTIN DEAN, insurance company executive; s. Hermann Henry and Marie (Knudsen) R.; m. Martha Jo Runyan, Dec. 29, 1941; children: Erik Knudsen, Barbara Jane Rivera; student Ind. U., 1938-40, grad. ins. mktg. Purdue U., 1947. Spl. agt. Northwestern Mut. Life, Indpls., 1946-56, dist. agt., 1956-58, gen. agt., Dallas, 1958-84, gen. agt. emeritus, 1984—; chmn. bd. dirs. Communication and Mgmt. Assocs., Ann Arbor, Mich. Bd. dirs., v.p. English Speaking Union, Dallas, 1972—; bd. dirs. Dallas Opera, 1984—, Taca Bd., Dallas Cultural Arts Assn. Served to capt. USAF, 1941-45, ETO. Decorated Purple Heart, Air Medal with Cluster, POW medal, Presdl. Unit citation Happy Warriors WWII Combat pilots, 8th Air Force Assn., 1995; recipient Trail Boss award S.W. Gen. Agts. and Mgrs. Assn., 1993. Mem. Dallas Estate Planning Coun. (pres. 1965-66), Dallas Assn. Life Underwriters (bd. dirs. 1960-63, Hall of Fame 1989), Million Dollar Roundtable (life), Dallas Knife and Fork (pres., bd. dirs. 1986—), Mil. Order World Wars, English-Speaking Union (dir., v.p. Dallas chpt. 1972—), Sertoma (pres. Dallas chpt. 1967-68, Sertoman of Yr. 1990), Phi Kappa Psi Alumni Assn. (pres. 1951-52), Ind. U. Alumni Assoc. (pres. Dallas/Ft. Worth 1968-69), Phi Kappa Psi (exec. council 1972-76, endowment bd. 1989—, Dallas sales and mktg. chpt. bd. 1969-72), Park City Club, Dallas Country Club, Northshore Club. Republican. Methodist. Home: 4311 Bordeaux Ave Dallas TX 75205-3719 Office: 3102 Oak Lawn Ave Ste 650 Dallas TX 75219-4271

RINSCH, CHARLES EMIL, insurance company executive; b. Vincennes, Ind., June 28, 1932; s. Emil and Vera Pearl (White) R.; m. Maryann Elizabeth Hitchcock, June 18, 1964; children: Christopher, Daniel, Carl. BS in Stats., Ind. U., 1953; MS in Bus., Butler U., 1959; MBA, Stanford U., 1960. Budget analyst Chrysler Corp., Indpls., 1955-57; sr. fin. analyst Ford Motor Co., Indpls., 1957-59; budget dir. Nat. Forge Co., Warren, Pa., 1960-61; div. controller and asst. to v.p., fin. Norris Industries, L.A., 1961-65; v.p., treas., sec. Teledyne Inc, L.A., 1965-88; pres., chief exec. officer Argonaut Group Inc., L.A., 1988—. Cubmaster Pack 721, Boy Scouts Am., L.A., 1987-88, treas. 1981-87; mem. dean's adv. coun. Ind. U. Sch. Bus. 1st lt. U.S. Army, 1953-55. Mem. Acad. Alumni Fellows Ind. U. Sch. Bus., L.A. Treas.'s Club. Avocations: photography, travel. Home: 19849 Greenbriar Dr Tarzana CA 91356-5428 Office: Argonaut Group Inc Ste 1175 1800 Avenue Of The Stars Los Angeles CA 90067-4213

RINSCH, MARYANN ELIZABETH, occupational therapist; b. L.A., Aug. 8, 1939; d. Harry William and Thora Analine (Langlie) Hitchcock; m. Charles Emil Rinsch, June 18, 1964; children: Christopher, Daniel, Carl. BS, U. Minn., 1961. Registered occupational therapist, Calif. Staff occupational therapist Hastings (Minn.) State Hosp., 1961-62, Neuropsychiat. Inst., L.A., 1962-64; staff and sr. occupational therapist Calif. Children's Svcs., L.A., 1964-66, head occupational therapist, 1966-68; researcher A. Jean Ayres, U. So. Calif., L.A., 1968-69; pvt. practice neurodevel. and sensory integraton Tarzana, Calif., 1969-74; pediat. occupational therapist neurodevel. & sensory integration St. Johns Hosp., Santa Monica, Calif., 1991-95; pvt. practice, cons. Santa Monica-Malibu Unified Sch. Dist., 1994—. Mem. alliance bd. Natural History Mus., L.A. County, 1983—; cub scouts den mother Boy Souts Am., Sherman Oaks, Calif., 1986-88, advancement chair Boy Scout Troop 474, 1989-92; mem. vol. League San Fernando Valley, Van Nuys, Calif., 1985-93; trustee Viewpoint Sch., Calabasas, Calif., 1987-90, Valley Women's Ctr., 1990-91. Mem. Am. Occupational Therapy Assn., Calif. Occupational Therapy Assn. Home: 19849 Greenbriar Dr Tarzana CA 91356-5428

RINSKY, ARTHUR C., lawyer; b. Cin., July 10, 1944. AB with honors, U. Cin., 1966; JD cum laude, U. Mich., 1969; LLM in Taxation, NYU, 1974. Bar: Fla. 1969, Calif. 1975, U.S. Tax Ct. 1974; cert. tax specialist. Atty. Gray, Cary, Ware & Freidenrich, P.C., Palo Alto, Calif. Mem. ABA, State Bar Calif., Phi Beta Kappa, Phi Eta Sigma. Office: Gray Cary Ware & FreidenrichPC 400 Hamilton Ave Palo Alto CA 94301-1809

RINSKY, JOEL CHARLES, lawyer; b. Bklyn., Jan. 29, 1938; s. Irving C. and Elsie (Millman) R.; m. Judith L. Lynn, Jan. 26, 1963; children: Heidi M., Heather S., Jason W. BS, Rutgers U., 1961, LLB, 1962, JD, 1968. Bar: N.J. 1963, U.S. Dist. Ct. N.J. 1963, U.S. Supreme Ct. 1967, U.S. Ct. Appeals (3d cir.) 1986; cert. civil trial atty., N.J. Sole practice Livingston, N.J., 1964—. Dem. committeeperson Millburn-Short Hills, N.J., 1982—, vice chmn., 1983-87; trustee Student Loan Fund, Millburn, 1983-91. Fellow Am. Acad. Matrimonial Lawyers; mem. N.J. Bar Assn., Essex County Bar Assn. (exec. com. sect. family law). Jewish. Avocations: tennis, running, chess, golf, piano. Home: 23 Winthrop Rd Short Hills NJ 07078-1411 Office: 66 W Mount Pleasant Ave Livingston NJ 07039-2930

RINSKY, JUDITH LYNN, foundation administrator, educator consultant; b. Sept. 12, 1941; d. Allen A. and Sophie (Schwartz) Lynn; m. Joel C. Rinsky, Jan. 29, 1963; children: Heidi Mae Schnapp, Heather Star Maxon. Jason Wayne. BA in Home Econs., Montclair State U., 1963. Notary pub., N.J. Tchr. home econs. Florence Ave. Sch., Irvington, N.J., 1963-66; substitute tchr. Millburn-Short Hills Sch. System, Millburn Twp., N.J., 1978-82, 90—, sr. citizen coord., 1982-87, home instruction, 1997—; respite care coord. Essex County Divsn. on Aging, East Orange, N.J., 1988-90; pvt. practice educator Short Hills, N.J., 1990—; bd. mem. adv. com. gerontology Seton Hall U., 1984-90; coord. Mayor's Adv. Bd. Sr. Citizens, Millburn-Short Hills, 1982-87; home instrn. Millburn-Short Hills Sch. Sys., 1997—. Pres. Deerfield Sch. PTA, 1979-80, Millburn H.S. PTA, 1983-85; co-chmn. dinner dance Charles T. King Student Loan Fund, 1981; active Handicapped Access Study Com., 1983-85; bd. dirs. Coun. on Health and Human Svcs., 1985-90, 94—; acting dir. B'nai Israel Nursery Sch., 1994. Mem. Lake Naomi Assn. (chmn. sailing com. 1981), N.J. Home Econs. Assn., Am. Home Econs. Assn., Rotary (pres. Millburn chpt. 1992-93, bd. dirs. 1992—, advisor Millburn interact club 1987—, chair Internat. Interact dist. 7470 1993-95, advisor 1995—). Home and Office: 23 Winthrop Rd Short Hills NJ 07078-1411

RINSLAND, ROLAND DELANO, retired university official; b. Low Moor, Va., Apr. 11, 1933; s. Charles Henry and Lottie (Parks) R.; A.B. with distinction, Va. State U., 1954; A.M., Tchrs. Coll., Columbia U., 1959, profl. diploma, 1960, Ed.D., 1966. Asst. to dean of men Va. State Coll., Petersburg, 1952-54; asst. purchasing agt. Glyco Products Co., Inc., N.Y.C., 1956-57; asst. office of registrar Tchrs. Coll., Columbia U., N.Y.C., 1957-66, tchr. cert. advisor, 1959-95, registrar, 1966-71, asst. dean for student affairs, also registrar, dir. office doctoral studies, 1971-95, ret., 1995; mem. Tchrs. Coll. Devel. Council, 1974-76, 91-95; rep., presenter of degrees Tchrs. Coll.,

Japan, 1989, 91, 93, 94. Served to 1st lt. AUS, 1954-56. Designated Important and Valuable Human Resource of USA Am. Heritage Research Assn. First Am. Bicentenium. Mem. N.Y. State Personnel and Guidance Assn., Am. Coll. Personnel Assn., Nat. Soc. Study Edn., Am. Ednl. Research Assn., Middle States, Am. assns. collegiate registrars and admission officers (inter-assn. rep. to state edn. depts. on tchr. cert. 1973-74, mem. com. on orgn. and adminstrn. registrars activities 1973, 74-76), Assn. Records Execs. and Adminstrs. (charter mem., by-laws and program chmn. 1969), Am. Acad. Polit. and Social Sci., Am. Assn. Higher Edn., Assn. Instl. Research, Internat. Assn. Applied Psychology, Soc. Applied Anthropology, Am. Assn. Counseling and Devel., Assn. Study of Higher Edn., AAAS, N.Y. Acad. Scis., Met. Opera Guild, NEA (Leah B. Sykes award for life mem.), Scabbard and Blade, Kappa Phi Kappa, Phi Delta Kappa, Kappa Delta Pi. Home: 25 W 68th St New York NY 10023-5302

RINTA, CHRISTINE EVELYN, nurse, air force officer; b. Geneva, Ohio, Oct. 4, 1952; d. Arvi Alexander and Catharina Maria (Steenbergen) R. BSN, Kent State U., 1974; MSN, Case Western Res. U., 1979. CNOR. Staff nurse in oper. rm. Euclid (Ohio) Gen. Hosp., 1974-76, oper. rm. charge nurse, 1977-79; commd. 1st lt. USAF, 1979, advanced through grades to lt. col.; staff nurse oper. rm. Air Force Regional Hosp., Sheppard AFB, Tex., 1979-82; staff nurse oper. rm., asst. oper. rm. supr. Regional Med. Ctr. Clark, Clark Air Base, Philippines, 1982-83; chief, nurse recruiting br. 3513th Air Force Recruiting Squadron, North Syracuse, N.Y., 1983-87; nurse supr. surg. svcs. 432d Med. Group, Misawa Air Base, Japan, 1987-89; course supr./instr. oper. rm. nursing courses 3793d Nursing Tng. Squadron, Keesler Med. Ctr., Keesler AFB, Miss., 1989-92; asst. dir., then dir. oper. rm. and ctrl. sterile supply Keesler Med. Ctr., Keesler AFB, Miss., 1992-93; comdr., enlisted clin. courses flight 383d Tng. Squadron, Sheppard AFB, Tex., 1993-94; comdr., officer clin. courses flight 383rd Tng. Squadron, Sheppard AFB, Tex., 1994-95; comdr. enlisted courses flight 383rd Tng. Squadron, Sheppard AFB, Tex., 1995-96; ops. officer, oper. rm. svcs. 74th Med. Squdron, Wright-Patterson AFB, Ohio, 1996—. Decorated Air Force Commendation medal, Air Force Achievement medal, Meritorious Svc. medal. Mem. ANA, Ohio Nurses Assn., Assn. Operating Rm. Nurses, Air Force Assn., Sigma Theta Tau. Home: 3110 Cymar Dr Beavercreek OH 45434-6355 Office: 74th Med Group SGOSB Wright Patterson AFB OH 45433

RINZEL, DANIEL FRANCIS, lawyer; b. Hartford, Wis., Dec. 30, 1942; s. Arthur Zeno and Marie Rose (Lorenz) R.; m. Kathleen Marie Saunders, Aug. 31, 1968 (div. 1987); children—Daniel, Laura, Joseph. B.A., Marquette U., 1965; J.D., U. Wis., 1968. Bar: Wis. 1968, D.C. 1982. Staff atty. Wis. Legis. Council, Madison, 1968-69; trial atty. U.S. Dept. Justice, Washington, 1969-79; chief criminal sect. U.S. Dept. Justice, 1979-83, dep. asst. atty. gen., 1984; staff dir., chief counsel U.S. Senate Permanent Subcom. on Investigations, 1984-86, chief counsel for minority, 1986-94; ptnr. Leonard, Ralston, Stanton & Remington, 1995-97; adj. faculty Columbia Sch. Law Cath. U. Am., 1989—. Supr., Dane County Bd. Suprs., Wis., 1968-69. Recipient Atty. Gen.'s Disting. Service award U.S. Dept. Justice, 1983. Mem. Wis. Bar Assn., D.C. Bar Assn. Republican. Roman Catholic.

RIOPELLE, ARTHUR JEAN, psychologist; b. Thorp, Wis., Apr. 22, 1920; s. Wilfred Gaspar and Ann Marie (Schroeder) R.; m. Mary Jane Astell, May 2, 1942; children—Mary Ann, James Michael, Jean Elizabeth. B.S., U. Wis., 1941, M.S., 1948, Ph.D., 1950. Asst. prof., then assoc. prof. Emory U., 1950-57; dir. psychology div. U.S. Army Med. Research Lab., Ft. Knox, Ky., 1957-59; dir. Yerkes Labs. Primate Biology, Orange Park, Fla., 1959-62, Delta Regional Primate Research Ctr., Covington, La., 1962-71; prof. psychology La. State U., Baton Rouge, 1972—, Boyd prof., 1977-89, Boyd prof. emeritus, 1989—; mem. NRC panel on manganese, Com. on Med. and Biol. Effects of Environ. Pollutants. Editor Jour. Gen. Psychology, 1978-95; asst. editor Animal Behavior, 1962-65; cons. editor Jour. Genetic Psychology and Genetic Psychology Monograph, 1978-95; contbr. chpts. to books. La. Bd. Examiners of Psychologists, 1972-75; mem. panel on Air Force tng. Nat. Acad. Sci.-NRC, 1955-56; primate research study sect. Am. Inst. Biol. Scis.-NASA, 1959-63; chmn. sub-com. on man Lunar Receiving Lab. Study, 1970-71; chmn. U.S.-Japan Conf. Primate Research, 1963-64; chmn. sub-com. primate standards Inst. Lab. Animal Resources, NRC, 1964-69. Served with USAAF, 1942-46, ETO. Mem. Am. Psychol. Assn., Am. Physiol. Soc., So. Soc. Philosophy and Psychology, Internat. Primatological Soc., AAAS, Psychonomic Soc., Southeastern Psychol. Assn., Sigma Xi, Phi Kappa Phi, Sigma Chi. Home: 9710 Highland Rd Baton Rouge LA 70810-4031 Office: La State U Dept Psychology Baton Rouge LA 70803

RIORDAN, GEORGE NICKERSON, investment banker; b. Patchogue, N.Y., May 16, 1933; s. E. Arthur and Constance E. (Whelden) R.; m. Ann Wiggins, Jan. 4, 1958; children—Susan M., Peter G. B.S., Cornell U., 1955; M.B.A., Harvard U., 1960. Vice-pres. Lehman Bros., N.Y.C., 1960-71; mng. dir. Blyth Eastman Paine Webber, Los Angeles and N.Y.C., 1971-81, Prudential-Bache Securities, Los Angeles, 1981-88, Bear Stearns & Co., Inc., L.A., 1988-89, Dean Witter Reynolds Inc., 1989-91; bd. dirs. MacNeal Schwendler Corp., L.A., chmn. bd. 1997—; bd. dirs. Pancho's Mexican Buffet, Inc., Ft. Worth. Served to capt. USAF, 1955-57. Mem. Calif. Club, Quoque Field Club (L.I., N.Y.), Athenaeum Club, Valley Hunt Club (Pasadena, Calif.). Office: 815 Colorado Blvd Ste 104 Los Angeles CA 90041-1720

RIORDAN, JAMES QUENTIN, retired company executive; b. Bklyn., June 17, 1927; s. James A. and Ruth M. (Boomer) R.; m. Gloria H. Carlson, June 23, 1951; children: Harris, Susan, James, Ruth. BA, Bklyn. Coll., 1945; LLB, Columbia U., 1949. Bar: N.Y. 1951, U.S. Supreme Ct 1954. Atty. Winthrop, Stimson, Putnam & Roberts, N.Y.C., 1949-51; mem. staff Ways and Means sub-com., Washington, 1951-52; atty. tax div. Justice Dept., Washington, 1952-55; atty. Chadbourne, Parke, Whiteside & Wolff, N.Y.C., 1955-57; various positions to vice chmn., chief fin. officer Mobil Corp., 1957-89; pres. Bekaert Corp., 1989-92; ret., 1992; bd. dirs. Dow Jones & Co., Inc., The Bklyn. Union Gas Co., The Houston Exploration Co., Tri-Continental Corp. and other J & W Seligman mutual funds, Pub. Broadcasting Svc. Bd. dirs. Com. Econ. Devel., Tax Foun., Inc.; trustee Bklyn. Mus. Mem. Rembrandt Club (N.Y.C.), Blind Brook Club, Sailfish Point (Fla.), Stockbridge Club. Office: 675 3rd Ave New York NY 10017-5704

RIORDAN, JOHN THOMAS, trade association executive; b. Newark, June 5, 1937; s. Daniel Francis and Kathleen May (Hanan) R.; m. Mary Theresa Fleming, Sept. 19, 1966; children: Sheila, Patrick, Aidan, Meghan, Brendan, Caitlin. BA, Montclair St. Coll., 1959; MA, Laval U., Que., Can., 1963; postgrad., Harvard U., 1980. Tchr. Princeton (N.J.) Pub. Schs., 1959-64; instr. SUNY, Cortland, 1965; editor McGraw-Hill Book Co., St. Louis, 1966; assoc. examiner Ednl. Testing Service, Princeton, 1967-68; mgr. Houghton Mifflin Co., Boston, 1968-73, editorial dir., 1973-74; v.p. Hougton Mifflin Co., Boston, 1974-75, dir., 1975, sr. v.p., 1975-81; dir. programs Internat. Council Shopping Ctrs., N.Y.C., 1982-83, gen. mgr., 1983-85, exec. v.p., 1986—. Cons., leader Experiment in Internat. Living, Brattleboro, Vt., 1961-64; mem. adv. bd. Sch. Internat. Tng., Brattleboro, 1971-79, Real Estate Ctr. U. Pa., 1991—, Ctr. for Real Estate MIT, 1992—; mem. fin. adv. bd. City of Georgetown, Mass., 1972-75; trustee The Pike Sch., Andover, Mass., 1973-76. Mem. Assn. Am. Pubs. (bd. dirs. 1978-80), Am. Soc. Assn. Execs. Office: Internat Council Shopping Ctrs 665 Fifth Ave New York NY 10022-5305

RIORDAN, RICHARD J., mayor; b. Flushing, N.Y., 1930; m. Eugenia Riordan; 6 children (2 dec.); m. Jill Riordan. Attended, U. Calif., Santa Clara; grad., Princeton U., 1952; JD, U. Mich., 1956. With O'Melveny & Myers, L.A.; owner, operator Original Pantry Cafe; founder Total Pharmaceutical Care, Tetra Tech; mayor L.A., 1993—. Co-founder LEARN, 1991; sponsor Writing to Read computer labs Riordan Found.; active Eastside Boys and Girls Club. Lt. U.S. Army, Korea. Office: Los Angeles City Hall 200 N Spring St Ste 305 Los Angeles CA 90012-4805*

RIOS, ALBERTO ALVARO, English educator; b. Nogales, Ariz., Sept. 18, 1952; s. Alberto Alvaro and Agnes (Fogg) R.; m. Maria Guadalupe Barron, Sept. 8, 1979; 1 child, Joaquin. BA in Lit. & Creative Writing with honor, U. Ariz., 1974, BA in Psychology with honors, 1975, MFA in Creative Writing, 1979. Asst. prof. English Ariz. State U., Tempe, 1982-85, assoc. prof., 1985-89, prof., 1989-94, regent's prof., 1995—, dir. creative writing program, 1986-89, 92—; mem. editorial bd. New Chicano Writing, 1990—; corr. editor Manoa, 1989—; bd. dirs. Libr. of Congress/Ariz. Ctr. for the Book, 1988—, vice chair, 1989—. Author: Elk Heads on the Wall, 1979, Sleeping on Fists, 1981, Whispering to Fool the Wind, 1982, The Iguana Killer, 1984, Five Indiscretions, 1985, The Lime Orchard Woman, 1988, The Warrington Poems, 1989, Teodoro Luna's Two Kisses, 1990 (Pulitzer prize nomination), Pig Cookies, 1995; editor Ploughshares, 1991-92, adv. editor, 1992—; poetry editor Colorado Review, 1993; editl. bd. New Chicana/Chicano Writing, 1990—, Equinox, 1992—; contbr. poems and stories to numerous jours. and anthologies. Guggenheim fellow, 1988-89; recipient Western States Book award for Fiction, Walt Whitman award Acad. Am. Poets, Pushcart Prize, 1986, 88, 89, 93, Community Appreciation award Chicanos Por La Causa, 1988, Gov.'s Arts award State of Ariz., 1991; named Author of Yr. Mountain Plains Libr. Assn., 1991; NEA fellow; Ariz. State U. grantee. Office: Ariz State U Dept English Tempe AZ 85287-0302

RIOS, EVELYN DEERWESTER, columnist, musician, artist, writer; b. Payne, Ohio, June 25, 1916; d. Jay Russell and Flossie Edith (Fell) Deerwester; m. Edwin Tietjen Rios, Sept. 19, 1942 (dec. Feb. 1987); children: Jane Evelyn, Linda Sue Rios Stahlman. BA with honors, San Jose State U., 1964, MA, 1968. Cert. elem., secondary tchr., Calif. Lectr. in music San Jose State U., 1969-75; bilingual cons., then assoc. editor Ednl. Factors, Inc., San Jose, 1969-76, mgr. field research, 1977-78; writer, editor Calif. MediCorps Program, 1978-85; contbg. editor, illustrator The Community Family Mag., Wimberly, Tex., 1983-85; columnist The Springer, Dripping Springs, Tex., 1985-90; author, illustrator, health instr. textbooks elem. schs., 1980-82. Choir dir. Bethel Luth. Ch., Cupertino, Calif., 1965-66, Bethel Luth. Ch., 1968-83; dir. music St. Aban's Ch., Bogota Colombia; organist Holy Spirit Episcopal Ch., Dripping Springs, Tex., 1987-94; music dir. Cambrian Park (Calif.) Meth. Ch., 1961-64; chmn. Dripping Springs Planning and Zoning Commn., 1991-93. Mem. AAUW, Am. Guild Organists (dean 1963-64), Phi Kappa Phi (pres. San Jose chpt. 1973-74). Episcopalian. Avocations: weaving, stitching, painting. Home and Office: 23400 FM 150 Dripping Springs TX 78620

RIOUX, ROCH, lawyer, government official; b. Sayabec, Que., Can., July 16, 1935; s. Albert and Aline (Mercier) R.; m. Camille Savard, Sept. 4, 1961 (div. Aug. 1991); children: Elaine, Denis, Marie-Claude; m. Francine Marcour, May 8, 1987; children: Sophie, Philippe. BA, St. Charles Garnier Coll., Quebec City, Que., 1956; M.Comml. Scis., Laval U., 1960, Licence in Law, 1963. Bar: Que. 1964. Dir. companies br. Dept. Justice, Quebec City, 1968-72, dep. minister, 1982-89; dir. legal svc. Dept. Fin. Instns., Quebec City, 1972-74, dep.minister, 1974-81; pres. Commn. of Statues Revision, Quebec City, 1981-86, Agrl. Complaint Commn., Quebec City, 1989-92, Rev. Bd. Mental Disorder, Quebec City, 1992—. Mem. Can. Bar, Que. Bar, Inst. Pub. Adminstrn. of Can. Roman Catholic. Avocations: cross-country skiing, reading, computers. Home: 982 Beaulieu St, St Jean Chrysostome, PQ Canada G6Z 2L1

RIP, GERALD J., federal judge; b. Montreal, Canada, Dec. 7, 1940; s. Harry and Pauline (Karcynel) R.; m. Brenda E. Saslove, Apr. 5, 1970; 1 child, Eytan. BA, Sir George Williams U., 1962; LLM, U. Montreal, 1965. Spl. asst. Min. Justice, Ottawa, Canada, 1966-67; tax litigation sect. Dept. Justice, Ottawa, 1967-72; tax specialist Soloway, Wright & Assocs., Ottawa, 1973-83; judge Tax Ct. Canada, Ottawa, 1983—. Office: Tax Ct Canada, 200 Kent St, Ottawa, ON Canada K1A 0M1

RIPINSKY-NAXON, MICHAEL, archaeologist, art historian, ethnologist; b. Kutaisi, Georgia, USSR, Mar. 23, 1944; s. Pinkus and Maria (Kokielov) R.; 1 child, Tariel. AB in Anthropology with honors, U. Calif.-Berkeley, 1966, PhD in Archeology and Art History, 1979. Rsch. asst. Am. Mus. Natural History, N.Y.C., 1964, U. Calif.-Berkeley, 1964-66; mem. faculty dept. anthropology and geography of Near East, Calif. State U.-Hayward, 1966-67; asst. prof. Calif. State U.-Northridge, 1974-75; rschr., assoc. UCLA, 1974-75, sr. rsch. anthropologist Hebrew U., Hadassah Med. Sch., Jerusalem, 1970-71; curator Anthropos Gallery of Ancient Art, Beverly Hills, Calif., 1976-78; chief rsch. scientist Archaeometric Data Labs., Beverly Hills, 1976-78; dir. Ancient Artworld Corp., Beverly Hills, 1979-82; dir. prehistoric studies Mediterranean Rsch. Ctr., Athens, 1989-91; prof., chairperson, Dept. Cultural Studies, Pedagogical U., Kielce, Poland, 1993-95; conducted excavations Israel, Egypt, Jordan, Mesopotamia, Mexico, Cen. Am; specialist in the development of early religions and shamanism, phenomenon of origins of domestication and camel ancestry; expert on art works from French Impressionists to ancient Egypt and classical world; research in evolution of consciousness, ethnogenesis and the origins of religion, shamanism and ecstatic states. Author: The Nature of Shamanism, 1993; contbr. articles to sci. and scholarly jours. dir. Cen. Am. Inst. Prehistoric and Traditional Cultures, Belize; chmn. bd. Am. Found. for Cultural Studies. Recipient Cert. of Merit for Sci. Endeavour, Dictionary of Internat. Biography, 1974. Fellow Am. Anthropol. Assn., Royal Asiatic Soc.; mem. Archaeol. Inst. Am. (life), Soc. for Am. Archaeology, Royal Anthropol. Inst., Am. Ethnol. Soc., History of Sci. Soc., Am. Chem. Soc., Assn. for Transpersonal Psychology, Soc. Ethnobiology, Soc. Anthropology of Consciousness, Soc. Archeol. Scis. (life). Office: Ctrl Am Inst, PO Box 59, San Ignacio Cayo Dist, Belize

RIPKEN, CALVIN EDWIN, JR. (CAL RIPKEN), professional baseball player; b. Havre de Grace, Md., Aug. 24, 1960. Player minor league teams Bluefield, Miami, Charlotte, Rochester, 1978-81; player Balt. Orioles, 1978—. Recipient Rookie of Yr. award Internat. League, 1981, Rookie of Yr. award Baseball Writers Assn., Am. League, 1982, Silver Slugger award, 1983-86, 89, 91, 93-94, Gold Glove award, 1991-92; named Am. League Rookie of the Yr., The Sporting News, 1982, Player of the Yr., 1983, 91, Am. League MVP, 1983, 91, Major League Player of Yr., Sportsman of the Year, (1995) The Sporting News, 1983, 91; named to Am. League All-Star Team, 1983-96. Holder major league record for consecutive games played; broke Lou Gehrig's record of 2131 consecutive games played, 1995; maj. league record home runs by shortstop; highest single season fielding percentage (.996), 1990; most consecutive errorless games at shortstop (95). Office: care Balt Orioles Oriole Pk at Camden Yards 333 W Camden St Baltimore MD 21201-2435*

RIPLEY, ALEXANDRA BRAID, author; b. Charleston, S.C., Jan. 8, 1934; m. Leonard Ripley, 1958 (div. 1963); m. John Graham, 1981; children Elizabeth, Merrill. BA in Russian, Vassar Coll., 1955. Former tour guide, travel agent, underwear buyer; former manuscript reader, publicity director N.Y.C. Author: Charleston, 1981, On Leaving Charleston, 1984, The Time Returns: A Novel of Friends and Mortal Enemies in Fifteenth Century Florence, 1985, New Orleans Legacy, 1987, Scarlett: The Sequel to Margaret Mitchell's Gone With the Wind, 1991, From Fields of Gold, 1994, A Divine Love, 1996. Office: care Sterling Lord Literistic 65 Bleecker St New York NY 10012-2420

RIPLEY, JOHN WALTER, academic administrator; b. Welch, W.Va., June 29, 1939; m. Molin B. Ripley, May 9, 1964; children: Stephen B., Mary D., Thomas H., John M. BSEE, U.S. Naval Acad., 1962; MS, Am. U., 1976. Commd. 2d lt. USMC, 1962, advanced through grades to col., 1984, ret., 1992; polit./mil. planner Office of Joint Chiefs of Staff, Washington; asst. prof. history Oreg. State U., Corvallis, 1972-75; dir. divsn. English and history U.S. Naval Acad., Annapolis, Md., 1984-87; commanding officer Naval ROTC unit Va. Mil. Inst., Lexington, 1990-92; pres. So. Va. Coll., Buena Vista, 1992-96, chancellor, 1992—; lectr. in field. Decorated Navy Cross, Legion of Merit (2), Silver Star, Bronze Star (2), Purple Heart. Mem. Phi Alpha Theta. Office: Southern Virginia College One College Hill Dr Buena Vista VA 24416

RIPLEY, RANDALL BUTLER, political scientist, educator; b. Des Moines, Jan. 24, 1938; s. Henry Dayton and Aletha (Butler) R.; m. Grace A. Franklin, Oct. 15, 1974; children: Frederick Joseph, Vanessa Gail. B.A., DePauw U., 1959; M.A., Harvard, 1961, Ph.D., 1963. Teaching fellow Harvard, 1960-62; mem. staff Brookings Inst., Washington, 1963-67; research asst. Brookings Inst., 1963-64, research asso., 1964-67; intern Office of Democratic Whip, U.S. Ho. of Reps., Washington, 1963; assoc. prof. dept. polit. sci. Ohio State U., Columbus, 1967-69, prof., 1969—, chmn., 1969-91, dean Coll. Social and Behavioral Scis., 1992—; lectr. Cath. U., Washington, 1963-64; professorial lectr. Am. U., Washington, 1964-67; vis. prof. U. Okla., 1969-91. Author: Public Policies and Their Politics, 1966, Party Leaders in the House of Representatives, 1967, Majority Party Leadership in Congress, 1969, Power in the Senate, 1969, The Politics of Economic and Human Resource Development, 1972, Legislative Politics U.S.A, 1973, American National Government and Public Policy, 1974, Congress: Process and Policy, 1975, 4th edit., 1988, Policy-making in the Federal Executive Branch, 1975, Congress, the Bureaucracy, and Public Policy, 1976, 5th edit., 1991, National Government and Policy in the United States, 1977, A More Perfect Union, 1979, 4th edit., 1989, Policy Implementation and Bureaucracy, 1982, 2d edit., 1986, CETA: Politics and Policy, 1973-82, 1984, Policy Analysis in Political Science, 1985, Readings in American Government and Politics, 1989, 2d edit. 1993, Congress Resurgent, 1993, U.S. Foreign Policy After the Cold War, 1997; contbr. articles to profl. jours. Bd. govs. Stratford Festival, Ont., Can., 1994—. Woodrow Wilson fellow, 1959-60; Danforth fellow, 1959-63; recipient Sumner prize Harvard, 1963. Mem. Am. Polit. Sci. Assn. (sec. 1978), Midwest Polit. Sci. Assn., Phi Beta Kappa. Democrat. Home: 2685 Berwyn Rd Columbus OH 43221-3207

RIPP, BRYAN JEROME, geological engineer; b. Tucson, Dec. 22, 1959; s. Jerome Peter and Helen Marie (Bussmuss) R.; m. Susan Sorensen, Nov. 7, 1987; children: Aaron, Nathan. BS in Geol. Engring., S.D. Sch. Mines, 1982; MS in Geol. Engring., U. Mo., Rolla, 1984. Registered profl. engr., Ill., Mo., profl. geologist, Ark., Mo., Am. Inst. Profl. Geologists. Roustabout Shell Oil Co., Yorba Linda, Calif., 1980; geol. engr. Tenneco Oil Co., Lafayette, La., 1981; staff engr. Shannon and Wilson, Inc., St. Louis, 1984-88; prin. engr. Geotechnology, Inc., St. Louis, 1988-94; sr. geol. engr. Weir Internat. Mining Cons., Des Plaines, Ill., 1994—; cons. Consolidation Coal Co., St. Louis, 1986—, Union Pacific RR, Omaha, 1985-88, Mallinckrodt Chem., Inc., St. Louis, 1992-94, Met. Water Reclamation Dist. of Greater Chgo, 1994—, Robbins, Kaplan, Miller and Ciresi, 1994, Ill. Office of Mines and Minerals, 1996—, Ill. Divsn. Abandoned Mined Lands Reclamation. Author: Underground Storage Tank Closure Manual, 1992, The Geo-Environmental Design of Coal Refuse Impoundment in Illinois, 1997, Hydrocarbon Assessment Manual, 1992, Urbanization in Karst Terrain- A St. Louis Perspective; reviewer WASTECH Innovative Site Remediation Tech. monographs; author reports. Mem. ASCE contbg. author ethics sect.), Soc. Mining Engrs. (St. Louis sect. chmn. 1992-93, Chgo. sect. programs chmn. and newsletter editor 1995-97, co-chmn. environ. assessments com. environ. divsn., mem. sci. tchrs. workshop com.), Assn. Engring. Geologists (St. Louis sect. treas. 1990-94), Order of Engr., Ill. Mining Inst., Sigma Xi. Home: 1280 W New Britton Dr Hoffman Estates IL 60195-1732 Office: Weir Internat Mining Cons 2340 S River Rd Ste 203 Des Plaines IL 60018-3223

RIPPE, PETER MARQUART, museum administrator; b. Mpls., Dec. 16, 1937; s. Henry Albert and Zelda (Marquart) R.; m. Maria Boswell Wornom, Aug. 10, 1968. BA, U. Puget Sound, 1960; MA, U. Del., 1962. Dir. Confederate Mus., Richmond, Va., 1962-68; exec. dir. Harris County Heritage Soc., Houston, 1968-79, Roanoke Mus. Fine Arts (Va.), 1979-89, P. Buckley Moss Mus., Waynesboro, Va., 1989—; mem. Roanoke Arts Commn., 1983-90. Author: P. Buckley Moss, Painting the Joy of the Soul, 1997. Fellow Old Deerfield Found., 1958, H.F. duPont Winterthur Mus., 1960-62; bd. dirs. Augusta-Staunton-Waynesboro Visitors Bur. Mem. Am. Assn. Mus. (chmn. small mus. com. 1981-83, sr. examiner, 1983—, councillor-at-large 1985-88), Tex. Assn. Mus. (pres. 1975-77, Tex. award 1979), Va. Assn. Mus. (pres. 1983-84), Southeast Mus. Conf. (chmn. awards com. 1986-89), Shanandoah Valley Travel Assn. (Augusta County rep. 1995-97), Rotary (Waynesboro chpt.), Waynesboro Club. Democrat. Lutheran. Home: 149 Brook Ct Waynesboro VA 22980-5559 Office: P Buckley Moss Mus 150 P Buckley Moss Dr Waynesboro VA 22980-9406

RIPPEL, CLARENCE W., academic administrator. Acting pres. Lincoln U. Office: Lincoln U Office of President 281 Masonic Ave San Francisco CA 94118-4416*

RIPPEL, HARRY CONRAD, mechanical engineer, consultant; b. Phila., Feb. 19, 1926; s. Philip and Emma (Metzger) R.; m. Dorothy Ann Tartala, Nov. 20, 1948; children—Linda Jean, Richard Peter. B.M.E., Drexel U., Phila., 1952, M.S., 1957. Registered profl. engr., Pa. With Franklin Research Center, div. Franklin Inst., Phila., 1952-87, Inst. fellow, 1978—; cons. in tribology, 1987—; resident consultant Rotor Bearing Tech. & Software Inc., 1987—; mem. Com. on Sci. and the Arts, Franklin Inst., Phila. Author manuals and articles in field. Sunday sch. tchr., layreader St. James Episcopal Ch., Phila.; bd. dirs. Turbo Rsch. Found. With AUS, WWII, ETO. Decorated Bronze Star. Fellow ASME, Soc. Tribologists and Lubrication Engrs.; mem. Sigma Xi, Pi Tau Sigma. Home: 1434 Sharon Park Dr Sharon Hill PA 19079-2218 Office: Rotor Bearing Tech & Software Inc Lee Park 1100 E Hector St Conshohocken PA 19428-2374

RIPPER, RITA JO (JODY RIPPER), strategic planner, researcher; b. Goldfield, Iowa, May 8, 1950; d. Carl Phillip and Lucille Mae (Stewart) Ripper; BA, U. Iowa, 1972; MBA, NYU, 1978. Contracts and fin. staff Control Data Corp., Mpls., 1974-78; regional mgr. Raytheon Corp., Irvine, Calif., 1978-83; v.p. Caljo Corp., Des Moines, Iowa, 1980-84; asst. v.p. Bank of Am., San Francisco, 1984-88; pres. The Northhaven Co., 1988—, The Boardroom Adv. Group, 1990-93. Am. United; vol. Cancer, Heart, Lung Assns., Edina, N.Y.C., Calif., 1974-78, 84—. Mem. Amnesty Internat., Internat. Mktg. Assn., World Trade Ctr. Assn., Acctg. Soc. (pres. 1975-76), World Trade Club, Intertel, Mensa, Beta Alpha Psi (chmn. 1977-78), Phi Gamma Nu (v.p. 1971-72) Presbyterian. Club: Corinthian Yacht. Home and Office: 1730 Marguerite Ave Corona Del Mar CA 92625-1121

RIPPETEAU, DARREL DOWNING, architect; b. Clay Center, Nebr., Jan. 14, 1917; s. Claude LaVerne and Eva (Downing) R.; m. Donna Doris Hiatt, Jan. 8, 1939 (dec. 1988); children: Bruce Estes, Darrel Downing, Jane Upson Heffron; m. Joyce Spencer, May 18, 1991. B.A. in Architecture, U. Nebr., 1941. Staff architect FHA, Omaha, 1941-42; project mgr., mng. ptnr. Sargent-Webster-Crenshaw & Folley, Archs. and Engrs., Watertown, Buffalo, Syracuse, N.Y., Burlington, Vt, Bangor, Maine, 1946-81; treas., dir. Empire Forest System, Albany, N.Y., 1984-89; ret., 1990; bd. dirs. Archtl. Corp. Atlanta, Key Bank No. N.Y., Watertown, Assn. Island Recreational Corp.; commr. N.Y. State Coun. Architecture, 1975-85; mem. N.Y. State Forest Practice Bd., 1980—, chmn., 1994—; nat. adv. bd. mem. Remington Art Mus., Ogdensburg, N.Y., 1983-95. Prin. works include Justice Bldg, Albany, N.Y. State Office Bldg Watertown, Toomey Abbott Towers Syracuse, State U. N.Y. Cortland, U.S. P.O. Facility Syracuse. Mem. nat. fin. com. Rep. Party, 1971-73; bd. trustees The Antique Boat Mus., Clayton, N.Y., 1973—, Glenn Curtiss Mus., Hammondsport, N.Y. Maj. U.S. Army, 1942-46; lt. col. Corps of Engrs. retired, 1977. Recipient North Country citation St. Lawrence U., Canton, N.Y., 1971; Sears-Roebuck scholar, 1936-37; U. Nebr. Dept. Architecture grantee, 1940-41; Nebr. master U. Nebr., 1971; Disting. Alumni award Coll. of Architecture Alumni Assn., U. Nebr., 1996. Fellow AIA (nat. dir. 1969-73, trustee AIA Found. 1970-73); mem. Greater Watertown C. of C. (past pres.), N.Y. State Assn. Indsl. Devel. Agys. (past v.p.), N.Y. State Assn. Architects (pres. 1968-69, polit. action com. 1980—, James Kideney award 1987), Bldg. Rsch. Inst., Res. Officers Assn. (past pres.), Am. Tree Farm Assn., Jefferson County Hist. Soc. (dir. 1974-78), OX-5 Aviation Pioneers (chpt. pres.), Assn. U.S. Army (chpt. pres. 1985-86). Republican. Presbyterian. Home: 1011 NW 3rd Ave Delray Beach FL 33444-2938 Home and Studio: River Oaks 45650 Landon Rd Wellesley Island NY 13640-2112

RIPPLE, KENNETH FRANCIS, federal judge; b. Pitts., May 19, 1943; s. Raymond John and Rita (Holden) R.; m. Mary Andrea DeWeese, July 27, 1968; children: Gregory, Raymond, Christopher. AB, Fordham U., 1965; JD, U. Va., 1968; LLM, George Washington U., 1972, LLD (hon.), 1992. Bar: Va. 1968, N.Y. 1969, U.S. Supreme Ct. 1972, D.C. 1976, Ind. 1984, U.S. Ct. Appeals (7th cir.), U.S. Ct. Mil. Appeals, U.S. Dist. Ct. (no. dist.) Ind. Atty. IBM Corp., Armonk, N.Y., 1968; legal officer U.S. Supreme Ct., Washington, 1972-73, spl. asst. to chief justice Warren E. Burger, 1973-77; prof. law U. Notre Dame, 1977—; judge U.S. Ct. Appeals (7th cir.), South Bend, 1985—; reporter Appellate Rules Com., Washington, 1978-85; commn. on mil. justice U.S. Dept. Def., Washington, 1984-85; cons. Supreme Ct. Ala., 1983, Calif. Bd. Bar Examiners, 1981; cons. Anglo-Am. Jud. Exch., 1977, mem., 1980; adv. com. Bill of Rights to Bicentennial Constn. Commn., 1989; mem. adv. com. on appellate rules Jud. Conf. U.S., 1985-90, chmn., 1990-93; chmn. adv. com. on appellate judge edn. Fed. Jud. Ctr., 1996—.

Author: Constitutional Litigation, 1984. Mem. bd. visitors Sch. Law, Brigham Young U., 1989-92. Served with JAGC, USN, 1968-72. Mem. ABA, Am. Law Inst., Phi Beta Kappa. Office: US Ct of Appeals 208 US Courthouse 204 S Main St South Bend IN 46601-2122 also: Fed Bldg 219 S Dearborn St Ste 2660 Chicago IL 60604-1803

RIPPLEY, ROBERT, wholesale distribution executive; b. 1968. BS in Bus. pub. adminstn., U. Mo., 1972. Pres., CEO Affiliated Food Stores Inc., Tulsa, Okla., 1989—. Office: Affiliated Food Stores Inc 4433 W 49th St Tulsa OK 74107-7313

RIPPON, THOMAS MICHAEL, art educator, artist; b. Sacramento, Apr. 1, 1954; s. Samuel Joseph Jr. and June Evelyn (Garnet) R.; m. Sarah Sterrett, Dec. 22, 1980; children: Adam Michael, Peter Thomas. MFA, Art Inst. Chgo., 1979. Instr. Columbia Coll., Chgo., 1978-79; asst. prof. Montana State U., Bozeman, 1980, Calif. State U., Sacramento, 1981; assoc. prof. Tenn. Tech. U., Cookeville, 1982-87; asst. prof. U. Nev., Reno, 1987-89; assoc. prof. U. Montana, Missoula, 1989—, chair dept. art, 1990—; artist in residence U. Nevada, Reno, 1988; vis. prof. U. Calif., Davis, 1989; lectr. in field, 1973—. Solo exhbns. include Quay Gallery, San Francisco, 1975, 77, 81, 85, Rochester (Minn.) Art Ctr., 1979, Betsy Rosenfield Gallery, Chgo., 1980, 82, 84, Drake U., Des Moine, Iowa, 1985, Cross Creek Gallery, Malibu, Calif., 1987, 88, Judith Weintraub Gallery, Sacramento, 1990, 91, Huntington (W.Va.) Mus. Art, 1991, Kohler Art Ctr., Sheboygan, Wis., 1992, Yellowstone Art Ctr., Billings, Mont., 1993, Missoula Mus. Arts, 1994, Holter Mus. Art, Helena, Mont., 1995, John Natsovlas Gallery, 1995, 97, others; group exhbns. include San Francisco Mus. Modern Art, 1972, Davis (Calif.) Art Ctr., 1973, Oakland Mus., 1974, Evanston (Ill.) Art Ctr., 1974, Fendrick Gallery, Washington, 1975, Campbell Mus., Camden, N.J., 1976, Montana State U., Bozeman, 1976, De Young Mus., San Francisco, 1978, Am. Craft Mus., N.Y.C., 1978, 81, Phila. Mus. Modern Art, 1980, Craft and Folk Mus., L.A., 1980, Indpls. Mus. Art, 1982, Impressions Today Gallery, Boston, 1982, Elements Gallery, N.Y.C., 1983, Tampa (Fla.) Mus., 1983, Hyde Park Art Ctr., Chgo., 1983, 85, Traver-Sutton Gallery, Seattle, 1984, Erie (Pa.) Art Mus., 1985, Fay Gold Gallery, Atlanta, 1986, Seattle Art Mus., 1987, Candy Store Art Gallery, Folsom, Calif., 1987, Crocker Art Mus., Sacramento, 1988, Lang Gallery Scripps Coll., Claremont, Calif., 1988, Sherley Koteen & Assoc., Washington, 1989, 90, Eve Mannes Gallery, Atlanta, 1989, Art Gallery Western Australia, 1989, Joanne Rapp Gallery, Scottsdale, 1990, Missoula Mus. of Arts, 1991, 92, Sutton West Gallery, Missoula, 1992, Yellowstone Art Ctr., 1992, Natsoulas Gallery, Davis, Calif., 1993, many others; represented in pvt. collections; pub. collections include San Francisco Mus. Art, L.A. County Mus. Art, Sheldon Meml. Collection U. Nebr., Mus. Fine Arts, Salt Lake City, Ch. Fine Arts Collection U. Nev., Reno, Kanzawa-Shi, Hokkoku Shinbun, Kyoto, Japan, Renwick Gallery Smithsonian Institution, Contemporary Art Mus., Honolulu, J.B. Speed Art Mus., Louisville, Ky., U. Iowa, Ames, Missoula Mus. Arts, others. Recipient Kingsley Art Club award Crocker Art Mus., Sacramento, 1971, Crocker-Kingsley award, 1972; NEA fellow, 1974, 81, Nelson Raymond fellow Art Inst. Chgo., 1979. Office: Univ of Montana Dept Of Art Missoula MT 59812

RIPPY, FRANCES MARGUERITE MAYHEW, English language educator; b. Ft. Worth, Sept. 16, 1929; d. Henry Grady and Marguerite Christine (O'Neill) Mayhew; m. Noble Merrill Rippy, Aug. 29, 1955 (dec. Sept. 1980); children: Felix O'Neill, Conrad Mayhew, Marguerite Hailey. BA, Tex. Christian U., 1949; MA, Vanderbilt U., 1951, PhD, 1957; postgrad., U. London, 1952-53. Instr. Tex. Christian U., 1953-55; instr. to asst. prof. Lamar State U., 1955-59; asst. prof. English Ball State U., Muncie, Ind., 1959-64; assoc. prof. English, Ball State U., 1964-68, prof., 1968—, dir. grad. studies in English, 1966-87; editor Ball State U. Forum, 1960-89; vis. asst. prof. Sam Houston State U., 1957; vis. lectr., prof. U. P.R., summers 1959, 60, 61; exch. prof. Westminster Coll., Oxford, Eng., 1988; cons.-evaluator North Cen. Assn. Colls. and Schs., 1973—, commn.-at-large, 1987-91; cons.-evaluator New Eng. Assn. Schs. and Colls., 1983. Author: Matthew Prior, 1986; contbr. articles to profl. jours., encys., ref. guides, chpts. to anthology; contbr. to Dictionary of Literary Biography. Recipient McClintock award, 1966; Danforth grantee, 1964, Ball State U. Rsch. grantee, 1960, 62, 70, 73, 76, 87, 88, 89, 90, 92, 93, 95, 96, 98, Lilly Libr. Rsch., 1978; Fulbright scholar U. London, 1952-53; recipient Outstanding Faculty award Ball State U., 1992, Ind. Coll. Tchr./Scholar of 1994, Ind. Coll. English Assn., 1994. Mem. MLA, AAUP, Coll. English Assn, Nat. Coun. Tchrs. English, Am. Soc. 18th Century Studies, Am. Fedn. Tchrs., Ind. Coll. English Assn. (pres. 1984-85) Johnson Soc. Midwest (sec. 1961-62). Home: 4709 W Jackson St Muncie IN 47304-3514 *I have found all of the worlds which the above biographical paragraph touches upon—familial, academic, literary—lively and stimulating and thoroughly satisfying. Each world demands a great deal and offers a great deal in return.*

RIPSTEIN, CHARLES BENJAMIN, surgeon; b. Winnipeg, Man., Can., Dec. 13, 1913; came to U.S., 1949; s. Hyman Mendel and Bertha (Benjamin) R.; m. Barbara Adelman, Dec. 26, 1950; children: Ellen Joan, Linda Hope. B.S., U. Ariz., 1936; M.D., C.M., McGill U., 1940. Diplomate: Am. Bd. Surgery, Am. Bd. Thoracic Surgery, Am. Bd. Colon and Rectal Surgery. Intern medicine Royal Victoria Hosp., Montreal, 1940-41; residency in surgery Royal Victoria and Montreal Gen. hosps., 1945-48; demonstrator surgery McGill U., 1948-49; asso. prof. surgery SUNY, Bklyn., 1949-52; prof. surgery SUNY, 1952-54; prof. surgery, also exec. officer dept. surgery Albert Einstein Coll. Medicine, Yeshiva U., 1954-58, prof. clin. surgery, 1958—; clin. prof. surgery U. Miami Sch. Medicine, 1972; chief divs. gen. and thoracic surgery Bronx Mcpl. Hosp. Center, N.Y.C., 1954-58; dir. surg. service Beth-El Hosp., Bklyn., 1958—; dir. surgery Brookdale Hosp. Center, Bklyn.; cons. in surgery Maimonides Hosp., Bklyn., Bronx VA Hosp., surgeon Miami Heart Inst.; attending surg. Lebanon Hosp.; clin. prof. surgery U. Miami, Fla.; cons. cardiac surgery Health Ins. Plan N.Y.; vis. prof. surgery U. Tel Aviv, 1969-70. Author chpt. on cardiac surgery in textbook. Served as squadron leader RCAF, 1941-45. Fellow ACS, Royal Coll. Surgeons (Can.), N.Y. Acad. Medicine, Am. Coll. Chest Physicians; mem. AMA, Soc. Univ. Surgeons, Am. Assn. Thoracic Surgery, Am. Heart Assn., N.Y. Surg. Soc., Alpha Omega Alpha, Zeta Beta Tau. Home: 500 Bayview Dr Apt 932 Miami FL 33160-4749

RIRIE, CRAIG MARTIN, periodontist; b. Lewiston, Utah, Apr. 17, 1943; s. Martin Clarence and VaLera (Dixon) R.; m. Becky Ann Ririe, Sept. 17, 1982; children: Paige, Seth, Theron, Kendall, Nathan, Derek, Brian, Amber, Kristen. AA, San Bernadino Valley Coll., 1966; DDS, Creighton U., 1972; MSD, Loma Linda U., 1978. Staff mem. Flagstaff (Ariz.) Med. Ctr., 1974—; pvt. practice dentistry specializing in periodontics Flagstaff, 1974—; assoc. prof. periodontics No. Ariz. U., Flagstaff, 1979—, chmn. dept. dental hygiene, 1980-81; med. research cons. W.L. Gore, Flagstaff, 1983—. Contbr. articles to profl. jours. Vice pres. bd. dirs. Grand Canyon coun. Boy Scouts Am., 1991—. Lt. col. USAFR. Health professions scholarship Creighton U., Omaha, 1969-71; recipient Mosby award Mosby Pub. Co., 1972; research fellowship U. Bergen, Norway, 1978-79. Mem. ADA, Am. Acad. Periodontology (cert.), Western Soc. Periodontology (chmn. com. on rsch. 1982—, bd. dirs. 1983—), No. Ariz. Dental Soc. (pres. 1994-96), Am. Acad. Oral Implantologists, Internat. Congress Oral Implantologists, Ariz. Dental Assn., Am. Cancer Soc. (bd. dirs.), Flagstaff C. of C., Rotary. Republican. Mem. LDS Ch. Avocations: skiing, tennis, golf. Home: 1320 N Aztec St Flagstaff AZ 86001-3004 Office: 1050 N San Francisco St Flagstaff AZ 86001-3259

RIS, HANS, zoologist, educator; b. Bern, Switzerland, June 15, 1914; came to U.S., 1938, naturalized, 1945; s. August and Martha (Egger) R.; m. Hania Wislicka, Dec. 26, 1947 (div. 1971); children: Christopher Robert, Annette Margo; m. Theron Caldwell, July 14, 1980. Diploma high sch. teaching, U. Bern, 1936; Ph.D., Columbia, 1942. Lectr. zoology Columbia U., 1942; Seessel fellow in zoology Yale U., 1942; instr. biology Johns Hopkins U., 1942-44; asst. Rockefeller Inst., N.Y.C., 1944-46; assoc. Rockefeller Inst., 1946-49; assoc. prof. zoology U. Wis., Madison, 1949-53; prof. U. Wis., 1953-84, prof. emeritus, 1984—; hon. prof. Peking U., Beijing, 1995—. Fellow AAAS; mem. Am. Acad. Arts and Scis., Nat. Acad. Scis., Electron Microscopy Soc. Am. (Disting. Investigator award 1983), Am. Soc. for Cell Biology (E.B. Wilson award 1993). Achievements include research on mechanisms of nuclear division, chromosome structure, nuclear envelope, cell ultrastructure, electron microscopy. Office: U Wis Zoology Rsch 1117 W Johnson St Madison WI 53706-1705

RIS, WILLIAM KRAKOW, lawyer; b. Dubuque, Iowa, June 11, 1915; s. Rinehart F. and Anna W. (Krakow) R.; m. Patty S. Nash, Dec. 28, 1940; children: Frederic N., William Krakow Jr. AB, U. Colo., 1945, LLB, 1939. Bar: Colo. 1939. Practice in Denver, 1939-43, 46-86; with firm Wood, Ris & Hames, P.C., 1948-86, of counsel, 1986—; mem. Commn. on Jud. Qualifications, 1973-77, chmn., 1977. Served with AUS, 1943-46. Fellow Am. Bar Found., Am. Coll. Trial Lawyers (bd. regents 1982-83); mem. Colo. Bar Assn. (pres. 1962-63), Denver Law Club (pres. 1956-57), Order of Coif. Episcopalian. Home: Unit 114 2800 S University Blvd Denver CO 80210 Office: 1775 Sherman St Ste 1600 Denver CO 80203-4317

RISCH, JAMES E., lawyer; b. Milw., May 3, 1943; s. Elroy A. and Helen B. (Levi) R.; m. Vicki L. Choborda, June 8, 1968; children—James E., Jason S., Jordan D. B.S. in Forestry, U. Idaho, 1965, J.D., 1968. Dep. pros. atty. Ada County, Idaho, 1968-69, chief dep. pros. atty., 1969-70, pros. atty., 1971-75; mem. Idaho Senate, 1974-88, 95—, majority leader, 1977-82, 97—, pres. pro tem, 1983-88, asst. majority leader, 1996; ptnr. Risch Goss & Insinger, Boise, Idaho, 1975—; prof. law Boise State U., 1972-75. Bd. dirs. Nat. Dist. Attys. Assn., 1973; pres. Idaho Prosecuting Attys. Soc., 1973; chmn. George Bush Presdl. Campaign, Idaho, 1988; mem. Gen. Coun. Idaho Rep. Party, 1991-95. Mem. ABA, Idaho Bar Assn., Boise Bar Assn., Am. Judicature Soc., Ducks Unlimited, Nat. Rifle Assn., Nat. Cattlemans Assn., Idaho Cattlemans Assn., Am. Angus Assn., Idaho Angus Assn., Am. Legis. Exch. Coun., Boise Valley Angus Assn., Phi Delta Theta, Xi Sigma Pi. Republican. Roman Catholic. Avocations: hunting; fishing; skiing; horseback riding; tennis. Home: 5400 S Cole Rd Boise ID 83709-6401 Office: Risch Goss & Insinger 407 W Jefferson St Boise ID 83702-6049

RISCH, MARTIN DONALD, marketing-management consulting company executive; b. Bklyn., Oct. 7, 1929; s. Rene and Lillian (Grant) R.; m. Joan Nattrass, Dec. 26, 1955; children: Lillian, David. BA, Colgate U., 1951; MBA, Harvard U., 1955. Dir. mktg. devel. Riegel Paper Co., N.Y.C., 1950-60, Fitchburg (N.Y.) Paper Co., 1960-64; dir. planning speciality paper div. Litton Industries, Fitchburg, 1965-69, 70-71, v.p. planning paper printing div., 1971-76; pres. Lincoln Assocs., Lexington, Mass., 1976—. 1st lt. USAF, 1951-53, Korea. Mem. TAPPI, Graphic Arts Tech. Found., Packaging Internat., Harvard Club, Oak Hill Country Club. Home: 71 Winter St Lincoln MA 01773-3502 Office: Lincoln Assocs 35 Bedford St Ste 4 Lexington MA 02173-4400

RISEBROUGH, DOUG, professional hockey team executive; b. 1954; m. Marilyn Risenbrough; children: Allison, Lindsay. Former player Montreal (Que.) Canadiens, for 8 years; former player Calgary (Alta., Can.) Flames, for 5 years, former asst. coach, 1987-89, asst. gen. mgr., 1989-90, head coach, 1990-92; General Manager Calgary (Alt., Can.) Flames, 1992—. Office: Calgary Flames, PO Box 1540 Sta M, Calgary, AB Canada T2P 3B9*

RISELEY, MARTHA SUZANNAH HEATER (MRS. CHARLES RISELEY), psychologist, educator; b. Middletown, Ohio, Apr. 25, 1916; d. Elsor and Mary (Henderson) Heater; BEd, U. Toledo, 1943, MA, 1958; PhD, Toledo Bible Coll., 1977; student Columbia U., summers 1943, 57; m. Lester Seiple, Aug. 27, 1944 (div. Feb. 1953); 1 child, L. Rolland, III; m. Charles Riseley, July 30, 1960. Tchr. kindergarten Maumee Valley Country Day Sch., Maumee, Ohio, 1942-44; dir. recreation Toledo Soc. for Crippled Children, 1950-51; tchr. trainable children Lott Day Sch., Toledo, 1951-57; psychologist, asst. dir. Sheltered Workshop Found., Lucas County, Ohio, 1957-62; psychologist Lucas County Child Welfare Bd., Toledo, 1956-62; tchr. educable retarded, head dept. spl. edn. Maumee City Schs., 1962-69; pvt. practice clin. psychology, 1956—; instr. spl. edn. Bowling Green State U., 1962-65; instr. Owens Tech. Coll., 1973-78; interim dir. rehab. services Toledo Goodwill Industries, summer 1967, clin. psychologist Rehab. Center, 1967—; staff psychologist Toledo Mental Health Center, 1979-84. Dir. camping activities for retarded girls and women Camp Libbey, Defiance, Ohio, summers 1951-62; group worker for retarded women Toledo YWCA, 1957-62; guest lectr. Ohio State U., 1957. Health care profl. mem. Nat. Osteoporosis Found., 1988—. Mem. Ohio Assn. Tchrs. Trainable Youth (pres. 1956-57), NW Ohio Rehab. Assn. (pres. 1961-62), Toledo Council for Exceptional Children (pres. 1965), Greater Toledo Assn. Mental Health, Nat. Assn. for Retarded Children, Ohio Assn. Tchrs. Slow Learners, Am. Assn. Mental Deficiency, Am. Soc. Psychologists in Marital and Family Counseling, Psychology and Law Soc. Am. (assoc.), Ohio, NW Ohio (sec.-treas. 1974-77, pres. 1978-79), Am. Theater Orgn. Soc., Ohio Psychol. Assn. (continuing edn. com. 1978—), NEA, AAUW, Am. Soc. Psychologists in Pvt. Practice (nat. dir. 1976—), State Assn. Psychologists and Psychol. Assts., Bus. and Profl. Women's Club, (pres. 1970-72), Ohio Fedn. Bus. and Profl. Women's Clubs (dist. sec. 1970-71, dist. legis. chmn. 1972-74), Toledo Art Mus., Women's Aux. Toledo Bar Assn., League Women Voters (pres. Toledo Lucas County 1991-93), Y Matrons (pres. 1993—), Toledo Area Theater Orgn. Soc. (sec. 1991—), Zonta Internat. (local pres. 1973-74, 78-79, area dir. 1976-78, Maumee River Valley Woman of Yr. for svc. to community and Zonta, 1992), Maumee Valley Hist. Soc., MBLS PEO (chpt. pres. 1950-51), Toledo Council on World Affairs, Internat. Platform Assn. Baptist. Home and Office: 2816 Wicklow Rd Toledo OH 43606-2833

RISEN, WILLIAM MAURICE, JR., chemistry educator; b. St. Louis, July 22, 1940. ScB, Georgetown U., 1962; PhD, Purdue U., 1967. Asst. prof. chemistry Brown U., Providence, 1967-72, assoc. prof. chemistry, 1972-75, prof. chemistry, 1975—, chmn. chemistry dept., 1972-80, chmn. of faculty, 1993-94; cons. in field. Contbr. over 100 articles to profl. jours. Grantee in field. Mem. Am. Chem. Soc., Am. Phys. Soc., Am. Ceramic Soc. Office: Brown U Dept of Chemistry 324 Brook St Providence RI 02912-9019

RISHEL, JAMES BURTON, manufacturing executive; b. Omaha, Apr. 27, 1920; s. James Blaine and Elizabeth Helen (Kerr) R.; m. Alice Jane Snyder, June 30, 1945; children: James Richard, Sara Jane Rishel Fields. BSME, U. Nebr., 1946. Profl. engr., Ohio. Pres. Corp. Equipment Co., Cin., 1962-82; chmn. bd. Systecon Inc., Cin., 1982—. Author: The Water Management Manual, HVAC Pump Handbook, 1996; patentee hydraulic systems; contbr. numerous articles to profl. jours. Capt. USAF, 1942-46, 51-52. Fellow ASHRAE; mem. Am. Water Works Assn., Water Environment Fedn. Avocations: philanthropy, golf, walking. Home: 7570 Thumbelina Ln Cincinnati OH 45242-4937 Office: Systecon Inc 9750 Crescent Park Dr West Chester OH 45069-3894

RISHEL, RICHARD CLINTON, banker; b. Oreland, Pa., June 7, 1943; S. Herbert Beale and Evelyn (Lauer) R.; m. Carol Staub, Apr. 3, 1965; children: Christian Daniel, Peter James. B.A., Pa. State U., 1965; postgrad., Drexel Inst. Tech., 1965-66. Credit analyst 1st Pa. Banking & Trust Co., Phila., 1965-69; comml. lending officer Nat. Bank of Chester County, West Chester, Pa., 1969; asst. v.p. Continental Bank of Norristown, Pa., 1969-70; sec. Continental Bank of Norristown, 1970-71, v.p., 1971-73, sr. v.p., chief fin. officer, 1973-75, exec. v.p., chief fin. officer, 1975-81, vice chmn., 1981-83, pres., chief adminstrv. officer, 1984-89, also dir.; pres., chief exec. officer Continental Bank, Continental Bancorp, 1990-92; vice chmn. bd. Continental Bank, 1981-84; pres. parent co. Continental Bancorp., 1981-92; dir. Barnett Inst. U. North Fla., 1993-94; sec. of banking Commonwealth of Pa., 1995—. Office: 4567 Saint Johns Bluff Rd S Jacksonville FL 32224-2646

RISHER, JOHN ROBERT, JR., lawyer; b. Washington, Sept. 23, 1938; s. John Robert and Yvonne Gwendolyn (Jones) R.; m. Carol Adrienne Seeger, June 9, 1974; children—John David, Michael Temple, Mark Eliot, Conrad Zachary. B.A., Morgan Coll., 1960; LL.B., U. So. Calif., 1963; postgrad., John F. Kennedy Sch., Harvard U., 1977. Bar: Calif. 1963, D.C. 1967, U.S. Supreme Ct. 1975. Mem. staff Pres.'s Com. on EEO, Washington, 1965; atty. criminal fraud sect. Dept. Justice, Washington, 1965-68; assoc. Arent, Fox, Kintner, Plotkin & Kahn, Washington, 1968-75; ptnr. Arent, Fox, Kintner, Plotkin & Kahn, 1975-76; corp. counsel D.C., 1976-78; ptnr. Arent, Fox, Kintner, Plotkin & Kahn, Washington, 1978—; chmn. D.C. Criminal Justice Coord. Bd., 1976-78, D.C. Bar spl. com. on federal judiciary, 1985-87; trustee, exec. com. Supreme Ct. Hist. Soc., 1990—; fellow Am. Bar Found., 1994—; trustee Frederick B. Abramson Meml. Found., 1996—; exec. com. The Smithsonian Instn. Washington Coun., 1997—. Chmn. budget com. Jewish Social Svc. Agy., 1980-85; chmn. D.C. Commn. on Licensure to Practice Healing Arts, 1976-78; chmn. nominating com. D.C. Bd. Elections and Ethics, 1974-76; bd. dirs. D.C. Pub. Defender Svc., 1974-76; chmn. Montgomery County Civil Liberties Union, 1970-71; mem. exec. com. Nat. Capital Area Civil Liberties Union, 1969-71; pres. D.C. Jewish Cmty. Ctr., 1985-87, bd. dirs., 1985—; trustee, bd. dirs. capital camps United Jewish Appeal Fedn., 1987-93; bd. dirs. Washington Symphony Orch., 1990—. Mem. ABA, Bar Assn. D.C., Calif. Bar Assn., Fed. Bar Assn., Washington Bar Assn.. DePriest 15. Democrat. Jewish. Home: 3311 Cleveland Ave NW Washington DC 20008-3456 Office: Arent Fox Kintner Plotkin Kahn 6th Floor 1050 Connecticut Ave NW Washington DC 20036-5339

RISHER, STEPHAN OLAF, investment officer; b. Santa Ana, Calif., Jan. 12, 1951; s. Joseph Leo and Catherine Minnie (Selle) R.; m. Kimberly Jo Hought, May 10, 1984 (div. 1992); 1 child, Jordan Stephan; m. Susan Ekberg, 1995. Miles C.C., Miles City, Mont., 1970, U. Mont., Missoula, 1972. Tech. asst. Polizbohn Farms, Kermanshah, Iran, 1972-73; sales mgr. B & B Signs, Missoula, 1973-75; asst. mgr. and sales Northwest Indsl., Billings, Mont., 1975-79; dist. mgr. Power River Explosives, Williston, N.D., 1979-83; investment officer Dain Bosworth, Inc., Fargo, N.D., 1983—. Mem. Cass County Commn., Fargo, 1991-95; pres. Hospice Red River Valley, Fargo, 1992; vice chair Lake Agassiz Regional Solid Waste, Fargo, 1992; mem. steering com. Nat. Assn. Counties, Washington, 1991; bd. dirs. Cass County Social Svcs., Fargo, 1991. Mem. Cass County Econ. Devel., Williston Petroleum Club, Masons, Shriners, Toastmasters. Lutheran. Avocations: hunting, fishing. Office: Dain Bosworth Inc 74 Broadway Fargo ND 58102-4934

RISHER, WILLIAM HENRY, cardiothoracic surgeon; b. New Orleans, Oct. 3, 1958; m. Michele Helene Risher; children: Amelia Alexandra, Jordan Prescott, Olivia Leigh. Student, U. New Orleans; BS in Biomed. Engring., Tulane U., 1981; MD, La. State U., 1985. Diplomate Am. Bd. Surgery, Am. Bd. Thoracic Surgery; lic. surgeon, N.Y.; cert. ACLS, advanced trauma life support, pediatric advanced life support provider, basic life support provider. Resident in gen. surgery Alton Ochsner Med. Found., New Orleans, 1985-90, chief resident, 1989-90, resident and fellow in cardiovascular surgery, 1990-92, chief resident, 1991-92; flight care physician Ochsner Flight Care, 1986-92; asst. prof. cardiothoracic surgery Med. Ctr. U. Rochester, N.Y., 1992—; presenter in field. Contbr. 23 articles to med. and sci. jours. T.H. Harris scholar Tulane U, 1977-79, full scholar, 1979-81. Fellow ACS, Am. Coll. Cardiology (assoc.); mem. AMA, Am. Coll. Chest Physicians, Soc. Thoracic Surgeons, Internat. Soc. Heart and Lung Transplantation, S.E. Surg. Congress, So. Med. Assn., Med. Soc. County Monroe, Rochester Acad. Medicine, Rochester Cardiovascular Soc., Upstate Soc. Thoracic Surgeons, Rochester Surg. Soc., Assn. for Advancement of Med. Instrumentation, Alton Ochsner Med. Soc., Tau Beta Pi, Alpha Omega Alpha. Home: 90 Rhinecliff Dr Rochester NY 14618-1506

RISI, LOUIS J., JR., business executive; b. Highland Park, Ill., July 2, 1936; s. Louis J. and Ann E. R.; m. Mary Jean Anson, Jan. 15, 1957; children: Steven, Janet, Andrew. B.S., Bradley U., 1958; MBA, U. Chgo. Pres., bd. dirs., mem. exec. com. Norin Corp., Miami, Fla., 1969-81; exec. com. dir. Maple Leaf Mills Ltd., Toronto, Can., 1970-81, Corp. Foods, Inc., 1970-81; chmn. bd. dirs. Louis Sherry, Inc., 1976-81; chmn. bd., chief exec. officer Nat. Investors Fire & Casualty Co., 1975-77; exec. com. dir. Investors Equity Life Ins. Co. of Hawaii, 1970-75; pres., dir. The Abbey, Lake Geneva, 1970-75; exec. comm., dir. Upper Lakes Shipping, Ltd., Toronto, Can., 1970-76; pres., dir. The Pioneer, Lake Oshkosh, 1971-76; exec. comm., dir. Port Weller and St. Lawrence Dry Dock, Ltd., St. Catharines, Can., 1971-76; pres., dir. Homosassa Springs, Fla., 1971-78; exec. v.p., dir. Ivan Tors Films Inc., Culver City, Calif., 1972-76, Ivan Tors Studios Inc., Miami, Fla., 1976-80; exec. com. dir. Midland Nat. Bank, 1976-80; pres., dir. Norris Grain Co., 1980-82; chmn. bd., CEO CTC Corp., 1981-83; pres. Victory Industries, Inc.; chmn. bd. dirs. Red Wing Co., Oklawaha Farms, Inc., Assured Security Co.; dir. Breckinridge Resorts Group; exec. v.p., bd. dirs. Detroit Red Wings Hockey Club, Inc., 1976-82; bd. govs. Nat. Hockey League, 1976-82; bd. dirs. Chgo. Rock Island and Pacific R.R., dir. exec. com., Bankmgrs. Corp.; lt. comdr. U.S.N.R., 1959-67; U.S. rep. Grain negotiations with USSR; U.S. rep. Feedstuffs negotiations with China; mem. adv. coun. Am. Stock Exch.; mem. Agrl. Processors Liaison com. FTC; mem. adv. bd. Nat. Millers Assn.; exec. v.p., bd. dirs. Adirondack Red Wings Hockey Club, Inc., 1976-82, Ft. Worth Red Wings Hockey Club, Inc., 1975-78; bd. govs. Internat. Hockey League, 1978-82, Am. Hockey League, 1975-79; dir. Nashville Country Club, Inc. Trustee Fairchild Tropical Garden, Miami, Fla. Mem. Ocean Reef Yacht Club (Key Largo, Fla.), Santa Rosa (Calif.) Country Club, Riviera Country Club (Coral Gables, Fla.), Anabelle's Club (London), St. James Club (London). Home: 10915 SW 53rd Ave Miami FL 33156-4209 Office: 200 NE 2nd Dr Homestead FL 33030-6119 also: 4535 E Elwood St Phoenix AZ 85040

RISIN, JACK See BUTCHER, JACK ROBERT

RISINGER, C. FREDERICK, social studies educator; b. Paducah, Ky., July 15, 1939; s. Charles Morris and Mary Neal (Barfield) R.; m. Margaret M. Marker, July 4, 1994; children: Donna Lyne, Alyson, Laura, John. BS in Edn., So. Ill. U., 1961; MA in History, No. Ill. U., 1968. Newscaster, disc jockey WMOK Radio, Metropolis, Ill., 1955-61; tchr., adminstr., coach Lake Park H.S., Roselle, Ill., 1962-73; coord. sch. social studies Ind. U., Bloomington, 1973-86, assoc. dir. social studies devel. ctr., 1986-90, dir. nat. clearinghouse for U.S.-Japan studies, 1990-95, assoc. dir. tchr. edn., 1995—; mem. adv. bd. Learning Mag., Boston, 1988—; pres. Nat. Coun. for the Social Studies, 1990-91. Co-author: America! America!, 1974, America's Past and Promise, 1995; editor jour. News and Notes on the Social Sciences, 1973-86. Pres. Social Studies Suprs. Assn., Washington, 1985-86; exec. dir. Ind. Coun. for Social Studies, Bloomington, 1975-87. Recipient numerous pub. and pvt. edn1. grants; named Tchr. of Yr. DuPage County Edn. Assn., 1973. Mem. ASCD, Nat. Coun. for Social Studies, Ind. Assn. Historians, Phi Delta Kappa. Democrat. Home: 7039 E State Rd 45 # E Bloomington IN 47408-9580

RISK, JOHN FRED, banker, investment banker; b. Ft. Wayne, Ind., Dec. 1, 1928; s. Clifford and Estella (Kline) R.; m. Viola Jean Tompt, July 12, 1953; children: Nancy Jean, John Thomas. B.S. cum laude, Ind. U., 1949, LL.B., J.D., 1951; postgrad., Nortwestern U.; LL.D., Ind. State U. With Harris Trust & Savs. Bank, Chgo., 1951-54, W.T. Grimm & Co., 1954-56; with Ind. Nat. Bank of Indpls., 1956-76, exec. v.p. dir., 1965-68, pres., 1968-76, chmn., 1971-76; chmn. Forum Group, Inc., 1976-91, Sovereign Group Inc., 1980—, Sargent & Greenleaf Inc., 1993—; bd. dirs. Steak 'n Shake, Inc., Standard Locknut, Inc., Somerset Corp., Nat. Homes Corp., Amli Realty Co., Security Group, Inc., Keystone Distbn., Inc. Lacy Diversified Industries, Inc., Excepticon, Inc., L. R. Nelson Corp., Breckenridge Corp., Canterbury Corp., Cygnet Enterprises, Inc., Franklin Corp., Haag Drug Co., Inland Container Corp., Ind. Bell Tel. Co., Ransburg Corp., Hook Drug Co., Northwestern Mut. Life Ins. Co., Consolidated Products Inc., Safemasters Co., Inc., Howard Sams Co. Bd. dirs. Hanover Coll., 1966-72, Ind. U. Found., 1968—, United Student Aid Fund; chmn. Indpls. Ctr. for Advanced Rsch., Ind. State Scholarship Com., 1968-72. Capt. inf. U.S. Army, 1950-51. Mem. Am. Bankers Assn., Ind. Bankers Assn., Res. City Bankers Assn., Ind. Bar Assn., Indpls. Bar Assn., Meridian Hills Country Club (Indpls.), Royal Poinciana Golf Club (Naples, Fla.), Quail Creek Country Club (Naples), Naples Sailing and Yacht Club. Methodist.

RISK, RICHARD ROBERT, health care executive; b. Chgo., Sept. 15, 1946; s. Clement Albert and Mary Catherine (Clarke) R.; m. Rebecca Ann Sandquist, Jan. 11, 1969 (div. Sept. 1984); children: Michael, Daniel, Laura; m. Louise L. Lawson, Dec. 1, 1984; stepchildren: Carrie Lawson, Valerie Lawson. BS in Econs., U. Ill., 1968; MBA in Health Adminstrn., U. Chgo., 1971. Asst. adminstr. U. Ill. Hosp., Chgo., 1969-72, Ctrl. DuPage Hosp., Winfield, Ill., 1972-74; mgmt. cons., v.p. Tribrook Group, Inc., Oak Brook, Ill., 1974-81; v.p. cons. svcs. Parkside Med. Svcs., Park Ridge, Ill., 1981-83; prin. health and med. divsn. Booz, Allen, & Hamilton, Inc., Chgo., 1983-84; exec. v.p. EHS Health Care, Oak Brook, 1984-92, pres., CEO, 1992-95; pres., CEO Advocate Health Care, Oak Brook, 1995—; mem. faculty Healthcare Fin. Mgmt. Assn., 1978-86, Am. Assn. Hosps. Cons., 1978-84; bd. dirs., mem. ad hoc ins. com., fin. com. Premier; lectr. grad. program social scis. No. Ill. U., 1982-88; lectr., adv. bd. multi-hosp. system study Kellogg Sch.

Health Mgmt. Program Northwestern U., 1985—; lectr. Grad. Program in Health Adminstrn. U. Chgo., 1982-94. Mem. access com. Gov.'s Task Force on Health Reform, 1992-94; mem. chancellor's adv. bd. U. Ill. at Chgo.; mem. dean's adv. bd. coll. of commerce DePaul U. Sgt. USAR, 1968-74. Fellow Am. Assn. Hosp. Cons. (bd. dirs., treas., chmn. govt. rels. com., chmn. membership task force, liaison Nat. Coun. Cmty. Hosps.); mem. Am. Hosp. Assn. (del. healthcare systems sect.), Ill. Hosp. Assn. (chmn. coun. on health fin., mem. strategic plan com., bd. dirs.), U. Chgo. Hosp. Adminstrn. Alumni Assn. (pres. exec. com. alumni coun., chmn. 50th ann. com.), Chgo. Health Policy Rsch. Coun. Home: 801 Clinton Pl River Forest IL 60305-1501 Office: Advocate Health Care 2025 Windsor Dr Oak Brook IL 60523-1586

RISKE, WILLIAM KENNETH, producer, cultural services consultant; b. Lamont, Alta., Can., May 9, 1949; s. Norman Elmer and Clara Jeanette (Krause) R.; m. Barbara Elizabeth Malcolm, Apr. 28, 1973; children: Elizabeth Nicola, William Norman Malcolm. BFA, U. Alta., 1969. Stage mgr. Royal Winnipeg Ballet, Man., Can., 1971-73; prodn. stage mgr. Royal Winnipeg Ballet, 1973-76, prodn. mgr., 1976-77, assoc. gen. mgr., 1978-79, gen. mgr., 1979-92, cultural svcs. cons., 1992—; assoc. prodr., gen. mgr. Cirque Du Soleil-Mystère, 1994-96; gen. mgr. Cirque du Soleil U.S., Inc., 1996—. Mem. Assn. Cultural Execs., Can. Assn. Profl. Dance Orgns. (pres. 1985-88), Dancevision (pres. 1990). Home: 227 Deer Crossing Way Henderson NV 89012

RISKO, JAMES RICHARD, business executive; b. Allentown, Pa., Feb. 8, 1953; s. John and Armida (Michetti) R.; m. Johanne Morin, May 2, 1981; 1 child, Steven; m. Heather Renee Todd, May 4, 1991; 1 child, Kyla Marie. Student in mining engring. program, Pa. State U., 1971-73; BS in Edn./Math., Kutztown (Pa.) U., 1976, BS in Bus. Acctg., 1984; MBA in Mgmt., Wilkes U., 1989. Sales trainee Sarco, Allentown, 1977-79, with dist. sales dept., 1979-81; with dist. sales dept. SKF Bearing, King of Prussia, Pa., 1981-82; engr./constrn. sales mgr. Spirax Sarco, Allentown, 1982-83, tech. mgr., 1983-85, major accounts mgr., 1985-86, regional sales mgr., 1986-92; pres. TLV Am., Charlotte, N.C., 1992—. Contbr. articles to profl. juors. With USMC, 1974-75. Presbyterian. Avocations: basketball, volleyball. Office: TLV Am Corp 6701 Northpark Blvd Ste K Charlotte NC 28216-2383

RISLEY, GREGORY BYRON, furniture company executive, interior designer; b. Vincennes, Ind., Feb. 2, 1949; s. Jack Byron and Elizabeth Louise (Rockwell) R.; children: Christopher Byron, Timothy Neal. BS, Oakland City (Ind.) Coll., 1973; postgrad., Butler U., 1973-74. Pres. Risley Furniture & Design, Bicknell, Ind., 1974—, Risley Enterprises Inc., Bicknell, Ind., 1979—. Co-author: Preview IV The Home Furnishings Store. Pres. Better Bicknell Club, 1971; coach Pee Wee League, Bicknell, 1975-77; leader cub pack Boy Scouts Am., Bicknell, 1977; chmn. Queen Pageant, Bicknell, 1978-85. Mem. Nat. Home Furnishings Assn. (chmn. nat. execs. 1978-80), Am. Contract Bridge League (life master, unit sec. 1986-88, v.p. 1989, pres. 1991-92, bd. dirs. unit 193, 1993-95), Bicknell Mchts. Assn., Interior Design Soc. (outstanding rm. design award 1980), Knox County Assn. Retarded Citizens, French Club, Masons, Scottish Rite, Old Town Players (charter), Elks (past exalted ruler Bicknell 1976-77). Avocations: bridge, golf, reading. Office: 114 S Main St Bicknell IN 47512-2626

RISLEY, ROD ALAN, education association executive; b. Hutchinson, Kans., Oct. 17, 1954; s. Ralph Edward and Patricia Ann (Gaulding) R.; m. Lynn René Plimpton, Mar. 13, 1963. AA, San Jacinto Coll., 1975; BBA, Sam Houston State U., 1982; AA (hon.), Austin (Tex.) Community Coll., 1991; MBA, Millsap Coll., 1995; PhD (hon.), Highpoint U., 1996, Mt. Ida Coll., 1996. Dir. alumni affairs Phi Theta Kappa, 1976-82; assoc. dir. Phi Theta Kappa Internat. Hdqrs., Jackson, Miss., 1982-85, exec. dir., 1985—. Mem. Millsaps Coll. Second Century Planning Com.; judge Truman Scholarship Found., 1993, 94. Named one of Outstanding Young Men Am., 1982, 83, 84, 85, 86, 87, 88, 89, Top Bus. Leaders Miss., 1994. Mem. Am. Soc. Assn. Execs., Jackson C. of C. (edn. com.), Am. Assn. of Cmty. Colls. (disting. alumnus award 1996), Phi Theta Kappa (sec., pub. jour.). Episcopalian. Office: Phi Theta Kappa Soc PO Box 13729 Jackson MS 39236-3729

RISLEY, TODD ROBERT, psychologist, educator; b. Palmer, Alaska, Sept. 8, 1937; s. Robert and Eva Lou (Todd) R.; 1 child, Todd Michael. A.B. with distinction in Psychology, San Diego State Coll., 1960; M.S., U. Wash., 1963, Ph.D., 1966. Asst. prof. psychology Fla. State U., Tallahassee, 1964-65; research assoc. Bur. Child Research, U. Kans., Lawrence, 1965-77, sr. scientist, 1977—, asst. prof. dept. human devel., 1967-69, assoc. prof., 1969-73, prof., 1973-84; prof. psychology U. Alaska, Anchorage, 1982—; pres. Ctr. for Applied Behavior Analysis, 1970-82; dir. Johnny Cake Child Study Ctr., Mansfield, Ark., 1973-74; vis. prof. U. Auckland (N.Z.), 1978; acting dir. Western Carolina Ctr., Morgantown, N.C., 1981; dir. Alaska Div. Mental Health and Devel. Disabilities, 1988-91; cons. in field to numerous orgns. and instns. Co-author: The Infant Center, 1977, Shopping with Children: Advice for parents, 1978, The Toddler Center, 1979, Meaningful Differences, 1995; editor: Jour. Applied Behavior Analysis, 1971-74; mng. editor: Behavior Therapy, The Behavior Therapist, Behavioral Asessment, 1977-80; mem. editl. bds. of numerous profl. jours.; contbr. revs. and numerous articles. Co-chmn. Fla. task force on use of behavioral procedures in state programs for retarded, 1974—; mem. resident abuse investigating com. div. retardation Fla. Dept. Health and Rehab. Services, 1972—; mem. adv. com. Social Research Inst., U. Utah, 1977—; mem. Alaska Gov.'s Council on Handicapped and Gifted, 1983-88, NIH Mental Retardation Research Com., 1987-88, Alaska Mental Health Bd., 1988. Grantee NIMH, 1971-72, 72-73; research grantee Nat. Ctr. Health Services, 1976-79; grantee Nat. Inst. Edn., 1973, NIH, 1967—. Fellow Am. Psychol. Assn. (coun. of reps. 1982-85, pres. div. 25, 1989); mem. AAAS, Am. Psychol. Soc., Am. Assn. Mental Deficiency, Assn. Advancement of Behavior Therapy (dir. 1975-80, pres. 1976-77, chmn. profl. rev. com. 1977—, series editor Readings in Behavior Therapy 1977—), Soc. Behavioral Medicine, Assn. Behavior Analysis, Sigma Xi. Office: U Alaska-Anchorage Dept Psychology 3211 Providence Dr Anchorage AK 99508-4614

RISMAN, MICHAEL, lawyer, business executive, securities company executive; b. Everett, Mass., Apr. 2, 1938; s. Morris Charles and Doris (Rosenbaum) R.; m. Rebecca R. Fuchs, Mar. 23, 1974; 1 stepchild, Ian Carlton Murray; children: Matthew Craig, Deborah Gayle, Jared Evan. BA, U. Mich., 1960; LLB, Georgetown U., 1964. Bar: D.C. 1964. Staff mem. Democratic Nat. Com., Washington, 1964; atty. U.S. Fgn. Claims Settlement Commn., Washington, 1964-66, SEC, Washington, 1966-67; counsel Seaboard Planning Corp., Beverly Hills, Calif., 1967-72, pres., 1970-72; v.p. Seaboard Corp., Beverly Hills, Calif., 1970-72; sec. B.C. Morton Realty Trust, 1967-71; with Arlington Investments Corp., Santa Monica, Calif., 1979-86; founder The Quincey Group, 1986; owner, pres. Armstrong Kitchens, San Francisco, 1988-90; sr. v.p. AFC Am. Housing Corp., L.A., Calif., 1991-97; bd. dir. Competitive Capital Fund, Income Fund Boston, Inc., Admiralty Fund. Home: 1133 Centinela Ave Santa Monica CA 90403-2316

RISOM, JENS, furniture designer, manufacturing executive; b. Copenhagen, May 8, 1916; came to U.S., 1939; naturalized, 1944; s. Sven J. and Inger Risom; m. Iben Haderup, Dec. 12, 1939 (dec. Jan. 1977); children: Helen Ann, Peggy Ann, Thomas Christian, Sven Christian; m. Henny Panduro, May 12, 1979. Student, Krebs, Denmark, 1922-27, St. Anne, 1927-32, Niels Brock Bus. Coll., 1932-34, Sch. for Fine Arts and Indust., Denmark, 1935-38. With design and decorating divsn. Nordiska Kompanet, Stockholm, 1934-35; with Inge Westin, Stockholm, 1935-36, Ernst Kühn, Arch., Copenhagen and N.Y.C., 1939, Dan Cooper, Inc., N.Y., 1939-41; freelance furniture designer, 1941-46; founder, pres. Jens Risom Design Inc., 1946-71; pres. Jens Risom Design, Inc. (became subs. Dictaphone Corp. 1971), N.Y.C., 1946-73; v.p. Dictaphone Corp., 1971-73; pres. Design Control, New Canaan, Conn., 1973—; cons. design, mktg., space planning. Trustee RISD, New Canaan Libr., Indsl. Design Soc. Am. With U.S. Army, 1943-45, ETO. Decorated Cross of Dannebrog', Queen of Denmark; recipient awards Archtl. League, Am. Inst. Internat. Design, Lifetime Achievement award Bklyn. Mus. Art, 1994, numerous Danish and Am. design awards. Home and Office: 103 Chichester Rd New Canaan CT 06840-3913 also: PO Box 596 Block Island RI 02807-0596

RISOM, OLE CHRISTIAN, publishing company executive; b. Copenhagen, Denmark, Oct. 3, 1919; came to U.S., 1941, naturalized, 1942; s. Sven and Inger (Henriques) R.; m. Agnes Grafin von Rechberg u Rothenloewen, May, 1947; children: Christopher, Camilla, Charles Nicholas. Art dir. Interior Design Mag., N.Y.C., 1948-50; assoc. art dir. McCall, Better Living Mag., N.Y.C., 1950-52; v.p., art dir. Golden Press Western Pub., N.Y.C., 1952-72; v.p., assoc. pub. juvenile div. Random House, N.Y.C., 1972-90. Author: I Am a Bunny, 1963 Little Bunny Follows its Nose, 1971, Max the Nosey Bear, 1972, Do You Know Colors, 1979, others. Served to sgt. U.S. Army, 1942-46, ETO. Decorated Bronze Star. Mem. Nat. Arts Club, Soc. Illustrators, Racquet and Tennis Club, Seawanhaka Corinthian Yacht Club, Royal Danish Yacht Club. Lutheran. Home: 160 Harbor Ln Roslyn NY 11576-1119

RISS, ERIC, psychologist; b. Vienna, Austria; s. David S. and Rebecca (Schneider) R.; came to U.S., 1940, naturalized, 1945; B.A., Bklyn. Coll., 1950; Ph.D., NYU, 1958; diplomate Am. Bd. Psychotherapy; m. Miriam Barbara Schoen, July 22, 1956; children: Arthur, Suzanne, Wendy. Pvt. practice psychotherapy, family therapy, marriage counseling, N.Y.C., 1952—; sr. psychologist N.Y.C. Diagnostic Center, 1954-57; with Marriage and Family Life Inst., N.Y.C., 1956-92; cons., 1956-58, dir. pub. edn., 1960-73, chmn. bd. dirs., 1961-73, dir., 1973-92; mem. attending staff, supr. psychotherapy and family therapy Payne Whitney Psychiat. Clinic, N.Y. Hosp., N.Y.C., 1971-78; clin. instr. psychology and psychiatry Cornell U. Med. Coll., 1971-72, clin. asst. prof., 1973-78; dir. Inst. for Exploration of Marriage, 1976-84; chief psychologist Artists, Writers and Performers Psychotherapy Center, 1978-92; lectr. Bklyn. Coll., 1955-62; cons. Fordham Hosp., 1956-68; psychotherapist N.Y. Neuropsychiat. Center, 1958-60; psychotherapist Community Guidance Service, N.Y.C., 1958-61. Mem. Am. Acad. Psychotherapy, N.Y. State Marriage, Family and Child Counseling Assn. (pres. 1971-72), Acad. Family Psychology, Am., N.Y. State psychol. assns. Contbr. numerous articles to profl. jours. Office: 174 E 73rd St New York NY 10021-4352

RISS, MURRAY, photographer, educator; b. Stryj, Poland, Feb. 6, 1940; came to U.S., 1951, naturalized, 1958; s. Elias and Dora (Feit) R.; m. Karen Mason; children: Shanna, Adya. Student, CCNY, 1958-63; B.A., Cooper Union, 1966; M.F.A., R.I. Sch. Design, 1968. Prof., chmn. dept photography Memphis Acad. Arts, 1969—; lectr. film and photography Southwestern U., Memphis, 1972—; artist-in-residence U. Syracuse, N.Y., 1980, U. Haifa, Israel, 1976. One man shows include Art Inst., Chgo, 1971, Mpls. Inst. Fine Arts, 1971, U. Rochester, N.Y., 1975, Photographers Gallery, London, 1977, Afterimage Gallery, Dallas, 1979, Visual Studies Workshop, Rochester, 1980, Hampshire (Mass.) Coll., 1981, Loomis Inst., Conn., 1984; group shows include Mus. Modern Art, N.Y.C., 1970, 71, New Orleans Mus. Art, 1975, Nexus Gallery, Atlanta, 1981, Askew Nixon Gallery; touring show So. Arts Fedn., 1985-86; conceived, organized, dir. Southern Eye, Southern Mind, A Photographic Inquiry, Memphis, 1981; illustrator: History of Memphis Architecture until 1900, 1983, Guide to Mud Island, 1989; curator, dir. Emerging Southern Photographers, Memphis Coll. Art Gallery, 1992, Memphis Brooks Mus. Art, 1994. Nat. Endowment for Arts fellow, 1979. Mem. Soc. Photographic Edn. Home: 1306 Harbert Ave Memphis TN 38104-4514 Office: Murray Riss Photography 516 S Main St Memphis TN 38103-4443 *Had I designed the events and outcomes of my life I would not have done as well as my fate has done for me.*

RISS, RICHARD MICHAEL, research economist, church history educator; b. Rochester, N.Y., May 22, 1952; s. Walter and Barbara Ann (Johnson) R.; m. Kathryn Janet Grieser, Mar. 3, 1979. BA, U. Rochester, 1974; MCS, Regent Coll., Vancouver, B.C., Can., 1979; MA, Trinity Evang. Div. Sch., Deerfield, Ill., 1988; postgrad., Drew U., 1990—. Instr. ch. history Christian Life Coll., Mt. Prospect, Ill., 1980-83; data base mgr. Systems and Mgmt. Infor. Svcs. 1st Chgo. Corp., 1980-85; rsch. assoc. to chief economist Prudential Securities, N.Y.C., 1988-91, C.J. Lawrence/Deutsche Bank Securities Corp., N.Y.C., 1991-96; prof. ch. history Zarephath (N.J.) Bible Sem., 1989—. Author: The Evidence for the Resurrection of Jesus Christ, 1977, Latter Rain, 1987, A Survey of Twentieth Century Revival Movements in North America, 1988, A History of the Worldwide Awakening, 1992-95, 1995, The Characteristics and Purpose of Revival, 1997, Images of Revival, 1997; also articles to Zondervan Dictionary of Pentecostal and Charismatic Movements, Ency. Hanoverian Eng. and The Library of Christian Worship. Mem. Soc. for Pentecostal Studies, Conf. on Faith and History, Evang. Theol. Soc., Soc. Christian Philosophers, Am. Soc. Ch. History. Presbyterian. Avocation: playing violin. Home: 290 River Rd Apt M-1 Piscataway NJ 08854-3566

RISS, ROBERT BAILEY, real estate investor; b. Salida, Colo., May 27, 1927; s. Richard Roland and Louise (Roberts) R.; married; children: Edward Stayton, G. Leslie, Laura Bailey, Juliana Warren. BSBA, U. Kans., 1949. Pres. Riss Internat. Corp., Kansas City, Mo., 1950-80, chmn. bd., 1964-86; founder, chmn. bd., pres. Republic Industries, Inc., Kansas City, Mo., 1969-86; chmn. bd. Grandview Bank and Trust Co., 1969-86, Commonwealth Gen. Ins. Co., 1986-93; Chmn. bd. dirs., exec. com. Heart of Am. Fire and Casualty Co.; chmn. bd. dirs. Comml. Equipment Co. Vice chmn. bd. trustees Kansas U. Endowment Assn., 1980-89. Recipient Silver Beaver award Kansas City Area coun. Boy Scouts Am., 1972; Disting. Svc. citation U. Kans., 1976; Fred Ellsworth medal U. Kans., 1979; named Most Outstanding Young Man in Mo. U.S. Jr. C. of C., 1956. Mem. Kans. U. Alumni Assn. (nat. pres. 1969-70), Sigma Nu. Episcopalian.

RISSANEN, JORMA JOHANNES, Scientist; b. Pielisjarvi, Finland, Oct. 20, 1932; arrived in U.S. 1964; m. Riitta T. Åberg, Nov. 6, 1956; children—Juhani, Natasha. Ph.D., Finland Inst. Tech., 1960. Mem. research staff IBM, San Jose, Calif., 1960—. Editor: Jour. Statistical Planning and Inference; contbr. articles to profl. jours. Patentee in field. Assoc. editor jour. of Control and Info. Recipient Outstanding Innovation award, IBM Research div., 1980, Best paper award Automatica, 1982, Corp. award, 1991, Richard W. Hamming medal, 1993. Mem. IEEE. Home: 140 Teresita Way Los Gatos CA 95032-6040

RISSE, GUENTER BERNHARD, physician, historian, educator; b. Buenos Aires, Argentina, Apr. 28, 1932; s. Francisco B. and Kaete A. R.; m. Alexandra G. Paradzinski, Oct. 14, 1961; children—Heidi, Monica, Alisa. MD, U. Buenos Aires, 1958; PhD, U. Chgo., 1971. Intern Mercy Hosp., Buffalo, 1958-59; resident in medicine Henry Ford Hosp., Detroit, 1960-61, Mt. Carmel Hosp., Columbus, Ohio, 1962-63; asst. dept. medicine U. Chgo., 1963-67; asst. prof. dept. history of medicine U. Minn., 1969-71; asso. prof. dept. history of medicine and dept. history of sci. U. Wis., Madison, 1971-76; prof. U. Wis., 1976-85, chmn. dept. history of medicine, 1971-77; prof., chmn. dept. history health scis. U. Calif., San Francisco, 1985—; Mem. project com. Ctr. for Photog. Images in Medicine and Health Care. Author: Paleopathology of Ancient Egypt, 1964, Hospital Life in Enlightenment Scotland, 1986; editor: Modern China and Traditional Chinese Medicine, 1973, History of Physiology, 1973, Medicine Without Doctors, 1977, AIDS and the Historian, 1991; mem. editl. bd. Jour. History of Medicine, 1971-74, 90-93, Clio Medica, 1973-88, Bull. History of Medicine, 1980-94, Medizinhistorisches Jour., 1981—, Med. History, 1989-95, History of Philos. Life Scis., 1993—, Asclepio, 1995—. Served with Argentine Armed Forces, 1955. Recipient NIH grants, 1971-73, 82-84, WHO grant, 1979, named Logan Campbell Disting. Lectr., New Zealand, 1994. Mem. Am. Assn. History of Medicine (pres. 1988-90, William H. Welch medal 1988), History Sci. Soc., Internat. Acad. History Medicine, Deutsche Gesellschaft fur Geschichte der Medizin, European Assn. History of Medicine and Health, Internat. Network for History of Pub. Health, Mex. Soc. History and Philosophy of Medicine, Peruvian Assn. Med. Ethnology and History, Brit. Soc. for Social History of Medicine, Argentine Ateneo de Historia de la Medicina, AIDS History Group (co-chair 1988-94), Internat. Network for History of Hosps. (convenor 1995—), Bay Area Med. Hist. Club (pres. 1994-96). Home: 600 Noriega St San Francisco CA 94122-4616 Office: Univ of Calif Dept History Health Scis 513 Parnassus Ave San Francisco CA 94122-2722

RISSER, ARTHUR CRANE, JR., zoo administrator; b. Blackwell, Okla., July 8, 1938; s. Arthur Crane and Mary Winn (Stevenson) R.; children: Michelle W., Stephen C., Michael R. BA, Grinnell Coll., Iowa, 1960; MA, U. Ariz., Tucson, 1963; PhD, U. Calif., Davis, 1970. Mus. technician, Smithsonian Instn., Washington, 1963-64; research assoc. Sch. Medicine U. Md., Balt., 1964-65; grad. teaching asst. U. Calif., Davis, 1965-70; asst. prof. biology U. Nev.-Reno, 1970-74; asst. curator birds Zool. Soc. San Diego, 1974-76, curator birds, 1976-81, gen. curator birds, 1981-86; gen. mgr. San Diego Zoo, 1986—; co-chmn. Calif. Condor Working Group on Captive Breeding and Reintroduction, 1983-85; mem. Calif. Condor Recovery Team, 1984-86. Treas., Planned Parenthood, Reno, 1972; bd. dirs. Internat. Found. Conservation Birds, 1979-88, Conservation Rsch. Found. of Papua New Guinea, 1991—. Fellow Am. Assn. Zool. Parks and Aquariums. Office: San Diego Zoo PO Box 551 San Diego CA 92112-0551

RISSER, JAMES VAULX, JR., journalist, educator; b. Lincoln, Nebr., May 8, 1938; s. James Vaulx and Ella Caroline (Schacht) R.; m. Sandra Elizabeth Laaker, June 10, 1961; children: David James, John Daniel. BA, U. Nebr., 1959, cert. in journalism, 1964; JD, U. San Francisco, 1962. Bar: Nebr. 1962. Pvt. practice law Lincoln, 1962-64; reporter Des Moines Register and Tribune, 1964-85, Washington corr., 1969-85, bur. chief, 1976-85; dir. John S. Knight fellowships for profl. journalists, prof. communication Stanford U., 1985—; lectr. Wells Coll., 1981; mem. com. on agrl. edn. in secondary schs. Nat. Acad. Scis., 1985-88. Trustee Reuter Found., 1989—; mem. Pulitzer Prize Bd., 1990—. Profl. Journalism fellow Stanford U., 1973-74; recipient award for disting. reporting public affairs Am. Polit. Sci. Assn., 1969; Thomas L. Stokes award for environ. reporting Washington Journalism Center, 1971, 79; Pulitzer prize for nat. reporting, 1976, 79; Worth Bingham Found. prize for investigative reporting, 1976; Raymond Clapper Meml. Assn. award for Washington reporting, 1976, 78; Edward J. Meeman award for Conservation Reporting, 1985. Mem. Nebr. Bar Assn., Soc. Environ. Journalists, Soc. Profl. Journalists (Disting. Svc. award 1976), Investigative Reporters and Editors Assn. Club: Gridiron. Home: 394 Diamond St San Francisco CA 94114-2821 Office: Stanford U Communication Dept Stanford CA 94305-2050

RISSMAN, BURTON RICHARD, lawyer; b. Chgo., Nov. 13, 1927; s. Louis and Eva (Lyons) R.; m. Francine Greenberg, June 15, 1952; children: Lawrence E., Thomas W., Michael P. BS, U. Ill., 1947, JD, 1951; LLM, NYU, 1952. Bar: Ill. 1951, U.S. Dist. Ct. (no. dist.) Ill. 1954, U.S. Ct. Appeals (7th cir.) 1978, U.S. Supreme Ct. 1982. Assoc. Schiff, Hardin & Waite, Chgo., 1953-59, ptnr., 1959—, mem. mgmt. com., 1984-92, chmn. mgmt. com., 1986-90; mem. faculty Practicing Law Inst. Bd. editor U. Ill. Law Forum, 1949-51; contbr. articles to profl. jours. Trustee Crow Canyon Archaeol. Ctr. 1st lt. JAGC, USAF, 1952-54. Food Law fellow, 1951. Mem. ABA, Ill. State Bar Assn., Chgo. Bar Assn., Chgo. Coun. Lawyers, Am. Judicature Soc., Met. Club, Carlton Club. Office: Schiff Hardin & Waite 233 S Wacker Dr Chicago IL 60606-6306

RISTAU, KENNETH EUGENE, JR., lawyer; b. Knoxville, Tenn., Feb. 14, 1939; s. Kenneth E. and Frances (Besch) R.; m. Mary Emily George, Nov. 27, 1967 (div. Apr. 1985); children: Heidi, Mary Robin, Kenny, Michael, Robert; m. Emily Pettis, Mar. 31, 1990; 1 child, James Patrick. BA, Colgate U., 1961; JD, NYU, 1964. Bar: U.S. Ct. Appeals (9th cir.) 1968, U.S. Ct. Appeals (D.C. cir.) 1974, U.S. Supreme Ct. 1974, U.S. Dist. Ct., Southern Dist. of Calif., 1993. Assoc. Gibson, Dunn & Crutcher, L.A., 1964-69; ptnr. Gibson, Dunn & Crutcher, Newport Beach, Calif., 1969—. Fellow Coll. Labor and Employment Lawyers (charter); mem. Employers Group (adv. bd.), Orange County Indsl. Rels. Rsch. Assn. (pres. 1992-93), Big Canyon Country Club, Rancho Las Palmas Country Club, Newport Beach Tennis Club, Santa Fe Hunt Club (pres., bd. dirs.). Office: Gibson Dunn & Crutcher Jamboree Ctr 4 Park Plz Irvine CA 92614-8557

RISTINE, JEFFREY ALAN, reporter; b. Ann Arbor, Mich., Apr. 21, 1955; s. Harold G. and Amelita (Schmidt) R.; m. Karen Lin Clark, Oct. 27, 1996. BA, U. Mich., 1977. Reporter The Midland (Mich) Times, 1978-79, Johnstown (Pa.) Tribune-Dem., 1979-80, San Diego Tribune, 1980-92, San Diego Union-Tribune, 1992—. Recipient Appreciation award Am. Planning Assn., San Diego sect., 1988; named Best polit./govt. reporter San Diego Press Club, 1986. Avocations: puzzle-solving, bicycling, cat photography. Office: San Diego Union-Tribune 350 Camino De La Reina San Diego CA 92108-3003

RISTOW, GEORGE EDWARD, neurologist, educator; b. Albion, Mich., Dec. 15, 1943; s. George Julius and Margaret (Beattie) R.; 1 child, George Andrew Martin. BA, Albion Coll., 1965; DO, Coll. Osteo. Medicine and Surgery, Des Moines, 1969. Diplomate Am. Bd. Psychiatry and Neurology. Intern, Garden City Hosp., 1969-70; resident Wayne State U., 1970-74; fellow U. Newcastle Upon Tyne, 1974-75; asst. prof. dept. neurology Wayne State U., Detroit, 1975-77; assoc. prof. Mich. State U., East Lansing, Mich., 1977-83, prof., 1983-84, 95—, prof., chmn., 1984-95. Fellow Am. Acad. Neurology, Royal Soc. Medicine; mem. AMA, Am. Osteo. Assn., Pan Am. Med. Assn., Am. Coll. Neuropsychiatrists (sr.). Home: 2070 Riverwood Dr Okemos MI 48864-2814 Office: Mich State U Dept Internal Medicine 305 E Fee Hall East Lansing MI 48824-1316

RITCH, HERALD LAVERN, finance company executive; b. Los Angeles, Feb. 13, 1951; s. Herald Lester and Caroline (Lillevold) R.; m. Linda Suzanne Lundberg, June 11, 1972; children: Eleanor Loring, Seth Alden. BA in Econs., Stanford U., 1973; MBA, U. Pa., 1975. Assoc. Dean Witter Reynolds Inc., N.Y.C., 1975-79, v.p., 1979-82, mng. dir., mgr. merger and acquisition dept., 1982-83; v.p. Kidder, Peabody & Co Inc., N.Y.C., 1983-86, mng. dir., 1987-88; gen. ptnr. Freeman Spogli & Co., N.Y.C., 1988-90; managing dir. Donaldson Lufkin & Jenrette, N.Y.C., 1991-94, mng. dir. and dir. mergers and acquisitions, 1994—. Contbr. articles to profl. jours. Dir. Greenwich Assn. Retarded Citizens; elder 1st Presbyn. Ch., Greenwich. Mem. Stanwich Club, Met. Club. Avocations: tennis, skiing, reading. Office: Donaldson Lufkin & Jenrette 277 Park Ave New York NY 10172

RITCH, KATHLEEN, diversified company executive; Harbor Beach, Mich., Jan. 23, 1943; d. Eunice (Spry) R.; B.A., Mich. State U., 1965: student Katharine Gibbs Sch., 1965-66. Exec. sec., adminstrv. asst. to pres. Katy Industries, Inc., N.Y.C., 1969-70; exec. sec., adminstrv. asst. to chmn. Kobrand Corp., N.Y.C., 1970-72; adminstrv. asst. to chmn. and pres. Ogden Corp., N.Y.C., 1972-74; asst. sec., adminstr. office services, asst. to chmn. Ogden Corp., N.Y.C., 1974-81, corporate sec., adminstr. office services, 1981-84, v.p., corporate sec., adminstr. office services, 1984-92, v.p. corp. sec., 1992—; part-owner Unell Mfg. Co., Port Hope, Mich., 1966-87. Bd. dir. Young Concert Artists, Inc., 1991—. Mem. Am. Soc. Corporate Secs. Home: 500 E 77th St New York NY 10162-0025 Office: Ogden Corp Two Pennsylvania Pla New York NY 10121

RITCHESON, CHARLES RAY, university administrator, history educator; b. Maysville, Okla., Feb. 26, 1925; s. Charles Frederick and Jewell (Vaughn) R.; m. Shirley Marie Spackman, June 13, 1953 (div. July 1964); children: Charles Brendan, Mark Frederick; m. Alice Luethi, Oct. 11, 1965; children: Philip Luethi, Steven Whitefield, Andrew Shepherd, Peter Lorentz. B.A., Okla. U., 1946; postgrad., Zurich U., Switzerland, 1946-47, Harvard U., 1947-48; Ph.D. (Fulbright fellow), Oxford U., Eng., 1951; D.Litt. (hon.), Leicester U., Eng. Asst. prof. history Okla. Coll. for Women, 1951-52, asso. prof., 1952-53; assoc. prof. Kenyon Coll., Gambier, Ohio, 1953-60; prof. Kenyon Coll., 1960-64, chmn. dept. history, 1964; chmn., dir. grad. studies in history So. Meth. U., 1965-70; dir. Center Ibero-Am. Civilization, 1967-68; dir. with rank of dean Library Advancement, 1970-71; Colin Rhys Lovell Prof. Brit. history U. So. Calif., 1971-74, Lovell Disting. prof., 1977-84, The Univ. Prof., univ. libr., dean, vice provost, spl. asst. to pres., 1984-90, The Univ. Prof. emeritus, Univ. libr. emeritus, 1990—; cultural attaché Am. Embassy, 1974-77; pres. So. Conf. on Brit. Studies, 1967-70, Pacific Coast br. Conf. on Brit. Studies, 1971-73; exec. sec. Nat. Conf. Brit. Studies, 1973-74; presdl. appointee Nat. Council on Humanities, 1982-86, Bd. of Fgn. Scholarships, 1986-88, Nat. Council on Humanities, 1988-90; Fulbright prof. Edinburgh U., Cambridge U., 1963-64. Author: British Politics and the American Revolution, 1954, Era of the American Revolution, 1968, British Policy Toward the U.S, 1783-1795, 1968; Contbr. articles to learned jours. Chmn. U.S.-U.K. Ednl. Commn., 1974-77; ofcl. observer Brit. Bicentennial Liaison Com., 1974-76; mem. internat. adv. coun. U. Buckingham, Eng.; v.p. Am. Friends of Covent Garden, 1982-85, Fund for Arts and Culture in Ea. Europe, 1992-96, exec. v.p.; mem. adv. coun. Ditchley Found.; chmn. Brit. Inst. U.S., 1978-81. Lt. (j.g.) USNR, 1942-45. Univ. award for creative scholarship, 1980; Social Sci. Research Council Faculty fellow, 1956-59; Eli

Lilly-Clements Library fellow, 1960; Am. Council Learned Socs. fellow, 1963-64. Fellow Royal Hist. Soc.; mem. Tex. Inst. Letters, Soc. Francaise d'Archeologie, Phi Beta Kappa. Clubs: Brooks, Beefsteak (London), Cosmos (Washington).

RITCHEY, HAROLD W., retired chemical engineer; b. Kokomo, Ind., Oct. 5, 1912; s. Glen Robert and Mabel Ann (Wilson) R.; m. Helen Hively, Aug. 29, 1941; children: Stephen, David. BSChemE, Purdue U., 1934, MS in Chemistry, 1936, PhD in Chemistry, 1938; MSChemE, Cornell U., 1945. Rsch. chemist Union Oil Corp., Calif., 1938-41, 46-47; nuclear reactor engr. GE Co., Richland, Wash., 1947-49; tech. dir. rocket divsn. Thiokol Corp., Huntsville, Ala., 1949-60; v.p. rocket divsn. Thiokol Corp., Ogden, Utah, 1960-64; pres. Thiokol Corp., Bristol, Pa., 1964-70; CEO, chmn. bd. dir. Thiokol Corp., Newtown, Pa., 1970-77. Mem. Rotary Club, Ogden, 1974—. Lt. comdr. USN, 1941-46. Named Outstanding Chem. Engr., Purdue U., 1994. Mem. AIAA, ADPA, AUSA, AIA, AFA, Purdue Rsch. Found., Am. Rocket Soc. (bd. dirs. 1956-60, v.p. 1960, pres. 1961, C.N. Hickman award 1954), Sigma Xi, Phi Lambda Upsilon. Patentee in rocketry, astronautics, and petroleum and nuclear energy fields. Home: 1756 Doxey St Ogden UT 84403-0524

RITCHEY, PATRICK WILLIAM, lawyer; b. Pitts., July 9, 1949; s. Joseph Frank and Patricia Ann (Giovengo) R. BA, Haverford Coll., 1971; JD, Yale U., 1974. Bar: U.S. Dist. Ct. (we. dist.) Pa. 1974, U.S. Ct. Appeals (3d. cir.) 1976, U.S. Supreme Ct. 1980, U.S. Ct. Appeals (4th cir.) 1981, U.S. Ct. Appeals (6th cir.) 1982, U.S. Dist. Ct. (ea. dist.) Wis. 1987, U.S. Ct. Appeals (7th cir.) 1991, U.S. Ct. Appeals (D.C. cir.) 1993, U.S. Ct. Appeals (8th cir.) 1993. Assoc. Reed Smith Shaw & McClay, Pitts., 1974-82, ptnr., 1982—; mem. Pitts. Personnel Assn., Pitts., 1982—, U.S. Dist. Ct. Rules Task Force, Pitts., 1988. Mem. ABA (labor law sect.), Allegheny County Bar Assn. (labor law and fed. ct. sects.), Harvard-Yale-Princeton Club, Duquesne Club. Office: Reed Smith Shaw & McClay James H Reed Bldg 435 6th Ave Pittsburgh PA 15219-1809

RITCHEY, WILLIAM MICHAEL, chemistry educator; b. Mt. Vernon, Ohio, June 2, 1925; s. Joseph David nd Minnie (Tanury) R.; m. Minetta Hoover, July 27, 1947 (dec. Aug. 1992); children: Stephen, Joseph, Mark; m. Mary E. Golambush, Aug. 28, 1993. With Standard Oil of Ohio Research Ctr., Clev., 1955-68; prof. chemistry and macromolecular sci. Case Western Res. U., Cleve., 1968—; researcher nuclear magnetic resonance; cons. Co-editor: Atlas of Spectral Data and Physical Constants for Organic Compounds, 1978. Asst. scoutmaster Troop 424, Greater Clev. Council; active Lyndhurst Baptist Ch., (Ohio). Served with U.S. Army, 1943-46. Mem. Am. Chem. Soc., Soc. Applied Spectroscopy, Sigma Xi. Home: 851 Haywood Dr South Euclid OH 44121-3403 Office: Millis Sci Center Adelbert Rd Cleveland OH 44106-7078

RITCHIE, ALBERT, lawyer; b. Charlottesville, Va., Sept. 29, 1939; s. John and Sarah Dunlop (Wallace) R.; m. Jennie Wayland, Apr. 29, 1967; children: John, Mary. BA, Yale U., 1961; LLB, U. Va., 1964. Bar: Ill. 1964. Assoc. Sidley & Austin, Chgo., 1964-71, ptnr., 1972—. Bd. dirs. Erie Neighborhood House, Chgo., 1978-88; bd. dirs. United Charities of Chgo., 1979-90; trustee U. Va. Law Sch. Found., 1997—. Capt. U.S. Army, 1965-67. Mem. ABA, Am. Coll. Real Estate Lawyers, Chgo. Legal Aid Soc., Legal Club Chgo. (pres. 1986-87), U. Va. Law Sch. Alumni Assn. (v.p. 1989-93, pres. 1993-95), LaSalle Club, Indian Hill Club. Episcopalian. Office: Sidley & Austin 1 First Natl Plz Chicago IL 60603-2003

RITCHIE, ANNE, educational administrator; b. Grants Pass, Oreg., July 1, 1944; d. William Riley Jr. and Allie Brown (Clark) R.; m. Charles James Cooper, Sept. 4, 1968 (div. 1985); children: Holly Anne, Wendy Nicole. BA in Edn. with honors, Calif. State U., Sacramento, 1981. Cert. elem. tchr., Calif. CEO El Rancho Schs., Inc., Carmichael, Calif., 1981—; citizen amb. del. People to People Internat., Russia, Lithuania, Hungary, 1993, China, 1994. Active Crocker Art Mus.; mem. Rep. Senatorial Inner Circle, Washington, 1997. Mem. AAUW, Nat. Assn. Edn. for Young Children, Profl. Assn. Childhood Educators, Nat. Child Care Assn. Episcopalian. Avocations: traveling, skiing, reading.

RITCHIE, DANIEL LEE, academic administrator; b. Springfield, Ill., Sept. 19, 1931; s. Daniel Felix and Jessie Dee (Binney) R. B.A., Harvard U., 1954, M.B.A., 1956. Exec. v.p. MCA, Inc., Los Angeles, 1967-70; pres. Archon Pure Products Co., Los Angeles, 1970-73; exec. v.p. Westinghouse Electric Corp., Pitts., 1975-78; pres. corp. staff and strategic planning Westinghouse Broadcasting Co., 1978-79, pres., chief exec. officer, 1979-81, chmn., chief exec. officer; chmn., chief exec. officer Westinghouse Broadcasting & Cable, Inc., 1981-87; owner Grand River Ranch, Kremmling, Colo., 1977—, Rancho Cielo, Montecito, Calif., 1977—; chancellor U. Denver, 1989—. With U.S. Army, 1956-58. Office: U Denver Office of the Chancellor University Park Denver CO 80208*

RITCHIE, J. MURDOCH, pharmacologist, educator; b. Aberdeen, Scotland, June 10, 1925; came to U.S. 1956; s. Alexander Farquharson and Agnes Jane (Bremner) R.; m. Brenda Rachel Bigland; children: Alasdair J., A. Jocelyn. BSc, Aberdeen (Scotland) U., 1944, U. Coll. London, 1949; PhD, U. Coll. London, 1952, DSc, 1960; MA, Yale U., 1968; DSc, Aberdeen U., 1987. Lectr. physiology U. Coll. London, 1949-51; sci. staff Nat. Inst. Med. Rsch., London, 1951-55; asst. prof. to prof. Albert Einstein Coll. Medicine, N.Y.C., 1954-63, prof. pharmacology, 1963-68; prof. and chmn. pharmacology Yale U., New Haven, 1968-74, dir. biol. scis., 1975-78, prof. pharmacology, 1968—. Contbr. articles to profl. jours.; editor sci. books and jours. Fellow Royal Soc., Univ. Coll. London, Inst. Physics London. Home: 47 Deepwood Dr Hamden CT 06517-3414 Office: Yale Univ Sch Medicine 333 Cedar St New Haven CT 06510-3206

RITCHIE, RICHARD LEE, media company executive; b. Grand Rapids, Mich., July 20, 1946; s. Robert George and Gertrude (Dryer) R.; m. Marlene Barton, Nov. 16, 1969; children: Gabrielle Gay, Steven Barton. B.A., Mich. State U., 1968, M.B.A., 1972; P.M.D., Harvard U., 1982. C.P.A., Mich. Sr. acct. Peat, Marwick, Mitchell & Co., Detroit, 1968-69, 72-74; mgr. corp. acctg. Grand Trunk Western R.R., Detroit, 1974-76; treas. Grand Trunk Western R.R., 1976-79, asst. v.p., treas., 1980-83; v.p., treas. James River Corp., Richmond, Va., 1984-86; sr. v.p. fin., chief fin. officer Harte Hanks Communications, San Antonio, 1987-96; exec. v.p., CFO Big Flower Press Holdings, Inc., N.Y.C., 1997—; prof. Oakland Community Coll., Farmington, Mich. Served with AUS, 1969-71. Mem. AICPA, Mich. Assn. CPAs, Am. Acctg. Assn., Beta Alpha Psi, Beta Gamma Sigma. Jewish. Office: Big Flower Press Holdings Inc 3 E 54th St New York NY 10022-3108

RITCHIE, ROBERT OLIVER, materials science educator; b. Plymouth, Devon, U.K., Jan. 2, 1948; came to U.S., 1974; s. Kenneth Ian and Kathleen Joyce (Sims) R.; m. Connie Olesen (div. 1978); 1 child, James Oliver; m. HaiYing Song, 1991. BA with honors, U. Cambridge, Eng., 1969, MA, PhD, 1973, ScD, 1990. Cert. engr., U.K. Goldsmith's rsch. fellow Churchill Coll. U. Cambridge, 1972-74; Miller fellow in basic rsch. sci. U. Calif., Berkeley, 1974-76; assoc. prof. mech. engring. MIT, Cambridge, 1977-81; prof. U. Calif., Berkeley, 1981—; dep. dir. Materials Scis. Divsn. Lawrence Berkeley Nat. Lab., Cambridge, 1990-94, dir. Ctr. for Advanced Materials, 1987-95, head Structural Materials, Materials Scis. Divsn., 1987-95; head Structural Materials Dept., Materials Scis. Divsn. Lawrence Berkeley Nat. Lab., 1995—; cons. Alcan, Allison, Boeing, Chevron, Exxon, GE, Grumman, Instron, Northrop, Rockwell, Westinghouse, Baxter, Carbomedics, Med. Inc., Shiley, St. Jude Med. Editor 10 books; contbr. more than 285 articles to profl. jours. Recipient Curtis W. McGraw Rsch. award Am. Soc. Engring. Educators, 1987, Rosenhain medal Inst. Materials London, 1992, G.R. Irwin medal ASTM, Van Horn Disting. Lectr. award Case Western Res. U., 1997; named one of Top 100 Scientists, Sci. Digest mag., 1984. Fellow Inst. Materials (London), Am. Soc. Metals Internat., Internat. Congress on Fracture (hon., pres. 1997—); mem. Am. Orchid Soc., Am. Soc. Materials, Materials Rsch. Soc., Minerals, Materials and Metals Soc. (Mathewson Gold medal 1985, Disting. Structural Materials Scientist/Engr. award 1996). Avocations: skiing, antiques, orchids, tennis. Home: 590 Grizzly Peak Blvd Berkeley CA 94708-1238 Office: U Calif Dept Materials Sci & Mineral Engring Berkeley CA 94720

RITCHIE, STAFFORD DUFF, II, lawyer; b. Buffalo, June 13, 1948; s. Stafford Duff Ritchie and A. Elizabeth Smith Cavage; m. Rebecca P. Thompson, June 27, 1975; children: Stafford D. III, Thompson C., Glynis A. Student, Rensselaer Poly. Inst., Troy, N.Y., 1966-68; BS in Econs., U. Pa., 1970, JD, 1974. Bar: N.Y. 1975. Atty./advisor, asst. gen. counsel, spl. asst. gen. counsel Adminstrv. Office of U.S. Cts., Washington, 1974-82, assoc. gen. counsel, to 1982; gen. counsel Cavages, Inc., Buffalo, 1982-94; pvt. practice Buffalo, 1994—; counsel Coms. of Jud. Conf. of U.S., Jud. Conf. Com., Jud. Conf. of 9th Cir. of U.S.; spl. counsel for major procurement Supreme Ct. of U.S. Trustee Calasanctius Sch., Buffalo, 1990-92; dir. Crisis Svcs. Inc., Buffalo, 1997—. Sgt. USMCR, 1970-76. Mem. ABA, Fed. Bar Assn., N.Y. State Bar Assn. Avocation: computers. Office: Law Office S D Ritchie II 200 Olympic Towers 300 Pearl St Buffalo NY 14202-2501

RITCHIE, WALLACE PARKS, JR., surgeon, educator; b. St. Paul, Nov. 4, 1935; s. Wallace Parks and Alice Ransome (Otis) R.; m. Barbara Carey Jewell, Aug. 10, 1960; children: Stephanie, David, Jessica. BA, Yale U., 1957; MD, Johns Hopkins U., 1961; PhD, U. Minn., 1971. Diplomate Am. Bd. Surgery. Intern, resident in surgery Yale U., New Haven, 1961-63; resident in surgery U. Minn. Hosps., Mpls., 1963-69, instr. in surgery, 1969-70; from asst. prof. to prof. surgery U. Va. Sch. Medicine, Charlottesville, 1973-83; prof., chmn. dept. surgery Temple U. Sch. Medicine, Phila., 1983-93; exec. dir. Am. Bd. Surgery, Phila., 1994—. Editor textbook: Essentials of Surgery, 1994; contbr. over 125 sci. articles to profl. jours. Lt. col. Med. Corps U.S. Army, 1970-73. USPHS grantee, 1974-85. Office: Am Bd Surgery Inc 1617 John F Kennedy Blvd Philadelphia PA 19103-1821

RITCHLIN, MARTHA ANN, occupational therapist; b. Jacksboro, Tex., Oct. 20, 1953; d. Carl Alton and Julia Ann (Jones) Rumage; divorced; children: Carl Allen, Julie Marie. BS, Tex. Women's U., 1976, postgrad., 1986. Occupational therapist Wichita Gen. Hosp., Wichita Falls, Tex., 1977-79; dir. occupational therapy Red River Hosp., Wichita Falls, 1979-83, Bethania Regional Health Care Ctr., Wichita Falls, 1983-87; occupational therapist Girling Home Health, Wichita Falls, 1984-85, Wichita Home Health, Wichita Falls, 1984-86, Outreach Home Health Svcs., Seymour, Tex., 1987—, N. Tex. Easter Seal Rehab. Ctr., Wichita Falls, 1988—; owner, therapist Community Occupational Therapy Svcs., Wichita Falls, 1988—; dir. occupational therapy Wichita Falls (Tex.) State Hosp., 1991—; cons., speaker Muscular Dystrophy Assn., Wichita Falls, 1986, Advantage Sr. Citizens Club, Wichita Falls, 1988, Stroke Club, 1986; cons., activity dir. Clay County Hosp., Henrietta, Tex., 1986-87. Cons., vol. Wichita County Juvenile Detention Svcs., Wichita Falls, 1980; mem. task force State Task Force on Assistive Tech., Tex., 1989—; bus. mem. Ptnrs. in Edn. Named Notable Women of Tex., 1985. Mem. Tex. Occupational Therapy Assn., Am. Occupational Therapy Assn., World Fedn. Occupational Therapy. Baptist. Avocations: reading, horseback riding, swimming, gardening. Home: 107 N 12th St Jacksboro TX 76458 Office: Graham Gen Hosp Graham TX 76458

RITER, STEPHEN, university administrator, electrical engineer; b. Providence, Mar. 7, 1940; s. Max and Jeannette (Finn) R.; m. Eve R. Hirsch, Aug. 11, 1963; children—Heidi L., Theodore H. B.A., Rice U., Houston, 1961, B.S. in Elec. Engring, 1962; M.S., U. Houston, 1967, Ph.D., 1968. Registered profl. engr., Tex. Dir. Center Urban Programs, Tex. A&M U., 1974-76, mem. univ. faculty, 1968-80, prof. elec. engring., 1976-80; dir. Tex. Energy Extension Service, 1976-79; prof. elec. engring., chmn. dept. elec. engring. and computer sci. U. Tex., El Paso, 1980-89, dean engring., 1989-95, dir. Ctr. for Environ. Resource Mgmt., 1989-95; interim v.p. acad. affairs U Tex, El Paso, 1995-96, provost, v.p., 1996—; Active El Paso Utility Regulatory Bd., 1982-89; cons. in field. Author papers in field.; Editor: Trans. Geosci. Electronics, 1972-76. Mem. policy adv. com. Tex. Dept. Community Affairs, 1979-81; Tex. Border Health and Environ. Issues Task Force, 1990—. Served with U.S. Army, 1962-64. Mem. IEEE, Am. Soc. Engring. Edn. Home: 836 Cherry Hill Ln El Paso TX 79912-3325 Office: Univ Tex Office of VP Acad Affairs El Paso TX 79968

RITSCH, FREDERICK FIELD, academic administrator, historian; b. Covington, Va., Nov. 25, 1935; s. Frederick Field and Harriet Curtis (Miller) R.; m. Jeannette McClung, June 14, 1957 (dec.); children: Frederick Field III, Lise Catherina; m. Debra Ronning, Dec. 21, 1991; 1 child, Anne Ronning. BA, U. Va., 1956, MA, 1959, PhD, 1962; student, Univ. de Strasbourg, France, 1957-58. Instr. Randolph-Macon Women's Coll., Lynchburg, Va., 1959; vis. lectr. Sweet Briar (Va.) Coll., 1959-60; from asst. prof. to prof. Dana history and humanities Converse Coll., Spartanburg, S.C., 1960-83, dir. ctr. for humanities, head div. humanities; dean of faculty Elizabethtown (Pa.) Coll., 1984-85, provost, 1986-96, prof., 1997—; cons. Ednl. Services, Inc., Washington, 1975-77; vice chmn. Communication Services, Inc., Spartanburg, 1978-82; dir. Ctr. for Study Contemporary Humanities, Spartanburg, 1972-81. Author: French Left and European Idea, 1967; author, editor: Issues and Commitment, 1976; editor: (with M. Goldberg) Probes and Projections, 1974; contbr. articles to profl. jours. and collections. Elder Donegal Presbyn. Ch., Mt. Joy, Pa. Fulbright fellow, 1957-58; NEH grantee, 1969; recipient Cert. Merit, Inst. Internat. Edn., 1978. Mem. Am. Hist. Assn., Pa. Acad. Deans Conf. (program chmn. 1984), So. Humanities Conf. (editor jour. Humanities in the South 1971-83, chmn. 1984), Phi Beta Kappa. Home: 600 S Spruce St Elizabethtown PA 17022-2552 Office: Elizabethtown Coll 1 Alpha Dr Elizabethtown PA 17022-2298

RITSEMA, FREDRIC A., lawyer; b. Kansas City, Mo., Feb. 12, 1951. AB, Calvin Coll., 1973; JD, U. Colo., 1976. Bar: Colo. 1976. Mem. Hall & Evans, Denver; mem. subcoms. Workers' Compensation. Mem. Denver Bar Assn., Colo. Def. Lawyers Assn. Office: Ritsema & Lyon PC 999 18th St Ste 3100 Denver CO 80202

RITT, PAUL EDWARD, communications and electronics company executive; b. Balt., Mar. 3, 1928; s. Paul Edward and Mary (Knight) R.; m. Dorothy Ann Wintz, Dec. 30, 1950; children: Paul Edward, Peter M., John W., James T., Mary Carol, Matthew J. B.S. in Chemistry, Loyola U., Balt., 1950, M.S. in Chemistry, 1952; Ph.D. in Chemistry, Georgetown U., 1954. Research asso. Harris Research Lab., Washington, 1950-52; aerospace research chemist Melpar, Inc., Falls Church, Va., 1952-60; research dir. Melpar, Inc., 1960-62, v.p. research, 1962-65, v.p. research and engring., 1965-67; v.p., gen. mgr. Tng. Corp. Am., 1965-67; pres. applied sci. div., applied tech. div. Litton Industries, 1967-68; v.p., dir. research GTE Labs., Waltham, Mass., 1968-86; dir. acad. affairs Babson Coll., Wellesley, Mass., 1986—; bd. dirs. Abex Inc., N.Y.C. subs. IC Industries, 1983-89; bd. dirs. Pneumo/Abex Inc., Boston, 1986-89. Contbr. articles to profl. jours. Mem. dean's adv. coun. U. Mass. Sch. Engring.; mgmt. bd. advs. Worcester Poly. Inst.; adv. coun. Stanford U.; mem. Mass. High Tech. Coun.; trustee Waltham-Weston Hosp., 1983—, New Eng. Coll. Fund., 1980-86. Fellow Am. Inst. Chemists, AAAS; mem. Am. Phys. Soc., Royal Soc. Chemistry, IEEE, Am. Inst. Physics, Electrochem. Soc., Am. Vacuum Soc., Am. Ceramic Soc., Am. Chem. Soc., Washington Acad. Sci., N.Y. Acad. Sci., Tech. Transfer Soc., Sigma Xi. Patentee in field. Home: 36 Sylvan Ln Weston MA 02193-1028 Office: Babson Coll Wellesley MA 02154

RITT, ROGER MERRILL, lawyer; b. N.Y.C., Mar. 26, 1950; m. Mimi Santini, Aug. 25, 1974; children: Evan Samuel, David Martin. BA, U. Pa., 1972; JD, Boston U., 1975, LLM, 1976. Bar: Mass. 1977, Pa. 1975, U.S. Tax Ct. Sr. ptnr. Hale and Dorr, Boston; adj. prof. grad. tax program Boston U., 1979-92; panelist Am. Law Inst., Mass. Continuing Legal Edn., World Trade Inst., NYU Inst. on Fed. Taxation; mem. exec. com. Fed. Tax Inst. New Eng. Treas. Found. for Tax Edn. Mem. ABA (tax sect.), Boston Bar Assn. Office: Hale and Dorr 60 State St Boston MA 02109-1800

RITTBERG, ERIC DONDARO, political consultant; b. Queens, N.Y., Nov. 21, 1962; s. Samuel Herman and Ida Gerri (Turk) R.; m. Barbara Jean Carpenter, Jan. 28, 1982. BA in Polit. Sci., Fla. State U., 1990. Mem. rep. Fla. C. of C., Tallahassee, 1991-93; advance man/travel aide Ron Paul for Pres., Houston, 1987-88; condr. campaign Ron Paul for Congress, Tallahassee; exec. dir. Republican Liberty Caucus, Tallahassee, 1993—; dist. rep. U.S. Congressman Ron Paul. Author: Activism for Liberty, 1995. Nat. committeeman Libertarian Party, 1986-87; precinct committeeman Leon County Rep. Party, Tallahassee, 1992—; chmn. County Conservation Dist. Bd. of Suprs., 1995—. With USN, 1981-85. Decorated Expiditiary medal USN, 1984. Mem. Young Reps. Republican. Avocations: books, traveling. Home: 1549 A Willow Bend Way Tallahassee FL 32301 Office: Rep Libery Caucus 1717 Apalachee Pkwy # 434 Tallahassee FL 32301-3009

RITTENHOUSE, NANCY CAROL, elementary education educator; b. Humeston, Iowa, May 26, 1941; d. Myrl Matthews and Opal L. (McCartney) Hixson; m. J. Kent Rittenhouse, Dec. 18, 1960 (div. Mar. 1984); children: Brenda L. Carroll, J. Aaron, Timothy K. Student, St. Mary of the Plains Coll., 1984-87; degree in elem. edn., Ft. Hays State Coll., 1989. Cert. tchr., Kans. Reading instr. Sacred Heart Sch., Dodge City, Kans., 1984; elem. tchr. Miller Sch., Dodge City, Kans., 1985-86, Washington Sch., Hays, 1987; city-county recreation dir. Sherman County, Goodland, 1988; elem. tchr. Northside Sch., Larned, 1989-90; with Great Bend (Kans.) Tribune. Artist numerous paintings; author poetry. Mem. Menninger Found., Topeka, 1984—; hon. mem. Boy Scouts Am., 1978; camp instr. Spl. Olympics Blind Found., Junction City, Kans., 1985-90, Dodge City, 1984; leader Girl Scouts USA, 1975-77. Recipient Hon. award Spl. Olympics, 1984, 1st pl. poetry award, 1990, watercolor award, 1990, oils award, 1988, pen and ink award, 1984. Mem. AAAS, Nat. Trust for Hist. Preservation, Nat. Geog. Soc., Planetary Soc., Smithsonian Assn., MIT. Republican. Avocations: painting, drawing, walking, swimming, writing prose. Home: PO Box 1872 Great Bend KS 67530-1872 Office: Great Bend Tribune 2012 Forest Ave Great Bend KS 67530-4014

RITTER, ALFRED, aerospace consultant; b. Bklyn., Mar. 15, 1923; s. Max and Anna Ritter; m. Joyce Rimer, June 15, 1947; children: Michael Glenn, Erica Anne, Theodore William. BS in Aerospace Engring., Ga. Inst. Tech., 1943, MS in Aerospace Engring., 1947; PhD, Cornell U., 1951. Rsch. engr. Office of Naval Rsch., Washington, 1951-54; supr. aerophysics Rsch. Inst. Ill. Inst. Tech., Chgo., 1954-58, instr. calculus and fluid mechanics, 1956-58; pres. Therm Advanced Rsch., Inc., Ithaca, N.Y., 1958-68; asst. head applied mechanics dept. Calspan Corp. (formerly Cornell Aero. Lab.), Buffalo, 1968-70, asst. head aerodynamic rsch. dept., 1970-78, head aerodynamic rsch. dept., 1978-80; dir. tech. Arnold Engring. Devel. Ctr. div. Calspan Corp. (formerly Cornell Aero. Lab.), Tullahoma, Tenn., 1980-86; sr. assoc. Booz Allen & Hamilton, Huntsville, Ala., 1986-88; pres. A. Ritter, Inc., Huntsville, 1988—; vis. lectr. Cornell U., 1965; instr. aerospace U. Ala., Huntsville, 1985, 87, 88, adj. prof. aerospace engring., 1988—; exec. dir. Calspan Ctr. for Aerospace Rsch., U. Tenn., 1984-86, chmn. nat. adv. bd. Space Inst., 1987—; mem. gov.'s task force So. Mid. Tenn. High Tech. Initiative, 1985-86; reviewer Applied Mechanics Revs., 1955-84; presenter seminars many ednl. instns. Contbr. articles to profl. publs. Mem. Ithaca (N.Y.) Bd. Edn., 1967. 2nd lt. U.S. Army AC, 1943-46. Named Ga. Inst. Tech. Coll. of Engring. Hall of Fame, 1995. Fellow AIAA (nat. v.p. tech. activities 1981-85, bd. dirs. 1981-85, mem. various coms., participant confs.); mem. AAAS (rep. to atmospheric and hydrospheric scis. sect. 1978-80), U.S. Air Force Assn. (pres. Gen. H.H. Arnold chpt. 1985-86, medal of merit 1986), Internat. Coun. Aero. Scis., Nat. Rsch. Coun. (mem. earthquake engring. com. 1984, mem. assessment of nat. aero. wind tunnel facilities com. 1987-88), Strategic Def. Initiative Orgn. (blue ribbon panel to review missile programs 1989, 92), N.Y. Acad. Scis., Rotary, Sigma Xi. Avocations: reading, music, sports, swimming, cross-country skiing. Home: 10044 Meredith Ln Huntsville AL 35803-2632

RITTER, ALFRED FRANCIS, JR., communications executive; b. Norfolk, Va., Dec. 31, 1946; s. Alfred Francis Ritter and Lucile Grey (Thomas) Woodward; m. Caroline Buchanan O'Keefe, Aug. 10, 1968; children: Alfred F. III, Caroline O'Donnell. BA, Coll. of William and Mary, 1968. CPA, Va. Staff acct. Goodman & Co. CPAs, Norfolk, Va., 1971-76; corp. contr. Landmark Communications, Norfolk, 1976-78, v.p., contr., 1978, v.p. fin., 1978; v.p. fin. TeleCable Corp., Norfolk, 1983-89, exec. v.p., 1989-96; exec. v.p. Landmark Comms., Inc., Norfolk, 1996—. Trustee Norfolk Acad., 1991—. Lt. USN, 1968-71. Mem. AICPAs, Va. Soc. CPAs, Bayville Golf Club (pres. 1995—). Episcopalian. Avocations: fishing, golf, Americana. Home: 1133 S Bay Shore Dr Virginia Beach VA 23451-3807 Office: Landmark Comms Inc 150 W Brambleton Ave Norfolk VA 23510-2018

RITTER, ANN L., lawyer; b. N.Y.C., May 20, 1933; d. Joseph and Grace (Goodman) R. B.A., Hunter Coll., 1954; J.D., N.Y. Law Sch., 1970; postgrad. Law Sch., NYU, 1971-72. Bar: N.Y. 1971, U.S. Ct. Appeals (2d cir.) 1975, U.S. Supreme Ct. 1975. Writer, 1954-70; editor, 1955-66; tchr., 1966-70; atty. Am. Soc. Composers, Authors and Pubs., N.Y.C., 1971-72, Greater N.Y. Ins. Co., N.Y.C., 1973-74; sr. ptnr. Brenhouse & Ritter, N.Y.C., 1974-78; sole practice, N.Y.C., 1978—. Editor N.Y. Immigration News, 1975-76. Mem. ABA, Am. Immigration Lawyers Assn. (treas. 1983-84, sec. 1984-85, vice chair 1985-86, chair 1986-87, chair program com. 1989-90, chair speakers bur. 1989-90, chair media liaison 1989-90), N.Y. State Bar Assn., N.Y. County Lawyers Assn., Assn. Trial Lawyers Am., N.Y. State Trial Lawyers Assn., N.Y.C. Bar Assn., Watergate East Assn. (v.p., asst. treas. 1990—). Democrat. Jewish. Home: 47 E 87th St New York NY 10128-1005 Office: 420 Madison Ave New York NY 10017-1107

RITTER, CHARLES EDWARD, lawyer; b. Detroit, July 24, 1938; s. Kenneth Eugene and Mary Elizabeth (Klinsmann) R.; m. Donna Lou Monroe, Mar. 20, 1965; children: Jeffrey Munro and Matthew Alan. B in Archtl. Engring., U. Detroit, 1961; JD, Wayne State U., 1966. Bar: Mich. 1966, U.S. Dist. Ct. (we. dist.) Mich. 1967, U.S. Ct. Appeals (6th cir.) 1988, U.S. Supreme Ct. 1988. Assoc. Adams, Burgie, Scott, Ritter & Brenton, P.C. and predecessors, Kalamazoo, 1966-69, ptnr., 1970-83; ptnr. Brown, Colman & DeMent, P.C., Kalamazoo, 1983-84; sr. ptnr. Miller, Canfield, Paddock and Stone, Kalamazoo, 1984—, resident dirs., 1988-90; group leader Western Mich. Litigation, 1994—. Sr. warden St. Martin of Tours Episc. Ch., Kalamazoo, 1990. Fellow Mich. Bar Found.; mem. Fed. Bar Assn., Kalamazoo Bar Assn. (bd. dirs. 1985--89, pres. 1988-89), Def. Rsch. Inst., Nature Conservancy (life). Avocations: cross country skiing, photography, outdoor activities. Office: Miller Canfield Paddock & Stone 444 W Michigan Ave Kalamazoo MI 49007-3714

RITTER, DALE WILLIAM, obstetrician, gynecologist; b. Jersey Shore, Pa., June 17, 1919; s. Lyman W. and Weltha B. (Packard) Ritter; m. Winnie Mae Bryant, Nov. 13, 1976; children: Eric, Lyman, Michael, Gwendolyn, Daniel. AB, UCLA, 1942; MD, U. So. Calif., 1946. Diplomate Am. Bd. Obstetrics and Gynecology. Intern Los Angeles County Hosp., L.A., 1945-46, resident, 1948-52, admitting room resident, 1948-52; pvt. practice medicine specializing in obstetrics and gynecology, Chico, Calif., 1952—; founder, mem. staff, past chmn. bd. dirs. Chico Cmty. Meml. Hosp.; guest lectr. Chico State Coll., 1956—; mem. staffs Enole Hosp., Chico, 1952—, Glenn Gen. Hosp., Willows, Calif., 1953—, Gridley Meml. Hosp., Calif., 1953-80; spl. cons. obstetrics Calif. Dept. Pub. Health, No. Calif., 1958-70. Contbr. articles to med. and archeol. jours. Bd. dirs. No. dist. Children's Home Soc., Chico, 1954-70. Served with AUS, 1943-45, with M.C., AUS, 1946-48. Recipient Pro-Life award Calif. KC; Paul Harris fellow Rotary Internat. 1989. Fellow ACS, Am. Coll. Obstetrics and Gynecology; mem. AMA, SAR, Calif. Med. Assn., Internat. Soc. Hypnosis, Am. Soc. Clin. Hypnosis, Am. Fertility Soc., Pacific Coast Fertility Soc., Assn. Am. Physicians and Surgeons, Pvt. Drs. of Am., Butte-Glenn County Med. Soc. (past pres.), Am. Cancer Soc. (former bd. dirs. Butte County), AAAS, Christian Med. Soc., Am. Assn. Pro-Life Obstetricians and Gynecologists, Butte-Glenn County Tumor Bd., Anthrop. Assn. Am., Archaeol. Inst. Am., Soc. Calif. Archaeology, Oreg. Archaeology Soc., Archeol. Survey Assn., Southwestern Anthrop. Soc., Am. Rock Art Rsch. Assn.(Pioneer award), Australian Rock Art Rsch. Assn., Internat. Assn. for Study of Prehistoric and Ethnologic Religions, Fretted Instrument Guild Am. (dir. Banjo Kats 'n Jammers), North Valley Banjo Band, Am. Philatelic Soc., Am. Horse CouncilPeruvian Paso Horse Registry of N.Am., Assn. Owners Breeders Peruvian Paso Horses, Phi Chi, Lambda Sigma, Zeta Beta Sigma. Republican. Lodge: Rotary. Office: Box 156 975 East Ave Chico CA 95926-1851

RITTER, DANIEL BENJAMIN, lawyer; b. Wilmington, Del., Apr. 6, 1937; s. David Moore and Bernice Elizabeth (Carlson) R.; m. Shirley F. Sether, Jan. 29, 1971; 1 child, Roxane Elise. AB with honors, U. Chgo., 1957; LLB, U. Wash., 1963. Bar: Wash. 1963, U.S. Dist. Ct. (we. dist.) Wash. 1963, U.S. Tax Ct. 1965, U.S. Ct. Appeals (9th cir.) 1963. Assoc. Davis, Wright Tremaine (formerly Davis, Wright and Jones), 1963-69, ptnr., 1969—; lectr. Bar Rev. Assocs. Wash., Seattle, 1964-86; chmn. internat. dept. Davis, Wright and Jones, Seattle, 1984-85, chmn. banking dept., 1986-89. Casenote editor U. Wash. Law Rev., 1962-63; contbg. author: Washington Commercial Law Desk Book, 1982, rev. edit., 1987, Washington Community Property Desk Book, 1977. Trustee Cathedral Assoc., Seattle, 1980-86; legal counsel Wash. State Reps., Bellevue, 1983-92; bd. dirs. U. Chgo. Club Puget Sound, Seattle, 1982—, pres., 1984-86; bd. dirs. Am. Lung Assn. Wash., Seattle, 1983-92; mem. vis. com. U. Wash. Law Sch., 1984-88; trustee U. Wash. Law Sch. Found., 1989-92; chmn. alumni rels. coun. U. Chgo., 1986-88; mem. statute law com. State of Wash., 1978-87; bd. dirs. Seattle Camerata, 1991-93; bd. dirs. Early Music Guild, Seattle, 1993-96. Mem. ABA (bus. law sect.), Wash. State Bar Assn. (chmn. bus. law sect. 1988-89, uniform comml. code com. 1980—, chmn. 1980-86, chmn. internat. law com. 1979-81, judicial recommendations com. 1991-93), Seattle-King County Bar Assn. (chmn. internat. and comparative law sect. 1980-82), Rainier Club, Order of Coif. Republican. Lutheran. Avocation: reading, theater, early music. Home: 1204 22nd Ave E Seattle WA 98112-3535 Office: Davis Wright Tremaine 2600 Century Sq 1501 4th Ave Seattle WA 98101-1662

RITTER, DEBORAH ELIZABETH, anesthesiologist, educator; b. Phila., May 16, 1947; d. Charles William and Elizabeth Angeline (Coffman) R. BA, Susquehanna U., 1968; MS, U. Pa., 1969; MD, Med. Coll. Pa., 1973. Diplomate Am. Bd. Anesthesiology (assoc. examiner oral bds. 1990, 92). Intern Thomas Jefferson Univ. Hosp., Phila., 1973-74, resident in anesthesia, 1974-76, clin. fellow in anesthesiology, 1976-77; affiliate resident in anesthesia Children's Hosp. Pa., Phila., 1975; assoc. in anesthesiology Frankford Hosp., Phila., 1977-78; clin. instr. anesthesiology Med. Coll. Pa., Phila., 1977-78; clin. instr. anesthesiology Thomas Jefferson U., 1978-80, clin. asst. prof., 1980-86, clin. assoc. prof., 1986—, vice chmn. dept. anesthesiology, 1985—. Contbr. articles to profl. jours. Named Top Doc, Phila. Mag., 1994, 96. Mem. AMA, Am. Women's Med. Assn., Am. Soc. Anesthesiologists, Internat. Anesthesia Rsch. Soc., Soc. Edn. Anesthesia, Assn. Anesthesia Clin. Dirs. Lutheran. Avocations: gardening, music, history, wilderness preservation, American Indian culture. Office: Thomas Jefferson U Dept Anesthesiology 111 S 11th St Ste 6460G Philadelphia PA 19107-4824

RITTER, DONALD LAWRENCE, environmental policy institute executive; b. N.Y.C., Oct. 21, 1940; s. Frank and Ruth R.; m. Edith Duerksen; children: Jason, Kristina. BSMetE, Lehigh U., 1961; MS in Phys. Metallurgy, MIT, 1963, ScD, 1966. Mem. faculty Calif. State Poly. U., also contract cons. Gen. Dynamics Co., 1968-69; mem. faculty dept. metallurgy and materials scis., asst. to v.p. for research Lehigh U., 1969-76; mgr. research program devel., 1976-79, mem. 96th-102d congresses from 15th Pa dist., 1979-93; scientist, chmn., pres. Nat. Environ. Policy Inst., Washington, 1994—; mem. energy and commerce com. and subcoms. telecommunications and fin.; ranking minority mem. transp. and hazardous materials; mem. sci., space and tech. com. and subcoms. environment and tech. and competitiveness; chmn. house Rep. task force on tech. and policy; co-chair Cngl. High Tech. Caucus; ranking minority mem. house Commn. on Security and Cooperation in Europe (Helsinki Commn.), mem. 1980-93; co-chmn. ad hoc com. on Baltic sttes and Ukraine; treas. Congl. steel caudus; mem. Congl. textile and apparel caucus; mem. environ. and energy study conf.; sci. echange fellow U.S. Nat. Acad. Scis.-Soviet Acad. Sci., Baikov Inst., Moscow, 1966-67. Contbr. articles to environmental sci., engring. and quality jours. Recipient award for disting. pub. svc. IEEE, 1990. Fellow Am. Inst. Chemists (honor scroll award); mem. NSPE, Am. Soc. for Metals (disting. life), Sigma Xi, Tau Beta Pi, Pi Mu Epsilon. Unitarian. Home: 2746 Forest Dr Coopersburg PA 18036-9253 Office: Nat Environ Policy Inst 1100 17th St NW Ste 330 Washington DC 20036-4631

RITTER, FRANK NICHOLAS, otolaryngologist, educator; b. New Albany, Ind., July 30, 1928; s. Carl Joseph and Kathleen Mary (Wolfe) R.; m. Gertrude Erlacher; children: Raymond, Kathleen, Lawrence, Mary Elizabeth, Teresa, Joseph, Sharon, Michael. BS, Notre Dame U., 1949; MD, St. Louis U., 1953; MS, U. Mich., 1959. Diplomate Am. Bd. Otolaryngology (pres. 1990-93). Intern Mercy Hosp., Ohio, 1953-54; resident in otorhinolaryngology U. Mich. Hosp., 1954-60; asst. prof. otolaryngology U. Mich., Ann Arbor, 1960-65, assoc. prof., 1966-70, clin. prof., 1971—. Author: The Surgical Anatomy and Technique of Surgery on the Paranasal Sinuses, 1978, 3d edit. 1992; contbr. articles to profl. jours. Capt. USAF, 1955-57. Recipient Sr. award Med. Sch., U. Mich., 1965, Shovel award U. Mich. Med. Students, 1967. Mem. Am. Laryngol. Assn., Am. Otological Soc., Am. Acad. Otolaryngology, Head and Neck Surgery, Am. Bronchoesophagological Assn. (pres. 1985), Mich. Otolaryn. Soc. (pres. 1968), Soc. Univ. of Otolaryngologists, Triological Soc. (exec. sec. 1985-89, pres. 1993), Centurian (pres. 1984), Walter Wark Soc. (pres. 1986). Roman Catholic. Avocations: golf, fishing. Office: Reichert Health Bldg 5333 Mcauley Dr Rm 4016R Ypsilanti MI 48197-1001

RITTER, FREDERICK EDMOND, plastic surgeon, educator; b. Cin., Aug. 21, 1959; s. Edmond J. and Alexandra (Engel) R.; m. Christina Weltz, Aug. 2, 1993. BS, U. Cin., 1980; MD, Washington U., St. Louis, 1984. Intern, resident U. Medicine and Dentistry N.J., 1984-90; resident in plastic and reconstructive surgery U. Calif., San Francisco, 1990-92; asst. prof. surgery Duke U., Durham, N.C., 1992—. Contbr. chpts. in books and articles to profl. jours. Republican. Achievements include reducing thrombogenicity biomaterials in contact with blood, innovations in reconstructive and asthetic surgery, tissue bioengineering. Office: Duke Univ Med Ctr Rm 142 Baker House Durham NC 27710

RITTER, HAL, newspaper editor. Mng. editor money sect. USA Today, Arlington, Va., now mng. editor news, 1995—. Office: USA Today 1000 Wilson Blvd Arlington VA 22209-3901*

RITTER, JAMES WILLIAM, architect, educator; b. Richmond, Va., June 14, 1942; s. James William and Catherine (Luck) R.; m. Betty Ann Mauck, June 19, 1965; 1 child, Mark Channing. BArch., Va. Poly. Inst. and State U., 1965. Registered architect Va., Md., D.C., Del., Ky., W.Va., N.C., Pa. Assoc. Wilkes and Faulker, Architects, Washington, 1967-70, Winesett/Duke,Architects, Springfield, Va., 1970-74; prin. James William Ritter Architect, Alexandria, Va., 1974–; adj. prof. architecture Va. Poly. Inst. and State U., 1981—. 1st lt. U.S. Army, 1965-67. Recipient Design award Masonry Inst., 1987, 1st Pl. Residential award Va. Masonry Coun., 1989, Grand award for nat. housing innovations, 1984; included in Am. Architects, 1989. Fellow AIA (bd. dirs. No. Va. chpt. 1976-78, 83-85, pres. 1988-89, bd. dirs., 1st v.p. Va. Soc. 1990-91, pres. 1993, various awards 1977—); mem. Am. Arbitration Assn. (mediator 1984—), Alexandria C. of C., Mensa. Avocation: leader Buck Creek Jazz Band. Office: 705 King St Alexandria VA 22314-3014

RITTER, ROBERT FORCIER, lawyer; b. St. Louis, Apr. 7, 1943; s. Tom Marshall and Jane Elizabeth (Forcier) R.; m. Karen Gray, Dec. 28, 1966; children: Allison Gray, Laura Thompson, Elisabeth Forcier. BA, U. Kans., 1965; JD, St. Louis U., 1968. Bar: Mo. 1968, U.S. Dist. Ct. (ea. and we. dists.) Mo. 1968, U.S. Ct. Mil. Appeals 1972, U.S. Supreme Ct. 1972, U.S. Ct. Appeals (8th cir.) 1980, U.S. Dist. Ct. (so. dist.) Ill. 1982. Assoc. Gray & Sommers, St. Louis, 1968-71; ptnr. Gray & Ritter, 1974—; bd. dirs. United Mo. Bank of St. Louis, Marine Bank and Trust Co.; adv. com. 22d cir. Supreme Ct., 1985-92; mem. Supreme Ct. com. on civil jury instrns., U.S. Dist. Ct. adv. com., 1993-95; lectr., author in field. Bd. dirs., Cystic Fibrosis Found., Gateway chpt. (pres. 1991). Served to capt. USAR, 1968-74. Recipient Law Week award Bur. Nat. Affairs, 1968. Fellow Internat. Soc. Barristers (bd. govs. 1994—), Am. Coll. Trial Lawyers, Internat. Acad. Trial Lawyers; mem. Bar Assn. Met. St. Louis (chmn. trial sect., 1978-79, exec. com. 1980-82, award of merit 1976, award of achievement 1982, chmn. bench bar conf. 1983), Mo. Bar Assn. (coun. practice and procedure com. 1972—, coun. tort law com. 1982—, bd. govs. 1984-91, fin. com. 1984-91), Mo. Bar Found. (outstanding trial lawyer award, 1978), ABA, Lawyers Assn. St. Louis (exec. com. 1976-81, pres. 1977-78), Mo. Assn. Trial Attys. (bd. govs. 1984—), Am. Judicature Soc., Assn. Trial Lawyers Am., Am. Bd. of Trial Advocates (advocate, award of merit Nat. Conf. Met. Cts. 1995), Noonday Club, Old Warson Country Club, Bellerive Country Club, John's Island Club, Racquet Club (bd. govs. 1988-93, pres. 1991-92). Presbyterian (elder 1992—). Contbr. articles to law jours. Office: Gray & Ritter PC 701 Market St Fl 8 Saint Louis MO 63101-1850

RITTER, ROBERT JOSEPH, lawyer; b. N.Y.C., Aug. 11, 1925; s. Robert Reinhart and Mary (Mandracchia) R.; m. Barbara Willis Foust, Oct. 1, 1955 (div. May 1977); children: Robert Thornton, Jan Willis Ritter Kelly, Nancy Carol Ritter dePoortere. Student, Bklyn. Poly. Inst., 1943; BA cum laude, Queens Coll., 1949; JD, NYU, 1953, LLM in Internat. Law, 1955. Bar: N.Y. 1953. Acct. UN Secretariat, N.Y.C., 1949-54; asst. counsel RCA Corp., N.Y.C., 1955-58; atty. CIBA-GEIGY Corp., Ardsley, N.Y., 1958-60, AT&T Bell Tel. Labs., Inc., Murray Hill, N.J., 1960-70; tax atty. AT&T Techs., Inc., N.Y.C., 1970-85; mgr. fin. AT&T Corp. Hdqrs., Parsippany, N.J., 1985-87; asst. sec. 14 subs. telephone cos. AT&T, 1985-87; v.p. CPPS Tax Cons., N.Y.C., 1987—. Contbr. articles to legal jours. Pres. Harry B. Thayer chpt. Tel. Pioneers Am., N.Y.C., 1983-84; trustee, sec. United Way Ctrl. N.J., Milltown, 1989—, chmn. cmty. divsn. govt. rels. allocations coms., 1990—; corp. program dir. Vol. Action Ctr. of Middlesex County, N.J., 1988; mem. adv. bds. Dept. Human Svcs., State of N.J. and Middlesex County, N.J., 1991—; mem. adv. coun. Project Resources, State of N.J., 1987—; bd. dirs. Somerset Hills YMCA, Bernardsville, N.J., 1971-73; bd. dirs., mem. Greater Raritan Pvt. Industry Coun./Workforce Investment Bd., New Brunswick, N.J., 1989—; Dem. candidate N.Y. State Assembly, Westchester County, N.Y., 1965; chmn. fund dr. Am. Cancer Soc., Bronxville, N.Y., 1964. With USAAF, 1943-46. Recipient Crusade award Am. Cancer Soc., 1965, Masonic Svc. award, 1947, Am. Legion Citizenship award, 1943, Vol. of Yr. award United Way, 1991. Mem. ABA (sr. lawyers divsn. 1990—), Nat. Tax Assn.-Tax Inst. Am. (chmn., advisor state sales and use taxation com. 1984-88, chmn. prodn. exemption subcom. 1978-84), Am. Soc. Internat. Law, Nat. Eagle Scout Assn., Assn. of Bar of City of N.Y., Internat. Platform Assn., Legal Aid Soc., NYU Law Alumni Assn., Rossmoor Old Guard (pres. 1994-95), Perth Amboy (N.J.) C. of C. (exec. dir. 1988-89), Rossmoor Tennis Club (pres. 1987-88), Church Club of N.Y., Kiwanis (1st v.p. 1970-71), Sigma Alpha. Democrat. Episcopalian. Home: 3-N Village Mall Jamesburg NJ 08831-1534 Office: CPPS Tax Cons Yorkville Sta PO Box 7022 New York NY 10128-0010

RITTER, SALLIE, painter, sculptor; b. Las Cruces, N.Mex., May 9, 1947; d. John Barnes Ritter and Billie Ruth (Carter) Simpson; m. Kent Frederick Jacobs, Apr. 13, 1971. Student, U. Rome Coll. Art History, 1965, Edinburgh (Scotland) Coll. Art, 1967-68; BA, Colo. Coll., 1969. One-woman shows include Lubbock (Tex.) Art Ctr., 1970, N.Mex. Arts Commn., Santa Fe, 1974, Las Cruces Cmty. Ctr., 1975, Aldridge Fine Arts, Albuquerque, 1980, Woodrow Wilson Fine Arts, Santa Fe, 1989, Adobe Patio Gallery, Mesilla, N.Mex., 1991, 93, Contemporary Southwest Galleries, Santa Fe, 1996, Adair Margo Gallery, 1997; exhibited in group shows at El Paso (Tex.) Mus. Art, 1988, Colorado Springs (Colo.) Fine Arts Ctr., 1995, Laguna Gloria Mus., Austin, Tex., 1979, Santa Fe Festival of the Arts, 1979, 83, The Governor's Gallery, Santa Fe, 1987, 94, Pioneer's Mus., Colo. Springs, 1985, 86, 88, N.Mex. State U., Las Cruces, 1988, 89, Dona Ana Arts Coun., Las Cruces, 1992, Tex. Commn. Arts, Austin, 1987, Tucson Mus. Art, 1995, Nat. Cowboy Hall of Fame, Oklahoma City, 1996, Autry Mus. Western Art, L.A., 1996, Albuquerque Mus. Art, 1996; represented in permanent collections U. Tex. Sch. of Law, Phelps Dodge Corp., Sunwest Bank, Albuquerque, N.Mex. State U., N.Mex., Santa Fe, Nat. Mus. Women in Arts, Washington; featured in Contemporary Women Artists, 1984, Contemporary Western Artists, 1985. Bd. dirs. Women's Bd., Mus. N.Mex., Santa Fe, 1987—, Dona Ana Arts Coun., Las Cruces, 1990—. Mem. Nat. Mus. of Women in the Arts. Episcopalian. Home and Studio: 3610 Southwind Rd Las Cruces NM 88005-5556 also: 1114 Main Rd Ruidoso NM 88345

RITTER, SANDRA HELEN, psychotherapist, counselor; b. Kingston, Pa., Dec. 31, 1947; d. Earl Jean and Lois Mae (Hartley) R.; stepfather Harry R. Smith; m. Billy Lee Ferguson, May 23, 1995; children: Christopher Andrew Hawkins, Alexander Cameron Hawkins (dec.); stepchildren: William Lee Ferguson, Ann Ferguson Bishop. BSME, Villanova U., 1969; MBA, Ctrl. Mich. U., 1981; MEd in Counseling, U. N.C., Greensboro, 1994, PhD in Counseling, 1997. Nat. cert. counselor; lic. profl. counselor. Engr. Automation Industries, Silver Spring, Md., 1974-83; sr. engr. Naval Sea Sys. Command, Alexandria, Va., 1983-85; ptnr. Clemmons (N.C.) Primary Care, 1987-91; owner, proprietor Serendipity Resource Ctr., Clemmons, 1985-91; mental health asst. Charter Hosp., Greensboro, N.C., 1992-94; pvt. practice Greensboro, 1994—. Co-author: Assessment in Counseling and Therapy, 1995; sr. author: Leadership Development on a Shoestring, 1995; mem. edtl. bd. Jour. Addictions and Offenders Counselors, 1995—. Vol. hospice, Winston-Salem, N.C., 1990-92; vol. counselor The Listening Post, Greensboro, 1993-94; mem. worship com. Unitarian Universalist Fellowship, Greensboro, 1993-95, svc. leader coord., 1994-95. Mem. ACA (mem. adv. coun. 1996—), Assn. for Adult Devel. and Aging (Midlife chair 1996—), , Internat. Assn. Addictions and Offenders Counselors (chair addictions com. 1993-96, mem. accreditation com. 1995-96, pres. 1997—), Am. Mental Health Counselors Assn., Assn. for Counseling Edn. and Supervision (Outstanding Doctoral Student 1995), C.G. Jung Soc., N.C. Assn. for Adult Devel. and Aging (pres. 1995-96), N.C. Assn. for Specialists in Group Work (pres. 1996-97), N.C. Counseling Assn. (co-chair spl. task force 1995-96, treas. 1995-96, exec. coun. 1994—, chair strategic planning com. 1996-97, pres.-elect 1997—), Chi Sigma Iota (fellow, mem. Upsilon Nu Chi chpt., treas. 1993-94, awards chair 1993-96, pres.-elect 1994-95, pres. 1995-96, Internat. Outstanding Master's Student 1994). Avocations: reading, vol. work, duplicate bridge, traveling. Home: 5000 Edinborough Rd Greensboro NC 27406 Office: 200 E Bessemer Ave Greensboro NC 27401-1416

RITTER-CLOUGH, ELISE DAWN, consultant, private investor; b. Balt., Aug. 14, 1952; d. Nelson Fred and Marjorie Jean (Corke) Ritter; m. Philip Anthony Gibson, Apr. 7, 1979 (div. Feb. 1990); 1 child, Christopher Ritter Gibson; m. Victor Wayne Clough, Jr., Mar. 3, 1990; stepchildren: Wesley T., Lindsay, Sharon. Student, Austro-Am. Inst., Vienna, Austria, 1973; BS, U. Kans., 1974. Researcher, Impeachment Inquiry Staff U.S. Ho. of Reps., Washington, 1974; researcher APA, Washington, 1975; editor prodn. The New Republic Mag., Washington, 1976-77; copy editor Time-Life Books, Alexandria, Va., 1977-79, assoc. editor, 1979-83, adminstrv. editor, 1983-87, asst. dir. editorial resources, 1988-90; dir. editorial resources Time Warner, Time-Life Books, Alexandria, 1990-94. Bd. Arlingtonians Ministering to Emergency Needs (AMEN), 1995—; chairperson outreach commn. Mt. Olivet Meth. Ch., Arlington, 1994—; vol. Mental Health Program, Visiting Nurse Assn., 1996—, Women's Ctr., 1997—.

RITTERHOFF, C(HARLES) WILLIAM, retired steel company executive; b. Balt., Nov. 1, 1921; s. Ernest F. and Anna M. (Luerssen) R.; m. Margery A. McKenney, June 24, 1944 (dec. May 1987); children: Leslie, William, James; m. Marita C. Halsey, Feb. 20. 1988. B.S. in Mech. Engring, Mass. Inst. Tech., 1947; grad., Advanced Mgmt. Program, Harvard, 1973. Asst. engr. mech. dept., then various supervisory positions Bethlehem Steel Co., Sparrows Point, Md., 1948-57; asst. supt. Sparrows Point plate mills, 1957-60, asst. chief engr. plant engring. dept., 1960-63; asst. chief engr. Burns Harbor project, 1963, asst. gen. mgr., 1963-67; gen. mgr. Burns Harbor plant, 1967-70; v.p. manufactured products and West Coast steel plants, 1970-71, v.p. steel operations-prodn., 1971-74, dir., 1974-82, exec. v.p., 1974-77, vice chmn., 1977-80, exec. v.p. steel ops., 1980-82. Served to 1st lt. U.S. Army, 1943-46. Mem. NAM (past bd. dirs.), Am. Iron and Steel Inst., Assn. Iron and Steel Engrs., Hwy. Users Fedn. (past bd. dirs.), Moorings Club, Bridgehampton Club (N.Y.). Home: 150 Anchor Dr Vero Beach FL 32963-2957

RITTERHOUSE, KATHY LEE, librarian; b. Hutchinson, Kans., May 24, 1952; d. Fayne Lee and Elizabeth Rose (Tener) R.; m. Michael Raymond Demmitt, July 8, 1972 (div. Apr. 1990). BA in English, Kans. State U., 1974; MLS, U. Okla., 1979. Circulation libr. Grand Prairie (Tex.) Meml. Libr., 1979-80, libr. dir., 1980—. Bd. dirs. Grand Prairie Arts Coun., 1980-97, pres., 1989. Named Pub. Svc. Employee of Yr. Grand Prairie C. of C., 1989. Mem. ALA, Tex. Libr. Assn. (Tex./SIRS Intellectual Freedom award 1993), Metro Rotary Club (bd. dirs. 1992-97), Beta Phi Mu. Office: Grand Prairie Meml Libr 901 Conover Dr Grand Prairie TX 75051-1521

RITTERSKAMP, DOUGLAS DOLVIN, lawyer; b. St. Louis, July 7, 1948; s. James Johnstone Jr. and Linn M. (Dolvin) R.; m. Linda S. Vansant, Mar. 23, 1974; 1 child, Tammy. AB, Washington U., 1970, JD, 1973; LLM in Taxation, NYU, 1978. Bar: N.Y. 1974, Mo. 1979. Assoc. Patterson, Belknap, Webb & Tyler, N.Y.C., 1974-78; jr. ptnr. Bryan Cave LLP (and predecessors), St. Louis, 1978-82; ptnr. Bryan Cave LLP, St. Louis, 1983—. Trustee Scottish Rite Clinic for Childhood Lang. Disorders of St. Louis, Inc., 1982—, St. Louis Mission and Ch. Ext. Soc., United Meth. Ch., 1987—, Mo. United Meth. Found., 1994—, The Coll. Sch., 1995—. Capt. USAR, 1970-79, active duty tng., 1973. Mem. ABA (employee benefits com. sect. taxation 1987-91, 96—), Bar Assn. Met. St. Louis (steering com. employee benefits 1989—), Masons (32d degree, knight comdr. ct. of honor), Shriners. Methodist. Home: 5223 Sutherland Ave Saint Louis MO 63109-2338

RITTINGER, CAROLYNE JUNE, newspaper editor; b. Swift Current, Sask., July 19, 1942; d. George Kelly Gaetz and Eva Evelyn (Hiebert) Olson; m. Robert Edward Rittinger, Aug. 16, 1958; children: Robert Wade, Angela Alison, Lisa Michelle. Women's editor Swift Current Sun, 1967-68; city editor Medicine Hat (Alta.) News, 1969-70; reporter Kitchener-Waterloo Record, Kitchener, Ont., 1972-75, copy editor, 1976, women's editor, then dist. editor, entertainment editor, wire editor, 1976-85, city editor, 1985-86, asst. mng. editor, 1986-89, mng. editor, 1989-92, editor, 1992—. Recipient News Story of Yr. award Calgary Women's Press Club, 1969, Best Feature Story on Fine Art award, 1970, Honorable Mention for A.R. McKenzie award for Info. Story, 1970; named Oktoberfest Woman of Yr., 1992. Avocations: downhill skiing, travel, live theatre. Office: Kitchener-Waterloo Record, 225 Fairway Rd, Kitchener, ON Canada N2G 4E5

RITTMER, ELAINE HENEKE, library media specialist; b. Maquoketa, Iowa, Feb. 4, 1931; d. Herman John and Clara (Luett) Heneke; m. Sheldon Lowell Rittmer, June 11, 1950; children: Kenneth, Lynnette, Robyn (dec.), infant son (dec.). BA, Marycrest Coll., 1973; MS, Western Ill. U., 1980. Permanent teaching cert. K-14, Iowa; cert. libr. media specialist K-14, Iowa. Sch. libr. Calamus-Wheatland (Iowa) Community Schs., 1970-74; high sch. libr. media specialist, libr. coord. Camanche (Iowa) Community Sch., 1974-96; legis. asst. State Capitol, Des Moines, 1997—; ind. tech. cons., 1988—. Mem. Iowa Edn. Media Assn., Iowa State Edn. Assn., Camanche Edn. Assn., Camanche Cmty. Schs. Tech. Com., Media Tech. Cons. Republican. Avocations: reading, walking, education, political activities, future technology developments. Home: 3539 230th St De Witt IA 52742-9208 Office: State Capitol Des Moines IA 50319

RITTMER, SHELDON, state senator, farmer; b. DeWitt, Iowa, Sept. 5, 1928; s. Elmer and Lois (Hass) R.; m. Elaine Heneke, June 11, 1950; children: Kenneth S., Lynnette Rittmer Jones, Robyn Jon (dec.), infant son (dec.). County supr. Clinton (Iowa) Conty Bd. Suprs., 1978-90; chmn. Clinton County Title III Com., 1987-90; v.p. Iowa Assn. County Suprs., Des Moines, 1989-90; mem. from 19th dist. Iowa Senate, 1990—; Iowa Senate coms. include small bus.-econ. devel., tourism, health and human rights, transp., state govt., appropriations com., local govt. com. Chmn. 1st Luth. Ch., Maquoketa, Iowa, 1964-68; active Clinton County Hist. Soc., 1980—. Recipient Spl. Recognition award Nat. Fedn. Ind. Bus., 1991-92, Spl. Recognition Iowa Soil Conservation award, 1994. Mem. Izaak Walton League Iowa, DeWitt Lions, Ducks Unlimited U.S.A, Clinton County Pork Prodr's. Assn., Clinton County Cattlemen's Assn., Pheasants Forever, City of Clinton C. of C., DeWitt C. of C., Bettendorf C. of C. Republican. Avocations: public speaking, governmental research, reading, agriculture. Home: 3539 230th St De Witt IA 52742-9208 Office: State Senate of Iowa State Capital Des Moines IA 50319

RITTNER, CARL FREDERICK, educational administrator; b. Boston, Feb. 28, 1914; s. Philip and Augusta (Beich) R.; m. Eunice Carin, 1940; 1 child, Stephen. BS in Edn., Boston U., 1936, EdM, 1937. Ednl. cons. Boston, 1940's; founder, dir. Rittners Floral Sch., Boston, 1947—. Co-author: Flowers for the Modern Bride, 1965, Arrangements for All Occasions, 1966, Flowers for the Modern Bride (In Living Color), 1968, Rittner's Silver Anniversary Book, 1972, Dried Arrangements, 1978, Rittners Guide to Permanent Flower Arranging, 1978, Vase Arrangements for the Professional Florist, 1979, Christmas Designs, 1979, Flowers for Funerals, 1980, Manual of Wedding Design Styles, 1980, Contemporary Floral Designs, 1983, Floral Designs for That Special Occasion, 1985, Inexpensive Bread & Butter Designs, 1986. Mem. Soc. Am. Florists, Florist Transworld Delivery Svc., Phi Delta Kappa. Office: 345 Marlborough St Boston MA 02115-1799

RITTNER, EDMUND SIDNEY, physicist; b. Boston, May 29, 1919; s. Philip and Augusta (Beich) R.; m. Marcella Weiner, Oct. 6, 1942; 1 child, Leona. B.S., MIT, 1939, Ph.D., 1941. Research assoc. MIT, Cambridge, 1942-45; sect. chief Philips Labs., Briarcliff Manor, N.Y., 1946-62; dir. Dept. Physics, 1962-67, dir. exploratory research, 1967-69; exec. dir. phys. scis. COMSAT Labs., Clarksburg, Md., 1969-84; A.D. Little postdoctoral fellow MIT, 1941-42. Contbr. articles to profl. jours. Fellow Am. Phys. Soc., IEEE (Photovoltaic Founders award, 1985). Home: 700 New Hampshire Ave NW 116-S Washington DC 20037

RITTNER, STEPHEN LEE, academic administrator; b. Boston, Oct. 31, 1952; s. Carl Frederick and Eunice (Carin) R. BS in Biology, BA in Religion, Tufts U., 1974, EdM, 1977; EdD, Boston U., 1981. Assoc. dir. Rittners Floral Sch., Boston, 1974—; producer videotapes on floral design. Author: Window Display for the Retail Florist, A Philosophy of Floral Designing, 1989, Introductory Floral Designing, 1992, A Bibliography of Floral Design Books for Teachers of Floral Designing, 1992; co-author: Vase Arrangements for the Professional Florist, 1979, Dried Arrangements, 1978, Christmas Designs, 1979, A Manual of Wedding Design Styles, 1980, Contemporary Floral Designs, 1983, Floral Designs for that Special Occasion, 1985, Inexpensive Bread and Butter Designs, 1986. Mem. Soc. Am. Florists, Assn. Ednl. Comms. and Tech., Florists Transworld Dslivery Svc., Redbook, Phi Beta Kappa, Phi Delta Kappa, Pi Lambda Theta. Office: Rittners Floral Sch 345 Marlborough St Boston MA 02115-1799

RITTS, JIM, professional sports team executive; b. Dallas, Tex., 1955. BS in Advt./Mktg., U. Tex.; MS in Journalism, Northwestern U. former rschr. ABC Sports, statistician NCAA Coll. Football and Monday Night Football; operator scoring system for ABC Sports telecasts of PGA Tour events and the U.S. Open. Prior various positions to pres./network affirs Channel One Comms. (subs. K-III Comms.), 1984-96; commr. Ladies Profl. Golf Assn., Daytona, Fla., 1996—. Avocation: golf. Office: Ladies Profl Golf Assn 100 International Golf Dr Daytona Beach FL 32124

RITVO, EDWARD ROSS, psychiatrist; b. Boston, June 1, 1930; s. Max Ritvo; m. Riva Golan, Sept. 11, 1989; children: Deborah, Eva, Anne, Matthew, Victoria, Skylre, Max. BA, Harvard U., 1951; MD, Boston U. Sch. Medicine, 1955. Diplomate Am. Bd. Psychiatry and Neurology, Am. Bd. Child Psychiatry. Prof. UCLA Sch. Medicine, 1963—. Author 4 books; contbr. over 150 articles to profl. jours. Capt. U.S. Army, 1959-61. Recipient Blanche F. Ittleson award Am. Psychiat. Assn., 1990. Mem. Nat. Soc. for Autistic Children, Profl. Adv. Bd. (chmn.). Office: UCLA Sch Medicine Dept Psychiatry 760 Westwood Plz Los Angeles CA 90024-8300

RITVO, ROGER ALAN, university dean, health management-policy educator; b. Cambridge, Mass., Aug. 12, 1944; s. Meyer and Miriam R.S. (Meyers) R.; m. Lynn Lieberman; children: Roberta, Eric. BA, Western Res. U., 1967; MBA, George Washington U., 1970; PhD, Case Western Res. U., 1976. Asst. adminstr. N.Y. Mental Health System, 1968-70; asst. prof., asst. dean Sch. Applied Social Scis. Case Western Res. U., Cleve., 1976-79, assoc. prof., 1981-84; assoc. prof., founding dir. Grad. Program in Health Adminstrn. Cleve. State U., 1984-87; prof. health mgmt. and policy, dean Sch. Health and Human Svcs. U. N.H., Durham, 1987-97; sr. health policy analyst to sec. DHHS, Washington, 1980-81; vice chancellor acad. and student affairs Auburn U., Montgomery, Ala., 1997—; vis. rsch. scholar WHO, Copenhagen, 1978; vis. prof. Am. U., Washington, 1980-81, U. W.I., 1993; vis. scholar U. Sheffield, Eng., 1985; cons. to numerous orgns. on profit and non-profit strategic planning. Editor, author 5 books, including Managing in the Age of Change, Improving Governing Board Effectiveness; contbr. articles to profl. jours. Trustee Hosp. Sisters of Charity, Cleve., 1980-85, Greater Seacoast United Way, 1991-93; chmn. health care adv. com. Ohio Senate, 1983-85; bd. mem. Fairmount Temple, Beachwood, Ohio, 1980-85; trsutee Leadership Seacoast, 1991-93, bd. dirs., 1992-95; bd. dirs. N.H. chpt. United Way, 1992-95. Recipient Outstanding Adminstr. award, 1982, Cert. of Merit U. N.H. Pres.'s Commn. on Women, 1994; Govt. fellow Am. Coun. Edn., 1980-81. Mem. Nat. Tng. Labs. Inst. (bd. dirs. 1981-85, 92-96), Cert. Cons. Internat., Jewish Philatelic, Hist. Soc. N.Y.C. Avocations: collecting flat irons and masks, philatelist, white water rafting. Office: Auburn U 7300 University Dr Montgomery AL 36117-3531

RITZ, ESTHER LEAH, civic worker, volunteer, investor; b. Buhl, Minn., May 16, 1918; d. Matthew Abram and Jeanette Florence (Lewis) Medalie; m. Maurice Ritz, Apr. 8, 1945 (dec. 1977); children—David Lewis, Peter Bruce. B.A. summa cum laude, U. Minn, 1940, postgrad., 1940-41; postgrad., Duke U., 1941-42. Adminstrv. analyst, economist Office of Price Adminstrn., N.Y., Washington and Chgo., 1942-46. Pres., Nat. Jewish Welfare Bd., 1982-86; v.p. Council of Jewish Fedns., 1981-84; pres. World Conf. Jewish Community Ctrs., 1981-86; bd. dirs. Am. Jewish Joint Distbn. Com., 1977-93, bd. dirs. (hon. life mem.) Joint Distbn. Com., 1994; trustee United Jewish Appeal, 1982-87; vice-chmn. bd. dirs. Jerusalem Ctr. Pub. Affairs, 1984—; bd. dirs. Wurzweiler Sch. Social Work Yeshiva U., 1984-89, HIAS, 1983-86; mem. Jewish Agy. Com. on Jewish Edn., 1984-90, bd. govs., 1988-92; bd. dirs. Legal Aid Soc., Milw. County, 1983-85; mem. Community Issues Forum, Milw.; vice chmn. bd. United Way Greater Milw., 1977-81; pres. Florence G. Heller Jewish Welfare Bd. Research Ctr., 1979-83; pres. Mental Health Planning Council of Milw. County, 1976-79; vice chmn Large City Budgeting Conf., 1976-82; pres. Jewish Community Ctr. Milw., 1966-71; pres. Milw. Jewish Fedn., 1978-81; bd. dirs. Shalom Hartman Inst., 1989—; bd. dirs.; mem. exec. com., policy com. Nat. Jewish Dem. Coun., 1991—, vice-chmn. bd. dirs., 1994-96; bd. dirs. Nat. Jewish Ctr. for Learning and Leadership, 1988-92, Ams. Peace Now, 1989—, vice-chmn. bd. dirs., 1995-96, Coun. Initiatives Jewish Edn., 1990—, Friends of Labor Israel (steering com. 1988—, chair 1988-90); bd. vis. Ctr. for Jewish Studies U. Wis., Madison, 1994—. Named to Women's Hall of Fame YWCA, 1979; recipient Cmty. Svc. award Wis. Region NCCJ, 1977, William C. Frye award Milw. Found., 1984, Telesis award Alverno Coll., Milw., 1984, Hannah G. Solomon award. Nat. Coun. Jewish Women, ProUrbe award Mt. Mary Coll., Evan P. Helfer award Milw. chpt. Nat. Soc. of Fund Raising Execs., 1994, Margaret Miller award Planned Parenthood of Wis., 1994. Mem. LWV, NAACP, NOW, Hadassah, Na'amat, Common Cause, Nat. Women's Polit. Caucus, Nat. Coun. Jewish Women, Planned Parenthood. Democrat. Avocations: music, bridge, art collecting. Home: 626 E Kilbourn Ave Milwaukee WI 53202-3235

RITZ, LORRAINE ISAACS, nursing administrator; b. Wheeling, W.Va.; d. John and Anna (Julian) Isaacs; m. Robert H. Ritz, Apr. 24, 1953; children: Chris Casuccio, Bonnie, Amy. Diploma nursing, Wheeling Hosp.; BS in Nursing, W. Liberty State Coll.; MS in Nursing, W.Va. U. Staff nurse Wheeling Hosp., supr.; DON Wheeling (W.Va.) Hosp., 1980-88, asst. adminstr. nursing, 1988-96; mem. adv. bd. West Liberty State Coll., 1984-96, W.Va. No. C.C., 1981-96; pres. W.Va. Bd. Examiners, 1993, 94; bd. dirs. Wheeling Health Right, sec., 1992, 93, 95-96. Bd. dirs. Florence Crittenton, 1984-91, sec., 1990-91. Mem. ANA, Nat. League Nurses, W.Va. Orgn. Nurse Execs. (v.p. 1988-89, pres., 1991, 92, 93, W.Va. Exec. of Yr. 1991), Am. Orgn. Nurse Execs. Office: Wheeling Hosp Inc Med Park Wheeling WV 26003

RITZ, RICHARD ELLISON, architect, architectural historian, writer; b. Colfax, Wash., Dec. 8, 1919; s. Henry Clay and Katharine Fredericka (Failing) R.; m. Evelyn R. Robinson, Sept. 21, 1940; children: Margaret Karen Ritz Barss, Susan Elizabeth Ritz Williams. Student, Whitman Coll., 1936-37. Registered architect, Oreg. Draftsman, job capt. Pietro Belluschi, Architect, Portland, Oreg., 1946-51; project mgr., chief prodn. Belluschi and Skidmore, Owings & Merrill, Portland, 1951-56; project mgr., then gen. mgr. Skidmore, Owings & Merrill, Portland, 1956-82; pvt. practice architecture Portland, 1982—; founder Greenhills Press, 1991. Author: A History of the Reed College Campus, 1990, An Architect Looks at Downtown Portland, 1991, The Central Library Portland's Crown Jewel, 1997; editor: A Guide to Portland Architecture, 1968; contbr. articles to profl. jours. Bd. dirs. Architecture Found., Portland, 1982-85; mem. Portland Hist. Landmarks Commn., 1987—. Sgt. USAF, 1942-45. Fellow AIA (bd. dirs. Portland chpt. 1975-79, pres. 1978, mem. handbook com. Fin. Mgmt. for Architects 1980); mem. Soc. Archtl. Historians, Oreg. Coun. Architects (del. 1975-79), Portland Art Mus., Oreg. Hist. Soc., Lang Syne Soc., City Club Portland, Univ. Club (Portland), Multnomah Athletic Club. Republican. Presbyterian. Home and Office: 4550 SW Greenhills Way Portland OR 97221-3214

RITZ, STEPHEN MARK, financial advisor, lawyer; b. Midland, Mich., Aug. 23, 1962; s. Alvin H. and Patricia M. (Padway) R. BA, Northwestern U., 1985; JD, Ind. U., 1989. Bar: Ill. 1990, U.S. Dist. Ct. (no. dist.) Ill. 1990. Atty. Chapman & Cutler, Chgo., 1990-93; pres., CEO S.M. Ritz and Co., Inc., Indpls., 1994—; dir. Indsl. Logistics, Inc., Indpls., 1994—. Mem. ABA, Inst. CFPs, Registry CFPs, Internat. Assn. Fin. Planners. Office: SM Ritz and Co Inc 9465 Counselors Row Ste 108 Indianapolis IN 46240-3816

RITZENTHALER, PATTY PARSONS, lawyer; b. Pocomoke City, Md., Feb. 20, 1954; d. E. Carmel Wilson (stepfather) and Evelyn Gay (Carter) Parsons-Wilson; m. John Paul Ritzenthaler, Oct. 30, 1993. BA in Psychology, U. Md., Balt., 1976; JD, U. Balt., 1979. Bar: Md. 1981, US. Dist. Ct. Md. 1981, U.S. Bankruptcy Ct. Md. 1981, Md. Ct. Appeals 1981, U.S. Ct. Appeals (4th cir.) 1984, D.C. Ct. Appeals 1989, D.C. 1989, Supreme Ct. Va. 1991, Va. 1991. Residential counselor U. Md., Balt., 1973-76; adminstr. Juvenile Law Clinic, Balt., 1979-80; legal asst. Edelman & Rubenstein P.A., Balt., 1979-81; labor atty. Edelman & Rubenstein, P.A., Balt., 1981-85; labor atty. Abato, Rubenstein and Abato, P.A., Balt., 1985-87, ptnr., 1988-89; pvt. practice, 1989-92; ptnr. Abato, Rubenstein & Abato, P.A., Balt., 1992—, pres., 1996—. Drug counselor Open Arms Community Counseling Ctr., Balt., 1972-73; vol. Domestic Violence Legal Clinic. Recipient Md. Poetry Soc. award, 1972; Outstanding Adv. award, U. Balt., 1977-78. Mem. Md. State Bar Assn. (adv. bd. labor sect.), ABA (developing labor law com., labor and employment sect.), Va. State Bar, Va. Bar Assn., D.C. Bar, Indsl. Rels. Rsch. Assn., Coalition Labor Union Women. Democrat. Home: 1309 Dartmouth Ave Baltimore MD 21234 Office: 809 Glen Eagles Ct Ste 320 Baltimore MD 21286-2230

RITZHEIMER, ROBERT ALAN, educational publishing executive; b. Trenton, Ill., Dec. 29, 1931; s. Leslie H. and Hilda M. (Fochtmann) R.; m. Shirley Ann Wharrie, Sept. 11, 1954; children: Kim E. Ritzheimer Chase, Gina C. Ritzheimer Hartle, Scott D., Susan L. Ritzheimer Kelly. BS in Edn., Ill. State Normal U., 1953, MS in Edn., 1960; postgrad., Columbia U., 1955. Cert. tchr., supr., k-12, Ill. Tchr. Bloomington (Ill.) Pub. Schs., 1955-57; prin., elem. and jr. high sch. Wesclin Community Unit #3, New Baden, Ill., 1957-62; ednl. sales rep. Scott Foresman Co., Bradford Woods, Pa., 1962-81; field sales mgr. Scott Foresman Co., Sunnyvale, Calif., 1981-91; mgr. sales support Scott Foresman Co., Sunnyvale, 1992-93; ret., 1993; cons., pub. Calif. State Bd. Edn., Sacramento, 1981-93; guest lectr. Stanford U., Palo Alto, Calif., 1983, Santa Clara (Calif.) U., 1992. Treas. Little League, New Baden, Ill., 1958-62; pres. Ill. Edn. Assn., Kaskaskia Div., E. St. Louis, 1961. With U.S. Army, 1953-55. Mem. ASCD, NEA (life), Calif.Sci. Teachers Assn. Republican. Avocations: travel, swimming, plate collecting. Home: 1566 Deerfield Dr San Jose CA 95129-4707

RIVA, J. MICHAEL, art director, production designer. Prodn. designer: (films) I Never Promised You a Rose Garden, 1977, Bare Knuckles, 1978, Fast Charlie...the Moonbeam Rider, 1979, Halloween II, 1981, The Hand, 1981, Bad Boys, 1983, The Adventures of Buckaroo Banzai: Across the 8th Dimension, 1983, The Goonies, 1985, The Slugger's Wife, 1985, The Color Purple, 1985 (Academy award nomination best art direction 1985), The Golden Child, 1986, Lethal Weapon, 1987, Scrooged, 1988, Lethal Weapon 2, 1989, Tango & Cash, 1989, Radio Flyer, 1992, Dave, 1992, A Few Good Men, 1992, (TV movies) Callie & Son, 1981; art dir.: (films) Ordinary People, 1980, Brubaker, 1980; visual cons.: (films) Stranger's Kiss, 1984. Office: Innovative Artists Ste 2850 1999 Avenue Of The Stars Los Angeles CA 90067-6082*

RIVARD, WILLIAM CHARLES, mechanical engineering educator; b. Detroit, Sept. 2, 1942; s. William John and Ruby Marie (Theel) R.; m. Betty L. Slocum, Nov. 21, 1964; children: Michele, Traci. BS, U. Detroit, 1965, MS, 1966; PhD, Ill. Inst. Tech., 1968. Staff mem. explosive systems div. Los Alamos (N.Mex.) Nat. Lab., 1968-71, assoc. group leader theoretical div., 1971-80; v.p., co-owner Flow Sci., Inc., Los Alamos, 1980-87; Arthur O. Willey prof. mech. engring. U. Maine, Orono, 1987—; pres. Fluid Systems, Inc., East Holden, Maine, 1988—; cons. Exxon Rsch. Ctr., Florham Park, N.J., 1989—, McDonnell Douglas Space Systems, Huntington Beach, Calif., 1987—, Aerospatiale, Les Mereaux, France, 1989—, Technischer Uberwachungs-Verein, Hanover, Fed. Republic of Germany, 1985-88. Contbr. articles to profl. jours. Grad. fellow NSF, 1967, NASA, 1968. Office: U Maine Mech Engring Dept Orono ME 04469

RIVAS, ERNESTO, newspaper columnist; b. N.Y.C., Dec. 19, 1924; s. Gabry and Sara (Solis) R.; m. Cocó, Dec. 8, 1969; children from previous marriage: Sara, Patricia, Estrella, Ernesto Jr., Rene, Regina; children: Martín Javier, Gabriela. B of Arts and Sci., Colegio Centroamérica, Granada, Nicaragua. Press div. clk. UN, N.Y.C., 1947-48; reporter La Nueva Prensa, Managua, Nicaragua, 1949-52; dir. Radio Panamericana, Managua, 1952-60; with pub. rels. dept. Nicaragua Mission to UN, N.Y.C., 1960-62; dir. news Radio 590, Managua, 1963-66; columnist La Noticia, Managua, 1967-77; with pub. rels. dept. Emp. Nacional de Luz y Fuerza, Managua, 1978-79; UPI corr., Managua, 1979-80; columnist Diario Las Américas, Miami, Fla., 1981—. Mem. UDN 1981-86, Acción Democrética, Miami, 1986—. Republican. Roman Catholic.

RIVE, SARELLE ROSELYN, manufacturing company executive; d. Max and Ruth Rae (Goldring) Riave; m. Norman E. Friedmann, June 22, 1952 (div. Nov. 1985); children: Marc David, Lance Alan, Keyla Ilene Treitman; m. Robert A. Suhosky, July 4, 1986 (div. July 1994). BA with honors, Barat Coll., 1977. Owner, dir. Gallerie Sarelle, Highland Park, Ill., 1977-78, L.A., 1982-84, 86-90; owner, dir. A Neat Idea By Sarelle, L.A., 1992—; silver level exec. Quorum Internat., L.A., 1992—; pres. Internat. Export Concepts, L.A., 1994—; CFO Universal Diesel Products, Inc. USA subs., Vancouver, B.C., Can., 1995—. Den mother, pack leader cub scout troop Boy Scouts Am., 1959-63; day camp dir., leader Girl Scouts U.S., L.A., 1966-73; bd. dirs. YWCA, Highland Park, Ill., 1974-77; docent Mus. of Contemporary Art, L.A., 1985-88; assoc. Older People in a Caring Atmosphere (OPICA), L.A., 1981—; founding mem. Nat. Mus. Women in Arts, Washington, 1993—, Mus. Contemporary Art, L.A., 1985-93; mem. president's cir. L.A. County Mus. of Art, 1987—, mem. president's cir. of patrons. 1993-95. Mem. City of Hope (life), Kappa Gamma Pi, Delta Epsilon Sigma. Jewish. Avocations: travel, walking, jigsaw puzzles, biking, swimming. Home and Office: 401 N Carmelina Ave Los Angeles CA 90049-2703

RIVELLI, WILLIAM RAYMOND ALLAN, photographer; b. Providence, May 10, 1935; s. William and Virginia C. (Capece) R.; m. Margaret A. Cronin, June 2, 1963 (dec. 1973); children: William Dante, Sarah Kerry; m. Cynthia Jean Lepore, Sept. 7, 1974; 1 child, Taylor Elia. BA in Philosophy, Brown U., 1957. Asst. to photographer Nina Leen Life Mag., N.Y.C., 1959-60, asst. to photographer Ralph Steiner, 1960-61; photographer Rivelli Photography, N.Y.C., 1963—; instr. Sch. Visual Arts, N.Y.C., 1991—. Subject/photographer profile and portfolio Communication Arts, 1982; dir. photography, photographer multi-media slide presentation Naked Chambers, 1987; chosen contbr.: American Photography, 1990, Graphis Photo, 1994, Communication Arts Photography Ann., Graphis Fine Art Photography, 1995; artist, photographer exhbn. Cathedral Portfolio, 1988-92; exhibited in groups shows Art Dirs. Club Exhbns., N.Y., N.J., Mass., Can., 1976-86, Advt. Photographers Awards Ann. Exhbn., 1988-91, 95. Recipient Cert. of Excellence award Art Dirs. Club, 1976-82, Creativity Cert. of Excellence award Art Dir. Mag., 1976-77, 80, Ann. Report Photography award Mead Corp., 1974, Outstanding Achievement award Champion Internat., 1995. Mem. Am. Soc. Media Photographers (nat. bd. dirs. 1987-89, chosen contbr. Kodak Traveling Exhbn. 1986-87, 89), Indsl. Photographers Assn. (bd. dirs. 1979-80). Home and Office: 303 Park Ave S Studio 508 New York NY 10010-3625

RIVENBARK, JAN MEREDITH, corporate executive; b. Spartanburg, S.C., Feb. 22, 1950; s. George Meredith and Audrey Isabel (Frady) R.; m. Barbara N. Newton, Sept. 25, 1976; children: Abigail, Justin, Patrick. BS in Math., Duke U., 1972; postgrad., Ga. State U., 1980. Mgmt. trainee Citizens & So. Nat. Bank, Atlanta, 1972, br. mgr., 1974, employee relations mgr., 1975-77, v.p. compensation, benefits, payroll and data mgmt., 1977-80; mgr. personnel First Tenn. Bank, Memphis, 1980-81; dir. compensation and benefits Hanes Group, Consol. Foods Corp. (now Sara Lee Corp.), Winston-Salem, N.C., 1981-83, exec. dir. compensation and benefits, Chgo., 1983-84; exec. dir. internat. staff Sara Lee Corp., 1985, exec. dir. corp. planning, 1985-87; sr. v.p., PYA/Monarch div. Sara Lee Corp., Greenville, S.C., 1987-89; pres., chief oper. officer JP Foodservice, Hanover, Md., 1989-92; COO, PCA Internat., Inc., Charlotte, N.C., 1992—. Mem. Alpha Tau Omega (chpt. pres. 1971-72). Republican. Home: 2500 Greenbrook Pky Matthews NC 28105-7790 Office: PCA International Inc 815 Matthews Mint Hill Rd Matthews NC 28105-1705

RIVERA, ANGEL (ANDY) MANUEL, retired career officer, city official; b. Arecibo, P.R., Dec. 24, 1942; s. Ramon and Domitila (Viruet) R.; m. Rose Marie Wuchina; children: Tina Nikkole, Marc Anthony. BBA, U. P.R., Rio Pedras, 1960; MBA, Inter-Am. U. P.R., San German, 1969. Commd. 2d lt. USAF, 1965, advanced through grades to col., 1987; various positions SAC, Tng. Command Airlift Command, 13th Air Force, Vietnam and U.S., 1965-77; wing exec. 1605th Air Base Wing Lajes Field, Azores, Portugal, 1978; instr., liaison officer U.S. Army Sch. Ams., Ft. Gulick, Panama, 1978-79; sec. joint staff U.S. So. Command, Quarry Heights, Panama, 1979-80; ops. officer U.S./Panama NG Combined Bd. U.S. So. Command, Quarry Heights, Republic of Panama, 1980-82; chief pers. divsn. 42d Combat Support Group, Loring AFB, Maine, 1982-84; asst., dep. chief staff for pers. 8th Air Force, Barksdale AFB, La., 1984-87; comdr. 7th Combat Support Group, Carswell AFB, Tex., 1987-89; comdr., prof. aerospace studies Tex. Christian U., Ft. Worth, 1989-91; ret., 1991; exec. asst. to chancellor U. North Texas, Denton, 1991-92; dir. airport sys., CEO City of Ft. Worth, 1992—; adj. faculty La. Tech. U., Barksdale AFB, 1986-87, U. Md. Lajes Field Azores, 1976-78, Ctrl. Tex. Coll., Lajes Field, 1976-78, Park Coll., Lajes Field, 1975-76, Big Bend C.C., Scott AFB, 1974-75; mem. civilian adv. coun. No. Maine Vocat. Tech. Inst., Presque Isle, 1983-84; instr. mgmt. and logistics U.S. Army Sch. Ams., 1978-79. Mem. Ft. Worth Airshow Com., Airport Minority Adv. Coun., Vets. Adv. Com., 12th Congl. Dist., Def./Mil. Adv. Com., 6th Congl. Dist. Adv. Com., Ft. Worth Lulac Coun. 601, Image of Ft. Worth, Am. G.I. Forum of Tarrant County, Forum Ft. Worth, Hispanics Friends of U. North Tex.; v.p. North Tex. Cemetary Commn., past mem. Metroplex Fed. Exec. Bd., Ft. Worth Crimestoppers Com., Star-Telegram Citizens Adv. Bd., Pres.'s Coun. U. North Tex.; past athletic trustee U. North Tex.; past exec. bd. dirs. Longhorn coun. Boy Scouts Am., past chmn. Silver Star dist.; past bd. dirs. Frontiers of Flight Mus., Love Fields, Dallas; past chmn. subcom. Ft. Worth chpt. Rev Com.; assoc. Greater Ft. Worth Civil Leaders Assn., United Hispanic Coun. Ft. Worth; past mem. exec. com. Sunshine dist. Girl Scouts Am., Panama Canal Zone; mem. Big Bros. and Big Sisters of Tarrant County, Ft. Worth Citizens Organized Against Crime, Alzheimers Assn. Tarrant County, Multiple Sclerosis Assn. Tarrant County. Decorated Legion of Merit with oak leaf cluster, Bronze Star, Def. M.S.M., A.F. M.S.M. with 3 oak leaf clusters, A.F.C.M. with oak leaf cluster, Armed Forces Honor medal 1st class, Air Svc. medal honor class, Gallentry Cross with palm (Vietnam), Air Force Achievement medal. Mem. Tex. Assn. Airport Execs., Am. Assn. Airport Execs., Air Force Assn. (life), Navy League, Ft. Worth Airpower Coun., Ft. Worth Hispanic C. of C., Ft. Worth C. of C., Forum Ft. Worth (chmn.), U. North Tex. Parents Assn., Rotary, Phi Beta Delta. Republican. Avocations: golf, sports. Office: Rsch Pk Devel Corp 7170 Research Rd Mansfield TX 76063

RIVERA, ANGEL LUIS, chemical engineer; b. Bayamon, P.R., Oct. 7, 1950; s. Luis and Felicita (Lopez) R.; m. Marta V. Rivera, Mar. 21, 1975; children: Luis E., Mayra Lynn, Carlos A. BAChemE, U. P.R., Mayaquez, 1974, MS in Nuclear Engring., 1976; PhD in Environ. Engring., Northwestern U., Evanston, Il., 1981; MBA, U. Tenn., 1986. Devel. engr. Oak Ridge (Tenn.) Nat. Lab., 1980-84, group leader, 1984-86, project mgr., 1986-89, program mgr., 1990—. Contbr. articles to profl. jours. and publs. Mem. Am. Chem. Soc., Am. Inst. Chem. Engrs., Am. Assn. Cost Engrs., Am. Mgmt. Assn., IEEE Computer Soc., Tau Beta Pi. Home: 107 Garnet Ln Oak Ridge TN 37830-5601 Office: Oak Ridge Nat Lab PO Box 2003 Oak Ridge TN 37831-2003

RIVERA, CHITA (CONCHITA DEL RIVERO), actress, singer, dancer; b. Washington, Jan. 23, 1933; d. Pedro Julio Figuerva del Rivero; m. Anthony Mordente. Student, Am. Sch. Ballet, N.Y.C. Broadway debut: Call Me Madam, 1952; appeared on stage in: Guys and Dolls, Can-Can, Seventh Heaven, Mister Wonderful, West Side Story, Father's Day, Bye Bye Birdie, Three Penny Opera, Flower Drum Song, Zorba, Sweet Charity, Born Yesterday, Jacques Brel is Alive and Well and Living in Paris, Sondheim-A Musical Tribute, Kiss Me Kate, Ivanhoe, Chicago, Bring Back Birdie, Merlin, Jerry's Girls, 1985, The Rink, 1984 (Tony award 1984), Can-Can, 1988, Kiss of the Spider Woman (Tony award, Best Actress in a musical), 1993; performs in cabarets and nightclubs around world; starred in: film Sweet Charity, 1969; numerous TV appearances include Kojak and the Marcus Nelson Murders, 1973, The New Dick Van Dyke Show, 1973-74, Kennedy Ctr. Tonight-Broadway to Washington!, Pippin, 1982, The Mayflower Madam, 1987, Sammy Davis Jr.'s 60th Birthday Celebration, 1990. Mem. AFTRA, SAG, Actors Equity Assn. Office: William Morris Agy care Gayle Nachlis 1325 Ave Americas New York NY 10019*

RIVERA, GERALDO, television personality, journalist; b. N.Y.C., July 4, 1943; s. Cruz Allen and Lillian (Friedman) R.; m. Sheri Rivera (div. 1984); m. C.C. Dyer, 1987; children: Gabriel Miguel Cruz, Isabella, Simone. BS, U. Ariz., 1965; JD, Bklyn. Law Sch., 1969; postgrad., U. Pa., 1969, Sch. Journalism, Columbia U., 1970. Bar: N.Y. 1970. Mem. anti-poverty neighborhood law firms Harlem Assertion of Rights and Community Action for Legal Svcs., N.Y.C., 1968-70; with Eyewitness News, WABC-TV, N.Y.C., 1970-75; reporter Good Morning America program ABC-TV, 1973-76, corr., host Good Night America program, 1975-77, corr., sr. producer 20/20 Newsmag., 1978-85; host syndicated talk show The Geraldo Rivera show, N.Y.C., 1987—; host investigative show on cable CNBC Rivera Live, N.Y.C., 1994—. Author: Willowbrook, 1972, Island of Contrasts, 1974, Miguel, 1972, A Special Kind of Courage, 1976, Exposing Myself, 1991; host numerous syndicated TV spls.; film appearances: The Bonfire of the Vanities, 1990; television movie: Perry Mason: The Case of the Reckless Romeo. Recipient 7 Emmy awards, Peabody award, Kennedy Journalism award, 1973, 75, numerous others; named Broadcaster of Yr. N.Y. State AP, 1971, 72, 74; Smith fellow U. Pa., 1969. Jewish. Office: Geraldo Investigative News Group 555 W 57th St New York NY 10019-2925

RIVERA, MARIANO, professional baseball player; b. Panama City, Panama, Nov. 29, 1969. Baseball player N.Y. Yankees, 1995—. Achievements include member of 1996 World Series Champions. Office: New York Yankees East 161St and River Ave Bronx NY 10451

RIVERA, RICHARD E., food products executive; b. Jan. 6, 1947; m. Leslie Suzanne Pliner, Nov. 18, 1984. BA, Washington & Lee U., 1968. Credit analyst Nat. Bank Commerce, Dallas, 1970-71; from mgmt. trainee to exec. v.p., dir. Steak Ale Restaurants of Am., Dallas, 1971-80; pres. restaurant div. El Chico Corp., 1980-82; exec. v.p., chief operating officer T.J. Applebee's and Taco Villa Mexican Restaurant, Dallas, 1982-87; exec. v.p. ops. TGI Friday's Inc., Dallas, 1987-88, pres., chief exec. officer, 1988-94; pres., CEO RARE Hosp. Inernat., Inc., Atlanta, 1994—. Office: Longhorn Steaks 8215 Roswell Rd Bldg 200 Atlanta GA 30350-2808

RIVERA, SOPHIE, photographer. Student, New Sch. for Social Rsch., N.Y.C. lectr. in field; photography resident, Syracuse, N.Y., 1987, SUNY, Buffalo, N.Y., 1987. Solo exhbns. include: Internat. Photo Optical Exhibit, N.Y.C., 1979, El Museo del Barrio, N.Y.C., 1987, En Foco Arts for Transit, N.Y.C., 1989, Windows on White, N.Y.C., 1990, Wilmer Jennings Gallery, N.Y.C., 1995, U. Conn., West Hartford, 1996, Studio Mus. Harlem, N.Y.C., 1997; dual exhbns. include Cork Gallery, N.Y.C., 1980, Casa Aboy, P.R., 1981; group shows include: El Museo del Barrio, 1984, 87, El Museo Nat. del Bellas Artes, Havana, Cuba, 1984, Bronx Mus. Arts, N.Y.C., 1986, Salmagundi Club, N.Y.C., 1987, Camera Club N.Y., 1987, Goddard-Riverside Cmty. Ctr., N.Y.C., 1987, John Jay Coll. Criminal Justice, 1988, Intar Gallery, N.Y.C., 1988, Blum-Helman Warehouse Gallery, N.Y.C., 1989, Mus. Sci. and Industry, Chgo., 1989, Dia Art Found., N.Y.C., 1989, Flossie Martin Gallery, Radford, Va., 1990, Purdue Univ. Galleries, Lafayette, Ind., 1990, En Foco Gallery, 1990, Galleria El Bohio, N.Y.C., 1990, Kince Gallery, N.Y.C., 1990, Ctr. for Book Arts, N.Y.C., 1990, 80 Washington Sq. East Galleries, N.Y.C., 1991, 93, CCNY, 1991, Ctr. for Photography at Woodstock, N.Y., 1991, Scott Alan Gallery, N.Y.C., 1991, Rutgers U., N.J., 1991, Monasterio de Santa Clara, Spain, 1992, Tweed Gallery, N.Y.C., 1993, Mus. at Stony Brook, N.Y., 1993, Kenkeleba Gallery, N.Y.C., 1994, Foto Fest '94, Houston, Hostos Art Gallery, 1995, Marymont Coll., 1997, Smithsonian Inst., 1997. Recipient awards Pub. Art Fund, 1989, N.Y. Found. for the Arts (Photography), 1989. Home and Studio: 31 Tiemann Pl New York NY 10027-3309

RIVERA-MARTINEZ, SOCORRO, retired educator, assistant principal; b. Mayagüez, P.R., Apr. 19, 1942; d. Sotero R. and Rafaela Martinez; m. Carmelo Torres, Dec. 26, 1965; 1 child, Yolivette. AEd., Catholic U., 1963, BA in Elem. Edn., 1980. Cert. tchr., mentor tchr. Tchr. 1-6 grades P.R. Dept. Edn., Mayagüez, 1962-93; auxilliary adminstr. Colegio San Agustin, Cabo Rojo, P.R., 1993-94, asst. principal, 1994-97; tchr. in charge Rio Hondo Sch. Mayagüez, 1964-70, 73-93, gifted children club, 1990-91, dir.'s resource for tng., 1985-93; math and sci. counselor Rio Hondo, Sch., Castillo Sch., 1971-93. Co-leader troop 384 Girl Scouts Am., Rio Hondo Sch., Mayagüez, P.R., 1975-79; vol. leader Catholic Ch. Summer camp, Cabo Rojo, P.R., 1990-92. Recipient Presidential award Excellence in Sci. and Math. Tchg. The White House, 1993, State award Excellence in Math. Nat. Coun. Math. Tchrs., 1993, Excellence in Math. award Dept. Edn., 1993; named Tchr. of the Year Dept. Edn., 1975, 82. Mem. Educadores Puertorriqueños en Acción, Coun. Elem. Sci. Internat., Coun. Presidential Awardees. Roman Catholic. Avocations: reading, poetry, writing, wire craft, gardening. Home: L22 Calle 3 Borinquen Cabo Rojo PR 00623-3324 Office: Colegio San Agustin Cabo Rojo PR 00623

RIVERS, JOAN, entertainer; b. N.Y.C., June 8, 1937; d. Meyer C. Molinsky; m. Edgar Rosenberg, July 15, 1965 (dec.); 1 child, Melissa. BA, Barnard Coll., 1958. Formerly fashion coordinator Bond Clothing Stores. Debut entertaining, 1960; mem. From Second City, 1961-62; TV debut Tonight Show, 1965; Las Vegas debut, 1969; nat. syndicated columnist Chgo. Tribune, 1973-76; creator: CBS TV series Husbands and Wives, 1976-77; host: Emmy Awards, 1983; guest hostess: Tonight Show, 1983-86; hostess The Late Show Starring Joan Rivers, 1986-87, Hollywood Squares, 1987—, (morning talk show) Joan Rivers (Daytime Emmy award 1990), 1989—, Can We Shop? Home Shopping Netwrok, 1994—; originator, screenwriter TV movie The Girl Most Likely To, ABC, 1973; other TV movies include: How to Murder A Millionaire, 1990, Tears and Laughter: The Joan and Melissa Rivers Story, 1994; cable TV spl. Joan Rivers and Friends Salute Heidi Abromowitz, 1985; film appearances include The Swimmer, 1968, Uncle Sam, The Muppets Take Manhattan, 1984; co-author, dir.: (films) Rabbit Test, 1978 (also acted), Spaceballs, 1987; actress: theatre prodn. Broadway Bound, 1988, Sally Marr...and her escorts, 1994; recs. include: comedy album What Becomes a Semi-Legend Most, 1983; author: Having a Baby Can be a Scream, 1974, The Life and Hard Times of Heidi Abromowitz, 1984, (autobiography with Richard Meryman) Enter Talking, 1986, (with Richard Meryman) Still Talking, 1991; debuted on Broadway (play) Broadway Bound, 1988, creator Seminar You Deserve To Be happy, 1995. Nat. chmn. Cystic Fibrosis, 1982—, benefit performer for AIDS, 1984. Recipient Cleo awards for commls., 1976, 82, Jimmy award for best comedian, 1981; named Hadassah Woman of Yr., 1983, Harvard Hasty Pudding Soc. Woman of Yr., 1984. Mem. Phi Beta Kappa. Office: William Morris Agy 151 S El Camino Dr Beverly Hills CA 90212-2704*

RIVERS, KENNETH JAY, judicial administrator, consultant; b. N.Y.C., Feb. 13, 1938; s. Alexander Maximillian and Albertina Ray (Gay) R.; m. Leah B. Files, Sept. 21, 1957 (div.); children: Londa Denise, Nancy Laura, Terrie Ruth, Kenneth J. Jr. AAS in Criminal Justice, St. Francis Coll., Bklyn., 1978, BS in Criminal Justice, 1978; MPA, L.I. Univ., 1981. Correction officer N.Y.C. Dept. Correction, 1965-69; ct. officer N.Y. State Unified Ct. System, N.Y.C., 1969-71, asst. ct. clk., 1971-73, sr. ct. clk., 1973-85, assoc. ct. clk., 1985-88, prin. ct. clk., 1988-90, dep. chief clk., 1991-93; ret., 1993; tng. instr. N.Y. State Unified Ct. System, N.Y.C., 1985—, pers. assessor, 1985—; lectr. John Jay Coll. NYU, N.Y.C., 1987. Author: Juvenile Crime Survey, 1982, New York State Jury Selection, 1984. Bd. dirs. Parkway Consumers Med. Coun., Bklyn., 1983—, Cen. Bklyn. Tenant's Rights, 1988—. Recipient Leadership award Tribune Soc., N.Y. State Cts., 1987, Svc. award, 1988, Cert. of Merit award Fedn. Afro-Am. Civil Svc.

Orgns., 1987. Mem. ASPA, Internat. Pers. Mgmt. Assn., Acad. Polit. Sci., Conf. Minority Pub. Adminstrs., Masons. Democrat. Methodist. Avocation: jazz musician.

RIVERS, LARRY, artist; b. N.Y.C., 1923; m. Augusta Berger, 1945 (div.); 2 sons; m. Clarice Price, 1961; 2 children. Grad., N.Y. U.; student painting with, Hans Hofmann. Exhibited one-man shows including: N.Y.C. galleries, 1949—, Kestner Gesellschaf, 1980-81, Staatliche Kunsthalle, Berlin, 1981, 82, Galerie Biederman, Munich, 1981, Hirshhorn Mus. and Sculpture Garden, Washington, 1981, Marlborough Gallery, N.Y.C., 1982, Gloria Loria Gallery, Bay Harbor, Islands, Fla., 1982, Lowe Art Mus., U. Miami, 1983, Guild Hall Mus., East Hampton, N.Y., 1983, Jewish Mus., N.Y.C., 1984, Hooks-Epstein Galleries, Houston, 1984; exhibited group shows: Vanguard Gallery, Paris, France, 1953, Am. Fedn. Arts traveling exhbn., 1954-55, Mus. Modern Art, N.Y.C., 1956, Museum de Arte Moderne, São Paulo, Brazil, 1957, Art Inst. Chgo., Mpls. Inst. Arts, La Jolla Mus. Art, 1980, Bklyn. Mus., 1980, 81, N.Y.U., 1981, Allen Mus., Berlin, 1981, Marquette U., Milw., 1981, Whitney Mus. Am. Art, 1981, 82, Los Angeles County Mus. Art, 1982, Nat. Gallery of Victoria, B.C., 1982, spl. exhbn. sponsored, Mus. Modern Art, Japan, Mus. Mexico City, Hirshhorn Gallery, Washington, Los Angeles County Mus., Mus. Caracas, Venezuela, 1979-80, Hanover (Ger.) Mus., 1980, permanent works in collections, William Rockhill Nelson Gallery Art, Kansas City, Mpls. Inst. Arts, State U. Coll. Edn., New Paltz, N.Y., Bklyn. Mus. Art, Met. Mus. Art, Mus. Modern Art, Whitney Mus. Am. Art, N.Y.C., R.I. Sch. Design, Providence, N.C. Mus. Art, Raleigh, Corcoran Gallery Art, Washington, also pvt. collections; stage designer: play The Toilet; appearance: film Pull My Daisy; executed mural History of the Russian Revolution.; Author: Drawings and Digressions, 1979, (with Arnold Weinstein) What Did I Do?, 1993. Recipient spl. awards Corcoran Gallery Art, 1954, spl. awards Arts Festival, Spoleto, Italy, also; Newport, R.I., 1958. Mem. NAD (assoc.). Address: Marlborough Gallery 41 W 57th St New York NY 10019-4001*

RIVERS, LYNN N., congresswoman; b. Augres, Mich., Dec. 19, 1956; married; 2 children. BA, U. Mich., 1987; JD, Wayne State U., 1992. Mem. sch. bd. City of Ann Arbor, Mich., 1984-92; mem. Mich. House of Reps., 1992-94; mem. 104th Congress from 13th dist., 1994, mem. budget/science basic rsch., technology, 1994. Office: US House Reps 1724 Longworth Bldg Washington DC 20515-2213

RIVERS, MARIE BIE, broadcasting executive; b. Tampa, Fla., July 12, 1928; d. Norman Albion and Rita Marie (Monroe) Bie; m. Eurith Dickinson Rivers, May 3, 1952; children—Eurith Dickinson, III, Rex B., M. Kells, Lucy L., Georgia. Student, George Washington U., 1946. Engaged in real estate bus., 1944-51, radio broadcasting, 1951—; pres., CEO, part owner Sta. WGUN, Atlanta, 1951—, Stas. KWAM and KJMS, Memphis, Sta. WEAS-AM-FM, Savannah, Ga., Stas. WGOV and WAAC, Valdosta, Ga., Sta. WSWN and Sta. WBGF, Belle Glade, Fla.; owner, chairperson, pres., CEO Sta. WCTH, Islamorado, Fla.; pres., CEO The Gram Corp., real estate com. Creative Christian Concepts Corp., 1985, pres., CEO Ocala, 1986; owner Suncoast Broadcasting Inc. Author: A Woman Alone, 1986; contbr. articles to profl. jours. Mem. Fla. Assn. Broadcasters (bd. dirs.), Ga. Assn. Broadcasters (bd. dirs., William J. Brooks award for exceptional svc. to radio broadcasting 1995), Coral Reef Yacht Club (Coconut Grove, Fla.), Palm Beach Polo and Country Club, Kappa Delta. Roman Catholic. Avocations: travel, music, writing, competitive ballroom dancing. Office: 11924 Forest Hill Blvd Ste 1 West Palm Beach FL 33414-6257 *It is my hope in life that no one will ever be worse off for having known me.*

RIVERS, WILGA MARIE, foreign language educator; b. Melbourne, Australia, Apr. 13, 1919; came to U.S., 1970; d. Harry and Nina Diamond (Burston) R. Diploma in edn, U. Melbourne, 1940, BA with honours, 1939, MA, 1948; License es L., U. Montpellier, France, 1952; PhD, U. Ill., 1962; MA (hon.), Harvard U., 1974; D Langs. (hon.), Middlebury Coll., 1989. High sch. tchr. Victoria, Australia, 1940-48; asst. in English lang. France, 1949-52; tchr. prep. schs., 1953-58; asst. prof. French No. Ill. U., DeKalb, 1963-64; assoc. prof. Monash U., Australia, 1964-69; vis. prof. Columbia U., 1970-71; prof. French U. Ill., Urbana-Champaign, 1971-74; prof. Romance langs. and lit., coord. lang. instrn. Harvard U., 1974-89, prof. emerita, 1989—; cons. NEH, Ford Found., Rockefeller Found., others; lectr 41 countries and throughout U.S.; adv. coun. Modern Lang. Ctr., Ont. Inst. for Studies in Edn., Nat. Fgn. Lang. Ctr., Lang. Acquire Rsch. Ctr., San Diego. Author: The Psychologist and the Foreign-Language Teacher, 1964, Teaching Foreign-Language Skills, 1968, 2d edit., 1981, A Practical Guide to the Teaching of French, 1975, 2d edit., 1988; co-author: A Practical Guide to the Teaching of German, 1975, 2d edit., 1988, A Practical Guide to the Teaching of Spanish, 1976, 2d edit., 1988, A Practical Guide to the Teaching of English as a Second or Foreign Language, 1978, Speaking in Many Tongues, 1972, 3d edit., 1983, Communicating Naturally in a Second Language, 1983, Teaching Hebrew: A Practical Guide, 1989, Opportunities for Careers in Foreign Languages, 1993, others; editor, contbr. Interactive Language Teaching, 1978, Teaching Languages in College: Curriculum and Content, 1992; writing translated into 10 langs.; edtl. bd. Studies in Second Language Acquisition, Applied Linguistics, Language Learning, Mosaic, System; adv. com. Can. Modern Lang. Rev.; contbr. articles to profl. jours. Recipient Nat. Disting. Fgn. Lang. Leadership award N.Y. State Assn. Fgn. Lang. Tchrs., 1974. Decorated Chevalier des Palmes Académiques, 1995. Mem. MLA, Am. Assn. Applied Linguistics (charter pres.), Am. Coun. on Teaching Fgn. Langs. (Florence Steiner award 1977, Anthony Papalia award 1988), Mass. Fgn. Lang. Assn. (Disting. Svc. award 1983), Tchrs. of English to Speakers of other Langs., Am. Assn. Tchrs. French, Linguistic Soc. Am., Am. Assn. Univ. Suprs. and Coords. Fgn. Lang. Programs Northeast Conf. (Nelson Brooks award 1983), Internat. Assn. Applied Psycholinguistics (v.p. 1983-89), Japan Assn. Coll. English Tchrs. (hon.), Am. Assn. Tchrs. German (hon.), Internat. Assn. Lang. Labs. (hon.). Episcopalian. Home and Office: 84 Garfield St Watertown MA 02172-4916

RIVES, STANLEY GENE, university president emeritus; b. Decatur, Ill., Sept. 27, 1930; s. James A. and Frances (Bunker) R.; m. Sandra Lou Belt, Dec. 28, 1957; children: Jacqueline Ann, Joseph Alan. B.S., Ill. State U., 1952, M.S., 1955; Ph.D., Northwestern U., 1963. Instr. W. Va. U., 1955-56, Northwestern U., 1956-58; prof. Ill. State U., Normal, 1958-80, Am. Council on Edn. Fellows Program, 1969-70, assoc. dean faculties, 1970-72, dean undergrad. instrn., 1972-80, assoc. provost, 1976-80, acting provost, 1979-80; provost, v.p. acad. affairs, prof. Eastern Ill. U., Charleston, 1981-83, pres., 1983-92, pres. emeritus, 1992—; vis. prof. U. Hawaii, 1963-64. Author: (with Donald Klopf) Individual Speaking Contests: Preparation for Participation, 1967, (with Gene Budig) Academic Quicksand. Trends and Issues in Higher Education, 1973, (with others) Academic Innovation: Faculty and Instructional Development at Illinois State University, 1979, The Fundamentals of Oral Interpretation, 1981; contbr. articles to profl. jours. Bd. dirs. Ill. State Univs. Retirement System, 1992—, treas., 1995—, Ea. Ill. Univ. Found., 1993—, also pres., 1996—, East Ctrl. Ill. Devel. Corp., 1983-92, Charleston Area Econ. Devel. Found., 1986-92, Coles Together, 1988-92; mem. pres. commn. NCAA, 1986-91; trustee Nat. Debate Tournament, 1967-75. With U.S. Army, 1952-54. Mem. Am. Assn. State Colls. and Univs., Ill. State C. of C. (bd. dirs. 1990-92), Charleston C. of C. (bd. dirs. 1985-88), Rotary, Theta Alpha Phi, Phi Kappa Delta, Pu Gamma Mu. Home: 2231 Andover Pl Charleston IL 61920-3807

RIVEST, ANNE-MARIE THERESE, post-anesthesia nurse; b. Springfield, Mass., Dec. 25, 1959; d. Robert Frances and Marguerite Marie (Dupuis) R. BSN, Fitchburg State Coll., 1982. Cert. post anesthesia nurse; cert. in pediat. advanced life support. Staff nurse med./surg. fl. Baystate Med. Ctr., Springfield, Mass., 1982-86, staff nurse post anesthesia care unit, 1986—; annual conf. program dir. post anesthesia care unit Baystate Med. Ctr., Springfield, 1989-93, co-unit educator, 1992—; rep., sec. Intensive Peer Rev. Bd., 1992-95. Solicitor local United Way, Baystate Med. Ctr., 1986—; mem. Nat. Wildlife Fedn., Washington, 1994—, Nat. Arbor Day Found., Nebraska City, 1994—. Mem. Am. Soc. Post Anesthesia Nurses, Mass. Soc. Post Anesthesia Nurses. Roman Catholic. Avocations: camping, baking, crafts. Home: 166 Line St Easthampton MA 01027-2620 Office: Baystate Med Ctr 759 Chestnut St Springfield MA 01199-1001

RIVET, DIANA WITTMER, lawyer, developer; b. Auburn, N.Y., Apr. 28, 1931; d. George Wittmer and Anne (Jenkins) Wittmer Hauswirth; m. Paul Henry Rivet, Oct. 24, 1952; children: Gail, Robin, Leslie, Heather, Clayton, Eric. BA, Keuka Coll., 1951; JD, Bklyn. Law Sch., 1956. Bar: N.Y. 1956, U.S. Dist. Ct. (ea. and so. dists.) N.Y. 1975. Sole practice, Orangeburg, N.Y., 1957—; county atty. Rockland County (N.Y.), 1974-77; asst. to legis. chmn. Rockland County, 1978-79; counsel, adminstr. Indsl. Devel. Agy., Rockland County, 1980-91, Rockland Econ. Devel. Corp., 1981-90; counsel, exec. dir. Pvt. Industry Coun. Rockland County, 1980-90; pres., CEO Environ. Mgmt. Ltd., Orangeburg, 1980—; mem. air mgmt. adv. com. N.Y. State Dept. Environ. Conservation 1984-92, Orangetown Planning Bd., 1993—; pres. Indoor Enviroment Ltd. Pres. Rockland County coun. Girl Scouts U.S., 1981-84; chmn. Rockland County United Way, 1996-97, mem. campaign com., 1983-84, 88-89, 93, sec., 97—, bd. dirs. 1988-94, 95—; bd. dirs. Rockland Bus. Assn., West Nyack, 1981—, Leadership Rockland, 1991-94. Recipient Cmty. Svc. award Keuka Coll., 1965, Disting. Svc. award Town of Orangetown, 1970, Disting. Svc. award Rockland County, 1989, Econ. Devel. award Rockland Econ. Devel. Corp., 1990; named Businessperson of Yr., Jour. News, Rockland County, 1982. Mem. ABA, N.Y. State Bar Assn. (mcpl. law sect. exec. com. 1976-83, environ. law sect. exec. com. 1974-86), Rockland County Bar Assn. (chair environ. law com. 1994-96). Democrat. Mem. Religious Soc. of Friends. Home: 1 Lester Dr Orangeburg NY 10962-2316

RIVETTE, GERARD BERTRAM, manufacturing company executive; b. Syracuse, N.Y., May 18, 1932; s. George Francis and Helen (McCarthy) R.; m. Patricia Anne Yates, June 20, 1953; children: Kevin Gerard, Brian Yates. A.B., Syracuse U., 1954; postgrad., U. Buffalo, 1957-59, Rutgers U., 1962-65. Owner-mgr. Rivette Sales and Svc., Syracuse, 1950-54; sales rep. Sperry-Rand, Inc., Elmira, N.Y., 1954-55; with Hewitt-Robins Inc., Buffalo, 1955-62; mgr. conveyor equipment sales Hewitt-Robins Inc., Passaic, N.J., 1962-65; pres. Hewitt-Robins (Can.) Ltd., Montreal, 1965-69, also dir.; Can. regional mgr. Hewitt-Robins Inc., 1965-69; pres. Conergics Corp., Kansas City, Kans., 1970-86, Mid-West Conveyer Co., 1970-86, Alpine Metals Co., Salt Lake City, Con Cal Corp., Orange, Calif.; chmn. bd. Versa Corp., Mt. Sterling, Ohio, 1972-86, Baker Erection Co., Kansas City, Mo., 1971-86, Arrowhead Conveyer Corp., Oshkosh, Wis., 1979-86, Conveyer Sales and Mfg., Seattle, 1983-86; chmn. bd., pres. Conveyer Corp. Am., Ft. Worth, 1978-86, Mayfran Internat. Inc., Cleve., 1984-86, Mayfran Limburg B.V., The Netherlands, 1984-86, Guardian Devel. Corp., Palo Alto, Calif., 1982—; chmn. bd. Jeffrey Chain Co., Morristown, Tenn., 1985-96, Whitney Chain Corp., Morristown, 1985—; chmn. bd., pres. Guardian Resources Ltd., Redwood City, 1966-91, Jeffrey Chain Can. Inc., Toronto, 1987-96; chmn. bd. Intelligent Software Internat. Inc., Redwood City, 1985-96, Tsubakimoto Mayfran, Osaka, Japan, 1984-86, Greaves Midwest Engring. Ltd., Bangalore, India, 1977-86; bd. dirs. Jeffrey Chain Can., Toronto. Trustee U. Kansas City, 1983-95, Midwest Rsch., Inst., 1983-93; bd. dirs. Monterey Inst. Internat. Studies, 1989—. Mem. AIME. Office: PO Box 205 Pebble Beach CA 93953-0205

RIVKIND, PERRY ABBOT, federal railroad agency administrator; b. Boston, Jan. 22, 1930; s. Samuel Alexander and Mae Edna (Polisnor) R.; m. Dolores Russo; children: Robert Douglas, Valerie Jean; m. Kathleen Marie Lysher, Aug. 14, 1989. AA, Miami (Fla.) Community Coll., 1963; BA, Fla. State U., 1965; MA, Fla. Atlantic U., 1966; postgrad., Nat. War Coll., Washington, 1981. Comml. charter pilot, 1956-58; police officer Met. Police Dept., Miami, 1958-61; chief investigator Dade County State Atty. Office, Miami, 1961-67; prof., dir. dept. Cen. Piedmont Coll., Charlotte, N.C., 1967-68; asst. dir. Fed. Bur. Narcotics, Washington, 1968-74; asst. adminstr. Law Enforcement Assistance Adminstrn., Washington, 1974-81; assoc. commr. U.S. Immigration and Naturalization Svc., Washington, 1981-84; dist. dir. U.S. Immigration and Naturalization Svc., Miami, 1984-88; safety mgr. Miami Herald Pub. Co., 1988-89; dep. adminstr. Fed. R.R. Adminstrn., Washington, 1989—; chmn. com. on tng. Pres.'s Coun. on Drug Abuse, Washington, 1971-74, chmn. com. on rsch. Working Group on Terrorism Nat. Security Coun., Washington, 1978-81. With U.S. Army, 1951-53. Perry A. Rivkind Day established in his honor City of Miami/Dade County/City of Miami Beach, 1985-89. Republican. Avocations: boating, hunting, fishing, motorcycling, camping.

RIVLIN, ALICE MITCHELL, federal agency administrator, economist; b. Phila., Mar. 4, 1931; d. Allan C. G. and Georgianna (Fales) Mitchell; m. Lewis Allen Rivlin, 1955 (div. 1977); children: Catherine Amy, Allan Mitchell, Douglas Gray; m. Sidney Graham Winter, 1989. B.A., Bryn Mawr Coll., 1952; Ph.D., Radcliffe Coll., 1958. Mem. staff Brookings Instn., Washington, 1957-66, 69-75, 83-93; dir. econ. studies Brookings Inst., 1983-87; dir. Congl. Budget Office, 1975-83; prof. pub. policy George Mason U., 1992; dep. dir. U.S. Office Mgmt. and Budget, 1993-94, dir., 1994-96; vice chmn. Fed. Res. Sys., Washington, 1996—; dep. asst. sec. program coordination HEW, Washington, 1966-68, asst. sec. planning and evaluation, 1968-69; mem. Staff Adv. Commn. on Intergovtl. Rels., 1961-62. Author: The Role of the Federal Governemnt in Financing Higher Education, 1961, (with others) Microanalysis of Socioeconomic Systems, 1961, Systematic Thinking for Social Action, 1971, (with others) Economic Choices 1987, 1986, (with others The Swedish Economy, 1987, (with others) Caring for the Disabled Elderly: Who Will Pay?, 1988, Reviving the American Dream, 1992. MacArthur fellow, 1983-88. Mem. Am. Econ. Assn. (nat. pres. 1986). Office: Fed Res Sys Office of Chmn 20th and C Sts NW Washington DC 20551*

RIVLIN, BENJAMIN, political science educator; b. Bklyn., July 10, 1921; s. Moses and Esther (Ribnick) R.; m. Leanne Green, July 9, 1957; 1 child, Marc Alexander. BA, Bklyn. Coll., 1942; MA, Harvard U., 1947, PhD, 1949. With OSS, 1943-45; teaching fellow Harvard U., 1948; mem. trusteeship dept. UN Secretariat, 1948, 50, 52; research assoc. Hoover Commn., 1948; mem. faculty Bklyn. Coll. of CUNY, 1949-75, prof. polit. sci., 1962-70, chmn. dept., 1966-70; mem. Grad. Sch. faculty CUNY, 1970-85, exec. officer Ph.D. program, 1970-75, dean research and univ. programs Grad. Sch. and Univ. Center, 1975-78, dir. Ralph Bunche Inst. on UN; vis. lectr. Johns Hopkins Sch. Advanced Internat. Studies, 1956; vis. prof. African and Middle East Insts., Columbia U., 1963-68. Author: The United Nations and The Italian Colonies, 1950, Self-Determination and Dependent Areas, 1955, (with J.S. Szyliowicz) The Contemporary Middle East: Tradition and Innovation, 1965, Ralph Bunche: The Man and His Times, 1990, (with Leon Gordenker) The Challenging Role of the UN Secretary-General, 1993; also articles. Served with AUS, 1942-45. Grantee Social Sci. Research Council, 1951, 54, 64; Fulbright scholar France and N. Africa, 1956-57. Fellow African Studies Assn., Middle East Studies Assn.; mem. Internat. Studies Assn. (pres. Middle Atlantic region 1978-80), Am. Polit. Sci. Assn., Acad. Coun. on UN System (vice chair 1990-91, dir. N.Y. liaison office). Office: CUNY 33 W 42nd St New York NY 10036-8003

RIVLIN, RACHEL, lawyer; b. Bangor, Maine, Sept. 1, 1945; d. Lawrence and A. Sara (Rich) Lait. BA, U. Maine, 1965; MA, U. Louisville, 1968; JD, Boston Coll., 1977. Bar: Mass. 1977, U.S. Dist. Ct. Mass. 1978, U.S. Ct. Appeals (1st cir.) 1983, U.S. Supreme Ct. 1985. Audiologist Boston City Hosp., 1969-72; dir. audiology Beth Israel Hosp., Boston, 1972-74; atty. Legal Systems Devel., Boston, 1977-78, Liberty Mutual Ins., Boston, 1978-82; counsel, sec. Lexington Ins. Co., Boston, 1982-85, v.p., assoc. gen. counsel, sec., 1985—. Mem. Civil Rights Com. Anti-Defamation League, Boston, 1982—; bd. dirs. DanceArt, Inc., Boston, 1985-92. Mem. ABA (com. on pub. regulation of ins. 1980—, vice chmn. 1980-81, vice chmn. pub. rels 1981-84, chmn. elect 1984-85, chmn. 1985-86, sr. vice chmn. 1989-90; excess surplus lines and reins. com. 1983—, vice chmn. 1986-87, chair-elect 1987-88, chmn. 1988-89; internat. ins. law com. 1983—; 1988 ann. meeting arrangements chmn. for TIPS; nat. inst. insurer involvency 1986, 89, nat. inst. reins. collections and involvency 1988), Boston Bar Assn. (council 1983-86; chmn. corp. counsel com., 1987, chmn. membership com. 1978-83, subcom. on ABA model rules of profl. conduct 1980-81; chmn. ins. law com. 1987-90; chmn. profl. liability ins. com. 1990—; steering com. corp. bus. law and fin. sect. 1987-89; edn. com. 1987-89, 90-91; nominating com. 1988; dinner dance com. 1989, 94; ethics com. 1993—), Boston Coll. Law Sch. Alumni Assn. (ann. fund com. 1981-89, council 1983-87; chmn. telethon com. 1989-94; leadership gifts exec. com. 1994—; search com. for dean 1993; search com. for law sch. fund dir. 1993; nominating com. 1990; search com. for dir. of instl. advancement, 1995, Father James Malley award 1996). Home: 122 Lincoln St Newton MA 02161-1528 Office: Lexington Ins Co 200 State St Boston MA 02109-2605

RIVLIN, RICHARD SAUL, physician, educator; b. Forest Hills, N.Y., May 15, 1934; s. Harry Nathaniel and Eugenie (Graciany) R.; m. Barbara Melinda Pogul, Aug. 28, 1960 (div.); children: Kenneth Stewart, Claire Phyllis; m. Rita Klausner, Feb. 29, 1976; children: Michelle Elizabeth, Daniel Elliott. A.B. cum laude in Biochem. Scis., Harvard U., 1955; M.D. cum laude in Biochem. Scis., 1959. Diplomate Am. Bd. Internat Medicine. Intern Bellevue Hosp., N.Y.C., 1959-60; asst. resident in medicine Johns Hopkins U. Hosp., Balt., 1960-61; asst. resident Johns Hopkins U. Hosp., 1963-64; clin. assoc. endocrinology br. Nat. Cancer Inst., NIH, Bethesda, Md., 1961-63; fellow dept. physiol. chemistry, medicine Johns Hopkins U. Sch. Medicine, Balt., 1964-66; lectr. clin. medicine Johns Hopkins U. Sch. Medicine, 1965-66; attending physician med. service Balt. City Hosps., 1964-66; assoc. in medicine Columbia U. Coll. Physicians and Surgeons, N.Y.C., 1966-67; asst. prof. medicine Columbia U. Coll. Physicians and Surgeons, 1967-71, assoc. prof. medicine, 1971-79; mem. Inst. Human Nutrition, 1972-79; chief endocrinology, asst. physician Francis Delafield Hosp., N.Y.C., 1966-75; asst. physician Presbyterian Hosp., N.Y.C., 1966-73; assoc. attending physician Presbyterian Hosp., 1973-79; chief nutrition service Meml. Sloan-Kettering Cancer Ctr., N.Y.C., 1979-90; prof. medicine Cornell U. Med. Coll., 1979—; chief div. nutrition dept. medicine N.Y. Hosp. -Cornell Med. Center, 1979—; NSF grant reviewer, 1970—; vis. prof. Creighton U., 1974, U. Guadalajara (Mexico), 1974; vis. prof. N.J. Coll. Medicine and East Orange VA Hosp., Newark Med. Sch., N.J., 1974, 1976, 1983; Upjohn vis. prof. in nutrition Med. Coll. Ga., 1976; vis. prof. Syracuse U., 1980; Nat. Dairy Council vis. prof. in nutrition U. Mich., Ann Arbor, 1982; vis. prof. Washington U.-Jewish Hosp., St. Louis, 1983; external examiner in physiology Calcutta U., India; vis. physician Rockefeller U., N.Y.C., 1979—; prin. investigator clin. nutrition rsch. unit Meml. Sloan-Kettering Cancer Ctr., N.Y.C., 1980—; rsch. program oversight com. Am. Inst. Cancer Rsch., 1995—; Sypen Stricker lectr. Med. Coll. Ga., 1989. Editor: Riboflavin, 1975; referee numerous profl. jours.; contbr. articles to profl. jours. Served with USPHS, 1961-63. Recipient Grace A. Goldsmith Lectre award Am. Coll. Nutrition, 1981. Fellow ACP; mem. Am. Soc. Clin. Nutrition (v.p. 1992-93, pres. 1993-94), Am. Fedn. Clin. Rsch., Endocrine Soc., AAAS, Harvey Soc., Am. Thyroid Assn., Am. Physiol. Soc., Am. Soc. Clin. Investigation, Am. Inst. Nutrition, Soc. Exptl. Biology & Medicine. Home: 30 Farragut Rd Scarsdale NY 10583-7206

RIVLIN, RONALD SAMUEL, mathematics educator emeritus; b. London, May 6, 1915; came to U.S., 1952, naturalized, 1955; s. Raoul and Bertha (Aronsohn) R.; m. Violet Larusso, June 16, 1948; 1 son, John Michael. BA, St. John's Coll., Cambridge U., 1937, MA, 1939, ScD, 1952; D.Sc. h.c., Nat. U. Ireland, 1980, Nottingham U., 1980, Tulane U., 1982; Dr. h.c., Sch. Tech. U. Thessaloniki, 1984. Rsch. physicist GE, Eng., 1937-42; sci. officer Telecom. Rsch. Establishment, Ministry Aircraft Prodn., Eng., 1942-44; rsch. physicist, head phys. rsch., supt. rsch. Brit. Rubber Prodrs. Rsch. Assn., 1944-52; head rsch. group Davy-Faraday Lab., Royal Instn., London, 1948-52; cons. Naval Rsch. Lab., Washington, 1952-53; prof. applied math. Brown U., 1953-63, L. Herbert Ballou U. prof., 1963-67, prof. applied math. and engring sci., 1963-67, chmn. divsn. applied math., 1958-63; professeur associé U. Paris, 1966-67; Centennial Univ. prof., dir. Ctr. for Application of Math. Lehigh U., Bethlehem, Pa., 1967-80; prof. emeritus Lehigh U., Bethlehem, 1980—, adj. Univ. prof., 1980-88; co-chmn. Internat. Congress Rheology, 1963; Russell Severance Springer vis. prof. U. Calif.-Berkeley, 1977; fellow Inst. Advanced Study, Berlin, 1984-85; Disting. vis. prof. U. Del., 1985-86. Contbr. articles profl. jours.; mem. editorial com. Jour. Rational Mechanics and Analysis, 1952-57, Archive for Rational Mechanics and Analysis, 1957-72, Jour. Math. Physics, 1960, Jour. Applied Physics, 1960-63, Acta Rheologica, 1963—, Internat. Jour. Biorheology, 1972-74, Mechanics Research Communications, 1974—, Jour. Non-Newtonian Fluid Mechanics, 1975—, Meccanica, 1975-94, Internat. Jour. Solids and Structures, 1990-95, Zietschrift für Angewandte Mathematik und Mechanik, 1992—. Recipient Panetti prize, 1975, von Humboldt Sr. award, 1981, Charles Goodyear medal Am. Chem. Soc., 1992, von Karman medal ASCE, 1993; Guggenheim fellow, 1961-62. Fellow ASME (mem. exec. com. applied mechanics divsn. 1975-80, vice-chmn. and sec. 1978-79, chmn. 1979-80, Timoshenko Medal 1987), Acad. Mechanics, Am. Phys. Soc.; mem. NAE, Soc. Natural Philosophy (chmn. 1963-64), Am. Acad. Arts and Scis., Inst. Physics (gov. 1974-76), Soc. Rheology (exec. com. 1957-59, 71-77, Bingham medal 1958, v.p. 1971-73, pres. 1973-75, nat. com. theoretical and applied mechanics 1973-82, chmn. 1976-78, vice chmn. 1978-80), Internat. Union Theoretical and Applied Mechanics (gen. assembly 1975-82, chmn. U.S. del. 1978), Coun. Sci. Pres. (sec.-treas. 1975, exec. bd. 1975-77), Mex. Soc. Rheology (hon.), Accademia Nazionale dei Lincei (fgn.), Royal Irish Acad. (hon.). Home: 1604 Merryweather Dr Bethlehem PA 18015-5249

RIVNER, MICHAEL HARVEY, neurologist; b. Bklyn., Sept. 26, 1950; s. Norman and Carol (Simson) R.; m. Roberta Fran Gottlieb, Aug. 13, 1978; children: Asher, Joshua, Peter, Harold. BA, Duke U., 1972; MD, Emory U., 1978. Diplomate Am. Bd. Psychiatry and Neurology, added qualifications in clin. neurophysiology; diplomate Am. Bd. Electrodiagnostic Medicine. Intern, resident in neurology Med. Coll. Ga., Augusta, 1978-82; from fellow to assoc. prof. neurology Med. Coll. Ga., 1982—; cons. neurology Eisenhower Med. Hosp., Ft. Gordon, Ga., 1982—, VA Med. Ctr., Augusta, 1982—. V.p., campaign chmn. Augusta Jewish Found., 1994, pres., 1995-97; treas. CSRA Swim League, Augusta, 1993—; treas. Augusta Jewish C.C. Fellow Am. Acad. Neurology; mem. Am. Assn. Electrodiagnostic Medicine (equipment com. 1984-87, tng. program com. 1989-92, edn. com. 1992—, chmn. edn. com. 1994—), Southeastern Neuromuscular Group (pres. 1996—). Avocations: computer programming, bicycling. Office: Med Coll Ga EMG Lab Augusta GA 30912

RIZER, FRANKLIN MORRIS, physician, otolaryngologist; b. Gallipolis, Ohio, Aug. 13, 1953; s. Franklin Morris and Wanda Mae (Potts) R.; m. Maria Nicolette Guglielmi, Feb. 8, 1986. BS cum laude, Ohio State U., 1975; MD, U. Cin., 1979; M in Med. Mgmt., Tulane U., 1997; MBA, YSU, 1997. Diplomate Am. Bd. Otolaryngology. Intern U. Calif., Davis, 1979-80; resident U. Wash., Seattle, 1980-81, Ea. Va. U. Coll. of Medicine, Norfolk, 1981-84; fellow House Ear Inst., 1984-87; chief otology St. Joseph's Riverside Hosp., Warren, Ohio, 1989—; assoc. prof. Ea. Va. Coll. of Medicine, Norfolk, 1987—, Northeastern Ohio U. Coll. of Medicine, Rootstown, 1987—, Ohio State U., Columbus, 1995—; fellowship dir. Warren Otologic Group, Warren, 1991—. Contbr. articles to profl. jours. Trustee Makoning Valley Macintosh Users Group, Warren, 1989-92; active Leadership Warren, 1989; bd. dirs. Humility of Mary Integrated Delivery Network, 1995—. With USAF, 1971-73. Fellow Am. Acad. Otolaryngology; mem. Am. Acad. Facial Plastics, Am. Coll. Physician Execs., Soc. of Wilderness Medicine, Undersea and Hyperbaric Med. Soc. United Methodist. Avocations: scuba diving, bicycling, camping, gardening. Home: 469 Country Club Dr NE Warren OH 44484-4616 Office: Warren Otologic Group 3893 E Market St Warren OH 44484-4706

RIZIO, RONALD R., writer, information specialist; b. Paterson, N.J., May 26, 1958; s. Ronald Francis and Lorraine Francis (Morosco) R.; m. Karen Schuster, Apr. 30, 1988; children: Douglas, Elaine. BA in Polit. Sci. & History, Ramapo Coll., 1980; MS in Info. Sci., Columbia U., 1990. Asst. editor Ridgewood (N.J.) Fin. Inst., 1980-82; reporter Ridgewood News, 1980; news libr. Bergen Record, Hackensack, N.J., 1983-87; dir. Med. Libr., Sch. Nursing Libr. Holy Name Hosp., Teaneck, N.J., 1989—; pres. Bergen-Passaic Health Scis. Librs., 1992. Contbr. news articles to Ridgewood News, Bergen Record; editor (newsletter) Med. Dialogue, 1990-93. Chmn. N.J. Internat. Rels. Com., 1995-96. Mem. Spl. Libr. Assn., Med. Libr. Assn. (publs. com. 1994—), N.J. Libr. Network, Health Librs. Assn. N.J. (info. tech. com., edn. com.). Office: Holy Name Hosp 718 Teaneck Rd Teaneck NJ 07666-4245

RIZZI, DEBORAH L., public relations professional; b. Jersey City, N.J., Feb. 26, 1955; d. Edwin Joseph and Beulah Marie (Ardoin) R. BA, Rutgers U., 1977. Program dir. Am. Cancer Soc., Jersey City, 1977-79; internat. program asst. Stevens Inst. Tech., Hoboken, N.J., 1980; dir. pub. rels. United Hosps. Med. Ctr., Newark, 1981-90; dir. practice devel. Stryker Tams & Dill, Newark, 1990-92; comm. mgr. United Water, Harrington Park, N.J., 1992—; adv. bd. Nat. Boxing Safety Ctr., Newark, 1984-88; sr. producer Children's Miracle Network Telethon, N.J., 1985-90. Contbg. author: (book) Children With HIV Source Book, 1990, (booklet) Guide for Victims of Sexual Assualt, 1985, Child With AIDS . . . Guide for the Family, 1986; co-producer: (video) Diagnosing Sexual Assault in Children, 1990. Recipient

Mercury award Internat. Acad. Comm. Arts and Scis., 1993, 94, 95, Galaxy award, 1993, 94, 95, ARC award, 1994, 95, Jaspar award Jersey Shore Pub. Rels. and Advt. Assn., 1994, 95. Mem. Internat. Assn. Bus. Communicators (Ace award N.Y. chpt. 1993, 94, 95, EPIC award Phila. chpt. 1994, Silver Quill award U.S. Dist. I 1994, 95, Iris award N.J. chpt. 1994, 95), Am. Hosp. Assn. (Nat. Touch Stone award 1987), Pub. Rels. Soc. Am., Nat. Assn. Law Firm Marketers, N.J. Hosp. Assn. (Percy award 1986, 88, 90), Literacy Vols. of N.J. (bd. dirs. 1997—). Avocation: bicycling. Office: United Water 200 Old Hook Rd Harrington Park NJ 07640

RIZZI, TERESA MARIE, bilingual speech and language pathologist; b. Denver, Aug. 8, 1964; d. Theophilus Marcus and Maudie Marie (Pitts) R. BA in Speech Pathology, U. Denver, 1986, BA in Spanish, 1986; MS in Speech Pathology, Vanderbilt U., 1988. Pediatric speech-lang. pathologist Rose Med. Ctr., Denver, 1988-90; pvt. practice Denver, 1990—; Spanish tchr. Temple Emanual, Denver, 1992-95; owner, operator Niños De Colo., Denver, Talk of The Town Speech-Lang. Pathologists; Spanish tutor and interpreter, Denver, 1988—; bilingual pediatric speech-lang. pathologist The Children's Hosp., Denver, 1994—; presenter in field. G'arin grantee Ctrl. Agy. Jewish Edn., 1993, grantee U. No. Colo. Grad. Sch., 1994. Mem. Am. Speech-Lang.-Hearing Assn. (Continuing Edn. award 1991), Colo. Speech-Lang.-Hearing Assn., Internat. Assn. Orofacial Myology, Phi Sigma Iota. Avocations: computers, chess. Office: Talk of the Town Speech-Lang Pathologists 695 S Colorado Blvd Ste 410 Denver CO 80246-8014

RIZZO, FRANCIS, arts administrator, writer, stage director; b. N.Y.C., Nov. 8, 1936; s. Patrick Charles and Mary Katherine (McTigue) R. AB, Hamilton Coll., 1958; student, Yale Sch. Drama, 1958-60. Gen. dir. (U.S.) Festival of Two Worlds, Spoleto, Italy, 1968-71; artistic adminstr. Wolf Trap Farm Park for the Performing Arts, Vienna, Va., 1972-78, artistic cons., 1985-94; artistic dir. The Washington Opera, 1977-87; free-lance stage dir. various U.S. cos. including N.Y.C. Opera, Houston Grand Opera, Santa Fe Opera, Opera Theater of St. Louis, others; cons. NEA, Washington, 1974—. Contbr. articles to Opera News, 1968—; translator supertitles, various U.S. opera cos., 1984—. Mem. Am. Guild Mus. Artists. Home: 590 W End Ave New York NY 10024-1722

RIZZO, JOANNE T., family nurse practitioner; b. Boston, Feb. 20, 1950; d. Anthony M. and Barbara A. Rizzo. BS, Northeastern U., 1972; MS, U. Colo., Denver, 1976. ACLS; cert. family nurse practitioner. RN pediatrics Mass. Gen. Hosp., Boston, 1972-75; family nurse practitioner Frontier Nursing Svc., Hyden, Ky., 1976-78; nurse practitioner migrant health program U. Colo., Alamosa, 1978-79; family nurse practitioner, clinic mgr. Plan de Salud del Valle, Ft. Lupton, Colo., 1979-82; family nurse practitioner Family Health Svc., Worcester, Mass., 1982-89; fgn. svc. nurse practitioner State Dept., Washington, 1989—; fgn. svc. nurse practitioner Am. Embassy, Bucharest, Romania, 1989-91, Lima, Peru, 1991-96; fgn. svc. Am. Embassy, Kathmandu, Nepal, 1996—; nurse practitioner preceptor Robert Wood Johnson plan de salud del valle, Platteville, Colo., 1980-81, U. Lowell, Worcester, 1984-88, U. Wash., 1995. Recipient Cert. of Appreciation, Agy. Internat. Devel., Romania, 1990, Meritorious Honor award & Group Valor award, Romania, 1990, Dept. of State Health Practitioner of Yr. award, 1995. Mem. Sigma Theta Tau. Avocations: reading, scuba diving, traveling, photography. Address: Dept State/Kathmandu Washington DC 20521-6190

RIZZO, RAYMOND S., advertising executive. Pres., CEO Clarion Mktg. and Comm., Inc., Greenwich, Conn. Office: Clarion Mktg & Comm Inc Greenwich Office Park S Greenwich CT 06831-5159

RIZZO, RONALD STEPHEN, lawyer; b. Kenosha, Wis., July 15, 1941; s. Frank Emmanuel and Rosalie (Lo Cicero); children: Ronald Stephen Jr., Michael Robert. BA, St. Norbert Coll., 1963; JD, Georgetown U., 1965, LLM in Taxation, 1966. Bar: Wis. 1965, Calif. 1967. Assoc. Kindel & Anderson, L.A., 1966-71, ptnr., 1971-86; ptnr. Jones, Day, Reavis & Pogue, L.A., 1986-93, Chgo., 1993—; bd. dirs. Guy LoCicero & Son Inc., Kenosha, Wis. Contbg. editor: ERISA Litigation Reporter. Schulte zur Hausen fellow Inst. Internat. and Fgn. Trade Law, Washington, 1966. Fellow Am. Coll. Tax Counsel; mem. ABA (chmn. com. on employee benefits sect. on taxation 1988-89, vice chair com. on govt. submissions 1995—), Los Angeles County Bar Assn. (chmn. com. on employee benefits sect. on taxation 1977-79, exec. com. 1977-78, 90-92), State Bar Calif. (co-chmn. com. on employee benefits sect. on taxation 1980), Nat. Ctr. Employee Ownership, West Pension Conf. (steering com. L.A. chpt. 1980-83). Avocations: reading, golf, travel. Home: 1040 N Lake Shore Dr Apt 19C Chicago IL 60611-1107 Office: Jones Day Reavis & Pogue 77 W Wacker Dr Chicago IL 60601

RIZZO, THOMAS DIGNAN, orthopedic surgeon; b. N.Y.C., May 25, 1931; s. Peter-Cyrus and Rose Ann (Dignan) R.; m. Jean Foley; children: Thomas D. Jr., Peter F., James G., Kathryn Anne Marie, William J., Francis V. BS cum laude, Georgetown U., 1958, MD cum laude, 1956. Diplomate Am. Bd. Orthopedic Surgery, Nat. Bd. Med. Examiners. Intern Georgetown U. Med. Ctr., Washington, 1956-57; asst. resident surgeon St. Vincent's Hosp., N.Y.C., 1957-58; resident in orthopedic surgery Hosp. for Spl. Surgery, N.Y.C., 1958-59, fellow in orthopedic surgery, 1961-62; resident fellow in orthopedic surgery Newington Hosp. for Crippled Children, Conn., 1962; pvt. practice Bronxville, N.Y., 1962—; clin. cons. orthopedic surgery N.Y. State Dept. Health, 1965; assoc. dir. orthopedics Lawrence Hosp., Bronxville, 1970-79, attending staff, 1963—; asst. attending St. John's Riverside Hosp., Yonkers, N.Y., 1963-74, sr. attending surgeon, 1974-87, dir. dept. orthopedic surgery, 1975-86, courtesy staff, 1987-96; assoc. attending Dobbs Ferry Hosp., 1970-73, cons. staff, 1973—; asst. attending Hosp. for Spl. Surgery, N.Y.C., 1963, Doctors Hosp., 1973-80; asst. attending surgeon N.Y. Hosp., 1981-83. Mem. adv. bd. Bapt. Home for Aged; trustee Fordham Prep. Sch., 1987-93; mem. Westchester Health Planning Coun., 1983-96, sec., 1988-89; bd. dirs. Hudson Valley Health Sys. Agy., 1988-96. Fellow ACS, Am. Acad. Orthopedic Surgeons, Am. Acad. Legal and Indsl. Medicine, N.Y. Acad. of Medicine, Westchester Acad. Medicine (bd. trustees 1968—), Am. Orthopedic Foot and Ankle Soc.; mem. AMA, N.Y. State Med. Soc. (county del. 1975-87), Westchester County Med. Soc. (bd. dirs. 1968—, pres. 1975-76), Irish Am. Orthopedic Soc., N.Y. State Soc. Orthopedic Surgeons, Ea. Orthopedic Assn., Georgetown U. Alumni Assn. (bd. govs. 1970-73, chpt. v.p. 1970-72), KC, Knight of Malta, Knight of Holy Sepulchre, Lotos Club (N.Y.C.), Cottage Club (Sea Island, Ga.), Lawrence Beach Club (Atlantic Beach, N.Y.), Bronxville (N.Y.) Field Club, Alpha Omega Alpha. Home: 633 California Rd Bronxville NY 10708-2311 also: 349 Cook Ave Sea Island GA 31561 Office: 77 Pondfield Rd Bronxville NY 10708-3809 also: Hosp for Spl Surgery 535 E 70th St New York NY 10021-4892

RIZZO, WILLIAM OBER, lawyer; b. Boston, Aug. 19, 1948; s. Nicholas Daniel and Edith Katherine (Kepler) R.; m. Susan J. Parker, May 17, 1984; 1 child, Aura E.P. AB, Lawrence U., 1970; JD, Columbia U., 1973. Bar: Mass. 1974, U.S. Dist. Ct. (fed. dist.) Mass. 1975. Law clk. to Hon. Irving R. Kaufman U.S. Ct. Appeals (2nd cir.), N.Y., 1973; assoc. Ropes & Gray, Boston, 1974-81; ptnr. McDermott & Rizzo, Boston, 1981-90, Kirkpatrick & Lockhart, Boston, 1990-96, Cherwin, Glickman & Theise, LLP, Boston, 1996—. Bd. dirs. Lawrence U. Alumni Assn., 1980-86, Beacon Hill Civic Assn., 1977-91, chmn. zoning and licensing com., 1977-84, pres., 1984-86, chmn. bd. dirs., 1986-88; trustee Thompson Island Edn. Ctr., 1981—; chmn. Boston Groundwater Trust, 1986-91; mem. Beacon Hill Archtl. Commn., 1991-93. Avocations: reading, Italian opera, collecting prints and antiques, tennis. Office: Cherwin Glickman & Theise LLP One Internat Pl 11th Fl Boston MA 02110

RIZZOLO, LOUIS B. M., artist, educator; b. Ferndale, Mich., Oct. 8, 1933; s. Louis and Bella (Bronson) R.; m. Patricia Ann, June 30, 1956 (div. 1982); children: Connie Lucille, Louis Matthew, Marc Angelo; m. Linda Talbot, Dec. 3, 1982; stepchildren: Heather MacIntyre, Cameron Smith, Jennifer Talbot, Meghan Smith. BS in Art, Western Mich. U., 1956; MA in Fine Art, U. Iowa, 1960; postgrad., U. Ga., 1969. Tchr. art Petoskey (Mich.) Pub. Schs., 1956-64; tchr. art history, art studio North Ctrl. Mich. Coll., Petoskey, 1959-64; grad. teaching asst. U. Iowa, Iowa CIty, 1958-60; tchr. painting Kalamazoo Inst. Art, 1970-85; prof. art Western Mich. U., Kalamazoo, 1964—; tchr. painting, drawing, interdisciplinary/multi media, installation/performance/exhbn. juror, lectr. and tchr. internat. workshops, Switzerlan, Austria, Can., France, Scotland, Hawaii, Norway, 1989—; artistic and gen. dir. Rizzolo and Assocs.: Inflatale Light Workshop Collaborative, Kalamazoo, 1980-92; co-dir. rsch. Creative Learning Program, Kalamazoo, 1986-92; R.W.S. London Watercolor del. Rep. of China (Best of Watercolor Book 1995). Capt. AUS, 1958-68. Grantee Ford Found., Dow Corning, Du Pont, Upjohn, Mich. Coun. Arts, Mich. Millenium Project, 1995-2000, Mich. Found. Arts, 1996, Edn. for the Arts, W.K. Kellogg, Kalamazoo Arts Coun., Nat. Exhbn./Collections: Western Mich. U. fellow. Mem. Internat. Soc. Art & Tech., Mich. Watercolor Soc., World Forum of Acoustic Ecology. Independent. Home: PO Box 62 Glenn MI 49416-0062

RIZZUTO, PHILIP FRANCIS (SCOOTER), sports broadcaster, former professional baseball player; b. Brooklyn, N.Y., 1917; s. Fiore Francesco Rizzuto and Rose. m. Cora, 4 children, 2 grandchildren. Shortstop N.Y. Yankees, N.Y.C., 1941-43, 46-56; radio and TV broadcaster, 1956-94. USN, Pacific theatre, 1943-45. MVP 1950; Baseball Hall of Fame, 1994. Office: care NY Yankees Yankee Stadium E 161 St & River Ave Bronx NY 10451*

RO, JAE YUN, pathologist; b. Seoul, Korea, Oct. 7, 1945; s. Kyeung-Yong and Soon Ie (Ha) R.; m. Jung-sil Cho, Oct. 23, 1972; 1 child, Bobby W. MD, Yonsei U. Sch. of Medicine, Seoul, Korea, 1969, MS, 1971, PhD, 1974. Diplomate Am. Bd. Pathology in Anatomic and Clin. Pathology; Korean Bd. Pathology in Anatomic Pathology; MD, Ohio, Tex., Ind. Resident dept. pathology Yonsei U., Seoul, Korea, 1969-73; chief dept. pathology Korean Army Hosp., Seoul, Korea, 1973-76; instr. dept. pathology Yonsei U., Seoul, 1976-78, asst. prof. dept. pathology, 1978-80; resident in anat. and clin. pathology Inst. Pathology Case Western Res. U., Cleve., 1980-84; fellow in pathology U. Tex./M.D. Anderson Cancer Ctr., Houston, 1984-85, asst. prof., 1987-89, assoc. prof., 1989-92, prof., 1992—. Author: Atlas of Surgical Pathology of the Male Reproductive Tract, 1997; mem. editorial bd. Internat. Jour. Surg. Pathology, 1993—, Advances in Anatomic Pathology, 1994—; guest editor Seminars in Diagnostic Pathology, 1988; contbr. over 300 articles to profl. jours., numerous abstracts to profl. publs., and numerous chpts. to books. Bd. dirs. Youth Meml. Mission Fund, Houston, 1990—. Maj. Korean Army, 1973-76. Named Top Honor Student, Yonsei U., 1969, Tchr. of Yr. M.D. Anderson Cancer Ctr., 1992, 94, 95, 96; grantee NIH, 1988-92, 91-95, 93-96. Mem. AMA, Am. Soc. Clin. Pathologists (chmn. short courses 1993—), Ohio Med. Assn., Coll. Am. Pathologists, Houston Soc. Pathologists (co-chmn. spring seminar 1991), Cleve. Soc. Pathologists, Internat. Acad. Pathology, Korean Soc. Pathology (chmn. short course 1994), Arthur Purdy Stout Soc. Surg. Pathologists. Baptist. Avocations: reading, golf. Office: The Univ of Tex MD Anderson Cancer Ctr 1515 Holcombe Blvd Houston TX 77030-4009

ROACH, ARVID EDWARD, II, lawyer; b. Detroit, Sept. 6, 1951; s. Arvid Edward and Alda Elizabeth (Buckley) R. BA summa cum laude, Yale U., 1972; JD cum laude, Harvard U., 1977. Bar: D.C. 1978, N.Y. 1978, U.S. dist. ct. D.C. 1978, U.S. dist. ct. (so. dist.) N.Y. 1978, U.S. Ct. Appeals (10th cir.) 1980, U.S. Ct. Appeals (2d cir.) 1981, U.S. Ct. Appeals (D.C. cir.) 1981, U.S. Ct. Appeals (7th and 9th cirs.) 1982, U.S. Supreme Ct. 1983, U.S. Dist. Ct. Md., 1985, U.S. Ct. Appeals (3d, 4th, 5th, 6th, 8th, 11th cirs.) 1988, U.S. Ct. Appeals (1st cir.) 1992. Law clk. to judge U.S. Dist. Ct., 1977-78; assoc. Covington & Burling, Washington, 1978-85, ptnr., 1985—. Mem. ABA, Am. Law Inst. Contbr. articles to legal jours. Office: Covington & Burling PO Box 7566 Washington DC 20044-7566

ROACH, EDGAR MAYO, JR., lawyer; b. Pinehurst, N.C., June 2, 1948; s. Edgar Mayo Sr. and Rhuamer (Richardson) R.; m. Deborah Day, Oct. 10, 1970; children: Edgar Mayo III, John Clifton. BA, Wake Forest U., 1969; JD with honors, U. N.C., 1974. Bar: N.C. 1974, Va. 1976, U.S. Ct. Appeals (4th cir.) 1976. Law clk. to judge U.S. Ct. Appeals (4th cir.), Abingdon, Va., 1974-75; assoc. Hunton & Williams, Richmond, Va., 1975-80; ptnr. Hunton & Williams, Raleigh, N.C., 1981-94; sr. v.p. Va. Power, Richmond, 1994—. Home: 3142 Monument Ave Richmond VA 23221-1457 Office: Va Power 1 James River Plz Richmond VA 23219-3229

ROACH, JAMES CLARK, government official; b. Charleston, W. Va., Sept. 29, 1943; m. Susan Roelke Roach, June 27, 1970; children: Edward J., Andrew A. BA in Social Studies and History, W. Va. Wesleyan Coll., 1965; MA in Am. History, W. Va. U. Historian Harpers Ferry (W. Va.) Nat. Hist. Pk., 1967-68, 70-72; chief interpretation resource mgmt. Ft. Frederica Nat. Monument, St. Simons Island, Ga., 1972-74; asst. chief interpretation visitor svcs. Colonial Nat. Hist. Pk., Yorktown, Va.; asst. chief interpretation, visitor svc. Colonial Nat. Hist. Pk., Jamestown, Va.; chief interpretation visitor svcs. Gettysburg (Pa.) Nat. Mil. Pk., Eisenhower Nat. Hist. Site, 1981-94; site mgr. Eisenhower Nat. Hist. Site, 1995—. Sec. Gettysburg Peace Celebration Commn. Inc. (former bd. dirs.). With U.S. Army, 1968-70, Vietnam. Recipient Freeman Tilden award Mid-Atlantic Region Interpreter of Yr., 1984, Ea. Superior Performance award Nat. Park and Monument Assn., 1985, Spl. Events award GETT Travel Coun. award, 1986, 87. Mem. Assn. Nat. Pk. Rangers, Lincoln Fellowship Pa. (past pres.), Adams County Torch Club (past pres.), Rotary. Lutheran. Avocations: gardening, reading, fishing, stamp collecting. Home: 84 Knoxlyn-Orrtanna Rd Gettysburg PA 17325 Office: Eisenhower Nat Hist Site 97 Taneytown Rd Gettysburg PA 17325-2804

ROACH, JAMES R., university president; married. BS in Edn. cum laude, Boston Coll., 1957; postgrad., St. John's Coll., Brighton, Mass., 1963; certificat d'etude, U. Geneva, Switzerland, 1969; PhD in World Religions, Boston U., 1972; postgrad., Harvard U. Inst. Ednl. Mgmt., summer 1978. Tchr. Annotto Bay Coll., Jamaica, West Indies, 1957-58, Coll. Ctr., Salem State Coll., 1965-69; tchr. grad. sch. St. John's and Boston Univs., 1970-72; tchr. divsn. grad. studies Salem State Coll., 1972-73; tchr. divsn. grad. studies North Adams State Coll., 1974-75, tchr. dept. philosophy, 1973-76, dir. acad. counseling svcs., 1973-76, acad. dean, 1976-78, v.p. acad. affairs, 1978-86, acting pres., 1984; interim vice chancellor acad. affairs Mass. Bd. Regents, 1980-81; pres. U.Maine, Presque Isle, 1986-92, Western Conn. State U., Danbury, 1992—; bd. dirs. Savs. Bank Danbury; state rep. Am. Assn. State Colls. and Univs., chair com. acad. affairs, 1991-92, mem. task force on bldg. polit. support, 1991-92; chmn. reaccreditation vis. com. Castleton (Vt.) State Coll., 1991; mem Trustee Task Force on Rsch. and Grad. Edn.; mem. State of Maine Legislature's Spl. Commn. to Study and Evaluate the Status of Edn. Reform in Maine, 1990; mem. Univ. Sys./State Govt. Partnership Policy Group, 1989—, Mass.Bd. Regents Design Team for Collective Bargaining, 1983, Gov.'s Edn. Task Force, 1982-86, Mass. Bd. Regents Adv. Task Force on Program Rev., 1982-86; mem. Mass. State Coll. Sys. Task Force for Devel. Skills, 1977, Task Force for Profl. Devel., 1978, Pers. Mgmt. Adv. Com., 1979; dir. Maine Devel. Found., 1989-92; pres. Maine Higher Edn.Coun., 1989-92; chmn. bd. dirs. Maine Rsch. and Productivity Ctr., 1988-92; coord.-tchr. Monroe Ednl. Release Program, 1973-77; chmn. Mass. State Coll. Ad Hoc Com., 1979; corporator North Adams State Coll. Found., 1981-86; dir. acad. program evaluation project North Adams State Coll., 1977-82; cons. Wang Inst. Grad. Studies, 1983; state rep. Am. Assn. State Colls. and Univs. Acad. Affairs Resource Ctr. Assocs., 1982-86; presenter papers, spkr. various orgns. and confs. Bd. trustees United Way of No. Fairfield County, Inc.; mem. exec. bd. dirs. No. Maine Regional Planning Commn./Econ. Devel. Dist., 1987—; bd. dirs. Maine/Loring Assn., 1986—; bd. dirs. Croissant Club No. Berkshire County, 1984-86. With USN. Mem. Danbury C. of C. (bd. dirs.), Am. Acad. Religion, Am. Assn. Higher Edn.,Am. Assn. Colls. Tchr. Edn., Assn. Am. Colls., Internat. Assn. Univ. Pres., Pi Lamba Theta. Home: 177 Lake Pl S Danbury CT 06810-7264*

ROACH, JAMES RICHARD, academic administrator. V.p. acad. affairs North Adams State Coll., Mass., until 1986; pres. U. Maine, Presque Isle, 1986-92, Western Conn. State U., Danbury, 1992—. Office: Western Conn State Univ 181 White St Danbury CT 06810

ROACH, JAMES ROBERT, retired political science educator; b. Rock Rapids, Iowa, Aug. 25, 1922; s. Paul Ramsey and Doris (Kline) R. BA, U. Iowa, 1943; AM, Harvard U., 1948, PhD, 1950. Mem. faculty, adminstrn. U. Tex., Austin, 1949—, prof. govt., 1965-95, prof. emeritus, 1995—, dir. spl. programs, 1965-69, vice provost, dean interdisciplinary programs, 1971-72, dean divsn. gen. and comparative studies, 1972-74; counselor for cultural affairs Am. embassy, New Delhi, 1974-78; Fulbright vis. lectr. polit. sci. Rajasthan U., India, 1961-62; mem. Bd. Fgn. Scholarships, 1965-74, chmn., 1969-71; mem. U.S. Commn. for UNESCO, 1966-69. With USNR, 1943-46. Fulbright rsch. grantee, Australia, 1951-52, Ford Found. fgn. fellow, India, 1956-57. Mem. Assn. Asian Studies, Phi Beta Kappa, Kappa Tau Alpha, Sigma Delta Chi, Phi Kappa Psi. Democrat. Conglist. Home: 8604 Dorotha Ct Austin TX 78759-8113 Office: U Tex Dept Of Govt Austin TX 78712-1087

ROACH, SISTER JEANNE, nun, hospital administrator; b. Denver, Aug. 25, 1934. Diploma, Regina Sch. Nursing, 1956; BS, Coll. Mt. St. Joseph, 1964; MS, Trinity U., 1973. Joined Sisters of Charity, Roman Cath. Ch., 1951; RN. Med. supr. St. Mary-Corwin Hosp., Pueblo, Colo., 1956-58; oper. rm. supr. San Antonio Hosp., Kenton, Ohio, 1958-61; dir. nursing svc. Mt. San Rafael Hosp., Trinidad, Colo., 1961-67; splty. supr. Penrose Hosp., Colorado Springs, Colo., 1967-69, dir. nursing svc., 1969-70, asst. adminstr., 1970-71, asst. adminstr. profl. svcs., 1973-75; assoc. adminstr. and coord. St. Joseph Hosp., Mt. Clemens, Mich., 1975-78; v.p. Good Samaritan Hosp., Cin., 1978-82; adminstr. Our Lady of the Way Hosp., Martin, Ky., 1982-85, Mother Margaret Hall Nursing Home, 1990—, Bayley Place Nursing Home, 1995—; CEO St. Joseph Hosp., Huntingburg, Ind., 1985-89. Trustee, treas. Ohio Valley Renal Disease Network, Inc., Louisville, 1981-83; bd. dirs. Mud Creek Clinic, Grethel, Ky., 1982-85, St. Mary-Corwin, Pueblo, Colo., Sunny Acres, Denver, St. Joseph's Home, Cin. Fellow Am. Coll. Health Care Adminstrs.; mem. Am. Mgmt. Assn., Am. Hosp. Assn., Cath. Health Assn., Ky. Hosp. Assn., Nat. League for Nursing. Office: Mother Margaret Hall 5900 Delhi Rd Mount Saint Joseph OH 45051-1500

ROACH, JOHN D. C., manufacturing company executive; b. West Palm Beach, Fla., Dec. 3, 1943; s. Benjamin Browning and Margaret (York) R.; m. Pam Flebbe, Dec. 29, 1967 (div. Aug. 1981); children: Vanessa, Alexandra; m. Elizabeth Louise Phillips, Aug. 28, 1982; children: Bruce Phillips, Bryce Phillips, Brian Phillips. BS in Indsl. Mgmt., MIT, 1965; MBA, Stanford U., 1967. Dir. mgmt. acctg. and info. systems Ventura div. Northrop Corp., Thousand Oaks, Calif., 1967-70; co-founder, mgr. Northrop Venture Capital, Century City, Calif., 1970-71; v.p., dir. Boston Consulting Group, Boston and Menlo Park, Calif., 1971-80; v.p., world-wide strategic mgmt. practice mng. officer Booz, Allen, Hamilton, San Francisco, 1980-82; Houston, 1982-83; vice chmn., mng. dir. Braxton Assocs., Houston, 1983-87; sr. v.p., chief fin. officer Manville Corp., Denver, 1987-88, exec. v.p. ops., 1988-91; pres. Manville Sales Corp., Denver, 1988-90, Manville Mining and Minerals Group, Denver, 1990-91, Celite Corp., Denver, 1990-91; chmn., pres., chief exec. officer Fibreboard Corp., Dallas, Calif., 1991—; bd. dirs. Magma Power, Thompson PBE, Morrison Knudsen, PMI Group, Am. Stock Exch. Author: Strategic Management Handbook, 1983. Bd. dirs. Opera Colo., Denver, 1987-91, Bay Area Coun., San Francisco, Dallas Symphony; bd. trustees Alta Bates Med. Ctr.; med. exec. com. San Francisco Opera Assn. Mem. N.Am. Soc. Strategy Planners, Greater Denver C. of C. (bd. dirs.), Geol. Energy and Minerals Assn. (bd. dirs.), Colo. Forum, Soc. Corp. Planners (charter), Fin. Execs. Inst., Stanford Grad. Sch. Bus. Club, MIT Alumni Club, Cherry Hills Country Club (Englewood, Colo.), Claremont Country Club (Oakland, Calif.), TPC Sports Country Club, Beaver Creek (Colo.) Country Club. Avocations: running, bicycling, golf, snow skiing, hunting. Home: 4278 Bordeaux Dallas TX 75205

ROACH, JOHN HENDEE, JR., bank executive, investment banker, financial service executive; b. N.Y.C., Oct. 24, 1941; s. John Hendee and Julia (Casey) R.; m. Joan Hayden Muchmore, Sept. 23, 1972; children: Hayden, Cameron, John, Lauriston, Schuyler. BA, Washington and Jefferson Coll., 1964; postgrad., Aspen Inst., 1987, Harvard U., 1989. With Chem. Bank, N.Y.C., 1968-71, sr. v.p. corp. bank, 1972-87, mng. dir. corp. fin., 1987-92; ret., 1992; sr. mng. dir., vice chmn. The Geneva Cos., N.Y.C., 1992-94; sr. mng. dir., client mgmt. and mktg. Am. Internat. Group, N.Y.C., 1994—. Capt. U.S. Army, 1964-66. Mem. Racquet and Tennis Club, Chgo. Club, Round Hill Club. Republican. Roman Catholic. Home: 16 Oakwood Ln Greenwich CT 06830-3831 Office: American Internat Group 70 Pine St New York NY 10270-0002

ROACH, JOHN ROBERT, retired archbishop; b. Prior Lake, Minn., July 31, 1921; s. Simon J. and Mary (Regan) R. B.A., St. Paul Sem., 1946; M.A., U. Minn., 1957; L.H.D. (hon.), Gustavus Adolphus Coll., St. Mary's Coll., St. Xavier U., Villanova U., U. St. Thomas, Coll. of St. Catherine. Ordained priest Roman Catholic Ch., 1946; instr. St. Thomas Acad., 1946-50, headmaster, 1951-68; named domestic prelate, 1966; rector St. John Vianney Sem., 1968-71; aux. bishop St. Paul and Mpls., 1971; consecrated bishop, 1971; pastor St. Charles Borromeo Ch., Mpls., 1971-73, St. Cecilia Ch., St. Paul, 1973-75; archbishop of St. Paul, 1975-95; appointed vicar for parishes, 1971, vicar for clergy, 1972—; Episc. moderator Nat. Apostolate for Mentally Retarded, 1974; Mem. Priests Senate, 1968-72; pres. Priests Senate and Presbytery, 1970; chmn. Com. on Accreditation Pvt. Schs. in Minn., 1952-57; mem. adv. com. Coll. Entrance Exam. Bd., 1964; Episc. mem. Bishops and Pres.'s Com.; chmn. Bishops Com. to Oversee Implementation of the Call to Action Program, 1979-80; chmn. priestly formation com.; mem. Cath. Charity Bd. Trustee St. Paul Sem. Sch. Div., 1971-75, chmn., 1975-95; trustee Cath. U. Am., 1978-81, Coll. St. Catherine, 1975-95; chmn. bd. trustees St. Thomas Acad., U. St. Thomas, St. John Vianney Sem.; v.p. Nat. Conf. Cath. Bishops, 1977-80, pres., 1980-83, chmn. ad hoc com. on call to action, 1977; chair internat. policy com. U.S. Catholic Conf., 1990-93. Mem. Am. Coun. Edn. (del. 1963-65), Minn. Cath. Edn. Assn. (past pres.), Assn. Mil. Colls. and Schs. U.S. (past pres.), North Cen. Assn. Colls. and Secondary Schs., Nat. Conf. Cath. Bishops (adminstrv. com., priestly formation com., chmn. vocations com., priorities and plans com., com. on sexual abuse), U.S. Cath. Conf. (com. on social devel. and world peace 1990-93, priorities and plans com.), Nat. Cath. Edn. Assn. (chmn. bd. dirs.), Nat. Cath. Rural Life Conf. (past chmn. task force on food and agr. 1987-89). Address: Chancery Office 226 Summit Ave Saint Paul MN 55102-2121

ROACH, JOHN VINSON, II, retail company executive; b. Stamford, Tex., Nov. 22, 1938; s. John V. and Agnes M. (Hanson) R.; m. Barbara Jean Wiggin, Mar. 31, 1960; children: Amy, Lori. BA in Physics and Math., Tex. Christian U., 1961, MBA, 1965. V.p. Radio Shack, 1972-75, Radio Shack Mfg., 1975-78; exec. v.p. Radio Shack, 1978-80; gen. mgr. data processing Tandy Corp., Ft. Worth, 1967-73, pres., 1980—, chief exec. officer, 1981—, chmn., 1982—, also bd. dirs.; bd. dirs. Justin Industries. Bd. dirs. Van Cliburn Found.; chmn. bd. Tex. Christian U. Mem. Ft. Worth Club, City Club, Colonial Country Club. Office: Tandy Corp 1800 1 Tandy Ctr Fort Worth TX 76102

ROACH, MARGOT RUTH, biophysicist, educator; b. Moncton, N.B., Can., Dec. 24, 1934; d. Robert Dickson and Katherine (McMillan) R.; m. Franklyn St. Aubyn House, Dec. 20, 1994. B.Sc. in Math. and Physics with honors, U. N.B., Fredericton, Can., 1955; M.D., C.M. cum laude, McGill U., Montreal, Can., 1959; Ph.D. in Biophysics, U. Western Ont., Can., 1963; D.Sc. (hon.), U. N.B., St. John, Can., 1981. Jr. intern Victoria Hosp., London, Ont., Can., 1959-60, fellow in cardiology, 1962-63, asst. resident in medicine, 1963-64; asst. resident in medicine Toronto Gen. Hosp., 1964-65; mem. faculty, dept. biophysics U. Western Ont., London, Ont., Can., 1965—, head dept. biophysics, 1970-78, prof., 1971—, asst. prof. medicine, 1965-72, assoc. prof., 1972-78, prof., 1978—; mem. staff dept. medicine Victoria Hosp., 1967-72, U. Hosp., London, 1972—; Commonwealth vis. sci., dept. applied math. theoretical physics Cambridge U., 1975; vis. sci. Bioengring. Inst., Chonqing U., People's Republic of China, 1991; mem. bioengring. grants com. Med. Rsch. Coun. Can., 1993-96; cons. and lectr. in field. Active civic orgns. and coms. including Univ. Rsch. Coun., 1976-79; mem. interview bd. London Conf. of United Ch., 1967-90; steward United Ch. Can., 1967-73, elder, 1973—; chmn. stewardship devel. com. Colborne St. United Ch., 1990-93. Recipient A. Wilmer Duff prize in physics U. N.B., 1955, Cushing prize in pediatrics, 1959, Ciba Found. award for research in aging, 1959, Teaching award Faculty of Medicine U. Western Ont., 1990, Dean's award, 1997, Women of Distinction award YWCA, 1997; Med. Research Council fellow U. Western Ont., 1960-62; numerous other fellowships and grants in medicine. Fellow Royal Coll. Physicians (Can.), Am. Coll. Cardiology (Young Investigator's award 1963); mem. Can. Physiol. Soc., Can. Cardiovascular Soc. (off council), Can. Clin. Investigation Soc. (council 1980-84), Can. Biophys. Soc., Can. Soc. Internal Medicine. Home: 223 University Crescent, London, ON Canada N6A 2L7

ROACH, MAXWELL LEMUEL, musician; b. Elizabeth City, N.C., Jan. 10, 1924; s. Alphonzo and Cressie (Saunders) R.; m. Mildred Wilkinson, Jan.

14, 1949 (div.); children: Daryl, Maxine; m. Abbey Lincoln, Mar. 3, 1962 (div.). Student, Manhattan Sch. Music, N.Y.C.; Mus.D. (hon.), New Eng. Conservatory Music, 1982. Prof. music U. Mass., from 1973. Adapted use of tympani in jazz; musician specializing percussion instruments; with Charlie Parker, 1946-48, later appeared with Thelonious Monk, Bud Powell, Dizzy Gillespie; co-leader Max Roach-Clifford Brown Quintet; with Sonny Rollins, Harold Land, 1954-56, later with Booker Little, Ray Bryant, Eric Dolphy; appearances at Paris Jazz Festival, 1949, Newport Jazz Festival, 1972; composer: integration of jazz and dance Freedom Now suite; albums include: Percussion Bitter Sweet, It's Time, Drums Unlimited, Speak Brother Speak, The Loadstar, Conversations, Long as You're Living, Survivors, The Long March, Jazz in 3/4 Time, Scott Free, To the Max!, 1991, It's Time, 1996, The New Orchestra of Boston and The So What Brass Quintet, 1996 (with Dizzy Gillespie) Max and Dizzy: Paris 1989; producer, dir. and choreographer. Recipient Best Record of Year award Down Beat mag. 1956; winner Down Beat poll 1955, 57, 58, 59, 60, 84, metronome poll 1951-54. Mem. Jazz Artists Guild Inc. (organizer), Am. Acad. and Inst. of Arts and Letters (Hon.), 1992. Office: Blue Note Records 810 7th Ave 4th Fl New York NY 10019*

ROACH, RALPH LEE, human services and rehabilitation consultant; b. Silver Spring, Md., Mar. 27, 1957; s. William A. and Mary B. (Collins) R.; m. Susan Diane Schirmacher, Aug. 17, 1985. BA, Messiah Coll., 1982; MS, Shippensburg U., 1985; PhD, Kennedy-We. U., 1995. Inventory controller Messiah Coll., Grantham, Pa., 1977-85; therapist, crisis interviewer Stevens Mental Health, Carlisle, Pa., 1983-86; psychotherapist Holy Spirit Community Mental Health Inst., Camp Hill, Pa., 1986—; presentor, cons. Lebanon (Pa.) Valley Coll., 1986; vocat. tng. mgr. Ctr. for Indsl. Tng., Mechanicsburg, Pa., 1985-87; program mgr. living unltd. program univ. hosp. rehab. ctr. for children and adults Pa. U. Hosp. Milton S. Hershey Med. Ctr., Hershey, Pa., 1987-92; corp. officer, clin. dir. Avalon Affiliates Rehab. Consultants, Inc. (now MRW, Inc.), Duncannon, Pa., 1993-96, MRW, Inc., 1995—; adj. faculty Elizabethtown Coll., 1987; presenter at profl. confs. Edn. dir. Cumberland Valley Ch., Dillsburg, Pa., 1980-83; presentor Gov.'s Com. on Handicapped, Harrisburg, Pa., 1986; presentor Office of Spl. Edn. and Rehab., Harrisburg, 1987. Mem. ACA, Am. Acad. Rehab. Medicine, Pa. Specialists in Group Work, Pa. Crisis Intervention Assn., Pa. Assn. Rehab. Facilities, Keystone State Head Injury Found. Presbyterian. Avocations: boating, fishing, black powder hunting, gardening, horticulture. Home: 101 Jefferson St Duncannon PA 17020-9675 Office: MRW Inc 101 Jefferson St Duncannon PA 17020

ROACH, ROBERT MICHAEL, JR., lawyer; b. Bronxville, N.Y., May 27, 1955; s. Robert M. and Mary Dee R.; m. Marcia E. Backus, June 14, 1986. BA, Georgetown U., 1977; JD, U. Tex., 1981. Bar: Tex. 1981, U.S. Dist. Ct. (so. dist.) Tex. 1982, U.S. Ct. Appeals (5th cir.) 1982, U.S. Dist. Ct. (we. dist.) Tex. 1984, U.S. Supreme Ct. 1986, U.S. Dist. Ct. (ea. dist.) 1986, U.S. Dist. Ct. (no. dist.) Tex. 1988. Assoc. Vinson & Elkins, Houston, 1981-83, Ryan & Marshall, Houston, 1983, Mayor, Day & Caldwell, Houston, 1983-88; ptnr. Mayor, Day, Caldwell & Keeton, Houston, 1989-93; founding ptnr. Cook & Roach LLP, Houston, 1993—; dir. appellate advocacy U. Houston Law Ctr., 1994—; adj. prof. law U. Houston, 1990; lectr. continuing legal edn. U. Houston Law Ctr., 1989—; lectr. continuing legal edn. State Bar Tex., U. Tex., South Tex. Coll. Law, So. Meth. U., ABA; rschr., editor U.S. Senate Com. on Nutrition, 1975, 76, 77; rschr. U.S Supreme Ct., Washington, 1977; mem. Tex. Law Rev., 1979-81. Editor Def. Counsel Jour., 1990-93. Active U.S. Supreme Ct. Hist. Soc. Mem. Internat. Assn. Def. Counsel, Fedn. Ins. and Corp. Counsel, Def. Rsch. Inst. (grievance com.), Tex. Assn. Def. Counsel, State Bar Tex. (appellate sect. coun. officer 1989—), Houston Bar Assn. (officer, appellate sect.), Houston Club, Houston Met. Racquet Club, Houston Ctr. Club. Avocations: music, travel, oenology, tennis. Office: Cook & Roach LLP Texaco Heritage Plz 1111 Bagby St Ste 2650 Houston TX 77002-2546

ROACH, THOMAS ADAIR, lawyer; b. Akron, Ohio, May 1, 1929; s. Edward Thomas and Mayme Bernice (Turner) R.; m. Sally Jane Bennett, July 11, 1953; children: Thomas, David, James, Dorothy, Steven, Patrick. AB, U. Mich., 1951, JD with distinction, 1953. Bar: Mich. 1953. Assoc. McClintock, Fulton, Donovan & Waterman (and successor firms), Detroit, 1956-62, ptnr., 1962-87; counsel Bodman, Longley & Dahling, Detroit and Ann Arbor, Mich., 1988-90; ptnr. Bodman, Longley & Dahling, Detroit and Ann Arbor, Mich., 1990—; bd. dirs. Ferndale Labs. Inc., Acme Abrasive Co. Contbr. articles to profl. jours. Vice chmn. 14th Congl. Dist. Democratic Orgn., 1971-75; chmn. platform and resolution com. Mich. Dem. Party, 1971-74, treas., 1975-87; permanent chmn. Dem. State Conv., 1976; mem. platform com. and drafting subcom. Dem. Nat. Conv., 1972, mem. rules com., 1980, alt. del., 1984; bd. regents U. Mich., 1975-90; bd. dirs. Mich. Tech. Coun., 1983-92, vice chmn. 1984-86, south-ctrl. region 1992-95; pres. 9th Dist. Res. Policy Bd. 1976-77; nat. chmn. Ann. Giving, U., Mich., 1987—; mem. Mich. Higher Edn. Assistance Authority, Mich. Higher Edn. Student Loan Authority, 1990-94, Great Sauk Trail Coun., 1993—; bd. dirs. Wolverine Coun. Boy Scouts Am., 1991-93; officer Compensation Commn. Pittsfield Twp., 1991-93. Served to capt. USCGR, 1953-56; res. group comdr., 1974-77. Mem. ABA, Fed. Bar Assn., Mich. Bar Assn. (chmn. constrn. law com. 1983-85), Detroit Bar Assn., Washtenaw County Bar Assn., Res. Officers Assn., Order of Coif, Thomas M. Cooley Club, U. Mich. Club (gov. 1970-74), U. Mich. Alumni Assn. (bd. dirs. 1991-94, 95—, pres. 1995-97), Rotary Club (bd. dirs. Ann Arbor chpt. 1991-96, pres. 1994-95). Anglican. Home: 11825 Durston St Pinckney MI 48169-9502 Office: Bodman Longley & Dahling 110 Miller Ave Ste 300 Ann Arbor MI 48104-1391

ROACH, WESLEY LINVILLE, lawyer, insurance executive; b. Norlina, N.C., Oct. 8, 1931; s. Joseph Franklin and Florence G. (Sink) R.; m. Mary Jon Gerald, Aug. 13, 1955; children: Gerald, Mary Virginia. B.S., Wake Forest U., 1953, J.D., 1955. Bar: N.C. 1955. With Pilot Life Ins. Co., Greensboro, N.C., 1958-86, also bd. dirs.; sr. v.p., gen. counsel Jefferson-Pilot Life Ins. Co., Greensboro, 1986-88; sec. Great Ea. Lif. Ins. Co., 1975-85; of counsel Smith, Anderson, Blount, Dorsett, Mitchell & Jernigan, Attys. at Law, Raleigh, N.C., 1988—; former chmn. bd. dirs. N.C. Life and Accident and Health Ins. Guaranty Assn., Va. Life, Accident and Health Guaranty Assn., S.C. Life, Accident and Health Guaranty Assn.; sec. JP Investment Mgmt. Co., Jefferson-Pilot Equity Sales, Inc., Spl. Services Agy., Inc., 1974-84; mem. exec. com., bd. dirs. N.C. Ins. Edn. Found., 1978—. Mem. fin. com. Greensboro United Fund, 1964-65; mem. fin. com. Greensboro 1st Bapt. Ch., 1963-66, 83-86, chmn., 1983-85, chmn. bd. deacons, 1974-76, 80-81; nat. chmn. alumni coun. coll. fund Wake Forest U., 1971-76, pres. nat. alumni coun., 1975-76, trustee univ., 1978-82; trustee So. Bapt. Theol. Sem., Louisville, 1973-84; trustee Bapt. Retirement Homes N.C., Inc., 1992—, chmn., 1993-94 With USNR, 1955-58. Mem. ABA, N.C. Bar Assn., Raleigh Bar Assn., Assn. Life Ins. Counsel (bd. govs. 1984-88), Greensboro C. of C. (chmn. nat. legis. com. 1973—), Nat. Orgn. Life Guaranty Assn. (bd. dirs. 1982-87). Democrat. Home: PO Box 1490 601 Selma Rd Wendell NC 27591-8648 Office: 2500 First Union Capitol Ctr PO Box 2611 Raleigh NC 27602-2611

ROACH, WILLIAM RUSSELL, training and education executive; b. Bedford, Ind., Jan. 1940; s. George H. and Beatrice M. (Schoenlaub) R.; m. Margaret R. Balogh, 1961 (div. 1994); children: Kathleen L., Keith W. BS in Fin. and Acctg., UCLA, 1961. CPA, Calif. Internal auditor Hughes Aircraft Co., L.A., 1961-62, Lockheed Aircraft Corp., L.A., 1962; sr. acct. Haskins & Sells, L.A., 1962-66; asst. to group v.p., asst. corp. contr. Lear Siegler, Inc., Santa Monica, Calif., 1966-71; exec. v.p., corp. sec., dir. Optimum Systems Inc., Santa Clara, Calif., 1972-79; pres., dir. Banking Systems Inc., subs. Optimum Systems Inc., Dallas, 1976-79, BancSystems, Inc., Santa Clara, 1976-79, DMA/Optimum, Honolulu, 1978-79; v.p. URS Corp., San Mateo, Calif., 1979-81; pres. URS Internat., Inc., 1980-81; pres., CEO, dir. Advanced Systems, Inc., from 1981, Applied Learning Internat., Inc. (formed from merger of Advanced Systems, Inc. and Deltak Training Corp.), Naperville, Ill., 1981-88; sr. v.p., bd. dirs. Nat. Edn. Corp. (parent co. Applied Learning Internat.), Irvine, Calif., 1989—; chmn. bd., pres., chief exec. officer TRO Learning Inc., (acquisition tng. and edn. group Control Data Corp.), Hoffman Estates, Ill., 1989—; bd. dirs. Mil. Profl. Resources, Inc.; guest speaker numerous industry related funtions including Rep. Platform Com., 1988. Mem. AICPA, Calif. Soc. CPAs, Theta Delta Chi, Commonwealth Club (San Francisco); The Meadow Club (Chgo.). Office: TRO Learning Inc Poplar Creek Office Plz 1721 Moon Lake Blvd Ste 555 Hoffman Est IL 60194-1074

ROACHE, EDWARD FRANCIS, retired manufacturing company executive; b. Morristown, N.J., May 2, 1923; s. Vincent D. and Cecelia R. (Kennedy) R.; m. Beth Davidson, Aug. 8, 1948; children: Marc E., Steven P., Kevin J. B.S. in Economics, Fordham U., 1947; postgrad., Sienna Coll., 1953. With Gen. Electric Co., 1947—; mem. fin. mgmt. program, corporate audit staff, mgr. fin. various depts., gen. mgmt. assignments in electronics, computers, aircraft engine and intern Gen. Electric Co., Syracuse, N.Y., Phoenix, Lynn, Mass., Fairfield, Conn., 1978-83; v.p., gen. mgr. internat. constrn. bus. div. Gen. Electric Co., 1978-83, ret., 1983; dir. Gen. Electric Co., Italy, Australia, S. Korea, U.K. Served with USMC, 1943-46. Mem. Fin. Execs. Inst. Clubs: Pinnacle; Landmark (Stamford, Conn.). Home: 1161 Mill Hill Rd Southport CT 06490-3020

ROADEN, ARLISS LLOYD, retired higher education executive director, former university president; b. Bark Camp, Ky., Sept. 27, 1930; s. Johnie Samuel and Ethel Nora (Killian) R.; m. Mary Etta Mitchell, Sept. 1, 1951; children: Janice Arletta Roaden Skelton, Sharon Kay Roaden Hagen. Grad., Cumberland Coll., 1949; AB, Carson Newman Coll., 1951; MS, U. Tenn., 1958, EdD, 1961; PhD (hon.), Cumberland Coll., 1986; DLitt (hon.), Tusculum Coll., 1992. With Oak Ridge Inst. Nuclear Studies, 1957-59, Auburn U., 1961-62; mem. faculty Ohio State U., 1962-74, prof. edn., 1967-74, acting dean Coll. Edn., 1968-70, vice provost for research, dean Grad. Sch., 1970-74; pres. Tenn. Tech. U., 1974-85, pres. emeritus, 1985—; dir. Tenn. Higher Edn. Commn., Nashville, 1985-95, exec. dir. emeritus, 1995—; summer vis. prof. Marshall U., 1961, U. So. Calif., 1964, Ind. U., 1967; cons. edni. instns., 1961—; pres. Tenn. Coll. Assn., 1978; chmn. sci. and tech. com. Am. Assn. State Colls. and Univs., 1980; chmn. task force on program and instl. assessment State Higher Edn. Exec. Officers', 1987, pres. 1993-94, chmn. coun. postsecondary accreditation liaison com., 1986-88, exec. com., 1988-95, pres. elect 1992-93; mem. exec. bd. trustees Southern Assn. Colls. and Schs., 1986—, chair communications com., 1990—, mem. task force, 1990—; mem. Southern Regional Edn. Bd., 1985—, chmn. procedures com. for reviewing bylaw changes and revisions, 1988-89; mem. exec. com., state rep., treas., chair Internal Audit Com., 1990-91, Edn. Commn. States, 1987-90; mem. Tenn. Econ. Cabinet Coun., 1988—, chmn.m 1988-91, bd. dirs. 1988—, Fgn. Lang. Inst.; treas., chair Internal Audit Com., 1990-91; mem. Performance Standards in Vocat.-Tech. Edn. Working Group, U.S. Dept. Edn., 1990. Co-author: The Research Assistantship: Recommendations for Colleges and Universities, 1975; editor: Problems of School Men in Depressed Urban Areas, 1967; contbr. articles to profl. jours. State chmn. Tenn. Cancer Soc. Crusade, 1986-88, bd. dirs., 1987—; mem. exec. bd., commr. Mid. Tenn. coun. Boy Scouts Am., 1987-88, mem. nat. coun., 1988—, chmn. scouts membership rels. com.; mem. Phi Delta Kappa Found., 1965—, past chmn. bd. govs., mem. futures and diamond jubilee coms., 1989—; chmn. Blue Ribbon Com. To Respond to Edn. Goals, 1990; bd. dirs. Nat. Project 714, 1986—, pres.-elect, 1987-88, chmn., 1988-89; pres. alumni assn. bd. Cumberland Coll., 1987-88, chmn. devel. bd., 1994—; adult Sunday sch. tchr. Woodmont Bapt. Ch., chmn. pers. com. , 1989—. With U.S. Army, 1951-53. Research grantee Phi Delta Kappa Internat., 1968; named Distinguished Alumnus Cumberland Coll., 1970; recipient Distinguished Alumni and Faculty Centennial medallion Coll. Edn., 1970, Distinguished Service award Council Grad. Students, 1974; both Ohio State U.; recipient Silver Beaver award Boy Scouts Am., Rotarian of Yr., 1984; Eagle Scout honoree Middle Tenn. Coun. Boy Scouts Am., 1989, others. Fellow Oxford Soc. Scholars; mem. AAAS, Am. Assn. Higher Edn., Acad. Polit. and Social Scis., Am. Ednl. Rsch. Assn. (chmn. publs. com. 1979-80), Nat. Soc. Study Edn., Nat. Assn. State Colls. and Land Grant Univs.,, Lions (bd. dirs. Nashville 1988-90, pres. 1991-92, zone chmn. 1992-93, vice dist. gov. 1995), Rotary (bd. dirs.), Order of Lion and Eagle, Phi Kappa Phi, Phi Delta Kappa (Disting. Svc. award Ohio State U. chpt. 1974), Kappa Phi Kappa, Kappa Delta Pi. Baptist.

ROAF, ANDREE LAYTON, judge; b. Mar. 31, 1941; m. Clifton G. Roaf; 4 children. BS in Zoology, Mich. State U., 1962; JD with high honors, U. Ark., 1978; LLD (hon.), Mich. State U., 1996. Bar: Ark. 1978. Bacteriologist Mich. Dept. Health, Lansing, 1963-65; rsch. biologist FDA, Washington, 1965-69; staff asst. Pine Bluff (Ark.) Urban Renewal Agy., 1971-75; biologist Nat. Ctr. for Toxicological Rsch., Jefferson, Ark., 1978-79; assoc. Walker, Roaf, Campbell, Ivory & Dunklin, Little Rock, 1979-86, ptnr., 1986-95; assoc. justice Ark. Supreme Ct., Little Rock, 1995-96; appellate judge Ark. Ct. Appeals, 1997—. Editor Ark. Law Rev. Mem. PTA bd. Forest Park Elem. Sch., 1972-74, 34th Ave Sch., 1974-76, 80-83, Southeast Jr. High, 1976-77; mem. ad hoc com. for voter registration Jefferson County, 1972-73; bd. dirs. Ark. Coun. on Human Rels., 1972-73, Ark. for Arts, 1983, Ark. Student Loan Authority, 1977-81, Vocals, 1989—; bd. trustees Southeast Ark. Arts and Sci. Ctr., 1972-75, sec., 1974-75; sec. Pine Bluff OIC Bd., 1972-78, Pine Bluff Police-Cmty. Rels. Task Force, 1973; mem. Jefferson County Com. on Black Adoptions, 1973-75, chmn., 1974-75; mem. Ark. Code of Ethics Commn., 1987, Friends of Sta. KRLE-FM, 1982-88, 90-94, pres., 1985-86; mem. Jefferson County Dem. Com., 1980-82; trustee Winthrop Rockefeller Found., 1990-94; mem. vestry Grace Episcopal Ch., 1995—. Recipient disting. alumni award Mich. State U., 1996; inducted Ark. Black Hall of Fame, 1996; named Gayle Pettus Pontz outstanding Ark. woman lawyer, 1996. Mem. ABA, Ark. Bar Assn. (chmn. youth edn. com. 1979-80), Pulaski County Bar Assn. (chmn. hist. com. 1986-87), Jefferson County Bar Assn., W. Harold Flowers Law Soc., Debtor-Creditor Bar Ctrl. Ark. Office: Justice Bldg 625 Marshall St Little Rock AR 72201-1054

ROAF, WILLIAM LAYTON, professional football player; b. Pine Bluff, Ark., Apr. 18, 1970; s. Clifton George and Andree Yvonne (Layton) R. Left offensive tackle New Orleans Saints, 1993—. Named All-American, Sports Writers, 1993, finalist Outland Trophy, Sports Writers, 1993; named to All-Rookie Team, Football News, 1994, Pro-Bowl Alt., 1994. Episcopal. Dr. Z's All-Pro team, 1994. Office: New Orleans Saints 7800 Airline Hwy Metairie LA 70003-6480*

ROAN, JAMES CORTLAND, JR., air force officer; b. St. Louis, Apr. 10, 1937; s. James Cortland and Marguerite L. (Johnson) R.; m. Connie R. Brown, Nov. 10, 1962; children: James Bradley, Brian Edward. BSBA, JD, Washington U., St. Louis, 1960. Bar: Mo. 1960. Commd. 1st lt. USAF, 1960, advanced through grades to brig. gen., 1990; staff judge adv. Air Force Aero. Systems Div., Dayton, Ohio, 1982-85, Hdqrs. Air Force Logistics Command, Dayton, 1991-92, Hdqrs. Air Force Systems Command, Washington, 1985-87, 1990-91; staff judge adv. Air Force Electronic Systems Div., Boston, 1987-90; comdr. Hdqrs. Air Force Contract Law Ctr., Dayton, 1991-92; staff judge adv. Hdqrs. Air Force Materiel Command, Dayton, 1992-95; ret., 1995. Recipient Stuart R. Reichart award as outstanding sr. atty. in USAF, Air Force Assn., 1989. Mem. Fed. Bar Assn. (pres. Beverly Hills chpt. 1980-81). Avocation: woodworking. Home: 267 Smith Creek Rd Warrenton MO 63383-6401*

ROARK, CHARLES ELVIS, healthcare executive; b. Port Arthur, Tex., Feb. 11, 1946; s. Chris C. and Alene (Adams) R.; m. Marlene Jones, Jan. 18, 1969; children: Cari Joann, Carolyn Dianne, Charles Eric. BBA, Lamar U., Beaumont, Tex., 1969; MS, Trinity U., San Antonio, 1971; EdD, Tex. Tech U., 1994. Asst. adminstr. Hotel Dieu Hosp., El Paso, 1969-76; dir. planning Tex. Hosp. Assn., Austin, 1976-79; adminstr. Gulf Coast Hosp., Wharton, Tex., 1979-81; pres. Charles E. Roark & Assocs., El Paso, 1980—; exec. dir. Hospice of El Paso Inc., 1990—; bd. dirs. El Paso Ind. Sch. Dist., 1995—. Pres. N.E. Civic Leaders Coun., Inc., 1986-90; mem. adv. bd. Anytown USA, 1987-88; mem. City of El Paso Sanitation Adv. Bd., 1987-88; bd. dirs. Keep El Paso Beautiful, 1986-88. Fellow Am. Coll. Healthcare Execs. (cert.); Mem. Rotary Club of El Paso, N.E. Civitan (pres. 1975-76, dist. gov. 1988-89), S.W. Healthcare Execs. (pres. 1991-92), Leadership El Paso Alumni Assn. (pres. 1996). Baptist. Avocations: sports, hunting, fishing. Office: Hospice of El Paso Inc 3901 N Mesa St Ste 400 El Paso TX 79902-1540

ROARK, EDITH HUMPHREYS, private school language arts educator, reading specialist; b. Raleigh, N.C., Jan. 26, 1943; d. Sidney Frederick and Jennie Mildred (Swain) Humphreys; m. Larry Alden Roark, Nov. 27, 1964; children: Jonathan Laurance, Nancy Elaine, Naomi Elizabeth. BS, Appalachian State U., 1965; MA, East Tenn. State U., 1980, postgrad., 1986-88. Cert. elem. tchr., Tenn. Tchr. Memphis City Schs., 1966, Wake County Schs., Garner, N.C., 1967, Dover (N.J.) Twp. Schs., 1968, Kingsport (Tenn.) Christian Sch., 1974-77; tchr. Tri-Cities Christian Sch., Kingsport, 1983-84, reading tutor, 1980-84; reading tutor Ashley Acad., Johnson City, Tenn., 1984-87, tchr., 1987—; ofcl. judge Odyssey of the Mind, Tenn., coach, 1992, regional judge, 1991-96, state judge, 1994-96; leader Gt. Books, Johnson City, 1988; participant NIE Playshop, Kingsport, summers 1989-95, Slingerland Multisensory Reading Tchr. Tng. Mem. Internat. Reading Assn., Orton Dyslexia Soc., Kappa Delta Pi, Delta Kappa Gamma (chair literacy com. 1991—, corr. sec. 1994-96). Baptist. Avocations: reading, collecting newspaper trivia, gardening, decorating, teaching Sunday school. Home: 222 Norwood Dr Johnson City TN 37615-3858 Office: Ashley Acad 816 Lacy St Johnson City TN 37604-3728

ROARK, TERRY PAUL, academic administrator, physicist; b. Okeene, Okla., June 11, 1938; s. Paul J. and Erma K. (Morrison) R.; m. Beverly Brown, Sept. 7, 1963; 1 child, David. C. BA in Physics, Oklahoma City U., 1960; MS in Astronomy, Rensselaer Poly. Inst., 1962, PhD in Astronomy, 1966. Asst. provost for curricula Ohio State U., Columbus, 1977-79, assoc. provost for instrn., 1979-83; prof. physics Kent (Ohio) State U., 1983-87, v.p. acad. and student affairs, 1983-87, provost, 1985-87; pres. U. Wyo., Laramie, 1987-97, prof. physics and astronomy, 1997—; bd. dirs. Rocky Mountain Fed. Savs. Bank, chmn. audit com., 1989-93; commr. Western Interstate Commn. for Higher Edn., 1987-97, chmn., 1991; bd. dirs. Associated Western Univs., 1987-94, chmn., 1991, bd. trustees, 1994-97, chmn. 1996; adv. bd. Wyo. Geol. Survey, 1987-97; mem. Warren AFB Civilian Adv. Coun., 1987-97; bd. dirs. First Interstate Bank of Wyo. Mem., treas. Ctr. for Pub. Edn., Columbus, 1980-83; mem. fin. adv. com. LWV, Kent, 1986; mem. long range planning com. Cleve. Urban League, 1985-86; mem. adv. com. Battelle youth sci. program Columbus and Ohio Pub. Schs., 1982; bd. dirs. Ivinson Hosp. Found., 1987—. Mem. Am. Astron. Soc., Internat. Astron. Union, Nat. Assn. State Univs. and Land Grant Colls. (bd. dirs. 1994-96, chair commn. on intenat. affairs 1995), Sigma Xi, Phi Kappa Phi, Omicron Delta Kappa. Avocations: photography, music, hiking. Home: 1752 Edward Dr Laramie WY 82070-2331 Office: U Wyo Dept Physics and Astronomy PO Box 3905 Laramie WY 82071-3434

ROATH-ALGERA, KATHLEEN MARIE, massage therapist; b. Binghamton, N.Y., Feb. 7, 1952; d. Stephen James and Virginia Mary (Purdy) Roath; m. Parker Newcomb Wheeler Jr., Sept. 18, 1971 (div. June 1976); 1 child, Colleen Marie Wheeler; m. John M. Algera, Feb. 14, 1981. AS in Phys. Edn., Dean Jr. Coll., Franklin, Mass., 1971; BS in Edn., Boston U., 1977; postgrad., U. Ctrl. Fla., Orlando, 1981-82; grad., Reese Inst. Massage Therapy, Oviedo, Fla., 1988. Lic. massage therapist; master practitioner in myofascial release. Counselor Dept. Def., Orlando, 1979-84; tchr. Divine Mercy Cath. Sch., Merritt Island, Fla., 1984-85; courier Emery Worldwide, Orlando, 1985-89; massage therapist, dir., owner Massage Therapy Clinic of Titusville, Fla., 1989—; instr., supr. clin. internship Reese Inst., 1992-95; assoc. Todd Jaffe, M.D., 1995—. Mem. Am. Massage Therapy Assn., Fla. State Massage Therapy Assn. (pres. Brevard County 1992—, Therapist of Yr. 1991-92), Nat. Cert. Bd. Therapeutic Massage and Bodywork (recert. chair 1994-97). Home: 5538 River Oaks Dr Titusville FL 32780 Office: Massage Therapy Clinic Titusville 3410 S Park Ave Titusville FL 32780-5139

ROBAK, KIM M., state official; b. Columbus, Nebr., Oct. 4, 1955; m. William J. Mueller; children: Katherine, Claire. BA with distinction, U. Nebr., 1977, JD with high distinction, 1985. Tchr. Lincoln (Nebr.) Pub. Schs., 1978-82; clerk Cline Williams Wright Johnson & Oldfather, Lincoln, 1983; summer assoc. Cooley Godward Castro Huddleson & Tatum, San Francisco, 1984, Steptoe & Johnson, Washington, 1985; ptnr. Rembolt Ludtke Parker & Berger, Lincoln, 1985-91; legal counsel Gov. E. Benjamin Nelson/State of Nebr., Lincoln, 1991-92, chief of staff, 1992-93; lt. gov. State of Nebr., Lincoln, 1993—; chair Prairie Fire Internat. Symposium on Edn., 1986. Fellow Leadership Lincoln, 1986-87, program com., 1987-90; chair program com. Leadership Lincoln Alumni Assn., 1987, selection com., 1990; chair Landfill Alternatives and Ops. Task Force, 1986-87; chair Gladys Forsyth award subcom. YWCA Tribute! to Women, 1987, chair nominations, 1991; mem. adv. com. U.S. Constn. Bicentennial Competition, 1987; gen. Dem. counsel, Nebr., 1985-92; mem. bd. women's ministries First Plymouth Congl. Ch., 1988-91, trustee, 1991-94; mem. Toll Fellowship Program, 1995; chair Nat. Conf. Lt. Govs., 1996; hon. chair Daffodil Day campaign Am. Cancer Soc.; hon. chair Walktoberfest, Am. Diabetes Assn.; hon. chair Nebr.'s campaign Prevent Blindness; hon. mem. Red Ribbon campaign Mothers Against Drunk Driving, 1994-95. Mem. Nat. Conf. Lt. Govs. (fed. practice com. 1986-92), Nat. Inst. Trial Advocacy, Nebr. State Bar Assn. (ethics com. 1987-92, vice chair com. on pub. rels. 1988-92, chair com. on yellow pages advt. 1988, ho. of dels. 1988-95), Lincoln Bar Assn., U. Nebr. Coll. Alumni Assn. (bd. dirs. 1986-89), Updowntowners, Order of Coif. Office: Lt Gov's Office Rm 2315 State Capitol Bldg Lincoln NE 68509-4863

ROBARDS, BOURNE ROGERS, elementary education educator; b. Milw., Jan. 5, 1950; s. William Simpson and Janet (Cross) R.; m. Martha Jane Snider, Oct. 29, 1977; children: Jonathan Matthew, Sara Elizabeth. BS, U. Mo., 1971; MAT, Webster U., St. Louis, 1989. Cert. elem. tchr., Mo. Classroom tchr. 4th and 6th grades Hazelwood Sch. Dist., Florissant, Mo., 1971-73; classroom tchr. 4th grade Jennings (Mo.) Sch. Dist., 1986—. Troop leader Boy Scouts Am., St. Louis, 1972-73; ch. leader St. Mark's Episcopal Ch., St. Louis, 1977—. Mem. Omicron Delta Kappa. Avocations: travel, reading, swimming, bicycling, music, photography. Home: 6320 Monterey Dr Saint Louis MO 63123-1510 Office: Northview Elem Sch Jennings Sch Dist 8920 Cozens Ave Jennings MO 63136-3921

ROBARDS, JASON NELSON, JR., actor; b. Chgo., July 26, 1922; s. Jason Nelson and Hope (Glanville) R.; m. Eleanore Pitman, May 7, 1948; children: Jason III, Sarah Louise, David; m. Lauren Bacall, July 4, 1961 (div.); 1 son, Sam; m. Lois O'Connor, 1970; children: Shannon, Jake. Student, Am. Acad. Dramatic Arts, 1946; DHL, Fairfield U., 1982; DFA, Williams Coll., 1983. Bd. dirs. Am. Acad. Dramatic Arts, 1957—. Broadway plays include Stalag 17, 1951-53, The Chase, 1952, The Iceman Cometh, 1956, Long Day's Journey Into Night, 1956-58, 76, 88, The Disenchanted, 1958, 1958-59, Toys in the Attic, 1960, Big Fish, Little Fish, 1961, A Thousand Clowns, 1962, After the Fall, 1964, But for Whom, Charlie, 1964, Hughie, 1964, The Devils, 1965, We Bombed in New Haven, 1968, The Country Girl, 1972, A Moon for the Misbegotten, 1973, A Touch of the Poet, 1977-78, A Month of Sundays, 1987, No Man's Land, 1993; other plays include Henry IV, Part I, Stratford (Ont., Can.), 1958, Macbeth, Cambridge, Mass., You Can't Take It With You, 1983, Iceman Cometh, 1985, Love Letters, 1989, A Month of Sunday, 1990, Ah Wilderness, 1988, Park Your Car in Harvard Yard, 1991, No Man's Land, 1995, Molly Sweeny, 1996, Moonlight, 1997; motion picture appearances include The Journey, 1959, No Mans Land, 1993, By Love Possessed, 1961, Long Day's Journey into Night (Cannes Internat. Film Festival, Best Actor Award, 1962), A Thousand Clowns, Big Hand for the Little Lady, 1966, Any Wednesday, 1966, St. Valentine's Day Massacre, 1967, Night They Raided Minsky's, 1968, Hour of the Gun, 1967, Loves of Isadora, 1969, Once Upon a Time in the West, 1969, Ballad of Cable Hogue, 1970, Julius Caesar, 1970, Tora, Tora, Tora, 1970, Fools, 1970, Johnny Got His Gun, 1971, Murders in the Rue Morgue, 1971, The War Between Men and Women, 1972, Pat Garrett and Billy the Kid, 1973, Mr Sycamore, 1975, A Boy and His Dog, 1975, All the President's Men, 1976, Julia, 1977, Comes a Horseman, 1978, Hurricane, 1979, Raise The Titanic, 1990, Melvin and Howard, 1979, Something Wicked This Way Comes, 1983, Max Dugan Returns, 1983, Square Dance, 1987, The Good Mother, 1988, Parenthood, 1989, Quick Change, 1990, Storyville, 1992, The Trial, 1993, The Adventures of Huck Finn, 1993, Philadelphia, 1993, Little Big League, 1994, The Paper, 1994, Crimson Tide, 1995, Thousand Acres, 1997; TV appearance Roberto in For Whom the Bell Tolls, CBS, 1959; starred in TV films including: The Iceman Cometh, 1961, One Day in the Life of Ivan Denisovitch, 1963, Washington Behind Closed Doors, 1977, F.D.R.: The Last Year, 1980, The Day After, 1983, Sakharov, 1984, Johnny Bull, 1986, Inherit the Wind, 1988 (Emmy award, 1988), The Christmas Wife, 1988, Chernobyl: The Final Warning, 1991; appeared in TV miniseries Haywire, 1980, The Atlanta Child Murders, 1985. Served with USN, 1939-46. Recipient ANTA award for outstanding contbn. to living theater, 1959, Antoinette Perry award as best actor, 1959, Obie award, 1956, Tony award for best dramatic actor, 1959, Acad. awards for best supporting actor, 1976-77, N.Y. Film Critics Circle award for best supporting actor, 1976, Emmy as best actor, 1988. Mem. Players Club, Century Club, N.Y. Athletic Club. Address: care Paradigm Talent Agy 200 W 57Th St Ste 900 New York NY 10019

ROBB, BRUCE, former insurance company executive; b. Norman, Okla., July 28, 1919; m. Betty Jane Sharrar, May 6, 1950; children: Elizabeth (dec.), Bruce. B.S., U.S. Naval Acad., 1941; M.B.A., Columbia U., 1949. Security analyst Clark, Dodge & Co., Inc., N.Y.C., 1948-52, 53-62; asst. treas. SAFECO Corp., Seattle, 1962-66; v.p., treas. SAFECO Corp., 1966-72, sr. v.p., treas., 1972-84. Mem. Wash. State Fin. Adv. Com., 1970-80; mem. investment com. Diocese of Olympia, 1964-94. Mem. Sand Point Country Club, Beta Gamma Sigma. Home: 6307 NE 57th St Seattle WA 98105-2011

ROBB, CHARLES SPITTAL, senator, lawyer; b. Phoenix, AZ, June 26, 1939; s. James Spittal and Francis Howard (Woolley) R.; m. Lynda Bird Johnson, Dec. 9, 1967; children: Lucinda Desha, Catherine Lewis, Jennifer Wickliffe. Student, Cornell U., 1957-58; B.B.A., U. Wis., 1961; J.D., U. Va., 1973. Bar: Va. 1973, U.S. Supreme Ct. 1976. Law clk. to presiding justice U.S. Ct. Appeals, 1973-74; atty. Williams Connolly & Califano, 1974-77; lt. gov. Va., 1978-82, gov., 1982-86; ptnr. Hunton & Williams, Richmond, Norfolk, and Fairfax, Va., Washington; U.S. Senator from Va., 1989—; mem. armed svcs. com., fgn. rels. com., intelligence com., senate Dem. policy com., senate Dem. tech. and comm. com.; chmn. Nat. Conf. Lt. Govs., 1979-80, Am. Coun. Young Polit. Leaders Dels. to Peoples Republif of China, 1979, edn. Commn. of the States, 1985; vis. prof. pub. affairs George Mason U., spring 1987. Chmn. Jobs for Am.'s Grads. Inc., 1985-90, Dem. Leadership Coun., 1986-88; gov. Atlantic Inst. for Internat. Affairs, 1987. With USMC 1961-70. Decorated Bronze Star, Vietnam Service medal with 4 Stars; Vietnamese Cross of Gallantry with Silver Star; recipient Raven award, 1973, Seven Soc. award U. Va. Mem. ABA, Va. Bar Assn., So. Govs. Assn. (chmn.), Dem. Govs. Assn. (chmn.), Coalition for Dem. Majority, Res. Officers Assn., USMC Res. Officers Assn., U.Fa. La. Alumni Assn. (bd. dirs. 1974-85), Am. Legion, Raven Soc., Navy League U.S., Coun. on Fgn. Rels., Omicron Delta Kappa. Episcopalian. Office: US Senate 154 Russell Senate Office Bldg Washington DC 20510-4603*

ROBB, DAVID BUZBY, JR., financial services company executive, lawyer; b. Phila., Nov. 30, 1935; s. David Buzby and Sarah Whelan (Carson) R.; m. Patricia Ann Irons, Sept. 14, 1979; children: Steven C., David S.; stepchildren: Donald Irons, Steven Irons. B.A., Princeton U., 1958; J.D., U. Va., 1963; A.M.P., Harvard Bus. Sch., 1978. Bar: Pa., 1963. Assoc. firm Ballard, Spahr, Andrews, Ingersoll, Phila., 1963-69; sr. v.p., chief operating officer trust div. Provident Nat. Bank, Phila., 1976-82, sr. v.p., gen. counsel Provident Nat. Corp., Phila., 1970-76; dir., vice chmn. Provident Instl. Mgmt. Corp., 1977-82; dir., chmn., chief exec. officer Provident Capital Mgmt., 1978-82; exec. v.p. SEI Corp., Wayne, Pa., 1982-89; pres., chief exec. officer Trust Funds Group, 1982-89; dir., pres., chief exec. officer Premier Systems, Inc., Wayne, Pa., 1989-91; dir., pres., CEO J.P. Morgan Fla., 1991—. Bd. dirs. Landmark Soc., Phila. City Inst., Friends Hosp., Pa. Acad. Fine Arts, ARC S.E. Pa., 1981-93, Econ. Coun. Palm Beach County, Intracoastal Health Systems Found., Civic Assn. Palm Beach, Preservation Found. Served to lt. USN, 1958-60. Mem. ABA, Pa. Bar Assn., Phila. Bar Assn., Sunnybrook G.C., P.G.A. Nat. G.C., City Club. Breakers Club, Club Colette. Republican. Episcopalian. Office: JP Morgan Florida FSB 109 Royal Palm Way Palm Beach FL 33480-4249

ROBB, DAVID METHENY, JR., art historian; b. Mpls., Apr. 12, 1937; s. David Metheny and Jane (Howard) R.; m. Frances Louise Osborn, Feb. 12, 1965; children: Andrew Osborn, Matthew Howard. BA, Princeton U., 1959; MA, Yale U., 1967; mus. mgmt. inst., U. Calif., Berkeley, 1983. Research asst. Soc. for Preservation of New Eng. Antiquities, Boston, 1959, Nat. Gallery Art, Washington, 1963; curator Paul Mellon Collection, Upperville, Va., 1963-65; curatorial fellow Walker Art Ctr., Mpls., 1967-69; research curator Kimbell Art Mus., Ft. Worth, 1969-74, chief curator, 1974-83, acting dir., 1979-80; dir. Telfair Acad. Art & Scis., Savannah, Ga., 1983-85; dir. Huntsville (Ala.) Mus. Art, 1985-94, dir. emeritus, 1995; mus. cons., 1992—. Co-author: Star-Spangled History—Joseph Boggs Beale, 1975; editor: Kimbell Art Museum: Catalogue of the Collection, 1972, Kimbell Art Museum: Handbook of the Collection, 1981; author: catalogue Louis J. Kahn: Sketches for the Kimbell Art Museum, 1978, preface Elisabeth Louise Vigée Le Brun, Ft. Worth, 1982. Mem. adv. com. S.E. Inst. for Edn. in Visual Arts, Chattanooga, 1987-92, Leadership 2000 Program, Huntsville, 1989-90. Comdr. USNR, 1960-63. Heritage Found. fellow, 1958, Ford Found. fellow, 1967-69. Mem. Am. Assn. Mus. Coll. Art Assn., Ala. Mus. Assn. (chmn. long-range plans com. 1989), Tallulah Bankhead Soc. (treas. 1991—), Huntsville Club, Rotary, Princeton Alumni Schs. Com. Home: 506 Lanier Rd SW Huntsville AL 35801-3214

ROBB, JAMES ALEXANDER, lawyer; b. Huntingdon, Que., Can., May 3, 1930; s. Alexander George and Irma Mary (Martin) R.; m. Katherine Ann Teare, June 26, 1960; children: Laura, John, Andrew. B.A., McGill U., 1951, B.C.L., 1954; postgrad., U. Montreal, 1961-63. Bar: Que. 1955, queen's counsel 1970. Lectr. comml. law and taxation Sir George Williams U., 1958-60; ptnr. Stikeman, Elliott and predecessor firm Stikeman, Elliott, Tamaki, Mercier & Robb, Montreal, 1967—; bd. dirs. Henry J. Kaiser Co. (Can.) Ltd., Multiquip Constrn. Equipment Can. Inc., State Internat. (Can.) Ltd., The Quebec Japan Bus. Forum, Robapharm (Can.), Inc., Itochu Can. Ltd., Majorich Investments Inc., YKK Can. Inc,. Hitachi (HSC) Can. Inc., NGK Spark Plugs Can. Ltd., Hitachi Credit Can. Inc., Klockner Stadler Hurter Ltd., Bilwyn Franchise Concepts Inc.; pres. Que-Japan Bus. Forum, 1993-95. Mem. Protestant Sch. Bd. Greater Montreal, mem. ctrl. parents com.; chmn. bd. trustees Martlet Found., 1967-69; v.p. Que. Liberal Party, 1976-79; mem. adv. com. McGill Ctr. for Study of Regulated Industries; bd. dirs. Montreal Mus. Fine Arts, 1987-90; bd. govs. McGill U., 1991-95. Mem. Bar Que., Consumers Assn. Can. (pst chmn. regulated industries program), McGill Alumni Assn. (pres. 1996—), Can. Club Montreal (bd. dirs. 1988, pres. 1990-91), Univ. Club, Kanawaki Golf Club (Que.), Royal Montreal Curling Club, Hillside Tennis Club. Home: 9 Renfrew Ave, Westmount, PQ Canada H3Y 2X3 Office: 1155 René Lèvesque, Blvd W Ste 4000, Montreal, PQ Canada H3B 3V2

ROBB, JAMES WILLIS, Romance languages educator; b. Jamaica, N.Y., June 27, 1918; s. Stewart Everts and Clara Johanna (Mohrman) R.; m. Cecilia Uribe-Noguera, 1972. Student, Inst. de Touraine, Sorbonne, 1937-38; BA cum laude, Colgate U., 1939; postgrad., U. Nacional de Mex., 1948; MA, Middlebury Coll., 1950; PhD, Cath. U. Am., 1958. Instr. Romance langs. Norwich U., 1946-50; asst. prof. Romance langs. George Washington U., Washington, 1950-58, assoc. prof., 1958-66, prof., 1966-88, prof. emeritus, 1988—. Author: El Estilo de Alfonso Reyes, 1965, 78, Repertorio Bibliográfico de Alfonso Reyes, 1974, Prosa y Poesia de Alfonso Reyes, 1975, 84, Estudios sobre Alfonso Reyes, 1976, Por los Caminos de Alfonso Reyes, 1981, Imágenes de América en Alfonso Reyes y en Germán Arciniegas, 1990; contbr. articles to profl. jours. With USNR, 1942-44, Brazil, 1944-46, PTO. Recipient Alfonso Reyes Internat. Lit. prize, 1978; Lit. Diploma of Merit, State of Nuevo León and City of Monterrey, Mex., 1979; OAS grantee, 1964; Am. Philos. Soc. grantee, 1977. Mem. MLA, Internat. Assn. Ibero-Am. Lit., Am. Assn. Tchrs. Spanish and Portuguese, N.Am. Assn. Colombianistas, Phi Beta Kappa. Office: George Washington U Romance Langs Dept Washington DC 20052

ROBB, JOHN WESLEY, religion educator; b. Los Angeles, Dec. 1, 1919; s. Edgar Milton and Alta (Boger) R.; m. Ethel Edna Tosh, June 13, 1942; children: Lydia Joan Robb Durbin, Judith Nadine Robb Eggerman. A.B., Greenville Coll., 1941; Th.M., U. So. Calif., 1945, Ph.D., 1952; L.H.D., Hebrew Union Coll.-Jewish Inst. Religion, 1977. Asst. prof. philosophy and religion Dickinson Coll., Pa., 1948-51; fellow Fund for Advancement Edn., 1951-52; assoc. prof. U. So. Calif., L.A., 1954-62, chmn. dept. religion, 1954-67, assoc. dean humanities Coll. Letters, Arts and Scis., 1963-68, Leonard K. Firestone prof., 1974-75, prof., 1962-87, prof. emeritus, 1987—; prof. Sch. Medicine U. So. Calif., 1981-87; coun. mem. Inst. of Lab. Animal Resources Nat. Acad. Scis. Nat. Rsch. Coun., 1986-93; prof. emeritus U. So. Calif., 1991—; vis. disting. prof. USAF Med. Ctr., Wilford Hall, Tex., 1985; mem. rev. com. NIH Guide for the Care and Use of Lab. Animals, NRC, NAS, 1993-96; advisor/tutor Med. Quality Assurance Commn., Dept. Health, State of Wash., 1994—; adj. prof. bioethics Sch. Medicine, U. So. Calif., 1989-91, prof. emeritus, 1991—. Author: Inquiry Into Faith, 1960; co-editor: Readings in Religious Philosophy; The Reverent Skeptic, 1979. Served as lt. (j.g.) USNR, 1945-47; to lt. 1952-54. Recipient award for excellence in tchg. U. So. Calif., 1960, 74, Dart award for acad. innovation, 1970, Raubenheimer Disting. Faculty award divsn. humanities, 1980, Outstanding Faculty award Student Senate, 1981, Disting. Emeritus award, 1995; Robert Fenton Craig award Blue Key, 1980. Fellow Soc. for Values in Higher Edn.; mem. Am. Acad. Religion (v.p. 1966, pres. 1967), Am. Philos. Assn., AAUP (v.p. Calif. Conf. 1977, pres. 1978-79), Phi Beta Kappa (hon.), Phi Kappa Phi, Phi Chi Phi. United Methodist. Home: 8001 Sand Point Way NE Apt C35 Seattle WA 98115-6356

ROBB, LYNDA JOHNSON, writer; b. Washington, Mar. 19, 1944; d. Lyndon Baines and Claudia Alta (Taylor) Johnson; m. Charles Spittal Robb, Dec. 9, 1967; children: Lucinda Desha, Catherine Lewis, Jennifer Wickliffe. BA with honors, U. Tex., 1966. Writer, McCall's mag., 1966-68; contbg. editor Ladies Home Jour., 1968-80; lectr. bd. dirs. Reading Is Fundamental, 1968—, Lyndon B. Johnson Family Found., 1969-95; nat. chair Reading is Fundamental, 1996. past mem. Va. State Coun. on Infant Mortality, Va. Maternal & Child Health Coun.; mem. Nat. Commn. to Prevent Infant Mortality, 1987-93; chmn. Pres.'s Adv. Com. for Women, 1979-81; chmn. bd. dirs. Nat. Home Libr. Found., Ford Theatre; chmn. Va. Women's Cultural History Project, 1982-85. Mem. Nat. Wildflower Rsch. Ctr. (bd. dirs.), Zeta Tau Alpha. Democrat. Episcopalian.

ROBB, NATHANIEL HEYWARD, JR., remote sensing company executive; b. Columbia, S.C., Sept. 10, 1942; s. Nathaniel Heyward Robb and Dorothy Claiborne (Cabell) Dortch; m. Louise Taber Rivers, Sept. 26, 1964; children: Elizabeth T., Nathaniel Heyward III, Catherine Pease. BSBA, The Citadel, 1964; grad. Realtors Inst., U. N.C., 1972; grad., Command and Gen. Staff Coll. Pres. Robb Realty, Raleigh, N.C., 1972-95; adj. gen. State of N.C., 1989-93; dep. comdr. in chief U.S. Atlantic Command, 1993-96; v.p. Ariel Images, Inc. and Spin-2 Digital Imagery, Raleigh, N.C., 1996—; exec. sec. Gov.'s Adv. Commn. Mil. Affairs, 1985-89; mem. Raleigh Bd. Realtors, 1975-85; dir. state property office N.C. Dept. Adminstrn., 1975-77; pres., founding mem. Raleigh Comml. Listing Svc., 1975-85; asst. sec. N.C. Dept. Crime Crontrol and Safety, Raleigh, 1985-89; bd. dirs. Aerial Images, Inc., Raleigh. Dir. Mordecai Sq. Hist. Soc.; mem. Raleigh Hist. Dists. Commn., 1973-78; dir., v.p. Raleigh Hist. Properties Commn., 1973-78; mem. Gov.'s Mgmt. Coun., Raleigh, 1985-89, Gov.'s Waste Mgmt. Bd., 1985-89; mem. Gov.'s Drug Cabinet, 1988-89; mem. Nat. Rep. Com., 1970—. Maj. gen. inf., U.S. Army N.G., 1964-70, Vietnam; N.C. N.G., 1970-96. Decorated D.S.M., N.C. D.S.M. with one device, Legion of Merit, Bronze Star with v device and one oak leaf cluster, Meritorious Svc. medal; Nat. Def. medal with star, USAR Components Achievement medal with four oak leaf clusters; Republic Vietnam Cross of Gallantry with bronze and silver stars and palm, other mil. awards; recipient Disting. Milit. Grad. award The Citadel, Humanitarian Svc. medal, Legion de Lafayette of Hist. Socs. of Militia and N.G. Mem. N.G. Assn. U.S., N.C. N.G. Assn., 2500 Club. Episcopalian. Avocations: skiing, pistol shooting. Home: 2115 Banbury Rd Raleigh NC 27608-1123 Office: Aerial Images Inc 615 Hillsborough St Raleigh NC 27603-1731

ROBB, WALTER LEE, retired electric company executive, management company executive; b. Harrisburg, Pa., Apr. 25, 1928; s. George A. and Ruth (Scantlin) R.; m. Anne Gruver, Feb. 27, 1954; children: Richard, Steven, Lindsey. BS, Pa. State U., 1948; MS, U. Ill., 1950, PhD, 1951; DEng (hon.), Milw. Sch. Engring., 1994; Worcester Poly. Inst., 1988. With GE, 1951-93; mgr. R & D dept. silicone products GE, Waterford, N.Y., 1966-68; venture mgr. med. devel. ops. GE, Schenectady, N.Y., 1968-71; sr. v.p., group exec. med. sys. group GE, Milw., 1973-86; sr. v.p. corp. R & D GE, Schenectady, 1986-93; cons., pres. Vantage Mgmt., Schenectady, N.Y., 1993—; bd. dirs. Celgene Corp., Marquette Electronics, Inc., Cree Rsch., Inc., Mech. Tech., Inc.; chmn. Neopath, Inc. Recipient Nat. Tech. medal, 1993, Indsl. Rsch. Inst. medal, 1994. Mem. NAE. Achievements include patentee in field of membranes and gas separation; rsch. in permeable membranes, diagnostic imaging equipment. Home: 1358 Ruffner Rd Niskayuna NY 12309-2500 Office: Vantage Mgmt 3000 Troy-Schenectady Rd Schenectady NY 12309

ROBBEN, MARY MARGARET, portrait artist; b. Bethesda, Md., Oct. 30, 1948; d. John Otto and Mary Margaret (McConnaughy) R. Student, Ohio U., 1967-71; B.Visual Art, Ga. State U., 1984. Visual merchandising staff Macy's Dept. Store, Union City, Ga., 1985-86; embroidery designer So. Promotions, Peachtree City, Ga., 1987-90; portrait artist Personal Touch Portraits, Peachtree City, Ga., 1991-95, Margy's Portraiture, Peachtree City, 1996—. Mortar Bd. scholar, 1984. Fellow Internat. Biographical Ctr. (life); mem. AAUW, Internat. Platform Assn., Ga. State U. Alumni Assn., Golden Key, Am. Bus. Women's Assn., Nat. Mus. of Women in the Arts. Avocations: cooking, gardening, reading. Home and Office: 207 Battery Way Peachtree City GA 30269-2126

ROBBINS, ALLEN BISHOP, physics educator; b. New Brunswick, N.J., Mar. 31, 1930; s. William Rei and Helen Grace (Bishop) R.; m. Shirley Mae Gernert, June 14, 1952 (div. 1978); children: Catherine Jean, Marilyn Elizabeth, Carol Ann, Melanie Barbara; m. Alice Harriet Ayars, Jan. 1, 1979. Student, Oberlin Coll., 1948-49; B.S., Rutgers U., 1952; M.S., Yale U., 1953, Ph.D., 1956. Research fellow U. Birmingham (Eng.), 1957-58, lectr., 1960-61; instr. physics Rutgers U., New Brunswick, N.J., 1956-57; asst. prof. physics Rutgers U., 1957-60, assoc. prof., 1960-68, prof., 1968—, chmn. dept. physics and astronomy, 1979-95. Contbr. articles on nuclear physics to profl. jours. Recipient Lindbach Christian and Mary F. Lindbach Found., Rutgers U., 1975. Fellow Am. Phys. Soc.; mem. Am. Assn. Physics Tchrs., AAAS, Phi Beta Kappa, Sigma Xi. Office: Rutgers U Dept Physics & Astronomy PO Box 849 Piscataway NJ 08855-0849

ROBBINS, ANNE FRANCIS See REAGAN, NANCY DAVIS

ROBBINS, BRENDA SUE, early childhood educator; b. Langdale, Ala., June 28, 1950; d. Richard Cecil and Audrey Millicent (Smallwood) R. Student, Mich. State U., 1968-72; BS in Edn., Auburn U., 1974, MS in Edn., 1977. Title 1 reading, math tchr. Muscogee Co. Sch. Dist., Columbus, Ga., 1977-78, fed. preschool tchr., 1978-80, tchr. grade 1, 1980-81, 1984-85, tchr. kindergarten, 1981-84, 1985—; staff devel. instr. Muscogee County Sch. Dist., Columbus, Ga., 1994; presenter in field. Mem. Georgia Assn. Educators, Nat. Edn. Assn. Avocations: snorkeling, whitewater rafting, traveling, reading. Office: Saint Marys Elem Sch 4408 Saint Marys Rd Columbus GA 31907-6286

ROBBINS, CHANDLER S(EYMOUR), research biologist; b. Belmont, Mass., July 17, 1918; s. Samuel Dowse and Rosa Margaret (Seymour) R.; AB, Harvard U., 1940; MS, George Washington U., 1950, ScD (hon.), U. Md., 1995; m. Eleanor Graham Cooley, Apr. 16, 1948; children: Jane S., Stuart B., George C., Nancy E. Wildlife rsch. biologist U.S. Fish and Wildlife Svc., U.S. Geol. Survey, Patuxent Wildlife Rsch. Ctr., Laurel, Md., 1945—; bd. dirs. Hawk Mountain Sanctuary Assn. Recipient Arthur A. Allen award Cornell Lab. Ornithology, 1979; Paul Bartsch award Audubon Naturalist Soc., 1979; Disting. Service award U.S. Dept. Interior, 1979, 87; Ludlow Griscom award Am. Birding Assn., 1984; Eugene Eisenmann medal Linnaean Soc. N.Y., 1987, Chuck Yeager award Nat. Fish and Wildlife Found., 1990. Fellow Am. Ornithologists' Union; mem. Am. Meteorol. Soc., Assn. Field Ornithologists, Wilson Ornithol. Soc., Cooper Ornithol. Soc., Brit. Trust for Ornithology, Nature Conservancy, Democrat. Author: Birds of North America, 1966; co-author: Birds of Maryland and the District of Columbia, 1958. Editor: Maryland Birdlife, 1947—; tech. editor Audubon Field Notes/American Birds, 1954-89, sr. editor Atlas of the Breeding Birds of Maryland and the District of Columbia, 1996. Home: 7900 Brooklyn Bridge Rd Laurel MD 20707-2822 Office: Patuxent Wildlife Research Ctr Laurel MD 20708-4015

ROBBINS, CONRAD W., naval architect; b. N.Y.C., Oct. 11, 1921; s. Girard David and Ethyl Rae (Bergman) R.; m. Danae Gray McCartney, Jan. 8, 1923 (dec. Jan. 1971); children: Lorraine, Linton, Jennifer; m. Melissa Jahn, Apr. 15, 1971 (dec. Mar. 1992). BSE, U. Mich., 1942. Estimator Pacific Electric Co., Seattle, 1946-47; pres. Straus-Duparquet, Lyons-Alpha, Albert Pick, N.Y.C. and Chgo., 1947-67, C.W. Robbins, Inc., Carefree, Ariz., 1967—; cons. in field. Capt. floating drydock USN, 1942-46. Avocations: travel, gardening, gourmet cooking. Home: 4401 E Mountainview Rd Phoenix AZ 85028 Office: CW Robbins Inc 7500 Stevens Rd Carefree AZ 85377

ROBBINS, CORNELIUS (VAN VORSE), education administration educator; b. Wilmington, Del., Nov. 2, 1931; s. Cornelius V. and Irene (Tatman) R.; m. Janet Porter, Aug. 1953; children: Eva Robbins Burke, Susan Robbins, Laurel Robbins, Melissa Robbins Beegle. B.A. in Polit. Sci, U. Del., 1953, M.Ed. in Social Scis, 1961; Ed.D. in Ednl. Adminstrn, U. Pa., 1964. Mem. faculty U. Del., 1957-58; tchr. Marshallton (Del.) Sch. Dist., 1958-60, Mt. Pleasant (Del.) Sch. Dist., 1960-62; asst. to dir. sch. study councils U. Pa., 1962-64; dean instrn. Ocean County Coll., 1965-67; dean of coll. Community Coll. of Delaware County, Pa., 1967-69; sr. assoc., coll. div. dir. McManis Assocs., Washington, 1969-70; pres. Genesee Community Coll., 1970-75; assoc. chancellor for community colls. SUNY, 1975-85; acting pres. Potsdam State Coll. (N.Y.), 1982-83; pres. Cobleskill (N.Y.) Coll. Agr. & Tech., 1985-92; prof. edn. adminstrn. SUNY, Albany, N.Y., 1992—; cons. Middle States Assn. Colls.; area liaison officer U.S. Mil. Acad., 1971-75; chmn. SUNY West Pres.'s Council and mem. Chancellor's Council, 1973-91. Contbr. articles to profl. publs. Served with U.S. Army, 1954-56. Recipient Outstanding Educator's award N.Y. State Assn. Jr. Colls., 1975, Disting. Svc. award Faculty Coun. Community Colls., 1988. Mem. Am. Assn. Higher Edn., State Dirs. of Community Colls. Assn., Phi Delta Kappa. Office: SUNY Albany ED329 Albany NY 12222

ROBBINS, DARRYL ANDREW, pediatrician; b. Modesto, Calif., Sept. 16, 1945; s. Jerome and Grace (Bass) R.; m. Harriette Lee Eisenberg, June 12, 1971; children: Jennifer Lynn, Julie Ellen, Allison Beth. BS, Dickinson Coll., 1967; DO, Phila. Coll. Osteo. Medicine, 1971. Diplomate Am. Bd. Pediatrics. Intern Doctor's Hosp., Columbus, Ohio, 1971-72; resident in pediatrics Children's Hosp. Med. Ctr., Cin., 1972-75; practice medicine specializing in pediatrics Columbus, 1975—; vice chairperson Diocesan Child Guidance Ctr., Columbus, 1986, bd. dirs., 1983-88; mem. genetics svcs. adv. com. Ohio Dept. Health, 1978-86; pres. med. staff Columbus Children's Hosp., 1996. Recipient Samuel Dalinsky Meml. award for Outstanding Graduating Resident Cin. Children's Hosp., 1975; named Pediatrician of Yr., Columbus Children's Hosp., 1982, 90. Fellow Am. Acad. Pediatrics; mem. Cen. Ohio Pediatric Soc. (pres. elect 1988, pres. 1989-90). Jewish. Home: 953 Old Farm Rd Columbus OH 43213-2674 Office: 3341 E Livingston Ave Columbus OH 43227-1949

ROBBINS, DONALD KENNETH, real estate investment advisor, consultant; b. Portland, Oreg., Sept. 21, 1928; s. Joseph and Anna Mae (Dexter) R.; m. Helen Virginia Holder (div. 1974); children: Beverly, Roland, Sandra, Debra, Roxanne; m. Barbara Ann Rabel, Mar. 10, 1976; children: Gia, Lisa. BS in Engring., U.S.. Naval Acad., 1950; AA in Real Estate, Mt. Hood C.C., Gresham, Oreg., 1968. Cert. real estate cons., review appraiser, mortgage underwriter. Enlisted USN, 1945, commn. ensign, 1950, advanced through grades to lt. (j.g.), 1953, resigned, 1955; founder Realty Exch., Portland, 1955—; real estate broker Realty Exch., Portland, 1970-86; registered rep. Omega Securities, Portland, 1973; registered prin. Real Estate Securities Exch. Co., Portland, 1983; exec. dir. Better Housing Trustcorp, Portland, 1988-93; cons. in field; bd. dirs. Realty Factors, Inc., REO Properties, Ltd., Estate Liquidators, Inc., Realty Remodeling Contractors Inc., Realty Trustcorp, USA Bldg. Maintenance Systems Corp., Project 2000, Eagles' Co., Eagles Net. Com., Inc., C-Lee, Inc., ATV Technologies, Genesis Group, LLC; exec. mgr. Eagles' Investment Club, LLC, Portland, 1994—, ATM Ventures, LLC, 1996—, C-Lee Mfg. Inc., 1997—, Opportunity Place, LLC, 1997—, Money Place, LLC, 1997—; State of Oreg. System of Higher Edn. accredited instr. U. Oreg., Eugene. Author, editor (newsletter) Investors' Clinic, 1970—; author DPP Study Outline (NASD), 1980; editor (newsletter) Eagles' Edge, 1995—; editor, pub. (electronic mag.) Eagles Network, 1995—; contbr. articles to Update newsletter, 1980-82. Mem. legis. coun. Oreg. Assn. Realtors, Salem, 1982-85; bd. dirs. Oreg. Housing Now!, Portland, 1990-92, Third Sector, Portland, 1991-92; regional v.p. for 5 Western states Real Estate Securities and Syndication Inst. of the Nat. Assn. Realtors, Chgo., 1981. Mem. Nat. Assn. Securities Dealers, Oreg. Mortgage Brokers Assn., Royal Rosarians of Portland, Oreg., Eagles' Network. Home and Office: 10285 NW Flotoma Dr Portland OR 97229-6218

ROBBINS, DOROTHY ANN, foreign language educator; b. Little Rock, Mar. 17, 1947; d. W.E. and Ina (Spencer) R. BA in Sociology, U. Ark., 1971; MS, U. Heidelberg, Germany, 1975; PhD, U. Frankfurt, Germany, 1981; postgrad., U. Hamburg, Germany, 1994—. Cert. state translator, Germany. Lectr. U. Heidelberg, 1977; head English dept. European Bus. Sch., Germany, 1978-80; dir. Inst. German Studies, Minn., 1985-87; asst. prof., then assoc. prof. fgn. lang. Ctrl. Mo. State U., Warrensburg, 1988—; Am. liaison Tolstoy Inst. Fgn. Langs., Moscow. Contbr. articles to profl. publs. Mem. Am. Assn. Applied Linguistics, Deutsch als Fremdsprache, Phi Beta Delta (pres. 1994-95). Avocations: travel to Russia, Russian language and literature, writing prose, trips to the sea, candlelight meals. Office: Ctrl Mo State U Martin 236 Warrensburg MO 64093

ROBBINS, EARL L., oil operator; b. Detroit, Mar. 9, 1921; s. Louis and Ida Robbins; m. Dorothy D. Robbins, Nov. 12, 1949 (div. Mar. 1974); children—T. Paul, Louis J., Loralee. BA, Wayne State U., 1949; MBA, U. Chgo., 1951. Owner, Enurtone of Tex., Houston, 1951-55; v.p. Continental Securities Co., Houston, 1955-57; owner, mgr. Robbins & Co., Houston, 1957-59; div. mgr. Great Books, Houston, 1960-96; owner, mgr. Robbins Oil Co., Houston, 1996—; exec. v.p. Solar Contractors, Inc.; CEO Wealth Co. Bus. Cons. Bd. dirs. Cancer League, Houston, 1983-84, Children's Resource and Info. Soc.; chmn. Alley Theater Gala, Houston, 1983; life mem. Houston Livestock Show, 1978-81; chmn. Cheesecake Hall of Fame. Served to maj. USAAF, 1941-46. Decorated Air medal; recipient Disting. Service award Am. Diabetes Assn., Houston, 1982. Mem. Associated Builders and Contractors Greater Houston (membership dir.), Wealth Corp. Sales and Bus. Conss. Office: Robbins Oil Co PO Box 35322 Houston TX 77235-5322

ROBBINS, ELIZABETH, stained glass artist, designer; b. N.Y.C., Dec. 17, 1941; d. Victor Ganales and Sylvia Sherrie (Woolf) R.; m. Jarvis Myers; children: Lorraine, Benjamin. BS in Art Edn., So. Conn. State Coll.; attended, Yale U., Cooper Union, N.Y.C., Silvermine (Conn.) Guild, Betzalel Art Sch., Jerusalem, Israel, Victoria & Albert Mus., London, Northeastern U., Boston, Wolverhampton (Eng.) Coll. Staff graphic layout and design Jarrett Press, N.Y.C., 1960-63; owner, operator Unique Boutique, Jerusalem, Israel, 1964-66; mem. staff, trainer Isratypeset, Jerusalem, 1967-72; costume designer MGM, Israel, 1967-72; graphic designer Time-Life Book Divsn., Amsterdam, Holland, 1973; originator, operator The Darkroom, Cambridge, Mass., 1976-82; owner, operator Elizabeth Robbins Studios, 1982-96. Gallery showings include Hartford (Conn.) Courant Art Competition, 1956-59 (Best in Show award (sculpture) 1957, 2d Place award (painting) 1958, (sculpture) 1959, 3d Place award (sculpture) 1956), So. Conn. State Coll., New Haven, 1965, Yale, New Haven Group Show, 1965, Betzalel, Israel Group Show, 1970, Amalgamated Gallery, N.Y.C., 1984, Art on the Green, Newton, Mass., 1982-86, Abrams Gallery, Cambridge, Mass., 1987, Corning (N.Y.) Show, 1988, Metro Show, Washington D.C., 1988 (Hon. Mention), Goldmine Gallery, Manchester, Vt., 1988, Catamount Gallery, St. Johnsbury, Vt., 1989, New England Art Glass Show, Derby Line, Vt., 1990-93, Pitts., The Orchid As Art, 1992, 94, Ventura, Calif. Group Show, 1992, 94, San Francisco Harvest Show, Calif. 1993, 95; represented in various pub. collections, including Amchad/Assn. for Hollocaust Survivors, Ramat Gan, Israel, Cobleigh Libr., Lyndonville, Vt., No. Vt. Regional Hosp., St. Johnsbury, Vt.; represented in numerous pvt. collections. Mem. Stained Glass Assn. Am., Vt. Coun. on the Arts, Vt. Handcrafters. Home: PO Box 1001 Lyndonville VT 05851-1001 Office: Elizabeth Robbins Studio Vail Circle Lyndonville VT 05851

ROBBINS, FRANCES ELAINE, educational administrator; b. Prescott, Mich., Oct. 27, 1928; d. Arlington Clifford and Anna Maria (Melrose) Osborne; m. Robert Allen Robbins, July 29, 1950 (dec. Feb. 1992); children: Gloria Jean, Reginald David, Eric Lynn. Student, Cen. Mich. U., 1948; BS, No. Mich. U., 1967, MA, 1974. Cert. elem. tchr., prin., Mich. Tchr. kindergarten Rose City (Mich.) Elem. Sch., 1948-51; tchr. Rudyard (Mich.) Elem. Sch., 1961-62, Pickford (Mich.) Elem. Sch., 1962-64, Skandia (Mich.) Elem. Sch., 1964-66; tchr. kindergarten Brimley (Mich.) Elem. Sch., 1966-69, tchr., coord., 1969-70, prin., 1970-95; mem. Ea. Upper Peninsula Substance Abuse Adv. Bd., Sault Ste. Marie, Mich., 1975-77; owner Robbins Refinishing and Repair, Brimley, 1985-95; adj. prof. Mich. State U., 1997—. Dir. choir, Sunday sch. tchr. Brimley Congl. Ch., 1970—; vol. Superior Twp. Ambulance Corp., Brimley, 1972-91. Recipient Celebrate Literacy award Internat. Reading Assn., 1986. Mem. NAESP, MARSP (life), Mich. Elem. and Mid. Sch. Prins. Assn., Ea. Upper Peninsula Reading Assn., Ea. Upper Peninsula Elem. Prins. Assn. (pres. 1990-91), Brimley Hist. Soc., Delta Kappa Gamma (state rec. sec. 1989-91, Woman of Distinction award Alpha Tau chpt. 1988), Chippewa Mackinaw Area Ret. Sch. Pers. Avocations: knitting, travel, grandchildren.

ROBBINS, FRANK EDWARD, lawyer; b. Hamilton, Ont., Can., Nov. 25, 1924; came to U.S., 1938; s. Frank E. and Mary Swann (Boyd) R.; m. Beatrice Noback, Dec. 20, 1944; children: R. Bruce (dec.) Mary E. Robbins Collina, B. Joanne Robbins Hicken, Frank E. Jr., Jacqueline, John C., George R. B Chem. Engring., Rensselaer Poly. Inst., 1944; JD, George Washington U., 1953. Bar: D.C. 1953, U.S. Ct. Appeals (fed. cir.) 1982, N.Y. 1958, Ill. 1968. Ptnr. Beale & Jones, Washington, 1953-56; pvt. practice, Rochester, N.Y., 1956-60; gen. counsel Photostat div. Itek Corp., Rochester, 1960-63; dir. patents and licensing Kennecott Corp., N.Y.C., 1963-66; patent and trademark counsel CPC Internat., Inc., N.Y.C., 1966-76; assoc. Irons & Sears, Washington, 1976-79, ptnr., 1979-81; sr. ptnr. Robbins & Laramie, Washington, 1981-90; ptnr. Venable, Baetjer, Howard & Civiletti, Washington, 1990-94; sr. of counsel Roylance, Abrams, Berdo & Goodman, Washington, 1994—. Author: The Defense of Prior Invention, 1977; author, editor: Candor in Prosecution, 1985. Treas. Quaint Acres Civic Assn., Silver Spring, Md., 1984-89. Lt. (j.g.) USNR, 1944-47. Mem. ABA, Am. Arbitration Assn., Assn. Corp. Patent Counsel, Am. Intellectual Property Law Assn., Md. Patent Law Assn. (past pres., bd. govs. 1985—), D.C. Bar Assn., Assn. Bar D.C. Democrat. Unitarian. Avocation: gardening. Office: Roylance Abrams Berdo & Goodman 1225 Connecticut Ave NW Washington DC 20036-2604

ROBBINS, FREDERICK CHAPMAN, physician, medical school dean emeritus; b. Auburn, Ala., Aug. 25, 1916; s. William J. and Christine (Chapman) R.; m. Alice Havemeyer Northrop, June 19, 1948; children: Alice, Louise. AB, U. Mo., 1936, BS, 1938; MD, Harvard U., 1940; DSc (hon.), John Carroll U., 1955, U. Mo., 1958, U. N.C., 1979, Tufts U., 1983, Med. Coll. Ohio, 1983; LLD, U. N.Mex., 1968. Diplomate Am. Bd. Pediatrics. Intern Children's Hosp., Boston, 1941-42, resident, 1940-41, resident pediatrican, 1946-48; sr. fellow virus disease Nat. Rsch. Coun., 1948-50; staff rsch. div. infectious diseases Children's Hosp., Boston, 1948-50, assoc. physician, assoc. dir. isolation svc., asso. rsch. div. infectious diseases, 1950-52; instr., assoc. in pediatrics Harvard Med. Sch., 1950-52; dir. dept. pediatrics and contagious diseases Cleve. Met. Gen. Hosp., 1952-66; prof. pediatrics Case Western Res. U., 1950-80, dean Sch. Medicine, 1966-80, univ. prof., dean emeritus, 1980—, univ. prof. emeritus, 1987—; pres. Inst. Medicine, NAS, 1980-85; vis. scientist Donner Lab., U. Calif., 1963-64. Served as maj. AUS, 1942-46; chief virus and rickettsial disease sect. 15th Med. Gen. Lab. investigations infectious hepatitis, typhus fever and Q fever. Decorated Bronze Star, 1945; recipient 1st Mead Johnson prize application tissue culture methods to study of viral infections, 1953; co-recipient Nobel prize in physiology and medicine, 1954; Med. Mut. Honor Award for, 1969; Ohio Gov.'s award, 1971. Mem. Assn. Am. Med. Colls. (Abraham Flexner award 1987), Nat. Acad. Scis., Am. Acad. Arts and Scis., Am. Soc. Clin. Investigation (emeritus mem.), Am. Acad. Pediatrics, Soc. Pediatric Research (pres. 1961-62, emeritus mem.), Am. Pediatric Soc., Am. Philos. Soc., Phi Beta Kappa, Sigma Xi, Phi Gamma Delta. Office: Case Western Res U Sch Med 10900 Euclid Ave Cleveland OH 44106-1712*

ROBBINS, HAROLD, author; b. N.Y.C., May 21, 1916; m. Lillian Machnivitz (div.); m. Grace Palermo (div.); children: Caryn, Adreana; m. Jann Stapp. Student pub. schs., N.Y.C. In food factoring bus., until 1940; shipping clk. Universal Pictures, N.Y.C., 1940-46. Author: Never Love a Stranger, 1948, The Dream Merchants, 1949, A Stone for Danny Fisher, 1951, Never Leave Me, 1953, 79 Park Avenue, 1955, Stiletto, 1953, The Carpetbaggers, 1961, Where Love Has Gone, 1962, The Adventurers, 1966, The Inheritors, 1969, The Betsy, 1971, The Pirate, 1974, Lonely Lady, 1976, Dreams Die First, 1977, Memories of Another Day, 1979, Goodbye, Janette, 1981, Spellbinder, 1982, Descent for Xanadu, 1984, The Storyteller, 1985, The Piranhas, 1991, The Raiders, 1994, The Stallion, 1996, Tycoon, 1997. Office: McIntosh & Otis 310 Madison Ave New York NY 10017-6009 also: care Simon & Schuster 1230 6th Ave New York NY 10020-1513*

ROBBINS, HARVEY ARNOLD, textile company executive; b. N.Y.C., Apr. 29, 1922; s. Ira B. and Mildred (Lowy) R.; student U. Mich., 1940-42, Cornell U., 1943, Columbia U., 1945; m. Carolyn Edith Goldsmith, June 8, 1947; children—Margaret Ann (Mrs. Jay Jacobson), James Andrew. Vice pres. Silberstein-Goldsmith, N.Y.C., 1946-50, North Advt., Chgo., 1950-59; v.p. M. Lowenstein & Sons, Inc., N.Y.C., also pres. Wamsutta/Pacific Domestic div., 1959-69; pres. Burlington Domestics div. Burlington Industries, N.Y.C., 1969-73; v.p. United Mchts. & Mfrs., N.Y.C., 1973-78; v.p. PRF Corp., 1978-80; exec. v.p. Whisper Soft Mills, N.Y.C., 1980-84; dir. product devel. Springs Industries, N.Y.C., 1984-85, textile cons., 1985—. Bd. dirs. Ednl. Found. for Fashion Industries; corp. mem. Lesley Coll., Cambridge, Mass. Served with U.S. Army, 1942-45. Decorated Purple Heart, Combat Inf. badge. Mem. Am. Mgmt. Assn., Am. Arbitration Assn., Textile Distbrs. Assn. Club: U. Mich. Alumni. Home and Office: 35 Brook Rd Valley Stream NY 11581-2401

ROBBINS, HENRY ZANE, public relations and marketing executive; b. Winston-Salem, N.C., Jan. 17, 1930; s. Romulus Mayfield and Vera Ethel (Daniel) R.; m. Barbara Anne Brown, Jan. 19, 1955; children: Zane Scott, Jill Stewart, Gail Ruth. AB, U. N.C., 1952; student, Emory U., 1952. Reporter Atlanta Constn., 1952; exhibit specialist Gen. Electric Co., Schenectady, 1952; employee relations specialist Gen. Electric Co., Cin., 1955; editor Gen. Electric Co., Schenectady, 1955; account supr. Gen. Electric Co., Winston-Salem, 1956-58; group supr. Gen. Electric Co., Schenectady, 1958-60; v.p., gen. mgr. Burson-Marsteller, Pitts. and Chgo., 1960-70, sr. v.p., 1970; pres., chief exec. officer SL&H-Robbins Inc., Chgo., 1970-72; also dir.; pres., chief exec. officer Beveridge Kraus Robbins & Manning, Chgo., 1973-75; also dir.; pres., dir., chief exec. officer Beveridge and Robbins Inc., Chgo., 1975-77; pres., chief exec. officer Financial Advt. of Ill., Inc., Chgo.; mng. dir. Sports Mgmt. Group, Chgo., 1975-77; dir. communications Arthur Andersen & Co., Chgo. and Geneva, Switzerland, 1977-81; dir. mktg. support services Arthur Andersen & Co., Chgo. and Geneva, 1981-89, dir. mktg. and comms., 1989-91; mem. Worldwide Alpha Group, 1991-96, exec. dir. global 1000 program, 1995—; prin. Arthur Andersen & Co., 1980—; mem. journalism adv. com. Harper Coll.; pub. relations com. Chgo. Met. Crusade Mercy; mem. Nat. Task Force on Environment; cons. sec. Dept. Health, Edn. and Welfare, 1970; chmn. pub. relations com. Honor Am. Day Com., 1970. Author: Vision of Grandeur, 1988; contbr. articles to profl. jours. Counselor Council of Mojave, 1972-74; gen. chmn. Chgo. Children's Classic Golf Tournament, 1974-77; chmn. Chgo. fin. com. Am.'s Freedom Train, 1976; chmn. fund devel. com. Presbytery of Chgo., 1977-83, maj. mission fund, 1977-79; dist. commr. Boy Scouts Am., 1976-79, chmn. Wildcat dist., 1980-83; mem. exec. bd. N.E. Ill. council, 1980-85; mem. Republican Citizens Com. Ill., 1960-61, Allegheny County (Pa.) Rep. Com., 1962-65; Trustee Roycemore Sch., Evanston, 1971-74; trustee, v.p. devel. Child and Family Services Chgo.; bd. dirs. Fellowship of Christian Athletes, U. N.C. Alumni Ill., Stockbrokers Assn. Chgo. Served to 1st lt. AUS, 1952-54. Elected to N.C. Pub. Rels. Hall of Fame, 1994. Mem. Pub. Relations Soc. Am., Nat. Investor Relations Inst., Midwest Travel Writers Assn., Chgo. Ednl. TV Assn., Pub. Relations Counselors Roundtable, Am. Mgmt. Assn., Environ. Writers Assn. Am., Chgo. Assn. Commerce and Industry, Art Inst. Chgo., Univ. Club, Sunset Ridge Country Club, Chi Psi. Republican. Presbyterian. Home: 2759 Broadway Ave Evanston IL 60201-1556 Office: 33 W Monroe St Chicago IL 60603-5300

ROBBINS, HULDA DORNBLATT, artist, printmaker; b. Atlanta, Oct. 19, 1910; d. Adolph Benno and Lina (Rosenthal) Dornblatt. Student, Phila. Mus's. Sch. Indsl. Art, 1928-29, Prussian Acad., Berlin, 1929-31, Barnes Found., Merion, Pa., 1939. Poster designer and maker ITE Circuit Breaker Co. Inc., Phila., 1944; instr. serigraphy Nat. Serigraph Soc. Sch., N.Y.C., 1953-60; instr. creative painting Atlantic County Jewish Community Centers, Margate and Atlantic City, N.J., 1960-67; represented by WIlliam P. Carl, Fine Prints, Boston, The Picture Store, Boston. One-man shows, Lehigh U. Art Galleries, 1933, ACA Galleries, Phila., 1939, 8th St. Gallery, N.Y.C., 1941, Serigraph Gallery, N.Y.C., 1947, Atlantic City Art Center, 1961, 71, numerous group shows, 2d Nat. Print ann. Bklyn. Mus., Carnegie Inst., Library of Congress, LaNapoule Art Found., Am. Graphic Contemporary Art; represented in permanent collections, including, Met. Mus. Art, N.Y.C., Mus. Modern Art, N.Y.C., Bibliotheque Nationale, Smithsonian Instn., Art Mus. Ont., Can., Victoria and Albert Mus., London, U.S. embassies abroad, Lehigh U., Princeton (N.J.) Print Club. Recipient Purchase prize Prints for Children, Mus. Modern Art, N.Y.C., 1941; prize 2d Portrait of Am. Competition, 1945; 2d prize Paintings by Printmakers, 1948. Mem. Am. Color Print Soc., Print Club, Graphics Soc., Serigraph Soc. (mem. founding group, charter sec., Ninth Ann. prize 1948, 49). Home and Office: 16 S Buffalo Ave Ventnor City NJ 08406-2635 *To cherish and express living through devotion to art.*

ROBBINS, JAMES O., advertising executive. Pres., dir. Cablerep, Inc., Atlanta; CEO, pres. Cox Comm., Inc., Atlanta. Office: Cablerep Inc 1400 Lake Hearn Dr NE Atlanta GA 30319-1464*

ROBBINS, JANE BORSCH, library science educator, information science educator; b. Chgo., Sept. 13, 1939; d. Reuben August and Pearl Irene (Houk) Borsch; married; 1 child, Molly Warren. BA, Wells Coll., 1961; MLS, Western Mich. U., 1966; PhD, U. Md., 1972. Asst. prof. library and info. sci. U. Pitts., 1972-73; assoc. prof. Emory U., Atlanta, 1973-74; cons. to bd. Wyo. State Libr., 1974-77; assoc. prof. La. State U., Baton Rouge, 1977-79; dean La. State U. Sch. Library and Info. Sci., 1979-81; prof., dir. Sch. Library and Info. Studies U. Wis., Madison, 1981-94; dean, prof. Fla. State U. Sch. Info. Studies, Tallahassee, 1994—. Author: Public Library Policy and Citizen Participation, 1975, Public Librarianship: A Reader, 1982, Are We There Yet?, 1988, Libraries: Partners in Adult Literacy, 1990, Keeping the Books: Public Library Financial Practices, 1992, Balancing the Books: Financing American Public Library Services, 1993, Evaluating Library Programs and Services: A Manual and Sourcebook, 1994, Tell It! The Complete Manual of Library Evaluation, 1996; editor Libr. and Info. Sci. Rsch., 1982-92; contbr. articles to profl. jours. Mem. ALA (councilor 1976-80, 91-95), Am. Soc. Info. Sci., Assn. for Libr. and Info. Sci. Edn. (dir. 1979-81, pres. 1984), Wis. Libr. Assn. (pres. 1986), Fla. Libr. Assn. (bd. dirs. 1997—). Democrat. Episcopalian. Office: Fla State U Sch Info Studies Louis Shores Bldg Tallahassee FL 32306

ROBBINS, JEFFREY HOWARD, media consultant, research writer, educator; b. N.Y.C., Mar. 29, 1941; s. Stanley Samuel and Miriam (Cooper) R.; m. Marsha Sue Rimler, Nov. 3, 1984 (div. Dec. 1996); 1 child, Nina Camille. BSME, Carnegie Mellon U., 1962; MS in Physics, U. N.Mex., 1966, ABD in Physics, 1967; postgrad., U. Calif., Berkeley and L.A., 1963-64. Summer rsch. assoc. Linde Co., Tonawanda, N.Y., 1961; rsch. engr. N.Am. Aviation (Rockwell), Downey, Calif., 1962-64; summer rsch. assoc. Los Alamos (N.Mex.) Nat. Lab., 1965; sr. engr. Radio Engring. Labs., L.I., N.Y., 1968-70; engring. cons. PRD Electronics, Syosset, N.Y., 1972-73; sr. cons. Bendix Corp., Teterboro, N.J., 1974-76; sr. engr. Giordano Assocs., Franklin Lakes, N.J., 1977-81; sr. applications engr. Racal-Redak, Mahwah, N.J., 1981-83; tech. media cons. Allied Signal Corp., Teterboro, 1983-92, U.S. Army, Picatinny Arsenal, N.J., 1992, Ford Motor Co., Lansdale, Pa., 1992—; cons., rsch. writer media literacy programs Packer Collegiate Inst., Bklyn., N.Y.C., 1992-93, On TV, Inc., N.Y.C., 1992—; initiator, moderator Media Literacy Forum, 1995; evening sch. instr. New Sch. for Social Rsch., N.Y.C., 1979-85; presenter in field. Author: On Balance and Higher Education, 1970; contbr. articles to profl. jours. Organizer, co-moderator Future Impact of Artificial Intelligence, Robotics Forum, 1984. Recipient 1st prize for essay The World and I Mag., 1990; nominee Grawemeyer award in Edn., 1988; NDEA fellow, 1966-67, others; feature essay premier issue Plain mag., 1994. Mem. IEEE (presenter Internat. Symposium in Tech. and Soc. 1993, 96, Internat. Soc. Sys. Scis. Conf. 1993, 95, initiator, moderator, media literacy forum Packer Collegiate Inst. 1995), N.Y. Acad. Scis., Sigma Xi, Phi Kappa Phi, Pi Tau Sigma. Home: 133 E Penn St Long Beach NY 11561 Office: Cassiopeia Cons Inc PO Box 335 Long Beach NY 11561-0335

ROBBINS, JEROME, choreographer, director; b. N.Y.C., Oct. 11, 1918; s. Harry and Lena (Rips) R. Student, NYU, 1935-36, hon. degree, 1985; D.F.A. (hon.), Ohio U., 1975; studied ballet, modern, Spanish and Oriental dance.; hon. degree, CUNY, 1980. Mem. panel N.Y. Council on Arts, 1973-77, Nat. Council on Arts, Nat. Endowment for Arts, 1974-80; Ballet Theatre (N.Y.C.), 1940-44, soloist, 1941-44; choreographer N.Y.C. Ballet, 1944—, assoc. artistic dir., 1949-59, ballet master, 1969-83, co-ballet master-in-chief, 1983-89; dir., Ballet U.S.A., 1958-61, Jerome Robbins Chamber Dance Co., tour Peoples' Republic of China (sponsored by U.S. Internat. Communications Agency), 1981; ballets also in repertories of Am. Ballet Theatre, Joffrey Ballet, Royal Swedish Ballet, Batsheva Ballet, Royal Danish Ballet, Boston Ballet, Nat. Ballet of Canada, Harkness Ballet, Royal Winnipeg Ballet, London Ballet, Australian Ballet, San Francisco Ballet, Pennsylvania Ballet, Dance Theatre of Harlem, Paris Opera Ballet, Bayerischen Staatsoper (Munich), La Scala, Opernhaus (Surich), Finnish Ballet, Star Dancers Kinov Foundation. Debut as dancer Sandor-Sorel Dance Center, 1937; dancer Broadway musicals Great Lady, 1939, Straw Hat Review, 1939, Keep Off the Grass, 1940; dancer ballets Helen of Troy, 1942, Petrouchka, 1944, Three Virgins and a Devil, 1944, Romeo and Juliet, 1944, Concert Varieties, 1945, Summer Day, 1947, Facsimile, 1947, Bouree Fantasique, 1949, The Prodigal Son, 1950, The Age of Anxiety, 1950, The Pied Piper, 1951, Circus Polka, 1971, George Abbott...A Celebration, 1976; tours include Gypsy, 1959, 81, Fiddler on the Roof, 1964, 80, Peter Pan, 1981, Jerome Robbins Chamber Dance Company, 1981; ballets choreographed include Fancy Free, 1944, Interplay, 1945, Afterthought, 1946, Facsimile, 1946, Summer Day, 1947, Pas de Trois, 1948, The Guests, 1949, (with Balanchine) Jones Beach, 1950, Age of Anxiety, 1950, Pied Piper, 1951, The Cage, 1951, Ballade, 1952, Fanfare, 1953, Afternoon of a Faun, 1953, Wonderful Town, 1953, The Tender Land, 1954, Quartet, 1954, The Concert, 1956, N.Y. Export: Opus Jazz, 1958, Moves, 1959, Les Noces, 1965 (City of Paris award, Internat. Dance Festival 1971), 3X3, 1961, Events, 1961, (with Balanchine) Firebird, 1970, Dances at a Gathering, 1969, In the Night, 1970, The Goldberg Variations, 1971, Requiem Canticles, 1972, (with Balanchine) Dumbarton Oaks, 1972, (with Balanchine) Pulcinella, 1972, Watermill, 1972, Scherzo Fantastique, 1972, Circus Polka, 1972, Interplay, 1972, An Evening's Waltzes, 1973, Celebration: The Art of the Pas de Deux, 1973, Beethoven Pas de Deaux, 1973, Dybbuk Variations, 1974, Introduction & Allegro for Harp, 1975, Une Barque Sur L'Ocean, 1975, Concerto in G (later in G Major), 1975, Ma mere l'oye, 1975, Chansons Madecasses, 1975, Concert for the Royal Ballet, 1975, Introduction, 1975, Allegro For Harp, 1975, Mother Goose, 1975, Other Dances, 1976, A Sketchbook, 1978, (with Peter Martins and Jean-Pierre Bonnefous) Tricolore, 1978, The Dreamer, 1979, Le Bourgeois Gentilhomme, 1979, The Four Seasons, 1979, Opus 19: The Dreamer, 1979, Suite of Dances, 1980, Rondo, 1981, Andantino, 1981, Piano Pieces, 1981, (with Pulchinella 1972 and Firebird 1970) Allegro con Grazia, 1981, The Gershwin Concerto, 1982, Four Chamber Works, 1982, Glass Pieces, 1983, I'm Old Fashioned, 1983, Antique Epigraphs, 1984, (with Twyla Tharp) Brahms/Handel, 1984, Eight Lines, 1985, In Memory Of..., 1985, Quiet City, 1986, Piccolo Balletto, 1986, Ives, Songs, 1988, N.Y.C. Retrospective of Jerome Robbins' Ballets, 1989, (with Mikhail Baryshnikov) A Suite of Dances, 1994, 2+3 Part Inventions, 1994; choreographer of Broadway musicals Billion Dollar Baby (Donaldson award 1946), 1946, High Button Shoes (Tony award best choreographer 1948, New York Drama Critics' award 1948), 1947, Miss Liberty, 1949, The King and I, 1951 (Donaldson award 1951), Two's Company (Donaldson award 1952), 1952; dir. and choreographer stage musicals Look Ma, I'm Dancin', 1948, Call Me Madam, 1950, Peter Pan, 1954, Bells Are Ringing, 1956 (Tony award nomination best choreographer 1957), West Side Story, 1957 (Tony award best choreographer 1958, London Evening Standard Drama award 1958), Gypsy (Tony award nomination best director of musical 1960), 1959, Fiddler on the Roof (Drama Critics' Circle award best musical 1965, Tony award best choreographer 1965, Tony award best director of musical 1965), 1964, Jerome Robbins' Broadway (Tony award best director of musical 1989), 1989-90; dir. plays that include That's the Ticket, 1948, The Pajama Game (Donaldson award 1954), 1954, Oh Dad, Poor Dad, Mama's Hung You in the Closet and I'm Feelin So Sad, 1962; choreographer and creator On the Town, 1944; creator of The Small House of Uncle Thomas, 1951; dir. and producer (with Cheryl Crawford) Mother Courage and Her Children (Tony award nomination best play 1963, Tony award nomination best producer 1963), 1963; choreographer motion pictures The King and I (Box Office Blue Ribbon award 1956), 1956, West Side Story, 1960 (SBI Gold Owl award 1961, Outstanding Directorial Achievement award for feature films Directors Guild of Am. 1961, Academy award best director 1961, Laurel award Writer's Guild of Am. West 1961); TV credits include Ford 50th Anniversary Show (Sylvania award 1953), 1953, Peter Pan (Emmy award best choreographer 1955), 1955, 56, 60, Two Duets, 1980, Live from Studio 8H: An Evening of Jerome Robbins' Ballets, 1980. Decorated chevalier Order of Arts and Letters (France), comdr., 1964; chevalier Legion of Honor (France); Dance Magazine award for outstanding achievement 1950, 57, City of New York Citation, 1959, Hon. Award for Brilliant Achievements in the Art of Choreography on Film, Acad. Motion Picture Arts and Scis., 1961, Capezio Dance award, 1976, recipient Handel medallion N.Y.C., 1976, American-Israel Arts, Sciences, and Humanities award, 1979, Kennedy Ctr. honors, 1981, Brandeis U. Creative Arts award, 1984, Astaire Lifetime Achievement award, 1985, Nat. medal of Arts, 1988, H.C. Andersen Ballet Prize, Royal Danish Theatre, 1988, Drama Desk award, 1989, Commonwealth award of distinguished svc. in the dramatic arts, Bank of Delaware, 1990; named best choreographer Theatre des Nations, 1959. Mem. Am. Acad. and Inst. Arts and Letters (hon., Commonwealth award 1990, Commandeur de l'Ordre des Arts et des Lettres 1990), French Legion of Honor, 1993. Office: care NYC Ballet NY State Theater Lincoln Ctr Plz New York NY 10023*

ROBBINS, JERRY HAL, educational administration educator; b. DeQueen, Ark., Feb. 28, 1939; s. James Hal and Barbara I. (Rogers) R. B.A. in Math, Hendrix Coll., 1960; M.Ed., U. Ark., 1963, Ed.D., 1966. Tchr. math. and music Clinton (Ark.) pub. schs., 1960-61; prin. Adrian (Mo.) High Sch., 1961-63; exec. sec. Ark. Sch. Study Council, Fayetteville, 1963-65; mem. faculty U. Miss., University, 1965-74; prof. ednl. adminstrn. U. Miss., 1970-74, chmn. dept. ednl. adminstrn., 1970-74; dean Coll. Edn., U. Ark., Little Rock, 1974-79; asso. v.p. for acad. affairs Ga. State U., Atlanta, 1979-84, dean Coll. Edn., 1984-90, prof. ednl. adminstrn., 1990-91; dean. Coll. Edn. Ea. Mich. U., Ann Arbor, 1991—. Co-author: (with S. B. Williams Jr.) Student Activities in the Innovative School, 1969, School Custodian's Handbook, 1970, Administrator's Manual of School Plant Administration, 1970. Mem. NEA, Am. Assn. Sch. Adminstrs., Am. Assn. Colls. Tchr. Edn. (dir. 1979-82), Nat. Assn. Secondary Sch. Prins., So. Regional Council Ednl. Adminstrn. (pres. 1970-71), Phi Delta Kappa, Kappa Delta Pi (v.p. chpt. devel. 1978-80, pres. elect 1980-82, pres. 1982-84, past pres. 1984-86). Mem. United Meth. Ch. Home and Office: 3384 Bent Trail Ann Arbor MI 48108 Office: Ea Mich U Boone Hall Ypsilanti MI 48197

ROBBINS, JOHN BENNETT, medical researcher; b. Bklyn., Dec. 1, 1932. BA, NYU, 1956, MD, 1959; MD (hon.), U. Goteborg, Sweden, 1976. Intern, resident Children's Med. Svc. Mass. Gen. Hosp., Boston, 1959-60; rsch. fellow dept. pediatrics U. Fla., 1961-64; guest scientist dept. chem. immunology Weizmann Inst. Sci., Rehovot, Israel, 1965-66; asst. prof. pediatrics and microbiology U. Fla., Gainesville, 1964-67; from asst. prof. to assoc. prof. pediatrics Albert Einstein Coll. Medicine, 1967-70; clin. dir. Nat. Inst. Child Health and Human Devel. NIH, 1970-72; chief devel. immunology br. NIH, 1971-74; dir. divsn. bacterial products FDA, 1974-83; chief lab. devel. and molecular immunity Nat. Inst. Child Health and Human Devel. NIH, 1983—; Henry Bale Meml. lectr. Nat. Inst. Biol. Stds. and Control, 1979, Erwin Neter Meml. lectr. U. Buffalo, 1984, Henry L. Barnett lectr. Albert Einstein Coll. Medicine, 1985, Maxwell Finland lectr. Infectious Disease Soc. Am., 1989, Louis Weinstein lectr. Tufts U., 1989. Recipient E. Mead Johnson award Am. Acad. Pediatrics, 1975. Fellow Am. Acad. Microbiology; mem. Inst. Med.-Nat. Acad. Sci., Soc. Pediatric Rsch., Soc. Infectious Disease, Am. Soc. Clin. Investigation, Assn. Am. Physicians, Am. Assn. Immunologists, Nat. Inst. Medicine, Nat. Acad. Svc. Office: Nat Inst of Child Hlth & Hum Dev Developmental Molecular Imm Lab 31 Center Dr Bldg 31 Bethesda MD 20892-0001

ROBBINS, JOHN CLAPP, management consultant; b. Cleveland, Jan. 22, 1921; s. John Clapp and Esther Turner (Holland) R.; m. Louise Severance Nash, Jan. 10, 1951 (div. Oct. 1974); children: Anne Millikin, Julia Severance, John Nash; m. Beatrice Blair, Aug. 2, 1975 (dec. July 1994). A.B., Harvard U., 1942. Copy boy, reporter, writer, promotion editor Cleve. Press, 1946-57; exec. internat. div. Mobil Oil Corp., N.Y.C., Istanbul, 1957-70; chief exec. officer Planned Parenthood/World Population, N.Y.C., 1970-75; prin. mgmt. cons. Stanford Research Inst., 1976-83; v.p. GPA Inc., N.Y.C., 1983—; pres. John Robbins Assocs.; spl. fin. cons. Internat. Helsinki Fedn., Vienna. Author: Too Many Asians, 1959. Bd. dirs., pres. Am. Hosp.. Istanbul; treas. Sex Info. and Edn. Coun. U.S., Harvard Libr. in N.Y.C. Capt. AUS, 1942-45. Decorated Bronze Star, Purple Heart; Reid fellow, 1953. Mem. Internat. Planned Parenthood Fedn. London, N.Y. State Republican Family Com. Unitarian. Home: 115 E 9th St New York NY 10003-5414 Office: 98 Riverside Dr New York NY 10024-5323

ROBBINS, KAREN DIANE, editor; b. Bloomington, Ill., Nov. 25, 1959; d. Harley Edward and Geraldine Elayne (Abell) H; m. Craig Douglas Robbins, May 25, 1992. Cert. Office Adminstrn./Info. Processing, Riverside (Calif.) C.C., 1993, Cert. Graphics Tech., 1993. Temp. Olsten Temp. Svcs., Riverside, 1982-83; inventory auditor RGIS, San Bernardino, Calif., 1984; messenger The Hammond Co., Riverside, 1984-87; data collector grocery stores INFOMAX Retail Auditing Co., Chino, Calif., 1988-90; mktg. auditor RGIS Inventory Specialists, Riverside, Calif., 1988-91. Editor Rat and Mouse Tales, AFRMA Yearbook, Rulebook and Show Regulations/Standards book. Mem. Am. Fancy Rat and Mouse Assn. (founder). Home: PO Box 2589 Winnetka CA 91396-2589

ROBBINS, LANNY ARNOLD, chemical engineer; b. Wahoo, Nebr., Apr. 3, 1940; s. Earl Willard and Mildred Irene (Hanson) R.; m. Connie Lou Polich, Feb. 24, 1962; children: James Alan, Debra Renea. BS, Iowa State U., 1961, MS, 1963, PhD, 1966. Rsch. engr., project leader Dow Chem. Co., Midland, Mich., 1966-73, rsch. specialist, 1973-76, assoc. scientist, 1976-83, rsch. scientist, 1983-88, sr. rsch. scientist, 1988-97, rsch. fellow, 1997—; adj. prof. Va. Poly. Inst., Blacksburg, 1973-76, Mich. State U., Lansing, 1983; mem. indsl. adv. bd. Iowa State U., Ames, 1994—. Author (chpt.) Schweitzer's Handbook of Separation Techniques, 1979, Perry's Chemical Engineer's Handbook, 1984. Recipient H.H. Dow medal, 1993. Mem. AIChE. Republican. American Baptist. Achievements include patents for AquaDetox Aqueous Purification stripping devices and process, Sorbathene pressure swing adsorption vent emission control processes, liquid distributors for packed distillation. Avocations: genealogy rsch., maple syrup by mech. vapor recompression evaporation. Home: 4101 Old Pine Trl Midland MI 48642-8892 Office: Dow Chem Co 1319 Bldg Midland MI 48667

ROBBINS, LAWRENCE HARRY, anthropologist; b. Washington, Nov. 22, 1938; s. Maurice and Edith R.; m. Martha Ann Edwards, Dec. 16, 1967; children: Daniel, Brian, Michael, Mark. A.B., U. Mich., 1961, A.M., 1962; Ph.D., U. Calif., Berkeley, 1968. Asst. prof. U. Utah, 1967; mem. faculty Mich. State U., East Lansing, 1968—; prof. anthropology and African studies Mich. State U., 1977—, chairperson ANP dept., 1992-95; vis. research asso. U. Nairobi, Kenya, 1969-70, Nat. Mus. Kenya, 1975-76; Fulbright vis. prof. U. Botswana, 1982-83; vis. archaeologist Nat. Mus. and Art Gallery, Botswana, 1982-83. Author: Stones, Bones and Ancient Cities, 1990; contbr. articles to profl. jours. Grantee NSF, 1965-66, 69-70, 75-77, 91—, Nat. Geographic Soc., 1987, 89. Mem. Am. Anthropol. Assn., Soc. Africanist Archeologists in Am., So. African Archeol. Soc., Botswana Soc. Office: Dept Anthropology Mich State U East Lansing MI 48824

ROBBINS, MARION LERON, agricultural research executive; b. Inman, S.C., Aug. 18, 1941; s. Jack Dennis and Christina (Champion) R.; m. Margaret Elanor Wilson, Sept. 25, 1965 (wid. Feb. 1995); children: Jack, Rona, Jeff, Kyle; m. Jeanette Rogers Robbins, May 10, 1996. BS, Clemson U., 1964; MS, La. State U., 1966; PhD, U. Md., 1968. Asst. prof. Iowa State U., Ames, 1968-72; rsch. scientist Clemson U., Charleston, S.C., 1972-83; resident dir. Sweet Potato Rsch. Sta., Chase, La., 1984-88, Calhoun (La.) Rsch. Sta., 1988—; advisor Farm Bur., Monroe, La., 1988-90, Agribus. Coun., Monroe, 1988—. Editor Jour. Vegetable Crop Prodn., 1992—; assoc. editor Crop Prodn. jour., 1972-90; contbr. more than 200 articles, abstracts, rsch. papers and revs. to profl. and trade jours. Delegation leader People to People Internat., Spokane, Wash., 1985—. Mem. Am. Soc. for Hort. Sci. (dir., pres. so. region 1982-83), Rsch. Ctr. Adminstrs. Soc. (dir. 1985),

Calhoun Civic Club (pres. 1994-95) Rotary Club (pres. 1987-88), Exch. Club (pres. 1976-77). Presbyterian. Achievements include development of 22 varieties and genetic lines of crop plants, including 2 All-American winners and an All-Am. designate. Office: Calhoun Rsch Sta 321 Highway 80 E PO Box 539 Calhoun LA 71225-9703

ROBBINS, MARJORIE JEAN GILMARTIN, elementary education educator; b. Newton, Mass., Sept. 19, 1940; d. John and Helen (Arbuckle) Gilmartin; m. Maurice Edward Robbins, Aug. 1, 1962; children: John Scott, Gregory Dale, Kris Eric. BS in Edn., Gordon Coll., 1962; postgrad., U. Maine, Augusta, 1976, U. Maine, Orono, 1986, U. Maine, Portland, 1987. Cert. tchr. Tchr. Ctr. St. Sch., Hampton, N.H., 1962-64, Claflin Sch., Newton, 1965-66, Israel Loring Sch., Sudbury, Mass., 1966-67, Cheney Sch., Orange, Mass., 1967-69, Palermo (Maine) Consolidated Sch., 1975—; founder, tchr. Primary Edn. Program, Palmero, 1990—; dir., author Child Sexual Abuse Program, Palmero, 1988—; mem. Title I Com., 1995—, Health Curriculum Com., 1995—. Mem. bd. Christian edn. Winter St. Bapt. Ch., Gardiner, Maine, 1993—, mem. bd. missions, 1993-94; bd. dirs. Hillside Christian Nursery Sch., 1994—; coord. student assistance team Maine Sch. Union #51, 1993—, bd. dirs. United Team, 1993—, mem. publicity com., 1991-92; coord. Nursing Home Ministry, Gardiner. Mem. NEA, Maine Tchrs. Assn., Palermo Tchrs. Assn. (pres. 1984-86), Maine Educators of the Gifted and Talented, Maine Sch. Union 51 (sec. certification steerin g com. 1988—, rep. gifted-talented com. 1976—), Palermo Sch. Club (exec. bd. 19 85-88. Avocations: travel, swimming, camping, basketball. Home: 204 Dresden Ave Gardiner ME 04345-2618 Office: Palermo Consolidated Sch RR 3 Palermo ME 04354

ROBBINS, N. CLAY, foundation administrator; b. Indpls., May 30, 1957; m. Amy Robbins; 3 children. BA, Wabash Coll., Crawfordsville, Ind., 1979; JD, Vanderbilt U., 1982. Exch. assoc. European Econ. Cmty. law dept. Rycken Burlion Bolle & Houben, Brussels, 1985-86; assoc. Baker & Daniels, 1982-85, ptnr., 1985-93; v.p. cmty. devel. Lilly Endowment Inc., Indpls., 1993-94, pres., 1994—; mem. bd. Nat. City Bank, Ind.; mem. draftin com. Ind. Nonprofit Corp. Act 1991. Past dir., pres. Indpls. Chamber Orch.; past dir. Greater Indpls. Progress Com., Damar Homes, Inc.; mem. bd. Corp. Cmty. Coun.; vice chmn. policy planning exec. com. United Way Ctrl. Ind., chair strategic planning com. Mem. ABA, Ind. State Bar Assn., Indpls. Bar assn. (chair internat. law sect. 1987-88), Indpls. C. of C. Methodist. Office: Lilly Endowment Inc 2801 N Meridian St PO Box 88068 Indianapolis IN 46208

ROBBINS, NANCY LOUISE See **MANN, NANCY LOUISE**

ROBBINS, OREM OLFORD, insurance company executive; b. Mpls., Feb. 5, 1915; s. Douglas Ford and Grace (Rorem) R.; m. Annette Strand Scherer, May 17, 1992; children: Ford M., Ross S., Gail R. Tomei, Cynthia R. Rothbard. BBA with distinction, U. Minn., 1936; BS in Law, William Mitchell Coll. Law, 1946, JD, 1948. Comml. rep. NW Bell Telephone Co., Mpls., 1936-48; dep. dir. U.S. Treas. Dept., Mpls., 1948-49; sales rep. Conn. Gen. Life Ins. Co., Mpls., 1949-56; founder, chmn. Security Life Ins. Co. Am., Mpls., 1956—. Bd. dirs., past pres. Family and Children's Svcs., Mpls., 1968—; bd. govs., past chmn. Meth. Hosp., Mpls., 1960-90; past treas., bd. dirs. Goodwill/Easter Seals, St. Paul, 1958-68, 75-88; life trustee Hamline U., St. Paul, 1979—, chmn. bd. trustees, 1990-91. Col. U.S. Army, 1941-46. Decorated Legion of Merit. Fellow Life Mgmt. Assn.; mem. Am. Soc. CLU (pres. Mpls. chpt. 1959), Health Underwriters Assn., Chartered Fin. Cons., Am. Legion, Skylight Club (Mpls.), Hole in the Wall Golf Club, Naples Yacht Club, Masons. Republican. Methodist. Office: Security Life Ins Co Am 10901 Red Circle Dr Minnetonka MN 55343-9304

ROBBINS, RAY CHARLES, manufacturing company executive; b. Syracuse, N.Y., Sept. 15, 1920; s. Frederick and Mary Elizabeth (Field) R.; children: Sandra Robbins Jannetta, Ray Charles Jr., Eric L. With Lennox Internat. Inc. (formerly Lennox Furnace Co.), 1940-48; asst sales mgr. Lennox Industries Inc. (formerly Lennox Furnace Co.), Syracuse, 1948-52; gen. mgr. new factory and sales office, Lennox Industries, Inc. (formerly Lennox Furnace Co.), Toronto, Ont., Can., 1952-67; dir. Lennox Can. and Timeplan Fin. Co. Ltd., 1953-65; pres. Lennox Can., 1965-69; exec. v.p. Lennox-Worldwide, 1969-70, pres., CEO, 1970-77; chmn. bd. Lennox Can., 1976-92; chmn. bd., chief exec. officer Lennox Industries Inc., 1977-80, chmn. bd., 1980-91, chmn. emeritus, 1991—; bd. dirs. Lennox Internat., First Interstate of Iowa, Inc., Hawkeye Security Ins. Co., Des Moines, Fin. Security Group, Inc., Des Moines, Q-Dot, Garland, Tex.; pres., founder, bd. dirs. Exec. Inst., Inc., Dallas, 1983—; bd. advisor Internat. Exec. Svc. Corp., 1993—. Bd. dirs. Metro Toronto Big Bros., 1964-69, Queensway Gen. Hosp., 1957-69, Texx Found., 1979-81, Bus. Industry Polit. Action Com.; bd. govs., mem. exec. com. Iowa Coll. Found., 1975-78; v.p., mem. exec. bd. Mid-Iowa County Boy Scouts Am., 1972-78; mem. Pres.' Phys. Fitness Council, from 1979; exec. bd. Circle 10 council Boy Scouts Am., from 1979; mem. Dallas Citizens Council; bd. of govs. Nat. Women's Econ. Alliance Found.; bd. dirs. North Tex. Commn. Served with AUS, 1942-45, PTO. Mem. ASHRAE (life), Am. Refrigeration Inst. (bd. dirs. 1973-74, 78, life from 1979, v.p. 1975-76, chmn. 1977), NAM (bd. dirs. 1974-75, dir. at large 1976, dir. State of Iowa 1977-78, dir. State of Tex. 1979-92), Nat. Mgmt. Assn. (exec. adv. com. 1979-92), Gas Appliance Mfrs. Assn. (past bd. dirs.), Can. Gas Assn. (pres.), Can. Mfg. Assn. (chmn. Toronto dist.), U.S. C. of C. (Can.-U.S. sect.), Bus.-Industry Polit. Action Com. (bd. dirs. 1991), Internat. Exec. Svc. Corps (bd. advs. 1993). Clubs: Park Cen., Landmark Athletic, Aerobics Activity Ctr. (Dallas); Canyon Creek Country (Richardson, Tex.). Office: Lennox Internat Inc PO Box 799900 Dallas TX 75379

ROBBINS, RICHARD, composer. Film scores include The Europeans, 1979, Jane Austen in Manhattan, 1980, Quartet, 1981, Heat and Dust, 1983, The Bostonians, 1984, A Room with a View, 1986, My Little Girl, 1986, Sweet Lorraine, 1987, Maurice, 1987, The Perfect Murder, 1988, Slaves of New York, 1989, Bail Jumper, 1990, Mr. and Mrs. Bridge, 1990, The Ballad of the Sad Cafe, 1991, Howards End, 1992 (Academy award nomination best original score 1993), The Remains of the Day, 1993 (Academy award nomination best original score 1993), Jefferson in Paris, 1995. Office: Creative Artists Agency 9830 Wilshire Blvd Beverly Hills CA 90212-1804*

ROBBINS, ROBERT B., lawyer; b. Canton, Ohio, Aug. 31, 1951; s. Nathan H. and Evelyn (Cohen) R.; m. Melinda Abbot Street, Oct. 18, 1981; children: Julia Bates, Katherine Melinda, Caroline Rachel, Eli Street. AB, Cornell U., 1972; JD, Harvard U., 1975. Bar: D.C. 1975. Ptnr. Shaw, Pittman, Potts & Trowbridge, Washington, 1976—, also vice chmn. corp. group; chmn. D.C. Bar Commn. on Broker-Dealer Regulation, 1985-90; co-chmn. Ann. Course Study on Pvt. Placements, Am. Law Inst.-ABA, 1992—. Mem. D.C. Bar (steering com., sect. corp., fin. and securities law 1991-94, chmn. 1993-94). Office: Shaw Pittman Potts & Trowbridge 2300 N St NW Washington DC 20037-1122

ROBBINS, STEPHEN J. M., lawyer; b. Seattle, Apr. 13, 1942; s. Robert Mads and Aneita Elberta (West) R.; children: Sarah E.T., Alicia S.T. AB, UCLA, 1964; JD, Yale U., 1971. Bar: D.C. 1973, U.S. Dist. Ct. D.C. 1973, U.S. Ct. Appeals (D.C. cir.) 1973, U.S. Ct. Appeals (3d cir.) 1973, U.S. Dist. Ct. (ea. and no. dists.) Calif. 1982, U.S. Dist. Ct. (cen. dist.) Calif. 1983, Supreme Ct. of Republic of Palau, 1994. Pres. U.S. Nat. Student Assn., Washington, 1964-65; assoc. Steptoe & Johnson, Washington, 1972-75; chief counsel spl. inquiry on food prices, com. on nutrition and human needs U.S. Senate, Washington, 1975; v.p., gen. counsel Straight Arrow Pubs., San Francisco, 1975-77; dep. dist. atty. City and County of San Francisco, 1977-78; regional counsel U.S. SBA, San Francisco, 1978-80; spl. counsel Warner-Amex Cable Communications, Sacramento, 1981-82; ptnr. McDonough, Holland and Allen, Sacramento, 1982-84; v.p. Straight Arrow Pubs., N.Y.C., 1984-86; gen. legal counsel Govt. State of Koror, Rep. of Palau, Western Caroline Islands, 1994-95; pvt. practice law, 1986—. Staff sgt. U.S. Army, 1966-68. Mem. ABA (sect. urban, state and local govt. law-land use, planning and zoning com., sect. real property, probate and trust law, sect. natural resources energy, environ. law, forum com. on affordable housing and cmty. devel.), Internat. Mcpl. Lawyers Assn., D.C. Bar, State Bar of Calif., Urban Land Inst. (assoc.), Am. Planning Assn. (planning and law divsn., internat. divsn.), Internat. Urban Devel., Law Assn. for Asia and the Pacific (Law Asia), Chamber Music Soc. of Sacramento, Oreg. Shakespeare Festival, Shaw Island Hist. Soc. Unitarian. Avocations: theatre, art, hiking. Office: 3300 Douglas Blvd Ste 365 Roseville CA 95661-3829

ROBBINS, THOMAS EUGENE, author; b. Blowing Rock, N.C., 1936; m. Terrie Hemingway (div.); m. Alexa d'Avalon, 1995; 1 child, Fleetwood Starr. Student, Washington and Lee U., 1954-56, U. Wash., 1963; degree in social sci., Va. Commonwealth U., 1959. Former copy editor Richmond (Va.) Times-Dispatch, Seattle Post-Intelligencer; art critic Seattle Times. Author: Guy Anderson, 1965, Another Roadside Attraction, 1971, Even Cowgirls Get the Blues, 1976 (Best Am. Short Story 1977), Still Life with Woodpecker, 1980, Jitterbug Perfume, 1984, Skinny Legs and All, 1990, Half Asleep in Frog Pajamas, 1994. With USAF. Office: PO Box 338 La Conner WA 98257-0338

ROBBINS, VERNON EARL, lawyer, accountant; b. Balt., Aug. 16, 1921; s. Alexander Goldborough and Anne Jeanette (Bubb) R.; m. Ruth Adele Holland, Oct. 21, 1941; m. 2d, Alice Sherman Meredith, Feb. 17, 1961; 1 dau., Sharon R. Fick; 1 stepdau., Susan V. Henry. A.B.A., Md. Sch. Acctg., 1941; J.D., U. Balt., 1952. Bar: Md. 1952. Internal revenue agt. IRS, Balt., 1945-52; ptnr. Robbins, Adam & Co., C.P.A. firm, Cambridge, Md., 1952—; sole practice law, Cambridge, 1952—; bd. dirs. Bank of Eastern Shore. Served with U.S. Maritime Service, 1941-45. Named Boss of Yr., Tidewater chpt. Nat. Secs. Assn., 1978. Mem. ABA, Md. bar Assn., Am. Inst. C.P.A.s, Md. Assn. C.P.A.s, Am. Assn. Atty.-C.P.A.s, Am. Judicature Soc., Navy League, Dorchester County Hist. Soc., Dorchester Art Center. Democrat. Methodist. Club: Cambridge Yacht. Lodges: Elks, Masons, Shriners. Office: PO Box 236 126 Market Square Cambridge MD 21613

ROBBINS-WILF, MARCIA, educational consultant; b. Newark, Mar. 22, 1949; d. Saul and Ruth (Fern) Robbins; 1 child, Orin. Student, Emerson Coll., 1967-69, Seton Hall U., 1969, Fairleigh Dickinson U., 1970; BA, George Washington U., 1971; MA, NYU, 1975; postgrad., St. Peter's Coll., Jersey City, 1979, Fordham U., 1980; MS, Yeshiva U., 1981, EdD, 1986; postgrad., Monmouth Coll., 1986. Cert. elem. tchr., N.Y., N.J., reading specialist, N.J., prin., supr., N.J., adminstr., supr., N.Y. Tchr. Sleepy Hollow Elem. Sch., Falls Church, Va., 1971-72, Yeshiva Konvitz, N.Y.C., 1972-73; intern Wee Folk Nursery Sch., Short Hills, N.J., 1978-81, dir. day camp, 1980-81, tchr., dir., owner, 1980-81; adj. prof. reading Seton Hall U., South Orange, N.J., 1987, Middlesex County Coll., Edison, N.J., 1987-88; asst. adj. prof. L.I. U., Bklyn., 1988, Pace U., N.Y.C., 1988—; ednl. cons. Cranford High Sch., 1988; presenter numerous workshops; founding bd. dirs. Stern Coll. Women Yeshiva U., N.Y.C., 1987; adj. vis. lectr. Rutgers U., New Brunswick, N.J., 1988. Chairperson Jewish Book Festival, YM-YWHA, West Orange, N.J., 1986-87, mem. early childhood com., 1986—, bd. dirs., 1986—; vice chairperson dinner com. Nat. Leadership Conf. Christians and Jews, 1986; mem. Hadassah, Valerie Children's Fund, Women's League Conservative Judaism, City of Hope; assoc. bd. bus. and women's profl. divsn. United Jewish Appeal, 1979; vol. reader Goddard Riverside Day Care Ctr., N.Y.C., 1973; friend N.Y.C. Pub. Libr., 1980—; life friend Millburn (N.J.) Pub. Libr.; pres. Seton-Essex Reading Coun., 1991-94. Co-recipient Am. Heritage award, Essex County, 1985; recipient Award Appreciation City of Hope, 1984, Profl. Improvement awards Seton-Essex Reading Council, 1984-86, Cert. Attendance award Seton-Essex Reading Council, 1987. Mem. N.Y. Acad. Scis. (life), N.J. Council Tchrs. English, Nat. Council Tchrs. English, Am. Ednl. Research Assn., Coll. Reading Assn. (life), Assn. Supervision and Curriculun Devel., N.Y. State Reading Assn. (council Manhattan), N.J. Reading Assn. (council Seton-Essex), Internat. Reading Assn., Nat. Assn. for Edn. of Young Children (life N.J. chpt., Kenyon group), Nat. Council Jewish Women (vice chairperson membership com. evening br. N.Y. sect. 1974-75), George Washington U. Alumni Club, Emerson Coll. Alumni Club, NYU Alumni Club, Phi Delta Kappa (life), Kappa Gamma Chi (historian). Club: Greenbrook Country (Caldwell, N.J.); George Washington Univ. Avocations: reading, theatre. Home: 242 Hartshorn Dr Short Hills NJ 07078-1914 also: 820 Morris Tpke Short Hills NJ 07078-2619

ROBE, LUCY BARRY, editor, educator; b. Boston, Jan. 15, 1934; d. Herbert Jr. and Lucy (Brown) Barry; m. Robert S. Robe Jr., Feb. 6, 1971; 1 child, Parrish C. BA, Harvard U., 1955; MA in Med. Writing, Pacific Western U., 1992. Writer Alcoholism Update Biomed. Info. Corp., N.Y.C., 1979-85; editor newsletter Am. Soc. of Addiction Medicine News, Washington, 1985-95; conf. mgr. Fla. Soc. of Addiction Medicine News; v.p. L.I. Coun. on Alcoholism, Mineola, N.Y., 1978-92. Author: Just So It's Healthy, 1978, Haunted Inheritance, 1982, Co-Starring: Famous Women & Alcohol, 1986; editor numerous books. Mem. Authors Guild of Am., Am. Med. Writer's Assn. Office: 509-D1 Sea Oats Dr Juno Beach FL 33408

ROBE, THURLOW RICHARD, engineering educator, university dean; b. Petersburg, Ohio, Jan. 25, 1934; s. Thrulow Scott and Mary Alice (McKibben) R.; m. Eleanora C. Komyati, Aug. 27, 1955; children: Julia, Kevin, Stephen, Edward. B.S.C.E., Ohio U., 1955, M.S. in Mech. Engring., 1962; Ph.D. in Applied Mechanics, Stanford U., 1966. Engr. Gen. Electric Co., Niles, Ohio, Cleve., Erie, Pa., Evendale,Ohio, 1954-60; instr. Ohio U., Athens, 1960-63; asst. prof to prof., assoc. dean U. Ky., Lexington, 1965-80; dean Ohio U., Athens, 1980-96, Cruse W. Moss prof. Engring. Edn., 1992-96; dir. Innovation Ctr. Authority Ohio U., 1983-96; dean emeritus, Moss prof. emeritus Russ Coll. Engring. and Tech., U. Ohio, Athens, 1996—; pres., chmn. bd. Q.E.D. Assocs., Inc., Lexington, 1975-83; dir. Databeam Corp., Lexington; bd. dirs. Assn. Ohio Commodores; trustee Engring. Found. Ohio, 1988-94; bd. govs. Edison Materials Tech. Ctr., 1987-96; dir. T. Richard and Eleanora K. Robe Leadership Inst. Contbr. articles to profl. jours.; patentee trailer hitch. Bd. dirs. Athens County Cmty. Redevel. Corp., 1980-86; treas. South Lexington Little League, 1976-80; vice chmn. Thoroughbred dist., Boy Scouts Am., 1975-77; pres. Tates Creek H.S. PTA, Lexington, 1975-76; bd. dirs. U. Ky. Athletics Ass.n, 1975-80. Served to maj. USAF Res., 1955-85. Recipient Alumni medal of merit Ohio U., 1993; named Am. Coun. on Edn. Adminstrn. fellow, 1970-71, Ohio U. Alumnus of Yr., 1996. Mem. ASME, NSPE (Profl. Engring. in Edn. exec. bd., ctrl. region vice-chmn. 1987-89), Am. Soc. Engring. Edn. (Outstanding Contbn. in Rsch. award 1966), Athens Country Club, Athens Reading Club, Athens Symposiarchs, Assn. of Ohio Commodores, Rotary, Sigma Xi, Tau Beta Pi Omicron Delta Kappa, Alpha Lambda Delta. Office: Russ Coll Engring & Tech Ohio U Athens OH 45701

ROBECK, MILDRED COEN, educator, writer; b. Walum, N.D., July 29, 1915; d. Archie Blain and Mary Henrietta (Hoffman) Coen; m. Martin Julius Robeck, Jr., June 2, 1936; children: Martin Jay Robeck, Donna Jayne Robeck Thompson, Bruce Wayne Robeck. BS, U. Wash., 1950, MEd, 1954, PhD, 1958. Ordnance foreman Sherman Williams, U.S. Navy, Bremerton, Wash., 1942-45; demonstration tchr. Seattle Pub. Schs., 1946-57; reading clinic dir. U. Calif., Santa Barbara, 1957-64; rsch. cons. State Dept. Edn., Sacramento, Calif., 1964-67; prof., head early childhood edn. U. Oreg., Eugene, Oreg., 1967-86; vis. scholar West Australia Inst. Tech., Perth, 1985; v.p. acad. affairs U. Santa Barbara, Calif., 1987-95; vis. prof. Victoria Coll., B.C. Can., summer 1958, Dalhousie U., Halifax, summer 1964; trainer evaluator U.S. Office of Edn. Head Start, Follow Thru, 1967-72; cons., evaluator Native Am. Edn. Programs, Sioux, Navajo, 1967-81; cons. on gifted Oreg. Task Force on Talented and Gifted, Salem, 1974-76; evaluator Early Childhood Edn., Bi-Ling. program, Petroleum and Minerology, Dhahran, Saudi Arabia, 1985. Author: Materials KELP: Kgn. Evaluation Learning Pot, 1967, Infants and Children, 1978, Psychology of Reading, 1990, Oscar: His Story, 1997; contbr. articles to profl. jours. Evaluation cons. Rosenburg Found. Project, Santa Barbara, 1966-67; faculty advisor Pi Lambda Theta, Eugene, Oreg, 1969-74; guest columnist Oreg. Assn. Gifted and Talented, Salem, Oreg., 1979-81; editorial review bd. ERQ, U.S. Calif., L.A., 1981-91. Recipient Nat. Dairy award 4-H Clubs, Wis., 1934, scholarships NYA and U. Wis., Madison, 1934-35, faculty rsch. grants U. Calif., Santa barbara, 1958-64, NDEA Fellowship Retraining U.S. Office Edn., U. Oreg., 1967-70. Mem. APA, Am. Ednl. Rsch. Assn., Internat. Reading Assn., Phi Beta Kappa, Pi Lambda Theta. Democrat. Avocations: dyslexia research, historical research, duplicate bridge, writing. Home: 95999 Highway 101 S Yachats OR 97498-9714

ROBEK, MARY FRANCES, business education educator; b. Superior, Wis., Jan. 30, 1927; d. Stephen and Mary (Hervert) R. BE, U. Wis., 1948; MA, Northwestern U., 1951; MBA, U. Mich., 1962, PhD, 1967. Tchr. Bergland (Mich.) High Sch., 1948, Tony (Wis.) High Sch., 1948-50, Sch. Vocat. and Adult Edn., Superior, 1950-58; prof. bus. edn. and office tech. Ea. Mich. U., Ypsilanti, 1958-93; instr. Jazyckova Gymnasium, Banská, Štiavnicá, Slovakia, 1994. Author: Information and Records Management, 1995. Assn. of Records Mgrs. and Adminstrs. fellow, 1992. Mem. Assn. Records Mgrs. and Adminstrs. (life), Inst. Cert. Mgrs. (pres. 1980-81), Cath. Daus. Am., Delta Pi Epsilon, Delta Kappa Gamma, Pi Lambda Theta. Republican. Roman Catholic. Home: 10844 S Nakoda Rd Solon Springs WI 54873-8413 *Opportunity to do creative and innovative things without infringing on the rights of others is limited only by priorities set considering people and technology.*

ROBENALT, JOHN ALTON, lawyer; b. Ottawa, Ohio, May 2, 1922; s. Alton Ray and Kathryn (Straman) R.; m. Margaret Morgan Durbin, Aug. 25, 1951 (dec. July 1990); children: John F., William A., James D., Robert M., Mary K., Margaret E., Thomas D.; m. Nancy Leech Kidder, Sept. 21, 1991. B.A., Miami U., 1943; LL.B., Ohio State U., 1948, J.D., 1948. Bar: Ohio 1948. Asst. atty. gen. Ohio, 1949-51; practice in Lima, Ohio, 1951-59; acting municipal judge Lima Municipal Ct., 1955-59; partner Robenalt, Daley, Balyeat & Balyeat, 1959-82; ptnr. Robenalt, Kendall & Robenalt, 1983-85, Robenalt, Kendall, Rodabaugh & Staley, 1985-92, Robenalt & Robenalt, 1993—. Chmn. Lima March of Dimes, 1957-58; Bd. dirs. Lima Civic Center, pres., 1971-72; bd. dirs. Lima Rotating Fund; trustee Allen County Regional Transit Authority, Lima, pres., 1975—. Served with AUS, 1943-45. Mem. ABA, Ohio Bar Assn., Allen County Bar Assn. (pres. 1969-70), Am. Legion, Lima Automobile Club (bd. dirs., pres. 1975-82), Shawnee Country Club (pres. 1968-70), Ohio Automobile Club (trustee 1982—, chmn. 1995—), Elks (bd. trustees 1991—), Rotary, Delta Tau Delta, Phi Delta Phi. Home: 1755 Shawnee Rd Lima OH 45805-3857 Office: 211215 N Elizabeth St Lima OH 45801-4300

ROBERSON, BRUCE H., lawyer; b. Wilmington, Del., Mar. 7, 1941; s. A. L. and Virginia Amelia (Heerdt) R.; m. Mary E. Abrams; children: Cheryl Anne, David B., Douglas M. B.S. cum laude, Washington and Lee U., 1963; J.D., U. Va., 1966. Bar: Va. 1966, Del. 1966, Fla. 1969. Mem. Morris, Nichols, Arsht & Tunnell, Wilmington, 1966-67; with Holland & Knight LLP, Tampa, Fla., 1969—; ptnr. Holland & Knight, Tampa, Fla., 1975—. Contbg. editor Warren, Gorham and Lamont Banking and Lending Institution Forms, 1992-97. Served to capt. U.S. Army, 1967-69. Decorated Bronze Star. Fellow Am. Bar Found., Fla. Bar Found.; mem. ABA (bus. law sect. com. on consumer fin. svcs. 1976—, banking law com. 1980—, savs. instns. com. 1989-96), Am. Judicature Soc., Fla. Bar Assn. (corp. banking and bus. law sect. exec. coun. 1978-86, chmn. banking law com. 1982-84), Del. Bar Assn., Va. Bar Assn., Hillsborough County Bar Assn., Univ. Club, Tampa Yacht and Country Club, Lambda Chi Alpha. Republican. Methodist. Office: Holland & Knight LLP 400 N Ashley Dr Ste 2300 PO Box 1288 Tampa FL 33601-1288

ROBERSON, DEBORAH KAY, secondary school educator; b. Crane, Tex., Jan. 15, 1955; d. David B. and Virginia L. (King) Cole; m. Larry M. Roberson; children: Justin, Jenai, Julie. BS in Secondary Edn., Coll. S.W., 1981; MA in Sch. Adminstrn., Sul Ross State U., 1991. Cert. biology and history tchr., mid-mgmt. cert., supt. cert., Tex., biology and history tchr., Okla. Sci. and social studies tchr. Andrews (Tex.) Ind. Sch. Dist., 1987-95; forum tchr.- gifted social studies program, social studies dept. chair Ctrl. Mid. Sch. Broken Arrow (Okla.) Pub. Schs., 1995—; mem. 7th grade history curriculum com. Andrews Ind. Sch. Dist., 1988, mem. outdoor classroom com., 1989-90, chair sci. curriculum com., 1989-90, chair health curriculum com., 1990-91, mem. Tex. pub. schs. open house com., 1989-90, 92-93, mem. dist. textbook com., 1990-91; secondary edn. rep. Ptnrs. in Parliament, Berlin, 1993; site-based com. Broken Arrow Pub. Schs., 1995—, B.A.S.I.S. com., 1995—, nat. history day coord. Ctrl. Middle Sch., 1995, geography bee coord., 1995—, tech. com., 1996—, mem. discipline com., 1996, mem. remediation com., 1996—, Tools for Tomorrow Conf. com., 1996—, others; mem. state geography com. Okla. State Dept. Edn., 1997. Prodr., dir.: Real History Radio, Broken Arrow Hist. Soc., 1997. Livestock leader Andrews County 4-H Program, 1985-89; vol. Am. Heart Assn., Andrews, 1988; vol., team mother Little League, Andrews, 1990; vol., treas. Mustang Booster Club, Andrews, 1993-95. Recipient Appreciation awards Mustang Booster Club, 1993, 94, VFW Ladies Aux. Post 10887 award, Broken Arrow, 1996—, Tchr. of Today award Masons, Broken Arrow, 1997, Nat. History Day Outstanding Tchr. award Tulsa C.C., 1997. Mem. AAUW, Nat. Assn. Secondary Sch. Prins., Nat. Staff Devel. Coun., Assn. Tex. Profl. Educators (pres. local unit 1992-93, mem. resolutions com. 1994-95, appreciation award 1993, sec. region 1993-94, v.p. region 1994-95), ASCD, Tex. Assn. Supervision and Curriculum Devel., Tex. Network for Continuous Quality Improvement, Nat. Coun. Social Studies, Okla. Assn. Supervision and Curriculum Devel., Okla. Alliance Geographic Edn., Union Redskins Booster Club (sec. 1996-97). Avocations: meeting people, travel, golf, rafting, hiking. Home: 708 N Sweet Gum Ave Broken Arrow OK 74012 Office: Broken Arrow Pub Schs Ctrl Mid Sch 210 N Main St Broken Arrow OK 74012-3939

ROBERSON, JAMES O., foundation executive; m. JoAnn Roberson; children: Melanie Merrill, Sharyl Ritucci, James Jr., Trisha Sermersheim, Joel. AB in Journalism, Baylor U., 1956; student Indsl. Devel. Inst., U. Okla.; student Inst. Orgnl. Mgmt., U. Houston. Cert. econ. developer. Dir. info. West Tex. C. of C., Abilene, 1956-59; area devel. mgr. Mo.-Kans.-Tex. R.R., 1959-63; exec. dir. Albuquerque Indsl. Devel. Svc., 1963-65; dir. N.Mex. Dept. Devel., Santa Fe, 1965-69; mgr. Forward Metro Denver, 1969-72; dir. R.I. Dept. Econ. Devel., Providence, 1972-77; v.p., dir. new bus. devel. Howard Rsch. and Devel. Corp. subs. Rouse Co., Columbia, Md., 1977-79; sec. Md. Dept. Econ. and Community Devel., Annapolis, 1979-83; pres. Louisville C. of C., 1983-88; pres., CEO Rsch. Triangle Found. N.C., 1988—; chmn. bd. dirs. Charlotte br. Fed. Res. Bank Richmond; cons., speaker in field. Editor West Tex. Today mag., 1956-59. Bd. dirs. N.C. Citizens for Bus. and Industry, N.C. Biotech. Ctr. Fellow Am. Econ. Devel. Coun. (past chmn.); mem. Indsl. Devel. Rsch. Coun., Nat. Assn. State Devel. Agys. (past pres.), Assn. Univ. Related Rsch. Parks (pres.).

ROBERSON, LINDA, lawyer; b. Omaha, July 15, 1947; d. Harlan Oliver and Elizabeth Aileen (Good) R.; m. Gary M. Young, Aug. 20, 1970; children: Elizabeth, Katherine, Christopher. BA, Oberlin Coll., 1969; MS, U. Wis., 1970, JD, 1974. Bar: Wis. 1974, U.S. Dist. Ct. (we. dist.) Wis. 1974. Legis. atty. Wis. Legis. Reference Bur., Madison, 1974-76, sr. legis. atty., 1976-78; assoc. Rikkers, Koritzinsky & Rikkers, Madison, 1978-79; ptnr. Koritzinsky, Neider, Langer & Roberson, Madison, 1979-85, Stolper, Koritzinsky, Brewster & Neider, Madison, 1985-93, Balisle & Roberson, Madison, 1993—; lectr. U. Wis. Law Sch., Madison, 1978—. Co-author: Real Women, Real Lives, 1981, Wisconsin's Marital Property Reform Act, 1984, Understanding Wisconsin's Marital Property Law, 1985, A Guide to Property Classification Under Wisconsin's Marital Property Act, 1986, 2d edit., 1997, Workbook for Wisconsin Estate Planners, 2d edit., 1993, 3rd edit., 1997, Look B efore You Leap, 1996, Family Estate Planning in Wis., 1992, rev. edit. 1996. Fellow Am. Acad. Matrimonial Lawyers; mem. ABA, Wis. Bar Assn., Dane County Bar Assn., Legal Assn. Women, Nat. Assn. Elder Law Attys. Office: Balisle and Roberson 217 S Hamilton # 302 PO Box 870 Madison WI 53701-0870

ROBERSON, MARK ALLEN, physicist, educator; b. Lufkin, Tex., Nov. 12, 1961; s. Roy and Thelma (Weist) R. AAS, Angelina County Jr. Coll., 1982; BSEE, Tex. A&M U., 1984; MS, Stephen F. Austin State U., 1989; PhD, Tex. Tech. U., 1994. From rsch. asst. to instr. Tex. Tech. U., Lubbock, 1990-95; instr. Vernon (Tex.) Regional Jr. Coll., 1995—. Robert A. Welch Found. fellow, 1991-94. Mem. AAAS, Am. Phys. Soc., Materials Rsch. Soc., Sigma Pi Sigma. Avocation: books. Office: Vernon Regl Jr Coll Vernon TX 76384-4092

ROBERSON, NATHAN RUSSELL, physicist, educator; b. Robersonville, N.C., Dec. 13, 1930; s. Nathan Russell and Myrtle (Taylor) R.; m. Ruth Haislip, June 19, 1954; children: David Wintner, Michael Taylor, Mary Russell. BS, U. N.C., 1954, MS, 1955; PhD, Johns Hopkins U., 1960. Jr. instr. Johns Hopkins U., Balt., 1955-60; research assoc. Princeton (N.J.) U., 1960-63; asst. prof. physics Duke U., Durhan, N.C., 1963-68, assoc. prof., 1968-74, prof., 1974—; bd. dirs. Triangle Univs. Computation Ctr., 1975-81; mem. instrumentation subcom. Nuclear Sci. Adv. Com., 1982-85; mem.

energy sci. network steering com. Dept. Energy, 1987-90, nuclear physics panel on computer networks, 1988-90, dep. dir. Triangle U. Nuclear Lab., 1990-92; dir. Triangle Univs. Nuclear Lab., 1992-96, assoc. dir., 1996—. Contbr. articles on physics to profl. jours. Treas. N.C. Council Chs., 1974-79. Fellow Am. Phys. Soc.; mem. IEEE, Am. Assn. Physics Tchrs., Phi Beta Kappa. Presbyterian. Home: 3406 Ogburn Ct Durham NC 27705-5427 Office: Dept Physics Duke U Durham NC 27708

ROBERSON, PATT FOSTER, mass communications educator; b. Middletown, N.Y., Dec. 3, 1934; d. Gilbert Charles and Mildred Elizabeth (O'Neal) Foster; m. Murray Ralph Roberson Jr., May 10, 1963 (dec. 1968). AA, Canal Zone Jr. Coll., 1954; BA in Journalism, La. State U., 1957, MA in Journalism, 1973; MA in Media, So. U., Baton Rouge, 1981; PhD in Mass Communication, U. So. Miss., 1985. Exec. sec. Lionel H. Abshire and Assocs., AIA, Architects, Baton Rouge, 1958-60, Murrell and Callari, AIA, Architects, Baton Rouge, 1960-63; bus. mgr. So. Rev. La. State U., Baton Rouge, 1963-69; free-lance researcher, ind. contractor Baton Rouge, 1969-74; rep. dept. info. State of La., Baton Rouge, 1974-75; asst. prof. mass. comm. So. U., 1976-86, assoc. prof. mass comm., 1986-93, prof. mass comm., 1993-96, prof. emeritus, 1996—; reviewer Random House Pubs., N.Y.C., 1981; profl. devel. intern Baton Rouge Morning Advocate, 1991, Baker Observer, 1991-92; cons. advt. Baton Rouge Little Theater, 1971-96; reporter-photographer Canal Record, Seminole, Fla., 1967—; biographer of Edward Livermore Burlingame, John H. Johnson, Daniel Kimball Whitaker, (book) American mag. journalists series, Dictionary Literary Biography, Detroit, 1986-87; tutor Operation Upgrade, 1978-82; vol. reporter, photographer, proofreader The Platinum Record, Baton Rouge, 1996—. Co-editor: La. State U. cookbook Tiger Bait, 1976; biographer Frank E. Gannett in Biographical Dictionary of American Journalism, 1987; freelance writer/editl. cons.; editl. bd. Am. Journalism, 1986-87; reviewer Longman Publs. 1991-92; contbr. articles to profl. jours. Mem. poll commn. East Baton Rouge Parish Govt., 1978-95; pres. Our Lady Lake Regional Med. Ctr., 1971-72; bd. dirs. Dist. Atty.'s Rape Crisis Commn., 1976-79, Plan Govt. Study Commn., 1973-76, Selective Svc. System Bd. 8, Baton Rouge, 1986—; docent Greater Baton Rouge Zoo, 1974-77; vol. ARC, 1989—; mem. East Baton Rouge Parish Commn. on Govtl. Ethics, 1992-93; mayoral appointee Baker Mobile Home Rev. Bd., 1990—; v.p. Baker Hist. and Cultural Found., 1990-93; mem. Baker Interclub Coun., 1990-91; organizer human-animal therapy svc. Baker Manor Nursing Home, 1994; mem. 1st class Citizens Basic Police Tng. Acad., Baton Rouge Police Dept., 1994. Mem. AAUP (sec.-treas. La. conf. 1988-89, sec. 1992-93, chmn. pub. rels. 1994-95), Assn. Edn. Journalism and Mass Comm., Am. Newspapers Pubs. Assn. (nat. coop. com. on edn. in journalism 1989-92), Women in Comm. (pres. Baton Rouge chpt. 1982, nat. judge Clarion awards 1987), Pub. Rels. Assn. La., La. State U. Journalism Alumni Assn. (pres. 1977), Soc. Profl. Journalists (pres. S.E. La. chpt. 1982), Am. Journalism Historians Assn., La. State U. Alumni Assn. (pres. East Baton Rouge Parish chpt. 1978-80), Popular Culture Assn., Investigative Reporters and Editors Assn., Baker C. of C., Toasmasters (adminstrv. v.p. Baton Rouge 1977), Pilot Club. Home: 2801 Allen Ct Baker LA 70714-2253

ROBERSON, ROBERT S., investment company executive; b. Mt. Kisco, N.Y., Nov. 30, 1942; s. Robert and Mercedes (Stack) R.; m. Barbara Drane, Oct. 21, 1967; children: Elizabeth de V., Merritt B., Barbara D. BS, NYU, 1964; MBA, Coll. William and Mary, 1973. Various positions in fin. and bldg. industries, 1964-67; mem. N.Y. Produce Exchange, 1965-66; with Weaver Bros., Inc., Newport News, 1967—, now pres., dir.; bd. dirs. First Peninsula Bank & Trust Co., Hampton, Va., 1977-78. Active Newport News Rep. City Com.; past dir. Peninsula Unit Am. Cancer Soc., Newport News; past dir. Heritage Coun. Girl Scouts U.S.A., Hampton; former trustee Newport News Pub. Libr., Va. Living Mus., Am. Assn. Mus., Newport News; former trustee Hampton Roads Acad., Newport News; former mem. bd. visitors to George Washington's Mt. Vernon Nat. Shrine; hon. dep. chief N.Y.C. Fire Dept. Decorated officer Order of St. John (England). Mem. S.R., Newcomen Soc. of the U.S., Hon. Fire Officers Assn., Gen. Soc. Colonial Wars, St. Nicholas Soc. of the City N.Y., Colonial Order Acorn, Sovereign Mil. Order of the Temple of Jerusalem (comdr.), Mil. Order Fgn. Wars of U.S., Squadron A Assn., Pilgrims of the U.S., Blue Key, Union Club, Church Club (N.Y.C.), Fishers Island (N.Y.) Club, James River Country Club, Hampton Roads German Club, The Hundred Club (Newport News, Va.), N.Y. Yacht Club, Fishers Island Yacht Club, Rotary Internat. (Paul Harris fellow), Delta Sigma Pi. Episcopalian. Home: PO Box 66 Williamsburg VA 23187-0066

ROBERT, JOSEPH CLARKE, historian, consultant; b. State College, Miss., June 2, 1906; s. Joseph Clarke and Hallie Christian (Cavett) R.; m. Evelyn Mercer Bristow, June 15, 1931 (dec.); children: Frank Chambers, Carol Mercer Robert Armstrong; m. Sara Cross Squires, May 12, 1985 (dec.). AB magna cum laude, Furman U., 1927, LLD, 1959; MA, Duke U., 1929, PhD, 1933; LittD, Washington and Lee U., 1958; LHD, Med. Coll. Va., 1962. Ranger-historian Nat. Park Service, Yorktown, Va., 1934; instr. history Ohio State U., Columbus, Ohio, 1934-38; from asst. prof. to prof. Duke U., 1938-52, assoc. dean Grad. Sch., 1949-52; pres. Coker Coll., Hartsville, S.C., 1952-55, Hampden-Sydney Coll., Va., 1955-60; prof. history U. Richmond, Va., 1961-67, William Binford Vest prof. history, 1967-71, prof. history emeritus, 1972—; cons. Psychol. Cons., Inc., Richmond, 1966, Newport News Shipbldg. & Dry Dock Co. (Va.), 1961-64, others. Author: The Tobacco Kingdom, 1938; The Road From Monticello, 1941; The Story of Tobacco in America, 1949; Ethyl: A History of the Corporation and the People Who Made It, 1983; Gottwald Family History, 1984; contbr. articles to profl. jours. Pres. S.C. Asssn. Colls., 1952-53. Watauga fellow Harvard U., 1929-30, Duke U. fellow, 1930-31, Fund for Advancement of Edn. travel and study grantee, 1960-61, Humanities fellow U. N.C., Duke U., 1966-67. Fellow Am. Coll. Dentists (hon.); mem. So. Hist. Assn. (life), Va. Hist. Soc. (pres. emeritus), Richmond Acad. Medicine (sect. on history of medicine, hon.), Commonwealth Club, Forum Club, Phi Beta Kappa, Omicron Delta Kappa, Sigma Chi. Presbyterian. Avocation: letter-press printing. Home: 103 Tuckahoe Blvd Richmond VA 23226-2224

ROBERT, LESLIE (LADISLAS), research center administrator, consultant; b. Budapest, Hungary, Oct. 24, 1924; s. Louis and Elizabeth (Bardos) R.; m. Barbara Klinger, Nov. 19, 1949 (dec.); children: Marianne, Catherine, Elisabeth; m. Jacqueline Labat, Dec. 20, 1976. Student, U. Szeged, Budapest, Hungary, 1944-48; MD, U. Paris, 1953; PhD, U. Lille, France, 1977; D (hon.), Med. U. Budapest, 1991. Mem. med. faculty dept. biochemistry U. Paris, 1949-59; postdoctoral rsch. fellow dept. biochemistry Sch. Medicine U. Ill., 1959-60; postdoctoral rsch. assoc., spl. fellow Columbia U., N.Y.C., 1960-61; 67; dir. biochemistry lab. Inst. for Immunobiology INSERM/CNRS, Broussais Hosp., Paris, 1962-66; founder 1st rsch. ctr. on connective tissue biochemistry CNRS, U. Paris XII, Créteil, France, 1966-94; adminstr. connective tissue unit Cell Biology Lab. U. Paris VII, 1995—; rsch. dir. French Nat. Rsch. Ctr., Paris, 1974-94, hon. rsch. dir., 1995—; founder rsch. ctr. for clin. and biol. rsch. on aging Charles Foix-Jean Rostand Hosp., Ivry, France, 1993—; cons. several pharm. firms; mem. Sci. Coun. Arteriosclerosis Rsch. Inst., U. Munster, Germany, 1970-96. Author 5 books on biology of aging, monograph series: Frontiers of Matrix Biology, 11 vols.; mem. editorial bd. several sci. jours.; contbr. more than 850 articles on connective tissues, biochemistry and pathology and aging to sci. jours. Recipient Spl. Sci. prize Sci. Writer, 1966, Reiss prize in Ophthalmology, 1970, Sandoz prize gerontol. rsch. Internat. Assn. Gerontology, 1977, Verzar medal for gerontol. rsch. U. Vienna, Austria, 1994. Mem. French Atherosclerosis Soc. (pres. 1993-97), Hungarian Acad. Sci. (fgn.), Acad. Scis. Westphalie-Rhen, Germany (corr.). Home: 7 Rue Lully, 94440 Santeny France Office: Univ Paris Dept Cell Biology, 2 Pl Jussieu-Tour 23/33, 75005 Paris France

ROBERT, PATRICK, playwright; b. Kilgore, Tex., Sept. 27, 1937; s. Robert and Beulah (Goodson) O'Connor. Author numerous plays produced off-off Broadway, off-Broadway, Broadway, also abroad including Robert Patrick's Cheep Theatricks (23 plays), 1972, Simultaneous Transmissions, 1973, Play-By-Play, 1975, The Golden Circle, 1975, Kennedy's Children, 1975, Let Me Tell It To You, Dr. Paroo, 1976, One Man, One Woman (6 plays), 1978, T-Shirts, 1979, Mutual Benefit Life, 1980, Mercy Drop and Other Plays (5 plays), 1980, My Cup Ranneth, 1984, Big Sweet, 1985, Untold Decades (7 plays), 1988, Drowned Out, 1990, Connie, 1991, Michaelangelo's Models, 1994, Bread Alone, 1994, The Trial of Socrates, 1994, Evan on Earth, 1995, Pouf Positive (CD), 1996; author: (novels) Temple Slave, 1986, Echo, 1990; teleplays include: High Tide, 1994, Robin's Hoods, 1995; contbr. poems, articles, stories to profl. jours. Rockefeller grantee, 1974, N.Y. State CAPS grantee, 1975; recipient Show Bus. Best Playwright award 1968-69, Glasgow Citizens' Theatre Best World Playwright award, 1974, Omni-Act One award, 1975, Robbie award, 1976, Founders award Internat. Thespians Soc., 1980, Blue is for Boys weekends in Manhattan, 1983, 86, Lifetime Achievement award for Gay Playwriting Robert Chesley Found., 1996, Robert Chesley Found. Lifetime Achievement in Gay Playwrighting award, 1996. Home: 1837 N Alexandria Ave Apt 211 Los Angeles CA 90027-4068 *No object or action has any meaning except that given to it by a writer. Writers create the consciousness of humanity, which in turn creates our world. Writers write the world.*

ROBERT, STEPHEN, investment firm executive; b. Haverhill, Mass., June 13, 1940; s. Samuel R.; m. Catherine Price; children: Tracey Alexandra, Elisabeth Amory. A.B. with honors, Brown U., 1962; postgrad., London Sch. Econs., 1962-63, Columbia Bus. Sch., 1963-65. Security analyst Faulkner Dawkins and Sullivan, 1965-67; v.p. Oppenheimer Funds, N.Y.C., 1968-76, chief portfolio mgr., 1969-76; gen. ptnr. Oppenheimer & Co., Inc., N.Y.C., 1970-82, dir. research, 1976-78, pres., 1979-83, chmn., chief exec. officer, 1983—; dir. NacRe Corp. Bd. dirs., chmn. fin. com. Wiltwyck Sch., 1968-78; bd. dirs. Joffrey Ballet, 1981—; trustee The Dalton Sch., 1984—, Brown U., 1984—. Club: Harmonie (N.Y.C.). Office: Oppenheimer & Co Inc Oppenheimer Tower World Fin Ctr New York NY 10281

ROBERTI, MARIO ANDREW, lawyer, former energy company executive; b. Denver, May 12, 1935; s. Emil and Elvira (Ligrano) R.; m. Patricia Ann Ludwig, Apr. 27, 1963; children: Andrea Louise, Paul Richard, Robert Raymond. B.S., Loyola U. (now Loyola Marymount U.), Los Angeles, 1957, J.D., 1960. Bar: Calif. 1961, Hawaii 1977, D.C. 1985. Dep. atty. gen. State of Calif., 1961-69; atty. Pacific Lighting Corp., Los Angeles, 1969-71; asst. gen. counsel, asst. sec. McCulloch Oil Corp., Los Angeles, 1971-76; v.p., gen. counsel Pacific Resources, Inc., Honolulu, 1976-88, sr. v.p., gen. counsel, 1988-92; with Reinwald, O'Connor & Playdon, Honolulu, 1993-97; bd. dirs. St. Francis Med. Ctr., Honolulu. Trustee Hawaii Sch. Girls, 1979-87; regent Loyola Marymount U., Chaminade U. Of Honolulu, 1982-93, chmn. bd. regents, 1987-89; adv. bd. Internat. Oil and Gas Ednl. Ctr., Southwestern Legal Found. Mem. ABA, D.C. Bar Assn., Hawaii Bar Assn. (chmn. corp. counsel sect. 1979), Calif. Bar Assn., Outrigger Canoe Club, Pacific Coast Gas Assn. (life, chmn. legal adv. com. 1983-84), Phi Alpha Delta, Phi Kappa Theta. Office: 24th Fl 733 Bishop St Fl 24 Honolulu HI 96813-4022

ROBERTI, WILLIAM VINCENT, retail executive; b. Bridgeport, Conn., Oct. 18, 1946; s. Armand E. and La Junta Juanita (Swindle) R.; m. Christina Gura, May 30, 1970; children—Jennifer A., Jessica M. BA, Sacred Heart U., Bridgeport, 1969; MBA, So. Meth. U., 1987. Buyer, D.M. Read's div. Allied Corp., Bridgeport, 1968-73; div. mdse. mgr. Robinson's Fla. div. Associated Dry Goods Co., St. Petersburg, 1973-77; exec. v.p. Maas Bros. div. Allied Corp., Tampa, Fla., 1977-83; v.p., gen. mdse. mgr. Mervyn's, Hayward, Calif., 1983-84; chmn., CEO Diversified Group Zale Corp., Dallas, 1984-87; pres., chief exec. Brooks Brothers, 1987-95; pres., CEO Plaid Clothing Group, Inc. (divsn. Hartmarx Corp.), 1995—. Trustee Sacred Heart U., 1989—; bd. govs. N.Y. chpt. Assn. U.S. Army; mem. Dept. Def. Clothing and Textile Bd.; mem. Nat. Multiple Sclerosis Soc.; Col. USAR, 1966—. Roman Catholic. Mem. Assn. U.S. Army. Union League Club (N.Y.C.), St. Petersburg Yacht Club (Fla.), Brooklawn C.C. Office: Plaid Clothing Group, Inc 730 5th Ave New York NY 10019-4105

ROBERTS, ALFRED WHEELER, III, law firm executive; b. N.Y.C., Aug. 3, 1938; s. Alfred Wheeler and Florence Henley (Kirk) R.; m. Pamela Anne Stover, June 29, 1967; children: Ashley Anne, Alfred Kirk, Michael Tyler. BA, Dartmouth Coll., 1960, MBA, 1961. CPA, N.Y. With Arthur Young & Co., N.Y.C., 1961-89, ptnr., 1971-89, vice chmn., 1982-88; ptnr. RFE Investment Ptnrs., New Canaan, Conn., 1989-90; exec. dir. Winthrop, Stimson, Putnam & Roberts, N.Y.C., 1991—. Bd. dirs., treas. Legal Aid Soc. N.Y., 1981-88; bd. dirs. YMCA of Greater N.Y., 1983-89, vice chmn., 1987-89. Mem. AICPA, Univ. Club. Congregationalist.

ROBERTS, ALICE NOREEN, educational administrator; b. Los Lunas, N.Mex., July 1, 1947; d. Earnest Lee and Lora Mae (Leatherman) Mayo; m. David Ivan Roberts, Apr. 18, 1975; children: Debra, Danielle, David II, Diana, Earnest. BA, Brescia Coll., 1970; MA, U. N.Mex., 1974. Cert. elem. tchr., adminstr., Calif. 5th and 6th grade tchr. St. John's Parochial Sch., Plattsmouth, Nebr., 1970-71; 5th grade tchr. Sacred Heart Parochial Sch., Farmington, N.Mex., 1971-72; 4th-6th grade tchr. Our Lady of Assumption Sch., Albuquerque, 1972-75; correctional officer Calif. Dept. Corrections, San Quentin, 1975-82; adult edn. tchr. Calif. Dept. Corrections, Soledad, 1983-86, San Luis Obispo, 1984; supr. acad. instrn. Calif. Dept. Corrections, Norco, 1986-90; supr. correctional edn. programs Calif. Dept. Corrections, Corcoran, 1990—; 6th grade tchr. St. Catherine's Parochial Sch., Martinez, Calif., 1981-82; mem. curriculum adv. com. Calif. Dept. Corrections, Sacramento, 1984-86, mem. computer adv. com., 1984-88, mem. literacy adv. com., 1990-94. Candidate for King City (Calif.) Bd. Edn., 1985; vol. Youth for Understanding rep., Hanford, 1994—. Mem. ASCD, Am. Vocat. Assn., Correctional Edn. Assn., Calif. Literacy, Inc., Calif. Coun. for Adult Edn., Hanford Emblem Club (rec. sec. 1994—). Roman Catholic. Avocations: computers, pencil puzzles, video games, crocheting. Office: Calif State Prison Visions Adult Sch PO Box 8800 Corcoran CA 93212

ROBERTS, ALIDA JAYNE, elementary school educator; b. Bristol, Conn., Aug. 11, 1967; d. James and Barbara Mae (Carlson) R. BA in Elem. Edn., Anna Maria Coll., Paxton, Mass., 1990; MS in Reading and Lang. Arts, Calif. State U., Fullerton, 1992. Cert. tchr., Conn., Mass., Calif. Elem. tchr. Rowland Unified Sch. Dist., Rowland Heights, Calif., 1990-94, Edgewood Elem. Sch., Bristol, Conn., 1994-95, Clara T. O'Connell Elem. Sch., Bristol, Conn., 1995-96, Edgewood Elem. Sch., Bristol, 19966; tchr. Gifted and Talented Edn. After Sch. Program, West Covina, Calif., 1993-94, Chpt. 1 After Sch. Program, West Covina, 1993-94; intramural coach After Sch. Program Edgewood Elem. Sch., Bristol, Conn., 1994-95. Tchr. advisor PTA, La Puente, 1992-93, Clara T. O'Connell PTA, 1995-96. Scholar Bristol Fedn. Tchrs., 1986; grantee Anna Maria Coll., 1986-90. Mem. NEA, ASCD, Internat. Reading Assn., Calif. Reading Assn., Calif. Tchrs. Assn., Orange County Reading Assn., Bristol Fedn. Tchrs. Avocations: reading, physical fitness. Home: 291 Morris Ave Bristol CT 06010-4418

ROBERTS, ANNA RUTH, financial consultant; b. Sweetwater, Tex., Apr. 10, 1942; d. Charles Heddington and Ethel Dorothy (Harris) Elliott; m. David Ira Roberts, Apr. 10, 1960; children: Craig Spencer, Edward Aaron. BA in Edn., Ariz. State U., 1976. CFP. Acct. Miller-Wagner & Co. Ltd., Phoenix, 1982-87; asst. v.p., sr. fin. cons. Merrill Lynch, Sun City, Ariz., 1987—; organizer, presenter seminars Pres.'s Club. Recipient Dist. Merit award Boy Scouts Am., Flagstaff, Ariz., 1975. Mem. Am. Bus. Women Assn., B'nai B'rith Women (Edith K. Baum chpt., Woman of Yr. 1976), Kiwanis (Disting. Svc. award 1991). Avocations: hiking, white-water rafting. Home: 6090 W Lone Cactus Dr Glendale AZ 85308-6280 Office: Merrill Lynch 9744 W Bell Rd Sun City AZ 85351-1343

ROBERTS, ANTONETTE, special education educator; b. San Francisco, Nov. 14, 1940; d. Anthony Francis and Lois Wilma (Litton) Jacklevich; m. Raymond Daly Roberts, Feb. 1, 1964; children: Shirley Lois Roberts Murphy, Alice Evelyn, Daniel Anthony. BA, U. Calif., Davis, 1962; MS, U. Nebr., 1971. Cert. elem. and spl. edn. tchr., Iowa. Elem. educator Esparto (Calif.) Unified Sch. Dist., 1962-66; itinerant resource educator Pottawattamie County Schs., Council Bluffs, Iowa, 1972-75; multi-categorical resource educator Lewis Cen. Community Sch. Dist., Council Bluffs, 1976—. mem. tchr. cadre U. No. Ioa, Cedar Falls and Lewis Ctrl. Cmty. Schs., Council Bluffs, 1990—; sponsor Lakeview Sch. Student Coun., Council Bluffs, 1990-92; mem. Lewis Ctrl. Instructional Coun., 1992-96, Lakeview Sch. Bldg. Cadre, 1994-95. Mem. NEA, Iowa State Edn. Assn., Lewis Cen. Edn. Assn., Coun. for Exceptional Children, Iowa Coun. Tchrs. of English, Phi Delta Kappa. Avocations: reading, writing, swimming, sewing, gardening. Office: Lakeview Sch Piute and Wright Rds Council Bluffs IA 51501

ROBERTS, ARCHIBALD EDWARD, retired army officer, author; b. Cheboygan, Mich., Mar. 21, 1915; s. Archibald Lancaster and Madeline Ruth (Smith) R.; grad. Command and Gen. Staff Coll., 1952; student U.S. Armed Forces Inst., 1953, U. Md., 1958; m. Florence Snure, Sept. 25, 1940 (div. Feb. 1950); children—Michael James, John Douglas; m. 2d, Doris Elfriede White, June 23, 1951; children—Guy Archer, Charles Lancaster, Christopher Corwin. Enlisted U.S. Army, 1939, advanced through grades to lt. col., 1960; served in Far East Command, 1942, 1953-55, ETO, 1943-45, 57-60; tech. info. officer Office Surgeon Gen., Dept. Army, Washington, 1950, Ft. Campbell, Ky., 1952-53, info. officer, Camp Chicamauga, Japan, Ft. Bragg, N.C., Ft. Campbell, Ky., 1953-56, Ft. Campbell, 1956-57, Ft. Benning, Ga., Wurzburg, Germany, 1957-58, spl. projects officer Augsburg, Germany, 1959-60, U.S. Army Info. Office, N.Y.C., 1960-61; writer program precipitating Senate Armed Services Hearings, 1962; ret., 1965; mgr., salesman Nu-Enamel Stores, Ashville, N.C., 1937-38; co-owner, dir. Roberts & Roberts Advt. Agy., Denver, 1946-49; pres. Found. for Edn., Scholarship, Patriotism and Americanism, Inc.; founder, nat. bd. dirs. Com. to Restore Constn., Inc., 1965—. Recipient award of merit Am. Acad. Pub. Affairs, 1967; Good Citizenship medal SAR, 1968; Liberty award Congress of Freedom, 1969; Man of Yr. awards Women for Constl. Govt., 1970, Wis. Legislative and Research Com., 1971; medal of merit Am. Legion, 1972; Speaker of Year award We, The People, 1973; Col. Arch Roberts Week named for him City of Danville, Ill., 1974; recipient Spl. Tribute State of Mich., 1979. Mem. Res. Officers Assn., Airborne Assn., SAR, Sons Am. Colonists. Author: Rakkasan, 1955; Screaming Eagles, 1956; The Marne Division, 1957; Victory Denied, 1966; The Anatomy of a Revolution, 1968; Peace: By the Wonderful People Who Brought You Korea and Viet Nam, 1972; The Republic: Decline and Future Promise, 1975; The Crisis of Federal Regionalism: A Solution, 1976; Emerging Struggle for State Sovereignty, 1979; How to Organize for Survival, 1982; The Most Secret Science, 1984; also numerous pamphlets and articles. Home: 2218 W Prospect PO Box 986 Fort Collins CO 80522-0986

ROBERTS, BERT C., JR., telecommunications company executive; b. 1942; married. BS, Johns Hopkins U., 1965. Project dir., mgr. Westinghouse Electric Corp., 1960-69; dir. Leasco Response Inc., 1969-72; with MCI Communications Corp., Washington, 1972—, v.p., 1974-76, sr. v.p., 1976-83, pres., 1983-85; chief operating officer MCI Telecommunications Corp., Washington, 1985-91, chief exec. officer, 1991—, chmn., 1992—. Office: MCI Comm Corp 1801 Pennsylvania Ave NW Washington DC 20006-3606*

ROBERTS, BILL GLEN, retired fire chief, investor, consultant; b. Deport, Tex., June 2, 1938; s. Samuel Westbrook and Ann Lee (Rhodes) R.; m. Ramona Ryall, June 1, 1963 (dec. Nov. 1988); 1 child, Renee Ann. Student, So. Meth. U., 1968, North Tex. State U., 1974; grad. paramedic course, U. Tex. Southwestern Med. Sch., 1974; grad. Exec. Program for Fire Service, Tex. A&M U., 1978; AAS, El Centro Jr. Coll., Dallas, 1980; grad. exec. fire officer program, Nat. Fire Acad., 1989. With Dallas Fire Dept., 1958-82, lt., 1964-67, capt., 1967-71, div. fire chief, 1971-79, asst. fire chief, 1979-83; fire chief Austin (Tex.) Fire Dept., 1983-94; tech. bd. dirs. Found. Fire Safety, Washington, 1982-85; adj. faculty Nat. Fire Acad., 1981-86; aft. State Life of Indpls., Dallas, 1962; owner Personnel Testing Lab., Dallas, 1963; real estate salesman Dale Copus Realtor, Dallas, 1963-66; salesman intercommunications equipment Chandler Sound, Dallas, 1966-67; field engr. IBM Corp., Dallas, 1968; cons. U. Tenn., 1974, Ga. Inst. Tech., 1974, Tex. Dept. Health Resources, 1973-78, Rand Corp., Washington, Mission Rsch., Santa Barbara, Calif., Macro. Author: EMS Dallas, 1978; (with others) Anesthesia for Surgery Trauma, 1976, EMS Measures to Improve Care, 1980; contbr. articles to periodicals. Com. chmn. Dallas Jaycees, 1962-65; mem. task force Am. Heart Assn., Austin, 1973-83; bd. dirs. Brackenridge Hosp., 1989, Rehab. Hosp. Austin, 1992-94, Austin Police Pensions Bd., 1989, Capitol Area coun. Boy Scouts Am., 1989-92. Recipient John Stemmons Service award Dallas Fire Dept., 1979; Internat. Assn. Fire Chiefs scholar, 1967. Mem. Internat. Assn. Fire Chiefs, Nat. Fire Protection Assn., Nat. Critical Care Inst., Am. Heart Assn., Am. Trauma Soc. (founder), Am. Assn. Trauma Specialists, Nat. Assn. Emergency Med. Technicians, Tex. Assn. Emergency Med. Technicians, ACS, North Tex. Coun. of Govts. (regional emergency svc. adv. coun. 1973-79), Internat. Rescue and First Aid Assn., Found. Fire Safety (tech. bd. dirs. 1982-85), Tex. Assn. Realtors, Austin World Affairs Coun., People to People Internat. Methodist. Home: 3 Highlander Rd Asheville NC 28804-1112

ROBERTS, BRIAN LEON, communications executive; b. Phila., June 28, 1959; s. Ralph J. and Suzanne F. Roberts; m. Aileen Kennedy, Dec. 28, 1985; children: Sarah, Tucker, Amanda. Student, U. Pa., 1981. V.p. opns. Comcast Cable Communications, Inc., Phila., 1985-86; exec. v.p. Comcast Corp., 1986—, also bd. dirs., now pres.; bd. dirs. Turner Broadcasting System, QVC Network, Viewer's Choice, Calbe Labs. Vice chmn. The Walter Katz Found. Mem. Nat. Cable TV Assn. (bd. dirs., exec. com.). Office: Comcast Corp 1500 Market St Philadelphia PA 19102*

ROBERTS, BURTON BENNETT, administrative judge; b. N.Y.C., July 25, 1922; s. Alfred S. and Cecelia (Schanfein) R.; m. Gerhild Ukryn. B.A., NYU, 1943, LL.M., 1953; LL.B., Cornell U., 1949. Bar: N.Y. 1949. Asst. dist. atty. N.Y. County, 1949-66; chief asst. dist. atty. Bronx County, Bronx, N.Y., 1966-68; acting dist. atty. Bronx County, 1968-69, dist. atty., 1969-72; justice Supreme Ct. State N.Y., 1973—, adminstrv. judge criminal br. Bronx County 12th Jud. Dist., 1984—, adminstrv. judge civil br. Bronx County 12th Dist., 1988—. Pres. Bronx div. Hebrew Home for Aged, 1967-72. With U.S. Army, 1943-45. Decorated Purple Heart, Bronze Star with oak leaf cluster. Mem. Assn. Bar City N.Y., Am. Bar Assn., N.Y. Bar Assn., Bronx County Bar Assn., N.Y. State Dist. Attys. Assn. (pres. 1971-72). Jewish (exec. bd. temple). Home: 215 E 68th St Apt 19A New York NY 10021-5727 Office: Supreme Ct Bronx County 851 Grand Concourse Bronx NY 10451-2937

ROBERTS, CALVIN, materials engineer; b. Savannah, Ga., Oct. 28, 1945; s. Fred and Hattie (Leach) R. AAS, Norwalk (Conn.) State Coll., 1968; BS in Civil Engring., NYU, 1971; MS in Civil Engring., Pa. State U., 1973. Registered profl. engr. N.Y., Conn., Mich. Sr. project engr. Wilbur Smith & Assocs., New Haven, 1979-81; project mgr. URS Co. Inc., N.Y.C., 1981-83; v.p. Salmon Assocs., P.E., L.I., N.Y., 1983-85; traffic and safety engr. State of Mich. Dept. Transp., Lansing, 1985-92, exec. office mgmt. assessment, 1992-94, engr. materials and tech., 1994—; engr. Frederic R. Harris Inc., Stamford, Conn., 1973-79. Mem. fin. com. Mich. Capital coun. Girl Scouts U.S., Lansing, 1988—; chmn. com. on minority engring. activities Pa. State U. Coll. Engring., University Park, 1988—. Mem. Transp. Rsch. Bd., Inst. Transp. Engrs., Nat. Com. on Uniform Traffic Control Devices (sec. signs tech. com. 1986-93), Am. Assn. State Hwy. Ofcls. (standing com. on hwy. traffic safety). Avocations: photography, sports, classical music, art collector. Home: 3928 Hemmingway Dr Okemos MI 48864-3773 Office: Mich Dept Transp 425 W Ottawa St # 30050 Lansing MI 48933-1532

ROBERTS, CARL GEOFFREY, lawyer; b. Boston, June 17, 1948; s. Simon Matthew and Ruth (Gorfinkle) R.; m. Sharon Ash, Mar. 24, 1979. BA, Harvard U., 1970; JD, U. Pa., 1974. Bar: Pa. 1974, U.S. Dist. Ct. (ea. dist.) Pa. 1974, U.S. Ct. Appeals (3d cir.) 1978, U.S. Supreme Ct. 1980, U.S. Ct. Claims 1980, U.S. Dist. Ct. (mid. dist.) Pa. 1986. Law clk. U.S. Dist. Ct. (ea. dist.) Pa., Phila., 1974-76; assoc. Dilworth, Paxson, Kalish & Kauffman, Phila., 1978-82, ptnr., 1982-92; ptnr. Ballard, Spahr, Andrews & Ingersoll, Phila., 1992—. Bd. dirs. Phila. Chamber Ensemble, sec., 1977-92, pres., 1992-95. Mem. ABA (law practice mgmt. sect., coun. computer divsn., vice chmn. techs. and facilities group). Office: Ballard Spahr Andrews & Ingersoll 1735 Market St Ste 51 Philadelphia PA 19103-7501

ROBERTS, CAROL ANTONIA, county commissioner, real estate associate; b. Miami, Fla., June 22, 1936; d. Milton R. and Betty Shirley (Pallot) Klein; m. Aug. 9, 1953; children: David, Jonathan, Mark, Stephen, Scott, Pamela. Student, Tuft U., 1953-54, Palm Beach (Fla.) Jr. Coll., 1960-62, Palm Beach Atlantic Coll., 1971-72. Host radio program Sta. WPBR, Palm Beach, Fla., 1976-83; co-founder Denman Roberts & Ross, West Palm Beach, Fla., 1978-80; pres. Sunshine Acad. Press, Inc., West Palm Beach, 1978-82; pres., broker VIP Mgmt. and Realty, Inc., West Palm Beach, 1980—. Commr. City of West Palm Beach, Fla., 1975, 77, 82, 84, vice mayor, 1976-77, 84-85, mayor, 1985-86; chair Palm Beach County Bd. Commrs., 1987, 88, bd. dirs., chair women's div. Palm Beach County Comprehensive Community Mental Health Ctr. Bd., 1978-80, Jewish Fedn. Palm Beach County, 1978-80, Palm Beach Inst. Med. Rsch., Goodwill Industries,

Cities in Schs., Anti-Defamation League, Adopt-A-Family; chair Tri-County Rail Authority, chmn. mktg. com.; vice chair Solid Waste Authority, 1977-78; pres. Fla. Assn. Counties, 1996-97; chair Art in Pub. Places, Artificial Reef com., Intracoastal Waterway com.; co-chair Water Resources Mgmt. Adv. Bd.; vice chair Fla. League of Cities Intergovtl. Rels. com.; mem. Palm Beach Sports Authority, So. Fla. Mental Health Consortium, Treasure Coast Regional Planning Coun.; mem Fla. Crime Prevention Commn., 1985; founder Jewish Cmty.Day Sch.of the Palm Beaches. John and Mabel Ringling Mus. Art grantee, Norton Art Gallery grantee, U. Ga. grantee, U. Fla. grantee, Tufts U. grantee, Fla. A&M U. grantee; named Woman of the Yr., Bus. and Profl. Women Palm Beaches, 1985, Leading Lady in Mcpl. Govt., Network Connection, 1985; recipient Appreciation award Tri-County Nat. Bus. League, 1985, Woman of the Yr. award Temple Beth El Sisterhood, 1986, Disting. medal Palm Beach Atlantic Coll., 1986, Disting mem. of Pres. Coun. U. Fla.; honoree as cmty. advocate Jewish Family and Children's Svc. of Palm Beach County, 1997; inducted into Fla.'s Hall of Fame, 1986. Mem. Fla. League of Cities (vice chair intergovtl. rels. com.), Fla. Assn. Counties (social svcs. policy com., pres. 1996—), Fla. Assn. Counties Bd. Dirs., Nat. Assn. Counties (intergovtl. rels. com., vice chair transp. and telecomms. steering com.), South Fla. Mental Health Consortium. Democrat. Jewish. Home: 6708 Pamela Ln West Palm Beach FL 33405-4175 Office: Office Bd County Commrs PO Box 1989 301 N Olive Ave West Palm Beach FL 33402-1989

ROBERTS, CASSANDRA FENDLEY, investment company executive; b. Port St. Joe, Fla., Sept. 24, 1951; d. Pope and Sophie Virginia (McGee) Fendley; m. Charles Stanton Roberts, Aug. 7, 1971; 1 child, Davis McGee. BSBA, Edison State Coll., 1983. Sales assoc., v.p. Cooper Corp., Atlanta, 1979-85; sales assoc., broker WTM Investments, Atlanta, 1985-92, v.p., 1992—. Mem. Nat. Bd. Realtors, Ga. Bd. Realtors, Atlanta Bd. Realtors. Avocations: mathematics, reading. Office: WTM Investments Inc PO Box 13256 Atlanta GA 30324-0256

ROBERTS, CECIL KENNETH, lawyer; b. Tyler, Tex., Mar. 31, 1930; s. Cecil Kelly and Blanche Lulu (Cash) R.; m. Cary N. Thornton, Sept. 1, 1951; children: Kenneth Kelly, Cristina Cary. BBA, U. Tex., Austin, 1950, JD, 1951; LLM, U. Tex., 1953; AMP, Harvard U., 1971. Bar: Tex. 1952. Atty. Exxon Co., U.S.A., Houston, 1954-64, N.Y.C., 1964-65; chief atty. refining, environment and labor rels. law Houston, 1965-67, adminstrv. mgr. Baytown refinery, 1967-68, mgr. pub affairs dept., 1969-72; exec. asst. to pres. Exxon Corp., N.Y.C., 1972-73, dep. mgr. pub. affairs dept., 1973-74, assoc. gen. counsel, 1974-79; gen. counsel Exxon Co., U.S.A., Houston, 1979-92; v.p., gen. counsel Exxon Corp., Dallas, 1993-95; of counsel Fulbright & Jaworski, Houston, 1995—; bd. dirs. Nat. Ctr. for State Cts., 1986-89; mem. steering com. Com. for Jud. Merit Election. Trustee Southwestern Legal Found., 1993-96, U. Tex. Law Found., 1992—; bd. dirs. Landmark Legal Found., Kansas City, Mo., 1980-96, vice chmn., 1987-93; mem. bd. visitors U. Tex. Law Sch., Austin; mem. bd. visitors Stanford U. Law Sch., 1980-84, mem. law and econs. adv. com., 1983-87. Recipient Paul C. Reardon award Nat. Ctr. for State Cts., 1990; named Outstanding Alumni, U. Tex. Sch. Law, 1993. Fellow Am. Bar Found.; mem. ABA, Tex. Bar Assn., Houston Bar Assn., Am. Law Inst., Am. Petroleum Inst. (gen. com. on law), Assn. Gen. Counsel, Am. Arbitration Assn. (bd. dirs. 1993—), Petroleum Club (bd. dirs.), River Oaks Country Club, Las Colinas Country Club, Univ. Club (N.Y.C.), Monterey Peninsula Country Club. Office: Fulbright & Jaworski 1301 Mckinney St Ste 5100 Houston TX 77010-3095

ROBERTS, CHALMERS MCGEAGH, reporter; b. Pitts., Nov. 18, 1910; s. Franklin B. and Lillian B. (McGeagh) R.; m. Lois Hall, Sept. 11, 1941; children: David H., Patricia E. Roberts Monahan, Christopher C. A.B., Amherst Coll., 1933, L.H.D., 1963. Reporter Washington Post, 1933-34, Asso. Press., Pitts. bur., 1934-35, Toledo News-Bee, 1936-38, Japan Times, Tokyo, 1938-39; asst. mng. editor Washington Daily News, 1939-41; Sunday editor Washington Times-Herald, 1941; staff OWI, London, Washington, 1941-43, Life mag., 1946-47, Washington Star, 1947-49; staff writer Washington Post, 1949-71, reporter local and nat. news, 1949-53, chief diplomatic corr., 1953-71, contbg. columnist, 1971—; contbg. columnist San Diego Union, 1971-86. Author: Washington Past and Present, 1950, Can We Meet the Russians Half Way?, 1958, The Nuclear Years: The Arms Race and Arms Control 1945-70, 1970, First Rough Draft: A Journalist's Journal of Our Times, 1973, The Washington Post: The First 100 Years, 1977, rev. In the Shadow of Power: The Story of the Washington Post, 1989, How Did I Get Here So Fast? Rhetorical Questions and Available Answers from a Long and Happy Life, 1991; contbr. articles to popular mags. Capt. USAAF, 1943-46. Decorated Order of Merit (Germany); recipient Sigma Delta Chi award, 1953, nat. news award Washington Newspaper Guild, 1954, 60; citation Overseas Press Club, 1955, front page grand prize Washington Newspaper Guild, 1957, 60, Raymond Clapper Meml. award, 1957, Edward Weintal prize for diplomatic reporting, 1975, Frank Luther Mott Rsch. award Kappa Tau Alpha, 1978; named to Washington Journalism Hall of Fame, Sigma Delta Chi, 1982. Mem. Am. Newspaper Guild, State Dept. Corrs. Assn. (pres. 1958-59), Coun. Fgn. Rels., Nat. Book Critics Cir. Home: 6699 MacArthur Blvd Bethesda MD 20816-2247

ROBERTS, CHARLES A., construction safety/accident prevention expert; b. Washington, Feb. 20, 1935; s. John Avon and Marion (Lewis) R.; m. Edith Emily Lanier, Aug. 12, 1940; children: Pamela Ruth Roberts Schweitzer, Michelle G. BA, Md. U., 1967; MBA, Antioch Sch. Law, 1984. Cert. safety profl. with constrn. and product liability specialist; cert. hazard control mgr.; cert. instr. OSHA constrn. safety courses; DDC cert. instr.-trainer Nat. Safety Coun.'s Defensive Driver course; cert. ARC instr.; cert. Bur Mine rescuer; cert. video prodr.; DOE-Dept. Energy nuclear site top secret security clearance; lic. single-engine pvt. pilot. Dir. safety Kora and Williams, 1981-83; nat. dir. safety and health Associated Builders and Contractors, 1983-84; pres. Roberts Safety Cons., Kensington, Md., 1983-88; safety dir. SMC Concrete Constrn. Inc., Va., 1988-95; pres. Constrn. Safety Inst., Inc., Kensington, 1990-93, 94—; safety mgr. Hyman Constrn. Co., 1993-94; tunnel safety mgr. Kiska Kajima, N.Y., 1994-95; safety coord. Mortenson Constrn., Richmond, Va., 1995-96. Author: Construction Safety Manual, 1989-97; contbr. articles to profl. jours. Coun. mem. City of Hyattsville, Md., 1973-78. With USN, 1953-58. Mem. Am. Soc. Safety Engrs. Republican. Avocations: crafts, woodworking, home repair, traveling. Office: Constrn Safety Inst 11401 Woodson Ave Kensington MD 20895-1433

ROBERTS, CHARLES PATRICK, senator; b. Topeka, Kans., Apr. 20, 1936; m. Franki Fann, 1969; children: David, Ashleigh, Anne-Wesley. BS, Kans. State U., 1958. Pub. Litchfield Park, Ariz., 1962-67; adminstrv. asst. to U.S. Senator Frank Carlson, U.S. Senate, Washington, 1967-68; adminstrv. asst. to U.S. Congressman Keith Sebelius U.S. Ho. of Reps., Washington, 1968-80; mem. 97th to 104th Congresses from 1st Kans. Dist., Washington, 1980-96, U.S. Senate from Kans., Washington, 1997—. Served with USMC, 1958-62. Office: US Senate 302 Hart Senate Off Bldg Washington DC 20510-1605

ROBERTS, CHARLES S., software engineer; b. Newark, Sept. 25, 1937; s. Ben and Sara (Fasten) R.; m. Wendy Shadlen, June 8, 1959; children: Lauren Roberts Gold, Tamara G. Roberts. BS in Chemistry, Carnegie-Mellon U., 1959; PhD in Physics, MIT, 1963. MTS, radiation physics rsch. AT&T Bell Labs., Murray Hill, N.J., 1963-68, head info. processing rsch., 1968-73, head interactive computer systems rsch., 1973-82; head, advanced systems dept. AT&T Bell Labs., Denver, 1982-87; head software architecture planning dept. AT&T Bell Labs., Holmdel, N.J., 1987-88; R&D mgr., system architecture lab. Hewlett-Packard Co., Cupertino, Calif., 1988-90, R&D mgr. univ. rsch. grants, 1990-92; prin. lab. scientist Hewlett-Packard Labs., Palo Alto, Calif., 1992—. Contbr. articles to profl. jours. Westinghouse scholar Carnegie Mellon U., 1955-59; NSF fellow MIT, 1959-63. Mem. IEEE, Assn. for Computing Machinery, Am. Phys. Soc., Sigma Xi, Tau Beta Pi, Phi Kappa Phi. Achievements include 2 patents on associative information retrieval and dithered display system; development of early UNIX operating system for 32-bit computers; research on theory to explain electron loss in Van Allen Belts, on superimposed code techniques for associative information retrieval. Home: 210 Manresa Ct Los Altos CA 94022-4623 Office: Hewlett-Packard Labs PO Box 10490 1501 Page Mill Rd Palo Alto CA 94303-0969

ROBERTS, CLYDE FRANCIS, business executive; b. Lawrence, Mass., Sept. 10, 1924; s. Clyde F. and Blanche (Fellows) R.; May 18, 1947; 1 dau., Michele. B.S.B.A., Boston U., 1947; postgrad., Am. U., Beirut, 1954. Commd. fgn. affairs officer Dept. State, 1948-57; v.p. NAM, Washington, 1957-75; pres. Indsl. Fasteners Inst., Cleve., 1975-82; founding ptnr. RBJ Technologies, 1982—; pres. Nat. Assets Mgmt. Enterprises, 1984—; mem. instl. rev. bd. Fairview Gen. Hosp., 1985-96; mem. adv. bd. Tabac Assocs., 1986-90, Phoenix Corp, 1989-96. Served with U.S. Army, 1943-45, Africa, Sicily, Italy, Greece. Mem. Nat. Indsl. Coun., Coun. Small Enterprise. Roman Catholic. Office: 4601 N Park Ave Chevy Chase MD 20815

ROBERTS, CORINNE BOGGS (COKIE ROBERTS), correspondent, news analyst; b. New Orleans, Dec. 27, 1943; d. Thomas Hale and Corinne Morrison (Claiborne) Boggs; m. Steven V. Roberts, Sept. 10, 1966; children: Lee Harriss, Rebecca Boggs. BA in Polit. Sci., Wellesley Coll., 1964; hon. degrees, Amherst Coll., Columbia Coll., Loyola U. of the South, Manhattanville Coll., Gonzaga U., Boston Coll., Hood Coll., Chestnut Hill Coll., Miss. Women's U., Notre Dame U. Md. Assoc. prodr., host Altman Prodns., Washington, 1964-66; prodr. Altman Prodns., L.A., 1969-72; reporter, editor Cowles Communications, N.Y.C., 1967; prodr. Sta. WNEW-TV, N.Y.C., 1968, Sta. KNBC-TV, L.A., Greece, 1972-74; reporter CBS News, Athens, Greece, 1974-77; corr. Nat. Pub. Radio, Washington, 1977—, MacNeil/Lehrer Newshour, Washington, 1984-88; spl. Washington corr. ABC News, Washington, 1988—; interviewer, commentator This Week With David Brinkley, Washington, 1992-96; co-anchor This Week, 1996—; lectr. in field. Co-host weekly pub. TV program on Congress, The Lawmakers, 1981-84; producer, host pub. affairs program Sta. WRC-TV, Washington; producer Sta. KNBC-TV Serendipity, L.A. (award for excellence in local programming, Emmy nomination for children's programming); contbr. articles to newspapers, mags. Bd. dirs. Dirksen Ctr., Pekin, Ill., 1988-95, Everett Dirksen award, 1987; bd. dirs. Fgn. Students Svc. Ctr., Washington, 1990—, Manhattanville Coll., Purchase, N.Y., 1991—, Children's Inn at NIH, Bethesda, Md., 1992—. Recipient Broadcast award Nat. Orgn. Working Women, 1984, Everett McKinley Dirksen disting. reporting of Congress, 1987, Weintal award Georgetown U., 1988, Corp. Pub. Broadcasting award, 1988, Edward R. Murrow award Corp. Pub. Broadcasting, 1990, Broadcast award Nat. Women's Polit. Caucus, 1990, David Brinkley Comm. award, 1992, Mother of Yr. award Nat. Mothers' Day Com., 1992, Emmy award news and documentary, 1992. Mem. Radio-TV Corrs. Assn. (pres. 1981-82, bd. dirs. 1980-94), U.S. Capitol Hist. Soc. Roman Catholic. Office: ABC News 1717 Desales St NW Washington DC 20036-4401 Office: Nat Pub Radio 635 Massachusetts Ave NW Washington DC 20001-3752

ROBERTS, DAVID, airport executive. Dir. Indpls. Internat. Airport. Office: Indpls Internat Airport Indpls Airport Authority Box 100 2500 S High School Rd Indianapolis IN 46241

ROBERTS, DAVID AMBROSE, lawyer; b. Pascagoula, Miss., Apr. 27, 1962; s. James Elmer and Edna Louise (Scott) R.; m. Elizabeth Anne Knecht, June 29, 1990. BA, U. Miss., 1985, JD, 1988. Bar: Miss. 1988, U.S. Dist. Ct. (no. dist.) Miss. 1988, U.S. Ct. Appeals (5th cir.) 1991, U.S. Dist. Ct. (so. dist.) Miss. 1991, U.S. Supreme Ct. 1996. Asst. dist. atty. Office of Dist. Atty., State of Miss., Pascagoula, 1988-90; ptnr. Gordon, Myers, Frazier & Roberts, Pascagoula, 1991-94; pvt. practice Pascagoula, 1994—. Recipient Am. Jurisprudence award, 1988; named to Outstanding Young Men in Am. Mem. Miss. Bar Assn., Jackson County Bar Assn., 5th Cir. Bar Assn., Nat. Assn. Criminal Def. Lawyers, Elks. Office: PO Box 2009 Pascagoula MS 39569-2009

ROBERTS, DAVID GLENDENNING, state supreme court justice; b. Fort Fairfield, Maine, July 17, 1928; s. Melvin Philip and Ethel (Chamberlain) R.; m. Rose Marie Downie, Feb. 9, 1952; children: Michael, Mary, Dorothy, Catherine, Sarah, Joseph, Susan. A.B., Bowdoin Coll., 1950; LL.B., Boston U., 1956. Bar: Maine 1956, U.S. Dist. Ct. Maine 1959, U.S. Ct. Appeals (1st cir.) 1964. Ptnr. Pendleton and Roberts, Caribou, Maine, 1956-61; asst. U.S. atty. U.S. Dept. Justice, Bangor, Maine, 1961-66; pvt. practice Bangor, 1966-67; justice Maine Superior Ct., Bangor, 1967-80; assoc. justice Supreme Jud. Ct., Portland, 1980—; mem. Maine Jud. Council, Augusta, 1969-77, 80-86. Served to lt. U.S. Army, 1951-53. Democrat. Roman Catholic. Office: ME Supreme Jud Ct PO Box 269 142 Federal St Portland ME 04112

ROBERTS, DAVID LOWELL, journalist; b. Lusk, Wyo., Jan. 12, 1954; s. Leslie James and LaVerne Elizabeth (Johns) R. BA, U. Ariz., 1979; postgrad., U. Nebr., 1992—. Founder, editor, publisher Medicine Bow (Wyo.) Post, 1977-88; journalism instr. U. Wyo., Laramie, 1987-92; adviser U. Wyo. Student Publs., Laramie, 1987-92; gen. mgr. Student Media Corp U No. Colo., Greeley, 1995—; founder, publisher Hanna Herald, Wyo., 1979-80; exch. reporter The Washington Post, 1982; freelance reporter Casper (Wyo.) Star-Tribune, 1978-83, various publs.; founder, The Hanna Herald, 1979-80. Co-author: (book) The Wyoming Almanac, 1988, 90, 94, 96; author: (book) Sage Street, 1991; columnist Sage Street, 1989-92. Chmn. Medicine Bow Film Commn., 1984; treas. Friends of the Medicine Bow Mus., 1984-88; pres. Medicine Bow Area C. of C., 1984; dir. Habitat for Humanity of Albany County, Laramie, 1991-92. Recipient Nat. Newspaper Assn. awards, over 40 Wyo. Press. Assn. awards, Five Editorial awards U. Wyo., Citizen of Yr. award People of Medicine Bow, 1986, Student Publs. awards U. Wyo., 1990, 92. Mem. Friends of Medicine Bow Mus., Habitat for Humanity of Albany County. Democrat. Methodist. Avocations: writing, golf, visiting museums, photography. Home: 4966 W 8th St Greeley CO 80631

ROBERTS, DELMAR LEE, editor; b. Raleigh, N.C., Apr. 9, 1933; s. James Delmer and Nellie Brockelbank (Tyson) R. BS in textile mgmt., N.C. State U., 1956; MA in journalism, U. S.C., 1974. Product develop. engr. U.S. Rubber Co. (Uniroyal), Winnsboro, S.C., 1959-64; process improvement engr. Allied Chemical Co., Irmo, S.C., 1965-67; assoc. editor S.C. History Illustrated Mag., Columbia, 1970; editor-in-chief, editl. v.p. Sandlapper-The Mag. of S.C., Columbia, 1968-74; mng. editor, art dir. Law Practice Mgmt. Mag. of the ABA, Chgo., Ill., 1975—. Editor: The Best of Legal Economics, 1979; freelance editor and/or designer of over 35 books. Active World Affairs Coun. Columbia, 1997—; 1st v.p. English-Speaking Union, 1996-97, pres. 1997—. With U.S. Army, 1956-58. Hon. fellow Coll. of Law Practice Mgmt., Ann Arbor, Mich., 1995—. Mem. Soc. Profl. Journalists, Capital City Club (Columbia), Phi Kappa Tau, Kappa Tau Alpha. Avocations: European travel, Turkish carpet/Kilim collecting, antique collecting.

ROBERTS, DENNIS WILLIAM, association executive; b. Chgo., Jan. 7, 1943; s. William Owen and Florence Harriet (Denman) R. BA in Journalism, U. N.Mex., 1968; MA in Legal Studies, Antioch U., 1982; MA, St. John's Coll., 1984. Cert. assn. exec. Gen. assignment reporter Albuquerque Pub. Co., 1964, sports writer, 1960-64, advt. and display salesman, 1967-68; dir. info. N.Mex. bldg. br. Assoc. Gen. Contractors Am., Albuquerque, 1968-79, asst. exec. dir., 1979-82, dir., 1982—. Active United Way, Albuquerque, 1969-78; chmn. Albuquerque Crime Prevention Council, 1982; bd. dir. ARC (Rio Grande chpt., 1992—). Recipient Pub. Relations Achievement award Assoc. Gen. Contractors Am., 1975, 78. Mem. N.Mex. Pub. Relations Conf. (chmn. 1975, 82-83), Pub. Relations Soc. Am. (accredited, pres. N.Mex. chpt. 1981, chmn. S.W. dist. 1984, chmn. sect. 1988), Am. Soc. Assn. Execs. (cert.), Contrn. Specifications Inst. (Outstanding Industry Mem. 1974, Outstanding Com. Chmn. 1978), Sigma Delta Chi (pres. N.Mex. chpt. 1969). Republican. Lutheran. Clubs: Toastmasters (dist. gov. 1977-78, Disting. Dist. award 1978, Toastmaster of Year 1979-80), Masons, Shriners, Elks. Home: #210 1520 University Blvd NE Albuquerque NM 87102 Office: Assn Gen Contractors 1615 University Blvd NE Albuquerque NM 87102-1717 *Personal philosophy: Set your priorities in life, then your goals. In pursuing your goals, visualize their accomplishment. Be persistent, and you will accomplish what you set out to accomplish. Learn to be fair to others and empathetic.*

ROBERTS, DONALD FRANK, JR., communications educator; b. Seattle, Mar. 30, 1939; s. Donald Frank Sr., and Ruth Amalia (Geiger) R.; m. Karlene Hahn, 1963 (div. 1981); 1 child, Donald Brett; m. Wendy G. Roberts, Aug. 26, 1983; stepchildren: Richard L., David L., Katherine M. AB, Columbia U., 1961; MA, U. Calif., Berkeley, 1963; PhD, Stanford U., 1968. Instr., dept. English U. Hawaii, Honolulu, 1963-64; asst. dir. ednl. svc. bur. The Wall Street Jour., Princeton, N.J., 1964-65; asst. prof., rsch. assoc. dept. Comm., Inst. Comm. Rsch. Stanford (Calif.) U., 1970-76, assoc. prof., 1976-84, prof. Comm., 1984—, dir. Inst. Comm. Rsch., 1985-90, chmn. dept. Comm., 1990-96, Thomas More Storke Prof., 1991—; cons. NIMH, 1970-71, Rand Corp., 1972-74, Sta. KQED-TV, 1975-77, Far West Lab. Ednl. Rsch. and Devel., 1978-79, FTC, 1978-80, Westinghouse Broadcasting, 1983-86, Soc. Nutrition Edn., 1984-86, The Disney Channel, 1986-87, WHO, 1988-89, SRI Internat., 1988-89, Carnegie Coun. Adolescence, 1989-90, NBC, 1992, Ctr. Disease Control, 1992, Children Now, 1992—, Software Pubs. Assn., 1994, Nickelodeon, 1994; bd. advisors Media Scope, 1992-94; v.p. Recreational Software Adv. Coun., 1994—; proposal reviewer NIMH, NSF, U.S. Agy. Internat. Devel., Can. Coun., John and Mary R. Markle Found., W.T. Grant Found.; speaker numerous seminars, confs., symposia. Co-author: Process and Effects of Mass Communication, 1971, Television and Human Behavior, 1978, It's Not ONLY Rock and Roll, 1997; mem. editl. bd. Jour. Broadcasting, 1980-88, Pub. Opinion Quarterly, 1981-86, Communicare, 1986—; editl. reviewer Commn. Rsch., Comm. Monograph, Comm. Yearbook, Human Comm. Rsch., Jour. Comm., Jour. Quarterly, Child Devel., Jour. Applied Psychology, Jour. Ednl. Psychology, Psychology Bull., Jour. Adolescent Health; contbr. articles to profl. jours., also monographs and book chpts. Fellow Human Scis. Rsch. Coun., Pretoria. South Africa, 1985, 1987, Fullbright Teaching fellow Inst. for Unterrichtstechnologie Und Medienpadagogic, Austria, 1987. Mem. APA, Internat. Comm. Assn., Assn. Edn. in Journalism and Mass Comm., Soc. Rsch. Child Devel., Soc. Personality and Soc. Psychology. Office: Stanford U Dept Comm McClatchy Hall Stanford CA 94305-2050

ROBERTS, DONALD JOHN, economics and business educator, consultant; b. Winnipeg, Man., Can., Feb. 11, 1945; came to U.S., 1967; s. Donald Victor and Margaret Mabel (Riddell) R.; m. Kathleen Eleanor Taylor, Aug. 26, 1967. B.A. (honours), U. Man., 1967; Ph.D., U. Minn., 1972. Instr. dept. managerial econs. and decision scis. J.L. Kellogg Grad. Sch. Mgmt., Northwestern U., Evanston, Ill., 1971-72, asst. prof., 1972-74; assoc. prof. J. L. Kellogg Grad. Sch. Mgmt., Northwestern U., Evanston, Ill., 1974-77; prof. J.L. Kellogg Grad. Sch. Mgmt., Northwestern U., Evanston, Ill., 1977-80, Grad. Sch. Bus., Stanford U., Calif., 1980; Jonathan B. Lovelace prof. grad. sch. bus. Stanford U., 1980—, assoc. dean grad. sch. of bus., 1987-90; dir. exec. program in strategy and orgn., 1992—; dir. global mgmt. program Stanford U., 1994—; prof. (by courtesy) dept. econs. Stanford U., 1986—; vis. rsch. faculty U. Catholique de Louvain, Belgium, 1974-75; cons. bus., econs. and antitrust, 1976—; vis. fellow All Souls Coll., Oxford U., 1995. Co-author: Economics, Organization and Management, 1992;; assoc. editor Jour. Econ. Theory, 1977-92, Econometrica, 1985-87, Games and Economics Behavior, 1988—; mem. editl. bd. Am. Econ. Rev., 1991-95, Jour. Econs. and Mgmt. Strategy, 1991—, Orgns. and Markets Abstracts, 1996—; contbr. articles to profl. jours. NSF grantee, 1973-93; rsch. fellow Ctr. Ops. Rsch. and Econometrics, Heverlee, Belgium, 1974, fellow Ctr. for Advanced Study in the Behavioral Scis., 1991-92. Fellow Econometric Soc. (coun. 1994-96); mem. Am. Econ. Assn., Beta Gamma Sigma. Home: 835 Santa Fe Ave Palo Alto CA 94305-1022 Office: Stanford U Grad Sch Bus Stanford CA 94305

ROBERTS, DONALD MUNIER, retired banker, trust company executive; b. Paterson, N.J., Aug. 3, 1935; s. Edward and Dorothy (Munier) R.; m. Sally D. Ingram, Sept. 6, 1958 (dec. Feb. 1978); 1 dau., Sarah M.; m. Mary Ayer Gordon, June 23, 1978; children: Edward (dec.), John, Martha. B.S., Yale U., 1957; M.B.A., NYU, 1961. Exec. v.p., 1979-90; vice chmn., treas. U.S. Trust Co. N.Y., N.Y.C., 1990-95; retired, 1995; bd. dirs. York (Pa.) Internat. Corp., Burlington Resources, Inc. Trustee, pres. St. Bernards Sch. Mem. N.Y. Road Runners Club Inc. (chmn.), Tau Beta Pi. Republican. Club: Links (N.Y.C.). Home: 10 Gracie Sq New York NY 10028-8031 Office: 430 Park Ave Ste 600 New York NY 10022-3505

ROBERTS, DORIS, actress; b. St. Louis, Nov. 4, 1930; d. Larry and Ann (Meltzer) R.; m. William Goyen, Nov. 10, 1963 (dec.); m. Michael E. Cannata, June 21, 1950; 1 child, Michael R. Student, NYU, 1950-51; studies with, Sanford Meisner, Neighborhood Playhouse, N.Y.C., 1952-53, Lee Strasberg, Actors' Studio, N.Y.C., 1956. Ind. stage, screen and TV actress, 1953—. Profl. stage debut, Ann Arbor, Mich., 1953; appeared in summer stock Chatham, Mass., 1955; Broadway debut in The Time of Your Life, 1955; other Broadway and off-Broadway appearances include The Desk Set, 1955, The American Dream, 1961, The Death of Bessie Smith, 1961, The Office, 1965, The Color of Darkness, 1963, Marathon 33, 1963, Secret Affair of Mildred Wilde, 1972, Last of the Red Hot Lovers, 1969-71, Bad Habits, 1973 (Outer Circle Critics award 1974), Cheaters, 1976, Fairie Tale Theatre, 1985, The Fig Tree, 1987, It's Only a Play, 1992; movie debut Something Wild, 1961, movies include Barefoot in the Park, 1968, No Way to Treat a Lady, 1973, A Lovely Way to Die, 1969, Honeymoon Killers, 1969, A New Leaf, 1970, Such Good Friends, 1971, Little Murders, 1971, Heartbreak Kid, 1972, Hester Street, 1975, The Taking of Pelham, One, Two, Three, 1974, The Rose, 1979, Good Luck, Miss Wyckoff, 1979, Rabbit Test, 1979, Ordinary Hero, 1986, #1 with a Bullet, 1987, For Better or for Worse-Street Law, 1988, National Lampoon's Xmas Vacation, 1989, Used People, 1992, The Night We Never Met, Momma Mia, 1994, Walking to Waldheim, 1995, The Grass Harp, 1995; TV debut on Studio One, 1958, Mary Hartman, Mary Hartman, 1975, Mary Tyler Moore Hour, 1976, Soap, 1978-79, Angie, 1979-80, Remington Steele, 1984-88, Lily Tomlin Comedy Hour, Barney Miller, Alice, Full House, Perfect Strangers, Sunday Dinner, A Family Man, The Fig Tree (Pub. Broadcasting System), 1987, (TV films) The Story Teller, 1979, Ruby and Oswald, 1978, It Happened One Christmas, 1978, Jennifer: A Woman's Story, 1979, The Diary of Anne Frank, 1982, A Letter to Three Wives, Blind Faith, 1989, The Sunset Gang, 1990, Crossroads, 1993, Dream On, 1993, The Boys, 1993, A Time To Heal, 1994, A Mom For Christmas, Murder She Wrote, Step By Step, Burk's Law Walker, Texas Ranger, 1994, Amazing Grace, 1995, High Society, 1996, Everybody Loves Raymond, 1996. Recipient Emmy award Nat. Acad. TV Arts and Scis., 1984, 85, Emmy nominations, 1986, 88, 91. Mem. SAG, AFTRA, Actors Equity Assn., Dirs. Guild Am.

ROBERTS, DORIS EMMA, epidemiologist, consultant; b. Toledo, Dec. 28, 1915; d. Frederic Constable and Emma Selina (Reader) R. Diploma, Peter Bent Brigham Sch. Nursing, Boston, 1938; BS, Geneva Coll., Beaver Falls, Pa., 1944; MPH, U. Minn., 1958; PhD, U. N.C., 1967. RN, Mass. Staff nurse Vis. Nurse Assn., New Haven, 1938-40; sr. nurse Neighborhood House, Millburn, N.J., 1942-45; supr. Tb Baltimore County Dept. Health, Towson, Md., 1945-46; Tb cons. Md. State Dept. Health, Balt., 1946-50; cons., chief nurse Tb program USPHS, Washington, 1950-57; cons. divsn. nursing USPHS, 1958-63; chief nursing practice br. Health Resources Adminstrn., HEW, Bethesda, Md., 1966-75; adj. prof. U. N.C. Sch. Pub. Health, 1975-92; cons. WHO, 1961-82. Contbr. articles to profl. jours. With USPHS, 1945-75. Recipient Disting. Alumna award Geneva Coll., 1971, Disting. Svc. award USPHS, 1971, Outstanding Achievement award U. Minn., 1983. Fellow APHA (v.p. 1978-79, Disting. Svc. award Pub. Health Nursing sect. 1975, Sedgwick Meml. medal 1979), Am. Acad. Nursing (hon. fellow); mem. Inst. Medicine of NAS, Common Cause, LWV, Delta Omega. Democrat. Episcopalian. Avocations: reading, needlepoint, gardening. Home: Apt 1112 9707 Old Georgetown Rd Bethesda MD 20814-1727

ROBERTS, DWIGHT LOREN, engineering consultant, novelist; b. San Diego, June 3, 1949; s. James Albert and Cleva Lorraine (Conn) R.; B.A., U. San Diego, 1976, M.A., 1979; m. Phyllis Ann Adair, Mar. 29, 1969; children: Aimee Renee, Michael Loren, Daniel Alexandr. Engring. aide Benton Engring. Inc., San Diego, 1968-73; pres. Robert's Tech. Research Co., also subs. Marine Technique Ltd., San Diego, 1973-76; pres. Research Technique Internat., 1978—; freelance writer, 1979—; owner Agrl. Analysis, 1985-88; constrn. mgr. Homestead Land Devel. Corp., 1988-92; sr. engr. cons. Morrison Knudson, 1992-95; sr. soils analyst Geotechnics, Inc., 1995—. Served with U.S. Army, 1969-71. Mem. ASTM, AAAS, Nat. Inst. Sci., N.Y. Acad. Scis., Nat. Inst. Cert. in Engring. Techs., Soil and Found. Engr. Assn., Phi Alpha Theta. Baptist. Author: Geological Exploration of Alaska, 1898-1924, Alfred Hulse Brooks, Alaskan Trailblazer, Papaveraceae of the World, Demarchism, Arid Regions Gardening, Visions of Dame Kind: Dreams, Imagination and Reality, Antal's Theory of the Solar System, Science Fair-A Teacher's Manual, Common Ground: Similarities of the World Religions, Black Sheep-Scientific Discoveries From the Fringe, After Manhattan, The Christofilos Effect; and others; contbr. articles to profl. jours. Office: 3111 E Victoria Dr Alpine CA 91901-3679 *Personal philosophy: Honesty and ethical behavior at all times. Trueness of being throughout my life. Love of my* *wife and children makes my life worth living and is always a light when there is darkness. God watches over my shoulder.*

ROBERTS, EDWARD BAER, technology management educator; b. Chelsea, Mass., Nov. 18, 1935; s. Nathan (dec.) and Edna (Podradchik) R.; m. Nancy Helen Rosenthal, June 14, 1959; children: Valerie Jo Roberts Friedman, Mitchell Jonathan, Andrea Lynne. BS and MS in Elec. Engring., MIT, 1958, MS in Mgmt., 1960, PhD in Econs., 1962. Founding mem. system dynamics program MIT, 1958-84, instr., 1959-61, asst. prof., 1961-65, assoc. prof., 1965-70, prof., 1970—, David Sarnoff prof. mgmt. of tech., 1974—, assoc. dir. research program on mgmt. of sci. and tech., 1963-73, chmn. tech. and health mgmt. group, 1973-88, chmn. mgmt. of tech. and innovation, 1988—, chmn. ctr. for entrepreneurship, 1992-94, co-dir. internat. ctr. rsch. mgmt. tech., 1993—, dir. mgmt. of tech. program, 1980-89, co-chmn., 1989—; co-founder, dir. Med. Info. Tech., Inc., Westwood, Mass., 1969—; co-founder, gen. ptnr. Zero State Capital Group, 1981—; bd. dirs. Advanced Magnetics, Inc., Cambridge, Selfcare, Inc., Waltham, Pegasystems, Inc., Cambridge, High Point Sys., Inc., Cambridge, Internet Techs. China, Inc., Cambridge. Author: The Dynamics of Research and Development, 1964, Systems Simulation for Regional Analysis, 1969, The Persistent Poppy, 1975, The Dynamics of Human Service Delivery, 1976, Entrepreneurs in High Technology, 1991; prin. author, editor: Managerial Applications of System Dynamics, 1978; editor (with others) Biomedical Innovation, 1981; editor: Generating Technological Innovation, 1987; mem. editorial bd. IEEE Trans. on Engring. Mgmt., Internat. Jour. Tech. Mgmt., Indsl. Mktg. Mgmt., Jour. Engring. and Tech. Mgmt., Jour. Product Innovation Mgmt., Tech. Forecasting and Social Change. Mem. IEEE, Inst. Mgmt. Sci., Sigma Xi, Tau Beta Pi, Eta Kappa Nu, Tau Kappa Alpha. Home: 300 Boylston St Apt 1102 Boston MA 02116-3923 Office: MIT 50 Memorial Dr Cambridge MA 02142-1347

ROBERTS, EDWARD GRAHAM, librarian; s. Samuel Noble and Frances Johnson (Boykin) R.; m. Anna Jean Walker, Nov. 12, 1949; children: Galer Walker, Edward Graham, John Boykin. B.A., U. South, 1943; B.A. in Library Sci., Emory U., 1948; Ph.D., U. Va., 1950. Curator manuscripts Duke U., Durham, N.C., 1948-52; dir. libraries (Drake U.), Des Moines, 1952-56; dir. Southeastern Interlibrary Research Facility, Atlanta, 1956-59; asst. prof. info. sci. Ga. Inst. Tech., Atlanta, 1963-66, assoc. prof., 1966-69, prof., 1969-73, assoc. dir. libraries, 1966-71, dir. libraries, 1971-84; dir. emeritus Ga. Inst. Tech., 1984—; chmn. info bank com. Ga. Tech. Service Program, Atlanta, 1965-67; mem. exec. bd. Southeastern Library Network, Atlanta, 1973-74; library cons. So. Regional Edn. Bd., Atlanta, 1958-59. Compiler, editor: Southeastern Supplement to the Union List of Serials, 1959; author: Literature of Science and Engineering, 1966, 2d edit.,1969. Served with U.S. Army, 1942-43. Mem. ALA, Southeastern Library Assn., Ga. Library Assn. Democrat. Episcopalian. Home: 1639 Adelia Pl NE Atlanta GA 30329-3807

ROBERTS, EDWIN ALBERT, JR., newspaper editor, journalist; b. Weehawken, N.J., Nov. 14, 1932; s. Edwin Albert and Agnes Rita (Seuferling) R.; m. Barbara Anne Collins, June 14, 1958; children: Elizabeth Adams, Leslie Carol, Amy Barbara, Jacqueline Harding. Student, Coll. William and Mary, 1952-53, NYU, evenings 1955-58; AA in Coll. & Cmty. Svc., St. Petersburg Jr. Coll., 1994. Reporter N.J. Courier, Toms River, 1953-54, Asbury Park (N.J.) Press, 1954-57; reporter Wall Street Jour., N.Y.C., 1957, editorial writer, 1957-63; news editor Nat. Observer, Silver Spring, Md., 1963-68, columnist, 1968-77; editorial writer, columnist Detroit News, 1977-78, editorial page editor, 1978-83; editor editorial page Tampa Tribune, 1983—. Author: Elections, 1964, 1964, Latin America, 1965, The Smut Rakers, 1966, Russia Today, 1967; Editor anthology: America Outdoors, 1965. Recipient Disting. Reporting Bus. award U. Mo., 1969; Pulitzer prize for distinguished commentary, 1974. Mem. Am. Soc. Newspaper Editors, Nat. Conf. Editorial Writers. Office: 202 S Parker St Tampa FL 33606-2308

ROBERTS, ELIZABETH MCCREERY, magazine editor; b. Jacksonville, Fla., Aug. 31, 1956; d. Edward McCreery and Joan Marie (Warthling) R. BA, Trinity Coll., Washington, 1977. Assoc. editor Pan Am Clipper mag., N.Y.C., 1977-84; copy editor Fortune mag., N.Y.C., 1984-86; editor-in-chief Facets mag., N.Y.C., 1987-89; editor Collier's Ency., N.Y.C., 1993-95; mng. editor Child mag., N.Y.C., 1995—. Democrat. Roman Catholic. Office: Child Mag 110 5th Ave New York NY 10011-5601

ROBERTS, ERIC, actor; b. Biloxi, Miss., Apr. 18, 1956. Ed., Royal Acad. Dramatic Art, London, 1973-74, Am. Acad. Dramatic Art, N.Y.C. Appeared in stage prodns. Rebel Women, Streetcar Named Desire, others; TV appearances include Another World; films include King of the Gypsies, 1978, Raggedy Man, 1981, Star 80, 1983, The Pope of Greenwich Village, 1984, The Coca-Cola Kid, 1985, Runaway Train, 1985, Nobody's Fool, 1986, Rude Awakening, 1989, Blood Red, 1989, The Best of the Best, 1989, Final Analysis, 1992, The Best of the Best 2, 1993, Babyfever, 1994, The Specialist, 1994, It's My Party, 1996; TV films include Paul's Case, Miss Lonelyhearts, A Time to Heal, 1988, Love, Honor & Obey: The Last Mafia Marriage, 1993, Love, Cheat and Steal, 1993, In Cold Blood, 1996, The Odyssey, 1997, others; Broadway plays include Burn This, 1988 (Theatre World award 1988). Office: United Talent Agency (UTA) 9560 Wilshire Blvd Fl 5 Beverly Hills CA 90212-2401

ROBERTS, ERNST EDWARD, marketing consultant; b. Wheeling, W.Va., Dec. 19, 1926; s. Charles Emmitt and Virginia Mae (Stephenson) R.; m. Donna Clare Davis, Dec. 27, 1949; children: Ernst Edward II, Carol Lee Roberts Gaydac. BS, U.S. Mil. Acad., 1949; MBA, Xavier U., Cin., 1954; MS in Mech. Engring., U. So. Calif., 1957; grad. with distinction, Air War Coll., 1970. Commd. 2nd lt. U.S. Army, 1949, advanced through grades to brig. gen., 1971; served as officer in combat U.S. Army, Korea, 1950-52; prof. mil. sci. Xavier U., Cin., 1952-54; mgmt. asst. to asst. comdt. U.S. Army Air Def. Sch., Fort Bliss, Tex., 1957-60; admissions officer U.S. Mil. Acad., West Point, N.Y., 1961-62, asst. to supt. (pres.), 1962-64, dir. admissions, 1964-65; comdg. officer 3d Missile Battalion, 71st Arty., Fed. Republic of Germany, 1965-67; staff officer Gen. Staff U.S. Army, Washington, 1968-70; comdg. officer NATO Air Defense Arty. Group, Fed. Republic of Germany, 1970-71; comdg. gen. 38th Air Def. Arty. Bridgade, Korea, 1971-72; asst. comdt. U.S. Army Air Def. Sch. and Ctr., Fort Bliss, Tex., 1972-74; retired U.S. Army, 1974; v.p. bldg. and property mgr. El Paso (Tex.) Nat. Bank and Corp., 1974-79, sr. v.p., dir. personnel and tng., 1979-83, exec. v.p., dir. mktg., 1983-92; mktg. cons., 1992—; mem. exec. mgmt. com. Tex. Commerce Bank, El Paso, 1983-92; vis. lectr. mktg. Webster U. Mem. bd. advisors SBA; mem. mayor's Citizens Com. on Police Dept. Matters, El Paso; mem. Task Force to Evaluate Mgmt. of Sheriff's Dept.; head bond-issue campaign, El Paso.; adv. dir. Armed Services YMCA, past pres.; adv. dir. nat. bd. dirs. Armed Svcs. YMCA, El Paso Community Found.; past pres. U. Tex.-El Paso Eldorados; mem. bd., trustee Found. Lighthouse for Blind; chmn. adv. bd. dirs. El paso Bus. Com. for Arts; chmn. capital fund drive com. Rio Grande Girl Scouts Am., Plaza Theatre-Plaza Park Restoration bd.; past mem. campaign cabinet United Way El Paso County; chmn. Capital Fund Drive, Air Def. Artillery Mus., Ft. Bliss, Tex.,; bd. dirs. City of El Paso, mem. steering com. Safe 2000; bd. dirs. Crimestoppers of El Paso. Decorated D.S.M., Legion of Merit, Silver Star, Meritorious Svc. medal; recipient Pro Eclesio Et Pontifice, Vatican, 1971; Conquistator award City of El Paso, Liberty Bell award Legal Community El Paso, 1988. Mem. Am. Inst. Banking, Assn. U.S. Army (gen. army Omar N. Bradley chpt.), El Paso C. of C. (mem. armed forces com., chmn. spl. task force to evaluate chamber mgmt.), El Paso Club (past pres., bd. dirs.), Rotary (past pres.), U.S. Army Air Def. Artillery Assn. (pres.). Republican. Roman Catholic. Home: 8212 Antero Pl El Paso TX 79904-2401

ROBERTS, EUGENE LESLIE, JR., newspaper executive, editor; b. Goldsboro, N.C., June 15, 1932; s. Eugene Leslie and Margaret (Ham) R.; m. Susan Jane McLamb, Feb. 23, 1957; children: Leslie Jane, Margaret Page, Elizabeth Susan, Polly Ann. AA, Mars Hill Jr. Coll., 1950-52; BA, U. N.C., 1952-54; postgrad., Harvard U., 1961-62; LLD (hon.), Colby Coll., 1989. Local govt. reporter Goldsboro News Argus, N.C., 1956-58; maritime reporter Norfolk Virginian-Pilot, Va., 1958-59; state capitol corr. Raleigh (N.C.) News & Observer, 1959-61, Sunday editor, 1962-63; labor writer Detroit Free Press, 1963-64, city editor, 1964-65; chief So. corr. N.Y. Times, 1965-67; war corr. N.Y. Times, Vietnam, 1968-69; nat. editor N.Y. Times, 1969-72; exec. editor, v.p. Phila. Inquirer and Phila. Newspapers, Inc., 1972-80, exec. editor, sr. v.p., 1980-86, exec. editor, pres., 1986-90; mng. editor New York Times, 1994—; mem. Pulitzer Prize bd., Columbia U., 1982-91, chmn., 1989-90; chmn. Am. com. Internat. Press Inst., 1987-93, internat. bd., 1990—; chmn. nat. adv. bd. UPI, Washington, 1986-91; bd. visitors Sch. Journalism U. Md., 1983-91, Sch. Journalism Pa. State U., 1983-89; chmn. bd. visitors Sch. Journalism U. N.C., 1989-91; chmn. bd. dirs. Knight Ctr. for Specialized Journalism, U. Md., 1987-91; bd. visitors U. Mich. Journalist-in-Residence program; bd. govs. Columbia U. Seminars and News Media on Soc., Grad. Sch. Journalism; bd. advisors Ctr. for Fgn. Journalists, 1987—; bd. dirs. World Press Freedom Com., 1986-93; bd. dirs. Arthur Burns Fellowship, 1990—; chmn. Woods Hole sci. writing fellowship Marine Biol. Lab., 1993-95; bd. dirs. Universal Press Syndicate, 1992-94; vice-chmn. Com. to Protect Journalists, 1995—. Author (with Jack Nelson) The Censors and the Schools, 1963; editor (with David R. Jones) Assignment America, 1973. With the counter intelligence corps, U.S. Army, 1954-56. Recipient William Allen White award U. Kans., 1985, John Peter Zenger award for Freedom of Press, U. Ariz., 1987, Disting. Contbns. to Journalism award Nat. Press Found., 1989, Elijah Parish Lovejoy award for Freedom of the Press, 1989; Disting. Achievement in Journalism award U. So. Calif., 1989, Reuben award for Disting. Contbns. to Newspaper Features, 1991, Fourth Estate award Nat. Press Club, 1993, Columbia Journalism award Columbia U., 1996; Nieman fellow, 1961-62. Mem. Am. Soc. Newspaper Editors, Soc. Profl. Journalists, Cosmos Club, Am. Antiquarian Soc., North Caroliniana Soc. Home: 113 E 81st St New York NY 10028-1403 Office: NY Times 229 W 43rd St New York NY 10036-3913

ROBERTS, FRANCES CABANISS, history educator; b. Gainesville, Ala., Dec. 19, 1916; d. Richard H. and Mary (Watson) R. B.S., Livingston State U., 1937; M.A., U. Ala., 1940, Ph.D., 1956, LHD, 1993; postgrad., Vanderbilt U., 1949-50. Tchr. pub. schs. Huntsville, Ala., 1937-52; teaching fellow U. Ala., 1952-53; mem. faculty U. Ala. at Huntsville, 1953-80; prof. history U. Ala., 1961-80, prof. emeritus, 1980—, chmn. dept., 1966-70, dir. Acad. Advisement Center, 1972-80. Author: Shadows on the Wall, The Life and Works of Howard Weeden, 1962, Civics for Alabama Schools, 1968, rev., 1970, History of the Church of the Nativity, 1843-1993, 1992; editor Huntsville Historical Review, 1989—. Bd. mem. Huntsville Civic Symphony, 1958-85; Bd. mem. Twickenham Hist. Preservation Assn., pres., 1983-84; Ala. state dir. on exec. bd. So. Heritage Found., 1964-65; bd. dirs. Burritt Mus., Huntsville, 1958-80; mem. Huntsville Historic Preservation Commn., 1972—, Commn. Restoration Capitol Bldg., 1973, Ala. Com. on Humanities and Pub. Policy, 1972-79; chmn. bd. Constitution Hall Park, 1979-83, Cahaba Hist. Commn., 1980-90; chair edn. com. for Vision 2000, Huntsville, 1988-90; chair edn. Summit, Huntsville, 1991; chair adv. com. Coll. Liberal Arts U. Ala., Huntsville, 1988—. Recipient Livingston State U. Alumni award, 1964; Ala. Historic Commn. award, 1969, 78; N.Ala. Bar Assn. Liberty Bell award, 1970; Life Sharer's award Kiwanis, 1973; Service award U. Ala., Huntsville, 1975; award of merit Am. Assn. State and; Alumni Faculty Appreciation award, 1976, 80; Disting. Citizen award Huntsville C. of C., 1990; Favorite Tchr. award TV Channel 19, 1991; Chapel of the Four Chaplins Legion of Honor award, 1992. Mem. Ala. Ednl. Assn., Huntsville Hist. Soc. (exec. bd. 1950—, pres. 1987-89), Ala. Council Social Studies (pres. 1947-48), Am. Hist. Assn., Ala. Hist. Assn. (pres. 1968-69, exec. bd. 1951-79), So. Hist. Assn., N. Hist. Assn. (exec. bd. 1956-64), Golden Key, Kappa Delta Pi, Phi Alpha Theta (scholarship award 1973), Phi Kappa Phi. Home: 603 Randolph Ave SE Huntsville AL 35801-4159

ROBERTS, FRANCIS JOSEPH, retired army officer, retired educational administrator, global economic advisor; b. Holyoke, Mass., July 26, 1918; s. Francis Raymond and Mary (Curry) R.; m. Mary Murray Prickett, May 30, 1942; children: Murray Francine Roberts Mux, Laurel Virginia Roberts Manning, Randall Curry, Phillip Raymond. BS, U.S. Mil. Acad., 1942; postgrad., George Washington U., 1960, Harvard U., 1964. Commd. 2d lt. U.S. Army, 1942, advanced through grades to brig. gen., 1966; comdg. officer (B Battery, 358th F.A.), 1942-43; ops. and tgn. staff 358th F.A., 1943-45; ops. and tng. staff officer (Hdqrs. III Corps), 1946; instr. tactics (U.S. Mil. Acad.), 1946, instr. academics, 1950-53, grad. mgr. athletics, dir. athletics, 1956-59; intelligence staff officer, plans officer (Amphibious Force U.S. Atlantic Fleet), 1946-48; pers. staff officer (Hdqrs. 101st Airborne Div.), 1948; dep. chief of staff 101th Airborne Divsn., 1948-49; plans and ops. staff officer (Hdqs. I Corps), Korea, 1953-54; comdg. officer (159th F.A.), Korea, 1954; plans and policy staff officer (J-3, Hdqs. Far East Command), Japan, 1954-55; chief pers. services div. (Office Asst. Chief of Staff for Pers.), Washington, 1960-61; mil. asst. to dep. sec. def. Washington, 1961-64; comdg. officer (4th Inf. Div. Arty.), 1964-66; chief war plans (SHAPE), 1966, chief strategic plans br., 1966-68; chief of staff (Alaskan Command), 1968-69; comdg. gen. (II Field Force Arty. Vietnam), 1969-70; chief of staff (Hdqs. II Field Force), Vietnam, 1970-71; chief (Europe-Middle East-Africa Div. Orgn. Joint Chiefs Staff), 1971-72, ret., 1972; dean of cadets N.Y. Mil. Acad., 1972, supt., 1972-82. Bd. dirs. Global Econ. Action Inst., 1980-93, Am. Child Guidance Found., 1966-74; v.p. AMP 45, Harvard; bd. dirs., mem. exec. com. U.S. Olympic Com.; mem. exec. com. Ea. Collegiate Athletic Conf.; mem. Western Alaska coun. Boy Scouts Am.; mem. nat. bd. trustees Boys and Girls Clubs Am.; mem. panel Golf Digest. Decorated D.S.M., D.F.C., Silver Star, Legion of Merit with 3 oak leaf clusters, 10 Air medals, Croix de Guerre avec Etoile de Argent, Legion of Honor, Army Disting. Order 1st Class medal Vietnam, Vietnam Gallantry Cross with Palm, Nat. Honor medal Vietnam, Royal Army Aiguillette Thailand, others; first inductee Nat. Alumni Hall of Fame, Boys and Girls Clubs Am. Mem. Assn. Grad. West Point, Harvard Alumni Assn., Grads. Nat. War Coll., U.S. Golf Assn. (sectional affairs com.), U.S. Srs. Golf Assn. (bd. govs., sec. internat. golf team), Internat. Srs. Amateur Golf Soc., Assn. U.S. Army (chpt. pres., chmn. nat. resolution com., bd. advisors), Ret. Officers Assn.(bd. dirs., exec. com.), So. Srs. Golf Assn., N.C. Srs. Golf Assn., Global Econ. Action Inst. (bd. dirs.). Clubs: Army-Navy Country (Washington); Pinehurst (N.C.) Country; Union League (N.Y.C.); Harvard-Radcliffe of Hudson Valley (pres. 1976-80), Touchdown of Am. (dir.), Bryce Mountain (Va.) Golf and Country, Ambs. Club-Duke U. Address: PO Box 2017 Pinehurst NC 28374-2017

ROBERTS, FRANCIS JOY, educational consultant; b. Marblehead, Mass., July 19, 1931; s. Roland Merritt and Carrie (Ramsdell) R.; m. Patricia Zanio, Dec. 25, 1953; children: Elizabeth, Katherine, Cynthia. BS, Mass. State Coll., 1953; MA, Wesleyan U., 1957; EdD, Harvard U., 1959. Cert. tchr., N.Y., Conn. Tchr. Middlefield (Conn.) Pub. Schs., 1952-53, 55-56; prof. Springfield (Mass.) Coll., 1957-60; prin. Cold Spring Harbor (N.Y.) High Sch., 1960-66; rsch. fellow Yale U., New Haven, 1973; supt. Stony Brook, N.Y., 1966-73; pres. Bank St. Coll., N.Y.C., 1973-79; asst. dir. NEH, Washington, 1980-83; supt. NEH, Cold Spring Harbor, 1983-95; prof. Long Island U., 1996—; cons. various ednl. orgns. Contbg. editor (columns and features) Parents mag., 1978—. Trustee Heckscher Mus. of Art, Huntington, N.Y., 1985—, vice chmn., 1990—. With U.S. Army, 1953-55. Recipient Golden Apple award, 1988. Mem. Am. Assn. Sch. Adminstrs., Nat. Soc. for Study Edn., Marblehead Arts Assn., Harvard Club (bd. dirs. Washington chpt. 1982-83). Democrat. Avocations: painting, travel, gardening, writing.

ROBERTS, FRANCIS STONE, advertising executive; b. Scranton, Pa., Aug. 15, 1944; s. Gordon Link and Eleanor Swartz (Stone) R.; m. Anne Carter Housh, Dec. 21, 1974; children: Francis Stone, Link McGregor. B.A., Grove City (Pa.) Coll., 1966; A.M.P., U. Chgo., 1984. With media dept., then account exec. Compton Advt. Inc., N.Y.C., 1966-69; account exec. Tatham-Laird & Kudner Advt., N.Y.C., 1969-70; account supr., v.p. SSC&B Advt. Inc., N.Y.C., 1970-78, sr. v.p., mgmt. supr., 1994; group exec. v.p. SSC&B: Lintas Advt. Worldwide, 1987-89; COO, pres. Lintas, N.Y., 1990-94; mem. policy and ops. coms., chmn. strategy rev. bd. Lintas N.Y.; also dir. Lintas N.Y. and U.S.A.; CEO, chmn. The CEO-Gotham Grp., N.Y.C., 1994-95; chmn., CEO Gotham Inc., N.Y.C., 1995—; mng. dir. Gotham Ltd., London, 1996—. Emergency rm. com. Lenox Hill Hosp. Mem. William Penn Charter Alumni Assn. (pres. N.Y. chpt. 1984-88), Ad Club N.Y., New Canaan Country Club, The Union League N.Y. Republican. Presbyterian. Club: New Canaan Field, New Canaan Winter, New Canaan Country. Home: 208 Canoe Hill Rd New Canaan CT 06840-3707 Office: Gotham Inc 260 Madison Ave New York NY 10016-2401 also: Gotham Ltd, 68 Knightsbridge, London SW1X 7LT, England

ROBERTS, GEORGE BERNARD, JR., business and government affairs consultant, former state legislator; b. Andover, Mass., June 13, 1939; s. George Bernard and Helene F. (Eversen) R.; m. Margaret Fay Edmunds, Aug. 26, 1967; children: Abigail Emerson, Jessica Swift. B.S., U. N.H., 1964, M.P.A., 1967. Ptnr. Roberts Real Estate Assocs., Gilmanton, N.H., 1966—; mem. N.H. Ho. of Reps., from 1967, majority leader, 1971-74, speaker, 1975-76, 77-78, 79-80; pres. Policy Mgmt. Assocs., govt. rels. cons., Concord, Concord Coach Soc. Del. Nat. Rep. Conv., 1972-76; mem. N.H. Constl. Conv., 1974, 84, N.H. Rep. Party Fin. Com.; pres. Nat. Conf. State Legislatures, 1979-80; chmn. exec. com. 1st Congl. Soc. Gilmanton. Mem. Nat. Rep. Legislators Assn. (founding, past pres.), Masons, Sigma Alpha Epsilon. Republican. Office: 4 Park St Ste 100 Concord NH 03301-6313

ROBERTS, GEORGE R., investment banking company executive; married; 3 children. JD, U. Calif., San Francisco. With Bears, Stearns, New York, until 1976; founding ptnr. Kohlberg, Kravis, Roberts, San Francisco; dir. Beatrice Co., Chgo., Houdaille Industries Inc., Northbrook, Ill., Malone and Hyde, Memphis, Union Tex. Petroleum Holdings Inc., Houston. Office: Kohlberg Kravis Roberts & Co 2800 Sand Hill Rd Ste 200 Menlo Park CA 94025-7055*

ROBERTS, GLYN CAERWYN, psychology educator; b. Chester, England, Jan. 13, 1940; came to U.S., 1965; s. Daniel and Myfanwy (Ingman) R.; m. Norma, Apr. 3, 1965 (div. Feb. 1993). MS, U. Mass., 1966; PhD, U. Ill., 1969. Asst. prof. Kent (Ohio) State U., 1969-73; from asst. prof. to prof. U. Ill., Champaign, 1973—. Author: Motivation in Sports Psychology and Exercise, 1992; editor The Sport Psychologist Jour., 1988-93. Kinesiology scholar U. Ctr. Ga., Atlanta, 1986. Fellow Assn. for Advancement of Sport Psychology; mem. N.Am. Soc. Sports Psychology (pres. 1981-82), Internat. Soc. Sports Psychology (sec. gen. 1985-93), Internat. Assn. Applied Psychology (pres. divsn. sport psychology 1994-98), Lions. Home: 7B Evergreen Cir Savoy IL 61874 Office: U Ill 906 S Goodwin Ave Urbana IL 61801-3841

ROBERTS, HARRY HEIL, geological research administrator; b. Huntington, W.Va., Feb. 2, 1940; m. Mary S. Hamb, 1963; 1 child, Andrew. BS, Marshall U., 1962; MS, La. State U., 1966, PhD in Giology, 1969. Asst. prof. geol. rsch. Coastal Studies Inst./La. State U., Baton Rouge, 1969-74, assoc. prof., 1974-78, prof. marine sci., 1978—, dir., 1987-96. Mem. Soc. Econ. Paleontologists and Mineralogists, Am. Assn. Petrol Geologists, Coastal Soc., Internat. Assn. Sedimentol. Office: Louisiana State Univ Coastal Studies Inst Howe Russell Geoscience Complex Baton Rouge LA 70803 also: Coastal Studies Inst La State Univ Baton Rouge LA 70803*

ROBERTS, HARRY MORRIS, JR., lawyer; b. Dallas, June 10, 1938; s. Harry Morris and La Frances (Reilly) R.; m. Nancy Beth Johnson, Mar. 7, 1964; children: Richard Whitfield, Elizabeth Lee. BBA, So. Meth. U., 1960; LLB, Harvard U., 1963. Bar: Tex. 1963, U.S. Dist. Ct. (no. dist.) Tex. 1964, U.S. Ct. Appeals (5th cir.), 1972, U.S. Supreme Ct. 1971. Assoc. Thompson & Knight, Dallas, 1963-69, ptnr., 1970-75, sr. ptnr., 1975—; chmn. real estate, probate and trust law sect. State Bar Tex., 1984-85; vis. scholar U. Tex. Law Sch., 1986. Contbr. articles to legal jours. Trustee Shelter Ministries of Dallas, 1982— (chmn. bd. trustees 1992-95). Mem. ABA, Dallas Bar Assn. (chmn. real estate sect. 1981), Am. Bar Found., Tex. Bar Found., Dallas Bar Found., Am. Coll. Real Estate Lawyers, Tex. Coll. Real Estate Attys. (vice chair, bd. dirs. 1990-93). Episcopalian. Clubs: Salesmanship (Dallas), Dallas Country. Office: Thompson & Knight 1700 Pacific Ave Ste 3300 Dallas TX 75201-4656

ROBERTS, HARRY VIVIAN, statistics educator; b. Peoria, Ill., May 1, 1923; s. Harry V. and Mary (Pickels) R.; m. June H. Hoover, Nov. 19, 1943; children: Andrew H., Mary D. BA, U. Chgo., 1943, MBA, 1947, PhD, 1955. Market researcher McCann-Erickson, Inc., Chgo., 1946-49; mem. faculty Grad. Sch. Bus., U. Chgo., 1949—, prof. stats., 1959-88, Sigmund E. Edelstone prof. of stats. and quality mgmt., 1988-93, emeritus, 1993—; cons. in field, 1950—. Author: (with James Lorie) Basic Methods of Marketing Research, 1951, (with Allen Wallis) Statistics: A New Approach, 1956, Converstaional Statistics, 1974, Time Series Analysis and Forecasting with IDA, 1983, Data Analysis for Managers with Minitab, 2d edit., 1991 (with Bernard Sergesketter) Quality is Personal, 1993; editor: Academic Initiatives in Total Quality for Higher Education, 1995; contbr. articles to profl. publs. Mem. rezoning commn. Village of Homewood, Ill., 1956-60, 71-73, mem. zone bd. appeals, 1962-75, chmn. zone bd. appeals, 1973-75, mem. plan commn., 1970-73; mem. mfg. bd., mem. sci. bd. Dept. Def., 1988-90. With AUS, 1943-45. Fellow AAAS (stats. sect.), Am. Statis. Assn. (census adv. com. 1973-78, asso. editor Jour. 1977-82); mem. Royal Statis. Soc., Inst. Math. Stats., Am. Econ. Assn. Home: 1353 Burr Oak Rd Homewood IL 60430-1908 Office: Univ Chgo Grad Sch Bus Chicago IL 60637

ROBERTS, HOWARD RICHARD, food scientist, association administrator; b. Eldred, Pa., July 6, 1932; s. Edward Euclid and Irene Victoria (Bills) R.; m. Marylyn Ann Morrissey, Dec. 28, 1957; children: Cynthia Anne, Mark Edward, Mary Beth, John Michael. BS, George Washington U., 1955, MS, 1957, PhD, 1962. Cert. quality engr., D.C. Instr. George Washington U., Washington, 1958-59; ops. analyst Johns Hopkins U., Bethesda, Md., 1958-59; rsch. dir. Booz, Allen & Hamilton, Washington, 1959-67; v.p. Booz, Allen & Hamilton, Kansas City, Mo., 1967-72; dir. bur. foods FDA, Washington, 1972-78; dir. sci. affairs Nat. Soft Drink Assn., Washington, 1978-85, sr. v.p., 1986—; cons. George Washington U. Med. Sch., Washington, 1958-59; adv. panel AMA, Chgo., 1974-80; food expert panel FDA, Washington, 1990-91. Author: Food Safety, 1981; co-author: Caffeine - Perspectives from Recent Research, 1984, Agricultural & Food Chemistry, 1978, Mycotoxins in Human and Animal Health, 1977; contbr. articles to Food Tech. Jour., Food Drug Cosmetic Jour., Food and Chem. Toxicology. Coach, official Vienna (Va.) Youth Inc., 1971-74. With USNR, 1950-54. George Washington U. fellow, 1957; recipient FDA award of Merit, 1978. Fellow Am. Soc. Quality Control (chmn. 1968-70, Svc. award 1971); mem. AAAS, ASTM, Am. Coll. Toxicology (coun. 1985-87), Inst. Food Technologists (profl.), N.Y. Acad. Scis., Internat. Food and Beverage Techs., Internat. Soc. Regulatory Toxicology and Pharmacology, Assn. Food and Drug Officials, Internat. Ozone Assn., Sigma Xi, Omicron Delta Kappa. Republican. Achievements include rsch. in risk assessment, consumption estimation. Office: Nat Soft Drink Assn 1101 16th St NW Washington DC 20036

ROBERTS, HUGH EVAN, business investment services company executive; b. Marion, Ind., Aug. 29, 1923; s. Arthur Edwin and Georgina (Fankboner) R.; m. Ellen Langtree Gordon, Sept. 16, 1950; children: Ellen Langtree, Daniel Evan, Robert Gordon. BSME, U. Cin., 1950. With Procter & Gamble Co., 1950-63, Monsanto Co., 1963-69; with Binkley Co., 1969-81, v.p., div. mgr., 1971-73, pres., 1973-79; chief exec. officer Binkley Co., Warrenton, Mo., 1971-81, chmn. bd., 1979-81; assoc. Capital Assocs. Fund, St. Louis, 1982-85; chmn. bd. Grant Cooper & Assocs., St. Louis, 1985-90; ptnr. Lockett, McNearney & Roberts Inc., St. Louis, 1990-94; retired. Mem. bd. St. Louis County Spl. Sch. Dist., 1973-79, pres., 1976-79. Served to 1st lt., pilot USAAF, World War II. Decorated D.F.C., Air medal with 4 oak leaf clusters. Republican. Episcopalian. Clubs: Mo. Quail and Gun; Univ. (St. Louis). Patentee chemistry, mech. devices. Home: 17 Frontenac Est Dr Saint Louis MO 63131-2613

ROBERTS, HYMAN JACOB, internist, researcher, author, historian, publisher; b. Boston, May 29, 1924; s. Benjamin and Eva (Sherman) R.; m. Carol Antonia Klein, Aug. 9, 1953; children: David, Jonathan, Mark, Stephen, Scott, Pamela. M.D. cum laude, Tufts U., 1947. Diplomate Am. Bd. Internal Medicine. Intern, resident Boston City Hosp., 1947-49; resident Mcpl. Hosp., Washington, 1949-50; rsch. fellow, instr. med. Tufts Med. Sch., Boston, 1948-49, Georgetown Med. Sch., Washington, 1949-50; fellow in medicine Lahey Clinic, Boston, 1950-51; mem. active staff Good Samaritan and St. Mary's Hosps., West Palm Beach, Fla., 1955—; dir. Palm Beach Inst. Med. Rsch., West Palm Beach, 1964—, pres., Sunshine Sentinel Press, Inc. lectr. two day seminar on The New Frontiers in Legal Medicine, Seminar on Defense Against Alzheimer's Disease. U.S. rep. Council of Europe for Driving Standards, 1972. Author: Difficult Diagnosis, Spanish and Italian edits, 1958; The Causes, Ecology and Prevention of Traffic Accidents, 1971, Is Vasectomy Safe?, 1979, Aspartame (NutraSweet): Is It Safe?, 1989, Sweet'ner Dearest, 1992, Is Vasectomy Worth the Risk?, 1993, Mega

Vitamin E: Is It Safe?, 1994, The Spirit of Modern Taiwan, 1994, West Palm Beach: Centennial Reflections, 1994, A Guide to Personal Peace, 1994, Defense Against Alzheimers Disease, 1995, Health and Wealth, Palm Beach Style, 1997; (play) My Wife, The Politician; assoc. editor: Tufts Med. Alumni Bull, Boston, 1978-87, Nutrition Health Rev.; contbr. sci. and med. articles to profl. and theol. jours. Pres. Jewish Community Day Sch., West Palm Beach, Fla., 1975-76; disting. mem. pres. council U. Fla., Gainesville, 1974—; founder Atlantic U., 1958; founder, dir. Jewish Fedn. Palm Beach County, West Palm Beach, 1960-72. Served to lt. USNR, 1951-54. Named Fla. Outstanding Young Man Jr. C. of C. Fla., 1958; hon. Ky. col.; Grantee Norton Art Gallery, U. Fla. Art Mus., U. Georgia Art Mus., Fla. A & M U., Tufts. Med Schs., (Roberts Core Libr.), Ringling Art Mus., Northwood U., recipient Gold Share cert. and silver certs. Inst. Agr. and Food Scis., U. Fla., 1974-78; Paul Harris fellow Rotary Found., 1980. Fellow ACP, Am. Coll. Chest Physicians, Am. Coll. Nutrition, Stroke Council; mem. AMA, AAAS, Am. Acad. Neurology, Endocrine Soc., Am. Diabetes Assn., Am. Fedn. Clin. Research, Am. Coll. Angiology (gov. 1981), Am. Coll. Legal Medicine, Pan Am. Med. Assn. (chmn. endocrinology 1982), So. Med. Assn., N.Y. Acad. Scis., Confrerie de la Chaine des Rotisseurs, Alpha Omega Alpha, Sigma Xi. Club: Governors of West Palm Beach (a founder), Executive (founder). Lodges: Rotary; B'nai B'rith, Order St. George (knight of magistral grace 1992). Research in med. diagnosis, diabetes, hypoglycemia, postvasectomy state, Vitamin E metabolism, pentachlorophenol, heavy metal toxicity, narcolepsy, traffic accidents, thrombophlebitis, aspartame, Alzheimer's disease, brain tumors, nutrition and bioethics. Home: 6708 Pamela Ln West Palm Beach FL 33405-4175 Office: Palm Beach Inst Med Rsch 300 27th St West Palm Beach FL 33407-5202 also: Sunshine Sentinel Press Inc PO Box 17799 West Palm Beach FL 33416

ROBERTS, J. WENDELL, federal judge; b. Somerset, Ky., May 1, 1943; s. Earl C. and Dorothy (Whitaker) R.; children: Stephen A., Shannon L. BA, Ea. Ky. U., 1964; JD, U. Ky., 1966. Bar: Ky. 1966, U.S. Dist. Ct. (we. dist.) Ky. 1978, U.S. Ct. Appeals (6th cir.) 1983. Atty. Ky. Dept. Revenue, Frankfort, 1966; law clk. Ky. Supreme Ct., Frankfort, 1966-67; atty. Charles A. Williams & Assoc., Paducah, Ky., 1967, Westberry & Roberts, Marion, Ky., 1968-87; city atty. City of Marion, 1968-84; judge U.S. Bankruptcy Ct. Western Dist. Ky., Louisville, 1987—, chief judge, 1988-95. Vice chmn. Pennyrile Area Devel. Dist., Hopkinsville, Ky., 1968-72. Mem. Ky. Bar Assn., Louisville Bar Assn., Nat. Conf. Bankruptcy Judges (bd. govs. 1991-94), Mcpl. Attys. Assn. Ky. (pres. 1983). Methodist. Avocations: travel, antiques. Office: US Bankruptcy Ct 528 US Courthouse 601 W Broadway Louisville KY 40202-2238

ROBERTS, JACK EARLE, lawyer, ski resort operator, wood products company executive, real estate developer; b. L.A., Nov. 5, 1928; s. James Earle and Illa Ann (Morgan) R.; m. Marilyn Humphreys, Sept. 13, 1954; children: Ronda, Cyndi, Scott, Robynne, Craig. B.S. in Accounting and Bus. Adminstrn, Brigham Young U., 1952; J.D., George Washington U., 1955, LL.M. in Taxation (Teaching fellow), 1956. Bar: Calif. 1957; CPA, Ariz. Pvt. practice L.A.; atty. Office Chief Counsel, IRS, L.A., 1956-60; mem. firm Roberts, Carmack, Johnson, Poulson & Harmer, L.A., 1961-78; pres. Park West Ski Resort, Park City, Utah, 1975-88; pres., dir. Accudyne Corp., Los Angeles, 1972-89, Richmark Corp., Los Angeles, 1972-77; chmn., dir. Comml. Wood Products Co., Los Angeles, 1968—; pres., dir. Snyderville Devel. Co., Inc., Utah, 1978-94, Community Water Co., Salt Lake City, 1987—, Roberts Mgmt. Corp., Salt Lake City, 1988—, Ste. Vacations, Inc., Salt Lake City, 1989—. Contbr. articles on legal subjects to tech. jours. Pres. Westwood Rep. Club, 1968; mem. cen. coms. Calif. State, L.A. County Rep. Party, 1974-77; mem. Utah State Cen. and Exec. Coms., 1981-96, Summit County Rep. cen. and exec. coms., 1978-84; state sec. Utah Rep. Com., 1985-88, chmn., 1989; mem. Rep. Nat. Com., 1988-96; chmn. Summit County Rep. Com., 1981-83. Mem. Calif. Bar Assn., D.C. Bar Assn. Office: 150 Virginia St Salt Lake City UT 84103-4315

ROBERTS, JAMES ALLEN, urologist; b. Beach, N.D., May 31, 1934; s. Earl Fernando and Maria Ellen R.; m. Hilda Peachy, Nov. 29, 1987; children from previous marriage: Jennifer Lou Roberts Walsh, Mary Ellen Roberts Wargo, Thomas J. M.D., U. Chgo., 1959. Diplomate: Am. Bd. Urology. Intern U. Chgo. Sch. Medicine, 1959-60, resident in urology, 1961-65; mem. faculty Tulane U. Med. Sch., New Orleans, 1971—; prof. urology Tulane U. Med. Sch., 1975—, assoc. chmn., 1986—; sr. research scientist, head dept. urology Tulane Regional Primate Research Center, Covington, 1972—; fellow Fogarty Sr. Internat. NIH, 1984. Mem. editorial bd. Am. Jour. Kidney Diseases and Urol. Rsch.; contbr. articles to profl. jours. Bd. dirs. Highland Park Hosp., 1985-87. Recipient grants NIH, Original Rsch. award Southern Med. Assn., 1990, Cert. Achievement Am. Urological Assn., 1997. Fellow ACS; mem. St. Tammany Parish Med. Soc. (pres. 1979), Soc. Rsch. on Calculous Kinetics, La. Urol. Soc., Am. Urol. Assn., Soc. Univ. Urologists, Nat. Kidney Found., Soc. Exptl. Biology and Medicine, Nat. Inst. Health (SAT study sect. 1995-99), Sigma Xi. Office: 1323 S Tyler St Covington LA 70433-2338

ROBERTS, JAMES CARL, communications executive, engineer; b. Orlando, Fla., May 6, 1953; s. James Ira and Avis Jean (Marg) R.; m. Lynne K. Lovvorn, Sept. 29, 1980; children: William D, Christine N., Jameson S., Michael B. BSEE, U. Miss., 1974; MBA, Newport (Calif.) U., 1988, DBA, 1992. Registered profl. engr., Kans. Pres. Accent Communications, Lakeland, Fla., 1977-80; engring. mgr. Motorola Corp., Foster City, Claif., 1980-83; regional mgr. MCI, Washington, 1983-84; dir. McCaw Communications, Denver, 1984-86; pres., chief exec. officer Communications Group Internat., Denver, 1986—; chief exec. officer Metro Page of Fla., Boca Raton, 1988—, Metrotek Ariz., Phoenix, 1988—; chief operating br. Tri-Pro, Denver, 1988—, CGI, Inc., Denver, 1986—, Metro, Inc., Ft. Meyers, Fla., 1988—, CGI, Denver, 1992—, Albania, 1992—; bd. dirs. Malta Cellular, Valeta; chmn., gen. dir. CGI-MT of Serbia, Yugoslavia, 1990-92; gen. dirs., chmn. Serbia Cellular, 1989-92. Author: Cellular for Malta, 1987. Staff sgt. USAF, 1969-77. Mem. Cellular Telephone Industry Assn., Telocator, Colo. Arabian Assn., Intercircle, Internat. Arabian Assn., Met. Club, St. James Club. Republican. Baptist. Office: CGI Worldwide Inc 11413 E Hilltop Rd Parker CO 80138-6007

ROBERTS, JAMES DONZIL, lawyer; b. St. Louis, Mo., Apr. 4, 1957; s. Donzil D. and Barbara V. Malona; m. Jody A. Garcia, Dec. 7, 1985; children: James D. Jr., Jessica E. Student, Calif. State U., Northridge, 1976-79, Calif. State U., Dominguez Hills, 1981; JD, U. LaVerne, 1985. Bar: Calif. 1985, U.S. Dist. Ct. (ctrl. dist.) Calif. 1986. Staff and supr. atty. Bollington Stilz & Bloeser, Woodland Hills, Calif., 1985-90; mng. atty. Bollington and Roberts, Long Beach, Calif., 1990—; judge pro tem Long beach Mcpl. Ct., Long Beach, 1992—; lectr. extension program UCLA, 1994—. Trustee U. LaVerne San Fernando Valley Coll. Law, Encino, 1984-85; active West L.A. County Coun., Boy Scouts Am., West Hills, Calif., 1995. Mem. Assn. Calif. House Counsel (founding mem.); mem. L.A. County Bar Assn., Long Beach Bar Assn., Assn. So. Calif. Def. Counsel, Long Beach Barristers Assn., Am. Inn Ct. (Long Beach, barrister). Avocations: baseball/softball, bowling, golf. Office: Bollington & Roberts 3780 Kilroy Airport Way Ste 540 Long Beach CA 90806-2459

ROBERTS, JAMES G., foundation executive; b. Lincoln, Nebr., May 20, 1922; s. Ellsworth James and Anna (Gillette) R.; m. Eleanor Ramsey, July 28, 1945; children—Kenneth James, Ellen Margaret. Student, Nebr. Wesleyan U., 1939-41; B.A., Colo U., 1942. Mgr. Littlefield C. of C., Tex., 1948-50; mgr. indsl. div. Amarillo C. of C., Tex., 1950-51; mgr. Plainview C. of C., Tex., 1951-53; mgr. Tulsa dist. U.S. C. of C., 1953-54; mgr. Southwestern div. U.S. C. of C., Dallas, 1954-58; gen. mgr. Greater Boston C. of C., 1958-59, exec. v.p., 1959-64; v.p. pub. info. New Eng. Mut. Life Ins. Co., Boston, 1964-67; pres. Roberts Assocs., 1968-72; exec. v.p. Greater Pitts. C. of C., 1972-75; gen. mgr. N.H. Bus. and Industry Assn., 1975-77, exec. v.p., 1977-83; pres. Gordon Coll. Found., Wenham, Mass., 1983-87; adminstr. St. Andrews Estates South, Boca Raton, Fla., 1988-91; 1st pub. Boston mag., 1962; pres. Back Bay Planning & Devel. Corp., Boston, 1965-67; bd. dirs. Wellesley Nat. Bank. Mem. exec. com. Billy Graham Crusade, Boston, 1964; trustee Gordon Coll., Joslyn Diabetes Found., Historic Park Street Ch.; bd. dirs. Salvation Army; deacon Presbyn. Ch.; active Pensacola Mayor's com. for Elderly Affairs; state dir. Fla. Life Care Residents Assn., 1995—. 1st lt. USAAF, World War II. Mem. Soc. Advancement of Mgmt. (v.p. pub. rels.), Fla. Life Care Residents Assn. (bd. dirs., mem. exec. com. 1995—), Boston BBB (bd. dirs.), No. Shore C. of C. (bd. dirs., Wellesley Club, Algonquin Club, Greater Boston Execs. Club (pres.), Ea. Yacht Club, Duquesne Club.

ROBERTS, JAMES HAROLD, III, lawyer; b. Omaha, Aug. 11, 1949; s. James Harold Jr. and Evelyn Doris (Young) R.; m. Marilyn Novak, June 29, 1974; children: Jessica Noël, Meredith Caitlin. BA, U. Notre Dame, 1971; JD, St. Louis U., 1974. Bar: Iowa 1974, U.S. Ct. Mil. Appeals 1974, U.S. Supreme Ct. 1979, D.C. 1981. Govt. contract atty. U.S. Gen. Acctg. Office, Washington, 1978-83, U.S. Dept. Treasury, Washington, 1983-88; pvt. practice Manatt Phelps & Phillips, Washington, 1988—. Editor St. Louis U. law rev., 1973-74. Served to capt. JAGC, U.S. Army, 1974-78, lt. col. USAR/NG, 1978—. Mem. ABA (pub. contract law sect.), D.C. Bar Assn., Fed. Bar Assn. Roman Catholic. Home: 308 N Monroe St Arlington VA 22201-1736 Office: Manatt Phelps & Phillips 1501 M St NW Ste 700 Washington DC 20005-1700

ROBERTS, JAMES MCGREGOR, retired professional association executive; b. Moncton, N.B., Can., Nov. 24, 1923; came to U.S., 1949, naturalized, 1956; s. Roland M. and Edith M. (Shields) R.; m. Thelma E. Williams, May 6, 1944; 1 dau., Jana M. B.Commerce, U. Toronto, Ont., Can., 1949. Auditor Citizens Bank, Los Angeles, 1949-54; auditor Acad. Motion Picture Arts and Scis., Hollywood, Calif., 1954—; controller Acad. Motion Picture Arts and Scis., 1956-71, exec. dir., 1971-89, exec. sec. acad. found., 1971-89; exec. cons. Acad. Motion Picture Arts and Scis., Hollywood, Calif., 1989-92; exec. cons., 1990-93, ret., 1994. Served as pilot Royal Can. Air Force, World War II. Home: 4968 Lerkas Way Oceanside CA 92056-7428

ROBERTS, JAMES MILNOR, JR., professional society administrator; b. Pitts., Sept. 16, 1918; s. James Milnor and Elizabeth (Bennett) R.; m. Virginia Lee Sykes, Mar. 15, 1947 (dec. Apr. 1995); children: James Milnor III, Mary Lee Roberts Newman, Deborah Lee Roberts Gillespie, Todd Osborn; m. Priscilla Bruce, Nov. 24, 1995. Student, Lehigh U., 1936-40, U.S. Army Command and Gen. Staff Coll., 1962, Nat. Def. U., 1963, Army War Coll., 1970. Commd. 2d lt. inf. U.S. Army, 1940, advanced through grades to maj., 1944, discharged, 1945; mem. U.S. Army (Res.), 1946-70; with 1st battle group U.S. Army Res. 314th Inf. Regt., Pitts., 1947-62; comdr. combat command sect. 79th Command Hdqrs., Pitts., 1962-64; with Office Chief Info., Dept. Army, Washington, 1964-67; comdr. 99th Army Res. Command, Pitts., 1967-70; promoted to maj. gen. 99th Army Res. Command, 1971; dep. chief U.S. Army Res., Washington, 1970-71; chief U.S. Army Res., 1971-75; exec. dir. Res. Officers Assn. U.S., Washington, 1975-84; pub. The Officer mag., 1975-84; pres. Nat. Intelligence Study Ctr.; sec., treas. High Frontier, Arlington, Va., 1994—, dir., 1995—. Chmn. Young Reps., Allegheny County, Pa., 1952-54; exec. v.p. Wind Symphony Orch., Pitts., 1961-62; bd. dirs. Pitts. Civic Light Opera, 1958-70; chmn. Com. for Free Afghanistan, 1983-93; pres. Nat. Hist. Intelligence Mus. Decorated D.S.M., Legion of Merit, Bronze Star; Croix de Guerre with silver star France; Mil. Cross Czechoslovakia; recipient USN Disting. Pub. Svc. award, USCG Disting. Pub. Svc. award, USAF Exceptional Svc. award; named Significant Sig Sigma Chi, 1973. Mem. Res. Officers Assn. (past chpt. officer), Am. Security Council, Assn. U.S. Army, Mil. Order World Wars, Ret. Officers Assn., The Dwight D. Eisenhower Soc. (chair 1992—), Soc. of Cin., SAR, VFW, Am. Legion, Army-Navy Club (Washington), Ft. Myer (Va.) Officers Club, Capital Hill Club, Masons. Home: 105-S 5501 Seminary Rd Falls Church VA 22041 Office: High Frontier 2800 Shirlington Rd Ste 404 Arlington VA 22206-3601

ROBERTS, JAMES OWEN, financial planning executive, consultant; b. Madison, Wis., Aug. 19, 1930; s. John William and Sada (Buckmaster) R.; m. Georgianna Timmons, Jan. 30, 1954; children: Stephen, Susan, Ellen, Timmons. BS, Ohio State U., 1952; MBA, Case Western Res. U., 1970. With Owens-Ill., Inc., Toledo, Ohio, 1952, 54-55, salesman, Atlanta, 1955-58, N.Y.C., 1958-62, food div. mgr., N.Y.C., 1963-66, br. mgr., Cleve., 1966-71; mgr. corp. fin. Stone & Webster Securities Corp., Cleve., 1971-74; regional dir. Mgmt. Planning, Inc., Cleve., 1976-80, v.p., 1980-86, sr. v.p., 1986, pres., 1986-96, chmn., 1996—; lectr. valuation and bus. ownership succession. Contbr. articles to profl. jours. Trustee Soc. for the Blind, Cleve., 1983-86, Ohio Motorists Assn., 1985-94, chmn., 1990-92; pres. Children's Svcs., Inc., 1986-88; trustee Great Lakes Theater; elder Fairmount Presbyn. Ch. 1st Lt. USAF, 1952-54. Mem. Fin. Analysts Fedn., Cleve. Skating Club, Nassau Club, Huron Yacht Club, Chgo. Athletic Assn. Republican. Avocations: sailing, skiing, flying, hiking, photography. Home: 2323 Stillman Rd Cleveland OH 44118-3520 Office: Mgmt Planning Inc 545 Hanna Bldg Cleveland OH 44115 also: 101 Poor Farm Rd Princeton NJ 08540-1941

ROBERTS, JARED INGERSOLL, lawyer; b. Phila., Mar. 20, 1946; s. Brooke and Anna (Ingersoll) R.; m. Katherine Marx Sherwood, May 17, 1986. BA, Princeton U., 1968; JD, U. Va., 1974. Bar: Pa. 1974, U.S. Dist. Ct. (ea. dist.) Pa. 1975, U.S. Ct. Appeals (3d cir.) 1978, U.S. Supreme Ct. 1978, D.C. 1985. Assoc. Duane, Morris & Heckscher, Phila., 1974-82; spl. counsel U.S. Dept. Transp., Washington, 1982-84; assoc. gen. counsel Nat. R.R. Passenger Corp., Washington, 1984—. Served to lt (j.g.) USN, 1968-70. Mem. ABA, Pa. Bar Assn., D.C. Bar Assn. Republican. Episcopalian. Avocations: sailing, skating, railroads. Home: 3607 N Glebe Rd Arlington VA 22207-4316 Office: Amtrak Law Dept 60 Massachusetts Ave NE Washington DC 20002-4225

ROBERTS, JAY, pharmacologist, educator; b. N.Y.C., July 15, 1927; s. Harry and Evelyn R.; m. Marion Camenson, June 18, 1950; children—Hunt, Kathy. B.S., L.I. U., 1949; Ph.D., Cornell U., 1953. Asst. prof., then asso. prof. pharmacology Cornell U. Med. Coll., 1956-66; prof. pharmacology U. Pitts. Med. Sch., 1966-70; prof. pharmacology, chmn. dept. Med. Coll. Pa., 1970—; chmn. dept. Med. Coll. Pa.-Hahneman U. Sch. Medicine, 1994—; cons. to industry; mem. NIH Study Sect. Contbr. numerous articles to profl. jours.; reviewer for numerous sci. jours.; assoc. editor (Pharmacology) Jour. Gerontology; asst. editor Jour. Pharmcol. and Exptl. Therap.; editor Jour. Gerontology & Biol. Scis. Served with USNR, 1945-46. Postdoctoral fellow N.Y. Heart Assn., 1953-57; Postdoctoral fellow USPHS, 1953-55; recipient Lindback Disting. Teaching award Med. Coll. Pa., 1973. Fellow Am. Coll. Cardiology, Am. Coll. Clin. Pharmacology, Coll. Physicians Phila. (chmn. geriatric sect. 1986-88), Gerontol. Soc. Am. (chmn. biol. sect. 1984); mem. Internat. Study Group Research Cardiac Metabolism, Am. Fedn. Clin. Research, AAAS, Am. Soc. Pharmacology and Exptl. Therapeutics, Soc. Exptl. Biology and Medicine, Cardiac Muscle Soc., Am. Heart Assn., Southeastern Pa. Heart Assn. (peer reviewer grants 1973-94, Sr. Investigation Achievement award 1990), Harvey Soc., Assn. Med. Sch. Pharmacology, Am. Coll. Clin. Pharmacology (charter), AAUP, U.S. Pharmacopeial Conv. (chmn. geriatric adv. panel 1980-90), Mid-Atlantic Pharmacology Soc. (pres. 1990-92), Sigma Xi. Home: Benson House 930 Montgomery Ave Bryn Mawr PA 19010-3044 Office: Med Coll Pa-Hahnemann Sch Med Allegheny U Health Sci 3200 Henry Ave Philadelphia PA 19129-1137

ROBERTS, JEANNE ADDISON, literature educator; b. Washington; d. John West and Sue Fisher (Nichols) Addison; m. Markley Roberts, Feb. 19, 1966; children: Addison Cary Steed Masengill, Ellen Carraway Masengill Coster. A.B., Agnes Scott Coll., 1946; M.A., U. Pa., 1947; Ph.D., U. Va., 1964. Instr. Mary Washington Coll., 1947-48; instr., chmn. English Fairfax Hall Jr. Coll., 1950-51; tchr. Am. U. Assn. Lang. Center, Bangkok, Thailand, 1952-56; instr. Beirut (Lebanon) Coll. for Women, 1956-57, asst. prof., 1957-60, chmn. English dept., 1957-60; instr. lit. Am. U., Washington, 1960-62; asst. prof. Am. U., 1962-65, assoc. prof., 1965-68, prof., 1968-93; dean faculties Am. U., 1974; lectr. Howard U., 1971-72; seminar prof. Folger Shakespeare Libr. Inst. for Renaissance and 18th Century Studies, 1974; dir. NEH Summer Inst. for High Sch. Tchrs. on Teaching Shakespeare, Folger Shakespeare Libr., 1984, 85, 86; dir. NEH summer inst. Va. Commonwealth U. 1995, 96 Writings By and About Women in The English Renaissance. Author: Shakespeare's English Comedy: The Merry Wives of Windsor in Context, 1979, The Shakespearean Wild: Geography, Genus and Gender, 1991; editor: (with James G. McManaway) A Selective Bibliography of Shakespeare: Editions, Textual Studies, Commentary, 1975; (with Peggy O'Brien) Shakespeare Set Free, vol. 1, 1993, vol. 2, 1994, vol. 3, 1995; contbr. articles to scholarly jours. Danforth Tchr. grantee, 1962-63; Folger Sr. fellow, 1969-70, 88. Mem. MLA (chmn. Shakespeare div. 1981-82), Renaissance Soc. Am., Milton Soc., Shakespeare Assn. Am. (trustee 1978-81, 87-89, pres. 1986-87), AAUP (pres. Am. U. chpt. 1966-67), Southeastern Renaissance Conf. (pres. 1981-82), Phi Beta Kappa, Mortar Board, Phi Kappa Phi. Episcopalian. Home: 4931 Albemarle St NW Washington DC 20016-4359 Office: Am U Dept Lit Washington DC 20016

ROBERTS, JIMMY, sports correspondent; b. Jan. 25, 1957. BA in Radio/TV/Film, U. Md., 1979. Staff reporter Westchester/Rockland (N.Y.) Newspaper, 1975-77; writer, prodr. Howard Cosell show ABC's SportBeat, 1985-87; writer, prodr. features ABC Sports, 1987-88; reporter, writer, prodr., corr. ESPN, 1988—; contbr. Outside the Line series ESPN, World News Tonight, ABC. Recipient 13 sports Emmys. Office: ESPN ESPN Plaza Bristol CT 06010

ROBERTS, JO ANN WOODEN, school system administrator; b. Chgo., June 24, 1948; d. Tilmon and Annie Mae (Wardlaw) Wooden; m. Edward Allen Roberts Sr. (div.); children: Edward Allen Jr., Hillary Ann. BS, Wayne State U., 1970, MS, 1971; PhD, Northwestern U., 1977. Speech, lang. pathologist Chgo. Bd. Edn., 1971-78, adminstr., 1978-88; dir. spl. svcs. Rock Island (Ill.) Pub. Schs., 1988-90; supt. Muskegon Hts. (Mich.) Pub. Schs., 1990-93; deputy supr. Chgo. Pub. Schs., 1993-96; supt. of schs. Hazel Crest (Ill.) Sch. Dist. #152 1/2, 1996—; instr. Chgo City Community Coll., 1976-77; project dir. Ednl. Testing Svc., Evanston, Ill., 1976-77; exec. dir. Nat. Speech, Lang. and Hearing Assn., Chgo., 1984-86; hon. guest lectr. Govs. State U., University Park, Ill., 1983-86; cons. in field. Author: Learning to Talk, 1974. Trustee Muskegon County Libr. Bd., 1990, Mercy Hosp. Bd., Muskegon, 1990, St. Mark's Sch. Bd. Dirs., Southborough, Mass., 1989, United Way Bd., Muskegon, 1990; mem. Mich. State Bd. Edn. Systematic Initiative in Math and Sci., 1991, Gov. John Engler Mich. 2000 Task Force, 1991, Chpt. II Adv. Commn., 1991. Recipient Leadership award Boy Scouts Am., 1990; named finalist Outstanding Young Working Women, Glamour Mag., 1984, Outstanding Educator, Blacks in Govt., 1990. Mem. Am. Assn. Sch. Adminstrs., Nat. Alliance Black Sch. Educators, Mich. Assn. Sch. Adminstrs., Assn. Supervision & Curriculum Devel., Phi Delta Kappa. Avocations: creative writing, peotry, modern dance, theater, drawing. Office: Hazel Crest Pub Schs Dist 152 1/2 170th and Dixie Hwy Hazel Crest IL 60429

ROBERTS, JOAN I., social psychologist, educator. BA in English, U. Utah, Salt Lake City, 1957; MA in Social Psychology, Columbia U., 1960, EdD in Social Psychology, 1970. Teaching asst. in English U. Utah, Salt Lake City, 1956-57; cons. psychologist Herrold Assocs. Mgmt. Cons., N.Y.C., 1958-61; research staff mem. Makerere Coll., Kampala, East Africa, 1961-63; research assoc. Hunter Coll., N.Y.C., 1964-67; coordinator Tng. Project and Research in Intergroup Relations, Madison, Wis., 1970-73; asst. prof. dept. ednl. policy studies U. Wis., Madison, 1968-75; assoc. prof. social scis. Upstate Med. Ctr./SUNY, Syracuse, 1976-79; chairperson dept. child, family, and community studies Syracuse (N.Y.) U., 1978-80, assoc. prof. dept. child, family, and community studies, 1978-84, prof. dept. child, family, and community studies, 1985—, prof. emerita, 1994—; prof. internat. programs abroad Syracuse U., London, 1984-85, 1990; adj. prof. Syracuse U. Sch. Nursing, N.Y., 1976—; adj. assoc. prof. social scis. SUNY, 1979-83; project dir. model caregivers tng. project N.Y. State Dept. Social Services, 1981; lectr. and presenter of papers to various academic and profl. groups; coordinator, mem. Wis. Coordinating Council of Women in Higher Edn., 1971-74. Author: School Children in the Urban Slum: Readings in Social Science Reseach, 1966, 2d rev. edit., 1968, Group Behavior in Urban Classrooms, 1968, Scene of the Battle: Group Behavior in Urban Classrooms, 1970; Beyond Intellectual Sexism: A New Woman, A New Reality, 1976; author: (with Prof. Sherri Akinsanya) Educational Patterns and Cultural Configurations: The Anthropology of Education, Vol. I, 1976, Schooling in the Cultural Context: Anthropological Studies of Education, Vol. II, 1975, Feminism and Nursing: Historical Perspectives on the Status, Power, and Political Activism in Nursing Profession, 1995. Mem. APA, Am. Anthrop. Assn., Brit. U. Womens Club.

ROBERTS, JOHN BENJAMIN, II, public policy consultant, television producer, writer; b. Albrook AFB, C.Z., Oct. 4, 1955; s. Robert Benjamin and Mary Pauline (Porath) R.; m. Elizabeth Ann Levandoski, 1996; 1 child, John Benjamin III. BA, U. Calif., Irvine, 1973; MA with honors, Oxford U., Eng., 1978. Assoc. editor Handgunner, Ltd., London, 1979—, British Rifleman, 1995—; press aide Reagan-Bush Campaign, Arlington, Va., 1980, sr. policy analyst, Washington, 1984; dep. dir. communications Rep. Nat. Com., Washington, 1981, Nat. Rep. Congl. Com., 1991; dir. editorial policy U.S. Dept. Edn., Washington, 1981-83; assoc. dir. office planning and evaluation White House, Washington, 1983-84, assoc. dir. office polit. and govtl. affairs, 1985-86; sr. v.p. Russo, Watts & Rollins Inc., Washington, 1986-88, pres. Roberts Communications, Inc., 1988—; v.p. programming Oliver Prodns., Inc., 1996—; TV producer McLaughlin Group, One on One, CNBC, 1986-96. Author: Entitlement Spending, 1984, Sons of Cincinnatus, 1996. Contbr. articles to newspapers, mags. Bd. dirs. Inst. for Rsch. on Small Arms in Internat. Security, Washington, 1989. Internat. Exch. Coun. (bd. dirs.), Oxford U. Pistol Club (Half-Blue Varsity award 1978), U.K. Practical Shooting Assn. (founder, life mem.), Oxford Soc . Avocations: competitive marksmanship, backpacking, photography.

ROBERTS, JOHN CHARLES, law school educator; b. Aberdeen, S.D., Feb. 29, 1940; s. Jacob John Schmitt and Leona (Blethen) Blake; m. Kathleen Kelly (div. 1985); children: Katherine, John Charles Jr.; m. Lynn Dale Friedman, Dec. 22, 1985; 1 child, Emily Sara. B.S., Northwestern U., 1961; LL.B., Yale U., 1968. Bar: U.S. Dist. Ct. D.C. 1969, Mich. 1981. Assoc. Covington & Burling, Washington, 1968-71; assoc. dean, lectr. Yale U. Law Sch., New Haven, 1971-77; gen. counsel U.S. Senate Com. on Armed Services, 1977-80; adj. prof. law Washington Coll. Law, Am. U., 1978-80; dean, prof. law Wayne State U. Law Sch., Detroit, 1980-86; prof., dean Law Sch. DePaul U., Chgo., 1986-96, v.p. for univ. advancement, 1996-97, prof. law, 1997—; mem. exec. com. Inst. for Continuing Legal Edn., Chgo., 1988-91. Mem. adv. com. Mich. Psychiat. Soc., 1980-86; bd. dirs. Constl. Rights Found., 1992-96. Lt. USN, 1961-65. Mem. ABA, Chgo. Bar Assn., Chgo. Coun. Lawyers, Assn. Am. Law Schs. (mem. exec. com., chmn. sect. instn. advancement 1987-88, chmn., sec. adminstrn. law schs. 1993-94), Order of Coif. Democrat. Avocations: collecting modern first editions. Office: DePaul U Coll Law 25 E Jackson Blvd Chicago IL 60604-2201

ROBERTS, JOHN D., chemist, educator; b. L.A., June 8, 1918; s. Allen Andrew and Flora (Dombrowski) R.; m. Edith Mary Johnson, July 11, 1942; children: Anne Christine, Donald William, John Paul, Allen Walter. AB, UCLA, 1941, PhD, 1944; D in Natural Scis. (hon.), U. Munich, 1962; D.Sc. (hon.), Temple U., 1964, Notre Dame U., 1993, U. Wales, 1993; student, Scripps Rsch. Inst., 1996. Instr. chemistry UCLA, 1944-45; NRC fellow chemistry Harvard U., 1945-46, instr. chemistry, 1946; instr. chemistry MIT, 1946, asst. prof., 1947-50, assoc. prof., 1950-52; vis. prof. Ohio State U., 1952, Stanford U., 1973-74; prof. organic chemistry Calif. Inst. Tech., 1953-72, inst. prof. chemistry, 1972-88, inst. prof. chemistry emeritus, lectr., 1988—, dean of faculty, v.p., provost, 1980-83, lectr., 1988—, chmn. divsn. chemistry and chem. engring., 1963-68, acting chmn., 1972-73; Foster lectr. U. Buffalo, 1956; Mack Meml. lectr. Ohio State U., 1957; Falk-Plaut lectr. Columbia U., 1957; Reynaud Found. lectr. Mich. State U., 1958; Bachmann Meml. lectr. U. Mich., 1958; J.D. Roberts Symp lectr. Harvard U., 1995; Rhodes-Rawlin lectr. U. Wyo., 1995; Bristol-Meyers Squibb lectr. Syracuse U., 1995;.vis. prof. Harvard, 1958-59, M. Tishler lectr., 1965; Reilly lectr. Notre Dame U., 1960; Am.-Swiss Found. lectr., 1960; O.M. Smith lectr. Okla. State U., 1962; M.S. Kharasch Meml. lectr. U. Chgo., 1962; K. Folkers lectr. U. Ill., 1962; Phillips lectr. Haverford Coll., 1963; vis. prof. U. Munich, 1962; Sloan lectr. U. Alaska, 1967; Disting. vis. prof. U. Iowa, 1967; Sprague lectr. U. Wis., 1967; Kilpatrick lectr. Ill. Inst. Tech., 1969; Pacific Northwest lectr., 1969; E.F. Smith lectr. U. Pa., 1970; vis. prof. chemistry Stanford U., 1973-74; S.C. Lind lectr. U. Tenn.; Arapahoe lectr. U. Colo., 1976; Mary E. Kapp lectr. Va. Commonwealth U., 1976; R.T. Major lectr. U. Conn., 1977; Nebr. lectr. Am. Chem. Soc., 1977; Leermakers lectr. Wesleyan U., 1980; Iddles Meml. lectr. U. N.H., 1981; Arapahoe lectr. Colo. State U., 1981; Winstein lectr. UCLA, 1981; Gilman lectr. Iowa State U., 1982; Marvel lectr. U. Ill., 1982; vis. lectr. Inst. Photog. Chemistry, Beijing, People's Republic of China, 1983, King lectr. Kans. State U., 1984, Lanzhou U., People's Republic of China, 1985, Davis lectr. U. New Orleans, 1986, Du Pont lectr. Harvey Mudd Coll., 1987, 3M vis. lectr. St. Olaf Coll., 1987, Swift lectr. Calif. Inst. Tech., 1987, Berliner lectr. Bryn Mawr Coll., 1988; Friend E. Clark lectr. W. Va. U., 1990; George H. Büchi lectr. MIT,

1991; Henry Kuivala lectr. SUNY Albany, 1991, Fuson lect. U. Nev., 1992; dir., cons. editor W.A. Benjamin, Inc., 1961-67; cons. E.I. du Pont Co., 1950—; mem. adv. panel chemistry NSF, 1958-60, chmn., 1959-60, chmn. divisional com. math., phys. engring. scis., 1962-64, mem. math. and phys. sci. div. com., 1964-66; chemistry adv. panel Air Force Office Sci. Research, 1959-61; chmn. chemistry sect. Nat. Acad. Scis., 1968-71; chmn. Nat. Acad. Scis. (Class I), 1976-78, councillor, 1980-83, nominating com., 1992; dir. Organic Syntheses, Inc. Author: Basic Organic Chemistry, Part I, 1955, Nuclear Magnetic Resonance, 1958, Spin-Spin Splitting in High-Resolution Nuclear Magnetic Resonance Spectra, 1961, Molecular Orbital Calculations, 1961, (with M.C. Caserio) Basic Principles of Organic Chemistry, 1964, 2d edit., 1977, Modern Organic Chemistry, 1967, (with R. Stewart and M.C. Caserio) Organic Chemistry-Methane To Macromolecules, 1971; (autobiography) At The Right Place at the Right Time, 1990; cons. editor: McGraw-Hill Series in Advanced Chemistry, 1957-60; editor in chief Organic Syntheses, vol. 41; mem. editorial bd. Spectroscopy, Organic Magnetic Resonance in Chemistry, Asymmetry, Tetrahedron Computer Methodology. Trustee L.S.B. Leakey Found., 1983-92; bd. dirs. Huntington Med. Rsch. Insts., Organic Syntheses Inc., Coleman Chamber Music Assn.; mem. Calif. Competitive Tech. adv. com., 1989—. Guggenheim fellow, 1952-53, 55-56; recipient Am. Chem. Soc. award pure chemistry, 1954, Harrison Howe award, 1957, Roger Adams award in organic chemistry, 1967, Alumni Profl. Achievement award UCLA, 1967, Nichols medal, 1972, Tolman medal, 1975, Michelson-Morley award, 1976, Norris award, 1978, Pauling award, 1980, Theodore Wm. Richards medal, 1982, Willard Gibbs Gold medal, 1983, Golden Plate award Am. Acad. Achievement, 1983, Priestley medal, 1987, Madison marshall award, 1989, (with W. V.E. Doering) Robert A. Welch award, 1990, Nat. Medal Sci. NSF, 1990, Glenn T. Seaborg medal, 1991, Award in nuclear magnetic resource, 1991, Svc. to Chemistry award, 1991, Arthur C. Cope award Am. Chem. Soc. 1994, Chem. Pioneer award, 1994, History Maker award from Pasadena Hist. Soc., 1994; named hon. alumnus Calif. Inst. Tech., 1990, SURF dedicatee, 1992. Mem. NAS (mem. com. on sci. and engring. pub. policy 1983-87), AAAS (councillor 1992-95), Am. Chem. Soc. (chmn. organic chemistry divsn. 1956-57), Am. Philos. Soc. (mem. coun. 1983-86), Am. Acad. Arts and Scis., Sigma Xi, Phi Lambda Upsilon, Alpha Chi. Sigma. Office: Calif Inst Tech Crellin Lab Pasadena CA 91125

ROBERTS, JOHN DERHAM, lawyer; b. Orlando, Fla., Nov. 1, 1942; s. Junius P. and Mary E. (Limerick) R.; m. Malinda K. Swineford, June 11, 1965; 1 child, Kimberlyn Amanda. Cert., Richmond (Va.) Bus. Coll., 1960; BS, Hampden-Sydney (Va.) Coll., 1964; LLB, Washington & Lee U., 1968. Bar: Va. 1968, Fla. 1969, U.S. Supreme Ct. 1969, U.S. Ct. Customs and Patent Appeals 1970, U.S. Tax Ct. 1970, U.S. Ct. Appeals (5th cir.) 1970, U.S. Ct. Appeals (9th cir.) 1974, U.S. Supreme Ct. 1969. Law clk. U.S. Dist. Ct., Jacksonville, Fla., 1968-69; assoc. Phillips, Kendrick, Gearhart & Aylor, Arlington, Va., 1969-70; asst. U.S. Atty. mid. dist. Fla. U.S. Dept. Justice, Jacksonville, 1970-74; asst. U.S. Atty. Dist. of Alaska, Anchorage, 1974-77, U.S. magistrate judge, 1977—. Bd. dirs. Teen Challenge Alaska, Anchorage, 1984-93; chmn. Eagle Scout Rev. Bd., 1993—; bd. dirs. Alaska Youth for Christ, 1993-96; govs.'s Prayer Breakfast Com., 1994—. Recipient Citizenship award DAR, Anchorage, 1984, plaque, U.S. Navy, Citizen Day, Adak, Alaska, 1980. Mem. ABA, Nat. Conf. Spl. Ct. Judges (exec. bd. 1985-92), 9th Cir. Conf. Magistrates (exec. bd. 1982-85, chmn. 1984-85), Alaska Bar Assn., Anchorage Bar Assn., Chi Phi, Psi Chi, Phi Alpha Delta. Republican. Office: US Magistrate Judge 222 W 7th Ave Unit 46 Anchorage AK 99513-7504

ROBERTS, JOHN GLOVER, JR., lawyer; b. Buffalo, Jan. 27, 1955; s. John Glover and Rosemary (Podrasky) R. AB summa cum laude, Harvard U., 1976, JD magna cum laude, 1979. Bar: D.C. 1981, U.S. Ct. Appeals (fed. cir.) 1982, U.S. Ct. Appeals (D.C., 5th, 9th cirs.) 1988, U.S. Ct. Appeals (3d, 7th , and 10th cirs.) 1996, U.S. Ct. Claims 1982, U.S. Supreme Ct. 1987. Law clk. U.S. Ct. Appeals 2d cir., N.Y.C., 1979-80; law clk. to Justice William H. Rehnquist U.S. Supreme Ct., Washington, 1980-81; spl. asst. to U.S. atty. gen. Dept. Justice, Washington, 1981-82; assoc. counsel to Pres. U.S., Washington, 1982-86; assoc. Hogan & Hartson, Washington, 1986-87, ptnr., 1988-89, 93—; dep. solicitor gen. U.S. Dept. Justice, Washington, 1989-93. Editor: Harvard Law Rev., 1977-79. Mem. Am. Law Inst., Phi Beta Kappa. Republican.

ROBERTS, JOHN PETER LEE, cultural advisor, administrator, educator, writer; b. Sydney, Australia, Oct. 21, 1930; s. Noel Lee and Myrtle Winifred (Reid) R.; m. Christina Van Oordt, July 28, 1962; children—Noel, Christina, Olga. Student, State Conservatorium Music, New South Wales; MA, Carleton U., 1988; DFA (hon.), U. Victoria, 1992. With CBC Radio, Toronto, Can., 1955—; producer CBC Radio, 1955—, head music and variety, 1971—, spl. adv. music and arts, 1975; sr. advisor cultural devel., head office Ottawa, 1983-87; mem. exec. bd. Internat. Music Centre, Vienna, 1968-80, first chmn. radio and comml. rec. group, 1969-70, hon. mem., 1980; mem. exec. bd. Internat. Inst. Music Dance and Theatre, Vienna, 1969-75; bd. govs. Can. Conf. Arts, 1970-76; exec. bd. Internat. Music Coun., Paris, 1973-79; v.p. Internat. Music Council, 1975, pres., 1978-79; pres. Can. Music Centre, Toronto, 1971-77; dir. gen. Can. Music Centre, 1977-81; pres. Can. Music Council, 1968-71, 75-77; dir. Festival Singers of Can., 1965-78, Elmer Iseler Singers, 1979-81, Toronto Mendelssohn Choir, 1969-81, Nat. Youth Orch. Can., 1973-80; chmn. 1st World Music Week, 1975, Internat. Music Day, 1975-82; v.p. Internat. Inst. Audio-Visual Communication and Cultural Devel. (Mediacult), Vienna, 1976-87, pres., 1987-93; pres. Internat. Rsch. Inst. for Media, Communication, Cultural Devel., Vienna, 1993-95; v.p. Musicians Internat. Mus. Aid Fund., Geneva, 1978, 79; pres. Les Jeunesses Musicales du Can., 1979-83; chmn. Internat. Vocal Competition, Rio de Janeiro, 1979; spl. advisor to chmn. Can. Radio-TV and Telecomms. Commn., 1981-83; sr. advisor cultural devel. CBC, 1983-87; dean of faculty of fine arts U. Calgary, 1987-95; vis. fellow McGill Inst. for Study of Can. McGill U., Montreal, 1995-96; adj. prof. U. Calgary, 1995—; bd. dirs. Nickle Arts Mus., 1987-95, Calgary Philharm. Orch., 1988-94, Ester Honen's Internat. Piano Competition, 1994. Mem. editorial bd. Can. Music Book, 1970-77. Mem. exec. bd. dirs. Can. Nat. Commn. for UNESCO, 1976-80; founding pres. Glenn Gould Found., Toronto, 1983—. Decorated Order of Can. (mem., 1983, officer, 1996); Cross of Honour for Sci. and the Arts (Austria). Mem. Can. assn. Fine Arts Deans (chmn. 1989-93), Internat. Coun. Fine Arts Deans (bd. dirs. 1992-94). Office: U Calgary Faculty Fine Arts, 2500 University Dr NW, Calgary, AB Canada T2N 1N4

ROBERTS, JULIA FIONA, actress; b. Smyrna, Ga., Oct. 28, 1967; d. Betty and Walter Motes; m. Lyle Lovett, Jun. 27, 1993 (div. 1995). Film appearances include Blood Red, 1986, Satisfaction, 1987, Mystic Pizza, 1988, Steel Magnolias, 1989 (Acad. Award nominee, Golden Globe award), Pretty Woman,1990 (Acad. Award nominee, Golden Globe Award), Flatliners, 1990, Sleeping With the Enemy, 1991, Hook, 1991, Dying Young, 1991, The Player, 1992, The Pelican Brief, 1993, I Love Trouble, 1994, Ready to Wear (Prêt-à-Porter), 1994, Something To Talk About, 1995, Mary Reilly, 1996, Everybody Says I Love You, 1996, Michael Collins, 1996, My Best Friend's Wedding, 1997; TV movies include Baja Oklahoma, 1988. Named Female Star of the Yr., Nat. Assn. Theatre Owners, 1991. Office: ICM 8942 Wilshire Blvd Beverly Hills CA 90211*

ROBERTS, KATHLEEN MARY, school system administrator; b. Syracuse, N.Y., Apr. 15, 1947; d. Casimer and Lorrayne Arletta (Molloy) Piegdon; m. James C. Roberts, June 29, 1968 (div. Sept. 1988). BA, Cen. State U., Edmond, Okla., 1968, MEd, 1971; PhD, U. Okla., 1977. Cert. tchr., prin., supt., Okla.; cert. supt., N.Y. Tchr. Putnam City Schs., Oklahoma City, 1960-72; reading specialist Moore (Okla.) Pub. Schs., 1973-74; reading specialist Crooked Oak Pub. Schs., Oklahoma City, 1974-77, supt., 1990-95; rsch. assoc. Oklahoma City Pub. Schs., 1977-80; supt. Okla. Dept. Corrections, Oklahoma City, 1980-86, Healdton (Okla.) Pub. Schs., 1986-90, Piedmont (Okla.) Pub. Schs., 1995—. Contbr. articles to profl. publs. Bd. dirs. United Meth. Prism Ministry, Oklahoma City, 1986—, Children's Shelter, Ardmore, Okla., 1989-90; mem. State Vocat. Edn. Coun., Oklahoma City, 1980-85. Recipient citation Okla. State Senate, 1986. Mem. ASCD, Internat. Reading Assn., Am. Assn. Sch. Adminstrs., Okla. Assn. Sch. Adminstrs., Piedmont C. of C. (v.p. 1997—), Phi Delta Kappa, Alpha Chi, Kappa Delta Phi. Democrat. Roman Catholic. Avocations: furniture refinishing, reading, gardening. Office: Piedmont Schs 713 Piedmont Rd N Piedmont OK 73078-9248

ROBERTS, KEITH EDWARD, SR., lawyer; b. White Hall, Ill., Apr. 27, 1928; s. Victor Harold and Ruby Harriet (Kelsey) R.; m. Marthan Dusch, Sept. 4, 1954; 1 child, Keith Edward. Student, Western Ill. U., 1946-47, George Washington U., 1947-48; BS, U. Ill., 1951, JD, 1953. Bar: Ill. 1953, U.S. Dist. Ct. (no. dist.) Ill. 1957, U.S. Dist. Ct. (so. dist.) Ill. 1961, U.S. Dist. Ct. (no. dist.) Ohio 1960, U.S. Ct. Mil. Appeals 1954, U.S. Ct. Appeals (7th cir.) 1968. Assoc. J.D. Quarant, Elizabethtown, Ill., 1953-54; staff atty. Pa. R.R. Co., Chgo., 1957-60; assoc. Henslee, Monek & Henslee, Chgo., 1960-67; sole practice, Naperville, Ill., 1967-68; ptnr. Donovan, Atten, Mountcastle, Roberts & DaRosa, Wheaton, Ill., 1968-77; pres. Donovan & Roberts, P.C., Wheaton, 1977—. Served to capt. U.S. Army, 1954-57. Mem. ABA, Internat. Soc. Barristers, Assn. Trial Lawyers Am., Ill. Bar Assn., DuPage County Bar Assn. (gen. counsel 1976-86). Presbyterian. Office: Donovan & Roberts PC PO Box 417 Wheaton IL 60189-0417

ROBERTS, KENNETH LEWIS, investor, lawyer, foundation administrator; b. Dungannon, Va., Dec. 12, 1932; s. Clarence Eugene and Katherine (Osborne) R.; m. Anne Foster Cook, Sept. 10, 1955; children—Kenneth L., Patrick Hagan Foster. B.A., Vanderbilt U., 1954, LL.B., 1959. Bar: Tenn. Assoc. prof. law Vanderbilt U., 1959-60; assoc. Waller, Lansden & Dortch, Nashville, 1960-66; exec. v.p. Commerce Union Bank, Nashville, 1966-71; pres., chief exec. officer, dir. Cen. Nat. Bank, Richmond, Va., 1971-76; pres., chief exec. officer First Am. Nat. Bank, Nashville, 1976-90; dir. First Am. Corp., Nashville, 1976-90, vice chmn., 1976-77, pres., chief exec. officer, 1977-79, chmn., chief exec. officer, 1979-90; pres., exec. dir. HCA Found., Nashville, 1991—; past pres., dir. Cen. Nat. Corp. Trustee Vanderbilt U.; bd. dirs. Leadership Nashville, Montgomery Bell Acad. Lt. Chem. Corps, AUS, 1955-57. Mem. ABA, Tenn. Bar Assn., Nashville Bar Assn., Nashville C. of C., Cumberland Club, Belle Meade Country Club, Univ. Club, Ponte Vedra (Fla.) Inn & Club. Office: FRIST Found 3319 W End Ave Ste 900 Nashville TN 37203-1076

ROBERTS, KEVIN, recreational facility executive. Pres. American Golf Corp., Santa Monica, Calif. Office: Am Golf Corp 2951 28th St Santa Monica CA 90405-2961

ROBERTS, LARRY SPURGEON, biological sciences educator, zoologist; b. Texon, Tex., June 30, 1935; s. E. Fowler and Frances Wray (Huggins) R.; m. Maria Elek, Feb. 7, 1962; children: Gregory Lorinc, Bruce Tibor, Teresa Margit, Eric Miklos. B.S., So. Meth. U., 1956; M.S. (NSF predoctoral fellow), U. Ill., 1958; D.Sc. (NIH predoctoral fellow), Johns Hopkins U., 1961. Cert. scuba instr. Nat. Assn. Underwater Instrs. Asst. prof. zoology U. Mass., Amherst, 1963-69, assoc. prof., 1969-75, prof., 1975-79; prof. biol. scis. Tex. Tech U., Lubbock, 1979-90; chmn. dept. Tex. Tech U., 1979-84; adj. prof. biol. scis. U. Miami, 1990—, Fla. Internat. U., 1990-93. Author: (with others) Foundations of Parasitology, 1977, 5th edit., 1996, Integrated Principles of Zoology, 1979, 10th edit., 1997, Biology of Animals, 1982, 6th edit., 1994, The Underwater World of Sport Diving, 1991, Animal Diversity, 1994. Mem. Amherst Dem. Town Com., 1968-79, vice chmn., 1972-76; mem. Amherst Town Meeting, 1966-76; mem. Amherst Zoning Bd. Appeals, 1972-75, vice chmn., 1972-75; recorder West Tex. Dems., 1985-86; mem. Dade County Dem. Exec. Com., 1991—. NIH postdoctoral trainee, 1961-63; NIH fellow, 1969-70; recipient Disting. Service cert. Mass. Tchrs. Assn., 1979. Mem. AAAS, ACLU (vice chmn. Hampshire County chpt. 1966-68, bd. dirs. Lubbock chpt. 1985-89, vice chmn. 1988-89, bd. dirs. Miami, Fla. chpt. 1991—, Fla. State bd. dirs.), Am. Soc. Parasitologists (Henry Baldwin Ward medal 1971, council mem. at large 1980-83, v.p. 1984-85, 96—), Am. Micros. Soc. (v.p. 1974-75, exec. com. 1978-81), Mass. Soc. Profs. (pres. 1977-78), Soc. Protozoologists, Am. Soc. Tropical Medicine and Hygiene, Wildlife Disease Assn., Southwestern Assn. Parasitologists (v.p. 1982, pres. 1983), Southeastern Soc. Parasitologists (pres. elect 1993, pres. 1994), Internat. Soc. Reef Studies, Crustacean Soc., Am. Acad. Underwater Scis., Sigma Xi. Home: 27700 SW 164th Ave Homestead FL 33031-2846

ROBERTS, LAWRENCE GILMAN, telecommunications company executive; b. Dec. 21, 1937; s. Elliott John and Elizabeth (Gilman) R.; m. June Ellen Stuller, 1959 (div. 1973); children: Paul, Kenny. BS, MIT, 1959, MS, 1960, PhD, 1963. Dir. info. proc. Advanced Rsch. Projects Agy. U.S. Dept. Def., Arlington, Va., 1969-73; dir. info. proc. ARPA U.S. Dept. Defense, Arlington, Va., 1969-73; pres., CEO GTE Telenet Corp., Vienna, Va., 1973-82; pres. DHL, Redwood City, Calif., 1982-83; chmn., CEO NetExpress, Inc., Foster City, Calif., 1983-93; pres. ATM Systems, Foster City, Calif., 1993—. Recipient L.M. Ericsson award for comms. Mem. IEEE, IEEE Computer Soc., Am. Fedn. Info. Processing (Harry Goode award, W. Wallace McDowell award), Assn. Computing Machinery, Sigma Xi. Office: ATM Systems 989E W Hillsdale Blvd # 290 San Mateo CA 94403-3839

ROBERTS, LEIGH MILTON, psychiatrist; b. Jacksonville, Ill., June 9, 1925; s. Victor Harold and Ruby Harriet (Kelsey) R.; m. Marilyn Edith Kadow, Sept. 6, 1946; children: David, Carol Roberts Mayer, Paul, Nancy Mills. B.S., U. Ill., 1945, M.D., 1947. Diplomate: Am. Bd. Psychiatry and Neurology. Intern St. Francis Hosp., Peoria, Ill., 1947-48; gen. practice medicine Macomb, Ill., 1948-50; resident in psychiatry U. Wis. Hosps., Madison, 1953-56; staff psychiatrist Mendota (Wis.) State Hosp., 1956-58; mem. faculty U. Wis. Med. Sch., Madison, 1959-89; prof. psychiatry U. Wis. Med. Sch., 1971-89, acting chmn. dept., 1972-75; mem. spl. rev. bd. Wis. Parole Bd. Sex Crimes Law, 1962-88, forensic cons., 1988—; mem. Dane County Devel. Disabilities Bd., 1962-66, Wis. Planning Com. Mental Health, 1963-65, Wis. Planning Com. Health, 1969-71, Wis. Planning Com. Vocat. Rehab., 1966-68, Wis. Planning Com. Health Centers, 1967-71, Wis. Mental Health Adv. Com., 1973-78; bd. dirs. Methodist Hosp., Madison, Dane County Rehab. House, Dane County Assn. Mental Health; cons. in field. Editor: Community Psychiatry, 1966, Comprehensive Mental Health, 1968; contbr. articles profl. jours. Pres. Wis. Council Chs., 1976-78; bd. dirs. Madison Campus Ministry, St. Benedict Center; trustee N.Central Coll., Naperville, Ill. Served with USNR, 1943-45, 50-53. Decorated Bronze Star, Purple Heart. Fellow Am. Psychiat. Assn. (bd. trustees 1981-84), Wis. Psychiat. Assn. (pres. 1967). Methodist. Home and Office: 722A Sauk Ridge Trl Madison WI 53705-1155 *Life is a precious gift whose journey is molded and shaped by cumulative experiences and relationships. Religious belief and practice which provides future-oriented hope, disciplined accountability and living service are balanced by professional psychiatric vistas on the uniqueness and worth of each human person.*

ROBERTS, LEONARD H., retail executive; b. Chgo., Feb. 19, 1949; s. Jack and Goldie (Solomon) R.; m. Laurie Susan Osser, Aug. 20, 1967; children: Dawn, Adina, Melissa. BS in Chemistry and Mktg., U. Ill., 1971; JD, DePaul U., 1974. Food scientist Armour Foods, Chgo., 1968-71, Cen. Soya, Chgo., 1971-74; govt. lobbyist Ralston Purina Co., St. Louis, 1974-76, dir. mktg., 1976-78; mng. dir. Raltech Ralston Purina Co., Madison, Wis., 1978-81; v.p. food service ops. Ralston Purina Co., St. Louis, 1981-85; pres., chief exec. officer Arby's Inc., Atlanta, 1985-89; chmn. bd., chief exec. officer Shoney's Inc., 1989-93; pres. Radio Shack, Fort Worth, TX, 1993—, Tandy Corp., Fort Worth, 1996—; bd. dirs. Ghirardelli Chocolate Co., Tandy Corp. Holder numerous patents on Soya protein research. Active United Way Met. Tarrant County, 1994, Nat. Crime Prevention Coun., 1994, Clark U. Students in Free Enterprise, Girl Scouts U.S., Harris Meth. Bd.; mem. exec. com. Fort Worth Symphony. Recipient Pvt. Sector Initiative award Office Pres. of U.S., Washington, 1987, Disting. Achievement award B'nai B'rith, Restaurant Bus. Leadership award, 1991, Golden Plate award Nations Restaurant News, 1991, Wall St. Bronze Critics award, 1992. Mem. ABA, Ill. Bar Assn. Home: 3516 Briarhaven Rd Fort Worth TX 76109-3128 Office: Radio Shack 100 Throckmorton St Ste 1900 Fort Worth TX 76102-2802

ROBERTS, LORIN WATSON, botanist, educator; b. Clarksdale, Mo., June 28, 1923; s. Lorin Cornelius and Irene (Watson) R.; m. Florence Ruth Greathouse, July 10, 1967; children: Michael Hamlin, Daniel Hamlin, Margaret Susan. BA, U. Mo., 1948, MA, 1950; PhD in Botany, U. Mo.-Columbia, 1952. Asst. prof., then assoc. prof. botany Agnes Scott Coll., Decaur, Ga., 1952-57; vis. asst. prof. Emory U., 1952-55; mem. faculty U. Idaho, 1957—, prof. botany, 1967-91, prof. botany emeritus, 1991—; Fulbright research prof. Kyoto (Japan) U., 1967-68; research fellow U. Bari, Italy, 1968; Cabot fellow Harvard, 1974; Fulbright teaching fellow North-Eastern Hill U., Shillong, Meghalaya, India, 1977; Fulbright sr. scholar and fellow Australian Nat. U., Canberra, 1980; sr. researcher U. London, 1984; pres. botany sect. 1st Internat. Congress Histochemistry and Cytochemistry, Paris, 1960; Alexander von Humboldt vis. fellow Australian Nat. U., 1992. Author: Cytodifferentiation in Plants, 1976 (with J.H. Dodds) Experiments in Plant Tissue Culture, 1982, 2d edit., 3d edit. 1995, 1985 (with P.B. Gahan and R. Aloni) Vascular Differentiation and Plant Growth Regulators, 1988; contbr. articles to profl. jours. Served with USAAF, 1943-46. Decorated chevalier de l'Ordre du Merit Agricole France, 1961; Alexander von Humboldt fellow, 1992. Fellow AAAS; mem. N.W. Sci. Assn. (pres. 1970-71), Bot. Soc. Am., Am. Soc. Plant Physiologists, Internat. Assn. Plant Tissue Culture, Am. Inst. Biol. Scis., Idaho Acad. Scis., Sigma Xi, Phi Kappa Phi, Phi Sigma. Home: 920 Mabelle St Moscow ID 83843-3834

ROBERTS, LOUIS DOUGLAS, physics educator, researcher; b. Charleston, S.C., Jan. 27, 1918; s. Louis Wigfall and Evelyn (Douglas) R.; m. Marjorie Violette Staveley-Lawson, Aug. 29, 1942; 1 child, Joyce Carol. AB with honors, Howard Coll., 1938; postgrad., John Hopkins U., 1938-39; PhD, Columbia U., 1941. Rockefeller Found. fellow Cornell U., Ithaca, N.Y., 1941-42; rsch. physicist GE, Schenectady, N.Y., 1942-46, U. Calif. at Berkeley, 1944-45; prin. physicist Oak Ridge (Tenn.) Nat. Lab., 1946-68; Ford Found. prof. U. Tenn., Knoxville, 1963-68; prof. physics U. N.C., Chapel Hill, 1968—, Alumni Disting. prof., 1980—. Contbr. articles on physics to profl. jours.; holder numerous patents in semiconductor devices, magnetron design, nuclear power, metals and alloys, etc. Recipient Tanner teaching award U. N.C., 1977; Fulbright fellow Oxford U., 1958-59, Guggenheim Found. fellow, 1958-59. Fellow Am. Phys. Soc. (mem. Southeastern sect., 1948—, vice chmn. 1954-55, chmn. 1955-56). Republican. Avocations: reading, music, travel, garden, photography. Home: 1116 Sourwood Cir Chapel Hill NC 27514-4912 Office: Univ NC Dept Physics and Astronomy Chapel Hill NC 27599-3255

ROBERTS, LOUISE NISBET, philosopher; b. Lexington, Ky., Apr. 21, 1919; d. Benjamin and Helen L. Nisbet; m. Warren Roberts, June 14, 1952; children: Helen Ward Roberts Hill, Valeria Lamar Roberts Emmett. AB, U. Ky., 1942, MA, 1944; PhD, Columbia U., 1952. Instr. philosophy Fairfax Hall, Waynesboro, Va., 1943-44, Fairmount Casements, Ormond Beach, Fla., 1944-45; mem. faculty Newcomb Coll., Tulane U., 1948—, prof. philosophy, 1969-85, dept. head, prof. emeritus, 1985—. Chmn. Episc. Diocese HIV/AIDS Commn., 1993-96. Contbr. articles to profl. jours. Univ. scholar, 1945-46. Mem. AAUW (fellow 1947-48, pres. New Orleans chpt. 1986-88), DAR (vice regent New Orleans chpt. 1987-90), So. Soc. Philosophy and Psychology, Phi Beta Kappa (chpt. pres. 1956-57), Delta Delta Delta (fellow 1946-47). Democrat. Episcopalian. Office: Tulane U Dept Of Philosophy New Orleans LA 70118

ROBERTS, LYNN ERNEST, theoretical physicist, educator; b. N.Y.C., Aug. 10, 1948; s. Lynn Ernest Roberts and Dorothy Elizabeth (Mobile) Woods; m. Brenda Joyce James, Aug. 1985; children: Natasha, Timothy, Lynn, Brendan, Ashleigh. BS in Physics, SUNY, Stony Brook, 1972; MS in Physics, Adelphi U., 1976, PhD in High Energy Theory, 1981. Teaching asst. Adelphi U., Garden City, N.Y., 1973-77, rsch. fellow, 1977-79; rsch. fellow Ford Found., Atlanta, 1977-79; rsch. collaborator Brookhaven Nat. Lab., Upton, N.Y., 1979-81, rsch. assoc., 1981-83, physicist, 1983-85; assoc. prof. physics Lincoln U., Lincoln University, Pa., 1985-90, prof., 1991—, acting chair, 1992-94; chair, 1995—; vis. rsch. scientist Argonne (Ill.) Nat. Lab., 1986-88; rschr. NSF, Washington, 1989-92, proposal reviewer, 1990, 93; specializing in lattice gauge theory, ultra-relativistic heavy ion collisions, phenomenology, relativistic field theory, math. physics, phase transitions and compositeness. Contbr. articles to sci. jours. Mem. Rotary (pres. Oxford, Pa. 1990), Inst. Advanced Sci. Studies (founding mem. and prin. officer). Home: 2501 Baynard Blvd Wilmington DE 19802-2961 Office: Lincoln U Dept Physics Wright Hall Lincoln University PA 19352

ROBERTS, LYNNE JEANINE, physician; b. St. Louis, Apr. 19, 1952; d. H. Clarke and Dorothy June (Cockrum) R.; m. Richard Allen Beadle Jr., July 18, 1981; children: Richard Andrew, Erica Roberts. BA with distinction, Ind. U., 1974, MD, 1978. Diplomate Am. Bd. Dermatology, Am. Bd. Pediatrics, Am. Bd. Laser Surgery. Intern in pediats. Children's Med. Ctr., Dallas, 1978-79, resident in pediats., 1979-80; resident in dermatology U. Tex. Southwestern Med. Ctr., Dallas, 1980-83, chief resident in dermatology, 1982-83, asst. instr. dermatology and pediatrics, 1983-84, asst. prof., 1984-90, assoc. prof., 1990—; physician Cons. Dermatol. Specialists, Dallas, 1990-93; pres. Lynne J. Roberts, MD, PA, Dallas, 1993—; dir. dermatology Children's Med. Ctr., Dallas, 1986—; dermatology sect. chief Med. City Dallas Hosp., 1994-95, 95-97. Contbr. articles to profl. jours., chpts. to books. Recipient Scholastic Achievement Citation Am. Med. Women's Assn., 1978. Fellow Am. Acad. Dermatology, Am. Acad. Pediatrics, Am. Soc. Laser Medicine and Surgery (bd. dirs. 1994-97); mem. Soc. Pediatric Dermatology, Am. Soc. Dermatologic Surgery, Tex. Med. Assn., Dallas Zool. Soc., Dallas Arboretum, Kappa Alpha Theta, Alpha Omega Alpha. Avocations: horseback riding, reading, fishing, swimming, camping. Office: 7777 Forest Ln Ste B314 Dallas TX 75230-2510

ROBERTS, MADELYN ALPERT, publishing executive. Assoc. pub. McCall's Gruner & Jahr USA Pub., N.Y.C. Office: Gruner & Jahr USA Pub 375 Lexington Ave New York NY 10017*

ROBERTS, MARGARET HAROLD, editor, publisher; b. Aug. 18, 1928. A.B., U. Chattanooga, 1950. Editor, pub. series Award Winning Art, 1960-70, New Woman mag., Palm Beach, Fla., 1971-84; editor, pub. Going Bonkers mag., 1992—. Author: juvenile book series Daddy is a Doctor, 1965. Office: PO Box 189 Palm Beach FL 33480-0189

ROBERTS, MARGOT MARKELS, business executive; b. Springfield, Mass., Jan. 20, 1945; d. Reuben and Marion (Markels) R.; children: Lauren B. Phillips, Debrah C. Herman. B.A., Boston U. Interior designer Louis Legum Furniture Co., Norfolk, Va., 1965-70; buyer, mgr. Danker Furniture, Rockville, Md., 1970-72; buyer W & J Sloane, Washington, 1972-74; pres. Bus. & Fin. Cons., Palm Beach, Fla., 1976-80, Margot M. Roberts & Assocs., Inc., Palm Beach, 1976—; dealer 20th century Am. art and wholesale antiques Margot M. Roberts, Inc., Palm Beach, 1989—; v.p., dir. So. Textile Svcs. Inc., Palm Beach. Pres. Brittany Condominium Assn., Palm Beach, 1983-87; v.p. South Palm Beach Civic Assn., 1983-88, South Palm Beach Pres.'s Assn., 1984-88; vice chmn. South Palm Beach Planning Bd., 1983-88, 90-91; elected town commr. Town South Palm Beach, Fla., 1991-92, elected vice mayor, 1992-93, elected mayor, 1993—; apptd. Commn. on Status of Women of Palm Beach County, 1992-95; voting mem. Palm Beach County Mcpl. League, 1991—; vice chair Commn. Status of Women of Palm Beach County, 1994-95. Mem. Nat. Assn. Women in Bus., Palm Beach C. of C. Republican. Office: Town Hall South Palm Beach 3577 S Ocean Blvd Palm Beach FL 33480-5706

ROBERTS, MARIE DYER, computer systems specialist; b. Statesboro, Ga., Feb. 19, 1943; d. Byron and Martha (Evans) Dyer; BS, U. Ga., 1966; student Am. U., 1972; cert. systems profl., cert. in data processing; m. Hugh V. Roberts, Jr., Oct. 6, 1973. Mathematician, computer specialist U.S. Naval Oceanographic Office, Washington, 1966-73; systems analyst, programmer Sperry Microwave Electronics, Clearwater, Fla., 1973-75; data processing mgr., asst. bus. mgr. Trenam, Simmons, Kemker et al, Tampa, Fla., 1975-77; mathematician, computer specialist U.S. Army C.E., Savannah, Ga., 1977-81, 83-85, Frankfurt, W. Ger., 1981-83; ops. rsch. analyst U.S. Army Contrn. Rsch. Lab., Champaign, Ill., 1985-87; data base adminstr., computer systems programmer, chief info. integration and implementation div. U.S. Army Corps of Engrs., South Pacific div., San Francisco, 1987-93; computer specialist, IDEF repository coord., Functional Process Improvement Expertise, Defense Info. Systems Agy., Arlington, Va., 1993-95; computer specialist Ctr. Integration Def. Info. Systems Agy., MacDill AFB, Fla., 1995—. instr. computer scis. City Coll. of Chgo. in Franfurt, 1982-83. Recipient Sustained Superior Performance award Dept. Army, 1983, 2 Nat. Performance Rev. Hammer awards V.P. Gore, 1996. Mem. Am. Soc. Hist. Preservation, Data Processing Mgmt. Assn., Assn. of Inst. for Cert. Computer Profls., Assn. Women in Computing, Assn. Women in Sci., NAFE, Am. Film Inst., U. Ga. Alumni Assn., Sigma Kappa, Soc. Am. Mil. Engrs. Author: Harris Computer Users Manual, 1983. *Best is the eye of the beholder. I have learned that the perspective or view point of the customer is critical to providing acceptable service to that customer. Beware of being* *called an expert as you may eventually believe you are. Arrogence is a barrier to providing good customer service.*

ROBERTS, MARK SCOTT, lawyer; b. Fullerton, Calif., Dec. 31, 1951; s. Emil Seidel and Theda (Wymer) R.; m. Sheri Lyn Smith, Sept. 23, 1977; children: Matthew Scott, Meredith Lyn, Benjamin Price. BA in Theater, Pepperdine U., 1975; JD, Western State U., 1978; cert. civil trial advocacy program, U. Calif., San Francisco, 1985; cert. program of instrn. for lawyers, Harvard U., 1990. Bar: Calif. 1980, U.S. Dist. Ct. (cen. dist.) Calif. 1980, U.S. Supreme Ct. 1989, U.S. Ct. Mil. Appeals 1989, U.S. Tax Ct. 1990. Concert mgr. Universal Studios, Hollywood, Calif., 1973-74; tchr. Anaheim (Calif.) Union Sch Dist., 1979-80; prin. Mark Roberts & Assocs., Fullerton, Calif., 1980—; instr. bus. law Biola U., La Mirada, Calif., 1980-84; judge pro tem Orange County Superior Ct., Santa Ana, 1989—. Co-author: Legacy-Plan, Protect and Preserve Your Estate, 1996. Mem. Calif. State Bar Assn., Orange County Bar Assn. Avocations: snow and water skiing. Office: Mark Roberts & Assocs 1440 N Harbor Blvd Ste 900 Fullerton CA 92835-4122

ROBERTS, MARKLEY, economist, educator; b. Shanghai, China, Sept. 3, 1930; s. Donald and Frances Charlotte (Markley) R.; m. Jeanne Addison, Feb. 19, 1966; children: Addison, Ellen. A.B., Princeton U., 1951; M.A., Am. U., 1960, Ph.D., 1970. Reporter Washington Star newspaper, 1952-57; legis. asst. Office of Senator Hubert Humphrey of Minn., Washington, 1957-62; legis. asst., economist AFL-CIO, Washington, 1962-96, asst. dir. econ. rsch. dept., 1989-96; bd. dir., vice chmn. Econ. Edn. Found. for Clergy, 1972-80; chmn. labor research adv. council Bur. Labor Stats.-Dept. Labor, 1972-96; adj. prof. econs. U. Md., 1966—, George Washington U., 1972-96. Contbr. numerous articles on labor and econ. affairs, tech., productivity to various publs.; author monographs in field. Mem. D.C. Democratic Central Com., 1964-68; ward III coordinator Washington Mayor Walter Washington, 1974-78; bd. dirs. Laymen's Nat. Bible Com. Inc., N.Y.C., 1972-82. Mem. UN Assn. (bd. dirs. nat. capitol area chpt. 1995—), Am. Econ. Assn., Indsl. Rels. Rsch. Assn. (exec. bd. 1975-77), Am. Polit. Sci. Assn., Nat. Acad. Social Ins., Assn. Evolutionary Econs., Am. Statis. Assn., Nat. Consumers League (bd. dirs. 1991—), Newspaper Guild, Ams. for Dem. Action (exec. bd. 1992—), Social Democrats USA. Democrat. Episcopalian. Home: 4931 Albemarle St NW Washington DC 20016-4359

ROBERTS, MAURA M., secondary school educator; b. Washington, Mar. 2, 1944; d. John E. and Mary M. (McCann) Martin; m. Charles D. Roberts, Aug. 15, 1987; 1 child, Caragh M. McLaughlin. AB, U. Mass. at Lowell, 1965; MAT, Salem State Coll., 1973. Cert. tchr. English, Mass., S.C. Tchr. English Hilton Head (S.C.) Prep Sch.; with Concord (Mass.)-Carlisle Sch. Dist.; tchr. English Concord-Carlisle Sch. Dist. Mem. edn. adv. bd. Orchard House Mus., Concord, 1994—. Mem. ASCD, Nat. Coun. Tchrs. of English, Concord Carlisle Tchrs. Assn., Mass. Tchrs. Assn.

ROBERTS, MELVILLE PARKER, JR., neurosurgeon, educator; b. Phila., Oct. 15, 1931; s. Melville Parker and Marguerite Louise (Reimann) R.; m. Sigrid Marianne Magnusson, Mar. 27, 1954; children: Melville Parker III, Julia Pell, Erik Emerson. BS, Washington and Lee U., 1953; MD, Yale U., 1957. Diplomate: Am. Bd. Neurol. Surgery. Intern Yale Med. Ctr., 1957, neurosurg. resident, 1958-60, 62-64, Am. Cancer Soc. fellow in neurosurgery, 1962-64, instr., 1964; asst. prof. surgery Sch. Medicine U. Va., Charlottesville, 1965-69; practice medicine specializing in neurol. surgery Hartford, Conn., 1970—; mem. sr. staff Hartford Hosp., John Dempsey Hosp.; asst. prof. surgery Sch. Medicine U. Conn., Farmington, 1970-71; assoc. prof. U. Conn., 1972-75, assoc. prof. neurology, 1974-77, chmn. divsn. neurosurgery, 1971-84, prof. surgery, 1975—, acting chmn. dept. neurology, 1973-77, acting chmn. dept. surgery, 1974-77, William Beecher Scoville prof. neurosurgery, 1976—; James Hudson Brown rsch. fellow Yale U., 1957. Author: Atlas of the Human Brain in Section, 1970, 2d edition, 1987; mem. editorial bd.: Conn. Medicine, 1973—; contbr. articles to profl. jours. Capt. M.C., U.S. Army, 1960-61. Fellow ACS, Royal Soc. Medicine (London); mem. AAUP, Am. Assn. Neurol. Surgeons, Soc. Neurol. Surgeons, Congress Neurol. Surgeons (bd. dirs. joint spinal sect. with Am. Assn. Neurol. Surgeons, chmn. ann. meeting 1987, sci. program chmn. ann. meeting 1988), Assn. for Rsch. in Nervous and Mental Diseases, New Eng. Neurosurg. Soc. (bd. dirs. 1976-79, pres. 1989-91), Soc. Brit. Neurol. Surgeons, Rsch. Soc. Neurol. Surgeons, Soc. Rsch. into Hydrocephalus and Spina Bifida, Conn. Acad. Arts and Sci., Vereingung Schweizer Neurochirugen, Mory's Assn., Graduate Club, Beaumont Med. Club (pres. 1988), Sloane Club, Naval Club, La Grande Mare Golf Club, Farmington Golf Club. Episcopalian. Office: 85 Seymour St Ste 707 Hartford CT 06106-5526

ROBERTS, MERRILL JOSEPH, economist, educator; b. Glendive, Mont., Aug. 10, 1915; s. Merrill Joseph and Inez (Ludgate) R.; m. Janet Hunter Dion, Aug. 31, 1941; children: David, Michael, James, Patricia. B.A., U. Minn., 1938; M.B.A., U. Chgo., 1939, Ph.D., 1952. Transp. economist OPA, Washington, 1941, USDA, Washington, 1942-46, TVA, 1946-48; asst. prof. transp. and econs., then assoc. prof. U. Fla., Gainesville, 1948-54, prof., 1955-58; assoc. prof. transp. UCLA, 1954-55; vis. prof. econs. Mich. State U., 1956-57; prof. transp. and pub. utilities Grad. Sch. Bus., U. Pitts., 1958-72, head dept. transp. and pub. utilities, 1958-61, prof. econs., 1960-72, chmn. faculty, 1960-63; dir. Bur. Bus. Research, 1963-66; v.p., dir. econs. div. Wilbur Smith and Assocs., 1972-75; prof., chmn. transp., bus. and pub. policy U. Md., 1975-79, prof., 1979-82, prof. emeritus, 1983—; research cons. Nat. Transp. Policy Study Commn., 1977-79; cons. ICC, 1979-84, Dept. Transp., Washington, 1982-84, Md. Dept. Transp., 1987-88; Disting. Research lectr., Iowa State U., 1986; econ. adv. Estudio Integral de Transport de Bolivia, 1979; mem. adv. panel, R.R. merger project Rail Services Planning Office, ICC; dir. study Penn Central R.R. bankruptcy U.S. Senate, 1971-72; Econ. cons. numerous fgn. govts. including, New Zealand, Thailand, Singapore, Hong Kong, Korea, Spain, Nicaragua, Algeria; cons. transp. to bus. and govt. agys.; research staff Commn. Money and Credit, 1959-60; mem. Venezuelan Commn. Economica Ferroviaria Nacional, 1959-60; participant transp. study conf. Nat. Acad. Sci.-NRC, 1960; research staff Nat. Planning Assn. study, 1962-63; participant Am. Assembly Conf. on the Future of Am. Transp., 1971; mem. research com. Transp. Assn. Am., 1965-72; v.p. Am. Transp. Research Forum, 1960-63; mem. legis. com. Allegheny Regional Adv. Bd., 1959-72; mem. com. applications of econs. Transp. Research Bd., Nat. Acad. Scis., 1973-80. Author: (with T.C. Bigham) Citrus Fruit Rates, 1950, Transportation, 1952, Taxation of Railroads and Other State-Assessed Companies in Florida, 1957, Evaluation of Rate Regulation, 1959, Transportation in Region in Transition, 1962, Freight Transport Coordination, 1966, The Penn Central and Other Railroads, 1973; contbr. numerous articles to profl. jours. Bd. dirs. Port Authority Allegheny County, 1962-69; Bd. visitors Amy Transp. Sch., 1959-60. Served to lt. (s.g.) USNR, 1942-46. Recipient Johnson award for outstanding research, Transp. Research Bd., Nat. Acad. Scis., 1986. Mem. Am. Econs. Assn. (sec.-treas. transp. and pub. utilities group 1957-61, chmn. 1963), Am. Soc. Traffic and Transp. (founder mem.), Nat. Def. Transp. Assn. (life), Delta Nu Alpha, Phi Delta Theta, Beta Gamma Sigma. Presbyterian. Club: Cosmos (Washington). Home: #113 3749 Sarasota Square Blvd Sarasota FL 34238

ROBERTS, MICHAEL FOSTER, biology educator; b. Guatemala City, Guatemala, Aug. 8, 1943; s. Ralph Jackson and Arleda (Allen) R.; m. Mary Sherill Noe, Dec. 27, 1966; children: Rosemary, Amelia. BA, U. Calif., Berkeley, 1966; MA, U. Wis. (Madison), 1968, PhD, 1972. Fellow John B. Pierce Found. Lab., Yale U., New Haven, Conn., 1972-76; asst. prof. Yale U., New Haven, 1976-81, Linfield Coll., McMinnville, oreg., 1981-84; assoc. prof. Linfield Coll., McMinnville, 1984-90, prof. biology, 1990—; guest referee editor Am. Physiol. Soc., Bethesda, Md., 1974—; peer rev. com. Am. Heart Assn., Portland, Oreg., 1982-87. Contbr. articles to profl. jours. Named NIH Predoctoral Fellow, 1969-72, Postdoctoral fellow, 1972-76; recipient NIH Rsch. grant, 1982-85, Am. Heart Assn. rsch. grant, 1985-86. Mem. Am. Physiol. Soc., Sigma Xi. Office: Linfield Coll Dept Biology McMinnville OR 97128

ROBERTS, MORTON SPITZ, astronomer; b. N.Y.C., Nov. 5, 1926; m. Josephine Taylor, Aug. 2, 1951; 1 dau., Elizabeth Mason. B.A., Pomona Coll., 1948; Sc.D. (hon.), 1979; M.Sc., Calif. Inst. Tech., 1950; Ph.D. (Lick Obs. fellow), U. Calif., Berkeley, 1958. Asst. prof. physics Occidental Coll., 1949-52; lectr. astronomy dept. U. Calif., Berkeley, 1959-60; lectr., research asso. Harvard Coll. Obs., Harvard U., 1960-64; scientist Nat. Radio Astronomy Obs., Charlottesville, Va., 1964-78; dir. Nat. Radio Astronomy Obs., 1978-84, sr. scientist, 1978—; Sigma Xi nat. lectr., 1970-71; vis. educator SUNY, Stony Brook, 1968, Cambridge U., 1972, 86-87, U. Groningen, 1972. Bd. editors: Astronomy and Astrophysics, 1971-80; asso. editor: Astron. Jour, 1977-79. NSF postdoctoral fellow, 1958-59. Fellow AAAS; mem. NAS, Am. Astron. Soc. (vis. prof. program 1965-73, v.p. 1971-72, mem. coun. 1983-86, publs. bd. 1979-80), Internat. Astron. Union (v.p. 1988-94, treas. 1993—), Internat. Sci. Radio Union. Home: 1826 Wayside Pl Charlottesville VA 22903-1631 Office: Nat Radio Astronomy Obs Edgemont Rd Charlottesville VA 22903

ROBERTS, NANCY, computer educator; b. Boston, Jan. 25, 1938; d. Harold and Annette (Zion) Rosenthal; m. Edward B. Roberts, June 14, 1959; children: Valerie Friedman, Mitchell, Andrea. AB, Boston U., 1959, MEd, 1961, EdD, 1975. Elem. tchr. Sharon (Mass.) Pub. Schs., 1959-63; asst. prof. Lesley Coll., Cambridge, Mass., 1975-79, assoc. prof., 1980-83; prof., 1983—; dir. grad. programs in tech. in edn. Lesley Coll., Cambridge, Mass., 1980—, dir. Project Bridge,, 1987-92; dir. Ctr. for Math., Sci. and Tech. in Edn., Cambridge, Mass., 1990-91; rsch. assoc. MIT, Cambridge, 1976-79;mem. nat. steering com. Nat. Edn. Computing Conf., Eugene, Oreg., 1979—, co-chmn. nat. conf., 1989, vice chmn. steering com., 1991-95. Author: Dynamics of Human Service Delivery, 1976, Practical Guide to Computers in Education, 1982, Computers in Teaching Mathematics, 1983, Introduction to Computer Simulation, 1983 (J.W. Forrester award 1983), Integrating Computers into the Elementary and Middle School, 1987, Computers and the Social Studies, 1988, Integrating Telecommunications into Education, 1990; mem. editorial bd. Jour. Ednl. Computing, 1983—, Jour. Rsch. in Sci. Teaching; editor Computers in Edn. book series, 1984-89. Mem. Computer Policy Com., Boston, 1982-84, mem. adv. bd. Electronic Learning, 1989-91; bd. dirs. Computers for Kids, Cambridge, 1983-85; mem. State Ednl. Tech. Adv. Coun., 1990-93. NSF grantee, 1985-96. Mem. System Dynamics Soc. (bd. dirs. policy com. 1987-89). Republican. Jewish. Home: 300 Boylston St Apt 1102 Boston MA 02116-3923 Office: Lesley Coll 29 Everett St Cambridge MA 02138-2702

ROBERTS, NANCY MIZE, retired librarian, composer, pianist; b. Corsicana, Tex., Apr. 19, 1931; d. Edward Harvey and Llora Inez (Huffman) Mize; m. Sam Butler Roberts, Jan. 27, 1928 (dec.); children: Sam Butler Roberts Jr., John Daniel Roberts (dec.). Attended, Corsicana H.S. Cert. county librarian. Inventory clerk Oil City Iron Works, Corsicana, 1949-51; programmer KAND Radio, Corsicana, 1959-60; librarian Corsicana Public Library, 1966-69; owner dress shop Hang-Up, Corsicana, 1969-70; librarian Corsicana Public Library, 1970-73; women's editor Corsicana Daily Sun, 1973-75; librarian Corsicana Public Library, 1975-96. Composer: (church anthems) Clap Your Hands, Two Commandments, God Moves in A Mysterious Way, I Must Tell Jesus. Mem. bd. dirs. Warehouse Living Arts, Women's Clubhouse Assn., 1996—, Consicana Pub. Libr. Bd., 1997—. Recipient Lifetime Achievement award Northeast Tex. Library Assn., 1996. Mem. Women's Clubhouse Orgn. Democrat. Baptist. Avocations: playing piano, arranging music, writing reviews, directing plays, singing. Home: 1443 W 3d Ave Corsicana TX 75110

ROBERTS, (GRANVILLE) ORAL, clergyman; b. nr. Ada, Okla., Jan. 24, 1918; s. Ellis Melvin and Claudius Priscilla (Irwin) R.; m. Evelyn Lutman, Dec. 25, 1938; children: Rebecca Ann (dec.), Ronald David (dec.), Richard Lee, Roberta Jean. Student, Okla. Bapt. U., 1942-44, Phillips U., 1947; LLD (hon.), Centenary Coll., 1975. Ordained to ministry Pentecostal Holiness Ch., 1936, United Meth. Ch., 1968. Evangelist, 1936-41; pastor Fuquay Springs, N.C., 1941, Shawnee, Okla., 1942-45, Toccoa, Ga., 1946, Enid, Okla., 1947; began worldwide evangelistic ministry thru crusades, radio, TV, printed page, 1947; founder Oral Roberts Evangelistic Assn., Inc., Tulsa, 1948, Univ. Village Retirement Center, 1970, City of Faith Med./Research Ctr., 1981, Healing Outreach Ctr., 1986; founder, pub. Abundant Life mag., Daily Blessing (quar. mag.); founder, chancellor Oral Roberts U., Tulsa, 1963—; founding chmn. Internat. Charismatic Bible Ministries. Author: over 50 books including: If You Need Healing, Do These Things, 1947, God is a Good God, 1960, If I Were You, 1967, Miracle of Seed-Faith, 1970, autobiography The Call, 1971, The Miracle Book, 1972, A Daily Guide to Miracles, 1975, Better Health and Miracle Living, 1976, How to Get Through Your Struggles, 1977, Receiving Your Miracle, 1978, Don't Give Up, 1980, Your Road to Recovery, 1986, Attack Your Lack, 1985, How I Learned Jesus Was Not Poor, 1989, How to Resist the Devil, 1989, Fear Not!, 1989, A Prayer Cover Over Your Life, 1990, Is God Your Source?, 1992, 11 Major Prophecies For You in 1992, 1992, Unleashing the Power of Praying in the Spirit, 1993; also numerous tracts and brochures, Bible commentaries. Recipient Indian of Yr. award Am. Broadcasters Assn., 1963; Okla. Hall of Fame, 1973; Oklahoman of Yr., 1974. Club: Rotary. Office: Oral Roberts U 7777 S Lewis Ave Tulsa OK 74171-0003

ROBERTS, PATRICK KENT, lawyer; b. Waynesville, Mo., Feb. 9, 1948; s. J. Kent and Winona (Clark) R.; m. Jeanne Billings, April 17, 1976; children: Christopher, Kimberly, Courtney. Student, U. Ill., Urbana, 1970; AB, U. Mo., 1970, JD, 1973. Bar: Mo. 1974, U.S. Dist. Ct. (we. dist.) Mo. 1974, U.S. Ct. Appeals (8th cir.) 1979. Lawyer U.S. Senator Stuart Symington, Columbia, Mo., 1973-76; ptnr. Daniel, Clampett, Powell & Cunningham, Springfield, Mo., 1976—. Mem. cen. com. Greene County Dems., Springfield, 1982-84, 88-90. Mem. Def. Res. Inst., Mo. Orgn. Def. Lawyers, Mo. Bar Assn., Greene County Bar Assn. Democrat. Methodist. Lodge: Rotary. Office: Daniel Clampett Powell & Cunningham PO Box 10306 3171 E Sunshine Springfield MO 65808

ROBERTS, PAUL CRAIG, III, economics educator, author, columnist; b. Atlanta, Apr. 3, 1939; s. Paul Craig and Ellen Lamar (Dryman) R.; m. Linda Jane Fisher, July 3, 1969; children: Pendaran Struan Sherman, Becky Ellen, Stephanie Bradford. BS, Ga. Inst. Tech., 1961; postgrad., U. Calif., Berkeley, 1962-63, Merton Coll., Oxford (Eng.) U., 1964-65; PhD (Earhart fellow), U. Va., 1967. Asst. prof. econs. Va. Poly. Inst., 1965-69; assoc. prof. U. N.Mex., 1969-71; rsch. fellow Hoover Instn., Stanford U., 1971-77, sr. rsch. fellow, 1978—; mem. U.S. Congl. Staff, 1975-78; asst. sec. of treasury for econ. policy Dept. Treasury, Washington, 1981-82; William E. Simon prof. polit. economy Georgetown U. Ctr. for Strategic and Internat. Studies, Washington, 1982-93; chmn. Inst. for Polit. Economy, 1985—, John M. Olin fellow, 1994—; disting. adj. scholar Ctr. Strategic and Internat. Studies Georgetown U., Washington, 1993-96; adj. scholar Cato Inst., 1987-93, disting. fellow, 1993-96; assoc. editor, columnist Wall St. Jour., N.Y.C., 1978-80; columnist Bus. Week, 1983—, Fin. Post, Can., 1988-89, Liberation, Paris, 1988-89, Erfolg, Fed. Rep. of Germany, 1988, Washington Times, 1988—, San Diego Union, 1988-92, Le Figaro, Paris, 1992-96; nationally syndicated columnist Scripps Howard News Svc., 1989-97, Creators Syndicate, 1997—; contbr. editor: Nat. Rev., 1993—, Reason Mag., 1993-95—, Creators Syndicate, 1997—; mem. Pres.-elect Reagan's Task Force on Tax Policy, 1980; dir. Value Line Investment Funds, N.Y.C., A. Schulman, Akron, Ohio; cons. Morgan Guaranty Trust Co., Lazard Freres Asset Mgmt., 1983-87; pres. Econ. & Communication Svcs. Inc.; cons. Dept. Commerce, 1983, Dept. Def., 1983-84; mem. adv. bd. Marvin and Palmer, 1986-96; mem. Wright Investors' Svc. Internat. Bd. Econ. and Invesmtent Advisors; bd. dirs. Com. on Present Danger; trustee Intercollegiate Studies Inst., Com. on Developing Am. Capitalism; mem. selection com. Frank E. Seidman disting. award in Polit. Economy. Author: Alienation and the Soviet Economy, 1971, new edit., 1990, Marx's Theory of Exchange, 1973, new edit., 1983, The Supply-Side Revolution: An Insider's Account of Policymaking in Washington, 1984, The Cost of Corporate Capital in the U.S. and Japan, 1985, Meltdown: Inside the Soviet Economy, 1990, The New Color Line: How Quotas and Privilege Destroy Democracy, 1995; The Capitalist Revolution in Latin America, Oxford U. Press, 1997—; mem. editl. bd. Modern Age, Intercollegiate Rev.; contbg. editor Harper's Mag. Drafted original Kemp-Roth Bill, 1976. Recipient Meritorious Svc. award Dept. Treasury, 1982, Pub. Svc. award GSA, 1991, Warren Brookes award for Excellence in Journalism, 1992; Am. Philos. Soc. grantee, 1968; named to Chevalier de la Légion d'Honneur, 1987; Nat. Chamber Found. fellow, 1984-85. Mem. Mont Pelerin Soc., Beethoven Soc., Am. Soc. French Legion of Honor, U.S. C. of C. (taxation com.).

ROBERTS, PAUL DALE, health services administrator; b. Fresno, Calif., Jan. 17, 1955; s. Paul Marceau and Rosemarie Roberts; m. Patricia Mary Mitchell, Mar. 24, 1964; 1 child, Jason Randall Porter. AA, Sacramento City Coll., 1977; diploma in pvt. investigations, Ctrl. Investigation & Security, 1984. Office asst. I Dept. Benefit Payments, Sacramento, Calif., 1976-77; firefighter Calif. Divsn. Forestry, Colfax, 1977; key data operator Dept. Justice, Sacramento, 1977-78; intelligence analyst, spl. forces instr. U.S. Army Mil. Intelligence, Seoul, Korea, 1979-84; law libr. Employment Devel. Dept., Sacramento, 1989-92; office asst. II Dept. Health Svcs., Sacramento, 1992—; disaster courier dept. social svcs. Gov.'s Office of Emergency Svcs., L.A., 1994; chief cert. support Dept. Health Svcs., Sacramento, 1992—. Author: Organization of D.E.A.T.H. (Destroy Evildoers and Teach Harmony), 1984, The Cosmic Bleeder, 1991, Madam Zara, Vampiress, 1993, People's Comic Book Newsletter, 1996, The Legendary Dark Silhouette, 1997, Vacationing in Dublin, Ireland and Newry, Northern Ireland, 1997; (jour.) Memoirs of Paul Roberts, 1991; prodr.: (book) Villalobos Family, 1993. Sgt. U.S. Army Mil. Police, 1973-76. Democrat. Roman Catholic. Avocations: private pilot, tennis, photography, hot air balloon/glider riding, sky diving. Home: 60 Parkshore Cir Sacramento CA 95831-3061 Office: Dept Health Svcs Radiologic Health Br 601 N 7th St Sacramento CA 95814-0208

ROBERTS, PETER CHRISTOPHER TUDOR, engineering executive; b. Georgetown, Demerara, Brit. Guiana, Oct. 12, 1945; came to U.S., 1979; s. Albert Edward and Dorothy Jean (Innis) R.; m. Julia Elizabeth Warner, Nov. 10, 1984; children: Kirsta Anne, Serena Amanda, Angelee Julia, Zephanie Elizabeth, Fiona Ann, Emrys Tudor, Peter Christopher Tudor Roberts II. BSc with honors, Southampton (Eng.) U., 1969, PhD in Microelectronics, 1975. Rsch. fellow dept. electronics Southampton U., 1974-77; prof. microcircuit dept. electronics INAOE, Tonantzintla, Mexico, 1977-79; staff scientist Honeywell Systems & Rsch. Ctr., Mpls., 1979-84; dir. advanced tech. Q-Dot Inc. R&D, Colorado Springs, Colo., 1984-86; program mgr. Honeywell Opto-Electronics, Richardson, Tex., 1986; vis. prof. U. N.Mex. CHTM, Albuquerque, 1987; supr. engring. Loral Inc. (formerly Honeywell), Lexington, Mass., 1988-90; mgr. engring. Litton Systems Inc., Tempe, Ariz., 1990-96; staff engr. Motorola Space and Systems Tech. Group, Scottsdale, Ariz., 1996—; dir. Pi-Rho Technics Internat., Inc., Gilbert, Ariz., 1996—; cons. engr. Q-Dot, Inc. R&D, Colorado Springs, 1982—, pvt. stockholder, 1984—. Author: (with P.C.T. Roberts) Charge-Coupled Devices and Their Applications, 1980; contbr. articles to Boletin del INAGE, IEEE Transactions on Electron Devices, Procs. of the IEE (UK), Procs. of the INTERNEPCON, Internat. Jour. Electronics,IEEE Electron Device Letters, Electronics Letters, Solid State and Electron Devices, IEEE Jour. Solid State Circuits, others. Republican. Achievements include patent for VHSIC bipolar ROM and RAM ciruits; patents pending for GaAs 2 GHz by 16-Bit Digital Active Backplane; random access image readout, others. Home: 1418 N Cliffside Dr Gilbert AZ 85234-2659 Office: Motorola Space and Systems Tech Grp 8201 E Mcdowell Rd Scottsdale AZ 85257-3812

ROBERTS, PHILIP JOHN, history educator, editor; b. Lusk, Wyo., July 8, 1948; s. Leslie J. and LaVerne Elizabeth (Johns) R. BA, U. Wyo., 1973, JD, 1977; PhD, U. Wash., 1990. Bar: Wyo. 1977. Editor Lake Powell Chronicle, Page, Ariz., 1972-73; co-founder, co-pub. Medicine Bow (Wyo.) Post, 1977; pvt. practice in law Carbon and Laramie County, Wyo., 1977-84; historian Wyo. State Hist. Dept., Cheyenne, 1979-84; editor Annals of Wyo., Cheyenne, 1980-84, 95—; owner, pub. Capitol Times, Cheyenne, 1982-84; co-editor Wyo. History Jour., 1995-96; editor, 1996—; owner, pub. Skyline West Press, Seattle, 1985-90; asst. prof. history U. Wyo., Laramie, 1990—; indexer Osborne-McGraw-Hill, Berkeley, 1988—; guest lectr. media law, Dubai, United Arab Emirates, 1996; mem. editl. bd. Annals of Wyo., 1990-95. Author: Wyoming Almanac, 1989 (pub. annually), Buffalo Bones: Stories from Wyoming's Past, 1979, 82, 84, Readings in Wyoming History, 1994-96; contbr. articles to profl. jours. Mem. Wyo. State Hist. Soc. (life), Wyo. State Bar, Pacific N.W. Historians' Guild, 9th Judicial Cir. Hist. Soc., Western History Assn., Am. Hist. Assn., Orgn. of Am. Historians. Avocations: hiking, fishing, golf, photography. Office: U Wyo Univ Sta PO Box 4286 Laramie WY 82071

ROBERTS, PRISCILLA WARREN, artist; b. Montclair, N.J., June 13, 1916; d. Charles Asaph and Florence (Berry) R. Student, Art Students League, 1937-39, Nat. Acad., 1939-43. Represented in permanent collections Met. Mus., Cin. Art Mus., Canton Art Inst., Westmoreland County Mus. Art, Pa., IBM, Dallaas Mus., Walker Art Ctr., Mpls., Butler Inst., Youngstown, Ohio, Nat. Mus. Am. Art, Washington. Recipient Proctor prize, 1947, popular prize Corcoran Biennial, 1947, prize Westmoreland County Mus., 3d prize Carnegie Internat., Pitts., 1950, Nat. Mus. Women in Arts, Washington, Snite Mus., U. Notre Dame, Ind. Mem. NAD (Hallgarten prize 1945), Allied Artists Am. (Zabriskie prize 1944, 46), Catherine Lorillard Wolfe Assn. (hon.). Address: PO Box 716 Georgetown CT 06829-0716

ROBERTS, RALPH JOEL, telecommunications, cable broadcast executive; b. N.Y.C., Mar. 13, 1920; s. Robert and Sara (Wahl) Roberts; m. Suzanne Fleisher, Aug. 23, 1942; children: Catherine, Lisa, Ralph Jr., Brian, Douglas. BS in Econs., U. Pa., 1941. Account exec. Aitken Kynett Advt., Phila., 1946-48; v.p. Muzak Corp., N.Y.C., 1948-50; pres., chief exec. officer Pioneer Industries, Inc., Darby, Pa., 1950-61; pres. Internat. Equity Corp., Bala Cynwyd, Pa., 1961-83; chmn. bd., Comcast Corp., Phila., 1969—; chmn., chief exec. officer Sural Corp. (merger with Internat. Equity Corp. 1983); trustee, chmn. conflict interest com. Albert Einstein Med. Ctr. Bd. dirs. regional NCCJ; trustee Brandywine Mus. and Conservancy, charter mem. World Bus. Coun.; past mem. mentor program and Benjamin Franklin assocs. U. Pa.; bd. dirs. Phila. Orch., 1993; past v.p. Family Svc. Phila.; past bd. dirs., mem. budget and fees com. State Coll. and Univ. Dirs.; mem. regulation and legis. affairs coms. Nat. Cable TV Assn.; past mem. Gov.'s Rev. of Govt. Mgmt., Inc. Lt. USNR, 1942-45. Reipient americanism award Anti-Defamation League of B'nai B'rith, Brotherhood award NCCJ, 1989, award for outstanding svc. to cable TV industry Walter Kaitz Found., 1990, Acres of Diamonds Entrepreneurioal Excellence award Entrepreneurial Inst. Temple U., 1991, Disting. Vanguard award for leadership Nat. Cable TV Assn., 1993; named to Broadcasting and Cable Hall of Fame, 1993. Avocations: tennis, travel. Home: Sural Farm 505 Fairview Rd East Fallowfield Township PA 19320-4431 Office: Comcast Corp 1500 Market St Philadelphia PA 19102*

ROBERTS, RANDOLPH WILSON, health and science educator; b. Scranton, Pa., Oct. 8, 1946; s. S. Tracy and Alecia Francis (Sullivan) R.; m. Martha Jeanne Burnite, July 12, 1969 (div. Dec. 1985); children: Gwendolyn Suzanne, Ryan Weylin; m. Ava Elaine Brown, June 17, 1989. AB in Biology, Franklin & Marshall Coll., 1968, MA in Geoscis., 1974; MS in Sci. Teaching, Am. U., 1977; MS in Counseling, Western Md. Coll., 1990; CHES, Towson State U., 1993; postgrad., U. Md., Johns Hopkins U., Loyola Coll., Md. Cert. tchr., counselor, health educator, health edn. specialist (CHES), tax cons. Tchr. sci. Woodlawn Jr. High Sch., Balt., 1968-73, Deer Park Jr. High/Mid. Sch., Randallstown, Md., 1973-87, Franklin Mid. Sch., Reisterstown, Md., 1987-89; counselor and chmn. health/sci. dept. Balt. County Home & Hosp. Ctr., 1989—; math and sci. tchr. Loyola H.S., Towson, Md., 1981-86, Talmudical Acad., Pikesville, Md., 1983-86; health educator Loyola Coll., Md., 1994; ednl. cons. Scott Fetzer co., Chgo., 1981-86; founder, pres. Tax Assistance, Ltd., Owings Mills, Md., 1981—; curriculum cons. Balt. County Bd. Edn., Towson, 1977, 78, 93, 95, 96; founder Building Children, 1982—. Author: Earth Sciences Workbook, 1979. Mem. Glyndon (Md.) Meth. Ch., 1993—, handbell choir mem., Christian edn. com., liturgist, Sunday sch. coord., adminstrv. coun. mem.-at-large; treas. Boy Scouts Am. Pack 315, Reis, Md., 1986-90, Webelos Den leader, 1987-90, advancement chmn., com. mem. Troop 315, 1990-93; fin. ptnr./treas. Bare Hills Investment Group. Mem. NEA, ACA, Am. Assn. Health Edn., Balt. Rd. Runners, Nature Conservancy, Chesapeake Bay Found., Phi Delta Kappa, Mu Upsilon Sigma, Eta Sigma Gamma. Avocations: traveling, gardening, running, bowling, investing. Home: 9 Indian Pony Ct Owings Mills MD 21117-1210 Office: Home and Hosp Ctr 6229 Falls Rd Baltimore MD 21209-2120

ROBERTS, RICHARD, mechanical engineering educator; b. Atlantic City, N.J., Feb. 16, 1938; s. Harold and Marion (Hofman) R.; m. Rochelle S. Perelman, Oct. 2, 1960; children: Lori, Lisa, Scott. BSME, Drexel U., 1961; MSME, Lehigh U., 1962, PhD in Mech. Engring., 1964. Asst. prof. mech. engring. Lehigh U., Bethlehem, Pa., 1964-68, assoc. prof., 1968-75, prof., 1975—. Editor: Proceedings of the Thirteenth Nat. Symposium on Fracture Mechanics, 1980, ASME PVP Division's Design Handbook, Materials and

Fabrication, Vol. III. Recipient W. Sparagen award Am. Welding Soc., 1972, Adams Meml. award, 1981. Home: 317 Bierys Bridge Rd Bethlehem PA 18017-1142 Office: Lehigh Univ MSE/200 W Packer Bethlehem PA 18015

ROBERTS, RICHARD JOHN, molecular biologist, consultant, research director; b. Derby, Eng., Sept. 6, 1943; came to U.S., 1969; s. John Walter and Edna Wilhelmina (Allsop) R.; m. Elizabeth Dyson, Aug. 21, 1965 (dec.); children: Alison, Andrew; m. Jean E. Tagliabue, Feb. 14, 1986; children: Christopher, Amanda. BS, Sheffield (Eng.) U., 1965, PhD, 1968. Rsch. fellow Harvard U., Cambridge, Mass., 1969-70, rsch. assoc., 1971-72; sr. staff investigator Cold Spring Harbor Lab., N.Y., 1972-87, asst. dir., 1987-92; rsch. dir. New England Biolabs, 1992—, cons. New Eng. Biolabs, Beverly, Mass., 1974-92; sci. adv. bd. Genex, Rockville, Md., 1977-85, Molecular Tool, Balt., 1994—. Contbr. articles to profl. jours. Recipient Nobel prize in Physiology and Medicine, Nobel Foundation, 1993. John Simon Guggenheim Found. fellow, 1979. Fellow Royal Soc.; mem. Am. Soc. Microbiology, Am. Soc. Biol. Chemists. Office: New Eng Biolabs 32 Tozer Rd Beverly MA 01915-5510*

ROBERTS, ROBERT CHADWICK, ecologist, environmental scientist, consultant; b. Yakima, Wash., Jan. 6, 1947. BA in Zoology, Humboldt State Coll., 1969; PhD in Ecology, U. Calif., Davis, 1976. Instr. U. Calif., Davis, 1971-73, 76-77; asst. prof. Western Mich. U., Kalamazoo, 1978-79; ind. cons. Eureka, Calif., 1979-80; instr. Humboldt State U., Arcata, Calif., 1982-83, 97—; dir. environ. svcs. Oscar Larson & Assocs., Eureka, 1980—; cons. Nat. Audubon Soc., Sacramento, 1984—, Calif. Native Plant Soc., Sacramento, 1987-89, U.S. forest Svc., Eureka and Sacramento, 1988—; mem. Outer Continental Shelf Adv. Com., County of Humboldt, 1987-91, Creeks/Wetlands Adv. Com., City of Arcata, 1989-93; chair Calif. steering com. Pacific Coast Venture, N.Am. Waterfowl Plan; expert witness in 7 legal actions, 4 legis. hearings. Contbr. articles to profl. jours., chpts. to books; author, editor numerous tech. reports and environ. documents. Cons. Ballot Proposition 130 Steering Com., Sacramento, 1990. Grantee F.M. Chapman Fund., 1974; sci. trainee NSF, 1970-75. Mem. Ecol. Soc. Am. (cert. sr. ecologist), Soc. Wetland Scientists (profl. wetland scientist), Cooper Ornithol. Soc., Wildlife Soc., Soc. Conservation Biology, Assn. of State Wetlands Mgrs., Phi Kappa Phi. Office: Oscar Larson & Assocs 317 3rd St Eureka CA 95501-0427

ROBERTS, ROBERT WINSTON, social work educator, dean; b. Balt., July 23, 1932; s. Kelmer Swan Roberts and Lettie Mae (Collins) Johnston; m. Helen Elizabeth Perpich, Mar. 4, 1964. BA with high honors, San Francisco State U., 1957; MSW, U. Calif., Berkeley, 1959; D in Social Welfare, Columbia U., 1970. Caseworker Edgewood Protestant Orphanage, San Francisco, 1959-62, Jewish Family Service, San Francisco, 1962-63; research assoc. U. Calif., Berkeley, 1963-65; research analyst Family Service Assn. Am., N.Y.C., 1965-69; asst. prof. U. Chgo., 1967-70; prof. U. So. Calif., Los Angeles, 1970-90, dean sch. social work, 1980-88, dean emeritus, prof. emeritus, 1990—; vis. prof. Western Australia Inst. Tech., Perth, 1976-77, Chinese U. Hong Kong and U. Hong Kong, 1980; cons. Crittenton Services, Los Angeles, 1970-72, James Weldon Johnson Community Ctr., N.Y., 1966-67; bd. dirs. El Centro, Los Angeles. Editor: The Unwed Mother, 1966; co-editor: Theories of Social Casework, 1970, Child Caring: Social Policy and the Institution, 1973, Theories of Social Work with Groups, 1976, Theory and Practice of Community Social Work, 1980; editorial bd. Social Work Jour.; contbr. articles to profl. jours. Staff sgt. USAF, 1950-54; sgt. 1st class USAR, 1956-59. Fellow NIMH, 1957-58, 65-67, Crown Zellerbach Found., 1958-59; recipient Outstanding Educator award Los Amigos de la Humanidad, 1979; named Disting. Assoc., Nat. Acad. Practice in Social Work, 1985. Mem. Nat. Assn. Social Workers (chmn. social action com. 1960-61), Council on Social Work Edn. (bd. dirs. 1970-73, del. to assembly 1971-72, commn. minority groups 1972-73), Sons of Confederate Vets. Avocations: cooking, reading, travel, photography. Office: Univ So Calif Sch Social Work Rm 214 Montgomery Ross Fisher Bldg Los Angeles CA 90089-0411

ROBERTS, ROBIN, sportcaster; b. Nov. 23, 1960. BA in Comms. cum laude, Southeastern La. U., 1983. Sports dir. WHMD/WFPR Radio, Hammond, La., 1980-83; spl. assignment sports reporter KSLU-FM, 1982; sports anchor, reporter WDAM-TV, Hattiesburg, Miss., 1983-84, WLOX-TV, Biloxi, Miss., 1984-86, WSMV-TV, Nashville, 1986-88, WAGA-TV, Atlanta, 1988-89; with WVEE-FM, Atlanta; host. Sunday SportsDay, contbr. NFL Prime Time, reporter, interviewer ESPN, Bristol, Conn., 1990-95, host, anchor SportsCenter, host In the SportsLight, 1995—; host Wide World of Sports ABC, 1995—. Apptd. adv. bd. Women's Sports Found., 1991; spkr. charity, civic functions. Recipient DAR T.V. Award of Merit, 1990, Women at Work Broadcast Journalism award, 1992, Excellence in Sports Journalism award Broadcast Media Northeastern U. Ctr. Study of Sport in Society and Sch. Journalism, 1993; inducted to Hall of Fame Women's Inst. Sport and Edn. Found., 1994. Office: ESPN Inc Comms Dept ESPN Plz Bristol CT 06010*

ROBERTS, ROSE HARRISON, social services administrator, consultant; b. Ripley, Miss., Mar. 30; d. Charles Edgar and Rosa Nell (Smith) Dickerson; m. Bobby R. Harrison, June 9 (div. 1972); children: Pat, Ava Jordan, Kim; m. James L. Roberts, Jr., Sept. 30, 1984. BS, Blue Mountain (Miss.) Coll., 1957; MSW, Tulane U., 1970. Lic. clin. social worker, Miss.; qualified clin. social worker, Nat. Assn. Social Workers, diplomate clin. social worker. Social worker Miss. Dept. Pub. Welfare, Ripley, 1963-68; dist. supr. Miss. Dept. Pub. Welfare, Pontotoc, 1970-85; EEO coord. Miss. Dept. Pub. Welfare, Jackson, 1985-86, bur. dir., 1986-88; dir. New Beginnings, Inc., Tupelo, Miss., 1988—; adj. assoc. prof. U. Miss., Oxford, 1974-83; field instr. Miss. So. U., Hattiesburg, 1985-88; cons. nursing homes, Ripley, 1975—; Pontotoc County bd. dirs. Region III Mental Health Com., Tupelo, 1990—. Mem. Blue Print for Hope. Mem. Acad. Cert. Social Workers. Home: PO Box 485 Pontotoc MS 38863-0485

ROBERTS, ROSEMARY, journalist, columnist; b. Albertville, Ala., Apr. 1, 1938; d. James Bailey Jr. and Mildred (Smith) R.; m. Jonathan Yardley, June 14, 1961 (div. 1975); children: James B., William W. II; m. Donald Arthur Boulton, Apr. 30, 1988. BA, U. N.C., 1960; MA, U. N.C., Greensboro, 1978. Staff writer The Charlotte (N.C.) Observer, 1960-61; editorial asst. The N.Y. Times, N.Y.C., 1962-64; staff writer The Greensboro (N.C.) News and Record, 1974-78, editorial writer, 1978-88, editorial columnist, 1988—; mem. faculty English dept. U. N.C., Greensboro, 1990—. Contbr. articles, book revs. to various publs. Bd. dirs. Weatherspoon Art Mus. U. N.C., Greensboro, 1986—, U. N.C. Journalism Found., 1985-93, Weatherspoon Art Found., 1989—, Friends U. Libr., Greensboro, 1994—, Ea. Music Festival, Greensboro, 1984-88; bd. dirs. English Speaking Union, Greensboro, 1995—. Recipient Awards N.C. Press Assn., 1976, 87, 95, 96; John S. Knight fellow Stanford U., 1980-81; Bosch Found. travel fellow, 1990, Atlantik Bruke Found. travel fellow, 1988. Democrat. Presbyterian. Home: 223 Elmwood Dr Greensboro NC 27408-5829 Office: The Greensboro News and Record 200 E Market St Greensboro NC 27401-2910

ROBERTS, RUBY ALTIZER, poet, author; b. Floyd Co., Vt., Apr. 22, 1907; d. Waddy William and Dana Adeline (Cummings) Altizer; m. Laurence Luther Roberts, July 23, 1927; 1 child, Heidi. Grad., Christianburg (Va.) High Sch.; nursing course, Norfolk (Va.) Protestant Hosp.; DHL, Coll. William and Mary, 1961. Freelance writer, 1939—, newspaper corr.; rep. of Spirit of Va., 1993. Author: (with Rosa Altizer Bray) Emera Altizer and His Descendants, 1937, 2 vols. poetry, Forever is Too Long, Command the Stars, (biography) The Way It Was, 1979, The Way It Is, 1992, Look Down at the Stars, 1994; editor juvenile verse dept. Embers Mag., Batavia, N.Y., 1944—; owner, editor, pub. The Lyric Mag.; poetry columnist Va. newspaper; contbr. over 120 poems to anthologies, newspapes, mags., numerous articles to profl. jours. Recipient First Poetry prize Sanctuary Mag., Ballaman award Disting. Svc. to Poetry, 1956, citation Disting. Svc. Poetry Khalsa Coll.; named poet laureate Va. Gen. Assembly, 1950, poet laureate Va. emeritus Gen. Assembly Va., 1992. 1st Woman to be named Poet Laureate of state. Home: 301 Roanoke St Christiansburg VA 24073-3150

ROBERTS, SAMUEL ALDEN, secondary school educator; b. Kansas City, Kans., Oct. 30, 1930; s. Elester and Sadie Lillian (Lewis) R.; m. Sallie Senora, Aug. 26, 1962; children: Sadie, Alden, Samuel Jr., William, Tyrone;. AB, Knoxville Coll., 1954; MDiv, Interdenominational Theol. Ctr, 1960; MS, Ind. State U., 1974; DMin, Chgo. Theol. Sem., 1981; EdS, Ind. State U., 1986. Cert. secondary English tchr., secondary prin. Supt. Lott Carey Bapt. Mission Sch., Haiti, 1964-68, Hardy Jr. High Sch., Chattanooga; tchr. Wirt High Sch., Gary, Ind.; asst. prin. Elston Jr. High Sch., Michigan City, Ind., athletic dir., 1976-80; tchr. Rogers High Sch., Michigan City. Mem. ASCD, Internat. Reading Assn., Nat. Coun. Tchrs. English, Michigan City Area Coun. (past pres.), Fedn. Block Units of Urban League N.W. Ind. (pres.), Ind. State Reading Assn. (secondary curriculum com.), Fedn. Block Clubs, Phi Delta Kappa (v.p., U. Chgo./DePaul U. chpt.). Home: 2721 W 65th Pl Merrillville IN 46410

ROBERTS, SAMUEL SMITH, television news executive; b. Port Chester, N.Y., Feb. 8, 1936; s. Robert M. and Lillian (Smith) R.; m. Harriet Rubin, July 27, 1975; children: Rachel, David; children by previous marriage: Nancy, Pamela. BS, Northwestern U., 1957. With UPI, N.Y.C., 1961, Capital Cities Broadcasting, Providence, 1962, CBS News, 1962-95; sr. prodr. CBS Evening News, N.Y.C., 1978-81, nat. editor, 1982-84, fgn. editor, 1984-87; exec. prodr. CBS News Prodns., 1992-95, 20th Century, 1994-95; pres. Roberts Media Internat., N.Y.C., 1995-96; v.p., gen. mgr. TV programming Electronic Media Co., N.Y. Times, 1996—. Served to lt. USN, 1957-61. Office: 1120 Avenue Of The Americas New York NY 10036-6700

ROBERTS, SANDRA, editor; b. Humboldt, Tenn., July 22, 1951; d. Harold and Margaret (Headrick) R.; m. Parker W. Duncan Jr., Aug. 11, 1990. Student, Tex. Christian U., 1969-70; BS, U. Tenn., 1972; MLS, Peabody Coll. Libr. The Tennessean, Nashville, 1975-82, editorial writer, 1982-87, editorial editor, 1987—. Pres. Women's Polit. Caucus, Nashville, 1982. Recipient John Hancock award John Hancock Co., 1983, Freedom award Tenn. Trial Laywers Assn., 1988. Mem. Am. Soc. Newspaper Editors, Nat. Conf. Editorial Writers, Sigma Delta Chi (Nat. Headliner award 1982). Mem. Christian Ch. Office: The Tennessean 1100 Broadway Nashville TN 37203-3116

ROBERTS, SEYMOUR M. (SKIP ROBERTS), advertising agency executive; b. Detroit, Aug. 11, 1934; s. Jacob and Florence Rabinowitz; m. Carol Knight, Dec. 16, 1956; children: Bradley Alan, Tracey Knight, Kristen Sophia. B.S. in Advt., Mich. State U., 1955; M.A. in Journalism, Wayne State U., Detroit, 1956. With W.B. Doner & Co., Southfield, Mich., 1956-91; exec. v.p. W.B. Doner & Co., Southfield, 1973-84, exec. v.p., gen. mgr., 1984-91; dir. strategic planning N.W. Ayer, Detroit, 1992—, sr. v.p., sr. ptnr., 1995—. Chmn. Vis. Nurse Assn. of Southeastern Mich. With AUS, 1957-59. Mem. NATAS, Am. Assn. Advt. Agys. (past chmn. Mich. coun.), Adcraft Club Detroit (pres. 1995-96), Franklin Hills Country Club. Office: NW Ayer 2000 W Fisher Bldg Detroit MI 48216-1287

ROBERTS, SIDNEY, biological chemist; b. Boston, Mar. 11, 1918; s. Samuel Richard and Elizabeth (Gilbert) R.; m. Clara Marian Szego, Sept. 14, 1943. B.S., Mass. Inst. Tech., 1939; postgrad., Harvard U., 1939-41; M.S., U. Minn., 1942, Ph.D., 1943. Instr. physiology U. Minn. Med. Sch., 1943-44, George Washington U. Med. Sch., 1944-45; rsch. assoc. Worcester Found. Exptl. Biology, Shrewsbury, Mass., 1945-47; asst. prof. physiol. chemistry Yale U. Med. Sch., 1947-48; mem. faculty U. Calif. Med. Sch., Los Angeles, 1948—; prof. biol. chemistry U. Calif. Med. Sch., 1957—; chmn. acad. senate UCLA, 1989-90; mem. adv. panel regulatory biology NSF, 1955-57, adv. panel metabolic biology, 1957-59; mem. metabolism study sect. NIH, 1960-63; basic sci. study sect. Los Angeles County Heart Assn., 1958-63; cons. VA Hosp., Long Beach, Calif., 1951-55, Los Angeles, 1958-62; air conservation tech. adv. com. Los Angeles County Lung Assn., 1972-76. Author articles, revs.; editor med. jours. Served to 2d lt. AUS, 1944-48. Guggenheim fellow, 1957-58. Fellow AAAS; mem. Am. Physiol. Soc., Endocrine Soc. (v.p. 1968-69, Ciba award 1953), Brit. Biochem. Soc., Soc. Neurosci., Am. Chem. Soc. (exec. com. div. biol. chemistry 1956-59), Am. Soc. Biol. Chemists, Am. Soc. Neurochemistry, Internat. Soc. Neurochemistry, Sigma Xi (pres. UCLA chpt. 1959-60). Home: 1371 Marinette Rd Pacific Palisades CA 90272-2627 Office: UCLA Sch Med Dept Biol Chemistry Los Angeles CA 90095-1737

ROBERTS, SIDNEY I., lawyer; b. Bklyn., Nov. 29, 1913; s. David I. and Ray (Bleicher) Robinovitz; m. Arlene Lee Aron, June 4, 1961; 1 son, Russell Lewis. B.B.A., CCNY, 1935; LL.B. magna cum laude, Harvard U., 1938. Bar: N.Y. 1938; C.P.A., N.Y. With Michael Schimmel & Co. (C.P.A.s), N.Y.C., 1938-39, S.D. Leidesdorf & Co. (C.P.A.s), N.Y.C., 1939-49; with firm Roosevelt, Freidin & Littauer, N.Y.C., 1950-56, Anderson & Roberts, N.Y.C., 1956-57, Roberts & Holland, N.Y.C., 1957-94; adj. prof. law Columbia U., 1971-78; mem. adv. council Internat. Bur. Fiscal Documentation. Author: (with William C. Warren) United States Tax Income Taxation of Foreign Corporations and Nonresident Aliens, 1966, (with others) Annotated Tax Forms: Practice and Procedure, 1970; editor: Legislative History of United States Tax Conventions, 16 vols., 1986—; contbr. articles to profl. jours. Mem. Internat. Bar Assn., ABA (sect. on taxation, council dir. 1970-73, chmn. com. on cooperation with state and local bar assns. 1968-70, chmn. com. on taxation of fgn. income 1963-64), N.Y. State Bar Assn. (tax sect. exec. com. 1967-87, chmn. com. on tax sect. planning 1968-70, chmn. com. on tax policy 1970-72), Assn. of Bar of City of N.Y., N.Y. State Soc. CPA's, Internat. Fiscal Assn. (mem. exec. com. 1972-77, pres. U.S.A. br. 1972-73). Jewish. Office: 145 Central Park W New York NY 10023-2004

ROBERTS, THEODORE HARRIS, banker; b. Gillett, Ark., May 14, 1929; s. D. Edward and Gertrude (Harris) R.; m. Elisabeth Law, July 17, 1953; children: Susan, William (dec.), Julia, John. BA in Govt., Northwestern State U., 1949; MA in Polit. Sci., Okla. State U., 1950; attended, U. Chgo. Grad. Sch. Bus., 1956. With Harris Trust and Savs. Bank, Chgo., 1953-82; exec. v.p., sec., treas. Harris Bank and Harris Bankcorp Inc., 1971-82, dir., exec. com., 1975-82; pres. Fed. Res. Bank St. Louis, 1983-85; chmn. bd., chief exec. officer Talman Home Fed. Savs. & Loan, Chgo., 1985-92; pres. LaSalle Nat. Corp., 1992-95 retired. Mem. Chgo. Club, Comml. Club Chgo., Econ. Club Chgo., Exmoor Country Club (Highland Park, Ill.). Office: 135 S La Salle St Ste 1162 Chicago IL 60603-4501

ROBERTS, THOMAS GEORGE, retired physicist; b. Ft. Smith, Ark., Apr. 27, 1929; s. Thomas Lawrence and Emma Lee (Stanley) R.; m. Alice Anne Harbin, Nov. 14, 1958 (dec. 1994); children: Lawrence Dewey, Regina Anne; foster child, Marcia Roberts Dale; m. Betty Howard McElyea, July 28, 1995. AA, Armstrong Coll., 1953; BS, U. Ga., 1956, MS, 1957; PhD, N.C. State U., 1967. Research physicist U.S. Army Missile Command, Huntsville, Ala., 1958-85; cons. industry and govt. agys., 1970—, SAIC, Huntsville, Ala., 1997—; owner Technoco, Huntsville. Contbr. articles to profl. jours. Patentee in field. Served to sgt. USAF, 1948-52. Fellow Am. Optical Soc.; mem. Am. Phys. Soc., IEEE, Huntsville Optical Soc. Am. (pres. 1980, 92). Episcopalian. Club: Toastmaster Internat. (pres. 1963). Current work: Laser physics, optics, particle beams and instrumentation; diagnostic devices and techniques development. Subspecialties: Laser physics; Plasma physics. Office: Technoco PO Box 4723 Huntsville AL 35815-4723

ROBERTS, THOMAS MORGAN, former government official; b. Memphis, Apr. 14, 1937; s. James T. and Emily K. (Allen) R.; m. Margaret Elizabeth Boyle, Jan. 14, 1967 (div. Aug. 1992); children: André Lovell, Elizabeth Boyle, Elinor Edgeworth. B.S., Ga. Inst. Tech., 1959. Asst. v.p. So. Boiler & Tank Works, Inc., Memphis, 1962-68, v.p., 1968-69, chmn. bd., pres., 1969-78; treas. George Bush for Pres. campaign, Houston, 1979-80; pvt. investor Washington, 1980-81; mem. U.S. Nuclear Regulatory Commn., Washington, 1981-90; underwriting mem. Lloyd's of London, 1979-94. Pres. Memphis Orchestral Soc., 1975-76; trustee Washington Opera, 1982-95. Lt. (j.g.) USN, 1959-62. Mem. James Smithson Soc. (life). Republican. Presbyterian. Clubs: Memphis Country, Memphis Hunt and Polo; Chevy Chase; Met.

ROBERTS, VIRGIL PATRICK, lawyer, business executive; b. Ventura, Calif., Jan. 4, 1947; s. Julius and Emma D. (Haley) R.; m. Eleanor Green, Aug. 28, 1973; m. Brenda Cecilia Banks, Nov. 10, 1979; children: Gisele Simone, Hayley Tasha. AA, Ventura Coll., 1966; BA, UCLA, 1968; JD, Harvard U., 1972. Bar: Calif. 1972. Assoc. Pacht, Ross, Warne Bernhardt & Sears, L.A., 1972-76; ptnr. Manning, Reynolds & Roberts, L.A., 1976-79, Manning & Roberts, 1980-81; mng. ptnr. Bobbitt & Roberts, 1996—; exec. v.p., gen. counsel Solar Records, L.A., 1981—; pres. Dick Griffey Prodns., L.A., 1982—, Solar Records, 1988—; judge pro tem L.A., Beverly Hills Mcpl. Cts., 1975—. Past bd. dirs. L.A. Black Leadership Coalition, L.A. Mus. African Am. Art, Beverly Hills Bar Assn., L.A. Legal Aid Found.; bd. dirs. Coro Found., 1984—, Calif. Cmty. Found., 1991—, L.A. Ednl. Alliance for Restructuring Now, Cmty. Build; past pres. Beverly Hills Bar Scholarship Found.; commr. Calif. Commn. for Tchr. Credentialing, 1980-83; chmn. L.A. Ednl. Partnership, 1989—, v.p. 1983-89; vice-chmn. Nat. Pub. Edn. Fund Network; chmn. bd. dirs. L.A. Annenberg Metropolitan Project. Trustee, Comm. Econ. Devel., 1991—. Recipient NAACP Legal Def. Fund Equal Justice award, 1988. Mem. Recording Industry Assn. Am., Black Entertainment and Sports Lawyers (treas., bd. dirs. 1982—). Lead atty. for NAACP in Crawford vs. Bd. Edn. desegregation case, L.A., 1979-80. Address: 4820 Vista De Oro Ave Los Angeles CA 90043-1611 Office: Bobbitt & Roberts 1620 26th St Ste 150 S Santa Monica CA 90404-4013

ROBERTS, WALTER HERBERT BEATTY, anatomist; b. Field, B.C., Can., Jan. 24, 1915; came to U.S., 1956, naturalized, 1965; s. Walter McWilliam and Sarah Caroline (Orr) R.; m. Olive Louise O'Neal, Sept. 1, 1937; children: Gayle, Sharon, David. M.D., Coll. Med. Evangelists (later Loma Linda U.), 1939. Intern St. Paul's Hosp., Vancouver, B.C., 1938-40; med. dir. Rest Haven Hosp. Sanitarium and Hosp., Sidney, Vancouver Island, B.C., 1940-53; post doctoral trg. White Meml. Hosp., Los Angeles, 1946-47, hosp., Edinburgh, Scotland, 1953-55; instr. in anatomy Loma Linda U., 1955-58, asst. prof. anatomy, 1959-62, asso. prof., 1962-70, prof., 1971—, chmn. dept. anatomy, 1974-81; prof. emeritus. Mem. Am. Assn. Anatomists, Sigma Xi, Alpha Omega Alpha. Adventist. Home: 11366 Campus St Loma Linda CA 92354-3302 Office: Loma Linda Univ Dept Path & Human Anatomy Divsn Human Anatomy Loma Linda CA 92350

ROBERTS, WALTER RONALD, political science educator, former government official; b. Waltendorf, Austria, Aug. 26, 1916; came to U.S., 1939, naturalized, 1944; s. Ignatius and Elizabeth (Diamant) R.; m. Gisela K. Schmarak, Aug. 22, 1939; children: William M., Charles E., Lawrence H. MLitt, Cambridge (Eng.) U., 1940, PhD, 1980. Research asst. Harvard U. Law Sch., 1940-42; writer, editor Voice of Am., 1942-49; press officer U.S. del. to Austrian Treaty talks, 1949, 55; fgn. affairs officer Dept. State, 1950-53; dep. asst. dir. USIA, 1954-60; counselor of embassy for pub. affairs Am. Embassy, Belgrade, Yugoslavia, 1960-66; diplomat-in-residence Brown U., Providence, 1966-67; counselor U.S. Mission to Internat. Orgns., Geneva, 1967-69; dep. assoc. dir. USIA, Washington, 1969-71, assoc. dir., 1971-74; dir. diplomatic studies Ctr. Strategic and Internat. Studies Georgetown U., Washington, 1974-75; exec. dir. Bd. Internat. Broadcasting, Washington, 1975-85; diplomat-in-residence George Washington U., Washington, 1986—. Author: Tito, Mihailovic and the Allies, 1941-45, 73, paperback, 1987, (with Terry L. Deibel) Culture and Information: Two Foreign Policy Functions, 1976; contbr. articles to profl. pubs. Apptd. mem. U.S. Adv. Commn. on Pub. Diplomacy, 1991—; bd. dirs. Salzburg Seminar, 1993—, Pub. Diplomacy Found., 1996—. Recipient Disting. Honor award USIA, 1974. Mem. Washington Inst. Fgn. Affairs, Coun. Fgn. Rels., Oxford-Cambridge Com., USIA Alumni Assn. (bd. dirs. 1995—), Met. Club. Home: 4449 Sedgwick St NW Washington DC 20016-2713 Office: George Washington U Elliott Sch Internat Affairs 2013 G St NW Washington DC 20006-4205

ROBERTS, WESS, author; b. Cedar City, Utah, Oct. 8, 1946; s. Lester Wyatt and Lura Virginia (Russell) R.; m. Cheryl Louise Barron, Mar. 22, 1968; children: Justin, Jaime, Jeremy. BS in Psychology, So. Utah U., 1970; MS in Psychology, Utah State U., 1972, PhD in Psychology, 1974. Project dir. Courseware, Inc., San Diego, 1976-78; project engr., tng. sys. specialist Northrop Svcs., Inc., San Diego, 1978-79; dir. ops. tng. Am. Express, N.Y.C., 1979-81; v.p. human resources Am. Express, Ft. Lauderdale, Fla., 1981-82, Salt Lake City, 1982-85; v.p. human resources devel. Firemans Fund Ins. Cos., Novato, Calif., 1985-91; pvt. practice lectr. Sandy, Utah, 1991—; ad hoc prof. Utah State U., Logan, 1970-73, mem. dean's adv. coun., 1984-85; cons. Utah State U. Devel. Ctr., Logan, 1970-75, INSGROUP, Inc., Huntington Beach, Calif., 1979; mem. evaluation com. Project EVE, Columbus, Ga., 1975; adj. prof. Nova U., Ctr. for the Study of Adminstrn., Ft. Lauderdale, 1981-85; mem. adv. bd. Inst. for Human Resource Mgmt., U. Utah, Salt Lake City, 1983-85; bd. advisors Sch. Profl. Studies, Westminster Coll., Salt Lake City, 1983-85; presenter in field; others. Author: Leadership Secrets of Attila the Hun, 1989, Straight A's Never Made Anybody Rich, 1991, Victory Secrets of Attila the Hun, 1993, Make It So: Leadership Lessons For The Next Generation, 1995, Protect Your Achilles Heel, 1997; editorial rev. bd.: The Pers. Adminstr., 1982-84; contbr. articles to profl. jours. Trustee The Discovery Ctr., Ft. Lauderdale, 1981-82, The Chord, Inc., Pompano Beach, Fla., 1981-83; mem., loaned exec. Nat. Alliance Bus., Western Region, 1983-85; mem. comm. com. Great Salt Lake United Way, 1984; bd. dirs. Health Plan of the Redwoods, Santa Rosa, Calif., 1987. Maj. U.S. Army, 1973-76. Recipient two Bronze medals Internat. Film and TV Festival of N.Y., 1982, Patriotic Svc. award U.S. Dept. Treasury, Washington, 1984, Silver medal and cert. of merit INTERCOM, Chgo. Internat. Film Festival, 1986, Cert. for Creative Excellence, U.S. Film and Video Festival, 1988, others; named to U.S. Army Field Artillery OCS Hall of Fame, 1995. Mem. APA.

ROBERTS, WILLIAM B., lawyer, business executive; b. Detroit, Aug. 23, 1939; s. Edwin Stuart and Marjorie Jean (Wardle) R.; m. Cathleen Anne Thompson, Sept. 1, 1962; children: Bradford William, Brent William, Katrina Marjorie. BA, Mich. State U., 1961; JD with distinction, U. Mich., 1963; China law diploma, U. East Asia, Macau, 1989. Bar: Mo. 1964, Fla. 1983, U.S. Dist. Ct. (ea. dist.) Mo., U.S. Dist. Ct. (mid. dist.) Fla. Mem. firm Thompson & Mitchell, St. Louis, 1963-67; atty. Monsanto Co., 1967-70; sr. exec. v.p. adminstrn., sec., gen. counsel Chromalloy Am. Corp. (successor Segua Corp. N.Y.), St. Louis, 1970-78; exec. v.p.-adminstrn., gen. counsel, sec. Chromalloy Am. Corp. (successor Segua Corp. N.Y.), Clayton, Mo., 1978-82; pvt. practice law, 1983-87; mng. ptnr. Roberts and Nordahl, St. Louis and Naples, Fla., 1988-89, Law Offices of William B. Roberts, St. Louis and Naples, 1989-90, Darrow & Roberts, P.A., Naples, 1992-93; pres., mng. dir. Law Offices of William B. Roberts, Naples, 1994—; pres., mng. dir. The Fairborne Group, Ltd., St. Louis and Naples, 1988-91, William B. Roberts & Assocs. Co., Merger and Acquisitions Specialists, 1982—; mem. exam. com. of policyowners Northwestern Mut. Life Ins. Co., Milw., 1978; del. to U.S.-China Joint Session on Trade Investment and Econ. Law, Beijing, 1987; sports rep. Steve Carlton, St. Louis Cardinals, Phila. Phillies baseball clubs, 1987-89; pres., CEO Tropical Tracks, Inc., Naples, 1994—; pres.-CEO Glouchestershire Ltd., Naples, Fla., 1996—. Mem. ABA, Fed. Bar Assn. (so. dist. Fla.), Mo. Bar Assn., St. Louis Bar Assn. (chmn. antitrust sect. 1973), Fla. Bar Assn., Collier County Bar Assn., Delta Theta Phi. Methodist. Home: 2294 Royal Ln Naples FL 34112-5323 Office: 4995 Tamiami Trl E Naples FL 34113-4131

ROBERTS, WILLIAM D., broadcasting executive; b. Drummondville, Que., Can., Sept. 3, 1952; s. William Henry and Freda Joyce (Crook) R.; m. Catherine Allman, July 15, 1990; children: Kristian, Nora, Craig. BA, Trent U., Peterborough, Ont., 1973; MBA, St. Mary's U., Halifax, N.S., 1976; MA, Sorbonne, Paris, 1977; Diploma in Broadcast Mgmt., U. Notre Dame, Ind. Sr. policy analyst CRTC, Ottawa, Ont., 1980-84; sr. v.p. Can. Assn. of Broadcasters, Ottawa, 1984-89; sr. dir. gen. TV Ontario, Toronto, 1989-96; sec. gen. N.Am. Nat. Broadcasters Assn., Toronto, 1996—; v.p. Couchiching Inst. for Pub. Affairs, Toronto, 1993—; fellow Calumet Coll., York U., Toronto, 1996—. Constnl. advisor Govt. of Sask., Regina, 1977-80; mem. Foster Parents Plan, Outward Bound. Swedish Inst. fellow, Stockholm, 1995; Banff Ctr. scholar, 1974. Mem. Broadcast Execs. Soc., Acad. Can. Cinema and TV, Amnesty Internat., Variety Club. Avocations: mountain climbing, karate, scuba diving, cooking. Office: North American National Broadcasters Assn, PO Box 500 Sta A, Toronto, ON Canada M5W 1E6

ROBERTS, WILLIAM EVERETT, lawyer; b. Pierre, S.D., May 12, 1926; s. Everett David and Bonnie (Martin) R.; m. Cynthia Cline, July 18, 1953; children: Catherine C. Roberts-Martin, Laura M., Nancy F., David H. BS, U. Minn., 1947; LLB, Yale U., 1950. Bar: Ind. 1950, U.S. Supreme Ct. 1964. Employee, ptnr. Duck and Neighbours, Indpls., 1950-58; ptnr. Cadick, Burns, Duck & Neighbours, Indpls., 1958-60, Roberts, Ryder, Rogers & Scism, Indpls., 1960-85; ptnr. Barnes & Thornburg, Indpls., 1986-93, of counsel, 1994—. Pres., bd. dirs. Park-Tudor Sch., Indpls., 1982-83; elder Second Presbyn. Ch., Indpls., 1962—; trustee Indpls. Mus. Art,

1978—; pres. New Hope of Ind., Indpls., 1986-87. Fellow Am. Bar Found.; mem. ABA, Ind. Bar Assn., Indpls. Bar Assn., Rotary, Meridian Hills Country Club (pres. 1983-84), Skyline Club. Republican. Home: 10466 Spring Highland Dr Indianapolis IN 46290-1101 Office: Barnes & Thornburg 1313 Mchts Bank Bldg 11 S Meridian St Indianapolis IN 46204-3506

ROBERTS, WILLIAM SMITHSON, gynecologic oncologist; b. Charlottesville, Va., Dec. 14, 1949; s. Paul Smithson and Cynthia (Larkum) R.; m. Virginia Ann Cummins, Dec. 30, 1981 (div. Apr. 1991); 1 child, William Miles; m. Sineath Gaynell Luzey, July 25, 1991; children: Seneca Leigh, Stratton Smithson. BA, Rutgers Coll., 1972; MD, Coll. of Medicine of N.J., 1976. Diplomate Am. Bd. Ob-gyn. Resident in ob-gyn. U. Fla. Coll. Medicine, Gainesville, 1976-80; fellow gynecologic oncology U. Calif. Irvine Coll. Medicine, Orange, 1980-82; asst. prof. ob-gyn. U. South Fla. Coll. Medicine, Tampa, 1982-87, assoc. prof. ob-gyn., 1987-94, prof. ob-gyn., 1995—; program leader gynecologic oncology H. Lee Moffitt Cancer Ctr., Tampa, 1993-96; chief gynecologic oncology Watson Clinic, Lakeland, Fla., 1996—; mem.-at-large bd. dirs. physicians group U. South Fla., 1992—, faculty senator, 1988-91; chief of staff H. Lee Moffitt Cancer Ctr., 1994-96. Author: (chpt.) Invasive Corcinoma of the Vulva: A Diseas of the Aged, 1987, (chpt.) Management of Malignant and Premalignant Lesion of the Female Genital Tract During Pregnancy, 1992, (chpt.) Ovarian Cancer Screening, 1996. Chmn. cancer control Hillsborough County Am. Cancer Soc., Tampa. 1991-93. Fellow Am. Coll. Ob-gyns., Am. Coll. Surgeons; mem. Soc. Gynecologic Oncologists, Fla. Soc. Gynecologic Oncologist (pres.-elect 1994—), Western Assn. Gynecologic Oncologists (v.p. 1992, James F. Nolan award 1986). Republican. Avocations: running, fishing, reading. Home: 4814 Highlands Place Dr Lakeland FL 33813-2163 Office: Watson Clinic 1600 Lakeland Hills Blvd Lakeland FL 33805-3019

ROBERTS HARVEY, BONITA, secondary school educator; b. Detroit, June 24, 1947; d. Walter James and Mattie Louise (Pacely) Hall; father, Dolphus Hall Sr.; m. Paul Randall Harvey, June 13, 1970 (div. Aug. 1980); 1 child, Paula Renee. BA, Grand Valley State U., 1974; cert. in continuing edn., Western Mich. U., 1987; postgrad, Mich. State U., 1995—. Art specialist Jenison (Mich.) Pub. Schs., 1974—, pub. rels. rep., 1994—; visual/performing artist Summer at Arts Place-Grand Rapids C.C., 1980-92; cons. art edn. Detroit Inst. Art, 1988. Bd. dirs., performing artist Robeson Players, Grand Rapids, Mich., 1973-94, Cmty. Cir. Theatre, Grand Rapids, 1981-84, Coun. Performing Arts for Children, Grand Rapids, 1981-88, Grand Rapids Art Mus., 1997; active First Cmty. African Meth. Episc. Ch., NAACP. Mem. ASCD, Nat. Art Edn. Assn., Mich. Art Edn. Assn., Mich. Edn. Assn. (tri-county pub. rels. 1994-95, regional del.), Mich. Alliance Arts Edn., Nat. Mus. Womenin Arts, Jenison Edn. Assn. (pub. rels. 1993—), Delta Sigma Theta. Avocation: performing/visual arts advocate. Office: Jenison Pub Schs 8375 20th Ave Jenison MI 49428-9230

ROBERTSON, A. HAEWORTH, actuary, benefit consultant, foundation executive; b. Oklahoma City, May 10, 1930; s. Albert Haeworth and Bonnie Tennessee (Duckett) R.; m. Mary Adeline Kissee, Feb. 3, 1952 (div. July 1979); children—Valerie Lynn, Alan Haeworth, Mary Kathryn. B.A. in Math., U. Okla., 1951; M.A. in Actuarial Sci., U. Mich., 1953. Actuary Wyatt Co., Washington and Dallas, 1955-58; actuary Bowles, Andrews & Towne, Dallas, 1958-60; v.p., actuary W. Alfred Hayes & Co., St. Louis, 1960-63; pres. First Am. Security Life Ins. Co. Mo., St. Louis, 1964-68; pvt. practice internat. cons. actuary Barbados and Ghana, 1969-72; sr. actuary ILO, Geneva, Switzerland, 1973-75; chief actuary U.S. Social Security Adminstrn., Balt., 1975-78; mng. dir. William M. Mercer, Inc., Washington, 1978-88; pvt. practice, internat. cons., actuary Washington, Kuwait, Turkey, Guyana, Zimbabwe, China, The Philippines, 1988—; chmn. Retirement Bd. Actuaries, Dept. Def., 1984-95; mem. Edn. Benefits Bd. Actuaries, 1985-95; pres., founder Retirement Policy Inst. Inc., 1986—. Author: The Coming Revolution in Social Security, 1981, Social Security: What Every Taxpayer Should Know, 1992, The Big Lie: What Every Baby Boomer Should Know About Social Security and Medicare, 1997. Served to 2d lt. USAF, 1953-55. Recipient Commrs. Citation, Social Security Adminstrn., Washington, 1976, Arthur J. Altmeyer award HEW, Washington, 1978. Fellow Soc. Actuaries (bd. govs. 1979-81, v.p. 1985-87), Conf. Cons. Actuaries; mem. Am. Acad. Actuaries, Internat. Actuarial Assn., Internat. Assn. Cons. Actuaries, U.K. Inst. Actuaries (assoc.), Cosmos Club, Phi Beta Kappa, Phi Eta Sigma, Phi Kappa Sigma. Republican. Methodist.

ROBERTSON, ABEL L., JR., pathologist; b. St. Andrews, Argentina, July 21, 1926; came to U.S., 1952, naturalized, 1957; s. Abel Alfred Lazzarini and Margaret Theresa (Anderson) R.; m. Irene Kirmayr Mauch, Dec. 26, 1958; children: Margaret Anne, Abel Martin, Andrew Duncan, Malcolm Alexander. BS, Coll. D.F. Sarmiento, Buenos Aires, Argentina, 1946; MD suma cum laude, U. Buenos Aires, 1951; PhD, Cornell U., 1959. Fellow tissue culture div. Inst. Histoloty and Embryology, Sch. Medicine Inst. Histology and Embryology, 1947-49; surg. intern Hosp. Ramos Mejia, Buenos Aires, 1948-50; fellow in tissue culture research Ministry of Health, Buenos Aires, 1950-51; resident Hosp. Nacional de Clinicas, Buenos Aires, 1950-51; head blood vessel bank and organ transplants Research Ctr. Ministry of Health, Buenos Aires, 1951-53; fellow dept. surgery and pathology Sch. Medicine Cornell U., N.Y.C., 1953-55; asst. vis. surgery U. Hosp. N.Y., N.Y.C., 1955-60; asst. prof. research surgery Postgrad. Med. Sch. NYU, N.Y.C., 1955-56; asst. vis. surgeon Bellevue Hosp., N.Y.C., 1955-60; assoc. prof. research surgery NYU, 1956-60, assoc. prof. pathology Sch. Medicine and Postgrad Med. Sch., 1960-63; staff mem. div. research Cleve. Clinic Found., 1963-73, prof. research, 1972-73; assoc. clin. prof. pathology Case Western Res. U. Sch. Medicine, Cleve., 1968-72, prof. pathology, 1973-82, dir. interdisciplinary cardiovascular research, 1975-82; exec. head dept. pathology Coll. Medicine, U. Ill., Chgo., 1982-88; prof. pathology Coll. Medicine U. Ill., 1982-93, prof. emeritus, 1993—; vis. prof. emeritus in cardiovascular medicine Stanford U. Coll. Medicine, 1995—; rsch. fellow N.Y. Soc. Cardiovasc. Surgery, 1957-58; mem. rsch. study subcom. of heart com. N.E. Ohio Regional Med. Program, 1969—. Mem. internat. editorial bd.: Atherosclerosis, Jour. Exptl. and Molecular Pathology, 1964—, Lab. Investigation, 1989—, Acta Pathologica Japonica, 1991—; contbr. articles to profl. jours. Recipient Research Devel. award NIH, 1961-63. Fellow Am. Coll. Cardiology, Am. Coll. Clin. Pharmacology, Am. Heart Assn. (established investigator 1956-61, nominating com. council on arteriosclerosis 1972), Royal Microscopical Soc., Royal Soc. Promotion Health (Gt. Britain), Am. Geriatrics Soc., N.Y. Acad. Scis., Cleve. Med. Library Assn.; mem. AMA, AAAS, AAUP, Am. Soc. for Investigative Pathology, Am. Inst. Biol. Scis., Am. Judicature Soc., Am. Soc. Cell Biology, Am. Soc. Pathologists, Am. Soc. Nephrology, Assn. Am. Physicians and Surgeons, Assn. Computing Machinery, Electron Microscopy Soc. Am., Assn. Pathology Chmn., Internat. Acad. Pathology, Soc. Cardiovascular Pathology, Internat. Cardiovascular Soc., Internat. Soc. Cardiology (sci. council on arteriosclerosis and ischemic heart disease), Internat. Fed. on Genetic Engrng. and Biotechnology, Internat. Soc. for Heart Rsch., Internat. Soc. Nephrology, Internat. Soc. Stereology, Pan Am. Med. Assn. (life, councillor in angiology 1966), Ill. Registry Anatomical Pathology (treas. 1985-87), Chgo. Pathology Soc., Reticuloendothelial Soc. Leucocyte Biology, Soc. Cryobiology, Tissue Culture Assn., Ohio Soc. Pathologists, Electron Microscopy Soc. Northeastern Ohio (pres., trustee 1966-68), Heart Assn. Northeastern Ohio, N.Y. Soc. Cardiovascular Surgery, N.Y. Soc. Electron Microscopists, Cuyahoga County Med. Soc., Cleve. Soc. Pathologists, The Oxygen Soc., Sigma Xi. Home: 415 Lee Ave Half Moon Bay CA 94019-1367

ROBERTSON, ARMAND JAMES, II, judge; b. San Diego, Sept. 23, 1937; s. Armand James and Muriel H. R.; m. Marion Sperry, Aug. 11, 1962; children: Armand James, Laura Marie. A.M. in Econs, Stanford U., 1960; LL.B., Harvard U., 1965. Bar: Calif. 1966. Law clk. to Charles M. Merrill, U.S. Ct. Appeals (9th cir.), 1965-66; assoc. firm Howard, Prim, Rice, Nemerovski, Canady & Pollak, San Francisco, 1966-71; ptnr. Howard, Prim, Rice, Nemerovski, Canady & Pollak, 1971-77; dir. Howard, Rice, Nemerovski, Canady, Robertson & Falk (P.C.), San Francisco, 1977-95; judge of the Superior Ct. City and County of San Francisco, 1995—. Dir. St. Francis Found., 1996—. Lt. (j.g.) USN, 1960-62. Mem. Am. Law Inst., ABA (antitrust sect.), Ct. for Pub. Resources, Phi Beta Kappa. Home: 178 Edgewood Ave San Francisco CA 94117-3713 Office: San Francisco Superior Ct Dept 26 850 Bryant St Ste 26 San Francisco CA 94103-4603

ROBERTSON, BEVERLY CARRUTH, steel company executive; b. Texarkana, Ark., May 16, 1922; s. Glenn C. Robertson (dec.); m. Ruth Mulcare, Oct. 31, 1945 (dec. Oct. 1993); children: Glenn J., Beverly R. Dodds, Rebecca A. Robertson Deans; m. Charlotte Doty Lawler, June 2, 1995. In sales Nat. Supply Co., Laurel, Miss., 1941-51; purchasing agt. Kirby Petroleum co., Houston, 1951-54; exec. v.p. mktg. Lone Star Steel Co., Dallas, 1954-85; exec. v.p. Lone Star Steel Co., 1985-86; pres., dir., chief exec. officer LSSCO Trading Corp., 1985-86; owner BSEER Enterprises, Dallas, 1986—; ptnr. Clayton Equipment Co., Dallas, 1992—; chmn. Sir Alec Inc., 1985-94; cons. Pipeco, Inc., Houston, 1986-88; exec. v.p. mktg. and procurement Nat. Pipe and Tube Co., Houston, 1988-89; pres., CEO Tex. Am. Pipe & Supply Co., Inc., Dallas, 1989—; cons. Ipsco Steel, Inc., Camanche, Iowa, 1991-92. Served to capt. USAF, 1943-46, ETO. Named Supplier of Yr. Petroleum Industry Buyers group Nat. Assn. Purchasing Mgmt., 1982. Mem. Dallas Country Club, Dallas Petroleum Club. Republican. Episcopalian. Home: PO Box 12688 Dallas TX 75225-0688

ROBERTSON, CLIFF, actor, writer, director; b. La Jolla, Calif., Sept. 9, 1925; s. Clifford Parker and Audrey (Willingham) R.; m. Dina Merrill, Dec. 21, 1966 (div.); children: Heather, Stephanie. DFA (hon.), Bradford Coll., 1981, MacMurray Coll., 1986, Susquehanna U., 1988. Contbr. articles to various publs.; stage appearances include Late Love, Wisteria Trees, Orpheus Descending; films include Picnic, 1956, Autumn Leaves, 1956, The Naked and the Dead, 1958, The Girl Most Likely, 1958, Gidget, 1959, All in a Nights Work, 1961, The Big Show, 1961, Under-World, U.S.A., 1961, As the Sea Rages, 1961, The Interns, 1962, PT 109, 1963, Sunday in New York, 1964, The Best Man, 1964, 633 Squadron, 1964, Love Has Many Faces, 1965, Masquerade, 1965, Up From the Beach, 1965, The Honey Pot, 1967, The Devil's Brigade, 1968, Charly, 1968, (Academy award for Best Actor 1969), The Great Northfield Minnesota Raid, 1972, Ace Eli and Rodger of the Skies, 1973, Too Late the Hero, 1970, Man on a Swing, 1974, 3 Days of the Condor, 1975, Out of Season, Obsession, 1976, Shoot, 1976, Star 80, 1983, Brainstorm, 1983, Malone, 1987, Wild Hearts Can't Be Broken, 1991, Wind, 1992, The Sunset Boys, 1995, Escape from L.A., 1996, Assignment Berlin, 1997; TV movies and miniseries appearances include The Days of Wine and Roses, 1958, The Sunshine Patriot, 1968, The Game, 1968 (Emmy award) The Man Without a Country, 1973, A Tree Grows in Brooklyn, 1974, My Father's House, 1975, Return to Earth, 1976, Washington: Behind Closed Doors, 1977, Overboard, 1978, Two of a Kind, 1982, The Key to Rebecca, 1985, Dreams of Gold, 1986, Ford: The Man and The Machine, 1987, Dead Reckoning, 1990, Dazzle, 1995, The Last Best Place; appeared in TV series Falcon Crest; writer, dir.: play The V.I.P.'s, 1981; J. W. Coop. Served to lt. (j.g.) USNR. Recipient Wallace award Am. Scottish Found., 1984, Sharples aviation award AOPA, 1983, Theatre World award, 1970, award Advt. Age, 1985. Mem. SAG (bd. dirs. N.Y. chpt. 1980—), Dirs. Guild, Writers Guild Am., Bath & Tennis Club Palm Beach, Maidstone Club (East Hampton), River Club (N.Y.C.), Brook Club (N.Y.C.), Players (N.Y.C.), River Club, Wings Club. Presbyterian. Avocations: flying, skiing, soaring, tennis.

ROBERTSON, DAVID, pharmacologist, educator; b. Sylvia, Tenn., May 23, 1947; s. David Herlie and Lucille Luther (Bowen) R.; m. Rose Marie Stevens, Oct. 30, 1976; 1 child, Rose. B.A., Vanderbilt U., 1969, M.D., 1973. Diplomate Am. Bd. Internal Medicine, Am. Bd. Clin. Pharmacology. Intern, Johns Hopkins U., Balt., 1973-74, asst. resident, 1974-75, asst. chief service in medicine, 1977-78; fellow in clin. pharmacology Vanderbilt U., Nashville, 1975-77, asst. prof. medicine and pharmacology, 1978-82, assoc. prof., 1982-86, prof., 1986—, prof. neurology, 1991—; dir. clin. research ctr., 1987—; dir. Ctr. for Space Physiology and Medicine, 1989—; dir. Med. Sci. Tng. Program, 1993—; pclin. rsch. specializing in gene therapy and disorders of blood pressure regulation, Nashville, 1978—; mem. staff Vanderbilt Hosp., Burroughs Wellcome scholar in clin. pharmacology, 1985-91. Author: (with B.M. Greene and G.J. Taylor) Problems in Internal Medicine, 1980, (with C.R. Smith) Manual of Clinical Pharmacology, 1981, (with Italo Biaggioni) Disorders of the Autonomic Nervous System, 1995, Primer on the Autonomic Nervous System, 1996; editor-in-chief Drug Therapy, 1991-94; editorial bds. Jour. Autonomic Nervous System, Clin. Pharm. and Therapeutics, Clin. Autonomic Rsch., Am. Jour. Med. Sci., Current Topics in Pharmacology. Recipient Research Career Devel. award NIH, 1981, Grant W. Liddle award for leadership in rsch., 1991; Adolph-Morsbach grantee Bonn, Germany, 1968; Logan Clendening fellow Reykjavik, Iceland, 1969. Fellow Am. Heart Assn. Council Hypertension and Circulation, ACP (teaching and research scholar 1978-81); mem. Am. Autonomic Soc. (pres. 1992-94), Am. Acad. Neurology, Soc. Neurosci., Am. Inst. Aeronautics and Astronautics, U.S. Pharmacopeial Conv., Nat. Bd. Med. Examiners, Aerospace Med. Assn. (space station sci. and applications com.), FDA Consortium Rare Disorders, Rare Disorder Network, Am. Fedn. for Clin. Research, Am. Soc. Clin. Investigation, Assn. Am. Physicians, So. Soc. for Clin. Investigation, Am. Soc. for Clin. Pharmacology and Therapeutics, Phi Beta Kappa, Alpha Omega Alpha (hon., bd. dirs. 1995—). Baptist. Home: 4003 Newman Pl Nashville TN 37204-4308 Office: Vanderbilt U Clin Rsch Ctr 21st Ave S Nashville TN 37232-2195

ROBERTSON, DAVID WAYNE, pharmaceutical company executive; b. Dumas, Tex., July 30, 1955; s. R.L. and N.C. R. BS, Stephen F. Austin State U., 1977; MS, U. Ill., 1978, PhD, 1981. Sr. medicinal chemist Eli Lilly and Co., Indpls., 1981-84, rsch. scientist, 1985-87, sr. rsch. scientist, 1988-89, rsch. group leader, 1988-89, dir. cen. nervous system rsch., 1990-91; v.p. medicinal chemistry Ligand Pharms., Inc., San Diego, 1991-92, v.p. rsch., 1992-93, v.p. discovery rsch., 1993-96; sr. dir. R & D DuPont Merek Pharm. Co, Wilmington, 1996—. Contbr. articles to profl. jours. Mem. Soc. for Neurosci., Am. Soc. Pharmacology and Exptl. Therapeutics, Am. Chem. Soc. Office: DuPont Merck Pharm Co Exptl Sta Bldg 500 3604B PO Box 80500 Wilmington DE 19880-0500

ROBERTSON, DOUGLAS STUART, lawyer; b. Portland, Oreg., Jan. 9, 1947; s. Stuart Neil and Mary Katherine (Gates) R.; m. Nan Reinhorn, Dec. 27, 1970; 1 child, Lauren Amanda. BS, Oreg. State U., 1969, MA in Bus. Adminstrn., 1970; JD U. Denver, 1973. Bar: Oreg. 1973, U.S. Dist. Ct. Oreg. 1974, U.S. Ct. Appeal (9th cir.) 1977, U.S. Supreme Ct. 1977. Staff atty. Multnomah County Bar Assn. Legal Aid, Portland, 1973-75; ptnr. Bouneff, Chally & Marshall, Portland, 1975-80; asst. gen. counsel Orbanco Fin. Services, Portland, 1980-83; gen. counsel Hyster Credit Corp., Portland, 1983-86; v.p., gen. counsel PacifiCorp Credit Inc., 1986-90; ptnr. Lane, Powell, Spears Lubersky, Portland, 1990-91; v.p., gen. counsel, sec., In Focus Systems, Inc., Wilsonville, Oreg., 1991-96, v.p. chief ops. officer, bd. dirs. Lightware, Inc., 1996—; chmn. bd., CEO Deschutes River Preserve, Inc., Portland, 1982—. Mem. editl. bd. Denver Jour. of Internat. Law and Policy, 1971. Served with U.S. Army 1968-70. Mem. ABA, Comml. Law League, Multnomah County Bar Assn., Am. Assn. of Equipment (lessor's law forum), Am. Corp. Counsel Assn. (bd. dirs., treas. N.W. chpt.). Republican. Club: Flyfisher's of Oreg., Oreg. Trout. Home: 29 Hillshire Dr Lake Oswego OR 97034-7375 Office: Lightware Inc 9875 SW Sunshine Ct Ste 200 Beaverton OR 97005

ROBERTSON, EDWARD D., JR., state supreme court chief justice; b. Durham, N.C., May 1, 1952; m. Renee Ann Beal; two children. BA, U. Mo., 1974, JD, 1977. Asst. atty. gen. Mo., 1978-79; assoc. mcpl. judge City of Belton, Mo., 1980-81; dep. atty. gen. City of Belton, 1981-85; justice Mo. Supreme Ct., Kansas City, 1985—; former chief justice, now judge Mo. Supreme Ct. Office: Mo Supreme Ct PO Box 150 Jefferson City MO 65102-0150*

ROBERTSON, EDWIN DAVID, lawyer; b. Roanoke, Va., July 5, 1946; s. Edwin Traylor and Norma Burns (Bowles) R.; m. Anne Littelle Ferratt, Sept. 7, 1968, 1 child, Thomas Therit. BA with honors, U. Va., 1968, LLB, 1971. Bar: N.Y. 1972, U.S. Ct. Appeals (2d cir.) 1972, U.S. Dist. Ct. (ea. and so. dists.) N.Y. 1973, U.S. Supreme Ct. 1975, U.S. Dist. Ct. (ea. dist.) Mich. 1986. Assoc. Cadwalader, Wickersham & Taft, N.Y.C., 1972-80; ptnr. Cadwalader, Wickershaft & Taft, N.Y.C., 1980—. Bd. dirs. Early Music Found. N.Y.C., 1983—, chmn., 1993—; bd. dirs. Oratorio Soc. of N.Y.C., 1988—, sec., 1991—. 1st lt. USAF, 1971-72. Mem. ABA, Fed. Bar Coun., N.Y. County Lawyers Assn. (chmn. bankruptcy com. 1983-87, bd. dirs. 1985-88, 95—, investment com. 1992—, exec. com. 1996—), Assn. of Bar of City N.Y., Soc. Colonial Wars, Down Town Assn., Jefferson Soc., Phi Beta Kappa, Phi Kappa Psi. Republican. Episcopalian. Home: 315 E 72nd St New York NY 10021-4625 Office: Cadwalader Wickersham & Taft 100 Maiden Ln New York NY 10038-4818

ROBERTSON, EDWIN OSCAR, banker; b. Speedwell, Tenn., May 28, 1923; s. John M. and Etta (Mayes) R.; m. Althea Maxine Moyers, June 3, 1948 (dec. Nov. 1970); children: Edwin Glenn, Craig Eric; m. Sarah Alice Parkman, Nov. 16, 1974. BS in Agr., U. Tenn., 1950; LLD (hon.), Lincoln Meml. U., 1984. Supr. vets. farm tng. County of Claiborne, Tazewell, Tenn., 1950-52; agr. rep. Citizens Bank, New Tazewell, Tenn., 1952; v.p., agr. rep. Nat. Bank, Middlesboro, Ky., 1953-57; chmn. bd., chief exec. officer Comml. Bancgroup, Inc., Harrogate, Tenn., 1976—; pres., chief exec. officer Comml. Bank, Middlesboro, 1958—; chmn., CEO Comml. Bank, Harrogate, 1988—; chmn. bd. Comml. Bank, Harrogate, 1976—; mem. Govt. Task Force on Banking, Ky., 1983; trustee Lincoln Meml. U., Harrogate, 1974—; bd. dirs. Cumberland Devel. Corp., Middlesboro. Gov. Ruritan Nat. Tenn. Dist., 1954-55; bd. dirs. Middlesboro Indsl. Commn., 1962—, Ky. C. of C., 1983-84. With USAF, 1943-45. Mem. Rotary. Republican. Baptist. Avocations: farming, horseback riding. Home: 125 St Johns Pl PO Box 100 Harrogate TN 37752-0100

ROBERTSON, GEORGE LEVEN, retired association executive; b. Alexandria, La., Feb. 7, 1921; s. Ernest E. and Cornelia (La Croix) R.; m. Florence Horne, Feb. 7, 1943; children—Dana Carleton, Linda, Malcolm Ernest, Judy Elaine. B.S., La. State U., 1941; M.S., A. and M. Coll. Tex., 1947; Ph.D. (Gen. Edn. Bd. fellow 1949-50), U. Wis., 1951. Grad. asst. animal husbandry A. and M. Coll. Tex., 1941-42, instr., then asst. prof., 1946-49, assoc. prof., 1951-55; grad. asst. U. Wis., 1949-51; prof. animal sci., head dept. La. State U., 1955-77, chmn. grad. council, 1961; exec. dir. Honor Soc. of Phi Kappa Phi, 1977-92. Trustee Baton Rouge Gen. Hosp.; deacon, trustee First Bapt. Ch., Baton Rouge. Served to capt. AUS, 1942-46; col. Res. Named Outstanding Tchr. A. and M. Coll. Tex. Sch. Agr., 1948-49. Fellow AAAS; mem. Am. Soc. Animal Sci. (pres. So. sect. 1967-68), AAUP, Assn. Coll. Honor Socs. (v.p. 1987-89, pres. 1989-91), Sigma Xi, Alpha Zeta, Phi Kappa Phi (nat. pres.-elect 1974-77), Gamma Sigma Delta, Omicron Delta Kappa. Clubs: Masons, Kiwanis. Home: 7017 Perkins Rd Baton Rouge LA 70808-4320

ROBERTSON, HORACE BASCOMB, JR., law educator; b. Charlotte, N.C., Nov. 13, 1923; s. Horace Bascomb and Ruth (Montgomery) R.; m. Patricia Lavell, Aug. 11, 1947; children—Mark L., James D. B.S., U.S. Naval Acad., 1945; J.D., Georgetown U., 1953; M.S., George Washington U., 1968. Commd. ensign U.S. Navy, 1945, advanced through grades to rear adm., 1972; line officer, 1945-55, law specialist, 1955-68; spl. counsel to sec. Navy, Washington, 1964-67; judge adv. Navy, 1968-76; spl. counsel to chief naval ops. Washington, 1970-72; dep. judge adv. gen. Navy Dept., Washington, 1972-75; judge adv. gen. Navy Dept., 1975-76; prof. law Duke U., 1976-89, sr. assoc. dean, 1986-89, ret., 1990; Chas H. Stockton chair of internat. law Naval War Coll., Newport, R.I., 1991-92. Decorated D.S.M. Mem. ABA, Am. Soc. Internat. Law. Methodist. Home: 5 Stoneridge Cir Durham NC 27705-5510 Office: Duke U Sch Law Durham NC 27708

ROBERTSON, HUGH DUFF, lawyer; b. Grosse Pointe, Mich., Mar. 14, 1957; s. Hugh Robertson and Louise (Grey) Bollinger. BBA in Fin., U. Wis., Whitewater, 1978; JD, Whittier Coll., 1982. Bar: Calif. 1983, U.S. Tax Ct. 1984. Pres., CEO, A. Morgan Maree Jr. & Assocs., Inc., L.A., 1979—. Mem. ABA (forum com. on entertainment 1982—), State Calif., L.A. County Bar Assn., Beverly Hills Bar Assn., Acad. TV Arts and Scis., Am. Film Inst., Phi Alpha Delta. Republican. Episcopalian. Avocations: sports, swimming, reading. Office: A Morgan Maree Jr & Assocs 4727 Wilshire Blvd Ste 600 Los Angeles CA 90010-3875

ROBERTSON, JACK CLARK, accounting educator; b. Marlin, Tex., Apr. 27, 1943; s. Rupert Cook and Lois Lucille (Rose) R.; m. Caroline Susan Hughes, Oct. 23, 1965; children: Sarah Ellen, Elizabeth Hughes. Student, Rice U., 1961-63; BBA with honors, U. Tex., Austin, 1965, M in Profl. Acctg., 1967; PhD, U. N.C., 1970. C.P.A., Tex. Tax acct. Humble Oil and Refining Co., Houston, 1964-65; auditor Peat, Marwick, Mitchell & Co., Houston, 1965-66; acct. Wade, Barton, Marsh C.P.A.s, Austin, Tex., 1966-67; asst. prof. U. Tex., Austin, 1970-74; assoc. prof. U. Tex., 1974-79, Price Waterhouse auditing prof., 1979-84, C.T. Zlatkovich Centennial prof. acctg., 1984—; acad. assoc. Coopers & Lybrand, N.Y.C., 1975-76; acad. fellow U.S. Securities and Exchange Commn. Office of the Chief Acct., Washington, 1982-83; Erskine fellow U. Canterbury, Christchurch, New Zealand, 1988; lectr. in field. Contbr. articles to profl. jours. Lay reader St. Matthews Episcopal Ch., Austin, 1972-75, mem. vestry, 1973-75, 77-79, 84-86, treas., 1974-75, 77-96, chmn. bldg. fund, 1976-87, chmn. everymen. canvass, 1980, sr. warden, 1986; del. Diocese of Tex. Coun., 1993-95. Mem. AICPA, Am. Acctg. Assn. (chmn. auditing sect. 1978-79, chmn. auditing stds. com. 1980-81, chmn. SEC liaison com. 1983-84), Tex. Soc. CPAs (vice chmn., profl. ethics com. 1986-94, 95-97, Presdl. citation 1994), Assn. Cert. Fraud Examiners (regent emeritus, cert.), Phi Kappa Phi, Beta Gamma Sigma, Beta Alpha Psi. Office: Univ of Tex CBA 4M 202 Dept Accounting Austin TX 78712

ROBERTSON, JAMES, judge; b. Cleve., May 18, 1938; s. Frederick Irving and Doris Mary (Byars) R.; m. Berit Selma Persson, Sept. 19, 1959; children: Stephen Irving, Catherine Anne, Peter Arvid. AB, Princeton U., 1959; LLB, George Washington U., 1965. Bar: D.C. 1966, U.S. Supreme Ct. 1969. Assoc. Wilmer, Cutler & Pickering, Washington, 1965-69, ptnr., 1973-94; U.S. dist. judge D.C., 1994—; chief counsel Lawyers Com. for Civil Rights Under Law, Jackson, Miss., 1969-70; dir. Lawyers Com. for Civil Rights Under Law, Washington, 1970-72, co-chmn., 1985-87; co-chmn. D.C. Lawyers Com. for Civil Rights Under Law, Washington, 1982-84; mem. com. on grievances U.S. Dist. Ct., 1988-92, vice chmn., 1989-92; bd. dirs. South Africa Legal Svcs. and Edn. Project, Inc., 1987—, pres., 1989-94; bd. dirs. D.C. Prisoners Legal Svcs., Inc., 1992-94. Editor in chief George Washington Law Rev., 1964-65. Lt. USN, 1959-64. Fellow Am. Coll. Trial Lawyers, Am. Bar Found.; mem. ABA, D.C. Bar (bd. govs. 1986-93, pres.-elect 1990-92, pres. 1991-92). Home: 11300 Cushman Rd North Bethesda MD 20852-3606 Office: Rm 6315 US Courthouse Washington DC 20001

ROBERTSON, JAMES COLVERT, insurance company executive; b. Takoma Park, Md., Feb. 2, 1932; s. Charles Edwin and Mary Louise (Colvert) R.; m. Grace A. Shuler, May 7, 1971. BS in Econs., U. Md., 1957; LLB, George Washington U., 1959. Bar: D.C. 1960, Pa. 1965. Atty./analyst SEC, Washington, 1959-64; atty. McNees, Wallace & Nurick, Harrisburg, Pa., 1964-67; gen. counsel Consumers Life, Camp Hill, Pa., 1967-68; pres., chmn. bd. Consumers Life & Consumers Fin. Corp., Camp Hill, 1968—; dir. Consumers Fin. Bd. dirs. Harrisburg Hosp., 1982-86, Elizabethtown Coll., 1982—, Keystone Sports Found., 1983-88; treas. Susquehanna Art Mus. 1988—. With U.S. Army, 1951-53. Mem. Pa. Bar Assn., Fed. Bar Assn. West Shore Country Club (bd. dirs.). Republican. Home: 86 Greenwood Cir Wormleysburg PA 17043-1140 Office: Consumers Life Ins Co PO Box 26 1200 Camp Hill By-Pass Camp Hill PA 17001-0026

ROBERTSON, JAMES IRVIN, JR., historian, educator; b. Danville, Va., July 18, 1930; s. James Irvin and Mae (Kympton) R.; m. Elizabeth Green, June 1, 1952; children—Mae Elizabeth, James Irvin III, Howard Wells. BA, Randolph-Macon Coll., 1955, LittD, 1980; MA, Emory U., 1956, PhD, 1959. Ordained deacon Anglican Cath. Ch. Editor Civil War History, U. Iowa, 1959-61; exec. dir. U.S. Civil War Centennial Commn., 1961-65; assoc. prof. history U. Mont., 1965-67; prof. Va. Poly. Inst. and State U., Blacksburg, 1967-76, chmn. dept. history, 1969-77, C.P. Miles prof. history, 1977-92, Alumni disting. prof., 1992—. Author: Civil War Sites in Virginia, 1982, General A.P. Hill, 1987, Soldiers Blue and Gray, 1988, Civil War Virginia, 1991, Civil War! America Becomes One Nation, 1992, Jackson & Lee: Legends in Gray, 1995, Stonewall Jackson: The Man, The Soldier, The Legend, 1997; contbr. articles to profl. jours. Recipient Harry S. Truman Hist. award, Bruce Catton award, Nevins Freeman award. Outstanding Faculty award Va. State Coun. Higher Edn., 1991, others. Mem. So. Hist. Assn., Va. Hist. Soc. Home: 405 Stonegate Dr Blacksburg VA 24060-3243 Office: Va Poly Inst History Dept Blacksburg VA 24061

ROBERTSON, JAMES MAGRUDER, geological research administrator; b. Port Clinton, Ohio, Sept. 24, 1943; married. BA, Carleton Coll., 1965; MS, U. Mich., 1968, PhD in Econ. Geology, 1972. Asst. prof. geology

Mich. Technol. U., 1972-74; mining geologist N.Mex. Bur. Mines and Mineral Resources, 1974-86, sr. econ. geologist, 1986-88, assoc. dir., 1988-92; geologist Wis. Geol. Survey, Madison, 1992—. Mem. Geochem. Soc., Geol. Soc. Am., Soc. Econ. Geology, Sigma Xi. Office: Univ Wisconsin Geol & Natural History Survey 3817 Mineral Point Rd Madison WI 53705-5121 also: Wis Geol Survey 3817 Mineral Point Rd Madison WI 53705-5121*

ROBERTSON, JAMES WOOLSEY, lawyer; b. Ft. Sam Houston, Tex., Aug. 6, 1942; s. Robert Charles Lee and Marjorie Evelyn (Woolsey) R.; 1 child, William Angus; m. Laura Ann Koons, Apr. 24, 1993. BBA, U. Tex., 1966, JD, 1967. Bar: Tex.; cert. real estate law specialist. Ptnr. Liddell, Sapp, Zivley, Hill & Laboon, L.L.P., Houston, 1971—, chmn. fin. com., 1985-90, chmn. banking and real estate sect., 1992—. Chancellor Episc. Ch. Holy Spirit, Houston, 1984-92, trustee, 1984-87. Lt. comdr. USCGR, 1968-71. Mem. State Bar Tex., Houston Bar Assn., Houston Real Estate Lawyers Coun. Republican. Avocations: golf, fly fishing, skiing, hunting. Office: Liddell Sapp Zivley Et Al 3400 Tex Commerce Tower 600 Travis St Houston TX 77002

ROBERTSON, JERALD LEE, physicist; b. Webbs Cross Roads, Ky., Oct. 4, 1935; s. Marvin Lee and Eva Lee (Wheat) R.; m. Carol Ann Sanderson, Aug. 29, 1963 (div. Jan. 1970). BS in Physics and Chemistry, Wilmington (Ohio) Coll., 1960; postgrad., Amherst (Mass.) Coll., 1961, U. Dayton, 1964-65. Cert. hazardous materials mgr. Trainee, indsl. mgr. Ralston Purina, Sharonville, Ohio, 1961-63; rsch. physicist Monsanto Rsch., Dayton, 1963-68; graphic arts engr. Formica Corp., Evendale, Ohio, 1968-70; tech. svcs. mgr. Color Pac Inc., Franklin, Ohio, 1970-73; tech. svcs. rep. GE, Coshocton, Ohio, 1972-77; tech. svcs. mgr. Cin. Milacron, 1978-82; mgr. R&D Kornylak Corp., Hamilton, Ohio, 1983-97; sec. E.P.C.O.R.P., 1983; mem. citizen adv. bd. Henkel Corp., Cin., 1994-96; chmn. M.C. Watershe Coun., 1996-97; mem. consensus Forum H.C.E.P.P., 1996-97; bd. dirs. Hamilton Safety Coun., Rivers Unltd.-MCRP, Cin. Author: (with others) Pulp and Paper, 1980; columnist (weekly article) Suburban Press, 1983-85; contbr. articles to profl. jours.; photo exhibit Urban Appalachian Mus. Councilman Village of Elmwood Place, Ohio, 1992-96, candidate for mayor, 1983, 87, 93; chmn. Mill Creek Watershed Steering Com., Cin., 1994-96; chmn. Citizens for Sensible Waste Mgmt., Cin., 1990-93; chmn. cmty. panel Bicentennial Commn., Cin., 1987; mem. sr. olympics basketball, 1992-97. Recipient C.U.F.A. Environ. award, 1997. Mem. Nature Conservancy, Am. Assn. for Ind. Investors. Avocation: wine tasting. Home: 111 Township Ave Cincinnati OH 45216-2425 Office: Kornylak Corp 400 Heaton St Hamilton OH 45011-1872

ROBERTSON, JERRY D., lawyer; b. Port Clinton, Ohio, Dec. 16, 1948; s. Edgar N. and Delores E. (Brough) R.; m. Kathryn A. Behlmer, Aug. 1, 1970; children: Matthew, Adam. BS, Bowling Green State U., 1971; JD, U. Toledo, 1974. Bar: Ohio 1974, U.S. Ct. Mil. Appeals 1974, U.S. Dist. Ct. (no. dist.) Ohio 1977, U.S. Supreme Ct. 1980. Pvt. practice Oak Harbor, Ohio, 1977—; instr. real estate law Terra tech. Coll., Fremont, Ohio, 1978-82; asst. pros. atty. Ottawa County, Ohio, 1980-84; law dir. Village of Oak Harbor, Ohio, 1982—; bd. dirs. Luther Home of Mercy, Williston, Ohio. Capt. U.S. Army, 1974-77. Decorated Meritorious Svc. medal. Mem. ABA, Nat. Network of Estate Planning Attys., Nat. Acad. Elder Law Attys., Ohio Bar Assn., Toledo Estate Planning Coun., Am. Legion. Lutheran. Home: 520 E Water St Oak Harbor OH 43449-1535 Office: PO Box 26 132 W Water St Oak Harbor OH 43449

ROBERTSON, JERRY EARL, retired manufacturing company executive; b. Detroit, Oct. 25, 1932; s. Earl Howard and Nellie (Wright) R.; m. Joanne Alice Wesner, Sept. 3, 1955; children: Scott Clark, Lisa Kay, Stuart Todd. B.S., Miami U., Oxford, Ohio, 1954; M.S., U. Mich., 1956, Ph.D., 1959. With Minn. Mining & Mfg. Co., St. Paul, 1963-94, tech. dir. med. products div., 1973-74, dept. mgr. surg. products dept., 1974-75, gen. mgr. surg. products div., 1975-79, div. v.p. surg. products div., 1979-80, group v.p. health care products and services, 1980-84, exec. v.p. life scis. sector, 1984-86, exec. v.p. life scis. sector and corp. svcs., 1986-94; ret., 1994; bd. dirs. Coherent, Inc., Cardinal Health Distbn., Inc., Haemonetics Corp., Braintree, Mass., Allianz Life Ins. Co. of N.Am., Choice Hotels Internat., Steris Corp., Medwave, Inc.; trustee Minn. Med. Found., Mpls., 1981-87. Bd. reference MAP Internat., Brunswick, Ga., 1986-94; bd. dirs. Project HOPE, 1988—, Manor Care Inc., 1989—. Mem. Pharm. Mfrs. Assn. (bd. dirs. 1984-89), Health Industry Mfrs. Assn. (bd. dirs. 1982-91, chmn. 1990-91). Unitarian. Office: Minn World Trade Ctr 30 Seventh St E Ste 3050 Saint Paul MN 55101-4901

ROBERTSON, JOHN ARCHIBALD LAW, nuclear scientist; b. Dundee, Scotland, July 4, 1925; s. John Carr and Ellen (Law) R.; m. Betty-Jean Moffatt, June 26, 1954; children: Ean Stuart, Clare Deborah, Fiona Heather. B.A., Cambridge (Eng.) U., 1950, M.A., 1953. Sci. officer U.K. Atomic Energy Authority, Harwell, Eng., 1950-57; research officer Atomic Energy Can. Ltd., Chalk River, Ont., 1957-63; head reactor materials br. Atomic Energy Can. Ltd., 1963-70, dir. fuels and materials div., 1970-75, asst. to v.p., 1975-82; dir. program planning Atomic Energy Can. Ltd. (Research Co. Head Office), 1982-85; cons., 1985—; mem. Atomic Energy Control Bd.'s Adv. Com. on Nuclear Safety, 1988-97. Author: Irradiation Effects in Nuclear Fuels, 1969; editor: Jour. Nuclear Materials, 1967-71. Served to capt., Royal Engrs. Brit. and Indian armies, 1943-47. Recipient W.B. Lewis medal Can. Nuclear Assn., 1987, W.J. Kroll Zirconium medal W.J. Kroll Inst. for Extractive Metallurgy, 1993. Fellow Royal Soc. Can.

ROBERTSON, JOSEPH EDMOND, grain processing company executive; b. Brownstown, Ind., Feb. 16, 1918; s. Roscoe Melvin and Edith Penina (Shields) R.; m. Virginia Faye Baxter, Nov. 23, 1941; 1 son, Joseph Edmond. BS, Kans. State U., 1940, postgrad., 1940. Cereal chemist Ewing Mill Co., 1940-43, flour milling engr., 1946-50, feed nutritionist, 1951-59; v.p., sec. Robertson Corp., Brownstown, Ind., 1960-80, pres., 1980—. Mem. Kans. State U. Varsity Basketball Team, 1937-40; pres. Jackson County (Ind.) Welfare Bd., 1948-52; mem. Ind. Port Commn., 1986-91; mem. Ind. Gov.'s Coun. of Sagamores of the Wabash. Forest products tech. writer Forest Prodn. Jour., 1973-78. Served with USAAF, 1943-45. Named to Hon. Order Ky. Cols. Mem. Hardwood Plywood Mfrs. Assn. (v.p. affiliate div. 1971-73, 87-88, internat. lectr. forest prodn. industry 1973-94), Am. Assn. Cereal Chemists, Assn. Operative Millers, Am. Legion, Brownstown C. of C. (dir. All Am. city program 1955), Kans. State U. Alumni Assn. (life), Blue Key, Phi Delta Theta, Phi Kappa Phi, Alpha Mu. Presbyterian. Clubs: Harrison Lakes Country Club, Internat. Travelers Century (Los Angeles), Circumnavigators Club (N.Y.C.). Lodge: Elks. Home: Lake and Forest Club 1268 E Lake Shore Dr PO Box A Brownstown IN 47220 Office: 200 N Front St Brownstown IN 47220-1040

ROBERTSON, LEON H., management consultant, educator; b. Atlanta, Jan. 25, 1934; s. Grady Jospeh and Pearline (Chandler) R.; m. S. Ann Parker, Aug. 27, 1971; children: Sharon, Michael. B.S. in Indsl. Mgmt., Ga. Inst. Tech., 1957, M.S., 1959; postgrad., U. Okla.-Norman, 1958, U. Mich., 1961; Ph.D. in Bus. Adminstrn., Ga. State U., 1968. Mgr. mgmt. cons. div. Arthur Anderson & Co., Atlanta, 1960-65; prof. bus. adminstrn. Ga. State U., 1965-75; corp. v.p. Tex. Gas Corp., Owensboro, Ky., 1975-78, sr. v.p., 1982-83; chmn., chief exec. officer Am. Carriers, Inc., Overland Park, Kans., 1978-88; chmn. bd. dirs. Midwest Coast Transport, Overland Park, 1988-89; prof. mgmt., dir. div. bus. adminstrn. U. Mo., Kansas City, 1990-96, dir. Internat. Acad. Programs, 1996—. Office: Univ of Mo-Kansas City Henry W Bloch Sch Bus & Pub Admn 5110 Cherry St Kansas City MO 64110-2426

ROBERTSON, LESLIE EARL, structural engineer; b. Los Angeles, Feb. 12, 1928; s. Garnett Roy and Tina (Grantham) R.; m. Saw-Teen See, Aug. 11, 1982; children: Jeanne, Christopher Alan, Sharon Miyuki, Karla Mei. BS, U. Calif., Berkeley, 1952; D in Engring. (hon.), Rensselaer Polytech. Inst., 1986; DSc (hon.), U. Western Ont., Can., 1988; DEng (hon.), Lehigh U., 1991. Lic. arch., Japan. Structural engr. Kaiser Engrs., Oakland, Calif., 1952-54, John A. Blume, San Francisco, 1954-57, Raymond Internat. Co., N.Y.C., 1957-58; mng. ptnr. Skilling, Helle, Christiansen, Robertson, N.Y.C., Seattle and Anchorage, 1958-82; chmn. Robertson, Fowler & Assocs., P.C., N.Y.C., 1982-85, Leslie E. Robertson Assocs., structural engrs., 1986—; chmn. Coun. on Tall Bldgs. and Urban Habitat; mem. Com. on Natural Disasters; commr., mem. U.S. Nat. Com. for the Decade for Natural Disasters Reduction; dir. Wind Engring. Rsch. Coun.; lectr. Rensselaer Poly. Inst., 1984, Johns Hopkins U., 1985, Nat. Bur. Standards, 1986, Cornell U., Hong Kong U., 1986, Technischische U., Delft, Holland, 1991, 93, Waseda (Japan) U., Musashi Inst. Tech., 1993, others; James L. Sherard lectr. U. Calif., Berkeley, 1991. Author papers in field. Bd. dirs. Architects/Designers/Planners for Social Responsibility; mem. Japan Structural Cons. Assn.; mem. human rights of scientists com. N.Y. Acad. Scis.; mem. U.S. Nat. Com. for Decade for Nat. Disaster Reduction; mem. engring. coll. coun. Cornell U. Served with USNR, 1944-46. Fellow The MacDowell Colony; recipient Inst. Honor award AIA, 1989, Mayor's award for excellence in sci. and tech. Mayor of City of N.Y./N.Y. Acad. Scis., 1993, John R. Parmer award, 1991, Disting. Engring. Alumnus award U. Calif., Berkeley, 1991, Prof. Gengo Matsui prize, Japan, 1993, World Trade Ctr. Individual Svc. medal, 1993, Citation of Excellence, ENR, 1993, named Constrn. Man of Yr., 1989. Fellow ASCE (Raymond C. Reese Rsch. prize 1974), Singapore Structural Steel Soc.; mem. Nat. Acad. Engring. Archtl. League of N.Y. (v.p.), N.Y. Acad. of Scis. (Mayor Award Excellence in Sci. and Tech. 1993, 95), Tokyo Soc. Architects (Disting. Hon. fellow). Home: 45 E 89th St Apt 25C New York NY 10128-1230 Office: 211 E 46th St New York NY 10017-2935

ROBERTSON, LINDA L., federal agency administrator. BS with honors, U. So. Ill., 1976; JD, U. Tulsa, 1979; LLM in Taxation, U. Georgetown, 1986. Bar: Okla. 1980, D.C. 1987. From staff counsel to tax counsel Rep. James Jones, 1976-87; ptnr. Powell, Goldstein, Frazer and Murphy, Washington, 1987-93; dep. asst. sec. legis. affairs Dept. of the Treasury, Washington, 1993—; asst. sec. legis. affairs & public liason Dept. Treasury, Washington. Mem. ABA (taxation sect.). Office: Legis Affairs Treasury Department 15th & Pennsylvania Ave NW Washington DC 20220*

ROBERTSON, MARK WAYNE, investment specialist; b. St. Louis, June 28, 1929; s. Harold LaGrand and Mabel Margaret (Mangels) R.; 1 child, A. Rafael Nuncio. Student, U. Houston, 1949-51. Cost acct. Mo. Pacific Railroad, Houston, 1951-55; contract adminstr. Air Cruisers Co., Belmar, N.J., 1955-57; right of way cons. Tex. Hwy. Dept., Houston, 1957; land mgr. Houston Natural Gas Co., 1957-71; adminstrv. asst. Houston Pile Line Co., 1971-84; real estate broker, investor, 1975—; pvt. practice as investor Kerrville, Tex., 1984—; co-owner several small businesses and distributorships. Profl. artist. Fundraiser John Tower for Senator, Houston, Am. Heart Assn., Houston, 1971-81; officer Mended Hearts Assn., Houston, 1971-81; 2d v.p. Hill County Art Foun., Kerrville, 1989-92, treas., 1990-91, adv. bd. 1996—; sr. mem. Soc. Ambs. St. Joseph Hosp., 1989—; adv. Butt Holdworth Libr., 1991; cultural adviser to mayor. Cpl. U.S. Army, 1951-53. Mem. Internat. Right of Way Assn. (officer 1958-83), Kerrville Art Club (pres. 1990), Art League of Houston, Nat. Soc. Painters in Casein and Acrylic, Allied Artists in Am., River Art Group. Roman Catholic. Avocation: owner of a small ranch resort.

ROBERTSON, MARY LOUISE, archivist, historian; b. L.A., May 19, 1945; d. Snell and Dorothy (Tregoning) R. BA, UCLA, 1966, MA, 1968, PhD, 1975. Teaching asst. dept. history UCLA, 1967-70; acting instr. UCLA Extension, 1973-74; acting instr. dept. history Pepperdine U., L.A., 1970, Calif. State U., Northridge, 1972-73; asst. curator manuscripts Huntington Libr., San Marino, Calif., 1975, assoc. curator, 1977, chief curator, 1979—; adj. prof. English Claremont Grad. Sch., 1994. Author: Guide to British Historical Manuscripts in the Huntington Library, 1982; co-author, editor: Guide to American Historical Manuscripts in the Huntington Library, 1979; contbr. articles on Tudor history to profl. jours. Mabel Wilson Richards dissertation fellow, 1970-72. Mem. Am. Hist. Assn., Soc. Am. Archivists, Soc. Calif. Archivists, N.Am. Conf. on Brit. Studies, Pacific Coast Conf. on Brit. Studies (treas. 1986-88, pres. 1988-90), Phi Beta Kappa. Office: Huntington Libr 1151 Oxford Rd San Marino CA 91108-1218

ROBERTSON, MARY VIRGINIA, retired elementary education educator; b. Lincoln, Nebr., Oct. 1, 1925; d. Dean Leroy and Anna Charlotte (Boge) R. AB in Philosophy and Psychology, U. Nebr., Lincoln, 1949, BS in Elem. Edn., 1953; postgrad., U. Toronto, Ont., Can., 1949. Cert. elem. tchr., Nebr. Country sch. tchr. Lancaster County schs., Nebr., 1943-44, Otoe County schs., Palmyra, Nebr., 1944-45; 3d-5th grade tchr. Palmyra Schs., 1945-46; 3d grade tchr. Valley (Nebr.) Schs., 1953-57, Lincoln Pub. Schs., 1957-81; ret.; leader workshop in field; math. coord. Riley Elem. Sch., Lincoln, 1970-71. Author pamphlet A Letter for You, 1954. Mem. NEA, AAUW, Nebr. State Edn. Assn., Nat. Coun. Math. Tchrs., Am. Child Edn. Internat., Belmont PTA (life), Eastern Star, Lincoln Women's Club. Methodist. Avocations: reading, cats, rocks, bridge, writing children's stories.

ROBERTSON, MICHAEL SWING, religious association administrator; b. Boston, July 20, 1935; s. Charles Stuart and Elizabeth (Swing) R.; m. Margaret Filoon, Sept. 17, 1960 (dec. Oct. 1996); children: Michael Swing, Ashlee Whipple, Christopher Filoon, Andrew Stuart. A.B., Harvard U., 1957, grad. Advanced Mgmt. Program, 1979. With Robertson Factories, Inc., 1957-80, exec. v.p., 1968-73, pres., 1973-79, chmn. bd., 1979-80; dir. Robertson-Swing Co., 1980—; pres. The Berkley Co. Inc., 1981-90, Reactions Inc., 1985-90; treas. Falmouth Marine Inc., 1981-88; pres., treas. Orchard Computer Inc., 1984-91, chmn., treas., 1991-93; exec. sec. Nat. Assn. Congl. Christian Chs., Oak Creek, Wis., 1991—. v.p. adv. coun. Coll. of Bus. and Industry, Southeastern Mass. U., North Dartmouth, Mass., 1979-91; selectman, Town of Berkley, Mass., 1974-80, chmn. 1979-80; mem. Pres.'s Adv. Com. for Trade Negotiations, 1983-86; bd. dirs. Mass. Easter Seal Soc., 1977-91, pres. 1982-83; bd. dirs. Nat. Easter Seal Soc., 1985-91, Wis. Easter Seal Soc., 1994-95; chmn. Berkley Rep. Town com., 1977-91; mem. Pilgrim Congl. Ch., Taunton, North Shore Congrl Ch., Fox Point, Wis.; Rep. nominee U.S. Senate from Mass., 1976, nominee for Mass. state auditor, 1982; co-chmn. Mass. Reagan for Pres. Com., 1980; Bristol County coord. Reagan/Bush campaign; co-chmn. Mass. Dole for Pres. Commn., 1987; chmn. Southeastern Mass. campaign Harvard Coll., 1981; chmn. Friends of Harvard Track, 1986-91; trustee Barnstable County Hosp., 1985-90, chmn., 1988. Mem. Harvard Varsity Club, Harvard Bus. Sch. Alumni Club of Wis. Home: 500 W Bender Rd Unit 51 Milwaukee WI 53217-4173 Office: Nat Assn Congl Christian Ch 8473 S Howell Ave Oak Creek WI 53154-2922 *Accept responsibility with enthusiasm and gratitude. Our individual freedom is unmatched in history, compelling us to remain true to our heritage and our God.*

ROBERTSON, NAT CLIFTON, chemist; b. Atlanta, July 23, 1919; s. Henry Booker and Eura Allen (Williams) R.; m. Elizabeth Bates Peck, Nov. 29, 1946; children: Henry Bartlett, Mary Amanda, Paul Edward. A.B., Emory U., 1939, Sc.D., 1970; Ph.D., Princeton U., 1942. Research asso. OSRD, 1942-43; chemist Standard Oil Co., N.J., 1943-47; group leader Celanese Corp. Am., 1947-51; dir. petrochems. dept. Nat. Research Corp., 1951-55; v.p., dir. research Escambia Chem. Corp., 1955-58; v.p. Spencer Chem. div. Gulf Oil Corp. (formerly Spencer Chem. Co.), Kansas City, Mo., 1958-66, Air Products & Chems., Inc., Allentown, Pa., 1966-69; sr. v.p. Air Products & Chems., Inc., 1969-77, also bd. dirs.; dir. Marion Labs., 1963-89. Trustee Midwest Research Inst.; bd. dirs. Kans. Research Found., 1963-66, pres., 1963-64. Mem. Am. Chem. Soc., Dirs. Indsl. Research, Indsl. Research Inst., Phi Beta Kappa, Sigma Xi. Democrat. Presbyterian. Club: Princeton (N.Y.C.). Home: 156 Philip Dr Princeton NJ 08540-5423

ROBERTSON, OSCAR PALMER (BIG O ROBERTSON), former professional basketball player, chemical company executive; b. Charlotte, Tenn., Nov. 24, 1938. BBBA, U. Cin., 1960. Player U.S. Olympic Basketball Team, 1960; basketball player Cin. Royals, 1960-70, Milw. Bucks, 1970-74; founder, pres., CEO, Orchem, Inc., Cin., 1981—, Orpack-Stone Corp., Herrin, Ill., 1990—, Oscar Robertson Constrn., Indpls., 1975—; player NBA Championship Team, 1971. Named Sporting News Coll. Player of Yr., 1958, 59, 60, Sporting News All-Star Fitrst Team, 1958, 59, 60, NBA Rookie of Yr., 1961, All NBA First Team, 1961-69; player NBA All Star Games, 1961-72; named MVP, NBA, 1964, M VP in NBA All-Star Games, 1961, 64, 69; named to NBA 35th Anniversary All-Star Team, 1980; elected to Naismith Meml. Basketball Hall of Fame, 1979. Office: Orchem Inc 4293 Mulhauser Rd Fairfield OH 45014-5450*

ROBERTSON, PAT (MARION GORDON ROBERTSON), religious broadcasting executive; b. Lexington, Va., Mar. 22, 1930; s. A. Willis and Gladys (Churchill) R.; m. Adelia Elmer; children: Timothy, Elizabeth, Gordon, Ann. BA, Washington and Lee U., 1950; JD, Yale U., 1955; MDiv, N.Y. Theol. Sem., 1959; ThD (hon.), Oral Roberts U., 1983. Ordained minister So. Bapt. Conv., 1961-87. Founder, CEO Christian Broadcast Network, Virginia Beach, Va., 1960—; host 700 Club, 1968—; founder, chancellor Regent Univ. (formerly CBN Univ.), 1977—; founder, chmn. Operation Blessing Internat. Relief and Devel. Inc., 1978—, Internat. Family Entertainment, Inc., 1990—, Asia Pacific Media Corp., 1993—; chmn. Starguide Digital Networks, Inc., 1995—, Porchlight Entertainment, Inc., 1995—; founder, pres. The Christian Coalition, 1989—, The Am. Ctr. for Law and Justice, 1990—; bd. dirs. United Va. Bank, Norfolk; mem. Pres. Task Force on Victims of Crime, Washington, 1982. Author: (with Jamie Buckingham) Shout It From the Housetops: The Story of the Founder of the Christian Broadcasting Network, 1972, My Prayer for You, 1977, The Secret Kingdom, 1982, Answers to 200 of Life's Most Probing Questions, 1984, Beyond Reason, 1984, 85, America's Dates with Destiny, 1986, The Plan, 1989, The New Millennium, 1990, The New World Order, 1991, The End of the Age, 1995. Candidate for Rep. nomination for Pres. U.S., 1988. Recipient Disting. Merit citation NCCJ, Knesset medallion Israel Pilgrimage Com., Faith and Freedom award Religious Heritage Am., Bronze Halo award So. Calif. Motion Picture Council, Humanitarian award Food for the Hungry, 1982, George Washington Honor medal Freedoms Found. at Valley Forge, 1983; named Internat. Clergyman of Yr. Religion in Media, 1981, Man of Yr. Internat. Com. for Goodwill, 1981. Mem. Nat. Broadcasters (bd. dirs. 1973—), Kentucky Colonels. Office: The Christian Broadcasting Network 977 Centerville Tpke Virginia Beach VA 23463-1001*

ROBERTSON, PAUL JOSEPH, lawyer, educator; b. Chgo., Dec. 31, 1963; s. Mary Ellen (Statom) R. BSBA in Mktg., Georgetown U., Washington, 1985; BA in Sociology, St. Leo (Fla.) Coll., 1988; MBA, U. Ill., 1992, JD, 1992. Bar: Ill. 1992, U.S. Dist. Ct. (no. dist.) Ill. 1992, U.S. Ct. Appeals (7th cir.) 1992. Counsel Region V U.S. Dept. Health and Human Svcs., Chgo., 1992-93, staff atty. Social Security Adminstrn., 1993-94; atty. Office Gen. Counsel U.S. Dept. Health and Human Svcs., Bethesda, Md., 1994—; lectr. NIH, Found. for Advanced Edn. in Scis., Bethesda, 1995—; mem. black employees fed. adv. com. NIH, 1994—. Campaign aide, FEC compliance, com. to elect Carol Moseley-Braun for U.S. Senate, Chgo., 1992. 1st lt. USAF, 1985-88. Decorated Air Force Meritorious Medal; recipient Joseph W. Rickert Award for Cmty. Svc., Faculty of Law, U. Ill., 1992. Mem. ABA, Nat. Bar Assn., Chgo. Bar Assn., Am. Legion, Masons. AME Ch. Avocations: Lacrosse, basketball, travel, reading, wine tasting. Office: NIH Bldg 31 Rm 2B-50 Bethesda MD 20892-2111

ROBERTSON, PETER BARRIE, mayor; b. N.Y.C., Nov. 4, 1938; s. Robert Barrie and Rosemary (Mecca) R.; m. Jo-Anne Chalmers; children: Scott, Kirk, Jodi. B Phys. Edn., U. Toronto, Ont., Can., 1961, BA in Psychology, 1964; MEd, Ont. Inst. Studies in Edn., Toronto, 1967. Tchr., coach Etobicoke Bd. Edn., 1962-66; cons. Toronto Bd. Edn., 1967-71; prof. faculty of edn. U. Toronto, 1972-95; councillor City of Brampton, Ont., 1974-91, mayor, 1991—; chmn. Greater Toronto Area Mayor's Com. on Mcpl. Tax Reform, 1994-95; rschr. on assisting street children; spkr. and workshop leader in field. Co-author: Health for Life, 1984, (multimedia kit) Sexually Transmitted Diseases, 1979, (video and teaching kit) Taking Control Family Violence, 1986. Sch. trustee, councillor Castlemore and Toronto Gore, Peel County, 1968-74; mem. nat. edn. nucleus com. Can. Cancer Soc.; founder Castlemore Cmty. Sch., Peel Dist. Health Coun., Victim Svcs. in Peel, Peel Drinking and Driving Awareness Com.; nat. bd. dirs. Inst. Prevention Child Abuse. Recipient Ministry of Health recognition Peel Dist. Health Coun., 1977-84, Silver Pin for Vol. Svc., Can. Cancer Soc., 1979-85, Multi Cultural award North American Sikh League, 1990. Mem. Can. Assn. Phys. Health and Recreation (nat. membership chmn.), Can. Mental Health Assn. (nat. bd. dirs.). Home: 11570 McVean Dr RR 9, Brampton, ON Canada L6T 3Z8 Office: City of Brampton, 2 Wellington St W, Brampton, ON Canada L6Y 4R2

ROBERTSON, RALPH S., secondary school principal. Prin. Richmond Sr. High Sch., Rockingham, N.C. Recipient Blue Ribbon Sch. award U.S. Dept. Edn., 1990-91, Nat. award Dale Parnell Tech. Prep Program of Excellence, 1991; named Prin. of Yr., N.C. Burger King/Nat. Assn. of Secondary Sch. Prin., 1987. Office: Richmond Sr High Sch PO Box 1748 US Hwy 1 North Rockingham NC 28379

ROBERTSON, RICHARD BLAKE, management consultant; b. Ahoskie, N.C., July 28, 1929; s. James Henry and Janie Bell (Baker) R.; m. Elizabeth Parker Gardner, Aug. 19, 1941. BSEE, N.C. State U., 1951; MBA, U. Md., 1956. Design engr. Westinghouse Electric Co., Friendship Airport, Md., 1951-54; product planner Gen. Electric Co., Lynchburg, Pa., 1956-59; dir. mktg. Gen. Motors Corp., Milw., 1959-60; pres. Robertson and Assocs., Pinetops, N.C., 1960—. Mem. Phi Kappa Phi, Tau Beta Pi, Phi Eta Sigma, Theta Tau, Eta Kappa Nu. Office: Robertson & Assocs Inc PO Drawer B Pinetops NC 27864

ROBERTSON, RICHARD EARL, physical chemist, educator; b. Long Beach, Calif., Nov. 12, 1933; s. Earl Austin and A. Isobel (Roberts) R.; m. Joyce W. Conger, Sept. 4, 1955 (div. 1972); children: Christopher, Jill; m. Patricia L. Richmond, Apr. 20, 1974. BA, Occidental Coll., L.A., 1955; student, UCLA, 1955-56; PhD, Calif. Inst. Tech., 1960. Phys. chemist rsch. lab. GE, Schenectady, N.Y., 1960-70; staff scientist Ford Motor Co., Dearborn, Mich., 1970-86; prof. materials sci. and engring. U. Mich., Ann Arbor, 1986—, dir. Macromolecular Sci. and Engring. Ctr., 1995—. Contbr. articles to profl. jours. Postdoctoral fellow Washington U., St. Louis, 1959-60. Fellow Am. Phys. Soc.; mem. Am. Chem. Soc., Sigma Xi. Office: U Mich Dept Materials Sci Eng Ann Arbor MI 48109-2136

ROBERTSON, RICHARD STUART, insurance holding company executive; b. Spokane, Wash., June 14, 1942; s. Stuart A. and Marjory (Moch) R.; m. Trudy Ann Prendergast, July 31, 1976; children: Thomas Stuart, Richard Andrew. BS, Calif. Inst. Tech., 1963. Chief reinsurance actuary Lincoln Nat. Life Ins. Co., Ft. Wayne, Ind., 1963-74; sr. v.p., chief fin. officer Lincoln Nat. Corp., Ft. Wayne, 1974-86, exec. v.p., CFO,, 1986-92, exec. v.p., corp. risk officer, 1992—; bd. dirs. 1st Penn-Pacific, Linsco Reins. Co. Fellow Soc. Actuaries (pres. 1985-86); mem. Am. Acad. Actuaries (v.p. 1980-81), Actuarial Stds. Bd. (chmn. 1996—). Episcopalian. Home: 12618 Aboite Center Rd Fort Wayne IN 46804-9725

ROBERTSON, R(ITA) KAE, nurse, administrator; b. Richland, Wash., Aug. 14, 1954; d. Richard Grant and Rita Ione (Woffinden) R. Diploma, Highland Hosp. Sch. Nursing, Rochester, N.Y., 1978; BSN, Alfred U., 1980; MS, SUNY, Buffalo, 1986; MBA, U. Rochester, 1992. RN, N.Y. Head nurse U. Rochester (N.Y.)-Strong meml. Hosp.; asst. v.p. nursing Highland Hosp., Rochester, 1986-88, v.p. nursing, 1988-93; ptnr. Ernst & Young LLP, Cleve., 1993—. Mem. Am. Orgn. Nurse Execs., Western N.Y. League Nursing (bd. dirs.).

ROBERTSON, ROBBIE, musician, popular; b. Toronto, 1943. Guitarist Ronnie Hawkins and The Hawks, 1959-63, The Hawks, 1963-65, The Band (with Bob Dylan), 1965-68; guitarist, songwriter The Band, 1968-76; solo performer, 1976—. Albums: (with The Band) Music from Big Pink, 1968, The Band, 1969, Stage Fright, 1970, Cahoots, 1971, Rock of Ages, 1972, Moondog Matinee, 1973, Northern Lights—Southern Cross, 1975, The Best of The Band, 1976, Islands, 1977, The Last Waltz, 1978, Anthology, 1978, (with Bob Dylan) Planet Waves, 1974, Before the Flood, 1974, The Basement Tapes, 1975, (solo) Robbie Robertson, 1987, Storyville, 1991, Robbie Robertson and the Red Road Ensemble Music for the Native Americans, 1994; record prodr. for artists including: Neil Diamond, Jesse Winchester, Hirth Martinez; exec. prodr.: Casino soundtrack, 1995, Phenomenon soundtrack, 1996; film composer: Raging Bull, 1980, The King of Comedy, 1983, The Color of Money, 1986; appearances in films, prodr.: The Last Waltz, 1978, Carny, 1980; appeared in film: The Crossing Guard, 1996. Group The Band inducted into Rock & Roll Hall of Fame, 1994. Office: Capitol Records 1750 Vine St Hollywood CA 90028-5209*

ROBERTSON, ROBERT GORDON, retired Canadian government official; b. Davidson, Sask., Can., May 19, 1917; s. John Gordon and Lydia Adelia (Paulson) R.; m. Beatrice Muriel Lawson, Aug. 14, 1943; children: John Lawson, Karen Martha. B.A., U. Sask., 1938; B.A. Juris, Oxford U., 1940, D.C.L., 1983; M.A., U. Toronto, 1941; L.L.D., U. Sask., 1959, McGill U., 1963, U. Toronto, 1973, U. Dalhousie, 1977; Di de l'univ., U. Laval, 1975,

Ottawa U., 1982, Carleton U., 1990. Mem. staff Dept. External Affairs, Govt. of Can., 1941-45; sec. to Office of Prime Minister, 1945-49; mem. staff Privy Council Office, 1949-53; dep. minister of No. Affairs and Nat. Resources; commr. Northwestern Territories, 1953-63; clk. Privy Council, sec. to cabinet, 1963-75, sec. to cabinet for fed.-provincial relations, 1975-79; chancellor Carleton U., 1980-90; ret., 1990; mem. Queen's Privy Coun. for Can., 1982. Decorated Companion of Order of Can. Fellow Royal Soc. Can. Mem. United Ch. of Can. Home: 20 Westward Way, Ottawa, ON Canada K1L 5A7

ROBERTSON, ROBERT GRAHAM HAMISH, physicist; b. Ottawa, Ont., Can., Oct. 3, 1943; came to U.S., 1971; s. Hugh Douglas and Alice Madeleine (Bell) R.; m. Peggy Lynn Dyer, July 4, 1980; 1 child, Ian. BA, MA, Oxford (Eng.) U., 1965; PhD, McMaster U., Hamilton, Ont., Can., 1971. Rsch. assoc. Mich. State U., East Lansing, 1971-72, asst. rsch. prof., 1972-73, asst. prof., 1973-78, assoc. prof., 1978-81, prof., 1981-82; mem. staff Los Alamos (N.Mex.) Nat. Lab., 1981—, fellow, 1988—; prof. U. Washington, Seattle, 1994—; rsch. assoc. Princeton (N.J.) U., 1975-76; vis. scientist Argonne (Ill.) Nat. Lab., 1979, Chalk River (Ont., Can.) Nuclear Lab., 1980. Contbr. over 40 articles to profl. jours. Alfred P. Sloan Found. fellow Mich. State U., 1976; Trevelyan scholar Eng., 1962-65, NRC scholar McMaster U., 1965-69, Oriel Coll. scholar, 1962-65. Fellow Am. Phys. Soc. (Tom W. Bonner prize 1997); mem. Inst. Physics of Eng. (assoc.), Can. Assn. Physicists. Achievements include first observation of nuclear isobaric quintet; development of technique for precise measurement of neutrino mass, determination of Lithium-6 synthesis in early universe. Office: Dept Physics U Washington Seattle WA 98195

ROBERTSON, RUTH ANN, systems analyst, engineer; b. Oak Ridge, Tenn., Nov. 20, 1959; d. Arnold Powell and Beatrice (Lazaroff) L. BME, Ga. Inst. Tech., 1982; postgrad., U. Redlands, Calif., 1991. Engring. intern IBM, Gaithersburg, Md., 1980-81; packaging engr. Hughes Aircraft Co., El Segundo, Calif., 1982-85; field engr. Spectrum Control, Inc., Valencia, Calif., 1985-86; pres. Precision Jaunt, El Segundo, 1986-87; sr. systems analyst Marquardt Co., Van Nuys, Calif., 1987-91, Axcom Computer Cons., Springfield, Mo., 1991-92; open systems product mgr. DataTrade, Inc., Springfield, 1992-96; mgr.product realization Dayco Products, Inc., Springfield, 1996—. Mem. Whitehead Leadership Soc., Tau Beta Pi, Phi Tau Sigma. Office: Dayco Products Inc Tech Ctr 2601 W Battlefield St Springfield MO 65807-4009

ROBERTSON, SAMUEL LUTHER, JR., special education educator, therapist; b. Houston, Apr. 28, 1940; s. Sam L. and Portia Louise (Burns) R.; children: Samuel Luther IV, Sean Lee (dec.), Ryan William, Susan Elizabeth (dec.), Henry Philmore. BS, McMurry U., 1969; MA, Hardin-Simmons U., 1973; PhD, U. Tex., 1993. Cert. tchr., adminstr., counselor, Tex.; lic. chem. dependency counselor, lic. clin. mental health counselor, alcoholism and drug counselor, Tex. Instr., coach, athletic dir. Tex. and La. schs., 1969-94; social worker, supr. Children's Protective Svcs., Abilene, Tex., 1978-79; instr., adminstr. Harlandale Sch. Dist., San Antonio, 1980-84, 87-90; adminstr. night sch. Harlandale Ind. Sch. Dist., San Antonio, 1988-89; instr. Edgewood Ind. Sch. Dist., San Antonio, 1985-87; developer, instr., integrated unit program San Antonio, 1990—; CEO The Educative Inst., San Antonio, 1992—; CEO Educative Therapeutic Processes, San Antonio, 1972—. Author: (play) The Challenged, 1965: (poem) Trains in the Night, 1969. State co-chmn. Youth for Kennedy-Johnson, Tex., 1960; mem. W. Tex. Dem. Steering Com., Abilene, 1962-63; founding dir. Way Off Broadway Community Theater, Eagle Pass, Tex., 1971-72; founding bd. dirs. Battered Women's Shelter, Abilene, 1978-79; v.p. bd. dirs. Mental Health Assn., San Antonio, 1980-83, bd. dirs Palmer Drug Abuse Program, San Antonio, 1985-87; pres., bd. dir. Alcoholic Rehab. Ctr., 1985-86, 1987-92; mem., vice chmn. Civilian and Mil. Addictive Programs, San Antonio, 1991-92; author, implementer Community Vitalization Program, 1994—. Named Tchr. of Yr. Southside Ind. Sch. Dist., San Antonio, 1970-71, Harlandale Alternative Ctr., San Antonio, 1987-88; Vol. of Yr., Mental Health Assn., San Antonio, 1982, Alcoholic Rehab. Ctr., San Antonio, 1992-93. Mem. ACA, NEA, Am. Mental Health Counseling Assn., Tex. State Tchrs. Assn., Am. Ednl. Rsch. Assn., Am. Assn. Sch. Adminstrs., Tex. Assn. Alcoholism and Drug Abuse Counselors, Nat. Alcoholism and Drug Abuse Counselors, N.Mex. Mental Health Counselors Assn., N.Mex. Profl. Counselors Assn., Phi Kappa Phi, Kappa Delta Pi. Episcopalian. Avocations: reading, writing, travel, theater, sports. Home: 14015 Big Tree San Antonio TX 78247 Office: Educative Therapeutic Processes 339 E Hildebrand Ave San Antonio TX 78212-2412 *I have participated in my life, my family's life, and my community's life in a responsible fashion through the Grace of God.*

ROBERTSON, SARA STEWART, portfolio manager; b. N.Y.C., Feb. 4, 1940; d. John Elliott and Mary Terry (Schlamp) Stewart; m. James Young Robertson, Nov. 29, 1975 (dec. Mar. 1988). BA, Conn. Coll., 1961; MBA, Am. U., 1969. From trainee to officer First Nat. Bank/First Chgo. Corp., 1969-75, v.p., 1975-92; prin. Royall Enterprises, Chgo., 1992—; prin., dir. Zeppelin Press, Inc., Miami, Fla., 1995—; bd. dirs. Youth Guidance, Chgo., 1982-85, 92-95, chair individuals fundraising, mem. exec. com., 1993-95. Bd. dirs. Harbor House Condominium Assn. Chgo., 1990-92; bd. trustees Sherwood Conservatory Music, 1993—, chair bd. devel., 1993-95; mem. allocations com. and family priority grants com. United Way-Chgo., 1992-95, resource devel. com., 1996—. Mem. Club 13 Palm Beach (pres. 1996—). Home and Office: 122 Peruvian Ave PH Palm Beach FL 33480-4477

ROBERTSON, STEWART, conductor; b. Glasgow, Scotland; m. Meryl Owen; children: Keren, Niel. Music dir. Glimmerglass Summer Opera Festival, 1988; past music dir., prin. condr. Santa Fe (N.Mex.) Symphony; music dir. Inland Empire Symphony Orchestra, San Bernardino, Calif.; guest condr. BBC Scottish Symphony, Ukraine State Philharmonic, Buenos Aires Philharmonic, Lille Festival, Fla. Philharmonic, Louisville Orchestra, Chgo. Lyric, N.Y.C. Opera, Cologne, Zurich, Scottish Opera, recordings Verdi-EMI. Home: 81 Poppy Rd Carmel Valley CA 93924-9619 Office: Inland Empire SympOrchestra 362 W Court St San Bernardino CA 92401-1608*

ROBERTSON, SUSAN JOYCE COE, special education educator; b. Pinedale, Wyo., May 22, 1954; d. Cecil James and Geraldine Ada (Greene) Coe; children: Jamie Michelle, Mark David. BS in Edn., Chadron (Nebr.) State Coll., 1976, MS in Counseling and Guidance, 1977; specialist in emotionally disturbed, U. No. Colo., 1982. Cert. crisis prevention intervention master trainer, peer mediation facilitator. Elem. tchr. pub. schs., Alliance, Nebr., 1976-77; social worker Community Action, Cheyenne, Wyo., 1978-79; Chpt. 1 tchr. Laramie County Sch. Dist. 1, Cheyenne, 1979-81, elem. tchr., 1981-84, tchr. severely emotionally disturbed, 1984-89, cons., specialist for severely emotionally disturbed, 1989-92, behavior intervention team specialist, 1992-95, tchr. learning disabled, 1995—; mem. Dist. Placement Com., 1981-92. Mem. Cmty. Commn., Cheyenne, 1981-92; basketball coach YMCA, 1994; deacon Presbyn. Ch. Mem. NEA, Am. Guidance and Counseling Assn., Coun. for Exceptional Children (faculty adviser 1991), Wyo. Edn. Assn., Cheyenne Tchr. Edn. Assn., Trailblazer Parent Assn., PEO. Presbyterian. Avocations: reading, swimming, racquetball, music. Home: 5425 Gateway Dr Cheyenne WY 82009-4035 Office: 6000 Education Dr Cheyenne WY 82009-3991

ROBERTSON, SUZANNE MARIE, primary education educator; b. Canton, Ohio, Nov. 21, 1944; d. Jules Michael and Emma Louise (Olmar) Franzen; m. William K. Robertson, June 30, 1973 (dec. 1979). BS in Early Childhood Edn., Kent State U., 1966; M in Early Childhood Edn., Southern Conn. U., 1976; postgrad., Fairfield U. and U. Bridgeport, 1981-82. Kindergarten tchr. Ridgefield (Conn.) Bd. Edn., 1966—, Internat. Sch. Basel, Switzerland, 1993-94; children's gymnastics instr. Ridgefield (Conn.) YMCA, 1982-83, Sherman Parks and Recreation, Conn., 1983-85; mem. com., facilitator Young Writer's Conf., Ridgefield, Conn., 1996. Toy designer; mem. nat. adv. bd. Learning Mag. Campaign vol. Cancer Fund of Am., Sherman, 1980-81. Awarded Honorable Mention Learning Mag., 1989; recipient Profl. Best Teaching awards. Mem. NEA, Tchrs. Assn. Supporting Children (chmn. 1986-89, Fairfield County pub. rels. com. 1986-89), Conn. Edn. Assn., Internat. Platform Assn., Sherman Hist. Soc., Phi Delta Kappa (historian 1989-90, rsch. rep. 1990-91). Avocations: collector children's books, water color painting, photography, winter skiing. Office: Farmingville Elem Sch 324 Farmingville Rd Ridgefield CT 06877-4241

ROBERTSON, TED ZANDERSON, judge; b. San Antonio, Sept. 28, 1921; s. Irion Randolf and Aurelia (Zanderson) R.; m. Margie Gardner. Student, Tex. A&I, 1940-42; LL.B., St. Mary's U., San Antonio, 1949. Bar: Tex. 1949. Chief civil dept. Dist. Atty.'s Office, Dallas County, Tex., 1960-65; judge Probate Ct. 2, Dallas County, 1965-69, Juvenile Ct. 2, Dallas County, 1969-75, 95th Dist. Ct., Dallas County, 1975-76, Ct. Civil Appeals, 5th Supreme Jud. Dist., Dallas, 1976-82, Supreme Ct. Tex., Austin, 1982; of counsel Frank Branson P.C., Dallas, 1989—; guest lectr. So. Meth. U., Dallas, Dallas County Juvenile Bd., Tex. Coll. of the Judiciary, 1970-82. Active Dallas Assn. for Retarded Children; active Dallas County Commn. on Alcoholism, Dallas County Mental Health Assn. Served as yeoman USCG, 1942-46. Recipient Golden Gavel St. Mary's U., San Antonio, 1979; named Outstanding Alumnus St. Mary's U., 1981. Mem. Am. Judicature Soc., Tex. Bar Assn., Dallas Bar Assn., Dallas County Juvenile Bd. Democrat. Methodist. Lodges: Masons; Lions. Home: 6233 Highgate Ln Dallas TX 75214-2157 Office: Frank Branson 4514 Cole Ave Ste 1800 Dallas TX 75205-4185

ROBERTSON, TIMOTHY B., cable television executive; b. 1954. With Christian Broadcasting Network, Inc., Virginia Beach, Va.; with Internat. Family Entertainment, Inc., Virginia Beach, 1989—, pres., CEO. Office: Internat Family Entertainment 2877 Guardian Ln Virginia Beach VA 23452-7328

ROBERTSON, TIMOTHY JOEL, statistician, educator; b. Denver, Oct. 4, 1937; s. Flavel P. and Helen C. (Oliver) Girdner; m. Joan K. Slater, Aug. 18, 1959; children—Kelly, Jana, Doug, Mike. B.A. in Math., U. Mo., 1959, M.S. in Math., 1961, Ph.D. in Stats., 1966. Asst. prof. Cornell Coll., Mt. Vernon, Iowa, 1961-63; prof. stats. U. Iowa, Iowa City, 1965—; vis. prof. U. N.C., Chapel Hill, 1974-75, U. Calif.-Davis, 1983-84; Eugene Lukacs Disting. vis. prof. Bowling Green State U., 1991-92; vis. lectr. Com. Pres. Statis. Soc., 1971-74. Author: (with F.T. Wright and R.L. Dykstra) Order Restricted Statistical Inference; assoc. editor Am. Math. Monthly, 1977-81; mem. editl. bd. Comms. in Stats., 1981-92; assoc. editor Jour. Am. Statis. Assn., 1990-96; contbr. numerous articles to profl. jours. Recipient Collegiate Teaching award U. Iowa, 1990. Fellow Am. Statis. Assn. (council 1974-75), Inst. Math. Stats., Internat. Statis. Inst.; mem. Math. Assn. Am., Sigma Xi, Sierra Club. Democrat. Avocations: canoeing, camping, bicycling, walking. Home: 1811 Kathlin Dr Iowa City IA 52246-4617 Office: University of Iowa Dept Stats/Actuarial Sci Iowa City IA 52242

ROBERTSON, VICKI DAWN, adminstrative secretary, writer; b. Miami, Okla., May 17, 1961; d. Elmer Dewitt and Wanda Jean (Stanley) Wynn; m. Stephen Matthew Robertson, June 9, 1984; 1 child, Christopher Michael. AA, Northeastern Okla. A&M U., 1981; BA, Okla. Bapt. U., 1984. Vol. Bapt. Student Union dir. Mission Svc. Corps. So. Bapts., San Francisco, 1984-86; pharmacy technician St. Francis Hosp., Tulsa, Okla., 1986-88; adminstrv. sec. The Williams Cos., Tulsa, Okla., 1988—. Active Chinese children's ministry Nichols Hills Bapt. Ch., Oklahoma City, 1982; Sunday sch. tchr., summer camp tchr. First Assembly, Miami, Okla., 1994; asst. Acteens leader First Bapt. Ch., Miami, 1983-84; active hosp. and deaf ministry Victory Christian Ctr., Tulsa, 1990-92; notary pub. Tulsa County, 1996; fund raising vol. United Way, Tulsa, 1992-94, Muscular Dystrophy Assn., Tulsa, 1995-96. Mem. Williams Office Network, Nat. African Violet Soc., Ministerial Alliance, Phi Theta Kappa. Avocations: growing violets, reading, camping, 4-wheel driving, gardening. Home: 4209 E 85th Tulsa OK 74137 Office: The Williams Cos PO Box 2848 Tulsa OK 74101

ROBERTSON, WILLIAM FRANKLIN, publishing executive; b. Richmond, Va., Sept. 1, 1917; s. Joseph William and Nancy Lucretia (Brooks) R.; m. Avis Dorothy Stillman, Aug. 7, 1943; children: Lynne Brooks, William Elden. BS, U. Richmond, 1938. Mgr. office Richmond Newspapers, Inc., 1941-46, credit mgr., contr., 1946-66, asst. treas., 1966-68, treas., asst. sec., 1968-87, cons., 1987-94; v.p., treas., asst. sec. Media Gen., Inc., 1977-87; cons. 1987-94. Past trustee Va. Bapt. Homes; trustee, treas. Bapt. Mins. Relief Fund Va.; endowment fund trustee Richmond Bapt. Assn. Mem. Inst. Newspaper Contrs. and Fin. Officers (past dir.), Adminstrv. Mgmt. Soc. (pres. Richmond chpt. 1964-65), Fin. Execs. Inst., Phi Delta Theta. Avocation: private pilot. Home: 4 Ralston Rd Richmond VA 23229-8022 Office: 333 E Grace St Richmond VA 23293-1000

ROBERTSON, WILLIAM RICHARD, banker, holding company executive; b. Schenectady, N.Y., July 26, 1941; s. Bruce Manson and Mary Jo (Gillam) R.; m. Sarah Reed Parker, June 20, 1964; children: Deborah Graham, John William, Julie Elizabeth. AB, Colgate U., 1964; MBA, Case Western Res. U., 1967. Nat. City Bank/Nat. City Corp., 1964—; Exec. v.p., chief fin. officer Nat. City Corp., Cleve., 1982-89, dep. chmn. bd. dirs., 1986-95; pres., 1995—; bd. dirs. Nat. City Corp., Kirtland Capital Corp. Trustee Coll. of Wooster, Ohio, 1982-91, Fairmount Presbyn. Ch., Cleve., 1983-86, St. Luke's Hosp., Cleve., 1984-97, Cleve. Ballet, 1985-89, United Way, 1986-97, Karamu House, 1988-95, Western Res. Hist. Soc., 1990—, Cleve. Mus. Art, 1991—, Salvation Army, 1985—, chmn. adv. bd., 1991-93; pres., trustee Big Bros. and Big Sisters, Cleve., 1973-80; chmn., bd. trustees United Way of Cleve., 1995-97, trustee Musical Arts Assn., 1994—, chmn. vis. com. of Case Western Res. U. Weatherhead Sch. Mgmt., 1995-97. Mem. Fin. Execs. Inst., Bankers Roundtable, Am. Bankers Assn., Cleve. Skating Club (pres. 1980-82), Union Club, Country Club, Pepper Pike Club, Ottawa Club, Desert Mountain Club. Republican. Avocations: travel, skiing, shooting, golf, history. Home: 2700 Chesterton Rd Shaker Heights OH 44122-1805 Office: Nat City Corp Nat City Ctr 1900 E 9th St Cleveland OH 44114-3401

ROBERTSON, WILLIAM WITHERS, lawyer; b. Morristown, N.J., Nov. 3, 1941; s. Thomas Withers and Jessie (Swain) R.; children: Barbara Ellen, William Withers, Jessie Swain. B.A., Rutgers U., 1964, LL.B., 1967. Bar: N.J. 1968. Law sec. to judge Superior Ct. N.J., 1967-68; asst. U.S. atty., 1972-76, 1st asst. U.S. atty., 1978-80; U.S. atty. Dist. N.J., 1980-81; chief Newark Organized Crime Strike Force, 1976-78; ptnr. firm Hannoch Weisman, Roseland, N.J., 1981—. Mng. editor Rutgers Law Rev., 1966-67. Trustee Rutgers U., 1984-88. Served to capt. JAGC USAR, 1968-72. Mem. Nat. Assn. Former U.S. Attys. (bd. dirs. 1990-93), Rutgers U. Law Sch. Alumni Assn. (pres. 1990-91), Rutgers U. Alumni Fedn. (pres. 1981-83). Office: Hannoch Weisman PO Box 1040 Newark NJ 07101-1040 also: Hannoch Weisman 4 Becker Farm Rd Roseland NJ 07068

ROBERTSON, WILLIAM WRIGHT, JR., orthopedic surgeon educator; b. Mayfield, Ky., Dec. 26, 1946; s. William Wright and Dorothy Frances (Beadles) R.; m. Karel Virginia Dierks, Jan. 26, 1974; children: Anna Elizabeth, Claire Alexandra. BA, Rhodes Coll., 1968; MD, Vanderbilt U., 1972. Intern U. Calif., San Diego, 1972-73, resident, 1975-76; resident Vanderbilt U., Nashville, 1976-79; asst. prof. orthopedics Tex. Tech U., Lubbock, 1979-86; assoc. prof. U. Pa., Phila., 1986-90; prof. orthopedic surgery George Washington U., Washington, 1990—; chair pediatric orthopedics Children's Nat. Med. Ctr., Washington, 1990—. Lt. USN, 1973-75. Fellow AMA, Am. Acad. Orthopedic Surgeons, Am. Acad. Cerebralpalsy Devel. Medicine, Am. Acad. Pediatrics, Am. Orthopedic Assn., Pediatric Orthopedic Soc. (bd. dirs. 1993—). Avocations: gardening, music. Office: Childrens Nat Med Ctr 111 Michigan Ave NW Washington DC 20010-2916

ROBERTSON, WYNDHAM GAY, university official; b. Salisbury, N.C., Sept. 25, 1937; d. Julian Hart and Blanche Williamson (Spencer) R. AB in Econs., Hollins Coll., Roanoke, Va., 1958. Rsch. asst. Standard Oil Co., N.Y.C., 1958-61; rschr. Fortune Mag., N.Y.C., 1961-67, assoc. editor, 1968-74, bd. of editors, 1974-81, asst. mng. editor, 1981-86; bus. editor Time Mag., N.Y.C., 1982-83; v.p. comm. U. N.C., Chapel Hill, 1986-96; bd. dirs. Wachovia Corp., Media Gen. Inc. Contbr. numerous articles to Fortune Mag. Bd. dirs. Mary Reynolds Babcock Found.; trustee U. N.C. Ctr. for Pub. TV.; trustee Thomas S. Kenan Inst. for the Arts, Nat. Humanities Ctr., Hollins Coll., chair. Recipient Gerald M. Loeb Achievement award, U. of Conn., 1972. Mem. Phi Beta Kappa. Episcopalian.

ROBEY, KATHLEEN MORAN (MRS. RALPH WEST ROBEY), civic worker; b. Boston, Aug. 9, 1909; d. John Joseph and Katherine (Berrigan) Moran; B.A., Trinity Coll., Washington, 1933; m. Ralph West Robey, Jan. 28, 1941. Actress appearing in Pride and Prejudice, Broadway, 1935, Tomorrow is a Holiday, road co., 1935, Death Takes a Holiday, road co., 1936, Left Turn, Broadway, 1936, Come Home to Roost, Boston, 1936; pub. relations N.Y. Fashion Industry, N.Y.C., 1938-43. Mem. Florence Crittenton Home and Hosp., Women's Aux. Salvation Army, Gray Lady, ARC; mem. Seton Guild St. Ann's Infant Home. Mem. Christ Child Soc., Fedn. Republican Women of D.C. English-Speaking Union. Republican. Roman Catholic. Clubs: City Tavern, Cosmos (Washington), Nat. Woman's Republican. Home: 4000 Cathedral Ave NW Washington DC 20016-5249

ROBEY, SHERIE GAY SOUTHALL GORDON, secondary education educator, consultant; b. Washington, July 7, 1954; d. James Edward and Gene Elizabeth (Gray) Southall; children: m. Robert Jean Claude Robey; children: Michael Aaron Gordon, Robert Eugene Robey, Jamie Lea Robey. BS, U. Md., 1976; MA in Edn. and Human Devel., George Washington U., 1988. Tchr. Esperanza Mid. Sch., Hollywood, Md., 1980-84, Chopticon High Sch., Morganza, Md., 1984—; coach Odyssey of the Mind, 1985-95; sponsor Future Tchrs. Am., Morganza, 1990—, S.H.O.P/S.A.D.D., Morganza, 1990—; cons. Ednl. Cosn., Waldorf, 1980—; pres. BNA Swim Team, 1992—; driver edn. classroom and lab instr. Choptican High Sch. Mem. Ednl. Rep. Assn. St. Mary's County, Lighthouse Hist. Soc. Methodist. Avocations: swimming, writing, visiting lighthouses, collection miniature lighthouses. Home and Office: 11181 Carroll Dr Waldorf MD 20601-2656

ROBFOGEL, SUSAN SALITAN, lawyer; b. Rochester, N.Y., Apr. 4, 1943; d. Victor and Janet (Rosenthal) Salitan; m. Nathan Joshua Robfogel, July 12, 1965; children: Jacob Morris, Samuel Salitan. BA cum laude, Smith Coll., 1964; JD, Cornell U., 1967. Bar: N.Y.1967, U.S. Dist. Ct. (we. dist.) 1968, U.S. Ct. Appeals (2d cir.) 1971, U.S. Supreme Ct. 1971, U.S. Dist. Ct. (no. dist.) 1974, D.C. 1982. Asst. corp. counsel, then sr. asst. corp. counsel City of Rochester, N.Y., 1967-70; assoc. Harris, Beach & Wilcox, Rochester, 1970-75; ptnr. Harris, Beach, Wilcox, Rubin & Levey, Rochester, 1975-85; ptnr., chair health svcs. practice Nixon, Hargrave, Devans & Doyle, LLP, Rochester, 1985—; panel mem., Fed. Svc. Impasses Panel, Washington, 1983-94; mem., past chair Data Protection Rev. Bd., Albany, N.Y., 1984—. Mem. trustees vis. com. U. Rochester Med. Sch., 1990; mem. mgmt. adv. panel SUNY, 1990. Recipient Brockport Coll. Found. Community award, 1989. Fellow Am. Bar Found., N.Y. State Bar Found., Coll. Labor and Employment Lawyers; mem. ABA, N.Y. State Bar Assn., Washington D.C. Bar Assn., Monroe County Bar Assn. (Rodenbeck award 1988). Home: 1090 Park Ave Rochester NY 14610-1728 Office: Nixon Hargrave Devans & Doyle LLP Clinton Sq PO Box 1051 Rochester NY 14603-1051 also: 437 Madison Ave New York NY 10022

ROBICHAUD, FERNAND, Canadian government official. Sec. of state for parliamentary affairs Govt. of Can., 1993—. Office: Sec of State, 507 Confederation Bldg, Ottawa, ON Canada K1A 0A6*

ROBICHAUD, LOUIS JOSEPH, Canadian senator; b. St. Anthony, N.B., Oct. 21, 1925; s. Amedee and Annie (Richard) R.; m. Lorraine Savoie, Aug. 9, 1951; children: Jean Claude (dec.), Paul, Louis-Rene, Monique. B.A., Sacred Heart U., 1947, Dr. Polit. Sci., 1960; postgrad., Laval U., 1947-49; LL.D., U. N.B., 1960, St. Joseph's U., 1961, U. Montreal, 1961, U. Ottawa, 1962, St. Dunstan's U., 1964, U. St. Thomas, 1965, McGill U., 1967, Dalhousie U., 1969; D.C.L., Mt. Allison U., 1961, Moncton U., 1973. Bar: N.B. bar, Queen's counsel 1960. Practiced in Richibucto, N.B., 1952-60; mem. N.B. Legislature, 1952-71, financial critic, 1957-58, leader of opposition, 1958-60, 70-71, premier, 1960-70, atty. gen. N.B., 1960-65; minister of youth, 1968-70; mem. Privy Council, 1967—; chmn. Canadian sect. Internat. Joint Commn., 1971-73; summoned to Senate of Can., 1973—; leader Liberal Party of N.B., 1958-71. Past pres. Ottawa Valley chpt. Kidney Found. Can., bd. dirs. found. Decorated companion Order of Canada; recipient gold medal Laval U. Alumni Assn., 1963. Mem. N.B. Barristers Soc. Mem. Liberal Party. Roman Catholic. Home: 7 Pineland Ave, Nepean, ON Canada K2G 0E5 Office: Senate of Ont, 266 East Block, Ottawa, ON Canada K1A 0A4

ROBIE, JOAN, elementary school principal. Prin. Monteith Elem. Sch., Grosse Pointe, Mich. Recipient Elem. Sch. Recognition award U.S. Dept. Edn., 1989-90. Office: Monteith Elem Sch 1275 Cook Rd Grosse Pointe MI 48236-2511

ROBILLARD, LUCIENNE, federal official; b. Montreal, Canada. BA, Coll. Basile-Moreau, 1965; MA in Social Work, U. Montreal, 1967; Diploma in Adminstrn., École des hautes études commerciales, Montreal, 1983, MBA, 1986. Social worker, clin. practitioner Maisonneuve-Rosemont Hosp.; sr. adminstr. Centre de svcs. sociaux Richelieu; youth leader in a kibutz Israel, 1969-72; apptd. pub. curator City of Quebec, Canada, 1986-89; elected mem. Quebec Nat. Assembly for Chambly, 1989; apptd. min. cultural affairs, 1989-90, apptd. min. higher edn. and science, 1990-92, apptd. min. of edn., 1992-93, min. edn. and science, 1993-94, min. health and social svcs., 1994-95; elected mem. parliament Saint-Henri-Westmount, 1995—; min. citizenship and immigration, 1996—; mem. Corp. professionelle des travailleurs sociaux de Québec, 1967—; mem. editl. com. (book) Le travail social et la santé au Québec, 1984-86; pres. Commn. adminstrv. des svcs. de santé mentale de Conseil régional de la Montérégie, 1983-86; cons. mental health dossier Rochon Commn., 1986. Office: 365 Laurier Ave W 21st Flr, Ottawa, ON Canada K1A 1L1

ROBIN, CLARA NELL (CLAIRE ROBIN), English language educator; b. Harrisonburg, Va., Feb. 19, 1945; d. Robert Franklin and Marguerite Ausherman (Long) Wampler; m. Phil Camden Branner, June 10, 1967 (div. May 1984); m. John Charles Robin, Nov. 22, 1984 (div. Dec. 1990). BA in English, Mary Washington Coll., 1967; MA in English, James Madison U., 1974; postgrad., Jesus Coll., Cambridge, Eng., 1982, Princeton U., 1985-86; Auburn U., 1988, U. No. Tex., 1990-91. Cert. tchr. English, French, master cert., Tex. Tchr. 7th grade John C. Myers Intermediate Sch., Broadway, Va., 1967-68; tchr. 10th grade Waynesville (Mo.) H.S., 1968-70; tchr. 6th, 7th, 8th grades Mary Mount Jr. Sch., Santa Barbara, Calif., 1970-72; tchr. 9th grade Forest Meadow Jr. H.S. Richardson (Tex.) Ind. Sch. Dist., 1972-78, tchr. 10th grade Lake Highlands H.S., 1972-84; tchr. 11th, 12th grades Burleson (Tex.) H.S. Burleson Ind. Sch. Dist., 1986—; instr. composition Hill Coll., 1992-94. Contbg. author: (book revs.) English Journal, 1989-94, (lit. criticism) Eric, 1993. Vol. Dallas Theater Ctr., 1990-96; mem. Kimbell Art Mus., Ft. Worth, 1990—, Modern Art Mus., Ft. Worth, 1992—, KERA Pub. TV, Dallas, 1990—. Fellow NEH, 1988, 89, 92, 95, Fulbright-Hays Summer Seminar, 1991; ind. study grantee Coun. Basic Edn., 1990; recipient Honorable Mention Tex. Outstanding Tchg. of the Humanities award, 1995. Mem. ASCD, NEA, Nat. Coun. Tchrs. English, Tex. State Tchrs. Assn., Epsilon Nu of Delta Kappa Gamma (1st v.p. 1988-94, v.p. 1992-94). Avocations: bicycling, traveling, reading, writing, theater. Home: 4009 W 6th St Fort Worth TX 76107-1619 Office: Burleson High Sch 517 SW Johnson Ave Burleson TX 76028-5312

ROBIN, RICHARD C., lawyer; b. Brownwood, Tex., July 12, 1945; s. Milton and Bernice F. (Fine) R.; children: Gregory, Max. B.A., Tulane U.; J.D., DePaul U. Bar: Ill. 1970, U.S. Dist. Ct. (no. dist.) Ill. 1971, U.S. Ct. Appeals (6th cir.), U.S. Ct. Appeals (7th cir.), Trial Bar (no. dist.) Ill. 1982. With civil trial div. Ill. Atty. Gen. Office, Chgo., 1970-74; assoc. firm Vedder Price Kaufman & Kammholz, Chgo., 1974-76, ptnr., 1976—. Mem. ABA, (com. on litigation), Chgo. Bar Assn. Office: Vedder Price Kaufman & Kammholz 222 N La Salle St Chicago IL 60601-1002

ROBIN, RICHARD SHALE, philosophy educator; b. Stamford, Conn., Apr. 18, 1926; s. Edwin Joseph and Eva (Effron) R.; m. Joann Wilma Cohan, Jan. 29, 1961; children: David Seth, Deborah Elizabeth. B.A., Harvard U., 1948, Ph.D., 1958. Instr. philosophy U. Conn., Storrs, 1958-62; asst. prof. Mt. Holyoke Coll., South Hadley, Mass., 1962-66; assoc. prof. Mt. Holyoke Coll., 1966-71, prof., 1971—, chmn. dept., 1968-83; mem. grad. faculty U. Mass. at Amherst, 1963—. Co-editor, co-author: Studies in the Philosophy of Charles Sanders Peirce, 1963, From Time and Chance to Consciousness, 1994; editor: Annotated Catalogue of the Papers of Charles S. Peirce, 1967; editor trans.: Charles S. Peirce Soc., bd. advs.; Peirce edit. project; bd. cons. Arisbe Papers; mem. editorial bd. Jour. Speculative Philosophy; adv. bd. The Peirce Seminar Papers. Grantee Harvard, 1960-61, Henry P. Kendall Found., 1962, Mt. Holyoke Coll., 1969-70, 75-76; Danforth assoc., 1967—; John Dewey sr. research scholar, 1983-84; Fulbright sr. lectr. Tohoku U., 1984-85; lectr. Kyoto Am. Studies Seminar, 1984, Charles Warren Ctr., Harvard U., 1991. Mem. Charles S. Peirce Soc. (pres. 1965-67), Charles S. Peirce Found., Am. Philos. Assn., AAUP, Soc. Advancement Am. Philosophy (exec. circle). Home: 78 Woodbridge St South Hadley MA 01075-1129

ROBINER, DONALD MAXWELL, federal official, lawyer; b. Detroit, Feb. 4, 1935; s. Max and Lucia (Chassman) R.; divorced; children: Steven Ralph, Lawrence Alan. BA, U. Mich., 1957; postgrad., Wayne State U., 1957-58; JD, Case Western Res. U., 1961. Bar: Ohio 1961, U.S. Supreme Ct. 1964, U.S. Ct. Appeals (6th cir.) 1965; bd. cert. civil trial adv. emeritus Nat. Bd. Trial Advocacy. Assoc. Metzenbaum, Gaines, Schwartz, Krupansky & Stern, Cleve., 1961-67; ptnr. Metzenbaum, Gaines, Krupansky, Finley & Stern, Cleve., 1967-72; v.p. Metzenbaum, Gaines, Finley & Stern Co., L.P.A., Cleve., 1972-77, Gaines, Stern, Schwarzwald & Robiner Co., Cleve., 1977-81; exec. v.p., sec. Schwarzwald, Robiner & Rock, Cleve., 1981-90; prin. Buckingham, Doolittle & Burroughs, Cleve., 1991-94; U.S. trustee Ohio and Mich. region 9 U.S. Dept. of Justice, 1994—; v.p., sec. Richard L. Bowen & Assocs., Inc., Cleve., 1969-94; acting judge Shaker Heights Mcpl. Ct., 1973; mem. Bd. Bar Examiners, State of Ohio, Columbus, 1974-79; life mem. 6th Cir. Jud. Conf.; mediator alt. dispute resolution panel U.S. Dist. Ct. (no. dist.) Ohio, 1993-94. Sec. Friends of Beachwood (Ohio) Libr., Inc., 1981-88, trustee, 1981-96. Recipient Cert. of Appreciation Ohio Supreme Ct., 1974-79, Appreciation award Am. Soc. of Appraisers 1975. Mem. ABA (forum com. on the constrn. industry 1980-94), Cleve. Bar Assn., Cuyahoga County Bar Assn. (Cert. of Appreciation 1986-87), Ohio State Bar Assn. (coun. dels. 1987—, legis. screening com. 1987-89, 91, sch. law com. 1981-94, legal edn. com. 1987-92), Am. Arbitration Assn. (Svc. award 1975), Ohio Coun. Sch. Bd. Attys. (exec. com. 1990-94), Jud. Conf. 8th Appellate Dist. Ohio (charter, life), KP. Home: 23512 E Silsby Rd Beachwood OH 44122-1266 Office: US Dept Justice Office of US Trustee BP America Bldg 200 Public Sq Ste 20-3300 Cleveland OH 44114-2301

ROBINETT, BETTY WALLACE, linguist; b. Detroit, June 23, 1919; d. Henry Guy and Beulah (Reid) Wallace; m. Ralph F. Robinett, Apr. 10, 1952 (dec. div. 1960); 1 child, Richard Wallace. BA, Wayne State U., 1940; MA, U. Mich., 1941, PhD, 1951. Instr., adminstrv. asst. English Lang. Inst., U. Mich., Ann Arbor, 1945-50; cons. Dept. Edn., San Juan, P.R., 1950-51, 52-57; lectr. English, U. Mich., 1951-52, 55-56; asso. prof. English InterAm. U., San German, P.R., 1957-59; asst. prof. English and linguistics Ball State U., Muncie, Ind., 1959-63; assoc. prof. English and linguistics English and linguistics Ball State U., 1963-67, prof., 1967-68; prof. dept. linguistics U. Minn., Mpls., 1968-88, dir. program in English as a second lang., 1968-80, acting asst. v.p. acad. affairs, 1979-80, asst. v.p. acad. affairs, 1980-84, assoc. v.p. acad. affairs, 1984-88, prof. emerita, 1988, Morse alumni disting. tchg. prof. emerita, 1996; chmn. Univ. Senate Consultative Com., 1977-78; vis. prof. Pa. State U., 1994-95; chmn. adv. panel on English tchg. USIA, 1988-93. Author: (with C.H. Prator) Manual of American English Pronunciation, 1972, 4th edit., 1985, Teaching English to Speakers of Other Languages, Substance and Technique, 1978, (with J. Schachter) Second Language Learning: Contrastive Analysis, Error Analysis and Related Aspects, 1983; editor Tesol Quar., 1967-72. Internat. Programs travel grantee, 1972, 77; recipient Morse-Amoco award for Excellence in Teaching, 1977. Mem. Tchrs. English to Speakers of Other Langs. (pres. 1974, James Alatis Svc. award 1990), Assn. Tchrs. ESL (chmn. 1976-77), Am. Assn. Applied Linguistics (v.p., pres. 1980-82), Linguistic Soc. Am. (life). Home: 1936 Park Forest Ave State College PA 16803-1329

ROBINETT, RUSH DALETH, III, robotics research manager; b. Albuquerque, July 14, 1960; s. Rush Daleth Jr. and Dorothy (Sohl) R.; m. Laurie Ellen Bowman, Dec. 28, 1993; 1 child Rush Daleth IV. Student, U. Notre Dame, 1978-80; BS magna cum laude, Tex. A&M U., 1982, PhD, 1987; MS, U. Tex., 1984. Teaching asst. U. Notre Dame, South Bend, Ind., 1979-80; rsch. asst. Tex. A&M U., College Station, 1981-82, U. Tex., Austin, 1983-84; rsch. assoc. Ctr. for Strategic Tech., College Station, 1984-87; rsch. mgr. Sandia Nat. Lab., Albuquerque, 1988—, disting. mem. tech. staff, 1995; student intern NASA Hdqs. Washington, 1981; rsch. engr. Northrop Aircraft Divsn., Hawthorne, Calif., summer, 1983; adj. prof. U. N.Mex., Albuquerque, 1994—; cons. Corning, Elmira, N.Y., 1993-95, Albuquerque Pub. Schs. Budget Rev. Bd., 1990; sci. advisor Albuquerque Pub. Schs., 1990-94, sci. instr., summer, 1988-90; presenter, cons. Explora, Albuquerque, 1992. Inventor: two axis hydraulic joint, sway suppressed crane control, moving mass spacecraft attitude control system; contbr. articles to profl. jours. Mentor Valley Acad., Albuquerque, 1989-92. Fellow AIAA (assoc., tech. com. 1991-93, student v.p. 1981-82, Best Presentation award 1992); mem. N.Y. Acad. Scis., Am. Helicopter Soc., Phi Kappa Phi, Sigma Gamma Tau. Avocations: softball, volleyball, ice hockey, fishing, hunting. Home: PO Box 1661 Tijeras NM 87059-1661 Office: Sandia Nat Lab MS 1003 PO Box 5800 Albuquerque NM 87185

ROBINOWITZ, CAROLYN BAUER, psychiatrist, educator; b. Bklyn., July 15, 1938; d. Milton Leonard and Marcia (Wexler) Bauer; m. Max Robinowitz, June 10, 1962; children—Mark, David. A.B., Wellesley Coll., 1959; M.D., Washington U., 1964. Diplomate Am. Bd. Psychiatry and Neurology. Chief physician tng. NIMH, Bethesda, Md., 1968-70; dir. pediatric liaison U. Miami Sch. Medicine, Fla, 1970-72, dir. child psychiatry tng., 1971-72; dir. edn. George Washington U. Sch. Medicine, Washington, 1972-74; project dir. Psychiatrist as Tchr., Washington, 1973-75; dep. med. dir. Am. Psychiat. Assn., Washington, 1976-86, dir. Office Edn., 1976-87, sr. dep. med. dir. & COO, 1986-94, COO, 1986-94; assoc. dean Georgetown U. Sch. Medicine, 1995—, professorial lectr., 1982-94, prof., 1995—; dir. Am. Bd. Psychiatry and Neurology, Evanston, Ill., 1979-86, sec., 1984, v.p., 1985, pres., 1986; clin. prof. psychiatry and behavioral scis., child health and devel. George Washington U., 1984—. Editor: Women in Context, 1976; contbr. articles to jours., chpts. to books. Admissions com. Wellesley Coll. Club, Washington, 1983-84; active Boy Scouts Am. Served with USPHS, 1966-69. Recipient NIMH Mental Health Career Devel. award, 1966-70, NIMH grantee, 1974-94. Fellow Am. Psychiat. Assn. (Disting. Svc. award 1991, Vestermark award 1995), Am. Coll. Psychiatrists (bd. dirs. 1993-96, 1st v.p. 1997—, pres. elect 1997, Bowis award 1994); mem. Group for Advancement of Psychiatry (dir. 1982-84, pres. 1989-91), Coun. Med. Splty. Socs. (dir. 1977-82, pres. 1981-82). Home: 7204 Helmsdale Rd Bethesda MD 20817-4624 Office: Georgetown U Sch medicine 3900 Reservoir Rd NW Rm NE 113 Washington DC 20007-2195

ROBINOWITZ, STUART, lawyer; b. Port Chester, N.Y., Apr. 6, 1929; s. Sam and Rose (Goldstein) R.; m. Anne, July 15, 1952; children: Cathy, Susan, Richard, Robert, Jane. B.A., Williams Coll.; LL.B., Yale U. Bar: N.Y. 1953. Ptnr. Rosenman, Colin, Kaye, Petscheck & Freund, N.Y.C., 1961-70, Paul Weiss, Rifkind, Wharton & Garrison, N.Y.C., 1970—; vis. lectr. Yale U. Law Sch., 1981-83, 90-92, NYU Law Sch., 1996. Mem. ABA, N.Y. State Bar Assn., N.Y. County Lawyers Assn., Assn. of Bar of City of N.Y., Phi Beta Kappa. Office: Paul Weiss Rifkind Wharton & Garrison 1285 Avenue Of The Americas New York NY 10019-6028

ROBINS, GERALD BURNS, education educator; b. Salem, Ark., Jan. 24, 1924; s. Gerald Alfred and Lucille (Burns) R.; m. Fay Ann Kennan, Sept. 1, 1946; children: Gerald Kennan, James Dow. B.S. in Edn. cum laude, U. Ark., 1948, M.S., 1950; Ed.D., U. Ga., 1954. Asst. prof., chmn. dept. distbv. edn., chmn. dept. bus. edn. U. Ga., 1950-57, prof. higher edn., 1970-73; pres. Augusta (Ga.) Coll., 1957-70; pres. Tex. A&I U., Kingsville, 1973-77, sr. prof., 1977-89, prof. emeritus, 1994—; owner RobArt Sculpture; cons. Air Force ROTC, 1954; chmn. edn. com. Ga.-S.C. Nuclear Council, 1969; acad. dean CAP Cadet Officers Sch., 1970-71. Author: Understanding the College Budget, 1973, Campus, 1980, 1975. Trustee Lawton B. Evans Ednl. Fund, Barrett Sch. Nursing, Augusta Prep. Sch.; bd. dirs., pres. Tex. A & I Fed. Credit Union; mem. Friends of John E. Conner Mus. Served with USAAF, 1943-46; lt. col. USAF Res. (ret.). Decorated Air medal; recipient Commendation Resolution, Ga. Ho. of Reps., 1965, Disting. Svc. award Tex. Hist. Commn., 1987, Disting. Alumnus award U. Ark., 1974, Silver Spur award Tex. A & I U.; named Col. Aide de Camp, Ga. Govs. Office, 1963; named to Hall of Honor, U. Ark., 1992; Donaghey fellow, 1943, Kellogg fellow, 1953-54, Paul Harris fellow. Mem. Am. Assn. State Colls. and Univs. (com. on studies), Assn. Tex. Colls. and Univs. (commn. on acad. affairs), Internat. Assn. U. Pres.'s, Internat. Council Edn. for Teaching, Nat. Collegiate Athletic Assn. (pres. Lone Star Conf.), U. Ark. Alumni Assn. (life), Kleberg (Tex.) Hist. Commn. (chmn.), So. Tex. Hist. Soc. (dir.), 8th Air Force Hist. Soc. (life), Ret. Officers Assn. (life, pres.), Navy League, Res. Officers Assn. (life), Ga. Ret. Tchrs. Assn. (life), Pinnacle Club, Kingsville Country Club, Javelina Club, Victory Club, Century Club, Masons (32d deg.), Rotary (pres. local club, pres. rep. 1992, dist. parliamentarian, 1991—, dist. gov. 1982-83, scholarship trustee, instr. internat. assembly 1985, faculty Tex. pres.'s tng. 1987-89, 93, 95, del. coun. on legis. 1992, 95, benefactor), Kappa Sigma (alumni advisor), Kappa Delta Pi, Phi Kappa Phi, Omicron Delta Kappa, Psi Chi, Phi Delta Kappa (emeritus mem., charter chpt. pres.); charter mem. Tex. State Aquarium. Methodist (bd. higher edn., campus ministry). Home: 515 University Blvd Kingsville TX 78363-4242

ROBINS, H(ENRY) IAN, medical oncologist; b. N.Y.C., Feb. 17, 1945; s. Edwin and Matilda (Morgenstern) R. AB in Biology, Boston U., 1966, AM in Biochemistry, 1968, PhD in Molecular Biology, 1971, MD, 1976. Diplomate Am. Bd. Internal Medicine, Am. Bd. Med. Oncology, Am. Bd. Forensic Medicine, Am. Bd. Forensic Examiners. Intern in internal medicine Univ. Hosps., Madison, Wis., 1976-77, resident in internal medicine, 1977-79; fellow in clin. oncology Wis. Clin. Cancer Ctr., Madison, 1979-81, fellow in rsch. oncology, 1981-82; instr. dept. human oncology, dept. medicine Dept. Human Oncology, Dept. Medicine U. Wis. Sch. Medicine, Madison, 1982-83, asst. prof., 1983-86, assoc. prof., 1986—; chief sect. med. oncology, dir. U. Wis. Sch. Medicine, Madison, 1990-95, prof. dept. human oncology, medicine and neurology, 1992—; chmn. Systemic Hyperthermia Oncology Working Group. Contbr. numerous articles to profl. jours.; reviewer numerous sci. jours. including Biochem. Pharmacology, Internat. Jour. Radiation Biology, Jour. Clin. Oncology, New Eng. Jour. Medicine, others. Mem. N.Y. Acad. Scis., AAAS, ACP, Internat. Clin. Hyperthermia Soc. , Radiation Rsch. Soc., N.am. Hyperthermia Group, Oncology Group, Am. Fedn. clin. Rsch., Ea. Coop. Oncology Group, European Soc. Hyperthermic Oncology, Vet. Cancer Soc., Transplantation Soc., Collaborative Ocular Melanoma Study Group, Am. Soc. Clin. Hypnosis, Minn. Soc. Clin. Hypnosis, Sigma Xi. Office: Clin Sci Ctr K4/662 600 Highland Ave Madison WI 53792-0001

ROBINS, LEE NELKEN, medical educator; b. New Orleans, Aug. 29, 1922; d. Abe and Leona (Reiman) Nelken; m. Eli Robins, Feb. 22, 1946 (dec. Dec. 1994); children: Paul, James, Thomas, Nicholas. Student, Newcomb Coll., 1938-40; BA, Radcliffe Coll., 1942, MA, 1943; PhD, Harvard U., 1951. Mem. faculty Washington U., St. Louis, 1954—, prof. sociology in psychiatry, 1968-91, prof. sociology, 1969-91, univ. prof. social sci., prof. social sci. in psychiatry, 1991—; past mem. Nat. Adv. Coun. on Drug Abuse; past mem. task panels Pres.'s Commn. on Mental Health; mem. expert adv. panel on mental health WHO; Salmon lectr. N.Y. Acad. Medicine, 1983; Cutter lectr. Harvard U., 1997. Author: Deviant Children Grown Up, 1966; editor 11 books; N.Am. Assoc. editor Internat. Jour. Methods in Psychiat. Rsch.; mem. editl. bd. Psychol. Medicine, Jour. Child Psychology and Psychiatry, Devel. and Psychopathology, Jour. Studies on Alcohol, Epidemiol. e Psochiat. Sociale, ; contbr. articles to profl. jours. Recipient Rsch. Scientist award USPHS, 1970-90, Pacesetter Rsch. award Nat. Inst. Drug Abuse, 1978, Radcliffe Coll. Grad. Soc. medal, 1979, Sutherland award Soc. Criminology, 1991, Nathan B. Eddy award Com. on Problems of Drug Dependence, 1993; rsch. grantee NIMH, Nat. Inst. on Drug Abuse, Nat. Inst. on Alcohol Abuse and Alcoholism. Fellow Am. Coll. Epidemiology, Royal Coll. Psychiatrists (hon.); mem. APHA (Rema Lapouse award 1979, Lifetime Achievement award sect. on alcohol and drug abuse 1994), World Psychiat. Assn. (sect. com. on epidemiology and cmty. psychiatry, treas.), Soc. Life History Rsch. in Psychopathology, Am. Coll. Neuropsychopharmacology, Am. Sociol. Assn., Internat. Sociol. Assn., Inst. Medicine, Internat. Epidemiol. Assn., Am. Psychopath. Assn. (pres. 1987-88, Paul Hoch award 1978). Office: Washington U Med Sch Dept Psychiatry Saint Louis MO 63110

ROBINS, MARJORIE KAPLAN, newspaper editor. Entertainment editor Saturday edit., travel editor Sunday edit. Newsday, Melville, N.Y. Office: Newsday Inc 235 Pinelawn Rd Melville NY 11747-4226*

ROBINS, NORMAN ALAN, strategic planning consultant, former steel company executive; b. Chgo., Nov. 19, 1934; s. Irving and Sylvia (Robbin) Robins; m. Sandra Ross, June 10, 1956; children: Lawrence Richard, Sherry Lynn. BS in Chem. Engring., MIT, 1955, MS in Chem. Engring., 1956; PhD in Math., Ill. Inst. Tech., 1972. Asst. mgr. process systems and controls Inland Steel Co., East Chicago, Ind., 1962-67, assoc. mgr. process systems and controls, 1967-72, dir. process research, 1972-77, v.p. research, 1977-84, v.p. technol. assessment, 1984-86, v.p. strategic planning, 1986-91, ret., 1991; ind. cons. in strategic planning, 1991—. Mem. bd. edn. Homewood-Flossmoor High Sch., Ill., 1974-77. Mem. AIME (Nat. Open Hearth Conf. award 1972), AIChE, Midwest Soc. Profl. Cons., Strategic Leadership Forum.

ROBINS, ROBERT SIDWAR, political science educator, administrator; b. Spangler, Pa., Apr. 20, 1938; s. Sydney and Katherine (Sidwar) R.; m. Marjorie McGann, Nov. 25, 1959; children: Anthony P., Nicholas A. BA, U. Pitts., 1959; MA, Duke U., 1961, PhD, 1963. Prof. polit. sci. Tulane U., New Orleans, 1965—, chmn. dept. polit. sci., 1979-90, dep. provost, 1991—; acad. visitor Inst. Commonwealth Studies, U. London, 1969-70, 78-79, mem. 1987-88; sr. assoc. mem. St. Antony's Coll., Oxford, Eng., 1972-73; vis. scholar Hastings Ctr., 1982; vis. scientist Tavistock Clinic, London, 1987-88. Author: Political Institutionalization and the Integration of Elites, 1976 (Carnegie Commn. report) Legislative Attitudes Toward Higher Education in Louisiana, 1968, Psychopathology and Political Leadership, 1977, Disease and Political Leadership, 1990; co-author: When Illness Strikes the Leader, Political Paranoia; contbr. articles to profl. publs. Vice chmn. Elections Integrity Commn., State of La., 1981-82. Recipient Excellence in Teaching award Tulane U., 1978; Fulbright scholar, 1961-62. Mem. Am. Polit. Sci. Assn., Internat. Soc. Polit. Psychology, New Orleans Fgn. Relations Assn. (bd. dirs.). Avocations: carpentry; gardening. Home: 727 Pine St New Orleans LA 70118-5118 Office: Tulane U Gibson Hall Office of the Provost New Orleans LA 70118

ROBINS, W. RONALD, lawyer; b. Hope, Ark., Dec. 4, 1943. BSChE, Lamar U., 1966; JD, U. Houston, 1969. Bar: Tex. 1969, U.S. Patent and Trademark Office. Mem. Vinson & Elkins L.L.P., Houston. Mem. Phi Delta Phi, Tau Beta Pi. Office: Vinson & Elkins 2500 First City Tower 1001 Fannin St Houston TX 77002-6706

ROBINSON, ADELBERT CARL, lawyer, judge; b. Shawnee, Okla., Dec. 13, 1926; s. William H. and Mayme (Forston) R.; m. Paula Kay Settles, Apr. 16, 1988; children from previous marriage: William, James, Schuyler, Donald, David, Nancy, Lauri. Student Okla. Baptist U., 1944-47; JD, Okla. U., 1950. Bar: Okla. 1950. Pvt. practice, Muskogee, Okla., 1956—; with legal dept. Phillips Petroleum Co., 1950-51; adjuster U.S. Fidelity & Guaranty Co., 1951-54, atty., adjuster-in-charge, 1954-56; ptnr. Fite & Robinson, 1956-62, Fite, Robinson & Summers, 1963-70, Robinson & Summers, 1970-72, Robinson, Summers & Locke, 1972-76, Robinson, Locke & Gage, 1976-80, Robinson, Locke, Gage & Fite, 1980-83, Robinson, Locke, Gage, Fite & Williams, Muskogee, 1983-95, Robinson, Gage, Fite & Williams, 1995—; police judge, 1963-64; mcpl. judge, 1964-70; prin. justice Temp. Div. 36 Okla. Ct. Appeals, 1981—; pres., dir. Wall St. Bldg Corp., 1969-78, Three Forks Devel. Corp., 1968-77, Rolo Leasing, Inc., 1971—, Suroya II, Inc., 1977—; sec. Muskogee Tom's Inc., Blue Ridge Corp., Harborcliff Corp.; bd. dirs. First Bancshares of Muskogee, Inc., First of Muskogee Corp., First City Bank, Tulsa; adv. dir. First Nat. Bank & Trust Co. of Muskogee; mng. ptnr. RLG Ritz, 1980—; ptnr. First City Real Estate Partnership, 1985-94. Del. to U.S./China Joint Session on Trade, Investment and Econ. Law, Beijing, 1987; chmn. Muskogee County (Okla.) Law Day, 1963; chmn. Muskogee Area Redevel. Authority, 1963; chmn. Muskogee County chpt. Am. Cancer Soc., 1956; pres. bd. dirs. Muskogee Cmty. Coun.; bd. dirs. United Way of Muskogee, Inc., 1980-88, v.p., 1982, pres. 1983; bd. dirs. Muskogee Cmty. Concert Assn., Muskogee Tourist Info. Bur., 1964-68; bd. dirs., gen. counsel United Cerebral Palsy Eastern Okla., 1964-68; trustee Connors Devel. Found., Connors Coll., 1981—, chmn., 1987-89; active Muskogee Housing Authority, 1992-95. With if. AUS, 1945-46. Mem. ABA, Okla. Bar Assn. (chmn. uniform laws com. 1970-72, chmn. profl. coop. com. 1965-69, past regional chmn. grievance com.), Muskogee County Bar Assn. (pres. 1971, mem. exec. coun. 1971-74), Okla. Assn. Def. Counsel (dir.), Okla. Assn. Mcpl. Judges (dir.), Muskogee C. of C., Delta Theta Phi. Methodist. Club: Rotary (pres. 1971-72). Home: 2408 Saint Andrews Ct Muskogee OK 74403-1657 Office: 530 Court St # 87 Muskogee OK 74401-6033

ROBINSON, ALEXANDER JACOB, clinical psychologist; b. St. John, Kans., Nov. 7, 1920; s. Oscar Frank and Lydia May (Beitler) R.; m. Elsie Louise Riggs, July 29, 1942; children: Madelyn K., Alicia A., David J., Charles A., Paul S., Marietta J., Stephen N. BA in Psychology, Ft. Hays (Kans.) State U., 1942, MS in Clin. Psychology, 1942; postgrad., U. Ill., 1942-44. Cert. psychologist, sch. psychologist. Chief psychologist Larned (Kans.) State Hosp., 1948-53, with employee selection, outpatient services, 1953-55; sch. psychologist County Schs., Modesto, Calif., 1955-61, Pratt (Kans.) Jr. Coll., 1961-66; fed. grantee, writer assoc. dir. Exemplary Federally Funded Program for Spl. Edn., Pratt, 1966-70; dir. spl. edn., researcher Stafford County Schs., St. John, 1970-81, ret., 1981; supr. testing and data Incidence of Exceptional Children in Kansas, Kans. State U., Ft. Hays, 1946; writer, asst. dir. Best Exemplary Federally Funded Program on Spl. Edn., Pratt, 1966-70; fed. grantee, researcher, writer, study dir. Edn. for the High-Performance Child, St. John, 1970—, Psychogenesis of the Sociopathic Personality, a longitudinal study. Minister, The Ch. of Jesus Christ. Served to 2d lt. U.S. Army, 1944-46, PTO. Mem. N.Y. Acad. Scis. Lodge: Lions (program chmn. St. John 1974-76). Avocations: history, ethnology, cultural anthropology, music, literature. Home and Office: 202 Grandview Saint John KS 67576-9801

ROBINSON, ANGELA TOMEI, clinical laboratory scientist; b. Bklyn., June 5, 1957; d. Leo James and Nina Angela T.; m. John C. Robinson, Sept. 27, 1987. BS, St. John's U., 1979, MS, 1985. Cert. lab. technologist Nat. Cert. Agy. for Med. Lab. Personnel. Exec. sec. Stead-fast Temporaries, Inc., N.Y.C., 1975-79; chief med. technologist Winthrop-U. Hosp., Mineola, N.Y., 1979—; coord., founder Nat. Med. Lab. Week, Mineola, N.Y., 1981—; tech. supr., lab. mgr., cons. Hilton Med. Group, Hempstead, N.Y., 1993-96; staff contbr. newsletter Winthrop-U. Hosp., Mineola, 1981—, in pub. rels., 1981—, mem. numerous coms., clin. instr. for retng. personnel in lab., chmn. com. to petition salary increases, 1987-90; guest lectr. seminar C.W. Post Coll., Westbury, N.Y., 1986—, adj. prof., 1992—; guest lectr. SUNY, Stony Brook, 1995—; rep. Nassau Suffolk Health Manpower Plan, 1991. Author: (poetry) Our World's Best Loved Poems, 1984 (2d place merit cert. 1983) contbr. articles to profl. jours.; lectr. ednl. seminars and confs. Singer Blessed Sacrament Ch. Choir, Bklyn., 1971-73, coord., singer ch. folk group, 1971-79; mem. Mothers Against Drunk Driving, 1985-87, Nat. Rep. Congl. Com., 1984-86, Am. Health Found., 1986-87, DAV, 1984-87; fundraiser Statue of Liberty/Ellis Island Found., 1985-86, 95-96, Hands Across Am., 1986, U.S. Olympic Team Spirit, 1992—, U.S. English First, Nat. Mus. Am. Indians. Recipient cert. of merit N.Y. State Senate, 1985, citation Gov. N.Y. State Pres. Soc., 1975; award St. John's U. Med. Tech. Alumni, 1992. Mem. Am. Soc. Clin. Lab. Sci., Profl. Stds. Coalition Clin. Lab. Pers., Am. Soc. Clin. Pathologists (registered), Made in the U.S. Found., N.Y. State Soc. Clin. Lab. Sci. (chmn. govt. liason com., state bd. dirs. 1988—, Outstanding Med. Tech. Student award 1979, Member of Yr. award 1995, founding officer Nassau-Suffolk chpt. 1985-86, bd. dirs., seminar moderator 1985-87, pres.-elect 1986-87, 90-91, pres. 1991—, membership com. 1991, state chairperson 1993—), Profl. STDS Coalition (pub. rels. chair 1993—, co-chair 1997—), Theta Phi Alpha (alumni chmn. 1976-77, alumni-collegiate rep. 1986-87). Avocations: piano, guitar, gardening, singing, tennis.

ROBINSON, ARTHUR HOWARD, geography educator; b. Montreal, Que., Can., Jan. 5, 1915; s. James Howard and Elizabeth (Peavey) R.; m. Mary Elizabeth Coffin, Dec. 23, 1938 (dec. Jan. 1992); children: Stephen Michael, Patricia Anne; m. Martha Elizabeth Rodabaugh Phillips, Feb. 6, 1993. BA, Miami U., Oxford, Ohio, 1936, LittD, 1966; MA, U. Wis., 1938; PhD in Geography, Ohio State U., 1947, DSc (hon.), 1984. Sec. to mem. Ohio Bd. Liquor Control, 1936; asst. geography U. Wis., 1936-38, Ohio State U., 1938-41; chief map div. OSS, 1941-46; mem. faculty U. Wis., 1945—, prof. geography, 1951-80, prof. emeritus, 1980—, chmn. dept., 1954-58, 66-68, Lawrence Martin prof. cartography, 1967—; dir. Univ. Cartographic Lab., 1966-73; hon. cons. cartography Library of Congress, 1974-80; Chief map officer U.S. Delegation Quebec and Cairo confs., World War II; pres. Internat. Cartographic Assn., 1972-76. Author: Look of Maps, 1952, Early Thematic Mapping in the History of Cartography, 1982; co-author: Elements of Geography, 4th edit., 1957, Elements of Cartography, 6th edit., 1995, Fundamentals of Physical Geography, 3rd edit., 1977, The Nature of Maps, 1976; co-editor: Cartographical Innovations, 1987; editor Am. Cartographer, 1974-76; also articles; designer Robinson map projection, 1963. Served to maj. AUS, 1944-45. Decorated Legion of Merit; recipient Carl Mannerfelt medal Internat. Cartographic Assn., 1981, Helen Culver Gold Medal Geog. Soc. Chgo., 1983, John Oliver LaGorce medal Nat. Geog. Soc., 1988, Silver medal Brit. Cartographic Soc., 1991; Guggenheim rsch. fellow, 1964, 78. Mem. Assn. Am. Geographers (council 1960-65, pres. 1963), Am. Congress Surveying and Mapping (hon.; chmn. cartography div. 1971). Home: 7802 Courtyard Dr Madison WI 53719-3517

ROBINSON, BARBARA PAUL, lawyer; b. Oct. 19, 1941; d. Leo and Pauline G. Paul; m. Charles Raskob Robinson, June 11, 1965; children: Charles Paul, Torrance Webster. AB magna cum laude, Bryn Mawr Coll., 1962; LLB, Yale U., 1965. Bar: N.Y. 1966, U.S. Dist. Ct. (so. and ea. dists.) N.Y. 1975, U.S. Tax Ct. 1972, U.S. Ct. Appeals (2d cir.) 1974. Assoc. Debevoise & Plimpton (formerly Debevoise, Plimpton, Lyons & Gates), N.Y.C., 1966-75, ptnr., 1976—; mem. adv. bd., lectr. Practicing Law Inst.; arbitrator Am. Arbitration Assn., 1987—, bd. dirs. Contbr. articles to profl. jours. Mem. adv. coun., bd. visitors CUNY Law Sch., Queens, 1984-90; trustee Trinity Sch., 1982-86, pres., 1986-88; bd. dirs. Found. for Child Devel., 1989—, chmn., 1991—; mem. Coun. on Fgn. Rels.; bd. dirs. Catalyst, 1993—, Am. Judicature Soc., Fund Modern Cts., 1990—, Wave Hill, 1994—, Garden Conservancy, 1996—; trustee The William Nelson Cromwell Found., 1993—; active Am. Irish Legal Rsch. Found. Inc., Citizens Union Found. Inc. Recipient Laura Parsons Pratt award, 1996. Fellow Am. Coll. Trust and Estate Counsel, Am. Bar Found., N.Y. Bar Found.; mem. ABA, N.Y. State Bar Assn. (vice chmn. com. on trust adminstrn., trusts and estates law sect. 1977-81, ho. of dels. 1984-87, 90-92, mem. com. ann. award 1993-94), Assn. of Bar of City of N.Y. (chmn. com. on trusts, estates and surrogates cts. 1981-84, judiciary com. 1981-84, coun. on jud. adminstrn. 1982-84, chair nominating com. 1984-85, mem. exec. com. 1986-91, chair 1989-90, v.p. 1990-91, pres. 1994-96, chair com. on honors 1993-94, mem. com. on long-range planning 1991-94), Assn. of Bar of City of N.Y. Fund Inc. (bd. dirs., pres.), Women's Forum, Yale Coun., Yale Law Sch. Assn. N.Y. (mem. devel. bd., exec. com. 1981-85, pres. 1988-93), Yale Club, Washington Club. Office: Debevoise & Plimpton 875 3rd Ave New York NY 10022-6225

ROBINSON, BARRY R., lawyer; b. Dover, Ohio, Dec. 8, 1946. AB, Princeton U., 1969; JD cum laude, Ohio State U., 1972. Bar: Ohio 1972. Ptnr. Baker & Hostetler, Columbus, Ohio. Fellow Am. Coll. Trust and Estate Counsel; mem. ABA, Ohio State Bar Assn., Columbus Bar Assn. Office: Baker & Hostetler Capital Sq 65 E State St Ste 2100 Columbus OH 43215-4213

ROBINSON, BERNARD LEO, retired lawyer; b. Kalamazoo, Feb. 13, 1924; s. Louis Harvey and Sue Mary (Starr) R.; m. Betsy Nadell, May 30, 1947; children: Robert Bruce, Patricia Anne, Jean Carol. BS, U. Ill., 1947, MS, 1958, postgrad. in structural dynamics, 1959; JD, U. N.Mex., 1973. Rsch. engr. Assn. Am. Railroads, 1947-49; instr. architecture Rensselaer Poly. Inst., 1949-51; commd. 2d lt. Corps Engrs., U.S. Army, 1945, advanced through grades to lt. col., 1965, ret., 1968; engr. Nuclear Def. Rsch. Corp., Albuquerque, 1968-71; admitted to N.Mex. bar, 1973, U.S. Supreme Ct. bar, 1976; practiced in Albuquerque, 1973-85, Silver City, N.Mex., 1985-89, Green Valley, Ariz., 1989-90, Sierra Vista, Ariz., 1990-91; pres. Robinson Fin. Svcs., 1993-95. Dist. commr. Boy Scouts Am., 1960-62; vice chmn. Rep. Dist. Com., 1968-70. Decorated Air medal, Combat Infantry badge. Mem. ASCE, ABA, Ret. Officers Assn., DAV, Assn. U.S. Army, VFW. Home: 1037 W Eagle Look Ln Tucson AZ 85737-6986

ROBINSON, BERNARD PAHL, thoracic surgeon, educator; b. N.Y.C., Apr. 12, 1919; s. Nathaniel and Augusta (Strauss) R.; m. Gloria Joyce Rehfuss, Oct. 3, 1943; children: Lawrence, Andrew. BS, NYU, 1938; MD, L.I. Coll. Medicine, 1942. Diplomate Am. Bd. Surgery, Am. Bd. Thoracic

Surgery. Intern Mount Sinai Hosp., N.Y.C., 1942-43, resident in surgery, 1946-47; resident in surgery Beth Israel Hosp., Boston, 1948-49; resident in thoracic surgery VA Hosp, Castle Point, N.Y., 1949-50; assoc. attending surgeon Mt. Sinai Hosp., N.Y.C., 1956—; asst. clin. prof. surgery Mt. Sinai Sch. Medicine, N.Y.C., 1968—. Capt. U.S. Army, 1943-46. Fellow Am. Coll. Surgeons, Am. Coll. Chest Physicians; mem. N.Y. Soc. for Thoracic Surgery. Jewish. Avocations: sailing, golf, photography, travel. Home: 4601 Henry Hudson Pky W Bronx NY 10471-3801 Office: 8 E 83rd St New York NY 10028-0418

ROBINSON, BINA AITCHISON, publisher, newsletter editor; b. Schenectady, N.Y., Aug. 31, 1923; d. Thomas Cant and Winifred Maud (Binless) Aitchison; m. David Dunlop Robinson, May 14, 1944; children: Challice Binless, Jean Aitchison, Andrew McLeod, Janet Davison. BA with honors, U. Rochester, 1944. Tchr. Phila. Pub. Schs., 1944-45, Brockport (N.Y.) Cen. Sch., 1946-47, Harley Sch., Rochester, N.Y., 1947-52; engrng. asst. GE, Pittsfield, Mass., 1945-46; entrepreneur, developer, mgr. Swain (N.Y.) Ski Ctr., 1947-77; founder, coord., editor, prin. writer Coalition to Protect Animals in Parks & Refuges, Swain, 1985—; editor, prin. writer The Civil Abolitionist, 1985—; Am. cons. Drs. and Lawyers for Responsible Medicine; vis. lectr. schs. and colls. Contbr. articles to publs. Past pres. Allegany County Soc. Prevention Cruelty Animals, Wellsville, N.Y., 1978—. Mem. Am. Anti-Vivisection Soc., Nat. Resources Def. Coun., Internat. Primate Protection League, Nat. Alliance for Animals, N.Y. State Coalition for Animals, Action on Smoking and Health, Union Concerned Scientists, Civis/Civitas (exec. dir. 1983-91), Citizens for Planetary Health (exec. dir. 1994—). Avocations: skiing, mountain hiking, swimming, canoeing, gardening. Home and Office: 1 Main St Swain NY 14884-0026

ROBINSON, BOB LEO, international investment services executive; b. Franklin, Tenn., Sept. 9, 1933; s. W.A. and Cornelia Irene (Lampley) R.; m. Carolyn Overton, Dec. 18, 1955; children: Richard Glenn, Leigh Ann, Elizabeth Lynne. BS in Indsl. Mgmt, Tenn. Tech. U., 1955. Cert. property mgr. Quality control engr. Gates Rubber Co., Nashville, 1960; tech. rep. Home Ins. Co., 1961-65; civilian staff adminstrv. asst. Dept. Army, Nashville, 1965; exec. asst. to pres. Sullivan's Dept. Stores, Nashville, 1966-69; dir. engring. and devel. Venture Out in Am., Knoxville, Tenn., 1969; v.p., then exec. v.p. Hosp. Corp. Am., Nashville, 1970-79; pres., chief exec. officer Real Estate Group Inc., Nashville, 1974—, Fidelity Title Co., Nashville, 1974-83; pres. Internat. Bus. and Investment Services, Orlando, 1978—; gen. partner Union Sq. Ltd., Jacksonville, Fla., 1973-79; dir. Am. Travel Service, World Health Cons.; chmn. bd. emeritus Arnold Palmer Devel. Co., Orlando, Fla., 1988—; past vice chmn. bd. dirs., chief exec. officer Clin. Diagnostic Systems, Inc., Orlando, 1988-89; past vice chmn. Space Rail Corp., Orlando, 1991; speaker in field. Mem. Mayor Nashville Blue Ribbon Com., 1975-77; commr. City of Brentwood, Tenn., 1969-71, vice mayor, 1969-71, mayor, 1971, mem. planning commn., 1970-71; bd. dirs. Goodwill Industries Ctrl. Fla., exec. com., chmn. ops. com.; chmn. bldg. fund St. Cecilia Acad., Nashville, 1978; vice chmn. Audubon council Boy Scouts Am., 1968; founder Tenn. Tech. ROTC Gen.'s Cup Scholarship Found., 1986; aide U.S. Com. for Normandy Meml. Mus., Caen, France, 1987—; parachutist Israeli Def. Forces, 1989, Royal Thai Spl. Warfare Command, 1990; campaign dir. Drage for County Chmn., Orange County, Fla., 1990; bd. dirs. Camp Blanding Mus. Found., 1995—. Served as officer, master army aviator, parachutist, U.S. Army, 1955-60, USAR, 1960-83; maj. gen. (brevet) USAR, 1990. Decorated Army Commendation medal, Meritorious Service medal; recipient numerous public service awards; named to Tenn. Tech. ROTC Hall of Fame, 1988. Mem. Internat. Inst. Hosp. Cons., Inst. Real Estate Mgmt., Army Aviation Assn. Am., Res. Officers Assn., Internat. Assn. Airborne Vets., 82d Airborne Divsn. Assn. Republican. Baptist (past v.p. bd. trustees). Clubs: Arnold Palmer's Bay Hill (Orlando); Shriners.

ROBINSON, BROOKS CALBERT, JR., former professional baseball player, TV commentator, business consultant; b. Little Rock, May 18, 1937; s. Brooks Calbert and Ethel (Denker) R.; m. Constance Louise Butcher, Oct. 8, 1960; children—Brooks David, Christopher Leslie, Michael Patrick, Diana Agnes. Student, U. Little Rock, 1956-57. Profl. baseball player Balt. Orioles, 1955-77; sports commentator for Baltimore Oriole Games Sta. WMAR-TV, Balt., 1978-90; spl. asst. mktg. dept. Crown Central Petroleum Corp., 1979—; v.p. Personal Mgmt. Assocs., 1979—. Selected Most Valuable Oriole, 1960, 62, 64, 71; named Am. League's Most Valuable Player, 1964, Most Valuable Player in Major League All-Star game at St. Louis, 1966; Most Valuable Player, 1970 World Series; recipient Hickock Athlete of Yr. award, 1970; Balt. Decade award, 1970; mem. World Series Championship Team, 1965, 70; named to Baseball Hall of Fame, Cooperstown, N.Y. Office: care Crown Central Petroleum Corp/Dept Mktg 1 N Charles St Ste 1168 Baltimore MD 21201-3740

ROBINSON, BRUCE BUTLER, physicist; b. Chester, Pa., Oct. 13, 1933; s. George Senior and Dorothy Conerly (Butler) R.; m. Dorothy Ross, June 4, 1960; children: Douglas Ross, Christopher Scott. BS in Physics, Drexel U., 1956; PhD in Physics, Princeton U., 1961; MBA, Rider U., 1977. Rsch. assoc. U. Calif., San Diego, 1961-63; rsch. scientist RCA David Sarnoff Lab., RCA, Princeton, N.J., 1963-73; exec. dir., mem. commerce tech. adv. bd. U.S. Dept. Commerce, Washington, 1973-75; dir. policy integration, dir. coal and synfuels policy U.S. Dept. Energy, Washington, 1975-81; sr. science advisor to v.p. rsch. Exxon Rsch. and Engring. Co., Linden, N.J., 1981-84; dep. dir. Office Naval Rsch., Arlington, 1984-87, dir. rsch., 1987-94, dep. dir. sci. and tech., 1994-96; assoc. tech. dir. for sci. and tech. Office Naval Rsch., 1996—; prin. author nat. energy policy plan U.S. Dept. Energy, 1981; U.S. rep. to internat. energy agy., govt. expert group on tech., Paris, 1979-81; mem. internat. team to rev. R&D programs Dutch Ministry Econs. and Fin., The Hague, The Netherlands, 1979; presenter sci. lectures. Contbr. articles to sci. jours. NSF fellow Princeton U., 1956-58, NSF internat. summer fellow, Varenna, Italy, 1962; recipient Meritorious Presdl. Rank award Pres. of U.S., 1989, Disting. Civilian Svc. medal Sec. of the Navy, 1997. Mem. IEEE, Am. Phys. Soc., The Oceanography Soc. (founding).

ROBINSON, CHARLES E., building materials executive; b. 1941. BA, Northwestern U., Evanston, Ill., 1963; JD, U. Mich., 1966. V.p., gen. coun. Jim Walter Corp., Tampa, Fla., 1990. Office: Jim Walter Corp 4010 W Boy Scout Blvd Tampa FL 33607-5727

ROBINSON, CHARLES EMANUEL, systems engineer, consultant; b. Hayes, Clarendon, Jamaica, Jan. 14, 1946; came to U.S., 1986; s. Charles E. and Ethlyn C. (Singh) R.; m. Joy B. Cassanova, July 31, 1971; children: Sonya, Monique, Nicole, Kimberley. Student, Nat. Tech. Schs., L.A., 1966. Radio technician Chin's Radio & TV, Kingston, Jamaica, 1964-66; solid state technician Wonards Radio Engring., Kingston, 1966-68; instrument technician Ewarton Plant, Aluminum Co. Can., Jamaica, 1968-69; sr. field tech. engr. Ruel Samuels Ltd., Kingston, 1969-77; mng. dir. MSS Ltd., Kingston, 1977-80, Robinson Assocs., Mandeville, Jamaica, 1980-86; design engr. Seaboard Electronics, New Rochelle, N.Y., 1986-95, mgr. tech. svc., 1988-95; sys. engr. MobileComm, Ridgeland, Miss., 1995—. Mem. IEEE, Am. Mgmt. Assn. Avocations: photography, reading, electronic circuit design and simulation, writing computer programs in C++. Home: 424 Red River Trail 1084 Irving TX 75063 Office: MobileComm 6221 N O Connor Blvd Ste 116 Irving TX 75039-3515

ROBINSON, CHARLES PAUL, nuclear physicist, diplomat, business executive; b. Detroit, Oct. 9, 1941; s. Edward Leonard and Mary Opal (Edmondson) R.; m. Barbara Thomas Woodard; children by previous marriage: Paula S., Colin C. BS in Physics, Christian Bros. U., 1963; PhD in Physics, Fla. State U., 1967. Mem. nuclear test staff Los Alamos (N.Mex.) Nat. Lab., 1967-69, chief test operator, 1969-70, mem. advanced concepts staff, 1971-72, assoc. div. leader, lasers, 1972-76, div. leader, 1976-79, assoc. dir., 1980-85; sr. v.p., bd. dirs. Ebasco Services Inc. subs. Enserch Corp., N.Y.C., 1985-88; ambass. to nuclear testing talks U.S. Dept. State, Geneva, 1988-90; v.p. Sandia Nat. Labs., Albuquerque, 1990-95, pres., 1995—; mem. sci. adv. group Def. Nuclear Agy., Washington, 1981-86; mem. nat. security bd. Los Alamos Nat. Lab., 1985-88; chmn. Presdl. Tech. Adv. Bd., 1991; mem. U.S. Strategic Command Adv. Bd. Pres. Student Concerts Inc., Los Alamos, 1972-74; instr. U. N.Mex., Los Alamos, 1974-76; exec. bd. Boy Scouts of N.Mex. Recipient Outstanding Pub. Svc. medal Joint Chiefs of Staff, 1996. Mem. Am. Phys. Soc., Am. Nuclear Soc. Avocation: choral singing. Office: Sandia Nat Labs Albuquerque NM 87185-0101

ROBINSON, CHARLES WARREN, controller; b. Steubenville, Ohio, Sept. 8, 1948; s. Arthur Henry and Thelma L. (Lewis) R.; m. Donna Lee Valko, Dec. 9, 1972; children: Jeffrey, Jason, Jared. Student, Jefferson Tech. Coll., 1968-71, 80-84, West Liberty State Coll., 1984. Tripper operator Ohio Power Co., Brilliant, 1966-71; loan officer Heritage Bank, Steubenville, Ohio, 1971-73; divsn. mgr. Carlisle's Dept. Store, Steubenville, 1973-75; asst. dir. Hancock County Sheltered Workshop, Weirton, W.Va., 1975-80; contr. Snyder Distbg., Wintersville, Ohio, 1980-84, Collier Industries, Collier, W.Va., 1984-89, Weir-Cove Moving & Storage, Weirton, W.Va., 1989—. Pres. St. Paul Sch. Bd., Weirton, W. Va., 1989-92, No. Panhandle Soccer Assn., Weirton, 1986-87; mem. Madonna High Sch. Athletic Bd., Weirton, 1992-93. Mem. Inst. Mgmt. Acctg., Am. Trucking Assn. Nat. Acctg. and Fin. Coun., Weirton Rotary Club (bd. mem. 1990—, Community Svc. award 1989, Rotarian of Year 1992, pres. 1996). Avocations: coaching youth soccer and basketball, community service. Office: Weir-Cove Moving & Storage 4224 Freedom Way Weirton WV 26062-5212

ROBINSON, CHARLES WESLEY, energy company executive; b. Long Beach, Calif., Sept. 7, 1919; s. Franklin Willard and Anna Hope (Gould) R.; m. Tamara Lindovna, Mar. 8, 1957; children: Heather Lynne, Lisa Anne, Wendy Paige. AB cum laude in Econs., U. Calif., Berkeley, 1941; MBA, Stanford U., 1947. Asst. mgr. mfg. Golden State Dairy Products Co., San Francisco, 1947-49; v.p., then pres. Marcona Corp., San Francisco, 1952-74; undersec. of state for econ. affairs Dept. State, Washington, 1974-75, dep. sec. of state, 1976-77; sr. mng. partner Kuhn Loeb & Co., N.Y.C., 1977-78; vice chmn. Blyth Eastman Dillon & Co., N.Y.C., 1978-79; chmn. Energy Transition Corp., Santa Fe and Washington, 1979-82; pres. Robinson & Assocs., Inc., Santa Fe, 1982—; pres. Dyna-Yacht, Inc., San Diego, 1982—; bd. dirs. The Allen Group, NIKE, Inc. Patentee slurry transport., Brookings Instn., Washington, 1977—. Served to lt. USN, 1941-46. Recipient Disting. Honor award Dept. State, 1977. Republican. Methodist. Office: Robinson & Assocs Inc PO Box 2224 Santa Fe NM 87504-2224

ROBINSON, CHARLOTTE HILL, artist; b. San Antonio, Nov. 28, 1924; d. Lucius Davis and Charlotte (Moore) Hill; m. Floyd I. Robinson, Mar. 1943; children: Floyd I. Jr., Lawrence H., Elizabeth H. Student, Incarnate Word Coll., 1943, 44, 45, NYU, 1947, 48, Corcoran Sch. Art, 1951-52. Painting instr. Art League No. Va., Alexandria, 1967-75; Condr. Art World Seminar Washington Women's Art Ctr., 1975-80, drawing workshop Smithsonian Instn. Resident Assocs. Program, Washington, 1977; program dir. Nat. Women's Caucus for Art, 1979; project coord., exhbn. curator The Artist and the Quilt, nat. mus. traveling exhbn., 1983-86; vis. artist S.W. Craft Ctr., San Antonio, 1983-85; lectr. WFUV 90 FM, Fordham U., N.Y.C., 1990, San Antonio Art Inst., 1991, Nat. Mus. for Women in Arts, Washington, 1991, Iowa State U., Ames, 1991. Editor: The Artist & The Quilt, 1983; one-person shows include Thames Sic. Ctr., New London, Conn., 1991, Brunner Gallery & Mus., Iowa State U., 1991, 92, San Antonio Art. Inst., 1991, de Andino Fine Arts, Washington, 1992, Masur Mus. Art, Monroe, La., 1993, 96, Lee Hansley Art Gallery, Raleigh, N.C., 1993, 97, Sol Del Rio, San Antonio, 1995, 1812 Artic Gallery, Virginia Beach, Va., 1995, Savannah Coll. Art and Design, 1997; exhibited in group shows at Franklin Square and Watkins Gallery, Washington, 1992, Rutgers U., New Brunswick, N.J., 1992, 96, Brody's Gallery, Washington, 1992, Lee Hansley Art Gallery, Raleigh, 1993, 96, Emerson Gallery, McLean, 1993, 95, No. Va. C.C., 1994, Harvard U., 1996. Trustee Bronx (N.Y.) Mus., 1977; bd. dirs. Washington Women's Art Ctr., 1977; nat. bd. dirs. Women's Caucus for Art, 1983-84; bd. dirs. New Art Examiner, 1985-86. Recipient Concourse award Corcoran Sch. Art, 1952, Scholarship award Telfair Acad. Art, Savannah, Ga., 1959; Nat. Endowment for Arts grantee, 1977, 78-81; fellow Va. Ctr. for Creative Arts, Sweet Briar, Va., 1985.

ROBINSON, CHESTER HERSEY, retired dean; b. Yonkers, N.Y., Nov. 8, 1918; s. Sherman Alexander and Alice (Hersey) R.; m. Marguerite Davis, Dec. 14, 1945 (div. Oct. 1976); children—Barry, Roslyn; m. Heidemarie Höfler, Dec. 30, 1976. A.B., Union Coll., Schenectady, 1940; Ph.D., Stanford U., 1950. Asst. registrar Stanford U., 1949-50; dir. div. extension and summer session Miami U., Oxford, Ohio, 1950-54; assoc. dir. Sch. Gen. Studies, Hunter Coll., 1954-60; dir. Sch. Gen. Studies, Bronx campus, 1960-66, dean, 1966-68; dean Sch. Gen. Studies, Herbert H. Lehman Coll. CUNY, 1968-82, dean Continuing Edn., 1982-86; prof. emeritus, 1986—. Served to lt. USNR, 1942-46. Mem. NEA, Beta Theta Pi, Phi Delta Kappa. Presbyterian. Lodge: Elks. Home: 87 Roses Grove Rd Southampton NY 11968

ROBINSON, CHRISTOPHER THOMAS, artist; b. Cold Spring Harbor, N.Y., Mar. 18, 1951; s. Fred Marlin and Gladys (Langford) R.; m. Janet Thompson, Jan. 17, 1972; children: Justin Christopher, Sarah Williams. BFA, Fla. State U., 1973; MFA, U. Mass., 1975. Teaching assoc. U. Mass., Amherst, 1973-75; assoc. prof. U. S.C., Columbia, 1975—, dir. grad. studies; vis. artist U. Ala., Huntsville, 1977, U. Cen. Ark., Conway, 1986, McDowell Tech., Marion, N.C., 1986—, Coll. of Charleston, S.C., 1987, U. N.C., 1987, Clemson U., 1989; ops. leader Operation Raleigh, Chile, 1985; expdn. leader U.S. Sci. Expdn., London, 1987-88, Global Patriots climb of Orizaba, Mex., 1990, Global Patriots climb of Aconcagua, Argentina, 1992; cons. S.C. State Mus., Columbia, 1986—; seminar speaker Internat. Leadership Seminar; guest artist Meadow Creek Project, Honors Program, Conway, 1987. Solo exhbns. include U. Mass., Amherst, 1974, 75, Heath Gallery, Atlanta, 1977, Greenville County Mus. Art, 1978, U. S.C. Museums, 1978, U. of the South, Sewanee, Tenn., 1980, Atlanta Art Workers Coalition Gallery, 1980, Columbia Coll., 1983, Coll. Charleston, S.C., 1987, U. N.C., Chapel Hill, 1987, S.C. State Mus., Columbia, 1989, Carolighting State House, Columbia, N.C., 1991, Fayetteville St. Mall, Raleigh, N.C., 1991, So. Bell Regional Hdqrs., Charlotte, N.C., 1991; exhibited in group shows at Seven Hills Gallery, Tallahassee, Fla., 1973, Fla. State U., 1973, Archives of Am. Art, 1975, Columbia Mus. of Art, 1976-77, 9th Nat. and Internat. Sculpture Conf., 1976, Southeastern Coll. Art, 1976, New Orleans Mus. Art, 1977, Nat. Sculpture Conf., Jonesboro, 1977, Arcosanti Festival, Cordes Junction, Ariz., 1978, 19th Nat. Art Roundup Las Vegas Mus. Art, 1979, Coll. Art Assn. Ann. Meeting, 1980, Appalachian State U., 1981, Eastern Ill. U., 1981, Southeastern Ctr. Contemporary Art, Winston-Salem, N.C., 1981, Netherlands/American Contemporary Print Exchange Exhibition, 1982, S.C. Arts Commn. Ann. Exhbn., 1976, 81, 83 (Purchase award-State Collection), Friends of Arts First Regional Juried Exhbn., Spartanburg, S.C., 1983, U.S. Nat. Fine Arts Competition, Tallahassee, Fla., 1984, Southeastern Ctr. Contemporary Art, Winston-Salem, N.C., 1984, Portrait of the South, Rome Exhibition, Palazzo Venezia, Rome Italy, 1984, Fact, Fiction and Fantasy: Recent Narrative Art in the S.E., Ewing Art Gallery, U. Tenn., 1987, Art in Transit, Arts Festival of Atlanta, 1989, Austin Peay State U., Clarksville, Tenn., 1993, Anderson County Arts Ctr., 1993 (Merit award 1993), S.C. State Mus., Columbia, 1994, Arts Festival Atlanta, 1994, Emblems, Yale U. Art Gallery. d. dirs. Lexington County Sch. Dist. 5, Ballentine, S.C., 1986-89; vice chmn. sch. bd., Sch. Dist. 5, Lexington and Richland counties, chmn. bd. trusteees, 1993-96; mem. boardmanship tng. cadre S.C. Sch. Bds. Assn., 1990; seminar speaker Hugh O'Brian Youth Found., Denver, 1987; pres.-elect exec. bd. S.C. Sch. Bds. Assn., 1993—. Lt. candidate, USN, 1978. Artist grant S.C. Arts Com., 1976; grantee Southern Regional Edn. Bd., Atlanta, 1985-86; Faculty Devel. grantee U. S.C., 1986-87; recipient Merit award 18th Ann. Juried Show Anderson County Arts Ctr.; Venture Fund grantee U. S.C. Mem. Southern Assn. Sculptors, Nat. Sculpture Exhbn., World Coun., Sci. Exploration Soc. (hon. 1987-89). Youth Svc. Internat. (bd. dirs. 1991—). Avocations: flying, mountain climbing. Leader Global Patriots climb of south ridge St. Elias, 1993. Home: 300 Lost Creek Dr Columbia SC 29212-2487 Office: U SC Dept Art Columbia SC 29208

ROBINSON, DANIEL BARUCH, banker; b. Hamilton, Ont., Can., Dec. 4, 1937; s. David A. and Zelda (Frank) R.; m. Marta A. Calero, May 7, 1960; children—Allegra, Robert. B.Commerce, McMaster U., Hamilton, Ont., 1960; postgrad., U. Mich., 1969, Harvard U., 1971, Pontif Universidade Católica do Rio de Janeiro, 1979, Georgetown U., 1994, 96. Chartered acct. Vice pres. fin. Comsur, La Paz, Bolivia, 1971-72; fin. dir. Light Servicos, Rio De Janeiro, Brazil, 1972-78; sr. fin. analyst The World Bank, Washington, 1978-79; v.p. fin. Jari Florestal, Rio De Janeiro, 1979-80, Manalta Coal, Calgary, Alta, Can, 1981-82; exec.v.p. Atomic Energy Can. Ltd., Mississauga, Ont., 1983-85; rep. Interam. Devel. Bank, Barbados, 1985-89, Washington, 1989—. Pres. Canadian Club, Rio de Janeiro, 1974-75. Recipient Highest Standing prize Chartered Accts. Assn., 1961; Price, Waterhouse and Co. scholar, 1959. Mem. Inst. Chartered Accts. Ont., Canadian Inst. Chartered Accts., Fin. Execs. Inst. Clubs: Rio de Janeiro Yacht, Jockey Club do Rio de Janeiro, Itanhangá Golf (Rio de Janeiro), Sandy Ln. Property Owners Assn. (Barbados). Avocations: reading; translating from Spanish and Portuguese to English. Home: 12 4th St NE Washington DC 20002-5930 Office: Interam Devel Bank Washington DC 20577

ROBINSON, DANIEL N., psychology educator; b. N.Y., Mar. 9, 1937; s. Henry S. and Margaret R.; children from a previous marriage: Tracey, Kimberly; m. Francine Malasko, 1967. BA, Colgate U., 1958; MA, Hofstra U., 1960; PhD, CUNY, 1965. Rsch. psychologist, electronics rsch. labs. Columbia U., 1960-65, asst. dir. sci. honors program electronics rsch. labs., 1964-68, sr. rsch. psychologist, electronics rsch. labs., 1965-68, asst. dir. of life scis. electronics rsch. labs., 1967-68; asst. prof. dept. psychology Amherst Coll., 1968-70, assoc. prof., 1970-71; dir. grad. program dept. psychology Georgetown Univ., 1981-83, chmn. dept. psychology, 1973-76, 85-91, assoc. prof., 1971-74, prof., 1974—; adj. prof. philosophy Georgetown Univ., Washington, 1996—; vis. lectr. in Psychol. Princeton U., 1965-68; vis. prof. Folger Shakespeare Inst., 1977; vis. sr. mem. Linacre Coll., vis. lectr. in philosophy, U. Oxford, 1991—; cons. NIH, 1967-70, NSF, 1965-75, PBS, 1978-84, 1985-88, MacArthur Found., 1985, Atty. Gen.'s. Task Force on Crime, 1980, Dept. Health and Human Svcs., NIH, 1988. Author: Psychology: A Study of Its Origins and Principles, 1972, The Enlightened Machine: An Anlytical Introduction to Neuropsychology, 1973, 80, Psychology: Traditions and Perspectives, 1976, An Intellectual History of Psychology, 1976, The Mind Unfolded: Essay's on Psychology's Historic Texts, 1978, Systems of Modern Psychology: A Critical Sketch, 1979, Psychology and Law: Can Justice Survive the Social Sciences?, 1980, An Intellectual History of Psychology-Revised Edition, 1981, 3rd edit., 1995, Toward A Science of Human Nature: Essays on the Psychologies of Hegel, Mill, Wundt, and James, 1982, Philosophy of Psychology, 1985, Aristotle's Psychology, 1989, (with William R. Uttal) Foundations of Psychobiology, 1983, (with Sir John Eccles) The Wonder of Being Human: Our Mind and Our Brain, 1984; editor Heredity and Achievement, 1970, Readings in the Origins and Principles of Psychology, 1972, Significant Contributions to the History of Psychology, 1977-78, Annals of Theoretical Psychology, 1990, Social Discourse and Moral Judgment, 1992, Wild Beasts and Idle Humours: Legal Insanity from Antiquity to the Present, 1996; contbr. chpts. to books, reference books, articles to profl. jours. Recipient Inst. for Advanced Study in the Humanities fellow, U. Edinburgh, 1986-87; Pres's. medal Colgate U., 1986, Pub. Svc. award Gen. Svcs. Adminstrn., 1986. Fellow Am. Psychol. Assn. (divsns. 3, 24, 26), British Psychol. Soc.; mem. Sigma Xi, Psi Chi. Home: 300 E Main St Middletown MD 21769-7927 Office: Georgetown U Dept Psychology Washington DC 20057

ROBINSON, DANIEL THOMAS, brokerage company executive; b. Los Angeles, June 17, 1925; s. George Thomas and Helen Theresa (Walsh) R.; m. Diane W. Robinson; children—Marc David, Matthew Curtis. B.S., U. So. Calif., 1948, M.B.A., 1950. Pres. Horton & Converse Inc., 1961—; v.p. Dart Industries, Inc., Los Angeles, 1962-63; sr. v.p. Bergen Brunswig Corp., Los Angeles, 1972-80; dir. bus. devel. Merrill Lynch, Los Angeles, 1981-82; with Internat. Network Brokerage, 1983—; bd. dirs. K.D.L. Corp., Home Interstate Bank Fin. Svcs., Healthbank Corp. Author: Medical Marketing of Seventies, 1968, Marketing Challenges of Biomedical Industry, 1969, Biomedical Marketing, 1975, Biomedical Representation, 1976, Real Estate Funding Principles, 1988, Desert Properties for a Future, 1988, Sea and Desert Investments, 1989, Principles of Network Brokerage Marketing, 1991, Medical Products Brokerage Avocation, 1993, Brokerage Marketing Through Network Brokers, 1996. Past pres., bd. dirs. Trojan Club, U. So. Calif.; past pres. Cardinal and Gold; past pres. U. So. Calif., bd. councillors. Mem. Am. Coll. Pharmacists (dir., past pres.), Am., Man. surg. trade assns., Health Industries Assn. Office: 32081 Via Flores San Juan Capistrano CA 92675-3867

ROBINSON, DAVID ADAIR, neurophysiologist; b. Boston, Dec. 9, 1925; s. Edwin Whitmore and Gladys (Mansley) Colby; m. Ellen Marie Rogus, June 13, 1980. B.A., Brown U., 1947; M.S., Johns Hopkins U., 1956, Dr.Engring., 1958. Project engr., dir. engring., v.p. charge research Airpax Electronics Inc., Ft. Lauderdale, Fla., 1951-61; mem. faculty Johns Hopkins U. Med. Sch., 1961—, prof. ophthalmology depts. ophthalmology and biomed. engring., 1975-93, prof. emeritus, 1993—; mem. vis. sci. study sect. div. research grants NIH, 1966-70, engring. in biology and med. tng. com., 1971-73; mem. communicative sci. cluster President's Biomed. Research Panel, 1975; mem. planning com. sensori-motor disorders vision Nat. Eye Inst., NIH, 1976, 81; cons. in field. Editorial bd.: Investigative Ophthalmology, Exptl. Brain Research, Vision Research, Jour. Neurophysiology. Served to ensign USN, 1947-49. Rsch. grantee Nat. Eye Inst., 1969—, Rsch. to Prevent Blindness, 1975-77. Mem. Am. Inst. Med. Biol. Engring., Assn. Research Vision and Ophthalmology, Soc. Neurosci., Bárány Soc. Democrat. Research and publs. on neurophysiology oculomotor system.

ROBINSON, DAVID BRADFORD, poet, scientific writer; b. Richmond, Va., Apr. 14, 1937; s. Albert Lewis and Martha Ellen (Lovern) R. BS, U. Miami, 1959, MS, 1961; AA, Miami-Dade Community Coll., 1970; DSc, Northwestern Coll., 1978, PhD, 1979. Author: Characteristics of Cesium, 1978, Collected Poems, 1987. Founder Ronald Reagan Rep. Ctr., Washington; exhibitor Statue of Liberty, Port of N.Y., 1986; mem. Heritage Found., 1989; sustaining sponsor Ronald Reagan Presdl. Found., 1987; charter mem. Ronald Reagan Trust; charter mem. Honor Roll Rep. Presdl. Task Force, 1990, life mem., 1989, Commemorative Honor Roll, 1991; mem. Nat. Rep. Senatorial Com. with Presdl. Commn., 1992; founding sponsor, founding mem. Space Life Sta., 1990; spkrs. citizen task force Inaugural Mem. Cert. of Honor, 1996. Recipient 2d pl. Amateur Trophy, Capablanca Chess Club, 1964, Presdl. Sports award bicycling, 1976, Presdl. Achievement award Rep. Nat. Com., 1982, Cert. Good Standing Rep. Presdl. Task Force, 1982-85, Presdl. Merit medal, 1982, Appreciation cert. Sen. Paula Hawkins, 1986, Golden Poet Trophy award World of Poetry, 1987k, Silver Anniversary Album, Nat. Geog. Soc., 1987, Pres. Ronald Reagan Appreciation cert., 1988, Pres. Bush Congl. Victory Squadron Recognition cert., 1989, Bush Inaugural/Freedom medal, 1989, World Time-Capsule cert., 1990, Am. in Space medal, 1990, Pegasus Time Capsule plaque, 1991, Congl. Merit cert. Nat. Rep. Congl. Com., 1992, Battle of Normandy Found. Appreciation award, 1993, Presdl. Legion of Merit medal, 1993, Congl. Order of Liberty award, 1993, Appreciation cert. Sen. Kay Bailey Hutchinson, 1993, Rep. Presdl. award, 1994, Albert Einstein medal Brit. Bur. Degree Promotion, 1994, Cert. of Appreciation, The Golden Heart Club, Mil. Order of Purple Heart Svc. Found., Congl. Order of Freedom, 1995, Cert. of Meritorious Svc. Rep. Party Planning Com., 1996, Chmn.'s Honor Roll cert., Rep. Nat. Com., 1997, others.$Dr commn. Rep. Nat. Com. Com., polit. orgns. Mem. Am. Air Mus. (Brit., founder 1991), Battle of Normandy Meml. Mus. (charter 1988), Sigma Xi, Russian Club, Phi Theta Kappa. Avocation: chess. Home: 715 NE 92nd St Apt 1A Miami FL 33138

ROBINSON, DAVID BROOKS, retired naval officer; b. Alexandria, La., Oct. 26, 1939; s. Donald and Marion (Holloman) R.; m. Gene Kirkpatrick, Aug. 1, 1964; children: Kirk, David. Student, Tex. A&M U., 1958-59; BS, U.S. Naval Acad., 1963; MS in Physics, Naval Postgrad. Sch., Monterey, Calif., 1969. Commd. ensign USN, 1963, advanced through grades to vice admiral, 1993; comdg. officer USS Canon and USS Ready, Guam, 1969-71; adminstrv. aide to Chmn. Joint Chiefs Staff, Washington, 1971-74; comdg. officer USS Luce, Mayport, Fla., 1976-78; surface comdr. assignment officer and dir. fiscal mgt. and procedural control divsn. Naval Mil. Pers. Cmd., 1979-81; mem. Fgn. Service Inst. Exec. Seminar, Washington, 1982; comdg. officer USS Richmond K. Turner, Charleston, S.C., 1983-84; chief of staff, comdr. Naval Surface Force, Atlantic Fleet, Norfolk, Va., 1984; exec. asst. and sr. aide to vice chief Naval Ops., Washington, 1985, dir. Manpower and Tng. div., 1986, dir. Surface Warfare div., 1987-88; cmdr. cruiser destroyer group 8, 1988-89; vice dir. and subsequently dir. operational plans and interoperability directorate Joint Staff, Washington, 1989-91; dep., chief of staff to comdr. U.S. Pacific Fleet, 1991-93, comdr. naval surface force, 1993-96; ret. USN, 1996. Decorated Navy Cross, Def. D.S.M., D.S.M., Legion of Merit with 4 gold stars, Bronze Star, Purple Heart. Mem. Optimists (pres. Oakton, Va. 1986-87). Methodist. Avocations: golf, cycling, stamp collecting, reading. Office: 1001 B Ave Ste 200 Coronado CA 92118-3424

ROBINSON, DAVID CLINTON, reporter; b. Goffstown, N.H., Nov. 5, 1963; s. Clinton and Barbara Lee (Ploss) R.; m. Karen Ruth Eckhardt, July 3, 1992; children: Laura Lee, Lindsay Lee, Clinton Nelson. AB, Syracuse U., 1985. Reporter The Buffalo News, 1985—. Mem. Buffalo Newspaper Guild (exec. com. 1989—, vice chmn. 1991-92). Office: The Buffalo News 1 News Plz Buffalo NY 14203-2930

ROBINSON, DAVID MAURICE, professional basketball player; b. Key West, Fla., Aug. 6, 1965. Grad., U.S. Naval Acad., 1987. Commd. ensign USN, 1987; with San Antonio Spurs, 1989—; mem. U.S. Olympic Basketball Team, 1988, 92. Recipient Naismith award, 1987, Wooden award, 1987, IBM award, 1990, 91, 94, Schick Pivotal Player award, 1990, 91; named to Sporting News All-Am. First Team, 1986, 87, Sporting News Coll. Player of Yr., 1987, NBA Rookie of Yr., 1990, All-NBA First Team, 1991, 92, All-Star team, 1990-94; named NBA Defensive Player of Yr., 1992, MVP, 1994-95, season MVP, 1995. Holder NCAA Divsn. 1 single season record most block shots per game (5.91), most blocked shots in 1 game (14), 1986, NBA career record most blocked shots per game (3.65). Office: care San Antonio Spurs 100 Montana St San Antonio TX 78203-1033*

ROBINSON, DAVID WEAVER, surgeon, educator; b. Kansas City, Mo., Nov. 15, 1914; s. David Beach and Aileen (Weaver) R.; m. Margaret Sherwood, June 20, 1940 (dec. Feb. 1986); children: David S., Nancy K., Peter B., Mary A.; m. Alma L. Dallas Horner, Aug. 26, 1987 (dec. 1991). A.B., U. Kans., 1935, M.S., 1948; M.D., U. Pa., 1938. Diplomate: Am. Bd. Surgery, Am. Bd. Plastic Surgery. Intern Phila. Gen. Hosp., 1938-40; surg. trainee U. Kans. Med. Ctr., Kansas City, 1940-43, instr., 1941-43, asst. prof., 1948-50, assoc. prof., 1951-54, prof. surgery, 1954-85, Regents prof., 1973-85; disting. prof. emeritus U. Kans. Med. Ctr., 1985—, chmn. sect. plastic surgery, 1947-72, dir. U. Kans. Burn Ctr., 1972-83, vice chancellor clin. affairs, 1974-80, acting vice chancellor, 1975-76; mem. surg. study sect. NIH Research Council, 1962-65. Contbr. articles to med. jours. Trustee Kansas City Philharm. Assn., Kans., 1963—. Served to capt. M.C. AUS, 1943-45. Decorated Croix de Guerre France; recipient disting. alumni citation U. Kans., 1969. Mem. Am. Assn. Plastic Surgeons (honoree of yr. award 1982), Am. Assn. for Surgery Trauma, ACS (gov. 1973-79 honoree of yr. award), Am. Soc. Plastic and Reconstructive Surgery (pres. 1966), Am. Trauma Soc. (founding mem.), Am. Surg. Assn. (2d v.p. 1965), Central Surg. Assn., Western Surg. Assn., AMA, Assn. for Cleft Palate Rehab., Kans. Med. Soc. Plastic Surgery Research Council, Rocky Mountain Traumatological Soc., Soc. for Surgery Head and Neck, Soc. Univ. Surgeons, Am. Bd. Plastic Surgery (chmn. examining bd. 1966—), Societe Internationale de Chirurgie, Sigma Xi, Nu Sigma Nu, Alpha Omega Alpha, Beta Theta Pi. Republican. Presbyterian (ruling elder 1953—). Home: 7930 Bristol Ct Shawnee Mission KS 66208-5220 Office: U Kans Med Ctr Kansas City KS 66103

ROBINSON, DAVID ZAV, non-profit agency consultant; b. Montreal, Que., Can., Sept. 29, 1927; s. Benjamin and Antonia (Seiden) R.; m. Nan Senior, Sept. 6, 1954; children: Marc, Eric. AB, Harvard U., 1946, AM, 1947, PhD, 1950. Asst. dir. rsch. Baird-Atomic Inc., Cambridge, Mass., 1949-59, 60-61; sci. liaison officer Office Naval Rsch., London, 1959-60; sci. advisor staff Office of Pres., Washington, 1961-67; v.p. acad. affairs NYU, 1967-70; v.p. Carnegie Corp. N.Y., N.Y.C., 1970-80, exec. v.p., 1981-85, exec. v.p., treas., 1986-88; exec. dir. Carnegie Commn. on Sci Tech. and Govt., 1988-97; dir. Urban Research Corp., Chgo., 1968-75; cons. Congressional Office of Tech. Assessment, 1975-78; mem. com. women in sci. NRC, 1975-82; mem. vis. com. dept. chemistry Harvard U., 1977-83; physics dept. Princeton U., 1970-76. Mem. N.Y. Energy Rsch. and Devel. Authority, 1971-77; trustee CUNY, 1976-81, Amideast, 1983-88, Citizen Union Found., 1985—, Inst. Schs. of the Future, 1986—, N.C. Sch. Sci. and Math., 1989—, Santa Fe Inst., 1987—, Prep for Prep, 1989—. Mem. AAAS, Optical Soc. Am., Coun. on Fgn. Rels., Am. Contract Bridge League, Harvard Club (N.Y.C.). Office: 437 Madison Ave New York NY 10022-7001

ROBINSON, DAVIS ROWLAND, lawyer; b. N.Y.C., July 11, 1940; s. Thomas Porter and Cynthia (Davis) R.; m. Suzanne Walker, June 11, 1966; children: Christopher Champlin II, Gracyn Walker. BA magna cum laude, Yale U., 1961; LLB cum laude, Harvard U., 1967. Bar: N.Y. 1968, D.C. 1971, U.S. Supreme Ct. 1972. Fgn. svc. officer U.S. Dept. State, Washington, 1961-69; assoc. Sullivan & Cromwell, N.Y.C., 1969-71; assoc., then ptnr. Leva, Hawes, Symington, Martin and Oppenheimer, Washington, 1971-81; legal adviser U.S. Dept. State, Washington, 1981-85; ptnr. Pillsbury, Madison & Sutro, Washington, 1985-88, Le Boeuf, Lamb, Greene & MacRae, Washington, 1988—; adj. prof. Georgetown Univ. Law Ctr.; dir. Mid. East Inst. Pres. Harvard Legal Aid Bur., 1966-67. Mem. ABA, Assn. of Bar of City of N.Y., Am. Law Inst. (adviser fgn. rels. law of U.S.), Am. Soc. Internat. Law, Coun. on Fgn. Rels., Phi Beta Kappa. Office: Le Boeuf Lamb Greene & MacRae 1875 Connecticut Ave NW Washington DC 20009-5728

ROBINSON, DIXIE FAYE, school system administrator; b. Lexington, Ky., Feb. 7, 1944; d. John David and Betty Lou (Taylor) Moore; m. Jim Darrell Robinson, June 25, 1978. BA, Georgetown (Ky.) Coll., 1966; MA in Edn., Ball State U., 1972; postgrad., Miami U., Oxford, Ohio, 1989—, Ind. U., 1990-92. Cert. tchr., Ind. Tchr. Richmond (Ind.) Community Schs., 1966-91, adminstr., 1991—; team leader Richmond Community schs., 1983-90, mentor tchr., 1989-91, coop. learning staff devel. mem., 1989-91, coord. ptnrship in edn., 1990-91, site-base convenor, 1990-91; v.p. Richmond Area Reading Coun., 1984. Pres. Historic Richmond, Inc., 1982; tour guide Richmond-Wayne County Tourism Bur., 1986-87; vice-chmn. Richmond Area Rose Festival, 1988-89; adv. bd. Palladium Item, Richmond, 1990. Recipient Hoosier Meritorious award Ind. Sec. of State, 1986, Nat. Energy Edn. Devel. award, Washington, 1991; grantee Newspapers in Edn., 1986. Mem. NEA, NAFE, ASCD, Nat. Middle Sch. Assn., Assn. Tchr. Educators, Nat. Assn. Secondary Sch. Prins., Nat. Coun. Tchrs. English (Ctr. of Excellence award 1988-91), Ind. Coun. Tchrs. of English (Hoosier Tchr. English 1991), Ind. Middle Level Inst., Richmond Area Reading Coun., Kappa Delta Gamma, Phi Delta Kappa. Avocations: historic preservation, antiques, community affairs, reading, travel. Home: 100 NW 8th St Richmond IN 47374-4055

ROBINSON, DONALD LEONARD, social scientist, educator; b. Buffalo, Dec. 28, 1936; s. Sidney Smith and Marion Esther (Hershiser) R.; m. Molly McCaslin Jahnige, Jan. 1, 1983; children: John Samuel, David Wynn; stepchildren: Katherine Jahnige, Paul Jahnige. BA, Yale U., 1958; MDiv, Union Theol. Sem., 1962; PhD, Cornell U., 1966. Instr. govt. Cornell U., Ithaca, N.Y., 1965-66; asst. prof. Smith Coll., Northampton, Mass., 1966-71, assoc. prof., 1971-78, prof., 1978—, Sylvia Dlugasch Bauman chair Am. studies, 1990-93, dir. Am. studies, 1979-85; cons. Ford Found., 1986-88, 91-92, Media and Society, 1986-87, Comm. on Operation of U.S. Senate, 1976; dir. Project '87, 1977-78; vis. prof. Doshisha U., Kyoto, Japan, 1989. Author: Slavery in the Structure of American Politics, 1765-1820, 1971, To the Best of My Ability: The Presidency and the Constitution, 1987, Government for the Third American Century, 1989; mem. editorial bd. Presdl. Studies Quar., 1987—; editor: Reforming American Government: The Bicentennial Papers of the Committee on the Constitutional System, 1985. Adminstr. New Eng. Regional Commn., 1973; chmn. Dem. City Com., 1978-80, Northampton Planning Bd., 1980-82; warden St. John's Episcopal Ch., 1981-85; trustee Diocese of Western Mass., 1988—; bd. selectmen, Ashfield, Mass., 1992—. Rockefeller Bros. fellow, 1958-59; Kent fellow, 1962-66; Project '87 fellow, 1980; fellow Ctr. for Study Democratic Insts., 1971; Phi Beta Kappa vis. scholar, 1988-89; recipient Anisfield-Wolf award, 1971. Mem. Am. Polit. Sci. Assn., Cosmos Club, Phi Beta Kappa. Home: Norton Hill Rd Ashfield MA 01330 Office: Smith Coll Dept Govt Northampton MA 01063

ROBINSON, DONALD PETER, musician, retired electrical engineer; b. Phila., Jan. 27, 1928; s. Warren Frederick and Marcella Theresa (Derry) R.; m. Beatrice Graves, Sept. 22, 1951 (dec.); children: Donald, Stephen, Sharon Robinson-Byrd, Michael; m. Mary Katherine Robertson, June 9, 1990. A.A., Temple U. Sch. Tech., 1956. Sr. engr./technician Gen. Electric Co., Utica, N.Y., 1956-89, ret., 1989; organist emeritus St. Joseph-St. Patrick's Ch., Utica, 1983—; minister music/organist St. Paul's Baptist Ch., Utica, 1961-88; organist Utica Council K.C., 1969—; organist/choir dir. 4th degree assembly Central N.Y. dist. K.C., 1985—; producer, host Organ Loft radio program WLFH, Little Falls, N.Y., 1962-90; pipe organ cons. Served with AUS, 1948-54. Mem. Am. Guild Organists (past dean central N.Y. chpt.), Am. Theatre Organ Soc., Nat. Assn. R.R. Passengers (bd. dirs.), K.C. (past faithful navigator 4th degree assembly). Roman Catholic. Home: 715 Garfield Ave Rockford IL 61103-6023

ROBINSON, DONALD WALTER, university dean; b. Rockford, Ill.; s. Walter John and Viola (Anderson) R.; m. Betty Jane Zink, May 30, 1948; children: Deborah Beth, Galen Don, Darci Lynn, Gregory John. A.B., Carthage Coll., 1950; M.A., Bradley U., 1951, Ph.D., 1957. Various positions coll. and pub. sch. adminstrn., 1952-58; specialist in coll. adminstrn. U.S. Office of Edn., Washington, 1959-62; dir. mental retardation research centers program Nat. Inst. Child Health and Human Devel., Bethesda, Md., 1962-65; asst. dean, prof. higher edn. So. Ill. U., Carbondale, 1965-70; dean, prof. Coll. Edn. Youngstown (Ohio) State U., 1970-72; dean Coll. Edn., prof. psychology and higher edn. Okla. State U., Stillwater, 1972-88, dean, prof. emeritus, 1988; dean, prof. Sch. Edn. U. Mo., St. Louis, 1988-92, dean emeritus, 1967-93; cons. examiner North Ctrl. Assn. Schs. and Colls., 1967-93; bd. examiners Nat. Coun. Accreditation/Tchr. Edn., 1990-93; cons. New Eng. Assn. Schs. and Colls., USPHS, U.S. Office Edn., World Bank; bd. dirs. Holmes Group, 1987-88. Bd. dirs. Marymount U., Arlington, Va., 1962-66, St. Louis Sci. Ctr., 1989-92, Teen Challenge Ark., 1994—, St. Louis Regional Edn. Partnership, 1989-92; pres. bd. dirs. Cmty. Counseling Found., Hot Springs, Ark.; ruling elder John Calvin Presbyn. Ch., Bridgeton, Mo., Kirk in Pines, Hot Springs Village, Ark. With USAAF, 1944-46. Mem. Am. Assn. Colls. Tchr. Edn. (govt. rels. com. 1977-79, 88-91, bd. dirs. 1988-90), North Ctrl. Assn. Colls. and Schs. (dir. 1975-79, chmn. coun. rsch. and svc. 1977-79), Am. Psychol. Assn., Am. Ednl. Rsch. Assn., Am. Assn. Higher Edn., Assn. Colls. and Schs. Edn. in State Univs., Land Grant Colls. and Affiliated Pvt. Univs. (sec. 1985-86, pres. elect 1987-88, pres. 1988-90, past pres., bd. dirs. 1990-92), Kiwanis. Home: 2 Caribe Ln Hot Springs Village AR 71909

ROBINSON, DOROTHY K., lawyer; b. New Haven, Feb. 18, 1951; children: Julia Robinson Bouwsma, Alexandra Toby Bouwsma. BA in Econs. with honors, Swarthmore Coll., 1972; JD, U. Calif.-Berkeley, 1975, MA (hon.) Yale U., 1987. Bar: Conn. 1981, N.Y. 1976, Calif. 1975, U.S. Ct. Appeals (2d cir.) 1975, U.S. Dist. Ct. (so. dist.) N.Y. 1978, U.S. Dist. Ct. Conn. 1981, U.S. Tax Ct. 1981. Assoc. Hughes Hubbard & Reed, N.Y.C., 1975-78; asst. gen. counsel Yale U., New Haven, 1978-79, assoc. gen. counsel, 1979-84, dep. gen. counsel, 1984-86, gen. counsel, 1986-95, dir. fed. relations, 1986-88, acting sec., 1993, v.p., gen. counsel, 1995—. Trustee Hopkins Grammar Day Prospect Hill Sch., New Haven, 1983-88, sec., 1986-88; trustee Wenner-Gren Found. Anthrop. Rsch.,1991—; bd. dirs. Cold Spring Sch., New Haven, 1990-95; mem. adv. bd. Conn. Mental Health Ctr., New Haven, 1979-89; bd. dirs. Nat. Assn. Coll. and U. Attys., 1987-90, Nat. Assn. Indep. Coll. and U., 1994—. Editor articles and book revs. Calif. Law Rev. Fellow Ezra Stiles Coll. Yale U. Fellow Am. Bar Found.; mem. ABA, Nat. Assn. Coll. and Univ. Attys., Conn. Bar Assn., Calif. Bar Assn., Assn. of Bar of City of N.Y., New Eng. Assn. Schs. and Colls. Commn. on Instns. Higher Edn., Phi Beta Kappa. Office: Yale U Office of Gen Counsel PO Box 208255 Yale Sta New Haven CT 06520-8255

ROBINSON, DOUGLAS GEORGE, lawyer; b. Hamilton, Mont., Feb. 24, 1943; s. Clarence Elijah and Frances Carolina (Alonzo) R.; m. Julia Elizabeth Sullivan, 1995; children by previous marriage: Stephen Douglas, Katherine Marielle. B.A. in Econs, U. Wash., 1965; J.D., George Washington U., 1969. Bar: D.C. Legis. asst. Wash. State Legis. Council, Olympia, 1965-66; assoc. firm Arnold & Porter, Washington, 1969-74; dep. gen. counsel Fed. Energy Adminstrn., Washington, 1974-76; mem. issues staff Carter-Mondale Presdl. Campaign, Atlanta, 1976; mem. Carter-Mondale Transition Group, Washington, 1976-77; spl. asst. to adminstr. for maj. energy projects Fed. Energy Adminstrn., Washington, 1977; asst. adminstr. for regulations and emergency planning Econ. Regulatory Adminstrn., U.S. Dept. Energy, Washington, 1977-78; dep. adminstr. for policy Econ. Regulatory Adminstrn., U.S. Dept. Energy, 1978-80, spl. asst. to sec., dep. sec., 1980-81; ptnr. Skadden, Arps, Slate, Meagher & Flom, Washington, 1981—. Editor-in-chief: George Washington Law Rev, 1968-69. Recipient John B. Larner medal George Washington U. Law Sch., 1969; cert. of superior service Fed. Energy Adminstrn., 1974; Outstanding Service medal Dept. Energy, 1979; Disting. Service medal Sec. of Energy, 1981. Mem. ABA (Nat. Pro Bono Publico award 1994), D.C. Bar Assn., Fed. Energy Bar Assn. Office: Skadden Arps Slate Meagher & Flom 1440 New York Ave NW Washington DC 20005-2111

ROBINSON, DWIGHT P., federal agency administrator; m. Linda; 1 child, Noah. BS in Urban Planning and Cmty. Devel., Mich. State U., 1975; postgrad., Ctrl. Mich. U. Various positions City of Flint, City of Ann Arbor, Mich.; with Mich. State Housing Devel. Authority, 1976—, dep. dir., chief mortgage underwriter, 1986-90; dir. single family affordable housing initiatives dept. Fed. Home Loan Mortgage Corp., 1990-93; pres. govt. nat. mortgage assn. U.S. Dept. Housing and Urban Devel., 1993—; deputy sec. HUD, Washington. Office: Dept Housing & Urban Devel 451 7th St SW Washington DC 20410-1047*

ROBINSON, EARL, JR., marketing and economic research executive, transportation executive, business educator, retired air force officer; b. St. George, Bermuda, Nov. 5, 1954; s. Willie Earl and Jeanette (Wilson) R.; m. Mildred Carter, Mar. 21, 1975; children: Aiyana Spring, Jasmine Summer, Earl III. BA in Radio, TV, U. Detroit, 1976; MS in Mgmt., Troy State U., 1986; postgrad., Old Dominion U., 1986—. Commd. lt. USAF, 1976, advanced through grades to lt. col., 1992; gen. officer aide, adminstrv. staff officer USAF, Sembach, Germany, 1982-85; with tactical air command USAF, Hampton, Va., 1986-88; mem. faculty Air Command and Staff Coll. USAF, Montgomery, Ala., 1989-92; comdr. recruiting squadron USAF, Clinton Twp., Mich., 1992-94; ret. USAF, 1994; pres. Power-Base USA, 1994—; chief advisor solar energy co., 1994—; exec. dir. Detroit Tranist Authority, 1994-95, 1995—; maj. prof. Spring Arbor (Mich.) Coll., 1992—; adj. prof. Faulkner U., Montgomery, 1991—; pres., CEO ERJ Corp. Ltd., Hampton, Va., 1986-88; pres. Paddle King Corp., Zaragoza, Spain, 1980-82; cons. Inst. Def. Analysis. Inventor info. resource mgmt. system. Mem. Nat. Tech. Assn. (publicity chmn. 1984-85), Urban Youth Action (case worker 1984-85), Housing Opportunity, Inc., Hampton Host Lions Club, Tuskegee Airmen (past chpt. pres.). Avocations: computers, reading, table-trennis, team sports, fishing, golf. Home: 1035 Roslyn St Mount Clemens MI 48043-2934

ROBINSON, EDDIE GAY, college football coach; m. Doris Robinson; children: Lillian Rose, Eddie Jr. BA, Leland Coll., 1940; MS, U. Iowa; LLD (hon.), La. Tech. Coach football Grambling U., La., 1941—, v.p. athletics; head coach East-West Shrine Game, 1977. Recipient Horatio Alger award, Nat. Football Found. award, NAACP award, VFW award, Bear Bryant award, Liberty Bowl award, others, Spl. Commendations from Pres. Ronald Reagan, Nat. Collegiate Athletic Assn., U.S. Congress, State of La., B'nai B'rith; holds record of most college football victories. Mem. Nat. Assn. Sports & Phys. Edn., Nat. Assn. Intercollegiate Athletics, Southwestern Athletic Conf., La. Sports Hall of Fame, Pop Warner, Sugar Bowl, Black Coll. Winner 10 nat. Black coll. football championships. Office: Grambling State Univ Athletic Dept Grambling LA 71245*

ROBINSON, EDGAR ALLEN, oil company executive; b. Boston, Dec. 12, 1933; s. Herbert and Ruth (Solomon) R.; m. Ruth Enid Schwartz, July 24, 1956; children: Jeffrey Michael, Laurie Karen. AB, Brown U., 1955; MBA, Harvard U., 1960. Fin. analyst Exxon Corp., N.Y.C., 1960-66, asst. treas., 1966-70; corp. planning mgr. Esso Europe Inc., London, 1970-72; pres. Esso Africa Inc., London, 1972-75; dep. contr. Exxon Corp., N.Y.C., 1975-79; sr. v.p. Exxon Co. U.S.A., Houston, 1979-83; v.p., treas. Exxon Corp., Irving, Tex., 1983—. Bd. dirs. bus. Arts Fund, Houston, 1980-83, chmn., 1983; trustee Houston Ballet Found., 1980-83, Brown U., Providence, 1982-88; mem. Dean's adv. com. U. Chgo. Bus. Sch., 1984—, chmn., 1990-94; bd. dirs. Dallas Zoo, 1992—; bd. govs. Dallas Symphony, 1993—. Office: Exxon Corp 5959 Las Colinas Blvd Irving TX 75039-4202

ROBINSON, EDWARD LEE, retired physics educator, consultant; b. Clanton, Ala., Nov. 6, 1933; s. Alonzo Lee and Ollie Sarah (Mims) R.; m. Shirley Anne Burnett (div. Sept. 1972); children: Edward Lee Jr., James Allan, Paul David; m. Linda G. Moon, 1990. AB with honors, Samford U., 1954; MS, Purdue U., 1958, PhD, 1962. Dir. Cyclotron Lab. Samford U., Birmingham, Ala., 1961-66, asst. prof. physics, chmn. dept., 1961-62; dir. cyclotron lab., 1961-67; assoc. prof., chmn. dept. Samford U., Birmingham, Ala., 1962-66, prof., chmn. dept., 1966-67; assoc. prof. U. Ala., Birmingham, 1967-77, co-radiation safety officer, 1967-85; dir. Van de Graaff Accelerator Lab., 1970-91, Samford U., Birmingham, Ala., 1969-91; acting chmn. dept. U. Ala., Birmingham, 1973-74, prof. physics, 1977-91, adj. prof. forensic sci., 1983-91; cons. in applied physics and accident reconstrn., 1991—; dir. Cyclotron Lab., Samford U., Birmingham, 1961-67, Van de Graff Accelerator Lab., U. Ala., Birmingham, 1970-91; cons. Hayes Internat. Corp., Birmingham, 1963-68, So. Research Inst., Birmingham, 1968-69; researcher Oak Ridge (Tenn.) Nat. Lab., 1968, 74-75, 82, U. Md., College Park, 1966, 67. Active Birmingham YMCA. Mem. Am. Phys. Soc., Soc. Automotive Engrs., AAAS, Ala. Acad. Sci. (v.p. 1964-65), N.Y. Acad. Sci. Baptist. Achievements include discovery, co-discovery of six radioisotopes. Avocations: handball, scuba diving. Home: 233 Oakmont Rd Birmingham AL 35244-3264

ROBINSON, EDWARD T., III, lawyer; b. Glen Cove, N.Y., May 23, 1932; s. Edward Jr. and Helen (Rahilly) R.; m. Lynn Simmons; children: Edward IV, Wendy, Christopher, Jeffrey, Lesley, Michael. AB, Holy Cross Coll., 1954; JD, Georgetown U., 1960. Bar: N.Y. 1961, U.S. Ct. Appeals (2d cir.) 1966. Counsel Royal-Globe Ins. Co., Mineola, N.Y., 1960-64; pvt. practice, Oyster Bay, N.Y., 1964-70, 91-94; ptnr. Robinson & Cincotta, Oyster Bay, 1970-85, Robinson & Lynch, Oyster Bay, 1985-91, Robinson, Bermingham & Donegan, Oyster Bay, 1994—; mem. adv. bd. Chgo. Title Ins. Co., N.Y.C., 1982—, Fleet Bank, 1989-95, United Cerebral Palsy, 1980—; mem. Nassau County Commn. on Govt. Revision, 1983—; mem. County Exec. Blue Ribbon Panel on Criminal Justice; mem. exec. coun. N.Y. State Conf. Bar Leaders, 1986-90; counsel Oyster Bay-East Norwich Ctrl. Sch. Dist., 1966—. Mem. Nassau County Traffic and Parking Violations Bur.; pres. Holy Cross Coll. Club, L.I., 1989-90; trustee Nassau County coun. Boy Scouts Am.; chmn. Forget-Me-Not Ball, United Cerebral Palsy. Recipient Community Svc. award Nassau County coun. Boy Scouts Am.; named Man of Yr. United Cerebral Palsy, Nassau County, 1979. Mem. N.Y. State Bar Assn. (del., v.p. 1992—), Nassau County Bar Assn. (pres. 1986-87), C. of C. (past pres.), Meadowbrook Hunt Club. Republican. Roman Catholic. Avocations: golf, tennis, jazz music. Home: 60 Calvin Ave Syosset NY 11791-2106 Office: 34 Audrey Ave Oyster Bay NY 11771-1548

ROBINSON, ENDERS ANTHONY, geophysics educator, writer; b. Boston, Mar. 18, 1930; s. Edward Arthur and Doris Gertrude (Goodale) R.; m. Eva Arborelius, Sept. 9, 1962 (div. 1973); children: Anna, Erik Arthur, Karin; m. Joyce McPeake, Aug. 8, 1992. BS in Math., MIT, 1950, MS in Econs., 1952, PhD in Geophysics, 1954. Dir. geophys. analysis group MIT, Cambridge, Mass., 1952-54; geophysicist Gulf Oil Corp., Pitts., 1954-55; instr. math. MIT, Cambridge, Mass., 1955-56; petroleum economist Standard Oil Co. N.J., N.Y.C., 1956-57; asst. prof. stats. Mich. State U., East Lansing, 1958; asst. prof. math. U. Wis., Madison, 1958-61, assoc. prof. math. (with tenure), 1961-62; dep. prof. stats. Uppsala (Sweden) U., 1960-64; v.p., dir. Digicon, Inc., Houston, 1965-70; pres. Robinson Rsch. Inc., Houston, 1970-82; vis. prof. theoretical and applied mechanics Cornell U., Ithaca, N.Y., 1981-82; McMan prof. geophysics U. Tulsa, 1983-93; Maurice Ewing and J.L. Worzel prof. geophysics Columbia U., N.Y.C., 1993—. Author 25 books on sci. and tech, including Einstein's Relativity in Metaphor and Mathematics, 1990; editor: Internat. Jour. of Imaging Systems & Tech., 1988—; assoc. editor: Jour. of Time Series Analysis, 1984—; editorial bd. Multidimensional Systems and Signal Processing, An Internat. Jour., 1990—. 2d lt. U.S. Army, 1950-51. Recipient Conrad Schlumberger award European Assn. of Exploration Geophysicists, 1969, Donald G. Fink Prize award IEEE, 1984. Mem. NAE, Nat. Rsch. Coun. (com. on undiscovered oil and gas resources), Soc. Exploration Geophysicists (hon., Best Paper award, 1964, medal 1969). Home: 560 Riverside Dr Apt 20J New York NY 10027-3236 Office: Columbia U Krumb Sch Mines New York NY 10027

ROBINSON, ESTHER MARTIN, secondary school educator; b. Buffalo, N.Y., Sept. 19, 1956; d. Douglas Charles and Esther (Hagen) Martin; m. Stephen Mark Robinson, May 6, 1978; children: Rachel Anne, Sarah Elizabeth. BA, Oral Roberts U., 1978; MA, U. Tulsa, 1983. Tchr. secondary sch. history Tulsa Pub. Schs., 1978-80; tchr. secondary sch. history Jenks (Okla.) High Sch., 1980-92, chair dept. social studies, 1990-92; tchr. world history, advanced placement U.S. history Langham Creek High Sch., Houston, 1992—; adj. prof. U.S. history Houston C.C., 1995—; presenter in field. Mem. Nat. Coun. Social Studies, Tex. Coun. Social Studies, Cypress Fairbanks Coun. for Social Studies, Tex. Assn. Gifted and Talented. Home: 8022 Null Ct Spring TX 77379-6141 Office: Langham Creek High Sch 17610 Fm 529 Rd Houston TX 77095-1004

ROBINSON, FARREL RICHARD, pathologist, toxicologist; b. Wellington, Kans., Mar. 23, 1927; s. Farrel Otis and Norine (Sloan) R.; m. Mimi Agatha Hathaway, June 5, 1949; children—Farrel Richard, Kelly S., E. Scott, Brian A. B.S., Kans. State U., 1950, D.V.M., M.S., 1958; Ph.D., Tex. A&M U., 1965. Diplomate: Am. Coll. Vet. Pathologists, Am. Bd. Vet. Toxicology (v.p. 1971-74, pres. 1976-79). Served with USN, 1945-46; commd. 2d lt. USAF, 1951, advanced through grades to lt. col., 1971; vet. pathologist Aerospace Med. Research Labs., Wright-Patterson AFB, Ohio, 1958-68; chief Vet. Pathology div. Armed Forces Inst. Pathology, Washington, 1968-74; ret., 1974; scientist assoc. Univs. Associated for Research and Edn. in Pathology, Inc., 1972-74; asst. clin. prof. pathology George Washington U. Sch. Medicine, 1972-74; instr. NIH Grad. Program, 1973-74; prof. toxicology-pathology Sch. Vet. Medicine, Purdue U., 1974-93; dir. Animal Disease Diagnostic Lab., 1978-85, head dept. vet. sci., 1978-85, head dept. vet. microbiology, pathology and pub. health, 1986-88, chief toxicology service, 1984-93: emeritus, 1993; cons. vet. pathology USAF surg. gen. and asst. surg. gen. for vet. services, 1970-74. Mem. editorial bd. Human and Vet. Toxicology, 1976—. Contbr. sci. articles to profl. jours. Decorated USAF Commendation medal, Meritorious Service medal; recipient Aerospace Med. Research Labs. Scientist of Year award, 1967. Mem. AVMA, Am. Bd. Vet. Toxicology, Am. Coll. Vet. Pathology, Am. Assn. Vet. Lab. Diagnosticians (bd. govs.1980-85, v.p. 1986, pres. 1987), Wildlife Disease Assn., Conf. Rsch. Workers in Animal Disease, Soc. Toxicology, U.S. Animal Health Assn., Sigma Xi, Phi Kappa Phi, Alpha Zeta, Phi Zeta. Democrat. Methodist. Home: 201 W 600 N West Lafayette IN 47906-9727 Office: Purdue U Animal Disease Diagnostic Lab West Lafayette IN 47907

ROBINSON, FRANK, professional baseball team executive, former coach, former player; b. Beaumont, Tex., Aug. 31, 1935; s. Frank and Ruth (Shaw) R.; m. Barbara Ann Cole, Oct. 28, 1961; children: Frank Kevin, Nichelle. Student, Xavier U., Cin. Baseball player Cin. Reds, 1956-65, Balt. Orioles, 1966-71, L.A., 1972, Calif. Angels, 1973-74; baseball player Cleve. Indians, 1974-76, mgr., 1975-77; coach Calif. Angels, 1977; coach Balt. Orioles, 1978-80, 85-87, mgr., 1988-91, asst. to gen. mgr., 1991-95; mgr. San Francisco Giants, 1981-84; batting coach Milw. Brewers, 1984; dir. baseball ops. Arizona Fall League Major League Baseball, 1997—. Author: (with Al Silverman) My Life is Baseball, 1967, (with Barry Steinbach) Extra Innings, 1989, Frank the First Year, 1976. Named Rookie of Yr. Nat. League, 1956, Most Valuable Player, 1961, Am. League, 1966, Am. League Mgr. of Yr., 1982, 89; mem. World Series Championship Team, 1966, 70, Nat. League All-Star Team, 1956-57, 59, 61.62, 65, Am. League All-Star Team, 1966-67, 69-71, 74; inducted into Baseball Hall of Fame, 1982. Office: care Major League Baseball 350 Park Ave New York NY 10022-6022

ROBINSON, FRANKLIN WESTCOTT, museum director, art historian; b. Providence, R.I., May 21, 1939; s. Charles Alexander Robinson Jr. and Celia (Sachs) Stillwell; m. Margaret Dredge, Aug. 14, 1967; 1 child, John Alexander. BA, Harvard U., 1961, MA, 1964, PhD, 1970. Instr. Wellesley Coll., 1968-69; asst. prof. Dartmouth Coll., 1969-75; assoc. prof. Williams Coll., 1975-79; dir. Williams Coll. Mus., 1976-79, Mus. of Art, R.I. Sch. Design, Providence, 1979-92, Herbert F. Johnson Mus. Art, Cornell U., Ithaca, N.Y., 1992—. Author: Gabriel Metsu, 1975, Seventeenth Century Dutch Drawings from American Collections, 1977, Dutch and Flemish Paintings from the Ringling Mus, 1980. Fulbright fellow, 1961-62; recipient Clairborne Pell award R.I. State Coun. Arts, 1992. Mem. Assn. Art Mus.

Dirs., Coll. Art Assn. Clubs: Century, Hope. Office: Herbert F Johnson Mus Art Cornell University Ithaca NY 14853-4001

ROBINSON, FRED COLSON, English language educator; b. Birmingham, Ala., Sept. 23, 1930; s. Emmett Colson and Morwenna Hope (Bennett) R.; m. Helen Caroline Wild, June 21, 1959; children: Lisa Karen, Eric Wild. BA, Birmingham So. Coll., 1953; MA, U. N.C., 1954, PhD, 1961; DLitt (hon.), Williams Coll., 1985; MA (hon.), Yale U., 1989. Instr. Stanford (Calif.) U., 1960-61, asst. prof., 1961-65, assoc. prof., 1967-71, prof. English philology, 1971-72; asst. prof. Cornell U., Ithaca, N.Y., 1965-66, assoc. prof., 1966-67; prof. Yale U., New Haven, 1972-83, Douglas Tracy Smith prof., 1983—, chmn. medieval studies, 1975-78, 80; vis. prof. Harvard U., Cambridge, Mass., 1983; mem. pub. com. Medieval Acad. Monographs, Cambridge, 1987-90. Author: Old English Literature: Select Bibliography, 1970, Beowulf and the Appositive Style, 1985, The Tomb of Beowulf, 1993, The Editing of Old English, 1994; co-author: A Bibliography...on Old English Literature, 1980, Old English Verse Texts from Many Sources: A Comprehensive Collection, 1991, A Guide to Old English, 5th edit., 1992; editor Old English Newsletter, 1966-73, Early English MSS in Facsimile, 1971—, Anglo-Saxon England, 1972—, Anglistica, 1981—; contbr. over 70 articles to scholarly jours. Trustee Yale Univ. Library Assocs., New Haven, 1986-89, 91-95. With U.S. Army, 1954-56. Fellow Guggenheim Found., 1974-75, Am. Coun. Learned Socs., 1968-69, Inst. Social and Econs. Rsch., Rhodes U., 1978, Japan Soc. for Promotion Sci., 1989; grantee NEH, 1976, 79, 81, 85, Am. Philos. Soc., 1973, 85. Fellow AAAS, Medieval Acad. Am. (pres. 1983-84, Haskins medal 1984), Brit. Acad. (corr.), Meddeleeue-verenigung van Suidelike Afrika (corr.); mem. New Eng. Medieval Conf. (pres. 1982-83), Conn. Acad. Arts and Scis. (pres. 1980-85), Elizabethan Club (bd. govs. 1986—, v.p. 1989-90, pres. 1990-92), Manuscript Club (v.p. New Haven chpt. 1990-92), Phi Beta Kappa. Episcopalian. Office: Yale Univ Dept of English New Haven CT 06520

ROBINSON, G. WILSE, molecular physicist, educator; b. Kansas City, Mo., July 27, 1924; s. George Wilse, Jr. R. and Elizabeth (Millett) Ivison; m. Ellen Elizabeth Johnson, June 5, 1950. B.S. in Chemistry, Ga. Inst. Tech., 1947, M.S. in Chemistry, 1949; Ph.D. in Chemistry, U. Iowa, Iowa City, 1952. Research asst. phys. chemistry U. Iowa, 1950-52; research fellow in chemistry U. Rochester, N.Y., 1952-54; asst. prof. chemistry Johns Hopkins U., Balt., 1954-59; assoc. prof. phys. chemistry Calif. Inst. Tech., Pasadena, 1959-61; prof. Calif. Inst. Tech., 1961-75; prof. phys. chemistry, dept. chmn. U. Melbourne, Australia, 1975-76; Robert A. Welch prof. chemistry, prof. physics Tex. Tech U., Lubbock, 1976—; FMC lectr. Princeton U., 1964; Bourke lectr., 1967, A.D. Little lectr., 1967; adv. to U.S. Army Research Office, Durham, 1969-72; Erskine fellow U. Canterbury, 1971; Guggenheim fellow, 1971-72. Author: (with S.-B. Zhu, S. Singh, M.W. Evans) Water in Biology, Chemistry and Physics. Experimental Overviews and Computational Methodologies, 1996; editor Chem. Physics, 1972-75; assoc. editor Jour. Chem. Physics, 1963-65; editl. adv. bd. Chem. Physics Letters, 1966-84, Jour. Molecular Spectroscopy, 1967-71, Photochemistry and Photobiology, 1971-75, Chem. Physics, 1975—, Jour. Phys. Chemistry, 1988-94; mem. editl. com. Ann. Rev. Phys. Chemistry, 1966-71; contbr. 280 sci. articles to profl. jours. Served with USN, 1944-46. Recipient Alexander von Humboldt prize, 1984. Fellow Am. Phys. Soc. Home: 4810 1st Pl Lubbock TX 79416-3150 Office: Tex Tech U Dept Chemistry PO Box 41061 Lubbock TX 79409-1061 *Many scientists are pioneers. A few are explorers. I like to think of myself as being in the latter category. It greatly increases the fun of doing science, but diminishes somewhat the recognition. Scientific developments are easy to remember. Not many persons remember the footprints.*

ROBINSON, GAIL PATRICIA, mental health counselor; b. Medford, Oreg., Dec. 31, 1936; d. Ivan T. and Evelyn H. (Hamilton) Skyrman; m. Douglas L. Smith; children: Shauna J., James D. BS in Edn., Oreg. State U., 1958, PhD in Counseling, 1978; MS in Counseling, Western Oreg. State Coll., 1974. Lic. profl. counselor, Oreg. Tchr. Monterey (Calif.) Pub. Schs., 1958-59; tchr. Corvallis (Oreg.) Pub. Schs., 1959-62, 69-75, counselor, 1977-81; pvt. practice Corvallis, 1977-95; vol. therapist Children's Svcs. divsn., Linn and Benton Counties, 1982-83; asst. prof. Western Oreg. State coll., 1977, counselor, 1982-83; mem. grad. faculty Oreg. State U., Corvallis, 1978-95; presenter workshops, lectr. in field. Contbr. articles to profl. jours. Mem. Benton County Mental Helath Citizens Adv. Bd., 1979-85, chair, 1982-83; trustee WCTU Children's Farm Home, 1978-84, chair child welfare com., 1982-83, pres., 1984; mem. Old Mill Sch. Adv. Bd., 1979-85, chair, 1979-81; bd. dirs. Cmty. Outreach, 1979-83; mem. Benton Com. for Prevention of Child Abuse, 1979-85, v.p., 1982; mem. Oreg. Bd. Lic. Profl. Counselors and Therapists, 1989-95, chair, 1989-90. Mem. ACA (govt. rels. com. 1988-91, professionalization com. 1988-92, pres. 1996-97), Am. Mental Health Counselors Assn. (chair consumer and pub. rels. com. 1988-91, bd. dirs. Western region 1989-91, chair strategic planning com. 1994-95, pres. 1992-93), Oreg. Counseling Assn. (chair licensure liaison com. 1985-91, exec. bd. 1985-88, steering com. 1986-87, register editorial com. 1985-86, Disting. Svc. award 1985, 87, Leona Tyler award 1989), Oreg. Mental Health Counselors Assn., Assn. Religion and Values in Counseling, Phi Delta Kappa (chpt. pres. 1979-80).

ROBINSON, GARY DAVID, principal; b. Altoona, Pa., Oct. 6, 1953; s. Donald R. and Theada (Brooks) R.; m. Nancy L., Aug. 15, 1981; children: Melissa, Brooke, David. BS, Pa. State U., 1975, MEd, 1979; EdD, Temple U., 1991. Grad. instr. Pa. State U., Altoona, 1978-83; math. tchr. Altoona Area Sch. Dist., 1975-83; asst. prin. Downingtown (Pa.) Area Sr. High Sch., 1983-88, athletic dir., 1983-86; high sch. prin. Octorara Area High Sch., Parkesburg, Pa., 1988-90, Hollidaysburg (Pa.) Area Sr. High Sch., 1990—; vocat. adv. com. Pa. Dept. Edn., 1991-96, prins. adv. com. 1987-91; pres. Prins. Adv. to Ctr. Arts/Tech, Brandywine Campus, 1988-90. Active Jail and Bail project Am. Cancer Soc., Chester County, 1988; vol. Pa. State Sen. and Ho. of Reps., AAU Jr. Olympics, 1982; active student coun. activities, Hollidaysburg Area Sch. Dist., 1982; bd. dirs. Am. Heart Assn., Altoona, 1992; established Heart of Tiger Found. for Hollidaysburg Area Sch. in cooperation with area alumni assn., 1991-92; pres. Blair County chpt. Am. Heart Assn., 1993—; numerous community activities. Mem. ASCD, Pa. Assn. Supervision and Curriculum Devel., nat. Assn. Secondary Sch. Prins., Pa. Assn. Secondary Sch. Prins. (mem. com. 1986-90), Pa. Sch. Bd. Assn., Chester County Prins. Orgn. (chmn. 1989-90), Phi Delta Kappa. Avocations: staff devel., sch. climate and culture, student employment and self-esteem. Home: 211 Bristol Ln Hollidaysburg PA 16648-2937 Office: Hollidaysburg Area Sr High 1510 N Montgomery St Hollidaysburg PA 16648-1909

ROBINSON, GWENDOLYN POWELL, savings and loan executive, church executive. BS in Orgnl. Behavior and Pers., Northwestern U., 1979; MS in Cmty. Bank Mgmt., U. Tex., 1995. With Ill. Svc. Fed. Savs. and Loan Assn., Chgo., 1969—, asst. supr. mortgage loan scs., 1972-74, supr. teller ops., 1974-79, staff advisor and trainer, 1979-80, br. mgr., 1980-81, asst. v.p. adminstrv. svcs. and pers., br. coord., 1984-88, v.p., COO, pers. dir., 1988-91, sr. v.p., COO, 1991-92, exec. .p., COO, compliance officer, 1992—, also bd. dirs.; gen. sec. Ch. of Living God, Cin., 1994—; mem. Smith and Smith CPA Firm, Chgo., 1985—; mem. ad hoc com. Chgo. Mayor's Office Employment Tng., 1984. Mem. adv. coun. Jones Comml. H.S., Chgo. Bd. Edn.; deacon Chgo. United. Recipient Black and Hispanic achievers award, award Jr. Achievement, Leadership award, Cmty. and Bus. Leadership award. Mem. Ill. Svc. Fed. Savs. and Loan Assn. Chgo., Chgo. Urban League, Sigma Gamma Rho. Office: Ill Svc Fed Savs and Loan Assn 4619 S King Dr Chicago IL 60653-4107 also: Ch of Living God Christian Workers Fellowship Workers Fellowship 430 Forest Ave Cincinnati OH 45229

ROBINSON, HERBERT HENRY, III, educator, psychotherapist; b. Leavenworth, Wash., Mar. 31, 1933; s. Herbert Henry II and Alberta (Sperber) R.; m. Georgia Muriel Jones, Nov. 24, 1954 (div. 1974); children: Cheri Dean Asbury, David Keith, Peri Elizabeth Layton, Tanda Rene Graff, Gaila Daire. Grad. of Theology, Bapt. Bible Coll., 1959; BA in Philosophy/Greek, Whitworth Coll., 1968; MA in Coll. Teaching, Ea. Wash. U., 1976; postgrad., Gonzaga U., 1980—. Cert. psychotherapist, perpetrator treatment program supervision. Choir dir. Twin City Bapt. Temple, Mishawaka, Ind., 1959-61; min. Inland Empire Bapt. Ch., Spokane, 1961-73; tchr. philosophy Spokane (Wash.) C.C., 1969-72; dir. Alternatives to Violence, Women in Crisis, Fairbanks, Alaska, 1985-87; tchr. pub. rels. U. Alaska, Fairbanks, 1986-87; dir. Alternatives to Violence Men Inc., Juneau, 1988-89; tchr. leadership mgmt. U. Alaska S.E., Juneau, 1988-89; min. Sci. of Mind Ctr., Sandpoint, Idaho, 1989-92; dir., therapist Tapio Counseling Ctr., Spokane, 1991—; cert. psychotherapist, supr. perpetrator treatment program Wash.; cons. Lilac Blind/Alpha Inc./Marshall Coll., Spokane, 1975-85, Alaska Placer Mining Co., Fairbanks, 1987; tchr. Spokane Falls C.C., Spokane, 1979-85; seminar, presenter Human Resource Devel., Spokane and Seattle, Wash., Pa., 1980; guest trainer United Way/Kellogg Found. Inst. for Volunteerism, Spokane, 1983. 1st trombone San Diego Marine Band, 1953-56, Spokane Symphony, 1961; bd. dirs. Tanani Learning Ctr., Fairbanks, 1987; mem. consensus bldg. team Sci. of Mind Ctr., Sandpoint, 1989-92. Cpl. USMC, 1953-56. Mem. ACA, Assn. for Humanistic Edn. and Devel., Assn. for Religious Values in Counseling, Internat. Assn. Addictions and Offender Counselors, Internat. Assn. Marriage and Family Counselors, Am. Assn. Profl. Hypnotherapists, Masterson Inst. Home: 11611 E Maxwell Ave Spokane WA 99206-4867 Office: Tapio Counseling Svcs Red Flag Bldg # 101A 104 S Freya Tapio Ctr Spokane WA 99202

ROBINSON, HOBART KRUM, management consulting company executive; b. Quincy, Mass., Oct. 8, 1937; s. Hobart Krum and Charlotte Elizabeth (Hall) R.; m. Gerd Ingela Janhede, Oct. 17, 1964; children: Steven Whitney, Karina Jill, Peter Danforth. BA, Williams Coll., 1959; MBA, Columbia U., 1964. Market analyst Mobil Chem. Co., Richmond, Va., 1964-67; mgr. program analysis and control Polaroid Corp., Cambridge, Mass., 1967-69; exec. v.p., dir. Simplex Wire and Cable, Inc., North Berwick, Maine, 1969-73; sr. engagement mgr. McKinsey and Co., Inc., N.Y.C., 1973-76; prin. McKinsey and Co., Inc., Copenhagen, 1977-81, N.Y.C., 1985-89; prin. McKinsey and Co., Inc., Stockholm, 1989-95, dir. adminstrn. Eastern Europe, 1993-95; dir. adminstrn. McKinsey and Co., Inc., N.Y.C., 1995—; pres. and chief exec. officer Brink's Inc., Darien, Conn., 1981-84; dir. Burlington No. Air Freight, Inc., Newport Beach, Calif., 1982-84. Pres. Am. Club in Copenhagen, 1980-81; dir. Fulbright Commn., Copenhagen, 1980-81. Served as lt. USNR, 1959-62. Mem. Innis Arden Golf Club (Old Greenwich, Conn.) (gov. 1982-87, prse. 1986-87), Tournament Players Club (Ponte Vedra, Fla.), Taconic Golf Club (Williamstown, Mass.), Sky Club (N.Y.C.). Republican. Episcopalian. Home: 14 Old Farm Ln Old Greenwich CT 06870-1021 Office: McKinsey & Co Inc 55 E 52nd St New York NY 10055-0002

ROBINSON, HUGH GRANVILLE, consulting management company executive; b. Washington, Aug. 4, 1932; s. James Hill and Wilhelmina (Thomas) R.; m. Matilda Turner; 1 stepdau., Mia; children by previous marriage—Hugh Granville, Susan K. Student, Williams Coll., 1949-50; B.S., U.S. Mil. Acad., 1954; M.S., MIT, 1959; LL.D., Williams Coll., 1983. Commd. 2d lt. U.S. Army, 1954, advanced through grades to maj. gen., 1983; platoon leader, co. comdr. Co. B, 185th Engrs. Bn., Korea, 1955; platoon leader, ops. officer 74th Engr. Co., Korea, 1955-56; br. chief Engr. Supply Control Office, St. Louis, 1956-58; chief Catalog and Authorization div. Engr. Supply Control Agy., Orleans, France, 1960-62; co. comdr. 553d Engr. Bn., Orleans, 1962-63; chief combat br. War Plans div. Engr. Strategic Studies Group, Washington, 1963-65; Army asst. to armed forces aide to Pres. Washington, 1965-69; comdr. 39th Engr. Bn., Vietnam, 1969-70; br. chief war plans div. Office Dep. Chief Staff for Ops., Washington, 1970-71; assigned Nat. War Coll., 1972; comdr. 3d regt. U.S. Corps Cadets, West Point, N.Y., 1973-74, U.S. Army Engr. Sch. Brigade, Fort Belvoir, Va., 1974-76; dist. engr. U.S. Army Engr. Dist., Los Angeles, 1976-78; dep. dir. civil works office Chief of Engrs., Washington, 1978-80; comdr. Southwestern Div., U.S. Army C.E., 1980-83; ret., 1983; v.p. Southland Corp., Dallas, 1983-88; pres. Cityplace Devel. Corp.; sr. v.p. Grigsby Brandford Powell, Inc., 1988-94; now chmn., chief executive officer The Tetra Group, Inc., Dallas, 1989—; mem. Mississippi River Commn., 1980-83, bd. engrs. for rivers and harbors, 1980-83, Coastal Engring. Rsch. Bd., 1980-83; bd. dirs. Belo Corp., TU-Electric, Smith Environ. Tech., Inc., Columbus Realty Trust, Circuit City Stores, Inc., Guaranty Fed.; chmn. Dallas Fed. Res. Bd., 1991; with Tex. pub. broadcasting LBJ Fedn., 1989—. Mem. nat. bd. dirs. Keep Am. Beautiful, 1981-85; bd. dirs. Dallas Symphony, 1981-85, Dallas United Way, 1984-92, Baylor U. Med. Ctr. Found., 1983-91, Dallas Opera, 1983-90, Dallas Citizens Coun., 1987-91, Greater Dallas C. of C., 1986-91, Vietnam Vets Meml. Fund Tex.; chmn. African Am. Mus., Dallas Youth Svcs. Corp.; trustee Dallas Mus. Fine Arts, 1988-93; mem. adv. coun. U. Tex. Engring. Fedn., 1991—. Mem. Am. Soc. Mil. Engrs. (past sec. Orleans chpt., regional v.p. Tex.), Assn. U.S. Army, Dallas Black C. of C., ASCE. Methodist. Office: The Tetra Group Inc 8150 N Central Expy Ste 550 Dallas TX 75206-1815

ROBINSON, HUGH R., retired marketing executive; b. Syracuse, N.Y., Sept. 18, 1922; s. Frank J. and Gladys (Hunt) R.; m. Evelyn De Mattia, Nov. 24, 1949; children: Susan, Hugh R., Patrice. BS, Syracuse U., 1949. Dist. mgr. Syracuse China, 1949-59; with Royal Worcester Porcelain Co., N.Y.C., 1959-77; v.p. sales Royal Worcester Porcelain Co., 1971-75, pres., 1975-76; pres. Royal Worcester Spode, Inc., 1977, Lance Internat., N.Y.C., 1977-84; v.p., dir. Caithness Glass Inc., N.Y.C., 1980-84; v.p. sales amnd mktg. Weil Ceramics & Glass Inc., 1985-86, CEO, exec. v.p., 1986-88; CEO LLadro U.S.A. Inc., 1988-91; v.p. Lladro Realty, Inc., 1988-94, Lladro Galleries, Inc., 1988-94; retired, 1994; advisor Lladro Group, Valencia, Spain, 1991-97; cons. in giftware industry. Served with USAAF, 1942-46. Mem. Alumni Assn. Syracuse U. Home: 4723 61st Ave Dr W Bradenton FL 34210

ROBINSON, IRWIN JAY, lawyer; b. Bay City, Mich., Oct. 8, 1928; s. Robert R. and Anne (Kaplan) R.; m. Janet Binder, July 7, 1957; children: Elizabeth Binder Schubiner, Jonathan Meyer, Eve Kimberly Wiener. AB, U. Mich., 1950; JD, Columbia U., 1953. Bar: N.Y. 1956. Assoc. Breed Abbott & Morgan, N.Y.C., 1955-58; asst. to ptnrs. Dreyfus & Co., N.Y.C., 1958-59; assoc. Greenbaum Wolff & Ernst, N.Y.C., 1959-65; ptnr. Greenbaum Wolff & Ernst, 1966-76; sr. ptnr. Rosenman & Colin, N.Y.C., 1976-90; of counsel Pryor, Cashman, Sherman & Flynn, 1990-92; sr. ptnr. Phillips, Nizer, Benjamin, Krim & Ballon, N.Y.C., 1992—; treas. Saarsteel, Inc., Whitestone, N.Y., 1970—. Bd. dirs. Henry St. Settlement, N.Y.C., 1960-85, Jewish Cmty. Ctr. Assn. N.Am., N.Y.C., 1967-94; bd. dirs. Heart Rsch. Found., 1989-94, pres., 1991-93. Mem. ABA, N.Y. State Bar Assn., Assn. Bar City of N.Y., Internat. Bar Assn., Thai-Am. C. of C. (founder, bd. dirs. 1992-95, pres. 1992-95), Vietnam-Am. C. of C. (founder, bd. dirs. 1992-95, pres. 1992-95), Philippine-Am. C. of C. (bd. dirs. 1960—, v.p. 1960—), Sunningdale Country Club (Scarsdale, N.Y.). Jewish. Home: 4622 Grosvenor Ave Riverdale NY 10471-3305 Office: Phillips Nizer Benjamin Krim & Ballon 666 5th Ave New York NY 10103-0001

ROBINSON, JACK ALBERT, retail drug stores executive; b. Detroit, Feb. 26, 1930; s. Julius and Fannie (Aizkowitz) R.; m. Aviva Freedman, Dec. 21, 1952; children: Shelby, Beth, Abigail. B in Pharmacy, Wayne State U., 1952. Founder, chief exec. officer, chmn. bd. Perry Drug Stores, Inc., Pontiac, Mich., 1957-95; founder, chmn., pres. JAR Group LLC, Bloomfield, Mich., 1996; bd. dirs. Riser Foods, Inc.; corp. dir. R & B, Inc. Chmn. Wayne State U. Fund, Detroit, 1986, Concerned Citizens for the Arts in Mich., 1990, 91—; chmn. ann. fund Detroit Symphony Orch.; bd. dirs. United Way of Pontiac, Mich., 1986, United Found. of Detroit, 1986, Pontiac Area Urban League, Cmty. Found., S.E. Mich., Detroit Svc. Group, Save Orch. Hall, Inc., Cranbrook Inst. Sci., Jewish Fedn. Apts., Wetzman Inst. Sci., Holocaust Meml. Ctr., Harper-Grace Hosp., Detroit; past dir. Pontiac Symphony Boys Club, Detroit Osteo. Hosp.; pres. United Jewish Found. Met. Detroit, 1992, Greater Detroit Interfaith Round Table NCCJ, 1994-95, co-chmn., 1992; pres. Jewish Fedn. Met. Detroit, 1992-94. Recipient Disting. Alumni award Wayne State U. Coll. Pharmacy, 1975, Eleanor Roosevelt Humanities award from State of Israel, 1978, B'nai B'rith Youth Svcs. Am. Tradition award, 1982, Wayne State U. Disting. Alumni award, 1985, Tree of Life award Jewish Nat. Fund, 1985, Disting. Citizen award Pontiac Boy Scouts Am., 1985, Corp. Leadership award Wayne State U., 1985, Booker T. Washington Bus. Assn. Brotherhood award, 1986, Humanitarian award March of Dimes, 1987, award Weizmann Rsch. Inst., 1987, Humanitarian award Variety Club, 1988, Fred M. Butzel award Jewish Fedn. Met. Detroit, 1991, B'nai B'rith Great Am. Traditions award, 1991, Cmty. Svc. award Am. Arabic and Jewish Friends, 1995; named Entrepreneur of Yr. Harvard U. Bus. Sch., Detroit, 1982. Mem. Nat. Assn. Chain Drug Stores (chmn. 1987, Lifetime Achievement award 1995, Robert B. Begley award 1995), Am. Pharm. Assn., Am. Found. for Pharm. Edn. (bd. dirs.), Econ. Club (bd. dirs. Detroit chpt.). Avocations: skiing, jogging, photography, classical music, glass collecting. Office: JAR Group LLC 500 N Woodward Ave Ste 220 Bloomfield Hills MI 48304-2963

ROBINSON, JACK F(AY), clergyman; b. Wilmington, Mass., Mar. 7, 1914; s. Thomas P. and Ethel Lincoln (Fay) R.; A.B., Mont. State U., 1936; D.B., Crozer Theol. Sem., 1939; A.M., U. Chgo., 1949, postgrad., 1950-52; m. Eleanor Jean Smith, Sept. 1, 1937 (dec. 1966); 1 dau., Alice Virginia Dungey; m. Lois Henze, July 16, 1968. Ordained to ministry Bapt. Ch., 1939; minister Bethany Ch., American Falls, Idaho, 1939-41, 1st Ch., Coun. Grove, Kans., 1944-49; ordained (transfer) to ministry Congregational Ch., 1945; minister United Ch., Chebanse, Ill., 1949-52, 1st Ch., Argo, Ill., 1954-58, Congl. Ch., St. Charles, Ill., 1958-64; assoc. minister Plymouth Congregational Ch., Lansing, Mich., 1964-66; tchr. Chgo. Pub. Schs., 1966-68; minister Waveland Ave. Congl. Ch., Chgo., 1967-79, interim pastor Chgo. Met. Assn., 1979—, First Congl. Ch., Des Plaines, Ill., 1979, Bethany United Ch., Chgo., 1980, Eden United Ch. of Christ, Chgo., 1983-84, St. Nicolai Ch., Chgo., 1984, Grace United Ch. of Christ, Chgo., 1985-86, Christ Ch. of Chgo., 1987-87, First Congl., Evanston, Ill., 1987-88, First Congl. Ch., Brookfield, Ill., 1988-89, First Congl. Ch., Steger, Il., 1990-91, First Congl. Ch., Berwyn, Ill., 1992, Immanual V.C.P. Ch., Streamwood, Ill., 1993—, Immanuel United Ch. of Christ, Bartlett, 1994; assoc. pastor, calling, min. of visitation People's Ch., Chgo., 1990-93; hist. cons. Bell & Howell Co., Chgo., 1981-82. Assoc. Hyde Park dept. Chgo. YMCA, 1942-44. U. Chgo. Libr. 1952-54; chmn. com. evangelism Kans. Congl. Christian Conf., 1947-48; city chmn. Layman's Missionary Movement, 1946-51; trustee Congl. and Christian Conf. Ill., v.p., 1963-64; mem. exec. coun. Chgo. Met. Assn. United Ch. of Christ, 1968-70, sec. ch. and ministry com., 1982-88 ; mem. gen. bd. Ch. Fedn. Greater Chgo., 1969-71; mem. Libr. Bd. Coun. Grove, 1945-49; city chmn. NCCJ, 1945-49; dean Northside Mission Coun. United Ch. of Christ, 1975-77, sec. personnel com. Ill. Conf. United Ch. of Christ, 1986-88. Recipient Pres'. award Congl. Christian Hist. Soc. Mem. Am. Soc. Ch. History, Am. Acad. Polit. Sci., Am. Hist. Assn., C. of C. (past dir.), Internat. Platform Assn. Author: The Growth of the Bible, 1969; From A Mission to a Church, 1976; Bell & Howell Company: A 75 Year History, 1982, (co-author) Harza: 65 Years, 1986, History of the Illinois Conference, United Church of Christ, 1990. Home: 321 E Morse Ave Bartlett IL 60103-4168

ROBINSON, JAKIE LEE, human services administrator; b. Santee, S.C., Feb. 16, 1951; s. Booker T. and Luciel (Holmon) R.; m. Anita Lynne Williams, Aug. 1, 1992; children: Joi Lynne Nakia, Jakquelynn Leona. AS in Electronic Instrumentation Tech., Orangeburg Calhoun Tech. Coll., Orangeburg, S.C., 1982; BS in Elec. Engring. Tech., S.C. State U., 1993, MA in Rehab. Counseling, 1994. Cert. Rehab. Counselor. Sr. devel. technician McDonnell Douglas Astronautics Co., Titusville, Fla., 1982-85; tech. publ. analyst Lockheed Space Ops. Co., Kennedy Space Ctr., Fla., 1985-88; tech. tng. instr. Orangeburg Calhoun Tech. Coll., 1989-90; computer room student asst. S.C. State U. Sch. Engring., Orangeburg, 1991-93; vol. clin. counselor Tri-County Alcohol and Drug Commn., Orangeburg, 1993-94; manpower case mgr. Charleston (S.C.) County Grants Adminstrn., 1994-96; mem. adv. com. Project Transition-Edisto Health Dist., Orangeburg, 1993-94; bd. dirs. The Bonds Wilson Collier Corp., Charleston. Vice-chair, co-founder Concerned Citizens in Action, Summerville, S.C., 1993; bd. dirs. S.C. Coalition Black Voters Participation Dorchester County, 1997. With USAF, 1971-74. Mem. Nat. Rehab. Assn. (life), Charleston Trident Assn. Realtors (lics. 1995), Commn. Notary Pub., Alpha Phi Alpha (chpt. corres. sec. 1995—), Alpha Kappa Mu, Chi Sigma Iota (life). Avocations: reading, cooking. Home: 8515 Kennestone Ln Charleston SC 29420

ROBINSON, JAMES ARTHUR, university president emeritus, political scientist; b. Blackwell, Okla., June 9, 1932; s. William L. and Ethel Bell (Hicks) R.; children: Adelaide Ethel, William Luke Walton. AB, George Washington U., 1954, DPS (hon.), 1977; MA, U. Okla., 1955; PhD, Northwestern U., 1957; LLD (hon.), Kyungpook (Korea) Nat. U., 1979; cert. Inst. for Ednl. Mgmt., Harvard U., 1986. Instr. polit. sci. Northwestern U., 1958-59, asst. prof., 1959-62, assoc. prof., 1962-64; prof. polit. sci. Ohio State U., Columbus, 1964-71; dir. Mershon Center, 1967-70, v.p. acad. affairs, provost, 1969-71; pres., prof. polit. sci. Macalester Coll., St. Paul, 1971-74; pres. U. West Fla., Pensacola, 1974-88, pres. emeritus, 1988—, Regents prof. polit. sci., mgmt., ednl. leadership, 1988—. Author: (with R. C. Snyder) National and International Decision Making, 1961, Congress and Foreign Policy Making, rev. edit, 1967, House Rules Committee, 1964. Recipient Manning Dauer award Fla. Polit. Sci. Assn., 1992; Congl. fellow Am. Polit. Sci. Assn., 1957-58. Club: Cosmos (Washington).

ROBINSON, JAMES D., III, corporate executive; b. Atlanta, Nov. 19, 1935; m. Bettye Bradley (div.); 2 children; m. Linda Gosden, 1984. BS, Ga. Inst. Tech., 1957; MBA, Harvard U., 1961. Officer various depts. Morgan Guaranty Trust Co. of N.Y., N.Y.C., 1961-66, asst. v.p., staff asst. to chmn. bd. and pres., 1967-68; gen. ptnr. White, Weld & Co., 1968-70; exec. v.p. Am. Express Co., N.Y.C., 1970-75, pres., dir., 1975-77, chmn. bd. dirs., CEO, dir., 1977-93; pres. J.D. Robinson, Inc., N.Y.C., 1993—; pres., CEO Am. Express Internat. Banking Corp., 1970-73; chair Am. Express Credit Corp., 1973-75; chair, CEO RRE Investors, 1994—; sr. advisor Trust Co. of the West, 1993; bd. dirs. Coca Cola Co., Bristol-Myers Squibb Co., Cambridge Tech. Ptnrs., First Data Corp., New World Comms. Group, Inc., Alexander & Alexander Svcs., Inc., Union Pacific Corp., Internat. Equity Ptnrs., MagiNet Corp., Iterated Sys., Inc. Kenny Rogers Roasters, Giga Info. Group, Inc. Author: Inflation Overkill, 1994. Active Bus. Coun., Adv. Coun., Trust Co. of Ga., Inter-Am. Devel. Bank, U.S.-Canada Private Sector Adv. Bd., Coun. on Fgn. Rels., U.S. Japan Bus. Coun., Dean's Adv. Coun. Roberto C. Goizueta Sch. Bus. Emory U., Exec. Adv. Bd., Ivan Allen Coll.; chair bd. overseers and mgrs. Meml. Sloan-Kettering Cancer Ctr.; hon. mem. The Brookings Instn.; mem., bd. dirs. Nat. Acad. Found.; mem. Pres.' Cir. The Asia Soc.; bd. dirs., chair emeritus N.Y.C. Partnership and C. of C., Inc.; chair emeritus World Travel & Tourism Coun.; former co-chair Internat. Trade and Investment Task Force of the Bus. Roundtable; mem. adv. com. on trade and policy negotiations United Way of Am.; former mem. Coun. on Competitiveness, Mayor's Coun. of Econ. Advisors, Gov.'s coun. on Fiscal & Econ. Policy; former trustee Alfred P. Sloan Found. Lt. USNR, 1957-59. Mem. Bus. Roundtable (former co-chmn.), N.Y.C. C. of C. and Industry (bd. dirs.), Brookings Inst., Japan Soc. (bd. dirs.), Coun. on Competitiveness, Econ. Club (N.Y.C.), Pilgrims of U.S. Club. Office: J D Robinson Inc 126 E 56th St 22nd Fl New York NY 10022 also: RRE Investors 126 E 56th St New York NY 10022

ROBINSON, JAMES G., film production executive; five children. Former owner automobile distributorship; businessman Balt.; founder, now chmn., chief exec. officer Morgan Creek Prodns. Co-exec. producer films Young Guns, 1988, Skin Deep, 1989, Enemies A Love Story, 1989, Renegades, 1989, Major League, 1989, Coupe de Ville, 1990, Nightbreed, 1990, Young Guns II, 1990, Pacific Heights, 1990, The Exorcist III, 1990, Robin Hood: Prince of Thieves, 1991, Freejack, 1992, White Sands, 1992, Stay Tuned, 1992, The Crush, 1993, True Romance, 1993, Ace Ventura: Pet Detective, 1994, Major League II, 1994, Trial By Jury, 1994, Silent Fall, 1994. Office: Morgan Creek Prodns 4000 Warner Blvd Bldg 76 Burbank CA 91522-0001*

ROBINSON, JAMES KENNETH, lawyer, educator; b. Grand Rapids, Mich., Nov. 27, 1943; s. Kenneth and Marguerite (Anderson) R.; m. Marietta Sebree; children: Steven James, Renee Elizabeth. BA with honors, Mich. State U., 1965; JD magna cum laude, Wayne State U., 1968. Bar: Mich. 1968, U.S. Dist. Ct. (ea. and we. dists) Mich. 1969, U.S. Ct. Appeals (6th cir.) 1969, U.S. Supreme Ct. 1977. Law clk. to judge U.S. Ct. Appeals (6th cir.), 1968-69; assoc. Miller, Canfield, Paddock & Stone, Detroit, 1969-71; assoc., then ptnr. Honigman Miller Schwartz and Cohn, Detroit, 1972-77, ptnr., 1981-93, chmn. litigation dept.; U.S. atty. Ea. Dist. Mich., 1977-80; prof., dean Law Sch. Wayne State U., Detroit, 1993—; adj. prof. Detroit Coll. Law, 1970-73, Wayne State U. Law Sch., 1973-84; mem. evidence test drafting com.-multistate bar exam Nat. Conf. Bar Examiners, 1975—; mem. adv. com. on evidence rules Jud. Conf. U.S., 1993—; chmn. com. on rules of evidence Mich. Supreme Ct., 1975-78; lectr. Mich. Jud. Inst., 1977—, Mich. Inst. Continuing Legal Edn. Author: (with others) Introducing Evidence-A Practical Guide for Michigan Lawyers, 1988, Scope of Discovery, 1986, Michigan Court Rules Practice - Evidence, 1996; contbg. author Evidence in America - The Federal Rules in the States, 1987; also articles; editor in chief Wayne Law Rev., 1967-68. Chmn. Gov.'s Commn. on Future Higher Edn.

in Mich., 1983-84; pres. State Bar of Mich., 1990-91, commr. 1980-81, 83-91. Recipient Disting. Alumni award Wayne State U. Law Sch., 1979, 1986. Fellow Am. Bar Found., Mich. Bar Found., Am. Coll. Trial Lawyers, Internat. Soc. Barristers, Am. Acad. of Appellate Lawyers; mem. ABA (litigation and criminal justice sects., lectr.), Fed. Bar Assn. (dir. 1975-81), Detroit Bar Assn. (bd. dirs. 1975-81), Nat. Assn. Former U.S. Attys. (pres. 1984-85), Am. Law Inst., 6th Cir. Jud. Conf., Wayne U. Law Alumni Assn. (pres. 1975-76), Detroit Athletic Club, Detroit Yacht Club. Office: Wayne State U Law Sch Detroit MI 48202

ROBINSON, JAMES WILLIAM, retired management consultant; b. Bklyn., Feb. 22, 1919; s. Charles Edward and Adelaide (Reimer) R.; m. Dorothy L. Luckow, July 5, 1946; 1 child, Joan Barbara. AB, Cornell U., 1940, LLB, 1942. Bar: N.Y. 1942. Assoc. atty. Whitman, Ransom & Coulson, 1946-57; with Westvaco Corp., N.Y.C., 1957-69, sec., 1966-69; prin., mng. dir. Georgeson & Co. Inc., N.Y.C., 1969-82; mng. dir. Morrow & Co., N.Y.C., 1982-90; pres. J.W. Robinson Assocs., Inc., Gig Harbor, Wash., 1990—; mem. adv. com. shareholder comms. SEC; com. on shareowner comms. N.Y. Stock Exch., 1986-92. Editor: Tender Offers Handbook, Proxy Rules Handbook. Capt. AUS, 1942-46. Decorated Bronze (V) Star medal. Mem. ABA, N.Y. State Bar Assn., Assn. Bar City N.Y., Am. Soc. Corp. Secs., Canterwood Country Club, Phi Delta Phi, Lambda Chi Alpha. Home and Office: 4820 Old Stump Dr NW Gig Harbor WA 98332-8899

ROBINSON, JANIE MONETTE, education educator; b. Merkel, Tex., Oct. 20, 1941; d. Orvin Leon and Velma Cleone (Rutledge) R.; div.; children: Gregory Blake Keller, Karel Blynn Keller. BS, Howard Payne U., 1963; MEd, U. Nev., Las Vegas, 1990; postgrad., U. Nev., Reno, 1991-92, Brigham Young U., 1990-91. Cert. tchr., Tex., N.Mex. Tchr., coach Eula Rural Sch., Clyde, Tex., 1961-63; tchr. Grand Lake High Sch., Lake Charles, La., 1964; instr. history Colo. Bapt. Coll., Denver, 1977-78; tchr. Lincoln County Sch. Dist., Caliente, Nev., 1978-86, Abilene (Tex.) Ind. Sch. Dist., 1986-87, Lander County Sch. Dist., Battle Mountain, Nev., 1990-93, Raton (N.Mex.) Mcpl. Sch. Dist., 1993—; instr. edn. Trinidad Jr. Coll., 1995; dir. day care A Child's World, North Las Vegas, Nev., 1988-89; dir. girls' group home Regina Hall, Henderson, Nev., 1989-90. em. NEA, ASCD, Coun. for Exceptional Children. Baptist. Avocations: quilting, camping, reading. Home: PO Box 522 Raton NM 87740 Office: Raton High Sch 1535 Tiger Cir Raton NM 87740-4300

ROBINSON, JAY (THURSTON), artist; b. Detroit, Aug. 1, 1915; s. Carter Boston and Marie Rose (Steger) R.; m. Dorothy June Whipple, Sept. 15, 1937 (dec. 1968); children: Theodore Carter, Thomas Whipple, James Jay; m. Anne Frances Helen Posch, Nov. 5, 1970. BA, Yale U., 1937; MFA, Cranbrook Acad. Art, 1943. Illustrator: (books) Seventeenth Summer (Maureen Daly), 1948, The New York Guide Book, 1964; contbr. illustrations to others; one-man shows include, Guggenheim Mus. Non-Objective Painting, N.Y.C., 1947, Milch Galleries, N.Y.C., 1948, 51, 53, 54, 55, 56, J.B. Speed Art Mus., Louisville, 1953, Dayton Art Inst., 1953, Phila. Art Alliance, 1957, Monede Gallery, N.Y.C., 1961, 62, Raymond Burr Galleries, Beverly Hills, Calif., 1963, xxth Century West Gallery, N.Y.C., 1968, E. Kuhlik Gallery, N.Y.C., 1971, New Canaan Soc. for Arts, 1983, Broome St. Gallery, N.Y.C., 1994, group shows include, Guggenheim Mus., 1947, 49, Carnegie Inst., Pitts., 1949, Des Moines Art Center, 1950, Butler Inst., Youngstown, Ohio, 1953, also Audubon Artists, N.Y.C., Corcoran Gallery, Washington, Mich. Artists, Detroit, NAD, N.Y.C., Pa. Acad., Phila., Provincetown (Mass.) Annual, Va. Biennial, Richmond; represented in permanent collections, including, Detroit Inst. Art, Houston Mus. Fine Art, Witte Meml. Mus., San Antonio, Philbrook Art Center, Tulsa; Berea Coll., Goucher Coll., Fisk U.; represented in also corp. collections, including, IBM; Republic Steel Co., Prentice-Hall Pub., portrait painter, designer china and textiles. Served with OSS, 1943; Served with USN, 1943-46. Louis Comfort Tiffany Found. award, 1950; various purchase awards Am. Acad. Arts and Letters, 1951-64; Outstanding Alumnus award Detroit Country Day Sch., 1966. Mem. Artist Equity Assn. N.Y. Home and Studio: 305 East Landing Williamsburg VA 23185-8254 *I have always been drawn to the theme of Man in His Environment. By extension to our own, I love jazz music, many of whose players I have painted; classic cars; Japanese gardens; good company and active social life. Travel enables me to see what others have done and are doing, all of us alike in trying to cope as best we can. In painting, I can not only portray but participate in what goes on on our planet.*

ROBINSON, JEFFERY HERBERT, transportation company executive; b. Atlanta, Nov. 30, 1956; s. Herbert W. and Annie Hue (Maxey) R.; children: Angela Marie, David Clifton, John William; m. Cynthia Moss Geeslin, Spet. 1991; adopted chidlren: William Damon Geeslin, Taylor Lauren Geeslin. AA, DeKalb Coll., Clarkston, Ga., 1979; BBA in Mktg., Ga. State U., 1980. Data comm. specialist GE, Atlanta, 1980-81; account exec. Burlington No. Air Freight, Atlanta, 1981-82; br. mgr. Spacemaster Internat., Charlotte, N.C., 1982-84; regional sales mgr. Profit Freight Systems, Atlanta, 1984-87; v.p. sales Eden Air Freight, Inc., Atlanta, 1987-93; v.p. sales & mktg. Amerford Internat. Corp., Atlanta, 1993-95; pres. Alpha Air Logistics, Atlanta, 1996—. With U.S. Army, 1974-77. Lewis Gordon Meml. scholar Sales and Mktg. Execs. Atlanta, 1980. Baptist. Office: Alpha Air Logistics Inc 2043 Lawrence St Atlanta GA 30344-1733

ROBINSON, JOE SAM, neurosurgeon; b. Atlanta, Ga., July 21, 1945; s. Joe Sam and Nell (Mixon) R.; m. Elixabeth Ann Moate, Apr. 3, 1982; children: Joe Sam III, Edward Richard, Thomas McRae. AB cum laude, Harvard Coll., 1967; MD, U. Va., 1971; MS, Northwestern U., 1975. Internship in surgery Emory Univ., 1971-72, residency in surgery, 1972-73; residency in neurosurgery Northwestern Univ., 1973-78; instr. Univ. Ill., 1978-79, Yale Univ., 1979-81; pres. Neurol. Inst. Ctrl. Ga., Macon, 1981—; prof., chief neurosurgery Mercer U. Sch. Medicine, Macon, 1986; chief surgery Med. Ctr. Ctrl. Ga., Macon, 1989-91, 97, vice chmn. surgery, 1991-97; vis. neurosurgeon China, 1992, Konaus Acad. Neurosurgery Inst., Lithuania, 1992. Lt. col. USANG, 1972-95. Fellow Internat. Coll. Surgeons (vice regent 1983-93); mem. Am. Assn. Neurol. Surgeons, Congress Neurol. Surgeons, AAAS, Ga. Neurosurg. Soc., Alpha Omega Alpha. Republican. Methodist. Office: Neurol Inst 840 Pine St Ste 880 Macon GA 31201-2197

ROBINSON, JOHN ALAN, logic and computer science educator; b. Halifax, Eng., Mar. 9, 1930; came to U.S., 1952; naturalized citizen, 1990.; s. Harry and Clara (Pilkington) R.; m. Gwen Groves, Dec. 18, 1954; children: Alan Groves, Hugh Parke Custis, Gwen Owen. B.A. in Classics with honours, Corpus Christi Coll., Cambridge (Eng.) U., 1952; M.A., 1955; M.A. in Philosophy, U. Ore., 1953; M.A., Princeton, 1955, Ph.D., 1956; D in Applied Sci. honoris causa, Leuven, 1988; D in Philosophy honoris causa, Uppsala, 1994. Operations research analyst E.I. du Pont de Nemours & Co., Inc., 1956-60; post-doctoral research fellow U. Pitts., 1960-6l; mem. faculty Rice U., 1961-67, prof. philosophy, 1964-65, prof. computer sci. and philosophy, 1965-66, prof. computer sci., 1966-67; disting. prof. logic and computer sci. Syracuse U., 1967-84, Univ. prof., 1984-92, univ. prof. emeritus, 1993—; cons. in applied math. divsn. Argonne Nat. Lab., 1961-67, Stanford Linear Acceleration Ctr., 1966-68; vis. rsch. fellow Australian Nat. U., 1989; Fujitsu vis. prof. U. Tokyo, 1991-92. Author: Logic: Form and Function, 1979; founder, editor-in-chief Jour. Logic Programming, 1984-86; contbr. articles to profl. jours. Served with RAF, 1948-49. Recipient Sr. U.S. Scientists prize Humboldt Found., 1995, Herbrand award, 1996; Guggenheim Found. fellow, 1967-68; hon. rsch. fellow U. Edinburgh, 1967—. Fellow Am. Assn. for Artificial Intelligence; mem. Kokusai Bunka Kaikan (Tokyo). Home and Office: 96 Highland Ave Greenfield MA 01301-3606

ROBINSON, JOHN BECKWITH, development management consultant; b. Portland, Oreg., May 23, 1922; s. Jewell King and Arvilla Agnes (Beckwith) R.; m. Dilys Walters, Sept. 8, 1945; children—John Gwilym, David Gwyn. B.A., U. Oreg., 1944; postgrad., U. Shrivenham, Eng., 1945, U. Oxford, Eng., 1946, Am. U., 1947. Staff Bur. Budget, 1948, 51-52; sr. program and budget officer UNESCO, 1948-51; chief personnel policy Mut. Security Agy., Washington, 1952-54; program officer Mut. Security Agy., Guatemala, 1954-59; planning officer, later acting asst. dep. dir. for program and planning Mut. Security Agy., Washington, 1959-61; dep. U.S. rep. devel. assistance com. OECD, 1961-64; asst. dir. devel. policy Pakistan, 1964-68; dep. dir. North Coast Affairs, AID, State Dept., Washington, 1969-71; dep. mission dir. U.S. Econ. Aid Program, Colombia, 1971-73; mission dir. U.S. Econ. Aid Program, Dominican Republic, 1973-76, Honduras, 1976-79; privatization adviser Gov. of Costa Rica, 1986-88; prin. assoc. J.B. Robinson & Assocs. (devel. mgmt. cons.), 1979—; mem. faculty, fellow Harvard U., 1968-69; cons. NATO, 1951, UN, 1959. Served to 1st lt., inf. AUS, 1943-46, ETO. Mem. Oriental Club (London), DACOR BACON House (Washington), Minchinhampton Golf Club, Minchinhampton Probus Club (pres. 1983-84). Episcopalian. Address: Anglezarke The Hithe, Rodborough Common, Stroud GL5 5BN Gloucestershire, England also: 7130 SW Gable Pky Portland OR 97225-2620 *Summary: always do more than what is asked for the task at hand. The extra effort always leads to unexpected opportunities for career advancement. Helping others to realize their potential has its own rewards and their success helps to realize your own hopes and aspirations, and improve your own quality of life and satisfaction in a life well-spent. Never underestimate the contribution of your wife and family.*

ROBINSON, JOHN BOWERS, JR., bank holding company executive; b. Laconia, N.H., Oct. 9, 1946; s. John Bowers and Lee (Osborn) R.; m. Jane Frances Moore, Aug. 31, 1968; children: John Paul, Claire Frances, David Moore, Leanne Elizabeth, Gregory Joseph, Peter August. BA, Fairfield U., 1968; MBA, Adelphi U., 1977. V.p., asst. to pres. Hempstead Bank, N.Y., 1977-79, exec. v.p., 1979-81, pres., 1981-82; v.p. planning Norstar Bancorp, Inc., Albany, N.Y., 1982-84, exec. v.p., 1984-87, pres., 1987-88; mng. dir. govt. banking Fleet Fin. Group, Albany, 1988—; bd. dirs. Fleet Securities, Inc.; mem. N.Y. State Banking Bd., 1990—, N.Y. State Bus. Coun., 1990—, Albany Med. Ctr., 1989—, Siena Coll., Loudonville, N.Y., 1989—. Pres. bd. trustees Doane Stuart Sch., Albany, N.Y., 1996—. Mem. Ft. Orange Club, Schuyler Meadows Club. Home: 81 Old Niskayuna Rd Loudonville NY 12211-1349 Office: Fleet Fin Group Peter D Kiernan Plz Albany NY 12207

ROBINSON, JOHN DAVID, retired army officer; b. Concord, Mass., June 9, 1937; m. Roberta Jean Small; children: Mark D., Karen L. BA, U. Maine, 1961; MBA, U. Ala., 1972. Commd. 2d lt. U.S. Army, 1961, advanced through grades to maj. gen., 1990; student Naval War Coll., Newport, R.I., 1979-80; asst. tng. and doctrine, command systems mgr. U.S. Army Aviation Ctr., Ft. Rucker, Ala., 1980; dir. army model improvement program U.S. Army Combined Arms Ctr., Ft. Leavenworth, Kans., 1980-83; comdr. 9th Cav. Brigade, 9th Inf. Div., Ft. Lewis, Wash., 1983-85; dep. asst. comdt. U.S. Army Aviation Ctr., Ft. Rucker, 1985-86; comdg. gen. Tng. and Doctrine Analysis Command, Ft. Leavenworth, 1986-88; dep. dir. for force structure, resource and assessment Joint Staff, Washington, 1988-89, dir., 1989-91; comdg. gen. U.S. Army Aviation Ctr., Ft. Rucker, 1991-94; v.p. ops. Raytheon Aerospace, Madison, Miss., 1994—. Decorated Def. D.S.M., Army D.S.M., Legion of Merit (2), Air medal with V device, Bronze Star with oak leaf. Mem. Assn. U.S. Army (sr. v.p.), Army Aviation Assn. Am. (nat. exec. bd.). Home: 109 Clairemont Dr Ridgeland MS 39157-9765 Office: Raytheon Aerospace 555 Industrial Dr S Madison MS 39110-9072

ROBINSON, JOHN GWILYM, conservationist; b. Paris, Nov. 22, 1949; s. John Beckwith and Dilys (Walters) R.; m. Linda Cox, June 8, 1974; children; David Andrew Cox, Amandia Siân Cox. BA in Zoology with honors, Swarthmore Coll., 1971; PhD in Zoology, U. N.C., 1977. Postdoctoral fellow dept. zool. rsch. Nat. Zool. Park, Smithsonian Instn., Washington, 1977-80, zoologist, 1980-83; affiliate assoc. curator Fla. Mus. Natural History, Gainesville, 1983—; affiliate assoc. prof. dept. wildlife and range scis. U. Fla., 1983-85, assoc. prof., 1985-90, courtesy prof., 1990—, dir. program for studies in tropical conservation, 1980-90; dir. wildlife conservation internat. Wildlife Conservation Soc. (former N.Y. Zool. Soc.), Bronx, N.Y., 1990-93, v.p. internat. conservation, 1993—; program dir. integrated approaches to tng. in conservation and sustainable devel. Pew Charitable Trusts, Phila., 1988-93; chmn. adv. group Sustainable Use Initiative, World Conservation Union, 1995—, mem. steering com. Species Survival Commn., 1991—, regional mem. N.Am. and Caribbean, 1991—, primate specialist Species Survival Commn., 1985—, sustainablue use specialist group, 1992—. Mem. editl. bd. Primates, 1991—; bd. editors Conservation Biology, 1993—; sci. com. Conservation and Mgmt., 1993—; editor: (with L.D. Navarro) Diversidad Biologica en La Reserva de la Biosphera de Sian Ka'an, 1990, (with K. H. Redford) Neotropical Wildlife Use and Conservation, 1991; contbr. articles to profl. jours., chpts. to books. Mem. tech. adv. bd. Fundaçao Biodiversitas, Brazil, 1989—; mem. coun. advisors Branger Found., Venezuela; bd. dirs. Wild Things Inc., 1992—, Global Coral Reef Alliance, 1992—, Greentree Group, Inc., 1993—, Sociedade Civil Mamirauá, Brazil, Sócio Efetivo, 1993—; bd. dirs. World Parks Endowment, Inc., 1994—. Mem. AAAS, Am. Soc. Primatologists (conservation com. 1984-88), Internat. Primatological Soc. (election com. 1990—, Martha T. Galante endowment overview com. 1989—, conservation com. 1986-92), Assn. Tropical Biology, Fauna and Flora Preservation Soc. Office: Wildlife Conservation Soc 185th St and Southern Blvd Bronx NY 10460

ROBINSON, JOHN LEWIS, geography educator; b. Leamington, Ont., Can., July 9, 1918; s. William John and Emily Laverne (Dunphy) R.; m. Josephine Rowan, Oct. 14, 1944; children: David, Jo-Anne, Patricia. B.A., Western Ont. U., 1940; M.A., Syracuse U., 1942; Ph.D., Clark U., 1946; LLD (hon.), Western Ont. U., 1984; DSc (hon.), U. B.C., 1994. Geographer N.W.T. Adminstrn., Ottawa, Ont., 1943-46; prof., head dept. geography U. B.C., Vancouver, 1946-68, prof. geography, 1968-85, prof. emeritus, 1985—. Author 14 books on aspects of regional geography of Can., including British Columbia: 100 Years of Geographical Change, 1973, Themes in the Regional Geography of Canada, 1983, 2d edit., 1989; contbr. articles to profl. jours. Recipient citation of merit Assn. Am. Geographers, 1966; Massey medal Canadian Geog. Soc., 1971. Mem. Canadian Assn. Geographers (pres. 1956, citation for service to profession 1976). Office: U BC, Dept Geography, Vancouver, BC Canada V6T 1Z2

ROBINSON, JOHN MINOR, lawyer, retired business executive; b. Uniontown, Pa., Mar. 18, 1910; s. John M. and Martha (Downs) R. A.B., Harvard U., 1932, LL.B, 1935. Bar: Calif. 1936. Assoc. firm Macdonald & Pettit, 1935-41; partner firm Musick, Peeler & Garrett, 1947-77; v.p., sec. Consol. Western Steel div. U.S. Steel Corp. (and predecessors), 1941-57. Clubs: Calif. (past pres. L.A.), Pacific Union (San Francisco); Cypress Point (Pebble Beach, Calif.); The Old Capital (Monterey, Calif.); Royal and Ancient Golf of St. Andrews (Fife, Scotland). Office: 9500 Center St Carmel CA 93923

ROBINSON, JOHN PETER, film composer, keyboardist; b. Fulmer, Eng., Sept. 16, 1945; s. John Lacey and Winifred Gertrude (Hayes) R.; m. Cecilia Karin Angela Gardtman, Nov. 4, 1983 (div. Jan. 1988); 1 child, Aimee-Jane Dadswell. Diploma, Royal Acad. Music, London, 1967. Founding mem., keyboardist Quatermass, 1969-71; keyboardist Stanley Clarke's School Days Band, 1977-78, Al Stewart, 1978-79; keyboardist Shawn Phillips, 1971-76, Stomu Yamashta, 1976-77, Al Jarreau, 1980-81, Eric Clapton, 1984, Phil Collins/Brand X, 1978-85. Composer for films The Wraith, 1986, The Gate, 1987, The Believers, 1987, Cocktail, 1988 (Box Office award ASCAP 1988), Return of The Living Dead Part II, 1988, The Kiss, 1988, The Wizard, 1989, Blind Fury, 1989, Cadillac Man, 1990, Wayne's World, 1992 (Box Office award ASCAP 1992), Encino Man, 1992, Wes Craven's New Nightmare, 1994, Highlander 3, 1995, Vampire in Brooklyn, 1995, TV films Deadly Encounter, 1982, Kate's Secret, 1986, J. Edgar Hoover, 1987, Bates Motel, 1987, Desert Rats, 1988, The Gifted One, 1989, Deadly Intentions...Again?, 1991, Hell Hath No Fury, 1991, Lighting Field, 1991, Are You Lonesome Tonight, 1992, The President's Child, 1992, The Night My Parents Ran Away, 1993. Recipient Best Music award nomination Acad. Sci. Fiction Fantasy/Horror Films, 1988. Home: care FMA 4146 Lankershim Blvd Ste 400 North Hollywood CA 91602-2832*

ROBINSON, JOHN WILLIAM, IV, lawyer; b. Atlanta, Apr. 29, 1950; s. J. William III and Elizabeth (Smith) R.; m. Ellen Showalter, Dec. 28, 1976; children: William, Anna. BA with honors, Washington & Lee U., 1972; JD, U. Ga., 1975. Bar: Fla., Ga., U.S. Dist. Ct. (no., so. and mid. dists.) Fla., U.S. Ct. Mil. Appeals, U.S. Ct. Appeals (5th and 11th cirs.), U.S. Supreme Ct.; cert. civil trial and bus. litigation lawyer, Fla., Nat. Bd. Trial Advocacy. Trial atty. Nat. Labor Rels. Bd., New Orleans, 1975-76; trial def. counsel 8th infantry U.S. Army, Mainz, Germany, 1977-78, trial counsel 8th infantry, 1979; law clerk, commr. Ct. Mil. Review, Washington, 1980; atty. Fowler, White, Gillen, Boggs, Villareal & Banker, P.A., Tampa, Fla., 1980—, head labor and employment law dept., 1993—; mem. faculty U. Md., 1977-79; arbitrator U.S. Dist. Ct. (mid. dist.) Fla. Editor-in-chief: Employment & Labor Relations Law, 1991-95; contbg. editor: Developing Labor Law, 1982—, Model Jury Instructions for Employment Litigation, 1994—, Employment Litigation Deskbook, 1997. Chmn. Tampa Bay Internat. Trade Coun., 1990-91, Rough Riders Dist. Boy Scouts Am., 1990, Drug Free Workplace Task Force, Greater Tampa C. of C., 1996. Capt. U.S. Army, 1976-80. Mem. ABA (chmn. employment and labor rels. com., litigation sect.), Fla. Bar Assn. (chmn. labor and employment law sect. 1992-93), Wash. & Lee U. Bd. (pres. nat. alumni bd. 1990-91, trustee 1995—), Rotary (pres. Tampa Bay chpt.), Am. Inn of Ct. (pres., dir. and barrister). Avocations: tennis, history. Office: Fowler White Gillen Boggs Villareal & Banker PA 501 E Kennedy Blvd Tampa FL 33602-5200

ROBINSON, JOSEPH EDWARD, geology educator, consulting petroleum geologist; b. Regina, Sask., Can., June 25, 1925; came to U.S., 1976; s. Webb Gabriel Wilton and Blanche Marion (Schiefner) R.; m. Mary Corrine Maclaughlin, Nov. 1, 1952 (div. 1977); children: Joseph Christopher, John Edward, Timothy Webb. B.Eng., McGill U., 1950, M.Sc., 1951; Ph.D., U. Alta., 1968. Registered profl. engr., Que., Can. Geophysicist Imperial Oil Ltd., Can., 1951-68; sr. geologist Union Oil Co. Can., Calgary, Alta., Can., 1968-76; cons. geologist J.E. Robinson & Assocs., Syracuse, N.Y., 1976—; prof. geology Syracuse U., 1976-91, prof. emeritus, 1991—. Author: Computer Applications in Petroleum Geology, 1982. Served with Can. Navy, 1943-46, ETO. Mem. Am. Assn. Petroleum Geologists, Soc. Exploration Geologists, Soc. Ind. Profl. Earth Scientists, Can. Assn. Petroleum Geologists, Internat. Assn. Math. Geology (assoc. editor 1976-78). Home: 837 Ackerman Ave Syracuse NY 13210-2906 Office: Syracuse U Dept Geology Syracuse NY 13244

ROBINSON, JULIAN B., church administrator. Dir. of bus. and records Ch. of God. Office: PO Box 2430 Cleveland TN 37320-2430*

ROBINSON, JUNE KERSWELL, dermatologist, educator; b. Phila., Jan. 26, 1950; d. George and Helen S. (Kerswell) R.; m. William T. Barker, Jan. 31, 1981. BA cum laude, U. Pa., 1970; MD, U. Md., 1974. Diplomate Am. Bd. Dermatology, Nat. Bd. Med. Examiners, Am. Bd. Mohs Micrographic Surgery and Cutaneous Oncology. Intern Greater Balt. Med. Ctr., Hanover, N.H., 1974; resident in medicine Greater Balt. Med. Ctr., 1974-75; resident in dermatology Dartmouth-Hitchcock Med. Ctr., Hanover, N.H., 1975-78, chief resident, clin. instr., 1977-78; instr. in dermatology Dartmouth-Hitchcock Med. Ctr., Hanover, 1978; fellow Mohs; chemosurgery and dermatologic surgery NYU Skin and Cancer Clinic, N.Y.C., 1978-79; instr. in dermatology NYU, N.Y.C., 1979; asst. prof. dermatology Northwestern U. Med. Sch., Chgo., 1979, asst. prof. surgery, 1980-85, assoc. prof. dermatology and surgery, 1985-91, prof. dermatology and surgery, 1991—; mem. consensus devel. conf. NIH, 1992; lectr. in field. Author: Fundamentals of Skin Biopsy, 1985, also audiovisual materials; editor: (textbooks) Atlas of Cutaneous Surgery, 1996, Cutaneous Medicine and Surgery: An Integrated Program in Dermatology, 1996; mem. editl. bd. Archives of Dermatology, 1988—; sect. editor The Cutting Edge: Challenges in Med. and Surg. Therapeutics, 1989-97; contbg. editor Jour. Dermatol. Surgery and Oncology, 1985-88; mem. editl. com. 18th World Congress of Dermatology, 1982; contbr. numerous articles, abstracts to profl. publs., chpts. to books. Bd. dirs. Northwestern Med. Faculty Found., 1982-84, chmn. com. on benefits and leaves, 1984, nominating com. 1988. Grantee Nat. Cancer Inst., 1985-91, Am. Cancer Soc., 1986-89, Skin Cancer Found., 1984-85, Dermatology Found., 1981-83, Northwestern U. Biomed. Rsch., 1981, Syntex, 1984. Fellow Am. Coll. Chemosurgery (chmn. sci. program ann. meeting 1983, chmn. publs. com. 1986-87, chmn. task force on ednl. needs 1989-90, co-editor bull. 1984-87); mem. AMA, Am. Cancer Soc. (pres. Ill. divsn. 1996-98), Am. Dermatol. Assn., Am. Acad. Dermatology (asst. sec. treas. 1995—, bd. dirs., 1993-95, Stephen Rothman Lectr. award 1992, Presdl. citation 1992), Dermatology Found. (trustee 1995—), Internat. Soc. Dermatol. Surgery, Am. Soc. Dermatol. Surgery (pres. 1994-95), Soc. Investigative Dermatology, Women's Dermatol. Soc. (pres. 1990-92), Chgo. Dermatol. Soc. Home: 132 E Delaware # 5806 Chicago IL 60611-1533

ROBINSON, KENNETH LEONARD, JR., trade association executive; b. Lynn, Mass., Feb. 14, 1929; s. Kenneth Leonard Sr. and Frances Ruth (Leighton) R.; m. Marie Louise Cormier, Sept. 1, 1951; children: Edward K., Elaine F., Ruth M., Doris A., Gordon M. BA, Boston Coll., 1950; MS, George Washington U., 1969. Advanced through grades to maj. gen. USMC, 1979; commdg. gen. Marine Corp. Base USMC, Camp Butler, Okinawa, 1977-79; commdg. gen. 3d Marine div. USMC, Okinawa, 1980; commdg. gen. Marine Corp. Base USMC, Camp Pendleton, Calif., 1980-83; ret. USMC, 1983; pres., chief exec. officer Nat. Assn. Fed. Credit Unions, Washington, 1984—; bd. dirs. San Diego (Calif.) Navy Fed. Credit Union, San Diego, Calif., 1981-83, Washington, 1975-77. Columnist on fin. topics for trade mags.; contbr. articles to trade publs. Mem. Far East Coun. Boy Scouts Am., Okinawa, 1977-80, San Diego Coun., 1980-83. Recipient Golden Eagle award Far East Coun. Boy Scouts Am., 1980, Silver Beaver award San Diego Coun., 1982. Mem. Am. Soc. Assn. Execs., Greater Washington Soc. Assn. Execs., USMC Hist. Soc. (bd. dirs. 1987—, chmn. audit com. 1987—), Army-Navy Club, Exchequer Club (Washington). Republican. Roman Catholic. Avocations: tennis, golf, bowling, chess. Home: 2538 N Vermont St Arlington VA 22207-4126 Office: Nat Assn Fed Credit Unions PO Box 3769 Washington DC 20007*

ROBINSON, LARRY CLARK, professional hockey coach; b. Winchester, Ont., Can., June 2, 1951. Head coach L.A. Kings, 1995—. Office: LA Kings Great Western Forum 3900 W Manchester Blvd Inglewood CA 90305-2200*

ROBINSON, LARRY ROBERT, insurance company executive; b. Indpls., Feb. 7, 1936; s. Manuel H. Robinson and Barbara Dawson Robinson Trees; m. Sharon Moore, Aug. 3, 1957; children: Christopher, Lizbeth, Lara, Jeremy. BA, DePauw U., Greencastle, Ind., 1957. Actuarial trainee State Life Ins. Co., Indpls., 1957-63, asst. actuary, 1963-66, actuary, 1966-67, asst. v.p., actuary, 1967-70, v.p., actuary, 1970-80, sr. v.p., actuary, 1980-83, exec. v.p., 1983—, also bd. dirs.; chmn. cost disclosure com. Am. Coun. Life Ins., Washington, 1985-87, chmn. actuarial com., 1990-91. Bd. dirs. Marion County Assn. Retarded Citizens, Indpls., 1980-86. With U.S. Army, 1961-62. Fellow Soc. Actuaries; mem. Am. Acad. Actuaries, Indpls. Actuarial Club (past pres.), Actuarial Club Ind., Ky. and Ohio (past pres.), Phi Beta Kappa. Office: State Life Ins Co 141 E Washington St Indianapolis IN 46204-3614

ROBINSON, LAURIE OVERBY, assistant attorney general; b. Washington, July 7, 1946; d. Kermit and Ethel Esther (Schlasinger) Overby; m. Craig Baab, Oct. 22, 1977; (div. 1991); 1 child, Teddy Baab; m. Sheldon Krantz, Dec. 8, 1991. BA in Polit. Sci. magna cum laude, Brown U., 1968. Desk editor Cmty. News Svc., N.Y.C., 1968-71; asst. staff dir. sect. criminal justice ABA, Washington, 1972-74, dir. sect. criminal justice, 1979-93; assoc. dep. atty. gen. U.S. Dept. Justice, Washington, 1993-94, asst. atty. gen. Office Justice Programs, 1994—; mem. ex-officio, bd. regents Nat. Coll. Dist. Attys., Houston, 1979-93; mem. adv. bd. Fed. Sentencing Reporter, N.Y.C., 1990—; chair Nat. Forum on Criminal Justice, Washington, 1991-93. Active Clinton Campaign Criminal Justice Com., 1992, Clinton Transition Com. Dept. Justice, 1992. Mem. ABA, Phi Beta Kappa. Democrat. Office: US Dept Justice 633 Indiana Ave NW Washington DC 20531-0001

ROBINSON, LAWRENCE PHILLIP, television engineer, inventor, consultant; b. Detroit, Feb. 10, 1933; s. Leroy Percival and Vida Irene (Thompson) R. Grad., DeVry Inst. Tech., Chgo., 1955-57; AS, Delta Coll., University Center, Mich., 1968; DD, Modern Apostles Sch., North Miami Beach, Fla., 1982; BS, Mich. State U., 1984. TV engr. Sta. WNEM-TV, Bay City, Mich., 1953-56, Sta. WKNX-TV, Saginaw, Mich., 1956-62, Sta. WUCM-TV, University Center, 1966-68, Sta. WEYI-TV, Flint, Mich., 1969-73; electronics tech. Am. Machine & Foundry, Saginaw, 1962-64; radio technician Sta. WBCM, Bay City, 1964-66; radio engr. Sta. WSGW, Saginaw, 1968, Sta. WKMF, Flint, 1968-69; TV engr. Sta. WKAR-TV, Mich. State U., East Lansing, 1973-96, ret., 1996. Author: The Stress-Strain Connection, 1981, Thoughts on the Nature of Matter, 1982, 3d rev. edit., 1988. With USNR, 1950-53. Recipient new product award Inventors Clubs Am., 1989, 90. Mem. AAAS, N.Y. Acad. Scis., Mich. State U. Alumni Assn. (life), Mensa (life), Camelo Pards, Am. Legion (life), Masons, Order of the Iron Test Pattern. Orthodox. Achievements include patents for shortened vertical antenna and the disk antenna for UHF-VHF. Home: Village Green of

Lansing Apt 5A3 5316 West Mall Dr Lansing MI 48917-1924 Office: Mich State U Sta WKAR-TV Comm Arts Bldg East Lansing MI 48824

ROBINSON, LEONARD HARRISON, JR., international government consultant, business executive; b. Winston-Salem, N.C., Apr. 21, 1943; s. Leonard Harrison and Winnie Cornelia (Thomas) R.; children: Kimberly Michelle, Rani Craft. NSF cert., Bennett Coll., Greensboro, N.C., 1959; BA, Ohio State U., 1964; postgrad., SUNY, Binghamton, 1966-67, Am. U., 1982-89, Harvard U., 1991; LLD (hon.), Shaw U., Raleigh, N.C., 1983; LHD (hon.), Huston-Tillotson Coll., 1991. Vol. Peace Corps., Bihar, India, 1964-66; assoc. dir. for India Peace Corps, Madras, 1967-70; dir. recruitment Peace Corps., Washington, 1970-71; dir. inner-city programs EPA, Washington, 1971-72; dir. mgmt. Family Planning Internat. Assistance, N.Y.C., 1972-74; Africa dir. Family Planning Internat. Assistance, Accra, Ghana and Nairobi, Kenya, 1974-77; task force dir. U.S. Ho. Reps., Washington, 1977-78; dir. population Africa AID, Washington, 1978-79; dir. Internat. Devel. Ctr. Battelle Inst., Washington, 1979-83; dep. asst. sec., sr. exec. svc. Dept. State, Washington, 1983-85; pres. African Devel. Found., Washington, 1985-90; dep. asst. sec. state, sr. exec. svc. Dept. State, Washington, 1990-93; vice chmn., COO Washington Strategic Consulting Group, Inc., Washington, 1993—; cons. area studies U. Mo. Peace Corps, summer 1966; mgmt. analyst ATAC, Washington, 1971; mem. U.S. presdl. del. to Dakar, Senegal, 1987, to Malawi, Mozambique, and Uganda, Sept. 1988, to Mali, Uganda, and Kenya, Dec. 1988, v.p.'s visit to Africa, 1991; hon. consul Govt. Sao Tome and Principe, 1996—. Author: monographs Assessment and Analysis of Population Attitudes in Tanzania, 1981, Analyze African Official Attitudes Concerning U.S. Population Assistance in Lesotho, Tanzania, Senegal and Togo, 1981. Adviser Population Resource Ctr., N.Y.C., 1978-82; adviser internat. program for health and tng., U. N.C., Chapel Hill, 1980-84; vice-chmn. New Directions Task Force Rep. Party, Montgomery County (Md.), 1982-83; adv. coun. Nat. Coun. Returned Peace Corps Vols., 1987—; bd. dirs. Washington Ballet, 1982-85, 86-91, v.p. bd. dirs. 1988-90; bd. dirs. Friends of Smithsonian Mus. African Art, Washington, 1982-84, Coalition for Equitable Representation in Govt., Montgomery County, Montgomery County Bd. Soc. Svcs., 1986-89, Joint Agrl. Consultative Corp., 1985-86, Alan Gutmacher Inst., 1992-96, Friends of the U. of Natal, South Africa, 1995—. Decorated commandeur de l'Ordre National du Niger, 1989; recipient Africare Disting. Svc. award, 1990, Key to the City of Greensboro, N.C., 1991, Christian D. Maxwell Disting. Svc. award Liberian Com. for Relief, Resettlement and Reconstruction, 1993; hon. counsel for the Govt. of Sao Tome and Principe, Ctrl. Africa. Mem. Soc. Internat. Devel. (dir. 1982), Am. Pub. Health Assn. (sec. population sect. 1979-81), Coun. on Fgn. Rels., C. of C. of D.C. (dir. 1979-82), Metro Club Washington, Kappa Alpha Psi, Sigma Pi Phi. Office: Washington Strategic Consulting Group 805 15th St NW Fl 10 Washington DC 20005-2207 *Human life is precious and extraordinary. I have strived to live to the fullest, by being productive, impact-oriented, and successful in contributng to the improvement of people's lives. This quest has brought me happiness and fulfillment.*

ROBINSON, LINDA GOSDEN, communications executive; b. L.A., Jan. 10, 1953; d. Freeman Fisher and Jane Elizabeth (Stoneham) Gosden; m. Stephen M. Dart (div. June 1977); m. James Dixon Robinson III. Student, UCLA, 1970-72; BA summa cum laude in Psychology, U. So. Calif., 1978. Dep. press sec. Reagan Presdl. Campaign, L.A., 1979; press sec., dir. pub. relations Rep. Nat. Com., Washington, 1979-80; dir. pub. affairs U.S. Dept. Transp., Washington, 1981-83; ptnr. pub. and govt. affairs Heron, Burchette, Ruckert & Rothwell, Washington, 1983; dep. to spl. envoy Office of the Pres., N.Y.C., 1985; sr. v.p. corp. affairs Warner Amex Cable Communications, N.Y.C., 1983-86; chmn., CEO Robinson Lerer & Montgomery, N.Y.C., 1986—; bd. dirs. Revlon Group, Inc., N.Y.C., VIMRx Pharms., Inc., Stamford Conn. Trustee NYU Med. Ctr., N.Y.C.; del. Rep. Nat. Conv., 1985. Mem. Nat. Women's Econ. Coun., Phi Beta Kappa. Avocations: horse showing, tennis, golf.

ROBINSON, MALCOLM, gastroenterologist; b. Amarillo, Tex., July 25, 1942; s. H. Malcolm and Frances Pauline (Kohn) R.; m. Susan Laird Robinson, June 22, 1969. BS with honors, Tulane U., 1964; MD, Okla. U., 1968. Diplomate in internal medicine and gastroenterology Am. Bd. Internal Medicine. Intern Cleve. Clinic, 1968-69; sr. resident, internal medicine U. Okla., Oklahoma City, 1974-75; GI fellow Duke U., Durham, N.C., 1969-71; sr. resident internal medicine U. Okla., Oklahoma City, 1974-75, asst. prof., 1975-76; chief GI Oklahoma City Clinic, 1976-89, Presbyn. Hosp., Oklahoma City, 1976-96; pres., dir. Okla. Found. for Digestive Rsch., Oklahoma City, 1989-96, also bd. dirs.; chief GI Presbyn. Hosp.; clin. assoc. prof. U. Okla., Oklahoma City, 1976-92, clin. prof., 1992—; mem. adv. bd. Procter and Gamble, Inc., TAP Pharm., Inc., Wyeth-Ayerst, Inc., Otsuka Am. Pharm., Eisai, Inc.; reviewer Am. Jour. Gastroenterology, Gastroenterology, Digestive Diseases and Sci., Gastrointestinal Endoscopy. Mem. internat. editl. bd. Alimentary Pharmacology and Therapeutics. Maj. M.C., U.S. Army, 1971-74. Benefactor Okla. State Bd. Regents for Higher Edn. chair in Gastroenterology, U. Okla. Coll. of Medicine, 1996; recipient Blesh-Rucks award for Outstanding Physician, Oklahoma City Clinic, 1982. Fellow ACP, Am. Coll. Gastroenterology; mem. Am. Soc. Gastrointestinal Endoscopy, Am. Gastroent. Assn. (Janssen award for outstanding lifetime achievement in clin. gastroenterology 1995). Office: Okla Found Digestive Rsch 6th Fl Tower 700 NE 13th St Oklahoma City OK 73104-5004

ROBINSON, MARGUERITE STERN, anthropologist, educator, consultant; b. N.Y.C., Oct. 11, 1935; d. Philip Van Doren and Lillian (Diamond) Stern; m. Allan Richard Robinson, June 12, 1955; children: Sarah Penelope, Perrine, Laura Ondine. BA, Radcliffe Coll., 1956; PhD, Harvard U., 1965. Assoc. scholar Inst. for Ind. Study (now Bunting Inst.) Radcliffe U., Cambridge, Mass., 1964-65; asst. prof. anthology Brandeis U., 1965-72, assoc. prof., 1972-78, prof., 1978-85, dean Coll. Arts and Scis., 1973-75; assoc. fellow Inst. Internat. Devel. Harvard U., Cambridge, 1978-80, fellow Inst. Internat. Devel., 1980-85, inst. fellow Inst. Internat. Devel., 1985—; dir. Cultural Survival Inc., 1981—; dir. Am. Inst. Indian Studies, Chgo., 1977—, chmn., 1983-84; cons. Ministry of Fin., Govt. of Indonesia, Jakarta, 1979-92, USAID, 1992-95, Banco Solidario, Bolivia, 1993-95, Bank Rakyat Indonesia, 1994-96, World Bank, 1994-95, Bank Danamon Indonesia, 1995-96. Author: Political Structure in a Changing Sinhalese Village, 1974, Local Politics: The Law of the Fishes, 1988, Pembiayaan Pertanian Pedesaan, 1993; contbg. author: Cambridge Papers in Social Anthropology 3, 1962, Cambridge Papers in Social Anthropology 5, 1968, Enterprises for the Recycling and Composting of Municipal Solid Waste, 1993, The New World of Microenterprise Finance, 1994, New Perspectives on Financing Small Business in Developing Countries, 1995; contbr. articles to profl. jours. Mem. internat. coun. advisors Calmeadow Found., 1996—; pres. The Greatest Gift Corp. Fellow NIH, 1964-65; grantee NSF, 1966-70, Ford Found., 1972-74, 79, Calmeadow Found., 1994; fellow Indo-Am. Fellowship Program-Indo-U.S. Subcommn. on Edn. and Culture, 1976-77, Am. Inst. Indian Studies, 1976-77; grantee Calmeadow Found., 1994. Fellow Am. Anthrop. Assn., Soc. Bunting Inst. Fellows; mem. Assn. Asian Studies, India Internat. Centre. Office: Harvard U Inst Internat Devel One Eliot St Cambridge MA 02138

ROBINSON, MARSHALL ALAN, economics educator, foundation executive; b. Berkeley, Calif., Feb. 16, 1922; s. Webster Richard and Evelyn (Casey) R.; m. Ynid Douglas Rankin, June 5, 1944 (div. 1973); children: Joan Douglas, Margaret Elaine, Richard Webster; m. Flavia Derossi, Oct. 1974. A.B., U. Calif.-Berkeley, 1943; M.A., Ohio State U., 1948, Ph.D., 1950. Instr. econs. Ohio State U., 1948-50; asst. prof. econs. Tulane U., 1951-53; research asso. Nat. Bur. Econ. Research, 1951-52; asst. prof. econs. Dartmouth Coll., 1953-55; sr. staff mem., asst. to pres. Brookings Instn., 1955-60; prof. econs., dean Grad. Sch. Bus., U. Pitts., 1960-63; dir. econ. devel. and adminstrn. program Ford Found., 1964-67, program officer in charge higher edn. and research, 1967-71, dep. v.p. edn. and research, 1971-73, v.p. resources and environ., 1973-79; pres. Russell Sage Found., N.Y.C., 1979-86; vis. prof. Grad. Sch. CUNY, 1986-89; fellow Inst. Social and Policy Studies Yale U., 1989-91; v.p. Daniele Agostino Found., 1992—. Author: An Introduction to Economic Reasoning, 1956, 5th edit., 1981, The National Debt Ceiling, 1959. Bd. dirs. Belgium-Am. Ednl. Found., 1981-96; trustee Antioch U., 1987-90. Served to 1st lt. USMCR, 1943-45, PTO. Decorated Royal Order of Leopold, Belgium. Mem. Am. Econs. Assn., N.Y. Sci. Policy Assn., Coun. on Fgn. Rels., Century Assn., Alpha Delta Phi.

ROBINSON, MARTHA STEWART, retired legal educator; b. Topeka, Mar. 2, 1914; d. Robert Bigger and Lenora (Stubbs) Stewart; m. Albrecht Marburg Yerkes, July 3, 1940 (dec. 1963); children: Robert Stewart, William Marburg; m. Stephan B. Robinson, Jr., July 17, 1971. A.B. cum laude, Washburn U., 1934, LL.B., 1940; LL.M., Stanford U., 1953. Bar: Kans. 1940, Calif. 1945. Individual practice law Los Angeles, 1946-55; instr. law Southwestern U. Sch. Law, Los Angeles, 1946-55; cons. Los Angeles Superior Ct. Com. on Standard Jury Instrns., 1957-64; prof. law Loyola U. Sch. Law, Los Angeles, 1965-84, prof. emeritus, 1984—; judge pro tempore Los Angeles County Superior Ct., 1963. Mem. Am. Law Inst., Calif. Bar Assn., L.A. County Bar Assn. (trustee 1976-78), Women Lawyers Assn. L.A. (past pres.). Home: 625 Old Mill Rd Pasadena CA 91108-1737 Office: Loyola U Law Sch 1441 W Olympic Blvd Los Angeles CA 90015-3903

ROBINSON, MARTIN (MARTY), television and radio broadcaster, media consultant; b. Chgo., Sept. 7, 1932; s. Edward Emmanuel Robinson and Florence Ruth (Cohen) Mayer; m. Mary Alice Wellingham, May 31, 1959; children: Paul Edward, Jill Marie. Broadcaster, host WAAF, WGN and WNIB, Chgo., 1956-58, WFMT, Chgo., 1958-93, WTTW-TV, Chgo., 1971—; speaker, concert narrator; lectr. Lyric Opera Chgo.; media cons. J. Walter Thompson, Hill & Knowlton, Burson Marsteller, Newell & Matthews, 1973—. Host, narrator programs (Peabody award, 15 Emmy awards, 8 Ohio State awards, Chgo. and San Francisco Film Festival Gold medals); prodr., host nationally syndicated opera program The First Fifty Years, 1967-93. Served with USN, 1950-53. Recipient 2 Emmy awards. Avocations: biking, weight training, the Internet. Office: WTTW-TV 5400 N Saint Louis Ave Chicago IL 60625-4623

ROBINSON, MARY JO, pathologist; b. Spokane, Wash., May 26, 1954; d. Jerry Lee and Ann (Brodie) R. BS in Biology, Gonzaga U., 1976; DO, Coll. Osteo. Medicine and Surgery, U. Med. Health Scis., 1987. Diplomate Nat. Bd. Osteo. Med. Examiners, Am. Osteo. Bd. Pathology; cert. anatomic pathology and dermatopathology. Med. technologist Whitman Comty. Hosp., Colfax, Wash., 1977-81, Madigan Army Med. Ctr., Ft. Lewis, Wash., 1981-83; intern Des Moines Gen. Hosp., 1987-88; resident in pathology Kennedy Meml. Hosp., Stratford, N.J., 1988-92; asst. prof. pathology Sch. Medicine U. Medicine and Dentistry of N.J., Stratford, 1995—; staff pathologist Kennedy Meml. Hosp., Cherry Hill, N.J., 1995—; fellow in dermatopathology Jefferson Med. Coll., Phila., 1994. Fellow Coll. Am. Pathologists; mem. AMA, Am. Osteo. Coll. Pathologists (1st prize resident paper 1992), Am. Osteo. Assn., Am. Soc. Clin. Pathologists, N.J. Assn. Osteo. Physicians and Surgeons. Avocations: astronomy, antiques, science fiction. Office: Kennedy Meml Hosp U Med Ctr 2201 Chapel Ave W Cherry Hill NJ 08002-2048

ROBINSON, MARY KATHERINE, school system administrator; b. Asheville, N.C., Sept. 11, 1943; d. William Robert Jr. and Iris Myrtle (Holden) Sherrill; m. Marcus William Sumner, Oct. 26, 1962 (div. June 1973); 1 child, Marcus Kevin; m. Frank Pearson Robinson, Jr., Oct. 26, 1974 (div. Jan. 1997). BS in Edn., Western Carolina U., Cullowhee, N.C., 1968, MA in Edn., 1983. Cert. tchr., N.C. Tchr. reading Jackson County Bd. Edn., Sylva, N.C., 1968-69, elem. tchr., 1970-76; instr. reading Western Carolina U., 1968, instr. remedial reading, 1972; Reading Program developer Haywood County Bd. Edn., Waynesville, N.C., 1976-82, Resource and Program developer, 1982—; cons. divsn. health, safety and phys. edn. N.C. Dept. Pub. Instrn., Raleigh, 1974-75; mem. adv. bd. Haywood Tech. Inst., Clyde, N.C., 1978-79; mem. N.C. Textbook Commn., Raleigh, 1989-93; mem. curriculum rev. com. in mktg. edn., bus. edn. N.C. Dept. Pub. Instrn., 1992, health edn., 1993. Compiler: Robert Lee Holden Family, 1993; contbr. to periodical; creator vocabulary game Jaw Breakers, 1977. Vol. Reading Is Fundamental project Haywood County Libr., 1978-79; treas. PTO, 1971-72; active Haywood County Found. Bd., 1995—. Recipient Gold Key award N.C. State Supt., 1991. Mem. NEA, ASCD, N.C. Assn. Educators (sec. 1977, v.p./pres. elect 1994-95, pres. 1995-96), Internat. Reading Assn. (v.p. 1978-79, pres. 1979-80), Bus. and Profl. Women's Orgn., Friends of Haywood County Libr., Delta Kappa Gamma (corr. sec. 1988-90, v.p. 1990-92, pres. 1992-94), Phi Delta Kappa, Kappa Delta Pi. Democrat. Avocations: genealogy, travel. Home: PO Box 1017 Lake Junaluska NC 28745

ROBINSON, MARY LOU, federal judge; b. Dodge City, Kans., Aug. 25, 1926; d. Gerald J. and Frances Strueber; m. A.J. Robinson, Aug. 28, 1949; children: Rebecca Aynn Gruhlkey, Diana Ceil, Matthew Douglas. B.A., U. Tex., 1948, LL.B., 1950. Bar: Tex. 1949. Ptnr. Robinson & Robinson, Amarillo, 1950-55; judge County Ct. at Law, Potter County, Tex., 1955-59, (108th Dist. Ct.), Amarillo, 1961-73; assoc. justice Ct. of Civil Appeals for 7th Supreme Jud. Dist. of Tex., Amarillo, 1973-77; chief justice Ct. of Civil Appeals for 7th Supreme Jud. Dist. of Tex., 1977-79; U.S. dist. judge No. Dist. Tex., Amarillo, 1979—. Named Woman of Year Tex. Fedn. Bus. and Profl. Women, 1973. Mem. Nat. Assn. Women Lawyers, ABA, Tex. Bar Assn., Amarillo Bar Assn., Delta Kappa Gamma. Presbyterian. Office: US Dist Ct Rm 226 205 E 5th Ave # F13248 Amarillo TX 79101-1559

ROBINSON, MICHAEL FRANCIS, private art dealer and appraiser; b. London, Oct. 6, 1954; came to U.S., 1978; s. Canon Joseph and Anne (Antrobus) R. Student, The King's Sch., Canterbury, Eng., 1968-72; LLB, King's Coll., London U., London, 1976; postgrad., The Coll. Law, London, 1976-77, Centre Study European Law, London & Luxembourg. Head rare books Brentano's, Inc., N.Y.C., 1978-81; head rare books Phillips Auctioneers, N.Y.C., 1981-85, auctioneer fine arts, 1982-85; pres. M.F. Robinson & Assocs., N.Y.C., 1985—; cons. to mus. and pvt. collectors, IRS, 1989—; Prforzheimer lectr. N.Y. Pub. Libr., N.Y.C., 1989; chmn. writers panel San Francisco Internat. Antique Fair, 1989, 90. Author articles Archtl. Digest, Connosieur, Art and Auction, Manuscripts and other mags.; contbg. editor The Am. Book Collector, 1985-89, Art and Auction, 1989-96; assoc. editor Jour. Guild of Bookworkers; editor Treasures of Eton College, The Pierpont Morgan Library, 1990; joinr editor, co-author: In August Co. The Collections of the Pierpont Morgan Library, 1991-92, Mark Twain: An American Voice to the World, 1996. Chmn. The Bach Ensemble, N.Y., 1984—. Mem. The Hon. Soc. Inner Temple (Duke of Edinburgh Scholar 1974), The Manuscript Soc., The Hardwick Soc. Episcopalian. Club: The Worshipful Co. of Wax Chandlers (London), Westside (Georgetown). Lodge: Masons (curator 1984—). Avocation: music before 1800. Office: PO Box 1947 Middleburg VA 20118-1947

ROBINSON, MICHAEL HILL, zoological park director, biologist; b. Preston, Eng., Jan. 7, 1929; came to U.S. 1984; s. Samuel and Ethel (Hill) R.; m. Barbara Cragg Robinson, May 19, 1955 (divorced). B.S., U. Wales, U.K., 1963; D.Phil., U. Oxford, Eng., 1966. Tchr. sci. U.K. Secondary Schs., 1953-60; sr. sci. master Camborne Grammar Sch., 1958-60; biologist Smith. Tropical Research Inst., Panama, 1966-71; vis. lectr. U. Pa., Phila., 1969; reader in biology New U. Ulster, No. Ireland, 1971; biologist Smithsonian Tropical Research Inst., Panama, 1971-84; asst. dir. Smithsonian Tropical Research Inst., 1980, acting dir., 1980-81, dep. dir., 1981-84; adj. prof. U. Miami, Coral Gables, Fla., 1981—; dir. Nat. Zool. Park, Washington, 1984—. Contbr. articles to profl. jours. Sci. fellow Zool. Soc. London, 1956. Fellow Linnean Soc., Royal Entomol. Soc.; mem. soc. for Study of Animal Behavior. Home: 2729 Ordway St NW Apt 5 Washington DC 20008-5052 Office: Nat Zool Pk 3000 Connecticut Ave NW Washington DC 20008

ROBINSON, MICHAEL R., aeronautical engineer. Dir. bus. devel. Boeing N.Am. (formerly Rockwell Internat. Corp.), Seal Beach, Calif.; co-originator and first program manager of the X-31 enhanced maneuverability fighter demonstrator and originator of the international team to conduct the program. Recipient DGLR Team award in recognition of exceptional achievements in the field of Aeronautics, 1996. Fellow Am. Inst. Aeronautics & Astronautics (aircraft design award 1994). Office: Boeing North American PO Box 3644 2600 Westminster Blvd Seal Beach CA 90740-7644

ROBINSON, MICHAEL R., advertising executive. Sr. ptnr., rsch. and planning dir. Tatham Euro RSCG, Chgo. Office: Tatham Euro RSCG 980 N Michigan Ave Chicago IL 60611-4501

ROBINSON, NAN SENIOR, not-for-profit organization consultant; b. Salt Lake City, Jan. 11, 1932; d. Clair Marcil Senior and Lillian (Worlton) Senior Davis; m. David Zav Robinson; Sept. 6, 1954; children: Marc S. Robinson, Eric S. Robinson. BA with hons., Mills Coll., 1952; MA, Harvard U., 1953. Spl. asst. to undersec. Dept. Housing and Urban Devel., Washington, 1966-69; asst. to the pres. U. Mass. Statewide System, Boston, 1970-73, v.p. for planning, 1973-78; dep. commr. Conn. Bd. Higher Edn., Hartford, 1978-81; v.p. adminstrn. The Rockefeller Found., N.Y.C., 1981-90; mem. governing coun. Rockefeller Archive Ctr., Pocantico Hills, N.Y., 1986-89; com. mem. Coun. on Founds. N.Y. Regional Assn. Grantmakers, 1985-89; mem. nat. advisory panel on governance Carnegie Found. for the Advancement of Teaching, Princeton, N.J., 1980-82. Trustee, chmn. fin. com. Inst. for Current World Affairs, Hanover, N.H., 1987-90; trustee Calif. Sch. Profl. Psychology, San Francisco, 1985-96; vice chair, bd. dirs. Fed. to Preserve the Greenwich Village Waterfront, 1996—. Recipient Centennial award Am. Assn. U. Women Hartford Br., 1981; named Woman of Yr. Hartford YWCA, 1980; named to Centennial Honor List of 100 Women Barnard Coll., 1989. Mem. Soc. for Coll. and U. Planning (com. chmn. 1985-86, nominating com. 1980-85, regional rep. 1975-77), Phi Beta Kappa. Home: 622 Greenwich St Apt 5B New York NY 10014-3305

ROBINSON, NEIL CIBLEY, JR., lawyer; b. Columbia, S.C., Oct. 25, 1942; s. Neil C. and Ernestine (Carns) R.; m. Judith Ann Hunter, Sept. 4, 1971 (div. Nov. 1979); 1 child, Hunter Leigh; m. Vicki Elizabeth Kornahrens, Mar. 2, 1985; children: Neil C. III, Taylor Elizabeth. BS in Indsl. Mgmt., Clemson U., 1966; JD, U. S.C., 1973. Bar: S.C. 1974, U.S. Ct. Appeals (4th cir.) 1974, U.S. Dist. Ct. S.C. 1976. Asst. to dean U. S.C. Law Sch., Columbia, 1973-74; law clk. to judge Charles E. Jr. Simons Jr. U.S. Dist. Ct. S.C., Aiken, 1974-76; assoc. Grimball & Cabaniss, Charleston, S.C., 1976-78; ptnr. Grimball, Cabaniss, Vaughan & Robinson, Charleston, 1978-84; ptnr., pres. Robinson, Wall & Hastie, P.A., Charleston, 1984-91; ptnr., mem. exec. com. Nexsen, Pruet, Jacobs, Pollard & Robinson, Charleston, 1991—; permanent mem. 4th Cir. Jud. Conf., 1982—; pres. Coastal Properties Inst., Charleston, 1981—. Bd. dirs. Southeastern Wildlife Exposition, Charleston, 1987—, pres. 1994—, Charleston Maritime Festival, 1993—, pres. 1994—, Parklands Found. of Charleston County; pres. S.C. Tourism Coun., Columbia, 1991—. Cpl. USMCR, 1960-66. Recipient Order of Palmetto, Gov. David Beasley, S.C., 1996. Mem. ABA, Urban Land Inst. (recreational devel. coun.), S.C. Bar Assn., Fed. Bar Assn., S.C. Def. Trial Lawyers Assn., Hibernian Soc. (mem. mgmt. com. 1984—), Kiawah Club, Haig Point Club, Country Club of Charleston, Phi Delta Phi. Presbyterian. Avocations: golf, hunting. Home: PO Box 121 Charleston SC 29402-0121 Office: Nexsen Pruet Jacobs Pollard & Robinson 200 Meeting St Ste 301 Charleston SC 29401-3156

ROBINSON, NELL BRYANT, nutrition educator; b. Kopperl, Tex., Oct. 15, 1925; d. Basil Howell and Lelia Abiah (Duke) Bryant; m. Frank Edward Robinson, July 14, 1945 (dec.); 1 child, John Howell Robinson. B.S., N. Tex. State U., 1945; M.S., Tex. Woman's U., 1958, Ph.D., 1967. Registered dietitian, Tex. Tchr. Comanche High Sch., Tex., 1945-46, Kopperl High Sch., Tex., 1946-48; county extension agt. Agrl. Extension Service, Tex., 1948-56; prof. nutrition Tex. Christian U., Fort Worth, 1957-92, chmn. dept. nutrition and dietetics, 1985-91, ret., 1992. Pres., bd. dirs. Sr. Citizens Svcs. of Greater Tarrant County, 1990-91. Contbr. chpt. to book. Named Top Prof., Tex. Christian U. Mortar Bd., 1978. Mem. Am. Dietetic Assn. (del. 1983-88, ethics com. 1985-88, coun. edn. 1988-90, chmn. coun. on edn. divsn. edn. accreditation/approval 1989-90, medallion award 1990), Am. Assn. Family and Consumer Scis., Tex. Dietetic Assn. (pres., 1972-73, Disting. Dietitian 1981), Tex. Assn. Family and Consumer Scis. (pres. 1978-80, Home Economist of Yr. 1975). Club: Fort Worth Women's. Lodge: Order Eastern Star. Home: 5729 Wimbleton Way Fort Worth TX 76133-3651

ROBINSON, PAMELA, dancer. Attended, Ctrl. Pa. Youth Ballet, Cin. Conservatory of Music, Lexington Ballet, Nat. Acad. Arts, Chempaign, Ill. Dancer Cleve. Ballet, Ala. Ballet, 1982-85; dancer Ballet West, Salt Lake City, 1985-88, prin. dancer, 1988—. Dance performances include Anna Karenina, Rosalinda, Lady of the Camellias, The Nutcracker, Sleeping Beauty, Swan Lake, Giselle, Carmina Burana (John Butler). Office: Ballet West 50 W 200 S Salt Lake City UT 84101-1642*

ROBINSON, PATRICIA ELAINE, women's health nurse practitioner; b. St. Louis, June 30, 1955; d. Harold Winford and Robbie LaVeal (Ferguson) Hammett; m. Kenneth M. Robinson, Nov. 18, 1978 (div.); children: Barry Christopher, Emily Vanessa; m. C. gilbert, Nov. 20, 1990. ADN, St. Louis Community Coll., 1987; student, Webster U., 1990—; cert. in forensic pathology, St. Louis U., 1975; cert. in pharmacology, St. Louis Coll. Health, 1984; womens health nurse practioner, U. Mo., 1995. Per diem float nurse St. Louis U. Hosp.; coord. ob-gyn. unit Group Health Plan, St. Louis; staff nurse Barnes Hosp., St. Louis; staff nurse dept. ob-gyn. Washington U. Sch. Medicine, St. Louis, 1990-93; chief exec. study coord. women's health rsch. Obstetric & Gynecologic Diagnosis & Consultation, Florissant, Mo., 1992-96; nurse practitioner and exec. study coord. women's health rsch. Women's HealthPartners, 1996—; acting dir. Nurses for Reproductive Health Svcs., St. Louis, 1990-93. Mem. NAFE, Nurse Assn. Am. Coll. Obstetrics and Gynecologists, Med. Group Mgmt. Assn., Nat. Assn. Nurse Practitioners Reproductive Health, Phi Theta Kappa. Office: James L Ottolini MD Inc 222 S Woods Mill Rd Ste 360 Chesterfield MO 63017-3425

ROBINSON, PATRICIA SNYDER, lawyer; b. Hoboken, N.J., Dec. 5, 1952; d. Anthony James and Agnes Loretta (Riordan) Snyder; m. Daniel Lewis Robinson, Aug. 27, 1978. BA summa cum laude, Montclair State U., 1975; MSc, Rutgers U., 1980; JD, Rutgers U., Newark, N.J., 1986. Bar: N.J. 1986, U.S. Dist. Ct. N.J. 1986, D.C. 1992, U.S. Ct. Appeals (3d cir.) 1992. Grad. asst. Rutgers U., New Brunswick, N.J., 1975-77; chemist AT&T Bell Labs., Murray Hill, N.J., 1977-80; mgr. AT&T, Bedminster, N.J., 1980-87; assoc. Norris, McLaughlin & Marcus, Somerville, N.J., 1987; assoc. Collier, Jacob & Mills, Somerset, N.J., 1987-92, ptnr., 1993—. Contbr. articles to profl. jours. Mem. ABA, N.J. State Bar Assn., D.C. Bar Assn., Somerset County Bar Assn., N.Y. Acad. Sci., Phi Kappa Phi. Office: Collier Jacob & Mills 580 Howard Ave Somerset NJ 08873-1136

ROBINSON, PAUL ARNOLD, historian, educator, author; b. San Diego, Oct. 1, 1940; s. Joseph Cook and Beryl Marie (Lippincott) R.; m. Ute Brosche, Aug. 3, 1964 (div. Aug. 1967); 1 child, Susan Marie. B.A., Yale U., 1962; postgrad., Free U. Berlin, 1962-63; PhD, Harvard U., 1968. Asst. prof. history Stanford U. (Calif.), 1967-73, assoc. prof., 1973-80, prof. history, 1980—, Richard W. Lyman prof. in the humanities, 1994—. Author: The Freudian Left, 1969, The Modernization of Sex, 1976, Opera and Ideas: From Mozart to Strauss, 1985, Freud and His Critics, 1993, Ludwig van Beethoven: Fidelio, 1996; editor: Social Thought in America and Europe, 1970; contbg. editor The New Republic, 1979-85. Guggenheim fellow, 1970-71, Stanford Humanities Ctr. fellow, 1984-85, 96-97, Inst. for Advanced Study fellow, 1990-91. Fellow Am. Acad. Arts and Scis.; mem. Am. Hist. Assn. Home: 671 Santa Ynez St Palo Alto CA 94305-8542 Office: Stanford Univ Dept History Stanford CA 94305

ROBINSON, PETER, paleontology educator, consultant; b. N.Y.C., N.Y., July 19, 1932; s. Edward and Carol Nye (Rhoades) R.; m. Patricia Ellen Fisher, Sept. 11, 1954 (div. Mar. 1980); children: Diane Elizabeth, Nathan; m. Paola D'Amelio Villa, Dec. 8, 1984. BS, Yale U., 1954, MS, 1958, PhD, 1960. Instr. Harpur Coll. SUNY, Binghamton, 1955-57; rsch. assoc. Yale Peabody Mus., New Haven, 1960-61; curator geology U. Colo. Mus., Boulder, 1961—, asst. prof. natural history, 1961-67, assoc. prof., 1967-71, prof., 1971—, dir. mus., 1971-82, prof. geol. sci., 1971—; geologist Colo. Nubian Expdn., Sudan, 1962-66; chief Colo. Paleontol. Expdn., Tunisia, 1967-81 ; mem. geol. adv. group Colo. Bur. Land Mgmt., Denver, 1983-91. Mem. AAAS, Soc. Vertebrate Paleontology (pres. 1977-78), Australian Mammal Soc., Soc. Española Paleontologia, Sigma Xi. Democrat. Home: 5110 Williams Fork Trl Apt 204 Boulder CO 80301-3408 Office: Campus Box 315 Mus U Colo Boulder CO 80309

ROBINSON, PETER CLARK, general management executive; b. Brighton, Mass., Nov. 16, 1938; s. Richard and Mary Elizabeth (Cooper) R.; m. Sylvia Phyllis Petschek, Aug. 26, 1961 (div. 1973); children: Marc Louis, Nicholas Daniel, Andrea Suzanne; m. Sarah Lingham, Jan. 1, 1984. B.S. in Fgn. Service, Georgetown U., 1961; M.B.A., Babson Inst., 1963; AMP, Harvard U., 1986. Asst. supt. prodn. Mass. Broken Stone Co., Weston, 1961-62; night shift supt. Mass. Broken Stone Co., 1962-65, v.p. ops., 1968, v.p., 1969-75, 85-94, sr. v.p., 1995—, also dir.; gen. supt. Berlin Stone Co., 1965-

67, v.p. ops., 1968; v.p. Holden Trap Rock Co., to 1975, also dir., v.p., 1985-94, sr. v.p., 1995—; pres. Blount Materials Inc., Saginaw, Mich., 1975-81; v.p. corp. mktg. Blount, Inc., Montgomery, 1978-79, v.p. corp. planning and mktg., 1979-92, v.p. corp. planning and devel., 1992-94; group exec., pres. Blount Agri/Indsl. Corp., 1984-90; pres. P.C. Robinson & Co., Montgomery, 1994—; bd. dirs. Mass. Broken Stone Co. Mem. Nat. Stone Assn. (dir., exec. com., chmn. govt. affairs com., chmn. bd.), Am. Mgmt. Assn., Am. Soc. Agrl. Engrs., Newcomen Soc., Engring. Soc. Detroit, Pres. Assn., SME-AIME. Clubs: Montgomery Country, Capital City (Montgomery), Harvard (Boston). Home: 1822 Galena Ave Montgomery AL 36106-1910 Office: Robinson & Co 1067 Woodley Rd Ste C Montgomery AL 36106-2414

ROBINSON, PHIL ALDEN, director; b. Long Beach, Mar. 1, 1950; s. S. Jesse and Jessie Francis (Roth) Robinson. BA, Union Coll., 1971. Newscaster Stas. WGY/WRGB-TV, Schenectady, 1969-71; freelance filmmaker Los Angeles, 1974—. Screenwriter All of Me, 1984, (with others) Rhinestone, 1984, (TV) 2 episodes Trapper John, M.D., 1981-82; writer, dir. In the Mood, 1987; dir. (TV) 2 episodes George Burns Comedy Week, 1986; screenwriter, dir. Field of Dreams (nomination Writers Guild, Dirs. Guild, Best Picture and Best Screenplay Adaption Acad. award nominations); co-screenwriter, dir. Sneakers. Served to 1st lt. USAF, 1971-74. Named Screenwriter of Yr. Nat. Assn. Theatre Owners, 1990. Mem. Acad. Motion Picture Arts and Scis., Writers Guild Am. West, Dirs. Guild Am., ASCAP. *

ROBINSON, PREZELL RUSSELL, academic administrator; b. Batesburg, S.C., Aug. 25, 1922; s. Clarence and Annie (Folks) R.; m. Lulu Harris, Apr. 9, 1950; 1 dau. A.B. in Econs. and Social Sci., St. Augustine's Coll., 1946; M.A. in Sociology and Econs., Cornell U., 1951, Ed.D. in Sociology-Ednl. Adminstrn., 1956; D.C.L. (hon.), U. of the South, 1970; L.H.D., Cuttington U. Coll., Monrovia, Liberia, Voorhees Coll., 1981, Episcopal Theol. Sem., 1982; LL.D. (hon.), Bishop Coll., 1979; D.C.L., Columbia U., 1980; DHL (hon.), Kenyon Coll., 1988. Tchr. social sci., French Bettis Jr. Coll., Trenton, S.C., 1946-48; sucessively registrar, tchr., acting prin. high sch., acting dean jr. coll., instr., dir. adult edn. Voorhees Jr. Coll., Denmark, S.C., 1948-56; prof. sociology, dean coll. St. Augustine's Coll., Raleigh, N.C., 1956-64, exec. dean, 1964-66, acting pres., 1966-67, pres., 1967—; pres. United Negro Coll. Fund, Inc., 1978-81, Nat. Assn. Equal Opportunity Higher Edn., 1981-84, N.C. Assn. Coll. & U., Cooperating Raleigh Colls., 1981, 86—; bd. dirs. Learning Inst. N.C.; scholar-in-residence Nairobi (Kenya) U., 1973; vis. lectr. Dept. State del. to African nations, 1971, 73, 78; dir. Wachovia Bank & Trust Co.; vice chmn. N.C. State Bd. Edn. Contbr. articles to profl. publs. Mem. exec. com. N.C. Edn. Com. on Tchr. Edn.; mem. N.C. Bd. Edn.; chmn. bd. Assn. Episcopal Colls.; mem. Mayor's Community Relations Com.; vice chmn. Wake County div. Occoneechee coun. Boy Scouts Am., 1959-67; chmn. Wake Occoneechee coun., 1963-66, mem. exec. com., from 1965; vice chmn. Wake County chpt. ARC; chmn. edn. div. United Fund of Raleigh, mem. budget com., 1965—; mem. exec. com. Wake County Libraries.; trustee Voorhees Coll. Fulbright fellow to India, summer 1965; former U.S. Pres. George Bush appointee U.S. Alt. Rep. or Public Member Amb. Gen. Assembly of U.N., N.Y., 1992, 96. Served with AUS, 1942. Recipient Distinguished Alumni award Voorhees Coll., 1967, Silver Anniversary award N.C. Community System, 1989; decorated Star of Africia Liberia; recipient numerous service awards and citations; named one of the most effective coll. pres.s in U.S. Coun. for Advancement and Support of Edn., Washington, 1986; Univ. fellow Cornell U., 1954, rsch. fellow, 1955, 56; Fulbright fellow, 1965. Mem. AAAS, Nat. Assn. Collegiate Deans and Registrars, Am. Acad. Polit. and Social Sci., Am. Sociol. Soc., N.C. Sociol. Soc. (exec. com.), Ctrl. Intercollegiate Athletic Assn. (exec. com.), N.C. Assn. Ind. Colls. and Univs. (dir.), Raleigh C. of C. (A.E. Finley Disting. Svc. award 1989), So. Sociol. Assn., Am. Acad. Polit. Sci., N.C. Lit. and Hist. Soc., N.C. Hist. Soc., Delta Mu Delta, Phi Delta Kappa, Phi Kappa Phi, Alpha Kappa Mu, Phi Beta Lambda. Protestant Episcopalian (lay reader). Home: 821 Glascock St Raleigh NC 27604 Office: St Augustine's Coll 1315 Oakwood Ave Raleigh NC 27610-2247

ROBINSON, R. CLARK, mathematician, educator; b. Seattle, Dec. 29, 1943; s. Rex J. and Ruth C. (Clark) R.; m. Peggie Crose, Aug. 20, 1966. From asst. prof. to assoc. prof. Northwestern U., Evanston, Ill., 1969-78, prof., 1978—. Author: Dynamical Systems: Stability Symnolic Dynamics, and Chaos, 1995; contbr. numerous articles to profl. jours. Mem. Am. Math. Soc., Math. Assn. Am., Soc. Indsl. and Applied Math. Presbyterian. Office: Math Dept Northwestern U 2033 Sheridan Rd Evanston IL 60208-0830

ROBINSON, RAYMOND EDWIN, musician, music educator, writer; b. San Jose, Calif., Dec. 26, 1932; s. Elam Edwin and Zula Mai (Hatley) R.; m. Ruth Aleen Chamberlain, Mar. 12, 1954; children: Cynthia Rae, Greg Edwin, David L., Brent Steven, Jeffrey Vernon. BA, San Jose State U., 1956; MMus, Ind. U., 1958, D in Mus. Edn., 1969; LHD, Westminster Choir Coll., 1987; postdoctoral study, Cambridge U., England, 1987-89, Jagiellonian U., Poland, 1995. Instr. music Ind. U., Bloomington, 1958-59; music critic Portland Reporter, 1962-63, Balt. Evening Sun, 1964-68; founder, tchr. seminar for music adminstrs., 1972—; chmn. divsn. fine arts Cascade Coll., Portland, Oreg., 1959-63; dean Peabody Inst., Balt., 1963-69; pres. Westminster Choir Coll., Princeton, N.J., 1969-87; vis. fellow Wolfson Coll. U. Cambridge, Eng., 1987-89; disting. prof. choral studies, choral condr. Palm Beach Atlantic U., West Palm Beach, Fla., 1989—; pres. Prestige Publs. Inc., 1978—; 1992-95; music critic Palm Beach (Fla.) Post, 1991—; prof. Sch. Ch. Music Knox Theol. Sem., Ft. Lauderdale, Fla., 1989—; choral condr. Palm Beach C.C., Lake Worth, Fla., 1992-93; condr.-in-residence, dir. music First Presbyn. Ch., West Palm Beach, 1989-97; dir. music Coral Ridge Presbyn. Ch., Ft. Lauderdale, Fla., 1997—; spl. guest choral condr. Palm Beach Opera, 1990—; interim condr. Choral Soc. Palm Beaches, 1992; condr. Ray Robinson Chorale, 1994—, Kiev, Ukraine, 1997, Budapest, 1997, Coral Ridge Presbyn. Ch., 1997—. Author: The Choral Experience, 1976, Choral Music, 1978; Krzysztof Penderecki, A Guide to His Works, 1983, A Study of the Penderecki St. Luke Passion, 1983, John Finley Williamson: A Centennial Appreciation, 1987; co-author: German Diction for the Choral Singer, 1992, A Bach Tribute: Bach Essays in Honor of William H. Scheide, 1993; editor The Choral Tradition Series, Hinshaw Music Inc., 1978—, Studies in Penderecki, 1994—. Bd. dirs. Balt. Symphony Orch., 1967-69, Am. Boy Choir Sch., 1970-73, N.Y. Choral Soc., 1972—, Palm Beach Atlantic U. choral series Hinshaw Music Inc., 1990—; bd. dirs. Palm Beach County Coun. Arts, chmn. profl. artists com., mem. task force for master plan, 1990-92; mem. cultural plan com. Palm Beach County Cultural Coun., 1992—; mem. task force for edn. Fla. Philharm. Orch., 1994—. Recipient Disting. Alumni Merit award Ind. U., 1975, Disting. Alumni award Sch. Music, 1973, Disting. Alumni award San Jose State U., 1990. Mem. Coll. Music Soc. (life), Am. Choral Dirs. Assn. (life, chmn. rsch. and publs. com. 1986—), Internat. Heinrich Schütz Soc. (chmn. Am. sect. 1984-87), Univ. Club N.Y., Nassau Club Princeton, Govs. Club West Palm Beach. Presbyterian. Home: 2413 Medina Way West Palm Beach FL 33401-8019

ROBINSON, RICHARD FRANCIS, writer, author; b. Passaic, N.J., June 13, 1941; s. Francis Ward and Evelyn (Burnett) R.; m. Brenda Kay Moore, Feb. 6, 1970; 1 child, Kelly. Student, Coll. of William & Mary, 1959-60; BA in Journalism, Mich. State U., 1964. Reporter, columnist North Jersey Herald News, Passaic, 1964-67; med. writer, reporter The Oakland Press, Pontiac, Mich., 1967-75; staff reporter Nat. Enquirer, Lantana, Fla., 1975-79; staff writer Hank Meyer Assocs., Miami, Fla., 1987-88; pres. Dick Robinson Co., Delray Beach, Fla., 1979—; bd. dirs. Krynova Enterprises, Inc., St. Petersburg, Fla., Windemere House Inc., Delray Beach, Fla. Editor: Foot & Leg Function, 1988-90; contbr. numerous articles to publs. Delegate Mich. State Rep. Conv., Detroit, 1970; mem. exec. bd. Mich. Fedn. Young Reps., 1970. Recipient First Pl. award AP, 1973. Mem. Am. Med. Writers Assn. (bd. dirs. 1984-85, chmn. trade book awards com. 1986, founding pres. Fla. chpt. 1983-84, pres. 1986-88), Nat. Assn. Sci. Writers, Athletic Club Boca Raton, Delray Beach Tennis Ctr. Avocations: tennis, computers, photography. Home and Office: 250 S Ocean Blvd Apt 252 Delray Beach FL 33483-6752 *To succeed at anything in life, honestly believe you can do it well-and you will.*

ROBINSON, RICHARD M., technical communication specialist; b. Bklyn., Nov. 28, 1934; s. Allen and Syd (Bell) R.; m. Rochelle Wolf, Dec. 25, 1967; children: Michelle P., Steven E. BS in Physics, Rensselaer Poly. Inst., Troy, N.Y., 1956, MS in Tech. Comm., 1959. Assoc. engr. Convair-Astronautics, San Diego, 1956-57; tech. writer Raytheon, Andover, Mass., 1957-58; pubs. engr. Hazeltine Electronics, Little Neck, N.Y., 1959-61; sr. pubs. engr. Sperry Gyroscope, Great Neck, N.Y., 1961-68; mgr. editl. svcs. Grumman Corp., Bethpage, N.Y., 1968-94; tech. comm. specialist/cons. Setauket, N.Y., 1995—; adj. faculty Suffolk County C.C. Contbr. articles to profl. jours.; referee papers IEEE Trans. on Profl. Comm. Mem. IEEE (sr. mem., tech. activities bd., conf. chmn., pres., adminstrv. com. Profl. Comm. Soc., Alfred N. Goldsmith award 1983), Soc. Tech. Comms. (sr. mem.), Miramar Ski Club (pres.), Amateur Ski Instrs. Assn. (cert. instr.). Home and Office: 10 Penelope Dr Setauket NY 11733

ROBINSON, ROBERT ARMSTRONG, pension fund executive; b. Waterbury, Conn., Sept. 11, 1925; s. Robert and Ethel (Armstrong) R.; m. D. Ann Harding, June 7, 1947; 1 child, Gayllis Robinson Ward. A.B. magna cum laude, Brown U., 1950, M.A., 1952; postgrad., U. Ill., 1954-55; Litt. D., Episcopal Theol. Sem. Ky., 1971; D.C.L., U. South, 1972; LL.D., Nashotah House, Oconomowoc, Wis. Instr. English Brown U., 1950-53; instr. English, asst. prof. rhetoric U. Ill., 1953-56; trust officer Colonial Bank & Trust Co., Waterbury, 1956-63; v.p., trust officer Colonial Bank & Trust Co., 1963-65, sr. trust officer, 1965-66; v.p., sec. Ch. Pension Fund and Affiliates, Ch. Life Ins. Corp., Ch. Ins. Co., Ch. Agy. Corp., Ch. Hymnal Corp., 1966-67, exec. v.p., 1967-68, pres., dir., 1968-91; pres. emeritus Ch. Pension Fund and Affiliates, Ch. Life Ins. Corp., et al., 1991—; mgr. East Side House Settlement; bd. dirs. Seabury Press, Inc., Mariners Instl. Funds, Inc., Mariner Tax Free Instl. Fund, UST Master Funds, Morehouse Pub. Co., Inc., Mariner Funds Trust, Mariner Equity Trust, Pigmy Corp., U.S.T. Master Tax Free Funds, U.S.T. Master Variable Series, Inc., Rosiclare Lead and Fluorspar Mining Co., Infinity Funds, Inc., others; cons. to exec. dir. Pension Benefit Guaranty Corp.; dir. Infinity Mutual Funds. Trustee Hillspeak, Eureka Springs, Ark., Canterbury Cathedral Trust in Am., Hoosac Sch. Washington Nat. Cathedral, Nashotah Theol. Sem., Wis., H.B. and F.K. Bugher Found., Living Ch. Found.; mem. exec. com. N.Y. couns. Boy Scouts Am., Ch. Pensions Conf.; mem. econ. adv. bd. Columbia U. Grad. Sch. Bus. Adminstrn, mem. John Carter Brown Libr. Assoc. With inf. AUS, 1943-46. Decorated Bronze Star, Purple Heart with oak leaf cluster, Mil. Order of the Purple Heart, Knights of Malta, Order St. John. Mem. Am. Numis. Soc. (councillor), Conn. Bankers Assn. (v.p., head trust divsn.), Am. Numis. Assn., Newsomen Soc., St. Andrew's Soc. (N.Y.C.), Brown Club (N.Y.C.), Union League Club (N.Y.C.), Church Club (N.Y.C.) (pres. 1991—), Country Club of New Canaan, Athenaeum Club (London), Pilgrims, Union, Met. Clubs (Washington), Yeaman's Hall Club (Charleston, S.C.), Phi Beta Kappa. Republican. Episcopalian (vestryman). Clubs: St. Andrew's Soc. (N.Y.C.), Brown (N.Y.C.), Union League (N.Y.C.), Church (N.Y.C.), Country of New Canaan, Athenaeum (London), Pilgrims, Union, Met. (Washington), Yeaman's Hall (Charleston, S.C.). Home: 2 Hathaway Common New Canaan CT 06840-5737 Office: 800 2nd Ave New York NY 10017-4709

ROBINSON, ROBERT BLACQUE, foundation administrator; b. Long Beach, Calif., Apr. 24, 1927; s. Joseph LeRoi and Frances Hansel R.; m. Susan Amelia Thomas, Jan. 21, 1960; children: Victoria, Shelly, Blake, Sarah. Student, Oreg. State Coll., 1946; BA, UCLA, 1950; student, U. Hawaii. Partner, Pritchard Assocs. (Mgmt. Cons.), Honolulu, 1956-58; asst. dir. Econ. Planning and Coordination Authority, Hawaii, 1959; dep. dir. dept. econ. devel. State of Hawaii, 1960-63; asst. mgr. Pacific Concrete and Rock Co., Ltd., Honolulu, 1963-66, exec. v.p. and gen. mgr., 1966-68, pres. and gen. mgr., 1968-75; chmn. Pacific Concrete and Rock Co., Ltd., 1976-77; pres. C. of C. of Hawaii, Honolulu, 1977—. Bd. govs. Hawaii Employers Coun., 1969-74, mem. exec. com., 1969-74, vice chmn., 1973-74; bd. dirs. Pacific Aerospace Mus., 1982-86; mem. Hawaii Tourism Conf., 1977, chmn., 1981-82; bd. dirs. Aloha United Fund, 1970-76, sec., 1972, v.p., 1973-76; bd. dirs. Oahu Devel. Conf., 1970-75; treas., bd. dirs. Crime Stoppers Hawaii, 1981—; mem. Hawaii Joint Coun. on Econ. Edn., 1985—; bd. dirs. Jr. Achievement Hawaii, 1967-73, pres., 1969; bd. dirs. Hawaii Ednl. Coun., 1974-75, Health and Community Services Coun. Hawaii, 1982-84; mem. exec. com. Hawaii Conv. Ctr. Coun., 1984—, Interagency Energy Conservation Coun., State of Hawaii, 1978—; trustee Cen. Union Ch., 1983-86; bd. dirs. Waikiki Improvement Assn. Inc., 1986—; mem. Ctr. for Tropical and Subtropical Aquacultute industry Adv. Coun., 1987—; chmn. Mayor's Adv. Com. on Pacific Nations Ctr., 1988-89. Lt. comdr. USNR, 1945-46, ret. Mem. Japan-Am. Conf. of Mayors and C. of C. Pres. (mem. Am. exec. com. 1974—), Am. Soc. Assn. Execs. (past dir. Hawaii chpt.), Hawaii Execs. Coun. (found. , Young Pres. Assn. (past mem.), Aloha Soc. Assn. Execs., C. of C. Hawaii (dir. 1972-75, chmn. 1975), Coun. of Profit Sharing Industries (past dir. Hawaii sect.), Cement and Concrete Products Industry of Hawaii (pres. 1968), Hawaii Mfrs. Assn. (past dir.), Navy League of U.S. (Hawaii council), Engring. Assn. Hawaii, Pacific Club, Rotary, Sigma Chi. Home: 1437 Kalaepohaku St Honolulu HI 96816-1804 Office: C of C Hawaii 735 Bishop St Ste 220 Honolulu HI 96813-4816

ROBINSON, ROBERT CRIBBEN, librarian, information company executive; b. Madison, Wis., June 16, 1950; s. Robert Cribben and Elizabeth (Mahoney) R.; m. Julie Baxter, June 10, 1978; children: Megan, Kerry. BA, Allegheny Coll., 1972; MLS, U. Md., 1973. Asst. program libr. Nat. Pub. Radio, Washington, 1974-75, news libr., 1975—, sr. libr., 1994—; pres. Robinson Info. Co., Arlington, 1985—. Mem. Spl. Libr. Assn., Nat. Genealogical Soc., Photographic Soc. Am., Investigative Reporters and Editors, Soc. Am. Archivists, Potomac Soc. Stereo Photographers (pres. 1985—). Home: 6231 21st St N Arlington VA 22205-2036 Office: Nat Pub Radio 635 Massachusetts Ave NW Washington DC 20001-3752

ROBINSON, ROBERT GEORGE, psychiatry educator; b. Pitts., May 22, 1945; s. Robert Campbell and Rosetta M. (Martindale) R.; m. Gretchen Priscilla Smith, Jan. 5, 1974; children: Christopher, Jonathan. BS in Engring. Physics, Cornell U., 1967, MD, 1971. Intern Montefiore Hosp. and Albert Einstein Med. Ctr., 1971-72; resident Cornell U., White Plains, 1972-73; rsch. assoc. NIMH, Washington, 1973-75; resident Johns Hopkins U., 1975-77, asst. prof. to assoc. prof., 1977-90, prof., 1990-91; prof., head of dept. U. Iowa Coll. Medicine, Iowa City, 1991—; mem. editorial bds. Jour. Neuropsychiatry & Clinical Neurosciences, Int. Jour. Psychiatry in Medicine, Psychiatry. Editor: Depression and Coexisting Disease, 1989, Depression in Neurologic Disease, 1993; contbr. 220 articles and chpts. to publs. Mullen Engring. scholar Cornell U., 1967; recipient Sandra Lee Shaw award for rsch. in neurology and pharmacology, Cornell U., 1969, Research Scientist award, NIMH, 1989; Mellon fellow Johns Hopkins U., 1977. Fellow APA; mem. Soc. for Neuroscience, Royal Coll. of Psychiatrist, AAAS, Soc. of Biological Psychiatry, Johns Hopkins Soc. Scholars, 1997. Office: U Iowa Coll Med 200 Hawkins Dr Iowa City IA 52242-1009

ROBINSON, ROBERT JAMES, retired manufacturing exeuctive; b. Pitts., Dec. 19, 1935; s. Robert S. and Mary Hazel (Beale) R.; m. Joyce Ann Cordt, Aug. 12, 1961; children: Wende Lynne, Brittany D., Robert S. II. BS, Carnegie Inst. Tech., 1957; MBA, U. Chgo., 1977. From engr. to gen. supt. Allegheny Ludlum Industries, Dunkirk, N.Y., 1957-74; from v.p. ops. to COO, exec. v.p. Axia Inc., Oak Brook, Ill., 1974-92; mgmt. cons. Colorado Springs, 1992—. Co-inventor bag closing machine. Mem. Union League. Republican. Methodist. Avocations: hunting, fishing, skiing, sport cars. Home and Office: 8315 Bluffview Way Colorado Springs CO 80919-4501

ROBINSON, ROBERT L., financial service company executive, lawyer; b. Ridgeway, Va., Feb. 22, 1936; s. Gerald L. and Annie (McBride) R.; m. Audrey M. Allen, July 30, 1960; children: Robert, Diane, Kelly. B.A., Va. State Coll., 1957; LL.B., Harvard U., 1960; M.B.A., U. Conn., 1976. Bar: N.Y. 1961, Pa. 1978. Atty. N.Y. Central Ry. Co., N.Y.C., 1960-63; asst. gen. counsel Crane Co., N.Y.C., 1963-71; counsel Xerox Corp., Stamford, Conn., 1971-77; v.p., asst. gen. counsel and sec. INA Corp., Phila., 1977-82; sr. v.p., gen. counsel investment group CIGNA Corp., Bloomfield, Conn., 1982-84, sr. v.p., asst. gen. counsel, corp. sec., 1984-87; sr. v.p., gen. counsel property & casualty group CIGNA Corp., Phila., 1987-88, sr. v.p., chief counsel litigation, 1988—. Dir. Com. of Seventy. Served to lt. U.S. Army, 1957. Mem. ABA, Pa. Bar Assn., Westchester-Fairfield Corp. Counsel Assn. (founder, bd. dirs. pres. 1976-77), Great Oak Yacht Cub, Harvard Club (N.Y.C.), Merion Cricket Club, Phila. Club. Republican. Office: CIGNA Corp 1601 Chestnut St Philadelphia PA 19192-0003

ROBINSON, RONALD ALAN, manufacturing executive; b. Louisville, Mar. 23, 1952; s. J. Kenneth and Juanita M. (Crosier) R.; m. Joan Parker, 1986; children: Rex., Jay. BS, Ga. Inst. Tech., 1974; MBA, Harvard U., 1978. Staff engr., asst. to exec. v.p. ops. Dual Drilling Co., Wichita Falls, Tex., 1978-80; v.p. Dreco, Inc., Houston, 1980-84, pres., dir. subs. Triflo Industries Internat. Inc.; pres., COO Ramteck Systems, Inc., 1984-87; chmn. and CEO Denver Techs. Inc., 1988-95; pres. Svedala Industries, Inc., 1996—; bd. dirs. Dreco Energy Svcs., Ltd., Edmonton, 1984—. Recipient Optimist Internat. Citizenship award, 1970; Gardiner Symonds fellow, 1977. Mem. Harvard Alumni Assn. Home: 4815 Newstead Pl Colorado Springs CO 80906-5935 Office: Denver Equipment Co 621 S Sierra Madre St Colorado Springs CO 80903-4021

ROBINSON, RONALD MICHAEL, health care financial executive, financial consultant; b. N.Y.C., May 1, 1942; s. Arthur John and Matilda (Siegel) R.; m. Mary Jane Reemelin, Feb. 25, 1972; children: Scott Edward, Elizabeth Drew. BS, Ohio State U., 1964; MBA, U. Pa., 1966. CPA, Pa. Fin. mgr. Am. Airlines, Inc., N.Y.C., 1969-72; mgmt. cons. Coopers & Lybrand, Phila., 1973-75; pres. Robinson Assocs., Inc., Paoli, Pa., 1975-81; dir. fin. and adminstr., chief fin. officer Decision Scis. Corp., Jenkintown, Pa., 1981-82; sr. v.p. fin., chief fin. officer Presbyn. Homes, Inc., Camp Hill, Pa., 1982—. Bd. dirs. Healthamerica. Mem. Carlisle (Pa.) Borough Council, 1988-92. Home: PO Box 908 Carlisle PA 17013-5908 Office: Presbyn Homes Inc 1217 Slate Hill Rd Camp Hill PA 17011-8012

ROBINSON, ROSCOE ROSS, nephrologist, educator; b. Oklahoma City, Aug. 21, 1929; s. Roscoe and Tennie (Ross) R.; m. Ann Allen, Aug. 24, 1952; children: Susan, Brooke. BS, U. Ctrl. Okla., 1949; MD, U. Okla., 1954, LHD, 1994. Diplomate: Nat. Bd. Med. Examiners, Am. Bd. Internal Medicine (asso. mem. bd. govs. 1975-78, mem. 1979-82, chmn. test com. on nephrology 1979-82). Intern in medicine Duke U. Med. Ctr., Durham, N.C., 1954-55, jr. asst. resident in medicine, 1955-56, chief resident, instr. medicine, 1957-58, assoc. in medicine, 1960-62, asst. prof. medicine, dir. div. nephrology, 1962-65, assoc. prof. medicine, dir. div. nephrology, 1965-69, prof. medicine, dir. div. nephrology, 1969-78, Florence McAlister prof. medicine, dir. div. nephrology, 1978-81, asso. v.p., 1976-81; chief exec. officer Duke U. Hosp., 1976-81; prof. medicine, vice chancellor health affairs Vanderbilt U. Med. Ctr., Nashville, 1981—; Am. Heart Assn. rsch. fellow, vis. fellow dept. medicine Columbia-Presbyn. Med. Ctr., N.Y.C., 1956-57; clin. investigator Durham VA Hosp., 1960-62, attending physician, 1962-81; cons. nephrology Fayetteville and Asheville, N.C.; cons. nephrology Research Triangle (N.C.) Inst., 1964-81; nat. cons. to surgeon gen. USAF, 1970-89; chmn. N.C. Kidney Coun. Region 21, Dept. HEW, 1977-81; bd. dirs. Research!America, 1993—. Mem. editorial bd. Archives Internal Medicine, 1970-80, Seminars in Nephrology, 1972-93, Mineral and Electrolyte Metabolism, 1977—; mem. editorial com. Fogerty internat. com. Monograph on Prevention of Kidney and Urinary Tract Disease; cons. editor renal diseases: Cecil Textbook of Medicine, 15th edit., 16th edit.; contbr. articles to profl. jours. Bd. dirs. SunHealth Corp., 1986-92, 1st Am. Corp., Tenn., 1992—; trustee Montgomery Bell Acad., Nashville, 1983—, Duke U., 1994—. Fellow ACP; mem. Am. Clin. and Climatol. Assn., Am. Fedn. Clin. Rsch. (councillor So. sect. 1968-71), Assn. Am. Physicians, European Dialysis and Transplant Assn., Am. Heart Assn., N.C. Heart Assn. (sr. investigator 1962-74, exec. com., bd. dirs. 1971-72), Am. Soc. Clin. Investigation, So. Soc. Clin. Investigation (councillor 1977-80), Am. Physiol. Soc., Am. Soc. Artificial Internal Organs (councillor 1968-71), Internat. Soc. Nephrology (editor Kidney Internat. jour. 1971-84, exec. com. 1972-95, v.p. 1984-87, pres.-elect 1987-90, pres. 1990-93), Am. Soc. Nephrology (councillor 1977-80, pres.-elect 1980-81, pres. 1981-82), Nat. Kidney Found. (sci. adv. bd. 1970-75), Kidney Found. N.C., Assn. Acad. Health Ctrs. (bd. dirs. 1985-91, chmn. 1989-90), Soc. Med. Adminstrs. (pres.-elect 1989-91, pres. 1991-93), Nat. Inst. Diabetes, Digestive and Kidney Diseases (nat. adv. coun. 1987-90), Alpha Omega Alpha. Home: 501 Jackson Blvd Nashville TN 37205-3427 Office: Vanderbilt U Med Center Dept Health Affairs Nashville TN 37232

ROBINSON, SALLY WINSTON, artist; b. Detroit, Nov. 2, 1924; d. Harry Lewis and Lydia (Kahn) Winston; m. Eliot F. Robinson, June 28, 1949; children: Peter Eliot, Lydia Winston, Sarah Mitchell, Suzanne Finley. BA, Bennington Coll., 1947; postgrad. Cranbrook Acad. Art, 1949; grad. Sch. Social Work, Wayne U., 1948, MA, 1972; MFA, Wayne State U., 1973. Psychol. tester Detroit Bd. Edn., 1944; pyschol. counselor and tester YMCA, N.Y.C., 1946; social caseworker Family Service, Pontiac, Mich., 1947; instr. printmaking Wayne State U., Detroit, 1973—. One person shows U. Mich., 1973, Wayne State U., 1974, Klein-Vogol Gallery, 1974, Rina Gallery, 1976, Park McCullough House, Vt., 1976, Williams Coll., 1976, Arnold Klein Gallery, 1977; exhibited group shows Bennington Coll., Cranbrook Mus., Detroit Inst. Art, Detroit Artists Market, Soc. Women Painters, Soc. Arts and Crafts, Bloomfield Art Assn., Flint Left Bank Gallery, Balough Gallery, Detroit Soc. Women Painters, U. Mich., U. Ind., U. Wis., U. Pittsburg, Toledo Mus., Krannert Mus.; represented in permanent collections, Detroit, N.Y.C., Birmingham, Bloomfield Hills; tchr. children's art Detroit Inst. Art, 1949-50, now artistic advisor, bd. dirs. drawing and print orgn. Bd. dirs. Planned Parenthood, 1951—, mem. exec. bd., 1963—; bd. dirs. PTA, 1956-60, Roeper City and Country Sch., U. Mich. Mus. Art, 1978; trustee Putnam Hosp. Med. Research Inst., 1978; mem. Gov.'s Commn. Art in State Bldgs., 1978-79; mem. art and devel. coms. So. Vt. Art Ctr., 1987-88; mem. vol. com. Marie Selby Gardens; patron Graphic Art Studio, U. So. Fla., Tampa. Fellow Williams Coll. Mus. Art (mem. visiting com.); mem. Detroit Artists Market (dir. 1956—), Bennington Coll. Alumnae Assn. (regional co-chmn. 1954), Detroit Soc. Women Painters, Birmingham Soc. Women Painters (pres. 1974-76), Bloomfield Art Assn. (program co-chmn. 1956), Founders Soc. Detroit Inst. Art., Village Women's Club (Birmingham, Mich.), Women's City Club (co-ordinator art shows Detroit 1950), Garden Club, Am. Club (Bennington, Vt., Sarasota, Fla.), Cosmopolitan (N.Y.C.). Unitarian. Home: 7 Monument Cir Bennington VT 05201-2134 also: 840 N Casey Key Rd Osprey FL 34229-9779 also: 200 E 69th St Apt 7B New York NY 10021

ROBINSON, SMOKEY, singer, composer; b. Detroit; m. Claudette Rogers (div.); children: Berry William, Tamla Claudette. V.p. Motown Record Corp. Formed group, Smokey Robinson and the Miracles, with Miracles, 1957-72, performed Detroit nightclubs, co-founder, Tamla record label, 1959; numerous singles and album recs. including: Sweet Harmony, 1973, Virgin Man, 1974, Agony and the Ecstasy, 1975, Quiet Storm, 1976, Open, 1976, There will Come a Day (I'm Gonna Happen to You), 1977; appearances at clubs, colls., also network TV shows including Shindig; star own TV spl., 1971; solo albums include Smokey, 1973, A Quiet Storm, Smokey's Family Robinson, Deep in My Soul, Smokin', Warm Thoughts, Being with You, 1989, Smokey's World, Shop Around, One Heartbeat, 1987, Love Smokey, 1990, Blame It on Love & All the Great Hits, 1990, Double Good Everything, 1992, Motown Legends, 1995; appeared on Broadway in An Evening with Smokey Robinson, 1985; author: (autobiography with David Ritz) Smokey: Inside My Life, 1989. Inducted Rock 'n Roll Hall of Fame, 1986, Songwriters Hall of Fame, 1986; recipient Grammy award for best male rhythm & blues vocal perfomance, 1987, Founders award ASCAP, 1988. Office: Motown Record Co 5750 Wilshire Blvd Ste 300 Los Angeles CA 90036-3697*

ROBINSON, SPENCER, JR., retired service club executive, accountant; b. Bridgeport, Conn., Apr. 16, 1942; s. Spencer Robinson and Helen (Diesinger) McNeill; m. Sally Emptage, June 21, 1963; children: David Spencer, Todd Wallace, John Marshall, Sarah Ann. BSIM, Ga. Tech. U., 1963; BS in Acctg., Jacksonville U., 1969; MSHA, U. Ala., Birmingham, 1989. Mng. ptnr. Deloitte Haskins & Sells, N.Y.C., 1963-85; exec. v.p., chief operating officer U. Ala. Health Svcs. Found., Birmingham, 1985-90; gen. sec., chief adminstrv. officer Rotary Internat., Evanston, Ill., 1990-94; adj. prof. Montreat Coll. Sch. Profl. and Adult Studies, 1995-97. Contbr. articles to profl. jours. Gen. sec. Rotary Found., Evanston, 1990-94; mem. Gov.'s Com. of 100, La., 1985; trustee Nat. Multiple Sclerosis Soc., La., 1984; sec., treas. Crimestoppers, Inc., New Orleans, 1983. Recipient Razzberry award Birmingham Press Club, 1989, Disting. Alumni award Jacksonville U., 1993. Republican. Presbyterian. Home: PO Box 280 Montreat NC 28757-0280

ROBINSON, SPENCER T. (HERK ROBINSON), professional baseball team executive; b. June 25, 1940; m. Kathy Robinson; children: Ashley,

Amanda. Student, U. Miami, Washington U., St. Louis. With Cin. Reds., 1962-67; asst. Baltimore Orioles, 1968; asst. scouting dir. Kansas City Royals, 1969-72, dir. stadium ops., 1973-74, v.p., 1975-85, exec. v.p. adminstrn., 1985-90, v.p., 1975-85, exec. v.p., gen. mgr., 1990—, former mem. bd. dirs. Office: Kans City Royals PO Box 419969 Kansas City MO 64141-6969*

ROBINSON, STEPHEN MICHAEL, applied mathematician, educator; b. Columbus, Ohio, Apr. 12, 1942; s. Arthur Howard and Mary Elizabeth (Coffin) R.; m. Chong-Suk Han, May 10, 1968; children: Diana Marie, James Andrew. BA, U. Wis., 1962, PhD, 1971; MS, NYU, 1963; Doctor honoris causa, Univ. Zürich, 1996. Adminstr. U. Wis., Madison, 1969-72, asst. prof., 1972-75, assoc. prof., 1975-79, prof. indsl. engrng. and computer scis., 1979—, chmn. dept. indsl. engrng., 1981-84; cons. to various agys. Dept. Def., 1971—. Editor: Math. of Ops. Rsch., 1981-86, assoc. editor, 1975-80, Jour. Ops. Rsch., 1974-86, Math. Programming, 1986-91; mem. bd. editors Annals Ops. Rsch., 1984—, Set-Valued Analysis, 1992—, Jour. Convex Analysis, 1994—; adv. editor Math. of Ops. Rsch., 1987—; contbr. numerous articles to profl. jours. Trustee Village of Shorewood Hills, Wis., 1974-76, mem. fin. com. , 1973-87; bd. overseers Simon's Rock Coll., Great Barrington, Mass., 1991—. Served to capt. U.S. Army, 1963-69, Korea, Vietnam. Decorated Legion of Merit, Bronze star, Air medal, Army Commendation medal with 2 oak leaf clusters. Mem. Inst. for Ops. Rsch. and Mgmt. Scis. (mem. Ops. Rsch. Soc. Am. coun. 1991-94), Inst. Indsl. Engrs., Soc. Indsl. and Applied Math., Math. Programming Soc. (mem.-at-large of coun. 1991-94), Madison Club. Home: 1014 University Bay Dr Madison WI 53705-2251 Office: U Wis Dept Indsl Engring 1513 University Ave Madison WI 53706-1539

ROBINSON, SUE L(EWIS), federal judge; b. 1952. BA with highest honors, U. Del., 1974; JD, U. Pa., 1978. Assoc. Potter, Anderson & Corron, Wilmington, Del., 1978-83; asst. U.S. atty. U.S. Attys. Office, 1983-88; U.S. magistrate judge U.S. Dist. Ct. (Del. dist.), 1988-91, dist. judge, 1991—. Mem. Del. State Bar Assn. (sec. 1986-87). Office: US Dist Ct J Caleb Boggs Fed Bldg 844 N King St Lockbox 31 Wilmington DE 19801-3519*

ROBINSON, SUSAN MITTLEMAN, data processing executive; b. Bklyn., Nov. 18, 1941; d. Samuel and Ida (Priest) Mittleman; m. Sheldon N. Robinson, June 5, 1962; children: Edward Bruce, Nancy Michelle, Jonathan Scott, Karen Barbara, Judith Lynn. AAS in Computer Sci., BCC, Lincroft, N.J., 1981; BBA, CUNY, 1962; MS in Computer Sci., Fairleigh Dickinson U., 1983; postgrad., Seton Hall U., 1983-85. Engr. asst. United Technologies, East Hartford, Conn., 1962-64; programmer, sys. analyst Litton Industries (Sweda), Pine Brook, N.J., 1981-83; asst. prof. data processing Mercer Coll., West Windsor, N.J., 1983-85; adj. instr. data processing Brookdale C.C., Lincroft, N.J., 1983—; coord. MIS N.J. Dept. Health and Sr. Svcs., Trenton, 1985—; Lan adminstr. N.J. Dept. Health and Sr. Svcs., Trenton, N.J., 1994—; world wide web webmaster N.J. Dept. Health and Sr. Svcs., Trenton; med. data set liaison N.J. Dept. Health and Sr. Svcs. and HCFA, 1996—; outsource cons. Medicare/Medicaid, Trenton, 1989—; cons. Health Care Fin. Authority, Balt., 1995—. Author (reference material) Info-Henco, 1987, Automated Survey Processing Environment Users Training Manual, 1993; developer computerized sys. to help patients and their family select a nursing home. Exec. bd. Temple Beth Am, Parsippany, N.J., 1972-80. Mem. SAS Users Group, N.J. DOH Prime Users Group. Avocations: knitting, puzzle-solving, travel. Office: NJ Dept Health and Sr Svcs CN 367 Trenton NJ 08625

ROBINSON, THEODORE CURTIS, JR., lawyer; b. Chgo., Jan. 22, 1916; s. Theodore Curtis and Edna Alice (Willard) R.; m. Marynel Werner, Dec. 28, 1940; children: Theodore Curtis III, Peter S. BA, Western Res. U., 1938, LLB, 1940. Bar: Ohio 1940, U.S. Dist. Ct. (no. dist.) Ohio 1946, U.S. Ct. Appeals (8th cir.) 1948, U.S. Dist. Ct. (we. dist.) Wis. 1950, U.S. Dist. Ct. (we. dist.) N.Y. 1950, U.S. Ct. Appeals (6th cir.) 1950, Ill. 1957, U.S. Dist. Ct. (no. dist.) Ill. 1957, U.S. Ct. Appeals (7th cir.) 1964, U.S. Supreme Ct. 1972. Assoc. Davis & Young, Cleve., 1940; law clk. no. dist. ea. divsn. U.S. Dist. Ct., Cleve., 1940-42; assoc. Leckie, McCreary, et al, Cleve., 1945-52; ptnr. McCreary, Hinslea & Ray, Cleve., 1953-57, McCreary, Hinslea, Ray & Robinson, Chgo., 1957-90; counsel Ray, Robinson, Hannin & Carle, Chgo., 1990-91, Ray, Robinson, Carle, Davies & Snyder, Chgo., 1991—; mem. exec. com. Maritime Law Assn. of U.S., N.Y.C., 1981-83; pres. Propellor Club of U.S., Chgo., 1966-67; sec., treas. Internat. Shipmasters Assn., Chgo., 1958-91. Contbr. articles to profl. law reviews. Lt. USCG, 1943-45. Fellow Am. Coll. Trial Lawyers; mem. ABA, Chgo. Bar Assn. (com. chmn. 1973), Internat. Assn. Def. Counsel, Order of Coif, Traffic Club Chgo. (dir. 1986, 87), Whitehall Club (N.Y.), Nat. Eagle Scout Assn. Republican. Avocations: gardening, golf, reading. Office: Ray Robinson Carle Davies & Snyder 850 W Jackson Blvd Chicago IL 60607-3025

ROBINSON, THOMAS NATHANIEL, pediatrician, educator, researcher; b. Detroit, May 11, 1960; s. Kenneth J. and Judith R. Robinson. BS in Biol. Scis., Stanford U., 1983, MD with rsch. honors, 1988; MPH in Maternal and Child Health, U. Calif., Berkeley, 1987. Diplomate Nat. Bd. Med. Examiners, Am. Bd. Pediatrics. Intern dept. medicine Children's Hosp. and Harvard Med. Sch., Boston, 1988-89, jr. asst. resident, 1989-90, sr. asst. resident, 1990-91; clin. fellow in pediatric medicine Harvard Med. Sch., Boston, 1988-91; Robert Wood Johnson clin. scholar Sch. Medicine Stanford U., Palo Alto, 1991-93, clin. instr. divsn. gen. pediatrics dept. pediatrics, acting dir. youth studies Ctr. for Rsch. in Disease Prevention Sch. Medicine, 1992-93, acting. asst. prof. divsn. gen. pediatrics dept. pediatrics, co-dir. youth studies Ctr. for Rsch. in Disease Prevention, 1993—; asst. prof. pediatrics and medicine Stanford U., 1996—; attending physician divsn. gen. pediatrics dept. pediatrics Stanford U. Hosp., Palo Alto, 1992—, Lucile Salter Packard Children's Hosp., Palo Alto, 1992—; clinician scientist Am. Heart Assn., 1993—; presenter in field. Contbr. articles to med. and sci. jours. Alumni Med. scholar Stanford U., 1985; grantee Met. Life Found., 1985-87. Fellow Am. Acad. Pediatrics (sch. health com. No. Calif. dist. 1992—, chair 1993-97), Am. Heart Assn. (grantee 1993—, phys. activity subcom. 1993—). Office: Stanford U Sch Med Ctr for Rsch Disease Prevention 1000 Welch Rd Palo Alto CA 94304-1811

ROBINSON, TONI, lawyer, educator; b. New Rochelle, N.Y.; d. Benjamin Mag and Eugenie (Lee) R.; m. Michael P. Plouf, Feb. 3, 1968. BA, Sarah Lawrence Coll., 1972; JD, Columbia U., 1976; LLM in Taxation, NYU, 1985. Bar: N.Y. 1977, U.S. Dist. Ct. (so. dist.) N.Y. 1977, U.S. Tax Ct. 1987. Assoc. Roberts & Holland, N.Y.C., 1976-79, Battle, Fowler, Jaffin & Kheel, N.Y.C., 1979-82; asst. prof. law U. Bridgeport, Conn., 1982-85, assoc. prof., 1985-88, prof., 1988-95, dir. tax clinic, 1987-93; prof. law, dir. Tax Clinic Quinnipiac Coll., Hamden, Conn., 1993—; tax adviser Conn. Small Bus. Adv. Svc., Bridgeport, 1987-92; asst. sec. UN Expert Group on Tax Treaties, N.Y.C., 1978-79, dep. sec., 1979-82; legal adviser Internat. Percy Grainger Soc., White Plains, N.Y., 1985-91; presenter, author study materials continuing legal edn. programs; vis. prof. law Coll. of William and Mary, Williamsburg, Va., 1989-90. Contbr. articles on taxes to profl. publs. Founding bd. dirs. Laurel Shelter, Inc. Mem. ABA (tax sect.), N.Y. State Bar Assn. (tax sect.), Assn. of Bar of City of N.Y., Conn. Women's Bar Assn., Phi Delta Phi. Democrat. Mem. Soc. of Friends. Avocations: sailing, horses. Office: Quinnipiac Coll Sch Law 275 Mt Carmel Ave Hamden CT 06518-1961

ROBINSON, W. LEE, lawyer; b. Rome, Ga., Sept. 24, 1943; m. Irene Scales, 1966; children: Christine, Jacquelyn. BS, Ga. Tech.; MBA, Mercer Univ., 1985, JD, 1985. With Robinson Hardware Store, Macon, Ga., 1954-86; former mem. Ga. Senate, Atlanta, 1975-83; mayor City of Macon, Macon, 1988-92; pvt. practice law Macon, 1985—. 2d. lt. U.S. Army, col. U.S. Army Res. Decorated 3 Bronze Stars. Mem. Macon C. of C. (former bd. dirs.). Address: 3824 Overlook Ave Macon GA 31204-1325 Office: 201 2nd St Ste 580 Macon GA 31201-2738 also: PO Box 4852 Macon GA 31208-4852

ROBINSON, WALTER GEORGE, arts management and funding consultant; b. London, June 18, 1911; s. Walter and Annie (Ledger) R.; m. Ruth V. Holden, Sept. 14, 1941 (dec. Mar. 1987); stepchildren: Malcolm D. Whitman III, Gail W. Hughes; m. Vesta H. Bogle, May 31, 1990. Student, NYU, 1943; D.F.A. (hon.), Mpls. Coll. Art and Design, 1975. Engaged in investment bus. N.Y.C., 1928-33; with Bass River Savs. Bank, South Yarmouth, Mass., 1934-60, pres., 1952-60; dir. Cape & Vineyard Electric Co., 1958-60, Hyannis Trust Co., until 1960; pres. Mpls. Soc. Fine Arts, governing and supporting orgn. for Mpls. Inst. Arts, Mpls. Coll. Art and Design, Children's Theatre Co., 1960-72, vice chmn., treas., sec., 1972-75; acting dir. Mpls. Sch. Art, 1962-63; acting pres. Mpls. Coll. Art and Design, 1974-75; dir. resource devel. Mus. Fine Arts, Boston, 1975-77; arts mgmt. and funding cons., 1977—; pres. Am. Art Advocates, Inc., 1984-87; trustee Farmers & Mechanics Savs. Bank. Vice pres. Cape Cod Hosp., 1955-60; chmn. Mpls. Com. for Urban Environment, 1968-70, 72-74; mem. Minn. State Arts Council, 1967-73, Minn. Heritage Preservation Commn., 1972-75; chmn. Mpls. Bicentennial Commn., 1974-75; mem. Minn. Com. on Esthetic Environment, 1973-75; founding dir. E.B. Kelley Found., Hyannis, Mass., 1954-87, v.p., 1985-87; bd. dirs. Tyrone Guthrie Theatre Found., Mpls., 1960-70; trustee Northwestern Hosp., 1967-74, Am. Assn. Museums, 1973-75. Clubs: Skylight, Minneapolis, Minnesota (Mpls.). Home: PO Box 490 Damariscotta ME 04543-0490

ROBINSON, WALTER STITT, JR., historian; b. Matthews, N.C., Aug. 28, 1917; s. Walter Stitt and Mary Irene (Jamison) S.; m. Constance Lee Mock, Mar. 18, 1944; children—Ethel Barry, Walter Lee. B.A. summa cum laude, Davidson (N.C.) Coll., 1939; M.A., U. Va., 1941, Ph.D., 1950. Asst. prof., then assoc. prof. history Florence (Ala.) State Coll., 1946-48; mem. faculty U. Kans., Lawrence, 1950—; prof. history U. Kans., 1959-88, prof. emeritus, 1988—, chmn. dept., 1968-73; mem. Nat. Civil War Centennial Commn., 1961-65, Kans. Com. Humanities, 1971-78, chmn., 1976-77. Author: Land Grants in Virginia, 1607-1699, 1957, The Southern Colonial Frontier, 1607-1763, 1979, James Glen: From Scottish Provost to Royal Governor of South Carolina, 1996; editor: Indian Treaties of Colonial Virginia, 2 vols., 1983, Indian Treaties of Colonial Maryland, 1987; mem. editl. bd. 18th century bibliography in Philos. Quar., 1975-78; contbr. articles to profl. jours. Mem. adminstrv. bd. First United Methodist Ch., Lawrence, 1952—; exec. com., bd. dirs. Kans. Sch. Religion, pres., 1983-86. Served to capt. AUS, 1941-45. Decorated Bronze Star; recipient Disting. Scholarship award U. Kans., 1976; grantee Social Sci. Rsch. Coun., 1959-60, Am. Philos. Soc., 1967, 83, NEH, 1994. Mem. Orgn. Am. Historians (chmn. program com. 1959), So. Hist. Assn., Kans. Hist. Soc. (bd. dirs., exec. com. 1989—, v.p. 1997), Douglas County Hist. Soc. (pres. 1979-81, pres. 1995-96, bd. dirs.), Raven Soc., Phi Beta Kappa, Phi Alpha Theta (internat. coun. 1978-80, adv. bd. 1980-81, 86-87, pres. 1984-85). Home: 801 Broadview Dr Lawrence KS 66044-2490 Office: Dept History U Kans Lawrence KS 66045

ROBINSON, WILKES COLEMAN, federal judge; b. Anniston, Ala., Sept. 30, 1925; s. Walter Wade and Catherine Elizabeth (Coleman) R.; m. Julia Von Poellnitz Rowan, June 24, 1955; children: Randolph C., Peyton H., Thomas Wilkes Coleman. AB, U. Ala., 1948; JD, U. Va., 1951. Bar: Ala. 1951, Va. 1962, Mo. 1966, Kans. 1983. Assoc. Bibb & Hemphill, Anniston, Ala., 1951-54; city recorder City of Anniston, 1953-55; judge Juvenile and Domestic Relations Ct. of Calhoun County, Ala., 1954-56; atty. legal dept. GM&O R.R., Mobile, Ala., 1956-58; commerce counsel, asst. gen. atty. Seaboard Air Line R.R., Richmond, Va., 1958-66; commerce counsel Monsanto Co., St. Louis, 1966-70; gen. counsel, v.p. Marion Labs., Inc., Kansas City, Mo., 1970-79; pres. Gulf and Gt. Plains Legal Found., Kansas City, Mo., 1980-85; atty. Howard, Needles, Tammen & Bergendoff, Kansas City, 1985-86, also bd. dirs.; v.p. S.R. Fin. Group, Inc., Overland Park, Kans., 1986-87; judge U.S. Ct. Fed. Claims, Washington, 1987—. Bd. govs. Kansas City Philharmonic Orch., 1975-77. Served with USNR, 1943-44. Mem. Skyline Club, Univ. Club, Mason, Scottish Rite, Phi Beta Kappa (past treas. Kansas City, Mo. chpt.), Phi Eta Sigma, Phi Alpha Theta, Kappa Alpha. Episcopalian. Home: 2353 S Queen St Arlington VA 22202-1550 Office: US Ct Fed Claims 717 Madison Pl NW Washington DC 20005-1011

ROBINSON, WILLIAM ANDREW, health service executive, physician; b. Phila., Jan. 31, 1943; s. Colonial Washington and Lillian Dorothy (Ivey) R.; m. Jacqueline Ellen Garcia, Mar. 28, 1980; 1 child, David Alan; 1 child by previous marriage, William Andrew Jr. BA, Hampton U., 1964; MD, Meharry Med. Coll., 1971; MPH, Johns Hopkins U., 1973. Diplomate Nat. Bd. Med. Examiners; lic. physician, Md. Rotating intern George W. Hubbard Hosp., Nashville, 1971-72, emergency rm. physician, 1972; med. officer gastrointestinal drug sect., bur. drugs FDA USPHS, Dept. Health, Edn. and Welfare, Rockville, Md., 1973-75; dep. dir. office health resources opportunity USPHS, Dept. Health and Human Svcs., Rockville, 1975-80, dep. dir. bur. health professions health resources adminstn., 1980-87, chief med. officer health resources and svcs. adminstn., 1987-89; dep. asst. sec. minority health, dir. office minority health USPHS, Dept. Health and Human Svcs., Washington, 1989-91; acting adminstr. health resources and svcs. adminstn. USPHS, Dept. Health and Human Svcs., Rockville, 1993-94, chief med. officer health resources and svcs. adminstrn., 1991—, dir. Office Pub. Health Affairs, 1996—; chmn. sr. execs. performance rev. bd. Office of Asst. Sec. for Health, 1990-91; pub. health svc. rep. 2d Internat. Conf. on Health Promotion, Adelaide, South Australia; health cons. com. on interior and insular affairs U.S. Ho. of Reps., Washington, 1982-83; appointed field faculty dept. family and comty. health Meharry Med. Coll., 1979; U.S. rep. to WHO Primary Health Care Conf., Alma Ata, Kazakhstan. Mem. nat. editl. bd. Jour. Health Care for the Poor and Underserved, 1991; contbr. articles to profl. jours. Capt. U.S. Army, 1964-67. Recipient Nat. Urban Coalition Comty. Health Svc. award, 1972, Letter of Appreciation, Chmn. Congl. Black Caucus Health Braintrust, U.S. Ho. of Reps., 1988. Mem. AMA, APHA, Am. Acad. Family Physicians, Blacks in Govt., Fed. Physicians Assn., Nat. Med. Assn., Sr. Execs. Assn., Delta Omega (Alpha chpt.). Office: 5600 Fishers Ln Rm 14-39 Rockville MD 20857-0001

ROBINSON, WILLIAM FRANKLIN, retired legal consultant; b. Hammond, Ind., Feb. 10, 1916; s. William P. and Pauline M. (Hopkins) R.; m. Betty Jo Powell, Sept. 15, 1946; children: William Franklin, Stephen Powell, Michael Paul. BA with high honors, Ind. U., 1942, JD, 1944. Bar: Ind. 1944, Mich. 1946, Calif. 1957. Spl. atty. Office Chief Counsel IRS, Washington, Detroit, 1944-46; pvt. practice Detroit, 1946-51; asst. gen. counsel, asst. sec. Montgomery Ward & Co. Inc., Chgo., 1951-56; v.p., gen. counsel, asst. sec., dir. Transam. Fin. Corp., L.A., 1956-82, ret., 1982; legal cons., 1982-83; spl. instr. Wayne State U. Law Sch., U. Detroit, 1947-51. Contbr. articles to profl. jours., chpts. to textbooks. Mem. sch. bd., Calumet City, Ill., 1954-55; apptd. to Gov.'s Credit Retail Adv. Com., 1981; mem., bd. dirs., past pres. Ocean Hills Country Club Homeowners' Assn. Mem. Calif. Loan and Fin. Assn. (chmn. laws and regulations com.), Nat. Consumer Fin. Assn., Conf. Personal Fin. Law, Am., L.A. County bar assns., Acacia, Phi Beta Kappa, Phi Delta Phi. Home: 4136 Andros Way Oceanside CA 92056-7401

ROBINSON, WILLIAM J., health facility adminstrator; b. 1951. Controller Meml. Hosp., Worcester, Mass., 1972-82, Leonard Morse Hosp., Methuen, Mass., 1982-85, Valley Regional Health Sys., Inc., Methuen, Mass., 1985-88; treas. New England Daconess Hosp., Boston, 1988—. Office: Beth Israel Deaconess Med Ctr Stoneman Bldg # 203 330 Brookline Ave Boston MA 02215-5400

ROBINSON, WILLIAM P., academic administrator, consultant, speaker; b. Elmhurst, Ill., Sept. 30, 1949; s. Paul Frederick and Lillian (Horton) R.; m. Bonnie Van Laan, Aug. 10, 1974; children: Brenna Kay, Benjamin Paul, Bailley Kay. Student, Moody Bible Inst., Chgo., 1967-70; AB, U. No. Iowa, 1972; postgrad., Princeton (N.J.) Theol. Sem., 1972-73; MA, Wheaton Coll., 1975; PhD, U. Pitts., 1979. Assoc. minister First Presbyn. Ch., Pitts., 1975-77; instr. U. Pitts., 1977-79; asst. prof. sch. continuing studies Nat. Coll. Edn., Evanston, Ill., 1979-80, dean sch. continuing studies, 1980-84, sr. v.p., 1984-86; pres. Manchester Coll., North Manchester, Ind., 1986-93, Whitworth Coll., Spokane, Wash., 1993; bd. dirs. Coun. Indep. Colls., Ind. Colls. Wash., Whitworth Coll.; cons., speaker for U.S. corps. and svc. orgns. Bd. dirs. Wash. Friends of Higher Edn., Spokane Symphony; vol. various orgns., especially prion work and hunger projects. Recipient various acad. awards. Mem. Nat. Assn. Ind. Colls. and Univs., Coun. Ind. Colls., Spokane Country Club, Spokane Club. Presyterian. Avocation: sports. Home: 215 Hawthorne Rd Spokane WA 99218 Office: Whitworth Coll Office of Pres Spokane WA 99251*

ROBINSON, WILLIAM PHILIP, III, lawyer; b. Providence, Jan. 30, 1940; s. William Philip and Dorothy Frances (Hayes) R.; m. Marlene H. Zieky, Sept. 1, 1974; children: Jeffrey, Kevin, Courtney. BA, U. de Louvain, Belgium, 1962; MA, U. R.I., 1966; PhD, U. Conn., 1971; JD, Boston Coll., 1975. Bar: R.I. 1975, Mass. 1985, U.S. Ct. Appeals (1st cir.) 1977, U.S. Supreme Ct. 1989. Instr. U. Conn., Storrs, 1967-71; law clk. U.S. Ct. Appeals, Boston, 1975-77; assoc. Edwards & Angell, Providence, 1977-81, ptnr., 1981—; bd. trustees Providence Country Day Sch., East Providence, 1991—. Mem. East Greenwich Sch. Com., 1988-96, vice chmn., 1990-94; mem. exec. com. R.I. Assn. of Sch. Coms.; mem. East Greenwich Dem. Town Com., 1988—; mem. Fed. Bd. Bar Examiners, R.I., 1994—; mem. R.I. Jud. Performance Evaulation Com., 1993—. Mem. Boston Coll. Law Sch. Alumni Assn. (v.p. R.I. chpt. 1990-93, pres. 1993—), Order of Coif, Phi Beta Kappa. Democrat. Roman Catholic. Avocations: reading, skiing, golf. Office: Edwards & Angell 2700 Hospital Trust Tower Providence RI 02903

ROBINSON, WILLIAM WHEELER, editor; b. Elizabeth, N.J., Oct. 4, 1918; s. Henry Pearson and Clare Stearns (Wheeler) R.; m. Jane Dimock, Feb. 27, 1942 (dec. 1997); children: William Wheeler Jr., Martha Robinson Bliss, Alice. B.A., Princeton U., 1939. Traffic rep., traffic dept. Eastern Airlines, N.Y.C., 1939-41; mgr. pub. relations Elco Yacht Div., Bayonne, N.J., 1945-47; sportswriter Newark Evening News, 1947-55; sportswriter, syndicated columnist Newark Star-Ledger, 1955-57; assoc. editor Yachting Mag., N.Y.C., 1957-67; editor, exec. v.p. Yachting Mag., 1967-78, editor-at-large, 1979-86; editor-at-large Cruising World Mag., 1987—; mem. exec. bd. Sea Ventures, Ft. Hancock, N.J., 1974-77; writer radio, TV shows on boating; freelance writer. Author: The Science of Sailing, 1960, New Boat, 1961, A Berth to Bermuda, 1961, Where the Trade Winds Blow, 1963, Expert Sailing, 1965, Over the Horizon, 1966, The World of Yachting, 1966, Better Sailing for Boys and Girls, 1968, (with H.L. Stone) The America's Cup Races, 1970, Legendary Yachts, 1971, rev., 1978, The Sailing Life, 1974, Right Boat For You, 1974, Great American Yacht Designers, 1974, America's Sailing Book, 1976, A Sailor's Tales, 1978, Cruising, the Boats and the Places, 1981, South to the Caribbean, 1981, Where to Cruise, 1984, Islands, 1985, Caribbean Cruising Handbook, 1986, 80 Years of Yachting, 1987, Cruising the Easy Way, 1990, Best Sailing Spots Worldwide, 1991, Destruction at Noonday, 1992, The Sailing Mystique, 1994, A Winter in the Sun, 1995; contbr. numerous articles to profl. jours. Vice pres. Rumson (N.J.) Community Appeal, 1952; mem. Rumson-Fair Haven (N.J.) Regional Bd. Edn., 1955-60, Rumson Environ. Commn., 1973-77. Served with USNR, 1941-45. Decorated Bronze Star with gold star. Mem. Met. Squash Racquets Assn. (v.p. 1973-75), Cruising Club Am. (historian 1972-77), Corinthians (master afterguard 1951-52). Clubs: Princeton of N.Y. (pres. 1984-87), N.Y. Yacht. Avocation: squash. Home: 14 Oyster Bay Dr Rumson NJ 07760-1822 *The key to a "good life" is to enjoy going to work each morning and to enjoy coming home in the evening. Combining vacation and avocation is extremely rewarding, and there is great satisfaction in the list of books that resulted.*

ROBINSON, ZELIG, lawyer; b. Balt., July 7, 1934; s. Morton Matthew and Mary (Ackerman) R.; m. Karen Ann Bergstrom (div. Oct. 1987); children: John, Christopher, Kristin; m. Linda Portner Strangmann, Dec. 23, 1987. BA, Johns Hopkins U., 1954; LLB, Harvard U., 1957. Bar: Md. 1958. Legis. analyst Md. House of Dels., Annapolis, 1958; tech. asst. IRS, Washington, 1958-60; pvt. practice Balt., 1960-62; assoc. gen. counsel commerce com. U.S. Ho. of Reps., Washington, 1962-64; assoc. Weinberg & Green, Balt., 1964-66; special legal cons. commerce com. U.S. Ho. of Reps., Washington, 1966-68; pvt. practice Balt., 1966-72; mem. Gordon, Feinblatt, Rothman, Hoffberger & Hollander, LLC, 1972—; bd. dirs. Durapak Mfg. Co., Balt., Vac Pac, Inc., Balt., Universal Die Casting Co., Inc., Saline, Mich.; chmn. Md. Pub. Broadcasting, 1991-95; mem. Gov.'s Commn. to revise Md. Code, Annapolis, 1968-89. Contbr. articles to profl. jours. Bd. dirs., v.p./sec. Gov.'s Mansion Found., Annapolis, Md.; v.p. bd. dirs. Md. Cmtys. and Citizens Fund, Chestertown, Md.; sec. bd. dirs. William Donald Schaefer Civic Fund; bd. dirs. Md. Arts Pl., Balt.; mem. Found. for Md. Pub. Broadcasting. With U.S. Army, 1958. Mem. ABA, Md. State Bar Assn. (laws com., internat. law com.). Democrat. Office: Gordon Feinblatt Rothman Hoffberger & Hollander LLC 233 E Redwood St Baltimore MD 21202-3306

ROBINSON-PETERSEN, CAROLE ANN, insurance executive, retired; b. Omaha, Dec. 21, 1935; d. Harry B. and Mildred (Daley) Baker; widowed Mar. 1989; 1 child, Pamela Fleming. Clk. Blue Cross/Blue Shield Colo., Denver, 1969-70; mgr. Blue Cross/Blue Shield Colo., 1970-72, asst. to treas., 1972-74, dir., 1974-79, treas., 1980-86, sr. v.p., treas., 1986-90; v.p., treas., chief investment officer Rocky Mountain Health Care (Holding Co.), Denver, 1991-93, sr. v.p., chief investment officer, CFO, 1986-93; ret., 1993; bd. dirs. Denver, Colo. Compensation Ins. Authority, Denver, Combined Health Appeal, Denver. Mem. investment com. City and County of Denver, 1988. Mem. Colo. Cash. Mgmt. Assn., Nat. Cash Mgmt. Assn., Life Office Mgmt. Assn. (treasury ops. com. 1985-93). Republican. Avocations: cooking, entertaining, gardening, reading. Office: Rocky Mountain Health Care 700 Broadway Ste 990 Denver CO 80203-3421

ROBISON, ANDREW CLIFFE, JR., museum curator; b. Memphis, May 23, 1940; s. Andrew Cliffe and Elfrieda (Barnes) R.; 1 child, Claire Catherine. A.B., Princeton U., 1962, Ph.D., 1974; B.A. (Marshall scholar), Oxford U., 1965, M.A., 1968. Instr. philosophy U. Ill., 1970-73, asst. prof. philosophy, 1973-75; curator, head dept. prints and drawings Nat. Gallery Art, Washington, 1974—, sr. curator, 1983-91, Andrew W. Mellon sr. curator, 1991—; Fulbright research scholar, India, 1965-66. Author: Giovanni Battista Piranesi: Prolegomena to the Princeton Collections, 1970, Paper in Prints, 1977, Master Drawings, 1978, Giovanni Battista Piranesi: The Early Architectural Fantasies, 1978, The Museum Curator and Fine Prints: Past, Present and Future, 1984, German Expressionist Prints from the Collection of Ruth and Jacob Kainen, 1985, Piranesi: Early Architectural Fantasies: A Catalogue Raisonné of the Etchings, 1986, Dürer to Diebenkorn, 1992, The Glory of Venice, 1994; contbr. articles and revs. to lit. Danforth fellow, 1966-70. Mem. Print Council Am. (pres. 1975-81), Master Drawings Assn. (internat. editorial adv. bd. 1981—), Drawing Soc. (bd. dirs. 1984—), Internat. Adv. Com. of Keepers of Pub. Collections of Graphic Art (pres. 1984-88), Ateneo Veneto, Phi Beta Kappa. Club: Grolier. Office: Nat Gallery of Art Washington DC 20565

ROBISON, BARBARA ANN, retired newspaper editor; b. Portland, Oreg., July 15, 1933; d. Louis Keith and Marjorie (Work) R.; 1 child, Nancy Fisher. Student, Coll. Idaho, 1951-54, U. Utah, 1968-70. Reporter Caldwell (Idaho) News Tribune, 1951-54; sports editor LaGrande (Oreg.) Evening-Observer, 1954-55; reporter Idaho Daily Statesman, Boise, 1955-57; asst. women's editor Tacoma (Wash.) News Tribune, 1958-59; lifestyle editor Salt Lake Tribune, 1967-93. Episcopalian. Avocations: reading, walking, animals. Home: 4210 Caroleen Way Salt Lake City UT 84124-2507

ROBISON, CLARENCE, JR., surgeon; b. Tecumseh, Okla., Dec. 9, 1924; s. Clarence Sr. and Margaret Irene (Buzzard) R.; m. Patricia Antoinette Hagee, May 27, 1951; children: Timothy D., Paul D., John D., Rebecca A. AS, Stanford U., 1943; MD, U. Okla., 1948. Intern Good Samaritan Hosp., Portland, Oreg., 1948-49; fellow pathology and oncology U. Okla., 1949-51; pathologist USAF Hosp., Cheyenne, Wyo., 1951-53; resident in surgery Okla. U. Health Scis.-Va. Svc., Oklahoma City, 1953-56; mem. faculty surgery dept. Okla. U. Health Scis., Oklahoma City, 1956-57, clin. prof. surgery, 1957—; mem. bd. advisors Mercy Health Ctr., Oklahoma City, 1974-81, sec. of staff, 1974-84, chief surgery, 1992-95; bd. dirs. Okla. Found. for Quality Assurance, Oklahoma City. Mem. Commn. on Mission Indian Nations Presbytery, 1980-91; bd. dirs. Found. Sr. Citizens, 1964—; elder Presbyn. Ch.; presdl. elector Dem. Party, 1960. Capt. USAF, 1951-53. Fellow ACS, Southwestern Surg. Soc., Am. Cancer Soc. (past pres. Okla. divsn., exec. com., bd. dirs., nat. del. dir.); mem. AMA (del. organized med. staff sect. Oklahoma City 1989—, alt. del. AMA from Okla. 1991-93, 96—), SAR, Oklahoma County Med. Soc. (bd. dirs. 1989-93), Okla. State Med. Assn. (alt. trustee Okla. 1989-92, trustee 1993-96), Okla. Surg. Assn. (sec., treas. 1966-68), Oklahoma City Surg. Soc. (pres. 1967-69), Oak Tree Sportsman's Club, Petroleum Club, Men's Dinner Club, Masons (32d degree), Shriners, Knights Templar. Office: 4200 W Memorial Rd Ste 805 Oklahoma City OK 73120-8305

ROBISON, FREDERICK MASON, financial executive; b. Danville, Ill., May 30, 1934; s. Frederick A. and Katherine L. (Mason) R.; m. Nancy Jane Potter, Aug. 18, 1956; children: Frederick B., Christopher M. BS, U. Ill., 1956, JD, 1959. Tax mgr. Arthur Andersen & Co., Chgo., 1959-65; treas.

Warnaco, Inc., Bridgeport, Conn., 1965-76; v.p. Emery Air Freight, Wilton, Conn., 1976-86, treas., 1976-79, sec., 1979-82, controller, 1979-86; v.p., controller Burlington Air Express, Irvine, Calif., 1986-88; sr. v.p. fin., chief fin. officer Sebastain Internat., Inc., Woodland Hills, Calif., 1988-96. Vice chmn. Town Council, Monroe, Conn., 1971-73, mem., 1969-73, bd. edn., Monroe, 1973-79, chmn., 1975-79. Mem. Fin. Execs. Inst. (dir. So. Conn. chpt. 1973-83, pres. 1977-78). Republican. Congregationalist. Home: 935 Triunfo Canyon Rd Westlake Village CA 91361-1826

ROBISON, JAMES EVERETT, management consulting company executive; b. Alfred, N.D., Nov. 22, 1915; s. John J. and Myrtle (Klundt) R.; m. Jeanette Hoffman, June 6, 1942 (dec.); 1 child, Martha Ann Davies. A.B., U. Minn., 1938; M.B.A., Harvard U., 1940; Sc. D. (hon.), Suffolk U., 1968. Salesman Nashua Mfg. Co., N.Y.C., 1940-41, Textron, Inc., N.Y.C., 1947-53; chief textile br. OPS, Washington, 1951; pres., chief exec. officer, dir. Indian Head, Inc., N.Y.C., 1953-67; chmn. bd., chief exec. officer Indian Head, Inc., 1967-72, chmn. fin. com., 1971-75; pres. Lonsdale Enterprises, Inc., 1975—. Mem. com. univ. resources Harvard U., 1966-69, mem. vis. com. Grad. Sch. Bus. Adminstrn., 1966-72, 73-79; chmn. bd. Assocs. Harvard Bus. Sch., 1968-70, bd. dirs., 1988-92; trustee Air Force Aid Soc., 1968-94, mem. fin. com., 1969-94; bd. dirs. Bus. Com. for Arts, 1973-80; trustee Com. Econ. Devel., 1965-74, Calif. Inst. Tech., 1970—; vice chmn. president's coun. U. Vt. Sch. Bus., 1982-89. Maj. USAAF, 1942-46. Decorated D.F.C., Air Medal with three oak leaf clusters; recipient Distinguished Service award Harvard Bus. Sch. Assn., 1969; Outstanding Alumni award U. Minn., 1974. Mem. Conf. Bd., Am. Textile Mfrs. Inst. (bd. dirs. 1961-64), Harvard Bus. Sch. Assn., Soaring Soc. Am., U.S. C. of C., Air Force Res. Assn., Harvard Club, Harvard Bus. Sch. Club Greater N.Y. (past bd. dirs., pres. 1967-68), Stanwich Club (Greenwich, Conn.), Bedford Golf and Tennis Club (N.Y.), Lyford Cay Club (Bahamas), Phi Delta Theta. Avocations: golf, skiing, soaring.

ROBISON, PAULA JUDITH, flutist; b. Nashville, June 8, 1941; d. David Victor and Naomi Florence R.; m. Scott Nickrenz; Dec. 29, 1971; 1 child, Elizabeth Hadley Amadea Nickrenz. Student, U. So. Calif., 1958-60; B.S., Juilliard Sch. Music, 1963. Founding artist, player Chamber Music Soc., N.Y.C., 1970-90, NY ChôroBand, 1994; co-dir. chamber music Spoleto Festival, Charleston, S.C., 1978-88; Filene artist-in-residence Skidmore Coll., Saratoga Springs, N.Y., 1988-89; mem. faculty New Eng. Conservatory Music, 1991—; co-dir. (with Leon Kirchner) Gardner Chamber Orch., Boston, 1995—. Soloist with various major orchs., including N.Y. Philharm., London Symphony Orch.; player, presenter Concerti di Mezzogiorno, Spoleto (Italy) Festival, 1970—; commd. flute concertos by Leon Kirchner, Toru Takemitsu, Oliver Knussen, Robert Beaser, Kenneth Frazelle; premiered works by Pierre Boulez, Elliott Carter, William Schuman, Thea Musgrave, Carla Bley; author: The Paula Robison Flute Warmups Book, 1989, The Andersen Collection, 1994, Paula Robison Masterclass: Paul Hindemith, 1995, The Sidney Lanier Collection, 1997; recos. on CBS Masterworks, Music Masters, Vanguard Classics, New World Records, Omega, Arabesque, Sony Classical, King Recs., Mode Recs. Recipient First prize Geneva Internat. Competition, 1966, Adelaide Ristori prize, 1987; named Musician of Month, Musical Am., 1979, House Musician for Isamu Noguchi Garden Mus., N.Y.C., 1988; Martha Baird Rockefeller grantee, 1966; Nat. Endowment for Arts grantee, 1978, 86; Fromm Found. grantee, 1980; Housewright Eminent scholar Fla. State U., 1990-91. Mem. Sigma Alpha Iota (hon.). Office: care Matthew Sprizzo 477 Durant Ave Staten Island NY 10308-3006

ROBISON, RICHARD EUGENE, architect; b. Wichita, Kans., Oct. 30, 1951; s. Robert Dale and Corene (Tiffany) R.; m. Manola Cristina Gomez Pantoja, Dec. 20, 1975; children: Amy Elizabeth, Harriet Paige. Student, Baker U., 1969-71; B Environ. Design, U. Kans., 1974. Lic. profl. architect, Kans.; cert. constrn. specifier. Architect U.S. Peace Corps, Khouribga, Morrocco, 1974-75, OFESUR, Valencia, Venezuela, 1975-78; instr. U. Carabobo, Valencia, 1979-80; architect, ptnr. R.G. Asessores SRL, Valencia, 1978-83; architect Van Doren-Hazard-Stallings, Inc., Topeka, 1983-87, Heery Internat., Inc., Atlanta, 1987-92; architect Lord, Aeck, and Sargent, Inc., Atlanta, 1992-94, prin., 1994—; instr. So. Coll. Tech., 1992. Co-author automated specifications writing system Sweet Spec, 1989, Spec System, 1990. Mem. AIA, Constrn. Specifications Inst. Avocations: music, theater. Home: 7484 Waters Edge Dr Stone Mountain GA 30087-6132 Office: Lord Aeck and Sargent Inc 1201 Peachtree St NE 400 Colony Sq NE Ste 300 Atlanta GA 30361-6303

ROBISON, SUSAN MILLER, psychologist, educator, consultant; b. Chgo., Nov. 15, 1945; d. William Louis and Constance Mary (Maloney) Miller; m. Philip Dean Robison, Dec. 27, 1969; 1 child, Christine Alyssa. BS, Loyola U., Chgo., 1967; MS, Ohio U., 1969, PhD, 1971. Lic. psychologist, Md. Asst. prof. psychology Ohio U., Lancaster, 1970-72; prof. psychology Coll. Notre Dame, Balt., 1972—; pvt. practice Ellicott City, Md., 1982—; leadership cons. Nat. Coun. Cath. Women, Washington, 1987—. Author: Sharing Our Gifts, 1987, 2d edit., 1992, Discovering Our Gifts, 1989, Thinking and Writing in College, 1991. Troop leader Girl Scouts U.S.A., Ellicott City, 1982-85, mem. adv. bd. Girl Scouts Central Md., 1987-88; mem. adv. bd. Archdiocese of Balt., 1986. Mem. Am. Psychol. Assn., Am. Assn. Sex Educators, Counselors and Therapists, Assn. for Advancement Behavior Therapy. Avocations: writing, skiing, dancing, jogging, sewing. Home: 3725 Font Hill Dr Ellicott City MD 21042-4932

ROBITAILLE, LUC, professional hockey player; b. Montreal, P.Q., Can., Feb. 17, 1966. With Hull Olympiques Major Jr. Hockey League, Que., 1983-84, L.A. Kings, 1984-94, Pitts. Penguins, 1994-95, N.Y. Rangers, 1995; scored winning goal for nat. team of Can. at 1994 World Hockey Championship. Recipient Guy LaFleur trophy, 1985-86, Can. Hockey Player of Yr. award, 1985-86, Calder Meml. trophy, NHL Rookie of Yr., 1986-87; named to NHL All-Star team, 1987, 88, 90-91, 92-93. Office: NY Rangers 4 Pennsylvania Plz New York NY 10001*

ROBLIN, DUFF, former Canadian senator, health facility administrator; b. Winnipeg, Man., Can., June 17, 1917; s. C.D. and Sophia May (Murdoch) R.; m. Mary Linda MacKay, Aug. 30, 1958; children—Andrew, Jennifer. Student, St. John's Coll. Sch., U. Chgo.; LL.D., McGill U., Man. U., Winnipeg U. Mem. Man. Legislature, Can., 1949-68, premier, 1958-67, sworn to privy council, 1967; appointed companion Order of Can., 1970; senator Can. Parliament, 1978-82, dep. leader opposition, 1980-84, leader of Govt. in Senate, 1984-86; pres. Canadian Pacific Investments Ltd., 1970-75. Progressive Conservative. Anglican. Office: 977 Century St, Winnipeg, MB Canada R3H 0W4*

ROBOCK, STEFAN HYMAN, economics educator emeritus; b. Redgranite, Wis., July 31, 1915; s. Samuel and Elizabeth (Kushner) R.; m. Shirley Bernstein, June 17, 1946 (div. Mar. 1980); children: Alan David, Jerry, Lisa (Mrs. Stephen Shaffer). B.A., U. Wis., 1938; M.A. (Adminstrn. fellow), Harvard U., 1941, Ph.D., 1948; Prof. Honoris Causa, U. Recife, Brazil, 1956; M. Honoris Causa, E.S.T.E., San Sebastian, Spain, 1974. Economist Nat. Resources Planning Bd., Washington, 1940-41; antitrust div. U.S. Dept. Justice, Washington, 1941-42, Boston, 1948-49; chief economist TVA, Knoxville, 1949-54; devel. adviser UN, Brazil, 1954-56; tech. asst. missions UN, Chile, 1955; Colombia, 1956; with Midwest Rsch. Inst., 1956-58; mem. Com. Econ. Devel., 1958-60; prof. internat. bus. Ind. U., Bloomington, 1960-67; R.D. Calkins prof. internat. bus. Columbia U., N.Y.C., 1967-84, prof. emeritus, 1984—; internat. economist Dept. Commerce, 1975-76; trustee Inst. Current World Affairs, 1981-86; cons. fgn. countries, 1959—; bd. dirs. Econs. Inst., Boulder, Colo., 1984-89; adv. bd. World Trade Inst., 1974-95; mem. bd. sci. and tech. NAS, 1969-72; vis. prof. Beijing Mgmt. Inst., 1985, U. Internat. Bus. and Econ., Beijing, 1989, Internat. Mgmt. Ctr., Budapest, Hungary, 1992. Author: Brazil's Developing Northeast, 1963, Brazil: A Study in Development Progress, 1975, International Business and Multinational Enterprises, 4th edit., 1989; Editorial bd.: Columbia Jour. World Bus, 1975-85. Served with USNR, 1942-46. Mem. Soc. Internat. Devel. (mem. council 1966-69), Am. Econ. Assn., Acad. Internat. Bus. (v.p. 1983-85), Phi Kappa Phi, Beta Gamma Sigma, Phi Eta Sigma. Club: Columbia Tennis. Home: 560 Riverside Dr Apt 21J New York NY 10027-3237

ROBOL, RICHARD THOMAS, lawyer; b. Norfolk, Va., Feb. 8, 1952; s. Harry James and Lucy Henley (Johnson) R.; m. Melissa Janet Sengstack, June 3, 1978; children: Thomas Coke, Robert Talbot, Charles Taliaferro. BA, U. Va., 1974; JD, Harvard U., 1978. Bar: Va. 1979, Ohio 1996, U.S. Dist. Ct. (ea. dist.) Va. 1979, U.S. Ct. Appeals (4th cir.) 1979, U.S. Dist. Ct. (we. dist.) Va. 1981, U.S. Supreme Ct. 1982, D.C. 1991, U.S. Ct. Appeals (6th and 9th cirs.) 1995. Law clk. to presiding justice U.S. Dist. Ct. (ea. dist.) Va., 1978-79; ptnr. Seawell, Dalton, Hughes & Timms, Norfolk, 1979-87, Hunton and Williams, Norfolk, 1987-92; exec. v.p., gen. counsel Columbus Am. Discovery Group, Inc., 1992—; pro bono counsel Nat. Commn. for Prevention Child Abuse, Norfolk, 1983, Tidewater Profl. Assn. on Child Abuse, 1983, Parents United Va., 1981-82, Sexual Abuse Help Line, 1983-86; mem. Boyd-Graves Conf. on Civil Procedure in Va., 1981-87. Contbr. articles to law revs.; contbg. editor: International Law for General Practitioners, 1981. Bd. dirs. Va. Opera Assn. Guild, Norfolk, 1983-87, Tidewater br. NCCJ, 1991-92; deacon Ctrl. Bapt. Ch., Norfolk, 1980-83. Capt. USAR, 1992—. Fulbright scholar, 1974. Mem. Va. State Bar Assn. (bd. dirs. internat. law sect. 1984-87, chmn. 1982-83), Va. Young Lawyers Assn. (cir. rep. 1984-88), Va. Assn. Def. Attys., Maritime Law Assn., Norfolk-Portsmouth Bar assn. (chmn. speakers bur. 1987-88), Assn. Def. Trial Attys. (chmn. Va. 1987), Def. Rsch. Inst., 1982-88. Avocations: camping, rowing, scuba diving. Home: 60 Kenyon Brook Dr Worthington OH 43085-3629 Office: Columbus Am Discovery Group 433 W 6th Ave Columbus OH 43201-3136

ROBOLD, ALICE ILENE, mathematician, educator; b. Delaware County, Ind., Feb. 7, 1928; d. Earl G. and Margaret Rebecca (Summers) Hensley; m. Virgil G. Robold, Aug. 21, 1955; 1 son, Edward Lynn. B.S., Ball State U., 1955, M.A., 1960, Ed.D., 1965. Substitute elem. tchr. Am. Elem. Sch., Augsburg, Germany, 1955-56; instr. Ball State U., Muncie, Ind., 1960-61; teaching fellow Ball State U., 1961-64, asst. prof. math. scis., 1964-69, assoc. prof., 1969-76, prof., 1976—. Mem. Nat. Coun. Tchrs. Math., Ind. Coun. Tchrs. Math., Sch. Sci. and Math. Assn., Pi Lambda Theta. Mem. Ch. of God. Office: Ball State U Dept Math Scis Muncie IN 47306

ROBRENO, EDUARDO C., federal judge; b. 1945. BA, Westfield State Coll., 1967; MA, U. Mass., 1969; JD, Rutgers U., 1978. With antitrust divsn. U.S. Dept Justice, Phila., 1978-81; ptnr. Meltzer & Schiffrin, Phila., 1981-86, Fox, Rothschild, O'Brien & Frankel, Phila., 1987-92; judge U.S. Dist. Ct. for Ea. Dist. Pa., Phila., 1992—; mem. Jud. Conf. Com. on Bankruptcy Rules. Fellow Am. Bar Found., Am. Law Inst. Office: US Courthouse Rm 3810 Philadelphia PA 19106

ROBSON, DONALD, physics educator; b. Leeds, Eng., Mar. 19, 1937; came to U.S., 1963; s. Albert and Rose Hannah (Parbutt) R.; m. Joy Olivia Burkitt Findlay, Aug. 1960 (div. May 1971); children: Donald Peter, David Ian, Karen Joy; m. Martha Breitenlohner, Aug. 26, 1971. BSc, U. Melbourne, Australia, 1959, MSc, 1961, PhD, 1963. Rsch. assoc. Fla. State U., Tallahassee, 1963-64, asst. prof. physics, 1964-65, assoc. prof., 1965-67, prof., 1967—, chmn. dept. physics, 1985-91, Disting. prof., 1990—. Editor: (with J.D. Fox) Isobaric Spin in Nuclear Physics, 1966, Nuclear Analogue States, 1976; assoc. editor Nuclear Physics A., 1972-96; contbr. more than 100 articles to profl. jours. Chmn. bd. trustees Southeastern Univ. Rsch. Assn., 1996—. Fulbright scholar, 1963-64; A.P. Sloan fellow, 1966-67; Alexander Von Humboldt sr. scientist, 1976-77. Fellow Am. Phys. Soc. (co-recipient Tom W. Bonner prize 1972). Avocations: chess, golf, running. Office: Fla State U Dept Physics Tallahassee FL 32306

ROBSON, JOHN MERRITT, library and media administrator; b. Gordon, Nebr., Sept. 22, 1930; s. John Wesley Robson and Martha Mildred (Shook) Belknap; m. Kathryn Mae Baker, Aug. 26, 1951; children: Deborah Dawn, Diana Lynn, Denise Anne. BS in Edn., U. Nebr., 1953; MA in Librarianship, Denver U., 1959. Ordained deacon Episc. Ch., 1991. Ref. asst. Lincoln (Nebr.) City Librs., 1957-58; ref. and inter libr. loan Denver U. Libr., 1958-59; cataloger humanities USAF Acad. Libr., Colo., 1959-61; cataloger St. Cloud (Minn.) U., 1961-63, acquisitions libr., 1963-66; libr. dir. Southwest State U., Marshall, Minn., 1966-71, dir. media svcs., 1971-81; head libr., prof. libr. and instructional tech. Nebr. Wesleyan U., Lincoln, 1981-91, dir. media svcs., 1991-95; ret., 1995; mem. S.E. Nebr. Regional Libr. Bd., Lincoln, 1983-84; steward teamsters Faculty /Adminstrv. Bargaining Unit, Marshall, 1977-78. Author: Index to Publications of the Hakluyt Society, 1963; contbr. articles to profl. jours. Mem. gov's. task force on librs. State of Minn., St. Paul, 1973. Mem. Nebr. Libr. Assn. (Mentor of Yr. 1989), Nebr. Ednl. Media Assn. (conv. planning com. 1984—), Nebr. Assn. for Ednl. Data Processing. Avocations: stained glass, wood working, photography. Home: 1620 Atlas Ave Lincoln NE 68521-1654

ROBSON, MARIAN LORRAINE, Canadian federal official. BA in English, U. Saskatchewan, Can., 1964; postgrad. in Polit. Sci., U. B.C., Can., 1965-67, U. Saskatchewan, 1965-67. Spl. asst. to Hon. Otto Lang Transport Can., 1970's; corp. sec. B.C. Railway, 1977-80; chmn. Vancouver Port Corp., 1983-84; dir. Can. Ports Corp., 1983-84; trans. and econ. devel. cons., 1984-89; mgr. pub. affairs CN Rail B.C., 1990-93; dir. Cascadia Inst., 1993-94; v.p. Hill and Knowlton, 1994-95; mem. Nat. Transp. Agy., Vancouver, B.C., Can., 1995-96; chm. Canadian TransportationAgy., Ottwa, O.N., Can., 1996—.

ROBSON, MARTIN CECIL, surgery educator, plastic surgeon; b. Lancaster, Ohio, Mar. 8, 1939; children: Karen Iredell, Douglas Spears, Martin Cecil III. Student, Northwestern U., 1957-59; B.A., Johns Hopkins U., 1961, M.D., 1964. Diplomate Am. Bd. Surgery, Am. Bd. Plastic Surgery (chmn. 1996-97). Intern U. Chgo. Hosps. and Clinics, 1964-65; resident in surgery Balt. City Hosp., 1965-67, Brooke Gen. Hosp., Ft. Sam Houston, Tex., 1967-69; resident in plastic surgery Yale-New Haven Hosp., 1971-73; instr. dept. surgery Yale U. Sch. Medicine, New Haven, 1973-74, asst. prof. plastic surgery, 1973-74, assoc. prof., 1974; assoc. prof., chief plastic surgery U. Chgo., 1974-77, prof. and chief plastic surgery, 1977-83, dir. Burn Center, 1976-83; prof., chmn. divsn. plastic and reconstructive surgery Wayne State U., Detroit, 1983-88; dir. Detroit Med. Ctr. Burn Ctr., 1983-88; Truman Blocker Disting. prof., chief divsn. plastic surgery U. Tex. Med. Br., 1988-93; dir. surg. svcs. Shriners' Burn Inst., Galveston, Tex., 1988-93; prof. surgery, chair divsn. surg. rsch. U. South Fla., Tampa, 1993—; chair surg. svc. Bay Pines (Fla.) VA Med. Ctr., 1993—. Mem. editl. bd. Jour. Burn Care and Rehab.; editl. cons. bd.: Jour. Trauma. Served to maj. M.C. U.S. Army, 1967-71; col. USAR Med. Corps, 1991—. Fellow ACS, Royal Australian Coll. Surgeons (hon.); mem. Plastic Surgery Rsch. Coun. (chmn. 1983-84), Am. Burn Assn. (pres. 1985-86, Disting. Svc. award), Am. Surg. Assn., Am. Assn. Plastic Surgery, Am. Soc. Plastic and Reconstructive Surgeons (chmn. residency rev. com. for plastic surgery 1993-95), Nu Sigma Nu, Phi Delta Theta, Alpha Omega Alpha. Office: Bay Pines VA Med Ctr Bay Pines FL 33504

ROBY, JASPER, bishop. Sr. bishop, exec. head Apostolic Overcoming Holy Ch. of God, Inc., Birmingham, Ala. Office: Apostolic Overcoming Holy Church God Inc 1120 24th St N Birmingham AL 35234-3131

ROBY, REGINALD HENRY, professional football player; b. Waterloo, Iowa, July 30, 1961. Student, U. Iowa. With Miami (Fla.) Dolphins, 1983-92, Washington Redskins, 1993-94; punter Tampa Bay (Fla.) Buccaneers, 1995-96; now with Houston Oilers. Named to The Sporting News NFL All-Pro Team, 1984, 94; selected to Pro Bowl, 1984, 89, 94. Achievements include leading NFL in net punting average, 1984, 86. Office: Houston Oilers 8030 El Rio Houston TX 77054*

ROCCO, DOMENIC PATRICK, JR., trust company executive, retired army officer; b. Bakerton, Pa., Mar. 17, 1937; s. Domenic Joseph and Nancy Marie (Gemus) R.; divorced; children: David M., Domenic Rocci III (dec.). Commd. 2d. lt. U.S. Army, 1963, advanced through grades to brig. gen., 1987-86; asst. divsn. comdr. 1st Armoured Divsn. and Cmty. Comdr. U.S. Army, Bamberg, Germany, 1987; dep. comdg. gen. U.S. Army Tng. Ctr. U.S. Army, Ft. Dix, N.J., 1989; command dir. N.Am. Aerospace Def. Command U.S. Army, Colorado Springs, Colo., 1984; inspector gen. 7th Army U.S. Army, Heidelberg, Germany, 1976; exec. officer to Comdr. in Chief UN Command U.S. Army, 1970; dep. dir. Combined Mil. Interrogation Ctr. U.S. Army, Vietnam; ret. U.S. Army, 1990; pres., CEO First Commonwealth Trust Co., Indiana, Pa., 1990—. Commr. Southwestern Pa. Heritage Preservation Commn.; bd. dirs., mem. exec. com., chmn. strategic planning com. Found. of Indiana U. of Pa.; vol. cons. Jr. Achievement, S.W. Pa., chmn. fund dr., 1985-86; mem. adv. bd. Indiana chpt. ARC; mem. com. Indiana County Heritage Preservation Com.; bd. dirs. Indiana Hosp., Indiana County Devel. Corp.; mem. Greater Indiana Strategic Planning Study Commn.; mem. Senator Rich Santorum of Pa. Vet.'s Adv. Bd. Decorated Legion of Merit with 3 oak leaf clusters, Bronze Star, Purple Heart. Mem. Indiana C. of C. (chmn. bd. dirs.), Indiana Country Club (sec.-treas. bd. govs.). Home: 90 Byrons Place Indiana PA 15701 Office: 614 Philadelphia St Indiana PA 15701-3904

ROCCO, RON, artist; b. Ft. Hood, Tex., Nov. 21, 1953; s. Raymond Anthony and Dorothy Ann (D'Angelo) R. Student, Fordham U., 1972; BFA, SUNY, Purchase, 1976; MS in Visual Studies, MIT Ctr. for Advanced Visual Studies, 1983. Artist-in-residence Exptl. TV Ctr., Owego, N.Y., 1982-87; guest lectr., artist-in-residence The Banff (Alta., Can.) Ctr., 1987; artist-in-residence Kunstlerhaus Bethanian, Berlin, 1991; artist-in-residence inter. studio program Kunst and Complex, Rotterdam, Netherlands, 1993; guest lectr. various univs., 1977-90; mem. UN Internat. Conf. on Communication Tech. and Traditional Cultures, N.Y.C., 1983, Art Corp. Am., N.Y.C., 1979-81. Performance at The Solomon R. Guggenheim Mus., N.Y.C., 1983; works exhibited: UN Comm. Ctr. of Population Inst., N.Y.C., 1983, The Asia Soc., N.Y.C., 1985, Internat. Exhibit of Computer Art Forms, Kortijk, Belgium, 1986, P.S.1/Inst. for Art and Urban Resources, N.Y.C., 1987, Found. Artgarden, Amsterdam, The Netherlands, 1989, The Katonah (N.Y.) Mus. Art, 1990, The Bklyn. Mus., 1990, Fundacao Rocha, Fortalesca, Brazil, 1991, Kunstlerhaus Bethanien, Berlin, 1991, Amerika Haus, Berlin, 1992, Rotunda Gallery, N.Y.C., 1996; artistic dir. Laser Sculpture/Dance, 1981; producer, dir. Zaroff's Tale, 1983 (N.Y. State Coun. on Arts grantee); co-dir., collaborator Buddah Meets Einstein at the Great Wall, 1985 (Nat. Endowment Arts award); collaborator, sculptor Light and Sound Sphere Study, 1986 (N.Y. State Coun. on Arts grantee). Founder, dir. Ithaca Artists Coop., 1977-80; pub. commns. Metro. Transit Authority, N.Y.C., project for Long Beach, L.I. LIRR station, 1996; N.J. Light Rail Project, West Ave. Station, 1997. Creative and Performing Arts Coun. grantee Cornell U., Ithaca, N.Y., 1977, expansion arts program grantee Nat. Endowment Arts, 1977-79; recipient Netherland-Am. Found. award, 1989, Art Matters award, 1989, N.Y. Found. for the Arts award, 1989, The Found. for Contemporary Performance Arts award, 1989. Mem. ACLU. Buddhist. Studio: 59 Harrison Ave Brooklyn NY 11211-8115

ROCEK, JAN, chemist, educator; b. Prague, Czech Republic, Mar. 24, 1924; came to U.S., 1960, naturalized, 1966; s. Hugo and Frida (Loebl) Robitschek; m. Eva Trojan, June 26, 1947; children: Martin, Thomas. M.S., Tech. U., Prague, 1949, Ph.D., 1953. Scientist Czechoslovak Acad. Sci., Prague, 1953-57; sr. scientist Czechoslovak Acad. Sci., 1957-60; vis. scientist U. Coll., London, 1958; research fellow Harvard U., 1960-62; asso. prof., then prof. Cath. U. Am., 1962-66; prof. chemistry U. Ill., Chgo., 1966-95; acting head dept. U. Ill., 1980-81, head dept., 1981-93; vice chancellor rsch., dean grad. coll. U. Ill., Chgo., 1993-95; acting dean Grad. Coll. U. Ill., 1969-70, dean Grad. Coll., 1970-79, asso. mem. Ctr. for Advanced Studies, 1968-69; ret., 1995; vis. scholar Stanford U., 1979-80, Cambridge U., 1980. Contbr. articles to profl. jours. Mem. Am. Chem. Soc., AAAS, Czechoslovak Soc. Arts and Scis. in Am., AAUP, Sigma Xi (pres. chpt. 1976-77, 85-86), Phi Kappa Phi. Home: 2636 Laurel Ln Wilmette IL 60091-2202

ROCHA, GUY LOUIS, archivist, historian; b. Long Beach, Calif., Sept. 23, 1951; s. Ernest Louis and Charlotte (Sobus) R. BA in Social Studies and Edn., Syracuse U., 1973; MA in Am. Studies, San Diego State U., 1975; postgrad., U. Nev., 1975—. Cert. archivist Am. Acad. Cert. Archivists. Tchr., Washoe County Sch. Dist., Reno, Nev., 1975-76; history instr. Western Nev. C.C., Carson City, 1976; curator manuscripts Nev. Hist. Soc., Reno, 1976-81, interim asst. dir., 1980, interim dir., 1980-81; state administr. archives and records Nev. State Libr. and Archives, Carson City, 1981—; hist. cons. Janus Assocs., Tempe, Ariz., 1980, Rainshadow Assocs., Carson City, 1983—; mem. State Bd. Geographic Names. Co-author The Ignoble Conspirancy: Radicalism on Trial in Nevada, 1986, The Earp's Last Frontier: Wyatt and Virgil Earp in Nevada 1902-1905, 1988; contbr. to book and govt. study; host weekly radio talk show Sta. KPTL, Carson City, 1988—; hist. cons. to film Las Vegas, 1996. Ex-officio mem. Nev. Commn. Bicentennial U.S. Constitution, 1986-91. Mem. Washoe Heritage Council, Reno, 1983-85; editorial bd. Nev. Hist. Soc., Reno, 1983—; mem. Washoe County Democratic Central Com., Reno, 1984-87. Mem. Conf. Intermountain Archivists (Council mem 1979-87, v.p. 1984-85, pres. 1985-86), No. Nev. Pub. Adminstrs. Group (pres. 1986-87), S.W. Labor Studies Assn., State Hist. Records Adv. Bd. (dep. coordinator 1984-86, coordinator 1986—), Westerners Internat. Nev. Corral (dep. sheriff 1980-81, sheriff 1984-85, mem. state coordinators steering com. 1985-87, vice chmn. 1986-87), Soc. Am. Archivists, Western History Assn., Nat. Assn. Govt. Archives and Records Adminstrs., Orgn. Am. Historians. Democrat. Home: 1824 Pyrenees St Carson City NV 89703-2331 Office: Nev State Libr & Archives 100 Stewart St Carson City NV 89710

ROCHA, MARILYN EVA, clinical psychologist; b. San Bernardino, Calif., Oct. 23, 1928; d. Howard Ray Gonding and Laura Anne (Johanson) Walker; m. Hilario Ursala Rocha, Mar. 25, 1948 (dec. Feb. 1971); children: Michael, Sherry, Teri, Denise. AA, Solano Jr. Coll., 1970. BA, Sacramento State U., 1973, MA, 1974; PhD, U.S. Internat. U., 1981. Psychologist, Naval Drug Rehab. Ctr., U.S. Navy, San Diego, 1975-85, chief psychologist, 1983-84; staff clin. psychologist Calif. Youth Authority No. Reception Ctr. Clinic, 1985-92, El Paso de Robles Sch., 1992—; dir. Self-Help Agys., San Diego. Author short story. Vol. counselor Hamonium, San Diego, 1976-77; SMRC Planning Group Scripps/Miramar Ranch, 1982-85; leader Vacaville council Cub Scouts Am., Calif., 1957-62, 4-H, also Brownie's. Recipient Outstanding Svc. award CYA, 1993, Woman of the Yr. award CYA, 1995. Mem. APA, PTA (hon., life), Calif. Scholastic Fedn., Am. Assn. Suicidology, Friends of the Libr. (sec.), Bus. and Profl. Women, Kiwanis Internat., Delta Zeta. Democrat. Unitarian. Home: Morning Glory Ranch 4625 Ross Dr Paso Robles CA 93446-9379

ROCHA, PEDRO, JR., academic administrator; b. Indé, México, Dec. 25, 1939; came to U.S., 1955; s. Pedro Sr. and Maria (Hernández) R.; m. Maria-Cruz Molina, Dec. 6, 1969; children: Diana-Marie, Delma-Irene, Pedro-Hugo. BA in History, U. Tex., El Paso, 1967, MA in Spanish, 1969; PhD in Edn. Adminstrn., U. Tex., 1981. Cert. secondary tchr., supr., adminstr., supt., Tex. Textbook adminstr. Ysleta Jr. High Sch., El Paso, 1976; secondary tchr. Ysleta Ind. Sch. Dist., El Paso, 1969-77; grad. student asst. U. Tex., El Paso, 1976-77; rsch. assoc. U. Tex., Austin, 1979-80; adminstrv. intern Austin (Tex.) C.C., 1978, substitute assoc. dean, 1981-83; rsch. intern S.W. Ednl. Devel. Lab., Austin, 1980-81; tax examiner div. clk. IRS, Austin, 1982; dir., coord. Cook Community Sch., Austin, 1982-85; from ESL instr. to dir., coord. Brooke Community Sch., Austin, 1985-86; dean Mesabi C.C., Virginia, Minn., 1987-92; v.p. for instrn. Trinidad (Colo.) State Jr. Coll., 1992-96; provost Union County Coll., Elizabeth, N.J., 1996—; instr. Spanish Vermilion C.C., Ely, Minn., 1990; adj. instr. Spanish Trinidad State Jr. coll., 1995, 96, Union County Coll., N.J., 1997—; cons.-evaluator for Commn. on Instns. of Higher Edn. of North Ctrl. Assn. Colls. and Schs.; cons. Raton (N.Mex.) Arts and Humanities Coun., 1993, U. Tex., Austin, 1982-86, Tex. Assn. Chicanos in Higher Edn., Denton, 1982, Mexican Am. Legal Def. & Edn. Fund, San Antonio, 1982, Intercultural Rsch., Inc., El Paso, 1981. Author: Staff Orientation Program: Welcoming the Employee to Our Team, (calendar) Historic Trinidad 1996: Hispanic Contributions to Las Animas County. Active mem., bd. dirs. So. Colo. Coal Miners Meml. and Scholarship Fund, 1994; pres. Marquette Sch. Bd., Virginia, 1991-92; active San Juan Coun. Cmty. Agencies, Farmington, 1986-87; leader Quarterly Dates Group, Farmington, 1986-87; adv. bd. Austin Cmty. Gardens, 1985-86. With USAF, 1961-65. Richardson fellow U. Tex., 1977-79; nominated and selected for Nat. Cmty. Coll. Hispanic Coun. Leadership Tng. Program for Hispanic C.C. Adminstrs., 1994. Mem. Am. Assn. for Higher Edn., Am. Assn. Cmty./Jr. Coll., Genealogical Soc. Hispanis Am., Minn. Chief Acad. Adminstrs., Colo. Coun. Acad. Deans and Vice Pres., Colo. Ednl. Svcs. Coun., Kiwanis Club (first v.p. Trinidad 1995), Hispanic C. of C. (bd. dirs. Trinidad-Las Animas County Hispanic C. of C., pres. 1995-96), Elizabeth C. of C., K.C. (mem. coun. 1072, 1995—), Rotary, Kappa Delta Pi, Sigma Delta Pi. Democrat. Roman Catholic. Avocations: bowling, basketball, walking, travel. Home: 330 Jerusalem Rd Scotch Plains NJ 07076-1437 Office: Union County Coll 12 W Jersey St Elizabeth NJ 07201-2314

ROCHBERG, GEORGE, composer, educator; b. Paterson, N.J., July 5, 1918; s. Morris and Anna (Hoffman) R.; m. Gene Rosenfeld, Aug. 18, 1941; children: Paul Bernard (dec.), Frances Ruth. BA, Montclair State Tchrs. Coll., 1939, LHD, 1962; BMus, Curtis Inst. Music, 1948; MA, U. Pa., 1949, MusD (hon.), 1988; MusD (hon.), Phila. Mus. Acad., 1964, Curtis Inst. Music, 1988. Mem. faculty Curtis Inst. Music, 1948-54; Fulbright fellow Am. Acad., Rome, 1950-51; editor, dir. publs. Theo. Presser Co., Bryn Mawr, Pa., 1951-60; chmn. Music dept. U. Pa., 1960-68; ret., 1983; Annenberg prof. humanities U. Pa., 1979. Commd. to compose ballet music for Anna Sokolov, Lincoln Center Fund, 1965; recordings include numerous others; (recipient Gershwin Meml. award 1952, Soc. for Publ. Am. Music award 1956, Koussevitzky commn. 1957, Naumberg Rec. award 1961); Composer: Symphony No. 1, 1948-49, Night Music, 1949, String Quartet No. 1, 1952, Serenata d Estate, 1955, Symphony No. 2, 1956, La Bocca della Verita, 1958, String Quartet No. 2, 1959-61, Blake Songs, 1961, Time-Span (II), 1962, Trio for Violin, Cello and Piano, 1963, Zodiac, 1964, Black Sounds, 1965, Contra Mortem et Tempus, 1965, Music for the Magic Theater, 1965, Symphony No. 3, 1969, Tableaux for chamber ensemble, 1968, String Quartet No. 3, 1972, Violin Concerto premiered by Isaac Stern, 1975, Piano Quintet (Nat. Endowment for Arts commn.), 1975, Symphony No. 4, 1976; monodrama Phaedra, 1976, String Quartet No. 4, 1979 (1st place Kennedy Center Friedheim award), The Confidence Man, an Opera, 1981, Piano Trio No. 2 (for Beaux Arts Trio), 1983, Symphony No. 5, Chgo. Symphony, 1986, Symphony No. 6, Pitts. Symphony, 1987, Muse of Fire for flute and guitar, 1989, Piano Trio No. 3 (for Beaux Arts Trio), 1991, Sonata for Violin and Piano, 1988, Sonata-aria for Cello and Piano, 1992, Concerto for Clarinet and Orchestra, 1994-95, Chromaticism: Symmetry in Atonal and Tonal Music, 1996, Circles of Fire for 2 Pianos, 1997. Served to 2d lt., inf. AUS, 1942-45, ETO. Decorated Purple Heart with cluster; gold medal in music Brandeis Creative Arts award, 1985; Nat. Inst. Arts and Letters grant, 1962; Fromm Found. commn., 1965; Guggenheim fellow, 1957, 1966-67; Nat. Endowment for Arts grantee, 1972-73. Mem. Am. Acad. Arts and Scis., Am. Musicological Soc., ASCAP, Am. Acad. Arts and Letters. *I have always clung fast to these fundamentals: that music was given man so he could express the best he was capable of; that the best he was capable of had to do with his deepest feelings; that his deepest feelings are rooted in what I believe to be a moral order in the universe which underlies all real existence.*

ROCHE, DOUGLAS DAVID, lawyer, bar examiner; b. Detroit, Oct. 29, 1936; s. James Michael and Louise Carolyn (McMillan) R.; widowed; children: Douglas Jr., Michael, Daniel, Thomas, Robert, Barbara. AB with honors, Holy Cross Coll., Worcester, Mass., 1958; JD, Harvard U., 1963. Bar: Mich. 1963, U.S. Supreme Ct., 1978. Ptnr. Dickinson, Wright, Moon, Van Dusen & Freeman, Detroit, 1963—. Lt. (j.g.) USNR, 1958-60. Mem. ABA, Can. Bar Assn., Fed. Bar Assn. (chmn. Detroit chpt. bankruptcy sect. 1991-92), Mich. Bar Assn., Detroit Bar Assn., Nat. Conf. Bar Examiners (chmn. 1987-88, bd. mgrs. 1981-89, chmn. multistate bar examination policy com. 1988-94), Mich. Bd. Law Examiners (pres. 1975-77), Orchard Lake (Mich.) Country Club, Detroit Athletic Club. Republican. Office: Dickinson Wright 500 Woodward Ave Ste 4000 Detroit MI 48226-3423

ROCHE, GEORGE CHARLES, III, college administrator; b. Denver, May 16, 1935; s. George Charles, Jr. and Margaret (Stewart) R.; m. June Bernard, Feb. 11, 1955; children: George Charles, IV, Muriel Eileen, Margaret Clare, Jacob Stewart. B.S., Regis Coll., Denver, 1956; M.A., U. Colo., 1961, Ph.D., 1965. Tchr. jr. and sr. high schs. Salida, Colo., 1958-60; mem. faculty U. Colo., 1963-64, Colo. Sch. Mines, 1964-66; pres. Hillsdale (Mich.) Coll., 1971—; dir. seminars Found. Econ. Edn., N.Y.C., 1966-71, trustee, 1971-90. Author: Power, 1967, American Federalism, 1967, Education in America, 1969, Legacy of Freedom, 1969, Frederic Bastiat: A Man Alone, 1971, The Bewildered Society, 1972, The Balancing Act: Quota Hiring in Higher Education, 1974, America by the Throat: The Stranglehold of Federal Bureaucracy, 1983, Going Home, 1986, A World Without Heroes, 1987, A Reason for Living, 1989, One By One, 1990, The Fall of the Ivory Tower: Government Funding, Corruption, and the Bankrupting of American Higher Education, 1994; also articles, newspaper column. Chmn. acad. adv. council Charles Edison Meml. Youth Bd., Nat. Council Ednl. Research, 1982-85. Served to 1st lt. USMCR, 1956-58. Recipient Freedom Leadership award Freedoms Found., 1972. Mem. Am. Hist. Assn., Am. Acad. Polit. and Social Sci., Am. Assn. Pres.'s Ind. Colls. and Univs., Mt. Pelerin Soc., Phila. Soc. Office: Hillsdale Coll 33 E College St Hillsdale MI 49242-1205

ROCHE, GERARD RAYMOND, management consultant; b. Scranton, Pa., July 27, 1931; s. Joseph Arthur and Amelia Jane (Garcia) R.; m. Marie Terotta, Apr. 27, 1957; children: Mary Margaret, Anne Elizabeth, Paul Joseph. B.S. in Acctg., U. Scranton, 1953; M.B.A., NYU, 1958. Mgmt. trainee AT&T, Phila., 1955-56; account exec. ABC-TV, N.Y.C., 1956-58; sales and mktg. positions Kordite Corp. subs. Mobil Oil Co., Macedon, N.Y., 1959-63; assoc. Heidrick & Struggles, Inc., N.Y.C., 1964-68, ptnr., 1968—, mgr. N.Y., 1968-73, mgr. East, 1973-77; pres., chief exec. officer Heidrick & Struggles, Inc., N.Y.C., 1978-81; chmn. Heidrick & Struggles, Inc., N.Y.C., 1981—; bd. dirs. Gulfstream Aerospace Corp. Former trustee Cath. U. Am., U. Scranton; bd. dirs. Covenant House, N.Y.C. Served to lt. USN, 1953-55. Mem. Univ. Club, Sky Club, Yale Club, Sleepy Hollow Country Club (bd. govs.), Blind Brook Club, Loxahatchee Club, Loblolly Pines C. C., Knights of Malta, Alpha Sigma Nu (past treas.). Roman Catholic. Home: 111 Paulding Dr Chappaqua NY 10514-2817 Office: Heidrick & Struggles Inc 245 Park Ave New York NY 10167-0002

ROCHE, JAMES MCMILLAN, lawyer; b. Detroit, Apr. 16, 1934; s. James Michael and Louise Cullen (McMillan) R.; m. Laura Jane McMillion, Oct. 27, 1962; children: James, Laura, David, Elizabeth. AB, Holy Cross Coll., 1956; LLB, Harvard U., 1959; LLM, Georgetown U., 1962. Bar: Mich. 1959, Ill. 1962. Ptnr., mem. mgmt. com. McDermott, Will & Emery, Chgo., 1962—; bd. dirs. Time Med Labeling, Inc., Burr Ridge, Ill. Contbr. articles to profl. jours. Chmn. Chgo. Econ. Devel. Corp., 1979-81; pres. Village of Kenilworth, Ill., 1982-85; bd. dirs. St. Francis Hosp., Evanston, 1987-97. Served to capt. USAF, 1959-62. Mem. ABA, Ill. Bar Assn., Chgo. Bar Assn., Mich. Bar Assn., Glen View (Ill.) Golf Club, Monroe Club (Chgo.), The Boulders Club (Ariz.), Desert Forest Club. Roman Catholic. Avocations: golf, Indian art, wine. Office: McDermott Will & Emery 227 W Monroe St Chicago IL 60606-5016

ROCHE, JAMES RICHARD, pediatric dentist, university dean; b. Fortville, Ind., July 17, 1924; s. George Joseph and Nelle (Kinnaman) R.; m. Viola Marie Morris, May 15, 1949; 1 child, Ann Marie Roche Potter. DDS, Ind. U., 1947, MS in Dentistry, 1983. Diplomate Am. Bd. Pediat. Dentistry (exec. sec.-treas. 1982—). Prof. emeritus Ind. U. Sch. Dentistry, Indpls., 1968—, chmn. divsn. grad. pediat. dentistry, 1969-76, asst. dean faculty devel., 1976-80, assoc. dean faculty devel., 1980-87, assoc. dean for acad. affairs, 1987-88; cons. Coun. Dental Edn., Hosp. Dental Svc. and Commn. Accreditation, Chgo., 1977-83. Capt. U.S. Army, 1952-54. Recipient Disting. Teaching Recognition award Ind. U., 1976. Fellow Internat. Coll. Dentists, Am. Coll. Dentists, Am. Acad. Pediat. Dentistry (bd. dirs. 1967-70), Pierre Fauchard Acad.; mem. ADA (cons. Bur. Dental Health Edn. 1977), Am. Soc. Dentistry for Children (award of excellence 1993), Ind. Dental Assn. (v.p. 1973-74, chmn. legis. com. 1968-77, lobbyist 1970-77), Indpls. Dist. Dental Assn. (pres. 1967-68), Ind. U.-Purdue U. Indpls. Sr. Acad. (charter), Masons, Omicron Kappa Upsilon. Home and Office: 1193 Woodgate Dr Carmel IN 46033-9232

ROCHE, JOHN EDWARD, human resources management consultant, educator; b. St. Albans, N.Y., Nov. 11, 1946; s. John F. and Carolyn C. (Miller) R.; m. Valerie Vastola; children: Christopher B., Danielle, Ryan J., Jennifer M. BA, Marist Coll., 1968, MBA, 1975; MS in Edn., SUNY, New Paltz, 1974; postgrad., Nova Southeastern U. Tchr. Kingston (N.Y.) City Schs., 1968-76; employment supr. ACLI Internat. Inc., N.Y.C., 1976-78; dir. pers. Balfour MacLaine Internat., N.Y.C., 1978-80; mgr. employee rels. Harcourt Brace Jovanovich, N.Y.C., 1980-82; nat. dir. pers. Hayt, Hayt & Landau, Great Neck, N.Y., 1982-86; pres. Pers. Mgmt. Svcs., Great Neck, N.Y., 1983-86, Martin-Roche Assocs., Inc., Levittown, N.Y., 1986-92; prof. instrnl. tech. N.Y. Inst. Tech., Old Westbury, 1989—; pres. Human Resources Dept. Inc., Syosset, N.Y., 1994—, L.I. Bus. Network, Inc., 1995—; pres. Martin-Roche Internat. Ltd., Plainview, N.Y., 1992-94. Exec. dir. Jr. Achievement, Kingston, 1972-76, coach Syosset Basseball Assn., CYO Basketball Assn.; human resource com. mem. Adults and Children with Learning and Devel. Disabilities, 1990—. Mem. ASTD, Am. Compensation Assn. (cert. compensation profl.), Soc. for Human Resource Mgmt. (cert. sr. profl. in human resources), KC (grand knight 1967-68). Republican. Roman Catholic. Avocations: astronomy, photography. Home: 17 Meadow Ln Syosset NY 11791-4126 Office: Human Resources Dept Inc 43 Berry Hill Rd Ste 101 Syosset NY 11791-2624 also: NY Inst Tech Dept Instrnl Tech Old Westbury NY 11568-8000

ROCHE, JOHN JEFFERSON, lawyer; b. N.Y.C., Apr. 12, 1934; s. William and Florence E. (Garvey) R.; m. Judith J. Stackpole, Sept. 4, 1980; 1 child from previous marriage, Forrest B. A.B., Brown U., 1957; LL.B., Boston U., 1964. Bar: Mass. 1964, U.S. Tax Ct. 1976. Asst. atty. gen. Dept. Atty. Gen., Boston, 1964-67; ptnr. Hale and Dorr, Boston, 1967-90; pvt. practice Cambridge, Mass., 1991—. Trustee The Hotchkiss Sch., 1986-91; bd. dirs. Indian Soc. Served with U.S. Army, 1959-62. Fellow Am. Coll. Probate Counsel, Internat. Acad. Estate and Trust Law; mem. ABA, Mass. Bar Assn., Boston Bar Assn. Republican. Congregationalist. Club: Wig and Penn (London); Winchester Country. Lodge: Masons. Office: John J Roche & Assocs Ste 405 One Cambridge Ctr Cambridge MA 02142

ROCHE, (EAMONN) KEVIN, architect; b. Dublin, Ireland, June 14, 1922; came to U.S., 1948, naturalized, 1964; s. Eamon and Alice (Harding) R.; m. Jane Tuohy, June 10, 1963; children: Eamon, Paud, Denis, Anne, Alice. B.Arch., Nat. U. Ireland, 1945; D.Sc. (hon.), Nat. U. Ireland, 1977; postgrad., Ill. Inst. Tech., 1948; D.F.A. (hon.), Wesleyan U., 1981, Yale U., 1995. With Eero Saarinen and Assocs., Hamden, Conn., 1950-66; partner Kevin Roche John Dinkeloo and Assocs., Hamden, from 1966. Prin. works include Ford Found. Hdqs., 1967, Oakland (Calif.) Mus, 1968, Met. Mus. Art, N.Y.C., Creative Arts Ctr., Wesleyan U., Middletown, Conn., 1971, Fine Arts Ctr., U. Mass., 1971, Union Carbide Corp. World Hdqs., Conn., Gen. Foods Corp. Hdqs., Rye, N.Y., 1977, 1978, Conoco Inc. Hdqs., Houston, 1979, Central Pk. Zoo, N.Y.C., 1980, DeWitt Wallace Mus. Fine Arts, Williamsburg, Va., 1980, Bouygues World Hdqs., Paris, 1983, J.P. Morgan and Co. Hdqs., N.Y.C., 1983, UNICEF Hdqrs., N.Y.C., 1984, Leo Burnett Co. Hdqs., Chgo., 1985, Corning (N.Y.) Inc. Hdqs., 1986, Merck & Co. Headquarters, N.J., 1987, Dai Ichi Hdqs./Norinchukin Bank Hdqrs., Tokyo, 1989, Nations Bank Hdqs., Atlanta, 1989, Pontiac Marina Pvt. Ltd., Singapore, 1990, Metropolitano, Madrid, 1990, Borland Internat. Headquarters, Scotts Valley, Calif., 1990, Tanjong & Binariang/Ampang Tower, Kuala Lumpur, Malaysia, 1993, Mus. of Jewish Heritage Holocaust Meml., N.Y.C., 1993, Tata Cummins Pvt. Ltd., Jamshedpur, India, 1994, Vis. Ctr., Columbus, Ind., 1994, Cummins Engine Co. APEX Mfg. Facility, 1994, Lucent Techs. Hdqs., Murray Hill, N.J., 1996, Wuxi Newage Cummins, Wuxi, China, 1996, Total Sys. Svcs. Corp. Headquarters, Columbus, Ga., 1997. Mem. Fine Arts Commn., Washington; trustee Am. Acad. in Rome, 1968-71, Woodrow Wilson Center for Scholars in Smithsonian Instn. Recipient Creative Arts award Brandeis U., 1967; A.S. Bard award City Club N.Y., 1968, 77, 79; award Gov. of Calif., 1968; N.Y. State award Citizens Union N.Y., 1968; total design award Am. Soc. Interior Design; Pritzker Archtl. prize, 1982; Albert S. Bard award, 1990. Fellow AIA (medal of honor N.Y. chpt. 1968, Gold Medal award 1993, 25-yr. award 1995), AAAS; mem. NAD (academician), AAAL (pres. 1994-97), Am. Acad. Arts and Letters (Brunner award 1965, Gold medal 1990), Académie d'Architecture (Grand Gold medal 1977), Mcpl. Art Soc. N.Y. (Brendan Gill prize 1989), Acad. di San Luca. Office: Kevin Roche John Dinkeloo & Assoc PO Box 6127 20 Davis St Hamden CT 06517-0127

ROCHE, MARK WILLIAM, German language educator; b. Weymouth, Mass., Aug. 29, 1956; s. Jason Bernard and Joan (Murphy) R.; m. Barbara Hampshire, June 13, 1981. BA, Williams Coll., 1978; MA, U. Tübingen, Germany, 1980, Princeton (N.J.) U., 1982; PhD, Princeton (N.J.) U., 1984. Asst. prof. German Ohio State U., Columbus, 1984-90, assoc. prof., 1990-96, chair dept. German, 1991-96; prof. German lang. and lit. U. Notre Dame, South Bend, Ind., 1996—. Author: Dynamic Stillness, 1987, Gottfried Benn's Static Poetry, 1991. Fulbright fellow Germany, 1978-80, Whiting fellow, 1983-84, ACLS fellow, 1985; NEH Summer Stipend grantee, 1991, DAAD Study Visit Rsch. grantee, 1991; Humboldt fellow, 1997. Mem. Soc. for Philosophic Study of contemporary Visual Arts (vice pres. 1990-92). Home: 12418 Range Line Rd Berrien Springs MI 49103-9632 Office: U Notre Dame 318 O Shaugnessy Hall Notre Dame IN 46556-5639

ROCHELEAU, JAMES ROMIG, academic administrator; b. Anchorage, Mar. 21, 1940; s. James Albert and Sophia (Rivord) R.; m. Margaret Anne Sheehan, Nov. 28, 1981; children from previous marriage: Renee, Tanya, Andrea. BA, U. Idaho, 1968, MA, 1969; PhD, Wash. State U., Pullman, 1975. Account exec. Spokesman Rev., Spokane, Wash., 1963; sales rep. RJR Nabisco, Inc., Spokane, 1963-66; grad. asst. U. Idaho, Moscow and Wash. State U., Pullman, 1967-70; instr. history Wash. State U., 1970-71; asst. prof. history Buena Vista Coll., Storm Lake, Iowa, 1971-76, dir., 1976-81, dean continuing edn., 1981-84; pres. Upper Iowa U., Fayette, 1984-94, pres. emeritus, 1994—; cons. North Cen. Assn., Chgo., 1981—, Kellogg Found., 1994—. Active N.E.-Midwest Leadership Coun. Served with U.S. Army, 1958-61. Mem. Nat. Assn. Ind. Colls. and Univs., Iowa Assn. Ind. Colls. Univs., Coun. Ind. Colls., Iowa Coordinating Coun. for Post-High Sch. Edn., C. of C. Home: 14455 90th Ave Seminole FL 33776-1925 Office: PO Box 373 Indian Rocks Beach FL 33785-0373

ROCHER, LUDO, humanities educator; b. Hemiksem, Belgium, Apr. 25, 1926; s. Jules and Anna Van Den (Bogaert) R.; m. Rosane Debels, Apr. 1, 1961. B.A., U. Ghent, Belgium, 1946, M.A., 1948, LL.D., 1950, Ph.D., 1952. Agrege U. Ghent, 1958-59; prof. Sanskrit and comparative philology U. Brussels, 1959-67; prof. Sanskrit U. Pa., Phila., 1966—, W. Norman Brown prof. South Asian studies, 1981—; chmn. dept. Oriental studies U. Pa., 1967-75, 88-94, chmn. dept. South Asia regional studies, 1975-78; dir. Center for Study of South and S.E. Asia, U. Brussels, 1961-67. Author: A Hindu Legal Digest, 1956, Manual of Modern Hindi, 1958, Bibliography of Hindu Law, 1963, Smrticintamani, 1976, Paulinus a S. Bartholomaeo on the Sanskrit Language, 1977, Ezourvedam, 1984, The Puranas, 1985; contbr. articles to profl. jours. Served with Belgian Army, 1950-52. Research fellow Nat. Found. for Sci. Research, Belgium, 1952-58. Fellow Royal Acad. for Overseas Scis. Belgium, Asiatic Soc. Calcutta; mem. Am. Philos. Soc., Am. Oriental Soc. (pres. 1985-86), Assn. for Asian Studies, Royal Asiatic Soc. (Eng.). Home: 226 W Rittenhouse Sq Apt 1506 Philadelphia PA 19103-5747

ROCHESTER, MICHAEL GRANT, geophysics educator; b. Toronto, Ont., Can., Nov. 22, 1932; s. Reginald Baillie Rochester and Ruth Ellen (Bonwick) Rochester Konrad; m. Elizabeth Manser, May 9, 1958; children—Susan, Fiona, John. BA with honors, U. Toronto, 1954, MA, 1956; PhD, U. Utah, 1959. Aerodynamicist A. V. Roe Can. Ltd., Malton, Ont., 1954-55; lectr. geophysics U. Toronto, 1959-60, asst. prof., 1960-61; asst. prof. U. Waterloo, Ont., 1961-65; assoc. prof. U. Waterloo, 1965-67, Meml. U. Nfld., St. John's, Can., 1967-70; prof. Meml. U. Nfld., 1970—, univ. research prof., 1986—. Mem., officer Nat. Spiritual Assembly of Baha'is of Can., 1963-92. Grantee NRC, Natural Scis. and Engring. Research Council Can. Fellow Royal Soc. Can.; mem. Internat. Union Geodesy and Geophysics (Can. nat. com. 1971-75, 84-88), AAAS, Am. Geophys. Union, Can. Assn. Physicists, Can. Geophys. Union (Tuzo Wilson medal, 1986), Internat. Astron. Union (commn. rotation of the Earth 1973—), Royal Astron. Soc. London, Sigma Xi. Avocations: hiking, swimming, history. Office: Meml Univ Nfld, Dept Earth Scis, Saint Johns, NF Canada A1B 3X5

ROCHETTE, EDWARD CHARLES, retired association executive; b. Worcester, Mass., Feb. 17, 1927; s. Edward Charles and Lilia (Viau) R.; m. Mary Ann Ruland, July 29, 1978; children by previous marriage—Edward Charles, Paul, Philip. Student, Washington U., St. Louis, Clark U. Exec. editor Krause Publs., Iola, Wis., 1960-66; acting exec. dir. Am. Numismatic Assn., Colorado Springs, Colo., 1967-68, exec. v.p., 1972-87, ret., 1987; editor jour. The Numismatist, Colorado Springs, Colo., 1968-72. Bd. overseers Inst. Philatelic and Numismatic Studies, Adelphi U., Garden City, N.Y., 1979-81; chmn. medals com. Colo. Centennial Bicentennial Commn., 1976; mem. adv. panel Carson City Silver Dollar program Gen. Services Adminstrn., 1979-80; mem. U.S. Assay Commn., 1965. Served with USN, 1944-46. Recipient Gold medal for syndicated column Numismatic Lit. Guild, 1980, 86-88. Mem. Am. Numis. Assn. (life, medal of merit 1972), Am. Soc. Assn. Execs., Colo. Soc. Assn. Execs. (pres. 1988-89). Democrat. Roman Catholic. Lodge: Pikes Peak Kiwanis (pres. 1987-88). Office: Am Numis Assn PO Box 7083 Colorado Springs CO 80933-7083

ROCHETTE, LOUIS, retired shipowner and shipbuilder; b. Quebec City, Que., Can., Feb. 19, 1923; s. Evariste and Blanche (Gaudry) R.; m. Nicole Barbeau, Oct. 12, 1968; children: Louise, Ann, Guy. M. Commerce, Laval U., Que., 1948. Chartered Accountant, Que. Chief auditor retail sales tax Govt. Que. Quebec City, 1953-55; treas. Davie Shipbldg., Ltd., Lauzon, Que., 1955-65; exec. v.p. Marine Industries, Ltd., Montreal, Que., 1965-76; chmn., CEO Davie Shipbldg. Ltd., Lauzon, Que., 1976-82; pres., CEO Soconav Inc., Quebec, 1982-86; pres. Gesconav Inc., 1986—; bd. dirs. Hawker Siddeley Can. Inc., Leader Industries, Inc; past chmn. Lloyd's Com. for Can. Author: Le Reve Separatiste, 1969. Bd. dirs. Gov. Coun. for Can. Unity; gov. Laval U. Found, Quebec Opera Found. Pilot RCAF, 1943-45, ETO. Named Hon. Col., Royal Can. Artillery. Fellow Inst. Chartered Accts. Can., Que. C. of C., Can. Inst. of Mgmt. Accts. Home and Office: 1155 Turnbull St #1002, Quebec, PQ Canada G1R 5G3 *Whatever success I have met with throughout my career was mainly achieved through perseverance in the face of what often looked like insurmountable obstacles.*

ROCHLIS, JAMES JOSEPH, manufacturing company executive; b. Phila., Apr. 12, 1916; s. Aaron and Gussie (Pearlene) R.; m. Riva Singer, Mar. 21, 1943; children: Jeffrey A., Susan J. Ed. pub. schs. Salesman Mid-City Tire Co., Phila., 1945-46, gen. mgr., 1946-49; pres. Ram Rubber Co., Phila., 1948-49; rep. Blair & Co., Phila., 1949-61, bus. analyst, 1955-61; pres., chief exec. officer Baldwin-Montrose Chem. Co., Inc., N.Y.C., 1961-68; v.p. Chris-Craft Industries, Inc., N.Y.C., 1968-69; pres. Chris-Craft Corp., Pompano Beach, Fla., 1969-71; exec. v.p. Chris-Craft Industries, Inc., N.Y.C., 1969-87, also bd. dirs.; pres. Baldwin-NAFI Industries div. Chris-Craft Industries, 1968—, Chris-Craft Internat., 1977-87; pres. Chris-Craft Indsl. Products, Inc., Pompano Beach, 1981-86, chmn., bd. dirs., cons., 1986—; bd. dirs. Montrose Chem. Co. Calif., Torrance and Mex., So. Mass. Cablevision Corp., N.Y.C., Piper Aircraft Corp., Lock Haven, Pa., Chris-Craft Pacific, Inc., Calif. Mem. AIAA, Fin. Analysts Soc. Phila., Soc. Naval Architects and Marine Engrs., Antique and Classic Boat Soc. Club: Lotus (N.Y.C.). Home: 150 E 69th St New York NY 10021-5704 also: 10601 Wilshire Blvd Los Angeles CA 90024-4518 Office: Chris-Craft Industries Inc 767 5th Ave New York NY 10153-0001

ROCHON, JEAN, government official; b. Montreal, Que., Can., July 29, 1938; s. Albert and Germaine (Laliberte) R.; m. Thérèse Morais, Aug. 31, 1963. BA, U. Montreal, 1958, LLL, 1961; MD, U. Laval, 1966; MPH, Harvard U., 1968, DPH, 1973; LLD honoris causa, U. Catholique de Louvain, Belgium, 1988. Dir. cmty. health univ. tchg. hosp., 1973-79; head dept. social and preventative medicine U. Laval, 1970-79, dean medicine, 1979-85; asst. dir. European regional office WHO, 1987-90, dir. health protection and promotion divsn. hdqs., 1990-93; chair Commn. d'enquete sur les serv de sante et svc. sociaux Que Govt., 85-87; min. health and social svcs. Nat. Assembly of Que., 1994—. Recipient R.D. Defries prize for contbn. to advancement of pub. health Can. Pub. Health Assn., 1994. Office: Min Health & Social Svcs, 1075 Chemin Ste-Foy, Quebec, PQ Canada G1S 2M1

ROCHON, JOHN PHILIP, cosmetics company executive; b. Sept. 20, 1951; s. Philip Benjamin and Helena Sylvia (McCullough) R.; m. Donna J. Hewitt, Dec. 15, 1972; children: Heidi C., William J., Lauren. BS, U. Toronto, Ont., 1973, MBA, 1976. Plant mgr. Econs. Lab. Ltd., Toronto, 1976-80; dir. mfg. Mary Kay Cosmetics, Ltd., Toronto, 1980-82; contr. mfg. group Mary Kay Cosmetics, Inc., Dallas, 1982-84, corp. contr., 1984, v.p. fin., chief fin. officer, 1984-85, exec. v.p., chief fin. officer, 1986-87, vice chmn. bd., 1987-93; pres., CEO Mary Kay Cosmetics Corp., Dallas, 1993-95; also bd. dirs. Mary Kay Cosmetics, Ltd., Dallas; CEO Mary Kay Holding Co., 1995—; bd. dirs. Mary Kay Holding Corp., Dallas, Strategic Assessment, Inc.; mem. fin. com. U. Tex., Dallas, 1985—. Mem. Cosmetic, Toiletry and Fragrance Assn., Direct Selling Assn., Verandah Club. Republican. Home: 4315 Firebrick Ln Dallas TX 75287-5138*

ROCHOWICZ, JOHN ANTHONY, JR., mathematician, mathematics and physics educator; b. Reading, Pa., Mar. 20, 1950; s. John Anthony and Sara Jane (Binckley) R. BS in Math., Albright Coll., 1972; MS in Math., Lehigh U., 1974; secondary edn. cert. math., Albright Coll., 1975; EdD in Ednl. Tech., Lehigh U., 1993. Cert. secondary teaching, Pa. Math. tchr. Bethlehem (Pa.) Cath. High Sch., 1980-81; instr. math. Pa. State U.-Berks, Reading, 1982-84, Kutztown (Pa.) U., 1983-84, Lehigh County C.C., Schnecksville, Pa., 1984, Alvernia Coll., Reading, 1984, Reading (Pa.) Area C.C., 1984-86; prof. math. Alvernia Coll., 1985—. Recipient Alumni Educator award Albright Coll., Reading, 1987. Mem. AAUP, Math. Assn. Am., Assn. for the Advancement Computing in Edn., Assn. for Ednl. Communications and Tech., Nat. Coun. Tchrs. Math.; contbr. articles to scientific jours. Democrat. Roman Catholic. Avocations: collecting music, computers, calculators, billiards, swimming. Home: 41 Columbia Ave SCM Reading PA 19606-1316 Office: Alvernia College 400 Saint Bernardine St Reading PA 19607-1756

ROCHWARGER, LEONARD, former ambassador; b. Buffalo, Aug. 3, 1925; s. Max and Sarah (Wallace) R.; m. Arlene Bassuk, June 19, 1949 (dec. Nov. 1996); children: Jeffrey Alan, Michelle. BS, U. Buffalo, 1949; PhD (hon.), Canisius Coll. Chief auditor Western N.Y. State, Buffalo, 1949-61; sr. ptnr. S. L. Horowitz & Co., Buffalo, 1961-65; chmn., chief exec. officer Rockmont Corp., Buffalo, 1965-87, 90—; U.S. amb. to Fiji Republic of Kiribati, Kingdom of Tonga and Tuvalu, 1987-89; chmn. bd. Indpls. Morris Plan Corp., Firstmark Fin. Corp., 1972-87; chmn. bd. Israel Am. Leasing Ltd., 1971-87; dir. Marine Midland Bank-Western, Nat. Fuel Gas Co.; adj. prof. SUNY, Buffalo; bd. chmn. Menorah Campus, 1993-96. Past gen. chmn. United Way Buffalo and Erie Co., 1973; past trustee, past chmn. bd. regents Canisius Coll.; past chmn. United Jewish Appeal, Buffalo, 1969; past. pres., life dir. Buffalo Jewish Ctr.; past mem. nat. bd. dirs. NCCJ; past bd. dirs., hon. life pres. Nat. Jewish Welfare Bd.; life mem., past pres. Jewish Fedn. Greater Buffalo; past bd. dirs. Coun. Jewish Fedns.; mem. adv. coun. Johns Hopkins U. Sch. Adv. Internat. Studies, Washington, 1986-88, 90-96; past pres. Found. Jewish Philanthropies, Buffalo; trustee U. Buffalo Found., Inc. With AUS, 1943-46. Decorated Bronze Star, Conspicous Svc. Cross, Combat/Infantryman's Badge. Jewish. Home: 81 Nottingham Ter Buffalo NY 14216-3620

ROCK, ALLAN MÍCHAEL, Canadian government official; b. Ottawa, Ont., Can., Aug. 30, 1947; s. James Thomas and Anne (Dane) R.; m. Deborah Kathleen, June 24, 1983; children: Jason, Lauren, Andrew, Stephen. BA, U. Ottawa, 1968, LLB, 1971. Certified specialist in civil litigation. Min. of justice, atty. gen. Govt. of Can., 1993—; treas. Law Soc. Upper Can., 1992-93; bencher Law Soc., 1983, 87, 91; former chmn. discipline and legal edn. coms.; past chmn. litigation dept. Fasken Campbell Godfrey. Fellow Am. Coll. Trial Lawyers. Office: Justice Canada, Justice Bldg 239 Wellington St, Ottawa, ON Canada K1A 0H8

ROCK, ANGELA, volleyball player; b. Carlsbad, Calif., Oct. 15, 1963. BA in Psychology, San Diego State U., 1994. Fire-fighter San Diego; profl. volleyball tour player; mem. U.S.A. Nat. Team, 1987-90; bd. dirs. Women's Profl. Volleyball Assn., El Segundo, Calif. Winner bronze medal Pan Am. Games, 1987; named USVBA Most Valuable Player, 1987, WPVA Best Hitter, 1991, Winner of the Miller Lite Ice Cup. Mem. Assn. Volleyball Profls., Women's Profl. Volleyball Assn. Competed Goodwill Games, 1987, Olympic, Seoul, 1988; compiled 18 WPVA Open Wins; won AVP Women's Tour Event with Linda Hanley, Ocean City, 1993, 1st ever with Holly McPeak, Phoenix, Miller Lite Opens, (receipient Miller Lite Ice Cup), Grand Haven and Nestea Opéns, Atlanta, Dallas with Nancy Reno, Phoenix, 1994. Office: care Womens Profl Volleyball Assn Ste 205 840 Apollo El Segundo CA 90245-4701*

ROCK, ARTHUR, venture capitalist; b. Rochester, N.Y., Aug. 19, 1926; s. Hyman A. and Reva (Cohen) R.; m. Toni Rembe, July 19, 1975. BS, Syracuse U., 1948; MBA, Harvard U., 1951. Gen. ptnr. Davis & Rock, San Francisco, 1961-68, Arthur Rock & Assocs., San Francisco, 1969-80; bd. dirs. Argonaut Group, Inc., L.A., Echelon, Palo Alto, Calif., AirTouch Comm., San Francisco; mem. exec. com. Teledyne, Inc., L.A., 1961-94; founder, chmn. exec. com., bd. dirs., past chmn. bd. dirs. Intel Corp., Santa Clara, Calif. Trustee Calif. Inst. Tech.; bd. dirs. San Francisco Opera Assn.,

1970-92, San Francisco Mus. Modern Art; mem. vis. com. Harvard U. Bus. Sch., 1982-88. Recipient Medal of Achievement Am. Electronics Assn., 1987, Am. Acad. Achievement, 1989; named to Jr. Achievement Hall of Fame, 1990, Calif. Bus. Hall of Fame, 1990, Bay Area Bus. Coun. Hall of Fame, 1995, Arents Pioneer medal Syracuse U., 1997. Office: 1 Maritime Plz Ste 1220 San Francisco CA 94111-3502

ROCK, DOUGLAS LAWRENCE, manufacturing executive; b. Glen Cove, N.Y., Jan. 25, 1947; s. Herb and Beatrice (Vyse) R.; m. Cindy Pegoraro, May 11, 1967 (div. Apr. 1973); 1 child, Jason; m. Mary Sue Bell, Mar. 23, 1991 (div. Jan. 1996). BS in Psychology and Chemistry, Pa. State U., 1968; postgrad., U. Chgo., 1971-73. Rsch. chemist FMC Corp., Princeton, N.J., 1968-69; mfg. system project leader A.O. Smith Corp., Erie, Pa., 1969-71; dir. materials and info. systems Joy Mfg., Michigan City, Ind., 1971-74; dir. info. systems Smith Tool div. Smith Internat. Inc., Irvine, Calif., 1974-75, dir. materials, 1975-77, v.p. mfg., 1977-80, sr. v.p. ops., 1980-82, pres., 1985-87; pres. Drilco div. Smith Internat. Inc., Houston, 1982-85; pres., chief exec. officer Smith Internat. Inc., Houston, 1987—, chmn. bd., 1991—; bd. dirs. Viad Corp. Named Golden Knight, Nat. Mgmt. Assn., 1983. Mem. Internat. Assn. Drilling Contractors, Am. Petroleum Inst., Petroleum Equipment Suppliers Assn. (bd. dirs. Houston chpt. 1987—, 1st v.p. 1996), Nat. Offshore Industries Assn. (fin. com. 1988, audit com. 1989), Greenspoint Club . Avocations: golf, racquetball, reading. Office: Smith Internat PO Box 60068 16740 Hardy Rd Houston TX 77205-0068

ROCK, GAIL ANN, obstetrical/gynecological nurse; b. Maquokela, Iowa, Mar. 24, 1960; d. Robert William and Mary Anne (Franzen) Scheckel; m. William Beale Rock III, June 6, 1981; 1 child, William Beale IV. Chiropractic Asst., Palmer Coll. Chiropractic, Davenport, Iowa, 1979; AAS in Nursing, North County Community Coll., Saranac Lake, N.Y., 1987; BSN, SUNY, Plattsburg, 1992-95. Cert. resolve thru sharing counselor, inpatient obstet. nurse; cert. childbirth educator; cert. lactation cons. Staff nurse ob-gyn. Adriondack Med. Ctr., Saranac Lake, N.Y., 1987-90, nurse mgr. ob-gyn., 1990-95; nurse mgr. birth ctr. Preston Meml. Hosp., Kingwood, W.Va., 1995—; group educator sibling and new parent classes, Saranac Lake, 1991-95; mem. Garrett County Pub. Health Childbirth Edn., 1995—. Mem. Assn. Women's Health Obstetric & Neonatal Nurses, NAFE, Sigma Theta Tau. Home: 880 Trap Run Rd Friendsville MD 21531 Office: Preston Meml Hosp 300 S Price St Kingwood WV 26537-1442

ROCK, HAROLD L., lawyer; b. Sioux City, Iowa, Mar. 13, 1932; s. Harold L. and Helen J. (Gormally) R.; m. Marilyn Beth Rock, Dec. 28, 1954; children: Michael, Susan, John, Patrick, Michele, Thomas. BS, Creighton U., 1954, JD, 1959. Bar: Nebr., N.Y., Minn., Mont., Wyo. Law clk. to judge U.S. Ct. Appeals 8th Circuit, Omaha, 1959-60, Fitzgerald Hamer Brown & Leahy, Omaha, 1960-65; ptnr. Kutak Rock, Omaha, 1965—; chmn. Nebr. Bd. Bar Examiners, 1989-96; bd. dirs. Mid City Bank, Omaha. Bd. dirs. Douglas County Hist. Soc., 1992—, Nat. Equal Justice Libr., 1995—. Served to 1st lt. U.S. Army, 1954-56. Recipient Alumni Achievement award Creighton U., 1995. Mem. ABA (ho. of dels. 1990-96, bd. govs. 1992-95), Nebr. Bar Assn. (ho. of dels., bd. dirs. 1985—, pres. 1988, Nebr. Bar found. bd. dirs., 1982—), Omaha Bar Assn. (pres. 1972-73), Omaha Legal Aid Soc. (pres. 1969-72), Nebr. State Bd. Pub. Accts. (bd. dirs. 1981-85). Roman Catholic. Office: Kutak Rock The Omaha Bldg 1650 Farnam St Omaha NE 68102-2104

ROCK, JOHN AUBREY, gynecologist and obstetrician, educator; b. Corpus Christi, Tex., Oct. 21, 1946; s. William A. and Burta (Wheeler) R.; m. Barbara McAlpine, Oct. 8, 1976; children: John Aubrey Jr., Deborah Ellen, Daniel Authur. BS in Zoology, La. State U., Baton Rouge, 1968; MD, La. State U., New Orleans, 1972. Asst. prof. Johns Hopkins U. Sch. Medicine, Balt., 1978-80, assoc. prof., 1980-87, prof. ob-gyn, 1987-92, prof. pediatrics, 1988-92, dir. reproductive endocrinology, 1979-91, dep. dir. med. sch., 1985-88; chmn. Union Meml. Hosp., Balt., 1991-92; James Robert McCord prof., chmn. dept. ob-gyn. Emory U. Sch. Medicine, Atlanta, 1992—; cons. Dept. Army, Washington, 1982-93, NASA, Houston, 1988—; chmn. ad hoc com. on in vitro fertilization State of Md., 1985. Author: Reparative and Constructive Surgery of the Female Generative Tract, 1983, Endometriosis, 1988, TeLinde's Operative Gynecology, 1991, 95; mem. editl. bd. Fertility and Sterility jour., 1986-94, Gynecology Surgery, 1989—. Fellow ACOG; mem. Am. Gynecol. and Obstet. Soc., Soc. Gynecol. Surgeons, Am. Fertility Soc. (bd. dirs. 1989-92), Soc. Gynecologic Investigation, Soc. Reproductive Surgeons (pres. 1986), Am. Soc. for Reproductive Medicine (pres. 1996-97), Rotary Club, Phi Kappa Phi. Methodist. Office: Emory Univ WMB Dept OB-GYN 1639 Pierce Dr Rm 4208 Atlanta GA 30322

ROCK, KENNETH WILLETT, history educator; b. Abilene, Kans., Dec. 12, 1938; s. Kenneth Melvin and Marjorie (Taylor) R.; m. Mercedes Alice de Sola, Aug. 22, 1964; children: Kenneth Teodoro, Laurel Elizabeth. BA, U. Kans., 1960; MA, Stanford U., 1962, PhD, 1969. From instr. history to asst. prof. Colo. State U., Ft. Collins, 1965-72, advisor Fulbright, Marshall, Rhodes scholarships, 1968-80, assoc. prof., 1972-83, prof., 1983—, acting dir. office internat. edn., 1984-85; vis. scholar Tech. U., Budapest, Hungary, 1993. Author (booklet) German Footprints in Colorado, 1983; contbr. articles to profl. jours.; chpts. to books. Fulbright scholar Inst. Internat. Edn., Vienna, Austria, 1964-65; fellow NEH, Vienna, 1972-73, NEH, U. Va., 1978; assoc. Danforth Found., 1978-84. Mem. Am. Assn. Advancement Slavic Studies, Conf. Group Cen. European History, Am. Hist. Assn., Am. Hist. Soc. Germans from Russia, Rocky Mountain Slavic Studies Assn., Phi Beta Kappa, Phi Alpha Theta. Democrat. Avocations: reading, historical miniatures, travelling, photography, painting. Home: 3212 Shore Rd Fort Collins CO 80524-1688 Office: Colo State U Dept History Fort Collins CO 80523

ROCK, RICHARD RAND, lawyer, former state senator; b. Wichita Falls, Tex., Sept. 27, 1924; s. Parker Francis and Ruth Ann (Phillips) R.; m. Rosalee Deardorff, Aug. 23, 1947; children: Richard R. II, Darci Lee, Devon Ray, Robert Regan. BA, Washburn U., 1948, LLB, 1950, JD, 1970. Bar: Kans., U.S. Dist. Ct. Kans., U.S. Ct. Appeals (4th and 10th cirs.). Dir. indsl. rels. Maurer-Neuer Packers, Arkansas City, Kans., 1950-52, plant supt., 1952-54; atty. Rock, Smith & Mason, Arkansas City, Kans., 1955-95; pres., owner Shreveport (La.) Packing Co., 1972-83, Amarillo (Tex.) Beef Processors, 1977-82, Lubbock (Tex.) Beef Processors, 1978-81, Montgomery (Ala.) Food Processors, 1978-91, Humboldt (Iowa) Sausage Co., 1985-92, Great Bend (Kans.) Packing Co., 1984-95; state senator, asst. minority leader State of Kans., 1988-96; chmn. bd. dirs. Rockgate Mgmt. Co., Overland Park, Kans. Judge Cowley County, Kans., 1952-56; state rep. State of Kans., 1957-61; authority mem. Kans. Turnpike Authority, 1980-83, chmn., 1993-97; commr. Children with Spl. Health Care Needs, Kans., 1993-95. Served USN Air Corps, 1943-45. Mem. Kans. Bar Assn., Nat. Counsel State Legislatures, Kans. C. of C., VFW. Democrat. Mem. Disciples of Christ. Avocations: golf, yard work.

ROCKART, JOHN FRALICK, information systems reseacher; b. N.Y.C., June 20, 1931; s. John Rachac and Janet (Ross) R.; m. Elise Jean Feldmann, Sept. 16, 1961; children: Elise B. Liesl, Scott F. AB, Princeton U., 1953; MBA, Harvard U., 1958; PhD, MIT, 1968. Sales rep. IBM, 1958-61, dist. med. rep., 1961-62, fellow in Africa, 1962-64; instr. MIT, Cambridge, Mass., 1966-67; asst. prof. IBM, Cambridge, Mass., 1967-70, assoc. prof., 1970-74, sr. lectr., 1974—; dir. MIT, Cambridge, 1976—; bd. dirs. Keane, Inc., Boston, Comshare, Inc., Ann Arbor, Mich., Transition Systems, Inc., Boston, Multiplex, St. Louis, Renaissance Solutions, Lincoln, Mass., Synon, Inc., Larkspur, Calif. Co-author: Computers & Learning Process, 1974, Rise of Managerial Computing, 1986, Executive Support Systems, 1988 (Computer Press Assn. 1989); contbr. articles to profl. jours. Trustee New Eng. Med. Ctr., Boston; mem. Mass. Gov. Adv. Coun. on Info. Tech., Boston. Lt. USN, 1953-56. Mem. Assn. for Computing Machinery, Inst. for Mgmt. Sci., Ops. Rsch. Soc. Am., Soc. for Info. Mgmt. (bd. dirs. mem. at large 1989-94), New Eng. Med. Ctr. Audit Com., Weston (Mass.) Golf Club, Lake Sunapee Country Club (New London, N.H.). Republican. Unitarian. Home: 150 Cherry Brook Rd Weston MA 02193-1308 Office: CISR MIT Sloan Sch Mgmt E40-187 77 Massachusetts Ave # E40-187 Cambridge MA 02139-4301

ROCKBURNE, DOROTHEA GRACE, artist; b. Montreal, Que., Can, Oct. 18, 1934. Student, Black Mountain Coll. Milton and Sally Avery Disting. prof. Bard Coll., 1986; trustee Ind. Curators Inc., N.Y., Art in Gen.; artist in residence Am. Acad. in Rome, 1991; vis. artist Skowhegan Sch. Printing and Sculpture, 1984; Rockefeller Found. resident Bellagio (Italy) Conf. and Study Ctr., 1997. One-person shows include Sonnabend Gallery, Paris, 1971, New Gallery, Cleve., 1972, Bykert Gallery, N.Y.C., 1970, 72, 73, Galleria Toselli, Milan, Italy, 1972, 73, 74, Galleria D'Arte, Bari, Italy, 1972, Lisson Gallery, London, 1973, Daniel Weinberg Gallery, San Francisco, 1973, Galerie Charles Kriwin, Brussels, 1975, Galleria Schema, Florence, Italy, 1973, 75, 92, John Weber Gallery, N.Y.C., 1976, 78, Galleria la Polena, Geona, Italy, 1977, Tex. Gallery, Houston, 1979, 80, 81, Xavier Fourcade Gallery, N.Y.C., 1980, 82, 83, 85, 86, David Bellman, Toronto, 1980, 81, Margo Leavin, Calif., 1982, Arts Club of Chgo., 1987, André Emmerich Gallery, N.Y.C., 1988, 89, 91, 92, 94, 95, 10 yr. retrospective Rose Art Mus., 1989, P. Fong & Spratt Galleries, San Jose, Calif., 1991, Sony Music Hdqs., N.Y.C., 1993, Frederick Spratt Gallery, San Jose, 1994, Guild Hall Mus., Easthampton, N.Y., 1995; group shows include Whitney Mus. Am. Art, 1970, 73, 77, 79, 82, Mus. Modern Art, N.Y.C., 71, 73, 84, 86, 93, 94, Buenos Aires, 1971, Kolner Kunst Market, Cologne, Germany, 1971, Stedelijk Mus., Holland, 1971, Spoleto (Italy) Festival, 1972, Palazzo Taverna, Rome, 1973, Nat. Gallery Victoria, Melbourne, Australia, 1973, Art Gallery NSW, Sydney, 1973, Auckland (New Zealand) City Art Gallery, 1973, Inst. Contemporary Art, London, 1974, Mus. d'Arte de la Ville, Paris, 1975, Galerie Aronowitsch, Stockholm, 1975, Stadtiches Mus., Manchengladbach, Germany, 1975, Galleria D'Arte Moderna, Bologna, Italy, 1975, Art Gallery Ont., Toronto, Can., 1975, Mus. Fine Art, Houston, 1975, Contemporary Arts Ctr., Cin., 1973, 75, 81, Mus. Contemporary Art, Chgo., 1971, 77, 86, Corcoran Gallery of Art, Washington, 1975, 87, Städtisches Mus., Leverkusen, Germany, 1975, Cannaviella Studio d'Arte Rome, 1976, Phila. Coll. Art, 1976, 83, Balt. Mus. Art, 1976, New Mus., N.Y.C., 1977, 80, 84, 83, Renaissance Soc. of U. Chgo., 1976, Lowe Art Mus., U. Miami, Fla., 1976, Inst. Contemporary Art, Boston, 1976, Seibu Mus. Art, Tokyo, 1976, N.Y. State Mus., Albany, 1977, Drawing Ctr., 1977, Kansas City (Mo.) Art Inst., 1977, Smithsonian Inst., Washington, 1977, Kassel, Fed. Republic Germany, 1972, 77, Ackland Art Ctr., Chapel Hill, N.C., 1979, 84, Milw. Art Ctr., 1978, 81, Biblioteca Nacional, Madrid, 1980, Gulbenkian Mus., Lisbon, Portugal, 1980, Bklyn. Mus., 1981, 89, Guggenheim Mus., 1982, 88, 89, Albright Knox Art Gallery, Buffalo, 1979, 80, 88, 89, Kuustforeningen Mus., Copenhagen, 1980, Venice Biennale, 1980, Cranbrook (Mich.) Acad. Art, 1981, Mus. Fine Arts, Boston, 1983, Contemporary Arts Mus., Houston, 1983, Norman Mackenzie Art Gallery, U. Regina, Sask., Can., 1983, Galleriet, Sweden, 1983-84, Seattle Art Mus., 1979-84, Nat. Mus. Art., Osaka, Japan, 1984, Fogg Art Mus., Cambridge, Mass., 1984, Am. Acad. and Inst. Arts and Letters, N.Y.C., 1984, 87, L.A. County Mus. Art, 1984, 86, Wadsworth Atheneum, Hartford, Conn., 1981, 84, Evehart Mus., Pa., 1984, Grey Art Gallery, NYU, 1977, 84, 87, Avery Ctr. Arts, Bard Coll., N.Y., 1985, 87-88, Stamford (Conn.) Mus., 1985, Aldrich Mus., Conn., 1979, 82, Bronx Mus. Arts, N.Y.C., 1985, High Mus., Atlanta, 1975, 81, Phila. Mus. Art, 1986, Nat. Gallery Art, Washington, 1984, Mus. Art, Ft. Lauderdale, Fla., 1986, Nat. Mus. Women in Art, Washington, 1987, Xavier Fourcade Gallery, 1983, 87, L.A. County Mus. Modern Art, 1986-87, The Hague, The Netherlands, 1986, Carnegie-Mellon Art Gallery, Pitts., 1979, 87, Balt. Mus. Art, 1975, 76, 88, Ctr. for Fine Arts, Miami, 1989, Milw. Art Mus., 1989, Cin. Art Mus., 1989, New Orleans Mus., 1989, Denver Art Mus., 1989, Parrish Art Mus., South Hampton, N.Y., 1990, 91, Margo Leavin Gallery, L.A., 1991, Mus. of Modern Art, N.Y.C,, 1991, Guild Hall Mus., East Hampton, N.Y., 1991, Am. Acad., Rome, 1991, Mus. Contemporary Art, L.A., 1991, Hunter Coll., N.Y., 1991, Centro Cultural/Arte Contemporanea, Mexico City, 1991, Hilton, San Jose, Calif., 1992, Hillwood Art Mus., L.I., N.Y., 1992, Am. Acad. and Inst. Arts and Letters, 1992, Neuberger Mus., 1992, Statue of Liberty Group, 1993, Foster Harmans Galliers of Am. Art, Sarasota, Fla., 1993, Kohn-Abrams Gallerie, L.A., 1993, The Gallery at Bristol Myers Squibb, N.J., 1993, Friends of Art and Preservation in Embassies, N.Y.C., 1993, Just Art, N.Y.C., 1993, Mus. Modern Art, N.Y.C., 1994, TZ Art and Co., N.Y.C., Andre Emmerich Gallery, N.Y.C., 1993, Nat. Gallery of Art, Washington, 1994, Fred Spratt Gallery, San José, Calif., 1994, RAAB Galarie, Berlin, 1994, Gallary at Bristol Myer Squibb, N.J., 1994, Moma, N.Y.C., 1994, N.Y. Studio Sch., N.Y.C., 1995, Aldrich Mus., Conn., 1995, Rose Art Mus., Brandeis U., 1996; represented in permanent collections Milw. Art Ctr., Mus. Modern Art N.Y.C., Fogg Mus., Cambridge, Mass., Phila. Mus. Art, High Mus. Art, Atlanta, Houston Mus. Fine Arts, Corcoran Gallery, Washington, Mpls. Art Inst., Mpls. Art Mus., Met. Mus. Art, N.Y.C., Guggenheim Mus., N.Y.C., Ludwig Mus., Aachen, Fed. Republic Germany, Holladay, Washington, Saatchi, London, Bard, Albright-Knox Art Gallery, Buffalo, Whitney Mus. Am. Art, N.Y.C., U. Mich., Ann Arbor, Ohio State U., Columbus, Gilman Paper Co., N.Y., Auckland (New Zealand) City Art Mus., Portland (Oreg.) Art Mus., Aaken Art Mus., Oberlin, Ohio, Highhold Internat., S. Africa, U. Ohio Art Gallery, Columbus, HHK Charitable Found., Milw., Art Gallery Ont., Toronto, Can., Nat. Mus. Women in Art, Washington, Chase Manhattan Bank, N.Y.C.; installations: Hilton Hotel, San Jose, Calif., Sony Music Hdqs., Aldridge Mus., Conn., Edward T. Gignoux Courthouse, Portland, Maine. Recipient Witowsky prize 72d Am. Exhbn., Art Inst., Chgo., 1976, Creative Arts award Brandeis U., 1985, Bard Coll., 1986; Guggenheim fellow, 1972; Nat. Endowment Arts grantee, 1974, Am. Acad., Rome, 1991.

ROCKE, DAVID MORTON, statistician, educator; b. Chgo., June 4, 1946; s. Sol J. and Verva (Coleman) R.; m. Carrie Clausen, Dec. 30, 1971; children: Emily Carolyn, Miriam Ruth. AB, Shimer Coll., 1966; PhD, U. Ill., Chgo., 1972, postdoctoral, 1977-79. Vis. lectr. math. dept. U. Ill., Chgo., 1972-74; prof. Govs. State U., Park Forest South, Ill., 1974-80; assoc. prof. grad. sch. mgmt. U. Calif., Davis, 1980-86, prof., 1986—, dir., Ctr. for Stats. in Sci. and Tech., 1995—; cons. Calif. State Water Bd., Sacramento, 1987—, Calif. Air Resources Bd., Sacramento, 1988—, U.S. Bur. Reclamation, Sacramento, 1986, Sherwin-Williams Rsch. Ctr., Chgo., 1980. Contbr. articles to profl. jours. Recipient Youden prize for articles Technometrics, 1983. Fellow Am. Statis. Assn. (Interlab. Testing award 1985); mem. AAAS, Inst. Math. Stats., Royal Statis. Soc., Am. Soc. for Quality Control (Shewell award 1987), Biometric Soc., Bernoulli Soc., Am. Math. Soc., Soc. for Indsl. and Applied Math., Math. Assn. Am. Office: U Calif Sch Mgmt Davis CA 95616

ROCKEFELLER, DAVID, banker; b. N.Y.C., June 12, 1915; s. John Davison Jr. and Abby Greene (Aldrich) R.; m. Margaret McGrath, Sept. 7, 1940 (dec. Mar. 1996); children: David, Abby A., Neva, Margaret D., Richard G., Eileen M. BS, Harvard Coll., 1936; student, London Sch. Econs.; LLD (hon.), Harvard U., 1969; PhD, U. Chgo., 1940; LLD (hon.), Columbia U., 1954, Bowdoin Coll., 1958, Jewish Theol. Sem., 1958, Williams Coll., 1966, Wagner Coll., 1967, Rockefeller U., 1980, Pace Coll., 1970, St. John's U., 1971, Middlebury, 1974, U. Liberia, 1979, Am. U., 1987, U. Miami, 1988; DEng (hon.), Colo. Sch. Mines, 1974, U. Notre Dame, 1987. Sec. to Mayor Fiorello H. La Guardia, 1940-41; asst. regional dir. Office Def., Health and Welfare Services, 1941-42; asst. mgr. for. dept. Chase Nat. Bank, N.Y.C., 1946-47, asst. cashier, 1947-48, 2d v.p., 1948-49; v.p. Chase Nat. Bank, 1949-51, sr. v.p., 1951-55; exec. v.p. Chase Manhattan Bank (Chase Nat. Bank merged with Bank of Manhattan), 1955-57; vice chmn. bd. Chase Manhattan Bank, 1957-61, pres., chmn. exec. com., 1961-69, chmn., 1969-81, CEO, 1969-80; chmn. bd. dirs. Chase Internat. Investment Corp., 1961-81, Chase Internat. Adv. Com., 1980—, Rockefeller Group, Inc., 1981-94, Rockefeller Ctr. Properties, Inc., 1986-92, N.Y. Clearing House, 1971-78, Ctr. for Intern-Am. Rels., 1966-70, Overseas Devel. Coun., U.S.-USSR Trade and Econ. Coun. Inc.; chmn. Internat. Exec. Svc. Corps., 1964-68. Author: Unused Resources and Economic Waste, 1940, Creative Management in Banking, 1964. Active Urban Devel. Corp., N.Y. State Bus. Adv. Coun., 1968-72, U.S. Adv. Com. on Reform on Internat. Monetary System, 1973-77, U.S. exec. com. Dartmouth Conf. Bd. Inst. Internat. Econs., Am. Friends of LSE, U.S. Hon. Fellows LSE, Bus. Com. for Arts; founding mem. Commn. on White House Fellows, hon. mem., 1964-65; exec. com., chmn. Downtown Lower Manhattan Assn., 1958-75; trustee Rockefeller U., 1940-95, Carnegie Endowment Internat. Peace, Hist. Hudson Valley, 1981—; chmn. Rockefeller Bros. Fund, 1981-87, vice-chmn., 1968-80; hon. trustee Rockefeller Family Fund; life trustee U. Chgo.; trustee, chmn. bd., exec. com. Mus. Modern Art, 1962-72, 87-93; bd. overseers Harvard Coll., 1954-60, 62-68; co-founder Trilateral Commn., 1973-91, N.Am. chmn. 1981-92, hon. chmn., 1992; hon. chmn. Internat. House, 1940—, dir., 1940-63; pres. Morningside Heights, Inc., 1947-57, chmn., 1957-65; chmn. Am. Soc., 1981-92, hon. chmn., 1992—, N.Y.C. Partnership, 1979-88. Capt. AUS, 1942-46, NATOUSA, ETO. Decorated Legion of Honor France; Order of Merit, Italy, Order of Southern Cross, Brazil, Order of the White Elephant and Order of Crown, Thailand, Order of the Cedar, Lebanon, Order of the Sun, Peru, Order of the Humane African Redemption, Liberia, Order of the Crown, Belgium, Nat. Order of Ivory Coast, Grand Cordon Order of Sacred Treasure, Japan, Order Bernardo O'Higgins, Chile; recipient Merit award N.Y. chpt. AIA, 1965, Gold medal Nat. Inst. Social Scis., 1967, AIA medal of Honor for City Planning N.Y.C., 1968, Charles Evans Hughes award NCCJ, 1974, World Brotherhood award Jewish Theol. Sem, 1953, C. Walter Nichols award NYU, 1970, Regional Planning Assn. award, 1971; Hadrian award, World Monuments Fund, 1994. Mem. Internat. Exec. Service Corps (dir., chmn. 1964-68), Center Inter-Am. Relations (dir., hon. chmn.), Council Fgn. Relations (dir. 1949-51 , v.p. 1951-70, chmn. 1970-85), Century Club, Harvard, River Club, Univ. Club. Links Club, Knickerbocker Club, N.Y. Yacht Club. Avocation: sailing. Address: 30 Rockefeller Plz New York NY 10112

ROCKEFELLER, EDWIN SHAFFER, lawyer; b. Harrisburg, Pa., Sept. 10, 1927; s. Edwin S. and Nancy Rhea (McCullough) R.; m. Marilie Gould Wallace, Dec. 22, 1952; children: Ben Wallace, Edwin Palmer. AB, Yale U., 1948, LLB, 1951, M in Internat. Pub. Policy, Johns Hopkins U., 1989. Bar: Conn. 1951, D.C. 1956, U.S. Supreme Ct. 1957. Atty., FTC, 1956-61, asst. to gen. counsel, 1958-59, exec. asst. to chmn., 1960-61; pvt. practice, Washington, 1961—; ptnr. Schiff Hardin & Waite, Washington, 1981-93, of counsel, 1994—; mem. USIA Inspection Team, Pakistan, 1971; adj. prof. Georgetown U. Law Ctr., Washington, 1985-87. 1st lt. JAGC, U.S. Army, 1953-56. Mem. ABA (chmn. sect. antitrust law 1976-77, ho. of dels. 1979-82), Chevy Chase Club, Met. Club (Washington), Yale Club (N.Y.C.). Author: Antitrust Questions & Answers, 1974; Desk Book of FTC Practice & Procedure, 3d edit., 1979; Antitrust Counseling for the 1980s, 1983. Office: Schiff Hardin & Waite 1101 Connecticut Ave NW Ste 600 Washington DC 20036-4348

ROCKEFELLER, JOHN DAVISON, IV (JAY ROCKEFELLER), senator, former governor; b. N.Y.C., NY, June 18, 1937; s. John Davison III and Blanchette Ferry (Hooker) R.; m. Sharon Percy, Apr. 1, 1967; children: John, Valerie, Charles, Justin. B.A., Harvard U., 1961; student, Japanese lang. Internat. Christian U., Tokyo, 1957-60; postgrad. in Chinese, Yale U. Inst. Far Eastern Langs., 1961-62. Apptd. mem. nat. adv. council Peace Corps, 1961, spl. asst. to dir. corps, 1962, ops. officer in charge work in Philippines, until 1963; desk officer for Indonesian affairs Bur. Far Eastern Affairs, U.S. State Dept., 1963; later asst. to asst. sec. state for Far Eastern affairs; cons. Pres.'s Commn. on Juvenile Delinquency and Youth Crime, 1964; field worker Action for Appalachian Youth program, from 1964; mem. W.Va. Ho. of Dels., 1966-68; sec. of state W.Va., 1968-72; pres. W.Va. Wesleyan Coll., Buckhannon, 1973-75; gov. State of W.Va., 1976-84; U.S. senator from W.Va., 1985—, mem. vets. affairs com., fin. com., commerce, sci. and transp. com., chmn. Sen. steel caucus, Bipartisan Com. on Comprehensive Health Care; chmn. Nat. Commn. on Children, natural resources and environ. com. Nat. Govs. Assn., 1981-84. Contbr. articles to mags. including N.Y. Times Sunday mag. Trustee U. Chgo., 1967—; chmn. White House Conf. Balanced Nat. Growth and Econ. Devel., 1978, Pres.'s Commn. on Coal, 1978-80, White House Adv. Com. on Coal., 1980; active Commerce, Sci., and Transp. Com., Fin. Com.; ranking mem. Vet. Affairs Com. Office: US Senate 531 Hart Senate Bldg Washington DC 20510

ROCKEFELLER, LAURANCE S., business executive, conservationist; b. N.Y.C., May 26, 1910; s. John Davison, Jr. and Abby Greene (Aldrich) R.; m. Mary French, Aug. 15, 1934; children—Laura Rockefeller Chasin, Marion French Rockefeller Weber, Lucy Rockefeller Waletzky, Laurance. BA, Princeton U., 1932; LLD (hon.), SUNY Sch. Forestry at Syracuse U., 1961, U. Vt., 1968; D.Pub. Svc. (hon.), George Washington U., 1964; LHD (hon.), Tex. Tech. Coll., 1966, Duke U., 1981, Marymount Coll., 1983; HHD (hon.), Princeton U., 1987. Chmn. Rockefeller Center, Inc., 1953-56, 58-66, dir., 1936-78; founding trustee, pres., chmn. Rockefeller Bros. Fund, 1958-80, vice chmn., 1980-82, adv. trustee, 1982-85; dir. Ea. Airlines, 1938-60, 77-81, adv. dir., 1981-87; chmn. Woodstock Resort Corp.; bd. dirs. Readers Digest Assn., 1973-93. Mem. Nat. Cancer Adv. Bd., 1972-79; hon. chmn. N.Y. Zool. Soc., 1975; life trustee Wildlife Conservation Soc.; Meml. Sloan-Kettering Cancer Ctr., 1947-60, chmn. 1960-82, hon. chmn. 1982—; chmn. Citizens Adv. Com. on Environ. Quality, 1969-73, Jackson Hole Preserve, Inc., pres., 1940-87, chmn. and trustee, 1987-96, chmn. emeritus and trustee, 1997—; pres. Palisades Interstate Pk. Commn., 1970-77, commr. emeritus, 1978—; chmn. Outdoor Recreation Resources Rev. Commn., 1958-65, White House Conf. on Natural Beauty, 1965; life mem. corp. MIT; trustee emeritus Princeton U.; hon. trustee Nat. Geog. Soc.; trustee Alfred P. Sloan Found., 1950-82, Greenacre Found., Nat. Pk. Found., 1968-76, Sleepy Hollow Restorations, 1975-87, Hist. Hudson Valley, 1987—; chmn. Woodstock Found., 1968—; hon. dir. Nat. Wildflower Ctr., 1988—. Decorated commandeur de Ordre Royal du Lion, Belgium, 1950; comdr. most excellent Order Brit. Empire, 1971; recipient Conservation Service award U.S. Dept. Interior, 1956, 62, Horace Marden Albright Scenic Preservation medal, 1957, Disting. Service medal Theodore Roosevelt Assn., 1963, Audubon medal, 1964, Nat. Inst. Social Scis. award, 1959, 67, Alfred P. Sloan, Jr. Meml. award Am. Cancer Soc., 1969, Medal of Freedom, 1969, Cert. of Award, Am. Assn. for Cancer Research, 1980, James Ewing Layman's award Soc. Surg. Oncology, 1980, Congl. gold medal, 1990, McAneny Hist. Pres. medal, 1993, Chmn.'s award Nat. Geograph. Soc., 1995, Theodore Roosevelt Nat. Park medal of honor, 1995. Mem. Am. Conservation Assn. (pres. 1958-80, chmn. 1980-85, hon. chmn. 1985—). Clubs: River, Princeton, University, Brook, Capitol Hill, Links, Boone and Crockett, Knickerbocker, Lotos (N.Y.C.), Sleepy Hollow (Tarrytown). Office: 30 Rockefeller Plz Rm 5600 New York NY 10112

ROCKEFELLER, MARGARETTA FITLER MURPHY (HAPPY ROCKEFELLER), widow of former vice president of U.S.; m. Nelson Aldrich Rockefeller (dec.); children: James B. Murphy, Margaretta H. Bickford, Carol Murphy Lyden, Malinda Murphy Menotti, Nelson A. Rockefeller, Jr., Mark F. Rockefeller. Dir. Archer-Daniels-Midland Co., Decatur, Ill.; alt. rep. of U.S. to 46th Session of UN Gen. Assembly, 1991, 47th Session, 1992. Address: ADM Co 4666 Faries Pkwy Decatur IL 62526*

ROCKEFELLER, SHARON PERCY, broadcast executive; b. Oakland, Calif., Dec. 10, 1944; d. Charles H. and Jeanne Dickerson Percy; m. John D. Rockefeller IV; children: John, Valerie, Charles, Justin. BA cum laude, Stanford U.; LLD (hon.), U. Charleston, 1977, Beloit Coll., 1978; LHD (hon.), West Liberty State Coll., 1980, Hamilton Coll., 1982, Wheeling Coll., 1984. Founder, chmn. Mountain Artisans, 1968-78; chmn. Corp. Pub. Broadcasting, Washington, 1981-84; bd. dirs. Stas. WETA-TV-FM, Washington, 1987-89, pres., 1989—; bd. dirs. State. WETA-TV-FM, Washington, 1987-89, pres., 1989—; bd. dirs. Pub. Broadcasting Svc., W.Va. Edn. Broadcasting Authority. Mem.-at-large Dem. Nat. Conv., del., 1976, 80, 84; bd. dirs. Rockefeller Bros. Fund. Office: Sta WETA-FM 3700 S Four Mile Run Dr Arlington VA 22206-2304*

ROCKEFELLER, WINTHROP P., state official; b. Sept. 17, 1948; s. Winthrop Rockefeller Sr.; m. Lisenne Rockefeller; children: Andrea, Katherine, Winthrop Jr., William, Colin, John, Louis. Student, Oxford U.; grad. Ranch Mgmt. Program, Texas Christian U., 1974. Lt. gov. State of Ark., 1996; chmn. Pres. Coun. on Rural Am., 1991-93, Juvenile Justice Adv. Group; bd. dirs. Ark. Crime Commn., Tex. Christian U.; mem. Ark. State Police Commn., 1981-95; pres. Ark. Cattlemen's Assn., 1976-78. Vice-chmn. Winthrop Rockefeller Found., Ark. Cancer Rsch. Ctr., Ark. Arts Found.; founder, chmn. Internat. Billfish Conservation, U.S. Marshal's Assn.; trustee Winthrop Rockefeller Charitable Trust. Mem. Ducks Unlimited (trustee emeritus). *

ROCKENSIES, JOHN WILLIAM, mechanical engineer; b. N.Y.C., May 30, 1932; s. John William and Wilma (Mercz) R.; m. Marion Pauline Peachman, Sept. 16, 1956; children: Kenneth John, Karen Martha Rockensies Steinbeck. B of Mech. Engring., CCNY, 1954, M of Mech. Engring., 1960; postgrad., Bklyn. Polytechnic Inst., 1955, Columbia U., 1956. Registered prof. engr., N.Y. Jet engine performance and compressor devel. Curtiss Wright Corp., Woodridge, N.J., 1954-56; product devel. engr. Sperry Gyroscope Corp., Lake Success, N.Y., 1956-60; sr. exptl. test engr. Pratt & Whitney Corp., East Hartford, Conn., 1960-62; project engr. Stratos Corp., Bayshore, N.Y., 1962; prin. propulsion engr. Republic Aviation Corp.,

Farmingdale, N.Y., 1963-64; power plant design engr., group and project leader, project engr., engr. specialist and mgr. Grumman Aerospace Corp., Bethpage, N.Y., 1964-95; retired, 1995; contract staff engr. Northrop-Grumman Corp., Bethpage, N.Y., 1996—; mem. SAE E-32 Engine Condition Monitoring com., 1983; instr. navigation Smithtown Bay Power Squadron. Author tech. papers in field. Deacon, trustee, elder First Presbyn Ch. of Smithtown. Recipient Apollo Achievement award NASA, Washington, 1970. Assoc. fellow AIAA (mem. air breathing propulsion tech. com. 1996—); mem. NSPE, ASME, U.S. Power Squadrons (sr.). Avocations: sailing/boating, jogging, tennis, camping, model aircraft, travel. Home: 65 Parnell Dr Smithtown NY 11787-2428 Office: Grumman Aircraft Systems MS B69-001 Bethpage NY 11713-5820

ROCKENSIES, KENNETH JULES, physicist, educator; b. N.Y.C., June 10, 1938; s. John William and Wilma (Mercz) R.; m. Eileen Regina Dros, June 6, 1970; children: Kevin John, Patricia Ann, Regina Marie. BS in Physics, Polytech. U. Bklyn., 1960, MS in Physics, 1962; postgrad., NYU, 1965-67, Adelphi U., 1969-75, Nova U., 1992—. Physicist We. Union Telegraph, N.Y.C., 1962-63; prof. CUNY, Bklyn., 1963-93, Coll. Misericordia, Dallas, Pa., 1993—. Author: The Rotational Interferometer, 1962, The Effect of Class Size on Achievement in College Physics, 1995; contbr. articles to profl. publs. Mem. NSTA, Am. Assn. Physics Tchrs., Soc. Coll. Sci. Tchrs., Optical Soc. Am. Achievements include rsch. in interferometry, relativistic optics, electrostatic data storage, electrosensitive recording papers and statis. studies in edn. Office: Coll Misericordia 301 Lake St Dallas PA 18612-1008

ROCKENSTEIN, WALTER HARRISON, II, lawyer; s. Walter Harrison and Martha Lee (Morris) R.; m. Jodell Lynn Steinke, July 29, 1972; children: Martha Liv, Andrew Harrison. BA cum laude, Coll. of Wooster, 1965; LLB, Yale U., 1968. Bar: Minn. 1968, U.S. Dist. Ct. Minn. 1968, U.S. Ct. Appeals (8th crct.) 1977. Spl. asst. atty. gen., chief antitrust divsn. Office of Minn. Atty. Gen., 1970-72; assoc. Head & Truhn, 1972-73; alderman 11th ward Mpls. City Coun., 1974-83; assoc. Faegre & Benson, Mpls., 1984-85, ptnr., 1986—; mem. Capital Long-Range Improvements Com., 1974-82, Gov.'s Econ. Roundtable, 1980-82, Hennepin County Waste Disposal & Energy Recovery Adv. Com., 1976-77; chmn. devel. strategies com. League of Minn. Cities, 1979-80, bd. dirs., 1980-83; Mpls. del. Metro. Aircraft Sound Abatement Coun., 1977-90, chmn., 1982-90; mem. aviation subcom. of transp. tech. adv. com. Metro. Coun., 1977-83; mem. airport noise adv. bd. Minn. Pollution Control Agy., bd. dirs. noise com., 1982-85, mem. tech. adv. com., 1990; adv. com. Nat. League of Cities, steering com. Environmental Quality, 1975-79, vice chmn., 1976, chmn., 1978, steering com. Energy, Environment and Natural Resources, 1980-83, Energy Task Force, 1977-79, Nat. Urban Policy Com., 1978; mem. Noise Task Force, Nat. League of Cities/Nat. Assn. of Counties, 1977-80; regional dir. Nat. Org. to Insure a Sound-Controlled Environment, 1976-90, v.p. legal affairs, 1983-90; cons. group nuclear waste mgt., U.S. Dept. Energy, 1978. Elder Westminster Presbyn. Ch., 1975-80, 95—, trustee, 1982-87, chair stewardship com., 1989, chair pastor nominating com., 1992-94; bd. dirs. Loring Nicollet-Bethlehem Cmty. Ctrs., Inc., 1984—, pres., 1988-92; bd. dirs. U. Minn. Underground Space Ctr. Adv. Bd., 1985-95, chair, 1988-95; bd. dirs. Minn. Ctr. for Book Arts, 1988-93; com. mem. Cub Scout pact 196, Diamond Lake Luth Ch., 1988-91, com. chair, 1990-91; alumni trustee, alumni bd. dirs. The Coll. of Wooster, 1990-96; com. mem. Boy Scout Troop 187. Recipient Cert. of Appreciation, Upper Midwest chpt. Acoustical Soc. Am., 1977, Resolution of Appreciation, City of Mpls., 1983, Citation of Honor, Hennepin County, 1983, Cert. of Recognition, League of Minn. Cities, 1983, Hope of Rotary award City of Lakes Rotary Club, 1989, WCCO Good Neighbor award, 1992. Mem. Minn. State Bar Assn., Hennepin County Bar Assn., Delta Sigma Rho-Tau Kappa Alpha, Phi Sigma Alpha. Republican. Presbyterian. Avocations: reading, backpacking, cross-country skiing, woodworking. Office: Faegre & Benson 2200 Norwest Ctr 90 S 7th St Minneapolis MN 55402-3903

ROCKETT, D. JOE, lawyer; b. Cushing, Okla., May 3, 1942; s. Gordon Richard and Hazel Peggy (Rigsby) R.; m. Mary Montgomery, Aug. 31, 1963; children: David Montgomery, Ann Morley. BA, U. Okla., 1964, JD, 1967. Bar: Okla. 1967, U.S. Dist. Ct. (we. dist.) Okla. 1968. Assoc. Kerr, Davis, Irvine & Burbage, Oklahoma City, 1967-69; assoc. Andrews Davis Legg Bixler Milsten & Price, Oklahoma City, 1969-73, mem., 1973—, also bd. dirs., pres., 1986-90; securities law advisor Oil Investment Inst., Washington, 1984-87. Bd. dirs. Myriad Gardens Conservatory, Oklahoma City, 1987—, chmn., 1991-92. Mem. ABA (fed. regulation of securities and partnership coms. of bus. law sect. 1984), Okla. Bar Assn. (securities liaison com. 1983, chmn. bus. assocs. sect. 1985, securities adminstr.'s select com. 1986—). Avocations: sailing, fishing, skiing. Office: Andrews Davis Legg Bixler Milsten & Price 500 W Main St Oklahoma City OK 73102-2253

ROCKEY, PAUL HENRY, physician, medical educator, university official; b. Idaho Falls, Idaho, Apr. 3, 1944; m. Linda Marie Miller, Dec. 27, 1964; 3 children. MD with honors, U. Chgo., 1970; BS in Biochemistry with high honors, Mich. State U., 1966; MPH, U. Wash., 1978. Diplomate Am. Bd. Internal Medicine, Nat. Bd. Med. Examiners, Am. Bd. Med. Mgmt. Rotating intern Harborview Med. Ctr., Seattle, 1970-71; dir. Indian Health Ctr., Rocky Boy Reservation, Box Elder, Mont., 1971-73; resident, chief resident in medicine U. Wash. affiliated hosps., Seattle, 1973-76; Robert Wood Johnson clin. scholar, acting instr. U. Wash. Sch. Medicine, Seattle, 1976-78, instr., 1978-79, asst. prof., 1979-85, assoc. prof., 1985-88, asst. dean, 1983-87; adj. asst. prof., adj. assoc. prof. dept. health svcs. U. Wash. Sch. Pub. Health and Cmty. Medicine, 1980-88; chief resident USPHS Hosp. (name now Pacific Med. Ctr.), Seattle, 1975-76, asst. chief medicine, residency coord., 1978-80, med. dir., 1980-86; assoc. prof., assoc. dean U. Mass. Med. Sch., Worcester, 1988-90; prof. depts. medicine and med. humanities So. Ill. U. Sch. Medicine, Springfield, 1991—, assoc. dean for clin. affairs, 1991—, acting chmn. dept. family practice, 1991-93; mem. med. staff No. Mont. Hosp., Havre, 1971-73, v.p. med. staff, 1973; mem. med. staff Pacific Med. Ctr., Seattle, 1976-88, U. Wash. Hosp., Seattle, 1978-87, Providence Med. Ctr., Seattle, 1987-88, Madigan Army Med. Ctr., Ft. Lewis, Wash., 1986-88, Meml. Med. Ctr., Springfield, 1991—, St. John's Hosp., Springfield, 1991—; sr. v.p. for med. affairs St. Vincent Healthcare Sys., Inc. and St. Vincent Hosp., Worcester, 1988-90; coord. rev. Joint Commn. on Accreditation Hosps., 1980-83, 88-90; mem. exec. com. of med. staff St. Vincent Hosp., 1988-90; pres. Pacific Health Assocs. of Seattle, 1981-87; dir., vice chmn., bd. dirs. Pacific Health Plans, HMO, 1985-87; mem. Group Health Plan Credentialing Com. for Ctrl. Ill., 1994—; cons. in quality assurance and utilization mgmt. Westminster Hosp., London, 1988; mem. mgmt. adv. team to U. del Norte and Hosp. Infantal San Francisco de Paula, Barranquilla, Colombia, 1989-90; presenter in field. Contbr. articles and abstracts to med. jours., chpts. to books. Pres., bd. dirs. N.W. GIRLCHOIR, 1982-85, mem., 1985-88; mem. steering com. Seattle Area Program for Affordable Health Care, 1983; mem. Alpental Doctor Patrol, 1975-86, Ski Acres Doctor Patrol, Snoqualmie Pass, Wash., 1982-86; trustee Ill. Cancer Coun., 1991-92; bd. dirs. Ancilla Sys., Hobart, Ind., 1993—, mem. compensation com., 1995—; vol. physician Health First Clinic, 1994—; mem. Golden Rule Aard Panel Springfield, 1994; participant med. edn. subcom. Ill. Gov.'s Medicaid Adv. Com., 1994-95; chmn. bd. dirs. Ancilla Med. Found., 1995-97; regional interviewer student selection com. U. Chgo. Pritzker Sch. Medicine, 1978-88. With USPHS, 1971-81; maj. Wash. Army N.G., 1986-88; lt. col. Mass. Army N.G., 1988-96; lt. col. Ill. Army N.G., 1996—. Alumni disting. scholar Mich. State U., 1962-66, scholar U. Chgo., 1966-70. Fellow ACP, Am. Coll. Physician Execs.; mem. AMA, Soc. Gen. Internal Medicine, Ill. Med. Soc., Sangamon County Med. Soc., Alpha Omega Alpha, Phi Kappa Phi. Home: 1433 Williams Blvd Springfield IL 62704-2344 Office: So Ill U Sch Medicine PO Box 19230 Springfield IL 62794-9230

ROCKHILL, JACK KERRIGAN, collections company executive; b. Alliance, Ohio, Sept. 10, 1930; s. Carl Columbus and Lovell Fanny (Brown) R.; m. Karen Sue Rocki, Aug. 30, 1969; children: Michele, Martin. Student, Canton Actual Bus. Coll., Ohio, 1955, Internat. Corr. Schs., 1960, Kent State U., Canton, Ohio, 1962-65. Player Washington Senators, 1948-49; collection unit mgr. Nationwide Audit & Investigations, Canton, Ohio, 1960-66; pres., PVT. INVESTIGATOR Fidelity Collections & Investigations, Alliance, 1960—; cons. Fidelity Properties, Inc., Alliance, 1980—, pres., 1984—. With USMC, 1950-58. Republican. Methodist. Avocations: golfing, yachting, scuba diving. Home: 1487 Glenking Ln Alliance OH 44601-3666 Office: Fidelity Collections PO Box 2055 Alliance OH 44601-0055

ROCKLEN, KATHY HELLENBRAND, lawyer, banker; b. N.Y.C., June 30, 1951. BA, Barnard Coll., 1973; JD magna cum laude, New England Sch. Law, 1977. Bar: N.Y. 1978, U.S. Dist. Ct. (so. and ea. dists.) N.Y. 1982, U.S. Dist. Ct. (no. dist.) Calif. 1985. Interpretive counsel N.Y. Stock Exchange, N.Y.C.; 1st v.p. E.F. Hutton & Co. Inc., N.Y.C.; v.p., gen. counsel and sec. S.G Warburg (U.S.A.) Inc., N.Y.C.; counsel Rogers & Wells, N.Y.C; pvt. practice N.Y.C. Office mgr. Com. to elect Charles D. Breitel Chief Judge, N.Y.; mem. exec. com. lawyers divsn. Am. Friends Hebrew U. Mem. N.Y. State Bar Assn., N.Y. Women's Bar Assn., Assn. Bar City N.Y. (exec. com., chmn. drugs and law com., fed. legis. com., securities law com., sec. 2d century com., sex and law com., young lawyers'com., corp. law com.). Avocation: running. Office: Law Office 515 Madison Ave New York NY 10022-5403

ROCKLER, WALTER JAMES, lawyer; b. Nov. 25, 1920; s. Nathan Rockler and Evelyn (Terfansky) Norian; m. Elsie Spira, June 14, 1942 (div. 1946); m. Aino Allekand, Aug. 16, 1949; children: Elliot, James, Nicolas, Julia. BA, U. Chgo., 1940; JD, Harvard U., 1943. Bar: Ill. 1947, N.Y. 1950, D.C. 1953. Pros. atty. Nuremberg (Germany) War Crimes Trials, 1947-49; assoc. Chapman, Bryson, et al., N.Y.C., 1949-51, Paul, Weiss, et al., N.Y.C. and Washington, 1951-53; ptnr. Lederer, Livingston, et al., Chgo., 1954-60, Pennish, Steele & Rockler, Chgo., 1961-63, Cotton, Watt, Rockler & Jones, Chgo., 1964-66, Arnold & Porter, Washington, 1966—; dir. Office of Spl. Investigations U.S. Dept. Justice, Washington, 1979-80. Contbr. articles to profl. jours. 1st lt. USMC, 1943-46. Decorated Bronze Star. Mem. Chgo. Bar Assn. (chmn. tax com. 1958-59), ABA (mem. tax com. 1964—), Phi Beta Kappa. Democrat. Jewish. Avocations: bridge, piano. Home: 11129 Stephalee Ln Rockville MD 20852-3655 Office: Arnold & Porter 555 12th St NW Washington DC 20004-1200

ROCKOFF, MARK ALAN, pediatric anesthesiologist; b. Jersey City, Apr. 13, 1948; s. Aaron and Rose (Drescher) R.; m. Elizabeth Sceery, Aug. 6, 1978; children: Benjamin, Jillian, Michael. BS, MIT, 1969; MD, Johns Hopkins U., 1973. Diplomate Am. Bd. Pediatrics, Am. Bd. Critical Care Pediatrics, Am. Bd. Anesthesiology. Pediatric intern and resident Mass. Gen. Hosp., Boston, 1973-75, anesthesia resident, 1975-77, assoc. dir. pediatric ICU, 1979-81; neuroanesthesia fellow U. Calif., San Diego, 1978-79; assoc. dir. ICU Children's Hosp., Boston, 1981-89, assoc. anesthesiologist-in-chief, 1988—; med. dir. operating rm., 1992—; assoc. prof. anesthesia/pediatrics Harvard Med. Sch., Boston, 1987—. Editor jours. Survey of Anesthesiology, 1984-94, Jour. Neurosurg. Anesthesiology, 1994—. Fellow Am. Soc. Anesthesiologists, Am. Acad. Pediats., Soc. Critical Care Medicine; mem. Soc. Pediat. Anesthesia (pres. 1996—). Office: Children's Hosp 300 Longwood Ave Boston MA 02115-5724

ROCKOFF, S. DAVID, radiologist, physician, educator; b. Utica, N.Y., July 21, 1931; s. Samuel and Sarah (Rattinger) R.; m. Jacqueline Garsh; children—Lisa E., Todd E., Kevin D. A.B., Syracuse U., 1951; M.D., Albany Med. Coll., 1955; M.Sc. in Medicine, U. Pa., 1961. Diplomate: Am. Bd. Radiology. Intern U.S. Naval Hosp., Bethesda, Md., 1955-56; resident and fellow in radiology, USPHS trainee dept. radiology p. of U. Pa., Phila., 1958-61; staff radiologist NIH, Bethesda, Md., 1961-65; asst. prof. radiology Yale U. Sch. Medicine, New Haven, 1965-68; assoc. prof. Yale U. Sch. Medicine, 1968; asst. attending radiologist Yale-New Haven Med. Center, 1965-68; assoc. prof. radiology Washington U. Sch. Medicine, St. Louis, 1968-71; asst. radiologist Barnes and Allied Hosps., St. Louis, 1969-71; cons. radiologist VA Hosp., St. Louis, 1969-71, Homer G. Phillips Hosp., St. Louis, 1968-71; prof. radiology George Washington U. Sch. Medicine, Washington, 1971—; chmn. dept. radiology George Washington U. Sch. Medicine, 1971-77, head pulmonary radiology, 1978—, interim chmn. dept. radiology, 1989-90, prof. emeritus radiology, 1993—; cons. NIH, 1972—; vis. prof. Hadassah U., Beersheba U., Rambam Hosp., Israel, 1977; cons. in radiology VA Hosp., Washington, 1972-77, U.S. Naval Med. Center, Bethesda, 1973-77; mem. diagnostic radiology adv. com. NIH, 1973-76; mem. Cancer Research Manpower Rev. Com., NIH, 1978. Editor-in-chief: Investigative Radiology, 1965-76; editor-in-chief emeritus, 1976—; editor Jour. Thoracic Imaging, 1985; Contbr. numerous articles to med. jours. Served with USN, 1955-58; Served with USPHS, 1961-63. Recipient numerous USPHS grants. Fellow Am. Coll. Radiology (pres.-elect D.C. chpt. 1976), Am. Coll. Chest Physicians; mem. Am. Fedn. Clin. Research, D.C. Med. Soc. (mem. med.-legal com. 1975-78), AMA, Radiol. Soc. N.Am., Assn. Univ. Radiologists, Soc. Thoracic Radiology (pres. 1983-84, exec. dir. 1984-87). Home: PO Box 675650 Rancho Santa Fe CA 92067-5650

ROCKOFF, SHEILA G., nursing and health facility administrator, nursing and health occupations educator; b. Chgo., Mar. 15, 1945; d. Herbert Irwin and Marilyn (Victor) R.; divorced. ADN, Long Beach City Coll., 1966; BSN, San Francisco State U., 1970; MSN, Calif. State U., L.A., 1976; EDD, South Ea. Nova U., 1993. RN, pub. health nurse, nursing instr., prof., health facility supr., Calif. Staff nurse Meml. Hosp., Long Beach, Calif., 1966-67, Mt. Zion Med. Ctr., San Francisco, 1967-69; instr. nursing Hollywood Presbyn. Med. Ctr., L.A., 1970-74; nursing supr. Orthop. Hosp., L.A., 1974-76; instr. nursing Ariz. State U., Tempe, 1976-78; nurse supr. Hoag Meml. Hosp., Newport Beach, Calif., 1977-78; nurse educator U. Calif., Irvine and Orange, 1978-80; nursing prof. Rancho Santiago Coll., Calif., 1980-89, dir. health svcs., 1989-95, dir., chair Health Occupations, 1995—; nursing prof. Rancho Santiago C.C., Santa Ana Campus; nurse cons. Home Health Care Agy., Irvine, 1983; educator, cons. Parenting Resources, Tustin, Calif., 1985-89. Contbr. articles to profl. jours. Mem. Nat. Assn. Student Personal Adminstrs., Am. Coll. Health Assn., Calif. Nurses Assn. (chmn. com. 1970-73), Assoc. of Calif. C.C. Administr., Calif C.C. Health Occpl. Educators, Assn. (bd. dirs.), Pacific Coast Coll. Health Assn., Soroptomist Internat., Phi Kappa Phi. Democrat. Jewish. Office: Rancho Santiago CC 1530 W 17th St Santa Ana CA 92706-3398

ROCKRISE, GEORGE THOMAS, architect; b. N.Y.C., Nov. 25, 1916; s. Thomas S. and Agnes M. (Asbury) R.; m. Margaret Lund Paulson, June 12, 1948 (dec. Aug. 1957); children: Christina, Peter; m. Sally S. Griffin, Dec. 1959 (div.); 1 child, Celia; m. Anneliese Warner, Nov. 27, 1985. B.Arch., Syracuse U., 1938; M.S. in Architecture, Columbia U., 1941. Fellow architecture Columbia U., 1940-41; architect Army and Navy, Panama, 1941-45; designer Edward D. Stone, N.Y.C., 1945-46, UN Hdqrs. Planning Commn., 1946-47; archtl. assoc. Thomas D. Church, San Francisco, 1948-49; pvt. practice architecture San Francisco, 1949-86, Glen Ellen, Calif., 1986-87; chmn. bd. Rockrise, Odermatt, Mountjoy Assocs. (architects and planners); lectr. Sch. Architecture, U. Calif., 1949-53; adviser to faculty com. Sch. Architecture, U. Venezuela, Caracas, 1954; mem. San Francisco Art Commn., 1952-56; cons. architect U.S. Dept. State, Japan, 1957-58, Fed. Republic Germany, Venezuela, Brazil, 1978-80, Bahrain, Brazil, Venezuela, Fed. Republic of Germany, 1981; architect U.S. embassy, Bahrain; vis. lectr. Cornell U., Clemson Coll., 1961, Syracuse U., U. Utah, Stanford U., 1962-65, Nat. U. Mex.; lectr. urban design Spanish Ministry Housing and Devel., Madrid, 1978; mem. San Francisco Planning Commn., 1961-62; adviser to Sec. for design HUD, 1966-67; participant State Dept. AID Urban Seminars Latin Am., 1971; mem. U.S. del. Pan Am. Congress Architects, Caracas, 1980; vis. prof. Universidad Central, Mex., 1985. Mem. pres.'s adv. com. U. Mass., 1971; mem. adv. council San Francisco Planning Urban Renewal Assn.; bd. dirs. Telegraph Hill Dwellers Assn., 1985-86, v.p.; pres. Archtl. Found. No. Calif., 1986; apptd. San Francisco Art Commn., 1986-87. Recipient AIA nat. award for residential work, 1953, 59, prog. architecture award citation, 1956, award of honor and award of merit AIA Homes for Better Living Program, 1956, regional awards for residential architecture AIA, 1957, Silver Spur award for Disting. Cmty. Cmty. Svc., San Francisco Planning and Urban Renewal Assn., 1996, others; Fulbright fellow in urban design U. Rome, 1978-79. Fellow AIA (pres. No. Calif. chpt. 1961, nat. v.p. 1969-72, mem. nat honor awards jury, mem. nat. commn. urban design and planning 1978); mem. Am. Soc. Planning and Housing Ofcls., Am. Inst. Cert. Planners, Am. Soc. Landscape Architects, Nat. Assn. Housing and Redevel. Ofcls., Glen Ellen (Calif.) Hist. Soc. (housing coord., dir. com. migrant housing workers), Delta Kappa Epsilon, Tau Sigma Delta, Lambda Alpha. Home and Studio: 1280 Hill Rd Glen Ellen CA 95442-9658 *My adult life as architect and planner has been devoted to the construction and improvement of the man-made environment. I have come to believe through this endeavor, that it is the concern and responsibility of all thinking persons, whether professional or lay person to comprehend the forces for change in the environment and to work for the protection and enhancement of our cities and the natural environment.*

ROCKSTEIN, MORRIS, science writer, editor, consultant; b. Toronto, Ont., Can., Jan. 8, 1916; came to U.S., 1923; s. David and Mina (Segal) R.; children: Susan M. Bumgarner, Madelaine Jo Sottile. AB magna cum laude, Bklyn. Coll., 1938; MA, Columbia U., 1941; PhD, U. Minn., 1948; cert., Oak Ridge (Tenn.) Inst. Nuclear Studies, 1950. Research asst. entomology U. Minn., St. Paul, 1941-42; asst. prof., assoc. prof. zoophysiology Wash. State U., Pullman, 1948-53; asst. prof., then assoc. prof. physiology NYU Sch. Medicine, N.Y.C., 1953-61; prof. physiology U. Miami Sch. Medicine, 1961-81, chmn. dept., 1967-71; pres. Cortisol Med. Research, Inc., 1983-85; chmn. sci. adv. bd. Anorexia Nervosa Inst., Melbourne, Fla., 1983-85, Fla. Med. Ctr., Lauderdale Lakes, 1971-78; cons. entomology APHA, 1961-78; del. White House Conf. on Aging, Washington, 1961, 71; cons. insect physiology Sect. Tropical Medicine and Parasitology NIH, Washington, 1962-66, NASA, 1980-92, BIOS, 1983-85; mem. corp. Marine Biol. Lab., 1961—, trustee, 1961-93, life mem., trustee emeritus, 1993—; vis. lectr. Minority Insts. FASEB MARCPROG, 1983-88. Sr. author: Biology of Human Aging, 1978; editor: (with G.T. Baker) Molecular Genetic Mechanisms in Development and Aging, 1972, Development and Aging in the Nervous System, 1973, Physiology of Insecta, 6 vols., 1973-74, Theoretical Aspects of Aging, 1977; (with R.T. Goldman) Physiology and Pathology of Human Aging, 1978, Biochemistry of Insects, 1978; editor Miscellaneous Publs. and Thos Say Found. Monographs, 1983-92; contbr. articles to profl. jours. Mem. resource and mgmt. com. Area Agy. on Aging, 1988-90. Served with USAAF, 1942-46, lt. comdr., USPHS res., 1951-81. NRC fellow in natural scis. U. Minn., 1946-48; recipient Disting. Alumnus award Bklyn. Coll., 1959, Outstanding Alumnus Achievement award U. Minn., 1977; named knight comdr. of merit Knights of Malta, 1982. Fellow AAAS (life, mem. coun. 1962-64), Gerontol. Soc. (pres. 1965-66), Entomol. Soc. Am. (life mem.); mem. Internat. Assn. Gerontology (mem. exec. coun. 1963-66), Internat. Assn. Prolongation of Human Life Span (v.p. 1974-92), Am. Physiol. Soc., Am. Soc. Zoologists, Soc. Gen. Physiologists, Sunflower Soc. Miami (v.p. 1986-88), People to People Fla., Army-Navy Club, Miami Internat. Press Club, Coral Gables Country Club (bd. dirs. Fleet 1994-96, 97—), PHi Beta Kappa, Sigma Xi.

ROCKSTROH, ROBERT JOHN, broadcast television executive; b. St. Paul, Aug. 2, 1952; s. Robert John Jr. and Helen Louise (Devaney) R.; m. Stephanie Abrams, Apr. 16, 1988. BA, U. Minn., 1975. Anchor, prodr. Sta. KXON-TV, Mitchell, S.D., 1976-77, Sta. WBAY-TV, Green Bay, Wis., 1977-80; prodr. Sta. KFMB-TV, San Diego, 1980-83; prodr., exec. prodr. Sta. KCST-TV, San Diego, 1983-85; prodr. Sta. KPIX-TV, San Francisco, 1985-88, Sta. KRON-TV, San Francisco, 1988-93; asst. news dir. Sta. KSTP-TV, St. Paul, 1994—. Recipient Emmy award NATAS, 1980, 81, 88, 90. Office: KSTP TV 3415 University Ave W Saint Paul MN 55114-1019

ROCKWELL, ALVIN JOHN, lawyer; b. Kalamazoo, Dec. 29, 1908; s. John S. and L. B. (DeVall) R.; m. Anne Hayward, Aug. 24, 1933; 1 son, John Sargent. A.B., DePauw U., 1929, LLD (hon.), 1991; postgrad., London Sch. Econs., 1929-30; J.D., Harvard U., 1933. Bar: Mass. 1933, Calif. 1948. Spl. asst. to U.S. atty. gen., 1940-43; gen. counsel NLRB, 1944-45; legal adviser to U.S. Mil. Govt., Germany, 1946-48; partner firm Brobeck, Phleger & Harrison, San Francisco, 1948-79; of counsel Brobeck, Phleger & Harrison, 1979—. Trustee De Pauw U., 1958-80, life trustee, 1980—; trustee San Francisco Law Library, 1975-81; trustee, later pres. San Francisco Bar Assn. Found., 1976-80; mem. Commn. on Uniform State Laws, 1962-69. Fellow Am. Bar Found.; mem. Am. Law Inst, Harvard Law Sch. Assn. No. Calif. (past pres.), World Affairs Council No. Calif. (past pres.), Phi Beta Kappa. Clubs: Commonwealth (San Francisco), Pacific-Union (San Francisco), Bohemian (San Francisco); Cosmos (Washington). Home: 1400 Geary Blvd Apt 2403 San Francisco CA 94109-6574 Office: Spear St Tower 29th Floor One Market Plaza San Francisco CA 94105

ROCKWELL, BRUCE MCKEE, retired banker, retired foundation executive; b. Denver, Dec. 18, 1922; s. Robert B. and Florence (McKee) R.; m. Virginia Packard, Apr. 22, 1950; children—David, Jane, Sarah. BA, Yale U., 1945. Exec. sec. to mayor City of Denver, 1947-51; pub. rels. and advt. account exec. William Kostka & Assocs., 1952-53; with Colo. Nat. Bank, Denver, 1953-85; pres. Colo. Nat. Bank, 1970-75, chmn., CEO, 1975-85, also dir.; pres. Colo. Trust, Denver, 1985-91; sr. cons. BBC, Inc., Denver, 1991. Chmn., bd. dirs. The Denver Partnership, Inc., Kaiser Permanente, 1980-92; bd. dirs. Am. Pub. Welfare Assn., 1989-91; chmn. Denver Urban Renewal Authority, 1958-68; nat. coun. Salk Inst., 1978-84; trustee C.C. Denver, Com. Econ. Devel., 1979-85, Denver Symphony Orch., 1974-77, Denver Art Mus., 1965-72, 82-86, Denver Health & Hosp., 1995—; mem. Colo. Moffat Tunnel Commn., 1997—. Ensign USNR, 1945-46. Named Colo. Bus. Man of Yr., Colo. Bus. Mag., 1976. Mem. Assn. Res. City Bankers (dir. 1975-85), Denver C. of C. Clubs: University, Tennis (Denver). Home: 815 Vine St Denver CO 80206-3741

ROCKWELL, BURTON LOWE, architect; b. Utica, N.Y., June 3, 1920; s. Burton Lowe and Blanch Louise (Taylor) R.; m. Ruth Aldrich, May 19, 1949; children: Peter Grant, Abbie. BArch, MIT, 1946, MArch, 1947. Registered architect, Calif., N.Y., Vt., Mich., Ind. Project architect John Lyon Reid, Architect, San Francisco, 1947-53; ptnr. John Lyon Reid & Ptnrs., San Francisco, 1953-60, Reid Rockwell Banwell & Tarics, San Francisco, 1960-62, Rockwell & Banwell, San Francisco, 1962-70; pvt. practice Burton Rockwell, FAIA, San Francisco, 1970-88; ptnr. Rockwell, Chatham, Marshall, San Francisco, 1977-88, Rockwell & Rockwell, Architects, San Francisco, 1987—; faculty mem. U. Calif. Berkeley, Coll. Environ. Design, 1962-71; guest prof. MIT, 1969-70; juror Calif. Coalition for Adequate Sch. Housing, Archtl. Competition, 1991; chmn. Calif. Coun. Architects and Engrs., 1965. Architect-designer: Med. Rsch. Facilities, U. Calif., San Francisco, 1968 (AIA honor 1968), ch. sanctuary Lafayette Orinda Presbyn. Ch., 1968 (AIA Bay Area Honor 1974), Ct. House, Govt. Ct., Santa Cruz County, 1967 (Progressive Architecture award); contbr. articles to profl. jours. Bd. dirs. Community Music Ctr., San Francisco, 1972-74, Eastshore Pk. Project, San Francisco, 1975-80, Friends of Recreation and Parks, San Francisco, 1993—; mem. citizens' adv. com. San Francisco Bay Conservation and Devel. Commn., 1966—; mem. archtl. edn. com. Calif. Coun. Higher Edn., Sacramento, 1968-70; mem. bd. examiners Dept. Pub. Works, San Francisco, 1977-78; chair Golden Gate Pk. Master Plan Task Force, 1997—. Served to capt. U.S. Army, 1942-46. Recipient 22 nat. awards for archtl. excellence San Francisco Art Commn., 1953—. Fellow AIA (pres. San Francisco chpt. 1965, bd. dirs., other officers); mem. ASTM, Calif. Coun. Architects (pres. 1968, bd. dirs., other offices 1965—), Constrn. Specification Inst., Am. Soc. Testing and Materials, Internat. Coun. Bldg. Officials. Avocations: Morgan and Lancia automobiles, Scottish deerhounds. Home: 150 Edgewood Ave San Francisco CA 94117-3713 Office: Rockwell & Rockwell Architects 888 Post St San Francisco CA 94109-6013

ROCKWELL, DON ARTHUR, psychiatrist; b. Wheatland, Wyo., Apr. 24, 1938; s. Orson Arthur and Kathleen Emily (Richards) R.; m. Frances Pepitone-Arreola, Dec. 23, 1965; children: Grant, Chad. BA, Wash. U., 1959; MD, U. Okla., 1963; MA in Sociology, U. Calif., Berkeley, 1967. Diplomate Am. Bd. Psychiatry and Neurology. Intern in surgery San Francisco Gen. Hosp., 1963-64; resident in psychiatry Langley-Porter Neuropsychiatric Inst. U. Calif. Med. Ctr., San Francisco, 1964-67; instr. dept. psychiatry U. Calif. Sch. Medicine, Davis, 1969-70, asst. prof., 1970-74, assoc. prof., 1974-80, acting. assoc., dean curricular affiars, 1979-80, acting assoc. dean student affairs, 1980, assoc. dean student affairs, 1980-82, prof., 1980-84; career tchr. NIMH, 1970-72; assoc. psychiatrist Sacramento Med. Ctr.; med. dir. U. Calif. Med. Ctr., Davis, 1982-84; prof., vice chmn. dept. psychiatry and biobehavioral scis. UCLA, 1984-96, dir. of ops. svcs., 1996—, chief profl. staff Neuropsychiat. Inst.,, 1984-85, also dir. outpatient svcs.; chmn. U. Calif. Hosp. Dirs. Council, 1988-89; cons. Nat. Commn. on Marijuana, Washington, 1971-73. Co-author: Psychiatric Disorders, 1982; contbr. chpts. to books; articles to profl. jours. Bd. dirs. Bereavement Outreach, Sacramento, 1974-84, Suicide Prevention, Yolo County, 1969-84; bd. visitors U. Okla. Sch. Medicine; chmn. hosp. dirs. coun. U. Calif. Hosp.; governing coun. AHA Psychiat. Hosp. Fellow Am. Psychiat. Assn., Am. Coll. Psychiatrists, Am. Coll. Mental Health Adminstrs.; mem. AMA (gov.

coun. psych. hosp.), Am. Sociologic Assn., Calif. Med. Assn. (med. staff survey com.), Cen. Calif. Psychiat. Assn. (sec.-pres. 1977-78), U. Okla. Alumni Assn. (trustee 1981-86), Alpha Omega Alpha. Home: 1816 E Las Tunas Rd Santa Barbara CA 93103-1744

ROCKWELL, ELIZABETH DENNIS, retirement specialist, financial planner; b. Houston; d. Robert Richard and Nezzell Alderton (Christie) Dennis. Student Rice U., 1939-40, U. Houston, 1938-39, 40-42. Purchasing agt. Standard Oil Co., Houston, 1942-66; v.p. mktg. Heights Savs. Assn., Houston, 1967-82; sr. fin. planner Oppenheimer & Co., Inc., Houston, 1982—; 2d v.p. Desk and Derrick Club Am., 1960-61. Contbr. articles on retirement planning, tax planning and tax options, monthly article 50 Plus sect. for Houston Chronicle newspaper. Bd. dirs. ARC, 1985-91, Houston Heights Assn., 1973-77; named sr. v.p. Oppenheimer, 1986—; mem. Coll. Bus. U. found. bd. Houston, 1990, mem. million dollar roundtable, 1991—, mem. ct. of the table, 1991—, Top of Table, 1996—, mem. U. Houston Sys. Planned Giving Coun., 1992—, mem. coll. bus. adv. bd., 1992—, mem. alumni bd., 1987-95; appointed trustee U. Houston Sys. Found., Inc., 1992; bd. gov. The Houston Forum; active Tex. Leader's Round Table, 1994; pres. U. Houston Coll. Bus. Adminstrn. Found.; mem. Houston C.C. Adv. Bd. for Ednl. TV. Named Disting. Alumnae Coll. Bus. Alumn. Assn. U. Houston, 1992, Disting. Alumna U. Houston Alumni Orgn., 1996; named YWCA Outstanding Woman of Yr., 1978. Mem. Am. Savs. and Loan League (state dir. 1973-76, chpt. pres. 1971-72; pres. S.W. regional conf. 1972-73; Leaders award 1972), Savs. Inst. Mktg. Soc. Am. (Key Person award 1974), Inst. Fin. Edn., Fin. Mgrs., Soc. Savs. Instns., U.S. Savs. and Loan League (com. on deposit acquisitions and adminstrn.), Houston Heights Assn. (charter, dir. 1973-77), Friends of Bayou Bend, Harris County Heritage Soc., U. Houston Alumni Orgn. (life), Rice U. Bus. and Profl. Women, River Oaks Bus. Womens Exchange Club, U. Houston Bus. Womens Assn. (pres. 1985), Forum Club, Greater Houston Women's Found. (charter). Office: Oppenheimer & Co Inc 1600 Smith St Ste 3100 Houston TX 77002-7347

ROCKWELL, ELIZABETH GOODE, dance company director, consultant, educator; b. Portland, Oreg., Sept. 10, 1920; d. Henry Walton and Elizabeth (Harmon) Goode; m. William Hearne Rockwell, Feb. 3, 1948; children: Enid, Karen, William. BA, Mills Coll., 1941; MA, NYU, 1946. Instr. dance Monticello Jr. Coll., Alton, Ill., 1941-42; dir. masters program in dance Smith Coll., Northampton, Mass., 1946-48; 1st dir. dance dept. High Sch. of Performing Arts, N.Y.C., 1948-51, 53-54; dir. Elizabeth Rockwell Sch. Dance, Bedford, N.Y., 1956-86, Rondo Dance Theater, Bedford, 1971-93; tchr. continuing dance classes CCAE, 1994—; with Martha Graham, 1944-46, with Hanya Holm, 1946-48, with José Limon, 1949-52; mem. adv. ednl. com. Calif. Ctr. for Arts, Escondido, Calif., 1993-95, dir. dance workshops, 1994—. Choreographer (suite of dances) Jazz Suite, 1966, (50-minute dances) Catch the Wind, 1969, Genesis, 1972, (narrative modern ballet) The Executioner, 1974, Decathalon, 1982; dir. (subscription series) Dance-Art-Poetry-Jazz, 1978-79, (dance/music 1600-1900) Stages in Ages, 1981, (Am. dance revivals) Masterpieces of American Dance, 1982-84, Dances of the Decades, 1985-90, (revival & new choreography) Dances of Our Times, 1991; dir. dance workshops for Calif. Ctr. Arts, 1994, 95, 96; creator, founder performing group of older dancers Golden Connections Dance Ensemble of Women, CCAE, 1996, 97. Bd. dirs. Coun. for Arts in Westchester, White Plains, N.Y., 1978-79, affiliate, 1978—. Recipient Medal for Performance, Israeli Army, 1966, Award for Excellence in Arts Edn. Alumnae of High Sch. of Performing Arts, 1990, various grants N.Y. State Coun. on Arts, 1971-93, Coun. Arts in Westchester, 1973-92, dance touring program grant Nat. Endowment for Arts, 1975-79. Mem. Am. Dance Guild, Westchester Dance Coun. (program dir. 1965-69), Assn. Am. Dance Cos., San Diego Area Dance Alliance (bd. dirs. 1995—). Avocations: writing, swimming, touring, reading. Home: 205 Tampico Glen Escondido CA 92025-7359

ROCKWELL, GEORGE BARCUS, financial consultant; b. Chgo., Jan. 5, 1926; s. Thomas S. and Irene G. (Barcus) R.; m. Lois Ladd, Sept. 30, 1950; children: Susan, Cynthia. A.B. in Econs, Harvard U., 1949, grad. Advanced Mgmt. Program, 1967. Salesman IBM, 1949, products mgr., 1956; asst. mgr. IBM, Boston, 1958; mgr. IBM, Albany, N.Y., 1960; v.p., div. head computer services State St. Bank & Trust Co., Boston, 1963; v.p., head mut. funds div. State St. Bank & Trust Co., 1966, sr. v.p., 1968, bank sales coordinator, 1968, exec. v.p., 1968, pres., 1970-75; vice chmn. bd. State St. Boston Fin. Corp., 1975-76; also industry dir.; v.p., mng. dir. fin. industries Arthur D. Little, Inc., Cambridge, Mass., 1976-89; v.p., dir. Webster-Atlas Bldg. Corp., Keane Assocs., Inc., 1970-75; pres., dir. State St. Bank Boston Internat., State St. Boston Securities Svcs. Corp., State St. Boston Credit Co., Inc., SSB Investments, Inc.; dir., exec. com. Nat. BankAmericard Inc., 1970-75, Royal Bus. Group, Inc., 1980-84, Computer Ptnrs., 1983-86; bd. dirs. Sandwich Coop. Bank. Bd. overseers Boys' Clubs Boston, 1969-75; trustee coun. Boston U. Med. Ctr., 1969-74, trustee Lahey Clinic, 1973-95, Lahey Hitchcock Clinic, 1995—. Served to 1st lt., inf. AUS, 1944-46. Mem. Greater Boston C. of C. (bd. dirs. 1969-76), Harvard Bus. Sch. Assn. Boston (bd. govs. 1969-72). Clubs: Wellesley Country, Rio Verde Country Club, Rotary. Home: 376 Glen Rd Weston MA 02193-1403

ROCKWELL, HAYS HAMILTON, bishop; b. Detroit, Aug. 17, 1936; s. Walter Francis and Kathryn (McElroy) R.; m. Linda Hullinger, Sept. 7, 1957; children: Keith, Stephen, Sarah, Martha. AB, Brown U., 1958; BD, Episcopal Theol. Sch., Cambridge, Mass., 1961; DD (hon.), Episcopal Theol. Seminary SW, Austin, Tex., 1984; BD, Kenyon Coll., 1974; HHD, St. Louis U., 1994. Ordained to ministry Episcopal Ch. as deacon, 1961, as priest, 1962; ordained bishop, 1991. Chaplain St. George's Sch., Newport, R.I., 1961-69, Univ. of Rochester, N.Y., 1969-71; dean Bexley Hall, Rochester, 1971-76; rector St. James' Ch., N.Y.C., 1976-91; bishop coadjutor Diocese of Mo., St. Louis, 1991-93, bishop, 1993—; dir. Union Theol. Seminary, N.Y.C., 1976, 87, 91. Author: Steal Away, Steal Away Home, 1985. Mem. Coun. on Fgn. Rels., N.Y.C., 1988; former trustee U. Rochester, N.Y.C.; trustee Mo. Bot. Garden, St. Luke's Hosp., Mo. Mem. Century Assn. (N.Y.C.). Office: Diocese of Missouri 1210 Locust St Saint Louis MO 63103-2322

ROCKWELL, KAY ANNE, elementary education educator; b. Brighton, Mich., Feb. 12, 1952; d. Philip Oscar and Patricia Irene (Bennett) Newton; m. Lawrence Edward Rockwell, Aug. 23, 1975. BA in Social Sci. & Elem. Edn. cum laude, Spring Arbor Coll., 1974; MA in Early Childhood Edn., Ea. Mich. U., 1981. Dir. child care St. Luke's Luth. Day Care Ctr., Ann Arbor, Mich., 1980-82; tchr. 3d grade Colo. Christian Sch., Denver, 1982-94; tchr. 1st grade Front Range Christian Sch., Littleton, Colo., 1994—; chmn. Nat. Children's Book Week Colo. Christian Sch., 1993-94, chmn. ACSI spelling bee, 1991-94, chmn. ACSI speech meet, 1985-86. Spring Arbor Coll. scholar, 1972-74. Office: Front Range Christian Sch 4001 S Wadsworth Blvd Littleton CO 80123-1358

ROCKWELL, R(ONALD) JAMES, JR., laser and electro-optics consultant; b. Cin., May 7, 1937; s. Ronald James and Mary Cornelius (Thornton) R.; m. Diane Lundin, Feb. 3, 1968; children: James Gregory, Christopher Derrick. BS, U. Cin., 1960, MS, 1964. Directing physicist, assoc. prof. laser scis., laser research labs. Med. Center, U. Cin., 1963-76; dir. continuing edn. services Electro-Optical Systems Design Jour., Cin., 1976-77; v.p. laser/electro-optics Control Dynamics, Inc., Cin., 1977-79; pres. Rockwell Assocs., Inc. (cons. lasers, optics and electro-optics), Cin., 1979-89; pres., chief exec. officer Rockwell Laser Industries (cons. lasers, optics and electro-optics), Cin., 1989—; exec. com. sate use lasers com. Am. Nat. Standards Inst., 1971—; exec. sec. Laser Inst. Am., 1976-77, dir., 1972-92, pres., 1974; mem. adv. com. Laser History Project, 1983-89; dir. Laserworks, Inc., Rockwell Devel. Co.; cons. WHO, Internat. Electrotechnical Commn., founder Consortium of Laser and Tech. Cons., 1988; mem. tech. com. Laser Fire Protection of the Nat. Fire Protection Assn., 1991—. Co-author: Lasers in Medicine, 1971; author: Laser Safety Training Manual, 1982, Laser Safety in Surgery and Medicine, 1985, Laser Safety: Concepts, Analysis and Controls, 1992, Laser Safety: Modularized Training Package, 1994, Users Guide for Laser Safety, 1997; created software program: Laser Hazard Analysis, 1987, LAZAN for Windows, 1995, SKYZAN for Windows, 1996; co-developer: LASERNET page on the World-Wide Web (Internet), 1966; contbr. chpts. to books and articles to profl. jours.; editor jours. in field; mem. editl. bd. Jour. Laser Applications, 1994—. Co-chmn. Internat. Laser Safety Conf., 1990, 92, mem. planning com., keynote spkr., 1997. Recipient Pres.' award Laser Inst. Am., 1985. Mem. IEEE, N.Y. Acad. Scis., Am. Soc. Laser Medicine and Surgery, Midwest Bio-Laser Inst., Internat. Laser Display Assn., Newcomen Soc., Sigma Xi (nat. lectr. 1971-75), Delta Tau Delta (D.S.C. award 1985, dir. acad. affairs, nat. bd. dirs. 1975-83). Methodist. Designer, builder portable laser entertainment system in laser light artistic shows; patentee in field. Home: 6282 Coachlite Way Cincinnati OH 45243 Office: PO Box 43010 7754 Camargo Rd Cincinnati OH 45243

ROCKWELL, THEODORE, nuclear engineer; b. Chgo., June 26, 1922; s. Theodore G. and Paisley (Shane) R.; m. Mary Juanita Compton, Jan. 25, 1947; children—Robert C., W. Teed, Lawrence E., Juanita C. B.S. in Engring, Princeton U., 1943, Chem.E. (M.S.), 1945; grad. courses, Oak Ridge, 1944-49; D.Sc. (hon.), Tri-State U., 1960. Registered profl. engr., D.C. Process improvement engr. Manhattan Project, Oak Ridge, 1944-45; head shield engring. group Oak Ridge Nat. Lab., 1945-49; nuclear engr., naval reactors br. AEC, also nuclear propulsion divs. Navy Bur. Ships, 1949-55, tech. dir., 1955-64; founding officer, dir. MPR Assos., Inc., Washington, 1964—; research asso. Johns Hopkins U. Center Fgn. Policy Research, 1965-66; Chmn. Atomic Indsl. Forum Reactor Safety Task Force, 1966-72; mem. adv. group artificial heart program NIH, 1966; cons. to Joint Congl. Com. on Atomic Energy, 1967; scientific adv. bd. Nat. Inst. Discovery Sci., 1996—; v.p., founding dir. Radiation, Sci. & Health, Inc., 1996—. Author: The Rickover Effect: How One Man Made a Difference, 1992; co-author: Shippingport Pressurized Water Reactor, 1958, Arms Control Agreements/Designs Verification, 1968; co-founder Princeton Engr.; editor: Reactor Shield Design Manual, 1956; contbg. editor New Realities, 1988-92; contbr. sci. articles to profl. publs., non-tech. articles nat. mags.; holder patents, patent applications for neutron-absorbing cermets, process for leaching uranium from slags, process for prodn. boron-containing plastic sheet, others. Mem. adv. council dept. chem. engring. Princeton U., 1966-72. Recipient Disting. Civilian Svc. medal USN, 1960, Disting. Svc. medal AEC, 1960, Lifetime Contbn. award Am. Nuclear Soc. (1st, now known as Rockwell award), 1986. Fellow Am. Soc. Psychical Rsch. (life); mem. AAAS (rep. of Parapsychol. Assn. to AAAS 1975-87), Soc. for Sci. Exploration, U.S. Psychotronic Assn. (dir. 1988-91), Authors Guild, Writers Ctr., Washington Ind. Writers, Cosmos Club (Washington), Nat. Press Club. Presbyterian (elder). Address: 3403 Woolsey Dr Chevy Chase MD 20815-3924

ROCKWELL, WINTHROP ADAMS, lawyer; b. Pittsfield, Mass., May 7, 1948; s. Landon Gale Rockwell and Ruth (Adams) Lonsdale; m. Barbara Washburn Wood, June 20, 1970; children: Samuel Adams, Madeleine McCord. AB, Dartmouth Coll., 1970; JD, NYU, 1975. Bar: Minn. 1975, U.S. Dist. Ct. Minn. 1975. Asst. newsman fgn. desk N.Y. Times, N.Y.C., 1970-71; asst. to pres. Dartmouth Coll., Hanover, N.H., 1971-72; assoc. Faegre & Benson, Mpls., 1975-79; assoc. chief counsel Pres.'s Commn. on Accident at Three Mile Island, Washington, 1979; assoc. Faegre & Benson, Mpls., 1979-82, ptnr., 1983—, chmn. diversity com., 1990-95, head gen. litigation group, 1995—. Bd. dirs., v.p. Children's Theatre, Mpls., 1982-83; bd. dirs. Actors Theatre St. Paul, 1975-79, Trinity Films, Mpls., 1978-82, Minn. Ctr. for Book Arts, 1996—. With U.S. N.G., 1970-76. Brit.-Am. Project fellow, 1987. Mem. ABA, Minn. Bar Assn., Hennepin County Bar Assn., Am. Agrl. Law Assn., Adirondack 46ers, Adirondack Mountain Club. Avocations: writing, tennis, mountaineering, gardening. Home: 1901 Knox Ave S Minneapolis MN 55403-2840 Office: Faegre & Benson 2200 Norwest Ctr 90 S 7th St Minneapolis MN 55402-3903

ROCKWOOD, RUTH H., former library science educator; b. Chgo., Oct. 15, 1906; d. Charles Edward and Myrtle Isabelle (Wheeler) Humiston; m. George Herbert Rockwood, Apr. 14, 1928 (dec.); children: Charles Edward, Nancy Hoyt Rockwood Haigh, Alice Frances Rockwood Bethke. A.B., Wellesley Coll., 1927; M.S., U. Ill., 1949; Ed.D., Ind. U., 1960. Adminstrv. asst., instr. U. Ill. Library Sch., 1949-52; Fulbright lectr. Chulalongkorn U., Bangkok, Thailand, 1952-53; vis. asst. prof. Ind. U. Library Sch., 1958-59; prof. library sci. Fla. State U., 1953-79, prof. emeritus, 1979—. Mem. Fla. Trail Assn., Sierra Club, Beta Phi Mu. Club: Pilot (Tallahassee). Home: 4449 Meandering Way #PC408 Tallahassee FL 32308-5740 Office: Sch Library Sci Fla State U Tallahassee FL 32306

ROCKWOOD, THOMAS JULIAN, management services executive, information technolgy consultant; b. Cleve., May 16, 1942; s. Charles W. and Marjorie J. (Engert) R.; m. Janet L. Hess, Nov. 26, 1966; children: Kim, Kevin. BS in Acctg., Lehigh U., 1965, BS in Mech. Engring., 1966; MBA in Corp. Fin., NYU, 1971. Engr. U.S. Steel, Homestead, Pa., 1966-67, Western Electric Co., N.Y.C., 1967-84; mgr. AT&T Network Systems, Morristown, N.J., 1984-89; pres. Rockwood Mgmt. Svcs., Chatham, N.J., 1989—. Mem. ASME, Am. Mktg. Assn., Am. Mgmt. Assn., Soc. Telecom. Cons. Office: Rockwood Mgmt Svcs 52 Johnson Dr Chatham NJ 07928-1168

ROCO, MIHAIL CONSTANTIN, mechanical engineer, educator; b. Bucharest, Romania, Nov. 2, 1947; came to U.S., 1980; s. Constantin M. and Armande Ch.-Ad. (Cantacuzino) R.; m. Ecaterina (Cathy) Roco, July 24, 1986; children: Constance-Armanda M., Charles Michael. PhD, Polytechnic Inst., Bucharest, 1976; diploma strat. planning/exec. leadership, U.S. OPM, Washington, 1992; diploma leadership program, U. Md., 1994. Prof. U. Ky., Lexington, 1981—; program dir. engring. NSF, Arlington, Va., 1990—, coord. "Grant Opportunities for Acad. Liaison with Industry", 1994—; part-time prof. Johns Hopkins U., Balt., 1993; vis. prof. U. Paderborn, Fed. Republic of Germany, 1979, U. Sask., Can., 1990, Tohoku U., Sendai, Japan, 1988-89, Calif. Inst. Tech., Pasadena, 1988-89, Delft (The Netherlands) U. Tech., 1997—; cons. to industry in U.S., Can., Europe and Australia, 1981-92; cons. to U.S. govt. agys., 1983-89; lectr. postgrad. engring. Japan, Chile, Ga., Fla., 1982-91. Author: (with others) Principles and Practice of Slurry Flow, 1991, Particulate Two-Phase Flow, 1993; assoc. tech. editor Jour. Fluids Engring., 1985-89; contbr. over 100 articles to sci. and engring. jours and several articles symbolist poetry in literary jours. Recipient Carl Duisberg Soc. award, Fed. Republic Germany, 1979, Outstanding Rsch. Professorship award U. Ky., 1986-87, Outstanding Performance award NSF, 1994; grantee NSF, Rsch. Founds. USA, Can., Fed. Republic Germany, OAS, 1979-91. Fellow ASME (editor internat. symposium series 1984-94, chmn. multiphase flow com. 1992-94, chmn. internat. multiphase flow award com. 1995—), Particle Tech. Forum (vice chmn. 1994-96, chmn. 1996—); mem. AIChE (Gary Leach award 1996), AIAA, Soc. Rheology, Acad. Mechanics, N.Y. Acad. Scis. Achievements include formulation of innovative numerical methods for fluid and particulate flows (finite volume, probabilistic, marching), computer-aided-engineering for centrifugal slurry pumps, hydrotransport of solids through pipelines, and electro-imaging (fast laser printers); 13 inventions of fluid machineries, wear resistant equipment, methods to increase pipe transport capacity, viscosimeter; research on multiphase flow modeling, laser Doppler anemometry, flow visualization, power stations, pumps, and wear mechanisms. Office: NSF 4201 Wilson Blvd Rm 525 Arlington VA 22230-0001

ROCQUE, VINCENT JOSEPH, lawyer; b. Franklin, N.H., Nov. 27, 1945; s. Francis Albert and Mary Helen (O'Grady) R.; m. Emily Adams Arnold, May 31, 1969; children: Amanda Adams, Peter O'Connor, Caroline Quin. AB magna cum laude, Georgetown U., 1967; JD, Columbia U., N.Y.C., 1970. Bar: D.C. 1971, U.S. Supreme Ct., 1973. Assoc. Hogan & Hartson, Washington, 1970-73; counsel, spl. asst. to commr. Barbara Franklin U.S. Consumer Product Safety Commn., Washington, 1973-77; asst. dir. bur. trade regulation U.S. Dept. Commerce, Washington, 1977-80; ptnr. Sullivan & Worcester, Washington, 1980-90; pvt. practice law Washington, 1990—. V.p., co-pres. Janney Pub. Elem. Sch. PTA, Washington, 1982-84; vol. coord. homeless shelters Cath. Charities, Washington and Silver Spring, Md., 1984-90. Staff sgt. USAR, 1969-75. Mem. ABA (adminstrv. law and regulatory practice sect., internat. law and practice sect., bus. law sect.), Fed. Bar Assn. (adminstrv. law and internat. law sects.), Mid-Atlantic Literary Edification Soc., Nat. Capital YMCA, Phi Beta Kappa. Catholic. Avocations: reading, travel, American Civil War history, basketball. Office: 1155 Connecticut Ave NW Ste 400 Washington DC 20036-4306

RODALE, ARDATH, publishing executive. Chmn. Prevention Mag. Office: Rodale Press Inc 33 E Minor St Emmaus PA 18098-0001*

RODBELL, CLYDE ARMAND, distribution executive; b. Atlanta, Aug. 16, 1927; s. Joseph Hirsch and Fannie (Turetzky) R.; m. Cecile Rosenson, Mar. 27, 1949 (div.); children: Marsha, Jeffrey, Keith, Kim; m. Robin Graham McKenzie Rodbell, Dec. 15, 1974; 1 child, Lindsey. BBA, Emory U., 1949. Pres. Apex Supply Co. Inc., Atlanta, 1949—. Co-chmn. George Bush Presdl. Fund Raising, Ga., 1988-89; mem. State of Ga. Electoral Coll., 1989, exec. commr. Am. Bicentenial Pres. Inaugural Bus. Adv., 1989, Pres' Commn. on White House Fellowships, 1989-92. With U.S. Army, 1945. Mem. Wholesale Assn. Ga., Southern Wholesalers Assn., Am. Supply Assn., Standard Club, Rotary Club. Republican. Jewish. Avocations: reading, gardening, antiquing, politics, fund raising.

RODBELL, MARTIN, biochemist; b. Balt., Dec. 1, 1925; s. Milton William and Shirley Helen (Abrams) R.; m. Barbara Charlotte Ledermann, Sept. 10, 1950; children: Paul, Suzanne, Andrew, Phillip. BA, Johns Hopkins U., 1949; PhD, U. Wash., 1954; DSc (hon.), U. Montpelier, 1992, U. Wash., 1996, U. Geneva, 1996, Va. Commonwealth U., 1996. Nutrition and endocrinology chemist NIH, Bethesda, Md., 1956—; chief lab. nutrition and endocrinology NIAMD, Bethesda, Md., 1972-84; sci. dir. Nat. Inst. Environ. Health Scis., Rsch. Triangle Park, N.C., 1985-89, chief sect. signal transduction, 1989-94; scientist emeritus Nat. Inst. Environ. Health Scis., Rsch. Triangle Park, 1994—. Recipient Supr. Svc. award HHS, 1974, Gairdner Found. award, 1984, Jacobeus award, 1973, Nobel Prize for Physiology or Medicine, 1994. Mem. AAAS, NAS (Richard Lounsbery award 1987), Am. Soc. Biol. Chemists., Am. Acad. Arts and Scis., Japanese Biochem. Soc., European Assn. Study of Diabetes, Hungarian Acad. Sci., Belgian Royal Soc. Medicine, Am. Acad. Achievement. Office: NIH Environmental Health Scis Research Triangle Park NC 27709

RODDENBERRY, STEPHEN KEITH, lawyer; b. Aguadilla, P.R., Sept. 20, 1948; s. Harry H. and Gladys (Davis) R.; m. Bonnie Lindquist, June 26, 1948; children—Thomas D., David A., Samuel C. A.B., Harvard U., 1970, J.D., 1973. Bar: Fla. 1974, N.Y. 1974. Assoc. firm Davis Polk & Wardwell, N.Y.C., 1973-78, McConnell Valdes & Kelley, Miami, Fla., 1978-83, Holland & Knight, Miami, 1984-88, Akerman, Senterfitt & Eidson, Miami, 1988—. Mem. Fla. Bar (chmn. corp. sect. 1984—). Home: 14140 SW 69th Ave Miami FL 33158-1316 Office: Akerman Senterfitt & Eidson 1 SE 3rd Ave Miami FL 33131-1700

RODDIS, RICHARD STILES LAW, insurance company executive, consultant, legal educator; b. Washington, Mar. 18, 1930; s. Louis Harry and Winifred Emily (Stiles) R.; m. Joanne Margreta Hagen, Aug. 16, 1953; children: Kathryn Hazel Roddis Meyer, Linda Marie Roddis McGinley, Victoria Anne Roddis Hoefer, Margaret Mae Roddis Rumpeltes, Richard Louis Martin. A.B., San Diego (Calif.) State Coll., 1951; J.D., U. Calif.-Berkeley, 1954. Bar: Calif. 1955, Wash. 1981, U.S. Supreme Ct. 1959. Dep. atty. gen. Calif. San Francisco, 1954-58; dep. atty. gen., chief sect. bus. law and investment frauds unit Los Angeles, 1961-63; practiced law San Diego, 1958-61; chief dep. ins. commr. Calif. Los Angeles, 1963-65; ins. commr., 1966-68; prof. law U. Wash., Seattle, 1968-95; prof. emeritus U. wash., Seattle, 1995—; dean U. Wash. (Sch. Law), 1970-78; chmn., chief exec. officer Unigard Security Ins. Co., Seattle, 1984-88; cons. Stewart Econs., Inc., 1988—; adviser U.S. Dept. Transp., 1968-70, Nat. Conf. Commrs. on Uniform State Laws, 1971-72; chmn. Gov. Wash. Task Force on Catastrophic Health Care Costs, 1973-74; mem. steering com. Med. Injury Compensation Study, Inst. Medicine NAS, 1976. Bd. dirs. Saul Haas Found.; bd. dirs. Crista Ministries, 1986-91. Mem. ABA (com. to improve liability ins. system 1988), State Bar Calif., State Bar Wash., Nat. Assn. Ins. Commrs. (chmn. blanks com., chmn. laws and legis. com., vice chmn. exec. com. 1966-68). Republican. Lutheran. Home: 15524 SE 53rd Pl Bellevue WA 98006-5102

RODE, HELEN JANE, special education educator; b. N.Y.C., Apr. 25, 1949; d. David Edward and Celia Zelda (Sandek) Gould; m. Robert Rode, Aug. 13, 1972; children: Rachel Beth, Jason Scott. BA in Psychology, Hofstra U., Hempstead, N.Y., 1972, MS in Elem./Spl. Edn., 1976. Cert. tchr. elem. edn. K-6, spl. edn. N-12, edn. of orthopedically impaired and learning disabled, N.Y. Learning disabilities cons. Hauppauge (N.Y.) Sch. Dist., 1977-78; tchr. Middle Country Sch. Dist., Centereach, N.Y., 1979; tchr./chair Island Trees Mid. Sch., Levittown, N.Y., 1979—, team leader grade 7, 1993-94, tchr. mem. com. on spl. edn., 1992—. Mem. ASCD, United Tchrs. Island Trees, Nassau Reading Coun., PTA, Island Trees Spl. Edn. PTA. Avocations: piano playing, reading, travel. Office: Island Trees Middle School 45 Wantagh Ave S Levittown NY 11554

RODE, LEIF, real estate personal computer consultant; b. Copenhagen, Aug. 24, 1926; came to U.S., 1948, naturalized, 1960; s. Stig and Kirsten (Bay) R.; m. Elsa B. Ringressy, Feb. 14, 1992; children from previous marriage: Christian, Lise. BS magna cum laude, Columbia U., 1959. ChFC; CLU; cert. internal auditor; lic. realtor assoc. GRI. Mgr. East Asiatic Co., N.Y.C., 1952-54; various auditing positions N.Y. Life Ins. Co., N.Y.C., 1954-70, asst. gen. auditor, 1970-71, gen. auditor, 1971-82, sr. v.p., gen. auditor, 1982-87, cons., 1987-89; real estate agt., Weichert Realtors, Holmdel, N.J., 1989-90, Frayberg Realtors, Holmdel, 1990-92, Colts Neck Realty, Colts Neck, 1992—. Bd. dirs. Sports Found., Inc., Colts Neck, N.J., 1973-75, pres., 1975-77; mem. Bd. Edn., Colts Neck, 1975-76, v.p., 1976-78; trustee Bayshore Community Hosp., Holmdel, N.J., 1986-87; mcpl. liaison to Colts Neck Twp. for N.J. Assn. Realtors, 1989-94, real estate personal computer cons., 1995—. Served with Royal Danish Navy, 1946-47. Recipient award of honor N.Y. State Soc. CPA's, 1960; Merle M. Hoover scholar, 1960. Mem. Inst. Internal Auditors, Am. Soc. of CLU and Chartered Fin. Cons., Monmouth County Bd. Realtors (constn. and by-laws com. 1989-92, co-chair 1991-92, strategic planning com. 1992-93), N.J. Assn. Realtors (bd. dirs. 1993, legis. com. 1990-93, vice-chair 1992, chmn. 1993, new products and tech. com. 1990-92), Nat. Assn. Realtors. Republican. Lutheran. Home: 47 Blackbriar Dr Colts Neck NJ 07722-1203 Office: Colts Neck Realty PO Box 128 Colts Neck NJ 07722-0128

RODEFER, JEFFREY ROBERT, lawyer, prosecutor; b. Santa Fe, Mar. 29, 1963; s. Robert Jacob and Joanne D. (Thomas) R. BS, U. Nev., 1985; JD, Willamette U., 1988, cert. dispute resolution, 1988. Bar: Calif. 1990, Nev. 1990, U.S. Dist. Ct. Nev. 1990, U.S. Dist. Ct. (ea. dist.) Calif. 1990, U.S. Ct. Appeals (9th cir.) 1990, Colo. 1991, Oreg. 1997, U.S. Supreme Ct. 1997; cert. arbitrator, Nev. Legal intern Willamette U. Legal Aid Clinic, Salem, Oreg., 1987-88; legal rschr. transp. divsn. Nev. Atty. Gen. Office, Carson City, 1989-90, dep. atty. gen. taxation divsn., 1990-93, dep. atty. gen. gaming divsn., 1993—. Author: Nevada Property Tax Manual, 1993; contbr. articles to Nev. Lawyer. Contbg. mem. U. Nev. Coll. Bus. Adminstrn. and Athletic Dept., Reno, 1992, Willamette U. Coll. Law, Ann. Law Fund, Salem, 1992; active Nat. Parks and Recreation Assn., Washington, 1991; mem. First Christian Ch. Mem. Internat. Assn. Gaming Attys., U. Nev. Coll. Bus. Alumni Assn., Am. Inns of Ct. (Bruce R. Thompson chpt.), State Bar Nev. (functional equivalency com. 1994—), Phi Delta Phi. Republican. Office: Nev Atty Gen Office Capitol Complex Carson City NV 89710

RODEFFER, STEPHANIE LYNN HOLSCHLAG, archaeologist, government official; b. Newark, Ohio, Oct. 5, 1947; d. Jerry Bernard and Joan Elizabeth (Dasher) Holschlag; m. Michael Joe Rodeffer, Sept. 11, 1971. BA, U. Ky., 1969; PhD, Wash. State U., 1975. Instr., then asst. prof. anthropology Lander Coll., Greenwood, S.C., 1974-77; archaeologist interagy. archaeol. svcs. Nat. Park Svc./Heritage Conservation and Recreation Svc., Atlanta, 1977-80; archaeologist divsn. cultural programs Heritage Conservation and Recreation Svc./Nat. Park Svc., Albuquerque, 1980-81; archaeologist div. cultural programs Nat. Park Svc., Santa Fe, N.Mex., 1981-82; archaeologist, acting chief preservation planning br. Nat. Park Svc., Phila., 1982-86; chief interagy. archaeol. svcs. br. div. nat. register programs Nat. Park Svc., San Francisco, 1986-90; chief mus. collections repository Western Archaeol. and Conservation Ctr. Nat. Park Svc., Tucson, 1990—. Muster Chmn. Star Ft. Hist. Com., Ninety Six, S.C., 1975. Recipient spl. achievement award Nat. Park Svc., 1980, 82, mgmt. award So. Ariz. Fed. Execs. Assn., 1992; Woodrow Wilson fellow, 1969. Mem. Soc. for Hist. Archeology (membership chmn. 1976-78, sec.-treas. 1978—, Carol Ruppé Disting. Svc. award 1994), Soc. for Am. Archaeology, Soc. Profl. Archaeologists, Phi Beta Kappa, Zeta Tau Alpha (pres. 1995-97, historian 1994). Roman Catholic. Avocations: genealogical research, quilting. Office: Nat Park Svc Western-Archaeol Cons Ctr 1415 N 6th Ave Tucson AZ 85705-6643

RODEMEYER, MICHAEL LEONARD, JR., lawyer; b. Balt., May 25, 1950; s. Michael Leonard and Claire Isabel (Gunther) R.; m. Dorrit Carolyn Green, June 7, 1975; children: Justin, Christopher. AB, Princeton U., 1972; JD, Harvard U., 1975. Bar: Md. 1977, D.C. 1980, U.S. Ct. Appeals (10th cir.) 1980. Atty. Fed. Trade Commn., Washington, 1976-81, atty. advisor, 1981-84; counsel Subcom. on Natural Resources, Agr. Rsch. & Environ., Washington, 1984-88; staff dir., counsel U.S. Ho. of Reps., Washington, 1988-90, house com. on sci., chief dem. counsel, 1990—. Bd. dirs. Glen Echo (Md.) Park Found., 1991. Democrat. Avocations: computing, bicycling. Home: 6000 Harvard Ave Glen Echo MD 20812-1114 Office: Com on Sci 822 O'Neill HOB Washington DC 20515

RODEN, DAN MARK, cardiologist, medical educator; b. Montreal, Can., Apr. 15, 1950; came to U.S., 1978; s. Rudolph George and Eva (Vonchovsky) R.; m. Rosemary Wetherill, Dec. 29, 1972; children: Mark McKenzie, Paul Joseph, Rosemary Claire. BSc, McGill U., 1970, MD, 1974. Diplomate Am. Bd. Internal Medicine, Am. Bd. Cardiovascular Disease, Am. Bd. Clinical Cardiac Electrophysiology, Am. Bd. Clinical Pharmacology; Lic. physician, Quebec, Canada and Tenn.; Cert. Med. Coun. of Canada, Nat. Bd. Med. Examiners. Intern Royal Victoria Hosp., Montreal, Can., 1974-75, resident, 1975-76, 77-78; pvt. practice Montreal, Can., 1976-77; rsch. fellow clin. pharmacology Vanderbilt U., Nashville, 1978-81, fellow cardiol., 1980-81, asst. prof., 1981-85, assoc. prof., 1985-89, prof. Med. and Pharmacology, 1989—, also dir. divsn. clin. pharmacology, 1992—; del. 4th U.S.-USSR Symposium on Sudden Death, Birmingham, Ala., 1985; mem. Nat. VA Merit Review Cardiovasc. Disease com., 1986-88, chmn. 1988-89; ad hoc reviewer, Pharmacology Study and Cardiovasc. and Pulmonary Study sects., NIH, mem. Cardiovasc. and Pulmonary Study sect., 1991-94, chmn. 1994-96; adv. panel cardiovasc. and renal drugs, U.S. Phamacopeial Conv., 1990-95; mem. external adv. com., Pharmacological Scis. Tng. Grant, Columbia U., 1992—; mem. Clin. Cardiac Electrophysiology Test Writing com., Am. Bd. Internal Medicine, 1992—; mem. adv. com., Vanderbilt Clin Rsch. Ctr., 1989-91, chmn. 91-92, faculty appointments and promotions, Vanderbilt U. Dept. Med., 1992-95; mem. instl. review bd., Vanderbilt U. Dept. Health Scis., 1991-93, chmn. 1993-94. Author 27 book chpts., over 150 abstracts and 130 articles to profl. jours.; mem. editl. bd. Jour. Cardiovasc. Electrophys., 1990—; mem. adv. bd. The Med. Letter (newsletter), 1991—. Fellow Am. Coll. Physicians, Am. Coll. Cardiology (annual scientific session program com. 1992-93), Royal Coll. Physicians of Can.; mem. Am. Fedn. Clin. Rsch., Am. Soc. Clin. Pharmacology Therapeutics (bd. dirs. 1994—, chmn. cardiovasc. and pulmonary sect., 1995—), North Am. Soc. Pacing and Electrophysiol., Cardiac Electrophysiol. Soc., Biophysical Soc., Am. Soc. Pharmacol. and Experimental Therapeutics, So. Soc. Clin. Investigation, Am. Soc. Clin. Investigation, Am. Heart Assn. (clinician-sci.t award, 1981-86, long-range planning com. 1995—, basic sci. coun. exec. com. 1995—). Office: Vanderbilt U 532B Medical Rsch Bldg I Nashville TN 37232-6602*

RODEN, JON-PAUL, computer science educator; b. Vernon, Conn., July 15, 1943; s. Paul James and Evelyn Mary (McCarthy) R. BS, SUNY, Oswego, 1965; MS, Cen. Conn. State U., 1970. Cert. pioneer in professionalism Nat. Bd. Profl. Tchg. Stds. Tchr. elem. sch. Vernon Pub. Schs., 1965-68, tchr. anatomy and physiology, 1969-79, tchr. computer sci., 1980-82, dist. chmn. computer sci., 1982—, staff devel. presentor, 1986—; tech. advisor Capitol Region Edn. Coun., 1981-85; presenter Inst. for Tchrs. and Learning, Conn. Dept. Edn., 1990-91, N.E. Holmes Group, Boston, 1994; mem. adv. com. Affiliate Newsletter Svc., 1992—; provider mgr. Conn. Dept. Edn., 1994—; mem. Legis. Task Force on ednl. tech., 1995-97; mem. Conn. stakeholders com. Nat. Bd. Profl. Tchg. Stds, 1995—, cons. 1995; mem. tchr. preparation program rev. com. Conn. State Bd. Edn.; mem. nat. parent-tchr. adv. coun. Am. Online; presenter Nat. Sch. Bd. Assn. Tech. Conf., 1995; keynote spkr. Minn. High Success Consortium, 1997. Assoc. editor: Logo Activities, 1985; writer, editor numerous teaching guides. Pres. U. Conn. Friends of Soccer, 1987-89; corporator Newington (Conn.) Children's Hosp., 1978—; mem. bd. govs. Conn. Children's Hosp., 1988-95; mem. Vernon Rep. Town Com., 1978—; celebrant Celebration of Excellence Conn. State Dept. Edn., 1991, 95; bd. govs. Conn. Children's Hosp., 1995—. Recipient Ofcl. Citation of Recognition Conn. Gen. Assembly, 1991, 95, 96. Mem. ASCD, NEA (design com. 1995, conv. del. 1995, 96, presenter 1995, tchr./cons. Ctr. Edn. Tech, Washington, 1995—, panelist N.E. regional leaders conf. Phila. 1997), Conn. Edn. Assn. (editorial bd. 1991—, presenter Mid-winter confs. 1995 and Summer Leadership confs., 1993—), New Eng. Assn. Tchr. Educators, Conn. Computer Educators, Phi Delta Kappa (chpt. pres. 1994—, exec. bd. 1991—, selection com. 1995), Delta Kappa Epsilon. Roman Catholic. Lodges: Elks, Masons, Shriners. Avocations: racquetball, cycling, skiing. Home: 105 Maple Ave Vernon Rockville CT 06066-5400 Office: Vernon Pub Schs 777 Hartford Tpke Vernon Rockville CT 06066-5126

RODENBACH, EDWARD FRANCIS, lawyer; b. Phillipsburg, N.J., Apr. 16, 1951; s. L. Ernst and Harriett T. (Reinbold) R.; m. Joanne B. Pursell, Aug. 18, 1973; children: Megan, Kyle. AB, Lafayette Co., Easton, Pa., 1973; JD, Cornell U., 1976. Bar: Conn. 1976, U.S. Dist. Ct. Conn. 1976, U.S. Tax Ct. 1976. Assoc. Cummings & Lockwood, Stamford, Conn., 1976-84, ptnr., 1984-87; ptnr. in charge fiduciary acctg. group, 1984-90; ptnr. Cummings & Lockwood, Greenwich, Conn., 1987—, mng. ptnr. Greenwich office, 1988—; v.p., mem. exec. com. Cummings & Lockwood, 1988—, mem. fin. com., 1993—. Mem. stewardship com. 1st Congl. Ch., Ridgefield, Conn., 1987-90, chmn. 1988-90; mem. endowment com. YMCA of Ridgefield, 1986-90. Mem. ABA (estates and real property sect.), Conn. Bar Assn. (estates and probate sect.), Estate Planning Coun. Lower Fairfield County (exec. com. 1985-89, pres. 1988-89). Republican. Avocation: skiing. Home: 44 Golf Ln Ridgefield CT 06877-4819 Office: Cummings & Lockwood 2 Greenwich Plz Greenwich CT 06830-6353

RODENBECK, SVEN E., environmental engineer, consultant; b. Ft. Eustis, Va., Oct. 2, 1955; s. Eric Otto and Herma (Grawi) R.; m. Pamela Jo Foster, July 27, 1991. AA in Gen. Studies, St. Petersburg Jr. Coll., 1975; BS in Gen. Studies, U. Ctrl. Fla., 1978, BS in Environ. Engring., 1978; MS in Environ. Engring., U. Md., 1983; postgraduate Sch. Pub. Health, Tulane U., 1991-93. Registered profl. engr., Md., Fla. Commd. USPHS, 1979; field engr. Indian Health Svc. USPHS, Billings, Mont., 1979; field engr. Rocky Boy (Mont.) Indian Reservation USPHS, 1979-81; environ. engr. pollution control sect., environ. protection br. Divsn. Safety, NIH, Bethesda, Md., 1981-86, environ. compliance officer environ. protection br., 1986-87; environ. engr. office health assessment Agy. for Toxic Substances and Disease Registry, Atlanta, 1987-89, environ. engr. med. waste group, office of assoc. adminstr., 1989-90, environ. engr. cons. divsn. health assessment and cons., 1990-91; environ. engr. cons. Tulane U. Sch. Pub. Health and Tropical Medicine, New Orleans, 1991-93; environ. engr. cons., divsn. health assessment and cons. Agy. for Toxic Substances and Disease Registry, Atlanta, 1993-95, acting sect. chief assessment and cons. divsn. health, 1995-96; environ. engr. cons. divsn. health assessment and cons., 1996—; water quality officer Nat. Scout Jamboree, Ft. A.P. Hill, Va., 1989. Contbr. articles to profl. publs.; author report to congress: The Public Health Implications of Medical Waste, 1990. Recipient numerous USPHS awards, including Commendation medal, 1987, 90, Achievement medal, 1984, 89, citation, 1981, Outstanding Unit citation, 1995, 96, Unit Commendation, 1984, 88, 89, 90, 96, Surgeon Gen.'s Exemplary Service medal, 1996, Field Med. Readiness badge, 1996, Engring. Literary awards, 1995. Mem. ASCE, Soc. for Risk Analysis, Water Environ. Fedn., Nat. Wildlife Fedn., Assn. of Mil. Surgeons of U.S. (life), Nat. Audubon Soc., Ret. Officers Assn., Assn. Commd. Corps USPHS, Consumers Union (life), UCF Alumni Assn., Delta Tau Delta (life). Lutheran. Home: 1229 Hadaway Ct Lawrenceville GA 30243-4668 Office: Agy Toxic Substances Disease Registry Mailstop E-32 1600 Clifton Rd NE Atlanta GA 30329-4018

RODENBERGER, CHARLES ALVARD, aerospace engineer, consultant; b. Muskogee, Okla., Sept. 11, 1926; s. Darcy Owen and Kathryn Martha (Percival) R.; m. Molcie Lou Halsell, Sept. 3, 1949; children: Kathryn Sue Wilcox, Charles Mark. Student, U. Ark., 1944-45; B.S. in Gen. Engring., Okla. State U., 1948; M.S.M.E., So. Meth. U., 1959; Ph.D. in Aero. Engring., U. Tex.-Austin, 1968. Registered profl. engr., Tex. Petroleum engr. Amoco Oil Co., Levelland, Tex., 1948-51; chief engr. McGregor Bros., Odessa, Tex., 1953; petroleum engr. Gen. Crude Oil Co., Hamlin, Tex., 1954; sr. design engr. Gen. Dynamics, Ft. Worth, 1954-60; aerospace engr. NASA, Houston, summer 1962; prof. aerospace engring. Tex. A&M U., College Station, 1960-82, prof. emeritus, 1982—; chmn. bd. Meiller Research, Inc., College Station, 1967-82; pres. JETS, Inc., N.Y.C., 1977-79; cons. Southwest Research Inst., Gen. Motors Corp., Gen. Dynamics. Patentee hypervelocity gun and orthotic device. Served with USAAF, 1945; served with USAF, 1951-53. NSF fellow, 1964-65; recipient Disting. Teaching award Tex. A&M U., 1962. Fellow AIAA (assoc.); mem. Nat. Soc. Profl. Engrs. (v.p. 1980-81), Tex. Soc. Profl. Engrs., ASME, Am. Soc. for Engring. Edn., Sigma Xi. Methodist. Home: 8377 FM 2228 Baird TX 79504-4813

RODENBERG-ROBERTS, MARY PATRICIA, advocacy services administrator, lawyer; b. New Ulm, Minn., July 13, 1963; d. Richard Theodore and Patricia Rae (Malone) Rodenberg; m. Richard Lee Roberts, Oct. 28, 1989; 9 children. BS in Corrections, Law Enforcement, Mankato State U., 1985; JD, Hamline U., 1989. Bar: Wis. 1991. Shift supr. Reentry Svcs., Inc., St. Paul, 1986-87; coord. REM Lyndale, Inc., Mpls., 1987-89; dir. advocacy REM Minn., Inc., Edina, 1989—; case mgr. REM Consulting and Svcs., Edina, 1991—. Mem. ABA, Am. Assn. Mental Retardation, Coalition on Sexuality and Disability, Minn. Social Svcs. Assn., Wis. Bar Assn., Assn. Residential Resources Minn. Republican. Lutheran. Avocations: reading, sewing, crafts, dog training.

RODENHUIS, DAVID ROY, meteorologist, educator; b. Michigan City, Ind., Oct. 5, 1936; married; 2 children. BS, U. Calif., Berkeley, 1959, Pa. State U., 1960; PhD in Atmospheric Sci., U. Wash., 1967. From asst. prof. to assoc. prof. dept. meteorology U. Md., College Park, 1968-75, assoc. prof. meteorology, 1976-84, dir. Climate Analysis Ctr., 1985-95, dir. Aviation Weather Ctr., 1996—; exec. scientist U.S. com. global atmospheric rsch. program NAS, 1972; sci. officer World Meteorol. Orgn., 1975—; U.S.-U.S.S.R. exchange scientist, 1980. Mem. Am. Geophys. Union, Am. Meteorol. Soc. Achievements include research in tropical meteorology, convection models, dynamic climate models. Office: NOAA-Nat Weather Svc Nat Ctrs Environ Prediction 601 E 12th St Kansas City MO 64106

RODENKIRK, ROBERT FRANCIS, JR., journalist; b. Evanston, Ill., Apr. 28, 1952; s. Robert Francis and Joan Marie (Wolter) R. BA in History and Journalism, Ind. U., 1974; postgrad., Northwestern U., 1976. Program dir., pub. affairs dir. WIUS Radio, Bloomington, Ind., 1972-74; reporter City News Bur. of Chgo., 1974-77; news dir. WNUR Radio, Evanston, Ill., 1977; announcer WDHF Radio, Chgo., 1977; news dir. WMET Radio, Chgo., 1977-78; Chgo. corr. AP Radio Network, 1978-79; reporter, anchor WINS Radio, N.Y.C., 1984-88, WMAQ Radio, Chgo., 1979-84, 88—. Recipient Nat. Broadcast awards UPI, 1979, 81, 83, 90, Nat. award Sigma Delta Chi, 1996, others. Mem. Ill. News Broadcasters Assn. (bd. dirs. 1988—, v.p. 1994-96, pres. 1996—), Soc. Profl. Journalists, Radio-TV News Dirs. Assn., Chgo. Headline Club (bd. dirs. 1993—, pres.-elect 1995-96, pres. 1996—, Peter Lisagor award 1988, 96), Branford Electric Ry. Assn., Ill. Ry. Mus., Fox River Trolley Mus. (publicity dir.). Roman Catholic. Avocations: railroading, bicycling. Office: WMAQ Radio News 455 N Cityfront Plaza Dr Chicago IL 60611-5503

RODER, RONALD ERNEST, accountant; b. Milw., Nov. 8, 1948; m. Marilyn L. Frederick, June 13, 1970; children: Lori A., Ronald J. BBA, U. Wis., 1970. CPA, Wis. Fin. svcs. officer U. Wis., Milw., 1970-73; asst. v.p. 1st Wis. Corp., Milw., 1973-79; sr. v.p., contr. 1st Wis. Nat. Bank, Madison, 1979-87; 1st v.p. mergers and acquisitions 1st Wis. Corp., Milw., 1987-88; sr. v.p. info. svcs. 1st Wis. Nat. Bank, Milw., 1988-89; pres. Firstar Info. Svcs. Corp., Milw., 1990—. Mem. Wis. Inst. CPAs. Office: Firstar Info Svcs Corp 16900 W Capitol Dr Brookfield WI 53005-2188

RODERICK, ROBERT LEE, aerospace executive; b. Chgo., Oct. 19, 1925; s. Albert Lee and Betha Manilla (Powers) R.; m. Lisa Wolf, Dec. 28, 1950; children: Diane Gale, Robert Kirk. Student, Iowa State U., 1943; BSEE, Ill. Inst. Tech., 1948; PhD, Brown U., 1951. V.p. Litton Industries, Beverly Hills, Calif., 1968-73; group v.p. Hughes Aircraft Co., Canoga Park, Calif., 1973-87; v.p. corp. tech. ctrs. Hughes Aircraft Co., L.A., 1987-90. Patentee instanteous vertical speed indicator. With USN, 1943-46. Recipient Spl. Recognition award Ill. Inst. Tech., 1967, named to Hall of Fame, 1983; recipient Pub. Svc. award NASA, 1967, Am. Machinist's award Am. Machinists Assn., 1970. Mem. Assn. U.S. Army, Am. Def. Preparedness Assn., Sigma Xi, Tau Beta Phi, Eta Kappa Nu. Avocations: tennis, personal computing. Home: 3426 Alginet Dr Encino CA 91436-4124

RODERICK, WILLIAM RODNEY, academic administrator; b. Chgo., Aug. 6, 1933; s. William Forrest and June Hazel (Kurtz) R.; m. Dorothy Jean Paetel, Oct. 21, 1965. BS in Chemistry, Northwestern U., 1954; SM in Chemistry, U. Chgo., 1955, PhD in Chemistry, 1957. Prof. chemistry U. Fla., Gainesville, 1958-62; rsch. chemist Abbott Labs., North Chicago, Ill., 1962-71; prof. chemistry Roosevelt U., Chgo., 1972—; assoc. dean Roosevelt U., Albert A. Robin Campus, Schaumburg, Ill., 1992—. Mem. AAAS, Am. Chem. Soc. (Tour Speaker of Yr. award 1969, 71), Sigma Xi, Phi Beta Kappa. Home: 15193 W Redwood Ln Libertyville IL 60048-1447 Office: Roosevelt Univ Albert A Robin Campus 1651 Mcconnor Pkwy Schaumburg IL 60173-4344

RODGERS, BERNARD F., JR., academic administrator, dean; b. Hazleton, Pa., Mar. 21, 1947; s. Bernard F. and Anna V. (Gulla) R.; m. Patricia Hick, Dec. 6, 1969 (div. June, 1982); m. Jane Powell, Oct. 27, 1984. BS in English and Edn., Mt. St. Mary's Coll., 1969; MA in English, U. Bridgeport, 1972; PhD in English with honors, U. Chgo., 1975. Tchr. Eng., dir. drama Somers Ctrl. High Sch., Lincolndale, N.Y., 1969-72; seminar coord. Shakespeare Inst. U. Bridgeport, 1972; lectr. Am. Lit. U. Chgo. Extension, 1975; instr., asst. prof. lit. and humanities City Colls. Chgo., 1975-82, spl. asst. to chancellor, 1984-85; faculty Eng. Simon's Rock Coll. of Bard, Great Barrington, Mass., 1985—, dean acad. affairs, 1985-87, v.p., dean, 1987—; chair lit. and humanities sect. coll. accreditation program Chgo. City-Wide Coll., 1977-78, chair coll. acceleration program, 1977-78, mem. adminstrv. coun., 1980-81; bd. overseers Simon's Rock Coll. of Bard, 1987—; evaluator NEH Summer Insts. H.S. English Tchrs., 1985, 86; proposal evaluator Fund for Empprovement Postsecondary Edn., 1984; mem. planning com. humanists Write On, Chgo., 1982-83; mem. nom. com. Eisenhower Fellowship, Am. Embassy, Warsaw, Poland, 1980; mem. writing panel artists-in-residence program Chgo. Coun. Fine Arts, 1978. Author: Philip Roth: A Bibliography, 1974, 2d edit., 1984, Philip Roth, 1978, Contemporary American Fiction 1944-79: A Chronology, 1980; essayist, reviewer in field; contbr. essays, reviews Art in Review, 1980-85; assoc. prodr. TV talk show U. Chgo., 1974-75, prodr., 1975-76; prodr., host interview program City Colls. Chgo., 1981-82; spkr. in field. Bd. dirs. Fairview Hosp., Great Barrington, Mass. Found. for Humanities, chair, 1992-94, vice chair, 1991-92, chair program com., 1990-92, Friends of Chgo. Pub. Libr., 1982; mem. South County cabinet Berkshires United Way, 1988, mem. planning com. humanists Read Ill., 1984-85, ad hoc com. excellence Ill. C.C. Trustees Assn., 1984-85. U. Chgo. fellow, 1973, Ford Found. fellow, 1974-75, Fulbright-Hays sr. lectr. to Poland, 1979-80, Chgo. Pub. Libr. assoc. scholar, 1976-78. Mem. So. Berkshire C. of C. (bd. dirs. 1987-90), New Eng. Assn. Schs. and Colls. (evaluation team chair commn. instns. higher edn. 1986—), North Ctrl. Assn. Colls. and Schs. (asst. chair commn. instns. higher edn 1982-84), Soc. Midland Authors (chair fiction award com. 1985), Lambda Iota Tau, Pi Delta Epsilon, Delta Epsilon Sigma. Home: PO Box 778 Great Barrington MA 01230-0778 Office: Simon's Rock Coll of Bard 84 Alford Rd Great Barrington MA 01230-1559

RODGERS, BILLY RUSSELL, chemical engineer, research scientist; b. Fitzgerald, Ga., Sept. 5, 1936; s. Jimmie R. and Ruby Doris (Morris) R.; divorced; children: Cheryl, Donna, Angie, Rusty. AA, U. Fla., 1956, BSChemE with high honors, 1966, MS in Engring., 1967; PhD, U. Tenn., 1980. Project leader Shell Devel. Co., 1968-72; group leader Keene Corp. Fluid Handling, Cookeville, Tenn., 1972-74, Oak Ridge (Tenn.) Nat. Lab., 1974-92; sr. engr. Walk Haydel & Assocs., New Orleans, 1992-94; pres. Rodgers USA Enterprises, Orange Park, Fla., 1992—, Intelligent Cons., Orange Park, 1993—; qualifying agt./mgr. Rodgers Constrn. Co., 1996—. Author 3 books in field; contbr. articles to profl. publs. Fellow AIChE (bd. dirs. 1993-97, chmn. fuels and petrochem. divsn. 1992-95, chmn. program com. fuels and petrochem. divsn. 1990-92). Republican. Achievements include 1 patent in field. Avocation: computers. Office: Rodgers USA Enterprises 794 Foxridge Center Dr Orange Park FL 32065-5776

RODGERS, DANIEL TRACY, history educator; b. Darby, Pa., Sept. 29, 1942; s. Oliver Eliot and Dorothy (Welch) R.; m. Irene Wylie, 1971; children: Peter Samuel, Dwight Oliver. AB, BS in Engring., Brown U., 1965; PhD in History, Yale U., 1973. Instr. history U. Wis., Madison, 1971-73, asst. prof., 1973-78, assoc. prof., 1978-80; assoc. prof. history Princeton (N.J.) U., 1980-86, prof., 1986—, chair, 1988-95, 97-98; Fulbright lectr., Frankfurt, Fed. Republic Germany, 1983-84. Author: The Work Ethic in Industrial America, 1860-1920 (Frederick Jackson Turner award 1978), 1978, Contested Truths: Keywords in American Politics since Independence, 1987. Recipient Chancellor's award U. Wis., Madison, 1978; Am. Coun. Learned Socs. fellow, 1976, NEH fellow, 1987-88, Ctr. for Advanced Study in Behavioral Scis. fellow, 1991-92. Office: Princeton U Dept History Princeton NJ 08544

RODGERS, DIANNA SUE, private school educator; b. Mineral Wells, Tex., Feb. 18, 1953; d. William Floyd and Nellie Rose (Frazier) R. Student, Glassboro State Coll., 1971-73; BA, Southeastern Coll. Assemblies of God, 1975; postgrad., Rollins Coll., 1976-77. Cert. tchr., N.J. 6th grade tchr. First Christian Assembly Acad., Memphis, 1975-81; kindergarten tchr. Ambassador Christian Acad., Glassboro, N.J., 1981-85; dir. Children's Edn. Ctr., Upland, Pa., 1985-86; 7th and 8th grade tchr. Ambassador Christian Acad., Glassboro, 1986-87, presch. tchr., 1987-88; 3d-6th grade tchr. Cen. Jersey Christian Sch., Asbury Park, N.J., 1988-94, elem. prin., 1990-93; tchr. 2d grade Calvary Acad., Lakewood, N.J., 1994—. Asst. Brownie leader Girl Scouts Am., Glassboro, 1971-72; dir., organizer Vacation Bible Sch., Calvary Hill Assembly of God, Glassboro, 1988, Children's Ch. leader, 1981-88; tchr. Vacation Bible Sch., First Assembly of God, Shrewsbury, N.J., 1991, 92, 93, sec., bd. dirs., 1991-96, toddler ch. tchr., 1989—; Sunday Sch. tchr. First Christian Assembly, Memphis, 1975-81. Mem. Delta Kappa Gamma (Mu chpt.), Alpha Zeta. Avocations: reading, arts and crafts, volleyball. Home: 96 Wallace St Red Bank NJ 07701-1811 Office: Calvary Acad 1133 County Line Rd E Lakewood NJ 08701-2115

RODGERS, EUGENE, writer; b. Bklyn., July 22, 1939; s. Thomas Aquinas and Catherine (Slattery) R.; m. Carol Diane Huber, 1977; children: Eric Eugene, Catherine Huber. BS, Villanova U., 1961; postgrad., U. Wis., 1961-63; MS, Va. Commonwealth U., 1991. Research asst. sci. writing U. Wis., Madison, 1961-63; pub. info. officer U.S. Antarctic Research Program, 1963-65; freelance writer Washington, 1965-67; mgr. sci. pub. relations Westinghouse Electric Corp., Pitts., 1967-75; editor Atomic Indsl. Forum Inc., Washington, 1975-76; speechwriter ERDA, Washington, 1976, IBM, Armonk, N.Y., 1977-79, United Techs. Corp., Hartford, Conn., 1979-82; free-lance writer, 1982-84; sr. writer Virginia Power, Richmond, VA, 1984-87; editor, pub. Electric RD&D Newsletter, Midlothian, Va., 1987-88; freelance writer Midlothian, 1988—; adj. instr. Va. Commonwealth U., Richmond, 1991-92. Author: Beyond the Barrier: The Story of Byrd's First Expedition to Antarctica, 1990, Flying High: The Story of Boeing and the Rise of the Jetliner Industry, 1996. Home: 2621 Ellesmere Dr Midlothian VA 23113-3939

RODGERS, FRANK, librarian; b. Darlington, Eng., July 28, 1927; came to U.S., 1956; s. Charles Bede and Frances (Page) R.; m. Sarah Louise Edelson, Dec. 18, 1971; children: Hilda Marie, Norah Frances. BA with honors, King's Coll., U. Durham, 1947; diploma librarianship, London U., 1952. Libr. Poplar Tech. Coll., London, 1951-53, St. Martin's Sch. Art, 1953-56; sr. libr. adult svcs. divsn. Akron (Ohio) Pub. Libr., 1956-59; asst. reference libr. U. Ill., 1959-64; chief reference libr., then asst. dir. pub. svcs. Pa. State U. Librs., 1965-69; dir. Portland (Oreg.) State U. Libr., 1969-79; dir. librs. U. Miami, Fla., 1979-97; mem. Oreg. adv. coun. librs., 1973-74; bd. dirs. Pacific N.W. Bibliog. Ctr., 1973-77; tech. adv. com. librs. Columbia Regional Assn. Govts., 1976-79; vis. fellow U. Southampton Eng., 1975-76; pres. Oreg. Libr. Assn., 1974-75; mem. nominating com. Southeastern Libr. Network, 1984-85; bd. dirs. S.E. Fla. Libr. Info. Network, 1984-97, pres. 1991-92; mem. exec. coun. Assn. Caribbean U. Rsch. and Instl. Librs., 1985-88; chmn. local organizing com. for 1981 and 1987 confs. in Miami; mem. Fla. Libr. Network Coun., 1985-91; NEH challenge grant rev. panel, 1987, Howard U. ann. inspection team, 1989, Reaffirmation com., Tex. Christian U., 1993. Author, editor various libr. publs., guides. Sr. fellow Grad. Sch. Libr. and Info. Sci. UCLA, 1983; grantee Coun. Libr. Resources, 1975-76. Fellow Libr. Assn. U.K.; mem. ALA, Assn. Rsch. Librs. (office mgmt. studies adv. com. 1981-83, stats. and measurements com. 1993-96), Assn. Specialized and Coop. Libr. Agys. (membership promotion com. 1994-96, chair 1990 program com.), Assn. Southeastern Rsch. Librs. (chmn. membership com. 1982-97). Home: 5630 Twin Lakes Dr Miami FL 33143-2038 Office: U Miami Library Coral Gables FL 33124

RODGERS, FREDERIC BARKER, judge; b. Albany, N.Y., Sept. 29, 1940; s. Prentice Johnson and Jane (Weed) R.; m. Valerie McNaughton, Oct. 8, 1988; 1 child: Gabriel Moore. AB, Amherst Coll., 1963; JD, Union U., 1966. Bar: N.Y. 1966, U.S. Ct. Mil. Appeals 1968, Colo. 1972, U.S. Supreme Ct. 1974, U.S. Ct. Appeals (10th cir.) 1981. Chief dep. dist. atty., Denver, 1972-73; commr. Denver Juvenile Ct., 1973-79; mem. Mulligan Reeves Teasley & Joyce, P.C., Denver, 1979-80; pres. Frederic B. Rodgers, P.C., Breckenridge, Colo., 1980-89; ptnr. McNaughton & Rodgers, Central City, Colo., 1989-91; county ct. judge County of Gilpin, 1987—; presiding mcpl. judge cities of Breckenridge, Blue River, Black Hawk, Central City, Edgewater, Empire, Idaho Springs, Silver Plume and Westminster, Colo., 1978-96; chmn. com. on mcpl. ct. rules of procedure Colo. Supreme Ct., 1984—; mem. gen. faculty Nat. Jud. Coll. U. Nev., Reno, 1990—, elected to faculty coun., 1994—. Author: (with Dilweg, Fretz, Murphy and Wicker) Modern Judicial Ethics, 1992; contbr. articles to profl. jours. Mem. Colo. Commn. on Children, 1982-85, Colo. Youth Devel. Coun., 1989—, Colo. Family Peace Task Force, 1994—. Served with JAGC, U.S. Army, 1967-72; to maj. USAR, 1972-88. Decorated Bronze Star with oak leaf cluster, Air medal. Recipient Outstanding County Judge award Colo. 17th Judicial Dist. Victim Adv. Coalition, 1991; Spl. Community Service award Colo. Am. Legion, 1979. Fellow Colo. Bar Found.; mem. ABA (jud. div. exec. coun. 1989—, vice-chair 1996—, ho. dels. 1993—), Colo. Bar Assn. (bd. govs. 1986-88, 90-92, 93—), Continental Divide Bar Assn., Denver Bar Assn. (bd. trustees 1979-82), First Jud. Dist. Bar Assn., Nat. Conf. Spl. Ct. Judges (chmn. 1989-90), Colo. County Judges Assn. (pres. 1995-96), Colo. Mcpl. Judges Assn. (pres. 1986-87), Colo. Trial Judges Coun. (v.p. 1994-95, sec. 1996—), Denver Law Club (pres. 1981-82), Colo. Women's Bar Assn., Am. Judicature Soc., Nat. Coun. Juvenile and Family Ct. Judges, Univ. Club (Denver), Arlberg Club (Winter Park), Marines Meml. Club (San Francisco), Westminster Rotary Club (Paul Harris fellow 1996). Episcopalian. Office: Gilpin County Justice Ctr 2960 Dory Hill Rd Golden CO 80403-8768

RODGERS, JAMES FOSTER, association executive, economist; b. Columbus, Ga., Jan. 15, 1951; s. Laban Jackson and Martha (Jackson) R.; m. Cynthia Lynne Bathurst, Aug. 20, 1975. B.A., U. Ala., Tuscaloosa, 1973; Ph.D., U. Iowa, 1980. Fed. intern Office Rsch. and Stats., Social Security Adminstrn., Washington, 1976-77; rsch. assoc. Ctr. Health Policy Rsch., AMA, Chgo., 1979-80, rsch. dir., 1980-82, asst. to dep. exec. v.p. AMA, 1982-85; dir. AMA Ctr. Health Policy Rsch., Chgo., 1985-96, v.p. health policy, 1996—. Contbr. articles on health econs. to profl. jours. Pharm. Mfrs. Assn. grantee, 1978; NSF grantee, 1978; Hohenberg fellow, 1969-70. Mem. Am. Econ. Assn., Am. Soc. Assn. Exec., Am. Statis. Assn., So. Econ. Assn., Western Econ. Assn. Home: 2233 N Orchard St Chicago IL 60614-3713 Office: AMA Ctr for Health Policy Rsch 515 N State St Chicago IL 60610-4325

RODGERS, JOHN, geologist, educator; b. Albany, N.Y., July 11, 1914; s. Henry D. and Louise W. (Allen) R. B.A., Cornell U., 1936, M.S., 1937; Ph.D., Yale U., 1944. Geologist, U.S. Geol. Survey, 1938-46, intermittently, 1946-95; sci. cons. U.S. Army Engrs., 1944-46; instr. geology Yale U., New Haven, 1946-47; asst. prof. Yale U., 1947-52, assoc. prof., 1952-59, prof., 1959-62, Silliman prof., 1962-85, Silliman prof. emeritus, 1985—; vis. lectr. Coll. de France, Paris, 1960; sec.-gen. commn. on stratigraphy Internat. Geol. Congress, 1952-60; commr. Conn. Geol. and Natural History Survey, 1960-71. Author: (with C.O. Dunbar) Principles of Stratigraphy, 1957, The Tectonics of the Appalachians, 1970; also articles in field.; editor Symposium on the Cambrian System, 3 vols., 1956, 61; recording artist: (with W. Ruff) The Harmony of the World, 1979; asst. editor Am. Jour. Sci., 1948-54, editor, 1954—. NSF sr. postdoctoral fellow France, 1959-60; exchange visitor Geol. Inst., Acad. Scis. USSR, 1967; Guggenheim fellow Australia, 1973-74; recipient Medal of Freedom U.S. Army, 1947, James Hall medal N.Y. State Geol. Survey, 1986; exchange scholar Inst. of Geology Academia

Sinica (Beijing) 1986; recipient Médaille Paul Fourmarier Académie Royale des Sciences, Lettres et Beaux-Arts de Belgique, 1987, William Clyde DeVane medal Phi Beta Kappa, 1990. Fellow AAAS, Geol. Soc. Am. (councillor 1962-65, pres. 1970, Penrose medal 1981), Am. Geophys. Union; mem. NAS, Am. Acad. Arts and Scis., Am. Assn. Petroleum Geologists, Conn. Acad. Sci. and Engring. (charter), Conn. Acad. Arts and Scis. (pres. 1969), Geol. Soc. London (hon.), Société géologique de France (assoc. mem., v.p. 1960, Prix Gaudry 1987), Am. Philos. Soc., Russian Acad. Scis. (hon. fgn. mem.), Academia Real de Ciencias y Artes Barcelona (fgn. corr. mem.), Sigma Xi, Phi Beta Kappa. Club: Elizabethan (New Haven). Office: Dept Geology Yale U PO Box 208109 New Haven CT 06520-8109

RODGERS, JOHN JOSEPH, III, school administrator; b. Jamaica, N.Y., Oct. 13, 1941; s. John Joseph Jr. and Edith (McInerney) R.; children: Janet, John Joseph IV. BS, Fordham U., 1962; Profl. diploma, St. Johns U., 1970, EdD, 1979; postgrad., CUNY, Flushing. Asst. prin. N.Y.C. Bd. Edn., 1972-82; prin. Howard T. Herber Sch., Malverne, N.Y., 1982-85, Norman Thomas High Sch., N.Y.C., 1988-96, Matawan Regional H.S., Aberdeen, N.J., 1996—. Mem. ASCD, Nat. Assn. Secondary Sch. Prins. Home: 82 Cloverdale Rd Clifton NJ 07013 Office: 450 Atlantic Ave Matawan NJ 07747-2326

RODGERS, KIRK PROCTER, international organization executive, environmentalist; b. Balt., Oct. 15, 1932; s. Samuel Procter and Florence Eugenia (Besley) R.; m. Karen Frances Johnson, Jan. 3, 1959; children: Brian Kirk, Kimberly Paige. BA in Geography, Yale U., 1954, MS in Natural Resource Conservation, 1956. Timber surveyor U.S. Forest Svc., Colo., Calif., 1953-54; land use planner Balt. (Md.) County Planning Commn., 1955; natural resources specialist, dept. econ. affairs Orgn. of Am. States, Washington, 1960-63, chief natural resources unit, dept. econ. affairs, 1963-69, dir. dept. regional devel. and environment, 1970-96, dir. unit of sustainable devel. and environ., 1996—; mem. strategic policy coun. Yale U. Sch. Forestry and Environ. Studies, 1992-97; permanent sec. Interamerican Travel Congress, Washington, 1986-96; pres. Besley and Rodgers Inc., Woolford, Md., 1988—; mem. U.S. com. Sci. Com. on Problems of the Environment, Washington, 1990-93; advisor UN Environment Program, 1986; mem. internat. bd. advisors UN Internat. Environ. Tech. Ctr., Osaka, Japan, 1995—; bd. advisors Jour. Environ. and Devel., 1992—. Author: Physical Resource Investigations for Economic Development, 1969, Integrated Regional Development Planning, 1984, Conservation in the Big Picture - Development Approaches for the Next Decade, 1992, The Interamerican Water Resources NEtwork: A Tool for Concept Builders, 1996; contbr. The Careless Technology-Ecological Consequences of Internat. Development, 1970, Managing the Environment in Developing Countries, 1992, Fovernance in the Western Hemisphere, 1982. Mem. nat. bd. dirs. Fla. Mus. Sci. and Tech., 1994—. Lt. (j.g.) USNR, 1956-58. Recipient Grad. fellowship Conservation Found., Yale U., 1955-56, Population Workshop fellowship Ford Found., Washington, 1956. Mem. Am. Soc. for Internat. Devel., Forest Landowners Assn. (chair govtl. affairs 1993-95, pres. 1997-98), Am. Forest Paper Assn. (mem. pvt. forestry bd. dirs.), Am. Water Resources Assn. (hon. mem. 1996). Avocations: white water canoeing, hunting, fishing, skiing. Home: 3508 Stoneybrae Dr Falls Church VA 22044-1229 Office: Orgn American States 1889 F St NW Washington DC 20006

RODGERS, LAWRENCE RODNEY, physician, educator; b. Clovis, N.Mex., Mar. 9, 1920; s. Samuel Frank and Lillian (O'Connor) R.; m. Ivy Lorna Piper, Aug. 6, 1943; children: Lawrence Rodney (dec.), Ivy Elizabeth, George Piper. B.S., West Tex. State U., 1940; M.D., U. Tex., 1943. Diplomate Am. Bd. Internal Medicine. Intern Phila. Gen. Hosp., 1943-44, resident in medicine, 1946-49; assoc. internist Tumor Inst., U. Tex. M.D. Anderson Hosp., Houston, 1949—; chmn. dept. medicine Hermann Hosp., Houston, 1966-71; assoc. prof. clin. medicine Baylor U., 1949—; prof. clin. medicine U. Tex., 1972—. Editor: Harris County Physician, 1976-80. Bd. dirs. Tex. Med. Found.; trustee Houston Mus. Med. Sci., 1981. Served to maj. M.C. AUS, 1944-46. Decorated Bronze Star with two oak leaf clusters; recipient Ashbel Smith Disting. Alumnus award U. Tex. Med. Br.-Galveston, 1993, Mastership award Am. Coll. Physicians, 1996. Fellow ACP (gov. for Tex. 1979-83, Laureate Internist Tex. award 1994); mem. AMA (del.), Tex. Med. Assn. (elected emeritus), Harris County Med. Soc. (exec. bd. 1978-82, v.p. 1984), Am. Heart Assn., Houston Soc. Internal Medicine (pres. 1974), Houston Acad. Medicine (pres. 1981), Houston Philos. Soc. (pres. 1993-94), Doctor's Club Houston (bd. govs. 1984-88, pres. 1986).

RODGERS, LOUIS DEAN, retired surgeon; b. Centerville, Iowa, Nov. 24, 1930; s. John James and Anna Alice (Spraguer) R.; m. Gretchen Lynn Hendershot, Feb. 19, 1954; children—Cynthia Ann, Elizabeth Dee. M.D., U. Iowa, 1960. Diplomate Am. Bd. Surgery. Intern, Broadlawns Hosp., Iowa, 1960-61; resident Meth-Hosp., Des Moines, 1961-65; practice medicine specializing in gen. surgery, Des Moines, 1965-95; chmn. dept. surgery Iowa Methodist Ctr., Des Moines, 1980-84, chief gen. surgery, 1982-95; clin. assoc. prof. surgery U. Iowa, Iowa City, 1983-95, ret., 1995. Mem. steering com. Gov.'s Campaign, Republican Party, Iowa, 1982; bd. dirs. Iowa Meth. Med. Found., Des Moines, 1983, Des Moines Symphony, 1984—, Des Moines Children's Home, 1987. Served to staff sgt. U.S. Army, 1951-54. Named Surg. Tchr. of Yr., Iowa Meth. Med. Ctr. Dept. Surgery, 1978, 84. Fellow ACS (liaison to cancer com. 1973); mem. Western Surg. Assn. (mem. Iowa trauma com. 1983), Iowa Acad. Surgery (pres. 1982-83), Throckmorton Surg. Soc. (pres. 1986). Republican. Club: Des Moines Golf and Country. Home: 715 53rd St Des Moines IA 50312-1820

RODGERS, MARY COLUMBRO, academic administrator, English educator, author; b. Aurora, Ohio, Apr. 17, 1925; d. Nicola and Nancy (DeNicola) Columbro; m. Daniel Richard Rodgers, July 24, 1965; children: Robert, Patricia, Kristine. AB, Notre Dame Coll., 1957; MA, Western Res. U., 1962; PhD, Ohio State U., 1964; postgrad., U. Rome, 1964-65; EdD, Calif. Nat. Open U., 1975, DLitt, 1978. Tchr. English Cleve. elem. schs., 1945-52, Cleve. secondary schs., 1952-62; supr. English student tchrs. Ohio State U., 1962-64; asst. prof. English U. Md., 1965-66; assoc. prof. Trinity Coll., 1967-68; prof. English D.C. Tchrs. Coll., 1968—; pres. Md. Nat. U., 1972—; chancellor Am. Open U., 1965—; dean Am. Open U. Acad. Author numerous books and monographs, latest works include: A Short Course in English Composition, 1976, Chapbook of Children's Literature, 1977, Comprehensive Catalogue: The Open University of America System, 1978-80, Open University of America System Source Book, V, VI, VII, 1978, Essays and Poems on Life and Literature, 1979, Modes and Models: Four Lessons for Young Writers, 1981, Open University Structures and Adult Learning, 1982, Papers in Applied English Linguistics, 1982, Twelve Lectures on the American Open University, 1982, English Pedagogy in the American Open University, 1983, Design for Personalized English Graduate Degrees in the Urban University, 1984, Open University English Teaching, 1945-85: Conceptual History and Rationale, 1985, Claims and Counterclaims Regarding Instruction Given in Personalized Degree Residency Programs Completed by Graduates of California National Open University, 1986, The American Open University, 1965 t0 1985: History and Sourcebook, 1986, New Design II: English Pedagogy in the American Open University, 1987, The American Open University, 1965 to 1985: A Research Report, 1987, The American Open University and Other Open Universities: A Comparative Study Report, 1988, Poet and Pedagogue in Moscow and Leningrad: A Travel Report, 1989, Foundations of English Scholarship in the American Open University, 1989, Twelve Lectures in Literary Analysis, 1990, Ten Lectures in Literary Production, 1990, Analyzing Fact and Fiction, 1991, Analyzing Poetry and Drama, 1991, Some Successful Literary Research Papers: An Inventory of Titles and Theses, 1991, A Chapbook of Poetry and Drama Analysis, 1992, Convent Poems, 1943-61, 93, Fables for Fiction Analysis, 3d edit., 1993, First Access List to the Open University Literary Trust, 1993, Catholic Marriage Poems, 1962-79, 1993, New Design Responses 1945-1993, 10 vols., 1993, Catholic Widow with Children Poems, 1979-93, 1994, Journals: Reflections and Resolves, 1984-1995, 16 vols., 1995, Biographical Sourcebook: Mary Columbro Rodgers, 1969-1995, 1995, Catholic Teacher Poems, 1945-1995, 1995, Second Access List to the Mary Columbro Rodgers Literary Trust, 1995, Defending English 211 and 212: Fourteen Research Directives, 1996, Mary Columbro Rodgers, Catholic Teacher and Writer: Bio-Bibliography for Researchers, 1996. Fulbright scholar U. Rome, 1964-65. Fellow Cath. Scholars; mem. Poetry Soc. Am., Nat. Coun. Tchrs. English, Am. Ednl. Rsch. Assn., Am. Acad. Poets, Ohioana Libr. Assn., Friends John Henry Newman Assn., Writer's Ctr. Md., Pi Lambda Theta. Home and Office: Coll Heights Estates 3916 Commander Dr Hyattsville MD 20782-1027 *My life as a Catholic scholar has focused on the literate and humane. Both as a student and as a scholar I have made my work a disciplined commitment to English literature, English language, and English pedagogy. My life's goal has been the effective, everyday transmission of humane values defined in my Catholic heritage to younger generations through my teaching, research and writing. My epitaph should read: She saw with the writer's eye and worked with the scholar's tools before she spoke with the teacher's tongue.*

RODGERS, NANCY LUCILLE, corporate executive; b. Denver, Aug. 22, 1934; d. Francis Randolph and Irma Lucille (Budy) Baker; student public schs.; m. George J. Rodgers, Feb. 18, 1968; children by previous marriage: Kellie Rae, Joy Lynn, Timothy Francis, Thomas Francis. Mgr., Western Telearm, Inc., San Diego, 1973-93; pres. Rodgers Police Patrol, Inc., San Diego, 1973-80; br. mgr. Honeywell Inc., Protection Services div., San Diego, 1977-80; pres. Image, Inc., Image Travel Agy., Cairo, Egypt, 1981-83, Western Solar Specialties, 1979-80; founder, pres. Internat. Metaphysicians Associated for Growth through Edn., San Diego, 1979; founder, dir. Point Loma Sanctuary, 1983-86; co-founder, producer Zerciee Prodns. Unltd., 1986—, co-founder, producer, dir. mktg., 1986—; co-founder Philae West, Breeder of Am. Bashkir Curleys. Bd. dirs. Cen. City Assn. Named Woman of Achievement Cen. City Assn., 1979. Mem. Nat. Assn. for Holistic Health, Am. Bus. Women's Assn. (Woman of Yr. 1980), Am. Union Metaphysicians, Inst. Noetic Scis. Republican.

RODGERS, RICHARD MALCOLM, management accountant; b. Montgomery, Ala., June 23, 1949; s. Charles Malcolm and Betty Jean (Gilbert) R.; m. Linda Joyce Meeks, Dec. 9, 1966 (div. Mar. 1970); 1 child, Angela Christina Rodgers Bolin; m. Sharon Lynn Thomas, May 10, 1992. Student, Emory U., 1967-69; BBA magna cum laude, Ga. State U., 1988. Cert. mgmt. acct. Staff acct. Charter Enterprises, Inc., College Park, Ga., 1971-72; contr. Royal Arts & Crafts, Inc., Atlanta, 1972-73; justice of peace Justice's Ct. Dist. 531, Decatur, Ga., 1973-76; chief cost acct. Gen. Assembly Mission Bd., Presbyn. Ch. U.S., Atlanta, 1974-80; internal audit mgr. Waffle House, Inc., Norcross, Ga., 1980-87; acctg. mgr. W.L. Thompson Cons. Engrs., Inc., Atlanta, 1988-90; contr. Hudson Everett Simonson Mullis & Assocs., Inc., Atlanta, 1990-96; instr. Gwinnett Coll. Bus., Lilburn, Ga., 1997—; freelance cons. and writer, 1995—; instr. Gwinnett Coll. Bus., Lilburn, Ga., 1997—. Poet, contbg. editor Archon mag., 1968-70 (Anthology award 1970); composer, lyricist: (musical play) Many a Glorious Morning, 1971; playwright, composer, lyricist: (musical play) Take the Money and Run!, 1979, 91. Exec. com. mem. DeKalb County Rep. Party, Decatur, 1969-76; v.p. Ga. Assn. Justices of the Peace and Constables, Warner Robbins, Ga., 1973-74; treas., founding dir. Ga. Bus. Com. for Arts, Inc., Atlanta, 1981-86; sec. Ga. State Poetry Soc., Inc., Atlanta, 1986 (Judge for Chapbook award 1991, 96). Stipe scholar Emory U., 1968. Mem. AAAS, Inst. Mgmt. Accts., N.Y. Acad. Scis., Idealists Internat. (charter), The Dramatists Guild, Golden Key Nat. Honor Soc. (charter), Beta Gamma Sigma, Phi Kappa Phi. Democrat. Episcopalian. Avocations: field archeology, geophysical rsch., acting, bridge, playing jazz on trumpet. Home and Office: 1111 Clairmont Rd # K-2 Decatur GA 30030

RODGERS, ROBERT AUBREY, physicist; b. Huntsville, Ala., May 10, 1967; s. Aubrey and Peggy Joyce (Hairald) R. BS, U. Ala., Huntsville, 1990, MS, 1992; MS in Health Physics, Ga. Inst. Tech., 1993. Grad. student physics rschr. Polarization and Lens Design Lab., U. Ala., Huntsville, 1991-92; grad. student med. physics rschr. Emory U.-Ga. Inst. Tech., Atlanta, 1992-94; staff med. health physicist, officer USAF, Lackland AFB, Tex., 1996—; diagnostic med. physics fellow USAF, Lackland AFB, 1997—. U. Ala.-Huntsville Honor scholar, 1988-89, scholar, 1986-87; USAF Diagnostic Med. Physics fellow, 1997—. Mem. Am. Assn. Physicists in Medicine, Health Physics Soc. (med. sect.), Optical Soc. Am., Soc. Nuclear Medicine, Air Force Assn. Baptist. Achievements include research on development of scattering polarimeter and measurement/analysis of diffraction grating polarization and efficiency properties, validation of compton scatter and attenuation correction methods for cardiac SPECT imaging. Home: 9898 Colonnade Blvd 16202 San Antonio TX 78230

RODGERS, RONALD CARL, psychometrician; b. Allentown, Pa., Jan. 9, 1948; s. LeRoy Clarence and Dolly Nouritza (Phillips) R.; m. Mary Ann Brady, June 23, 1979; 1 child, Brian. BS in Math Edn., Northwestern U., 1970, MA in Ednl. Psychology, 1972, PhD in Ednl. Rsch., 1975. Sportswriter, columnist The Herald-Tribune, Sarasota, Fla., 1964-67; edn. editor, reporter Lerner Newspapers, Chgo., 1967-73; grad. asst. Northwestern U., Evanston, Ill., 1971-75, asst. prof., 1975-77; rsch. psychologist Ednl. Testing Svc., Evanston, 1977-83, asst. dir., 1981-83; pres. Rodgers & Assocs., Wilmette, Ill., 1983—; Cons. City of Chgo., 1983-91, D.C. Pub. Schs., Washington, 1991-94; psychometrician Ill. Dept. Profl. Regulation, Springfield, 1984—; pres. Employment R & D Inst., Wilmette, 1986—. Editor: Measurement Trends in Career Education, 1983; assoc. editor: Jour. Econ. Devel., 1985-92; contbr. articles to profl. jours. Trustee Wilmette Pub. Libr. Bd., 1984—, v.p., 1987-89, pres., 1989—; trustee North Suburban Libr. Systems, Wheeling, Ill., 1991-97, v.p., 1993-94, pres. 1994-96; asst. scoutmaster Troop 11 Boy Scouts Am., 1992-93, 95-96, scoutmaster, 1993-94. Recipient Writer's award Chgo. Heart Assn., 1970. Mem. APA, ALA, Ill. Libr. Assn., Nat. Coun. Measurement in Edn. Avocations: politics, scouting, computers, libraries. Home: 200 Millbrook Ln Wilmette IL 60091-2939 Office: Employment R & D Inst 809 Ridge Rd Ste 201 Wilmette IL 60091-2480

RODGERS, STEVEN EDWARD, tax practitioner, educator; b. Pierre, S.D., Feb. 8, 1947; s. Thomas Edward and Dorothy Zoe (Barker) R.; m. Donna Lynn Joyner, June 10, 1984; 1 child, Michelle Ann. Student, State U. S.D., 1964-65, U. Calif., Berkeley, 1968-72; cert., Coll. for Fin. Planning, 1986-87; fellow, Nat. Tax Practice Inst., 1988-89. CFP, Enrolled Agent. Collection mgr. Cenval Leasing-Ctrl. Bank, Long Beach, Calif., 1972-77; tax preparer Rodgers Tax Svc., Las Vegas, 1977-78; CEO Rainbow Tax Svc. Inc., Las Vegas, 1978—; pres. Rainbow Tax Svc., Inc., Las Vegas, 1978-90. Author: Marketing To Build Your Tax Practice, 1994. Active Amnesty Internat., Mensa; chmn. Best in the West Edn. Found., Las Vegas, 1994—, Nat. Assn. Enrolled Agents Edn. Found., 1995-96. With U.S. Army, 1965-68, Vietnam. Mem. Nat. Assn. Enrolled Agts. (nat. sec. 1989-90, nat. treas. 1991-92, nat. edn. chair 1994-95, named Tax Educator of the Yr., 1995), Nat. Assn. Enrolled Agents Edn. Found. (chair 1995-96), Nev. Soc. Enrolled Agts. (charter pres. 1985-86, fellow edn. found.), So. Nev. Assn. Tax Cons. (pres. 1981-82), Nat. Soc. Pub. Accts., Vietnam Vets. Am. Home: 1101 Cahill Ave Las Vegas NV 89128-3335 Office: Rainbow Tax Svc Inc 6129 Clarice Ave Las Vegas NV 89107-1401

RODGMAN, ALAN, chemist, consultant; b. Aberdare, Wales, Feb. 7, 1924; came to U.S., 1954, naturalized, 1961; s. Arch and Margaret (Llewellyn) R.; m. Doris Curley, June 7, 1947; children: Eric, Paul, Mark. B.A. in Chemistry, U. Toronto, 1949, M.A. in Organic Chemistry, 1951, Ph.D. in Organic Chemistry, 1953. Rsch. asst. med. rsch. dept. U. Toronto, 1947-51, rsch. assoc., 1951-54; tchr., courses in organic chemistry, phys. chemistry, math. Chem. Inst. Can., 1951-54; sr. rsch. chemist R.J. Reynolds Tobacco Co., Winston-Salem, N.C., 1954-65; head smoke rsch. sect. R.J. Reynolds Tobacco Co., 1965-75, mgr. analytical rsch., 1975-76, dir. rsch., 1976-80, dir. fundamental rsch. and devel., 1980-87; cons. in field, 1987—; adj. prof. Wolfe's U., Maple, Ont., Canada, 1993—. Mem. editorial bd. Tobacco Sci., 1963-67 (Vol. 31 Tobacco Sci. dedicated in his name 1987), Beitrage zur Tabakforschung Internat., 1978-87. Mem. Tobacco Working Group, Nat. Cancer Inst., 1976-77, Tech. Study Group on Cigarette and Little Cigar Fire Safety, 1984-87, Sci. Commn. Cooperation Ctr. for Sci. Rsch. Relative to Tobacco, 1982-84. With Can. Navy, 1942-45. Mem. Chem. Inst. Can., Am. Chem. Soc., N.Y. Acad. Scis., N.C. Acad. Sci., Sigma Xi. Episcopalian. Club: Winston-Salem Sertoma (award 1972). Home: 2828 Birchwood Dr Winston Salem NC 27103-3410

RODIBAUGH, ROBERT KURTZ, judge; b. Elkhart County, Ind., July 2, 1916; s. Ralph Leedy and Rose (Kurtz) R.; m. Doris Ann Siekemeyer, Jan. 1, 1942 (dec.); children—David L., Bob K. m. 2d, Eunice Margaret Room, Nov. 25, 1972. B.S.C., U. Notre Dame, 1940, J.D., 1941. Bar: Ind. 1941, U.S. Dist. Ct. (no. dist.) Ind. 1946, U.S. Ct. Appeals (7th cir.) 1972, U.S. Supreme Ct. 1965. Dep. pros. atty. Ind. 60th Jud. Cir., St. Joseph County, 1948-50, 53-57; judge U.S. Bankruptcy Ct., No. Dist. Ind., South Bend, 1960—; lectr. in law U. Notre Dame, 1973; atty. St. Joseph County Bd. Zoning Appeals, 1958-60. V.p. No. Ind. council Boy Scouts Am., 1967-77; bd. dirs. St. Joseph County chpt. ARC, 1970-77. Capt. U.S. Army, 1941-46; PTO. Recipient Silver Beaver award Boy Scouts Am., 1969. Mem. ABA, Seventh Fed. Cir. Bar Assn., Ind. Bar Assn., St. Joseph County Bar Assn. (gov. 1953-56), Am. Judicature Soc., Comml. Law League, Nat. Conf. Bankruptcy Judges (dir. 1977-79), Exchange Club, Masons, DeMolay Club (Legion of Honor), Shriners. Office: US Bankruptcy Ct PO Box 7003 401 S Michigan St South Bend IN 46634-7003

RODIGER, WILLIAM KING, telecommunications and media industry consultant; b. Norwalk, Conn., Oct. 6, 1961; s. Walter Gregory and Elizabeth (King) Rodiger; m. Heather L. McKinney, Oct. 20, 1990; 1 child, Jonathan Amory. BS in Physics, Dickinson Coll., 1984; MS in Computer Engring., Syracuse U., 1986. Grad. rsch. asst. N.Y. State Ctr. for Computer Applications/Software Engring., Syracuse, 1985-86; staff engr. IBM Data Systems Divsn., Kingston, N.Y., 1986-89; systems engr. IBM Nat. Sci. Mktg., White Plains, N.Y., 1989-91; mktg. cons. IBM North Am., Waltham, Mass., 1991—. Patentee NxM round robin switching matrix; coherence control; look-ahead priority arbitration. Trustee Sudbury (Mass.) United Meth. Ch., 1994-97. Mem. IEEE Computer Soc., Assn. Computing Machinery, Boston Computer Soc. Home: 193 Morse Rd Sudbury MA 01776-1716 Office: IBM 404 Wyman St Waltham MA 02154-1264

RODIMER, FRANK JOSEPH, bishop; b. Rockaway, N.J., Oct. 25, 1927; s. Frank Grant and Susan Elizabeth (Hiler) R. Student, St. Charles Coll., Catonsville, Md., 1944-45; B.A., St. Mary's Coll.-Sem., Balt., 1947; postgrad., Immaculate Conception Sem., Darlington, N.J., 1947-50; S.T.L., Cath. U. Am., 1951, J.C.D., 1954. Ordained priest Roman Catholic Ch., 1951; asst. chancellor, 1954-64, chancellor, 1964-77, apptd. papal chaplain, 1963; apptd. 6th Bishop of Paterson, N.J., 1977; consecrated 6th Bishop of Paterson, 1978, ordained, 1978—. Office: 777 Valley Rd Clifton NJ 07013-2205*

RODIN, ALVIN ELI, retired pathologist, medical educator, author; b. Winnipeg, Man., Can., Mar. 25, 1926; came to U.S., 1963; s. Paul and Bessie (Oretsky) R.; m. Bernice Block, Dec. 15, 1951 (div. Dec. 1973); children: Beverly, Paula, Mindy, Lisa; m. Jean Colladay, Feb. 10, 1974. MD, U. Man., Winnipeg, 1950, MSc in Medicine, 1960. Diplomate Am. Bd. Pathology, Am. Bd. Clin. Pathology. Sr. intern Shaughnessy Hosp., Vancouver, B.C., Can.; asst. resident in pathology, demonstrator in parasitology Deer Lodge Hosp., U. Man., Winnipeg, 1955-56, resident in clin. pathology, demonstrator in parasitology, 1957-58, rsch. assoc., 1958-59; resident in pathology, teaching fellow in pathology Queen's U., 1956-57; pvt. practice medicine Minitonas, Man., 1951-54; asst. pathologist Royal Alexander Hosp., Edmonton, Alta., Can., 1959-60; dir. labs. Misericordia Hosp., Edmonton, 1960-63; prof. pathology, dir. pathology edn. U. Tex. Med. Br., Galveston, 1963-75; prof. pathology, chmn. dept. postgrad. edn. Sch. Medicine, Wright State U., Dayton, Ohio, 1975-88, chmn. dept. pathology, 1976-77; dir. med. edn. Green Meml. Hosp., Xenia, Ohio, 1976-92; mem. Miami Valley Health Improvement Coun., Dayton, 1986—. Author: 11 books; contbr. numerous articles to profl. jours. Recipient Golden Apple award Student Am. Med. Assn., 1969, 73-74, Tchr. of Month award Rotary, Galveston, 1974, Outstanding Community Svc. award United Health Svcs., Dayton, 1980. Fellow Royal Soc. Medicine; mem. Am. Osler Soc. (pres. 1992), Soc. for Health and Human Values, Group for Rsch. in Pathology Edn. (pres. 1971-73), Internat. Acad. Medicine, Toastmasters (pres. Galveston club 1968-70). Home: 4440 Pavlov Ave San Diego CA 92122-3712

RODIN, JUDITH SEITZ, academic administrator, psychology educator; b. Phila., Sept. 9, 1944; d. Morris and Sally R. (Winson) Seitz. AB, U. Pa., 1966; PhD, U. Columbia, 1970. Asst. prof. psychology NYU, 1970-72; assoc. prof. Yale U., 1975-79, prof., dir. grad. studies, 1982-89, Philip R. Allen prof. psychology, medicine and psychiatry, 1984-94, chmn. dept. psychology, 1989-91, dean Grad. Sch., 1991-92, provost, 1992-94; pres. U. Pa., Phila., 1994—, prof. psychology, medicine and psychiatry, 1994—; chmn. John D. and Catherine T. MacArthur Found. Rsch. Network on Determinants and Consequences of Health-Promoting and Health-Damaging Behavior, 1983-93; vice chair coun. pres. U. Rsch. Assn., 1994-95, chair, 1995-96; mem. Ind. Panel to Review Safety Procedures at The White House, 1994-95; chair adv. com. Robert Wood Johnson Found., 1994—; mem. Pres. Clinton's Com. Advisors Sci. and Tech., 1994—; bd. dirs. Aetna Life & Casualty Co., Air Products, Allentown, Pa. Author: (with S. Schachter) Obese Humans and Rats, 1978, Exploding the Weight Myths, 1982, Body Traps, 1992; chief editor Appetite Jour., 1979-92; contbr. articles to profl. jours. Mem. Pa. Task Force on Higher Edn. Funding, 1994; bd. dirs. Catalyst, N.Y.C., 1994—; trustee Brookings Inst., 1995—. Fellow Woodrow Wilson Found., 1966-67, John Simon Guggenheim Found., 1986-87; grantee NSF, 1973-82, NIH, 1981—. Fellow AAAS, Am. Acad. Arts and Scis., Am. Psychol. Assn. (bd. sci. affairs 1979-82), Soc. Behavioral Medicine; mem. Am. Philosophical Soc., Inst. Medicine of NAS, Acad. Behavioral Medicine Rsch., Ea. Psychol. Assn. (exec. bd. 1980-82, pres. divsn. 38 health psychology 1982-83, Outstanding Contbn. award 1980, Disting. Sci. award 1977), Phi Beta Kappa, Sigma Xi (pres. Yale chpt. 1986-87). Office: U Pa 121 College Hall Philadelphia PA 19104-6380*

RODIN, MICHAEL F., lawyer, corporate; b. Norwalk, Conn., Sept. 18, 1954. AB with honors, U. Chgo., 1975; JD cum laude, NYU, 1979. Bar: Pa. 1979, U.S. Dist. Ct. (mid. dist.) Pa. 1979, Wash. 1981, U.S. Dist. Ct. (mid. dist.) Wash. 1981. Law clk. to Hon. Malcolm Muir U.S. Dist. (mid. dist.) Pa., 1979-81; assoc. Preston Thorgrimson, Seattle, 1981-86, ptnr., 1987-90; gen. counsel Puget Sound Bancorp, Tacoma, Wash., 1990-93, Key Bank of Washington, Tacoma, 1993—; regional gen. counsel/N.W. region Key Corp, 1995—; speaker in field. Author: (with others) Washington Practice Manual, 1986-89. Fellow securities inst., NYU, 1979. Mem. ABA, Wash. State Bar Assn. (chair ad hoc securities com. bus. law sect. 1990, mem. opinion letter com. 1991—), Seattle-King County Bar Assn. Office: Key Bank Washington 700 5th Ave Seattle WA 98104-5000

RODITE, ROBERT R.R., engineering scientist; b. Easton, Pa., Oct. 17, 1942; s. Victor James and Alice Cecilia (Zatovich) R.; m. Patricia Ann Sule, Apr. 8, 1967; children: Colleen P., Robert J. BSEE, Lafayette Coll., 1964; MSEE, Caif. Inst. Tech., 1965. Rsch. engr., mgr. mfg. rsch. lab. IBM, Endicott, N.Y., 1965-70, mfg. engring. mgr. electronic packaging mfg., 1970-72, devel. engring. mgr. electronic packaging engring., 1972-77; program dir. corp. engring., programming & tech. staff IBM, Armonk, N.Y., 1977-79; product engring. mgr., sr. engr. multichip module devel. IBM, East Fishkill, N.Y., 1979-81; system mgr., sr. tech. staff mem. fin. industry devel. IBM, Charlotte, N.C., 1981-92; sr. tech. staff mem. corp. tech. strategy devel. staff IBM, Armonk, 1992-93; pres. Rodite Assocs., Inc., Charlotte, N.C., 1993—; workgroup mem. Am. Nat. Standards Inst. Com. X9B Stds. Com., 1991—; chmn. IBM Image Processing and Visualization Interdivisional Tech. Liaison Com., 1992-93. Contbr. articles to profl. jours.; patentee in field. Asst. scoutmaster Boy Scouts Am., Charlotte, 1991, 92; mid. sch. basketball coach, Charlotte, 1991-92, 93-94; com. mem. Town County Consolidation Com., Endicott, 1970s; Cath. sch. bd. mem. Diocese of Charlotte, 1988-90. Tau Beta Pi fellow Calif. Inst. Tech., 1964. Mem. IEEE (sr.), Assn. for Info. and Image Mgmt. Internat. (designated Master Info. Tech. 1997), Phi Beta Kappa, Tau Beta Pi, Eta Kappa Nu. Avocations: personal computers, camping. Home: 10022 Thomas Payne Cir Charlotte NC 28277-8872

RODMAN, ALPINE CLARENCE, arts and crafts company executive; b. Roswell, N.Mex., June 23, 1952; s. Robert Elsworth and Verna Mae (Means) R.; m. Sue Arlene Lawson, Dec. 13, 1970; 1 child, Connie Lynn. Student, Colo. State U., 1970-71, U. No. Colo. Ptnr. Pinel Silver Shop, Loveland, Colo., 1965-68, salesman, 1968-71; real estate salesman Loveland, 1971-73; mgr. Traveling Traders, Phoenix, 1974-75; co-owner Deer Track Traders, Loveland, 1975-85; pres. Deer Track Traders, Ltd., 1985—. Author: The Vanishing Indian: Fact or Fiction?, 1985. Mem. Civil Air Patrol, 1965-72, 87-92, dep. comdr. for cadets, 1988-90; cadet comdr. Ft. Collins, Colo., 1968, 70, Colo. rep. to youth tng. program, 1969, U.S. youth rep. to Japan, 1970. Mem. Bur. Wholesale Sales Reps., Western and English Salesmen's Assn. (bd. dirs. 1990), Internat. Platform Assn., Indian Arts and Crafts Assn. (bd. dirs. 1988-94, exec. com. 1989-92, v.p. 1990, pres. 1991, market chmn. 1992), Crazy Horse Grass Roots Club. Republican. Office: Deer Track Traders

Ltd PO Box 448 Loveland CO 80539-0448 *Personal philosophy: I believe that most good and bad in the world comes out of respect or lack of respect for one's self, fellow man, environment and creator.*

RODMAN, DENNIS KEITH, basketball player; b. Trenton, May 13, 1961. Student, Cooke County Jr. Coll., Gainesville, Tex., 1982-83, Southeastern Okla. State U., 1983-86. With Detroit Pistons, 1986-93; forward San Antonio Spurs, 1993-95, Chicago Bulls, 1995—. Author: (with Tim Keown) Bad As I Wanna Be, 1996. Named NBA Defensive Player of Yr., 1990, 91, NBA All-Defensive First Team, 1989, 90, 91, 92, 93, All-Star team, 1990, 92, NBA All-Defense Second Team, 1994; mem. NBA chmpionship team, 1989-90, 96. Office: Chgo Bulls United Ctr 1901 W Madison St Chicago IL 60612-2459*

RODMAN, JAMES PURCELL, astrophysicist, educator; b. Alliance, Ohio, Nov. 11, 1926; s. Clarence James and Hazel (Purcell) R.; m. Margaret Jane Kinsey, Aug. 14, 1950; children: William James, Jeffrey Kinsey, David Lawrence, Gretchen. B.S. in Physics, Chemistry and Math, Mt. Union Coll., 1949; M.A. in Nuclear Physics, Washington U., St. Louis, 1951; Ph.D. in Astrophysics, Yale U., 1963. Sec. Alliance Ware, Inc., 1954-55, Alliance Machine Co., 1959-69; v.p., treas. Alliance Tool Co., 1951-54, pres., 1954-59; instr. dept. physics and math. Mt. Union Coll., Alliance, 1951-59; assoc. prof. physics Mt. Union Coll., 1962-66, prof., 1966-92, head dept. physics, 1963-65, head dept. physics and astronomy, 1965-74, 77-85, staff astronomer, 1992—; dir. Clarke Obs., 1953—, Computer Center, 1967-74, 77; coll. marshal, 1990-92, prof. emeritus, 1993; rsch. assoc. astronomy Yale U., 1963-68, rsch. fellow, 1982; cons. astrophys. engr. astron. instrumentation, 1962—; chief engr., owner Rodman Rsch., 1988—; v.p. and chmn. bd. Westmont Inc., 1984—. Author books; also contbr. articles to profl. jours.; leader JR4 Musical Combo, 1962—. Mem. Alliance Bd. Edn., 1957-59, pres., 1959; exec. com. Buckeye coun. Boy Scouts Am., 1963-77, mem. nat. scouting com., 1973-77; dept. sheriff Stark County, 1972-73; spl. police officer Alliance Police Dept., 1974-90, tech. insp., 1976-90; exec. com. Stark County Disaster Svcs., 1976-78, chmn., 1979; trustee Western Res. Acad., 1969-92, Alliance Comty. Hosp., Inc., 1980-87, pres., 1986; mem. Cape May Cottagers Assn. Inc., 1967—; grand marshal Carnation City Parade, 1986. With USNR, 1944-45. Recipient Gt. Tchr. award, 1976, Alliance Mayor's Award as outstanding citizen, 1978. Fellow AAAS, Royal Astron. Soc.; mem. Am. Phys. Soc., Am. Astron. Soc., Astron. Soc. Pacific, Am. Assn. Physics tchrs., Optical Soc. Am., Nantucket Maria Mitchell Assn. (pres. 1974), Masons (32 degree), Shriners, Corinthian Yacht Club, Beach Cape May Club, Alliance Country Club, Wranglers Club (pres. 1986—), Sigma Xi. Home: 1125 Fernwood Blvd Alliance OH 44601-3764 also: 1613 Beach Dr Cape May NJ 08204-3608

RODMAN, LEIBA, mathematics educator; b. Riga, Latvia, June 9, 1949; came to U.S., 1985; s. Zalman and Haya Rodman; m. Ella Levitan, Feb. 2, 1983; children: Daniel, Ruth, Benjamin, Naomi. Diploma in maths., Latvian State U., 1971; MA in Statis., Tel Aviv (Israel) U., 1976, PhD in Maths., 1978. Instr. Tel Aviv U., 1976-78, sr. lectr., 1981-83, assoc. prof., 1983-85; postdoctoral fellow U. Calgary, Can., 1978-80; from assoc. to full prof. Ariz. State U., Tempe, 1985-87; prof. math. Coll. William and Mary, Williamsburg, Va., 1987—. Author: Introduction to Operator Polynomials, 1989, (with others) Matrix Polynomials, 1982, Matrices and Indefinite Scalar Products, 1983, Invariant Subspaces of Matrices with Applications, 1986, Interpolation of Rational Matrix Functions, 1990, Algebraic Riccati Equations, 1995; co-editor: Contributions to Operator Theory and Its Applications, 1988. Mem. IEEE, Am. Math. Soc., Math. Assn. Am., Internat. Linear-Algebra Soc., Soc. Indsl. and Applied Maths. Office: Coll of William & Mary Dept Of Math Williamsburg VA 23187

RODMAN, LEROY ELI, lawyer; b. N.Y.C., Feb. 22, 1914; s. Morris and Sadie (Specter) R.; m. Toby Chertcoff, Mar. 14, 1943; children: John Stephen, Lawrence Bernard. AB, CCNY, 1933; J.D. (James Kent scholar), Columbia, 1936. Bar: N.Y. 1937. Practiced in N.Y.C., 1937-43, 46—; law sec. to U.S. dist. judge Bklyn., 1936; law asst. Am. Law Inst., N.Y.C., 1937; chief food enforcement unit N.Y. Regional Office, OPA, 1942-43; mem. firm Lawrence R. Condon, N.Y.C., 1937-42; ptnr. Joseph & Rodman, N.Y.C., 1946-53; sr. ptnr. Rodman, Maurer & Dansker, N.Y.C., 1964-73, Carro, Spanbock, Londin, Rodman & Fass, N.Y.C., 1973-78, Rodman & Rodman, N.Y.C., 1978-89, Teitelbaum, Hiller, Rodman, Paden & Hibsher, P.C., N.Y.C., 1990-96; of counsel Morrison, Cohen, Singer & Weinstein LLP, N.Y.C., 1996—; tchr. fed. taxation Pace Coll., N.Y.C., 1953-55; bd. dirs., v.p., sec. Francosteel Corp., N.Y.C.; sec. Ameribrom, Inc. Editorial bd.: Columbia Law Rev, 1934-36; Contbr. articles to legal jours. Bd. dirs. Manhattan coun. Boy Scouts Am., 1960—, v.p., 1961-68, pres., 1972-75; exec. bd. Greater N.Y. coun., 1972—. Capt. JAGD AUS, 1943-46. Recipient Certs. Svc., Silver Beaver award Boy Scouts Am., 1962. Fellow Am. Coll. Trust and Estate Counsel; mem. ABA, N.Y. County Lawyers Assn., Assn. of Bar of City of N.Y., Judge Adv. Assn., Phi Beta Kappa. Jewish (trustee, v.p. synagogue, pres. brotherhood 1958-60). Clubs: Univ. (N.Y.C.); Metropolis Country (White Plains, N.Y.) (sec. 1976-77, 80-82, v.p. 1977-78, bd. govs. 1976-82). Home: 535 E 86th St New York NY 10028-7533 Office: 750 Lexington Ave New York NY 10022-1200

RODMAN, PETER WARREN, foreign policy specialist; b. Boston, Nov. 24, 1943; s. Sumner and Helen Rhoda (Morris) R.; m. F. Veronique Boulad, Apr. 13, 1980; children: Theodora, Nicholas. BA summa cum laude, Harvard U., 1964, JD, 1969; BA, MA, Oxford (Eng.) U., 1966. Staff mem. NSC, Washington, 1969-77; fellow in diplomatic studies Ctr. for Strategic and Internat. Studies, Washington, 1977-83; dir. rsch. Kissinger Assocs., Washington, 1982-83; mem. policy planning council Dept. of State, Washington, 1983-84, dir. policy planning staff, 1984-86; dep. asst. to pres. for nat. security affairs (fgn. policy) NSC, Washington, 1986-87, counselor, spl. asst. to pres. for nat. security affairs, 1987-90; fellow Johns Hopkins Fgn. Policy Inst., Washington, 1990-93; dir. Middle East and Eurasian studies Ctr. for Strategic and Internat. Studies, Washington, 1994-95; dir. nat. security programs Nixon Ctr. for Peace and Freedom, Washington, 1995—. Author: More Precious Than Peace: The Cold War and the Struggle for the Third World, 1994; sr. editor Nat. Rev., 1991—; contbr. articles to profl. jours. V.p. World Affairs Coun., Washington, 1996—; trustee Freedom House, 1997—. Mem. Coun. on Fgn. Rels., Internat. Inst. for Strategic Studies, Atlantic Coun. U.S., Cosmos Club. Office: Nixon Ctr for Peace and Freedom 1620 I St NW Ste 900 Washington DC 20006-4005

RODMAN, SUE ARLENE, wholesale Indian crafts company executive, artist; b. Fort Collins, Colo., Oct. 1, 1951; d. Marvin F. Lawson and Barbara I. (Miller) Lawson Shue; m. Alpine C. Rodman, Dec. 13, 1970; 1 child, Connie Lynn. Student Colo. State U., 1970-73. Silversmith Pinel Silver Shop, Loveland, Colo., 1970-71; asst. mgr. Traveling Traders, Phoenix, 1974-75; co-owner, co-mgr. Deer Track Traders, Loveland, 1975-85, v.p. Deer Track Traders, Ltd., 1985—. Author: The Book of Contemporary Indian Arts and Crafts, 1985. Mem. U.S. Senatorial Club, 1982-87, Rep. Presdl. Task Force, 1984-90; mem. Civil Air Patrol, 1969-73, 87-90, pers. officer, 1988-90. Mem. Internat. Platform Assn., Indian Arts and Crafts Assn., Western and English Sales Assn., Crazy Horse Grass Roots Club. Mem. Am. Baptist Ch. Avocations: museums, piano, recreation research, fashion design, writing. Office: Deer Track Traders Ltd PO Box 448 Loveland CO 80539-0448

RODMAN, SUMNER, insurance executive; b. Malden, Mass., Aug. 5, 1915; s. Nathan Markel and Sara Ruth (Slater) R.; m. Helen Rhoda Morris, July 2, 1942; children: Peter Warren, John Slater. A.B. cum laude, Harvard, 1935. C.L.U. Agt. Aetna Life Ins. and Annuity Co., Boston, 1935—; with Rodman Ins. Agy., Inc., Newton Ctr., Mass.; life ins. adviser, 1953—; Pres. Boston Life Ins. and Trust Council, 1958-59. Bd. dirs. Jewish Family and Children's Service, Boston, 1953-85, Boston Estate Planning Council, 1960-85, Youth Tennis Found. New Eng., 1963-85, Simons-Gutman Found., 1965—, Alzheimers Assn. Ea. Mass., 1990—; hon. trustee Combined Jewish Philanthropies of Greater Boston, 1967—; mem. Am. Jewish Com., Anti-Defamation League of B'nai Brith; mem. World Affairs Coun. Boston; hon. trustee Temple Israel, Boston.. Served to capt. AUS, 1941-46, ETO. C.L.U. Inst. fellow, 1952, 61; named to New Eng. Tennis Assn. Hall of Fame, 1992. Mem. The Am. Coll. (trustee 1971-74), Boston Life Underwriters Assn. (pres. 1965-66), Am. Soc. CLUs (pres. 1972-73), Million Dollar Round Table (life), New Eng. Lawn Tennis Assn. (bd. dirs. 1966-68), Golden Key Soc. Jewish (trustee temple). Clubs: Harvard (Boston), Harvard Varsity (Boston); Newton (Mass.) Squash and Tennis; Wightman Tennis Center (Weston, Mass.). Lodge: Masons. Home: 94 Vine St Chestnut Hill MA 02167-3050 Office: 75 Wells Ave Newton MA 02159-3214

RODNEY, JOEL MORRIS, dean; b. Bklyn., Nov. 9, 1937; s. Samuel Seymour and Jane (Loorya) R.; m. Judith DeStefano, July 22, 1994; children from previous marriage: Jonathan, Adam, Benjamin. BA cum laude, Brandeis U., 1959; PhD, Cornell U., 1965; attended, Inst. Ednl. Mgmt. Harvard U., 1976. From instr. to assoc. prof. Wash. State U., Pullman, 1963-70; chmn. div. social scis., assoc. prof. history Elmira (N.Y.) Coll., 1970-72, coordinator flood relief and community planning, 1973; dean arts and sci., prof. history Widener Coll., Chester, Pa., 1973-76, acting chief acad. officer, dean, 1976-77, chief acad. officer, dean, 1977-81, dir. univ. grad. programs, 1979-81; v.p. acad. affairs Salisbury (Md.) State Coll., 1981-86; provost Rockford (Ill.) Coll., 1986-90; dean U. Wis. Ctr.-Washington County, West Bend, 1990—. Editor Albion, 1967-78; contbr. articles to profl. jours. Vice chmn. Md. Gov.'s Com. on Employment of Handicapped, 1985-86, chmn. and mem. Lower Shore divsn., 1983-86; chmn. adv. bd., mem. Crozer-Chester Med. Health Ctr., Chester, 1974-77; project evaluator NEH, 1986, RSA, 1993; mem., sec. Delaware County Mental Health/Mental Retardation Bd., 1975-81; adv. bd. Rehab. Inst. of Chgo., 1988-94; mem. coun. Ct. of Gov.'s Regents Coll., London, 1986-90, Rock Valley Coll. Indsl. Coun., Rockford, 1989-90; bd. dirs. Moraine Symphony Orch., 1990-93, Welcome Holme, Inc., 1990, pres., 1992; citizens adv. bd. West Bend Bank One, 1991, Washington County Vol. Ctr., 1991-92; bd. dirs. The Threshold, 1992; apptd. to State Wis. Coun. Phys. Disabilities, 1994, vice chmn., 1995, chmn., 1996; exec. com. Moraine area Tech. Prep. Coun., 1994; mem. Wis. Gov.'s Com. on Persons with Disabilities, 1994, vice chmn., 1996; mem. adv. bd. S.E. Wis. Area Health Edn. Coun., 1995-96; mem. West Bend C. of C. Ambs., 1995, Washington County Growth Mgmt. Task Force, 1996; pres. adv. bd. West Bend Art Mus., 1996; del. Washington County, 1997. Recipient Disting. Service award Widener Meml. Sch., 1978, Award of merit Md. Gov.'s Com. on Employment of Handicapped, 1984; named to Legion of Honor, Chapel of Four Chaplains, 1978; honoree West Phila. Vets. and Handicapped Employment Com., 1977. Mem. Am. Assn. Acad. Deans, Conf. on Brit. Studies, Am. Assn. Univ. Adminstrs., Nat. Spinal Cord Injury Assn. (bd. dirs. Ill. chpt. 1988-90), Rotary, Phi Alpha Theta. Republican. Home: 229 Bittersweet Dr West Bend WI 53095-4907 Office: U Wis Ctr Washington County 400 S University Dr West Bend WI 53095-3619

RODNICK, ELIOT HERMAN, psychologist, educator; b. New Haven, Nov. 27, 1911; s. Louis D. and Bertha (Caplan) R.; m. Helen Percival Hollander, Nov. 20, 1940; children: Jonathan Eliot, Marion Percival Rodnick Bell. AB with high oration, Yale U., 1933, PhD, 1936. Asst. research Yale U., 1934-36; research psychologist, research service Worcester (Mass.) State Hosp., 1936-46, dir. psychol. research, chief psychologist, 1946-49; acting dir. Worcester Child Guidance Clinic, 1946-47; instr. Mt. Holyoke Coll., 1939; asst. prof. psychology Clark U., 1942-46, assoc. prof., 1946-49; vis. lectr. summer session U. Wis., 1949, Harvard U., 1952, U. Colo., 1958; prof. psychology, dir. clin. tng. psychology Duke U., 1949-61, chmn. dept. psychology, 1951-61; prof. psychology, dir. clin. tng. psychology U. Calif. at Los Angeles, 1961-79, prof. emeritus, 1979—; cons. psychologist VA, 1949-79, mem. central office adv. com. to chief, dept. psychiatry and neurology, 1957-61; mem. mental health study sect. NIH, 1954-57, behavorial sci. study sect., 1957, mental health projects rev. commn., 1957-60, chmn. spl. mental health grants rev. com., 1960-62; bd. dirs. Los Angeles Psychiat. Service, 1961-66, Didi Hirsch Mental Health Center, 1973-82, Calif. Sch. Profl. Psychology, 1981-83; cons. Calif. Dept. Mental Hygiene; mem. com. on research tng. in biol. scis. Nat. Inst. Mental Health, 1962-66, chmn., 1965-66; mem. mental health council Western Commn. Higher Edn., 1961-66; adv. com. abuse of stimulant and depressant drugs FDA, 1966-68; sci. adv. com. on drug abuse U.S. Dept. Justice, 1968-75; Cons. Narcotics Control Commn. N.Y., 1969-75; cons. Calif. Sch. Profl. Psychology. Editorial bd.: Am. Jour. Orthopsychiatry, 1954-57, Jour. Personality, 1955-60, Jour. Abnormal and Social Psychology, 1957-62, Am. Jour. Community Psychology, 1972-77, Family Process, 1977-81. Trustee Calif. Sch. Profl. Psychology, 1981-83. Commd. officer USPHS Res. Recipient Stanley Dean prize for outstanding research in schizophrenia, 1967; Wilbur Lucius Cross medal for outstanding profl. performance Yale Grad. Sch. Assn., 1975. Fellow AAAS, APA (bd. dirs. 1962-65, Disting. Contbn. to Clin. Psychology award 1976), Western Psychol. Assn. (pres. 1966-67), Am. Psychol. Soc. (James McKeen Cattell fellow award), Calif. Psychol. Assn. (Disting. Sci. Contbns. in Psychology award 1975), Los Angeles County Psychol. Assn., N.C. Psychol. Assn. (past pres.), Am. Orthopsychiat. Assn. (bd. dirs. 1966-69, pres. 1967-68); mem. Cosmos Club (Washington), Phi Beta Kappa, Sigma Xi. Home: 7577 Oak Leaf Dr Santa Rosa CA 95409-6254 Office: U Calif Dept Psychology 405 Hilgard Ave Los Angeles CA 90095-9000

RODNING, CHARLES BERNARD, surgeon; b. Pipestone, Minn., Aug. 4, 1943; s. Selmer Bernard and Ida Amanda (Selness) R.; m. Mary Elizabeth Lipke, June 15, 1968; children: Christopher Bernard, Soren Piers, Kai Johannes. BS, Gustavus Adolphus Coll., St. Peter, Minn., 1965; MD, U. Rochester, 1970; PhD, U. Minn., 1979. Diplomate Am. Bd. Med. Examiners, Am. Bd. Surgery. Intern, asst. resident dept. surgery U. Rochester Sch. Medicine and Dentistry, 1970-72; assoc. resident to chief resident, med. fellow dept. surgery U. Minn. Health Scis. Ctr., Mpls., 1972-79; asst. prof. dept structural and cellular biology U. South Ala., Mobile, 1981—, prof. dept. surgery, 1981—, vice chmn. dept. surgery, 1981—; field liaison physician Commn. on Cancer-ACS, Chgo., 1984—; mem. med. adv. bd. Ala. Organ & Tissue Ctr., Birmingham, 1988—. Author: Elan Vital, Wode and Ston, Sorrowful Wheel, Ponderings, The Sea Rises in the West, Stepping Stones, Snowbound Below the Firn Line; reviewer Jour. Histochem. Cytochem., 1988—; contbr. numerous articles to Clin. Anatomy, Surg. Endoscopy, Pharos, Jours. Thoracic Cardiovascular Surgery, So. Med. Jours., others. Bd. dirs. Mobile Mental Health Ctr., Mental Health Found. of S. Ala., Eichold-Henstis Med. Mus. Comdr. USN, 1974-81. Recipient Physicians Recognition award AMA, 1980, 85, 88, 91, Bacaner Rsch. award Minn. Med. Found., 1979; named Disting. Faculty U. South Ala., 1990, 91, 92, 93. Fellow ACS, Internat. Coll. Surgeons (vice regent Ala. chpt. 1989—); mem. Iota Delta Gamma, Alpha Omega Alpha, Phi Kappa Phi. Office: Med Ctr USA 2451 Fillingim St Mobile AL 36617-2238

RODNUNSKY, SIDNEY, lawyer, educator; b. Edmonton, Alta., Can., Feb. 3, 1946; s. H. and I. Rodnunsky; m. Teresita Asuncion; children: Naomi, Shawna, Rachel, Tevie, Claire, Donna, Sidney Jr. BEd, U. Alberta, 1966, LLB, 1973; MEd, U. Calgary, 1969, grad. diploma, 1990; BS, U. of State of N.Y., 1988; MBA, Greenwich U., 1990. Served as regional counsel to Her Majesty the Queen in Right of the Dominion of Can.; former gov. Grande Prairie Regional Coll.; now prin. legal counsel Can.; Alta. coord. for gifted children Mensa Can., nat. exec.; past pres. Grande Prairie and Dist. Bar Assn. Author: Breathalyzer Casebook; editor: The Children Speak. Decorated knight Grand Cross Sovereign and Royal Order of Piast, knight Grand Cross Order of St. John the Baptist; knight Hospitaller Order St. John of Jerusalem; Prince of Kiev, Prince of Trabzon, Prince and Duke of Rodori, Duke of Chernigov, Count of Riga, County of St. John of Alexandria; named to Honorable Order of Ky. Colonels; named adm. State of Tex.; recipient Presdl. Legion of Merit. Mem. Law Soc. Alta., Law Soc. Sask., Can. Bar Assn., Inst. Can. Mgmt., Phi Delta Kappa. Home: 3 Grandview Garden Ct, 4802-46A Ave, Athabasca, AB Canada T9S 1H9

RODOVICH, ANDREW PAUL, lawyer, federal magistrate; b. Hammond, Ind., Feb. 24, 1948; s. Andrew H. and Julia (Makar) R.; m. Gail Linda Patrick, May 27, 1972; children: Caroline Anja, Mary Katherine, James Patrick. BA, Valparaiso (Ind.) U., 1970, JD, 1973. Bar: Ind. Ptnr. Hand, Muenich & Rodovich, Hammond, 1973-78; chief dep. prosecutor Lake County Prosecutor's Office, Crown Point, Ind., 1979-82; U.S. magistrate U.S. Dist. Ct., Hammond, 1982—; referee Hammond City Ct., 1978; adj. prof. Valparaiso Law Sch., 1985—. Fellow Ind. Bar Found.; mem. Nat. Coun. U.S. Magistrates, Delta Theta Phi. Republican. Avocations: sports. Home: 7207 Baring Pky Hammond IN 46324-2218 Office: US Dist Ct 136 Federal Bldg Hammond IN 46320-1529

RODOWSKY, LAWRENCE FRANCIS, state judge; b. Balt., Nov. 10, 1930; s. Lawrence Anthony and Frances (Gardner) R.; m. Colby Fossett, Aug. 7, 1954; children: Laura Rodowsky Ramos, Alice Rodowsky-Seegers, Emily Rodowsky Savopoulos, Sarah Jones Rodowsky, Gregory, Katherine Rodowsky O'Connor. A.B., Loyola Coll., Balt., 1952; LL.B., U. Md., 1956. Bar: Md. 1956. Ct. crier, law clk. U.S. Dist. Ct. Md., 1954-56; asst. atty. gen. State of Md., 1960-61; assoc., ptnr. firm Frank, Bernstein, Conaway & Goldman, Balt., 1956-79; assoc. judge Ct. Appeals Md., Annapolis, 1980—; mem. rules com. Ct. Appeals Md., 1969-80; lectr., asst. instr. U. Md. Law Sch., 1958-68, 87-91; reporter jud. dept. Md. Constl. Conv. Commn., 1966-67. Chmn. Gov. Md. Commn. Racing Reform, 1979. Fellow Am. Coll. Trial Lawyers; mem. Md. Bar Assn., Balt. Bar Assn. Roman Catholic. Home: 4306 Norwood Rd Baltimore MD 21218-1118 Office: Ct Appeals Md 620 C M Mitchell Jr CTHS Baltimore MD 21202

RODRICKS, DANIEL JOHN, columnist, television commentator; b. Brockton, Mass., Mar. 8, 1954; s. Joseph Allen and Rose Mary (Popolo) R.; m. Lillian M. Donnard, Sept. 6, 1980. B.A., U. Bridgeport, 1976. Reporter The Patriot Ledger, Quincy, Mass., 1973-75; wire editor Middletown Times Record, N.Y., 1975; reporter Balt. Evening Sun, 1976-79, columnist, 1979—; reporter, commentator Sta. WBAL-TV, Balt., 1980—. Recipient Heywood Broun award Newspaper Guild, 1983, Front Page award, 1983; awards from Sigma Delta Chi, Md.-Del.-D.C. Press Assn., Firefighters Internat., also others. Mem. Sigma Delta Chi. Democrat. Roman Catholic. Avocations: cooking, fishing, theater, operetta. Office: Baltimore Sun 501 N Calvert St Baltimore MD 21202-3604*

RODRIGUE, CHRISTINE M(ARY), geography educator, business consultant; b. L.A., Oct. 27, 1952; d. John-Paul and Josephine Genevieve (Gorsky) R. AA in French, German, L.A. Pierce Coll., 1972; BA in Geography summa cum laude, Calif. State U., Northridge, 1973, MA in Geography, 1976; PhD in Geography, Clark U., 1987. Computer analyst Jet Propulsion Labs., Pasadena, Calif., 1977; teaching asst. Clark U., Worcester, Mass., 1976-79, rsch. asst., 1977-78; instr. geography L.A. Pierce Coll., Woodland Hills, Calif., 1981—; cons. Area Location Systems, Northridge, 1984—, tech. writer, 1990—; asst. prof. urban studies and geography Calif. State U., Northridge, 1980-89; asst. prof. geography and planning Calif. State U., Chico, 1989-94, assoc. prof., 1994—; co-dir. Ctr. for Hazards Rsch., 1994—; faculty senator Calif. State U., Chico, 1990-92, grad. geog. adviser, 1992-93, 96—, dir. rural and town planning program, grad. advisor, 1996—; ptnr. Carmel Poster Gallery and Framing, Carmel, Calif., 1989-96; owner Nomad Arabians. Exhibited in L.A. Mcpl. Art Show, 1996, Faculty-Staff Art Show, Chico, 1994, 97; contbr. numerous articles to refereed profl. publs. Mem. bd. advisers So. Calif. Environment and History Conf., 1995—; founder, mem. bd. advisers No. Calif. Environment and History Conf., 1996—. Recipient Meritorious Performance and Profl. Promise award Calif. State U., 1987, 88, 89, Calif. State U. summer scholar grant, 1990, 92, 94. Mem. NOW, Am. Statis. Assn., Assn. Am. Geographers (chmn. splty. group 1983-84, councillor splty. group 1994—), Capitalism Nature Socialism (mem. editl. bd. 1991—), L.A. Geog. Soc. (v.p. 1987, pres. 1988, editor 1981-84), Planetary Soc., Internat. Arabian Horse Assn., Arabian Horse Registry. Democrat. Avocations: Arabian horses, science fiction, hiking, art, baroque music. Office: Calif State U Dept Geography & Planning Chico CA 95929-0425

RODRIGUES, ALFRED BENJAMIN KAMEEIAMOKU, marketing consultant; b. Honolulu, Jan. 23, 1947; s. Alfred Benjamin Kameeiamoku and Ruth Shiegeko (Kameda) R. BA, U. San Francisco, 1969; postgrad. U. Wis., 1977. Pub. info. mgr. Hawaiian Tel.-GTE, Honolulu, 1979-80, pub. affairs program mgr., 1980-84, dir. pub. affairs, 1984-85, dir. mktg. communications, 1986-87, dir. mktg. communications and svcs., 1987-89 sr. v.p., Milici, Valenti and Gabriel Advt., Inc., 1989-91, exec. v.p., 1991-92; pres. Al Rodrigues & Assocs., 1992—. Bd. dirs., pub. rels. chmn. Am. Lung Assn., 1981-88; trustee, v.p. Hawaii Army Mus. Soc., 1982—; bd. dirs. ARC Hawaii, 1983-85; budget com. Aloha United Way. Maj. USAR, 1969-89. Decorated Bronze Star with three oak leaf clusters, Meritorious Svc. medal with oak leaf cluster, Army Commendation medal with 2 oak leaf clusters, Purple Heart with oak leaf cluster, Air medal with oak leaf cluster. Mem. Am. Mktg. Assn. (bd. dirs. Hawaii chpt.), Am. Advt. Fedn., Hawaii Advt. Fedn. (bd. dirs., pres., Advt. Man of Yr., 1989), Pub. Rels. Soc. Am. (pres. Hawaii), Res. Officers Assn., Hawaii C. of C., Rotary. Republican. Roman Catholic.

RODRIGUES, MARK, financial executive, manpower consultant; b. Jhansi, India, Oct. 7, 1948; came to U.S., 1983; s. Basil and Monica (Dasgupta) R.; m. Sandra Williams, Mar. 27, 1976; children: Sarah, Daniel. BTech, Loughborough U., Leicester, Eng., 1970; MBA, Strathclyde U., Glasgow, Scotland, 1971. Cert. Acct., Eng. Fin. analyst Ford Europe, Inc., London, 1971-73; mgmt. cons., London mgr. Mann Judd Mgmt. Cons., 1973-78; pres. Bur. and Industry Svcs. Ltd., London, 1978-81; mng. dir. Indsl. Engring. Svcs., London, 1981-83; v.p. Internat. Staffing Cons., Newport Beach, Calif., 1983-88; pres. Brit. Workforce, Inc., Mission Viejo, Calif., 1988—; chmn. Euro Precision Inc., Mission Viejo, Calif., 1992—; pres. Computer Workforce, 1997—. Fellow Assn. Cert. Accts.; mem. Royal Oriental Club. Avocations: skiing, sailing, horseback riding, sail plane pilot. Office: Brit Workforce Inc 26012 Marguerite Pkwy Ste 234 Mission Viejo CA 92692-3263

RODRIGUEZ, ADOLFO, library director, historian; b. Piedras Negras, Coahuila, Mex., Mar. 28, 1942; s. José Valentín Rodríguez González and Guadalupe Gallardo de Rodríguez; m. María Mercedes del Carmen Villatoro A.; children: Ernesto Rodríguez Villatoro, Diego Rodríguez Villatoro. M History, El Colegio de México, México City, 1964; MLS, U. Texas, 1970. Info. coord. Armo Industry, Mexico City, 1970-73; subdir. Sec. de Edn. Pub. Nat. Sch. Libr. Scis., Mexico City, 1971; dir. Sec. de Edn. Pub. Nac. Sch. Libr. Scis., Mexico City, 1972-76, 1977; dir. Univ. Nac. Autonoma de Mex. Gen. Dir. of Librs., Mexico City, 1973-77, acad. coord., 1977-81, libr. assessor faculty Philosophy and Letters, 1979-81, dir. Centro Universitario de Investigaciones Bibliotecológicas, 1982-84, dir., 1985—. Author: Las bibliotecas en los informes presidenciales, 1990, Historia de la legislacion bibliotercaria de la UNAM, 1994, El regazo en las bibliotecas, 1996; co-author Bibliografía comentada sobre educacion bibliotecologica en Mexico, 1987; contbr. articles to profl. jours. Named 1st level Nat. Investigator Nat. System Investigators, México, 1991, named 2d level, 1994. Mem. Internat. Fedn. Documentation (rep. 1973), Am. Libr. Assn., Internat. Fedn. Assns. Librs. (Comité para Am. Latina com. 1987-92), Nat. Assn. Librs. (pres. 1981-83). Home: Cerrada de Iliada # 24, Col Axomiatla, DF 01820, Mexico Office: Dir Gen de Bibliotecas, Ciudad Universitaria, 04510 Mexico City Mexico

RODRIGUEZ, AGUSTIN ANTONIO, surgeon; b. Hato Rey, P.R., Aug. 20, 1961; s. Agustin and Esther Rodriguez (Gonzalez) R.; m. Liana Esther Lopez, 1993; 1 child, Agustin Andrés. AB in Biology, Harvard Coll., 1982; MD, U. P.R., San Juan, 1986. Diplomate Nat. Bd. Med. Examiners, Am. Bd. Surgery. Intern Boston U. Med. Ctr., 1986-87, resident in surgery, 1988-93, acad. trainee surgery; vascular fellow Tufts U., New England Med. Ctr., 1993-95; asst. prof. surgery Tufts U. Sch. Medicine, Boston, 1995—; assoc. prof. surgery Sch. Medicine U. P.R., San Juan, 1996—. Contbr. articles to profl. jours. Mem. AMA, Am. Numismatic Soc., Am. Numismatic Assn., Mass. Med. Soc., N.Y. Acad. Scis., European Soc. Vascular Surgery (assoc.), Am. Venous Forum, Interam. Coll. Physicians and Surgeons, Am. Soc. Clin. Vascular Surgery, Assn. Acad. Surgery, Soc. Am. Gastrointestinal and Endoscopic Surgeons, Coll. Med. Surgeons Puerto Rico, Ciruganos Vasculares de Habla Hispana, Alpha Omega Alpha. Republican. Home: 1483 Ashford Ave #702 San Juan PR 00907-1533 Office: U PR Sch Medicine Dept Surgery San Juan PR 00936-5067

RODRIGUEZ, ALEXANDER EMMANUEL, professional baseball player; b. N.Y.C., July 27, 1975. Grad. high sch., Miami. Baseball player Seattle Mariners, 1995—. Named Winner Am. League Batting Title, 1996.

RODRIGUEZ, ANTONIO JOSE, lawyer; b. New Orleans, Dec. 7, 1944; s. Anthony Joseph and Josephine Olga (Cox) R.; m. Virginia Anne Soignet, Aug. 23, 1969; children: Henry Jacob, Stephen Anthony. BS, U.S. Naval Acad., 1966; JD cum laude, Loyola U. of the South, New Orleans, 1973. Bar: La. 1973, U.S. Dist. Ct. (ea. dist.) La. 1973, U.S. Ct. Appeals (5th cir.) 1973, U.S. Dist. Ct. (mid. dist.) La. 1975, U.S. Dist. Ct. (we. dist.) La. 1977, U.S. Ct. Appeals (11th cir.) 1981, U.S. Supreme Ct. 1987, U.S. Dist. Ct. (so. dist.) Miss. 1991, U.S. Ct. Appeals (4th cir.) 1991, U.S. Ct. Internat. Trade, 1991. Assoc. Phelps, Dunbar, Marks, Claverie & Sims, New Orleans, 1973-

77; ptnr. Phelps Dunbar, New Orleans, 1977-92, Rice Fowler, New Orleans, 1992—; prof. law Tulane U., New Orleans, 1981—; mem. nat. rules of the road adv. coun. U.S. Dept. Transp., Washington, 1987-90, chmn. nat. navigation safety adv. coun., 1990-94; spkr. on admiralty and environ. Co-author: Admiralty-Limitation of Liability, 1981—, Admiralty-Law of Collision, 1990—; author: (chpt.) Benedict on Admiralty, 1995—; assoc. editor Loyola Law Rev., 1971-73; contbr. articles to profl. maritime and environ. jours. Bd. dirs. Greater New Orleans Coun. Navy League, 1988—. Lt. USN, 1966-70; capt. USNR, 1970-95. Decorated Navy Commendation medal; recipient Disting. Pub. Svc. award U.S. Dept. Transp., 1993. Fellow La. Bar Found.; mem. ABA, La. Bar Assn., La. State Law Inst., Maritime Law Assn. U.S. (proctor 1975—), New Orleans Bar Assn., Southeastern Admiralty Law Inst., Assn. Average Adjusters U.S., Assn. Average Adjusters U.K., Naval Res. Assn. (chpt. pres. 1982-84), U.S. Naval Acad. Alumni Assn. (chpt. pres. 1981-83), Bienville club, Phi Alpha Delta, Alpha Sigma Nu. Republican. Roman Catholic. Home: 4029 Mouton St Metairie LA 70002-1303 Office: Rice Fowler 201 Saint Charles Ave Fl 36 New Orleans LA 70170-1000

RODRIGUEZ, ARTURO SALVADOR, labor union official; b. San Antonio, June 23, 1949; s. Arthur Salvador and Felice (Quintero) R.; m. Linda Fabela Chavez, Mar. 30, 1974; children: Olivia, Julie, Arthur. BA in Sociology, St. Mary's U., 1971; MSW, U. Mich., 1973. Various positions United Farm Workers of Am., Keene, Calif., 1973-90, v.p., 1981-93, organizer, 1990-92; pres. United Farm Workers Am. AFL-CIO, Keene, 1993—. Chief instr. UFW Sch., Keene, 1978-79; coord. Edward Kennedy Presdl. Dr., San Antonio, 1980. Office: United Farm Workers Am AFL-CIO PO Box 62-La Paz 29700 Woodford Tehachapi Rd Keene CA 93531

RODRIGUEZ, BEATRIZ, ballerina; b. Ponce, P.R.. Attended, Newark Acad. Ballet, N.J. Sch. of Ballet; scholarship student, Joffrey Ballet Sch. Former dancer N.J. Ballet; dancer Richard Englund's Dance Repertory Co., 1970; mem. Joffrey II Dancers, 1971-72; mem., sr. dancer Joffrey Ballet, N.Y.C., 1972—. Repertory includes: Cakewalk, Dream Dances, Illuminations, Love Songs, Offenbach in the Underworld, Petrouchka, Return to the Strange Land, Rodeo, and The Green Table, Moves, Interplay, Deuce Coupe, As Time Goes By, Billy the Kid, The Dream, Taming of the Shrew, Wedding Bouquet, Force Field, Concerto Grosso, Valentine, Trinty, Kettentans, Fanfarita, The Rite of Spring, Cotillion, Romeo and Juliet, Forgotten Land, Le Sacre du Printemps, The Green Table. Recipient Dance Mag. award, 1993. Office: The Joffrey Ballet 130 W 56th St New York NY 10019-3803

RODRIGUEZ, CARLOS AUGUSTO, lawyer; b. Havana, Cuba, Sept. 1, 1954; came to U.S., 1960; s. Urbano and Estela (Cardenas) R.; m. Valerie Carr, May 27, 1989. BA magna cum laude, Furman U., 1977; JD, U. Fla., 1980. Bar: Fla. 1980, U.S. Ct. Appeals (5th cir.) 1981, U.S. Dist. Ct. (so. dist. and trial bar) Fla. 1984, U.S. Ct. Appeals (11th cir.) 1995; bd. cert. civil trial atty. Asst. pub. defender Broward County Pub. Defender's Office, Ft. Lauderdale, Fla., 1980-83, chief asst. pub. defender, 1983-85; assoc. Fazio, Dawson & DiSalvo, Ft. Lauderdale, Fla., 1985-87; sole practice Ft. Lauderdale, Fla., 1987—; assoc. prof. U. Miami Sch. Law, Miami, 1983-85; lectr. criminal procedure Nova Law Cen., Ft. Lauderdale, 1983-85, lectr. on law Broward Community Coll., Ft. Lauderdale, 1983-87; mem. Nuisance Abatement Bd., 1989—, chmn., 1996—; vice chmn. Marine ADv. Bd., 1990. Mem. Marine Adv. Bd., Broward, Fla., 1986-96; rep. Primary Rep. Port Everglades Commn., Broward, 1984. Mem. ABA, Assn. Trial Lawyers Am., Acad. Fla. Trial Lawyers, Broward County Bar Assn., Phi Beta Kappa. Republican. Roman Catholic. Avocations: scuba diving, fishing, water and snow skiing. Home: 2424 SE 13th Ct Pompano Beach FL 33062-7211 Office: 633 S Andrews Ave Ste 300 Fort Lauderdale FL 33301-2849

RODRIGUEZ, CARMEN VILA, artist, art educator, art historian; b. N.Y.C., July 16, 1927; d. Manuel and Julia (Lopez) Vila; m. Sabino Rodriquez Jr., Aug. 22, 1948; children: Sabino III, Manuel. BA in Art, Hunter Coll., 1948; studied with muralist Raul Anguiano, U. Mexico, 1966; student in advanced Ceramics and Jewelry, Calif. Coll. Arts and Crafts, 1966; student, U. Madrid, Spain, 1968; MA in Art and Art History, Columbia U., 1969, EdD in Art and Art Edn., 1977; postgrad., Fairfield U., 1982-93. Cert. in adminstrn. and supervision, Conn., art tchr., Conn., N.Y. Art tchr. Yorkville Vocat. H.S., N.Y.C., 1951-52; art history lectr. Instituto de Bellas Artes, Caracas, Venezuela, 1953-55; art tchr., dept. chmn. Eastchester (N.Y.) Sch. Dist. 1, 1958-92; cons., pres. VILA, Inc., Visual Instrnl. Libr. Art, Inc., 1981—; art edn. leader, lectr. art history Discovery Mus., Bridgeport, Conn., 1992—, Mus. Arts and Scis., Daytona Beach, Fla., 1997—; co-chair ednl. programs Lockwood-Mathews Manor Mus., Norwalk, Conn., 1992-94; adj. faculty Daytona Beach C.C., 1993—, Norwalk (Conn.) Cmty. Tech. Coll., 1996—; art instr. Norwalk Sr. Citizen Ctr., 1992-95, New Canaan (Conn.) Sr. Ctr., 1993—, Girl Scouts USA, Norwalk, 1990-93. Author: Tracy Loves Picasso, 1993; one-woman shows include Picture This Gallery, Westport, Conn., 1995, 1st Fidelity Bank, Norwalk, 1995, Sun Trust Bank, Daytona Beach, Fla., Sun Trust Bank, Daytona Beach, Fla., 1996, First Union Bank, Daytona Beach, 1997; group shows include Rowayton (Conn.) Arts Ctr., 1994, 96 (ribbon 1994), Bonnie Blair Country Club, Scarsdale, N.Y., 1962, N.Y. Gallery, 1970, Scarsdale Pub. Libr., 1975, Portland Gallery, Norwalk, Conn., 1996, Sun Trust Bank, 1996, Artist Workshop Inc., New Smyrna, Fla., 1997; editor J. Walter Thompson Advt., N.Y.C., 1970; editor, head stylist Trimble Studios, N.Y.C., 1949-53; contbr. articles to profl. jours. Art instr. Norwalk (N.Y.) Sr. Citizen Ctr., 1992—, Girl Scouts USA, Norwalk, Conn., 1990-93. Recipient Painting ward Eastchester Womens Club, 1964, Premio Major de Arte U. Mex., 1961. Mem. NEA, AAUW, NOW, Nat. Art Edn. Assn., Rowayton Art Assn., Art League Daytona Beach, Port Orange Art Assn., Artists Workshop Inc. Avocations: painting, travel, sculpture, writing, art history. Home: Oceans Seven-1906 2947 S Atlantic Ave Daytona Beach Shores FL 32118 Office: VILA Inc PO Box 466 466 E Norwalk South Norwalk CT 06856

RODRIGUEZ, CESAR, librarian; b. Callao, Peru, Oct. 23, 1945; came to U.S., 1957; s. Jose Rodriguez and Angela (Seminario) Tabarne; m. Daisy Rodriguez, June 21, 1969. AA, Concordia Coll., 1965; BA, Queens Coll., 1972, MLS, 1975; M in Internat. Affairs, Columbia U., 1983. Libr. acquisitions asst. McKinsey & Co., Inc., N.Y.C., 1971-73; acquisitions libr. Info. for Bus., Inc., N.Y.C., 1973-76; acquisitions libr. Yale U. Libr., New Haven, Conn., 1976-86, curator L.Am. Collection, 1986—; mem. exec. bd. Casa Cultural Julia De Burgos, New Haven, 1993—. Contbr. to profl. books. Corp. U.S. Marines, 1965-68, Vietnam. Mem. ALA, L.Am. Studies Assn., Seminar of L.Am. Libr. Materials (exec. bd. 1993—, chair coms. 1979—). Episcopalian. Office: Yale U L Am Collection Box 208240 130 Wall St New Haven CT 06520

RODRIGUEZ, CHI CHI (JUAN RODRIGUEZ), professional golfer; b. Bayamon, P.R., Oct. 13, 1935. Profl. golfer, 1960—. Contbg. columnist golf. mags. Winner PGA Tour Denver, 1963, Lucky Internat., 1964, Western Tour, 1964, Tex. Tour, 1967, Sahara Tour, 1968, Byron Nelson Tour, 1973, Greater Greensboro, 1973, KO Olina Invitational, 1992; named to Ryder Cup Team, 1973.Inducted into the World Sports Humanitarian Hall of Fame, 1994. Leading money winner on sr. tour, 1987; represented P.R. in 12 world cups; ranked # 5 on PGA sr. tour, 1992; ranked # 4 among scoring leaders PGA sr. tour, 1992. Office: PGA 100 Avenue Of Champions Palm Beach Gardens FL 33418-3653*

RODRIGUEZ, DAVID G., JR., art and religion educator, priest; b. San Antonio, Tex., June 9, 1947; s. David Campos and Maria Beatrice (Gonzalez) R. BFA, Coll. St Francis, 1979; M in pastoral studies, Loyola U., 1984; M in divinity, Cath. Theo. Union, 1988; M in arts inter-discipline, Columbia Coll., 1993; MFA, Md. Inst. Coll. Art, 1995. Cert. elem. tchr., art tchr., Ill. Clk. USAF, 1968-72; tchr. St. Ann's Cath. Sch., Great Falls, Mont., 1969-72; sales & design Gen. Men's Wear, San Antonio, 1972-73; tchr. art and religon St. Jude's Cath. Sch., New Lenox, Ill., 1974-79; tchr. cont. edn. Joliet Jr. Coll., New Lenox, 1976-77; tchr., chair fine arts Providence H.S., New Lenox, 1979-84; tchr., chair arts & religion Hales Francisan H.S., Chgo., 1984—; priest Chgo. and Joliet Dioc., Chgo., 1989—; chaplain Cruise Lines, Fla., 1989—; art teach core mem. Chgo. Cath. H.S., 1989—; art dept. evaluator Ill. North Cen., Chgo., 1990—; curriculum staff and evaluator Hales Franciscan H.S., 1990—; adj. faculty art edn. dept. The Sch. of Art Inst. Chgo., 1994—, apprentice tchr. supr., 1995—. Represented in permanent collections at Mus. Sci. & Industry, Chgo., Sco. of Art Inst. Chgo., Columbia Coll., Chgo. Juror fine arts Art Reach, Chgo., 1990—; mem. Arts Basics, Art. Inst. Chgo., 1990—; mem. Gt. Falls Symphony Chorus. With USAF, 1968-72. Coca-Cola fellow Md. Inst. Coll. Art, 1991-95. Mem. NCEA, Nat. Cath. Edn. Assn., Nat. Art Edn. Assn., Cath. Edn. Archdiocese of Chgo., Facets Cinema, Art Inst. Chgo., Mex. Fine Arts Mus. Roman Catholic. Avocations: dance, remodeling design, floral design, cooking, choreography, painting. Home: 4930 S Cottage Grove Ave Chicago IL 60615-2616 Office: Hales Franciscan HS Province 4930 S Cottage Grove Ave Chicago IL 60615-2616

RODRIGUEZ, ELENA GARCIA, retired pension fund administrator; b. Havana, Cuba, Mar. 21, 1944; came to U.S., 1959; d. Eliseo and Elena (Suarez) Garcia; divorced; children: Victor, Yvonne, Daniel. B in Profl. Studies, Barry U., 1983; MS in Mgmt., St. Thomas U., 1985; postgrad., U. Phila., 1989, UCLA, 1990. With City of Miami, Fla., 1969-95, pension adminstr., 1978-95, ret., 1995. Author: General and Sanitation Pension Benefit Booklet, 1982, Fire and Police Pension Benefit Booklet, 1982, Retirement Planning Booklet, 1985; author numerous programs dealing with pension and acctg. for pension assets. Mem. Leadership Miami, 1985—; mediator Cir. Ct., family, County Ct., NASD. Mem. NASD (arbitrator), Internat. Found. Employee Benefit Plans, Internat. Pers. Mgmt. Assn., Inst. Fiduciary Edn., Fla. Assn. City Clks., New York Stock Exch. (arbitrator), Am. Stock Exch. (arbitrator), Am. Arbitration Assn., Better Bus. Bur. (arbitrator, mediator). Republican. Roman Catholic. Avocations: growing orchids, stained glass, tile mosaics, painting.

RODRIGUEZ, ELIAS C., judge; b. Dallas, Sept. 7, 1919; s. Elias S. and Anna (Fernandez) R.; m. Alberta Lenore Durbin, Jan. 1, 1949; children—Michael, Robert, Richard. B.A., So. Meth. U., 1941; J.D., Georgetown Law Sch., 1948, LL.M., 1953. Bar: Tex. 1948, D.C. 1948. Atty. IMF, Washington, 1948-51; fgn. service officer Dept. State, Washington, 1952-69; 1st sec. Am. Embassy Rome, Italy, 1960-65; atty. CAB, Washington, 1971-78, adminstrv. law judge, 1977-84; chief adminstrv. law judge, CAB, 1982-84; chief adminstrv. law judge Dept. Transp., Washington, 1984-87. Served to lt. col. U.S. Army, 1942-46, ETO.

RODRÍGUEZ, FERDINAND, chemical engineer, educator; b. Cleve., July 8, 1928; s. José and Concha (Luís) R.; m. Ethel V. Koster, July 28, 1951; children: Holly Edith, Lida Concha. B.S., Case Western Res. U., 1950, M.S., 1954; Ph.D., Cornell U., 1958. Devel. engr. Ferro Corp., Bedford, Ohio, 1950-54; asst. prof. chem. engring. Cornell U., 1958-61, asso. prof., 1961-71, prof., 1971—; on sabbatic leave at Union Carbide Corp., 1964-65, Imperial Chem. Industries, Ltd., 1971, Eastman Kodak Co., 1978-79; cons. to industry. Author: Principles of Polymer Systems, 4th edit., 1996; contbr. numerous articles to profl. jours.; songwriter. Served with U.S. Army, 1954-56. Recipient Excellence in Teaching award Cornell Soc. Engrs., 1966, Edn. Achievement award Hispanic Engr. Mag., 1991. Fellow Am. Inst. Chem. Engrs.; mem. Am. Chem. Soc., Soc. Hispanic Profl. Engrs., Soc. Plastics Engrs. Lutheran. Home: 107 Randolph Rd Ithaca NY 14850-1720 Office: 230 Olin Hall Cornell U Ithaca NY 14853

RODRIGUEZ, GENO (EUGENE RODRIGUEZ), artist, arts administrator; b. N.Y.C., June 2, 1940; s. Eugenio and Juana (Lopez) R.; m. Janice Rooney, Oct., 1966; 1 dau., Samantha Marisol. Student, Internat. Peoples Coll., Elsinor, Denmark, 1961-62; nat. diploma in art, Hammersmith Coll. Art, London, 1966. Founder, pres., exec. dir. Alternative Center for Internat. Arts Alternative Museum, N.Y.C., 1975—; instr. photography Sch. Visual Arts, N.Y.C., 1978-82, Rutgers U., 1977-79; mem. Artists Cert. Appeals Bd., N.Y.C., 1979, spl. artist task force N.Y. State Council on Arts, 1981; panelist, cons. NEA, Dept. Cultural Affairs N.Y.C.; lectr. in field. Exhibited in one-man shows Il Diaframa Gallery, Milan, Italy, 1979, Mus. Contemporary Arts, Caracas, Venezuela, 1979, Real Art Ways Gallery, Hartford, Conn., 1980, Cayman Gallery, N.Y.C., 1980, CEPA Gallery, Buffalo, 1987, Sheldon Meml. Art Gallery U. Nebr., Lincoln, 1989; group shows include Autoren Gallery, Munich, 1980, Miss. Mus. Art, Jackson, 1981, Palacio de Minerias, Mexico City, 1981, J.A.M. Gallery, N.Y.C., 1981, Chrysler Mus., Norfolk, Va., 1981, Am. Indian Gallery, 1982, Roger Litz Gallery, N.Y., 1982, Tweed Gallery, N.J., 1983, Baumgartner Gallery, Washington, 1983, Municipality of Genoa, Italy, 1984, Phila. Arts Alliance, 1985, Jayne H. Baum Gallery, N.Y.C., 1985-86, Gerald Melberg Gallery, Charlotte, N.C., 1985, Eupherat Gallerty, Calif., 1986, N.Y. State Mus., Albany, 1986, Hillwood Art Gallery, N.Y., 1986, Stux Gallery, Boston, 1986, San Diego Mus. Art, 1987, Alternative Mus., N.Y.C., 1987, Graham Modern, N.Y.C., 1987, Internat. Ctr. Photography, N.Y.C., 1987, Haggerty Mus. Art Marquette U., Milw., 1988, Herter Art Gallery U. Mass., 1989, Nat. Mus. Am. Art Smithsonian Instn., 1989; represented in permanent collections Internat. Ctr. Photography, N.Y.C., Mus. City of N.Y., Met. Mus. Art, N.Y.C., Everson Mus. Art, Syracuse, N.Y., Am. Mus. Natural History, N.Y.C., Mus. Contemporary Art, Caracas, Venezula; author: The Islands: Worlds of the Puerto Ricans, 1974, Mira, Mira, Mira Puerto Rican New Yorkers, 1975. Active Clinton/Gore Presdl. Transition Team for Arts and Humanites, 1992. Served with USN, 1959-63. Recipient Phelps-Stokes Fund award, 1977; Ludwig Vogelstien Found. award, 1981; Nat. Endowment for Arts fellow, 1979. Mem. Am. Assn. Mus. (exec. mem. curators com. 1985). Office: Alternative Museum 594 Broadway Rm 408 New York NY 10012-3234*

RODRIGUEZ, IVAN, professional baseball player; b. Vaga Baja, P.R., Nov. 30, 1971. With Tex. Rangers, 1988—; mem. Am. League All-Star Team, 1992-96, Am. League Silver Slugger Team The Sporting News, 1994-96. Recipient Gold Glove award, 1992-96. Office: Tex Rangers 1000 Ballpark Way Arlington TX 76011-5168*

RODRIGUEZ, J. LOUIS, civil engineer, land surveyor; b. N.Y.C., Sept. 8, 1920; s. Cesar and Carmen (Quintero) R.; m. Rita Victoria Fradera, Sept. 4, 1948; children: Carmen Brana, Christina McCarthy, Robert. BCE, City Coll. N.Y., 1942. Lic. profl. engr., N.Y., Conn., Ohio, Miss., Mass., Maine, Ontario, Alberta; lic. land surveyor, Conn. Office engr. Arthur A. Johnson Co., L.I., N.Y., 1945-48; project engr. Merritt Chapman & Scott Corp., N.Y.C., 1948-54; chief engr. Merritt Chapman & Scott Corp. of the Dominican Republic, Santo Domingo, Dominican Republic, 1954-55; estimator Hoggson Bros./F. H. McGraw, N.Y.C., 1956-59; mgr. engring. Diamond Internat. Corp., N.Y.C., 1959-86; owner North Stamford (Conn.) Surveyors, 1986—; constrn. adminstr. Holy Spirit Parish, Stamford, 1986-88; bldg. planning coord. Drug Liberation Program, Stamford, 1989-91. Stamford rep. S.W. Regional Planning Agy, Norwalk, Conn., 1973-75; bd. dirs. Drug Liberation Program, Inc., Stamford, 1987-91; keynote speaker Vets. Day Program, Stamford, 1982. 1st lt. USAAF, 1942-45, maj. USAFR. Decorated Air medal with oak leaf cluster; recipient Air Commendation medal, 1970. Fellow ASCE (life); mem. NSPE (life), Profl. Engrs. Ontario, Conn. Soc. Profl. Engrs. (chpt. pres., state dir. 1963), Conn. Assn. Land Surveyors, North Stamford Exch. Club (bd. dirs., past pres., Man of Yr. award 1989), Eighth Air Force Hist. Soc., Air Force Escape and Evasion Soc., Tau Beta Pi. Republican. Roman Catholic. Achievements include designing structures for Molded Pulp Plant, Natchez, Miss., Tissue Mill, Old Town, Maine, 600 Ton Recovery Boiler, Old Town. Home and Office: 237 Russet Rd Stamford CT 06903-1823

RODRIGUEZ, JOSEPH H., federal judge; b. 1930; m. Barbara Marriner. AB, La Salle Coll., 1955; JD, Rutgers U., 1958. Assoc. Brown, Connery et al, Camden, N.J., 1959-82; pub. advocate, pub. defender State of N.J., 1982-85; judge U.S. Dist. Ct. N.J., Camden, 1985—; instr. law Rutgers U., N.J., 1972-82, 93—; chmn. State Commn. Investigation, N.J., 1974-79. Chmn. State Bd. of Higher Edn., N.J., 1971-73. Mem. N.J. State Bar Assn. (pres. 1978-79). Office: US Dist Ct PO Box 886 One John F Gerry Plz Camden NJ 08101-0886*

RODRIGUEZ, JUAN ALFONSO, technology corporation executive; b. Santiago, Cuba, Feb. 10, 1941; came to U.S., 1953; s. Alfonso and Marie Madeleine (Hourcadette) R. BEE, CCNY, 1962; MEE, NYU, 1963. Engr. IBM, Poughkeepsie, N.Y. and Boulder, Colo., 1963-68; engring. mgr. IBM, 1968-69; dir. tech. Storage Tech. Corp., Louisville, Colo., 1969-74, v.p. engring., 1974-77, v.p., gen. mgr. disk, 1977-79; v.p., gen. mgr. optical disk Storage Tech. Corp., Longmont, Colo., 1979-85; pres., CEO Exabyte Corp., Boulder, 1985-87, CEO, 1987-90; chmn., 1987-92; pres. Sweetwater Corp., 1992-93, chmn., 1992-95, also bd. dirs.; prof. elec. and computer engring. and engring. mgmt. U. Colo., 1992—, co-exec. dir. Ctr. for Entrepreneurship, 1994—; chmn. Datasonix, 1992-96, Vixel, 1995—; chmn., CEO Ecrix Corp., 1996—; mem. devel. coun. Coll. Engring. U. Colo., 1990-92; Kapre Corp.; mem. engring. adv. bd. CCNY, bd. dirs. Colo. Advanced Tech. Enterprise, 1994—, co-exec. dir. Joint Ctr. for Entre Preneurship, U. Colo., 1994—; Robert J. Appel Disting. lectr. law and tech. Law Sch. U. Denver, 1990. Patentee in field. Bd. dirs. Boulder YMCA, 1982-87, U. Colo. Artist Series, 1988—; mem. bd. govs. Boulder County United Way, 1989-93, chairperson campaign, 1992; commr. Colo. Advance Tech. Inst., 1988-92. Recipient Ind. Quality award Rocky Mountain sect. Am. Soc. Quality Control, 1990, Gen. Palmer award for Outstanding Engr. in Industry The Am. Cons. Engrs. Coun. of Colo., 1995; named Boulder Spirit Entrepreneur of Yr., 1989, Entrepreneur of the Decade Boulder C. of C., 1994, Hispanic Engr. of Yr., Entrepreneur Hispanic Engr. Nat. Achievement Awards Coun., 1995; finalist Entrepreneur of Yr., Arthur Young & Inc Mag., 1989. Fellow IEEE; mem. Computer Soc. of IEEE (mem. steering com. on mass storage 1981-93), Soc. Photo-Optical Instrumentation Engrs., Boulder C. of C. (chmn. entrepreneurs support program 1989), Greater Denver C. of C. (bd. dirs. 1990-91). Office: Univ Colo PO Box 425 Boulder CO 80309-0425

RODRIGUEZ, JUAN GUADALUPE, entomologist; b. Espanola, N.Mex., Dec. 23, 1920; s. Manuel D. and Lugardita (Salazar) R.; m. Lorraine Ditzler, Apr. 17, 1948; children: Carmen, Teresa, Carla, Rosa. BS, N.Mex. State U., 1943; MS, Ohio State U., 1946, PhD, 1949. Asst. entomologist U. Ky., Lexington, 1949-55, assoc. entomologist, 1955-61, prof. entomology, 1961—; adv. entomology U. de San Carlos, Guatemala, 1961; vis. scientist Warsaw U., 1961; sec. V Internat. Congress Acarology, 1978; del. internat. confs. Vienna, Moscow, San Jose, Costa Rica, Nottingham, Eng., Prague, Saalfelden, Austria, Kyoto, Japan, Edinburgh, Scotland, Hamburg, Fed. Republic Germany; bd. dirs. Ky. Sci. & Tech. Coun., 1990—; cons. to food industry, 1989—. Ky. steering com. Eisenhower Math/Sci. Consortium Appalachia Ednl. Lab., 1992—. Bd. dirs. Lexington chpt. NCCJ, Ky. Sci. & Tech. Coun., 1989—, Ky. steering com. of Appalachia Edn. Lab., 1993—. Served with inf., AUS, World War II; ex POW. Recipient Disting. Research award U. Ky. Alumni Assn., 1963; Thomas Poe Cooper award U. Ky. Coll. Agr., 1972, Outstanding Acarologist award Am. Registry Profl. Entomologists, 1984. Fellow AAAS, Royal Entomol. Soc. London; mem. Nat. Assn. Acads. Sci. (pres., 1997), Am. Inst. Biol. Scis., Acarol. Soc. Am. (governing bd.), Ky. Acad. Sci. (pres. 1982-83; pres. Found. 1982—, Disting. Scientist award 1985, exec. sec. 1988—), Can. Entomol. Soc., Ont. Entomol. Soc., Entomol. Soc. Am. (br. sec.-treas. 1963-65, br. com. man at large 1968-71, br. pres. 1982-83, North Cen. States br. rep. to governing bd. 1984-87, chmn. centennial com. 1987-89, hon. mem. 1989), Order Ky. Cols., Ky. Dept. Am. ex-POWs (comdr. 1992-94), Sigma Xi (pres. U. Ky. chpt. 1977), Gamma Alpha, Gamma Sigma Delta. Roman Catholic. Editor: Insect and Mite Nutrition, 1972, Recent Advances in Acarology, vols. I and II, 1979; co-editor: Current Trends in Insect Endocrinology and Nutrition, 1981, Leafhoppers and Planthoppers, 1985, Nutritional Ecology of Insects, Mites and Spiders, 1987; mem. editorial bd. Internat. Jour. Acarology; contbr. articles to profl. jours. Home: 1550 Beacon Hill Rd Lexington KY 40504-2304

RODRIGUEZ, LINDA TAKAHASHI, secondary school educator, administrator; b. L.A., June 22, 1941; d. Edward S. and Mary Takahashi; divorced; children: Regina Marie, Marla Sari. AA, Trinidad (Colo.) Jr. Coll., 1961; BA, We. State Coll., Gunnison, Colo., 1963; MA, U. Colo., Denver, 1991. Cert. tchr., adminstr., Colo. Tchr. Stratton (Colo.) Jr./Sr. High Sch., 1964-65, Pikes Peak Elem. Sch., Colorado Springs, 1966-68, Prince Sch., Tucson, 1968-70, Ipava (Ill.) Grade Sch., 1970-72, Macomb (Ill.) Schs., 1972-74, Colchester (Ill.) Jr./Sr. High Schs., 1979-83, Hazel Park (Mich.) Alternative Sch., 1984-85; tchr. 8th grade lang. arts and social studies Denver Pub. Schs., 1986-95, chair lang. dept., 1987-96, tchr. reading resource, 1987-92; asst. prin. Martin Luther King Jr. Efficacy Acad.-Middle Sch.; creator, dir. Reading Summer Sch., 1987-95; presenter insvcs. Denver Pub. Schs., 1987-94; mentor Alternative Tchr. Cert. Program; mem. bd. dirs. Asian Cultural Ctr. Advisor Asian Edn. Adv. Bd., Denver, 1989-95; bd. dirs. Colo. Youth-at-Risk, Denver, 1992-93, Colo. Aids Project. Mem. Landmark Edn. Forum, Highland Park Optimists, Delta Kappa Gamma. Avocations: reading, skiing, personal growth, swimming, socializing. Home: 1617 Daphne St Broomfield CO 80020-1155

RODRIGUEZ, LOUIS JOSEPH, university president, educator; b. Newark, Mar. 13, 1933; m. Ramona Dougherty, May 31, 1969; children: Susan, Michael, Scott. BA, Rutgers U., 1955; MA, La. State U., 1957, PhD, 1963. Dean, Coll. Bus. Adminstrn., Alcee Fortier Disting. prof. Nicholls State U., Thibodaux, La., 1958-71; dean Coll. Bus. U. Tex.-San Antonio, 1971-72, v.p. acad. affairs, dean faculty, 1972-73; dean Sch. Profl. Studies U. Houston-Clear Lake City, 1973-75, vice-chancellor, provost, 1975-80; pres. Midwestern State U., Wichita Falls, Tex., 1981—, Hardin Found. prof., 1994—; vice chmn. Coun. Tex. Pub. Univ. Pres. and Chancellors, 1992-93; mem. formula and health professions edn. adv. coms. Tex. Higher Edn. Coordinating Bd. Author 4 books; contbr. over 50 articles to profl. jours. Chmn. bd. Tex. Council on Econ. Edn., Houston, 1981-83; bd. dirs. Joint Council on Econ. Edn., N.Y.C., 1981-83, Goodwill Industries Am., Washington, 1976-82, Robert Priddy Found., 1993-96; pres. Wichita Falls Bd. Commerce and Industry, 1988-89, Clear Lake City Devel. Found., Houston, 1976-77, Goals for Wichita Falls, Inc., 1983; mem. internat. adv. com. Tex. Higher Edn. Coordinating Bd. Recipient Tchr. Edn. Supportive Pres. award Am. Assn. Colls. Tchr. Edn., 1991; named Wichitan of the Yr., 1987; Ford Found. grantee, 1964; Fulbright fellow, 1976. Mem. Am. Assn. State Colls. and Univs. (bd. dirs.), So. Assn. Colls. and Schs. (Commn. on Colls.), Assn. Tex. Colls. and Univs. (pres. 1988-89), Rotary (pres. Downtown Wichita Falls club 1990-91). Mem. Ch. of Christ. Home: 2405 Midwestern Pky Wichita Falls TX 76308-2811 Office: Midwestern State U 3410 Taft Blvd Wichita Falls TX 76308-2095

RODRIGUEZ, MANUEL ALVAREZ, pathologist; b. Guantanamo, Cuba, Nov. 12, 1946; came to U.S., 1961, naturalized, 1970; s. Mauel and Maria Teresa (Alvarez) R.; divorced; children: Austin B., Matthew J. BSc in Biology, U. Nev., 1966; MT, St. Alexius Hosp., Bismarck, N.D., 1969; BSc in Medicine, U. N.D., 1971; MD, U. Tex., Galveston, 1973. Diplomate Am. Bd. Pathology. Rotating intern Meml. Med. Ctr., Corpus Christi, Tex., 1973-74; commd. USPHS, 1974, advanced through grades to comdr., 1993; gen. surgery resident USPHS Hosp., New Orleans, 1974-75, anatomic/clin. pathology resident, 1975-76; anatomic/clin. pathology resident U. N.D. Sch. Medicine, Grand Forks, 1976-77, Touro Infirmary Hosp., New Orleans, 1977-79; pvt. practice Houston, 1979-89; sr. med. officer USPHS-USCG Med. Clinic, New Orleans, 1990-92; flight surgeon, sr. med. officer USPHS-Brooks AFB, San Antonio, 1992, USPHS-USCG Air Sta. Med. Clinic, Sitka, Alaska, 1992-96, USPHS-USCG Miami Air Sta. Med. Clinic, Miami Lakes, Fla., 1996; sr. staff med. officer USPHS, San Pedro, Calif., 1996-97; clin. dir. USPHS, El Centro, Calif., 1997—; instr. pathology La. State U. Med. Sch., Baton Rouge, 1979-80; tchg. fellow pathology U. N.D. Med. Sch., Grand Forks, 1976-77. Contbr. articles to profl. jours. Dir. charitable donations mil. ann. drive USPHS-USCG, New Orleans, Sitka, 1990-96, Miami Lakes, Fla., 1996. Fellow Am. Acad. Family Practice, Coll. Am. Pathologists, Aerospace Med. Assn. Roman Catholic. Avocation: writing professional articles. Home: 6941 Holly Rd Miami Lakes FL 33014

RODRIGUEZ, MATT L., protective services professional. AA in Bus. Adminstrn. with high honors, Wright Coll., 1972; BS in Pub. Adminstrn. with honors, Roosevelt U., 1975, MPA with honors, 1976; postgrad., Northwestern U., 1976-77. Joined Chgo. Police Dept., 1959, advanced through grades to capt., 1988, patrolman, 1959-60, investigator Organized Crime sect., 1960-70, patrol sgt., 1970-71, investigative sgt. Criminal Investigation div., 1971-73, watch comdr., coord. gambling unit Vice Control div., 1973-76, 77-78, field lt. Patrol div., 1979, commanding officer area 6 youth div. Bur. Investigative Svcs., 1979, commanding officer gambling sect. Vice Control div., 1979-80, adminstrv. asst. to supt., 1980, dep. supt. Bur. Tech. Svcs., 1980-92, supt., 1992—; adj. prof. criminal justice dept. U. Ill., Chgo., 1979—, mem. adv. com. office internat. criminal justice; mayoral appointee Chgo. Emergency Telephone Systems Bd.; chmn. bd. Hispanic Inst. Law Enforcement; mem. adv. coun. Atty. Gen./State of Ill. Victim Assistance Program; lectr. Pub. Svcs. U., Beijing, 1984, Acad. Criminal Justive Scis., Orlando, Fla., 1984, Bramshill Police Coll., Hampshire, Eng., 1986, Am. Soc. Criminology ann. conf., Chgo., 1988, numerous others; keynote speaker

IRS, Chgo., 1987, Northwestern U. Traffic Inst., 1989; panelist Nat. Conf. Criminal Justice Info. Law and Policy, CHgo., 1984, U.S. Dept. Justice Community Rels. Svcs.; participant numerous seminars and internat. confs. Contbr. articles to profl. jours. Bd. advisors Cath. Charities, Archdiocese of Chgo.; bd. dirs. Chgo. chpt. March of Dimes Birth Defects Found., Mental Health Assn. Greater Chgo., Law Found. Ill.; mem. community adv. com. Sta. WYCC-TV; mem. adv. bd. Malcom X Coll. Recipient Man or Yr. award Puerto Rican Congess Law and Order, 1983, Man of Yr. award Mex. Am. Legal Def. Ednl. Fund, 1987, Outstanding Achievement award Puerto Rican Congress Mut. Aid, Inc., 1987, Outstanding Support award Mex. Civic Soc. Ill., Inc., 1987, Cert. Appreciation Near North Kiwanis Chgo., 1988, Man of Yr. award Polonia Cares Found., 1989, Outstanding Alumnus award Wright Coll., 1989, Alumni award Holy Trinity High Sch., 1989, Citation of Honor Jewish Nat. Fund, 1991, Cert. Appreciation Drug Enforcement Adminstrn., 1991. Mem. Hispanic Am. Police Command Officers Assn. (1st v.p., bd. dirs.), Internat. Assn. Chiefs of Police (com. on civil rights, Cert. Appreciation for Outstanding Contbns. Towards Professionalization Law Enforcement 1990, coms. on cmty. policing and comms.), Latin Am. Police Assn. (bd. dirs., Man of Yr. award 1984). Office: Chgo Police Dept Office of Supt 1121 S State St Rm 400 Chicago IL 60605-2304*

RODRIGUEZ, NORA, social worker; b. Bklyn., Nov. 27, 1958; d. Carlos and Luz Ilia (Morales) R.; m. Manuel Rodriguez, Oct. 8, 1983; children: Eva Luisa, Esteban Manuel. BA, BSW, Seton Hall U., 1980; MSW, Columbia U., 1982. Social worker Puerto Rican Family Inst., Inc., N.Y.C., 1982-84; pediatric social worker Raritan Bay Med. Ctr., Perth Amboy, N.J., 1984-87; sr. social worker Children's Specialized Hosp., Mountainside, N.J., 1987-91; CPL Union County, 1991—; cons. Community Svc. Advisor Tng. Prog., New Brunswick, N.J., 1981—; guest Healthscope & Health Lifestyles/Cablevision, 1991. Editor: newsletter Puerto Rican Family Inst., Alianza, 1983-84. Vol. probationer Middlesex County Probation Dept., New Brunswick, 1979-80. Mem. NASW, Seton Hall Alumni Assn., Columbia U. Alumni Assn., Columbia U. Hispanic Caucus, Alpha Delta Mu. Democrat. Roman Catholic. Avocations: crafts, indoor gardening, cooking.

RODRIGUEZ, PLACIDO, bishop; b. Celaya, Mex., Oct. 11, 1940; came to U.S., 1953; s. Eutimio and Maria Concepcion (Rosiles) R. STB, STL, Cath. U., Washington, 1968; MA, Loyola U., 1971. Ordained priest Roman Cath. Ch., 1968, ordained to bishop, 1983. Pastor Our Lady Guadalupe Ch., Chgo., 1972-75, Our Lady of Fatima Ch., Perth Amboy, N.J., 1981-83; vocat. dir. Claretians, Chgo., 1975-81; bishop aux. Archdiocese of Chgo., 1983-94; bishop Diocese of Lubbock, Tex., 1994—. Office: The Catholic Ctr PO Box 98700 Lubbock TX 79499-8700*

RODRIGUEZ, RAY, broadcast executive; b. Camaguey, Cuba, Jan. 31, 1951; s. Ray Sr. and Maria Patricia (Tobin) R.; m. Liana Silvia Garcia, July 27, 1975; children: Liana Marie, Rainaldo Gabriel, Claudia Marie. BBA, U. Miami, 1973. Mgr. Deloitte Haskins & Sells CPAs, Miami, Fla., 1973-83; mgr., chief exec. officer Julio Iglesias, Miami, Fla., 1983-88; pres. Ray Rodriguez Co., Miami, Fla., 1988-90; pres., chief exec. officer Univision Holdings, Miami, 1990—. Mem. Rep. Bd. Govs. Dade County, Fla., 1989—. Mem. Kiwanis Little Havana Found. (chpt. pres. 1987—, trustee, bd. dirs. 1974-88). Roman Catholic. Avocations: golf, boating, tennis. Office: Univision 9405 NW 41st St Miami FL 33178-2301*

RODRIGUEZ, RITA MARIA, banker; b. La Havana, Cuba, Sept. 6, 1944; came to U.S., 1960; Tomas and Adela (Mederos) R.; m. E. Eugene Carter, Jan. 7, 1972; 1 child, Adela-Marie R. Carter. BBA, U. Puerto Rico, 1964; MBA, NYU, 1968, PhD, 1969. Bus. adminstrn. asst. prof., then assoc. prof. Harvard Bus. Sch., Cambridge, Mass., 1969-74, 74-78; fin. prof. U. Ill., Chgo., 1978-82; dir. Export-Import Bank of U.S., Washington, 1982—; cons. Polaroid Corp. and Indsl. Devel. Bank in Ecuador (Corporacion Financiera Nacional), 1978-82, U.S. IRS, 1982; bd. dirs. Acad. Ednl. Devel., Washington, 1989-93; bd. advisors Pew Econ. Freedom Fellows, Washington, 1991—. Author: (with E. Eugene Carter) International Financial Management, 1976, 2d edit., 1979, 3rd edit., 1984, (with Heinz Riehl) Foreign Exchange Markets: A Guide to Foreign Currency Operations, 1977, Foreign Exchange Management in U.S. Multinationals, 1980 (with Heinz Riehl) Foreign Exchange and Money Markets, 1983, Japanese, Spanish, Portuguese translations, The Export-Import Bank at Fifty, 1987; contbr. numerous fin. articles to profl. publs. Recipient Outstanding Achievement award, Nat. Coun. of Hispanic Women, 1986; Outstanding Hispanic Achievement award, Hispanic Corp. Achievers, 1988; National Leadership award-Government, The Nat. Network of Hispanic Women, 1989. Mem. Coun. Foreign Rels., Am. Econ. Assn. Roman Catholic. Avocations: gardening, music. Home: 3075 Ordway St NW Washington DC 20008-3255 Office: Export-Import Bank of U.S. 811 Vermont Ave NW Washington DC 20571-0001

RODRIGUEZ, ROBERT, filmmaker; b. 1969; s. Cecilio and Rebecca Rodriguez; m. Elizabeth Avellan. Student, U. Tex. Prodr. (films) El Mariachi, 1993, Desperado, 1995, Four Rooms, 1995, From Dusk Till Dawn, 1995. Office: care Internat Creative Mgmt 8942 Wilshire Blvd Beverly Hills CA 90211

RODRIGUEZ, TERESA IDA, elementary education educator, educational consultant; b. Levittown, N.Y., Oct. 10, 1951; d. George Arthur and Frieda (Diaz) R. BA in Secondary Edn., Hofstra U., 1973, MA in Bilingual Edn., 1978; profl. diploma in multicultural leadership, L.I. U., 1990. Cert. permanent nursery, kindergarten, elem. Spanish, bilingual K-6, ESL tchr., sch. dist. adminstr., sch. adminstr., supr., N.Y. Bilingual elem. tchr. Long Beach (N.Y.) Pub. Schs., 1973-76, Hempstead (N.Y.) Pub. Schs., 1976-79; account exec. Adelante Advt., N.Y.C., 1979-81; adminstrv. asst. Assocs. and Nadel, N.Y.C., 1981-84; freelance outside prop and set decorator for TV commls. N.Y.C., 1984-88; tchr. ESL Central Islip (N.Y.) Pub. Schs., 1988-92; ednl. cons. Houghton Mifflin Co., 1992-95; tchr. 5th grade Central Islip (N.Y.) Pub. Schs., Princeton, N.J., 1995—; cons. on tchr. tng. Staff Devel. Ctr. Islips, Central Islip, 1989—; cons. on staff devel. Nassau Bd. Coop. Ednl. Svcs., Westbury, N.Y., 1990—, edn. instrn. specialist IBM, 1991; presenter confs., workshops, seminars; cons. and grant writer, N.Y.C. and suburbs. Grantee N.Y. State Div. Bilingual Edn., 1988-90, Staff Devel. Ctr. Islips, 1988, Suffolk Bd. Coop. Ednl. Svcs., 1989; WLIW Pub. TV mini grantee; Pres.'s fellow L.I.U., 1989-90. Mem. ASCD, Nat. Assn. Bilingual Educators, State Assn. Bilingual Educators, Internat. Reading Assn. (presenter nat. conf. 1992, 93), N.Y. State ASCD, Suffolk Reading Coun., Smithtown Township Arts Coun. Avocations: tennis, photography, bicycling, swimming. Home: 30 Wheelwright Ln Levittown NY 11756-5233 Office: 545 Clayton St Central Islip NY 11722-3021

RODRIGUEZ, VINCENT ANGEL, lawyer; b. Cayey, P.R., 1921; s. Vicente and Maria (Antongiorgi) R. B.S., Harvard U., 1941; LL.B., Yale U., 1944. Bar: N.Y. 1947. Assoc. Sullivan & Cromwell, N.Y.C., 1944-56, ptnr., 1956—; dir. Deltec Internat. Ltd., Eng., Am. Investors, Inc., Bermuda. Mem. Council Fgn. Relations, ABA, Assn. Bar City N.Y., Am. Soc. Internat. Law. Club: River (N.Y.C.). Home: 4521 Fisher Island Dr Fisher Island FL 33109-0156 Office: Sullivan & Cromwell 125 Broad St New York NY 10004-2400

RODRIGUEZ, WILLIAM JULIO, physician; b. Ponce, P.R., June 18, 1941. BS, MD, Georgetown U., Washington, 1967; PhD, Georgetown U., 1975. Intern and resident Univ. Hosp., San Juan, P.R., 1967-72; fellow Children's Hosp., Washington, 1972-75; attending in infectious disease Children's Hosp. Nat. Med. Ctr., Washington, 1975—; assoc. chief infectious disease and microbiology rsch. Children's Hosp. Med. Ctr., 1979-80, chief infectious disease and microbiology, 1980-83, chmn. infectious disease dept., 1983—; cons. staff Hosp. for Sick Children, Washington, 1985—; cons. staff Shady Grove Adventist Hosp., Rockville, Md., 1988—, Holy Cross Hosp., Silver Spring, Md., 1988—, Columbia Hosp. for Women, 1990—. contbr. articles to profl. jours. MARC fellow, XIII, 1973-76. Fellow Infectious Disease Soc.; mem. AAAS, Am. Fedn. Clin. Rsch., Am. Soc. Microbiology, Assn. of Puerto Ricans in Sci. & Engring. Office: Childrens Nat Med Ctr 111 Michigan Ave NW Washington DC 20010-2916

RODRÍGUEZ-ARIAS, JORGE HERMINIO, retired agricultural engineering educator; b. Ponce, P.R., Apr. 24, 1915; s. Herminio Rodriguez Colón and Rosa Maria Arias Ríos; m. Carmen Teresa Quiñones Sepúlveda, May 9, 1948; children: Jorge H., Jaime Osvaldo, Nelson Rafael. BS in Agriculture, U. P.R., Mayaguez, 1936; BS in Agrl. Engring., Tex. A&M U., 1945; MS in Agrl. Engring., Kans. State U., 1947; PhD in Agrl. Engring., Mich. State U., 1956; D (hon.), U. P.R., Mayaguez, 1986. Instr. vocat. agriculture P.R. Reconstruction Adminstrn., Aibonito, 1936-37; instr. horticulture U. P.R., Mayaguez, 1937-43, from asst. to assoc. to prof. agrl. engring., 1947-77, dir. agrl. engring. dept., 1948-77; panelist UN Program for Devel., Lima, Peru, 1959. With USN, 1945-46. Fellow Am. Soc. Agrl. Engrs. (life), Instn. of Agrl. Engrs.; mem. Am. Soc. for Engring. Edn. (life), Inst. of Food Technologists (profl.). Home and Office: U PR PO Box 5158 College Station Faculty Residences # 3-B Mayaguez PR 00681

RODRIGUEZ-CAMILLONI, HUMBERTO LEONARDO, architect, historian, educator; b. Lima, Peru, May 30, 1945; came to U.S., 1963; s. Alfonso and Elda (Camilloni) R.; m. Mary Ann Alexanderson, July 1, 1972; children: Elizabeth Marie, William Howard. BA magna cum laude, Yale U., 1967, MArch, 1971, MPhil, 1973, PhD, 1981. Rsch. asst. Sch. Architecture Yale U., 1964-70, teaching fellow dept. history art, 1971-72, 74-75; chmn. research dept. Centro de Investigacion y Restauracion de Bienes Monumentales Instituto Nacional de Cultura, Lima, 1973; restoration architect OAS, Washington, 1976—; asst. prof. Sch. Architecture Tulane U., New Orleans, 1975-82; assoc. prof., dir. Henry H. Wiss Ctr. Theory and History of Art and Architecture, Coll. Architecture and Urban Studies Va. Poly. Inst. and State U., Blacksburg, 1983—, dir. Ctr. for Preservation and Rehab. Tech., Coll. Architecture, 1986—; vis. prof. U. Ill., Chgo., 1982-83; reviewer, cons. Choice, 1975—; mem. interim bd. dirs. Ctr. Planning Handbook Latin-Am. Art, 1978-87; cons., adviser Internat. Exhbn. and Symposium Latin-Am. Baroque Art and Architecture, 1980; mem. adv. bd. Mountain Lake Symposium on Art and Architecture Criticism, 1985—, Internat. Symposium Luis Barragan, 1990; coord., advisor exhbn. Tradition and Innovation: Painting, Architecture and Music in Brazil, Mex. and Venezuela between 1950-80, 1991, Internat. Art History Colloquium, 1993, 48th Internat. Congress of Americanists, 1994, Congress Internat. Union Architects, 1996; coord., adv. exhbn. Frank Lloyd Wright: An Architect in America, 1995. Author: (with Walter D. Harris) The Growth of Latin American Cities, 1971; (with Charles Seymour, Jr.) Italian Primitives, The Case History of a Collection and its Conservation, 1972, Religious Architecture in Lima of the Seventeenth and Eighteenth Centuries: The Monastic Complex of San Francisco el Grande, 1984; contbg. editor Handbook of Latin American Studies, 1987—, The Retablo Facade as Transparency: A Study of the Frontispiece of San Francisco, Lima, 1991, Tradición e Innovación en la Arquitectura del Virreinato del Perú: Constantino de Vasconcelos y la Invención de la Arquitectura de Quincha en Lima Durante el Siglo XVII, 1994; contbg. editor: The Dictionary of Art, 1991-96. Named Ellen Battell Eldridge fellow, 1970-72, Robert C. Bates Jr. fellow Jonathan Edwards Coll., Yale U., 1970-71, Social Sci. Rsch. Coun. fellow, 1972-74, Yale Concilium Internat. Studies fellow, 1972-73, Giles Whiting fellow, 1974-75, NEH fellow Columbia U., 1983, Hobart and William Smith Colls. fellow, 1987, U. Ill. fellow, 1990, Edilia De Montequin fellow, 1991, NEH fellow U. N.Mex., 1992. Mem. Soc. Archtl. Historians (bd. dir. 1977-80, past. pres., past sec. South Gulf chpt.) SE sect. Soc. Archtl. Historians, Coll. Art Assn. Am., SE Coll. Art Conf., Latin Am. Studies Assn., Assn. Latin Am. Art, Assn. Preservation Va. Antiquities, New River Valley Preservation League (bd. dir. 1987—), Nat. Trust Historic Preservation, Save our Cemeteries (past dir.), Preservation Resource Ctr. (past bd. dir.), Assn. for Preservation Tech., Blacksburg Regional Art Assn. (bd. dir), Inter-Am. Inst. Advanced Studies in Cultural History (bd. dirs. 1996—), Tau Sigma Delta. Roman Catholic. Office: Va Poly Inst and State U Coll Architecture & Urban Studies Blacksburg VA 24061-0205 *As an educator across the years, I have come to realize that the true art of teaching consists of reaching both the human mind and the human heart.*

RODRIGUEZ-ERDMANN, FRANZ, physician; b. Mexico City, Feb. 2, 1935; came to U.S., 1961; m. Irma Villarreal; 1 child, Foro. M.B., U. Heidelberg, Germany, 1958, M.D., 1960. Diplomate: Am. Bd. Internal Medicine. Intern Univ. Hosps., Heidelberg, 1958-61, Mercy Hosp., Detroit, 1962-63; research assoc. Wayne State U. Med. Sch., Detroit, 1961-62; jr. asst. resident in medicine Tufts U. New Eng. Med. Center, Boston, 1964-65; research fellow hematology Tufts U. New Eng. Med. Center, 1964, clin. fellow cardiology, 1965-66; resident in medicine Boston City Hosp., 1966-67; sr. resident in medicine Georgetown U., Washington, 1967-68; fellow in hematology Peter Bent Brigham Hosp., Boston, 1968-69; assoc. in medicine Peter Bent Brigham Hosp., 1969-71; practice medicine specializing in internal medicine and hematology; attending physician Boston City Hosp.; instr., then asst. prof. Harvard U. Med. Sch., 1969-71; prof. medicine U. Ill. Med. Sch., 1971—; chief hematology sect. and hemostasis unit Edgewater Hosp., Chgo., 1979-82. Contbr. numerous articles to profl. jours. Fellow A.C.P.; mem. Internat. Soc. Hematology, Am. Fedn. Clin. Research, Am. Soc. Hematology, Internat. Soc. Hemostasis and Thrombosis, Council on Thrombosis, World Fedn. Hemophilia, Brazilian Coll. Hematology, Mex. Nat. Acad. Medicine, Bolivian Soc. Internal Medicine, Colombian Soc. Hematology, Alpha Omega Alpha. Home: 3255 Brookdale Rd Northbrook IL 60062-7501 Address: 5015 N Paulina St Chicago IL 60640-2717

RODRIGUEZ-SAINS, RENE S., physician, surgeon, educator; b. Santiago, Cuba, July 25, 1952; came to U.S., 1960, naturalized, 1968; s. Emilio Rene Rodriguez and Caridad Sains; m. Juanita Laszlo, Aug. 31, 1974; children: Daniel Rene, Diana. BA cum laude, CUNY, 1973; MD, NYU, 1977. Diplomate Nat. Bd. Med. Examiners, Am. Bd. Ophthalmology. Dermatology rsch. fellow NYU Med. Ctr., N.Y.C., 1973-77, intern dept. medicine, 1977-78; resident in ophthalmology Manhattan Eye, Ear and Throat Hosp., 1978-81, chief resident in ophthalmology, 1980-81, asst. attending surgeon, 1981-85, assoc. attending surgeon Ophthalmic Plastic & Reconstructive Surgery, Ocular Tumor & Orbital Clinic, 1985-89, surgeon dir. Ophthalmic Plastic & Reconstructive Surgery Clinic, 1989-93, surgeon dir., chief Ocular Tumor & Orbital Clinic, 1989-93; attending surgeon, chief Manhattan Eye, Ear And Throat Hosp., N.Y.C., 1993—, attending surgeon ophthalmic plastic and reconstructive surgery clinic, 1993—, dir. internat. fellowship program, 1991—. Heed Ophthalmic Found. fellow Manhattan Eye, Ear and Throat Hosp.-N.Y. Hosp., Cornell U. Med. Ctr., 1981-82, resident instr. dept. ophthalmology, 1983-85; adj. asst. prof. dermatology NYU, 1981-88; clin. asst. prof. ophthalmology, Mt. Sinai Med. Ctr.; attending surgeon Dept. Ophthalmology, Plastic and Reconstructive Surgery divsn., Bronx VA Hosp., 1985-88; clin. asst. prof. Dept. Ophthalmology, NYU Med. Ctr., 1988—. Mem. med. adv. bd. Skin Cancer Found., 1980—; mem. NYU Malignant Melanoma Clin. Coop. Group, 1981—; bd. dirs. Orbital Disease Found., 1994—; mem. Barraquer Inst. Barcelona, Spain, N.Y. Soc for Clin. Ophthalmology. Contbg. editor Jour. Dermatologic Surgery ad Oncology, 1980-90; co-author: Malignant Melanoma, 1979; contbr. articles to med. jours. Fellow Am. Coll. Surgeons, Am. Acad. Facial Plastic and Reconstructive Surgery, Am. Soc. Ophthalmic Plastic and Reconstructive Surgery, N.Y. Acad. Medicine; mem. AMA, N.Y. State Ophthalmol. Soc., Am. Assn. Ophthalmology, Assn. Rsch. in Vision and Ophthalmology, Manhattan Ophthalmologic Soc., N.Y. County Med. Soc., Med. Soc. State N.Y., Am. Acad. Ophthalmology. Office: 178 E 71st St New York NY 10021-5119

RODRIK, DANI, economics and international affairs educator; b. Istanbul, Turkey, Aug. 14, 1957. AB in Govt. and Econs. summa cum laude, Harvard U., 1979; MPA with distinction, Princeton U., 1981, PhD in Econs., 1985. Asst. econ. affairs officer UN Conf. on Trade and Devel., Geneva, 1980, 81-82; asst. prof. pub. policy Kennedy Sch. Govt. Harvard U., Cambridge, Mass., 1985-89, assoc. prof. pub. policy, 1989-92; prof. econs. and internat. affairs Columbia U., N.Y.C., 1992-96; Rafiq Hariri prof. internat. polit. econs. Kennedy Sch. Govt., Harvard U., 1996—; mem. adv. bd. METU Studies in Devel., New Perspectives on Turkey; Wei Lun vis. prof. Chinese U. of Hong Kong, 1992-93; vis. scholar fiscal affairs dept. Internat. Monetary Fund, 1990, Internat. Fin. div. Bd. Govs. Fed. Reserve System, 1987; advisor Ministry of Fgn. Econ. Rels., Govt. of Poland, 1990; rsch. assoc. Nat. Bur. Econ. Rsch.; rsch. fellow Ctr. Econ. Policy Rsch.; cons. in field. Author: Has Globalization Gone Too Far?, 1997; co-author: Eastern Europe and the Soviet Union in the World Economy, 1991, External Debt, Adjustment and Burden Sharing: A Unified Framework, 1992; co-editor: The Political Economy of Turkey: Debt, Adjustment and Sustainability, 1990, The Economics of Middle-East Peace, 1993; assoc. editor Jour. Internat. Econs., Jour. Devel. Econs., Econs. & Politics; contbr. articles to profl. publs., chpts. to books. Sr. rsch. fellow Inst. for Policy Reform, vis. fellow Inst. for Internat. Econs., NBER Olin fellow, 1990-91, Robert S. McNamara fellow, 1987-88, Hoover Instn. Nat. fellow, 1991-92, Harbison fellow, 1980-81; recipient Raymond Vernon prize Assn. for Pub. Policy Analysis and Mgmt., 1988. Office: Harvard U Kennedy Sch Govt 79 Jfk St Cambridge MA 02138-5801

RODWELL, JOHN DENNIS, biochemist; b. Boston, Oct. 9, 1946; s. William Joseph and Lillian Catherine (Cunningham) R.; m. Ellen M. McCaffrey, Dec. 18, 1971; children: Elizabeth Ann, Sarah Catherine. BA in Chemistry, U. Mass., 1968; MS in Organic Chemistry, Lowell Technol. Inst., 1971; PhD in Biochemistry, UCLA, 1976. Postdoctoral fellow Sch. Medicine U. Pa., Phila., 1976-80; rsch. asst., prof. U. Pa. Sch. Medicine, 1980-81; with Cytogen Corp., Princeton, N.J., 1981—; v.p. discovery rsch. Cytogen Corp., 1987-88, v.p. R & D, 1989-96, sr. v.p., chief sci. officer, 1996—; adj. asst. prof., then adj. assoc. prof. Sch. Medicine, U. Pa., 1981—; series editor, Marcel Dekker, Inc., N.Y.C., 1988—; bd. dirs., treas. Biotech. Consortium, 1994—; bd. dirs., chief sci. officer AxCell Bioscis. Corp., 1996—. Patentee, antibody conjugates for compound delivery, antibody metal ion complexes; editor: Antibody Mediated Delivery Systems, 1988; co-editor: Covalently Modified Antigens and Antibodies in Diagnosis and Therapy, 1989. Recipient Nat. Rsch. Svc. award NIH, 1978-80, Thomas Alva Edison Patent award, 1993. Mem. AAAS, Am. Assn. Immunologists, Am. Chem. Soc. (assoc. editor 1989-93), N.Y. Acad. Scis., Soc. Nuc. Medicine, Indsl. Rsch. Inst. Democrat. Avocations: gardening, photography. Home: 1340 Eagle Rd New Hope PA 18938-9222 Office: Cytogen Corp 600 College Rd E Princeton NJ 08540-6636

RODWELL-BELL, REGINA, museum director; b. Casablanca, Morocco, Aug. 19, 1954; came to U.S., 1955; d. Richard Francis and Roxie Jean (Fletcher) Rodwell; m. Jack D. Bell, Apr. 4, 1981; children: Spencer Bell, Noel R. Bell. BS in Orgnl. Mgmt., Nyack Coll., 1993; cert. in fund raising, Marymount Coll., 1994. Lic. real estate broker, N.Y. Profl. dancer, actress N.Y.C., 1977-81; dance tchr., choreographer Coll. Ozarks, Point Lookout, Mo., 1981-82; real estate broker Baer & McIntosh Real Estate, Nyack, N.Y., 1986-93; founder, pres. Hudson Valley Children's Mus., Nyack, N.Y., 1993-95, exec. dir., 1995—. Author, editor Big Ideas, 1995. Bd. dirs. Rockland Coun. Young Children, 1994—; bd. trustees Hudson Valley Childen's Mus., 1993-95. Recipient Appreciation cert. Town Orangetown, 1996, Group Study Exch. award Rotary Internat., 1997. Mem. Assn. Youth Mus. (assoc.), New Eng. Mus. Assn. (assoc.). Democrat. Presbyterian. Avocations: hiking, travel, theater, museums, historical sites. Office: Hudson Valley Childrens Mus Nyack Seaport 21 Burd St Nyack NY 10960

RODZIANKO, PAUL, energy and environmental company executive; b. Washington, Oct. 22, 1945; s. Paul and Aimee Rodzianko; m. Chauncie McKeever, May 1987; children: Marina, Alexander. BA, Princeton U., 1967; MA, Inst. Critical Langs., 1967. With GE Co., 1967-76; pres. U.S. Geothermal Corp., N.Y.C., 1976-77, Geothermal Energy Corp., N.Y.C., 1977-83, Geothermal Food Processors, Inc., Fernley, Nev., 1979-82; exec. v.p. Grace Geothermal Corp., 1981-83, bd. dirs., 1981-83; pres. Bay Capital Corp., Oyster Bay, N.Y., 1983-85, Data Port Co., 1985-86; v.p. spl. projects Kvaerner Energy Devel., Inc., Dover, N.J., 1992-95; pres., CEO Tuxedo Venture Mgmt. Group Inc., 1995—; bd. dirs. McGill Environ. Sys., Inc., Fresh Creek Technologies, Inc.; chmn. bd. dirs. Mt. Hope Hydro, Inc., 1986-92, Halecon, Inc., 1986-92, Kvaerner Venture Inc., 1992-95; v.p. Little Horn Energy Who., 1993; v.p., dir. energy, mining and environ. ops. Access Industries, 1996—; dir. Bogatyr Coal Co., Ekibastuz, Rep. of Kazakstan, 1996—. Vice chmn. Russian Orthodox Theol. Fund, 1978—; chmn., CEO Mt. Hope Waterpower Project, 1989-92; dir. energy, mining and environ. ops. Access Industries, 1996—; mem. Town Coun., Tuxedo, N.Y., 1992—, co-chmn. revitatlization com., mem. Rockaway Twp. Econ. Devel. Com., 1995. Fellow Royal Geog. Soc., Explorers Club, New Eng. Soc.; mem. Geothermal Resources Coun. (bd. dirs., chmn. audit com. 1980-82), Nat. Inst. Social Scis., Rockaway Area C. of C. (bd. dirs. 1988-92), Camp Fire Club, Tuxedo Club, Rotary (hon., Paul Harris fellow 1988-92), Lions (mem.-at-large). Office: 627 Mount Hope Ave Wharton NJ 07885-2811

ROE, BENSON BERTHEAU, surgeon, educator; b. L.A., July 7, 1918; s. Hall and Helene Louise (Bertheau) R.; m. Jane Faulkner St. John, Jan. 20, 1945; children: David B., Virginia St. John. AB, U. Calif., Berkeley, 1939; MD cum laude, Harvard U., 1943. Diplomate Am. Bd. Surgery, Am. Bd. Thoracic Surgery (dir. 1971-83, chmn. bd. 1981-83, chmn. exam. com. 1978, chmn. long-range planning com. 1980, chmn. program com. 1977). Intern Mass. Gen. Hosp., Boston, 1943-44, resident, 1946-50; nat. rsch. fellow dept. physiology Med. Sch., Harvard U., Boston, Mass., 1947, instr. surgery, 1950; Moseley Traveling fellow Harvard. U. at U. Edinburgh, Scotland, 1951; asst. clin. prof. surgery U. Calif., San Francisco, 1951-58, chief cardiothoracic surgery, 1958-76, prof. surgery, 1966-89, emeritus prof., 1989—; pvt. practice medicine specializing in cardiothoracic surgery San Francisco, 1952-85; cons. thoracic surgery VA Hosp., San Francisco Gen. Hosp., Letterman Army Hosp., St. Lukes Hosp., Blue Shield of Calif., Baxter Labs., Ethicon, Inc.; bd. dirs. Control Laser Corp.; vis. prof. U. Utah, U. Ky., U. Gdansk, Poland, Nat. Heart Hosp., London, U. Ibadan, Nigeria, Sanger Clinic, Charlotte, Rush-Presbyn. Hosp., Chgo., Penrose Hosp., Colorado Springs. Mem. editl. bd. Annals of Thoracic Surgery, 1969-82, Pharos; editor 2 med. texts; author 21 textbook chpts.; contbr. 174 articles to profl. jours. Bd. dirs. United Bay Area Crusade, 1958-70, mem. exec. com., 1964-65; bd. dirs. chmn. exec. com. San Francisco chpt. Am. Cancer Soc., 1955-57; bd. dirs. San Francisco Heart Assn., 1964-72, pres., 1964-65, chmn. rsch. com., 1966-71; mem. various coms. Am. Heart Assn., 1967-70; pres. Miranda Lux Found., 1982-94; trustee Avery Fuller Found.; bd. dirs. Internat. Bioethics Inst., Point Reyes Bird Observatory. Served with Med. Svc. Corps, USNR, 1944-46. Fellow Am. Coll. Cardiology, ACS (chmn. adv. coun. thoracic surgery, program chmn. thoracic surgery, cardiovascular com.), Polish Surg. Assn. (hon.); mem. Am. Assn. Thoracic Surgery (chmn. membership com. 1974-75), AMA (residency rev. com. for thoracic surgery), Am. Surg. Assn., Pacific Coast Surg. Assn., Calif. Acad. Medicine (pres. 1974), Calif. Med. Assn., Soc. Univ. Surgeons, Soc. Throacic Surgerons (pres. 1972, chmn. standards and ethics com.), Soc. Vascular Surgery (v.p.). Clubs: Cruising of Am, Pacific Union, St. Francis Yacht, Calif. Tennis. Office: U Calif Div Cardiothoracic Surgery U Calif M593 San Francisco CA 94143-0118

ROE, BYRON PAUL, physics educator; b. St. Louis, Apr. 4, 1934; s. Sam S. and Gertrude Harriet (Claris) R.; m. Alice Susan Krauss, Aug. 27, 1961; children: Kenneth David, Diana Carol. B.A., Washington U., St. Louis, 1954; Ph.D., Cornell U., 1959. Instr: physics U. Mich., Ann Arbor, 1959-61, asst. prof., 1961-64, assoc. prof., 1964-69, prof., 1969—; guest physicist SSC Lab., 1991. Author: Probability and Statistics in Experimental Physics, 1992, Particle Physics at the New Millennium, 1996 (Libr. Sci. Book Club selection). CERN vis. scientist Geneva, 1967, 89; Brit. Sci. Rsch. Coun. fellow, Oxford, 1979; recipient inventor's prize CDC Worldtech, Edina, Minn., 1982, 83. Fellow Am. Phys. Soc. Home: 3610 Charter Pl Ann Arbor MI 48105-2825 Office: U Mich Physics Dept 500 E University Ave Ann Arbor MI 48109-1120

ROE, CLIFFORD ASHLEY, JR., lawyer; b. Elyria, Ohio, Nov. 5, 1942; s. Clifford A. and Betty (Humphrey) R.; m. Mary Jo Loparo, Aug. 29, 1964; children: Mary, Kip, Michael, Cathleen, Danny, Beth. BS in English, Xavier U., Cin., 1964; JD, Notre Dame (Ind.) U., 1967. Bar: Ohio 1967, U.S. Dist. Ct. (so. dist.) Ohio 1970, U.S. Ct. Appeals (6th cir.) 1968. Assoc. Dinsmore & Shohl, Cin., 1967-74, ptnr., 1974—. Author: The Ohio Corporation - Legal Aspects of Organization and Operation, 1989. Mem. Ohio Bar Assn., Cin. Bar Assn. (chmn. various coms.), Queen City Club, Western Hills Country Club. Republican. Roman Catholic. Avocations: tennis, golf, sailing, jogging. Home: 2089 Beech Grove Dr Cincinnati OH 45233-4915 Office: Dinsmore & Shohl 1900 Chemed Ct 255 E 5th St Cincinnati OH 45202-4700

ROE, MARK J., law educator; b. N.Y.C., Aug. 8, 1951; m. Helen Hsu, Aug. 12, 1974; children: Andrea Hsu, Jessica Hsu. BA, Columbia U., 1972; JD, Harvard U., 1975. Bar: N.Y. 1976. Atty. Fed. Res. Bank, N.Y.C., 1975-77; assoc. Cahill Gordon & Reindel, N.Y.C., 1977-80; prof. Rutgers U. Law Sch., Newark, 1980-86, prof. U. Pa. Law Sch., 1986-88; prof. Sch. Law Columbia U., N.Y.C., 1988—. Author: Strong Managers, Weak Owners: The Political Roots of American Corporate Finance, 1994. Office: Columbia U Sch Law 435 W 116th St New York NY 10027-7201

ROE, RICHARD C., industry consultant, former home furnishings manufacturing executive; b. Des Moines, Jan. 4, 1930; s. Lloyd E. and Mary E. (Nuzum) R.; m. Sally McGlothlen, Dec. 27, 1952; children: Stephen James, Julie Ann. B.S. in Gen. Engring, Iowa State U., 1952. Registered profl. engr., Iowa, Ind., Ill. Indsl. engr. Maytag Co., Newton, Iowa, 1952-56; gen. mgr. mfg. Schnadig Corp., Chgo., 1956-66; v.p. mfg. Sealy Inc., Chgo., 1966-76, group v.p., 1976-86; pres. Sealy Inc., 1987-89; cons. to industry, 1989—; bd. dirs. Schnadig Corp., Chgo., Serta, Inc., Chgo. Former chmn. adv. com. dept. mgmt. Iowa State U., mem. adv. council coll. bus. Recipient profl. achievement citation in engring. Iowa State U., 1989. Mem. NSPE, Am. Inst. Indsl. Engrs., Internat. Sleep Products Assn. (Exceptional Svc. award 1989). Republican. Clubs: Merchants and Mfrs. (Chgo.); Elks. Patentee in field. Home: 2435 Hamilton Dr Ames IA 50014-8203 Office: 225 S Rohlwing Rd Apt 101 Palatine IL 60067-6468

ROE, ROGER ROLLAND, lawyer; b. Mpls., Dec. 31, 1947; s. Roger Rolland Roe; m. Paula Speltz, 1974; children: Elena, Madeline. BA, Grinnell Coll., 1970; JD, U. Minn., 1973. Bar: Minn. 1973, U.S. Dist. Ct. Minn. 1974, U.S. Ct. Appeals (8th cir.) 1977, U.S. Supreme Ct. 1978, Wis. 1988, U.S. Dist. Ct. Nebr. 1995, U.S. Dist. Ct. (ea. and we. dists.) Wis. Law clk. to Hon. Judge Amdahl Hennepin County Dist. Ct., Mpls., 1973-74; from assoc. to ptnr. Rider, Bennett, Egan & Arundel, Mpls., 1974-91; mng. ptnr. Yaeger, Jungbauer, Barczak & Roe, Ltd., Mpls., 1992—; mem. nat. panel arbitrators Am. Arbitration Assn.; judge trial practice class and moot ct. competitions law sch. U. Minn.; guest lectr. Minn. Continuing Legal Edn. courses. Fellow Internat. Soc. Barristers; mem. ATLA (guest lectr.), Am. Bd. Trial Advs. (diplomat, Mass. chpt. pres. 1996-97), Minn. Trial Lawyers Assn., Million Dollar Round Table. Avocations: golfing, downhill skiing. Office: Yaeger Jungbauer Barczak & Roe Ltd 701 4th Ave S Ste 1400 Minneapolis MN 55415-1816

ROE, THOMAS ANDERSON, building supply company executive; b. Greenville, S.C., May 29, 1927; s. Thomas Anderson and Leila (Cunningham) R.; m. Shirley Marie Waddell, Aug. 2, 1980; children: Elizabeth Overton Roe Mason, Thomas Anderson, Philip Stradley, John Verner; 1 stepchild, Amy Elizabeth Waddell Willcox. BS, Furman U., 1948, LLD, 1980; diploma in bus. mgmt., LaSalle Extension U., 1956. Cancer rsch. asst. Furman U., 1947-48; with Builder Marts of Am., Inc., Greenville, S.C., 1948-87, pres., 1961-69, chmn., 1969-87, CEO, 1969-78; chmn. 1st Piedmont Corp., 1967-74, 1st Piedmont Bank & Trust Co., 1967-74; bd. dirs. Swiss Tex.; bd. govs. Atlas Econ. Rsch. Found., Fairfax. Mem. Greenville County Redevel. Authority, 1971-75; vice chmn. S.C. Republican Com., 1963-64, fin. chmn. 1986—; mem. Nat. Rep. Fin. Com., 1963-64; hon. asst. sgt.-at-arms Rep. Nat. Conv., Chgo., 1960; past bd. dirs. Nat. Found. Ileitis and Colitis, Greenville United Cerebral Palsy, Greenville chpt. ARC; past chmn. adv. council Furman U.; pres. S.C. Policy Council, Columbia, 1986-90, now founding chmn., bd. dirs.; bd. govs. Council for Nat. Policy, 1984-94; past trustee Greenville Symphony, 1985-93, Inst. Rsch. on Econs. of Taxation, 1983-90; trustee Christ Ch. Episc. Sch., 1970-72, Coker Coll., 1975-81, Intercollegiate Studies Inst., 1983—, Heritage Found., 1985—, Free Congress Rsch. and Edn. Found., Washington, 1987-96; mem. bd. govs. Found. Francisco Marroquin, Guatemala, Internat. Policy Forum, Washington, 1984-90; bd. dirs., mem. exec. com. Peace Ctr. for Performing Arts, Greenville; founding chmn., bd. dirs. State Policy Network, Ft. Wayne, Ind.; pres. Charity Ball Bd., Rose Ball, Greenville, S.C., 1996. Named builder of yr. Greenville Home Builders Assn., 1962. Mem. Nat. Assn. Home Builders (internat. housing com.), Greenville Home Builders Assn. (v.p. 1962-63), Nat. Lumber Bldg. Material Dealers Assn., Carolina Bldg. Material Dealers Assn. (pres. 1965-66), Greenville Bldg. Materials Assn. (pres.), Mont. Pelerin Soc., Greenville C. of C. (dir. 1967-70, pres. 1970), Players Club (pres. 1951), Sertoma Club (pres. local club 1960-61, disting. svc. award 1959, superior leaderhsip award 1961), World Trade Ctr. Club, Poinsett Club. Home and Office: 712 Crescent Ave Greenville SC 29601-4350

ROE, THOMAS COOMBE, former utility company executive; b. Dover, Del., Sept. 22, 1914; s. John Moore and Elizabeth Lindale (Cooper) R.; m. Emma Lillian Scotton, Oct. 16, 1937; children: Thomas C., Margaret Ruth (dec.). B.S. in Elec. Engring, U. Del., 1935; DHL (hon.), Wesley Coll., 1987. With Eastern Shore Public Service, 1936-43; with Delmarva Power & Light Co., 1943—; pres. subs. Delmarva Power & Light Co., 1971-76, chmn. bd., 1976-79, dir., 1971-80, ret., 1980. Hon. trustee Peninsula Regional Med. Ctr., Salisbury, Md.; trustee Wesley Coll., Dover, Del.; former chmn. Wesley Coll.; former trustee Wesley Theol. Sem., Washington. Served with AUS, 1941-45. Republican. Methodist. Club: Rotary (past pres.).

ROE, THOMAS LEROY WILLIS, pediatrician; b. Bend, Oreg., Sept. 1, 1936. MD, U. Oregon Health Scis. U., Portland, 1961. Diplomate Am. Bd. Pediatrics. Intern U. Calif., San Francisco, 1961-62, resident, 1962-64; physician Sacred Heart Med. Ctr., Eugene, Oreg.; pvt. practice Peace Health Med. Group, Eugene, 1985—; clin prof. pediatrics U. Oregon, Eugene, 1985—. Fellow Am. Acad. Pediatricians; mem. AMA, North Pacific Pediatrics Soc. Office: Eugene Clin 1162 Willamette St Eugene OR 97401-3568

ROE, WANDA JERALDEAN, artist, retired educator, lecturer; b. Batesville, Ark., Nov. 9, 1920; d. William Melvin and Luna Eva (Cockrum) Finley; m. Roy A. Roe, Dec. 25, 1940; children: Ramona Jeraldean, Roy A. II. BS in Edn., U. Cen. Ark., Conway, 1954; MS in Edn., Ark. State U., 1965; diploma Exec. Devel. Ctr., U. Ill., 1984; postgrad., U. Ark., 1981. Cert. educator, Ark.; lic. profl. counselor, Ark. Counselor Fountain Lake H.S., Hot Springs, Ark., 1965-68; instr. art and home econs. Foreman (Ark.) H.S., 1968-72; profl. counselor Pea Ridge (Ark.) H.S., 1972-83; instr. art No. Ark. C.C., Rogers, 1980-90; profl. artist Rogers (Ark.) Art Guild Gallery, 1983—, Big Spring Gallery, Neosho, Mo., 1989—, Ark. Artists Registry, Little Rock, 1983—; instr. art Wishing Springs Gallery, Bella Vista, Ark.; dir. workshops State Dept. Edn., Little Rock, 1965-83; supr. for practice tchrs. and counselor interns. Ark. Colls. and Univs., 1968-83; art instr. War Eagle Seminar, 1996; presenter in field. Exhibited in one-person show at Walton Art Ctr., 1996; contbr. poetry to mags.; mem. editorial adv. bd. Cmty. Pubs. Inc., 1994-97. Mem. State Adv. Coun. for Gifted/Talented Edn., Little Rock, 1989-96; mem. Ark. Leadership Acad., 1996, G/T Coalition, 1996-97; juror for art contests; guide for County Constn. Day, Benton County, 1987; pres. United Meth. Women, Pea Ridge, 1973-75; cmty. vol.; sec. Benton County Dem. Ctrl. Com., 1996—; White House vol., 1996. Travel Study grantee Delta Kappa Gamma, 1987; named Art Educator of Yr., N.W. Art Educators Assn., 1983; recipient numerous art awards. Mem. AAUW (state exec. bd., state pres. 1985-87), Nat. Art Educators Assn., Ark. Art Educators Assn., Spiva Art Ctr., Ozark Pastel Soc. (Signature mem., pres. 1990-93), Rogers Art Guild (pres. 1991-92), Dem. Women's Club (v.p. 1996—), Delta Kappa Gamma (state exec. bd., state pres. 1983-85). Democrat. Methodist. Avocations: music, lecturing, directing workshops.

ROE, WILLIAM THOMAS, behaviorial engineer, educator, researcher; b. N.Y.C., July 7, 1944; s. William T. and Harriet E. (Higgins) R.; m. Susan C. Kane, Aug. 30, 1972. BA in Engining./Indsl. Psychology, Calif. State U.-Northridge, 1971, MA in Human Factors and Applied Exptl. Psychology, 1978; postgrad., Walden U.; Rsch. asst. XYZYX Info. Corp., Canoga Park, Calif., 1973-74; mem. psychol. staff Manned Systems Scis. Inc., Northridge, 1974-75; rsch. psychologist Inst. Safety and Systems Mgmt., U. So. Calif., L.A., 1975-76; mgr., acct. exec. systems and data processing Mgmt. Recruiters So. Calif., Encino, 1976-79; resource evaluation analyst Samaritan Health Svc., Phoenix, 1979; sr. methods analyst Valley Nat. Bank, Phoenix, 1979-81; indsl. engr. City of Scottsdale, Ariz., 1981-84; prof. psychology Phoenix Coll., 1984—; editorial reviewer numerous major text publs. Author: Ergonomic Models of Human Performance: Source Materials for the Analyst, 1975, Behavioral Engineering:Paradigm for Human Transformation, 1988, Mind-Body Psychology: Source Materialsfor Medical Education, 1995; contbr. articles to profl. jours. With USN, 1961-67, Vietnam. Recipient Recognition certs. San Fernando Valley chpt. Data Data Processing Mgmt. Assn., 1978, Phoenix chpt. 1983, NISOD Teaching Excellence award, 1996. Mem. APA (divsns. 2, 21, 24, 27, 30, 46), AACD, Am. Psychol. Soc., Am. Inst. Indsl. Engrs., Human Factors Soc., World Future Soc., Western Psychol. Assn., Ariz. Counselors Assn., Ariz. Mental Health Counselors Assn. Office: Phoenix Coll 1202 W Thomas Rd Phoenix AZ 85013-4208

ROEBUCK, JUDITH LYNN, secondary school educator; b. Huntington, W.Va., Jan. 1, 1946; d. Russell Vance and Janice Lee (Adams) Dickey; m. William Benjamine Roebuck Jr., Mar. 28, 1970; children: Lisa, Paul. AB, Marshall U., 1968; MA, W.Va. U., 1973; postgrad., Marshall U., W.Va. U., 1973—. Cert. tchr., adminstr., W.Va. Tchr. art, English Vinson High Sch., Huntington, 1967-68; tchr. art Wayne (W.Va.) and Crockett Elem. Sch., 1968-69; tchr. art, speech Ona (W.Va.) Jr. High/Mid. Sch., 1969-91; tchr. speech, debate Huntington High Sch., 1991-92; tchr. art Barboursville (W.Va.) High Sch., 1992-94, Midland H.S., Ona, W.Va., 1994—; chmn. related arts team Ona Mid. Sch., 1988-91, mem. sch. improvement team, 1990-91; ret., 1996; mem. adv. bd. Teen Inst., Huntington, 1990—, W.Va. Teen Inst., 1995, leader, 1990—; mem. drama and debate program, Huntington, 1991-92, Invitationalism Coun., Huntington, 1990—, Cabell County Curriculum Coun., Huntington, 1991-92, Cabell County Reading Coun., 1991-92, Cabell County Tchrs. Acad., Tchr. Expectancy Student Achievement, W.Va. Health Schs. Program; mediator, trainer Healping Improve Peace, 1994; mentor, tchr. Impact. Contbr. articles to endl. jours. Counselor, Coll. Scouts Program, 1994—. Mem. NEA, DAR (sec. 1988—), Nat. Art Edn. Assn. (curriculum coun., art chmn. 1993-96, county del. 1994), W.Va. Edn. Assn., Cabell Edn. Assn. (membership chmn. 1989-91), Horizons, Phi Delta Kappa. Avocation: crafts, sewing, reading, diet and health, walking. Home: 30 Chris Ln Rt 2 Milton WV 25541

ROEDDER, EDWIN WOODS, geologist; b. Monsey, N.Y., July 30, 1919; s. Hans and Edna (Woods) R.; m. Kathleen Rea; children: Spencer, Lucy. BA, Lehigh U., 1941; MA, Columbia U., 1947, PhD, 1950; DSc (hon.), Lehigh U., 1976. Rsch. engr. Bethlehem Steel Corp., Bethlehem, Pa., 1941-46; predoctoral fellow Geophys. Lab., Carnegie Inst., Washington, 1946-47; asst. in geology Columbia U., N.Y.C., 1946-49; asst. prof., assoc. prof. U. Utah, Salt Lake City, 1950-55; chief solid state group U.S. Geol. Survey, Washington, 1955-60, staff geologist, 1960-62, geologist, 1962-73, rsch. geologist, 1974-87; assoc. Harvard U., 1987—; scientist emeritus U.S. Geol. Survey, Washington, 1987—; mem. or cons. various adv. bds, vis. coms., panels for U.S. govt. and several universities. Author: Composition of Fluid Inclusions, 1972, Fluid Inclusions, 1984; editor: Research on Mineral Forming Solutions, 1965, Fluid Inclusion Research (ann. book), 1968—; patentee in field. Recipient Exceptional Sci. Achievement medal NASA, 1973, Disting. Svc. medal U.S. Dept. Interior, 1978, Abraham Gottlob-Werner medaille Deutschen Min. Gesellschaft, 1985, Cyril Purkyne medal Czech Geol. Survey, 1991; first H.C. Sorby medal, 1993; grantee NSF, others. Fellow AAAS, Am. Geophys. Union (pres. V.G. and P. sect. 1978-80), Mineral Soc. Am. (v.p. 1981-82, pres. 1982-83, Washington A. Roebling medal 1986); mem. NAS, Geochem. Soc. (sec. 1967-70, v.p. 1975-76, pres. 1976-77), Soc. Econ. Geologists (R.A.F. Penrose medal 1988). Avocations: music, travel, stamp collecting. Office: Harvard U Dept Earth & Planetary Scis Cambridge MA 02138

ROEDDER, WILLIAM CHAPMAN, JR., lawyer; b. St. Louis, June 21, 1946; s. William Chapman and Dorothy (Reifeiss) R.; m. Gwendolyn Arnold, Sept. 13, 1968; children: William Chapman, Barcley Shane. BS, U. Ala., 1968; JD, Cumberland U., 1972. Bar: Ala. Law clk. to chief justice Ala. Supreme Ct., Montgomery, 1972; ptnr. McDowell Knight Roedder & Sledge, L.L.C., Mobile, Ala., 1997—. Comments editor Cumberland-Samford Law Rev. Contbr. articles to legal publs. Mem. ABA (vice-chair com. trial tactics, torts and ins. practice 1995-96, Ala. State Bar, Mobile County Bar Assn. (past sec., past chmn. ethics com. 1988-90, grievance com. 1994-96, Fed. Ins. and Corp. Counsel (chmn. products liability sect. 1990-93, regional v.p. 1994-96, bd. dirs. 1996—), Ala. Def. Lawyers Assn., Curia Honoris, Order of Barristers, Def. Rsch. Inst., Phi Alpha Delta (pres. 1971-72). Home: 211 Levert Ave Mobile AL 36607-3219 Office: McDowell Knight Roedder & Sledge LLC PO Box 350 Mobile AL 36601

ROEDEL, PAUL ROBERT, steel company executive; b. Millville, N.J., June 15, 1927; s. Charles Howard and Irene (Voorhees) R.; m. June Gilbert Adams, June 25, 1951; children—Beth Anne, Meg Adams. B.S. in Accounting, Rider Coll., 1949. With Carpenter Tech. Corp., Reading, Pa., 1949—; asst. controller Carpenter Tech. Corp., 1957-65, controller, 1965-72, treas., 1972-73, v.p. fin., treas., 1973-75, exec. v.p., 1975-79, pres., 1979—, chief operating officer, 1979-81, chief exec. officer, 1981-92, dir., 1973—, chmn., CEO, 1987-92; dir. Gen. Public Utilities Corp., 1979—, P.H. Glatfelter Co., 1992—. Bd. dirs. Hawk Mountain coun. Boy Scouts Am., Pa. 2000 Edn. Coalition; trustee Gettysburg Coll.; treas. Wyomissing Found. With USNR, 1945-46. Home: 416 Wheatland Ave Reading PA 19607-1326 Office: Carpenter Tech Corp 101 Bern St Reading PA 19601-1203

ROEDER, REBECCA EMILY, software engineer; b. Findlay, Ohio, Nov. 2, 1959; d. Brian Eldon and Barbara Lee (Melton) R.; m. Stephen William Bigley, May 28, 1983. BS in Edn. and Computer Sci., Bowling Green State U., 1983, MS in Computer Sci., 1993. Sys. analyst NCR Corp., Dayton, Ohio, 1983-84; sr. sys. analyst Unisys (Burroughs) Corp., Detroit, 1984-88; asst. dir. St. Vincent Med. Ctr., Toledo, 1988-95; sr. cons. Advanced Programming Resources, Inc., Columbus, Ohio, 1996; sr. sys. analyst LCI Internat., Dublin, Ohio, 1996—. Active Sta. WGTE/WGLE Pub. Radio, Toledo, 1984-96, Sta. WOSU Pub. Radio, Columbus, 1996—, Sta. WCBE Pub. Radio, Columbus, 1996—, Toledo Mus. Art, 1988-96, Toledo Zoo, 1993-96, Columbus Zoo, 1997—; presenter Women in Sci. Career Day, Lourde's Coll., 1992. Marathon scholar Marathon Oil Co., Findlay, 1978, Hancock scholar Findlay Area C. of C., 1978. Mem. AAUW, Assn. for Computing Machinery, Columbus Computer Soc. Episcopalian. Avocations: instrumental and choral music, drum and bugle corps, reading. Home: 4964 Vicksburg Ln Hilliard OH 43026-5740 Office: LCI Internat 4650 Lakehurst Ct Dublin OH 43016-3252

ROEDER, RICHARD KENNETH, business owner, lawyer; b. Phila., Oct. 11, 1948; s. Walter August and Gloria (Miller) R.; m. Frederika Anne Beesemyer, June 25, 1983; 1 child, William Frederick. AB, Amherst Coll., 1970; JD, U. Calif., Berkeley, 1973, Cambridge U., 1973-74. Assoc. Paul, Hastings, Janofsky & Walker, L.A., 1974-81, ptnr., 1981-90; ptnr. Aurora Capital Ptnrs., L.A., 1990—. Office: Aurora Capital Ptnrs 1800 Century Park E Ste 1000 Los Angeles CA 90067-1513

ROEDER, ROBERT GAYLE, biochemist, educator; b. Boonville, Ind., June 3, 1942; s. Frederick John and Helene (Bredenkamp) R.; m. Suzanne Himsel, July 11, 1964 (div. 1981); children: Kimberly, Michael; m. Cun Jing Hong, June 2, 1990. BA summa cum laude (Gilbert scholar), Wabash Coll., 1964, DSc (hon.), 1990; MS, U. Ill., 1965; PhD (USPHS fellow), U. Wash., 1969. Am. Cancer Soc. fellow dept. embryology Carnegie Instn. Washington, Balt., 1969-71; asst. prof. biol. chemistry Washington U., St. Louis, 1971-75; assoc. prof. Washington U., 1975-76, prof., 1976-82, prof. genetics, 1978-82, James S. McDonnell prof. biochem. genetics, 1979-82; prof. lab. biochemistry and molecular biology Rockefeller U., N.Y.C., 1982—; Arnold O. and Mabel S. Beckmann prof. molecular biology and biochemistry Rockefeller U., 1985—; cons. USPHS, 1975-79, Am. Cancer Soc., 1983-86. Recipient Dreyfus Tchr.-Scholar award Dreyfus Found., 1976, molecular biology award NAS-U.S. Steel Found., 1986, outstanding investigator award Nat. Cancer Inst., 1986—, Rosensteil award for disting. work in basic med. scis. Brandeis U., 1995, Passano award Passano Found., Inc., 1995; grantee NIH, 1972—, NSF, 1975-79, Am. Cancer Soc., 1979-85. Fellow AAAS, Am. Acad. Arts & Scis., Am. Acad. Microbiology, N.Y. Acad. Scis.; mem. NAS, Am. Chem. Soc. (Eli Lilly award 1977), Am. Soc. Biol. Chemists, Am. Soc. Microbiologists, Harvey Soc. (pres. 1994), Phi Beta Kappa. Home: 504 E 63rd St Apt 36P New York NY 10021-7933 Office: Rockefeller University 1230 York Ave New York NY 10021-6307

ROEDER, STEPHEN BERNHARD WALTER, chemistry and physics educator; b. Dover, N.J., Aug. 26, 1939; s. Walter Martin and Katherine E.R. (Holz) R.; m. Phoebe E. Barber, June 28, 1969; children: Adrienne H.K., Roland K.W. B.A., Dartmouth Coll., 1961; Ph.D., U. Wis., 1965. Postdoctoral fellow Bell Telephone Labs., Murray Hill, N.J., 1965-66; lectr. physics U. Oreg., Eugene, 1966-68; asst. prof. chemistry and physics San Diego State U., 1968-72, assoc. prof., 1972-75, prof., 1975—, chmn. dept. physics, 1975-78, chmn. dept. chemistry, 1979-86, acting dir. Master of Liberal Arts Program, 1987, 89, chmn. dept. physics, 1991-94, chmn. dept. of chemistry, 1995—; vis. staff mem. Los Alamos Nat. Labs., 1974-92; vis. assoc. prof. chemistry U. B.C., Vancouver, Can., 1974-75; vis. prof. physics Tex. A&M U., College Station, 1982; cons. Lovelace Med. Found., 1985-90. Author: (with others) Experimental Pulse NMR, 1981. Recipient Outstanding Teaching award San Diego State U., 1971, Outstanding Prof. award San Diego State U., 1992; grantee Rsch. Corp., 1968, 71, 72. Mem. AAAS, Am. Chem. Soc., Am. Phys. Soc., Sigma Xi. Republican. Home: 6789 Alamo Way La Mesa CA 91941-5874 Office: San Diego State U Dept of Chem San Diego CA 92182-1030

ROEDERER, JUAN GUALTERIO, physics educator; b. Trieste, Italy, Sept. 2, 1929; came to U.S., 1967, naturalized, 1972; s. Ludwig Alexander and Anna Rafaela (Lohr) R.; m. Beatriz Susana Cougnet, Dec. 20, 1952; children: Ernesto, Irene, Silvia, Mario. Ph.D., U. Buenos Aires, 1952. Research scientist Max Planck Inst., Gottingen, W.Ger., 1952-55; group leader Argentine Atomic Energy Commn., Buenos Aires, 1953-59; prof. physics U. Buenos Aires, 1959-66, U. Denver, 1967-77; prof. physics U. Alaska, Fairbanks, 1977-93, prof. emeritus, 1993—, dir. Geophys. Inst., 1977-86, dean Coll. Environ. Scis., 1978-82; vis. staff Los Alamos Nat. Lab., 1969-81; chmn. U.S. Arctic Research Com., 1987-91. Author: Dynamics of Geomagnetically Trapped Radiation, 1970, Physics and Psychophysics of Music, 1973, 3d edit., 1995; contbr. articles to profl. jours. Nat. Acad. Sci. NASA sr. research fellow, 1964-66. Fellow AAAS, Am. Geophys. Union; mem. Assn. Argentina de Geodestas y Geofisicos, Nat. Acad. Sci. Argentina (corr.), Nat. Acad. Sci. Austria (corr.), Third World Acad. Scis. (assoc.). Lutheran. Research on plasma and energetic particles in earth's magnetosphere, policy issues for Arctic, perception of music. Home: 105 Concordia Dr Fairbanks AK 99709-3029 Office: Geophys Inst U Alaska Fairbanks AK 99775-7320

ROEDIGER, JANICE ANNE, artist, educator; b. Trenton, N.J.; d. John and Anne Balint; m. Paul Margerum Roediger; children: Pamela Anne, Matthew Paul, Joan Margaret. Student, Beaver Coll., 1975-78; grad. cert., Pa. Acad. Fine Arts, 1988. Instr. multi-media Jane Law Long Beach Island Gallery, Surf City, N.J., 1992-97, 94-97; instr. drawing Long Beach Island Found., Loveladies, N.J., 1994-96; docent Mus. Am. Art, Pa. Acad. Fine Arts, Phila., 1992-96. Exhibited in group shows at Rittenhouse Galleries, Phila., 1988-94, Phila. Mus. Art, ASR Gallery, 1992-96, Schaff Gallery, Cin., 1995-96. Mem. vestry, rector's warden St. Anne's Episcopal Ch., Abington, Pa., 1970-73; chair med. staff aux. Abington Meml. Hosp., 1973-7, chair scholarship com., 1974; coord. student com. Pa. Acad. Fine Arts, Phila., 1986-88; active Phila. Mus. Art, 1972—. Recipient Rohm & Haas Outstanding Achievement award Pa. Acad. Fine Arts, 1987, Pearl Van Sciver award Woodmere Mus., 1991, Blumenthal award Cheltenham Ctr. for Arts, 1991, Lance Lauffler award for visionary painting Pa. Acad. Fine Arts, 1988, Award of Merit Long Beach Island Found., 1994, 96. Mem. Nat. Mus. Women in Arts, Phila. Art Alliance, Artists Cultural Exch. (bd. dirs. 1989—). Episcopalian. Avocations: writing, collecting, golf, walking, travel. Home: 1244 Rydal Rd Rydal PA 19046-1415 Studio: 1010 Arch St Philadelphia PA 19107-3003

ROEDIGER, PAUL M., hospital administrator; b. Princeton, N.J., June 30, 1932; s. Paul Otto and Helen Mae (Margerum) R.; m. Janice Ann Balint, Aug. 18, 1956; children: Pamela, Matthew, Joan. AB, Princeton U., 1954; MD, Jefferson Med. Coll., 1958. Dir. med. edn. Abington (Pa.) Meml. Hosp., 1965—, chief divsn. gen. internal medicine, 1972—. Vestry mem. St. Ann's Episcopal Ch., Abington, 1965—. Fellow ACP, Coll. Physicians of Phila. Home: 1244 Rydal Rd Rydal PA 19046 Office: 1235 York Rd Abington PA 19001-3800

ROEG, NICOLAS JACK, film director; b. London, Aug. 15, 1928; s. Jack Nicolas and Mabel Getrude (Silk) R.; m. Susan Rennie Stephen, May 12, 1957; children: Joscelin Nicolas, Nicolas Jack, Lucien John, Sholto Jules; m. Theresa Russell, 1985; children: Maximilian Nicolas Sextus, Statten Jack. Student Brit. schs.; LittD honoris causa, Hull (Eng.) U., 1995. Cinematographer films The Caretaker, 1963, Masque of Red Death, 1964, Fahrenheit 451, 1966, A Funny Thing Happened on the Way to the Forum, 1966, Far from the Madding Crowd, 1967, Petulia, 1968; co-dir. film Performance, 1970; dir. films Walkabout, 1970, Don't Look Now, 1973, Glastonbury Fayre, 1973, The Man Who Fell to Earth, 1976, Bad Timing, 1980, Eureka, 1982, Insignificance, 1985, Castaway, 1986, 89, Track 29, 1987, Aria, 1987, The Witches, 1988-89, Cold Heaven, 1990, Heart of Darkness, 1994, Two Deaths, 1994, Hotel Paradise, 1995, Full Body Massage, 1995, Samson & Delilah, 1996; dir. TV films: Sweet Bird of Youth, 1989, Heart of Darkness, 1994; exec. producer Without You I'm Nothing, 1989, Young Indy, 1991. Decorated comdr. Brit. Empire. Fellow Brit. Film Inst.; mem. Dirs. Guild Am., Dir. Guild Gt. Britain, Acad. Motion Picture Arts and Scis., Assn. Cinematograph, TV and Allied Technicians. Office: care Robert Littman Beverly Hills CA 90210

ROEGNER, GEORGE PETER, industrial designer; b. Flushing, N.Y., Sept. 3, 1932; s. George Elmer and Margaret (Hanna) R.; B.F.A., Pratt Inst., 1954; m. Jane R. Kramer, Aug. 29, 1959; children—George Curtis, John Hanson, Nicholas Meade. Staff designer Gen. Motors Corp., 1954-55, Raymond Loewy Assocs., N.Y.C., Westinghouse Corp., Metuchen, N.J., 1960-66; product design mgr. RCA, Indpls., 1966-70; dir. design Lenox Inc., Trenton, 1972-74; pres. Curtis Hanson Meade Inc., Far Hills, N.J., 1974—; ptnr. Furniture Concepts Internat. Ltd.; dir. Cove House Corp. Bd. dirs. Clarence Dillon Library; vice chmn. Far Hills Bd. Adjustment; councilman Borough of Far Hills, 1982—, police chmn., 1984—. Served with U.S. Army, 1956-58. Recipient design awards ID Mag., Nat. Paper Box, Consumer Electronics Show, Printing Industries, Print Mag., Wescon. Mem. Indsl. Designers Soc. Am. (past nat. com. chmn.), Somerset Hills Assn., Raritan Valley Watershed Assn. Republican. Clubs: Eastward Ho Country, Stage Harbor Yacht. Designs shown at Mus. Modern Art, Smithsonian Instn., N.Y. World's Fair, Brussels, Zagreb Fairs, Indpls. Art Mus.

ROEHL, JERRALD J(OSEPH), lawyer; b. Austin, Tex., Dec. 6, 1945; s. Joseph E. and Jeanne Foster (Scott) R.; m. Nancy J. Meyers, Jan. 15, 1977; children: Daniel J., Katherine C., J. Ryan, J. Taylor. BA, U. N.Mex., 1968; JD, Washington and Lee U., 1971. Bar: N.Mex. 1972, U.S. Ct. Appeals (10th cir.) 1972, U.S. Supreme Ct. 1977. Practice of Law, Albuquerque, 1972—; pres. Roehl Law Firm P.C. and predecessors, Albuquerque, 1976—; lectr. to profl. groups; real estate developer, Albuquerque. Bd. dirs. Rehab. Ctr. of Albuquerque, 1974-78; mem. assocs. Presbyn. Hosp. Ctr., Albuquerque, 1974-82; incorporator, then treas. exec. com. Ctr. City Coun., 1991—. Recipient award of recognition State Bar N.Mex., 1975, 76, 77. Mem. ABA (award of achievement Young Lawyers div. 1975, council econs. of law practice sect. 1978-80, exec. council Young Lawyers div. 1979-81, fellow div. 1984—, council tort and ins. practice sect. 1981-83), N.Mex. Bar Assn. (pres. young lawyers sect. 1975-76), Albuquerque Bar Assn. (bd. dirs. 1976-79), N.Mex. Def. Lawyers Assn. (pres. 1983-84), Sigma Alpha Epsilon, Sigma Delta Chi, Phi Delta Phi. Roman Catholic. Clubs: Albuquerque Country, Albuquerque Petroleum. Bd. advs. ABA Jour., 1981-83; bd. editors Washington and Lee Law Rev., 1970-71. Home: 4411 Constitution Ave NE Albuquerque NM 87110-5721 Office: Roehl Law Firm PC 300 Central Ave SW Albuquerque NM 87102-3249

ROEHL, KATHLEEN ANN, financial executive; b. Chgo., June 1, 1948; d. Walter Steven and Catherine (Puss) Kalchbrenner; m. Eric C. Roehl, June 28, 1969; children: Aaron C., Marc E. BA with honors, U. Ill., 1969. Registered investment advisor. Tchr. Ft. Huachuca (Ariz.) Accomodation Schs., 1969-70; interior designer Key Kitchens, Dearborn Heights, Mich., 1979-80; stockbroker, fin. cons. Merrill Lynch, Dearborn, Mich., 1980-81; v.p., registered investment advisor Merrill Lynch, Northbrook, Ill., 1982—; bd. dirs. ATA Info. Systems. Mem. Ill. Govt. Fin. Officers Assn., Internat. Assn. for Fin. Planning (bd dirs. 1987-88), Northbrook C. of C. (bd. dirs. 1991-93), Northbrook Early Risers Rotary (charter mem.). Avocations: horticulture, architecture. Office: Merrill Lynch 400 Skokie Blvd Northbrook IL 60062-2816

ROEHLING, CARL DAVID, architect; b. Detroit, June 25, 1951; m. Barbara K. Jeffries; children: Carl Robert, Kristin Virginia. BS in Architecture, U. Mich., 1973, MArch, 1975. Registered arch., Mich.; cert. Nat. Coun. Archtl. Registration Bd. Architect Minoru Yamasaki and Assocs., Inc., Troy, Mich., 1976-77; TMP Assocs., 1977-81; architect Harley Ellington Pierce Yee Assocs., Inc., Southfield, Mich., 1981-83, Giffels/Hoyem Basso Assocs., Troy, 1983-87, Smith, Hinchman & Grylls Assocs., Inc., Detroit, 1987—; with Chrysler World Hdqs., 1994. Prin. works include CBS/Fox Video Hdqrs., Livonia, Mich. (Honor award Mich. Masonry Inst., 1985), First Ctr. Office Bldg., Southfield, Mich. (Honor award AIA Mich.,

1988), Ind. U. Chemistry Bldg., Bloomington (Honor award AIA Detroit, 1990, AIA Mich., 1990), U. Mich. Aerospace Lab. Bldg., Ann Arbor, 1993, Los Alamos (N.Mex.) Materials Sci. Lab., 1993, others. Mem. AIA (Mich. chpg. pres. bd. dirs. 1989, mem. nat. com. on environ. 1991, Detroit chpt. pres. 1994, Young Arch. of Yr., AIA Detroit, 1986, AIA Mich., 1991, regional dir. 1996—, nat. bd. dirs.), Am. Archtl. Found. (bd. dirs. 1997—), Mich. Archtl. Found. (chmn. pres. scholarship program 1990). Office: Smith Hinchman & Grylls 150 W Jefferson Ave Ste 100 Detroit MI 48226-4415

ROEHM, MACDONELL, JR., retail executive; b. Semerang, Indonesia, July 6, 1939; s. MacDonell and Mary Bennett (Cobb) R.; m. Nedra Ann Zeth, May 11, 1974. B.A., Colgate U., 1961; M.B.A., Harvard U., 1966. Fin. analyst Exxon Corp., 1966-68; asso. Lazard Freres, N.Y.C., 1968-71; gen. partner J. Bush & Co., N.Y.C., 1971-73; v.p. planning and devel. Cerro Corp., N.Y.C., 1973-75; v.p., treas. N L Industries, Inc., N.Y.C., 1976-79; sr. v.p. ops., devel. and planning N L Petroleum Services/N L Industries, Inc., Houston, 1979-80; pres. N.L. Shaffer/NL Industries, Inc., 1980-82; exec. v.p. NL Industries, Inc., 1982-85; ptnr. AEA Investors, Inc., 1985-95; chmn., pres., CEO Bill's Dollar Stores, Inc., 1995—. Served with USN 1961-64. Decorated Silver Star, Bronze star, Purple Heart. Office: Bills Dollar Stores Inc 3800 I 55 N Jackson MS 39211-6324

ROEHRIG, C(HARLES) BURNS, internist, health policy consultant, editor; b. Brookline, Mass., Jan. 21, 1923; s. Gilbert Haven and Helen (Burns) R.; m. Patricia Joan Orme, July 22, 1952; children—Joan Russell Roehrig Vater, Jennifer Orme Roehrig Munn, Charles Burns, Jr. Student, Amherst Coll., 1941-43, Vanderbilt U., 1943-44; M.D., U. Md., 1949; cert. in internal medicine, U. Pa. Grad. Sch. Medicine, Phila., 1953. Diplomate Am. Bd. Internal Medicine. Intern Boston City Hosp., 1949-50; resident in internal medicine and diabetes Joslin Clinic, New Eng. Deaconess Hosp., Boston, 1952-54; practice medicine specializing in internal medicine and diabetes Boston, 1954—; chief of staff, pres. med. adminstrv. bd. New Eng. Deaconess Hosp., Boston, 1972-75; dir., mem. exec. com. Blue Shield of Mass., Inc., Boston, 1977-88, dir., 1989—; mem. exec. com. Met. Boston Hosp. Coun., 1982-86; mem. physician adv. council Mass. Hosp. Assn., Burlington, 1982-86. Editor: The Today's Internist, Washington, 1987—; contbr. med. articles to profl. jours. Bd. dirs. Camping Svcs. Bd., Greater Boston YMCA, 1966—; mem. physician adv. group Health Care Financing Adminstrn., Washington, 1983-88; mem. adv. panel on physician payment and med. tech. Office of Tech. Assessment, U.S. Congress, Washington, 1984-85; chmn. Federated Coun. for Internal Medicine, Washington, 1985-86; trustee New Eng. Deaconess Hosp. Capt. (flight surgeon) USAF, 1949-52. Fellow ACP; mem. AMA (chmn. coun. on long range planning and devel., Chgo.), New Eng. Diabetes Assn. (pres. 1963-64), Mass. Soc. Internal Medicine (pres. 1971-72), Am. Soc. Internal Medicine (pres. 1984-85), Country Club of Hilton Head. Republican. Episcopalian. Club: Wellesley Country (Mass.).

ROEHRKASSE, PAULINE CATHERINE HOLTORF, retired secondary education educator; b. Malmo, Nebr., Sept. 14, 1909; d. Jurgen Heinrich and Wiebke (Knuth) Holtorf; m. Raymond Roehrkasse, June 11, 1935; children: Paula Joan Knepper, Claire Rae Eason, Kathryn Grace Trebelhorn. Grad. in Music, Luther Jr. Coll., Wahoo, Nebr., 1929; BS in Edn., U. Nebr., 1967; postgrad., Kearney State U., Nebr., 1970. Tchr. Grand Island (Nebr.) pub. schs., 1951-72; pipe organist Trinity Luth. Ch., 1938-53. Author: A Flowering: A Festival, 1984. V.p. Ctrl. States Coalition on Aging, 1989-90; elected U.S. Silver Haired Senator from Nebr., 1988—; sec. steering com. Nat. Silver Haired Congress, 1988-95, Nebr. chair, 1997; publicity chmn. Nat. Coun. Silver Haired Legislators, 1985-93; organizer Internat. Luth. Women's Missionary League, Chgo., 1942, corr. sec., 1942-52, pres. Nebr. South dist., 1948-52. Mem. AAUW (legis. chmn., program chmn.), Am. Assn. Ret. Persons (program chmn. 1983-85, legis. chmn. 1985-92), Ret. Tchrs. Assn., Alpha Delta Kappa (pres. Epsilon chpt.). Democrat. Lutheran. Home: 503 S Broadwell Ave Grand Island NE 68803-5951

ROEL, RON, newspaper editor. Dep. bus. editor Newsday, Inc., Melville, N.Y., now dep. nat. editor, 1995—. Office: Newsday Inc 235 Pinelawn Rd Melville NY 11747-4226*

ROELLIG, LEONARD OSCAR, physics educator; b. Detroit, May 17, 1927; s. Oscar Otto and Laura K. (Rutz) R.; m. B. Pauline Cowdin, June 20, 1952; children: Thomas Leonard, Mark Douglas, Paul David. A.B., U. Mich., 1950, M.S., 1956, Ph.D., 1959. From asst. prof. to prof. physics Wayne State U., Detroit, 1958-78; dean Wayne State U., 1971-72, asso. provost, 1972-76; pres. Central Solar Energy Research Corp., Detroit, 1977; prof. physics CCNY, 1978-96, prof. emeritus, 1996—; vice chancellor acad. affairs CUNY, 1978-83; vis. prof. Univ. Coll., London, 1968-69, Tata Inst. Fundamental Rsch., Bombay, India, 1973, Paul Scherrer Inst., Villigen, Switzerland, 1991-92; chmn. bd. advisers Midwest Regional Solar Energy Planning Venture, 1977. Co-author: Positron Annihilation, 1967; contbr. articles to profl. jours. Bd. dirs. Luth. Publicity Bur., 1981-91, v.p., 1984-85, pres., 1985-89; v.p. Grosse Pointe (Mich.) Human Rels. Coun., 1969-70. With USN, 1945-46, U.S. Army, 1950-52. Recipient Wayne State U. Fund Research Recognition award, 1963, Probus Club award for acad. achievement, 1968, Probus Club award for acad. leadership, 1977. Mem. Am. Phys. Soc. Home: 4520 Sioux Dr Boulder CO 80303 Office: U Colo Dept Physics Boulder CO 80302

ROELOFS, WENDELL LEE, biochemistry educator, consultant; b. Orange City, Iowa, July 26, 1938; s. Edward and Edith (Beyers) R.; m. Donna R. Gray, Dec. 23, 1989; children by previous marriage: Brenda Jo, Caryn Jean, Jeffrey Lee, Kevin Jon. BA, Central Coll., Pella, Iowa, 1960, DSc (hon.), 1985; PhD, Ind. U., 1964, DSc (hon.), 1986; DSc (hon.), Hobart and William Smith Colls., 1988, U. of Lund, Sweden, 1989, Free U. Brussels, 1989. Asst. prof. Cornell U., Geneva, N.Y., 1965-69, assoc. prof., 1969-76, prof., 1976—, Liberty Hyde Bailey prof. insect biochemistry, 1978—, chmn. dept., 1991—. Contbr. over 300 articles to sci. jours. Recipient Alexander von Humboldt award in Agr., 1977, Outstanding Alumni award Central Coll., 1978, Wolf prize for agr., 1982, Disting. Alumnus award Ind. U., 1983, Nat. Medal of Sci., 1983, Disting. Svc. award USDA, 1986, Silver medal Internat. Soc. Chem. Ecology, 1990; postdoctoral fellow MIT, 1965. Fellow AAAS, Entomol. Soc. Am. (J. Everett Bussart Meml. award 1973, Founder's Meml. award 1980, Disting. Achievement award Ea. br. 1983); mem. NAS, Am. Chem. Soc. (Sterling B. Hendricks award 1994), Am. Acad. Arts and Sci., Sigma Xi. Republican. Presbyterian. Patentee in field (10). Home: 4 Crescence Dr Geneva NY 14456-1302 Office: Cornell Univ Insect Biochemistry Geneva NY 14456

ROELS, OSWALD ALBERT, oceanographer, educator, business executive; b. Temse, Belgium, Sept. 16, 1921; came to U.S., 1958, naturalized, 1965; s. Ghisleen and Elvire (Heirwegh) R.; m. Dorothy Mary Broadhurst, Sept. 16, 1950; 1 dau., Margaret Ann Roels Talarico. B.S., U. Louvain, Belgium, 1940, M.S., 1942; Ph.D., 1944. Prof. Columbia U., N.Y.C., 1960-75, CCNY, 1969-76; prof., dir. dept. marine sci. U. Tex., Austin, 1976-80; chmn. Maritek Corp., Corpus Christi, Tex., 1980-92; pres. Bradley Barges Inc.; adj. prof. Rockefeller U., N.Y.C., 1969-80; vis. research prof. Laval U., Que., Can., 1972-80; dir. mariculture research Port Aransas (Tex.) Marine Lab., U. Tex. Marine Sci. Inst., 1976-80. Author numerous articles in field.; assoc. editor: Nutrition Revs., 1961-68. Served with Belgian Army, 1940. Recipient Postdoctoral award U. Brussels, 1945, Postdoctoral award U. Liverpool, Eng., 1946, Postdoctoral award Sorbonne, 1957; Research Career Devel. award NIH, 1962-65; WHO fellow, 1957; Hoffman-LaRoche vis. lectr., 1974. Mem. AAAS, Am. Chem. Soc., Am. Inst. Nutrition, Am. Soc. Biol. Chemists, Am. Soc. Limnology and Oceanography, Chemici Lovanienses, Inst. Environ. Scis., Inst. Food Tech., Internat. Conf. Biochem. Lipids, Marine Tech. Soc., N.Y. Acad. Scis., N.Y. Lipid Club, Photoelectric Spectrometry Group Gt. Britain, World Mariculture Soc. Home: 4345 Rosecliff Dr Charlotte NC 28277-8657

ROEMER, EDWARD PIER, neurologist; b. Milw., Feb. 10, 1908; s. John Henry and Caroline Hamilton (Pier) R.; m. Helen Ann Fraser, Mar. 28, 1935 (dec.); children: Kate Pier, Caroline Pier; m. Marion Clare Zimmer, May 24, 1980. BA, U. Wis., 1930; MD, Cornell U., 1934. Diplomate Am. Bd. Neurology. Intern Yale-New Haven Hosp., 1934-36; resident internal medicine N.Y. Hosp., 1936; resident neurology Bellevue Hosp., N.Y.C., 1936-38; instr. Med. Sch. Yale U., New Haven, 1935-36; asst. prof. neurology Cornell U., N.Y.C., 1936-41; prof. neurology U. Wis., Madison, 1946-64; chief of neurology Huntington Meml. Hosp., Pasadena, Calif., 1964-78; pvt. practice Capistrano Beach, Calif., 1978—; founder, dir. Wis. Neurol. Found., Madison, 1946-64; dir. Wis. Multiple Sclerosis Clinic, Madison, 1946-64; adv. bd. Inst. Antiquities and Christianity, Claremont Grad. Sch., 1970—; dir. found. Univ Good Hope, S.Africa. Contbr. rsch. articles on multiple sclerosis, neuropathies to profl. jours. Lt. col. med. corps U.S. Army, 1941-46, ETO. Fellow ACP, Royal Coll. Medicine, L.S.B. Leakey Found.; mem. Rotary Internat., Annandale Golf Club, El Niguel Country Club, Nu Sigma Nu, Phi Delta Theta. Republican. Achievements include significant findings in field of anthropology and archaeology in Egypt and southwest U. S. relative to prehistory and PreColumbian European influences. Home: 35651 Beach Rd Capo Beach CA 92624-1710

ROEMER, ELAINE SLOANE, real estate broker; b. N.Y.C., Apr. 23, 1938; d. David and Marion (Frauenthal) Sloane; m. David Frank Roemer, June 21, 1959; children: Michelle Sloane Wolf, Alan Sloane Roemer. BBA, U. Fla., 1959; MEd, U. Miami, 1963. CFP; cert. tchr. Tchr. math. and bus. Dade County Pub. Schs., Miami, 1959-80, Miami Dade Community Coll., 1968-80; tchr. edn. Fla. Internat. U., Miami, 1977-80; real estate broker Miami, 1978—; tchr. math. St. Leo's Coll., Miami, 1991-92; mortgage broker, Miami, 1986—; speaker in field. Contbr. articles to profl. jours. Mem. Kendall-Perrine Assn. Realtors (sec., treas. 1992-93, bd. dirs. 1991-92, grievance com. 1990, arbitration com. 1991, pres.-elect 1994, pres. 1995), Fla. Assn. Realtors (rep. dist. 4 1992-95, honor soc. 1995), Nat. Assn. Realtors, NEA, Fla. Edn. Commn., Classroom Tchrs. Assn., Dade County Edn. Assn., Fla. Coun. Tchrs. Math., Fla. Bus. Edn. Assn., Assn. Classroom Educators, Dade County Assn. Ednl. Adminstrs., ASCD, Alpha Delta Kappa. Home: 7705 SW 138th Ter Miami FL 33158-1120 Office: 9036 SW 152nd St Miami FL 33157-1928

ROEMER, ELIZABETH, astronomer, educator; b. Oakland, Calif., Sept. 4, 1929; d. Richard Quirin and Elsie (Barlow) R. BA with honors, U. Calif., Berkeley, 1950, PhD (Lick Obs. fellow), 1955. Tchr. adult class Oakland pub. schs., 1950-52; lab technician U. Calif. at Mt. Hamilton, 1954-55; grad. research astronomer U. Calif. at Berkeley, 1955-56; research asso. Yerkes Obs. U. Chgo., 1956; astronomer U.S. Naval Obs., Flagstaff, Ariz., 1957-66; asso. prof. dept. astronomy, also in lunar and planetary lab. U. Ariz., Tucson, 1966-69; prof. U. Ariz., 1969—; astronomer Steward Obs., 1980—; Chmn. working group on orbits and ephemerides of comets commn. 20 Internat. Astron. Union, 1964-79, 85-88, v.p. comm. 20, 1979-82, pres., 1982-85, v.p. commn. 6, 1973-76, 85-88, pres., 1976-79, 88-91; mem. adv. panels Office Naval Research, Nat. Acad. Scis.-NRC, NASA; researcher and author numerous publs. on astrometry and astrophysics of comets and minor planets including 79 recoveries of returning periodic comets, visual and spectroscopic binary stars, computation of orbits of comets and minor planets. Recipient Dorothea Klumpke Roberts prize U. Calif. at Berkeley, 1950, Mademoiselle Merit award, 1959; asteroid (1657) named Roemera, 1965; Benjamin Apthorp Gould prize Nat. Acad. Scis., 1971; NASA Spl. award, 1986. Fellow AAAS (council 1966-69, 72-73), Royal Astron. Soc. (London); mem. Am. Astron. Soc. (program vis. profs. astronomy 1960-75, council 1967-70, chmn. div. dynamical astronomy 1974), Astron. Soc. Pacific (publs. com. 1962-73, Comet medal com. 1968-74, Donohoe lectr. 1962), Internat. Astron. Union, Am. Geophys. Union, Brit. Astron. Assn., Phi Beta Kappa, Sigma Xi. Office: U Ariz Lunar and Planetary Lab Tucson AZ 85721-0092

ROEMER, MILTON IRWIN, physician, educator; b. Paterson, N.J., Mar. 24, 1916; s. Jacob and Mary (Rabinowitz) R.; m. Ruth Rosenbaum., Sept. 1. 1939; children: John, Beth. B.A., Cornell U., 1936, M.A., 1939; M.D., NYU, 1940; M.P.H., U. Mich., 1943. Diplomate: Am. Bd. Preventive Medicine. Intern Barnert Meml. Hosp., Paterson, 1940-41; with N.J. Health Dept., Trenton, 1941-42, USPHS, Washington, 1943-48; mem. faculty Yale U. Med. Sch., 1949-51; with WHO. Geneva, 1951-53, Sask. (Can.) Health Dept., 1953-56; mem. faculty Cornell U., 1957-61; prof. health adminstrn. U. Calif. Sch. Pub. Health, Los Angeles, 1962—; cons. in field. Author: numerous books, including Health Care Systems in World Perspective, 1976, Comparative National Policies on Health Care, 1977, Ambulatory Health Services in America, 1981, National Health Systems of the World: Vol. 1: The Countries, 1991, Vol. 2: The Issues, 1993. Mem. Inst. Medicine, Am. Pub. Health Assn. (award for excellence in internat. health 1977, Sedgwick medal 1983), Am. Coll. Preventive Medicine, Internat. Epidemiol. Assn., Physicians Forum, Group Health Assn. Am., Phi Beta Kappa, Sigma Xi, Alpha Omega Alpha, Phi Kappa Phi, Delta Omega. Home: 365 S Westgate Ave Los Angeles CA 90049-4207 Office: Univ Calif Sch Pub Health Los Angeles CA 90095

ROEMER, TIMOTHY J., congressman; b. South Bend, Ind., Oct. 30, 1956; m. Sarah Lee Johnston, 1989. BA in pol. sci, U. Calif., San Diego, 1979; MA, PhD in internat. rels., U. Notre Dame, 1986. Staff asst. to congressman John Brademas U.S. Congress; def., trade and fgn. policy advisor to senator Dennis DeConcini; mem. prof. 102nd-103rd Congresses from 3rd Ind. dist., 1991—; mem. economic and ednl. opportunity com., mem. sci. com.; adj. prof. Am. U. Office: 2348 Rayburn Bldg Ofc B Washington DC 20515-1403 also: 217 N Main St South Bend IN 46601-1216

ROEMING, ROBERT FREDERICK, foreign language educator; b. Milw., Dec. 12, 1911; s. Ferdinand August and Wanda E. (Radtke) R.; m. Alice Mae Voss, Aug. 30, 1941; 1 child, Pamela Alice. BA in Econs./Acctg., U. Wis., 1934, MA in Italian, 1936, PhD in French, 1941. Mem. faculty U. Wis.-Milw., 1937—, prof. French and Italian, 1956—, assoc. dean Coll. Letters and Sci., asst. to provost for devel. of spl. programs, 1957-62, sole dir. dept. lang. labs., 1964-70, dir. English as 2d lang., 1967-70, founder and dir. Ctr. Twentieth Century Studies, 1970-74, prof. emeritus, 1980—; founder, chief investigator Camus Bibliography Research Collection, Golda Meir Library, 1985; rep. D.C. Heath Co., 1943-46; cons., 1946-50; cons. computer systems Harnischfeger Corp., Milw., 1953-57; chmn. tech. sect. Internat. Congress on Fgn. Lang. Tchg., Pädagogisches Zentrum, Berlin, summer 1964; guest InterAm. Congress of Linguists, Montevideo, Uruguay, 1966; ofcl. guest Romanian govt. 10th Internat. Congress Linguists, summer 1967; dir. Insts. in Adult Basic Edn., 1969, U.S. Office Edn.; pres., treas. Electronic Rsch. Instruments Co., Inc., Nashotah, Wis., 1969-93. Author: (with C.E. Young) Introduction to French, 1951, Camus, A Bibliography, 1969, rev. and augmented computer-microfiche, 13th edit., 1997, Little Magazine Catalog, 1976, 77 (NEH grantee); editor: Modern Lang. Jour, 1963-70; contbr. numerous monographs and articles to profl. jours., 72 taped radio programs on French Black lit. Chmn. bldg. commn. Village of Chenequa, Wis., 1972-88; trustee, chmn. Midwest chpt. Jose Greco Found. for Hispanic Dance, Inc., 1970-76; mem. Wis. Bd. Nursing, 1977-79, chmn., 1979; mem. numerous nat. conservation orgns. and local civic groups. Decorated chevalier, officier, commandeur Ordre Palmes Académiques (France); recipient Travel award Italian Govt., 1934. Mem. MLA (life, index com. 1970-79), Nat. Fedn. Modern Lang. Tchrs. Assn. (exec. com. 1963-70), Verband Deutscher Schriftsteller, Wis. News Photographers Assn. (hon. life, Pres.'s award 1972), Soc. des Etudes Camusiennes, Am. Assn. of French Acad. Palms, Wis. Assn. for the Blind and Physically Handicapped, Chenequa Country Club, Lake Country Racquet and Athletic Club, Phi Eta Sigma, Phi Kappa Phi, Tau Kappa Epsilon. Research in application of the computer to humanities, applied linguistics and contemporary French and Italian Lit. Home: 6078 N Oakland Hills Rd Nashotah WI 53058 Office: U Wis-Milw Golda Meir Libr W240 2311 E Hartford Ave Milwaukee WI 53211-3175

ROEMMELE, BRIAN KARL, electronics, publishing, internet, financial and real estate executive; b. Newark, Oct. 4, 1961; s. Bernard Joseph and Paula M. Roemmele. Grad. high sch., Flemington, N.J. Registered profl. engr., N.J. Design engr. BKR Techs., Flemington, N.J., 1980-81; acoustical engr. Open Reel Studios, Flemington, 1980-82; pres. Ariel Corp., Flemington, 1983-84, Ariel Computer Corp., Flemington, 1984-89; pres., chief exec. officer Ariel Fin. Devel. Corp., N.Y.C., 1987-91; pres., CEO Avalon Am. Corp., Temecula, Calif., 1990—; CEO United Credit Card Acceptance Corp., Beverly Hills, 1992—, United ATM Card Acceptance Corp., Beverly Hills, 1992—; pres. Multiplex Media Corp., Beverly Hills, 1993—; pres., CEO Coupon Book Ltd., 1987-89, Value Hunter Mags., Ltd., AEON Cons. Group, Beverly Hills; bd. dirs. The Emporium Network, 1995, Beverly Hills, Waterman Internat., Whitehouse Station, N.J.; electronic design and software cons., L.A., 1980—. Pub., editor-in-chief: Computer Importer News, 1987—. Organizer Internat. Space Week or Day, 1978-83, Internet Engrs. Soc., 1993, Internet Soc., Geneva, 1993—; lectr. Trenton (N.J.) State Mus., 1983; chmn. Internet tech. com. Safe Water Internat., Paris; assoc. dir. World Payment Assn., Geneva. Mem. AAAS, AIAA, ABA, IEEE, World Wide Web Assn. (founder), Am. Bankers Assn., Bankcard Svcs. Assn., Boston Computer Soc., Ford/Hall Forum, Am. Soc. Notaries, Planetary Soc. Avocations: musician, surfing, cycling, reading, numismatics. Office: Avalon Am Corp PO Box 1615 Temecula CA 92593-1615

ROEN, PHILIP RUBEN, urologist, surgeon, medical educator; b. N.Y.C., Aug. 5, 1914; s. Nathaniel and Ida (Brickman) R.; m. Florence Sonia Gluck, Dec. 23, 1944; children: Janet Leslie. BA, Columbia Coll., 1934, MD, 1938. Diplomate Am. Bd. Urology. Fellow Cleve. Clinic; resident in urology N.Y. Hosp.; dir. urology St. Clare's Hosp., N.Y.C., 1959—; attending urologist Roosevelt Hosp., N.Y.C., 1980—; prof. clin. urology N.Y. Med. Coll., Valhalla, 1980—. Author: Atlas of Genitourinary Surgery, 1951, Atlas of Urologic Surgery, 1967, Male Sexual Health, 1974; contbr. articles to profl. jours. Chmn. profl. rels. Blue Shield, N.Y.C., 1978-80. Mem. ACS, Am. Urol. Assn., N.Y. Urol. Assn., Princeton Club N.Y.C. Office: 220 Madison Ave New York NY 10016-3422

ROEN, SHELDON R., publisher, psychologist; b. N.Y.C.; s. Morris Rosenthal and Gussie (Weininger) R.; m. Selma Lois Pollets, Feb. 21, 1954; children—Randa M., Marjorie A., Harris L. B.S., City U. N.Y., 1950, M.A., 1951; Ph.D., Columbia U., 1955; postgrad., New Sch. Social Research, 1951-53, Harvard Sch. Pub. Health, 1961-62. Diplomate: Am. Bd. Examiners in Profl. Psychology. Tchr. pub. schs. N.Y.C., 1950-53; chief Clin. Psychology Svc., Ft. Sill, Okla., 1955-58; instr. Cameron Coll., Okla. A. and M. U., 1956-58; asst. prof. U. N.H., 1958-60; asst. chief psychol. services Mass. Mental Health Center, Boston, 1960-63; instr. Harvard, 1961-63; rsch. assoc. Med. Sch., 1960-63; dir. rsch. S. Shore Mental Health Center, Quincy, Mass., 1962-66; assoc. prof. dept. psychology Tchrs. Coll., Columbia, N.Y.C., 1966-72; dir. Psychol. Consultation Center, 1966-72; chmn. bd., pres., psychologist Human Scis. Press, N.Y.C., 1972—; Lectr. L.I. U., summer 1958, Tufts U., 1961-62; mem. N.H. Gov.'s Com. on Spl. Edn., also Study Com. on Mental Health Reorgn., 1961-62; cons. VISTA program OEO, 1966-67; mem. juvenile problems research rev. com. NIMH, 1968-69; mem. research rev. com. Title III Elementary and Secondary Edn. Act project application Ohio Dept. Edn., 1969-72; mem. mental health coordinating com. local sch. dist. 5, N.Y.C., 1969-72; mem., research dir. work incentive program for welfare recipients Wharton Sch. Pa., U.S. Dept. Labor, 1969-72; mem. mental health and community control com. N.Y. Psychologists for Social Action, 1969-72. Authors, editor books.; Editor: Mass. Psychol. Assn. Newsletter, 1963-65, Community Mental Health Jour; contbr. articles to profl. jours. and chpts. to books. Chmn. bd. trustees Bristol Acres Sch., Taunton, Mass., 1965-67. Fellow Am. Psychol. Assn. (mem. com. pre-coll. behavioral scis. 1968-71, founder div. 27 community psychology div. 1969, chmn. subcom. pre-high sch. behavioral sci. 1969-72), Am. Pub. Health Assn., Am. Orthopsychiat. Assn. (com. on research edn. 1965-67), Am. Sociol. Assn.; mem. New Eng. Psychol. Assn. (steering com. 1965-68), N.H. Psychol. Assn. (legis. chmn. 1961-62). Office: 3205 Beacon St Pompano Beach FL 33062-1207

ROENICK, JEREMY, professional hockey player; b. Boston, Jan. 17, 1970. Center Chgo. Blackhawks, 1988—. Named The Sporting News NHL Rookie of the Yr., 1989-90. Played in NHL All-Star Games, 1991-94. Office: Chgo Blackhawks 1901 W Madison St Chicago IL 60612-2459*

ROEPER, RICHARD, columnist; b. Chgo., Oct. 17, 1959; s. Robert and Margaret R. BA, Ill. State U., 1982. Freelance writer, 1982-87; columnist Chgo.-Sun Times, 1987—; talk show host Sta. WLS-FM, Chgo.; commentator Fox Thing in the Morning, Sta. WFLD-TV, Fox TV, Chgo. Recipient Outstanding Columnist Ill. Press Assn., 1992, Nat. Headliner award for top columnist Atlantic City Press Club, 1992, Emmy award, 1994. Mem. Am. Fedn. TV & Radio Artists, Chgo. Newspaper Guild. Office: Chgo Sun-Times 401 N Wabash Ave Chicago IL 60611-5642*

ROER, ROBERT DAVID, physiologist, educator; b. N.Y.C., Oct. 15, 1952; s. Edwin Marvin and Dorothy Barbara (Blaymore) R.; m. Marjorie Elizabeth Smith, May 29, 1976; 1 child, Sara Elizabeth. BS, Brown U., 1974; PhD, Duke U., 1979. Asst. prof. U. N.C., Wilmington, 1979-85, assoc. prof., 1985-90, prof., 1990—. Contbr. articles to various jours. and publs. Grantee NSF, NASA, N.C. Biotech. Ctr., N.C. Sea Grant. Mem. AAUP, Am. Physiol. Soc., Soc. Interactive & Comp. Biology, Crustacean Soc., Sigma Xi. Office: Univ North Carolina 601 S College Rd Wilmington NC 28403-3297

ROESCH, CLARENCE HENRY, banker; b. Egg Harbor City, N.J., Aug. 22, 1925; s. Joseph Aloysius and Bertha (Heumann) R.; m. Helen Regina Owens, Sept. 25, 1954; children: Kathleen Marie, Helena Patricia, Maryanne Cornelia. BBA, Rutgers U., 1949, postgrad., 1961; certificate, Am. Inst. Banking, 1961; grad., Trust Sch., Bucknell U., 1971. Cert. internal auditor, data processing auditor. Bookkeeper, teller, head teller, asst. sec., trust officer, auditor Egg Harbor Bank & Trust Co., 1949-61; bank examiner Phila. Fed. Res. Bank, 1962-65; chief auditor Am. Bank & Trust Co. of Pa. (name changed to Meridian Bancorp Inc. 1985), Reading, 1966—, v.p. audit dept., 1968-88; ret. officer Am. Bank & Trust Co. of Pa. (name changed to Meridian Bancorp Inc. 1985), 1988; parish sec. St. Benedict Ch., Plowville, 1989—; sr. staff auditor Nat. Penn Bank, Boyertown, 1990—; mem. faculty Berks County chpt. Am. Inst. Banking, 1966-68; instr. bank auditing Bank Adminstrn. Inst., U. Richmond, 1968; pres., past mems. chpt. Am. Banking Inst., Atlantic County, N.J., 1958-59. Budget com. Berks County chpt. United Way, 1967-73; bd. dirs. Berks Reading Coun. Camp Fire, 1966-93, chmn. fin. com., 1973, 75, treas., 1974-84; instr. 55 Alive Program AARP, 1989-93. Recipient John Johnston award as outstanding banker N.J., 1955; award U.S. Savs. Bond Com., 1961; Luther Halsey Gulick award for vol. services Camp Fire, 1975; John C. Collier award for outstanding bus. and fin. services, 1981, Blue Ribbon award for vol. services Camp Fire, 1984, award for corp. vol. of yr. Meridian Bancorp Inc., 1984, 85, Outstanding Svc. in Fin. Mgmt. award Camp Fire, 1988. Mem. Inst. Internal Auditors (dir. ctrl. Pa. chpt.), Berks County Bankers Assn., Travelers Protective Assn., Berks Reading C. of C., Bank Administration Inst. (past pres., dir. Penn-Jersey chpt.), Spring Lawn Optimist Club (bd. dirs. 1992, Key Mem. award 1992, chmn. fin. and budget com. 1992-94). Home: 24 Medinah Dr Flying Hills Reading PA 19607

ROESELER, WOLFGANG GUENTHER JOACHIM, city planner; b. Berlin, Mar. 30, 1925; s. Karl Ludwig and Therese (Guenther) Ph.D., Philipps State U. of Hesse, Marburg, W.Ger., 1946-49; LL.B., Blackstone Sch. Law, Chgo., 1958; m. Eva Maria Jante, Mar. 12, 1947; children—Marion, Joanie, Karl. Asso. planner Kansas City (Mo.) Planning Commn., 1950-52; city planning dir. City of Palm Springs, Calif., 1952-54; sr. city planner Kansas City, 1954-56; prin. assoc. Ladislas Segoe & Assos., Cin., 1956-64; dir. urban and regional planning Howard, Needles, Tammen & Bergendoff, cons. Kansas City, N.Y.C., 1964-68; owner W.G. Roeseler, Cons. City Planner and Transp. Specialist, Bryan, Tex., 1969—; head dept. urban and regional planning Tex. A&M U., 1975-81, 85-88, prof., 1975-90, dir. Tex. A&M Ctr. Urban Affairs, 1984-88, exec. officer for edn. College of Architecture, 1987-88, prof. emeritus, 1990—. Fellow Inst. Transport Engrs.; mem. Am. Inst. Cert. Planners (life mem.), Am. Planning Assn., Transport Planners Coun., Urban Land Inst. Author: Successful American Urban Plans, 1982. Contbr. articles to profl. jours. Home: 2508 Broadmoor PO Box 4007 Bryan TX 77805-4007 Office: Tex A&M U PO Box 4007 College Station TX 77844-4007

ROESLER, JOHN BRUCE, lawyer; b. Portland, Oreg., Oct. 9, 1943; s. Bruce Emil Roesler and Charlotte Amanda (Naess) Ledger; m. Kathryne Elise Nilsen, Aug. 14, 1965 (dec. July 1974); children: Paul, Mark; m. Gloria Ruiz, Oct. 15, 1988; children: Joaquin, Nico. BA, U. Kans., 1966, JD, 1971. Bar: Mo. 1971, N.Mex. 1979, U.S. Dist. Ct. (we. dist.) Mo. 1971, U.S. Dist. Ct. N.Mex. 1979, U.S. Ct. Appeals (10th cir.) 1979, U.S. Ct. Appeals (5th cir.) 1988, U.S. Ct. Appeals (4th cir.) 1992, U.S. Supreme Ct. 1987. Assoc. Gage & Tucker, Kansas City, Mo., 1971-74; civil rights advocate State of N.Mex. Human Rights, Santa Fe, 1977-78; law clk. Hon. Edwin L. Felter N.Mex. Supreme Ct., Santa Fe, 1978-79; asst. dist. atty. Taos (N.Mex.) Dist. Atty.'s Office, 1979-80; asst. spl. pros. Santa Fe Dist. Atty.'s Office, 1980-82;

pvt. practice, 1982—; instr. John Marshall Law Sch., Chgo., summer 1974; spkr. civil rights and children's rights issues U. Miami Sch. Law, 1991, U. Miami Sch. Medicine, 1991. Author: (books) How To Find the Best Lawyers, In Harm's Way: Is Your Child Safe in School; mem. law rev. com. U. Kans. Sch. Law, 1970-71; contbr. articles to profl. jours. and treatise. Speaker convention Nat. Com. for the Prevention of Child Abuse, 1988, 89, 90. Mem. N.Mex. Bar Assn., N.Mex. Trial Lawyers Assn. Democrat. Roman Catholic. Avocation: skiing. Home: 1384 Santa Rosa Dr Santa Fe NM 87505 Office: 347 E Palace Ave Santa Fe NM 87501-2275

ROESLER, ROBERT HARRY, city official; b. Hammond, La., Oct. 5, 1927; s. Albert N. and Hilda (Schwartz) R.; m. Cloe Alferez, May 7, 1955; children: Kim, Bob, Toby. Student, Tulane U. Mem. sports staff Times Picayune, New Orleans, 1949-94, sports editor, 1964-80; exec. sports editor Times Picayune and States-Item, 1980-94; sports coord. New Orleans Met. Conv. and Visitors Bur., 1994—; CEO Roesler Media Cons. Vice chmn. Navy Recruiting Dist.; mem. assistance coun., New Orleans, 1992—. With USN, WWII, Korean conflict. Mem. Profl. Football Writers Assn. Am. (pres. 1976-77), Nat. Turf Writers Assn., Football Writers Am., Am. Legion, Navy League U.S., New Orleans Press Club (pres. 1959-60, sports writing awards). Home: 6958 Colbert St New Orleans LA 70124-2334 Office: 1520 Sugar Bowl Dr New Orleans LA 70112-1255

ROESNER, LARRY AUGUST, civil engineer; b. Denver, Mar. 14, 1941; s. Walter George and Sarah Jane (Merrick) R.; m. Kathleen Ann Fahrenbruch, Dec. 13, 1964; children: David John, Kevin Walter, Nathan August, Melissa Jane. B.S., Valparaiso (Ind.) U., 1963; M.S., Colo. State U., 1965; Ph.D., U. Wash., Seattle, 1969. Registered profl. engr., Calif., Mich., Va., Md., Fla., Ohio. Part-time grad. research asst. Colo. State U., 1963-65, U. Wash., 1965-68; assoc. engr., then prin. engr. Water Resources Engrs., Inc., Walnut Creek, Calif., 1968-77; assoc., then v.p. Camp Ovesser & McKee Inc., Annandale, Va., 1977-85; sr. v.p. and dir. water resources Camp Ovesser & McKee Inc., Maitland, Fla., 1985-92, chief tech. officer, 1992—; chmn. Engr. Found. Conf. on Current Practice and Design Criteria Urban Runoff Quality Controls, 1988; guest lectr., cons. urban hydrology and surface water quality; invited lectr. NATO Adv. Rsch. Conf. on Urban Runoff Pollution, 1985; NRC exec. com. Wastewater Mgmt. in Urban Coastal Areas, 1992; urban wet weather adv. com. Water Environ. Rsch. Fedn.; U.S. del. to joint IHR/IAWQ com. on urban drainage. Author rsch. reports, tech. revs., contbg. author on urban hydrology in several books. Fellow ASCE (chmn. 1995 water resources planning and mgmt. div. splty. conf., nat. Walter L. Huber civil engrng. rsch. prize 1975); mem. NAE, Am. Acad. Environ. Engrs. (diplomate), Am. Water Resources Assn., Am. Cons. Engrs. Assn., Water Environ. Fedn. (chmn. urban quality runoff task force), Tau Beta Pi (eminent engr.). Republican. Lutheran. Achievements include development of several widely used mathematical models for U.S. government agencies including QUAL-II stream quality model for the EPA; STORM, an urban stormwater management model for the U.S. Army CE; SWMM-EXTRAN, a dynamic hydraulics model for storm drainage and sewer systems for the EPA. Home: 205 Wild Creek Ct Longwood FL 32779-3351 Office: Camp Dresser & McKee Inc Ste 300 2301 Maitland Center Pkwy Maitland FL 32751-7422 *An environmental engineer is a caretaker in God's garden, the earth. The challenge for the environmental engineer is to maintain a balance between the needs of man and those of nature so that man may both use and enjoy the garden. It is the responsibility of the environmental engineer to leave the garden a little nicer than he found it.*

ROESNER, PETER LOWELL, manufacturing company executive; b. Winchester, Ind., July 3, 1937; s. Lowell LeClair and Martha Christine (Overmyer) R.; children: Peter Lowell II, David Brandon, John Franklin. Student, Durham (Eng.) U., 1957-58; B.A., DePauw U., 1959; J.D., U. Mich., 1962; M.B.A., Harvard U., 1964. Bar: Ind. 1962, N.J. 1992. Asst. to pres. Overmyer Corp., Muncie, Ind., 1964-65, corp. sec., 1965-69, pres., 1969-84, also dir.; pres. Clinitemp Inc., Indpls., 1985-88; pres., owner Middletown (N.J.) Interiors Inc., 1993—; dir. Mchts. Nat. Bank, 1974-84. Trustee Purdue U., 1978. Mem. Ind. Mfrs. Assn. (dir. 1970-82, pres. 1975, chmn. Phoenix Award com. 1974), Glass Packaging Inst. (trustee 1981-84), ABA. Episcopalian. Office: Middletown Interiors 1270 Highway 35 Middletown NJ 07748-2014

ROESS, ROGER PETER, engineering educator; b. Flushing, N.Y., Dec. 12, 1947; s. Charles Gordon and Theresa (Welchner) R.; m. Janet Elaine Mitchell, July 4, 1970; children: Roger Michael, Christopher John. BCE, Poly. Inst. N.Y., Bklyn., 1968, MS in Transp. Planning, 1969, PhD in Transp. Planning, 1972. Instr. Poly. Inst. N.Y., 1969-72, asst. prof., 1972-77, assoc., 1977-83, prof., 1983-86; prof. Poly. U., Bklyn., 1986—, dean engrng., 1984-95, 96—, assoc. provost acad. affairs, 1990-93; v.p. for academic affairs Poly U., Bklyn., 1993-95, v.p. acad. ops., 1996—. Contbr. articles to profl. jours. Vice pres. Garden City South Little League, N.Y., 1981-87; trustee Franklin Sq. Bd. Edn., N.Y., 1984-90, 94—. Recipient D. Grant Mickle award Transp. Research Bd., 1979. Mem. Transp. Rsch. Bd (hwy. capacity and quality service com. 1985-96), Inst. Transp. Engrs. (assoc.),Sigma Xi, Chi Epsilon, Tau Beta Pi. Office: Poly U Dept Civil-Environ Engring Brooklyn NY 11201-2907

ROESSER, JEAN WOLBERG, state legislator; b. Washington, May 8, 1930; d. Solomon Harry Wolberg and Mary Frances Brown; m. Eugene Francis Roesser, Aug. 3, 1957; children: Eugene Francis, Jr., Mary Roesser Calderon, Anne. BA, Trinity Coll., Washington, 1951; postgrad. in econs., Cath. U. of Am., 1951-53. Congl. relations asst. U.S. Info. Agy., Washington, 1954-58; news reporter for Montgomery County Coun., Suburban Record, 1983-86; del. Md. Gen. Assembly, Annapolis, 1986-94; mem. State Senate, Md. Gen. Assembly, Annapolis, 1994—, mem. fin. com., ethics com., 1994—; joint comm. state econ. devel. initiatives 1995—; joint com. welfare reform 1996—; spl. joint com. on group homes, 1995—, joint com. health-care delivery & financing, 1996—, joint budget & audit com., 1997—. Former mem. Md. Gov.'s Task Force on Energy; former pres. Montgomery County Fedn. Rep. Women, Potomac Women's Rep. Club; former 3d v.p. Md. Fedn. Rep. Women; founding mem. Montgomery County Arts Coun.; alt. del. Rep. Nat. Conv., 1992, del., 1996. Recipient Cmty. Achievement awrd Washington Psychiat. Soc., 1994, Trinity Coll. Leadership award, 1994, Common Cause Md. award, 1993, Md. Underage Drinking Preventio Coalition award, 1994, Legislator of the Yr. award Montgomery County Med. Soc., 1996. Mem. Women Legislators Md., also area citizens assns. and chambers commerce. Republican. Roman Catholic. Home: 10830 Fox Hunt Ln Potomac MD 20854-1553 Office: James Senate Office Bldg 110 College Ave Annapolis MD 21401-8012

ROESSLER, CAROL ANN, state senator; b. Madison, Wis., Jan. 16, 1948; d. John J. and Lucile E. (Kraner) Murphy. BS, U. Wis., Oshkosh, 1972. Dir. nutrition program for older adults County of Winnebago, Wis., 1973-82; mem. Wis. Ho. of Reps., Madison, 1983-87, Wis. Senate, Madison, 1987—; instr. pre-retirement planning Fox Valley Tech. Inst., 1978-81. Bd. dirs. Oshkosh Found., 1976-82. Home: 1506 Jackson St Oshkosh WI 54901-2942 Office: State Senate State Capital Madison WI 53707

ROESSLER, RONALD JAMES, lawyer; b. Kansas City, Mo., Aug. 10, 1939; s. Robert Louis and Eleanor Florence (Ramsdell) R.; m. Sally Jo Canfield, Aug. 18, 1962; children: Martha Lee, Elizabeth Ramsdell. BA in Govt., Miami U., 1961; postgrad. Law Sch., Duke U., 1961-62; JD, Wis. Law Sch., 1964; LLM, George Washington U., 1968. Bar: Wis. 1964, D.C. 1970, W.Va. 1971, Md. 1972, N.Y. 1985. Atty. Dept. Agr., Washington, 1964-66, Office Gen. Counsel, CIA, Washington, 1966, 68-69, C & P Tel. Co., Washington, 1969-72; sr. v.p., gen. counsel Alexander & Alexander Services Inc., N.Y.C., 1972-94; sr. counsel Rollins Hudig Hall, N.Y.C., 1995—; adj. prof. bus. law Towson State U., 1981-82. Trustee Bryn Mawr Sch., Balt., 1980-83. Served with USAF, 1966-68. Mem. ABA, Wis. Bar Assn., D.C. Bar Assn., W. Va. Bar Assn., Md. Bar Assn., Assn. of Bar of City of N.Y. Home: 15 Ferncliff Rd Cos Cob CT 06807-1206 Office: Rollins Hudig Hall Two World Trade Ctr New York NY 10048

ROESSNER, BARBARA, journalist; b. Elizabeth, N.J., Sept. 16, 1953; d. Gilbert George and Dorothy Anne (Hector) R.; m. Craig William Baggott, Jan. 20, 1982; children: Craig, Taylor, Liam, Katherine, Elizabeth. BA, Wesleyan U., 1975. Reporter, editor Meriden (Conn.) Record-Jour., 1975-78; reporter The Hartford (Conn.) Courant, 1978-81, chief polit. writer, 1981-86, columnist, 1986—; column distributed worldwide by L.A. Times-Washington Post News Svc. Recipient Best Mag. Column award Soc. Profl. Journalists, 1993, Best Mag. Feature award, 1993. Home: 22 Vanderbilt Rd West Hartford CT 06119-1341 Office: Hartford Courant Co 285 Broad St Hartford CT 06115-2500*

ROETHE, JAMES NORTON, lawyer; b. Milw., Jan. 27, 1942; s. Arthur Frantz and Bess Irma (Norton) R.; m. Nita May Dorris, July 15, 1967; children: Melissa Dorris, Sarah Rebecca. BBA, U. Wis.-Madison, 1964, JD, 1967. Bar: Wis. 1967, U.S. Dist. Ct. (we. dist.) Wis. 1967, Calif. 1968, U.S. Dist. Ct. (no. dist.) Calif. 1972, U.S. Ct. Claims 1975, U.S. Ct. Appeals (9th cir.) 1980, U.S. Dist. Ct. (ea. dist.) Calif. 1982, U.S. Dist. Ct. (cent. dist.) Calif. 1986, U.S. Ct. Appeals (4th cir.) 1988, U.S. Ct. Appeals (2nd cir.) 1989. Assoc., Pillsbury, Madison & Sutro, San Francisco, 1971-77, ptnr., 1978-92; sr. v.p., dir. litigation, Bank of Am., San Francisco, 1992-96, exec. v.p., gen. counsel, 1996—; staff atty. Commn. on CIA Activities within U.S., Washington, 1975. Editor: Africa, 1967; editor-in-chief Wis. Law Rev., 1966-67. Bd. dirs. Orinda Assn. (Calif.), 1984-85, pres. 1986. Commr. City Orinda Planning Commn., 1988-94, chmn., 1990, 93; bd. dirs. Calif. Shakespeare Festival, 1993—; bd. visitors U. Wis. Law Sch., 1994—. Served to lt. USNR, 1967-71. Fellow Am. Bar Found.; mem. ABA, Wis. Bar Assn., Calif. Bar Assn., Bar Assn. San Francisco, Orinda Country Club, Phi Kappa Phi, Order of Coif. Republican. Home: 36 Fallen Leaf Ter Orinda CA 94563-1209 Office: Bank of Am Legal Dept 555 California St San Francisco CA 94104

ROETHEL, DAVID ALBERT HILL, consultant; b. Milw., Feb. 17, 1926; s. Albert John and Elsie Margaret (Hill) R.; children: Elizabeth Jane, Susan Margaret. BS, Marquette U., 1950, MS, 1952; cert., Oak Ridge Sch. Reactor Tech., 1953. Chem. engr. naval reactors br. AEC, Washington, 1952-57; mgr. profl. relations, asst. to exec. sec. Am. Chem. Soc., Washington, 1957-72; exec. dir. Nat. Registry in Clin. Chemistry, Washington, 1967-72, Am. Assn. Clin. Chemists, Washington, 1968-70, Am. Orthotic and Prosthetic Assn., 1973-76, Am. Acad. Orthotists and Prosthetists, Am. Bd. Cert. in Orthotics and Prosthetics, 1973-76; exec. dir., fellow Am. Inst. Chemists, Washington, 1977-90; bd. dirs., exec. com. Am. Inst. Chemists, 1981-90, exec. dir. Nat. Certification Commn. in Chemistry and Chem. Engring., 1977-90, exec. dir., trustee Am. Inst. Chemists Found., 1982-90, sec., 1990; pres. Peachtree Promotions, 1991—; dir. Chemical Heritage Found., 1992—; v.p., treas. Cons. Consortium, 1994—; sec., vice chmn., then chmn. Intersoc. Com. on Health Lab. Svcs., 1966-72; v.p. Pensions for Profls., Inc., Washington, 1970-72; vice chmn., then chmn. Engrs. and Scientists Joint Commn. on Pensions, 1978-80, vice chmn., 1985-87, chmn., 1988-90, 94-95, sec., 1996—; mem. Commn. Profls. in Sci. and Tech., 1978-96, sec.-treas., 1979-82, bd. dirs., 1989-96, v.p., 1990-91, exec. com., 1990-93, 95; sec. gen. 7th Internat. Congress in Orthotics and Prosthetics, 1975-76, 2d World Congress in Prosthetics and Orthotics, 1975-77; chmn. U.S. arrangements Can.-Am. Chem. Congress, 1982-84; bd. dirs. China-U.S. Sci. Exchanges, 1985-89. Editor: Almanac, 1973-76, Chemist, 1977-90. Mem. Md. Gov.'s Com. on Sci. Devel., 1969; bd. dirs. Episcopal Ctr. for Children, 1991-97, sec., 1992-93, pres., 1993-95. Served with U.S. Army, 1944-46, CBI. Recipient Outstanding Svc. award Intersoc. Com. on Health Lab. Svcs., 1972, Appreciation awards Nat. Reg. in Clin. Chemistry, 1972, Engrs. and Sci. Ctr. on Pensions, 1996. Mem. Am. Chem. Soc. (dir. fed. credit union 1967-70, pres. 1968-70), Coun. Engring. and Sci. Soc. Execs. (bd. dirs. 1983-86), Am. Inst. Chemists, D.C. Inst. Chemists (sec. 1992-94, pres.-elect 1995—), Sports Car Am. Club (bd. dirs. 1964-67, 75-77, vice chmn., sec. 1967, 75-76, local officer 1960-74, historian 1989—), Alpha Chi Sigma (pres. Washington profl. chpt. 1963-64, 89-90, 95—, bd. dirs. 1991—, Profl. Achievement award 1986, bd. mgrs. 1986-90, dist. counselor 1964-68, nat. profl. rep. 1986-92, 96—, grand prof. alchemist 1992-94), Sigma Gamma Chi, Pi Mu Epsilon.

ROETHENMUND, OTTO EMIL, financial and banking executive; b. Thun, Switzerland, Sept. 1, 1928; came to U.S., 1951, naturalized, 1957; s. Franz and Berta (Dallenbach) R.; m. Ermina Grassi, May 7, 1955; children—Robert, Denise. M.A., U. Neuchatel, 1948. Mgmt. trainee Kantonalbank, Bern, 1948-51; exec. trainee J. Henry Schroeder Banking and Trust Corp., N.Y.C., 1951-56; with Deak-Perera Group, N.Y.C., 1956—; vice chmn., group partner Deak-Perera Group, 1962—; v.p., then sr. v.p. Deak & Co. (holding co.), 1962-74, exec. v.p., 1974-80, pres., chief exec. officer, 1980-86; pres., dir. Inter-Nation Capital Mgmt. Corp., 1986—; lectr. internat. monetary and investment seminars. Served to lt. Swiss Army, 1948-51. Decorated knight Mil. Order Sts. Salvador and Brigitta (Sweden). Mem. Explorers Club, Met. Club (N.Y.C.), Westchester Country Club. Home: 2 Shore Rd Rye NY 10580-1031 Office: Inter-Nation Capital Mgmt Corp 230 Park Ave Rm 650 New York NY 10169-0699

ROETMAN, ORVIL M., retired airplane company executive; b. Slayton, Minn., Aug. 28, 1925; s. Ernest Gilbert and Olava (Christianson) R.; m. Lavera Jones, Mar. 14, 1948; 1 child, Debra Roetman Caldwell. BA, U. Minn., 1950; BS in Aerospace Engring., U.S. Naval Post Grad. Sch., 1955; JD, George Washington U., 1965; postgrad. Naval War Coll., 1961. Bar: D.C., 1966. Commd. ensign U.S. Navy, 1945, advanced through grades to comdr., 1962, ret., 1965; sole practice law, Washington, 1965-66; in legal services Boeing Co., Seattle, 1966-67, dir. contract adminstrn., 1968, dir. internat. sales, 1971-79, v.p. internat. sales, 1979-83, v.p. contracts, 1983-87, corp. v.p. govt. and internat. affairs, 1988-90, ret., 1990; bd. dirs. higher edn. Concordia U. Sys.

ROETT, RIORDAN, political science educator, consultant; b. N.Y.C., Sept. 10, 1938; s. Riordan Jr. and Marion (Underwood) R. BA, Columbia U., 1959; MIA, 1962, PhD, 1968. Postdoctoral fellow Ctr. for Internat. Studies, MIT, Cambridge, Mass., 1966-67; asst. prof., assoc. prof. polit. sci. Vanderbilt U., Nashville, 1967-73; prof. polit. sci. Sch. Advanced Internat. Studies, Johns Hopkins U., Washington, 1973—; sr. polit. analyst internat. capital markets Chase Manhattan Bank, N.Y.C., 1983-95; sr. advisor World Econ. Forum, Geneva; bd. dirs. Global Ptnrs. Income Fund, Emerging Markets Income Fund I & II, Salomon Bros. Worldwide Income Fund, Emerging Markets Floating Rate Fund, Salomon Bros. 2008 Worldwide Dollar Govt. Term Trut. Editor, co-author: Latin America, Western Europe, and the U.S.: Reevaluating the Atlantic Triangle, 1985, Mexico and the U.S.: Managing the Relationship, 1988, Paraguay: The Legacy of Personalist Politics, 1990, Mexico's External Relations in the 1990's, 1991, Political and Economic Liberalization in Mexico, 1993, The Challenge of Institutional Reform in Mexico, 1995. Fulbright fellow, 1962. Mem. Latin Am. Studies Assn. (v.p. 1977, pres. 1978), Coun. on Fgn. Rels., Cosmos Club. Democrat. Roman Catholic. Home: 2301 Connecticut Ave NW Apt 1B Washington DC 20008-1730 Office: Johns Hopkins U SAIS 1740 Massachusetts Ave NW Washington DC 20036-1903

ROETZEL, DANNY NILE, lawyer; b. Hancock, Mich., July 6, 1952; s. J.D. and Deva Dale (Butler) R.; m. Zenobia Ann Kennedy, Sept. 30, 1973. BS, SUNY, 1980; MA, Ctrl. Mich. U., 1987; JD cum laude, St. Louis U., 1987, MA, 1989. Bar: Mo. 1987. Youth counselor Mo. Divsn. Youth Svcs., Jefferson City, 1973-77; juvenile parole officer Mo. Divsn. Youth Svcs., Kansas City, 1977-79; facility mgr. II Mo. Divsn. Youth Svcs., Jefferson City, 1979-84; spl. cons. to dean Sch. Bus. and Adminstrn. St. Louis U., 1984-87; law clk. to chief magistrate U.S. Dist. Ct. (ea. dist.) Mo., St. Louis, 1987-89; staff atty. U.S. Ct. Appeals (8th cir.), St. Louis, 1989-90; spl. asst. U.S. Atty. U.S. Dist. Ct. (ea. dist.) Va., 1990-91; trial atty. criminal enforcement sect. tax divsn. U.S. Dept. Justice, Washington, 1990, 91—; spl. asst. U.S. Atty. U.S. Dist. Ct. (so. dist.) Calif., 1992—. Active White County Young Dems., Searcy, Ark., 1970-71, Harding U. Young Dems., 1970-71; exec. officer North St. Louis County Young Dems., 1985-87. Mem. Mo. Bar Assn., Sigma Iota Epsilon, Phi Alpha Delta. Avocations: reading history, travel. Home: 6107 Havener House Way Centreville VA 20120-3270 Office: US Dept Justice Tax Divsn Criminal Enforcement Sect Tenth Constitution Ave NE Washington DC 20530-0001

ROFF, ALAN LEE, lawyer, consultant; b. Winfield, Kans., July 2, 1936; s. Roy Darlis and Mildred Marie (Goodaile) R.; m. Sonyia Ruth Anderson, Feb. 8, 1954; 1 child, Cynthia Lee Roff Edwards; m. Molly Gek Neo Tan, July 21, 1980. BA with honors and distinction, U. Kans., 1964, JD with distinction, 1966. Bar: Okla. 1967. Staff atty. Phillips Petroleum Co., Bartlesville, Okla., 1966-75, sr. atty., 1976-85, sr. counsel, 1986-94; cons. in Asia, 1995—. Mem. editl. bd. Kans. Law Rev., 1965-66. Precinct com. man Rep. Party, Lawrence, Kans., 1963-64; assoc. justice Kans. U. Chancery Club; mem. Kans. U. Young Reps. Elizabeth Reeder scholar U. Kans., 1965-66, Eldon Wallingford award, 1964-66. Mem. ABA, Okla. Bar Assn., Washington County Bar Assn., Phoenix Club (Bartlesville) (bd. dirs. 1985-86, gen. counsel 1986-91), Order of the Coif, Masons, Phi Alpha Delta, Pi Sigma Alpha. Mem. First Christian Ch. Avocation: travel. Home and Office: 2247 Mountain Dr Bartlesville OK 74003-6924

ROFF, J(OHN) HUGH, JR., energy company executive; b. Wewoka, Okla., Oct. 27, 1931; s. Hugh and Louise Roff; m. Ann Green, Dec. 23, 1956; children—John, Charles, Andrew, Elizabeth, Jennifer. A.B., U. Okla., 1954, LL.B., 1955. Bar: Okla., Mo., N.Y. Law clk. to presiding justice U.S. Ct. Appeals (10th cir.), 1958; atty. Southwestern Bell Telephone Co., St. Louis, 1959-63, AT&T, N.Y.C., 1964-68; v.p., gen. atty. Long Lines, N.Y.C., 1969-73, gen. atty., 1973-74; chmn., pres., chief exec. officer United Energy Resources, Houston, 1974-86; chmn. PetroUnited Terminals Inc., Houston, 1986—. Past chmn. Cen. Houston Inc.; mem. adv. bd. Ctr. for Strategic and Internat. Studies, Washington; mem. coun. overseers Jones Sch. Bus. Adminstrn., Rice U.; trustee Baylor Coll. Medicine; chmn. adv. bd. The Salvation Army, Houston. 1st lt. JACG, U.S. Army, 1955-58. Mem. Order of Coif, Phi Beta Kappa, Beta Theta Pi. Clubs: Houston Country, Coronado, Houstonian. Office: 333 Clay St Ste 4300 Houston TX 77002-4103

ROFF, WILLIAM ROBERT, history educator, writer; b. Glasgow, Scotland, May 2, 1929; came to U.S., 1969; s. Robert Henry William and Isabella (Anderson) R.; m. Susanne Rabbitt, Aug. 2, 1978; children: Sarah, Emily. B.A., U. New Zealand, 1957, M.A., 1959, Ph.D., Australian Nat. U., 1965. Lectr. history Monash U., Australia, 1963-66; lectr., sr. lectr. U. Malaya, Malaysia, 1966-69; assoc. prof. Columbia U., N.Y.C., 1969-73, prof., 1973-90, prof. emeritus, 1990—; vis. prof. Yale U., 1971, L'Ecole des Hautes Etudes en Sciences Sociales, Paris, 1985; vis. fellow Australian Nat. U., 1974, Trinity Coll., Oxford U., Eng., 1981; hon. fellow Edinburgh U., Scotland, 1992—. Author: The Origins of Malay Nationalism, 1967, (with others) In Search of Southeast Asia, 1971, Bibliography of Malay and Arabic Periodicals, 1972; author, editor: Kelantan: Religion, Society and Politics, 1973; editor: Islam and the Political Economy of Meaning, 1987. Guggenheim Found. fellow 1973; Rockefeller Found. fellow, 1982. Mem. Royal Asiatic Soc. (life), Assn. for Asian Studies, Asian Studies Assn. Australia, Brit. Soc. for Middle East Studies, Middle East Studies Assn. Avocation: parenting. Home: 29 Shore St, Cellardyke Fife, Scotland

ROFFE-STEINROTTER, DIANN, Olympic athlete. Silver medalist, Giant Slalom Albertville Olympic Games, 1992. Silver medalist Giant Slalom, Albertville Olympic Games, 1992, Gold medalist Super-G, Lillehammar Olympic Games, 1994. Address: PO Box 611 Potsdam NY 13676-0611 Office: US Skiing 1500 Kearns Blvd PO Box 100 Park City UT 84060*

ROFFMAN, HOWARD, motion picture company executive; b. Phila.. Student, U. Pa.; JD, U. Fla. Assoc. Morgan, Lewis & Bockius, Washington; from legal counsel to gen. counsel Lucasfilm, Ltd., San Rafael, Calif., 1980-84, acting chief operating officer, 1984-85, v.p. licensing, 1986—. Author: Presumed Guilty, 1974, Understanding the Cold War, 1976, The Edge of Desire, 1995, Three, 1996. Mem. Calif. Bar Assn., Washington Bar Assn., Licensing Industry Merchandising Assn. Office: Lucasfilm Ltd PO Box 2009 San Rafael CA 94912-2009

ROGAL, PHILIP JAMES, physician; b. N.Y.C., Dec. 23, 1939; s. Abraham and Cecilia (Sandor) R.; m. Susan Regan, June 17, 1967; Michael James, Elizabeth. BA, Princeton (N.J.) U., 1960; MD, Columbia U., 1964. Diplomate Am. Bd. Internal Medicine, Am. Bd. Cardiology. Intern Yale-New Haven Hosp., 1964-65; resident Bellevue Hosp., N.Y.C., 1965-67, Presbyn. Hosp., N.Y.C., 1967-68; fellow Bronx Mcpl. Hosp., 1970-71; pvt. practice internist, cardiologist N.Y.C., 1971-88, Tampa, Fla., 1988—; admissions com. Albert Einstein Coll. of Medicine, N.Y.C., 1983-88; chief of medicine Meml. Hosp., Tampa, 1995—. Capt. USAF, 1968-70. Fellow Am. Coll. Cardiology; mem. ACP, Alpha Omega Alpha. Avocations: squash racquets, tennis, travel, music. Office: Palma Ceia Med Group 2919 W Swann Ave Ste 106 Tampa FL 33609-4049

ROGALSKI, CAROL JEAN, clinical psychologist, educator; b. Chgo., Sept. 25, 1937; d. Casimir Joseph and Lillian Valentine Rogalski. BS, Loyola U., Chgo., 1961; PhD, NYU, 1968; cert. in psychoanalysis, Postgrad. Ctr. Mental Health, 1973. Lic. clin. psychologist, N.Y., Ill. Rsch. assoc. William Alanson White Inst., N.Y.C., 1961-66; rsch. asst., intern Hillside Hosp., Glen Oaks, N.Y., 1966-68; cons. Mt. Sinai Hosp., N.Y.C., 1968-73; staff psychologist Westside VA Hosp., Chgo., 1974—; clin. asst. prof. psychiatry Med. Sch. U. Ill., 1996—. Mem. editorial bd. Internat. Jour. Addictions, 1994—; contbr. articles to profl. publs. Mem. APA, Communal Studies Assn., Chgo. Soc. for Psychotherapy Rsch. (chair 1988-91). Avocation: watercolors. Office: Westside VA Hosp 820 S Damen Ave Chicago IL 60612-3728

ROGALSKI, EDWARD J., university administrator; b. Manville, N.J., Feb. 16, 1942; s. Joseph Stanley and Wladyslawa (Kraszewski) R.; m. Barbara Ann Bogk, June 01, 1968; children: Edward, James, Daniel, David, Christopher. BA, Parsons Coll., 1965; MA, U. Iowa, 1968, PhD, 1985; LittD (hon.), Loras Coll., 1990. Dean of men, asst. dean of students Parsons Coll., Fairfield, Iowa, 1965-67; dean of students St. Ambrose Coll., Davenport, Iowa, 1968-74, v.p. adminstrn., 1974-80, sr. v.p., 1980-86, exec. v.p., 1986-87; pres. St. Ambrose U., Davenport, 1987—; bd. dirs., corp. sec. Genesis Med. Ctr., 1994—; bd. dirs. Firstar Bank Davenport N.A.; corp. sec. ednl. div. Marriott Corp., 1988—. Vice chairperson Civil Rights Commn., Davenport, 1975; bd. dirs. Handicapped Devel. Ctr., Davenport, 1987, Jr. Achievement, 1988, Big Brothers-Big Sisters, 1988, Iowa Coll. Found., 1992—. Grantee Kettering Found., 1968. Mem. Iowa Assn. Ind. Colls. and Univs. (exec. com., treas. 1992—), Am. Assn. Higher Edn., Davenport C. of C. (bd. dirs. 1992), Rotary, Phi Delta Kappa. Roman Catholic. Home: 806 W Rusholme St Davenport IA 52804-1928 Office: St Ambrose U 518 W Locust St Davenport IA 52803-2829*

ROGALSKI, LOIS ANN, speech and language pathologist; b. Bklyn.; d. Louis J. and Filomena Evelyn (Maro) Giordano; m. Stephen James Rogalski, Jun e 27, 1970; children: Keri Anne, Stefan Louis, Christopher James, Rebecca Blair, Gregory Alexander. BA, Bklyn. Coll., 1968; MA, U. Mass., 1969; PhD., NYU, 1975. Lic. speech and lang. pathologist, N.Y. Speech, lang. and voice pathologist Rehab. Ctr. of So. Fairfield County, Stamford, Conn., 1969, Sch. Health Program-P.A. 481, Stamford, 1969-72; pvt. practice speech, lang. and voice pathology Sch. Health Program-P.A. 481, Scarsdale, N.Y., 1972—; cons. Bd. Coop. Ednl. Svcs., 1976-79, Handicapped Program for Preschoolers for Alcott Montessori Sch., Ardsley, N.Y., 1978—; rsch. methodologist Burke Rehab. Ctr., 1977. Mem. profl. adv. bd. Found. for Children with Learning Disabilities, 1978—; bd. dirs. United Way of Scarsdale-Edgemont, 1988-89; instr. religious instr. CCD Immaculate Heart of Mary Ch., Scarsdale, 1991—. Fellow Rehab. Svcs. Adminstrn., 1968-69; N.Y. Med. Coll., 1972-75. Mem. N.Y. Speech & Hearing Assn., Westchester Speech & Hearing Assn., Am. Speech, Hearing & Lang. Assn. (cert. clin. competence), Coun. for Exceptional Children, Assn. on Mental Deficiency, Am. Acad. Pvt. Practice in Speech Pathology & Audiology (bd. dirs., treas. 1983-87, pres. 1987-89), Internat. Assn. Logopedics & Phoniatrics, Sigma Alpha Eta. Office: PO Box 1242 Scarsdale NY 10583-9242

ROGAN, ELEANOR GROENIGER, cancer researcher, educator; b. Cin., Nov. 25, 1942; d. Louis Martin and Esther (Levinson) G.; m. William John Robert Rogan, June 12, 1965 (div. 1970); 1 child, Elizabeth Rebecca. AB, Mt. Holyoke Coll., 1963; PhD, Johns Hopkins, 1968. Lectr. Goucher Coll., Towson, Md., 1968-69; rsch. assoc. U. Tenn., Knoxville, 1969-73; rsch. assoc. U. Nebr. Med. Ctr., Omaha, 1973-76, asst. prof., 1976-80, assoc. prof. Eppley Inst., dept. pharm. scis. and dept. biochemistry and molecular biology scis., U. Nebr., 1980-90, prof., 1990—. Contbr. articles to profl. jours. Predoctoral fellow USPHS, Johns Hopkins U., 1965-68. Mem. AAAS, AAUP, Am. Assn. Cancer Rsch., Am. Soc. Biochem. Molecular Biology. Democrat. Roman Catholic. Home: 8210 Bowie Dr Omaha NE 68114-1526 Office: U Nebr Med Ctr Eppley Inst 600 S 42nd St Omaha NE 68198-1002

ROGATZ, PETER, physician; b. N.Y.C., Aug. 5, 1926; s. Julian and Sally (Levy) R.; m. Marjorie Plaut, June 10, 1949; children—Peggy Joy, William Peter. B.A., Columbia Coll., 1945; M.D., Cornell U., 1949; M.P.H., Columbia U., 1956. Intern Lenox Hill Hosp., N.Y.C., 1949-50; resident Lenox Hill Hosp., 1950-51, VA Hosp., Bronx, N.Y., 1951-52, N.Y. Hosp., N.Y.C., 1952-53; dep. dir. Montefiore Hosp., N.Y.C., 1960-63; dir. L.I. Jewish Med. Center, 1964-68, Univ. Hosp., SUNY, Stony Brook, 1968-71; sr. v.p. Blue Cross/Blue Shield of Greater N.Y., 1971-76; prin., founding ptnr. RMR Health and Hosp. Mgmt. Cons., Inc., Roslyn Heights, N.Y., 1976-84; v.p. med. affairs Vis. Nurse Service, N.Y., 1984-91; med. dir. Staff Builders, Inc., 1992—; prof. cmty. medicine SUNY, Stony Brook, 1968—; mem. N.Y.C. Mayor's Commn. on Delivery of Health Svcs., 1967; v.p. Health and Welfare Coun. of Nassau County, 1968-72; bd. dirs. Cmty. Coun. Greater N.Y., 1974-77; mem. Task Force on N.Y.C. Crisis, 1976-81; chmn. bd. dirs. Cmty. Health Program (affiliated with L.I. Jewish Med. Ctr.), 1989-94; chmn. bd. dirs. Managed Health Inc., 1990-94. Author: Organized Home Medical Care in New York City, 1956, (with Eli Ginzberg) Planning for Better Hospital Care, 1961; mem. editorial bd.: Preventive Medicine, 1975-81; contbr. articles to profl. jours. Bd. dirs. Choice in Dying, 1994—. Commonwealth Fund fellow, 1955; recipient Dean Conley award Am. Coll. Hosp. Adminstrs., 1975. Fellow ACP, N.Y. Acad. Medicine, Am. Public Health Assn., Am. Coll. Preventive Medicine; mem. Am. Hosp. Assn., N.Y. Public Health Assn., AMA, N.Y. State Med. Soc., N.Y. County Med. Soc. Home and Office: 76 Oakdale Ln Roslyn Heights NY 11577-1535

ROGENESS, MARY SPEER, state legislator; b. Kansas City, Kans., May 18, 1941; d. Frederic A. and Jeannette (Hybskmann) Speer; m. Dean Rogeness, Aug. 31, 1964; children: Emily, James, Paul. BA, Carleton Coll., 1963. Computer analyst Dept. Def., Ft. Meade, Md., 1963-66; freelance writer, editor Longmeadow, Mass., 1982-91; mem. Mass. Ho. of Reps., Boston, 1991—. Editor: Reflections of Longmeadow, 1983. Mem. Longmeadow Rep. Town Com., 1983—; Mass. alt. del. Rep. Nat. Conv., Houston, 1992. Mem. Am. Legis. Exch. Coun., World Affairs Coun. of Western Mass. (bd. dirs. 1990-96—), Goodwill-Industries Hartford-Springfield (bd. dirs. 1996—). Office: Mass House of Reps State House Boston MA 02133

ROGER, JERRY LEE, school system administrator; b. Chase, Kans., Mar. 11, 1945; s. LeRoy J. and Lottie E. (Maphet) R.; m. Tucky Saint Smith, 1995. BS, U. Tulsa, 1966, MA, 1969, EdD, 1975. Cert. tchr., supt., Okla. Math. tchr. Kansas City (Mo.) Pub. Schs., 1966-67, Shawnee Mission (Kans.) Pub. Schs., 1967-71; rsch. asst. Tulsa Pub. Schs., 1972-73, rsch. coord., 1973-81, adminstrv. asst., 1981-90, rsch. dir., 1990-95, dir. planning and assessment, 1995—; adj. instr. Tulsa Jr. Coll., 1975-88; adj. asst. prof. U. Tulsa, 1980-85. Contbr. book revs. to Tulsa Sunday World, 1990-92. Paul Harris fellow; Rotary benefactor. Mem. NEA, Nat. Book Critics Ctr., Nature Conservancy, The Nat. Conf., Phi Delta Kappa. Home: 3538 S Winston Ave Tulsa OK 74135 Office: Tulsa Pub Schs 3027 S New Haven Ave Tulsa OK 74114-6131

ROGERS, ALAN VICTOR, former career officer; b. Hannibal, Mo., Nov. 13, 1942; s. Julian Alan and Gladys Cuneo R.; m. Linda Rae Peterson, May 8, 1966; children: Kimberly Rae, Krista Anne, Peter Alan. BS in Mil. Sci., USAF Acad., 1964; MBA with distinction, Harvard Bus. Sch., 1972; grad. with distinction, Air War Coll., 1980. Commd. 2d lt. USAF, 1964, advanced through grades to maj. gen., 1989, ret., 1993; combat fighter pilot 355th Tactical Fighter Wing, Takhli, Thailand, 1966-67; jet pilot instr. Flying Tng. Wing, Williams AFB, Ariz., 1967-69; student Harvard Bus. Sch., Cambridge, Mass., 1970-72; pers. officer Cols. Group USAF Pentagon, Washington, 1972-75; student Air War Coll., Maxwell AFB, Ariz., 1980; wing comdr. 5th Bomb Wing, Minot AFB, N.D., 1982-84, 96th Bomb Wing (1st B-1 Wing), Dyess AFB, Tex., 1984-86; dir. ops. SAC, Offutt AFB, Nebr., 1986-89; asst. chief of staff ops. Supreme HQ Allied Powers Europe, Mons, Belgium, 1989-91; dir. J-7 Joint Staff, Washington, 1991-93; assoc. Burdeshaw Assocs., Ltd., Bethesda, Md., 1993-94; prin. Gemini Consulting, Morristown, N.J., 1994—. Mem., mil. adviser C. of C., Minot, N.D., 1982-84, Abilene, Tex. 1984-86. Decorated D.S.M., Legion of Merit, D.F.C. with two oak leaf clusters, Purple Heart. Mem. Air Force Assn., Red River Valley Fighter Pilots Assn., Nat. Eagle Scout Assn., Daedalians (chpt. pres. 1986). Republican. Roman Catholic. Avocations: skiing, travel, antiques. Home: 4600 N 32rd Rd Arlington VA 22207 Office: Gemini Consulting 25 Airport Rd Morristown NJ 07960-4624

ROGERS, ARTHUR HAMILTON, III, lawyer; b. Florence, S.C., Apr. 19, 1945; s. Arthur Hamilton Jr. and Suzanne (Wilson) R.; m. Karen Lyn Hess, June 22, 1968; children: Sarah Elizabeth, Thomas Hess. BA, Rice U., 1967; JD, Harvard U., 1970. Bar: Tex. 1970. Assoc. Fulbright & Jaworski LLP, Houston, 1970-74; participating assoc. Fulbright & Jaworski L.L.P., Houston, 1974-77; ptnr. Fulbright & Jaworski, L.L.P., Houston, 1977—; gen. counsel Lifemark Corp., Houston, 1981-82; sec. Mosher, Inc., Houston, 1984—. Dir. Alley Theatre, Houston, 1990—, Autry House, 1994-97; mem. exec. com. Rice U. Fund Coun., Houston, 1993—, vice-chair, 1996—. Mem. ABA, State Bar Tex., Assn. of Rice Alumni (treas. 1995—), Ramada-Tejas Club. Episcopalian. Home: 5309 Bordley Dr Houston TX 77056-2323 Office: Fulbright & Jaworski LLP 1301 Mckinney St Fl 51 Houston TX 77010-3031

ROGERS, BERNARD WILLIAM, military officer; b. Fairview, Kans., July 16, 1921; s. William Henry and Lora (Haynes) R.; m. Ann Ellen Jones, Dec. 28, 1944; children: Michael W., Diane E., Susan A. Student, Kans. State Coll., 1939-40; BS, U.S. Mil. Acad., 1943; BA (Rhodes scholar), Oxford (Eng.) U., 1950, MA, 1954, DCL (hon.), 1983; grad., Command and Gen. Staff Coll., 1954-55, Army War Coll., 1959-60; LLD, Akron U., 1978, Boston U., 1981. Commd. lt. U.S. Army, 1943, advanced through grades to gen., 1974; aide to supt. U.S. Mil. Acad., 1945-46, comdt. cadets, 1967-69; aide to high commr. Austria Gen. Mark W. Clark, 1946-47; bn. comdr. Korea, 1952; exec. to comdr.-in-chief Far East Command, 1953-54; mil. asst. to Chief Staff U.S. Army, 1956-59; exec. to chmn. (Joint Chiefs of Staff), 1962-66; asst. div. comdr. (1st Inf. Div.), Vietnam, 1966-67; comdg. gen. (5th Inf. Div.), Ft. Carson, Colo., 1969-70; chief legis. liaison Dept. Army, 1971-72, dep. chief of staff for personnel, 1972-74; comdg. gen. U.S. Army Forces Command, 1974-76; chief of staff U.S. Army, 1976-79; supreme allied comdr. Europe; comdr. in chief (U.S. European Command), 1979-87; ret. U.S. Army, 1987; former bd. dirs. Atlantic Coun. U.S., George C. Marshall Found., Gen. Dynamics Co., Kemper Nat. Ins. Co., Thomas Industries; former sr. cons. The Coca-Cola Co.; chmn. USO World Bd. of Govs., 1988-94. Decorated DSC, Def. DSM, DSM of Army, Navy and Air Force, Silver Star, Legion of Merit with 3 oak leaf clusters, D.F.C. with 2 oak leaf clusters, Bronze Star medal with V device; hon. fellow Univ. Coll., Oxford U.; recipient Disting. Svc. Citation U. Kans., 1984, Disting. Grad. award U.S. Mil. Acad., 1995. Mem. VFW, Assn. U.S. Army (bd. dirs.), Assn. Am. Rhodes Scholars, Soc. 1st Inf. Divsn., Am. Soc. French Legion of Honor, Ret. Officers Assn., Mil. Order of World Wars, The Pilgrims, Army-Navy Country Club, Army and Navy Club, Alfalfa, Phi Delta Theta.

ROGERS, BRIAN DEANE, librarian; b. New London, Conn., June 26, 1937; s. Albert Nash and Janette (Loofboro) R.; m. Carol Priscilla Mallett, May 18, 1962; children: Alison, Paul, Amy. BA, Alfred U., 1959; MLS, Rutgers U., 1967. Asst. registrar Salem (W. Va.) Coll., 1964-66; reference librarian Wesleyan U., Middletown, Conn., 1967-69, head pub. services, 1969-75; librarian Conn. Coll., New London, 1975-93, spl. collections libr., 1993—; Mem. State Adv. Council on Libraries, Hartford, 1976, chair 1977; mem. library bd. Mystic Seaport Maritime Mus., Mystic, Conn., 1987—. Mem. accreditation teams New England Assn. Sch. & Colls., 1985-90. Served with U.S. Army, 1961-64. Mem. ALA, Assn. Coll. and Research Libraries (com. on coll. library standards 1982-86), Beta Phi Mu. Clubs: Columbiad (Meriden, Conn.); Acorn (Hartford, Conn.). Home: 114 Library St Mystic CT 06355-2420 Office: Conn Coll Library 270 Mohegan Ave New London CT 06320-4125

ROGERS, BRYAN LEIGH, artist, art educator; b. Amarillo, Tex., Jan. 7, 1941; s. Bryan Austin and Virginia Leigh (Bull) R.; m. Cynthia Louise Rice; 1 child, Kyle Austin Rogers. BE, Yale U., 1963; MS, U. Calif., Berkeley, 1966, MA, 1969, PhD, 1971. Design engr. Monsanto Co., Texas City, Tex., 1962; research engr. Rocketdyne, Canoga Park, Calif., 1963-64; research scientist Lawrence Livermore (Calif.) Lab., 1966; lectr. U. Calif., Berkeley, 1972-73; fellow Akademie der Bildenden Künste, Munich, 1974-75; prof. art San Francisco State U., 1975-88; head profd. sch. art Carnegie Mellon U., Pitts., 1988—, dir. Studio for Creative Inquiry, 1989—; fellow Ctr. Advanced Visual Studies MIT, Cambridge, Mass, 1981. Editor Leonardo Jour., San Francisco, 1982-85. One-man shows include: Laguna Beach (Calif.) Mus. Art, 1974, DeSaisset Art Gallery U. Santa Clara, Calif., 1974, San Francisco Mus. Modern Art, 1974, Baxter Art Gallery Calif. Inst. Tech., Pasadena, 1979, Contemporary Crafts gallery, Portland, Oreg., 1987; group exhbns. include: Berkeley (Calif.) Art Ctr., 1969, Hansen-Fuller Gallery, San Francisco, 1970, San Francisco Arts Commn. Gallery, 1984, Clocktower Gallery, N.Y.C., 1984, Otis-Parsons Gallery, L.A., 1985, P.P.O.W. Gallery, N.Y.C., 1985, 18th Internat. Bienal, São Paulo, Brazil, 1985, MIT, Cambridge, 1990, Objects Gallery, Chgo., 1992, ARTEC 93 Internat Biennale, Nagoya, Japan, 1993, Chgo. Cultural Ctr., 1993, Am. Iron and Steel Expo., Pitts., 1993, Pitts. Ctr. for Arts, 1994, Allegheny Coll. Gallery, Meadville, Pa., 1997. Fellow NEA, Washington, 1981, 82, Deutscher Akademischer Austauschdienst, Fed. Republic of Germany, 1974, NSF, Washington, 1965-69; recipient SECA award San Francisco Mus. Modern Art, 1974. Office: Carnegie Mellon U Art Dept Pittsburgh PA 15213

ROGERS, C. B., lawyer; b. Birmingham, Ala., July 10, 1930; s. Claude B. Rogers and Doris (Hinkley) Rogers Lockerman; m. Patricia Maxwell DeVoe, Dec. 22, 1962; children: Bruce Lockerman, Evelyn Best, Brian DeVoe. A.B., Emory U., 1951, LL.B., 1953. Bar: Ga. 1953. Adj. prof. litigation Emory U., 1968-70; assoc., then partner firm Powell, Goldstein, Frazer & Murphy, 1954-76; partner firm Rogers & Hardin, Atlanta, 1976—. Fellow Am. Coll. Trial Lawyers; mem. Am. Law Inst., Capital City Club (Atlanta). Democrat. Episcopalian. Home: 1829 W Wesley Rd NW Atlanta GA 30327-2019 also: Brandon Mill Rd Lakemont GA 30335 Office: Rogers & Hardin 2700 International Tower 229 Peachtree St NE Atlanta GA 30303-1601

ROGERS, CHARLES EDWIN, physical chemistry educator; b. Rochester, N.Y., Dec. 29, 1929; s. Charles Harold and Maybelle (Johnson) R.; m. Barbara June Depuy, June 12, 1954; children: Gregory Newton, Linda Frances, Diana Suzanne. BS in Chemistry, Syracuse U., 1954; PhD in Phys. Chemistry, SUNY at Syracuse U., 1957. Rsch. assoc. dept. chemistry Princeton U., 1957-59, Goodyear fellow, 1957-59; mem. tech. staff Bell Telephone Labs., Murray Hill, N.J., 1959-65; assoc. prof. macromolecular sci. Case Western Res. U., Cleve., 1965-74, prof., 1974—; sr. vis. fellow Imperial Coll., U. London, 1971; assoc. dir. Ctr. for Adhesives Sealants Coatings, Case Western Res. U., 1984-88, dir., 1988-91; co-dir. Edison Polymer Innovation Corp., Ctr. for Adhesives, Sealants and Coatings, 1991—; cons. to polymer and chem. industries; devel. overseas ednl. instns. Editor: Permselective Membranes, 1971, Structure and Properties of Block Copolymers, 1977; contbr. numerous articles to profl. jours.; patentee in field. Served with U.S. Army, 1946-49. Mem. Am. Chem. Soc., Am. Phys. Soc., N.Am. Membrane Soc., Cleve. Coatings Soc., The Adhesion Soc. Home: 8400 Rockspring Dr Chagrin Falls OH 44023-4645 Office: Case Western Reserve U Dept Macromolecular Sc Cleveland OH 44106-7202

ROGERS, CHARLES RAY, minister, religious organization administrator; b. Grapevine, Tex., Nov. 26, 1935; s. Arlin Avery and Bessie Lorene (Deaton) R.; m. Oma Fay Hines, Aug. 21, 1954; children: Sheree Gay Rogers Saberjissa, Charles Denne Ray, Robin Celeste Rogers Eddins. MS in Christian Edn., Faith Bible Coll., 1980, DD in Humanities (hon.), 1981; D of Ministry in Humanities (hon.), Sem. of Theol. Missions, Escuintla, Guatemala, 1992. Pastor various Bapt. chs., Athens, Dallas, Ft. Worth, 1960-64, various interdenominational chs., Houston, Longview, 1965-69; pres. Evangelism in Action, Ft. Worth, 1969—; bd. dirs. World Ministry Fellowship, Plano, Tex., dir. world missions, 1970—; leader Over 100 Mission, humanitarian trips Evangelism in Action, Ft. Worth, 1976—. Author: Joy, 1979, Handbook for Victorious Living, 1980, How to Develop Christian Love, 1981; vocalist (rec.) Charlie, 1981. Republican. Avocations: golf, tennis, swimming, running, computers. Home: 6417 Rogers Dr Fort Worth TX 76180-4807 Office: Evangelism in Action PO Box 820724 Fort Worth TX 76182-0724

ROGERS, CHARLIE ELLIC, entomologist; b. Booneville, Ark., Aug. 13, 1938; s. Robert Wesley and Parthenia Fern (Mahoney) R.; m. Donna Carol Ray, Jan. 29, 1971; children: Christian Edward, Cheryl Elaine. BS, Northern Ariz. U., 1964; MS, U. Ky., 1967; PhD in Entomology, Okla. State U., 1970. Cert. entomologist. Tchr. biology, social studies Dysart Pub. Sch., Glendale, Ariz., 1964-65; grad. rsch. asst. U. Ky., Lexington, 1965-67; grad. rsch. asst. Okla. State U., Stillwater, 1967-70, postdoctoral rsch. assoc., 1970-71; asst. prof. agrl. exptl. station Tex. A&M U., College Station, 1971-75; rsch. entomologist SW Gt. Plains Rsch. Ctr., USDA Agrl. Rsch. Svc., Bushland, Tex., 1975-80; supervisory rsch. entomologist, rsch. leader Conservation & Prodn. Rsch. Ctr., USDA, Bushland, Tex., 1980-83; dir. Insect Biology and Population Mgmt. Rsch. Lab. Agrl. Rsch. Svc.-USDA, Tifton, Ga., 1983—; editor Biol. Control Acad. Press, San Diego, 1990—; rsch. com. Sunflower Assn. Am., Fargo, N.D., 1981-83; dir. elect Bd. Cert. Entomologist Entomol. Soc. Am., Lantham, Md., 1992. Author: Sunflower Species of the United States, 1982; co-editor: The Entomology of Indigenous and Naturalized Systems in Agriculture, 1988; editor: Biological Control, 1990—; contbr. articles to profl. publs. Sch. bd. mem. Bushland Ind. Sch. Dist., 1981-83; tchr. First Bapt. Ch., Tifton, 1986-91; mem. Rotary Club, Vernon, Tex., 1974-76. With U.S. Army, 1958-61. Recipient Profl. Excellence award Am. Agrl. Econ. Assn., 1979, Leadership award USDA, 1987, Profl. Svc. award Am. Registered Profl. Entomologists, 1987, Outstanding Performance award USDA, 1991, 95, Disting. Alumni award 1992. Mem. Entomol. Soc. Am. (bd. cert. entomologist, Disting. Svc. award certification program 1996), Ga. Entomol. Soc., Entomol. Soc. S.C, Sigma Xi, Tifton Club (pres. 1992-93). Republican. Baptist. Achievements include study of biology, ecology, and control of sheep nose bot, oestrus ovis; biology and augmentation of Propylea 14-punctata against the green bug; control of guar midge Conterina texana; control of insect pests of sunflowers; biology, taxonomy and pathogenicity of the nematode Noctuidonema. Home: 1711 Sarah Dr Tifton GA 31794-4287 Office: USDA/ARS Insect Biology & Population Mgmt Rsch Lab PO Box 748 Tifton GA 31793

ROGERS, DAVID, apparel executive. With Pickwick Internat., Mpls.; pres. Wilson's The Leather Experts, Inc., Brooklyn Park, Minn., 1979—. Office: Wilsons The Leather Experts Inc 7401 Boone Ave N Brooklyn Park MN 55428-1007

ROGERS, DAVID, playwright, novelist, actor; b. N.Y.C.; s. George and Deborah (Samuels) Rosenberg; m. June Lois Walker, Oct. 14, 1962; children—Dulcy Dru, Amanda Brooke. Student, Am. Theatre Wing Sch., 1948, 49. N.Y.C. prodns. include Ziegfld Follies, 1957, Vintage '60, 1960, New Faces of 1962, Fun City, 1967, Charlie and Algernon, 1980 (Tony award nomination); London prodns. include Jubilee Girl, 1956, Young at Heart, 1961, Flowers for Algernon, 1979, Killing Jessica, 1986; pub. plays include Tom Jones, 1964, Flowers for Algernon, 1969, Brave New World, 1970, F.L.I.P.P.E.D, 1971, Here and Now, 1973, Soft Soap, 1982, Rehearsal for Murder, 1983; pub. musicals include Best of Broadway, 1961, Cheaper by the Dozen, 1969, The Hobbit, 1972, The Truth About Cinderella, 1974, The Dream on Royal Street, 1981; TV The Hero; opera, 1966 (winner Prix d'Italia Concorso Internat. Per Opere Radiofoniche e Televisive), Carol Burnett show, 1970; novels Oh Eden, 1974, The Bedroom Set, 1976, Somewhere There's Music, 1977, The Great American Alimony Escape, 1979, The In-Laws, 1979; actor Broadway prodns. Doubles, 1985, George Abbott's Broadway, 1987, internat. tour Grand Hotel, 1991; regional theatre appearances include Players Theatre, Columbus, 1992, Birmingham (Mich.) Theatre, Jupiter (Fla.) Theatre, 1993, Great Lakes Theatre Festival, Cleve., 1994, Phoenix Theatre, Purchase, N.Y., 1995, Denver Ctr. Theatre Co., 1996. Served with U.S. Army, 1951-52, Korea. Mem. Dramatists Guild, Writers Guild Am. East, AFTRA, Broadcast Music Inc., Actors Equity. Club: Theatre Artists Workshop (Westport, Conn.) (bd. dirs. 1985).

ROGERS, DAVID HUGHES, finance executive; b. Chgo., May 21, 1947; s. Joseph Gordon and Viola Winifred (Hughes) R.; Bonnie Hope Sinai, 1997; children: Kristen Morgan, Loren Avery, Daniel Jay. BA, U. Mich., 1968; PhD, Columbia U., 1975. Economist Fed. Res. Bank of Cleve., 1974-75; asst. treas. B.F. Goodrich Co., Akron, Ohio, 1975-82; exec. v.p., chief fin. officer First Tex. Savs. Assn., Dallas, 1982-83; sr. exec. v.p., chief operating officer PriMerit Bank, Las Vegas, 1984-87, pres., dir., 1987-91; vice chmn., 1991-92; chief oper. officer The Baird Cos., Las Vegas, Nev., 1992—. Author: Consumer Banking in New York, 1975; also articles. Mem. exec. bd. Boulder Dam Area coun. Boy Scouts Am., 1986—; bd. dirs. Nev. Sch. arts, 1988—, Hebrew Acad., 1996—; chmn. Las Vegas Bus. Bank, 1995—. Office: The Baird Cos 1160 Town Center Dr Las Vegas NV 89134-0561

ROGERS, DESIREE GLAPION, utilities executive; b. New Orleans, June 16, 1959; d. Roy and Joyce Glapion; m. John Rogers, Jr.; 1 child, Victoria. B in Polit. Sci., Wellesley Coll., 1981; MBA, Harvard U., 1985. Customer svc. mktg. mgr. AT&T, N.J., 1985-87; dir. devel. Levy Orgn., Chgo., 1987-89; founder, pres. Mus. Ops. Consulting Assocs., Chgo., 1989-91; dir. Ill. State Lottery, Chgo., 1991-97; v.p. Peoples Energy Corp., Chgo., 1997—. Chmn. of the bd. The Chgo. Children's Mus.; bd. dirs. Mus. Sci. and Industry, Frances Xavier Warde Sch., WTTW/Ch. 11; bd. trustees Harvard Bus. Sch. Club Chgo.; bd. trustees Mus. Contemporary Art; sec. Marwen Found.; bd. dirs. Smithsonian, Nat. Mus. Nat. History. Mem. The Econ. Club, Harvard Bus. Sch. Club, Wellesley Club. Office: Peoples Energy Corp 130 E Randolph St Fl 18 Chicago IL 60601

ROGERS, DONALD ONIS, language educator; b. Springfield, Mo., Oct. 9, 1938; s. Onis Lee and Wilma (Gideon) R.; m. Mora Jeannine, Aug. 19, 1961; children—Donald Scott, Anne Margaret. B.S., SW Mo. State U., 1961; M.A., La. State U., 1968; Ph.D., Southwestern La. U., 1978. Lang. coordinator Ralls County Pub. Schs., Mo., 1961-66; grad. teaching asst. La. State U., Baton Rouge, 1966-68; asst. prof. La. State U., Eunice, 1968-74, assoc. prof., 1974-79, head div. liberal arts, dir. acad. affairs, 1973-78, prof. English, dean acad. affairs and services, 1979-91, prof. English, vice chancellor for acad. affairs, 1991-95. Bd. dirs. Bayouland Library System, 1974-78. Served with USNR, 1957-59. Mem. Ralls County Tchrs. Assn. (pres. 1965-66), Coll. English Assn., La. Council Tchrs. English, S.W. Regional Conf. English in 2-Yr. Colls., MLA, South Central MLA. Democrat. Home: PO Box 301 Cheneyville LA 71325-0301 Office: PO Box 1129 Eunice LA 70535-1129

ROGERS, DONALD PATRICK, business administration educator; b. Tucson, Aug. 28, 1947; s. Patrick Joseph and Pearl Anna (Howarter) R.; m. Fran Carlin, Aug. 3, 1974; children: Tracy Lynn, Anne Marie. BS, U. Ariz., 1969; MBA, Ohio U., 1971, PhD, 1973. Sales rep. TMC, Tucson, 1966-68; asst. prof. SUNY, Buffalo, 1972-78; assoc. prof. SUNY, Genesseo, 1978-87; prof. human resource mgmt. Rollins Coll., Winter Park, Fla., 1987—; dir. Survey Info. Rsch. Ctr., Geneseo, N.Y., 1978-87, dir. masters in human resources Rollins Coll., Winter Park, 1993—; rsch. cons. various cos., Winter Park, 1976—. Co-author: Auditing Organizational Communications, 1978; editor: Fundamental Concepts of Business, 1984, Contemporary Issues in Human Resource Management, 1994, Cases in Human Resource Management, 1995; co-editor: Integrated Business Analysis, 1985; contbr. articles to profl. publs. Mem. Acad. Mgmt. (divsn. chmn. 1982-83, svc. award 1993), Soc. Human Resource Mgmt., Am. Compensation Assn. Democrat. Office: Rollins Coll Holt Ave Winter Park FL 32789

ROGERS, EARL LESLIE, artist, educator; b. Oakland, Calif., July 8, 1918; s. Robert Ray and Addie Myrtle (Dice) R.; m. Eileen Estelle MacKenzie, Apr. 9, 1945; children: Leslie Eileen, Brian Donald (dec.). Student, L.A. Valley Coll., 1949-52, Northridge State U., 1958-59, UCLA Extension, 1967, Sergei Bongart Sch. Art, 1967-68; AA, Pierce Coll., 1958. Cert. tchr., Calif. Various positions City of L.A., Van Nuys, Calif., 1948-55, Reseda, Calif., 1955-68; pvt. practice Canoga Park, Calif., 1948-68; art tchr. Mariposa (Calif.) County High Sch., 1969-70; art instr. Merced (Calif.) County Coll., 1970—; instr. Earl Rogers Studio Workshop, Mariposa, Calif., 1969—; art dir. Yosemite Nat. Park, Calif., 1973; instr. art Asilomar Conf. Grounds, Pacific Grove, Calif., 1980; juror various art orgns., 1971-95; demonstrator Clovis (Calif.) Art Guild, 1971, 89, Sierra Artists, Mariposa, 1972, 81, 82, 84, 91, Merced Art League, 1976, Yosemite Western Artists, Oakhurst, Calif., 1973, Madera (Calif.) Art Assn., 1978, Chowchilla (Calif.) Art Guild, 1983, 86, 87, 89, 91, Soc. Western Artists, 1981, 89, 93. One-man shows include L.A. City Hall, 1968, Merced Coll., 1969, 95, Mariposa Title Co. Bldg., 1969, Coffee's Gallery, 1970, others; exhibited in group shows including West Valley Artists Assn., 1966-68, L.A. City Hall, 1967, Yosemite Nat. Park, 1973, Soc. Western Artists, 1977-78, Cannon Bldg. Rotunda, Washington, 1982, Mother Lode Gallery, Columbia, Calif., 1977, 78, Arbor Gallery, Merced, 1988, 96, Gold Country Gallery, 1990, 91, Merced Coll., 1969-92, 96, others; represented in permanent collections including John C. Freemont Hosp., Mariposa, Mariposa County Arts Coun., Mariposa Mus. and History Ctr. Asst. scout master Boy Scouts of Am., Canoga Park, Calif., 1956-58; art instr. L.A. Recreation Corps, L.A. Parks and Recreation Dept., 1967. Mem. Soc. Western Artists (Neva Rall Meml. award 1978), Mariposa Mus. and Hist. Ctr. (life), Pastel Soc. West Coast, Oil Painters of Am. Avocations: piano and books. Home and Office: 5323 State Highway 49 N Mariposa CA 95338-9503

ROGERS, EDWARD SAMUEL, communications company executive; b. Toronto, May 27, 1933; s. Edward Samuel and Velma Melissa (Taylor) R.; m. Loretta Anne Robinson, Sept. 25, 1963; children: Lisa Anne, Edward Samuel, Melinda Mary, Martha Loretta. BA, Trinity Coll., U. Toronto, 1956; LLB, Osgoode Hall Law Sch., 1961; DSc (hon.), Clarkson U., 1989; LLD (hon.), U. Victoria, 1990; LLD, York U., 1994. Bar: Ont., 1962. Founder, prin. Rogers Telecomm. Ltd., Toronto, 1960—; pres., CEO Rogers Comm. Inc., 1978—; vice-chmn. Rogers Cablesystems Ltd., Rogers Broadcasting Ltd.; bd. dirs. The Hull Group, The Toronto Dominion Bank, Can. Pub. Corp., Mercedes-Benz Can., Inc., Rogers Cable TV Ltd., Rogers Cablesystems Ltd., Rogers Broadcasting Ltd. Bd. dirs. Jr. Achievement Can. Mem. Royal Can. Yacht Club, Albany Club, Granite Club, York Club, Muskoka Golf & Country Club, Rideau Club Ottawa, Lyford Cay Club (gov.), Balboa Bay Club, Sigma Chi (Beta Omega chpt.). Progressive Conservative. Mem. Anglican Ch. Office: Rogers Comms Inc PO Box 1007, 40 King St W Ste 6400 Scotia Plz, Toronto, ON Canada M5H 3Y2

ROGERS, EDWIN EARL, newspaper editor; b. Carbondale, Pa., Sept. 7, 1929; s. William Earl and Jessie (Pethick) R.; m. Eleanor Louise Hopkins, Feb. 28, 1959; children: Karen, Kevin, Kyle, Kathryn. Sports editor News-Leader, Carbondale, Pa., 1944-46; bur. reporter, photographer The Scranton (Pa.) Tribune, 1946-51; bur. reporter, photographer The Scranton Times, 1953-54, reporter, 1954-66, state editor, 1966-73, city editor, 1973-80, mng. editor, 1980-95, editor Good Times for Srs., 1995—. Trustee Steamtown Found., Scranton, 1984; bd. dirs. Lackawanna County R.R. Authority, Scranton, 1984. Cpl. U.S. Army, 1951-53. Mem. Pa. Assn Press Mng. Editors (pres. 1985). Republican. Methodist. Avocations: railroading, travel. Office: The Scranton Times PO Box 3311 149 Penn Ave Scranton PA 18503

ROGERS, ELIZABETH BARLOW, urban planner, municipal park administrator; b. San Antonio, Feb. 6, 1936; d. Caleb Leonidas and Elizabeth (Ewing) Browning; m. Edward Lee Barlow, July 6, 1957 (div. 1979); children: Elizabeth Ewing, David Browning; m. Theodore Courtney Rogers, June 28, 1984. BA in Art History, Wellesley Coll., 1957; MA in City Planning, Yale U., 1964. Open space cons. Parks Council N.Y., 1965-69; legis. asst. N.Y. State Senate, 1967-68; freelance journalist, author, 1969-74; screenwriter Time-Life Film Series, N.Y.C., 1974-75; exec. dir. Central Park Task Force, N.Y.C., 1975-79; adminstr. N.Y.C. Dept. Parks and Recreation, 1979-95; founder, pres. Cen. Park Conservancy, 1980-95; pres. Cityscape Inst., 1996—. Author: The Forests and Wetlands of New York City, 1971, Frederick Law Olmsted's New York, 1972; co-author: East Hampton, A History and Guide, 1976, The Central Park Book, 1978, Rebuilding Central Park, A Management and Restoration Plan, 1985, others. Ptnr. N.Y.C. Partnership. Recipient John Burroughs medal, 1971, Honor award AIA, 1985, Urban Beautification award Am. Hort. Soc., 1987, Disting. Alumnae Achievement award Wellesley Coll., 1989, Hist. Preservation award and medal Garden Club Am., 1992, Citizen Leadership medal Nat. Park Found., 1994. Mem. Century Assn., Cosmopolitan Club, Georgica Assn. Home: 7 W 81st St New York NY 10024 Office: 121 Avenue Of The Americas New York NY 10013-1510

ROGERS, ERNEST MABRY, lawyer; b. Demopolis, Ala., Sept. 22, 1947; s. James B. and Ernestine B. (Brewer) R.; m. Jeanne Edwards, Dec. 15, 1979; children—Gilbert B., Katherine B., Mary C. B.A., Yale U., 1969; J.D., Harvard U., 1974. Bar: Ala. 1974, U.S. Dist. Ct. (no. dist.) Ala. 1975, U.S.

Ct. Appeals (5th cir.) 1976, U.S. Ct. Appeals (11th cir.) 1981, U.S. Supreme Ct. 1981, U.S. Ct. Claims 1983, U.S. Ct. Appeals (6th cir.) 1987. Law clk. to judge U.S. Dist. Ct. (no. dist.) Ala., 1974-75; ptnr. Bradley, Arant, Rose & White, Birmingham, Ala., 1981—. Contbr. articles to profl. jours. Fellow, Am. Coll. of Constrn. Lawyers. Episcopalian. Lodge: Kiwanis. Office: Bradley Arant Rose & White PO Box 830709 Birmingham AL 35283

ROGERS, EUGENE CHARLES, investment firm executive; b. Bklyn., Sept. 29, 1932; s. Eugene Aloysius and Agnes Hilda (Scharbach) R.; m. Anita Therese Tobin, May 13, 1961; 1 son, Eugene Charles. B.B.A., St. John's U., Bklyn., 1954; M.B.A., N.Y. U., 1960. C.P.A., N.Y. Staff accountant Haskins & Sells (C.P.A.s), N.Y.C., 1954-60, Bache & Co., N.Y.C., 1960-62; controller, then chief fin. officer Reynolds Securities Inc., N.Y.C., 1962-72; v.p., treas. Reynolds Securities Inc., 1972—; 1st v.p., treas. Dean Witter Reynolds Inc., 1978-81, sr. v.p., treas., 1981—; guest lectr., panelist in field. Bd. advisors Coll. Bus. Adminstrn., St. John's U. Served with U.S. Army, 1954-56. Mem. N.Y. State Soc. C.P.A.'s, Fin. Execs. Inst., Fin. Club of N.Y. U. Grad. Sch. Bus., Securities Industry Assn. (past pres. fin. mgmt. div.), Sun and Surf Beach Club, World Trade Ctr. Club, Hempstead Golf and Country Club. Roman Catholic. Home: 15 Whitby Ct Rockville Centre NY 11570-1641 Office: Dean Witter Reynolds Inc 2 World Trade Ctr New York NY 10048-0203

ROGERS, EUGENE JACK, medical educator; b. Vienna, Austria, June 13, 1921; came to U.S., 1937; s. Louis and Malvina (Haller) R.; m. Joyce M. Lighter, Feb. 9, 1952; children: Jay A., Robert J. B.S., CCNY; M.B., Chgo. Med. Sch., 1946, M.D., 1947. Diplomate Am. Bd. Phys. Medicine and Rehab. Intern Our Lady of Mercy Med. Ctr. and Cabrini Meml. Hosps., N.Y.C., 1946-48; resident Madigan Hosp., Tacoma, 1951, Mayo Clinic, Rochester, Minn., 1951, N.Y. Med. Coll. Met. Med. Ctr., 1953-55; USPHS fellow, 1955-56; ship's surgeon U.S. Lines, Grace Lines, N.Y.C., 1948-49; indsl. physician Abraham & Strauss Stores, Bklyn., 1949-51; practice medicine specializing in phys. medicine and rehab. Bklyn., 1956-73; dir. rehab. service, attending physician N.Y. City Hosp. Dept., 1955-73; prof. and chmn. dept. rehab. medicine Chgo. Med. Sch., North Chicago, Ill., 1973—; cons. N.Y.C. Mayor's Adv. Com. for Aged, 1957; asst. prof. SUNY Downstate Med. Sch., Bklyn., 1958-73; med. dir. Schwab Rehab. Hosp., Chgo., 1973-75; acting chief rehab. service VA Center, North Chicago, 1975-77; chmn. Ill. Phys. Therapy Exam. Com., 1977-78; examiner Am. Bd. Phys. Medicine and Rehab., 1983; sec., dir. Microtherapeutics, Inc., 1972. Editor: Total Cancer Care, 1975; contbr. articles to med. jours.; contbg. editor Ill. Med. Jour., 1983-89. Served to capt. U.S. Army, 1951-53. Recipient Bronze medal Am. Congress Rehab. Medicine, 1974. Fellow ACP, Am. Acad. Phys. Medicine and Rehab. (Cert. of Appreciation 1993); mem. Ill. Med. Soc. (chmn. workmen's compensation com. 1980-83), Ill. Soc. Phys. Medicine and Rehab. (pres. 1983-84), Chgo. Med. Sch. Faculty Assembly (spkr. 1978-80), Chgo. Med. Sch. Alumni Assn. (exec. com., asst. treas. 1983-93, treas. 1993—, sec. 1995—, Presdl. plaque Greater N.Y. chpt., Disting. Alumnus award 1980), Odd Fellows (pres. 1961-62), Alpha Omega Alpha, Phi Lambda Kappa (trustee 1980). Home: 1110 N Lake Shore Dr Chicago IL 60611-1054 Office: Finch U Health Scis Chgo Med Sch 3333 Green Bay Rd North Chicago IL 60064-3037 *To render good medical care: Prevent disease, evaluate the patient, treat the condition, educate patient and family, restore function.*

ROGERS, FRANCES NICHOLS, assistant principal; b. Fontana Dam, N.C., July 25, 1944; d. Fred Edward and Violet Bernice (Slagle) Nichols; m. Terry William Rogers, July 3, 1970. BA in English, Berea Coll., 1966; MA in Elem. Edn., U. Ky., 1968; postgrad., U. N.C., 1992. Tchr. intern Breathitt County Schs., Jackson, Ky., 1966-68; tchr. elem. sch. Haywood County Schs., Waynesville, N.C., 1968-72, resource program developer, 1972-75, 77-83, asst. prin., 1983-89, 92—, prin., 1989-92; pres. Haywood County Chpt. N.C. Edn. Assn., 1969-70. Author: Mount Zion United Methodist Church: A History 1850-1982, 1982; author of poems; contbr. articles to profl. jours. Mem. Friends of Libr., Waynesville, 1980—, Haywood Animal Welfare Assn., Waynesville, 1980—, Youth for Christ, Waynesville, 1980—. Named Outstanding Young Educator Waynesville Jaycees, 1968-69, Leader of Am. Elem. Edn., 1971. Mem. ASCD (N.C. sect.), Tarheel Assn. Prins. and Adminstrs., Haywood County Prins. Assn., Internat. Reading Assn. (sec. local chpt. 1973-74). Methodist. Avocations: travel, reading, gardening. Home: 120 Arrowood Acres Rd Clyde NC 28721-9751

ROGERS, FRED BAKER, medical educator; b. Trenton, N.J., Aug. 25, 1926; s. Lawrence H. and Eliza C. (Thropp) R. A.A., Princeton U., 1947; M.D., Temple U., 1948; M.S. in Medicine, U. Pa., 1954; M.P.H., Columbia U., 1957; spl. student, Johns Hopkins U., 1962. Diplomate: Am. Bd. Preventive Medicine. Intern Temple U. Hosp., Phila., 1948-49; chief resident physician Temple U. Hosp., 1953-54; USPHS fellow Temple U. Sch. Medicine, 1954-55, asst. prof. preventive medicine, 1956-58, assoc. prof., 1958-60, prof., 1960-90, prof. emeritus, 1991—, chmn. dept., 1970-77; lectr. epidemiology Columbia U. Sch. Pub. Health, 1957-68, Sch. Nursing, U. Pa., 1964-67; cons. USN Hosp., Phila., 1964-73. Author: A Syllabus of Medical History, 1958, Help-Bringers: Versatile Physicians of N.J, 1960, Epidemiology and Communicable Disease Control, 1963, Studies in Epidemiology, 1965, (with A.R. Sayre) The Healing Art, 1966, (with M.E. Cashel) Your Body is Wonderfully Made, 1974; mem. editorial bd. Am. Jour. Pub. Health, 1967-73; contbr. articles to profl. jours. Served with M.C. USNR, 1950-53, Korea. Recipient Chapel of Four Chaplains award, 1982. Fellow ACP; mem. AMA (past chmn. sect. preventive medicine), Am. Pub. Health Assn., Royal Soc. Medicine of London (hon.), Sigma Xi, Alpha Omega Alpha, Phi Rho Sigma. Clubs: Campus (Princeton); Franklin Inn (Phila.); Charaka (N.Y.C.); Osler (London). Home: 333 W State St Trenton NJ 08618-5722 Office: Temple U Sch Medicine Philadelphia PA 19140

ROGERS, FRED MCFEELY, television producer and host; b. Latrobe, Pa., Mar. 20, 1928; s. James Hillis and Nancy (McFeely) Flagg; m. Sara Joanne Byrd, July 9, 1952; children: James Byrd, John Frederick. MusB, Rollins Coll., 1951; MDiv, Pitts. Theol. Sem., 1962; DHL (hon.), Thiel Coll., 1969; HHD (hon.), Eastern Mich. U., 1973; LittD (hon.), St. Vincent Coll., 1973; DD (hon.), Christian Theol. Sem., 1973, Washington and Jefferson Coll., 1984, Westminster Coll., 1987; LHD (hon.), Yale U., 1974, Lafayette Coll., 1977, Washington and Jefferson Coll., 1984, Linfield Coll., 1982, Duquesne U., 1982, Slippery Rock Coll., 1982, U. S.C., 1985, MacMurray Coll., 1986, Drury Coll., 1986, Bowling Green State U., 1987; DFA (hon.), Carnegie-Mellon U., 1976; MusD (hon.), Waynesburg Coll., 1978, U. Ind., 1988; LLD (hon.), Hobart and William Smith Colls., 1985, U. Conn., 1991, Ind. U., Pa., 1992, Boston U., 1992, Moravian Coll., 1992; hon. degree, Goucher Coll., 1993, U. Pitts., 1993, N.C. State, 1996; DHL(hon.), U. W.Va., 1995. Adj. prof. U. Pitts., 1976; pres. Family Communications, Inc., Pitts.; asst. producer NBC, N.Y.C., 1951-53; exec. producer Sta. WQED, Pitts., 1953-62; producer, host CBC, Toronto, Ont., 1962-64; exec. producer, host Mister Rogers' Neighborhood (PBS), Pitts., 1965—; prodr., host Old Friends, New Friends PBS interview series, 1979-81; host Fred Rogers' Heros PBS, 1994. Author: Mister Rogers Talks with Parents, 1983, Mister Rogers' First Experiences Books, 1985, Mister Rogers' Playbook, 1986, Mr. Rogers Talks About Divorce, 1987, Mister Rogers-How Families Grow, 1988, You are Special, 1994, Let's Talk About It: Divorce, 1995, Let's Talk About It: Adoption, 1996, Dear Mister Rogers, 1996; producer five audio cassettes of original songs-Many Ways to Say I Love You, audio cassettes Bedtime, 1992, Growing, 1992, You Are Special, 1995; composer: Mr. Rogers' Songbook; host, writer, producer five one hour videocassettes home videos CBS, 1987-88, eight 30 minute home videos, 1995-96. Chmn. child devel. and mass media forum White House Conf. on Children; mem. Esther Island Preserve Assn.; bd. dirs. McFeely Rogers Found.; hon. chmn. Nat. PTA, 1992-94. Recipient Peabody award for finest children's TV program; award for excellence in children's programming Nat. Ednl. TV; Emmy award, 1980; Ohio State award, 1983, ACT award, 1984, The Christopher award, 1984, Ga. Assn. Broadcasters award, 1984; Lamplighter award Ednl. Press. Assn. Am., 1985; Disting. Service award Spina Bifida Assn. Am., 1985; Children's Book Council award, 1985, Emmy award for outstanding writing in children's series, 1985, Assn. Childhood Edn. award, 1986; Director's award-Ohio State award, 1986; Gold medal Internat. Film and TV Festival, 1986, award Nat. Assn. State Dirs. Migrant Edn., 1987, Ollie award Am. Children's TV Festival, 1987, Immaculata (Pa.) Coll. medal, 1988, Bronze medal Internat. Film and TV Festival, 1988, Outstanding Pa. Author award, 1988, Parent's Choice award, 1987, 88, Spl. Recognition award Nat. Assn. Music Mchts., 1989, PBS award in recognition of 35 yrs. in pub. TV, 1989, Hall of Fame award Action for Children's TV, 1988, Man. of Yr. award Pitts. Vectors, 1990, Peabody award, 1993, Disting Svc. medal, Colgate Rochester Divinity Sch., 1994, Eleanor Roosevelt Val-Kill medal, 1994, Joseph F. Mulach, Jr. award, 1995, Great Friend to Kids award Coun. and Membership of Assn. of Youth, 1996, Chmn.'s award NATPE, 1997, Outstanding Achievement award Pitts. Film Workers Assn., 1997, Lifetime Achievement Emmy award, 1997, Emmy for outstanding performer in children's series, 1997. Mem. Luxor Ministerial Assn., Nat. Assn. TV Program Execs. Presbyterian. Office: 4802 5th Ave Pittsburgh PA 15213-2957 *Every person in this life is so much more than meets the eye or ear. I'm continually surprised at the complexity of all those whom I'm fortunate enough really to get to know.*

ROGERS, GARTH WINFIELD, lawyer; b. Fort Collins, Colo., Nov. 4, 1938; s. Harlan Winfield and Helen Marie (Orr) R.; m. Joanne Kathleen Rapp, June 16, 1962; children: Todd Winfield, Christopher Jay, Gregory Lynn, Clay Charles. BS, U. Colo., 1958, LLB, 1962. Bar: Colo. 1962; U.S. Dist. Ct. Colo. 1962. Law clk. to presiding justice U.S. Dist. Ct., Denver, 1962-63; assoc. Allen, Stover & Mitchell, Ft. Collins, 1963-68; ptnr. Allen, Rogers & Vahrenwald, Ft. Collins, 1968—. Articles editor Rocky Mountain Law Rev., 1961-62. Bd. advs. Salvation Army, Ft. Collins; past bd. dirs. United Way of Ft. Collins, Trinity Luth. Ch., Ft. Collins, others. Mem. Ft. Collins C. of C. (past bd. dirs.), ABA, Colo. Bar Assn., Larimer County Bar Assn. Avocations: Nicaragua projects, participative sports, amateur writing, reading. Office: Allen Rogers & Varenwald 125 S Howes St Fort Collins CO 80521-2737

ROGERS, HAROLD DALLAS (HAL ROGERS), congressman; b. Barrier, KY, Dec. 31, 1937; m. Shirley McDowell, 1957; children: Anthony, Allison, John Marshall. BA, U. Ky., 1962, LLB, 1964. Bar: Ky. 1964. Pvt. practice Somerset, Ky., 1967-69; Commonwealth atty. Pulaski and Rockcastle counties, Ky., 1969-80; mem. 97th-105th Congresses from 5th Dist. Ky., 1981—; mem. appropriations com., subcom. commerce and justice, energy and water. Mem. appropriations coms. Ky. N.G., 1957-64. Republican. Office: US Ho of Reps 2468 Rayburn Bldg Washington DC 20515-1705*

ROGERS, HOWARD H., chemist; b. N.Y.C., Dec. 26, 1926; s. Julian Herbert and Minnie (Jaffa) R.; m. Barbara Kniaz, Mar. 27, 1954 (div. 1978); children: Lynne, Mark David, Susan; m. Maureen Dohn, Dec. 28, 1978. BS in Chemistry, U. Ill., 1949; PhD in Inorganic Chemistry, MIT, 1953. Research group leader Allis-Chalmers Mfg. Co., West Allis, Wis., 1952-61; sr. tech. specialist Rocketdyne div., Rockwell, Canoga Park, Calif., 1961-70; chief research scientist Martek Instruments, Newport Beach, Calif., 1970-73; sr. scientist, engr. Hughes Electronics Co., Torrance, Calif., 1973—. Developer nickel-hydrogen battery; patentee; contbr. sci. papers to profl. publs. in field. Served with USN, 1944-46. Recipient Lawrence A. Hyland Patent award Hughes Aircraft Co., 1987. Mem. Electrochem. Soc. (chmn. So. Calif./Nev. sect. 1976-78), Am. Chem. Soc., Sigma Xi. Home: 18361 Van Ness Ave Torrance CA 90504-5309 Office: Hughes Electronics Co B231/1720 PO Box 2999 Torrance CA 90509-2999 *In my 70 years of living experience I have found that these two items are vital: focus on what you intend to do, not what you have already done; complete honesty to yourself and to others in interpreting and reporting results is mandatory.*

ROGERS, ISABEL WOOD, religious studies educator; b. Tallahassee, Aug. 26, 1924; d. William Hudson and Mary Thornton (Wood) R. BA, Fla. State U., 1945; MA, U. Va., 1947; MRE, Presbyn. Sch. Christian Edn., 1949; PhD, Duke U., 1961; DD (hon.), Austin Coll., 1986; LLD (hon.), Westminster Coll., 1988; LHD, Centre Coll., 1989. Campus min. 1st Presbyn. Ch., Milledgeville, Ga., 1949-52; campus chaplain Ga. Coll., Milledgville, 1952-61; prof. of applied Christianity Presbyn. Sch. Christian Edn., Richmond, Va., 1961—; elder Ginter Pk. Presbyn. Ch., Richmond, 1976-79, 89—; moderator of Gen. Assembly, Presbyn. Ch. U.S.A., 1987-88; lectr. Presbyn. chs. Author: The Christian and World Affairs, 1965, In Response to God, 1969, Our Shared Earth, 1980, Sing A New Song, 1981. Vol. Richmond Community Action Program, 1968-75, YWCA, Women's Advocacy Program, 1982—; bd. dirs. Presbyn. Outlook Found., Richmond, 1987—. Du Pont fellow U. Va., 1946. 47, Kearns fellow Duke U. Mem. Soc. Christian Ethics, Phi Kappa Phi, Phi Beta Kappa. Democrat. Avocations: hiking, jogging, tennis, gardening, stamp collecting. Home and Office: Presbyn Sch Christian Edn 1205 Palmyra Ave Richmond VA 23227-4417

ROGERS, JACK DAVID, plant pathologist, educator; b. Point Pleasant, W.Va., Sept. 3, 1937; s. Jack and Thelma Grace (Coon) R.; m. Belle C. Spencer, June 7, 1958. BS in Biology, Davis and Elkins Coll., 1960; MF, Duke U., 1960; PhD, U. Wis., 1963. From asst. prof. to prof. Wash. State U., Pullman, 1963-72, chmn. dept. plant pathology, 1986—. Contbr. articles to profl. jours. Recipient William H. Weston Teaching Excellence award Mycological Soc. Am., 1992. mem. Mycological Soc. of Am. (pres., 1977-78), Am. Phytopathol. Soc., Botanical Soc. Am., British Mycological Soc.

ROGERS, JAMES ALBERT, lawyer; b. Chgo., May 15, 1944; s. Albert Lee and Edith Jane (Magee) R.; m. Jane Austin Pughe, May 14, 1967 (div. 1980); m. Ellen Sheriff, Sept. 26, 1987; children: Alison Sheriff, Emily Sheriff. B.A., Carleton Coll., 1966; J.D., U. Mich., 1969. Bar: Minn. 1969, Wis. 1971, D.C. 1975. Law clk. Justice C. Donald Peterson, Supreme Ct. of Minn., 1969-70; asst. atty. gen. State of Wis., 1971-73; assoc. gen. counsel water and solid waste U.S. EPA, 1977-80; ptnr., head environment dept. Skadden, Arps, Slate, Meagher & Flom, Washington, 1981-91; ptnr., head environment group Wilmer, Cutler & Pickering, Washington, 1991—. Contbr. articles to profl. jours. Recipient Presidential award for meritorious sr. exec. service Pres. Carter, 1980. Mem. D.C. Bar Assn., Minn. Bar Assn., Wis. Bar Assn., Environ. Law Inst. (bd. dirs. 1982—, chmn. bd. 1987-90), Am. Law Inst. Democrat. Office: Wilmer Cutler & Pickering 2445 M St NW Washington DC 20037-1435

ROGERS, JAMES CURTIS, publisher, psychologist, screenwriter; b. Sandston, Va., May 21, 1930; s. James Allen and Julia Pollard (Curtis) R. BA, U. Calif., Berkeley, 1961; BS, William and Mary Coll.; MA, Columbia Pacific, PhD. Sec., treas., CEO Rojet Theatre Co., Atlanta, 1954; prof. Capitol Radio and Electronics Inst., Washington, 1955; tech. writer Guided Missile Rocket dept. RCA Svc. Co., Alexandria, Va., Cherry Hill, N.J.; sec., treas., CEO Hawkeye Records, Iowa City, Iowa, 1961-63; tchr. Calvert County H.S., Prince Frederick, Md., 1964; child protective officer Social Svc. Bur., Richmond, Va., 1964-68; head master Lyceum Ednl. Com., Gloucester, Va., 1968-70; pub. Lyceum Publs., Richmond, Va., 1968-92; producer, agt. YoungStar Prodns., Richmond, 1989-91; pub., editor FutureWend Publs., Richmond, 1991—; ethics cons. The Matrism Orgn., Richmond, 1988—; publs. officer U.S. Coast GuardAux., Richmond, 1986-87. Author: Foreign Language With a Smile, 1965—, The Kidnapping, 1995; editor It's Your Choice Mag., 1993; author plays. Adminstr. Julie and Jim Rogers scholarship fund, Richmond, 1988—; scoutmaster Robert E. Lee Coun., Boy Scouts Am., Richmond, 1948-52, sea scout skipper, 1948-52; dir. Children's Theatre Project, Berkeley, 1959. Mem. Thalian Soc., Am. Inst. Hypnosis, Coll. Med. Hypnotists. Avocations: piano/organ public performance, foreign languages. Office: FutureWend Publs 733 Hindry Ave Inglewood CA 90301-3005

ROGERS, JAMES DEVITT, judge; b. Mpls., May 5, 1929; s. Harold Neil and Dorothy (Devitt) R.; m. Leanna Morrison, Oct. 19, 1968. AB, Dartmouth Coll., 1951; JD, U. Minn., 1954. Bar: Minn. 1954, U.S. Supreme Ct. 1983. Assoc. Johnson & Sands, Mpls., 1956-60; sole practice Mpls., 1960-62; judge Mpls. Municipal and Dist. Ct., 1959-91; mem. faculty Nat. Judicial Coll. Bd. dirs. Mpls. chpt. Am. Red Cross, chmn. service to mil. families and vets. com.; bd. dirs. Minn. Safety Council, St. Paul, 1988-91. Served to sgt. U.S. Army, 1954-56. Mem. ABA (chmn. nat. conf. spl. ct. judge, spl. com. housing and urban devel. law, traffic ct. program com., chmn. criminal justice sect., jud. adminstrn. div.), Nat. Jud. Coll. (bd. dirs.), Nat. Christmas Tree Grower's Assn. (pres. 1976-78), Mpls. Athletic Club. Congregational. Office: 14110 Prince Pl Minnetonka MN 55345-3027

ROGERS, JAMES EDWARD, paper company executive; b. Richmond, Va., Aug. 13, 1945; s. Olin Adair and Marjorie (Aiken) R.; children: James Edward Jr., Catherine, Margaret. BS in Physics, Va. Mil. Inst., 1967; MS in Nuclear Engring., U. Va., 1969; postgrad., Harvard U., 1987. Licensing engr. Va. Electric and Power Co., Richmond, 1969-71; sales engr., sales mgr., v.p. sales and mktg. James River Paper Co., Richmond, 1971-77, 79-82, sr. v.p., gen. mgr., 1977-82; v.p. corp. devel., 1982-87; sr. v.p., group exec., specialty paper bus. James River Corp., Richmond, 1987-92; pres., CEO Specialty Coatings Intl., Richmond, 1992-93; pres. SCI Investors Inc., Richmond, 1993—; chmn., bd. dirs. Custom Papers Group Inc., Richmond; bd. dirs. Owens and Minor, Inc., Richmond, Wellman, Inc., Shrewsbury, N.J., Caraustar Industries, Inc., Austell, Ga., Marine Devel. Corp., Richmond, Mohawk Paper Mills., Inc., Cohoes, N.Y., Wilson Paper Co., Richmond, Robert Bryan Ltd., Port Royal, Va. 5d. dirs. Richmond Cerebral Palsy Ctr., Richmond Childrens Mus., Maymont Found., Richmond, 1987; mem. men's adv. coun. Va. Home, Richmond, Commonwealth Girl Scouts. Mem. Soc. Internat. Bus. Fellows, Pub. Affairs Group, Storm Trysail Club, Commonwealth Club, Fishing Bay Yacht Club (past commodore), N.Y. Yacht Club. Republican. Clubs: Commonwealth (Richmond); Fishing Bay Yacht (Deltaville, Va.) (commodore 1980); N.Y. Yacht (N.Y.C.). Office: SCI Investors Inc 101 Shockoe Slip Ste O Richmond VA 23219-4144

ROGERS, JAMES EUGENE, electric and gas utility executive; b. Birmingham, Ala., Sept. 20, 1947; s. James E. and Margaret (Whatley) R.; m. Robyn McGill (div.); children: Chrissi, Kara, Ben; m. Mary Anne Boldrick, Oct. 28, 1977. BBA, U. Ky., 1970, JD, 1974. Asst. atty. gen. Commonwealth Ky., Louisville; asst. chief trial atty. Fed. Energy Regulation Commn., Washington, dep. gen. counsel litigation and enforcement; law clk. to presiding justice Supreme Ct Ky., Louisville; ptnr. Akin, Gump, Strauss, Hauer & Feld, Dallas, Akin Gump Strauss Hauer & Feld, Houston, 1985-86; formerly pres. Transwestern Pipeline, Houston; pres., CEO CINergy Corp. (formerly PSI Resources, Inc.), Cin.; bd. dirs. CINergy Corp., A O Irkutsk Energo, Fifth Third Bank, Bankers Life Holding, Inc., Edison Electric Inst., Duke Realty Investments, Inc. Trustee Nat. Symphony Orch.; bd. dirs. Cin. Mus. Assn., The Nature Conservancy-Ind. chpt., Butler U., Indpls., U. Ky. Bus. Partnership Found. Mem. FBA, Young Pres.' Orgn., Ky. Bar Assn., D.C. Bar Assn., Skyline Club, Meridian Hills Country Club, Crooked Stick Golf Club, Queen City Club, Bankers Club, Met. Club. Baptist. Avocations: tennis, biking, skiing, golf. Office: CINergy Corp PO Box 960 Cincinnati OH 45201

ROGERS, JAMES FREDERICK, banker, management consultant; b. Centerville, Iowa, June 27, 1935; s. John W. and Mildred Holly (Morris) R.; m. Janet L. Marsden, June 27, 1957; children: Jennifer Burke, John William. AB, U. Mo., 1957; postgrad., Rutgers U. Grad. Sch. Banking, 1970-72. With Am. Security and Trust Co., Washington, 1959-85; exec. v.p. Am. Security and Trust Co., 1980-83; bd. dirs., pres. Am. Security Corp., 1983-85; cons. B.E.I.-Golembe Assoc., 1985-93; chmn. Nat. Bank of No. Va., 1988-89. Commr. Arlington County Planning Commn., 1979-80; asst. treas. Kennedy Ctr. Performing Arts; pres., trustee Leonard Wood Found.; trustee Friends of Nat. Zoo, Greater Washington Rsch. Ctr., Washington Dulles Task Force, Arena Stage, Sch. Commerce U. Va. Officer AUS, 1958-59. Mem. D.C. Bankers Assn. (pres. 1984-85), Davenport Soc., U. Mo., Met. Club (Washington), Chevy Chase Club. Presbyterian. Home: 4201 38th Rd N Arlington VA 22207-4554

ROGERS, JAMES GARDINER, accountant, educator; b. St. Louis, May 6, 1952; s. Gardiner and Virginia Joy (Goodbar) R.; m. Barbara May Baird, Feb. 14, 1976; children Andrew Baird, Benjamin Baird, Samuel Baird. BA, Washington and Lee U., 1973; MBA, Am. U., 1975. CPA, Pa. Credit officer loan workout div. Phila. Nat. Bank, Phila., 1975-78; mgr. cash and banking Gen. Waterworks Corp., Phila., 1978-81, asst. treas., 1981-85; v.p. fin., treas. Phila. Presbyn. Homes, Inc., Phila., 1985-88; dir. devel. Eastern Coll., St. Davids, Pa., 1988—; ptnr., bd. dirs. PC Mgmt. Enterprises, Inc., Bryn Mawr, Pa.. Treas. Lower Merion Bapt. Ch., Bryn Mawr, 1978-85; v.p. Lupus Foundn. of Am., Inc., Washington, 1985-87, asst. v.p., 1982-85, bd. dirs., 1977—; pres., bd. dirs. Pa. Lupus Foundn., Wayne, 1973—, bd. dirs.; elder Proclamation Presbyn. Ch., 1996—. Mem. Mensa. Republican. Club: Merion Cricket (Haverford, Pa.). Avocations: reading, microcomputers, tennis, skiing. Home: 308 Chamounix Rd Wayne PA 19087-3612 Office: Eastern Coll Saint Davids PA 19087

ROGERS, JAMES THOMAS, lawyer; b. Denver, Oct. 3, 1941; s. John Thomas and Elizabeth (Milligan) R. JD, U. Wis., 1966. Bar: Wis. 1966, U.S. Tax Ct. 1976, U.S. Ct. Claims, 1975, U.S. Ct. Customs and Patent Appeals, 1975, U.S. Supreme Ct. 1973. Chmn., Madison (Wis.) Legal Aid Soc., 1965-66; dist. atty. Lincoln County (Wis.), 1967, 69-73; spl. dist. atty. pro tem Oneida County (Wis.), 1972, Price County (Wis.), 1972-76, Lincoln County (Wis.), 1976-84; spl. city atty. City of Wausau (Wis.), 1973, 74, 77; ptnr. Rogers & Bremer, Merrill, Wis., 1973-89; prin. Rogers Criminal Law Offices, Merrill, 1989—. bd. dirs. Merrill Fed. Savings & Loan Assn., 1990—. Chmn. Judiciary Com., N.E. Crime Control Commn., 1971-72. Chmn., Lincoln County Republican Com., 1971-73; pub. defender bd. State of Wis., 1988—, 2d vice chmn., 1989-93, 1st vice chmn., 1993—. Bd. dirs. Wis. Judicare, 1990-92. Mem. State Bar Wis. (spl. com. on prosecutorial improvements 1983-89, spl. com. to rev. criminal sanctions 1987-88, conv. and entertainment com. 1989-93), Lincoln County Bar Assn. (pres. 1969-70), Wis. Dist. Attys. Assn. (life), ABA (liaison drunk driving com. of criminal justice sect., vice chmn. asset and investment mgmt. com. sec. econs. of law practice, marriage and cohabitation com. family law sect., def. svcs. commn. criminal law sect., liaison criminal justice sect.), Nat. Assn. Criminal Def. Lawyers (state and local def. bar liaison com., ad hoc subcom. on property of DNA evidence), Assn. Trial Lawyers Am. (constl. challenge com. 1988-92), Wis. Acad. Trial Lawyers (chmn. constl. challenge com. 1988-91), bd. dirs. 1985-91), Tex. Trial Lawyers Assn., N.Y. State Trial Lawyers Assn., Wis. Assn. Criminal Def. Lawyers (sec. 1986-87, pres.-elect 1987-88, pres. 1988-89, bd. dirs. 1986—, liaison to ABA criminal justice sect.), Wausau Club. Home: PO Box 438 1408 E 8th St Merrill WI 54452-0438 Office: Rogers Criminal Law Offices 301 Grand Ave PO Box 1085 Wausau WI 54402-1085

ROGERS, JAMES WILSON, church official; b. Vancouver, BC, Canada, Feb. 18, 1943; m. Carol Haney; children: Amy, Darren. Student, L.I.F.E. Bible Coll. With real estate profession, 1963-69; br. mgr. Wall & Redekop Realty, 1969-74, v.p., gen. mgr., 1974-90; exec. asst. to pres. Internat. Ch. of Foursquare Gospel, 1990—; dir. bus. devel. Realty World Can.; con. to numerous offices, Western Can.; Western regional dir. Comml. Divsn. Coun. mem. Kingsway Foursquare Ch., Vancouver, B.C.; bd. dirs. Youth for Christ Greater Vancouver; mem. pres.'s adv. com. Trinity Western U.; bd. dirs., bd. regents L.I.F.E. Bible Coll. Can.; founding dir., officer Foursquare Ch. Can., nat. bd. dirs., 1979-90. Office: Internat Ch Foursquare Gospel 1910 W Sunset Blvd Ste 200 Los Angeles CA 90026-3247

ROGERS, JEANNE VALERIE, art educator, artist; b. Islip, N.Y., Dec. 1, 1935; d. Joseph Oliver and Louise Valerie (Bayer) Fields; m. James Aubrey Rogers, Jan. 1, 1956; children: Bradley, Tyler, Lisa, Todd. BFA in Ceramics Design, Alfred U., 1957; MS in Art Edn., SUNY, New Paltz, 1962; postgrad., L.I. U., 1986-90, Parsons Sch. Design, 1988-90. Cert. art edn. tchr. K-12, elem. tchr., N.Y. Elem. art tchr. Sayville (N.Y.) Sch. Dist., 1957-61, high sch. art tchr., 1987-90; art tchr. Bayport (N.Y.)/Bluepoint Sch. Dist., 1980; art dir., art tchr. The Hewlett Sch., East Islip, N.Y., 1984-87; field supr. of student tchrs. Dowling Coll., Oakdale, N.Y., 1990—; high sch. art tchr. Torah Acad., Commack, N.Y., 1991—; instr. watercolor painting Staff Devel. Ctr. of The Islips, East Islip 45, N.Y.C., N.Y., 1996—; instr. oil painting adult edn. East Islip High Sch., 1961-62; dir. children's art Summer Outdoor Art Workshops, East Islip, 1967-78; adj. prof. Dowling Coll., 1991-92, art cons., 1990—; instr. watercolor painting for tchrs. Staff Devel. Ctr. of the Islips, East Islip H.S., N.Y., 1996—. Co-author/illustrator: Suffolk Scribes Calligraphic Poetry, 1980 (Libr. award East Islip, 1980); exhibited juried show at Babylon (N.Y.) Citizens Coun. Arts, 1994 (Best in Show award), Invitational Exhibit of Women Artists, Patchogue, N.Y., 1995; reader children's poetry Women in the Arts cable TV show, 1974; contbr. painting as cover design Suffolk Woman Watch Newspaper (premier issues), 1994. Instr. life saving and water safety ARC, Islip, 1955-61; tchr. Sunday sch. Presbyn. Ch., Islip, 1957-63; instr., dir. lifesaving and water safety Shoreham Beach Club, Sayville, 1965-70; instr. preschool, youth and adult swimming Bayshore YMCA, Lasalle Acad., Oakdale, 1971-88, instr., swim dir., 1983-88; art judge C. of C. Summerfest, Sayville, 1990. Recipient award of merit in painting, Nat. League Am. PEN Women, Vanderbilt Mus., Centerport, N.Y., 1993, 94, Chem. Bank award for painting Arts Coun.,

1992, East Islip Pub. Libr., 1992, hon. mention Huntington Township Art League, Northport Spoke Gallery N.Y., 1991, HTAL winners show Hutchins Gallery, CW Post Campus/L.I. U., 1991, Honorable Mention Huntington Twp. Art League, Northport Spoke Gallery, N.Y., 1991, others. Mem. AAUW (implementation chair soc.'s reflection in arts study 1972-74, legis. chair Islip area br. 1972-74, cultural interests chair 1973-75), summer socials chmn. General and Ednl. grants Fundraising, 1995—, historian 1996—), Suffolk Scribes (charter mem., corr. sec. 1988-89), Nat. League Am. PEN Women (corr. sec. 1996-97), South Shore Watercolor Soc., South Bay Art Assn., N.Y. State Tchrs. Assn., L.I. Art Tchrs. Assn. Republican. Presbyterian. Avocations: tennis, swimming, ballroom dancing, reading, travel. Home: 274 Marilynn Ct East Islip NY 11730-3315

ROGERS, JEFFREY, dancer. Attended, Sch. Am. Ballet. Dancer Ballet West, Salt Lake City, 1984-89; soloist Ballet West, 1989-91, prin. artist, 1991—; instr., guest artist Ballet West Conservatory. Dance performances include The Dream, Abdallah, Romeo & Juliet, Giselle, Sleeping Beauty, The Age of Anxiety (John Neumeier). Recipient Princess Grace Found. award, 1984. Office: Ballet West 50 W 200 S Salt Lake City UT 84101-1642*

ROGERS, JERRY L., federal agency administrator; b. Tex., Dec. 22, 1938; s. Ancell Robert and Grace Evalena (Coin) R.; m. Peggy Floretta Sifford, Apr. 6, 1963; children: Tiana Lynne Conklin, Elvin Houston, Jeffrey Martin. BA in History, Tex. Tech, 1962, MA, 1965. Historian Nat. Park Svc., Ft. Davis, Tex., 1965-66; historian Nat. Register Nat. Park Svc., Washington, 1967-69, chief registration, 1972-73, chief grants divsn., 1973-75, chief archeology and hist. preservation, 1975-79, assoc. dir. cultural programs, 1981-83, assoc. dir. cultural resources, 1983-94; regional dir. S.W. region, 1994-95, supt. S.W. office, 1995—; dir. Ranching Heritage Ctr. Tex. Tech Mus., Lubbock, 1969-72; dep. assoc. dir. Heritage Conservation Svc., Washington, 1979-81; internat. cons. in hist. preservation to Italy, Russia, Spain, China, India, Egypt. Contbr. articles to prof. jours. Mem. adv. com. on cemeteries and memls. VA, Washington, 1987-94. Recipient Meritorious Svc. award Dept. Interior, 1992. Mem. AIA (mem. com. hist. resources, ex-officio mem. 1979-94), Nat. Trust Hist. Preservation (trustee 1981-94), Civil War Trust. N.Mex. Heritage Preservation Alliance (bd. dirs. 1996—), Coun. on Am.'s Mil. Past (bd. dirs. 1997—). Avocations: geneology, classic automobiles. Home: 27 Bosque Loop Santa Fe NM 87505-2231 Office: Nat Park Svc 1100 Old Santa Fe Trail PO Box 728 Santa Fe NM 87504

ROGERS, JOHN JAMES WILLIAM, geology educator; b. Chgo., June 27, 1930; s. Edward James and Josephine (Dickey) R.; m. Barbara Bongard, Nov. 30, 1956; children: Peter, Timothy. BS, Calif. Inst. Tech., 1952, PhD, 1955; MS, U. Minn., 1952. Lic. geologist, N.C. From instr. to prof. Rice U., Houston, 1954-75, master Brown Coll., 1966-71, chmn. geol. dept., 1971-74; W.R. Kenan Jr. prof. geology U. N.C., Chapel Hill, 1975-97. Author: A History of the Earth, 1993; co-author: Fundamentals of Geology, 1966, Precambrian Geology of India, 1987; co-editor: Holocene Geology of Galveston Bay, 1969, Precambrian of South India, 1983, Basalts, 1984, African Rifting, 1989; regional editor Jour. African Earth Scis., 1982-93; contbr. articles to profl. jours. Fellow Geol. Soc. Am., Geol. Soc. India, Geol. Soc. Africa (hon.); mem. Mineral. Soc. Am., Am. Assn. Petroleum Geologists, Soc. Econ. Paleontologists and Mineralogists. Home: 1816 Rolling Rd Chapel Hill NC 27514-7502 Office: U of NC Dept Geology CB #3315 Chapel Hill NC 27599-3315

ROGERS, JOHN S., retired union official; b. Scranton, Pa., Nov. 19, 1930. Student, U. Wis., 1959-61, U. Mich., 1963; student spl. studies, Am. U., 1965-66, Harvard U. Bus. Sch., 1967. Internat. rep. United Brotherhood of Carpenters and Joiners of Am., Washington, 1958-65, asst. to gen. pres., 1966-74, dir. edn., 1971-82, mem. gen. exec. bd., 1974-78, gen. sec., 1978-91, ret., 1992; sec.-treas. Suffolk County (N.Y.) Dist. Coun. Carpenters, 1957-58; v.p. N.Y. State Bldg. and Constrn. Trades Council, 1974-78, N.Y. State Fedn. Labor, 1974-78; pres. N.Y. State Coun. Carpenters, 1974-78; vice chmn. N.Y. State Commn. Jobs and Energy; mem. Suffolk County Pub. Employment Rels.s Bd.; vis. lectr. George Meany Ctr. Labor Studies. Author numerous trade union leadership mans. and instructional materials, 1966-79. Bd. dirs. L.I. action com. Assn. Help for Retarded Children, 1956-60; labor co-chmn United Cerebral Palsy, N.Y.C., 1977-78; v.p. Leukemia Soc. Mem. Harvard Trade Union Alumnae Assn. Home: 2713 SW Cranbrook Dr Boynton Beach FL 33436

ROGERS, JOHN WASHINGTON, JR., investment management company executive; s. John W. Sr. and Jewel (Mankarious) R.; m. Desiree Glapion. BS in Econs., Princeon U. Broker William Blair & Co.; now pres. Ariel Capital Mgmt., Inc., Ariel Mut. Funds, Chgo.; bd. dirs. Am. Nat. Bank, Burell Comms. Group, Aon Corp. Bd. dirs. Chgo. Urban League, Chgo. Park Dist., Chgo. Symphony Orch., Rush Presbyn. St. Luke's Hosp. Office: Ariel Capital Mgmt Ariel Mut Funds 307 N Michigan Ave Ste 500 Chicago IL 60601-5305

ROGERS, JUDITH W., federal circuit judge; b. 1939. AB cum laude, Radcliffe Coll., 1961; LLB, Harvard U., 1964; LLM, U. Va., 1988; LLD (hon.), D.C. Sch. Law, 1992. Bar: D.C. 1965. Law clk. Juvenile Ct. D.C., 1964-65; asst. U.S. atty. D.C., 1965-68; trial atty. San Francisco Neighborhood Legal Assistance Found., 1968-69; atty. assoc. atty. gen.'s office U.S. Dept. Justice, 1969-71, atty. criminal divsn., 1969-71; gen. counsel Congl. Commn. on Organization of D.C. Govt., 1971-72; coordinator legis. program Office of Dep. Mayor D.C., 1972-74, spl. asst. to mayor for legis., 1974-79, corp. counsel, 1979-83; assoc. judge D.C. Ct. Appeals, 1983-88, chief judge, 1988-94; cir. judge U.S. Ct. Appeals-D.C. Cir., 1994—; mem. D.C. Law Revision Commn., 1979-83; mem. grievance com. U.S. Dist. Ct. D.C., 1982-83; mem. exec. com. Conf. Chief Justices, 1993-94. Bd. dirs. Wider Opportunities for Women, 1972-74; mem. vis. com. Harvard U. Sch. Law, 1984-90; trustee Radcliffe Coll., 1982-88. Recipient citation for work on D.C. Self-Govt. Act, 1973, Disting. Pub. Svc. award D.C. Govt., 1983, award Nat. Bar Assn., 1989; named Woman Lawyer of Yr., Women's Bar Assn. D.C., 1990. Fellow ABA; mem. D.C. Bar, Nat. Assn. Women Judges, Conf. Chief Justices (bd. dirs. 1988-94), Am. Law Inst., Phi Beta Kappa. Office: US Ct Appeals 333 Constitution Ave NW Washington DC 20001-2802*

ROGERS, JUSTIN TOWNER, JR., retired utility company executive; b. Sandusky, Ohio, Aug. 4, 1929; s. Justin Towner and Barbara Eloise (Larkin) R. AB cum laude, Princeton U., 1951; JD, U. Mich., 1954. Bar: Ohio 1954. Assoc. Wright, Harlor, Purpus, Morris & Arnold, Columbus, 1956-58; with Ohio Edison Co., Akron, 1958-93, v.p., then exec. v.p., 1970-79, pres., 1980-91, chmn. bd., 1991-93; ret., 1993; bd. dirs. 1st Nat. Bank Ohio, 1st Merit Corp; past mem. coal adv. bd. Internat. Energy Agy. Past pres., trustee Akron Cmty. Trusts, Akron Child Guidance Ctr.; past chmn. Akron Assoc. Health Agys., U. Akron Assocs., Ohio Electric Utility Inst.; past chmn., trustee, mem. exec. com. trustees Akron Gen. Med. Ctr., Health Network Ohio; trustee Sisler McFawn Found., VNS-Hospice Found.; past dir. Edison Elec. Inst., Elec. Power Rsch. Inst., Assn. of Edison Illuminating Co.'s. Mem. Portage Country Club, Mayflower Club, Rockwell Springs Trout Club (Castalia, Ohio), Princeton Club (N.Y.C.), Phi Delta Phi, Beta Gamma Sigma.

ROGERS, KATE ELLEN, interior design educator; b. Nashville, Dec. 13, 1920; d. Raymond Lewis and Louise (Gruver) R.; diploma Ward-Belmont Jr. Coll., 1940; BA in Fine Arts, George Peabody Coll., 1946, MA in Fine Arts, 1947; EdD in Fine Arts and Fine Arts Edn., Columbia U., 1956. Instr., Tex. Tech. Coll., Lubbock, 1947-53; co-owner, v.p. Design Today, Inc., Lubbock, 1951-54; student asst. Am. House, N.Y.C., 1953-54; asst. prof. housing and interior design U. Mo., Columbia, 1954-56, assoc. prof., 1956-66, prof., 1966-85, emeritus, 1985—, chmn. dept. housing and interior design, 1973-85; mem. accreditation com. Found. for Interior Design Edn. Rsch., 1975-76, chmn. stds. com., 1976-82, chmn. rsch., 1982-85. Mem. 1st Bapt. Ch., Columbia, Mo.; bd. dirs. Meals on Wheels, 1989-91. Nat. Endowment for Arts rsch. grantee, 1981-82. Fellow Interior Design Educators Coun. (pres. 1971-73, chmn. bd. 1974-76, chmn. rsch. com. 1977-78); mem. Am. Soc. Interior Designers, (hon., medal of honor 1975), Am. Home Econs. Assn., Columbia Art League (adv. bd. 1988-93), Pi Lambda Theta, Kappa Delta Pi, Phi Kappa Phi (hon.), Gamma Sigma Delta, Delta Delta Delta (Phi Eta chpt.), Phi Upsilon Omicron, Omicron Nu (hon.). Democrat. Author: The Modern House, USA, 1962; editor Jour. Interior Design Edn. and Research, 1975-78.

ROGERS, KENNETH RAY, entertainer, recording artist; b. Houston, Aug. 21, 1938; s. Edward Floyd and Lucille (Hester) R.; 1 child by 1st marriage, Carol; 1 child by 2d marriage, Kenneth; m. Marianne Gordon; 1 child, Christopher Cody; m. Wanda Miller, June 1, 1997. Student, U. Houston. Founder Kenny Roger's Roasters, 1991—. Appeared on American Bandstand, 1958; mem. Bobby Doyle Trio, 1959-66, Christy Minstrels, 1966-67, The First Edition, 1967-69, Kenny Rogers and The First Edition, 1969-75, pursued solo career, 1975—; performed numerous concerts in U.S., Can., Eng., Scotland, New Zealand, Australia, Japan; hosted TV spls. Kenny Rogers Classic Weekend, 1988, 89, 90, Kenny, Dolly & Willie, 1989, Kenny Rogers in Concert, 1989, Goodwill Games, 1990; starred in TV series Rollin' with The First Edition, 1972; appeared in movies Six Pack, 1982; appearances Tonight Show; appeared in TV movies: Kenny Rogers as the Gambler, 1980, Coward of the County, 1981, Gambler, Part II, 1983, Gambler III: The Adventure Continues, 1987, Christmas in America, 1989, The Gambler Returns, The Luck of the Draw (Gambler IV), 1991, Rio Diablo, 1993, Gambler V, 1994, Big Dreams & Broken Hearts: The Dottie West Story, 1995; appeared in TV spl. Very Special Arts; (TV series): MacShayne, 1994—; rec. artist with Liberty Records, 1976-82, RCA Records, 1983—; toured Kenny & Dolly, Dollywood, 1990, British Isles, 1990; recs. include That Crazy Feeling (Gold single), I Don't Need You (Brit. Country Music Assn. award, Acad. Country Music award), Love is What We Make It, 1985, The Heart of the Matter, 1985, They Don't Make Them Like They Used To, What About Me, I Prefer the Moonlight, 1987, When You Put Your Heart in It, 1988 (ofcl. theme song U.S. Gymnastics Fedn.), Christmas in America, 1989, Love Is Strange, 1990, Greatest Country Hits, 1990, If Only My Heart Had a Voice, 1993, Greatest Hits, 1994; number #1 albums include Kenny Rogers-Lucille, 1976, Love or Something Like It, 1978, The Gambler, 1978, Kenny, 1979, Gideon, 1980, Share Your Love, 1981, Eyes That See in the Dark, 1983, Something Inside So Strong, 1989, Timepiece, 1994, (christian album) The Gift, 1996; author photographic works Kenny Roger's America, 1986, Your Friends and Mine, 1987; rec. artist Warner/Reprice, 1988—; TV host A&E The Real West, 1993. Hon. capt. 1988 U.S. Gymnastics Team. Named Cross-Over Artist of Year Billboard mag., 1977, named Top Male vocalist People mag., 1979, 80; recipient Country Music Assn. award, 1978, 79, Am. Music award, Best Male Vocalist, Best Album, 1984, Am. Music award, Best Male Country Vocalist, Best Album, 1985, Country Music Found. Roy Acuff award, 1985, UN Peace award, 1984, Rec. Industry Assn. Am. Most Awarded Artist award, 1984 (11 platinum, 18 gold albums), Grammy award for best male country vocal, 1977, 79, co-recipient (with Ronnie Milsap) for best country vocal duet, 1987, 1st Harry Chapin award for humanitarianism ASCAP, 1988, Horation Alger award, 1990; numerous other music awards. Address: care Kragen & Co 1112 N Sherbourne Dr Los Angeles CA 90069-2202 also: Capitol/Liberty Records 1750 Vine St Los Angeles CA 90028

ROGERS, KENNETH SCOTT, professional baseball player; b. Savannah, Ga., Nov. 10, 1964. Ed., Plant City, Fla. Pitcher Tex. Rangers, 1989-95, NY Yankees, 1996—. Named to Am. League All-Star Team, 1995; pitched perfect game against Calif. Angels, 1994. *

ROGERS, LAWRENCE H., II, retired television executive, investor, writer; b. Trenton, N.J., Sept. 6, 1921; s. Norman Tallman and Nancy (Titus) R.; m. Suzanne Long; children: Hallie, Suzanne, Lawrence H. III, Campbell, Natalie, Christian. Grad., Lawrenceville Sch., 1939; BA with honors in history, Princeton U., 1943; student, Harvard U., 1963. A pioneer broadcast editorials; built sta. WSAZ-TV Inc.; with Taft Broadcasting Co., Cin., 1960-76; pres. Taft Broadcasting Co., 1963-76; pres., CEO Omega Comms., Inc., Orlando, Fla., 1977-92; chmn. bd. dirs. Cin. br. Fed. Res. Bank of Cleve., 1975-82; bd. dirs. Cin. Fin. Corp., Cardinal Group of Funds, Columbus, Ohio; past mem. TV Code Rev. Bd.; treas. TV Bur. Advt., then chmn. bd. dirs.; vice chmn. bd. Sta. NBC-TV Affiliates; v.p., dir. Assn. Maximum Svc. Telecaster, Washington; mem. info. com. Nat. Assn. Broadcasters, then editl. com.; mem. TV Code Rev. Bd.; cons. to USIA, Africa, 1967, USSR and Ea. Europe, 1971; mem. summit trip and SALT signing with Pres. Richard Nixon, 1972. Author: Business of Broadcasting, 1963, Orlando Shoot-Out, 1990. Vice chmn. trustees distbn. com. Greater Cin. Found.; Former Gov. W.Va. Econ. Devel. Agy.; Bd. dirs. Theatre Devel. Fund; gen. chmn. Greater Cin. Fine Arts Fund. Served to capt. F.A. AUS, World War II, ETO. Recipient Distinguished Service award U.S. Jr. C. of C., 1956. Mem. Internat. Radio TV Exec. Soc., Newcomen Soc. Clubs: Queen City (Cin.); Camargo, N.Y. Yacht, Brook (N.Y.C.); Rolling Rock (Ligonier, Pa.); Commonwealth (Cin.). Home and Office: 4600 Drake Rd Cincinnati OH 45243-4118

ROGERS, LEE FRANK, radiologist; b. Colchester, Vt., Sept. 24, 1934; s. Watson Frank and Marguerite Mortimer (Cole) R.; m. Donna Mae Brinker, June 20, 1956; children: Michelle, Cynthia, Christopher, Matthew. BS, Northwestern U., 1956, MD, 1959. Commd. 2d lt. U.S. Army, 1959, advanced through grades to maj., 1967; rotating intern Walter Reed Gen. Hosp., 1959-60; resident radiology Fitzsimons Gen. Hosp., 1960-63; ret., 1967; radiologist Baptist Meml. Hosp., San Antonio, 1967-68, U. Tex. Med. Sch., San Antonio, 1968-71; dir. residency tng., radiologist U. Tex. Med. Sch., Houston, 1972-74; prof., chmn. dept. radiology Northwestern U. Med. Sch., Chgo., 1974-95; editor-in-chief Am. Jour. Roentgenology, Winston-Salem, N.C., 1995—; prof. radiology Bowman Gray Sch. Medicine Wake Forest Univ. Fellow Am. Coll. Radiology (past pres.), Am. Roentgen Ray Soc. (past pres.); mem. Assn. U. Radiologists (past pres.), Radiol. Soc. N.Am., Am. Bd. Radiology (past pres.), Alpha Omega Alpha. Episcopalian. Office: Am Jour Roentgenology 101 S Stratford Rd Ste 303 Winston Salem NC 27104-4224 *The source of most problems is previous solutions.*

ROGERS, LEE JASPER, lawyer; b. Fort Monmouth, N.J., May 6, 1955; s. Peter and Ethel Mae (Williams) R.; m. Vanessa Walisha Yarbrough, Apr. 18, 1981 (div. Oct. 1988); 1 child, Stephanie Alexandria. Student, Drew U., 1975, Monmouth Coll., 1975; BA in History, Hampton Inst., 1977; JD, Howard U., 1980. Pvt. practice Red Bank, N.J., 1981-91, 95—; asst. dep. pub. defender Ocean County region, Toms River, N.J., 1991-92; mortgage loan officer Allied Fin. Svcs., Neptune, N.J., 1992-93, Mortgage Money Mart, Edison, N.J., 1993-94, Residential First, Inc., Shrewsbury, N.J., 1994-95, Fairmont Funding, Lakewood, N.J., 1995-96; vol. counsel Pro Bono Legal Svcs., Red Bank, N.J., 1982-91; pres., chmn. bd. Jay-Mar Entertainment Enterprises, Inc., 1986—; mem. vocal group, Pizazz, 1996—. Author numerous poems; vocal singing group Pizazz, 1991-94, 96—, Nu Eara, 1992; vocalist Piyayz, 1996—. Pres., bd. dirs. Ct. Basie Learning Ctr., Red Bank, N.J.; chmn. Red Bank Republican Club, 1994-95. Mem. ABA, NAACP (exec. com. Red Bank chpt. 1983-88), Assn. Trial Lawyers Am., Elks (sec. ho. com. Bates lodge #220 1988-90, loyal knight 1990-91, esteemed loyal knight 1993-94, chmn. by-laws com. 1993-94, mem. house com.). Baptist. Home: 298 Shrewsbury Ave Apt 3 Red Bank NJ 07701-1319 *Mastery is achieved through the development of the spirit, and the resulting obtainment of bliss. We should all seek to be at one within ourselves and with the world around us. To do this, we must walk with God. Only then can we find true happiness!.*

ROGERS, LON B(ROWN), retired lawyer; b. Pikeville, Ky., Sept. 5, 1905; s. Fon and Ida (Brown) R.; BS, U. Ky., 1928, LLB, 1932; LHD (hon.), Pikeville Coll., 1979, LHD (hon.) Centre Coll. of Ky., 1992; m. Mary Evelyn Walton, Dec. 17, 1938; children: Marylon Walton, Martha Brown, Fon II. Bar: Ky. 1932. Practiced law in Lexington, 1932-38, Pikeville, 1939-80. Dir. East Ky. Beverage Co., Pikeville, 1940-90, Pikeville Nat. Bank & Trust Co., 1979-95. Elder, 1st Presbyterian Ch, Pikeville, Ky., 1947-75; mem. Pikeville City Council, 1951; mem. local bd. SSS, 1958-69; mem. Breaks Interstate Park Commn., Ky.-Va., 1960-68, chmn., 1960-62, 64-66, vice chmn., 1966-68; chmn. Community Services Commn., Pikeville Model Cities, 1969-71; mem. Ky. Arts Commn., 1965-72, Ky. Travel Council, 1967-70, 73-75; pres. Ky. Mountain Laurel Festival Assn., 1971-72. Chmn. bd. trustees Presbytery Ebenezer, U.S.A., 1950-71; trustee Pikeville Coll., 1951-72, 73-79, trustee emeritus, 1979—; trustee Presbytery of Transylvania, 1971-83; mem. bd. nat. missions United Presbyn. Ch. USA, 1954-66; trustee Appalachian Regional Hosps., Inc., 1963-67, Ky. Ind. Coll. Fund., 1973-82; bd. dirs. Meth. Hosp. of Ky., 1966-82; mem., Presbyn. Ch., Lexington, 1982—, trustee, 1989-91, 2nd Presbyterian Ch. Mem. Ky. C. of C. (regional v.p. 1962-64, 69-74), Ky. Hist. Soc., S.A.R., Civil War Round Table, Blue Grass Kiwanis (past lt. gov.), Filson Club, Blue Grass Automobile (pres. 1971-74, dir.), Sigma Alpha Epsilon, Phi Delta Phi. Republican. Home: 505 E Main St Lexington KY 40508-2309 Office: 300 E Main St Ste 403 Lexington KY 40507-1539

ROGERS, LORENE LANE, university president emeritus; b. Prosper, Tex., Apr. 3, 1914; d. Mort M. and Jessie L. (Luster) Lane; m. Burl Gordon Rogers, Aug. 23, 1935 (dec. June, 1941). B.A., N. Tex. State Coll., 1934; M.A. (Parke, Davis fellow), U. Tex., 1946, Ph.D., 1948; D.Sc. (hon.), Oakland U., 1972; LL.D. (hon.), Austin Coll., 1977. Prof. chemistry Sam Houston State Coll., Huntsville, Tex., 1947-49; research scientist Clayton Found. Biochem. Inst. U. Tex., Austin, 1950-64, asst. dir., 1957-64, prof. nutrition, 1962-80, assoc. dean Grad. Sch., 1964-71, v.p. univ., 1971-74, pres., 1974-79, mem. exec. com. African grad. fellowship program, 1966-71; research cons. Clayton Found. for Research, Houston, 1979-81; Vis. scientist, lectr., cons. NSF, 1959-62; cons. S.W. Research Inst., San Antonio, 1959-62; mem. Grad. Record Exams Bd., 1972-76, chmn., 1974-75; adv. com. ITT Internat. Fellowship, 1973-83; dir. Texaco, Inc., Gulf States Utilities, Republic Bank, Austin. Bd. dirs. Tex. Opera Theatre, Austin Lyric Opera; chmn. bd. trustees Texaco Philanthropic Found.; chmn. council of presidents Nat. Assn. State Univs. and Land-Grant Colls., 1976-77, mem. exec. com., 1976-79; mem. com. on identification of profl. women Am. Council on Edn., 1975-79, mem. com. on govt. relations, 1978-79; mem. target 2000 project com. Tex. A&M U. System; mem. ednl. adv. bd. John E. Gray Inst., Lamar U., Beaumont, Tex. Eli Lilly fellow, 1949-50; Recipient U. Tex. Students Assn. Teaching Excellence award, 1963; Disting. Alumnus award N. Tex. State U., 1972; Outstanding Woman of Austin award, 1950, 60, 71, 80; Disting. Alumnus award U. Tex., 1976; Honor Scroll award Tex. Inst. Chemists, 1980. Fellow Am. Inst. Chemists; mem. AAAS, Am. Chem. Soc. (sec. 1954-56), Am. Inst. Nutrition, Am. Soc. Human Genetics, Nat. Soc. Arts and Letters, Assn. Grad. Schs. (internat. edn. com. 1967-71), Sigma Xi, Phi Kappa Phi, Iota Sigma Pi, Omicron Delta Kappa. Research in hydantoin synthesis, intermediatry metabolism, biochem. nutritional aspects of alcoholism, mental retardation, congenital malformations. Home: 4 Nob Hill Cir Austin TX 78746-3650

ROGERS, MALCOLM AUSTIN, museum director, art historian; b. Scarborough, Yorkshire, Eng., Oct. 3, 1948; s. James Eric and Frances Anne (Elsey) R. M.A., Magdalen Coll., U. Oxford , Eng., 1973; D. Phil., Christ Ch., U. Oxford, 1976. Asst. keeper Nat. Portrait Gallery, London, 1974-83, dep. dir., 1983-94; dir. Mus. Fine Arts, Boston, 1994—. Mem. Harvard overseers' com. Visit the Art Mus.; trustee Found. for the Arts, Nagoya. Author: Blue Guide: Museums and Galleries of London, 1983; also articles. Fellow Soc. Antiquaries. Avocations: wine and food; travel; opera. Home: 20 Charles River Sq Boston MA 02114-3266 Office: Mus Fine Arts 465 Huntington Ave Boston MA 02115-5523

ROGERS, MARGARET ELLEN JONSSON, civic worker; b. Dallas, Aug. 7, 1938, d. John Erik and Margaret Elizabeth (Fonde) Jonsson; m. Robert D. Rogers; children: Emily, Erik, Laura. Student Skidmore Coll., 1956-57, So. Methodist U., 1957-60. Civic worker, Dallas; dir. Sta. KRLD radio, Dallas, 1970-74; dir. 1st Nat. Bank, Dallas, 1976-85, vice-chmn. dirs. trust com.; trustee Meth. Hosps., 1972-82, mem. exec. com., 1977-82, corp. bd. mem., 1990-94, mem. fin. com., 1990-93. Bd. dirs. Lamplighter Sch., 1967—; past mem. vis. com. dept. psychology MIT; mem. vis. com. Stanford U. Librs., 1984-90; bd. dirs. Callier Ctr. Communication Disorders, 1967-90, Winston Sch., 1973-85; bd. dirs., mem. exec. com. Episc. Sch., 1976-83; chmn. Crystal Charity Ball; co-chmn. nat. major gifts com. Stanford Centennial Campaign; bd. dirs. Children's Med. Center, Hope Cottage Childrens' Bur., Baylor Dental Sch., Dallas Health and Sci. Mus., Dallas YWCA, Day Nursery Assn.; mem. devel. bd. U. Tex., Dallas, 1988-90; bd. govs. The Dallas Found., 1988-95, chmn. investment com. 1991-92; trustee So. Meth. U., mem. investment com., 1988—, chmn. investment com., 1992—; mem. visiting com. Dedman Coll., 1989-90; life trustee Dallas Mus. Art, mem. investment com.; mem. collectors com. Nat. Gallery Art; bd. dirs. Dallas Arboretum, 1991-92; trustee Monterey Bay Aquarium, 1995—. Margaret Jonsson Charlton Hosp. of Dallas named in her honor, 1973. Mem. Internat. Coun. Mus. of Modern Art., MJR Fund (pres.), Jonsson Fund.

ROGERS, MARK CHARLES, physician, educator; b. N.Y.C., Oct. 25, 1942; s. Gerald and Inez (Kaufman) R.; m. Elizabeth Ann London, Dec. 30, 1972; children: Bradley, Meredith. BA, Columbia U., 1964; MD, SUNY, Syracuse, 1969; MBA, U. Pa., 1991; PhD (hon.), U. Ljubljana Slovenia, 1995. Diplomate Am. Bd. Anesthesiology (examiner 1982—), Am. Bd. Pediatrics. Intern Mass. Gen. Hosp., Boston, 1969-70, resident, 1973-75; resident Boston Children's Hosp., 1970-71; fellow Duke U. Med. Ctr., Durham, N.C., 1971-73; asst. prof. dept. anesthesiology and critical care medicine Johns Hopkins U., Balt., 1977-79, assoc. prof., 1979-80, prof., chmn. dept., 1980-93, assoc. dean Sch. Medicine, 1990-93, dir. pediatric ICU, 1977-93; CEO Duke Hosp. and Health Network, 1993-96; sr. v.p. Perkin Elmer, Wilton, Conn., 1996—; pres. Critical Care Found., Balt., 1981-96; cons. WHO, Bangkok, 1982-83. Editor in chief: Yearbook of Critical Care, 1983-96, Textbook of Pediatric Intensive Care, 1987, 91, 96, Principles and Practices of Anesthesiology, 1990; editor: Perioperative Management, 1989, dep. editor in chief Critical Care Medicine Jour., 1990-96. Maj. U.S. Army, 1975-77. Recipient Club of Mainz award, Mainz, Fed. Republic of Germany, 1981, award Assn. Univ. Anesthetists, 1980; Fulbright scholar, Ljubljana, Yugoslavia, 1990. Mem. Inst. Medicine. Home: 85 Lukeswood Rd New Canaan CT 06840 Office: Perkin Elmer 50 Danbury Rd Wilton CT 06897-4406

ROGERS, MARY MARTIN, publishing company executive; b. Nov. 22, 1945; married; 3 children. BA in English, U. Hawaii, 1967. Prodn. editor Academic Press, N.Y.C., 1968-70; asst. prodn. mgr. U. Miami Press, Coral Gables, Fla., 1970-75; mng. editor Am. Statis. Assn., Washington, 1976-78; prodn. mgr. Am. Anthropological Assn., Washington, 1978-79; prodn. editor, books Raven Press, Ltd., N.Y.C., 1981-84, book prodn. mgr., 1984-85, acquisitions editor, 1985-87, exec. editor acquisitions, 1986-87, v.p., editor-in-chief, acquisitions, 1987-91, pres., 1991-95; pres., CEO Lippincott-Raven Publ., Phila., 1995—; comms. specialist So. Fla. Regional Planning Coun., Miami, 1970-75. Office: Lippincott Raven Publ 227 E Washington Sq Philadelphia PA 19106-3713

ROGERS, MICHAEL ALAN, writer; b. Santa Monica, Calif., Nov. 29, 1950; s. Don Easterday and Mary Othilda (Gilbertson) R.; m. Suzanne Elaine Lavoie, May 21, 1995. BA in Creative Writing, Stanford U., 1972. Assoc. editor Rolling Stone Mag., San Francisco, 1972-76; editor-at-large Outside mag., San Francisco, 1976-78; sr. writer Newsweek mag., San Francisco, 1983—; mng. editor Newsweek InterActive, San Francisco, 1993—; exec. prodr. broadband divsn. The Wash. Post Co., 1995-96; v.p. Post-Newsweek New Media, 1996—; vis. lectr. fiction U. Calif., Davis, 1980. Author: Mindfogger, 1973, Biohazard, 1977, Do Not Worry About The Bear, 1979, Silicon Valley, 1982, Forbidden Sequence, 1988; contbr. articles to mags., newspapers. Recipient Disting. Sci. Writing award AAAS, 1976, Best Feature Articles award Computer Press Assn., 1987. Mem. Author Guild, Sierra Club. Avocations: backpacking, horses.

ROGERS, MILLARD FOSTER, JR., retired art museum director; b. Texarkana, Tex., Aug. 27, 1932; s. Millard Foster and Jessie Bell (Hubbell) R.; m. Nina Olds, Aug. 3, 1963; 1 son, Seth Olds. BA with honors, Mich. State U., 1954; MA, U. Mich., 1958; studied with, John Pope-Hennessy; LHD, Xavier U., 1987. Gosline fellow Victoria and Albert Mus., London, Eng., 1959; curator Am. art Toledo Mus. Art, 1959-67; coord. Ford Found. intern program; dir. Elvehjem Art Ctr., prof. art history U. Wis., Madison, 1967-74; dir. Cin. Art Mus., 1974-94, dir. emeritus, 1994—; vis. scholar Principia Coll., Elsah, Ill., 1982, 84; pres. Mariemont Preservation Found., Ohio, 1982-91, 95—; adj. prof. U. Cin., 1987-91. Author: Randolph Rogers, American Sculptor in Rome, 1971, Spanish Paintings in the Cincinnati Art Museum, 1978, Favorite Paintings from The Cincinnati Art Museum, 1980, Sketches and Bozzetti by American Sculptors, 1800-1950, 1988. With AUS, 1954-56. Named Outstanding Citizen of Mariemont, 1991. Mem. Assn. Art Mus. Dirs. (hon.), Am. Assn. Mus., Ohio Mus. Assn., Phi Beta Kappa. Office: Cin Art Mus Eden Park Cincinnati OH 45202-1596

ROGERS, NATHANIEL SIMS, banker; b. New Albany, Miss., Nov. 17, 1919; s. Arthur L. and Elizabeth (Bouton) R.; m. Helen Elizabeth Ricks,

July 3, 1942; children—Alice, John, Lewis. AB, Millsaps Coll., 1941; MBA, Harvard U., 1947. With Deposit Guaranty Bank and Trust Co., Jackson, Miss., 1947-69, 1st v.p., 1957-58, pres., dir., 1958-69; pres., dir. 1st City Nat. Bank Houston, 1969-81, chmn., 1982-84; pres. 1st City Bancorp. of Tex., Houston, 1970-83, chmn., 1983-85, also bd. dirs. Chmn. Jackson United Givers Fund, 1957, pres., 1959, bd. dirs., 1958-61; pres. Andrew Jackson area coun. Boy Scouts Am., 1962; trustee Miss. Found. Ind. Colls., 1959-69; past pres., trustee Millsaps Coll.; trustee Methodist Hosp., Houston; chmn. ofcl. bd. Meth. ch. Lt. (s.g.) USNR, 1942-46. Named Outstanding Young Man of Year Jackson Jr. C. of C., 1955. Mem. Am. Bankers Assn. (pres. 1969-70), Miss. Bankers Assn. (pres. jr. banker sect. 1952-53, pres. 1964-65), Robert Morris Assocs. (pres. S.E. chpt. 1954-55, nat. dir. 1959-62), Assn. Res. City Bankers (bd. dirs. 1980-83), Jackson C. of C. (pres. 1962), Houston C. of C. (chmn. 1979-80), Young Pres.'s Orgn., Millsaps Coll. Alumni Assn. (pres. 1955-56), Newcomen Soc., Phi Beta Kappa, Omicron Delta Kappa, Kappa Alpha. Methodist.

ROGERS, OSCAR ALLAN, JR., college president; b. Natchez, Miss., Sept. 10, 1928; s. Oscar Allan and Maria Pinkie (Jackson) R.; m. Ethel Lee Lewis, Dec. 20, 1950; children—Christopher, Christian, Christoff. A.B., Tougaloo Coll., 1950; S.T.B., Harvard U., 1953, M.A.T., 1954; Ed.D., U. Ark., 1960; postgrad. U. Wash., 1968-69; LHD (hon.), Oklahoma City U., 1992.. Ordained to ministry Congl. Ch., 1953, Baptist Ch., 1955, Methodist Ch., 1962. Asst. pastor St. Mark Congl. Ch., Roxbury, Mass., 1951-54; dean-registrar Natchez Jr. Coll., Miss., 1954-56; pres. Ark. Bapt. Coll., Little Rock, 1956-59; dean students prof. social sci. and edn. Jackson State U., Miss., 1960-68, dean Grad. Sch., 1969-84; pres. Claflin Coll., 1984-94, pres. emeritus, 1994—; postdoctoral fellow U. Wash., Seattle, 1968-69; pastor Asbury-Kingsley Charge, Bolton and Edwards (Miss.) United Meth. Ch., 1962-84, Merton (Miss) Cir. United Meth. Chs., 1994-96. Served with USN, 1946-47. Recipient Order of the Palmetto Gov. Campbell (S.C.), 1994. Mem. Conf. Deans of Black Grad. Schs. (pres. 1975-76, treas. 1979-84), AAUP, NAACP, Phi Delta Kappa, Kappa Delta Pi, Alpha Phi Alpha. Democrat. Author: My Mother Cooked My Way Through Harvard with These Creole Recipes, 1973; Mississippi: The View from Tougaloo, 1979. Home and Office: 5932 Holbrook Dr Jackson MS 39206-2003

ROGERS, PAUL GRANT, lawyer, former congressman; b. Ocilla, Ga., June 4, 1921; s. Dwight L. and Florence (Roberts) R.; m. Rebecca Bell, Dec. 15, 1962; 1 child, Rebecca Laing. BA, U. Fla., 1942, JD, 1948, LLD; LLD (hon.), Fla. Atlantic U., U. Md., Duke U., L.I. U.; DSc (hon.), George Washington U., U. Miami, Albany Med. Coll. of Union U.; D.Sc. (hon.), Commonwealth U. Va.; H.H.D. (hon.), Nova U.; L.H.D. (hon.), N.Y. Med. Coll., N.Y. Coll. Podiatric Medicine, Hahnemann Med. Coll.; D.Med. Sci. (hon.), Med. U. S.C. Bar: Fla. 1948. Partner Burns, Middleton, Rogers, Farrell & Faust, 1952-69; mem. 84th-95th congresses from 11th Dist. Fla., 1955-79; chmn. house subcom. on health and environ. Hogan & Hartson, Washington, 1979—, ptnr., 1979—. Trustee Cleve. Clinic Found.; chmn. The Scripps Rsch. Inst.; bd. dirs. Am. Cancer Soc.; co-chmn. nat. Leadership Coalition on Health Care Reform; chmn. bd. dirs. Nat. Coun. Patient Info. and Edn.; chmn. Nat. Osteoporosis Found., Friends of Nat. Libr. Medicine; mem. health scis. coun. Sch. Medicine, U. Va.; mem. nat. coun. Washington U. Sch. Medicine; mem. coun. for the div. biol. scis. U. Chgo.; mem. dean's coun. Harvard Sch. Pub. Health. Recipient Pub. Welfare medal Nat. Acad. Scis., 1982, Sea Grant award, 1985, Yr. 2000 award Nat. Cancer Inst., 1987, Albert and Mary Lasker Found. award for pub. svc., 1993, Hugo Schaefer award APHA, 1994, NOF Leadership award, 1995, Maxwell Finland award, 1996. Mem. ABA, Fla. Bar Assn. (gov. jr. sect. 1952-53), Palm Beach County Bar Assn., D.C. Bar Assn., Inst. Medicine of NAS, Phi Delta Phi, Phi Delta Theta. Methodist (steward). Office: Hogan & Hartson 555 13th St NW Ste 1200 Washington DC 20004-1109

ROGERS, PAULA ANN, secondary school educator; b. Springfield, Ill., July 21, 1954; d. Paul I. and Pearl L. (Montgomery) R. BS in Math. Edn., Ill. State U., 1976; postgrad., Murray State, 1977; MS in Animal Sci., U. Ill., 1981. Cert. math. tchr., Ill. Math. tchr. Griffin High Sch., Springfield, Ill., 1976-78; adult educator Urbana, Ill., 1981-83; math. tchr. Danville (Ill.) High Sch., 1983-85, Urbana High Sch., 1985—; tutor Urbana Sch. Dist., 1985—; Job Tng. Partnership Act summer youth worksite coord. Urbana Adult Edn., 1983—; coach math. team competitions Urbana H.S., 1985—, booster pal participant, 1992-93. Contbr. articles to profl. jours. Mem. Math. Assn. Am., Ill. Coun. Tchrs. Math., Delta Kappa Gamma. Methodist. Avocations: horseback riding, piano playing, reading, running, aerobics. Office: Urbana High Sch 1002 S Race St Urbana IL 61801-4957

ROGERS, PETER PHILIPS, environmental engineering educator, city planner; b. Liverpool., England, Apr. 30, 1937; came to U.S., 1960, naturalized, 1977; s. Edward Joseph and Ellen (Duggan) R.; m. Rosemarie Rogers, July 11, 1964; children: Christopher, Justin. B in Engring., Liverpool U., 1958; MS, Northwestern U., 1961; PhD, Harvard U., 1966. Asst. engr. Sir Alfred McAlpine & Sons Ltd., Cheshire, Eng., 1958-60; mem. faculty Harvard U., 1966—, Gordon McKay prof. environ. engring., 1974—, prof. city planning, 1974—; mem. Center Population Studies, Harvard U. Sch. Pub. Health, 1974—; cons. World Bank, UN, U.S. Agy. for Internat. Devel., Govt. India, Govt. Pakistan, Govt. Bangladesh, Govt. Nepal, Govt. Italy, Govt. Costa Rica, Commonwealth P.R. Co-author: Urbanization and Change, 1970, Land Use and The Pipe: Planning for Sewerage, 1975, Resource Inventory and Baseline Study Methods for Developing Countries, 1983, Systems Analysis for River Basin Management, 1985, Evaluacion de Projectos de Desarrollo, 1990, America's Waters, 1993, Water in the Arab World, 1994. Gordon McKay tchg. fellow 1961; Radley rsch. student, 1962-64; doctoral dissertation fellow Resources for Future 1964-65; recipient Clemens Herschel prize Harvard U., 1964; Guggenheim fellow, 1973, 20th Century Found. fellowship, 1989. Mem. Third World Acad. Scis. (corr.), Indian Inst. Agrl. Engring. (life), Cosmos Club (Washington), Sigma Xi. Home: 20 Berkeley St Cambridge MA 02138-3410 Office: Harvard U 116 Pierce Hall Cambridge MA 02138

ROGERS, RALPH B., industrial business executive; b. Boston, 1909; married. Ed., Northeastern U. With Cummins Diesel Engine Corp., Edwards Co., Hill Diesel Engine Co., Ideal Power Lawnmower Co., Indian Motocycle Co., Rogers Diesel & Aircraft Corp., Rogers Internat. Corp., Armstrong Rubber Export Corp.; with Tex. Industries Inc., Dallas, 1950—, chmn. bd., pres., CEO, 1951-75, chmn. bd., 1975—; dir. numerous subsidiaries. Chmn. bd. dirs. Tex. Industries Found.; chmn. emeritus Pub. Communication Found. North Tex., Pub. Broadcasting Svc., Univ. Med. Ctr., Inc.; past bd. dirs. Nat. Captioning Inst.; trustee Northeastern U.; trustee, chmn. emeritus St. Mark's Sch. of Tex.; former chmn. bd. mgrs. Dallas County Hosp. Dist.; founding chmn., chmn. emeritus Dallas Arboretum and Bot. Soc.; pres. Dallas Found. for Health, Edn. and Rsch.; co-founder Children's TV Workshop; founder, chmn. Zale Lipshy Univ. Hosp. Mem. Masons. Office: Tex Industries Inc 1341 W Mockingbird Ln Ste 700W Dallas TX 75247-6905

ROGERS, RAYMOND JESSE, federal railroad associate administrator; b. Eugene, Oreg., Mar. 1, 1941; s. Raymond Everett and Virginia Elaine (Simpkins) R.; m. Joan Katherine Peterson, June 6, 1964 (div. Aug. 1974); 1 child, Virginia Arlene; m. Kim Lien Nguyen, Dec. 26, 1974; children: Kim Lan, Vincent Minh. Student, Santa Rosa (Calif.) Jr. Coll., 1960-61, U.S. Army Non-commd. Officer Acad., Anchorage, Alaska, 1963, U. Md., 1967-74, Fed. Exec. Inst., Charlottsville, Va., 1981. Lic. real estate agt., Va. Sr. asst. mgr. Household Fin. Corp., Md., 1964-67; contract specialist Dept. Navy, Washington, 1967-71; contract svcs. officer AID, Saigon, Vietnam, 1971-76; contracting officer Dept. Transp., Fed. R.R. Adminstrn., Washington, 1976-80, dir. fin. svcs., 1980-84, assoc. adminstr. for adminstrn., 1984—. Leader local group Boy Scouts Am., Vienna, Va., 1987-92, Izaac Walton League of Am., Am. Legion, Am. Assn. of Retired Persons. Sgt. U.S. Army, 1961-64. Decorated Vietnam Civilian Svc. medal. Mem. U.S. Sr. Exec. Svc., Fed. Exec. Inst. Alumni Assn. Avocations: fishing, hiking, camping, waterskiing. Home: 102 Yeonas Dr SW Vienna VA 22180-6557 Office: Dept Transp Fed RR Adminstrn 400 7th St SW Washington DC 20590-0001

ROGERS, RICHARD DEAN, federal judge; b. Oberlin, Kans., Dec. 29, 1921; s. William Clark and Evelyn May (Christian) R.; m. Helen Elizabeth Stewart, June 6, 1947; children—Letitia Ann, Cappi Christian, Richard Kurt. B.S., Kans. State U., 1943; J.D., Kans. U., 1947. Bar: Kans. 1947. Ptnr. firm Springer and Rogers (Attys.), Manhattan, Kans., 1947-58; instr. bus. law Kans. State U., 1948-52; partner firm Rogers, Stites & Hill, Manhattan, 1959-75; gen. counsel Kans. Farm Bur. & Service Cos., Manhattan, 1960-75; judge U.S. Dist. Ct., Topeka, Kans., 1975—. City commr., Manhattan, 1950-52, 60-64, mayor, 1952, 64, county atty., Riley County, Kans., 1954-58, state rep., 1964-68, state senator, 1968-75; pres. Kans. Senate, 1975. Served with USAAF, 1943-45. Decorated Air medal, Dfc. Mem. Kans., Am. bar assns., Beta Theta Pi. Republican. Presbyterian. Club: Masons. Office: US Dist Ct 444 SE Quincy St Topeka KS 66683

ROGERS, RICHARD F., construction company executive, architect, engineer; b. Chgo., July 25, 1942; s. Frank S. and Emily H. (Novak) R.; m. Christina L. Rogers, June 30, 1963; children: Mitchell, Cynthia. B in Architectural Engineering, U. Ill., Chgo., 1964. Registered architect, Ill., Wis., Mich., profl. engr., Ill. Architect Einstein Assocs. Inc., Skokie, Ill., 1963-69; v.p. Land Am. Corp., Chgo., 1969-70; project architect M.A. Lombard Constrn. Co., Alsip, Ill., 1970-73; sr. project mgr. W.E. O'Neil Constrn. Co., Chgo., 1973-78; pres. A.C.M. Assocs. Inc., Mt. Prospect, Ill., 1978—. Mem. AIA, Builders Assn. Chgo. Office: ACM Assocs Inc 322 N Wolf Rd Mount Prospect IL 60056-2724

ROGERS, RICHARD HUNTER, lawyer, business executive; b. Flushing, N.Y., Sept. 11, 1939; s. Royden Harrison and Frances Wilma (Hunter) R.; children: Gregory P., Lynne A., Reade H. B.S. in Bus. Adminstrn, Miami U., 1961; J.D., Duke, 1964. Bar: Ill. 1964, Ohio 1973. Atty. Continental Ill. Nat. Bank, Chgo., 1964-65; sr. atty. Brunswick Corp., Chgo., 1965-70; corporate counsel The A. Epstein Cos., Inc. (real estate developers), Chgo., 1970-73; v.p., gen. counsel, sec. Price Bros. Co., Dayton, Ohio, 1973-82; v.p., div. mgr. Water Systems Tech. div. Price Bros. Co., Dayton, Ohio, 1982-85; v.p., div. mgr. Internat. div. Price Bros. Co., Dayton, Ohio, 1986-88; chmn. Rogers Internat. Inc., 1988—; pvt. practice law Dayton, 1988—. Pres. adv. coun. Miami U. Bus. Sch.; bd. dirs. Red and White Club, Miami U.; mem. Washington Twp. Task Force on Future Govt.; trustee Woodhaven, Inc.; mem., vice chmn. Washington Twp. Zoning Commn. Mem. ABA (forum com. on constrn.), Ill. Bar Assn., Ohio Bar Assn., Dayton Bar Assn. (chmn. corp. law dept. com. 1983-84, exec. com. 1986-87, editor Bar Briefs 1990-91), Miami U. Alumni Assn. (pres.), Miami U. Pres.'s Club., Sycamore Creek Country Club. Office: 7333 Paragon Rd Ste 200 Dayton OH 45459-4157 Address: PO Box 751144 Dayton OH 45475-1144

ROGERS, RICHARD LEE, educator; b. N.Y.C., Sept. 17, 1949; s. Leonard J. and Beverly (Simon) R.; m. Susan Jane Thornton, Aug. 14, 1976; children: Caroline, Meredith. BA, Yale U., 1971, MA in Religion, 1973; postgrad., U. Chgo., 1977-80; MS in Edn., Bank St. Coll. Edn., N.Y.C., 1989. Tchr. Foote Sch., New Haven, 1974-77; devel. assoc. U. Chgo., 1980-81, spl. asst. to v.p. planning, 1981-82; spl. asst. to pres. New Sch. Social Rsch., N.Y.C., 1982-83, sec. of corp., then v.p., sec., 1983-94; pres. Ctr. for Creative Studies, Detroit, 1994—. Mem. Univ. Cultural Ctr. Assn. (v.p., bd. dirs.). Office: Ctr Creative Studies 201 E Kirby St Detroit MI 48202-4048

ROGERS, ROBERT BURNETT, naval officer; b. Plainfield, N.J., May 25, 1931; s. Jack Willoughby and Margaret (Snyder) R.; m. Jeanne Weaver, Mr. 15, 1956 (dec. Sept. 1978); children: Robert Burnett, Steven Michael, John Weaver, Kathryn Patricia; m. Marolyn Maybelline Templeton, May 25, 1981. B.S., U.S. Naval Acad., 1954; M.S., George Washington U., 1968. Commd. ensign U.S. Navy, 1954, advanced through grades to rear adm., 1981; comdg. officer U.S.S. Austin, Norfolk, Va., 1977-78; asst. chief of staff Naval Surface Force Atlantic, Atlantic Fleet, Norfolk, 1978-80; dep. comdr. Naval Surface Force Atlantic, Norfolk, 1982-83; comdr. Destroyer Squardron Eight, Mayport, Fla., 1980-81; dep. chief of staff Supreme Allied Command Atlantic, Norfolk, 1981-82; comdr. Amphibious Group Two, Norfolk, 1983-86; dir. logistics Atlantic Fleet, Norfolk, 1986, ret., 1986. City Commr. Fernandina Beach, 1994, mayor, 1996-97. Decorated Legion of Merit with 4 gold stars; recipient William S. Sims award Navy League U.S. Mem. U.S. Naval Inst., Marine Corps. Assn. Roman Catholic. Home: 2056 Oak Marsh Dr Fernandina Beach FL 32034-2407

ROGERS, ROBERT ERNEST, medical educator; b. West Palm Beach, Fla., Nov. 16, 1928; s. Jessie H. and Willie L. (Bahr) R.; m. Barbara Ann Hill, May 16, 1950; children: Robert E. Jr., Stephanie Ann Thompson, Cheri Lee Heck. BS, John B. Stetson U., 1949; MD, U. Miami, 1957. Diplomate Am. Bd. Ob-Gyn. Commd. 1st lt. M.C., U.S. Army, 1952, advanced through grades to col., 1971; intern Brooke Gen. Hosp., San Antonio, 1957-58, chief resident ob-gyn, 1960-61; resident in ob-gyn Jackson Meml. Hosp., Miami, Fla., 1958-60; fellow gynecology M.D. Anderson Hosp., Houston, 1965-66; asst. chief ob-gyn Tripler Army Med. Ctr., Honolulu, 1966-69; chmn. ob-gyn Walter Reed Med. Ctr., Washington, 1969-70, Madigan Army Med. Ctr., Tacoma, Wash., 1970-74; ret. U.S. Army, 1974; prof. Ind. U. Sch. Medicine, Indpls., 1974—, also chief gynecol. div., 1974—; chief ob-gyn svd. Wishard Meml. Hosp., Indpls., 1983-87. Contbr. articles on ob-gyn to profl. jours. Mem. AMA, Am. Coll. Ob-Gyn (chmn. gynecol. practice com., commr. practice), Soc. Gynecol. Surgeons (pres. 1983-84), Soc. Gynecol. Oncologists. Office: Ind U Sch Medicine 550 University Blvd Indianapolis IN 46202-5149

ROGERS, ROBERT MARK, physician; b. Upper Darby, Pa., June 9, 1933; s. John Francis and Clara (Baumann) R.; m. Sandra Betz, Feb. 14, 1968; children: Janet Marie, Robert Mark, Linda, William Bradford, David Philip. BA cum laude, LaSalle Coll., Phila., 1956; MD, U. Pa., 1960. Intern Hosp. of U. Pa., 1960-61, chief emergency svcs., 1968-69, founder, dir. respiratory ICU, 1968-72, dir. pulmonary disease sect. tng. program, 1970-72; resident Case Western Res. U. Hosps., Cleve., 1961-63; fellow in pulmonary disease VA Hosp., Cleve., 1963-64; fellow in pulmonary disease U. Pa., 1964-65, postdoctoral trainee in physiology, 1966-68, asst. prof. medicine and assoc. in physiology, 1968-72; prof.medicine, assoc. prof. physiology Okla. Health Scis. Ctr. Coll. Medicine, 1972-80, also chief pulmonary disease sect., dept. medicine, dir. clin. pulmonary physiology lab. hosp. and clinics; prof. medicine, chief pulmonary, allergy & critical care medicine U. Pitts. Med. Sch., 1980-96, dir. Comprehensive Lung Ctr., 1990—. Editor: Respiratory Intensive Care, 1977; mem. editl. bd. Current Opinion in Pulmonary Medicine and Critical Care; contbr. rsch. articles to profl. pubs. Mem. ACP (U.S. rep. to Chinese Med. Assn. 1979, founding editor-in-chief audio cassettes program 1978-80), Am. Thoracic Soc. (founding dir. Learning Resources Ctr. 1971-77, Presdl. commendation 1977), Am. Fedn. Clin. Rsch., Am. Coll. Chest Physicians, Am. Physiol. Soc., Soc. Critical Care Medicine, Am. Heart Assn., Ctrl. Soc. Clin. Rsch., So. Soc. Clin. Rsch., Pa. Thoracic Soc. (pres. 1985-88), Coll. Physicians Phila. Home: 4116 Bigelow Blvd Pittsburgh PA 15213-1408 Office: U Pitts Sch Medicine 440 Scaife Hall Pittsburgh PA 15261-2004

ROGERS, RODDY, civil and geotechnical engineer; b. Springfield, Mo.. BSCE cum laude, U. Mo., 1981, MSCE, 1983, MS in Engring. Mgmt., 1990. Registered profl. engr., Mo. Asst. and staff engr. Dames and Moore Consulting Firm, Phoenix, Ariz., 1983-85; project mgr. City Utilities, Springfield, 1985-90, sr. engr. civil engring. sect. system engring., 1990—; teaching asst. soil mechanics U. Mo., 1981-83, rsch. asst. soil mechanics lab., 1982-83; 4 time gov. appointee to Mo. Dam and Reservoir Safety Coun.; presented numerous papers. Contbr. articles to profl. jours. Trustee missions com. 1st Bapt. Ch., Springfield, 1989-94; judge sci. fair Springfield Pub. Schs., 1988-89; bd. dirs. Jr. Achievement, 1986-87; vol. Engring. Ministries Internat., 1988, 90-93. Needles scholar, Curators scholar; Recipient Young Engr. Awd., 1991, Nat. Soc. Profl. Engr. Mem. NSPE (chpt. treas. 1988-89, chpt. sec. mem. various coms., chpt. pres.-elect 1990-91, pres. 1991-92, Young Engr. of Yr. award Ozark chpt. 1990, Young Engr. of Yr. award 1991, Edmund Friedmund Young Engr. award for svc. to global cmty. 1991), ASCE, Am. Water Works Assn., Nat. Water Well Assn., Assn. State Dam Safety Ofcls. (award of excellence in dam safety), Mo. Soc. Profl. Engrs. (ethics task force chmn., Young Engr. of Yr. award 1990, Extra Mile Resolution award), Mid-Mo. Soc. Civil Engrs. (3d v.p. 1989-90, 2d v.p. 1990-91, 1st v.p. 1991-92, pres. 1992-93), U. Mo.-Rolla Civil Engrs. Alumni Adv. Coun., Tau Beta Pi, Chi Epsilon. Home: 2241 E Powell St Springfield MO 65804-4692 Office: City Utilities Springfield PO Box 551 Springfield MO 65801-0551

ROGERS, RODNEY ALBERT, biologist, educator; b. Lucas, Iowa, Aug. 24, 1926; s. Harold A. and Ardis (Allen) R.; m. Frances A. Ritchey, July 1, 1956; children—Robert, William. B.A., Drake U., 1949, M.A., 1951; Ph.D., U. Iowa, 1955. Asst. prof. biology Drake U., Des Moines, 1955-60; asso. prof. Drake U., 1961-64, prof., 1965—, chmn. biology dept., 1966-92; asso. program dir. NSF, 1967-68. Served with AUS, 1944-46, PTO. Mem. A.A.A.S., Am. Inst. Biol. Sci., Am. Soc. Parasitologists, Soc. Am. Microbiologists, Am. Soc. Zoologists, Am. Assn. U. Profs., Am. Soc. Tropical Medicine and Hygiene, Sigma Xi, Omicron Delta Kappa. Home: 4203 40th St Des Moines IA 50310-3702

ROGERS, ROSEMARY, author; b. Panadura, Ceylon, Dec. 7, 1932; came to U.S., 1962; naturalized citizen.; d. Cyril Allan and Barbara (Jansze); m. Summa Navaratnam (div.); children: Rosanne, Sharon; m. Leroy Rogers (div.); children: Michael, Adam; m. Christopher Kadison (div.). B.A., U. Ceylon. Writer features and pub. affairs info. Associated Newspapers Ceylon, Colombo, 1959-62; sec. billeting office Travis AFB, Calif., 1964-69; sec. Solano County (Calif.) Parks Dept., Fairfield, 1969-74; part-time reporter Fairfield Daily Republic. Author: (novels) Sweet Savage Love, 1974, The Wildest Heart, 1974, Dark Fires, 1975, Wicked Loving Lies, 1976, The Crowd Pleasers, 1978, The Insiders, 1979, Lost Love, Last Love, 1980, Love Play, 1981, Surrender to Love, 1982, The Wanton, 1985, Bound by Desire, 1988, The Tea Planter's Bride, 1995, A Dangerous Man, 1996. Mem. Authors Guild of Authors League Am., Writers Guild Am. *

ROGERS, ROY (LEONARD FRANKLIN SLYE), country musician, actor; b. Cin., Nov. 5, 1911; s. Andrew E. and Mattie Martha (Womach) Slye; m. Arlene Wilkins, 1936 (dec. Nov. 1946); children: Cheryl Darlene, Linda Lou, Roy Jr., Marion, Scottish Ward; m. Dale Evans; children: Robin (dec.), John (dec.), Mary Little Doe, Deborah (dec.). pres. Roy Rogers Enterprises; past owner Roy Rogers Apple Valley Inn; owner Roy Rogers Western World and Mus., Victorville, Calif.; franchised Roy Rogers Family Restaurants. Organized western group Sons of the Pioneers; appeared in numerous films including Under Western Stars, 1938, The Old Corral, Frontier Pony Express, Silver Spurs, My Pal Trigger, Son of Paleface, Mackintosh & T.J.; former radio singer; TV series, spls.; actor, prodr. TV films; host TV show The Great Movie Cowboys, 1975; many personal appearances rodeos, fairs; rec. artist Capitol Records, 20th Century Records, RCA Records; albums include, Best Of, 1990, Tribute, 1991, Rhythm & Groove, 1996; author: (with Dale Evans) Happy Trails: Our Life Story, 1994. Mem. AFTRA, SAG, Am. Guild Variety Artists, Musicians Union, Masons. Address: RCA/BMG Music 1 Music Cir N Nashville TN 37203-4310*

ROGERS, ROY STEELE, III, dermatology educator, dean; b. Hillsboro, Ohio, Mar. 3, 1940; s. Roy S. Jr. and Anna Mary (Murray) R.; m. Susan Camille Hudson, Aug. 22, 1964; children: Roy Steele IV, Katherine Hudson. BA, Denison U., 1962; MD, Ohio State U., 1966; MS, U. Minn., 1974. Cert. dermatologist, dermatopathologist and immunodermatologist. Intern Strong meml. Hosp., Rochester, N.Y., 1966-67; resident Duke U. Med. Ctr., Durham, N.C., 1969-71; resident Mayo Clinic, Rochester, Minn., 1972-73, cons., 1973—, prof. dermatology, 1983—, dean Sch. Health Related Scis., 1991—; adv. coun. Rochester Community Coll., 1991—. Contbr. over 170 sci. articles to publs. Capt. USAF, 1967-69. Recipient Alumni Achievement award Ohio State U. Coll. of Medicine, 1991, Alumni citation Denison U., 1993, Faculty Svc. award Mayo Med. Sch., 1993. Mem. Am. Acad. Dermatology (bd. dirs. 1988-91), Am. Soc. Dermatologic Allergy and Immunology (sec.-treas. 1988—), Am. Dermatologic Assn., Soc. Investigative Dermatology, Assn. Schs. Allied Health Professions, Dermatology Found. Avocations: travel, family, reading. Home: 1101 7th Ave SW Rochester MN 55902-6333 Office: Mayo Clinic 200 1st St SW Rochester MN 55902-3008

ROGERS, RUTHERFORD DAVID, librarian; b. Jesup, Iowa, June 22, 1915; s. David Earl and Carrie Zoe (Beckel) R.; m. E. Margaret Stoddard, June 4, 1937; 1 child, Jane Shelley. B.A., U. No. Iowa, 1936, Litt.D., 1977; M.A., Columbia, 1937, B.S. (Lydia Roberts fellow), 1938; D.Library Adminstrn. (hon.), U. Dayton, 1971. Asst. N.Y. Pub. Library, 1937-38; reference librarian Columbia Coll. Library, Columbia U., 1938- 41, acting librarian, 1941-42, librarian, 1942-45; research analyst Smith, Barney & Co., N.Y.C., 1946-48; dir. Grosvenor Library, Buffalo, 1948-52, Rochester Pub. Library, 1952-54; chief personnel office N.Y. Library, 1954-55; chief reference dept., 1955-57; chief asst. librarian of Congress, Washington, 1957-62; dep. librarian of Congress, 1962-64; dir. univ. libraries Stanford U., 1964-69; univ. librarian Yale U., 1969-85, univ. librarian emeritus, 1985—; dir. H.W. Wilson Co., 1969—; founder, chmn. bd. dirs. Rsch. Librs. Group, Inc.; mem. Exam. Com. for Pub. Librarians' Certs., N.Y. State, 1951-54; mem. U.S. Adv. Coun. Coll. Libr. Resources; bd. govs. Yale U. Press; bd. dirs., v.p. H.W. Wilson Found., 1995—; chmn. program mgmt. com. Internat. Fedn. Libr. Assns. Author: Columbia Coll. Library Handbook, 1941, (with David C. Weber) University Library Administration, 1971; also articles in profl. jours. Served from pvt. to 1st sgt. Air Transp. Command USAAF, 1942-43; from 2d lt. to capt., planning officer, chief, spl. Planning Div., Office Asst. Chief Staff, Plans, Air Transport Command 1943-46. Decorated officier de L'Ordre de la Couronne Belge; recipient U. No. Iowa Alumni Achievement award, 1958, Disting. Alumni award Columbia U. Sch. Libr. Svc., 1992. Fellow Am. Acad. Arts and Scis.; mem. A.L.A. (chmn. com. Intellectual Freedom 1950-51), (1950-60), (2d v.p. 1965-66), (mem. exec. bd. 1961-66), (trustee endowment fund), Assn. Research Libraries (dir., pres. 1967-68), N.Y. Library Assn., AAUP, Bibliog. Soc. Am., Assn. Coll. and Reference Libraries, Blue Key, Kappa Delta Pi, Sigma Tau Delta, Theta Alpha Phi. Clubs: Grolier; N.Y. Library (N.Y.C.), Columbia U. (N.Y.C.), Yale (N.Y.C.); Cosmos (Washington), Kenwood Country (Washington); Roxburghe (San Francisco); Book of Calif. Home: 1111 S Lakemont Ave Apt 605 Winter Park FL 32792-5474

ROGERS, RYNN MOBLEY, community health nurse; b. Georgetown, S.C., Aug. 2, 1950; d. Ralph Edward and Pearl (Hill) Mobley; m. C. Rogers Jr., July 3, 1971 (div. Mar. 1992); 1 child, Julie Pearl. Student, Georgetown County Sch. Nursing, 1970; AS, SUNY, Albany, 1982; AS in Criminal Justice, Georgetown Tech. Coll., 1992; postgrad., 1994. Cert. community nurse, med. asst. Mem. staff Georgetown Meml. Hosp., 1969-71; office nurse Dr. L. Benton Williams, Georgetown, 1971—; jail nurse Georgetown County Detention Ctr., 1991-92; staff devel. nurse Prince George Village, 1992—. Mem. ANA, Am. Assn. Office Nurses, Nat. Assn. Physicians Nurses, S.C. Nurses Assn., Order Ea. Star. Baptist. Avocations: crafts, cross stitch, photography, fabric painting, wedding photography. Home: 217 Beneventum Rd Georgetown SC 29440-9461 Office: 1743 N Fraser St Georgetown SC 29440-6407 also: Prince George Village 901 Maple St Georgetown SC 29440

ROGERS, SAMUEL SHEPARD See SHEPARD, SAM

ROGERS, SHARON J., education consultant; b. Grantsburg, Wis., Sept. 24, 1941; d. Clifford M. and Dorothy L. (Beckman) Dickau; m. Evan D. Rogers, June 15, 1962 (div. Dec. 1980). BA summa cum laude, Bethel Coll., St. Paul, 1963; MA in Libr. Sci., U. Minn., 1967; PhD in Sociology, Wash. State U., Pullman, 1976. Lectr., instr. Alfred (N.Y.) U., 1972-76; assoc. prof. U. Toledo, 1977-80; assoc. dean Bowling Green (Ohio) State U. Librs., 1980-84; univ. libr. George Washington U., Washington, 1984-92, asst. v.p. acad. affairs, 1989-92, assoc. v.p. acad. affairs, 1992-97, co-dir. Univ. Teaching Ctr., 1990-97; mem. Online Computer Libr.Ctr. Users Coun., 1985-92, pres., 1989-90, mem. rsch. adv. com., 1990-92, trustee, 1992—, chair, 1997; exec. dir. Assn. for Libr. and Info. Sci. Edn., 1997—. Contbr. articles to profl. jours. Bd. dirs. ACLU, Toledo, 1978-84, CapAccess, 1993—, treas., 1993-95. Jackson fellow U. Minn., 1964-65; NSF trainee Wash. State U., 1969-72. Mem. ALA (exec. coun. 1987-91, pub. com. 1989-93, chair 1990-93), Assn. Coll. and Rsch. Librs. (pres. 1984-85), Am. Sociol. Assn., Washington Rsch. Libr. Consortium (bd. dirs 1987-90), Universal Serials and Book Exch. (bd. dirs., treas. 1987).

ROGERS, SHERRY ANNE, physician; b. Syracuse, N.Y., Apr. 15, 1943; d. Rodney Wellington and Hayne (Marshall) Hammond; m. Robert Hamilton Rogers, June 30, 1970. BA, Syracuse U., 1965; MD, SUNY, 1969-70. Pediatrician pvt. practice, Auburn, N.Y., 1970-71; emergency physician Cmty. Gen. Hosp., Syracuse, N.Y., 1971-72; family physician pvt. practice, Syracuse, N.Y., 1972-85, physician environ. medicine, 1978—. Author. (Books) Depression Cured At Last, Wellness Against All Odds, Tired of Toxic, You Are What You Ate, The EF Syndrome Chemical Sensitivity,

Contbr. articles to profl. jours. Office: Northeast Ctr Environ Med 2800 W Genesee St Syracuse NY 13219-1451

ROGERS, STEPHEN, newspaper publisher; b. Lansing, Mich., Feb. 24, 1912; s. Anthony and Anna (Kruszewska) R.; m. Athenia A. Andros, Oct. 19, 1935; children: Stephen A., Christopher A., Elizabeth A. A.B., Mich. State Coll., 1933; LLD (hon.), Syracuse U., 1988. Writer Detroit Times, 1934-35; copy editor N.Y. Herald-Tribune (European edit.), Paris, France, 1936-37; spl. writer Newark Ledger, 1937-38; editorial writer, city editor Long Island Daily Press, 1938-41; editor Long Island Star-Jour., 1941-55; pub. Post Standard, Syracuse, N.Y., 1955-58, Herald-Journal, Herald-Am., Syracuse; and pres. The Herald Co., 1958—; dir. N.Y. Dental Service Corp., N.Y.C., Mchts. Nat. Bank; pres. Met. Devel. Assn., 1980—. Bd. dirs. Crouse-Irving Hosp., Syracuse. Mem. N.Y. State Pubs. Assn. (pres. 1963), Am. Newspaper Pubs. Assn. Roman Catholic. Office: Syracuse Newspapers Ltd Clinton Sq PO Box 4915 Syracuse NY 13221-4915

ROGERS, STEPHEN HITCHCOCK, former ambassador; b. Flushing, N.Y., June 21, 1930; s. Francis Walker and Julia (Wheeler) R.; m. Kent Brain, June 23, 1956; children: Kryston R. Fischer, F. Halsey, Julia L., John H. BA, Princeton U., 1952; MA, Columbia U., 1956; MPA, Harvard U., 1962. Fgn. svc. officer Dept. of State, 1956-93; econ. counselor Am. Embassy, London, 1970-72; counselor U.S. Mission to OECD, Paris, 1972-75; office dir. Bur. Inter.-Am. Affairs Dept. of State, Washington, 1975-78; econ. counselor Am. Embassy, Mexico City, 1978-82; prof. Nat. Def. U., Washington, 1982-85; econ. counselor Am. Embassy, Pretoria, South Africa, 1986-90; amb. Am. Embassy, Mbabane, Swaziland, 1990-93. Lt. (jg) USN, 1952-55. Mem. United Ch. of Christ. Home: 3803 Ivydale Dr Annandale VA 22003-2006

ROGERS, STEVEN RAY, physicist; b. Tachikawa, Honshu, Japan, Dec. 6, 1952; came to U.S., 1953; s. Culis Doyle Martin and Mary Lu (Bowles) Rogers; m. Robina Rae Behel, Dec. 27, 1975; children: Miranda Rae, Kellina Gail. BA in Math./Physics magna cum laude, U. No. Colo., 1975; MS in Physics, Kans. State U., 1977. Rschr., instr. Kans. State U., Manhattan, 1975-79; tech. staff ElectroMagnetic Applications, Lakewood, Colo., 1979-82; lead engr. MITRE Corp., Colorado Springs, Colo., 1982—; cons., advisor on system survivability and hardening North Am. Aerospace Def. Command * U.S. Space Command, Colorado Springs, 1982—; adj. prof. Webster U., Colorado Springs, 1994. Contbr. articles to Jour. Physics: Atomic & Molecular, IEEE Transactions on Nuclear Sci. and other profl. jours. Mentor for gifted students Colorado Springs Schs. #20, 1992-93; host family for cadet USAF Acad., Colorado Springs, 1994—. Recipient Program Recognition award MITRE Corp., 1988, 1996. Mem. IEEE (sr., chmn. Pikes Peak sect. 1993-94), Sigma Pi Sigma, Lambda Sigma Tau. Achievements include co-invention of global situation awareness information distribution system (patent pending); co-founder of programs that sustain the survivability of NORAD and U.S. Space Command systems; evaluation and integration of NORAD systems. Home: 5510 Broadmoor Bluffs Dr Colorado Springs CO 80906-7971 Office: MITRE Corp 1150 Academy Park Loop Ste 212 Colorado Springs CO 80910-3716

ROGERS, THEODORE COURTNEY, investment company executive; b. Lorain, Ohio, Aug. 25, 1934; s. William Theodore and Leona Ruth (Gerhart) R.; m. Elizabeth B. Barlow, June 28, 1984; children by previous marriage: Pamela Anne Rogers Harmon, Theodore Courtney Jr. BS in Social Sci., Miami U., Oxford, Ohio, 1956; postgrad. Johns Hopkins U., 1957; MBA summa cum laude, Marquette U., 1968. With Armco Inc., 1958-80; pres. Olympic Fastening Systems, 1970-74, with Bathey Mfg. Co. subs., 1970, group v.p. indsl. products, 1971-74, exec. v.p. Nat. Supply Co. subs., Houston, 1974-76, pres., 1976-80, v.p. parent co., 1976-79, group v.p. parent co., 1979-80; pres., COO NL Industries, Inc., N.Y.C., 1980-82, pres., CEO, 1982-83, chmn., pres., CEO, 1983-87; ptnr. Am. Indsl. Ptnrs., N.Y., 1987—; bd. dirs. Sweetheart Cup, Day Internat., Derby Internat., Nottingham, Eng.; chmn. bd. Sunshine Materials, Easco Aluminum, RBX Corp. Bd. dirs. United Cerebral Palsy Rsch. and Ednl. Found., Inc., Ballet Rev., Lincoln Ctr. for Performing Arts, City Ctr. for Music and Drama, Poets & Writers, Nat. Ocean Industries Assn.; chmn. bd. Theatre for New Audience, Ctr. Cmty. Interests; former chmn. N.Y.C. Ballet; trustee Ballet Review. Lt. USN, 1956-58. Mem. Petroleum Equipment Suppliers Assn. (bd. dirs.), N.Y. Soc. Libr. (trustee), World Pres. Orgn., Century Assn. (N.Y.), Bus. Roundtable, Poets and Writers (bd. dirs.), Achilles Track Club (founder, bd. dirs.), Ramada Club, Houston Country Club, Links Club, Sky Club, Econ. Club (N.Y.), Met. Club (Washington), The Union Club (Cleve.), Century Assn., Beta Gamma Sigma (bd. dirs.), Kappa Phi Kappa, Sigma Chi. Office: Am Indsl Ptnr 551 5th Ave Ste 3800 New York NY 10176-0001

ROGERS, THEODORE OTTO, JR., lawyer; b. West Chester, Pa., Nov. 17, 1953; s. Theodore Otto and Gladys (Bond) R.; m. Hope Tyler Scott, Nov. 7, 1981; children: Helen Elliot, Theodore Scott, Robert Montgomery Bond. AB magna cum laude, Harvard U., 1976, JD cum laude, 1979. Bar: N.Y. 1980, U.S. Ct. Appeals (2nd cir.) 1980, U.S. Dist. Ct. (so. and ea. dists.) N.Y. 1980, D.C. 1981, U.S. Ct. Claims, 1982, U.S. Supreme Ct. 1983, U.S. Ct. Appeals (6th and 10th cirs.) 1983, U.S. Ct. Appeals (1st cir.) 1984, U.S. Ct. Appeals (fed. cir.) 1986. From assoc. to ptnr. Sullivan & Cromwell, N.Y.C., 1979—. Co-author: Employment Litigation in New York, 1996. Mem. U.S. Presdl. Transition Team, 1980. Mem. ABA, Assn. of Bar of City of N.Y. (labor and employment law), Down Town Assn. Republican. Home: 535 E 86th St New York NY 10028-7533 Office: Sullivan & Cromwell 125 Broad St New York NY 10004-2400

ROGERS, THOMAS FRANCIS, foundation administrator; b. Providence, Aug. 11, 1923; s. Thomas Francis and H. Ann (Flaharty) R.; m. Estelle E. Hunt, July 6, 1946; children: Clare, Judith Reynolds, Hope Grove. BS cum laude, Providence Coll., 1945; MA, Boston U., 1949. Rsch. assoc. Radio Rsch. Lab. Harvard U., Cambridge, Mass., 1944-45; TV engr. Bell and Howell Co., Chgo., 1945-46; electronics scientist AF Cambridge Rsch. Ctr., Cambridge, Mass., 1946-54; assoc. group leader MIT Lincoln Lab., Cambridge, 1951-53; lab. head AF Cambridge Rsch. Ctr., Bedford, Mass., 1954-59; div. head and steering com. mem. MIT Lincoln Lab., Bedford, 1959-64; asst. dir. def. rsch. and engring. Office of Sec. Def., Washington, 1964-65, dep. dir. def. rsch. and engring., 1965-67; dir. rsch. and tech. Office of Sec. HUD, Washington, 1967-69; v.p. The Mitre Corp., Washington, Bedford, 1969-72; pres. The Sophron Found., McLean, Va., 1980—; dir. U.S. Congress Office of Tech. Assessment Study on Civilian Space Stas. and U.S. Future in Space, Washington, 1982-84; pres. The Space Transp. Assn., Arlington, 1992—; founding chmn. bd. dirs. External Tanks Corp., Boulder, Colo.; bd. dirs. Internat. Radio Satellite Corp., Washington, Space Destinations Svcs., Inc., 1994—; chmn. bd. dirs. Luna Corp., Great Falls, Va., 1991—; chmn. POLARIS Command-Comm. Co., USN, 1960-64; mem. Satellite Comm. Panel, Pres.'s Sci. Adv. Com., 1961-63; mem. Dept. Def. NASA Satellite Comm. Com., 1961-64; U.S.A. del. UN Conf. on Applications of Sci. and Tech. by Lesser Developed Nations, Geneva, 1963; mem. Fed. Aeronautics and Astronautics Coordinating Bd., 1965-67, Fed. Coun. on Sci. and Tech., 1967-69; mem. Space Program Adv. Coun., NASA, 1971-73, chmn. applications com., 1972-73; mem. NAS com. on regional emergency med. comm. systems, 1976-78, space applications bd. com. on NASA space comms. 1986-87, com. on antenna, satellite broadcasting and emergency preparedness for Voice of Am., 1986-88, adv. com. study space transp. U.S. Congrl. Office Tech. Assessment, 1994-95. Contbr. articles to jours., chpts. to books. Trustee X-Prize Found., 1995—. Recipient Outstanding Performance award CSC, 1957, cert. commendation Sec. Navy, 1961, Meritorious Civilian Svc. award and medal, Sec. Def., Constrn.'s Man of Yr. award Engring. News Record, 1969, Space Pioneer award Nat. Space Soc., 1988. Fellow IEEE (past chmn. aerospace R&D policy com. 1991-95, Profl. Achievement award 1995); mem. Cosmos Club (Washington). Home and Office: 7404 Colshire Dr Mc Lean VA 22102-7404

ROGERS, VANCE DONALD, former university president; b. Frontenac, Minn., May 16, 1917; s. Azzy Floyd and Mary C. (Martinson) R.; m. Barbara Marie Yarwood, June 22, 1940; children: Nancy Ann Rogers Steele, Mary Lou Rogers Frederickson. Student, Gustavus Adolphus Coll., St. Peter, Minn., 1934-36; A.B., Hamline U., 1938, LL.D., 1976; postgrad., Northwestern U., 1940-41; M.Div., Garrett Bibl. Inst., 1941; D.D., Nebr. Wesleyan U., 1955; LL.D., Mt. Union Coll., 1958; L.H.D., Morningside Coll., 1960; Litt.D., Lane Coll., 1966; L.H.D., U. Nebr., 1968; S.T.D., Oklahoma City U., 1984. Ordained to ministry Methodist Ch., 1941; minister Meth. Ch., Dundee, Ill., 1941-43, Brookfield, Ill., 1946-53; minister Trinity Meth. Ch., Lincoln, Nebr., 1953-57; pres. Nebr. Wesleyan U., Lincoln, 1957-77; chmn. bd. Pure Water, Inc., 1978-80; ret., 1981; staff cons. Lincoln Found., Inc. (Nebr.), 1981-86; sr. assoc., v.p. Larry Price & Assocs., Lincoln, 1986-87; adv. dir. Nat. Bank Commerce, Lincoln, 1986-94. Served as lt. comdr. Chaplains Corps, USNR, 1943-46. Mem. Nebr. Acad. Scis., Newcomen Soc. N.Am., Am. Legion, Blue Key, C. of C., Phi Kappa Phi, Phi Eta Sigma, Pi Kappa Delta. Clubs: Mason (Lincoln) (Shriner, K.T.), Univ. (Lincoln), Lincoln Country (Lincoln), Rotary (Lincoln). Home: 3741 Faulkner Dr Apt 307 Lincoln NE 68516-4746 *A successful life is one that is: disciplined (body, mind, and spirit); adventuresome (seeking new ideas, innovative approaches to problem solving, and new areas of exploration); dedicated (to personal standards that call for mature responses-to ideal patterns of behavior-to moral and spiritual ideals rooted in the Judeo-Christian tradition).*

ROGERS, VERN CHILD, engineering company executive; b. Salt Lake City, Aug. 28, 1941; s. Vern S. and Ruth (Child) R.; m. Patricia Powell, Dec. 14, 1962. BS, U. Utah, 1965, MS, 1965; PhD, MIT, 1969. Registered profl. engr. Assoc. prof. Brigham Young U., Provo, Utah, 1969-73; vis. assoc. prof. Lowell Tech. Inst., 1970-71; mgr. IRT Corp., San Diego, 1973-76; v.p. Ford, Bacon & Davis, Salt Lake City, 1976-80; pres. Rogers & Assocs. Engring. Corp., Salt Lake City, 1980—. Contbr. articles to profl. jours. Mem. Health Physics Soc., Am. Soc. Profl. Engrs., Am. Nuclear Soc., Am. Chem. Soc. Mormon. Office: Rogers & Assocs Engring Corp PO Box 330 Salt Lake City UT 84110-0330

ROGERS, WARREN JOSEPH, JR., journalist; b. New Orleans, May 6, 1922; s. Warren Joseph and Rose Agatha (Tennyson) R.; m. Hilda Kenny, Dec. 23, 1943 (dec.); children: Patricia Ann, Sean; m. Alla Bilajiw, Dec. 26, 1973; 1 son, Michael (dec.). Student, Tulane U., 1940-41, La. State U., 1951. Copy boy, cub reporter New Orleans Tribune, 1939-41; copyreader, columnist New Orleans Item, 1945-47; reporter A.P., Baton Rouge, 1947-51; reporter A.P., Washington, 1951-53, diplomatic corr., 1953-59; mil., fgn. affairs corr. assignments abroad Wash. Bur. N.Y. Herald Tribune, 1959-63; chief Washington corr. Hearst Newspapers, assignments abroad, 1963-66; Washington editor LOOK mag., 1966-69, chief, 1969-70; mil., fgn. affairs corr. Washington bur. Los Angeles Times, 1970-71; Washington columnist Chgo. Tribune-N.Y. News syndicate, 1971-73; v.p. pub. affairs Nat. Forest Products Assn., Washington, 1973-76; editorial dir. Plus Publs., Washington, 1977-78; v.p., editor-in-chief Plus Publs., 1978-79; free-lance, 1979—; Washington bur. chief The Trib of N.Y., 1977-78; editor White House Weekly, 1981-89; exec. editor Associated Features, Inc., Washington editor, 1992—; editor This Week in the White House, 1989-90, Georgetown Courier, 1991-92; bd. dirs. Nat. Press Found.; founder Robert F. Kennedy Journalism awards; lectr. presdl. politics, mil. and fgn. affairs. Author: The Floating Revolution, 1962, Outpost of Freedom, 1965, (with others) An Honorable Profession: A Tribute to Robert F. Kennedy, 1968, (with Paul Watson) Sea Shepherd, 1982, When I think of Bobby: A Personal Memoir of the Kennedy Years, 1993. Served with USMCR, 1941-45. Recipient citation Overseas Press Club N.Y., 1963, Disting. Svc. award Nat. Press Found., 1991. Clubs: Nat. Press (pres. 1972), Federal City Club, Gridiron Club, Washington Ind. Writers. Home: 1622 30th St NW Washington DC 20007-2903 *In more than 50 years of reporting, I have learned that people yearn for the truth, as long as it is about somebody else. But they go to almost any length to conceal it or put a spin on it when it is about themselves. Yet, telling the truth is what a reporter must do. No wonder we rank behind Congress in the popularity polls.*

ROGERS, WERNER, state superintendent schools. State supt. schs. Ga. Dept. Edn., Atlanta, 1995; exec. dir. Georgia Public Broadcasting, 1995—. Office: Georgia Public Broadcasting 260 14th St NW Atlanta GA 30390*

ROGERS, WILLIAM, psychologist, consultant, writer, lecturer, journalist. BA in Broadcast Journalism, L.A. Inst. Arts, 1970; BA in Psychology, We. Ill. U., Macomb, 1979; MS in Counseling Psychology, Our Lady of the Lake U., San Antonio, 1989; PhD in Psychology, Columbia Pacific U., San Rafael, Calif., 1993; postgrad., Rollo May Ctr. Social Rsch. Saybrook Inst., San Francisco, 1994. Fgn. and domestic correspondent ABC News, NBC News, UPI Internat., KTRH Radio News, WOAI Radio News, 1970-85. Author: The Technology of Behavior, 1993, The Behavior Management Handbook, 1994, Creating Positive Behavior, 1995, Recovered Memory and Other Assaults Upon the Mysteries of Consciousness, 1995, Behavior and Consequences, 1997, Kids in Chaos, 1997; feature stories include Cmty. Responsibility, Behavior and Consequences, 1974, Missing Children, 1984; contbr. articles to profl. jours., TV and radio shows. Recipient George Foster Peabody Nomination Tex. Med. Assn., Wendall mays Pub. Svc. award Tex. Bar Assn., Gov.'s award AP, Tex. Assn. Broadcasters, Radio-T.V. News Dirs. Assn., Tex. Legislature Commendation, League of United Lat. Am. Citizens award Tex. State Network News, Coastal Bend Planning Commn. Spl. Svc. award, Headliner's News award; citation ABA, U.S. Senate, Spl. Citation City of Corpus Christi, Tex., Spl. Resoultion of Commendation Tex.Ho. Reps., Exceptional Recognition Entered Into Perpetuity State of Tex. Archives; recognized as founder of Behavior Mgmt. Philosophy and Methodology (Existential-Realism). Office: Behavior Rsch Inst 7201 Broadway St San Antonio TX 78209-3743

ROGERS, WILLIAM BROOKINS, financial consultant, business appraiser; b. Atlanta, Mar. 31, 1938; s. William Brookins and Mildred (LaHatte) R.; m. Carolyn Ansley Duren, May 28, 1966; children: W. Brandon, Alicia Deanne. BBA in Acctg., Ga. State U., 1965, MBA in Fin., 1968, PhD student in fin., 1968-70. CPA Ga., cert. mediator, arbitrator; state registered nutral mediator and arbitrator. Sr. acct. A.M. Pullen & Co. CPA's, Bus. Appraisers, Atlanta, 1964-69; pres., chmn. Ponderosa Internat., Inc., Atlanta, 1970-76; exec. v.p., chief op. ofcr. GRC/Tidewater Group, Atlanta, 1976-79; pres., CEO Atlanta Bil, Inc., 1979-86, Brookins Mgmt. Co., Inc., Atlanta, 1979—, Hilton Enterprises, Inc., Atlanta, 1981-96; bd. dirs. Ranick Ltd., Athens, Ga., 1981-96; lectr. Am. Mgmt. Assn., Atlanta, 1969-75, Bus. Grad. Sch. U. Ala., Tuscaloosa, 1970, Bus. Sch. Augusta State Coll., 1971; mem. nat. panel of comml. arbitrators Am. Arbitration Assn. With U.S. Army, 1959-61. Fellow AICPA; mem. Am. Arbitration Assn. (arbitrator nat. panel), Inst. Bus. Appraisers, Beta Gamma Sigma, Omicron Delta Kappa, Beta Alpha Psi. Republican. Episcopalian. Avocations: family, business. Home: 5425 Heathridge Terr Duluth GA 30155-5702 Office: Brooking Mgmt Co Inc PO Box 2198 Duluth GA 30136-8449

ROGERS, WILLIAM CECIL, political science educator; b. Manhattan, Kans., 1919; s. Charles Elkins and Sadie (Burns) R.; m. Mary Jane Anderson, Aug. 31, 1941; children: Shelley, Faith, Mary Sarah. B.A., U. Chgo., 1940, M.A., 1941, Ph.D., 1943. Asst. to dir. Pub. Adminstrn. Clearing House, Chgo., 1943-47; lectr. internat. relations U. Chgo., 1945-47; asst. prof. U. Va., 1947-48; asso. prof. polit. sci. Western Res. U., 1948-49; dir. World Affairs Center, U. Minn., Mpls., 1949-84; cons. Minn. Internat. Ctr., 1984—; dir. Program Info. on World Affairs, Mpls. Star and Tribune, 1951-73. Author: Community Education in World Affairs, 1956, A Guide to Understanding World Affairs, 1966, Global Dimensions in U.S. Education: The Community, 1972; co-author: The Winter City Book, 1980. Pres. Minn. Jazz Sponsors, 1966-67; chmn. Mpls. Com. on Urban Environ., 1976-80. Mem. Nat. Univ. Extension Assn. (past sec.-treas.), Winter Cities Assn. (co-founder 1982). Home: 3510 Mckinley St NE Minneapolis MN 55418-1511 Office: 711 E River Rd Minneapolis MN 55455-0369

ROGERS, WILLIAM DILL, lawyer; b. Wilmington, Del., May 12, 1927; m. Suzanne Rochford, Sept. 7, 1926; children: William Rogers, Daniel. B.A., Princeton U., 1948; LL.B., Yale U., 1951. Bar: D.C. 1952, U.S. Supreme Ct. 1954. Ptnr. Arnold & Porter, Washington, intermittently 1953—; dep. U.S. coordinator Alliance for Progress, AID, 1962-65; pres. N.Y. Ctr. Inter.-Am. Relations, 1965-72; asst. sec. of state inter-Am. relations Dept. State, 1974-76, undersec. of state for econ. affairs, 1976-77; mem. law faculty Cambridge U., Eng., 1982-83; sr. counselor Bipartisan Commn. on Central Am., 1983-84; vice chmn. Kissinger Assocs. Inc. Author: The Twilight Struggle: The Alliance for Progress and U.S.-Latin-American Relations, 1967. Co-chmn. U.S.-Mexico Binat. Commn.; bd. dirs. Coun. Fgn. Rels., 1981-90. Mem. Am. Soc. Internat. Law (pres. 1971-73), ABA. Office: Arnold & Porter 555 12th St NW Washington DC 20004-1200

ROGERS, WILLIAM RAYMOND, college president emeritus, psychology educator; b. Oswego, N.Y., June 20, 1932; s. William Raymond and A. Elizabeth (Hollis) R.; m. Beverley Claire Partington, Aug. 14, 1954; children: John Partington, Susan Elizabeth Howell, Nancy Claire Glassman. BA magna cum laude, Kalamazoo Coll., 1954; BD, U. Chgo. and Chgo. Theol. Sem., 1958; PhD, U. Chgo., 1965; MA (hon.), Harvard U., 1970. Cons., staff counselor Counseling and Psychotherapy Rsch. Ctr., U. Chgo., 1960-62; tchg. fellow, counselor to students Chgo. Theol. Sem., 1961-62; asst. prof. psychology and religion, dir. student counseling Earlham Coll., Richmond, Ind., 1962-68; assoc. prof. psychology and religion, assoc. dean of Coll. Earlham Coll., 1968-70; vis. lectr. pastoral counseling Harvard U. Div. Sch., Cambridge, Mass., 1969-70, prof. religion and psychology Div. and Edn. Schs., 1970-80, faculty chmn. clin. psychology and pub. practice, 1970-72, chmn. counseling and cons. psychology, 1979-80; prof. psychology and religious studies Guilford Coll., Greensboro, N.C., 1980—, pres., 1980-96, pres. emeritus, 1996—; bd. dirs. Br. Bank and Trust. Author: The Alienated Student, 1969, Project Listening, 1974, Nourishing the Humanistic in Medicine, 1979; Contbr. articles to profl. jours. Bd. dirs. Greensboro Symphony Soc., Canterbury Sch.; pres. Mary Reynolds Babcock Found., Cemala Found., Wesley Long Cmty. Health Found. Danforth Found. fellow, Blatchford Traveling fellow U. Chgo. and Chgo. Theol. Sem., 1958. Mem. Soc. Values in Higher Edn., Friends Assn. Higher Edn., Nat. Assn. Ind. Colls. and Univs., So. Assn. Colls. and Schs., Rotary (club pres.). Mem. Soc. of Friends. Home: 5400 Westfield Dr Greensboro NC 27410-9223

ROGGE, RICHARD DANIEL, former government executive, security consultant, investigator; b. N.Y.C., July 5, 1926; s. Daniel Richard and Bertha (Sarner) R.; m. Josephine Mary Kowalewska, June 6, 1948 (dec. June 1995); children: Veronica Leigh Rogge-Erbeznik, Richard Daniel, Christopher Ames, Meredith Ann Rogge-Pierce. BS in Bus. Adminstrn., NYU, 1952. Cert. profl. investigator. Clerical worker FBI, N.Y.C., 1947-52, spl. agt., Phila., 1952-54, Washington, 1954-58, supr., 1958-65, asst. spl. agt. in charge, Richmond, Va., 1965-66, Phila., 1966-67, L.A., 1967-69, inspector, 1969, spl. agt. in charge, Honolulu, 1969-72, Richmond, 1972-74, Buffalo, 1974-77, now security cons., investigator, Calif.; police tng. instr.; writer, lectr. in field. With USMC, 1944-46; PTO. Recipient Order of Arrow award Boy Scouts Am., 1943, Svc. to Law Enforcement awards Va. Assn. Chiefs Police, 1975, N.Y. State Assn. Chiefs Police, 1977, others. Mem. Calif. Assn. Lic. Investigators, Calif. Peace Officers Assn., Peace Officers Assn. of Los Angeles County, World Assn. Detectives, Inc., Soc. Former Agts. FBI, Inc., FBI Agents Assn., Am. Legion, K.C., Elks. Republican. Roman Catholic. Home and Office: 32010 Watergate Ct Westlake Village CA 91361

ROGGER, HANS JACK, history educator; b. Herford, Germany, Sept. 9, 1923; s. Max and Berni (Heilbronn) R.; m. Claire Ryan, Jan. 2, 1955; 1 son, Alexander. B.A., Sarah Lawrence Coll., 1948; Ph.D., Harvard U., 1956. Asst. prof. Sarah Lawrence Coll., Bronxville, N.Y., 1953-58; asso. prof. Sarah Lawrence Coll., 1958-61; asso. prof. UCLA, 1961-66, prof. history, 1966-92, chmn. dept., 1978-83, dir. Russian and East European Studies Center, 1962-66, prof. emeritus, 1992—; fellow Russian Rsch. Ctr., Harvard U., 1962; sr. mem. St. Antony's Coll., Oxford U., 1972; vis. scholar George Kennan Ctr. Advanced Russian Studies, 1975, mem. acad. coun., 1984-88; sr. assoc. fellow Oxford Ctr. Postgrad. Hebrew Studies, 1984—; co-dir. Rand/UCLA Ctr. Soviet Studies, 1989-93. Author: (with E. Weber) The European Right, 1965, 66, 74, (with H. Hyman) Heard Round the World, 1969, National Consciousness in 18th Century Russia, 1960, 70, Russia in Modernization and Revolution, 1881-1917, 1983, Jewish Policies and Right-Wing Politics in Imperial Russia, 1985; contbr. chpts. to book: Shared Destiny: Fifty Years of Soviet-American Relations, 1985, Pogroms: Anti-Jewish Violence in Modern Russia History, 1991, Hostages of Modernization, 1993, Guerre et Culture, 1994; mem. editl. bd.: Am. Hist. Rev., 1982-85, Slavic Rev., 1985-91, Contention, 1992-96, also assoc. editor, 1993-96. Served with USN, 1943-46. Recipient Guggenheim fellowship, 1964-65; Am. Council Learned Socs. fellow, 1962; Nat. Endowment Humanities fellow, 1975-76. Mem. AAUP, Am. Assn. Advancement Slavic Studies (bd. dirs. 1982-85), Am. Hist. Assn. Office: Dept History UCLA Los Angeles CA 90024

ROGIN, GILBERT LESLIE, editor, author; b. N.Y.C., Nov. 14, 1929; s. Robert I. and Lillian Carol (Ruderman) R. Student, State U. Iowa, 1947-49; A.B., Columbia, 1951. Editor-at-large Time Inc. Ventures, N.Y.C., 1955—. Author: The Fencing Master, 1965, What Happens Next?, 1971, Preparations for the Ascent, 1980. Served with AUS, 1952-54. Recipient award for creative work in lit. Am. Acad. Inst. Arts and Letters 1972. Home: 43 W 10th St New York NY 10011-8701 Office: Time Pub Ventures Time & Life Bldg New York NY 10020

ROGLIANO, ALDO THOMAS, publishing executive; b. Tuckahoe, N.Y., Mar. 7, 1925; s. Alfred and Nancy (Morrone) R.; m. Bettie Eleanor Fehrs, June 13, 1948; children: Susan Rogliano Shortley, Betsy Rogliano Dyer, Guy, Barbara Rogliano Tracy, Robert. Student, Syracuse U., 1946-49. Newsstand promotion mgr. Fawcett Publs. Inc., Greenwich, Conn., 1949-54; promotion mgr. Fawcett Publs. Inc., 1957-68, MacFadden Pub. Co., N.Y.C., 1954-57; account exec., promotion mgr. Dell Pub. Co., 1968-71; v.p., dir. pub. relations MacFadden-Bartell Corp., N.Y.C., 1971-74; promotion dir. Internat. Circulation Distbrs., N.Y.C., 1974-77, Kable News Co., 1977-78; v.p., dir. promotion and publicity Publishers Distbg. Corp. (a Filmways co.), N.Y.C., 1978-80; advt. and promotion dir. Flynt Distbg. Co., Los Angeles, 1980-83. Served with USMCR, 1943-45. Decorated Purple Heart; recipient Pub. Relations Gold Key award, 1971. Home: 4417 San Lucian Ln Fort Myers FL 33903-1360

ROGLIERI, JOHN LOUIS, health facility administrator; b. Plainfield, N.J., June 24, 1939; s. Vito and Grace Mary (DeCristofaro) R.; m. Geraldine Ann Piller, June 15, 1963; children: Maria Roglieri Friedman, Anna Roglieri Healy, John. BSChemE, Lehigh U., 1960, AB in Applied Scis., 1960; MD, Harvard U., 1966; MS in Bus., Columbia U., 1978. Diplomate Nat. Bd. Med. Examiners. Intern Bellevue Hosp., Columbia Svc., 1966-67; resident Presbyn. Hosp., N.Y.C., 1969-71, dir. divsn. ambulatory medicine, 1973-75, v.p. ambulatory svcs., 1975-82, dir. employee health svc., 1988-92; fellow Harvard Med. Sch., Boston, 1971-73; asst. dir. lab. computer sci. Mass. Gen. Hosp., 1972-73, dir. ambulatory screening clinic, 1972-73; med. dir. N.Y. Health Plan, Inc., N.Y.C., 1988-92; corp. med. dir. Sanus Corp. Health Sys., Ft. Lee, N.J., 1992-95, NYL Care Health Plans Inc., N.Y.C., 1996—; cons. Nat. Ctr. Health Svc. Rsch. and Devel., 1973-75; dir. clin. scholar program Columbia U., 1975-77, asst. prof. clin. medicine Coll. Physicians and Surgeons, 1973—; health edn. cons. Basic Internat. Investments, 1975-76; v.p., bd. dirs. AMARCO Internat., N.Y.C., 1975-85; mem. adv. bd. Western and Upper Manhattan Regional Perinatal Network, Coll. Physicians and Surgeons, N.Y.C., 1975-80; appeared in various TV and radio programs. Author: Odds on Your Life, 1980; mem. editl. bd. Managed Care, 1992—, Jour. Applied Rsch. in Health Adminstrn., 1979-81, Hosp. Physician, 1997—; book rev. cons. Acad. Press, Inc., N.Y.C.; contbr. articles to profl. publs.;. Capt. USPHS, 1967-69. Mem. APHA, Am. Fedn. Clin. Rsch., Am. Soc. Internal Medicine, N.Y. State Soc. Internal Medicine, Soc. for Rsch. and Edn. in Primary Care Internal Medicine, Nat. Assn. Managed Care Physicians. Roman Catholic. Avocations: surfcasting, woodworking. Office: NYL Care Health Plan 1 Liberty Plz New York NY 10006-1404

ROGO, KATHLEEN, safety engineer; b. Carrollton, Ohio, Sept. 28, 1952; d. Silvio and Mary (Siragusano) R. Grad. high sch., Carrollton; PhD in Med. Sci. (hon.), Ohio Valley Pathologists, Inc., 1992. Cert. histotechnologist, emergency med. technologist, safety engr. Rsch. pathology trainee Aultman Hosp., Canton, Ohio, 1970-75, supr. anatomic pathology, 1974-75; lab. mgr. W. Morgan Lab., Canton, 1973-74; supr. anatomic pathology Dr.'s Hosp., Massillon, Ohio, 1975-78; emergency med. technician Canton Fire Dept., 1976-81; safety engr. Ashland Oil Co., Canton, 1980-82; rsch. pathologist assoc., med. cons, v.p. Ohio Valley Pathologists, Inc., Wheeling, W.Va., 1990—. Mem. Am. Soc. Clin. Pathology (cert. histotechnician), Am. Soc. Safety Engrs. (cert.), Am. Soc. Emergency Med. Technicians (cert.), Ohio State Med. Soc., Internat. Platform Assn. Democrat. Roman Catholic. Avocations: professional model, dancer and musician.

ROGOFF, JEROME HOWARD, psychiatrist, psychoanalyst, forensic expert; b. Detroit, Dec. 21, 1938; s. Abraham Solomon and Sarah Riva

(Epstein) R.; (div. 1983); m. Erika Kathleen Keller, Sept. 25, 1983. BA cum laude, Harvard Coll., 1960; MD, Case Western Reserve U., 1965. Diplomate Am. Bd. Psychiatry and Neurology. Physician Peace Corps USPHS, Kathmandu, Nepal, 1966-68; clin. fellow psychiatry Harvard Med. Sch., Boston, 1975-79; staff psychiatrist Westwood (Mass.) Lodge Hosp., 1972-74; assoc. clin. prof. psych. Tufts Med. Sch., Boston, 1977-86; assoc. chief, psychiatry and dir., inpatient Psychiatry, day hosp. Faulkner Hosp., Boston, 1975-94; cons. psychiatrist Mass. Parole Bd. Probate Ct. Plymouth County, Mass., LEAA, Washington, 1971-78; med. psychiat. dir. ct. diversion program Boston TASC-A, 1974-75; treas., bd. dirs. Guild for Continuing Edn., Boston, 1981-95; founding dir. Law and Psychiatry Resource Ctr., Boston, 1983—; adj. prof. Simmons Sch. Social Work, Boston, 1981-85; lectr. on psychiatry Harvard Med. Sch., Boston, 1980-81, 84-94. Chmn. psychiatry team Combined Jewish Philanthropies, Boston, 1978-83, assoc. chmn. med. team, 1984-87, mem. social planning and allocations com., 1991—; bd. dirs. Jewish Vocat. Svc., Boston, 1987-91. Fellow Am. Psychiat. Assn. (pub. affairs rep. 1988-92, 93-94, mem. budget com. 1996—); mem. Mass. Psychiat. Soc. (councillor 1988-94, chair pub. affairs com. 1988-92, 93-94, chair nominating com. 1990), Am. Psychoanalytic Assn., Boston Psychoanalytic Soc., Am. Acad. Psychiatry and Law. Democrat. Avocations: cabinetry, carpentry, cooking, classical music, squash, languages. Home and Office: 659 Chestnut St Newton MA 02168-2035 *Two guiding principles, both from my father: "When in doubt, do the right thing." Sounds trite and naive, but turns out in the event to be profound; one almost always knows deep down what the right thing is. "When you are born, you cry, and everyone around you laughs. So live your life that when you come to leave it, you laugh, and everyone around you cries." On my profession of psychiatry and psychoanalysis: psychotherapy adds insight to injury.*

ROGOFF, KENNETH S., economics educator; b. Rochester, N.Y., Mar. 22, 1953; s. Stanley Miron and June Beatrice (Goldman) R.; m. Evelyn Jane Brody, Aug. 18, 1979 (div. 1989); m. Natasha Lance, June 25, 1995; 1 child, Gabriel. BA/MA in Econs., Yale U., 1975; PhD in Econs., MIT, 1980. Economist Internat. Monetary Fund, Washington, 1983; economist, sect. chief Internat. Fin. div., Bd. Govs. of the Fed. Res. Sys., Washington, 1979-84; assoc. prof. econs. U. Wis., Madison, 1985-89; prof. econs. U. Calif., Berkeley, 1989-92; prof. econs. and internat. affairs Princeton (N.J.) U., 1992—; Charles and Marie Robertson prof. of internat. affairs Princeton U., 1995—; vis. scholar San Francisco Fed. Res., 1990-92, World Bank, Washington, 1989, IMF, Washington, 1988-94. Author books and contbr. articles to profl. jours. Alfred P. Sloan Rsch. fellow, 1986-87, Hoover Instn. Nat. fellow, 1986-87, NSF fellow, 1985—. Fellow Econometric Soc.; mem. Am. Econ. Assn., Internat. Grandmaster Chess. Office: Princeton U Woodrow Wilson Sch Princeton NJ 08544-1013

ROGOLS, SAUL, food scientist; b. Cambridge, Mass., July 27, 1933; s. Barney Barkan and Dora (Cohen) R.; m. Donna Janelle, May 25, 1985. BSc in Biology and Chemistry, Antioch Coll., 1955; MSc in Bacteriology and Biochemistry, Ohio State U., 1958, postgrad., 1959-60; postgrad., Ohio State U., 1961-62; MBA, Ohio U., Lancaster, 1982. Cert. med. technician; cert. instr. ARC. Tech. dir. quality control/quality assurance A. E. Staley Mfg. Co., 1961-79; med. technologist Children's Hosp., Columbus, Ohio, 1961-75; materials control mgr. Essex Group div. United Technologies, 1979-80; dir. quality assurance Hexcel Corp., 1980-82; sr. scientist Amstar Corp., 1982-84; sr. food scientist Grain Processing Corp., 1986-91; dir. tech. svcs., prin. scientist Penwest Foods Co., Englewood, Colo., 1991—. Mem. adv. bd. Chem. Week Mag.; contbr. articles to profl. jours.; patentee in field. Fellow Am. Inst. Chemists; mem. TAPPI, Am. Assn. Cereal Chemists (charter mem. carbohydrate div.), Am. Chem. Soc. (biol. chemistry div.), Inst. Food Technologists (carbohydrate exec. com.), Am. Assn. Candy Technologists, N.Y. Acad. Sci., Sigma Xi. Avocation: model ship building. Home: 23573 Pondview Pl Golden CO 80401-5761 Office: Penwest Foods Co 11011 E Peakview Ave Englewood CO 80111-6808

ROGOSHESKE, WALTER FREDERICK, lawyer, former state justice; b. Sauk Rapids, Minn., July 12, 1914; m. Dorothy Heywood, Sept. 29, 1940; children: James, Thomas (dec.), Mark, Paul, Mary Alice. BA, U. Minn., 1937, LLB, 1939; LLD, William Mitchell Coll. Law. Bar: Minn. 1940. Gen. practice Sauk Rapids, 1940-50; dist. judge 7th Jud. Dist., 1950-62; assoc. justice Supreme Ct. Minn., 1962-80; lectr. law U. Minn. Law Sch., 1951-74, adj. prof., 1980-84; cons. arbitration and mediation proceedings, 1980-95. Chmn. Mpls.-St. Paul Met. Airports Commn., 1949-50; Mem. Minn. Ho. of Reps., 1943-49; Bd. dirs. Amicus, Inc.; past pres. Big Bros., St. Paul. Served with AUS, 1944-45. Fellow Am. Bar Found.; mem. ABA (mem. adv. com. prosecution and def. function, criminal law project 1968-71, chmn. 1969-71, mem. council sect. criminal justice 1970-74), Minn. Bar Assn., 7th Dist. Bar Assn., Am. Judicature Soc., Inst. Jud. Adminstrn., U. Minn. Law Alumni Assn. (dir.). Lutheran. Home and Office: 138 Canabury Ct Saint Paul MN 55117-1503

ROGOSKI, PATRICIA DIANA, financial executive; b. Chgo., Dec. 29, 1939; d. Raymond Michael and Bernice Rose (Konkol) R. BS in Acctg. and Econs., Marquette U., 1961, postgrad., 1965-66; postgrad., NYU, 1966-68, St. John's U., N.Y.C., 1975-76; cert. mgmt. acct., 1979. Sr. fin. analyst Blackhawk Mfg. Co., Milw., 1961-66; mgr., sr. analyst Shell Oil Co., N.Y.C., 1966-71; mgr. data processing Bradford Nat./Penn Bradford, Pitts., 1971-75; asst. mgr. fin. controls ITT, N.Y.C., 1975-79; v.p., comptr. ITT Consumer Fin. Corp., Mpls., 1979-80; sr. v.p. fin. ITT Fin. Corp., St. Louis, 1980-84; v.p., exec. asst., group exec. ITT Coins, Secaucus, N.J., 1984-85; pres. Patron S., Ltd., Wilmington, Del., 1986—; CFO, sr. v.p. Guardsmark, Inc., Memphis, 1989-94; sr. v.p. Peoplemark, Inc., Memphis, 1989-94. Bd. dirs. St. Louis Repertory Theater, 1983-84. Named to Acad. Women Achievers, YWCA, N.Y.C., 1980. Mem. Fin. Execs. Inst., Inst. Mgmt. Acctg., Econ. Club, Memphis Symphony Chorus. Avocation: duplicate bridge. Office: Patron S Ltd NE Hercules Plz 1313 N Market St Ste 3410 Wilmington DE 19801-6103

ROGOVIN, JOHN ANDREW, lawyer; b. Washington, July 10, 1961; s. Mitchell and Sheila Ann (Erder) R. AB, Columbia U., 1983; JD, U. Va., 1987. Bar: N.Y. 1989, D.C. 1990. Law clk. hon. Laurence Silberman U.S. Ct. Appeals (D.C. Cir.), Washington, 1987-88; assoc. Kramer, Levin et al, N.Y.C., 1988-89; assoc. O'Melveny & Myers, Washington, 1990-92, spl. counsel, 1996—; dep. transition counsel Presdl. Transition, Little Rock, 1992-93; asst. to atty. gen. U.S. Dept. Justice, Washington, 1993, dep. asst. atty. gen. Civil Divsn., 1993-96. Mem. ABA, D.C. Bar Assn. Office: O'Melveny & Myers LLP 555 13th St NW Ste 500 W Washington DC 20004-1109

ROGOVIN, MILTON, documentary photographer, retired optometrist; b. N.Y.C., Dec. 30, 1909; s. Jacob and Dora (Shainhouse) R.; m. Anne Setters, Apr. 7, 1942; children—Ellen, Mark, Paula. B.S. in Optics and Optometry, Columbia U., 1931; M.A. in American Studies, SUNY-Buffalo, 1972; DFA (hon.), U. Buffalo, 1994, Buffalo State Coll., 1994, Dyouville Coll., 1994. Optometrist, Buffalo, 1931-75; freelance documentary photographer, 1958—. Author: Milton Rogovin: The Forgotten Ones, 1985, Portraits in Steel, 1993, Triptychs Buffalo's Lower West Side Revisited, 1993. Served with U.S. Army, 1942-45. Recipient W. Eugene Smith Meml. Fund award, 1983. Home: 90 Chatham Ave Buffalo NY 14216-3109

ROGOWSKY, ROBERT ARTHUR, trade commission director; b. Vancouver, B.C., Can., Mar. 12, 1951; s. Michael Randall and Ruth Ann (Wellman) R.; m. Linda Sue George, June 17, 1972; children: Vanessa, Heather, Tara, Nichole, Alexis. BA in Econs., Boston U., 1973; MA in Econs., U. Va., 1975, PhD in Econs., 1982. Asst. prof. dept. econs. George Mason U., Fairfax, Va., 1977-78; rsch. economist Bur. Econs. FTC, Washington, 1979-83; econ. advisor to commrs. Consumer Product Safety Commn., Washington, 1983-84, acting exec. dir., asst. to dir., 1984; pres. Econ. Edn. for Clergy, Inc., Bethesda, Md., 1985-86; exec. asst. to chmn. Internat. Trade Commn., Washington, 1986-87; dep. dir. Bur. Consumer Protection FTC, Washington, 1987-89; dir. office of industries U.S. Internat. Trade Commn., Washington, 1989-92, dir. ops., 1992—; instr. U. Va., 1976-77; econ. rschr. Am. Enterprise Inst., 1976; econ. rsch. analyst Econ. Policy Office, U.S. Dept. Justice, 1974-75; presenter in field. Contbr. articles to profl. jours. Mem. Am. Mgmt. Assn., Am. Econs. Assn., Assn. Christian Economists. Lutheran. Home: 729 Forest Park Rd Great Falls VA 22066-2907 Office: US International Trade Comm Operations 500 E St NW Washington DC 20436-0003

ROGUL, JUNE AUDREY, fundraising executive, government relations specialist; b. N.Y.C., Dec. 30, 1942; d. Caroll Mitchell and Gail (Arkin) Silver; m. Marvin Rogul, Mar. 17, 1974; children: Jonathan, Daniel. BA, Tufts U., 1964; MS, Columbia U., 1966. Cmty. orgn. specialist D.C. Redevel. Land Agy., Washington, 1966-70; asst. to the dir. Prime Minister's Commn. on Disadvantaged Children & Youth, Jerusalem, Israel, 1971-72; rep. Nat. Conf. Soviet Jewry, Washington, 1973-75; lobbyist Am. Israel Pub. Affairs Com., Washington, 1975-77; dir. JWB, Washington, 1980-82, GNK Assocs., Washington, 1982-83; dir. Washington region Am. Com. for Weizmann Inst. Sci., Washington, 1983—, dir. govt. rels., 1992—; assoc. The Kahn Pub. Policy Report, Washington, 1982-83; cons., rep. Na'Amat U.S.A., Washington, 1982-89; cons. in field. Del. Allied Civic Group, Silver Spring, Md., 1978-79; chmn. Linden Civic Assn., Silver Spring, 1978-79; appointee Montgomery County Housing Policy Implementation Com., Rockville, Md., 1979; mem. Joint Action Com. for Polit. Affairs, Washington, 1982—, co-chmn., 1992. Mem. Nat. Soc. Fund Raising Execs., Nat. Jewish Dem. Coun., Washington Reps. Nat. Jewish Orgns. Democrat. Avocations: travel, foreign languages, jogging, skiing. Home: 6132 Roseland Dr North Bethesda MD 20852

ROGULA, JAMES LEROY, consumer products company executive; b. Rock Island, Ill., Nov. 8, 1933; s. Andrew and Nellie Pearl (Cook) R.; m. Adelaide F. Dittbrenner, May 29, 1960; children: James Lyle, Adelaide Ann, John Andrew. BA, Knox Coll., 1955; MBA, NYU, 1964. Group product mgr. Am. Chicle Co., Long Island City, N.Y., 1958-66; v.p. new product devel. Carter Wallace, Inc., N.Y.C., 1966-72; v.p. new products J.B. Williams Co., N.Y.C., 1972-74; sr. v.p. E.J. Brach & Sons, Chgo., 1974-77; v.p., gen. mgr. A.E. Staley Mfg. Co., Oak Brook, Ill., 1977-80; exec. v.p. Booth Fisheries Corp., Chgo., 1980-82; v.p., gen. mgr. Arm & Hammer div. Church & Dwight, Inc., Princeton, NJ, 1982-90; pres. Am. Candy Co., Richmond, Va., 1990-94; sr. v.p. consumer bus. group Scotts Co., Marysville, Ohio, 1994—. With U.S. Army, 1956-58. Mem. Sunset Ridge Country Club, Econ. Club Chgo., Wedgewood Country Club. Home: 10527 Cardigan Ridge Pl Powell OH 43065-8784 Office: Scotts Co 14111 Scottslawn Rd Marysville OH 43040-9506

ROHACK, JOHN JAMES, cardiologist; b. Rochester, N.Y., Aug. 22, 1954; s. John Joseph and Margaret Elizabeth (McLaughlin) R.; m. Charlotte McCown, Dec. 7, 1980; 1 child, Elisha Monique Feigle. BS, U. Tex., El Paso, 1976; MD, U. Tex., Galveston, 1980. Diplomate Am. Bd. Internal Medicine. Intern internal medicine U. Tex. Med. Br. Hosps., Galveston, 1980-81, resident internal medicine, 1981-83, chief resident internal medicine, 1983-84, fellow cardiology, 1984-86; instr. medicine U. Tex. Med. Br., Galveston, 1983-86; asst. prof. medicine Tex. A&M Coll. Medicine, College Station, 1986-95, assoc. prof., 1995—, sect. chief cardiology, 1989-97; assoc. med. dir. Scott and White Health Plan Bryan Coll. Sta., 1995-97, assoc. med. dir. for med. ops., 1997—; bd. dirs. Health for All Clinic, v.p., 1994-96; mem. Accreditation Coun. on Continuing Med. Edn., 1995—; med. dir. Fitlife Ctr. Tex. A&M U., College Station, 1990-97. Bd. dirs. Am. Heart Assn., Brazos Valley College Station, 1987—, Tex. affiliate Austin, 1991—, 1st v.p., 1994-95, pres.-elect, 1995-96, pres., 1996-97. Fellow ACP, Am. Coll. Cardiology (bd. dirs. Tex. chpt. 1992—); mem. AMA (alt del. ho. of dels. 1984-93, del. 1993—, coun. on med. edn. 1995-98, chair elect 1996-97, chair 1997—), Tex. Med. Assn. (exec. coun. med. student sect. 1981-82, ho. of dels. 1982—, trustee 1994—), U. Tex. Med. Br. Alumni Assn. (trustee 1989—, pres. 1996-97), Brazos Robertson County Med. Soc. (exec. com. 1989-97, pres. 1995-96). Avocations: golf, gardening, reading. Office: Scott and White Clinic 2401 S 31st St Temple TX 76508-0001

ROHAN, BRIAN PATRICK, lawyer; b. Bklyn., July 1, 1964; s. John Eamon and Janet Dee (Trebian) R.; m. Lori Lanahan, Aug. 18, 1990; children: Connor James, Taylor Kathleen. BS, SUNY, Plattsburgh, 1986; MBA, Union Coll., 1990; JD, Union U., 1990. Bar: N.Y. 1991, Mass. 1991, U.S. Dist. Ct. (no. dist.) N.Y. 1991. Atty. Waite & Assocs., P.C., Albany, N.Y., 1990-96; pvt. practice Brian P. Rohan Law Offices, Albany, N.Y., 1996—. Bd. dirs. Catholic Family & Cmty. Svcs., Albany, 1991-94. Mem. ATLA, N.Y. State Bar Assn., Albany County Bar Assn. Office: 1 Rapp Rd Albany NY 12203-4432

ROHATGI, RAJEEV, cardiologist; b. New Delhi, India, Dec. 5, 1953; married. MB, BS, Inst. Med. Scis., New Delhi, 1975. Diplomate Am. Bd. Internal Medicine. Intern All-India Inst. Med. Scis., 1976; resident in internal medicine Easton (Pa.) Hosp., 1977-80; fellow in cardiology U. Chgo. Med. Sch., 1980-82; cardiologist Easton Cardiovascular Assocs., Inc., 1982—. V.p. Am. Heart Assn., 1990-91. Mem. AMA, Am. Coll. Cardiology, Soc. Nuclear Medicine, Pa. Med. Soc., Am. Soc. Echocardiography. Home: 20 Tamarack Path Easton PA 18045-5572 Office: Easton Cardiovasular Assocs 2003 Fairview Ave Easton PA 18042-3915

ROHATYN, FELIX GEORGE, investment company executive; b. Vienna, Austria, May 29, 1928; came to U.S., 1942, naturalized, 1950; s. Alexander and Edith (Knoll) R.; m. Jeannette Streit, June 9, 1956; children: Pierre, Nicolas, Michael; m. Elizabeth Fly, May 31, 1979. BS, Middlebury (Vt.) Coll., 1948; LLD (hon.), Adelphi U., Bard Coll., Hofstra U., 1981, L.I. U., 1981, Middlebury Coll., 1982, Fordham U., 1983; LLB (hon.), NYU, 1979, Brandeis U., 1987. With Lazard Freres & Co., LLC, N.Y.C., 1948—, mng. dir., 1960—; bd. dirs. Pfizer Co., Gen. Instrument, Crown, Cork & Seal Corp. Served with AUS, 1951-53, Korea. Office: Lazard Freres & Co 30 Rockefeller Plz New York NY 10112

ROHE, WILLIAM MICHAEL, urban planning educator; b. N.Y.C., Apr. 23, 1950; s. Victor Joseph and Grace (White) R.; m. Jamie Stone, June 10, 1989. AAS, SUNY, Farmingdale, 1970; BS, SUNY, Buffalo, 1972; M Regional Planning, Pa. State U., 1975, PhD in Man Environ. Rels., 1978. Asst. prof. Pa. State U., University Park, 1977-78; asst. prof. city, regional planning U. N.C., Chapel Hill, 1978-85, assoc. prof., 1985-92; prof., 1992-94, Dean E. Smith prof., 1994—; dir. Ctr. for Urban and Regional Studies U. N.C., Chapel Hill, 1994—; cons. Rsch. Triangle Inst., Rsch. Triangle Park, N.C., 1979—; cons. Urban Systems Rsch. and Engring., Cambridge, Mass., 1985-87; HUD vis. scholar, Washington, 1984-85. Author: Planning with Neighborhoods, 1985; mem. editorial bd. Jour. Am. Planning Assn., Jour. Planning Lit., Jour. Planning Edn. and Rsch.; contbr. articles to profl. jours. Mem. Chapel Hill Planning Commn., 1980-86; Chapel Hill Small Area Planning Com., 1990-94. Grantee Nat. Inst. Justice, 1982, HUD, 1987, 95, rsch. grantee Ford Found., 1988, 91. Mem. AAUP (pres.-elect U. N.C. chpt. 1990-91, pres. 1991-93), Am. Planning Assn. (Best Paper award 1992, 95), Fed. Nat. Mortgage Assn., Assn. Collegiate Schs. of Planning (exec. com. 1993-95, Best Paper award 1996). Avocation: basketball. Office: U N C CB # 3140 Dept City Regional Planning Chapel Hill NC 25799

ROHLF, F. JAMES, biometrician, educator; b. Blythe, Calif., Oct. 24, 1936. BS, San Diego State Coll., 1958; PhD in Entomology, U. Kans., 1962. Asst. prof. biology U. Calif., Santa Barbara, 1962-65; assoc. prof. statis. biology U. Kans., 1965-69; assoc. prof. biology SUNY, Stony Brook, 1969-72, prof., 1972—, chmn. dept. ecology and evolution, 1975-80, 90-91; statis. cons. N.Y. Pub. Svc. Commn., 1975-78, IBM, 1977-81, U.S. EPA, 1978-80; vis. scientist IBM, Yorktown Heights, N.Y., 1976-77, 80-81. Mem. Biometric Soc., Soc. Systematic Biology, Classification Soc. Achievements include research and development of statistical methods and software for geometric morphometrics and applications of multivariate analysis to systematics and population biology. Office: SUNY at Stony Brook Dept Ecology and Evolution Stony Brook NY 11794-5245

ROHLF, ROBERT HENRY, retired library director, library consultant; b. Mpls., May 14, 1928; s. Henry E. and Helen (Mulcahy) R.; m. Joan Ann Peters, Sept. 17, 1949; children: Catherine Rohlf Stepanek, Cynthia Rohlf Molenaar, William R., John H., David R. BA, Coll. St. Thomas, St. Paul, 1949; BSLS, U. Minn., 1950, MA, 1953, cert. in pub. adminstrn., 1955. Libr. inst. agrl. U. Minn., 1950-51, libr., 1951-53; libr., adminstrv. asst. Mpls. Pub. Libr., 1953-58; dir. Dakota/Scott Regional Libr., West St. Paul, 1959-66, Ill. Libr. Devel. Project, Aurora, 1963; coord. of bldg. plan Libr. of Congress, Washington, 1966-68, dir. adminstrn., 1968-69; dir. Hennepin County Libr., Mpls., 1969-94; prin. ptnr. Profl. Libr. Cons., P.A.; mem. adj. faculty Coll. of St. Catherine; cons. libr. planning and mgmt., 1960—; U.S. rep. internat. exec. com. UNESCO, Alexandria, 1993—. Author: Plan for Public Library Development in Illinois, 1963, Public Libraries in San Diego, 1981. Active Met. Coun., Mpls. Citizens League, Gov.'s Adv. Com. on Youth, Minn. Bd. Edn. Adv. Coun. Named one of Outstanding Young Men, Mpls. Jaycees, 1954. Mem. ALA (life, divsn. pres. 1981) Minn. Libr. Assn. (life, pres., Libr. of Yr. 1967), Rotary (bd. dirs. Edina chpt. 1994—), Jaycees (sen.). Avocations: skiing, golf, reading, sailing, camping.

ROHLFING, FREDERICK WILLIAM, travel executive, consultant, retired judge; b. Honolulu, Nov. 2, 1928; s. Romayne Raymond and Kathryn (Coe) R.; m. Joan Halford, July 15, 1952 (div. Sept. 1982); children: Frederick W., Karl A., Brad (dec.); m. Patricia Ann Santos, Aug. 23, 1983. BA, Yale U., 1950; JD, George Washington U., 1955. Bar: Hawaii 1955, Am. Samoa 1978. Assoc. Moore, Torkildson & Rice, Honolulu, 1955-60; ptnr. Rohlfing, Nakamura & Low, Honolulu, 1963-68, Hughes, Steiner & Rohlfing, Honolulu, 1968-71, Rohlfing, Smith & Coates, Honolulu, 1981-84; sole practice Honolulu, 1960-63, 71-81, Maui County, 1988—; dep. corp. counsel County of Maui, Wailuku, Hawaii, 1984-87, corp. counsel, 1987-88; land and legal counsel Maui Open Space Trust, 1992—; pres. Rohlfing Consulting & Travel, Inc., 1985—; magistrate judge U.S. Dist. Ct. Hawaii, 1991-96; polit. cons., cruise travel adv. Mem. Hawaii Ho. Reps., 1959-65, 80-84; Hawaii State Senate, 1966-75; U.S. alt. rep. So. Pacific Commn., Noumea, New Caledonia, 1975-77, 1982-84. Capt. USNR, 1951-87. Mem. Hawaii Bar Assn., Maui Country Club, Outrigger Canoe Club. Avocation: ocean swimming. Home and Office: RR 1 Box 398 Kekaulike Ave Kula HI 96790

ROHM, ROBERT HERMANN, sculptor, educator; b. Cin., Feb. 6, 1934; s. Hermann George and Anna Katherine (Sager) R.; m. Patricia Jean Cutlip, Dec. 6, 1959 (div. 1978); children: Hans Tobin, Kyle Curtis. B in Indsl. Design, Pratt Inst., 1956; MFA in Sculpture, Cranbrook Acad. Art, 1960. Instr. Columbus (Ohio) Coll. Art and Design, 1956-59, Pratt Inst., Bklyn., 1960-65; prof. art U. R.I., Kingston, 1965-95; pres. emeritus U. R.I., Kingston, N.Y., 1996—. One-man shows: O.K. Harris Gallery, N.Y.C., 1970, 72, 73, 75, 77, 80, 83, 84, 86, 89, 92, 94, Parker St. 470 Gallery, Boston, 1970, 72, Univ. Rochester, N.Y., 1971, N.S. Coll. Art, Halifax, 1970, Worcester Art Mus. (Mass.), 1978, Univ. R.I., 1981, 88, 94, Nielsen Gallery, Boston, 1985, 86, 92, La Jolla Mus. Contemporary Art, Calif., 1985, Lenore Gray Gallery, Providence, 1990, 93, 95; group shows include Boston Mus., 1974, Whitney Mus., N.Y.C., 1962, 64, 69, 70, 73, 83, Va. Mus., Richmond, 1970, Fogg Mus., Cambridge, Mass., 1971, Seattle Art Mus., 1969, Vancouver Art Mus., B.C., Can., 1970, N.J. State Mus., Trenton, 1969, R.I. State Coun. on Arts, 1973, 82, Vassar Coll., 1971, Inst. Contemporary Art, Boston, 1975, Miss. Mus. Art, Jackson, 1979-80, Grey Art Gallery, NYU, 1980, Montclair (N.J.) Art Mus., 1978, Aldrich Mus. Contemporary Art, Ridgefield, Conn., 1981, 82, SUNY-Plattsburgh, 1981, Zone Gallery, Springfield, Mass., 1982, Cumberland Gallery, Nashville, 1986, 93, Allan Frumkin Gallery, N.Y.C., 1985, Beitzel Fine Arts Inc., N.Y.C., Addison Gallery Am. Art, Andover, Mass., 1989, Nielsen Gallery, Boston, 1990-91, Soma Gallery, San Diego, 1993, Palo Alto (Calif.) Cultural Ctr., Centre Coll., Danville, Ky.; represented in permanent collections Columbus Gallery Fine Art, Finch Coll., N.Y.C., Pa. State U., Kunsthalle, Zurich, Va. Mus. Fine Arts, Mus. Modern Art, N.Y.C., U. N.Mex., Albuquerque, Albright-Knox Gallery, Buffalo, Whitney Mus. Am. Art, N.Y.C., Met. Mus. Art, N.Y.C., Rose Art Mus., Brandeis U., Waltham Mass., Mus. Fine Art, Boston, Mus. of Contemporary Art, Chgo., Newport (R.I.) Art Mus. Grantee Guggenheim Found., 1964, R.I. State Council on Arts, 1973, 82, 93, NEA, 1974, 86; recipient Cassandra Found. award, 1967, award Boston 200 Bicentennial Commn., 1975. Subject of numerous articles in jours. and catalogues. Office: U RI Art Dept Fine Arts Ctr Kingston RI 02881

ROHN, REUBEN DAVID, pediatric educator and administrator; b. Israel, Apr. 12, 1945; came to U.S., 1954; s. Aryeh and Rachel (Brenner) R.; m. Judith Semel, Sept. 6, 1971; 1 child, Karen. BA cum laude, Bklyn. Coll., 1967; MD, N.Y. Med. Coll., 1971. Diplomate Am. Bd. Pediat., Am. Bd. Pediatric Endocrinology, Am. Bd. Pediatrics-Adolescent Medicine. Intern in pediatrics Montefiore Hosp., Bronx, N.Y., 1971-72, resident in pediatrics, 1972-74; fellow in adolescent medicine U. Md. Hosp., Balt., 1974-76; preceptor in pediatrics Johns Hopkins U. Sch. Health Svcs., Balt., 1975-76; asst. prof. dept. pediatrics Ea. Va. Med. Sch., Norfolk, 1976-82; coord. pediatric clerkship Ea. Va. Med. Sch., Children's Hosp. of King's Daughters, Norfolk, 1977-90; prof. dept. pediatrics Ea. Va. Med. Sch., Norfolk, 1989—; adj. prof. chemistry Old Dominion U., Norfolk, 1984—; dir. adolescent medicine/endocrinology Children's Hosp. of King's Daughters, Norfolk, 1976—; mem. curriculum com. Ea. Va. Med. Sch., 1977-79, clerkship coords. com. 1977-90, genetics com., 1978-80, evaluation com. 1979-91, chmn. selectives com., 1981-82, ad hoc com. on consultation, 1982-83, student progress com., 1983-85, student health com., 1985-87, LCME com. on curriculum, 1990-92; mem. child abuse com. Children's Hosp. of King 's Daus., 1976-80, chmn. adolescent adv. com., 1976-80, patient care com. 1980-94, nutrition com. 1980-94, utilization rev. com., 1980-82, med. records com., 1987-89, gen. med./surg. task force com., 1987-88, chmn. dept. promotions com., 1990—; bd. dirs. Pediatric Faculty Assocs., 1994—; spkr. in field. Reviewer Jour. Adolescent Health Care, 1986—, mem. editorial bd., 1989-92; contbr. articles to profl. jours. Mem. Norfolk Sch. Health Coun., 1977—, mem. ad hoc com. infant screening program for hypothroidism Commonwealth of Va., 1977-79, cons., 1979—; mem. cmty. adv. bd. Norfolk Adolescent Pregnancy Prevention Svc. Project, 1981-83; bd. dirs. Elizabeth River chpt. Am. Diabetes Assn., 1982-85, South Hampton Roads chpt. 1985-93; mem. adv. com. Norfolk-Virginia Beach Jr. League, 1987-88; judge ann. Health Edn. Fair, Norfolk Pub. schs., 1980-94. Recipient grant Bressler Rsch. Fund, 1975-76, Biomed. Rsch. Devel. grant Ea. Va. Med. Sch., 1978, 78-79, 79-80. 81-82, 83-84, Children's Health Found. grant, 1988-89. Fellow Am. Acad. Pediatrics (youth and adolescence com. Va. chpt. 1978—); mem. Soc. Adolescent Medicine (abstract reviewer 1984-91), Lawson Wilkins Pediatric Endocrine Soc., Sigma Xi. Avocations: photography, folk dancing. Home: 4653 Larkwood Dr Virginia Beach VA 23464-5815 Office: Childrens Hosp Kings Daus 601 Childrens Ln Norfolk VA 23507-1910

ROHNER, BONNIE-JEAN, small business owner, computer consultant; b. Waltham, Mass., Aug. 2, 1946; d. Gerrit John and Marjorie Lorraine (Hollis) R.; children: David Harrison Sackett, Amanda Marjorie Sackett. BFA in Fashion, Pratt Inst., Bklyn., 1967; BA in Biology, Adelphi U., Garden City, N.Y., 1983; MS, CIS, U. New Haven, Conn., 1993. Freelance fashion designer Garden City, 1971-76; owner, mgr. The Printing Workshop, Massapequa, N.Y., 1976-78; personnel mgr. Doron Ltd., Norwich, Conn., 1978-79; computer related trainer Gen. Dynamics, Groton, Conn., 1979-89; acad. computing coord. Three Rivers Com./Tech. Coll., Norwich, 1989-94; owner, mgr. bytestream, Norwichtown, Conn., 1993—; computer cons. U. New Haven, Groton, 1990-92; tech. advisor Countywide Network Com., 1989-90; sec. Connbug, Rocky Hill, Conn., 1992-93. Mem. NAFE, AAUW, AAUP, ACM, Women's Network of S.E. Conn. Avocations: creative writing, internet.

ROHNER, RALPH JOHN, lawyer, educator, university dean; b. East Orange, N.J., Aug. 10, 1938. A.B., Cath. U. Am., 1960, J.D., 1963. Bar: Md. 1964. Teaching fellow Stanford (Calif.) U., 1963-64; atty. pub. health div. HEW, 1964-65; prof. law Cath. U. Am. Sch. Law, Washington, 1965—, acting dean, 1968-69, assoc. dean, 1969-71, dean, 1987-95; staff counsel consumer affairs subcom. U.S. Senate Banking Com., 1975-76; cons. Fed. Res. Bd., 1976-83, chmn. consumer adv. council, 1981; cons. FDIC, 1978-80; spl. counsel Consumer Bankers Assn., 1984—; cons. U.S. Regulatory Coun., 1979-80; bd. dirs. Hanover Funds, Inc., N.Y.C. Co-author: Consumer Law: Cases and Materials, 1979, 2d edit., 1991; co-author, editor The Law of Truth in Lending, 1984. Bd. dirs. Migrant Legal Action Program, Inc., Washington, Automobile Owners Action Coun., Washington, Credit Rsch. Ctr., Purdue U. Mem. ABA, Am. Law Inst., Coll. of Consumer Fin. Svcs. Lawyers. Home: 10909 Forestgate Pl Glenn Dale MD 20769-2047 Office: Cath U Sch Law 620 Michigan Ave NE Washington DC 20064-0001 *We learn from those we teach, we are inspired to write by those who read, and we should serve as examples to those who aspire.*

ROHNER, THOMAS JOHN, JR., urologist; b. Trenton, N.J., Jan. 1, 1936; s. Thomas J. and Julia (Kanyo) R.; m. Jessie Rohner; children: Christopher, James. BA, Yale U., 1957; MD, U. Pa., 1961. Diplomate Am. Bd. Urology. Intern Hosp. U. Pa., Phila., 1961-62, resident in gen. surgery, 1962-64, resident in urology, 1964-67; asst. prof. surgery M.S. Hersey Med. Ctr., Pa. State U., Hershey, 1970-71, assoc. prof., 1971-75, prof., 1975—, chief urol. divsn., 1970-96; assoc. dean for clin. affairs M.S. Hershey Med. Ctr., Pa. State U., Hershey, 1996—; corp. mem. Pa. Blue Shield, 1991—, bd. dirs., 1993—. Contbr. articles to profl. jours. Served to maj. M.C., U.S. Army, 1967-69. USPHS fellow, 1969-70; grantee HEW, 1971-76, USPHS, 1971-76. Fellow ACS (pres. cen. Pa. chpt. 1983-84, bd. govs. 1991—); mem. AMA, Am. Urol. Assn. (pres. mid-Atlantic sect. 1986-87), Urol. Assn. Pa., Phila. Urol. Soc. (pres. 1980-81), Assn. Acad. Surgeons, Am. Bd. Urology (trustee 1995—), Pa. Med. Soc., Dauphin County Med. Soc., Soc. Pediat. Urology, Soc. Univ. Urologists (pres. 1990-91), Nat. Urol. Forum, Societe Internationale d'Urologie, Transamerican Urol. Rschrs., Internat. Continence Soc., Coll. Physicians of Phila. Home: 2907 Mt Gretna Rd Elizabethtown PA 17022-9689 Office: Milton S Hershey Med Ctr Pa State Univ PO Box 850 Hershey PA 17033-0850

ROHR, DAVIS CHARLES, aerospace consultant, business executive, retired air force officer; b. Burlington, Wis., Oct. 29, 1929; s. Charles Davis Rohr and Dorothy Elizabeth (Hahn) Rohr Larson; m. Gayle Lynn White, Aug. 22, 1959; children—Ellen Louise, Jean Elizabeth. Student, Northwestern U., 1947-48; B.Sc., U.S. Mil. Acad., 1952; M.A., U. Wash., 1960. Commd. 2d lt. USAF, 1952, advanced through grades to maj. gen, 1980; fighter pilot USAF, Ohio, Korea, Japan, 1954-58; asst. prof. history USAF Acad., Colo., 1960-64; fighter pilot, squadron ops. officer Idaho and, Fed. Republic Germany, 1965-69; fighter squadron comdr. Vietnam, 1969-70; country dir. S.Am. Office of Sec. of Def., Washington, 1970-73; exec. officer, dep. dir. maintenance Hdqrs. Tactical Air Command, 1973-75; tactical fighter wing comdr. Tex., Utah, 1976-79; chief Office of Mil. Coop., Cairo, 1979-81; dir. plans and policy U.S. European Command, Stuttgart, Fed. Republic Germany, 1981-84; dep. comdr. in chief U.S. Cen. Command, MacDill AFB, Fla., 1984-87, ret.; aerospace cons., 1988—; prof. history U.S. Air Force Acad. Decorated Def. D.S.M., 2 Def. Superior Service medals, Legion of Merit with cluster, D.F.C., Meritorious Service medal, Air medal with 14 clusters, Air Force Commendation medal, Purple Heart.

ROHR, DONALD GERARD, history educator; b. Toledo, Oct. 10, 1920; s. Lewis Walter and Marie (Pilliod) R.; m. Joan Willis Michener, Sept. 14, 1948; children: Karen, Kristin. B.A., U. Toronto, Ont., Can., 1943, M.A., 1949; Ph.D., Harvard U., 1958. Instr., then asst. prof. Williams Coll., 1953-59; mem. faculty Brown U., 1959—, prof. history, 1963-86, emeritus, 1986—, chmn. dept., 1960-65, 66-69, 72-74, sec. faculty, 1969-72, assoc. dean faculty and acad. affairs, 1976-81; adminstv. dir. Howard Fedn., 1989-92. Author: The Origins of Social Liberalism in Germany, 1963, (with Robert Ergang) Europe Since Waterloo, 1967. Served with AUS, 1943-46, ETO. Mem. Am. Hist. Assn., Conf. Group Ctrl. European History, Providence Com. Fgn. Rels. (sec. 1968-81, chmn. 1981-92), Thomas Becket Fedn. (v.p. 1983-84, pres. 1984-86), English Speaking Union (pres. Providence br. 1986-88), U. Club, Faculty Club (Providence, pres. 1981-83). Democrat. Roman Catholic. Home: 71 Grotto Ave Providence RI 02906-5609

ROHR, KAROLYN KANAVAS, school system administrator; b. Chgo., Dec. 10, 1947; d. John George and Lorraine Marian (Erickson) Kanavas; m. Stephen Mitchell Rohr, Oct. 8, 1983; stepchildren: Susan Anne, John S. BA, Conn. Coll., 1969, MAT, 1971. Cert. adminstrn. and supervision, secondary prin., supr., tchr., Md.; cert. assessor Md. State Dept. Edn. and Nat. Assn. Secondary Sch. Prins. Tchr. Norwich (Conn.) Free Acad., 1971-72; tchr., acting dept. chair Fairport (N.Y.) Ctrl. Schs., 1972-74; tchr. Montgomery County Pub. Schs., Rockville, Md., 1975-78, specialist gifted and talented edn., area office, 1978-79, specialist leadership tng. dept. staff devel., 1979-81, coord. adminstrv. programs, 1981-92, coord. systemwide tng. Office Pers. Svcs., 1992—; insvc. course instr. Montgomery County Pub. Schs., Rockville, 1979-83; sr. faculty assoc. Johns Hopkins U., Balt., 1991—; cons. on leadership and prins. tng., assessment, Mich., Fla., Md. Sch. Systems, 1980—. Author: (with others) Principal Selection Guide, 1987. Dir. Ijamsville (Md.) Community Assn., 1989-92. Recipient Showcase of Excellence Program award Nat. Coun. of States on In-Svc. Edn., 1988, Exemplary Leadership Devel. Program award Am. Assn. Sch. Adminstrs., 1988, Outstanding Achievement in Profl. Devel. award Am. Assn. Sch. Adminstrs. and Nat. Staff Devel. Coun., 1990. Mem. NAESP, ASCD, Nat. Staff Devel. Coun., Nat. Assn. Secondary Sch. Prins., Md. Coun. Staff Developers. Avocations: equine business, architectural design, travel. Office: Montgomery County Pub Schs 850 Hungerford Dr Rockville MD 20850-1718

ROHRABACHER, DANA, congressman; b. June 21, 1947; s. Donald and Doris Rohrabacher. Student, L.A. Harbor Coll., 1965-67; BA in History, Long Beach State Coll., 1969; MA in Am. Studies, U. So. Calif., 1976. Reporter City News Svc./Radio West, L.A., 4 yrs.; editorial writer Orange County Register, 1979-80; asst. press sec. Reagan for Pres. Campaign, 1976, 80; speechwriter, spl. asst. to Pres. Reagan White House, Washington, 1981-88; mem. 101st-102nd Congresses from Calif. dist., 1989-93, 103d-105th Congress from 45th dist. Calif., 1993—; U.S. del. Young Polit. Leaders Conf., USSR; disting. lectr. Internat. Terrorism Conf., Paris, 1985; mem. Internat. Rels. com.; chmn. sci. subcom. on space and aeronautics. Recipient Disting. Alumnus award L.A. Harbor Coll., 1987. Avocations: surfing, white water rafting. Office: US House of Reps Rayburn Bldg 2338 Washington DC 20515-0545

ROHRBACH, HEIDI A., lawyer; b. Buffalo, N.Y., Jan. 25, 1953; d. William R. and A.T. R.; m. Leonard Lance, Aug. 9, 1996; 1 child, Peter R. Frank. BA, Northwestern U., Evanston, Ill., 1974; JD, Vanderbilt U., Nashville, 1977. Bar: N.Y., 1978. V.p., and asst. gen. counsel Chase Manhattan Bank, N.Y.C., 1985—. Office: Chase Manhattan Bank 270 Park Ave Fl 40 New York NY 10017-2014

ROHRBACH, ROGER PHILLIP, agricultural engineer, educator; b. Canton, Ohio, Oct. 12, 1942; s. Clarence A. and Beatrice E. (Burens) R.; m. M. Jeanette Weishner, June 12, 1965; children: Sharon E., Gregory A., Sara L. BS in Agrl. Engring., Ohio State U., 1965, PhD, 1968. From asst. prof. to assoc. prof. N.C. State U., Raleigh, 1968-78, prof., 1978—. Author: Design in Agricultural Engineering, 1986, Engineering Principles of Agriculture Machines, 1993. Fellow Am. Soc. Agrl. Engrs. (Young Designer award 1981). Office: NC State U Biol and Agrl Engring Dept PO Box 7625 Raleigh NC 27695-7625

ROHRBOUGH, ELSA CLAIRE HARTMAN, artist; b. Shreveport, La., Sept. 26, 1915; d. Adolph Emil and Camille Claire (Francis) Hartman; m. Leonard M. Rohrbough, June 19, 1937 (dec. Jan. 1977); children: Stephen, Frank, Leonard. Juried exhbns. (painting) Massur Mus. Art, Monroe, La., Mobile (Ala.) Art Gallery, Gulf Coast Juried Exhibit, Mobile, Juried Arts Nat., Tyler, Tex., Greater New Orleans Nat., La. Watercolor Soc. Nat., Ky. Watermedia Nat., So. Watercolor Ann., La. Women Artist, many others. One-woman shows include Le Petit Theatre du Vieux Carre, New Orleans World Trade Ctr.'s Internat. House, Singing River Art Assn., Pascagoula, Miss., La. Font Inn, Pascagoula, Mandeville (La.) City Hall, St. Tammany Art Assn., Covington, La., others; exhibited in groups shows at 1st Guaranty Bank, Hammond, La., St. Tammany Art Assn., Ft. Isabel Gallery, Covington, S.E. La. State U. Mem. Nat. League Am. Pen Women (v.p. S.E. La. br. 1986-87, pres. 1987-92, 94-98), St. Tammany Art Assn. (bd. dirs. 1985-86, 87, instr. 1977-78, classes chmn. 1986-88). Republican. Roman Catholic. Avocations: sewing, flower arranging, gardening, ethnic cooking, American antiques. Home: 100 Christwood Blvd Apt 106 Covington LA 70433

ROHREN, BRENDA MARIE ANDERSON, therapist, educator; b. Kansas City, Mo., Apr. 18, 1959; d. Wilbur Dean and Katheryn Elizabeth (Albright) Anderson; m. Lathan Edward Rohren, May 10, 1985; 1 child, Amanda Jessica. BS in Psychology, Colo. State U., 1983; MA in Psychology, Cath. U. Am., 1986. Lic. mental health practitioner. Mental health therapist, sr. case mgr. Rappahannock Area Community Svcs. Bd., Fredericksburg, Va., 1986-88; mental health therapist, case mgmt. supr. Rappahannock Area Community Svcs. Bd., 1988; rsch. assoc. Inst. Medicine, NAS, Washington, 1988-89; supr. adult psychiat. program Lincoln (Nebr.) Gen. Hosp., 1989, program supr. mental health svcs., 1989-91; adj. instr. S.E. Community Coll., Lincoln, 1990—; assessment & referral specialist Rivendell Psychiat. Ctr., Seward, Nebr., 1993-95; therapist Lincoln Day Treatment Ctr., Lincoln, Nebr., 1993-95; adj. inst. Coll. of St. Mary, 1994—; therapist Rape/Spouse Abuse Crisis Ctr., Lincoln, 1996—; computer cons. Syscon Corp., Washington, 1983-84. Author: (report) Bottom Line Benefits: Building Economic Success Through Stronger Families; editor: (newsletter) Alliance for Mentally Ill, Lincoln. Active Lincoln Alliance for the Mentally Ill, Nebr. Domestic Violence/Sexual Assault Coalition. Mem. APA (assoc.), Nat. Alliance for Mentally Ill, Nebr. Psychol. Assn. (assoc.). Democrat. Roman Catholic. Avocations: interior decorating, reading, landscaping, camping. Home: 3821 S 33rd St Lincoln NE 68506-3806 Office: SE Community Coll 8800 O St Lincoln NE 68520-1227 also: Coll of St Mary 4600 Valley Rd Ste 403 Lincoln NE 68510-4844

ROHRER, GEORGE JOHN, retired lawyer; b. Elmira, N.Y., Oct. 24, 1931; s. George J. and Lois (Hess) R.; m. Martha M. Jacobs, Jan. 6, 1952; children: Jacquelyn D. Berbusse, Michael A., John S. JD with distinction, Pacific Coast U., 1967. Bar: Calif. 1969, U.S. Dist. Ct. (ctrl. dist.) 1969. Incentive dir. Blue Chip Stamp Co., L.A., 1963-69; gen. ptnr. Songer, Leavell Rohrer, Bellflower, Calif., 1969-80; sr. ptnr. Rohrer & Holtz, Anaheim, Calif., 1980-94; ret., 1994; panel atty. Calif. Assn. of Realtors/State, Hotline, Calif. 1977—; Founder/Dir. Midcities Nat. Bank, Bellflower, 1981-90; trustee S.E. area Bar Assn., Norwalk, Calif., 1974-75. Pres. Bellflower Kiwanis Club, 1972-73; dir. Los Cerritos Y.M.C.A., Bellflower, 1977-78; vol. counsel Am. Radio Relay League, 1987-92. Mem. Orange County Bar Assn., Los Angeles County Bar Assn., Orange County Amicus (pro bono), Bellflower C. of C. (pres. 1975-76), Masons, Shriners. Republican. Avocations: amature radio, fishing, travel.

ROHRER, MAURICE PIERRE, journalist; b. Geneva, July 8, 1931; s. Henri Louis Rohrer and Germaine Marie-Josèphine Rohrer-Joguin. Lic. in Econ. Geography, Geneva U., 1954, PhD in Econs., 1959. Tchr. Ecole Supérieure de Commerce Genève/Coll. Genève, Geneva, 1954-92; asst. dept. geography U. Geneva, 1959-62; dep. Gen. Dept. Secondary Edn., Geneva, 1965-93; freelance journalist numerous publs., Switzerland, France, Germany, 1975—; subs. prof. U. Geneva, 1962, Centre d'Etudes Industrielles, Geneva, 1962; expert economist commn. urbanization, Geneva, 1962-65; methodol. cons. pedagogical studies secondary education, Geneva, 1965-81; expert geographer fed. consultative commn. Schweizer Weltatlas, 1978-93. Author: Placez Mieux Votre Argent, 1966, L'Epargne-Investissement, 1969; editor econs. and fin. Jour. de Genève, 1960-72, L'Illustrè, 1962-75; contbr. articles to profl. jours. Roman Catholic. Avocations: fine arts, painting. Home: Rue d'Ermenonville 7, CH-1203 Geneva Switzerland

ROHRER, RICHARD JEFFREY, surgeon, educator; b. Columbus, Mar. 14, 1950; s. James William and Nancy Lenore (Acheson) R.; m. Jill Ellen Stein, Nov. 29, 1981; children: Benjamin, Noah. BS, Yale U., 1973; MD, Columbia U., 1977. Surgeon New England Deaconess and Harvard Med. Sch., Boston, 1984-87; surgeon, chief transplantation New Eng. Med. Ctr., Boston, 1988—; assoc. prof. surgery Tufts Sch. Medicine, Boston, 1988—. Trustee New Eng. Organ Bank, Boston, 1988—; councillor United Network for Organ Sharing, 1996—. Fellow ACS; mem. Am. Soc. Transplaant Surgeons, Transplantation Soc., Physicians for Social Responsibility, Assn. for Acad. Surgery, Assn. for Surg. Edn., Soc. Critical Care Medicine. Office: New England Med Ctr Box 40 750 Washington St Boston MA 02111-1526

ROHSENOW, WARREN MAX, retired mechanical engineer, educator; b. Chgo., Feb. 12, 1921; s. Fred and Selma (Gorss) R.; m. Katharine Towneley Smith, Sept. 20, 1946; children—John, Brian, Damaris, Sandra, Anne. B.S., Northwestern U., 1941; M.Eng., Yale, 1943, D.Eng., 1944. Teaching asst., instr. mech. engring. Yale, 1941-44; mem. faculty Mass. Inst. Tech., 1946-85, prof. mech. engring., 1955-85, dir. heat transfer lab., 1954-85, prof. emeritus, 1985; bd. dirs. Dynatech Corp., Thermal Process System. Author: (with Choi) Heat Mass and Momentum Transfer, 1961; Editor: Developments in Heat Transfer, 1964, (with Hartnett) Handbook of Heat Transfer, 1973, 2d edit., 1985. Served as lt. (j.g.) USNR, 1944-46; mech. engr. gas turbine div. Engring. Expt. Sta. Annapolis, Md. Recipient Pi Tau Sigma gold medal Am. Soc. M.E., 1951; award for advancement sci. Yale Engring. Assn., 1952; merit award Northwestern Alumni, 1955. Fellow Am. Acad. Arts and Scis., Nat. Acad. Engring., Am. Soc. M.E. (hon. mem., Heat Transfer Meml. award 1967, Max Jakob Meml. award 1970); mem. Sigma Xi, Tau Beta Pi, Pi Tau Sigma. Home: 32 Carroll St Falmouth ME 04105-1908 Office: MIT Cambridge MA 02139

ROHWER, WILLIAM D., JR., university dean; b. Denver, Oct. 2, 1937. AB, Harvard U., 1959; PhD, U. Calif., Berkeley, 1964. Asst. prof. education U. Calif., Berkeley, 1964-68, assoc. prof., 1968-70, prof., 1970-95, acting assoc. dean grad. div., 1969-70, assoc. dean, 1970, acting dir. Inst. Human Learning, 1971, chmn. div. ednl. psychology, vice-chmn. dept. edn., 1982, assoc. dean edn., 1983-86, acting dean, 1989-90, dean, 1990-95, prof. emeritus, dean emeritus, 1996—; acting dir. Inst. Human Devel., Berkeley, 1996—; vis. lectr. psychology U. Wis., Madison, 1967; rsch. psychologist U.S. Naval Pers. Rsch. Activity, San Diego, 1964. Contbr. articles to profl. jours.; ad hoc reviewer Child Develop., Devel. Psychology, Jour. Ednl. Psychology, Jour. Exptl. Child Psychology, Psychol. Rev., Sci. Recipient Palmer O. Johnson Meml. award Am. Ednl. Rsch. Assn., 1972; fellow Van Leer Jerusalem Found., 1974-75, Ctr. Advanced Study Behavioral Scis. Stanford U., 1979-80; scientific adviser Bernard Van Leer Found., 1974-75; grantee U.S. Office Edn., OEO, NSF, Nat. Inst. Child Health and Human Devel. Office: U Calif Tolman Hall Berkeley CA 94720-1671

ROISEN, FRED JERROLD, neurobiologist, educator, researcher, anatomy educator; b. N.Y.C., Sept. 12, 1941; s. Israel Jacob and Louise M. (Friedman) R.; m. Maxine G. Gerson, Mar. 28, 1965; children: Kim Felice, Alexandra Suzanne. PhD, Princeton U., 1966, 69. Asst. prof. Rutgers U., New Brunswick, N.J., 1969-72; asst. prof. Med. Sch. Rutgers U., Piscataway, N.J., 1972-75, assoc. prof. Med. Sch., 1975-80; prof. Med. Sch. U. Medicine & Dentistry of N.J., Piscataway, 1980-83, acting dept. chair, prof. Med. Sch., 1983-86; chmn., prof. dept anatomy, scis., and neurobiology U. Louisville, 1986—; chair ad hoc com. shared instrumentation NIH, Bethesda, Md., 1987-90. Author: Histology Review, 1980; contbr. over 100 articles to profl. jours. Pres., chair AAUP, Piscataway, 1977-80. Recipient numerous grants. Jewish. Home: 5800 River Knolls Dr Louisville KY 40222-5863 Office: U Louisville Sch Medicine Dept Anat Sci Neurobio Louisville KY 40292*

ROISLER, GLENN HARVEY, quality assurance professional; b. Milw., Apr. 6, 1952; s. George Harvey and Mayme Elvin (Salo) R.; m. Jacqueline Bout, July 27, 1971; 1 child, Renee Jenette. Student electronics tech., DeVry Inst. Tech., Chgo., 1976; student computer engring. tech., Capitol Radio Engring. Inst., Washington, 1980; BA in Econs., N.C. State U., 1992. Instr. scuba Pirate's Cove, Inc., Milw., 1969-70; sr. electronics technician Bendix Field Engring. Corp., Columbia, Md., 1977-79; field engr. Technicare, Inc., Solon, Ohio, 1979; supr. electronics Troxler Labs., Inc., Research Triangle Park, N.C., 1979-81; mgr. prodn. Matrix Corp., Raleigh, N.C., 1981; vendor surveillance specialist Carolina Power and Light Co., Raleigh, N.C., 1981-84, sr. quality assurance specialist, 1984-91, sr. systems analyst, 1991—. Contbr. articles to profl. publs. Served with USN, 1971-77. Mem. Am. Soc. Quality Control (crt. quality engr., reliability engr.), Gamma Beta Phi, Sigma Pi Sigma, Omicron Delta Epsilon. Methodist. Avocations: scuba diving, ice hockey. Office: Carolina Power & Light Co PO Box 1551 Raleigh NC 27602-1551

ROITMAN, JUDITH, mathematician; b. N.Y.C., Nov. 12, 1945; d. Leo and Ethel (Gottesman) R.; m. Stanley Lombardo, Sept. 26, 1978; 1 child, Ben Lombardo. BA in English, Sarah Lawrence Coll., 1966; MA in Math., U. Calif., Berkeley, 1971, PhD in Math., 1974. Asst. prof. math. Wellesley (Mass.) Coll., 1974-77; from asst. prof. to prof. math. U. Kans., Lawrence, 1977—. Author: Introduction to Modern Set Theory, 1990; contbr. articles to profl. jours. Grantee NSF, 1975-87, 92-95. Mem. Math. Assn. Am., Assn. Symbolic Logic, Am. Math. Soc., Assn. Women in Math. (pres. 1979-81, Louise Hay award 1996), Kans. Assn. Tchrs. Math., Nat. Assn. Tchrs. Math. Avocation: poetry.

ROITSCH, PAUL ALBERT, pilot; b. Hermosa Beach, Calif., Oct. 15, 1926; s. George Arthur and Margaret (Pattillo) R.; m. Phyllis T.A. McCoy, Aug. 26, 1955; children—Sharon Elise, Alison Carol, Paul Eric. BA, U. So. Calif., 1952; postgrad. U.S. Navy Test Pilot Sch., 1965. Copilot, navigator Pan Am. Airways, San Francisco, 1952-53, pilot, 1955-64, asst. chief pilot tech., Jamaica, N.Y., 1965-69, chief pilot tech., 1969-73, line pilot, 1973-86, pres. Paul Roitsch Assocs., Internat. Aviation Cons., Greenwich, Conn., 1986—, pilot Civil Air Transport, 1954-55; bd. dirs. Pan Am Hist. Found., 1993—, v.p., 1994—, exec. v.p., 1995—. With USN, 1944-49, 53-54. Mem. AIAA, Soc. Automotive Engrs. (safety standardization adv. com., airplane handling qualities and flight deck design com., recipient cert. of appreciation 1981), Internat. Soc. Air Safety Investigators. Home: 39 John St Greenwich CT 06831-2608 Office: PO Box 786 Greenwich CT 06836-0786

ROIZEN, NANCY J., physician, educator; b. Hartford, Conn.; m. Michael F. Roizen; children: Jeffrey, Jennifer. BS, Tufts U., 1968, MD, 1972. Diplomate Am. Bd. Pediats. Staff physician Oakland (Calif.) Children's Hosp., 1976-84; asst. prof. clin. pediats. Johns Hopkins Hosp., Balt., 1984-85; from asst. prof. to assoc. prof. pediats. and psychiatry U. Chgo., 1985—. Fellow Am. Acad. Pediats.; mem. Soc. for Devel. Pediats. (pres. 1996—). Office: U Chgo Hosps MC 1051 5841 S Maryland Ave Chicago IL 60637-1463

ROIZMAN, BERNARD, virologist, educator; b. Chisinau, Rumania, Apr. 17, 1929; came to U.S., 1947, naturalized, 1954; s. Abram and Liudmilla (Seinberg) R.; m. Betty Cohen, Aug. 26, 1950; children: Arthur, Niels. B.A., Temple U., 1952, M.S., 1954; Sc.D. in Microbiology, Johns Hopkins, 1956; D.H.L. (hon.), Gov.'s State U., 1984; MD (hon.), U. Ferrara (Italy), 1991; DSc (hon.), U. Paris, 1997. From instr. microbiology to asst. prof. Johns Hopkins Med. Sch., 1956-65; mem. faculty div. biol. scis. U. Chgo., 1965—, prof. microbiology, 1969-84, prof. biophysics, 1970—, chmn. com. virology, 1969-85, 88—, Joseph Regenstein prof., 1981-83, Joseph Regenstein Disting. Svc. prof., 1984—, chmn. dept. molecular genetics and cell biology, 1985-88; convener herpes virus workshop, Cold Spring Harbor, N.Y., 1972; lectr. Am. Found. for Microbiology, 1974-75; mem. spl. virus cancer program, devel. rsch. working group Nat. Cancer Inst., 1967-71, cons. inst., 1967-73; mem. steering com. human cell biology program NSF, 1971-74, cons. found., 1972-74; mem. adv. com. cell biology and virology Am. Cancer Soc., 1970-74; chmn. herpes virus study group Internat. Commn. Taxonomy of Viruses, 1971-93; mem. Internat. Microbiol. Genetics Commn. Internat. Assn. Microbiol. Scis., 1974-81; mem. sci. adv. coun. N.Y. Cancer Inst., 1971-88; med. adv. bd. Leukemia Rsch. Found., 1972-77; mem. herpes-virus working team WHO/FOA, 1978-81; mem. bd. sci. cons. Sloan Kettering Inst., N.Y.C., 1975-81; mem. study sect. exptl. virology NIH, 1976-80; mem. task force on virology Nat. Inst. Allergy and Infectious Disease, 1976-77; mem. external adv. com. Emory U. Cancer Ctr., 1973-81, Northwestern U. Cancer Ctr., 1979-89; cons. Inst. Merieux, Lyon, France, 1979-91; mem. com. to establish vaccine priorities Nat. Inst. Medicine, 1983-85; chmn. sci. adv. bd. Teiky-Showa Univs. Ctr., Tampa Bay Rsch. Inst., 1983—, chmn. bd. trustees, 1991—. Author sci. papers, chpts. in books; editor: Herpes Viruses, Vol. 1, 1982, Vol. 2, 1983, Vols. 3 and 4, 1985, The Human Herpesviruses, 1993, Infectious Diseases in an Age of Change, 1995; adv. editor Progress in Surface Membrane Science, 1972; editor-in-chief Jour. Infectious Agts. and and Disease, 1992—; mem. editl. bd. Jour. Hygiene, 1985-61, Infectious Diseases, 1965-69, Jour. Virology, 1970—, Jour. Intervirology, 1972-85, Archives of Virology, 1975-81, Virology, 1976-78, 83—, Microbiologica, 1978—, Cell, 1979-80, Gene Therapy, 1994. Trustee Goodwin Inst. for Cancer Rsch., 1977—. Recipient Lederle Med. Faculty award, 1960-61, Career Devel. award USPHS, 1963-65, Pasteur award Ill. Soc. Microbiology, 1972, Esther Langer award for achievement in cancer research, 1974, Outstanding Alumnus in Pub. Health award Johns Hopkins U., 1984; named hon. prof. Shandong Acad. Med. Scis., People's Republic of China, 1985; Am. Cancer Soc. scholar cancer research at Pasteur Inst. Paris, 1961-62; ICN Internat. prize in virology, 1988; faculty research assoc., 1966-71; traveling fellow Internat. Agy. Research Against Cancer, Karolinska Inst., Stockholm, Sweden, 1970; grantee USPHS/NIH, 1958—, Am. Cancer Soc., 1962-90, NSF, 1962-79, Whitehall Found., 1966-74. Fellow Japanese Soc. for Promotion of Sci., Pan Am. Cancer Soc. (hon.); mem. Nat. Acad. Scis., Hungarian Acad. of Scis. (hon.), Am. Acad. Arts and Scis., Am. Acad. Microbiology, Am. Assn. Immunologists, Am. Soc. Microbiology, Am. Soc. Virology, Am. Soc. Biol. Chemists, Brit. Soc. Gen. Microbiology, Johns Hopkins U. Soc. Scholars, Quadrangle Club (Chgo.). Home: 5555 S Everett Ave Chicago IL 60637-1968 Office: U Chgo MB Kouler Viral Oncology Labs 910 E 58th St Chicago IL 60637-1432

ROJAS, CARLOS, Spanish literature educator; b. Barcelona, Spain, Aug. 12, 1928; s. Carlos and Luisa (Vila) R.; m. Eunice Anne Mitcham, Mar. 19, 1966; children: Carlos, Eunice Anne. MA, U. Barcelona, 1951; PhD, U. Cen., Madrid, 1955; PhD (hon.), U. Simón Bólivar, Barranquilla, Colombia, 1985. Teaching asst. U. Barcelona, 1951-52; fgn. asst. U. Glasgow, Scotland, 1952-54; asst. prof. Rollins Coll., Winter Park, Fla., 1957-60; asst. prof. Emory U., Atlanta, 1960-63, assoc. prof., 1963-68, prof., 1968-80, Charles Howard Candler prof. Spanish lit., 1980-96, Charles Howard Candler prof. emeritus, 1996. Author: Auto de fe, 1968 (Premio Nacional de Literatura 1968), Azana, 1973 (Planeta award 1973), El Igenioso Hidalgo y Poeta F.G. asciende a los infiernos, 1980 (Nadal award 1980), El Sueno de Sarajevo, 1982, El Jardin de las Hespèrides, 1988, El Jardin de Atocha, 1990, Yo, Goya, 1990, Proceso A Godoy, 1992, Salvador Dali, or the Art of Spitting on Your Mother's Portrait, 1993, Alfonso de Borbón Habla Con El Demonio, 1995, !Muera La Inteligencia! !Viva La Muerte! Salamanca, 1995, The Garden of Janus, 1996, Crónica de la Guerra Civil Española, 1996; coauthor, contbg. editor Spanish Civil War documents, Momentos estelares de la guerra de España, 1996. Recipient Premio Espejo de España award, Madrid, 1984, Encomienda al Mérito Civil, King of Spain, 1986, Univ. Scholar/Tchr. award Emory U., 1987; honoree of yr. Philol. Assn. of Carolinas, 1987. Mem. MLA, Am. Assn. Tchrs. Spanish and Portuguese, Assn. Doctores y Licenciados Españoles en los Estados Unidos (bd. dirs.), South Atlantic MLA. Avocation: painting. Home: 1378 Harvard Rd NE Atlanta GA 30306-2413 Office: Emory U Dept Spanish Atlanta GA 30322

ROJAS, VICTOR HUGO MACEDO, retired vocational education educator; b. Mollendo, Peru, Jan. 11, 1923; came to U.S., 1944; s. Mariano A. and Maria Santos (Macedo) R.; m. Mary Emily Bush, Apr. 28, 1945 (dec. 1984); m. Ellen Manuel Proimos, Dec. 26, 1990. AA, Miami-Dade C.C., 1982; BS in Vocat. Edn., Fla. Internat. U., 1986. Cert. tchr., Fla. Automotive mechanic various Ford dealerships, Miami, Fla., 1945-60; automotive technician East Tenn. Motors, Knoxville, 1960-63; automotive technician Tally-Embry Ford, Inc., Miami, 1964-66, shop foreman, then mgr., 1966-75, master technician, automotive instr., 1973-75; instr. automotive tech. Dade County Pub. Schs., Miami, 1975-91; ret., 1991; adviser, sponsor Vocat.-Indsl. Clubs Am., Miami, 1988-91. With Armada Peruana, 1940-44, USN, 1945. Recipient Cert. of Achievement Motor Age mag., 1961, 62, St. Mary's Cathedral, Miami, 1988, Automotive Svc. Excellence award Nat. Inst. Automotive Svc., 1975. Mem. Am. Legion (historian 1989), Elks. Democrat. Roman Catholic. Avocations: music, art, camping, ballroom dancing, stock car racing. Home: 2365 Ainsworth Ave Spring Hill FL 34609-4402

ROJAS GUTIERREZ, CARLOS, Mexican government official. Degree in engring., Nat. U. Mex. With Nat. Indiginist Inst., 1978-82; dir. marginalized zones program Secretariat of Programmation and Budget, 1982-87; coord. for undersec. regional devel., coord. fed. decentralized program; coord. spl. events Office of Presdl. Candidate Salinas de Gortari; gen. coord. Nat. Program Solidarity; sec. social devel. Govt. of Mex., Mexico City, 1993—. Office: Avda Constituyentes 947 Edif B, Colonia Belen de las Flores, 01110 Mexico City Mexico*

ROJEK, KENNETH J., health facility administrator, hospital; b. Chgo., Aug. 6, 1953; m. Carol Rojek; 2 children. BS with honors, U. Ill., 1975; MBA with honors, Roosevelt U., 1980. Diplomate, cert. healthcare exec. Am. Coll. Healthcare Execs. Lab. mgr., tech. dir. Rush-Presbyn.-St. Lukes Med. Ctr., Chgo., 1977-80; adminstr. Wyler Children's Hosp., dept. pediatrics U. Chgo., 1980-86; v.p. Parkside Human Svcs., 1986-89, Luth. Gen. Med. Group, S.C., Chgo., 1989-92; sr. v.p. Luth. Gen. Hosp., Park Ridge, Ill., 1992-94, CEO, 1994—; adj. faculty U. Minn., St. Francis Coll., Joliet, Ill. Active numerous cmty. and civic orgns., cmty. devel. couns. Fellow Am. Coll. Med. Practice Execs. Med. Group Mgmt. Assn. Office: Luth Gen Hosp 1775 Dempster St Park Ridge IL 60068-1143

ROJHANTALAB, HOSSEIN MOHAMMAD, chemical engineer, researcher; b. Tehran, Iran, Sept. 26, 1944; came to U.S., 1964; s.

Mohammad Rojhantalab and (Fakhri-Molouk) Nasser-Ghandi; 1 child, Ayda. MS, Calif. State U., Hayward, 1972; PhD, Oreg. State U., 1976. Asst. prof. Ahwaz (Iran) U., 1976-77, Shiraz (Iran) U., 1977-82; cons., chemist Water-Con Co., Tehran, 1982-84; rsch. assoc. U. Oreg., Eugene, 1985-88; lithography engr. Intel Corp., Hillsboro, Oreg., 1988-91; thin film CVD, Aloha, Oreg., 1991-93; Tungsten polish team leader Intel Corp., Alpha, Oreg., 1993-97, oxide planarization rschr., 1997—; transl. Popular Sci. Pub. Co., Tehran, 1980-83, UNESCO workshop, 1984; editor, CEO, DNA Pub. Co., Tehran, 1982-84; vis. prof. chemistry Ore. State U., 1985. Editor, translator 4 books on genetic code, controlled nuclear fusion to Farsi, 1981-84; contbr. articles to sci. jours. Scholar Calif. State U., 1971-72; grantee Oreg. State U., 1975-76, CENTO, 1978-79. Mem. Electrochem. Soc. Am. Achievements include patent on single pass graded NSG/BPSG glass for deep trench fill; development of thin BPSG film for defect detection of O.2 - 10 microns. Home: PO Box 6652 Aloha OR 97007-0652

ROKKE, ERVIN JEROME, air force officer, university president; b. Warren, Minn., Dec. 12, 1939; s. Edwin K. and Joan (Ivery) R.; m. Pamela Mae Patterson, June 6, 1962; children: Lisa Mae, Eric Scott. Student, St. Olaf Coll., 1957-58; BS, USAF Acad., 1962; MPA, Harvard U., 1964, PhD in Polit. Sci., 1970. Commd. 2d lt. USAF, 1962, advanced through grades to lt. gen., 1994; intelligence officer Pacific Air Forces, Hawaii, Japan, 1965-68; assoc. prof. dept. polit. sci. USAF Acad., Colorado Springs, Colo., 1968-73, permanent prof., 1976-80, dean of faculty, 1982-86; plans officer NATO Hdqrs., Brussels, 1973-76; air attache Am. Embassy, London, 1980-82; def. attache Am. Embassy, Moscow, 1987-89; sr. staff Nat. Security Agy., Ft. Meade, Md., 1989-91; dir. intelligence Hdqrs. European Command, Stuttgart, Fed. Republic Germany, 1991-93; assigned to Hdqs. USAF, Washington, 1993-94; pres. Nat. Def. U., Ft. Lesley J. McNair, DC, 1994—; cons. Dept. State, 1969. Editor: American Defense Policy, 1973. Decorated Def. Disting. Svc. medal, Disting. Svc. medal, Def. Superior Svc. medal, Legion of Merit. Mem. Coun. on Fgn. Rels., Am. Polit. Sci. Assn. (assoc.). Lutheran. Avocations: reading, skiing, squash. Home: Qtrs 12 Ft Lesley J McNair Washington DC 20024 Office: Nat Def U 300 5th Ave Ft Lesley J McNair Washington DC 20319-6000

ROKOSZ, GREGORY JOSEPH, emergency medicine physician, educator; b. Passaic, N.J., Mar. 27, 1955; s. Ferdinand and Stella D. (Wirkowski) R.; m. Christine M. Muller, Oct. 1, 1983; 1 child, Stefanie Lee. BA in Biol. Scis. with honors, Rutgers U., 1977; DO, U. Osteo. Medicine/Health Sci., Des Moines, 1980; postgrad., Seton Hall U., 1995—. Diplomate Am. Bd. Emergency Medicine, Am. Bd. Osteo. Emergency Medicine, Am. Osteo. Bd. Family Physicians. Intern Met. Hosp., Phila., 1980-81; resident in family practice Union (N.J.) Hosp., 1981-82, emergency dept. physician, 1982-94, dir. med. edn., 1993—, v.p. med. affairs, 1994—; med. dir. N.J. Paramedic Registry Exam., 1990-94; mobile ICU insp. N.J. Dept. Health, Office EMS, Newark, 1990-94; mem. N.J. Bd. Med. Examiners, Trenton, 1994—; clin. instr. dept. emergency medicine U. Medicine and Dentistry Sch. Osteo. Medicine, Stratford, 1992-93, asst. clin. prof., 1993—; asst. prof. emergency medicine N.Y. Coll. Osteo. Medicine/N.Y. Inst. Tech., Old Westbury, 1994-96, assoc. prof., 1996— ; assoc. mem. PRO of N.J., 1991—; expert witness in emergency medicine. Contbg. author: Continuous Quality Improvement for Emergency Departments, 1994; mem. Seton Hall Law Rev., 1997—. Fellow Am. Coll. Emergency Physicians, Am. Coll. Osteo. Emergency Physicians; mem. ABA, Am. Osteo. Assn., Am. Coll. Osteo. Family Physicians, Assn. Osteo. Dirs. and Med. Educators, Am. Coll. Physician Execs., Assn. for Hosp. Med. Edn. Republican. Roman Catholic. Avocations: skiing, sports, cultural events, music, family activities. Home: 12 Ivy Ln Parsippany NJ 07054 Office: Union Hosp 1000 Galloping Hill Rd Union NJ 07083-7951

ROLAND, ANNE, registrar Supreme Court of Canada; b. Neuilly-sur-Seine, France, Feb. 27, 1947; d. Pierre Philippe Roland and Geneviève Lehman; m. Alphonse Morisette, Dec. 3, 1975; 1 child, Julien. BA Philosophy, Caen, France, 1965; diploma, Inst. Supérieur d'interprétation et de traduction, 1969; lic. in law, Paris, 1969; LLB, U. Ottawa, 1979. Bar: Quebec 1980. Legal trans., revisor Can., 1971-75; chief trans. svcs. customs and excise Sec. of State, Can., 1975-76; spl. asst. to chief justice Can., 1976-81; chief law editor Supreme Ct. Can., 1981-88, dep. registrar, 1988-90, registrar, 1990. Mem. Can. Bar Assn., Assn. Can. Ct. Adminstrs., Assn. Francophone Jurists, Can. Inst. Adminstrn. Justice, Assn. Reporters Jud. Decisions. Office: Supreme Ct of Can Office Reg, Wellington St., Ottawa, ON Canada K1A 0J1

ROLAND, BILLY RAY, electronics company executive; b. Grandview, Tex., June 12, 1926; s. Marvin Wesley and Minnie Mae (Martin) R.; m. Ruth Ranell Sheets, Mar. 9, 1950 (div. 1982); children: Carl Ray and Darla Kay (twins); m. Linda Sue Leslie, Feb. 21, 1986 (div. Nov. 1991); m. Martha Kay Redford, May 17, 1993. B.S., Tex. Christian U., 1954. C.P.A., Tex. Ticket and baggage agt. Southwestern Greyhound Co., Ft. Worth, 1943-44, 46-51; supr. acctg. dept. Tandy Leather Co., 1954-60; controller, asst. sec., treas. Tandy Corp., 1960-75, Tandy crafts, Inc., 1975-78; v.p. Tandy Corp., 1978-85, ret. V.p., treas. David L. Tandy Found., 1966—; mng. trustee James L. and Eunice West Charitable Trust, 1980-91; treas. Benjamin F. Johnston Found., 1984—. Served with inf. U.S. Army, 1944-46. Mem. Am. Inst. C.P.A.s, Tex. Soc. C.P.A.s, Ft. Worth Soc. C.P.A.s, Ft. Worth C. of C. Democrat. Methodist. Clubs: Colonial Country, Petroleum, Lake Country Golf and Country. Home: 8937 Random Rd Fort Worth TX 76179-2739

ROLAND, CHARLES GORDON, physician, medical historian, educator; b. Winnipeg, Man., Can., Jan. 25, 1933; s. John Sanford and Leona (McLaughlin) R.; m. Marjorie Ethel Kyles, 1953 (div. 1973); children: John Kenneth, Christopher Franklin, David Charles, Kathleen Siobhan; m. Connie Rankin, 1979. Student, U. Toronto, Ont., Can., 1952-54; MD, U. Man., 1958, BSc, 1958, DS (hon.), 1997. Intern St. Boniface Hosp., Man., 1958-59; pvt. practice medicine specializing in family medicine Tillsonburg, Ont., 1959-60, Grimsby, Ont., 1960-64; sr. editor Jour. Am. Med. Assn., Chgo., 1964-69; head sect. publs. Mayo Clinic, 1969-70, chmn. dept. biomed. communications, 1970-77; prof. history medicine, prof. biomed. communications, coordinator family practice track, chmn. adminstrv. com. dept. family medicine Mayo Med. Sch., 1971-77; mem. admissions, edn. and curriculum coordinators coms., hon. mem. med. staff West Lincoln Meml. Hosp., Grimsby; mem. grants com. Hannah Inst. History of Medicine, Toronto, 1974-77, 87-91, mem. publs. com., 1991-95; Jason A. Hannah prof. history of medicine McMaster U., Hamilton, Ont., Can., 1977—; assoc. mem. dept. history. McMaster U.; chmn. archives com. Faculty of Health Scis. McMaster U., Hamilton, Ont., Can., 1983—; chmn. spl. grants com. Hannah Inst. for History of Medicine, 1981-85; Sid W. Richardson vis. prof. Inst. Med. Humanities U. Tex. Med. Br., Galveston, 1984. Author: (with L.S. King) Scientific Writing, 1968, (with J.P. McGovern) William Osler, The Continuing Education, 1969, Good Scientific Writing, 1971, William Osler's The Master Word in Medicine: A Study in Rhetoric, 1972, (with L.S. Baker) You and Leukemia: A Day at a Time, 1976, (with P. Potter) An Annotated Bibliography of Canadian Medical Periodicals, 1826-1975, 1979, Clarence Meredith Hincks 1885-1964: Mental Health Crusader, 1990, Courage Under Seige:: Starvation, Disease and Death in the Warsaw Ghetto, 1992, Harold Nathan Segall: Pioneer Canadian Cardiologist, 1995; editor: (E.P. Scarlett) In Sickness and In Health, 1972; co-editor: An Annotated Checklist of Osleriana, 1976, Sir William Osler 1849-1919: A Selection for Medical Students, 1982, Health Disease and Medicine: Essays in Canadian History, 1984, Bibliography of Secondary Sources in Canadian Medical History, 1985, (with J.P. McGovern) The Collected Essays of Sir William Osler (3 vols.), 1985; editor, author introduction: Medical Topography of Upper Canada, 1985; (with Richard Golden) Sir William Osler: An Annotated Bibiography with Illustrations, 1987; co-editor: The Persisting Osler, 1984, The Persisting Osler II, 1994; editor in chief Can. Bulletin of Med. History, 1987-90; mem. editorial adv. bd. Canadian Family Physician, 1964-72, Chest, 1966—, Med. Communications, 1971-75, Postgrad. Med. Jour., London, 1967-72, Mayo Clinic Procs., 1969-77, Bioscis. Communications, 1975-80, Ont. Med. Rev., 1979-84, HSTC Jour., 1980-87, Can. Bull. Med. History, 1983-90, Med. History (London), 1982-87, Jour. History of Medicine and Allied Scis., 1991-94, 96—. Mem. bd. curators Osler Library, McGill U., Montreal, 1981—. Recipient Jason A. Hannah medal Royal Soc. Can., 1994. Fellow AAAS (council 1969-74), Am. Med. Writers Assn. (pres. 1969-70); mem. Can. Med. Assn., Am. Assn. History Medicine (sec.-treas. 1976-80, publs. com. 1979-85), Acad. Medicine Toronto (Grogan lecture com. 1978-83), Am. Mil. Inst., Internat. Inst. Prisoners of War, Soc. Internat. d'Histoire de la Medicine (internat. del. for Can. 1983-86), Can. Soc. for History of Medicine (v.p. 1982-87, pres. 1993-95), Soc. Med. History Chgo. (sec.-treas. 1966-69), Can. Ctr. for Studies in Hist. Horticulture (exec. com. 1982-89), Council Biology Editors, Med. Hist. Club Toronto (pres. 1977-78), Ont. Hist. Soc., Can. Hist. Assn., Bibliog. Soc. Can., Am. Osler Soc. (sec.-treas. 1975-85, v.p. 1985-86, pres. 1986-87), Japan Osler Soc. (hon.), Royal Soc. Medicine (London), Royal Can. Mil. Inst., Champlain Soc. (Toronto), History of Second World War (Can. com.), Soc. Army Hist. Research, Sigma Xi. Clubs: Univ. (Rochester); Osler (London); Alpine of Can.; Literary (Chgo.). Office: McMaster U, 3N10-HSC Med Ctr 1200 Main St W, Hamilton, ON Canada L8N 3Z5

ROLAND, DONALD EDWARD, printing company executive; b. Dalhart, Tex., Nov. 14, 1942; s. Vernon O. Roland and Doris M. (Cox) Roland Hutson; m. Kathleen Marie Bennett, Feb. 1, 1964; children—Aileen, Donald E., Jenny. B.S., Calif. State U.-Los Angeles, 1964; M.A., U. Calif.-Riverside, 1967; exec. mgmt. cert. UCLA, 1979, Claremont Grad. Sch., 1974. Dir. computer graphics Times Mirror Press, Los Angeles, 1966-78, plant mgr., 1978-81, v.p. prodn., 1981-83; group v.p. ops. Treasure Chest Advt., Glendora, Calif., 1983-84, sr. v.p. ops., 1984-93, exec. v.p. 1993-94, pres., CEO, 1995—. Republican. Home: 4 Norwood Rd Annapolis MD 21401 Office: Treasure Chest Advt 250 W Pratt St Baltimore MD 21201-2423

ROLAND, JOHN, newscaster; b. Pitts., Nov. 25, 1941; s. John Roland and Marion (Costlow) Gingher. BA in English., U. Calif., Long Beach, 1963. Rschr. NBC News, L.A., 1966-69; reporter KTTV, L.A., 1969; anchorman Fox News, N.Y.C., 1970—. Recipient Emmy award, 1978, 83, Pub. Svc. award Am. Fed. Govt. Employees Assn., 1974, Cert. of Appreciation, Goldwater Hosp., N.Y., 1975, N.Y. City Patrolman's Benevolent Assn. Journalism award, 1982, Good Samaritan award Bronx C. of C., 1983, Excelsior award N.Y.C. Coun., 1983, Man of the Yr. award N.Y.'s Finest Found., 1989; named Crimefighter of the Week, N.Y. Daily News, 1983. Mem. N.Y.C. Police Dept. Detective Endowment Assn. (hon.), Sigma Alpha Epsilon. Avocations: boating, tennis, golf. Office: Fox TV News 205 E 67th St New York NY 10021-6002*

ROLAND, RAYMOND WILLIAM, lawyer, mediator; b. Ocala, Fla., Jan. 3, 1947; s. Raymond W. and Hazel (Dunn) R.; m. Jane Allen, Dec. 28, 1968; children: John Allen, Jason William. BA, Fla. State U., 1969, JD, 1972. Bar: Fla. 1972, U.S. Dist. Ct. (no. dist.) Fla. 1973, U.S. Dist. Ct. (mid. dist.) Fla. 1985, U.S. Ct. Appeals (5th cir.) 1974, U.S. Ct. Appeals (11th cir.) 1983, U.S. Supreme Ct. 1985; cert. civil trial lawyer; cert. cir. ct. mediator. Assoc. Keen, O'Kelley & Spitz, Tallahassee, 1972-74, ptnr., 1974-77; ptnr., v.p. McConnaughhay, Roland, Maida & Cherr, P.A., Tallahassee, 1978-97; owner, mediator Roland Mediation Svcs. Bd. dirs. So. Scholarship Found., Tallahassee, 1985-89, v.p. 1989. Mem. Internat. Assn. Def. Coun., Def. Rsch. Inst., Fla. Bar (mem. Judicial Adminstrn., Selection and Tenure com.), Fla. Def. Lawyers Assn., Tallahassee Bar Assn. (treas. 1979), Kiwanis (life, lt. gov. 1984-85), Capital City Kiwanis Club (Kiwanian of Yr. 1978, pres. 1979), Fla. Kiwanis Found. (life fellow). Republican. Baptist. Avocations: reading, hiking, camping, golf. Home: 1179 Ox Bottom Rd Tallahassee FL 32312-3519

ROLANDI, GIANNA, coloratura soprano; b. N.Y.C., Aug. 16, 1952; d. Enrico G. and Jane E. (Frazier); m. Andrew Davis, 1 child, Edward. Mus.B., artist diploma, opera cert., Curtis Inst. Music, 1975. Made operatic debut at, N.Y.C. Opera, 1975; numerous appearances N.Y.C. Opera, made Met. Opera debut, 1979, numerous appearances Met. Opera, 1979—; star roles in: Tales of Hoffman, Ariadne auf Naxos, Rigoletto, The Barber of Seville, Daughter of the Regiment, Giulio Cesare, The Cunning Little Vixen, Marriage of FigAro, Lucia di Lammermoor, others; appeared with major opera cos. and symphonies throughout U.S., Eng., France, Italy, Switzerland; (rec.) Marriage of Figaro-Mozart; (video) Arabella; numerous appearances on Live from Lincoln Ctr., PBS, Including Lucia di Lammermoor, Cunning Little Vixen. Winner Met. Opera Audition; Rockefeller grantee; Nat. Opera Inst. grantee.

ROLETT, ELLIS LAWRENCE, medical educator, cardiologist; b. N.Y.C., July 10, 1930; s. Daniel Meyer and Mary Elaine (Warshaw) R.; m. Virginia Ann Vladimir, Mar. 25, 1956; children: Roderic Lawrence, Barry Vladimir, Daniel Alfred. B.S., Yale U., 1952; M.D. cum laude, Harvard U., 1955. Diplomate: Am. Bd. Internal Medicine, Am. Bd. Cardiovascular Disease. Intern, resident in medicine Mass. Gen. Hosp., Boston, 1955-56, 59-61; asst. resident N.Y. Hosp.-Cornell U. Med. Ctr., N.Y.C., 1956-57; Am. Heart Assn. research fellow Peter Bent Brigham Hosp., Boston, 1961-63; mem. faculty U. N.C., Chapel Hill, 1963-74, then prof., 1971-74; prof. UCLA, 1974-77; chief cardiology VA Wadsworth Hosp., Los Angeles, 1974-77; prof. Dartmouth Med. Sch., Hanover, N.H., 1977—; chief cardiology Dartmouth-Hitchcock Med. Ctr., Hanover, N.H., 1977-87; vis. scientist August Krogh Inst., Copenhagen, 1984; mem. merit rev. bd. Cardiovascular studies VA, 1976-79, chmn., 1978-79; mem. regional rsch. rev. com. New Eng. Am. Heart Assn., 1978-83; mem. sci. bd. Stanley J. Sarnoff Endowment for Cardiovascular Sci., 1992-97, chmn., 1994-95, also bd. dirs.; literature section review com. Nat. Library Medicine, 1995—; dir. Vt.-Karelia (Russia) Med. Project, 1992—. Bd. dirs. N.H. affiliate Am. Heart Assn., 1978-85; pres. N.H. affiliate Am. Heart Assn., 1983-85. Served to capt. M.C. USAF, 1957-59. Recipient Lederle Med. Faculty award, 1965-68, USPHS Career Devel. award, 1967-72; grantee USPHS/NIH, 1964-76, VA Merit Rev. Rsch. Program, 1975-77, Mathers Found., 1984-86, 93-96, Am. Heart Assn., 1989-91. Mem. AAAS, Am. Coll. Cardiology, Am. Fedn. Clin. Research, Am. Heart Assn., Am. Physiol. Soc., Internat. Soc. Heart Research, Phi Beta Kappa, Alpha Omega Alpha. Home: 4 Balch Hill Ln Hanover NH 03755-1622 Office: Dartmouth-Hitchcock Med Ctr Dept Cardiology Lebanon NH 03756

ROLEY, JERRY L., bank executive; b. San Francisco, Aug. 6, 1946. With Avco Corp., Silver Spring, Md., 1969-72, U.S. Ho. Rep. Credit Union, Washington, 1972-90; pres. U.S. Senate Credit Union, Washington, 1990—. With USAF, 1966-70. Office: US Senate FCU PO Box 77920 Washington DC 20013-8920

ROLF, HOWARD LEROY, mathematician, educator; b. Laverne, Okla., Nov. 25, 1928; s. James Walter and Edith (Yoho) R.; m. Anita Jane Ward, June 24, 1961; children: James Scott, Jennifer Jane, Stephanie Kaye, Rhonda Mary. BS, Okla. Baptist U., 1951; MA, Vanderbilt U., 1953, PhD, 1956. Instr. math. Vanderbilt U., 1954-56, asst. prof., dir. computer ctr., 1959-64; asst. prof. Baylor U., 1956-57, prof., 1964-98, dir. acad. computing, 1968-70, chmn. dept. math., 1971-97; assoc. prof. Georgetown (Ky.) Coll., 1957-59; cons. in field. Author: (with William C. Brown) Mathematics, 1982, Finite Mathematics, 1988, 91, 94, Mathematics for Management, Social and Life Sciences, 1991. Mem. Math. Assn. Am. (chmn. Tex. sect. 1977), Am. Math. Soc., Sigma Xi, Pi Mu Epsilon. Baptist. Home: 4096 Speegleville Rd Waco TX 76712-4033

ROLF, TOM, film editor. Editor: (with Melvin Shapiro) The Glory Guys, 1965, Clambake, 1968, The McKenzie Break, 1969, The Hunting Party, 1970, The Honkers, 1972, The Lollymadonna War, 1972, The Last American Hero, 1973, The Man Who Loved Cat Dancing, 1974, (films) Lucky Lady, 1975, French Connection II, 1975, (with Marcia Lucas and Melvin Shapiro) Taxi Driver, 1976, Black Sunday, 1976, (with Marica Lucas) New York, New York, 1977, Blue Collar, 1978, Prophecy, 1979, Hard Core, 1979, (with Lisa Fruchtman, Jerry Greenberg, and William Reynolds) Heaven's Gate, 1980, Ghost Story, 1981, (with Glenn Farr, Fruchtman, Stephan A. Rotter, and Douglas Stewart) The Right Stuff, 1983 (Acad. award best film editing 1983), Wargames, 1983, Thief of Hearts, 1984, 9 1/s Weeks, 1986, Quicksilver, 1986, Outrageous Fortune, 1987, (with Michael Ripps) Stakeout, 1987 (with Seth Flaum and William Gordean) The Great Outdoors, 1988, Black Rain, 1989, Jacob's Ladder, 1990, Sneakers, 1992, (with Trudy Ship) The Pelican Brief, 1993, Mr. Jones, 1993, Dangerous Minds, 1994 (with Dov Hoenig, Pat Bulba, Bill Goldenberg) Heat, 1995, (with Dennis Virkler) The Devils Own, 1996. Mem. Am. Cinema Editors (pres.). Office: Broder Kurland Webb Uffner Agency 9242 Beverly Blvd Ste 200 Beverly Hills CA 90210-3710

ROLFE, MICHAEL N., management consulting firm executive; b. Chgo., Sept. 9, 1937; s. Mark Alexander and Antoinette (Wittgenstein) R.; m. Judith Mary Lewis, June 16, 1959; children—Andrew, Lisa, James. A.B. in Econs., U. Mich., 1959; MBA, U. Chgo., 1996. Sales staff Lewis Co., Northbrook, Ill., 1961-62; systems mgmt. staff Brunswick Corp., Chgo., 1962-68; v.p. Kearney Mgmt. Cons., Chgo., 1968-81; ptnr. KPMG/Peat Marwick, Chgo., 1981-92; dir. Keystone Group, Evanston, Ill., 1992—. Author: AMA Management Handbook, 1969. Bd. dirs. Common, Chgo., 1972-75, U. Chgo. Cancer Rsch., 1985-88, Am. Cancer Soc., Chgo., 1985—; trustee Michael Reese Med. Ctr., 1986-91; pres. Sch. Bd. Dist. 113, Highland Park, Ill., 1977-83, Sch.Dist. 113 Found., 1993—; mem. Am. Jewish Com., 1996—. Lt. (j.g.) USNR, 1959-61. Clubs: Northmoor Country (Highland Park); Standard (Chgo.). Home: 800 Deerfield Rd Apt 109 Highland Park IL 60035-3550 Office: Keystone Group 1560 Sherman Ave Evanston IL 60201

ROLFE, ROBERT MARTIN, lawyer; b. Richmond, Va., May 16, 1951; s. Norman and Bertha (Cohen) R.; m. Catherine Dennis Stone, July 14, 1973; children: P. Alexander, Asher B., Joel A., Zachary A. BA, U. Va., 1973, JD, 1976. Bar: Va. 1976, N.Y. 1985, U.S. Dist. Ct. (ea. and we. dists.) Va. 1976, U.S. Supreme Ct. 1979, U.S. Ct. Appeals (4th cir.) 1976, U.S. Ct. Appeals (2d cir.) 1979, U.S. Dist. Ct. (ea. dist.) Mich. 1985, U.S. Ct. Appeals (D.C. cir.) 1985, U.S. Dist. Ct. (so. dist. and ea. dist.) N.Y. 1985; U.S. Ct. Appeals (7th cir.) 1995. Assoc. Hunton & Williams, Richmond, 1976-83, ptnr., 1983—. Contbr. articles to profl. jours. Bd. dirs. Jewish Family Svcs., Richmond, pres., 1993-95; bd. mgrs., 2d v.p. Congregation Beth Ahabah, 1995-97, 1st v.p., 1997—. Mem. ABA (litigation sect., natural resources, energy and environ. law sect.), Va. Bar Assn., Va. State Bar, Richmond Bar Assn., Am. Arbitration Assn. (comml. arbitrators panel), Order of Coif (Alumni award for acad. excellence U. Va. 1976). Home: 18 Greenway Ln Richmond VA 23226-1630 Office: Hunton & Williams Riverfront Plz East Tower 951 E Byrd St Richmond VA 23219-4040 also: 200 Park Ave New York NY 10166-0005

ROLFE, RONALD STUART, lawyer; b. N.Y.C., Sept. 5, 1945; s. Nat and Florence I. (Roth) R.; m. Yvonne Susan Quinn, Sept. 1, 1979; 1 child, Andrew Quinn. AB, Harvard U., 1966; JD, Columbia U., 1969. Bar: N.Y. 1969, U.S. Ct. Appeals (2d cir.) 1970, U.S. Dist. Ct. (so. and ea. dists.) N.Y. 1971, U.S. Supreme Ct. 1973, U.S. Ct. Appeals (9th cir.) 1977, U.S. Dist. Ct. (no. dist.) Calif. 1982, U.S. Ct. Appeals (5th cir.) 1982, U.S. Ct. Appeals (6th cir.) 1984, U.S. Dist. Ct. (ea. dist.) Ky. 1984, U.S Ct. Appeals (fed. cir.). Law clk. to judge U.S. Dist. Ct. (so. dist.) N.Y., 1969-70; assoc. Cravath, Swaine & Moore, 1970-77, ptnr., 1977—. Sec. bd. trustees Allen-Stevenson Sch., 1981-91, pres., 1992—; trustee Lawrenceville Sch., 1987—; v.p., trustee Prep for Prep. Kent and Stone scholar, 1969; mem. bd. visitors Columbia Law Sch. Fellow Am. Bar Found.; mem. ABA, N.Y. State Bar Assn., Assn. of Bar of City of N.Y., Fed. Bar Coun. (trustee 1989-94), Am. Law Inst., Union Club, Univ. Club, Stanwich Club (Greenwich, Conn.), Turf and Field Club (N.Y.C.), Royal Automobile Club (London). Office: Cravath Swaine & Moore Worldwide Plz 825 8th Ave New York NY 10019-7416

ROLFE, STANLEY THEODORE, civil engineer, educator; b. Chgo., July 7, 1934; s. Stanley T. and Eunice (Fike) R.; m. Phyllis Williams, Aug. 11, 1956; children: David Stanley, Pamela Kay, Kathleen Ann. B.S., U. Ill., 1956, M.S., 1958, Ph.D., 1962. Registered profl. engr., Pa., Kans. Supr. structural-evaluation sect. ordnance products div. U.S. Steel Corp., 1962-69, div. chief mech. behavior of metals div., 1969; A.P. Learned prof. civil engring. U. Kans., 1969—, chmn. civil engring. dept., 1975—; Chmn. metall. studies panel ship research com. Nat. Acad. Scis., 1967-70. Co-author: Fracture and Fatigue Control in Structures—Applications of Fracture Mechanics; co-author: textbook Strength of Materials; Contbr.: numerous articles to profl. jours. T.R. Higgins lectr., 1980; Recipient Sam Tour award Am. Soc. Testing Materials, 1971, H.E. Gould Distinguished Teaching award U. Kans., 1972, 75, AWS Adams Meml. Educator award, 1974; U. Ill. Civil Engring. Disting. Service award, 1985, U. Ill. Coll. Engring. Alumni Honor award Disting. Service in Engring., 1987; U. Kans. Irvin E. Youngberg research award, 1985. Mem. Nat. Acad. Engring., ASCE (chmn. task force on fracture, State of Art award 1983), Am. Soc. Testing Materials, ASME, Soc. Exptl. Stress Analysis, Am. Soc. Engring. Edn., Chi Psi. Presbyterian. Home: 821 Sunset Dr Lawrence KS 66044-2433

ROLL, DAVID LEE, lawyer; b. Pontiac, Mich., May 1, 1940; s. Everett Edgar and Garnette (Houts) R.; m. Nancy E. Roll, Aug. 17, 1963; children: Richard, Molly. BA cum laude, Amherst Coll., 1962; JD, U. Mich., 1964. Bar: Mich. 1965, U.S. Dist. Ct. (ea. dist.) Mich. 1965, U.S. Ct. Appeals (6th cir.) 1969, D.C. 1974, U.S. Dist. Ct. D.C. 1975, U.S. Supreme Ct. 1975, U.S. Ct. Appeals (4th cir.) 1976, U.S. Ct. Appeals (D.C. cir.) 1983, U.S. Ct. Appeals (3rd and 11th cirs.) 1985, U.S. Ct. Appeals (9th cir.) 1992, U.S. Ct. Appeals (fed. cir.) 1993. Assoc. Hill, Lewis, Detroit, 1965-70, ptnr., 1970-72; asst. dir. gen. litigation Bur. of Competition Fed. Trade Commn., Washington, 1972-75; ptnr. Steptoe & Johnson, Washington, 1975-93, chmn., 1993—. Mem. ABA (chair Robinson Patman Act com., antitrust sect. 1984-86, Clayton Act com., antitrust sect. 1986-88, Energy Litigation com., litigation sect. 1992—, mem. task force on indsl. competitiveness 1987, coun., antitrust sect. 1988-91, author, editor antitrust sect.). Office: 1330 Connecticut Ave NW Washington DC 20036-1704

ROLL, IRWIN CLIFFORD (WIN ROLL), advertising, marketing and publishing executive; b. N.Y.C., Aug. 21, 1925; s. Arnold and Bertha (Vogel) R.; m. Marilyn Witlin, Apr. 10, 1949; children: Richard J., Douglas W. B.B.A. magna cum laude, CCNY, 1948; postgrad., Columbia U., 1952. Asst. advt. mgr. Standard Motor Products, Inc., Long Island City, N.Y., 1948-50; advt. and sales promotion exec. RCA, Harrison, N.J., 1950-54; account exec. Fuller & Smith & Ross, Inc., N.Y.C., 1954-59; group v.p. Fuller & Smith & Ross, Inc., 1959-66; pres., dir. Henderson & Roll, Inc., advt. and pub. relations agy., 1966-77; pres., dir., chief exec. officer Henderson, Roll & Friedlich, Inc., 1977-79; chmn. bd., treas., chief exec. officer, dir. Listfax Corp., nat. computerized info. services co., 1966-79; pres., CEO Win Roll and Co., Inc., N.Y.C., 1979-89; chmn. bd. Roll-Bender Research, 1980-82, Devonshire Communications, Ltd., 1980-83; sr. v.p. Tradewell Industries, Inc., 1983-87; exec. v.p. Internat. Mktg. Sys. Inc., 1988-90; pres. Concord Cons. Group, 1990—; corp. devel. dir. Ind. Media Svcs., Inc., 1990-92; pres., chief oper. officer, treas., bd. dirs. Megaworld, Inc., 1993—. Mem. mktg. com. Nat. Multiple Sclerosis Soc.; bd. dirs. Westchester County chpt. Multiple Sclerosis Soc., 1983-89; pres. Rosedale Residential Assn., 1983-85, bd. dirs., 1980—. With U.S. Army, 1943-46, ETO. Mem. Ad-Net Nat. Advt. Orgn. (bd. dirs. 1983-90, pres. 1986-88), Adv. Club of N.Y., Beta Gamma Sigma (bd. dirs., v.p. N.Y. Alumni chpt. 1986-89, pres. 1989-91, adv. bd. 1991—), Alpha Delta Sigma. Home: 11 Cedarwood Rd White Plains NY 10605-5331

ROLL, JOHN MCCARTHY, judge; b. Pitts., Feb. 8, 1947; s. Paul Herbert and Esther Marie (McCarthy) R.; m. Maureen O'Connor, Jan. 24, 1970; children: Robert McCarthy, Patrick Michael, Christopher John. B.A., U. Ariz., 1969, J.D., 1972, LLM U. Va., 1990. Bar: Ariz. 1972, U.S. Dist. Ct. Ariz. 1974, U.S. Ct. Appeals (9th cir.) 1980, U.S. Supreme Ct. 1977. Asst. pros. atty. City of Tucson, 1973; dep. county atty. Pima County (Ariz.), 1973-80; asst. U.S. atty. U.S. Atty.'s Office, Tucson, 1980-87; judge Ariz. Ct. Appeals, 1987-91, U.S. Dist. Ct. Ariz., 1991—; lectr. Nat. Coll. Dist. Attys. U. Houston, 1976-87; mem. criminal justice mental health standards project ABA, 1980-83. Contbr. to Trial Techniques Compendium, 1978, 82, 84, Merit Selection: The Arizona Experience, Arizona State Law Journal, 1991, The Rules Have Changed: Amendments to the Rules of Civil Procedure, Defense Law Journal, 1994. Coach, Frontier Baseball Little League, Tucson, 1979-84; mem. parish coun. Sts. Peter and Paul Roman Catholic Ch., Tucson, 1983-91, chmn., 1986-91; mem. Roman Cath. Diocese of Tucson Sch. Bd., 1986-90. Recipient Disting. Faculty award Nat. Coll. Dist. Attys., U. Houston, 1979, Outstanding Alumnus award U. Ariz. Coll. Law, 1992. Mem. Fed. Judges Assn., Pima County Bar Assn. Republican. Lodge: K.C. (adv. coun. 10441). Office: US Dist Ct 55 E Broadway Blvd Tucson AZ 85701-1719

ROLLAND, DONALD F., printing company executive. CEO Big Flower Press, Glendora, Calif., until 1993; pres., CEO Treasure Chest Advt., Balt., 1993—. Office: Treasure Chest Advt PO Box 17102 Baltimore MD 21297*

ROLLAND, IAN MCKENZIE, insurance executive; b. Fort Wayne, Ind., June 3, 1933; s. David and Florence (Hunte) R.; m. Miriam V. Flickinger, July 3, 1955; children: Cheri L., Lawrence D., Robert A., Carol Ann, Sara

K. B.A., DePauw U., 1955; M.A. in Actuarial Sci., U. Mich., 1956. With Lincoln Nat. Life Ins. Co., Ft. Wayne, 1956—, sr. v.p., 1973-75, pres., 1977-81, chief exec. officer, 1977-91, chmn., pres., 1981-92, chmn., chief exec. officer, 1992—; pres. Lincoln Nat. Corp., 1975-91, CEO, 1977-91, chmn., CEO, 1992—; bd. dirs. Norwest Corp. Norwest Bank (Ind.), No. Ind. Pub. Svc., Lincoln Fin. Corp., GTE North, Inc., Tokh. Mem. adv. bd. Ind. U.-Purdue U., 1977, Fort Wayne Leadership, Fort Wayne Community Found., Corp. Innovation Devel. Ventures; bd. dirs. Associated Colls. Ind., Corp. Innovation Devel.; chmn. Ind. Fiscal Policy Com.; trustee Hudson Inst.; mem. Indiana Acad. Mem. Soc. Actuaries, Acad. Actuaries, Health Ins. Assn. Am., Am. Council Life Ins. (past chmn. bd. dirs.), Assoc. Ind. Life Ins. Cos. (exec. com.), Ind. Ins. Soc. (bd. dirs.), Internat. Ins. Soc. (bd. dirs.), Ind. C. of C. (mem. exec. com.). Office: Lincoln Nat Corp 200 E Berry St Fort Wayne IN 46802-2706

ROLLAND, LUCIEN G., paper company executive; b. St. Jerome, Que., Can., Dec. 21, 1916; s. Olivier and Aline (Dorion) R.; m. Marie de Lorimier, May 30, 1942; children: Nicolas, Natalie, Stanislas, Dominique, Christine, Etienne, David. Student, Coll. Jean de Brebeuf, Montreal, Loyola Coll., U. Montreal; B.A., B.A.Sc., C.E., also D.C.Sc. (hon.), Loyola Coll., U. Montreal, 1960. Registered profl. engr. With Rolland Paper Co. Ltd. (name changed to Rolland inc. 1979), 1942—, v.p., gen. mgr., 1952, pres., gen. mgr., 1952-78, pres., CEO, 1978—, chmn., pres., CEO, 1984, chmn., CEO, 1985, chmn., 1991; cons. in field, 1995; pres. Tarascon Holdings, Inc. Bd. govs. Notre-Dame Hosp., Montreal Children's Hosp., Montreal Gen. Hosp., Hôpital Marie Enfant. Decorated Knight Comdr. Order St. Gregory, officer Order of Can. Mem. Can. Pulp and Paper Assn. (hon.), Corp. Profl. Engrs., Montreal Bd. Trade, Province of Que., C of C, Montreal C. of C., Engring. Inst. Can. Home: Apt B-60, 1321 Sherbrooke St W, Montreal, PQ Canada H3G 1J4 Office: Rolland Inc, 2 Rolland Ave, Saint Jerome, PQ Canada J7Z 5S1 Office: Tarascon Inc, 1200 McGill College #1100, Montreal, PQ Canada H3B 4G7

ROLLANS, JAMES O., service company executive; b. Glendale, Calif., July 7, 1942; s. Henry Leo and Geraldine Ada (Berg) R.; children: Jodie Helene, Thomas James, Daniel Joseph. BS, Calif. State U., Northridge, 1967. Vice pres., dir. Chase Manhattan Bank, 1976-78; v.p. corp. communications Dart Industries, Los Angeles, 1978-80; v.p. bus. analysis and investor relations Dart & Kraft, Chgo., 1980-82; sr. v.p., chief adminstrv. officer Fluor Corp., Irvine, Calif., 1982—; bd. dirs. Plaza Comm., Lafayette Pharms. Corp., Irvine Med. Ctr. Mem. BW/IP, Inc. Episcopalian. Avocations: boating; skiing; fishing; hunting. Office: Fluor Corp 3353 Michelson Dr Irvine CA 92698-0010

ROLLASON, MARY KATHERINE, artist, art educator; b. Balt., Jan. 18, 1908; d. Clarence Irving and Mary Agnes (Sadler) Drenner; m. Fred Rollason, Sept. 27, 1941 (dec. Mar. 1994). Student, Sch. Music Arts, Balt., 1928-33; student in fgn. lang., Costa Rican Consulate, Balt., 1936-40, Italian Consulate, Balt., YMCA, Balt.; pvt. student of Clyde Taylor,, Carnegie Mellon Inst., Pa., Md., 1941-45. Coloratura soprano Balt. Civic Opera Co., 1930; singer WBAL Radio, Balt., 1930-32; art tchr., owner Kay's Art Gallery, Crossville, Tenn., 1980—. Exhbn.: Salon des Nations à Paris, Internat. D'Art Contemporium, 1985; founder,mem. Black-Eyed Susans chpt. Sweet Adelines, Catonsville, Md., 1959-65. Aide-de-camp Hon. Shirley Duer, Tenn. Ho. Rep., 1981. Named Artist of the Month Cumberland Cmty. Bank, Crossville, 1981. Mem. Nat. Mus. Women in the Arts (charter), N.Y. Internat. Soc. Artists, Women of Moose (libr. chmn. Balt., 1945, conservation chmn. Balt., 1946, Acad. Friendship degree). Avocations: bowling, singing, oil painting. Home and Office: RR 11 Box 99 Crossville TN 38555-8920

ROLLE, ANDREW F., historian, educator, author; b. Providence, Apr. 12, 1922; m. Frances Squires, Dec. 1945 (div.); children: John Warren, Alexander Frederick, Julia Elisabeth.; m. Myra Moss, Nov. 1983. B.A., Occidental Coll., 1943; M.A., UCLA, 1949, Ph.D., 1953; grad., So. Calif. Psychoanalytic Inst., 1976. Am. vice consul Genoa, Italy, 1945-48; editorial asso. Pacific Hist. Rev., 1952-53; from asst. prof. to Cleland prof. history Occidental Coll., 1953-88; rsch. scholar Huntington Libr., San Marino, Calif., 1988—. Author: Riviera Path, 1946, An American in California, 1956, reprinted, 1982, The Road to Virginia City, 1960, reprinted, 1989, Lincoln: A Contemporary Portrait, 1961, (with Allan Nevins, Irving Stone) California: A History, 1963, rev. edits., 1969, 78, 87, 97, Occidental College: The First Seventy-Five Years, 1963, The Lost Cause: Confederate Exiles in Mexico, 1965, 1992, The Golden State, 1967, rev. edit., 1978, 1989, California, A Student Guide, 1965, Los Angeles, A Student Guide, 1965; Editor: A Century of Dishonor (Helen Hunt Jackson), 1964, Life in California (Alfred Robinson), 1971; The Immigrant Upraised, 1968, The American Italians: Their History and Culture, 1972, Gli Emigrati Vittoriosi, 1973; (with George Knoles others) Essays and Assays, 1973, (with others) Studies in Italian American Social History, 1975, (with others) Los Angeles: The Biography of a City, 1976, 2d edit., 1991, (with Allan Weinstein and others) Crisis in America, 1977, The Italian Americans: Troubled Roots, 1980, 2d edit. 1985, Los Angeles: From Pueblo to Tomorrow's City, 1981, 2nd edit., 1995, Occidental College: A Centennial History, 1986, John Charles Frémont: Character as Destiny, 1991, Henry Mayo Newhall and His Times, 1992. Served to 1st lt. M.I. AUS, 1943-45, 51-52. Decorated Cavaliere Ordine Merito Italy; recipient silver medal Italian Ministry Fgn. Affairs; Commonwealth award for non-fiction; Huntington Library-Rockefeller Found. fellow; resident scholar Rockefeller Found. Center, Bellagio, Italy. Fellow Calif. Hist. Soc.; mem. Phi Beta Kappa. Office: Huntington Libr Rsch Div San Marino CA 91108

ROLLE, CHRISTOPHER DAVIES, lawyer; b. Tokyo, Dec. 25, 1951; s. Norman Benjamin and Mavis Cameron (Williams) R.; children: Christopher Davies Jr., Zachery B. BA, Ark. State U., 1974; JD, Stetson U., 1977. Bar: Fla. 1978, U.S. Dist. Ct. (mid. dist.) Fla. 1979, U.S. Dist. Ct. (no. and so. dists.) Fla. 1980, U.S. Ct. Appeals (5th cir.) 1979, U.S. Ct. Appeals (11th cir.) 1981, U.S. Supreme Ct. 1981. Asst. state's atty. 20th Jud. Cir., Ft. Myers, Fla., 1978; atty. securities fraud unit and office compt. State of Fla., Tampa, 1978-79; asst. atty. gen. adminstrv. law sect. State of Fla., Tallahassee, 1979-83; ea. regional counsel Nat. Med. Enterprises, Inc., Tampa, 1983-84; gen. counsel, v.p. Retirement Corp. Am., Bradenton, Fla., 1984-85; with Holland & Knight, Bradenton and Orlando, Fla., 1985-88; assoc. Baker & Hostetler, Orlando, Fla., 1988-90; ptnr. Foley & Lardner, Orlando, 1990—; mem. health com. Orlando Naval Tng. Ctr. Reuse Commn. Editorial bd. Physician's Mktg. and Mgmt. Chmn. Jim Smith's gubernatorial campaign, Bradenton, 1986; bd. dirs. Retirement Housing Coun., 1985-87, v.p., 1986-87, Health Care Ctr. for Homeless, Inc.; chmn. bd. dirs. Children's Wish Found., Orlando, 1988—, grad. Leadership Orlando, 1990-91; bd. dirs. Fla. C. of C. Mgmt. Corp., 1996—. Named one of Outstanding Young Men Am., 1988. Mem. ABA (forum on health law), Fla. Bar Assn. (vice chmn. commn. on elderly 1990-91, pub. rels. com. 1988-92, vice chmn. health law com. 1987-88, adminstrv. law sect. exec. coun., founding mem., exec. coun. health law sect. 1988-91, chmn. 1989-90), Manatee County Bar Assn. (treas. 1987-88), Orange County Bar Assn., Fla. Hosp. Assn., Fla. Acad. Healthcare Attys. (bd. dirs.), Am. Hosp. Assn., Am. Acad. Healthcare Attys., Nat. Health Lawyers Assn., Greater Orlando C. of C., Lambda Chi Alpha. Office: Foley & Lardner 111 N Orange Ave Ste 1800 Orlando FL 32801-2387

ROLLE, MYRA MOSS See MOSS, MYRA ELLEN

RÖLLER, HERBERT ALFRED, biology and medical scientist, educator; b. Magdeburg, Germany, Aug. 2, 1927; came to U.S., 1962; s. Alfred H. and Elfriede (Wartner) R.; m. Manuela R. Buresch, Dec. 20, 1957. Abiturium, Christian Thomasius Schule, Halle/Saale, 1946; Dr.rer.nat., Georg August U., Goettingen, 1962; MD, U. Muenster, 1955. Project assoc. zoology U. Wis., Madison, 1962-65; asst. prof. pharmacology U. Wis., 1965-66, research assoc. zoology, 1966-67, assoc. prof. zoology, 1967-68; prof. biology Tex. A&M U., 1968-83, prof. biochemistry and biophysics, 1974-83, dir. Inst. Devel. Biology, 1973-83, Disting. prof., 1977—, Alumni prof., 1980-85; v.p. rsch. Zoecon Corp., Palo Alto, Calif., 1968-72, sci. adv., 1972-85, chief scientist, Zoecon Rsch. Inst., Palo Alto, 1985-88; sci. advisor Syntex Rsch., Palo Alto, 1966-68, European Cmty., 1988—, Affymax Rsch. Inst., Palo Alto, 1989-96, Symyx Techs., Sunnyvale, Calif., 1996—; mem. adv. panel regulatory biology, divsn. biol. and med. scis. NSF, 1969-72; mem. Internat. Centre Insect Physiology and Ecology, Nairobi, Kenya, 1970—, dir. rsch., 1970-75. Editorial bd.: Jour. Chem. Ecology, 1974—; Contbr. articles to profl. publs. Recipient Disting. Achievement award for research Tex. A&M U., 1976. Fellow Tex. Acad. Sci.; mem. Deutsche Akademie Naturforscher Leopoldina, AAAS, Am. Soc. Zoologists, Entomol. Soc. Am., Am. Soc. Devel. Biology, Sigma Xi. Home: 824 N Rosemary Dr Bryan TX 77802-4309

ROLLER, ROBERT DOUGLAS, III, psychiatrist; b. Charleston, W.Va., Nov. 17, 1928; s. Francis Oliver and Mary Elizabeth (Rice) R.; m. Anthonia Ijsselstein, Mar. 7, 1970; children: Robert Douglas IV, Katherine Willis, David Nelson, Anthonia Elizabeth, Alexander Robert, John Richard. BA, U. Va., 1950, MD, 1960; postgrad. in philosophy, U. Pa., 1953-56. Tchr. Chestnut Hill Acad. Phila./Raven Soc., U. Va., 1953-56; intern U. N.C. Hosp., Chapel Hill, 1960-61, resident, 1961-62; resident Med. Coll. of Va., Richmond, 1963; NIMH research and teaching fellow U. Calif. Med. Ctr., San Francisco, 1963-66; pvt. practice Berkeley, 1966—; assoc. psychiatrist, rsch. psychiatrist U. Calif., Berkeley, 1965-71; clin. asst. prof. U. Calif. Med. Sch., San Francisco, 1970—; clin. instr. Stanford U. Med. Sch., Palo Alto, Calif., 1969-78, C.G. Jung Analytic Inst., 1964-72; mem. staff Alta Bates Hosp., 1971—, Lodi (Calif.) Meml. Hosp., 1971—, Cmty. Hosp., 1971-88; chief psychiatrist Clear Water Ranch for Children, Santa Rosa, Calif., 1964-71. Mem. Episcopal and Presbyn. Ch. With USNR, 1950-51. Mem. Farmington Country Club (Charlottesville, Va.), U. Calif. Faculty Club, St. Anthony Club of N.Y., St. Elmo Club (Va.), Sleepy Hollow Tennis Club, Bankers Club of San Francisco, Phila. Cricket Club. Home: 757 San Diego Rd Berkeley CA 94707-2025 Office: 2999 Regent St Ste 422 Berkeley CA 94705-2119

ROLLER, THOMAS BENJAMIN, manufacturing company executive; b. Phila., Mar. 4, 1950; s. Clarence Thomas and Anne Dolores (Marrese) R.; m. Christine Louise Rebman, Oct. 14, 1978; children: Thomas Nathaniel, Laura Anne, Elizabeth Anne. BA, Clemson U., 1972; MBA, Duke U., 1974. Fin. analyst E.I. duPont de Nemours & Co., Wilmington, Del., 1974-75; sr. fin. analyst Rockwell Internat. Corp., Pitts., 1975-77; mgr. acquisitions Rockwell Internat. Corp., Troy, Mich., 1978, mgr. bus. planning, 1979; dir. worldwide bus. devel. Rockwell Internat. Corp., London, 1979-81; v.p. mktg. automotive div. United Techs., Lausanne, Switzerland, 1981-83; v.p. corp. planning carrier United Techs., Syracuse, N.Y., 1984-85, v.p., gen. mgr. replacement components div., 1985-87, pres. residential products div., 1988-90; pres., CEO Plywood Panels, Inc., New Orleans, 1990-92; CEO Fruehauf Trailer Corp., Indpls., 1992-96, Wolverine Tube, Huntsville, Ala., 1996—. Com. mem. U.S. Dept. Commerce Indsl. Sector Adv. Com. Capital Goods, Washington, 1986-89; pres. adv. Clemson U., 1990—; bd. dirs. alumni coun. Fuqua Sch. Bus. Duke U., Durham, N.C., 1985-87. Republican. Avocations: fishing, N.Am. archaeology.

ROLLHAUS, PHILIP EDWARD, JR., manufacturing company executive; b. Phila., Sept. 29, 1934; s. Philip Edward and Elizabeth Snow (Bedford) R.; m. Jacqueline Merrill, Feb. 13, 1965 (div. 1975); children: Natalie, Philip Edward III; m. Barbara Lynn Walker, Oct. 8, 1983. BA in English Lit., Wesleyan U., 1956. Dir. gen. Société Rollhaus, Paris, 1960-64; regional mgr. Bus. Internat., Chgo., 1964-67; mgr. pvt. placements Woolard & Co., Chgo., 1967-69; founder, chmn., CEO Quixote Corp., Chgo., 1969—, pres., 1969-95; bd. dirs. Chgo. Capital Fund., 1986-91, DeVry, Inc., 1987-90, Keller Grad. Sch. Mgmt., Chgo., 1974-87, Alliance Francaise de Chicago, 1993-95; mem. Am. Bus. Conf., Washington, 1987—; chmn. Starlight Found., Chgo., 1986-88, Gastro-Intestinal Rsch. Found., Chgo., 1984-90; trustee Inst. Psychoanalysis, Chgo., 1983-89, Nat. Symphony Orch., Washington, 1989-92; bd. assocs. Gallaudet U., Washington, 1993—; mem. adv. bd. Inst. Internat. Edn., 1995—; active Wilson coun. Woodrow Wilson Internat. Ctr. for Scholars, Washington, 1995—. Served to lt. (j.g.) USN, 1956-60. Mem. Econ. Club of Chgo., Soc. Mayflower Descs., Chicago Club, Racquet Club, Tavern Club, Bath and Tennis Club (Palm Beach, Fla.), Palm Beach Yacht Club, Shelter Island (N.Y.) Yacht Club, Bohemian Club (San Francisco), Metro. Club (Washington). Home: 1500 N Lake Shore Dr Chicago IL 60610-1607 Office: Quixote Corp 1 E Wacker Dr Fl 30 Chicago IL 60601-1802

ROLLIN, BERNARD ELLIOT, philosophy educator, consultant on animal ethics; b. N.Y.C., Feb. 18, 1943; s. Phillip and Yetta Ethel (Bookchin) R.; m. Linda Mae Schieber, Aug. 30, 1964; 1 child, Michael David Hume. BA, CCNY, 1964; PhD, Columbia U., 1972. Preceptor Columbia U., N.Y.C., 1968-69; asst. prof. philosophy Colo. State U., Ft. Collins, 1969-73, assoc. prof., 1973-78, prof., 1978—, prof. physiology and biophysics, 1980—, dir. bioethical planning, 1981—; cons. Can., Australian, South African, The Netherlands, and U.S. govts., various univs. and agys. including U. Calif., Berkeley, Wash. State U., U. Fla., USDA, NIH, 1980—, United Airlines, Denver, 1985—, Nat. Livestock Ethics Coun., 1997—; lectr. on animal ethics, 1978—. Author: Natural and Conventional Meaning, 1976, Animal Rights and Human Morality, 1981, 2d edit., 1992 (Outstanding Acad. Book award Choice Mag. Am. Assn. U. Librs., 1982, Gustavus Meyers Ctr. award for study of human rights 1993), The Unheeded Cry, 1989, The Experimental Animal in Biomedical Research, 1990, vol. 2, 1995, The Frankenstein Syndrome: Ethical and Social Issues in the Genetic Engineering of Animals, 1995, Farm Animal Welfare, 1995; mem. editl. bd. Jour. AVMA, Between the Species, Agrl. Ethics, Acta Semiotica et Linguistica, Studies in Animal Welfare Sci., numerous others; contbr. articles to profl. jours. Recipient Harris T. Guard award Colo. State U., 1981, honors prof., 1983; Waco F. Childers award Am. Humane Assn., 1982, svc. award Colo. Vet. Med. Assn., 1983, Disting. Faculty award Colo. State U. Coll. Vet. Med., 1993, Gustavus Myers Human Rights award 1994, Brownlee award Animal Welfare Found. Can., 1994. Jewish. Avocations: weightlifting, horseback riding, motorcycles. Office: Colo State U Dept Philosophy Fort Collins CO 80523-1781

ROLLIN, BETTY, author, television journalist; b. N.Y.C., Jan. 3, 1936; d. Leon and Ida R.; m. Harold M. Edwards, Jan. 21, 1979. BA, Sarah Lawrence Coll., 1957. Assoc. features editor Vogue mag., 1964; sr. editor Look mag., 1965-71; network corr. NBC News, N.Y.C., 1971-80, contbg. corr., 1985—; network corr. ABC News Nightline, 1982-84; lectr. in field. Profl. actress on stage and television, 1958-64; Author: I Thee Wed, 1958, Mothers Are Funnier Than Children, 1964, The Non-Drinkers' Drink Book, 1966, First, You Cry, 1976, reissue, 1993, Am I Getting Paid for This?, 1982, Last Wish, 1985; columnist Hers, N.Y. Times; Contbr. articles to popular mags. V.p. Death With Dignity Nat. Ctr., 1997—. Office: care NS Bienstock Inc 1740 Broadway New York NY 10019-4315

ROLLINS, ALDEN MILTON, documents librarian; b. Billerica, Mass., July 31, 1946; s. Alden Milton and Agnes Morgan (Simpson) R. BA, Am. U., 1968; MLS, U. R.I., 1973. Cert. geneal. record specialist, Bd. for Certification of Genealogists., Vt., N.H. Documents libr. U. Alaska Libr., Anchorage, 1973—. Author: The Fall of Rome: A Reference Guide, 1983, Rome in the Fourth Century A.D., 1991, Vermont Warnings Out, 1995. With U.S. Army, 1969-71. Mem. Nat. Geneal. Soc., Geneal. Soc. Vt., N.H. Geneal. Soc., New Eng. Hist. Geneal. Soc., N.H. Hist. Soc., Vt. Hist. Soc. (life), Piscataqua Pioneers (life). Avocation: genealogy. Home: 221 E 7th Ave Apt 114 Anchorage AK 99501-3639 Office: U Alaska Libr Govt Documents 3211 Providence Dr Anchorage AK 99508-4614

ROLLINS, ALFRED BROOKS, JR., historian, educator; b. Presque Isle, Maine, May 28, 1921; s. Alfred Brooks and Clarissa (Jack) R.; m. Ernestine Emma McMullin, Nov. 6, 1942 (dec. Aug. 28, 1972); children: John Douglas, Nancy Jane, James Scott; m. Faith Kenyon, June 16, 1973 (dec. Mar. 1979); m. Helen Anrod Jones, Feb. 28, 1981. BA, Wesleyan U., Middletown, Conn., 1942, MA, 1946; PhD, Harvard U., 1953. From instr. to prof. history State U., N.Y. at New Paltz, 1948-63; prof., chmn. dept. history State U. N.Y. at Binghamton, 1964-67; dean U. Vt., Burlington, 1967-70; v.p. acad. affairs U. Vt., 1970-76; pres. Old Dominion U., Norfolk, Va., 1976-85; prof. history Old Dominion U., Norfolk, 1976-91, pres. emeritus, prof. emeritus, 1991—; Cons. oral history project John F. Kennedy Library, 1965. Author: Roosevelt and Howe, 1962; Editor narrative: Franklin D. Roosevelt and the Age of Action, 1960, Woodrow Wilson and the New America, 1965; Contbr. articles to profl. jours. Served to 1st lt. USAAF, 1943-46. Decorated D.F.C., Air medal with four clusters. Mem. Am. Hist. Assn., Orgn. Am. Historians, Phi Beta Kappa, Chi Psi.

ROLLINS, ARLEN JEFFERY, osteopathic physician; b. Cleve., June 30, 1946; s. Lee Roy and Celia (Madorsky) R.; m. Deborah Joyce Gross, Dec. 18, 1971 (div.); children: Aaron Jason, Howard Philip, Lee Craig. AB, Miami U., Oxford, Ohio, 1968; DO, Chgo. Coll. Osteo. Medicine, 1973; MS in Occupl. Medicine, Environ. Health, U. Cin., 1984. Diplomate Am. Bd. Preventive Medicine. Intern, Phoenix Gen. Hosp., 1973-74; resident in environ. health/occupl. medicine Cin. Gen. Hosp.-U. Cin., 1974-77; plant physician Ford Motor Co., Cin., 1974-77, Walton Hills stamping plant divsn., Cleve., 1987—; assoc. med. dir. East Side Occupl. Health Ctr., Cleve., 1977-79; med. dir. Ferro Corp., Cleve., 1979—, S.K. Wellman Corp., Cleve., 1979-87, Morgan Matroc, 1979—; pres. Occupl. Health Mgmt. Cons.; cons. occupl. health Ohio Bell Telephone Co., Cleve., 1981-87; cons. Occupl. Health Ctr., Univ. Hosps. of Cleve.; dir. occupl. health program Bedford Med. Ctr. Univ. Hosps. Cleve. Fellow Am. Acad. Occupl. Medicine, Am. Occupl . Med. Assn., Am. Coll. Preventive Medicine; mem. Ohio State Med. Assn., Cleve. Acad. Medicine (pub. health and immunization com., med.-legal com.), Western Res. Med. Dirs. Assn., Am. Osteo. Assn., Am. Osteo. Acad. Pub. Health and Preventive Medicine (past bd. dirs.).

ROLLINS, EDWARD TYLER, JR., newspaper executive; b. Durham, N.C., May 23, 1922; s. Edward Tyler and Bessie (Steed) R.; m. Frances Louise Page, Oct. 5, 1963; children: Edward Tyler III, William Lawson. AB, U. N.C., 1947. V.p., asst. sec. Durham (N.C.) Herald Co., 1949-69, v.p., sec.-treas., 1969-81, pres., pub., 1982-88, chmn., bd. dirs., 1985—; pres. Durham Radio Corp. Stas. WDNC-AM, WDCG-FM, 1982-88. Bd. dirs. Chowan Coll. Graphic Arts Found., 1986—; bd. dirs. Sch. of Journalism Found. of N.C., 1982-88; mem. Friends of Duke Art Mus., mem. adv. bd. N.C. Nat. Bank, 1979-89; mem. Gov.'s Bus. Coun. on Arts and Humanities, 1989-90; mem. Duke Pres.'s Art Mus. com., 1994—; trustee Meredith Coll., Raleigh, N.C., 1966-69, Durham Pub. Libr., 1961-81; former bd. dirs. Durham Salvation Army; pres. Durham YMCA, 1952; former bd. dirs. Family Svc. Assn.; supporter N.C. Symphony. With U.S. Army, 1943-46. Mem. Newspaper Assn. Am., N.C. Press Assn., So. Newspaper Publs. Assn., The English Speaking Union, Durham C. of C. (bd. dirs. 1969), Kiwanis, Hope Valley Country Club, Treyburn Country Club, Univ. Club, Carolina Club. Presbyterian. Office: Durham Herald Co Inc 2828 Pickett Rd Durham NC 27705-5613

ROLLINS, HENRY, musician, author, publisher; b. Feb. 13, 1961. Prin., pub. 2.13.61 Records, L.A.; prin. Human Pitbull Music Pub. Formerly with Black Flag; now songwriter, lead singer Rollins Band; albums with Rollins Band include Hot Animal Machine, 1987, Drive By Shooting, 1987, Life Time, 1988, Do It, 1989, Hard Volume, 1989, Turned On, 1990, The End of Silence, 1992, Electro Convulsive Therapy, 1993, Weight, 1994; albums with Black Flag include My War, 1983, Family Man, 1984, Slip It In, 1984, Live '84, 1984, Loose Nut, 1985, The Process of Weeding Out, 1985, In My Head, 1985, Who's Got the 10, 1986; spoken word releases include Short Walk on a Long Pier, Big Ugly Mouth, Sweatbox, Live at McCabe's, Human Butt, The Boxed Life, Get in the Van; video Talking From the Box; author: High Adventure in the Great Outdoors, 1984, Hallucinations of Grandeur, 1986, You Can't Run from God, 1986, Pissing in the Gene Pool, 1987, Works, 1988, Art to Choke Hearts, 1989, Bang!, 1990, One From None, 1991, Black Coffee Blues, 1992, See a Grown Man Cry, 1992, Now Watch Him Die, 1993, Get in the Van, 1994, Eye Scream, 1996, Do I Come Here Often, 1997; contbr. Detals mag., Village Voice, Spin, Sounds, Melody Maker, The Face, various anthologies; film appearances include: The Chase, 1994, Johnny Mnemonic, 1995, Heat, 1996; spoken word performer, 1983—. Grammy nomination, Best Metal Performance for "Liar", 1995, Grammy award winner Best Spoken Word Album Get in the Van, 1995. Office: 2 13 61 PO Box 1910 Los Angeles CA 90078 also: care Imago Recording Co 152 W 57th St New York NY 10019-3310

ROLLINS, JAMES GREGORY, air force officer; b. Vandenberg AFB, Calif., Apr. 6, 1963; s. Clarence Leslie and Mary Ethel (Brooks) R. BS in Bus. Adminstrn., San Jose State U., 1985; MSA in Gen. Adminstrn., Ctrl. Mich. U., 1992; MBA in Aviation Mgmt., Embry-Riddle Aero. U., 1992. Commd. 2d lt. USAF, 1985, advanced through grades to maj., 1997; minuteman intercontinental ballistic missile dep. crew comdr. USAF, Grand Forks AFB, N.D., 1985-86, minuteman intercontinental ballistic missile instr. dep. crew comdr., 1986-87, minuteman intercontinental ballistic missile evaluator dep. crew comdr., 1987-88, strategic air command missile combat competition instr., 1987-88, intercontinental ballistic missile crew comdr., 1988-89, scheduling br. chief ops., 1989-90, order tng. officer emergecy war, 1990-91, intercontinental ballistic missile ops. plans officer, 1991-92; acquisition info. mgr. USAF, L.A. AFB, 1992-93, dep. dir. program control divsn., 1993-94, chief plans and analysis divsn., 1994-96; dep. chief Peace Shield Deployment USAF, Hanscom AFB, Mass., 1996, chief Peace Shield Sustainment, 1996—. Editor (newsletters) Families First, 1991, Vol. Network, 1990-91. Asst. project officer Project Sandbox fundraiser, 1986; founder Above and Beyond Vol. Tutoring, 1988, cons., 1988—; vol. staff Youth Ctr., Grand Forks AFB, 1988-91, Rebuild L.A. Edn. and Job Tng. Task Force; base project officer Rob's Coats for Kids, 1990, 91; vol. Grand Forks United Way Cmty. Svcs., 1990-91; mem. Points of Light Found., 1991—, Minn. Office Vol. Svcs., 1991-95, Commdrs. Cmty. Ptnrs. Program, 1994-96; project coord. L.A. Works, 1995-96; bd. dirs., vol. Habitat for Humanity, 1994—, vol. People Making a Difference, 1996—; vol. Boston Cares, 1996—. Decorated Air Force Achievement medal, 1990, Air Force Commendation medal, 1992; named Vol. of Yr., 321st Strategic Missile Wing, 42d Air Divsn., 8th Air Force, Strategic Air Command, 1990; recipient Presdl. award for volunteerism, 1991, Outstanding Vol. Svc. medal Mil., 1996. Mem. Air Force Assn., Air Force Cadet Officer Mentor Action Program, Performance Mgmt. Assn., Soc. Cost Estimating & Analysis, Tuskegee Airmen, Inc., Assn. of Air Force Missileers, Points of Light Found., Ctr. Corp. Cmty. Rels. Home: 176 East St # 202 Methuen MA 01844 Office: USAF ESC/ISD Hanscom AFB MA 01731-1644

ROLLINS, JIMMY DON, school system administrator. Supt. Springdale (Ark.) Sch. Dist. State finalist Nat. Supt. Yr. award, 1992. Office: Springdale Sch Dist 804 W Johnson St Springdale AR 72764-4159 also: Springdale Sch Dist PO Box 8 Springdale AR 72765-0008

ROLLINS, JUNE ELIZABETH, elementary education educator; b. Turin, N.Y., June 24, 1929; d. Jay Elihue and Mildred (Evans) Hoskins; m. Clair Austin Rollins, June 28, 1952; children: Timothy, Teri June, Scott, Tracy. BS in Music, Fredonia (N.Y.) State U., 1950. Cert. tchr. nursery, kindergarten, elem. edn., music, N.Y. Tchr. instrumental and vocal music Greenwood (N.Y.) Ctrl. H.S., 1968-71, Greenwood Ctrl. Sch., 1950-58, 59-68, Whitesville Ctrl., 1958-59; tchr. kindergarten Greenwood Ctrl. Sch., 1965-68, tchr. 3rd grade, 1971—; tchr. piano. Organist, choir dir., tchr. Bible sch. and Sunday sch. Greenwood Meth. Ch., 1972—; organist Andover Meth. Ch., 1995-97. Recipient Spl. Mission Recognition award Meth. Ch. for Music, 1981, Spl. Recognition award Music Dean Dist. United Meth. Houghton Coll., 1992, Gen. Douglas MacArthur Youth award Grand Lodge of State of N.Y., 1994, Outstanding Educator award Twin Tiers of N.Y. and Pa., 1995; named Outstanding Citizen West Greenwood Grange, 1992; featured in Evening Tribune, Hornell, N.Y., 1990. Mem. Delta Kappa Gamma (publicity chair 1989—, sec. 1994-95, 96-97). Methodist. Avocations: flower gardening, crafts, needlework, quilting, bike riding. Home: 2671 Main St Greenwood NY 14839 Office: Greenwood Ctrl Sch PO Box 936 Greenwood NY 14839-0936

ROLLINS, SANDRA L., academic administrator; b. Phila., May 16, 1952; d. Joseph and Leola Schuriq; divorced; 1 child, Gregory Clay Rollins. BA in Edn., LaSalle U., 1975; postgrad., Rider U., 1990—. Counselor fin. aid Jefferson Med. Coll., Thomas Jefferson U., Phila., 1975-77, asst. to dean of admissions, 1977-81; coord. admissions and fin. aid Coll. Grad. Studies, Thomas Jefferson U., 1984-90; asoc. dir. fin. aid U. Medicine and Dentistry N.J., Stratford, 1990—. Mem. AAUW, N.J. Assn. Student Fin. Aid Adminstrs. (tng. chair 1992-94, grad. and prof. concerns com. 1994-95), Nat. Assn. Student Fin. Aid Admsntrs., Middestates Assn. Coll. Registrars and Officers of Admission, com chair conf. 1987-90). Home: 2 Cobblestone Ln Shamong NJ 08088-8404 Office: U Medicine & Dentistry NJ 40 Laurel Rd E Stratford NJ 08084-1350

ROLLINS, SHERRIE SANDY, television executive; b. Roanoke, Va., June 11, 1958; d. William Gresham and Charlotte (Weeks) Sandy; m. Edward

John Rollins, Jr., May 2, 1987. BA, U. Va., 1980. Exec. v.p. ABC TV Network, N.Y.C., 1996—; advt. dir. Georgetown mag., Alexandria, Va., 1980-81; exec. dir. Bus. and Profl. Assn. Georgetown, Washington, 1981-84; v.p. communications The Oliver Carr Co., Washington, 1985-89; asst. sec. for pub. affairs HUD, Washington, 1989-90; dir. news info. ABC News, N.Y.C., 1990-92; asst. to Pres. of U.S. for pub. liason and intergovtl. affairs The White House, Washington, 1992; sr. v.p. U.S. News and World Report, Washington, 1992-94; sr. v.p. Network Comms. ABC TV Network, N.Y.C., 1994-96, exec. v.p. network comm., 1996—; bd. dirs. Am. Coun. Young Pol. Leaders, Cities in Schs. Mem. U. Va. Alumni Assn. (bd. mgrs.). Home: 107 Dellwood Rd Bronxville NY 10708 Office: Capital Cities/ABC 77 W 66th St New York NY 10023-6201

ROLLINS, (THEODORE) SONNY, composer, musician; b. N.Y.C., Sept. 7, 1930; s. Walter and Valborg (Solomon) R.; m. Dawn Finney, 1956 (div.); m. Lucille Pearson, Sept. 7, 1959. Ed. high sch., N.Y.C.; ArtsD, Bard Coll., 1992. Condr. Sonny Rollins & Co. Orch., concert tours in Europe, Far East, 1973—; composed, scored and played music for motion picture Alfie; more than 100 original compositions recorded for Milestone, Fantasy-Prestige compositions include Way Out West, also others. Recipient numerous awards Guggenheim fellow, 1972. Home: RR 9 # G Germantown NY 12526

ROLLMAN, CHARLOTTE, artist, educator; b. Harrisburg, Pa., Oct. 15, 1947; d. Joseph and Beulah (Overton) R.; m. Edward H. Shay, 1971 (div. 1982); m. William B. Holland, 1987; 1 child, Danielle Suzanne Holland. BFA, Murray State U., 1969; MFA, U. Ill., 1971. Instr. art Ball State U., Muncie, Ind., 1971-75; supr. hand-painted silk garments Nicole, Ltd., Chgo., 1980-84; textile designer, stylist Thybony Wallcovering, Chgo., 1983-88; prof. art No. Ill. U., DeKalb, 1987—. Exhibitions include New Harmony (Ind.) Gallery Art, Charlotte Brauer, Munster, Ind., Jan Cicero, Chgo., Roy Boyd, Chgo, Locus, St. Louis, Suzanne Brown, Scottsdale, Ariz, Nestle's Corp., DeKalb, Capitol State Bank, St. Louis, others; illustrator New Internat. Dictionary Music, 1991; AV coord. Women's Caucus Art, Beijing, 1995. Grad. Sch. Rsch. grantee No. Ill. U., 1993, Faculty Enhancement grantee, 1995, Undergrad. Improvement grantee No. Ill. U., 1996. Mem. AAUW, Women's Caucus Art, Nat. Mus. Women Arts, Chgo. Area Women's Studies, DeKalb Area Women's Ctr. Office: No Ill U Sch Art De Kalb IL 60115

ROLLMAN, STEVEN ALLAN, communication educator; b. N.Y.C., Aug. 3, 1947; s. Leo and Margot (Seelenberger) R.; m. Nancy Sue Toberen, June 15, 1973; 1 child, Benjamin Allan. BA, C.W. Post Coll., 1970; MA, Ohio U., 1972; PhD, Pa. State U., 1977. Instr. Pa. State U., University Park, 1976; asst. prof. James Madison U., Harrisonburg, Va., 1977-83, assoc. prof., 1983-95, coord. interpersonal communication, 1986-90, prof., 1995—; cons. various sch. dists., Va., 1978—, Swissair, Zurich, 1971-72; book reviewer Choice, 1982—. Contbr. articles to profl. jours.; editor: Virginia Journal of Communication, 1980-81. Mem. Speech Comm. Assn., So. States Comm. Assn., Va. Speech Comm. Assn., Internat. Listening Assn. Avocations: computers, music, film, automobiles, tennis. Home: 608 Wynhdam Woods Cir Harrisonburg VA 22801-1668 Office: James Madison U Sch Speech Comm Harrisonburg VA 22807

ROLLO, F. DAVID, hospital management company executive, health care educator; b. Endicott, N.Y., Apr. 15, 1939; s. Frank C. and Augustine L. (Dumont) R.; m. Linda Wood, June 1, 1991; children : Mindee, Alex. BA, Harpur Coll., 1959; MS, U. Miami, 1965; PhD, Johns Hopkins U., 1968; MD, Upstate Med. Ctr., Syracuse, N.Y., 1972. Diplomate Am. Bd. Nuclear Medicine. Asst. chief nuclear medicine services VA Hosp., San Francisco, 1974-77; chief nuclear medicine VA Hosp., Nashville, 1977-79; sr. v.p. med. affairs Humana Inc., Louisville, 1980-92; dir. nuclear medicine div. Vanderbilt U. Med. Ctr., Nashville, 1977-81; prof. radiology Vanderbilt U., Nashville, 1979—; pres., CEO Metricor Inc., Louisville, 1992-95; sr. v.p. med. affairs HCIA, Louisville, 1995-96; sr. v.p. med. affairs, med. dir. Raytel Med. Corp., Louisville, 1996—; mem. med. adv. com. IBT, Washington, 1984—; mem. pvt. sector liaison panel Inst. of Medicine, Washington, 1983—; bd. dirs. ADAC Labs., KBL Healthcare, Positron Corp., Inc., Raytel Med. Corp., Cambridge Heart. Editor: Nuclear Medicine Physics, Instruments and Agents, 1977; co-editor: Physical Basis of Medical Imaging, 1980, Digital Radiology: Focus on Clinical Utility, 1982, Nuclear Medicine Resonance Imaging, 1983; mem. editorial adv. bd. ECRI, 1981—. Pres. bd. dirs. Youth Performing Arts Coun., Louisville, 1984-85; bd. dirs. Louisville-Jefferson County Youth Orch., 1983-85; sr. v.p., exec. com. USA Internat. Harp Competition, 1992-94, chmn., 1994—. Fellow Am. Coll. Nuclear Physicians (profl. com. 1982-84, chmn. 1984); mem. AMA, Soc. Nuclear Medicine (trustee 1979-83, 84—, Cassen Meml. lectr. western region 1980, 84), Radiol. Soc. N.Am., Am. Coll. Radiology, Ky. Sci. Tech. Coun. (exec. bd. 1987—), Advancement Med. Instrumentation (bd. dirs. 1986—), Louisville C. of C. (chmn. MIC com. 1987—). Avocations: racquetball, squash. Home: 15735 Peach Hill Rd Saratoga CA 95070 Office: 2755 Campus Dr San Mateo CA 94403-2513

ROLNIK, ZACHARY JACOB, publishing company executive; b. Bayonne, N.J., Oct. 2, 1961; s. Joseph and Katie (Simon) R. BA, U. Rochester, 1982; M. in Pub. Policy, Harvard U., 1984. Ops. analyst, presdl. mgmt. intern U.S. Dept. Treasury, Washington, 1984-85; sr. editor, pub. Kluwer Acad. Pubs., Norwell, Mass., 1985-95, v.p., mng. dir., 1996—. Home: 146 Pleasant St Hanover MA 02339-1844 Office: Kluwer Acad Pubs 101 Philip Dr Norwell MA 02061-1615

ROLOF, MARCIA CHRISTINE, sales executive; b. Green Bay, Wis., Sept. 1, 1950; adopted d. William August Rolof and Marcella S. (Rantanen) R.; m. Gerald W. Mattson, July 5, 1969 (div. 1974); 1 child, Shannon M. Mattson; m. Louis Glenn Mitchell, Nov. 12, 1994. Mgr., sales rep. Cameo Photography, 1980-82; tchr., physically challenged resource coord. U. Wis., 1982-85; dist. mgr. Women's Specialty Retail Group, U.S. Shoe, 1985-90; regional sales dir. Decor/Claire Corp., 1990-93; corp. adminstr. FLC, Inc., Houston, 1994-97; writer, author, 1991—; tutor, reading and lang. Pasadena Ind. Sch. Dist., Houston. Author: Tie the Moon to Your Car (My Cancer, My Way), 1994; author short stories; spokesperson childrens radio program. Network vol. U. Tex. M.D. Anderson Cancer Ctr., Houston, 1993—; vol. counselor R to R Cancer Soc., Houston, 1994. Mem. Houston C. of C., Pasadena C. of C.

ROLSHOVEN, ROSS WILLIAM, legal investigator, art photographer; b. Mandan, N.D., Oct. 20, 1954; s. Raymond Paul and Bernice June (Mastel) R.; divorced; 1 child, Ashley Anna. BA in Bus. Adminstrn., U. N.D., 1976. Lic. pvt. investigator, N.D., Minn. Claims adjuster, investigator Border Area Adjustments, Grand Forks, N.D., 1976-84; owner, mgr. Great Plains Claims, Inc., Grand Forks, N.D., 1984—; chmn. N.D. Claims Seminar, Grand Forks, 1988; guest lectr. U. N.D. Law Sch., 1993-96. Photographic exhibits include Artifacts, 1992 (1st pl. award 1992), Spirit of the Buffalo, 1992 (1st pl. award 1992), Grey Morn' on the Red, 1991 (Merit award 1991); featured artist Custer County Art Show, Miles City, Mont., 1995; sculpture How the West Was Won, 1992 (2d pl. award 1992). Mem. N.D. Mus. Art; patron Grand Forks Fire Hall Theater, 1988-92; mem. Fargo/Moorhead Art Assn., 1992; mem. bldg. restoration com. North Valley Arts Coun. Recipient Svc. Recognition award United Way, 1984, Hist. Preservation award N.D. Hist. Soc., 1990, Buckskinner award Roughrider Internat. Art Show Com., 1994, 2d Pl. award Fargo Regional Art Show, 1994-95. Mem. Nat. Assn. Legal Investigators, Minn. Assn. Detectives, Red River Valley Claims Assn. (pres. 1986-87), Upper Red River Valley Claims Assn. (pres. 1988-89), Dakota Masters Club Swim Club. Avocations: photography, painting, horseback riding, swimming, archaeology. Office: Great Plains Claims Inc 220 S 3rd St Grand Forks ND 58201-4732

ROLSTON, HOLMES, III, theologian, educator, philosopher; b. Staunton, Va., Nov. 19, 1932; s. Holmes and Mary Winifred (Long) R.; m. Jane Irving Wilson, June 1, 1956; children: Shonny Hunter, Giles Campbell. BS, Davidson Coll., 1953; BD, Union Theol. Sem., Richmond, Va., 1956; MA in Philosophy of Sci., U. Pitts., 1968; PhD in Theology, U. Edinburgh, Scotland, 1958. Ordained to ministry Presbyn. Ch. (USA), 1956. Asst. prof. philosophy Colo. State U., Ft. Collins, 1968-71, assoc. prof., 1971-76, prof., 1976—; vis. scholar Ctr. Study of World Religions, Harvard U., 1974-75; lectr. Yale U., Vanderbilt U., others; official observer UNCED, Rio de Janiero, 1992. Author: Religious Inquiry: Participation and Detachment, 1985, Philosophy Gone Wild, 1986, Science and Religion: A Critical Survey, 1987, Environmental Ethics, 1988, Conserving Natural Value, 1994; assoc. editor Environ. Ethics, 1979—; mem. editorial bd. Oxford Series in Environ. Philosophy and Pub. Policy, Zygon: Jour. of Religion and Sci.; contbr. chpts. to books, articles to profl. jours. Recipient Oliver P. Penock Disting. Svc. award Colo. State U., 1983, Coll. award for Excellence, 1991, Univ. Disting. Prof., 1992; Disting. Russell fellow Grad. Theol. Union, 1991, Disting. Lectr., Chinese Acad. of Social Scis., 1991, Disting. Lectr., Nobel Conf. XXVII, Gifford Lectr., U. Edinburgh, 1997. Mem. AAAS, Am. Acad. Religion, Soc. Bibl. Lit. (pres. Rocky Mountain-Gt. Plains region), Am. Philos. Assn., Internat. Soc. for Environ. Ethics (pres. 1989-94), Phi Beta Kappa. Avocation: bryology. Home: 1712 Concord Dr Fort Collins CO 80526-1602 Office: Colo State U Dept Philosophy Fort Collins CO 80523

ROM, (MELVIN) MARTIN, securities executive; b. Detroit, Mar. 2, 1946; s. Jack and Thelma (Meyer) R.; m. Barbara Miller, July 12, 1970. BA magna cum laude, U. Mich., 1967. Founder MultiVest, Inc., Southfield, Mich., 1969; pres. MultiVest, Inc., Southfield, 1969-73; chmn. bd., chief exec. officer MultiVest, Inc., 1973-75; pres. Real Estate Securities and Syndication Inst., Nat. Assn. Realtors, Washington, 1975—; dir., bd. govs. Real Estate Securities and Syndication Inst., Nat. Assn. Realtors, 1972—; pres. Martin Rom Co., Inc., 1976—; vice chmn. Sports Illus. Ct. Clubs, Inc., 1977-79; bd. dirs. Mocatta Corp., Med. Informatics Corp.; mem. joint com. Nat. Assn. Securities Dealers-Nat. Assn. Realtors, 1975-76; mem. adv. com. on market instruments Commodity Futures Trading Commn. Author: Nothing Can Replace the U.S. Dollar . . . and It Almost Has, 1975; Adv. bd.: Housing and Devel. Reporter, Washington. Trustee U. Chgo. Found. Mem. Nat. Assn. Securities Dealers, Com. on Gold Regulations, Phi Beta Kappa. Home and Office: 60 Quarton Ln Bloomfield Hills MI 48304-3456

ROM, WILLIAM NICHOLAS, physician; b. San Francisco, July 6, 1945; s. William N. and Barbara J. (Berlin) R.; m. Holly Wight Meeker, Oct. 7, 1973; children: Nicole, Meredith. BA, U. Colo., 1967; MD, U. Minn., 1971; MPH, Harvard U., 1973. Diplomate Am. Bd. Internatl Medicine, Am. Bd. Pulmonary Disease, Am. Bd. Preventive Medicine, Occupational Medicine. Internship U. Calif.-Davis, 1971-72; residency, 1973-75; from asst. to assoc. prof. U. Utah, Salt Lake City, 1977-83; sr. investigator NIH, Bethesda, Md., 1983-89; chief Divsn. Pulmonary/Critical Care Medicine NYU Med. Ctr., 1989—. Author: Canoe Country Wilderness, 1987; editor: Environmental and Occupational Medicine, 1992. Capt. USAFR, 1972-77. Recipient Harriet Hardy award New Eng. Occupational Med. Assn., 1993. Fellow Explorer's Club, Pulmonary and Occupational Medicine, Mt. Sinai, N.Y., 1975-77. Democrat. Avocations: skiing, mountain climbing, canoeing, cabin building, travel. Home: 4 Stanley Keyes Ct Rye NY 10580-3259 Office: NYU Med Ctr 550 1st Ave New York NY 10016-6481*

ROMAGOSA, ELMO LAWRENCE, clergyman, retired editor; b. Thibodaux, La., Jan. 11, 1924; s. Lawrence Gabriel and Lydie (Achee) R. Ed., St. Joseph Sem., Notre Dame Sem., New Orleans, 1947. Ordained priest Roman Cath. Ch., 1947. Asst. pastor Cut Off, La., 1947-50, New Orleans, 1950-58; chaplain Ursuline Convent and Nat. Shrine Our Lady of Prompt Succor, 1958-63; pastor St. John's Ch., New Orleans, 1963-70; asst. dir. Soc. for Propagation of Faith, 1950-60, dir., 1962; communications dir. Archdiocese New Orleans, 1962; founding editor Clarion Herald newspaper, 1963-74; priest in residence Sts. Peter and Paul Ch., New Orleans, 1970-72; pastor Holy Trinity Ch., New Orleans, 1972-74, St. Rose of Lima Ch., New Orleans, 1974-76, St. Clement of Rome Ch., Metairie, La., 1976-84; chaplain Port of New Orleans, 1984-88; pastor Ch. of Infant Jesus, Harvey, La., 1988—; nat. sec. Cath. Broadcasters Assn., 1963-65; mem. U.S. Cath. bishops subcoms. on Cath.-Jewish relations, 1965; named prelate of honor, 1980. Editor Airtime, 1963-64. Dir. Stella Maris Maritime Ctr., 1984-88; chaplain Harbor Police, Port of New Orleans, 1984-88; mem. Nat. Conf. Seafarers, 1984, pres., 1986—, mem. legal adv. com. Ctr. for Seafarers Rights, 1986; mem. Nat. Cath. Conf. for Seafarers, 1984, pres., 1986-88. Recipient First Place award for best editorial and best feature photo Press Club New Orleans, 1965, First Place award for best column Press Club New Orleans, 1972; named Prelate of Honor, Pope John II, 1980. Mem. Cath. Press Assn. (1st Place awards for gen. excellence 1963-65), Sociedad Espanola New Orleans (founding sec.-treas.), Equestrian Order of Holy Sepulchre of Jerusalem (knight 1978, knight comdr. 1983, master of ceremonies 1986, Gold Palms of Jerusalem medallion 1993). Republican. Home and Office: Ch of the Infant Jesus 700 Maple Ave Harvey LA 70058-4008

ROMAGUERA, MARIANO ANTONIO, consulting engineer; b. Mayaguez, P.R., May 4, 1928; s. Jose Mariano and Aminta (Martinez) R.; BS, MIT, 1950; MS, U. P.R., 1975; m. Virginia Casablanca, July 3, 1952; children: Jose Mariano, Jorge Enrique, Alberto, Ana Maria. Asst. engr. Arturo Romaguera, Cons. Engr., Colombia, 1950-51; asst. engr. Ingenio Providencia, Palmira, Colombia, 1951; shift engr. Central Igualdad and Western Sugar Refinery, Mayaguez, 1954; erection engr., asst. project mgr., Pradera Valle, Colombia, 1954-55, plant supt., chief engr., 1955-57; project engr. Ingenior Providencia, Palmira, Colombia, 1957, chief engr. ops. and maintenance, 1958-64; exec. v.p. Romaguera & Vendrell Devel. Corp., Mayaguez, P.R., 1964-68; pres. RomaVel, Inc., Mayaguez, 1965-68, Yagueka Equipment, Inc., 1968-78, Mariano A. Romaguera and Assocs., Engrs., Appraisers and Cons., Mayaguez, 1974—; sr. ptnr. Camino, Romaguera & Assocs., 1976—; sr. ptnr. M/E Appraisers, 1976—; cons. engr. Sugar Corp. P.R., Commonwealth of P.R., Biomass Steam Generation Rsch.; bd. regents Cath. U. P.R. Pres., Yagueka dist. P.R. coun. Boy Scouts Am., 1965-69, mem. exec. bd. P.R. coun.; chmn. ARC, 1966; bd. dirs. Mayaguez YMCA; mem. MIT Ednl. Coun.; mem. bd. regents Catholic U. of P.R. With Army, 1952-54, Korea. Recipient Silver Beaver award P.R. coun.l Boy Scouts Am., 1969. Mem. NSPE, ASME (pres. S.W. P.R. group), Am. Soc. Appraisers, P.R. Bd. Appraisers and Examiners, Instituto de Evaluadores de P.R., Colegio Ingenieros y Agrimensores de P.R. (past pres. Mayaguez dist.), Instituto de Ingenieros Mecanicos de P.R., P.R. Soc. Profl. Engrs., Assn. Engring. Socs., Am. Right of Way Assn., Internat. Soc. Sugar Cane Technologists, P.R. Assn. Real Estate Bds., Mayaguez Bd. Realtors, M.I.T. Alumni Assn., Nu Sigma Beta, Alpha Phi Omega. Roman Catholic. Lodge: Rotary. Home: 16 Calle Peral N Mayaguez PR 00680-4855 Office: PO Box 1340 Mayaguez PR 00681-1340

ROMAIN, BELLA MARY, graphic designer; b. Oakland, Calif., June 16, 1949; d. John Thomas Kondrup and Anna (Rabinowitz) Friedman; m. Stewart Jay Romain, Mar. 19, 1972. Student, SUNY, Stony Brook, 1967-68, Sch. Visual Arts, 1973-75; BFA magna cum laude, West Ga. Coll., 1989. Asst. to editor Dell Pub. Co., N.Y.C., 1968-72; reporter, proofreader Local News, Long Island, N.Y., 1973-76; graphic designer, editor Yellow Book Corp., N.Y.C., 1976-78; freelance graphic designer, editor N.Y.C., 1978-82; owner, graphic designer, editor designplus, Carrollton, Ga., 1982—; publs. cons. West Ga. Coll., Carrollton, 1985—. Paintings exhibited in numerous juried shows, including Alexandria Mus. Art, 1992. Spkr. to civic groups, Carrollton, 1993; vol. Amateur Radio Emergency Svcs., Carrollton, 1985—; vol. ARC. Recipient Fine Arts Achievement award Binney & Smith, 1989. Mem. Nat. Mus. Women in Arts, Lions Internat., Am. Bus. Women's Assn., Toastmasters (chair membership local chpt. 1993), Carroll County C. of C., Phi Kappa Phi. Avocations: amateur radio, painting. Home and Office: 285 Timber Ridge Trl Carrollton GA 30117-8884

ROMAINE, HENRY SIMMONS, investment consultant; b. N.Y.C., May 30, 1933; s. Theodore Cole and Cornelia (Simmons) R.; m. Susan Donaldson; children: Henry, Hilary, Kathryn. BA, Harvard U., 1954. Asst. security analyst Mutual Life Ins. Co., N.Y.C., 1958-60, investment analyst, 1960-61, investment specialist, 1961-64, asst. dir. investments, 1964, dir. investments, 1964-66, asst. v.p. for securities investment, 1966-68, 2d v.p. for securities investment, 1969-71, v.p. for securities investment, 1971-72, sr. v.p., 1972-78, sr. v.p., chief investment officer, 1976-78, exec. v.p., 1978-81, pres., 1981-86; vice chmn., chief investment officer Am. Gen. Corp., Houston, 1986-93; dir. MONY Life Ins. Co. of Can.; chmn. bd. MONY Real Estate Investors, 1978-86; mem. adv. bd. Chem. Bank, 1974-93. Served with USN, 1954-57. Mem. Links Club, Harvard Club. Home: 7 Conquest Ave Sullivans Island SC 29482-9779

ROMAN, ANDREW MICHAEL, lawyer, educator; b. Pitts., Aug. 19, 1951; s. James Andrew and Lois Roman; m. Heather Lynne Harms; children: Rebecca Lynne, Carolyn Elizabeth. BA, Bucknell U., 1973; JD, Duquesne U., 1976. Bar: Pa. 1976. Law clk. U.S. Dist. Ct. (we. dist.) Pa., Pitts., 1976-77; assoc. Eckert Seamans Cherin & Mellott, Pitts., 1977-84, ptnr., 1985-91; dir. Cohen & Grigsby, P.C., Pitts., 1991—; adj. prof. law Duquesne U. Sch. Law, Pitts., 1993—; arbitrator Fed. Ct. Arbitration Panel, Pitts., 1991—; faculty mem. seminar on bad faith litigation in Pa. Nat. Bus. Inst., 1995. Editor-in-chief Duquesne Law Rev., 1976, A New Look at the Broad Form Nuclear Exclusion, Risk Management, 1995. Bd. dirs. Codes Rev. Bd., Mt. Lebanon, Pa., 1991—; mem. vestry St. Paul's Episcopal Ch., Mt. Lebanon, 1995—. Recipient Am. Jurisprudence awards Lawyers Coop. Pub. Co., 1974; T. Robert Brennan scholar Duquesne U. Sch. Law, 1974, Duquesne U. Sch. Law scholar, 1975. Mem. ABA, Am. Arbitration Assn. (mem. panel 1991—), Pa. Bar Assn., Allegheny County Bar Assn., Duquesne U. Law Alumni Assn. (treas. 1985-86, bd. dirs. 1988-90, pres. 1992-93). Office: Cohen & Grigsby PC 2900 CNG Tower 625 Liberty Ave Pittsburgh PA 15222-3110

ROMAN, KENNETH, JR., corporate communications executive; b. Boston, Sept. 6, 1930; s. Kenneth J. and Bernice (Freedman) R.; m. Ellen L. Fischer, Mar. 27, 1953. B.A., Dartmouth Coll., 1952. Asst. advt. promotion mgr. Interchem Crp., N.Y.C., 1952-55; mgr. advt. sales promotion RCA Distbrs., Phila., 1955-56; advt. mgr. Allied Chem. Corp., 1956-63; account mgr. Ogilvy & Mather, N.Y.C., 1963-79; pres. Ogilvy & Mather, U.S., 1979-85, Ogilvy and Mather Worldwide, 1985-89; chmn., chief exec. The Ogilvy Group, 1988-89; exec. v.p. Am. Express, N.Y.C., 1989-91; bd. dirs. Brunswick Corp., Compaq Computer Corp., Coty, Inc., IBJ Schroder Bank & Trust Co., Penncorp Fin. Group. Co-author: How to Advertise, 1992, Writing That Works, 1992. Bd. dirs. N.Y. Bot. Garden, Meml. Sloan-Kettering Cancer Ctr., Sheltering Arms Childrens Svcs. Mem. Univ. Club (N.Y.C.), The Century Assn. Home: 7 Gracie Sq New York NY 10028-8030 Office: 866 3rd Ave Fl 26 New York NY 10022-6221

ROMAN, STAN G., lawyer; b. Athens, Ga., Dec. 31, 1954; s. Costic and Marilyn (Gracey) R.; m. Elizabeth Ann Whelan, Sept. 18, 1982; children: John, Matthew, Nicholas. BA, U. N.C., 1976; JD with honors, U. Tex., 1979. Bar: Calif. 1979, U.S. Dist. Ct. (no., so., ctrl. and ea.) Calif. 1979, U.S. Ct. Appeals (9th cir.) 1979. Congl. intern Honorable John Buchanan, Washington, 1977; summer assoc. Bradley, Arant, Rose & White, Birmingham, Ala., 1978; assoc. Bronson, Bronson & McKinnon, San Francisco, 1979-85, ptnr., 1985—; arbitrator, mediator Calif. Superior Ct., San Francisco, 1989—. Mem. ABA, Assn. Bus. Trial Lawyers, Def. Rsch. Inst., Calif. Bar Assn., San Francisco Bar Assn. San Francisco Com. Urban Affairs, Phi Beta Kappa, Phi Eta Sigma. Avocations: running, golf, skiing, swimming. Office: Bronson Bronson & McKinnon 505 Montgomery St San Francisco CA 94111-2552

ROMAN, STANFORD AUGUSTUS, JR., medical educator, dean; b. N.Y.C.; s. Stanford Augustas and Ivy L. (White) R.; children: Mawiyah Lythcott, Jane E. Roman-Brown. AB, Dartmouth Coll., 1964; MD, Columbia U., 1968; MPH, U. Mich., 1975. Diplomate Nat. Bd. of Med. Examiners. Intern in medicine Columbia U.-Harlem Hosp. Ctr., 1966-69, resident in medicine, 1969-71, chief resident in medicine, 1971-73; assoc. dir. ambulatory care Columbia U. Harlem Hosp., N.Y.C., 1972-73; instr. in medicine Columbia U., N.Y.C., 1972-73; asst. physician Presbyn. Hosp., 1972-73; clin. dir. Healthco, Inc., Soul City, N.C., 1973-74; dir. ambulatory care, asst. prof. medicine/sociomed. scis. Boston City Hosp., 1974-78; asst. prof. medicine U. N.C., Chapel Hill, 1973-74; asst. dean Boston U. Sch. Medicine, 1974-78; med. dir. D.C. Gen. Hosp., Washington, 1978-81; assoc. dean acad. affairs Dartmouth Med. Sch., Hanover, N.H., 1981-86, assoc. prof., 1981-87, dep. dean, 1986-87; dean, v.p., prof. medicine Morehouse Sch. Med., Atlanta, 1987-89; sr. v.p., med. and profl. affairs Health and Hosps. Corp., N.Y.C., 1989-90; dean med. sch., prof. community health and social medicine CUNY, 1990—; dir. Boston Comprehensive Sickle Cell Ctr., 1975-78; bd. dirs. Nat. Bd. Med. Examiners, Phila., 1988-92, Winifred Masterson Burke Rehab. Hosp., White Plains, N.Y.; mem. Dartmouth Hitchcock Med. Ctr. Bd. of Medicine, N.Y.; trustee Dartmouth Coll., Hanover, N.H. Contbr. to book chpts. and profl. jours. and editls. Fellow N.Y. Acad. Medicine; mem. AMA, APHA, Nat. Med. Assn., N.Y. State Coun. Grad. Med. Edn., N.Y. State Dept. Edn. Bd. Medicine. Democrat. Episcopalian. Avocations: photography, travel, music. Office: CUNY Med Sch J 909 Convent Ave and 138th St New York NY 10031

ROMANELLI, G. JACK, journalist; b. San Benedetto Del Tronto, Ascoli Piceno, Italy, Oct. 16, 1959; arrived in Can., 1965; s. Martino and Ida (Michetti) R.; m. Lily Bramante, Aug. 30, 1985; children: Alexa, Julian. BA in Journalism, Loyalist Coll., 1983. Reporter Alliston (Ont.) Herald, Can., 1983; reporter, columnist Burlington (Ont.) Gazette, 1983-84; copy editor Montreal (Que.) Gazette, Can., 1984-88, asst. sports editor, 1988-91; exec. sports editor Montreal (Que.) Gazette, 1991-95, asst. mng. editor sports and projects, 1995-96, asst. mng. editor news dept., 1996—; chmn. sports editors' com. Southam Newspaper Group, 1993-95; chmn. Can. region AP Sports Editors, 1994-96. Avocations: reading, golf, racquetball, baseball stats. analysis. Home: 1538 Baxter St, LaSalle, PQ Canada H8N 2T5 Office: The Montreal Gazette, 250 St Antoine St W, Montreal, PQ Canada H2Y 3R7

ROMANI, JOHN HENRY, health administration educator; b. Milan, Italy, Mar. 6, 1925; s. Henry Arthur and Hazel (Pettengill) R.; m. Barbara A. Anderson; children: David John, Paul Nichols, Theresa A. Anderson. BA, U. N.H., 1949, MA, 1949; PhD, U. Mich., 1955. Instr. U. N.H., 1950-51; instr. U. Mich., Ann Arbor, 1954-55, assoc. prof., asst. to assoc. dean Sch. Pub. Health, 1961-69, assoc. v.p., 1971-75, chmn. health planning and adminstrn., 1975-80, prof., 1971-93, prof. emeritus pub. health adminstrn., 1993—; interim chair Pub. Health Policy and Adminstrn., 1991-92; asst. prof. Western Mich. U., 1956-57; assoc. dir. Cleve. Met. Svcs. Commn., 1957-59; assoc. prof. U. Pitts., 1959-61; vice chancellor, prof. U. Wis.-Milw., 1969-71; rsch. fellow Brookings Instn., 1955-56; mem. task force Nat. Commn. on Orgn. Cmty. Health Svcs., 1963-66; dir. staff Sec.'s Com. on Orgn. Health Activities, HEW, 1965-66; dir. Govtl. Affairs Inst., 1969-75, chmn., 1970-72; trustee Pub. Adminstrn. Svc., 1969-75, chmn., 1973-75; bd. dirs. Delta Dental Plan Mich., 1972-78, chmn. consumers' adv. coun., 1975-77; bd. dirs. Ctr. for Population Activities, 1975-81, chmn., 1975-81; lifetime vis. prof. Capital U. Economics and Bus., Beijing, 1996—. Author: The Philippine Presidency, 1956; editor: Changing Dimensions in Public Administration, 1962; contbr. articles to profl. jours. Mem. Citizens League, Cleve., 1957-59; mem. Ann Arbor Citizens Coun., 1965-69; bd. dirs. Southeastern Mich. Family Planning Project, 1975-77; trustee Congregational Summer Assembly, 1982-85; commr. Accrediting Commn. on Edn. for Health Svcs. Adminstrn., 1989-95. Served with AUS, 1943-46, ETO. Fellow Am. Pub. Health Assn. (chmn. program devel. bd. 1975-77, mem. exec. bd. 1975-80, mem. governing coun. 1975—, pres. 1979, chmn. publs. bd. 1984-88), Royal Soc. Health (hon.), Am. Polit. Sci. Assn. (life); mem. Am. Soc. Pub. Adminstrn. (past mem. coun.), Phi Kappa Phi, Pi Sigma Alpha, Pi Gamma Mu, Delta Omega. Home: 2670 Bedford Rd Ann Arbor MI 48104-4010 Office: PO Box 7903 Ann Arbor MI 48107-7903

ROMANI, PAUL NICHOLAS, government official; b. L.I., N.Y., May 14, 1943; s. Nicholas Oliver and Rita (Gripp) R.; m. Patricia Elsie Riley, July 26, 1968; children: Michele P., Christopher P. BBA, George Washington U., 1967, MBA, 1968, DPA with distinction, 1975. Lic. real estate broker, Va.; cert. EEO counselor; CFP, CNA; cert. nat. engr. Assoc. professorial lectr. George Washington U., 1970-72; sci. adminstr. NSF, Washington, 1972-82; sci. and tech. fellow The White House, Washington, 1982-83, dir. fin. and adminstrn. automated systems div., 1983-85, dir. adminstrv. ops., 1985-91; dir. Fed. Fin. Instns. Exams. Coun., Washington, 1991—; dir. adminstrn., comptr. Pres.' Edn. Summit with Govs., Charlottesville, Va., 1989; cons. to Pres. Nixon's Adv. Coun. on Mgmt. Improvement, 1970. Contbr. articles to profl. jours. Bd. dirs. scholarship fund City of Alexandria, Va., 1992—. Humble Oil fellow, 1968, McGraw-Edison fellow George Washington U., 1971-73; recipient Disting. Svc. award Exec. Office of the Pres., 1989, Disting. Svc. award Fed. Fin. Instns. Exam. Coun., 1992, Spl. Achievement award, 1995. Mem. Am. Soc. Pub. Adminstrn., Soc. Gen. Systems Rsch., Soc. Am. Value Engrs., Alpha Kappa Psi. Roman Catholic. Office: Fed Fin Instns Exam Coun 2100 Pennsylvania Ave NW Washington DC 20037-3202

ROMANKIW, LUBOMYR TARAS, materials engineer; b. Zhowkwa, Ukraine, Apr. 17, 1931. BSc, U. Alta., 1955; MSc and PhD in Metallurgy,

MIT, 1962. Mem. rsch. staff materials and processes, Thomas J. Watson Rsch. Ctr. IBM Corp, Yorktown Heights, N.Y., 1962-63, mgr. magnetic components divsn., 1965-68, mgr. magnetic material and devices, 1968-78, mgr. material and process studies, 1981-91, dep. mgr.; fellow IBM Corp, 1986; head Ctr. for Electrochem. Tech. and Microfabrication IBM Corp, Yorktown Heights, N.Y., 1991-95, project leader in magneto-micro-electromechanics, 1995—; instr. MIT, 1959-61; cons. East Fishkill Devel. Lab. & Mfg. IBM Corp, 1978-80, San Jose Devel. Lab. anf Mfg.; mem. Berkeley Indsl. Adv. Bd. on Sensors and Actuators Porgram; advisor chemistry dept. Pace U.; advisor chem. engring. dept. Tulane U., New Orleans, Columbia U., N.Y.C.; lectr. various univs. Author 4 book chpts.; 47 patents in field; 120 published inventions; N.Am. bd. of advisors Jour. of Processing of Advanced Material, 1993—; adv. annual book series Advances in Electrochemical Science and Engineering. Recipient Perkin medal Am. Chem. Soc., 1993, Vittorio de Nora medal and award Electrochem. Soc. Inc.; IBM fellow, 1986, ECS fellow, 1990, IBM Acad. Tech. fellow, 1987; named Disting. Chemist of Westchester, 1992. Fellow IEEE (Morris Liebman award 1994); mem. ISE, Electrochem. Soc. (sec.-treas. 1979-80, Vittorio de Nora medal and award 1994), Am. Electroplaters Soc. award, Acad. Engring. Sci. of Ukraine, Sigma Xi. Achievements include invention and development of laser enhanced plating and etching; invention and pioneer work on electrochemical processes for x-ray lithography masks, high aspect ratio plated x-ray structures, precursors of LIGA, thin film chip carriers, electrochemical flip-chip C-4 interconnects, eletroplated on chip wiring and throug-mask eletro etching; invention and development of fabrication processes for thin film inductive read-write heads, of integrated magnetoresistive read-inductive write head and proceses for their fabrication - these heads used in all hard disk magnetic storage devices; invention of high precision paddle plating tools, plating solutions and controls for Nife, CoNife, CoNiCu and others; research in magnetic thin films, deposition of thin films, x-ray lithography mask devel. dielectrics, magnetic device design, material selection and fabrication, electrodeposition, high moment magnetic materials, HIMEMS, UGA tech., magnetic materials, electronic and magnetic device fabrication, chemical engineering, and metallurgy; developed technology for high MEMS structure fabrication, integrated magnetic variable reluctance mini-motor. Office: IBM-Thomas J Watson Research Ctr PO Box 218 Yorktown Heights NY 10598-0218

ROMANO, ANTONIO, microbiologist; b. Penns Grove, N.J., Mar. 6, 1929; s. Antonio and Maria R.; m. Marjorie J. Backus, 1953; children: Stephen, James, Charles. BSc in Biology, Rutgers U., 1949, PhD, 1952. Assoc. microbiologist Ortho Rsch. Found., Raritan, N.J., 1952-54; instr. microbial biochemistry Waksman Inst. Microbiology, Rutgers U., 1954-56; sr. asst. scientist to sr. scientist R.A. Taft San. Engring. Ctr., USPHS, Cin., 1956-59; from assoc. prof. to prof. bacteriology U. Cin., 1959-71, head dept. biol. scis., 1964-66; prof. biology U. Conn., Storrs, 1971—, head microbiology sect., 1974-85, dean Coll. Liberal Arts and Scis., 1992-96; sr. vis. fellow dept. biochemistry U. Leicester, Eng., 1967-68; vis. fellow in biochemistry Clare Hall, U. Cambridge, Eng., 1979; program dir. for cell biology NSF, Washington, 1984-85; vis. scholar dept. biology U. Calif. San Diego, La Jolla, 1989; U.S. rep. NATO Adv. Panel on Collaborative Rsch. Grants, 1990-92. Author/co-author books and monographs; mem. editorial bd. Jour. Bacteriology, 1971-80, Applied and Environ. Microbiology, 1973-76; contbr. chpts. to books, numerous articles to profl. jours. N.J. State scholar, 1945-49, Rutgers Rsch. and Endowment Found. fellow, 1949-51; NSF sr. postdoctoral fellow, 1967-78. Mem. AAAS, Am. Soc. for Microbiology, Sigma Xi. Office: U Conn Box U-125 Storrs CT 06269-3125

ROMANO, JOHN FRANCIS, physician; b. S.I., N.Y., July 4, 1948; m. Catherine Theresa Marino, Mar. 5, 1977; children: Francesca, Caterina. BS in Biology, St. Peter's Coll., 1969; MD, Cornell U., 1973. Diplomate Am. Bd. Dermatology. Pratice medicine specializing in dermatology N.Y.C., 1979—; dir. dermatology Queens (N.Y.) Hosp. Ctr., 1980-83; attending St. Vincent's Hosp., N.Y.C., 1979—; clin. asst. prof. dermatology N.Y. Hosp.-Cornell, N.Y.C., 1979—; dermatology cons. Walsh Home, N.Y.C., 1983-92. Contbr. articles to profl. jours. Mem. Columbus Citizen's Found. Fellow Am. Acad. Dermatology, Manhattan Dermatology Soc. (pres., sec.), N.Y. Acad. Medicine, Am. Soc. Dermatol. Surgery, Soc. for Pediat. Dermatology, N.Y. State Dermatology Soc., Am. Order Malta. Avocation: sailing. Office: 36 7th Ave New York NY 10011

ROMANO, JOSEPH ANTHONY, marketing and consulting executive; b. Bklyn., Sept. 5, 1946; s. Anthony Wilbur and Anne (Fusco) R.; m. Linda Rose Giacalone, Sept. 23, 1972; children: Nicholas Joseph, Christine Dianne. Student, Villanova U., 1964-66; BS Pharm. Sci., Columbia U., 1970, D Pharmacy, 1972. Clin. resident Lenox Hill Hosp., N.Y.C., 1970-72; asst. dean, asst. prof. Columbia U., N.Y.C., 1972-76, SUNY, Buffalo, 1976-78; assoc. dean, assoc. prof. U. Wash., Seattle, 1978-83; assoc. dir. medicine Pfizer Labs., N.Y.C., 1983-85, product mgr., 1985, asst. to pres., 1985-87; sr. v.p., group dir. Hill & Knowlton, Inc., N.Y.C., 1987-88; exec. dir. external affairs Sandoz Pharm. Corp., N.Y.C., 1988-89; pres. Audio Visual Med. Mktg., N.Y.C., 1989-92; vice chair Nelson Communications, Inc., N.Y.C., 1992—; chmn., CEO Sciens Worldwide Healthcare Comms., 1996—; mem. U.S. Nat. Adv. Com. Health Profls., Washington, 1980-85. Co-author: Clinical Pharmacology, 1980, Pharmacy State Board Reviews, 1976, 78, 85, The Vitamin Book, 1985, 97; cons. editor Med. Intercom, N.Y.C., 1986-89; contbr. articles to profl. jours. Fellow Royal Soc. Health London; mem. Am. Pharm. Assn., Am. Soc. Healthcare Pharmacists, Am. Assoc. Study Headaches, Nat. Headache Found., Am. Assn. Colls. Pharmacy, U.S. Golf Assn., Rho Chi. Avocations: photography, philately, golf, music. Office: Sciens Worldwide Healthcare Comms Inc 41 Madison Ave New York NY 10010-2202

ROMANO, REBECCA KAY, counselor; b. Zanesville, Ohio, Mar. 26, 1958; Charles Ronald Fulkerson and Margaret Jane (Kiser) Williams; m. Richard Ralph Romano, May 24, 1986; children: Nicholas Robert, Kaitlin Kristine. BA, Walsh U., 1980; MEd, Bowling Green State U., 1981, 82. Lic. profl. counselor; nat. cert. counselor. Day program instr. Devel. Opportunities, Cañon City, Colo., 1983-85; clin. behavior specialist Pueblo Regional Ctr. Colo. Divsn. Devel. Disabilities, 1985-86; career devel. tchr. Colo. Dept. Corrections, Cañon City, 1986-87, facility mental health therapist, 1987—, devel. disabilities coord., 1991—, facility mental health coord., 1995—; therapist sex offender treatment team Colo. Dept. Corrections, 1986—; presenter in field. Mem. ACA, Am. Assn. Mental Retardation (past state bd. dirs. 1987-91), Am. Correctional Assn., Nat. Assn. for Dually Diagnosed, Women of the Evang. Luth. Ch. Am. (exec. bd. mem.). Lutheran. Avocations: reading, gardening, bicycling, volleyball, softball. Office: Colo Dept Corrections CTCF Mental Health PO Box 1010 Canon City CO 81215-1010

ROMANOFF, MILFORD MARTIN, building contractor, architectural designer; b. Cleve., Aug. 21, 1921; s. Barney Sanford and Edythe Stolpher (Bort) R.; student Coll. Arch., U. Mich., 1939-42; B.B.A., U. Toledo, 1943; m. Marjorie Reinwald, Nov. 6, 1945; children—Bennett S., Lawrence M., Janet Beth (dec.). Pres., Glass City Constrn. Co., Toledo, 1951-55, Milford Romanoff Inc., Toledo, 1956—. Co-founder, Neighborhood Improvement Found. Toledo, 1960; mem. Lucas County Econ. Devel. Com., 1979—; mem. citizens adv. bd. Recreation Commn. Toledo, 1973-86; mem. campus adv. com. Med. Coll. Ohio, 1980—; trustee Cummings Treatment Center for Adolescents, 1981—; mem. Children's Services Bd. Lucas County, 1981-97; pres. Ohio B'nai Brith, 1959-60, Toledo Lodge, 1958-59; bd. dirs. Anti-Defamation League, 1955-60, Ohio Hillel Orgns., Lucas County Dept. Human Svcs., Arthritis Assn., 1995—; chmn. Toledo Amateur Baseball and Softball Com., 1979-81; mem. Democratic Precinct Com., 1975-78, Arthritis Bd. Dirs.; trustee Temple Brotherhood, 1956-58, bd. dirs., 1981—; pres. Cherry Hill Nursing Home, 1964-85; cons. U.S. Care Corp., 1985—; mem. Crosby Gardens Bd. Advisors, 1983-96; bd. govs. Toledo Housing for Elderly, 1982-84, sec., 1989, pres. bd. govs., 1990—, pres, 1991—; bd. advisors Ret. Sr. Vol. Program, 1987-89, chmn. 1988-90, 93—, sec. adv. bd., 1990—; mem. adv. bd. Salvation Army (vice chmn. 1986-87, chmn. 1988-90, ct. apptd. spl. advocate adv., bd. treas. 1988—), chmn. Mental Health Adv. Bd., 1983-84, sec., 1989; bd. dirs. Kidney Found. Northwestern Ohio, 1986—, sec., 1989; bd. dirs. Toledo Urban Forestry Commn., 1991—, pres., 1993, 95, Lucas County Dept. Human Svcs. Bd.; bd. dirs. Arthritis Assn. Lt. (j.g.) USN, 1943-46, Toledo Met. area of Gov't Exec. Com., 1996—. Mem. U. Toledo Alumni Assn., Toledo Mus. Art (assoc.), Econ. Opportunity Planning Assn. Greater Toledo (adv. bd.), Juvenile Justice (adv. bd.) U. Mich. Alumni Assn., Toledo Zool. Soc., Zeta Beta Tau. Clubs: Masons; B'nai B'rith (pres. Toledo lodge 1958-59, statewide pres. 1959-60), Hadassah (assoc. Toledo chpt.). Home and Office: Milford Romanoff Inc 2514 Bexford Pl Toledo OH 43606-2414

ROMANOFF, STANLEY M., JR., human resource specialist; b. Toledo, Feb. 3, 1948; s. Stanley M. and Helen (Feinberg) R.; children: Erika Lee, Jennifer Lyn, Tara Marie, Erin Michele. BBA, U. Cin., 1970. Pers. supr. assembly div. GM, Norwood, Ohio, 1969-72; pers. mgr. Diamond Internat. Corp., Norwood, 1972-73; property mgr., investment counselor Romanoff Enterprises, Toledo, 1973-77; pers. adminstr. wage and salary United Telephone Co. Ohio, Mansfield, 1977-79; compensation and benefits mgr. United Inter-Mountain Telephone Co., Bristol, 1979-84, employee rels. mgr., 1984-86; human resources cons. Romanoff Enterprises, Bristol, Tenn., 1986-87; bus. mgr. Magna Internat., Livonia & Southfield, Mich., 1987-94, dir. human resources and bus. systems, 1994—. Mem. Am. Compensation Assn., Am. Mgmt. Assn., Soc. for Human Resource Mgmt., Am. Soc. of Employers, Human Resources Assn. of Greater Detroit. Office: Magna Internat 26200 Lahser Rd Ste 300 Southfield MI 48034-7157

ROMANOS, NABIL ELIAS, business development manager; b. Roumie, Metn, Lebanon, June 3, 1965; came to U.S., 1982; s. Elias Rachid and Kamale (Salame) R. BA in Econs. and History magna cum laude, Georgetown U., 1986; postgrad., Hautes Etudes Commerciales, France, 1989; MBA, U. Calif., Berkeley, 1989. Rsch. assoc. Am. Fin. Svcs. Assn., Washington, 1986-87; fin. analyst Varian Assocs., Palo Alto, Calif., 1988, sr. fin. analyst, 1989-91; mgr. fin. mkt. analysis Varian Oncology Systems, Palo Alto, 1991-92; mgr. bus. devel. Varian Health Care Systems, Palo Alto, 1992-94, Zug, Switzerland, 1994-95, São Paulo, Brazil, 1996—. Author: Finance Facts Yearbook, 1987. Vol. tutor for refugees Community Action Coalition, Washington, 1985-86; vol. interpreter emergency room Georgetown U., Washington, 1984-86; internat. vol. Internat. House U. Calif., Berkeley, 1987-89. Scholar Georgetown U., 1985-86, U. Calif., Berkeley, 1987-89. Mem. Phi Alpha Theta. Maronite Catholic.

ROMANOW, ROY JOHN, provincial government official, barrister, solicitor; b. 1939; s. Michael and Tekla R.; m. Eleanore Boykowich, 1967. Arts and Laws degrees, U. Sask. Mem. Sask. Legislative Assembly, 1967-82, 1986—, provincial sec., 1971-72, atty. gen. of province, 1971-82, minister of intergovernmental affairs, 1979-82, leader, Sask. New Dem. Party, 1987—, leader of the opposition, 1987-91, leader of the majority, 1991—, premier, 1991—; opposition house leader for New Dem. Party Caucus, 1986. Co-author: Canada Notwithstanding, 1984. Office: Legislative Bldg, Rm 226, Regina, SK Canada S4S 0B3

ROMANOWITZ, BYRON FOSTER, architect, engineer; b. Covington, Ky., Nov. 14, 1929; s. Harry Alex and Mildred (Foster) R.; m. Mildred Elaine Gize, June 15, 1957; children: Laura Ann, Mark Walter, Cynthia Ellen. B.S. in Civil Engring, U. Ky., 1951; M.F.A. in Architecture, Princeton, 1953. Instr. sch. architecture Princeton U., 1954; architect Brock & Johnson, Lexington, 1958-59, Johnson & Romanowitz, Architects, Lexington and Louisville, 1960—; pres. Ky. Bd. examiners and Registration of Archs., 1975-91; instr. U. Ky. Sch. Architecture, 1996, 97. Prin. works include U. Ky. campus bldgs., 1959-91, Ea. Ky. U. campus bldgs., 1959-77, Centre Coll., Danville, Ky., campus bldgs., 1967-89, Georgetown (Ky.) Coll. campus bldgs., 1964-84, Asbury Coll., Wilmore, Ky., 1972-78, Asbury Theol. Sem., 1978-93, Berea Coll. bldgs., 1978-91, Transylvania U. bldgs., 1974-90, U. Louisville, 1990, 11 downtown Lexington office bldgs. Mem. Lexington Urban Renewal Commn., 1963-69; chmn. adv. bd. Salvation Army, 1971-72; trustee Midway (Ky.) Coll., 1986-95. With USNR, 1955-58; lt. comdr. Res. Recipient award of merit nat. archtl. competition AIA/Ednl. Facilities Lab., 1966. Fellow AIA (1st honor awards Ky. archtl. competition 1959, 61, 68, 70, 73, 78, 80, 81, pres. East Ky. chpt. 1965); mem. Ky. Soc. Architects (pres. 1966), Masons, Rotary, Lexington Club, Cotillion Club, Tau Beta Pi, Phi Mu Alpha, Phi Sigma Kappa. Home: 2057 Lakeside Dr Lexington KY 40502-3016 Office: Johnson Romanowitz Arch & Assoc 300 E Main St Ste 301 Lexington KY 40507-1538

ROMANOWSKI, THOMAS ANDREW, physics educator; b. Warsaw, Poland, Apr. 17, 1925; came to U.S., 1946, naturalized, 1949; s. Bohdan and Alina (Sumowski) R.; m. Carmen des Rochers, Nov. 15, 1952; children—Alina, Dominique. B.S., Mass. Inst. Tech., 1952; M.S., Case Inst. Tech., 1956, Ph.D., 1957. Rsch. assoc. physics Carnegie Inst. Tech., 1956-60; asst. physicist high energy physics Argonne Nat. Lab., Ill., 1960-63; assoc. physicist Argonne Nat. Lab., 1963-72, physicist, 1972-78; prof. physics Ohio State U., Columbus, 1964-92, prof. emeritus, 1992—; sr. scientist Argonne Nat. Lab., 1992. Contbr. articles to profl. jours. and, and papers to sci. meetings, seminars and workshops. Served with C.E. AUS, 1946-47. Fellow Am. Phys. Soc., AAAS; mem. Lambda Chi Alpha. Achievements include research in nuclear and high energy physics. Home: 4408 Morgal St Rockville MD 20853-2162 Office: Dept Energy Div High Energy Physic Washington DC 20585

ROMANS, DONALD BISHOP, corporate executive; b. Louisville, Apr. 22, 1931; s. Albert D. and Moneta (Bishop) R.; m. Marilyn Yvonne Neff, June 13, 1953; children: Rebecca Ann, Jennifer. BS, U. Louisville, 1953; MBA, Harvard U., 1958. Mgr. internal auditing and data processing, mem. contr. staff Container Corp. Am., Chgo., 1958-62; successively asst. to pres., asst. treas., treas., v.p. fin., sr. v.p. fin., exec. v.p. Trans Union Corp., Chgo., 1962-81; exec. v.p., chief fin. officer Sunbeam Corp., Chgo., 1981-82, Bally Mfg. Corp., Chgo., 1982-87; fin. cons. Chgo., 1987; pres. Romans and Co., Chgo., 1987-93; chmn. Merlin Corp., Geneva, Ill., 1990; bd. dirs. Burnham Fund Inc., N.Y.C.; trustee Zweig Series Trust, N.Y.C.; life trustee St. Mary of Nazareth Hosp. Capt. USMCR, 1953-56. Mem. Econ. Club. Republican. Avocations: tennis, boating.

ROMANS, JOHN NIEBRUGGE, lawyer; b. Bklyn., May 23, 1942; s. John McDowell and Helen Pond (Niebrugge) R.; m. Caroline Ward; children: John A., Andrew C. BA, Williams Coll., 1964; LLB, Columbia U., 1967. Bar: N.Y. 1967, U.S. Dist. Ct. (so. and ea. dist.) N.Y. 1971, U.S. Ct. Appeals (2d cir.) 1971, U.S. Ct. Appeals (3rd cir.) 1976, U.S. Ct. Appeals (4th and 7th cirs.) 1987, U.S. Ct. Appeals (9th cir.) 1992, U.S. Ct. Appeals (11th cir.) 1996, U.S. Supreme Ct. 1971. Ptnr. Curtis, Mallet-Prevost, Colt & Mosle, N.Y.C., 1982-90, Katten Muchin & Zavis, N.Y.C., 1990-96, Biedermann, Hoenig, Massamillo & Ruff, P.C., N.Y.C., 1996—; lectr. on air law topics at various seminars. Contbr. articles to profl. jours. Trustee Summit (N.J.) Unitarian-Universalist Ch., 1978; bd. dirs. Robert Sterling Clark Found., 1989—; bd. trustees Mamaroneck Pub. Libr. Dist., 1990—. Lt. USNR, 1968-71. Mem. Internat. Assn. Def. Counsel, Assn. of Bar of City of N.Y. (mem. aero. com. 1983-85, chmn. 1986-89, 92-94, products liability com. 1989-91), Larchmont (N.Y.) Yacht Club. Avocations: sailing, tennis. Office: Biedermann Hoenig et al 90 Park Ave New York NY 10016

ROMANSKY, MONROE JAMES, physician, educator; b. Hartford, Conn., Mar. 16, 1911; s. Benjamin and Henrietta (Levine) R.; m. Evelyn Muriel Lackman, Jan. 10, 1943; children: Stephen, Gerald, Michael, Richard. A.B., U. Maine, 1933; M.D., U. Rochester, 1937. Diplomate: Am. Bd. Internal Medicine. Intern Strong Meml. Hosp.-U. Rochester, N.Y., 1937-38; asst. resident Strong Meml. Hosp.-U. Rochester, 1938-39, James Gleason Research fellow studies on relationship of kidneys to hypertension, 1939-40, chief resident, 1940-41, instr. in medicine, 1941-42; investigator Office Sci. Research and Devel., Surgeon Gen. U.S., 1941-42; chief biochemistry and antibiotic research Walter Reed Army Hosp., 1942-46; asso. prof. Sch. Medicine, George Washington U., Washington, 1946—; prof. medicine Sch. Medicine, George Washington U., 1957—; dir. George Washington U. med. div. D.C. Gen. Hosp., 1950-69; dir. infectious diseases research lab. and infectious diseases div. D.C. Gen. Hosp., 1950-69; cons. internal medicine antibiotics Walter Reed Army Hosp., Washington, 1946—; Cons. internal medicine antibiotics VA Hosp., Washington, 1952—, NIH, Bethesda, Md., 1953—, Surgeon Gen. USAF, 1966—; mem. Asian influenza adv. com. D.C., 1956-61; mem. ad hoc adv. com. Bur. Medicine FDA, 1966-67; examiner Am. Bd. Internal Medicine, 1965, 67, 69. Editorial bd.: Antimicrobial Agts. and Chemotherapy, 1961-72; Contbr. to profl. jours. Trustees council U. Rochester, 1965—. Served with M.C., AUS, 1942-46. Decorated Legion of Merit; recipient Founders award Tau Epsilon Phi, Disting. Career award U. Maine. Fellow ACP (adv. bd. to gov. D.C. 1969—); mem. Am. Soc. Internal Medicine, Am. Fedn. Clin. Research, Soc. Exptl. Biology and Medicine, Am. Soc. Microbiology, Infectious Diseases Soc. (founding council 1963-66), Soc. Med. Cons. to Armed Forces, Sigma Xi, Alpha Omega Alpha. Club: Woodmont Country. Pioneer work in prolonging action of penicillin, requiring only single daily injection, Romansky Formula, 1944; nutritional studies in obesity as related to weight reduction. Home: 5600 Wisconsin Ave Chevy Chase MD 20815-4408

ROMARY, JOHN M., lawyer; b. Paterson, N.J., Aug. 7, 1947. BSEE with honors, Lehigh U., 1969; JD, Georgetown U., 1973. Bar: D.C. 1973. Law clerk to Chief Judge James L. Latchum U.S. Dist. Ct. Del., 1973-75; ptnr. Finnegan, Henderson, Farabow, Garrett & Dunner, Washington. Editor-at-Large Law & Policy in Internat. Bus., 1972-73. Mem. ABA, Am. Intellectual Property Law Assn., U.S. C. of C. (govt. and regulatory affairs com. 1984-86), D.C. Bar, Bar Assn. D.C., Fed. Bar Assn., Licensing Execs. Soc., Tau Beta Pi, Eta Kappa Nu, Phi Eta Sigma. Office: Finnegan Henderson Farabow Garrett & Dunner 1300 I St NW Ste 700 Washington DC 20005-3314

ROMBERGER, JOHN ALBERT, scientist, historian; b. near Klingerstown, Pa., Dec. 25, 1925; s. Ralph T. and Carrie (Bahner) R.; student Hershey Jr. Coll., 1947-49; BA, Swarthmore Coll., 1951; MS, Pa. State U., 1954; PhD, U. Mich., 1957; postdoctoral, Calif. Inst. Tech., 1957-60; m. Margery Janet Davis, June 17, 1951; children: Ann I., Daniel D. Plant physiologist, Forest Physiology Lab., U.S. Forest Service, U.S. Dept. Agr., Beltsville, Md., 1961-82; vis. scientist Swedish U. Agrl. Scis., Alnarp, 1983, Inst. Agrl. Scis., Zamosc, Poland, 1985, Agrl. U., Warsaw, 1988. Served with AUS, 1945-46. Fellow Poland-U.S. Interacad. Exchange Program, U. Silesia, Katowice, 1981, 83. Fellow AAAS; mem. Am. Soc. Plant Physiologists, Bot. Soc. Am., Soc. for History Tech., Pa. German Soc., Sigma Xi. Author: Meristems, Growth, and Development in Woody Plants, 1963, (with Z. Hejnowicz and J.F. Hill) Plant Structure: Function and Development, 1993; editor: Internat. Rev. Forestry Research, 1963-70, Beltsville Symposia in Agrl. Research, 1976-78. Contbr. articles on devel. and theoretical biology to profl. jours. Home: 320 Tennessee Ave Elizabethville PA 17023

ROMBOUT, LUKE, museum designer, administrator; b. Amsterdam, Netherlands, May 4, 1933; emigrated to Can., 1954, naturalized, 1959; s. Louis and Aleida (VanBuren) R. B.F.A., Mt. Alison U., Sackville, N.B., 1967. Acting curator Owens Art Gallery/Mt. Allison U., 1965-67, dir., 1968-71; chmn., asst. prof. visual arts program York U., Toronto, Ont., 1972-74; mem. arts adv. panel Can. Council, Ottawa, Ont., 1969-70; dir. art bank Can. Council, 1972-74, head visual arts film sect., 1974-75; dir. Vancouver Art Gallery (B.C., Can.), 1975-84; lectr. Can. Art History/Mt. Allison U., 1968-71; lectr. art history N.S. Coll. Art Design (Can.), 1970-72; lectr. U. Ottawa, 1974-75; mem. adv. com. art Can. Dept. Pub. Works, 1973; mem. design adv. com. Can. Post., 1973; mem. fine arts com. Can. Dept. External Affairs, 1973-75; bd. dirs. Anna Wyman Dance Theatre, 1976-85; dir. McCord Mus. Can. History, Montreal, Can., 1990-94; dean, faculty of creative work George Brown Coll., Toronto, Can., 1994-96. Prin. works include Owens Art Gallery, Mt. Allison Univ., Sackville, N.B., 1970, Art Bank Repository, Can. Coun., Ottawa, Ont., 1972, Vancouver (B.C.) Art Gallery, 1983, Palais de la Civilisation Ville de Montréal, 1985, Expo'86 Contemporary Art Mus. Roundhouse Renovation, Vancouver, 1986, Expo'86 Ramses II Pavilion, Vancouver, 1986, McCord Mus. Can. History, Montréal, 1992. Fellow Royal Soc. Arts; mem. Order of Can., Assn. Internat. Critiques d'Art. Home and Office: 214 Blvd St Joseph E, Montreal, PQ Canada H2T 1H6

ROME, DONALD LEE, lawyer; b. West Hartford, Conn., May 17, 1929; s. Herman Isaac and Juliette (Stern) R.; m. Sheila Ward, Apr. 20, 1958; children: Adam Ward, Lisa, Ethan Stern. SB, Trinity Coll., 1951; LLB, Harvard U., 1954. Bar: Conn. 1954, U.S. Dist. Ct. 1955, U.S. Cir. Ct. Appeals 1965, U.S. Supreme Ct. 1965. Assoc. Ribicoff and Kotkin, Hartford, Conn., 1954-58, ptnr., 1958-67; ptnr. Rosenberg, Rome, Barnett, Sattin & Santos and predecessor, Hartford, 1967-83; now ptnr. Robinson & Cole, Hartford, 1983—; mem. Conn. Gov.'s Study Commn. on Uniform Consumer Credit Code, 1969-70; chmn. Conn. bar adv. com. of attys. to make recommendations to U.S. Dist. Ct. for proposed changed of bankruptcy rules in dist. Conn., 1975-77; mem. Bankruptcy Merit Screening Com. for Dist. Ct., 1980-81; mem. adv. com. Conn. Law Revision commn. on article 2A for Uniform Comml. Code, 1987-89; mem. CPR Inst. for Dispute Resolution Panel of Disting. Neutrals and CPR Fin. Svcs. Panel of Disting. Neutrals; mem. panel of mediators for U.S. Dist. Ct. and U.S. Bankruptcy Ct., Hartford, Am. Arbitration Assn. Nat. Panel Comml. Arbitrators and Mediators; lectr. law U. Conn., 1965-74, 81-83; mem. faculty Sch. Banking of South, La. State U., 1982-84; lectr. continuing legal edn. on secured creditors' rights, comml. fin., bankruptcy and uniform comml. code, 1958—. Prin. author, editor: Business Workouts Manual, 1985, 1992; co-author: A Comparative Analysis and Study of the Uniform Consumer Credit Code in Relation to the Existing Consumer Credit Law in Connecticut, 1970; contbg. author: Connecticut Practice Book, 1978, Collier Bankruptcy Practice Guide, 1981, Asset-Based Financing: A Transactional Guide, 1984, Controllers Business Advisor, 1994; mem. bd. editors Jour. Bankruptcy Practice, 1991—; contbr. articles to profl. jours. Past mem. bd. dirs. New Eng. region Am. Jewish Com., also Hartford chpt., Hebrew Home for Aged, Hartford; past mem. bd. trustees Temple Beth Israel, West Hartford. Mem. ABA (bus. bankruptcy com., uniform commercial code, and comml. fin. svcs. com., sect. on bus. law, mediation com., sect. on dispute resolution), Fed. Bar Assn. (bankruptcy law com.), Conn. Bar Assn. (chmn. sect. comml. law and bankruptcy 1977-80, exec. com. banking law sect. 1984-95, chmn. spl. com. scope and correlation 1983-84, exec. comm. 1996—, dispute resolution sect.), Hartford County Bar Assn., Conn. Bar Found., Assn. Comml. Fin. Attys. (pres. 1978-80), Am. Law Inst., Am. Coll. Comml. Fin. Lawyers (chmn. alternate dispute resolution com., bd. regents), Am. Bankruptcy Inst., Turnaround Mgmt. Assn., Harvard Law Sch. Assn. Conn. (pres. 1970-71), Hartford Club, Masons (32 deg., trial commn. Conn. grand lodge 1970-82). Home: 46 Belknap Rd West Hartford CT 06117-2819 Office: Robinson & Cole 1 Commercial Plz Hartford CT 06103-3599 *We are told by Kipling that success and failure are "imposters." I have found this fundamental teaching to be most helpful in the practice of law and in life generally. Concentration on long-term relationships and basic values is so much more important than ephemeral successes and failures.*

ROMEO, LUIGI, linguist, educator; b. Tropea, Italy, Sept. 20, 1926; came to U.S., 1953; s. Pasquale and Beatrice (Lo Torto) R.; m. Elenore Ruth Andersen, Aug. 10, 1983. B.A. in Fgn. Langs., Wash. State U., 1957; M.A. in Romance Langs., U. Wash., 1959, Ph.D., 1960. Instr. Romance langs. U. Wash., Seattle, 1959-60, acting asst. prof. Romance langs., 1960-61; asst. prof. Italian U. Toronto, 1961-65; assoc. prof. Italian U. Colo., Boulder, 1965-68, prof. linguistics, 1968-84, prof. linguistics emeritus, 1984—.

ROMEO, PETER JOHN, lawyer; b. Darby, Pa., Aug. 1, 1942; s. Joseph Paul and Rose Marie (Beckett) R.; m. Nancy Virginia Schmidt, July 15, 1972; children: Christopher, Jeffrey, Michael. BSBA, Georgetown U., 1964; JD, George Washington U., 1967, LLM, 1969. Bar; Va. 1968, U.S. Dist. Ct. D.C. 1969, U.S. Supreme Ct. 1972; CPA, D.C. Acct. Schumaker & Yates, Washington, 1964-69; atty. U.S. Securities and Exchange Com., Washington, 1969-72, spl. counsel, 1972-79, chief counsel div. corp. finance, 1980-84; ptnr. Hogan & Hartson LLP, Washington, 1984—. Author: Comprehensive Section 16 Outline, 1984 (updated annually), The Registration Process, 1985 (updated biannually); co-author: Section 16 Reporting Guide, 1989, Section 16 Forms and Filing Handbook, 1991 (updated 1993, 96), Section 16 Treatise and Reporting Guide, 1994; contbr. articles to profl. jours. Mem. ABA (mem. fed. regulation securities com., chmn. task force on sect. 16 devels.), D.C. Bar Assn., Va. State Bar. Roman Catholic. Office: Hogan & Hartson LLP 555 13th St NW Washington DC 20004-1109

ROMER, ROBERT HORTON, physicist, educator; b. Chgo., Apr. 15, 1931; s. Alfred Sherwood and Ruth (Hibbard) R.; m. Diana Haynes, June 12, 1953 (dec. Feb. 1992); children: Evan James, David Hibbard, Theodore Haynes; m. Betty Steele, June 25, 1994. B.A., Amherst Coll., 1952; Ph.D. in Physics, Princeton U., 1955. Faculty Amherst (Mass.) Coll., 1955—, prof. physics, 1966—, chmn. dept., 1966—; Research asso. Duke, 1958-59; guest physicist Brookhaven Nat. Lab., 1963—; vis. prof. physics Voorhees Coll., 1969-70. Author: Energy—An Introduction to Physics, 1976, Energy Facts and Figures, 1984. NSF fellow U. Grenoble, France, 1964-65. Fellow

AAAS, Am. Phys. Soc.; mem. Am. Assn. Physics Tchrs. (asso. editor jour. 1968, book rev. editor 1982-88, editor 1988—), Phi Beta Kappa, Sigma Xi. Research low temperature physics, solar energy, electromagnetic theory. Home: 104 Spring St Amherst MA 01002-2332

ROMER, ROY R., governor; b. Garden City, Kans., Oct. 31, 1928; s. Irving Rudolph and Margaret Elizabeth (Snyder) R.; m. Beatrice Miller, June 10, 1952; children: Paul, Mark, Mary, Christopher, Timothy, Thomas, Elizabeth. B.S. in Agrl. Econs., Colo. State U., 1950; LL.B., U. Colo., 1952; postgrad., Yale U. Bar: Colo. 1952. Engaged in farming in Colo., 1942-52; ind. practice law Denver, 1955-66; mem. Colo. Ho. of Reps., 1958-62, Colo. Senate, 1962-66; owner, operator Arapahoe Aviation Co., Colo. Flying Acad., Geneva Basin Ski Area; engaged in home site devel.; owner chain farm implement and indsl. equipment stores Colo.; commr. agr. State of Colo., 1975, chief staff, exec. asst. to gov., 1975-77, 83-84, state treas., 1977-86, gov., 1987—; chmn. Gov. Colo. Blue Ribbon Panel, Gov. Colo. Small Bus. Council; mem. agrl. adv. com. Colo. Bd. Agr. Bd. editors Colo. U. Law Rev., 1960-62. Past trustee Iliff Sch. Theology, Denver; mem., past chmn. Nat. Edn. Goals Panel; co-chmn. Nat. Coun. on Standards and Testing. With USAF, 1952-53. Mem. Dem. Gov.'s Assn. (chmn.), Nat. Gov.'s Assn. (former chmn.), Colo. Bar Assn., Order of the Coif. Democrat. Presbyterian. Office: Office of Gov State Capitol Bldg Rm 136 Denver CO 80203*

ROMERO, DANNY, JR., boxer; b. Albuquerque, July 12, 1974. named Jr. Bantamweight Champion, 1996, Flyweight Champion, 1995, Internat. Boxing Fedn. Office: Internat Boxing Fedn 134 Evergreen Pl Ste 9 East Orange NJ 07018-2012

ROMERO, GEORGE A., film director; b. N.Y.C., Feb. 4, 1940. Dir.: (films) Night of the Living Dead, 1968, There's Always Vanilla, 1972, The Crazies, 1972, Hungry Wives, 1973, Martin, 1978, Dawn of the Dead, 1979, Creepshow, 1982, Day of the Dead, 1985, Monkey Shines: An Experiment in Terror, 1988, Two Evil Eyes, 1990, The Dark Half, 1993; dir., screenwriter Knightriders, 1981; exec. producer, scriptwriter Tales from the Dark Side:The Movie, 1990, Night of the Living Dead, 1990; Television: (exec. prodr., screenwriter) Tales From the Darkside. Office: care The Gersh Agy 232 N Canon Dr Beverly Hills CA 90210-5302*

ROMERO, JEFF, lawyer; b. Albuquerque, Dec. 5, 1945; s. Efrain and Marguerite Gloria (Gallegos) R.; m. Evangeline Trujillo, Nov. 24, 1989; children: David A., Michael J., Rebecca J. BA, Mich. State U., 1967; JD, U. N.Mex., 1971. Bar: N.Mex. 1971, U.S. Dist. Ct. N.Mex. 1971, U.S. Ct. Appeals (10th cir.) 1975, U.S. Supreme Ct. 1993. Lawyer sole practice Jeff Romero, Atty. at Law, Albuquerque, 1972-75, 84-96; lectr. in law U. N.Mex. Law Sch., Albuquerque, 1975-77; asst. dist. atty. 2d Jud. Dist. Atty., Albuquerque, 1975-81; spl. prosecutor Atty. Gen. of N.Mex., Santa Fe, 1981-83; dist. atty. 2d Jud. Dist. of N.Mex., 1997—; bd. dirs. Employment Law Sect.-State Bar, Albuquerque, 1991. Mem. N.Mex. Trial Lawyers Assn., Assn. Trial Lawyers Am., Albuquerque Bar Assn., State Bar of N.Mex. Democrat. Office: Dist Atty 2d Judicial Dist 111 Union Square SE Albuquerque NM 87102

ROMERO, JORGE ANTONIO, neurologist, educator; b. Bayamon, P.R., Apr. 15, 1948; s. Calixto Antonio Romero-Barcelo and Antonia (de Juan) R.; m. Helen Mella, June 20, 1970 (div. 1983); children: Sofia, Jorge, Alfredo, Isabel; m. Cheryl Raps, Aug. 1994; 1 child, Jessica. SB, MIT, 1968; MD, Harvard U., 1972. Diplomate Am. Bd. Psychiatry and Neurology. Intern U. Chgo. Hosp. and Clinics, 1972-73; resident Mass. Gen. Hosp., Boston, 1975-78; rsch. fellow in pharmacology NIMH, Bethesda, Md., 1973-75; asst. prof. neurology Harvard Med. Sch., Boston, 1979-92; mem. staff VA Med. Ctr., Brockton, Mass., 1979-92; assoc. physician Brigham and Women's Hosp., Boston, 1980-92; chmn. dept. neurology Ochsner Clin. Baton Rouge, 1993—; cons. Mass. Mental Health Ctr., Boston, 1987-92. With USPHS, 1973-75. Recipient Career Devel. award VA, 1979. Mem. Am. Acad. Neurology. Office: Ochsner Clin Baton Rouge 9001 Summa Ave Baton Rouge LA 70809-3726

ROMERO, LYNETTE DENISE, news reporter, anchor; b. Denver, Feb. 2, 1967; d. Andy (Andelecio) and Viola Lydia (Nuanez) R. BS, Colo. U., 1989. Reporter, news writer 9KUSA TV, Denver, 1988-91, gen. assignment reporter, anchor, 1992—; gen. assignment reporter KVUE TV, Austin, Tex., 1991-92; mem. adv. bd. Denver Options, 1992—. Recipient 2nd Pl. Best Children's Program Colo. Broadcaster awards, 1990, Best Hard News Story award Tex. AP, 1991. Mem. NATAS (Emmy nominations), Colo. Hispanic Media Assn. Office: 9NEWS 500 E Speer Blvd # 9news Denver CO 80203-4187

ROMERO, PHILIP JOSEPH, economic and policy advisor; b. Abington, Pa., Mar. 22, 1957; s. Joseph John and Mildred Edith (Laundis) R.; m. Lita Grace Flores, Oct. 6, 1984. BA in Econs. and Polit. Sci., Cornell U., 1979; PhD in Policy Analysts, Rand Grad. Sch., 1988. Asst. to mayor Twp. of East Brunswick, N.J., 1977-78; policy analyst Sci. Applications Internat. Corp., Washington, 1980-83; rsch. assoc. RAND Corp., Santa Monica, Calif., 1983-88, assoc. economist, 1988-90; dir. strategic planning United Technologies/Carrier, Hartford, Conn., 1990-91; chief economist Gov.'s Office, Sacramento, Calif., 1991—, dep. cabinet sec., 1995—; exec. dir. Calif. Managed Health Care Improvement Task Force, 1996—; cons. Office of Tech. Assessment, Washington, 1989-90, RAND Corp., Washington, 1990-91, Sec. of Air Forces Sci. Adv. Bd., Washington, 1980-83, Undersec. of Def., Washington, 1985-86; adj. prof. U. So. Calif. and Calif. State U., 1994—; mem. Coun. on Fgn. Rels., 1994—; mem. econ. adv. coun. Calif. Congl. Delegation, 1993—. Co-author: (book) The Deescalation of Nuclear Crises, 1992; contbr. numerous reports and papers to profl. publs. Pres. RAND Grad. Sch. Alumni Assn., Santa Monica, 1989—; founder Adopt-A-School Honors Program, Pacific Palisades, Calif., 1986. Recipient Internat. Affairs fellowship Coun. on Fgn. Rels., N.Y.C., 1989. Mem. The Planning Forum, Am. Econ. Assn., Ops. Rsch. Soc. of Am., Pacific Coun. on Internat. Policy (founding), Acad. Pub. Policy Analysts and Mgmt., Inst. Mgmt. Sci. Avocations: designer of hist. games, musical theater. Home: 1587 Barnett Cir Carmichael CA 95608-5852 Office: Gov's Office State Capitol Sacramento CA 95814-4906

ROMERO-BARCELÓ, CARLOS ANTONIO, governor of Puerto Rico; b. San Juan, P.R., Sept. 4, 1932; s. Antonio S. Romero and Josefina Barceló; m. Kathleen Donnelly, Jan. 2, 1966; children: Juan Carlos, Melinda Kathleen; children by previous marriage: Carlos, Andrés. BA, Yale U., 1953; LLB, U. P.R., 1956; LLD (hon.), U. Bridgeport, 1977. Bar: P.R. 1956. Mem. Herrero-Frank & Romero-Barceló, 1956-58; ptnr. Rivera-Zayas, Rivera-Cestero & Rúa, San Juan, 1958-63, Segurola, Romero & Toledo, 1963-68; pres. Citizens for State 51, 1965-67; mayor, San Juan, 1969-77; gov. P.R., 1977-85, 92—; pres. New Progressive Party, 1974-85, 89-91; P.R.'s at-large rep. U.S. Ho. of Reps. Recipient Hoey award for Interracial Justice, Cath. Interracial Council of N.Y., 1977, Spl. Gold Medal award Spanish Inst., N.Y., 1979, U.S. Atty.-Gen.'s medal, 1981. Mem. Nat. Govs. Assn., So. Govs. Assn. (chmn. 1980-81), Conf., Nat. League Cities (pres. 1975), U.S. Conf. Mayors (bd. dir.). Roman Catholic. Author: Statehood is for the Poor; contbr. articles to profl. jours. Office: 2443 Rayburn Bldg Washington DC 20515-5401

ROMEY, WILLIAM DOWDEN, geologist, educator; b. Richmond, Ind., Oct. 26, 1930; s. William Minter and Grace Warring (Dowden) R.; m. Lucretia Alice Leonard, July 16, 1955; children—Catherine Louise, Gretchen Elizabeth, William Leonard. A.B. with highest honors, Ind. U., 1952; student, U. Paris, 1950-51, 52-53; Ph.D., U. Calif. at Berkeley, 1962. Asst. prof. geology and sci. edn. Syracuse U., 1962-66, assoc. prof., 1966-69; exec. dir. earth sci. ednl. program Am. Geol. Inst., 1969-72; prof., chmn. dept. geology St. Lawrence U., Canton, N.Y., 1971-76; prof. St. Lawrence U., 1976—, prof., chmn. dept. geography, 1983-93; prof. emeritus, 1993—; ednl. cons., 1962—; NAS visitor USSR Acad. Sci., 1967; vis. geoscientist Am. Geol. Inst., 1964-66, 71; earth sci. cons. Compton's Ency., 1970-71; adj. prof. Union Grad. Sch., 1974—; mem. bd. rsch. advisers and readers Walden U., 1981—; prof. Grad. Sch. Am., 1993—; travel writer and cruise ship lectr., 1990—. quthor: (with others) Investigating the Earth, 1967, (with J. Kramer, E. Muller, J. Lewis) Investigations in Geology, 1967, Inquiry Techniques for Teaching Science, 1968, Risk-Trust-Love, 1972, Consciousness and Creativity, 1975, Confluent Education in Science, 1976, Plus Ça Change..., 1996; co-editor: Geochemical Prospecting for Petroleum, 1959; assoc. editor: Jour. Coll. Sci. Tchg., 1972-74, Geol. Soc. Am. Bull., 1979-84, Jour. Geol. Edn., 1980—; editor-in-chief: Ash Lad Press, 1975—; contbr. articles on geology, geography and edn. to profl. publs. Bd. dirs. Onondaga Nature Centers, Inc., 1966-69. Served to lt. USNR, 1953-57; lt. comdr. Res. Woodrow Wilson Found. fellow, 1959-60, 61-62; NSF sci. faculty fellow U. Oslo, 1967-68. Fellow Geol. Soc. Am., AAAS; mem. Nat. Assn. Geology Tchrs. (v.p. 1971-72), N.Y. Acad. Scis., Nat. Assn. Geology Tchrs. (pres. 1972-73), Assn. Am. Geographers, Am. Geophys. Union, Geol. Soc. Norway, Assn. Educating Tchrs. of Sci., Can. Assn. Geographers, Assn. for Can. Studies in U.S., Phi Beta Kappa, Sigma Xi, Phi Delta Kappa. Home: PO Box 294 East Orleans MA 02643-0294 Office: St Lawrence U Dept Geography Canton NY 13617

ROMIG, ALTON DALE, JR., metallurgist, educator; b. Bethlehem, Pa., Oct. 6, 1953; s. Alton Dale and Christine (Groh) R.; m. Julie H. Romig. BS, Lehigh U., 1975, MS, 1977, PhD, 1979. Metallurgist, mem. tech. staff Sandia Nat. Labs., Albuquerque, 1979-87, supr. physical metallurgy, 1987-90, mgr. metallurgy, 1990-92, dir. materials and process scis., 1992-95; dir. Microelectronics and Photonics, 1995—; part time full prof. N.Mex. Inst. Mining and Tech., Socorro, 1981—; Acta/Scripta Metallurgica Lectr., 1993; Fellow Am. Soc. for Metals Internat. (trustee 1992—, v.p. 1996—, Outstanding Rsch. award 1992); mem. TMS, Electron Microscopy Soc. Am. (Burton Outstanding Young Sci. medal 1988), Microbeam Analysis Soc. (pres. 1990, Heinrich award for Outstanding Young Sci. 1991), Materials Rsch. Soc., Sigma Xi, Tau Beta Pi. Author: Principles of Analytical Electron Mecroscopy, 1986, Scanning Electron Microscopy, X-ray Microanalysis and Analytical Electron Microscopy, 1991, Scanning Electron Microscopy and Microanalysis, 1992; editor numerous procs. in phys. metallurgy and electron microscopy; contbr. over 160 articles to sci. jours. Home: 4923 Calle De Luna NE Albuquerque NM 87111-2916 Office: Sandia Nat Labs Sandia Nat Labs Ctr 1300 Albuquerque NM 87185

ROMINE, THOMAS BEESON, JR., consulting engineering executive; b. Billings, Mont., Nov. 16, 1925; s. Thomas Beeson and Elizabeth Marjorie (Tschudy) R.; m. Rosemary Pearl Melancon, Aug. 14, 1948; children—Thomas Beeson III, Richard Alexander, Robert Harold. Student, Rice Inst., 1943-44; B.S. in Mech. Engring, U. Tex., Austin, 1948. Registered profl. engr., Tex., Okla., La., Ga. Jr. engr. Gen. Engring. Co., Ft. Worth, 1948-50; design engr. Wyatt C. Hedrick (architect/engr.), Ft. Worth, 1950-54; chief mech. engr. Wyatt C. Hedrick (architect/engr.), 1954-56; chmn., chief mech. engr. Thomas B. Romine, Jr. (now Romine Romine & Burgess, Inc. cons. engrs.), Ft. Worth, 1956—; mem. heating, ventilating, and air conditioning controls com. NRC, 1986-88. Author numerous computer programs in energy analysis and heating and air conditioning field; contbr. articles to profl. jours. Mem. Plan Commn., City of Ft. Worth, 1958-62; mem. Supervisory Bd. Plumbers, City Ft. Worth, 1963-71, chmn., 1970-71; chmn. Plumbing Code Rev. Com., 1968-69; mem. Mech. Bd., City Ft. Worth, 1974-82, chmn., 1976-82; chmn. plumbing code bd. North Central Tex. Council Govts., Ft. Worth, 1971-75; Bd. mgrs. Tex. Christian U.-South Side YMCA, 1969-74; trustee Ft. Worth Symphony Orch., 1968—, Orch. Hall, 1975—. Served with USNR, 1943-45. Disting. fellow ASHRAE (pres. Ft. Worth chpt. 1958, nat. committeeman 1974—); fellow Am. Cons. Engrs. Coun., Automated Procedures for Engring. Cons. (trustee 1970-71, 75, 1st v.p. 1972-73, internat. pres. 1974); mem. NSPE, Tex. Soc. Profl. Engrs. (bd. dirs. 1956, treas. 1967), Cons. Engrs. Coun. Tex. (pres. North Tex. chpt., also v.p. state orgn. 1965, dir. state orgn. 1967), Starfish Class Assn. (nat. pres. 1970-73, nat. champion 1976), Delta Tau Delta (v.p. West div. 1980-90), Pi Tau Sigma. Episcopalian (vestryman). Clubs: Colonial Country, Rotary. Home: 3232 Preston Hollow Rd Fort Worth TX 76109-2051 Office: Romine Romine & Burgess 300 Greenleaf St Fort Worth TX 76107-2316 *It has long been my belief that, in this technological age, the general public can do little more than accept on faith the propriety of mechanical and electrical systems provided for use in their homes and businesses, and that without an understanding and knowledgeable agent to guide them this faith is often misplaced. It is thus incumbent upon the Professional Engineer to use his expertise in this field to insure competency and safety in those projects under his control, and to assist wherever possible in guiding and influencing appropriate legislation in this regard along sound engineering pathways.*

ROMINGER, RICHARD, federal agency administrator; b. Woodland, Calif., July 1, 1927; M. Evelyne Rowe; children: Richard S., Charles A., Ruth E., Bruce J. BS in Plant Sci., U. Calif., Davis, 1949. Farmer Calif.; dir. Dept. Food and Agriculture, Calif., 1977-82; dep. sec. USDA, 1993—. Recipient Disting. Svc. award Calif. Farm Bur. Fedn., 1991; named Agriculturalist of Yr. Calif. State Fair, 1992; numerous others. Office: US Dept of Agriculture Office of the Deputy Secy 14th & Independence Ave SW Washington DC 20250-0002

ROMLEY, RICHARD M., lawyer; b. Tucson, Apr. 28, 1949; s. Henry Romley and Margaret (Meyers) Madrid; m. Carol Ann Haight, July 20, 1985; children: Darin, David, Aaron. AA, Glendale (Ariz.) Community Coll., 1972; BS, Ariz. State U., 1974, JD, 1981. Bar: Ariz. 1981, U.S. Ct. Appeals (9th cir.) 1982. Spl. prosecutor City of Phoenix, 1981-83, spl. prosecutor sex crimes unit, 1984-86; prosecutor narcotics unit Maricopa County Atty's. Office, Phoenix, 1987-88; county atty. Maricopa County, 1989—; mem. Ariz. Criminal Justice Commn., Phoenix, 1989—; mem. policy/legis. com. Nat. Dist. Attys. Assn., Arlington, Va., 1989; co-chmn. Maricopa County Teen Substance Abuse Task Force, Phoenix, 1989; bd. dirs. Crime Victim Found., Phoenix; spl. law prof. Phoenix Coll., 1987. Active Gov's. Task Force on Domestic Violence, Ariz. Community Punishment Coun. With USMC, 1968-70. Recipient County Achievement award Nat. Assn. Counties, 1990-97; Refnes scholar Glendale C.C., 1971. Mem. Internat. Assn. Chiefs, Law Enforcement Intelligence, Assn. Govt. Attys. Republican. Office: Maricopa County Attys Office 301 W Jefferson St Phoenix AZ 85003-2143

ROMMER, JAMES ANDREW, physician; b. Newark, Aug. 22, 1952; s. Thomas Colman and Hortense (Marsh) R.; m. Linda Joan Anderson, Oct. 7, 1979; children: Elizabeth Anne, Nicole Marie. BS, Haverford Coll., 1974; MD, Cornell U., 1978. Diplomate Am. Bd. Internal Medicine. Intern N.Y. Hosp., Cornell Med. Ctr., N.Y.C., 1978-79; resident in internal medicine N.Y. Hosp., Cornell Med. Ctr., 1978-81; fellow in internal medicine Johns Hopkins Med. Sch., Balt., 1981-82; pvt. practice internal medicine Livingston, N.J., 1982—; attending physician St. Barnabas Med. Ctr., Livingston, 1984—, mem. exec. com., 1990, 94, 96; co-chief sect. of internal medicine, clin. chief dept. medicine, 1996; asst. clin. prof. Univ. Medicine and Dentistry N.J. Med. Sch., Newark, 1983—. Fellow Am. Coll. Physicians; mem. AMA, Am. Soc. Internal Medicine, Alpha Omega Alpha. Avocations: tennis, reading, jogging. Office: 349 E Northfield Rd Livingston NJ 07039-4802

ROMNEY, CARL F., seismologist; b. Salt Lake City, June 5, 1924; m. Barbara Doughty; children: Carolyn Ann, Kim. B.S. in Meteorology, Calif. Inst. Tech., 1945; Ph.D., U. Calif., Berkeley, 1956. Seismologist U.S. Dept. Air Force, 1955-58; asst. tech. dir. Air Force Tech. Applications Center, 1958-73; dep. dir. Nuclear Monitoring Research Office, Def. Advanced Research Projects Agy., 1973-75, dir., 1975-79; dep. dir. Def. Advanced Research Projects Agy., 1979-83; dir. Ctr. Seismic Studies, 1983-91; v.p. Sci. Applications Internat. Corp., 1987—; tech. adviser U.S. reps. in negotiations Test Ban Treaty; mem. U.S. del. Geneva Conf. Experts, 1958, Conf. on Discontinuance Nuclear Weapons Tests, 1959, 60; negotiations on threshold Test Ban Treaty, Moscow, 1974; mem. U.S. del. Peaceful Nuclear Explosions Treaty, Moscow, 1974-75. Contbr. articles to tech. jours. Recipient Exceptional Civilian Service awards Air Force, 1959, Exceptional Civilian Service awards Dept. Def., 1964, 79; Pres.'s award for Distinguished Fed. Civilian Service, for outstanding contbns. to devel. of control system for underground nuclear tests, 1967; Presdl. Rank of Meritorious Exec., 1980. Research on earthquake mechanism, seismic noise; generation, propagation, detection seismic waves from underground explosions. Home: 4105 Sulgrave Dr Alexandria VA 22309-2629 Office: Ste 1450 1300 N 17th St Arlington VA 22209-3801

ROMNEY, RICHARD BRUCE, lawyer; b. Kingston, Jamaica, Dec. 29, 1942; came to U.S., 1945, naturalized, 1956; s. Frank Oswald and Mary Ellen (Burton) R.; m. Beverly Cochran, Sept. 11, 1965 (dec. 1984); children: Richard Bruce, Jr., Stephanie Cochran; m. Lynthia H. Walker, Aug. 14, 1988; children: Alisa Dawn, Kristen Elizabeth. BA, U. Pa., 1964; JD, U. Va., 1972. Bar: N.Y. 1973, U.S. Ct. Appeals (2d cir.) 1975. Assoc. Dewey, Ballantine, Bushby Palmer & Wood, N.Y.C., 1972-80, ptnr., 1981—. Mem. editorial bd. U. Va. Law Rev., 1970-72. Served to lt. USN, 1964-68. Mem. ABA, N.Y. State Bar Assn., Assn. Bar City N.Y., Order of Coif. Republican. Home: Aleja Wojska Polskiego 37, 05 510 Konstancin Jeziorna Poland Office: Dewey Ballantine, SP 2 00 Ul Klonowa 8, 00-591 Warsaw Poland

ROMNEY, SEYMOUR LEONARD, physician, educator; b. N.Y.C., June 8, 1917; s. Benjamin and Anne (Senter) R.; m. Shirley Gordon, Nov. 4, 1945; children: Benjamin, Mary Clark, Tim Hayes, Anne. A.B., Johns Hopkins, 1938; M.D., N.Y. U., 1942. Intern Beth Israel Hosp., Boston, 1942-43; resident Boston Lying-in Hosp., Free Hosp. for Women, Boston, 1946-51; fellow, instr. Harvard Med. Sch., 1947-51, asst. prof. obstetrics and gynecology, 1951-57; prof., chmn. dept. gynecology and obstetrics Albert Einstein Coll. Medicine, N.Y.C., 1957-72; prof. Albert Einstein Coll. Medicine, 1972-89, prof. emeritus, 1989—, dir. research gynecol. oncology, 1972—; dir. obstetrics and gynecology Bronx Mcpl. Hosp. Ctr., N.Y.C., 1957-72; cons. WHO. Chair Soc. of Physicians for Reproductive Choice and Health; mem. med. adv. com. Maternity Ctr. Assn.; bd. dirs. Planned Parenthood, N.Y.C. Served to lt. comdr. M.C. USNR, 1943-45. Mem. ACOG, AAAS, Am. Assn. Med. Colls. (life), Am. Gynecol. and Obstet. Soc., Soc. Gynecologic Investigation, Am. Assn. Cancer Rsch., Maternity Ctr. Assn., Population Assn. Am., N.Y. Obstet. Soc., N.Y. Acad. Medicine, N.Y. Acad. Sci. Home: Glenbrooke Dr White Plains NY 10605-5008 Office: Einstein Coll Morris Park Ave East Bronx NY 10461

ROMOFF, JEFFREY ALAN, university officer, health care executive; b. N.Y.C., Nov. 30, 1945; s. Richard Warren and Evelyn (Alter) R.; m. Vivian Irene Goodman, Aug. 25, 1966 (dec. June 1983); children: Jennifer Ann, Rebecca Lynn; m. Maxine Ketterer, July 28, 1984 (div. July 1996). B.S. magna cum laude in Social Scis., CCNY, 1967; M.Phil. in Polit. Scis., Yale U., 1971. Teaching fellow Yale U., 1969-70, teaching assoc., 1970-71; exec. dir. Central Naugatuck Valley Mental Health Council, Waterbury, Conn., 1971-73; regional programing dir. Western Psychiat. Inst. and Clinic (U. Pitts.), 1973-74, assoc. dir. div. edn. and research, 1974-75; assoc. dir. Western Psychiat. Inst. and Clinic, 1975—; adj. asst. prof. pub. health U. Pitts., 1981—, instr. psychiatry, 1982—, assoc. v.p. health scis., 1984-86, vice chancellor health scis., 1986-92; exec. v.p. U. Pitts. Med. Ctr., 1986-92; sr. vice chancellor for Health Adminstrn. U. Pitts., 1992—; pres. U. Pitts. Med. Ctr. Sys., 1992—. N.Y.C. Regents scholar CCNY, 1963-67. Mem. Am. Hosp. Assn. (governing coun. sect. for mental health and psychiat. scvs. 1986-89), Am. Psychiat. Assn. (chmn. joint com. with Am. Hosp. Assn. 1983-84), Hosp. Assn. Pa., Coun. Psychiat. Svc. Providers (exec. com. 1981-84). Jewish. Home: 3208 Fox Run Rd Allison Park PA 15101 Office: U Pitts Medical Ctr Sys Forbes Tower 200 Lothrop St Ste 11045 Pittsburgh PA 15213-2546

ROMOND, JAMES, principal. Prin. La Salle Inst., Troy, N.Y. Recipient Blue Ribbon Sch. award U.S. Dept. Edn., 1990-91. Office: La Salle Inst 174 Williams Rd Troy NY 12180*

ROMOSER, GEORGE KENNETH, political science educator; b. Kingston, N.Y., Sept. 14, 1929; s. Carl August and Alva (Becker) R.; m. Mechthild von Tresckow, Apr. 30, 1967; children: Alexandra Ada, Valerie Anna. A.B., Rutgers U., 1951; A.M., U. Chgo., 1954, Ph.D., 1958. Research asst. Nat. Opinion Research Center, 1953; asst. Freiburg (Germany) U., 1955-56; instr. Ohio State U., 1957-61; asso. prof. Conn. Coll., 1963-67; asst. prof., asso. prof., prof. polit. sci. U. N.H., Durham, 1961-62, 67-96, chmn. dept., 1968-71, prof. Internat. Affairs, 1986-93, course dir. Internat. Perspective Ctr., 1986-88, dir. program on tech., society and values, 1996—; Fulbright prof. Faculty of Law, Mainz U., Fed. Republic Germany, 1962-63; dir. Emigre Meml. German Internship Programs, 1965—; vis. prof. Free U., Berlin, 1964, Mannheim U., 1968, 82-83, Johns Hopkins, Bologna, Italy, 1969, Munich U., 1973-74, U. Pa., 1986, Kobe U., Japan, 1988-89, Bowdoin Coll., 1990, Freiburg U., Germany, 1993-94, Fulbright Sr. Prof., 1993-94; adj. prof. Mannheim U., Fed. Republic Germany, 1983—; Fulbright sr. rsch. fellow Munich U., 1974; Rockefeller fellow Aspen Inst. for Humanistic Studies, 1978-79; cons. Com. on Internat. Exchange of Persons, 1965-66; NEH fellow Yale U., 1993; co-founder Conf. Group on German Politics, 1968—, chmn., 1968-84, regional dir., 1984-87; founder, dir. New Eng. Workshops on German Affairs, 1980—; co-founder Pacific Coast Workshops on German Affairs, 1983-93; commuting fellow Ctr. European Studies Harvard U., 1983—; founder The Japanese Circle, 1989—. Co-author: West German Politics in the Mid-Eighties, 1985, Germany's New Politics, 1995; contbr. articles to profl. jours., books. Chmn. com. on govtl. reorgn. Democratic party N.H., 1962. Decorated Civilian Knight's Cross Fed. Republic of Germany, 1972. Mem. Am. Coun. on Germany, Phi Delta Theta, Pi Sigma Alpha, Delta Phi Alpha, Phi Alpha Theta. Home: Worster Rd Eliot ME 03903 Office: U NH Huddleson Hall 334 Durham NH 03824

ROMSDAHL, MARVIN MAGNUS, surgeon, educator; b. Hayti, S.D., Apr. 2, 1930; s. Conrad Magnus and Hilda Johanna (Shelsta) R.; m. Virginia McElvany; children: Christine Ann, Laura Marie. AB, U. S.D., 1952, BS, 1954; MD, U. Ill., Chgo., 1956; PhD, U. Tex., Houston, 1968. Diplomate Am. Bd. Surgery. Clin. assoc. NIH, NCI, Bethesda, Md., 1958-60; instr. surgery U. Ill., Chgo., 1963-64; asst. surgeon, asst. prof. surgery U. Tex./M.D. Anderson Cancer Ctr., Houston, 1967-69; assoc. grad. faculty mem. Grad. Sch. Biomed. Sci., U. Tex., Houston, 1969-72; assoc. surgeon/asso. prof. surgery U. Tex./M.D. Anderson Cancer Ctr., Houston, 1969-75; dep. dept. head U. Tex./M.D. Anderson Cancer Ctr., 1979-85; grad. faculty mem. U. Tex. Health Sci. Ctr., Houston, 1972—; prof. surgery U. Tex. Med. Sch., Houston, 1975—; surgeon, prof. surgery U. Tex./M.D. Anderson Cancer Ctr., Houston, 1975—; lectr. in field. Contbr. articles to profl. jours. Pfizer scholar, 1953; recipient Sr. Clin. Traineeship award, USPHS, 1963, Spl. Fellowship award, 1964; ACS Mead Johnson award, 1965, Ann. Outstanding Tchr. award, Dept. Gen. Surgery, U. Tex. M.D. Anderson Cancer Ctr., 1988. Mem. ACS, AMA, Am. Assn. Cancer Rsch., Am. Radium Soc., Assn. for Acad. Surgery, Collegium Internationale Chirugiae Digestivae, Harris County Med. Soc., Houston Acad. Medicine, Houston Philos. Soc., Soc. for Surgery of Alimentary Tract, Soc. of Surg. Oncology, S.W. Sci. Forum, Tex. Med. Assn., Tex. Surg. Soc. (1st v.p. 1995-96), Houston Surg. Soc., W.H. Cole Soc. (1st v.p. 1995-96), Western Surg. Assn., Sigma Xi. Republican. Home: 4530 Verone St Bellaire TX 77401-5514 Office: UT M D Anderson Cancer Ctr 1515 Holcombe Blvd Houston TX 77030-4009

RONALD, ALLAN ROSS, internal medicine and medical microbiology educator, researcher; b. Portage, Man., Can., Aug. 24, 1938; s. David E. and Muriel M. (MacFarlane) R.; m. Myrna Jean Marchyshyn, Oct. 19, 1962; children: Wendy, Sandra, Vickie. BSc in Medicine, U. Man., Winnipeg, 1961, MD with honors, 1961. Resident in internal medicine U. Md., 1962-64; fellow in infectious disease and microbiology U. Wash., 1964-68; asst. prof. U. Man., 1968-72, assoc. prof., 1972-77, prof., head med. microbiology, 1976-85, Disting. prof., head dept. internal medicine, physician-in-chief Health Scis. Ctr., 1985-90; head infectious diseases St. Boniface Gen. Hosp., Winnipeg, 1991-94; assoc. dean rsch. faculty of medicine U. Manitoba, Winnipeg, 1993—; vis. prof., researcher AIDS epidemiology U. Nairobi, Kenya, 1980—; Malcolm Brown Meml. lectr. Can. Soc. Clin. Investigation, 1985; mem. Med. Rsch. Coun. Can., 1987-93. Contbr. articles to profl. jours. Decorated Officer of Order of Can., 1994; recipient Jubilee award U. Man. Alumni Assn., 1990, Thomas Parran award Am. Venereal Disease Assn., 1991, Ortho award Can. Infectious Disease Soc., 1991. Fellow ACP (gov. 1996—); mem. Infectious Disease Soc. Am. (councillor 1990-93), Internat. Soc. Infectious Diseases (pres. 1996—), Am. Soc. Clin. Investigation, Assn. Am. Physicians, Can. Inst. Acad. Medicine. Home: ADT 1102, 21 Roslyn Rd, Winnipeg, MB Canada R3L 2S8 Office: Sect Infectious Diseases, St Boniface Hosp C5124, 409 Tache Ave, Winnipeg, MB Canada R2H 2A6

RONALD, PAULINE CAROL, art educator; b. York, Yorkshire, Eng., Feb. 28, 1945; came to U.S., 1966; d. Peter Vincent Leonard and Doris Annie (Clark) Hume-Shotton; m. James Douglas Ronald, July 16, 1966 (div. 1986); 1 child, Alexia Denise; m. James Donald Wadsworth, Feb. 15, 1991 (div. July 1994). Diploma, Harrogate Sch. Art, Yorkshire, 1965, U. New Castle, Upon Tyne, 1966; MA, Ball State U., 1977. Cert. art tchr., Ind. Art tchr. Knightstown (Ind.) Schs., 1966-67, Dunkirk (Ind.) Schs., 1967-68, Richmond (Ind.) High Sch., 1968—; part time tchr. Ind. U., Earlham Coll.,

Richmond 1974-84; set painter Richmond Civic Theatre. Exhibited in numerous group shows; illustrator History of Wayne County, History of Centerville, 1996. Coach State Acad. Fine Arts State Team Champions, 1988, 96, 2d Pl. for the state, 1989, 95, 97; bd. dirs., mem. permanent collection com. Richmond Art Mus. Recipient Best Set Painting awards, also numerous awards for drawing and painting, Indpls. Art Mus. Mem. NEA, Ind. State Tchrs. Assn., Art Assn. Richmond, Indpls. Mus. Art. Avocations: painting, gardening, cooking, reading, travel. Home: 417 S 20th St Richmond IN 47374-5729

RONALD, PETER, utility executive; b. Duluth, Minn., Aug. 26, 1926; s. George W. and Florence (Jones) R.; m. Mary Locke Boyd, Nov. 25, 1950; children: Peter Webb, Pauline Morton, Samuel Herschel. B.A., U. Va., 1950. With Louisville Gas & Electric Co., 1950-88, treas., 1962—, v.p., 1969-82, sr. v.p., 1982-88, dir., 1979-89. Bd. dirs., mem. exec. com. Bus. Devel. Corp. Ky., 1967-75, pres., 1971-72; bd. dirs. Louisville Community Chest, 1967-72, v.p., 1969-72; bd. dirs., v.p. Louisville Rehab. Ctr., 1964-82, pres., 1970-71; bd. overseers Louisville Country Day Sch., 1967-70; trustee Children's Hosp. Found., 1978-81, sec.-treas., 1978-81; bd. govs. Captiva (Fla.) Civic Assn., 1990-94, v.p., 1992; commr. Captiva, Fla. Erosion Prevention Dist., 1996—. With USNR, 1945-46. Mem. Louisville Country Club, Pendennis Club, Captiva Yacht Club, Zeta Psi. Home: 43 Mockingbird Valley Dr Louisville KY 40207 also: 1112 Schefflera Ct PO Box 877 Captiva FL 33924-0877

RONALD, THOMAS IAIN, financial services executive; b. Glasgow, Scotland, Feb. 16, 1933; s. Newton Armitage and Elizabeth (Crawford) R.; m. Cristina de Yturralde, Aug. 30, 1962; children: Christopher, Isobel. B in Law, Glasgow U., 1956; MBA, Harvard U., 1963. Chartered acct. Pres., CEO Zellers, Inc., Montreal, Que., Can., 1982-85; exec. v.p., dir. Hudson's Bay Co., Toronto, Ont., Can., 1985-87; pres. Mgmt. Svcs. Group CIBC, Toronto, 1987-88, Adminstrv. Bank CIBC, 1988-92; vice chmn. CIBC, Toronto, 1992-95 (ret.), ret., 1995; dir. The North West Co. Inc., Loblaw Co. Ltd., Wittington Investments Ltd., Leon's Furniture Ltd., Mobil Oil Can. Ltd., Holt Renfrew & Co., Cambridge Shopping Ctrs., Covington Capital Corp., Smed Mfg. Inc., Alliance Gas Mgmt. Inc., Noma Industries, Ltd., Can. Life Assurance Co., T.A.L. Investment Counsel Ltd. Bd. dirs. Toronto Symphony Orch. Served as lt. Royal Navy, 1956-58. Fellow Inst. Chartered Accts. Ont.; mem. Inst. Chartered Accts. Scotland. Presbyterian. Club: Granite (Toronto). Avocations: music, squash, tennis. Office: Can Imperial Bank of Commerce, Commerce Court, Toronto, ON Canada M5L 1A2

RONALD, WILLIAM, artist; b. Stratford, Ont., Can., Aug. 13, 1926; came to U.S., 1954, naturalized, 1964; s. William Stanley and Lillian M. (Plant) R.; m. Helen Marie Higgins, Sept. 6, 1952 (div. 1988); children: Suzanne Marie, Dianna Louise, ; m. Alana Michelle Harris, 1989 (div. 1994). Grad. with honors, Ont. Coll. Art, Toronto, 1952; pupil, Jock Macdonald. founding mem. Painters Eleven Group, Toronto, 1952; radio and TV broadcaster, from 1966; newspaper columnist, book reviewer. One man shows include Hart House, U. Toronto, 1954, Greenwich Gallery, Toronto, 1957, Laing Galleries, Toronto, 1960, Douglass Coll., New Brunswick, N.J., Kootz Gallery, N.Y.C., 1957-60, 62, 63, Princeton Mus., 1963, Issacs Gallery, Toronto, 1963, David Mirvish Gallery, Toronto, 1965, Dunkelman Gallery, Toronto, 1970, Tom Thompson Meml. Gallery, Owen Sound, Ont., 1971, Brandon (Man.) U., 1972, Morris Gallery, Toronto, 1975, Gustafssen Gallery, Brampton, Ont., Brampton Pub. Libr. and Art Gallery, Bramlea, Ont., 1976; retrospective exhbn. Ronald-25 Yrs. at Robert McLaughlin Gallery, Oshawa, Ont., 1975, Musee d'Art Contemporain, Montreal, Que., Can., Rodman Hall Arts Centre, St. Catherines Art Gallery and Mus., Charlottetown, P.E.I., Edmonton (Alta.) Art Gallery, Burnaby (B.C.) Art Gallery, 1976, Art Gallery of Windsor, Ont., Morris Gallery, Toronto, 1977, 78, 79, 80, Wells Gallery, Ottawa, Ont., 1982, Quan-King Gallery, Toronto, ,Moore Gallery, Hamilton, Ont., 1990; exhbns. of work The Prime Ministers (of Can.) Art Gallery of Ont., 1984, Art Gallery of Windsor, 1984, Manulife Pl., Edmonton, 1984, The N.B. Mus., St. John, 1985, Art Gallery N.S., 1985, Can., Montreal Gallery of Contemporay Art, 1986, The Jolliette (Que.) Mus., 1988; group exhbns. include Trinity Coll., Toronto, 1951, Eglinton Gallery, Toronto, 1953, Biennial exhbns. Nat. Gallery Can., 1955, 57-58, Smithsonian Travelling Exhbn., 1956, Riverside Mus., N.Y.C., Contemporary Can. Painters, 1957, Carnegie Internat., 1957, Brussels World Fair and Travelling Show, Sao Paulo Biennale, 1959, Whitney Mus. Ann., Corcoran Biennial, 1962-63, Toysby Contemporary Artists, 1966, Artists on Campus, York U., Toronto, 1970, Toronto Painting, 1972, Robert McLaughlin Gallery, Oshawa, 1978; represented in permanent collections Art Gallery Ont., Bklyn. Mus., Carnegie Inst., Guggenheim Mus., Mus. Modern Art, Nat. Gallery Can., R.I. Sch. Design, Albright Knox Gallery, Buffalo, Aldrich Mus., Ridgefield, Conn., U. B.C., Art Inst. Chgo., Internat. Minerals and Chems. Corp., Skokie, Ill., James A. Michener Found., Allentown, Pa., Montreal Mus. Fine Arts, York U., David Rockefeller Collection, Nelson A. Rockefeller Collection, U. N.C., Phoenix Art Mus., Balt. Mus., Walker Art Ctr., Mpls., Williams Coll., Princeton Mus., Queens U., Kingston, Ont., Brandeis U., Wadsworth Atheneum, Hartford, Conn., Whitney Mus. Am. Art, Washington Gallery Modern Art, Newark Mus., N.J. State Mus., Trenton, U. Tex., Can. Coun. Collection, Can. Art Bank, Windsor Art Mus., Hudson River Mus., Pasadena (Calif.) Mus. Modern Art, Peel County Mus. Brampton, Wellington County Mus., Kitchener Waterloo Art Mus., Masters Sch. and Mercy Coll., Dobbs Ferry, N.Y., Toronto Dominion Bank, Notre Dame U., U. Okla. Art Mus., Norman, numerous others; commd. artist prime mins. Can. Recipient Hallmark Art award for watercolor, 1952, Guggenheim Mus. award Can. painting, 1956, Sr. Arts award Can. Coun., 1977; Ind. Order Daus. Empire scholar, Can., 1951, Can. Amateur Hockey Assn. scholar Can. Found., 1956. Mem. Royal Can. Acad. Home: 206 Robert St, Toronto, ON Canada M5S 2K7

RONAN, WILLIAM JOHN, management consultant; b. Buffalo, Nov. 8, 1912; s. William and Charlotte (Ramp) R.; m. Elena Vinadé, May 29, 1939; children: Monica, Diana Quasha. A.B., Syracuse U., 1934; Ph.D., N.Y. U., 1940, LL.D., 1969; certificate, Geneva Sch. Internat. Studies, 1933. Mus. asst. Buffalo Mus. Sci., 1928-30; with Niagara-Hudson Power Co., 1931; transfer dept. N.Y.C.R.R., 1932; Penfield fellow internat. law, diplomacy and belles lettres, 1935, Univ. fellow, 1936; editor Fed. Bank Service, Prentice-Hall, Inc., 1937; instr. govt. N.Y. U., 1938, exec. sec. grad. div. for tng. in pub. services, 1938, asst. dir., 1940, asst. prof. govt., dir. grad. div. for tng. pub. service, 1940, assoc. prof. govt., 1946-47, prof., 1947, dean, grad. sch. pub. adminstrn. and social service, 1953-58; Cons. N.Y.C. Civil Service Commn., 1938; prin. rev. officer, negotiations officer U.S. Civil Service Commn., 1942; prin. div. asst. U.S. Dept. State, 1943; cons. Dept. State, 1948, Dept. Def., 1954; dir. studies N.Y. State Coordination Commn., 1951-58; project mgr. N.Y. U.-U. Ankara project, 1954-59; cons. ICA, 1955, N.Y. State Welfare Conf.; adminstrv. co-dir. Albany Grad. Program in Pub. Adminstrn.; 1st dep. city adminstr. N.Y.C., 1956-57; exec. dir. N.Y. State Temporary Commn. Constl. Conv., 1956-58; sec. to Gov. N.Y., 1959-66; chmn. interdept. com. traffic safety, commr. Port Authority N.Y. and N.J., 1967-90, vice chmn., 1972-74, chmn., 1974-77; with UTDC Corp., West Palm Beach, Fla.; trustee Crosslands Savs. Bank; chmn. bd. L.I. R.R., 1966-74; chmn. Tri-State Transp. Com., N.Y., N.J., Conn., 1961-67; chmn. interstate com. New Haven R.R., 1960-63; chmn. N.Y. Com. on L.I. R.R., 1964-65; mem. N.Y. State Commn. Internstate Coop., 1961, N.Y. State Com. Fgn. Ofcl. Visitors, 1961, N.Y. State Coordination Commn., 1960; mem. N.Y. Civil Svc. Commn., Temporary State Commn. on Constl. Conv., 1966-67; chmn. N.Y. State Met. Commuter Transp. Authority, 1965-68, Met. Transp. Authority, 1968-74, Tri-Borough Bridge and Tunnel Authority, 1968-74, N.Y.C. Transit Authority, 1968-74, Manhattan and Bronx Surface Transit Operating Authority, 1968-74; chmn. bd., pres. 3d Century Corp., 1974-94; mem. Commn. Critical Choices for Am., 1973—, acting chmn., 1975—; mem. urban transp. adv. com. U.S. Dept. Transp.; sr. adviser Rockefeller family, 1974-80; pres. Nelson Rockefeller Collection, Inc., 1977-80; trustee Power Authority of State of N.Y., 1974-77; cons. to trustees Penn Ctrl. Transp. Co.; vice chmn. bd. CCX, Inc.; sec.-treas. Sarabam Corp. N.V.; chmn., dir. UTDC (U.S.A.) Inc., 1987-88; chmn. UTDC Corp., 1989-94, Transit Svcs. Corp., 1989-94; cons. Herzog Transit Svcs., 1995—, Dime Savs. Bank, Metal Powder Products Inc., Prometech, Inc., Internat. Mining and Metals Inc., Quadrant Mgmt. Inc., 1990—, Ohio Highspeed Rail Authority, 1991-93; chmn. N.Y. and N.J. Inland Rail Rate Com.; dir. Nat. Mgmt. Coun., 1951. Author: Money Power of States in International Law, 1940, The Board of Regents and the Commissioner, 1948, Our War Economy, 1943, (with others), articles in profl. jours.; adviser: Jour. Inst. Socio-Econ. Studies. Mem. U.S. FOA, Am. Public Health Assn.; staff relations officer N.Y.C. Bd. Edn.; Mem. Nat. Conf. Social Work, Nat. Conf. on Met. Areas, Citizens Com. on Corrections, Council on Social Work Edn.; bd. dirs. World Trade Club; adv. bd. World Trade Inst.; mem. 42d St. Redevel. Corp., chmn., 1980-94; mem. Assn. for a Better N.Y.; bd. advisers Inst. for Socioecon. Studies, 1977—; dir. Nat. Health Council, 1980-86; dep. dir. policy Nelson Rockefeller campaign for Republican presdl. nomination, 1964; mem. N.Y. State Gov.'s Com. on Shoreham Nuclear Plant, 1983-85, Nassau County Indsl. Devel. Authority, 1982-90, U.S. Dept. Transp. Com. on Washington and Capital Dist. Airports, 1985-86; bd. dirs. Ctr. Study Presidency, 1986-90, Alcoholism Council of N.Y., 1986—; trustee N.Y. Coll. Osteopathic Medicine, 1986-91. Served as lt. USNR, 1943-46. Mem. NEA, Am. Polit. Sci. Assn., Am. Acad. Pub. Adminstrn., Am. Soc. Pub. Adminstrn., Civil Svc. Assembly of U.S. and Can., Internat. Assn. Met. Rsch. and Devel., Nat. Mcpl. League, Mcpl. Pers. Soc., Citizens Union of N.Y., Nat. Civil Svc. League, Am. Acad. Polit. and Social Sci., L.I. Assn. Commerce and Industry (dir.), Internat. Inst. Adminstrv. Scis., Am. Fgn. Law Assn., Internat. Union Pub. Transport (mgmt. com., v.p.), Am. Pub. Transit Assn. (chmn. 1974-76), Nat. Def. Transp. Assn. (v.p. for Mass transit), Met. Opera Club, Maidstone Club, Devon Yacht Club, Knickerbocker Club, Hemisphere Club, Harvard Club, Creek Club, Wings Club, Traffic Club, Univ. Club, Am. Club Riviera, Beach Club (Palm Beach), Everglades Club. Home: 525 S Flagler Dr West Palm Beach FL 33401-5922 Home: Villa La Pointe Du Cap, Ave de La Corniche, 06230 Saint Jean Cap Ferrat France

RONAYNE, MICHAEL RICHARD, JR., academic dean; b. Boston, Apr. 29, 1937; s. Michael Richard and Margaret (Fahey) R.; m. Joanne Maria, Aug. 7, 1971; 1 child, Michelle Eileen. BS, Boston Coll., 1958; PhD, U. Notre Dame, 1962. Instr. chemistry Providence Coll., 1962-63, asst. prof. chemistry, 1963-64; rsch. chemist Panametrics, Inc., Waltham, Mass., 1964-66; asst. prof. chemistry Suffolk U., Boston, 1966-67, assoc. prof., 1967-70, prof., chmn. dept. chemistry, 1970-72, dean Coll. Liberal Arts and Sci., 1972—; reaccreditation vis. team mem. New Eng. Assn. Schs. and Colls., Winchester, Mass., 1974-80, Mass. Dept. Edn., Boston, 1975; mem. acad. adv. com. Mass. Bd. Higher Edn., Boston, 1977. Contbr. articles to sci. jours., profl. publs. Mem. Winchester Sch. Com., 1983-92, chmn., 1984-85, 86-87; mem. Winchester Town Meeting, 1983—, mem. town capital planning com., 1983-84, town coun. on youth, 1987-88, 89-90; mem. exec. com., bd. dirs. Mass. Bay Marine Studies Consortium, 1985-87; project dir. U.S. Dept. of Edn. Title III Grants. Shell Oil Corp. fellow, 1958-59, AEC fellow 1959-62; recipient Contbns. in Sci. and Edn. citation New Eng. Sch. Art and Design, Boston, 1991. Mem. AAAS, Am. Chem. Soc., Am. Conf. Acad. Deans, Coun. for Liberal Learning, Am. Assn. for Higher Edn., Sigma Xi, Phi Alpha Theta, Phi Gamma Mu, Sigma Tau Delta, Omicron Delta Epsilon, Sigma Zeta. Office: Suffolk U Beacon Hill Boston MA 02114

RONDEAU, CHARLES REINHARDT, lawyer; b. Jefferson, La., Oct. 14, 1966; s. Clement Robert and Irmtraut Juliana Rondeau. BA, Columbia U., 1988; JD, Southwestern U., L.A., 1992; diploma in Advanced Internat. Legal Stud, McGeorge Sch. Law, 1993. Bar: Calif. 1993, N.Y., N.J., U.S. Dist. Ct. N.J., U.S. Dist. Ct. (so. and ea. dists.) N.Y., U.S. Dist. Ct. (cent. dist.) Calif., U.S. Ct. Appeals (3rd cir.), U.S. Tax Ct. 1994. Visiting jurist Cabinet Berlioz et Cie, Paris, 1992-93; assoc. Stanley A. Teitler, P.C., N.Y.C., 1993-95; ptnr. Rondeau & Homampour, Beverly Hills, Calif., 1995—. Rsch. editor: Southwestern U. Law Rev., 1989-92. Mem. ABA, L.A. County Bar Assn., Beverly Hills Bar Assn. Avocations: jazz, skiing, sailing. Office: Rondeau & Homampour PLC 8383 Wilshire Blvd Ste 830 Beverly Hills CA 90211-2407

RONDEPIERRE, EDMOND FRANCOIS, insurance executive; b. N.Y.C., Jan. 15, 1930; s. Jules Gilbert and Margaret Murray (Moore) R.; m. M. Anne Lerch, July 5, 1952; children: Aimee S., Stephen C., Peter E., Anne W. BS, U.S. Mcht. Marine Acad., 1952; JD, Temple U., 1959. Bar: D.C. 1959, Conn. 1988, U.S. Supreme Ct. 1992. Third mate Nat. Bulk Carriers, 1952-53; field rep. Ins. Co. N.Am., Phila., 1955-59, br. mgr., 1959-61, asst. sec. underwriting, 1965-67, asst. gen. counsel, 1967-70, sr. v.p., gen. counsel, 1970-76; v.p., dep. chief legal affairs INA Corp., Phila., 1976-77; v.p., gen. counsel Gen. Reins. Corp., Stamford, Conn., 1977-79, sr. v.p., corp. sec., gen. counsel, 1979-94, sr. v.p., 1994-95; pres. ARIAS-US, 1994—; bd. dirs. Arias-US. Lt. USN, 1953-55. Mem. ABA, Conn. Bar Assn., D.C. Bar Assn., Inter-Am. Bar Assn., Soc. CPCU, Internat. Assn. Def. Counsel (past bd. dirs.), AIDA Reins. and Ins. Arbitration Soc. (dir., pres.), Stamford Yacht Club. Roman Catholic.

RONDINELLI, DENNIS A(UGUST), business administration educator, research center director; b. Trenton, N.J., Mar. 30, 1943; s. August P. and Vincentia Rondinelli; m. Soonyoung Chang, Dec. 19, 1976; children: Linda, Lisa. BA, Rutgers U., 1965; PhD, Cornell U., 1969. Asst. prof. urban affairs U. Wis., Milw., 1971-73; assoc. prof. grad. sch. of mgmt. Vanderbilt U., Nashville, 1973-76; assoc. prof. planning Maxwell Sch. of Citizenship and Pub. Affairs Syracuse U., N.Y., 1976-79, prof. social scis., 1979-86; prin. scientist and sr. policy analyst Office for Internat. Programs, Research Triangle Inst., Research Triangle Park, N.C., 1986-90; Glaxo Disting. Internat. Prof. Mgmt. Kenan-Flagler Bus. Sch.; dir. Ctr. Global Bus. Rsch., Kenan Inst. Pvt. Enterprise U. N.C., Chapel Hill, N.C., 1990—; cons. World Bank, U.S. Dept. State, UN Devel. Program, Govts. of Colombia, South Korea, Can., Indonesia, Philippines, China, India. Author: Decentralization and Development: Policy Implementation in Developing Countries, 1983, Applied Methods of Regional Analysis: The Spatial Dimensions of Development Policy, 1985, Development Administration and U.S. Foreign Aid Policy, 1987, Urban Services in Developing Countries: Public and Private Roles in Urban Development, 1988, Planning Education Reforms in Developing Countries, 1990, Development Projects as Policy Experiments, 1993, Privatization and Economic Reform in Central Europe, 1994, Expanding Sino-American Business and Trade: China's Economic Transition, 1994, Great Policies: Strategic Innovations in Asia and the Pacific, 1995, Policies and Institutions for Managing Privatization, 1996; mem. editl. adv. bd. Bangladesh Jour. of Pub. Adminstrn., 3d World Planning Rev., Bus. and the Contemporary World, Environ. Quality Mgmt. Captain U.S. Army, 1965-72. Decorated Julio Lieras Order of Merit (Colombia); recipient Rural Devel. medal Republic of Vietnam, 1971, Ethnic Minorities Devel. medal, 1971; East-West Ctr. sr. fellow, 1975-76, Pacific Basin Rsch. Ctr./Soka U. of Am./Harvard U. rsch. fellow, 1991-92. Avocations: gardening, writing nonfiction. Office: Kenan Inst Pvt Enterprise CB#3440 The Kenan Ctr U NC Chapel Hill NC 27599-3149

RONE, WILLIAM EUGENE, JR., newspaper editor, retired; b. Atlanta, Nov. 7, 1926; s. William Eugene and Marguerite (Kellett) R.; m. Margaret Louise Banks, July 17, 1953; 1 child, James Kellett. AB, Wofford Coll., 1949; LLB, U. S.C., 1951; grad., U.S. Army Command and Gen. Staff Coll., 1974. With The State (newspaper), Columbia, S.C., 1950-97, city editor, 1962-65, asso. editor, 1966-69, editorial page editor, 1969-90, sr. editor, 1990-93; consulting editor, 1993-97; S.C. corr. So. Edn. Reporting Service, Nashville, 1962-68; columnist Raleigh (N.C.) News & Observer, 1968-83, Atlanta Jour.-Constn., 1973-84. Author: Biography of Max Hirsch, 1956. Chmn. S.C. Athletic Hall of Fame, 1957-61. Served with USNR, 1945-46. Recipient S.C. AP award for reporting in depth, 1962. Mem. Am. Soc. Newspaper Editors, Nat. Conf. Editorial Writers, S.C. Bar, Phi Beta Kappa, Kappa Sigma, Phi Delta Phi. Episcopalian. Home: 726 Fairway Ln Columbia SC 29210-5715

RONEN, CAROL, state legislator. BS, Bradley U.; MA, Roosevelt U. Dir. legis. and cmty. affairs Chgo. Dept. Human Svcs., 1985-89; exec. dir. Chgo. Commn. on Women, 1989-90; dir. planning and rsch. Chgo.-Cook County Criminal Justice Commn.; asst. commn. Chgo. Dept. Planning, 1991, Chgo. Dept. Housing; mem. Ill. Ho. of Reps., 1993—. Former pres. Ill. Task Force on Child Support; bd. dirs. Cook County Dem. Women, St. Martin De Porres Shelter for Women and Children, Alternatives Youth Orgn., Citizen Action Consumer Rights Orgn.; governing coun. Am. Jewish Congress Midwest Region; mem. Coun. Jewish Women. Democrat. Home: 6033 N Sheridan Rd Chicago IL 60660-3003 Office: Ill Ho of Reps State Capitol Springfield IL 62706

RONEY, JOHN HARVEY, lawyer, consultant; b. L.A., June 12, 1932; s. Harvey and Mildred Puckett (Cargill) R.; m. Joan Ruth Allen, Dec. 27, 1954; children: Pam Roney Peterson, J. Harvey, Karen Louise Hanke, Cynthia Allen Harmon. Student, Pomona Coll., 1950-51; B.A., Occidental Coll., 1954; LL.B., UCLA, 1959. Bar: Calif. 1960, D.C. 1976. Assoc. O'Melveny & Myers, L.A., 1959-67, ptnr., 1967-94, of counsel, 1994—; gen. counsel Pa. Co., 1970-78, Baldwin United Corp., 1983-84; dir. Coldwell Banker & Co., 1969-81, Brentwood Savs. & Loan Assn., 1968-80; spl. advisor to dep. Rehab. of Mut. Benefit Life Ins. Co., 1991-94; cons., advisor to Rehab. of Confederation Life Ins. Co., 1994-95; mem. policy adv. bd. Calif. Ins. Commn., 1991-95. Served to 1st lt. USMCR, 1954-56. Mem. ABA, Calif. Bar Assn. (ins. law com. 1991-95, chmn. 1993-94), Los Angeles County Bar Assn., D.C. Bar Assn., N.Y. Coun. Fgn. Rels., Pacific Coun. on Internat. Policy, Conf. Ins. Counsel, Calif. Club, Sky Club (N.Y.), Gainey Ranch Golf Club (Scottsdale). Republican. Home: The Strand Hermosa Beach CA 90254 Office: 400 S Hope St Ste 1600 Los Angeles CA 90071-2801

RONEY, PAUL H(ITCH), federal judge; b. Olney, Ill., Sept. 5, 1921; m. Sarah E. Eustis; children: Susan M., Paul Hitch Jr., Timothy Eustis. Student, St. Petersburg Jr. Coll., 1938-40; B.S. in Econs, U. Pa., 1942; LL.B., Harvard U., 1948; LL.D., Stetson U., 1977; LL.M., U. Va., 1984. Bar: N.Y. 1949, Fla. 1950. Assoc. Root, Ballantine, Harlan, Bushby & Palmer, N.Y.C., 1948-50; ptnr. Mann, Harrison, Roney, Mann & Masterson (and predecessors), St. Petersburg, Fla., 1950-57; pvt. practice law, 1957-63; ptnr. Roney & Beach, St. Petersburg, 1963-69, Roney, Ulmer, Woodworth & Jacobs, St. Petersburg, 1969-70; judge U.S. Ct. Appeals (5th cir.), St. Petersburg, 1970-81; judge U.S. Ct. Appeals (11th cir.), St. Petersburg, 1981-86, chief judge, 1986-89, sr. cir. judge, 1989—; mem. adv. com. on adminstrv. law judges U.S. CSC, 1976-77; pres. judge U.S. Fgn. Intelligence Surveillance Ct. of Rev., 1994—. With U.S. Army, 1942-46. Fellow Am. Bar Found.; mem. ABA (chmn. legal adv. com. Fair Trial-Free Press 1973-76, mem. task force on cts. and public 1973-76, jud. adminstrn. div., chmn. appellate judges conf. 1978-79, mem. Gavel Awards com. 1980-83), Am. Judicature Soc. (dir. 1972-76), Am. Law Inst., Fla. Bar, St. Peterburg Bar Assn. (pres. 1964-65), Nat. Jud. Coll. (faculty 1974, 75), Jud. Conf. U.S. (subcom. on jud. improvements 1978-84, exec com. 1986-89, com. to review circuit coun. conduct and disability orders 1991-93). Home: Bayfront Tower 1 Beach Dr SE Saint Petersburg FL 33701-3963 Office: US Ct Appeals 11th Circuit 601 Federal Bldg 144 1st Ave S Saint Petersburg FL 33701-4311

RONEY, ROBERT KENNETH, retired aerospace company executive; b. Newton, Iowa, Aug. 5, 1922; s. Louie Earl and Hazel Iona (Cure) R.; m. Alice Lorraine Mann, Oct. 6, 1951; children: Stephen P., Karen Margaret Dahl. BSEE, U. Mo., 1944; MSEE, Calif. Inst. Tech., 1947, PhD, 1950. Engr. rsch. Jet Propulsion Lab. Calif. Inst. Tech., Pasadena, 1948-50; engr. rsch. Hughes Aircraft Co., Culver City, Calif., 1950-54, mgr. sys. analysis, 1955-59, dir. tech. R&D, 1960, assoc. mgr. space sys. divsn., 1961-68, mgr. space sys. divsn., 1968-70, v.p. asst. group exec., 1970-85, sr. v.p. corp. tech., 1986-88, ret., 1988. Mem. adv. bd. Dept. Transp. Comml. Space Transp., 1984-87, Engring. Sch. U. Kans., 1988-91. Lt. (j.g.) USNR, 1944-46, PTO. Recipient Honor award for Disting. Svc. in Engring. U. Mo.-Columbia, 1979. Fellow IEEE; mem. NAE, Caltech Assocs. Home: 1105 Georgina Ave Santa Monica CA 90402-2027

RONEY, SHIRLEY FLETCHER, retail company executive; b. Atlanta, Dec. 3, 1935; d. Grady Franklin and Grace Ilene (Camp) Fletcher; student public schs., Atlanta; m. Sept. 19, 1953 (div.); 1 son, Joseph Clay. Collection corr. GMAC, Atlanta, 1953-64; sales rep. Washburn Realty, Atlanta, 1964-67; sec.-treas. Frank Jackson Lincoln Mercury, Inc., Sandy Springs, Ga., 1967-79, sec. treas., 1971—, comptroller, 1979—, pres., gen. mgr., 1983—; v.p., dir. J&J Investment Corp., 1975—; v.p., dir. Rivergate Corp., 1979-86, pres. 1986—; sec. treas., dir. Ajax Rent a Car, Sandy Springs Toyota. Div. vice chmn. United Way, 1979; treas. Martins Landing Found., 1994—; bd. dirs. Ga. Spl. Olympics. Mem. Am. Bus. Womens Assn., Am. Contract Bridge League (life master). Office: 7555 Roswell Rd Atlanta GA 30350-4838

RONEY, WALLACE, musician; b. Phila., May 25, 1960. Studied with Sigmund Haring, Howard U.; student, Berklee Coll. Trumpeter Art Blakey's Jazz Messengers, Tony Williams Quintet. Recorded 8 albums under own name, Verses, 1987, Intuition, 1989, Obsession, 1991, Seth Air, 1992, Misterios, 1994, Munchin, 1995, The Wallace Roney Quintet, 1996; other recs. include Story of Neptune (with Tony Williams), Seth Air Tribute to Miles Davis (with Herbie Hancock, Wayne Sholter, Ron Carter and Tony Williams), Live at Montreux (with Miles Davis), Killer Joe (with Art Blakey). Nominee for Grammy award, 1994. Office: Warner Bros 75 Rockefeller Plz New York NY 10019*

RONNINGSTAM, ELSA FRIDEBORG, psychologist; b. Boden, Sweden, Oct. 17, 1950; came to U.S., 1985; d. Yngve Fritjof and Frideborg (Rönnberg) Karlsson. BA, U. Umeå, Sweden, 1971; MSc, U. Stockholm, 1976, PhD, 1988. Clin. psychologist dept. psychiatry Huddinge Hosp., Stockholm, 1980-85, 87-88; rsch. fellow in clin. psychology, psychosocial rsch. program McLean Hosp., Harvard Med. Sch., Belmont, Mass., 1985-87, rsch. and clin. fellow, 1989-90; instr. in psychology Harvard Med. Sch., 1990-95, asst. prof. psychology, 1996—; asst. psychologist McLean Hosp., 1990-95, assoc. psychologist, 1996—. Author: (in Swedish) Bereavement in Childhood, 1978; editor: Disorders of Narcissiou - Diagnostic Clinical and Eupinical Implication, 1997. Swedish Am. Found. scholar, 1989-91. Office: McLean Hosp Psychol Rsch Pr 115 Mill St Belmont MA 02178-1041

RONSMAN, WAYNE JOHN, insurance company executive; b. Milw., Jan. 21, 1938; s. Harry Martin and Martha Elizabeth (Popp) R.; m. Joan P. Murphy-Mays, Nov. 30, 1974; children: Allison, Alanna; children by previous marriage: Rosemary, Harry, Martha. Student Marquette U., 1955-58, U. San Francisco, 1960-66. CLU, CFP, chartered fin. cons. Acct. Otis McAllister & Co., 1960-62; acct., salesman of data processing Statis. Tabulation Corp., San Francisco, 1962-66; chief acct., gen. mgr. Dillingham Bros. Ltd., Honolulu, 1966-67; ins. salesman Mut. Benefit Life Ins. Co., 1968-91, mgr. Met Life Honolulu, 1991-93, gen. agt., Hawaii, Alaska, 1991; v.p. Brenno Assos., Honolulu, 1972-80; prin. Ronsman-Brenno, Anchorage, Alaska, 1980-90; owner Ronsman, Hammond & Assocs., 1991—; bd. dirs. Aloha Nat. Bank, Kihei, Maui, 1989-90; guest lectr. Chaminade U. Law Sch., Honolulu. Mem. Gov's Task Force to Program Correctional Facilities Land, 1970-72; mem. State Bd. Paroles and Pardons, 1972-75; treas. Spl. Edn. Ctr. Oahu, 1969-78; pres. Ballet Alaska, 1986-87, Maui Ballet Co. Ltd., 1992-93; v.p. devel. Make A Wish Hawaii, 1992—; chmn. Maui County Salary Commn., 1996—. Served with USMCR, 1958-60. Mem. Inst. Mgmt. Acct. (pres. Anchorage chpt. 1989-90), Am. Soc. CLUs, Hawaii Estate Planning Coun. (dir. 1994), Honolulu Assn. Life Underwriters (million dollar round table 1973—), Inst. Mgmt. Accts. (pres. Honolulu 1994-95, 95-96), Hawaii (state editor 1970-71, nat. dir. 1972-73), Kailua (pres. 1968-69) Jaycees, Hawaii C. of C., Nat. Assn. Securities Dealers, Kailua C. of C. (pres. 1977-78). Roman Catholic. Home: Ronsman-Hammond & Assocs 1099 Alakea St Ste 1500 Honolulu HI 96813-4500 Office: PO Box 336 Honolulu HI 96809-0336

RONSON, RAOUL R., publishing executive; b. Fiume, Italy, Mar. 22, 1931; came to U.S., 1951; s. Mirko and Margaret (Fischer) Ruzicka; m. Susan Kohn, July 22, 1962; 1 child, Paul. DBA, U. Rome, 1950; MA, New Sch Social Research, 1957; postgrad., Inst. for Advanced Internat. Studies, U. Miami, 1967-68, NYU, 1974. Fgn. corr., freelance writer, 1953-59; treas. Daron Enterprises, Inc., 1959-63; pres. Seesaw Music Corp., N.Y.C., 1963—, Okra Music Corp., N.Y.C., 1963-77, Ulsyra Prodn. Corp., N.Y.C., 1963—; pres. The Composers Press, 1972-76; acad. lectr. Am., Australian, New Zealand univs. and conservatories; vis. lectr. Youngstown (Ohio) State U., 1985—, Finch Coll., N.Y.C., Eastman Sch. Music, Rochester, N.Y., Wake Forest U., Winston-Salem, N.C. Producer documentary films, 1959—, classical music recs., 1963—, The Dana Recording Project (nominated 2 Grammy awards). Mem. Emergency Control Bd. Office of Mayor, N.Y.C., 1973-82, Fed. Emergency Mgmt. Agy., Washington, 1982-84; rsch. analyst Office of the Sec. Def., Res. Affairs, The Pentagon, Washington, 1984-91; liaison officer U.S. Mil. Acad., West Point, N.Y., 1988—. With M.I., AUS, 1952-54, USAR, 1955-91, ret. 1991. Decorated Legion of Merit, Def. Superior Svc. medal, Def. Meritorious Svc. medal, Army Meritorious Svc. medal, Army Commendation medal, Def. Identification badge Office Sec., Korean Svc. medal, UN Svc. medal; recipient numerous other awards and decorations; Grammy award nominee for Classical Prodr. of the Yr., 1993. Mem. Am. Polit. Sci. Assn., Am. Acad. Polit. and Social Sci., Internat. Platform Assn., Civil Affairs Assn., Sibelius Soc. (bd. dirs. 1978-85), Nat. Acad. Rec. Arts and Scis., Masons. Home: 825 W End Ave New York NY 10025-5349 Office: 2067 Broadway New York NY 10023-2806

RONSTADT, LINDA MARIE, singer; b. Tucson, July 15, 1946; d. Gilbert and Ruthmary (Copeman) R. Rec. artist numerous albums including Evergreen 1967, Evergreen Vol. 2, 1967, Linda Ronstadt, The Stone Poneys and Friends, Vol. 3, 1968, Hand Sown, Home Grown, 1969, Silk Purse, 1970, Linda Ronstadt, 1972, Don't Cry Now, 1973, Heart Like a Wheel, 1974, Different Drum, 1974, Prisoner In Disguise, 1975, Hasten Down the Wind, 1976, Greatest Hits, 1976, Simple Dreams, Blue Bayou, 1977, Living in the U.S.A., 1978, Mad Love, Greatest Hits Vol. II, 1980, Get Closer, 1982, What's New, 1983, Lush Life, 1984, For Sentimental Reasons, 1986, Trio (with Dolly Parton, Emmylou Harris), 1986, 'Round Midnight, 1987, Canciones de Mi Padre, 1987, Cry Like a Rainstorm-Howl Like the Wind, 1989, Mas Canciones, 1991, Frenesi, 1992, Winter Light, 1993, Feels Like Home, 1995, Dedicated to the One I Love, 1996; starred in Broadway prodn. of Pirates of Penzance, 1981, also in film, 1983, off Broadway as Mimi in La Boheme, 1984. Recipient Am. Music awards, 1978, 79, Grammy awards, 1975, 76, 87 (with Emmylou Harris and Dolly Parton), 1988, 89 (with Aaron Neville), 1990 (with Aaron Neville, 1992 (2), 1996, Acad. Country Music award, 1987, 88. Office: care Peter Asher Mgmt Inc 644 N Doheny Dr West Hollywood CA 90069-5526

ROOB, E. MITCHELL, healthcare administrator; b. Oct. 16, 1961; s. Edward and Barbara (Leske) R.; m. Sandy Matthys, Sept. 28, 1985; 1 child, Trey. BA in Polit. Sci. and History, DePauw U., Greencastle, Ind., 1983; MBA, U. Notre Dame, 1989. Field dir. Percy for U.S. Senate, Chgo., 1983-84; asst. to gov. State of Ill., Chgo., 1985-89; cons. Crowe Chizek, Indpls., 1989-92; dir. Dept. Transp., Indpls., 1992-94; pres. Health and Hosp. Corp. Marion County, Indpls., 1994—; bd. dirs. Ind. Health Care, Indpls., 1996—, CIMCO, 1994—. Policy dir. Goldsmith for Gov., Indpls., 1995-96; precinct committeeman Marion County Rep. Party, 1991-93. Named among 40 Under 40, I.B.J., Indpls., 1993, Up and Comers, Modern Healthcare, 1996. Avocations: reading, triathlons. Office: Wishard Meml Hosp 1001 W 10th St Indianapolis IN 46202-2859

ROOB, RICHARD, manufacturing executive; b. 1932. Degree, Hamilton Coll., 1953; JD, Columbia U., 1956. Assoc. Gifford, Woody, Palmer & Serles, N.Y.C., 1956-77; with Benjamin Moore & Co., Montvale, N.J., 1977—, vice chmn. bd., 1982-84, CEO, chmn. bd. dirs., 1984—. Office: Benjamin Moore & Co 51 Chestnut Ridge Rd Montvale NJ 07645-1801*

ROOBOL, NORMAN RICHARD, industrial painting consultant, educator; b. Grand Rapids, Mich., Aug. 19, 1934; s. Pleune and Henrietta (Sietsema) R.; m. Joan Lois Ezinga, Aug. 15, 1957; children—Kerri Linda, Michael Eric, Victoria May, Sara Elizabeth Angelique. B.S., Calvin Coll., 1958; Ph.D. in Organic Chemistry, Mich. State U., 1962. Rsch. chemist Shell Oil Co., Emeryville, Calif., 1962-65; asst. prof. chemistry GMI Engring. Inst., Flint, Mich., 1965-68, assoc. prof., asst. head dept. math., sci., 1968-72, prof., 1972-89; pres. NR Painting Cons. Co., Peachtree City, Ga., 1989—; Rhodes prof. Russelsheim, Fed. Republic of Germany, 1980-81; tchr. short course on paint; cons. on coatings application processes; frequent spkr. on indsl. painting methods to paint soc. meetings; painting advisor, instr. Bombardier of Can., 1988—, Compaq-Asia, Singapore, 1991—, Harley-Davidson, 1992—, Outboard Marine Corp., 1986—, Metagal Comercie e Industria, San Paulo, Brazil, 1996—; adj. prof. Kent (Ohio) State U., 1986—, Okla. State U., 1994—. Author: Painting Problems Solved, 1987, Industrial Painting Principles and Practices, 1991, 2nd edit., 1997; monthly columnist, tech. editor Industrial Finishing jour.; contbr. numerous articles to profl. jours.; patentee in field. Sr. adviser Flint Sci. Fair. Served with Signal Corps, U.S. Army, 1954-56. Johnson fellow, 1957-58; NSF fellow, 1960-62; Dow fellow, 1961-62. Fellow Am. Inst. Chemists; mem. AAUP, Am. Sci. Affiliation, Soc. Mfg. Engrs. (bd. dirs.), Assn. Finishings Proc. (v.p. profl. devel. council), Sigma XI, Alpha Tau Omega, Pi Tau Sigma (chpt. sr. adviser 1979-86). Home and Office: NR Painting Cons Co 507 Haddington Ln Peachtree City GA 30269-3340

ROOD, DAVID S., linguistics educator; b. Albany, N.Y., Sept. 14, 1940; s. J. Henry and Pearl B. (Stanley) R.; m. Juliette A. Victor; 1 child, Jennifer. AB, Cornell U., 1963; MA, U. Calif., Berkeley, 1965; PhD, U. Calif., 1969. Instr. U. Colo., Boulder, 1967-69, asst. prof., 1969-77, assoc. prof., 1977-82, prof., 1982—. Author: Wichita Grammar, 1975, Siouan Languages Archive, 1982; (with others) Beginning Lakhota, 1976; editor Internat. Jour. of Am. Linguistics, 1981—; contbr. numerous articles to profl. jours. NSF grantee, 1972-96, NEH grantee, 1972-96. Mem. Linguistic Soc. Am., Soc. for Study Indigenous Langs. Am., Soc. for Linguistic Anthropology, Tchrs. of English to Speakers Other Langs. Office: U of Colo Dept of Linguistics Campus Box 295 Boulder CO 80309-0295

ROOF, BETTY SAMS, internist; b. Columbia, S.C., Apr. 13, 1926; s. Grover Melton Saunders and Lucinda Wood (Sams) R.; m. Herman Hugh Fudenberg (div.); children: Drew Douglas, Brooks Roberts, David Melton, Hugh Haskell. BS, U. S.C., Columbia, 1944; MD, Duke U., 1949. Diplomate Am. Bd. Internal Medicine, Am. Bd. Endocrinology and Metabolism. Vol. vis. investigator Rockefeller Inst., N.Y.C., 1949-50; intern Presbyn. Hosp., N.Y.C., 1950-51, asst. resident, 1951-53, asst. physician, 1953-55; attending physician Francis Delafield Hosp., N.Y.C., 1954-55; clin. and research fellow dept. medicine Mass. Gen. Hosp., Boston, 1955-56, research fellow dept. pathology, 1957-58; research fellow Harvard U., 1955-56; research assoc. dept. microbiology and pathology Rockefeller Inst., 1958-59; asst. research physician Cancer Research Inst. U. Calif., San Francisco, 1962-63, assoc. research physician, 1967-71, lectr. medicine, 1971-74, assoc. clin. prof., 1974; assoc. prof. medicine Med. U. S.C., 1974-80, prof., 1980—, asst. dean, 1989—. Mem. Library Bd., Mill Valley, Calif., 1965-68; mem. Tamalpais Nursery Sch. Bd., Mill Valley, Calif., 1968. Am. Cancer Soc. trainee, 1953-55; grantee Am. Cancer Soc., USPHS, Koebig Trust Fund; USPHS fellow, 1949-50. Mem. Am. Assn. Cancer Research, Am. Diabetes Assn. (Woman of Valor award 1995), Western Soc. Clin. Research, Endocrine Soc., Internat. Endocrine Soc., Am. Soc. for Bone and Mineral Research, Charleston Med. Soc., ACP, Am. Fedn. Clin. Research, So. Soc. Clin. Investigation, Waring Library Soc., Soc. for Destitute Widows and Children of Dec. Physicians, Pilot Club of Charleston (S.C.) (v.p., 1988-89, pres. 1990-91), Phi Beta Kappa, Alpha Omega Alpha. Contbr. articles to profl. jours. Home: 675 Ft Sumter Dr Charleston SC 29412-4333 Office: Med U SC 171 Ashley Ave Charleston SC 29425-0001

ROOF, ROBERT L., broadcast executive, sales executive; b. Circleville, Ohio, Apr. 15, 1946; s. Roger D. and Doris (Kraft) R.; m. Linda Anderson, Nov. 28, 1969; children: Jennifer, Leslie. BA, Franklin U. Sales, disc jockey Sta. WPKO Radio, Waverly, Ohio, 1969-72, Sta. WSCR Radio, Scranton, Pa., 1972-75; sales Sta. WSPD Radio, Toledo, Ohio, 1975-78; sales Sta. WTVN Radio, Columbus, Ohio, 1978-81, local sales mgr., 1981-83, gen. sales mgr., 1984-87; v.p., gen. mgr. Sta. WDVE Radio, Pitts., 1987-93, pres., gen. mgr., 1993—. Bd. dirs. Southwest PA Jr. Achievement, Pitts., 1994—. Recipient Bronze Leadership award Jr. Achievement, Pitts., 1994. Mem. Columbus Sales Club (pres. 1982), Pitts. Sales Club (pres. 1989), Pitts. Radio Orgn. (pres. 1994). Methodist. Avocations: golf, hunting, Am. history. Home: 916 Summit Dr Wexford PA 15090-7580 Office: Sta WDVE-FM 200 Fleet St Pittsburgh PA 15220-2908

ROOK, JUDITH RAWIE, producer, writer; b. Long Beach, Calif., Jan. 25, 1942; d. Wilmer Ernest and Margaret Jane (Towle) Rawie; m. John Holland, July 11, 1964 (div. Feb. 1978); children: Daryn Kirsten, Dawn Malia; m. Timothy Daniel Rook. BBA, Loyola-Marymount Coll., 1964; BA in Visual Arts and Communications, U. Calif., San Diego, 1978. Producer/writer PBS series Focus, 1980, PBS series Achieving (Emmy award 1982, ACE nominee), dir. IABC, San Francisco, 1982; dir. programming Westinghouse Cable, 1983-85; dir. devel. Embassy/Nelson Home Entertainment, 1985-87; ptnr. Real Magic, 1988-89; ind. prodr.-screenwriter R2 Group, 1989—. Mem. adv. bd. U. Calif.-Irvine Screenwriting/Film Prodn., 1996—; mem. adv. bd. U. Art Mus., 1996-97; co-pres. Contemporary Coun., U. Art Mus., 1996-97; founder L.B. Mus. Art. Mem. Am. Film Inst., Women in Film, Found. Long Beach Mus. Art, Democrat. Episcopalian.

ROOKE, ALLEN DRISCOLL, JR., civil engineer; b. San Antonio, Oct. 5, 1924; s. Allen Driscoll and Jean Edna (Lackner) R.; m. Betty Ruth Whitson, Oct. 17, 1949; children: Victoria Lynn Lewis, Cornelia Ruth. BSCE, Tex. A&M U., 1957; MSCE, Miss. State U., 1980. Registered profl. engr., Miss. Enlisted U.S. Army, 1942, advanced through grades to brig. gen., ret., 1984; rsch. civil engr. U.S. Army Corps Engrs., Vicksburg, Miss., 1958-83; ptnr. F.B. Rooke & Sons, Woodsboro, Tex., 1964—; sr. engr. Sci & Tech. Corp., Vicksburg, Miss., 1984-95; bd. dirs. First Nat. Bank, Woodsboro, 1985—. Author/co-author numerous tech. publs. Mem. Res. Officers Assn. U.S. (dept. pres. 1980-82, svc. award 1980, 84), Assn. of U.S. Army, Ret. Officer's Assn. (chpt. v.p. 1985-86), Soc. Am. Mil. Engrs. (post v.p. 1979). Episcopalian. Club: Army and Navy Vicksburg (pres. 1980, 82). Avocation: chess. Home: PO Box 732 Woodsboro TX 78393-0732

ROOKE, DAVID LEE, retired chemical company executive; b. San Antonio, Tex., May 2, 1923; s. Henry Levi, Jr. and Annie (Davidson) R.; m. Esthermae Litherland, June 2, 1945; children—Eugene, Mark, Paul, Bruce. B.S. in Chem. Engring, Rice Inst., Houston, 1944; postgrad., U. Houston. With Dow Chem., Midland, Mich., 1946-88, v.p. ops., 1977-78; pres. Dow U.S.A., 1978-82; v.p. Dow Chem. Corp., 1978-82, exec. v.p., 1982-83, sr. v.p., 1983-86, sr. cons., 1986-88, ret., 1988, also bd. dirs.; bd. dirs. Dow Corning Corp., James Avery Craftsman, Inc. nat. exec. bd. Boy Scouts Am., 1979-86; bd. dirs. Meth. Mission Home, San Antonio. Served with USNR, 1944-46. Mem. AICE, United Meth. Reporter Found. (Dallas). Methodist.

ROOKLIDGE, WILLIAM CHARLES, lawyer; b. Portland, Oreg., Aug. 10, 1957; s. Chester Herbert and Barbara Kathryn (Dodson) R.; m. Kathryn Elaine Roosa, Aug. 20, 1983; children: Elizabeth Jill, Matthew Joseph. BS, U. Portland, 1979; JD, Lewis & Clark, 1984; LLM, George Washington U., 1985. Bar: Oreg. 1985, U.S. Patent Office 1985, U.S. Ct. Appeals (fed. cir.) 1985, Calif. 1988, U.S. Dist. Ct. (cen. dist.) Calif. 1988, U.S. Ct. Appeals (9th cir.) 1988, U.S. Supreme Ct. 1993, U.S. Dist. Ct. (so. dist.) Calif. 1992, U.S. Dist. Ct. (so. dist.) Calif. 1989. Engr. Tube Forgings Am., Inc., Portland, 1978-82; jud. clk. U.S. Ct. Appeals (fed. cir.), Washington, 1985-87; assoc. Knobbe, Martens, Olson & Bear, Newport Beach, Calif., 1987-89, ptnr., 1990-94; dir. Howard, Rice, Nemerovski, Canady, Falk & Rabkin, Newport Beach, Calif., 1995—. Contbr. articles to profl. jours. Recipient Joseph Rossman Meml. award Patent & Trademark Office Soc., 1988, Gerald Rose Meml. award John Marshall Law Sch., 1993. Mem. ABA (sect. intellectual property law, com. chair 1992-96), Am. Intellectual Property Law Assn. (com. chair 1988-93, dir. 1995—, Robert C. Watson award 198 7), Orange County Patent Law Assn. (bd. dirs. 1990-93, pres. 1994). Republican. Presbyterian. Office: Howard Rice Nemerovski Canady et al 610 Newport Center Dr Ste 450 Newport Beach CA 92660-6435

ROOKS, CHARLES S., foundation administrator; b. Whiteville, N.C., June 29, 1937. BA in English, Wake Forest Coll., 1959; Rockefeller Brothers fellow, Harvard U., 1959-60; MA in Polit. Sci., Duke U., 1964, PhD in Polit. Sci., 1968. Rsch. assoc. Voter Edn. Project, Atlanta, 1969-70, dir. tech. assistance programs, 1970-71, dep. dir., 1971-72; exec. dir. Southeastern Coun. of Founds., Atlanta, 1972-78; dir. mem. svcs. Coun. on Founds., Washington, 1979-80, v.p., 1981-82, acting CEO, 1981-82; exec. dir. Meyer Meml. Trust, Portland, Oreg., 1982—; instr. polit. sci. Duke U., Durham, N.C., 1963, 65-67; asst. prof. of govt. Lake Forest Coll., Ill., 1967-69; asst. prof. polit. sci. Clark Coll., Atlanta, 1969-71; bd. dirs. Pacific Northwest Grantmakers Forum; mem. adv. bd. Neighborhood Partnership Fund (Oreg. Cmty. Found.). Contbr. articles to profl. jours. Home: 2706 SW English Ct Portland OR 97201-1622 Office: Meyer Memorial Trust 1515 SW 5th Ave Ste 500 Portland OR 97201-5450

ROOKS, CHARLES SHELBY, minister; b. Beaufort, N.C., Oct. 19, 1924; s. Shelby A. and Maggie (Hawkins) R.; m. Adrienne Martinez, Aug. 7, 1946; children: Laurence Gaylord, Carol Ann. AB, Va. State U., 1949; MDiv, Union Theol. Sem., 1953; LHD (hon.), Howard U., 1981, Va. State U., 1984, Talladega Coll., 1989; DD (hon.), Coll. Wooster, 1968, Interdenominational Theol. Ctr., 1979, Va. Union U., 1980; LLD (hon.), Dillard U., 1986, Heidelberg Coll., 1990; LittD (hon.), Huston-Tillotson Coll., 1989. Ordained to ministry United Ch. of Christ, 1953. Pastor Shanks Village Ch., Orangeburg, N.Y., 1951-53; pastor Lincoln Meml. Congl. Temple, Washington, 1953-60; assoc. dir. Fund for Theol. Edn., Princeton, N.J., 1960-67, exec. dir., 1967-74; pres. Chgo. Theol. Sem., 1974-84; exec. v.p. United Ch. Bd. for Homeland Ministries, N.Y.C., 1984-92, ret., 1992; mem. exec. bd. dept. ministry Nat. Coun. Chs., 1962-70; chmn. bd. United Ch. of Christ Office of Comm., 1964-81, chmn. com. structure Ctrl. Atlantic Conf., 1962-64; mem. Union Theol Sem. Alumni Coun., 1968-70, Theol. Perspectives Comm. on Nat. Com. Black Churchmen, 1968-74; vis. fellow Episc. Theol. Sem. S.W., Austin, Tex., 1966; lectr. in field., 1960-94. Author: Rainbows and Reality, 1984, The Hopeful Spirit, 1987, Revolution in Zion, 1990; editor: Toward a Better Ministry, 1965; mem. editorial bd. Theology Today, 1966, New Conversations, 1977; contbr. articles to religious jours. Chmn. planning com. Nat. Consultation Negro in Christian Ministry, 1965; trustee Bexley Hall Theol. Sem., Colgate-Rochester Div. Sch., 1968-73, Lancaster Theol. Sem., Pa., 1969-74, Eastern Career Testing Ctr., Lancaster, 1969-74; mem. Princeton Regional Sch. Bd., 1969-70, exec. bd. Nat. Com. Religion and Labor, 1987-91; bd. dirs. The Africa Fund, 1987-91, Wash. Urban League, 1955-60, chmn. housing com., 1956-60; chmn. ednl. adv. com. Chgo. Urban League, 1978-84; pres. Communications Improvement, 1971-81; vice chair Nat. Com. for Full Employment, 1987-91. Served with AUS, 1943-46, PTO. Recipient Elizabeth Taylor Byrd Fund Outstanding Community Service award, 1969. Mem. Va. State U. Nat. Alumni Assn. (pres. 1966-67), Soc. for Study Black Religion (pres. 1970-74, 80-84), Assn. Theol. Schs. (cons. Black ch. studies 1970-71, mem. commn. on accrediting 1976-82, chmn. 1980-82, exec. com. 1982-84, Disting. Svc. medal 1992).

ROOKS, JUDITH PENCE, family planning, maternal health care, midwifery consultant; b. Spokane, Wash., Aug. 18, 1941; d. Lawrence Cyrus and Christine Atrice (Snow) Pence; m. Peter Geoffrey Bourne, Mar. 1972 (div.); m. Charles Stanley Rooks, Sept. 21, 1975; 1 child, Christopher Robert. BS, U. Wash., 1963; MS, Cath. U. Am., 1967; MPH, Johns Hopkins U., 1974. Cert. edpidemiology, nursing, nurse-midwife, mediator. Staff nurse The Clin. Ctr., NIH, Bethesda, Md., 1965; asst. prof. nursing dept. San Jose (Calif.) State Coll., 1967-69; epidemiologist Ctrs. for Disease Control, Atlanta, 1970-72, 74-78; asst. prof. dept. ob-gyn. Oreg. Health Sci. U., Portland, 1978-79; expert Office of the Surgeon Gen., Dept. HHS, Washington, 1979-80; project officer U.S. AID, Washington, 1980-82; prin. investigator Columbia U. Sch. Pub. Health, N.Y.C., 1988-89; cons. Portland, 1982—; mem. tech. adv. com. Family Health Internat., Research Triangle Park, N.C., 1986—; mem. midwifery adv. com. Frontier Nursing Svc., Hyden, Ky., 1997—; mem. com. Inst. of Medicine NAS, Washington, 1983-85; academic faculty cmty.-base nurse-midwifery edn. program Frontier Sch. Midwifery and Family Nursing, Hyden, Ky., 1993-95. Author: Midwifery and Childbirth in America, 1997; co-author: Nurse-Midwifery in America, 1986, Reproductive Risk in Maternity Care and Family Planning Services, 1992; contbr. articles to profl. jours. Mem bd. advisors World Affairs Coun. Oreg., Portland, 1987—; bd. dirs. Planned Parenthood of the Columbia/Willamette, Portland, 1987-90; chm. Ga. Citizens for Hosp. Abortion, Atlanta, 1969-70; assoc. Pacific Coun. on Internat. Policy, 1995—. Mem. APHA (chair com. on women's rights 1982-83, mem. governing coun. 1976-77, 79-82, Martha May Eliot award for svc. to mothers and children 1993), Am. Coll. Nurse-Midwives (life, pres. 1983-85). Avocations: gardening, running, reading, traveling, cooking. Home and Office: 2706 SW English Ct Portland OR 97201-1622

ROOMANN, HUGO, architect; b. Tallinn, Estonia, Mar. 25, 1923; came to U.S., 1951, naturalized, 1957; s. Eduard August and Annette (Kask) R.; m. Raja R. Suursoho, Sept. 15, 1945; children—Katrin-Kaja, Linda-Anu. B.S., Inst. Tech. Carolo Wilhelmina, Braunschweig, W. Ger., 1950; M.F.A. in Arch. (scholar 1956-57), Princeton U., 1957. Archtl. engr. Austin Co., Roselle, N.J., 1951-54; archtl. designer Epple & Seaman, Newark, 1954-55, 57-61; propr. Hugo Roomann, Cranford and Elizabeth, N.J., 1961-66; partner A.M. Kinney Assocs. (Architects and Engrs.), Cin., N.Y.C. and Chgo., 1966-89; dir. architecture, v.p. corp. ops. A.M. Kinney, Inc., Cin., 1967, 77, 89; dir. Walter Kidde Constructors, Inc., 1973, A.M. Kinney, Inc., A.M. Kinney Assocs. Inc., Chgo.; pres. Design Art Corp., 1986. Prin. works include Grad. Rsch. Ctr. for Biol. Scis., Ohio State U., 1970, Lloyd Libr., Cin., 1968, offices, labs. and mfg. facilities, Miles Labs., West Haven, Conn., 1969, Am. Mus. Atomic Energy, Oak Ridge, 1975, Renton K. Brodie Sci. Ctr., U. Cin., 1970, EPA Nat. Labs., Cin., 1975, NALCO Tech. Ctr., Naperville, Ill., 1979, Brown & Williamson Corp. Hdqrs., Louisville, 1983, U. Cin. Kettering Lab., 1989. Pres. Citizens League, Elizabeth, N.J., 1966, Estonian Heritage Assn. Cin., 1991-94; bd. dirs., pres. Inter-Ethnic Coun. of Greater Cin., 1992-95. Recipient Top Ten Plant award Factory mag., 1967, Top Ten Plant award Modern Mfg. mag., 1970. Mem. AIA (Ohio chpt. award for Renton K. Brodie Sci. Ctr. 1971, for NALCO Ctr. 1980), Soc. Archtl. Historians, Princeton Club. Lutheran. Office: 2856 Observatory Ave Cincinnati OH 45208-2340

ROOMBERG, LILA GOLDSTEIN, lawyer; b. Bklyn., Oct. 21, 1929; d. William H. and Mary (Abramowitz) Goldstein; m. Lawrence A. Simon (div. 1965); 1 child, Virginia Simon Feil; m. Gerald Armon Roomberg (dec. 1995). BA, NYU, 1949, JD, 1951. Bar: N.Y. 1952, Pa. 1963. Assoc. Ballard, Spahr, Andrews & Ingersoll, Phila., 1959-71, ptnr., 1971-91, of counsel, 1992—. Mem. ABA, Pa. Bar Assn., Phila. Bar Assn., Phila. Bar Found. (sec. 1984-87, trustee 1981-87). Home: 120 Spruce St Philadelphia PA 19106-4315 Office: Ballard Spahr Andrews & Ingersoll 1735 Market St Philadelphia PA 19103-7501

ROONEY, ANDREW AITKEN, writer, columnist; b. Albany, N.Y., Jan. 14, 1919; s. Walter S. and Ellinor (Reynolds) R.; m. Marguerite Howard, Mar. 21, 1942; children: Ellen, Martha, Emily, Brian. Student, Colgate U., 1942. Writer-producer CBS-TV News, 1959—; newspaper columnist Tribune Co. Syndicate, 1979—. Author: (with O.C. Hutton) Air Gunner, 1944, The Story of Stars and Stripes, 1946, Conquerors' Peace, 1947, The Fortunes of War, 1962, A Few Minutes with Andy Rooney, 1981, And More By Andy Rooney, 1982, Pieces of My Mind, 1984, Word for Word, 1986, Not That You Asked, 1989, Sweet and Sour, 1992, My War, 1995; TV programs include An Essay on War, Mr. Rooney Goes to Washington, Mr. Rooney Goes to Dinner; regular commentator-essayist: 60 Minutes, 1978—. Served with AUS, 1941-45. Decorated Air medal, Bronze Star.; recipient awards for best written TV documentary Writers Guild Am., 1966, 68, 71, 75, 76, Emmy awards, 1968, 78, 81, 82. Office: CBS News/60 Minutes 524 W 57th St New York NY 10019-2902

ROONEY, DANIEL M., professional football team executive; b. 1932; s. Arthur Joseph and Kathleen (McNulty) R. Former salesman advt., editor Pitts. Steelers Program; now pres. Pitts. Steelers; mem. exec. coms. NFL. Office: Three Rivers Stadium 300 Stadium Cir Pittsburgh PA 15212-5729*

ROONEY, GAIL SCHIELDS, college administrator; b. St. Francis, Kans., Feb. 15, 1947; d. Fred Harlan and Darlene Mary (Saint) Schields; m. Thomas Michael Rooney, June 27, 1970; children: Shane Michael, Shauna Meghan. BA, U. Colo., 1969; MS, George Williams Coll., 1974; PhD, U. Ill., 1982. Asst. dir. Spl. Svcs. Program Cleve. State U., 1970-71; admissions counselor George Williams Coll., Downers Grove, Ill., 1972-73; coord. of career exploration ctr. Women's Programs Cuyahoga Community Coll., Cleve., 1973-76; vis. asst. prof. Sch. Clin. Medicine U. Ill., Champaign, 1981-82; counselor, instr. Cuyahoga Community Coll., Cleve., 1982-84, dir. counseling, career and psychol. svcs., 1984-85; dir. career, counseling and health svcs. Briar Cliff Coll., Sioux City, Iowa, 1985-88, v.p. for student devel., 1988-95, ednl. cons. and adj. faculty, 1996—; mem. faculty psychology Mesa (Ariz.) C.C., 1995; adj. instr. counselor edn. Wayne (Nebr.) State Coll., 1988, 96; adj. grad. faculty U. S.D., 1996; program presenter Myers Briggs Type Indicator, Sioux City, 1986—. Bd. dirs. Gordon Chem. Dependency Ctr., Sioux City, 1986-89, St. Luke's Gordon Recovery Ctr., Sioux City, 1991-95. Mem. ACA, Am. Coll. Pers. Assn., Nat. Assn. Student Pers. Adminstrs. Home: 52 Red Bridge Dr Sioux City IA 51104-1061

ROONEY, GEORGE WILLARD, lawyer; b. Appleton, Wis., Nov. 16, 1915; s. Francis John and Margaret Ellen (O'Connell) R.; m. Doris I. Maxon, Sept. 20, 1941; children: Catherine Ann, Thomas Dudley, George Willard. BS, U. Wis., 1938; JD, Ohio State U., 1948. Bar: Ohio 1949, U.S. Supreme Ct. 1956, U.S. Ct. Appeals 1956. Assoc. Wise, Roetzel, Maxon, Kelly & Andress, Akron, Ohio, 1949-54; ptnr. Roetzel & Andress, and predecessor, Akron, 1954—; dir. Duracote Corp. Nat. bd. govs. ARC, 1972-78; trustee, mem. exec. bd. Summit County chpt. ARC, 1968, 1975—; v.p. Akron coun. Boy Scouts Am., 1975—; pres. Akron Automobile Assn., 1980-83, trustee, 1983—; chmn. bd. Akron Gen. Med. Ctr., 1981-86, trustee, mem. exec. com., 1986—; trustee Mobile Meals Found., Bluecoats, Inc. Maj. USAAF, 1942-46. Decorated D.F.C. with 2 oak leaf clusters, Air medal with 3 oak leaf clusters; recipient Disting. Community Svc. award Akron Labor Coun.; Disting. Svc. award Summit County chpt. ARC, 1978. Mem. ABA, Ohio Bar Assn. Akron Bar Assn. Am. Judicature Soc., Rotary (past pres.), Portage Country Club (past pres.), Cascade Club (past chmn., bd. govs.), KC. Republican. Roman Catholic. Avocations: golf, travel, gardening. Home: 2863 Walnut Ridge Rd Akron OH 44333-2262 Office: Roetzel & Andress 75 E Market St Akron OH 44308-2010

ROONEY, JOHN PHILIP, law educator; b. Evanston, Ill., May 1, 1932; s. John McCaffery and Bernadette Marie (O'Brien) R.; m. Jean Marie Kliss, Feb. 16, 1974 (div. Oct. 1988); 1 child, Caitlin Mairin. BA, U. Ill, 1953; JD, Harvard U., 1958. Bar: Ill. 1958, Calif. 1961, Mich. 1975, U.S. Tax Ct. 1973. Assoc. lawyer Chapman & Cutler, Chgo., 1958-60, Wilson, Morton, San Mateo, Calif., 1961-63; pvt. practice San Francisco, 1963-74; prof. law Cooley Law Sch., Lansing, Mich., 1975—. Author: Selected Cases (Property), 1985; contbr. articles to profl. jours. Pres. San Francisco coun. Dem. Clubs, 1970. 1st lt. U.S. Army, 1953-55. Recipient Beattie Teaching award Cooley Law Sch. Grads., 1979, 90, 92. Mem. ABA (real estate fed. tax problems com. 1986—, title ins. com.), Mich. Bar Title Stds. Com., Ingham County Bar Assn., Univ. Club. Democrat. Unitarian. Office: Cooley Law Sch 217 S Capitol Ave Lansing MI 48933-1503

ROONEY, KEVIN DAVITT, lawyer; b. Springfield, Mass., June 23, 1944; s. Davitt Michael and Elizabeth Isabel (Wlodyka) R.; m. Annette Eloise Benevento, Nov. 11, 1972; children: Kathryn Denise, Mary Elizabeth. B.A., St. Marys Coll., 1966; J.D., George Washington U., 1975. Bar: Va. 1975, D.C. 1977. Computer systems analyst VA, Washington, 1967-68, 70-73; chief legal programs and budget Dept. Justice, Washington, 1973-77, exec. asst. to assoc. atty. gen., 1977, asst. atty. gen. for adminstrn., 1977-84; prin. Rooney & Assocs, Washington, 1984-87, 90-94, Rooney & Barry, Washington, 1987-89; assoc. dir. Exec. Office for Immigration Rev., U.S. Dept. Justice, Falls Church, Va., 1995-97; asst. dir. Fed. Bur. Prisons, U.S. Dept. Justice, Washington, 1997—; bd. dirs., v.p. Joint Action in Cmty. Svcs., Inc., Washington, 1988-94. Served with U.S. Army, 1968-70. Mem. ASPA, Fed. Bar Assn., Va. Bar Assn., D.C. Bar Assn. Office: US Dept Justice Bur Prisons 500 1st St NW Washington DC 20001-2025

ROONEY, MARIA DEWING, photographer; b. N.Y.C., July 25, 1949; d. Madeleine L'Engle (Camp) Franklin; m. John Bryon Rooney, Jan. 21, 1984; children: Bryson, Alexander. BFA, Phila. Coll. Art, 1971. Tchr. photography Bishop Bright Grammar Sch., Leamington Spa, Eng., Mid-Warwickshire Sch. of Further Edn., Leamington Spa, 1976-80; photographer, owner The Studios, Shipston-on-Stour, Eng., 1977-80; photographer Gary Studios & Comini Studios, Dallas, 1980-83; owner, photographer studio, Essex, Conn., 1990—. Exhbns. include Warwick (Eng.) Gallery, Derby (Eng.) Coll. Art Gallery, Bath (Eng.) Place Cmty. Ctr., Midland Group Gallery, Nottingham, Eng., Wimbledon Sch. Art, London, Warwich U. Arts Ctr., Birmingham, Eng., Essex Art Assn.; photographer (book) Anytime Prayers, 1994, (book) Mothers and Daughters, 1997; photographs published in Co-Optic Publs., London, 1976-80. Mem. Child and Family Svcs. Mem. AAUW, Essex Art Assn. Avocation: sailing. Home and Office: 48 N Main St PO Box 340 Essex CT 06426

ROONEY, MATTHEW A., lawyer; b. Jersey City, May 19, 1949; s. Charles John and Eileen (Dunphy) R.; m. Jean M. Alletag, June 20, 1973 (div. Dec. 1979); 1 child, Jessica Margaret; m. Diane S. Kaplan, July 6, 1981; children: Kathryn Olivia, S. Benjamin. AB magna cum laude, Georgetown U., 1971; JD with honors, U. Chgo., 1974. Bar: Ill. 1975, U.S. Dist. Ct. (no. dist.) Ill. 1975, U.S. Ct. Appeals (7th cir.). 1990. Law clk. to cir. judge U.S. Ct. Appeals (7th cir.), Chgo., 1974-75; assoc. Mayer, Brown & Platt, Chgo., 1975-80, ptnr., 1981—. Assoc. editor U. Chgo. Law Rev., 1973. Mem. ABA, 7th Cir. Bar Assn., Order of Coif, Phi Beta Kappa. Democrat.

Roman Catholic. Avocations: jogging, golfing. Home: 2718 Sheridan Rd Evanston IL 60201-1754 Office: Mayer Brown & Platt 190 S La Salle St Chicago IL 60603-3410

ROONEY, MICKEY (JOE YULE, JR.), actor; b. Bklyn., Sept. 23, 1920; s. Joe and Nell (Carter) Yule; m. Ava Gardner, Jan. 10, 1942 (div. May 1943); m. Betty Jane Rase, Sept. 30, 1944 (div. 1949); children: Mickey Jr., Timothy; m. Martha Vickers, June 3, 1949 (div.); m. Elaine Mahnken (div. 1958); m. Barbara Thomason, Dec. 1958; children: Kerry, Kyle, Kelly Ann, Kimmy Sue; m. Margie Lang, Sept. 1966 (div. 1967); m. Carolyn Hockett, (div.); 1 adopted child, Jimmy, 1 child, Jonell; m. Jan Chamberlin, July 28, 1978; stepchildren: Chris Aber, Mark Aber. Ed. in, Dayton Heights and Vine Street grammar sch., Pacific Mil. Acad., under tutors. First appeared in vaudeville with parents; then appeared with Sid Gould, numerous TV programs; appeared in motion pictures Judge Hardy's Children, Hold That Kiss, Lord Jeff, Love Finds Andy Hardy, Boys Town, Stablemates, Out West With the Hardys, Huckleberry Finn, Andy Hardy Gets Spring Fever, Babes in Arms, Young Tom Edison, Judge Hardy and Son, Andy Hardy Meets Debutante, Strike Up the Band, Andy Hardy's Private Secretary, Men of Boystown, Life Begins for Andy Hardy, Babes on Broadway, A Yank at Eton, The Human Comedy, Andy Hardy's Blonde Trouble, Girl Crazy, Thousands Cheer, National Velvet, Ziegfeld Follies, The Strip, Sound Off, Off Limits, All Ashore, Light Case of Larceny, Drive A Crooked Road, Bridges at Toko-Ri, The Bold and Brave, Eddie, Private Lives of Adam and Eve, Comedian, The Grabbers, St. Joseph Plays the Horses, Breakfast at Tiffany's, Somebody's Waiting, Requiem For A Heavyweight, Richard, Pulp, It's a Mad, Mad, Mad, Mad World, Everything's Ducky, The Secret Invasion, The Extraordinary Seaman, The Comic, The Cockeyed Cowboys of Calico County, Skidoo, B.J. Presents, That's Entertainment, The Domino Principle, Pete's Dragon, The Magic of Lassie, Black Stallion, Arabian Adventure, Erik the Viking, My Heroes Have Always Been Cowboys, 1991, (voice) Little Nimo: Adventures in Slumberland, 1992, Long Road Home, 1996, Kings of the Court, 1997, Animals, 1997; starred in TV prodns. Pinocchio, 1957, Leave 'Em Laughing, 1981, Bill, 1981 (Emmy, Golden Globe), Senior Trip!, 1981, Bill on His Own, 1983, Little Spies (Acad. Hon. award 1982), It Came upon the Midnight Clear, 1984, Bluegrass, 1988, Legend of Wolf Mountain, 1992, That's Entertainment! III, 1994, Revente of the Red Baron, 1994, Radio Star-die AFN-Story, 1994, The Legend of O.B. Taggart, 1995; appeared on stage in Sugar Babies, 1979, The Will Rogers Follies, 1993; appeared in TV series A Year at the Top, The Mickey Rooney Show; author: I.E. An Autobiography, 1965, Life Is Too Short, 1991, Search for Sonny Skies, 1994; fgn. films: Midsummer Nights Dream, 1937, Words and Music, 1946, Rachels, 1973, To Hong Kong with Love, 1975, Oddessy of the Pacific, 1979. With AUS, WWII. Recipient Spl. Acad. Award, 1940, Tony award for best mus. actor, 1980; named One of Top 10 Money-Making Stars, Herald-Fame Poll, 1938-43. Office: PO Box 3186 Thousand Oaks CA 91359-0186*

ROONEY, PAUL C., JR., lawyer; b. Winnetka, Ill., Oct. 23, 1943; s. Paul C. and Mary K. (Brennan) R.; m. Maria Elena Del Canto, Sept. 6, 1980. BA, Harvard U., 1963, LLB, 1966. Bar: Mass. 1968, N.Y. 1972, Fla. 1980, Tex. 1980, U.S. Dist. Ct. (ea. and so. dists.) N.Y., U.S. Ct. Appeals (2d cir.). Ptnr. White & Case, N.Y.C., 1983—. Served to lt. USNR, 1966-69. Mem. ABA, N.Y. State Bar Assn., Fla. Bar Assn., Tex. Bar Assn., Dallas Bar Assn., Univ. Club (N.Y.C.), Harvard Club (N.Y.C.), Mashomack Preserve (N.Y.), Sharon Country Club (Conn.). Home: 417 Park Ave New York NY 10022-4401 also: 11 Lilac Ln Sharon CT 06069-2302 Office: White & Case 1155 Ave Of The Americas New York NY 10036-2711

ROONEY, PAUL GEORGE, mathematics educator; b. N.Y.C., July 14, 1925; s. Geoffrey Daniel and Doris Elizabeth (Babcock) R.; m. Mary Elizabeth Carlisle, June 20, 1950; children: Francis Timothy, Elizabeth Anne, Kathleen Doris, John Edward, James Carlisle. B.Sc., U. Alta., 1949; Ph.D., Calif. Inst. Tech., 1952. Asst. prof. math. U. Alta., 1952-55; asst. prof. U. Toronto, 1955-60, assoc. prof., 1960-62, prof., 1962-91, prof. emeritus, 1991—; dir. Commonwealth Petroleum Co., Calgary, 1946-59. Editor in chief Can. Jour. Math. 1971-75; contbr. articles to profl. jours. Bd. dirs. Francis F. Reeve Found., 1954-85. Served with Can. Army, 1943-45. Fellow Royal Soc. Can.; Mem. Can. Math. Soc. (councillor 1960-64, 66-70, 76-78, v.p. 1979-81, pres. 1981-83), Am. Math. Soc., Math. Assn. Am. Office: U Toronto, Dept Math, Toronto, ON Canada M5S 1A1

ROONEY, PAUL MONROE, former library administrator; b. Buffalo, Apr. 16, 1918; s. John Francis and Marguerite (Cass) R.; m. Elizabeth Dorsey, Jan. 22, 1955; children: James, Thomas. B.S., State Tchrs. Coll., Buffalo, 1938; B.S. in L.S, U. Buffalo, 1940. Br. librarian Buffalo Pub. Library, 1940-42; head reference dept. Grosvenor Library, 1945-59; head tech. dept. Buffalo and Erie County Pub. Library, 1959-61, asst. dep. dir., 1961-63, dep. dir., 1963-75, dir., 1975-83; chmn. N.Y. State Pub. Librarians Certification Com., 1959-60; trustee Western N.Y. Library Resources Council, 1966-83, pres., 1969-70. Served with USAF, 1942-45. Mem. ALA, N.Y. Libr. Assn. Roman Catholic. Home: 522 Ashland Ave Buffalo NY 14222-1307*

ROONEY, WILLIAM RICHARD, magazine editor; b. New Brunswick, N.J., Mar. 12, 1938; s. William Richard and Bernadette (Huether) R.; m. Rita Ann Scherer, July 20, 1963; children: Karen, Kevin, Brian, Kristin. BS in English, St. Peter's Coll., Jersey City, 1959. Asst., then assoc. editor Marine Engring./Log mag., N.Y.C., 1960-64; assoc. editor Outdoor Life mag., N.Y.C., 1964-72, mng. editor, 1972-76, sr. editor, 1976-77; editor articles Sports Afield ann. outdoor mags., 1983-90; editor Am. Forests mag., Washington, 1977-95, v.p. for publs., 1991-95; book editor Safari Press, 1996—; mng. editor Am. Guardian mag., Fairfax, Va., 1997—, Am. Hunter mag., 1997—. Contbr. to: Complete Outdoors Ency, 1972; others. With AUS, 1959-60. Mem. Outdoor Writers Assn. Am. Roman Catholic. Home: 7916 Carrie Ln Manassas VA 20111-2548 Office: 1516 P St NW Washington DC 20005-1910

ROOP, EUGENE FREDERIC, religion educator; b. South Bend, Ind., May 11, 1942; s. G. Frederic and Lois Elizabeth (Berkebile) R.; m. Delora Ann Mishler, Aug. 24, 1963; children: Tanya Marie, Frederic John. BS, Manchester (Ind.) Coll., 1964; MDiv, Bethany Theol. Seminary, Oakbrook, Ill., 1967; PhD, Claremont (Calif.) Grad. Sch., 1972. Asst. prof. Earlham Sch. Religion, Richmond, Ind., 1970-74, assoc. prof., 1975-77; assoc. prof. Bethany Theol. Seminary, 1977-78, prof. Bibl. studies, 1978-86, Wieand prof. Bibl. studies, 1987—; pres. Bethany Theol. Sem., 1992—; dir. Ch. of Brethren Outdoor Ministries Assn., Elgin, Ill., 1982-88; bd. dirs. Ecumenical Ctr. for Stewardship Studies, N.Y.C., 1979-92. Author: Coming Kingdom Teacher's Guide, 1982, Living the Biblical Story, 1979, Commentary on Genesis, 1987, Heard in our Hand, 1990, Let the Rivers Run, 1991. Active sch. bd. adv. com., Villa Park, Ill., 1981-85; bd. dirs. Richmond Symphony Orch., 1994—, Ind. U. East, 1996—. So. Ohio Seminary Consortium summer fellow, 1975, Assn. Theol. Schs. summer fellow, 1974, Sea-Atlantic Fund rsch. fellow, 1978-79. Mem. Soc. Bibl. Lit., Chgo. Soc. Bibl. Rsch., Assn. Case Tchrs. Avocations: photography, travel, tennis. Office: Bethany Theol Seminary 615 National Rd W Richmond IN 47374-4019

ROOP, JAMES JOHN, public relations executive; b. Parkersburg, W.Va., Oct. 29, 1949; s. J. Vaun and Mary Louise (McGinnis) R.; m. Margaret Mary Kuneck (div. 1982); m. Susan Lynn Hoell (div. 1989); m. Daisy P. Billue, 1990. BS in Journalism, W. Va. U., 1971. Various account mgmt. postions Ketchum Pub. Rels., Pitts., 1972-77, v.p., 1977-79; v.p. Burson-Marsteller, Chgo., 1979-81; sr. v.p. Hesselbart & Mitten/Watt, Cleve., 1981-84, exec. v.p., 1984-86, pres., 1986-87; pres. Watt, Roop & Co. (formerly Hesselbart & Mitten/Watt), Cleve., 1987-96; chmn., pres., CEO James J. Roop Co., Cleve., 1996—. Contbr. articles to profl. jours. Bd. dirs. Ctr. for Families and Children. Fellow Pub. Rels. Soc. Am. (chmn. investor rels. sect. 1984-85, chmn. honors and awards com. 1995); mem. Nat. Investor Rels. Inst. (chpt. pres. Cleve./Akron chpt., sr. investor rels. roundtable), Boys Hope, Police Athletic League, Econs. Am., Leadership Cleve., Cleve. Skating Club, Mayfield Country Club. Republican. Home: 2574 Fairmount Blvd Cleveland Heights OH 44106-3241 Office: James J Roop Co 650 Huntington Bldg 925 Euclid Ave Cleveland OH 44115

ROOP, RALPH GOODWIN, retired oil marketing company executive; b. Snowville, Va., June 23, 1915; s. Guy C. and Ora (Goodwin) R.; married; children: Nancie Roop Kennedy, Paterson Roop Webster. BS, Va. Poly. Inst., 1936; MS, Cornell U., 1937. Various positions So. States Corp., Richmond, Va., 1937-66; pres. and/or chmn. bd. Petroleum Marketers, Inc., Richmond, 1954-88, dir., mem. exec. com., 1988—; bd. dirs. Jefferson Nat. Bank, Charlottesville, Va., 1979—. Trustee Va. Wesleyan Coll., Norfolk, 1982—; bd. dirs. Suhor Found., 1988—, Trinity Found., Richmond, Va. Tech. Found., Blacksburg. Named Oil Man of Yr., Va. Petroleum Jobbers Assn., 1983. Mem. Va. Petroleum Council (chmn. 1964-67), Va. Oil Men's Assn. (pres. 1975-76), Am. Petroleum Inst., Richmond C. of C. (past bd. dirs.). Methodist. Avocations: travel, photography, fishing. Home: 2300 Cedarfield Pky Apt 363 Richmond VA 23233

ROORDA, JOHN FRANCIS, JR., business consultant; b. Evanston, Ill., Jan. 16, 1923; s. John Francis and Sadie M. (Daley) R.; m. Elizabeth Mulcahy, July 2, 1949; children: Elizabeth Roorda Barker, John F., Ann Roorda Hollis. B.S. in Chem. Engring, Purdue U., 1943, Ph.D., 1949. With Shell Oil Co., 1949-83; gen. mgr. combined oil products/chem. econs. dept., 1973-74, v.p. planning and econs., 1974-77; v.p. Shell Devel. Co., Houston, 1977-78; v.p. corp. planning Shell Oil Co., 1978-83; pres. John Roorda, 1983—; coordinator Exec. Service Corps, Houston, 1985—. Served to lt. (j.g.) USNR, 1943-46. Recipient Disting. Engring. Alumnus award Purdue U., 1976, Outstanding Chem. Engr. award Purdue U., 1993. Mem. Sigma Xi. Roman Catholic. Office: 2401 Fountainview Suite 910 Houston TX 77057

ROOS, CASPER, actor; b. N.Y.C., Mar. 21, 1925; s. Jacob and Sabina (Uhlenbusch) R.; m. Shirley Anne Nicholson, June 27, 1953; 1 child, Pieter Nicholson. Student, N.Y. Coll. Music. treas. Actors Equity Found., N.Y.C., 1982-88; co-chmn. research subcom. Nat. Theater Com., N.Y.C., 1983—. Prin. actor Shenandoah, N.Y.C., 1975-78, Brigadoon, N.Y.C., 1979-80, My One and Only, N.Y.C., 1982-85, Into the Light, 1986, Man of La Mancha, Zurich, 1988, (Broadway prodn.) Shenandoah Revival, 1989; numerous regional theater prodns. Served with U.S. Mcht. Marines, 1943-46. Mem. Actors Equity (treas. 1982-88, councilor 1964-79, 88-93). Home: PO Box 11 Gilbertsville NY 13776-0011 *Don Quixote wanted to 'add a little grace to the world.' I, too, would like to add a 'little' to this world, whether it be grace or laughter or tears to an audience or service to my colleagues. If, like Don Quixote, I look a little foolish, so be it. I prefer a life of striving for the ultimate to the easier smug acceptance of the status quo.*

ROOS, DANIEL, civil engineering educator; b. Bklyn., Apr. 12, 1939; s. Sigmund and Anita (Sperling) R.; m. Eva Bonis, June 1, 1969; children—Richard Joseph, Linda Suzanne. B.S. in Civil Engring, M.I.T., 1961, M.S., 1963, Ph.D., 1966. Mem. faculty MIT, Cambridge, 1963—, assoc. prof. civil engring., 1970-76, prof., 1976—, head transp. systems div., 1977-78, dir. Ctr. for Transp. Studies, 1978-85, dir. Ctr. Tech., Policy and Indsl. Devel., 1985—, Japan Steel Industry prof., 1985—; mem. Commn. on Indsl. Productivity MIT, 1987-89; founder, dir. Multisystems Inc., Cambridge, 1965-85; chmn. com. to assess advanced vehicle and hwy. techs., NRC, 1990-91; mem. com. on fuel economy NRC, 1991-92; dir. Internat. Motor Vehicle Program, 1980—; co-dir. Lean Aircraft Initiative, 1992—, coun. indsl. relationships MIT, 1996—. Author: ICES System Design, 1964; The Future of the Automobile, 1984, Auto Futures, 1990; co-author: Made in America, 1989, The Machine That Changed the World, 1990; contbr. articles to profl. jours. Mem. U.S. Task Force on Transp., 1969. Recipient Shingo Prize for Excellence in Mfg. Rsch., 1994. Mem. ASCE (Frank M. Masters Transp. Engring. award 1989), Assn. Computing Machinery, Ops. Research Soc. (treas. transp. sci. sect. 1970-71), Transp. Research Bd. (chmn. para-transit com. 1974-80, group coun. 1980-84), Coun. Univ. Transp. Ctrs. (pres. 1983). Developer Dial-A-Ride transp. concept, 1965; dir. Internat. Motor Vehicle. Home: 28 Baskin Rd Lexington MA 02173-6929 Office: MIT Ctr Tech Policy & Indsl Devel 77 Massachusetts Ave Cambridge MA 02139-4301

ROOS, ERIC EUGENE, plant physiologist; b. Charleroi, Pa., May 23, 1941; s. Carl F. and Isabelle (McPherson) R.; m. Lois Bonita Bruno, Aug. 24, 1964; children: Michael, Erin. BS, Waynesburg Coll., 1963; PhD, W.Va. U., 1967. Supr. plant physiologist, rsch. leader Nat. Seed Storage Lab, Agrl. Research Service of USDA, Ft. Collins, Colo., 1967—. Fellow Am. Soc. Agronomy, Am. Soc. Hort. Sci., Crop Sci. Soc. Am.; mem. Sigma Xi, Gamma Sigma Delta. Office: USDA Agrl Research Service 1111 S Mason St Fort Collins CO 80521-4500

ROOS, JOSEPH CHARLES, III, publisher, pastor; b. Kansas City, Mo., July 19, 1946; s. Joseph Charles and Juanita (Ladage) R. BS in Physics, U. Mo., Kansas City, 1968; MS in Atmospheric Sci., U. Mo., Columbia, 1970. Pub. Sojourners Mag., Washington, 1971—; bd. dirs. Assoc. Ch. Press, Phoenix, 1989—, pres., 1995—. Field organizer McGovern forPres., Chgo., 1992; bd. dirs. Evangs. for Social Action, Phila., 1983-86, vice-chmn., 1985-86. Avocations: astronomy, meteorology. Home: 1208 Fairmont St NW Washington DC 20009 Office: Sojourners 2401 15th St NW Washington DC 20009-4101

ROOS, NESTOR ROBERT, consultant; b. St. Louis, Aug. 19, 1925; s. Maurice and Fannie (Friedman) R.; m. Fay Weil, July 8, 1951; children: Marilyn Roos Hall, Eileen Roos Ruddell, Robert F. BBA, Washington U., St. Louis, 1948; MSBA, Washington U., 1949; D of Bus. Adminstrn., Ind. U., 1959. Instr. bus. La. State U., Baton Rouge, 1949-51; teaching fellow Ind. U., Bloomington, 1951-53; asst. prof. Ga. State U., Atlanta, 1953-55; prof. U. Ariz., Tucson, 1955-86, prof. emeritus, 1986; pres. Risk Mgmt. Pub. Co., Tucson, 1976-90, cons. editor, 1990—; cons., expert witness in field; bd. dirs. Blue Cross-Blue Shield Ariz., sec., 1993-95, vice chair, 1995—; mem. Ins. Dirs. Adv. Com., Phoenix, 1987—, Reverse Mortgage Adv. Com., Tucson, 1988-90. Author: (with others) Multiple Line Insurers, 1970, Governmental Risk Management Manual, 1976, Industrial Accident Prevention, 1980. Bd. dirs. Handmaker Geriatric Ctr., Tucson, 1987-92; pres. Temple Emanu-El, Tucson, 1981-83. With U.S. Army, 1943-45, ETO. Grantee Nat. Inst. Occupational Safety and Health, 1975. Mem. Risk and Ins. Mgmt. Soc., Western Risk and Ins. Assn. (pres. 1972-73), Public Risk and Ins. Mgmt. Assn. (dir. edn. and tng. 1982-89). Democrat. Jewish. Avocations: gardening, golf. Home: 7311 E Camino De Cima Tucson AZ 85715-2212 Office: Risk Mgmt Pub Co 2030 E Broadway Blvd Ste 106 Tucson AZ 85719-5908

ROOS, THOMAS BLOOM, biological scientist, educator; b. Peoria, Ill., Mar. 19, 1930; s. Seymour G. and Clara Gertrude (Bloom) R.; m. Marilyn A. Siker, June 14, 1953; children: David S., Sara D. AB, Harvard U., 1951; MS, U. Wis., 1953, PhD, 1960; MA (hon.), Dartmouth Coll., 1971. Instr. U. Wis., Madison, 1959-60; instr. Dartmouth Coll., Hanover, N.H., 1960-61, asst. prof., 1961-66, assoc. prof., 1966-71, prof., 1971—; vis. prof. St. George's Med. Sch., London, 1973-75; Fulbright lectr. U. Delhi, U. Calcutta, Bhabha Atomic Rsch. Centre, Coun. Indsl. and Sci. Rsch. Labs., Calcutta, Hyderabad; vis. scientist Harvard Med. Sch., 1988; cons. Commn. on Undergrad. Edn. in Biol. Scis., Washington, 1967-71, St. George's Med. Sch., 1974—, CSP, Inc., Billerica, Mass., 1986—. Inventor Master Scan Image Analyzing Computer. Mem. Dem. Town Com., Hanover, N.H., 1961-68. With U.S. Army, 1954-56. Spl. postdoctoral fellow NIH, Leyden, Netherlands, 1965-66; hon. fellow Univ. Coll., London, 1972-73. Mem. AAAS, Am. Soc. Zoologists. Club: Faculty (Hanover, N.H.) (pres. 1981-85). Avocations: music, computer programming, poetry. Home: 19 Rayton Rd Hanover NH 03755-2211 Office: Dartmouth Coll Dept Of Biology Hanover NH 03755

ROOSEVELT, EDITH KERMIT, journalist; b. N.Y.C., Dec. 19, 1927; d. Archibald Bulloch and Grace Stackpole (Lockwood) R. Grad., Barnard Coll., 1948. Reporter UPI, San Francisco, L.A., 1951-53, Siskiyou Daily News, 1953, UPI, Washington, 1953-55; writer McCann Erickson Co., N.Y.C., 1956-57; assoc. editor Spadea Syndicate, N.Y.C., 1957-59; reporter, feature writer Newark Star Ledger, 1959-63; syndicated columnist numerous newspapers, 1963-80; Washington editor, corr. Nutrition & Health Review, 1980—; lectr. in field. Contbr. numerous articles to profl. jours. Recipient J.C. Meriam, Ervin S. Cobb & Rupert Hughes award of merit Am. Acad. Pub. Affairs. Address: 1661 Crescent Pl NW Washington DC 20009-4048

ROOSEVELT, THEODORE, IV, investment banker; b. Jacksonville, Fla., Nov. 27, 1942; s. Theodore III and Anne Mason (Babcock) R.; m. Constance Lane Rogers, Aug. 1, 1970; 1 child, Theodore Roosevelt V. AB, Harvard U., 1965, MBA, 1972. Assoc. Lehman Bros., N.Y.C., 1972-76; corp. v.p. Lehman Bros. Kuhn Loeb, N.Y.C., 1976-82; sr. v.p. Lehman Comml. Paper Inc., N.Y.C., 1982-85; mng. dir. Lehman Brothers (formerly Shearson Lehman Bros., Inc.), N.Y.C., 1985—; bd. dirs. Lehman Bros. Fin. Products, Inc.; publ. bd. World Policy Jour. Bd. dirs. Trout Unltd., League of Conservation Voters; trustee of the Reservations, Mass.; mem. chmn.'s coun. Nat. Resource Def. Counsel, N.Y.C.; mem. N.Y. State Park Recreation and Hist. Preservation Commn. for City of N.Y.; trustee Am. Mus. Natural History. Mem. Coun. Fgn. Rels., Fgn. Policy Assn. (gov.), The Links (N.Y.C.), The Heights Casino Club (Bklyn.), Explorers Club, Harvard Club (N.Y.C.). Republican. Home: 1 Pierrepont St Brooklyn NY 11201-3361 Office: Lehman Brothers 3 World Fin Ctr New York NY 10285-1900

ROOT, ALAN CHARLES, diversified manufacturing company executive; b. Essex, Eng., Apr. 11, 1925; came to U.S., 1951, naturalized, 1959; s. Charles Stanley and Lillian (Collins) R. B.A., Oxford U., 1943; M.A., Cambridge U., 1951; M.B.A., Stanford U., 1953. Rsch. analyst Dow Chem. Co., Midland, Mich., 1954-55; mgr. mktg. rsch. Gen. Electric Co., 1955-61; v.p. bus. planning Mosler Safe Co., Hamilton, Ohio, 1961-70; v.p. corp. planning Am. Standard Inc., N.Y.C., 1970-76, sr. v.p. ops. svcs., 1976-86, sr. v.p., 1986-88, sr. advisor, 1989; trustee 1995 Trust Fund; sr. advisor Unit Ice, 1995—; bd. dirs. Am.-Standard Energy Inc., Amstan Trucking Inc., 1976-86. Bd. dirs., chmn. Brit. Schs. and Univs. Found.; trustee, treas. N.J. Chamber Music Soc., 1988-95. Served to capt. AUS, 1944-48. Admission to Order of St. John of Jerusalem sanctioned by Her Majesty Queen Elizabeth II, 1986, comdr., 1994. Mem. AIChE (assoc. producer TV series Midland sect. 1955), Pilgrims U.S., NEwcomen Soc. N.Am., Univ. Club (N.Y.C.), Order of St. John of Jerusalem (comdr. 1994). Home: 4934 Mount Pleasant Ln Las Vegas NV 89113-0114 *Good luck meant that my industrial career drew on the education I enjoyed as a young man. Professional advancement came by building on prior experience at each step and through long-term, managerial continuity.*

ROOT, ALLEN WILLIAM, pediatrician, educator; b. Phila., Sept. 24, 1933; s. Morris Jacob and Priscilla R.; m. Janet Greenberg, June 15, 1958; children: Jonathan, Jennifer, Michael. AB, Dartmouth Coll., 1955, postgrad. Med. Sch., 1954-56; MD, Harvard U., 1958. Diplomate Am. Bd. Pediatrics (mem. bd. 1986—), Am. Pediatric Endocrinology (mem. bd. 1985-90, chmn. 1990). Intern Strong Meml. Hosp., Rochester, N.Y., 1958-60; resident in pediatrics Hosp. U. Pa., Phila., 1960-62; fellow in pediatric endocrinology Children's Hosp. of Phila., 1962-65; assoc. physician in pediatrics U. Pa. Sch. Medicine, 1964-66, asst. prof. pediatrics, 1966-69; assoc. prof. pediatrics Temple U. Sch. Medicine, Phila., 1969-73; prof. Temple U. Sch. Medicine, 1973; asst. physician in endocrinology Children's Hosp. Phila., 1965-69; chmn. divsn. pediatrics Albert Einstein Med. Center., Phila., 1969-73; prof. pediatrics U. South Fla. Coll. Medicine, Tampa, 1973—, prof. biochemistry, 1987—, assoc. chmn. dept. pediatrics, 1974—, dir. sect. pediatric endocrinology, 1973-96; dir. univ. tchg. svcs. All Children's Hosp., St. Petersburg, 1973-89; mem. Fla. Infant Screening Adv. Coun., 1979—, chmn., 1994—; mem. Hillsborough County Thyroid Adv. Com., 1980; mem. med. adv. com. Nat. Pituitary Agy., 1974-78, mem. growth hormone subcom., 1972-79, 81-85. Author: Human Pituitary Growth Hormone, 1972; editor: (with C. La Cauza) Problems in Pediatric Endocrinology, 1980; mem. editl. bd. Jour. Pediats., 1973-81, Jour. Adolescent Health Care, 1979-95, Jour. Pediat. Endocrinology and Metabolism, 1985—, Jour. Clin. Endocrinology and Metabolism, 1993-96, Growth, Genetics and Hormones, 1993—, Pediats. in Rev., 1995—; assoc. editor Adolescent and Pediat. Gynecology, 1992—. USPHS grantee; Birth Defects Found. grantee. Mem. AAAS, Am. Pediatric Soc., Soc. Pediatric Rsch., Lawson Wilkins Pediatric Endocrine Soc. (treas. 1979-88, pres. 1988-89), Endocrine Soc., Am. Acad. Pediatrics, Am. Fedn. Clin. Rsch., Soc. Exptl. Biology and Medicine, Soc. Nuclear Medicine, N.Y. Acad. Scis., Phila. Coll. Physicians, Phila. Endocrine Soc. (bd. dirs. 1971-72, treas. 1973), Dartmouth Coll. Alumni Coun., Dartmouth Club. Office: 801 6th St S Saint Petersburg FL 33701-4816

ROOT, DORIS SMILEY, portrait artist; b. Ann Arbor, Mich., June 28, 1924; d. George O. and Hazel (Smith) Smiley. Student, Art Inst. of Chgo., 1943-45, N.Y. Sch. Design, 1976-77, Calif. Art Inst., 1984-85. Creative dir. All May Co.'s, L.A., 1962-63; advt. sales pro. dir. Seibu, L.A., 1963-64; v.p. Walgers & Assoc., L.A., 1964-70; owner, designer At The Root of Things, L.A., 1970-73; adv. sales pro. dir. Hs. of Nine, L.A., 1973-74; asst. designer MGM Grand, Reno, Nev., 1974-76; designer, office mgr. Von Hausen Studio, L.A., 1976-82; ABC libr. ABC/Cap Cities, L.A., 1982-89; portrait artist (also known as Dorian), AKA Dorian, art studio, L.A., 1982—. One-man shows include Cookeville, Tenn., 1989, Beverly Hills, Calif., 1991; artist in residence, Cookeville, 1989-90. Republican. Presbyterian. Avocations: painting, golf. *I'm one of the luckiest women alive. I love fun and found a little of it the best space to create in, in my career and in my personal life. People feel free to try things in a fun place to work. And I must admit, I'm still having fun with painting people's portraits!.*

ROOT, EDWARD LAKIN, education educator, university administrator; b. Cumberland, Md., Dec. 5, 1940; s. Lakin and Edna Grace (Adams) R. BS, Frostburg (Md.) State Coll., 1962, MEd, 1966; EdD, U. Md., 1970. Cert. tchr., Md. Tchr. Allegany County Bd. of Edn., Cumberland, 1962-66; grad. fellow U. Md., College Park, 1966-67, fellow, 1967-69; with Frostburg State U., 1969—, prof., head edn. dept., 1980-87, dean, 1987-95, prof., head MEd. adminstrn., 1995—; mem. Profl. Standards Bd. Md., Balt., 1980-87, 95—, Cert. Rev. Bd. Md., Balt., 1987-90, Md. Task Force Adminstrn., Balt., 1985-88, Md. Task Force: Essentials in Tchr. Edn., 1995, Md. Task Force: Prisoners of Time and Response; task force tchr. assessment, 1995—. Mem. Allegany County (Md.) Planning and Zoning Bd. Appeals, 1995-96. Mem. ASCD, Nat. Assn. Secondary Sch. Prins., Nat. Soc. for the Study of Edn., Mensa, Elks, Shriners, Masons, Phi Delta Kappa. Democrat. Methodist. Avocation: photography. Home: 100 Pennsylvania Ave Cumberland MD 21502-4236 Office: Frostburg State U College Ave Frostburg MD 21532-1724

ROOT, FRANKLIN RUSSELL, business educator; b. Hartford, Conn., Jan. 30, 1923; s. Albert Edward and Marie Rose (Benard) R.; m. Liliane Anny Weissbrod, Feb. 2, 1951 (dec. 1975); children: Michele, Peter, Valerie, Allan, Jonathan; m. Joyce Elinor Halfen, Aug. 1, 1976. BS, Trinity Coll., 1947; MBA, Wharton Sch., 1948; PhD, U. Pa., 1951. Instr. Wharton Sch. U. Pa., Phila., 1948-50; from assoc. to full prof. bus. Wharton Sch. U. Pa., 1956-93; asst. prof. U. md., College Park, 1951-55; rsch. economist UN, N.Y.C., summer 1949, 50; Fulbright prof. Copenhagen Sch. Econs. and Bus. Adminstrn., Denmark, 1963-64; prof. Naval War Coll., Newport, R.I., 1967-68; regional adv. UN, Santiago, Chile, 1970. Author: Strategic Planning for Export Marketing, 1964, International Trade and Investment, 1959, rev. edit., 1994, Entry Strategies for International Markets, 1982, rev. edit., 1994, International Strategic Management, 1992; contbr. articles to profl. jours. Cpl. AUS, 1943-46. Fellow Acad. Internat. Bus. (pres. 1981-83); mem. Internat. Trade and Fin. Assn. (pres. 1991), Phi Beta Kappa. Independent. Unitarian. Avocations: carpentry, swimming. Office: U Pa Wharton Sch Philadelphia PA 19104

ROOT, GERALD EDWARD, courts resource manager; b. Gridley, Calif., May 5, 1948; s. Loris Leo Root and Mary Helen (Wheeler) Murrell; m. Tricia Ann Caywood, Feb. 13, 1981; children: Jason Alexander, Melinda Ann. AA in Bus., Yuba C.C., Marysville, Calif., 1968; BA in Psychology, Calif. State U., Sonoma, 1974; MA in Social Sci., Calif. State U., Chico, 1977; EdD candidate orgn. and leadership, U. San Francisco, 1997. Gen. mgr. Do-It Leisure Therapeutic Recreation, Chico, 1977-79; CETA projects coord. City of Chico, 1980-81; exec. dir. Voluntary Action Ctr., Inc., South Lake Tahoe, Calif., 1981-83; devel. dir. Work Tng. Ctr., Inc., Chico, 1983-92; exec. dir. North Valley Rehab. Found., Chico, 1986-92; resource adminstrn. and devel. mgr. Sacramento Superior and Mcpl. Cts., 1992—; planning, resource devel. and project mgr. Juvenile Detention Alternatives Initiative, 1992-97, Feather River Industries Vocat. Tng., 1991, Creative Learning Ctr. Constrn., 1988, Correctional Options-Drug Ct., 1994, Violence Prevention Resource Ctr., 1995, Juvenile Delinquency Prevention Initiative, 1995, Securing the Health and Safety of Urban Children Initiative, 1995-97, Joint Cabinets Youth Work Group/Child Welfare League Am., 1996, Task Force on Fairness-The Juvenile Justice Initiative, 1994-97, SacraMentor, Inc., CA Wellness Found., 1994-97, Violent Injury Prevention Coalition/Calif. Dept. Health and Human Svcs., 1995-97, Domestic Violence Coordinating Coun., Sacramento County, 1995-97, Multicultural Perspectives on Family Violence

Conf., 1997, Family Violence Summit, 1997, Healthy Teen Mothers Program, 1997. Bd. dirs. Cmty. Action Agy., Butte County, Calif., 1990, ARC, Butte County, 1989, Sunrise Recreation and Park Dist., 1996—; adv. bds. Butte C.C. Dist., 1987-92, Cmty. Svcs. Planning Coun., 1994-96. Grantee Annie E. Casey Found., USDA, U.S. Bur. Justice, Robert Wood Johnson Found., Calif. Office Criminal Justice Planning, Office of Juvenile Justice & Delinquency Prevention. Phi Delta Kappa. Office: Sacramento Supr & Mcpl Cts Ct Resources 9555 Kiefer Blvd Sacramento CA 95827-3816

ROOT, JAMES BENJAMIN, landscape architect; b. Detroit, Jan. 26, 1934; s. William Jehial and Helen Elizabeth (English) R. BBA, Memphis State U., 1960; B in Landscape Architecture, U. Ga., 1966. Registered landscape architect; lic. real estate agt., Va. Asst. prof. W.Va. U., Morgantown, 1973-75, 93; pvt. practice Charlottesville, Va., 1976-85, 91—; site planner LBA, PH&R, Charles P. Johnson & Assocs., Fairfax, Va., 1986-90; pvt. practice as golf course architect, Charlottesville, 1976—; instr. Parkersburg C.C., 1975, Piedmont Va. C.C., 1981. Author: Fundamentals of Landscaping and Site Planning, 1985; contbr. articles to profl. jours. Mem. Planning Commn., Marietta, Ohio, 1972. Mem. Nat. Golf Found., Elks, Va. Writers Club. Avocation: playing piano. Office: PO Box 7017 Charlottesville VA 22906-7017

ROOT, M. BELINDA, chemist; b. Port Arthur, Tex., May 2, 1957; d. Robert A. and Charlene (Whitehead) Lee; m. Miles J. Root, Nov. 8, 1980; children: Jason Matthew, Ashley Erin. BS in Biology, Lamar U., 1979; MBA, U. Houston, 1994. Asst. chemist Merichem Co., Houston, 1979-81, project chemist, 1982-84, instrument chemist, 1984-85, quality assurance coord., 1986-89, product lab. supr., 1989-91; quality control supr. mfg. Welchem Inc. subs. Amoco, 1991—; mgr. Quality Control Petrolite Corp., 1993; mgr. quality control/quality assurance Akzo-Nobel Chems., Pasadena, Tex., 1994—. Editor (newsletter) Merichemer, 1989-91. Mem. MADD, 1989—, PTA, 1988—. Recipient Gulf Shore Regional award Cat Fanciers Assn., 1981, Disting. Merit award, 1990. Mem. NAFE, Am. Soc. Quality Control (cert. quality auditor, quality engr.), Am. Chem. Soc., United Silver Fancier (sec. 1980-82), Lamar U. Alumni Assn., Beta Beta Beta (sec. 1978-79), Beta Gamma Sigma. Avocations: camping, gardening. Office: Akzo-Nobel Chem Inc 13000 Baypark Rd Pasadena TX 77507-1104

ROOT, NILE, photographer, educator; b. Denver, Dec. 11, 1926; s. Victor Nile and Ella May (Holaway) R.; student U. Denver, 1968; MS in Instructional Tech., Rochester Inst. Tech., 1978; m. Abigail Barton Brown, Feb. 5, 1960; 1 child, James Michael. Microphotographer, U.S. Dept. Commerce, Field Info. Agy. Tech., Fed. Republic Germany, 1946-48; free-lance photographer, 1949-51; pres. Photography Workshop, Inc., Denver, 1952-60; dir. dept. biophotography and med. illustration Rose Meml. Med. Ctr., Denver, 1960-70; dir. med. illustration dept. Children's Hosp., Denver, 1970-71; dir. Photography for Sci., Denver, 1971-72; prof. biomed. photog. communications Rochester Inst. Tech. (N.Y.), 1972-86 , chmn. dept., 1974-86, prof. emeritus Coll. Imaging Arts and Scis., 1986—; travel writer, photographer, Japan, China, S.E. Asia, 1986-89; writer, photographer, Tucson, 1989—. dir. HEW project for devel. of field, 1974-77. Served with USN, 1945-46. Recipient numerous awards for sci. photographs; Eisenhart Outstanding Tchr. award Rochester Inst. Tech., 1986; 1st Ann. Faculty fellow Sch. Photog. Arts and Scis., Rochester Inst. Tech., 1979. Fellow Biol. Photog. Assn. (registered, emeritus, bd. govs. 1977-79, Louis Schmidt award 1986); mem. Ctr. Creative Photography. Democrat. Contbr. illustrations to med. textbooks; represented in numerous mus. photog. exhibits and numerous pvt. collections. Home and Office: 314 N Banff Ave Tucson AZ 85748-3311

ROOT, NINA J., librarian; b. N.Y.C., Dec. 22; d. Jacob J. and Fannie (Slivinsky) Root; BA, Hunter Coll.; MSLS, Pratt Inst.; postgrad. U.S. Dept. Agr. Grad. Sch., 1964-65, City U. N.Y., 1970-75. Reference and serials libr. Albert Einstein Coll. Medicine Libr., Bronx, N.Y., 1958-59; asst. chief libr. Am. Cancer Soc., N.Y.C., 1959-62; chief libr. Am. Inst. Aeros. and Astronautics, N.Y.C., 1962-64; head ref. and libr. svcs. sci. and tech. div. Libr. Congress, Washington, 1964-66; mgmt. cons. Nelson Assocs., Inc., N.Y.C., 1966-70; dir. libr. svcs. Am. Mus. Natural History, N.Y.C., 1970—; free-lance mgmt. cons. and libr. planning, 1970—. Trustee Barnard Found., 1984-91; mem. libr. adv. coun. N.Y. State Bd. Regents, 1984-89, trustee Metro, 1987-92; bd. dirs. Hampden/Booth Libr., Players, 1990—; trustee Mercantile Libr. N.Y., 1993-95. Recipient Meritorious Svc. award Libr. of Congress, 1965. Mem. ALA (preservation com. 1977-79, chmn. libr./binders com. 1978-80, chmn. preservation sect. 1980-81, mem. coun. 1983-86), Spl. Librs. Assn. (sec. documentation group N.Y. chpt. 1972-73, 2d v.p. N.Y. 1975-76, treas. sci. and tech. group N.Y. 1975-76, mus. arts and humanities div. program planning chairperson-conf. 1977), Archons of Colophon (convener 1978-79), Soc. Natural History (N.Am. rep. 1977-85), N.Y. Acad. Scis. (mem. publs. com. 1975-80, 89-91, archives com. 1976-78, search com. 1976), Univ. Club. Home: 400 E 59th St New York NY 10022-2342

ROOT, STANLEY WILLIAM, JR., lawyer; b. Honolulu, Mar. 2, 1923; s. Stanley William and Henrietta E. (Brown) R.; m. Joan Louise Schimpf, Sept. 3, 1949; children: Henry, Louise. AB, Princeton U., 1947; LLB, U. Pa., 1950. Bar: Pa. 1950, U.S. Ct. Mil. Appeals 1951, U.S. Supreme Ct. 1971. Ptnr. Foley, Schimpf & Steeley, Phila., 1952-69; ptnr. Ballard, Spahr, Andrews & Ingersoll, Phila., 1970-91, of counsel, 1992—; lectr. Pa. Bar Assn., 1970-80; bd. dirs. Boardman-Hamilton Co., sec. 1980—. Exec. v.p. Chestnut Hill Cmty. Assn., Phila., 1978; with Whitpain Farm Assn., Blue Bell, Pa., 1987, 90, pres., 1992-94; with St. Paul's Ch. Vestry, Phila., 1969-75; bd. dirs. Lansdale (Pa.) Med. Group, 1972-95, E.B. Spaeth Found. Wills Hosp., Phila., 1975-88, Chevalier Jackson Clinic, Phila., 1965-88; trustee Civil War Libr. and Mus., 1985-93, v.p., 1989, sec., 1992-93, mem. adv. bd., 1993-95; trustee Soc. Protestant Episc. Ch., Pa. Diocese, 1955-95. Lt. col. U.S. Army, 1942-45, ETO, 1950-52, Korea. Decorated Bronze Star; recipient Pa. Commendation medal State of Pa., 1962; named Comdr., Mil. Order Fgn. Wars, 1972. Mem. Union League (pres. 1983-85), Phila. Cricket Club, Sunnybrook Golf Club, Royal Poinciana Golf Club, Brit. Officers Club, Mil. Order Loyal Legion. Republican. Episcopalian. Avocations: golf, tennis, fishing. Home: 16 Hounds Run Ln Blue Bell PA 19422-2456 Office: Ballard Spahr Andrews & Ingersoll 51st Fl 1735 Market St Fl 51 Philadelphia PA 19103-7501

ROOT, WILLIAM ALDEN, export control consultant; b. Boston, Sept. 20, 1923; s. John Alden and Louise Joy (Eppich) R.; m. Constance Hilda Young, Dec. 14, 1945; children: Carl David, Margaret Anne Root Bruck, John Alden, Christine Eppich Root Wiley. B.A., Colo. Coll., 1943; M. Internat. Affairs, Columbia, 1948; certificate, Russian Inst., 1948. Budget examiner Bur. Budget, Washington, 1948-50; mgmt. and budget officer Dept. State, Washington, 1950-52, Bonn, Germany, 1952-55; budget officer for Europe Dept. State, 1955-59; economist Am. embassy, Copenhagen, Denmark, 1959-63; dep. dir. Office East-West Trade, Dept. State, 1964-69; econ. officer Am. embassy, Vietnam, 1969-71; econ. counselor U.S. Mission, Berlin, 1971-74; dir. Office Soviet and Eastern European Sci. and Tech. Affairs Dept. State, 1974-76, dir. Office East West Trade, 1976-83; export control cons., 1983—; mem. Tech. Adv. Com., 1989—. Author: United States Export Controls, Aspen Law and Business. Served to lt. (j.g.) USNR, 1943-46. Mem. Phi Beta Kappa. Address: 4024 Franklin St Kensington MD 20895-3826

ROOT, WILLIAM LUCAS, electrical engineering educator; b. Des Moines, Oct. 6, 1919; s. Frank Stephenson and Helen (Lucas) R.; m. Harriett Jean Johnson, Dec. 10, 1918; children: William Lucas Jr., Wendy Elizabeth Root Cate. BEE, Iowa State U., 1940; MEE, MIT, 1943, PhD in Math., 1952. Staff mem. MIT Lincoln Lab., Lexington, Mass., 1952-61, group leader, 1959-61; lectr. Harvard U., Cambridge, Mass., 1958-59; visitor U. Wis., Madison, 1963-64; vis. prof. Mich. State U., East Lansing, 1966, 68, U. Calif., Berkeley, 1966-67; prof. aerospace engring. U. Mich., Ann Arbor, 1961-87, prof. emeritus, 1988—; vis. fellow U. Cambridge (Eng.), 1970; mem. U.S. Army Sci. Bd., 1979-82. Co-author: Random Signals and Noise, 1958 (Russian and Japanese transls.); assoc. editor: (IEEE) Information Theory Transactions, 1977-79; Soc. Indsl. and Applied Math. Jour. Applied Mathematics, 1962-72; contbr. 65 articles to profl. jours., book chpts. and conf. procs. Served to lt. USMCR, 1943-45. NSF Sr. postdoctoral fellow, 1970, vis. fellow Cambridge Clare Hall, 1970; recipient Claude E. Shannon award IEEE Info. Theory Soc., 1986, Career Achievement award ComCon Conf. Bd., 1987. Life fellow IEEE (vice chmn. adminstrv. com. info. theory group 1965-66); mem. Am. Math. Soc. Home: PO Box 3785 Ann Arbor MI 48106-3785 Office: U Mich Dept Aerospace Engring Ann Arbor MI 48109

ROOT, WILLIAM PITT, poet, educator; b. Austin, Minn., Dec. 28, 1941; s. William Pitt and Bonita Joy (Hilbert) R.; m. Judith Carol Bechtold, 1965 (div. 1970); 1 dau., Jennifer Lorca; m. Pamela Uschuk, 1987. B.A., U. Wash., 1964; M.F.A., U. N.C. at Greensboro, 1967; postgrad. (Wallace Stegner Writing fellow), Stanford, 1968-69. Asst. prof. Mich. State U., 1967-68; tchr. writing Mid-peninsula Free U., 1969; writer-in-residence Amherst Coll., U. Southwestern La., 1976, U. Mont., 1978, 80, 83-84; with poet-in-schs. program state art councils Oreg., Miss., Idaho, Ariz., Vt., Mont., Wyo., Wash., Tex., 1971—; Distinguished writer-in-residence Wichita State U., 1976; vis. writer in residence U. Mont., 1978, 80, 83-86, Hunter Coll., N.Y.C., 1986—; vis. writer NYU, 1986; vis. writer Westside Young Men's Hebrew Assn., N.Y.C., 1988, Pacific Lutheran U., 1990. Author: The Storm and Other Poems, 1969, Striking the Dark Air for Music, 1973, The Port of Galveston, 1974, Coot and Other Characters, 1977, 7 Mendocino Songs, 1977, A Journey South, 1977, Fireclock, 1981, Reasons for Going It on Foot, 1981, In the World's Common Grasses, 1981, The Unbroken Diamond: Nightletter to the Mujahideen, 1983, Invisible Guests, 1984, Faultdancing, 1986; transl. Trace Elements from a Recurring Kingdom, 1994; collaborated (with filmmaker Ray Rice) on poetry films Song of the Woman and the Butterflyman (Orpheus award 1st Internat. Poetry Film Festival 1975), 7 For a Magician, 1976, Faces, 1981. Rockefeller Found. grantee, 1969-70; Guggenheim Found. grantee, 1970-71; Nat. Endowment for Arts grantee, 1973-74; U.S./U.K. Bicentennial Exchange Artist, 1978-79, Wallace Stegner creative writing fellow Stanford U., 1968-69; recipient 1st prize univ. poetry contest Acad. Am. Poets, 1966, Atlantic Young Poet award, 1967, Stanley Kunitz Poetry award, 1981, Guy Owen Poetry Prize, 1982, Pushcart Prize (Poetry), 1977, 1980, 1985. Address: CUNY Hunter Coll Dept Eng 695 Park Ave New York NY 10021-5024 *With Rilke I believe the measure of one's life consists in a growing capacity to change life even as one is changed by it, to engage ever more fully in that dance between what we call will and what we call fate until the result is a contagion of vitality powerful enough to dissipate the spell of habits and to recreate in oneself that first spirit which is intuitive, sympathetic, and clear. Poems simply record the complex effort.*

ROOT-BERNSTEIN, ROBERT SCOTT, biologist, educator; b. Washington, Aug. 7, 1953; s. Morton Ira and Maurine (Berkstresser) Bernstein; m. Michèle Marie Root-Bernstein, Sept. 2, 1978; children: Meredith Marie, Brian Robert. AB, Princeton U., 1975, PhD, 1980. Postdoctoral fellow Salk Inst. for Biol. Studies, La Jolla, Calif., 1981-82, rsch. assoc., 1983-84; from asst. to assoc. prof. Mich. State U., East Lansing, 1987-96, prof., 1996—; cons. Parke-Davis Pharm. Rsch. Divsn., Ann Arbor, 1990-96, Chiron Corp., 1992-96; mem. adv. bd. Soc. for Advancement Gifted Edn., Chgo., 1987-92; Sigma Xi nat. lectr., 1994-96. Author: Discovering, 1989, Rethinking AIDS, 1993, Honey, Mud, Maggots and Other Medical Marvels, 1997; columnist The Scis. mag., 1989-92; contbr. numerous articles to profl. jours. MacArthur Found. fellow, 1981-86; recipient D.J. Ingle Meml. Writing prize, 1988. Mem. Phi Beta Kappa (hon.), Sigma Xi. Avocations: drawing, painting, photography, cello. Office: Mich State U Dept Physiology Giltner Hall East Lansing MI 48824

ROOTMAN, JACK, ophthalmologist, surgeon, pathologist, oncologist, artist; b. Calgary, Alta., Can., June 22, 1944; s. Abraham S. and Lillian (Walman) R.; m. Jenny Puterman, June 20, 1965; children: Russel Mark, Kathryn Anne, Daniel Benson. MD, U. Alta., 1968. Res. ophthalmology U. Alta., Edmonton, 1973, clin. asst. prof. ophthalmology and pathology, 1973-75; from asst. prof. to assoc. prof. ophthalmology & pathology U. B.C., Vancouver, 1976-84, prof. ophthalmology & pathology, 1985—, chmn. ophthalmology, 1990—; cons. pathologist Vancouver Gen. Hosp., 1989; pathology cons. Can. Reference Ctr. Cancer Pathology, Ottawa, Ont., 1989; chmn. ocular & orb tumor group B.C. Cancer Agy., 1980—. Author: Diseases of the Orbit: A Multidisciplinary Approach, 1988, Orbital Surgery: A Conceptual Approach, 1995; contbr. chpts. to books, numerous articles to profl. jours.; inventor Rootman Orbital Surgery Set, numerous orbital surgical procedures; reviewer Can. Jour. Ophthalmology, 1981—, Survey Ophthalmology, 1990—, Am. Jour. Ophthalmology, 1992, Brit. Jour. Ophthalmology, 1993, others in field; paintings exhibited in group shows Vancouver Gen. Hosp. Gallery, 1988, Zack Gallery, Vancouver, 1989, N.W. Watercolor Soc. Nat. Exhibition, 1994; one-man shows include Taylor Gallery, Mayne Island, B.C., 1989, U. B.C. Faculty Club, 1990, C.J. Herman Galleries, Vancouver, 1991, 92, 93, Greenhill Galleries, Adelaide, Australia, 1997. Chmn. Vancouver Talmud Torah, 1982-84; bd. dirs. Contemporary Art Gallery, Vancouver, 1991; bd. mem. Emily Carr Found., Emily Carr Inst. Art and Design. Recipient 1st Prize (tied) Can. Fed. Artists 50th Anniversary Show, 1991; Can. Cancer Soc. fellow, 1974, Med. Rsch. Coun. fellow, 1977-78, E.A. Baker Found. fellow, 1978, 82, 91; Vancouver Found. grantee, 1978, B.C. Cancer Found. grantee, 1978, McLean Fund grantee, 1979, B.C. Health Care Rsch. Found. grantee 1979-81, 83-85, 87-89, 92, B.C. Med. Svcs. Found. grantee 1982-83, Med. Rsch. Coun. grantee, 1982-88, others. Fellow Royal College Surgeons; mem. Am. Bd. Ophthalmology (cert., diplomate), Royal Coll. Physicians and Surgeons (specialty com. ophthalmology, accrediation surveys), B.C. Soc. Eye Physicians and Surgeons, B.C. Med. Assn., Can. Ocular Pathology Study Group, Can. Oculoplastic Study Group, Can. Ophthalmol. Soc., Hogan Soc., Internat. Orbit Soc., N.Am. Skull Base Soc. (charter), Am. Assn. Ophthalmic Pathologists, others. Office: Univ BC Dept Ophthalmology, 2550 Willow St, Vancouver, BC Canada V5Z 3N9

ROOTS, ERNEST FREDERICK, scientific advisor emeritus; b. Salmon Arm, B.C., Can., July 5, 1923; s. Ernest and Margaret Frances (Sharpe) R.; m. June Christine Blomfield, Jan. 15, 1955; children: Charles, Frances, Hannah, Jane, Robin. BASc, U. B.C., Vancouver, 1946, MASc, 1947; PhD, Princeton U., 1949; DSc (hon.), U. Victoria, B.C., 1986. Asst. meteorologist Can. Meteorol. Br., Banff, Alta., 1938-40; topog. surveyor Nat. Parks Svc., various locations, B.C., various locations, Alta., 1940-41; student asst. Geol. Survey Can., Ottawa, Ont., 1942-46, geologist, 1947-49, 53-58; geologist Norwegian, Brit. and Swedish Antarctic Expdn., 1949-52; asst. prof. geology Princeton (N.J.) U., 1952-54; coord. polar continental shelf project Can. Dept. Energy, Mines and Resources, Ottawa, 1958-73; sci. advisor Dept. Environ. Can., Ottawa, 1973-90, spl. advisor, 1990—; chmn. Can. Environ. Assessment Rsch. Coun., Ottawa, 1986-91; co-chmn. environ. sci. rev. group Nuclear Waste Environ. Assessment Rev. Panel, Ottawa, 1990—; pres. Internat. Arctic Sci. Com., 1990-93; chmn. Man and Biosphere No. Sci. Network, UNESCO, Paris, 1992—. Contbr. over 130 articles to sci. jours., chpts. to books. Decorated officer Order of Can.; recipient Patron's medal Royal Geog. Soc., London, 1960, Polar medals, Norway, 1952, USSR, 1960, U.K., 1984, U.S., 1986. Fellow Royal Soc. Can. Home: RR 3, Wakefield, PQ Canada J0X 3G0

ROPER, BERYL CAIN, writer, publisher, retired library director; b. Long Beach, Calif., Mar. 1, 1931; d. Albert Verne and Ollie Fern (Collins) Cain; m. Max H. Young, Aug. 22, 1947 (div. 1958); children: Howard, Wade, Debra, Kevin, John R., Christopher; m. George Albert Roper, Mar. 24, 1962 (dec. July 1978); children: Ellen, Georgianne; m. Jack T. Hughes, Sept. 21, 1993. BA, West Tex. State U., 1986; MA, Tex. Womans U., 1989. Libr. clk. Cornette Libr., West Tex. State U., Canyon, 1981-87; dir. Clarendon (Tex.) Coll. Libr., 1988-96; lectr. in history and archaeology; co-owner Aquamarine Publs. Editor, pub.: In the Light of Past Experience, 1989, Transactions of the Southwest Federation of Archaeological Societies, 1993, Greenbelt Site, 1996; author, pub.: Trementina, 1990, Trementina Revisited, 1994; author articles on women and history. Mem. Clarendon Archaeol. Soc. (charter, v.p. 1990-91), Tex. Libr. Assn., Tex. Intertribal Indian Orgn., Pi Gamma Mu, Beta Phi Mu, Alpha Chi, Phi Alpha Theta. Republican. Mem. LDS Ch. Avocations: teaching Sunday school, music, gardening, decorating, remodeling old houses, genealogy. Office: Aquamarine Publs 1903 3rd Ave Canyon TX 79015-3030

ROPER, BURNS WORTHINGTON, retired opinion research company executive; b. Creston, Iowa, Feb. 26, 1925; s. Elmo Burns and Dorothy Camille (Shaw) R.; m. Elizabeth Kellock, Feb. 7, 1945 (div.); children: Bruce, David, Douglas; m. Helen Gillette Lanagan, Dec. 26, 1958 (dec. Apr. 1990); 1 child, Candace Gillette; m. Helen Grinnell Page, Sept. 19, 1991. Hon. doctorate, Colgate U., 1996. Rsch. asst. Elmo Roper, N.Y.C., 1946-48, project dir., 1948-55; ptnr. Elmo Roper & Assocs., N.Y.C., 1955-66; pres., chmn. bd. Roper Rsch. Assocs., N.Y.C., 1967-70, The Roper Orgn., Inc., N.Y.C., 1970-93; exec. v.p. Roper Starch Worldwide, Mamaroneck, N.Y., 1981-94; chmn. bd. The Roper Pub. Opinion Rsch. Ctr., Storrs, Conn., 1970-94, trustee 1947—. Contbr. numerous articles on polls to profl. jours., book chpts. Trustee Nat. Urban League, N.Y.C., 1955-64, UN Assn. Am., N.Y.C., 1964—, Freedom House, N.Y.C., 1970—. 1st lt. USAAF, 1943-45, ETO. Decorated DFC, Air medal with five oak leaf clusters. Mem. Am. Assn. Pub. Opinion Rsch. (nat. pres. 1982-83, award 1988), Nat. Coun. on Pub. Polls (bd. dirs. 1969—, chmn. bd. trustees 1980-93), Market Rsch. Coun. (pres. 1967-68, inducted into Hall of Fame 1990), Wings Club. Democrat. Home: 70 Old Dam Rd Bourne MA 02532-3749 *When public opinion differs from my opinion, the first thing I do is reassess my opinion. The public can be wrong but its track record is awfully good. Those you buy from should be treated in the same manner as those you sell to; those who work for you should be treated as those you work for.*

ROPER, JOHN LONSDALE, III, shipyard executive; b. Norfolk, Va., Jan. 19, 1927; s. John Lonsdale II and Sarah (Dryfoos) R.; m. Jane Preston Harman, Sept. 29, 1951; children: Susan Roper, John Lonsdale IV, Sarah Preston Roper Massey, Jane Harman Roper Van Sciver, Katherine Hayward Roper Stout. BSME, U. Va., Charlottesville, 1949; BS in Naval Architecture and Marine Engring., MIT, 1951. CEO, pres. Norfolk Shipbuilding & Drydock Corp., 1985-91, pres., CEO, 1991—, also bd. dirs.; dir. John L. Roper Corp., Cruise Internat., Inc., The Flagship Group Ltd.; pres., dir. Lonsdale Bldg. Corp. Marepcon Corp.-Internat. With USCG, 1945-46. Mem. Shipbuilders Coun. Am. (bd. dirs.). Episcopalian.

ROPER, JOHN MARLIN, federal magistrate judge; b. Greenville, Ala., Dec. 11, 1942; s. Marlin Ross and Ruby Lois (Martin) R.; m. Virginia Gene Kerth, Apr. 2, 1966; 1 son, John Marlin. B.S. Auburn U., 1964; J.D., Tulane U., 1968. Bar: Ala. 1968, Miss. 1974. Counselor/program dir. Juvenile Delinquency Instn., New Orleans, 1966-69; sr. law clk. to judge U.S. Dist. Ct. (so. dist.) Miss., 1969-75, magistrate judge, 1975—. Mem. Fed. Magistrate Judges Assn. (dir. 5th cir. 1976-82, nat. officer 1982-86, nat. pres. 1986-87, security com. jud. conf. 1987-89, budget com. jud. conf. 1989—). Methodist. Office: US District Court Ste 150 725 Washington Loop Biloxi MS 39530-2267

ROPER, WILLIAM LEE, physician, health care executive; b. Birmingham, Ala., July 6, 1948; s. Richard Barnard and Jean (Fyfe) R.; m. Maryann Roper, Jan. 14, 1978. A.A., Fla. Coll., 1968; B.S., U. Ala, 1970, M.D., 1974, M.P.H., 1981. Diplomate Am. Bd. Pediatrics, Am. Bd. Preventive Medicine. Intern, resident in pediatrics U. Colo. Med. Ctr., Denver, 1974-77; health officer Jefferson County Dept. Health, Birmingham, 1977-82, 83; White House fellow Washington, 1982-83, spl. asst. to Pres. for health policy, 1983-86; adminstr., Health Care Finance Adminstrn. HHS, Washington, 1986-89; dep. asst. to pres. for domestic policy The White House, Washington, 1989-90; adminstr. Agy. for Toxic Substances and Disease Registry and dir. Ctrs. for Disease Control and Prevention, Atlanta, 1990-93; pres. Prudential Ctr. for Health Care Rsch., 1993-95; sr. v.p. Prudential Health Care, 1994—. Mem. Inst. Medicine of NAS, Phi Beta Kappa, Alpha Omega Alpha. Republican. Home: PO Box 28 Green Village NJ 07935-0028

ROPSKI, GARY MELCHIOR, lawyer; b. Erie, Pa., Apr. 19, 1952; s. Joseph Albert and Irene Stefania (Mszanowski) R.; m. Barbara Mary Schleck, May 15, 1982. BS in Physics, Carnegie-Mellon U., 1972; JD cum laude, Northwestern U. Sch. Law, 1976. Bar: Ill. 1976, U.S. Patent and Trademark Office 1976, U.S. Dist. Ct. (no. dist.) Ill. 1976, U.S. Ct. Appeals (7th cir.) 1977, U.S. Dist. Ct. (ea. dist.) Wis. 1977, U.S. Ct. Appeals (3d cir.) 1981, U.S. Ct. Claims 1982, Pa. 1982, U.S. Ct. Appeals (Fed. cir.) 1982, U.S. Supreme Ct. 1982, U.S. Dist. Ct. (ea. dist.) Mich. 1984, U.S. Dist. Ct. (no. dist.) Calif. 1986. Assoc. Brinks Hofer Gilson & Lione, Chgo., 1976-81, shareholder, 1981—; adj. prof. patents and copyrights Northwestern U. Sch. Law, Chgo., 1982—. Contbr. numerous articles to profl. jours. Mem. ABA, IBA, INTA, Am. Intellectual Property Law Assn., Ill. Bar Assn., Intellectual Property Law Assn. Chgo., Chgo. Bar Assn. Roman Catholic. Clubs: University, Chgo. Yacht. Office: Brinks Hofer Gilson & Lione NBC Tower Ste 3600 455 N Cityfront Plaza Dr Chicago IL 60611-5503

ROREM, NED, composer, author; b. Richmond, Ind., Oct. 23, 1923; s. Clarence Rufus and Gladys (Miller) R. Student, Northwestern U., 1940-42, Curtis Inst., Phila., 1943; B.A., Juilliard Sch. Music, 1946, M.A., 1948; D.F.A. (hon.), Northwestern U., 1977. Slee prof., composer-in-residence Buffalo U., 1959-61; prof. composition U. Utah, 1965-67, Curtis Inst., 1980-94. Composer: symphonies No. 1, premiere Vienna, Austria, 1951, No. 2, premiere La Jolla, Calif., 1956, No. 3, premiere with Leonard Bernstein and N.Y. Philharmonic, 1959, Three Piano Sonatas, 1949, 50, 54, Lento for Strings, 1950, Design for Orch., 1954, Pilgrims for Strings, 1958, Eagles for Orch., 1958, Lions, 1964, Ideas for Easy Orch, 1961, Piano Concerto No. 2, 1951, 3d Piano Concerto, 1970, Eleven Studies, 1959, Water Music, 1966, Sun; for voice and orch., commd. by N.Y. Philharmonic, 1966, Air Music for Orch, 1974 (Pulitzer prize 1976), Assembly and Fall, 1975, Sunday Morning for Orch., 1977, Remembering Tommy, 1981; numerous chorus works, latest being Letters from Paris, 1965; for chorus and orch., commd. by Koussevitzky Found. in Library of Congress, Little Prayers, 1972, Whitman Cantata, 1982, An American Oratorio, 1983, Homer, 1986, Seven Motets, 1986, Te Deum, 1986, What is Pink?, 1987, The Death of Moses, 1987, Goodbye My Fancy, 1988; operas A Childhood Miracle, 1952, Three Sisters Who Are Not Sisters, 1969, Fables, 1970, Bertha, 1968, Miss Julie, 1964 (Ford Found. grantee), Hearing, 1976, Cycles: War Scenes, 1969, Six Songs for High Voice and Orchestra, 1954, Six Irish Poems, 1951, Poems of Love and the Rain, 1964, Ariel for Voice, clarinet and piano, 1971, Last Poems of Wallace Stevens for voice, cello and piano, 1971, Serenade for voice, violin, viola and piano, Women's Voices, 1975, The Nantucket Songs, 1979, Three Calamus Poems, 1982, The Schuyler Songs, 1987, Day Music and Night Music for Violin, 1972-73, Etudes for Piano, 1975, Book of Hours for flute and harp, A Quaker Reader for Organ, 1976, The Santa Fe Songs, 1980, Remembering Tommy, 1980, Views From the Oldest House for organ, 1981, Winter Pages, 1981, Picnic on the Marne, 1982, Dances for Cello, 1983, Violin Concerto, 1984, Organ Concerto, 1985, String Symphony, 1985, Septet: Scenes from Childhood, 1985, Trio: End of Summer, 1985, Quintet: Bright Music, 1988, Diversions for Brass Quintet, 1989, Trio (Spring Music), 1990, Three Organbooks; The Auden Poems, Trio for Violin, Cello, Piano, 1990, Swords and Plowshares (for 4 solo voices and orch.), 1991, Third Quartet, 1991, Fourth Concerto for Piano (left hand) and Orch., 1991, Present Laughter for mixed chorus, piano and brass, 1993, Fourth Quartet, 1994, Songs of Sadness for quartet of baritone, guitar, clarinet and cello, 1994, More Than a Day for countertenor and orch., 1995, Six Variations for Two Pianos, 1995; commns. for U.S. Bicentennial include compositions for, Cin. Symphony, N.C. Symphony, Nat. Endowment of the Arts, Am. Harp Soc.; Author: The Paris Diary of Ned Rorem, 1966, Music from Inside Out, 1967, The New York Diary, 1967, Music and People, 1968, Critical Affairs, 1970, Pure Contraption, 1973, The Later Diaries, 1974, An Absolute Gift, 1978, Setting the Tone, 1983, Paul's Blues, 1985, The Nantucket Diary, 1987, Settling the Score, 1988, Knowing When To Stop, 1994, Other Entertainment, 1996, also articles newspapers, mags., Recs. for, Columbia, Decca, Odyssey, Desto, Phillips, Premier, C.R.I., Westminster, Orion, New World Records. Recipient Music Libraries Assn. award for song Lordly Hudson 1948, Gershwin Meml. award 1949, Lili Boulanger award 1950, Nat. Inst. Arts and Letters award 1968, Pulitzer prize in music 1976, Grammy award for Best Orchestral Rec., 1989; Fulbright fellow Paris, 1951-52; Guggenheim fellow, 1957-58, 77-78. Mem. PEN, ASCAP, AAAL. Mem. Soc. of Friends. Address: PO Box 764 Nantucket MA 02554-0764

RORER, LEONARD GEORGE, psychologist, writer; b. Dixon, Ill., Dec. 24, 1932; s. Leonard Gleason and Marion Emma (Geyer) R.; m. Gail Evans, Apr. 30, 1958 (div. May 11, 1964); children: Liat, Eric Evans; m. Nancy McKimens, Jan, 9, 1969 (div. Jan. 19, 1976); 1 child, Mya Noelani. BA, Swarthmore Coll., 1954; PhD, U. Minn., 1963 . Rsch. assoc., then assoc. dir. Oreg. Rsch. Inst., Eugene, 1963-75; prof. psychology Miami U., Oxford, Ohio, 1975-93, dir. clin. psychology tng. program, 1976-86; pres. Oreg. Psychol. Assn., 1973-75. NIMH spl. rsch. fellow, 1967-68; fellow Netherlands Inst. Advanced Study, 1971-72; postdoctoral fellow Inst. for Rational-

Emotive Therapy, 1982-83. Fellow APA (coun. reps. 1968-72), Am. Psychol. Soc. (charter), We. Psychol. Assn.; mem. Midwestern Psychol. Assn., Assn. Advancement Behavior Therapy, Soc. Multivariate Exptl. Psychology. Author articles in field, mem. editorial bds. profl. jours. Home: 407 High Santa Cruz CA 95060-2613

RORICK, WILLIAM CALVIN, librarian, educator, portrait artist; b. Elyria, Ohio, June 23, 1941; s. Harold R. and Edythe E. (Harris) R.; m. Anne L. Sherbondy, Aug. 21, 1971. BA in Econs. and Bus. Adminstrn., Ohio Wesleyan U., 1963; MusB in Music History and Lit., U. Utah, 1968; MusM in Music History and Lit., Northwestern U., 1970; MLS, Pratt Inst., 1974; MA in Musicology, NYU, 1982; trainee in portraiture, various art schs., workshops, 1990—. Curator orchl.-choral libr., reference asst., office mgr. Manhattan Sch. Music Libr., N.Y.C., 1970-74; music reference libr. CUNY Queens Coll. Music Libr., Flushing, 1974-96, instr., 1974-79, asst. prof., 1979-96, asst. prof. emeritus, 1996—, mem. senate nominating com., del.-at-large arts divsn.v., 1984-86. Contbr. articles and revs. to profl. jours. Grantee Rsch. Found. CUNY, 1981-84; recipient art awards including Best in Show Conn. Classic Arts Assn. Mem. Am. Musicological Soc., Am. Printing History Assn., Assn. for Recorded Sound Collections, Internat. Assn. Music Librs., Libr. Assn. CUNY (chmn. grants com. 1978-80, mem. publs. com. 1979-81, editor Directory 1980-81, del. 1983-85), Music Libr. Assn. (program chmn. Greater N.Y. chpt. 1977-79, sec.-treas. 1979-81, chpt. chmn. 1983-85, mem. nat. subcom. on basic music collection 1977-79, chmn. nat. membership com. 1979-82, mem. Music Pubs. Assn. joint com. 1986-88), Am. Soc. Portrait Artists, Sonneck Soc., Conn. Classic Arts, Inc. (publicity chmn. 1996—), Beta Phi Mu. Home and Studio: 63 Beacon Hill Dr Southbury CT 06488-1914

RORIE, CONRAD JONATHAN, scientist, naval officer; b. Henning, Tenn., Oct. 28, 1930; s. Elvy and Lena (Jenkins) R.; m. Patricia Paris Cunliffe, Feb. 7, 1952; children: Michael Stephen, Catherine Jean, Patrick Jonathan. BS, Union U., Jackson, Tenn., 1952; MSEE, U.S. Naval Postgrad. Sch., 1961; PhD in EE, Vanderbilt U., 1970. Enlisted USN, 1952, advanced through grades to rear adm., 1971; comdg. officer various ships, 1957-72; comdr. U.S. Naval Surface Weapons Ctr., Dahlgren, Va., 1974-77; dep. comdr. for surface combatants and weapons systems engr. Naval Sea Systems Command, Washington, 1977-81; comdr. Naval Surface Forces Middle Pacific & Naval Base Pearl Harbr, Hawaii, 1981-84; planning dir. Johns Hopkins U., Applied Physics Lab., 1984—; mem. numerous naval bd. for officer career devel., chmn. Weapons Systems Mgr./Ordnance Adv. Bd. to Naval Postgrad. Sch. President Hawaii Navy Relief Soc. and Red Cross, 1980; chmn. Combined Fed. Campaign Charity Dr., 1981; bd. dirs. Govs. for Navy Charity Retail Store, 1981; commissioning chmn. USS Antietam, 1987, USS Arleigh Burke, 1991; mem. panel Navy/Civilian U. Lab., 1988; mem. curricula rev. com. Naval Postgrad. Sch., 1977-81. Decorated Legion of Merit (4), Meritorious Svc. medal with gold star; recipient Ann. Disting. Alumnus award Union U., 1975, Am. Spirit of Honor medal; named Tenn. Number One State Future Farmer, 1948; C.J. Rorie award for Excellence in his honor, 1987. Mem. Naval Inst., Am. Soc. Naval Engrs., Nat. Security Indsl. Assn., AIAA, Am. Astronaut. Soc., U.S. Navy League, Armed Forces Communications and Electronics Assn., Mil. Order of Carabao, Masons, Bapt. Club, Sigma Xi, Eta Kappa Nu, Alpha Tau Omega. Home: 12412 Hooper Ct Fulton MD 20759-9645 Office: Johns Hopkins U Applied Physics Lab Johns Hopkins Rd Laurel MD 20707

RORIE, NANCY KATHERYN, elementary and secondary school educator; b. Union County, N.C., May 31, 1940; d. Carl Van and Mary Mildred (Pressley) R. BA, Woman's Coll. U. N.C., 1962; MEd, U. N.C., 1967; EdD, Duke U., 1977. Cert. curriculum and instrnl. specialist, social studies tchr. for middle and secondary levels, English tchr., N.C. Social studies and English tchr. Guilford County Schs., Greensboro, N.C., 1962-67; social studies instr. Lees-McRae Coll., Banner Elk, N.C., 1967-76; social studies tchr. Monroe (N.C.) City Schs., 1977-93; curriculum instrnl. specialist, social studies tchr. Union County Schs., Monroe, N.C., 1993—. Mem. Prof. Educators N.C., Phi Alpha Theta, Kappa Delta Pi. Democrat. Baptist. Home: 2401 Old Pageland Rd Monroe NC 28112-8163

RORIG, KURT JOACHIM, chemist, research director; b. Bremerhaven, Germany, Dec. 1, 1920; came to U.S., 1924, naturalized, 1929; s. Robert Herman and Martha (Grundke) R.; m. Helen Yonan, Mar. 20, 1949; children: James, Elizabeth, Miriam. BS, U. Chgo., 1942; MA, Carleton Coll., 1944; PhD, U. Wis., 1947. Lectr. Loyola U., Chgo., 1950-62; chemist to dir. Chem. Research G.D. Searle & Co., Chgo., 1947-87; pres. Chemo-Delphic Cons. Ltd., Chgo., 1987—; adj. prof. chemistry U. Ill., Chgo., 1989—. Patentee in field. Mem. Sch. Bd., Wilmette, Ill., 1969-71. Mem. Am. Chem. Soc. (dir. Chgo. sect.), Am. Soc. Pharm. and Exptl. Therapeutics, N.Y. Acad. Scis., AAAS, Chgo. Chemists Club (past pres.). Presbyterian. Home and Office: 337 Hager Ln Glenview IL 60025-3329

RORKE, LUCY BALIAN, neuropathologist; b. St. Paul, June 22, 1929; d. Aram Haji and Karzouhy (Ousdigian) Balian; m. Robert Radcliffe Rorke, June 4, 1960. A.B., U. Minn., 1951, M.A., 1952, B.S., 1955, M.D., 1957. Diplomate Am. Bd. Pathology. Intern Phila. Gen. Hosp., 1957-58, resident anat. pathology and neuropathology, 1958-62, asst. neuropathologist, 1963-67, chief pediat. pathologist, 1967-68, chief neuropathologist, 1968-69, chmn. dept. anat. pathology and chief neuropathologist, 1969-73, chmn. dept. pathology, 1973-77, pres. med. staff, 1973-75; practice medicine specializing in neuropathology Phila., 1962—; neuropathologist Children's Hosp., Phila., 1965—, pres. med. staff, 1986-88, acting pathologist-in-chief, 1995—; cons. neuropathologist Wyeth Rsch. Labs., Radnor, Pa., 1961-87, Wistar Inst. Anatomy and Biology, Phila., 1967-93; assoc. prof. pathology U. Pa. Sch. Medicine, Phila., 1970-73, prof., 1973—, clin. prof. neurology, 1979—; forensic neuropathologist Office of Med. Examiner, Phila., 1977—. Author: Myelinization of the Brain in the Newborn, 1969, Pathology of Perinatal Brain Injury, 1982; mem. editl. bd. Jours. Neuropathology Exptl. Neurology, 1980-85, 93—, Pediatric neurosurgery, 1984—, Child's Nervous System, 1984-88, Brain pathology, 1990-95; contbr. articles to profl. jours. NIH fellow in neuropathology, 1961-62; NIH grantee for study of neonatal brain, 1963-68. Fellow Coll. Am. Pathologists; mem. Phila. Gen. Hosp. Med. Staff (pres. 1973-75), Phila. Neurol. Soc. (v.p. 1971-72, editor Transactions 1973, pres. 1975-76), Am. Assn. Neuropathologists (exec. council 1976-85, v.p. 1979-80, pres. 1981-82), Am. Neurol. Assn., AMA, Burlington County Med. Soc., Phila. Coll. Physicians. Home: 120 Chestnut St Moorestown NJ 08057-2937 Office: Childrens Hosp of Philadelphia 324 S 34th St Philadelphia PA 19104-4301

RORQUIST, IVOR CARL, mechanical engineer; b. Wadena, Sask., Can., Nov. 19, 1920; s. John Theodore and Alma (Samuleson) R.; m. Hazel Irene Bonney, June 9, 1947 (wid. May 1978); children: John Alan, Karen Janice; m. Gladys Kildoo, Nov. 12, 1983. B Engring., U. Saskatchewan, 1951. Registered profl. engr., Pa., Ont. Project engr. Steel Co. of Can., Hamilton, Ont., Can., 1951-58; projects mgr. steel plant constrn. and installation Aetna Std. Engring., Ellwood City, Pa., 1958-83; chief engr., cons. engr. Fabrimac, Inc., Ellwood City, Pa., 1983-88, Thimons, Inc., Ellwood City, Pa., 1988-91; cons. engr. ADS Machy, Thimons & others, Ellwood City, 1991—. Founding mem. Oakes/Adult Day Care Ctr., Ellwood, 1992-95. LAC RCAF, 1942-45. Mem. Rotary (treas. 1992—). Home: 111 2nd St Ellwood City PA 16117-2109

RORSCHACH, RICHARD GORDON, lawyer; b. Tulsa, Aug. 9, 1928; s. Harold Emil and Margaret (Hermes) R.; m. Martha Kay King, Dec. 23, 1979; children by previous marriage: Richard Helm, Reagan Cartwright, Andrew Maxwell. BS, MIT, 1950; MS, U. Okla., 1952; JD, U. Houston, 1961. Bar: Tex. 1961. Cons. civil engr. Freese & Nichols, Ft. Worth, 1955; cons. engr. Freese, Nichols & Turner, Houston, 1955-56; petroleum engr. Marathon Oil Co., Bay City, Tex., 1956-57, Houston, 1957-61; atty. Marathon Oil Co., 1961-64; ptnr. Broady, Kells & Rorschsch, Houston, 1964-68; ptnr. Ragan, Russell & Rorschach, Houston, 1968-80, Kilgore, Tex., 1980—; mem. exec. com. Colonial Royalties Co., Tulsa, 1970-77; officer Little River Oil &Gas Co., 1980-88; mng. ptnr. Pentagon Oil Co., 1988—; pres. Nat. Assn. Royalty Owners-Tex., 1993-96; chmn. Nat. Assn. Royalty Owners, Inc., 1996—; mem. exec. com. Nat. Assn. Royalty Owners, Inc.; owner, breeder, exhibitor Arabian Horses Shadowbrook Farm, Kilgore, Tex., 1980—. Served to 1st lt. C.E., AUS, 1952-54, Korea. Mem. ASME, ASCE, Tex. Bar Assn., Rotary Club (pres. Kilgore chpt. 1984-85), Sigma Xi, Sigma Alpha Epsilon. Republican. Presbyterian. Home: RR 4 Box 210 Kilgore TX 75662-9023 Office: 1100 Stone Rd PO Box 1934 Kilgore TX 75663-1934

ROSA, FREDRIC DAVID, construction company executive; b. Monroe, Wis., Oct. 31, 1946; s. Fredric Carl Rosa and Irene (Sommers) Rosa Figi; m. Melanie A. Downs, May 31, 1986; children: Mark, Katherine. BBA in Mktg., U. Wis., 1968. Dir. mktg. Swiss Colony Stores, Inc., Monroe, 1968-80; pres. Videotape Indsl. Prodns., Inc., Madison, Wis., 1980-82; agt. VR Bus. Brokers, Colorado Springs, Colo., 1982-83; sales rep. NCR Corp., Denver, 1983-85; prin. F. D. Rosa & Assocs., Denver, Aspen and Eagle, Colo., 1985-89; pres. Peak Benefit Cons., Colorado Springs, 1989-95; registered prin. Nexus Fin. Programs, Inc., Colorado Springs, Colo., 1990-92, Nutmeg Securities Ltd., Colorado Springs, 1992-94; sales staff Am. Airlines, Colorado Springs, Colo., 1993-95; cons. Kolb-Lena Cheese Co., Lena, Ill., 1983-85; instr. The Am. Coll., Bryn Mawr, Pa., 1990-91, A.D. Banker & Co., Overland Park, Kans., 1995—; owner Rosa Constrn., Colorado Springs, 1990-94, Lakewood, Colo., 1995—. Contbr. articles to trade publs. and newspapers. Mem. Am. Soc. CLU and Chartered Fin. Cons., Mensa, Internat. Legion of Intelligence, Delta Sigma Pi (life). Methodist. Avocations: big game hunting, skiing, camping, travel. Home and Office: Fred Rosa Constrn 1270 Cody St Lakewood CO 80215-4897

ROSA, MARGARITA, agency chief executive, lawyer; b. Bklyn., Jan. 5, 1953; d. Jose and Julia (Mojica) R.; 1 child, Marisol Kimberly Rosa-Shapiro. BA in History cum laude, Princeton U., 1974; JD, Harvard U., 1977. Bar: N.Y. Assoc. Rosenman & Colin, N.Y.C., 1977-79, Rabinowitz & Boudin, N.Y.C., 1981-84; staff atty. Puerto Rican Legal Def. Edn. Fund, N.Y.C., 1979-81; teaching fellow Urban Legal Studies program CUNY, 1984-85; gen. counsel N.Y. State Div. Human Rights, N.Y.C., 1985-88, exec. dep. commr., 1988-90, commr., 1990-95; exec. dir. Grand St. Settlement, 1995—; vice chmn. N.Y. State Task force on ADA Implementation, 1991-95; mem. N.Y. Gov.'s Task Force on Sexual Harassment, 1992; bd. dirs. Pub. Interest Law Found., NYU Law Sch., 1982-84; adj. prof. of law Fordham Law Sch., 1995; adj. prof. pub. policy Wagner Sch. NYU, 1995—; mem. bd. dirs. Martin Luther King Jr. Commn. N.Y. State, 1990-95, Feminist Press CUNY, 1990-95. Bd. dirs. N.Y. Civil Liberties Union, 1981-86, Lower East Side Family Union, N.Y.C., 1982-84. Recipient Hispanic Women Achievers award N.Y. State Gov.'s Office Hispanic Affairs, 1990, Woman of Excellence award CUNY, 1992, Oscar García Rivera award P.R. Bar Assn., 1996; Lombard Assn. fellow Office of U.S. Atty., So. Dist. N.Y., 1975; Revson Teaching fellow Charles Revson Found., 1984-85. Office: Grand St Settlement 80 Pitt St New York NY 10002-3516

ROSA, RAYMOND ULRIC, retired banker; b. New Britain, Conn., Jan. 30, 1927; s. Kenneth E. and Regina (Chenette) R.; m. Irene M. Asselin, Feb. 5, 1949; children: R. James, David M., Cathryn P., Michael F., Nancy A., Kenneth E. AS, Hillyer Coll., 1949. CPA, Conn. Pvt. practice pub. accounting Manchester, Conn., 1949-52; auditor Auditors of Pub. Accounts, State of Conn., Hartford, 1952-65; dir. Fed.-State Relations Dept. Finance and Control, Conn., 1965-69; dep. commr. Finance and Control, Conn., 1969-71; sr. v.p., auditor Soc. Savings, Hartford, 1971-90, ret., 1990; mem. Windsor Locks (Conn.) Bd. Fin., 1973-81; pres. Savs. Bank Forum, 1981-82; trustee, sec.-treas. Mease Manor, Inc., Dunedin, Fla., 1995—. Treas. Mental Health Assn. Conn., 1974-77, v.p., 1977-80, pres., 1980-83; bd. dirs. Nat. Assn. Mental Health, 1977-85, v.p. region 1, 1982-83; bd. dirs. Combined Health Appeal of Greater Hartford, 1982-90. Served with USNR, 1944-46. Mem. AICPA, Conn. Soc. CPAs, Conn. Soc. Govtl. Accts., KC, Dunedin Country Club, Suffield Country Club (bd. govs. 1984-91). Home: 2060 Golf View Dr Dunedin FL 34698-2330

ROSADO-MAY, FRANCISCO JAVIER, agricultural studies educator, researcher; b. Felipe Carrillo Puerto, Mex., Apr. 26, 1955; s. Alfredo Rosado Esquivel and Lilia May Tiran; m. Silvia Cuellar; 1 child, Silvia R. Rosado Cuellar; m. Patricia Salvidar Garcia, Aug. 2, 1989; 1 child, Francisco A. Rosado-May. BA in Tropical Agriculture, Colegio Superior de Agricultura Tropical, Cardenas, Tabasco, Mex., 1979, MSc in Tropical Ecology, 1980; PhD in Biology, U. Calif., Santa Cruz, 1991. Rsch. asst. Nat. Inst. Agrl. Rsch., Oaxaca, Mex., 1977; prof., rschr. dept. crop prodn. Colegio Superior de Agricultura Tropical, H. Cardenas, Tabasco, Mex., 1981-85, coord. agrl. prodn. courses, 1982-83, coord. extension program, 1984-85; founder U. Quintana Roo, 1991; rschr. Centro de Investigaciones de Quintana Roo, Chetumal, Quintana Roo, Mex., 1991-93, chair terrestial ecology dept., 1991-93; prof., acad. coord., rschr. Universidad de Quintana Roo, Chetumal, 1993—, gen. sec., 1993, acad. sec., 1993-94, dir. scis. and engring. divsn., 1994—; mem. coun. teaching and rsch. Colegio Superior de Agricultura Tropical, H. Cardenas, Tabasco, 1980, undergrad. seminars coord. dept. crop prodn., 1981, 82, 83, asst. to rsch. subdir., 1983-84, mem. editl. com., 1983-85; founder U. Quintanta, Roo, Mex. Contbr. articles to profl. jours. Nat. Coun. Sci. and Tech. fellow, 1979-81, 85-89, 92-96, U. Calif.-Mexus Consotrium fellow, 1989, Secretaria de Educacion Publica fellow, 1992, 94, 95, 96. Mem. Ecol. Soc. Am., Botanical Soc. Am., Econ. Botany Soc. Am., Sigma Xi. Avocations: dancing, music, racket ball. Home: Ave Benito Juarez # 775, 77200 Felipe Carrillo Puerto Mexico Office: U de Quintana Roo, Boulevard Bahia & I Comonfort, Chetumal Mexico

ROSALDO, RENATO IGNACIO, JR., cultural anthropology educator; b. Champaign, Ill., Apr. 15, 1941; s. Renato Ignacio and Mary Elizabeth (Potter) R.; m. Michelle Sharon Zimbalist, June 12, 1966 (dec. Oct. 1981); children: Samuel Mario, Manuel Zimbalist; m. Mary Louise Pratt, Nov. 26, 1983; 1 child, Olivia Emilia Rosaldo-Pratt. AB, Harvard U., 1963, PhD, 1971. Asst. prof. cultural anthropology Stanford (Calif.) U., 1970-76, assoc. prof., 1976-85, prof., 1985—, Mellon prof. interdisciplinary studies, 1987-90, dir. Ctr. for Chicano Rsch., 1985-90, chair anthropology, 1994-96, Lucie Stern prof. social scis., 1993—. Author: Ilongot Headhunting 1883-1974, 1980, Culture and Truth, 1989. Recipient Harry Benda prize Assn. for Asian Studies, 1983; Guggenheim fellow, 1993. Fellow Am. Acad. Arts and Scis. Avocations: swimming, drawing, dancing. Home: 2520 Cowper St Palo Alto CA 94301-4218 Office: Stanford U Dept Anthropology Stanford CA 94305-2145

ROSALES, SUZANNE MARIE, hospital coordinator; b. Merced, Calif., July 23, 1946; d. Walter Marshall and Ellen Marie (Earl) Potter; children: Anita Carol, Michelle Suzanne. AA, City Coll., San Francisco, 1966. Diplomate Am. Coll. Utilization Review Physicians. Utilization review coord. San Francisco Gen. Hosp., 1967-74; mgr. utilization review/discharge planning UCLA Hosp. and Clinics, 1974-79; nurse III Hawaii State Hosp., Kaneohe, 1979-80; review coord. Pacific Profl. Std. Review Orgn., Honolulu, 1980-81; coord. admission and utilization reviewq The Rehab. Hosp. of the Pacific, Honolulu, 1981-85; coord. Pacific Med. Referral Project, Honolulu, 1985-87; dir. profl. svcs. The Queen's Healthcare Plan, Honolulu, 1987-88; utilization mgmt. coord. Vista Psychiat. Physician Assocs., San Diego, 1989; admission coord. utilization review San Francisco Gen. Hosp., 1989-91, quality improvement coordinator, 1991—; cons. Am. Med. Records Assn. Contbr. articles to profl. jours. Mem. Nat. Assn. Utilization Review Profls. Home: 138 Alta Vista Way Daly City CA 94014 Office: San Francisco Gen Hosp 1001 Potrero Ave San Francisco CA 94110-3518

ROSAN, RICHARD MARSHALL, real estate executive, architect; b. Bronxville, N.Y., Jan. 15, 1942; s. Richard A. and Helen (Marshall) R.; m. Nancy Davis, Apr. 12, 1969; children—Elizabeth, Christina, Peter. B.A., Williams Coll., 1964; M.Arch., U. Pa., 1967. Registered architect, N.Y. Chmn., dir. Office of Downtown Bklyn. Devel., N.Y.C., 1972-75; dir. office of Devel., City of N.Y., 1975-80; pres. Real Estate Bd. N.Y., N.Y.C., 1980-86; sr. v.p. Silverstein Properties, 1986—; trustee Lincoln Savs. Bank, Turner Equity Investors. Pres. bd. trustees Berkeley-Carroll Street Sch., Bklyn., 1977—; bd. dirs. Bklyn. Acad. Music, 1980—; pres. bd. Park Slope Neighborhood Family Care Ctr., Bklyn., 1982—. Mem. AIA. Democrat. Congregationalist. Home: 2950 Davenport St NW Washington DC 20008-2165*

ROSAND, DAVID, art history educator; b. Bklyn., Sept. 6, 1938; s. Johan Herbert and Frieda (Grotenstein) R.; m. Ellen Fineman, June 18, 1961; children: Jonathan, Eric. AB, Columbia Coll., 1959; MA, Columbia U., 1962, PhD, 1965. Instr. art history Columbia U., N.Y.C., 1964-67, asst. prof., 1967-69, assoc. prof., 1969-73, prof., 1973-95, chmn. Soc. of Fellows in the Humanities, 1979-83, Meyer Schapiro prof. art history, 1995—. Author: (with Michelangelo Muraro) Titian and the Venetian Woodcut, 1976, Titian, 1978, Painting in Cinquecento Venice: Titian, Veronese, Tintoretto, 1982, rev. edit., 1997, Interpretazioni Venezione, 1984, The Meaning of the Mark: Leonardo and Titian, 1988, (with Robert Cafritz and Lawrence Gowing) Places of Delight: The Pastoral Landscape, 1988, Robert Motherwell on Paper, 1997; editor: (with Robert W. Hanning) Castiglione: The Ideal and the Real in Renaissance Culture, 1983, Titian: His World and His Legacy, 1982; editorial bd. Arion, Imago Musicae, Venezia Cinquecento. Mem. bd. advisors CASVA Nat. Gallery Art., 1990-94. Fulbright Commn. fellow, 1962-63; NEH fellow, 1971-72, 85-86, 91-92; John S. Guggenheim Meml. Found. fellow, 1974-75. Mem. Coll. Art Assn. Am., Renaissance Soc. Am. (mem. exec. bd. 1981—), Save Venice, Inc. (mem. gen com. 1992—), Ateneo Veneto (fgn.). Home: 560 Riverside Dr New York NY 10027-3210 Office: Columbia U Dept Art History & Archaeology 826 Schermerhorn Hall New York NY 10027

ROSAR, VIRGINIA WILEY, librarian; b. Cleve., Nov. 22, 1926; d. John Egbert and Kathryn Coe (Snyder) Wiley; m. Michael Thorpe Rosar, April 8, 1950 (div. Feb. 1968); children: Bruce Wiley, Keith Michael, James Wilfred. Attended, Oberlin Coll., 1944-46; BA, U. Puget Sound, 1948; MS, C.W. Post Coll., L.I.U., Greenvale, N.Y., 1971. Cert. elem. and music tchr., N.Y.; cert. sch. library media specialist, N.Y. Music programmer Station WFAS, White Plains, N.Y., 1948; prodn. asst. NBC-TV, N.Y.C., 1948-50; tchr. Portledge Sch., Locust Valley, N.Y., 1967-70; librarian Syosset (N.Y.) Schs., 1970-71, Smithtown (N.Y.) Schs., 1971-92; ret., 1992; pres. World of Realia, Woodbury, N.Y., 1969-86; founder Cygnus Pub., Woodbury, 1985-87. Active local chpt. ARC, 1960-63, Community Concert Assn., 1960-66, Leukemia Soc. Am., 1978—. Mem. AAAS, N.Y. Acad. Scis., L.I. Alumnae Club of Pi Beta Phi (pres. 1964-66). Republican. Presbyterian. Avocations: music, sewing, gardening, writing. Home: 10 Warrenton Ct Huntington NY 11743-3750

ROSAS, SUSAN JANE, designer, graphic artist, illustrator, art director; b. Oakland, Calif., June 30, 1937; d. Clarence Francis and Barbara Hischier Matthews; m. John Anthony Roach, July 28, 1958 (div. 1968); children: Jennifer, Adam; m. Gilbert Joseph Rosas, June28, 1975. BA, U. Calif., Santa Barbara, 1961; postgrad., Ventura Coll., 1993-94. With La Cumbre Animal Hosp., Santa Barbara, 1967-76; artist Rood Assocs., Santa Barbara, 1969-71. Designer, artist: (seasonal brochures) Ventura County Chamber Orchestra, 1994-95; designer: (nutcracker collectibles featured in Hammacher Schlemmer catalog and Collector's Mart Mag.) "Nutcracker Prince" for Adrian Taron & Sons and "Clara," 1994-95. Recipient Best of Show award Fine Arts Exhibit-Acrylics U. Calif., Santa Barbara, 1961, Fine Arts Exhibit-Oils, 1961. Mem. AAUW (sec. 1961-62), Nat. Mus. Women in the Arts, U. Calif. Santa Barbara Alumni Assn., Buenaventura Art Assn., Carmel Art Assn. Avocations: painting and creating: watercolor, oils, pastel paintings, mixed media creations. Home: 1131 Windward Way Oxnard CA 93035-2459 Office: Adrian Taron & Sons 801 Linden Ave Carpinteria CA 93013-2042

ROSATI, MARIO, mathematician, educator; b. Rome, Jan. 5, 1928; s. Aristide and Maria (Gabrielli) R.; m. Maria Luisa Marziale, Aug. 3, 1968; children: Francesca, Nicoletta, Giulio. Laurea in Math., U. Rome, 1950. Asst. prof. U. Rome, 1952-66; prof. math. U. Padua, Italy, 1966—; dir. Applied Math. Inst., Padua U., 1978-86, Dept. Pure Applied Math., 1987-92, Seminario Matematico, 1994—. Co-editor: (with G. Tedone) Collana di Informazione Scientifica, 1965-78; contbr. books and articles in field. Fellow U. Goettingen 1955. Mem. Italian Math. Union, Am. Math. Soc., Nat. Rsch. Ctr. Roman Catholic. Home: 43 G Leopardi, 35126 Padua Italy Office: Dept Pure Applied Math, 7 GB Belzoni, 35131 Padua Italy

ROSATO, ANTHONY DOMINICK, mechanical engineer, educator; b. Bklyn., Aug. 28, 1953; s. Michael Joseph and Betty (Rispoli) R. BME, Pratt Inst., 1975; MS in Theoretical and Applied Mechanics, Northwestern U., 1979; MS in Applied Maths., Carnegie Mellon U., 1981, PhD in Mech. Engring., 1985. Devel. engr. Green Fan Co., Beacon, N.Y., 1975-77; rsch. asst. dept. civil engring. Northwestern U., Evanston, Ill., 1977-79; tchg. asst. mech. engring. and maths. Carnegie Mellon U., Pitts., 1979-82, rsch. asst., 1981-84, rsch. assoc. dept. mech. engring., 1985-86; adj. faculty dept. exact scis. Carlow Coll., Pitts., 1986; asst. prof. divsn. mech. engring. N.J. Inst. Tech., Newark, 1987-93, assoc. prof. mech. engring., 1993—, dir. Particle Tech. Ctr., 1995—; faculty Gov.'s Sch. in Scis., Drew U., Madison, N.J., 1988; vis. faculty fellow, physicist dept. earth scis. Lawrence Livermore (Calif.) Nat. Lab., 1989, 90; Joliot professorship Ecole Superieure de Physique et de Chimie Industrielles, Laboratoire H.M.P., Paris, 1994; mem. nat. materials adv. bd. NRC, 1995; vis. scientist The Lovelace Insts., Albuquerque, 1995-96; vis. assoc. prof. mech. engring. Worcester Poly. Inst., 1995. Reviewer Jour. Computational Physics, Applied Mechanics Reviews, EuroPhysics Letters, Powder Tech., Jour. Fluid Mechanics, Physics of Fluids, Mechanics Rsch. Comm., NSF, Phys. Rev. Letters; contbr. articles to profl. jours. Recipient grants Dept. Energy, 1990-95, Sun Microsys. Acad. Equip., 1992, NATO, 1992-94, Nat. Supercomputing Ctr. for Energy and the Environ., 1992-93, State of N.J., 1994-95, NSF, 1989-91, 92-93, 94-96, Exxon, 1994-96, NSF Combined Rsch. and Curriculum Devel., 1994-97, NSF Small Grants for Exploratory Rsch., 1996-97. Mem. AICE (particle tech. forum), ASME, Am. Soc. Engring. Edn. (program chair elect grad. studes divsn. 1995), Am. Acad. Mechanics, N.J. Inst. Tech. Ctr. for Applied Maths. and Stats., Assn. Pour L'Etude de la Micromechanique des Mileux Granulaires, Sigma Xi, Tau Beta Pi, Pi Tau Sigma. Roman Catholic. Achievements include research on modeling the effects of vibrating boundaries in a non-cohesive particle assembly; simulation of vibratory transport of bulk solids; experimental study to measure the collisional properties of spheres using automated high-speed motion analysis; development of a non-intrusive particle tracing technique for inclined chute flows and vibrated beds; developed Brazil Nuts model to explain size segregation of particulates; developed experimental and computational study of vibratory size segregation and induced convection; particle percolation in a packed bed. Avocations: classical piano, pen and ink illustrations. Office: NJ Inst Tech Mech Engring Dept University Heights Newark NJ 07102

ROSATO, LAURA MARIE, toxicologist, educator; b. Pitts., Jan. 13, 1958; d. William A. and Mary (Wachter) R. BS, U. Pitts., 1981, MS, 1985, PhD, 1990. Grad. student rschr. U. Pitts., 1983-85, rsch. asst. III, 1982-83, coord. & lectr., 1987-89, grad. student rschr., 1985-90; divsnl. toxicologist Procter & Gamble Co., Cin., 1990-92; prin. toxicologist Millennium Petrochem. Inc. (formerly Quantum Chem. Corp.), Cin., 1992-94, sr. prin. toxicologist, 1994—; adj. prof., cons. toxicologist U. Cin., 1995—; ind. cons. Pitts., 1985-90; provider internat. toxicity estimates for risk peer review bd., 1997. Contbr. numerous articles to sci. jours. Recipient Student Leadership award U. Pitts., 1989, Leading Women in Cin. award for rsch. and tech., 1997, Great Rivers Girl Scout Coun. Woman of Distinction award, 1997. Mem. Ohio Valley Soc. Toxicology, Greater Cin. Women's Network (bd. dirs. 1996—, chair awards and recognition com. adv. coun., co-chair leading women corp. sponsorship com. 1997, co-chair Cin./No. Ky. United Way mgmt. cabinet for cmty. outreach 1997), Internat. Soc. Regulatory Toxicology and Pharmacology, Ohio Valley Soc. Environ. Toxicology and Chemistry, Soc. Toxicology, Vinyl Acetate Toxicology Group (v.p. and treas. 1994—), Diethyl Ether Prodrs. Assn. (chair 1995—), Toastmasters Internat. (sec.), Leading Women, Inc. (trustee, pres.-elect exec. com. 1997—). Avocations: reading, walking, teaching, mentoring. Home: 7027 Waterview Way Apt 13 Cincinnati OH 45241-4510 Office: Millennium Petrochemicals Inc 11530 Northlake Dr Cincinnati OH 45249-1642

ROSBERG, DAVID WILLIAM, plant sciences educator; b. Superior, Wis., Jan. 3, 1919; s. Albert and Hulda (Sundin) R.; m. Helen Dana McDonald, Nov. 8, 1941; children—David William, Dana Karin. B.A., St. Olaf Coll., 1940; postgrad., Tex. A&M Coll., 1940-41; M.S., Ohio State U., 1947, Ph.D., 1949. Grad. asst. biology dept. Tex. A&M U., College Station, 1940-42, lab asst. Tex. Agrl. Exptl. Sta., 1942, asst. prof. plant physiology and pathology dept., 1949-54, asso. prof., 1954-58, prof., 1958-60, prof., head dept. plant scis., from 1960, prof. emeritus, 1981—; insp. R.R. Perishable Inspection Agy., N.Y.C., 1941; grad. asst. dept. botany Ohio State U., 1946-48, research asst.; Research Found., 1948-49; lab. asst. Battelle Meml. Inst., Columbus, O., 1948. Named Disting. Alumnus Ohio State U., 1972. Mem. AAAS, Am. Phytopath. Soc., Tex. Acad. Sci., Sigma Xi, Phi Kappa Phi, Gamma

Sigma Delta. Home: 11630 Sh # 30 College Station TX 77845 Office: Dept Plant Scis Tex A&M U College Station TX 77843

ROSBERG, MERILEE ANN, education educator; b. Oak Park, Ill., June 1, 1942; d. Andrew Clark and Martha (Kester) Adamson; m. William H. Rosberg, Aug. 17, 1963; children: Peter E., Trent W. AB, Augustana Coll., 1963; MA, U. Iowa, 1971, PhD, 1985. Tchr. Cedar Rapids (Iowa) Pub. Schs., 1963-65, Internat. Sch. Kuwait, 1965-67, N. Winnishoik Cmty. Schs., Decorah, Iowa, 1967-69, St. Mark's Luth. Ch. Presch., Cedar Rapids, 1969-71; staff tng. specialist Linn County Day Care Svcs., Cedar Rapids, 1971-76; dir. early childhood program Jane Boyd Comty. House, Cedar Rapids, 1976-86; prof., divsn. chair Mt. Mercy Coll., Cedar Rapids, 1986—; vis. prof. U. Sts. Cyril & Methodius, Veliko Turnovo, Bulgaria, 1992, Czech Tech. U., Prague, Czech Rep., 1990. Fulbright scholar U. Brunei Darusalam, 1994-95. Mem. Nat. Assn. Early Childhood Edn., Nat. Coun. Tchrs. English, Internat. Readign Assn., Orgn. Mondiale Pour L'Education Prescolaire (U.S. nat. com.). Avocations: reading, travel. Home: 1900 Bever Ave SE Cedar Rapids IA 52403-2715 Office: Mt Mercy Coll 1330 Elmhurst Dr NE Cedar Rapids IA 52402-4763

ROSBOTTOM, RONALD CARLISLE, French, arts and humanities educator; b. New Orleans, July 15, 1942; s. Albert Carlisle and Marjorie Catherine (Chavez) R.; m. Betty Elane Griffin, Sept. 5, 1964; 1 child, Michael K. B.A., Tulane U., 1964; M.A., Princeton U., 1966, Ph.D., 1969; MA (hon.), Amherst Coll., 1990. Instr. U. Pa., Phila., 1967-69, asst. prof., 1969-73; assoc. prof. Ohio State U., Columbus, 1973-78, prof. French lit., 1978-89, chmn. Romance langs., 1982-88; dean of faculty Amherst (Mass.) Coll., 1989-95, prof. French lit. and European studies, 1989—, Winifred E. Arms prof. arts and humanities, 1996—, chair European Studies program, 1996—. Author: Marivaux's Novels, 1974, Choderlos de Laclos, 1979 (Havens prize 1980); editor: Studies in 18th Century Culture, 1975, 76, Essays in the French Enlightenment, 1991; mem. editorial bds. Eighteenth Century: Theory & Interpretation, Romance Quarterly. Decorated Ordre des Palmes Académiques; Woodrow Wilson Found. fellow, 1964-65, 66-67; Am. Council Learned Socs. summer fellow, 1970. Mem. MLA, Internat. Soc. 18th Century Studies (exec. com. 1978-83), Am. Soc. 18th Century Studies (exec. sec. 1978-83, 2d v.p. 1992-93, 1st v.p. 1993-94, pres. 1994-95), Am. Assn. Tchrs. French, Phi Beta Kappa. Democrat. Home: 326 Shays St Amherst MA 01002-2943 Office: Amherst Coll Box 2255 Amherst MA 01002-5000

ROSCH, JOHN THOMAS, lawyer; b. Council Bluffs, Iowa, Oct. 4, 1939; s. H.P. and Phebe Florence (Jamison) R.; m. Carolyn Lee, Aug. 18, 1961; children: Thomas Lee, Laura Lee. BA, Harvard U., 1961, LLB, 1965. Bar: Calif. 1966, U.S. Dist. Ct. (no. dist.) Calif. 1966, U.S. Dist. Ct. (ea. dist.) Calif. 1967, U.S. Ct. Appeals (9th cir.) 1966. Assoc. McCutchen, Doyle, Brown & Enersen, San Francisco, 1965-72, ptnr., 1972-73, 75-93; office mng. ptnr. Latham & Watkins, San Francisco, 1994—; dir. Bur. Consumer Protection, FTC, Washington, 1973-75. Contbr. articles profl. jours. Fellow Am. Bar Found., Am. Coll. Trial Lawyers; mem. ABA (past chmn. antitrust sect.), State Bar Calif., San Francisco Bar Assn., Calif. State and Antitrust and Trade Regulation Sect. (past sect. chair). Republican. Episcopalian. Office: Latham & Watkins 505 Montgomery St San Francisco CA 94111-2552

ROSCH, PAUL JOHN, physician, educator; b. Yonkers, N.Y., June 30, 1927; s. Samuel Joseph and Mary (Gang) R.; m. Lorraine Marie Hunt, June 27, 1951; children: David Carl, Jonathan Hunt, Jane Ellen, Michael Edward, Richard Joseph, Donna Marie; m. Marguerite Delamater, Sept. 12, 1972. AB, Brown U., NYU, 1948; MA, NYU, 1950; MD, Albany Med. Coll., 1954. Diplomate Am. Bd. Internal Medicine. Fellow Inst. Exptl. Medicine and Surgery, U. Montreal, Que., Can., 1951-52; intern, asst. resident in medicine Johns Hopkins Hosp., 1954-56; resident in medicine, then chief dept. metabolism Walter Reed Med. Ctr., 1956-58; physician-in-charge nuclear medicine St. John's Riverside Hosp., Yonkers, 1959-67, dir. endocrine clinic, sr. attending physician, 1959-96, vice chief of staff, 1977; chief endocrine clinic St. Joseph's Hosp., 1959, sr. cons. in medicine, 1980—; pres. Am. Inst. Stress, Yonkers, 1978—, sr. cons. in medicine, 1980—; clin. prof. medicine and psychiatry N.Y. Med. Coll., 1980—; asst. clin. prof. medicine Mt. Sinai Hosp. Sch. Medicine, 1963-67; former adj. prof. medicine in psychiatry U. Md. Sch. Medicine. From asst. to assoc. editor Health Comm. and Informatics; editor-in-chief Stress Medicine, 1990—; mem. editorial bd. AMA Archives Internal Medicine, Folia Clinica Internat, Jour. Human Stress, Internat. Jour. Psychosomatics, Am. Jour. Health Promotion, Cardiovascular Revs. & Reports, Internat. Jour. Stress Mgmt., Comprehensive Therapy, Jour. Human Behavior; contbg. editor Creative Living; contbr. articles to profl. jours. Bd. govs. Jewish Community Ctr.; bd. dirs. Family Svc. Soc., Mensana Clinic, 1980—; chmn. bd. Internat. Found. Biosocial Devel. and Human Health, 1980—; mem. adv. bd. Image Inst., 1980—. Capt. AUS, 1956-58. Fellow ACP, Internat. Stress Mgmt. Assn. (hon. v.p. 1991—), Am. Coll. Cardiology, Internat. Acad. Medicine, Am. Coll. Angiology, N.Y. Diabetes Assn.; mem. Westchester Diabetes Assn. (pres. 1968), Internat. Law Enforcement Stress Assn. (adv. bd. 1980—), Yonkers Acad. Medicine (bd. govs., pres. 1971), N.Y. Cardiology Soc., Acad. Psychosomatic Medicine, Soc. Behavioral Medicine, N.Y. Acad. Scis., Endocrine Soc., Am. Diabetes Assn., Westchester Soc. Internat. Medicine (past pres.), Stress Mgmt. Assn. (hon. v.p.), N.Y. State Soc. Internal Medicine (pres. 1974), Soc. Nuclear Medicine (bd. dirs.), Am. Fedn. Clin. Rsch., Am. Soc. Internal Medicine, Am. Geriatrics Soc., Elmwood Country Club, Atlantis Golf Club, Breakers Golf Club, St. Andrews Golf Club, La Coquille Club (Palm Beach, Fla.). Home: 10 Old Jackson Ave Hastings On Hudson NY 10706 also: 221 N Country Club Dr Atlantis FL 33462-1113

ROSCHER, NINA MATHENY, chemistry educator; b. Uniontown, Pa., Dec. 8, 1938; d. Charles Kenneth and Wilma Pauline (Solomon) Matheny; m. David Roscher, Dec. 27, 1964. BS in Chemistry, U. Del., 1960; PhD in Chemistry, Purdue U., 1964. Phys. chemist Nat. Bur. of Standards, 1958-61; rsch. and teaching asst. Purdue U., West Lafayette, Ind., 1960-64, fellow in chemistry, instr. chemistry, 1964-65; instr. U. Tex., Austin, 1965-67; sr. staff chemist Coca-Cola Export Corp., 1967-68; asst. prof. Douglass Coll., Rutgers U., The State U., 1968-74, asst. dean, 1971-74; dir. acad. adminstrn. Am. U., Washington, 1974-76, assoc. prof. chemistry, 1974-79, prof., 1979—, assoc. dean grad. affairs Coll. Arts and Scis., 1976-79, vice-provost acad. svcs., 1979-82, vice provost for acad. affairs, 1982-85, dean faculty affairs, 1981-85, chair chemistry dept., 1991—; program dir. sci. edn., NSF, 1986—; lectr. in field. Contbr. articles to profl. jours. Recipient Disting. Alumna award Purdue Univ. Sch. Sci., 1996, Am. Chem. Soc. award for encouraging women into careers in the chem. scis. Camille and Henry Dreyfus Found., 1996; Standard Oil fellow, 1961-62, David Ross fellow, 1963-64, Rutgers U. Rsch. Fund, Biomed. Support grantee. Fellow AAAS, Am. Inst. Chemists (profl. opportunities for women com., pres. dist. inst. chemists 1978-79, sec. 1976-77, fin. com. 1983-87, exec. com., bd. dirs. 1986), Assn. Women in Sci.; mem. Am. Chem. Soc. (treas. Monmouth County sect. 1970-72, chair 1974, pres. Washington sect. 1995, profl. programs planning and coord. com. 1976-78, admissions com. 1981-89, 91-96, GM scholar 1956-60, Virgil F. Payne award, others), N.Y. Acad. Scis., AAUA, Assn. Women in Sci., Soc. Applied Spectroscopy, Sci. Manpower Commn. Profls. in Sci. Home: 10400 Hunter Ridge Dr Oakton VA 22124-1616 Office: Am Univ Dept Chemistry Washington DC 20016-8014

ROSCOE, STANLEY NELSON, psychologist, aeronautical engineer; b. Eureka, Calif., Nov. 4, 1920; s. Stanley Boughton and Martha Emma (Beer) R.; m. Margaret Hazel Brookins, Dec. 21, 1948 (dec.); children: Lee Marin Roscoe Bragg, Jack; m. Elizabeth Frances Lage, Mar. 12, 1977 (dec.); 1 child, Catherine Marie; m. Gayle Buchanan Karshner, Mar. 15, 1990. AB in Speech and English, Humboldt State U., 1943; postgrad., U. Calif., Berkeley, 1942, 46; MA in Psychology, U. Ill., 1947, PhD in Psychology, 1950. Cert. psychologist, Calif. Research asst. U. Ill., Champaign, 1946-50, research assoc., 1950-51, asst. prof., 1951-52; assoc. dir. Inst. Aviation, head aviation research lab., Champaign, 1969-75, prof. psychology and aero. and astronautical engring., 1969-79, prof. emeritus, 1979—; prof. N.Mex. State U., Las Cruces, 1979-86, prof. emeritus, 1986—; with Hughes Aircraft Co., Culver City, Calif., 1952-69, 75-77, dept. mgr., 1962-69, sr. scientist, 1975-77; tech. adviser, cons. in field; pres. Illiana Aviation Scis. Ltd., Las Cruces, N.Mex., 1976—; v.p. Aero Innovation, Inc., Montreal. Author: Aviation Psychology, 1980, Flightdeck Performance: The Human Factor, 1990; editor: Aviation Research Monographs, 1971-72, Heydays in Humboldt, 1991, From Humboldt to Kodiak, 1992; assoc. editor: Human Factors Jour., 1982—; cons. editor Internat. Jour. Aviation Psychology, 1991—; contbr. numerous articles to profl. jours. 1st lt. AC, U.S. Army, 1943-46. Fellow APA (divsn. of applied and engring. psychology, Franklin V. Taylor award 1976), Human Factors Soc. (pres. 1960-61, Jerome H. Ely award 1968, 73, 89, 91, Alexander C. Williams award 1973, Paul M. Fitts award 1974, Pres.'s award 1990), Royal Aero Soc. (Eng.); mem. IEEE, AIAA, Inst. Navigation, Assn. Aviation Psychologists (ann. career award 1978), Aerospace Human Factors Assn. (Paul T. Hansen award 1994), Sigma Xi, Phi Kappa Phi, Phi Sigma, Chi Sigma Epsilon. Patentee, inventor in field. Home: 2750 Sunnygrove Ave Mckinleyville CA 95519 Office: PO Box 4498 Las Cruces NM 88003-4498

ROSCOPF, CHARLES BUFORD, lawyer; b. Marvell, Ark., Apr. 21, 1928; s. Emmett Lee and Sally Virginia (King) R.; m. Mary Anne Maddox, Aug. 22, 1954; children—Charles David; Ann Karen. Student, Hendrix Coll., 1948-50; J.D., U. Ark., 1954. Bar: Ark. bar 1954, U.S. Dist. Cts 1955, 64, U.S. Supreme Ct. bar 1965. Pvt. practice Helena, Ark., 1954—; assoc. firm Burke, Moore & Burke, 1954-58; ptnr. firm Burke & Roscopf, 1958-64; sr. ptnr. Roscopf and Roscopf, P.A., 1964—; mem. Ark. Ho. of Reps., 1953-58; del. Ark. Constl. Conv., 1968; mem. Ark. Probate Drafting Com.; mem. Ark. State Bd. Law Examiners, 1973-79; spl. justice Ark. Supreme Ct. Served with USN, 1946-48; served with USAFR, 1962-68. Fellow Ark. Bar Found. (pres. 1995-96); mem. ABA, ATLA, Ark. Bar Assn. (pres. 1990-91), Am. Law Inst., Rotary (Paul Harris fellow), Masons, Shriners, Kappa Sigma. Methodist. Home: 117 Avalon Pl Helena AR 72342-1722 Office: Nat Bank Bldg 408 Helena PO Box # 610 Helena AR 72342

ROSDEITCHER, SIDNEY SAMUEL, lawyer; b. Bayonne, N.J., June 2, 1936; s. Morris and Lee (Rosenbluth) R.; m. Linda Latter, Aug. 28, 1960; children: Elizabeth, David, Emily. AB, Columbia U., 1958; LLB magna cum laude, Harvard U., 1961. Bar: N.Y., 1963, D.C., 1961, U.S. Dist. Ct. (so. and ea. dists.) N.Y., U.S. Claims Ct., U.S. Tax Ct., U.S. Ct. Appeals (1st, 2d, 3d, 4th, 5th, 8th, 9th, 10th, 11th, D.C. and fed. cirs.), U.S. Supreme Ct. Atty. office of legal counsel U.S. Dept. Justice, Washington, 1961-62; advisor to commr. FTC, Washington, 1965-66; assoc. Paul, Weiss, Rifkind, Wharton & Garrison, N.Y.C., 1962-65, 66-72, ptnr., 1972—; adj. prof. civil liberties Bklyn. Law Sch., 1974-75; lectr. profl. responsibility Columbia Law Sch., 1990-93. Article editor Harvard U. Law Rev., 1960-61; contbr. articles to legal jours. Trustee Lawyers Com. for Civil Rights Under Law, 1992—; bd. dirs. NAPIL Fellows, 1992-96; governing coun. Internat. League Human Rights, 1996—. Mem. D.C. Bar Assn. (model rules spl. com. 1982-85), Assn. of Bar of City of N.Y. (chmn. profl. and jud. ethics com. 1979-82, fed. cts. com. 1982-85, chmn. com. on internat. human rights 1991-94, chmn. coun. on internat. affairs 1995—, civil rights com. 1994—). Home: 90 Riverside Dr New York NY 10024-5306 Office: Paul Weiss Rifkind Wharton & Garrison 1285 Avenue Of The Americas New York NY 10019-6064

ROSE, ADAM ZACHARY, economist, educator; b. Bergen-Belsen, Germany, Jan. 5, 1948; s. Isaac and Gusta Eugenia (Kaiser) R.; m. Anne Lynn Carver, Oct. 15, 1972; children: Eleanor, Jonathan. BA, U. Utah, 1970; MA, Cornell U., 1972, PhD, 1974. Sr. economist N.Y. Council Econ. Advisers, N.Y.C., 1974-75; asst. prof. U. Calif., Riverside, 1975-81; assoc. prof. W.Va. U., Morgantown, 1981-84; faculty assoc. Regional Research Inst., Morgantown, 1981-88; vis. assoc. EQL, Calif. Inst. Tech., Pasadena, 1986; prof. mineral econs. W.Va. U., 1984-88, chmn. dept., 1981-83, 86-88; prof. mineral econs., head dept. energy, environ. & mineral econs. Pa. State U., University Park, 1988—, faculty assoc. Earth System Sci. Ctr., 1993—, faculty assoc. Environ. Pollution Control Program, 1995—; cons. Mayor's Office, City of L.A., 1980, NSF, Washington, 1980, U.S. Forest Svc., 1982-83, So. Calif. Gas Co., 1983, 85, U.S. Corps of Engrs., 1984, 92-93, San Francisco City Atty's Office, 1986, Nat. Coal Assn., 1990, U.S. Dept. Energy, 1990, EUREMCO, 1991-92, UNCTAD, 1991-92, Foster Wheeler, Inc., 1992, Air Products & Chemicals Inc., 1992-93, Ctr. Energy and Econ. Devel., 1994-95, EQE Internat., 1996; expert witness U.S. Senate, Washington, 1985, W.Va. Pub. Svc. Commn., 1991, Pa. Pub. Utility Commn., 1992. Sr. author: Forecasting Gas Demand, 1987, Natural Resource Policy and Income Distribution, 1988, Combating Global Warming: A Global System of Tradeable Carbon Emission Entitlements, 1992; editor, author: Geothermal Energy and Regional Development, 1979, Frontiers of Input-Output Analysis, 1989; author (monograph): Dynamic Interindustry Model of Pollution Abatement, 1976; guest editor: Jour. Policy Modeling, 1989; Resource and Energy Economics, 1993, Energy Policy, 1996; assoc. editor: Jour. Regional Sci., 1985—; editorial bd. mem. Resources Policy, 1989—, Resource and Energy Economics, 1993—, Pacific & Asian Jour. Energy, 1996. Recipient Outstanding Planning Program Honor award Am. Planning Assn., 1983; Woodrow Wilson Found. fellow, Cornell U., 1970-71; grantee U.S. Dept. Energy, 1983-84, 92-95, grantee NSF, Washington, 1987-88, 90-91, 93—; grantee Nat. Ctr. Earthquake Engring. Rsch., 1992-96; grantee Argonne Nat. Lab., 1992-94. Mem. Am. Econ. Assn. (rep. to AAAS 1986-92), AAAS (mem. sect. K exec. com.), Regional Sci. Assn., Internat. Assn. Energy Economists, Assn. Resource & Environ. Economists, Mineral Econs. and Mgmt. Soc. Democrat. Jewish. Home: 1702 Princeton Dr State College PA 16803-3259 Office: Pa State U 222 Walker Bldg University Park PA 16802-5010

ROSE, ALAN DOUGLAS, lawyer; b. Flushing, N.Y., Dec. 22, 1945; s. William Allen and Josephine (Grohe) R.; m. Janet Louise Clift, Aug. 20, 1966; children: Alan Douglas Jr., Windsor, Ainsley, Vanessa, Hillary, Lacey. BA, Harvard U., 1967; MSc, London Sch. Econs., 1969; JD, U. Va., 1972. Bar: Mass. 1974, U.S. Dist. Ct. Mass. 1975, U.S. Ct. Claims 1983, U.S. Ct. Appeals (1st cir.) 1976, U.S. Ct. Appeals (fed. cir.) 1986, U.S. Supreme Ct. 1991. Law clk. to judge U.S. Dist. Ct. Mass., Boston, 1972-73; assoc. Choate Hall & Stewart, Boston, 1973-75; asst. U.S. Atty. Dept. Justice, Boston, 1975-80; ptnr. Nutter McClennen & Fish, Boston, 1980-95; mgr. litigation dept., 1991-93; ptnr. Rose & Assocs., Boston, 1995—; lectr. Law Sch. Harvard U., Cambridge, Mass., 1981-82; spl. asst. atty. gen. Commonwealth Mass., 1991-92; mem. U.S. Dist. Ct. Civil Justice Adv. Bd., 1995—. Mem. ABA, Boston Bar Assn. (vice chair joint bar com. on jud. appointments 1991-92), City Mission Soc. (chmn., bd. dirs.). Democrat. Mem. United Ch. Christ. Home: 50 Bristol Rd Wellesley MA 02181-2728 Office: Rose & Assocs One Boston Pl Boston MA 02108-4400

ROSE, BEATRICE SCHROEDER (MRS. WILLIAM H. ROSE), harpist, educator; b. Ridgewood, N.J., Nov. 15, 1922; d. Henry William and Ida (LeHovey) Schroeder; m. William Harrison Rose, Apr. 10, 1954; 1 child, Daniel. Student, Inst. Musical Art, 1940-41, Mannes Coll. Music, 1942-44; studies with, Lucile Lawrence and Carlos Salzedo. Concert and radio debut N.Y. World's Fair, 1939; soloist Damrosch Music Appreciation Hour broadcast, 1940, Duke of Windsor's Save the Children Fund, Nassau, The Bahamas, 1941; assoc. harpist Radio City Music Hall Orch., N.Y.C., 1944-50; various radio and solo performances N.Y. area, 1944-51; concert artist Italy, U.S. and Can., 1952; prin. harpist Houston Symphony, 1953-84; prof. harp Moores Sch. Music, U. Houston, 1953—; soloist Contemporary Music Soc., 1959, 60, Houston Chamber Orch., 1969; dir. Christmas Festival of Harps, Houston Harp Ensemble, PBS, 1978, Harps of Gold, 1983; staff harpist, Heritage club, 1987-95; High Tea Ritz Carlton, 1996—. Author: Troubadour Harp: A Guide for Teachers and Students, 1976, rev. edits., 1982, 92; co-author; Outline of Six-Year Harp Course for Elementary, Junior and Senior High School, 1966; composer works include Enchanted Harp, rev. edit., 1975; recs. for Houston Symphony, Stokowski, Everest, Capitol, Comissiona, Vanguard Records. Recipient 1st prize Federated Music Clubs Contest, 1936; N.Y. Hour of Music award, 1945. Mem. Am. Harp Soc., Tex. Music Educators Assn. (adjudicator All-State competitions), Nat. Fedn. Music Clubs (harp adviser 1991—), Phi Beta. Home: 1315 Friarcreek Ln Houston TX 77055-6714 Office: U Houston Sch Music Houston TX 77004

ROSE, BEVERLY ANNE, pharmacist; b. Lewiston, Idaho, June 11, 1950; d. Burton Roswell and Nell Dora (Greenburg) Stein; m. Fred Joseph Rose, July 21, 1973 (div. Aug. 1980). BS in Pharmacy, Ohio No. U., 1973; MBA, Cleve. State U., 1987. Registered pharmacist, Ohio, N.Y. Staff pharmacist Lorain (Ohio) Community Hosp., 1973-79, dir. pharmacy, 1979-91; dir. dept. pharmacy svcs. The House of the Good Samaritan Health Care Complex, Watertown, N.Y., 1991-93; adj. faculty, clin. tng. specialist U. Toledo Coll. Pharmacy, 1980-91; computer cons. Hosp. Pharmacy Network; mem. State Bd. Legis. Rule Rev., Ohio State Bd. Pharmacy, 1987, 88; mem. pres. adv. bd. Ohio No. U., Ada, 1990—. Mem. editl. bd. Aspen Publs., 1992—. Mem. Am. Soc. Health Sys. Pharmacists (apptd. coun. legal and pub. affairs 1988-89, 89-90, state del. ho. of dels. Ohio 1984, 85, 86, 87, 88, 89, mem. psychotherapeutics-spl. practice group 1990—), Adminstrs. Practice Mgmt. Group, Am. Pharm. Assn., Ohio Soc. Hosp. Pharmacists (pres. 1985-89, Squibb Leadership award 1988, Ciba-Geigy Svc. award 1988, Evlyn Gray Scott award 1987), N.Y. State Coun. Hosp. Pharmacists, Am. Soc. Parenteral and Enteral Nutrition, Fedn. Internat. Pharmaceutique, N.Y. Chpt. Am. Coll. Clin. Pharmacy, others. Avocations: computers, photography, classical music, singing. Home: 20 Cambridge Dr Apt 4 Georgetown OH 45121-9737

ROSE, CHARLES, television journalist. B in History, Duke U., JD; post-grad., NYU. Interviewer Sta. WPIX-TV, N.Y.C., 1972; mng. editor Bill Moyers Internat. Report, from 1974; exec. producer Bill Moyers Jour., from 1975; corr. U.S.A.: People in Politics, PBS, 1976; polit. corr. NBC News, 1976-77; co-host A.M. Chgo., 1978; host The Charlie Rose Show Sta. KXAS-TV, Dallas, Ft. Worth, 1979-81; host nationally syndicated The Charlie Rose Show Sta. WRC-TV, Washington, 1981-83; former host, interviewer CBS News Nightwatch, Washington, from 1984; now host "Charlie Rose" Rose Comms., Inc for PBS, N.Y.C., 1994—. Producer: (TV program) A Conversation with Jimmy Carter (Peabody award). Recipient News and Documentary Emmy award for Conversation with Roger Payne, 1992, 14th Annual Cable ACE award, 1992. Office: 499 Park Ave New York NY 10022-1240*

ROSE, CHARLES DAVID, consulting company executive; b. Corpus Christi, Dec. 28, 1939; s. Robert Chester and Gladys (Blackmon) R.; m. Mary Ann McKinney, Apr. 23, 1965; children: David, Elizabeth, Katherine. BS in Physics magna cum laude, La. Tech. U., 1964; postgrad., Iowa State U. From engr. to dist. level supr. staff ops. South Ctrl. Bell Telephone Co., 1964-70; mgr. sales and engring. Hycaloader Co., 1970-74; owner Charles Rose Cons., Monroe, La., 1974—. Contbr. numerous articles to profl. jours. Mem. ASTM (various coms.), Am. Statis. Assn., Am. Soc. for Quality Control. Achievements include devel. of fractal variogram model for use in geostatistics; designated U.S. expert for ISO on coal sampling. Home: 4404 Landlewood Ct Dallas TX 75287 Office: Charles Rose Cons PO Box 797425 Dallas TX 75379-7425

ROSE, CHARLES GRANDISON, III (CHARLIE ROSE), former congressman; b. Fayetteville, N.C., Aug. 10, 1939; s. Charles Grandison Jr. and Anna Frances (Duckworth) R.; m. Stacye Hefner; children: Charles Grandison IV, Sara Louise, Kelly Josephine. AB, Davidson Coll., 1961; LLB, U. N.C., 1964. Bar: N.C. 1964. Chief prosecutor Dist. Ct., 12th Jud. Dist., 1967-70; mem. 93nd-104th Congresses from 7th N.C. dist., Washington, 1972-96; mem. agrl. com., subcom. Specialty Crops and Natural Resources, Gen. Farm Commodities 93nd-104th Congresses from 7th N.C. dist.; co-founder Congl. Rural Caucus; founder Congl. Clearing House on the Future. Pres. N.C. Young Democrats, 1968. Presbyterian. Home: 3413 S Wakefield St Arlington VA 22206

ROSE, DANIEL, real estate company executive, consultant; b. N.Y.C., Oct. 31, 1929; s. Samuel B. and Belle (Bernstein) R.; m. Joanna Semel, Sept. 16, 1956; children: David Semel, Joseph Benedict, Emily, Gideon Gregory. Student, Yale U., 1947-50; cert. of proficiency in Russian lang., U.S. Air Force Program, 1951; B.A., Syracuse U., 1952; postgrad., U. Paris. With Dwelling Mgrs., Inc., N.Y.C., 1954—; pres. Dwelling Mgrs., Inc., 1960—, vice chmn., sec.-treas. Baltic-Am. Enterprise Fund, 1994—; dir. Dreyfus Tax Exempt Bond Fund Inc., 1976-82, Dreyfus Money Market Fund, Inc., 1980-82; pres., CEO Rose Assocs., Inc., N.Y.C., 1980—; 22 Dreyfus Funds, 1992—; assoc. fellow Pierson Coll. Yale U., 1974—; bd. govs., hon. life mem. Technion-Israel Inst. Tech.; bd. dirs., mem. grants com. Realty Found. N.Y.; vice chmn. Lionel Trilling seminars Columbia U., 1977—; bd. dirs. Nat. Humanities Ctr., Ventures in Edn.; trustee, mem. exec. and compensation and benefits coms. U.S. Trust Co. of N.Y., 1982-92; trustee, vice chmn. mixed use devel. coun. Urban Land Inst., 1986-93; trustee, mem. investment and compensation coms. Corp. Property Investors; mem. exec. com. Urban Land Found., 1989—, gov., 1993—; designated Cert. Property Mgr. Inst. for Real Estate Mgmt. Expert adv. to sec. HUD, 1972; expert/cons. to commr. edn. HEW, 1974; cons. HUD panel on urban devel., 1984-86; dir. N.Y. Coun. Humanities, 1980-86, N.Y. Conv. Ctr. Devel. Corp., 1980-90, Get Ahead Found., 1989—, Fifth Ave. Assn., 1989—; mem. Governor's Task Force on Housing, 1975, Task Force on Taxation, Mcpl. Assistance Corp., 1976-77, Planning Commn. Theatre Adv. Group, coun. of fellows, vis. com. to grad. faculty, bd. overseers Ctr. for Study of N.Y.C. affairs New Sch. for Social Rsch.; overseers com. to visit Ctr. Internat. Affairs Harvard U., 1992—; mem. adv. bd. CUNY-TV channel A, 1986—, Mcpl. Broadcasting System, 1977-78, MIT Ctr. for Real Estate Devel.; donor Daniel Rose chair urban econs., trustee NYU N.Y. Inst. for Humanistic Studies, Mus. of City of N.Y., 1984-90, Jewish Publ. Soc., Com. for Econ. Devel., N.Y.C. Rand Inst.; chmn. bd. trustees, Horace Mann-Barnard Sch., 1971-74, trustee, 1962-89, hon. trustee, 1989— ; v.p., assoc. treas., bd. dirs. Police Athletic League of N.Y., vice chmn. Cen. Harlem Facility; pres. Harlem Ednl. Activities Fund Inc., YM & YWHA of the Bronx, 1963-67; v.p. N.Y. Landmarks Conservancy, bd. dirs. 1977-90; bd. dirs. Jewish Cmty. Ctrs. Assn., 1970—, pres. 1974-78, hon. pres. 1978—; v.p. World Confedn. of Jewish Cmty. Ctrs., 1977-83; former trustee and exec. com. mem. Fedn. of Jewish Philanthropies of N.Y., chmn. standing functional com. on cmty. ctrs., 1969-73; ptnr. N.Y.C. Partnership, 1990—; treas., bd. dirs. Citizens Housing and Planning Coun. of N.Y., 1972-90; chmn. Dem. platform adv. com., 1984 Nat. Conv.; bd. advisors Dem. Leadership Coun., 1992—, Progressive Policy Inst.; trustee Dem. Nat. Com., 1988; chmn. Del. Svcs. Host Com., N.Y.C.; bd. trustees MBA of N.Y. Scholarship Found., Inc., 1996—. Served with USAF, 1951-54. Mem. Internat. Inst. Strategic Studies (dir. Am. com. for IISS 1987—), Coun. on Fgn. Rels., Fgn. Policy Assn. (bd. dirs. 1971—, chmn. fgn. policy assocs. 1972-75), Inst. for East-West Security Studies (bd. dirs. 1982—, treas. 1988—, co-chmn. fin. com. 1990—), Am. Soc. Real Estate Counselors (mem. publs.-rsch. com.), Real Estate Bd. of N.Y. Inc. (chmn. housing com. 1975—, mem. bd. govs. 1977-80, 90—, mem. REBNY Found.), Assn. of Yale Alumni (del.-at-large 1978-81, class of 1951 del. 1986-89), Century Assn. (N.Y.C.), Coffee House, Yale Union League Club, Cosmos (Washington), Racquet and Tennis, Quaker Ridge Country Club, Noyac Country Club, Econ. Club N.Y. Home: 895 Park Ave New York NY 10021-0327 Office: Rose Associates Inc 200 Madison Ave New York NY 10016-3903

ROSE, DAVID ALLAN, investment manager; b. N.Y.C., Feb. 15, 1937; s. Edward William and Marion (Nadelstein) R.; m. Frances Helaine Dushman, Aug. 16, 1959; children: Evan Denali, Mitchell Franklin. BS in Acctg., Queens Coll., 1958; MBA, Syracuse U., 1968. Fin. mgr. U.S. Army, Fort Richardson, Alaska, 1961-75; comptroller U.S. Army, Fort Richardson, 1975; exec. dir. Alaska Mcpl. Bond Bank Authority, Anchorage, 1975-82, Alaska Indsl. Devel. Authority, Anchorage, 1980; co-owner Downtown Investment Co., Anchorage, 1980—, Downtown Delicatessen, Inc., Anchorage, 1976—; CEO, Alaska Permanent Fund Corp., Juneau, 1982-92; chmn., CEO, Alaska Permanent Capital Mgmt. Co., Inc., Anchorage, 1992—; ptnr. Russian Alaska Export/Import Co., Anchorage, 1993—; fin. advisor Fin. Green Lake Dam, Sitka, Alaska, 1977, Fin. Dutch Harbor Port, Unalaska, Alaska, 1979-80, Fin. Kenai-Anchorage Pipeline, Anchorage, 1979-80, Fin. Pulp Mill Pollution Control, Ketchikan, Alaska, 1979-80. Mem. City Coun., Anchorage, 1971-75, Borough Assembly, Anchorage, 1971-75, Mcpl. Assembly, Anchorage, 1975-80; pres. Alaska Mcpl. League, 1975, Mcpl. Assembly, Anchorage, 1975-77; vice chmn. endowment fund Alaska Pacific U., 1994—. Recipient Golden Man award Boys Club Alaska, Anchorage, 1974, Decoration for Meritorious Civilian Service, U.S. Army, 1975, Pub. Service award City and Borough, Juneau, 1986, Lions Internat. awards, awards for fundraising Am. Diabetes Assn.; named Pub. Adminstr. Yr. Am. Soc. Pub. Adminstrn., Alaska chpt., 1986. Mem. Rotary (awards). Republican. Jewish. Avocations: boating, gardening. Office: Alaska Permanent Capital 900 W 5th Ave Ste 601 Anchorage AK 99501-2029

ROSE, DAVID L., lawyer; b. Ft. Monmouth, N.J., Feb. 18, 1955; s. Llewellyn Paterson and Bebe (Faulk) R.; m. Laura Marie Jarvis, Sept. 3, 1989; children: Allison Michelle, Jessica Morgan, Ashley Elizabeth. BA in Comm., U. Colo., 1980; JD, Ariz. State U., 1991. Bar: Ariz., U.S. Dist. Ct.

Ariz., U.S. Ct. Appeals (9th cir.), U.S. Supreme Ct. Law clk. Bonn & Anderson, Phoenix, 1988-91, Maricopa County Superior Ct., Phoenix, 1990-91; lawyer Anderson, Brody, Levinson, Weiser & Horwitz, Phoenix, 1991-92, Brandes, Lane & Joffe, Phoenix, 1992-93; pvt. practice Phoenix, 1993—; gen. counsel Counsel for Children's Rights, Ariz. Editor: Missive, 1992. Bd. dirs. Maricopa County Family Support Adv. Com., Phoenix; adv. coun. Washington Sch. Dist., Phoenix; mem. Ariz. State Legis., Domestic Rels. Reform Com., Phoenix. Mem. Maricopa County Bar Assn. (adv. family law com.), ABA (adv. family law sect.), Nat. Congress for Men (pres.), Father's for Equal Rights of Colo. (pres.). Avocations: aviation, computer systems. Office: 1221 E Osborn Rd Ste 101 Phoenix AZ 85014-5540

ROSE, DONALD JAMES, computer science educator; b. Santa Ana, Calif., May 25, 1944; 1 child, Tamar Rose. BA, U. Calif., Berkeley, 1966; AM, Harvard U., 1967, PhD, 1970. Instr. applied math. Harvard U., Cambridge, Mass., 1970; asst. prof. math. U. Denver, 1970-72; asst. prof. applied math. Harvard U., 1972-74, assoc. prof., 1974-77; prof., chmn. dept. computer sci. Vanderbilt U., Nashville, 1977-78; researcher Bell Labs., Murray Hill, N.J., 1978-84; prof., chmn. dept. computer Sci. Duke U., Durham, N.C., 1984-91, prof., 1991—; cons. MCNC, Research Triangle Park, 1984-89, Bell Labs, Murray Hill, 1984—, Tanner Rsch. Pasadena, Calif., 1993-94. Co-editor: Sparse Matrices and Their Applications, 1972, Sparse Matrix Computations, 1976; contbr. more than 50 articles to profl. jours. Mem. IEEE, Am. Math. Soc., Math. Assn. Am., Assn. Computing Machinery, Soc. Indsl. Applied Math. Office: Duke U Dept Computer Sci D112A LSRC Box 90129 Durham NC 27708-0129

ROSE, DONALD L., physician, educator; b. St. Charles, Mo., July 20, 1911; s. William Albert and Estelle Mattie (Sherry) R.; m. Martha Jane Koontz, Mar. 6, 1937; children: Nancy Kathryn Rose Harling, William Donald. BA, U. Colo., 1933, MA, MD, 1936. Diplomate Am. Bd. Phys. Medicine and Rehab. Intern Miami Valley Hosp., Dayton, Ohio, 1936-37, resident, 1937-38; rsch. assoc. Kettering Inst. Med. Rsch., Dayton, 1938-41; asst. prof. sch. medicine Univ. Kans., Kansas City, 1947-49, assoc. prof., 1949-51, prof., 1951-74, prof. emeritus, 1974—; cons. Phys. Med. Surgeon Gen.'s Office, Washington, 1957-65, nat. cons. USAF, 1959-61; bd. govs. Am. Bd. Phys. Medicine and Rehab., Rochester, Minn., 1957-67. Contbr. chpt. An Atlas of Amputations, 1947, Postgraduate Medicine and Surgery, 1951, Therapeutic Heat, 1958. Med. advisor NFIP Wyandotte County, Kansas City, 1947-60, Johnson County chpt., 1950-60, MDA Kansas City, 1965-74. Fellow Baruch Found., Boston, 1946-47. Mem. AMA, Am. Acad. Phys. Medicine and Rehab. (pres. 1953-54, Disting. Clin. award 1983), Am. Congress Rehab. Medicine (pres. 1957-58), Kans. Med. Soc., Wyandotte County Med. Soc. Republican. Methodist. Avocations: golf, boating. Home: 16 Eaton Cir Bella Vista AR 72715-5513

ROSE, DONALD MCGREGOR, lawyer; b. Cin., Feb. 6, 1933; s. John Kreimer and Helen (Morris) R.; m. Constance Ruth Lanner, Nov. 29, 1958; children: Barbara Rose Mead, Ann Rose Weston. AB in Econs., U. Cin., 1955; JD, Harvard U., 1958. Bar: Ohio 1958, U.S. Supreme Ct. 1962. Asst. legal officer USNR, Subic Bay, The Philippines, 1959-62; with Office of JAG USNR, The Pentagon, Va., 1962-63; assoc. Frost & Jacobs, Cin., 1963-70, ptnr., 1970-93; sr. ptnr., 1993—; co-chmn. 6th Cir. Appellate Practice Inst., Cin., 1983, 90, mem. 6th Cir. adv. com., chmn. subcom. on rules, 1990-94, chmn., 1994-96. Trustee, chmn. Friends of Cin. Pks., Inc., 1986-89, pres. 1980-86; trustee Am. Music Scholarship Assn., Cin., 1985-88; pres. Social Health Assn. Greater Cin. Area Inc., 1969-72; co-chmn. Harvard Law Sch. Fund for So. Ohio, Cin., 1985-87; pres. Meth. Union, Cin., 1983-85; chmn. trustees Hyde Pk. Cmty. United Meth. Ch., Cin., 1974-76, chmn. coun. on ministries, 1979-81, chmn. adminstrv. bd., 1982-84, chmn. mem. canvass, 1985, chmn. staff parish rels. com., 1988-90, chmn. commn. missions, 1993-95; trustee Meth. Theol. Sch. Ohio, vice chmn. devel. com., 1990-94, sec. 1992-94, chmn. devel. com., 1994—. Lt. USNR, 1959-63. Mem. ABA (co-chmn. advocacy tng. subcom., appellate practice com., litigation sect. 1988—), Ohio Bar Assn., Cin. Bar Assn., U. Club (Cin.), Cin. Country Club. Republican. Avocations: sailing, golf. Home: 8 Walsh Ln Cincinnati OH 45208-3423 Office: Frost & Jacobs 2500 PNC Ctr 201 E 5th St Cincinnati OH 45202-4117

ROSE, EDWARD W. (RUSTY ROSE), professional sports team executive. Gen. partner Texas Rangers, Arlington, TX. Office: care Texas Rangers 1000 Ballpark Way Arlington TX 76011-5168*

ROSE, ELIHU, real estate executive; b. N.Y.C., Mar. 30, 1933; s. Samuel B. and Belle (Bernstein) R.; m. Susan Wechsler, Feb. 6, 1965; children: Amy, Isabel, Abigail. BS, Yale U., 1954; MA, NYU, 1969, PhD, 1978. Ptnr. Rose Assocs., N.Y.C., 1956—; trustee Tchrs. Coll., Columbia U. Contbr. articles to profl. mil. jours. Trustee Jewish Mus. of N.Y., 1992—, Internat. Ctr. Photography; bd. visitors Boston U. Med. Sch., 1978—, past chmn.; bd. dirs. Sta. WNET (PBS), Lincoln Ctr. Theater, 1992—; bd. dirs. N.Y. State Archives Partnership Trust. Mem. Internat. Inst. Strategic Studies, Council Fgn. Relations, Century Assn., Union League Club, Yale Club of N.Y., Army and Navy Club (Washington). Office: Rose Assocs 200 Madison Ave New York NY 10016-3903

ROSE, ELIZABETH, author, satirist, poet, publisher; b. N.Y.C., 1941. BA summa cum laude, U. Redlands, 1976. Pub. Butterfly Pub. Co., Santa Monica, 1985; radio and TV personality L.A., 1985—. Author: Sainthood and Single Motherhood, 1990. Avocations: plays and movies, ice skating, crossword puzzles, dancing.

ROSE, ERNST, dentist; b. Oldenburg, Germany, July 22, 1932; s. William and Elsie (Lowenbach) R.; came to U.S., 1940, naturalized, 1946; m. Shirley Mae Glassman, Dec. 24, 1960; children: Ruth Ellen, Michele Ann, Daniel Scot, Seth Joseph. BS, Georgetown U., 1955; DDS, Western Res. U., 1963. Intern, Waterbury (Conn.) Hosp., 1964; pvt. practice dentistry, Hubbard, Ohio, 1964-96; pres., treas. Dr. Ernst Rose, Inc. Lab. instr. Ohio State U., Columbus, 1956-57; dental adviser Assoc. Neighborhood Ctr. Mem. Liberty Twp. Zoning Commn., 1967-74, 1988-92, vice chmn.; chmn., 1970-74, chmn., 1990; chmn. Hubbard (Ohio) Urban Renewal Com., 1968-74. Mem. brotherhood bd., 1967—, treas. 1971-73, 88-90, pres. 1975-77, 90-92, temple bd. dirs. 1975-84, 89-95. Served with AUS, 1957-59. Mem. ADA, Ohio Dental Assn., Corydon Palmer Dental Soc. (mem. coun. 1983-87), Warren Dental Soc., Hubbard C. of C. (bd. dirs. 1967—, v.p. 1995—), Jewish Chatauqua Soc. (life), Alpha Omega (council mem. 1968—, sec. 1970-71, v.p. 1971-72, pres. 1972-73, pres. 1989-90). Lodges: B'nai B'rith (pres. 1970-71, trustee 1971—), Rotary (vice chmn. Kashrut com. 1983-85, chmn. Kashrut com. 1985—, vice chmn. Mikvah com. 1983-93, Paul Harris Fellow). Home and Office: 30 N Main St Hubbard OH 44425-1697

ROSE, FREDERICK PHINEAS, builder and real estate executive; b. N.Y.C., Nov. 16, 1923; s. Samuel and Belle (Bernstein) R.; m. Sandra Priest, June 28, 1948; children: Deborah, Jonathan Frederick Phineas, Samuel P. (dec.), Adam Raphael. B.C.E., Yale U., 1944. V.p. Rose Assocs., Inc., N.Y.C., 1946-60, pres., 1960-80, chmn., 1980—; vice chmn. N.Y. State Facilities Devel. Corp., 1970-75, Phoenix Home Life Mut. Ins. Co., 1972-93; mem. publs. com. Commentary Mag., 1964—, chmn. publs. com., 1979-84; trustee United Mut. Savs. Bank, 1977-82, Consol. Edison Co. N.Y., 1977-96; gov. N.Y. Real Estate Bd., 1972-75, 86-89, 94—; mem. Coun. Fgn. Rels.; U.S. del. to UN Conf. on Housing, Planning, and Bldg. Rsch., 1962-63, 67; bd. dirs. Olympia & York Co. Pres. Fedn. Jewish Philanthropies of N.Y., 1974-77, chmn. bd. dirs., 1981-83, hon. chmn., 1983—; vice chmn. Greater N.Y. Fund, 1974-76; bd. dirs. Henry Kaufmann Campgrounds, 1950-66, pres., 1962-66; trustee Lexington Sch. for Deaf, 1954-70, Mills Coll. Edn., 1960-68, Children's Aid Soc., 1964-75; trustee Scarsdale (N.Y.) Bd. Edn., 1966-71, pres., 1969-70; trustee Mt. Sinai Sch. Medicine, Hosp. and Med. Ctr., 1966-73, Rockefeller U., 1984—, Citizens Budget Commn., N.Y.C., 1969-94, Energy Fund, 1970-75, Inst. Pub. Adminstrn., 1970-81, Asia Soc., 1976-82, 94—, Philharm. Symphony Soc. N.Y., Inc., 1979-96, hon. trustee 1997—, trustee Aspen Inst. Humanistic Studies, 1979-91, Met. Mus. Art, 1981—, Manhattan Inst., 1987—, Yale U., 1989-94, Am. Mus. Natural History, 1991—; trustee, treas. Jewish Communal Fund, 1982-85; trustee Inst. Internat. Edn., 1984-89; chmn. bd. govs. Assn. Yale Alumni, 1972-75; bd. dirs. N.Y.C. Partnership, Inc., 1982-90, Lincoln Ctr. for the Performing Arts, Inc., 1984—, vice chmn., 1991—; mem. Univ. Council Yale U., 1976-81; trustee Rye Hist. Soc., 1992-94. Served to lt. (j.g.) USNR, World War II. Recipient Yale medal, 1976, Urban Leadership award N.Y. U., 1978, Patron of Art award Yale Sci. and Engring. Soc., 1991; Jonathan Edwards Coll. fellow. Mem. Union League Club N.Y. Clubs: Century Assn., Beach Point Yacht, Century Country; Yale (N.Y.C.). Home: 8 S Manursing Is Rye NY 10580-4310 Office: Rose Assocs Inc 200 Madison Ave New York NY 10016-3903

ROSE, GREGORY MANCEL, neurobiologist; b. Eugene, Oreg., Feb. 3, 1953; s. Mancel Lee and Ilione (Schenk) R.; m. Kathleen Ann Frye, June 30, 1979; 1 child, Julian Mancel. BS cum laude, U. Calif., Irvine, 1975, PhD, 1980. Research fellow M.P.I. for Psychiatry, Munich, 1976; rsch. assoc. Miescher Labor, M.P.I., Tuebingen, Republic of Germany, 1980-81; regular fellow dept. pharmacology U. Colo. Health Sci. Ctr., Denver, 1981-84, asst. prof., 1984-89, assoc. prof., 1989—; rsch. biologist VA Med. Ctr., Denver, 1981—, co-dir. neurosci. tng. program, 1986-89, assoc. rsch. career scientist, 1989—. Achievements include discovery of importance of stimulus patterning for induction of hippocampal synaptic plasticity. Bd. dirs. Greater Park Hill Community, 1987-90. VA Rsch. Svc. grantee, 1984, 86, 89, 93, NSF grantee, 1988, 90, NIMH grantee, 1989, 94, NIA grantee, 1991. Mem. AAAS, Am. Aging Assn., Soc. Neurosci., Internat. Brain Rsch. Orgn., N.Y. Acad. Sci. Democrat. Episcopalian. Avocations: fine woodworking, fly fishing. Office: VA Med Ctr Med Rsch 151 1055 Clermont St Denver CO 80220-3808

ROSE, HENRY, lawyer; b. Olean, N.Y., Mar. 28, 1927; s. Irving and Sarah Rose; m. Norma Lefcowitz, Feb. 16, 1957 (div. 1981); children: Benjamin, Andra, Jonathan. BA cum laude, U. Buffalo, 1950, LLB cum laude, 1951. Bar: N.Y. 1951, D.C. 1953, U.S. Ct. Appeals (D.C., 2nd, 3d, 4th, 5th, 6th, 9th, 10th cirs.), U.S. Dist. Ct. (we. and so. dists.) N.Y., U.S. Dist. Ct. (so. dist.) Tenn., U.S. Supreme Ct. 1956. Sterling fellow Yale U., New Haven, 1956-57; atty. NLRB, 1952-53; pvt. practice Buffalo, 1953-56; assoc. prof. U. Toledo, Ohio, 1957-58, Rutgers U., Camden and Newark, N.J., 1958-62; from spl. asst. to solicitor, dep. assoc. solicitor for legislation and legal counsel U.S. Dept. Labor, Washington, 1962-70, assoc. solicitor, 1970-74; gen. counsel Pension Benefit Guaranty Corp., Washington, 1974-84; ptnr., chmn. employee benefits dept. Epstein Becker & Green, P.C., Washington, 1985-92, of counsel, 1993-95; pvt. practice, Washington, 1995—; teaching assoc. Northwestern U., 1951-52; part-time lectr. U. Buffalo, 1954-56, U. Va., 1968; guest lectr. Harvard U., Am. U., Cath. U., Georgetown U., George Washington U.; acad. visitor London Sch. Econs., 1971-72; speaker in field. Contbr. articles to profl. jours. Asst. spl. counsel emergency crime com. Chgo. City Coun., 1952. Rsch. grantee Ford Found., 1959. Mem. ABA (chmn. joint com. on employee benefits 1995-96), D.C. Bar Assn. Home: 700 New Hampshire Ave NW Washington DC 20037-2406

ROSE, HUGH, management consultant; b. Evanston, Ill., Sept. 10, 1926; s. Howard Gray and Catherine (Wilcox) R.; m. Mary Moore Austin, Oct. 25, 1952; children: Susan, Nancy, Gregory, Matthew, Mary. BS in Physics, U. Mich., 1951, MS in Geophysics, 1952; MBA with highest distinction, Pepperdine U., 1982. Mgr. Caterpillar, Inc., Peoria, Ill., 1952-66; v.p., mktg. mgr. Cummins Engine Co., Columbus, Ind., 1966-69; pres., CEO Cummins Northeastern, Inc., Boston, 1969-77; pres. Power Systems Assocs., L.A., 1980-83, C.D. High Tech., Inc., Austin, Tex., 1984-87; mgmt. cons. Rose and Assocs., Tucson, 1984, 87—. Contbr. paleontol. articles to various publs. Bd. dirs. Raymond Alf Mus., Claremont, Calif., 1975—, Comstock Found., Tucson, 1988, Environ. Edn. Exch., 1991, Heart Ctr. U. Ariz., Tucson, 1992. With USAAF, WWII. Fellow AAAS; mem. Acacia, Soc. Vertebrate Paleontology, Beacon Soc. Boston (pres. 1979-80), Algonquin Club Boston (v.p., bd. dirs. 1974-80), Duxbury Yacht Club, Longwood Cricket Club, Cum Laude Soc., Phi Beta Kappa, Delta Mu Delta, Sigma Gamma Epsilon, Beta Beta Beta, Cum Laude Soc. Republican. Presbyterian. Office: Rose & Assocs 5320 N Camino Sumo Tucson AZ 85718-5132

ROSE, HUGH, retired economics educator; b. London, July 20, 1920; came to U.S., 1960, naturalized, 1977; s. William and Ann (Ogus) R. Student, Oxford (England) U., England, 1939-40, 45-47, Nuffield Coll., England, 1950-52. Lectr. in econs. Rhodes U., South Africa, 1947-50, lectr., 1952-53; lectr. in econs. Exeter U., England, 1954-60; assoc. prof. econs. U. Rochester, N.Y., 1961-63, prof., 1965-70; assoc. prof. econs. U. Toronto, Can., 1963-65; hon. rsch. assoc. Harvard U., Cambridge, Mass., 1969-70; prof. econs. Johns Hopkins U., Balt., 1970-91. Author: Macroeconomic Dynamics, 1991; contbr.a rticles to profl. jours. With British Army, 1940-45. Home: 112 Cross Keys Rd Apt D Baltimore MD 21210-1536 Office: Johns Hopkins U Dept Econs 3400 N Charles St Baltimore MD 21218-2608

ROSE, ISRAEL HAROLD, mathematics educator; b. New Britain, Conn., May 17, 1917; s. Abraham and Dora (Dubrow) R.; m. Pearl Nitzberg, Jan. 24, 1942 (div. Feb. 1956); 1 son, Steven Philip; m. Susan Ann Lazarus, Mar. 26, 1961; children: Dora, Eric. Student, CCNY, 1934-36; A.B., Bklyn. Coll., 1938, A.M., 1941; Ph.D., Harvard, 1951. Tutor, instr. Bklyn. Coll., 1938-41; instr. Pa. State Coll., 1942-46; asst. prof. U. Mass., 1948-54, assoc. prof., 1954-60; faculty Hunter Coll., 1960-68, prof. math., 1965-68, chmn. dept., 1966-68; prof. math. Lehman Coll., CUNY, 1968-82, prof. emeritus, 1983—, chmn. dept., 1968-72, 80-82, resident prof., 1983—; Vis. asst. prof. Mt. Holyoke Coll., 1951-52, vis. assoc. prof., 1954-55, 58-59; sci. cons. AID, India, summer 1965. Author: A Modern Introduction to College Mathematics, 1959, Algebra: An Introduction to Finite Mathematics, 1963, Vectors and Analytic Geometry, 1968, Elementary Functions: A Precalculus Primer, 1973, (with Esther R. Phillips) Elementary Functions, 1978. NRC predoctoral fellow Harvard, 1946-48; fellow Fund Advancement Edn., 1952-53. Mem. Am. Math. Soc., Math. Assn. Am. (chmn. Met. N.Y. sect. 1973-75), Nat. Council Tchrs. Math., Assn. Tchrs. Math. New Eng. (pres. Conn. Valley sect. 1956-57), Sigma Xi (pres. Hunter Coll. chpt. 1966-67). Home: 18 Floral Dr Hastings On Hudson NY 10706-1202 Office: Lehman Coll Bedford Park Blvd W Bronx NY 10468

ROSE, JALEN, professional basketball player; b. Detroit, Jan. 30, 1970; s. Jeanne R. Student, U. Mich. Guard Denver Nuggets, 1994-96, Ind. Pacers, 1996—. Named Honorable Mention All-Am., AP, 1991; set Michigan freshman scoring record, 1991; selected as All-Am., Parade Magazine, Third-Team All-Am., USA Today; set Nuggets' rookie record for assists, 1994-95 season; named to All-Rookie Second Team, NBA, 1995;. Office: Ind Pacers 300 E Market St Indianapolis IN 46204*

ROSE, JAMES MCKINLEY, JR., lawyer, government official; b. N.Y.C., 1927; m. Anne Louise Bourne, Aug. 19, 1960; children: Anne Clark, Louise Barnes. Grad., Phillips Exeter Acad., 1946; BA, Princeton U., 1951; JD, Harvard U., 1954. Bar: N.Y. 1955, D.C. 1977. With Dewey, Ballantine, Bushby, Palmer & Wood, N.Y.C., 1954-57; asst. U.S. atty. U.S. Dist. Ct. (so. dist.) N.Y., 1957-61; legal asst. to pres. Atlantic Mut. Ins. Co., 1961-65, sec., counsel, 1965-71; asst. fed. ins. adminstr. U.S. HUD, Washington, 1971-81; exec. asst. to adminstr. Fed. Ins. Adminstrn., Fed. Emergency Mgmt. Agy., Washington, 1981-93. Mem. men's com. Am. Mus. Natural History, 1968-71; sr. warden Episcopal ch. With AUS, 1946-47. Mem. D.C. Bar Assn., Assn. of Bar of City of N.Y., St. Nicholas Soc., Prouts Neck Assn. (pres. 1979-85), Prouts Neck Country Club, Chevy Chase Club. Republican. Home: 4913 Rodman St NW Washington DC 20016-3238

ROSE, JAMES TURNER, aerospace consultant; b. Louisburg, N.C., Sept. 21, 1935; s. Frank Rogers and Mary Burt (Turner) R.; m. Daniele Raymond, Sept. 15, 1984. BS with high honors, N.C. State U., 1957. Aero. rsch. engr. NASA, Langley Field, Va., 1957-59; project engr. NASA (Mercury and Gemini), Langley Field, Va. and Houston, 1959-64; program sys. mgr. McDonnell Douglas Astronautics Co (MDAC), St. Louis, 1964-69; mgr. shuttle ops. and implementation (MDAC) McDonnell Douglas Astronautics Co., St. Louis, 1969-72, mgr. shuttle support (MDAC), 1972-74, mgr. space processing programs, 1976-83; dir. electrophoresis ops. in space McDonnell Douglas Astronautics Co (MDAC), St. Louis, 1983-86; dir. space shuttle engring. NASA, Washington, 1974-76, asst. adminstr. comml. programs, 1987-91; aerospace cons., 1992—; chmn. Fla. Space Bus. Roundtable, 1995—. Recipient Lindberg award for mgmt. leadership AIAA, 1983, Presdl. Meritorious Rank award, 1989, NASA Exceptional Svc. medal, 1990, Laurels award Aviation Week, 1990, Aerospace Contribution to Soc. award AIAA, 1993. Mem. Phi Kappa Phi. Episcopalian.

ROSE, JEFFREY RAYMOND, economist, educator, negotiator; b. Toronto, Ont., Can., Sept. 23, 1946; s. Albert and Thelma (Harris) R.; m. Sandra Black; 1 child, Adam. B.A. with honors, U. Toronto, 1968, M.Indsl. Relations, 1983; postgrad., London Sch. Econs., 1968-69. Planner planning dept. City of Toronto, 1976-80; pres. local 79 Can. Union Pub. Employees, Toronto, 1980-83; nat. pres. Can. Union Pub. Employees, Ottawa, Ont., 1983-91; dep. min. intergovtl. affairs Govt. of Ont., Toronto, 1991-95; sr. fellow Harrowston program in conflict mgmt.-negotiation U. Toronto, 1995—; gen. v.p. Can. Labour Congress, 1983-91. Exec. mem. Ont. New Dem. Party, 1982-91; bd. dirs. Inst. for Rsch. on Pub. Policy, 1988-91; mem. fed. coun. New Dem. Party, 1988-91; co-chmn. Ont.-Que. Commn. for Cooperation, 1991-95. Home: 55 Sunnydene Crescent, Toronto, ON Canada M4N 3J5 Office: U Toronto Faculty Law, Rm 3029 Laskin Libr, Toronto, ON Canada M5S 2C5

ROSE, JENNIFER JOAN, lawyer; b. Dayton, Ohio, Oct. 25, 1951; d. Virginia Rose Kelly Apaydin. BA, Tarkio Coll., 1972; JD, Drake U., 1976. Bar: Iowa 1977, U.S. Dist. Ct. (so. and no. dists.) Iowa 1977, U.S. Ct. Appeals (8th cir.) 1978, U.S. Supreme Ct. 1980, Nebr. 1984. Adminstrv. asst. State Ombudsman, Des Moines, 1975; spl. asst. county atty. Page and Taylor Counties, Iowa, 1977-80; city atty. Imogene, Iowa, 1977-78, 85-87; city atty. Essex, Iowa, 1981-88; pvt. practice, Shenandoah, Iowa, 1977-81; dir. Southwest Iowa Family Systems Project, 1978-80; adv. council southwest region Legal Svcs. Corp. Iowa, 1983-88. Contbr. articles to profl. jours. and popular press. Vice-pres. vol. coun. Planned Parenthood Mid Iowa, 1980-83. Fellow Am. Acad. Matrimonial Lawyers, Internat. Acad. Matrimonial Lawyers; mem. Page County Bar Assn. (pres. 1978-80, v.p. 1988—), Southwest Iowa Bar Assn., Iowa State Bar Assn. (sec. coun. family law sect. 1989-93, chmn. 1992-93, spl. com. family law, young lawyers com. law and mental health, spl. com. on family law 1977-81, liaison to family law sect. 1991-92), ABA (chair GPS task force on sole & small firms 1991-92, mem. gen. practice sect., chmn. membership com. 1992-94, nominating com. 1993-94, Mead Data Task Force 1993-94, vice-chmn. family law com. 1988-91, chmn. family law com. 1989-91, editor Family Law Update 1990-92, GPS coun. 1993—, juvenile law com., exec. mem. marital property com. family law sect., newsletter editor 1989—; editor-in-chief: Compleat Lawyer, 1995—; mem. editl. bd. Matrimonial Strategist, 1993-95. Mem. Inter-Am. Bar Assn., Am. Orthopsychiat. Assn., Nat. Coun. Juvenile and Family Ct. Judges, Nat. Assn. Counsel for Children, Nat. Assn. Vol. in Criminal Justice (bd. dirs.), Iowa Law Alert (family law editor 1990-94), Internat. Soc. Family Law, Delta Theta Phi. Jewish. Home: RR 1 Shenandoah IA 51601-9801 Office: Rose Law Offices PO Box 616 Shenandoah IA 51601-0616

ROSE, JOAN L., computer security specialist; b. N.Y.C., June 27, 1946; d. Vincent A. LaVertu and Joan (Mileti) Ellis; children: Robert, Lauren. BA, Bklyn. Coll./CUNY, Bklyn., 1967. Cert. Info. Sys. Security Profl. Internat. Info. Sys. Security Cert. Consortium. Programmer Met. Life Ins., N.Y.C., 1967-68; sys. analyst Western Electric, Oklahoma City, 1968-74, Pacific Intermountain Express, Oakland, Calif., 1974-78, Chevron, San Francisco, 1978—; project mgr. GUIDE (IBM Users Group), Chgo., 1983—. Participant Habitat for Humanity, 1995—. Mem. Info. Sys. Security Assn. (Bay Area chpt. treas. 1983—). Democrat. Home: 3299 Pine Valley Rd San Ramon CA 94583 Office: Chevron H2196 6001 Bollinger Canyon Rd # H2196 San Ramon CA 94583-2324

ROSE, JOANNA SEMEL, cultural activist; b. Orange, N.J., Nov. 22, 1930; d. Philip Ephraim and Lillian (Mindlin) Semel; m. Daniel Rose, Sept. 16, 1956; children: David S., Joseph B., Emily, Gideon G. Cert. Shakespeare Inst., U.K., 1951; BA summa cum laude, Bryn Mawr Coll., 1952; postgrad. St. Hilda's Coll., Oxford U., 1953. Chmn. adv. bd. Partisan Rev., N.Y.C.; mem. exec. com. Am. Friends of St. Hilda's Coll., former chmn.; former pres. bd. dirs., current bd. dirs. Paper Bag Players, N.Y.C.; bd. dirs., former pres., mem. adv. coun. Poets and Writers, Inc., N.Y.C.; bd. dirs. Bay Street Theatre, Sag Harbor, Nat. Dance Inst., N.Y.C., British Inst., N.Y.C., Eldridge St. Project, N.Y.C., Ctr. for Visual History, N.Y.C.; bd. dirs., mem. adv. coun. Am. Friends Jewish Mus. Greece; former bd. dirs. N.Y. Pub. Libr., Guild Hall East Hampton, Musical Theatre Works, N.Y.C. Home: 895 Park Ave New York NY 10021-0327 also: 1 Lily Pond Ln East Hampton NY 11937

ROSE, JODI, opera company founder and artistic director; b. Phila., Nov. 27, 1952; d. Hubert Michael and Rita Gervase (Schubert) Rosenberger; m. Edward A. Caycedo; children: Gervase-Teresa, Thomas Schubert, Tanya-Katrina, Edward-Michael. Student, Vienna (Austria) Hochshule, 1973; BS in Edn. and Music, Chestnut Hill Coll., Phila., 1974; postgrad. in performing arts, NYU, 1976-77. Vocalist various musicals and operas, various cities, 1974-88; founder, artistic dir. Opera on the Go, Ltd., Jamaica Estates, N.Y., 1988—. Produced, staged and choreographed many children's and adult operas, including Goldilocks, Little Red Riding Hood, The Tortoise and the Hare, The Pirate Captains, Telephone, Sweet Betsy from Pike, The Medium, and La Pizza Con Funghi. Exec. chair PTA cultural com., Jamaica Estates, 1990—; founder, dir. musical theater workshops for youths, Queens Theater, N.Y., 1993—;. Recipient numerous cmty. and corp. grants, as well as grants from N.Y. State Coun. on Arts; selected as guest performers at Lincoln Ctr., N.Y.C.; recipient 3-yr. grant N.Y.C. Dept. Youth Svcs. Republican. Roman Catholic. Avocations: ballroom dancing, scuba diving, water skiing, swimming, horseback riding. Home and Office: 184-61 Radnor Rd Jamaica Estates NY 11432

ROSE, JOEL ALAN, legal consultant; b. Bklyn., Dec. 26, 1936; s. Edward Isadore and Adele R.; BS in Econs., N.Y.U., 1958; MBA, Wharton Grad. Sch., U. Pa., 1960; m. Isadora Fenig, Apr. 12, 1964; children: Susan, Terri. Asst. purchasing agt. Maidenform, Inc., N.Y.C., 1960-62; personnel dir. E.J. Korvette, Inc., N.Y.C., 1962-66; mgmt. cons. Daniel J. Cantor & Co., Inc., Phila., 1966—, sr. v.p., 1987—; prin. Joel Alan Rose & Assocs. Inc., Cherry Hill, N.J., 1987—; mgmt. cons. to legal profession; coordinator Ann. Conf. on Law Firm Mgmt. and Econs. Served with U.S. Army, 1960, Res. 1960-66. Fellow Coll. of Law Practice Mgmt.; mem. Inst. Mgmt. Cons., Am. Arbitration Assn. (nat. panel), ABA (chmn. acquisition and mergers com., practice mgmt. sect., large law firm interest group), Adminstrv. Mgmt. Soc. (past chpt. pres.), Am. Mgmt. Assn., Assn. Legal Adminstrs. Author: Managing the Law Office; mem. adv. bd. Law Office Economics and Management, 1987; contbg. columnist N.Y. Law Jour., 1984—, Nat. Law Jour.; also articles; bd. editors Acctg. For Law Firms; editl. adv. bd. Corp. Counsel's Guide to Law Dept. Mgmt. Office: Joel A Rose & Assoc Inc 1766 Rolling Ln PO Box 162 Cherry Hill NJ 08003-0162

ROSE, JOHN CHARLES, physician, educator; b. N.Y.C., Dec. 13, 1924; s. Hugh Stanley and Marie-Louise (Delury) R.; m. Dorothy Anne Donnelly, June 26, 1948; children—Nancy, Ellen, John Charles, Richard, Christopher. B.S., Fordham U., 1946; M.D. magna cum laude, Georgetown U., 1950, D.Sc. (hon.), 1973; LL.D. (hon.), Mt. St. Mary's Coll., 1973. Diplomate: Am. Bd. Internal Medicine, Am. Bd. Family Practice. Intern Walter Reed Army Hosp., 1950-51; resident, research fellow Georgetown U., VA hosps., Washington, 1950-54; established investigator Am. Heart Assn., 1954-57; instr., asst. prof. medicine Georgetown U., 1954-57, coord. med. edn., 1957-58, assoc. prof. physiology and biophysics, 1958-60, prof., 1960-91, chmn. dept. physiology and biophysics, 1958-63, dean Sch. Medicine, 1963-73, 78-79, prof. medicine, 1973-91, prof. emeritus, 1991—, vice chancellor Med. Ctr., 1984-87. Assoc. editor Am. Family Physician, 1955-62, chief med. editor, 1962-88; assoc. editor Acad. Medicine, 1992-95; contbr. articles to sci. pubs. Bd. dirs. Charles E. Culpeper Found., 1986-96. Served to 2d lt. USAAF, 1943-45. Decorated Air medal. Fellow A.C.P.; mem. Am. Physiol. Soc., Soc. Exptl. Biology and Medicine (nat. councillor 1962-63), Am. Heart Assn. (fellow sect. circulation). Club: Cosmos (Washington). Home: 5710 Surrey St Chevy Chase MD 20815-5520

ROSE, JOHN THOMAS, finance educator; b. Ft. Worth, Aug. 20, 1943; s. Paul Pittman and Francis Nan (White) R.; m. Sandra Kaye Rolen, Sept. 5, 1969; children: Melanie Ann, Leah Nan, Lynnelle Renee. BA with honors, Tex. A&M U., 1965; MA, Washington U., St. Louis, 1968, PhD, 1976. Economist Bd. Govs. of FRS, Washington, 1972-82, sr. economist, 1982-84; prof. fin., Harriette L. & Walter G. Lacy, Jr. chair banking Baylor U., Waco, Tex., 1984—, acting chair dept. fin. ins. and real estate, 1996-97; chmn. dept. Baylor U., Waco, 1997—. Contbr. articles to profl. jours. Bd. visitors Abilene (Tex.) Christian U., 1989-92. Capt. U.S. Army, 1969-71. Decorated

Bronze Star U.S. Army; recipient Disting. Bus. Prof. award, 1988, Hankamer Sch. Bus. Baylor U., 1988; Econ. Devel. Adminstrn. U.S. Dept. of Commerce fellow, 1968-69; Ernst & Young Found. Rsch. grantee, 1991. Mem. Am. Fin. Assn., So. Fin. Assn., Southwestern Fin. Assn., Fin. Mgmt. Assn., Omicron Delta Epsilon, Beta Gamma Sigma. Mem. Ch. of Christ. Office: Baylor U Hankamer Sch of Bus Dept Fin Ins and Real Estate PO Box 98004 Waco TX 76798-8004

ROSE, JONATHAN CHAPMAN, lawyer; b. Cleve., June 8, 1941; s. Horace Chapman and Katherine Virginia (Cast) R.; m. Susan Anne Porter, Jan. 26, 1980; 1 son, Benjamin Chapman. A.B., Yale U., 1963; LL.B. cum laude, Harvard U., 1967. Bar: Mass. 1968, D.C. 1972, U.S. Supreme Ct. 1976, Circuit Ct. Appeals 1977, Ohio 1978. Law clk. Justice R. Ammi Cutter, Mass. Supreme Jud. Ct., 1967-68; spl. asst. to U.S. pres., 1971-73; gen. counsel Council on Internat. Econ. Policy, 1973-74; assoc. dept. atty. gen. U.S. Dept. Justice, 1974-75; dept. asst. atty. gen. U.S. Dept. Justice (Antitrust Div.), 1975-77; asst. atty. gen. Office of Legal Policy, 1981-84; ptnr. firm Jones, Day, Reavis & Pogue, Washington, 1977-81, 84—. Prin. Ctr. for Excellence in Govt.; pres. Yale Daily News Found. 1st lt. U.S. Army, 1969-71. Mem. ABA, D.C. Bar Assn., Mass. Bar Assn., Ohio Bar Assn., Fed. Bar Assn., Am. Law Inst. Republican. Episcopalian. Clubs: Met, Chevy Chase, Union, Yale, Harvard. Office: Jones Day Reavis & Pogue 1450 G St NW Ste 600 Washington DC 20005-2001

ROSE, JOSEPH HUGH, clergyman; b. Jewett, Ohio, Nov. 21, 1934; s. Joseph Harper and Lottie Louella (VanAllen) R.; m. Nila Jayne Habig, Feb. 14, 1958; children: J. Hugh II, Stephanie Jayne, David William, Dawnella Jayne. ThB, Apostolic Bible Inst., St. Paul, 1955, DD, 1990. Ordained United Pentecostal Ch. Assoc. min. Calvary Tabernacle, Indpls., 1956-73; Ind. youth sec. United Pentecostal Ch., 1958-60, Ind. youth pres., 1960-72; bd. edn. United Pentecostal Ch., Hazelwood, Mo., 1974—; presbyter Ohio dist. United Pentecostal Ch., 1975-97, hon. life presbyter Ohio, 1997; pastor Harrison Hills Ch., Jewett, Ohio, 1973—. Editor, Ind. Dist. News, 1959-70; narrator radio svc. Harvestime, 1961—. Republican. Avocations: travel. Office: United Pentecostal Ch 8855 Dunn Rd Hazelwood MO 63042-2212

ROSE, L. STEVEN See **JASHEL, LARRY STEVEN**

ROSE, LEATRICE, artist, educator; b. N.Y.C., June 22, 1924; d. Louis Rose and Edna Ades; m. Sol Greenberg (div.); children: Damon, Ethan; m. Joseph Stefanelli, Oct. 10, 1975. Student, Cooper Union, 1941-45, Arts Students League, 1946, Hans Hoffman Sch., 1947. Solo exhbns. include Hansa Gallery, N.Y.C., 1954, Zabriskie Gallery, N.Y.C., 1965, Landmark Gallery, N.Y.C., 1974, Tibor de Nagy Gallery, N.Y.C., 1975, 78, 81, 82, Elaine Benson Gallery, Bridgehampton, N.Y., 1980, Armstrong Gallery, N.Y.C., 1985, Benton Gallery, Southampton, N.Y., 1987, Cyrus Gallery, N.Y.C., 1989; group exhbns. include Sam Kootz Gallery, N.Y.C., 1950, Peridot Gallery, N.Y.C., 1952, Poindexter Gallery, N.Y.C., 1959, Tanager Gallery, N.Y.C., 1960, 62, Riverside Mus., N.Y.C., 1964, Frumkin Gallery, N.Y.C., 1964, Pa. Acad. Fine Arts, Phila., 1966, N.Y. Cultural Ctr., 1973, The Queens (N.Y.) Mus., 1974, 83, Nat. Acad. Design, N.Y.C., 1974, 75, 76, 92, 93, Weatherspoon Art Gallery, Greensboro, N.C., 78, 81, Whitney Mus. Am. Art, N.Y.C., 1978, Albright-Knox Gallery, Buffalo, 1978, 81, Met. Mus. Art, 1979, Vanderwoude Tananbaum Gallery, N.Y.C., 1982, Benton Gallery, 1986, 87.; public collections include Albrect Gallery, St. Joseph, Mo., Guild Hall Mus., East Hampton, N.Y., Tibor de Nagy, Met. Mus. Art. Grantee N.Y. State Coun. Arts, 1974, The Ingram Merrill Found., 1974, AAUW, 1975, NEA, 1977, Esther and Aldolph Gottlieb Found., 1980, 88; recipient Altman prize NAD, 1974, Phillips prize NAD, 1992, award AAAL, 1992, Am. Inst. Art award. Mem. NAD. Avocations: reading, walking. Office: 463 West St Apt A924 New York NY 10014-2038

ROSE, LLOYD, theatre critic. Office: The Washington Post 1150 15th St NW Washington DC 20071-0001*

ROSE, MARGARETE ERIKA, pathologist; b. Esslingen, Germany, Feb. 12, 1945; came to U.S., 1967; d. Wilhelm Ernst and Lina (Schurr) Pfisterer; m. Arthur Caughey Rose, Feb. 3, 1967; children: Victoria Anne, Alexandra Julia, Frederica Isabella. MD, U. So. Calif., L.A., 1972. Diplomate Am. Bd. Anatomic and Clin. Pathology. Pathologist St. Joseph Med. Ctr., Burbank, Calif., 1977-78, Glenview Pathology Med. Ctr., Culver City, Calif., 1979—; dir. anatomic pathology Glenview Meml. Pathology, Culver City, 1988—; dir. Life Chem. Lab., Woodland Hills, Calif.; co-dir., lab. Holy Cross Med. Ctr., Mission Hills, Calif., 1994-95. Mem. Because I Love You, L.A., 1994. Fellow Am. Soc. Pathology, Coll. Am. Pathology. Avocations: cross-stitching, gardening, traveling. Office: Brotman Med Ctr Dept Pathology 3828 Hughes Ave Culver City CA 90232-2716

ROSE, MARIAN HENRIETTA, physics researcher; b. Brussels, Belgium; (parents Am. citizens); m. Simon Rose, Oct. 20, 1948 (dec. Jan. 1981); children: Ann, James, David, Simon. BA, Barnard Coll., 1942; MA, Columbia U., 1944; PhD, Harvard U., 1947. Teaching fellow Harvard U., Cambridge, Mass., 1945-46; adj. asst. prof. Courant Inst., N.Y.C., 1947-48, rsch. assoc., 1951-65, sr. rsch. scientist, 1965-75; vis. fellow Yale U., New Haven, Conn., 1981-93; bd. dirs. Minna-James-Heineman Stiftung, Essen, Fed. Republic of Germany. Contbr. articles to profl. jours. Bd. dirs. Jay Heritage Ctr., Rye, N.Y.; mem. Wetlands Control Commn., Bedford, N.Y., 1992—, Conservation Bd., Bedford, 1989-93; pres. Croton Watershed Clean Water Coalition, 1997—. Mem. Sierra Club (conservatin chair Atlantic chpt. 1992-95, chair N.E. regional conservation com. 1995—, del. at large to Westchester County Environ. Mgmt. Coun. 1994—), Phi Beta Kappa, Sigma Xi. Avocations: skiing, hiking.

ROSE, MARIANNE HUNT, business educator; b. Portsmouth, Ohio, Nov. 6, 1940; d. Harry Duke and B. Marie (Craycraft) Hunt; m. W. Craig Rose, Aug. 9, 1958 (dec. 1988); children: W. Stuart, Deirdre Anne. BS in Edn., Ohio U., 1962; postgrad., U. Va., James Madison U., George Mason U. Cert. tchr., Va., Ohio. Asst. editor Morehead (Ky.) News, 1962-63; mgr. Birthday Calendar Co., Morehead, 1963-64; bus. tchr. Clay Twp. Schs., Portsmouth, 1964-65, Prince William County Adult Edn., Woodbridge, Va., 1977-80, Prince William County Schs., Woodbridge, 1973-94; retired, 1994; co-sponsor Future Bus. Leaders Am., Gar-Field Sr. H.S., Woodbridge, mentor TLC program, 1990-94; team mem. Tech.-Prep. Consortium, No. Va. C.C., Woodbridge, 1992-94. Mem. Dale City Civic Assn., Woodbridge; elder, sec. 1st United Presbyn. Ch., Dale City, 1972—. Recipient Professionalism award Tchr. Recognition Com./Gar-Field, 1993. Mem. NEA, AAUW, Va. Edn. Assn., Va. Bus. Edn. Assn., Prince William Edn. Assn. (bldg. rep.). Avocations: reading, music, dancing. Home: 14415 Fairview Ln Woodbridge VA 22193-2045

ROSE, MARK ALLEN, humanities educator; b. N.Y.C., Aug. 4, 1939; s. Sydney Aaron and Rose (Shapiro) R.; m. Ann Bermingham; 1 son, Edward Gordon. AB summa cum laude, Princeton, 1961; LittB, Merton Coll., Oxford (Eng.) U., 1963; PhD, Harvard, 1967. From instr. to assoc. prof. English Yale U., 1967-74; prof. English U. Ill., Urbana, 1974-77; prof. U. Calif., Santa Barbara, 1977—, chmn. dept. English, 1987-89; dir. U. Calif. Humanities Rsch. Inst., 1989-94. Author: Heroic Love, 1968, (fiction) Golding's Tale, 1972, Shakespearean Design, 1972, Spenser's Art, 1975, Alien Encounters, 1981, Authors and Owners, 1993; editor: Twentieth Century Views of Science Fiction, 1976, Twentieth Century Interpretations of Antony and Cleopatra, 1977, (with Slusser and Guffey) Bridges to Science Fiction, 1980, Shakespeare's Early Tragedies, 1994. Woodrow Wilson fellow, 1961, Henry fellow, 1961-62, Dexter fellow, 1966, Morse fellow, 1970-71, NEH fellow, 1979-80, 90-91. Mem. MLA, Renaissance Soc. Am., Shakespeare Soc. Am., Phi Beta Kappa. Home: 1135 Oriole Rd Montecito CA 93108-2438

ROSE, MARY PHILOMENA, business educator; b. Detroit, Sept. 27, 1943; d. Henry Joseph and Marie Frances (Wilt) Mueller; m. Robert Henry Rose, June 24, 1966; children: Christopher, Jennifer, Matthew. BS, U. Detroit, 1966; MA in Tchg., Oakland U., 1992. Cert. secondary tchr., Mich.; adminstrv. cert. Vocat. tchr. Detroit Public Schs., 1966-70; tchr. presch. Utica Cmty. Schs., Sterling Heights, Mich., 1980-82, tchr. computers, 1982-92, tchr. in charge, computers adult edn., acad. adv., 1992-97, coord. bus. partnership programs, 1992-94; instr. Lotus Macomb Intermediate Sch. Dist., Clinton Twp., Mich., 1988-90; adj. faculty Oakland Cmty. Coll., Auburn Hills, Mich., 1991; co-chairperson UCS Adult Edn. Sch. Improvement team, Sterling Heights, Mich., 1992-96; coord. Skills Enhancement Ctr., Ford Mich. Proving Grounds (Romeo Cmty. Schs.), 1997—. Mem. Utica Cmty. Schs. Citizen's adv. com., Sterling Heights, Mich., 1975-85; pres. PTO, Shelby Twp., Mich., 1980-83. Mem. Mich. Assn. Acad. Adv. Adult and Cmty. Edn. (pres. 1994-95), Grtr. Detroit Employment Opportunity Assn., Macomb County Assn. Placement Personnel, Mich. Assn. Cmty. and Adult Edn., Nat. Ctr. Cmty. Edn. Avocations: reading, dancing, walking, traveling. Office: Mich Proving Grounds SEP 74240 Fisher Rd Romeo MI 48065-2908

ROSE, MELISSA EVA ANDERSON, small business owner; b. Grayson, Ky., Sept. 24, 1959; d. Thomas Erwin and Betty Jane (Mauk) Hall; m. William David Rose, June 19, 1992. Student, Araphoe Bus. Coll., Denver, 1976-78; BA, Morehead State U., 1979-84. Sales clk. Cases Hardware and Antiques, Olive Hill, Ky., 1970-72; waitress Los Gringitos, Morehead, Ky., 1975; tele-mktg. operator Citi-Corp Fin. Svcs., Denver, 1977-78; model, spokeswoman Ford Agy. NY, N.Y.C., 1979-81; counselor Christian Social Svcs., 1979-81; activities coord. Dept. Corrections, Denver, 1979; pres. ops. Dimensions Unltd. Inc., Denver, 1981—; owner, pres. Dimensions Unltd. Inc., Huntington, W.Va., 1985-96, Unlimited Expressions, Olive Hill, Ky., 1996—; cons. Home Interior Designs, Inc., Denver, 1985-86; sec. Denver County Real Estate Commn., 1987-88; bd. dirs. Found. for Human Concerns, Morehead, Ky., 1987-90, Excalibur Fin. Svc., Olive Hill, Ky., Melissa E. Rose Inc., Internat. Mgmt. Specialists; cons. Ky. C. of C., Glasgow, 1988—; founder, pres. Unified Fortress Group, Inc., 1989, Gold Link Publs., 1991-92; contr. Alpha Mktg. Corp., 1992-95; owner Mystic Limousine, 1992—, Four Dragon Internat., Inc., 1997—. Author: Business Ethics 2nd Moral Values, 1987, Life After Death 2 Cultural Explorations, 1987, Business Marketing-Sales for the 90s, 1992, Secrets Through the Eyes of Stone, 1996 (autobiography). Spokesperson Nat. Rep. Group, Morehead, 1981; chairperson Tiffany's Gold Charity Soc., Denver 1986; sec. Bus. Devel. Soc., Las Vegas, 1987; charter sponsor NATO Culture Exch. in W.Va., NY, 1989. Named Dutchess Hutt River Province, Australia, 1996. Mem. NAFE, Am. Music Assn., Dunn V. Bradstree, Inc., Nat. Assn. Mchts., Encore Gold Purchasing Club, League Human Rights, Nat. Assn. Euroeoan Bus. Cmtys., Met. Mus. Art, Smithsonian Instn., Citizens for a Better Govt. (chair), Country Music Assn. (Pres. award for Excellence, 1997), Olive Hill C. of C. Avocations: painting, sculpting, reading, swimming, travelling. Office: Four Dragons Internat Inc PO Box 869 Olive Hill KY 41164 also: Golden Link Publs PO Box 869 Olive Hill KY 41164-0869

ROSE, MERRILL, public relations counselor; b. Beaufort, N.C., Apr. 20, 1955; d. Robert Lloyd Rose and Betty Lou (Merrill) Ellis. Student, U. N.C., 1977. Reporter, editor Consumer News, Washington, 1978-79; v.p. Fraser/Assocs., Washington, 1979-82; sr. assoc. Porter/Novelli, Washington, 1982-85, v.p., 1985-87; sr. v.p., food practice leader Porter/Novelli, N.Y.C., 1989-91, exec. v.p., 1990—; gen. mgr. Chgo. Porter/Novelli, 1991-96; dir. Europe Porter Internat., Brussels, 1996—. Bd. dirs. CARE, 1991—; bd. visitors U. N.C. Sch. Journalism, Chapel Hill, 1992—; bd. dirs. Friends of Prentice affiliate Northwestern Meml. Hosp., 1993—; mem. accrediting com. Accrediting Coun. for Edn. in Journalism and Comm., 1994—. Mem. Am. Inst. of Wine and Food, Pub. Rels. Soc. Am. Office: Porter Novelli Internat, rue d'Arlon 50, 1000 Brussels Belgium

ROSE, MICHAEL DEAN, lawyer, educator; b. Johnstown, Pa., Oct. 22, 1937; s. Theodore Earl and Geraldine Ethel (Boyer) R.; m. Veda Sue Garber, June 27, 1959 (dec.); children: Christopher John, Susan Elizabeth. BA, Ohio Wesleyan U., 1959; JD, Case Western Res. U., 1963; LLM, Columbia U., 1967. Bar: Ohio 1963. Assoc. firm Porter, Stanley, Treffinger & Platt, Columbus, Ohio, 1963-66; asst. prof. law Ohio State U., Columbus, 1967-69, assoc. prof., 1969-72, prof., 1972—, Lawrence D. Stanley prof. law, 1987—; staff asst. to chief counsel IRS, Washington, 1970-71. Author: (with Leo J. Raskind) Advanced Federal Income Taxation: Corporate Transactions, 1978, (with Joseph S. Platt) A Federal Taxation Primer, 1973, Hornbook on Federal Income Taxation, 3d edit., 1988; editor Selected Federal Taxation Statutes and Regulations, 1973—, Ohio Will Manual, 1986—. Fellow Am. Coll. Trust and Estate Counsel; mem. Am. Law Inst. Home: 1327 Friar Ln Columbus OH 43221-1527 Office: Ohio State U 55 W 12th Ave Columbus OH 43210-1338

ROSE, NOEL RICHARD, immunologist, microbiologist, educator; b. Stamford, Conn., Dec. 3, 1927; s. Samuel Allison and Helen (Richard) R.; m. Deborah S. Harber, June 14, 1951; children: Alison, David, Bethany, Jonathan. BS, Yale U., 1948; MA, U. Pa., 1949, PhD, 1951; MD, SUNY, Buffalo, 1964; MD (hon.), U. Cagliari, Italy, 1990; ScD (hon.), U. Sassari, Italy, 1992. From instr. to prof. microbiology SUNY Sch. Medicine, Buffalo, 1951-73; dir. Center for Immunology SUNY Sch. Medicine, 1970-73, dir. Erie County Labs., 1964-70; dir. WHO Collaborating Center for Autoimmune Disorders, 1968—; prof. immunology and microbiology, chmn. dept. immunology and microbiology Wayne State U. Sch. Medicine, 1973—82; prof., chmn. dept. immunology and infectious diseases Johns Hopkins U. Sch. Hygiene and Pub. Health, Balt., 1982-93, prof. medicine and environ. health scis., 1982—, prof. molecular microbiology and immunology, 1993—; prof. pathology, dir. immunology Johns Hopkins U. Sch. Medicine, 1994—; cons. in field. Editor: (with others) International Convocation on Immunology, 1969, Methods in Immunodiagnosis, 1973, 3d rev. edit., 1986, The Autoimmune Diseases, 1986, 2d edit., 1992, 3d edit., 1997, Microbiology, Basic Principles and Clinical Applications, 1983 Principles of Immunology, 1973, 2d rev. edit., 1979, Specific Receptors of Antibodies, Antigens and Cells, 1973, Manual of Clinical Laboratory Immunology, 1976, 2d rev. edit., 1980, 4d edit. 1992, 5th edit., 1997, Genetic Control of Autoimmune Disease, 1978, Recent Advances in Clinical Immunology, 1983, Clinical Immunotoxicology, 1992, Manual of Human Immunology, 1997; editor in chief Clin. Immunology and Immunopathology, 1988—; contbr. articles to profl. jours. Recipient award Sigma Xi, 1952, award Alpha Omega Alpha, 1976, Lamp award, 1975, Faculty Recognition award Wayne State U. Bd. Govs., 1979, Pres.'s award for excellence in teaching, 1979, Disting. Service award Wayne State U. Sch. Medicine, 1982, U. Pisa medal, 1986; named to Acad. Scholars Wayne State U., 1981; Josiah Macy fellow, 1979. Fellow APHA, Am. Acad. Allergy and Immunology, Am. Acad. Microbiology; mem. AAAS, Acad. Clin. Lab. Physicians and Scientists, Am. Assn. Immunologists, Am. Soc. Investigative Pathology, Am. Soc. Clin. Pathologists, Am. Soc. Microbiology (Abbott Lab. Clin. and Diagnostic Immunology award 1993), Brit. Soc. Immunology, Coll. Am. Pathologists, Société Française d'Immunologie, Can. Soc. Immunology, Soc. Exptl. Biology and Medicine Coun., Clin. Immunology Soc. (sec., treas., pres. 1993), Austrian Immunology Soc. (hon. mem.), Sigma Xi (pres. Johns Hopkins U. chpt. 1988), Alpha Omega Alpha, Delta Omega. Office: Johns Hopkins U Sch Hygiene & Pub Health Dept Molecular Microbiology & Immunology 615 N Wolfe St Baltimore MD 21205-2103

ROSE, PETER EDWARD, former professional baseball player and manager; b. Cin., Apr. 14, 1941; s. Harry Rose; m. Karolyn Ann Englehardt (div.); children: Fawn, Peter; m. Carol Woliung, Apr. 1984; children: Cara, Tyler. Player Cin. Reds, 1963-78, player mgr., 1984-87, mgr., 1987-89; player Phila. Phillies, 1979-83, Montreal Expos, 1984; host weekly radio show Pete Rose on Baseball Sta. WCKY, Cin., 1992; now host syndicated show Talk Sports with Pete Rose Sta. WGTO-AM, Orlando, Fla. Author: (with Bob Hertzel) Charlie Hustle, 1975, Winning Baseball, 1976, (with Peter Golenback) Pete Rose on Hitting, 1985, (with Roger Kahn) Pete Rose: My Story, 1989. Named Nat. League Rookie of Yr., 1963, Most Valuable Player, 1973, Most Valuable Player World Series, 1975, Nat. League Player of Yr. The Sporting News, 1968, Ball Player of Decade, 1979; named to Nat. League All-Star Team, 1965, 67-71, 73-79, 80-81. Second player in baseball history to exceed 4000 hits, all time leader in hits. also: care Sta KCKY-AM 219 Mcfarland St Cincinnati OH 45202-2614*

ROSE, PETER ISAAC, sociologist, writer; b. Rochester, N.Y., Sept. 5, 1933; s. Aaron E. and Lillian (Feld) R.; m. Hedwig Hella Cohen, Mar. 25, 1956; children: Elisabeth Anne, Daniel Eric. AB, Syracuse U., 1954; MA, Cornell U., 1957, PhD, 1959. Instr. Goucher Coll., 1958-60; mem. faculty Smith Coll., Northampton, Mass., 1960—; prof., 1967-73; chmn. dept. sociology and anthropology Smith Coll., 1967-74, 79-80, Sophia Smith prof., 1973—; dir. Am. Studies Diploma program, 1975—; mem. grad. faculty U. Mass., 1961—; Fulbright prof. U. Leicester, Eng., 1964-65, Kyoto (Japan) Am. Studies Inst., Flinders U., Australia, 1970; vis. prof. Wesleyan U., Middletown, Conn., 1966-67, U. Colo., 1968, Yale U., 1970, Clark U., 1970-71; vis. scholar Harvard U., 1983, 84-85, vis. prof., spring 1984; vis. scholar Chinese Acad. Social Sci., Beijing, 1986; resident scholar Rockefeller Study Ctr., Bellagio, Italy, summer 1987; vis. fellow St. Catherine's Coll., Oxford, spring, 1995, Hoover Instn., Stanford U., 1996. Author: They and We, 1964, 5th edit., 1997, The Subject is Race, 1968, Strangers in Their Midst, 1977, Mainstream and Margins, 1983, Tempest-Tost, 1997; co-author: Sociology, 1977, 2d edit., 1982, Understanding Society, 1978, 3d edit., 1968; editor: The Study of Society, 1967, 4th edit., 1977, The Ghetto and Beyond, 1969, Americans From Africa, 1970, Nation of Nations, 1972, reissued, 1981, Seeing Ourselves, 1972, rev. edit., 1975, Socialization and the Life Cycle, 1979, Working With Refugees, 1986, Interminority Relations in the U.S., 1993; co-editor: Through Different Eyes, 1973. Mem. Am. Sociol. Assn. (mem. coun. 1974-77), Mass. Sociol. Assn. (pres. 1967-68), Soc. Study of Social Problems (v.p. 1968-69), Ea. Sociol. Soc. (v.p. 1970-71, pres. 1991-92). Home: 66 Paradise Rd Northampton MA 01060-2907

ROSE, PHYLLIS, English language professional, author; b. N.Y.C., Oct. 26, 1942; d. Eli and Minnie Davidoff; m. Mark Rose, (div. 1975); 1 son, Ted.; m. Laurent de Brunhoff, 1990. BA summa cum laude, Radcliffe Coll., 1964; M.A., Yale U., 1965; Ph.D., Harvard U., 1970. Teaching fellow Harvard U., Cambridge, Mass., 1966-67; acting instr. Yale U., New Haven, 1969; asst. prof. Wesleyan U., Middletown, Conn., 1969-76, assoc. prof., 1976-81, prof. English, 1981—; vis. prof. U. Calif., Berkeley, 1981-82; chmn. fiction jury Nat. Book Awards, 1993; bd. dirs. Wesleyan Writers Conf. Author: Woman of Letters: A Life of Virginia Woolf, 1978, Parallel Lives: Five Victorian Marriages, 1983, Writing of Women, 1985, Jazz Cleopatra: Josephine Baker in Her Time, 1989, Never Say Goodbye: Essays, 1991, The Year of Reading Proust, 1997; editor: The Norton Book of Women's Lives, 1993; book reviewer N.Y. Times Book Rev., The Atlantic; essayist; contbr. editor Civilization mag. Nat. Endowment for Humanities fellow, 1973-74; Rockefeller Found. fellow, 1984-85; Guggenheim fellow, 1985. Mem. PEN, Nat. Book Critics Circle, Authors Guild. Home: 1225 Smith St Key West FL 33040 Office: Wesleyan U Dept English Middletown CT 06457

ROSE, REGINALD, television writer, producer; b. N.Y.C., Dec. 10, 1920; s. William and Alice (Obendorfer) R.; children: Jonathan, Richard, Andrew and Steven (twins); m. Ellen McLaughlin, July 6, 1963; children—Thomas, Christopher. Student, Coll. City N.Y., 1937-38. pres. Defender Prodn., Inc., 1961—. Author TV plays, 1951—, including: Twelve Angry Men, 1954, The Sacco Vanzetti Story, 1959, The Defenders, 1961-65, Escape From Sobibor, 1987; film scripts include: Crime in the Streets, 1956, Twelve Angry Men, 1957, Baxter!, 1973, Somebody Killed Her Husband, 1978, The Wild Geese, 1978, The Sea Wolves, 1980, Whose Life Is It Anyway?, 1981; plays include Black Monday, 1962, Twelve Angry Men, 1958, The Porcelain Year, 1965, Principals Only, 1995; books include Six TV Plays, 1956, The Thomas Book, 1972. Pres. Reginald Rose Found., 1963—. Served to 1st lt. AUS, 1942-46. Recipient Emmy awards, 1954, 62, 63; numerous others including Laurel award Writers Guild Am., 1987. Address: 20 Wedgewood Rd Westport CT 06880-2735

ROSE, RICHARD LOOMIS, lawyer; b. Long Branch, N.J., Oct. 21, 1936; s. Charles Frederick Perrott and Jane Mary (Crotta) R.; m. Marian Frances Irons, Apr. 1, 1960; children: Linda, Cynthia, Bonnie. BA, Cornell U., 1958; JD, Washington and Lee U., 1963. Bar: N.Y. 1963, Conn. 1965, U.S. Dist. Ct. (so. dist.) N.Y. 1964, U.S. Dist. Ct. Conn. 1965, U.S. Ct. Appeals (2d cir.) 1965, U.S. Supreme Ct. 1970. Assoc. Cummings & Lockwood, Stamford, Conn., 1965-71; ptnr. Cummings & Lockwood, Stamford, 1971-91, Kleban & Samor, P.C., Southport, 1991-93; of counsel Whitman Breed Abbott & Morgan, Greenwich, Conn., 1993-95; prin. Roberts, Kambas, Rose & Bates, P.C., Stamford, Conn., 1995—; bd. dirs. and sec. Index Corp.; mem. adv. com. Conn. Banking Commr. on Conn. Securities Laws, 1982—; dir. Conn. World Trade Assn. Editor: Washington and Lee Law Rev. Chmn. Fgn. Trade Zone Com. to Mayor of City of Bridgeport, Conn., 1988-90; mem. fgn. trade awareness com. S.W. Area Industry and Commerce Assn., Task Force, 1987-88. 1st lt. U.S. Army, 1958-60, Korea. Mem. ABA, Conn. Bar Assn. (exec. com. corp. sect.), Internat. Bar Assn., New Canaan Country Club, Campfire Club Am. (bd. govs.), Phi Delta Phi, Omicron Delta Kappa, Phi Delta Theta. Republican. Office: Roberts Kambas Rose & Bates PC PO Box 15630 1055 Washington Blvd Stamford CT 06901

ROSE, ROBERT CARLISLE, retired banker; b. Gutheria, Okla., Aug. 14, 1917; s. Warren Glenn and Elizabeth Aileen (Landenberger) R.; m. Maejeanne Harker, June 17, 1939; children—Sharon Sue, Barbara Ann. Student public schs.; diploma, Sch. Banking, U. Wis., 1962. With Am. Nat. Bank, Vincennes, Ind., 1935—; chmn. bd. dirs. Am. Nat. Bank, 1975—, also dir.; now ret. Bd. dirs. Vincennes Community Sch. Corp.; sec. Harmony Soc., Vincennes. Served with USNR, World War II. Mem. Ind. Bankers Assn., Independent Bankers Assn. (dir.), Am. Legion, Vincennes C. of C. (dir.). Democrat. Baptist. Club: Elks. Office: Am Nat Bank 302 Main St Vincennes IN 47591

ROSE, ROBERT E(DGAR), state supreme court justice; b. Orange, N.J., Oct. 7, 1939. B.A., Juniata Coll., Huntingdon, Pa., 1961; LL.B., NYU, 1964. Bar: Nev. 1965. Dist. atty. Washoe County, 1971-75; lt. gov. State of Nev., 1975-79; judge Nev. Dist. Ct., 8th Jud. Dist., Las Vegas, 1986-88; justice Nev. Supreme Ct., Carson City, 1989—, chief justice, 1993-94. Office: Nev Supreme Ct 201 S Carson St Carson City NV 89701-4702

ROSE, ROBERT GORDON, lawyer; b. Newark, June 25, 1943; s. Harry and Ann Shirley (Gordon) R.; m. Ellen Nadley Berkowitz, July 2, 1966; children: Lisa Pauline, Michael Allan. BA, SUNY, Buffalo, 1965; MA, Columbia U., 1969; JD, Seton Hall U., 1974. Bar: N.J. 1974, U.S. Dist. Ct. N.J. 1974, U.S. Ct. Appeals (3rd cir.) 1974, U.S. Ct. Appeals (2nd cir.) 1975. Law clk. to Hon. John J. Gibbons U.S. Ct. Appeals (3rd cir.), Newark, 1974-75; assoc. Pitney, Hardin, Kipp & Szuch, Morristown, N.J., 1975-80, ptnr., 1980—. Contbr. articles to profl. jours. Mem. ABA, N.J. Bar Assn., Morris County Bar Assn. (trustee 1989-90). Avocations: travel, philately. Office: Pitney Hardin Kipp & Szuch Park Ave at Morris County PO Box 1945 Morristown NJ 07962-1945

ROSE, ROBERT HENRY, arts education administrator; b. Butler, Pa., Sept. 10, 1948; s. Robert C. and Olga (Matzko) R.; m. Melanie Sue McKamish, Sept. 12, 1987; children: Aaron, Joseph, Julie. BS, Geneva Coll., Beaver Falls, Pa., 1991; MEd, Pa. State U., 1993. Cert. in environ. protection CDC; cert. in human resource devel. With Armco Steel Corp., Butler, Pa., 1978-83; commd. U.S. Army, 1983, advanced through grades to master sgt., 1992; ret., 1995; dir. Oakbridge Acad. Arts, 1995—. Decorated Purple Heart; Vets. grantee PHEAA, 1990. Mem. Masons, Elks (lecturing knight 1983-84), Strategic Planning Com. Plum Boro Sch. Dist., Pi Lambda Theta. Avocations: running, writing, golf, tennis. Home: 155 Shearer Rd New Kensington PA 15068-9320 Office: 1309 Greensburg Rd Lower Burrell PA 15068-3843

ROSE, ROBERT JOHN, bishop; b. Grand Rapids, Mich., Feb. 28, 1930; s. Urban H. and Maida A. (Glerum) R. Student, St. Joseph Sem., 1944-50; B.A., Seminaire de Philosophie, Montreal, Que., Can., 1952; S.T.L., Pontifical Urban U., Rome, 1956; M.A., U. Mich., 1962. Ordained priest Roman Catholic Ch., 1955; dean St. Joseph Sem., Grand Rapids, 1966-69; dir. Christopher House, Grand Rapids, 1969-71; rector St. John's Sem., Plymouth, Mich., 1971-77; pastor Sacred Heart Parish, Muskegon Heights, Mich., 1977-81; bishop Diocese of Gaylord, Mich., 1981-89, Diocese of Grand Rapids, Mich., 1989—. Mem. Nat. Conf. Cath. Bishops. *

ROSE, ROBERT LAWRENCE, financial services company executive; b. N.Y.C., Mar. 10, 1945; s. Martin and Helen (Diamond) R.; m. Andrea Joan Hoffman, Dec. 27, 1964 (div. June 1972); 1 child, Dawn; m. Julia Frances Knipl, Jan. 2, 1974 (div. Mar. 1991); children—Justin, Adam, Andrew. BS, Mich. State U., 1966; JD, U. Mich., 1969; LLM in Taxation, NYU, 1978. Bar: N.Y., Conn., Calif. Assoc. Kindel & Anderson, 1969-72; owner, mgr. Carol's Restaurant, N.Y.C., 1972-74; assoc. gen. counsel Equitable Life Ins. Co., N.Y.C., 1974-77; tax counsel Conn. Gen. Life Ins. Co., Bloomfield, 1977-80, assoc. gen. counsel, 1980-82; chief counsel employee benefits and fin. services CIGNA Corp., Bloomfield, 1982-84, sr. v.p., chief counsel investment group, 1984-89; v.p. corp. acctg. and planning CIGNA Corp., Phila., 1989-95, v.p. strategic growth and devel., 1995—. Author: Group Insurance Tax, 1980, Annual Meeting-Annuity Taxation, 1983, Tax Shelters, 1984; editor U. Mich. Law Rev., 1968-69, Duke U. Law Jour., 1978. Mem. Leadership Greater Hartford, 1984, Am. Leadership Forum, 1986. Mem. Am. Council Life Ins. (fin. regulatory policy subcom.), U. Conn. Sch. of Law Ins. Inst. (chmn.), Assn. Life Ins. Counsel, Calif. Bar Assn., Conn. Bar Assn., N.Y. Bar Assn. Avocations: skiing, tennis, travel. Office: CIGNA Corp 1 Liberty Pl PO Box 7716 1650 Market St Philadelphia PA 19192-1520

ROSE, ROBERT MICHAEL, materials science and engineering educator; b. N.Y.C., Apr. 15, 1937; s. Lawrence Lapidus and Lillian (Rosen) R.; m. Martha Gibbs, Oct. 15, 1961; children: Cynthia J., James L., Joshua S. S.B., MIT, 1958, Sc.D., 1961. Registered profl. engr., Mass. Asst. prof. materials sci. and engring MIT, Cambridge, 1961-66, assoc. prof., 1966-72, prof., 1972—; dir. MIT Concourse program, 1988—; prof. health scis. and tech. Harvard Med. Sch.- MIT, 1978-90; dir. Cryoelectro Assocs., Wenham, Mass., 1978-90; mem. Mass. Bd. Registration of Profl. Engrs. and Land Surveyors, 1991-93; adj. prof. Tufts U. Sch. Vet. Medicine. Author: Structure and Properties of Materials, 1964, Practical Biomechanics for the Orthopedic Surgeon, 1979, 92, The Chicken From Minsk, 1995. Recipient Kappa Delta prize Am. Acad. Orthopedic Surgeons, 1973. Mem. Am. Soc. Metals (vice chmn. 1971-72, Bradley Stoughton prize, chmn. 1972-73), Metal Soc. AIME, Dolphin Yacht Club (Marblehead, Mass.), Boston Yacht Club. Jewish. Home: 18 Morgan St Wenham MA 01984-1114 Office: Room 4-132 MIT 77 Massachusetts Ave Cambridge MA 02139-4301 *I would share my thoughts with you if I were satisfied with what I am. But I submit to you that anyone who is truly satisfied with his personal success doesn't understand the nature of his own achievement. Distrust all advice (including this!).*

ROSE, ROBERT NEAL, brokerage house executive; b. Chgo., Feb. 27, 1951; s. James Allan Rose and Hazel (Gordon) Kaufman; m. Anna Yvette Trujillo, Aug. 23, 1981; children: David James, Michelle Elizabeth, Daniel Jonathan. BS, Georgetown U., 1973; MPA, Harvard U., 1995. Trader Salomon Bros., N.Y.C., 1974-75; regional coord. Latin Am. Merrill Lynch Govt. Securities, N.Y.C., 1975-76; dir. fed. govt. affairs Pub. Service of N.Mex., Albuquerque, 1977-78; exec. dir. Gov. Jerry Apodaca, Washington, 1979-80; expert cons. U.S. Dept. Commerce, Washington, 1980-81; asst. treas. Am. Express Internat. Bank, N.Y.C., 1981-82; sr. v.p. Refco, Inc., N.Y.C., 1982-84; v.p., mgr. Thomson McKinnon Securities, N.Y.C., 1984-88; sr. v.p. Lehman Bros., N.Y.C., 1988-92; mng. dir. Credit Agricole Futures Inc., N.Y.C., 1992-95, Bear Stearns, N.Y.C., 1995—; cons. BDM Corp., McLean, Va., 1981-88; Presdl. appointee J. William Fulbright Fgn. Scholarship Bd., 1993-97. Mem. conv. site selection com., 1989-90; mem. arrangements com. Dem. Conv., San Francisco, 1984; mem. Dem. Town Com., Westport, 1990-96; fin. chmn. Conn. Dem. State Ctrl. Com., 1993; event chmn. N.Y. Presdl. Gala, N.Y.C., 1993; chmn. Dem. Gov.'s Assn. Presdl. Dinner, 1994. Wexner Heritage Found. fellow, 1992-94. Jewish. Avocation: skiing. Office: 245 Park Ave New York NY 10167-0002

ROSE, ROBERT R., JR., lawyer; b. Evanston, Ill., Nov. 1, 1915; s. Robert R. and Eleanor B. R.; m. Kathryn Lorraine Warner, June 14, 1948; children: Robert R. III, Cynthia Ann. JD, U. Wyo., 1941. Bar: Wyo. bar 1941. Atty. Dept. Justice, 1941; with UNRRA, China; asst. sec. Dept. Interior, 1951-52; sr. partner firm Rose, Spence, Dobos and Duncan, Casper, Wyo., 1968-75; justice Wyo. Supreme Ct., 1975-85, chief justice, 1981-82; assoc. Spence, Moriarity and Schuster, Cheyenne, Wyo., 1985-95; ptnr. Rose, Rose & O'Donnell, L.L.C., 1995-96, Rose & Rose, 1996—; organizer, past pres., chmn. bd. Title Guaranty Co. Wyo.; faculty Nat. Coll. Criminal Def., 1977-90; founder, instr. Western Trial Advocacy Inst., 1977-93; founder Western Trial Advocacy Inst., 1977—; vis. prof. trial practice U. Wyo. Coll. Law, 1985-86; Milward Simpson chair in polit. sci. U. Wyo., 1985-86; Gerry Spence faculty, corp. officer Trial Lawyer's Coll., 1994, 95. Author legal articles. Past chmn. fund drive Casper Community Chest, Am. Cancer Soc.; mem. Wyo. Ho. of Reps., 1949-51; mayor of, Casper, 1950-51; past trustee Casper Coll. Served with USAAF, World War II. Recipient Jud. Achievement award Nat. Assn. Criminal Def. Lawyers, 1983. Mem. Am. Law Inst., Order of Coif (hon.), Trial Lawyers Coll. (founder, treas. bd. dirs. 1994—), Land and Water L. Rev. (bd. advs.). Episcopalian. Address: PO Box 1006 Cheyenne WY 82003-1006

ROSE, ROSLYN, artist; b. Irvington, N.J., May 28, 1929; d. Mark and Anne Sarah (Green) R.; m. Franklin Blou, Nov. 26, 1950; 1 child, Mark Gordon Blue (dec.). Student, Rutgers U., 1949-51, Pratt Ctr. for Contemporary, Printmaking, N.Y.C., 1967; BS, Skidmore Coll., 1976. Artist. One-person shows include Midday Gallery, Caldwell, N.J., 1972, Caldwell Coll., 1972, Kean Coll., Union, N.J., 1973, Art Corner Gallery, Millburn, N.J., 1974, Brandeis U., Mass., 1974, Newark (N.j.) Mus., 1974, George Frederick Gallery, Rochester, N.Y., 1981, Robbins Gallery, Washington, 1981, Signatures Gallery, Washington, 1981, Arnot Art Mus., Elmira, N.Y., 1982, Douglas Coll. Rutgers U., New Brunswick, 1987, Nathans Gallery, West Paterson, N.J., 1984, 86, 89, 96; exhibited in group shows at Seattle Art Mus., Portland (oreg.) Mus., NYU U. Small Works Show, Montclair Art Mus., N.J., Middlesex County Mus., Piscataway, N.J., and others; permanent collections include N.J. State Mus., Trenton, Citibank of N.Y., Russia, N.J. State Libr., Trenton, Roddenbery Meml. Libr., Cairo, Ga., Rosenberg Libr., Galveston, Tex., Newark Mus., Newark Pub. Libr., AT&T, BASF Wyandotte Corp., Canon Calculator Systems, N.Y.C., First Fed. Bank, Rochester, Gulf & Western Industries, Irving Trust Co., N.Y., Kidder, Peabody & Co., N.Y., McAllen Internat. Mus., Tex., Nabisco Brands Corp., East Hanover, N.J., N.J. Bell, Readers Digest Collection, Voorhees-Zimmerli Mus., Rutgers U., New Brunswick, N.J., others; creator UNCIF cards, 1979-80. Recipient graphic award Westechester (N.Y.) Art Soc., 1973, Best-in-Show award Livingston (N.J.) Art Assn., 1971, Best-in-Show award N.J. Ctr. for Visual Arts, Summit, 1969, Mixed Media Merit award Salmagundi Club, N.Y.C., 1995; numerous others. Mem. Nat. Assn. Women Artists (v.p. 1997—, Innovative Painting award 1990), N.Y. Artists Equity, Pen and Brush Club (N.Y.C. Stauffer Mixed Media award 1996, 97). Avocation: tennis. Office: Atelier Rose PO Box 5095 Hoboken NJ 07030-5095

ROSE, RUDOLPH L., lawyer; b. Milan, Tenn., 1943. BS, Loyola Coll., 1967; JD, Catholic U., 1973. Bar: Md. 1973. Law clk. Judge C. Awdry Thompson Md. Ct. Special Appeals, 1973-74; mem. Semmes, Bowen & Semmes, Balt. Assoc. editor: Catholic U. Law Review, 1972-73. Mem. ABA, Internat. Assn. Defense Counsel (exec. com. 1993-96, chair, products liability com., 1990-93), Defense Rsch. Inst., Md. Assn. of Defense Trial Counsel, Md. Self Insurers and Employers Compensation Assn. (chmn. legis. subcommittee, 1987—), Md. C. of C. (chmn. workers compensation 1986—). Office: Semmes Bowen & Semmes 250 W Pratt St Baltimore MD 21201-2423

ROSE, SARA MARGARET, English as a second language educator; b. Johnstown, Pa., Sept. 22, 1950; d. William S. and Mary Margaret (Leberknight) R.; m. Akbar Ahamadian (common law, separated); 1 child, Meryem Rose. Student Sociology, Univ. Copenhagen, Denmark, 1971-73; MEd, Blagard Tchrs. Seminarium, Copenhagen, 1981. Cert. tchr., Denmark. Lang. tchr. and cons. Adult Edn., Hillerød, Denmark, 1981-90; cons. on immigrant and refugee issues Danish Dept. Welfare, Hillerød, 1983-88; ESL instr. Balt. City C.C., 1991-94, Catonsville C.C., Balt., 1992-96, Balt. Hebrew U., 1993-95; ESL instr. Balt. County Adult Edn., 1990-96, ESL facilitator, adminstr., 1994-96; dir. English Lang. Inst. Coll. Notre Dame of Md., Balt., 1996—; cmty. coord. Au Pair Care, Balt., 1991—. Lectr. on Immigrant and Refugee Issues, AOF Hillerød, 1983-90; founder, adminstr. Fgn. Women's Social Club, Hillerød, 1985-87; mem. People's Movement Against Racial Hatred and Discrimination, Denmark, 1983-90. Recipient Study Tour to Turkey, Danish Ministry of Edn., 1986, Cert. of Appreciation Balt. City C.C., 1993. Mem. TESOL, Balt. Assn. TESOL, Amnesty Internat., Greenpeace. Methodist. Avocations: reading, travel, music, theater, ne with daughter. Home: 3905 Darleigh Rd Unit 2H Baltimore MD 236 Office: English Lang Inst Coll Notre Dame of Md 4701 N Charles St ltimore MD 21210-2404

ROSE, SELWYN H., chemical company executive; b. N.Y.C., May 1, 1933; s. Rubin and Ruth Rosenthal; BS, CCNY, 1954; MS, Ohio State U., 1958, PhD, 1961; MBA with honors, U. Chgo., 1979; CFP, Coll. Fin. Planning, 1994; m. Helen Diana De Mov, July 25, 1957; children: Michelle, Wendy, Suzanne. Sr. rsch. chemist Pennwalt Corp., King of Prussia, Pa., 1961-65; dept. mgr. Horizons Inc., Beachwood, Ohio, 1965-72, dir. rsch., 1972-74; mgr. long range rsch. De Soto Inc., Des Plaines, Ill., 1974-79; dir. rsch., cen. rsch. lab. Borg-Warner Chems., Des Plaines, 1979-85; v.p. tech. Parker Chem. Co., Madison Heights, Mich., 1985-88; gen. mgr. rsch. and devel. Himont Inc., Wilmington, Del., 1988-91, v.p. product devel., 1991-93; pres. SHR Fin. Advisors, Wilmington, 1993—. 1st lt. U.S. Army, 1954-56. Recipient IR 100 award Indsl. Rsch. mag., 1971; award Roon Found., 1979. Mem. Am. Chem. Soc., Internat. Assn. Fin. Planners, Inst. Cert. Fin. Planners. Contbr. articles to profl. jours.; patentee in field. Achievements include development of polyphosphazene polymers. Home: 1704 N Park Dr Wilmington DE 19806-2144

ROSE, SHARON MARIE, critical care nurse; b. Big Spring, Tex., Feb. 16, 1958; d. William Coleman Smith and Grace Marie (Arnett) Karns; m. Christopher Robin Rose, Jan. 21, 984; children: Crystal Alyss, Nasson Andrew. AAS, Odessa Coll., 1981; BS in Occupational Edn., Wayland Bapt., 1987. Cert. nephrology nurse. Critical care RN Univ. Med. Ctr., Lubbock, Tex., 1981-88; med-surg. instr. Lubbock (Tex.) Gen. Hosp., 1988-89; dialysis RN St. Mary of the Plains Hosp., 1989-91; asst. CCU mgr. St. Mary of the Plains Hosp., Lubbock, 1990-91; health occupations instr. Lubbock Ind. Sch. Dist., 1991-94; in-svc. coord. Dialysis Ctr. Lubbock, Tex., 1994—; tchr. summer session Asst. for Med. Terminology course, 1993; mem. Health Occupations Adv. Com., Lubbock, 1988. Mem. Nat. Kidney Found. Mem. Tex. Health Occupations Assn. (v.p. 1993-94), Health Occupation Students Am. (advisor 1991-94), Tex. Tech. Med. Alliance, Nat. Kidney Found. (coun. nephrology nurses and technicians). Baptist. Avocations: jigsaw puzzles, reading, family, skiing. Home: 4708 31st St Lubbock TX 79410 Office: Dialysis Ctr Lubbock 4110 22nd Pl Lubbock TX 79410-1122

ROSE, SUSAN CAROL, restaurant executive, chef, consultant; b. Rochester, N.Y., Jan. 29, 1942; d. Frederick Raymond Smith and Grace Eunice (Read) Smith Drum; m. Larry Anthony Rose, Jan. 5, 1963 (div. Jan. 1976); children: John David, Karen Michelle Haines, Patricia Anne. Student, Monroe Community Coll., Rochester, 1959-60; cert. exec. steward, Innisbrook Resort, 1976; student, St. Petersburg Jr. Coll., Tarpon Springs, Fla., 1978-80, Pinellas Voc. Tech., 1987—. With Blue Cross-Blue Shield, Rochester, 1959-67; from coffee service mgr. to exec. steward Innisbrook Resort, Tarpon Springs, 1974-84; catering team supr. Bon Appetit Restaurant, Dunedin, Fla., 1984, Bounty Caterers, Dunedin, 1984; asst. mgr. trainee Wendy's Internat., Largo, Fla., 1984; store mgr. Long John Silver's, Largo, 1984-85; exec. steward, banquet chef, room service mgr., cons. Sandestin Beach Hilton, Destin, Fla., 1985; day mgr. Shells Restaurant, Clearwater, Fla., 1986-87; sous chef, kitchen mgr. Saltwaters Seafood Grille, Palm Harbor, Fla., 1987; exec. steward Adam's Mark Caribbean Gulf Resort, Clearwater Beach, 1987—; chef/kitchen mgr. Seafood Broiler, 1990-91; chef Hwy. Ribbery Restaurant, 1991, Boomerangs Cafe, 1992; galley supr., cook Empress Cruise Lines, 1992-94; chef Wards Seafood, 1994—; garde manger 94th Aero Squadron Restaurant, Las Fontanas Restaurant; mgr. Beef O'Brady's, 1997; cons. restaurant mgmt. Mem. Nat. Assn. Female Execs., Hospitality Industry Assn., Smithsonian Inst. Assocs., Holiday Inn Priority Club, Internat. Travel Club, Encore Travel Club, Clearwater Jaycees. Democrat. Roman Catholic. Avocations: school, music, reading, bowling. Home: 1162 Jackson Rd Clearwater FL 34615-4605 Office: Adam's Mark Caribbean Gulf Resort Gulfview Blvd Clearwater FL 34616

ROSE, SUSAN PORTER, federal commissioner; b. Cin., Sept. 20, 1941; d. Elmer Johnson and Dorothy (Wurst) Porter; m. Jonathan Chapman Rose, Jan. 26, 1980; 1 child, Benjamin Chapman. BA, Earlham Coll., 1963; MS, Ind. State U., Terre Haute, 1970. Staff asst. Congressman Richard L. Roudebush, Washington, 1963-64; asst. dean George Sch., Bucks County, Pa., 1964-66; asst. dir. admissions Mt. Holyoke Coll., South Hadley, Mass., 1966-71; asst. dir. correspondence First Lady (Mrs. Nixon) The White House, 1971-72, dir. of scheduling to First Lady (Mrs. Nixon), 1972-74, to First Lady (Mrs. Ford), 1974-77; spl. asst. to asst. atty. gen. Office Improvements in Adminstrn. Justice, Washington, 1977-79, Justice Mgmt. div. U.S. Dept. Justice, 1979-81; chief of staff to Mrs. Bush, asst. to v.p. Office of V.P. of U.S. Washington, 1981-89; dep. asst. to Pres. of U.S., chief of staff to First Lady (Mrs. Bush) The White House, 1989-93; commr. U.S. Commn. Fine Arts, 1993—. Bd. dirs. Barbara Bush Found. for Family Literacy; bd. trustees Bush Presdl. Libr. and Ctr. Recipient Dist. Alumni award Earlham Coll., 1992, Ind. State U., 1991. Mem. Ind. Acad. Home: 501 Slaters Ln Apt 1001 Alexandria VA 22314-1118

ROSE, T. T., bishop. Bishop of Cen. Ill., Ch. of God in Christ, Springfield. *

ROSE, THOMAS ALBERT, artist, art educator; b. Washington, Oct. 15, 1942; s. Francis John and Ann Elizabeth (Voelkel) R.; m. Mary Melinda Moyer, Aug. 21, 1965; children: Sarah, Jessica. Student, U. Wis., 1960-62; BFA, U. Ill., 1965; MA, U. Calif., Berkeley, 1967; postgrad., Lund (Sweden) U., 1967-68. Instr. U. Calif., Berkeley, 1968-69, N.Mex. State U., Las Cruces, 1969-72; faculty mem. U. Minn., Mpls., 1972—, prof. art, 1983—. Author: Winter Book, 1995; one-man shows include Clock Tower, N.Y.C., 1977, Truman Gallery, N.Y.C., 1977-78, Rosa Esman Gallery, N.Y.C., 1979, 81, 82, Marianne Deson Gallery, Chgo., 1984-86, Robert Thomson Gallery, Mpls., 1986, 91, 92, 95, Deson Saunders Gallery, Chgo., 1989, Mpls. Inst. Art, 1992, Weisman Art Mus., Mpls., 1994, Tweed Mus., Duluth, Minn., 1995, Steinbaum/Krauss Gallery, N.Y., 1996; exhibited in group shows at Walker Art Ctr., Mpls., 1974, 76, 77, Whitney Mus. Downtown, N.Y.C., P.S. #1, N.Y.C., 1978, Wave Hill, Bronx, N.Y., 1981, Hirshhorne Mus., Washington, 1981, Am. Ctr. in Paris, 1982, Harvard U. Sch. Architecture, 1983, Cultural Ctr., Chgo., 1983, Hal Bromm Gallery, N.Y.C., Sheldon Mus., Lincoln, Nebr., 1989, Tampa (Fla.) Mus., 1988, MCAD, Mpls., 1996, Minn. Mus. Art, 1996, Socrates Sculpture Park, N.Y.C.; represented in permanent collections Walker Art Ctr., Joslyn Mus., Omaha, Park St. Lofts, Springfield, Mass., U. Minn., Mpls., Am. Lung Assn. Target Ctr., Mpls., St. Lukes Episcopal Ch., Mpls.; set designer: Fool for Love, Cricket Theater, Mpls., 1985, Circus, Theater de Jeune Lune, 1986; project dir. Works of Art in Pub. Places for Humphrey Inst. Pub. Affairs, Mpls., 1988. Fellow Nat. Endowment for Arts, 1977, 81, Bush Found., 1979, Minn. State Arts Bd., 1979, 84, McKnight Found., 1981, McKnight Found. Rsch., 1993-96; McKnight Artist fellow, 1995, travel fellow Dayton-Hudson/Jerome, 1990, 95, Jerome Found. Arts, 1993-94, Mellon Found., 1993; grantee Arts Bd. Opportunities, 1993; Rockefeller resident Bellagio, Italy, 1993. Home: 91 Nicollet St Minneapolis MN 55401-1513 Office: Univ Minn 208 Studio Arts 23d Ave SE Minneapolis MN 55455

ROSE, VICTORIA LASDON, retired magazine publisher. Pub. YM/Young & Modern mag., N.Y.C. Office: YM/Young & Modern 685 3rd Ave New York NY 10017-4024

ROSE, W. AXL (WILLIAM BRUCE BAILEY), singer; b. Lafayette, Ind., Feb. 6, 1962; s. L. Stephen (stepfather) and Sharon Bailey; m. Erin Everly, 1991 (div. 1992). Lead singer (band) Guns N' Roses; albums include Live Like A Suicide, 1986, Appetite For Destruction, 1987, GN'R Lies, 1988, Use Your Illusion I, 1991, Use Your Illusion II, 1991, The Spaghetti Incident?, 1993. Office: care of David Geffen Co 9130 W Sunset Blvd West Hollywood CA 90069-3110*

ROSE, WIL, foundation executive; b. Townsend, Ohio, Sept. 13, 1931; s. William Marion and Dorothy Louise (Arnold) R.; m. Anna Marie Thielmann, Mar. 4, 1952 (div. 1976); children: Sharon, Dan; m. Princess Pale Moon, Oct. 7, 1977; children: Michael, Robert, John Mark. AA in Comml. Photography, Santa Monica City Coll., 1956; LitD, Ashland U., 1982. With motion picture prodn. dept. Moody Inst. Sci., Santa Monica, Calif., 1955-57; pres., founder DATA Internat., Palo Alto, Calif., 1958-66; pres. People to People, Inc., Kansas City, 1966-67; CEO Am. Indian Heritage Found., Falls Church, 1973—; pres., founder PlanAm. Consulting, Falls Church, Va., 1981—. Charitable devel. officer Nat. Heritage Found. Inc., Falls Church, Va., 1968—; pres., founder Nat. Found. Philanthropy, Mpls., 1978-80; bd. devel. officer Congrl. Awards for Youth, Fairfax, Va., 1978—; mem. presdl. task force Reagan Adminstrn., Washington, 1984. Staff sgt. USMC, 1950-54, Korea. Decorated Purple Heart; recipient Nat. Achievement award SERTOMA Internat., 1964; named Outstanding Young Man, Calif. Jaycees, 1962, Outstanding Young Man in U.S., U.S. Jaycees, 1966. Mem. Rotary Club (various com. chmn.). Avocations: writing, speaking.

ROSE, WILLIAM ALLEN, JR., architect; b. Flushing, N.Y., Nov. 26, 1938; s. William Allen and Josephine (Grohe) R.; m. Sandra L. Latham, June 24, 1961; children: Lindsay E., Lesley A. AB cum laude, Harvard U., 1960; MArch, Columbia U., 1964; DHL (hon.), Mercy Coll., 1997. Architect Rose Beaton Corsbie Dearden & Crowe, N.Y.C. and White Plains, N.Y., 1964-69; ptnr. Rose Beaton & Rose, White Plains, 1969-92; prin. Einhorn Yaffee Prescott, White Plains, 1993-96. Chmn. White Plains Citizens Adv. Com., 1970-73; pres. Hillair Circle Civic Assn., White Plains, 1972-76, Am. Inst. Architects Rsch. Corp., 1980-81; mem. White Plains City Coun., 1974-78, pres., 1976-78; mem. White Plains Urban Renewal Agy., 1988—, White Plains Comprehensive Plan Management Group, 1994-95; bd. dirs. White Plains YMCA, 1970-73, chmn. bd. trustees, 1981-83; bd. govs. YMCA Cen. and No. Westchester, 1983—, vice-chmn., 1983-85, chmn., 1985-87; chmn. bd. mgrs. McBurney Sch., N.Y.C., 1973-76, trustee, 1981-85; trustee Rye Country Day Sch., N.Y., 1981-87; trustee Baldwin League of Ind. Schs., 1986-88; trustee Mercy Coll., 1980-91, vice-chmn., 1982-88, chmn. 1988-91; bd. dirs. Burke Rehab. Inst., 1979-84, v.p., 1981-84; chmn. Commn. Fed. Procurement of Archtl. and Engring. Svcs., 1983-84. Recipient Robert Ross McBurney medal McBurney Sch., 1956, Design award Bell Sys., 1971, 76, Honor award for Archtl. Excellence L.I. Assn., 1971, 76, award Westchester Easter Seals, 1976, Outstanding Citizenship award United Way White Plains, 1980, World Fellowship award YMCA, 1988. Fellow AIA (pres. chpt. 1975-76, regional dir. 1978-81, nat. v.p. 1982, Upjohn fellow, 1991, trustee polit. action com. 1981-82, bursar Coll. of Fellows 1986-88, vice chancellor 1989, chancellor 1990, gold medal Westchester chpt. 1983); mem. N.Y. State Assn. Architects (pres. 1977-78, trustee polit. action com. 1981-84, Del Gaudio award 1982, James W. Kideney award 1988), Columbia Archtl. Alumi Assn. (v.p. 1969), Am. Archtl. Found. (regent 1990), St. Andrew's Soc. N.Y., Rotary, N.Y. Athletic Club (N.Y.C.), Harvard of Westchester Club, Sunningdale Golf Club (U.K.), Royal & Ancient Golf Club (St. Andrews, Scotland), John's Island Club, Winged Foot Golf Club (pres. 1997—). Republican. Congregationalist. Office: Einhorn Yaffee Prescott 81 Main St White Plains NY 10601-1711

ROSE, WILLIAM SHEPARD, JR., lawyer; b. Columbia, S.C., Mar. 9, 1948; s. William Shepard and Meta Cantey (Boykin) R.; m. Frances John Hobbs, Aug. 11, 1973; children: Katherine Cummings, William Shepard, III, Whitaker Boykin. BA in English, U. South, 1970; JD, U. S.C., 1973; LLM in Taxation, Georgetown U., 1976. Bar: S.C. 1973, Ohio 1977, D.C. 1974, U.S. Dist. Ct. D.C. 1976, U.S. Tax Ct. 1976, U.S. Supreme Ct. 1976, U.S. Claims Ct. 1978, U.S. Ct. Appeals (10th cir., 5th cir., 4th cir.) 1987, U.S. Ct. Appeals (3d, 6th, 7th, 8th, 9th and 11th cirs.) 1988. Trial atty. Office of Chief Counsel IRS, Washington, 1973-77; assoc. Frost & Jacobs, Cin., 1977-80, McNair Law Firm, PA, Hilton Head Island, S.C., and Washington, 1980-83, ptnr., 1983-87, 89—; asst. atty. gen., tax div. U.S. Dept. of Justice, Washington, 1987-89; chmn. and dir. Sea Pines Montessori Sch., 1983-86, Hilton Head Broadcasting, 1983-87, Hilton Head Planned Parenthood, 1985-87, MBR Corp., Adwell Corp., Links Group Inc., Hilton Head Prep. Sch., 1986-87, 89-93, dir. Boys & Girls Club of Hilton Head Island, 1992—, Hilton Head Humane Soc., 1985. Contbr. articles to profl. jours. Asst. to chmn. of bus. fund raising Beaufort County United Way, Hilton Head Island, 1984; vice-chmn. Beaufort County Rep. Party, 1991-92, 93, chmn. 1992-93, vice chmn. 1993-95; mem. Beaufort County Transportation Com., 1994-95; commr. Sea Pines Pub. Svc. Dist., South Island Pub. Svc. Dist. Mem. ABA (past co-chmn. subcom. tax sect.), Am. Coll. Tax Counsel, Ohio Bar Assn., D.C. Bar Assn., S.C. Bar Assn., Beaufort County Bar Assn., Hilton Head Bar Assn. Republican. Episcopalian. Clubs: S.C. Yacht Club (bd. govs. 1989-94, exec. com. 1993-94, rear commodore 1993-94), Hilton Head Cotillion, Ducks Unltd., Caroliniana Ball. Home: 11 Jessamine Pl Hilton Head Island SC 29928-4255 Office: PO Drawer 7787 52 New Orleans Rd Ste 204 Hilton Head Island SC 29938

ROSE-ACKERMAN, SUSAN, law and political economy educator; b. Mineola, N.Y., Apr. 23, 1942; d. R. William and Rosalie (Gould) Rose; m. Bruce A. Ackerman, May 29, 1967; children: Sybil, John. B.A., Wellesley Coll, 1964; Ph.D., Yale U., 1970. Asst. prof. U. Pa., Phila, 1970-74; lectr. Yale U., New Haven, Conn., 1974-75, asst. prof., 1975-78, assoc. prof., 1978-82; prof. law and polit. economy Columbia U., N.Y.C., 1982-87, dir. Ctr. for Law and Econ. Studies, 1983-87; Ely prof. of law and polit. econ. Yale U., New Haven, 1987-92, Luce prof. jurisprudence (law and polit. sci.), 1992—; rev. panelist Program on Regulation and Policy Analysis, NSF, Washington, 1982-84, Am. studies program Am. Coun. Learned Socs., 1987-90; review panelist, faculty Fulbright Commn., 1993-96; vis. rsch. fellow World Bank, 1995-96. Author: (with Ackerman, Sawyer and Henderson) Uncertain Search for Environmental Quality, 1974 (Henderson prize 1982); Corruption: A Study in Political Economy, 1978; (with E. James) The Nonprofit Enterprise in Market Economies, 1986; editor: The Economics of Nonprofit Institutions, 1986; (with J. Coffee and L. Lowenstein) Knights, Raiders, and Targets: The Impact of the Hostile Takeover, 1988, Rethinking the Progressive Agenda: The Reform of the American Regulatory State, 1992, Controlling Environmental Policy: The Limits of Public Law in Germany and the United States, 1995; contbr. articles to profl. jours.; bd. editors: Jour. Law, Econs. and Orgn., 1984—, Internat. Rev. Law and Econs., 1986—, Jour. Policy Analysis and Mgmt., 1989—, Polit. Sci. Quar., 1988—. Guggenheim fellow 1991-92, Fulbright fellow, Free U. Berlin, 1991-92. Mem. Am. Law and Econs. Assn. (bd. dirs. 1993-96), Am. Econ. Assn. (mem. exec. com. 1990-93), Am. Polit. Sci. Assn., Assn. Am. Law Schs., Assn. Pub. Policy and Mgmt. (mem. policy coun. 1984-88). Democrat. Office: Yale U Law Sch PO Box 208215 New Haven CT 06520-8215

ROSEANNE, actress, comedienne, producer, writer; b. Salt Lake City, Nov. 3, 1952; d. Jerry and Helen Barr; m. Bill Pentland, 1974 (div. 1989); children: Jessica, Jennifer, Brandi, Buck, Jake; m. Tom Arnold, 1990 (div. 1994); m. Ben Thomas, 1994. Former window dresser, cocktail waitress; prin. Full Moon & High Tide Prodns., Inc. As comic, worked in bars, church coffeehouse, Denver; produced showcase for women performers Take Back the Mike, U. Boulder (Colo.); performer The Comedy Store, L.A.; showcased on TV special Funny, 1986, also The Tonight Show; featured in HBO-TV spl. On Location: The Roseanne Barr Show, 1987 (Am. comedy award Funniest Female Performer in TV spl., 1987, Ace award Funniest Female in Comedy, 1987, Ace award Best Comedy Spl. 1987); star of TV series Roseanne ABC, 1988— (U.S. Mag. 2nd Ann. Readers Poll Best Actress in Comedy Series, 1989, Golden Globe nomination Outstanding Lead Actress in Comedy Series 1988, Emmy award Outstanding Lead Actress in Comedy Series, 1993); actress: (motion pictures) She-Devil, 1989, Look Who's Talking Too (voice), 1990, Freddy's Dead, 1991, Even Cowgirls Get the Blues, 1994, Blue in the Face, 1995; TV movies: Backfield in Motion, The Woman Who Loved Elvis, 1993; appeared in TV spl. Sinatra: 80 Years My Way, 1995; exec. prodr. Saturday Night Spl., Fox-TV; author: Roseanne: My Life as a Woman, 1989, My Lives, 1994. Active various child advocate orgns. Recipient Peabody award, People's Choice award (4), Golden Globe award (2), Am. Comedy award, Humanitas award, Nickelodeon Kids Choice award, 1990, Eleanor Roosevelt award for Outstanding Am. Women. Office: Full Moon & High Tide Prodns 4024 Radford Ave # 916 917 Studio City CA 91604-2101

ROSEBERG, CARL ANDERSSON, sculptor, educator; b. Vinton, Iowa, Sept. 26, 1916; s. Swan Bernard and Selma (Olson) R.; m. Virginia M. Gorman, Aug. 23, 1942. B.F.A., U. Iowa, 1939, postgrad., 1939-41, M.F.A., 1947; postgrad., Cranbrook Acad. Art, summers 1947-48, U. Hawaii, 1950-51, U. Va., summer 1964, Mysore (India) U., summer 1965, Tyler Sch. Art, Temple U., summer 1967. Faculty Coll. William and Mary, Williamsburg, Va., 1947—; prof. fine arts Coll. William and Mary, 1966-82, prof. emeritus, 1982—, William and Mary Heritage fellow, 1968-82; founding bd. mem. 20th Century Gallery, Williamsburg.; active judge various art groups. Exhibited one man shows at Radford Coll., 1962, Roanoke Fine Art Gallery, 1962-63, Norfolk Mus., 1963, Asheville (N.C.) Gallery Art, 1963, Longwood Coll., 1966, Phi Beta Kappa Hall, William and Mary Coll., 1970; 35 yr. retrospective William and Mary Coll., 1982; retrospective Twentieth Century Gallery, 1983; exhibited in numerous group shows; represented in permanent collections at U. Iowa, Springfield (Mo.) Mus., Va. Mus. Fine Arts, Colonial Williamsburg, Chrysler Mus. Norfolk, Rockingham County Citizens Com., Longwood Coll., Farmville, Va., Thalhimer Bros., Inc., Swem Libr., Coll. William and Mary, others; designer, creator bronze meml. plaque honoring Donald W. Davis for, Millington Hall, Coll. William and Mary, 1970, bronze plaque honoring William G. Guy, Rogers Hall, 1975; I.L. Jones, Jr., Bruton Parish Ch., 1985. designer: James City County Bicentennial Medallion, 1976; designer, creator Carter O. Lowance Bronze Medallion Marshall-Wythe Sch. Law Coll. William and Mary, 1989, Bronze Medallion honoring 300th Ann. Coll. William and Mary, 1991, Bronze Medallion honoring L. I'Anson Marshall-Wythe Sch. Law, 1991. Served to comdr. USNR, 1941-45, 50-52; ret. Res. Recipient Thomas Jefferson award, 1971, numerous art awards, Cheek award William & Mary, 1993. Fellow Internat. Inst. Arts and Letters; mem. Am. Audubon Artists, Fulbright Assn., Res. Officers Assn. Am., Va. Watercolor Soc., Navy League U.S., Williamsburg German Club, Mid. Plantation Club, Masons, Lambda Chi Alpha. Presbyterian. Home: PO Box 1468 Williamsburg VA 23187-1468

ROSEBUSH, JAMES SCOTT, international management and public affairs consultant, former government official; b. Flint, Mich., June 1, 1949; s. Kenneth F. and Jacqueline (Porter) R.; m. Nancy Paull, May 18, 1974; children: Claire Haisley, Lauren Culver. BA, The Principia, Elsah, Ill., 1971; MA, Boston U., 1973. Cons. Boston, 1972-76; v.p. Nat. Chamber Found., Washington, 1976-79; assoc. dir. corp. contbn. Standard Oil Co., Cleve., 1979-81; dir. Office Bus. Liaison, U.S. Dept. Commerce, Washington, 1981, spl. asst. to pres. for pvt. sector initiatives, Washington, 1981-82; dept. asst. to pres., chief staff for First Lady The White House, Washington, 1982-86; pres. James Rosebush & Co., 1986—; lectr. Georgetown U., Washington, 1977-79, George Washington U., Washington, 1977-79; presdl. appointee Nat. Mus. Svcs. Bd. Author: First Lady, Public Wife, 1987; contbr. articles to profl. jours. Mem. rev. com. United Way, Cleve., 1979; mem. community relations com. Cleve. Orch., 1979; bd. mem. Concord Art Assn., 1972. Recipient Internat. award Rotary Internat., 1970. Republican. Avocations: tennis, skiing, reading, travelling. Office: 1250 24th St NW Ste 350 Washington DC 20037-1124

ROSEFSKY, JONATHAN BENENSOHN, pediatrician; b. Johnson City, N.Y., June 28, 1939; s. I.J. and Elsie S. Rosefsky; m. Sue Perel, 1964; children: Katherine, Douglas, Matthew. AB, Cornell U., 1960; B in Med. Sc., Dartmouth U., 1962; MD, Harvard U., 1964. Diplomate Am. Bd. of Pediatrics; lic. Pa., Va. Intern in surgery Vanderbilt Univ. Hosp., Nashville, 1964-65; resident in pediatrics Children's Hosp. Med. Ctr., Boston, 1965-67; pediatrician USAF Med. Corps, Langley AFB, Va., 1967-69; dir. neonatal ICU United Health Svcs. Hosp., Johnson City, N.Y., 1969-74; pvt. practice pediatrics Binghamton, N.Y., 1969-86; pres. Notation Systems, Inc., Binghamton, 1981-89; asst. dir. clin. devel. McNeil Consumer Products Co., Ft. Washington, Pa., 1986-89; sr. dir. med. affairs Wyeth-Ayerst Labs., St. David's, Pa., 1990—; cons. in pediatrics, N.Y. State Dept. Social Svcs., Albany, 1976-86, FDA adv. com. on Gen. Hosp. and Personal Use Devices, Rockville, Md., 1986; industry rep. FDA adv. com. on immunology devices, Rockville, 1987-93; asst. prof. pediatrics, Jefferson Med. Sch., Phila., 1987—. Inventor: back wedge, 1981, mole marker, 1982; contbr. articles to profl. jours. Chmn. Citizen's Adv. Com. to Mayor of Binghamton, N.Y., 1971; active chmn.'s coun. Phila. Mus. of Art. Capt. USAF Med. Corps, 1967-69. Recipient Physician's Recognition award AMA, 1995. Fellow Am. Acad. Pediatrics, Am. Coll. Nutrition, Am. Coll. Physician Execs., Am. Acad. Pharm. Physicians; mem. Harvard Club (N.Y.C.), Green Valley Country Club. Avocations: skiing, swimming, photography, fgn. langs., travel. Home: 251 W Montgomery Ave Haverford PA 19041

ROSEGGER, GERHARD, economist, educator; b. Bruck/Mur, Austria, July 28, 1930; came to U.S., 1954, naturalized, 1961; s. Walter and Irmgard Elsa (Stark) R.; m. Clara Louise Tretter, July 17, 1954; children: Karin Andrea, Michael Lorenz, Nora Lynn, Thomas Martin. Dr.iur., U Graz, Austria, 1953; MBA, U. Pa., 1954. From instr. to asst. prof. Rutgers U. Coll. of S. Jersey, Camden, N.J., 1956-61; asst. prof. Case Inst. Tech., Cleve., 1962-65; assoc. prof. Case Western Res. U., 1965-75, prof. econs., 1975—, Frank Tracy Carlton prof. econs., 1978—; Fulbright vis. prof. U. Innsbruck, Austria, 1983-84, 91; vis. prof. U. Cin., 1988, U. Kassel, Germany, Helsinki (Finland) Sch. Econs., 1991, Vienna Tech. U., 1995; vis. rsch. scholar U. Waikato, Hamilton, N.Z. Author: The Economics of Production and Innovation, 1980, 2d edit., 1986, 3d edit., 1995, (with others) Evaluating Technological Innovations, 1980, Technological Progress and Industrial Leadership, 1984; contbr. chtps. to books, numerous articles to profl. jours. Fulbright scholar, 1950-51; recipient research and travel grants. Mem. Am. Econ. Assn., Inst. Mgmt. Scis., Sigma Xi. Mem. Christian Ch. (Disciples of Christ). Home: 15719 Chadbourne Rd Cleveland OH 44120-3333 Office: Case Western Reserve Univ Economics Dept Cleveland OH 44106

ROSEHART, ROBERT GEORGE, university president, chemical engineer; b. Owen Sound, Ont., Can., July 29, 1943; s. Clarence Daniel and Evaline (Sutton) R.; m. Rita June Purvis, Aug. 26, 1967; children—Robert George, William, Karen Ann. Ch.E., B.A.Sc., U. Waterloo, 1967, M.A.Sc., 1968, Ph.D., 1970. Registered chem. engr. Assoc. prof. chem. engring Lakehead U., Thunder Bay, Ont., Can., 1970-77, dean univ. schs., 1977-84, pres., 1984—; sci. counsellor Porter Royal Commn. on Electric Power Planning, 1975-77; mem. Thunder Bay waferboard study Govt. of Ont., 1986-87; chmn. Ont. Forest Resources Inventory Com.; govt. reviewer No. Labour Mgmt. Issues. Contbr. articles to profl. jours. Chmn. com. on resource coms., 1985, Premiers Coun. Sci. and Tech. Grantee in field. Mem. Can. Pulp and Paper Assn., Assn. Profl. Engrs. Ont. Roman Catholic. Avocations: curling, skiing, boating. Home: 588 Riverview Dr, Thunder Bay, ON Canada P7C 1R7 Office: Lakehead U, Off of Pres, Thunder Bay, ON Canada P7B 5E1

ROSEL, CAROL ANN, artist; b. Dodge City, Kans., June 12, 1944; d. John Elbert and Mary Claire (Wetmore) Frazier; m. Herbert Carey Zortman, Aug. 21, 1960 (div. Jan. 1989); children: Elaine Marie, Anita Louise, Stanley Dale; m. George D. Rosel, Sept. 22, 1990 (dec. June 1995). Student, Ctrl. Coll., McPherson, Kans., 1961; BFA cum laude, Ft. Hays State U., 1994. Cert. machine embroidery instr. Dress designer Ms. Cosmo Ltd., Wichita, Kans., 1975-76; designer artistic embroidery garments, 1977-80; owner Carol Ann's Gallery, Liberal, Kans.; part-time art tchr. C.C.s, Baker Art Ctr., Seward County C.C., U.S. D 480, Liberal; singer A Touch of Class. One-woman show Ft. Hays Libr., 1993. Mem. Baker Art Ctr., Liberal, 1989—, Hays (Kans.) Arts Coun., 1993; tchr. Sunday sch.; counselor girls ch. camp; solo pianist ch. weddings and comty. functions. Recipient All Am. Scholar Collegiate award, 1994, Grand Champion award State Fair, 1989, 90, 95, Purple Champion award, 1990, others; named Woman of World, 1995-96, Internat. Women of World, 1996-97, Internat. Woman of Yr., 1995-96. Mem. Mid. Am. Arts and Crafts Assn., Pinnacle Honor Soc., Art Club, Christian Life Drama Club, Lions Club. Republican. Avocations: piano, singing, dramatics. Home and Office: 406 Harvard Ave Liberal KS 67901-3024

ROSELL, SHARON LYNN, physics and chemistry educator, researcher; b. Wichita, Kans., Jan. 6, 1948; d. John E. and Mildred C. (Binder) R. BA, Loretto Heights Coll., 1970; postgrad., Marshall U., 1973; MS in Edn., Ind. U., 1977; MS, U. Wash., 1988. Cert. profl. educator, Wash. Assoc. instr. Ind. U., Bloomington, 1973-74; instr. Pierce Coll. (name formerly Ft. Steilacoom (Wash.) Community Coll.), 1976-79, 82, Olympic Coll., Bremerton, Wash., 1977-78; instr. physics, math. and chemistry Tacoma (Wash.) Community Coll., 1979-89; instr. physics and chemistry Green River Community Coll., Auburn, Wash., 1983-86; researcher Nuclear Physics Lab., U. Wash., Seattle, 1986-88; asst. prof. physics Cen. Wash. U., Ellensburg, 1989—. Lector and dir. Rite of Christian Initiation of Adults, St. Andrew's Ch., Ellensburg, Wash., 1993—, mem. parish coun., 1995—. Mem. Am. Phys. Soc., Am. Assn. Physics Tchrs. (rep. com. on physics for 2-yr. colls. Wash. chpt. 1986-87, v.p. 1987-88, 94-95, pres. 1988-89, 95-96, past pres. 1996-97), Am. Chem. Soc., Internat. Union Pure and Applied Chemistry (affiliate), Pacific Northwest Assn. Coll. Physics (bd. dirs. 1997—). Democrat. Roman Catholic. Avocations: leading scripture discussion groups, reading, writing poetry, needlework. Home: 1100 N B St Apt 2 Ellensburg WA 98926-2570 Office: Cen Wash U Physics Dept Ellensburg WA 98926 *Personal philosophy: Every human being is born with a unique set of talents and gifts with which to serve the Lord and other people; the greater the gift, the greater the obligation to serve.*

ROSELLA, JOHN DANIEL, clinical psychologist, educator; b. Phila., Sept. 12, 1938; s. Orazio and Angela Theresa (Cardone) R.; B.S. in Psychology, Villanova U., 1961; cert. in Edn., St. Joseph's U., 1963; M.Ed., Temple U., 1966, postgrad., 1969-72; Ph.D., Walden U., 1981; Diplomate Am. Bd. Forensic Examiners; cert. hynotherapist; m. Rose Mary Theresa Malloy, Nov. 14, 1964; children—Anne-Marie, John Daniel Jr. Tchr., counselor Father Judge High Sch., Phila., 1962-67; counselor Bristol Twp. Sch. Dist., Bucks County, Pa., 1967-69; prof. Bucks County Community Coll. Divsn. Social & Behavioral Scis., 1994, subject area coord., 1995, Newtown, Pa., 1968—, founder coll. reading and study skills program, 1968-70, founding chmn. dept. basic studies, 1970-76; dir. psychol. services Fairless Hills (Pa.) Med. Center, 1978-89, dir. clin. svcs., 1989-96; asst. clin. prof. Widener U., 1990; cons. Office of Vocat. Rehab., 1977—; psychol. cons. Eugenia Hosp., 1980—, Bur. Disability Determination, 1982—, Human Growth Center, Inc., 1987—, Crestview North Nursing Home and Rehab. Ctr., 1990—, cons. staff psychologist, Attleboro Nursing Home and Rehabilitation Ctr., 1993, cons. staff psychologist; clin. assoc. prof. Dept. Mental Health Scis. Hahnemann U., 1982-94; cons. Bucks County (Pa.) Family Ct., 1985—; grad. clin. supr. Coll. of N.J., 1985-86; grad. counseling intern supr. Rider Coll., 1988-95; participant 1st Internat. Colloquium on Family Health, Sri Lanka, 1983, Australia, 1988, ednl. profl. travel, Italy and Switzerland, 1991; Bd. dirs. Valley Day Sch., 1978-81, Bucks County Community Centers, 1980-85; co-founder Newtown Twp. Dem. Party, 1978, 1st vice chmn., 1979-80, Dem. committeeman, 1989-92; active Right to Read Task Force, 1972-73; mem. 8th Congressional Dist. Adv. Council on Health Care, 1981-83; project dir. Fairless Hills Psychiat. Hosp. bldg. program, 1982-83; pres. bd. trustees Friends of the Library Found., Bucks County Community Coll., 1984—. Recipient Man of Yr. award Assn. to Advance Ethical Hypnosis, 1976, Disting. Teaching recognition Phi Theta Kappa, 1981, 83, Faculty Svc. award, 1989, Profl. Achievement award Bucks County Community Coll. Alumni Assn., 1991. Lic. psychologist, Pa. Fellow Internat. Council for Sex Edn. and Parenthood of Am. U., Pa. Psychol. Assn.; mem. Am. Psychol. Assn., Am. Assn. Marriage and Family Therapy (clin.), Pa. Assn. Marriage and Family Therapy, Am. Legion. Roman Catholic, Profl. Acad. Custody Evaluators (registered custody evaluator 1993), . Clubs: KC, Sons of Italy. Author: Reading and Study Skills: A Counseling Approach, 1970; Effects of the Basic Studies Program on the Academic Achievement of High Risk Students, 1973-74; The Professor and the Law, 1975; Research in Hypnosis for Students, 1976; Marriage and Family Therapy: Its Evolution from Revolution, 1980; others; (audio-tapes) Developing Successful Study Skills, Guided Imagery Exercises; also articles. Office: Offices at Oxford Crossing 333 N Oxford Valley Rd Ste 202 Fairless Hills PA 19030-2626

ROSELLE, DAVID PAUL, university president, mathematics educator; b. Vandergrift, Pa., May 30, 1939; s. William John and Esther Suzanne (Clever) R.; m. Louise Helen Dowling, June 19, 1967; children—Arthur Charles, Cynthia Dowling. BS, West Chester State Coll., 1961; PhD, Duke U., 1965; LLD, West Chester U., 1994. Asst. prof. math. U. Md., College Park, 1965-68; assoc. prof. math. La. State U., Baton Rouge, 1968-73, prof., 1973-74; prof. Va. Poly. Inst. and State U., Blacksburg, 1974-87, dean grad. sch., 1979-81, dean research and grad. studies, 1981-83, provost, 1983-87, chmn. Commn. on Rsch., 1981-83, chmn. Commn. on Grad. Studies, 1983-87; prof. U. Ky., 1987-90, pres., 1987-90; prof. math., pres. U. Del., 1990—; pres. COMAP, Inc., Lexington, Mass., 1986-95; bd. dirs. William Trust Corp., VTLS, Inc. Editor: Proc. of the First Louisiana Conf. on Combinatorics, Graph Theory and Computing, 1970, Proc. of the Second Louisiana Conf. on Combinatorics, Graph Theory and Computing, 1971; mem. editorial bd. The Bicentennial Tribute to American Mathematics, 1977; contbr. numerous research articles to profl. jours. Mem. Del. Roundtable, 1990—, Bus.and Pub. Edn. Coun., 1990—; trustee Winterthur Mus., 1991—; bd. dirs. Del. Acad. Medicine, 1991—, Med. Ctr. Del., 1991—. Named Outstanding Alumnus West Chester State Coll., 1979; Westinghouse Coop. scholar, 1957; NSF grantee, 1965-75; Teaching Excellence Cert., 1978; Digital Equipment grant, 1984; Nat. Coun. Tchrs. Math. Cert. of Appreciation, 1984; founding fellow of Inst. for Combinatorics and Its Applications, 1990; numerous invited addresses at univs. and profl. soc. meetings. Mem. Am. Math. Soc., Math. Assn. Am. (sec., fin. com., exec. com., com. on publs. 1975-84; com. on spl. funds 1985—; chmn. com. on accreditation 1985; numerous other coms.). Home: 47 Kent Way Newark DE 19711-5201 Office: U Del Hullihen Hall Newark DE 19716

ROSELLE, WILLIAM CHARLES, librarian; b. Vandergrift, Pa., June 30, 1936; s. William John and Suzanne Esther (Clever) R.; m. Marsha Louise Lucas, Aug. 2, 1959; 1 child, Paul Lucas. BA, Thiel Coll., 1958; MLS, U. Pitts., 1963. Lic. profl. guide State of Mont., 1978. Mem. faculty Milton Hershey (Pa.) Sch., 1960-62; trainee Pa. State Library, 1962-63; asst. catalog librarian Pa. State U., 1963-65; engring., math. librarian U. Iowa, 1965-66, library adminstrv. asst., 1966-69, asst. dir. libraries, 1969-71; prof., dir. library U. Wis.-Milw., 1971-89; dir. univ. library system U. Pitts., 1989-90; pvt. cons. Thiensville, Wis., 1991—; chmn. Morris Fromkin Meml. Lectr. Com., 1972-89; chmn. planning task force on computing U. Wis. System, 1973-74, mem. library planning study com., 1978-79, co-chmn. library automation task force, 1983-85; chmn. computing mgmt. rev. team U. Wis.-Stout, 1976; chmn. Council for U. Wis. Libraries, 1981-82; library cons. Grambling (La.) State U., Viterbo Coll., LaCrosse, Wis., N.C. A&T U., Greensboro, Mt. Mary Coll., Milw., U. Ill. at Chgo., Milw. Sch. Engring., Bklyn. Coll., U. South Ala., Concordia Coll., Milw., Metrics Rsch. Corp., Cardinal Stritch Coll., Milw., N.Y. Inst. Tech., Indiana U. of Pa., Med. Coll. Wis., Wis. Luth. Coll., Milw.; participant Library Adminstrs. Devel. Program, U. Md., 1973, micrographics seminar Nat. Microfilm Assn., 1973, Mgmt. Skills Inst., Assn. Rsch. Libraries, Kansas City, Mo., 1977, Meadowbrook Symposium Midwest Library Network, 1976; mem. sect. geography and map libraries Internat. Fedn. Library Assns. and Instns., 1978-83; mem. bldg. com. Ctr. for Rsch. Libraries, 1980-82. Editorial cons. The Quest for Social Justice, 1983, Current Geographical Publications, 1978-89; contbr. articles to profl. jours. Pres. Thiensville (Wis.) Village Bd., 1987; bd. dirs. Charles Allis Art Mus., 1979-84. Served with AUS, 1958-60. Named Disting. Alumnus, Thiel Coll., 1985. Hon. fellow Am. Geog. Soc.; mem. Spl. Libraries Assn. (spl. citation 1979), ALA (life), Iowa Library Assn. (chmn. audit com. 1968-70, chmn. intellectual freedom com. 1969-70), Wis. Library Assn., Midwest Acad. Librarians Conf. (chmn. 1969-71), AAUP (treas. U. Iowa chpt. 1969-70), Coun. Wis. Libraries (chmn. 1973-74), Soc. Tympanuchus Cupido Pinnatus, Milw. Civil War Round Table, Ozaukee Corvette Club, Beta Beta Beta, Beta Phi Mu, Phi Alpha Theta, Phi Kappa Phi, Phi Delta Kappa. Lutheran. Home: 324 Sunny Ln Thiensville WI 53092-1334

ROSELLI, RICHARD JOSEPH, lawyer; b. Chgo., Mar. 2, 1954; s. H. Joseph and Dolores Roselli; m. Lisa McNelis; children: Nicholas Joseph, Christiana Elise, Alexandra Grace, Michaela Luciana. BA, Tulane U., 1976, JD, 1980. Bar: Fla. 1981, U.S. Dist. Ct. (so. dist.) Fla. 1981, U.S. Ct. Appeals (5th and 11th cirs.); bd. cert. civil trial lawyer. Assoc. Krupnick & Campbell, Ft. Lauderdale, Fla., 1981-84; ptnr. Krupnick, Campbell, Malone Roselli, Ft. Lauderdale, 1984-91, Krupnick Campbell Malone Roselli Buser Slama & Hancock P.A., Ft. Lauderdale, 1991—. Trustee Fla. Dem. Party, 1992-95. Mem. ATLA, Am. Bd. Trial Advocates, Am. Soc. Law and Medicine, So. Trial Lawyers Assn. (founder), Acad. Fla. Trial Lawyers (bd. dirs. 1987—, exec. com. 1990—, sec. 1993, treas. 1994, pres. 1996—, chmn. Fla. lawyers action group-PAC 1996, Golden Eagle award, 1989, 1996, Silver Eagle award, 1990, Crystal Eagle award 1995), Trial Lawyers for Pub. Justice, Lawyer Pilots Bar Assn., St. Jude Catholic Ch. Office: 700 SE 3rd Ave Fort Lauderdale FL 33316-1154

ROSEMAN, JACK, computer services company executive; b. Lynn, Mass., June 13, 1931; s. Abraham and Bessie (Guz) R.; m. Judith Ann Rosenthal, Feb. 21, 1960; children: Laura, Alan, Shari. BA, Boston U., 1954; MS, U. Mass., 1955. Instr. U. Mass., 1958-60; dir. info. processing CEIR, Inc., Washington, 1960-66; v.p. KMS Tech. Ctr., Washington, 1966-70; pres. On-Line Systems, Inc., Pitts., from 1970-79 also bd. dirs.; pres., chmn. United Computing Internat. subs. of SPRINT, 1992—; pvt. investor, ptnr. J.R. Assocs., Pitts, 1988—; Donald H. Jones Disting. adj. prof. in entrepreneurship, Carnegie Mellon U., 1985—; assoc. dir. Donald H. Jones Ctr. Entrepreneurship, 1992—; dir. emeritus Pitts. High Tech. Coun.; rsch. staff mem. whilwind project computation ctr. MIT; chmn. bd. dirs. Omega Systems, Inc., 1994—, chmn., 1994-96; bd. dirs. Vision Systems, 1996—, Cybergenetics, 1996—. Recipient Judges' award for Entrepreneurship Ernst & Young, and Merill Lynch Inc. mags. Mem. AAUP, Am. Assn. Advancement Sci., Assn. Computing Machinery.

ROSEMAN, SAUL, biochemist, educator; b. Bklyn., Mar. 9, 1921; s. Emil and Rose (Markowitz) R.; m. Martha Ozrowitz, Sept. 9, 1941; children: Mark Alan, Dorinda Ann, Cynthia Bernice. B.S., CCNY, 1941; M.S., U. Wis., 1944, Ph.D., 1947; (hon.) M.D., U. Lund, Sweden, 1984. From instr. to asst. prof. U. Chgo., 1948-53; from asst. prof. to prof. biol. chemistry, also Rackham Arthritis Research Unit, U. Mich., 1953-65; Ralph S. O'Connor prof. biology Johns Hopkins U., Balt., 1965—, chmn. dept., 1969-73; dir. McCollum-Pratt Inst., 1969-73, chmn. dept. biology , dir., 1988-90; cons. NIH, NSF, Am. Cancer Soc., Hosp. for Sick Children, Toronto; sci. counselor Nat. Cancer Inst.; Lynch lectr. U. Notre Dame, 1989; Van Niel lectr. Stanford U., 1992. Author articles on metabolism of complex molecules containing carbohydrates and on solute transport.; former mem. editorial bd.: Biochemistry, Jour. Biol. Chemistry. Served with AUS, 1944-46. Recipient Sesquicentennial award U. Mich., 1967, T. Duckett Jones Meml. award Helen Hay Whitney Found., 1973, Rosenstiehl award Brandeis U., 1974, Internat. award Gairdner Found. award, 1981, Townsend Harris award CUNY, 1987, Spl. award 11th Internat. Symposium on Glycoconjugates, 1991, Karl Meyer award Soc. Glycobiology, 1993. Fellow Am. Acad. Microbiology; mem. Am. Soc. Biol. Chemists, Am. Soc. Cell Biology, Am. Acad. Arts and Scis., Nat. Acad. Scis., Am. Chem. Soc., Am. Soc. Microbiologists, Biochem. Soc. Japan (hon.). Office: Johns Hopkins U 34th Charles St Baltimore MD 21218

ROSEMARIN, CAREY STEPHEN, lawyer; b. Englewood, N.J., Aug. 19, 1950; s. Jack L. and Muriel Ruth (Gordon) R.; m. Joan Maxine Lafer, June 17, 1973; children: Benjamin Joseph, Meryl Ruth. BS, U. Mich., 1972; MS, Pa. State U., 1974; JD, U. Tenn., 1978. Bar: Tenn. 1978, Ill. 1982, U.S. Dist. Ct. (ea. dist.) Tenn. 1978, U.S. Dist. Ct. (no. dist.) Ill. 1982. Rsch. assoc. Union Carbide Corp., Oak Ridge Nat. Lab., 1974-80; asst. regional counsel U.S. EPA, Chgo., 1980-86; ptnr. Katten, Muchin, & Zavis, Chgo., 1986-90, Jenner & Block, Chgo., 1990—. Mem. ABA, Tenn. Bar Assn., Chgo. Bar Assn. (chmn. environ. law com. 1985-86), Environ. Law Inst. (assoc.). Jewish. Avocations: licensed glider pilot, bicycling. Office: Jenner & Block 1 E Ibm Plz Chicago IL 60611-3586

ROSEMBERG, EUGENIA, physician, educator, medical research administrator; b. Buenos Aires, Argentina, Apr. 25, 1918; came to U.S., 1948, naturalized, 1956; d. Pedro and Fanny (Hestrin) R. BS, Liceo Nacional de Senoritas, Buenos Aires, 1936; MD, U. Buenos Aires, 1944. Intern Hosp. Pirovano, Buenos Aires, 1940-41; resident Hosp. Nacional de Clinicas, U. Hosp., U. Buenos Aires, 1941-44, assoc. in pediatrics, 1943-48; instr. in anatomy Hosp. Nacional de Clinicas, U. Hosp., U. Buenos Aires (Med. Sch.), 1940-46, instr. pediatrics, 1946-48; practice medicine specializing in pediatrics, 1946-48; research in endocrinology Balt., 1948-51, Worcester, Mass., 1955—; Mead Johnson fellow dept. endocrinology Johns Hopkins Med. Sch., Balt., 1948-49; vis. scientist Med. Sch., U. Montevideo, Uruguay, 1950; research fellow NIH, Bethesda, Md., 1951-53, Nat. Inst. Arthritis and Metabolic Diseases, 1951-53, Med. Research Inst. and Hosp., Oklahoma City, 1953; mem. staff Worcester Found. Exptl. Biology, Shrewsbury, Mass., 1953-62; research dir. Med. Research Inst. of Worcester, Inc., 1962—; cons. Center for Population Research, Nat. Inst. Child Health and Human Devel., NIH, 1969-70, chief contraceptive devel. br., 1970-71; prof. pediatrics U. Md. Hosp., Balt., 1970-73; prof. medicine U. Mass. Med. Sch., Worcester, 1972—; mem. staff Worcester City Hosp., 1955-85, sec. human experimentation com., 1965-83, chmn., 1984-85, dir. clin. research, 1972-85; Sec. subcom. on gonadotropins Nat. Hormone and Pituitary Program, Nat. Inst. Arthritis, Diabetes, Digestive and Kidney Diseases, 1965-69, chmn., 1969-85, mem. med. adv. bd., 1969-72, 73-85, sec. subcom. on standards endocrinology study sect., 1968. Author: Gonadotropins, 1968, (with C.A. Paulsen) The Human Testis, 1970, Gonadotropin Therapy in Female Infertility, 1973, (with C. Gual) Hypothalamic Hypophysiotropic Hormones—Physiological and Clinical Studies, 1973; Mem. editorial bd.: Giner, 1970—, Procs. 1st Ann. Meeting Am. Soc. Andrology, supplement, Vol. 8, 1976, Andrologia, 1978—, Jour. Andrology, 1979-82, Internat. Jour. Andrology, 1978—; assoc. editor: Reproduccion, 1970—, Andrologia jour, 1974-77; Contbr. articles and book chpts. on research in endocrinology to med. texts and jours.; Translator: from Spanish Diagnosis and Treatment of Endocrine Disorders in Childhood and Adolescence (L. Wilkins). Patentee in field, U.S., Can., Europe. Fellow AAAS; mem. Am. Med. Women's Assn., Endocrine Soc. U.S. (mem. com. pub. affairs 1971, v.p. 1975-76), Soc. for Research in Biology of Reproduction, Soc. for Study of Reproduction, Am. Fertility Soc., Peru Fertility Soc. (fgn. corr.), N.Y. Acad. Scis., New Eng. Cardiovascular Soc., Am., Mass. heart assns., Argentine Endocrine Soc., Argentine Pediatric Soc., Sociedad Argentine Para El Estudio de la Esterilidad., Pan Am. Med. Women's Alliance, Am. Soc. Andrology (program chmn. 1975-76, exec. council 1976-78, chmn. publ. com. 1975-80, Disting. Andrologist award 1982), Internat. Com. for Study Andrology (exec. council 1976-79).

ROSEMONT, NORMAN, television and feature producer; b. N.Y.C., Dec. 12, 1924. Prodns. include A Tale of Two Cities, Brigadoon, Carousel, Kiss Me Kate, Kismet, Stiletto, The Man Without a Country, Miracle on 34th Street, A Tree Grows in Brooklyn, The Red Badge of Courage, The Count of Monte Cristo, The Man in the Iron Mask, The Mad Mad Mad Mad World of the Super Bowl, Captains Courageous, The Court Martial of George Armstrong Custer, Four Feathers, Les Miserables, All Quiet on the Western Front, Pleasure Palace, Little Lord Fauntleroy; TV miniseries: Master of the Game, 1984, Camille, 1985, The Secret Garden, 1987, The Tenth Man, 1988, Ironclads, 1991, Long Road Home, 1991, Shadow of a Doubt, 1991, Fergie and Andrew, 1992, Harmful Intent, 1993. •

ROSEN, ALEXANDER CARL, psychologist, consultant; b. L.A., Feb. 2, 1923; s. Benjamin and Pauline (Katz) R.; m. Florence Friedman, Mar. 18, 1951 (div. Nov. 1973); children: Diane, Judith; m. Susan Margaret Gersbacher, Nov. 4, 1973; 1 child, Rebecca. AA, U. Calif., L.A., 1943; AB, U. Calif., Berkeley, 1946, PhD, 1953. Diplomate clin. psychology Am. Bd. Profl. Psychology; lic. psychologist. Psychologist Contra Costa County, Martinez, Calif., 1953-56; asst. rsch. psychologist Office Naval Rsch. and San Francisco State Coll., 1953-56, UCLA-Neuropsychiat. Inst., L.A., 1956-57; asst. prof. to prof. psychiatry and behavioral sci. UCLA Sch. Medicine, L.A., 1956-89; chief psychology UCLA Neuropsychiatric Inst., L.A., 1958-89; prof. emeritus UCLA Sch. Medicine, L.A., 1989—; pvt. practice psychology cons. L.A., 1973—; instr. San Francisco State Coll., 1955; instr. psychology Calif. Inst. Tech., Pasadena, 1969; staff assoc. Nat. Tng. Lab. Inst. Applied Behavioral Sci., 1962—; cons. tng. U.S. Veteran's Assn., Sepulveda (Calif.) Hosp., 1966—; bd. mem. L.A. Group Psychotherapy Tng. Inst., 1972-75; bd. mem., trustee Calif. Sch. Profl. Psychology, 1974-76, 78; nat. bd., regional bd. Cert. Cons. Internat. Cons. Cons. editor: Jour. Genetic Psychology and Genetic Psychology Monograph, 1984—; contbr. articles to profl. jours. Mem. gov. bd. Hillel Coun., So. Calif.; cons. San Fernando Valley Counseling Ctr., 1991-92, Pacific Ctr. for AIDS, L.A., 1991-94; adv. bd. mem. CSN Valley Youth Orch.; docent Pacific Asia Mus., 1997—; co-chair College-Park Neighborhood Assn., 1997—. Fellow APA, AAAS; mem. Calif. State Psychology Assn. (pres. 1977-78), Western Psychol. Assn. Avocations: photography, music, drama. Home: 6247 Sunnyslope Ave Van Nuys CA 91401-2411

ROSEN, ANA BEATRIZ, electronics executive; b. Guayaquil, Ecuador, May 16, 1950; came to U.S., 1962; d. Luis A. and Luz Aurora (Rodriguez) Moreira; m. Manuel Jose Farina, Dec. 15, 1979 (dec. Apr. 1990); children: Kevin, Mark; m. Michael G. Rosen, June 6, 1992. AA, Latin-Am. Inst., 1971. Adminstr. asst. M&T Chem. Inc., N.Y.C., 1971-75; mgr. sales Singer Products Co., N.Y.C., 1975-78; v.p. Argil Internat. Ltd., N.Y.C., 1978-83; pres. KMA Enterprises Inc., Bklyn., 1983-94, KMA Industries Inc., Palm Beach Gardens, Fla., 1994—; mem. U.S Trade Adv. Bd. Mem. ARC. Mem. ARC, NAFE, World Trade Coun. (Palm Beach County), Gold Coast Bus. and Profl. Women of the Palm Beaches. Roman Catholic.

ROSEN, ARTHUR MARVIN, advertising executive; b. N.Y.C., Dec. 28, 1930; s. Joseph and Cornelia (Grob) R.; m. Maureen Elizabeth Reilly; children: Ellen Jessica, Deborah Lynn, Daniel Joshua. BA, Cuny, 1952; MA, Yale U., 1953; postgrad., Columbia U., 1955-57. Analyst research Dancer-Fitzgerald-Sample, N.Y.C., 1955-56; supr. research Benton and Bowles, N.Y.C., 1956-61; account exec. Young and Rubicam, N.Y.C., 1961-66; v.p. account supr. Grey Advt., N.Y.C., 1966-69; pres. Met. Diagnostic, N.Y.C., 1969-73; v.p. group mgmt. Grey Advt., N.Y.C., 1973-81; exec. v.p. Sudler and Hennessey, N.Y.C., 1981-94; mktg. cons. Himmel Nutrition, Inc., 1994-

95, Martin Himmel, Inc., 1994-95; spkr. in field. Contbr. articles to profl. jours. Pres. Temple Beth Or, Washington Twp., N.J., 1973-74; chmn. Soc. Families, Colgate U., 1983-84; served as cpl. U.S. Army, 1953-55. Republican. Jewish.

ROSEN, ARYE, microwave, optoelectronics and medicine researcher; b. June 26, 1937. BSEE cum laude, Howard U., 1963; MScE, Johns Hopkins U., 1965; MSc in Physiology, Thomas Jefferson U., 1975; PhD in Elec. Engring., Drexel U., 1993. Registered profl. engr., B.C., Can. Sr. mem. tech. staff David Sarnoff Rsch. Ctr. (subs. of SRI), Princeton, N.J., 1967—; assoc. in medicine Jefferson Med. Coll., Phila., 1977—; adj. prof. elec. and computer engring. Drexel U., Phila., 1981—. Co-editor: High-Power Optically Activated Solid-State Switches, 1993, New Frontiers in Medical Device Technology, 1995; contbr. more than 150 articles to profl. jours. Recipient Microwave prize 16th European Microwave Conf., 1986. Fellow IEEE (mem. MTT-S tech. com. for light-wave tech. 1979—, mem. MTT-S tech. program com., chmn. MTT-S tech. com. on biol. effects and med. applications, mem. editorial bd., assoc. editor IEEE Jour. Light-Wave Tech., editorial bd. Transactions on Microwave Theory and Techniques, editorial bd. Microwave and Optical Tech. Letters, mem. tech. com. IEEE Internat. Conf. Microwaves in Medicine 1991, ednl. activities bd., mem.-at-large health care engring. policy com., Region One award for significant contbns. to microwave tech.by the invention and devel. of microwave balloon angioplasty, 1989, Disting. Microwave lectr. 1997—), N.Y. Acad. Scis. Achievements include 45 patents in the fields of engineering and medicine, including Percutaneous Transluminal Microwave Catheter Angioplasty, Method and Apparatus for High Frequency Catheter Ablation, Catheter with Distally Located Integrated Circuit Radiation Generator, Electrical Phase Shifter Controlled by Light, Direct DC to RF Conversion by Impulse Excitation, Light Controlled Antennas, High Power Optical Switch, Radiation Protection Circuit for Protection Against Gamma Ray and Neutron Radiation. Office: David Sarnoff Rsch Ctr CN 5300 Princeton NJ 08543-5300

ROSEN, BENJAMIN MAURICE, venture capitalist, computer company executive; b. New Orleans, Mar. 11, 1933; s. Isidore J. and Anna Vera (Leibof) R.; m. Alexandra Ebere, Sept. 29, 1967; children—Jeffrey Mark, Eric Andrew. B.S., Calif. Inst. Tech., 1954; M.S., Stanford U., 1955; M.B.A., Columbia U., 1961. Engr. Raytheon Corp., Oxnard, Calif., 1955-56; engr. Sperry Corp., Great Neck, N.Y., 1957-59; v.p. Quantum Sci. Corp., N.Y.C., 1961-65; ptnr. Coleman & Co., N.Y.C., 1965-75; v.p. Morgan Stanley & Co. Inc., N.Y.C., 1975-80; pres. Rosen Research Inc., N.Y.C., 1980-83; ptnr. Sevin Rosen Mgmt. Co., N.Y.C., 1981—, chmn. bd., 1982—; also chmn. Compaq Computer Corp, Houston, TX; former founder dir. Lotus Devel. Corp.; mem. bd. overseers and mgrs. Meml. Sloan Kettering Cancer Ctr., N.Y.C.; mem. bd. overseers Columbia U. Grad. Sch. Bus., N.Y.C. Trustee Calif. Inst. Tech., Pasadena. Office: Sevin Rosen Mgmt Co 200 Park Ave New York NY 10166-0005 also: Compaq Computer Corp PO Box 692000 B Houston TX 77269-2000*

ROSEN, BENSON, business administration educator; b. Detroit, Oct. 9, 1942; s. David and Laura R.; m. Brenda M. Leibroder, Dec. 17, 1966; children: Gregory Scott, David Loren. BS, Wayne State U., 1964, MA, 1968, PhD, 1969. Asst. prof. U. N.C., Chapel Hill, 1969-74, assoc. prof., 1974-80, prof. bus. adminstrn., 1980—, Hanes prof., 1992, sr. assoc. dean acad. affairs, 1995—; vis. prof. U. Minn., 1981; cons. to bus., industry, govt.; cons. EEOC. Author: Becoming Aware, 1976; Older Employees: New Roles for Valued Resources, 1985; mem. editorial rev. bd. Acad. Mgmt. Jour., 1978-84; contbr. articles to profl. jours. Bd. dirs. SHRM Found., 1994—. Recipient Young Scholars award Spencer Found., 1976, 78, Disting. Rsch. award, 1993, PhD Teaching award, 1994; NSF grantee, 1973-75; Adminstrn. on Aging grantee, 1978-80. Fellow APA; mem. Acad. Mgmt., Soc. Human Resource Mgmt. Office: Kenan Flagler Bus Sch U NC Chapel Hill NC 27599-3490

ROSEN, BERNARD H., chemical engineer; b. N.Y.C., Sept. 29, 1922; s. Max and Dorothy (Hildebr) R.; m. Anita Ruth Greenberg, Aug. 26, 1947; children: Jeffrey Paul, Seth Gordon, Lise Ann. B.S. in Chem. Engring., CCNY, 1943; M.S., NYU, 1947; postgrad., Harvard U., 1943-44, Okla. A&M U., 1949, Ill. Inst. Tech., 1949-50, Columbia U., 1955-56. Grad. asst. NYU, 1946-47; with Cities Service Research and Devel. Co., 1947-82; successively research chem. engr. Cities Service Research and Devel. Co., Tallant, Okla.; asso. chemist Cities Service Research and Devel. Co., East Chicago, Ind.; chem. engr. Cities Service Research and Devel. Co., Camden, N.J.; asst. v.p. Cities Service Research and Devel. Co., N.Y.C., 1947-57; mgr. products devel. Cities Service Research and Devel. Co., Cranbury, N.J., 1957-58; mgr. Cranbury Lab., 1958-65; dir. product and process research Cities Service Oil Co., 1965-71; mgr. research and planning, chems. and metals group Cities Service Co., N.Y.C., 1971-72; dir. research Cities Service Co., 1972-76; pres. Cities Service Research & Devel. Co., Cranbury, 1972-76; gen. mgr. tech. systems div. Cities Service Research & Devel. Co., Tulsa, 1976-78; gen. mgr. metal fabrication Cities Service Research & Devel. Co., Chester, N.Y., 1978-80; cons. Cities Service Research & Devel. Co., 1980-81; gen. engr. U.S. Army, Ft. Monmouth, N.J., 1982-91; cons., 1992—. Contbr. articles to profl. jours. Served as 1st lt. AUS, 1943-46; capt. Res. Mem. Sigma Xi. Patentee in field. Home: 13 Buena Vista Ave Rumson NJ 07760-1109

ROSEN, CAROL MENDES, artist; b. N.Y.C., Jan. 15, 1933; d. Bram de Sola and Mildred (Bertuch) Mendes; m. Elliot A. Rosen, June 30, 1957. BA, Hunter Coll., 1954; MA, CUNY, 1962. Tchr. art West Orange (N.J.) Pub. Schs., 1959-85; co-curator exhibit Printmaking Coun. N.J., Somerville, 1981; exhibit curator 14 Sculptors Gallery, N.Y.C, 1988, Collection: Nat. Collection of Fine Arts, Smithsonian Instn., Newark Mus., N.J. State Mus., Bristol-Myers Squibb, AT&T, Noyes Mus; guest curator Hunterdon Art Ctr., 1998. Contbr. articles to arts mags. Fellow N.J. State Coun. on Arts, 1980, 83; recipient Hudson River Mus. award, Yonkers, 1983. Jewish. Avocations: gardening, reading. Home: 10 Beavers Rd Califon NJ 07830-3433

ROSEN, CAROLE, cable television executive. BS, Russell Sage Coll., 1966; MS, Hunter Coll., N.Y.C., 1969. Tchr. N.Y.C. Pub. Schs.; v.p. family programming HBO, N.Y.C. Originator, exec. prodr.: (animated series) Happily Ever After: Fairy Tales for Every Child, Babar, Tintin, Cirque du Soleil (Emmy award), Lifestories: Families in Crisis (Emmy award, ACE award), Shakespeare: The Animated Tales (Emmy award), Going, Going, Gone: Animals in Danger (Emmy award Outstanding Children's Spl.). Office: HBO Time Warner Entertainment 1100 6th Ave New York NY 10036-6712

ROSEN, CHARLES, production designer. Prodn. designer: (films) Charly, 1968, A Separate Peace, 1972, Heroes, 1977, Empire of the Ants, 1977, Big Wednesday, 1978, Invasion of the Body Snatchers, 1978, Last Embrace, 1979, The Main Event, 1979, Inside Moves, 1980, My Favorite Year, 1982, The Entity, 1983, Flashdance, 1983, The Whoopee Boys, 1986, Broadcast News, 1987, Touch & Go, 1987, My Stepmother Is an Alien, 1988, My Blue Heaven, 1990, Downtown, 1990, The Butcher's Wife, 1991, Stop! or My Mon Will Shoot, 1992, Free Willy, 1993, My Girl 2, 1993, Mother, 1996, Private Parts, 1996; (TV movies) City in Fear, 1981. Office: care Lawrence Mirisch Innovative Artists Agy 1999 Ave of the Stars Ste 2850 Los Angeles CA 90067*

ROSEN, CHARLES, II, lawyer; b. New Orleans, Jan. 29, 1925; s. Louis Leucht and Nita (Silverstein) R.; m. Mary Alice Waldauer (div. 1976); children: Charles III, Virginia, Jane, James Louis; m. Sandra Reed (div. 1995); m. Emily Hart, 1995. BA, Tulane U., 1948, LLB, 1951. Bar: La. 1951. Assoc. Rosen, Kammer, Wolff, Hopkins & Burke, New Orleans, 1951-55; assoc. Jones, Walker, Waechter, Poitevent, Carrere & Denegre, New Orleans, 1955-58, ptnr., 1958-90; spl. counsel Locke, Purnell, Rain, Harrell, New Orleans, 1990—; mem. exec. com., past chmn. Golf & Sports Attractions, Inc. Past trustee Touro Synagogue; hon. trustee Touro Infirmary; chmn. lawyers div. Jewish Fedn. Greater New Orleans, 1969; past chmn. lawyers div. United Fund. 1st lt. U.S. Army, 1944-46, PTO. Mem. ABA, La. Bar Assn., New Orleans Bar Assn., Am. Coll. Real Estate Attys., Anglo Am. Real Property Inst., So. Golf Assn. (past bd. dirs.), New Orleans Golf Assn. (past pres., past bd. dirs.), Tulane Green Wave Club (past bd. dirs.), Lakewood Country Club (past pres., bd. dirs.). Republican. Avocation: golf. Home: 410 Northline Metairie LA 70005 Office: Locke Purnell Rain Harrell 601 Poydras St Ste 2400 New Orleans LA 70130-6029

ROSEN, CHARLES ABRAHAM, electrical engineer, consultant; b. Toronto, Ont., Can., Dec. 7, 1917; came to U.S., 1950; s. Morris and Ida (Muscet) R.; m. Blanche Jacobson, May 15, 1941; children: Hal, Steven, Naomi, Sema. BEE, Cooper Union, 1940; M in Engring., McGill U., 1950; PhD, Syracuse U., 1957. Founder, CEO Electrolabs Registered, Montreal, Can., 1946-50; semiconductor designer GE, Syracuse, N.Y., 1950-52, mgr. dielectrics group, 1952-57; mgr. applied physics SRI Internat., Menlo Park, Calif., 1957-62, dir. artificial intelligence, 1962-78; founder, chmn. Machine Intelligence Corp., Sunnyvale, Calif., 1980-85; co-founder, dir. Ridge Vineyards, Cupertino, Calif., 1962-87; CEO Cultured Foods Corp., San Francisco, 1988-92, also bd. dirs.; pvt. practice cons. Atherton, Calif., 1988—; cons. Ricoh Rsch., Menlo Park, 1989—, Food Machinery, Sunnyvale, 1989—; adv. com. Nat. Rsch. Coun., Washington, 1990-92. Coauthor Principles of Transistor Circuits, 1953, Solid State Dielectric Design, 1959; contbr. articles to profl. jours.; patentee in field. P.O., Air Force, Can., 1944-45. Recipient Engelberger award Robot Inst. Am., 1982. Fellow IEEE (Taylor award 1975), Am. Assn. Artificial Intelligence; mem. AAAS, Am. Physical Soc. Avocations: winemaking, horticulture, hydroponics, inventions. Home: 139 Tuscaloosa Ave Atherton CA 94027-4016

ROSEN, COREY M., professional association executive; b. Denver, Nov. 26, 1948; s. Abraham and Dorothy Lillian (Bernstein) R.; m. Karen Young, Aug. 4, 1979; 1 child, Jessica. BA, Wesleyan U., 1970; MA, Cornell U., 1972, PhD, 1973. Asst. prof. govt. Ripon (Wis.) Coll., 1973-75; congressional fellow U.S. Senate, Washington, 1975-76; staff profl. Sen. James Abourezk, Washington, 1976-78; com. staff Senate Sm. Bus. Com., Washington, 1978-81; exec. dir. Nat. Ctr. for Employer Ownership, Oakland, Calif., 1981—. Author: Employee Ownership in America, 1986, Employee Ownership at Work, 1986, Understanding Employee Ownership, 1991. Democrat. Jewish. Avocations: running, bicycling, racquetball, reading. Office: Nat Ctr Employee Ownership 1201 Martin Luther King Jr Way Oakland CA 94612-1217

ROSEN, DAVID MATTHEW, education educator; b. Hagerstown, Md., Dec. 29, 1948; s. Norman and Lois (Barbanell) R.; m. Elizabeth Randall Kindleberger, Dec. 29, 1975; children: Louis Wardlaw, Samuel Barbanell. BA in Eng., Haverford Coll., 1971; MA, John Hopkins U., 1974, PhD, 1979. Prof. English and drama, chair divsn. arts and letters U. Maine, Machias, 1994—, co-chair divsn. scis., 1994—. Author: Changing Fictions of Masculinity, 1993, Embodying Masculinity, 1994. Founder, exec. dir. Maine Youth Summer Theater Inst.; mem. exec. bd. Acadia Annex Repertory. Mem. Nat. Coun. Tchrs. Eng., Modern Lang. Assn., Maine Humanities Coun. (chair exec. bd.). Home: Maple Tree Farm RR 1 Box 4100 Lubec ME 04652 Office: Univ Maine Machias ME 04654

ROSEN, DAVID PAUL, book editor; b. Buffalo, May 23, 1959; s. Paul Maurice and Ethel A. (Witt) R. BA summa cum laude, Elmira Coll., 1981; MA, Temple U., 1984. Mktg. assoc. Temple U. Press, Phila., 1982-85; editor The Advocate, L.A., 1985-87, Ziff-Davis, N.Y.C., 1987-89; sr. editor Book-of-the-Month Club/Time Warner, N.Y.C., 1989-95; exec. editor Book-of-the-Month Club, N.Y.C., 1995-96, editl. dir. Quality Paperback Book Club, 1996—; lectr. pub. course NYU, 1994-97. Editor (book series) Triangle Classics, 1993—. Recipient Robertson prize Temple U., 1984, GLAAD award, 1994. Mem. Pub. Triangle, Wallace Stevens Soc., Phi Beta Kappa. Office: BOMC QPB Rm 308 1271 Avenue Of The Americas Lbby 3 New York NY 10020-1302

ROSEN, ELLEN FREDA, psychologist, educator; b. Chgo., Jan. 28, 1941; d. Samuel Aaron and Clara Laura (Pauker) R. BA, Carleton Coll., 1962; MA, U. Ill., 1965, PhD, 1968. Instr. psychology U. Ill., Urbana, 1966-67; prof. Coll. William and Mary, Williamsburg, Va., 1967—; cons. Ctr. for Teaching Excellence Hampton (Va.) U., 1988-94. Author: Ednl. Computer Software, (with E. Rae Harcum) The Gatekeepers of Psychology, 1993; contbr. articles to profl. jours. Mem. Soc. for Computers in Psychology (bd. dirs.), Psychonomic Soc., Va. Psychol. Assn., Ea. Psychol. Assn., C.G. Jung Soc. of Tidewater (treas.), Am. Psychol. Soc. Office: Coll of William and Mary Dept of Psychology Williamsburg VA 23187

ROSEN, FRED SAUL, pediatrics educator; b. Newark, May 26, 1930; s. Philip and Amelia (Feld) R. AB, Lafayette Coll., 1951; MD, Western Res. U., 1955; MA (hon.), Harvard U., 1970; DSc (hon.), Lafayette Coll., 1978. From asst. to assoc. prof. pediatrics Harvard Med. Sch., Boston, 1966-72, James L. Gamble prof. pediatrics, 1972—; chief. div. immunology Children's Hosp., Boston, 1968-85, program dir. Gen. Clin. Rsch. Ctr., 1977-91; pres. Ctr. for Blood Rsch., Boston, 1987—; chmn. sci. com. on immunodeficiencies WHO, Boston, 1988—. Author: Dictionary of Immunology, 1989. Pres. Am. Friends of Jenner Appeal, Boston, 1985—; Sr. asst. surgeon USPHS, 1957-59. Recipient E. Mead Johnson award for pediatric rsch. Am. Acad. Pediatrics, 1970, Gen. Clin. Rsch. Ctrs. Program 4th Ann. award NIH, 1992; John Simon Guggenheim Meml. Found. fellow, 1974. Mem. Am. Assn. Immunology, Am. Soc. Clin. Investigation, Am. Pediatric Soc., Assn. Am. Physicians, NAS Inst. Medicine, St. Botolph Club, Harvard Club, Somerset Club. Home: 101 Chestnut St Boston MA 02108 Office: The Ctr for Blood Rsch 800 Huntington Ave Boston MA 02115-6303*

ROSEN, GEORGE, economist, educator; b. St. Petersburg, Russia, Feb. 7, 1920; s. Leon and Rebecca (Rosenoer) R.; m. Sylvia Vatuk; 1 son, Mark. B.A., Bklyn. Coll., 1940; M.A., Princeton U., 1942, Ph.D., 1949. Prof. econs. Bard Coll., Annandale-on-Hudson, N.Y., 1946-50; economist Dept. State, Washington, 1951-54, Council Econ. Indsl. Research, Washington, 1954-55, MIT, Cambridge, 1955-59, UN, N.Y.C., 1959-60, Ford Found., N.Y.C., India, 1960-62, Rand Corp., Santa Monica, Calif., 1962-67; chief economist Asian Devel. Bank, Manila, Philippines, 1967-71; prof. econs. U. Ill.-Chgo., 1972-85, prof. econs. emeritus, 1985—, head dept., 1972-77; fellow Woodrow Wilson Internat. Ctr., Washington, 1989-90; adj. prof. Johns Hopkins U.-Nanjing U. Ctr. Chinese-Am. Studies, 1986-87; cons USAID, Egypt, 1994; book rev. editor Econ. Devel. and Cultural Change, 1988—; treas. Am. Com. for Asian Econ. Studies, 1990-95. Author: Industrial Change in India, 1958, Some Aspects of Industrial Finance in India, 1962, Democracy and Economic Change in India, 1966, 67, Peasant Society in a Changing Economy, 1975, Decision-Making Chicago-Style, 1980, Western Economists and Eastern Societies, 1985, Industrial Change in India 1970-2000, 1988, Contrasting Styles of Industrial Reform: China and India in the 1980s, 1992, Economic Development in Asia, 1996. Ford Found. fellow NYU, 1971-72; grantee U. Ill., 1977-78, Social Sci. Research Council and Am. Inst. Indian Studies, 1980-81, Am. Inst. Indian Studies, 1983-84, 87-88, Rockefeller Found. Bellagio Study Ctr., 1984. Office: U Ill Dept Econs M/C 144 601 S Morgan St Chicago IL 60607-3401

ROSEN, GERALD ELLIS, federal judge; b. Chandler, Ariz., Oct. 26, 1951; s. Stanley Rosen and Marjorie (Sherman) Cahn; m. Laurie DeMond. BA, Kalamazoo Coll., 1973; JD, George Washington U., 1979. Researchist Swedish Inst., Stockholm, 1973; legis. asst. U.S. Senator Robert P. Griffin, Washington, 1974-79; law clk. Seyfarth, Shaw, Fairweather & Gerardson, Wash., 1979; from assoc. to sr. ptnr. Miller, Canfield, Paddock and Stone, Detroit, 1979-90; judge U.S. Dist Ct. (ea. dist.) Mich., Detroit, 1990—; mem. Jud. Evaluation Com. (co-chmn. 1983-88), Detroit; adj. prof. law Wayne State U., 1992—, U. Detroit Law Sch., 1992—; mem. U.S. Jud. Conf. Com. on Criminal Law; lectr. CLE confs., others. Contbr. articles to profl. jours. Rep. candidate for U.S. Congress, Mich., 1982; chmn. 17th Congl. Dist. REp. Com., 1983-85; mem. Mich. Criminal Justice Commn., 1985-87; mem. Birmingham Athletic Club. Fellow Kalamazoo Coll. (sr. 1972). Jewish. Office: US Courthouse Rm 802 231 W Lafayette Blvd Detroit MI 48226-2799

ROSEN, GERALD HARRIS, physicist, consultant, educator; b. Mount Vernon, N.Y., Aug. 10, 1933; s. David A. and Shirley (Schapiro) R.; m. Sarah Louise Sweet, June 8, 1963; children: Lawrence Alexander, Karlyn Penelope Aires. B.S.E. (Guggenheim Jet Propulsion scholar, Whiton Engring.-Physics scholar), Princeton U., 1955, M.A. (NSF predoctoral fellow), 1956, Ph.D., 1958. NSF predoctoral fellow Inst. Theoretical Physics, Utrecht, Netherlands, 1957-58; research asso. dept. aero. engring. Princeton, 1958-59; NSF postdoctoral fellow Inst. Theoretical Physics, Stockholm, 1959-60; tech. cons. weapon systems evaluation div. The Pentagon, 1960; prin. scientist Martin-Marietta Aerospace div., Balt., 1960-63; cons. to a tech. v.p. Southwest Research Inst., 1963-66; prof. physics Drexel U., Phila., 1966-73; M.R. Wehr prof. physics Drexel U., 1973—; cons. fin., indsl. and govt. agys., 1966—. Author: Formulations of Classical and Quantum Dynamical Theory, 1969, A New Science of Stock Market Investing, 1990; assoc. editor Bull. Math. Biology, 1982—; contbr. revs., articles to Math. Revs., Am. Phys. Soc., other profl. jours. Sponsor San Antonio Chamber Music Soc., 1963-66; mem. Franklin Inst., 1967—; mem. publ. bd. Soc. Math. Biol., 1983—. Fellow Am. Phys. Soc., AAAS; mem. Am. Math. Soc. Patentee in field. Home: 415 Charles Ln Wynnewood PA 19096-1604 Office: Drexel U Dept Physics Philadelphia PA 19104 *The meaning of life has transcended human understanding up to the present time, but there are reasons to believe that future discoveries in science will illuminate the significance of life in nature. We must break completely free of non-rational dogma and illusion, and attempt to solve this mystery with factual clues revealed by scientific progress.*

ROSEN, GERALD ROBERT, editor; b. N.Y.C., Nov. 17, 1930; s. Sol and Essie (Shapiro) R.; m. Lois Lehrman, May 9, 1958; 1 son, Evan Mark. BS, Ind. U., 1951, MA, 1953. Intelligence analyst Dept. Def., N.Y.C., 1955-58; assoc. editor Challenge: The Mag. of Econ. Affairs, N.Y.C., 1959-61; mng. editor Challenge: The Mag. of Econ. Affairs, 1961-64, 65-66; sr. editor Dun's Rev., N.Y.C., 1964-65, nat. affairs editor, 1967—; exec. editor Dun's Rev. (now Bus. Month), 1978-90; editor IMF survey Washington, 1990-93; mng. dir. Global Insights Svcs., Washington, 1993—; fin. corr. Westinghouse Broadcasting Co. Served with CIC U.S. Army, 1953-55. Mem. Soc. Am. Bus. and Econ. Writers, N.Y. Fin. Writers Assn., White House Corrs. Assn. Club: Nat. Press. Home: 3210 Grace St NW Washington DC 20007-3628 Office: 1700 K St NW Washington DC 20006-3817

ROSEN, HOWARD ROBERT, lawyer; b. Montreal, Que., Can., Apr. 15, 1960; came to U.S. 1967; s. Kelvin and Binnie Lynn (Michaels) R. ; m. Adrienne Joy Unger, Apr. 11, 1987. BA, Emory U., 1982; JD, U. Miami, 1985. Bar: Fla. 1985. Asst. state atty. Dade County State Atty. Office, Miami, Fla., 1985—. Mem. ABA. Avocations: travel, sports. Home: 17931 NW 9th Ct Pembroke Pines FL 33029 Office: Dade County State Atty 1350 NW 12th Ave Miami FL 33136-2102

ROSEN, JAMES MAHLON, artist, art historian, educator; b. Detroit, Dec. 3, 1933; s. Joseph and Lillian Rosen; children: Shira Del, Phyllis Dresser, Jeremy-Joseph. Student, Cooper Union, 1956; BS, Wayne State U., 1957; MFA, Cranbrook Acad. Art, 1958. Mem. faculty dept. art Wayne State U., 1961-63, U. Hawaii, 1965-67; mem. faculty Santa Rosa (Calif.) Jr. Coll., 1967-84, U. Calif., 1987-88; Wm. Morris Eminent scholar in art Augusta Coll., 1989-96; prof., head Meyer Schapiro Program Augusta State U., 1996—; artist-in-residence, guest lectr. Deep Springs Coll., R.I. Sch. Design, Montclair State Coll., San Bernardino State Coll., Pa. Acad. Fine Arts; artist-in-residence Ferrara, Italy. Author: Notes From a Painter's Journal, 1960, An American Homage to Piero della Francesca, In the Realm of Light, William Bartram Sketches: The Field and the Image, Qualities of Camouflaging, 1970, On the Sheer Nonsense of Liking Anything, 1979; exhbns. include Betty Parsons Gallery, N.Y.C., Donald Morris Gallery, Detroit, Gallery Paule Anglim, San Francisco, Mus. Modern Art Penthouse Show, Eva Gelfman Gallery, Thomas Babeor Gallery, La Jolla, Calif., La Jolla Mus. Contemporary Art; dir., curator William Bartram Art Exhbn.; represented in permanent collections in Mus. Modern Art, N.Y.C., Whitney Mus. Am. Art, Ga. Mus. Art, Syracuse U., Ashmolean Mus., U. Calif. Berkeley Mus., San Francisco Mus. Modern Art, Met. Mus. of Art, Cranbrook Mus. Art, Victoria and Albert Mus., London; bd. dirs. Arts Meridian-A Cultural Jour. Ams.; commissions include Sheraton Hotel, Venice, Ascott Residencies, London, Occidental Grand Hotel, Atlanta, Fairmont Hotel, Chgo. Served with M.C. U.S. Army, 1953-55. Grantee Huntington Hartford Found., Yaddo, MacDowell Found., NEH, Djerassi Found. Arts, Ga. Coun. on Arts. Mem. Am. Soc. Art, Religion and Culture (bd. dirs.), Soc. So. Painters (pres., Painter of the Yr. award 1997), Soc. of Art, Religion and Contemporary Culture (bd. dirs.), Phi Kappa Phi. Home: 824 Johns Rd Augusta GA 30904-6116

ROSEN, JON HOWARD, lawyer; b. Bklyn., May 20, 1943; s. Eli and Vera (Horowitz) R.; m. Georgeanne Evans, 1993; children of a previous marriage: Jason Marc, Hope Terry. BA, Hobart Coll., 1965; JD, St. John's U., 1968; postgrad. Bernard Baruch Sch. Bus., CCNY, 1969-71. Bar: N.Y. 1969, Calif. 1975, Wash. 1977. Atty. FAA, N.Y.C., 1968-71; regional atty., contract adminstr. Air Line Pilots Assn., N.Y.C., Chgo., L.A., San Francisco, 1971-77; pvt. practice Seattle, 1977-80; ptnr. Frank and Rosen, Seattle, 1981—; instr. labor studies Shoreline Community Coll., 1978-90. Trustee Temple DeHirsch Sinai, 1992—. Fellow Coll. Labor and Employment Lawyers; mem. ABA (union co-chmn. com. on Employee Rights and Responsibilities 1992-96, co- regional EEOC liaison), Seattle-King County Bar Assn. (past chmn. aviation and space law sect., past chmn. Pacific Coast Labor Law Conf., past chmn. labor law sect.), Nat. Employment Lawyers Assn. (state steering com., chair 1990-95), Wash. State Trial Lawyer's Assn. (past chair employment law com.). Office: Frank & Rosen 705 2nd Ave Ste 1200 Seattle WA 98104-1729

ROSEN, JUDAH BEN, computer scientist; b. Phila., May 5, 1922; s. Benjamin and Susan (Hurwich) R.; children—Susan Beth, Lynn Ruth. BSEE, Johns Hopkins U., 1943; PhD in Applied Math., Columbia U., 1952. Rsch. assoc. Princeton (N.J.) U., 1952-54; head applied math. dept. Shell Devel. Co., 1954-62; vis. prof. computer sci. dept. Stanford (Calif.) U., 1962-64; prof. dept. computer sci. and math. rsch. ctr. U. Wis., Madison, 1964-71; prof., head dept. computer sci. U. Minn., Mpls., 1971—; fellow Supercomputer Inst. U. Minn., 1985—; sr. fellow Supercomputer Ctr., San Diego, 1993—; adj. rsch. prof. dept. computer sci. and engrin. U. Calif. San Diego, La Jolla, 1992—; Fulbright prof. Technion, Israel, 1968-69, Davis vis. prof. 1980; invited lectr. Chinese Acad. Sci., Peking, 1980, Guilin, 1996; lectr., cons. Argonne (Ill.) Nat. Lab.; mem. Nat. Computer Sci. Bd. Author: Topics in Parallel Computing, 1992; editor: Nonlinear Programming, 1970, Supercomputers and Large-Scale Optimization, 1988; assoc. editor Global Optimization, 1990—, Annals of Ops. Rsch., 1984—; contbr. articles to profl. jours. and procs. Grantee NSF, 1995—, ARPA/NIST, 1994-97. Mem. Assn. Computing Machinery, Soc. Indsl. and Applied Math., Math. Programming Soc. Research interests: supercomputers and parallel algorithms for optimization, computation of molecular structure by energy minimization, algorithms for structured approximation in signal processing. Home: 10305 28th Ave N Plymouth MN 55441-3219 also: 322 Prospect St La Jolla CA 92037 Office: EE/CSci Bldg U Minn Minneapolis MN 55455-0100 also: Univ Calif-San Diego Dept Computer Sci Engring 9500 Gilman Dr La Jolla CA 92093-5003

ROSEN, KAY, painter. BA, Tulane U.; MA, Northwestern U. adv. bd. Visual Arts Panel Ind. Arts Commn., 1986, Arts Midwest Focus Groups, 1988; curator, vis. artist Sch. Art Inst. Chgo., 1988, U. Chgo., 1990; lectr. Columbia Coll., 1989, Ind. U. N.W., Gary, 1992; panelist Midwest Coll. Art Assn. Conf., Cin., 1989, Mass. Artists Fellowship Program Painting Panel, 1990; graduate critique panelist, Sch. Art Inst. Chgo., 1989; rev. panelist, Arts Midwest New Partnership Grants Visual Artists, 1990; spkr., panelist, Mountain Cake Symposium, Va., 1990; grad. faculty advisor Sch. Art Inst. Chgo., 1992; spkr. Ind. State U., Terre Haute, 1993. Editor Spunky Internat., 1992; exhibited at Whitney Mus. Art, 1991, Mus. Contemporary Art, Chgo., Shoshana Wayne Gallery, Santa Monica, Calif., Forefront Gallery Indpls. Mus. Art, Victoria Miro Gallery, London, Galeria Massimo de Carlo, Milan, 1994, Galerie Erika & Otto Friedrich, Berne, Switzerland, 1995. Recipient Visual Arts award Hirshhorn Mus., Albequerque Mus., Toledo Mus. Art, 1991, Mus. Modern Art, Melbourne, Australia, various others. Address: 6925 Indian Boundary Gary IN 46403-1246*

ROSEN, LAWRENCE, anthropology educator; b. Cin., Dec. 9, 1941; s. George and Hannah (Persky) R. B.A., Brandeis U., 1963; M.A., U. Chgo., 1965, Ph.D., 1968, J.D., 1974. Bar: N.C. 1975, U.S. Supreme Ct. 1979. Asst. prof. anthropology U. Ill., Urbana, 1968-70; mem. Inst. for Advanced Study, Princeton, N.J., 1970-71; assoc. prof. anthropology Duke U., Durham, N.C., 1974-77; prof. anthropology Princeton U., N.J., 1977—; adj. prof. Columbia U. Law Sch., 1979—; vis. prof. Northwestern U. Law Sch.,

Chgo., 1985-87, U. Pa. Law Sch., Phila., 1985-86, Georgetown Law Ctr., 1994; Lewis H. Morgan lectr. U. Rochester, 1985. Co-author: Meaning and Order in Moroccan Society, 1978, Bargaining for Reality, 1984, The Anthropology of Justice, 1989; editor: The American Indian and the Law, 1974, Other Intentions, 1995. Legal asst. Native Am. Rights Fund., Boulder, Colo., 1973. Woodrow Wilson fellow, 1964, Guggenheim fellow, 1981, John & Catherine MacArthur Found. fellow, 1981, Fulbright fellow, 1991; recipient Princeton U. Women's Orgn. award, 1994; vis. scholar Phi Beta Kappa, 1997. Fellow Am. Anthrop. Assn.

ROSEN, LOUIS, physicist; b. N.Y.C., June 10, 1918; s. Jacob and Rose (Lipionski) R.; m. Mary Terry, Sept. 4, 1941; 1 son, Terry Leon. BA, U. Ala., 1939, MS, 1941; PhD, Pa. State U., 1944; DSc (hon.), U. N.Mex., 1979, U. Colo., 1987. Instr. physics U. Ala., 1940-41, Pa. State U., 1943-44; mem. staff Los Alamos Sci. Lab., 1944-90, group leader nuclear plate lab., 1949-65, alt. div. leader exptl. physics div., 1962-65, dir. meson physics facility, 1965-85, div. leader medium energy physics div., 1965-86, sr. lab. fellow, 1985-90, sr. fellow emeritus, 1990—; Sesquicentennial hon. prof. U. Ala., 1981; mem. panel on future of nuclear sci., chmn. subpanel on accelerators NRC of NAS, 1976, mem. panel on instnl. arrangements for orbiting space telescope, 1976; mem. U.S.A.-USSR Coordinating Com. on Fundamental Properties of Matter, 1971-90. Author papers in nuclear sci. and applications of particle accelerators.; bd. editors: Applications of Nuclear Physics; co-editor Climate Change and Energy Policy, 1992. Mem. Los Alamos Town Planning Bd., 1962-64; mem. Gov.'s Com. on Tech. Excellence in N.Mex.; mem. N.Mex. Cancer Control Bd., 1976-80, v.p., 1979-81; co-chmn. Los Alamos Vols. for Stevenson, 1956; Dem. candidate for county commr., 1962; bd. dirs. Los Alamos Med. Ctr., 1977-83, chmn., 1983; bd. govs. Tel Aviv U., 1986. Recipient E.O. Lawrence award AEC, 1963, Golden Plate award Am. Acad. Achievement, 1964, N.Mex. Disting. Pub. Svc. award, 1978; named Citizen of Yr., N.Mex. Realtors Assn., 1973; Guggenheim fellow, 1959-60; alumni fellow Pa. State U., 1978; Louis Rosen prize established in his honor by bd. dirs. Meson Facility Users Group, 1984; Louis Rosen Auditorium dedicated, 1995. Fellow AAAS (coun. 1989), Am. Phys. Soc. (coun. 1975-78, chmn. panel on pub. affairs 1980, div. nuclear physics 1985, mem. subcom. on internat. sci. affairs 1988). Home: 1170 41st St Los Alamos NM 87544-1913 Office: Los Alamos Sci Lab PO Box 1663 Los Alamos NM 87544-0600 *I have come to believe that only after one has learned to manage and set worthy goals for himself should he attempt to do so for others.*

ROSEN, MATTHEW STEPHEN, botanist, consultant; b. N.Y.C., Oct. 7, 1943; s. Norman and Lucille (Cass) R.; m. Deborah Louise Mackay, June 16, 1974 (div. Feb. 1983); children: Gabriel Mackay, Rebecca Mackay; m. Kay Eloise Williams, July 11, 1987. MFSc, Yale U., 1972; BS, Cornell U., 1967. Instr. ornamental horticulture SUNY-Farmingdale, 1968-69; landscape designer Manhattan Gardener, N.Y.C., 1969-70; instr. ornamental horticulture McHenry County Coll., Crystal Lake, Ill., 1972-74; coord. agrl. studies, asst. prof. biology, chemistry Mercer County Community Coll., West Windsor, N.J., 1974-79; adminstr. Des Moines Botanical Ctr., 1979-96, horticulture divsn. mgr., 1996—; consulting dir. West Mich. Horticultural Soc., 1993; cons. in field. Contbr. articles to profl. jours. Com. chmn. United Way Cen. Iowa, 1982, div. chmn. 1983-86, 88-89, 91, group chmn. 1987, chmn. arts adv. com. 1985-86, pres. 1986, bd. dirs. Arts and Recreation Council, 1985-86, com. chmn., 1992; mem. career vocat. com. Des Moines Indsl. Sch. Dist., 1986, co-chmn., 1987, mem. Ptnrs. for Progress com., 1988-90, mem. sci. monitoring program, 1991, 92; chmn. Two Rivers Festival, 1987-88; active Des Moines Sister City Program, Kofu, Japan, 1984, delegation, 1989, Naucalpan, Mexico, 1986, 87, Shijiazhuang, China, 1986, 90, 92, 95, 97; mem. edn. com. Am. Assn. Botanical Gardens & Arboretum, mem. membership com., mem. conservation com., bd. dirs., 1997—. Mem. Am. Assn. Botanical Gardens and Arboreta (edn. com.), Greater Des Moines C. of C. (team leader 1984—, chmn. new mem. sales, chmn. 8 O'clock new, Pres. Cabinet award 1983, 84, 85, Achievement award C. of C. Fedn. 1986, mem. exec. com. 1995, 96, 97), East Des Moines C. of C. (bd. dirs. 1992—, v.p., sec. 1993—, pres.- elect 1994, pres. 1995, 96, sister cities commn. 1994, china chair 1995, 96, 97, treas. 1995, 96, 97), Greater Des Moines Conv. and Visitors Bur. (chmn. new mem. sales com. 1988-89), Iowa Advt. Rev. Coun., Affiliate Pres.'s Coun. of Chambers (chair 1995, 97), bd. of dirs. DM Gen. Hosp., 1994-95, 96, 97, Rotary, Phi Kappa Phi, Pi Alpha Xi. Democrat. Jewish. Avocations: photography, reading, model trains, collecting old books, writing. Home: 1042 22nd St West Des Moines IA 50265-2219 Office: Des Moines Botanical Ctr 909 E River Dr Des Moines IA 50316-2854

ROSEN, MEYER ROBERT, chemical engineer; b. Bklyn., Mar. 9, 1943; s. Philip and Jeanne (Rosenzweig) R.; children: Carrie, David; m. Selma Mirman. BS, Poly. Inst. Bklyn., 1964, MS, 1966. Diplomate Am. Bd. Forensic Examiners; bd. cert. forensic examiner; cert. profl. chemist; cert. profl. chem. engr. Rsch. engr. Union Carbide Corp., Tonawanda, N.Y., 1966-73, project scientist, 1973-79; devel. scientist Union Carbide Corp., Tarrytown and Boundbrook, N.J., 1979-92; dir. chemistry and chem. engring. Inter-City Testing and Cons. Corp., Mineola, N.Y., 1993—; cons. Brookfield Engring. Labs., Stoughton, Mass., 1979-81; course dir. Ctr. for Profl. Advancement, East Brunswick, N.J., 1994; adj. prof. chemistry Westchester C.C., 1970-84; spkr. in field of chem. engring. and energy medicine. Contbr. articles to profl. pubs., including Polymer Plast. Tech. Engr., Jour. Coatings Tech., Jour. Coll. Interface Sci., Am. Jour. Acupuncture, Union Carbide World Mag.; author 2 books on Hyperacusis ear disorder. Fellow Royal Soc. Chemistry London (chartered chemist), Am. Inst. Chemists; mem. ASTM (mem. various subcoms.), Am. Chem. Soc. (divsn. colloid and surface chemistry, mem. noise com.), Am. Indsl. Hygiene Assn., Am. Soc. Safety Engrs., Assn. Cons. Chemists and Chem. Engrs. (dir. exec. coun.), Nat. Fire Protection Assn., Soc. Indsl. Chemistry (Am. sect.), Nat. Assn. Tchrs. Acupuncture and Oriental Medicine, Am. Assn. Acupuncture and Oriental Medicine, Acupuncture Soc. Pa., Nat. Dental Acupuncture Soc. (mem. exec. bd.), Acupuncture Soc. N.Y., Nat. Alliance of Acupuncture and Oriental Medicine (bd. cert. in pain mgmt.), Nat. Hearing Conservation Assn. Achievements include 19 patents for process for fire fighting foams, antifoams; flocculation of phosphatic slimes, high molecular weight water soluble polymers and flocculating method, process for producing polymer water-in-oil emulsion, process for agglomerating ore concentrate utilizing clay and dispersions of polymer binders or dry powder binders, removal of residual ethylene oxide from poly(ethylene oxide), development of treatment of previously incurable ear disorder, seminar leader in Reflex-Correspondence Training. Publications include Polyox R Water Soluble Resin Worldwide Technical Literature; Rheology of Non-Newtonian Fluids; Energy Medicine; Auriculotherapy; Korean Hand Therapy. Office: Inter-City Testing & Cons 167 Willis Ave Mineola NY 11501-2621

ROSEN, MOISHE, religious organization administrator; b. Kansas City, Mo., Apr. 12, 1932; s. Ben and Rose (Baker) R.; m. Ceil Starr, Aug. 18, 1950; children: Lyn Rosen Bond, Ruth. Diploma, Northeastern Bible Coll., 1957; DD, Western Conservative Bapt. Sem., 1986. Ordained to ministry Bapt. Ch., 1957. Missionary Am. Bd. Missions to the Jews, N.Y.C., 1956; minister in charge Beth Sar Shalom Am. Bd. Missions to the Jews, Los Angeles, 1957-67; dir. recruiting and tng. Am. Bd. Missions to the Jews, N.Y.C., 1967-70; leader Jews for Jesus Movement, San Francisco, 1970-73, exec. dir., 1973-96, founder, 1973—; speaker in field. Author: Saying of Chairman Moishe, 1972, Jews for Jesus, 1974, Share the New Life with a Jew, 1976, Christ in the Passover, 1977, Y'shua, The Jewish Way to Say Jesus, 1982, Overture to Armageddon, 1991, The Universe is Broken: Who on Earth Can Fix It?, 1991, Demystifying Personal Evangelism, 1992. Trustee Western Conservative Bapt. Sem., Portland, Oreg., 1979-85, 86-91, Bibl. Internat. Coun. on Bibl. Inerrancy, Oakland, Calif., 1979-89; bd. dirs. Christian Advs. Serving Evangelism, 1987-91. Named Hero of the Faith, Conservative Bapt. Assn. Am., 1997. Office: Jews for Jesus 90 Miraloma Dr San Francisco CA 94127-1641

ROSEN, MYOR, harpist, educator; b. N.Y.C., May 28, 1917; s. Caesar and Rose (Seidenberg) R.; m. Esther Rosen, May 25, 1941; children: Linda, David. Diploma, Juilliard Sch. Music, 1940. Faculty Juilliard Sch. Music, 1947-69. Prin. harpist, Mexico Symphony Orch., 1941-42, Indpls. Symphony Orch., 1941-42, Mpls. Symphony Orch., 1943-44, staff harpist, CBS, Columbia Records and free lanced, 1945-60, prin. harpist, N.Y. Philharm., 1960-87; Composer incidental music for; NBC series Arts and the Gods, 1946, CBS Camera Three, 1947, Solomon, The King, 1948. Served with U.S. Army, 1945. Mem. Am. Fedn. Musicians, Bohemians. *Having been the fortunate recipient of a 7-year scholarship through the New York Philharmonic Symphony Society and the Juilliard School of Music when I began my career as a harpist, I can think of no greater honor than my privilege in having been accepted as principal harpist with the same organization which trained me. I now bend my efforts to train future harpists to excel in like manner. In my opinion, the most important function of a teacher is to teach his students how to teach themselves; self-development.*

ROSEN, NATHANIEL KENT, cellist; b. Altadena, Calif., June 9, 1948; s. David Leon and Frances Jean (Kaufman) R.; m. Jennifer Langham, Aug. 27, 1976 (div. 1986); m. Margo Shohl, May 21, 1989; children: Samuel Gregory, Stella Rosalie. Student, Pasadena (Calif.) City Coll., 1965-67; Mus.B., U. So. Calif., 1971. Teaching asst. U. So. Calif., 1968-75, mem. faculty 7th ann. Gregor Piatigorsky Seminar Sch. Music, 1984; asst. prof. Calif. State U. at Northridge, 1970-76; mem. faculty Manhattan Sch. Music, N.Y.C., 1982-88, 94—; now mem. faculty U. Ill., Urbana, 1988-94. Prin. cellist, Los Angeles Chamber Orch., 1970-76, Pitts. Symphony, 1977-79, concert cellist worldwide; recordings include Orientale: Romantic Music for the Cello. Recipient 1st prize Naumburg Competition, 1977, 1st prize Moscow Tchaikovsky Competition, 1978; Ford Found. grantee, 1970-71; Rockefeller Found. grantee, 1973-74. Mem. Violoncello Soc. N.Y., Century Assn. N.Y. Office: John Gingrich Mgmt Inc PO Box 1515 New York NY 10023-7004 also: North Star Recordings 95 Hathaway St Providence RI 02907-3760*

ROSEN, RAYMOND, health facility executive; b. Louisville, Feb. 5, 1950; s. Sam and Olga Rosen; m. Deborah Joy Rubinow, June 25, 1972; children: Lisa, Jessica. BS, Pa. State U., 1972; MA, George Washington U., 1974. Adminstrv. resident York (Pa.) Hosp., 1973-74, asst. to pres., 1974-75, asst. adminstr.-adminstrn., 1975-77, asst. adminstr.-med. affairs, 1977-79, adminstr.-med. affairs, 1979-87, v.p. opers., 1987—. Pres. Young Adminstrs. Group Ctrl. Pa., 1980-82; pres. Community Transit, Inc., 1992—, vice chmn., 1989-92, chmn., 1992—; bd. dirs. Fedn. South Ctrl. Pa. Emergency Health Svcs., 1978-92, mem. adv. com., 1992-93, York County Emergency Health Svcs. Coun., 1978-92, Jewish Community Ctr., 1986-91; divsn. chmn. United Way York County, 1988, York County Transp. Auth., 1995—. Fellow Am. Coll. Healthcare Execs. (regent south ctrl. Pa. 1991-95), mem. Am. Hosp. Assn., Hosp. Assn. Pa. (planning com. 1992—). Office: York Health Sys 1001 S George St York PA 17403-3676

ROSEN, RHODA, obstetrician and gynecologist; b. Trenton, N.J., Jan. 17, 1933; d. Max and Gussie (Thierman) R.; m. Seymour Kanter, Aug. 19, 1956; children: Cynthia, Gregg, Larry, Brad. BA, U. Pa., 1954, MD, 1958. Diplomate Am. Bd. Obstetrics and Gynecology. Intern Albert Einstein Phila. Med. Ctr., 1958-59, resident, 1959-62; clin. prof. ob-gyn. Temple U. Med. Sch., Phila.; assoc. staff gyn. exec. com. Albert Einstein Med. Ctr., Phila.; attending physician Rolling Hill Hosp., Elkins Park, Pa.; pvt. practice obs/gyn Phila., 1962—; chmn. gynpathology com. Albert Einstein Med. Ctr., Phila. Bd. dirs. Joseph J. Peters Inst. Fellow ACOG, ACS; mem. AMA, Pa. Med. Soc., Phila. Colposcopy Soc. (past pres.), Ex-Residents Assn. (past pres. Albert Einstein Med. Ctr.), Philadelphia County Med. Soc. (com.), Phila. Bar Assn. (com.). Jewish. Avocations: tennis, biking, art, swimming, music. Home: 1011 Valley Rd Elkins Park PA 19027-3032

ROSEN, RICHARD LEWIS, lawyer, real estate developer; b. N.Y.C., Mar. 6, 1943; s. Morris and Lorraine (Levy) R.; m. Doris Ellen Bloom, Aug. 28, 1983. BA, Cornell U., 1965; JD, N.Y. Law Sch., 1968; cert. N.Y.U. Real Estate Inst., 1980. Bar: N.Y. 1968, U.S. Dist. Ct. (so. and ea. dists.) N.Y. 1972; lic. real estate broker. Sole practice, N.Y.C., 1971-73; ptnr. Rosen, Wise, Felzen & Salomon, N.Y.C., 1973-79; ptnr. Rosen & Felzen, N.Y.C., 1979-84, Rosen, Rudd, Kera, Graubard & Hollender, 1985-88, Bell, Kalnick, Klee and Green, N.Y.C., 1989-90, Rosen, Einbinder & Dunn, P.C., N.Y.C., 1990—. Mem. ABA (mem. Forum Commn. on Franchising.), Am. Assn. Franchisees and Dealers (mem. legal steering com., fair franchising stds. com.), N.Y. State Bar Assn. (mem. franchise law com.), Assn. Bar City N.Y. (panel mem. com. on franchising, panel com. on corp. law), Red Key Hon. Soc., Cornell U., Sphinx Head Hon. Soc., Cornell U., Spiked Shoe Soc., Cornell U., Ea. Intercollegiate Athletic Assn. (named Lightweight Football All Ea. Selection, 1963, 64). Named Ea. States Lightweight Weightlifting Champion, 1968; N.Y. State Regents scholar. Avocations: tennis, skiing, phys. fitness, guitar, reading. Home: 1 Old Jericho Tpke Jericho NY 11753-1205 also: Lamb Ave Quogue NY 11959 Office: Rosen Einbinder & Dunn PC 641 Lexington Ave New York NY 10022-4503 *While the shortest distance between two points is, invariably, a straight line, it is helpful if one has a good compass to guide one along the way. Further, detours are frequently necessary, even if only to view the scenery, while traveling towards our chosen destination.*

ROSEN, ROBERT THOMAS, analytical and food chemist; b. Concord, N.H., Nov. 5, 1941; s. Maurice J. and Miriam M. (Miller) R.; m. Sharon Lynne Beres, Apr. 23, 1972. BA (cum laude), Nasson Coll.; PhD, Rutgers U. Sr. rsch. scientist Chem. Rsch. and Devel. Ctr., FMC Corp., Princeton, N.J., 1966-84; program dir. analytical support facilities, 1984—; assoc. dir. Ctr. for Advanced Food Technology, Rutgers U., New Brunswick, N.J., 1993—; full mem. food sci. dept., grad. faculty Rutgers U., New Brunswick, N.J., 1996—; chmn. North Jersey ACS Mass Spectrometry Topical Group, 1987-88. Assoc. editor The Mass Spec Source, 1988-90; contbr. articles and book reviews to profl. jours. Fellow Am. Inst. Chemists; mem. Am. Soc. for Mass Spectrometry, Am. Chem. Soc. N.Y. Acad. Scis., N.Am. Native Fishes Assn., Inst. Food Technologists, Phi Lambda Upsilon (hon.). Achievements include research in gas and liquid chromatography, free and glycosidically bound organic compounds in fruits and vegetables, determination of non-volatile and thermally labile pesticides and phytochemicals in food, natural products and the environment by liquid chromatography and mass spectrometry. Home: Box 293 8 Keats Road Pottersville NJ 07979 Office: Rutgers U Cook Coll Ctr for Advanced Food Tech New Brunswick NJ 08903

ROSEN, SAM, economics educator emeritus; b. Balt., Apr. 1, 1920; s. Louis and Belle (Kurtz) R.; m. Mary Berman, Mar. 5, 1943; children—Michael David, Laura Elizabeth, Jonathan Donald. A.B., U. Wis., 1942; M.A., Harvard U., 1948, Ph.D., 1952. Asst. prof. econs. U. Wyo., Laramie, 1949-51, U. Del., Newark, 1952-57; assoc. prof. U. N.H., Durham, 1957-63; prof. U. N.H., 1963-74, Nashua Corp. prof. econs., 1974-85, emeritus prof. econs., 1985—; vis. prof. Inst. Social Studies, Holland, 1969, People's Republic China, 1987; vis. Fulbright prof., Malta, 1975. Author: National Income, 1963, National Income and Other Social Accounts, 1972; Contbr. articles to profl. jours. Served to lt. USN, 1942-45. Mem. AAUP (pres. U. N.H. chpt. 1962-63, 72-73), Am. Econ. Assn., Internat. Assn. Rsch. in Income and Wealth, Am. Fin. Assn., Ret. Faculty Assn. (chmn., bd. dirs.), N.H. Assn. for the Elderly, Seacoast Jazz Soc. (bd. dirs.). Office: Whittemore Sch Bus-Econs Mcconnell Hall Durham NH 03824

ROSEN, SANFORD JAY, lawyer; b. N.Y.C., Dec. 19, 1937; s. Alexander Charles and Viola S. (Grad) R.; m. Catherine Picard, June 22, 1958; children: Caren E. Andrews, R. Durelle Schacter, Ian D., Melissa S. AB, Cornell U., 1959; LLB, Yale U., 1962. Bar: Conn. 1962, U.S. Supreme Ct. 1966, D.C. 1973, Calif. 1974. Law clk. to Hon. Simon E. Sobeloff U.S. Ct. Appeals, Balt., 1962-63; prof. sch. law U. Md., Balt., 1963-71; assoc. dir. Coun. on Legal Edn. Opportunity, Atlanta, 1969-70; vis. prof. law U. Tex., Austin, 1970-71; asst. legal dir. ACLU, N.Y.C., 1971-73; legal dir. Mex.-Am. Legal Def. Fund, San Francisco, 1973-75; ptnr. Rosen, Remcho & Henderson, San Francisco, 1976-80, Rosen & Remcho, San Francisco, 1980-82; prin. Law Offices of Sanford Jay Rosen, San Francisco, 1982-86; sr. ptnr. Rosen & Phillips, San Francisco, 1986-89; prin. Rosen & Assocs., San Francisco, 1990; sr. ptnr. Rosen, Bien & Asaro, San Francisco, 1991—; mem. Balt. Cmty. Rels. Commn., 1966-69; mem. com. Patuxent Instn., Balt., 1967-69; ad hoc adminstrv. law judge Calif. Agrl. Labor Rels. Bd., San Francisco, 1975-80; interim monitor U.S. Dist. Ct. for no. dist. Calif., San Francisco, 1989, early neutral evaluator, 1987—, mediator, 1993—; judge pro tem San Francisco Superior Ct., 1991—; perm. atty. del. Jud. Conf. U.S. Ct. Appeal for 4th Cir., alt del. for 9th Cir., 1996-98. Contbr. articles to profl. jours. Mem. Com. on Adminstrn. of Criminal Justice, Balt., 1968; mem. adv. com. HEW, Washington, 1974-75. Mem. ABA, Assn. Trial Lawyers Am. (chair civil rights sect. 1993-94), D.C. Bar Assn., Calif. Bar Assn., Bar Assn. San Francisco. Avocations: reading, travel, movies. Office: Rosen Bien & Asaro 155 Montgomery St 8th Fl San Francisco CA 94104-4105

ROSEN, SAUL WOOLF, research scientist, health facility administrator; b. Boston, July 29, 1928; s. David Tsvi and Ida (Hannah) Sadwin; m. Mary Jean Westfall, June 14, 1959 (div. 1986); children: Craig, Laura, David; m. Deborah Susan Kieffer, Nov. 3, 1989. BA cum laude, Harvard U., 1947, MD, 1956; PhD, Northwestern U., 1955. Intern U. Calif. Med. Ctr., San Francisco, 1956-57, resident, 1957-58, sr. res., 1960-61; clin. assoc. Nat. Inst. Arthritis and Metabolic Diseases, Bethesda, Md., 1958-60; sr. investigator NIH Nat. Inst. Arthritis and Metabolism Disease, Bethesda, Md., 1961-84; dept. dir. Clin. Ctr. NIH, Bethesda, Md., 1984-90; acting dir. NIH, Bethesda, 1990-94; vis. scientist Nat. Inst. Med. Rsch., London, Eng., 1975-76. Contbr. articles to profl. jours. U.S. Rubber Co. fellow, Northwestern U., 1950. Fellow ACP; mem. Assn. Am. Physicians, Endocrine Soc. Avocations: opera, lexicography, philately, weightlifting. Home: 7401 Westlake Ter Apt 1104 Bethesda MD 20817-6531

ROSEN, SHERWIN, economist, educator; b. Chgo., Sept. 29, 1938; s. Joe W. and Nell (Rudy) R.; m. Sharon Ginsberg, June 11, 1961; children: Jennifer, Adria. BS, Purdue U., 1960; M.A., U. Chgo., 1962, Ph.D., 1966. Mem. faculty dept. econs. U. Rochester, N.Y., 1964-75, Kenan prof. econs., 1975-77; prof. econs. U. Chgo., 1977-83, Bergman prof. econs., 1984—, chmn. econ. dept., 1988-94; sr. fellow Hoover Instn.; vis. prof. U. Buffalo, 1970, Harvard U., 1971-72, Columbia U., 1973, Stanford U., 1976; bd. trustees Joint Coun. on Econ. Edn., 1990—; rsch. assoc. Nat. Bur. Econ. Rsch. Editor: Jour. of Polit. Economy, 1986—; contbr. articles to profl. jours. Fellow Am. Acad. Arts and Scis.; mem. Am. Econ. Assn. (exec. com. 1985--88, v.p. 1994). Office: U Chgo Dept Econs 1126 E 59th St Chicago IL 60637-1539

ROSEN, STANLEY HOWARD, humanities educator; b. Warren, Ohio, July 29, 1929; s. Nathan A. and Celia (Narotsky) R.; m. Francoise Harlepp, Sept. 5, 1955; children: Nicholas David, Paul Mark, Valerie. B.A., U. Chgo., 1949, Ph.D., 1955; student, Am. Sch. Classical Studies, Athens, Greece, 1955-56. Mem. faculty Pa. State U., 1956-94, prof. philosophy, 1966-94; Fulbright research prof. U. Paris, 1960-61; research fellow Humanities Research Inst., U. Wis., 1963-64; Inst. Arts and Humanities research sr. fellow Pa. State U., 1972—, Evan Pugh prof. philosophy, 1985-94; Bowne prof. philosophy Boston U., 1994—; vis. prof. U. Calif., San Diego, 1978, U. Nice, 1981, Scuola Superiore Pisa, 1989; vis. lectr. U. Barcelona, Spain, 1992. Author: Plato's Symposium, 1968, Nihilism, 1969, G.W.F. Hegel, 1974, The Limits of Analysis, 1980, Plato's Sophist: The Drama of Original and Image, 1983, Hermeneutics as Politics, 1987, The Quarrel Between Philosophy and Poetry, 1988, The Ancients and the Moderns, 1989, The Question of Being, 1993, Plato's Statesman: The Web of Politics, 1995, The Mask of Enlightenment, 1995. Research grantee Am. Philos. Soc., 1961; Research grantee Earhart Found., 1971, 73, 81. Mem. Metaphys. Soc. Am (pres. 1990-91). Home: 117 Brook St Wellesley MA 02181-6632 Office: 745 Commonwealth Ave Boston MA 02215-1401

ROSEN, STEVEN TERRY, oncologist, hematologist; b. Bklyn., Feb. 18, 1952; married, 1976; 4 children. MB, Northwestern U., 1972, MD, 1976. Genevieve Teuton prof., med. sch. Northwestern U., 1989—, dir. cancer ctr., 1989—; dir. clin. programs Northwestern Meml. Hosp., 1989—. Editor-in-Chief Jour. Northwestern U. Cancer Center, 1989—, Contemporary Oncology, 1990-95. Mem. AAAS, ACP, AMA, Am. Soc. Hematology, Am. Soc. Clin. Oncology, Ctrl. Soc. Clin. Rsch. Achievements include research in cutaneous T-cell lymphomas, biology of lung cancer, biologic therapies, and hormone receptors. Office: Northwestern U Robert H Lurie Cancer Ctr Olson Pavilion Rm 8250 303 E Chicago Ave Chicago IL 60611-3008

ROSEN, THOMAS J., food and agricultural products executive. CEO Rosen's Diversified, Fairmont, Minn. Office: Rosen's Diversified 1120 Lake Ave Fairmont MN 56031-1939*

ROSEN, WILLIAM, English language educator; b. Boston, July 1, 1926; s. Louis H. and Alice (Goldstein) R.; m. Barbara Cooper, Aug. 13, 1960; children: Judith Anne, Susan Eleanor. AB, Harvard U., 1948, AM, 1949, PhD, 1958. Instr. U. Wis., Madison, 1956-60; asst. prof. U. Conn., Storrs, 1960-63, assoc. prof., 1963-65, prof. English, 1965-92; prof. emeritus, 1992—; coordinator English grad. studies U. Conn., Storrs, 1979-80, 81-84, head English dept., 1987-92; Old Dominion prof. humanities Hampton Inst., Va., 1969-70; vis. fellow Clare Hall, Cambridge U., Eng., 1980-81, 88-89. Author: Shakespeare and the Craft of Tragedy, 1960; co-editor: Julius Caesar, 1963; contbr. articles to profl. jours. Vol. long term care adv., ombudsman program State of Conn., 1994—; mem. Town of Mansfield Commn. on Aging, 1995—. Pvt. U.S. Army, 1953-55. Mem. Am. Assn. Univ. Profs. (v.p. 1974-75, pres. 1975-76, chief negotiator U. Conn. chpt. 1976-77), Shakespeare Assn., MLA, Renaissance Soc. Am. Democrat. Jewish. Avocations: reading, gardening. Home: 233 Hanks Hill Rd Storrs Mansfield CT 06268-2333 Office: U Conn Dept English Storrs CT 06268

ROSEN, WILLIAM WARREN, lawyer; b. New Orleans, July 22, 1936; s. Warren Leucht and Erma (Stich) R.; m. Eddy Kahn, Nov. 26, 1965; children: Elizabeth K., Victoria A. BA, Tulane U., 1958, JD, 1964. Bar: La. 1964, U.S. Dist. Ct. (ea. dist.) La. 1965, U.S. Ct. Appeals (5th cir.) 1965, U.S. Supreme Ct. 1984, U.S. Dist. Ct. (mid. dist.) La. 1985, Colo. 1989. Assoc. Dodge & Friend, New Orleans, 1965-68, Law Office of J.R. Martzell, New Orleans, 1968-70; pvt. practice New Orleans, 1970-79, 89-90; ptnr. Lucas & Rosen (and predecessor firms), New Orleans, 1979-87, Herman, Herman, Katz & Cotlar, New Orleans, 1987-88, Rosen and Samuel, New Orleans, 1990-95; of counsel Rittenberg & Samuel, New Orleans, 1996—; founder & dir. Litigation Consultation Svcs., New Orleans, 1996—; adj. prof. trial advocacy Law Sch. Tulane U., 1988—, mem. adv. com. paralegal studies program, 1977-86, instr. bus. orgns., 1978, instr. legal interviewing, 1980-81; mem. adv. com. Paralegal Inst. U. New Orleans, 1990—, instr. legal interviewing and investigations, 1986-87; lectr. legal and paralegal fields; lectr. real and demonstrative evidence Nat. Edn. Network, 1993. Author: (with others) Trial Techniques publ. La. Trial Lawyers Assn., 1981; columnist Briefly Speaking publ. New Orleans Bar Assn., 1993—. Mem. budget and planning com. Jewish Welfare Fedn., 1970-73; mem. adv. coun. on drug edn. La. Dept. Edn., 1973; mem. profl. adv. com. Jewish Endowment Found., 1982—; mem. exec. com. U.S. Olympic Com., La., 1982-84; bd. dirs. Planned Parenthood La., 1994—; pres. Dad's Club, Isidore Newman Sch., 1984-85, Uptown Flood Assn., 1982-85; bd. dirs. Jewish Children's Home Svc., 1973-76, Met. Crime Commn. New Orleans, 1976-82; spl. agt. Office Spl. Investigations USAF, 1958-61. Fellow, Inst. of Politics. Loyola U. Mem. ABA (La. vice-chmn. pub. rels. com. 1970-73, 88-89, past chmn. state youth drugabuse edn. program, vol. lawyers for arts 1986—, chmn. sr. counsel com. 1995—), Assn. Trial Lawyers Am. (keyperson com. 1986-89), paralegal mem. com., vice chmn. 1989-91, family law adv. com. 1989-90, sec. family law sect. 1990-91, legal edn. lectr. 1979, 81, 83-83, 86, 88) Am. Arbitration Assn., Nat. Fedn. Paralegal Assn. (adv. coun. 1989—), Assn. Atty Mediators (pres. La. chpt. 1995), Nat. Choice in Dying (legal adv. com. 1992-96) Nat. Edn. Network (legal edn. lectr. 1993), New Orleans Bar Assn. (continuing legal edn. com. 1990-91, chmn. 1991-92, adv. com. 1993—, panel moderator 1997, Inn of Ct. master 1992—). Avocation: photography (included in Louisiana Photographers publ. Contemporary Arts Ctr. 1988). Office: Litigation Consultation Svcs 715 Girod St Ste 200 New Orleans LA 70130-3505

ROSENAU, JAMES NATHAN, political scientist, author; b. Philadelphia, Nov. 25, 1924; s. Walter Nathan and Fanny Fox (Baum) R.; m. Norah McCarthy, Aug. 5, 1955 (dec. July 1974); 1 child, Heidi Margaret; m. Pauline Vaillancourt, June 14, 1987 (div. 1993); m. Hongying Wang, Dec. 11, 1993. A.B., Bard Coll., 1948; A.M., Johns Hopkins U., 1949; Ph.D., Princeton U., 1957. Instr. Rutgers U., New Brunswick, N.J., 1949-54; asst. prof. Rutgers U., New Brunswick, 1954-60, assoc. prof., 1960-62, prof., 1962-70; prof. Ohio State U., Columbus, 1970-73; prof. polit. sci. U. So. Calif., Los Angeles, 1973-92; univ. prof. of internat. affairs George Washington U., 1992—; research asst. Inst. Advanced Study, Princeton, N.J., 1953-54; research assoc. Princeton U., N.J., 1960-70; dir. Sch. Internat. Relations U. So. Calif., Los Angeles, 1976-79; dir. Inst. for Transnat. Studies, U. Southern Calif., Los Angeles, 1973-92. Author: Public Opinion and Foreign Policy, 1961, National Leadership and Foreign Policy, 1963, The Dramas of Politics, 1973, Citizenship between Elections, 1974, The Scientific Study of Foreign Policy, 1980, Turbulence in World Politics, 1990, The United Nations in a Turbulent World, 1992, (play) Kwangju: An Escalatory Spree, 1991; co-author: American Leadership in World Affairs, 1984, Global Voices, 1993, Thinking Theory Thoroughly, 1995, International Political Economy, 1995, Along the Domestic-Foreign Frontier, 1997; co-editor: Journeys through World Politics, 1989, Global Changes and Theoretical Challenges, 1989, Governance without Government, 1992. Trustee Bard Coll., Annandale-on-Hudson, 1968-70, Odyssey Theater Ensemble, Los Angeles, 1987-88. Served with U.S. Army, 1942-46. Fellow Ford. Found., 1958-59, Guggenheim fellow, 1987-88; rsch. grantee NSF, 1970, 73, 78, 79, 83, 88, 92, 96, grantee NEH, 1976. Mem. Internat. Studies Assn. (pres. 1984-85), Am. Polit. Sci. Assn. (mem. exec. council 1975-77). Democrat. Office: 2130 H St NW Washington DC 20037-2521

ROSENBACH, LEOPOLD, engineer, consultant; b. Walbrzych, Poland, Jan. 10, 1947; came to the U.S., 1969; s. Samuel and Halina (Kormicz) R.; m. Pola Knott, Dec. 23, 1969; 1 child, Coleene Rosenbach. MSEE, Polytechnic, Wroclaw, Poland, 1968. Cert. mfg. engr. Mfg. mgr. Leviton Mfg. Co., Bklyn., 1973-77; mfg. engr. Eagle Electric, Long Island City, N.Y., 1977-78; electric mfg. engr. Standard Motor Products, Long Island City, 1979-83, product devel. mgr., 1984-87, design mgr., 1988-90, engring. mgr., 1991-93, dir. materials, 1994-96, dir. ops., 1996—. Contbr. numerous articles to sci. jours. Mem. IEEE, Am. Soc. Metals, Am. Purchasing Soc., Internat. Soc. for Hybrid Microelectronics (met. chpt. treas. 1988-89, sec. 89-90, pres. 90-91), Soc. Mfg. Engrs. Avocations: music, astronomy. Home: 7933 Bayside View Dr Orlando FL 32819 Office: Standard Motor Electronics 170 Sunport Ln Orlando FL 32809-7892

ROSENBAUM, ALVIN ROBERT, writer; b. Florence, Ala., Jan. 14, 1945; s. Stanley and Mildred Ruth (Bookholtz) R.; m. Susan F. Ladmer, Aug. 15, 1965 (div. July 1972); 1 child, Aaron David; m. Lydia F. Gillman, Sept. 8, 1988; 1 child, Samuel Marcus. AB, Bard Coll., 1968. Planner City Planning Dept., Poughkeepsie, N.Y., 1967-69; v.p. David L. Hackett Assocs., Washington, 1969-71; pres. Rosenbaum Group, Inc., Washington, 1971-89; chmn. Rosenbaum Group, Inc., Chevy Chase, Md., 1989—, Heritage Devel. Strategies, Chevy Chase, 1995—; mem. adv. bd. Ctr. for Nat. Policy, Washington, 1980—; exec. v.p. Chesapeake & Potomac Regional Alliance, 1992—; pres. Nat. Coalition of Heritage Areas, Washington, 1994—; pres., CEO Nat. Ctr. for Heritage Devel., Washington, 1996—; bd. dirs. Heritage Area Planners, Inc., Chevy Chase, Waterford (Va.) Found. Author: Young People's Yellow Pages, 1984, America's Meeting Places, 1985, White House Christmas, 1992, Usonia, 1993, Works in Progress, 1994, The Complete Home Office, 1995; one-man shows include Corcoran Gallery of Art, Washington, 1968. Mem. cultural tourism com. U.S. Com., Internat. Coun. Monuments and Sites; mem. Nat. Preservation Coord. Coun. Recipient Gold award Printing Industries Washington, 1989. Mem. Cosmos Club, Com. of 100 on The Fed. City, Am. Planning Assn., Travel Industry Assn. Am., Lambda Alpha Internat. Land. Econs. Soc. Democrat. Jewish. Home: 3107 Rolling Rd Chevy Chase MD 20815 Office: 5520 Connecticut Ave NW Washington DC 20015-2609

ROSENBAUM, ARTHUR ELIHU, neuroradiologist, educator; b. Cleve., June 30, 1935; s. Lionel Clarence and Dora Beatrice (Heldman) R.; m. Rona C. Rosenbaum, Dec. 25, 1981; children: Jeffrey Rosenbaum, Lisa L. Anne Rosenbaum, Michael Cader, Andrew Cader. Student, Case-Western Res. U., 1953-54, AB, 1958; student, U. Mex., 1954-56; MD, U. Miami, 1962. Diplomate Am. Bd. Radiology. Med. intern Jefferson Davis-Ben Taub Hosps., Houston, 1962-63; asst. resident, resident, then chief resident Montefiore Hosp. and Med. Center, N.Y.C., 1963-66; instr. in radiology Albert Einstein Coll. Medicine, N.Y.C., 1966-67; asst. vis. physician Bronx Mcpl. Hosp. Center, 1966-67; cons. in neuroradiology Bronx-Lebanon Hosps., 1966-67; radiologist-in-chief USPHS Hosp., S.I., N.Y., 1968-69; clin. instr. radiology Sch. Medicine, U. Calif., San Francisco, N.Y., 1969; asst. clin. prof. radiology Sch. Medicine U. Calif., San Francisco, 1969; vis. asst. prof. radiology Harvard Med. Sch., Boston, 1970, asst. to assoc. prof. radiology, 1970-75; chief neuroradiology sect. Peter Bent Brigham Hosp., Boston, 1970-75; lectr. radiology Tufts U. Sch. Medicine, Boston, 1974-75; chief neuroradiology sect. Beth Israel Hosp., Boston, 1971-75; prof. radiology U. Pitts. Sch. Medicine, 1975; chief neuroradiology div. Children's Hosp. of Pitts., 1977, dir. pediatric neuroradiology, from 1979; neuroradiologist-in-chief U. Pitts. Sch. Medicine and Affiliated Hosps. of U. Health Center, 1978-80; prof. radiology Johns Hopkins U. Sch. Medicine and Med. Instns., Balt., 1980-87; chmn. div. radiology Cleve. Clinic Found., 1988; prof. radiology, dir. neuroradiologic rsch. SUNY-Health Sc. Ctr., Syracuse, N.Y., 1989—; dir. neuroradiology div. SUNY Health Sci., Syracuse, 1992—, prof. neurosurgery, 1996, prof. pathology, 1996—; cons. Luth. Med. Ctr., Cleve., 1988-89, Cleve. Spine and Arthritis Inst., Siemens, Philips, Medvad, GE, Carl Zeiss, Inc.; spl. cons. to editor Neuroradiology, 1990—. Mem. editorial bd. Neuroradiology, 1974-82, Stroke, 1986-90; adv. editorial bd. Am. Jour. Neuroradiology, 1979-86; contbr. articles to profl. jours., presenter papers profl. confs. U.S., France, Mex., Uruguay, Can., Norway, Bermuda, Chile, lectr. in field, author (sci. exhibits profl. convs.), designer (radiologic equipment), developer (radiologic equipment and instrumentation). Trustee, mem. edn., benefits and devel. coms. Syracuse Symphony Orch., 1990-92, chmn. young orch. com., 1992—, chair youth orch., 1993-94, artistic divsn., 1993-95, mktg. divsn., 1995-96; sec. Performing Arts Medicine of Ctrl. N.Y., 1990-91, mem. exec. com., 1990—. With USPHS Res., 1967-69. Fellow Am. Coll. Radiology (diplomate); mem. AAAS, Am. Soc. Neuroradiology (nat. sec. 1974-77, pres. 1982-83), Radiol. Soc. N.Am. (chair neuroradiology program com. 1978-81), Assn. Univ. Radiologists, Soc. Photo-Optical Instrumentation Egnrs., Am. Soc. Stereotactic and Functional Neurosurgery, World Soc. Sterotactic and Functional Neurosurgery, Itnernat. Med. Soc. for Advancement of Sci., Phi Sigma, Alpha Omega Alpha. Fellow Am. Coll. Radiology (diplomate); mem. AAAS, Am. Soc. Neuroradiology (nat. sec. 1974-77, pres. elect 1981, pres. 1982-83), Radiol. Soc. N.Am., Assn. Univ. Radiologists, Soc. Photo-Optical Instrumentation Engrs., Am. Soc. for Stereotactic and Functional Neurosurgery, Internat. Med. Soc. for Advancement of Sci., Phi Sigma, Alpha Omega Alpha. Office: SUNY Health Sci Ctr 750 E Adams St Syracuse NY 13210-2306

ROSENBAUM, DAVID MARK, engineering executive, consultant, educator; b. Boston, Feb. 11, 1935; s. Frederick and Elizabeth (Gelman) R.; m. Karen Jeanne Smith, Dec. 27, 1964; children: Benjamin Micah, Shoshana Elizabeth. BSc, Brown U., 1956; MS, Renessaler Polytech. Inst., 1958; PhD, Brandeis U., 1964. Asst. rsch. prof. Boston U., 1964-65; assoc. prof. Polytech. U., Bklyn., 1969-70; pres. Network Analysis Corp., Glen Cove, N.Y., 1970-72; asst. dir. Office of Nat. Narcotics Intelligence, Washington, 1973-74; cons. to compt. gen. GAO, Washington, 1975-78; dir. Office of Radiation Programs EPA, Washington, 1978-81; pres. Tech. Analysis Corp., McLean, Va., 1981—; cons. Dir. of Licensing, AEC, Washington, 1972-73. Author: Super Hilbert Space and the Quantum Time Operator, 1969, Liquefield Energy Gases Safety, 1978, A Statistical Procedure for Testing Pacemakers, 1978, Health Effects of Low-Level Radiation, 1981, A Statistical Procedure for Cluster Recognition with Application to Atlanta Leukemia Data, 1983. Mem. IEEE (sr.), Am. Phys. Soc. Office: Tech Analysts Corp # 202 6723 Whittier Ave Mc Lean VA 22101-4533

ROSENBAUM, IRVING M., retail store executive; b. Dresden, Germany, Apr. 20, 1921; came to U.S., 1938, naturalized, 1943; s. Max and Clara (Koerner) R.; m. Hanni Schein, Oct. 15, 1953; children: Eli M., Daniel S., Michael J. B.A. in Econs., New Sch. Social Research, 1953; M.A. in Econs., NYU, 1956. Stockman, S.E. Nichols Inc., N.Y.C., 1938-40; asst. store mgr. S.E. Nichols Inc., 1940-43, store mgr., 1946-48, buyer, 1949-56, mdse. mgr., 1957-60, pres., 1960-72, chmn. bd., 1972-83, vice-chmn. bd., 1983-85, also bd. dirs.; v.p. Venture Israel Ltd., Balt., 1985—, Israel Pharms., Balt., 1976-83; chmn. bd. F.R. Schreiber Co., Lititz, Pa., 1975-82; adv. com. mem. AMIFID Ptnrs. L.P., N.Y.C. Bd. dirs., chmn. bd. overseers Solomon Schechter Day Sch., Nassau and Suffolk Counties, 1985-90; bd. dirs. United Jewish Appeal, Fedn. Jewish Philanthropies, Israel Bond Orgn. Greater N.Y.; nat. chmn. Friends of the Open U. Israel, 1989—. With U.S. Army, 1943-45. Recipient Prime Minister's medal Israel, 1976, 88. Mem. Nat. Mass Retailing Inst., U.S. C. of C. (govt. and regulatory affairs com. 1977-79, adminstrv. law coun. 1980-85). Club: Lake Mohawk Country (Sparta, N.J.). *Only a person who appreciates his own background, traditions and values is able to appreciate those of others.*

ROSENBAUM, JACOB I., lawyer; b. Cleve., Oct. 4, 1927; s. Lionel C. and Dora (Heldman) R.; m. Marjorie Jean Arnold, Apr. 20, 1952; children: Laura Rosenbaum, Alexander, Judith Bartell. JD, U. N.Mex., 1951. Bar: N.Mex. 1951, Ohio 1952. Pres. Ohio Savs. Assn., Cleve., 1955-60, sr. v.p., 1960-92, also dir.; ptnr. Burke, Haber & Berick, Cleve., 1955-79; chmn. bd. Mercury Holdings, Inc., Richmond Heights, Ohio, 1967—; ptnr. Arter & Hadden, Cleve., 1979—. Pres. Temple Emanu El, University Heights, Ohio, 1965-67, 95—, Kiwanis Found. of Cleve., 1994—; active Judson Retirement Cmty., Cleveland Heights, Ohio, 1990—, trustee, 1981-94, pres., 1990-92; trustee Cleve. Zool. Soc., 1983—, Golden Age Ctrs. of Cleve., 1995; pres. adv. bd. Cleve. Women's Orch., 1983—; trustee Cleve. Nat. Air Show, 1981—, pres., 1987-90, 94—, pres. Found., 1995—. Mem. Lawyer-Pilots Bar Assn. (pres. 1981-82, editor jour. 1982—), Ohio Bar Assn. (chmn. aviation law com. 1981-84), Greater Cleve. Bar Assn., Nat. Transp. Safety Bd. Bar Assn., Cleve. Execs. Assn. (pres. 1989, chmn. 1990), Kiwanis (pres. 1970-71). Democrat. Jewish. Avocation: flying. Home: 28050 N Woodland Rd Cleveland OH 44124-4521 Office: Arter & Hadden 1100 Huntington Bldg 925 Euclid Ave Cleveland OH 44115

ROSENBAUM, JAMES EDWARD, psychologist, educator; b. Plainfield, N.J., Dec. 11, 1943; s. Irving and Dorothy Louise (Berger) R.; m. Virginia Ruth Warcholik, Aug. 4, 1974; 1 child, Janet. BA, Yale Coll., 1966; PhD, Harvard U., 1973. Asst. prof. Yale U., New Haven, Conn., 1973-79; prof. Northwestern U., Evanston, Ill., 1979—; advisor commn. on youth and Am's. future, commn. on workforce quality U.S. Dept. Labor, Washington, 1988—, U.S. GAO, Washington, 1988—, U.S. Dept. HHD, Washington, 1990; cons. Leadership Coun., Chgo., 1982—. Author: Making Inequality, 1976, Careers in Corporations, 1984, Blacks in White Suburbs, 1990, Transition from High School to Work, 1990, Youth Apprenticeship in America, 1993. Grantee Spencer Found., 1982, Mott Found., 1989, Ford Found., 1989, U.S. Dept. Labor, 1977, Joyce Found., 1985. Mem. Am. Sociol. Assn., Am. Psychol. Assn. Office: Northwestern U Soc Dept 2040 Sheridan Rd Evanston IL 60208-0855

ROSENBAUM, JAMES MICHAEL, judge; b. Fort Snelling, Minn., Oct. 12, 1944; s. Sam. H. and Ilene D. (Bernstein) R.; m. Marilyn Brown, July 30, 1972; children: Alexandra, Victoria and Catherine (twins). BA, U. Minn., 1966, JD, 1969. Bar: Minn. 1969, Ill. 1970, U.S. Supreme Ct. 1979. VISTA staff atty. Leadership Council for Met. Open Communities, Chgo., 1969-72; assoc. Katz, Taube, Lange & Frommelt, Mpls., 1972-77; ptnr. Rosenbaum & Rosenbaum, Mpls., 1977-79, Gainsley, Squier & Korsh, Mpls., 1979-81; U.S. dist. atty. U.S. Dept. Justice, Mpls., 1981-85; judge U.S. Dist. Ct., Minn., 1985—. Author booklet: Guide to Practice Civil Rights Housing, 1972; co-author: U.S. Courts Design Guide, 1991-96. Campaign chmn. People for Boschwitz, Minn., 1978, bd. vis. U. Minn. Law Sch. (pres. 1996-97). Mem. Fed. Bar Assn. (bd. dirs., pres. 1992-93). Republican. Jewish. Office: US Dist Ct 669 US Courthouse 110 S 4th St Minneapolis MN 55401-2244

ROSENBAUM, JOAN HANNAH, museum director; b. Hartford, Conn., Nov. 24, 1942; d. Charles Leon and Lillian (Sharasheff) Grossman; m. Peter S. Rosenbaum, July 1962 (div. 1970). AA, Hartford Coll. for Women, 1962; BA, Boston U., 1964; student, Hunter Coll. Grad Sch., 1970-73; cert., Columbia U. Bus. Sch. Inst. Non Profit Mgmt., 1978; DHL (hon.), Jewish Theol. Sem., 1993. Curatorial asst. Mus. Modern Art, N.Y.C., 1966-72; dir. mus. program N.Y. Council on Arts, N.Y.C., 1972-79; cons. Michal Washburn & Assocs., N.Y.C., 1979-80; dir. Jewish Mus., N.Y.C., 1980—; mem. adv. bd. Pub. Ctr., N.Y.C. Bd. dirs. Artists Space, 1980-93 ; mem. coun. Am. Jewish Mus., 1981—; mem. policy panel Nat. Endowment Arts, 1982-83. Created knight (Denmark); recipient Disting. Alumni award Boston U. Coll. Libera Arts, 1994, Woman of Distinction award Hadassah, 1997; European travel grantee Internat. Coun. Mus., 1972. Mem. Am. Assn. Mus. (cons. 1979—), Assn. Art Mus. Dirs. (com. chair), N.Y. State Assn. Mus. (mem. coun. 1981-90), Art Table. Office: Jewish Mus 1109 Fifth Ave New York NY 10128-0118

ROSENBAUM, KENNETH E., journalist, editor; b. N.Y.C., Aug. 30, 1942; s. Abraham Rosenbaum and Lena (Sentner) Schroeder; m. Mary Hercelia Zeller, Aug. 30, 1964 (div. 1972); children: Sandra, Steven; m. Karen Marie Tiefenbach, June 14, 1980; stepchildren: Stephanie Kay Burket and Stacey Jo Burket. BA, Ohio State U., 1965. Editor Ohio Jewish Chronicle, Columbus, 1963-64; mng. editor Medina (Ohio) County Gazette, 1965-68; copy editor, reporter Akron (Ohio) Beacon Jour., 1968; news editor Cleve. Press, 1968-82; slotman, asst. news editor St. Louis Globe-Dem., 1982-84; systems editor Toledo Blade, 1984-87, asst. mng. editor, graphics, 1987-89, dir. photography, 1989-93, dir. news systems, 1993—; photography judge Medina Country Fair, 1977-82; instr. journalism Cuyahoga Community Coll., Cleve., 1982, Bowling Green State U., 1989, 91. Democrat. Jewish. Lodges: Lions (bd. dirs. Medina chpt. 1970-71), Masons (steward 1986-87), Shriner. Avocations: photography, golf, motorcycling, rotisserie baseball. Home: 7045 Leicester Rd Toledo OH 43617-1310

ROSENBAUM, LOIS OMENN, lawyer; b. Newark, Apr. 10, 1950; d. Edward and Ruth (Peretz) Omenn; m. Richard B. Rosenbaum, Apr. 4, 1971; children: Steven, Laura. AB, Wellesley Coll., 1971; JD, Stanford U., 1974. Bar: Calif. 1974, Oreg. 1977, D.C. 1974, U.S. Supreme Ct. 1990. Assoc., Fried, Frank, Harris, Shriver & Kampelman, Washington, 1974-75, Orrick, Herrington, Rowley & Sutcliffe, San Francisco, 1975-77, Stoel Rives LLP (formerly Stoel, Rives, Boley, Jones & Grey), Portland, Oreg., 1977-81, ptnr., 1981—; mem. U.S. Dist. Ct. Mediation Panel. Bd. dirs. Providence Med. Found., 1990-95; Robison Jewish Home; past mem. Nat. Legal Com. Am. Jewish Com. Wellesley Coll. scholar, 1971. Mem. ABA, Multnomah County Bar Assn. (arbitration panel), Am. Arbitration Assn (panel mem.). Clubs: Multnomah Athletic, Wellesley (Oregon) (pres. 1987-88). Office: Stoel Rives LLP 900 SW 5th Ave Ste 2300 Portland OR 97204-1232

ROSENBAUM, MICHAEL A., investor relations consultant; b. Chgo., May 13, 1953; s. Robert and Muriel (Caplan) R.; m. Jill Ann Rubenstein, Oct. 12, 1975; children: Susan Brooke, Stephanie Ilyse. BS in Communications, U. Ill., 1974; MBA, Roosevelt U., 1979. Reporter Peoria (Ill.) Jour. Star, 1974, Compass Newspaper, Hammond, Ind., 1974-75; corr. UPI, Chgo., 1975-78; mng. editor Purchasing World Mag., Barrington, Ill., 1978-79; chief Midwest bur. The Jour. of Commerce, Chgo., 1979-83; sr. assoc. The Fin. Rels. Bd., Inc., Chgo., 1983-85, ptnr., 1985-88, sr. ptnr., 1988-90, dep. mng. ptnr., chief oper. officer, 1990—. Author: Selling Your Story to Wall Street: The Art and Science of Investor Relations, 1994; contbr. articles to profl. jours. Chmn. capital campaign Congregation Beth Judea, Long Grove, Ill., 1984-87, v.p. programming & membership, 1993-94; mem. capital campaign com. Infant Welfare Soc., Chgo., 1990-92, dir., 1993—, v.p., 1994—. Recipient Ann. Report Excellence award Fin. World Mag., 1988-95, Nat. Assn. of Investment Clubs, 1986, 88-95, Assn. of Publicly Traded Cos., 1988-95, Publicity Club of Chgo., 1989, 96. Mem. Nat. Investor Rels. Inst., Nat. Assn. Corp. Dirs.. Jewish. Office: Financial Relations Bd John Hancock Ctr 875 N Michigan Ave Chicago IL 60611-1803

ROSENBAUM, MICHAEL FRANCIS, securities dealer; b. N.Y.C., Feb. 9, 1959; s. Francis Fels Jr. and Joyce (Keefer) R.; m. Elika Sosnick, Mar. 8, 1986; children: Erin Sosnick, Sarah Greer, Kira Keefer. AB, Princeton U., 1981. Cert. Nat. Assn. Securities Dealers. Product mgr. Sutro & Co., Inc., San Francisco, 1981-84; v.p. sales Pacific Securities, San Francisco, 1984-89; v.p., br. mgr. Rauscher Pierce Resfnes, San Francisco, 1989-92; v.p. sales Smith Mitchell Investment Group, San Francisco, 1992-93; sr. v.p. sales Gruntal & Co., Inc., San Francisco, 1993-94; sr. v.p. taxable fixed income Coast Ptnrs. Securities, San Francisco, 1994—; bd. dirs. S.G. Rosenbaum Found., N.Y.C. Patroller Nat. Ski Patrol, Northstar, Calif., 1988; trustee Princeton U. Democrat. Jewish. Avocations: skiing, sailing, dog breeding. Home: PO Box 1104 Ross CA 94957-1104

ROSENBAUM, RICHARD MERRILL, lawyer; b. Oswego, N.Y., Apr. 8, 1931; s. Jack M. and Shirley (Gover) R.; m. Judith Kanthor, June 1, 1958; children: Amy, Jill, Matthew, Julie. BA, Hobart Coll., 1952; JD, Cornell U., 1955. Bar: N.Y. 1956. Ptnr. Rosenbaum, Agnello, Agnello & Levine, Rochester, N.Y., 1955-70; justice Supreme Ct. N.Y. State, 1970-73; ptnr. Nixon, Hargrave, Devans & Doyle, Rochester, 1977-84, 88—; counsel to chmn. of bd., dir. govt. rels. and pub. affairs. Integated Resources, Inc., 1984-88, also bd. dirs.; dir. Integrated Resources, Inc.; past mem. econ. adv. bd. U.S. Dept. Commerce; bd. dirs., sec. Jonathan Inst. Contbr. writings in fields of politics and public affairs, legal opinions to publs., 1984-88. Trustee Hobart Coll., 1971-89; nat. committeeman N.Y. State Rep. Nat. Com., 1977—, rules rev. com., subcom. chmn. conv. procedures, 1977—; del.-at-large Rep. Nat. Conv., 1980, 84, 88, congl. dist. del., 1968, chmn. N.Y. State del., 1976; chmn. Monroe County Rep. Com., 1968-70, N.Y. Rep. State Com., 1973-77, Northeastern Rep. State Chairmen's Assn., 1973-76, Nat. Rep. State Chairmen's Assn., 1975-77; justice of peace Town of Penfield (N.Y.), 1962-66; mem. and asst. majority leader Monroe County Legislature, 1966-68; former mem. coun. SUNY, Brockport; dep. counsel U.S. Senate Majority, 1988; apptd. by Pres. Ronald Reagan, U.S. Holocaust Meml. Coun., reapptd. by Pres. George Bush; apptd. by U.S. Senate to Bd. of Fed. Jud. Ctr. Found., 1989—; bd. dirs. Cardozo Sch. Law Yeshiva U.; bd. dirs. Rochester Mus. & Sci. Ctr., 1978—, gen. chmn. devel. fund drive, 1977—; trustee Rochester Area Colls., 1979—; mem. coun. of governing bds. of Ind. Colls. of State of N.Y., 1979—; apptd. mem. N.Y. Mental Hygiene Council, 1973-77, Nat. Citizens Adv. Com. on Environ. Quality, 1977; past bd. dirs. Jewish Home for Aged, Rochester, bd. dirs. Rochester Philharmonic Orchestra; exec. com. Cornell Law Sch; Rep. candidate for nomination for N.Y. state gov., 1994. Recipient Congl. Medal Honor Ellis Island, 1992, Hobart Coll. Alumni citation. Mem. ABA, N.Y. State Bar Assn. Jewish. Clubs: Royal Order of Jesters, Masons, Shriners. Home: 19 Denonville Rdg Rochester NY 14625-1611 Office: Nixon Hargrave Devans & Doyle Clinton Sq PO Box 1051 Rochester NY 14603

ROSENBAUM, ROBERT ABRAHAM, mathematics educator; b. New Haven, Nov. 14, 1915; s. Joseph and Goldey (Rostow) R.; m. L. Louise Johnson, Aug. 1, 1942; children: Robert J., Joseph, David; m. Marjorie Rice Daltry, Aug. 26, 1980. A.B., Yale U., 1936, Ph.D., 1947; L.H.D. (hon.), St. Joseph Coll., 1970, Wesleyan U., Middletown, Conn., 1981; DSc (hon.), Conn. State U., 1993. Henry Fund fellow St. John's Coll., Cambridge (Eng.) U., 1936-37; Gen. Edn. Bd. fellow Reed Coll., 1939-40, from instr. to prof. math., 1940-53; prof. math. Wesleyan U., 1953-85, chmn. dept. math., 1953-63, dean sci., 1963-65, provost, 1965-69, v.p. for acad. affairs, 1967-69, chancellor, 1970-73, univ. prof., 1977-85, univ. prof. emeritus, 1985—; vis. prof. Swarthmore Coll., 1950-51, U. Mass., 1973, Coll. of St. Thomas, 1983; dir. Project to Increase Mastery Math. and Sci., 1979-95, chmn., 1995—; mem. exec. com. Hartford Alliance for Edn. in Math., Sci. and Tech., 1988-92, mem. coordinating com. Project CONNSTRUCT, 1991—; bd. dirs. Conn. Acad. for Edn. in Math., Sci. and Tech., 1991—, pres., 1992-96. Served with USNR, 1942-45. Named hon. alumnus Reed Coll.; recipient Baldwin medal Wesleyan U., 1985, Transylvania medal, 1992. Fellow AAAS, Soc. for Values in Higher Edn.; mem. AAUP (chpt. pres. 1959-61, coun. 1981-84), Math. Assn. Am. (2d v.p. 1961-62, editor 1966-68, Christie lectr. 1994), Am. Math. Soc., Conn. Acad. Sci. and Engring. (charter mem., treas., chair edn. com.), Phi Beta Kappa, Sigma Xi. Office: Wesleyan U Middletown CT 06459

ROSENBERG, ALAN DAVID, accountant; b. Mt. Vernon, N.Y., Apr. 11, 1946; s. Benjamin Bernard and Miriam Mickey (Nierenberg) R.; m. Wendy Patricia Cutler, May 25, 1975; children: Kerri L., Joshua Z., Brian S. BS in Acctg., NYU, 1967; MBA in Taxation, Baruch Coll., 1970. CPA, N.Y. Sr. acct. Ernst & Ernst, N.Y.C., 1967-70; dir. acctg., CFO various firms, N.Y.C., 1970-75; pres. Alan D. Rosenberg, CPA, P.C., N.Y.C., New Rochelle, N.Y., 1975—. Mem. AICPA (mem. tax practice mgmt. com. 1992—), N.Y. State Soc. CPAs, Inst. Mgmt. Accts., Nat. Conf. CPA Practitioners, Alliance of Practicing CPAs, Estate Planning Coun. Westchester County, Tax Soc. NYU. Jewish. Avocations: sports, reading, family activities. Office: 2 W 45th St Ste 1208 New York NY 10036-4212

ROSENBERG, ALAN GENE, newspaper editor; b. Chgo., Sept. 14, 1957; s. Earl David and Lorraine Faith (Blum) R.; m. Avis Beth Gunther-Rosenberg, Apr. 8, 1984; children: Ethan Elijah, Rebecca Greer, Jacob Sigmund. BS in Journalism, Northwestern U., 1978. From state staff reporter to asst. features editor Providence (R.I.) Jour.-Bulletin, 1978—. Mem. Am. Assn. Sunday and Feature Editors. Office: Providence Jour-Bulletin 75 Fountain St Providence RI 02902-0050

ROSENBERG, ALAN STEWART, lawyer; b. N.Y.C., Mar. 29, 1930; s. Louis and Sadye (Knobler) R.; m. Ilse Rosenberg/Klein, Aug. 15, 1963; children: Gary, Robert. BA, Stanford U., 1949; LLB, Columbia U., 1952; LLM, NYU, 1960. Bar: N.Y. 1955. Assoc. Wolf Haldenstein Adler & Freeman, N.Y.C., 1955-56; ptnr., chmn. tax dept. Proskauer Rose Goetz & Mendelsohn, N.Y.C., 1957-94; bd. dirs. PEC Israel Econ. Corp. Contbr. articles to profl. jours. Mem. exec. com., bd. visitors Stanford (Calif.) U. Law Sch., 1982-85, advisor Humanities Ctr., 1985—, Jewish studies program, 1986—; chmn. bd. N.Y. Alliance for the Pub. Sch., 1988-91; mem. adv. com. on pub. issues Advt. Coun., 1991-94; bd. dirs., sec. Univ.-Urban Schs. Nat. Task Force Inc., 1981-96; mem. bd. visitors Columbia U. Law Sch., 1991-96; mem. bd. advisors Ctr. Ednl. Innovation, 1994—; bd. dirs., treas. Justice Resource Ctr., 1994—; bd. dirs. The Abraham Fund; chmn. bd. dirs. Richalan Found. Lt. (j.g.) USN, 1952-55. Avocations: amateur opera singer; tennis. Home: 115 Central Park W New York NY 10023-4153

ROSENBERG, ALEX, mathematician, educator; b. Berlin, Germany, Dec. 5, 1926; came to U.S., 1949, naturalized, 1959; s. Theodore and Rela (Banet) R.; m. Beatrice Gershenson, Aug. 24, 1952 (div. Apr. 1985); children: Theodore Joseph, David Michael, Daniel Alex; m. Brunhilde Angun, June 14, 1985. B.A., U. Toronto, 1948, M.A., 1949; Ph.D., U. Chgo., 1951. From instr. to assoc. prof. math. Northwestern U., 1952-61; prof. math. Cornell U., Ithaca, N.Y., 1961-88, prof. emeritus, 1988—, chmn. dept., 1966-69; prof. U. Calif., Santa Barbara, 1986-94, chmn. dept., 1986-87, prof. emeritus, 1994—; mem. com. undergrad. program math. Math Assn. Am., 1966-76; mem. Inst. Advanced Study, 1955-57; vis. prof. U. Calif., Berkely, 1961, 1979, U. Calif., Los Angeles, 1969-70, 82, U. London, Queen Mary Coll., 1963-64, U. Munich, 1975-76, E.T.H Zurich, 1976, U. Dortmund, 1984-85; trustee Am. Math Soc., 1973-83. Editor: Proc. Am. Math. Soc., 1960-66, Am. Math. Monthly, 1974-77; Contbr. articles to profl. jours. Recipient Humboldt Stiftung Sr. U.S. Scientist award U. Munich, 1975-76, U. Dortmund, 1981. Home: 1225 Plaza Del Monte Santa Barbara CA 93101-4819

ROSENBERG, ALISON P., public policy official; b. Miami, Fla., Sept. 5, 1945; d. Mortimer I. and Gail (Sklar) Podell; m. Jeffrey Alan Rosenberg, May 4, 1969; 1 child, Robert Aaron. BS in Econs., Smith Coll., 1967. Mng. officer Citibank, N.Y.C., 1967-69; legis. aide Senator Charles Percy, Washington, 1969-80; profl. staff mem. Senate Fgn. Rels. Com., Washington, 1981-85; assoc. asst. adminstr. Agy. for Internat. Devel., Washington, 1985-87; dir. African affairs Nat. Security Coun., Washington, 1987-88; dep. asst. sec. for Africa State Dept., Washington, 1988-92; asst. admnstr. for Africa Agy. for Internat. Devel., Washington, 1992-93; regional co-financing advisor for Africa The World Bank, Washington, 1993—.

ROSENBERG, ARTHUR JAMES, company executive; b. Boston, Dec. 8, 1926; s. Benjamin R. and Lillian (Wolfson) R.; m. Naomi C. Solomon, Oct. 16, 1949; children: Deborah L., Janis E., Mia B. B.S. magna cum laude, Tufts U., 1948; M.A., Harvard U., 1951, Ph.D., 1952. Research scientist Merck & Co., Inc., 1951-54; mem. tech. staff Lincoln Lab., MIT, Cambridge, 1954-60; pres. Tyco Labs., Inc., Waltham, Mass., 1960-70, Epidyne, Inc., Hawthorne, Calif., 1972-79, Panatech R&D Corp., L.A., 1980-97. Office: 1208 Daskalos Dr NE Albuquerque NM 87123-1963

ROSENBERG, BRUCE ALAN, English language educator, author; b. N.Y.C., July 27, 1934; s. Howard Alyne and Audrey (Olenick) R.; m. Ann Harleman, June, 1981; children: Eric Peter, Seth Allan, Bradley Michael, Sarah Stewart. Student, Alfred U., 1952-54; B.A., Hofstra U., 1955; M.A., Pa. State U., 1962; Ph.D., Ohio State U., 1965. Mem. faculty U. Calif., Santa Barbara, 1965-67, U. Va., Charlottesville, 1967-69, Pa. State U., State College, 1969-77; prof. English lit. and Am. civilization Brown U., 1977—; Fulbright lectr., Warsaw, Poland, 1981. Author: The Art of the American Folk Preacher, 1970, Custer and the Epic of Defeat, 1976, The Code of the West, 1981, The Spy Story, 1987, Can These Bones Live?, 1988, Ian Fleming, 1989, Folklore and Literature, 1991, The Neutral Ground, 1994; asst. editor Chaucer Rev., 1967-69, Jour. Am. Folklore, 1970-79; contbg. editor Oral Tradition, 1985—. Served with U.S. Army, 1955-57. Recipient James Russell Lowell prize, 1970; Chgo. Folklore prize, 1970, 76; Am. Council Learned Socs. fellow, 1967; Nat. Endowment Humanities fellow, 1976-77; Guggenheim fellow, 1982-83. Mem. MLA, Folklore Fellows Internat., Am.

Folklore Soc. Jewish. Home: 55 Summit Ave Providence RI 02906-2709 Office: Brown U 82 Waterman St Brown Sta Providence RI 02912-0001

ROSENBERG, CHARLES ERNEST, historian, educator; b. N.Y.C., Nov. 11, 1936; s. Bernard and Marion (Roberts) R.; m. Carroll Ann Smith, June 22, 1961 (div. 1977); 1 child, Leah; m. Drew Gilpin Faust, June 7, 1980; 1 child, Jessica. B.A., U. Wis., 1956; M.A., Columbia U., 1957, Ph.D., 1961; DHL, U. Wis., 1997. Fellow Johns Hopkins U., Balt., 1960-61; asst. prof. U. Wis., 1961-63; assoc. prof. U. Pa., Phila., 1965-68; prof. history U. Pa., 1968—, chmn. dept., 1974-75, 79-83; Bd. dirs. Mental Health Assn. Southeastern Pa., 1973-76, Library Co. of Phila., 1980—. Author: The Cholera Years: The United States in 1832, 1849 and 1866, 1962, The Trial of the Assassin Guiteau: Psychiatry and Law in the Gilded Age, 1968, No Other Gods: On Science and Social Thought in America, 1976, The Care of Strangers: The Rise of America's Hospital System, 1987, Explaining Epidemics and Other Studies in the History of Medicine, 1992; editor Isis, 1986-89. Nat. Inst. Health Research grantee, 1964-70; Guggenheim Found. fellow, 1965-66, 89-90; Nat. Endowment Humanities fellow, 1972-73; Rockefeller Found. humanities fellow, 1975-76; fellow Inst. Advanced Study, 1979-80, Ctr. Advanced Study in Behavioral Scis., 1982-83. Fellow Am. Acad. Arts and Scis.; mem. Inst. Medicine of NAS, Am. Assn. History of Medicine (William H. Welch medal 1969, coun. 1974-76, pres. 1992-94), History of Sci. Soc. (George Sarton medal 1995, coun. 1972-75), Soc. Social History of Medicine (pres. 1981), Orgn. Am. Historians (exec. bd. 1985-88). Home: 746 Beacom Ln Merion Station PA 19066-1604 Office: U Pa Dept History & Sociology Philadelphia PA 19104-6310

ROSENBERG, CHARLES HARVEY, otorhinolaryngologist; b. N.Y.C., June 10, 1919; s. Morris and Bessie (Greditor) R.; m. Florence Rich, Dec. 27, 1942; children: Kenneth, Ina Garten. BA cum laude, Alfred U., 1941; MD, U. Buffalo, 1944. Intern Jewish Hosp. Bklyn., 1944-45; resident otolaryngology Mt. Sinai Hosp., N.Y.C., 1945-46, 48-50; teaching faculty, sr. clin. asst. Mt. Sinai Hosp. and Med. Sch., N.Y.C., 1950-72; attending surgeon Stamford (Conn.) Hosp., St. Joseph's Hosp., 1953—; dir. dept. otolaryngology Stamford Hosp. and St. Joseph's Hosp., 1973-79. Campaign chmn. United Jewish Fedn., Stamford, 1978-81, pres., 1981-83, exec. com., 1978—; bd. trustees Alfred (N.Y.) U., 1996—. Capt. U.S. Army, 1945-46. Fellow ACS; mem. AMA, Stamford Med. Soc., Fairfield Med. Soc., Conn. State Med. Soc., Am. Bd. Otolaryngology, Am. Acad. Ophthalmology and Otolaryngology. Democrat. Jewish. Home: 304 Erskine Rd Stamford CT 06903-1001 Office: 810 Bedford St Stamford CT 06901-1115

ROSENBERG, CHARLES MICHAEL, art historian, educator; b. Chgo., Aug. 3, 1945; s. Sandor and Laura (Fried) R.; m. Carol Ann Weiss, June 25, 1967; children: Jessica Rachel, Jasper Matthew. BA, Swarthmore Coll., 1967; MA, U. Mich., 1969, PhD, 1974. Asst. prof. SUNY, Brockport, 1973-80; assoc. prof. U. Notre Dame, Ind., 1980-96, prof., 1996—. Author: 15th Century North Italian Painting and Drawing: Bibliography, 1986, Art and Politics in Late Medieval and Early Renaissance Italy, 1990, Este Monuments and Urban Development in Renaissance Ferrara, 1997; contbr. articles to Art Bull., Renaissance Quar., others. Kress Found. fellow Kunsthistorisches Inst., Florence, Italy, 1971-73, Am. Coun. Learned Socs. fellow, 1977-78, NEH fellow, Brown U., 1979-80, Villa i Tatti, Florence, 1985-86. Mem. Coll. Art Assn., Renaissance Soc. Am., Centro di Studi Europa Della Corti, Italian Art Soc. Office: Notre Dame U Dept Art Art History & Design Notre Dame IN 46556

ROSENBERG, CLAUDE NEWMAN, JR., investment adviser; b. San Francisco, Apr. 10, 1928; s. Claude Newman and Elza (Wolff) R.; m. Louise Jankelson, Dec. 19, 1968; children: Linda Kay, Douglas Claude. BA, Stanford U., 1950, MBA, 1952. Research analyst J. Barth & Co., San Francisco, 1955-62; partner charge research J. Barth & Co., 1962-70; investment adviser, pres. Rosenberg Capital Mgmt., San Francisco, 1970—; lectr. and mem. adv. council Grad. Sch. Bus., Stanford. Author: Stock Market Primer, 1962, rev., 1970, 76, 81, 87, The Common Sense Way to Stock Market Profit, 1968, rev., 1978, Psycho-Cybernetics and the Stock Market, 1970, Investing with the Best, 1986, rev., 1993, Wealthy and Wise, 1994. Bd. dirs. Jewish Welfare Fedn., Presbyn. Children's Cancer Research Center, Internat. Hospitality Center, Jewish Community Center; trustee San Francisco Ballet Assn., Univ. High Sch., San Francisco.; chmn. adv. council Stanford U. Sch. Bus. Served with USNR, 1951-53. Recipient Arbuckle award Stanford U. Grad. Sch. Bus., 1984, Daniel I. Forrestal Leadership award Assn. of Investment and Mgmt. Rsch. 1992, Lilywhite award Employee Benefit Rsch. Inst., 1994, Bus. Statesman award Harvard Bus. Sch. Assn. of No. Calif., 1995. Mem. Financial Analysts San Francisco, Alumni Assn. Stanford U. Grad. Sch. Bus. (pres.). Republican. Jewish religion. Clubs: Family (San Francisco), Concordia-Argonaut (San Francisco), Calif. Tennis (San Francisco), Family (San Francisco). Home: 2465 Pacific Ave San Francisco CA 94115-1237 Office: Four Embarcadero Center 29th Floor San Francisco CA 94111

ROSENBERG, DALE NORMAN, retired psychology educator; b. St. Ansgar, Iowa, Dec. 12, 1928; s. Eddie Herman and Ella (Kirchgatter) R.; BS, Mankato State Coll., 1956; M.Ed., U. S.D., 1959; postgrad. Ball State Tchrs. Coll., 1962, U. Nebr., 1961, Colo. State Coll., 1963-67; D.Arts, U. Central Ariz., 1978; m. Delrose Ann Hermanson, Sept. 10, 1950; children—Jean Marie, James Norman, Julie Ann, Lisa Jo. Tchr. public schs., Holstein, Iowa, 1956-60; prin., guidance dir., Crystal Lake, Iowa, 1960-62; prin. Grafton (Iowa) Jr. High Sch., 1962-66; psychol. tester Dept. Rehab., State of Iowa, 1960-66; prof. psychology North Iowa Area Community Coll., Mason City, 1966-97 ; vis. lectr. Buena Vista Coll., Storm Lake, Iowa, 1984; invited speaker Inst. Advanced Philosophic Research, 1984-85. Served with USAF, 1949-53. Mem. NEA, Iowa Edn. Assn., Kappa Delta Pi, Phi Delta Kappa. Lutheran. Author multi-media curriculum for teaching disadvantaged introductory welding; author textbook-workbook, 1985. Recipient Golden Apple award Iowa TV Channel 3, 1994. Home: 100 Brook Terr Mason City IA 50401-9828

ROSENBERG, DAN YALE, retired plant pathologist; b. Stockton, Calif., Jan. 8, 1922; s. Meyer and Bertha (Naliboff) R.; AA, Stockton Jr. Coll., 1942; AB, Coll. Pacific, 1949; MS, U. Calif. at Davis, 1952; m. Marilyn Kohn, Dec. 5, 1954; 1 son, Morton Karl. Jr. plant pathologist Calif. Dept. Agr., Riverside, 1952-55, asst. plant pathologist, 1955-59, assoc. plant pathologist, 1959-60, pathologist IV, 1960-63, program supr., 1963-71, chief exclusion and detection, div. plant industry, 1971-76, chief nursery and seed svcs. div. plant industry, 1976-82, spl. asst. div. plant industry, 1982-87; pres. Health, Inc., 1972-73; agrl. cons., 1988—; mem. Citrus Rsch. Adv. com. U. Calif., Riverside, 1992—; mem. Gov.'s Interagy. Task Force on Biotech., 1986—; bd. dirs. Health Inc., Sacramento, 1967, pres., 1971-72, 79-81, 81-83. Contbr. articles to profl. jours. Served with AUS, 1942-46; ETO. Mem. Am. Phytopath. Soc. (fgn. and regulatory com. 1975—, grape diseases sect. 1977-79, grape pests sect. 1979—), Calif. State Employees Assn. (pres. 1967-69), Sacramento Met. C. of C. (internat. trade com. 1993—). Home and Office: 2328 Swarthmore Dr Sacramento CA 95825-6867

ROSENBERG, DAVID ALAN, military historian, educator; b. N.Y.C., Aug. 30, 1948; s. Sidney and Fay (Breitman) R.; m. Deborah Lee Haines, July 1, 1973; 1 child, Rebecca Haines. BA in History, Am. U., 1970; MA in History, U. Chgo., 1971, PhD in History, 1983. Asst. historian, cons. Lulejian & Assocs., Inc., Falls Church, VA., 1974-75; instr. history U. Wis., Milw., 1976-78; pvt. practice cons., researcher Chgo., Washington, 1978-82; asst. prof. history U. Houston, University Park, 1982-83; sr. fellow Strategic Concepts Devel. Ctr., Nat. Def. U., Washington, 1983-85; prof. strategy and ops. U.S. Naval War Coll., Newport, R.I., 1985-90; assoc. prof. history Temple U., Phila., 1990—; Admiral Henry W. Hill prof. of maritime strategy Nat. War Coll., Washington, D.C., 1996—; mem. U.S. exec. com. four Nation Nuclear History Program, project dir. Berlin Crisis, 1989-95; cons. Office of Sec. Def., 1991-93, Office of Chief of Naval Ops., 1991—, Office of Sec. of Navy, 1992—; mem., chair Sec. Nay's Adv. Subcom. of Naval History, 1995—. Co-editor: (15 vol. book set) U.S. Plans for War, 1945-1950, 1990; contbr. articles to Jour. Am. History (2 awards nat. hist. assns. 1980), 22 others, also 16 book chpts. With USNR, 1982—. Advanced rsch. scholar U.S. Naval War Coll., 1974-79; Ford Found grantee, 1985-86, MacArthur rsch. grantee 1987-88; MacArthur fellow 1988-93. Mem. Orgn. Am. Historians (Binkley-Stephenson article prize), Soc. for Historians of Am. Fgn. Rels. (Bernath article prize), Soc. for Mil. History, U.S. Naval Inst., Internat. Inst. for Strategic Studies. Jewish.

ROSENBERG, DOUGLAS OWEN, healthcare management executive; b. Chgo., July 13, 1941; s. Owen Carl and Doris Raven (Ambrose) R.; m. Deloris Anne Wimmer, Aug. 19, 1967; children: Kevin Douglas, Jeffrey Kendall. BS in Biology, U. Chgo., 1963, MBA in Hosp. Adminstrn., 1969. Adminstrv. asst., asst. adminstr., assoc. adminstr. Ohio State U. Hosps., Columbus, 1969-74; v.p. adminstrn. Ravenswood Hosp., Chgo., 1974-76; v.p. clin. svc. Evanston (Ill.) Hosp., 1976-78; exec. v.p. ops., pres. Glenbrook Hosp., 1978-92; pres., CEO Howard Young Health Care, Woodruff, Wis., 1994—; grad. student preceptor various univs., 1980-92. Pres. Glenview (Ill.) Safety Com., 1979-83; v.p. Glenview chpt. Am. Cancer Soc., 1979-86; budget chmn. United Way, Northbrook, Ill., 1986-94. Capt. U.S. Army, 1964-67, Vietnam. Decorated Bronze Star; Inst. Medicine fellow, 1977-92. Mem. Wis. Hosp. Assn. Methodist. Avocations: history, numismatics, canoeing, tennis. Home: 7066 Hwy J Saint Germain WI 54558 Office: Howard Young Health Care PO Box 470 Woodruff WI 54568

ROSENBERG, ELLEN Y., religious association administrator; married; 2 children. Student, Goucher Coll.; BS in Edn., Mills Coll.; postgrad., Columbia U. Assoc. dean for acad. affairs Marymount Manhattan Coll., N.Y.C.; assoc. dir. Nat. Fedn. Temple Sisterhoods; exec. dir. Women of Reform Judaism. V.p. Riverdale Temple, pres. Temple Sisterhood. Office: 838 5th Ave New York NY 10021-7012

ROSENBERG, GARY ARON, construction executive, lawyer; b. Green Bay, Wis., June 18, 1940; s. Ben J. and Joyce Sarah (Nemzin) R.; m. Gloria Davis, Nov. 1967 (div. 1975); children: Myra, Meredith; m. Bridgit A. Maile, Apr. 9, 1983. BS, Northwestern U., 1962, MBA, 1963; JD, U. Wis., 1966. Bar: Wis. 1966, Ill. 1967. Chmn., dir. The Rosenberg Found., 1960—; atty. U.S. SEC, Washington, 1966-67; pvt. practice Chgo., 1967-74; founder, chmn. bd., CEO UDC Homes, Inc. (formerly UDC-Universal Devel., L.P.), Chgo., 1968-1995; chmn., CEO, dir. Canterbury Devel. Corp., 1986—; vice-chmn., dir. Olympic Cascade Fin. Corp., 1996—; dir. Nat. Securities, 1996—; chmn., dir. Dimyon Multimedia Ltd., 1996—; mem. adv. bd. Kellogg Grad. Sch. Mgmt. Northwestern U., Evanston, Ill., 1985—, founder, chmn. adv. bd. Real Estate Rsch. Ctr., 1986—, adj. prof., 1982—; founder Shadow Hill Entertainment Corp., Beverly Hills, Calif., 1990. Recipient Arts Edn. Svc. award Ill. Alliance for Arts Edn., Chgo., 1988, Kellogg Schaffner Disting. Alumni award Kellogg Grad. Sch. Mgmt., 1993. Mem. Nat. Assn. Home Builders (coun. 1989-90), John Evans Club. Avocations: skiing, hiking, climbing, tennis, golf, reading. Office: Olympic Cascade Fin Corp The John Hancock Ctr 875 N Michigan Ave Ste 1560 Chicago IL 60611-1894

ROSENBERG, GEORGE A., public relations company executive; b. N.Y., Dec. 13, 1945. BA in Pub. Rels., The Am. U., 1967; student, Pace Coll. With Burson-Marsteller, 1969-85; pres., COO Cohn & Wolfe, 1986-92, pres., CEO, 1992-93; mng. dir. Ward Howell Internat., N.Y., 1993—. Office: Cohn & Wolfe 225 Peachtree St NE Atlanta GA 30303-1701

ROSENBERG, HENRY A., JR., petroleum executive; b. Pitts., Nov. 7, 1929; s. Henry A. and Ruth (Blaustein) R.; children: Henry A. III, Edward Lee, Frank Blaustein; m. Dorothy Lucibello, June 30, 1984. B.A. in Econs., Hobart Coll., 1952. With Crown Cen. Petroleum Corp., Balt., 1952—, pres., 1966-75, chmn. exec. com., 1966—, chmn. bd., 1975—, also chief exec. officer; dir. Am. Trading & Prodn. Corp., USF&G Corp., Signet Banking Corp. Bd. dirs. Johns Hopkins Hosp., Goucher Coll., McDonogh Sch., Nat. Flag Day Found., YMCA Greater Balt., United Way Ctrl. Md., Crohn's and Colitis Found. Md., Nat. Aquarium Balt.; mem. nat. exec. bd., mem. N.E. regional bd., v.p. program group nat. coun., past pres., exec. bd., adv. coun. Balt. Area coun. Boy Scouts Am.; past chmn., mem. adv. bd. William Donald Schaefer Ctr. for Pub. Policy; past chmn. bd. dirs. Balt. Area Conv. and Visitors Assn.; trustee Hobart and William Smith Colls. and Loyola Coll. Med. Mem. Nat. Petroleum Refiners Assn. (chmn., bd. dirs., exec. com.), Nat. Petroleum Coun., 25 Yr. Club Petroleum Industry, Nat. Assn. Mfrs. (bd. dirs.). Office: Crown Cen Petroleum Corp 1 N Charles St PO Box 1168 Baltimore MD 21203

ROSENBERG, HOWARD ANTHONY, journalist; b. Kansas City, Mo., June 10, 1942; s. Sherman Rosenberg and Claire (Kanchuk) Rosenberg Magady; m. Carol Finkel; 1 child, Kirsten. Journalist Los Angeles Times, now TV critic, columnist. Recipient Editorial award Los Angeles Times, 1981; Headliner award Atlantic City Press Club, 1984; Pulitzer prize Columbia U., 1985. Office: Los Angeles Times Times Mirror Sq Los Angeles CA 90053*

ROSENBERG, JEROME DAVID, physicist; b. N.Y.C., June 15, 1920; s. Hyman D. and Hilda (Cantor) R.; m. Shirley Sirota, 1947; children: Jonathan, Hindy. BS in Physics, CCNY, 1948; postgrad., Nat. Bur. Standards Grad. Sch., 1949-52, George Washington U., 1952, U. Md., 1951-53, Cath. U. Am., 1953-54. Engr. officer USCG Acad., 1942, APA-34, 1943-44; project mgr., adminstr. test nuclear reactor Harry Diamond Labs., Washington, 1950-62; ops. mgr. tech. utilization NASA, Washington, 1962-64; program and project mgr. space applications program NASA Nat. Geodetic Satellite Program Pageos, GEOS 1&2, Washington, 1964-69; dep. dir. comm. program NASA, Washington, 1969-74, dir. tech. applications divsn., 1974-77, dir. office energy programs divsn. bus. mgmt., 1977-78; spl. assignment to solar applications & conservation, barriers and incentive br. Dept. Energy, 1978-79; leader solar energy group Mitre Corp., McLean, Va., 1979-80; prin. cons. energy and environ. divsn. Booz, Allen & Hamilton, Washington, 1980-82; sr. staff officer Bd. Telecomm. and Computer Applications, NRC-NAS, Washington, 1982-85; exec. dir. NASA Alumni League, Washington, 1986—; mem. Outlook for Space Study Group, NASA planning group to develop U.S. space programs, 1975. Lt. (j.g.) USCG, 1943-44. Recipient NASA Exceptional Svc. medal, 1973. Mem. Fed. Exec. Inst., Sigma Pi Sigma. Office: NASA Alumni League 750 1st St NE Washington DC 20002-4241

ROSENBERG, JEROME I., lawyer; b. Passaic, N.J., June 9, 1931; s. Emanuel and Sylvia S. (Schwartz) R.; m. Dorothy Elaine Teninbaum, Aug. 21, 1955; children—Peter, Michael. B.A., NYU, 1953; LL.B., Harvard U., 1956. Bar: N.Y. 1966, D.C. 1957, U.S. Supreme Ct. Tax law specialist IRS, Washington, 1960-63; mem. firm Hughes Hubbard & Reed, N.Y.C., 1968—; lectr. NYU Tax Inst. Contbr. articles to Jour. of Taxation. Served as lt. USAF, 1957-60. Mem. N.Y. State Bar Assn., Assn. of Bar of City N.Y., D.C. Bar Assn., Phi Beta Kappa. Office: Hughes Hubbard & Reed One Battery Park Plz New York NY 10004-1466

ROSENBERG, JEROME LAIB, chemist, educator; b. Harrisburg, Pa., June 20, 1921; s. Robert and Mary (Katzman) R.; m. Shoshana Gabriel, Sept. 15, 1946; children—Jonathan, Judith. AB, Dickinson Coll., 1941; MA, Columbia U., 1944, PhD, 1948. Rsch. chemist S.A.M. Labs., 1944-46; Instr. chemistry Columbia U., 1946-48; rsch. assoc. (asst. prof.) inst. Radiobiology and Biophysics, U. Chgo., 1950-53; mem. faculty U. Pitts., 1953-91, chmn. dept. biophysics and microbiology, 1969-71, prof. biol. scis., 1976-91, dean faculty arts and scis., 1970-86, vice provost, 1978-89, chmn. biol. scis., 1989-90, interim chmn. communication, 1991, assoc. dean faculty arts and scis., 1991-92, rsch. integrity officer, 1992—, prof. emeritus biol. scis., 1991—, dir. Jewish studies program, 1991—. Author: Photosynthesis, 1965; editor, reviser: Outline Theory and Problems of College Chemistry (Schaum), 1949, 58, 66, 80, 90, 97; contbr. articles to profl. jours. NSF sr. fellow Technion Israel Inst. Tech., 1962-63, AEC fellow U. Chgo., 1948-50; recipient Pitts. award Am. Chem. Soc., 1987. Mem. AAUP (nat. coun. 1968-69, pres. Pa. div. 1968-69). Home: 1029 S Negley Ave Pittsburgh PA 15217-1045

ROSENBERG, JERRY MARTIN, business administration educator; b. N.Y.C., Feb. 5, 1935; s. Frank and Esther (Gardner) R.; m. Ellen Young, Sept. 11, 1960; children: Lauren, Elizabeth. BS, CCNY, 1956; MA, Ohio State U., 1957; cert., Sorbonne, 1958; PhD, NYU, 1963. Asst. prof. Sch. Indsl. and Labor Rels. Cornell U., 1961-64; asst. prof. Columbia U., N.Y.C., 1964-68; pvt. practice cons. N.Y.C., 1968-71; assoc. prof. CUNY, 1971-74; prof. mgmt., chmn. dept. Poly. Inst. N.Y., N.Y.C., 1974-77; prof. mgmt. Lehman Coll., CUNY; prof. bus. adminstrn. and mgmt., chmn. dept. bus. adminstrn. Rutgers U., Newark, 1977-88, prof. grad. sch. mgmt., chmn. dept. internat. bus., 1988—, dir. Ctr. for Middle East/North Africa Bus. Studies, 1996; testified before U.S. Senate on privacy; dir. Ctr. for Middle East-N. Africa Bus. Studies, 1996—. Author: Automation Manpower and Education, 1966, The Computer Prophets, 1969, The Death of Privacy, 1969, Dictionary of Business and Management, 1978, Dictionary of Banking and Financial Services, , 1982, Inside the Wall Street Journal, 1982, Dictionary of Computers, Data Processing and Telecommunications, 1983, Investor's Dictionary, 1986, Dictionary of Artificial Intelligence and Robotics, 1986, The New Europe, 1991, Dictionary of Business Acronyms, Abbreviations and Initials, 1992, Dictionary of Wall Street Acronyms, Abbreviations and Initials, 1992, Dictionary of Information Technology and Computer Acronyms, Abrreviations and Initials, 1992, The New American Community, 1992, Dictionary of International Trade, 1994, Encyclopedia of NAFTA, The New American Community and Latin-American Trade, 1994, Dictionary of Marketing and Advertising, 1995, Dictionary of Retailing and Merchandising, 1995, The Peace Dividend: Creating a Middle East/N. Africa Community, 1996. Recipient Fulbright and French Govt. awards, 1957. Known as Am.'s foremost bus. and tech. lexicographer. Home: 515 Tulfan Ter Bronx NY 10463-1705 Office: Rutgers U Mgmt Edn Ctr Newark NJ 07102

ROSENBERG, JILL, realtor, civic leader; b. Shreveport, La., Feb. 17, 1940; d. Morris H. and Sallye (Abramson) Schuster; m. Lewis Rosenberg, Dec. 23, 1962; children: Craig, Paige. BA in Philosophy, Tulane U., 1961, MSW, 1965; grad., Realtor Inst., 1994. Cert. residential specialist Residential Sales Coun.; grad. Realtor Inst. 1993. Social worker La. Dept. Pub. Welfare, 1961-62, 63-64; genetics counselor Sinai Hosp., Balt., 1967-69; ptnr. Parties Extraordinaire, cons., 1973-77; realtor assoc. Robert Weil Assocs., Long Beach, Calif., 1982—. Pres. western region Brandeis U. Nat. Women's Com., 1972-73; bd. dirs. Long Beach Symphony Assn., 1984-85; v.p. Jewish Cmty. Fedn. Long Beach and West Orange County, 1983-86, bd. dirs., 1982-86; pres. Long Beach Cancer League, 1987-88, exec. bd. dirs., 1984—; pres. Long Beach Jewish Cmty. Sr. Housing Corp., 1989-91; v.p. fundraising S.E. unit Long Beach Harbor chpt. Am. Cancer Soc., 1989-90; bd. dirs. Westerly Sch. Assoc., 1991—; bd. trustees St. Mary Med. Ctr. Found., 1991—; fund chair St. Mary Med. Ctr., 1992-94; pres. nat. conf. NCCJ, 1994-96; pres. Leadership Long Beach, 1994-95, Phoenix Long Beach Mus. Art, 1995—, Rotary Club of Long Beach, 1996—; bd. dirs. Am. Diabetes Assn., Long Beach, Calif., 1997—; numerous others. Recipient Young Leadership award Jewish Community Fedn. Long Beach and West Orange County, 1981, Jerusalem award State of Israel, 1989, Hannah G. Solomon award Nat. Coun. Jewish Women, 1992, Alumnus of Yr. award Leadership Long Beach, 1995, Humanitarian award The Nat. Conf., 1997; scholar La. Dept. Pub. Welfare, 1962, NIMH, 1964. Office: Robert Weil Assocs 5220 E Los Altos Plz Long Beach CA 90815-4251

ROSENBERG, JOHN DAVID, English educator, literary critic; b. N.Y.C., Apr. 17, 1929; s. David and Dorothy Lilian (Shatz) R.; m. Barbara E. Hatch, 1952 (div. 1969); m. Maurine Ann Hellner, June 11, 1972; 1 child, Matthew John. BA, Columbia U., 1950, MA, 1951, PhD, 1960; BA, Clare Coll., Cambridge U., 1953, MA, 1958. Editor-in-chief Columbia Rev., 1949-50; lectr. English Columbia U., N.Y.C., 1953-54, asst. prof., 1962-65, assoc. prof., 1966-67, prof. English, 1967—, William Peterfield Trent prof., 1994—; instr. CCNY, 1954-62; chmn. Columbia Coll. humanities program, 1970-73, dir. grad. studies in English, 1986-89; vis. prof. English, Harvard U., summer 1968, U. B.C., Summer 1970, Princeton U., 1978; vis. fellow Clare Hall, Cambridge (Eng.) U., 1969; guest lectr. U.S. Mil. Acad., Cambridge U., Queens U. Author: The Darkening Glass: A Portrait of Ruskin's Genius, 1961, The Fall of Camelot: A Study of Tennyson's Idylls of the King, 1973, Carlyle and the Burden of History, 1985; editor: The Genius of John Ruskin, 1963, Mayhew, 1968, Swinburne: Selected Poetry and Prose, 1968, The Poems of Alfred, Lord Tennyson, 1975; contbr. essays and reviews on English lit. to N.Y. Times Book Rev., Harper's mag., Hudson Rev. and profl. jours. Recipient Clarke F. Ansley award Columbia U., 1960, Disting. Svc. award Columbian Coll. Core Curriculum, 1997; Coun. for Rsch. in Humanities grant-in-aid, 1965; Euretta J. Kellett fellow Cambridge U., 1951-53, Edward Coe fellow, 1956-57, Samuel S. Fels fellow, 1959-60, Am. Coun. Learned Soc. fellow, 1965-66, 70, Lawrence H. Chamberlain fellow, 1965-66, Guggenheim fellow, 1968-69, NEH fellow, 1982-83. Mem. MLA (chmn. exec. com. Victorian divsn. 1970, exec. com. 1979-83), Tennyson Soc., Ruskin Assn., Camp Rising Sun Alumni Assn., Columbia Coll. Alumni Assn. (dir. 1980-82, Alexander Hamilton medal 1994), Phi Beta Kappa. Office: Columbia U Dept English 116 Broadway New York NY 10005-1007

ROSENBERG, JOHN K., lawyer; b. N.Y.C., May 13, 1945; s. Robert and Joyce (Kane) R.; m. Fern Kaufman; children: Joyce, Amie. BA, Pa. State U., 1967; JD, Columbia U., 1970. Bar: N.Y. 1971, Kans. 1980, U.S. Dist. Ct. (no. dist.) N.Y. 1971, U.S. Dist. Ct. Kans. 1980, U.S. Ct. Appeals (10th cir.) 1982, U.S. Ct. Appeals (5th cir.) 1986, U.S. Supreme Ct. 1990. Staff counsel N.Y. Pub. Svc. Commn., Albany, 1970-74; prin. atty. N.Y. Consumer Protection Bd., Albany, 1974-78; asst. gen. counsel The Kans. Power & Light Co., Topeka, 1979-87, v.p. gen. counsel, 1987-89, exec. v.p., gen. counsel, sec., 1989-92; exec. v.p., gen. counsel Western Resources, Inc., Topeka, 1992—; mem. legal com. Edison Elec. Inst., 1987—. Bd. dirs. Friends of the Topeka 20, 1983-89, 94—, pres., 1988; mem. Mayor's Commn. on Literacy, 1990-93; bd. dirs., sec. Concerned Citizens of Topeka, 1995—. Mem. Am. Gas. Assn. (legal mng. com. 1986—). Avocations: golf, flyfishing, hiking. Office: Western Resources Inc 818 S Kansas Ave Topeka KS 66612-1203

ROSENBERG, JUDITH LYNNE, middle school educator; b. Bklyn., Nov. 1, 1944; d. Benjamin and Rose (Delbaum) Jackler; m. Joel Barry Rosenberg, Aug. 26, 1965; children: Jeffrey Alan, Marc David. BA in Edn., Queens Coll., Flushing, N.Y., 1966, MS in Edn., 1972. Lic. advanced profl. elem. and mid. sch. math., Md., elem. edn., N.Y. Elem. tchr. N.Y.C. and Cranston, R.I., 1966-68; tchr. math. Earl B. Wood Mid. Sch., Rockville, Md., 1981-82, Walt Whitman High Sch., Bethesda, Md., 1982-83, Robert Frost Mid. Sch., Rockville, Md., 1983-89; math. and interdisciplinary resource Julius West Mid. Sch., Rockville, 1989—. Mem. NEA, Nat. Coun. Tchrs. Math., Md. State Tchrs. Assn. Home: 16 Flameleaf Ct Gaithersburg MD 20878-5216 Office: Julius West Mid Sch Great Falls Rd Rockville MD 20850

ROSENBERG, LEON JOSEPH, marketing educator; b. Atlanta, Oct. 9, 1918; s. Harry Manville and Gertrude Dora (Hassenbusch) R.; m. Phylis Jane Israel, Feb. 6, 1943 (dec. Mar. 1976); children: Joanne Rosenberg Larson, Paul Harvey; m. Louise Marjorie Nachman, Oct. 15, 1977. B.S. in Indsl. Mgmt, Ga. Inst. Tech., 1939; M.S. (Univ. scholar), Columbia U., 1940; Ph.D., N.Y. U., 1967. Mem. staff Nat. Retail Mchts. Assn., N.Y.C., 1947-49; sr. research analyst Federated Dept. Stores, Inc., Cin., 1949-52; research dir. Sanger Harris Dept. Store, Dallas, 1952-56; gen. supt. Sanger Harris Dept. Store, 1956-67; assoc. prof. Coll. Bus. Adminstrn., U. Ark., Fayetteville, 1967-74; prof., mktg. and transp. Coll. Bus. Adminstrn., U. Ark., 1975-89, dept. head, 1986-88; prof. emeritus U. Ark., 1989—; mktg. cons. Lindsey & Assocs. Inc., Fayetteville, 1990—; real estate cons., 1968—; disting. vis. prof. Calif. State U., San Bernardino, 1990. Contbr. articles to profl. jours. Pres. Jewish Family Svc., Dallas, 1960-62, Temple Shalom, Fayetteville, 1992-96; mem. exec. com. Dallas Jewish Fedn., 1963-67; bd. dirs. New Orleans Jewish Children's Regional Svc., 1962-73, 75—, Jewish Fedn. Ark., 1992-96; pres. N.W. Ark. unit B'nai B'rith, 1992—; bd. dirs. Washington County (Ark.) chpt. Am. Cancer Soc., 1979-86, pres., 1982-83. Capt. USAAF, 1940-46. Mem. Acad. Mktg. Sci., Am. Mktg. Assn., So. Mktg. Assn., S.W. Mktg. Assn., S.W. Small Bus. Inst. Assn., Econs. and Bus. History Soc. (trustee 1986-89), Masons, Alpha Phi Omega (svc. award 1971), Beta Gamma Sigma, Delta Nu Alpha. Home: 1124 Lakefront Dr Fayetteville AR 72703-2000 Office: Lindsey & Assocs Inc PO Box 1174 Fayetteville AR 72702-1174

ROSENBERG, LEONARD See RANDALL, TONY

ROSENBERG, MANUEL, retail company executive; b. Boston, Apr. 26, 1930; s. Israel and Lillian (Wirin) R.; m. Audray Merle Gold, Aug. 28, 1955; children: Peter Neal, Beth Susan. A.B., Harvard U., 1951, M.B.A., 1953. V.P. Filene's, Boston, 1967-73; pres., chief exec. officer Gimbel's, Phila., 1973-75, chmn. bd., chief exec. officer, 1975-77; exec. v.p. Garfinckel, Brooks Bros., Miller & Rhoads, Inc., Washington, 1977-79, pres., 1979-82, also dir.;

chmn. bd., chief exec. officer Morse Shoe, Inc., Canton, Mass., 1982-92. Trustee Beth Israel Hosp., Boston, Mass. Eye and Ear Infirmary, Boston. Lt. USN, 1953-56. Mem. Univ. Club, Harvard Club. Home: 370 Beacon St Boston MA 02116-1002

ROSENBERG, MARILYN ROSENTHAL, artist, visual poet; b. Phila., Oct. 11, 1934; m. Robert Rosenberg, June 12, 1955; 2 children. B in Profl. Studies in Studio Arts, SUNY, Empire State Coll., 1978; MA in Liberal Studies, NYU, 1993. Author, pub., creator unique and edit. poetry/painting books; solo exhbns. include Irvine Gallery, State U. Calif., Irvine, 1981, The Sandor Tezsler Libr. Gallery, Spartanburg, S.C., 1983, U. Wis., River Falls, 1984, 361 Degrees Gallery, Greenfield, Mass., 1987, UCLA Art Libr. Dickson Art Ctr., L.A., 1989-90, Marymount Coll., Tarrytown, N.Y., 1993, McHenry County Coll., Crystal Lake, Ill., 1997; two-person exhbns. include SUNY Purchase Libr., 1982, The Hudson River Mus., Yonkers, N.Y., 1984, Women's Studio Workshop Inskirts Gallery, Rosendale, N.Y., 1986, Brownson Art Gallery, Purchase, N.Y., 1988, (with collaborator) Westchester County Gallery, White Plains, N.Y., 1989; group exhbns. include Long Beach (Calif.) Mus. Art, 1977, Kathryn Markel Fine Arts Gallery, N.Y.C., 1978, Pratt Graphic Ctr. Gallery, N.Y.C., 1978, Polytechnic State U. Gallery, San Luis Obispo, Calif., 1979, Phila. Art Alliance, Glassboro State Coll., Pa., 1979, Ridotte del Teatro Comunale, Italy, 1980, SUNY Purchase Gallery, 1982, Galerie Caroline Corre, Paris, 1983, Thorpe Intermedia Gallery, Sparkhill, N.J., 1983, U. Rochester Gallery, Rochester, N.Y., 1984, 14 Sculptors Gallery, N.Y.C., 1984, Georgetown U., Washington, 1984, Franklin Furnace, N.Y.C., 1986, Douglas & Cook Colleges, New Brunswick, N.J., 1985, City Without Walls, Newark, 1986, Galleri T.V., Malmo, Sweden, Post Machina Group and Am. Consulate, Bologna, Italy, 1986, Technical U. of Nova Scotia, Halifax, 1986, Museu Municipal, Figuira Da Foz, Portugal, 1987, King Stephen Mus., Szekesfehrvar, Hungary, 1987, Allen Meml. Art Mus., Oberlin, Ohio, 1987, Cultural Centre of San Paulo, Brazil, 1988, Centro Cultural de la Caja de Ahorros de Valencia, Spain, 1988, Cooper Union Art, N.Y.C., 1989, San Francisco Craft and Folk Art Mus., 1990, Alternatives Gallery, San Luis Obispo, Calif., 1990-91, San Antonio Art Inst., 1991, Sazama Gallery, Chgo., 1992, SUNY Oneonta, 1992, Ralston Fine Arts, Johnson City, Tenn., 1993, Va. Ctr. for Craft Arts, 1993, Libr. Can., 1993, Muée de la Post, Paris, 1993, Pratt Inst., N.Y.C., 1993, Musée de la Poste, Paris, 1993-94, Papertrail, Ottawa, Can., 1993-94, Nexus Found. for Arts, Phila., 1994, Va. Ctr. for Craft Arts, Richmond, 1994, Ormond Meml. Art Mus., Fla., 1994, Libr. Nat. Mus. Women, Washington, 1994-95, Spirit Sq. Ctr. Arts, Charlotte, N.C., 1995, Ellipse Arts Ctr., Arlington, Va., 1995, Monterserrat Coll. Art Gallery, Beverly, Mass., 1995, Yale U. Art Gallery Sculpture Hall, New Haven, Conn., 1995, Harper Collins, N.Y.C., 1995, Brookfield Craft Ctr., Conn., 1995, Muscatine Art Ctr., Iowa, 1995, Sangre de Cristo Art Ctr., Pueblo, Colo., 1995, Lake George (N.Y.) Art Project, 1995, Mus. Nebr. Arts, U. Nebr., Kearney, 1995, The Battery, Hastings-on-Hudson, N.Y., 1996, Ctr. for Book Arts, N.Y.C., 1996, Franklin Furnace, N.Y.C., 1996, Rutgers U., New Brunswick, 1996, Harper Collins, N.Y., 1996, The Stamp Art Gallery, San Francisco, 1997, U. Alberta, Edmonton, Can., 1997; public collections and archives include Art Gallery New South Wales, Sydney, Australia, Artpool Art Rsch. Ctr., Budapest, Hungary, Bibliotheque Nationale, Paris, Canadian Postal Mus. Archive, Ottawa, Electrografia Museo Internacional, La Mancha, Cuenca, Spain, Fogg Art Mus., Cambridge, Mass., Mus. of Modern Art Libr., N.Y.C., The Ruth and Marvin Sackner Archive, Miami Beach, Fla., Tate Gallery Libr., London, Yale U. Libr., New Haven, Ct., Canberra Sch. Art Gallery, Australia, Cleve. Inst. Art Libr., Harvard U. Fogg Mus. and Houghton Libr., Cambridge, Mass., Rochester (N.Y.) Inst. Tech., Sch. Art Inst. Chgo. Libr., Amherst (Mass.) Coll. Libr., Atlanta Coll. of Art Libr., Brown U. Libr., Cleve. Inst. of Art Libr., Dartmouth Coll., Sherman Art Libr., Georgetown U. Library, The N.Y. Pub. Libr., Rhode Island Sch. of Design, Stanford U. Libr., Temple U. Library, Phila., U. Calif. at Davis, Santa Barbara Librs., U. Chgo. Libr., U. Utah, Mariott Libr., U. Va. Libr., Va. Commonwealth U. Libr., Wellesley Coll. Libr., Libr. Mus. Fine Arts, Boston, Sch. Mus. of Fine Art Libr., Boston, Nat. Art Libr., Victoria and Albert Mus., London; works included in various pubs., periodicals, web sites and exhibition catalogs. Studio: 67 Lakeview Ave West Peekskill NY 10566-6415

ROSENBERG, MARK B., think-tank executive; b. Athens, Ohio, Aug. 15, 1949; married; 2 children. BA, Miami U., Ohio; PhD in Polit. Sci., U. Pitts. Asst. prof. polit. sci. Fla. Internat. U., Miami, 1976—, chairperson Caribbean L.Am. studies coun., 1977-79, founding dir. L.Am. and Caribbean Ctr., 1979—, founding/acting dean Coll. Urban and Pub. Affairs, 1994—, vice provost for internat. studies; co-dir. Fla. Caribbean Inst., Fla. Mexico Inst. Author, editor, co-editor 6 books; contbr. articles to profl. jours. Mem. Greater Miami C. of C. (vice chairperson exec. com. for internat. econ. devel.). Office: Fla Int'l U Coll Urban & Pub Affairs North Miami Campus ACI-200 3000 NE 151st St Miami FL 33181-3605*

ROSENBERG, MARK L., health facility administrator; b. Newark, July 30, 1945; m. Jill Dimond; children: Julie, Ben. BA in Biology magna cum laude, Harvard Coll., 1967, MD cum laude, 1972, M of Pub. Policy, 1972. Diplomate Am. Bd. Internal Medicine, Am. Bd. Psychiatry and Neurology. Intern Mass. Gen. Hosp., Boston, 1972-73, resident in medicine, 1973-74; resident in preventive medicine Ctrs. for Disease Control, Atlanta, 1975-76; resident in psychiatry Beth Israel Hosp., Boston, 1980-83; clin. assoc. prof. dept. cmty. medicine & family practice Morehouse Sch. Medicine, Atlanta, 1984-93; clin. prof. psychiatry Emory U. Sch. Medicine, Atlanta, 1993—; dir. Nat. Ctr. for Injury Prevention and Control, Atlanta, 1994—, acting assoc. dir. for public health practice, 1992-93; dir. divsn. injury control Ctr. for Environ. Health and Injury Control, 1989-92; spl. asst. for behavioral sci. office of dep. dir. Ctrs. for Disease Control, Atlanta, 1989, advisor to dep. dir., 1988, asst. dir. for sci. divsn. injury epidemiology and control, 1986-88, liaison officer office program planning and evaluation, 1979-80; assoc. dir. office extramural health programs Harvard Sch. Pub. Health, Boston, 1979-80; clin. fellow in psychiatry Harvard Med. Sch., Boston, 1980-83; vis. prof. dept. cmty. health Emory U. Sch. Medicine, Atlanta, 1984-91, clin. asst. prof. psychiatry, 1985-87, clin. assoc. prof., 1988-93; adj. prof. Emory U. Sch. Public Health, Atlanta, 1991—; clin. prof. dept. cmty. health and preventive medicine Morehouse Sch. Medicine, Atlanta, 1993; staff physician Womens Med. Clinic, Atlanta, 1974-76, Harvard St. Neighborhood Health Ctr., Boston, 1976-77, Winchester (Mass.) Hosp., 1978-83; emergency rm. physician Burbank Hosp., Fitchburg, Mass., 1976-77, Harrington Hosp., Southbridge, Mass., 1976-77; vis. physician dept. psychiatry Grady Meml. Hosp., Atlanta, 1985—; lectr. and cons. in field. Author: Patients: The Experience of Illness, 1980, Violence in America: A Public Health Approach, 1990; mem. editl. bd. Violence and Victims, 1985-88, Violence, Aggression and Terrorism, 1986—; contbr. articles to profl. jours. Bd. dirs. southeastern divsn., sci. adv. coun. Am. Suicide Found., 1990—; active Calif. Wellness Found., 1993—. Mass. Gen. Hosp. fellow, 1977-78, Mead-Johnson fellow, 1982; John Harvard scholar, 1964; recipient Coulter Lecture award Am. Congress Rehab. Medicine, 1991, William S. Stone award Am. Trauma Soc., 1991, Outstanding Achievement award, 1994, World Health Day award Am. Assn. for World Health, 1993, Disting. Svc. award Ga. Assn. Family and Marital Therapists, 1994. Mem. Phi Beta Kappa, Alpha Omega Alpha. Avocation: photography. Home: 972 Oakdale Rd Atlanta GA 30307

ROSENBERG, MARK LOUIS, lawyer; b. Lexington, Ky., Sept. 21, 1947; s. Edward George and Shirley Lee (Berkin) R.; m. Betty Adler, May 16, 1982; stepchildren—Aaron and Sarah Claxton; children: Eli, Daniel. B.A., U. Mich., 1969; J.D., Harvard U., 1973, LL.M. in Taxation, Georgetown U., 1985. Bar: D.C. 1973, U.S. Dist. Ct. D.C. 1973, U.S. Ct. Appeals (D.C. cir.) 1973. Asst. to v.p. George Washington U., 1973-75; counsel U.S. Ho. of Reps., Washington, 1975-77; sr. atty. FTC, Washington, 1977-85; atty. Ross & Duerk, Washington, 1985-89; pntr. Gordon, Feinblatt et al, Washington, 1989-91; prin. Law Offices of Mark L. Rosenberg, 1991—; of counsel The Jacobovitz Law Firm, 1994—. Mem. Fed. Bar Assn. (Disting. Service award 1982, 83, 87, dep. sect. coordinator), ABA (legis. monitor adminstrv. law sect.). Democrat. Jewish. Home: 6101 Shady Oak Ln Bethesda MD 20817-6027 Office: The Jacobovitz Law Firm 1914 Sunderland Pl NW Washington DC 20036-1608

ROSENBERG, MICHAEL, lawyer; b. N.Y.C., Oct. 13, 1937; s. Walter and Eva (Bernstein) R.; m. Jacqueline Raymonde Combe, Apr. 29, 1966; children: Andrew James, Suzanne Jennifer. AB in Econs. with honors, Ind. U., 1959; LLB, Columbia U., 1962. Bar: N.Y. 1963, U.S. Dist. Ct. (so. and ea. dists.) N.Y. 1966, U.S. Ct. Appeals (2d cir.) 1975, U.S. Dist. Ct. (ea. dist. so. div.) Mich. 1989. From. dep. asst. atty. gen. to asst. atty. gen. N.Y. State Dept. Law, N.Y.C., 1963-66; assoc. Hellerstein, Rosier & Rembar, N.Y.C., 1966-73; assoc. gen. counsel Gen. Instrument Corp., N.Y.C., 1973-78; from assoc. gen. counsel to dep. gen. counsel U.S. Filter Corp., N.Y.C., 1978-82; v.p., gen. counsel, sec. Alfa-Laval Inc., Ft. Lee, N.J., 1982-88; counsel Becker Ross Stone De Stefano & Klein, N.Y.C., 1988-89; ptnr. Rosenberg & Rich, White Plains, N.Y., 1989-95, Quinn, Marantis & Rosenberg, LLP, White Plains, N.Y., 1995-97, Marantis, Rosenberg & van Nes, LLP, White Plains, 1997—. Mem. Zoning Bd. Appeals Town of North Castle, N.Y., 1995—. Mem. ABA, N.Y. State Bar Assn., Westchester County Bar Assn. Office: Marantis Rosenberg & van Nes LLP 3 Barker Ave White Plains NY 10601-1509

ROSENBERG, MICHAEL JOSEPH, financial executive; b. Passaic, N.J., Apr. 19, 1928; s. Emanuel and Sylvia Sarah (Schwartz) R.; m. Judith Ann Melnick, Dec. 6, 1964 (div. 1983); children: Ann Kirsten, Emily Jeanne; m. Kathleen Ann Jennings, Mar. 3, 1990. BS, Upsala Coll., 1951; MBA, NYU, 1955, postgrad., 1955-59. Asst. v.p. Meinhard & Co., N.Y.C., 1953-58, A.J. Armstrong Co., N.Y.C., 1958-59, Sterling Nat. Bank, N.Y.C., 1959-61; exec. v.p. Rosenthal & Rosenthal, Inc., N.Y.C., 1961-96; bd. dirs. D.V.L., Inc., N.Y.C.; dir. Am. com. Shenkar U. Contbr. numerous articles on comml. fin. to newspapers and mags. Bd. dirs., treas. Town Hall Found., N.Y.C., 1982—; treas. Citizens for Clean Air, N.Y.C., 1984; trustee NYU, 1997—. Capt. U.S. Army, 1951-53, Korea. Decorated Silver Star, Bronze Star; recipient Meritorious Svc. award NYU, 1983; Albert Gallatin fellow, 1981. Mem. Albert Gallatin Assocs. (chmn. 1984-87), NYU Bus. Forum (pres. 1981-82), NYU Grad. Sch. Bus. Adminstrn. Alumni Assn. (pres. 1978-79), NYU Ptnrs. (co-chmn. 1987-89, chmn. 1990-93), NYU Club (pres. 1975-77, 82-85). Avocations: skiing, tennis, running, sailing. Office: 53 Columbus Ave Ste 2 New York NY 10023-6917

ROSENBERG, NORMAN, surgeon; b. N.Y.C., Apr. 25, 1916; s. Leo and Rose (Kamerman) R.; m. Ruth Harriet Feller, Nov. 30, 1940; children: Lois A. Rosenberg Ebin, Ralph. BA, U. Pa., 1934; MD, NYU, 1938. Diplomate Am. Bd. Surgery, Am. Bd. Gen. Vascular Surgery. Intern Mt. Sinai Hosp., N.Y.C., 1939-41; resident Mt. Sinai Hosp., 1942-43; practice medicine, specializing in vascular surgery New Brunswick, N.J., 1946-80; sr. attending surgeon St. Peters Med. Center, New Brunswick, from 1946, now emeritus sr. attending surgeon; chief staff Middlesex Gen. Hosp., New Brunswick, 1959-66, chief vascular surgery, 1960-86, dir. dept. surgery, 1975-81; cons. surgeon Roosevelt Hosp., Metuchen, N.J., 1956-87 , Raritan Valley Hosp., Greenbrook, N.J., 1970-81, Somerset Hosp., Somerville, N.J., 1952-88 , J.F. Kennedy Hosp., Edison, N.J., 1969-88 ; clin. prof. surgery Robert Wood Johnson Med. Sch., U. Medicine and Dentistry N.J., New Brunswick, 1972-81, chief vascular surgery sect., 1981-86, prof. surgery, 1981-91, prof. emeritus, 1991—; cons. Johnson & Johnson Research Center, New Brunswick, 1954-78. Author: Handbook of Carotid Artery Surgery Facts and Figures, 1989, 2d edit., 1994; contbr. articles to books and profl. jours.; co-inventor modified bovine arterial graft. Trustee Robert Wood Johnson Found., 1958-96. Capt. M.C., AUS, 1943-46. Fellow A.C.S., Southeastern Surg. Congress; mem. Soc. Vascular Surgery, Internat. Soc. Cardiovascular Surgery, Soc. Surgeons N.J. Home: 48 North Dr East Brunswick NJ 08816-1122

ROSENBERG, NORMAN JACK, agricultural meteorologist, educator; b. Bklyn., Feb. 22, 1930; s. Jacob and Rae (Dombrowitz) R.; m. Sarah Zacher, Dec. 30, 1950; children: Daniel Jonathon, Alyssa Yael. BS, Mich. State U., 1951; MS, Okla. State U., 1958; PhD, Rutgers U., 1961. Soil scientist Israel Soil Conservation Service, Haifa, 1953-55, Israel Water Authority, Haifa, 1955-57; asst. prof. agrl. meteorology U. Nebr., Lincoln, 1961-64, assoc. prof., 1964-67, prof. agrl. meteorology, 1967—, prof. agrl. engring., 1975—, prof. agronomy, 1976—, George Holmes prof. agrl. meteorology, 1981-87, prof. emeritus, 1987—, leader sect. agrl. meteorology, 1975-79, acting asst. vice chancellor for research, 1983-85; sr. fellow, dir. climate resources program Resources for the Future, Washington, 1987-92; chief scientist integrated earth studies energy sci. divsn. Battelle Pacific N.W. Nat. Lab., Washington, 1992—; cons. Dept. State AID, NOAA, Oak Ridge Assoc. Univs., 1986-87, Elec. Power Rsch. Inst. 1989-92, Sandia Nat. Labs., 1990; mem. numerous ad hoc coms. and mem. standing com. on atmospheric sci. Nat. Acad. Scis./NRC, 1975-78, mem. bd. on atmospheric sci. and climate, 1982-85, mem. U.S. com. Internat. Geosphere-Biosphere Program, 1984-86, mem. panel on policy implications of climate change, 1990-91; mem. bd. coun. Agrl. Sci. and Tech.; vis. prof. agrl. meteorology Israel Inst. Tech., Haifa, 1968; trustee Nat. Inst. Global Environ. Change, 1992, vice-chmn., 1992—. Author: Microclimate: The Biological Environment, 1974, 2d edit., 1983, Chinese transl., 1983, Malay transl., 1987; also numerous articles in profl. jours.; editor: North American Droughts, 1978, Drought in the Great Plains: Research on Impacts and Strategies, 1980, Greenhouse Warming: Abatement and Adaptation, 1989; editor: Toward an Integrated Impact Assessment of Climate Change: The MINK Study, 1993; tech. editor Agronomy Jour., 1974-79; cons. editor Agrl. and Forest Meteorology, Climatic Change. Mem. Intergovernmental Panel on Climate Change, 1993—. Recipient Centennial medal Nat. Weather Svc., 1970; sr. fellow in sci., NATO, 1968, rsch. fellow U. Nebr., 1968, Lady Davis fellow Hebrew U., Jerusalem, 1977, nat. resources fellow Resources for Future, 1986; grantee State of Nebr., 1970-73, NSF, 1971-87, 96, U.S. Dept. Commerce, 1972-74, 80-82, 83-85, 88-89, NASA, 1972-73, 85-86, U.S. Dept. Interior, 1974-75, 77-79, 88—, USDA, 1979-82, 88-89, U. Nebr. Found., 1982, Nat. Ctr. Atmospheric Rsch., 1984-85, U.S. Dept. Energy, 1989-92, G. Gunnar Vetleson Found., 1987-92, UN Environ. Program, 1989, EPA, 1988-89, NASA, 1995—, NOAA, 1996. Fellow AAAS (com. climate 1984-89, com. global change 1992—, adv. panel Earth Explorer ency. 1992-95), Am. Soc. Agronomy, Am. Meteorol. Soc. (Outstanding Achievement in Bioclimatology award 1978, councillor 1981-84); mem. Am. Assn. State Climatologists (Nebr. rep. 1979-81), Arid Zone Soc. India, Sigma Xi, Alpha Zeta, Gamma Sigma Rho. Jewish. Club: Cosmos (Washington). Office: Battelle Pacific Northwest Nat Lab 901 D St SW Washington DC 20024-2169

ROSENBERG, PAUL, physicist, consultant; b. N.Y.C., Mar. 31, 1910; s. Samuel and Evelyn (Abbey) R.; m. Marjorie S. Hillson, June 12, 1943; 1 child, Gale B.E. AB, Columbia U., 1930, MA, 1933, PhD, 1941. Chemist Hawthorne Paint & Varnish Corp., N.J., 1930-33; grad. asst. physics Columbia U., 1934-39, lectr., 1939-41; instr. Hunter Coll., N.Y.C., 1939-41; rsch. assoc. elec. enging. MIT, Cambridge, 1941; mem. staff Radiation Lab., Nat. Def. Rsch. Com., 1941-45; pres. Paul Rosenberg Assocs. (cons. physicists), Larchmont, N.Y., 1945—, Inst. Nav., 1950-51; mem. war com. radio Am. Standards Assn., 1942-44; gen. chmn. joint meeting Radio Tech. Commn. for Aeros., Radio Tech. Commn. for Marine Services and Inst. of Nav., 1950; co-chmn. Nat. Tech. Devel. Com. for upper atmostphere and interplanetary nav., 1947-50; mem. maritime research adv. com. Nat. Acad. Scis.-NRC, 1959-60; chmn. cartography panel space programs Earth resources survey NRC, 1973-76; chmn. panel on nav. and traffic control space applications study Nat. Acad. Scis., 1968; bd. dirs. Ctr. for Environment and Man, 1976-85. Mem. editorial com. Jour. Aerospace Scis., 1952-60; contbr. chpts. to books, entries to encys., over 70 articles to sci. tech. publs.; patentee in field. Recipient James S. Cogswell award U.S. Dept. Def., 1986. Fellow AAAS (v.p. 1966-69, mem. coun. 1961-73), IEEE, AIAA (assoc.), Am. Inst. Chemists, Explorers Club; mem. Am. Phys. Soc., Am. Chem. Soc., Nat. Acad. Engring., Acoustical Soc. Am., Armed Forces Communication Assn., Optical Soc. Am., Am. Soc. Photogrammetry (Talbert Abrams Grand award 1955), Am. Assn. Physics Tchrs., N.Y. Acad. Scis., Inst. Navigation (hon., pres. 1950-51), Beach Point Yacht Club (Mamaroneck, N.Y.), Columbia U. Club, Sigma Xi, Zeta Beta Tau. Home: 53 Fernwood Rd Larchmont NY 10538-1705 Office: Paul Rosenberg Assocs PO Box 729 Larchmont NY 10538-0729

ROSENBERG, PHILIP, production designer. Prodn. designer: (films) The Anderson Tapes, 971, The Possession of Joel Delaney, 1972, Child's Play, 1972, From the Mixed-up Files of Mrs. Basil E. Frankweiler, 1973, The Gambler, 1974, Network, 1976, Next Stop, Greenwich Village, 1976, The Sentinel, 1977, (with Tony Walton) The Wiz, 1978 (Academy award nomination best art direction 1978), (with Tony Walton) All the Jazz, 1979 (Academy award best art direction 1979), Eyewitness, 1981, Soup for One, 1982, Lovesick, 1983, Daniel, 1983, Garbo Talks, 1984, The Manhattan Project, 1986, Moonstruck, 1987, Running on Empty, 1988, The January Man, 1989, Family Business, 1989, Q & A, 1990, Other People's Money, 1992, Beyond Innocence, 1993, Guilty as Sin, 1993, The Pelican Brief, 1993, Night Falls on Manhattan, 1995. Office: Art Directors 11365 Ventura Blvd Studio City CA 91604-3148*

ROSENBERG, PIERRE MAX, museum director; b. Paris, Apr. 13, 1936; s. Charles and Gertrude (Nassauer) R.; m. Beatrice de Rothschild, July 29, 1981. Baccalauréat, Lycée Charlemagne, Paris; Licence, Law Faculty, Paris; Diplome, Louvre Sch., Paris. Chief curator dept. paintings Musée du Louvre, Paris, 1982-94, pres., dir., Musée du Louvre, 1994—. Author: Chardin, 1963; Peyron, 1983; (catalogue) La peinture française du XVIIe siècle dans les coll. americaines, 1981; (catalogue) Watteau, 1984, 96, Fragonard, 1987, Fréres Le Nain, 1993, Poussin, 1994. Mem. Soc. Histoire Art Français (pres. 1982-84), Com. Français Histoire Art (pres. 1984), Acad. Française. Home: 35 rue de Vaugirard, 75006 Paris France Office: Musée du Louvre, 34 quai du Louvre, 75058 Paris France

ROSENBERG, RALPH, former state senator, lawyer, consultant, educator; b. Chgo., Oct. 7, 1949; s. Nathan Benjamin and Rhea (Matlow) R.; m. Teresa Marie Sturm, July 11, 1989; children: Jacob Louis, Joel Patrick. BS in Commerce and Bus. Adminstrn., U. Ill., 1972; JD, Drake Law Sch., 1974. Bar: Iowa 1974. Sole practice Rosenberg Law Firm, Ames, Iowa, 1974—; mem. Iowa Ho. of Reps., Des Moines, 1981-90, Iowa Senate, Des Moines, 1990-94; adj. faculty Des Moines Area C.C., 1980—, Drake Law Sch., 1992, Upper Iowa U., 1993, Iowa State U., 1994—; dir. Environ. Planning Rsch. Group, Ames, 1976-77; exec. dir. Story County Legal Aid Soc., Nevada, Iowa, 1977-78; asst. Story County atty. County Attys. Office, Nevada, 1979-81; exec. dir., mng. atty. Youth Law Ctr., Des Moines, 1989-92; coord. Inst. Pub. Leadership, 1994—; exec. dir. Coalition for Family and Childrens Svcs., 1995—. Author, editor: Public Interest Law, 1992; author: Family Theory, Law, Policy and Practice, 1994; editor: Descriptive Analysis of Iowa Environmental Agencies, 1977. Co-chair Midwest Leadership Inst. of Coun. of State Govt.; bd. dirs. Jewish Cmty. Rels. Commn., Iowa Protection and Advocacy, regional adv. bd. Legal Svcs. Corp. Iowa, Child and Family Policy Ctr.; past bd. dirs. Co-op. Child Care Svcs., Ames Cmty. Action Rsch. Group, Rural Iowa. Recipient Outstanding Contbn. to Well-being of Children award Youth and Shelter Svcs., 1992, Excellence in Svc. award Legal Svcs. Group, 1993, Iowa LWV Cornerstone award, 1994, Iowa Farmers' Union Friend of the Farmer award, 1994, Iowa Consumer Action Network Citizen Svc. award, 1994; named LEgislator of Yr., Sierra Club, 1988, Isaak Walton League, 1993; named Legis. Conservationist of Yr., Wildlife Soc., 1988, Elected Ofcl. of Yr., Iowa Corrections Assn., 1984. Mem. Iowa State Bar Assn. (family law com. 1993—), Nat. Conf. State Legislators (criminal justice com. 1986-94). Home: 1202 Northwestern Ave Ames IA 50010-5256 Office: 111 9th St Ste 200 Des Moines IA 50309-4210

ROSENBERG, RICHARD F., physician, radiologist; b. N.Y.C., June 13, 1942; s. Henry J. and Sylvia (Harris) R.; m. Judith Wolf, May 5, 1985; 1 child, Glen. BA, Colgate U., 1964; MD, N.Y. Med. Coll., 1968. Diplomate Am. Bd. Radiology. Intern Met. Hosp., N.Y.C., 1968-69; resident Montefiore Hosp. and Med. Ctr., Bronx, N.Y., 1969-70, 72-74, chief resident, 1974; radiologist Lipsay & Rosenberg, Great Neck, N.Y., 1974-78; dir. gastrointestinal radiology North Shore U. Hosp., Manhasset, N.Y., 1978-82; radiologist, owner Great Neck Radiologists, 1982—; mem. adv. bd. Bank of Great Neck, 1990-94. Contbr. articles to profl. jours. Lt. comdr. USN, 1970-72. Fellow Am. Coll. Gastroenterology; mem. Am. Coll. Radiology, Alpha Omega Alpha. Republican. Office: Great Neck Radiologists 935 Northern Blvd Great Neck NY 11021-5309

ROSENBERG, RICHARD MORRIS, banker; b. Fall River, Mass., Apr. 21, 1930; s. Charles and Betty (Peck) R.; m. Barbara K. Cohen, Oct. 21, 1956; children: Michael, Peter. BS, Suffolk U., 1952; MBA, Golden Gate U., 1962; LLB, Golden Gate Coll., 1966. Publicity asst. Crocker-Anglo Bank, San Francisco, 1959-62; banking services officer Wells Fargo Bank, N.A., San Francisco, 1962-65; asst. v.p. Wells Fargo Bank, N.A., 1965-68, v.p. mktg. dept., 1968, v.p., dir. mktg., 1969, sr. v.p. mktg. and advt. div., 1970-75, exec. v.p., from 1975, vice chmn., 1980-83; vice chmn. Crocker Nat. Corp., 1983-85; pres., chief operating officer Seafirst Corp., 1986-87, also dir.; pres., chief operating officer Seattle First Nat. Bank, 1985-87; vice chmn. bd. BankAm. Corp., San Francisco, 1987-90, chmn., CEO, 1990-96; dir. Airborne Express, Potlatch Corp., Northrop Cor., SBC Comms., Pacific Mut.; past chmn. Mastercard Internat. Bd. dirs. San Francisco Symphony, United Way; trustee Calif. Inst. Tech. Jewish. Office: BankAm Corp Dept 3001-B PO Box 37000 San Francisco CA 94137

ROSENBERG, ROBERT ALLEN, psychologist, educator, optometrist; b. Phila., July 31, 1935; s. Theodore Samuel and Dorothy (Bailes) R.; m. Geraldine Bella Tishler, Sept. 3, 1961; children: Lawrence David, Ronald Joseph. BA, Temple U., 1957, MA, 1964; BS, Pa. Coll. Optometry, 1960, OD, 1961. Lic. optometrist, psychologist, Pa. Instr. Pa. Coll. Optometry, Phila., 1962-65, asst. prof., 1965-67; asst. prof. psychology Community Coll. Phila., 1967-76, assoc. prof., 1976—; pvt. practice optometry, Roslyn, Pa., 1965-95; assoc. in practice optometry, Huntingdon Valley, Pa., 1995—. Contbr. articles to profl. jours. Named Humanitarian Chapel of Four Chaplains Bapt. Temple, 1980. Fellow Am. Acad. Optometry; mem. Am. Optometric Assn., Pa. Optometric Assn., Bucks-Montgomery Optometric Assn., Alumni Assn. Pa. Coll. Optometry (v.p. 1991—, sec. 1992—). Avocations: singing, acting, photography, writing, public speaking. Home: 970 Corn Crib Dr Huntingdon Valley PA 19006-3304 Office: Community Coll Phila 1700 Spring Garden St Philadelphia PA 19130-3936

ROSENBERG, ROBERT BRINKMANN, technology organization executive; b. Chgo., Mar. 19, 1937; s. Sidney and Gertrude (Brinkmann) R.; m. Patricia Margaret Kane, Aug. 1, 1959 (dec. Feb. 1988); children: John Richard Debra Ann; m. Maryann Bartoli Manrot, June 25, 1989. B.S. in Chem. Engring. with distinction, Ill. Inst. Tech., 1958, M.S. in Gas Tech, 1961, Ph.D. in Gas Tech, 1964. Registered profl. engr., Ill. Adj. asst. prof. Ill. Inst. Tech., 1965-69; mem. staff Inst. Gas Tech., Chgo., 1962-77; v.p. engring. research Inst. Gas Tech., 1973-77; v.p. research and devel. Gas Research Inst., Chgo., 1977-78; exec. v.p. Gas Research Inst., 1978-84, v.p., 1984-96; pres. RBR @ Vision, Oakbrook Terrace, Ill., 1996—; also bd. dirs. IEA Internat. Ctr. for Gas Tech. Info. Author. Mem. Hinsdale (Ill.) Home Rule Ad Hoc Com., 1975-77; bd. dirs. Hinsdale Arts Coun., 1977-85, dir. emeritus, 1985-95; pres. Triangle Frat. Edn. Found., 1974-96; mem. vis. com. dept. chemistry U. Tex.; mem. adv. coun. U. Tex. Coll. Natural Scis. Found., 1990-95. Recipient Gas Industry Research award, 1985, Energy Exec. of Yr. award, 1987, Triangle Frat. Svc. Key and Outstanding Alumnus awards, 1987. Mem. AIChE, Am. Gas Assn. (operating sect. award of merit 1989), Inst. Gas Engrs., Combustion Inst. (past treas. bd. cen. states sect.), Atlantic Gas Rsch. Exch. (chmn. mng. bd. 1980-96), Internat. Gas Union (U.S. rep. subcom. F-2 1974-83), Gas Appliance Engrs. Soc. (past trustee), Air Pollution Control Assn. (past sect. com. residential pollution sources). Patentee in field. Home: 28 Lake Ridge Club Dr Burr Ridge IL 60521-7937 Office: RBR @ Vision Ste 800 Two Mid America Plaza Oakbrook Terrace IL 60181

ROSENBERG, ROBERT CHARLES, housing corporation executive; b. Bronx, N.Y., Oct. 21, 1934; s. Bernard L. and Flora (Popiel) R.; BS, NYU, 1955, JD (hon.), 1995; LLB, Columbia U., 1958; m. Diane Stricof, Jan. 28, 1962 (dec.); children: Andrew, Scott; m. Frances Kaufman, Sept. 11, 1976; stepchildren: Michael Kaufman, Benjamin Kaufman. Bar: N.Y. 1959. Adminstrv. asst. N.Y. State Dept. Law, N.Y.C., 1957-58; assoc. firm Barron Rice & Rochmore, N.Y.C., 1959-62, Carro Spanbock & Londin, N.Y.C., 1962-68; first dep. commr. for devel. dept., N.Y.C. Housing and Devel. Adminstrn., 1968-73; dir., 1st sr. v.p. Starrett Corp., N.Y.C., 1973-97; gen. mgr. Starrett City; pres., chmn. bd. Grenadier Realty Corp., 1976-97; pres. Rosenberg Housing Group, 1997—; lectr. Practicing Law Inst., Real Estate Bd. N.Y.C., Harvard U. Kennedy Sch. of Govt., Beijing Inst. of Design, U. Nancy (France), Columbia U., N.Y.U and others; fed. receiver Chester (Pa.) Housing Authority, 1994—. Candidate for N.Y. State Assembly, 1958, 65; sec. N.Y. State Assn. Young Republican Clubs, 1959-61; bd. dirs., chmn. Bklyn. Philharmonic; corp. rep. Nat. Com. U.S.-China Rels.; mem. N.Y.C. Mayor's-Beijing (China) Sister City Com.; bd. dirs. Bklyn. Acad. Music; v.p. Citizen's Housing and Planning Council, exec. v.p. N.Y.C. Associated Builders and Owners; v.p., exec. commn. Nat. Housing Conf. Served with USAF, 1958. Mem. ABA, N.Y. State Bar Assn., N.Y. County Lawyers Assn., Nat. Assn. Housing and Renewal Ofcls., N.Y. State Assn. Housing and Renewal Ofcls., Urban Land Inst. Author N.Y. acts for residential constrn., rent. Home: 254 E 68 St New York NY 10021-1811 Office: 419 Park Ave S New York NY 10016-8410 also: 1230 Pennsylvania Ave Brooklyn NY 11239-1915

ROSENBERG, ROGER NEWMAN, neurologist, educator; b. Milw., Mar. 3, 1939; s. Sol J. and Cora D. (Newman) R.; m. Adrienne Turick, June 24, 1962; children—Jennifer, Lara. Student, Tufts U., 1957-60; BS, Northwestern U., 1961, MD with distinction, 1964. Diplomate Am. Bd. Psychiatry and Neurology. Intern Harvard Med. Service, Beth Israel Hosp., Boston, 1964-65; resident in neurology Neurol. Inst., Columbia U., N.Y.C., 1965-67, instr. neurology, 1967-68; research assoc. Lab. of Biochem. Genetics, NIH, Bethesda, Md., 1968-70; clin. instr. Howard U. Med. Sch., Washington, 1969-70; asst. prof. neuroscis. Sch. Medicine, U. Calif.-San Diego, 1970-71; assoc. prof. neuroscis. and pediatrics, attending neurologist Univ. Hosp., U. Calif.-La Jolla, 1971-74; prof., chmn. dept. neurology U. Tex. Southwestern Med. Ctr., Dallas, 1973-91, prof. physiology, 1976—, Zale Disting. chair, prof. neurology, 1990—, dir. Alzheimer's Disease Rsch. Ctr., 1989—; attending neurologist Parkland Meml. Hosp. and Children's Med. Ctr., Dallas, 1974—, Zale Lipshy Univ. Hosp., 1990—; mem. staff Presbyn. Hosp., Dallas, 1974—, St. Paul's Hosp., Dallas, 1974—; cons. staff VA Hosp., Dallas, 1974—; mem. nat. med. adv. bd. Nat. Ataxia Found., Mpls., 1971—, Myasthenia Gravis Found., 1973; chmn. med. adv. bd., dir. med. sci. research Internat. Joseph Diseases Found., Livermore, Calif., 1977—; lectr. Japanese Soc. Neurology, 1987, 94, Chinese Neurol. Soc., 1987, Spanish Neurol. Soc., 1992; chmn. bd. sci. councilors NIH, 1984-86; pres. (hon.), Intl. French Soc. of Neurology Charcot Centenary Symposium, 1993. Editor Jour. Neurogenetics; mem. editorial bd. Neurology, 1977-82, 91—, Trends in Neurosci., 1980-86, Current Opinion in Neurology & Neurosurgery, 1990—; chief editor Archives of Neurology, 1997—; contbr. articles to med. jours. Bd. dirs. Winston Sch., Dallas, 1974-80. 1st Woody Guthrie scholar, 1971; USPHS grantee; recipient Disting. Alumnus award Neurol. Inst., N.Y., 1994. Fellow AAAS; mem. Am. Acad. Neurology (chmn. sci. program com. nat. meetings 1979-84, elected councillor exec. bd. 1984-89, pres. 1991-93), Am. Neurochem. Soc., Tissue Culture Soc., Soc. Neurosci., Am. Fedn. Clin. Rsch., Soc. Pediat. Rsch., Internat. Child Neurology Assn., Am. Neurol. Assn. (1st v.p. 1987), Ctrl. Soc. Neurol. Rsch., Can. Congress Neurol. Scis. (hon.), Spanish Neurol. Soc. (hon. 1994), Sigma Xi, Alpha Omega Alpha (Merit award Northwestern U. Alumni Assn. 1986). Home: 4425 Wildwood Rd Dallas TX 75209-2801 Office: U Tex Southwestern Med Ctr Dallas TX 75235

ROSENBERG, RUTH HELEN BORSUK, lawyer; b. Plainfield, N.J., Feb. 23, 1935; d. Irwin and Pauline (Rudich) Borsuk; children—Joshua Cohen, Sarah, Rebecca, Daniel, Miriam, Tziporah, Isaac. A.B., Douglass Coll., 1956; J.D., U. Pa., 1963. Bar: Pa. 1964, N.Y. 1967, D.C. 1986, Md. 1987, Va. 1994, Mass. 1995, U.S. Ct. Appeals (3d cir.) 1969, U.S. Supreme Ct. 1969, U.S. Ct. Appeals (4th cir.) 1994. Law clk. Ct. Common Pleas, Phila., 1963-64; assoc. Blank, Rudenko, Klaus & Rome, Phila., 1964-67; atty. Office Corp. Counsel, City of Rochester, 1967-68; assoc. Nixon, Hargrave, Devans & Doyle, Washington, 1968-74, ptnr., 1975—; vice chairperson character and fitness com. Appellate divsn. 4th dept. 7th Jud. Dist. N.Y. Supreme Ct., 1976-80, mem. grievance com., 1981-84. Bd. dirs. Soc. Prevention Cruelty to Children, 1976-77, N.Y. Civil Liberties Union, 1972-85, v.p. 1976-85; bd. dirs. Jewish Home and Infirmary, 1978-83, pres., 1980-83; v.p. Jewish Fedn. Rochester, 1983, Yachad, Inc., Jewish Cmty. Housing Devel. Corp., 1990-94; bd. dirs. Jewish Cmty. Coun., Greater Washington, 1989-93, Leadership Washington, 1990-91, Libr. Theatre, 1994—, Op. Understanding, D.C., 1994-95. Mem. ABA, D.C. Bar Assn., Md. Bar Assn., Va. Bar Assn., Phi Beta Kappa. Office: Nixon Hargrave Devans & Doyle LLP 1 Thomas Cir NW Ste 700 Washington DC 20005-5802

ROSENBERG, SAMUEL NATHAN, French and Italian language educator; b. N.Y.C., Jan. 19, 1936; s. Israel and Etta (Friedland) R. AB, Columbia U., 1957; PhD, Johns Hopkins U., 1965. Instr. Columbia U., N.Y.C., 1960-61; lectr. Ind. U., Bloomington, Ind., 1962-65; asst. prof. Ind. U., Bloomington, 1965-69; assoc. prof. Ind. U., Bloomington, Ind., 1969-81; prof. dept. French and Italian Ind. U., Bloomington, 1981—, chmn. dept., 1977-84. Author: Modern French CE, 1970, (with others) Harper's Grammar of French, 1983, (with W. Apel) French Secular Compositions of the 14th Century, 3 vols., 1970-72, (with H. Tischler) Chanter m'estuet: Songs of the Trouveres, 1981; translator: (with S. Danon) Ami and Amile, 1981, revised edit., 1996, Lyrics and Melodies of Gace Brulè, 1985, (with H. Tischler) The Monophonic Songs in the Roman de Fauvel, 1991, Lancelor-Grail Cycle, vol. 2, 1993, Chansons des trouvères, 1995. Pres. Mid-Am. Festival of the Arts, Inc., Bloomington, Ind., 1984-85. Woodrow Wilson Found. fellow, 1959-60; Fulbright fellow, 1960-61; Lilly Faculty fellow, 1986-87. Mem MLA, Am. Assn. Tchrs. French; mem. Medieval Acad. Am., Internat. Courtly Lit. Soc., Am. Literary Translators Assn., Phi Beta Kappa. Home: PO Box 1164 Bloomington IN 47402-1164 Office: Dept French and Italian Ind U Bloomington IN 47405

ROSENBERG, SARAH ZACHER, institute arts administration executive, humanities administration consultant; b. Kelem, Lithuania, Jan. 10, 1931; came to U.S., 1938; d. David Meir Zacher and Rachel Korbman; m. Norman J. Rosenberg, Dec. 30, 1950; children: Daniel, Alyssa. BA in History, U. Nebr., 1970, MA in Am. History, 1973. Rsch. historian U. Mid-Am., Lincoln, Nebr., 1974-78, program developer dept. humanities, 1978-79, asst. dir. div. acad. planning, 1980-81, dir. program devel., 1981-82; exec. dir. Nebr. Humanities Coun., Lincoln, 1982-87, Nebr. Found. for Humanities, Lincoln, 1984-87; exec. dir. Am. Inst. for Conservation Hist. and Artistic Works, Washington, 1987—, exec. dir. found., 1991—; program officer, spl. cons. mus. div. NEH, Washington, 1987, external reviewer, 1981, 89; lay participant long-range planning conf. Nebr. Bar Assn., Hastings, 1986. Co-editor: The Great Plains Experience: Readings in the History of a Region, 1978; contbr. articles to profl. jours. Action mem. Haddasah, Lincoln, 1961-87, Tifereth Israel Synagogue, 1961-87, Beth El Congregation, Bethesda, Md., 1988—; bd. dirs. Sta. KUCV, affiliate Nat. Pub. Radio, Lincoln, 1986-87, Lincoln Community Playhouse, 1986-87. NEH grantee, 1981, 86, merit awards, 1983, 87; Humanities Resource Ctr. grantee, Peter Kiewit Found., 1984. Mem. Am. Hist. Assn., Western Hist. Assn., Alpha Theta. Democrat. Home: 8102 Appalachian Ter Potomac MD 20854-4050 Office: Am Inst for Conservation 1717 K St NW Ste 301 Washington DC 20006-1501

ROSENBERG, SAUL ALLEN, oncologist, educator; b. Cleve., Aug. 2, 1927. BS, Western Res. U., 1948, MD, 1953. Diplomate Am. Bd. Internal Medicine, Am. Bd. Oncology. Intern Univ. Hosp., Cleve., 1953-54; resident in internal medicine Peter Bent Brigham Hosp., Boston, 1954-61; research asst. toxicology AEC Med. Research Project, Western Res. U., 1948-53; asst. prof. medicine and radiology Stanford (Calif.) U., 1961-65, assoc. prof., 1965-79, chief div. oncology, 1965-93, prof., 1970-95; prof. emeritus, 1995—; Am. Cancer Soc. prof. Stanford (Calif.) U., 1983-89, assoc. dean, 1989-92; chmn. bd. No. Calif. Cancer Program, 1974-80. Contbr. articles to profl. jours. Served to lt. M.C. USNR, 1954-56. Master ACP; mem. Am. Assn. Cancer Research, Inst. Medicine Nat. Acad. Sci., Am. Fedn. Clin. Research, Am. Soc. Clin. Oncology (pres. 1982-83), Assn. Am. Physicians, Calif. Acad. Medicine, Radiation Research Soc., Western Soc. Clin. Research, Western Assn. Physicians. Office: Stanford U Sch Medicine Div Oncology M-211 Stanford CA 94305

ROSENBERG, SEYMOUR, psychologist, educator; b. Newark, Sept. 7, 1926; s. Morris and Celia (Weiss) R.; children: Harold Stanley, Michael Seth. B.S., The Citadel, 1948; M.A., Ind. U., 1951, Ph.D., 1952. Research psychologist USAF, San Antonio, 1952-58, U. Kans., Lawrence, 1958-59, Bell Telephone Labs., Murray Hill, N.J., 1959-65; vis. prof. psychology Columbia, N.Y.C., 1965-66; prof. psychology Rutgers U., New Brunswick, N.J., 1966—; chmn. dept. psychology Rutgers U., 1981-83, 94-95; adj. prof. Rutgers U. Med. Sch., 1974—; vis. scholar U. Leuven, Belgium, 1983, 92, Université de Provence, France, 1990; panel mem. NSF, 1970-72. Cons. editor Jours. Personality and Social Psychology, 1968-69; assoc. editor, 1970-73; contbr. articles to profl. jours. Served with USN, 1945-46. NSF grantee, 1965—; NIMH, 1966-68; NIMH research scientist grantee, 1968-73; Social Sci. Research Council fellow, 1973-74. Fellow Am. Psychol. Assn.; mem. Soc. Exptl. Social Psychology, Psychometric Soc., Classification Soc., N.Y. Acad. Sci., Eastern Psychol. Assn. Home: 689 Canal Rd Somerset NJ 08873-7327 Office: Rutgers U Dept Psychology ED Livingston Campus New Brunswick NJ 08903

ROSENBERG, SHIRLEY SIROTA, publications and public relations executive; b. Bklyn.; d. Charles and Donia (Rudoy) Sirota; m. Jerome D. Rosenberg; children: Jonathan, Hindy. BA, Bklyn. Coll. Freelance writer, 1968—; contract writer-editor Dept. HEW, Washington, 1968-72; writer, editor Smithsonian Instn., Washington, 1972-77; instr. George Washington U., 1979—, Georgetown U., Washington, 1992; pres. SSR, Inc., Washington, 1977—; Washington corr. Parent's mag.; cons. NSF, Nat. Task Force on Minorities, Women and the Handicapped in Sci. and Enging., Joseph P. Kennedy Inst., also bd. dirs.; cons. Office of Comm., U.S. Holocaust Meml. Coun., Humanities mag. NEH, George Washington U. Pubs. Specialist program, ARC Blood Svcs., Georgetown U. Pubs. Specialist Program. Author: The First Oil Rush, 1967, Code of Ethics and Professional Standards for Print Media Professionals, 1981, 92; contbr. articles to trade and profl. jours.; editor, coord. top level nat. and internat. position papers. Recipient 1st place award Soc. Tech. Communicators, 1983, Achievement award, 1990, Merit award Art Dirs. Club, 1984. Mem. Am. Soc. Journalists and Authors (past v.p.), Assn. Edit. Businesses (past v.p., bd. dirs.), Am. Med. Writers Assn., EdPress (past v.p., treas., bd. dirs. Silver award, 1992, 93, 96, Gold awards, 1995, 96), Nat. Assn. Govt. Communicators (sec., bd. dirs. 1997, 1st Pl. award 1981, 95, 2d Pl. award 1990), Washington Women in Pub. Rels. (past bd. dirs.).

ROSENBERG, STEPHEN, lawyer; b. N.Y.C., May 18, 1943; s. Leo A. and Freda (Block) R.; m. Lucille Susan Abrams, June 23, 1968; children: Jonathan Paul, Michele Sydney. AB, Columbia Coll., 1964; LLB, Harvard U., 1967. Bar: N.Y. Assoc. Delson & Gordon, N.Y.C., 1968-69; assoc. Carro, Spanbock, Kaster & Cuiffo, N.Y.C., 1969-76, ptnr., 1976-90, counsel, 1990-93; sec. Zahren Fin. Corp., Avon, Conn., 1990—, Zahren Alternative Power Corp., Avon, 1994—; ptnr. Newman Tannenbaum Helpern Syracuse & Hirschtritt, LLP, N.Y.C., 1993—; profl. lectr. in field. Contbr. articles to profl. jours. Pres. Old Bridge (N.J.) Theater Guild, 1984-85, Timber Glen Civic Assn., Old Bridge, 1985-87; trustee Temple Emanuel, Westfield, N.J., 1992-94, v.p. 94—. Mem. ABA, N.Y. Bar Assn., Columbia Coll. Alumni Assn., Harvard Law Sch. Alumni Assn., B'nai B'rith (trustee 1988-89). Avocations: travel, tennis. Office: Newman Tannenbaum Helpern Syracuse & Hirschtritt 900 3rd Ave New York NY 10022-4728

ROSENBERG, STEVEN AARON, surgeon, medical researcher; b. N.Y.C., Aug. 2, 1940; s. Abraham and Harriet (Wendroff) R.; m. Alice Ruth O'Connell, Sept. 15, 1968; children—Beth, Rachel, Naomi. B.A., Johns Hopkins U., 1960, M.D., 1963; Ph.D., Harvard U., 1968. Resident in surgery Peter Bent Brigham Hosp., Boston, 1963-64, 68-69, 72-74; resident fellow in immunology Harvard U. Med. Sch., Boston, 1969-70; clin. assoc. immunology br. Nat. Cancer Inst., Bethesda, Md., 1970-72; chief surgery Nat. Cancer Inst., 1974—, assoc. editor Jour., 1974—; mem. U.S.-USSR Coop. Immunotherapy Program, 1974—, U.S.-Japan Coop. Immunotherapy Program, 1975—; clin. assoc. prof. surgery George Washington U. Med. Ctr., 1976—; prof. surgery Uniformed Services U. Health Scis. Contbr. articles to profl. jours. Author: The Transformed Cell: Unlocking the Mysteries of Cancer, 1992. Served with USPHS, 1970-72. Recipient Meritorious Service medal Pub. Health Service, 1981; co-recipient Armand Hammer Cancer prize, 1985; named 1990 Scientist of the Yr., R&D magazine. Mem. Soc. Univ. Surgeons, Am. Surg. Assn., Soc. Surg. Oncology, Surg. Biology Club II, Halsted Soc., Transplantation Soc., Am. Assn. Immunologists, Am. Assn. Cancer Research, Phi Beta Kappa, Alpha Omega Alpha. Office: Nat Cancer Inst Clinical Sci 31 Center Dr Bldg 10 Bethesda MD 20892-0001*

ROSENBERG, STUART, film director; b. Bklyn., Aug. 11, 1927; s. David and Sara (Kaminsky) R.; m. Margot Pohoryles, Aug. 4, 1950; 1 son, Benjamin. B.A., NYU, 1949. Editor, producer, dir. over 300 TV shows, 1950-65, in films, 1965—; films directed include Murder, Inc., 1962, Cool Hand Luke, 1967, April Fools, 1969, WUSA, 1970, Voyage of the Damned, 1977, Amityville Horror, 1979, Brubaker, 1980, The Pope of Greenwich Village, 1984; (Recipient Emmy award for dramatic directing 1962, Dir.'s Guild award nominee (4). Served with USNR, 1945-47.

ROSENBERG, SUSAN, lawyer; b. Bklyn., July 24, 1945; d. Harold and Kitty (Paris) Schildkraut; m. Neil David Rosenberg, June 10, 1967; children—Lonnie Stuart, Seth Ian. A.B., Washington U., 1967; J.D. cum laude, Marquette U., 1983. Bar: Wis. 1983. Tchr. history Balt. City Pub. Schs., 1967-70; assoc. Samster, Aiken, & Mawicke, S.C., Milw., 1983-88; ptnr. Aiken & Mawicke, S.C., Milw., 1988-90, Domnitz Mawicke Goisman & Rosenberg SC, 1990—; Bd. dirs. Women to Women, Inc., Milw., 1984-86, Ctr. Pub. Representation, 1992-95. Thomas More scholar, 1981-83; Adolph I. Mandelker scholar, 1982-83. Mem. Wis. Acad. Trial Lawyers (bd. dirs. 1989—), Assn. Women Lawyers (bd. dirs. 1994—, pres. 1995-96). Jewish. Mem. Marquette U. Law Rev., 1981-83. Office: Domnitz Mawicke Golsman & Rosenberg S C 1509 N Prospect Ave Milwaukee WI 53202-2323

ROSENBERG, THEODORE ROY, financial executive; b. Nyack, N.Y., Aug. 6, 1933; s. Rebecca Sheer R.; m. Eleanor Schmalsteig, Feb. 19, 1956 (div. 1976); children: Bradley Scott, Martha Ann; m. Mary Frances McVay, Sept. 21, 1991. BS, U. Conn., 1955; MBA, U. Pa., 1964. Commd. 2nd lt. U.S. Army, 1955, advanced through grades to col., 1976, retired, 1982; portfolio mgr. The Burney Co., Falls Church, Va., 1979—, v.p. mktg., 1982-94, v.p., 1994-95; pres., 1995—. Active exec. com. Our Daily Bread, Fairfax, Va., 1991—; bd. dirs. Army Transp. Mus., U. Conn. Found., 1995—. Decorated Legion of Merit, Bronze Star; recipient Vietnam Medal of Honor, Govt. of Vietnam, 1966; inducted into Alumni Hall of Fame, U. Conn. Sch. Bus. Adminstrn., 1994. Mem. U. Pa. Mid-Atlantic Regional Adv. Bd., Wharton Club of Washington (Man of Yr. 1995). Avocations: scuba diving, snorkeling. Office: The Burney Co 121 Rowell Ct Falls Church VA 22046-3126

ROSENBERG, THOMAS FREDERICK, physician; b. St. Louis, June 17, 1941; s. William Lawrence Rosenberg and Gertrude Lubens; m. Adrienne Merle France, July 3, 1966; children: Lisa Jill, Jason Gregory. AB, Washington & Jefferson U., 1963. Physician Alergy and Asthma Ctr., Kans., 1974—; clin. asst. prof. pediatrics Sch. of Medicine U. Kans., Wichita, 1975-87, clin. assoc. prof. pediatrics Sch. of Medicine, 1987—; clin. asst. prof. Wichita State U., 1987-90. Maj. USAF, 1970-74. Fellow Am. Acad. Pediatrics, Am. Coll. Allergy & Immunology; mem. NASW (Citizen of the Yr. Kans. chpt. 1983). Avocations: golf, reading, travel. Office: Allergy and Asthma Ctr 8110 E 32nd St N Wichita KS 67226-2616

ROSENBERGER, BRYAN DAVID, lawyer; b. Johnstown, Pa., Oct. 8, 1950; s. Clarence Haines and Ida Rae (Neiderheiser) R.; m. Barbara Leah Byer, July 4, 1977; children: Laura Michelle, Lisa Renee. BS, Juniata Coll., 1971; JD, Coll. of William and Mary, 1974. Bar: Pa. 1974. Assoc. Eckert Seamans Cherin & Mellott, Pitts., 1974-82, ptnr., 1983—, chmn. corp. and bus. dept., 1992—; mem. exec. com., 1994—. Active new leadership bd. Pitts. Symphony Soc., 1990—. Mem. ABA, Pa. Bar Assn., Allegheny County Bar Assn. Home: 1358 Oakledge Ct Upper Saint Clair PA 15241-3540 Office: Eckert Seamans Cherin & Mellott 600 Grant St Ste 42 Pittsburgh PA 15219-2703

ROSENBERGER, CAROL, concert pianist; b. Detroit, Nov. 1, 1935; d. Maurice Seiberling and Whilamet (Gibson) R. B.F.A., Carnegie-Mellon U., 1955; postgrad., Acad. Performing Arts, Vienna, 1956-59. Mem. artist faculty U. So. Calif.; vis. artist numerous colls. and univs. Internat. concert career, 1964—; New York debut, 1970; appeared several times at Carnegie Hall; soloist Am. Symphony, Nat. Symphony, Royal Philharmonic, San Diego Symphony, Detroit Symphony, Houston Symphony, St. Louis Symphony, Indpls. Symphony, Los Angeles Chamber Orch.; performed world premiere of Buenaventura; piano concerts with Philippine Philharmonic, 1977, Am. Symphony, 1977; recital series in Am., European, Asian music capitals; recordings include Hindemith's Four Temperaments with London Royal Philharm., Water Music of the Impressionists, works of Beethoven, Schubert, Szymanowski, Night Moods, 1989, Perchance To Dream, 1989, Reveries: Music of Chopin, others; contbr. articles to music publs. Recipient Steinway Centennial medal, 1954, Critics Choice award Gramaphone mag., 1980. Mem. Nat. Acad. Rec. Arts and Scis. Chosen to represent Am. women musicians by Nat. Commn. on Observance Internat. Womens Year, 1976. Office: care Dorothy Cone Artist Rep 60 E 86th St New York NY 10028-1009 also: Delos Internat Inc 1645 Vine St Ste 340 Los Angeles CA 90028-8842*

ROSENBERGER, DAVID A., research scientist, cooperative extension specialist; b. Quakertown, Pa., Sept. 14, 1947; s. Henry and Ada C. (Geissinger) R.; m. Carol J. Freeman, July 28, 1973; children: Sara, Matthew, Nathan. BS in Biology, Goshen Coll., 1969; PhD in Plant Pathology, Mich. State U., 1977. Asst. prof. Hudson Valley lab. Cornell U., Highland, N.Y., 1977-84, assoc. prof., 1984—; supt. Hudson Valley Lab. Cornell U., Highland, 1990—. Mem. AAAS, Am. Phytopathological Soc., Coun. Agrl. Sci. and Tech. Avocations: church activities, gardening, hiking, jogging. Office: Cornell U Hudson Valley Lab PO Box 727 Highland NY 12528

ROSENBERGER, ERNST HEY, judge; b. Hamburg, Germany, Aug. 31, 1931; came to U.S., 1935, naturalized, 1943; s. Ferdinand and Edith (Heymann) R.; m. Judith Ann Brailey, June 10, 1978; children: John Brailey, Anne Elizabeth. BA, CCNY, 1955; JD, N.Y. Law Sch., 1958; cert. in criminal law and practice, Northwestern U., summer 1960; cert., Nat. Coll. State Judiciary, U. Nev., 1976; LLM, U. Va., 1996. Bar: N.Y. 1958, U.S. Dist. Ct. 1959, 61, U.S. Ct. Appeals 1962, U.S. Customs Ct 1962, U.S. Supreme Ct. 1970. Assoc. Kunstler & Kunstler, N.Y.C., 1958-59; pvt. practice N.Y.C., 1959-69; ptnr. Ordover, Rosenberger & Rosen, N.Y.C., 1970-72; judge Criminal Ct. City of N.Y., 1972-76; acting justice Supreme Ct. N.Y., 1973-76, justice, 1977—; presiding justice Extraordinary Spl. and Trial Term of Supreme Ct., 1978-85; justice Appellate divsn. Supreme Ct. N.Y., 1985—; instr. courses for N.Y. State Supreme Ct. Justices, N.Y. Civil and Criminal Ct.; mem. faculty Hastings Coll. Law, U. Calif., San Francisco, 1979; adj. prof. law N.Y. Law Sch., 1976—; guest lectr. Bklyn. Law Sch., St. John's Law Sch., John Jay Coll., New Sch., Pratt Inst., N.Y.C. Police Dept., NYU Postgrad. Med. Sch.; chmn. Criminal Trial Advocacy Course, Appellate divsn., 1st Jud. Dept.; tech. assistance and evaluations cons. to dir. legal svcs. OEO, Washington, 1970; U.S. rep. to study youth laws and cts., Germany, 1975. Editor in chief: N.Y. Law Rev. (Moot Ct. award); contbr. book reviews to profl. jours. Trustee N.Y. Law Sch., Tng. Inst. Mental Health Practitioners, Congregation Habonim; bd. dirs. Blue Card. With U.S. Army, 1949-51. N.Y. Law Sch. scholar, 1958, Northwestern U. scholar, summer 1960, U. Va. scholar, 1993-95. Mem. ABA, Am. Judicature Soc., Am. Soc. Legal History, N.Y. State Bar Assn. (mem. exec. com. criminal justice sect., award for work in Criminal Law Edn. 1980, award for Outstanding Jud. Contbn. to Criminal Justice 19890, Assn. Justices Supreme Ct. State of N.Y., NCYLA Am. Inn of Ct. (pres.), New York County Lawyers Assn. (guest lectr.), Assn. of Bar of City of N.Y., Scribes. Jewish. Home: 1165 Fifth Ave New York NY 10029 Office: Supreme Ct NY 27 Madison Ave New York NY 10010-2201

ROSENBERGER, JAMES LANDIS, statistician, educator, consultant; b. Hatfield, Pa., Nov. 15, 1946; s. Raymond Henning and Sallie Moyer (Landis) R.; m. Gloria Horst, June 14, 1970; children: Grant Horst, Laura Horst, Kurt Horst. BA in Math., Ea. Mennonite U., 1968; MS in Math., Polytechnic U., N.Y.C., 1972; PhD in Biometry, Cornell U., 1977. Programmer and statis. asst. NYU Med. Ctr., 1968-72; asst. prof. stats. Pa. State U., University Park, 1976-82, assoc. prof. stats., 1982-92, acting head stats. dept., 1990-91, head stats. dept., 1991—, prof. stats., 1992—; rsch. fellow in biostats. Harvard U. Sch. Pub. Health, Boston, 1980; vis. lectr. biometry U. Zimbabwe, Harare, 1984-86; statistician Strategic Hwy. Rsch. Program, Washington, 1986-92; cons. Minitab, Inc., State College, Pa., 1986-92, Pa. Dept. Revenue, Harrisburg, 1986-88. Editor newsletter Statis. Computing & Statis. Graphics, 1993-95; contbr. articles to profl. jours. Mem. citizen adv. com. State College Area Sch. Dist., 1989-90; bd. trustees Ea. Mennonite U., Harrisburg, 1989—, vice chair, 1995-97; treas. Boy Scout Troop 31, State College, 1992-95. Postdoctoral fellow Nat. Cancer Inst., 1980. Fellow Am. Statis. Assn. mem. The Biometry Soc. (program chair 1996), Inst. Math. Stats., Bernoulli Soc., Internat. Statis. Inst. Democrat. Mennonite. Avocations: sailing, skiing, jogging, biking, reading. Office: Pa State U Dept Stats University Park PA 16802-2111

ROSENBERRY, WILLIAM KENNETH, lawyer, educator; b. St. Louis, Aug. 14, 1946; s. William Hugh and Shirley Anne (Love) R.; m. Linda Lou Lang, Aug. 24, 1968 (div. 1985); children: Ashlie Anne, Allison Renee; m. Donna L. Pruitt; stepchildren: Corey David Pruitt, Lindsey Lee Pruitt. BBA, U. Tex., Arlington, 1967; JD, Baylor U., 1970. Bar: Tex. 1970, Colo. 1991, U.S. Dist. Ct. (no. dist.) Tex. 1971; bd. cert. specialist in comml. real estae law, residential real estae law, Tex. Assoc. Hinds & Chambers, Arlington, 1970-71; ptnr. Duke, Rosenberry, Duke & Jelinek, Arlington, 1971-76; pvt. practice, Arlington, 1976—; mem. faculty U. Tex., 1991—; bd. dirs. Equitable Bank, NA, Arlington, Equitable Bankshares, Dallas; gen. mgr. Triple R. Properties. Assoc. editor Baylor Law Rev., 1969. Pres. Pantego Christian Acad. Boosters, Arlington, 1990-92; mem. Arlington City Zoning Bd., 1989-92. Recipient oustanding part-time faculty teaching award dept. real estate and fin. U. Tex., 1992; named to Outstanding Young Men in Am., 1980. Mem. Arlington Bar Assn. (bd. dirs. 1987), Arlington Sportsmans Club, Baylor Bear Club, Arlington Republican Club. Mem. Pantego Bible Ch. Avocations: fishing, hunting, jogging. Office: 3010 W Park Row Dr Arlington TX 76013-2048

ROSENBLATT, ALBERT MARTIN, judge; b. N.Y.C., Jan. 17, 1936; s. Isaac and Fannie (Dachs) R.; m. Julia Carlson, Aug. 23, 1970; 1 dau., Elizabeth. BA, U. Pa., 1957; LLB (JD), Harvard U., 1960. Bar: N.Y. 1961. Dist. atty. Dutchess County, N.Y., 1969-75, county judge, 1976-81; justice N.Y. State Supreme Ct., 1982-89, appellate div., 1989—; chief adminstrv. judge N.Y. State, 1987-89; vis. prof. Vassar Coll., 1993—; mem. N.Y. State Fair Trial Free Press Conf., 1973-75; creator Dutchess County 1st consumer protection bur., 1973; instr. newly elected state supreme ct. judges and county judges; chmn., curriculum head tng. programs state dist. attys., asst. dist. attys., 1974, 75; instr. N.Y. State Police Acad. law tng., 1981; lectr. Nat. Dist. Attys. Assn., 1968-74. Area fund raising rep. Harvard U. Law Sch., 1974; alumni fund raising chmn. U. Pa., 1965, 66; bd. dirs. United Way Community Chest, 1970; bd. dirs. Bardavon 1869 Opera House, Dutchess County Hist. Soc.; mem. adv. bd. Jewish Cmty. Ctr., 1987—. With USAR, 1960-66. Mem. N.Y. State Bar Assn. (named Outstanding Prosecutor 1974, Outstanding Jud. Svcs. award 1994), N.Y. State Dist. Attys. Assn. (pres. 1974, Frank S. Hogan award 1987, Jud. Svcs. award, 1994), Profl. Ski Instrs. Am. (cert. 1984—). Republican. Jewish. Club: Baker St. Irregulars (former assoc. editor Baker St. Jour.). Mem. bd. editors N.Y. State Bar Jour., 1992—; contbr. to N.Y. State Bench Book for Trial Judges, 1986-87; contbr. articles on law to profl. jours. and popular mags. Home: 300 Freedom Rd Pleasant Valley NY 12569-5437 Office: Supreme Ct Chambers 40 Garden St Poughkeepsie NY 12601-3131

ROSENBLATT, ARTHUR ISAAC, architect, former museum director; b. N.Y.C., Aug. 31, 1931; s. Harry and Helen (Satz) R.; m. Ruth Anne Turteltaub, Aug. 5, 1956; children: Paul Mark, Judith Alice. Diploma in architecture, Cooper Union, 1952; BArch, Carnegie-Mellon U., 1956. Registered architect, N.Y. Designer Katzman Assocs., N.Y.C., 1956-57, Isadore & Zachary Rosenfield, N.Y.C., 1957-60, Skidmore, Owings & Merrill-Harrison, Abramovitz, Pomerance and Breines, N.Y.C., 1960-61; chief designer Irwing S. Chanin, Architect, N.Y.C., 1961-65; first dep. commr. N.Y.C. Dept. Parks, Recreation and Cultural Affairs, 1966-68; v.p., vice dir. Met. Mus. Art, N.Y.C., 1968-86; dir. capital projects N.Y. Pub. Libr., N.Y.C., 1982-86; dir. U.S. Holocaust Meml. Mus., Washington, 1986-88; v.p. Grand Cen. Partnership, N.Y.C.; assoc. dir. Bryant Park Restoration Corp., N.Y.C., 1989-95; v.p. 34th St. Partnership, N.Y.C., 1991-95; prin. RKK&G Mus. & cultural Facilities Cons., Inc., N.Y.C., 1995—; faculty Sarah Lawrence Coll., Bronxville, N.Y., 1967-69; dir. capital projects N.Y. Pub. Libr., N.Y.C., 1982-86; cons. arch. Butler Mus. Am. Art, 1980, Whitney Mus. Am. Art, N.Y.C., 1981, Chrysler Mus. Art, Norfolk, Va., 1982, Internat. Ctr. Photography, N.Y.C., 1985-86, Mus. and Archive Acad. Hebrew Lang., Jerusalem, Newport Harbor Art Mus., 1990-91, J.B. Speed Art Mus., Louisville, 1992, Museo de Arte de Ponce, Ponce, P.R., 1995, P.R. Tourism Co., Commonwealth of P.R., 1995, Museo de Arte de P.R., 1996, Songwriters Hall of Fame Mus., 1997. Author: Temple of Dendur, 1978; co-author: Movie Song Catalog, 1993; contbr. articles to mags. and jours. Vice chmn. cmty. planning bd. # 8, N.Y.C., 1964-66; trustee The Cooper Union, 1983-86; commr. N.Y.C. Coun. Environment; pres. Met. Hist. Structures Assn.; presl. appointee Nat. Mus. Svc. Bd., 1995. With U.S. Army, 1953-55. Nat. Endowment for the Arts grantee, 1981. Fellow AIA (pres. N.Y. chpt.

1982-83, spl. citation 1978), Nat. Inst. for Archtl. Edn. (bd. dirs. 1978); mem. Mcpl. Art Soc., Archtl. League N.Y. (pres. 1970-72). Home: 1158 5th Ave New York NY 10029-6917 Office: 48 W 25th St New York NY 10010-2708

ROSENBLATT, EDDIE, record company executive; b. Far Rockaway, N.Y., Nov. 6, 1934; m. Bobbie Rosenblatt, 1954; children: Michael, Steven, Peter, Gretchen. AA in Bus., Bklyn. Coll., 1954. With Macy's Dept. Store, 1956, Cosnat, Cleve., 1957-62; gen. mgr. Main Line, Cleve., 1962-67; sales mgr. A&M Records, Calif., 1967-70, TA Records, Calif., 1970; sales mgr. Warner Bros. Records, Calif., 1971-72, v.p., dir. nat. sales and promotion, then sr. v.p., 1972-80; pres. Geffen Records, Calif., 1980-90, DGC Records, Calif., 1990—; chmn. bd., CEO Geffen Records, 1995—; co-founder, developer WEA Distributing Corp. Served with U.S. Army, 1954-56. Mem. NARAS, Rec. Industry Assn. Am. Achievements include tennis, books, movies, professional basketball. Office: Geffen Records 1755 Broadway New York NY 10019-3743*

ROSENBLATT, JASON PHILIP, English language educator; b. Balt., July 3, 1941; s. Morris D. and Esther (Friedlander) R.; m. Zipporah Marton, June 2, 1964; children: Noah David, Raphael Mark. BA, Yeshiva U., 1963; MA, Brown U., 1966, PhD, 1969. Asst. prof. English U. Pa., Phila., 1968-74; asst. prof. English Georgetown U., Washington, 1974-76, assoc. prof., 1976-83, prof. English, 1983—; vis. lectr. English lit. Swarthmore (Pa.) Coll., 1972-73; cen. exec. com. Folger Inst./Folger Shakespeare Libr., Washington, 1976-88. Author: Torah and Law in "Paradise Lost", 1994; co-editor: Not in Heaven: Coherence and Complexity in Biblical Narrative, 1991; mem. editl. bd. Milton Studies, 1992—; contbr. articles to scholarly publs. Guggenheim Found. fellow, 1977-78; NEH fellow, 1990-91. Mem. MLA (del. assembly 1989-91, exec. com. div. religion and lit. 1982-86), Milton Soc. Am. (exec. com. 1977-80, James Holly Hanford award 1989), Milton Seminar, Phi Beta Kappa. Democrat. Jewish. Avocations: Talmud study, music, swimming. Office: Dept English Georgetown Univ 37th St at O St Washington DC 20057

ROSENBLATT, JOAN RAUP, mathematical statistician; b. N.Y.C., Apr. 15, 1926; d. Robert Bruce and Clara (Eliot) Raup; m. David Rosenblatt, June 10, 1950. AB, Barnard Coll., 1946; PhD, U. N.C., 1956. Intern Nat. Inst. Pub. Affairs, Washington, 1946-47; statis. analyst U.S. Bur. of Budget, 1947-48; rsch. asst. U. N.C., 1953-54; mathematician Nat. Inst. Standards and Tech. (formerly Nat. Bur. Standards), Washington, 1955—, asst. chief statis. engring., 1963-68, chief statis. engring. lab., 1969-78, dep. dir. Ctr. for Applied Math., 1978-88; dep. dir. Computing and Applied Math. Lab., Gaithersburg, 1988-93, dir., 1993-95; mem. com. on indsl. rels. Dept. Stats. Ohio State U., 1981-90; mem. adv. com. in math. and stats. USDA Grad. Sch., 1971—; mem. Com. Applied and Theoretical Stats., Nat. Rsch. Coun., 1985-88. Mem. editorial bd. Communications in Stats., 1971-79, Jour. Soc. for Indsl. and Applied Math., 1965-75, Nat. Inst. Stds. and Tech. Jour. Rsch., 1991-93; contbr. articles to profl. jours. Chmn. Com. on Women in Sci., Joint Bd. on Sci. Edn., 1963-64. Rice fellow, 1946, Gen. Edn. Bd. fellow, 1948-50; recipient Fed. Woman's award, 1971, Gold medal Dept. Commerce, 1976, Presdl. Meritorious Exec. Rank award, 1982. Fellow AAAS (chmn. stats. sect. 1982, sec. 1987-91), Inst. Math. Stats. (coun. 1975-77), Am. Statis. Assn. (v.p. 1981-83, dir. 1979-80, Founders award 1991), Washington Acad. Scis. (achievement award math. 1965); mem. AAUW, Royal Statis. Soc. London, Philos. Soc. Washington, Internat. Statis. Inst., Bernouilli Soc. Probability and Math. Stats., Caucus Women Stats. (pres. 1976), Assn. Women Math., Exec. Women Govt., Phi Beta Kappa, Sigma Xi (treas. Nat. Bur. Standards chpt. 1982-84). Home: 2939 Van Ness St NW Apt 702 Washington DC 20008-4628 Office: Nat Inst Stds and Tech Rm 353 NIST North Gaithersburg MD 20899-0001

ROSENBLATT, JOSEPH, poet, editor; b. Toronto, Ont., Can., Dec. 26, 1933; s. Samuel and Bessie (Tee) R.; m. Faye Carole Smith, Oct. 13, 1969; 1 son, Eliot Howard. Grad. pub. schs. Writer-in-residence U. Western Ont., 1979-80, U. Victoria, 1980-81, U. Rome and U. Bologna, Italy, 1987. Author: Voyage of the Mood, 1963, The LSD Leacock, 1966, Winter of the Luna Moth, 1968, Dream Craters, 1974, Top Soil, 1976, Loosely Tied Hands, 1978, Tommy and the Ant Colony, 1979, Sleeping Lady, 1979, Brides of the Stream, 1983, Escape from the Glue Factory, 1985, The Kissing Goldfish of Siam, 1989, Beds and Consenting Dreamers, 1994, Madre Tentacolare, 1995, Tentacled Mother, 1995, Joe Rosenblatt Reader, 1995; author, illustrator: Greenbaum, 1971, The Bumblebee Dithyramb, 1972, The Blind Photographer, 1972, Virgins and Vampires, 1975; illustrator: Dr. Anaconda's Solar Fun Club, 1978, Snake Oil, 1978, The Voluptuous Gardener, 1996; editor: Jewish Dialogue, 1969—; poems included in Oxford Book of Canadian Verse, 1968, Poets of the Sixties, 1973, Poets of Canada, 1978, Gridi nel buio (Italian), 1990, other anthologies; exhibited ink drawings one-man show Gadatsy Gallery. Can. Coun. grantee, 1966, 68, 73, 80, 86, 92; B.C. Arts Coun. grantee, 1991; recipient Ont. Arts Coun. poetry award, 1970, Gov. Gen.'s award for poetry, 1976, B.C. Book prize, 1986. Mem. Writers Union of Can.

ROSENBLATT, KARIN ANN, community health educator; b. Chgo., Apr. 22, 1954; d. Murray and Adylin Rosenblatt. BA, U. Calif., Santa Cruz, 1975; MPH, U. Mich., 1977; PhD, Johns Hopkins U., 1988. Postdoctoral fellow U. Wash., Seattle, 1987-89; staff scientist Fred Hutchinson Cancer Rsch. Ctr., Seattle, 1989-91; asst. prof. U. Ill., Champaign, 1991-97, assoc. prof., 1997—. Mem. APHA, Internat. Genetic Epidemiology Soc., Am. Coll. Epidemiology, Soc. for Epidemiologic Rsch. Home: 1603-A1 Valley Rd Champaign IL 61820 Office: Dept Comty Health 121 Huff Hall MC 588 1206 S 4th St Champaign IL 61820-6920

ROSENBLATT, LESTER, naval architect; b. N.Y.C., Apr. 13, 1920; s. Mandell and Rosa (Wolff) R. BS, CCNY; BS in Naval Architecture and Marine Engring., U. Mich., 1942; DSc (hon.), Webb Inst. Naval Architecture, 1993. Registered profl. engr., N.Y., Mass. Naval architect John H. Wells, Inc., 1942-47; naval acrhitect USN Pearl Harbor Navy Yard, 1944-46; co-founder, chmn., chief exec. officer, naval architect M. Rosenblatt & Son Inc., Naval Architects and Marine Engrs., N.Y.C. and throughout U.S., 1947—; designer maj. ships, U.S. and fgn. Contbr. numerous tech. papers. Trustee (hon.) Webb Inst. Naval Architecture; mem. United Jewish Appeal N.Y., Maritime Friends of Seamen's Ch. Inst. Recipient U. Mich. Sesquicentennial award in ship design, 1967, 1st Rosenblatt-Mich. award, U. Mich., 1992; Admiral's honoree SUNY Maritime Coll., 1992. Fellow Soc. Naval Architects and Engrs. (pres. 1978-80, nat. chmn. membership com. 1964-78, mem. coun. and exec. com., Land medalist, hon. mem., chmn. N.Y. sect. 1961-62); mem. Am. Bur. Shipping, Bur. Veritas, Am. Soc. Naval Engrs. (Harold Saunders award 1987), Marine Soc. N.Y. (hon.), Internat. Maritime Hall of Fame, Soc. Marine Cons., N.Y. Yacht Club, Tau Beta Pi. Home: 8 E 83rd St Apt 12B New York NY 10028-0418 Office: M Rosenblatt & Son Inc 350 Broadway New York NY 10013-3911

ROSENBLATT, MICHAEL, medical researcher, educator; b. Lund, Sweden, Nov. 27, 1947; s. Arthur Rosenblatt and Jean (Strosberg) Bialer; m. Patricia Ellen Regenbogen, Aug. 23, 1969; children: Anna Miriam, Adam Richard. AB summa cum laude, Columbia U., 1969; MD magna cum laude, Harvard U., 1973. Diplomate Am. Bd. Internal Medicine. Intern then resident Mass. Gen. Hosp., Boston, 1973-75, clin. rsch. fellow in endocrinology and metabolism, 1975-77, chief endocrine unit, 1981-84; instr. in medicine Harvard U., Boston, 1976-78, asst. prof. medicine, 1978-82, assoc. prof. medicine, 1982-85; v.p. for biol. rsch. Merck Sharp & Dohme Rsch. Labs., 1984-87, v.p. for biol. rsch. and molecular biology, 1987-89; sr. v.p. rsch. Merck Sharp & Dohme Rsch. Labs., West Point, Pa., 1989-92; Ebert prof. molecular medicine Harvard Med. Sch., Boston, 1992—; dir. div. health scis. and tech. Harvard-MIT, 1992—; chief div. bone and mineral metabolism Beth Israel Hosp., Boston, 1992-96; faculty dean acad. programs Beth Israel Hosp., Harvard Med., 1996; sr. v.p. acad. affairs Beth Israel Deaconess Med. Ctr., 1996; exec. dir. Harvard Med. Sch./Beth Israel Deaconess Mount Auburn Inst. for Edn. and Rsch., 1996. Editor: Atrial Natriuretic Factor Endocrinology and Metabolism Clinics of N.Am., 1987; contbr. numerous sci. articles on parathyroid hormone and calcium metabolism to leading sci. jours. Recipient Vincent du Vigneaud award Gordon Confs., Kingston, R.I., 1986, Fuller Albright award Am. Soc. for Bone and Mineral Rsch., 1986, citation Japan Endocrine Soc., Tokyo. Fellow AAAS; mem. The Endocrine Soc., Am. Soc. for Biochemistry and Molecular Biology, Am. Soc. for Clin. Investigation, Am. Soc. Bone and Mineral Rsch. (pres.-elect 1996), Assn. Am. Physicians (pres. 1997-98), Inter-Urban Clin. Club. Home: 130 Lake Ave Newton MA 02159-2108 Office: Harvard Med Sch HST MEC 213 260 Longwood Ave Boston MA 02115-5701

ROSENBLATT, MURRAY, mathematics educator; b. N.Y.C., Sept. 7, 1926; s. Hyman and Esther R.; m. Adylin Lipson, 1949; children—Karin, Daniel. B.S., CCNY, 1946; M.S., Cornell U., 1947, Ph.D. in Math., 1949. Asst. prof. statistics U. Chgo., 1950-55; assoc. prof. math. Ind. U., 1956-59; prof. probability and statistics Brown U., 1959-64; prof. math. U. Calif., San Diego, 1964—; vis. fellow U. Stockholm, 1953; vis. asst. prof. Columbia U., 1955; guest scientist Brookhaven Nat. Lab., 1959; vis. fellow U. Coll., London, 1965-66, Imperial Coll. and Univ. Coll., London, 1972-73, Australian Nat. U., 1976, 79; overseas fellow Churchill Coll., Cambridge U., Eng., 1979; Wald lectr., 1970; vis. scholar Stanford U., 1982. Author: (with U. Grenander) Statistical Analysis of Stationary Time Series, 1957, Random Processes, 1962, (2d edit), 1974, Markov Processes, Structure and Asymptotic Behavior, 1971, Studies in Probability Theory, 1978, Stationary Sequences and Random Fields, 1985, Stochastic Curve Estimation, 1991; editor: The North Holland Series in Probability and Statistics, 1980; mem. editorial bd. Jour. Theoretical Probability. Recipient Bronze medal U. Helsinki, 1978; Guggenheim fellow, 1965-66, 71-72. Fellow Inst. Math Statistics, AAAS; mem. Internat. Statis. Inst., Nat. Acad. Scis. Office: U Calif Dept Math La Jolla CA 92093 also: PO Box 2066 La Jolla CA 92038-2066

ROSENBLATT, PAUL GERHARDT, federal judge. AB, U. Ariz., 1958, JD, 1963. Asst. atty. gen. State of Ariz., 1963-66; adminstrv. asst. to U.S. Rep., 1967-72; sole practice, Prescott, 1971-73; judge Yavapai County Superior Ct., Prescott, 1973-84; judge, U.S. Dist. Ct. Ariz., Phoenix, 1984—. Office: US Dist Ct US Courthouse & Fed Bldg 230 N 1st Ave Ste 7012 Phoenix AZ 85025-0007*

ROSENBLATT, PETER RONALD, lawyer, former ambassador; b. N.Y.C., Sept. 4, 1933; s. William and Therese Amalia (Steinhardt) R.; m. Naomi Henriette Harris, July 1, 1952; children: Therese Sarah Sonenshine, Daniel Harris, David Steinhardt. B.A., Yale U., 1954, LL.B., 1957; postgrad. fellow, Tel-Aviv U., 1971. Bar: N.Y. 1959, D.C. 1969. Teaching asst. history Yale U., New Haven, 1954-55; asst. dist. atty. N.Y. County, 1959-62; asso. Stroock & Stroock & Lavan, N.Y.C., 1962-66; dep. asst. gen. counsel AID, Washington, 1966; mem. White House staff, Washington, 1966-68; jud. officer, chmn. bd. contract appeals U.S. Post Office Dept., Washington, 1968-69; v.p., dir. EDP Technology, Inc., Washington, 1969-71; chmn. bd. Internat. Devel. Services, Washington, 1969-71; spl. cons. to Senator Edmund S. Muskie, 1970-72; practice law Washington, 1972-77, 81-91; ptnr. Heller & Rosenblatt, Washington, 1991—; personal rep. of Pres. with rank amb. to conduct negotiations on future polit. status of Trust Ter. of Pacific Islands, Washington, 1977-81; mem. Mid. East study group Dem. Adv. Coun. Elected Ofcls., 1974-76; bd. dirs. MediSense, Inc., 1983-96. Sec., chmn. exec. com. Coalition for a Dem. Majority, 1973-77, pres., 1983-93; bd. dirs. Com. on Present Danger, 1976-77, 82-93; mem. U.S. Nat. Com. Pacific Econ. Cooperation, 1986, sec., 1987—; bd. govs. Haifa (Israel) U., 1990-94; sec.-treas. Fund for Democracy and Devel., 1991-94, pres., 1994—; mem. adv. coun. Nixon Ctr. for Peace and Freedom, 1994—; mem. task force on fgn. policy Dem. Policy Commn., 1986. Mem. ABA, N.Y., D.C. Bar, Coun. Fgn. Rels. Jewish. Office: Heller & Rosenblatt 1501 M St NW Ste 1175 Washington DC 20005-1700

ROSENBLATT, ROGER, writer; b. N.Y.C., Sept. 13, 1940; m. Virginia Rosenblatt; children: Carl, Amy, John. PhD in English and Am. Lit., Harvard U.; hon. doctorates, U. Md., Claremont Grad. Sch., U. Utah, Pace U. Tchr. lit. and creative writing Harvard U., 1968-73; dir. edn. NEH, 1973-75; lit. editor The New Republic, 1975-78; columnist Washington Post, mem. editorial bd., 1976-79; essayist, sr. writer Time, 1980-88; essayist MacNeil/Lehrer News Hour, PBS, 1983—; columnist, editor-at-large Life mag., 1989-92; contbg. editor Time Mag., New Republic, also others; Univ. Prof. writing L.I. U. Author: Black Fiction, 1974, Children of War, 1983 (Robert F. Kennedy Book prize), Witness: The World Since Hiroshima, 1985, Life Itself: Abortion in the American Mind, 1992 (Melcher award), The Man in the Water, 1994, Coming Apart, 1997, (plays) Free Speech in America, 1991, And, 1992, Bibliomania, 1993. Fulbright scholar, Dublin, Ireland, 1965; recipient numerous journalistic honors including two George Polk awards, George Foster Peabody award, Emmy award.

ROSENBLATT, STEPHEN PAUL, marketing and sales promotion company executive; b. N.Y.C., Feb. 13, 1935; s. Jack Aaron and Ruth (Kloth) R.; m. Dorothy Freedman, Apr. 7, 1962; children: Gregg, Amy, Robert. BEd, NYU, 1957. Tchr. art N.Y.C. Schs., 1957-78; art dir. Morse Internat., N.Y.C., 1958-65; v.p. L.C. Gumbinner Advt., N.Y.C., 1966-71; group mktg. dir. Norcliff Thayer, Tarrytown, N.Y., 1971-75; pres. BMS Mktg. Services, Inc., N.Y.C., 1975-89, The Promotion Group Inc. subs. Doctus PLC, N.Y.C., 1989-91, SPQR Inc., Yorktown Heights, N.Y., 1991—. Home and Office: 1451 White Hill Rd Yorktown Heights NY 10598-3543

ROSENBLEETH, RICHARD MARVIN, lawyer; b. Phila., Mar. 20, 1932; s. Morris B. and Henrietta (Friedman) R.; m. Judith A. Alesker, June 20, 1954; children—Dori, Lyn. BS in Econs., U. Pa., 1954, JD, 1957. Bar: Pa. 1958, U.S. Supreme Ct. 1961. Asst. dist. atty. City of Phila., 1957-62; assoc. Richman, Price & Jamieson, 1962-65; ptnr. Blank, Rome, Comisky & McCauley, Phila., 1965—; mem. Civil Justice Reform Act Adv. Group, U.S. Dist. Ct. (ea. dist.) Pa., 1991—; co-chair Mayor Rendell's Transition Task Force on the Law Dept., 1991; judge pro tem Phila. Ct. Common Pleas, 1992—. Pres. Merion Park Civic Assn., Pa., 1967; mem. Citizens Crime Commn., Phila., 1979-87; commr. Youth Svcs. Coordinating Commn., Phila., 1979-85; Pa. state mem. chair U.S. Supreme Ct. Hist. Soc., 1994-95; bd. dirs. Corp. Alliance for Drug Edn., 1995—, v.p., 1996; chmn. Pa. Conv. Ctr. Authority, 1996—. Fellow Am. Coll. Trial Lawyers (chmn. Pa. state com. 1993-94), Internat. Acad. Trial Lawyers, Am. Bar Found.; mem. ABA, Pa. Bar Assn., Phila. Bar Assn., Phila. Bar Found. (pres. 1994). Avocations: golf; art collecting. Office: Blank Rome Comisky et al 1200 Four Penn Ctr Plz Philadelphia PA 19103

ROSENBLITH, WALTER ALTER, scientist, educator; b. Vienna, Austria, Sept. 21, 1913; came to U.S., 1939, naturalized, 1946; s. David A. and Gabriele (Roth) R.; m. Judy Olcott Francis, Sept. 27, 1941; children: Sandra Yvonne, Ronald Francis. Ingenieur Radiotelegraphiste, U. Bordeaux, 1936; Ing. Radioelectricien, Ecole Supérieure d'Electricité, Paris, 1937; ScD (hon.), U. Pa., 1976, S.D. Sch. Mines, 1980, Brandeis U., 1988, U. Miami, Fla., 1992; PhD (hon.), Fed. U. of Rio de Janeiro, 1976. Research engr. France, 1937-39; research asst. N.Y. U., 1939-40; grad. fellow, teaching fellow physics U. Calif. at Los Angeles, 1940-43; asst. prof., asso. prof., acting head dept. physics S.D. Sch. Mines and Tech., 1943-47; research fellow Psycho-Acoustic Lab., Harvard U., 1947-51; lectr. otology and laryngology Harvard Med. Sch., 1969—; assoc. prof. comm. biophysics MIT, Cambridge, Mass., 1951-57, prof., 1957-84, inst. prof., 1975-84; inst. prof. emeritus MIT, Cambridge, 1984—; staff Research Lab. Electronics, 1951-69, chmn. faculty, 1967-69, assoc. provost, 1969-71, provost, 1971-80; dir. Kaiser Industries, 1968-76; chmn. com. electronic computers in life scis. Nat. Acad. Scis.-NRC, 1960-64, mem. brain scis. com., 1965-68, chmn., 1966-67; mem. cen. coun. Internat. Brain Rsch. Orgn., 1960-68, mem. exec. com., 1960-68, hon. treas., 1962-67; cons. life scis. panel Pres.'s Sci. Adv. Com., 1961-66; mem. coun. Internat. Union Pure and Applied Biophysics, 1961-69; inaugural lectr. Tata Inst. Fundamental Rsch., Bombay, 1962; Weizmann lectr. Weizmann Inst. Sci., Rehovoth, Israel, 1962; U.S. Nat. Commn. on Pure and Applied Biophysics, 1964-69; mem. Pres.'s Com. Urban Housing, 1967-68; cons. communications sci. WHO, 1964-65; mem. bd. medicine NAS, 1967-70; charter mem. Inst. Medicine, 1970—, mem. coun., 1970-76; mem. adv. com. to dir. NIH, 1970-74; mem. governing bd. NRC, 1974-76; mem. adv. com. med. sci. AMA, 1972-74; mem. selection com. Tyler Prize for Environ. Achievement, 1973—; chmn. sci. adv. coun. Callier Ctr. for Communication Disorders, 1968-85; chmn. rsch. com of the Health Effects Inst., 1981-89, bd. dirs., 1989—; chmn. internat. adv. panel of Chinese U. Devel. Project, 1986-91; mem. gov. coun. Internat. Centre Insect Physiology and Ecology, Kenya, 1987-90; mem. Am. and internat. panels on UNESCO (UN Assn. U.S. Am.), 1988-89; mem. Com. on Scholarly Communication with People's Republic of China, 1977-86, Coun. on Fgn. Rels., 1983-92. Bd. Fgn. Scholarships, 1978-81, chmn., 1980-81; co-chmn. NRC-IOM com. for study of saccharin and food safety policy, 1978-79; cons. Carnegie Corp. N.Y., 1986—, Carnegie Commn. on Sci., Tech. and Govt., 1988—; hon. consulting prof. U. of Electronic Sci. and Tech. of China, 1988. Editor: Sensory Communication, 1961; contbr. articles, chpts. to profl. publs. Bd. govs. Weizmann Inst. Sci., 1973-86; chmn. com. on rehab. of physically handicapped NRC, 1975-77; trustee Brandeis U., 1979—. Decorated croix du chevalier Legion d'Honneur (France); recipient Alexander von Humboldt medal, 1989; Rosenblith lectr. created in his honor NAS, 1992, Rosenblith chair of neuroscis. named in his honor MIT, 1995. Fellow Acoustical Soc. Am., World Acad. Art and Sci., Am. Acad. Arts and Scis. (exec. bd. 1970-77), AAAS, IEEE; mem. Internat. Council Sci. Unions (v.p. 1984-88), Biophys. Soc. (council 1957-61, 69-72, exec. bd. 1957-61), NAE, NAS (fgn. sec. 1982-86), Soc. Exptl. Psychologists, Engring. Acad. of Japan (fgn. assoc.). Office: MIT Cambridge MA 02139

ROSENBLOOM, ARLAN LEE, physician, educator; b. Milw., Apr. 15, 1934; s. Harris Phillip and Esther (Schneider) R.; m. Edith Kathleen Peterson, Sept. 14, 1958; children: Eric David, Maliah Jo, Disa Lynn, Harris Phillip. BA, U. Wis., 1955, MD, 1958. Diplomate Am. Bd. Pediatrics, Am. Bd. Pediatric Endocrinology, Am. Coll. Epidemiology. Intern Los Angeles County Gen. Hosp., 1958-59; resident in gen. practice Ventura County Hosp., Ventura, Calif., 1959-60; physician-in-chief Medico Hosp., Kratie, Cambodia, 1960-61; med. officer Pahang, Malaysia, 1961-62; resident in pediatrics U. Wis. Hosp., Madison, 1962-63, 64-65; fellow in pediatric endocrinology U. Wis. Hosp., 1963-64, 65-66; asst. prof. pediatrics U. Fla., Gainesville, 1968-71; assoc. prof. U. Fla., 1971-74, prof., 1974-96; disting. svc. prof. emeritus U. Fla., Gainesville, 1996—; founder, chief div. endocrinology U. Fla., 1977-94; dir. Office for Internat. Health Programs, 1995—; mem. Ctr. for African Studies U. Fla., mem. Ctr. for Latin Am. Studies; assoc. dir. Clin. Research Center, 1969-74, dir., 1974-80; dir. Nat. Found. March of Dimes Birth Defects Center, 1969-73; med. dir. Gainesville Youth Clinic, 1972-74; mem. adv. com. Nat. Disease and Therapy Index; mem. Fla. Com. Children and Youth, 1972; data work group chmn. Nat. Diabetes Commn., 1975; mem. epidemiology and disease control study sect. NIH, 1978-82; vis. prof. McMaster U. Med. Centre, 1974-75; cons. epidemiologist Boston U. Health Policy Inst., West Africa, 1983-84; mem. affiliate faculty dept. clin. psychology U. Fla., 1984—; pres., dir. Fla. Camp for Children and Youth with Diabetes, 1970-90; dir. N. Fla. Regional Diabetes Program Children and Youth, 1974-88; dir. U. Fla. Diabetes Rsch. Edn. and Treatment Ctr., 1977-90; clin. and sci. adv. bd. Children's Diabetes Found., Denver, 1978-86; dir. N. Fla. Regional Diabetes and Endocrine Program for Children and Youth, 1988-96; asst. med. dir. Children's Med. Svcs., Dist. 3/13, 1986—; mem. nat. diabetes adv. bd. NIH, 1990-94; internat. cons. Inst. for Endocrinology, Metabolism and Reproduction, Quito, Ecuador, 1990—. Editor Acta Paediactria Belgica, 1979-82, Today in Medicine (Diabetes), 1989—; mem. editl. bd. European Jour. Pediat., 1982—, Jour. Pediat. Endocrinology and Metabolism, 1983—, Clin. Pediat., 1989—, Diabetes Care, 1992-95, Jour. Clin. Endocrinology and Metabolism, 1995—, Clin. Diabetes, 1996—; contbr. numerous articles to profl. jours. Chief med. officer Hole in the Wall Gang Fund/South, 1990-95; bd. dirs. Chinn Med. Adv. Commn. Boggy Creek Gang Camp, 1995; epidemiologist smallpox eradication program USPHS, Yaounde, Cameroon, 1966-68, comdr. inactive Res., 1968-69, capt. Ready Res., 1987—. Recipient Best Drs. in Am., 1992-94, Faculty Rsch. prize U. Fla. Coll. Medicine, 1994, U. Wis. Med. Alumni Citation, 1995, U. Fla. Blue Key Disting. Faculty award, 1995. Mem. Am. Acad. Pediatrics, Am. Fedn. Clin. Rsch., Am. Diabetes Assn. (bd. dirs. 1986-90), Brit. Diabetic Assn., Fla. Diabetes Assn. (dir.), Alachua County Med. Soc., Internat. Soc. Pediatric Adolescent Diabetes, Endocrine Soc., Nat. Coun. for Internat. Health, Lawson Wilkins Pediatric Endocrine Soc., Am. Pediatric Soc., Internat. Diabetes Epidemiology Group, Soc. Pediatric Rsch. Home: 2902 SW 1st Ave Gainesville FL 32607-3002 Office: Children's Med Svcs Ctr 1701 SW 16th Ave Rm 2163 Gainesville FL 32608-1153

ROSENBLOOM, BERT, marketing educator, consultant, writer; b. Phila., Feb. 2, 1944; s. Max and Dora (Cohen) R.; m. Pearl Friedman, Aug. 18, 1968; children: Jack Alan, Robyn. B.S., Temple U., 1966, M.B.A., 1968, Ph.D., 1974. Instr. mktg. Rider Coll., Trenton, N.J., 1968-72, asst. prof., 1972-74; asst. prof. mktg. Baruch Coll. CUNY, 1974-76; assoc. prof. Drexel U., Phila., 1976-80, prof., 1980-85, G. Behrens Ulrich prof. mktg., 1985—, assoc. dean grad. programs, 1994—; cons. editor mktg. Random House, N.Y.C., 1977—; cons. in field; mem. bd. dirs. Reality Lndscaping Corp., 1991—, McKee Real Estate Devel. Corp., 1991—. Author: Marketing Channels, 1978, 3d edit., 1987, Market Functions and the Wholesaler Distribution, 1987, Marketing Channels: A Management View, 4th edit., 1991, 5th edit., 1995; Retail Marketing, 1981, Direct Selling Channels, 1993; editor: Journal of Marketing Channels, 1989—, Jour. Consumer Mktg., Jour. Global Mktg., Jour. Acad. Mktg. Sci.; contbr. articles to profl. jours. Named dist. Erskine fellow U. Canterbury, New Zealand, 1986; recipient outstanding educator award Chapel of Four Chaplains, 1984, rsch. award Distbn. Rsch. and Edn. Found., 1986, rsch. award Direct Selling Found., 1986, 91, 96; Nat. Assn. Wholesaler Distbrs. grantee, 1991; honored as disting. prof Retail Mktg. Inst. of Australia, 1985; Vis. scholar Ecole Superiore de Commerce de Paris, 1993. Fellow Acad. Mktg. Sci. (bd. govs. 1978-89); mem. Internat. Mgmt. Devel. Assn. (pres. 1992-94), Am. Mktg. Assn. (v.p. Phila. chpt. 1978-79), Beta Gamma Sigma. Office: Drexel U Sch Bus 32d and Market Sts Philadelphia PA 19104

ROSENBLOOM, DANIEL, investment banker, lawyer; b. N.Y.C., Feb. 11, 1930; s. Sol and Florence (Vogel) R. BA, U. Va., 1951, JD, 1954; LLM, NYU, 1960. Bar: Va. 1954, N.Y. 1956. Atty. Paskus, Gordon & Hyman, N.Y.C., 1956-61; v.p., sec., gen. counsel Phila. & Reading Corp., N.Y.C., 1962-67; ptnr. First Manhattan Co., 1967—. Trustee Nat. Found. for Facial Reconstruction, NYU Med. Ctr., Univ. Va. Law Sch. Found. 1st lt. AUS, 1954-56. Mem. Sunningdale Country Club, Farmington Country Club, Harmonie Club, City Athletic Club, Atlantic Golf Club, Phi Alpha Delta, Phi Epsilon Pi. Jewish. Office: First Manhattan Co 437 Madison Ave New York NY 10022-7001

ROSENBLOOM, H. DAVID, lawyer; b. N.Y.C., May 26, 1941; s. Milton M. and Rose Gold R.; m. Carla L. Peterson, June 23, 1968; children: Sarah Alix, Julia Micol. A.B., Princeton U., 1962; postgrad. (Fulbright scholar), U. Florence, Italy, 1962-63; J.D., Harvard U., 1966. Bar: N.Y. 1967, D.C. 1968. Spl. asst. to Arthur J. Goldberg U.S. amb. to UN, 1966-67; law clk. to Abe Fortas U.S. Supreme Ct., 1967-68; assoc. Caplin & Drysdale, Washington, 1968-72, ptnr., 1972-77, 81—; spl. asst. to dep. asst. sec. for tax policy Dept. Treasury, Washington, 1977, internat. tax counsel, 1978-81; lectr. Harvard U. Law Sch., 1984-87, 90-93, 95-96, Stanford U. Law Sch., 1988, Columbia U. Law Sch., 1997—. Mem. D.C. Bar. Home: 2948 Garfield Ter NW Washington DC 20008-3507 Office: One Thomas Circle NW Washington DC 20005

ROSENBLOOM, LEWIS STANLEY, lawyer; b. Fort Riley, Kans., Feb. 28, 1953; s. Donald and Sally Ann (Warsawsky) R.; m. Rochelle Leavitt, Dec. 16, 1973; children: Micah, Shaina. BA, Lake Forest Coll., 1974; JD with high honors, DePaul U., 1977. Bar: Ill. 1977, U.S. Dist. Ct. (no. dist.) Ill, 1977, U.S. Ct. Appeals (7th cir.) 1979, U.S. Supreme Ct. 1983, U.S. Ct. Appeals (9th cir.) 1987, U.S. Ct. Appeals (3rd cir.) 1993. Sr. acct. Gale, Takahasi & Channon, Chgo., 1973-74; law clk. to Hon. Robert L. Eisen U.S. Dist. Ct. (no. dist.) Ill., Chgo., 1976; assoc. Nachman, Munitz & Sweig, Ltd., Chgo., 1976-82, prin., 1982-87; ptnr., co-chmn. involvency, bankruptcy & bus. reorgn. dept. Winston & Strawn, Chgo., 1987-93; ptnr., sr. corp. reorgn. counsel McDermott, Will & Emery, Chgo., 1994—; co-chmn. distressed transactions SBU; mem. bd. advisors to bankruptcy, comml. law advisor Bus. Laws, Inc., 1988—; lectr. in field. Contbr. articles to profl. jours. Mem. adv. com. and fin. subcom. Ill. Bd. Higher Edn., Springfield; mem. state edn. and legal aid subcom. Ill. Coun. on Children and Youth Welfare, Chgo. Coll. scholar Lake Forest Coll., 1973-74. Fellow Am. Coll. Bankruptcy; mem. ABA (bus. bankruptcy com. 1982—, chmn. new and pending bankruptcy legis. subcom. 1982-85, chmn. transp. reorganizations subcom. 1985-88), Chgo. Bar Assn. (bankruptcy reorganization com., co-chmn. subcom. on retention and fees 1987-88). Office: McDermott Will & Emery 227 W Monroe St Chicago IL 60606-5016

ROSENBLOOM, MORRIS VICTOR, author, publisher, public relations executive, government official; b. Pitts., Oct. 25, 1915; s. Alfred A. and Corinne (Lorch) R.; m. Ronda Rose Robins, May 16, 1953 (div.

1975). B.A., U. Pitts., 1936. Dir. research stats. for Edward L. Bernays, N.Y.C., 1937; asst. to pres. Ruffsdale Distilling Co., Braddock, Pa., 1937-39; founder, dir. Am. Industries Surveys, N.Y.C., 1939-41; reactivated as Am. Surveys, 1947, dir., 1947-54, pres., 1955—; pres. Am. Surveys Internat., 1965—; sabbatical yr. as bus. liaison officer U.S. Customs Service, Washington, 1983-84; sr. economist OPM, 1941-42; prin. indsl. specialist, chief consumers durable goods and service equipment WPB, later asst. to vice chmn. civilian requirements, 1942-43; v.p. charge sales Diamond Prodns., Inc., 1946-47; mktg. and sales cons. to pres. Publicker Industries, Inc., Phila.; sales mgr. subs. Publicker Industries, Inc., 1947-50; program coordinator, asst. to chmn. NSRB, 1950; spl. asst. dep. adminstr. DPA, 1951-52; founder, exec. dir. Inst. on Econs. Def. Moblzn., sponsored by Am. U., ODM, 1951-52; exec. dir. def. materials operating and policy coms. ODM, 1953; asso. Coates & McCormick, Inc., Washington and N.Y.C., 1954. Author: The Liquor Industry, 1935, rev. edit., 1937; Bottling for Profit (with A.B. Greenleaf), 1940; Peace Through Strength: Bernard Baruch and a Blueprint for Security, 1953 (Warner award); contbr.: Profitable Pub. Rels.; contbr. articles to profl. jours.; lectr. Dir. ops. Nat. Citizens Com. for Hoover Report; sponsor Atlantic Council; mem. pub. relations adv. com. Fair Campaign Practices Com.; mem. Nat Council, nat. pub. rels. com. Boy Scouts Am.; also mem. adv. bd. and chmn. pub. relations com. Nat. Capital Area Council; chmn. alumni regional council U. Pitts., 1960-61. Served with USNR, 1943-46, comdg. officer submarine chaser PTO. Recipient Silver Beaver award Boy Scouts Am., 1963. Fellow Pub. Relations Soc. Am. (accredited, chmn. govt. affairs adv. com. 1969, mem. exec. com. counselors academy, dir. Washington chpt., David Apter Meml. award Pub. Svc. 1990, Paul M. Lund Pub. Svc. award 1990); mem. Nat. Eagle Scout Assn., Def. Orientation Conf. Assn. (life, charter, v.p. 1955-56), Internat. Pub. Relations Assn. (charter), Res. Officers Assn. U.S., U.S. Naval Inst., Friends of Kennedy Ctr. (founder), Dominion Found. for Natural Areas (hon.), Mil. Order of World Wars, Am. Legion Press Post 20 (commdg. officer), Internat. Platform Assn., Pi Lambda Phi (Big PII award 1973). Clubs: Army and Navy (Washington), Pitt. (Washington). Home: 4201 Butterworth Pl NW 321 Washington DC 20016-4538 *Since boyhood days, my lodestar has been to serve humanity in both my personal and business life. This rewarding objective has been realized with the warmth and encouragement from friends and associates over the years, for which I am deeply appreciative.*

ROSENBLOOM, SANFORD M., lawyer; b. Phila., Sept. 24, 1928; s. Fred L. and Pauline B. (Basen) R.; m. Irene Nelson, 1961 (div. 1974); m. Willa Glazer, Nov. 21, 1976. BS, U. Pa., 1951; JD, Rutgers U., 1955. Bar: Pa. 1956, U.S. Dist. Ct. (ea. dist.) Pa. 1956, U.S. Ct. Appeals (3d cir.) 1957. Ptnr. Schnader, Harrison, Segal & Lewis, Phila., 1955-93, ret., 1993. Mem. Phila. Bar Assn. (former officer and chmn. com. real estate sect.), Pa. Bar Assn. (ho. of dels., chmn. real property, probate and trust law sect. 1991-92), Am. Coll. Real Estate Lawyers, Bala Golf Club (Phila.), Palm Aire Golf Club (Pompano Beach, Fla.). Republican. Jewish. Avocations: tennis, golf. Home: The Philadelphian Apt 20B32 2401 Pennsylvania Ave Philadelphia PA 19130-3005 Office: Schnader Harrison Segal et al 1600 Market St Ste 3600 Philadelphia PA 19103-7286

ROSENBLOOM, STEVE, sportswriter. Sports columnist Chgo. Sun Times. Office: Chgo Sun-Times 401 N Wabash Ave Chicago IL 60611-5642*

ROSENBLUM, CONSTANCE, newspaper editor. Arts and leisure sect. editor N.Y. Times, N.Y.C. Office: The NY Times 229 W 43rd St New York NY 10036-3913*

ROSENBLUM, EDWARD G., lawyer; b. Union City, N.J., Aug. 2, 1944; s. Milton and Frances (Nardi) R.; m. Charis Ann Schlatter, Dec. 1, 1971; children: Deborah, Michelle. BA, Rutgers U., 1966, JD, 1969. Bar: N.J. 1969. Ptnr. Rosenblum & Rosenblum, P.A., Jersey City, 1971-79, Secaucus, N.J., 1979-93; Rosenblum Wolf & Lloyd, P.A., Secaucus, 1994—; lectr. in field. Author: N.J. Lawyer, 1980, N.J. Municipalities, 1987. Active Hudson County chpt. Am. Cancer Soc., Hoboken, N.J., 1987—. Mem. N.J. State Bar Assn. (vice chmn. tax ct. rules com. taxation sect. 1984—, chmn. real property tax com. 1984—, vice chmn. taxation sect. 1987—, chmn.-elect 1987, chmn. 1988-89, Supreme Ct. com. on tax ct. 1982-92). Office: One Harmon Plaza Secaucus NJ 07094

ROSENBLUM, HAROLD ARTHUR, grocery distribution executive; b. Sharon, Pa., Jan. 5, 1923; s. H. David and Carol (Thaler) R.; m. Irene F. Rosen, June 25, 1950; children—Julia M., Mark A., Lee S., Joel N., Ruth C. (dec.). Student, Western Res. U., 1939-40; A.B. cum laude, Harvard, 1943, J.D., 1949. Bar: Pa. 1949. With Sharon div. Peter J. Schmitt Co. (formerly Golden Dawn Foods, Inc.), Sharon, 1950-85; pres. Golden Dawn Foods, Inc., 1961-80, chmn. bd., 1980-83, treas., 1961-73; sec. H.M. Pollock Co., Kittanning, Pa., 1982-90. Mem. Mercer County Mental Health/Mental Retardation Bd., 1967-90, chmn., 1967-70, 80-81, sec., 1984-90; chmn. Community Council Com. Mental Health/Mental Retardation, 1965-67, Shenango Valley Jewish Fedn., 1964—; pres. Friends of Buhl Henderson Library, 1973-75; treas. Mercer County Mental Health Assn., 1964-66; bd. dirs. Mercer County Cmty. Mental Health & Counseling Ctr., 1959-82, sec., 1961-63, pres., 1963-65; v.p. Mercer County Drug and Alcohol Coun., Inc., 1973-74; mem. exec. bd. Shenango Valley Human Rels. Coun., 1960-68; mem. econ. devel. com. Multi-County Manpower Devel. Corp., 1972-73; mem. Sharon Human Relations Commn., 1969-88 , sec., 1984, chmn. 1985-86; sec. Mercer County Comprehensive Health Planning Bd., 1972-74, mem. adv. com., 1971-74; charter mem. Pa. Freedom of Choice in Family Planning; mem. Mercer County Commn. on Drug and Alcohol Abuse, 1973-78; mem. adv. bd. Shenango Valley Campus, Pa. State U., 1976; exec. com. Mercer County br. NAACP, 1964-71; pres. bd. dirs. Playhouse 600, 1973-76; bd. dirs. Sharon Regional Health System (formerly Sharon Gen. Hosp.), 1964—, sec., 1966-77, chmn., 1977-96, home health adv. com., 1973—; mem. Mayor's Com. for Arts, 1973-75; trustee-at-large Pa. council Union Am. Hebrew Congregations, 1966-76, 85-90; bd. dirs. Shenango Valley Urban League, 1971-73, Pa. Mental Health Assn., 1968-72; bd. dirs. Mercer County Edn. and Rehab. Ctr. (formerly Mercer County Crippled Children's and Adults Soc.), 1981-94, exec. com., 1983-94, sec., 1986-92; bd. dirs. Family and Children's Svc. of Youngstown Area Jewish Fedn., 1981—, sec., 1986-87, v.p., 1987-89, pres. 1990-92; bd. dirs. Temple Beth Israel, Sharon, 1951-63, 82-89, v.p., 1956-58, pres., 1958-63, 84-87 ; bd. dirs. Cmty. Food Warehouse, 1983-88 , pres., 1985-86; Youngstown State U. Human Services Devel. Adv. Bd., 1986-92; adv. bd. Behavioral Health Ctr., 1988—. Served with AUS, 1943-46. Buhl Day honoree, 1985. Mem. Nat. Am. Wholesale Grocers Assn. (bd. govs. 1964-66), Shenango Valley C. of C. (bd. dirs. 1969-71, treas. 1970, Person of Yr. 1985). Clubs: Rotary (Sharon) (pres. 1978-79), Sharon Country (Sharon), University (Sharon) (fin. sec., pres. 1978-79); F.H. Buhl (dir. 1977-79). Home: 1700 Hannah Ct Sharon PA 16146-3818

ROSENBLUM, JOHN WILLIAM, dean; b. Houston, Jan. 1, 1944; s. H. William and Susan (Ullmann) R.; m. Carolyn Edith Jones, Sept. 12, 1964; children: J. Christopher, Kathryn, Nicholas. A.B., Brown U., 1965; M.B.A., Harvard U., 1967, D.B.A., 1972. Instr. Harvard U. Bus. Sch., Boston, 1969-72, asst. prof., 1972-75, assoc. prof., 1975-79; prof. Darden Grad. Sch. Bus. Adminstrn., U. Va., Charlottesville, 1979-80, assoc. dean, 1980-82, dean, 1982-93; Tayloe Murphy prof., 1993—; dean Jepson Sch. Leadership Studies, U. Richmond, Va., 1996—; bd. dirs. Chesapeake Corp., Cadmus Comms., Inc., T. Rowe Price Assocs., Comdial Corp., Cone Mills Corp., The Providence Jour. Co. Co-author: Strategy and Organization, 1973, (2d edit.), 1977, Cases in Political Economy-Japan, 1980. Mem. Phi Beta Kappa, Omicron Delta Kappa. Home: RR 3 Box 530 Crozet VA 22932-9319 Office: Univ Richmond Jepson Sch Richmond VA 23173

ROSENBLUM, M. EDGAR, theater director; b. Bklyn., Jan. 8, 1932; s. Jacob and Pauline (Feldman) R.; m. Cornelia Hartmann, May 1, 1960; 1 child, Jessica Alex. Student, Bard Coll., 1951-55. Prodr. Folk Rock Chamber Music Series, Woodstock, N.Y., 1956-72; dir. Polari Gallery, Woodstock, 1959-72; asst. to mgr. Nat. Music League, N.Y.C., 1958-59; stage mgr. Joffrey Ballet Nat. Tour, 1960; prodr. When I Was a Child, 41st St Theatre, N.Y.C., 1960-61, Woodstock Playhouse, 1960-73; stage mgr. Turn of the Screw Nat. Tour, 1961; exec. dir. Hudson Valley Repertory Theatre, Woodstock, 1964-67; exec. prodr. The Shadow Box, N.Y.C., 1977; exec. dir. Long Wharf Theatre, New Haven, 1970-96; exec. prodr. Cir. in the Sq., N.Y.C., 1996—; producer and owner, Woodstock (N.Y.) Playhouse, 1959-73; cons. Fedn. for Ext. and Devel. of Am. Profl. Theatre, N.Y.C., 1970, Arts Couns. of New Haven, R.I., Alaska, Conn., Ohio, 1970—; bd. trustees Am. Arts Alliance, chmn of bd. 1982-84; vis. lectr. Yale U., New Haven, 1985-91. With U.S. Army, 1953. Recipient award New Haven Arts Coun., 1994; Ezra Stiles Coll. fellow Yale U., 1973. Mem. Am. Arts Alliance (chmn. 1982-84), League of Resident Theatres (mem. exec., liaison and negotiating coms. 1974, v.p. 1993-96, pres. 1996—), Nat. Corp. Theatre Fund (founding pres. 1976), Conn. Advocates for the Arts (bd. dirs. 1978—), Greater New Haven C. of C. (bd. dirs.). Office: Circle in the Square 1633 Broadway New York NY 10019-6708

ROSENBLUM, MARVIN, mathematics educator; b. Bklyn., June 30, 1926; s. Isidore and Celia (Mendelsohn) Rosenblum; m. Frances E. Parker, May 30, 1959; children: Isidore, Mendel, Jessie, Rebecca, Sarah. B.S., U. Calif.-Berkeley, 1949, M.A., 1951, Ph.D., 1955. Instr. math. U. Calif.-Berkeley, 1954-55; asst. prof. U. Va., Charlottesville, 1955-59, assoc. prof., 1960-65, prof., 1965—, now Commonwealth prof.; mem. Inst. Advanced Study, 1959-60. Served with USNR, 1944-46. Mem. Am. Math. Soc., Am. Math. Assn., Soc. Indsl. and Applied Math. Jewish. Office: U Va Dept Math Kerchof Hall Charlottesville VA 22903

ROSENBLUM, MINDY FLEISCHER, pediatrician; b. Bronxville, N.Y., June 5, 1951; d. Herman and Muriel (Gold) Fleischer; m. Jay S. Rosenblum, June 22, 1971; children: Meira, Tamar, Rafi, Rachel. BA, Yeshiva U., 1972; MD, Albert Einstein Coll., 1976. Diplomate Am. Bd. Pediatrics, Am. Bd. Pediatrics Endocrinology. Intern in pediatrics Bronx Mcpl. Hosp. Ctr., 1976-77, residency in pediatrics, 1977-79; fellow in pediatric endocrinology Children's Hosp. of Phila., 1981; asst. prof. U. Pa., Phila., 1981—; attending physician Bryn Mawr (Pa.) Hosp., 1981—, Lankenau Hosp., Wynnewood, Pa., 1983—. Fellow Am. Acad. Pediatrics; mem. Phila. Pediatrics Soc. (bd. dirs. 1988-92), Am. Diabetes Assn., Lawson Wilkins Pediatric Endocrine Soc.

ROSENBLUM, ROBERT, art historian, educator; b. N.Y.C., July 24, 1927; s. Abraham H. and Lily M. (Lipkin) R.; m. Jane Kaplowitz, June 23, 1977; children: Sophie Lila, Theodore Abraham. BA, Queens Coll., 1948; MA, Yale U., 1950; PhD, NYU, 1956; MA (hon.), Oxford U., 1972; ArtsD (hon.), Queens Coll., 1992. Mem. faculty U. Mich., Ann Arbor, 1955-56, Princeton (N.J.) U., 1956-66, Yale U., New Haven, 1966-67; mem. faculty NYU, N.Y.C., 1967—; prof. fine arts NYU, 1967—. Author: Cubism and Twentieth Century Art, 1960, Transformations in Late Eighteenth Century Art, 1967, Ingres, 1967, Frank Stella, 1971, Modern Painting and the Northern Romantic Tradition, 1975, The International Style of 1800, 1976, Andy Warhol: Portraits of the 70s, 1979, 19th Century Art, 1984, The Dog in Art From Rococo to Post-Modernism, 1988, The Romantic Child From Runge to Sendak, 1989, Paintings in the Musee d'Orsay, 1989, The Jeff Koons Handbook, 1992, Andy Warhol Portraits, 1993, Mel Ramos: Pop Images, 1994, The Paintings of August Strindberg, The Structure of Chaos, 1995. Served with U.S. Army, 1945-46. Recipient Frank Jewett Mather award for art criticism, 1981. Fellow Am. Acad. Arts and Scis.; mem. Coll. Art Assn. Am. Office: NYU Dept Fine Arts Washington Sq N New York NY 10003-6688

ROSENBLUM, SCOTT S., lawyer; b. N.Y.C., Oct. 4, 1949; s. Harold Lewis and Greta Blossom (Lesher) R.; m. Barbara Anne Campbell, Oct. 29, 1977; children: Harold, Emma, Casey. AB summa cum laude, Dartmouth Coll., 1971; JD, U. Pa., 1974. Bar. U.S. Dist. Ct. (so. dist.) N.Y. 1975. From assoc. to ptnr. Stroock & Stroock & Lavan, N.Y.C., 1974-91; ptnr. Kramer, Levin, Naftalis & Frankel, N.Y.C., 1991-93, mng. ptnr., 1994—; N.Y. Adv. Bd. Mid. East Quarterly, Phila., 1994—; bd. dirs. Dovenmuehle Mortgage, Inc., Schaumburg, Ill, Greg Manning Auctions, Inc., West Caldwell, N.J., Temco Svc. Industries, Inc., N.Y.C. Co-author: Public Limited Partnerships and Roll-Ups, Securities Law Techniques, The Practitioner's Guide to Transactions and Litigation, 1995. Trustee Village of Saltaire, N.Y., 1993—. Mem. ABA (high tech. com. 1983-84), Assn. Bar City N.Y. (corps. com. 1991-94), Phi Beta Kappa. Avocation: sailing. Home: 19 Wildwood Cir Larchmont NY 10538 Office: Kramer Levin Naftalis Frankel Kamin & Frankel 919 3rd Ave New York NY 10022

ROSENBLUM, VICTOR GREGORY, political science and law educator; b. N.Y.C., June 2, 1925; s. George and Vera (Minster) R.; m. Louise Rann, Feb. 21, 1946; children: Susan, Ellen, Laura, Keith, Jonathan, Peter, Warren, Joshua. A.B., Columbia U., 1945, LL.B., 1948; Ph.D., U. Calif.-Berkeley, 1953; D.H.L., Hebrew Union Coll., 1970; D.L., Siena Heights Coll., 1982. Bar: Ill., N.Y., U.S. Supreme Ct. Lectr. polit. sci. U. Calif., Berkeley, 1949-52, asst. prof. polit. sci., 1953-57; assoc. prof. polit. sci. Northwestern U., 1958-63, prof. polit. sci. and law, 1963-68, 70-88, Nathaniel L. Nathanson prof., 1988—; pres. Reed Coll., Portland, Oreg., 1968-70; sr. legal cons. project on bankruptcy govtl. studies div. Brookings Instn., 1964-69; vis. Fulbright lectr. Sch. Law U. Louvain, Belgium, 1966-67, vis. prof., 1978-79, 91-92; mem. Adminstrv. Conf. U.S., 1982—. Editor in chief Adminstrv. Law Rev., 1958-62; author: Law As A Political Instrument, 1955, (with A.D. Castberg) Cases on Constitutional Law: Political Roles of the Supreme Court, 1973, (with Frances Zemans) The Making of a Public Profession, 1981; contbr. to law revs., also law and polit. sci. books. Staff assoc. Govtl. Affairs Inst., Washington, 1952-53; cons., assoc. counsel Subcom. on Exec. and Legis. Reorgn., Com. on Govt. Ops., U.S. Ho. of Reps., 1956-57; bd. dirs. Center for Adminstrv. Justice, 1972-78. Mem. ABA (council sect. adminstrv. law 1962-65, 72-75, chmn. 1977-78), Fed. Bar Assn., Am. Polit. Sci. Assn., Law and Soc. Assn. (pres. 1970-72), Am. Judicature Soc. (dir. 1982-90, chmn. bd. 1985-86), Assn. Am. Law Schs. (exec. com. 1984-88, pres. 1987), Consortium of Social Sci. Assns. (pres. 1987-88), Phi Beta Kappa, Pi Sigma Alpha. Democrat. Jewish. Home: 2030 Orrington Ave Evanston IL 60201-2912 Office: Northwestern U Sch Law 357 E Chicago Ave Chicago IL 60611-3008

ROSENBLUTH, MARION HELEN, educator, consultant, psychotherapist; b. Chgo., Apr. 4, 1928; d. Edwin William and Louise (Sulzberger) Eisendrath; m. Paul Richard Rosenbluth, June 16, 1950 (dec. Nov. 1972); children: Daniel, Jane Baldwin, Thomas, James, Catherine Rothschild. BA, Harvard U., 1949; MSW, Cath. U. of Am., 1951; PhD, U. Ill., 1986. Lic. clin. social worker, Ill. Clin. therapist Chgo. Dept. of Health, 1973-80; pvt. practice Chgo., 1980—; prof. Loyola U., Chgo., 1986—; cons. Inst. for Clin. Social Work, Chgo., 1988—; cons. student health Loyola U., 1978-80. Bd. dirs. Chgo. Area Project, 1978—, Rec. for the Blind, Chgo., 1980—, Inst. Psychiatry Northwestern U. Mem. NASW, Coun. on Social Work Edn., Bd. Examiners Clin. Social Work (diplomate), Ill. Soc. Clin. Social Work, Arts Club of Chgo., Cliff Dwellers, Friday Club. Office: 676 N Saint Clair St Chicago IL 60611

ROSENBLUTH, MORTON, periodontist, educator; b. N.Y.C., Sept. 28, 1924; s. Jacob and Eva (Bigeleissen) R.; m. Sylvia Fradin, July 2, 1946; children: Cheryl Bonnie, Hal Glen. BA, NYU, 1943, grad. program in periodontia, oral medicine, DDS, 1946. Diplomate Am. Bd. Periodontology. Intern Bellevue Hosp. N.Y.C., 1946-47, resident, 1947; individual practice dentistry, N.Y.C., 1947-59; individual practice periodontia, North Miami Beach, Fla., 1960—, individual practice periodontia, TMJ, implantology, Bay Harbor Islands, Fla., 1995—; periodontist Mt. Sinai Hosp., N.Y., Polyclinic Hosp. and Med. Sch. N.Y., Mt. Sinai Hosp., Miami Beach, Fla., Parkway Gen. Hosp.; chief dental dept. North Miami Gen. Hosp.; chmn. periodontia sect. Dade County Research Ctr.; clin. assoc. prof. div. oral and maxillofacial surgery U. Miami Sch. Medicine; assoc. clin. prof. Southeastern U. Health Scis.; assoc. prof. Nova Southeastern U. Coll. Dental Medicine; lectr. throughout U.S.A., Israel, Mexico, Rome, Teheran, Bangkok, Hong Kong, Tokyo, Honolulu, Jamaica, Paris, London, Sicily, Budapest, Berlin, Luxembourg, South Africa, and others; vis. lectr. U. Tenn. Dental Coll., NYU Dental Coll.; cons. VA Hosp., Miami. Mem. adv. bd. U. Fla. Coll. Dentistry; mem. profl. adv. bd. North Dade Children's Center, Hope Sch. Mentally Retarded Children; mem. sci. adv. com. United Health Found.; chmn. Dental div. United Fund of Dade County, Combined Jewish Appeal; nat. chmn. Hebrew U. Sch. Dental Medicine; bd. dirs. Health Planning Council S. Fla. Contbr. articles to profl. jours. Pres. Condominium Assn.; bd. dirs. and bd. overseers Am. Friends of Hebrew U.; mem. med. adv. bd. Dade-Broward Lupus Found.; trustee Jewish Congregation, 1961-64. With AUS, 1943-44, as capt. USAF, 1951-52. Recipient Maimonides award State of Israel, 1979. Fellow Am. Coll. Dentists, Internat. Coll. Dentists; mem. ADA, Am. Acad. Periodontology, Am., Fla. socs. periodontists, Am. Assn. Hosp. Dental Chiefs, Am. Acad. Dental Medicine, Am. Soc. Advancement Gen. Anesthesia in Dentistry, Northeastern Soc. Periodontists, Fla. (chmn. council on legislation), Miami, Miami Beach, East Coast (sec.-treas. 1968, pres. 1971-72), North Dade (pres. 1963-64) dental socs., Fedn. Dentaire Internationale, Fla. Acad. Dental Practice Adminstrn., Alpha Omega (pres. 1967-68, internat. regent 1973-75, internat. editor 1975-77, internat. pres.-elect 1977-78, internat. pres. 1979, chmn. bd. Alpha Omega Found. 1985-90) Am. Dental Interfrat. Council (pres. 1981-82), Nocoma Club (pres. 1958-60), NYU Century Club (local chmn.), Jockey Club (bd. govs.), KP, Masons, Kiwanis (bd. dirs. 1965), Chaine Des Rotisseurs (Miami Beach charge de missions). Home: 11111 Biscayne Blvd Apt 857 Miami FL 33181-3404 Office: 1166 Kane Concourse Bay Harbor Is FL 33154-2000

ROSENDAHL, ROGER WAYNE, lawyer. B, U. So. Calif., 1965; JD, Georgetown U., 1969, LLM, 1971. Bar: N.Y. 1973, Calif. 1975. Mng. ptnr. Cadwalader, Wickersham & Taft, L.A.; lectr. law U. Frankfurt, Germany. Mng. editor Law and Policy in Internat. Bus. Mem. fgn. svc. adv. com. U.S. Trade Rep. Schulte zur Hausen fellow. Mem. ABA (past officer, coun.), Asia-Pacific Lawyers Assn. (founding coun. 1991-92), L.A. County Bar Assn. (bd. advisors, exec. com.), Am. Arbitration Assn. Office: Cadwalader Wickersham & Taft 660 S Figueroa St Fl 23 Los Angeles CA 90017-3442

ROSENDALE, SUZANNE MOORE, library media specialist; b. Utica, N.Y., July 12, 1942; d. Clark Wilbur and Lynda Louise (Hokerk) Moore; m. Walter R. Rosendale Jr., June 18, 1966; children: Kristen, Jennifer. AA, Penn Hall Jr. Coll., Chambersburg, Pa., 1962; BS in Elem. Edn. and BS in English 7-12, SUNY, Oswego, 1980; MLS, Syracuse U., 1986. Cert. elem. edn. tchr., N.Y. English tchr. VVS Middle Sch., Verona, N.Y., 1980-85; libr. media specialist VVS Middle Sch., Verona, N.Y., 1986—. Co-author: Creative Mathematics, 1980. Bd. dirs. Sherrill-Kenwood Community Chest, Sherrill, N.Y., 1980-84; trustee/regent Sherrill-Kenwood Free Libr., 1992—, chmn. pers. com. 1992-94; mem. beautification com. City of Sherrill, 1992. Named 1st runner-up Vol. Yr. Oneida (N.Y.) Daily Dispatch, 1970. Mem. ASCD, Cen. N.Y. State Libr. Assn., Sherrill, N.Y. Garden Club (sec., treas. 90-93). Republican. Methodist. Avocations: fishing, gardening, antiquing, boating, refinishing. Home: 177 Willow Pl Sherrill NY 13461-1056

ROSENDHAL, JEFFREY DAVID, federal science agency administrator, astronomer; b. Bklyn., June 21, 1941; s. Louis and Beulah (Goldsmith) R.; m. Sharon E. Katzman, Dec. 27, 1964 (div. Jan. 25, 1989); children: Martin Andrew, Rachel Lynn; m. Ellen R. Anderson, Feb. 14, 1992. BA, Williams Coll., 1962; MS, U. Ill., 1963; PhD, Yale U., 1968. Vis. asst. prof. astronomy U. Wash., Seattle, 1968-69; asst. prof. U. Wis., Madison, 1969-71, U. Ariz., Tucson, 1971-74; with NASA, Washington, 1974—, mgr. advanced programs and tech., astrophysics divsn., 1978-80, asst. assoc. adminstr. advanced planning Office Space Sci., 1980-81, asst. assoc. adminstr. sci. Office Space Sci., Applications, 1981-87, spl. asst. to assoc. adminstr. for space sci. and applications, 1987-89, 92-93, spl. asst. for policy Office for Exploration, 1989-90, asst. dir. exploration (internat.) Office Aeronautics, Exploration and Tech., 1990-91, asst. dir. strategic planning Astrophysics Divsn. Office of Space Sci., 1993-96, asst. assoc. adminstr./edn. and outreach Office Space Sci., 1996—; vis. prof. internat. rels. George Washington U., 1988-89; mem. staff energy subcom. House Sci. Space and Tech. Com., 1992. Mem. editl. adv. bd. Jour. Brit. Interplanetary Soc., 1988—; contbr. articles to Astrophys. Jour., Astrophysics and Space Sci., Physics Today, Issues in Sci. and Tech., Acta Astronautica, other jours. and conf. procs. Recipient NASA Sr. Exec. Svc. Performance awards, 1980, 82-86, 96, Outstanding Leadership medal, 1984, group achievement awards, 1986 (2), 95, 96, European Space Agy. Team Achievement award, 1983, 85, 86, Presdl. award of Meritorious Exec. in Sr. Exec. Svc., 1987; NSF grantee, 1971, 72-73; NASA fellow Yale U., 1966-68; hon. Woodrow Wilson fellow, 1962. Mem. AIAA (sr. mem.), Astron. Soc. Pacific, Am. Astron. Soc., Royal Astron. Soc., Internat. Acad. Astronautics, Internat. Astron. Union, Cosmos Club, Phi Beta Kappa. Achievements include discovery of the variability of the microturbulence in early-type high luminosity stars; direction of the selection of flight experiments for every major NASA scientific mission 1980-88; development of strategic and implementation plans for incorporating education and the public understanding of science into space science research programs and missions. Home: 11446 Links Dr Reston VA 20190-4813 Office: NASA Hdqrs Office Space Sci Code S Washington DC 20546

ROSENDIN, RAYMOND JOSEPH, electrical contracting company executive; b. San Jose, Calif., Feb. 14, 1929; s. Moses Louis and Bertha C. (Pinedo) R.; m. Jeanette Marie Bucher, June 30, 1951 (dec. Feb. 1967); children: Mark R., Patricia A., Debra M., Cynthia C., David R.; m. Nancy Ann Burke, July 6, 1984; children: Raymond M., Callie R., Blake W. Student engring., San Jose State U., 1947-48; B.S.E.E., Heald's Engring. Coll., San Francisco, 1950. V.p., CEO Rosendin Electric, Inc., San Jose, Calif., 1953-59, exec. v.p., CEO, 1969-75, pres., CEO, 1975-94, chmn., CEO, 1995—; former dir. Community Bank, San Jose. Bd. fellows U. Santa Clara, Calif., 1966-93, pres. bd., 1969-72, bd. regents, 1972-82; bd. dirs. United Way, Santa Clara, 1970-74; O'Connor's Hosp., San Jose, 1979-85, Community Hosp., Los Gatos, Calif., 1968-74. Recipient Man of Yr. award Santa Clara Valley Youth Village, 1963, Optimist of Yr. award Optimist Club, San Jose, 1970. Mem. C. of C. Greater San Jose (past dir.), Nat. Elec. Contractors Assn. (past pres., gov., dir.). Republican. Roman Catholic. Club: St. Claire (San Jose). Avocation: boating. Office: Rosendin Electric Inc 880 Mabury Rd San Jose CA 95133-1021

ROSENDORFF, CLIVE, cardiologist; b. Bloemfontein, South Africa, Mar. 28, 1938; s. Karl and Rachel (Elkon) R.; m. Daphne Avigail Lynn, Dec. 30, 1962; children: Bryan Peter, Nicola, Adam. BSc with honors, U. Witwatersrand, Johannesburg, South Africa, 1958, MBBCh, 1962, MD, 1977, DSc Medicine, 1984. Med. cert. South Africa, U.K., N.Y. Lectr., cons. medicine St. Thomas Hosp., London, 1965-69; prof., chmn. physiology U. Witwatersrand Med. Sch., Johannesburg, 1970-91, dean, 1987-90; prof., assoc. chmn. medicine Mt. Sinai Sch. Medicine, N.Y.C., 1991—; chief medicine VA Med. Ctr., Bronx, N.Y., 1991—; vis. prof. Yale U., 1969-70, U. Calif., San Francisco, 1977, Hosp. Lariboisiere, Paris, 1991; rsch. fellow Am. Heart Assn., Yale U., 1969-70. Author: Clincial Cardiovascular and Pulmonary Physiology, 1988; author over 160 rsch. papers. Fellow ACP, Royal Soc. South Africa, Royal Coll. Physicians, Am. Coll. Cardiology. Achievements include research in cardiovascular disease. Office: Mt Sinai Sch Medicine Dept Medicine 1 Gustave L Levy Pl New York NY 10029-6504 also: VAMC Med Ctr Med Svc 130 W Kingsbridge Rd Bronx NY 10468

ROSENFELD, ARNOLD SOLOMON, newspaper editor; b. N.Y.C., Apr. 18, 1933; s. William and Sarah (Cohen) R.; m. Ruth Doris Lilly, Sept. 30, 1956 (dec. Sept. 1996); children—William Bennett, Jonathan Andrew, Lauren. Student, U. Houston, 1951; Profl. Journalism fellow, Stanford U., 1967. Mem. staff Houston Post, 1953-67; assoc. editor Detroit mag., Detroit Free Press, 1967; editor Detroit mag., 1968; mng. editor Dayton Daily News, Ohio, 1968-76; editor Dayton Daily News, 1976-80, Dayton Daily News and Jour. Herald, 1980-84, Austin Am.-Statesman, Tex., 1984-88, Atlanta Jour.-Constitution, 1988-89; editor-in-chief Cox Newspapers, Atlanta, 1989—; dir. The Temple, Atlanta, 1994—. Editor: A Thomason Sketchbook, 1969. Pres. Temple Israel Dayton, 1984; bd. dirs. Antioch U., 1978-84, Huston-Tillotson Coll., 1987-89. With AUS, 1951-53. Recipient Editorial Writing award A.P. Mng. Editors Assn. Tex., 1966; Tex. Theta Sigma Phi award, 1969, 72; Media award Nat. Assn. Mental Health, 1976. Mem. Am. Soc. Newspaper Editors Found. (bd. dirs., treas. 1992—). Home: 5875 Riverwood Dr NW Atlanta GA 30328-3728 Office: Cox Newspapers PO Box 105720 Atlanta GA 30348-5720

ROSENFELD, ARTHUR H., lawyer, publisher; b. Bklyn., May 24, 1930; s. Abraham and Sadie (Albert) R.; m. Lois E. Glantz, Apr. 15, 1956; children: Felicia Ann, Carolyn Jane, Sara Ellen. Student, St. Andrew's U., 1950-51; AB, Union Coll., Schenectady, 1952; JD, Harvard U., 1955; postgrad., CCNY, 1962-63. Bar: N.Y. 1955. Pres. Warren, Gorham & Lamont, Inc., N.Y.C., 1970-81, Internat. Thomson Profl. Pub., N.Y.C., 1981-84; chmn. bd. Rosenfeld, Emanuel Inc., Larchmont, N.Y., 1984-88; pres. Prentice Hall Tax & Profl. Ref., N.Y.C., 1988-89, Maxwell Macmillan Profl. and Bus. Reference Div., Englewood Cliffs, N.J., 1989-92, Arthur H. Rosenfeld Assocs., 1991—; Civic Rsch. Inst., Inc., 1992—; of counsel Am. Assn. Legal Publishers, 1995—; exec. dir. Fund for Pub. Access to the Law, 1995—. Vice chmn., bd. dirs. Coun. Econ. Priorities, 1990—. Mem. ABA, N.Y. State Bar

Assn., Am. Assn. Pubs. (exec. coun. 1991). Democrat. Club: Harvard. Office: 330 W 72nd St New York NY 10023

ROSENFELD, AZRIEL, computer science educator, consultant; b. N.Y.C., Feb. 19, 1931; s. Abraham Hirsh and Ida B. (Chadaby) R.; m. Eve Hertzberg, Mar. 1, 1959; children—Elie, David, Tova. B.A., Yeshiva U., 1950, M.H.L., 1953, M.S., 1954, D.H.L., 1955; M.A., Columbia U., 1951, Ph.D, 1957; D.Tech. (hon.), Linkoping U., Sweden, 1980; D of Tech. (hon.), Oulu U., Finland, 1994. Ordained rabbi, 1952. Physicist Fairchild Controls Corp., N.Y.C., 1954-56; engr. Ford Instrument Co., Long Island City, N.Y., 1956-59; mgr. research electronics div. Budd Co., Long Island City and McLean, Va., 1959-64; prof., dir. Ctr. for Automation Rsch. U. Md., College Park, 1964—, Disting. univ. prof., 1995—; vis. asst. prof. Yeshiva U., N.Y.C., 1957-63; pres. ImTech, Inc., Silver Spring, Md., 1975-92. Author, editor numerous books; editor numerous jours. Fellow IEEE (Emanuel R. Piore award 1985), IEEE Computer Soc. (Harry Goode Meml. award 1995), IEEE Sys., Man and Cybernetics Soc. (Norbert Wiener award 1995), Washington Acad. Scis. (Sci. Achievement award 1988), Am. Assn. for Artificial Intelligence (founding), Assn. Computing Machinery (founding); mem. Math. Assn. Am., Machine Vision Assn. (bd. dirs. 1984-88, Pres.'s award 1987), Internat. Assn. Pattern Recognition (pres. 1980-82, K.S. fu award 1988, founding fellow 1994), Assn. Orthodox Jewish Scientists (pres. 1963-65), Nat. Acad. Engring. of Mex. (corr.). Home: 847 Loxford Ter Silver Spring MD 20901-1132 Office: U Md Ctr Automation Rsch Computer Vision Lab College Park MD 20742-3275

ROSENFELD, HARRY MORRIS, editor; b. Berlin, 1929; s. Sam and Esther Laja (Sherman) R.; m. Anne Hahn, Feb. 28, 1953; children: Susan, Amy, Stefanie. BA, Syracuse U., 1952; postgrad., NYU, 1954, Columbia U., 1955-59. With N.Y. Herald Tribune, 1954-66, fgn. editor, 1962-66; mng. editor Herald Tribune News Svc., 1959-62; with Washington Post, 1966-78, fgn. editor, 1967-69; asst. mng. editor Met. News, 1970-74, Nat. News, 1974-76, Outlook/Book World, 1976-78; editor Times Union and Knickerbocker News, Albany, N.Y., 1978-88, L.A. Herald Examiner, 1985, The Times Union and Sunday Times Union, 1978-96; editor-at-large The Times Union and Sunday Times Union, Albany, N.Y., 1996—; dir. daily Watergate coverage for Washington Post (newspaper award Pulitzer Gold medal for pub. svc.); vice chmn. N.Y. Fair Trial Free Press Conf., 1985-97; co-chmn. N.Y. State Reporters Com. for Freedom of Press; mem. adv. com. Harvard Journalism Fellowship for Advanced Studies in Pub. Health. Recipient Black United Front award, 1973, First Amendment award Anti-Defamation League-B'nai B'rith, L.A., Outstanding Alumni award, Syracuse U. Coll. of Arts and Scis., 1993, Media Responsibility award N.Y. State Martin Luther King Jr. Inst. for Non-Violence, 1993. Mem. Am. Soc. Newspaper Editors, N.Y. State AP Assn. (pres. 1983, 3d pl. column award 1983, 85, 1st pl. column award 1987), N.Y. State Soc. Newspaper Editors, Internat. Press Inst., UPI Fgn. News Com. (rep. for N.E., Pulitzer juror 1987-88, 96, 97), Soc. Profl. Journalists (adv. bd. Albany chpt.), and 3 commns. on Cameras in the Cts. (adv. comm.). Office: Times Union PO Box 15000 Albany NY 12212

ROSENFELD, JOEL, ophthalmologist, lawyer; b. Jan. 27, 1957; s. Jacques Maurice and Mazal (Attia) R.; m. Amy Beth Garon. BS with high honors, U. Mich., 1976, MD, 1980; JD cum laude, U. Detroit, 1993. Diplomate Nat. Bd. Med. Examiners, Am. Bd. Ophthalmology; bar: Mich. 1994. Intern Baylor Coll. Medicine, Houston, 1980-81; resident in ophthalmology Kresge Eye Inst./Wayne State U., Detroit, 1981-84; fellow in ultrasound U. Iowa, Iowa City, 1984; chief of ophthalmology Wheelock Hosp., Goodrich, Mich., 1984—, Huron Meml. Hosp., Bad Axe, Mich., 1988—; St. Joseph Mercy Hosp., Pontiac, Mich., 1989—; co-founder, pres., gen. counsel Mktg. Systems, Inc., 1994—. Author rsch. reports. Supporting mem. Boys and Girls Club Am., Pontiac, Mich., 1984—, Pontiac Rescue Mission, 1988—. Recipient Man of Yr. award Boys and Girls Clubs Am., 1988; named Hon. Citizen, Father Flanagan Boys Home, Boys Town, Nebr., 1991, Ptnr. of Conscience, Amnesty Internat., N.Y.C., 1991. Fellow AMA, Am. Acad. Ophthalmology, Am. Coll. Legal Medicine; mem. ABA, FBA, Am. Soc. Law, Medicine and Ethics, Mich. State Med. Soc., Nat. Health Lawyers Assn. Jewish. Avocations: internat. politics and fin., history, reading autobiographies, travel. Home: 4612 W Maple Rd Bloomfield Hills MI 48301-1415

ROSENFELD, JOEL CHARLES, librarian; b. Bklyn., June 16, 1939. BA, U. Mich., 1961, AM in L.S., 1964. Br. libr. Flint Pub. (Mich.) Libr., 1962-66; adult svcs. cons. Lincoln Trail Librs., Champaign, Ill., 1967-68; dir. Urbana (Ill.) Free Libr., 1968-74; exec. dir. Met. Libr. Svc. Agy., St. Paul, 1974-79; exec. dir. Rockford (Ill.) Pub. Libr. 1980—; pres. Rockford Area Literary Coun., 1986-88, 95-96. Mem. ALA (chmn. constl. and bylaws com. 1988-89), Ill. Libr. Assn., Pub. Libr. Assn. (dir.-at-large 1980-81, pres. met. library sect. 1979-80). Office: Rockford Pub Library 215 N Wyman St Rockford IL 61101-1023

ROSENFELD, MARK KENNETH, retired retail store executive; b. Jackson, Mich., Mar. 17, 1946; s. Nathan and Marjorie N. (Leopold) R.; children: Edward Robert, Zachary, Alix Caitlin. B.A., Amherst Coll., 1968; S.M., MIT, 1970. With Jacobson's, Jackson, 1972—, v.p., real estate group mgr., 1976-78, exec. v.p., 1978-82, pres, 1992-93; chmn., CEO Jacobson's, Jackson, Mich., 1993-96; bd. dirs. Jacobson Stores, Ramco-Gershenson Property Trust, TCF Fin. Corp., Gt. Lakes Nat. Bank. With U.S. Army, 1969-70. Jewish.

ROSENFELD, MICHAEL G., medical educator. Prof. dept. medicine U. Calif. Med. Sch., La Jolla. Mem. NAS. Office: U Calif San Diego Sch Medicine M-013 Dept Medicine La Jolla CA 92093*

ROSENFELD, SARENA MARGARET, artist; b. Elmira, N.Y., Oct. 17, 1940; d. Thomas Edward and Rosalie Ereny (Fedor) Rooney; m. Robert Steven Bach, June 1958 (div. 1963); children: Robert Steven, Daniel Thomas; m. Samson Rosenfeld III, June 5, 1976. Student, Otis/Parson Art Inst., L.A., 1994—, Idyllwild Sch. Music and Arts, 1994—. One-woman shows and group exhbns. include Robert Dana Gallery, San Francisco, Gordon Gallery, Santa Monica, Calif., Hespe Gallery, San Francisco, Gallery 444, San Francisco, Art Expressions, San Diego, Ergane Gallery, N.Y.C., Nat. Mus. of Women in the Arts, Washington, also in L.A., La Jolla, Calif., Aspen, Colo., New Orleans, Soho, N.Y.C., Santa Barbara, Calif., Tanglewood, Mass., Honolulu, Johannesburg, South Africa, La Sierra U., Riverside, Calif. Mem., vol., animal handler Wildlife Waysta., Angeles Nat. Forest, Calif. Recipient Best of Show award Glendale Regional Arts Coun., 1984-85, 1st pl. awards Santa Monica Art Festival, 1982, 83, 84, 85, 86, Sweepstakes award and 1st pl., 1986, Purchase prize awards L.A. West C. of C., 1986-87, Tapestry in Talent Invitational San Jose Arts Coun., 1986, 1st pl. awards Studio City and Century City Arts Couns., 1976-84. Mem. Nat. Mus. of Women in the Arts. Republican. Home: 6570 Kelvin Ave Canoga Park CA 91306-4021

ROSENFELD, STEPHEN SAMUEL, newspaper editor; b. Pittsfield, Mass., July 26, 1932; s. Jay C. and Elizabeth R.; m. Barbara Bromson, Oct. 28, 1962; children: David, Rebecca, Emmet, James. B.A., Harvard U., 1953; M.A., Columbia U., 1959. Reporter Berkshire Eagle, Pittsfield, 1955-57; successively reporter, fgn. corr., editorial writer, columnist, dep. editor editorial page Washington Post, 1959—. Co-author: (with Barbara Rosenfeld) Return from Red Square, 1967; author: The Time of Their Dying, 1977. Served to 1st lt. USMC, 1953-55. Mem. Coun. on Fgn. Rels., Alexandria Lit. Soc., Century Assn. Home: 202 S Saint Asaph St Alexandria VA 22314-3744 Office: Washington Post Co 1150 15th St NW Washington DC 20071-0001

ROSENFELD, STEVEN B., lawyer; b. N.Y.C., Apr. 12, 1943; s. Eugene David and Laura (Sipin) R.; m. Naomi Eve Winkler, Aug. 21, 1965; children: Kathryn Anne, Elizabeth Jane. BA, Columbia Coll., 1964; LLB, Columbia U., 1967. Bar: N.Y. 1967, D.C. 1984, U.S. Dist. Ct. (so. dist.) N.Y. 1969, U.S. Dist. Ct. (ea. dist.) N.Y. 1970, U.S. Ct. Appeals (2d cir.) 1971, U.S. Ct. Appeals (3d cir.) 1974, U.S. Ct. Appeals (Fed. cir.) 1978, D.C. 1979, U.S. Supreme Ct. 1979, U.S. Ct. Appeals (5th cir.) 1982, U.S. Ct. Appeals (6th and D.C. cirs.) 1984, U.S. Ct. Appeals (4th and 9th cirs.) 1987, U.S. Ct. Appeals (1st cir.) 1989, U.S. Ct. Appeals (10th cir.) 1991. Law clk. to Hon. Charles M. Metzner U.S. Dist. Ct. (so. dist.) N.Y., 1967-68; assoc. Rosenman & Colin, N.Y.C., 1968-71; dep. gen. counsel N.Y. State Commn. on Attica, N.Y.C., Batavia, N.Y., 1971-72; assoc. Paul, Weiss, Rifkind, Wharton & Garrison, N.Y.C., 1972-75, ptnr., 1976—; lectr. Columbia U. Sch. Law, 1995—. Contbr. articles to profl. jours. Bd. dirs. N.Y. Assn. New Ams., N.Y.C., 1973-95; trustee Dalton Sch., N.Y.C., 1988-94; trustee Putney Sch. Putney, Vt., 1995—. Mem. N.Y. State Bar Assn. (ho. of dels. 1996—), Assn. of Bar of N.Y.C. (exec. com. 1992-96, past mem. various coms.), Legal Aid Soc. (pres. 1989-91, bd. dirs., exec. com. 1978-95). Democrat. Jewish. Avocations: opera and chamber music, theatre, tennis. Office: Paul Weiss Rifkind Wharton & Garrison 1285 Avenue Of The Americas New York NY 10019-6028

ROSENFELD, STEVEN IRA, ophthalmologist; b. N.Y.C., Nov. 18, 1954; s. Frederick and Pearl (Stern) R.; m. Lisa Allyson Klar, June 24, 1978; children: Michael, Julie. BA, Johns Hopkins U., 1976; MD, Yale U., 1980. Diplomate Am. Bd. Ophthalmology, Nat. Bd. Med. Examiners. Intern Yale-New Haven Hosp., 1980-81; resident Barnes Hosp., St. Louis, 1981-84; fellow Bascom Palmer Eye Inst., Miami, Fla., 1984-85; ptnr. in pvt. practice Delray Eye Assocs., Delray Beach, Fla., 1985—; clin. instr. Bascom Palmer Eye Inst., 1985-90, asst. clin. prof., 1990-96, assoc. clin. prof., 1996—; assoc. examiner Am. Bd. Ophthalmology, Phila., 1993—. Author: The Eye in Systemic Disease, 1990, Lens and Cataract, 1996; contbr. articles to profl. jours. Recipient Harry Rosenbaum Rsch. award Washington U. Sch. Medicine, 1984; named one of Best Doctors in Am., 1996; Heed Ophthalmic Found. fellow, 1984. Fellow ACS, Am. Acad. Ophthalmology, Soc. Heed Fellows; mem. Castroviejo Corneal Soc., Eye Bank Assn. Am., Fla. Med. Assn., Fla. Soc. Ophthalmology, Assn. for Rsch. in Vision and Ophthalmology, Ocular Microbiology and Immunology Group, Phi Beta Kappa, Alpha Omega Alpha. Avocations: tennis, golf, fly fishing, lacrosse. Office: Delray Eye Assocs 16201 Military Trl Delray Beach FL 33484-6503

ROSENFELD, WALTER DAVID, JR., architect, writer; b. N.Y.C., May 30, 1930; s. Walter David and Florence (Romann) R.; m. Marilyn Smith, Oct. 15, 1954; children: John W., Sarah E., Susannah, Elizabeth A. AB, U. Pa., 1952; postgrad. Ind. U., 1953-54, Yale U., 1954-55, 57-60. Registered architect, Mass., N.H., Pa.; cert. Nat. Coun. Archtl. Registration Bds.; cert. constrn. specifier. Draftsman, specifier Perry Dean Stewart, Boston, 1960-67; architect, specifier, v.p., prin. The Architects Collaborative, Cambridge, 1967-86, also dir., 1980-84, consulting architect Walter Rosenfeld, CSI, Newton, Mass., 1986—. Author: The Practical Specifier, 1985. Contbg. editor Progressive Architecture mag., 1980-94; contbr. articles to profl. jours. Pres. Friends of Newton Free Libr., Mass, 1970-72; chmn. Newton Ward 1 Dem. Com., 1974-80; vice chmn. designer selection com. City of Newton, 1976-86; bd. dirs. Mass. Audubon Soc., 1987—. With U.S. Army, 1955-57, Fed. Republic Germany. Mem. Constrn. Specifications Inst. (bd. dirs. Boston chpt. 1980-86, pres. Boston chpt. 1987-88), AIA, Boston Soc. Architects. Avocation: sailing. Office: Walter Rosenfeld CSI PO Box 380909 Cambridge MA 02238-0909

ROSENFIELD, ALLAN, physician; b. Cambridge, Mass., Apr. 28, 1933; s. Harold Herman and Beatrice (Garber) R.; m. Clare Stein, July 31, 1966; children: Paul Allan, Jill Emilie. BA cum laude, Harvard U., 1955; MD, Columbia U., 1959. Diplomate Am. Bd. Ob-Gyn. Intern, surgical resident Beth Israel Hosp., Boston, 1959-61; resident in ob-gyn Boston Hosp. for Women (now Brigham and Woman's Hosp.), Boston, 1963-66; rep., med. advisor The Population Council and Ministry Pub. Health, Bangkok, 1967-73; asst. dir. tech. assistance div. The Population Council, N.Y.C., 1973-75; prof. ob-gyn Columbia U., N.Y.C., 1975-88, prof. pub. health, 1975-86, DeLamar Prof. pub. health, 1986—, dir. ctr. for population and family health, 1975-88, acting chmn. dept. ob-gyn., 1984-86, dean sch. pub. health, 1986—. Contbr. over 100 articles to profl. jours. Capt. USAF, 1961-63. Fellow Am. Coll. Obstetricians and Gynecologists; mem. Inst. Medicine of NAS (several coms. and bds.), Am. Pub. Health Assn. Jewish. Avocations: tennis, skiing, music. Home: 4 Crosshill Rd Hartsdale NY 10530-3014 Office: Columbia U Sch Pub Health 600 W 168th St New York NY 10032-3702

ROSENFIELD, BRUCE ALAN, lawyer; b. Mpls., Apr. 30, 1951; s. Arnold M. and Phyllis M. (Fruchtman) R.; m. Bonnie S. Brier, Aug. 15, 1976; children: Rebecca, Elizabeth, Benjamin. AB, Dartmouth Coll., 1973; JD, Stanford U., 1976. Bar: Pa. 1976, U.S. Dist. Ct. (ea. dist.) Pa. 1976. Law clk. to Hon. Raymond Broderick U.S. Dist. Ct. (ea. dist.) Pa., Phila., 1976-78; assoc. Schnader, Harrison, Segal & Lewis, Phila., 1978-85, ptnr., 1986—; cons. Pa. Joint State Govt. Adv. Com. on Decedent and Estate Laws, 1991—; bd. dirs. Rittenhouse Fin. Svcs.; counsel Settlement Music Sch. Phila. Fellow Am. Coll. Trust and Estate Coun.; mem. Pa. Bar Assn. (coun. real property and trust law sect. 1995—), Phila. Bar Assn. (chmn. probate sect. 1993). Home: 132 Fairview Rd Penn Valley PA 19072-1331 Office: Schnader Harrison Segal & Lewis 1600 Market St Ste 3600 Philadelphia PA 19103-7286

ROSENFIELD, JAMES HAROLD, communications executive; b. Boston, July 18, 1929; s. Harold and Beatrice (Garber) R.; m. Nancy Lee Stenbuck, Oct. 19, 1952; 2 children. BA, Dartmouth Coll., 1952; D of Comml. Sci. (hon.), St. John's U., 1981. TV network sales exec. NBC, N.Y.C., 1954-57; advt. mgr. Polaroid Corp., Boston, 1956-59; v.p. mktg. Airequipt, Inc., New Rochelle, N.Y., 1959-65; TV account exec. CBS, Inc., N.Y.C., 1965-67, dir. daytime sales, 1967-70, v.p. Ea. sales, 1970-75, v.p. network sales adminstrn., 1975-77, v.p., nat. sales mgr., 1977, pres. TV Network Div., 1977-81; exec. v.p. CBS/Broadcast Group, N.Y.C., 1981-83, sr. exec. v.p., 1983-86; chmn., CEO John Blair Communications, Inc., N.Y.C., 1987-93; pres. JHR Assocs., Consulting, N.Y.C., 1993; mng. dir. Veronis, Suhler & Assocs., N.Y.C., 1994—. Mem. nat. bd. dirs. Jr. Achievement, Inc.; past alumni trustee Roxbury (Mass.) Latin Sch.; bd. dirs., former chmn. Adv. Coun. With Signal Corps, AUS, 1950-53. Mem. NATAS (bd. internat. coun.), Internat. Radio TV Soc. (past pres.).

ROSENFIELD, JAY GARY, publisher; b. Roslyn, N.Y., June 25, 1948; s. Maurice Ullman and Harriet Jessica (Obstfeld) R.; m. Lily Schwartzberg, Aug. 23, 1975; children—Adam, Amanda. B.A. in History, Ithaca Coll., 1970. Pres. Reese Communications, N.Y.C., 1970-95, creator, founder, pub. Video mag., 1977—; pres. R.G.H. Pub. Inc., 1989-96; pres., mem. bd. dirs. Art Levis Found. Bd. dirs. Denton Green Sr. Dwellings, Inc., New Hyde Park, N.Y., 1979-95. Mem. Whipporwill Assn. (bd. dirs. 1988—), Internat. Motoring Press Assn. Office: Video Mag Hachette Filipacchi Mags 1633 Broadway New York NY 10019-6708

ROSENFIELD, ROBERT LEE, pediatric endocrinologist, educator; b. Robinson, Ill., Dec. 16, 1934; s. Irving and Sadie (Osipe) R.; m. Sandra L. McVicker, Apr. 14, 1973. BS, Northwestern U., 1956, MD, 1960. Diplomate Am. Bd. Pediatric Endocrinology. Intern, Phila. Gen. Hosp. and Children's Hosp., Phila., 1960-63, 65-68; practice medicine specializing in pediatric endocrinology; prof. pediatrics, medicine U. Chgo., 1968—. Contbr. research articles to profl. jours. Served to capt. USMC, 1963-65. Fogarty Sr. Internat. fellow, USPHS, Weizmann Inst., Israel, 1977-78. Mem. Am. Bd. Pediatrics (sub.-bd. pediatric endocrinology 1983-86), Am. Pediatric Soc., Lawson Wilkins Pediatric Endocrinology Soc., Endocrine Soc., Soc. Gynecol. Investigation, Chgo. Pediatric Soc. (pres. 1981). Democrat. Jewish. Avocation: photography. Home: 5474 S Greenwood Ave Chicago IL 60615-5104 Office: U Chgo Med Ctr 5841 S Maryland Ave Chicago IL 60637-1463

ROSENHEIM, DANIEL EDWARD, journalist, television news director; b. Chgo., Aug. 12, 1949; s. Edward W. and Margaret Morton (Keeney) R.; m. Christina J. Adachi, May 10, 1976 (div. 1979); m. Cindy Catherine Salans, June 20, 1980; children: Joseph Michael, James Salans, Nicholas Edward. BA, Wesleyan U., 1971. Factory worker Pitts. and Chgo., 1972-77; reporter Sun-Jour., Lansing, Ill., 1977; bus./labor editor Hammond (Ind.) Times, 1977-80; bus. writer Chgo. Sun Times, 1980-82, spl. writer, 1982-84; bus. writer Chgo. Tribune, 1984-85; econs. editor San Francisco Chronicle, 1985-87, city editor, 1987-94, mng. editor, 1994-96; news dir. KRON-TV, San Francisco, 1996—. Mem. Radio and TV News Dirs. Assn., San Francisco Tennis Club. Avocations: tennis, golf, fly fishing. Office: KRON-TV 1001 Van Ness Ave San Francisco CA 94109-6913

ROSENHEIM, DONALD EDWIN, electrical engineer; b. N.Y.C., Mar. 23, 1926; s. Seymour Lawrence and Leah Rebecca (Rosenberg) R.; m. Judith Comfort Hyman, June 22, 1958; children—Micah Robert, Jay Aaron. BSEE magna cum laude, Poly. Inst. Bklyn., 1949; M.S., Columbia U., 1957. Devel. engr. Servo Corp. Am., 1949-51; mem. rsch. staff IBM ., 1951—, asst. dir. rsch. divsn., 1972-73; dir. San Jose (Calif.) Rsch. Lab., 1973-83, dir. tech. coordination, 1983-84; asst. dir. Almaden Rsch. Ctr., San Jose, 1984-92. Fellow IEEE; mem. Sigma Xi, Tau Beta Pi, Eta Kappa Nu. Home: 128 Smith Creek Dr Los Gatos CA 95030-1634

ROSENHEIM, EDWARD WEIL, English educator; b. Chgo., May 15, 1918; s. Edward Weil and Fannie (Kohn) R.; m. Margaret Morton Keeney, June 20, 1947; children: Daniel Edward, James Morton, Andrew Keeney. B.A., U. Chgo., 1939, M.A., 1946, Ph.D., 1953. Publicity writer Pub. Relations Service, Chgo., 1939-40; instr. Gary (Ind.) Coll., 1946; faculty U. Chgo., 1947—, prof. English, 1962—, David B. and Clara E. Stern prof., 1980-88, prof. emeritus, 1988—, assoc. chmn. dept. English, 1967-75, dir. broadcasting for univ., 1954-57; dir. Nat. Humanities Inst., 1977-80; Disting. vis. prof. Pa. State U., 1961; Disting. lectr. Nat. Coun. Tchrs. English, 1967; mem. Ill. Humanities Coun., 1982—, pres., 1985-87. Author: What Happens in Literature, 1960, Swift and the Satirist's Art, 1963; editor: Selected Prose and Poetry of Jonathan Swift, 1958, Jour. Gen. Edn., 1954-56; co-editor: Modern Philology, 1968-88. Served to capt. inf. AUS, 1941-46. Recipient Alumni Svc. medal U. Chgo., 1990; Willet Faculty fellow, 1962, Guggenheim Meml. fellow, 1967. Mem. Am. Soc. 18th Century Studies, Johnson Soc. (pres. Central region 1971). Clubs: Quadrangle, Wayfarers, Caxton. Home: 5805 S Dorchester Ave Chicago IL 60637-1730 Office: 1050 E 59th St Chicago IL 60637-1512

ROSENHEIM, HOWARD HARRIS, management consultant; b. Williamson, W.Va., Oct. 1, 1915; s. William Spiller and Frances Minerva (Harris) R.; m. Marjorie Jane Griffin, June 30, 1945; children: Cathy (Mrs. Mark Bustamante), William Spiller. B.S., Northwestern U., 1936, M.B.A., 1954; grad., Advanced Mgmt. Program, Harvard U. Grad. Sch. Bus., 1956. Civilian dir. indsl. planning div. USAF, Dayton, Ohio, 1947; pres. Internat. Register Co., elec. mfg. co., Chgo., 1948-70; pres. home study sch. Internat. Accts. Soc., Chgo., 1971; pres. Denoyer-Geppert Co. ednl. pub. subs. Times Mirror Co., Chgo., 1972-79, Internat. Assocs., Ltd., cons., 1980—; chmn. Camelot Controls, Ltd. (Eng.), 1966-70; dir. Extel Corp., Chgo., Telecommunication Radio Inc., Chgo., Data One, Inc., Chgo.; Vis. prof. bus. Northwestern U., Evanston, Ill., 1956-71, trustee, 1968-70; cons. Presdl. Commn. Nat. Air Policy, 1947; adv. to ministry of edn. Kingdom of Saudi Arabia, 1976-79. Pub. over 800 titles of ednl. materials in Arabic for schs. in Saudi Arabia; author articles to profl. jours. Served to maj. USAF, 1942-46. Decorated Award of Merit; recipient Disting. Educator award Northwestern U., 1972. Mem. Am. Mktg. Assn., Northwestern U. Alumni Assn. (pres. 1966-67). Methodist (mem. ofcl. bd. 1965-70). Clubs: Union League (Chgo.); Park Ridge (Ill.) Country. Inventor various time switches. Home: 2411 Farrell Ave Park Ridge IL 60068-1167

ROSENHEIM, MARGARET KEENEY, social welfare policy educator; b. Grand Rapids, Mich., Sept. 5, 1926; d. Morton and Nancy (Billings) Keeney; m. Edward W. Rosenheim, June 20, 1947; children: Daniel, James, Andrew. Student, Wellesley Coll., 1943-45; J.D., U. Chgo., 1949. Bar: Ill. 1949. Mem. faculty Sch. Social Service Adminstrn., U. Chgo., 1950—, assoc. prof., 1961-66, prof., 1966—, Helen Ross prof. social welfare policy, 1975—, dean, 1978-83; lectr. in law U. Chgo., 1980—; lectr. in law U. Chgo., 1980—; vis. prof. U. Wash., 1965, Duke U., 1984; Helen Ross prof. emeritus U. Chgo., 1996—; acad. visitor London Sch. Econs., 1973; cons. Pres.'s Commn. Law Enforcement and Adminstrn. Justice, 1966-67, Nat. Adv. Commn. Criminal Justice Stds. and Goals, 1972; mem. Juvenile Justice Stds. Commn., 1973-76; trustee Carnegie Corp. N.Y., 1979-87, Children's Home and Aid Soc. of Ill., 1981—, chair, 1996—; dir. Nat. Inst. Dispute Resolution, 1981-89, Nuveen Bond Funds, 1982-97; mem. Chgo. Network, 1983—. Editor, contbr.: Justice for the Child, 1962, reprinted, 1977, Pursuing Justice for the Child, 1976, Early Parenthood and Coming of Age in the 1990s, 1992; contbr. articles and book revs. to profl. jours. Home: 5805 S Dorchester Ave Chicago IL 60637-1730 Office: 969 E 60th St Chicago IL 60637-2640

ROSENHOFFER, CHRIS, lawyer; b. Cin., Apr. 19, 1913; s. Joseph and Barbara (Stitzel) R.; m. Alberta Arlene Jarvis, Dec. 28, 1935 (div. Apr. 1992); children: Chris Jr., Dennis P., Gary A., John J., Nancy A., Todd D. BS Commerce, Salmon P. Chase Coll. Commerce, Cin., 1948; JD, Salmon P. Chase Coll. Law, Cin., 1951. Bar: Ohio, 1951, U.S. Dist. Ct. (so. dist.) Ohio 1952. Acct., log buyer Al J. Boehm Walnut Co., Kenova, W.Va., 1938-44; acct. The Green Embry Co., Cin., 1948-51; judge Clermont County Ct., Batavia, Ohio, 1958-62, 67-86; pvt. practice law Batavia, 1951—; spl. counsel Atty. Gen. of Ohio, Batavia, 1963-64. Treas. Clermont County Rep. Club, Batavia, 1957-58; team mem. Citizens Amb. Program, Seattle, 1988, 93; mem. sch. bd. West Clermont Local Sch. Dist., Amelia, Ohio, 1958-74. With U.S. Army, 1944-46. Mem. Ohio Bar Assn., Ohio Acad. Trial Lawyers, Clermont County Bar Assn. (pres. 1962), Cin. Bar Assn., Am. Legion. Methodist. Avocations: fishing, hunting. Office: 97 Main St Batavia OH 45103

ROSENHOUSE, IRWIN J., artist, designer; b. Chgo. B.F.A., Cooper Union, N.Y.C., 1950. Designer Mus. Modern Art, 1954-57, Harcourt, Brace & Co., 1957, Dell Books, 1963; tchr. art Mus. Modern Art, 1967-69, Pratt Graphic Center, N.Y.C., 1972, 85, Bklyn. Coll., 1972-73, Bklyn. Mus. Art Sch., 1974, Nassau C.C., 1972-97, N.Y. Tech. Coll., 1983-86; owner Rosenhouse Gallery, N.Y.C., 1963-72; lectr. art, book illustration, design; preparer graphics for Arab-Israeli peace confs.: The Road to Peace, Convocation for Peace, N.Y.C., 1989-90; dir. monthly ednl. lecture series N.Y. Artist Equity, 1989-91; adj. prof. Nassau C.C., 1997. One-man shows N.Y.C., Bklyn., Easthampton, N.Y., Dance Theater Workshop Art Gallery, N.Y.C., 1992, also various colls. and mus. in U.S.; exhibited in group shows numerous mus., painting socs. exhbns. throughout U.S.; represented in permanent collections Met. Mus., N.Y. Pub. Libr., Everhart Mus., Cooper Union Mus., Bklyn. Coll. Collection; illustrator: (juvenile) Have You Seen Trees?, The Rabbis Bible. Served with U.S. Mcht. Marine, 1944-51. Recipient Louis Comfort Tiffany Found. award, 2 Huntington Hartford Found. awards, Billboard Ann. award, Illustrators Club award, 1st prize Rome Collaborative; record cover designs included in Smithsonian ethnic music collection. Address: 256 Mott St New York NY 10012-3402
Humanist imagery has been my main concern and the pursuit of a simple, direct image of nature.

ROSENKER, MARK VICTOR, trade association executive; b. Balt., Dec. 8, 1946; s. Stanley and Irene (Moss) R.; m. Heather Beldon. BA in Communications, U. Md., 1969, postgrad., 1970-71; grad., USAF Air Command and Staff Coll., 1986, USAF Air War Coll., 1990. Asst. to events producer, relief engr. ABC-TV News, Washington, 1968-69; dep. dir. radio and TV Com. Reelect Pres., Washington, 1972; staff asst. to sec. U.S. Dept. Interior, Washington, 1972-73; account exec. Daniel Edelman Pub. Relations, Inc., Washington, 1973-75; dir. communications Motorized Bicycle Assn., Washington, 1975; dep. press sec. Pres. Ford Com., Washington, 1976; v.p. Electronic Industries Assn., Washington, 1977—; bd. of vis. Cmty. Coll. USAF, Maxwell, Ala., 1981-86; apptd. commr. Am. Battle Monument Commn., 1990-94. Active Campaign to Elect Reagan/Bush, Washington, 1980, 84, Campaign to Elect Bush/Quayle, 1988, 92—; sr. advisor Dole/Kemp Campaign, 1995-96. 1st lt. USAF, 1969-72, col. USAFR, 1972—. Recipient Chuck Docekal Meml. award, 1987, Am. Battle Monuments Commn. Meritious Svc. award, 1994. Mem. Am. Soc. Assn. Execs., Greater Washington Soc. Assn. Execs., Res. Officers Assn. Club, Capitol Hill Club, Army Navy Club. Avocations: sailing, tennis, skiing, golf. Home: 1626 Great Falls St Mc Lean VA 22101-5079 Office: Electronic Industries Assn 2500 Wilson Blvd Arlington VA 22201-3834

ROSENKOETTER, GERALD EDWIN, engineering and construction company executive; b. St. Louis, Mar. 16, 1927; s. Herbert Charles and Edna Mary (Englege) R.; m. Ruth June Beekman, Sept. 10, 1949; children: Claudia Ruth, Carole Lee. BSCE, Washington U., St. Louis, 1951; MSCE, Sever Inst. Tech., St. Louis, 1957. Registered profl. engr. Colo., Del., D.C., Fla., Ga., Idaho, Kans., Mass., Mich., Mo., N.C., N.J., Ohio, Pa., Tex., Utah, Wis. Sr. structural engr. Sverdrup & Parcel, Inc., St. Louis, 1951-56, project engr., 1956-60; engring. mgr. Sverdrup & Parcel, Inc., Denver, 1960-62; project mgr. Sverdrup & Parcel & Assocs., St. Louis, 1962-69, chief engr.,

1969-74, v.p., 1974-80; pres. SPCM, Inc., St. Louis, 1980-85; exec. v.p. Sverdrup Corp., St. Louis, 1985-88, vice-chmn., 1988-93; pres. Sverdrup Hydro, Inc., 1988-93; engr. and fin. cons. Sarasota, 1993—; asst. prof. Washington U., 1955-60; ptnr. 3 Sverdrup Partnerships, 1977-93; expert witness Sverdrup & Parcel & Assocs., 1970-75; cons. engring. and constrn. projects, 1993—. Councilman City of Berkeley, Mo., 1956-58, councilman-at-large, 1958-60, chmn. city planning and zoning com., 1963-65; dir. Conservatory and Sch. Arts, St. Louis, 1989-92. Sgt. U.S. Army, 1945-46. Engrs. Club of St. Louis scholar, 1950. Mem. ASCE (chmn. continuing edn. 1965-66, named Outstanding Sr. Engring. Student 1951), Bent Tree Country Club (Sarasota, Fla.). Lutheran. Avocations: golfing, sailing.

ROSENKRANS, KENNETH RAY, financial services; b. Waterloo, Iowa, Feb. 6, 1951; s. Frank Preston and Winona Marie (DeVore) R.; m. Francene Annette Maniscalco, June 23, 1989; children: Erin, Matthew, Melissa, Jennifer. BS in Mktg., U. No. Iowa, 1974. V.p. Norwest Mortgage, Waterloo, Iowa, 1977-82, Ticor Realty Tax Svcs., Chgo., 1982-87; sr. v.p. mktg. TRTS Data Svcs., L.A., 1987-92; sr. v.p. regional mgr. First Am. REal Estate Tax Svc., L.A., 1992—. With U.S. Army, 1976-79. Mem. Mortgage Bankers Assn. of Am., Orange County Mortgage Bankers Assn. Avocations: sports, wine, music.

ROSENKRANTZ, DANIEL J., computer science educator; b. Bklyn., Mar. 5, 1943; s. Harry and Ruth (Sirota) R.; m. Carole Jaffee, Aug. 2, 1969; children: Holly, Sherry, Jody, Andrew. BS, Columbia U., 1963, MS, 1964, PhD, 1967. With Bell Telephone Labs., Murray Hill, N.J., 1966-67; info. scientist GE Co. R & D Ctr., Schenectady, N.Y., 1967-77; prof. dept. computer sci. U. Albany-SUNY, Albany, 1977—, dept. chair, 1993—; prin. computer scientist Phoenix Data Systems, Albany, 1983-85. Author: (with P.M. Lewis II and R.E. Stearns) Compiler Design Theory, 1976. Fellow ACM (editor-in-chief jour. 1986-91, area editor for formal langs. and models of computation 1981-86, mem. numerous conf. coms.); mem. IEEE Computer Soc., ACM Spl. Interest Group on Automata and Computability Theory (sec. 1977-79). Home: 1261 Cranbrook Ct Niskayuna NY 12309-1203 Office: U at Albany SUNY Dept Computer Sci Albany NY 12222

ROSENKRANZ, HERBERT S., environmental toxicology educator, cancer researcher; b. Vienna, Sept. 27, 1933; came to U.S., 1948; s. Samuel and Lea Rose (Marilles) R.; m. Deanna Eloise Green, Jan. 27, 1959; children: Pnina Gail, Eli Joshua, Margalit E., Dara V., Jeremy Amiel, Sara C., Naomi, Tsilila. BS, CCNY, 1954; PhD, Cornell U., 1959. Postdoctoral fellow Sloan-Kettering Inst. for Cancer Rsch., 1959-60, U. Pa., Phila., 1960-61; asst. prof. microbiology Columbia U., N.Y.C., 1961-65, assoc. prof., 1965-69, prof., 1969-76; prof., chmn. microbiology dept. N.Y. Med. Coll., Valhalla, 1976-81; prof. Case Western Res. U., Cleve., 1981-90, dir. Ctr. Environ. Health Sci., 1981-84, chmn. dept. environ. health sci., 1985-90; prof., chmn. dept. environ. and occupational health U. Pitts., 1990—, dir. Ctr Environ. and Occupational Health and Toxicology. Lalor Found. awardee, 1963; Nat. Cancer Inst. Research Career Devel. awardee, 1965-75. Mem. AAAS, Am. Assn. Cancer Research, Am. Soc. Biol. Chemists, Environ. Mutagen Soc., Soc. Toxicology. Jewish. Office: U Pitts Grad Sch Pub Health Dept Environ and Occup Health 260 Kappa Dr Pittsburgh PA 15238-2818

ROSENKRANZ, ROBERT BERNARD, military officer; b. Paterson, N.J., Sept. 26, 1939; s. Irving Morton and Lucille (Kane) R.; m. Barbara Jean Larson, May 17, 1970; children: Stephen Robert, Deborah Anne, Diana Rebecca, Susan Leslie. BS, U.S. Mil. Acad., 1961; MA, U. Pa., 1969. Comd. 2d. lt. U.S. Army, 1961, advanced through grades to maj. gen., 1992; officer U.S. Army, Fed. Republic of Germany, 1962-65; battalion exec. officer U.S. Army, Korea, 1973-74; battery comdr. U.S. Army, Vietnam, 1966-67; battery and brigade comdr. U.S. Army, Fed. Republic of Germany, 1977-79, 83-85; assoc. prof. U.S. Mil. Acad., West Point, N.Y., 1969-72; dir. soviet studies U.S. Army War Coll., Carlisle, Pa., 1981-83; sr. mil. asst. under sec. of def. Pentagon, Washington, 1986-88; dep. dir. Army Ops., Readiness and Mobilization U.S. Army Pentagon, Washington, 1988-89, dir. force programs, 1989-92; comdr. U.S. Army Optec, Washington, 1992-95; v.p. test and evaluation/ranges Dyncorp, Reston, Va., 1995—. Decorated Bronze Star, Air medal; recipient Superior Svc. medal U.S. Dept. Def., 1988, D.S.M., 1992, 95. Mem. Internat. Inst. of Strategic Studies, Assn. of the U.S. Army, Internat. Test and Evaluation Assn. Republican. Jewish. Avocations: jogging, reading, woodworking, golf, racquetball. Home: 3222 Wynford Dr Fairfax VA 22031-2828

ROSENKRANZ, STANLEY WILLIAM, lawyer; b. N.Y.C., Aug. 20, 1933; s. Jacob and Adele R.; m. Judith Ossinsky, Aug. 14, 1960; children: Jack Michael, Andrew Lawrence. BS in Acctg, U. Fla., 1955, JD with honors, 1960; LLM (Kenneson fellow), NYU, 1961. Bar: Fla. 1960, Ga. 1970; cert. tax lawyer. Mem. firm Macfarlane, Ferguson, Allison & Kelly, Tampa, Fla., 1961-68, 71-79; with King & Spalding, Atlanta, 1969-71, Holland & Knight, Tampa, 1979-86, Shear, Newman, Hahn & Rosenkranz P.A., Tampa, 1986—; adj. prof. Grad. Sch. Law, U. Fla., 1975-79, Grad. Coll. Bus. Adminstrn., U. Tampa, 1989, 97—. Pres. Congregation Schaarai Zedek, Tampa, 1981-83; bd. dirs. Union Am. Hebrew Congregations, 1990—, v.p. S.E. region, 1988-90, pres., 1992-96. With U.S. Army, 155-57. Named Young Man of Year Tampa Jaycees, Fla., 1967. Mem. ABA, Am. Coll. Tax Counsel, Am. Law Inst., Fla. Bar Assn., Ga. Bar Assn., Greater Tampa C. of C. (bd. govs., chmn. anti-drug task force). Home: 1125 Shipwatch Cir Tampa FL 33602-5785 Office: 201 E Kennedy Blvd Tampa FL 33602

ROSENMAN, KENNETH D., medical educator; b. N.Y.C., Feb. 25, 1951. AB, Cornell U., 1972; MD, NYU, 1975. Bd. cert. internal medicine; bd. cert. occupational and preventive medicine. Asst. prof. U. Mass., Amherst, 1979-81; dir. occupational and environ. health N.J. Dept. Health, Trenton, 1981-86; pvt. practice Plainsboro, N.J., 1986-88; assoc. prof. Mich. State U., East Lansing, 1988-93, prof., 1993—. Office: Mich State U 117 W Fee Hall East Lansing MI 48824-1315

ROSENMAN, LEONARD, composer; b. Brooklyn, N.Y., Sept. 7, 1924. Condr. Rome, 1962-66; instr. U. So. Calif.; musical dir. New Muse Chamber Orch. Music dir., composer: (film scores) The Outsider, 1962, Barry Lyndon, 1975 (Academy award best adapted score 1975), Bound for Glory, 1976 (Academy award best adapted score 1976), The Lord of the Rings, 1978; music condr.: (TV movies) Sherlock Holmes in New York, 1976; composer: (film scores) The Cobweb, 1955, East of Eden, 1955, Rebel without a Cause, 1955, Bombers B-52, 1957, Edge of the City, 1957, The Young Stranger, 1957, Lafayette Escadrille, 1958, Pork Chop Hill, 1959, The Bramble Bush, 1960, The Crowded Sky, 1960, The Plunderers, 1960, The Rise and Fall of Legs Diamond, 1960, The Chapman Report, 1962, Convicts Four, 1962, Hell is for Heroes, 1962, A Covenant with Death, 1966, Fantastic Voyage, 1966, Countdown, 1968, The Savage Land, 1969, Beneath the Planet of the Apes, 1970, A Man Called Horse, 1970, The Todd Killings, 1971, Battle for the Planet of the Apes, 1973, Race with the Devil, 1975, Birch Interval, 1976, The Car, 1977, 9/30/55, 1977, An Enemy of the People, 1978, Promises in the Dark, 1979, Prophecy, 1979, Hide in Plain Sight, 1980, The Jazz Singer, 1980, Making Love, 1982, Cross Creek, 1983 (Academy award nomination best original score 1983), Heart of the Stag, 1984, Sylvia, 1985, Star Trek IV: The Voyage Home, 1986 (Academy award nomination best original score 1986), Robocop 2, 1990, Ambition, 1991, (TV movie scores) Banyon, 1971, In Broad Daylight, 1971, Vanished, 1971, The Bravos, 1972, The Cat Creature, 1973, Judge Dee and the Monastery Murders, 1974, Nakia, 1974, The Phantom of Hollywood, 1974, The First Thirty-Six Hours of Dr. Durant, 1975, Sky Heist, 1975, Kingston: The Power Play, 1976, Lanigan's Rabbi, 1976, Sybil, 1976 (Emmy award best music composition for dramatic underscore 1977), Mary White, 1977, The Possessed, 1977, The Other Side of Hell, 1978, Friendly Fire, 1979 (Emmy award best music composition for dramatic underscore 1979), Nero Wolfe, 1979, City in Fear, 1980, Murder in Texas, 1981, The Wall, 1982, Celebrity, 1984, Heartsounds, 1984, The Return of Marcus Welby, M.D., 1984, First Steps, 1985, Promised a Miracle, 1988, Where Pigeons Go to Die, 1990, Aftermath: A Test of Love, 1991, Keeper of the City, 1992, (TV series scores) Men from Shiloh, 1970, Primus, 1971, Nakia, 1974, Gibbsville, 1976, Holmes and Yoyo, 1976, Rafferty, 1977, Joshua's World, 1980, (musical works) Threnody on a Song of K.R., 1971, Chamber Music 5, 1979, Foci I, 1981. *

ROSENMAN, STEPHEN DAVID, physician, obstetrics, gynecology; b. Bklyn., Sept. 4, 1945; s. Bernard and Theresa (Marks) R. m. Arlette de Greef, Dec. 26m 1970; children: Burt, Joelle. BA in Biology, Hofstra U., 1967; MD magna cum laude, Cath. U. of Louvain (Belgium), 1972. Diplomate Am. Bd. Ob-Gyn., voluntarily re-cert. 1991; lic. N.Y., Conn. Rotating intern Dalhousie U., Canada, 1972-73; ob-gyn. resident Bridgeport (Conn.) Hosp., 1973-75, chief resident, 1976-77, sr. attending physician ob-gyn., 1986—; pvt. practice Fairfield, Stratford, Trumbull, Bridgeport, Conn., 1978—. Named Tchr. of Yr., Bridgeport (Conn.) Hosp. 1977, '78, '80, Best Doctors in Am., 1996-97; featured in Connecticut Mag. Fellow Am. Bd. Obstetrics, Am. Coll. Ob.-Gyn. Avocations: computer, reading. Office: Ob-gyn of FFLD County PC 1725 Post Rd Fairfield CT 06430-5715 also: 2499 Main St Stratford CT 06497-5843 also: 15 Corporate Dr Trumbull CT 06611-1351

ROSENMANN, DANIEL, physicist, educator; b. Lima, Peru, Sept. 6, 1959; came to U.S., 1991; s. Lothar and Eva (Roiter) R.; m. Patricia Edith Alvarado, Jan. 21, 1989. BS in Physics, U. Nac. Mayor de San Marcos, Lima, Peru, 1986; postgrad., No. Ill. U., 1991-93. Instr. U. Nacional Mayor de San Marcos, Lima, 1982-91; tchr. Coll. Leon Pinelo, Lima, 1986-91; teaching asst. No. Ill. U., DeKalb, 1991-93, grad. rsch. asst., 1993; lab. grad. participantship Argonne (Ill.) Nat. Lab., 1993-96; rsch. lab. mgr. physics dept. No. Ill. U., DeKalb, 1994-96; sci. assoc. Argonne Nat. Lab., 1996—. Author: Lab. guide book, 1988, 89. Scholar, fellow Argonne Nat. Lab. 1993-96. Mem. AAAS, Am. Phys. Soc., N.Y. Acad. Scis., Nat. Geographic Soc., Sigma Xi, Sigma Pi Sigma. Home: 2512 Bordeaux Ln Apt 204 Naperville IL 60540-1965

ROSENN, HAROLD, lawyer; b. Plains, Pa., Nov. 4, 1917; s. Joseph and Jennie (Wohl) R.; m. Sallyanne Frank, Sept. 19, 1948; 1 child, Frank Scott. BA, U. Mich., 1939, JD, 1941; LLD (hon.), Coll. Misericordia, 1991. Bar: Pa. 1942, U.S. Supreme Ct. 1957. Ptnr. Rosenn & Rosenn, Wilkes Barre, Pa., 1948-54; ptnr. Rosenn, Jenkins & Greenwald, Wilkes Barre, 1954-87, of counsel, 1988—; mem. Pa. State Bd. Law Examiners, 1983-93, Pa. Gov.'s Justice Commn., 1968-73, Pa. Crime Commn., 1968-73, Fed. Jud. Nominating Com., Pa., 1977-79, Appellate Ct. Nominating Com., Pa., 1979-81; asst. dist. atty. Luzerne County, Pa., 1952-54. Chmn. ARC, Wilkes-Barre, 1958-60 (life mem. bd.); pres. Pa. Coun. on Crime and Delinquency, Harrisburg, 1969-71; bd. dirs. Coll. Misericordia, Dallas, Pa., 1976-86, emeritus, 1986—, Hoyt Libr., Kingston, Pa., 1971-78, Nat. Coun. on Crime and Delinquency, N.Y.C., 1969-71; chmn. United Way Campaign of Wyoming Valley, 1978-80; pres. Temple Israel of Wilkes Barre, 1972-74 (chmn. bd. 1974-84, life mem. bd.); comdr. post 395 Am. Legion, Kingston, 1948; mem. bd. dirs. Keystone State Games, 1982—. Capt. USAAF, 1942-45, ETO. Decorated presdl. citation with cluster; recipient Erasmus medal Dutch Govt., Disting. Svc. award in Trusteeship, Assn. Governing Bds. Univs. and Colls., 1990; Disting. Community Svc. award Greater Wilkes-Barre Soc. Fellows Anti-Defamation League, 1991, Clara Barton honor award Wyoming Valley chpt. ARC, 1992, Lifetime Achievement award United Way of Wyoming Valley, 1992; honoree Wyoming Valley Interfaith Coun., 1986; named Golden Key Vol. of Yr., United Way of Pa., 1989; inductee Jr. Achievement Hall of Fame for N.E. Pa., 1997. Mem. ABA, Pa. Bar Assn., Am. Judicature Soc., The Pa. Soc. Republican. Jewish. Clubs: U. Mich. (N.E. Pa.) (pres. 1946-76), Westmoreland (Wilkes Barre). Lodge: B'nai Brith (pres. Wilkes Barre 1952-53, Community Service award 1976).

ROSENN, KEITH SAMUEL, lawyer, educator; b. Wilkes-Barre, Pa., Dec. 9, 1938; s. Max and Tillie R. (Hershkowitz) R.; m. Nan Raker, June 21, 1960; 1 child, Eva; m. Silvia R. Rudge, Mar. 21, 1968; children—Jonathan, Marcia. A.B., Amherst Coll., 1960; LL.B., Yale U., 1963. Bar: Pa. 1964, U.S. Ct. Appeals (3d cir.) 1979, Fla. 1981, U.S. Ct. Appeals (11th cir.) 1982. Law clk. to Judge Smith U.S. Ct. Appeals for 2d Circuit, 1963-64; asst. prof. law Ohio State U. Coll. Law, 1965-68, assoc. prof., 1968-70, prof., 1970-79; project assoc. Ford Found., Rio de Janeiro, 1966-68; assoc. Escritorio Augusto Nobre, Rio de Janeiro, 1979-80; prof. law U. Miami, Fla., 1979—; project coordinator Olin Fellowship Program Law and Econs. Ctr., U. Miami, Fla., 1980-81, assoc. dean Law Sch., 1982-83, dir. fgn. grad. law program, 1985—; cons. Hudson Inst., 1977, U.S. State Dept., 1981-82, World Bank, 1988-90; Fulbright lectr. Argentina, 1987, 88. Author: (with Karst) Law and Development in Latin America, 1975; Law and Inflation, 1982, Foreign Investment in Brazil, 1991; co-editor: A Panorama of Brazilian Law, 1992; advisor InterAm. Law Rev.; contbr. articles to law jours. Recipient Order of Democracy award Congress of Republic of Colombia, 1987, Lawyer of the Ams. award, 1989; grantee Social Sci. Rsch. Coun., 1970, Dana Found., 1982. Mem. ABA, Am. Law Inst., Inter-Am. Bar Assn., Fla. Bar, Am. Soc. Comparative Law (bd. dirs.). Jewish. Office: U Miami Law Sch PO Box 248087 Coral Gables FL 33124

ROSENN, MAX, federal judge; b. Plains, Pa., Feb. 4, 1910; s. Joseph and Jennie (Wohl) R.; m. Tillie R. Hershkowitz, Mar. 18, 1934; children: Keith S., Daniel Wohl. BA, Cornell U., 1929; LLB, U. Pa., 1932. Bar: Pa. 1932, U.S. Supreme Ct. 1955, Cts. of Philippines 1946. Gen. practice Wilkes-Barre, Pa., 1932-70; dir. Franklin Fed. Savs. & Loan, Wilkes-Barre, 1937-70; spl. counsel Pa. Dept. Justice, 1939; asst. dist. atty. Luzerne County, 1942-44; also solicitor various mcpl. boroughs, ptnr. firm Rosenn & Rosenn, 1947-54, Rosenn, Jenkins & Grenwald, Wilkes-Barre, 1954-66, 67-70; sec. pub. welfare Pa., 1966-67; judge U.S. Ct. Appeals (3d cir.), 1970-81, sr. judge, 1981—; former mem. criminal procedure rules com. Supreme Ct. Pa., 1958-85; mem. Pa. Commn. to Revise Pub. Employee Laws, 1968-69; Pa. chmn. White House Conf. on Children and Youth. Contbr. articles to legal publs. Mem. Pa. Bd. Pub. Welfare, 1963-66; chmn. Pa. Gov.'s Hosp. Study Commn., Pa. Gov.'s Coun. for Human Svcs., 1966-67; mem. exec. bd. Commonwealth of Pa., 1966-67; chmn. Commn. Met. Govt., 1957-58; pres. Property Owners Assn. Luzerne County, 1955-57; chmn. Pa. Human Rels. Commn., 1969-70, Pa. Comm. Children and Youth, 1968-70, Legis. Task Force Structure for Human Svcs., 1970; alt. del. Rep. Nat. Conv., 1964; pres. Wyoming Valley Jewish Com., 1941-42; life trustee Wilkes-Barre Jewish Community Ctr.; chmn. Flood Recovery Task Force, 1972. Max Rosenn U.S. Courthouse dedicated, 1996. Fellow Am. Coll. Trial Lawyers, Internat. Acad. Trial Lawyers; mem. ABA, Pa. Bar Assn., Luzerne County Bar Assn., Am. Law Inst., Am. Soc. Law and Medicine (charter mem., former assoc. editor jour.), Am. Judicature Soc., B'nai B'rith (pres. dist. grand lodge 1947-48, life bd. govs., former chmn. bd. dirs. Anti-Defamation League Pa., W.Va. and Del. 1955-58, nat. commr. 1964—), Westmoreland Club, Masons (33d degree), Alpha Epsilon Pi. Jewish. Office: US Ct Appeals 229 US Courthouse 197 S Main St Wilkes Barre PA 18701-1500

ROSENNE, MEIR, lawyer, government agency administrator; b. Iasi, Romania, Feb. 19, 1931; came to Israel, 1944; s. Jacob and Mina Rosenhaupt; m. Vera Ayal, June 9, 1959; children—Mihal, Dafna. MA in Polit. Sci., Inst. Polit. Sci., Paris, 1953; LLB, Sorbonne, U. Paris, 1955, PhD in Internat. Law with honors, 1957; grad., Inst. Internat. Studies, Paris, 1953. In govt. service Israel, 1953—; consul Israel Consulate, N.Y.C., 1967-69; sr. lectr. in polit. sci. U. Haifa, Israel, 1969-71; coordinator Atomic Energy Commn. Israel, 1969-71; chief legal adviser Fgn. Office Israel, Jerusalem, 1971-79; Israeli amb. to France, Paris, 1979-83; Israeli amb. to U.S. Washington, 1983-87; pres. State of Israel Bonds, N.Y., 1989-93; ptnr. Balter, Guth, Aloni & Co., Jerusalem, 1994—; chmn. overseas com. Jerusalem Bank; bd. dirs. IDB, Ltd., Israel Discount Bank Holding. Contbr. articles to N.Y. Times, Washington Post, N.Y. Herald Tribune, also others. Chmn. internat. bd. govs. Share-Zedek Hosp., Jerusalem, 1989-94. Sgt. Israeli Air Force, 1948-50. Recipient Harold Weil medal NYU Sch. Law, Elie Wiesel award. Mem. Internat. Law Soc. (France), Soc. Internat. Law, Israeli Bar Assn., Am. Soc. Internat. Law, French Assn. Internat. Law. Jewish. Club: Internat. (Washington). Avocations: volleyball; swimming. Office: Balter Guth & Aloni, 23 Hillel St, Jerusalem Israel

ROSENOF, HOWARD PAUL, electrical engineer; b. Newark, Dec. 26, 1948; s. Abraham and Zelda (Ginsberg) R.; m. Jane Emily Rosengarten, Mar. 3, 1990. BS, Cornell U., 1970; MSEE, Northeastern U., Boston, 1973. Registered profl. engr., Mass., N.Y. Engr. controls Stone & Webster Engring. Corp., Boston, 1972-78; from project engr. to mgr. The Foxboro (Mass.) Co., 1978-88; from sr. cons. to dir. consulting Gensym Corp., Cambridge, Mass., 1988-91; mktg. mgr. Gensym Corp., Cambridge, 1991—. Co-author: Batch Process Automation Theory and Practice, 1987; contbr. articles to profl. jours. Mem. Instrument Soc. Am. (sr., pres. Boston sect. 1985-86, com. SP88 1990-92). Achievements include producing a general software structure and engineering method for the automation of batch processing. Office: Gensym Corp 125 Cambridgepark Dr Cambridge MA 02140-2329

ROSENOW, EDWARD CARL, III, medical educator; b. Columbus, Ohio, Nov. 2, 1934; s. Oscar Ferdinand and Mildred Irene (Eichelberger) R.; m. Constance Donna Grahame, Sept. 7, 1957; children: Sheryl Lynn, Scott Edward. BS, Ohio State U., 1955, MD, 1959; MS in Medicine, U. Minn., 1969. Diplomate Am. Bd. Internal Medicine (mem. pulmonary subbd. 1982-88); cert. in Subspecialty Pulmonary Diseases. Intern Riverside Meth. Hosp., Columbus, Ohio, 1959-60; resident in internal medicine Mayo Grad. Sch. Medicine, Rochester, Minn., 1960-65, clin. fellow in thoracic diseases, 1965-66; cons. in internal medicine (pulmonary diseases) Mayo Clinic, Rochester, 1966; instr. in medicine Mayo Grad. Sch. Medicine, Rochester, 1969-73; asst. prof. medicine Mayo Med. Sch., Rochester, 1973-77, assoc. prof. medicine, 1977-80, prof. medicine, 1980; chmn. divsn. pulmonary and critical care medicine, 1987-94; assoc. dir. internal medicine residency program Mayo Clinic, Rochester, 1977-79, program dir. internal medicine residency program, 1979-84, sec. Mayo staff, 1979; pres. Mayo staff, 1986; Arthur M. and Gladys D. Gray prof. medicine Mayo Clinic, Rochester, 1987—; cons. NASA, Houston. Capt. M.C., U.S. Army, 1962-64. Recipient Alumni Achievement award Coll. Medicine Ohio State U., 1989, Disting. Mayo Clinician award, 1994, Henry S. Plummer Disting. Internist award, 1994, Karis award Mayo Clinic, 1996; Edward W. and Betty Knight Scripps Professorship named in his honor Mayo Med. Sch., 1994, Edward C. Rosenow, III, Outstanding Subspecialty fellow award established in his honor. Fellow ACP (gov. Minn. chpt. 1987-91, Ralph S. Claypoole Sr. award for Lifetime Dedication to Patient Care 1995, Minn. chpt. Laureate award 1994, Disting. Lectr. award 1996), Am. Coll. Chest Physicians (master fellow, editl. bd. CHEST 1973-78, editor spl. case reports 1975-90, com. on postgrad. med. edn. 1978-84, sci. program com. 1982, com. on undergrad. med. edn. 1981-82, co-chmn. sci. program com. Internat. Coll. Chest Physicians meeting, Sydney, Australia, 1985, regent 1984-88, pres. elect 1988-89, pres. 1989-90, Dist. Lectr. award); mem. AMA, So. Minn. Med. Assn., Minn. Thoracic Soc., Am. Thoracic Soc., Sigma Xi. Office: Mayo Clinic Div Pulmonary Diseases 200 1st St SW Rochester MN 55902-3008

ROSENOW, JOHN EDWARD, foundation executive; b. Lincoln, Nebr., Sept. 15, 1949; s. Lester Edward and Lucille Louise (Koehler) R.; m. Nancy Kay Hadley; children: Matthew, Stacy. BS in Agrl. Engring., U. Nebr., 1971. Dir. of tourism Nebr. Dept. Econ. Devel., Lincoln, 1971-79, interim dept. dir., 1985; founder Nat. Arbor Day Found., 1972; exec. dir. million-mem. Nat. Arbor Day Found., Lincoln and Nebraska City, 1979-94; pres. Nat. Arbor Day Found., 1994—. Co-author: (book) Tourism: the good, the bad, and the ugly, 1979. Democrat. Mem. United Ch. of Christ. Office: Nat Arbor Day Found 211 N 12th St Lincoln NE 68508-1422

ROSENOW, JOHN HENRY, surgeon, educator; b. Chgo., Sept. 16, 1913; s. Edward Carl and Lydia Barbara (Senty) R.; m. Jane Dexter, June 8, 1938; children: Joan (Mrs. Charles Jackson), Peter Dexter, Philip John, Charles Edward, Margaret (Mrs. Theodore Hope), Barbara (Mrs. Derek Von Schlegall). B.A., Carleton Coll., Northfield, Minn., 1934; M.D., Harvard U., 1938; M.S. in Surgery, Mayo Found., U. Minn., 1944. Diplomate: Am. Bd. Surgery. Intern Presbyn. Hosp., Chgo., 1939-40; fellow in surgery Mayo Clinic, 1941-43, 46-47; pvt. practice medicine specializing in gen. surgery Mpls., 1948-63; part-time editor Modern Medicine Publs., Inc., Mpls., 1955-63; sr. med. editor Modern Medicine Publs., Inc., 1963-75; clin. instr. surgery U. Minn. Med. Sch., 1955—; chief med. officer Mil. Entrance Processing Sta., Mpls., 1975-88; mem. staff Abbott-Northwestern Hosp., Fairview-Southdale hosps., Hennepin County Med. Center. Contbr. articles to med. jours. Mem. diocesan standing com. Episcopal Ch., 1961-64, 70-73. Served with M.C. USNR, 1943-46, PTO. Decorated Bronze Star. Fellow A.C.S.; mem. Am., Minn. med. assns., Hennepin County Med. Soc., Minn. Surg. Soc., Mpls. Acad. Medicine.

ROSENSAFT, MENACHEM ZWI, lawyer, author, foundation executive, community activist; b. Bergen-Belsen, Germany, May 1, 1948; came to U.S., 1958, naturalized, 1962; s. Josef and Hadassah (Bimko) R.; m. Jean Bloch, Jan. 13, 1974; 1 child, Joana Deborah. BA, MA, Johns Hopkins U., 1971; MA, Columbia U., 1975, JD, 1979. Bar: N.Y. 1980. Adj. lectr. dept. Jewish studies CCNY, 1972-74, professorial fellow, 1974-75; rsch. fellow Am. Law Inst., 1977-78; law clk. to judge U.S. Dist. Ct. (so. dist.) N.Y., N.Y.C., 1979-81; assoc. Proskauer, Rose, Goetz & Mendelsohn, N.Y.C., 1981-82, Kaye, Scholer, Fierman, Hays & Handler, N.Y.C., 1982-89; v.p., sr. assoc. counsel Chase Manhattan Bank, N.Y.C., 1989-93; spl. counsel Hahn & Hessen, N.Y.C., 1994-95; sr. internat. counsel Ronald S. Lauder Found., N.Y.C., 1995-97; exec. v.p. Jewish Renaissance Found., Inc., N.Y.C., 1996—. Author: Moshe Sharett, Statesman of Israel, 1966, Fragments, Past and Future (poetry), 1968, Not Backward to Belligerency, 1969; editor: Bergen Belsen Youth mag., 1965; book rev. editor Columbia Jour. Transnat. Law, 1978-79; co-editor (with Yehuda Bauer) Antisemitism: Threat to Western Civilization, 1988; contbg. editor: Reform Judaism, 1993—; contbr. to various publs. including N.Y. Times, Newsweek, N.Y. Post, L.A. Times, Phila. Inquirer, Miami Herald, Internat. Herald Tribune, Jerusalem Post, Liberation, Paris, Davar, Tel Aviv, El Diario, Santiago de Chile, Columbia Human Rights Law Rev., Jewish Social Studies, Leo Baeck Inst. Year Book XXI, Columbia Jour. Environ. Law, (with Michael I. Saltzman) Tax Planning Internat. Rev., Fellowship, Reform Judaism, United Synagogue Rev., Forward, Midstream, N.Y. Jewish Week, Jewish Telegraphic Agy. Bull.; subject of profile "Survivor's Son" in Present Tense mag., 1990. Chmn. Internat. Network Children Jewish Holocaust Survivors, 1981-84, founding chmn., 1984—; nat. pres. Labor Zionist Alliance, 1988-91; chmn. commn. human rights World Jewish Congress, 1986-91, chmn. exec. com. Am. sect., 1986-90; mem. Gen. Coun. World Zionist Orgn., 1987-92; mem. U.S. Holocaust Meml. Coun., 1994—, chmn. content com., 1994—, chmn. collections and acquisitions com., 1996—, chmn. task force on procedures for com. on conscience, 1996, mem. exec. com., 1996—; mem. N.Y.C. Holocaust Meml. Commn., 1982-96, chmn. collections com., 1987-89; bd. dirs., exec. com. Nat. Com. for Labor Israel, 1988-91, 95—; mem. Am. Zionist Tribunal, 1988-90, chmn., 1990; sec. Am. Zionist Fedn., 1990-93; bd. dirs. Am. Jewish Joint Distbn. Com., 1988-91, Mercaz, 1991—; mem. nat. adv. bd. United Synagogue Conservative Judaism, 1995—, also chmn. United Synagogue delegation to Nat. Jewish Cmty. Rels. Adv. Coun., 1994-97; mem. exec. com. Nat. Jewish Cmty. Rels. Adv. Coun., 1994-97; mem. N.Y. County Dem. Com., 1981-85; organizer, leader demonstration against Pres. Reagan's visit to Bitburg Cemetery and Bergen-Belsen concentration camp, 1985; del. meeting on recognition of Israel between five Am. Jews and leaders of Palestine Liberation Orgn., Stockholm, 1988; mem. adv. coun. Park Ave. Synagogue, 1993-94, trustee, 1994—, chmn. Sherr Inst. Adult Jewish Studies, 1993—. Recipient Abraham Joshua Heschel Peace award, 1989, Parker Sch. recognition of achievement with honors in internat. and fgn. law, 1979; Harlan Fiske Stone scholar, 1977-79. Mem. ABA, Phi Beta Kappa. Home: 179 E 70th St New York NY 10021-5154 Office: Jewish Renaissance Found 767 5th Ave Ste 4200 New York NY 10153-0001

ROSENSHIELD, GARY, Russian literature educator; b. Bklyn., May 14, 1944; s. Wolf Samuel R. and Bertha (Davis) Weiss; m. Jill Kathleen Bast; children: Mark, Adam. BA, Bklyn. Coll., 1965; MA, U. Wis., 1968, PhD, 1972. Asst. prof. Slavic langs. U. Wis., Madison, 1970-76, assoc. prof. Slavic langs., 1976-93, prof. Slavic langs., 1993—. Contbr. articles to profl. jours. Mem. N.Am. Dostocusky Soc. Office: U Wis Slavic Langs Dept Madison WI 53706

ROSENSTEEL, GEORGE THOMAS, physics educator, nuclear physicist; b. Balt., Sept. 30, 1947; s. Walter St. George and Marie Emily (White) R. BSc, U. Toronto, Ont., Can., 1973, PhD, 1975. Can. fellow NRC, 1976-78; prof. physics Tulane U., New Orleans, 1978—, chmn. dept., 1985-91; vis. fellow Brit. Sci. and Engring. Coun., U. Sussex, Eng., 1986; vis. prof. Nat. Inst. Nuclear Theory, U. Washington, 1992. Contbr. numerous articles to profl. jours. Delivered grad. sch. commencement address Tulane U., 1987; recipient 7 grants NSF, 1979—. Mem. Am. Phys. Soc., Am. Math. Soc., Sigma Xi (young scientist award 1987). Office: Tulane U Dept of Physics New Orleans LA 70118

ROSENSTEEL, JOHN WILLIAM, insurance company executive; b. Chgo., June 4, 1940; s. Harold Eugene and Alice (Shanahan) R.; m. Judith;

children: Elizabeth, Margaret, Jill. BS in Econs., Holy Cross Coll., 1962. Chartered life underwriter. Home office rep. Aetna Life and Casualty, Chgo., 1967-72, regional dir., 1972-75; dir. Aetna Life and Casualty, Hartford, Conn., 1975-81; nat. dir. Aetna Life and Casualty, Hartford, 1981-83, v.p., 1983-86; sr. v.p. European region Aetna Internat., Inc., Hartford, 1986-92; CEO Keyport Life Insurance Co., Boston, Mass., 1993—; bd. dirs. Keyport Life Ins. Co., Independence Life and Annuity Co. Lt. USN, 1963-66, Vietnam. Mem. Nat. Assn. Life Underwriters. Republican. Roman Catholic. Avocations: golf, swimming, reading. Home: 13 Glen Oak Dr Wayland MA 01778-3921 Office: Keyport Life 125 High St Boston MA 02110-2704

ROSENSTEIN, BERYL JOEL, physician; b. Boston, Jan. 5, 1937; s. Benjamin and Doris (Goldhagen) R.; m. Carolyn S., Aug. 31, 1958; children: Susan Eileen, Jonathan David. BA, Boston U., 1957; MD, Tufts U., 1961; M Adminstrv. Sci., Johns Hopkins U., 1987. Diplomate Am. Bd. Pediatrics. Intern in pediatrics Johns Hopkins Hosp., Balt., 1961-62, resident in pediatrics, 1962-64, dir. cystic fibrosis clinic, 1972—, v.p. med. affairs, 1994—; prof. pediatrics Johns Hopkins Sch. Med., Balt., 1989—; med. dir. Mt. Washington Pediatric Hosp., Balt., 1988-93; med. adv. coun. Cystic Fibrosis Found., Bethesda, Md., 1980-88, trustee, 1986—. Author: Pediatric Pearls: Handbook of Pediatrics, 1989, Primary Care of the Newborn, 1992; contbr. over 100 articles to profl. jours. and chpts. to books. Lt. comdr. USPHS, 1964-66. Fellow Am. Acad. Pediatrics, Ambulator Pediatric Assn.; mem. Am. Thoracic Soc., Am. Pediatric Soc., Alpha Omega Alpha. Avocations: tennis, bicycling, antique cars, travel, art. Office: Johns Hopkins Hosp 315 Park Ave Baltimore MD 21201-3611

ROSENSTEIN, JAMES ALFRED, lawyer; b. Phila., Jan. 4, 1939; s. Louis Charles and Natalie Selma (Stern) R.; m. Linda Merle Lederman, Sept. 7, 1969; 1 child, Judith Esther. A.B., Harvard U., 1961, J.D., 1968. Bar: Pa. 1968. Assoc. Wolf, Block, Schorr and Solis-Cohen, Phila., 1968-76; ptnr. Wolf, Block, Schorr and Solis-Cohen, 1976—; mem. adv. com. task force on condominiums Joint State Govt Commn., Pa. Gen. Assembly, 1977-79; mem. condominium-coop. steering com. Phila. City Planning Commn., 1980-81. Contbr. articles to profl. jours. Trustee exec. com. Jewish Fedn. of Greater Phila., 1977—, chmn. com. on local svcs., 1986-89, sec., 1987-88, v.p., 1988-94, chmn. com. on allocations and planning, 1989-92; v.p. jewish Cmty. Rels. Coun., 1982-85, 89-90, 96—; trustee United Way of Greater Phila., 1979-84, bd. dirs., 1982-85, 91-97. Lt. USN, 1961-64. Mem. ABA (chmn. devel. and financing of condominium projects 1993-97), Pa. Bar Assn. (chmn. common interest ownership com. 1980-93, chmn. real property divsn. 1993-95, chmn. real property, probate and trust law sect. 1995-96), Phila. Bar Assn. (chmn. legis. rels. com. 1996—), Am. Coll. Real Estate Lawyers, Coll. Cmty. Assn. Lawyers, Coun. Jewish Fedns. (bd. dirs. 1986—, chmn. com. on svcs. to aging 1991-94, chair nat. funding coun. 1996—, exec. com. 1997—). Office: Wolf Block Schorr and Solis-Cohen Packard Bldg 12th Fl 111 S 15th St Philadelphia PA 19102-2625

ROSENSTEIN, MARVIN, public health administrator; b. Sept. 5, 1939. BSChemE, U. Md., 1961; MS in Environ. Engring., Renssselaer Poly. Inst., 1966; PhD in Nuclear Engring., U. Md., 1971. Rschr. U.S. Bur. Mines/College Park (Md.) Metall. Rsch. Sta., 1961; commd. ensign Commd. Corps Pub. Health Svc., 1962, advanced through grades to capt., 1983; with N.E. Radiological Health Lab., Winchester, Mass., 1962, program coord. analytical quality control svc. divsn. radiological health, 1962; with data collation and analysis sect. radiation surveillance ctr. Divsn. Radiological Health, Washington, 1966; chief radiation exposure intelligence sect. standards and intelligence br. Nat. Ctr. for Radiological Health, Rockville, Md., 1967; dep. chief radiation measurements and calibration br. divsn. electronic products Bur. Radiological Health, Rockville, 1971, spl. asst. to dir. divsn. electronic products, 1972, dep. dir. divsn. electonic products, 1973; dep. assoc. commr. for policy coordination office policy coordination FDA, Rockville, 1978; sr. sci. advisor, 1979; dir. office health physics Ctr. for Devices and Radiological Health, Rockville, 1982-95; sr. staff fellow Ctr. for Devices and Radiol. Health, Rockville, Md., 1995—; mem. USASI Standards Com. N101, 1968-69; guest worker Ctr. for Radiation Rsch., Nat. Bur. Standards, 1969-74; faculty rsch. assoc. lab. for polymer and radiation sci. dept. chem. engring. U. Md., 1971-74; asst. clin. prof. radiology sch. medicine and scis. George Washington U., 1977-90. Contbr. over 70 publs. to profl. and sci. jours. Recipient Fed. Engr. of Yr. award NSPE/Dept. Health and Human Svcs., 1987. Mem. Nat. Coun. on Radiation Protection and Measurements (coun. 1988—, sci. com. 44 1976—, sci. com. 62 1980-85, chmn. sci. com. 46-12 1992-96), Health Physics Soc. (publs. com. 1967-77, del. to 4th internat. congress Internat. Radiation Protection Assn. 1977, contbg. editor newsletter 1982-97), Com. on Interagy. Radiation Rsch. and Policy Coord. (alt. HHS policy panel 1984-95, vice chmn. sci. panel 1985-94, exec. com. 1985-94, chmn. subpanel on use NAS com. on biol. effects of ionizing radiation report V and UN sci. com. on the effects of atomic radiation 1988, report in risk assessment 1989-92), Internat. Commn. on Radiol. Protection (com. 3 on radiol. protection in medicine 1985—, corr. mem. task group on rev. publ. 21 1979-88), Internat. Commn. on Radiation Units and Measurements (report com. on dosimetry in diagnostic radiology for the patient 1994—), Commd. Officers Assn., Sigma Xi. Achievements include patent for radiation dosimeter; research in absorbed dose from medical X rays, radiation risk estimates, dosimetry for epidemiological studies, absorbed dose to the public from radiation emergencies, electron depth-dose and dosimetry, radiochemistry and environmental health, radioactivity in food, general radiological health. Office: FDA (HFZ-60) Ctr Devices & Radiol Health 16071 Indsl Dr Gaithersburg MD 20877

ROSENSTEIN, NEIL, surgeon, genealogical researcher; b. Cape Town, South Africa, Oct. 31, 1944; came to U.S., 1969; s. Emanuel Boruchovich and Annie (Marine) R.; m. Mavis Joyce Naumann, Jan. 14, 1968; children: Joel, Ari, Moshe Baruch, Rafael Samuel, Jonathan Simcha. MD, U. Cape Town Med. Sch., 1967. Intern Tel Hashomer Hosp., Tel Aviv, Israel, 1968-69; surg. resident Mt. Sinai Hosp., Cleve., 1970-75, N.Y.C., 1970-75; mem. surg. staff St. Elizabeth Hosp., Elizabeth, N.J., 1975—, Elizabeth Med. Ctr., N.J., 1975—. Author: These Are the Generations, 1969, The Unbroken Chain, 1976, 90, The Margolis Family, 1984; co-author: From King David to Baron David—A Rothschild Saga, 1989; editor: Latter Day Leaders, Sages and Scholars, 1982, The Feast and the Fast, 1984. Founder, pres. Jewish Geneal. Soc., N.Y.C., 1977-79; bd. dirs. YMHA, Union, N.J., 1990—; founder, dir. Computer Ctr. for Jewish Geneaology. Mem. Med. Soc. N.J., Union County Med. Soc. N.J. Republican. Jewish. Home: 185 Shelley Ave Elizabeth NJ 07208

ROSENSTEIN, ROBERT BRYCE, lawyer; b. Santa Monica, Calif., Feb. 26, 1954; s. Franklin Lee and Queen Esther (Shall) R.; m. Resa Shanee Brookler, Nov. 30, 1980; children: Shaun Franklin, Jessica Laney, Madeline Frances. BA, Calif. State U., Northridge, 1976; JD, Southwestern U., 1979. Bar: Calif. 1979, U.S. Dist. Ct. (cen. and no. dists.) Calif. 1980, U.S. Tax Ct. 1981; registered environ. assessor. Service rep. Social Security Adminstrn., Los Angeles, 1974-77; tax cons. Am. Tax Assocs., Los Angeles, 1970-78, ptnr., 1978; prin., pres. Robert B. Rosenstein, PC, Los Angeles, 1979-84; ptnr. Rosenstein and Werlin, Los Angeles, 1984-87; pres. Robert Bryce Rosenstein Ltd., Temelula, 1987—; chief fin. officer BSE Mgmt. Inc., Los Angeles, 1987-90, corp. counsel, 1987-92, sr. v.p. corp. devel., acquisitions, 1990-92; bd. dirs. BSE Mgmt. Inc, Sirius Computer Corp., Spartan Computer, Unicomp, Inc., Diagnostic Engring. Inc.; pres. Will Find Inc., 1986-87. Recipient Am. Jurisprudence award Bancroft Whitney; Order of Cheviler. Mem. ABA (taxation and environ. coms., vice chmn. gen. bus. sect. 1995), Assn. Trial Lawyers Am., L.A. Bar Assn. Republican. Jewish. Lodges: Masons, Ionic, Composite. Avocations: sports, reading, golf. Office: 27450 Ynez Rd Ste 222 Temecula CA 92591-4680

ROSENSTOCK, SUSAN LYNN, orchestra manager; b. Bklyn., Nov. 2, 1947. BS, SUNY, Cortland, 1969; MBA, So. Meth. U., 1977, MFA, 1978. Asst. mgr. Columbus (Ohio) Symphony Orch., 1978-82; grants program dir., info. officer Greater Columbus Arts Coun., 1982-83, asst. dir. grants and adminstrn., 1983-84; dir. annual giving and spl. events Columbus Symphony Orch., 1984-86, dir. devel., 1986-90, orch. mgr., 1990—; panelist Ohio Arts Coun. Music Panel, 1986, 87, Challenge Grants Panel, 1991, J.C. Penney Gold Rule Award Judges Panel, 1993, 94. Mem. Am. Symphony Orch. League (devel. dirs. steering com. nat. conf. 1987, 88), Nat. Soc. Fund Raising Execs. (program com. Ctrl. Ohio chpt. 1988-94, chmn. program com. 1993, 94, bd. dirs. 1993-95, treas. 1995). Office: Columbus Symphony Orch 55 E State St Columbus OH 43215-4203

ROSENSWEIG, DAN, publishing executive. Pub. PC Mag. divsn. Ziff-Davis Pub. Co., N.Y.C.; exec. v.p. Ziff-Davis Pub. Co., 1996—. Office: PC Mag Ziff-Davis Pub Co 1 Park Ave New York NY 10016-5802*

ROSENSWEIG, RONALD ELLIS, scientist consultant; b. Hamilton, Ohio, Nov. 8, 1932; s. Herman and Deana (Meisel) R.; m. Ruth Evelyn Cohen, Sept. 5, 1954; children—Scott Elliot, Beth Ellen, Perry Ethan. Chem. Engr., U. Cin., 1955; S.M., MIT, 1956, Sc.D., 1959. Asst. prof. dept. chem. engring. MIT, Cambridge, 1959-62; prin. scientist Avco Corp., Wilmington, Mass., 1962-69; pres., tech. dir., co-founder Ferrofluidics Corp., Burlington, Mass., 1969-73, also dir., 1969-85; rsch. assoc. Exxon Corp., Annandale, N.J., 1973-78, sr. rsch. assoc., 1978-85, sci. advisor, 1985-95; internat. rsch. chair Blaise Pascal, Paris, 1996—; vis. prof. U. Minn., Mpls., 1980, U. Chgo., 1990, Weizmann Inst. Sci., Israel, 1997. Author: Ferrohydrodynamics, 1985; contbr. articles to profl. jours.; patentee in field. Fellow NSF, MIT, 1955-56; recipient IR-100 awards Indsl. Rsch. Pubs., 1968, 69, 71; named Young Engr. of Yr., Avco Corp., 1966, Disting. Engring. Alumnus U. Cin., 1986. Mem. Nat. Acad. Engring., Am. Inst. Chem. Engrs. (Alpha Chi Sigma award for rsch. 1985), Am. Phys. Soc., Magnetic Fluids Conf., Internat. Steering Com. (chmn. 1977-92). Jewish. Home: 34 Gloucester Rd Summit NJ 07901-3023

ROSENTHAL, AARON, management consultant; b. N.Y.C., July 12, 1914; s. Zelig and Sarah (Shapinsky) R.; m. Edna Blanche Finkel, Sept. 3, 1940; children—Stephen Mark, Marjorie Ann. B.A., Coll. City N.Y., 1934, M.S. in Edn, 1935; postgrad., Georgetown U. Law Sch., 1937-39, Am. U., 1950-53. Dir. Internal Audit Service, VA, Washington, 1953-58; controller VA, 1958-60; dir. financial mgmt. NASA, 1960-61; comptroller NSF, 1961-69, Nat. Acad. Scis., 1969-76; exec. cons. Coopers & Lybrand; fin. cons. to Ctr. for Devel. and Population Activities; fin. and mgmt. cons. to Joint Oceanographic Instns. Inc.; U.S. rep. supr. Radiation Effects Rsch. Found., Hiroshima, Japan; mem. nat. adv. coun. nat. Ctr. for Higher Edn. Mgmt. Systems; bd. dirs. TCOA, Inc., Manchester Center, Vt. Trustee Sci. Service Inc. Served with AUS, 1943-45. Recipient Exceptional Service award VA, 1960; Merit citation Nat. Civil Service League, 1957; Distinguished Service award NSF, 1969. Fellow AAAS; mem. Am. Soc. Pub. Adminstrn., Assn. Govt. Accts. Home: 3001 Veazey Ter NW Washington DC 20008-5454 Office: 2101 Constitution Ave NW Washington DC 20418-0007

ROSENTHAL, ALAN SAYRE, former government official; b. N.Y.C., Sept. 30, 1926; s. Morris S. and Elizabeth (Ralph) R.; m. Helen Miller, Sept. 8, 1951; children: Edward S., Susan L., Richard M., James M. A.B., U. Pa., 1948; LL.B., Yale U., 1951. Bar: N.Y. 1952. Asst. in instrn. Yale U. Law Sch., 1950-51; law clk. to U.S. Circuit Judge Henry W. Edgerton, Washington, 1951-52; atty. appellate sect., civil div. Justice Dept., 1952-72, asst. chief, 1958-72; admnstrv. judge atomic safety and licensing appeal panel AEC (now Nuclear Regulatory Commn.), Washington, 1972-91, chmn., 1972-88; adminstrv. judge pers. appeals bd. GAO, Washington, 1991-96, chmn., 1992-94; mem. ethics panel Montgomery County Bd. Edn., 1987-93; lectr. law U. Pa., 1981-83, Am. U., 1991-92. Pres. Kensington Elem. Sch. PTA, 1966-67; pres. North Chevy Chase Swimming Pool Assn., 1974-76; chmn. trustees Cedar Ln. Unitarian Ch., 1970-71; bd. dirs. Montgomery chpt. ACLU, 1967-69. Served with USAAF, 1944-46. Recipient John Marshall award Justice Dept., 1969, Disting. Svc. award Nuclear Regulatory Commn., 1988. Mem. Order of Coif, Phi Beta Kappa, Pi Gamma Mu, Delta Sigma Rho. Home: 3203 Kent St Kensington MD 20895-3210

ROSENTHAL, ALBERT JAY, advertising agency executive; b. Chgo., Sept. 30, 1928; s. Harry and Jennie (Comm) R.; m. Rhoda R. Rosenstein, June 18, 1950; children: Jayne, Michael, James, Nancy. BA, U. Ill., 1950. Reporter Transradio Press., Chgo., 1950-51; columnist Lerner Newspapers, Chgo., 1951-53; creative dir. Elliot, Jaynes & Baruch, Chgo., 1953-61; chmn. Albert Jay Rosenthal & Co., Chgo. and N.Y.C., 1961-85; chmn. Midwest div. HBM/Creamer-Albert Jay Rosenthal, Chgo., 1985-88, Della Femina, McNamee WCRS, Inc., Chgo., 1988-93; chmn. DFM/Tatham, Chgo., 1993; founder, pres. Franchising & Licensing World Ctr., Chgo., 1994—. Bd. dirs. Ill. Arts Alliance Found., Ill. Arts Alliance, Court Theatre U. Chgo.; mem. sustaining fund com. Ravinia Festival Assn.; mem. mktg. com. World Bus. Coun., Washington; vice chmn. Chgo. Internat. Film Festival; v.p. Gastro-Intestinal Rsch. Found. U. Chgo. Named one of Chgo. Ten Outstanding Young Men, Chgo. Jr. Assn. of Commerce, 1962, Advt. Man of Yr., Alpha Delta Sigma, 1978, Communicator of Yr., Jewish United Fund, 1988. Jewish. Home: 179 E Lake Shore Dr Chicago IL 60611-1351 Office: Franchising & Licensing World Ctr 239 Merchandise Mart Plz Chicago IL 60654

ROSENTHAL, ALBERT JOSEPH, university dean, law educator, lawyer; b. N.Y.C., Mar. 5, 1919; m. Barbara Snowden, June 30, 1953; children: Edward H., Thomas S., William I. B.A., U. Pa., 1938; LL.B., Harvard U., 1941. Bar: N.Y. 1942, U.S. Supreme Ct. 1947. Law clk. to judge U.S. Ct. Appeals 1st Circuit, Boston, 1941-42; spl. appellate atty. OPA, Washington, 1946-47; law clk. to Justice Frankfurter U.S. Supreme Ct., Washington, 1947-48; asst. loan officer IBRD, Washington, 1948-50; atty. Dept. Justice, Washington, 1950-52; gen. counsel Small Def. Plants Adminstrn., Washington, 1952-53; ptnr. Golden Wienshienk & Rosenthal, N.Y.C., 1953-64; prof. law Columbia U., N.Y.C., 1964-89, Maurice T. Moore prof., 1974-89, dean Sch. Law, 1979-84, prof. emeritus, dean emeritus, 1989—; hearing officer N.Y. State Dept. Environ. Conservation, 1975, 77; mem. N.Y. State Law Revision Commn., 1987—; vis. prof. law St. John's U., 1989-92, disting. prof. 1992—; spl. master U.S. Dist. Ct. N.Y., 1990—. Author: (with H. Korn and S. Lubman) Catastrophic Accidents in Government Programs, 1963, (with F. Grad and G. Rathjens) Environmental Control: Priorities, Policies and the Law, 1971, Federal Regulation of Campaign Finance, 1972, (with F. Grad and others) The Automobile and the Regulation of Its Impact on the Environment, 1975; editor: (with L. Henkin) Constitutionalism and Rights: The Influence of the U.S. Constitution Abroad, 1989; contbr. articles to law jours. Mem. Logan Airport Master Plan Study Team, 1975. Served to capt. U.S. Army Air Corps, 1942-45. Fellow Am. Acad. Arts and Scis., Am. law Inst. Home: 15 Oak Way Scarsdale NY 10583-1415 Office: Columbia U Law Sch 435 W 116th St New York NY 10027-7201

ROSENTHAL, AMNON, pediatric cardiologist; b. Gedera, Israel, July 14, 1934; came to U.S., 1949, naturalized, 1959; s. Joseph and Rivka Rosenthal; m. Prudence Lloyd, July 22, 1962; children: Jonathan, Eben, Nathaniel. M.D., Albany Med. Coll., 1959. Intern Buffalo Children's Hosp., 1959-60; resident in pediatrics Children's Hosp. Med. Center, Boston, 1960-62; resident in pediatric cardiology Children's Hosp. Med. Center, 1965-68; asso. prof. pediatrics Children's Hosp. Med. Center and Harvard U. Med. Sch., Boston, 1975-77; dir. pediatric cardiology, prof. pediatrics C.S. Mott Children's Hosp., U. Mich., Ann Arbor, 1977—, assoc. dir. dept. pediatrics, 1989-92. Served to capt. M.C. USAF, 1962-65. Amnon Rosenthal endowed professorship U. Mich., 1994. Mem. Am. Acad. Pediatrics, Soc. for Pediatric Rsch., Am. Pediatric Soc., Am. Heart Assn., Am. Coll. Cardiology, Am. Bd. Pediatrics, Am. Bd. Pediatric Cardiology (chmn. 1987-88). Office: CS Mott Children's Hosp Ann Arbor MI 48109-0204

ROSENTHAL, ANDREW, newspaper editor. Washington bur. editor N.Y. Times. Office: The NY Times Washington Bur 1627 I St NW Fl 7 Washington DC 20006-4007*

ROSENTHAL, ARNOLD H., film director, producer, writer, graphic designer, calligrapher; b. Chgo., Jan. 31, 1933; s. Gus and Sara (Ariel) R.; children: Michel, Jason, Anthony. B.A., U. Ill., 1954. Graphic designer Whitaker-Guernsey Studios, Chgo., 1954-55; art dir. Edward H. Weiss Advt., Chgo., 1956-60; owner Arnold H. Rosenthal & Assos., Chgo., 1960-70; partner, creative dir., pres. Meyer & Rosenthal Inc. (mktg. communications), Chgo., 1970-75; sr. v.p., creative dir. Garfield-Linn & Co. (Advt.), Chgo., 1975-81; pres., exec. prodr./dir. Film Chgo., 1981—; TV comml. jury chmn. Chgo. Internat. Film Festival, 1977, 78, 79, 87, mem. governing bd., 1984—; represented at Moscow Film Fest, 1990; TV jury chmn. U.S. Festival, 1980; lectr. Columbia Coll., Purdue U., U. Ill., Ohio State U. Contbr. articles to profl. publs. Bd. dirs. Jewish United Fund. Served with AUS, 1955-56. Recipient creative awards Communication Clubs Chgo., N.Y.C., 1960—, Silver medal N.Y. Film Festival, 1986, Clio award, 1981. Mem. Soc. Typographic Arts (design awards 1958—, pres. 1971-72), Am. Inst. Graphic Arts (spl. award 1974), Dirs. Guild Am., Jazz Inst. Chgo. (charter, jazz drummer), Tau Epsilon Phi, Alpha Delta Sigma.

ROSENTHAL, ARTHUR JESSE, publisher; b. N.Y.C., Sept. 26, 1919; s. Arthur J. and Grace (Ellinger) R.; m. Margaret Ann Roth, Dec. 12, 1975; children: James, Kathryn, Paul. BA, Yale U., 1941; postgrad., Harvard U. Bus. Sch., 1942. Spl. asst. to U.S. ambassador to Israel, Jerusalem, 1948; pres., editor in chief Basic Books, Inc., N.Y.C., 1949-72; dir. Harvard U. Press, Cambridge, 1972-90; pub. Hill and Wang, N.Y.C., 1990—; founding trustee Bank St. Coll. Edn., 1952-68. Editorial bd.: Pub. Interest, Harvard Bus. Rev, Family Process, Yale U. Press. Trustee Austen Riggs Center, Stockbridge, Mass. Served to capt., M.I. U.S. Army, 1942-46. Clubs: Century Assn. (N.Y.C.); St. Botolph (Boston).

ROSENTHAL, BRIAN DAVID, lawyer; b. Glen Ridge, N.J., May 1, 1952; s. Charles and Dorothy H. (Stanger) R.; m. Joy N. Weisman, Aug. 11, 1974; children: Adam M., Elizabeth J., Alexander H. BA magna cum laude, U. Pa., Phila., 1974; JD, Georgetown U., Washington, 1977. Bar: Pa. 1977, U.S. Dist. Ct. (ea. dist.) Pa. 1983, U.S. Ct. Appeals (3rd cir.) 1984. Asst. dist. atty. Phila. Dist. Attys. Office, 1977-82; assoc. atty. Ominsky Joseph & Welsh PC, Phila., 1982-85; ptnr. Ominsky Welsh & Rosenthal PC, Phila., 1986-92; pres., founding ptnr. Rosenthal & Weisberg PC, Phila., 1992—; commr. Bd. Commrs., Lower Merion Township, Pa., 1994—; settlement master Phila. Ct. Common Pleas, 1993—. Author: Medical Malpractice in Pennsylvania, 1993, Insurance Litigation in Pennsylvania, 1993. Pres. Lower Merion Little League, 1991—; dir. baseball Kaiserman J.C.C., Penn Wynne, Pa., 1985; bd. dirs. Nat. Multiple Sclerosis Soc., Phila., 1979-84. Named Outstanding Vol. Kaiserman Jewish Cmty. Ctr., Penn Wynne, 1985, Outstanding Adult Vol. Lower Merion Little League, 1993. Mem. ABA (sects. on litigation, tort and ins. practice, criminal justice), Assn. Trial Lawyers Am., Pa. Trial Lawyers Assn., Pa. Bar Assn., Phila. Bar Assn. (coms. medico legal com., state judiciary com. 1993—), Phi Beta Kappa. Avocations: baseball, reading, travel, coaching. Office: Rosenthal & Weisberg PC 2 Logan Sq Ste 1565 Philadelphia PA 19103-2707

ROSENTHAL, CHARLES MICHAEL, financial executive; b. Bklyn., Nov. 21, 1935; s. David B. and Edna (Lefcort) R.; m. Eva F. Sonnenberg, July 7, 1963; children: Andrea (dec.), Nicole. BA, Colgate U., 1957. Rsch. asst. Fed. Res. Bank N.Y., N.Y.C., 1960-62; v.p. L.M. Rosenthal & Co., Inc., 1962-74; ptnr. 1st Manhattan Co., N.Y.C., 1974—. Trustee Brown U., Providence, 1992—. Capt. USAF, 1957-60. Mem. Investment Assn. N.Y., Security Traders Assn. N.Y., Am. Coun. on Germany, East Hampton Tennis Club. Jewish. Home: 784 Park Ave New York NY 10021-3553 Office: 1st Manhattan Co 437 Madison Ave New York NY 10022-7001

ROSENTHAL, DAVID, media executive, publicist; b. Basel, Switzerland, Mar. 8, 1969; s. Moshe and Regula (Kreis) R. Grad., U. Basel Law Sch., 1997. Ptnr., CEO Insider Communications, Basel, 1989—; owner, CEO DCC Software, Basel, 1987—; ptnr. Rosenthal & Zehnder Media Ventures, Basel, 1995—; cons. Bank for Internat. Settlements, Basel, 1990—, Deutsche Telekom, Bonn, Germany, 1995-96; bd. dirs. Swiss Assn. Trade Press. Contbr. articles to profl. jours.; author: Skripten zum Schweizerischen Zivilgesetzbuch, 1995, Projekt Internet: Was Unternehmen ûber Internet und Recht wissen mûssen, 1997. Recipient Bedag Informatik Medienpreis, 1994. Mem. Swiss Fed. Commn. on Info. Soc., Swiss Assn. Sci. Writers. Avocation: fencing. Home: Leonhardsstrasse 24, 4051 Basel Switzerland Office: IPD Insider Presse Dienst, Postfach 228 Hans Huber-Str 15, 4003 Basel Switzerland

ROSENTHAL, DONALD B., political scientist, educator; b. N.Y.C., July 14, 1937; s. Max and Bessie Dora (Silverman) R. AB, Bklyn. Coll., 1958; AM, U. Chgo., 1960, PhD, 1964. Asst. prof. polit. sci. SUNY, Buffalo, 1964-68, assoc. prof., 1968-72, prof., 1972—, chmn. dept., 1978-80, 86-91. Author: The Limited Elite, 1970, The Expansive Elite, 1977, (monograph) Sticking Points and Ploys in Federal-Local Relations, 1979; Urban Housing and Neighborhood Revitalization, 1988; co-author: The Politics of Community Conflict, 1969, (monograph) Local Power and Comparative Politics, 1974; editor: The City in Indian Politics, 1976, Urban Revitalization, 1980; contbr. articles to profl. jours. Fellow Am. Inst. Indian Studies, 1963-64, 70, Nat. Assn. Schs. Pub. Affairs and Adminstrn., 1977-78, Rockefeller Inst., 1983; NSF grantee, 1974-75. Mem. Am. Polit. Sci. Assn., Am. Soc. Pub. Adminstrn. Democrat. Jewish. Office: SUNY Buffalo Amherst Campus Dept of Polit Sci Buffalo NY 14260

ROSENTHAL, DOUGLAS EURICO, lawyer, author; b. N.Y.C., Feb. 12, 1940; s. Jacob and Edna Louise (Muir) R.; m. Erica Switzen Kremen, Nov. 12, 1967; children: Benjamin Muir, Rachel Elizabeth. BA summa cum laude, Yale U., 1961, LLB, 1966, PhD in Polit. Sci, 1970; postgrad., Oxford (Eng.) U., 1962; MA, Columbia U., 1963. Bar: N.Y. 1968, U.S. Supreme Ct. 1976, D.C. 1980. Project dir. Russell Sage Found., N.Y.C., 1968-70; assoc. Fried, Frank, Harris, Shriver & Jacobson, N.Y.C., 1970-74; asst. chief fgn. commerce sect., antitrust div. Dept. Justice, Washington, 1974-77, chief, 1977-80; ptnr. Sutherland, Asbill & Brennan, Washington, 1980-88, Coudert Bros., 1989-94, Sonnenschein, Nath & Rosenthal, Washington, 1994—; reporter Am. Law Inst.-Am. Bar Assn. Model Lawyer Peer Rev. System, 1980; adj. prof. Tokyo U. Law Sch., 1992; speaker USIA, Australia, Eng., Can., Germany, Japan; escrow agt. Boesky settlement funds paid to U.S. Govt. Author: (with D. Baker and others) Antitrust Guide for International Operations, 1977; author: Lawyer and Client: Who's in Charge?, 1972, 2d rev. edit., (with Knighton) National Law and International Commerce: The Problem of Extraterritoriality, 1982, Competition Policy in Hufbauer, Europe, 1992: An American Perspective, 1990; co-editor (with Carl Green) Competition Regulation in the Pacific Rim, 1996; author (with others) Global Competition Policy, 1997; chmn. bd. advisor Euro Watch; mem. bd. advisors Antitrust and Trade Regulation Reporter, George Washington Jour. Law and Econs., Can. Competition Policy Record; contbr. articles to profl. publs. Committeeman Nassau County (N.Y.) Dem. Com., 1963-65; lifetime mem. corp. Culinary Inst. Am. Recipient Edward S. Corwin nat. award Am. Polit. Sci. Assn., 1971; Henry fellow Balliol Coll., Oxford U., 1962, Nobel Internat. and Woodrow Wilson fellow Columbia U., 1963. Mem. ABA (internat. law, litigation and antitrust sect.), Coun. on Fgn. Rels., The European Inst., Am. Law Inst. (adv. com. law governing lawyers), Confrerie des Chevaliers du Tastevin, Mory's Assn., Phi Beta Kappa. Jewish. Office: 1301 K St NW Ste 600 Washington DC 20005-3317

ROSENTHAL, ELIZABETH ROBBINS, physician; b. Bklyn., Feb. 10, 1943; d. Marc and Ruth Jackson (Oginz) Robbins; m. Samuel Leonard Rosenthal, June 26, 1940; children: Thomas, Benjamin, Marc. AB, Smith Coll., 1963; MD, NYU, 1967. Diplomate Am. Bd. of Dermatology. Intern in pediatrics Upstate Med. Ctr., Syracuse, N.Y., 1967-68; resident in dermatology Henry Ford Hosp., Detroit, 1968-69, Roosevelt Hosp., N.Y.C., 1969-70, Boston U. Med. Ctr., 1972-74; pvt. practice Mamaroneck, N.Y., 1976—; chief dermatology, attending United Hosp., Pt. Chester, N.Y., 1994—; asst. clin. prof. Albert Einstein Coll. Medicine, Bronx, 1978—. Bd. dirs. Community Counseling Ctr., Mamaroneck, N.Y., 1982—. Fellow Am. Acad. Dermatology; mem. N.Y. State Med. Soc., NOW, Westchester County Med. Soc., Am. Med. Women's Assn. Office: 1600 Harrison Ave Mamaroneck NY 10543-3145

ROSENTHAL, FRANZ, language educator; b. Berlin, Aug. 31, 1914; came to U.S., 1940, naturalized, 1943; s. Kurt W. and Elsa (Kirschstein) R. Ph.D., U. Berlin, 1935; DHL (hon.), Hebrew Union Coll., 1987; PhD (hon.), Hebrew U., 1987, Tel Aviv U., 1992, U. Tübingen, 1993; Columbia U., 1996. Asst. prof. Semitic langs. Hebrew Union Coll., Cin., 1940-48; prof. Arabic, U. Pa., 1948-56; Louis M. Rabinowitz prof. Yale U., 1956-67, Sterling prof. Near Eastern langs., 1967-85, prof. emeritus, 1985—. Author: Aramaistische Forschung, 1939, Technique and Approach of Muslim Scholarship, 1947, Hist. of Muslim Historiography, 1952, Humor in Early Islam, 1956, Ibn Khaldun, The Muqaddimah, 1958, The Muslim Concept of Freedom, 1960, Fortleben der Antike im Islam, 1965, Knowledge Triumphant, 1970, The Herb: Hashish versus Medieval Muslim Society, 1971, Gambling in Islam, 1975, Sweeter than Hope, 1983, History of al-Tabari, vols. 1 and 38, 1985, 89, Muslim Intellectual and Social History: A Collection of Essays, 1990. Served with AUS, OSS, 1943-45. Fellow AAAS, Brit. Acad. (corr.); mem. Am. Philos. Soc., Am. Oriental Soc. (pres. 1964-65),

Accademia Nazionale dei Lincei, Société Asiatique (hon.), Deutsche Morgenländische Ges (hon.). Home: 80 Heloise St Hamden CT 06517-3422

ROSENTHAL, HAROLD LESLIE, biochemistry educator; b. Elizabeth, N.J., Mar. 26, 1922; s. Isadore and Sophia (Shapiro) R.; m. Rose Schwartz, June 7, 1947; children: Jenifer Ann, Pamela Susan. B.Sc., U. N. Mex., 1944; Ph.D., Rutgers U., 1951. Rsch. asst. Rutgers U., New Brunswick, N.J., 1948-51; instr. Tulane U., New Orleans, 1951-53; chief biochemist Rochester Gen. Hosp., N.Y., 1953-58; prof. biomed. scis. Washington U., St. Louis, 1958-87, prof. emeritus, 1987—; vis. scientist Minerva Found., Finland, 1966, Nat. Acad. Sci., Hungary, 1974. Served with USN, 1943-46. Fellow AAAS; mem. Am. Chem. Soc. (emeritus), Am. Inst. Nutrition, Am. Soc. for Biochemistry and Molecular Biology, Sigma Xi. Avocations: gardening; oenology. Home: 7541 Teasdale Ave Saint Louis MO 63130-3923

ROSENTHAL, HELEN NAGELBERG, county official, advocate; b. N.Y.C., June 6, 1926; d. Alfred and Esther (Teichholz) Nagelberg; m. Albert S. Rosenthal, Apr. 10, 1949 (dec.); children: Lisa Rosenthal Michaels, Apryl Meredith Rosenthal Stuppler. BS, CUNY, 1948; MA, NYU, 1950; postgrad., Adelphia U., L.I. U., Lehman Coll., 1975. Cert. early childhood and gifted edn. tchr., N.Y., N.J., elem. and secondary tchr., Fla. Tchr. gifted students N.Y. Bd Edn., Bklyn., 1949-77, 79-87, Baldwin (N.Y.) Pub. Schs., 1977-79; rep. community affairs County of Dade, Fla., 1988-92; ret., 1992. Author: Criteria for Selection and Curriculum for the Gifted, 1977, Science Experiments for Young Children, 1982, Music in the Air...and in Our Minds. Dir. Condominium, 1989-91. Recipient Departmental award, 1948. Mem. Concerned Citizens for Educating Gifted and Talented (officer N.Y.C. chpt.), Assn. Gifted and Talented Edn. (N.Y. chpt.), Am. Inst. Cancer Rsch., Bklyn. Coll. Alumni Assn. (pres. Broward-Dade chpt. 1995-96, v.p. membership 1996—).

ROSENTHAL, HERBERT MARSHALL, legal association executive. BA, UCLA; JD, Hasting Coll. Law, U. Calif., San Francisco. Bar: Calif. 1962. Exec. dir. State Bar Calif., San Francisco. Office: State Bar Calif 555 Franklin St San Francisco CA 94102-4456

ROSENTHAL, HOWARD LEWIS, political science educator; b. Wilkinsburg, Pa., Mar. 4, 1939; s. Arnold Sidney R. and Elinor (Kaufman) (Rosenthal) Lewis; m. Annie Regine Lunel, June 30, 1960 (div. Nov., 1967); children: Illia Rebecca, Jean Laurent; m. Margherita Guastoni Spampinato, Feb. 6, 1968; 1 son, Gil Guastoni. B.S., MIT, 1960, Ph.D., 1964. Asst. prof. polit. sci. U. Calif.-Irvine, 1965-66; asst. prof. and assoc. prof. polit. sci. Carnegie-Mellon U., Pitts., 1966-71, prof., 1971-93; Roger Williams Straus prof. social scis. Princeton U., N.J., 1993—; vis. prof. Hebrew U., Jerusalem, 1968-69, U. Calif., San Diego, 1976-77, MIT, Cambridge, 1989-90, U. Paris I, 1990; Walras-Pareto lectr. U. Lausanne, Switzerland, 1996; vis. grad. lectr. Fondation Nat. des Scis. Politiques, Paris, 1972-73. Author: Prediction Analysis of Cross Classifications, 1977, Analysis of Ordinal Data, 1977, Partisan Politics, Divided Government and the Economy, 1995, Flexible Integration: Towards a More Effective and Democratic Europe, 1995, The Realignment of National Politics and Income Redistribution, 1997, Congress: A Political-Economic History of Roll Call Voting, 1997; mem. editl. bd. Pub. Choice, Econs. and Politics. Fellow NSF, 1969-92; fellow Ford Found., 1972-73, Social Sci. Rsch. Coun., 1964-65; Nat. fellow Hoover Instn., Stanford U., 1979-80; Sherman Fairchild disting. scholar Calif. Inst. Tech., 1982-83; fellow Internat. Ctr. for Econ. Rsch., Turin, Italy, 1991-93, Ctr. for Advanced Study in the Behavioral Scis., 1991-92, ECARE U. Libre de Brussels (Belgium), 1995. Fellow Am. Acad. Arts and Scis.; mem. Pub. Choice Soc. (Duncan Black award 1979), Am. Polit. Sci. Assn. (CQ Press award 1985), French Polit. Sci. Assn. Office: Princeton Univ Politics Dept Princeton NJ 08544

ROSENTHAL, IRA MAURICE, pediatrician, educator; b. N.Y.C., June 11, 1920; s. Abraham Leon and Jean (Kalotkin) R.; m. Ethel Ginsburg, Oct. 17, 1943; children: Anne, Judith. Student, CCNY, 1936-38; A.B., Ind. U., 1940, M.D., 1943. Intern Lincoln Hosp., N.Y.C., 1943-44; resident in pathology Albert Einstein Hosp., Phila., 1947-48; resident in pediatrics Fordham Hosp., N.Y.C., 1948-49; practice medicine specializing in pediatrics Bklyn., 1950-52; instr. U. Ill. Coll. Medicine, Chgo., 1953; asst. prof. U. Ill. Coll. Medicine, 1953-55, assoc. prof., 1955-63, prof. pediatrics, 1963-90, prof. emeritus, 1990—, head dept., 1973-82; clin. prof. pediatrics Stritch Sch. Medicine Loyola U., Chgo., 1990-91, lectr., 1991-93; clin. assoc. in pediatrics U. Chgo., 1990-91, clin. prof. pediatrics, 1991—; mem. med. service adv. com. Nat. Found. March of Dimes, 1975-80. Served to capt. U.S. Army, 1944-46. Mem. Am. Pediatric Soc., Soc. Pediatric Research, Acad. Pediatrics, Lawson Wilkins Pediatric Endocrine Soc., Endocrine Soc. Home: 5490 S South Shore Dr Chicago IL 60615-5984 Office: U Chgo Dept Pediats MC 5053 5841 S Maryland Ave Chicago IL 60637-1463

ROSENTHAL, JACOB (JACK ROSENTHAL), newspaper editor; b. Tel-Aviv, June 30, 1935; came to U.S., 1938, naturalized, 1943; s. Manfred and Rachel (Kaplan) R.; m. Holly Russell, Dec. 21, 1985; children by previous marriage: John, Ann; stepchildren: Christopher Russell, Andrew Russell. A.B., Harvard U., 1956. Reporter, editor Portland Oregonian, Reporter, 1950-61; asst. dir., dir. public info. U.S. Dept. Justice, Washington, 1961-66; exec. asst. to Undersec. of State, 1966-67; Kennedy fellow Harvard Inst. Politics, 1967-68; nat. urban corr. Life Mag., N.Y.C., 1968-69; urban corr. N.Y. Times, Washington, 1969-73; asst. Sun. editor, mag. editor N.Y. Times, N.Y.C., 1973-77, dep. editorial page editor, 1977-86, editorial page editor, 1986-93; mag. editor, 1993—. Prin. author: Kerner Commn. Report on Urban Riots, 1968. Mem. Harvard Crimson Grad. Bd. Recipient Best Editorial award Internat. Labor Press Assn., 1961, Loeb award, 1973, Pulitzer prize for editorials, 1982. Office: NY Times Co 229 W 43rd St New York NY 10036-3913

ROSENTHAL, JAMES D., retired federal official, former U.S. ambassador; b. San Francisco, Jan. 15, 1932. B.A., Stanford U., 1954; student Fgn. Service Inst., 1960-61, Nat War Coll., 1974-75. With U.S. Fgn. Service, 1956-90, adminstrv. officer, Port of Spain, Trinidad, 1958-60; polit officer, Saigon, Vietnam, 1961-65; faculty U.S. Mil. Acad., 1965-67; internat. relations officer Vietnam affairs Dept. State, 1967-70; mem. U.S. dele. to Vietnam Peace Talks, Paris, 1970-72; dep. chief of mission, Bangui, 1972-74; dir. Vietnam, Laos and Cambodia affairs Dept. State, 1975-77; dep. chief of mission Kuala Lumpur, Malaysia, 1977-79; dep chief mission, Manila, 1979-83; ambassador to Guinea, Conakry, 1983-86, dep. dir. mgmt. ops. Dept. State, Washington, 1986-90; exec. dir. Commonwealth Club of Calif., 1990-96.

ROSENTHAL, JULIAN BERNARD, association executive, lawyer; b. N.Y.C., July 4, 1908; s. Alex Sidney and Katherine (Goodman) R.; m. Frances Stone, Nov. 14, 1941; children—Brian, John L. Student, Columbia, 1925-26; LL.B., Fordham U., 1929. Bar: N.Y. 1931. Practiced in N.Y.C., 1931-72, Ga., 1972-78; mem. firm Javits & Javits, 1968-72, of counsel, 1972-74; mem. Air Force Assn., 1945—, life mem., 1946—, sec., 1946-59, chmn. bd. dirs., 1959-60, chmn. constn. com., 1946-71, chmn. resolutions com., 1946-61, permanent bd. dirs., 1960-84, dir. emeritus, 1984—; chmn. bd. dirs. Aerospace Edn. Council, N.Y.C., 1965-73; mem. Atlanta consumer adv. panel Gulf Oil Corp.; Govt. appeal agent SSS, 1943-44; chmn. steering com., Ga. joint legis. com. Am. Assn. Ret. Persons-Nat. Ret. Tchrs. Assn., 1975-78, mem. Ariz. joint state legis. com., 1978-81; mem. motion picture div. Dem. Nat. Com., 1940; past treas., dir. Lydia M. Morrison Found.; former sec. bd. dirs. Herbert I. and Shirley C. Rosenthal Found.; former v.p., treas., dir. Vanguard Found.; past trustee, sec. Aerospace Edn. Found.; mem. tech. adv. com. Health Planning Agy., Ga., 1987. Vol. legal aide North Cen. Legal Assistance Program, Durham, N.C., 1990—. Served with USAAF, 1944-45. Recipient Man of Yr. award Air Force Assn., 1953, Exceptional Svc. medal USAF, 1996. Mem. ABA, Am. Assn. Ret. Persons (mem. nat. legis. adv. com. 1977, capitol task force Ga. 1987-89). Address: 2701 Pickett Rd Apt 4014 Durham NC 27705-5652

ROSENTHAL, LAURENCE, composer; b. Detroit, Nov. 4, 1926. Numerous film scores include: A Raisin in the Sun, 1961, The Miracle Worker, 1962, Requiem for a Heavyweight, 1962, Becket, 1964, Man of La Mancha, 1972, Rooster Cogburn, 1975, The Return of a Man Called Horse, 1976, The Island of Dr. Moreau, 1977, Who'll Stop the Rain, 1978, Meteor, 1979, Clash of the Titans, 1981, Heart Like a Wheel, 1983, Easy Money, 1983; TV work includes: Fantasy Island, 1977, Peter the Great, 1986, The Bourne Identity, 1988, My Name Is Bill W., 1989, The Young Indiana Jones Chronicles, 1992 (Emmy award, Outstanding Achievement in Music Composition for a series 1995). Office: Gorfaine-Schwartz Agy 3301 Barham Blvd Ste 201 Los Angeles CA 90068-1477*

ROSENTHAL, LEE H., federal judge; b. Nov. 30, 1952; m. Gary L. Rosenthal; children: Rebecca, Hannah, Jessica, Rachel. BA in Philosophy with honors, U. Chgo., 1974, JD with honors, 1977. Bar: Tex. 1979. Law clk. to Hon. John R. Brown U.S. Ct. Appeals (5th cir.), 1977-78; assoc. Baker & Botts, 1978-86, ptnr., 1986-92; judge U.S. Dist. Ct. (so. dist.) Tex., 1992—. Editor topics and comments Law Rev. U. Chgo., 1977-78. Active vis. com. Law Sch. U. Chgo., 1983-86, 94—; mem. devel. coun. Tex. Children's Hosp., 1988-92; pres. Epilepsy Assn. Houston/Gulf Coast, 1989-91; trustee Briarwood Sch. Endowment Found., 1991-92; bd. dirs. Epilepsy Found. Am., 1993—. Fellow Tex. Bar Found.; mem. ABA, Am. Law Inst., Texas Bar Assn., Houston Bar Assn. Office: US Dist Ct US Courthouse Rm 8631 515 Rusk St Houston TX 77002-2600*

ROSENTHAL, LEIGHTON A., aviation company executive; b. Buffalo, Jan. 27, 1915; s. Samuel and Sadie (Dosberg) R.; m. Honey Rousuck, June 30, 1940; children: Cynthia, Jane. Student, Phila. Textile Sch.; grad. Wharton Sch., U. Pa.; hon. doctorate, Cleve. Coll. Jewish Studies, 1973. Pres. Cleve. Overall Co., 1956-61, Work Wear Corp., 1961-86, The Purity Uniform Service Inc., 1986-89, Lars Mgmt. div. Purity Uniform Service Inc., 1986-89, Lars Aviation Inc., 1990—; chmn. Architecture Commn., City of Palm Beach. Trustee Jewish Community Fedn. Cleve., Leighton A. Rosenthal Family Found., Samuel Rosenthal Found., Preservation Found. Palm Beach; bd. dirs. Ohio Motorists Assn. Fellow Am. Assn. Jewish Edn., Oakwood Club, Union Club, Poinciana Club, Marks Club, Annabels Club. Office: Lars Aviation Inc 1228 Euclid Ave Ste 310 The Halle Bldg Cleveland OH 44115

ROSENTHAL, LUCY GABRIELLE, writer, editor, educator; b. N.Y.C.; d. Henry Moses and Rachel (Tchernowitz) R. AB, U. Mich., 1954; MS in Journalism, Columbia U., 1955; MFA, Yale Sch. Drama, 1961; postgrad. Writers Workshop, U. Iowa, 1965-68. Asst. editor Radiology mag., Detroit, 1955-57; free-lance editorial cons. various pub. houses, lit. agts. N.Y.C., 1957-73; mem. admissions staff U. Iowa Writers Workshop, Iowa City, 1965-68; editor Book-of-the-Month Club, N.Y.C., 1973-74, mem. editorial bd. judges, 1974-79; sr. editorial advisor Book-of-the-Month Club, 1979-87; mem. biography jury Pulitzer Prize, 1980; mem. bd. Am. Book Awards, 1981-82; adj. prof. English, NYU, 1986—; mem. guest faculty in writing Sarah Lawrence Coll., 1988-96, regular faculty writing, 1996—; lectr. writing program Columbia U. Sch. Gen. Studies, 1990-96, Humanities faculty, 92nd St. YM/YWCA, 1987; fiction workshop The Writer's Voice, West Side YMCA, summer 1991; adj. prof. NYU Sch. Continuing Edn., 1988; adj. assoc. prof. writing Sch. of Arts, 1996—; mem. faculty Sarah Lawrence Ctr. for Continuing Edn., 1989, 90; instr. fiction writing course Art Workshop Internat., Assisi, Italy, summer 1993. Plays produced at Eugene O'Neill Meml. Theater Ctr., 1966, 67; author: The Ticket Out, 1983; editor: Great American Love Stories, 1988, The World Treasury of Love Stories, 1995; contbr. articles and revs. to various mags. and periodicals including Washington Post and Chgo. Tribune Book World, Saturday Rev., Ms. mag., Mich. Quar. Rev., N.Y. Times Book Rev.; contbr. fiction to Global City Rev., 1995. Pulitzer fellow critical writing, 1968. Mem. Authors Guild, Authors League, Nat. Book Critics Circle, Women's Media Group (bd. mem. 1979-81), PEN, Associated Writing Programs, Eugene O'Neill Meml. Theater Ctr., Phi Beta Kappa, Phi Kappa Phi. Office: care of Wendy Weil Agy Inc 232 Madison Ave Ste 1300 New York NY 10016-2901

ROSENTHAL, LYOVA HASKELL See GRANT, LEE

ROSENTHAL, MARVIN BERNARD, pediatrician, educator; b. Bklyn., Jan. 1, 1930; s. Robert Rosenthal and Elizabeth (Gartner) Rosenthal Dreyfuss; m. Janet H. Swerlick, dec. 31, 1959; 1 child, Robert G. BA, Alfred U., 1951; MD, Leiden U., The Netherlands, 1957. Diplomate Nat. Bd. Med. Examiners, Am. Bd. Pediatrics. Intern Kings County Hosp., Bklyn., 1957-58; resident in pediatrics SUNY Downstate Med. Sch., Bklyn., 1958-60; fellow in hematology Children's Hosp. Phila., 1962; pediatrician Somerset Pediatric Group, Bridgewater, N.J., 1963-84; chief pediatrics Somerset Hosp., Somerville, N.J., 1983-84; assoc. dir. family practice residency Warren Hosp., Phillipsburg, N.J., 1984—, chief pediatrics, 1991—, dir. med. edn., 1989—; mem. cons. staff Morristown (N.J.) Meml. Hosp., 1989—; clin. assoc. prof. Robert W. Johnson Med. Sch., UMDNJ, New Brunswick, N.J., 1980—; mem. adj. faculty U. New Eng. Coll. Osteopathics, Biddeford, Maine, 1988—. Capt. USAF, 1960-62. Recipient Silver medallion Am. Heart Assn., 1976, 78. Fellow Am. Acad. Pediatrics, Am. Acad. Family Practice; mem. N.J. Med. Soc., Acad. Medicine N.J., N.J. Pediatric Soc., Soc. Tchrs. Family Medicine, Ambulatory Pediatric Assn., Assn. Hosp. Med. Educators, Eagle Scout Assn. Home: 500 Spring Valley Rd Easton PA 18042-6872 Office: Warren Hosp Roseberry St Phillipsburg NJ 08865-1628

ROSENTHAL, MEYER L(OUIS), lawyer; b. Wilkes-Barre, Pa., May 27, 1944; s. Samuel J. and Lottie G. (Goncher) R.; m. Susan M., Aug. 19, 1967; children: Norman, Bonnie. BA, Rutgers U., 1966, JD, 1969. Bar: N.J. 1969, U.S. Dist. Ct. N.J. 1969, Calif. 1975, U.S. Dist. Ct. (cen. dist.) Calif. 1981, U.S. Dist. Ct. (ea. dist.) N.Y. 1980, U.S. Dist. Ct. (so. dist.) N.Y. 1981, U.S. Ct. Appeals (9th cir.) 1981. Law sec. Hon. Leon Milmed N.J. Superior Ct., Newark, 1969-70; assoc. Kaufman & Kaufman, Elizabeth, N.J., 1970-76; ptnr. Trueger & Rosenthal, Morristown, N.J., 1976-82; atty. pvt. practice, Morristown, N.J., 1982—. Editor Rutgers Law Rev. Cub scout leader Morris Area Boy Scouts Am., Randolph, N.J., 1980; chmn. Morris City Human Rels. Commn., Morristown, 1992-95. Recipient Comty. Hero award Morris County Orgn. Hispanic Affairs, 1996. Mem. Comml. Law League Am., Calif. Bar Assn., N.J. Bar Assn., B'nai B'rith (bd. govs. 1975—, pres. dist. 3 1988-89, Internat. Young Leadership award 1982, Internat. Founders award 1985). Office: 161 Washington St Morristown NJ 07960-3753

ROSENTHAL, MICHAEL ROSS, academic administrator, dean; b. Youngstown, Ohio, Dec. 2, 1939; s. Samuel Herman and Frances Vance (Schlesinger) R.; m. Linda Gabler, Sept. 6, 1963; children: Heidi, Erika, Nicolas Gabler. AB, Case Western Res. U., 1961; MS, U. Ill., 1963, PhD, 1965. Asst. prof. chemistry Bard Coll., Annandale, N.Y., 1965-68, assoc. prof. chemistry, 1968-73, prof. chemistry, 1973-84, assoc. dean acad. affairs, 1980-84; v.p. acad. affairs St. Mary's Coll. of Md., St. Mary's City, 1984-89; provost, dean faculty, prof. chemistry Southwestern U., Georgetown, Tex., 1989-96; dep. sec. Md. Higher Edn. Commn., Annapolis, 1996—; acad. cons., ind. and as rep. of Assn. Am. Colls. Author or co-author of numerous articles in jours. of inorganic chemistry and chem. edn. Chmn. Environ. Mgmt. Coun., Dutchess County, N.Y., 1978-84; founding chmn. Heritage Task Force for Hudson River Valley, 1980-84; pres., bd. dirs. Hudson River Heritage, N.Y., 1978-84; bd. dirs. Hudson River Rsch. Coun., 1976-84; teaching assoc. Danforth Found., 1980. Recipient Outstanding Community Svc. award, Dutchess County (N.Y.) Legislature, 1980. Mem. Am. Chem. Soc., The Royal Society (Chemistry, London), Am. Conf. Acad. Deans, Hudson River Environ. Soc., Sigma Xi, Phi Beta Kappa, Phi Lambda Upsilon. Democrat. Office: Md Higher Edn Commn 16 Francis St Annapolis MD 21401-1714 *Those of us who spend our professional lives as educators are subject to many pressures and influences - financial influences, political influences, intellectual influences. I try to remember that in the usually chaotic world of education the only really important thing is the welfare of the student.*

ROSENTHAL, MILTON FREDERICK, minerals and chemical company executive; b. N.Y.C., Nov. 24, 1913; s. Jacob C. and Louise (Berger) R.; m. Frieda Bojar, Feb. 28, 1943; 1 child, Anne Rosenthal Mitro. BA, CCNY, 1932; LLB, Columbia U., 1935. Bar: N.Y. 1935. Rsch. asst. N.Y. State Law Revision Commn., 1935-37; law sec. Fed. Judge William Bondy, 1937-40; assoc. atty. Leve, Hecht & Hadfield, 1940-42; sec., treas. Hugo Stinnes Corp., 1946-48, exec. v.p., treas., 1948-49, pres., dir., CEO, 1949-64; pres., dir., CEO Minerals and Chems. Philipp Corp., N.Y.C., 1964-67; pres., dir., COO Engelhard Minerals & Chem. Corp., N.Y.C., 1967-71; chmn., pres., CEO, dir. Engelhard Minerals & Chems. Corp., N.Y.C., 1971-81; dir. emeritus Salomon, Inc., N.Y.C., Ferro Corp., Cleve.; chmn. Engelhard Corp., N.J., 1981-86; ret. Trustee Mt. Sinai Med. Ctr. and Mt. Sinai Hosp.; bd. dirs. United Cerebral Palsy Rsch. and Ednl. Found., Inc.; ret. trustee Am. Fedn. Arts, Manhattanville Coll., Purchase Coll. Found. 1st lt. JAG dept. U.S. Army, 1942-45. Mem. Assn. of Bar of City of N.Y., Chgo. Bar Assn., Columbia Law Sch. Alumni Assn., Judge Adv. Assn., Phi Beta Kappa. Home: 450 Woodlands Rd Harrison NY 10528-1220 also: 1602 Quartz Valley Dr Carefree AZ 85377 Office: 450 Park Ave Ste 2701 New York NY 10022-2605

ROSENTHAL, MURRAY WILFORD, chemical engineer, science administrator; b. Greenville, Miss., Feb. 25, 1926; s. Monnie and Esther (Bernstein) R.; m. Miriam Sylvia Teplit, Aug. 7, 1949; children: Elaine, Douglas I. BSChemE, La. State U., 1949; PhDChemE, MIT, 1953. Devel. engr. heat transfer rsch., reactor exptl. engrng. div. Oak Ridge (Tenn.) Nat. Lab., 1953-55, group leader aqueous homogeneous reactor analysis, 1956-59, group leader analysis advanced reactors, reactor div., 1959-61, project engr., 1961-63, chief planning and analysis sect., 1963-65, dir. planning, 1965, dir. molten salt reactor program, 1966-73, acting dep. dir., 1973, assoc. dir. advanced energy systems, 1974-89, dep. dir., 1989-93, lectr. in reactor engrng. sch. reactor tech., 1955; cons., 1994—; vis. prof. chem. engrng. MIT, Boston, 1961; tech. asst. to asst. gen. mgr. AEC, Washington, 1966. Vice chmn. Oak Ridge Charter Commn., 1955-56, chmn., 1962-63; mem. Oak Ridge Human Rels. Adv. Bd., 1963-65, Adv. Task Force on Tenn. Energy Future, Oak Ridge, 1978. Lt. (j.g.) USN, 1943-46. Recipient Disting. Career award Fusion Power Assocs., 1993, Disting. Svc. award Nat. Mgmt. Assn., 1994; inducted into Engring. Hall of Distinction, La. State U., 1982; Humble fellow MIT, 1950, Std. Oil fellow, 1951, Pan Am. fellow, 1952. Fellow Am. Nuclear Soc. (bd. dirs. 1970-73, exec. com. 1971-73); mem. NAE, AAAS, Sigma Xi. Home and Office: 124 Carnegie Dr Oak Ridge TN 37830-7732

ROSENTHAL, MYER H., anesthesiologist; b. Boston, July 11, 1941. MD, U. Vt., 1967. Intern Naval Hosp. Bethesda, Md., 1967-68; resident Fell Critical Care Medicine Naval Hosp. San Diego, 1968-70; attending anesthesiologist Stanford (Calif.) Med. Ctr., 1975—, prof. anesthesiology; prof. Stanford U., 1975—. Office: Med Dir Intensive Care Stanford U Med Ctr 300 Pasteur Dr Stanford CA 94305*

ROSENTHAL, NAN, curator, author; b. N.Y.C., Aug. 27, 1937; d. Alan Herman and Lenore (Fry) R.; m. Otto Piene (div.); m. Henry Benning Cortesi, Sept. 5, 1990. BA, Sarah Lawrence Coll., 1959; MA, Harvard U., 1970, PhD, 1976. Asst. prof. art history U. Calif., Santa Cruz, 1971-77, assoc. prof., 1977-84, prof., 1985-86, chair dept. art history, 1976-80; curator 20th-century art Nat. Gallery Art, Washington, 1985-92; cons. Dept. of 20th Century Art, Metro. Mus. of Art, N.Y.C., 1993—; Lila Acheson Wallace vis. prof. of Fine Arts Inst. of Fine Arts, NYU, 1996; vis. prof. art history Fordham U., Lincoln Ctr., 1981, 85; vis. scholar N.Y. Inst. for Humanities, NYU, 1982-83; vis. lectr. visual arts Princeton U., 1985, 88, 92. Author: George Rickey, 1977; also exhbn. catalogues, catalogue essays and articles; art editor Show, 1963-64; assoc. editor, then editor at large and contbg. editor Art in Am., 1964-70. Radcliffe Inst. fellow, 1968-69, scholar, 1970-71; travelling fellow Harvard U., 1973-74, rsch. fellow U. Calif., 1978, Ailsa Mellon Bruce curatorial fellow Nat. Gallery of Art, 1988-89; rsch. and travel grantee U. Calif., Santa Cruz, 1974, 77-80, 82-85. Office: Met Mus of Art 20th Century Art 1000 Fifth Ave New York NY 10028-0113

ROSENTHAL, PETER, public relations executive; b. N.Y.C., Nov. 1, 1946; s. Walter and Rita (Horn) R.; m. Terri Thompson; children: Daniel, Joel. BA, Lehman Coll., 1969; MA, Ball State U., 1972. Tchr., N.Y.C. Bd. Edn., 1969-71; reporter Bklyn. Today, 1972-73; asst. dir. pub. rels. St. Vincents Hosp., N.Y.C, 1973-76; account exec. Howard Rubenstein Assocs., N.Y.C., 1976-78, v.p., 1978-81, sr. v.p., 1981-84, exec. v.p., 1984-87, sr. exec. v.p., 1987—; mem. bd. gov's. science and endowment fund Bronx H.S. Mem. Internat. Assn. Bus. Communications, Nat. Assn. Real Estate Editors, Nat. Assn. Real Estate Investment Trust, Urban Land Inst. (assoc.) Jewish. Avocations: reading, theater, travel. Office: Howard J Rubenstein Assocs Inc 1345 Avenue Of The Americas New York NY 10105-0302

ROSENTHAL, RICHARD JAY, real estate consultant, mediator, educator; b. N.Y.C., Mar. 10, 1940; s. David and Laura Rosenthal. BBA, Hofstra U., 1961; postgrad., U. So. Calif., 1966, NYU, 1978, U. Pa., 1976. Lic. real estate broker, Calif.; cert. counselor of real estate; cert. brokerage mgr.; grad. Realtor Inst. Pres., designated broker MDR Investment Co., L.A.; broker owner R.J. Rosenthal & Assocs., Realtors, L.A., 1975; CEO The Rosenthal Co., Real Estate Cons., L.A., 1975; mng. ptnr. The Rosenthal Group Real Estate Consultants, Mediators and Educators, L.A., 1990—; vis. lectr. State of Calif. Pers. Devel. Ctr.; guest lectr. Sch. Law, Whittier Coll.; master instr. Calif. Assn. Realtors; adj. prof. real estate Sch. Bus. Adminstrn., Calif. State U., Sacramento; chmn. exec. bd. Real Estate and Land Use Inst., Calif. State U.; cert. instr. for continuing edn. State of Calif. State of Hawaii; mediator L.A. Superior Ct. Panel, La. Supreme Ct. Panel, Calif. Assn. Realtors Panel; mediator and arbitrator NASDR; speaker in field. Contbr. articles to profl. jours. Commr. County of L.A., 1984—, chmn. commn. on local govt. svcs., 1992—; mediator L.A. Superior Ct. Panel, La. Supreme Ct. Panel. Recipient spl. honor and highest commendation, Calif. State Assembly, 1979, 86, commendation for Outstanding Leadership and Svc. to the People of Calif. and the Real Estate Industry, Senate Rules Com., 1986, Outstanding Svc. to the Community and Real Estate Industry, Bd. of Suprs., 1979, Outstanding Leadership and Svc. to Community and Field of Real Estate, 1985, Dedicated Svc. to County of Los Angeles, 1987, Mayor's Cert. of Appreciation, 1986, and others. Mem. ABA, Am. Soc. Real Estate Counselors, Nat. Assn. Realtors (bd. dirs. 1984—, regional vice pres. Calif., Hawaii and Guam 1991), Nat. Coun. Exchangors, Nat. Inst. for Dispute Resolution, Realtors Nat. Mktg. Inst., Calif. Real Estate Educators Assn., Calif. Assn. Realtors (bd. dirs. 1978—, pres. 1986), So. Calif. Mediation Assn., No. Calif. Mediation Assn., Los Angeles County Bar Assn., L.A. Bd. Realtors, Palm Desert-Rancho Mirage Bd. Realtors, Palm Springs Bd. Realtors, Beverly Hills Bd. Realtors, Los Angeles County Trial Lawyers Assn. (assoc.), Soc. Profls. in Dispute Resolution, Real Estate Educators Assn., Lambda Alpha Internat., Soc. Profls. in Dispute Resolution, Nat. Inst. for Dispute Resolution, Southern Calif. Mediation Assn., No. Calif. Mediation Assn. and others. Office: The Rosenthal Group Real Estate Cons PO Box 837 Venice CA 90294-0837

ROSENTHAL, ROBERT, psychology educator; b. Giessen, Germany, Mar. 2, 1933; came to U.S., 1940, naturalized, 1946; s. Julius and Hermine (Kahn) R.; m. Mary Lu Clayton, Apr. 20, 1951; children: Roberta, David C., Virginia. A.B., UCLA, 1953, Ph.D., 1956. Diplomate: clin. psychology Am. Bd. Examiners Profl. Psychology. Clin. psychology trainee Los Angeles Area VA, 1954-57; lectr. U. So. Calif., 1956-57; acting instr. UCLA, 1957; from asst. to assoc. prof., coordinator clin. tng. U. N.D., 1957-62; vis. assoc. prof. Ohio State U., 1960-61; lectr. Boston U., 1965-66; lectr. clin. psychology Harvard U., Cambridge, Mass., 1962-67, prof. social psychology, 1967—, chmn. dept. psychology, 1992-95, Edgar Pierce prof. psychology, 1995—. Author: Experimenter Effects in Behavioral Research, 1966, enlarged edit., 1976; (with Lenore Jacobson) Pygmalion in the Classroom, expanded edit., 1992, Meta-analytic Procedures for Social Research, 1984, rev. edit., 1991, Judgement Studies, 1987; (with others) New Directions in Psychology 4, 1970, Sensitivity to Nonverbal Communication: The Pons Test, 1979; (with Ralph L. Rosnow) The Volunteer Subject, 1975, Primer of Methods for the Behavioral Sciences, 1975, Essentials of Behavioral Research, 1984, 2d edit., 1991, Understanding Behavioral Science, 1984, Contrast Analysis, 1985, Beginning Behavioral Research, 1993, 2d edit., 1996, People Studying People: Artifact and Ethics in Behavioral Research, 1997; (with Brian Mullen) BASIC Meta-analysis, 1985; editor: (with Ralph L. Rosnow) Artifact in Behavioral Research, 1969, Skill in Nonverbal Communication, 1979, Quantitative Assessment of Research Domains, 1980, (with Thomas A. Sebeok) The Clever Hans Phenomenon: Communication With Horses, Whales, Apes and People, 1981; (with Blanck and Buck) Nonverbal Communication in the Clinical Context, 1986; (with Gheorghiu, Netter and Eysenck) Suggestion and Suggestibility: Theory and Research, 1989, (with Ralph L. Rosnow and Donald B. Rubin) Contrasts and Effect Sizes in Behavioral Research: A Correlational Approach. Recipient Donald Campbell award Soc. for Personality and Social Psychology, 1988, James McKeen Cattell Sabbatical award, 1995-96; co-recipient Golden Anniversary Monograph award Speech Comm. Assn., 1996; Guggenheim fellow, 1973-74, fellow Ctr. for Advanced Study in Behavioral Scis., 1988-89; sr. Fulbright

Scholar, 1972. Fellow AAAS (co-recipient Sociopsychol. prize 1960, co-recipient Behavioral Sci. Rsch. prize 1993), APA (co-recipient Cattell Fund award 1967, chmn. task force on statis. conf.), Am. Psychol. Soc. (charter); mem. Soc. Exptl. Social Psychology (Disting. Scientist award 1996), Ea. Psychol. Assn. (Disting. lectr. 1989), Mid-western Psychol. Assn., Mass. Psychol. Assn. (Disting. Career Contbn. award 1979), Soc. Projective Techniques (past treas.), Phi Beta Kappa, Sigma Xi. Home: 12 Phinney Rd Lexington MA 02173-7717 Office: Harvard U 33 Kirkland St Cambridge MA 02138-2044

ROSENTHAL, ROBERT JON, newspaper editor, journalist; b. N.Y.C., Aug. 5, 1948; s. Irving and Ruth (Moss) R.; m. Inez Katherina von Sternenfels, Nov. 22, 1985; children: Adam, Benjamin, Ariella. BA, U. Vt., 1970. News asst. N.Y. Times, N.Y.C., 1970-73; reporter Boston Globe, 1974-79; reporter Phila. Inquirer, 1979-82, Africa corr., Nairobi, Kenya, 1982-86, fgn. editor, Phila., 1986-91, city editor, 1991-93, asst. mng. editor, daily, 1993-94; assoc. mng. editor, 1994-96, exec. editor, 1996—. Recipient Third World Reporting award Nat. Assn. Black Journalists, 1983, Mag. award Overseas Press Club, 1985, Disting. Fgn. Corr. award Sigma Delta Chi, 1985, Mag. Writing award World Population Inst., 1986. Avocations: sports, painting, fishing, cooking. Office: Phila Inquirer 400 N Broad St Philadelphia PA 19130-4015*

ROSENTHAL, SOL, lawyer; b. Balt., Oct. 17, 1934; s. Louis and Hattie (Getz) R.; m. Diane Myra Sackler, June 11, 1961; children: Karen Abby, Pamela Margaret, Robert Joel. AB, Princeton U., 1956; JD, Harvard U., 1959. Bar: Md. 1959, Calif. 1961. Law clk. to chief judge U.S. Ct. Appeals, 4th cir., Balt., 1959-60; assoc. Kaplan, Livingston, Goodwin, Berkowitz & Selvin, Beverly Hills, Calif., 1960-66, ptnr., 1966-74; ptnr. Buchalter, Nemer, Fields & Younger, L.A., 1974-96; of counsel Blanc, Williams, Johnston & Kronstadt, L.A., 1996—; bd. dirs. Playboy Enterprises, Inc., Chgo.; arbitrator Dirs. Guild Am., L.A., 1976—, Writers Guild Am., L.A., 1976—, Am. Film Mktg. Assn., 1989—; negotiator Writers Guild-Assn. Talent Agts., L.A., 1978—; mem. entertainment panel Am. Arbitration Assn., 1997—. Founder Camp Ronald McDonald for Good Times, L.A., 1985; charter founder Mus. Contemporary Art, L.A., 1988. Mem. ABA, Calif. Bar Assn., L.A. County Bar Assn. (trustee 1981-82), L.A. Copyright Soc. (pres. 1973-74), Acad. TV Arts and Scis. (bd. govs. 1990-92), Beverly Hills Bar Assn. (pres. 1982-83), Phi Beta Kappa. Office: Blanc Williams Johnston & Kronstadt 1900 Ave Of Stars Ste 1700 Los Angeles CA 90067-4408

ROSENTHAL, STANLEY LAWRENCE, meteorologist; b. Bklyn., Dec. 6, 1929; s. Louis and Fay (Pokorne) R.; m. Mildred Farlow, Aug. 8, 1953; children—Russell K., Sarah Lynn, David Scott. B.S., CCNY, 1951; M.S., Fla. State U., 1953, Ph.D., 1958. With NOAA, Dept. Commerce, 1960-93; chief theoretical studies group Nat. Hurricane Research Lab., Miami, Fla., 1960-75, chief modeling group, 1975-77, chief analytical and theoretical studies group, 1977-93, dir., 1980-93; dir. Nat. Hurricane and Exptl. Meterology Lab., 1977-80; dep. dir. Atlantic Oceanographic and Meteorol. Labs., 1981; sr. rsch. assoc. Coop. Inst. for Marine & Atmospheric Scis. U. Miami, 1993—; adj. prof. meteorology U. Miami, Coral Gables, Fla., 1964-84. Contbr. articles to profl. jours. Served with U.S. Army, 1953-55. Recipient Gold medal U.S. Dept. Commerce, 1970. Fellow Am. Meteorol. Soc. (council 1980-83), mem. com. on hurricanes and tropical meteorology 1981-85, past chmn. Greater Miami br.), AAAS (past officer sect. W). Home: 13301 SW 99th Pl Miami FL 33176-6163

ROSENTHAL, STEVEN SIEGMUND, lawyer; b. Cleve., May 22, 1949; s. Fred Siegel and Natalie Josephine Rosenthal; m. Ilene Edwina Goldstein, Oct. 1, 1983; 1 child, Alexandra M. AB, Dartmouth Coll., 1971; JD, Harvard U., 1974. Bar: Fla. 1974, D.C. 1975, U.S. Supreme Ct. 1978, Calif. 1983. Law clk. U.S. Ct. Appeals (D.C. cir.), 1974-75; assoc. Covington & Burling, Washington, 1975-80; assoc. Morrison & Foerster, Washington, 1980-81, ptnr., 1981—; lawyer rep. Jud. Conf. D.C. Cir., 1981-83. Pres. Family and Child Services Washington, 1986-88, trustee, 1978—. Mem. ABA, Am. Law Inst., Phi Beta Kappa. Republican. Office: Morrison & Foerster Ste 5500 2000 Pennsylvania Ave NW Washington DC 20006-1831

ROSENTHAL, TONY (BERNARD), sculptor; b. Highland Park, Ill., Aug. 9, 1914; s. Nathan H. and Bessie (Baumgarden) R.; m. Halina Kotlowicz, Apr. 2, 1946 (dec. 1991); m. Cynthia Dillon, 1995. AB, U. Mich., 1936; student, Art Inst. Chgo., Cranbrook Acad. Arts; hon. doctorate, Hofstra U., 1989. Exhbns. include Art Inst. Chgo., Met. Mus. Art, Mus. Modern Art, N.Y., Whitney Mus. Am. Art, N.Y.C., Pa. Acad. Fine Arts, Archtl. League, N.Y., Yale U., U. Ill., U. Nebr., 100 Biennale Exhbn., Sao Paulo, Brazil, Brussel's Fair, 1958, others; one man shows include San Francisco Mus, Western Mus. Assn. Travel Exhbn., Santa Barbara (Calif.) Mus., Long Beach (Calif.) Mus., Catherine Viviano Gallery N.Y., Kootz Gallery, N.Y.C., M. Knoedler & Co., Denise Rene Gallery, Paris, 1988, others; archtl. commn. include Temple Emanuel, Beverly Hills, Calif., 1955, IBM Bldg., 1958, Southland Ctr., Dallas, IBM Western Hdqrs., Los Angeles, Police Plaza, N.Y.C., Fullerton (Calif.) State Coll., Fin. Ctr. Pacific, Honolulu, Holocaust Meml., Buffalo, Metro-Rail Sta., Miami, S.E. Nat. Bank, Miami, Grove Isle, Miami, Met. Hosp., Phila., 1010 Lamar, Houston, Crantsrook Acad. Art, Bloomfield Hills, Mich., Steelpark, 400 E. 80th St, N.Y.C., Alamo, Astor Pl., N.Y.C., Rondo, 111 E. 59th St., N.Y.C., U. Ind., Hofstra U., N.Y., others; works in permanent collections Milw. Art Ctr., Ill. State U., Los Angeles County Mus., Long Beach, Lincoln (Mass.) Mus., Ariz. State Coll., Mus. Modern Art, Whitney Mus. Art, Albright Knox Art Gallery, Buffalo, U. Ill., NYU, Yale U., Middelheim Mus., Antwerp, Belgium, Guggenheim Mus., N.Y.C., Hofstra U. Fashion Inst. Art, N.Y.C., others; pvt. collections. Served with AUS, 1942-46. Recipient awards, prizes San Francisco Mus., 1950, Los Angeles City Exhbn., 1951, 52, Audubon Artists, N.Y., 1953, Pa. Acad. Fine Arts, 1953, Los Angeles County Mus., 1950, 57, Santa Barbara Mus. Art, 1959, Art in Steel award Iron and Steel Inst., 1974-75, Disting. Alumni award U. Mich., 1977, Sculpture award Inst. Arts and Letters, N.Y.C., 1985. Mem. Nat. Acad. Design. Address: 173 E 73rd St New York NY 10021-3510

ROSENTHAL, WILLIAM J., lawyer; b. Balt., Nov. 4, 1920; s. Justin J. and Ray Marian (Stern) R.; m. Margaret Irwin Parker, July 4, 1956; children—Adriane Leigh, Jacqueline Rae, John Justin. A.B., Johns Hopkins U., 1941; LL.B., U. Balt., 1950. Bar: Md. 1950. Adminstrv. asst. Office Price Adminstrn., Washington, 1941-42; assoc. firm Earle K. Shawe (name changed to Shawe & Rosenthal 1967), Balt., 1951-67; ptnr. Shawe & Rosenthal, Balt., 1967—; lectr. U. Balt., 1952-56; mem. regional adv. council NLRB; vets. rep. Md. Constrn. Adv. Council, 1946-49; lectr. NYU Conf. Labor Relations, Boston U. Labor Law Seminar, 1985; expert witness on labor law, legis. and congl. coms. Contbg. author: The Developing Labor Law; contbr. articles to profl. jours. Served to lt. USNR, 1942-46, ETO. Mem. ABA, Md. Bar Assn., Balt. Bar Assn., Spiked Shoe Soc., Omicron Delta Kappa, Pi Delta Epsilon. Club: Suburban of Baltimore County (bd. govs., pres.). Home: 8207 Cranwood Ct Baltimore MD 21208-1823 Office: Shawe & Rosenthal Sun Life Bldg Charles Center Baltimore MD 21201

ROSENWASSER, LANNY JEFFREY, allergist, immunologist; b. N.Y.C., Mar. 3, 1948. MD, NYU, 1972. Cert. in allergy and immunology; cert. in internal medicine. Intern U. Calif.-HC Moffitt Hosp., San Francisco, 1972-73; resident U. Calif. Affiliated Hosps., San Francisco, 1973-74. Mem. Alpha Omega Alpha, Sigma Xi. Office: Nat Jewish Ctr Im/Resp Med 1400 Jackson St Denver CO 80206-2761

ROSENZWEIG, CHARLES LEONARD, lawyer; b. N.Y.C., Apr. 12, 1952; s. William and Frieda (Dechner) R.; m. Rya R. Mehler, June 14, 1975; children: Jessica Sara, Erica Danielle. AB cum laude, Princeton U., 1974; JD, NYU, 1977. Bar: N.Y. 1978, U.S. Dist. Ct. (ea. and so. dists.) N.Y. 1978, U.S. Ct. Appeals (7th cir.) 1980, U.S. Ct. Internat. Trade 1981, U.S. Ct. Appeals (2d cir.) 1985. Assoc. Graubard, Moskovitz et al, N.Y.C., 1977-85; ptnr. Rand, Rosenzweig, Smith, Radley, Gordon & Burstein LLP, N.Y.C., 1987—. Editor NYU Jour. Internat. Law. and Politics. Officer Jewish Cmty. Ctr., Harrison, 1994—. Mem. ABA (internat. law sect.), N.Y. State Bar Assn. (co-chair internat. litigation com.), Am. Arbitration Assn., NYU Alumni Assn. (chmn. jour. internat. law and politics alumni 1985-87), Princeton Club. Avocations: skiing, cycling, tennis, scuba diving. Home: 37 Franklin Rd Scarsdale NY 10583-7563 Office: Rand Rosenzweig et al 605 3rd Ave New York NY 10158

ROSENZWEIG, HERBERT STEPHEN, stockbroker; b. Phila., Aug. 5, 1943; s. Morton and Helen (Katzen) R.; m. Myra Pauline Saltzburg, June 7, 1964; children: Helene, Michael, Elisa, Jeffrey. BS in Fin., Temple U., 1965. CFP. Stockbroker Walston & Co., Phila., 1967-73, Reynolds Securities, Phila., 1974, Merrill Lynch, Riverside, Calif., 1974—. Vol. Spl. Olympics, 1980—; chmn. Pomona Valley Coun. Chs. Hunger Walk; pres. Upland Youth Accountability Bd. Mem. Kiwanis (past pres., lt. gov. Divsn. 15 1992-93, Club Kiwanian of Yr., Divsn. Kiwanian of Yr. 1992). Republican. Jewish. Office: Merrill Lynch PO Box 472 Riverside CA 92502-0472

ROSENZWEIG, MARK RICHARD, psychology educator; b. Rochester, N.Y., Sept. 12, 1922; s. Jacob and Pearl (Grossman) R.; m. Janine S.A. Chappat, Aug. 1, 1947; children: Anne Janine, Suzanne Jacqueline, Philip Mark. BA, U. Rochester, 1943, MA, 1944; PhD, Harvard U., 1949; hon. doctorate, U. René Descartes, Sorbonne, 1980. Postdoctoral rsch. fellow Harvard U., 1949-51; asst. prof. U. Calif., Berkeley, 1951-56, assoc. prof., 1956-60, prof. psychology, 1960-91, assoc. rsch. prof., 1958-59, rsch. prof., 1965-66, prof. emeritus, 1991—, prof. grad. sch., 1994—; vis. prof. biology U. Sorbonne, Paris, 1973-74. Author: Biologie de la Mémoire, 1976, (with A.L. Leiman) Physiological Psychology, 1982, 2nd edit., 1989, (with M.J. Renner) Enriched and Impoverished Environments: Effects on Brain and Behavior, 1987, (with D. Sinha) La Recherche en Psychologie Scientifique, 1988; editor: (with P. Mussen) Psychology: An Introduction, 1973, 2nd edit., 1977, (with E.L. Bennett) Neural Mechanisms of Learning and Memory, 1976, International Psychological Science: Progress, Problems, and Prospects, 1992, (with A.L. Leiman and S.M. Breedlove) Biological Psychology, 1996; co-editor: (with L. Porter) Ann. Rev. of Psychology, 1968-94; contbr. articles to profl. jours. Served with USN, 1944-46. Recipient Disting. Alumnus award U. Rochester; Fulbright rsch. fellow; faculty rsch. fellow Social Sci. Rsch. Coun., 1960-61; rsch. grantee NSF, USPHS, Easter Seal Found., Nat. Inst. Drug Abuse. Fellow AAAS, APA (Disting. Sci. Contbn. award 1982, Disting. Contbn. award for Internat. Advancement of Psychology 1997), Am. Psychol. Soc.; mem. NAS, NAACP (life), Am. Physiol. Soc., Am. Psychol. Soc., Internat. Union Psychol. Sci. (hon. life, mem. exec. com. 1972-96, v.p. 1980-84, pres. 1988-92, past pres. 1992-96, mem. U.S. nat. com. for Internat. Union Psychol. Sci., NRC and NAS 1984-96), Internat. Brain Rsch. Orgn., Soc. Exptl. Psychologists, Soc. for Neurosci., Société Française de Psychologie, Sierra Club (life), Common Cause, Fulbright Assn. (life), Phi Beta Kappa, Sigma Xi. Office: U Calif Dept Psychology 3210 Tolman Hall Berkeley CA 94720-1651

ROSENZWEIG, NORMAN, psychiatry educator; b. N.Y.C., Feb. 28, 1924; s. Jacob Arthur and Edna (Braman) R.; m. Carol Treleaven, Sept. 20, 1945; 1 child, Elizabeth Ann. MB, Chgo. Med. Sch., 1947, MD, 1948; MS, U. Mich., 1954. Diplomate Am. Bd. Psychiatry and Neurology. Asst. prof. psychiatry U. Mich., Ann Arbor, 1957-61, asst. prof., 1963-67, assoc. prof., 1967-73; prof. Wayne State U., Detroit, 1973—; chmn. dept. psychiat. Sch. Med. Wayne State U., Detroit, 1987-90, Sinai Hosp., Detroit, 1961-90; spl. cons., profl. advisor Oakland County Community Mental Health Services Bd., 1964-65; mem. protem med. adv. panel Herman Kiefer Hosp., Detroit, 1970, psychiat. task force N.W. Quadrangle Hosps., Detroit, 1971-78, planning com. mental health adv. council Dept. Mental Health State of Mich., Lansing, 1984-90, tech. adv.rsch. com., 1978-82; psychiat. bed need task force Office Health and Med. Affairs State of Mich., 1980-84; bd. dirs. Alliance for Mental Health, Farmington Hills, Mich., 1986-94; speaker in field. Author: Community Mental Health Programs in England: An American View, 1975; co-editor: Psychopharmacology and Psychotherapy-Synthesis or Antithesis?, 1978, Sex Education for the Health Professional: A Curriculum Guide, 1978; contbr. articles to profl. jours. and chpts. to books. Mem. profl. adv. bd. The Orchards, Livonia, Mich., 1963. Served as capt. USAF, 1955-57. Recipient Appreciation and Merit cert. Mich. Soc. Psychiatry and Neurology, 1970-71, Career Svc. award Assn. Mental Health in Mich., 1994. Fellow Am. Coll. Mental Health Adminstrn., fellow emeritus Am. Coll. Psychiatrists (hon. membership com., com. on regional ednl. programs, liaison officer to The Royal Australian and New Zealand Coll. Psychiatrists 1984-88), Am. Psychiat. Assn. (life fellow, coun. on internat. affairs 1970-79, chmn. 1973-76, assembly liaison to coun. on internat. affairs 1979-80, 82-84, reference com. 1973-76, nominating com. 1978-79, internat. affairs survey team 1973-74, assoc. representing Am. Psychiat. Assn. to Inter-Am. Coun. Psychiat. Assns. 1973-75, treas. APA lifers 1991-94, v.p. 1994-95, pres. 1995-96, com. on sr. psychiatrists 1993—, others, Rush Gold Medal award 1974, cert. Commendation, 1973-76, 78-80, Warren Williams award 1986); mem. AAUP, AMA (Physician's Recognition award 1971, 74, 77, 80-81, 84, 87, 90, 92), Am. Assn. Dirs. Psychiat. Residency Tng. (nominating com. 1972-74, task force on core curriculum 1972-74), Am. Assn. Gen. Hosp. Psychiatry, Puerto Rico Med. Assn. (hon., presdl. award 1981), Am. Hosp. Assn. (governing coun. psychiat. svcs. sect. 1977-79, ad hoc com. on uniform mental health definitions, chmn. task force on psychiat. coverage under Nat. Health Ins. 1977-79, others), Brit. Soc. Clin. Psychiatrists (task force on gen. hosp. psychiatry 1969-74), Can. Psychiat. Assn., Mich. Assn. Professions, Mich. Hosp. Assn. (psychiat. and mental health svcs. com. 1979-81), Mich. Psychiat. Soc. (com. on ins. 1965-69, chmn. com. on community mental health svcs. 1967-68, chmn. com. on nominations of fellows 1972-73, mem. com. on budget 1973-74, task force on pornography 1973-74, chmn. commn. on health professions and groups 1974-75, pres. elect 1974-75, pres. 1975-76, chmn. com. on liaison with hosp. assns. 1979-81, chmn. subcom. on liaison with Am. Hosp. Assn. 1979-81, numerous others, Past Pres. plaque, 1978, cert. Recognition, 1980, Disting. Service award 1986), Mich. State Med. Soc. (vice chmn. sect. psychiatry 1972-73, chmn. sect. psychiatry 1974-75, mem. com. to improve membership 1977-78, alt. del for Mich. Psychiat. Soc. to Ho. of Dels. 1978-79, del. from Wayne County Med. Soc. to Mich. Med. Soc. Ho. of Dels. 1982-88), N.Y. Acad. Scis., Pan Am. Med. Assn., Wayne County Med. Soc. (com. on hosp. and prof. rels., 1983-84, com. on child health advocacy 1983-87, med. edn. com. 1983-87, mental health com. 1983-87), Royal Australian and New Zealand Coll. Psychiatrists (hon.), Indian Psychiat. Soc. (hon. corr.), World Psychiat. Assn., Sect. Gen. Hosp. Psychiat. Avocations: music, films, reading. Home: 1234 Cedarholm Ln Bloomfield Hills MI 48302-0902 Office: 26211 Central Park Blvd Ste 602 Southfield MI 48076-4164

ROSENZWEIG, RICHARD STUART, publishing company executive; b. Appleton, Wis., Aug. 8, 1935; s. Walter J. and Rose (Bahcall) R. B.S., Northwestern U., 1957; Advanced Mgmt. Program, Harvard U., 1975. Credit rep. Dun & Bradstreet, Inc., 1958; with Playboy Enterprises, Inc., 1958—, exec. asst. to pres., 1963-73, sr. v.p., dir., 1973—, dir. mktg., 1974—, exec. v.p. publs. group, 1975-77, exec. v.p., head West Coast ops., 1977-80; exec. v.p. corp. affairs Playboy Enterprises, Inc., Los Angeles, 1980-82; exec. v.p., chmn. emeritus Playboy Enterprises, Inc., 1982—; pres. Playboy Jazz Festivals, 1989—; dir. I. Bahcall Industries, Appleton. Trustee L.A. Film Expn.; mem. 2d decade coun. Am. Film Inst.; bd. dirs. Mus. Contemporary Art, Chgo., Periodical and Book Assn. Am., Internat. Inst. Kidney Diseases of UCLA, Children of Night, Maple Ctr. Beverly Hills; mem., chmn. bd. UCLA Legis. Network, Town Hall of Calif.; adv. bd. West Hollywood Mktg. Corp., 1985—; bd. dirs. So. Calif. ACLU, 1985—; mem. Los Angeles County Mus.; apptd. to blue ribbon com. project West Coast Gateway. With AUS, 1957. Recipient Do-ers award, 1988, Beverly Hills medal Beverly Hills City Coun., 1993. Mem. Am. Mktg. Aslsn., L.A. Pub. Affairs Officers Assn., UCLA Chancellor's Assocs., Pres.'s Cir., Beverly Hills C. of C. (bd. dirs., visitors' bur., v.p.), Beverly Hills Fine Art Commn. (chmn.), Beverly Hills Econ. Devel. Coun., Founders Circle of Music Ctr., Pub. Affairs Coun., Craft and Folk Art Mus., Pres.' Coun. and Contemporary ARts Coun. L.A. Mus. Contemporary Art, The Am. Cinematheque (groundbreaker), Variety Club So. Calif. (bd. dirs.). Office: Playboy Enterprises Inc 9242 Beverly Blvd Beverly Hills CA 90210-3710

ROSENZWEIG, SAUL, psychologist, educator, administrator; b. Boston, Feb. 7, 1907; s. David and Etta (Tuttle) R.; m. Louise Ritterskamp, Mar. 21, 1941; children: Julia, Ann. A.B. summa cum laude, Harvard U., 1929, M.A., 1930, Ph.D., 1932. Research assoc. Harvard Psychol. Clinic, 1929-34, Worcester (Mass.) State Hosp., 1934-43; affiliate prof. Clark U., Worcester, 1938-43; chief psychologist Western State Psychiat. Ins. and Clinic, Pitts., 1943-48; lectr. psychology U. Pitts., 1943-48; assoc. prof. psychology and med. psychology Washington U., St. Louis, 1949-51; prof. Washington U., 1951-75, prof. emeritus, 1975—; chief psychologist Child Guidance Clinic, 1949-59; cons., mem. life scis. study sect. NIH, 1964-68; mng. dir. Found. for Idiodynamics and the Creative Process; adj. prof. psychology St. Louis U., 1996. Author: (with Kate L. Kogan) Psychodiagnosis, Grune and Stratton, 1949, Rosenzweig Picture-Frustration Study, 1948, Aggressive Behavior and the Rosenzweig Picture-Frustration Study, 1978, Freud and Experimental Psychology: The Emergence of Idiodynamics, 1986, Sally Beauchamp's Career, 1987, Freud, Jung, and Hall the King-Maker, 1992, 2d edit., 1994; assoc. editor: Jour. Abnormal and Social Psychology, 1950-56; cons. editor: Psychol. Monographs, 1948-57, Zeitschrift für Diagnostische Psychologie und Persönlichkeitsforschung, 1953-58, Diagnostica, 1959—; adv. editor: Jour. Cons. Psychology, 1959-64, Jour. Abnormal Psychology, 1965-67; mem. editorial bd. Aggressive Behavior, 1974—; contbr. articles to profl. jours. Fellow Am. Psychol. Assn. (rep. Internat. group for Coordination Psychiatry and Psychol. Methods 1955-61), Am. Psychopathol. Assn.; mem. Internat. Soc. for Research on Aggression (founding pres. 1972-73, archivist 1981-88), Soc. Prof. Emeriti Washington U. (founding pres. 1978), Sigma Xi, Phi Beta Kappa. Home: 8029 Washington Ave Saint Louis MO 63114-6333 Office: Washington U Box 1125 Saint Louis MO 63130

ROSES, ALLEN DAVID, neurologist, educator; b. Paterson, N.J., Feb. 21, 1943. BS in Chemistry summa cum laude, U. Pitts., 1963; MD, U. Pa., 1967. Diplomate Am. Bd. Psychiatry and Neurology. Intern Hosp. of the U. Pa., Phila., 1967-68; resident in neurology N.Y. Neurol. Inst., Columbia U., N.Y.C., 1968-70; chief resident divsn. neurology Duke U. Med. Ctr., 1970-71, assoc. in medicine divsn. neurology, 1970-73, asst. prof. medicine divsn. neurology, 1973-76, assoc. prof. medicine divsn. neurology, 1976-79, asst. prof. biochemistry, 1977-89, prof. neurology dept. medicine, 1979—, prof. neurobiology, 1989—, Jefferson-Pilot Corp. prof. neurobiology and neurology, 1990—, chief divsn. neurology dept. medicine, 1977—; fellow Nat. Multiple Sclerosis Soc., Lab. Neurochemistry, Divsn. Neurology, Duke U. Med. Ctr., Lab. Virology, Divsn. Pediat. Neurology, Duke U. Med. Ctr., 1971-73, dir. Duke Neuromuscular Rsch. Clinic, 1974—, dir. neurosciences study program Sch. Medicine, 1975-85, investigator Howard Hughes Med. Inst., 1977-81, dir. Duke Muscular Dystrophy Assn. Clinic, 1979—, Joseph and Kathleen Bryan Alzheimer's Disease Rsch. Ctr., 1985— ; cons. neurologist N.C. State Hosp. Sys., Cherry Hosp., Goldsboro, 1973-76, N.C. State Hosp. Sys., Lenox Baker Hosp., Durham, 1974—; chmn. internat. sci. adv. com. Australian Neuromuscular Rsch. Inst., 1989-92; sci. adv. Cyprus Isnt. Neurology and Genetics, 1990—; mem. external adv. com. Neonatal Neurology Ctr., SUNY, Stonybrook, Epidemiology of Dementia in an Urban Cmty. Program Project Renewal. Assoc. editor Molecular and Cellular Neuroscis., 1989-94; mem. editl. bd. Amyloidosis Jour., An Internat. Jour. Exptl. and Clin. Investigation, 1993—, Neurobiology of Disease, 1993—, Fondation Ipsen, Rsch. and Perspectives in Neuroscis., 1994—, Alzheimer's Rsch., 1995—, Contemporary Neurology, 1995—, Alezheimer's Disease Rev., 1995—; contbr. articles to profl. jours. Capt. USAFR, 1967-72. Recipient Rsch. Career Devel. award Nat. Inst. Neurol. and Communicative Disorders and Stroke, 1976, Best in the Triangle-Aerobics Instr. award Spectator Mag., 1986, Leadership in Excellence in Alzheimer's Disease award Nat. Inst. Aging, 1988, Met.-Life Found. prize for outstanding med. rsch., 1994, Potamkin prize for Alzheimer's Disease Rsch., 1994; Basil O'Connor Starter Rsch. grantee Nat. Found. March of Dimes. Fellow Am. Acad. Neurology; mem. Am. Soc. for Clin. Investigation, Am. Soc. for Clin. Rsch., Am. Neurol. Assn. (trustee 1982-84), Assn. Univ. Profs. Neurology, Assn. Brit. Neurologists (hon. fgn. mem.), Muscular Dystrophy Assn. (genetics task force and rev. com. 1989—, med. adv. com. 1990—, nat. v.p. nat. hdqrs. 1994—), Alzheimer's Assn. (med. sci. adv. com. 1989—, vice chair 1991—, Sigma Tau award 1990, Rita Hayward Gala award 1994), Phi Beta Kappa. Office: Duke Univ Med Ctr Durham NC 27710-7599 also: Divsn Neurology Box 2900 Durham NC 27710

ROSETT, ANN DOYLE, librarian; b. Valdosta, Ga., Jan. 9, 1955; d. David Spencer Doyle and Lois Annette Gray; m. Robert Allen Richardson, Aug. 1, 1976 (div. June 1981); children: Caitlin Ann, Brendan Wesley; m. John David Rosett, Aug. 6, 1983. Student, Kenyon Coll., 1972-75, U. Dayton, 1974, U. Ala., Birmingham, 1978; BA, Shepherd Coll., 1982; MLS, U. Wash., 1988. Cert. profl. libr., Wash. College libr. Northwest Coll., Kirkland, Wash., 1988—. Mem. ALA, Assn. Christian Librs. (dir.-at-large 1992-93), Assn. Coll. and Rsch. Librs., Am. Theol. Lib. Assn., N.W. Assn. Christian Librs. (treas. 1989-91, pres. 1991-93). Democrat. Office: NW Coll DV Hurst Libr PO Box 579 5520 108th Ave NE Kirkland WA 98033-7523

ROSETT, ARTHUR IRWIN, lawyer, educator; b. N.Y.C., July 5, 1934; s. Milton B. and Bertha (Werner) R.; m. Rhonda K. Lawrence; children: David Benjamin, Martha Jean, Daniel Joseph. A.B., Columbia U., 1955, LL.B., 1959. Bar: Calif. 1968, N.Y. State 1960, U.S. Supreme Ct. 1963. Law clk. U.S. Supreme Ct., 1959-60; asst. U.S. atty. So. Dist. N.Y., 1960-63; practice law N.Y.C., 1963-65; assoc. dir. Pres.'s Commn. on Law Enforcement and Adminstrn. Justice, 1965-67; acting prof. law UCLA, 1967-70, prof., 1970—. Author: Contract Law and Its Application, 1971, 5th revised edit., 1994, (with D. Cressey) Justice by Consent, 1976, (with E. Dorff) A Living Tree, 1987. Served with USN, 1956-58. Mem. Am. Law Inst. Home: 641 S Saltair Ave Los Angeles CA 90049-4134 Office: UCLA Law Sch 405 Hilgard Ave Los Angeles CA 90095-9000

ROSETT, RICHARD NATHANIEL, economist, educator; b. Balt., Feb. 29, 1928; s. Walter and Essie (Stofberg) R.; m. Madelon Louise George, June 24, 1951; children: Claudia Anne, Martha Victoria, Joshua George, Sarah Elizabeth, Charles Richard. B.A., Columbia U., 1953; M.A., Yale U., 1954, Ph.D., 1957. Instr. Yale U., 1956-58; mem. faculty U. Rochester, 1958-74, chmn. dept. econs., 1966-74, prof. econs., 1967-74, prof. preventive medicine and community health, 1969-74; prof. bus. econs. Grad. Sch. Bus., U. Chgo., 1974-84, dean, 1974-83; dean Faculty Arts and Scis. Washington U., 1984-87, prof. econs., 1984-90; dean Coll. Bus. Rochester (N.Y.) Inst. Tech., 1990-96, instr. tech., 1990-96, dir. quality cup programs, 1990—; pres. U.S. Bus. Sch. in Prague, Inc., 1990—; bd. dirs. Hutchinson Techs., Inc., Lumbermans Mut. Ins. Co., Smith Corona Corp., Nat. Bur. Econ. Rsch., chmn., 1986-89, ORMEC; trustee Keuka Coll., 1992—. Editor: The Role of Health Insurance in the Health Services Sector, 1976; Contbr. articles to profl. jours. Mem. Am. Econ. Assn., Mont Pelerin Soc., Chgo. Club, Phi Beta Kappa, Beta Gamma Sigma. Home: 26 Whitestone Ln Rochester NY 14618-4118 Office: Rochester Inst Tech Office of Dean 108 Lomb Meml Dr Rochester NY 14623-5608

ROSEWATER, ANN, federal official; b. Phila., July 30, 1945; d. Edward and Maxine (Friedmann) R. BA with distinction, Wellesley Coll., 1967; MA, Columbia U., 1969. Rsch. editl. asst. Tchrs. Coll. Columbia U., N.Y.C., 1969; rsch. asst. to pres., v.p. rsch. Met. Applied Rsch. Ctr., N.Y.C., 1969-70; asst. to v.p. Nat. Urban Coalition, Washington, 1970-73; nat. edn. staff Childrens Def. Fund, Washington, 1973-77; assoc. prodr. Smithsonian World Nat. Pub. TV Series, Washington, 1977-78; sr. legis. asst. U.S. Ho. of Reps., Washington, 1979-83, dep. staff dir. com. on children, youth and families, 1983-90; sr. assoc. Chapin Hall Ctr. for Children/U. Chgo., 1990-93; dep. asst. sec. for children and families Dept. Health & Human Svcs., Washington, 1993-96, dep. asst. sec. for human svcs. policy, 1996—; pub. policy and found. cons. in field, 1977-79, 90-93; grad. instr. Harvard Sch. Pub. Health, Nova U., George Washington U., 1977-79; mem. Nat. Adv. Com. on Svcs. for Families with Infants and Toddlers, Washington, 1994, Nat. Adv. Com. for Campaign Against Domestic Violence, 1992-93. Contbr. articles to profl. jours. Bd. dirs. Family Resource Coalition, Chgo., 1990-93, Youth Law Ctr., San Francisco, 1990-93, Jewish Fund for Justice, N.Y.C., 1990-93, Georgians for Children, Atlanta, 1990-93. Recipient Leadership award Leadership Atlanta, 1992-93, Pres. cert. for outstanding svc. Am. Acad. Pediat., 1990, Leadership in Human Svc. award Am. Pub. Welfare Assn., 1989-90. Mem. D.C. Bar Assn. (mem. citizens adv. com. 1974-79, fee conciliation svc., panel bd. on profl. responsibility). Office: 200 Independence Ave SW Washington DC 20201-0004

ROSHEL, JOHN ALBERT, JR., orthodontist; b. Terre Haute, Ind., Apr. 7, 1941; s. John Albert and Mary M. (Griglione) R.; B.S., Ind. State U., 1963; D.D.S., Ind. U., 1966; M.S., U. Mich., 1968; m. Kathy Roshel; children—John Albert III, James Livingston, Angela Kay. Individual practice dentistry, specializing in orthodontics Terre Haute, 1968—. Mem. ADA, Am. Assn. Orthodontists, Terre Haute C. of C., Lambda Chi Alpha, Delta Sigma Delta, Omicron Kappa Upsilon. Clubs: Terre Haute Country, Lions, Elks, K.C. Roman Catholic. Home: 15 E Wedgeway Dr Terre Haute IN 47802-4983 Office: 4241 S 7th St Terre Haute IN 47802-4367

ROSHON, GEORGE KENNETH, manufacturing company executive; b. Pottstown, Pa., July 30, 1942; s. George Washington III and Ellen Eleanor (Knopf) R.; B.S. in Elec. Engring., Pa. State U., 1964; M.S., Drexel U., Phila., 1974, postgrad., 1974-75; m. Ella Maye Barndt, Nov. 21, 1964; 1 child, Kirsten Renee. Sr. engr. Am. Electronics Labs., Inc., Colmar, Pa., 1966-69; v.p. engring. Acrodyne Industries, Inc., Montgomeryville, Pa., 1969-74; mgr. electric design W-J div. Hayes-Albion Corp., Norristown, Pa., 1974-78; mgr. quality assurance PSMBD, Gen. Electric Co., Phila., after 1978, mem. exec. com. electronics test council after 1980, mgr. advanced systems engring., 1983-84, mgr. communications engring., Malvern, Pa., 1984-86; v.p. quality assurance Hercules Aerospace Display Systems, Inc., Hatfield, Pa., 1986-88, v.p. engring., 1988-90; mgr. Electronics Group Westcode, Inc., Malvern, Pa., 1991-92; v.p. manufacturing Epitaxx Inc., West Trenton, N.J., 1992—. Patentee in field. Served to lt. USNR, 1964-66. Registered profl. engr., Pa. Mem. Nat. Soc. Profl. Engrs., Am. Soc. Quality Control (cert. quality engr.), Pa. Soc. Profl. Engrs., Gen. Electric Mgmt. Assn., Elfun Soc., Drexel U. Alumni Assn., Pa. State U. Alumni Assn., Tri-County Arabian Horse Assn. Home: 454 Eagle Ln Lansdale PA 19446-1547 Office: 7 Graphics Dr Trenton NJ 08628-1547

ROSICA, GABRIEL ADAM, corporate executive, engineer; b. N.Y.C., Jan. 9, 1940; s. Gabriel J. and Elma (P.) R.; m. Bettina R. Nardozzi, Sept. 8, 1962; children: Gregory A., Julie Ann, Mark A. BA in Math. and Physics, Columbia U., 1962, BSEE, 1963; MSEE, Rensselaer Poly. Inst., 1966; MBA, Boston U., 1971. Registered profl. engr., Mass. Rsch. engr. United Aircraft Research Labs., East Hartford, Conn., 1963-67; mgr. electronic devel. The Foxboro (Mass.) Co., 1967-75, gen. mgr. U.S. div., 1975-77, v.p., 1977-80; pres., chief operating officer Modular Computer Systems, Inc., Ft. Lauderdale, Fla., 1980-82, pres., chmn., chief exec. officer, 1982-88; pvt. practice bus. cons. Boca Raton, Fla., 1988-91; sr. v.p. Elsag Bailey Corp., Pepper Pike, Ohio, 1991-92; exec. v.p. Bailey Controls Co., Wickliffe, Ohio, 1993-94; COO Bailey Control Co., Wickliffe, Ohio, 1994-96; sr. v.p. Keithley Instruments, Solon, Ohio, 1996—; bd. dirs. Sturtevant Co., Dorchester, Mass., Keithley Instruments, Solon, Ohio; chmn. engring. adv. coun. U. Fla., Gainesville, 1987-90; chmn. hi tech adv. coun. Coll. Boca Raton, Fla., 1987-90. Mem. Pres.'s Coun. Fla. Atlantic U., Boca Raton, 1987-91; trustee Nova U., Ft. Lauderdale, Fla., 1987-94. Recipient Boston U. Chair, 1971, Outstanding Young Engr. of Year award Mass. Soc. Profl. Engrs., 1974. Mem. IEEE (sr. mem.), Am. Electronics Assn. (bd. dirs. 1987, chmn Fla. bd. dirs. 1987-88), Fla. High Tech. and Industry Coun. Home: 35640 Spicebush Ln Solon OH 44139-5063 Office: Keithley Instruments Inc 28775 Aurora Rd Solon OH 44139-1837

ROSICH, RAYNER KARL, physicist; b. Joliet, Ill., Aug. 28, 1940; s. Joseph F. and Gretchen (Cox) R.; BS in Physics cum laude with distinction and honors, U. Mich., 1962, MS in Physics, 1963; PhD, U. Colo., 1977; MBA, U. Denver, 1982; m. Judy Louise Jackson, Aug. 20, 1966; children: Heidi Ann, Kimberly Ann, Dawn Ann. Teaching fellow and rsch. asst. U. Mich., Ann Arbor, 1962-67; staff, Argonne (Ill.) Nat. Lab. Applied Math. Div., summers 1961-63; physicist, project leader Inst. for Telecommunication Sci., U.S. Dept. Commerce, Boulder, Colo., 1967-80; sr. scientist and program mgr. Electro Magnetic Applications, Inc., Denver, 1980-82; applications mgr. Energy Systems Tech., Inc., Denver, 1982-83, mgr. R&D, 1983; prin. scientist, program mgr. Contel Info. Systems, Inc., Denver, 1983-84, dir. tech. audits, 1985, dir. basic and applied R&D, 1986; lab. scientist for systems engring. lab. Hughes Aircraft Co., Denver, 1986, lab. scientist for data systems lab, 1986-90, lab. scientist for systems lab., 1990-92; prin. engr., Advanced System Techs., Inc., Denver, 1992-95; project mgr. Evolving Systems, Inc., 1995; network planning engr., project mgr. Apollo Travel Svcs., 1996—. instr. math. Arapahoe Cmty. Coll., 1987-97. Vol. judo instr., county recreation dist., 1976-77. Recipient Spl. Achievement award U.S. Dept. Commerce, 1974, Outstanding Performance award, 1978, Sustained Superior Performance award, 1979; Libbey-Owens-Ford Glass Co./U. Mich. Phoenix Meml. fellow, 1964-66; NSF Summer fellow, 1965. Mem. Am. Phys. Soc., AAAS, IEEE, Assn. Computing Machinery, Applied Computational Electromagnetics Soc., Soc. Computer Stimulation, Sigma Xi, Phi Kappa Phi. Home: 7932 W Nichols Ave Littleton CO 80123-5558 Office: Apollo Travel Svcs 5347 S Valentia Way Englewood CO 80111-3101

ROSIN, HENRY DAVID, physician; b. Bklyn., Apr. 1, 1931; s. Morris Bernard and Esther Harriet (Auerbach) R.; m. Nancy Claire Peikin; children: Diane, Matthew, Laura, Robert. BA, Syracuse U., 1951; MD, SUNY, Syracuse, 1956. Diplomat Am. Bd. Otolaryngology. Intern Mt. Sinai Hosp., N.Y.C., 1956-57, resident, 1959-63; dir. dept. otolaryngology & head & neck surgery Valley Hosp., Ridgewood, N.J., 1982-90; med. dir. Northwest Bergen Hospice, Ridgewood, N.J., 1982-90; otolaryngologist pvt. practice, 1964—. Pres. Physician Polit. Com., Midland Park, N.J. Capt. USAF, 1957-59. Fellow Am. Acad. Ophthalmology and Otolaryngology, Am. Coll. Surgeons, Am. Soc. Head and Neck Surgery, Am. Acad. Facial, Plastic and Reconstructive Surgery; mem. AMA, N.Y. Head and Neck Surgery, Med. Soc. N.J., N.J. Hospice Orgn. (past pres.), Bergen County Med. Soc. (trustee 1980-81), Soc. Fellows, Tower Club. Avocation: Japanese art. Home: PO Box 647 Franklin Lakes NJ 07417-0647 Office: 44 Godwin Ave Midland Park NJ 07432-1969

ROSIN, WALTER L., religious organization administrator. Sec. Luth. Ch.-Mo. Synod, St. Louis. Office: The Lutheran Ch-Missouri Synod 1333 S Kirkwood Rd Saint Louis MO 63122-7226

ROSINSKI, EDWIN FRANCIS, health sciences educator; b. Buffalo, June 25, 1928; s. Theodore Joseph and Josephine M. (Wolski) R.; m. Jeanne C. Hueniger, Oct. 27, 1951; children: John T., Mary E., Sarah J. BS, SUNY, Buffalo, 1950; EdM, U. Buffalo, 1957, EdD, 1959. Prof. health scis. Med. Coll. Va., Richmond, 1959-66; dep. asst. sec. HEW, Washington, 1966-68; exec. vice chancellor U. Calif., San Francisco, 1968-72, prof., 1972-94; prof. emeritus medicine & pharmacy, 1994—; adv. Rockefeller Found., N.Y.C., 1962-67, WHO, Geneva, 1962-78, Imperial Com. Health, Tehran, Iran, 1974-77; cons. Stanford Research Inst., Menlo Park, Calif., 1975-79. Author: The Assistant Medical Officer, 1965; contbr. over 100 articles to profl. jours. Served with USAF, 1950-54. Recipient spl. citation HEW, 1968, Merrell Flair award, 1991; named disting. prof. Australian Vice Chancellors Office, 1974, disting. vis. prof. Tulane U., New Orleans, 1983. Fellow AAAS; mem. Assn. Am. Med. Colls. (Merrel Flair award), Am. Ednl. Research Assn., Soc. Health and Human Values (founding mem.), Calif. Pharmacists Assn. (hon.), Phi Delta Kappa. Roman Catholic. Avocation: physical fitness. Home: 80 Sotelo Ave San Francisco CA 94116-1423

ROSINSKI, JAN, mathematics educator; b. Gorzow, Poland, May 18, 1950; came to U.S., 1983; s. Franciszek and Zofia (Mierzejewska) R.; m. Wanda Maria Kasprzak, 1977; 1 child, Marek. MA in Math., Wroclaw (Poland) U., 1974, PhD in Math., 1975. Asst. prof. math. dept. Wroclaw U., 1976-85; assoc. prof. math. dept. U. Tenn., Knoxville, 1985-91, prof., 1991—; vis. asst. prof. math. dept. La. State U., Baton Rouge, 1983, Case Westen Res. U., Cleve., 1983-84; vis. scientist Cornell U., Ithaca, N.Y., 1990, Ctr. Stochastic Processes U. N.C., Chapel Hill, 1984-85, 91; reviewer NSF, 1986—. Contbr. articles on probability and stochastic processes to profl. jours. Rsch. grantee, Air Force Office of Sci. Rsch., 1986-92, NSF, 1994—. Fellow Inst. Math. Stats.; mem. Am. Math. Soc., Bernoulli Soc. Avocations: travel, bridge. Office: U Tenn Dept Math Knoxville TN 37996

ROSKAM, JAN, aerospace engineer; b. The Hague, The Netherlands, Feb. 22, 1930; came to U.S., 1957, naturalized, 1962; s. Kommer Jan and Agatha (Bosman) R.; m. Janice Louise Thomas-Barron, Dec. 21, 1994. M.A. in Aerospace Engring, Tech. U. Delft, 1954; Ph.D. in Aeros. and Astronautics, U. Wash., 1965. Asst. chief designer Aviolanda Aircraft Co., Netherlands, 1954-57; sr. aerodynamics engr. Cessna Aircraft Co., Wichita, Kans., 1957-59; sr. group engr. Boeing Co., Wichita and Seattle, 1959-67; Ackers disting. prof. aerospace engring. U. Kans., Lawrence, 1967—; pres. Roskam Aviation and Engring. Corp., 1972—, Design, Analysis and Rsch. Corp., 1991—; cons. to govt. and industry. Author: Airplane Flight Dynamics and Automatic Flight Controls, 2 vols, 1979; co-author: Airplane Aerodynamics and Performance, 1981, Airplane Design, Parts I-VIII, 1986. Served to 1st lt. Royal Netherlands Air Force, 1954-56. Fellow AIAA, Soc. Automotive Engrs.; mem. Air Force Assn., Am. Def. Preparedness Assn., Aircraft Owners and Pilots Assn., Royal Aero. Soc., Koninklijk Instituut van Ingenieurs, U.S. Chess Fedn., Exptl. Aircraft Assn., Internat. Wildlife Assn., Sigma Xi, Tau Beta Pi, Sigma Gamma Tau, Omicron Delta Kappa. Office: U Kans 2004 Lea Hall Lawrence KS 66045

ROSKAM, PETER JAMES, state legislator, lawyer; b. Hinsdale, Ill., Sept. 13, 1961; s. Verlyn Ronald and Martha (Jacobsen) R.; m. Elizabeth Andrea Gracey, June 18, 1988; children: Gracey, James (dec.), Frances, Stephen, Alec. BA, U. Ill., 1983; JD, Ill. Inst. Tech., 1989. Bar: Ill. 1989. Tchr. All Saints Sch., St. Thomas, V.I., 1984-85; legis. asst. to Congressman Tom Delay U.S. Ho. of Reps., Washington, 1985-86, legal asst. to Congressman Henry Hyde, 1986-87; exec. dir. Ednl. Assistance Ltd., Glen Ellyn, Ill., 1987-93; ptnr. Salvi & Roskam, Wheaton, Ill., 1994—; mem. Ill. Gen. Assembly, Springfield, 1993—; legis. chmn. Ill. State Crime Commn. Republican. Mem. Evangelical Covenant Ch. Office: Salvi & Roskam 1755 S Naperville Rd Wheaton IL 60187-8132

ROSKENS, RONALD WILLIAM, international business consultant; b. Spencer, Iowa, Dec. 11, 1932; s. William E. and Delores A.L. (Beving) R.; m. Lois Grace Lister, Aug. 22, 1954; children: Elizabeth, Barbara, Brenda, William. BA, U. No. Iowa, 1953, MA, 1955, LHD (hon.), 1985; PhD, State U. Iowa, 1958; LLD (hon.), Creighton U., 1978, Huston-Tillotson Coll., 1981, Midland Luth. Coll., 1984, Hastings Coll., 1981; LittD (hon.), Nebr. Wesleyan U., 1981; PhD (hon.), Ataturk U., Turkey, 1987; LHD (hon.), U. Akron, 1987; DSc (hon.), Jayewardenepura U., Sri Lanka, 1991; LHD (hon.), Am. Coll. of Greece, Athens, 1994. Lic. min. United Ch. of Christ (Congl. and E&R). Tchr. Minburn (Iowa) High Sch., 1954, Woodward (Iowa) State Hosp., summer 1954; asst. counselor to men State U. Iowa, 1956-59; dean of men, asst. prof. spl. edn. Kent (Ohio) State U., 1959-63, assoc. prof., then prof., 1963-72, asst. to pres., 1963-66, dean for adminstrn., 1968-71, exec. v.p., prof. ednl. adminstrn., 1971-72; chancellor, prof. ednl. adminstrn. U. Nebr., Omaha, 1972-76; pres. U. Nebr. System, 1977-89, pres. emeritus, 1989; hon. prof. East China Normal U., Shanghai, 1985; adminstr. USAID, Washington, 1990-92; pres. Action Internat., Inc., Omaha, 1993-96, Global Connections, Inc., Omaha, 1996—; interim exec. officer Omaha Pub. Libr., 1996—; bd. dirs. ConAgra Inc., 1992—, MFS Comms. Co. Inc., 1993—, Enron Corp., 1979-90, Art's Way Mfg. Co., 1981-90, Guarantee Mut. Life Ins. Co., 1979-90, Am. Charter Fed. Savs. and Loan Assn., 1986-90; mem. Bus.-Higher Edn. Forum, 1979-89, exec. com., 1984-87; mem. govtl. relations com. Am. Council Edn., 1979-83, bd. dirs., 1981-86, vice chair, 1983-84, chair, 1984-85; chmn. com. on financing higher edn. Nat. Assn. State Univs. and Land Grant Colls., 1978-83, vice chmn. com. on financing higher edn., 1983-84, chmn. com. on fed. student fin. assistance, 1981-87; mem. nat. adv. com. on accreditation and instl. eligibility U.S. Dept. Edn., 1983-86, chmn., bd. dirs., 1986; exec. bd. North Cen. Assn., 1979-84, chmn. exec. bd., 1982-84, pres., 1989-90; active Environ. Ams. Bd., 1991-92, Strategic Command Consultation Commn., 1993—, Nat. Exec. Res. Corps, Fed. Office Emergency Preparedness, 1968-88; chmn. Omaha/Douglas Pub. Bldg. Commn., 1996—. Co-editor: Paradox, Process and Progress, 1968; contbr. articles profl. jours. Mem. Kent City Planning Commn., 1962-66; bd. dirs. United Ch. of Christ Bd. Homeland Ministries, 1968-74, Met. YMCA, Omaha, 1973-77, Mid-Am. council Boy Scouts Am., 1973-77, Midlands United Community Services, 1972-77, NCCJ, 1974-77, Omaha Rotary Club, 1974-77, Found. Study Presdl. and Congl. Terms, 1977-89, First Plymouth Congl. Ch., 1989-90, Midland Luth. Coll., 1993—, Coun. Aid to Edn., 1985-89, Russian Farm Cmty. Project; trustee Huston Tillotson Coll., Austin, Tex., 1968-81, chmn., 1976-78, Joslyn Art Mus., 1973-77, Nebr. Meth. Hosp., 1974-77, 1st Ctrl. Congregational Ch., Brownell-Talbott Sch., 1974-77, Harry S. Truman Inst., 1977-89, Willa Cather Pioneer Meml. and Ednl. Found., 1979-87; pres. Kent Area C. of C., 1966; active Met. Commn. Coll. Found., 1993-96. Decorated comdr.'s cross Order of Merit (Germany); recipient Disting. Svc. award for community svc., Kent, Ohio, 1967, Brotherhood award NCCJ, 1977, Americanism citation B'nai B'rith, 1978, Legion of Honor, Order of DeMolay, 1980, gold medal Nat. Interfrat. Coun., 1987, Agri award Triumph Agr. Expn., Omaha, 1989; named Nat. 4-H Alumnus, 1967, Outstanding Alumnus, U. No. Iowa, 1974, Midlander of Yr., Omaha World Herald, 1977, King Ak-Sar-Ben LXXXVI, 1980; named to DeMolay Hall of Fame, 1993. Mem. AAAS, APA, AAUP, Am. Coll. Pers. Assn., Assn. Urban Univs. (pres. 1976-77), Am. Ednl. Rsch. Assn., Coun. on Fgn. Rels., Chief Execs. Orgn., Young Pres. Orgn., Lincoln C. of C. (bd. dirs. 1989-90), Masons (33 deg.), Rotary (bd. dirs. Omaha 1974-77), Phi Delta Kappa, Phi Eta Sigma, Sigma Tau Gamma (pres. grand coun. 1968-70, Disting. Achievement award 1980, Disting. scholar 1981), Omicron Delta Kappa (nat. pres. 1986-90, Found. pres. 1986-96). Home: 1311 N 97th Plz Omaha NE 68114-2101

ROSKI, EDWARD P., professional sports team executive; s. Edward P. Roski, Jr.; m. Gayle Roski. BS in Fin. and Real Estate, U. So. Calif., 1962. Pres. So. Calif.-based Majestic Realty Co.; owner L.A. Kings, 1995—. Dir. Big Bros. of Greater L.A.; bd. govs. Natural History Mus. of L.A. County; bd. dirs. Comerica Bank, Calif. With USMC, 1962-66. Mem. Explorers Club, Soc. Indsl. Realtors. Avocations: cycling, mountain climbing. Office: Los Angeles Kings 3900 W Manchester Blvd Inglewood CA 90305-2200

ROSKIND, E. ROBERT, real estate company executive; b. N.Y.C., Mar. 18, 1945; s. Edward R. and Harriet (Weinberg) R.; m. Diane L. Albert, Aug. 4, 1966; children: Dina Lee Walsh, Scott. BA, U. Pa., 1966; JD, Columbia U., 1969. Mng. ptnr. The LCP Group, N.Y.C., 1974—; chmn. Lexington Corp. Prop., N.Y.C., 1993—; dir. Berkshire Realty, Boston, Krupp Govt. Income Trust, Krupp Govt. Income Trust II. Chmn. Babies Heart Fund, N.Y.C., 1984—; mem. health & scis. adv. com. Columbia Presbyn. Hosp., N.Y.C., 1990—. Office: The LCP Group 355 Lexington Ave New York NY 10017-6603*

ROSKOSKI, ROBERT, JR., biochemist, educator, author; b. Elyria, Ohio, Dec. 10, 1939; s. Robert and Mary R.; m. Laura Martinsek, Aug. 27, 1974. B.S., Bowling Green State U., 1961; M.D., U. Chgo., 1964, Ph.D., 1968. Asst. prof. U. Iowa, Iowa City, 1972-75; assoc. prof. U. Iowa, 1975-79; vis. prof. U. Iowa, Iowa City, 1993; prof., head dept. biochemistry and molecular biology Med. Center, La. State U., New Orleans, 1979—, Fred G. Brazda prof., 1991—; cons. biochemistry test com. Nat. Bd. Med. Examiners; mem. merit rev. bd. for basic scis. VA; mem. rev. com. biol. scis. U. South Fla., 1992. Served with USAF, 1966-69. NIH postdoctoral fellow U. Chgo., 1964-66; NIH spl. fellow Rockefeller U., 1969-71. Mem. Am. Chem. Soc., Am. Soc. Neurochemistry, Soc. for Neurosci., Am. Soc. Biol. Chemists, Am. Soc. Pharmacology and Exptl. Therapeutics, Internat. Soc. Neurochemistry, Assn. Med. and Grad. Depts. Biochemistry (sec. 1994-96, pres. 1997), Nat. Caucus Basic Biomed. Sci. Chairs. Condr. research enzymology. Home: 1206 Aline St New Orleans LA 70115-2421 Office: 1100 Florida Ave New Orleans LA 70119-2714

ROSKY, BURTON SEYMOUR, lawyer; b. Chgo., May 28, 1927; s. David T. and Mary W. (Zelkin) R.; m. Leatrice J. Darrow, June 16, 1951; children: David Scott, Bruce Alan. Student, Ill. Inst. Tech., 1944-45; BS, UCLA, 1948; JD, Loyola U., L.A., 1953. Bar: Calif. 1954, U.S. Supreme Ct 1964, U.S. Tax Ct 1964; C.P.A., Calif. Auditor City of L.A., 1948- 51; with Beidner, Temkin & Ziskin (C.P.A.s), L.A., 1951-52; supervising auditor Army Audit Agy., 1952-53; practiced law L.A., Beverly Hills, 1954—; ptnr. Duskin & Rosky, 1972-82; s Rosky, Landau & Fox, 1982-93; ptnr. Rosky, Landau, Stahl & Sheehy, Beverly Hills, 1993; lectr. on tax and bus. problems; judge pro tem Beverly Hills Mcpl. Ct., L.A. Superior Ct.; mem. L.A. Mayor's Community Adv. Council. Contbr. profl. publs. Charter supporting mem. Los Angeles County Mus. Arts; contbg. mem. Assocs. of Smithsonian Instn.; charter mem. Air and Space Mus; mem. Am. Mus. Natural History, L.A. Zoo; supporting mem. L.A. Mus. Natural History; mem. exec. bd. So. Calif. coun. Nat. Fedn. Temple Brotherhoods, mem. nat. exec. bd.; mem. bd. govs. Loyola Sch. Law, L.A. With USNR, 1945-46. Walter Henry Cook fellow Loyola Law Sch. Bd. Govs. Fellow Jewish Chautauqua Soc. (life mem.); mem. Am. Arbitration Assn. (nat. panel arbitrators), Am. Assn. Attys.-CPAs (charter mem. pres. 1968), Calif. Assn. Attys.-CPAs (charter mem., pres. 1963), Calif. Soc. CPAs, Calif., Beverly Hills, Century City, Los Angeles County bar assns., Am. Judicature Soc., Chancellors Assocs. UCLA, Tau Delta Phi, Phi Alpha Delta.; mem. B'nai B'rith. Jewish (mem. exec. bd., pres. temple, pres. brotherhood). Club: Mason. Office: Rosky Landau Stahl & Sheehy 8383 Wilshire Blvd Beverly Hills CA 90211

ROSKY, THEODORE SAMUEL, insurance company executive; b. Chgo., Apr. 14, 1937; s. Theodore and Lora Marie (O'Connell) R.; m. Jacqueline Reed, Apr. 19, 1958; 1 child, Laura Marie. B.A., State U. Iowa, 1959. Various actuarial positions Conn. Gen. Life Ins. Co., Hartford, 1959-66; assoc. actuary Conn. Gen. Life Ins. Co., 1967-70, controller, 1970-73, 2d v.p., actuary, 1973, v.p., 1973-78; exec. v.p. Capital Holding Corp., 1978-84, exec. v.p., CFO, 1984-91, exec. v.p., 1991-92; bd. dirs. Legend Funds, 1993—, SBM Mut. Funds, 1995—, SBM Certificate Co., 1996—; instr. State U. Iowa, 1958-59, U. Hartford, 1964-66, U. Conn., 1967-68. Bd. dirs. Hartford Coll. for Women, 1974-78, Macauley Theater, 1983-85, Louisville Fund for the Arts, 1980—, Louisville Luth. Home, 1983—, Louisville Orch., 1982-88, 89-95, Ky. Opera, 1992—, Lincoln Found., 1992—, Actors Theatre of Louisville, 1995—, New Performing Arts, 1996—, Oak and Acorn, 1995—; mem. bd. pensions Evangel. Luth. Ch. Am., 1974-82, 84-87, 89-95. Recipient award Soc. Actuaries, 1958. Fellow Soc. Actuaries; mem. Am. Acad. Actuaries, Southeastern Actuaries Club, Pendennis Club. Republican. Lutheran. Home: 2304 Speed Ave Louisville KY 40205-1642

ROS-LEHTINEN, ILEANA, congresswoman; b. Havana, Cuba, July 15, 1952; d. Enrique Emilio and Amanda (Adato) Ros; m. Dexter Lehtinen. AA, Miami (Fla.)-Dade C.C., 1972; BA, Fla. Internat. U., 1975, MS, 1987. Prin. Ea. Acad., from 1978; mem. Fla. Ho. of Reps., Tallahassee, 1982-86, Fla. Senate, 1986-89, 101st-105th Congresses from 18th Fla. Dist., 1989—; mem. govt. reform and oversight com. nat. security, internat. affairs and criminal justice internat. rels. - Africa 101st-104th Congresses from 18th Fla. Dist. Roman Catholic. Office: US Ho of Reps 2440 Rayburn Bldg Washington DC 20515-3301*

ROSMARIN, LEONARD ALAN, dermatologist; b. Bronx, May 29, 1950; s. Jack and Dorothy (Blumenstein) R.; m. Wendy Nevard, June 13, 1976; children: David, Deborah. BA, SUNY, Stony Brook, 1972; MD, NYU, 1976. Intern Montefiore Hosp., Bronx, 1976-77, resident, 1977-80; dermatologist pvt. practice, Whitestone, N.Y., 1981—; instr. dermatology Montefiore Hosp., Bronx, 1980-90; attending physician, cons. dermatology N.Y. Hosp. Med. Ctr. Queens County, 1980—. Fellow Am. Acad. Dermatology; mem. L.I. Dermatologic Soc., Greater N.Y. Dermatologic Soc., Soc. Tropical Dermatology. Jewish. Avocations: exercise, reading, photography, travel. Office: 18-15 Francis Lewis Blvd Whitestone NY 11357

ROSMINI, GARY DAVID, financial marketing executive, consultant; b. Sewickley, Pa., Dec. 20, 1952; s. Silvio and Evelyn (Casciola) R.; m. Vivian Hooks, Jan. 7, 1978 (div. July 1984). BA, Pa. State U., 1975. Acct. mgr. Atwood-Vandell Assocs., Inc., N.Y.C., 1976-80, Clayton Brokerage, N.Y.C., 1980-81; assoc. v.p. Whitehall Investors Internat., Inc., N.Y.C., 1981-82; v.p. Monetary Futures Inc., N.Y.C., 1982-84; regional mktg. dir. Barrick Group, New Haven, Conn., 1984-86; pres. Rosmini Assocs., San Raphael, Calif., 1986-88; regional mgr. Chilmark Commodities, Emeryville, Calif., 1987-88; exec. v.p. Calif. Custom Constrn., Ignacio, Calif., 1988-90; loan officer San Francisco Fed. Bank, Santa Rosa, Calif., 1991—; exec. v.p. BWT LLC, San Francisco, 1996—; mem. bd. advisors Pacific Investment Banking Group, Portland, Oreg., 1986—; bd. dirs. Superior Robotics Am., Petaluma, Calif., 1983-84; cons. in field. Creative dir. corp. brochure, 1986; copy writer bus. publ., 1983-84. Foster parent Save the Children, Ind., 1983-86, 88-90, Found. for Inner Peace, N.Y.C., 1976-78; choir dir. Saint Frances Cabrini Ch., Monaca, Pa., 1970-72; mem. Sewickley (Pa.) Civic Symphony, 1970-72, N.Y.C. Choral Soc., 1979-81, S.F. Choral Soc., 1990-95, Co-Opera of San Francisco, 1995—, Foster Parents Plan, 1988-90. Recipient Billy Mitchell award CAP, 1970, Life Master award ACBL, 1996. Mem. Internat. Assn. Fin. Planning. (bd. dirs. 1981-84), Pa. State Alumni Assn., Commonwealth Club of Calif. Avocations: art collecting, wine collecting, golf, tennis, hiking. Home & Office: 1004 Masonic Ave # 6 San Francisco CA 94117-2011

ROSMUS, ANNA ELISABETH, writer; b. Passau, Germany, Mar. 29, 1960; d. Georg Rudolf and Anna Johanna (Friedberger) R.; divorced; children: Dolores Nadine, Beatrice Salome Kassandra. M, U. Passau, 1994. speaker and organizer in field. Author: Resistance and Persecution, 1983 (Geschwister Scholl Preis 1984), Exodus In The Shadow of Mercy, 1988, Robert Klein A German Jew Looks Back, 1991, Wintergreen Suppressed Murders, 1993 (Concsience in Media award 1994), Pocking End and Renewal, 1995, What I Think, 1995; guest talk shows including Documentaries and Features in Germany, Austria, Great Britain, Denmark, Holland, France, Italy, Sweden, Poland, Can., U.S., South Am., Australia, 1983—. Fundraiser Anne Frank Found., Jewish Cmty. Ctrs., Holocaust Ctrs., others, 1992—. Recipient Achievement award Am. Immigration Lawyers Assn., 1997; named Best German Writer, European essay Competition, 1980; Oscar nomination for movie The Nasty Girl, 1991; Sarnat award Anti Defamation League, 1994; Anna Rosmus Day, City of Santa Cruz, 1994. Mem. PEN Internat., NAFE. Avocations: environment protection, multicultural projects, minority programs.

ROSNER, ANN See SEAMAN, BARBARA

ROSNER, FRED, physician, educator; b. Berlin, Oct. 3, 1935; came to U.S., 1949, naturalized, 1955; s. Sidney and Sara (Feingold) R.; m. Saranne Eskolsky, Feb. 24, 1959; children: Mitchel, Miriam, Aviva, Shalom. B.A. cum laude, Yeshiva Coll., 1955; M.D., Albert Einstein Coll., 1959. Diplomate: Am. Bd. Internal Medicine. Intern Maimonides Med. Center, Bklyn., 1959-60, resident in medicine, 1960-62, fellow in hematology, 1962-63, asst. dir. hematology, 1967-70; instr. SUNY Downstate Med. Center, Bklyn., 1968-70; asst. prof. medicine SUNY Downstate Med. Center, 1970; asso. prof. SUNY, Stony Brook, 1970-78, prof. medicine, 1978-89; asst. dean, prof. medicine Albert Einstein Coll. Medicine, 1989-93; prof. medicine Mt. Sinai Sch. Medicine, N.Y.C., 1993—; dir. hematology Queens Hosp. Center, Jamaica, N.Y., 1970-78; dir. medicine Queens Hosp. Center, 1978—. Author: Modern Medicine and Jewish Law, 1972, Medicine in the Bible and Talmud, 1977, 2d edit., 1995, Biblical and Talmudic Medicine, 1978, 2d edit., 1993, Jewish Bioethics, 1979, Modern Medicine and Jewish Ethics, 1986, 2d edit., 1991, Practical Medical Halachah, 1990, Medicine and Jewish Law vol. I, 1990, vol. II, 1993; translator, editor: several Moses Maimonides' works including Moses Maimonides' Treatise on Hemorrhoids and Responsa, 1969; Medical Aphorisms of Moses Maimonides, 1970, Sex Ethics in the Writings of Moses Maimonides, 1974, 94, Moses Maimonides' Introduction to the Mishnah, 1975, 95, Maimonides Glossary of Drug Names, 1979, Moses Maimonides' Commentary on Sanhedrin, 1981, Maimonides' Treatise on Resurrection, 1982, Medicine in the Mishneh Torah of Maimonides, 1984, Maimonides' Treatises on Poisons, Hemorrhoids and Cohabitation, 1984, Maimonides' Commentary on the Aphorisms of Hippocrates, 1987, Maimonides' Medical Aphorisms, 1990, The Existance and Unity of God: Three Treatises Attributed to Moses Maimonides, 1990, Moses Maimonides' Three Treatises on Health, 1990, Six Treatises Attributed to Maimonides, 1991, Maimonides: Physician, Philosopher and Scientist, 1993, Maimonides' Treatise on Asthma, 1994, Maimonides' Glossary of Drug Names, 1996; mem. editl. bd. Cancer Invest, Mt. Sinai Jour. Medicine; contbr.: Ency. Boethics; contbr. articles to tech. lit. Served with USPHS, 1963-65. Recipient Maimonides award Michael Reese Hosp., Chgo., 1969, Bernard Revel Meml. award Yeshiva U., 1971; Maimonides award of Wis., 1977. Fellow A.C.P., N.Y. Acad. Medicine; mem. AMA, Am. Assn. History Medicine, N.Y. Soc. Study of Blood, Am., Internat. socs. hematology, Am. Fedn. Clin. Research. Home: 750 Elvira Ave Far Rockaway NY 11691-5405 Office: Queens Hosp Ctr 82-68 164th St Jamaica NY 11432-1140

ROSNER, JONATHAN LINCOLN, physicist, educator; b. N.Y.C., July 23, 1941; s. Albert Aaron and Elsie Augustine (Lincoln) R.; m. Joy Elaine Fox, June 13, 1965; children: Hannah, Benjamin. BA, Swarthmore Coll., 1962; MA, Princeton U., 1963, PhD, 1965. Research asst. prof. U. Wash., Seattle, 1965-67; vis. lectr. Tel Aviv U., Ramat Aviv, Israel, 1967-69; asst. prof. physics U. Minn., Mpls., 1969-71, assoc. prof., 1971-75, prof., 1975-82; prof. U. Chgo., 1982—. Contbr. numerous articles to profl. and scholarly jours. Alfred P. Sloan fellow, 1971-73. Fellow Am. Phys. Soc. Democrat. Jewish. Avocations: fishing, hiking, skiing, amateur radio. Office: U Chgo Enrico Fermi Inst 5640 S Ellis Ave Chicago IL 60637-1433

ROSNER, LEONARD ALLEN, lawyer; b. N.Y.C., Apr. 13, 1967; s. Arnold and Betty (Zimmerman) R.; m. Rachel Stein, Nov. 19, 1994. AB in Polit. Sci., Syracuse U., 1989, AB in Pub. Rels., 1989, JD cum laude, 1992. Bar: N.Y. 1993. Assoc. Law Office Stephen D. Rogoff Esq., Rochester,

N.Y., 1992—. Fin. editor Syracuse Jour. Internat. Law and Commerce, 1991-92. Assigned coun. Monroe County Assigned Coun., Rochester, 1993-94. Mem. N.Y. Bar Assn., Monroe County Bar Assn. Avocations: golfing, reading, television sports, nautilus. Home: Apt # 5 150 French Woods Circle Rochester NY 14618 Office: 14 Franklin St Ste 900 Rochester NY 14604-1504

ROSNER, M. NORTON, business systems and financial services company executive; b. Camden, N.J., Aug. 17, 1931; s. Adolph and Anne (Cotler) R.; m. M. Patricia Eskin, Oct. 18, 1953; children—Robert, Susan, Jan. B.S. in Econs., U. Pa., 1953; M.B.A., U. Mich., 1965. From acct. to mgr. overhead standards RCA Corp., Camden, N.J., 1953-62; supr. methods and programs, then internal cons. forward model planning Ford Motor Co., Dearborn, Mich., 1962-66; asst. controller, then v.p. planning Singer Co., N.Y.C., 1966-70; treas., then v.p. fin. Popular Services, Passaic, N.J., 1970-72; dir. fin. planning, then asst. controller, then gen. mgr. GSD, then v.p. RE/GSD Xerox Corp., Rochester, N.Y., 1972-90; retired, 1990; bd. dirs., treas. Parcel Post Assn., N.Y.C., 1970-71; dir. Harbinger, Stamford, Conn.; chmn. Xerox Realty Corp., Stamford. Vice chmn. Compeer, Inc., Rochester, N.Y., 1981-87, chmn., 1987-89; chmn. DP2, Rochester, 1985-87; bd. dirs., treas. Rochester Blue Cross-Blue Shield, 1987-89; dir. Palm Beach County Mental Health Assn., 1992, treas., 1993, v.p., 1994-95, pres., 1995-96; dir. JARC, 1992, v.p., 1993, pres., 1994-96. Recipient Nat. Vol. Action award Pres. U.S. Clubs: U. Mich.; U. Pa. Home: 17831 Heather Ridge Ln Boca Raton FL 33498-6423

ROSNER, ROBERT, astrophysicist; b. Garmisch-Partenkirchen, Bavaria, Germany, June 26, 1947; came to U.S., 1959; s. Heinz and Faina (Brodsky) R.; m. Marsha Ellen Rich, Nov. 8, 1950; children: Daniela Karin, Nicole Elise. BA, Brandeis U., 1969; PhD, Harvard U., 1975. Asst. prof. Harvard U., Cambridge, Mass., 1978-83, assoc. prof., 1983-86; astrophysicist Smithsonian Astrophys. Observatory, Cambridge, 1986-87; prof. U. Chgo., 1987—; trustee Adler Planetarium, Chgo., 1989—, chmn. dept. astronomy and astrophysics, 1991-97. Contbr. more than 130 articles to profl. jours. Woodrow Wilson fellow, 1969. Fellow Am. Phys. Soc.; mem. Am. Astron. Soc., Soc. Indsl. and Applied Math. Home: 4950 S Greenwood Ave Chicago IL 60615-2816 Office: U Chicago Astrophysics 5640 S Ellis Ave Chicago IL 60637-1433

ROSNER, SETH, lawyer, educator; b. N.Y.C., Jan. 6, 1931; s. Oscar S. and Miriam (Reinhardt) R.; m. Sara Jane Sheldon, Dec. 4, 1970 (div. Mar. 1978); m. Ann E. Del Toro, June 23, 1983; 1 child, Rachel Ferrer. AB, Wesleyan U., Middletown, Conn., 1952; JD, Columbia U., 1955; LLM in Comparative Law, NYU, 1960; postgrad., U. Paris, 1960-61. Bar: N.Y. 1955, U.S. Dist. Ct. (so. and ea. dists.) N.Y. 1956, U.S. Supreme Ct. 1967. Ptnr. Rosner & Rosner, N.Y.C., 1955-80; sr. ptnr. Marchi Jaffe Cohen Crystal Rosner & Katz, N.Y.C., 1981-88; pvt. practice N.Y.C., 1989-97; counsel Jacobs Persinger & Parker, N.Y.C., 1997—; adj. prof. NYU Sch. of Law, N.Y.C., 1961-89. Trustee, v.p. exec. com. Fedn. Jewish Philanthropies, N.Y.C., 1977-86; pres., chmn. Jewish Home and Hosp. for Aged, N.Y.C., 1978-86; bd. trustees Conn. Wesleyan U. Middletown, 1977-80; bd. govs. Josephson Inst. of Ethics, Marina Del Rey, Calif., 1986—. Lt. USN, 1956-59. Fellow Am. Bar Found. (life); mem. ABA (chmn. gen. practice sect. 1980-81, ethics and profl. responsibility com. 1983-89, chmn. professionalism com. 1992-95, chmn. com. on scope, chmn. com. on lawyer competence 1995-97, bd. govs. 1997—), Assn. of Bar of City of N.Y. (ethics com. 1970-73), N.Y. State Bar Assn. (chmn. gen. practice sect. 1982-83). Avocations: writing, photography, Ferrari automobiles.

ROSOFF, JEANNIE I., foundation administrator; b. Clamart, France, Nov. 8, 1924; came to U.S., 1948; d. Georges Auguste Marie and Suzenne (Philomene) Martin; m. Morton Rosoff, Dec. 8, 1945 (div. 1958); 1 child, Ann Susan. BA in Law cum laude, U. Paris, 1946. Cmty. organizer East Harlem Project, N.Y.C., 1953-56; assoc. dir. N.Y. Com. for Dem. Voters, N.Y.C., 1960-64; spl. projects coord. Planned Parenthood Fedn. Am., N.Y.C., 1964-74, assoc. dir., 1968-74, assoc. dir. Ctr. for Family Planning Program Devel., 1968-74; v.p. govt. affairs Planned Parenthood Fedn. Am., Washington, 1974-77, dir., 1976-81; sr. v.p. Alan Guttmacher Inst., Washington, 1974-78, pres., 1978—; participant in UN Population Conf., Bucharest, 1974, UN Conf. on Internat. Women's Yr., Mexico City, 1975; ofcl. U.S. del. UN Conf. on Population and Devel., Cairo, 1994; del.-at-large Internat. Women's Yr. Conf., Houston, 1977. Author: Teenage Pregnancy in Industrialized Countries, 1986, Health Care Reform: A Unique Opportunity, 1993, (govt. publs.) Family Planning: An Analysis of Laws, 1974, Family Planning: Contraception, 1979. Recipient merit award Nat. Family Planning and Repro. Health Assn., 1980, Ten for Ten award Ctr. for Population Options, 1990. Mem. APHA (pres., chair population sect. 1976, Carl S. Schultz award 1980; maternal and child health sec. 1973-76), Nat. Health Lawyers Assn., Population Assn. Am., Nat. Inst. Child Health and Human Devel., Pathfinder Internat. (bd. dirs. 1993—). Office: Alan Guttmacher Inst 120 Wall St Fl 21 New York NY 10005-4001

ROSOFF, LEONARD, SR., retired surgeon, medical educator; b. Grand Forks, N.D., May 5, 1912; s. Albert and Sophie (Koblin) R.; m. Marie Louise Aronsfeld, June 1, 1935; 1 son, Leonard. BA, U. So. Calif., 1931; MD, U. Tex., 1935. Diplomate: Am. Bd. Surgery (dir. 1970-76). Intern, then resident gen. surgery Los Angeles County Hosp., 1935-40; from instr. to prof. surgery U. So. Calif. Sch. Medicine, 1946-80, emeritus, 1980—, chmn. dept., 1969-79; chief surg. services, dir. surgery Los Angeles County-U. So. Calif. Med. Center, 1955-77, sr. attending surgeon, 1977-80, ret., 1980; clin. prof. surgery U. Tex. Health Ctr., San Antonio, 1992—; hon. staff Hosp. Good Samaritan, Cedars-Sinai, Los Angeles Children's, Huntington Meml. hosps.; lectr. in field. Contbr. articles to med. jours., textbooks. Served with M.C., AUS, 1942-45. Recipient Outstanding Alumnus award U. Tex. Med. Br., 1971. Fellow ACS (bd. govs. 1975-81, 2d v.p. 1981), Tex. Surg. Soc. (hon.); mem. Am. Surg. Assn. (1st v.p. 1984), Western Surg. Assn. (2d v.p.), Pacific Coast Surg. Assn., L.A. Surg. Assn. (pres. 1970), Am. Assn. Endocrine Surgeons (bd. councilors 1980-87, pres. 1984), Am. Assn. Surgery Trauma, Soc. Surgery Alimentary Tract (pres. 1979-80), Internat. Soc. Surgery, L.A. Acad. Medicine, L.A. Athletic Club, Giraud Club (San Antonio). Research surgery parathyroids, thyroid gland and other endocrine systems, surgery peptic ulcer and other gastrointestinal diseases, studies in shock. Home: One Towers Park Ln # 1115 San Antonio TX 78209

ROSOFF, WILLIAM A., lawyer, executive; b. Phila., June 21, 1943; s. Herbert and Estelle (Finkel) R.; m. Beverly Rae Rifkin, Feb. 7, 1970; children: Catherine D., Andrew M. BS with honors, Temple U., 1964; LLB magna cum laude, U. Pa., 1967. Bar: Pa. 1968, U.S. Dist. Ct. (ea. dist.) Pa. 1968. Law clk. U.S. Ct. Appeals (3d cir.), 1967-68; instr. U. Pa. Law Sch., Phila., 1968-69; assoc. Wolf, Block, Schorr & Solis-Cohen, Phila., 1969-75, ptnr., 1975-96, chmn. exec. com., 1987-88; vice chmn. Advanta Corp., Spring House, Pa., 1996—; trustee RPS Realty Trust, 1990-96, Atlantic Realty Trust, 1996—; guest lectr. confs. and seminars on tax law; mem. tax adv. bd. Commerce Clearing House, 1983-94; mem. legal activities policy bd. Tax Analysts, 1978—; mem. Little, Brown Tax Adv. Bd., 1994-96; chmn. bd. dirs. RMH Televcs., Inc., 1997—. Editor U. Pa. Law Rev., 1965-67; mem. bd. contbg. editors and advisors Jour. Partnership Taxation, 1983—; author reports and papers on tax law. Bd. dirs., mem. com. on law and social action Phila. coun. Am. Jewish Congress. Fellow Am. Coll. Tax Counsel; mem. Am. Law Inst. (cons. taxation of partnerships 1976-78, assoc. reporter taxation of partnerships, 1978-82, mem. adv. group on fed. income tax project 1982—), Locust Club (dir.), Order of Coif, Beta Gamma Sigma, Beta Alpha Psi. Office: Advanta Corp Welsh Rd & McKean Rds Horsham PA 19044

ROSOVSKY, HENRY, economist, educator; b. Danzig, Sept. 1, 1927; came to U.S., 1940, naturalized, 1949; s. Selig S. and Sophie (Rosovsky) R.; m. Nitza Brown, June 17, 1956; children—Leah, Judith, Michael. A.B., Coll. William and Mary, 1949, LL.D., 1976; A.M. (John E. Thayer scholar), Harvard U., 1953; Ph.D., 1959; L.H.D. (hon.), Yeshiva U., 1977, Hebrew Union Coll., 1978, Colgate U., 1979, Brandeis U., 1984; Ph.D. (hon.), Hebrew U. of Jerusalem, 1982; LL.D. (hon.), Queen's U., Ont., 1984, U. Hartford, 1984, CUNY, 1986, U. Mass., 1986; DHL (hon.), Hebrew Coll., Brookline, Mass., 1987, NYU, 1993; DL, St. Mary's Coll. Md., 1989, Theol. Sem., 1995. From asst. prof. to prof. econs. and history U. Calif., Berkeley, 1958-65; chmn. Center Japanese and Korean Studies, 1962-65; prof. econs. Harvard U., 1965—, Walter S. Barker prof. econs., 1975-84, Geyser univ. prof., 1984-96, Geyser univ. prof. emeritus, 1996—, chmn. dept., 1969-72, dean Faculty Arts and Scis., 1973-84; assoc. dir. East Asia Research Center, 1967-69; mem. Harvard U. Corp., 1985—; vis. prof. Hitotsubashi U., Tokyo, 1957, Tokyo U., 1962, Hebrew U., Jerusalem, 1965; bd. dirs. Corning, Inc., Paine Webber Group, Japan Fund.; hon. prof. Centro U. Francisco, De Vitoria, Madrid, 1996. Author: Capital Formation in Japan, 1868-1940, 1961, Quantitative Japanese Economic History, 1961, (with K. Ohkawa) Japanese Economic Growth, 1973, The University: An Owner's Manual, 1990; editor: Explorations in Entrepreneurial History, 1954-56, Industrialization in Two Systems, 1966, Discord in the Pacific, 1972, (with H. Patrick) Asia's New Giant, 1976, (with P. Higonnet, D. Landes) Favorites of Fortune, 1991, (with S. Kumon) The Political Economy of Japan, Vol. 3: Cultural and Social Dynamics, 1992. Chmn. bd. trustees Am. Jewish Congress, 1975-88. Served to 1st lt. AUS, 1946-47, 50-52. Jr. fellow Soc. Fellows, 1954-57; recipient Schumpeter prize Harvard, 1963, Clark Kerr medal U. Calif., Berkeley, 1992. Fellow Am. Acad. Arts and Scis., Am. Philos. Soc.; mem. Am. Econ. Assn., Econ. History Assn., Assn. Asian Studies, Chevalier, Legion of Honor, Order of Sacred Treasure, Star (Japan). Home: 37 Beechcroft Rd Newton MA 02158-2403 Office: Harvard Univ 218 Littauer Ctr Cambridge MA 02138

ROSOW, JEROME MORRIS, institute executive; b. Chgo., Dec. 2, 1919; s. Morris and Mary (Cornick) R.; m. Rosalyn Levin, Sept. 28, 1941; children: Michael, Joel. BA cum laude, U. Chgo., 1942. Position classification analyst Dept. Army, Washington, 1942-43; orgn. and methods examiner, asst. mgr. wage and salary div. Dept. Army, 1948-51; dir. compensation War Assets Adminstrn., Washington, 1946-48; dir. policy, salary stblzn. bd. Econ. Stblzn. Agy., 1952-53; with Creole Petroleum Corp. subs. Standard Oil N.J., Caracas, Venezuela, 1953-55; various exec. positions including coord. of compensation, indsl. relations rsch. Standard Oil N.J., N.Y.C., 1955-66; mgr. employee relations dept. ESSO Europe, Inc., London, 1966-69; asst. sec. labor for policy, evaluation and rsch. Dept. Labor, 1969-71; planning mgr. pub. affairs. dept. Exxon Corp., 1971-77; founder, pres. Work in Am. Inst., 1976—; cons. fed. pay plans U.S. Bur. Budget and U.S. CSC, 1964; mem. bus. adv. rsch com. Bur. Labor Stats., 1958-65; chmn. coun. of compensation Nat. Indsl. Conf. Bd., 1959-66; assoc. seminar on labor, Columbia U., 1961—; dir. N.Y.C. Vocat. Adv. Service, 1961—, chmn. finance com., 1962-65; mem. White House Working Group on Welfare Reform, 1969-71; chmn. cabinet com. White House Conf. Children and Youth, 1970-71; chmn. subcabinet com. nat. growth policy; U.S. del OECD Ministers Conf., Paris, 1970, 74; vice-chmn. Nat. Productivity Commn., 1971; chmn. tech. experts multinat. indsl. relations OECD, Paris, 1972; chmn. subcom. manpower and social affairs; chmn. Pres.'s Adv. Com. Fed. Pay, 1971-82; adviser Pres. U.S.; chmn. Am. assembly The Changing World at Work. Editor: American Men in Government, 1949, The Worker and the Job: Coping with Change, 1974; Editor: (with Clark Kerr) Work in America: The Decade Ahead, 1979, Productivity: Prospects for Growth, 1981, Views from the Top, 1985, Teamwork: Joint Labor-Management Programs in America, 1986, Global Marketplace, 1988, Training-The Competitive Edge, 1988, Allies in Education Reform, 1988; contbr. articles on manpower, compensation, welfare reform, indsl. relations, orgn. transformation, labor mgmt. relations to profl. jours. Bd. dirs. Young Audiences; trustee Nat. Com. Employment of Youth; adviser Com. Econ. Devel., 1972—, Nat. Planning Assn., 1973—; mem. Nat. Commn. Productivity and Quality of Work, 1975; v.p. Population Edn. Inc., 1975—; mem. Study Group Work and Edn. in China, 1978; cons. comptroller gen. U.S., 1972—, Ford Found.; mem. Mayor's Commn. on Gainsharing, N.Y.C., 1993. With AUS, 1943-46. Recipient Comptroller Gen.'s Public Service award, 1980. Mem. Indsl. Relations Rsch. Assn. (life, exec. bd., pres. 1979). Jewish. Home: 117 Fox Meadow Rd Scarsdale NY 10583-2301 Office: 700 White Plains Rd Scarsdale NY 10583-5013

ROSOW, STUART L., lawyer; b. N.Y.C., Mar. 28, 1950; s. Bernard and Lillian (Bonime) R.; m. Amy Berk Kuhn. AB cum laude, Yale U.; JD cum laude, Harvard U. Law clk. to presiding justice U.S. Ct. Appeals (7th cir.), Chgo., 1975-76; assoc. Paul, Weiss et al, N.Y.C., 1976-79; assoc. Kaye, Scholer, Fierman, Hays & Handler, N.Y.C., 1979-84, ptnr., 1984—. Mem. ABA, N.Y. State Bar Assn., Assn. of Bar of City of N.Y. Office: Kaye Scholer Fierman Hays & Handler 425 Park Ave New York NY 10022-3506

ROSOWSKI, ROBERT BERNARD, manufacturing company executive; b. Detroit, July 23, 1940; s. Bernard and Anna (Maciag) R.; m. Kathleen Patricia Bates, Aug. 26, 1961; children: John, Paul, Mary, Judith. BS, U. Detroit, 1962; MBA, Mich. State U., 1974. CPA, Mich. Auditor, staff supr. Coopers and Lybrand, Detroit, 1962-71; fin. analyst Masco Corp., Taylor, Mich., 1971-73, controller, 1973-85, v.p., controller, 1985—. Bd. dirs. Econ. Devel. Coun. City of Taylor, 1983—, v.p., contr., treas., 1996; chmn. bd. dirs. Acctg. Aid Soc. Met. Detroit, 1987—; chmn. Oakwood Hosp. Found., 1990—. Mem. Am. Inst. CPA's, Mich. Assn. CPA's. Avocations: golf, fishing, boating, photography. Office: Masco Corp 21001 Van Born Rd Taylor MI 48180-1340

ROSS, ADRIAN E., drilling manufacturing company executive; b. Clintonville, N.Y., Mar. 6, 1912; s. James A. and Bertha (Beardsley) R.; B.S. in Elec. Engring., M.I.T., 1934, M.S. in Elec. Engring., 1935; m. Ruth T. Hill, Mar. 2, 1934; children—James A., Daniel R. Materials engr. USN, 1935-37; devel. engr. Electrolux Corp., 1937-41; chief engr. and asst. to pres. Sprague & Henwood, Inc., Scranton, Pa., 1946-53, dir., 1951—, pres., 1953-74, chmn. bd., 1963—; pres., dir. Sprague & Henwood de Venezuela; dir. Hands Eng. Ltd., Scranton Lackawanna Indsl. Bldg. Co. (emeritus), N.E. Bank of Pa. (emeritus), Penn Security Bank. Past chmn. bd., dir. emeritus Keystone Jr. Coll.; pres., dir. Ross Family Found.; former chmn. bd., dir. emeritus Johnson Sch. Tech. Served from lt. to lt. col. Air Communication. USAAF, 1941-46. Registered profl. engr., Pa. Mem. Diamond Core Drill Mfrs. Assn. (past pres.), AIME, ASCE, Soc. Profl Engrs., U.S. Nat. Council Soil Mechanics, Indsl. Diamond Assn. Am. (past pres.), C. of C. Presbyn. Clubs: Mining (N.Y.C.); Scranton, M.I.T. (Scranton, Pa.). Contbr. articles to Mining Congress Jour., Mining Engring., Engring. and Mining Jour., Diamond Drill Handbook. Home: 5 Overlook Rd Clarks Summit PA 18411-1121

ROSS, ALBERTA BARKLEY, retired chemist; b. Moores Hill, Ind., July 26, 1928; d. Lawrence Houston and Stella Olcott (Wright) Barkley; m. Joseph Hansbro Ross, June 2, 1956; children: Mary Angela, Joseph Hansbro Jr., Robert Barkley, Kathleen. BS, Purdue U., 1948, Wash. U., 1951; PhD, U. Md., 1957. Tech. libr. Monsanto Chem. Co., St. Louis, 1948-53; rsch. assoc. U. Mich., Ann Arbor, 1957-58; supr. Radiation Chemistry Data Ctr. U. Notre Dame (Ind.), 1964-95; ret., 1995. Mem. Am. Chem. Soc. (chmn. St. Joseph Valley chpt. 1977-78), Sigma Xi (chpt. pres. 1980-81), Iota Sigma Pi.

ROSS, ALLAN ANDERSON, music educator, university official; b. Amesbury, Mass., Jan. 16, 1939; s. Frank Albert and Ruth Ethel (Anderson) R.; m. Barbara Kay Bedford, Apr. 15, 1962; children: Karen Elizabeth, Judith Carol, Donna Susan, Linda Beth, Jason Andrew. A.B., U. Rochester, 1961; MusM, Ind. U., 1962, MusD, 1968. Asst. dir. music U. Rochester, N.Y., 1962-65; instr. music Ind. U., Bloomington, 1967-69, asst. prof. music, 1969-71, assoc. prof., dir. undergrad. studies, 1971-73, prof., 1977-79, asst. to dean, 1973-79; dean Shepherd Sch. Music, Rice U., Houston, 1979-81; prof. music U. Okla., Norman, 1981—, dir. music, 1981-92, devel. officer Coll. Fine Arts, 1992-93; condr. U. Okla. Symphony Orch., 1993—; dir. music Trinity Methodist Ch., Rochester, N.Y., 1963-65, First United Meth. Ch., Bloomington, Ind., 1969-79, 1st Christian Ch., Norman, Okla., 1981-91; bd. dirs. Riemenschneider Bach Inst.; bd. dirs., exec. bd. Okla. Summer Arts Inst. Guest condr. and adjudicator at music festivals throughout, U.S.; Author: Techniques for Beginning Conductors, 1976. Bd. dirs. United Way of Norman, Helpline of Norman, Okla. Arts Inst.; mem. gov.'s commn. for Okla. Symphony Orch. NDEA Title IV fellow, 1965. Mem. Music Educators Nat. Conf., Am. Choral Dirs. Assn., Coll. Music Soc., Nat. Assn. Schs. of Music (grad. commn., evaluator), Okla. Music Educators Assn., Phi Mu Alpha Sinfonia, Pi Kappa Lambda. Home: 1879 Rolling Hills St Norman OK 73072-6707 Office: U Okla Sch Music 560 Parrington Oval Norman OK 73019-3040

ROSS, ALLAN MICHAEL, physician, medical educator; b. N.Y.C., June 20, 1939; s. Irving and Rose Ross; m. Loleta Saylors, Nov. 1, 1965; children—Jenifer, Aaron, Jed. B.A., Northwestern U., 1960; M.D., Chgo. Med. Sch., 1964. Diplomate Am. Bd. Internal Medicine. Fellow in cardiology Yale U., New Haven, 1971-72; instr. medicine Yale U., 1972-73, asst. prof. medicine, 1975-77, assoc. prof., 1977-78; dir. cardiol. cath. lab. West Haven VA Hosp., 1973-75; prof. medicine, dir. div. cardiology George Washington U., Washington, 1979-94; prof./assoc. chmn. dept. medicine, dir. cardiovascular rsch. George Washington U., 1994—. Inventor spl. function cardiac catheters; designer cardiologic diagnostic algorhythms. Served with M.C. U.S. Army, 1968-71. Am. Heart Lung and Blood Inst. prin. investigator, 1983. Fellow Am. Coll. Cardiology (bd. govs. D.C. sect. 1982-85); mem. Am. Heart Assn. (fellow coun. on clin. cardiology, D.C. counsellor 1983). Office: George Washington U 2150 Pennsylvania Ave NW Washington DC 20037-3201

ROSS, ALLYNE R., federal judge; b. 1946. BA, Wellesley Coll., 1967; JD cum laude, Harvard Law Sch., 1970. Assoc. Paul, Weiss, Rifkind, Wharton & Garrison, 1971-76; asst. U.S. atty. U.S. Dist. Ct. (N.Y. ea. dist.), 2nd circuit, Brooklyn, 1976-83, chief, appeals div., 1983-86, magistrate judge, 1986-94, dist. judge, 1994—. Mem. Federal Bar Coun., New York City Bar Assn. Office: US District Court 225 Cadman Plz E Rm 252 Brooklyn NY 11201-1818*

ROSS, BEATRICE BROOK, artist; b. N.Y.C., Mar. 31, 1927; d. Alexander and Ray (Tennenbaum) Brook; m. Alexander Ross, Dec. 23, 1945; children: Robert Alan, Kenneth Jay, Stefani Lynn. Student, Hunter Coll., 1943, CCNY, 1944, Bklyn. Mus. Art Sch., 1959-60, 64-65; pupil of Ruben Tam, Wang Chi Yuan, Leo Manso; scholar, Sch. Chinese Brush Work, 1973. Owner, operator Jean Rosenthal Bea Ross Gallery, Jericho, 1961-64; represented by Gillary Gallery, Jericho, N.Y., Patrician Gallery, West Palm Beach, Fla.; founder Birchwood Art League, 1958-63; lectr. bd. edn., Ont., Can., 1972; mem. ad hoc com. with Lucy Lippard Women in Art, 1970-74. Exhbns. include Women in Art, Huntington, N.Y., 1972, C.W. Post Coll., 1972, 73-76, Guild Hall Mus., East Hampton, 1969-72, Lever House, Inc., 1969-72, J. Walter Thompson Loan Show, 1970, Whitehouse Gallery, 1970, Park Ave. Synagogue, 1970, Locust Valley Ann., 1970, Nat. Arts Club, 1970, Loeb Student Ctr., NYU, 1969, Suffolk Mus., Stony Brook, N.Y., 1969, Lynn U., Boca Raton, 1992, Suffolk Mus., Stony Brook, N.Y., 1971, NAD, 1968, Audubon Artists, 1968, 70, Silvermine Guild, 1968, 71, Port Washington (N.Y.) Library, 1968, 70, 76, Profl. Artists Guild L.I., 1968, Bklyn. Coll., 1968, Huntington Twp. Art League, Cold Spring Harbor, N.Y., 1967, Gillary Gallery, Jericho, N.Y., 1966, 68, 70, 72, 79, 83, Hecksher Mus., 1960, 63, 70, Ho. of Reps., 1965, Library of Congress, 1965, Merrick (N.Y.) Gallery, 1963, N. Shore Community Art Ctr. ann., Roslyn, N.Y., 1959, 62, Birchwood Art League, Jericho, N.Y., 1958, 61-62, Hofstra U., 1960, City Ctr., N.Y.C., 1960, Emily Lowe Gallery, 1960, Nassau Democratic County Com. ann., 1958, R.A.A. Gallery, N.Y.C., 1969-70, 77, Roosevelt Field Art Gallery, Garden City, N.Y., 1958, Boca Raton (Fla.) City Hall, 1991, Bryant Library, Roslyn, N.Y., 1973, Women's Interart Ctr., N.Y.C., 1974, Wantagh (N.Y.) Library, 1975, Port Washington Library, 1976, LIU, 1976, N.Y. Tech., 1974, C.W. Post Coll. Schwartz Library, 1976, St. Johns U., 1976, Union Carbide, N.Y.C., 1977, Harley U. Ctr. Gallery, Adelphi U., 1976, 82, Lincoln Ctr., N.Y.C., 1978, 82, Gallery 84, N.Y.C., 1981, Am. Properties Inc., Boca Raton, Fla., 1996; represented in pvt. collections, traveling shows in France, Italy and Japan; mus. curated show No. Trust Bank, Boca Mus., Fla., 1992, Nations Bank, Boca Raton Mus., Fla., 1995. Recipient 1st prize oil Birchwood Art League, 1958; certificate award outstanding contbn. Mid Island Plaza Art League, Hicksville, N.Y., 1961, 2d prize oil, 1962; hon. mention oil Operation Democracy, Inc. ann., Locust Valley, 1967, 1st prize oil, 1970; Benjamin Altman landscape prize N.A.D., 1968; 2d prize Heckscher Mus., Huntington, N.Y., 1970; hon. mention Port Washington Ann., 1971, Benjamin Altman Landscape prize, Nat. award Nat. Acad. Design, N.Y.C., 1969, RAA Gallery, 1967-78, Harbor Gallery, Glen Cove, N.Y., 1983-85, Gillary Gallery Jericho, N.Y., 1984, Judge's Recognition award Boca Raton Mus., 1989, 2d prize, 1990, others; named to Nat. Women's Hall of Fame; MacDowell fellow, 1975, 80. Mem. Profl. Artists Guild L.I. (v.p. admissions 1971-74, exec. v.p. 1975-77, Judge's Recognition award at Boca Raton Mus. 1989, 2d prize for group show 1990), Profl. Artists Guild Fla., Easthampton Guild-Women in Arts, N.Y. Artists Equity, Nat. Mus. Women in Arts (charter), Gallery 84 (N.Y. chpt. 1979-85). Home and Studio: 5253 Bolero Cir Delray Beach FL 33484

ROSS, BERNARD, engineering consultant, educator. BME, Cornell U., 1957; MSc in Aero. Engring., Stanford U., 1959, PhD in Aero. and Aerospace Engring., 1965; Diploma, Ecole Nat. Superieure L'Aero., France, 1960; cert., U. Edinburgh, Scotland, 1961. Registered profl. engr., Calif. Structural test engr. Gen. Dynamics Corp., Montreal, Quebec, Can., 1956; servomechanism and control sys. design engr. Marquardt Corp., Van Nuys, Calif., 1957; stress analyst Douglas Aircraft Co., Santa Monica, Calif., 1959; vibration and dynamics engr. ONERA, Paris, 1960; rsch. asst. Stanford U., 1961-63, rsch. assoc., 1963-65; sr. rsch. engr., program mgr. Stanford Rsch. Inst., Menlo Park, Calif., 1965-70; founder, chmn. emeritus Failure Analysis Assocs., San Francisco, 1967—; vis. prof. U. Santa Clara, Calif., 1970-79; adv. coun. Stanford U., 1991—, cons. prof., 1992—; pres. internat. adv. bd. structural failure, product liability and tech. ins. confs. U. Vienna, 1986—; mem. univ. coun. Cornell U., 1995; speaker and lectr. in field. Contbr. articles to Exptl. Mechanics, AIAA Jour., Israel Jour. Tech., Profl. Safety, others. Cons. U.S. Consumer Product Safety Commn., Washington. NATO scholar, 1960. Mem. ASME, NSPE, AIAA, AAAS, Am. Soc. Safety Engrs., Am. Soc. Agrl. Engrs., Calif. Soc. Profl. Engrs., Soc. Automotive Engrs., Soc. Exptl. Mechanics, Internat. Soc. for Law, Technology and Ins. Achievements include research in analysis of structural collapse, mechanics of impact and penetration, accident reconstruction, safety warning design for heavy equipment, mechanical failure of machine parts, transportation system design. Office: Failure Analysis Assocs PO Box 3015 149 Commonwealth Dr Menlo Park CA 94025

ROSS, CHARLES, artist; b. Phila., Dec. 17, 1937; s. Fred H. and Gertrude (Hill) R.; m. Elizabeth Ginsberg, 1977. A.B. in Math, U. Calif., Berkeley, 1960, M.A. in Sculpture, 1962. Exhibited in one-man shows: Dilexi Gallery, San Francisco, 1961, 65, 66, 68, Dwan Gallery, N.Y.C., 1968, 69, 71, Daytons Gallery 12, Mpls., 1968, John Weber Gallery, N.Y.C., 1972, 77, 79, 81, The Clocktower, N.Y.C., 1974, Utah Mus. Fine Arts, Salt Lake City, 1975, Mus. Contemporary Art, La Jolla, Calif., 1976, Chgo., 1976, Inst. Contemporary Art, Phila., 1977, Susan Caldwell Gallery, N.Y.C., 1977, MIT, 1977, Portland Center for Visual Arts, 1981, Sena Gallery, Santa Fe, 1991, Johnson Gallery U. N.Mex., 1992, Humphrey Gallery, N.Y.C., 1995, Mus. de Arte y Diseno Contemporaneo, San Jose, Costa Rica, 1996; exhibited in group shows: Archtl. League of, New York, 1967, Albright Knox Art Gallery, Buffalo, 1967, Finch Coll., N.Y.C., 1967, Aldrich Mus., Ridgefield, Conn., 1967, Nelson Atkins Mus., Kansas City, 1968, Milw. Art Center, 1968, Whitney Mus., N.Y.C., 1969, Art Inst. Chgo., 1969, Art Gallery of Ont., Toronto, 1969, Galeries-pilotes, Lausanne, Switzerland, 1970, Mus. Fine Arts, Boston, 1971, Indpls. Mus. Art, 1974, Neuberger Mus., SUNY, Purchase, 1975, Stadtisches Mus., Leverkusen, Germany, 1975, Phila. Coll. Art, 1977, Hirshhorn Mus., Washington, 1977, Old Customs House, N.Y.C., 1977, Mus. Natural History, N.Y.C., 1977, Leo Castelli Gallery, N.Y.C., 1978, Yale U. Art Gallery, 1978, Dartmouth Coll. Gallery, 1978, Aspen (Colo.) Center for Visual Arts, 1980, Centre Georges Pompidou, Paris, 1980, Renwick Gallery, Smithsonian Instn., Washington, 1980, Mus. Contemporary Art, Chgo., 1981, MIT, Cambridge, 1981, Bard Coll., 1984, Light Gallery, N.Y.C., 1985, Venice Biennale, 1986, Differentes Natures la Defense, Paris, 1992, Anchorage Mus. History & Art, 1994, Richard Humphrey Gallery, N.Y.C., 1995, Kunsthallen Brandts Klaedefabrik, Odense, Denmark, 1996, SITE Santa Fe, 1996; commn. include: prism and/or solar spectrum skylight sculpture for Fed. Bldg, Lincoln, Nebr., 1976, U. Pa., 1977, Dietrich Found., Phila., 1979, Spectrum Bldg, Denver, 1980, Grand Rapids Art Mus., Mich., 1982, Towson State U., Md., 1983, Cumberland Rapid Transit Sta., Chgo., 1983, Linay Corp., Kansas City, Mo., 1985, Plaza of the Americas, Dallas, 1985, Wells Fargo Bldg., San Diego, 1986, San Francisco Internat. Airport, 1987, Anchorage Internat. Airport, 1987, Naugatuck Higher Edn. Ctr., Conn., 1990, Harvard Bus. Sc. Chapel, 1992, French Ministry of Culture Chateau d'Oiron, 1993, Cook Inst., Grand Rapids, Mich., 1996, Light Sanctuary, United World Coll., Montezuma, N.Mex., 1996; represented in permanent collections Nelson Atkins Mus., Whitney Mus. Am. Art, Berkeley Art Mus., Indpls. Mus. Art, Butler Inst. Am. Art, Herbert F. Johnson Mus. Art Cornell U., GSA Art and Architecture Program, U. Pa., Dietrich Found., Grand Rapids Art Mus., Gen. Elec.

Corp., City Chgo., Towson State U., Becton Dickinson Corp., Security Pacific Bank, Found. Ctr., N.Y.C., Wynne Jackson Inc., Albuquerque Mus., Linclay Corp., Witco Chem. Corp., City of San Diego, Walker Art Ctr., City of San Francisco, State of Alaska, Koll Co., Los Angeles County Mus. Art, Mus.de Arte y Diseno Contemporaneo, San Jose, Kunsthallen Brandts Klaedefabrik, Odense, Des Moines Art Ctr., French Ministry of Culture, Frederick A. Weisman Mus., Mpls., Harvard Bus. Sch., Mus. Fine Arts, Santa Fe, United World Coll., N.Mex.; works in progress include: Star Axis, monumental sculpture/observatory atop a mesa in N.Mex. Author: Sunlight Convergence Solar Burn (Am. Inst. Graphic Arts award 1976); films Sunlight Dispersion, 1972, Solar Eclipse, 1972. Recipient Art and Architecture Collaborations award Boston Soc. Architects, 1993. Office: Richard Humphrey Gallery 250 E 51st St New York NY 10022-6501 also: Joyce Schwartz Ltd 17 W 54th St New York NY 10019 *As I work to focus light and energy into material form, my work has shown me that it is possible for us to gain an intimacy with the stars.*

ROSS, CHARLES ROBERT, lawyer, consultant; b. Middlebury, Vt., Feb. 24, 1920; s. Jacob Johnson and Hannah Elizabeth (Holmes) R.; m. Charlotte Sells Hoyt, Aug 28, 1948; children—Jacqueline Hoyt, Peter Holmes, Charles Robert. A.B., U. Mich., 1941, M.B.A., 1948, LL.B., 1948. Bar: Ky. 1949, Vt. 1954, U.S. Supreme Ct. 1968. Instr. Oreg. State Coll., 1948-49; practice law Louisville and Burlington, Vt., 1949-59; chmn. Vt. Pub. Service Commn., 1959-61; commr. FPC, 1961-68; mem. U.S. sect. Internat. Joint Commn., 1962-81; mem. Nat. Consumers Energy Com., 1973-74; pub. mem. Adminstrv. Conf. U.S., 1971-74; adj. prof. econs. U. Vt., 1969-74. Served to capt. USAAF, 1942-46. Home: 806 Wake Robin Dr Shelburne VT 05482-7582

ROSS, CHARLES WORTHINGTON, IV, metals company executive; b. Frederick, Md., Jan. 27, 1933; s. Charles Worthington and Priscilla Avis (Wilson) R., 3d; student U. Md., 1951-54; m. Betty Lou Waldvogel, May 26, 1956; children: Holly Theresa Ross-Hartung, Kristna Lynn Ross-Serpico, Amy Louise Ross-Drummond, Carol Ann. BA in Polit. Sci., Syracuse U., 1963; MA in Occupational Safety and Health, NYU, 1976. Commd. 2d lt. U.S. Air Force, 1954, safety officer, 1966-68; ret., 1968; gen. mgr. Mgmt. Recruiters, Inc., Norfolk, Va., 1968-71; regional safety mgr. Mobil Oil Corp., Scarsdale, N.Y., 1971-75; corp. safety mgr. Schering-Plough Corp., Kenilworth, N.J., 1975-79; corp. mgr. safety and health Westvaco Corp., N.Y.C., 1979-81; v.p. mktg., safety and health cons., dir. IHI-KEMRON, Huntington, N.Y., 1981-83, WAPORA, Inc., 1983-86, Essex Chem. Corp., Clifton, N.J., 1986-89; mgr. safety and loss control Handy & Harman, Rye, N.Y., 1989-96; ccons. indsl. safety and workers compensation, 1996—; instr. safety mgmt. Kean Coll., Union, N.J., 1978-79. Recipient 2d place award for tech. paper Am. Soc. Safety Engrs./Vets. Safety, 1980. Registered profl. engr., Calif.; cert. safety profl., hazard control mgr. (masters level). Mem. Am. Soc. Safety Engrs. (profl. mem.), System Safety Soc., Nat. Safety Mgmt. Soc., Am. Indsl. Hygiene Assn., Safety Execs. N.Y. (pres.). Democrat. Episcopalian. Author: Computer Systems for Safety and Health Management, 1984, 2d edit., 1991; contbr. articles to profl. jours. Home and Office: 35478 Occohannock Dr Belle Haven VA 23306

ROSS, CHARLOTTE PACK, suicidologist; b. Oklahoma City, Oct. 21, 1932; d. Joseph and Rose P. (Traibich) Pack; m. Roland S. Ross, May 6, 1951 (div. July 1964); children: Beverly Jo, Sandra Gail; m. Stanley Fisher, Mar. 17, 1991. Student U. Okla., 1949-52, New Sch. Social Rsch., 1953. Cert. tchr. Exec. dir. Suicide Prevention and Crisis Ctr. San Mateo County, Burlingame, Calif., 1966-88; pres., exec. dir. Youth Suicide Nat. Ctr., Washington, 1985-93; exec. dir. Death with Dignity Edn. Ctr., San Mateo, Calif., 1994—; pres. Calif. Senate Adv. Com. Youth Suicide Prevention, 1982-84; speaker Menninger Found., 1983, 84; instr. San Francisco State U., 1981-83; conf. coord. U. Calif., San Francisco, 1971—; cons. univs. and health svcs. throughout world. Contbg. author: Group Counseling for Suicidal Adolescents, 1984, Teaching Children the Facts of Life and Death, 1985; mem. editorial bd. Suicide and Life Threatening Behavior, 1976-89. Mem. regional selection panel Pres.'s Commn. on White House Fellows, 1975-78; mem. CIRCLON Svc. Club, 1979—, Com. on Child Abuse, 1981-85; founding mem. Women for Responsible Govt., co-chmn., 1974-79. Recipient Outstanding Exec. award San Mateo County Coordinating Com., 1971, Koshland award San Francisco Found., 1984. Fellow Wash. Acad. Scis.; mem. Internat. Assn. Suicide Prevention (v.p. 1985—), Am. Assn. Suicidology (sec. 1972-74, svc. award 1990), bd. govs. 1976-78, accreditation com. 1975—, chair region IX, 1975-82), Assn. United Way Agy. Execs. (pres. 1974), Assn. County Contract Agys. (pres. 1982), Peninsula Press Club.

ROSS, CHERI LOUISE, English language educator; b. Marion, Ind., Oct. 10; d. Kenneth Earl and Hazel Emma (DaWalt) Graves; m. James Brian Wagaman, Jan. 28, 1994. BA, Purdue U., 1970, MS, 1975, PhD, 1991. Cert. tchr., Ind. Asst. prof. Pa. State U., Mont Alto, 1992-95; asst. prof. humanities and English edn. Capital Coll., Pa. State U.-Harrisburg, Middletown, 1995—; assoc. English faculty Ind. Vocat. Tech. Coll., Lafayette, 1983-92; vis. asst. prof. Purdue U., West Lafayette, Ind., 1991-92; adv. bd. Collegiate Press, 1995—; manuscript referee Coll. Literature Jour., West Chester, Pa., 1992—; cons. U. Tenn. Press, Knoxville, 1989, Purdue U. Press, West Lafayette, 1991. Editor Mid-Atlantic Gazette; contbr. articles to profl. jours. Mem. MLA, Popular Culture Assn. (area chair of cultural conflict and women, Kathleen Gregory Klein award 1989, Jane Bakerman award 1990), N.E. MLA, Mid-Atlantic Popular Culture Assn., Mid-Atlantic Am. Culture Assn. (exec. bd.), Phi Kappa Phi, Phi Delta Kappa. Democrat. Home: 555 Mountainview Rd Middletown PA 17057 Office: Pa State U Harrisburg Divsn Humanities and Edn 777 W Harrisburg Pike Middletown PA 17057-4846

ROSS, CHESTER WHEELER, retired clergyman; b. Evansville, Ind., Nov. 3, 1922; s. Mylo Wheeler and Irma (Berning) R.; AB cum laude, Kans. Wesleyan U., 1952; MDiv, Garrett Theol. Sem., 1954; D Ministry, St. Paul Sch. Theology, 1979; postgrad. in Computers Kans. Vocat.-Tech, 1989.; m. Ruth Eulaine Briney, Aug. 30, 1949; children: James W., Deborah R., Judith R., Martha S., John W. Ordained to ministry United Meth. Ch., 1953; enlisted pvt. USAAF, 1942, advanced through grades to lt. col., 1968; chaplain, Africa, Europe, Alaska, Greenland, Taiwan; installation chaplain, Columbus AFB, Miss., 1972-75; ret., 1975; pastor Unity Parish, Iuka, Kans., 1975-80, Ness City (Kans.) United Meth. Ch., 1980-88. active ARC, Boy Scouts Am.; vol. parolee counselor; mem. USD 303 Sch. Bd. Paul Harris fellow Rotary Internat.; Decorated Air medal (2), Meritorious Svc. medal (2); recipient Silver Beaver award, Boy Scouts Am., 1975. Mem. Am. Police Assn., Rail to Trails, Ministers Assn., Mil. Chaplains Assn., Stephen Ministry, Rural Chaplins Assn., 301st Vets Assn., Acad. Parish Clergy, Ret. Officers Assn., Air Force Assn., Nat. Hist. Soc., Am. Assn. Christian Counselors, Cmty. Vol. Svcs., Air Force Gunners Assn., Appalachian Trail Conf., Menninger Found., Kans. Sheriffs Assn. Assn. Ret. Persons, Order Ky. Col., Am. Legion, VFW. Address: 1102 Arcade St Goodland KS 67735-3426

ROSS, CHRISTOPHER WADE STELYAN, diplomat; b. Quito, Ecuador, Mar. 3, 1943 (parents Am. citizens); s. Claude G. Anthony and Antigone Andrea (Peterson) R.; m. Carol Geraldine Canning, Nov. 30, 1968; 1 child, Anthony Gordon. AB summa cum laude, Princeton U., 1965; cert. Middle East Centre for Arab Studies, 1964; MA, Johns Hopkins U., 1967. Editorial asst. Middle East Jour., Washington, 1965-68; instr. Arabic lang. Columbia U., N.Y.C., 1966, Princeton U., 1967; pub. affairs trainee USIA, 1968-69; jr. officer trainee Am. Embassy, Tripoli, Libya, 1969-70; dir. Am. Cultural Ctr., Fez, Morocco, 1970-73; press attache Am. Embassy, Beirut, 1973-76; pub. affairs officer Am. Embassy, Algiers, Algeria, 1976-79, dep. chief mission and charge d'affaires, 1979-81; pub. affairs adviser Bur. Near Eastern and South Asian Affairs, Dept. State, Washington, 1981-82, spl. asst. to presdl. emissaries to Lebanon and Middle East, 1982-84, dir. regional affairs, 1984-85; exec. asst. to Under Sec. State for Polit. Affairs, Washington, 1985-88; amb. to Algeria, 1988-91; amb. to Syria, Damascus, 1991—; chmn. bd. trustees Am. Sch. Algiers, 1977-80; hon. chmn., bd. trustees Damascus Community Sch., 1991—. Contbr. articles to profl. jours. Recipient Superior Honor award U.S. Info. Agy., 1976, 83, Dept. State, 1988, Presdl. Meritorious Svc. award, 1983, 85, 89, 93. Mem. Coun. Fgn. Rels., Am. Fgn. Svc. Assn., Assn. for Diplomatic Studies and Tng., Middle East Inst., Middle East Studies Assn. of N.Am., Royal Soc. for Asian Affairs. Greek Orthodox. Club: Princeton (Washington). Avocations: classic cars; bicycling. Office: Damascus Dept State Washington DC 20521 also: Am Embassy, 2 al-Mansur St Abu Rumaneh, Damascus Syria

ROSS, COLEMAN DEVANE, accountant, insurance company consultant; b. Greensboro, N.C., Mar. 18, 1943; s. Guy Matthews and Nancy McConnell (Coleman) R.; m. Carol Louise Morde, Aug. 26 1965; children: Coleman, Jonathan, Andrew. BS in Bus. Adminstrn., U. N.C., 1965; postgrad. Grad. Sch. of Banking of South, 1982-84, U. N.C. Advanced Mgmt. Program, 1994. CPA, CLU, ChFC; cert. bank auditor; cert. fin. svcs. auditor. With Price Waterhouse, Tampa, 1965-76, Toronto, 1970, Hartford, Conn., 1976-93, N.Y.C., 1993—, ptnr., 1977—, chmn., mng. ptnr. Nat. Ins. Svcs. Group, 1988-94. Bd. dirs. N.E. Region Boy Scouts Am., 1988—, v.p., 1993-96, pres. New Eng. area, 1988-91; bd. dirs. Greater N.Y. Couns. Boy Scouts Am., 1994—; mem. exec. bd. Conn. Rivers coun. Boy Scouts Am., 1978—, pres. 1985-88, vice-chmn., 1996—; corporator Inst. Living, 1992—, Vis. Nurses Assn. Health Care Greater Hartford, 1992—, Hartford Hosp., 1995—; div. campaign chmn. United Way of Capital Area, 1984; bd. dirs., treas. Family Svc. Soc. Greater Hartford, 1977-80; participant Leadership Greater Hartford, 1977. Recipient Silver Beaver award Boy Scouts Am., 1987, Silver Antelope award, 1991. Fellow Life Mgmt. Inst.; mem. AICPA (ins. cos. com. 1985-88, reins. auditing and acctg. task force 1979-85, rels. with actuaries com. 1982-85), N.Y. Soc. CPAs, N.C. Assn. CPAs, Conn. Soc. CPAs, Soc. Ins. Fin. Mgmt., Am. Soc. CLUs and ChFCs, N.Y.C. Soc. CLUs and ChFCs, Internat. Ins. Soc., Nat. Soc. Cert. Fin. Svcs. Auditors, Nat. Soc. Chartered Bank Auditors, Assn. Mut. Ins. Accts., Assn. Investment Mgmt. and Rsch., N.Y. Soc. Security Analysts, Hartford Club (bd. govs. 1977-84). Home: 6 Wildflower Ln West Simsbury CT 06092-2434 Office: Price Waterhouse 1177 Avenue Of The Americas New York NY 10036-2714

ROSS, DANIEL R., lawyer; b. Stamford, Conn., Oct. 20, 1941; s. Adrian E. and Ruth (Hill) R.; m. Faye Zerwekh, Aug. 15, 1965; children: Kevin S., Eric D., David W. SB, MIT, 1963; LLB, U. Pa., 1966. Atty. adviser to Hon. Theodore Tannenwald, Jr. U.S. Tax Ct., Washington, 1966-68; assoc. Drinker, Biddle & Reath, Phila., 1970-77, ptnr., 1977—. Presenter in field. Pres. bd. trustees First United Meth. Ch. Germantown, 1984—. Capt. U.S. Army, 1968-70, Vietnam. Mem. ABA (chair com. on income of estates and trusts 1985-87, com. on govt. subcoms. 1988-91, taxation sect.). Avocations: bicycling, skiing, tennis, computers. Office: Drinker Biddle & Reath 1100 PNB Bldg 1345 Chestnut St Philadelphia PA 19107-3426

ROSS, DAVID A., art museum director; b. Malverne, N.Y., Apr. 26, 1949; s. Joshua and Grayce R.; m. Margaret Gronner; children—Lindsay, Emily. B.A., Syracuse U.; postgrad. Grad. Sch. Fine Arts, Syracuse. Curator video art Everson Mus. Art, Syracuse, N.Y., 1971-74; dep. dir. program devel. and TV Long Beach Mus. Art, Calif., 1974-77; chief curator Univ. Art Mus., Berkeley, Calif., 1977-82; dir. Inst. of Contemporary Art, Boston, 1982-91; dir., CEO Whitney Mus. Am. Art., 1991—. Active Fed. Adv. Com. om Internat. Exbns., 1990—. Contbr. articles to profl. jours. Mem. Assn. Art Mus. Dirs. Office: Whitney Museum Am Art 945 Madison Ave New York NY 10021-2701*

ROSS, DAVID EDMOND, church official; b. Lewiston, Maine, Oct. 1, 1950; s. Rev. and Mrs. Lorne Arla Collins R.; m. Shirley Evelyn Godin, Aug. 19, 1972. BA in Theology cum laude, Berkshire Coll., 1973; MPA, U. Maine, 1989. Ordained to ministry Advent Christian Ch., 1975. Pastor State Road Advent Christian Ch., Presque Isle, Maine, 1973-91; exec. dir. Advent Christian Ch. Gen. Conf., Charlotte, N.C., 1991—; v.p. Maine State Conf. Advent Christian Chs., 1975-76, pres., 1976-81, 86-91; mem. exec. coun. Advent Christian Ch., 1981-90, long range strategy com., 1986—; seminar leader Am. Festival of Evangelism, Kansas City, 1981; dir. Northern Lights Youth Choir, 1974-90. Office: Advent Christian Church PO Box 23152 Charlotte NC 28227-0272

ROSS, DELMER GERRARD, historian, educator; b. Los Banos, Calif., Nov. 5, 1942; s. Elmer G. and Orva Beth (Dickinson) R.; m. Karen Ann Gibson, June 17, 1977; children: Michelle, Richard. BA, Pacific Union Coll., 1965; MA, U. Calif., Santa Barbara, 1967, PhD, 1970. Instr. Pacific Union Coll., Angwin, Calif., 1968-69; from asst. to assoc. prof. Oakwood Coll., Huntsville, Ala., 1970-76; from assoc. prof. to prof. history Loma Linda U., Riverside, Calif., 1976-91, chmn. dept. history and polit. sci., 1986-90; prof. history and polit. sci. La Sierra U., Riverside, 1991—. Author: Visionaries and Swindlers, 1975, Rails Across Costa Rica, 1976, Rails in Paradise, 1991, Gold Road to La Paz, 1992; chmn. editorial bd. Adventist Heritage mag., 1987-90. Bd. dirs. Inst. for Research in Latin Am., Mobile, Ala., 1968-82. Mem. Am. Hist. Assn., Conf. Latin Am. History (Caribe-Centroamerica regional com. chmn. 1973-75), Assn. 7th Day Adventist Historians (exec. sec. 1973-74, sec.-treas. 1974-75, pres. 1981-82), Assn. Western Adventist Historians, Nat. Railway Hist. Soc., Colo. Railroad Hist. Found., Railway and Locomotive Hist. Soc. Republican. Office: La Sierra U Dept of History Riverside CA 92515

ROSS, DIANA, singer, actress, entertainer, fashion designer; b. Detroit, Mar. 26, 1944; d. Fred and Ernestine R.; m. Robert Ellis Silberstein, Jan. 1971 (div. 1976); children: Rhonda, Tracee, Chudney; m. Arne Naess, Oct. 23, 1985; 1 son: Ross Arne. Grad. high sch. Pres. Diana Ross Enterprises, Inc., fashion and merchandising, Anaid Film Prodns., Inc., RTC Mgmt. Corp., artists mgmt., Chondee Inc., Rosstown, Rossville, music pub. Started in Detroit as mem. the Primettes; lead singer until 1969, Diana Ross and the Supremes; solo artist, 1969—; albums include Diana Ross, 1970, 76, Everything Is Everything, 1971, I'm Still Waiting, 1971, Lady Sings The Blues, 1972, Touch Me In The Morning, 1973, Original Soundtrack of Mahogany, 1975, Baby It's Me, 1977, The Wiz, 1978, Ross, 1978, 83, The Boss, 1979, Diana, 1981, To Love Again, 1981, Why Do Fools Fall In Love?, 1981, Silk Electric, 1982, Swept Away, 1984, Eaten Alive, 1985, Chain Reaction, 1986, Diana's Duets, 1987, Workin' Overtime, 1989, Red Hot Rhythm and Blues, 1987, Surrender, 1989, Ain't No Mountain High Enough, 1989, The Force Behind the Power, 1991, Stolen Moment: The Lady Sings... Jazz & Blues, 1993, Musical Memories Forever, 1993, The Remixes, 1994; films include Lady Sings the Blues, 1972, Mahogany, 1975, The Wiz, 1978; NBC-TV spl., An Evening With Diana Ross, 1977, Diana, 1981, numerous others; TV movie Out of Darkness, 1994; album Endless Love, 1982; author: Secrets of a Sparrow, 1993. Recipient citation Vice Pres. Humphrey for efforts on behalf Pres. Johnson's Youth Opportunity Program, citation Mrs. Martin Luther King and Rev. Abernathy for contbn. to SCLC cause, awards Billboard, Cash Box and Record World as worlds outstanding singer, Grammy award, 1970, Female Entertainer of Year NAACP, 1970, Cue award as Entertainer of year, 1972, Golden Apple award, 1972, Gold medal award Photoplay, 1972, Antoinette Perry award, 1977, nominee as best actress of year for Lady Sings the Blues Motion Picture Acad. Arts and Scis., 1972, Golden Globe award, 1972; named to Rock and Roll Hall of Fame, 1988. Office: care Paul Bloch Rogers and Cowan 1888 Century Park E Ste 500 Los Angeles CA 90067-1709 also: care Shelly Berger 6255 W Sunset Blvd Los Angeles CA 90028-7403

ROSS, DONALD, JR., English language educator, university administrator; b. N.Y.C., Oct. 18, 1941; s. Donald and Lea (Meyer) R.; m. Sylvia Berger (div.); 1 child, Jessica; m. 2d, Diane Redfern, Aug. 27, 1971; children—Owen, Gillian. B.A., Lehigh U., 1963, M.A., 1964; Ph.D., U. Mich., 1967. Asst. prof. English U. Pa., Phila., 1967-70; prof. English U. Minn., Mpls., 1970—, dir. composition program, 1982-86, dir. Univ. Coll., 1984-89; ret., 1989. Co-author: Word Processor and Writing Process, 1984, Revising Mythologies: The Composition of Thoreau's Major Works, 1988; contbr. articles to profl. jours. Grantee Am. Coun. Learned Socs., 1976, 90, NSF, 1974, Fund for Improvement of Postsecondary Edn., 1982-85; recipient Disting. Teaching award U. Minn., 1992. Mem. Assn. for Computers and Humanities (exec. sec. 1978-88), MLA, Assn. for Lit. and Linguistic Computing. Office: U Minn Composition Program 209 Church St SE Minneapolis MN 55455-0152

ROSS, DONALD EDWARD, university administrator; b. Mineola, N.Y., June 29, 1939; s. Alexander Walker and Florence M. (Carville) R.; m. Helen Landgren, June 23, 1966; children: Ellen Ross Sarafian, Kevin McAndrew. BFA, N.Y. Inst. Tech., 1962, LLD (hon.), 1978; MS, Hofstra U., 1970. Dean of students N.Y. Inst. Tech., Old Westbury, 1962-68; pres. Wilmington (Del.) Coll., 1968-77; pres., CEO Lynn U. (formerly Coll. of Boca Raton), Fla., 1971—; chmn. adv. com. U.S. Army Command and Gen. Staff Coll. Bd. dirs. Fla. Endowment Fund, 1989—; trustee Boca Raton Community Hosp., 1990—; mem. governing bd. Philharmonic Orch. Fla., 1990—; mem. U.S. Mil. Screening Com. Named Industrialist of Yr., Greater Boca Raton C. of C., 1992, Man of the Yr., City of Hope; recipient Boy Scouts Am. Leadership Svc. award, Boca Raton award, 1991. Mem. Assn. Univ. Pres., Econ. Coun. of Palm Beach County, Royal Palm Yacht and Country, Loggerhead Club, Adirondack League Club, Old Forge Club, City (Boca Raton). Avocations: snowskiing, tennis, reading, travel. Home: 212 Coconut Palm Rd Boca Raton FL 33432 Office: Lynn Univ 3601 N Military Trl Boca Raton FL 33431-5507*

ROSS, DONALD EDWARD, engineering company executive; b. N.Y.C., May 2, 1930; m. Jeanne Ellen McKessy, Apr. 4, 1954; children: Susan, Christopher, Carolyn. BA, Columbia U., 1952, BS in Mech. Engring., 1953; MBA, NYU, 1960. Registered profl. engr., N.Y., 14 other states. Engr. Carrier Corp., N.Y.C., 1955-70; v.p. Dynadata, 1970-71; with Jaros, Baum & Bolles, N.Y.C., 1971—, ptnr., 1977—. Mem. adv. coun. Columbia U. Sch. Engring. and Applied Sci. Lt. (j.g.) USN, 1953-55. Fellow ASHRAE; mem. ASME, NSPE, Nat. Acad. Enrs. (mech. engring. peer com.), Am. Cons. Engrs. Coun., Nat. Bur. Engring. Registration, N.Y. Assn. Cons. Engrs. (pres. 1984-86), Coun. on Tall Bldgs. and Urban Habitat (vice chmn. N.Am., mem. steering group), Univ. Club (N.Y.C.), Columbia U. Sch. Engring. Alumni Assn. (pres.), Nassau Country Club, Columbia Sch. Engring. Alumni Assn. (pres.), Tau Beta Pi. Office: Jaros Baum & Bolles 345 Park Ave New York NY 10154-0004

ROSS, DONALD HUGH, fraternal organization executive; b. Delta, Ohio, Aug. 19, 1949; s. Hugh Archbald and Margaret Baker (Harlton) R.; m. Mary Lynn Feuerborn, Dec. 21, 1974; children: Jon, Michael. BS, Miami U., Oxford, Ohio, 1971. Auditor Moose Internat., Mooseheart, Ill., 1971-76, dep. supreme sec., 1976-78, asst. comptroller, 1978-83; supreme sec. Supreme Lodge, Mooseheart, Ill., 1983—; sec. Mooseheart Bd. Govs., Moosehaven Bd. Govs., 1983—. Mem. editorial bd. Moose Action publ.; contbr. articles to newspapers and profl. jours. Republican. Club: Interact (Delta) (pres. 1966-67). Lodge: Moose (past gov. 1976, Pilgrim Degree of Merit 1983). Avocations: golf, bowling. Home: 1119 Woodland Ave Batavia IL 60510-3049 Office: Supreme Lodge Moose Internat Mooseheart IL 60539

ROSS, DONALD KEITH, retired insurance company executive; b. Rochester, N.Y., July 1, 1925; s. Alexander L. and Althea G. (Granger) R.; m. Mary F. Fyffe, June 4, 1949; children: Catherine (Mrs. Charles P. Lesher), Susan (Mrs. William Gardner Morris, Jr.), Donald Keith, Deborah Anne (Mrs. Michael Holt). B.E., Yale U., 1946; M.B.A., Harvard U., 1948. With N.Y. Life Ins. Co., N.Y.C., 1948—, exec. v.p., 1974-79, vice chmn., 1979-80, pres., 1980-81, chmn. bd., CEO, 1981-90, chmn. exec. com., 1990-93, also bd. dirs.; ret., 1990; trustee Consol. Edison of N.Y. Office: NY Life Ins Co 51 Madison Ave New York NY 10010-1603

ROSS, DONALD KENNETH, consulting engineering executive; b. St. Louis, Apr. 15, 1925; s. Maurice James and Babe Cyril (Grodsky) R.; m. Peggy Grosberg, July 1, 1951; 1 dau., Pamela Toder. BSEE, U. Minn., 1946; MS, MIT, 1948; ScD, Washington U., St. Louis, 1960. Rsch., teaching asst. MIT, 1946-48; electronics engr. Mo. Rsch., Inc., 1949-51; prin. Donald Ross & Assocs., St. Louis, 1953-61; pres. Ross & Baruzzini, Inc., St. Louis, 1961-91, chmn., 1991—; pres. Hanlon & Assocs., Inc., St. Louis, 1976-85; profl. assoc. Bldg. Rsch. and Adv. Bd., Nat. Acad. Scis.; lectr. Washington U. Patentee to 3 U.S. Patents. With USNR, 1943-46, 1951-53 Korea. Recipient Outstanding Achievement award IEEE Industry Applications Soc., 1989, Engring. Alumni Achievement award Washington U., 1993. Fellow Am. Cons. Engrs. Council, IEEE; mem. Assn. Profl. Material Handling Cons. (pres. 1976-77), Mo. Assn. Cons. Engrs. (past pres.), Sigma Xi, Tau Beta Pi, Eta Kappa Nu. Office: 1300 Baur Blvd Saint Louis MO 63132-1903

ROSS, DONALD ROE, federal judge; b. Orleans, Nebr., June 8, 1922; s. Roe M. and Leila H. (Reed) R.; m. Janice S. Cook, Aug. 29, 1943; children: Susan Jane, Sharon Kay, Rebecca Lynn, Joan Christine, Donald Dean. JD, U. Nebr., 1948, LLD (hon.), 1990. Bar: Nebr. bar 1948. Practice law Lexington, Nebr., 1948-53; mayor City of Lexington, 1953; assoc. Swarr, May, Royce, Smith, Andersen & Ross, 1956-70; U.S. atty. Dist. Nebr., 1953-56; gen. counsel Rep. party, Nebr., 1956-58; mem. Rep. Exec. Com. for Nebr., 1952-53; nat. com. mem. Rep. Nat. Com., 1958-70, vice chmn., 1965-70; sr. judge U.S. Ct. Appeals 8th cir., 1971—.

ROSS, DOROTHY RABIN, history educator; b. Milw., Aug. 13, 1936; m. Stanford G. Ross, June 9, 1958; children: John, Ellen. BA, Smith Coll., 1958; MA, Columbia U., 1959, PhD, 1965. Fellow in history and psychiatry Cornell U. Med. Coll/Payne Whitney Clinic, N.Y.C., 1965-67; spl. asst. com. on women historians Am. Hist. Assn., Washington, 1971-72; asst. prof. Princeton (N.J.) U., 1972-76; from assoc. prof. to prof. U. Va., Charlottesville, 1978-90; Arthur O. Lovejoy prof. history Johns Hopkins U., Balt., 1990—; mem. adv. com. on women HEW, Washington, 1978. Author: G. Stanley Hall, 1972, The Origins of American Social Science, 1991; editor: Modernist Impulses in the Human Sciences, 1870-1930, 1994; adv. editor Isis, 1979-86; bd. editors Jour. of the History of Ideas, 1993—; contbr. articles to profl. jours. USPHS grantee, 1965-68, NSF grantee, 1980-81. Fellow Ctr. for Advanced Study in Behavioral Scis., Soc. Am. Historians; mem. Am. Studies Assn., History of Sci. Soc., Am. Hist. Assn., Orgn. Am. Historians (exec. bd. 1987-89). Office: Johns Hopkins U Dept Of History Baltimore MD 21218

ROSS, DOUGLAS, lawyer, legal academic administrator; b. L.A., July 12, 1948; s. Mathew and Brenda Butler (Boynton) R.; m. Lynne Rose Maidman, June 14, 1970. AB cum laude, Tufts U., 1970; JD with honors, George Washington U., 1973. Bar: Ohio 1973, D.C. 1980, U.S. Supreme Ct. 1976. Asst. atty. gen., antitrust sect. Office of Ohio Atty. Gen., Columbus, 1973-74; spl. asst. U.S. atty. Ea. Dist. Va., Alexandria, 1977; trial atty. antitrust divsn. U.S. Dept. Justice, Washington, 1975-82; atty. advisor Office of Legis. Affairs, 1984-86, Office of Legal Policy, 1987-89, Office Policy Devel., 1989-92; Supreme Ct. counsel Nat. Assn. Attys. Gen., 1982-91; ran advocacy project for states to enhance their effectiveness before Supreme Ct., 1982-91, operated clearinghouse on state constl. law, 1987-91; civil divsn. Appellate Staff, 1992-94, Office of Consumer Litigation, 1994—. Recipient Meritorious award Dept. Justice, 1979, Spl. Achievement award, 1984, 96. Mem. Supreme Ct. Hist. Soc., D.C. Bar Assn., Supreme Ct. Opinion Network (bd. dirs. 1989-91), Arlington County Sports Comm. (chair subcom. on swimming pools 1995—). Jewish. Home: 3153 19th St N Arlington VA 22201-5103 Office: US Dept Justice PO Box 386 Washington DC 20044-0386

ROSS, DOUGLAS TAYLOR, retired software company executive; b. Canton, Republic of China, Dec. 21, 1929; (parents Am. citizens); s. Robert Malcolm and Margaret (Taylor) R.; m. Patricia Mott, Jan. 24, 1951; children: Jane R. Yoos, Kathryn R. Chow, Margaret R. Thrasher. AB in Math. cum laude, Oberlin Coll., 1951; SM, MIT, 1954, postgrad. math., 1958. Head computer applications group elec. systems lab. MIT, Cambridge, 1952-69, lectr. dept. elec. engring. and computer sci., 1960-69, 83—, exec. com. MIT Enterprise Forum, 1984-89; pres. SofTech, Inc., Waltham, Mass., 1969-75, chmn. bd., 1975-89, 91-93, chmn. emeritus, 1989-91, 93-94, chmn. emeritus ret., 1994—. Mem. town meeting, Lexington, Mass., 1960-70; trustee, bd. dirs. Charles Babbage Inst., 1984—. Mem. United Ch. of Christ. Home and Office: 33 Dawes Rd Lexington MA 02173-5926

ROSS, E. EARL, small business owner; b. St. Louis, July 3, 1942; s. Edward Earl and Ruth Randles (Loewen) R.; B.A. in Psychology, Central Mo. State U., 1965; M.A. in Corrections, Webster U., Webster Groves, Mo., 1976; m. Mary Donna Moore, May 31, 1964; 1 son, Damon Moore. Reporter, Warrensburg (Mo.) Daily Star-Jour., 1965; social worker St. Louis County Welfare Div., Maplewood, Mo., 1966-68; asso. dist. scout exec. Boy Scouts Am., St. Louis, 1968; dep. juvenile officer St. Louis County Juvenile Ct., Clayton, Mo., 1969-72; program dir. St. Louis County Detention Center, Clayton, 1972—; asst. supt. St. Louis County Detention Center, Clayton, 1978—; trainer statewide detention staffs; past pres. Historygram, Inc. Recipient Outstanding Detention Program award Nat. Council Juvenile and Family Ct. Judges, 1982. Mem. St. Louis County Juvenile Justice Assn., Am. Corrections Assn., Mo. Juvenile Justice Assn., Am. Mgmt. Assn.

Home: 15333 Appalachian Trl Chesterfield MO 63017-1939 Office: 501 S Brentwood Blvd Clayton MO 63105-2522

ROSS, EDWARD, cardiologist; b. Fairfield, Ala., Oct. 10, 1937; s. Horace and Carrie Lee (Griggs) R.; BS, Clark Coll., 1959; MD, Ind. U., 1963; m. Catherine I. Webster, Jan. 19, 1974; children: Edward, Ronald, Cheryl, Anthony. Intern, Marion County Gen. Hosp., Indpls., 1963; resident in internal medicine Ind. U., 1964-66, 68, cardiology rsch. fellowship, 1968-70, clin. asst. prof. medicine, 1970; cardiologist Capitol Med. Assn., Indpls., 1970-74; pvt. practice medicine, specializing in cardiology, Indpls., 1974—; staff cardiologist Winona Meml. Hosp., Indpls.; staff Meth. Hosp., Indpls., chmn. cardiovascular sect., 1989-96; Chmn., Cardiovcascular sect., dir. cardiovascular ctr. Meth. Hosp., 1990-92; bd. dirs. Meth. Hosp. Heart-Lung Ctr., 1990—, med. dir. cardiovascular svcs., 1991—. Mem. Cen. Ind. Health Planning Coun., 1972-73; bd. dir. Ind. chpt. Am. Heart Assn., 1973-74, multiphasic screening East Side Clinic, Flanner House of Indpls., 1968-71; med. dir. Nat. Ctr. for Health Service Rsch. and Devel., HEW, 1970; consumer rep. radiologic device panel health, FDA, 1988-92; dir. hyptertensive screening State of Ind., 1974; J.B. Johnson Cardiovascular lectr. Nat. Med. Assn., 1991. Assoc. editor Angiology, Jour. Vascular Disease. Capt., MC, USAF, 1966-68. Woodrow Wilson fellow, 1959; Nat. Found. Health scholar, 1955, Gorgas Found. scholar, 1955. Diplomate Am. Bd. Internal Medicine. Fellow Royal Soc. Promotion of Health (Eng.), Am. Coll. Angiology (v.p. fgn. affairs, sec. 1993—), Internat. Coll. of Angiology, Am. Coll. Cardiology, Assn. Black Cardiologists (mem. bd. dirs. 1990-94); mem. AMA, Am. Soc. Contemporary Medicine and Surgery, Nat. Med. Assn. (council sci. assembly 1985-89), Ind. Med. Soc., Marion County Med. Soc., Am. Soc. Internal Medicine, Am. Heart Assn., Ind. Soc. Internal Medicine (pres. 1987-89), Ind. State Med. Assn. (chmn. internal medicine sect. 1987-89), Aesculapean Med. Soc., Hoosier State Med. Assn. (pres. 1980-85, 90—), NAACP, Urban League, Ind. Med. Soc., Alpha Omega Alpha, Alpha Kappa Mu, Beta Kappa Chi, Omega Psi Phi. Baptist. Sr. editor Jour. Vascular Medicine, 1983—. Office: 3737 N Meridian St Ste 400 Indianapolis IN 46208-4348

ROSS, EDWARD JOSEPH, architect; b. Everett, Mass., Dec. 13, 1934; s. Miriam R.; m. Gail Tishler, Feb. 2, 1963; children: Linda Joy, Melissa Carol. Student Boston Archtl. Ctr., 1952-55, 61-62, USAF Surveying Sch., 1955-56, Boston Soc. Civil Engrs., 1956-57, Carl Bolivar Structural Engring., 1962-63. Registered architect, Mass., Calif., N.Y., Fla., N.H., Vt.; cert. Nat. Coun. Archtl. Registration Bds.; lic. constrn. supr., Mass.; expert witness constrn. law. Draftsman, assoc. William W. Drummey, Architect, Boston, 1952-59; job capt., designer Drummey-Rosane-Anderson, Boston, 1959-64; projects architect Maginnis & Walsh & Kennedy, Boston, 1964-69; v.p. William Nelson Jacobs Assocs., Inc., Boston, 1969-73; staff architect, Robert Charles Assocs., Inc., Architects, Boston, 1973-74; office mgr. Charles F. Jacobs Assocs., Inc., Cambridge, Mass., 1974-76; cons. architect Linenthal, Eisenberg & Anderson, Boston, 1976-77; staff architect Eisenberg Haven Assocs., Inc., Boston, 1977-78; chief architect, chief inspector Boston Housing Authority, 1978-83; prin. Edward J. Ross, AIA/FARA, Randolph, Mass., 1983-84; architect, sr. assoc., dir. constrn. administrn., Stull and Lee, Inc., Boston, 1984-91; practice architecture, Randolph and Stoughton, 1963—; mem. fed. comm. commn. Tech Plus. Bd. dirs. Linderhof Property Owners Assn. Mem. N.Y. Soc. Security Analysis, Assn. Investment Mgmt. and Rsch., Ancient and Honorable Arty. Co. of Mass. Staff sgt. USAF; capt. Mass. Mil. Res. Fellow Soc. Am. Registered Architects; mem. Am. Assn. Retired Persons, Am. Arbitration Assn. (mem. nat. panel 1965—), AIA, Boston Soc. Architects (housing com. 1982-86), Mass. State Assn. Architects, Constrn. Specifications Inst., Air Force Assn. (pres. Boston chpt.), Mass. Air Nat. Guard Historical Assn., Assn. First Corps Cadets, Jewish War Vets. U.S.A. (capt.), Ten of Us Club, Linderhof Golf Course Site One Assn. (pres. 1980-86), Elks, Knights of Pythias, Am. Legion. Home and Office: 10 Patricia Dr Stoughton MA 02072-1223

ROSS, E(DWIN) CLARKE, association executive, educator; b. Balt., Sept. 21, 1948; s. Harry Edwin and Margaret Frances (Turner) R.; m. Elizabeth Christine Shannon, Mar. 26, 1988; 1 child, Andrew Clarke. BA, U. Md., 1970, MA, 1974; D of Pub. Adminstrn., George Washington U., 1981. Vol. VISTA, Washington, 1970-71; legis. asst. Nat. Assn. State Mental Health Program Dirs., Washington, 1971-72; from asst. dir. to dir. Govt. Rels. United Cerebral Palsy Assns., Washington, 1972-84; asst. prof. European region Troy State U., Weisbaden, Germany, 1984-86; asst. exec. dir. for fed. rels. Nat. Assn. State Mental Health Dirs., Washington, 1986-93, dep. exec. dir., 1993-95; exec. dir. Am. Managed Behavior Healthcare Assn., Washington, 1995—; adj. grad. faculty, Cen. Mich. U., Washington, 1983-84, 87-93; adj. assoc. prof. U. Md., College Park, 1992—. Contbr. articles to profl. jours. and chpts. to books; author: Endurance as a Virtue: Army of Northern Virginia Civil War Experiences. Vol. Com. for Legal Svcs., Washington, 1970-71; mem. U.S. Olympic Com. on Winter Sports for Disabled, Colo. Springs, Colo., 1983-84; mem. program com. Dem. Club, Annapolis, Md., 1984. Recipient Maternal and Child Health scholarship to Johns Hopkins U., State of Md., 1975. Mem. SAR, Am. Soc. Pub. Adminstrn., Am. Polit. Sci. Assn., St. Andrew's Soc., Sons of Confederate Vets, Sovereign Mil. Order of Temple of Jerusalem, Beta Gamma Sigma (life). Presbyterian. Avocations: Scottish country dancing, skiing, Scottish and U.S. history. Home and Office: 1718 Reynolds St Crofton MD 21114-2635

ROSS, EDWIN WILLIAM, rubber company executive; b. Phila., May 28, 1938; s. Edwin Morrison and Frances Louise (Ort) R.; m. Dorothy Anne Reilly, Sept. 24, 1966; children: E. William Jr., Catherine Anne, James David. BSBA, Lehigh U., 1960. Chmn. bd., CEO, Key Chems., Inc., Phila., 1965-87, Ross Enterprises, Inc., Villanova, Pa., 1987—; pres., CEO Pelmor Labs., Inc., Newtown, Pa., 1989—; mem. adv. bd. First Sterling Bank, Devon, Pa., 1995—. Deacon Bryn Mawr (Pa.) Presbyn. Ch., 1977-81, elder, 1985-91, trustee, 1997—. Recipient Alumni award Lehigh U., 1985. Mem. MidAtlantic Employers Assn. (chmn. 1995-96), Metal Finishing Suppliers Assn. (pres. 1986-88, 89-90, Munning award 1992), N.E. Phila. C. of C. (chmn. 1983), Lehigh U. Alumni Assn. (bd. dirs. 1997—), Exch. Club (pres. Frankford-Phila. 1972), Phila. Country Club (pres. 1986-89). Republican. Avocations: downhill skiing, hunting, travel, golf. Home: 1514 Willowbrook Ln Villanova PA 19085-1912 Office: Pelmor Labs Inc 401 Lafayette St Newtown PA 18940-2151

ROSS, ELINOR, soprano; b. Tampa, Fla., Aug. 1, 1932; d. Joe D. and Lillian Rosenthal; m. Aaron M. Diamond; 1 son, Ross. Student, Syracuse U. Debuts include: Turandot, Met. Opera, N.Y.C., Il Trovatore, Cin. Opera, Cavalleria Rusticana, La Scala, Milan, Tosca, Bolshoi, Moscow; leading soprano roles with, Met. Opera, LaScala, Bolshoi, Chgo. Lyric Opera, San Francisco Opera, Tulsa Opera, Cin. Opera, Staatsoper, Vienna, LaFenice, Venice, Teatro Colon, Buenes Aires, Argentina, Arena de Verona, Massimo de Palermo; inaugurated Rossini Festival in Pesaro; televised concert tour in Peoples Republic of China, Taiwan; appeared in concerts, opera, symphony in Hong Kong, Japan, Thailand, Korea; appeared with symphony orchs. throughout world. Recipient medal of honor Novosibiresk, Siberia. Jewish.

ROSS, ERIC ALAN, civil engineer; b. Mineola, N.Y., Sept. 11, 1961; s. Howard Edward and Marjorie Jean (Sheldon) R.; m. Lauren Elizabeth O'Connell, May 31, 1986. BA in Math., Hope Coll., 1983; BE, Hofstra U., 1985. Registered profl. engr., Mich. Asst. civil engr. N.Y.C. Dept. Environ. Protection, 1985-86; project mgr., estimator Angelo Iafrate Constrn., Warren, Mich., 1986-90, purchasing agt., 1990-91; civil engr. McNeely & Lincoln Assocs., Inc., Northville, Mich., 1991—. Vol. ARC, Oakland, Mich., 1988—; rep. Northfield Hills Homeowners Assn., Troy, Mich., 1988—, Coun. Troy Homeowners Assn. Mem. ASCE, Nat. Soc. Profl. Engrs., Mich. Soc. Planning Ofcls. Republican. Methodist. Home: 1860 Fordham Dr Troy MI 48098-2542

ROSS, EUNICE LATSHAW, judge; b. Bellevue, Pa., Oct. 13, 1923; d. Richard Kelly and Eunice (Weidner) Latshaw; m. John Anthony Ross, May 29, 1943 (dec. Jan. 1978); 1 child, Geraldine Ross Coleman. BS, U. Pitts., 1945, LLB, 1951. Bar: Pa. 1952. Atty., Pub. Health Law Research Project, Pitts., 1951-52; atty. jud. asst., law clk. Ct. Common Pleas, Pitts., 1952-70; adjunct law prof. U. Pitts., 1967-73; dir. family div. Ct. Common Pleas, Pitts., 1970-72; judge Ct. Common Pleas of Allegheny County, Pitts., 1972-96, Commonwealth Ct. of Pa., 1997—; mem. Bd. Jud. Inquiry and Rev., Commonwealth of Pa., 1984-89, Gov's Justice Commn., 1972-78. Author: (with others) Survey of Pa. Public Health Laws, 1952. Author: Justice, 1995; co-author: Will Contests, 1992; contbr. articles to legal publs. Com. person for 14th ward, vice chmn. Democratic Com., Pitts., 1972; exec. com. bd. trustees U. Pitts., 1980-86, bd. visitors law sch., 1985—, bd. visitors sch. health, 1986—; adv. bd. Animal Friends, Pitts., 1973—; bd. mem. The Program, Pitts., 1983-87, Pitts. History and Landmarks FDTN., West Pa. Hist. Soc., West Pa. Conservancy. Recipient Disting. Amumna award U. Pitts., 1973, Medal of Recognition, 1987, Susan B. Anthony award Womens' Bar Assn. Western Pa., 1993, Probate and Trusts award, 1994; named Girl Scout Woman of Yr., Pitts. coun. Girl Scouts U.S., 1975; cert. of Achievement Pa. Fedn. Women's Clubs, 1975, 77. Mem. Scribes, Allegheny County Bar Assn. (vice chmn., exec. com. young lawyers sect. 1956-59), Pa. State Trial Judges Conf., Order of Coif. Home: 1204 Denniston Ave Pittsburgh PA 15217-1329 Office: Frick Bldg 3d Fl 437 Grant St Pittsburgh PA 15219

ROSS, FRED MICHAEL, organic chemist; b. N.Y.C., Aug. 26, 1921; s. Albert N. and Shirley (Honig) R.; m. Nee Kilar, May 9, 1954; children: Robin, Bonnie, Richard. BS, Mich. Tech. U., 1943. Sr. gas analyst Pure Oil Co., Chgo., 1943-44; chief chem. engr. Multiplate Glass Corp., Jamaica, N.Y., 1945-51; founder, CEO Diamond Dust Co., Inc., Mineola, N.Y., 1952-80; chmn. bd. dirs. Portfolio Mgmt., Inc., Rochester, N.Y., 1976-80; founder, pres. Gemery Corp., Mineola, 1974-80; CEO, chmn. Robonard, Inc., Boca Raton, Fla., 1980—. Contbr. over 40 articles to profl. publs. Campaign co-chmn. for R. Shaw for Ariz. Ho. of Reps, 1994. Officer USN, 1944-45. Recipient Bd. of Control Silver medal for Outstanding Alumnus Mich. Tech. U., 1978. Fellow Am. Inst. Chemists. Achievements include development of process for manufacture of ovate diamonds for use in petroleum bits and geological core drills, process for reclamation and recovery of industrial diamond bearing waste materials. Office: Robonard Inc 10325 Crosswind Rd Boca Raton FL 33498-4757

ROSS, GEORGE MARTIN, investment banker; b. Phila., July 24, 1933; s. David L. and Beatrice (Rittenberg) Rosenkoff; m. Lyn Merry Goldberg, Nov. 26, 1959; children: Merry Beth, Michael John. BS, Drexel U., 1955. Mgmt. trainee Sears, Roebuck & Co., Phila., 1955-58; assoc. Goldman, Sachs & Co., Phila., 1959-68, v.p., 1968-70, gen. ptnr., 1971-90, ltd. ptnr., 1991—. Mem. Mayor's Cultural Adv. Coun., Phila., 1987-91, campaign steering com. Bus. Leadership Organized for Cath. Schs., 1983-89; campaign policy com. United Way Southeastern Pa., 1983-84, We the People 200 com., 1984-86, Gov.'s Pvt. Sector Initiatives Task Force, 1983-84, Gov.'s Commn. on Financing Higher Edn., 1983-84, Wills Eye Hosp. Adv. Coun., 1979-81, nat. bd. govs., exec. com., past pres., bd. dirs., past chmn. Phila chpt. Am. Jewish Com.; v.p., exec. com. Jewish Fedn. Greater Phila.; gov. Phila. Stock Exch., 1981-85; trustee Episcopal Acad., 1981-84; chmn. bd. trusts, mem. exec. com. Drexel U,. Phila., 1981—; bd. dirs. Ave. of the Arts, 1994—, Phila. Orch. Assn. and Acad. Music Phila., 1985-91, Cystic Fibrosis Found., 1978-83, Nat. Found. Jewish Culture, 1986-91; mem. nat. bd., Phila. co-chmn. One to One; mem. investment com. U.S. Holocaust Mus.; mem. Gov. Sports & Exposition Facilities Task Force, 1996. Mem. Urban Affairs Partnership (bd. dirs. 1978-83), Greater Phila. C. of C. (mem. exec. com. 1989—), Bond Club Phila., Sunday Breakfast Club (Phila.), Locust Club, Phila. Club. Home: 1116 Barberry Rd Bryn Mawr PA 19010-1908 Office: Goldman Sachs & Co Mellon Bank Ctr Fl 26 Philadelphia PA 19103

ROSS, GEORGE WILLIAM, social scientist, educator; b. Cambridge, Mass., Aug. 18, 1940; s. Donald Reynolds and Mabel (Cumming) R.; m. Anne Gillain, Aug. 12, 1964 (div. 1967); m. Jane Jenson, Jan. 18, 1978; 1 child, Bridget Jenson. AB, Williams Coll., 1962; MSc in Econs., London Sch. Econs., 1964; PhD, Harvard U., 1972. Asst. prof. dept. sociology Brandeis U., Waltham, Mass., 1971-76, assoc. prof., 1976-82, prof. sociology, 1982—, Morris Hillquit prof. in labor and social thought, 1986—, chmn. dept. sociology, 1987-90; sr. assoc. Ctr. European Studies, Harvard U., Cambridge, 1983—. Author: Workers and Communists in France, 1982, (with others) Unions, Crisis and Change, 1982, The View from Inside, 1984; editor: The Mitterrand Experiment, 1987, Searching for the New France, 1991, Jacques Delors and European Integration, 1994; corp. editor Theory and Society, 1978—; co-editor French Politics and Society, 1982—. Decorated officier Ordre des Palmes Académiques (France); German Marshall Fund of U.S. fellow, 1978-79, 91-92, Fulbright fellow, 1984-85; Bellagio resident, Rockefeller Found., 1987. Mem. Am. Sociol. Assn., Am. Polit. Sci. Assn., Coun. European Studies (exec. com., chair coun.), Conf. Group French Politics and Soc. (exec. sec. 1985—). Avocations: music, hiking, skiing. Office: Brandeis Univ Dept Of Sociology Waltham MA 02154

ROSS, GERALD FRED, engineering executive, researcher; b. N.Y.C., Dec. 14, 1930; s. Samuel Henry and Jenny (Saltzman) Rozansky; m. Vivian Ida Turkish, Dec. 24, 1953; children: Jayne T. Ross Kaufman, Steven A., Helene B. Ross Joseph. BEE, CCNY, 1952; MEE, Poly. U., 1955, PhD, 1963. Registered profl. engr., N.Y., Mass. Rsch. asst. U. Mich., Ann Arbor, 1952-53; sr. engr. W.L. Maxson Corp., N.Y.C., 1954-58; rsch. sect. head Sperry Gyroscope Co., Great Neck, L.I., N.Y., 1958-65; dept. mgr. Sperry Rsch. Ctr., Sudbury, Mass., 1965-81; CEO, chmn. ANRO Engring., Inc., Sarasota, Fla., 1981—; pres., v.p., treas. Adams Pool Corp., Lexington, Mass., 1968-81. Capt. USAFR, 1953—. Contbg. author 3 books, 1986, 90, 93; contbr. numerous articles to profl. jours.; 56 patents in field. Fellow Polytechnic U. Fellow IEEE (life, K.C. Black Nerem Best paper award 1974), Nat. Acad. Engring. (life); mem. Electromagnetics Acad., Res. Officers Assn., Lexington Golf Club, Longboat Key Club, Sigma Xi (sr.), Tau Beta Pi, Eta Kappa Nu. Republican. Jewish. Avocations: golf, tennis. Office: ANRO Engring Inc 1800 2nd St Ste 878 Sarasota FL 34236-5907

ROSS, GLORIA FRANKENTHALER, tapestry artist, consultant; b. N.Y.C., Sept. 5, 1923; d. Alfred and Martha (Lowenstein) Frankenthaler; m. John J. Bookman; children: Alfred Frankenthaler Ross, Beverly Ross, Clifford Ross. BA, Mt. Holyoke Coll., 1943. Owner, operator Gloria F. Ross Tapestries, N.Y.C., 1963—; lectr. Internat. Tapestry Symposium, Australian Bicentennial, Fashion Inst. Tech., N.Y., Harvard Club, Shared Horizons, Santa Fe. Exhibited at Rutgers Barclay Gallery, Santa Fe, Feigen Gallery, Chgo., Washington and N.Y., Pace Gallery, N.Y.C., Pace Edits., N.Y., The Ringling Mus., Sarasota, Fla., Lausanne Biennale, Kauffman Gallery, Houston; represented in permanent collections at IBM, J.C. Penney Co., Tougaloo (Miss.) Coll. Art Mus., Kennedy Internat. Airport, N.Y., Bank of Tokyo, N.Y., Citibank, N.Y., Metro. Mus. Art, Denver Art Mus., Wheelwright Mus., Wustum Mus.; comms. include Westinghouse Broadcasting Co., Phila., Winters Bank, Dayton, Ohio, Fed. Courthourse, Portland, Oreg., Mazza Gallery, Washington, Congregation Emanu-El, N.Y.; collaborator tapestries with various artists, including Avery Bearden, Stuart Davis, Hofmann Motherwell, Youngerman. Chmn. Child Devel. Ctr., N.Y.C., 1960's; trustee Mt. Holyoke Coll., South Hadley, Mass., 1986—. Avocation: sports.

ROSS, GLYNN, opera administrator; b. Omaha, Dec. 15, 1914; s. Herman and Ida (Carlson) R.; m. Angelamaria Solimene, Nov. 15, 1946; children: Stephanie, Claudia, Melanie, Anthony. Student, Leland Powers Sch. Theater, Boston, 1937-39. founder O.P.E.R.A. Am.; bd. dirs. Nat. Opera Inst., Soc. for Germanic Music Culture; founder, dir. Pacific N.W. Festival, 1975—. Opera stage dir., U.S., Can., 1939-63, debut, San Francisco Opera, 1948, gen. dir., founder Seattle Opera Assn., Inc., 1963-83; dir. Ariz. Opera, 1983—; founder Pacific N.W. Ballet. Served to 1st lt. AUS, 1942-47. Office: Ariz Opera Assn 3501 N Mountain Ave Tucson AZ 85719-1925

ROSS, GUY MATTHEWS, JR., international leaf tobacco executive; b. Guilford County, N.C., May 5, 1933; s. Guy Matthews and Nancy McConnell (Coleman) R.; m. Patricia Jane Fields, Aug. 27, 1955; children: Charles Alan, Steven York. BSBA, U. N.C., Chapel Hill, 1955. With fin. mgmt. program, then supr. sales acctg. and billing, corp. audit staff, fin. analyst Gen. Electric Co., Ft. Wayne, Ind., Schenectady, Pittsfield, Mass., 1955-56, 58-66; chief acct., v.p. fin. and adminstrn. Imperial Group Ltd., Am. Leaf Orgn., Wilson, N.C., 1966-80; treas., sec. Std. Comml. Corp., Wilson, 1980-92, v.p., sec., 1992—; bd. dirs. Wachovia Bank and Trust Co., Wilson. Pres., heart fund chmn. Wilson div. N.C. Heart Assn., 1967-68; dir., exec. com. Wilson United Way; instl. rep. East Carolina council Boy Scouts Am., 1967-76, mem. adminstrv. bd. and fin. com., 1971-78; pres. Men's Fellowship Class, First United Methodist Ch., 1975-76. Served with U.S. Army, 1956-58. Mem. U. N.C. Alumni Assn. (life; mem. Ednl. Found.), Fin. Execs. Inst. (dir. N.C. chpt., pres. 1993-94), Nat. Investor Relations Inst., Kiwanis (life mem., disting. lt. gov. 1978-79). Home: 1804 Chelsea Dr NW Wilson NC 27896-1412 Office: Standard Comml Corp 2201 Miller Rd S Wilson NC 27893-6860

ROSS, HENRY RAYMOND, advertising executive and legal counsel; b. Toronto, Ont., Can., Nov. 9, 1919; S. Joseph and Mary (Rotenburg) R.; m. Ann Clarfield, Nov. 5, 1944; children: Ellen Louise, Janice Carol. Grad., Ont. Coll. Art, 1936. Pres. Ferris Theaters, Toronto, 1937-39, Ross Enterprises, Toronto, 1939-44; with F.H. Hayhurst Co. Ltd., Toronto, 1944—, sr. v.p., dir. creative svcs., 1957-73, sr. v.p., dir. industry, govt. and corp. affairs, 1973-79; dir., pres. Contemporary Paintings, Toronto, 1969—; sr. ptnr. H.M.S. Investments, Toronto, 1975—; pres. Henry R. Ross Cons. Inc., Toronto, 1979—; chmn. broadcast com. Assn. Can. Advertisers, Toronto, 1970—; chmn. talent negotiation com., bd. dirs. Can. Advt. Rsch. Found.; trustee Am. Fedn. Musicians; resource advisor Fed. and Provincial Govts. in devel. advt. bus. practices laws. Contbr. articles to jours. in field. Served with Can. Armed Forces, 1943-44. Fellow Inst. Can. Advt. (chmn. broadcast com. 1970—); mem. Art Dirs. Club Toronto, Broadcast Execs. Soc., Donalda Country Club. Home: 127 Munro Blvd, Willowdale, ON Canada M2P 1C7 Office: 55 Eglinton Ave E, Toronto, ON Canada M4P 1G9 *If only we would realize that we are indeed the masters of our own life's accomplishments. And so every deed and thought must be considered in that light, long before life passes us by.*

ROSS, HERBERT DAVID, film director; b. Bklyn., May 13, 1927; m. Nora Kaye, Aug. 21, 1959 (dec. 1987); m. Lee Radziwill, Sept., 1988. Dir. motion pictures Goodbye Mr. Chips, 1969, The Owl and The Pussycat, 1970, T. R. Baskin, 1971, Play It Again Sam, 1972, The Last of Sheila, 1973, Funny Lady, 1975, The Sunshine Boys, 1975, The Seven Percent Solution, 1976, The Goodbye Girl, 1977, The Turning Point, 1977, California Suite, 1978, Nijinsky, 1980, Pennies From Heaven, 1981, I Ought To Be in Pictures, 1982, Max Dugan Returns, 1983, Footloose, 1984, Protocol, 1984, The Secret of My Success, 1987, Dancers, 1987, Steel Magnolias, 1988, Undercover Blues, 1993; dir., producer: My Blue Heaven, 1989, True Colors, 1990, Boys On The Side, 1995; exec. prodr. Soapdish, 1991, choreographer: Spoleto (Italy) Festival, Berlin (Germany) Festival; active in numerous Broadway prodns., including Anyone Can Whistle; dir.: Broadway Chpt. Two, I Ought to Be in Pictures, 1980; opera dir. La Boheme, L.A. Music Ctr., 1993; recipient Golden Globe award 1978, award of distinction Dance mag. 1980. Office: Int'l Creative Mgmt 8942 Wilshire Blvd Beverly Hills CA 90211-1934*

ROSS, HUGH COURTNEY, electrical engineer; b. Dec. 31, 1923; s. Clare W. and Jeanne F. Ross; m. Sarah A. Gordon (dec.); m. Patricia A. Malloy; children: John C., James G., Robert W. Student, Calif. Inst. Tech., 1942, San Jose State U., 1946-47; BSEE, Stanford U., 1950, postgrad., 1954. Registered profl. elec. engr., Calif. Instr. San Benito (Calif.) High Sch. and Jr. Coll., 1950-51; chief engr. vacuum power switches Jennings Radio Mfg. Corp., San Jose, Calif., 1951-62; chief engr. ITT Jennings, San Jose, Calif., 1962-64; pres. Ross Engring. Corp., Campbell, Calif., 1964—. Contbr. articles to tech. jours.; patentee in field. Fellow IEEE (life) (chmn. Santa Clara Valley subsect. 1960-61); mem. Am. Vacuum Soc., Am. Soc. Metals. Avocations: electronics, electric autos, camping, ranching, solar power. Office: 540 Westchester Dr Campbell CA 95008-5012

ROSS, IAN MUNRO, electrical engineer; b. Southport, Eng., Aug. 15, 1927; came to U.S., 1952, naturalized, 1960; m. Christina Leinberg Ross, Aug. 24, 1955; children: Timothy Ian, Nancy Lynn, Stina Marguerite. BA, Gonville and Caius Coll., Cambridge U., 1948; MA in Elec. Engring, Cambridge U., 1952, PhD, 1952; DSc (hon.), N.J. Inst. Tech., 1983, Poly. U., 1988; D of Engring. (hon.), Stevens Inst. Tech., 1983; DSc (hon.), Polytech. U., 1988. With AT&T Bell Labs. (and affiliates), 1952-92, exec. dir. network planning div., 1971-73, v.p. network planning and customer svcs., 1973-76; exec. v.p. systems engring. and devel. AT&T Bell Labs. (and affiliates), Holmdel, N.J., 1976-79, pres., 1979-91; pres. emeritus Lucent Technologies (formerly AT&T Bell Labs.), Holmdel, 1991—; dir. Thomas & Betts Corp., B.F. Goodrich Co.; chmn. Nat. Adv. Commn. on Semicondrs. Patentee in field. Recipient NASA Pub. Svc. award, 1969, 75, medal Ind. Rsch. Inst., 1987. Fellow IEEE (Founders' medal 1988, Am. Acad. Arts and Scis.; mem. NAS, NAE, Nat. Sci. Bd. Home: 5 Blackpoint Horseshoe Rumson NJ 07760-1500 Office: Lucent Technologies 101 Crawfords Corner Rd Holmdel NJ 07733-1900

ROSS, JAMES BARRETT, finance and insurance educator; b. Cleve., Apr. 25, 1930; s. James Barrett and Marjorie (Stutsman) R.; m. Ann Penney, July 1, 1950; children: James, Scott, Alison, Andrea, Alan, Dana, Ann Elizabeth, Brandon, Mary Ellen, Marjorie, Wendy. AB cum laude, Harvard Coll., 1951; MBA, U. R.I., 1988; PhD, U. Conn., 1992. CLU; CPCU; ChFC. With Conn. Gen. Life Ins. Co., 1951-62; pres., dir. Puritan Life Ins. Co., Providence, 1962-68; exec. v.p. mktg. Keystone Custodian Funds Inc., Boston, 1968-73; sr. v.p. Met. Life Ins. Co., N.Y.C., 1973-80; chmn., chief exec. officer INA Internat., 1980-83; sr. exec. v.p. Ins. Co. N.Am., 1980-83; pres. Continental Vision Fin. Svcs., 1983-86; vice chmn. Andersen & Walsh, 1986-91; assoc. prof. fin. and ins. Radford (Va.) U., 1992—. Fellow Soc. Actuaries, Life Mgmt. Inst.; mem. Am. Acad. Actuaries, Fin. Mgmt. Assn., Ea. Fin. Assn., Midwestern Fin. Assn., So. Fin. Assn., Southwestern Fin. Assn., Acad. Fin. Svcs., Am. Risk and Ins. Assn., So. Risk and Ins. Assn., Beta Gamma Sigma, Phi Kappa Phi. Congregationalist. Home: 1103 Scott Alan Cir Blacksburg VA 24060

ROSS, JAMES ELMER, economist, administrator; b. Danville, Ill., Jan. 15, 1931; s. Carl Henry and Lura Jane (Witherspoon) R.; m. Barbara Lou Becker, Dec. 24, 1958 (dec. Aug. 1982); 1 child, Candis Anne; m. Erin Elizabeth O'Shea, June 20, 1986. BS, U. Ill., 1953, MS, 1959, PhD, 1966. Agrl. counselor Am. Embassy, Caracas, Venezuela, 1976-78, Cairo, Egypt, 1978-81; asst. adminstr. Fgn. Agrl. Svc., Washington, 1981-83; mem. Sr. Exec. Seminar, Dept. State, 1983-84; alt. permanent rep. U.S. Mission to UN Agys., Rome, 1984-87; agrl. counselor U.S. Embassy, Seoul, Republic of Korea, 1987-88; dir. trade assistance and planning office Fgn. Agrl. Svc., Washington, 1988-92; courtesy prof. U. Fla., 1992—; v.p. J.E. Ross & Associates., Inc., 1993—; cons. Govt. of Ecuador, 1971-72; mem. internat. programs U. Fla., Costa Rica, 1966-69, Ghana, 1969-70; assoc. dir., 1970-72; asst. dean Fla. Coop. Extension Svc., 1972-75; spl. asst. to undersecretary USDA, 1975-76. Author: Cooperative Rural Electrification, 1972; co-author: Rural Electrification and Development, 1978. Col. USAR, ret. Mem. Internat. Assn. Agrl. Economists, Am. Agrl. Econs. Assn., Assn. for International Agriculture and Rural Devel., Assn. for the Study of the Cuban Economy, Internat. Agrl. Trade Rsch. Consortium, Internat. Agribus. Mgmt. Assn., Masons. Republican. Home: 206 Sunnyside Dr Hawthorne FL 32640-8116

ROSS, JAMES NEIL, JR., veterinary educator; b. Akron, Ohio, Dec. 18, 1940; s. James Neil and Ruth Evelyn (Gray) R.; m. Marcia Day Collins, June 27, 1964; children: Stephanie, Amy, Lisa. DVM, Ohio State U., 1965, MSc, 1967; PhD, Baylor Coll. Medicine, 1972. Diplomate in cardiology and internal medicine Am. Coll. Vet. Internal Medicine; diplomate Am. Coll. Vet. Emergency and Critical Care. Lectr., cardiologist Ohio State U. Vet. Sch., Columbus, 1965-67; asst. prof. surgery and physiology Baylor Coll. Medicine, Houston, 1967-74; assoc. prof. physiology Med. Coll. Ohio, Toledo, 1974-80; prof. and chmn. dept. medicine Tufts U. Sch. Vet. Medicine, North Grafton, Mass., 1981—; cons. Proctor & Gamble, Cin., 1976-84; mem. scientist rev. bds. of various jours. including Jour. of Investigative Surgery, Am. Jour. Vet. Rsch. 1983-86. Contbr. chpts. to books, articles to profl. jours. Named Veterninarian of the Yr. Animal Sci. Assn., 1972; grantee NIH, 1965-67; fellow NIH, 1969-71. Mem. AVMA (coun. on edn. 1989-95), Am. Bd. vet. spltys.), Am. Coll. Vet. Internat Medicine, Am. Heart Assn., Am. Animal Hosp. Assn., Vet. Emergency and Critical Care Soc. (pres. 1991-92), Phi Eta Sigma, Gamma Sigma Delta, Am. Coll. Vet. Emergency and Critical Care (treas. 1989—, exec. sec. 1993—), Omega Tau Sigma, Phi Gamma Delta. Methodist. Achievements include research in cardiovascular disease in animals; assisted circulation. Office: Tufts U Sch Vet Medicine 200 Westboro Rd North Grafton MA 01536-1828

ROSS, JAMES ULRIC, lawyer, accountant, educator; b. Del Rio, Tex., Sept. 14, 1941; s. Stephen Mabrey and Beatrice Jessie (Hyslop) R.; m. Janet S. Calabro, Dec. 28, 1986; children: James Ulric Jr., Ashley Meredith. BA, U. Tex., 1963, JD, 1965. Bar: Tex. 1965, U.S. Tax Ct. 1969; CPA, Tex.

Estate tax examiner IRS, Houston, 1965-66; tax acct. Holmes, Raquet, Harris & Shaw, San Antonio, 1966-67; pvt. practice law and acctg., Del Rio and San Antonio, 1968—; instr. St. Mary's U., San Antonio, 1973-75; assoc. prof. U. Tex., San Antonio, 1975—. Active Am. Cancer Soc., Residential Mgmt., Inc., Am. Heart Assn. Mem. ABA, Tex. Bar Assn., Tex. Soc. CPAs, San Antonio Bar Assn., San Antonio Estate Planners Coun. Contbr. articles on U.S. and Internat. Estate Planning and Taxation to legal and profl. jours. Home: 3047 Orchard Hl San Antonio TX 78230-3078 Office: 760 Tex Commerce Bank Bldg 7550 IH 10 W San Antonio TX 78229

ROSS, JEAN LOUISE, physical education educator; b. Lebanon, Pa., June 20, 1951; d. Jonas John and Eloise Mary (Miller) Walmer; m. Edward Richard Ross, Nov. 10, 1978; 1 child, Aaron Edward. BS in Health and Phys. Edn., West Chester U., 1973; MS in Phys. Edn., Pa. State U., 1979; MSEd in Counseling Psychology, St. Bonaventure U., 1992. Health and phys. edn. tchr. Lower Dauphin Sch. dist., Hummelstown, Pa., 1973-78; health and phys. edn. tchr., mentor tchr. Bradford Area Sch. Dist., Pa., 1978-80; health and phys. edn. tchr. Bradford Area Sch. Dist., 1986—; in-home edn. specialist SCAN/PEP Program, The Guidance Ctr., Bradford, 1985-86. Recipient mini-grants Rotary Club of Bradford, 1984, 86-88, 93, 95. Mem. NEA, AAHPERD, Pa. State Edn. Assn., Bradford Area Edn. Assn., Pa. State Alliance Health, Phys. Edn., Recreation and Dance. Democrat. Avocations: recreational activities, sewing, knitting. Office: Fretz Middle Sch 140 Lorana Ave Bradford PA 16701-1831

ROSS, JEFFREY ALAN, research biologist; b. Thayer, Mo., Oct. 19, 1955; s. Ralph and Naomi June (Jacobs) R.; m. Lisa Lynn Pnazek, Apr. 23, 1977; children: Trillian Elise, Jennifer Ariane, Marissa Kerowyn. BS, U. Dallas, 1977; PhD, U. Tex., Dallas, 1982. Predoctoral fellow Robert A. Welch Found., 1979-82; postdoctoral fellow Cancer Ctr. Rsch. div. U. Tex., Smithville, 1982-85; NRC fellow U.S. EPA, Research Triangle Park, N.C., 1985-86, rsch. biologist, 1986—. Contbr. articles to profl. jours. Bd. dirs. 1st Environments Early Learning Ctr., Research Triangle Park, 1989-90, 94-96, 94-96. John B. O'Hara Found. fellow, 1973-76. Mem. AAAS, Am. Assn. Cancer Rsch., N.Y. Acad. Scis., Genotoxicity and Environ. Mutagen Soc. (bd. dirs. 1991-94). Achievements include research on the formation, repair, and biological consequences of carcinogen DNA adducts. Office: US EPA MD-68 Research Triangle Park NC 27711

ROSS, JEFFREY ALLAN, political scientist, organization executive, educator; b. N.Y.C., Dec. 24, 1947; s. Joseph and Pearl (Epstein) R.; B.A. in Polit. Sci. summa cum laude with high honors, SUNY, Binghamton, 1969; Ph.D. in Polit. Sci. (Ford Found. fellow, Ford Found. grantee), U. Minn., 1982; m. Marjorie Appelson, Aug. 30, 1970; children—Craig, Eric, Brian, Allison. N.Y. State Regents' fellow, teaching asst. U. Minn., Mpls., 1969-71, research asst., 1971-73, instr., 1973; instr. Kirkland Coll., Clinton, N.Y., 1973-78, Huber Found. faculty research grantee, 1973, 74, 77, Mellon Found. grantee, 1974, research prof., 1975-76; instr. govt. Hamilton Coll., Clinton, 1978-80, asst. prof., 1980-82; vis. prof. polit. sci. Syracuse U., 1984; adj. prof. polit. sci. Queens Coll., CUNY, 1987-88; dir. campus affairs dept. Anti-Defamation League of B'nai B'rith, 1984—; v.p., bd. dirs. Research Ctr. for Religion and Human Rights in Closed Socs.; exec. bd. Com. for Pub. Higher Edn.; chmn., mem. various profl. panels; Mpls. Found., Frances E. Andrews Fund All-Univ. research fellow, surveyer Soviet Jewish emigrants, Israel, 1972. Precinct rep. Democratic Farm Labor Party, Mpls., 1972-73. Mem. Am. Polit. Sci. Assn., N.E. Polit. Sci. Assn. (exec. council), Internat. Polit. Sci. Assn., Internat. Studies Assn., Mongolia Soc., Can.-Mongolia Soc., Comparative Interdisciplinary Studies Soc. (exec. coun.), N.Y. State Polit. Sci. Assn. (v.p. 1982-83, pres. 1983-84), Sound Cyclists Bicycle Club (v.p. 1989-90, 94, pres. 1991-93), Norwalk Ski Club (v.p. 1992-93). Democrat. Author: (with Ann Cottrell) The Mobilization of Collective Indentity: Comparative Perspectives, 1980, Pamyat: Hatred Under Glasnost, 1989; contbr. articles to profl. jours.; mem. editorial bd. Teaching Polit. Sci., 1971-81; editor Hamilton Social Sci. Rev., 1977-79; reviewer manuscripts for profl. jours., book pubs. Home: 20 Soundview Loop South Salem NY 10590 Office: Anti-Defamation League 823 United Nations Plz New York NY 10017-3518 *A satisfying life must be multidimensional. One's community, family and recreation have a necessary place alongside one's career. A fully realized person becomes also a fully realized professional.*

ROSS, JIMMY DOUGLAS, army officer; b. Hosston, La., May 23, 1936; s. Horace Eugene and Lucile Marie (Pontious) R.; m. Patricia L. Cox., Dec. 18, 1955; children: Sabra, DiAnna, Tony. B.S., Henderson State U., 1958; M.A. in Bus. Mgmt., Central Mich. U., 1975. Commd. 2d lt. U.S. Army, 1958, advanced through grades to 4 Star Gen., 1994, served comdr. co., bn., brigade levels; comdg. gen. 2d Support Command (Corps) VII Corps U.S. Army, Nellingen, W. Ger., 1980-82; dir. transp., energy and troop support Office Dep. Chief of Staff for Logistics, U.S. Army, Washington, 1982-84; chief staff U.S. Army Materiel Command, Alexandria, Va., 1984-86; comdr. U.S. Army Depot System Command, Chambersburg, Pa., 1986-87; dep. chief of staff for logistics U.S. Army, Washington, 1987-92; commdg. gen. U.S. Army Materiel Command, Alexandria, Va., 1992-94; retired, 1994; bd. dirs. VSE Engring. Co.; chmn. Def. Industry Conf. Bd.; pres. bd. dirs. Indsl. Coll. of Armed Forces Assn. Dist. commr. Alpine dist. Boy Scouts Am., 1980-82; sr. v.p. Biomed. Svcs., ARC Nat. Hdqrs., 1994-97; chmn. Army Sci. Bd. Decorated D.S.M. with oak leaf cluster, Legion of Merit, Bronze Star, Air medal. Fellow Assn. U.S. Army (sr.); mem. Am. Def. Preparedness Assn., Nat. Def. Transp. Assn., Armed Forces Benefit Assn. (bd. dirs.). Methodist. Home: 9208 Cross Oaks Ct Fairfax Station VA 22039-3337

ROSS, JOHN, physical chemist, educator; b. Vienna, Austria, Oct. 2, 1926; came to U.S., 1940; s. Mark and Anna (Krecmar) R.; m. Virginia Franklin (div.); children: Elizabeth A., Robert K.; m. Eva Madarasz. BS, Queens Coll., 1948; PhD, MIT, 1951; D (hon.), Weizmann Inst. Sci., Rehovot, Israel, 1984, Queens Coll., SUNY, 1987, U. Bordeaux, France, 1987. Prof. chemistry Brown U., Providence, 1953-66; prof. chemistry MIT, Cambridge, 1966-80, chmn. dept., 1966-71; chmn. faculty of Inst. MIT, 1975-77; prof. Stanford (Calif.) U., 1980—, chmn. dept., 1983-89; cons. to industries, 1979—; mem. bd. govs. Weizmann Inst., 1971—. Author: Physical Chemistry, 1980; editor Molecular Beams, 1966; contbr. articles to profl. jours. 2nd lt. U.S. Army, 1944-46. Recipient medal Coll. de France, Paris. Fellow AAAS, Am. Phys. Soc.; mem. NAS, Am. Acad. Arts and Scis., Am. Chem. Soc. (Irving Langmuir Chem. Physics prize 1992). Home: 738 Mayfield Ave Palo Alto CA 94305-1044 Office: Stanford U Dept Chemistry Stanford CA 94305-5080

ROSS, JOHN, cultural organization administrator; b. Tahlequah, Okla., Feb. 16, 1955; s. John and Nancy (Augerhole) R.; m. Anita Faye Franklin, Jan. 1, 1976; children: Anthony John, Adam John. Student, U. Ark., 1976; degree, Nutrition and Diatetics Tng. Ctr., 1981; AA Health in Phys. Edn. and Recreation, Rogers State Coll., 1982; cert. in food svc. mgmt., St. Louis U., 1984; BA Social Sci., Northeastern State U., 1985. Cook Claremore Indian Hosp., Okla., 1979-86; asst. mgr. Horseshoe Bend Bingo, Sperry, Okla., 1986-87; owner/operator South Greasy Smokeshop, Stilwell, Okla., 1988; material handler Allied Signal, Tulsa, Okla., 1988-92; various elected and apptd. positions United Keetoowah Band of Cherokee Indians in Okla., 1985—, chief, 1992—. Office: United Keetoowah Cherokee Indians PO Box 746 Tahlequah OK 74465-0746

ROSS, JOHN, JR., physician, educator; b. N.Y.C., Dec. 1, 1928; s. John and Janet (Moulder) R.; children—Sydnie, John, Duncan; m. Lola Romanucci, Aug. 26, 1972; children: Adan, Deborah Lee. A.B., Dartmouth Coll., 1951; M.D., Cornell U., 1955. Intern Johns Hopkins Hosp., 1955-56; resident Columbia-Presbyn. Med. Center, N.Y.C., 1960-61, N.Y. Hosp.-Cornell U. Med. center, 1961-62; chief sect. cardiovascular diagnosis cardiology br. Nat. Heart Inst., Bethesda, Md., 1962-68; prof. medicine U. Calif., San Diego, 1968—, also dir. cardiovascular div., 1968-91; co-dir. for sci. affairs, 1991—; prof. cardiovascular research Am. Heart Assn. San Diego Co. Affiliate, San Diego, 1985—; co-dir. for scientific affairs divsn. cardiology U. Calif., San Diego, 1991—; mem. cardiology adv. com. Nat. Heart, Lung and Blood Inst., 1975-78, task force on arteriosclerosis, 1978-80, adv. council, 1980-84; bd. dirs. San Diego Heart Assn.; vis. prof. Brit. Heart Assn., 1990. Author: Mechanisms of Contraction of the Normal and Failing Heart, 1968, 76, Understanding the Heart and Its Diseases, 1976; mem. editorial bd. Circulation, 1967-75, 80-88, editor in chief 1988-93, Circulation Research, 1971-75, Am. Jour. Physiology, 1968-73, Annals of Internal Medicine, 1974-78, Am. Jour. Cardiology, 1974-79, 83-88; cons. editor Jour. Clin. Investigation, 1992—; contbr. chpts. to books, sci. articles to profl. jours. Served as surgeon USPHS, 1956-63. Recipient Ing. Enzo Ferrari prize Organizing Com. for Enzo Ferrari, Modena, Italy, 1989, James B. Herrick award Coun. Clin. Cardiology Am. Heart Assn., 1990. Fellow Am. Coll. Cardiology (v.p. trustee, pres. 1986-87, Disting. Scientist award 1990), ACP; mem. Am. Soc. Clin. Investigation (councillor), Am. Physiol. Soc., Assn. Am. Physicians, Cardiac Muscle Soc., Assn. Univ. Cardiologists, Assn. West. Physicians (councillor). Home: 8599 Prestwick Dr La Jolla CA 92037-2025 Office: Univ California Dept Med M # 013B San Diego CA 92037

ROSS, JOHN MICHAEL, editor, magazine publisher; b. Bklyn., Oct. 17, 1919; s. Albert Henry and Dorothy Veronica (Murray) R.; m. Kathleen M. Courtney; children: Donna Patricia Ross Easterbrook, Maureen Courtney Ross Fay. Student pub. schs., N.Y.C. Sports writer Bklyn. Eagle, 1937-41, The Newspaper PM, 1946-47; editor Am. Law Tennis mag., 1947-50, Macfadden Publs., 1950-51, 60-61; contbg. editor Am. Weekly, 1952-60; editor-in-chief Golf mag., 1961-67, Golf Bus. mag., 1963-65, Golfdom mag., 1965-67; v.p. Universal Pub. and Distbn. Corp., 1965-67; pres. Golf Promotions, Inc., 1967-70; pub. Golf Bus. Almanac, also Golf TV Guide, 1969; pub. relations dir. Profl. Golfers Assn. Golf Tour, 1970-71; editor-in-chief Golf mag., 1972-79, assoc. pub., 1979-84; publishing dir., v.p. The Golf Link, 1985-87; editorial dir. Am. Golf mag., 1990-94; sr. ptnr. J.M. Ross Assocs., Westport, Conn., 1994—; bd. dirs. World Golf Hall of Fame, 1974-83, mem. adv. bd. 1993—; chmn. Women's Golf Scholarship Fund, 1976-82; exec. dir. World Cup Golf Internat. Golf Assn., 1977-84. Co-author: Nothing But The Truth, 1960; editor: Encyclopedia of Golf, 1977; contbr. numerous articles to nat. publs. including Reader's Digest, Life, Sports Illustrated. Justice of peace, Newtown, Conn., 1960-64. Served with AUS, 1942-46. Recipient Christopher award for best mag. story, 1957; recipient Lincoln Werden award for golf journalism, 1991. Mem. U.S. Golf Assn. (nat. com. 1977—), Lawn Tennis Writers Assn. (sec. 1949-50), Golf Writers Assn. Am. (gov. 1966-67), Met. Golf Writers Assn. (pres. 1975-76), Assn. of Golf Writers (Great Britain), Am. Soc. Mag. Editors, Overseas Press Club (N.Y.C.), Patterson Club (Fairfield, Conn.). Roman Catholic. Home: 19 Riverfield Dr Weston CT 06883-2908 Office: J M Ross Assocs PO Box 774 Westport CT 06881-0774

ROSS, JOSEPH COMER, physician, educator, academic administrator; b. Tompkinsville, Ky., June 16, 1927; s. Joseph M. and Annie (Pinckley) R.; m. Isabelle Nevins, June 15, 1952; children: Laura Ann, Sharon Lynn, Jennifer Jo, Mary Martha, Jefferson Arthur. BS, U. Ky., 1950; MD, Vanderbilt U., 1954. Diplomate Am. Bd. Internal Medicine (bd. govs. 1975-81), with added qualifications in pulmonary disease. Intern Vanderbilt U. Hosp., Nashville, 1954-55; resident Duke U. Hosp., Durham, N.C., 1955-57, rsch. fellow, 1957-58; from instr. medicine to prof. Ind. U. Sch. Medicine, Indpls., 1958-70; prof., chmn. dept. medicine Med. U. of S.C., Charleston, 1970-80; vis. prof. Vanderbilt U. Sch. Medicine, Nashville, 1979-80, prof. medicine, 1981—, assoc. vice chancellor for health affairs, 1982—; mem. cardiovascular study sect. NIH, 1966-70, program project com., 1971-75; mem. adv. coun. Nat. Heart, Lung and Blood Inst., 1982-86; mem. ad hoc coms. NAS, 1966, 67; mem. Pres.'s Nat. Adv. Panel on Heart Disease, 1972; mem. merit rev. bd. in respiration VA Rsch. Svc., 1972-76, chmn., 1974-76. Mem. editorial bd. Jour. Lab. and Clin. Medicine, 1964-70, Chest, 1968-73, Jour. Applied Physiology,1968-73, Archives of Internal Medicine, 1976-82, Heart and Lung, 1977-86; contbr. articles to profl. jours. Bd. dirs., past pres. Nashville Ronald McDonald House; bd. dirs. Agape, Leadership Nashville; mem. adv. com. Davidson County Cmty. Health Agy.; active Tenn. Lung Assn. With U.S. Army, 1945-47. Fellow ACP, Am. Coll. Chest Physicians (gov. S.C. 1970-76, vice chmn. bd. govs. 1974-75, chmn. bd. govs. 1975-76, exec. council 1974-80, pres.-elect 1976-77, pres. 1978-79, chmn. sci. program com. 1973), Am. Coll. Cardiology; mem. AMA (sect. on med. schs.), Am. Fedn. Clin. Rsch. (chmn. Midwest sect.), Am. Physiol. Soc., Am. Soc. Clin. Investigation, Assn. Am. Physicians, Assn. Profs. Medicine, Cen. Soc. Clin. Rsch., S.C. Med. Soc., Am. Thoracic Soc. (nat. councillor 1972-76), So. Soc. Clin. Rsch., S.C. Lung Assn. (v.p. 1974-75), Am. Soc. Internal Medicine, Phi Beta Kappa, Alpha Omega Alpha. Mem. Ch. of Christ (elder). Office: Vanderbilt U 2000 Village at Vanderbilt Nashville TN 37232

ROSS, JOSEPH FOSTER, physician, educator; b. Azusa, Calif., Oct. 11, 1910; s. Verne Ralph and Isabel Mills (Bumgarner) R.; m. Eileen Sullivan, Dec. 19, 1942; children: Louisa, Elisabeth, Joseph, Jeanne, Marianne. AB with great distinction, Leland Stanford Jr. U., 1933; MD cum laude with spl. honors in Physiology, Harvard U., 1936. Diplomate Am. Bd. Internal Medicine (mem. 1973-83), Am. Bd. Nuclear Medicine (founding, sec. 1971-72, 79, chmn. 1973-77, pres., chief exec. officer 1980—). Asst. topographical anatomy Harvard U. Sch. Medicine, 1934-37, research fellow biochemistry, 1943-46; med. house officer Harvard cancer commn. Huntington Meml. Hosp., 1934-35; Palmer Meml., New Eng. Deaconess hosps., 1935-36; resident pathology Mallory Inst. Pathology, 1936-37; intern Harvard Med. Svc. Boston City Hosp., 1937-39; asst. pathology U. Rochester Sch. Medicine, 1939-40; resident pathology Strong Meml. Hosp., Rochester, N.Y., 1939-40; physician, dir. hematology and radioisotope divs. Mass. Meml. Hosp., 1940-54; instr., asst. prof., assoc. prof. medicine Boston U., 1940-54; dir. radioisotope unit Cushing VA, Boston VA hosps., 1948-54; prof. medicine UCLA, 1954—, prof. radiobiology, 1954-59, assoc. dean, 1954-58, chmn. dept. nuclear med. and radiation biology, 1958-60, dir. Lab. Nuclear Med. and Radiation Biology, 1958-65, prof., chmn. dept. biophysics and nuclear medicine, 1960-65, chief div. hematology, 1969-76; chief staff U. Calif. Hosp., Los Angeles, 1954-58; attending physician U. Calif. Hosp., 1954—, now pres.; U.S. del. Internat. Conf. Peaceful Uses Atomic Energy, Geneva, 1955; mem. U.S. Atoms for Peace mission to Latin Am., 1956, U.S. AEC Life Scis. Mission to, Greece, Turkey, 1961; mem. USA AEC sci. mission to USSR, 1966; mem. Calif. Adv. Council on Cancer, 1959-84, chmn., 1963-66, 74-77; mem. CENTO Sci. Mission Iran, Turkey, Pakistan, 1963; mem. nat. adv. cancer council Nat. Cancer Inst., 1956-60; Research preservation whole blood OSRD, World War II. Editorial bd.: Blood, Jour. Hematology, 1946-76, Annals Internal Medicine, 1960-70, Jour. Nuclear Medicine, 1968; med. book div., Little Brown Co., 1958-68, med. book series, U. Calif. Press, 1962-70; Contbr. articles to profl. jours. Recipient cert. of merit Pres. U.S., 1948, Van Meter award Am. Goiter Soc., 1953, Dorothy Kirsten French Meml. award for disting. contbn. to medicine French Found. for Alzheimer's Disease Rsch., 1994; Wilson medalist, lectr. Am. Clin. and Climatol. Assn., 1964; Disting. fellow Am. Coll. Nuclear Physicians, 1994. Fellow Am. Coll. Nuclear Medicine (Disting. fellow 1988); mem. ACP, AMA, Am. Soc. Exptl. Pathology, Am. Soc. Clin. Investigation, Assn. Am. Physicians, Am. Acad. Arts and Scis., Biophys. Soc., Radiation Research Soc. (council 1964-65), Internat. Soc. Hematology, Am. Soc. Hematology (pres. 1961-62), Western Assn. Physicians (pres. 1962-63), Am. Bd. Nuclear Medicine (co-founder 1972, sec. 1972-75, chmn., pres. 1975-78, exec. dir. 1978-79, pres. 1980—), Soc. Nuclear Med. (trustee 1962-72, pres. So. Calif. chpt. 1964-65, Nuclear Pioneer lectr. 1971, 77, Disting. Scientist award Western. sect. 1977, Disting. Svc. award 1984, Spl. Presdl. Recognition award 1991, Hevesy Nuc. Pioneer award and lectr., 1995), L.A. County Med. Assn. (dist. v.p. 1976-77, 78-79, del. to Calif. Med. Assn. 1978-79), Am. Bd. Med. Spltys. (exec. com. 1982-84), Council Med. Splty. Socs. (sec. 1981-82, dir. 1980-82), World Fedn. Nuclear Medicine and Biology (chmn. statutes com. 1980-84), Phi Beta Kappa, Sigma Xi, Alpha Omega Alpha, Theta Xi, Nu Sigma Nu. Presbyterian (exec. com. Westminster Found. So. Calif. 1962-72, pres. 1968). Clubs: Harvard (Boston); Cosmos (Washington). Home: 11246 Cashmere St Los Angeles CA 90049-3503 Office: Am Bd Nuclear Med 900 Veteran Ave Rm 12-200 Los Angeles CA 90024-2703*

ROSS, JUNE ROSA PITT, biologist; b. Taree, New South Wales, Australia, May 2, 1931; came to U.S., 1957; d. Bernard and Adeline Phillips; m. Charles Alexander, June 27, 1959. BS with honors, U. Sydney, New S. Wales, Australia, 1953, PhD, 1959, DSc, 1974. Research assoc. Yale U., New Haven, 1959-60, U. Ill., Urbana, 1960-65; research assoc. Western Wash. U., Bellingham, 1965-67, assoc. prof., 1967-70, prof. biology, 1970—, chair dept. biology, 1989-90; pres. Western Wash. U. Faculty Senate, Bellingham, 1984-85; conf. host Internat. Bryozoology Assn., 1986. Author: (with others) A Textbook of Entomology, 1982, Geology of Coal, 1984; editor (assoc.) Palaios, 1985-89; contbr. articles to profl. jours. NSF grantee; recipient Award of Excellence Sydney U. Grads. Union of N.Am., 1995. Mem. Australian Marine Scis. Assn., The Paleontol. Soc. (councillor 1984-86, treas. 1987-93), U.K. Marine Biol. Assn. (life), Microscopy Soc. of Am., Internat. Bryozoology Assn. (pres. 1992-95). Avocations: hiking, classical music. Office: Western Wash U Dept Biology Bellingham WA 98225-9160

ROSS, KATHLEEN ANNE, college president; b. Palo Alto, Calif., July 1, 1941; d. William Andrew and Mary Alberta (Wilburn) R. BA, Ft. Wright Coll., 1964; MA, Georgetown U., 1971; PhD, Claremont Grad. Sch., 1979; LLD (hon.) Alverno Coll. Milw., 1990, Dartmouth Coll., 1991, Seattle U., 1992; LHD (hon.) Whitworth Coll., 1992, LLD (hon.) Pomona Coll., 1993. Cert. tchr., Wash. Secondary tchr. Holy Names Acad., Spokane, Wash., 1964-70; dir. rsch. and planning Province Holy Names, Wash. State, 1972-73; v.p. acads. Ft. Wright Coll., Spokane, 1973-81; rsch. asst. to dean Claremont Grad. Sch., Calif., 1977-78; assoc. faculty mem. Harvard U., Cambridge, Mass., 1981; pres. Heritage Coll., Toppenish, Wash., 1981—; cons. Wash. State Holy Names Schs., 1971-73; coll. accrediting assn. evaluator N.W. Assn. Schs. and Colls., Seattle, 1975—; dir. Holy Names Coll., Oakland, Calif., 1979—; cons. Yakama Indian Nation, Toppenish, 1975—; speaker, cons. in field. Author: (with others) Multicultural Pre-School Curriculum, 1977, A Crucial Agenda: Improving Minority Student Success, 1989; Cultural Factors in Success of American Indian Students in Higher Education, 1978. Chmn. Internat. 5-Yr. Convocation of Sisters of Holy Names, Montreal, Que., Can., 1981, 96; TV Talk show host Spokane Council of Chs., 1974-76. Recipient E.K. and Lillian F. Bishop Founds. Youth Leader of Yr. award, 1986, Disting. Citizenship Alumna award Claremont Grad. Sch., 1986, Golden Aztec award Washington Human Devel., 1989, Harold W. McGraw Edn. prize, 1989, John Carroll award Georgetown U., 1991, Holy Names medal Ft. Wright Coll., 1981, Pres. medal Eastern Washington U., 1994; named Yakima Herald Rep. Person of Yr. 1987, First Annual Leadership award Region VIII Coun. Advancement and Support Edn., 1993; Wash. State Medal of Merit, 1995; numerous grants for projects in multicultural higher edn., 1974—. Mem. Nat. Assn. Ind. Colls. and Univs., Am. Assn. Higher Edn., Soc. Intercultural Edn., Tng. and Rsch., Sisters of Holy Names of Jesus and Mary-SNJM. Roman Catholic. Office: Heritage Coll Office of Pres 3240 Fort Rd Toppenish WA 98948-9562

ROSS, KATHLEEN MARIE AMATO, secondary school educator; b. Rochester, N.Y., June 14, 1947; d. Walter Charles Poff and Margaret Lorraine (Cummings-Amato) Herkimer; m. William Anthony Ross, Apr. 4, 1970; children: Jay William, Daniel Clark. BA in History, Nazareth Coll., Rochester, 1969; postgrad., SUNY, Brockport, 1970-72, SUNY, Oswego, 1972-75, U. Rochester, 1979-81. Cert. secondary social studies tchr., N.Y. Tchr. social studies Webster (N.Y.) Cen. Sch. Dist., 1969—. Home: 2757 Lake Rd Williamson NY 14589-9517

ROSS, LEONARD LESTER, anatomist; b. N.Y.C., Sept. 11, 1927; s. Aaron Theodore and Shirley (Smolen) R.; m. Marcella Gamel, June 23, 1951; children: Jane, Jill. A.B., NYU, 1946, Ph.D., 1954. Asst. prof. U. Ala. Med. Coll., 1954-57; assoc. prof. Cornell U. Med. Coll., 1957-69, prof., 1969-73; vis. prof. Cambridge U., 1967-68; prof., chmn. dept. anatomy Med. Coll. Pa., Phila., 1973-89; exec. v.p., Annenberg dean Med. Coll. Pa., 1989-93, pres. and Annenberg dean, 1993-94; provost Allegheny U., Phila., 1994; exec. v.p. Allegheny Health, Edn. and Rsch. Found. Assoc. editor: Anat. Record, 1976. Served with M.C., U.S. Army, 1946-47. Recipient Lindback award for teaching, 1976; NIH sr. research fellow, 1967-68. Mem. Am. Assn. Anatomists (exec. com. 1984-88), Soc. Neurosci., Soc. Cell Biology, N.Y. Soc. Electron Microscopists (pres. 1975-76), Assn. Anatomy Chairmen (pres. 1983-84), AAUP (nat. council 1974-77), Sigma Xi. Office: Broad and Vine St Philadelphia PA 19102-5087

ROSS, MADELYN ANN, newspaper editor; b. Pitts., June 26, 1949; d. Mario Charles and Rose Marie (Mangieri) R. B.A., Indiana U. of Pa., 1971; M.A., SUNY-Albany, 1972. Reporter Pitts. Press, 1972-78, asst. city editor, 1978-82, spl. assignment editor, 1982-83, mng. editor, 1983-93; mng. editor Pitts. Post-Gazette, 1993—; bd. dirs. PG Pub. Co.; instr. Community Coll. Allegheny County, 1974-81; Pulitzer Prize juror, 1989, 90. Mem. Task Force Leadership Pitts., 1985-92; v.p. Old Newsboys Charity Fund; bd. dirs. Dapper Dan Charity. Mem. Am. Soc. Newspaper Editors, Women's Press Club. Democrat. Roman Catholic. Avocations: tennis; piano; organ. Office: Pitts Post-Gazette 34 Blvd Of The Allies Pittsburgh PA 15222-1204

ROSS, MALCOLM, mineralogist, crystallographer; b. Washington, Aug. 22, 1929; s. Clarence Samuel and Helen Hall (Frederick) R.; m. Daphne Dee Virginia Riska, Sept. 1, 1956; children: Christopher A., Alexander MacC. BS in Zoology, Utah State U., 1951; MS in Chemistry, U. Md., 1959; PhD in Geology, Harvard U., 1962. Rsch. mineralogist U.S. Geol. Survey, Washington, 1954-5, 61-74, Reston, Va., 1974—; prin. investigator lunar sci. program NASA, 1969-74. Author: Asbestos and Other Fibrous Minerals, 1988; contbr. numerous articles to profl. jours. First Lt. U.S. Army, 1952-54. Recipient Disting. Svc. award, U.S. Dept. Interior, 1986. Fellow Mineral. Soc. Am., Geol. Soc. Am., AAAS; mem. Am. Geophys. Union, Clay Minerals Soc., Mineral Soc. Am. (bd. dirs. treas. 1976-80, v.p. 1990, pres. 1991, Pub. Svc. award, 1990). Avocation: long distance bicycling. Home: 1608 44th St NW Washington DC 20007-2025 Office: US Geol Survey MS 955 Reston VA 20192

ROSS, MARION, actress; b. Albert Lea, Minn.; children: Jim, Ellen. Grad., San Diego State U. Performed with Globe Theatre, San Diego, LaJolla Summer Theatre; Broadway debut in Edwin Booth; starred in touring prodns. of Never Too Late, Barefoot in the Park, The Glass Menagerie, Long Days Journey Into Night, Love Letter, Steel Magnolias, film debut in Forever Female, 1953; on woman show A Lovely Light, 1988—; TV series include Life with Father, 1953-55, Paradise Bay, 1965-66, Happy Days, 1974-84, Love Boat, 1985-86, Brooklyn Bridge, 1991-93 (Emmy nomination for lead actress in a comedy 1992, 93), Hidden in Silence, 1995, Evening Star, 1996. Office: Marion Ross Enterprises Inc 20929-47 Ventura Blvd # 144 Woodland Hills CA 91364-2334

ROSS, MARLENE, educator; b. Bklyn., May 13, 1939; d. Oscar and Minna (Buchweitz) Feldstein; m. Bernard H. Ross, June 2, 1963; children: Jeffrey Leonard, Joanne Sharon, Carolyn Suzanne. BA, Barnard Coll., 1959; MEd, Harvard U., 1960; PhD, Am. U., 1985. Tchr. grades P, 2, 3, 5 Greenburgh Sch. Dist. # 8, White Plains, N.Y., 1960-66; asst. dir. edn. Anti-Defamation League, N.Y.C., 1966-67; with U. Md., College Park, 1967-74; sr. assoc. Enterprises for New Directions, Inc., Washington, 1976-78; assoc. dir. Mid-Atlantic Ctr. Am. U., Washington, 1981-86; mgr. ann. meeting Am. Coun. on Edn., Washington, 1986-92, dep. dir. fellows program, 1988-90, dir. fellows program, 1990—; spkr., cons. in field. Author: The American College President, 1993, (with others) The Rules of the Game: Unwritten Code of Career Mobility, 1990, Administrative Internship Programs, 1993, So You Want To Be A College President, 1996. Recipient Phil Carroll Advancement of Mgmt. award in Mgmt. Edn., Soc. Advancement of Mgmt., 1993. Mem. Am. Assn. Higher Edn., Nat. Assn. Women in Edn., Leadership Greater Washington (bd. dirs.), Barnard-in-Washington, Women Adminstrs. in Higher Edn. Avocation: traveling. Office: Am Coun on Edn 1 Dupont Cir NW Washington DC 20036-1110

ROSS, MARTIN HARRIS, advertising executive; b. Phila., Dec. 7, 1937; s. Simon Max and Sarah (Tofsky) R.; m. Lorraine Rosenthal, Mar. 11, 1962; children: Bradley Allen, Steven Andrew. BS, NYU, 1959. Copywriter William Douglas McAdams, Inc., N.Y.C., 1959-66; sr. copywriter Robert A. Becker, Inc., N.Y.C., 1966-68; copy chief Sudler & Hennessey, Inc., N.Y.C., 1968-73; founder, exec. v.p. Dugan/Farley Comm. (divsn. Bozell Jacobs Kenyon & Eckhardt Healthcare), Upper Saddle River, N.J., 1973—. Mem. New Hyde Park Rep. Club, 1983—. Served with U.S. Army, 1959. Mem. Healthcare Mktg. Coun. (creative com. 1984—). Jewish. Avocations: tennis, golf, antique collecting. Home: 169 Lawrence St New Hyde Park NY 11040-2044 Office: Dugan Farley Comm Divsn Bozell Jacobs Kenyon & Eckhardt Healthcare 600 E Crescent Ave Saddle River NJ 07458-1846

ROSS, MARY O., religious organization administrator. Pres. Women's Auxiliary Convention of the Nat. Baptist Ch. USA, Detroit. Office: Women's Auxiliary Conv 584 Arden Park Blvd Detroit MI 48202-1304*

ROSS, MARY RIEPMA COWELL (MRS. JOHN O. ROSS), retired lawyer; b. Oklahoma City, Okla., Oct. 1, 1910; d. Sears F. and Elizabeth (Van Zwaluwenburg) Riepma; AB, Vassar Coll., 1932; LLB, Memphis State

U., 1938; LLD, U. Nebr., 1973; m. Richard N. Cowell, Mar. 1, 1946 (dec. Jan. 1953); m. 2d, John O. Ross, Mar. 31, 1962 (dec. June 1966). Bar: Tenn. 1938, D.C. 1944, N.Y. 1947. Atty. U.S. Govt., Washington, 1940-44; pvt. practice Cromelin & Townsend, Washington, 1944-46. Royall, Koegel & Rogers and predecessors, N.Y.C., 1946-61; individual practice law, 1961-88; dir. 39 E. 79th St. Corp., 1966-73; dir. 795 Fifth Ave. Corp., 1977-90; mem. adv. com. N.Y. Commn. on Estates, 1965-67. Bd. dirs. Silver Cross Day Nursery, N.Y.C., 1963-70, Cunningham Dance Found., 1969-72, Central Park Community Fund, 1977-81, Mary Riepma Ross Film Theatre, 1988—; trustee U. Nebr. Found., 1966—, bd. dirs., 1974-79; hon. trustee Nebr. Art Assn. Mem. Am. Bar Assn., N.Y. Women's Bar Assn. (pres. 1955-57, dir. 1957-63, 74-80, adv. coun. 1963—), Bar Assn. City N.Y. (surrogate cts. com. 1961-65, library com. 1965-78, com. on profl. responsibility 1972-75), Nat. Assn. Women Lawyers (assembly del. 1962-64, 73-74, UN observer 1965-67, v.p. 1967, chmn. 1971 ann. conv., distinguished service award 1973), Vassar Coll. Alumnae Assn., Phi Alpha Delta, Delta Gamma, Dinner Dances, Inc. (bd. govs. 1979-93). Address: 2 E 61st St Apt 2404 New York NY 10021-8402

ROSS, MATHEW, psychiatry educator; b. Boston, July 29, 1917; s. Abraham and Frances (Lampke) R.; m. Brenda Boynton, Dec. 24, 1946; children: Douglas Ross, Gail Ross, Craig Ross, Bruce Ross. BS, Tufts U., 1938, MD, 1942. Diplomate Am. Bd. Psychiatry and Neurology. Intern Kings County Hosp., N.Y.C., 1942-43; resident VA Med. Ctr., L.A., 1946-48; intern L.A. Psychoanalytic Inst., 1949-53; Prof. Sch. Medicine UCLA, 1953-58; prof. Sch. Medicine George Washington U., Washington, 1958-73; resident psychiat. adminstrn. U. Chgo., 1959; prof. Sch. Medicine Harvard U., Boston, 1963-73, Brown U., Providence, 1964-65, R.I. U., Providence, 1964-65, U. Calif., Irvine, 1974—; resident sch. alcoholism U. Utah, 1977; Fulbright prof., rsch. scholar U. Gronigen and U. Amsterdam, The Netherlands, 1962-63; med. dir. Am. Psychiat. Assn., Washington, 1958-62. Editor: Newsletter Am. Psychiat. Assn., 1958-62, Mental Hosp. & Community Psychiatry, 1958-62, PDE Scientific Journal, 1975—. Sr. legislator State of Calif., 1985-86; commr. Newport Beach (Calif.) Arts Commn., 1989—. Maj. U.S. Army, 1943-46, ETO. Fellow ACP, Am. Psychiat. Assn., Am. Assn. Psychiatrists, Am. Pub. Health Assn., So. Calif. Psychiat. Soc. (founding pres. 1953-60); hon. fellow Australia-New Zealand Coll. Psychiatrists. Home: Unit 1163 24055 Paseo Del Lago Laguna Hills CA 92653-2678

ROSS, MATTHEW, lawyer; b. N.Y.C., Dec. 28, 1953; s. Harvey and Cecile (Shelsky) R.; m. Susan Ruth Goldfarb, Apr. 20, 1986; children: Melissa Danielle, Henry Max, Thomas Frank. BS in Econs., U. Pa., 1975; JD, U. Va., 1978. Bar: N.Y. 1979, U.S. Dist. Ct. (so. dist.) N.Y. 1979. Assoc. Cravath, Swaine & Moore, N.Y.C., 1978-84; prin., assoc. gen. counsel KPMG Peat Marwick LLP, N.Y.C., 1984-90; prin., deputy gen. counsel Deloitte & Touche LLP, N.Y.C, 1990—. Mem. ABA (corp. law sect.), N.Y. State Bar Assn. (corp. banking and bus. law sect.), Assn. of Bar of City of N.Y. (corp. law com.), Beta Gamma Sigma. Avocations: basketball, tennis, skiing, travel. Home: 17 Carthage Ln Scarsdale NY 10583-7507 Office: Deloitte & Touche LLP 1633 Broadway New York NY 10019-6708

ROSS, MICHAEL FREDERICK, magistrate, lawyer; b. Coral Gables, Fla., Sept. 20, 1950; s. George Thomas and Frances (Brown) Skaro. BA, Yale U., 1973; JD, U. Conn., 1979; MLS, So. Conn. State U., 1981. Bar: Conn. 1979, Fla. 1979, N.J. 1983, Mass. 1984, V.I. 1985, U.S. Dist. Ct. Conn. 1979, U.S. Dist. Ct. N.J. 1983, U.S. Dist. Ct. Vt. 1984, U.S. Dist. Ct. V.I. 1985, U.S. Ct. Claims 1980, U.S. Tax Ct. 1980, U.S. Ct. Customs and Patent Appeals 1980, U.S. Ct. Mil. Appeals 1980, U.S. Ct. Appeals (1st, 2d and D.C. cirs.) 1980, U.S. Ct. Appeals (5th, 9th and 11th cirs.) 1981, U.S. Ct. Appeals (Fed. cir.) 1982, U.S. Ct. Appeals (3d, 4th, 6th, 7th, 8th and 19th cirs.) 1983, Temp. Emergency Ct. Appeals 1985, Mashantucket Pequot Tribal Ct. 1995, U.S. Supreme Ct. 1982. Pvt. practice New Haven, Conn., 1979-82, Madison, Conn., 1985—; chief of adjudications Conn. Motor Vehicle Dept., Wethersfield, 1980-82; adminstrv. law judge State of Conn. Motor Vehicle Dept., Wethersfield, 1985—; asst. atty. gen. State of Conn., Hartford, 1982-84, Dept. of Law, St. Croix, V.I., 1984-85; magistrate Superior Ct. of Middlesex, New Haven and New London Counties, Conn., 1988—; mem. faculty Conn. Bar Assn. Acad. Profl. Devel. of Continuing Legal Edn., 1987, 91. Chmn. Madison Zoning Bd. Appeals, 1991-95. Mem. ABA, Conn. Bar Assn., V.I. Bar Assn., Mensa, Am. Trial Lawyers Assn., Conn. Def. Lawyers Assn., Conn. Magistrates Assn., Fence Club, Morys Assn. Club, Madison Men's Club. Democrat. Jewish. Home: 48 Mohawk Trl Guilford CT 06437 Office: 74 Bradley Rd PO Box 1280 Madison CT 06443-1280

ROSS, MOLLY OWINGS, gold and silversmith, jewelry designer, small business owner; b. Ft. Worth, Feb. 5, 1954; d. James Robertson and Lucy (Owings) R. BFA, Colo. State U., 1976; postgrad., U. Denver, 1978-79. Graphic designer Amber Sky Illustrators and Sta. KCNC TV-Channel 4, Denver, 1977-79; art dir. Mercy Med. Ctr., Denver, 1979-83, Molly Ross Design, Denver, 1983-84; co-owner Deltex Royalty Co., Inc., Colorado Springs, Colo., 1981—, LMA Royalties, Ltd., Colorado Springs, 1993—; art dir., account mgr. Schwing/Walsh Advt., Mktg. and Pub. Rels., Denver, 1984-87, prodn. mgr., 1987-88; jewelry designer Molly O. Ross, Gold and Silversmith, Denver, 1988—. Pres. Four Mile Hist. Park Vol. Bd., Denver, 1985-87; bd. dirs. Four Mile Hist. Park Assn., 1985-86, Hist. Denver, Inc., 1986-87, Denver Emergency Housing Coalition, 1989-90; coun. mem. feminization of poverty critical needs area coun. Jr. League Denver, 1989-90, chmn. children in crisis/edn. critical needs area, 1990-91, chmn. project devel., 1991-92, co-chmn. Done in a Day Comty. Project 75th Anniversary Celebration, 1991-93; mem. bd. dirs., 1993-94, v.p. comty. projects, 1993-94; co-chmn. Project IMPACT, 1994-95; exec. v.p. external affairs Jr. League of Denver, 1995-96; co-chmn. Comty. Coalitions Com., 1996-97; bd. dirs. Rocky Mountain PREP, 1994—, pres. bd. dirs., 1997—; mem. steering com. Denver Urban Resources Partnership, 1995—. Named Vol. of Month (March), Jr. League Denver, 1990, Vol. of Yr., Four Mile Hist. Pk., 1988; recipient Gold Peak Mktg. award-team design Am. Mktg. Assn., 1986, Silver Peak Mktg. award-team design Am. Mktg. Assn., 1986, Gold Pick award-art dir. Pub. Rels. Soc. Am., 1980-81. Mem. Natural Resources Def. Coun., Physicians for Social Responsibility, Am. Farmland Trust, Nat. Trust for Hist. Preservation, Sierra Club, Environ. Def. Fund. Avocations: horseback riding, bicycling, hiking, backpacking, pastel drawing.

ROSS, MONTE, electrical engineer; b. Chgo., May 26, 1932; s. Jacob Henry and Mildred Amelia (Feller) R.; m. Harriet Jean Katz, Feb. 10, 1957; children—Karyn, Dianne, Ethan. B.S. in Elec. Engring., U. Ill., 1953; M.S., Northwestern U., 1962. Devel. engr. Chance Vought, Dallas, 1953-54; sr. electronics engr. Motorola, Chgo., 1955-56; project engr. Motorola, 1957-59, assoc. dir. research, 1960-63; dir. research Hallicrafters Co., Chgo., 1964-65; mgr. laser tech. McDonnell Douglas Astronautics Co., St. Louis, 1966-70, dir. laser communications; program mgr. Laser Space Communications, 1971-87; pres. Ultradata Sys., Inc. (formerly Laser Data Tech.), St. Louis, 1987—; mem. alumni bd. dept. elec. and computer engring. U. Ill., 1985-90; guest lectr. various univs.; cons. NSF. Author: Laser Receivers, 1966; tech. editor Laser Applications Series, vol. 1, 1971, vol. 2, 1974, vol. 3, 1977, vol. 4, 1980; patentee in field. Recipient St. Louis High Tech. Entrepreneur of Yr. award, 1995; McDonnell Douglas Corp. fellow, 1985. Fellow IEEE; mem. Internat. Laser Communications Soc. (pres. 1988-89), Sigma Xi. Home: 19 Beaver Dr Saint Louis MO 63141-7901 Office: Ultradata Sys Inc 9375 Dielman Industrial Dr Saint Louis MO 63132-2212

ROSS, MURRAY GEORGE, social science educator, university president emeritus; b. Sydney, N.S., Can., Apr. 12, 1910; s. George Robert and Catherine (MacKay) R.; m. Janet Kennedy Lang, May 10, 1940; children—Susan Janet, Robert Bruce. B.A., Acadia U., 1936, D.C.L., 1960; M.A., U. Toronto, 1938, LL.D., 1970; Ed.D., Columbia, 1948; D.Litt., York U., 1970; D.Un., U. York, Eng., 1973; LL.D., Laurentian U., 1977. Prof. U. Toronto, 1950-55, v.p., 1955-60; pres. York U., Downsview, Ont., 1960-70, prof. social sci., 1970—, pres. emeritus, 1972—; former dir. Continental Can Co., Can., McGraw Hill Ryerson, Ltd., Time Can., Capital Growth Fund Ltd., Walwyn, Que. and Toronto; mem. N.Am. adv. bd. Volvo Co. Author: Religious Beliefs of Youth, 1950, The Y.M.C.A. in Canada, 1951, (with C.E. Hendry) New Understanding of Leadership; A Survey and Application of Research, 1957, Case Histories in Community Organization, 1958, The New University, 1961, New Universities in the Modern World, 1965, Community Organization: Theory and Principles; and fgn. edits., 1955, 2d edit., 1965, The University: The Anatomy of Academe, 1976, Canadian Corporate Directors on the Firing Line, 1980, The WayMust Be Tried, 1992; editor: Towards Professional Maturity, 1948; contbr. articles to profl. jours. Past chmn. bd. trustees Hist. Series; trustee Sunnybrooke Hosp. Decorated officer Order of Can., Order of Ont.; recipient Book award Am. Coun. on Edn., 1976, Centennial medal, 1967, Queen's Jubilee medal, 1978, Commemorative medal 125th Anniversary of Can. Confedn. Fellow Am. Sociol. Soc. Home: 75 Highland Crescent, Willowdale, ON Canada M2L 1G7 Office: Glendon Coll, 2275 Bayview Ave, Toronto, ON Canada M4N 3M6

ROSS, MURRAY LOUIS, lawyer, business executive; b. Rochester, N.Y., Apr. 26, 1947; s. Charles Allen and Florence L. (Falk) R.; m. Linda Marie Wabschall, Dec. 26, 1970. AB in History, Lycoming Coll., 1969; JD, U. Toledo, 1972. Bar: Pa. 1976. Asst. to exec. v.p. Falk Machinery Inc., Rochester, 1972-74; asst. v.p. Phila. (Pa.) Stock Exch., 1975-78, dir. securities dept., 1978-79, dir. market surveillance, 1979-82, v.p., corp. sec., 1982—; exec. v.p. Shiffrin Selections, Ltd., 1994—; corp. sec. Phila. (Pa.) Bd. Trade Inc., 1984—, Phila. (Pa.) Depository Trust Co., 1986—, Stock Clearing Corp. Phila., 1986—. Mem. ABA, Phila. Bar Assn., Securities Assn. of Phila. Avocations: wine, golf, ice hockey. Home: 1126 Woodstock Ln West Chester PA 19382-7244 Office: Phila Stock Exchange Inc 1900 Market St Philadelphia PA 19103-3527

ROSS, NORMAN ALAN, publisher; b. Bklyn., Nov. 1, 1942; s. Robert E. and Bertha (Cohen) R.; m. Leslie Ann Sandler, Oct. 10, 1969; children: Caroline Beth, Juliet Michelle. B.B.A., CCNY, 1964, postgrad., 1967-74. Prodn. mgr. Thomas Pub. Co., 1964-67; systems analyst Reuben H. Donnelley Corp., 1968-70; project mgr. Holt Rinehart & Winston, 1971-73; pres. Clearwater Pub. Co., Inc., N.Y.C., 1973-88, Video Strategies USA, Inc., N.Y.C., 1981-84, Broadside Ltd. pub. Broadside Mag., 1983-87, Norman Ross Pub. Inc., 1987—. Author: Index to the Decisions of the Indian Claims Commission, 1973, Index to the Expert Testimony Before the Indian Claims Commission, 1973, Guide to Architectural Trade Catalogs from the Avery Library, 1989, Guide to Yiddish Children's Books from the Yivo Inst., 1989. Mem. Assn. Info. Mgmt. Home: 392 Central Park W Apt 20-c New York NY 10025-5860 Office: Norman Ross Pub Inc 330 W 58th St New York NY 10019-1827

ROSS, NORMAN ALEXANDER, retired banker; b. Miami, Fla., Jan. 30, 1922; s. Norman DeMille and Beatrice (Dowsett) R.; children: Isabel, Diana. A.B., Stanford U., 1946; postgrad., Trinity Coll., Oxford U., Eng., 1953; D.H.L., Lincoln Coll., Ill., 1959, Fisk U., 1978, Roosevelt U., 1979; Litt.D., Lake Forest Coll., 1967. Airport mgr. Pan Am. Airways, 1943; asst. to producer Metro-Goldwyn-Mayer, 1943-44; ptnr. Norman Ross & Co., 1947-50; owner Norman Ross Record Club, 1951-52; v.p. pub. affairs First Nat. Bank Chgo., 1968-79, sr. v.p. communications dept., 1979-81, sr. v.p. community affairs, 1981-86; pres. Ross-McElroy Prodns., Inc., 1962-68; sr. affairs commentator Sta. WLS-TV, Chgo., 1989—; radio-TV commentator NBC, ABC, Chgo., 1953-64, ABC, Stas. WGN and WBKB, Chgo., 1964-68; former columnist Chgo. Daily News. Served with inf. AUS, World War II. Decorated cavaliere Dell Ordine Repubblica Italiana, Knight 1st Class Republic of Austria, 1989; U.S. Army Outstanding Civilian Service medal; officier and cross of chevalier Legion of Honor France; recipient Peabody award for TV program Off the Cuff 1964. Mem. Phi Gamma Delta. Clubs: Chgo., Racquet, Oxford, Econ. (Chgo.), Wayfarers, Casino. Home: 1200 N Lake Shore Dr Apt 801 Chicago IL 60610-2347 Office: Pilot Knob Bed & Breakfast Inn PO Box 1280 Pilot Mountain NC 27041-1280 *"Doing onto others as you would have them do unto you" is even more important today than it was 2000 years ago.*

ROSS, PATTI JAYNE, obstetrics and gynecology educator; b. Nov. 17, 1946; d. James J. and Mary N. Ross; B.S., DePauw U., 1968; M.D., Tulane, U., 1972; m. Allan Robert Katz, May 23, 1976. Asst. prof. U. Tex. Med. Sch., Houston, 1976-82, assoc. prof., 1982—, dir. adolescent ob-gyn., 1976—, also dir. phys. diagnosis, dir. devel. dept. ob-gyn.; speaker in field. Bd. dirs. Am. Diabetes Assn., 1982—; mem. Rape Coun. Diplomate Am. Bd. Ob-Gyn, Children's Miracle Network Hermann's Children's Hosp; Olympic torch relay carrier, 1996; founder Women's Med. Rsch. Fund, U. Tex. Med. Sch., Houston. Mem. Tex. Med. Assn., Harris County Med. Soc., Houston Ob-Gyn. Soc., Assn. Profs. Ob-Gyn., Soc. Adolescent Medicine, AAAS, Am. Women's Med. Assn., Orgn. Women in Sci., Sigma Xi. Roman Catholic. Clubs: River Oak Breakfast, Profl. Women Execs. Contbr. articles to profl. jours. Office: 6431 Fannin St Houston TX 77030-1501

ROSS, PHILIP ROWLAND, library director; b. Indiana, Pa., Apr. 7, 1940; s. David Biddle and Miriam Elizabeth (Hill) R.; m. Elaine Lucille George, July 17, 1965; children: Mary Elizabeth, David Bruce. BA, Pa. State U., 1962; MSLS, U. Md., 1969. Postal fin. officer USAF, Tachikawa AFB Tokyo, 1963-65; chief data control and quality control Hdqrs. Air Force Systems Command, Andrews AFB, Md., 1965-68; asst. libr. acquisitions West Liberty (W.Va.) State Coll., 1969-86; dist. mgr. Wheeling (W.Va.) office First Investors Corp., 1986-89; divs. mgr. State of Ark. First Investors Corp., Little Rock, 1989-92; dir. Lonoke (Ark.) Prairie County Regional Libr. System, 1992—; founder, treas.-mgr. West Liberty (W.Va.) State Coll. Fed. Credit Union, 1977-82, chmn. bd., 1984-85; mem. Ark. On Line Network Adv. Com., Little Rock, 1993-96, Libr. Devel. Dist. State Coun., Little Rock, 1993—, vice chmn., 1996. Maj. USAF, 1962-68; maj. Res., 1968-84, ret. Maj. USAF, 1962-68; maj. Res., 1968-84, ret. Decorated various USAF medals and decorations. Mem. Assn. Ark. Pub. Librs. (treas.-sec. 1993, 94, v.p. pres.-elect 1995, prse. 1996), Ark. Libr. Assn. (com. mem. 1994-95, conv. com. 1996, 97), Lonoke, Ark. C. of C., Am. Legion, Lions. Republican. Methodist. Avocations: reading, gardening, refinishing antique furniture. Home: 691 Wayne Elmore Rd Lonoke AR 72086-9126 Office: Lonoke/Prairie County Regional Libr System 303 Court St Lonoke AR 72086-2858

ROSS, RHODA, artist; b. Boston, Dec. 24, 1941. Student, Skowhegan Sch. Painting; BFA, RISD, 1964; MFA, Yale U., 1966. tchr. NYU, 1994—, Chautauqua (N.Y.) Sch. Art; participant Art in Embassies Program Dept of State. One-woman shows include Frick Gallery, Belfast, Maine, Yale U., New Haven, Convent of the Sacred Heart, Mcpl. Art Soc., L.I. U., Emma Willard Sch. Dietal Gallery, Marymount Manhattan Coll., N.Y.C., N.Y.C. Landmarks Preservation Commn. 25th Silver Ann., numerous others; groups shows include The Crane Collection, Boston, Michael Ingbar Gallery, N.Y., N.Y. Studio Sch., N.Y.C., Am. U., Washington, Springfield (Mo.) Art Mus., numerous others; permanent collections include The White House, Gracie Mansion, N.Y.C., The Juilliard Sch., N.Y.C., Bankers Trust, Mus. City of N.Y., Chem. Bank Nat. Hqrs., Lehman Coll., Waldorf Astoria Hotel, N.Y.C., Russian Tea Rm., Rose Assocs., Bklyn. Union Gas, numerous other pvt. and pub. collections; artwork appears on New Sch. Social Rsch. catalog cover, Gifts and Decorative Accessories Mag. cover, UNICEF greeting card, The New York Times. Treas. R.I. Sch. Design Alumni Exec. Com. Fellow Va. Ctr. for Creative Arts. Mem. RISD Alumni Assn. (treas., mem. alumni exec. com.), Phi Tau Gamma. Home and Studio: 473 W End Ave New York NY 10024-4934

ROSS, RICHARD FRANCIS, veterinarian, microbiologist, educator; b. Washington, Iowa, Apr. 30, 1935; s. Milton Edward and Olive Marie (Bergren) R.; m. Karen Mae Paulsen, Sept. 1, 1957; children: Scott, Susan. D.V.M., Iowa State U., 1959, M.S., 1961, Ph.D., 1965. Rsch. assoc. Iowa State U., Ames, 1959-61, asst. prof., 1962-65, assoc. prof., 1966-72, prof., 1972—, assoc. dir., assoc. dean, 1990—, interim dean, 1992-93, dean, 1993—; oper. mgr. Vet. Lab. Inc., Remsen, Iowa, 1961-62; postdoctoral fellow Rocky Mountain Lab., NIAID, Hamilton, Mont., 1965-66; sr. U.S. scientist Alexander von Humboldt Found., Bonn, Fed. Republic Germany, 1975-76; chmn. Internat. Research Program on Comparative Mycoplasmology, 1982-86; pres. Iowa State U. Research Found., Ames, 1984-86; Howard Dunne meml. lectr. Am. Assn. Swine Practitioners, 1984; mem. adv. bd. Sec. Agr., 1996-97, mem. strat. pl. task force, 1997—. Contbr. numerous articles to profl. publs., 1963—. Named Disting. Prof., Iowa State U., 1982, Hon. Master Pork Producer, Iowa Pork Producers Assn., 1985; recipient faculty citation Iowa State U. Alumni Assn., 1984, Beecham award for rsch. excellence, 1985, Howard Dunne Meml. award Am. Assn. Swine Practitioners, 1988, Am. Feed Mfg. award for rsch.; 1995, Sec. of Agr. award for personal and profl. accomplishment, 1996. Mem. Am. Coll. Vet. Microbiologists (diplomate, vice chmn. 1974-75, sec.-treas. 1977-83), Am. Soc. Microbiology (chmn. div. 1985-86), Internat. Orgn. Mycoplasmology (chair 1990-92), AVMA, AAAS, Osborn Research Club, Conf. Rsch. Workers in Animal Diseases (coun. mem., pres. 1992), Assn. Am. Vet. Med. Colls. (pres.-elect 1996-97). Republican. Lutheran. Avocations: fishing, gardening, walking, reading. Home: 2003 Northwestern Ave Ames IA 50010-4522 Office: Iowa State U Coll Vet Medicine Ames IA 50011

ROSS, RICHARD STARR, medical school dean emeritus, cardiologist; b. Richmond, Ind., Jan. 18, 1924; s. Louis Francisco and Margaret (Starr) R.; m. Elizabeth McCracken, July 1, 1950; children: Deborah Starr, Margaret Casad, Richard McCracken. Student, Harvard U., 1942-44, M.D. cum laude, 1947; Sc.D. (hon.), Ind. U., 1981; LHD (hon.), Johns Hopkins U., 1994. Diplomate: Nat. Bd. Med. Examiners, Am. Bd. Internal Medicine. (subsplty. bd. cardiovascular disease). Successively intern, asst. resident, chief resident Osler Med. Service, Johns Hopkins Hosp., 1947-54; research fellow physiology Harvard Med. Sch., 1952-53; instr. medicine Johns Hopkins Med. Sch., 1954-56, asst. prof. medicine, 1956-59, assoc. prof., 1959-65, assoc. prof. radiology, 1960-71, prof. medicine, 1965—, Clayton prof. cardiovascular disease, 1969-75; dir. Wellcome Research Lab., Johns Hopkins; physician Johns Hopkins Hosp.; dir. cardiovascular div. dept. medicine, adult cardiac clinic Johns Hopkins Sch. Medicine and Hosp., dir. myocardial infarction research unit, 1967-75; dean med. faculty, v.p. medicine Johns Hopkins U., 1975-90, dean. emeritus, 1990—; Sir Thomas Lewis lectr. Brit. Cardiac Soc., 1969; John Kent Lewis lectr. Stanford U., 1972; bd. dirs. emeritus Johns Hopkins Hosp., Francis Scott Key Med. Ctr.; mem. cardiovascular study sect. Nat. Heart and Lung Inst., 1965-69, chmn. cardiovascular study sect., 1966-69, mem. tng. grant com., 1971-73, chmn. heart panel, 1972-73, adv. coun., 1974-78; mem. Inst. of Medicine, 1976—; chmn. vis. com. Harvard Med. and Dental Sch., 1979-86; bd. overseers Harvard U., 1980-86. Editor Modern Concepts Cardiovascular Disease, 1961-65, The Principles and Practice of Medicine, 17th-22nd edits., 1968-88; mem. editorial bd. Circulation, 1968-74; mem. editorial com. Jour. Clin. Investigation, 1969-73; contbr. numerous articles on cardiovascular disease and physiology to profl. jours. Served as capt. M.C. AUS, 1949-51. Flexner award, Assn Am. Med. Coll., 1994; hon. fellow UMDS, Guy's and St. Thomas's Hosps., London, 1996. Fellow Am. Coll. Cardiology; mem. ACP (master 1979), Boylston Med. Soc., Am. Fedn. Clin. Research, Am. Physiol. Soc., Assn. Am. Physicians, Am. Soc. Clin. Investigation (councillor 1967-69), Am. Clin. and Climatol. Assn. (pres. 1978-79, councillor 1979-83, Metzger lecture 1986), Assn. Univ. Cardiologists (councillor 1972-75), Am. Heart Assn. (chmn. sci. sessions program com. 1965-67, chmn. publs. com. 1970-73, pres. 1973-74, dir. 1974-77, Connor lectr. 1979, Gold Heart award 1976, James B. Herrick award 1982), Heart Assn. Md. (pres. 1967-68), Sigma Xi, Alpha Omega Alpha; corr. mem. Brit. Cardiac Soc., Sociedad Peruana de Cardiologie, Cardiac Soc. Australia and New Zealand. Clubs: Peripatetic, Interurban (pres. 1978), Elkridge, Blue Hill Country Club (Maine). Home: 901 Drohomer Pl Baltimore MD 21210 Office: Johns Hopkins U 1830 E Monument St Baltimore MD 21205-2114

ROSS, ROBERT, health agency administrator. Exec. dir. Muscular Dystrophy Assn., Tucson. Office: Muscular Dystrophy Assn 3300 E Sunrise Dr Tucson AZ 85718-3208*

ROSS, ROBERT DONALD, librarian; b. N.Y.C., Mar. 28, 1931; s. William and Ceceile (Cross) Rosenfeld; B.A., CCNY, 1954; postgrad. NYU, 1960-64, Columbia U., 1968; M.L.S., Rutgers U., 1966; m. Madeleine Ladner, May 28, 1961; children: Jeffrey Laurence, Jodie Dianne. Reference libr. Bklyn. Pub. Libr., 1965; reader svcs. libr., asst. prof. Suffolk County (N.Y.) Community Coll., 1966-69; dir. South Brunswick (N.J.) Pub. Libr., 1969-73, Ridgewood (N.J.) Pub. Libr., 1973-95; adj. prof. Middlesex County (N.J.) Community Coll., 1973-76. Mem. exec. bd. South Brunswick Community Coun., 1970-73, Human Rels. Coordinating Coun., Ridgewood, 1988-94; adv. com. Nat. Project Ctr. for Film and Humanities, N.Y.C., 1971-75; treas. Bergen-Passaic Regional Library Coop., 1987-88, mem. exec. bd., 1986-89; mem. Ridgewood Bicentennial Commn., 1975-76. Mem. ALA (chmn. discussion group com. fund raising and fin. devel. sect. libr. adminstrn. and mgmt. div. 1984-85), N.J. Libr. Assn. (libr. devel. com. 1977-93, chmn. edn. for librarianship com. 1982-83, govt. rels. com. 1982, 100th anniversary com. 1988-91), Librs. of South Middlesex (chmn. 1970-73), North Bergen Fedn. Librs. (chmn. dirs. coun. 1975), Bergen County Coop. Libr. System (pres., treas. 1982-83, 86-87, exec bd. computer consortium 1987-89, budget com. 1989-94), Ridgewood C. of C. (bd. dirs. 1983-93, treas. 1988-93), Soc. Valley Hosp. Club: Ridgewood Kiwanis (pres. 1982-83, treas. 1987-88, Disting. Club Pres. award 1983). Home: 1475 Grand Point Way Reno NV 89523-2573

ROSS, ROBERT E., psychologist, clergyman, counselor. ThB in Pastoral Counseling, BD, MA, PhD in Religion; postgrad. in Clin. Psychology, Alfred Adler Inst. of Counseling and Psychotherapy, Chgo. Ordained clergyman. Counselor psychiat. unit of the neuropsychiatry br. profl. div. of Dept. of Medicine and Surgery U.S. Navy; dir. Counseling Ctr. for Effective Living, Indpls.; participant in grad. rsch. program in Substance Abuse and the Family, Substance Abuse in Bus. and Industry, and the Psychology and Physiology of Substance AbuseNova U.; speaker in field; workshop leader; numerous appearances radio and TV shows. Author: Beyond the Rope's End. Lt. commdr. USNR. Fellow Am. Assn. of Pastoral Counselors; mem. Nat. Assn. Sch. Psychologists, Am. Counseling Assn., Am. Mental Health Counselors Assn. Office: Counseling Ctr for Effective Living 4321 E 82nd St Indianapolis IN 46250-1676

ROSS, ROBERT EVAN, bank executive; b. Alliance, Ohio, Sept. 22, 1947; s. James Jacob Ross and Eva Mae (Forsha) Bodo; m. Susan Margaret Burd, June 20, 1970; children: Margaret Mae, James William. BBA, Kent State U., 1970; MBA, U. Chgo., 1977. Advisor to fraternities, dean of men's office Kent (Ohio) State U., 1970-71; trainee, supr. of trainees Northern Trust Co., Chgo., 1971-73, jr. analyst, 1973-74, trust rep., 1974-77, trust officer, 1977-81, v.p., div. head for personal fin. planning, 1981-85; portfolio mgr., investment rep. Morgan Stanley, Chgo., 1985-89; pres. Northern Trust Bank in Winnetka, Ill., 1989-92; exec. v.p. Northern Trust Bank/Lake Forest, Ill., 1992-95; vice chmn. Northern Trust Bank/Lake Forest, 1995-97, pres., CEO, , 1997—; bd. dirs. No. Trust Bank, Lake Forest, O'Hare, Ill., DuPage, Ill. Bd. dirs. The Camerata Singers of Lake Forest, Lake Forest Symphony, 1992—; suburban chair United Way North Region, 1993—. Avocations: sports, reading, stock market, painting. Office: No Trust Bank Lake Forest Deerpath And Bank Ln Lake Forest IL 60045

ROSS, ROBERT JOSEPH, head professional football coach; b. Richmond, Va., Dec. 23, 1936; s. Leonard Aloysius and Martha Isabelle (MMiller) R.; m. Alice Louise Bucker, June 13, 1959; children: Chris, Mary Catherine, Teresa, Kevin, Robbie. BA, Va. Mil. Inst., 1959. Tchr., head football coach Benedictine High Sch., Richmond, 1959-60; tchr., coach Colonial Heights (Va.) High Sch., 1962-65; asst. football coach Va. Mil. Inst., Lexington, 1965-67, Coll. William and Mary, Williamsburg, Va., 1967-71, Rice U., Houston, 1971-72, U. Md., College Park, 1972-73; head football coach The Citadel, Charleston, S.C., 1973-77; head coach U. Md., College Park, 1982-87; head football coach Ga. Inst. Tech., Atlanta, 1987-91; asst. coach Kansas City (Mo.) Chiefs, 1978-82; head coach San Diego Chargers, 1992-96, Detroit Lions, 1997—. 1st lt. U.S. Army, 1960-62. Named Coach of Yr., Washington Touchdown Club, 1982, Kodak Coach of Yr., 1990, Bobby Dodd Coach of Yr., 1990, Bear Bryant Coach of Yr., 1990, Scripps-Howard Coach of Yr., 1990, Nat. Coach of Yr., CBS Sports, 1990, Coach of Yr., Walter Camp Football Found., 1990, NFL Coach of Yr. UPI, 1992, Pro Football Weekly, 1992, Pro Football Writers' Assn., 1992, Football News, 1992, Football Digest, 1992, Maxwell Football Club, 1992, AFC Coach of Yr. Kansas City 101 Banquet. Mem. Am. Football Coaches Assn., Coll. Football Assn. (coaching com. 1988-92). Roman Catholic. *

ROSS, ROBERT THOMAS, neurologist, educator; b. Winnipeg, Man., Can., June 25, 1924; s. John L. and Alberta I. (Gray) R.; m. Margot Joan Ellacott, May 27, 1950; children: Gray T., John L., Mary E.; m. Angela Morrow Brady, Aug. 14, 1970; children: Diana Gray Salter, Drew Garland Salter. MD, U. Man., 1948. Intern Winnipeg Gen. Hosp., 1947-50; resident Nat. Hosp. Queen Sq., London, 1950-52; lectr. dept anatomy U. Man., Winnipeg, 1953-55, asst. prof. dept. medicine, 1955-59, assoc. prof., 1959-77, prof. medicine, 1977—, head sect. neurology, 1971-84. Editor, pub., founder: Can. Jour. Neurol. Scis., 1972-81; author: How to Examine the

Nervous System, 1978, 2d edit., 1985; Syringobulbia-A Contribution to the Pathophysiology of the Brain Stem, 1986, Syncope, 1988. Trustee Man. Med. Svc., 1958-64; pres. United Health Found., Winnipeg, 1969-71; bd. dirs. Man. Med. Coll. Found., 1983-85; mem. senate U. Manitoba, 1988—. Recipient E.L. Drewry prize E.L. Drewry Found., 1948; recipient Can. Centennial Medal, 1967, Queen Elizabeth Jubilee Medal, 1977. Fellow Royal Coll. Physicians (Can. and London), Am. Acad. Neurology; mem. Can. Neurol. Soc. (pres. 1971), Coll. Physicians and Surgeons of Man (pres. 1971), Am. Neurol. Assn., Order of Can. Baptist. Home: 312 Park Blvd, Winnipeg, MB Canada R3P OG7 Office: U Man Sect Neurology, PGF535 820 Sherbrook St, Winnipeg, MB Canada R3A 1R9

ROSS, ROBINETTE DAVIS, publisher; b. London, May 16, 1952; d. Raymond Lawrence and Pearl A. (Robinette) Davis; m. William Bradford Ross, III, Mar. 16, 1979; children: Nellie Tayloe, William Bradford IV; 1 stepchild, Aviza Tayloe. Student, Am. U., 1977-78. Asst. to editor The Chronicle of Higher Edn., Washington, 1978, advt. mgr., 1978-82, advt. dir., 1983-88, assoc. pub., 1988-94; assoc. pub. The Chronicle of Philanthropy, 1988-94; publ. The Chronicle of Higher Edn., Washington, 1994—; pub. The Chronicle of Philanthropy, Washington, 1994—. Mem. Nat. Press Club, Am. News Women's Club, City Tavern Club. Episcopalian. Home: 3908 Virgilia St Chevy Chase MD 20815-5026 Office: The Chronicle of Higher Edn 1255 23rd St NW Washington DC 20037-1125

ROSS, RODERIC HENRY, insurance company executive; b. Jamestown, N.Y., July 14, 1930; s. Edwin A. and Mary (Dornberger) R.; m. Patricia Johnson, Aug. 6, 1955; children: Timothy, Amy, Jane, Christopher. BA, Hobart Coll., 1952, LLD (hon.), 1979. CLU, ChFC. Gen. agt. Phila. Life Ins. Co., 1957-70, sr. v.p. mktg., 1972-73, pres., 1973-83, vice chmn., 1983-84; chmn., CEO Keystone State Life Ins. Co., Phila., 1985—; bd. dirs. PNC Bank Corp., Pitts., Hunt Mfg. Corp., Phila., Pa. Mfrs. Corp., Phila., Ky. Home Capital Corp., Louisville, Ky. Home Mut. Life Ins. Co., Louisville; past chmn. Ins. Fedn. Pa.; dir. Intergroup Svcs. Corp., Malvern, Pa. Rector's warden St. David's Ch., Radnor, Pa., 1989-90; trustee Hobart-William Smith Colls., Geneva, N.Y., 1972—, chmn. bd., 1983-88. Sgt. U.S. Army, 1952-54. Mem. Am. Soc. CLUs, Nat. Assn. Life Underwriters, Million Dollar Round Table (life), Union League (former dir.), Orpheus Club, St. David's Golf Club (Wayne, Pa.), Pine Valley Golf Club (Clementon, N.J.). Republican. Episcopalian. Avocations: golf, tennis. Home: 770 Pugh Rd Wayne PA 19087-2011 Office: Keystone State Life Ins Co 1401 Walnut St Philadelphia PA 19102-3128

ROSS, RUSSELL, pathologist, educator; b. St. Augustine, Fla., May 25, 1929; s. Samuel and Minnie (DuBoff) R.; m. Jean Long Teller, Feb. 22, 1956; children: Valerie Regina, Douglas Teller. A.B., Cornell U., 1951; D.D.S., Columbia U., 1955; Ph.D., U. Wash., 1962; DSc (hon.P, Med. Coll. of Pa., 1987. Intern Columbia-Presbyn. Med. Ctr., 1955-56, USPHS Hosp., Seattle, 1956-58; spl. research fellow pathology sch. medicine U. Wash., Seattle, 1958-62, asst. prof. pathology and oral biology sch. medicine and dentistry, 1962-65, assoc. prof. pathology Sch. Medicine, 1965-69, prof. Sch. Medicine, 1969—, adj. prof. biochemistry Sch. Medicine, 1978—, assoc. dean for sci. affairs sch. medicine, 1971-78, chmn. dept. pathology sch. medicine, 1982-94; dir. Ctr. for Vascular Biology, 1991—; vis. scientist Strangeways Rsch. Lab., Cambridge, Eng.; mem. rsch. com. Am. Heart Assn.; mem. adv. bd. Found. Cardiologique Princess Liliane, Brussels, Belgium; life fellow Clare Hall, Cambridge U.; mem. adv. coun. Nat. Heart, Lung and Blood Inst., NIH, 1978-81; vis. prof. Royal Soc. Medicine, U.K., 1987, 95. Editorial bd. Procs. Exptl. Biology and Medicine, 1971-86, Jours. Cell Biology, 1972-74, Exptl. Cell Rsch., 1982-92, Jour. Exptl. Medicine, Growth Factors, Am. Jours. Pathology, Internat. Cell Biology Jour., Circulation, Arteriosclerosis & Thrombosis, Growth Regulation; assoc. editor Arteriosclerosis, 1982-92, Jours. Cellular Physiology, Jours. Cellular Biochemistry; exec. editor Trends in Cariovascular Medicine; reviewing editorial bd. Sci. mag., 1987-90; contbr. articles to profl. jours. Trustee Seattle Symphony Orch. Recipient Birnberg Rsch. award Columbia U., 1975, Nat. Rsch. Achievement award Am. Heart Assn., 1990, Rous-Whiple award Am. Assn. Pathologists, 1992, Glorney-Raisbeck award N.Y. Acad. Medicine, 1995, Gordon Wilson medal Am. Clin. and Climatol. Assn., 1981; named to Inst. Medicine, Nat. Acad. Scis., Japan Soc. Promotion of Sci. fellow, 1985, Guggenheim fellow, 1966-67. Fellow AAAS, Am. Acad. Arts and Scis.; mem. Am. Soc. Cell Biology, Tissue Culture Assn., Am. Assn. Pathologists (Rous-Whipple award 1992), Internat. Soc. Cell Biology, Electron Microscope Soc. Am., Am. Soc. for Investigative Pathology (pres. 1994-95), Am. Heart Assn. (fellow Coun. on Arteriosclerosis, Nat. Rsch. Achievement award 1990), Royal Micros. Soc., Harvey Soc. (hon.), Am. Soc. Biochemistry and Molecular Biology, Romanian Acad. Med. Scis. (hon.), Royal Belgian Acad. Scis. (fgn. corr. mem.), Sigma Xi. Home: 3812 48th Ave NE Seattle WA 98105-5227 Office: U Wash Sch Medicine 1959 NE Pacific St Seattle WA 98195-0004

ROSS, RUSSELL MARION, political science educator; b. Washington, Iowa, June 2, 1921; s. Harold Ellis and Lucille Carrie (Dorris) R.; m. Jo Ellen Rude; children: Sheryl Ross, Julie. BA, U. Iowa, 1942; cert., Harvard U., 1945; MA, U. Iowa, 1946, PhD, 1948. Instr. dept. polit. sci. U. Iowa, Iowa City, 1946-48, asst. prof., 1948-52, assoc. prof., 1952-60, research prof., 1963-64, prof., 1965—, chmn. dept., 1970-91; prof. emeritus, 1991—; adminstrv. asst. to atty. gen., Iowa, 1960; exec. asst. to Gov. Iowa, 1961-62. Author: Iowa Government and Administration, 1958, State and Local Government and Administration, 1966, Gubernatorial Transitions, 1985, Political Science at the University of Iowa, 1990. Chmn. Regional Planning Commn., 1966-68; pres. Iowa City Community Sch. Bd., 1969-70; chmn. Iowa Campaign Finance Disclosure Commn., 1973-77; Mayor University Heights, 1954-60; Bd. dirs. Goodwill Industries S.E. Iowa. Served to lt. USNR, 1942-45. Mem. AAUP, Internat. City Mgrs. Assn. (hon.), Am. Pub. Adminstrn. Soc., Am. Polit. Sci. Assn., Mid-West Polit. Sci. Assn., Phi Beta Kappa, Phi Delta Kappa, Pi Sigma Alpha, Alpha Sigma Lambda. Club: Kiwanian. Home: 315 Highland Dr Iowa City IA 52246-1602

ROSS, SALLY PRICE, artist, mural painter; b. Cleve., Oct. 25, 1949; d. Philip E. and Mimi (Einhorn) Price; m. Howard D. Ross, Mar. 3, 1979; children: Sasha, Emily. BFA, Kent State U., 1971; MA, U. Iowa, 1974, MFA, 1975; student, Art Students League, N.Y.C., 1976-78. art cons. Art Options, Cleve., 1990-94; 1st and only woman artist to paint murals in the U.S. Capital/Ho. of Reps. corridors, 1978-79. Art exhbns. include Cain Park Art Gallery, Cleve., 1967, Jewish Cmty. Ctr. Cleve., 1967, 86, Canton (Ohio) Art Inst., 1969, Studio Theatre, Iowa City, 1973; designed and executed murals Montefiore Nursing Home, Cleve., 2 murals Rainbow Babies and Children's Hosp. New Bldg., Cleve., 1996-97. Edwin Abbey scholar, 1975-77, Fresco scholar Skowhegan Sch. Painting and Sculpture, 1977. Home: 25 Millcreek Ln Chagrin Falls OH 44022-1265

ROSS, SHELDON JULES, dentist; b. N.Y.C., June 17, 1924; s. Sam and Regina (Rosner) R.; 1 stepson, Nathan Sudnow; m. Carolyn L. M. Loesch, Apr. 26, 1946; children: Jane, Eric, Ellen, Lisa. D.D.S., NYU, 1949. Diplomate: Am. Bd. Periodontology, Am. Bd. Oral Medicine (examiner 1980-85). Pvt. practice periodontology N.Y.C., 1949—; prof. periodontics and oral medicine N.Y. U. Sch. Dentistry, 1949—; resident oral medicine Montefiore Hosp., N.Y.C., 1956-57; charge periodontics Montefiore Hosp., 1951-70, oral medicine, 1951-81, cons., 1981-95; attending charge oral medicine and periodontics Beth Abraham Hosp., Bronx, N.Y., 1961-81, cons., 1981-87; cons. in oral medicine Goldwater Meml. Hosp., N.Y.C., 1982—; former cons., lectr. periodontics and oral medicine Cabrini Hosp. and Med. Ctr., N.Y.C.; lectr. in field; honored lectr. Internat. Odontological Congress, Maringa, Brazil, 1972. Editor Jour. Oral Medicine, 1971-88, Annals of Dentistry, 1971-88; contbr. articles to dental jours., chpts. to textbooks. Served with AUS, 1942-43. Fellow N.Y. Acad. Dentistry (v.p. 1989-90, pres.-elect 1990-91, pres. 1991-92), Am. Acad. Oral Medicine (pres. 1980); mem. ADA, Am. Assn. Dental Editors, Am. Acad. Oral Medicine, Am. Acad. Periodontology, N.E. Soc. Periodontists, Orgn. Tchrs. Oral Diagnosis, Am. Heart Assn., Omega Kappa Upsilon. Home and Office: 40 Twisting Ln Wantagh NY 11793-1947 *None admit to having any new ideals except loving redemption of some souls: Man expects rational and normal deliberation instead.*

ROSS, SHERMAN, psychologist, educator; b. N.Y.C., Jan. 1, 1919; s. Max R. and Rachel (Khoutman) R.; m. Jean Goodwin, Aug. 18, 1945; children: Norman Kimball, Claudia Lisbeth (Mrs. Overway), Michael Lachlan. B.S., CCNY, 1939; A.M., Columbia U., 1941, Ph.D., 1943. Asst. psychology, research psychologist Columbia U., 1941-44; asst., then assoc. prof. psychology Bucknell U., 1946-50; research fellow N.Y. Zool. Soc., 1948; guest investigator, sci. asso. Jackson Lab., 1947-77; assoc. prof., then prof. psychology U. Md., 1950-60; spl. cons. Psychopharmacology Svc. Ctr. NIMH, 1956-63; asst. chief NIMH, 1956-57; exec. sec. edn. and tng. bd., sci. affairs officer APA, 1960-68; prof. psychology Howard U., 1968-89, emeritus, 1989—; exec. sec., staff assoc., assembly of behavioral and social scis. Nat. Acad. Scis.-NRC, 1968-76; lectr. Himmelfarb Mobile U., 1994—; cons. VA, Human Ecology Fund, Stanford Research Inst., Office Naval Research, U.S. Sci. Exhibit, Am. U., HRB-Singer, Inc.; bd. dirs. Interdisciplinary Communications Assocs., Washington; adv. council Woodrow Wilson Rehab. Center Found.; mem. Md. Bd. Examiners Psychology, 1957-58, 84-89; chmn. bd. dirs. Inst. for Research, State Coll., Pa.; mem. Montgomery County Health Planning Commn.; mem. Md. Statewide Health Coordinating Coun., Met. Washington Area Council of Health Planning Agys., Emergency Med. Svcs. Adv. Council; commr. health emeritus Montgomery County, Md.; sec. bd. dirs. Mobile Med. Care, Inc., Kensington, Md. Trustee Carver Research Found., Tuskegee U. Served to lt. (j.g.) USNR, 1944-46; capt. USNR (ret.). Fellow APA, Am. Coll. Neuropsychopharmacology, Royal Soc. Health, Washington Acad. Scis.; mem. Aerospace Med. Assn., Am. Soc. Zoologists, Ecol. Soc., Ergonomics Rsch. Soc., Md. Psychol. Assn. (pres. 1973-74), D.C. Psychol. Assn. (pres. 1982), Cosmos Club (Washington), Bethesda Naval Club (Md.), Sigma Xi (pres. U. Md. 1957-58, pres. Howard U. 1983-84), Phi Kappa Phi, Psi Chi (nat. pres. 1964-68). Home: 382 Russell Ave Gaithersburg MD 20877-2863 also: Glen Mary Rd Bar Harbor ME 04609-1301

ROSS, SHIRLEY S., retired English educator; b. Hardy, Ky., Feb. 15, 1936; d. Thomas Jefferson and Margaret (Stiltner) Stacy; m. Clarence Edwin Ross, Aug. 17, 1957; children: Cheryl Ann, Elizabeth Kay, Naomi Ruth. BA, Milligan (Tenn.) Coll., 1958. 7th grade English tchr. Galion (Ohio) city schs.; part-time staff Lifeline Christian Mission, Haiti; lectr. in field. Mem. NEA, Nat. Coun. Tchrs. English, Ohio Edn. assn., Galion Edn. Assn., Order Ea. Star, Clan Ross Assn. U.S. (sec. commr. of Ohio). Home: 235 S Jefferson St Galion OH 44833-2417

ROSS, STAN, accounting firm executive; b. 1939. With Kenneth Leventhal & Co., L.A., 1964—, now mng. ptnr.; now vice chmn., mng. ptnr. real estate Ernst & Young, LLP, L.A., 1995—. Office: Kenneth Leventhal & Co 2049 Century Park E Ste 1700 Los Angeles CA 90067-3119*

ROSS, STANFORD G., lawyer, former government official; b. St. Louis, Oct. 9, 1931; m. Dorothy Rabin, June 9, 1958; children: John, Ellen. AB with honors, Washington U., 1953; JD magna cum laude, Harvard U., 1956. Bar: D.C. 1969, Calif. 1956, N.Y. 1959. Assoc. firm Irell & Manella, Los Angeles, 1956-57; teaching fellow, research asst. Harvard Law Sch., 1957-58; assoc. firm Dewey, Ballantine, Bushby, Palmer & Wood, N.Y.C., 1958-61; asst. tax legis. counsel U.S. Dept. Treasury, 1961-63; prof. law N.Y. U., 1963-67; White House staff asst. to Pres. Johnson, 1967-68; gen. counsel U.S. Dept. Transp., 1968-69; ptnr. Caplin & Drysdale, Washington, 1969-78; commr. Social Security Adminstrn., Washington, 1978-79; ptnr. Califano, Ross & Heineman, Washington, 1980-82, Arnold & Porter, Washington, 1983—; pub. trustee Social Security Trust Funds, Washington, 1990-95. Editor: Harvard Law Rev, 1954-56. Mem. ABA, Fed. Bar Assn., Internat. Fiscal Assn., Nat. Acad. Social Ins. (bd. dirs.). Office: Arnold & Porter 555 12th St NW Washington DC 20004-1200

ROSS, STANLEY RALPH, writer, publisher, producer, software manufacturing executive; b. N.Y.C., July 22, 1940; s. Morris Harvey and Blanche (Turer) R.; m. Neila Hyman, Dec. 14, 1957; children: Andrew Steven, Lisa Michelle Turer, Nancy Ellen. Student, Pratt Inst.; DD, Universal Life Ch., Modesto, Calif., 1973; PhD in Lit., L.A. U., 1976. Self-employed photographer N.Y.C., 1956; copywriter Fuller, Smith & Ross, Los Angeles, 1956-60, Universal Pictures, Los Angeles, 1960-61; advt. exec. Universal Studios, Universal City, Calif., 1960-62; program exec. ABC-TV, Los Angeles, 1961-63; creative dir. Cole, Fischer & Rogow, Beverly Hills, Calif., 1963-65, Becker Advt., Long Beach, Calif., 1964-65; pres., freelance film and TV writer Neila, Inc., Los Angeles, 1965—; Guest lectr. Calif. Luth. Coll., L.A. Coll., Sherwood Oaks U., others; tchr. writing, assoc. prof. U. So. Calif.; cons. in field; exec. v.p., bd. dirs. Crime Books, Wilmette, Ill., 1983—; bd. dirs. The Writers Group, L.A.; pres., CEO Comedy Software, Ltd., Disktop Pub., Inc.; pres. Hollywood Showcase, Inc.; new products cons. RJR Nabisco. Author: Games for Planes, 1974, Speak When You Hear the Beep, 1975, Swan Song, Any Port in a Storm, 1976; writer TV programs All in the Family, The Monkees, Batman, The Man from UNCLE; developer Wonder Woman, The Electric Company, That's My Mama, The Kallikaks, The Monster Squad, The Challenge of the Sexes; scriptwriter Banacek, Colombo, Kids, Inc., Tales from the Crypt, Coffee, Tea or Me?, Gold of the Amazon Women, Murder at the Mardi Gras, The Town That Went on a Diet, Three on a Date, Mrs. R., The Answer, Tomorrow's News, Jojo, Rodeo Drive, Follow Me, Saturday Matinee; editor, author: (with Jay Robert Nash) The Motion Picture Guide, feature film ency., 24 vols.; actor appeared in (TV) Punky Brewster, The Facts of Life, Falcon Crest, Ellery Queen, Hart to Hart, Bill Cosby Show, Double Life of Henry Phyfe, Divorce Court, Superior Court, Family Medical Center, Superman, The Munsters Today (films) Sleeper, Romantic Comedy, John Goldfarb Please Come Home, Tony Rome, Sideout (an Alan Smithee film), numerous commls.; voice over cartoons, commls.; columnist Restaurant Row mag. Vol. The Thalians, Beverly Hills, 1972—, Nosotros, Los Angeles, 1985—, The Soc. of Singers. Recipient UNICEF award, 1974, West Los Angeles Coll. Presdl. citation, 1974, Carson (Calif.) citation, 1973, Cert. Appreciation Personal Freedom Alliance, 1974, Inkpot award San Diego Comicon, 1977, Emmy award nomination Nat. Acad. TV Arts and Scis., 1970, 71, 72, Golden Eagle awards, Nat. Assn. Theater Owners awards, 3 Emmy nominations Nat. Acad. TV Arts and Scis.; named to Bklyn. Hall of Fame Celebrity Path, 1992. Mem. Writers Guild Am. West (award 1971, 72, 74, Family Film award 1990), Producers Guild, Dirs. Guild, Dramatists Guild, Screen Actors Guild, AFTRA, ASCAP, Hon. Order Ky. Cols, TV Acad., Beverly Hills C. of C. Republican. Mem. Universal Life Ch. Club: Saints and Sinners (Los Angeles). Avocations: composing, writing lyrics, baseball, oil painting. Home: 451 S Beverwil Dr Beverly Hills CA 90212-4209 also: Hollywood Showcase 11661 San Vicenti Blvd Ste 500 Los Angeles CA 90049 *My goal in life has been to have a good time and do only what I care to. I feel that I cannot do something that is alien to my nature and have so refused over the years until I discovered that writing was my true vocation. In the past three decades, I have enjoyed myself and had more success than in all my former work years due to this independence. The only other principle I espouse is the law of Karma. For every effect, there is a cause; and every good thing one does is noted in a grand book and the rewards for doing good are reaped here on earth.*

ROSS, SUE, entrepreneur, author, fundraising executive; b. Chgo., Feb. 2, 1948; d. Irving and Rose (Stein) R. BA in Secondary Edn., Western Mich. U., 1971; postgrad., Northwestern U., Chgo. State U., U. Ill., 1971-75. Dir. youth employment Ill. Youth Svcs. Bur., Maywood, Ill., 1978-79; exec. dir. Edn. Resource Ctr., Chgo., 1979-82; asst. dir. devel. Art Inst. Chgo., 1982-83, mgr. govt. affairs, 1983-84, dir. govt. affairs, 1984-85; v.p. devel. Spertus Inst. of Judaica, Chgo., 1985-90; mgmt. and fundraising counsel Sue Ross Enterprises, Chgo. and San Francisco, 1990—; founder, pres. Kid Angels Internat., San Francisco, 1994—; lectr. Sch. Art Inst., Chgo., 1982-85, Episcopalian Archdiocese, Chgo., 1984, Nat. Soc. Fund Raising Execs. and Donor's Forum, Chgo., 1987; instr. DePaul U. Sch. for New Learning, 1987-88, Columbia Coll., Chgo., 1980-91. Resident counsel for devel. The Joffrey Ballet, 1990-91; resident counsel for devel. The 1995 Children's World Peace Festival; adv. panelist Chgo. Office Fine Arts, 1981-82; v.p., bd. dirs. Lines Contemporary Ballet, 1995—; mem. adv. bd. Silkworm Found., 1996—; coord. Pacific Heights Neighborhood Emergency Response Teams, San Francisco, 1996—; mem. adv. coun. Greater Chgo. Food Depository, 1984-85; exec. com. Chgo. Coalition Arts in Edn., 1981-82; mem. info. svcs. com. Donors' Forum Chgo., 1986-88, mem. internationally renowned Gospel Choir of Glide Meml., 1991-93, San Francisco City Chorus, 1994; mem. com. Congregation Sherith Israel, 1996, San Francisco Angel Club, 1994, Angel Collector's Club of Am., 1994—, Angels of World, 1994—; resident counsel for devel. The 1995 Children's World Peace Festival. Mem. Nat. Soc. Fund Raising Execs. (mem. svcs. com. Golden Gate chpt. 1993). Democrat. Jewish. Avocations: community service, singing. Home and Office: 1807 Octavia St San Francisco CA 94109-4328

ROSS, TERRY D., lawyer; b. Glendale, Calif., Aug. 12, 1943. BA, U. Calif., Santa Barbara, 1965; JD, U. Calif., San Francisco, 1968. Bar: Calif. 1969. Ptnr. Gray, Cary, Ware & Freidenrich, San Diego; mem. panel arbitrators Am. Arbitration Assn. Note and comment editor Hastings Law Jour., 1967-68. Bd. dirs. Davis Grossmont YMCA. Mem. ABA (sect. litigation), State Bar Calif., San Diego County Bar Assn. (mem. arbitration panel, superior ct. com.), S.D. Marlin Club, SDMB Boat and Ski Club, Phi Delta Phi. Office: Gray Cary Ware & Freidenrich 401 B St Ste 1700 San Diego CA 92101-4240

ROSS, THOMAS BERNARD, communications company executive; b. N.Y.C., Sept. 2, 1929; s. Henry M. and Evelyn (Timothy) R.; m. Gunilla Ekstrand, Nov. 2, 1963; children: Maria, Anne, Kristina. BA, Yale, 1951. Reporter Internat. News Svc., 1955-58, UPI, 1958; mem. staff Chgo. Sun-Times, 1958-77, mem. staff Washington Bur., 1958-68; fgn. corr. Chgo. Sun-Times, Beirut and Paris, 1968-70; Washington bur. chief Chgo. Sun-Times, 1970-77; asst. sec. def. for pub. affairs, 1977-81; dir. corp. comm. Celanese Corp., 1981-82; sr. v.p. corp. affairs RCA Corp., 1982-86; sr. v.p. NBC News, 1986-90; sr. v.p., dir. media rels. worldwide Hill and Knowlton, N.Y.C., 1990-94; spl. asst. to pres., sr. dir. pub. affairs NSC, White House, Washington, 1994-95; v.p. govt. rels. Loral, N.Y.C., 1995—. Author: (with David Wise) The U-2 Affair, 1962, The Invisible Government, 1964, The Espionage Establishment, 1967. Lt. (j.g.) USNR, 1951-54. Nieman fellow Harvard U., 1964; recipient Marshall Field award, 1961, 71; decorated Def. Disting. Pub. Svc. medal. Mem. Coun. on Fgn. Rels., Elizabethan Club (New Haven), Gridiron Club (Washington), Century Club (N.Y.C.). Home: 1148 Fifth Ave New York NY 10128-0807

ROSS, THOMAS J., JR., personal finanical adviser; b. N.Y.C., Aug. 25, 1954; s. Thomas J. Sr. and Margaret (Byrne) R.; m. Elise Mary Bishop, Sept. 20, 1980; children: Kaitlyn Ann, John Patrick, Brendan Christopher. BA in English magna cum laude, Boston Coll., 1976; MBA in Fin., U. Pa., 1980. Cons. Wharton Applied Rsch. Ctr., Phila., 1978-80; part owner, v.p. Asset Mgmt. Group, Parsippany, N.J., 1980-86; dir. Coopers & Lybrand, Parsippany, 1986-89, ptnr., 1989-92, regional ptnr. personal fin. svcs. group, N.Y. Metro Area, 1992—; mem. adv. bd. Summit Bank, Chatham, N.J.; mem. nat. PFS steering com. Coopers & Lybrand, N.Y.C., 1987—, mem. investment policy com., 1996—. Editor newsletter Growing Your Wealth, 1992—; contbr. numerous tax and fin. articles to Chief Exec. Mag., Bottom Line Fin., N.J. Law Jour. Mem. Kickoff Classic Tix Com., Ind. Coll. Fund of N.J., Summit, 1990—; mem. Boston Coll. Alumni Admissions Coun., Chestnut Hill, Mass., 1976—; mem. exec. com. Boston Coll. Wall St. Coun.; mem. Boston Coll. Wall St. Coun., 1986—; soccer, baseball and lacrosse coach Mountain Lakes Youth Leagues, 1989—; mem. pre-cana team St. Catherine of Siena. Recipient scholarships Boston Coll., Imaculate Heart Guild, others, 1972-76; named Fin. Coun. of Yr., Asset Mgmt. Group, 1983-85. Mem. AICPAs, N.J. Soc. CPAs (com. mem. 1990-92), Wharton Bus. Club of N.Y., Rockaway River C. of C. (house mem. 1991—), Park Ave. Club, Boston Coll. Clubs of N.J. and N.Y.C. Avocations: golf, racquetball, coaching, reading. Home: 140 Kenilworth Rd Mountain Lakes NJ 07046-1156 Office: Coopers & Lybrand One Sylvan Way Parsippany NJ 07054

ROSS, THOMAS MCCALLUM, professional society administrator; b. Hamilton, Ont., Can., May 5, 1931; s. Laverne Robinson and Della Louise (McCallum) R.; m. Marguerite Hilda Ross, Aug. 14, 1954; children: Thomas Wayne, Gregory (dec.), Karyn. Mgr. Sutherland Pharmacy, Hamilton, 1955-60; assoc. sec. Can. Pharm. Assn., Toronto, Ont., 1960-63; mem. research staff Royal Commn. Health Services Govt. Can., Ottawa, Ont., 1963-64; exec. dir. Can. Retail Hardware Assn., Toronto, 1964—. Bd. dirs. People for Sunday Assn., pres. 1987-88. Founding fellow Hardware Mgmt. Inst.; mem. Internat. Fedn. Ironmongers Assn. (coun. 1970—), Can. Soc. Assn. Execs. (chmn. edn. com. 1986-88, bd. dirs. 1990-92, Pinnacle award 1989), Am. Soc. Assn. Execs., Can. C. of C. Home: 59 Walby Dr, Oakville, ON Canada Office: Can Retail Hardward Assn, 6800 Campobello Rd, Mississauga, ON Canada

ROSS, VONIA PEARL, insurance agent, small business owner; b. Taylorville, Ill., Dec. 4, 1942; d. Alvin Clyde and Lois Eva (Weller) Brown; m. Wyatt Gene Ross, Nov. 11, 1962 (Div. Nov. 1986); children: Craig Allen Ross, Cayle Allen Ross. Student, So. Ill. U., 1962-64, Palomar Coll., 1986-88, San Diego State U., 1988-90. Real estate agt. Joe Foster Agy., Collinsville, Ill., 1964-69; ofice mgr. real estate Bank of St. Louis, 1969-73; real estate agt. Palmer-Stelman, San Diego, 1986-89; office mgr. real estate McMillin Realty, San Diego, 1989-90; mgr., ins. agt. Calif. Plus Ins., San Diego, 1990-93; prin. Vonia Ross Ins. Agy., 1993—, Bernardo Flooring, 1993—; mem. Calif. Assn. Real Estate, Sacramento, 1986—, San Diego Bd. Realtors, 1986—, Health Underwriters, 1991—. Mem. adv. com. Rancho Bernardo Libr. Campaign, 1994—; active NOW, San Diego, 1988; mem. activist Barbara Boxer Campaign, San Diego, 1992, Susan Golding Campaign, San Diego, 1992, Barbara Warden Campaign for San Diego City Councilwoman. Scholar Ill. Assembly, 1962; named Philanthropy Coun. Vol. of the Year, 1996. Mem. Rancho Bernardo C. of C. (v.p., bd. dirs. 1993—, pres.-elect 1996—), Soroptimists (pres. Rancho Bernardo 1993-94, 95-96). Avocations: walking, biking, mountain climbing, hiking, golf. Home: 18284 Fernando Way San Diego CA 92128-1213

ROSS, WALTER BEGHTOL, music educator, composer; b. Lincoln, Nebr., Oct. 3, 1936; s. Robert Thurber and Barbara Adeline (Ellis) R.; m. Marion Helen Wright, July 22, 1960; 1 child, Douglas Campbell. BA, U. Nebr., 1960, MusM, 1962; student, Inst. Torcuato Di Tella, Buenos Aires, 1965-66; D of Mus. Arts, Cornell U., 1966. Asst. prof. music CUNY, Cortland, 1966-67; prof. U. Va., Charlottesville, 1967—; mem. judging panel symphonic awards ASCAP, 1978, Internat. Biennial Composition Contest, P.R., 1981, Va. chpt. Coll. Band Dir.'s Nat. Assn. Nat. Band Composition Contest, 1982, 88; bass Blue Ridge Chamber Orch., Charlottesville, 1992—. Composer over 100 works, including compositions for symphony orch., symphonic band, brass, chamber music, piano, voice, opera, theatre, and film; recs. include Concerto for Piano and Orch., Wind Quintet, Nos. 2 and 3, Harlequinade for piano and wind quintet, Escher's Sketches, Concerto for Wind Quintet and String Orch., also others. Nominee Pulitzer Prize, 1973; recipient ASCAP award, 1974—, 1st prize Internat. Trombone Assn., 1982; grantee Am. Music Ctr., 1983; fellow Presser Found., 1958, 59, Orgn. Am. States, 1965, NEA, 1975. Democrat. Avocations: chess, cooking, amateur astronomy. Office: U Va Music Dept Charlottesville VA 22903

ROSS, WENDY CLUCAS, newspaper editor, journalist; b. Balt., Apr. 15, 1942; d. Charles Max and Jean (Talbot) Clucas; m. David N. Ross, Sept. 5, 1964 (div. 1979). BA, Bradley U., 1964. Women's editor DeKalb (Ill.) Daily Chronicle, 1968-69; reporter Chgo. Tribune, 1969-70; copy editor, mag. editor Mpls. Tribune, 1970-72; copy editor Peoria (Ill.) Jour. Star, 1973-75, Miami (Fla.) Herald, 1975-77; asst. news editor Washington Post, 1977-83, dep. news editor, 1983-87, news editor, 1987-93; asst. mng. editor news desk, 1993—. Recipient award of excellence Soc. Newspaper Design, 1985, 87-91, Disting. Alumnae award Bradley U. Centurion Soc., 1994; Nieman fellow Harvard U., 1983-84. Avocations: skiing, sailing, reading, travel. Office: The Washington Post 1150 15th St NW Washington DC 20071-0001

ROSS, WILLIAM JARBOE, lawyer; b. Oklahoma City, May 9, 1930; s. Walter John and Bertha (Jarboe) R.; m. Mary Lillian Ryan, May 19, 1962; children: Rebecca Anne Roten, Robert Joseph, Molly Kathleen. B.B.A., U. Okla., 1952, LL.B., 1954. Bar: Okla. 1954. Since practiced in Oklahoma City; asst. municipal counselor Oklahoma City, 1955-60; mem. firm Rainey, Ross, Rice & Binns, 1960—, partner, 1965—; mem. admissions and grievences com. U.S. Dist. Ct. (we. dist.) Okla.; bd. dirs. PetroUnited Terminals, Inc.; bd. dirs., mem. exec. com. Boatmen's First Nat. Bank of Okla. v.p. exec. com., past pres. bd. dirs. St. Anthony's Hosp. Found.; bd. dirs. Harn Homestead; trustee Ethics and Excellence in Journalism Found., Inasmuch Found. Mem. Okla. Bar Assn., Okla. Heritage Assn. (vice chmn. edn. com.), The Newcomen Soc., Phi Alpha Delta, Beta Theta Pi. Clubs: Oklahoma City Golf and Country, Econ. (Okla.). Lodges: Rotary, K.C. Home: 6923 Avondale Ct Oklahoma City OK 73116-5008

ROSS, WILLIAM WARFIELD, lawyer; b. Washington, Oct. 3, 1926; s. W. Warfield and Vera Elfleda (Payne) R.; m. Jennie Fitch, Jan. 30, 1963; children—James, Mary, Billy. A.B., St. John's Coll., Annapolis, Md., 1948; LL.B., Yale U., 1951. Bar: D.C. 1951. Legal asst. Exec. Office Pres. Harry S. Truman, 1952-53, Pres. Dwight D. Eisenhower, 1953; atty. appellate sect. civil div. Dept. Justice, Washington, 1954-57; asst. to solicitor FPC, Washington, 1957-59; ptnr. Wald, Harkrader & Ross, Washington, 1963-87, Pepper, Hamilton & Scheetz, Washington, 1987-91; adj. prof. Cornell U. Grad. Sch. Bus. and Pub. Adminstrn., 1977-80; chmn. D.C. Council Commn. on Bd. Appeals and Rev. of D.C. Govt., 1972. Chmn. Nat. Capital area ACLU, 1966-68; chmn. audit hearing panel Title I ESEA of 1965, 1976-80. Served with USN, 1945-46. Mem. ABA (chmn. sect. adminstrv. law 1978-79), Bar Assn. D.C. (chmn. adminstrv. law sect. 1968-69, gov. 1969-70), D.C. Bar, Fed. Bar Assn., Fed. Energy Bar Assn. (contbr. articles to jour.). Club: Metropolitan (Washington). Home: 4978 Sentinel Dr Apt 303 Bethesda MD 20816-3573

ROSSANO, AUGUST THOMAS, environmental engineering educator; b. N.Y.C., Feb. 1, 1916; s. August Thomas and Rosa (Cosenza) R.; m. Margie Chrisney, Dec. 6, 1944; children: August Thomas III, Marilyn, Pamela, Jeannine, Renee, Christopher, Stephen, Teresa. B.S., M.I.T., 1938; M.S., Harvard U., 1941, S.D., 1954. Diplomate Am. Acad. Environ. Engrs., Am. Bd. Indsl. Hygiene. Commd. lt. (j.g.) USPHS, 1941, advanced through grades to capt., 1955; assigned Hdqrs. USPHS, 1941, 48, Taft Engring. Ctr., Cin., 1954-59; ret., 1963; prof. air resource engring. U. Wash., Seattle, 1963-81, prof. emeritus, 1981—; pres. Rossano Inc. Environ. Engring. Cons., 1982—; vis. prof. Calif. Inst. Tech., 1960-63; Mem. expert adv. panel on air pollution WHO, Geneva, 1960—, Pan Am. Health Orgn., 1975—; cons. European office WHO, 1960—, U.S. Dept. HEW, 1962—, U.S. Dept. State, 1962—, U.S. Dept. Commerce, 1962—, State of Wash., 1963—, Puget Sound Air Pollution Control Agy., 1967—; cons. govts. U.S., Can., Greece, Czechoslovakia, Republic of China, Peoples Republic of China, Belgium, Netherlands, Mexico, Syria, Iran, Egypt, Brazil, Peru, Chile, Barbados, P.R., Philippines, Venezuela, Curacao, also; Smithsonian Instn. and World Bank, various other nat. and multi-nat. corps.; mem. subcom. on hydrogen sulfide NRC.; Bd. dirs. Environ. Resources Assos., Bellevue Montessori Sch., Environ. Sci. Service div. E.R.A., N.W. Environmental Scis. Ltd., Inst. Exec. Research, Nat. Air Conservation Commn.; lectr. applied physics and environment Bellevue Montessori Sch., WAsh., 1981—, Arbor Elem. Sch., Issaquah, Wash., 1993—; lectr. in field; co-founder Internat. Environ. Inst., 1988. Author: (with Hal Cooper) Source Testing for Air Pollution Control, 1971; Editor: Air Pollution Control, 1969; Contbr. 115 articles to tech. jours. Patentee pollution control device. Served with C.E. AUS. Recipient Spl. Svc. award USPHS, 1958, Disting. Achievement award Pacific NW-Internat. sect. Air Pollution Control Assn., Lyman A. Ripperton award Air and Waste Mgmt. Assn., 1993, Disting. Achievement educator, 1993, Spl. Svc. award USPHS, 1958, Fulbright Travel Lectr. award to eight univs. and rsch. instns. Italy, 1987; HEW tng. grantee, 1964-70; EPA grantee, 1971—; cert. achievement for 45 Yrs. Continuous Svc., Am. Indsl. Hygiene Assn., 1995. Mem. Harvard Pub. Health Alumni Assn. (pres.), Sigma Xi, Delta Omega (prize essay, 1951), Tau Beta Pi. Clubs: Bellevue Triangle Pool, Bellevue Athletic, Alderbrook (Wash.) Golf and Yacht, Wapato Point Resort, Elliott Bay Yacht, Columbia Towers. Home and Office: Emerald Heights 10901 176th Cir NW Apt 4702 Redmond WA 98052

ROSSANT, JAMES STEPHANE, architect, artist; b. N.Y.C., Aug. 17, 1928; s. Marcus and Anne (Orbach) R.; m. Colette Solange Palacci, Sept. 7, 1955; children—Marianne, Juliette, Cecile, Thomas. B.Arch., U. Fla., 1950; M.City and Regional Planning, Harvard U., 1953. Registered architect, N.Y., Calif., Fla. Architect Mayer & Whittlesey, N.Y.C., 1956-60; assoc. Whittlesey & Conklin, N.Y.C., 1961-65; ptnr. Whittlesey Conklin Rossant, N.Y.C., 1966-67, Conklin Rossant, N.Y.C., 1967-94; prin. James Rossant Architects, N.Y.C., 1994—; prof. Pratt Inst., Bklyn., 1958-61, Columbia U., N.Y.C., 1968, NYU, 1976-81, Harvard U., Cambridge, Mass., 1985-89; architect art commn. City of N.Y., 1979-83. Prin. works include design of Reston, Va., Dodoma, Tanzania, Butterfield House, Ramaz Sch. at N.Y.C.; one man shows include Gallery of Architecture, N.Y., 1976, John Nichols Gallery, 1990, Gallery Ueda, Tokyo, 1991, Galeria Pecanins, Mexico City, 1993, Galerie Mantoux-Gignac, Paris, 1995. Fellow AIA (medal of honor N.Y. chpt. 1977). Democrat. Office: 114 Sullivan St New York NY 10012-3604

ROSSAVIK, IVAR KRISTIAN, obstetrician, gynecologist; b. Stavanger, Rogaland, Norway, Nov. 3, 1936; came to U.S., 1982; s. Andreas and Bergit (Berge) R.; divorced; children: Line, Anne Britt, Kirsten, Solveig; m. Claudia Lagos, May 23, 1987; children: Claudia Kristina, Eevar Benjamin. MD, U. Oslo, 1962, PhD, 1982. Pvt. practice, medicine Stavanger, 1974; asst. chief, acting chmn. U. Tromsoe, Norway, 1974-76; clin. fellow Nat. Hosp. of Norway, Oslo, 1976-81, Norwegian Radium Hosp./U. Oslo, 1981-82; pvt. practice Oslo, 1977-82; rsch. asst. prof. Baylor Coll. Medicine, Houston, 1983-86; assoc. prof. U. Okla., Oklahoma City, 1987-93, prof., 1993—; dir. Ultrasound Svcs., Dept. Ob/Gyn., U. Okla. Inventor Rossavik Growth Equation, 1980; author: (textbook) Practical Obstetrical Ultrasound: With and Without A Computer, 1991. Lt. Royal Norwegian Navy, 1964-65. Mem. AMA, Am. Fertility Soc., Am. Inst. Ultrasound in Medicine, Okla. State Med. Assn., Irish and Am. Paediatric Soc., Internat. Perinatal Doppler Soc., So. Med. Assn., AAAS. Lutheran. Avocations: ultrasonography technology, computer technology, fetal growth studies. Office: Univ Oklahoma Dept Ob-Gyn PO Box 26901 Oklahoma City OK 73126-0901

ROSSBACHER, LISA ANN, dean, geology educator, writer; b. Fredericksburg, Va., Oct. 10, 1952; d. Richard Irwin and Jean Mary (Dearing) R.; m. Dallas D. Rhodes, Aug. 4, 1978. BS, Dickinson Coll., 1975; MA, SUNY, Binghamton, 1978, Princeton U., 1979; PhD, Princeton U., 1983. Cons. Republic Geothermal, Santa Fe Springs, Calif., 1979-81; asst. prof. geology Whittier (Calif.) Coll., 1982-84; asst. prof. geology Calif. State Poly. U., Pomona, 1984-86, assoc. prof. geol. sci., 1986-91, assoc. v.p. acad. affairs, 1987-93, prof. geol. sci., 1991-93; v.p. acad. affairs, dean faculty Whittier (Calif.) Coll., 1993-95; dean of coll., prof. geology Dickinson Coll., Carlisle, Pa., 1995—; vis. researcher U. Uppsala, Sweden, 1984. Author: Career Opportunities in Geology and the Earth Sciences, 1983, Recent Revolutions in Geology, 1986; (with Rex Buchanan) Geomedia, 1988; columnist Geotimes, 1988—; contbr. articles to profl. jours. Recipient scholarship Ministry Edn. of Finland, Helsinki, 1984; grantee NASA, 1983-94. Mem. AAAS (geol. nominating com. 1984-87, chair-elect geology and geography sect. 1997—), Geol. Soc. Am., Sigma Xi (grantee 1976). Office: Dickinson Coll Dean of the Coll Carlisle PA 17013

ROSSE, JAMES N., newspaper publishing executive. CEO Freedom Comms., Irvine, Calif. Office: Freedom Comms PO Box 19549 Irvine CA 92762*

ROSSE, THERESE MARIE, reading and special education educator, curriculum and instruction specialist; b. Orleans, Nebr., Dec. 23, 1936; d. Ford Huston and Bertha Therese (Flamming) McCoy; m. John A. Rosse, Apr. 19, 1958 (div. 1979); children: Michelle, John, Robert, David. BS, Coll. St. Mary, Omaha, 1972; MS, U. Nebr., Omaha, 1973; PhD, U. Nebr., Lincoln, 1994. Cert. tchr. reading, spo. edn., history, elem. Tchr., reading clinician Omaha Pub. and Parochial Schs., 1958-72; grad. asst. U. Nebr., Omaha, 1972-73; reading cons. Ralston (Nebr.) Pub. Schs., 1973-75; reading and spl. edn. cons. Area Edn. Agy. 13, Council Bluffs, Iowa, 1975—; adj. prof. Buena Vista Coll., Storm Lake, Iowa, 1976-79, U. Nebr. Omaha, 1978-79, Marycrest Coll., Danveport, Iowa, 1985—, N.W. Mo. State U., Maryville, 1985—, Met. Cmty. Coll., Omaha, 1990—; tester Ednl. Testing Svcs., Princeton, N.J., 1972-73; cons. Creative Cons., Muncie, Ind., 1973-75, Midlands Ednl. Cons., Omaha, 1974-75; rschr. Iowa Dept. Pub. Instrn., Dept. Edn., Des Moines, 1980-82, advisor, 1987-89; text reviewer Scott Foresman, Glenview, Ill., 1980-82; evaluation team North Ctrl. Accredidation Assn., 1980-82. Author: Viewing Reading Comprehension as a Problem Solving Skill: Approaches to Developing Comprehensive Strategies, 1982, Breaking the Language Barrier of Mathematical Thought Problems, 1982, A Grounded Theory of An Organizaed Learner; A Balanced Ecological System, 1994. Advisor Mayor's Commn. on Status of Women Edn. Divsn., Omaha, 1973-75. Mem. ASCD, Internat. Reading Assn. (state bd. sec. 1973-75, v.p. local chpt., state co-chairperson, reading chairperson), Am. Ednl. Rsch. Assn., Coun. Exceptional Children, Phi Delta Kappa, Phi Delta Gamma (pres. local chpt. 1979-80, mem. nat. bd. 1980-82), Phi Alpha Theta. Avocations: travel, reading, classical music and art, writing/research, tennis. Home: 817 N 131 Plz Omaha NE 68154

ROSSEELS, GUSTAVE ALOIS, music educator; b. Malines, Belgium, Jan. 19, 1911; came to U.S., 1946; s. Karel Hubert and Elisabeth (Rooms) R.; m. Jacqueline Crepin, Sept. 5, 1944; children: Marc, Elisabeth, Susanne. Grad. with highest distinction, Royal Conservatory Music, Brussels. Lectr. violin & chamber music U. Mich. Sch. Music, 1957, prof., 1962, prof. emeritus, 1978; instr. violin and chamber music Mills. Coll., Brigham Young U., Aspen (Colo.), Inst., All-State Program Nat. Music Camp, Interlochen, Mich., summers 1981, 82. Violinist, Pro Nova Quartet, Paganini Quartet, Stanley Quartet, Baroque Trio; condr. Jackson (Mich.) Symphony, 1960; author: (autobiography) A Remembering Journey, 1981. Avocations: swimming, golf, reading. Home: 3076 Bolgos Cir Ann Arbor MI 48105-1513

ROSSELL, CHRISTINE HAMILTON, political science educator; b. Bklyn., Jan. 22, 1945; d. Robert Hamilton and Ann (Bezold) R.; 1 child, Elise. AB, UCLA, 1967; MA, Calif. State U., Northridge, 1969; PhD, U. So. Calif., 1974. Asst. prof. Pitzer Coll., Claremont, Calif., 1973-74; rsch. assoc. U. Md., College Park, 1974-75; asst. prof. Boston U., 1975-82, assoc. prof., 1982-89, prof., 1989—, chair dept. polit. sci., 1992-95; vis. asst. prof. Duke U., Durham, N.C., 1977-78, U. Calif., Berkeley, 1981; vis. lectr. Canberra (Australia) Coll., 1985. Author: (with others) Strategies for Effective Desegregation, 1983, Carrot or Stick for School Desegregation, 1990, Bilingual Education in Massachusetts: The Emperor Has No Clothes, 1996;; co-editor: Consequences of School Desegregation, 1983. Mem. Citywide Coord. Coun., Boston, 1976-77. Home: 44 High St Brookline MA 02146-7707 Office: Boston U Dept Polit Sci 232 Bay State Rd Boston MA 02215-1403

ROSSELLINI, ISABELLA, actress, model; b. Rome, June 18, 1952; d. Roberto Rossellini and Ingrid Bergman; m. Martin Scorsese, Sept. 1979 (div. Nov. 1982); m. Jonathan Wiedemann (div.); 1 child, Elettra Ingrid. Student, Finch Coll., 1972, New Sch. for Social Research, N.Y.C. Became model for Lancôme, 1982. Appeared in films A Matter of Time, 1976, Il Pap'occhio, 1980, The Meadow, 1982, White Nights, 1985, Blue Velvet, 1986, Siesta, 1987, Red Riding Hood, 1987, Tough Guys Don't Dance, 1987, Zelly and Me, 1988, Cousins, 1989, Wild at Heart, 1990, Les Dames Galantes, 1990, Death Becomes Her, 1992, The Pickle, 1992, Fearless, 1993, Wyatt Earp, 1994, Immortal Beloved, 1994, The Innocent, 1995, The Funeral, Crime of the Century, 1996, Big Night, 1996; TV films: The Last Elephant, 1990, Lies of the Twins, 1991. Office: United Talent Agency 9560 Wilshire Blvd Fl 5 Beverly Hills CA 90212-2401

ROSSELLÕ, PEDRO, governor of Puerto Rico; b. San Juan, P.R., Apr. 5, 1944; m. Maga Nevares, Aug. 9, 1969; children: Juan Oscar, Luis Roberto, Ricardo Antonio. BS, U. Notre Dame, 1966; MD, Yale U., 1970; MPH, U. P.R., 1981; LLD (hon.), U. Notre Dame, 1995, U. Mass., 1995. Intern straight surgery Beth Israel Hosp., Boston, 1970-71, resident gen. surgery, 1971-74; resident cardiac and burns Mass. Gen. Hosp., Boston, 1972; resident trauma San Francisco Gen. Hosp., 1973; sr. resident pediat. surgery Children's Hosp., Boston, 1974-75, chief resident, pediat. surgery-urology, 1975-76; instr. surgery Harvard Med. Sch., 1975-76; pvt. practice San Juan, 1976-92; asst. prof. surgery U. P.R., 1978-82, assoc. prof. surgery, 1982-92; dir. Dept. Health City of San Juan, 1985-87; chief surgery San Jorge Hosp., San Juan, 1989-92, med. dir., 1990; gov. Puerto Rico, 1993—; lead gov. So. Regional Project Infant Mortality, 1993-95; chair So. States Energy Bd., 1995-96; mem. intergovtl. policy adv. com. U.S. Trade Rep.; pres.-elect Coun. State Govts. Contbr. articles to profl. jours. Mem. P.R. Olympic Com., 1982-84, 87-88; v.p. New Progressive Party, 1988-91, pres., 1991—; mem. exec. com. Edn. Commn. States; bd. visitors Georgetown U. Law Ctr., Washington; del. Dm. Nat. Conv., Chgo., 1996. Capt. USNG, 1970-76. Mem. Nat. Govs. Assn. (host 1996 ann. meeting), So. Govs. Assn. (vice chair), Dem. Govs. Assn. (vice chmn.), P.R. Tennis Assn. (pres. 1982-84), Caribbean Tennis Assn. (pres. 1983-84), Alpha Omega Alpha. Avocations: jogging, tennis, ocean kayaking.

ROSSEN, JORDAN, lawyer; b. Detroit, June 13, 1934; s. Nathan Paul and Rebecca (Rizy) R.; m. Susan Friebert, Mar. 24, 1963 (div. June 1972); 1 child, Rebecca; m. M. Elizabeth Bunn, Jan. 3, 1981; children—N. Paul, Jordan David. B.A., U. Mich., 1956; J.D., Harvard U., 1959. Bar: Mich. 1960, U.S. Dist. Ct. (ea. dist.) Mich. 1960, U.S. Ct. Appeals (6th cir.) 1966, U.S. Ct. Appeals (7th cir.) 1974, U.S. Supreme Ct. 1966. Assoc. Sullivan, Elmer, Eames & Moody, Detroit, 1960-62; assoc. Sugar & Schwartz, Detroit, 1962-64; asst. gen. counsel UAW, Detroit, 1964-74, assoc. gen. counsel, 1974-83, gen. counsel, 1983—; vice pres. N.P. Rossen Agy., Inc., Detroit, 1960-83; gen. counsel Mich. Health & Social Security Research Inst., Inc., Detroit, 1965-83; dir. UAW Job Devel. & Tng. Corp., Detroit, 1984-90. Editor: Mich. Bar Labor Section Publication, 1961-64. Contbr. articles to profl. jours. Pres. Young Democrats, Mich., 1963-65; chmn. Americans for Democratic Action, Mich., 1966-68; chmn. Voter Registration Dem. Party, Mich., 1967. Recipient Human Rights award City of Detroit, 1978. Mem. ABA, Mich. Bar Assn., Nat. Bar Assn., Fed. Bar Assn., Wolverine Bar Assn., Women Lawyers Assn., Lawyers Guild. Jewish. Office: UAW Legal Dept 8000 E Jefferson Ave Detroit MI 48214-3963

ROSSER, ANNETTA HAMILTON, composer; b. Jasper, Fla., Aug. 28, 1913; d. Carlos Calvin and Jermai Reuben (Gilbert) Hamilton; m. John Barkley Rosser, Sept. 7, 1935 (dec. Sept. 1989); children: Edwenna Merryday, John Barkley Jr. BM, Fla. State U., 1932. Cert. tchr., Fla. Tchr. music Kirby-Smith Jr. High Sch., Jacksonville, Fla., 1932-35; 1st violinist Santa Monica (Calif.) Symphony, 1949-50; concertmaster Ithaca (N.Y.) Chamber Orch., 1948-56; concertmaster Cornell Univ. Orch., Ithaca, 1948-56, soloist, 1957; 1st violinist Princeton (N.J.) Symphony, 1959-61; concertmaster Madison (Wis.) Symphony Orch., 1963-66, 1st violinist, 1967-82. Composer of over 100 vocal and instrumental compositions including Meditations on Cross, song cycle for 2 voices, flute and piano, 1976, An Offering of Song, book of 48 songs, 1977, Songs of a Nomad Flute, song cycle for soprano, flute and piano, 1978, Six Songs of the T'ang Dynasty for soprano and violin, 1983, Nocturne for violin and piano, 1989, Trio for flute, violin and piano, 1991, Scherzo for flute ensemble, 1991. Bd. dirs. Madison Opera Guild, 1972-86, Madison Civic Music Assn., 1983-85; past pres. Madison Symphony Orch. League, Ithaca Federated Music Club, Ithaca Composers Club; trustee Madison Art Ctr., 1979-83, Madison Civics Club, 1976-79, Madison Woman of Distinction, 1980. Recipient Sr. Svc. award Rotary Club, 1994; original music manuscripts were added to archives of Wis. and women composers in U. Wis.-Madison Music Libr., 1996. Mem. AAUW, Univ. League, Univ. League Bird Study Group, Madison Club, Madison Federated Music Club, PEO, Phi Kappa Phi, Pi Kappa Lambda, Sigma Alpha Iota. Republican. Presbyterian. Avocations: Chinese snuff bottles, English brass rubbings, birding. Home: 4209 Manitou Way Madison WI 53711-3703

ROSSER, EDWIN MICHAEL, mortgage company executive; b. Denver, Oct. 11, 1940; s. Edwin Michael and Anne (Ratliff) R.; m. Keren Call, July 17, 1969; children: Kevin, William. BS, Colo. State U., 1964; MA, U. No. Colo., 1974. Cert. mortgage banker. Mktg. officer United Bank Mortgage, Denver, 1968-74; dir. nat. accounts PMI Mortgage Ins. Co., Denver, 1974-85; v.p. Moore Mortgage Co., Denver, 1985-87, Pacific First Mortgage Corp., Englewood, Colo., 1987-89; 1st v.p. 1st Nat. Bank, San Francisco, 1990-93; v.p. nat. accounts United Guaranty Corp., 1993—; bd. dirs. Rocky Mtn. Women's Inst. Photographer represented in Denver Art Mus., The Buffalo in Winter, (1st place award 1981). Steering com. Blueprint for Colo., Govs. Unified Housing Task Force; mem. Colo. Housing Coun. (chmn. 1986-87); bd. dirs. Colo. State Found. Mem. Mortgage Bankers Assn. Am. (bd. govs. 1986-90, state and local achievement award 1986, Ernest P. Schumacher award 1988, membership achievement award 1995, Burton Wood Legis. Svc. award), Colo. Mortgage Bankers Assn. (bd. dirs. 1979-88, pres. 1986, E.C. Spelman award 1978), Colo. Assn. Commerce and Industry, Denver Nat. Soc. Real Estate Fin., Mus. Natural History, Denver C. of C., Colo. State U. Alumni Assn. (nat. pres. 1985, bd. dirs. 1979-87, mem. found. bd. 1987-91, 93—, Honor Alumnus 1984, ha Sasso award Dept. Athletics 1993), City Club Denver, Commonwealth Club. Calif. Republican. Roman Catholic. Avocations: competitive swimming, photography. Home: 12478 E Amherst Cir Aurora CO 80014-3306 Office: United Residential Ins Co 6312 So Fiddlers Greencircle Englewood CO 80111

ROSSER, JAMES MILTON, academic administrator; b. East St. Louis, Ill., Apr. 16, 1939; s. William M. and Mary E. (Bass) R.; 1 child, Terrence. B.A., So. Ill. U., 1962, M.A., 1963, Ph.D., 1969. Diagnostic bacteriologist Holden Hosp., Carbondale, Ill., 1961-63; research bacteriologist Eli Lilly & Co., Indpls., 1963-66; coordinator Black Am. studies, instr. health edn. So. Ill. U., Carbondale, 1968-69; asst. prof. Black Am. studies dir. So. Ill. U., 1969-70, asst. to chancellor, 1970; asso. vice chancellor for acad. affairs U. Kans., Lawrence, 1970-74; assoc. prof. edn., pharmacology and toxicology U. Kans., 1971-74; vice chancellor dept. higher edn. State of N.J., Trenton, 1974-79; acting chancellor State of N.J., 1977; pres., prof. health care mgmt. Calif. State U., Los Angeles, 1979—; mem. tech. resource panel Ctr. for Research and Devel. in Higher Edn., U. Calif., Berkeley, 1974-76; mem. health maintenance orgn. com. Health Planning Coun., State of N.J., 1975-79; mem. standing com. on research and devel. bd. trustees Ednl. Testing Service, 1976-77; mem. steering com. and task force on retention of minorities in engring. Assembly of Engring. NRC, 1975-78; mem. Bd. Med. Examiners, State of N.J., 1978-79; vis. faculty mem. Inst. Mgmt. of Lifelong Edn., Grad. Sch. Edn., Harvard U., 1979; mem. Calif. State U. Trustees Spl. Long Range Fin. Planning Com., 1982-87; mem. Am. Coun. on Edn., 1979—, AFL/CIO Labor Higher Edn. Coun., 1983—, Nat. Commn. Higher Edn. Issues, 1981-82; mem. The Calif. Achievement Coun., 1983-89, strategic adv. counc. Coll. and Univs. Systems Exchange, 1988-91; bd. dirs. Am. Humanities Coun., So. Calif. Am. Humanics, Inc. Coun., Sanwa Bank Calif., 1993—, Edison Internat., 1985—, Fedco, Inc., 1987—. Author: An Analysis of Health Care Delivery, 1977. Mem. exec. bd., chmn. varisty scouting program L.A. area coun. Boy Scouts Am., 1980—; bd. dirs. Hispanic Urban Ctr., L.A., 1979—, L.A. Urban League, 1982-95, Cmty. TV of So. Calif., Sta. KCET, 1980-89, United Way, L.A., 1980-91, Orthopaedic Hosp., 1983-86, L.A. Philharm. Assn., 1986—, Nat. Health Found., 1990—, Calif. C. of C., 1993—; mem. Citizen's Adv. Coun. Congl. Caucus Sci. and Tech., 1983—; mem. performing arts coun./edn. coun. Music Ctr., 1984—; mem. minority bus. task force Pacific Bell, 1985-86; mem. bd. govs. Nat. ARC, 1986-91, Mayor's Blue Ribbon Task Force on Drugs, City of L.A., 1988, L.A. Annenberg Met. Project, 1994—; Nat. Adv. Coun. on Aging, 1989-93; bd. trustees Woodrow Wilson Nat. Fellowship Found., 1993—; mem. bd. advisors Historically Black Colls. and Univs. and Minority Insts., Dept. Air Force, 1997—. NSF fellow, 1961; NDEA fellow, 1967-68; recipient award of recognition in Edn. Involvement for Young Achievers, 1981, Pioneer of Black Hist. Achievement award Brotherhood Crusade, 1981, Alumni Achievement award So. Ill. U., 1982, Friend of Youth award Am. Humanics, Inc., 1985, Leadership award Dept. Higher Edn. Ednl. Equal Opportunity Fund Program, 1989, Medal of Excellence Gold State Minority Found., 1990, Take Charge of Learning Success award Inst. for Redesign of Learning. Mem. Calif. C. of C. (bd. dirs. 1993—), Alhambra C. of C. (bd. dirs. 1979—), Los Angeles C. of C. (bd. dirs. 1985-90), Am. Assn. State Colls. and Univs., Kappa Delta Pi, Phi Kappa Phi. Roman Catholic. Office: Calif State Univ Office of the Pres 5151 State University Dr Los Angeles CA 90032-4226

ROSSER, RHONDA LANAE, psychotherapist; b. Champaign, Ill., Aug. 29, 1953; d. Neill Albert and Grace Lee (Byers) R.; (div. June 1, 1993); children: Anthony Neill Williams, Joseph Neill Jackson Hogan. BS in Psychology, Guilford Coll., 1975; MEd in Edn., U. N.C., Greensboro, 1979, PhD in Counseling, 1991. Joined 3rd Order of Secular Franciscans/Order of St. Francis. Instr. U. N.C., Greensboro, 1985-88; dir. Montagnard Program Luth. Family Svcs., Greensboro, 1985-88; psychotherapist pvt. practice, Greensboro, 1989—. Contbr. articles to profl. jours. Recipient Presdl. citation U.S. Govt., 1987. Mem. Am. Counseling Assn. (Outstanding Rsch. award 1991), Chi Sigma Iota. Democrat. Roman Catholic (3d order of Secular Franciscans/Order of St. Francis). Avocations: fox hunting, bird watching, snow skiing, writing. Home and Office: 2318 W Cornwallis Dr Greensboro NC 27408-6802

ROSSER, RICHARD FRANKLIN, company executive; b. Arcanum, Ohio, July 16, 1929; s. Harold Arm and Margaret (Whitacre) R.; m. Donna Eyssen., Mar. 21, 1951; children—Eric, Carl, Edward. B.A., Ohio Wesleyan U., 1951; M.P.A., Syracuse U., 1952, Ph.D., 1961. Joined U.S. Air Force, 1952, advanced through grades to col., 1968; prof. polit. sci. U.S. Air Force Acad., Colorado Springs, Colo., 1959-73; head dept. U.S. Air Force Acad., 1967-73, ret., 1973; prof. polit. sci., dean Albion (Mich.) Coll., 1973-77; pres. DePauw U., Greencastle, Ind., 1977-86, chancellor, 1986; pres. Nat. Assn. Ind. Colls. and Univs., Washington, 1986-93; cons. in higher edn. pvt. practice, Traverse City, Mich., 1993—. Author: An Introduction to Soviet Foreign Policy, 1969; Contbr. articles to profl. jours. Mem. univ. senate United Meth. Ch., 1980-84; mem. spl. commn. of Chief of Staff on Honor Code U.S. Mil. Acad., 1989; bd. visitors Air U., 1991-94; bd. trustees Ohio Wesleyan U., 1991—; mem. nat. adv. com. Instnl. Quality and Integrity, 1994—; co-chair Citizens for Librs., Grand Traverse County, 1995-96. Decorated Legion of Merit with oak leaf cluster. Mem. Am. Polit. Sci. Assn., Phi Beta Kappa, Omicron Delta Kappa. Presbyterian. Home and Office: 2161 Harbor Reach Dr Traverse City MI 49686-9721

ROSSET, BARNET LEE, JR., publisher; b. Chgo., May 28, 1922; s. Barnet Lee and Mary (Tansey) R.; m. Joan Mitchell, 1950 (div. 1952); m. Hannelore Eckert, Aug. 1953 (div. 1957); 1 child, Peter; m. Cristine Agnini, Mar. 11, 1965 (div. 1979); children—Tansey, Beckett; m. Elisabeth Krug, 1980 (div. 1991; 1 child, Chantal. Ph.B., U. Chgo., 1947; B.A. New Sch. Social Research, N.Y.C., 1952. Pub., editor Grove Press, Inc., 1951-86, Evergreen Rev., Rosset and Co., Inc., 1957-73, Blue Moon Books, Inc., N.Y.C., 1987—. Served to 1st lt. Signal Corps AUS, 1942-46. Recipient Ninth Pub. citation PEN Am. Ctr., 1988. Mem. PEN, Overseas Press Club. Office: 61 4th Ave New York NY 10003-5204

ROSSET, LISA KRUG, editor; b. N.Y.C., Nov. 11, 1952; d. George William and Rita (Earle) Krug; m. Barney Rosset, Nov. 5, 1980 (div. Dec. 1990); 1 child, Chantal. B.A. magna cum laude, Smith Coll., 1974; M.A., Columbia U., 1976. Editor Latin Am. Series, N.Y.C., 1976-86; gen. editor Grove Press, N.Y.C., 1976-86; mng. editor Aperture, N.Y.C., 1987-90; pvt. practice N.Y.C., 1990—; cons. writer and editor UNICEF, N.Y.C., 1995—. Author: James Baldwin, 1989, Thurgood Marshall, 1993, Outstanding Book For Teenagers, 1994. Mem. Phi Beta Kappa.

ROSSETTI, LINDA ELAINE, special education educator; b. Boston, Sept. 17, 1946; d. Bert A. and Angela (Callionais) Badavas; m. John Peter Rossetti, Dec. 26, 1969; children: Lisa, Nicholas. BA in Sociology, U. Mass., Amherst, 1969; MA in Spl. Edn., W.Va. U., 1972. Cert. tchr., Md. Program dir. Zia Sch. for Children, Alamogordo, N.Mex., 1972-73; tchr., prescriptive specialist Alamogordo Ctr. for Exceptional Students, 1973-78; head tchr. Golden Hills Acad., Auburn, Calif., 1978-79; resource tchr., team leader Bushy Park Elem. Sch., Glenwood, Md., 1986—; mem. tchr. interview team Howard County Pub. Schs., Ellicott City, Md., 1990—; initiator and coord. Spl. Olympics, Alamogordo Pub. Schs., 1973-78; coord. Working on Wellness team Bushy Park Elem. Sch., 1990-92. Bd. dirs. Otero County Assn. Retarded Citizens, Alamogordo, 1973-77. Nominee for Md. Tchr. of Yr. Mem. Coun. for Exceptional Children (pres. 1973-77), Howard County Ednl. Assn., Phi Delta Kappa. Office: Bushy Park Elem Sch 2670 State Route 97 Glenwood MD 21738-9712

ROSSEY, PAUL WILLIAM, school superintendent, university president; b. Richmond, Ind., July 7, 1926; s. Chris C. and Lela (Longman) R.; m. Adelaide Elizabeth Finnegan; 1 dau., Joanne Rossey Sczubelek. B.S., Jersey City State Coll., 1952, Litt. D., 1971; M.A., NYU, 1953, Ed.D. (Kellogg Found. fellow 1955), 1958. Head jr. sch. Peddie Sch., Hightstown, N.J., 1952-53; cons., elem. sch. instr. West Hempstead, N.Y., 1953-55; prin. elem. sch. Dobbs Ferry, N.Y., 1955-58; supt. schs. Litchfield, Conn., 1958-60, Scotch Plains-Fanwood, N.J., 1960-67; dist. supt. schs. Nassau County, N.Y., 1967-69; pres. West Chester (Pa.) State U., 1969-74; supt. schs. Millburn-Short Hills, N.J., 1974-92; ret.; lectr. NYU, 1954-67. Contbr. articles to profl. jours. County dir. Boy Scouts Am.; v.p. YMCA; bd. dirs. Garbe Found., Community Fund; trustee NYU, 1970-74, The Peddie Sch., 1974-92; mem. exec. com. N.J. Coun. Edn., 1977-83. With USNR, 1944-46, USMCR, 1972-86; ret. Named Outstanding Alumnus, Jersey City State Coll., 1962; recipient NYU medallion, 1966, Ernest O. Melby award human relations, 1970. Mem. Am. Assn. Sch. Adminstrs. (chmn. N.J. 1965-67), Am. Council Edn., Aircraft Owners and Pilots Assn., N.J. Assn. Sch. Adminstrs. (exec. com. 1964-67, 81-85), Horace Mann League U.S. (nat. pres. 1977-78), Kappa Delta Pi, Phi Delta Kappa. Republican. Presbyn. Clubs: Exchange (dir.), N.J. Schoolmasters. Home: 219 Summit Ave Summit NJ 07901-2213

ROSSI, ALICE S., sociology educator, author; b. N.Y.C., Sept. 24, 1922; d. William A. and Emma (Winkler) Schaerr; m. Max Kitt, Dec. 1941 (div. Sept. 1951); m. Peter H. Rossi, Sept. 29, 1951; children: Peter Eric, Kristin Alice, Nina Alexis. BA, Bklyn. Coll., 1947; PhD, Columbia U., 1957; 9 hon. degrees. Rsch. assoc. Cornell U., Ithaca, N.Y., 1951-52, Harvard U., Cambridge, Mass., 1952-55, U. Chgo., 1961-67, Johns Hopkins U., Balt., 1967-69; prof. sociology Goucher Coll., Balt., 1969-74; prof. sociology U. Mass., Amherst, 1974-91, prof. emerita, 1991—. Author/editor: 11 books; contbr. numerous articles to profl. jours. Founder, bd. mem. NOW, 1966-70; pres. Sociologists for Women in Soc., 1971-72. Career grantee NIMH, 1965-69, rsch. grantee Rockefeller Found., Ford Found., NIH, NSF, others; CommonWealth Disting. Scholarship award, 1988. Mem. Am. Sociol. Assn. (pres. 1983-84), Ea. Sociol. Soc. (pres. 1973-74). Avocations: design, sewing, gardening, creative writing. Home: 34 Stagecoach Rd Amherst MA 01002-3527

ROSSI, ANTHONY GERALD, lawyer; b. Warren, Ohio, July 20, 1935; s. Anthony Gerald and Lena (Guarnieri) R.; m. Marilyn J. Fuller, June 22, 1957; children: Diana L., Maribeth, Anthony Gerald III. BS, John Carroll U., 1957; JD, Cath. U. Am., 1961. Bar: Ohio 1961. Ptnr. Guarnieri & Secrest, Warren, 1961—; former acting judge Warren Municipal Ct. Mem. Mahoning-Shenango Estate Planning Coun., 1968—, past sec.; past pres. Warren Olympic Club; past bd. govs. Cath. U. Am. Law Sch. Coun.; past trustee Trumbull Art Guild, Warren Civic Music Assn. Capt. Transp. Corps, AUS, 1957-65. Mem. ABA, Ohio Bar Assn., Trumbull County Bar Assn. (exec. com. 1975—, pres. 1976-77), Am. Arbitration Assn., Ohio Motorist Assn. (corp. mem., trustee 1980-86, 92—), Wolf's Club, KC, Elks. Home: 2500 Hidden Lakes Dr NE Warren OH 44484-4159 Office: 151 E Market St Warren OH 44481-1102

ROSSI, ENNIO C., physician, educator; b. Madison, Wis., Apr. 3, 1931; s. Joseph and Esther (D'Amelio) R.; m. Anna Maria Bianchi, June 22, 1957; children: Roberta, Marco. BA, U. Wis., 1951, MD, 1954. Diplomate Am. Bd. Internal Medicine. Intern Ohio State U. Hosps., 1954-55; resident medicine U. Wis. Hosps., 1958-61, fellow, 1961-63; instr. medicine Marquette U., Milw., 1963-64, asst. prof. medicine, 1964-66; assoc. prof. medicine Northwestern U., Chgo., 1966-72, prof. medicine, 1972-96, prof. emeritus, 1996—, chief hematology, 1967-84, chief transfusion medicine, 1984-96; v.p. med. affairs Life Source Blood Ctr., Glenview, Ill., 1988-93; vis. scientist Mario Negri Inst., Milan, 1977. Co-editor: Haemostasis and the Kidney, 1989; sr. editor: Principles of Transfusion Medicine, 1991, 2d edit., 1996. Capt. U.S. Army, 1956-58. Fulbright scholar, U.S. Dept. State, U. Rome, 1955; Nat. Heart, Lung Blood Inst. Transfusion Medicine Acad. awardee, 1983; WHO travelling fellow, 1985. Fellow ACP; mem. Am. Soc. Hematology, Am. Soc. Pharmacology and Exptl. Therapeutics, Am. Assn. Blood Banks (chmn. acad. transfusion medicine com. 1988-93), Internat. Soc. Blood Transfusion. Home: 1256 Forest Glen Dr N Winnetka IL 60093-1423

ROSSI, FAUST F., lawyer, educator; b. 1932. BA, U. Toronto, 1953; JD, Cornell U., 1960. Bar: N.Y. 1960. Tax trial atty., Dept. Justice, Washington, 1960-61; sole practice, Rochester, N.Y., 1961-66; assoc. prof. Cornell U., Ithaca, N.Y., 1966-69, prof. 1970—, assoc. dean, 1973-75, Samuel S. Leibowitz prof. trial techniques, 1982—; vis. fellow Wadham Coll., Oxford, 1987-88; vis. prof. Emory U., 1990; cons. report of fed. class actions Am. Coll. of Trial Lawyers, 1971-72; cons. com. on proposed fed. rules of evidence N.Y. Trial Lawyers Assn., 1970; cons., instr. annual seminar N.Y. State Trial Judges, 1970-78; cons., instr. Nat. Inst. for Trial Advocacy, 1974-75, 80-84, 88; cons. N.Y. Law Revision Commn. Project for N.Y. Code of Evidence, 1978-80. Lt. j.g. USN. Recipient Jacobsen prize for teaching trial advocacy, 1992. Mem. Order of Coif. Author: Study of the Proposed Federal Rules of Evidence, 1979, Report on Rule 23 Class Actions, 1972, The Federal Rules of Evidence, 1970, Expert Witnesses, 1991; co-author: New York Evidence, 1997; contbr. articles to profl. jours. Office: Cornell U Law Sch Myron Taylor Hall Ithaca NY 14853

ROSSI, HARALD HERMANN, retired radiation biophysicist, educator, administrator; b. Vienna, Austria, Sept. 3, 1917; came to U.S., 1939; s. Oswald J. and Hedwig E. (Braun) R.; m. Ruth Gregg, June 22, 1946; children: Gerald, Gwendolyn Gladstone, Harriet Furey. Student, U. Vienna, 1935-39, U. Bristol, Eng., 1939; Ph.D., Johns Hopkins U., 1942. Cert. in radiol. physics Am. Bd. Radiology. Instr. Johns Hopkins U., Balt., 1940-45; research physicist Nat. Bur. Standards, Washington, 1945; physicist and radiation protection officer Presbyn. Hosp., N.Y.C., 1954-60; rsch. scientist radiol. rsch. lab. Columbia U., N.Y.C., 1946-60, asst. prof. radiology, 1949-53, assoc. prof., 1953-60, prof. radiology and physics, dir. radiol. rsch. lab., 1960-84, prof. radiation oncology, 1984-87, prof. emeritus, 1988—; cons., 1988—; cons. NIH, NRC, Dept. Energy, FAA; chmn. tech. com. Radiation to Health Commr. of N.Y.C., 1978-82; mem. Internat. Com. on Radiation Units and Measurements, Main Com., Washington, 1959—, Nat. Coun. on Radiation Protection, Main Coun., 1954-83, hon. mem., 1983—. Co-author: Advances in Biological and Medical Physics, 1967, Radiation Dosimetry, 1968, Cancer: A Comprehensive Treatise, 1982. Trustee, pres. Upper Nyack sch. Bd., N.Y., 1957-60; trustee Rockland County Day Sch., 1961-63. Recipient Shonka Meml. Found. award, 1972, Gray medal Internat. Commn. on Radiation Units and Measurements, 1985, Disting. Scientific Achievement award Health Physics Soc., 1987. Fellow Am. Coll. Radiology; mem. AAAS, Radiation Research Soc. (pres. 1974-75), Am. Coll. Radiology, Radiol. Soc. N.Am., Sigma Xi. Office: 105 Larchdale Ave Nyack NY 10960-1003

ROSSI, MARIO ALEXANDER, architect; b. Chgo., Apr. 9, 1931; s. Gastone J. and Irma (Giorgi) R.; m. Jo Ann Therese Kneip, Apr. 12, 1958; children: John Vincent, Lyn Ann, Paul Alexander, Mara Ann. BArch, Ill. Inst. Tech., 1955. Architect Omnimetrics, L.A., 1967-78; pvt. practice Seal Beach, Calif., 1975—. Prin. works include fin. models for Calif. Fed. Bank, L.A., First Nat. City Bank, N.Y.C., Glendale (Calif.) Fed. Bank, Wailea, Alexander and Baldwin, Hawaii. Lt, (j.g.) USN, 1955-58. Research computerized techniques in architecture and economic feasibility land development. Home and Office: 1721 Catalina Ave Seal Beach CA 90740-5710

ROSSI, PETER HENRY, sociology educator; b. N.Y.C., Dec. 27, 1921; s. Peter Maxim and Elizabeth (Porcelli) R.; m. Alice Schaerr, Sept. 29, 1951; children: Peter Eric, Kristin Alice, Nina Alexis. B.S., CCNY, 1943; Ph.D., Columbia, 1951. Research asso. Bur. Applied Social Research, Columbia U., 1947- 51; asst. prof. Harvard U., 1951-55; prof. dept. sociology U. Chgo., 1955-67; dir. Nat. Opinion Research Center, 1960-67; prof. dept. social relations Johns Hopkins, 1967-74, chmn. dept., 1967-70; dir. research Center for Met. Planning and Research, 1972-74; prof. sociology, dir. Social and Demographic Research Inst., U. Mass., Amherst, 1974-92; Stuart A. Rice prof. sociology, dir. Social and Demographic Research Inst., U. Mass., 1984-92, prof. emeritus, 1992—; faculty assoc. Chapin Hall U. Chgo., 1994—. Author: Why Families Move, 1956, The Politics of Urban Renewal, 1962, The Education of Catholic Americans, 1966, New Media and Education, 1967, Ghetto Revolts, 1970, Cities Under Siege, 1971, Evaluating Social Programs, 1972, Roots of Urban Discontent, 1974, Reforming Public Welfare, 1976, Prison Reform and State Elites, 1977, Evaluation: A Systematic Approach, 1979, Money, Work & Crime, 1980, After the Clean-up, 1980, Social Science and Natural Hazards, 1981, Measuring Social Judgements, 1982, Natural Hazards and Public Choice, 1982, Under the Gun, 1983, Applied Sociology, 1983, Without Shelter, 1989, Down and Out in America, 1989, Of Human Bonding, 1990; editor: Am. Jour. Sociology, 1957-58; assoc. editor: Am. Sociol. Rev, 1957-60, Am. Sociologist, 1964-66; editor: Social Sci. Research, 1972-89; contbr. articles to profl. and popular jours. Served with AUS, 1942-45. Recipient Alvah and Gunnar Myrdal award for contbns. to evaluation research, 1981; Commonwealth award for contbns. to sociology, 1985; faculty research grantee Social Sci. Research Council, 1959; Carnegie sr. fellow, 1965. Fellow Am. Acad. Arts and Scis.; mem. Am. Sociol. Assn. (sec. 1968-72, pres.-elect 1979-80, pres. 1980-81), Am. Evaluation Assn.

ROSSI, RONALD ALDO, sports association administrator, Olympic athlete; b. Bronx, N.Y., Dec. 2, 1956; s. Aldo D. and Jeanette (Morretta) R.; m. Susan Veltman, Mar. 26, 1983; 1 child, Scott. BEE, Manhattan Coll., 1978. Registered profl. engr., N.Y. Mem. computer ops. staff John Blair and Co., N.Y.C., 1978-83, communications engr., 1984; sports program dir. U.S. Luge Assn., Lake Placid, N.Y., 1984-85, exec. dir., 1985—; com. mem. U.S. Luge Assn., 1978—, athlete's rep., 1980-83; com. mem. U.S. Olympic Com., Colorado Springs, Colo., 1989-90, 93—. Mem. U.S. Olympic Luge Team, Sarajevo, Yugoslavia, 1984; mem. Olympic team staff, Calgary, Can., 1988, Albertville, France, 1992, Lillehammer, Norway, 1994. Avocations: luge, golf, softball, movies, computers. Office: US Luge Assn PO Box 651 Lake Placid NY 12946-0651

ROSSI, STEVEN B., newspaper publishing executive. Grad., Ursinus Coll., 1971; MBA, U. Pa., 1974. With UI Internat. Corp., Phila., 1974-78, UGI Corp., Phila., 1978-87; with Phila. Newspapers, 1987—, exec. v.p., gen. mgr. Office: Phila Newspapers Inc 400 N Broad St Philadelphia PA 19130-4015*

ROSSIDES, EUGENE TELEMACHUS, lawyer, writer; b. N.Y.C., Oct. 23, 1927; s. Telemachus and Anna (Maravel) R.; m. Elinor Burcham (div.); 1 child, Gale; m. Aphrodite Macotsin, Dec. 30, 1961; children: Michael, Alexander, Eleni. AB, Columbia U., 1949, JD, 1952. Criminal law investigator Office of Dist. Atty., N.Y.C., 1952; assoc. Rogers & Wells, N.Y.C., 1954-56, 61-66, ptnr., 1966-69, 73-92, sr. counsel, 1993—; asst. atty. gen. State of N.Y., N.Y.C., 1956-58; asst. to undersec. Dept. Treasury, Washington, 1958-61, asst. sec., 1969-73; bd. dirs. Sterling Nat. Bank, N.Y.C. Author: U.S. Import Trade Regulation, 2d edit., 1986, Foreign Unfair Competition, 3d edit., 1991, United States Import Trade Law, 1992, also articles; chief import editor Internat. Trade Reporter, Bur. Nat. Affairs, 1980—; editor: Doing Business in Greece, 1996. Mem. Grace Commn., Washington, 1981-82; chmn. nationalities div. Reagan Bush Com., Washington, 1980; campaign mgr. N.Y.C. Nixon for Pres. Com., 1968, Keating for Senator Com., N.Y. State, 1964; bd. dirs. Eisenhower World Affairs Inst., Washington, Am. Hellenic Inst. Inc. Capt. USAF, 1952-60. Recipient Medal for Excellence, Columbia U., 1972, Young Lawyer's award Columbia Law Sch. Alumni Assn., 1972, Silver Anniversary award NCAA, 1974, John Jay award Columbia Coll. Alumni Assn., 1994. Mem. ABA, N.Y. State Bar Assn., Fed. Bar Assn. Republican. Greek Orthodox. Avocations: tennis, photography. Home: 3666 Upton St NW Washington DC 20008-3125 Office: Rogers & Wells 607 14th St NW Washington DC 20005-2000

ROSSIN, HERBERT YALE, television producer; b. Phila., May 15, 1936; s. Jack Rossin and Edna Wolinsky; m. Meryl Ann Barsky, Nov. 15, 1965; children: Abby Rae, Shane J.P. Degree in journalism, Temple U., 1958. Gen. mgr. KIKU TV/13, Honolulu, 1968-70; br. mgr. Columbia Pictures, Las Vegas, 1970-74; pres. Internat. TV Concepts, Las Vegas, 1974-78; sta. mgr. KUAM AM/FM/TV, Agana, Guam, 1978-80; v.p. Tag Mktg. and Advt., Cherry Hill, N.J., 1981-83; gen. mgr. WLXI-TV/61, Greensboro, N.C., 1983-85; v.p., gen. mgr. WHLL-TV/27, Boston, 1986-87; v.p. Home Shopping Network, L.A., 1987-88; owner A.S.A.P. Multi-Corp., Las Vegas, 1988—; broadcast cons. Fashion Channel-Video Mall, L.A., 1987-88, Las Vegas TV Network, 1987-88; script writer Four Star Pictures, L.A., 1988-89; pres. Video Music TV Stas. Am., 1984-88; network cons.; mem. Guam Gaming Commn., 1979. Prodr. motion picture Miss Conduct, 1957; creator TV shows New Millionaires, 1993, Slim Scents, 1995, Big Bucks Bingo, 1980, Sportalk, 1997, Football Weekly, 1996, Wireless Wonder, 1994, Las Vegas at Nite, 1997; editor Israel Mag., 1960. Prodr. telethon Heart Fund Am., Las Vegas, 1972. With Pa. Air Nat. Guard, 1954-59. Named Broadcaster of Yr., Video Music TV Stas. Am., 1985; recipient Edn. award Albert Einstein Acad., 1974, People Law Sch. award Nev. Trial Lawyers, 1992, others. Mem. Nat. Assn. TV Program Execs. Avocation: softball. Home and Office: ASAP Multi Corp 7704 Musical Ln Las Vegas NV 89128-4082

ROSSING, CATHERINE BARRETT SCHWAB, dental hygienist; b. San Francisco, Apr. 8, 1932; d. Richard James and Mary Ann (McAuliff) and Richard Thomas Barrett; m. Donald Theodore Schwab, Aug. 8, 1954 (div. 1965); 1 child, Carla Diane; m. Alan Robert Rossing, Mar. 31, 1989. AA, U. Calif., Berkeley, 1952, BS, 1954; MPA, Calif. State U., Long Beach, 1983. Registered dental hygienist, Calif. Preventive specialist Dr. Thomas Evans Office, Anaheim, Calif., 1968-72, 90; mem. T.E.A.M. program U. So. Calif., L.A., 1972-73; staff hygienist Dr. Joseph Berger Dental Office, Fountain Valley, Calif., 1974-88; pub. Rossing Enterprises, Pebble Beach, Calif., 1991—; co-founder Preventive Dental Care, L.A., 1985-90; co-owner Schwab/Flora Meeting Organizers, Anaheim, 1981-90. Mem. Calif. Dental Hygienists' Assn. (editor jour. 1974-76, 81-84, 89-95, Golden Pen award 1976), Am. Dental Hygienists' Assn. (trustee 1977-81, Recognition award 1981). Avocations: Monterey Bay Aquarium, gardening, orchids. Home: 1060 Old Dr Pebble Beach CA 93953-2509

ROSSING, THOMAS D., physics educator; b. Madison, S.D., Mar. 27, 1929; s. Torstein H. and Luella E. Rossing; children: Karen, Barbara, Erik, Jane, Mary. BA, Luther Coll., 1950; MS, Iowa State U., 1952, PhD, 1954. Rsch. physicist Univac div. Sperry Rand, 1954-57; prof. physics St. Olaf Coll., 1957-71, chmn. physics dept., 1963-69; prof. physics No. Ill. U., DeKalb, 1971—, Disting. Rsch. prof., chmn. dept., 1971-73; rschr. Microwave Lab., Stanford (Calif.) U., 1961-62, Lincoln Lab., MIT, Cambridge, Mass., summer 1963, Clarendon Lab., Oxford (Eng.) U., 1966-67, physics dept. MIT, 1976-77; rsch. assoc. Argonne (Ill.) Nat Lab., 1974-76, scientist-in-residence, 1990—; vis. lectr. U. New Eng., Armidale, Australia, 1980-81; vis. exch. scholar People's Republic of China, 1988; guest rschr. Royal Inst. Tech., Stockholm, 1983, 84, 85, Inst. Perception Rsch., Eindhoven, The Netherlands, 1984, 85, Physikalisch-Technische Bundesanstalt, Braunschweig, Germany, 1988-89; guest rschr. Ecole Nat. Superiéure des Telecomm., Paris, 1996. Author 10 books in field; contbr. more than 250 articles to profl. publs. Fellow AAAS, Acoustical Soc. Am. (Silver medal in mus. acoustics 1992); mem. IEEE, Am. Phys. Soc., Am. Assn. Physics Tchrs. (pres. 1991), Catgut Acoustical Soc., Percussive Arts Soc., Guild Am. Luthiers, Sigma Xi (nat. lectr. 1984-87), Sigma Pi Sigma. Achievements include research in musical acoustics, psychoacoustics, speech and singing, vibration analysis, magnetic levitation, environmental noise conrol, surface effects in fusion reactors, spin waves in metals, physics education; 9 U.S. and 11 foreign patents in field. Office: No Ill U Physics Dept De Kalb IL 60115

ROSSINGTON, DAVID RALPH, physical chemistry educator; b. London, July 13, 1932; s. George Leonard and Clara Fanny (Simmons) R.; children: Andrew, Carolyn, Nicholas, Philip. BSc with honors, U. Bristol, Eng., 1953, PhD, 1956. Postdoctoral research fellow N.Y. State Coll. Ceramics at Alfred (N.Y.) U., 1956-58; tech. officer Imperial Chem. Industries Ltd., Eng., 1958-60; asst. prof. phys. chemistry (emeritus) Alfred U., 1960-63, assoc. prof., 1963-69, prof., 1969-95, head div. ceramic engring., 1976-79, 82-84, dean sch. engring., 1984-91. Editor: Advances in Materials Characterization, 1983; contbr. numerous articles to profl. jours. Town Justice, Alfred, 1976-86. Fulbright scholar, 1956, 58. Fellow Am. Ceramic Soc.; mem. Am. Chem. Soc., Ceramic Edn. Coun., Am. Soc. Engring. Edn., Tau Beta Pi, Phi Kappa Phi. Democrat. Episcopalian. Office: Alfred U Sch Of Engring Alfred NY 14802

ROSSINI, JOSEPH, contracting and development corporate executive; b. New Rochelle, N.Y., Nov. 25, 1939; m. Antonia Rossini; children: Katherine, Anthony, Andrew. Student, Fordham U., 1965-66, Iona Coll., 1972. Pres. Rossini Contracting Corp., New Rochelle, 1963—; prin. Rossini Devel. Co., Monticello, N.Y., 1965—; bd. dirs. Circuit Realty Corp., New Rochelle, 1970-71. Mem. planning bd. City of New Rochelle, 1986-92, mem. bldg. dept. adv. com., 1985; vol. instr. N.Y. State Dept. Environ. Conservation, Albany, 1968-95; vice chmn. New Rochelle Conservative Party, 1984—; county committeeman Westchester County Conservative Party; v.p. bd. trustees Beechwoods Cemetery, New Rochelle; dir. New Rochelle Neighborhood Revitalization Corp., 1993-96. With USN, 1959-61. Mem. NRA (endowment mem.), Gen. Contractors Assn. N.Y., Constrn. Industry Coun. Westchester and Hudson Valley, Bldg. Trades Employers Assn., Soc. Explosives Engrs., Deep Founds. Inst., Young Ams. for Freedom, Am. Lauretana Assn., Mensa, Assoc. Gen. Contractors Am. Roman Catholic. Office: Rossini Contracting Corp 113 Edison Ave Mount Vernon NY 10550-5005

ROSSITER, ALEXANDER, JR., news service executive, editor; b. Elmira, N.Y., Mar. 2, 1936; s. Alexander H. and Eleanor (Howell) R.; m. Sylvia Lee Vanlandingham, June 11, 1960; children: Alexander H. III, Jill Jarrell. BA, Rutgers U., 1958; postgrad., Emory U., 1959. With UPI, 1959-92; newsman Atlanta, 1959-61, Richmond, Va., 1961-63; bur. mgr. Cape Canaveral, Fla., 1963-73; sci. editor Washington, 1973-87, exec. editor, 1987-88, exec. editor, sr. v.p., 1988-91, editor, exec. v.p., 1991-92; asst. v.p., dir. news svc. Duke U., Durham, N.C., 1992—; mem. nat. adv. bd. Knight Ctr. for Specialized Journalism, Colleg Pk., Md., 1988-92. Recipient Grady-Stack medal Am. Chem. Soc., 1987, other journalism awards. Mem. Nat. Assn. Sci. Writers, Edn. Writers Assn. Office: Duke U 615 Chapel Dr Durham NC 27706-2500
Enthusiasm is the key to success. Take on your education, your family responsibilities and your work with enthusiasm and good things will result.

ROSSITER, BRYANT WILLIAM, chemistry consultant; b. Ogden, Utah, Mar. 10, 1931; s. Bryant B. and Christine (Peterson) R.; m. Betty Jean Anderson, Apr. 16, 1951; children: Bryant, Mark, Diane, Steven, Linda, Karen, Matthew, Gregory. BA, U. Utah, 1954, PhD, 1957. Researcher Eastman-Kodak Co., Rochester, N.Y., 1957-63, head color phys. chem. lab., 1963-70, dir. chemistry div., 1970-84, dir. sci., tech. devel., 1984-86; pres. Viratek Inc., Costa Mesa, Calif., 1986-89; sr. v.p. ICN Pharms., Costa Mesa, 1989-90; ret., 1990; pres., CEO WRECON, Inc., Laguna Hills, Calif., 1991-96; sr. editor John Wiley & Sons, N.Y.C., 1970—; chmn. bd. Nucleic Acid Rsch. Inst., Costa Mesa, 1987-88; trustee Eastman Dental Ctr., Rochester, 1973-93 (bd. pres. 1982-85); bd. dirs. Verax & Corp. Editor: (chem. treatises) Physical Methods of Chemistry (11 vols.), 1970-76, Physical Methods, (12 vols.), 1986—, Chemical Experimentation Under Extreme Conditions, 1979. Mem. rsch. adv. com. U.S. Agy. for Internat. Devel., Washington, chmn. rsch. adv. com., 1989-92; mem. panel on biosci. Pres.' Coun. Advisors on Sci. and Tech., 1991; mem. adv com. Cornell Internat. Inst. for Food, Agr. and Devel., 1991; presiding officer Ch. Jesus Christ Latter Day Saints, Ea. U.S. and Can., 1959-86. 1st lt. USAFR, 1951-58. Named Hon. Alumni Brigham Young U., Provo, Utah, 1982. Fellow AAAS, Am. Inst. Chemists (lectr., Fellows award 1988, Will Judy award Juanita Coll. 1978); mem. Internat. Union Pure and Applied Chemistry (chmn. U.S. nat. com., orignator, chmn. Chemical Rsch. Applied to World Needs com. 1975-87, chmn. Chemical Rsch. Applied to World Needs II The Internat. Conf. on Chemistry and World Food Supplies, 1982), Am. Chem. Soc. (chmn. internat. activities). Avocations: horseback riding, reading, fishing. Home and Office: 25662 Dillon Rd Laguna Hills CA 92653-5800

ROSSLER, WILLIS KENNETH, JR., petroleum company executive; b. Houston, Nov. 17, 1946; BS in Indsl. Engring., Tex. Tech. U., 1969; postgrad. in bus. Stanford U.; s. Willis Kenneth and Fay Lee (Olle) R.; m. Jennifer Hill West; children: Nancy Rossler Ewing, Deborah Anne, Ryan Konrad, Eric George; 1 stepchild, Jason Hill Yelverton. Dist. mgr. Tex.-La. ops. Continental Pipe Line Co., Lake Charles, La., 1974-75, mgr. engring., Houston, 1976-77; asst. mgr. corp. planning and devel. Conoco, Inc., Houston, 1977-78; v.p. project devel. PetroUnited, Inc., Houston, 1978-80, pres., 1981-86, also dir. Pres., Village Pl. Community Assn., Houston, 1978, also partnership com. Antwerp Gas Terminal, V.G.N., 1982-85, v.p., gen. mgr., Pilko and Assoc., Inc., Houston, 1986-90; pres., CEO Houston Fuel Oil Terminal Co., 1990—; bd. dirs. Pilko and Assocs., Naylor Industries, Inc., Clean Channel Assn. (chmn.), Greater Houston Port Bur., Grace Presbyn. Sch. Mem. Am. Inst. Indsl. Engrs., Am. Petroleum Inst., Houston Mgmt. Council, Intensive Mgmt. Devel. Inst. (adv. dir. 1983-84), Ind. Liquid Terminals Assn. (vice chmn. 1986, chmn.-elect 1987), Am. Mgmt. Assn., Planning Forum (pres. chpt. 1985), Petroleum Club of Houston, Lakeside Country Club. Office: Houston Fuel Oil Terminal Co 16642 Jacintoport Blvd Houston TX 77015-6541

ROSSMAN, JANET KAY, architectural interior designer; b. Lansing, Mich., Feb. 13, 1954; d. Elmer Chris and Jean Elizabeth (Schell) R.; m. Farzad Moazed; children: Alexander, Christina. BA with High Honors, Mich. State U., 1976. Designer Tilton & Lewis Assocs., Inc., Chgo., 1977-79, Swanke Hayden Connell & Ptnrs., N.Y.C., 1979-81, Bonsignore Brignati & Mazzotta Architects, N.Y.C., 1982-84; dir. design, assoc. SPGA Group, Inc., N.Y.C., 1984—; instr. Design Edn. Ctr., Lansing, 1975-76. Fellow Mus. Modern Art, N.Y.C., 1977—. Mem. Am. Soc. of Interior Designers (chair. 1973-76, editor Collage 1973-76), Inst. Bus. Designers, Nat. Assn. for Female Execs., Omicron Nu. Republican. Club: Atrium, Landmark. Avocations: photography, equestrian activities, travel. Home: 367 W Hill Rd Stamford CT 06902-1709

ROSSMAN, RICHARD ALAN, lawyer; b. Albany, N.Y., June 16, 1939; s. Kenneth Fisher and Edith Bell (Wheeler) R.; m. Patricia Margaret Booth, Jan. 2, 1965; children: Lisa, Jeffrey. AB, U. Mich., 1961, JD, 1964. Asst. pros. atty. Oakland County, Pontiac, Mich., 1965-67, 70-71; chief dep. fed. defender, Detroit, 1972-75, sole practice, 1975-77; chief asst. U.S. Atty. Ea. Dist. Mich., Detroit, 1977-80, U.S. atty., 1980-81; ptnr. Butzel, Long, Gust, Klein & Van Zile, Detroit, 1981-86, Pepper, Hamilton & Scheetz, Detroit, 1986—. Mem. ABA, Fed. Bar Assn. (pres. Detroit chpt. 1982-83), Mich. Bar Assn. (chair standing com. on U.S. cts. 1996—, rep. assembly 1980-82), Oakland County Bar Assn., Detroit Bar Assn. (trustee found. 1984-86). Office: Pepper Hamilton & Scheetz 100 Renaissance Ctr Ste 3600 Detroit MI 48243-1101

ROSSMAN, ROBERT HARRIS, management consultant; b. Phila., Jan. 27, 1932; s. Benjamin Bernard and Vivian (Silnutzer) R.; m. Wanda Ward, Aug. 9, 1980; 1 child, Victoria Anne; children from previous marriage: Rodger Samuel, Robbi Jennifer, Ronni Esther. BS, U.S. Merchant Marine Acad., 1953; MSME with honors, U.S. Naval Postgrad. Sch., 1963; cert. advanced naval architecture, MIT, 1973. Cert. mgr. human resources; cert. value specialist. Commd. ensign USN, 1953, advanced through grades to comdr., 1967, shipboard engr., 1953-55, maintenance and repair officer Reserve Fleet, 1955-57; served as ship supt. Norfolk Naval Shipyard, Portsmouth, Va., 1957-60; maintenance and logistics planning officer Amphibious Squadron Twelve, Little Creek, Va., 1963-65; planning and estimating supt. U.S. Naval Ship Repair Facility, Yokosuka, Japan, 1965-67; design and planning advisor USN, Saigon, Republic Viet Nam, 1967-68; chief prodn. engring. Def. Contract Adminstrn. Svcs., Alexandria, Va., 1968-70; dir. cost reduction Naval Ship Systems Command, Washington, 1970-73; dep. program mgr. new ship class Naval Ship Engring. Ctr., Hyattsville, Md., 1973; ret. USN, 1973; ptnr. Kempter-Rossman Internat., Washington, 1974-91; owner Rossman Assocs. Internat., 1991—; cons. in cost and time reduction, mgmt. improvement, productivity and competition enhancement. Author: (textbook) Function Based Analysis, 1983, Total Cycle Time Reduction, 1992; editor mag. Performance, 1970-73; contbr. articles to profl. jours. Pres. PTA, Fairfax County, Va., 1969-70, Community Civic Assn., Fairfax County, 1970-71; chmn. Boy Scouts Am. and Weblos troops, 1969-71, del. at large 1st Congl. Dist. Rep. Com., N.C., 1989-90; chmn. Chowan County (N.C.) Rep. Com., 1990-92. Decorated USN Commendation medals, Honor medal-1st Class (Republic of Vietnam Armed Forces), Combat Action medal. Fellow Soc. Am. Value Engrs. (v.p. 1970-73, Disting. Svc. award 1976); mem. U.S. Merchant Marine Acad. Alumni Assn., Am. Legion, Sigma Xi. Jewish. Avocations: gardening, home remodeling, restoration, writing. Home: 110 Old Hertford Rd Edenton NC 27932-9608 Office: Rossman Assocs Internat Speight House 110 Old Hertford Rd Edenton NC 27932-9608

ROSSMAN, RUTH SCHARFF, artist, educator; b. Bklyn.; d. Joseph and Elsie (Frankel) Scharff; m. Phillip Rossman; 1 dau., Joanne. Grad., Cleve. Inst. Art, 1934; BS, Case Western Res. U., 1934; postgrad., Kahn Inst. Art, 1947-50, UCLA, 1960. Art instr. Canton (Ohio) public schs., 1934-39, Canton Art Inst., 1937-45, Rustic Canyon Art Center, Los Angeles, 1978-81. One-woman shows at Heritage Gallery, L.A., 1963, 66, Canton (Ohio) Community Ctr., 1967, Marymount Coll., U. Judaism, 1980, L.A. Fedn. Bldg., 1981, 89, Platt Gallery, 1986, 93, others; exhibited in group shows Mus. Modern Art, N.Y.C., Butler Mus., Washington and Jefferson Coll., Denver Mus., Space Mus., Mt. St. Mary's Coll., L.A., M.H. de Young Mus., San Francisco Mus. Art, Venice Art Walk, ann. 1981-94, 96, Univ. Judaism, 1986, 93, Brand Art Gallery, 1987, others; represented in permanent collections Pa. Acad. Fine Arts, Phila., Brandeis-Bardin Inst., U. Redlands, Calif., Nat. Watercolor Soc., Ahmanson Collection, Rocky Mt. Nat., others; paintings included in book The California Romantics: Harbingers of Watercolor, 1987. Chair selection com. for Platt Gallery, U. Judaism, L.A., 1986—.

Recipient purchase-cash awards Los Angeles All-City Art Exhbn. Mem. Nat. Watercolor Soc. (pres. 1974-75, juror 75th Ann. Exhbn. 1995).

ROSSMAN, TOBY GALE, genetic toxicology educator, researcher; b. Weehawken, N.J., June 3, 1942; d. Norman N. and Sylvia Betty (May) Natowitz; m. Neil I. Rossman, Sept. 16, 1962 (div. Sept. 1980); m. Gordon Rauer, Aug. 19, 1990. AB, NYU, 1964, PhD, 1968; postgrad., Brandeis U., 1964-65. Instr. Polytech. Inst. of N.Y., N.Y.C., 1968-69; postdoctoral dept. pathology NYU, N.Y.C., 1969-71; from asst. to assoc. prof. Inst. for Environ Medicine NYU Med Ctr, N.Y.C., 1974-85; prof. Inst. for Environ. Medicine, 1985—; dir. molecular and genetic toxicology Nelson Inst. Environ. Medicine, NYU Med. Ctr., N.Y.C., 1995—. Mem. editorial bd. Molecular Toxicology, 1989-91, Teratogenesis, Carcinogenesis, Mutagenesis, 1990-91, Environmental and Molecular Mutagenesis, 1994—, Mutation Research, 1994—; contbr. numerous articles to profl. jours. EPA grantee, NIH grantee. Mem. AAAS, Assn. for Women in Sci., Am. Assn. for Cancer Rsch., Am. Soc. for Microbiology, Environ. Mutagen Soc. (councilor 1990-93). Office: NYU Inst Environ Medicine Long Meadow Rd Tuxedo Park NY 10987

ROSSMANN, JACK EUGENE, psychology educator; b. Walnut, Iowa, Dec. 4, 1936; s. Wilbert C. Rossmann and Claire L. (Mickel) Walter; m. Marilyn Martin, June 14, 1958; children: Ann, Charles, Sarah. BS, Iowa State U., 1958, MS, 1960; PhD, U. Minn., 1963. Lic. cons. psychologist, Minn. Asst. prof. Macalester Coll., St. Paul, 1964-68, assoc. prof., 1968-73, prof., 1973—, v.p. acad. affairs, 1978-86; chair dept. psychology Macalester Coll., 1990—; cons. Pers. Decisions Inc., Mpls., 1989—; cons.-evaluator North Ctrl. Assn., 1975—. Author: (with others) Open Admissions at CUNY, 1975; contbr. articles to profl. jours. Bd. dirs. Twin City Inst. for Talented Youth, St. Paul, 1978-91; trustee United Theol. Sem., New Brighton, Minn., 1984-96. 2d lt. U.S. Army, 1959. Mem. APA, AAUP (pres. Minn. conf. 1993-95), Am. Psychol. Soc., Assn. for Instl. Rsch., Am. Assn. for Higher Edn. Home: 99 Cambridge St Saint Paul MN 55105-1947 Office: Macalester Coll 1600 Grand Ave Saint Paul MN 55105-1801

ROSSMANN, MICHAEL GEORGE, biochemist, educator; b. Frankfurt, Germany, July 30, 1930; s. Alexander and Nelly (Schwabacher) R.; m. Audrey Pearson, July 24, 1954; children—Martin, Alice, Heather. B.Sc. with honors, Polytechnic, London, 1951, M.Sc. in Physics, 1953; Ph.D. in Chemistry, U. Glasgow, 1956. Fulbright scholar U. Minn., 1956-58; research scientist MRC Lab. Molecular Biology, Cambridge, Eng., 1958-64; asso. prof. biol. scis. Purdue U., West Lafayette, Ind., 1964-67; prof. Purdue U., 1967-78, Hanley Disting. prof. biol. scis., 1978—, prof. biochemistry, 1975—. Editor: The Molecular Replacement Method, 1972; mem. editl. bd. Jour. Biol. Chemistry, 1975-80; contbr. over 300 articles to profl. jours. Grantee NIH, NSF; recipient Fankuchen award Am. Crystallographic Assn., 1986, Horwitz prize Columbia U., 1990, Gregori Arminoff prize Royal Swedish Acad. Sci., 1994, Stein & Moore award Protein Soc., 1994, Ewald prize Internat. Union Crystallography, 1996. Mem. Am. Soc. Biol. Chemists, Am. Chem. Soc., Biophys. Soc., Am. Crystallographic Assn., Brit. Biophys. Soc., Inst. Physics., Chem. Soc. (U.K.), AAAS, NAS, Indian Nat. Sci. Acad., Royal Soc. Democrat. Club: Lafayette Sailing. Home: 1208 Wiley Dr West Lafayette IN 47906-2434 Office: Dept Biol Scis Purdue Univ West Lafayette IN 47907-1392

ROSSMILLER, GEORGE EDDIE, agricultural economist; b. Gt. Falls, Mont., June 8, 1935; s. Albert E. and Romaine (Hennford) R.; m. Betty Ann Rinio, Dec. 20, 1955 (dec. Mar. 1990); children: David W., Diane J.; m. Frances Sandiford, May 22, 1996. BS, Mont. State U., 1956, MS, 1962; PhD, Mich. State U., 1965. Rsch. assoc. Mich. State U., East Lansing, 1965-66, asst. prof., 1967-71, assoc. prof., 1972-76, prof. agrl. econs., 1977-80; agrl. attache to OECD, Fgn. Agrl. Service, USDA, Paris, 1978-79; asst. adminstr. internat. trade policy Fgn. Agrl. Svc., USDA, Washington, 1979-81, dir planing and analysis, 1981-85; sr. fellow and dir. Nat. Ctr. Food and Agr. Policy, Resources for the Future, 1986-92; also exec. dir. Internat. Policy Council on Agr. and Trade, 1988-92; chief situation and policy studies svc. Food and Agr. Orgn. of UN, Rome, 1992-97. Author: The Grain-Livestock Economy of West Germany with Projections to 1970 and 1975, 1968, (with others) Korean Agricultural Sector Analysis and Recommended Development Strategies, 1971-1985, 1972; editor: (with others) Agricultural Sector Planning: A General System Simulation Approach, 1978. Served with U.S. Army, 1956-59. Recipient service citation Korean Ministry of Agrl. and Fisheries, 1973, service citation Office of Prime Minister of Korea, 1977, Superior Service award U.S. Dept. Agr., 1983, Fgn. Agrl. Service merit award, 1984. Mem. Am. Agrl. Econs. Assn. (Disting. Policy Contbn. award 1992), Internat. Assn. Agrl. Economists. Presbyterian. Home: The Conifers, Kennerleigh Devon EX17 4RS, England

ROSSOF, ARTHUR HAROLD, internal medicine educator; b. Chgo., Dec. 12, 1943; s. Jack and Libby (Gordon) R.; m. Rebecca Ann, Aug. 11, 1967 (div. 1983); children: Jacob Earl, Lizabeth Eva; m. Kristine Ann, Feb. 14, 1985. Student, Bradley U., 1961-64; MD, U. Ill., 1968. Diplomate Nat. Bd. Med. Examiners, Am. Bd. Internal Medicine, Am. Bd. Oncology, Am. Bd. Hematology. Fellow sect. neurobiology dept. neurology Presbyn.-St. Luke's Hosp., Chgo., 1965-68, intern straight medicine, 1968-69, resident dept. medicine, 1969-71, Eastern Coop. Oncology Group fellow sect. oncology, dept. medicine, 1971-72, asst. attending physician dept. internal medicine, 1976-80, assoc. attending physician, dept. internal medicine, 1980-82, sr. attending physician dept. internal medicine, 1982-90; med. dir. MacNeal Cancer Ctr., Berwyn, Ill., 1985—; asst. medicine U. Ill. Coll. Medicine, 1969-71; clin. asst. prof. medicine U. Tex. health Sci. Ctr., San Antonio, 1973-76; instr. medicine Rush Med. Coll., 1971-72, asst. prof. medicine, 1976-81, assoc. prof. medicine, 1981-90; assoc. prof. medicine Loyola U. Med. Ctr., Chgo., 1990-91, prof., 1991—; mem. resident selection com. Rush-Presbyn.-St. Luke's Med. Ctr., 1976-88, mem. ethics conf. planning group, 1981-90, tumor com., 1981-90, chmn. med. edn.com., continuing med. edn. subcom., 1982-90; mem. pharmacy and therapeutics com., chmn. instnl. rev. bd., chmn. cancer com. MacNeal Hosp.; cons. Cancer Info. Svcv., Ill. Cancer Coun., mem. clin. trials com. 1978—, credentials rev. com.; mem. adv. com. Lincoln Park Zoo, 1978—. Author: Lithium Effects on Granulopoiesis and Immune Function, 1980; contbr. articles in field to profl. jours.; patentee in field. Mem. exec. com. prevention com. Cancer Incidence & Ednl. Results com. Am. Cancer Soc.; mem. profl. adv. bd. Wellness House Med. Advisor. Maj. M.C., USAF, 1972-76. Fellow ACP; mem. Internat. Soc. Exptl. Hematology, Am. Soc. Clin. Oncology, Am. Fedn. Clin. Research, Am. Assn. Cancer Research, Am. Soc. Hematology, N.Y. Acad. Scis., Soc. Air Force Physicians, Cell Kinetic Soc., Internat. Assn. Study Lung Cancer, Soc. Med. History Chgo., Chgo. Soc. Internal Medicine, AAAS, Am. Assn. Cancer Edn., Assn. Community Cancer Ctrs., Alliance Continuing Med. Edn., Sigma Xi, Phi Eta Sigma, Alpha Omega Alpha. Republican. Jewish. Avocation: tennis. Office: MacNeal Cancer Ctr 3340 Oak Park Ave Berwyn IL 60402-3420

ROSSOLIMO, ALEXANDER NICHOLAS, management consultant; b. Paris, June 8, 1939; came to U.S., 1952; naturalized, 1958; s. Nicholas S. and Vera A. (Boudakovitch) R.; m. Meryl Louise Stowbridge, Sept. 10, 1977; children: Gregory, Katherine, Elizabeth. BEE, CUNY, 1962; MA in Applied Math., Harvard U., 1963, PhD in Applied Physics, 1973; MBA, MIT, 1973. Cert. in bus. French. Tchg. fellow Harvard U., 1963-65, rsch. asst., 1966-71; fin. analyst Péchiney, Paris, 1972; brand/advt. mgmt. The Clorox Co., Oakland, Calif., 1973-74; cons. The Boston Consulting Group, 1974-77; dir. planning and fin. analysis United Brands, Boston, 1977-80; sr. dir. Digital Equipment Corp., Maynard, Mass., 1980-92; pres. Internat. Strategy Assocs., Newton, Mass., 1992-94, pres., chief exec. officer, 1994—; vis. fellow Harvard U., Cambridge, Mass., 1991-93; bd. dirs. ACG Internat., Chgo., Ctr. for Security and Social Progress, Inc., Newton Consulting Group; founding dir. Forum 128, 1996—. Contbr. numerous articles to bus. and internat. newspapers. Mem. search com. Ecole Bilingue, French-Am. Internat. Sch. of Boston, 1991-93; fund raiser Milton (Mass.) Acad., 1994—. Recipient award in elec. engring. Blonder-Tongue Co., N.Y.C., 1961, Belden prize, gold medal in math., 1960; NSF fellow, 1962; Dealmaker Challenge winner, 1995. Mem. Nat. Assn. Corp. Dirs., Bus. Execs. for Nat. Security, Boston Security Analysts Soc., French Am. C. of C., Japan Soc. Boston, World Affairs Coun., Assn. for Corp. Growth Boston (chmn. 1995-96), Harvard Club Boston, Toastmasters Internat. (pres.), Tau Beta Pi, Eta Kappa Nu. Avocations: jogging, tennis, foreign languages, international organizations, theater. Office: International Strategy Associates PO Box 207 Waban MA 02168-0002

ROSSON, GLENN RICHARD, building products and furniture company executive; b. Galveston, Tex., Aug. 17, 1937; s. John Raymond and Elsie Lee (Reece) R.; m. Edwina Lucille Hart, June 2, 1956; children—Darrell Richard, Alex Mark. B.B.A., Tex. Tech U., 1959. C.P.A., Tex. Supr., accountant Axelson div. U.S. Industries Inc., Longview, Tex., 1960-67; controller U.S. Industries Inc., 1968; group financial v.p. U.S. Industries Inc., Dallas, 1969; group chmn. U.S. Industries Inc., 1969-72, v.p., 1973-74, sr. v.p., 1974, exec. v.p., 1974-80, also dir.; pres. Rosson Investment Co., 1980—; chmn. bd. Yorktowne Inc., 1988—. Mem. Am. Inst. C.P.A.s, Tex. Soc. C.P.A.s, Nat. Assn. Accts. (past nat. dir., past pres. E. Tex. chpt.), Assn. for Corp. Growth (past pres.). Club: Dallas Athletic, TBARM Raquet. Home: 11367 Drummond Dr Dallas TX 75228-1946 Office: 5910 N Central Expy Ste 1000 Dallas TX 75206-5142

ROSSOTTI, BARBARA JILL MARGULIES, lawyer; b. Englewood, N.J., Feb. 28, 1940; d. Albert and Loretta (Jill) Margulies; m. Charles Ossola Rossotti; children: Allegra Jill, Edward Charles. BA magna cum laude, Mount Holyoke Coll., 1961; LLB, Harvard U., 1964. Bar: D.C. 1966. Assoc. Nutter McClennen & Fish, Boston, 1964-65, Covington & Burling, Washington, 1965-72; assoc. Shaw, Pittman, Potts & Trowbridge, Washington, 1972-73, ptnr., 1973—. Trustee Mt. Holyoke Coll., South Hadley, Mass., 1984, vice chmn., 1989-94, chmn., 1994—; chmn. exec. com. Campaign for Mt. Holyoke Coll., 1986-91; trustee Legal Aid Soc., D.C., 1979-92, pres. 1985-89, mem. pres. coun., 1992—; trustee Choral Arts Soc., Washington, 1989-96, chair, 1993-95; bd. dirs. Washington Home, 1989—. Fellow Am. Bar Found.; mem. ABA, Am. Soc. Internat. Law, Internat. Law Assn., D.C. Bar. Office: Shaw Pittman Potts & Trowbridge 2300 N St NW Washington DC 20037-1122

ROSSOTTI, CHARLES OSSOLA, computer consulting company executive; b. N.Y.C., Jan. 17, 1941; s. Charles C. and V. Elizabeth (Ossola) R.; m. Barbara Jill Margulies, June 9, 1963; children: Allegra Jill, Edward Charles. AB magna cum laude, Georgetown U., 1962; MBA with high distinction, Harvard U., 1974. Mgmt. cons. Boston Cons. Group, 1964-65; prin. dep. asst. sec. Office of Systems Analysis, Dept. Def., Washington, 1965-70; prin. dep. asst. sec. of Def. Office of Systems Analysis, Dept. Def., 1969-70; pres. Am. Mgmt. Systems, Inc., Arlington, Va., 1970—, chief exec. officer, 1981—, chmn. bd., 1989—; bd. dirs. Intersolv, Inc. Bd. dirs. Georgetown U., 1969-77, 92—; chmn. Woodstock Theol. Ctr., 1990—. Mem. Coun. Fgn. Rels. Office: Am Mgmt Systems Inc 4050 Legato Rd Fairfax VA 22033-4087

ROSSTON, EDWARD WILLIAM, lawyer; b. San Francisco, Nov. 14, 1918; s. Ernest William and Goldah Ray (Charmak) R.; m. Maxine Goldmark Aaron, June 28, 1947; children—Edward William, Richard Mark, Ellen Maxine Rosston Neft, Jean Frances. A.B., U. Calif.-Berkeley, 1939, JD, 1947; LL.M., Columbia U., 1948. Bar: Calif. 1947. Assoc. Heller Ehrman White & McAuliff, San Francisco, 1948-58; ptnr. Heller Ehrman White & McAuliff, 1958—; instr. Hastings Coll. Law, U. Calif., San Francisco, 1949-51; bd. dirs. Consumer Credit Counsellors, San Francisco, 1965-95; sec. MPC Ins. Ltd., 1986-93. Nat. trustee Lawyers Com. for Civil Rights, 1977—; co-chmn., mem. exec. com. San Francisco Lawyers Com. for Urban Affairs, 1972-83; trustee The Mechanics Inst. and Chessroom, 1991—, v.p., 1993-97. Lt. USNR, 1941-46, PTO. Mem. ABA, State Bar Calif., Bar Assn. San Francisco (bd. dirs., com. chmn. 1959-65), Am. Arbitration Assn. (arbitrator and mediator, adv. coun. North Calif. chpt. 1988—), Boalt Hall Alumni Assn. (trustee 1977-79). Democrat. Jewish. Club: Commonwealth (San Francisco). Office: Heller Ehrman White & McAuliffe 333 Bush St San Francisco CA 94104-2806

ROST, PETER, pharmaceutical company executive; b. Bollebygd, Sweden, May 31, 1959; came to U.S., 1987; s. Siegfrid and Kathie (Zerne) R.; m. Tina Forssten, Apr. 21, 1984. MD, U. Gothenburg, Sweden, 1984. Intern anesthesiology dept. Ea. Hosp., Gothenburg, 1984, practice medicine specializing in anesthesiology, 1984; pres., CEO Bus. Lit. Inc., Gothenburg, 1985-87; copywriter Ehrenstrahle & Co., Gothenburg, 1985, Ogilvy & Mather, Gothenburg, 1985; account supr., copywriter Grey Gothenburg, Gothenburg, 1985-87; med. dir., account supr. Maher Kaump & Clark, Inc., L.A., 1987-92; assoc. dir. med. edn. Lederle Labs. divsn. Am. Cyanamid Co., Wayne, N.J., 1992, dir. med. edn., 1993; product mgr. Lederle Labs. divsn. Am. Cyanimid Co., Wayne, N.J., 1993-94; mkt. planning mgr. Wyeth-Ayerst Internat., St. Davids, Pa., 1995, dir. mktg internal medicine products, 1995-96; dir. comml. ops. Europe Wyeth-Ayerst Internat., St. Davids, 1996—; chmn., chief exec. officer W. Swedish Model Group, Gothenburg, 1985. Author: Emergency Surgery, 1985, The Art of Driving a Car Free, 1985. Mem. AMA, Am. Coll. Physician Execs., Pharm. Advt. Coun. Office: Wyeth-Ayerst Internat Inc PO Box 8616 Philadelphia PA 19101-8616 also: 150 Radnor-Chester Rd Saint Davids PA 19087

ROST, THOMAS LOWELL, plant biology educator; b. St. Paul, Dec. 28, 1941; s. Lowell Henry Rost and Agnes Marie (Wojtowicz) Jurek; m. Ann Marie Ruhland, Aug. 31, 1963; children: Christopher, Timothy, Jacquelyn. BS, St. John's U., Collegeville, Minn., 1963; MA, Mankato State U., 1965; PhD, Iowa State U., 1970. Postdoctoral fellow Brookhaven Nat. Lab., Upton, N.Y., 1970-72; asst. to full prof. dept. botany U. Calif., Davis, 1972-82, faculty asst. to chancellor, 1982-83, prof., chmn. plant biology sect., 1994-96, assoc. dean divsn. biol. sci., 1996—; cons. faculty of agronomy U. Uruguay, 1979, 89; vis. fellow Rsch. Soc. Biol. Sci., Canberra, Australia, 1979-80; vis. prof. U. Wroclaw, Poland, 1987, U. Exeter, Eng., 1993. Co-author: Botany: A Brief Introduction to Plant Biology, 1979, Botany: An Introduction on Plant Biology, 1982; co-editor: Mechanisms and Control of Cell Division, 1977; also numerous articles to profl. jours. Served to capt. U.S. Army, 1965-67. Fellow Japan Soc. Promotion of Sci.; mem. Bot. Soc. Am., Soc. Exptl. Biology, Am. Inst. Biol. Sci. Democrat. Roman Catholic. Avocation: community theatre. Office: U Calif Sect Plant Biology Davis CA 95616-8537

ROST, WILLIAM JOSEPH, chemist; b. Fargo, N.D., Dec. 8, 1926; s. William Melvin and Christine Ruth (Hamerlik) R.; m. Rita Cincoski, Sept. 15, 1951; children—Kathryn, Patricia, Carol. B.S., U. Minn., 1948, Ph.D., 1952. From asst. prof. to prof. pharm. chemistry Sch. Pharmacy U. Kansas City, Mo., 1952-63; prof. pharm. chemistry Sch. Pharmacy U. Mo., Kansas City, 1963—. Co-author: Principles of Medicinal Chemistry, 1974, 3d rev. edit., 1988; contbr. articles profl. jours. Mem. Am. Pharm. Assn., Am. Chem. Soc., Sigma Xi, Kappa Psi, Rho Chi, Phi Lambda Upsilon. Home: 709 W 115th Ter Kansas City MO 64114-5597 Office: U Mo Sch of Pharmacy Kansas City MO 64110

ROSTAGNO, DERRICK, professional tennis player; b. Los Angeles, Calif., Oct. 25, 1965; s. Juan and Helga R. Student, Stanford U. Mem. U.S. Olympic Team, 1984; 6th in U.S. Tennis Assn. rankings, 13th in world ranking, 1991, ranked 14th in U.S. Tennis Assn., 1993. Office: care US Tennis Assn 70 W Red Oak Ln White Plains NY 10604*

ROSTEN, IRWIN, writer, producer, director. Writer-producer news, pub. affairs Sta. KNXT-CBS, Los Angeles, 1954-60; dir. news, pub. affairs Sta. KTLA, Los Angeles, 1960-63; writer-producer, dir. Wolper Prodns., Inc., Los Angeles, 1963-67; chief documentary dept. MGM Studios, Culver City, Calif., 1967-72; pres. Ronox Prodns., Inc., Los Angeles, 1970-87. Writer-prodr.-dir. Nat. Geog. Soc. spls.: Splendid Stones, Elephant, Great Moments with National Geographic, The Thames, Mysteries of the Mind, Gold!, The Legacy of L.S.B. Leakey, The Volga, The Incredible Machine, Grizzly!, The Eerie World of Jacques-Yves Cousteau, National Parks: Playground or Paradise?, numerous other shows including Unsolved Mysteries, The Wolf Men, Ripley's Believe It or Not, Sports Illustrated, Trial by Wilderness, Hollywood: The Dream Factory, Kifaru: The Black Rhinoceros, Birds Do It, Bees Do It, Indestructible People, Journey Into Life, One Man's Noise: Stories of an Adventursome Oceanographer, Tiger: Lord of the Wild; video prodr. opening ceremonies 1984 Olympic Games, L.A., Interactive Multimedia: Columbus, Evolution/Revolution. Recipient Emmy award Acad. TV Arts and Scis.; recipient Writers Guild Am. award, Peabody award, Am. Med. Writers Assn. award, Christophers award, Ohio State U. award, Saturday Rev. award, CINE Golden Eagle award. Mem. Writers Guild Am., Dirs. Guild Am., Acad. TV Arts and Scis., Internat. Documentary Assn. Office: 2217 Chelan Dr Los Angeles CA 90068-2620

ROSTER, MICHAEL, lawyer; b. Chgo., May 7, 1945. AB, Stanford U., 1967, JD, 1973. Bar: Calif. 1973, D.C. 1980. Reporter UPI, Chgo., 1965; writer Time-Life, San Francisco, 1966-67; ptnr. McKenna, Conner & Cuneo, L.A. and Washington, 1973-87, Morrison & Foerster, L.A. and Washington, 1987-93; gen. counsel Stanford (Calif.) U., 1993—; bd. dirs. Silicon Valley Bancshares, vice chmn., 1995—, bd. dirs. Am. Corp. Counsel Assn., Washington. Contbr. articles to profl. jours. Chmn. Cityscape Panel of Strategic Planning Commn., Pasadena, Calif., 1985-86; bd. dirs. Pasadena Heritage, 1986-87. Lt. (j.g.) USN, 1969-71. Mem. ABA (chmn. com. on savs. instns. 1985-89, fin. svcs. com. 1981—, banking com. 1989—), Calif. Bar Assn. (chmn. banking com. 1978-79), Stanford U. Alumni Assn. (chmn. 1992), Univ. Club (Washington), L.A. Athletic Club. Office: Stanford U Gen Counsel Box N Stanford CA 94309

ROSTKER, BERNARD, federal official; m. Louise Cowen; children: David, Michael. BS in Econs. and Edn., NYU, 1964; M in Econs., Syracuse U., 1967, PhD in Econs., 1970. Economist Manpower Requirements Directorate Office of the Asst. Sec. of Def. for Sys. Analysis, 1968-70; rsch. economist RAND Corp., 1970-72, program dir. manpower per. and tng. program, 1972-77; prin. dep. asst. sec. for manpower and res. affairs USN, 1977-79, dir. Selective Svc., 1979-81, dir. navy mgmt. program Ctr. for Naval Analyses, 1981-83; dir. sys. mgmt. divsn. Sys. Rsch. and Applications Corp., 1983-84; program dir. force devel. and employment program RAND Corp.- The Arroyo Ctr., 1984-90, assoc. dir., 1984-90; dir. Def. Manpower Rsch. Ctr. RAND Nat. Def. Rsch. Ctr., 1990-94; asst. sec. for manpower and res. affairs USN, 1994—, spl. asst. to dep. sec. def. for Gulf War illnesses, 1996—. Office: Dept of the Navy Manpower and Res Affairs The Pentagon Washington DC 20350-1000

ROSTKY, GEORGE HAROLD, editor; b. N.Y.C., Feb. 28, 1926; s. Morris and Mary (Wyloge) R.; m. Rhoda Thelma Bornstein, June 29, 1950; children: Mark, Lisa. B.E.E., CCNY, 1957. Assoc. editor Electronic Design, N.Y.C., 1957-61; editor-in-chief Electronic Design, Rochelle Park, N.J., 1971-78; editorial dir./assoc. pub. Electronic Engring. Times, Manhasset, N.Y., 1978-85; cons., 1985—; founder George Rostky Assocs., Focus Rsch., Great Neck, N.Y.; securities analyst McDonnell & Co., N.Y.C., 1961-62; editorial dir. Mactier Pub. Co., N.Y.C., 1962-71; U.S. Dept. Commerce industry tech. rep. to U.S. Electronics Catalog Exhbn., India, 1980. Served with AUS, 1942-45. Recipient Indsl. Mktg. award for editorial excellence, 1964, Neal awards, 1967, 74, 75, 77. Home: 39 Cumberland Ave Great Neck NY 11020-1422 Office: 600 Community Dr Manhasset NY 11030-3847

ROSTOKER, GORDON, physicist, educator; b. Toronto, Ont., Can., July 15, 1940; s. Louis and Fanny (Silbert) R.; m. Gillian Patricia Farr, June 29, 1966; children: Gary David, Susan Birgitta, Daniel Mark. BSc in Physics, U. Toronto, 1962, MA in Physics, 1963; PhD in Geophysics, U. B.C., Can., 1966. Postdoctoral fellow Royal Inst. Tech., Stockholm, 1966-68; asst. prof. physics U. Alta., B.C., 1968-73, assoc. prof., 1973-79, prof., 1979—, McCalla Rsch. Prof., 1983-84, ann. Killam Prof., 1991-92, dir. Inst. Earth and Planetary Physics, 1985-91; assoc. chmn. dept. physics U. Alta., 1976-79, univ. rep. to bd. dirs. Can. Network for Space Rsch., 1992-94, mem. univ. rsch. policy com., 1987-91; cons. TRW Sys. Group, 1973, Dome Petroleum Ltd., 1981, U. Western Ont., 1983, York U., 1986; contract rschr. Energy, Mines and Resources, Can., Hydro-Québec; mem. assoc. com. space rsch. Nat. Rsch. Coun. Can., 1975-80, mem. com. on internat. sci. exchanges, 1977-79, others; mem. physics and astronomy com. Natural Scis. and Engring. Rsch. Coun., 1979-82, mem. spl. ad hoc com. on physics and astronomy, 1987-91, mem. grant selection com. for sci. publs., 1988-92; prin. investigator CANOPUS, 1989—; chmn. divsn. III Internat. Assn. Geomagnetism and Aeronomy, 1979-83; chmn. working group on data analysis phase of Internat. Magnetospheric Study Sci. Com. on Solar Terrestrial Physics of Internat. Coun. Sci. Unions, 1980-86, co-chmn. steering com. for Solar-Terrestrial Energy Program, 1987-89, chmn., 1989—. Editor Can. Jour. Physics, 1980-86, mem. editl. adv. bd., 1986-96; contbr. over 250 articles to profl. publs. Mem. pub. adv. com. Govtl. Environ. Conservation Authority of Province of Alta., Edmonton, 1973-74. Recipient Steacie prize EWR Steacie Meml. Fund, 1979, Geophys. Centenary medal Acad. Scis. USSR, 1984. Fellow Royal Soc. Can.; mem. Am. Geophys. Union (assoc. editor Jour. Geophys. Rsch. 1976-79, 92-94, Jour. Geomagnetism and Geoelectricity 1993-96), Can. Assn. Physicists (sec.-treas. Can. Geophys. Union 1973-74, chmn. divsn. aeronomy and space physics 1977-78, publs. com. 1980-86), Internat. Assn. Geomagnetism and Aeronomy (v.p. 1995—). Achievements include use of ground magnetometer arrays to discover stepwise evolution of electric current systems which flow in the ionosphere and magnetosphere during episodes of strong auroral disturbance. Office: U Alta, Dept Physics, Edmonton, AB Canada T6G 2J1

ROSTOKER, MICHAEL DAVID, micro-electronics company executive, lawyer; b. Quincy, Mass., Mar. 15, 1958; s. David and E. Louise (Berleue) R. Student, Carnegie-Mellon U., 1976-78; BS in Indsl. Engring., U. Pitts., 1980; JD, Franklin Pierce Law Ctr., 1984; PhD in Indsl. Engring., City U., L.A., 1992. Bar: U.S. Patent and Trademark Office 1983, N.H. 1984, U.S. Dist. Ct. N.H. 1984, Mass. 1985, Pa. 1985, U.S. Dist. Ct. D.C. 1985, U.S. Ct. Appeals (D.C. cir.) 1985. Lectr. in computer sci. Point Park Coll., Pitts., 1979-80; sys. analyst GE, Fitchburg, Mass., 1980-81; patent atty. Rines and Rines, Boston and Concord, N.H., 1983-85; patent counsel Schlumberger Well Svcs., Houston, 1985-87; sr. counsel intellectual property Intel Corp., Santa Clara, Calif., 1987-88; v.p. strategic alliances LSI Logic Corp., Milpitas, Calif., 1988-96; pres., CEO Microelectronics Rsch. Inc. subs. Kawasaki, Santa Clara, Calif., 1996—; cons. in field, Concord, 1981-85; mem. faculty computer sci. and math. Franklin Pierce Coll., Rindge, N.H., 1981-85; mem. adj. faculty law Franklin Pierce Law Ctr., 1983-85; edtl. bd. Software Protection Reporter, 1984-94; lectr. seminars in field. Author: Computer Jurisprudence: Legal Responses to the Information Revolution, 1985, Technology Management: Licensing and Protection for Computers in the World Market, 1993; contbr. articles to profl. jours.; patentee in field. Mem. ABA (patents, sci. and tech., litigation sects.), Am. Trial Lawyers Assn., Am. Intellectual Property Assn. Republican. Jewish. Avocations: volleyball, racquetball, weightlifting, theater, music. Home: 108 Mcpherson Ct Boulder Creek CA 95006-9203 Office: Microelectronics Rsch Inc 4655 Old Ironsides Dr Ste 264 Santa Clara CA 95054-1808

ROSTON, ARNOLD, information specialist, educator, advertising executive, artist, editor; b. Racine, Wis., June 29, 1923; s. Felix and Hannah (Epstein) R.; m. Evelyn Eisen, June 16, 1944 (dec.); children: Karen Laurie, Susan Joyce. Student, CCNY, New Sch., 1942, Harvard Grad. Sch., 1975. Info. specialist Exec. Office of the Pres. Office of Emergency Mgmt., 1942, Joint (U.S.) Army-Navy Intelligence Svc.-BSC, 1943; asst. to adminstrv. v.p., co-dir., advt. and promotion, creative dir. MBS-RKO, 1944-59; creative group head Grey Advt. Agy., 1959-60; dir. creative services Van Brunt & Co., 1961-64; pres. Roston & Co., 1965-76, chmn., 1979—; instr. secret U.S.A. Officer Tng. Sch. Marshall Field Estate, Oyster Bay, N.Y., 1943; exec. editor Budget Decorating Mag., 1973-76; dean Ctr. for Understanding Media of The New Sch., 1974-75; organizer, exec. sec. The Election Process and The New Media Workshop Conf., N.Y.C., 1975; dir. program devel. art therapy deg. program & accreditation Sch. Visual Arts, N.Y.C., 1976-77; cultural affairs corr. Broadcasting Co. of the Carolinas Inc., 1976-88; pres. Van Brunt/Roston Corp. Communications, 1977-78; instr. Cooper Union, 1947-53, Bklyn. Mus. Art Sch., 1949-51, Pratt Inst. Grad. Seminar, 1954-55, CUNY, 1973; designer 29th Art Dirs. ann., 1949-50; instr. workshop in advt. design Am. Inst. Graphic Arts, 1951; chmn. Great Neck Com. Art and Design, N.Y., 1967-77; chmn. 36th Ann. Nat. Exhbn. Art and Design, 1956-57; founder, pres., dir. Art Dirs. Scholarship Fund, Inc., 1971-93, also mem. bd., chmn. coms.; mem. pres.'s adv. commn. N.Y. H.S. of Art and Design, 1974-94; organizer N.Y.C. Bd. Edn. "Expo '74" in Times Sq. and Radio City; chmn. Vatican com. Justitia Et Pax, 1968-72. Exhbns. include Met. Mus. Art, Mus. Modern Art, Pa. Acad. Fine Arts, N.Y. World"s Fair, Bklyn. Mus., Heckscher Mus., Montclair Art Mus., N.Y. Mcpl. Art Galleries, Lever House, Cooper Hewitt Mus., others; represented in permanent collections: Met. Mus. Art, Mus. Modern Art, Libr. of Congress, N.Y. Pub. Libr., Aldridge Mus., Ridgefield, Conn., The Vatican; mural Great Neck Pub. Libr.; contbr. articles on design, advt., scholarship to profl. jours. Trustee, sec. Sch. Art League Bd. Edn., N.Y.C., 1969-79; chmn. Landmarks

Preservation Commn. Inc., Village of Great Neck, 1979-84; bd. dirs. Canterbury Crossing, 1984-85. George Foster Peabody-Yaddo Found. resident fellow; recipient awards including Suydam Silver medal NAD, Nat. Exhbn. Advt. and Editorial Art and Design awards, Certs. of Excellence and Gold medals Art Dirs. ann. nat. exhibits; Mus. Modern Art nat. hemispherical poster awards, 1940, 41, Certs. of Excellence Am. Inst. Graphic Arts, Ptnr. in Edn. award N.Y.C. Bd. Edn., 1979, Gt. Trademarks of World catalog, Milan, Italy, others. Mem. Princeton Club of N.Y., Art Dirs. Club. Studio: PO Box 717 Shrub Oak NY 10588-0717

ROSTON, DAVID CHARLES, lawyer; b. Evanston, Ill., Oct. 15, 1943. BA cum laude, Brandeis U., 1964; JD cum laude, Harvard U., 1967. Bar: Ill. 1967. Ptnr. Altheimer & Gray, Chgo.; mem. pres. coun. Brandeis U. Mem. ABA, Ill. State Bar Assn., Chgo. Bar Assn. (chmn. com,. on profl. responsibility 1997—). Office: Altheimer & Gray 10 S Wacker Dr Ste 4000 Chicago IL 60606-7407

ROSTOW, CHARLES NICHOLAS, lawyer, educator; b. Geneva, Switzerland, Mar. 3, 1950; s. Eugene Victor and Edna (Greenberg) R.; m. Heyden White, Oct. 31, 1987; children: Theodore Isaac, Celia A.M. BA, Yale U., 1972, PhD, 1979, JD, 1982. Assoc. Shearman & Sterling, N.Y.C., 1982-85; spl. asst. to legal adviser U.S. Dept. State, Washington, 1985-87; dep. legal adviser Nat. Security Coun., Washington, 1987, spl. asst. to Pres., legal adviser, 1987-93; Disting. rsch. prof. Coll. of Law, U. Tulsa, 1995—; exec. dir. Mass. Office Internat. Trade and Investment, 1995—. Author: Anglo-French Relations 1934-36, 1984; editor: Akten zur deutschen auswaertigen Politik: 1918-1945, vols. XIV-XXI, 1980-83; contbr. articles to prof. jours. Hon. dir. John Goodwin Tower Ctr. for Polit. Studies, So. Meth. U.; nat. adv. bd. Am. Jewish Com. Mem. Royal Inst. Internat. Affairs, Coun. Fgn. Rels., Assn. of Bar of City of N.Y., Phi Beta Kappa, Cosmos Club, Yale Club (N.Y.C.), Elizabethan Club (New Haven). Jewish. Home: 97 Hubbard St Concord MA 01742 Office: Mass Office Internat Trade 100 Cambridge St Ste 1302 Boston MA 02202-0044

ROSTOW, EUGENE VICTOR, lawyer, educator, economist; b. Bklyn., Aug. 25, 1913; s. Victor A. and Lillian (Helman) R.; m. Edna Berman Greenberg; children: Victor A. D., Jessica, Charles Nicholas. AB, Yale U., 1933, LLB, 1937, AM, 1944; postgrad., King's Coll., Cambridge (Eng.) U., 1933-34; M.A., Cambridge U., 1959, LL.D., 1962; LL.D., Boston U., 1976, U. New Haven, 1981, N.Y. Law Sch., 1984. Bar: N.Y. 1938. Practice in N.Y.C., 1937-38; mem. faculty Law Sch. Yale, 1938—, prof. law, 1944-84, prof. emeritus, sr. research scholar, 1984—, dean, 1955-65, Sterling prof. law and pub. affairs, 1964-84; master Trumbull Coll., 1966; dir. ACDA, 1981-83; Disting. vis. research prof. law and diplomacy Nat. Def. U., 1984-90, 92—; under-sec. state for polit. affairs, 1966-69; pres. Atlantic Treaty Assn., 1973-76; vis. prof. U. Chgo., 1941; Pitt prof. Am. history and instns., professorial fellow King's Coll., Cambridge U., 1959-60; William W. Cook lectr. Mich. U., 1958; John R. Coen lectr. U. Colo., 1961; Leary lectr. U. Utah, 1965; Brandeis lectr. Brandeis U., 1965; Rosenthal lectr. Northwestern U., 1965; George Eastman vis. prof., fellow Balliol Coll., Oxford (Eng.) U., 1970-71; Adviser Dept. State, 1942-44; asst. exec. sec. Econ. Commn. for Europe, UN, 1949-50; mem. Jud. Council of Conn., 1955-66, Atty. Gen.'s Nat. Com. Study Antitrust Laws, 1954-55; chmn. exec. com. Com. on the Present Danger, 1976-81, 86-92. Author: Planning for Freedom, 1959, The Sovereign Prerogative, 1962, Law, Power and the Pursuit of Peace, 1968, Peace in the Balance, 1972, The Ideal in Law, 1978, Toward Managed Peace, 1993, A Breakfast for Bonaparte, 1994; editor: Is Law Dead?, 1971. Decorated Chevalier Legion d'Honneur (France), Grand Cross Order of Crown (Belgium); recipient Disting. Civilian Svc. award U.S. Army, 1990; Guggenheim fellow, 1959-60, Randolph fellow U.S. Inst. Peace, 1990-92, hon. fellow Hebrew U. of Jerusalem, 1992—. Fellow Am. Acad. Arts and Scis.; mem. Am. Law Inst., Phi Beta Kappa, Alpha Delta Phi, Elizabethan Yale Club, Century Assn. N.Y.C. Club, Cosmos Club Washington. Democrat. Jewish. Home: 1315 4th St SW Washington DC 20024-2201 Office: Nat Def U Washington DC 20319-6000 also: Yale U Sch Law New Haven CT 06520

ROSTOW, WALT WHITMAN, economist, educator; b. N.Y.C., Oct. 7, 1916; s. Victor Aaron and Lillian (Helman) R.; m. Elspeth Vaughan Davies, June 26, 1947; children: Peter Vaughan, Ann Larner. BA, Yale U., 1936, PhD, 1940. Instr. econs. Columbia U., 1940-41; asst. chief German-Austrian econ. div. Dept. State, 1945-46; Harmsworth prof. Am. history Oxford (Eng.) U., 1946-47; asst. to exec. sec. Econ. Commn. for Europe, 1947-49; Pitt. prof. Am. history Cambridge (Eng.) U., 1949-50; prof. econ. history MIT, 1950-60; staff mem. Center Internat. Studies, 1951-60; dep. spl. asst. to Pres. for nat. security affairs, 1961; counselor, chmn. policy planning council Dept. State, 1961-66; spl. asst. to Pres., 1966-69; U.S. rep., ambassador Inter-Am. com. Alliance for Progress, 1964-66; now Rex G. Baker Jr. prof. polit. economy, depts. econs. and history U. Tex., Austin, prof. emeritus; mem. Bd. Fgn. Scholarships, 1969-72; chmn. bd., task force dir. Austin Project, 1982—. Author: The American Diplomatic Revolution, 1947, Essays on the British Economy of the Nineteenth Century, 1948, The Process of Economic Growth, 1953, 2d edit., 1960, (with A.D. Gayer, A.J. Schwartz) The Growth and Fluctuation of the British Economy, 1790-1850, 1953, 2d edit., 1975, (with A. Levin, others) The Dynamics of Soviet Society, 1953, (with others) The Prospects for Communist China, 1954, (with R.W. Hatch) An American Policy in Asia, 1955, (with M.F. Millikan) A Proposal: Key to an Effective Foreign Policy, 1957, The United States in the World Arena, 1960, The Stages of Economic Growth, 1960, 2d edit., 1971, 3d edit., 1990, A View from the Seventh Floor, 1964, A Design for Asian Development, 1965, (with William E. Griffith) East-West Relations: Is Detente Possible?, 1969, Politics and the Stages of Growth, 1971, The Diffusion of Power, 1972, How It All Began, 1975, The World Economy: History and Prospect, 1978, Getting From Here to There, 1978, Why the Poor Get Richer and the Rich Slow Down, 1980, Pre-Invasion Bombing Strategy: General Eisenhower's Decision of March 25, 1944, 1981, British Trade Fluctuations, 1868-1896: A Chronicle and a Commentary, 1981, The Division of Europe After World War II: 1946, 1981, Europe After Stalin: Eisenhower's Three Decisions of March 11, 1953, 1982, Open Skies: Eisenhower's Proposal of July 21, 1955, 1982, The Barbaric Counter-Revolution: Cause and Cure, 1983, Eisenhower, Kennedy, and Foreign Aid, 1985, The United States and the Regional Organization of Asia and the Pacific: 1965-1985, 1986, Rich Countries and Poor Countries, 1987, Essays on a Half Century: Ideas, Policies and Action, 1988, History, Policy, and Economic Theory, 1989, Theorists of Economic Growth From David Hume to the Present with a Perspective on the Next Century, 1990; editor: The Economics of Take-Off Into Sustained Growth, 1963. Maj. OSS, AUS, 1942-45. Decorated Legion of Merit, Hon. Order Brit. Empire (mil.); recipient Presdl. Medal of Freedom with distinction; Rhodes scholar Balliol Coll., 1936-38, Outstanding Work in Social Scis. award Assn. Am. Pubs., 1990. Mem. Am. Acad. Arts and Scis., Am. Philos. Soc., Mass. Hist. Soc., Tex. Philos. Soc., Cosmos Club, Elizabethan Club. Clubs: Cosmos (Washington); Elizabethan (New Haven). Home: 1 Wildwind Pt Austin TX 78746-2434

ROSTROPOVICH, MSTISLAV LEOPOLDOVICH, musician; b. Baku, USSR, Mar. 27, 1927; s. Leopold and Sofia (Fedotova) R.; m. Galina Pavlovna Vishnevskaya; children: Olga, Elena. Grad., Moscow Conservatory 1948; numerous hon. doctorate degrees. Faculty mem. Moscow Conservatory, 1953, prof., 1960; head cello and double-bass dept., formerly prof. Leningrad Conservatory; music dir., conductor Nat. Symphony Orch., Washington, 1977-94; hon. prof. Cuban Nat. Conservatory, 1960-78; pres. Evian Internat. Music Festival. Debut as violoncellist, 1940; performer world concert tours, Moscow Philharm. Orch.; recordings include (with various artists) Mstislav Rostropovich Melodiya Recordings, 1949-56, 48-59, The Young Rostropovich: Rare Recordings for the 1950-52 Years, Schnittke's Cello Concerto No. 2, In Memorium, Return to Russia. Decorated Hon. Knight of the Brit. Empire, 1987; Commdr. French Legion of Honor, 1987; Officer's Cross of Merit, Fed. Republic Germany, 1987; recipient Stalin prize, 1951, 53, Lenin prize, 1963, Life in Music prize, 1984, Albert Schweitzer Music award, 1985, Grammy awards, 1970, 77, 80, 84, Presdl. Medal Freedom, 1987, Ditson Condr.'s award, Columbia U., 1990, Four Freedoms award Franklin and Eleanor Roosevelt Inst., 1992; named Musician of Yr., Mus. Am., 1987. Mem. Am. Acad. Arts and Scis., Union Soviet Composers, Brit. Royal Acad. Music (hon.), Acad. Arts of French Inst.-Forty Immortals. address: CAMI 165 W 57th St New York NY 10019-2201*

ROSZTOCZY, FERENC ERNO, business executive; b. Szeged, Hungary, Aug. 16, 1932; came to U.S., 1957, naturalized, 1962; s. Ferenc Lipot and Edith Jolan (Kunzl) R.; m. Diane Elder, Dec. 21, 1963; children: Thomas Ferenc, Robert Anthony, Stephanie Elder, Edward Joseph. MS, U. Szeged, 1955; PhD, U. Calif., Berkeley, 1961. Phys. chemist Stanford Research Inst., Menlo Park, Calif., 1961-64; mem. tech. staff Bell Labs., Murray Hill, N.J., 1964-68; mgr. semicondr. materials Bell & Howell, Pasadena, Calif., 1968-69; mgr. semicondr. crystal growth and device engring. Varian Assos., Palo Alto, Calif., 1969-75; dir. Ariz. Machinery Co., Avondale, 1974—, pres., 1975—, chmn. bd., 1976—; pres. Stotz Farms, Inc., 1979—; dir. Ariz. Indsl. Machinery Co., 1975-91; cons. Siltec Corp., Menlo Park, Calif., 1971-72; mem. agribusiness adv. bd. 1st Interstate Bank Ariz., 1995-96. Bd. trustees Agua Fria High Sch., 1981-89, pres. 1986-87. Mem. United Dairymen Ariz. (dir. 1985—). Roman Catholic. Club: Wigwam Country. Contbr. articles to profl. jours. Patentee in field. Home: 1010 E Acacia Cir Litchfield Park AZ 85340-4529 Office: Ariz Machinery Co 11111 W Mcdowell Rd Avondale AZ 85323-5000

ROTBERG, EUGENE HARVEY, investment banker, lawyer; b. Phila., Jan. 19, 1930; s. Irving Bernard and Blanche Grace (Levick) R.; m. Iris Sybil Comens, Aug. 29, 1954; children—Diana Golda, Pamela Lynn. B.S., Temple U., 1951; LL.B., U. Pa., 1954; PhD (hon.), Salem-Teikyo U., 1992. Chief counsel Office Policy Research Securities and Exchange Commn., Washington, 1963-66; v.p., treas. World Bank, Washington, 1969-87; exec. v.p. Merrill Lynch & Co., N.Y.C., 1987-90. Served with U.S. Army, 1954-55. Decorated King Leopold II medal (Belgium); recipient Disting. Svc. award Securities and Exch. Commn., 1968; named Alumnus of Yr., Temple U., 1969. Home: 7211 Brickyard Rd Potomac MD 20854-4808 Office: 1250 24th St NW Ste 350 Washington DC 20037-1124

ROTBERG, IRIS COMENS, social scientist; b. Phila., Dec. 16, 1932; d. Samuel Nathaniel and Golda (Shuman) Comens; m. Eugene H. Rotberg, Aug. 29, 1954; children: Diana Golda, Pamela Lynn. BA, U. Pa., 1954, MA, 1955; PhD, Johns Hopkins U., Balt., 1958. Research psychologist Pres.'s Commn. on Income Maintenance Programs, Washington, 1968-69, Office Planning, Research and Evaluation, Office Econ. Opportunity, Washington, 1970-73; dep. dir. compensatory edn. study Nat. Inst. Edn., Washington, 1974-77, dir. Office Planning and Program Devel., 1978-82; program dir. NSF, Arlington, Va., 1985-87, 89-91, 1993-96; tech. policy fellow Com. on Sci., Space and Tech., U.S. Ho. of Reps., Washington, 1987-89; sr. social scientist RAND, Washington, 1991-93; rsch. prof. edn. policy Grad. Sch. Edn. and Human Devel. George Washington U., Washington, 1996—. NSF fellow, 1956-58. Home: 7211 Brickyard Rd Potomac MD 20854-4808

ROTCH, JAMES E., lawyer; b. Auburn, Ala., Mar. 26, 1945; s. Elroy B. and Martha (Ellisor) R.; m. Carolyn J. Kramer, July 29, 1995; children: Jamison B., Susannah R., Issac M. Craig. BS, Auburn U., 1967, postgrad., 1967-68; JD, U. Va., 1971. Bar: Ala. 1971, U.S. Dist. Ct. (no. dist.) Ala. 1973. Rsch. asst. Office Instl. Rsch. Auburn (Ala.) U., 1967-68; clk. U.S. Judiciary System, Birmingham, Ala., 1971-72; assoc. Bradley Arant Rose & White LLP, Birmingham, 1971-76; ptnr. Bradley, Arant, Rose & White, Birmingham, 1976—, administrv. ptnr., 1990-93; mem. adv. com. Bioelastics Rsch. Ltd., Birmingham, 1992—, Gov.'s Task Force on Biotechnology, Ala., 1993. Pres. adv. com. Birmingham Mus. Art, 1989-92; bd. dirs. Operation New Birmingham, 1990-91, 95—; mem. Newcomen Soc. Birmingham, 1980—, Coalition for Better Edn., Birmingham, 1990—; active Boy Scouts Am.; bd. dirs. The Birmingham Com. for Olympic Soccer, 1994—, Ala. Sports Found., 1994—, Birmingham Bus. Assistance Network, 1995—; mem. adminstrv. bd. Canterbury United Meth. Ch., 1991-93. Capt. USAR, 1972-78. Mem. ALA, Auburn U. Bar Assn., Birmingham Bar Assn., Internat. Bar Assn., Ala. State Bar Assn., Leadership Birmingham, Auburn Coll. Liberal Arts (adv. coun.), U. Va. Alumni Assn., Birmingham Venture Club (bd. dirs. 1990—, v.p. 1991, pres. 1992-93), Birmingham Area C. of C. (trustee 1992—), Country Club of Birmingham, Kiwanis Club (vice-chair membership), Auburn Alumni Assn., The Jockey Club, The Summit Club (charter mem.). Methodist. Avocations: horses, bird hunting, cattle farming, golf. Office: Bradley Arant Rose & White 2001 Park Pl Ste 1400 Birmingham AL 35203-2700

ROTCH, WILLIAM, business administration educator; b. Cambridge, Mass., Nov. 19, 1929; s. Charles Morgan and Helen Aldis (Bradley) R.; m. Jane Coolidge Whitehill, Dec. 20, 1952; children: Jane Revere, William Jr., Sarah Aldis. AB, Harvard U., 1951, MBA, 1956, DBA, 1959. Asst. auditor Ga. R.R. Bank, Augusta, 1953-54; rsch. assoc. Harvard Bus. Sch., Boston, 1956-57; mem. faculty Colgate Darden Grad. Sch. Bus. Adminstrn. U. Va., Charlottesville, 1959—, now Johnson and Higgins prof. bus. adminstrn.; vis. assoc. prof. Amos Tuck Sch., Dartmouth Coll., 1966-67; vis. prof. IMEDE Mgmt. Devel. Inst., Lausanne, Switzerland, 1973-75. Co-author: Executives Guide to Management Accounting and Control, 5th edit., 1993, Cases in Management Accounting and Control Systems, 3d edit., 1995. Vestryman St. Paul's Meml. Ch., Charlottesville, 1962-89; trustee World Learning, Brattleboro, Vt., 1957—, chmn. bd., 1988—. 2d lt. Signal Corps, U.S. Army, 1951-53. Recipient Experiment citation Experiment in International Living, 1986. Mem. Am. Acctg. Assn. (mem. various coms.), Inst. Mgmt. Accts., Somerset Club (Boston), Harvard Club (N.Y.). Avocations: sailing, photography. Home: 808 Fendall Ter Charlottesville VA 22903-1653 Office: U Va Darden Grad Bus Sch 520 Massie Rd Charlottesville VA 22903-1738

ROTE, NELLE FAIRCHILD HEFTY, business consultant; b. Watsontown, Pa., May 23, 1930; d. Edwin Dunkel and Phebe Hill (Fisher) Fairchild; m. John Austin Hefty, Mar. 20, 1948 (div. June 1970); children: Harry E. Hefty, John B. Hefty, Susan E. Hefty DeBartolo; m. Keith Maynard Rote, Dec. 16, 1983 (dec. Aug. 1985). Student, Bucknell U., 1961, Williamsport Sch. of Commerce, 1968-69, Pa. State U., 1971-72, 83, Susquehanna U., 1986. Typesetter, page designer Colonial Printing House, Inc., Lewisburg, Pa., 1970-76; account exec. Sta. WTGC Radio, Lewisburg, 1976-78; co-owner Colonial Printing Co., Lewisburg, 1978-83; temp. HATS-Temps, Lewisburg, 1986-89; artist, editor Create-A-Book, Inc., Milton, Fla., 1980-92; census crew leader, spl. svc. Dept. Commerce, Washington, 1990; cons. Personalized Books, Create-A-Book, Inc., Div. John B. Hefty Pub., Gulf Breeze, Fla., 1991—. Artist: Children's Playmate Mag., 1942, Christmas Wish, Big Parade, 1989-90. Vol. proofreader Lewisburg Bicentennial Commn., 1976; editor-poet Holiday Newspaper Bus. Assn., Lewisburg, 1987; charter mem. Women's Art Mus., Washington; charter sponsor and field rep. Women in Mil. Svc. Meml., Arlington, Va., 1991; chmn. Rooftop Garden Project Evang. Hosp., Pa., 1995—, Nelle Fairchild Rote Book Fund, Union County Libr. Recipient Humanitarian recognition Tri-County Fedn. Women's Clubs, Pa., 1965, Grand Prize in Cooking, Milton Std., 1966, Most Profl. Photo award, Lewisburg Festival of Arts, 1980, Hon. Mention Award Women in Arts, Harrisburg, Pa., 1981, Photo Contest award Congressman Allen Ertel, Washington, 1981, Photo awards 2d and 3d place Union County Fair, Laurelton, Pa., 1981, Hon. Mention Photo award Susquehanna Art Soc., Pa., 1981, Silver award for poetry World of Poetry, 1990. Mem. DAR (nat. def. reporter Shikelimo chpt. 1989-95, sec. 1992-95, regent 1995—), Civic Club Lewisburg (v.p. 1994-97), Orgn. United Environment, Nat. Wildlife Fedn. Assn.), Inst. Lifelong Learning Susquehanna U., Marine Corps League Aux. (life), Union County Hist. Soc., Warrior Run Heritage Soc. Home: 1015 Saint Paul St Lewisburg PA 17837-1213

ROTELL, THOMAS M., publishing executive. Dir. U of Penn. Press, Phila.; now dir. Texas A & M Press. Office: Texas A&M Press Lindsey Bldg Drawer C College Station TX 77843

ROTEMBERG, JULIO JACOBO, economist, educator, consultant; b. Buenos Aires, Argentina, Sept. 26, 1953; came to U.S., 1972; s. Salomon and Ellen (Wolf) R.; m. Analisa Lattes, Nov. 8, 1982; childrenL Veronica M., Martin S. BA, U. Calif., Berkeley, 1975; PhD, Princeton U., 1981. Researcher Banco Cen. De La Republica Argentina, Buenos Aires, 1976; from asst. prof. to assoc. prof. econs. Sloan Sch. Mgmt. MIT, Cambridge, 1980-89, prof., 1989—; rsch. assoc. Nat. Bureau of Econ. Rsch., Cambridge, 1986—; vis. prof., bus. adminstrn. Harvard Bus. Sch., Boston, 1994-95. Mem. bd. editors Rev. Econ. Studies, 1985-88, Econometrica, 1987—, Quarterly Jour. Econs., 1989—; contbr. articles to profl. jours. Fellow Econometric Soc.; mem. Am. Econ. Assn. Avocations: skiing, bicycling. Office: MIT Sloan Sch Mgmt Cambridge MA 02139

ROTENBERG, MANUEL, physics educator; b. Toronto, Ont., Can., Mar. 12, 1930; came to U.S., 1946; s. Peter and Rose (Plonzker) R.; m. Paula Weissbrod, June 23, 1952; children: Joel, Victor. BS, MIT, 1952, PhD, 1956. Mem. staff Los Alamos (N.Mex.) Nat. Lab., 1955-58; instr. physics Princeton (N.J.) U., 1958-59; asst. prof. U. Chgo., 1959-61; prof. applied physics U. Calif., San Diego, 1961-93, dean grad. studies and research, 1975-84, chmn. dept. elec. engring. and computer engring., 1988-93, rsch. prof., 1993—. Author: The 3-j and 6-j Symbols, 1959; founding editor: Methods of Computational Physics, 1963, Jour. of Computational Physics, 1962; editor: Biomathematics and Cell Kinetics, 1981. Fellow Am. Phys. Soc.; mem. AAAS, Sigma Xi. Office: U Calif San Diego La Jolla CA 92093-0407

ROTENBERG, SHELDON, violinist; b. Attleboro, Mass., Apr. 11, 1917; s. Joseph and Jennie (Almer) R.; m. Hilde Sussmann, Jan. 29, 1950; children: David, Steffi. A.B., Tufts U., 1939, grad. student, 1939-40; violin pupil of, Felix Winternitz, Georges Enesco, Maurice Hewitt. Tchr. violin, 1947—; music adviser, cons. pub. schs., Brookline, Mass.; archivist, cons. Boston Symphony Orch., 1992-93. Concertized extensively with the Boston String Quartet sponsored by Elizabeth Sprague Coolidge, including concerts and rec. at the Libr. of Congress, 1948-52, occupies endowed Kasdon-Paley chair, 1st violin sect., Boston Symphony Orch., 1948-91, solo performances with Boston Pops Orch., 1939-41; Boston Symphony rep. as soloist, tchr., mem. orch. in State Dept. cultural exch. program with Japan Philharm., Tokyo, 1968-69; mem. faculty Boston U. Tanglewood Inst., 1979—. Served to capt. AUS, 1942-46. Mem. Harvard Mus. Assn., Tufts U. Alumni Assn. Home: 60 Browne St Brookline MA 02146-3441 Office: care Boston Symphony Orch Symphony Hall Boston MA 02115

ROTENBERRY, CLINTON GRICE, state representative, real estate broker; b. Mendenhall, Miss., Jan. 12, 1953; s. Clinton Grice and Ethel Jane (Cobb) R; m. Christy Ann Stephens, Aug. 14, 1976; children: Jennifer Christine, Rebecca Kathleen, Natalie Jane. BA, Belhaven Coll., Jackson, Miss., 1975; postgrad., La. State U., 1976. Sales clk., buyer Stephens of Mendenhall, 1977-79; salesman, realtor Scothye Hooker Real Estate, Jackson, Miss., 1980-88; broker Rotenberry Realty, Mendenhall, 1988—; rep. Miss. Ho. of Reps., Jackson, 1992—; sec. pub. utilities com. Mass. Ho. Reps., Jackson, 1993—, sec. constn. com., 1995—, Banks & Banks. Youth vol. 1st Bapt. Ch., Mendenhall, 1977-80; pres. Mendenhall Jaycees, Mendenhall, 1980; grad. Simpson County Leadership, Mendenhall, 1993, Miss. Econ. Coun. Leadership, Jackson, 1994; mem. nat. policy forum Nat. Rep. Party, 1994—. Mem. Nat. Conf. State Legislators, So. Legis. Conf., Am. Legis. Exch. Coun. (comms. com. 1996—), Miss. Craftsman's Arts Guild (bd. dirs. 1994—). Baptist. Avocation: golf. Home: RR 5 Box 56 Mendenhall MS 39114-9102 Office: Rotenberry Realty PO Box 818 Mendenhall MS 39114

ROTERT, DENISE ANNE, occupational therapist, army officer, educator; b. Sioux Falls, S.D., Nov. 18, 1949; d. Leonard Joseph and Irene Winnifred (Jennings) R. BS, U. Puget Sound, 1971; MA, U. No. Colo., 1975. Commd. 2d lt. Med. Specialist Corps, U.S. Army, 1970, advanced through grades to lt. col. , 1990; staff occupational therapist Tripler Army Med. Center, Honolulu, 1973-76, officer in charge occupational therapy sect. Ireland Army Hosp., Fort Knox, Ky., 1976-77; clin. supr. occupational therapy sect. Letterman Army Med. Center, Presidio of San Francisco, 1977-79; chief instr. occupational therapy asst. course Acad. Health Scis., Ft. Sam Houston, Tex., 1979-84; chief occupational therapy Tri-Service Alcohol Recovery Dept., Naval Hosp., Bethesda, Md., 1984-89, Womack Army Hosp., Ft. Bragg, N.C., 1989-90, ret., 1990; therapist Charter Sioux Falls, 1996—; mem. faculty U. S.D., 1991—. Recipient Myra McDaniel Writer's award, 1989. Mem. Am. Occupational Therapy Assn., World Fedn. Occupational Therapists, S.D. Occupational Therapy Assn. Roman Catholic. Home: 2609 S Prairie Ave Sioux Falls SD 57105-4626 Office: USDSM OT Dept 414 E Clark St Vermillion SD 57069-2307

ROTH, ALAN J., lawyer; b. Bklyn., Feb. 18, 1955; s. Benjamin and Naomi (Wisler) R. BA, Am. U., 1976; JD, N.Y.U., 1979. Bar: Conn. 1979, U.S. Dist. Ct. Conn. 1979, D.C. 1980, U.S. Ct. Appeals (D.C. cir.) 1980, U.S. Ct. Appeals (2d cir.) 1982, U.S. Supreme Ct. 1983. Law clk. to Hon. M. Joseph Blumenfeld U.S. Dist. Ct., Hartford, Conn., 1979-80; assoc. Tyler, Cooper & Alcorn, New Haven, Conn., 1980-84; counsel com. energy and commerce U.S. Ho. of Reps., Washington, 1985-92, chief counsel com. energy and commerce, 1992, staff dir., chief counsel, 1993-95, minority staff dir., chief coun. com. on commerce, 1995-97; ptnr. Bryan Cave LLP, 1997—; adj. professorial lectr. sch. pub. affairs Am. U., Washington, 1989-92. Democrat. Jewish. Office: Bryan Cave LLP 700 13th St NW Ste 700 Washington DC 20005-3960

ROTH, ALEDA VENDER, business educator; b. Cleve., Oct. 8, 1945; d. Joseph Patrick and Beatrice Vender; m. G. Douglas Roth, Sept. 26, 1970; children: G. Brian, Lauren Carter. BS in Psychology with honors, Ohio State U., 1968; MSPH in Biostats., U. N.C., 1970; PhD in Ops. Mgmt., Ohio State U., 1986. Chief statistician Ark. Children's Colony Ark. State Dept. Human Svcs., 1968-69; rsch. assoc., epidemiologist Epidemiologic Field Sta. Greater Kansas City Mental Health Found., 1970-72, statis. cons. Epidemiologic Field Sta., 1972-74; nat. dir. stats. dept. ANA, 1972-79; grad. teaching and rsch. assoc. faculty mgmt. sci. Ohio State U., 1979-83, grad. teaching and rsch. assoc. acctg. dept., 1983, instr. computer and info. sys. Coll. Engring., 1983-84, instr. faculty mgmt. sci. Coll. Adminstrv. Sci., 1984-85; asst. prof. Sch. Mgmt. Boston U., 1985-89; prin. investigator retail banking futures project, 1986-94; co-investigator mfg.'s future rsch. Boston U., 1985-89; prin. co-investigator rsch. DTT-UNC global mfg. strategy and tech. vision project, 1989—, rsch. assoc. ctr. health rsch. and edn., 1989-93; assoc. prof. dept. health adminstrn. Duke U. Med. Ctr., Durham, 1989-91; assoc. prof. bus. Duke U., Durham, N.C., 1989-93, U. N.C., Chapel Hill, 1993—; prin. rsch. co-investigator Internat. Svc. Study, 1996—; adj. faculty mem. Sch. Pub. Health, U. N.C., Chapel Hill, 1972-74; mem. Coop. Health Stats. Sys. Adv. Com., Nat. Ctr. Health Stats., DHHS, 1974-76; membership svcs. com. Nat. Decision Scis. Inst., 1989-90; adj. rsch. faculty Boston U. Mfg. Roundtable, 1985-90; rsch. adv. com. U. N.C.-Ctr. for Mfg. Excellence, 1989-94; exec. com. U. N.C. Cato Ctr. Applied Bus. Rsch., 1994-97, rsch. com. 1997—. Author: (with M. van der Velde) The Future of Retail Banking Delivery Systems, 1988, Retail Banking Strategies, Opportunities for the 1990s, 1990, World Class Banking: Benchmarking the Market Leaders, 1992, (with C. Giffi and G. Seal) Competing in World Class Manufacturing: America's 21st Century Challenge, 1990; editor: Facts About Nursing, 1972-73 edit., 1974, 1974-75 edit., 1976, 1980-81 edit., 1981, (with J. Jaeger and A. Kaluzny) The Management of Continuous Improvement: Cases in Health Administration, 1993; sr. assoc. editor Mfg. and Svc. Ops. Mgmt., 1996—; assoc. editor Decision Scis., 1993—, Jour. Ops. Mgmt., 1993—; area editor Prodn. and Ops. Mgmt. Jour., 1993—, mem. editl. adv. bd. 191-93; assoc. editor OM Rev., 1992-94, Benchmarking for Quality and Tech. Mgmt., 1993—; mem. editl. bd. Internat. Jour. Prodn. and Ops. Mgmt., 1995—; ad hoc referee Mgmt. Sci., Jour. Ops. Mgmt., Decision Scis., Prodn. and Ops. Mgmt. Jour., IEEE Trans.; contbr. articles to profl. jours., chpts. to books. Recipient Book award of excellence Soc. for Tech. Comm., 1992, Kenan Inst. Faculty Rsch. award, 1994, Outstanding Paper award for excellence Literati Club, London, 1995, Kenan-Flagler Bus. Sch. Disting. Rsch. award 1996, Best Paper award Acad. Mgmt., 1996; winner Decision Scis. Inst.'s Interdisciplinary Paper award, 1996, Best Theoretical/Empirical Rsch. Paper award 1985, Doctoral Dissertation award 1985; Anna Dice scholar Ohio State U., 1985; mem. grantee U.S. Quality Coun. II of the Conf. Bd., 1991—, Quality Mgmt. Ctr., 1992—; NIMH fellow, 1969-70, U. N.C. Cato Ctr. fellow, 1995, Kenan Inst. fellow, 1995-96, O'Herron Faculty scholar, 1996. Mem. Prodn. and Ops. Mgmt. Assn. (sec. 1988-91, bd. dirs. 1988-94, planning com. ann. conf. 1990-91, session chair ann. mtg. 1991), Decision Scis. Inst. (bd. dirs. 1996—), Phi Kappa Phi, Delta Omega. Office: U NC Kenan-Flagler Bus Sch Chapel Hill NC 27599-3490

ROTH, ALLAN ROBERT, lawyer, educator; b. Newark, June 7, 1931; s. Michael H. and Belle F. (Rosenberg) R.; m. Deborah R. Comerford, Feb. 29, 1976; children: Joseph (dec.), Alexander, Charles (dec.), Sarah. AB, Rutgers U., 1953; LLB, Harvard U., 1956. Bar: D.C. 1956, N.J. 1959, N.Y. 1965. Assoc. Toner, Crowley, Woelper & Vanderbilt, Newark, 1956-61; staff atty. for Gen. Counsel, SEC, Washington, 1962-64; dir. legal and govt. affairs dept. Am. Stock Exch., N.Y.C., 1964-68; prof. grad. sch. mgmt. Rutgers U., Newark, 1969—; dir. Internat. Bus. Inst., 1969-87; coord.

Rutgers U. programs in China, 1993-97, dir. internat. programs, 1997—; mem. legal adv. coun. Mid-Atlantic Legal Found., 1978-81; cons. IFC, 1972, Asian Devel. Bank, 1990, 91, 93, AID, 1965, 67, 71, 72, 94, World Bank, 1994; cons. to fgn. govts., 1965—; UN advisor to Pakistan, 1968-69; Fulbright profl. scholar to Thailand, 1988; mem. adv. bd. BNA Direct Investment in N.Am., 1988-95; mem. N.Am. Free Trade and Investment Report, 1995—; mem. book rev. panel Am. Jour. Internat. Law, 1978. Edtl. bd. Jour. Internat. Bus. Studies, 1975-85; contbg. editor: Corp. Law Review, 1977-86; contbr. chpts. to books, articles to profl. jours. With U.S. Army, 1956-58. Mem. ABA (staff dir. study of regulation of fgn. investment in U.S. 1975-79, 87—), Soviet-Am. Securities Law Working Group, Am. Soc. Internat. Law, Am. Law Inst., Phi Beta Kappa. Home: 630 Prospect St Maplewood NJ 07040-2724 Office: Rutgers U Grad Sch Mgmt 180 University Ave Newark NJ 07102-1803

ROTH, ALVIN ELIOT, economics educator; b. N.Y.C., Dec. 18, 1951; s. Ernest and Lillian (Caesar) R.; m. Emilie Matarasso, May 22, 1977; children: Aaron Leon, Benjamin Nathaniel. B.S., Columbia U., 1971; M.S., Stanford U., 1973, Ph.D., 1974. Asst. prof. dept. bus. adminstrn. and dept. econs. U. Ill., Urbana, 1974-77, assoc. prof., 1977-79, prof., 1979-82; A.W. Mellon prof. econs. U. Pitts., 1982—. Author: Axiomatic Models of Bargaining, 1979, Game-Theoretic Models of Bargaining, 1985, Laboratory Experimentation in Economics, 1987, The Shapley Value, 1988; (with M. Sotomayor) Two-Sided Matching: A Study in Game Theoretic Modeling and Analysis, 1990; (with J. Kagel) Handbook of Experimental Economics, 1995. Recipient Founders' prize Tex. Instruments Found., 1980; Guggenheim fellow, 1983; A.P. Sloan research fellow, 1984; 10 Outstanding Young Ams. award, 1984; Lanchester prize Ops. Rsch. Soc. Am., 1991. Fellow Econometric Soc.; mem. AAAS, Am. Econ. Assn., Inst. Mgmt. Scis. Jewish. Home: 2061 Beechwood Blvd Pittsburgh PA 15217-1705 Office: U Pitts Dept Econs Pittsburgh PA 15260

ROTH, BERNARD, mechanical engineering educator, researcher; b. N.Y.C., May 28, 1933; s. Morris Michael and Sara (Goldfarb) R.; m. Ruth Ochs, June 24, 1954; children: Steven Howard, Elliot Marc. BS, CCNY, 1956; MS, Columbia U., 1958, PhD, 1962. Engr. Ford Instrument Co., L.I., N.Y., 1955, Lockheed Aircraft Co., Van Nuys, Calif., 1956, Atlantic Design Co., Newark, 1958; lectr. CCNY, 1956-59; rsch. asst. Columbia U., N.Y.C., 1959-62; prof. Stanford (Calif.) U., 1962—; guest prof. U. Paris, 1988-90; expert, team leader UN Devel. Orgn., Vienna, Austria, 1986-88; mem. tech. adv. bd. Adept Tech., Inc., San Jose, Calif., 1983—; mem. adv. bd. Ctr. for Econ. Conversion, Mountain View, Calif., 1988—; bd. dirs. Peace Rev. Jour., Palo Alto., Calif., 1988-93. Co-author: Theoretical Kinematics, 1979, 2d edit., 1990; contbr. numerous articles on kinematics, robotics and design to profl. jours. Recipient Joseph F. Engelberger award Robotics Industries Assn., 1986. Fellow ASME (Melville medal 1967, Best Papers award mechanism conf. 1978, 80, 82, 92, 94, Mechanisms Coms. award 1982, Machine Design award 1984, chair design engring. divsn. 1981-82), Japanese Soc. for Promotion Sci.; mem. IEEE, Internat. Fedn. for Theory of Machines and Mechanisms (pres. 1980-83, hon. chmn. 7th World Congress 1987). Office: Stanford U Dept Mech Engring Stanford CA 94305

ROTH, CAROLYN LOUISE, art educator; b. Buffalo, June 17, 1944; d. Charles Mack and Elizabeth Mary (Hassel) R.; m. Charles Turner Barber, Aug. 4, 1991. Student, Art Student's League N.Y., 1965, Instituto Allende, San Miguel de Allende, Mex., 1966; BFA, Herron Sch. Art, 1967; MFA, Fla. State U., 1969. Asst. prof. art U. Tenn., Chattanooga, 1969-72; lectr. art So. Ill. U., Carbondale, 1973-75; asst. prof. art U. Evansville, Ind., 1975-80; lectr. art U. So. Ind., Evansville, 1984—; exhbn. coord., gallery dir. Krannert Gallery, U. Evansville, 1977-79; exhbn. coord., conf. advisor Ind. Women in Arts Conf., Ind. Arts Commn., Evansville, 1978. Solo exhbns. include Wabash Valley Coll., Mt. Carmel, Ill., 1994, So. Ind. Ctr. for Arts, Seymour, Ind., 1996, Zionsville (Ind.) Munce Art Ctr., 1997; exhibited in group shows Liberty Gallery, Louisville, 1992, Artlink Contemporary Art Gallery, Ft. Wayne, Ind., 1994, S.E. Mo. Coun. on Arts, Cape Girardeau, 1994, Lexington (Ky.) Art League, 1996, Mills Pond Horse Gallery, St. James, N.Y., 1996, SOHO Gallery, Pensacola, Fla., 1996, Indpls. Art Ctr., 1996, Artemesia Gallery, Chgo., 1997; works appeared in Contemporary Batik and Tie-Dye, 1973, Kalliope: A Journal of Women's Art, vol. XIV, no. 1, 1992, Jour. Am. Vet. Med. Assn., vol. 203, no. 3, 1993, others. Malone fellow visitor to Morocco and Tunisia, 1996. Mem. Nat. Mus. Women in Arts, Met. Mus. Art, Evansville Mus. Arts and Sci., New Harmony Gallery of Contemporary Art. Democrat. Mem. Unity Ch. Avocation: travel to study art works in museums and galleries in Europe and Mex. Home: 10801 S Woodside Dr Evansville IN 47712-8422 Office: U So Ind 8600 University Blvd Evansville IN 47712-3534

ROTH, DANIEL BENJAMIN, lawyer, business executive; b. Youngstown, Ohio, Sept. 17, 1929; s. Benjamin F. and Marion (Benjamin) R.; m. Joann M. Roth; children: William M., Jennifer A., Rochelle. BS in Fin., Miami U., Oxford, Ohio, 1951; JD, Case-Western Res. U., 1956. Bar: Ohio 1956, D.C. 1983. Pres. Roth, Stephens, Blair, Roberts & Co., Youngstown, 1969—; co-founder, vice chmn. Nat. Data Processing Corp., Cin., 1961-69, Torent, Inc., Youngstown, 1971—; vice chmn. Morrison Metalweld Process Corp., 1979—, McDonald Steel Corp., 1980—, Torent Oil & Gas Co., 1979—, Vaughn Indsl. Car & Equipment Co., 1988—, DTS Explosive Hardening Co., 1988—, Nat. Heat Exch. Cleaning Corp., 1996—; bd. dirs., exec. com. Mahoning Nat. Bank, Gasser Chair Co., Jarret Corp., Metal Products Corp. Profl. singer: appearances including Steve Allen Show, 1952. bd. dirs. Youngstown Symphony, Stambaugh Auditorium; bd. dirs. Youngstown Playhouse, v.p., 1991-93; pres. Rodef Sholom Temple, Youngstown, 1982-84. 1st lt. USAF, 1951-53, lt. col. Res., ret. Recipient Mgr. of Yr. award Mahoning Valley Mgmt. Assn., 1989, Man of Yr. award Youngstown YWCA, 1995. Mem. ABA, D.C. Bar Assn., Ohio Bar Assn., Mahoning County Bar Assn., Lawyer-Pilots Bar Assn., Nat. Assn. Corp. Dirs., Soc. Benchers of Case Western Res. U. Law Sch., Youngstown Club, Squaw Creek Country Club, Pelican Isle Yacht Club (Naples, Fla.), Zeta Beta Tau (nat. v.p. 1964-66), Omicron Delta Kappa, Phi Eta Sigma, Tau Epsilon Rho. Jewish. Home: 150 Talsman Dr Canfield OH 44406-1228 Office: Bank One Bldg Youngstown OH 44503-1514

ROTH, ERIC, screenwriter. screenplays include: The Nickel Ride, 1975, The Concorde - Airport '79, 1979, Suspect, 1987, Memories of Me, 1988 (with Billy Crystal), Mr. Jones, 1993, Forrest Gump, 1994 (Acad. award Best Adapted Screenplay). Office: care CAA 9830 Wilshire Blvd Beverly Hills CA 90212-1804*

ROTH, ERIC M., lawyer; b. Bklyn., Jan. 16, 1954. BA with distinction in all subjects, Cornell U., 1974; JD, NYU, 1977. Bar: N.Y. 1978; U.S. Dist. Ct. (so., ea. dists.) N.Y. 1978, D.C. 1980; U.S. Supreme Ct. 1981; U.S. Ct. Appeals (2nd. cir.) 1984, (4th, 5th cirs.) 1985, (8th cir.) 1989, (9th cir.) 1997. Law clk. to Hon. Lee P. Gagliardi U.S. Dist. Ct., 1977-79; mem. Wachtell, Lipton, Rosen & Katz, N.Y.C. Note and comment editor: NYU Law Review, 1976-77. Mem. ABA, N.Y. State Bar Assn., The D.C. Bar Assn., The D.C. Bar, Fed. Bar Coun., NYU Law Alumni Assn. Inc. (former mem. bd. dirs). Office: Wachtell Lipton Rosen & Katz 51 W 52nd St New York NY 10019-6119

ROTH, EUGENE, lawyer; b. Wilkes-Barre, Pa., June 28, 1935; s. Max and Rae (Klein) R.; m. Constance D. Smulyan, June 16, 1957; children: Joan Roth Kleinman, Steven P., Jeffrey H., Lawrence W. BS, Wilkes U., 1957; LLB, Dickinson Sch. of Law, 1960. Bar: Pa. 1960, U.S. Dist. Ct. (mid. dist.) Pa. 1961. Assoc. Rosenn, Jenkins & Greenwald, Walkes-Barre, 1960-64, ptnr., 1964—; mem. adv. bd. 1st Union Bank; bd. dirs. C-Tec Inc.; chmn. Greater Wilkes-Barre Partnership, Inc., 1991-93. Trustee Wilkes U., 1979—, chmn. 1993—; chmn. United Way of Wyoming Valley, 1983; bd. dir. Geisinger-Wyoming Valley Hosp. Recipient Disting. Pennsylvanian award Phila. C. of C., 1980; named Outstanding Vol. Fund Raiser Nat. Soc. Fund Raising Exec., 1993; Community Svc. award B'nai B'rith, 1994. Mem. ABA, Pa. Bar Assn., Luzerne County Law and Libr. Assn., Wilkes-Barre C. of C. (chmn. 1980, vice com. for econ. growth), Wyo. Valley United Jewish Campaign (chmn. 1978 and 1993), B'nai B'rith. Republican. Jewish. Avocations: reading, community svc. Office: Rosenn Jenkins & Greenwald 15 S Franklin St Wilkes Barre PA 18711-0076

ROTH, EVELYN AUSTIN, elementary school educator; b. Coronado, Calif., May 31, 1942; d. Robert Emmett and Marjorie Eastman (Rice) Austin; m. John King Roth, June 25, 1964; children: Andrew Lee, Sarah Austin. BA, San Diego State U., 1964; MA, U. of LaVerne, Calif., 1984; postgrad., U. Calif., Riverside, 1985. Cert. elem. tchr., Calif. Elem. tchr. Poway (Calif.) Unified Schs., 1964, Wallingford (Conn.) Unified Schs., 1964-66, Ontario (Calif.) Montclair Sch. Dist., 1982-88, Claremont (Calif.) Unified Schs., 1966-67, 83-93, Foothill Country Day Sch., Claremont, 1993—. Pres., bd. trustees Friends of Stone Libr., Claremont, 1993-94. Mem. AAUW, NEA, Calif. Tchrs. Assn., Internat. Reading Assn. (treas. Foothill Reading Coun. 1985-86), Delta Kappa Gamma (v.p. 1991-92). Republican. Presbyterian. Avocations: travel, reading, gardening.

ROTH, GEORGE STANLEY, research biochemist, physiologist; b. Honolulu, Aug. 5, 1946; s. George Frederick and Laura Ann (Zembrzuski) R.; m. Mary Jane Fletcher, Mar. 11, 1972; children: Susan Marie, George William. BS, Villanova U., 1968; PhD, Temple U., 1971. Postdoctoral fellow Fels Rsch. Inst., Phila., 1971-72; staff fellow Gerontology Rsch. Ctr. NIH, Balt., 1972-76, rsch. chemist, 1976—, chief molecular physiology and genetics sect., 1984—; vis. prof. Mehary Med. Coll., Nashville, 1983; Alpha Omega Alpha prof. U. P.R. Med. Sch., San Juan, 1986; chmn. Gordon Rsch. Conf. on Biology of Aging, Oxnard, Calif., 1985; rsch. cons. George Washington U., 1977-82; lectr. Med. Sci. Ctr. Student Sci. Program, 1980, Sandoz lectr. gerontology, Basel, Switzerland, 1984, 86, 94, also various other nat. and internat. meetings and workshops including Gordon confs., NATO workshops, internat. congresses, etc. Contbr. numerous articles and papers to profl. publs.; editor Exptl. Gerontology, Exptl. Aging Rsch., Proc. Soc. Exptl. Biology and Medicine; co-editor Chem. Rubber Co. Press Series in Aging, 1981—; assoc. editor The Ency. of Aging, 1987—. V.p. Community Coalition Harford County, Bel Air, Md., 1988-90, bd. dirs., 1990-92; co-dir. Ea. Harford County Civic Assn., Bel Air, 1981—. Recipient Ann. Rsch. award Am. Aging Assn., 1981, Sandoz prize for gerontol. rsch. Sandoz Ltd., Basel, 1989, Third Age award Internat. Assn. Gerontology, 1989, Spl. award Balt. Longitudinal Study on Aging, 1991; Sigma Chi scholar in residence Miami U., Oxford, Ohio, 1989, Equal Employment Opportunity award NIH, 1995, merit award, 1996. Fellow Gerontol. Soc. Am. (chair biol. scis. sect. 1975-76, chair rsch. com. 1978-79, chair fellowship com. 1986-87); mem. Soc. Exptl. Biology and Medicine. Republican. Roman Catholic. Avocations: basketball, fishing, hiking, canoeing. Office: Gerontology Rsch Ctr Molecular Physiology & Gen Hopkins Bayview Campus Baltimore MD 21224

ROTH, HADDEN WING, lawyer; b. Oakland, Calif., Feb. 10, 1930; s. Mark and Jane (Haley) R.; m. Alice Becker, Aug., 1987; 1 child, Elizabeth Wing. AA, Coll. Marin, 1949; BA, U. Calif., Berkeley, 1951; JD, U. Calif., San Francisco, 1957. Bar: Calif. 1958, U.S. Dist. Ct. (no. dist.) Calif. 1958, U.S. Ct. Appeals (9th cir.) 1958, U.S. Supreme Ct. 1966. Pvt. practice San Rafael, 1970—; judge Marin County Mcpl. Ct., 1966-70; spl. cons. Marin Muni Water Dist., Corte Madera, Calif., County of Marin; atty. Bolinas Pub. Utility Dist., Ross Valley Fire Svc., Town of Ross and San Anselmo, Calif.; hearing officer dist. hosps., 1981—; lectr. law Golden Gate Coll. Law, San Francisco, 1971-73. Chmn. Marin County prison task force, 1973; bd. dirs. Marin Gen. Hosp., 1964-66. Named Outstanding Citizen of Yr., Coll. Marin, 1972. Mem. ABA, Am. Trial Lawyers Assn., Calif. Bar Assn., Marin County Bar Assn., San Francisco Trial Lawyers Assn., Am. Assn. Ind. Investors, Assn. Bus. Trial Lawyers. Avocations: running, weights, reading. Home: 343 Fairhills Dr San Rafael CA 94901-1110 Office: 1050 Northgate Dr San Rafael CA 94903-2544

ROTH, HAROLD, architect; b. St. Louis, June 30, 1934; s. Samuel and Dorothy (Yawitz) R.; m. Dvora Feigon, Dec. 6, 1959; children: Elizabeth, David. AB, Washington U., 1956; MArch, Yale U., 1957. Designer Warner Burns Toan & Lunde, N.Y.C., 1957; sr. designer Eero Saarinen & Assocs., Roche Dinkeloo & Assocs., Hamden, Conn., 1959-65; ptnr. Harold Roth - Edward Saad, Hamden, Conn., 1965-72; sr. ptnr. Roth & Moore Architects, New Haven, 1973—; critic archtl. design Yale U. Sch. Architecture, New Haven, 1964—; pres., trustee Perspecta, Yale Archtl. Jour. Trustee Long Wharf Theatre, New Haven, 1972—, Conn. Trust for Hist. Preservation, 1983-90; pres. bd. trustees Conn. Architecture Found., 1990-93. Officer U.S. Army, 1957-59, Korea. Recipient Design award Nat. Coun. Religious Arch., 1970, 96, Design award New Haven Preservation Trust, 1978, 88, Tucker award Bldg. Stone Inst., 1983, 88, Honor award Concrete Reinforcing Steel Inst., 1983, Design award Portland Cement Assn., 1984, Design award Archtl. Record, 1970, 80, Design award AIA/ALA, 1983, Faculty Design award Assn. Collegiate Schs. of Arch., 1988, Healthcare Facilities Design award Boston Soc. Archs., 1992; fellow Pierson Coll., Yale U., 1978—. Fellow AIA (chmn. nat. com. on design 1990, bd. dirs. 1992-94, sec. Coll. of Fellows 1997—, mem. Conn. chpt., bd. dirs. Conn. chpt. 1982-85, Design award Conn. chpt. 1974, 78, 83, 86, 88, 90, 92, 93, Design award New Eng. chpt. 1968, 84, 92)); mem. Elihu Club, Yale Club N.Y. Home: 37 Autumn St New Haven CT 06511-2220 Office: Roth & Moore Architects 108 Audubon St New Haven CT 06510-1206

ROTH, HAROLD PHILMORE, physician; b. Cleve., Aug. 2, 1915; s. Abraham J. and Ida (Harris) R.; m. Kelly Cecile Rabinovitch, Dec. 9, 1952; children: Anita Alix, Edward Harris. B.A., Western Res. U., Cleve., 1936, M.D., 1939; M.S. in Hygiene, Harvard U., 1967. Diplomate Am. Bd. Internal Medicine, Am. Bd. Gastroenterology. Intern Cin. Gen. Hosp., 1939-40; house officer Boston City Hosp., 1940-42; asst. resident in medicine Barnes Hosp., St. Louis, 1942-43; clin. instr. Western Res. U., Cleve., 1949-52; sr. clin. instr. Western Res. U., 1953-55, asst. prof., 1955-63, assoc. prof., 1963—; assoc. prof. dept. community health Case Western Res. U., 1971-74; chief gastroenterology service VA Hosp., Cleve., 1947-74; dir. gastroenterology tng. program Univ. Hosps. and VA Hosp., 1963-74; assoc. physician Univ. Hosps. of Cleve., 1969-74; cons., asst. physician Highland View Hosp.; vis. physician in gastroenterology dept. medicine Cleve. Met. Gen. Hosp.; assoc. dir. for Digestive Diseases and Nutrition Nat. Inst. Arthritis, Diabetes, Digestive and Kidney Disease, NIH, Bethesda, Md., 1974-85, dir. div. Digestive Disease and Nutrition, 1983-85, epidemiology and data systems program dir., div. digestive diseases and nutrition, 1985-91, sr. gastroenterologist emeritus, 1991—; mem. Nat. Commn. on Digestive Diseases, Nat. Digestive Diseases Adv. Bd. Contbr. articles to med. jours. Served with AUS, 1943-46. USPHS spl. fellow, 1966-67; awards from Coalition of Digestive Disease Orgns., 1984, and Am. Gastroent. Assn., 1984. Mem. Am. Gastroenterol. Assn., Am. Assn. Study of Liver Disease, Central Soc. Clin. Rsch., ACP, Soc. Clin. Trials (pres. 1978-80), Phi Beta Kappa. Home: 10319 Gary Rd Potomac MD 20854-4102 Office: NIH 9000 Rockville Pike Rm 9a47 Bethesda MD 20814-1436 *Fifty years ago when I graduated from medical school, the practice of medicine was primarily an art. The physician had a limited number of useful diagnostic tests and procedures and an even more limited number of effective treatments. Since then new diagnostic tests and procedures have been developed that make diagnosis more precise, and new treatments such as the antibiotics still seem miraculous. I was fortunate to have an opportunity to become involved in some of these developments in medicine.*

ROTH, HARVEY PAUL, publisher; b. N.Y.C., Feb. 20, 1933; s. Lewis Theodore and Harriet (Wallow) R.; m. Tanya Cohen; children by previous marriage: Andrea Warriner, Matthew Jay; stepchildren: Laura Meryl Becker, Matthew Robert. A.B., Bklyn. Coll., 1954; LL.B., N.Y. U., 1957. Bar: N.Y. bar 1959. Editor West Pub. Co., N.Y.C., 1959-61; pres. BFL Communications, Inc., Plainview, N.Y., 1961-76, Roth Pub., Inc., Great Neck, N.Y., 1976—; chmn. Alcove Press, London, 1970-75, Nash Pub. Corp., Los Angeles, 1971-75. Served with U.S. Army, 1957-58. Office: Roth Pub Inc 175 Great Neck Rd Great Neck NY 11021-3313

ROTH, HERBERT, JR., corporate executive; b. South Bend, Ind., Oct. 7, 1928; s. Gilbert and Vita (Augustienovicz) Shoemaker; m. Dolores Maloney, June 5, 1951; children: Christine, Diane, Carla. B.S., U.S. Mil. Acad., 1951; M.S., Newark Coll. Engring., 1959. Sr. product planner EDP div. RCA, 1956-61; v.p. Nuclear Corp. Am., Phoenix, 1961-62, GCA Corp., Bedford, Mass., 1962-66; pres., chief exec. officer Anelex Corp., Boston, 1966-67; dir., chmn. exec. com. Mohawk Data Scis., Corp., Boston, 1967-68; pres., chief exec. officer, dir. LFE Corp., Clinton, Mass., 1968-85; dir. Boston Edison Co., Landauer Inc., Tech/OpsSevcon Inc., Phoenix Mut. Life Ins. Co., Mark IV Ind. and Phoenix Series Funds. Served with U.S. Army, 1951-55. Mem. Boston C. of C. (pres. 1980-81).

ROTH, JACK ALAN, thoracic surgeon; b. Jan. 29, 1945; s. Richard and Bernice (Saperstein) R.; m. Elizabeth Ann Grimm, Nov. 24, 1978; children: Johanna, Katherine. BA, Cornell U., 1967; MD, Johns Hopkins U., 1971. Diplomate Am. Bd. Surgery, Am. Bd. Thoracic Surgery. Surg. intern Johns Hopkins Hosp., Balt., 1971-72, resident in surgery, 1972-73; postgrad. rsch. fellow div. surg. oncology UCLA Ctr. for Health Scis., 1973-75; resident in gen. surgery UCLA Sch. Medicine, 1975-77, resident, chief resident in thoracic surgery, 1977-79, chief resident in gen. surgery, 1979-80; sr. investigator surgery br. div. cancer treatment Nat. Cancer Inst., NIH, Bethesda, Md., 1980-86, head thoracic oncology sect., 1982-86; prof. tumor biology U. Tex.-M.D. Anderson Cancer Ctr., Houston, 1986—, Bud S. Johnson prof. thoracic surgery, chmn. dept., 1986—; prof. dept. surgery U. Tex., Houston, 1986—; apptd. faculty grad. sch. biomed. scis. U. Tex. Health Sci. Ctr., Houston, 1987—; tng. Ctr. for Advanced Tng. in Cell and Molecular Biology, Washington, 1985; lectr. surgery Johns Hopkins U. Sch. Medicine, 1980-86; clin. asst. prof. Georgetown U. Sch. Medicine, Washington, 1982-86; cons. cardiothoracic surgery svc. Walter Reed Army Hosp., Washington, 1984-86; cons. rsch. microbiology dept. George Washington U. Grad. Sch. Arts and Scis., 1986. Editor: Thoracic Oncology, 1989, 95; contbr. more than 500 articles to publs. including Cancer Rsch., Jour. Clin. Oncology, Nature Medicine. Recipient Mead Johnson Excellence of Rsch. award Nat. Rsch. Forum, 1980, spl. achievement award HHS, 1981, Lucy Wortham James Basic Rsch. award, E.J. Tabah award, Moertal Lectureship award, Cosbie lectr.; grantee NIH, 1987—. Achievements include development of combined modality therapies for lung and esophageal cancer; research in identification of factors important in prognosis following surgical resection of pulmonary metastases, identification of molecular events in development of lung and esophageal cancers, gene therapy of cancer. Office: Anderson Cancer Ctr 1515 Holcombe Blvd Houston TX 77030-4009

ROTH, JACK JOSEPH, historian, educator; b. Dec. 17, 1920; s. Max and Dinah (Kraus) R.; m. Sheilagh Goldstone. B.A., U. Chgo., 1942, Ph.D., 1955; postgrad., Inst. d'Études Politiques, Paris, 1949-50. Mem. faculty Roosevelt U., 1951-68, prof. history, chmn. dept., 1960-68; prof. history Case Western Res. U., Cleve., 1968—; chmn. dept. Case Western Res. U., 1968-73; vis. asso. prof. history U. Chgo., 1962, professorial lectr. history, 1968; vis. prof. history U. Wis., 1964-65. Project dir.: The Persistence of Surrealism, Nat. Endowment for Humanities, festival, 1979, film, 1982; Translator: (Georges Sorel): Reflections on Violence, 1951, Sorel und die Totalitären Systeme, 1958, Revolution and Morale in Modern French Thought: Sorel and the Sorelians, 1963, The First World War: A Turning Point in Modern History, 1967, The Roots of Italian Fascism, 1967, Georges Sorel: on Lenin and Mussolini, 1977, The Revolution of the Mind: The Politics of Surrealism Reconsidered, 1977, The Cult of Violence: Sorel and the Sorelians, 1980; Contbr. articles to profl. jours., chpts. to books. Served with AUS, 1942-46. Recipient Penrose Fund award Am. Philos. Soc., 1964. Home: 24301 Bryden Rd Beachwood OH 44122-4038 Office: Dept History Case Western Res U Cleveland OH 44106

ROTH, JAMES FRANK, manufacturing company executive, chemist; b. Rahway, N.J., Dec. 7, 1925; s. Louis and Eleanor R.; m. Sharon E. Mattes, June 20, 1969; children by previous marriage: Lawrence, Edward, Sandra. B.A. in Chemistry, U. W.Va., 1947; Ph.D. in Phys. Chemistry, U. Md., 1951. Research chemist Franklin Inst., Phila., 1951-53, mgr. chemistry lab., 1958-60; chief chemist Lehigh Paints & Chems. Co., Allentown, Pa., 1953-55; research chemist GAF Corp., Easton, Pa., 1955-58; with Monsanto Co., St. Louis, 1960-80, dir. catalysis research, 1973-77, dir. process sci. research, 1977-80; corp. chief scientist Air Products and Chems., Inc., Allentown, 1980-91; indsl. cons., 1991—. Contbr. articles to profl. jours.; mem. editl. bd. Jour. Catalysis, 1976-85, Catalysis Revs., 1973-93, Applied Catalysis, 1981-85; editor for Ams., 1985-88, assoc. editor, 1988-95. With USN, 1943-46. Recipient Richard J. Kokes award Johns Hopkins U., 1977, Chem. Pioneer award Am. Inst. Chemists, 1986, Perkin medal Soc. Chem. Industry, 1988. Mem. NAE, Am. Chem. Soc. (St. Louis sect. St. Louis award 1975, E.V. Murphree nat. award 1976, Indsl. Chemistry award 1991), Catalysis Soc. N.Am. (E.J. Houdry award 1991), Catalysis Club of Phila. (award 1981). Inventor process biodegradable detergents, for acetic acid; U.S., fgn. patents in field. Home: 5440 Eagles Point Cir #205 Sarasota FL 34231-9144

ROTH, JANE RICHARDS, federal judge; b. Philadelphia, Pa., June 16, 1935; d. Robert Henry Jr. and Harriett (Kellond) Richards; m. William V. Roth Jr., Oct. 9, 1965; children: William V. III, Katharine K. BA, Smith Coll., 1956; LLB, Harvard U., 1965; LLD (hon.), Widener U., 1986, U. Del., 1994. Bar: Del. 1965, U.S. Dist. Ct. Del. 1966, U.S. Ct. Appeals (3d cir.) 1974. Adminstrv. asst. various fgn. service posts U.S. State Dept., 1956-62; assoc. Richards, Layton & Finger, Wilmington, Del., 1965-73, ptnr., 1973-85; judge U.S. Dist. Ct. Del., Wilmington, 1985-91, U.S. Ct. Appeals (3d cir.), Wilmington, 1991—; adj. faculty Villanova U. Sch. Law. Hon. chmn. Del. chpt. Arthritis Found., Wilmington; bd. overseers Widener U. Sch. Law; bd. consultors Villanova U. Sch. Law; trustee Hist. Soc. Del. Recipient Nat. Vol. Service citiation Athritis Found., 1982. Fellow Am. Bar Found.; mem. ABA, Fed. Judges Assn., Del. State Bar Assn. Republican. Episcopalian. Office: US Ct House J Caleb Boggs Fed Bldg 844 N King St Rm 5100 Wilmington DE 19801-3519*

ROTH, JOE, motion picture company executive; b. 1948. Prodn. assistant various commls. and feature films, San Francisco; also lighting dir. Pitchel Players, San Francisco; then producer Pitchel Players, L.A.; co-founder Morgan Creek Prodns., L.A., 1987-89; chmn. 20th Century Fox Film Corp., L.A., 1989-92; founder Caravan Pictures, L.A., 1992-94; chmn. Walt Disney Motion Pictures Group, Burbank, 1994—, Walt Disney Studios, Burbank. Prodr. numerous films including Tunnelvision, Cracking Up, Americathon, Our Winning Season, The Final Terror, The Stone Boy, Where the River Runs Black, Bachelor Party, Off Beat, Streets of Gold (dir. debut), Revenge of the Nerds II (also dir.); exec. prodr. Young Guns, Dead Ringers, Skin Deep, Major League, Renegades, Coupe de Ville (also dir.), Enemies: A Love Story: Caravan Pictures releases include Walt Disney's The Three Musketeers, Angie, Angels in the Outfield, I Love Trouble, A Low Down Dirty Shame, Houseguest, The Jerky Boys, Heavyweights, Tall Tale, While You Were Sleeping. Office: Walt Disney Studio 500 S Buena Vista St Burbank CA 91521-0001*

ROTH, JOHN KING, philosopher, educator; b. Grand Haven, Mich., Sept. 3, 1940; s. Josiah V. and Doris Irene (King) R.; m. Evelyn Lillian Austin, June 25, 1964; children: Andrew Lee, Sarah Austin. BA, Pomona Coll., 1962; student, Yale U. Div. Sch., 1962-63; MA, Yale U., 1965, PhD, 1966; LHD, Ind. U., 1990. Asst. prof. philosophy Claremont McKenna Coll., Calif., 1966-71, assoc. prof., 1971-76, Russell K. Pitzer prof. philosophy, 1976—; vis. prof. philosophy Franklin Coll., Lugano, Switzerland, 1973; Fulbright lectr. Am. studies U. Innsbruck, Austria, 1973-74; vis. prof. philosophy Doshisha U., Kyoto, Japan, 1981-82; vis. prof. Holocaust studies U. Haifa, Israel, 1982; Fulbright lectr. in Am. studies Royal Norwegian Ministry of Edn., Oslo, Norway, 1995-96. Author: Freedom and the Moral Life, 1969, Problems of the Philosophy of Religion, 1971, American Dreams, 1976, A Consuming Fire, 1979, (with Richard L. Rubenstein) Approaches to Auschwitz, 1987, (with Frederick Sontag) The American Religious Experience, 1972, (with Frederick Sontag) The Questions of Philosophy, 1988, (with Robert H. Fossum) The American Dream, 1981, (with Fossum) American Ground, 1988, (with Rubenstein) The Politics of Latin American Liberation Theology, 1988, (with Michael Berenbaum) Holocaust: Religious and Philosophical Implications, 1989, Ethics, 1991, (with Carol Rittner) Memory Offended, 1991, (with Creighton Peden) Rights, Justice, and Community, 1992, (with Carol Rittner) Different Voices, 1993, American Diversity, American Identity, 1995, Inspiring Teaching, 1997, (with Carol Rittner) From the Unthinkable to the Unavoidable, 1997. Spl. advisor U.S. Holocaust Meml. Coun., Washington, 1980-85, mem., 1995—. Danforth grad. fellow, 1962-66; Graves fellow, 1970-71; NEH fellow, 1976-77; Faculty Pairing grantee Japan-U.S. Friendship Commn., 1981-83; named U.S. Prof. of Yr. Coun. Advancement and Support of Edn. and Carnegie Found. Advancement of Tchg., 1988. Mem Am. Philos. Assn., Am. Acad. Religion, Am. Studies Assn., Calif. Coun. for Humanities, Phi Beta Kappa.

Presbyterian. Home: 1648 N Kenyon Pl Claremont CA 91711-2905 Office: Claremont McKenna Coll 850 Columbia Ave Claremont CA 91711-3901

ROTH, J(OHN) REECE, electrical engineer, educator, researcher-inventor; b. Washington, Pa., Sept. 19, 1937; s. John Meyer and Ruth Evangeline (Iams) R.; m. Helen Marie DeCrane, Jan. 14, 1972; children: Nancy Ann, John Alexander. S.B. in Physics, MIT, 1959; Ph.D., Cornell U., 1963. Engring. aide Aerojet-Gen. Corp., Azusa, Calif., 1957, 58; aerospace engr. N.Am. Aviation, Canoga Park, Calif., 1959; prin. investigator NASA Lewis Research Ctr., Cleve., 1963-78; prof. elec. engring. U. Tenn., Knoxville, 1978—; hon. prof. U. Electronic Sci. and Tech. of China, Chengdu, 1992—; prin. investigator Office Naval Rsch., Washington, 1980-89, Air Force Office Sci. Rsch., Washington, 1981-95, Army Rsch. Office, 1988-93, NASA Langley Rsch. Ctr., Hampton, Va., 1995—, March Instruments, Inc., Concord, Calif., 1996—; cons. TVA, Chattanooga, 1982-84, BDM Corp., 1987-88, Tenn. Eastman, 1989-90, March Instruments, 1995—; speaker at profl. meetings; mem. NAS-NRC Com. on Aneutronic Fusion, 1986-87. Author: Industrial Plasma Engineering, Introduction to Fusion Energy; contbr. articles to profl. jours. Sloan scholar, 1955-59; Ford fellow, 1961-62. Fellow IEEE, AIAA (assoc.); mem. Am. Phys. Soc., Am. Nuclear Soc. (exec. com. No. Ohio sect. 1975-78), Nuclear and Plasma Scis. Soc., Am. Soc. Engring. Edn., Knoxville Art Gallery, East Tenn. Soc. of Archaeol. Inst. Am., Sigma Xi (pres. U. Tenn. Knoxville chpt. 1985-86). Club: U. Tenn. Faculty (Knoxville). Home: 12359 N Fox Den Dr Farragut TN 37922-3755 Office: U Tenn Dept Elec Engring 409 Ferris Hall Knoxville TN 37996-2100

ROTH, JUDITH SHULMAN, lawyer; b. N.Y.C., Apr. 25, 1952; d. Mark Alan and Margaret Ann (Podell) Shulman; m. William Hartley Roth, May 30, 1976; children: Andrew Henry, Caroline Shulman. AB, Cornell U., 1974; JD, Columbia U., 1977. Bar: N.Y. 1978, U.S. Dist. Ct. (ea. dist.) N.Y. 1978, U.S. Dist. Ct. (so. dist.) N.Y. 1978, U.S. Ct. Appeals (2d cir.) 1993. Assoc. Phillips Nizer Benjamin Krim & Ballon, N.Y.C., 1978-87, ptnr., 1988—; lectr. CLE Fordham Law Sch., N.Y.C., 1990. Mem. Cosmopolitan Club. Jewish. Avocations: reading, tennis, golf, art, gardening. Office: Phillips Nizer Benjamin Krim & Ballon 666 5th Ave New York NY 10103-0001

ROTH, KATHRYN GAIE, government executive; b. Torrejon, Spain, Mar. 19, 1964; came to U.S., 1964; d. Edwin Isaac and Deborah (Weissman) R.; m. Greg Douquet. BA, Bryn Mawr Coll., 1987; MPA, Princeton U., 1991. Founder, editor-in-chief Jour. for Pub. and Internat. Affairs, Princeton, N.J., 1989-91; asst. sec. to bd., dir. spl. projects Nathan Cummings Found., N.Y.C., 1991-92; assoc. dir. presdl. advance White House, Washington, 1993-95; v.p. Revlon Found. MacAndrews & Forbes Holding, Inc., N.Y.C., 1995-96; exec. dir. planning and integration U.S. Dept. Def. Indsl. Affairs and Installations, 1996—; polit. cons. Mondale Campaign, Dukakis Campaign, Simon Campaign, Clinton for Pres. Campaign and Transition. Contbg. author: Public Opinion in U.S. Foreign Policy: The Controversy Over Contra Aid, 1994; contbr. articles to profl. publs. Mem. Dem. Bus. Coun. Women's Leadership Forum; bd. dirs. N.Y. Dem. Leadership Coun. Recipient Conf. Paper award Assn. Profl. Schs. of Internat. Affairs, 1991; Woodrow Wilson fellow, 1989-91. Mem. Women in Philanthropy, Coun. Fgn. Rels. (term member), Dem. Bus. Coun. N.Y., Dem. Leadership Coun. Democrat. Jewish. Avocations: travel, art, scuba diving, flying. Home: 1657 31st St NW #205 Washington DC 20007 Office: DUSD IA&I/A&T 3300 Defense Pentagon Rm 3e1074 Washington DC 20301-3300

ROTH, LAURA MAURER, physics educator, researcher; b. Flushing, N.Y., Oct. 11, 1930; d. Keith Langden and Ruth (Oliphint) Maurer; m. Willard Dale Roth, June 6. 1952; children: Andrew Eric, Karen Elsa. AB, Swarthmore Coll., 1952; AM, Radcliffe Coll., 1953, PhD, 1957. Staff physicist Lincoln Lab., MIT, Lexington, Mass., 1956-63; lectr. Harvard U., Cambridge, Mass., summer 1959; assoc. prof., prof. physics Tufts U., Medford, Mass., 1963-67; physicist GE R & D Ctr., Schenectady, N.Y., 1967-72; lectr. Inst. for Theoretical Physics, U. Colo., Boulder, Colo., summer 1969; Abbey Rockefeller Mauze vis. prof. physics MIT, Cambridge, Mass., 1972-73; rsch. prof. SUNY, Albany, 1973-77, prof. physics, 1977-95, prof. emerita, 1995—; cons. Lincoln Lab., MIT, 1963. Co-author: Women in Physics, 1975; co-editor: Fundamental Questions in Quantum Mechanics, 1984, The Instructions of Gampupa, 1996; editor: Dharma Paths, 1993; contbr. 80 articles to physics jours., 1956—. Dir. Karma Thegsum Choling Buddhist Ctr., Albany, N.Y., 1979—; program dir. for publs. Karma Kagyu Inst., Woodstock, N.Y., 1988—. Recipient medal Radcliffe Grad. Soc., 1962; grantee Sloan Found., Tufts U., 1963-65, NSF, SUNY, Albany, 1976-81. Democrat. Buddhist. Home: 1270 Ruffner Rd Niskayuna NY 12309-4601 Office: SUNY Albany Dept Physics 1400 Washington Ave Albany NY 12222-0100

ROTH, LAWRENCE MAX, pathologist, educator; b. McAlester, Okla., June 25, 1936; s. Herman Moe and Blanche (Brown) R.; m. Anna Berit Katarina Sundstrom, Apr. 3, 1965; children—Karen Esther, David Josef. B.A., Vanderbilt U., 1957; M.D., Harvard U., 1960. Diplomate Am. Bd. Pathology. Rotating intern U. Ill. Research and Ednl. Hosps., Chgo., 1960-61; resident in anat. pathology Washington U. Sch. Medicine, St. Louis, 1961-64; resident in clin. pathology U. Calif. Med. Ctr., San Francisco, 1967-68; asst. prof. pathology Tulane U. Sch. Medicine, New Orleans, 1968-71; assoc. prof. pathology Ind. U. Sch. Medicine, Indpls., 1971-75, prof., 1975—, dir. div. surg. pathology. Series editor: Contemporary Issues in Surgical Pathology; mem. editl. bd. Am. Jour. Surg. Pathology, Human Pathology, Seminars in Diagnostic Pathology, Internat. Jour. Gynecol. Pathology, Endocrine Pathology; contbr. articles to med. jours. Served to capt. U.S. Army, 1965-67. Mem. Am. Assn. Investigative Pathologists, U.S. and Can. Acad. Pathology, Am. Soc. Clin. Pathologists, Internat. Soc. Gynecol. Pathologists, Arthur Purdy Stout Soc. Surg. Pathologists, Assn. Dirs. Anatomic and Surg. Pathology. Home: 7898 Ridge Rd Indianapolis IN 46240-2538 Office: 550 University Blvd Indianapolis IN 46202-5149

ROTH, LEE B(RITTON), lawyer; b. Perth Amboy, N.J., May 8, 1937; s. Alton James and Katherine (Crouse) R.; m. Nancy Hanawalt, Aug. 20, 1960; children: Barbara, Jon. BA, Oberlin Coll., 1959; JD, Cornell U., 1962. Bar: N.J. 1962, U.S. Dist. Ct. N.J. 1963. Assoc. Wharton, Stewart, Davis, Somerville, N.J., 1962-65; pvt. practice Flemington, N.J., 1965; sr. ptnr. Roth & Beeman and predecessor firm, Flemington, 1978—; of counsel Lee B. Roth Law Offices; mem. adv. coun. Summit Bank; lectr. in field. Author: Negotiating Residential Real Estate Contract, Resolving Disputes in Real Transactions; contbr. articles to profl. jours., chpts. to books. Fund drive chmn. Hunterdon Dr. Am. Cancer Soc., Flemington, past bd. dirs., N.J., past bd. mgrs., Hunterdon County, past spl. gifts chmn., past legacy chmn.; past pres. Raritan Twp. Rep. Club; eagle scout Boy Scouts Am.; past bd. dirs., past fin. chmn. Girl Scouts USA; founder, past bd. dirs., past H.S. lacrosse coach Hunterdon County Lacrosse Assn.; past mem. Branchburg Bd. Edn.; past chmn. Branchburg Recreation Commn. Mem. ABA (past chmn. com econ., tech. and practice methods), N.J. Assn. Real Estate Attys. (chmn. bd. dirs.), N.J. State Bar Assn. (trustee, past chmn. real property probate trust sect., mem. banking law sect., mem. family law sect., founder, bd. dirs. N.J. Lawyer newspaper, past chmn. com. specialization, past chmn. com. law office econs.), Hunterdon County Bar Assn. (pres. 1979-80), N.J. State Bar Assn. (trustee), Hunterdon County Bd. Realtors. Avocations: photography, LaCrosse, tennis, basketball, music. Home: 10 Birch St Flemington NJ 08822-4525 Office: Lee B Roth Law Offices 8 Main St Flemington NJ 08822-1468

ROTH, LOREN H., psychiatrist; b. May 9, 1939; m. Ellen A. Roth; children: Jonathan, Alexandra, Elizabeth. BA in Philosophy, Cornell U., 1961; MD cum laude, Harvard U., 1966, MPH, 1972; postgrad., Am. U., 1972-73. Diplomate Am. Bd. Psychiatry and Neurology; lic. physician, Conn., Md., Mass., Pa. Med. intern Univ. Hosps., Western Res. U., Cleve., 1966-67; resident psychiatry Yale U., New Haven, 1969-70, Mass. Gen. Hosp., Boston, 1970-72; staff psychiatrist Ctr. for Studies Crime and Delinquency, NIMH, Rockville, Md., 1972-74; co-dir., dir. law and psychiatry program Western Psychiat. Inst. and Clinic/U. Pitts., 1974—, chief adult clin. svcs., 1983-87, 88-89, chief clin. svcs., 1989-95, co-dir., dir. law and psychiatry program, 1974-94; vice-chmn. dept. psychiatry U. Pitts., 1988—, asst. prof., 1974-78, assoc. prof., 1978-82, prof., 1982—; v.p. for Managed Care U. Pitt. Med. Ctr., 1993—; assoc. vice chancellor for edn., health scis. U. Pitts. Sch. Medicine, 1995—; med. staff Presbyn.-Univ. Hosp., Pitts., 1983—; gen. med. officer Fed. Penitentiary, Lewisburg, Pa., 1967-69; William E. Schumacher disting. lectr. Maine Dept. Mental Health and Mental Retardation, Portland, 1982; mem. commn. on mentally disabled ABA, Washington, 1987; cons. law and psychiatry Dept. Welfare, Commonwealth Pa., 1974; cons. reviewer, site visitor crime and delinquency sect. NIMH, 1977; examiner Am. Bd. Psychiatry and Neurology, 1985. Author: (with others) Informed Consent: A Study of Decisionmaking in Psychiatry, 1984; editor: (with others) Psychiatry, Social, Epidemiologic and Legal Psychiatry, Vol. 5, 1986; contbr. articles to profl. jours., chpts. to books; editorial bd. Criminology, 1974-78, Law and Human Behavior, 1980-85, Internat. Jour. Law and Psychiatry, 1980-88, Behavioral Scis. and the Law, 1987-95; assoc. editor Am. Jour. Psychiatry, 1982-90; cons. editor Criminal Justice and Behavior, 1982-85. Lt. comrd. USPHS Res., 1967—. Recipient Steve Allen award United Mental Health, Inc., 1990; grantee NIMH, 1979, 80-81, 89, Founds. Fund for Rsch. in Psychiatry, 1980-82. Fellow Am. Psychiat. Assn. (Isaac Ray award 1988), Am. Coll. Utilization Rev. Physicians, Am. Coll. Psychiatrists; mem. AMA, Am. Acad. Psychiatry and Law (pres. 1983-84), Group for Advancement Psychiatry (com. on psychiatry and law 1979-80, chmn. 1981-84), Am. Soc. Criminology, Am. Soc. Law and Medicine (bd. dirs. 1982-85), Internat. Acad. Law and Mental Health (bd. dirs.), Am. Psychopath. Assn., Phi Beta Kappa, Phi Kappa Phi. Home: 6820 Edgerton Ave Pittsburgh PA 15208-2803 Office: Western Psychiat Inst 3811 Ohara St Pittsburgh PA 15213-2593

ROTH, MARJORY JOAN JARBOE, special education educator; b. Ranger, Tex., May 24, 1934; d. James Aloysius and Dorothy Knight (Taggart) Jarboe; m. Thomas Mosser Roth, Jr., Dec. 22, 1959; children: Thomas Mosser III, James Jarboe. BA in English, Rice U., 1957; MEd in Ednl. Adminstrn., U. N.C., Greensboro, 1981. Cert. tchr.-specific learning disabilities, middle grades lang. arts and social studies, intermediate grades, adminstr.-prin., N.C. Tchr. 4th grade Houston Ind. Sch. Dist., 1957-60; specific lang. disabilities instr. Forsyth Tech. C.C., Winston-Salem, N.C., 1976-77; specific learning disabilities tchr. Forsyth Country Day Sch., Winston-Salem, 1977-80; tchr. 5th grade Winston-Salem/Forsyth County Schs., 1982-83, specific learning disabilities tchr. Mt. Tabor High Sch., 1983-86; part time instr. English and Learning Disabilities Forsyth Tech. C.C., 1986-90; founding pres., prin. Greenhills Sch., Winston-Salem, 1990—. Co-author, co-editor booklets. Sunday Sch. dir., tchr. Galloway Meml. Episcopal Ch., 1960-70, pres., treas., sec. Churchwomen, 1963-74; treas. Elkin Jr. Woman's Club, 1962; chmn. Elkin Heart Fund Drive, 1968; bd. dirs. Hugh Chatham Hosp. Auxillary, 1968, Friends of the Elkin Pub. Libr., 1968-74, chmn., 1970-72, chmn., exhibits chmn. summer reading program; pres. South Surry Heart Assn., 1969; mem. Churchwomen of St. Paul's Episcopal Ch., Winston-Salem, 1982—, Fiddle and Bow Folk Music Soc., Winston-Salem, 1992—. Recipient June Lyday Orton award for outstanding svc. in the field of dyslexia, 1997; Forsyth fellow NEH, 1985; grantee in field. Mem. ASCD, Children with Attention Deficit Disorder (profl. adv. bd. N.C. Triad chpt. 1990—), Learning Disability Assn. N.C. (sec., bd. dirs. 1981-86), Orton Dyslexia Soc. (sec., bd. dirs. Carolinas br. 1981-85, founding pres. N.C. br. 1987-91, bd. dirs. 1987-96, nat. nominating com. 1992-94). Republican. Avocations: tennis, hiking, folk music. Home: 940 Fox Hall Dr Winston Salem NC 27106-4431 Office: Greenhills Sch 1360 Lyndale Dr Winston Salem NC 27106-9739

ROTH, MICHAEL, lawyer; b. N.Y.C., July 22, 1931; s. Philip Arthur and Mollie (Breitenbach) R.; m. Jeanny Macoir, Nov. 24, 1957; 3 children. B.A., Yale Coll., 1953; J.D., Columbia U., 1956, M. Internat. Affairs, 1964. Bar: N.Y. 1956. Law assoc. Stroock & Stroock & Lavan, N.Y.C., 1956-63; ptnr. Roth, Carlson, Kwit & Spengler, N.Y.C., 1964-74; chmn. N.Y. State Liquor Authority, N.Y.C., 1974-77; ptnr. Shea & Gould, N.Y.C., 1979-89; of counsel Rosenman & Colin, N.Y.C., 1989—. Mem. U.S. del. to UN Population Commn., 1969; Rep.-Conservative candidate for N.Y. State atty. gen., 1978; mem. Pres.' Task Force on Internat. Pvt. Enterprise, 1983-84, Pres.' Commn. on Mgmt. AID Programs, 1991-92. Mem. ABA, N.Y. State Bar Assn., Assn. Bar City N.Y., Sunningdale Country Club (Scarsdale, N.Y.). Republican.

ROTH, OLIVER RALPH, radiologist; b. Cumberland, Md., Nov. 30, 1921; s. DeCoursey Andrew and Mabel (Lathrum) R.; BS, Frostburg (Md.) State Coll., 1942, DSc (hon.), 1980; MD, U. Md., 1950; m. Virginia McBride, June 2, 1943; 1 child, Tiija. Diplomate Am. Bd. Radiology. Resident, Johns Hopkins Hosp., Balt., 1954-57; cancer research fellow Middlesex Hosp., London, 1957-58; founder dept. radiation oncology Presbyn. Hosp., Charlotte, N.C., 1958-62; attending radiologist King's Daus. Hosp., Ashland, Ky., 1962-80; radiologist Our Lady of Bellefonte Hosp., 1981-86; mem. faculty Sch. of Allied Health Shawnee State U., Portsmouth, Ohio, 1986-90; prof. radiology Sch. Medicine Marshall U., Huntington, W.Va., 1990—; mem. adv. com. Ky. Cancer Commn., 1978; bd. dirs. Boyd County chpt. Am. Cancer Soc., 1978. With USN, 1942-45. Commanded to Buckingham Palace, June 17, 1958; recipient Disting. Alumni award Frostburg State U., 1979. Mem. AMA, Am. Coll. Radiology, Radiol. Soc. N.Am., Am. Radium Soc., Royal Faculty Radiology, Brit. Inst. Radiology. Democrat. Lutheran. Club: Shriners (Cumberland, Md.). Book reviewer Radiology, 1954-55. Home: 2912 Cogan St Ashland KY 41102-5230

ROTH, PAMELA JEANNE, strategic marketing professional, web site developer and publisher; b. Huntington, N.Y., Sept. 9, 1955; d. Julius Leo and Constance Abby (Gettenberg) R. BA with honors, New Coll. Hofstra U., 1975; MS, Rensselaer Inst. Tech., 1977; JD, New England Sch. Law, 1983; postgrad., Sandler Sales Inst., 1996. Assoc. editor Functional Photography, Hempstead, N.Y., 1976; documentation specialist Allendale Ins., Johnston, R.I., 1977-78; systems analyst Comml. Union Ins., Boston, 1978-79; sr. software writer NEC Info. Systems, Lexington, Mass., 1979-82; pres. TEKDOC Tech. Communications, North Andover, Mass., 1978-86; sr. tech. writer Software Internat., Andover, Mass., 1983; pres., CEO SPIRAL Communications, Inc., SPIRAL Group, SPIRAL Books, Manchester, N.H., 1986—; developer Ofcl. Olympic Torch Relay event web site, Nashua, N.H., 1996; presenter in field. Author: The First Book of Adam, 1984, The Second Book of Adam, 1984, Using the PFS Family, 1985; editor: Data Warehousing and Decision Support-The State of the Art, 1995, Data Warehousing and Decision Support, vol. 2, 1997; contbr. articles to profl. jours. Gen. mgr. ImprovBoston, 1986. Mem. Women Owners Network (pres.). Avocations: sporting clays, travel, bicycling, dog training. Office: PO Box 5488 Manchester NH 03108-5488

ROTH, PAMELA SUSAN, lawyer; b. N.Y.C., Nov. 23, 1961; d. Edward Abraham and Susan Violet (Castro) R. BS in Biology, Adelphi U., 1982, MBA, 1986; JD, Pace U., 1990. Bar: N.Y. 1991, U.S. Dist. Ct. (ea. and so. dists.) N.Y. 1991, U.S. Ct. Appeals (10th cir.) 1993, Colo. 1995, U.S. Dist. Ct. Colo. 1995, U.S. Supreme Ct. 1995. Asst. gen. counsel N.Y.C. Dept. Probation, Bklyn., 1990-91; asst. dist. atty. Kings County Dist. Atty., Bklyn., 1992-93; assoc. Law Firm of Portales & Assocs., Denver, 1993-95; pvt. practice N.Y.C., 1995—; gen. counsel Hispano Crypto-Jewish Rsch. Ctr., Denver, 1994—. Mem. ABA, Am. Soc. Internat. Law, Hispanic Nat. Bar Assn., Bklyn. Bar Assn., Internat. Assn. Jewish Lawyers and Jurists, Kings County Criminal Bar Assn. Avocations: aerobics, skiing, roller blading, gourmet cooking. Office: 26 Court St Ste 2003 Brooklyn NY 11242-0103

ROTH, PAUL NORMAN, lawyer; b. N.Y.C., May 4, 1939; s. Sol and Florence (Glassman) R.; m. Ellen Joan Lipp, May 24, 1964; children: Stefanie H., Jessica A. AB, Harvard U., 1961, LLB, 1964. Bar: N.Y. 1966, U.S. Ct. Appeals (2d cir.) 1966, U.S. Dist. Ct. (so. and ea. dists.) N.Y. 1967, U.S. Supreme Ct. 1975. Assoc. Cleary, Gottlieb, Steen & Hamilton, N.Y.C., 1965-69; ptnr. Schulte Roth & Zabel, N.Y.C., 1969--. Trustee Ctrl. Synagogue, N.Y.C., 1987-95. Fulbright fellow, Netherlands, 1965. Mem. ABA, N.Y. State Bar Assn., Assn. of Bar of City of N.Y. (com. on securities regulation 1982-85, chmn. 1989-92), Harvard Law Sch. Assn. N.Y. (trustee 1987-90, v.p. 1992-93), Century Country Club. Office: Schulte Roth & Zabel 900 3rd Ave New York NY 10022-4728

ROTH, PETER, broadcast executive; b. Larchmont, N.Y.; m. Andrea Roth; 2 children. Student, U. Pa.; grad., Tufts U., 1972. From mgr. to dir. children's programs ABC TV Network, 1976, dir. current programs, 1979, v.p. current prime-time series, 1981; past pres. Stephen J. Cannell Prodns.; pres. prodn. Twentieth Network TV, 1992, pres., 1993; pres. 20th Century Fox TV, 1994, Fox Entertainment Group, N.Y.C., 1996—. Office: Fox Broadcasting Co 3d Fl 1211 Avenue of the Americas New York NY 10036-8795*

ROTH, PHILLIP JOSEPH, retired judge; b. Portland, Oreg., Feb. 29, 1920; s. Harry William and Minnie Alice (Segel) R.; m. Ida Lorraine Thomas, Feb. 22, 1957 (div. 1977); children: Phillip Joseph, David William; m. Allison Blake Ramsey, Feb. 14, 1978 (div. 1994). BA cum laude, U. Portland, 1943; JD, Lewis and Clark Coll., 1948. Bar: Oreg. 1948, U.S. Dist. Ct. Oreg. 1949, U.S. Ct. Appeals (9th cir.) 1959, U.S. Supreme Ct. 1962. Dep. atty. City of Portland, 1948-50; dep. dist. atty. Multnomah County, Portland, 1950-52; sole practice Portland, 1952-64; cir. judge Multnomah County State of Oreg., Portland, 1964-94, presiding cir. judge, 1970-71, 76-78; adj. prof. Lewis & Clark U. Law Sch., Portland, 1978-80, mem. standing com., 1972-90; mem. exec. com. Nat. Conf. State Trial Judges, 1980-91. Author: Sentencing: A View From the Bench, 1973; co-author: The Judicial Immunity Doctrine Today: Between the Bench and a Hard Place, 1984, The Brief Jour.; The Dangerous Erosion of Judicial Immunity, 1989. Mem. Oreg. Legislature, 1952-54; Rep. nominee for Congress, 1956; chmn. Oreg. Rep. Ctrl. Com., 1962-64; mem. adv. bd. Portland Salvation Army, 1976—; mem. bd. overseers Lewis and Clark Coll., 1972-90. Named Alumnus of Yr. U. Portland, 1963; named Alumnus of Yr. Lewis & Clark Law Sch., 1973. Fellow Am. Bar Found.; mem. ABA (chmn. jud. immunity com. jud. adminstrn. divsn. 1982-90, mem. commn. on standards jud. adminstrn. divsn. 1973-77, chmn. conf. state trial judges 1990-91, HBH Comm. on State Justice Initiatives 1994—, chmn. jud. adminstrn. divsn. 1994-95), Oreg. Bar Assn. (bd. govs. 1961-64), Multnomah County Bar Assn. (pres. 1959), Am. Judicature Soc., Oreg. Cir. Judges Assn. (pres. 1988-89), U. Portland Alumni Assn. (pres. 1967), Lewis and Clark Coll. Alumni Assn. (prs. 1974-76, 80-81), Multnomah Law Libr. Assn. (bd. dirs.), City Club, Univ. Club, Masons, Shriners, Rotary, B'nai B'rith, Delta Theta Phi. Jewish. Home: 2495 SW 73d Ave Portland OR 97225

ROTH, ROBERT ALLEN, systems consultant; b. Chgo., Oct. 26, 1947; s. Ralph Robert and Lucile Emily (Hence) R.; m. Betty Rae Wooten, July 23, 1968 (div. June 1975); children: Robert Allen III, Anna Katherine; m. Carolyn McConnell, Aug. 23, 1980. AA, St. Johns River Jr. Coll., Palatka, Fla., 1967; B Gen. Studies, Rollins Coll., 1969; MBA, U. North Fla., 1974. Cert. sys. profl., computing profl. Various positions, 1968-80; systems mgr. Charter Oil Co.-Alaska Oil Co., Jacksonville, Fla., 1980-81; project leader, lead analyst Halliburton Svcs., Duncan, Okla., 1982; mgr. data adminstrn. and software quality assurance Comm. Satellite Corp., Washington, 1982-83; div. mgr. Automated Scis. Group, Inc., Fairfax, Va., 1983-86; div. dir. Inf. Sys. and Networks (ISN) Corp., Sarasota, Fla., 1986-87; pres., owner, operator ROMAC Enterprises, Sarasota, 1987-92; hdqs. div. mgr. COMPEX Corp., Sarasota, 1987, v.p., gen. mgr. S.E. region, 1991-92; pres., dir. R&D Advanced Tech. Group, Jacksonville, Fla., 1992-96; prin. cons. Data Dimensions, Jacksonville, 1996—. Mem. Rotary (v.p. Sarasota 1991-92, pres. 1992-93, Paul Harris fellow 1992). Avocations: car rallies, golf, tennis, boating, shooting. Home and Office: Data Dimensions 3692 East Wexford Hollow Rd Jacksonville FL 32224-6678

ROTH, ROBERT EARL, environmental educator; b. Wauseon, Ohio, Mar. 30, 1937; s. Earl Jonas and Florence Lena (Mahler) R.; m. Carol Sue Yackee, Aug. 8, 1959; children: Robin Earl, Bruce Robert. BSc, Ohio State U., Columbus, 1959, BSc in Secondary Sci. Edn., 1960, MSc in Conservation Edn., 1960; PhD in Environ. Edn., U. Wis., Madison, 1969. Supr. conservation edn. Ethical Culture Schs., N.Y.C., 1961-63; naturalist, sci. tchr. Lakeside Sch., Spring Valley, N.Y., 1963-65; instr. No. Ill. U.-Oregon, 1965-67; asst. prof. Ohio State U., Columbus, 1969-73, assoc. prof., 1973-78, prof. environ. edn. and sci. edn., 1978—, chmn. div., 1973-84, coord. Office of Internat. Affairs, 1985-89, asst. dir., sch. sec., Sch. Natural Resources Coop. Extension Svc. 1989-93, acting dir. Sch. Natural Resources, 1993-94, assoc. dir., 1994—, state extension specialist Environ. Edn., 1993—; R&D assoc. Moseley & Assocs., Columbus, 1986-89; project cons. NARMA project, U.S. Agy. Internat. Devel., Santo Domingo, Dominican Rep., 1982-87; cons. Richard Trott and Assocs., 1988-90, Kinzelman and Kline, 1990-94, Midwest Consortium Internat. Activity, 1995; workshop leader Carribean Conservation Assn., Bridgetown, Barbados, 1981-83; vis. scholar Indonesian Second U. Devel. project, Jakarta, 1988; vis. scholar Uganda Makerere U., 1989, Pacific Cultural Found., Taipei, Taiwan, 1989; AID lectr., Thesolonika, Greece, 1992. Exec. editor Jour. Environ. Edn., 1974-91, Pub.'s prize 1970; contbr. article to profl. jours. Committeeman Boy Scouts Am., 1983-86; adv. council McKeever Environ. Learning Ctr., Pa., 1977-83. Recipient Pomerene Teaching Enhancement award, Ohio State U., 1986, 95, Environ. Edn. award Ohio Alliance for the Environ., 1992, Outstanding Advising award Coll. Food, Agrl. and Environ. Scis., 1996. Mem. N. Am. Assn. Environ. Edn. (life mem., bd. dirs. 1972-82, pres. 1977-78, Walt Jeske award 1988), Nat. Sci. Tchrs. Assn. (life), Sch. Nat., Resource Alumni Assn. (inducted hon. 100), Agrl. Faculty Coun. (elect-pres. 1989, pres. 1990), TBDBITL Alumni Club, Phi Beta Delta, Gamma Sigma Delta (treas. 1987-88, sec. 1988-89, pres.-elect. 1989-90, pres. 1990-91), Sigma Xi. Avocations: swimming, canoeing, camping, fishing, travel. Home: 570 Morning St Columbus OH 43085-3775 Office: Ohio State U Environ Edn Sch Natural Resources Columbus OH 43210

ROTH, SANFORD HAROLD, rheumatologist, health care administrator, educator; b. Akron, Ohio, June 12, 1934; s. Charles and Rose Marie (Zelman) R.; m. Marcia Ann, June 9, 1957; children: Shana Beth, Sari Luanne. B.Sc., Ohio State U., 1955, M.D., 1959. Intern Mt. Carmel, Columbus, Ohio, 1959-60; fellow Mayo Grad. Sch. Medicine, 1962-65; pvt. practice medicine specializing in rheumatology Phoenix, 1965—; med. dir. Arthritis Ctr., Ltd., Phoenix, 1983—; dir. Arthritis Program Healthwest Regional Medical Ctr., Phoenix, 1987-89; med. dir. Arthritis/Orthopedic Ctr for Excellence Humana Hosp., Phoenix, 1989—; dir. arthritis rehab. program St. Luke's Hosp., Phoenix, 1978-87; med. research dir. Harrington Arthritis Research Ctr., Phoenix, 1984-88; prof., dir. aging and arthritis program Coll. Grad. Program, Ariz. State U., Tempe, 1984—; dir. medicine Ariz. Insts., Phoenix, 1985—; past state chmn. Gov.'s Conf. on Arthritis in Ariz., 1967; cons., rep. arthritis adv. com. FDA, 1982—, chmn. anti-rheumatic new drug guidelines, 1984—; cons. Ciba-Geigy, 1983—, Upjohn, 1985-87, Pennwalt, 1985-88, Arthritis Found. Clinics, 3M-Riker Labs, Inc., 1981-89, VA, 1970-87, FTC, 1980—, Boots Pharm. Co., 1980-87, Greenwich Pharm., 1986-87, Hoffman-LaRoche, 1986—, FDA Office Compliance, 1987—, G.D. Searle, 1987—; prin. investigator Coop. Systematic Studies of Rheumatic Diseases; vis. scholar in rheumatology Beijing Med. Coll., People's Republic China, 1982; proctor, vis. scholar program U.S.-China Edn. Inst., 1982—; med. research dir., exec. bd., trustee Harrington Arthritis Research Ctr., 1983-88; co-chair PANLAR Collaborative Clin. Epidemiol. Group, 1989—; mem. com. on revision U.S. Pharmacopeial Conv., 1990—; mem. antirheumatic drug task force WHO-Internat. League Against Rheumatism, 1991—; med. dir. columbia ElderCare, 1997—; mem. com. revision U.S. Parmacopia, 1990. Author: New Directions in Arthritis Therapy, 1980; Handbook of Drug Therapy in Rheumatoloy, 1985; med. contbg. editor RISS, Hosp. Physician, 1960-68, Current Prescribing, 1976-80; hon. internat. cons. editor Drugs, 1977—; editor in chief Arthron, 1982-85; editor, contbg. author: Rheumatic Therapeutics, 1985; med. cons. editor Update: Rheumatism, 1985, AMA Drug Evaluations, 6th edit., 1986, 7th edit., 1990; mem. editorial bd. VA Practitioner, 1985—, Comprehensive Therapy, 1987; mem. internat. editorial bd. Jour. Drug Devel., 1988—, Practical Gastroenterology, 1989—; contbr. numerous articles to profl. jours., chpts. to books. Fellow Am. Coll. Rheumatology (founding, liaison com. to regional med. program 1974-76, co-dir. med. info. system ARAMIS, computer com., chmn. antiinflammatory drug study club 1974—, com. on clubs and councils 1977-80, western regional co-chmn. 1977—, therapeutic and drug com. 1979—, glossary com. 1981-83, ad hoc com. on future meeting sites 1983); mem. AMA, ACP (regional program com., ann. Philip S. Hench lectureship chmn. 1978-79), Arthritis Found. (dir. central Ariz. chpt. 1982-83, past chmn. med. and sci. com. 1967-72), Lupus Found. Am. (bd. 1981—), Internat. Soc. Rheumatic Therapy (sec.-gen. 1990—, bd. dirs. 1987—, pres. 1992—), Maricopa County Med. Soc. (rehab. com.), Am. Soc. Clin. Rheumatology (past pres. exec. council), Am. Coll. Clin. Pharmacology, Soc. Internal Medicine, Mayo Clinic Alumni Assn., Mayo Clinic Fellows Assn. (sec. 1964-65), Argentine Rheumatology Soc. (hon.), Mayo Clinic Fellows Rheumatology Soc. (pres. 1964-65), Mayo Clinic Film Soc. (bd. dirs. 1964-65), Pan Am. League Against Rheumatism (chmn. clin. trials com. 1987—). Office: Arthritis Ctr Ltd 3330 N 2nd St Ste 601 Phoenix AZ 85012-2371 *To reconcile research of* *the boundless limits of our restless science with the legacy of our ancient art as to be healer, educator, organizer--all the while blessed by the joys of family love and community service. We create our destiny not alone but with individual dedication.*

ROTH, SANFORD IRWIN, pathologist, educator; b. McAlester, Okla., Oct. 14, 1932; s. Herman Moe and Blanche (Brown) R.; m. Kathryn Ann Corliss, Sept. 3, 1961; children: Jeffrey Franklin, Elisabeth Francyne, Gregory James, Suzannah Joan. Student, Vanderbilt U., 1949-52; MD, Harvard U., 1956. Intern Mass. Gen. Hosp., Boston, 1956-57; resident in pathology Mass. Gen. Hosp., 1957-60, pathologist, 1962-75; pathologist Armed Forces Inst. Pathology, 1960-62; asst. prof. Med. Sch. Harvard U., 1962-69, assoc. prof. Med. Sch., 1969-75; pathologist, prof., chmn. dept. Coll. Medicine U. Ark., Little Rock, 1975-81; prof. Med. Sch. Northwestern U., Chgo., 1981—; chief lab. svc. VA Lakeside Med. Ctr., Chgo., 1981-86; attending pathologist Northwestern U. Hosp., 1981—. With M.C. U.S. Army, 1960-62. Mem. AMA, AAAS, Am. Soc. Cell Biology, Coll. Am. Pathology, U.S.-Can. Acad. Pathology, Soc. for Investigative Dermatology, Ill. Med. Soc., Mass. Med. Soc. Home: 920 Forest Glen Dr W Winnetka IL 60093-1430 Office: 303 E Chicago Ave Chicago IL 60611-3008

ROTH, SOL, rabbi; b. Rzeszow, Poland, Mar. 8, 1927; came to U.S., 1934, naturalized, 1939; s. Joseph and Miriam (Lamm) R.; m. Debra H. Stitskin, Nov. 26, 1957; children: Steven, Michael, Sharon. B.A., Yeshiva U., 1948, D.D. (hon.), 1977; M.A., Columbia U., 1953, Ph.D., 1966; Rabbi, Yeshiva U. Theol. Sem., 1950. Ordained rabbi Orthodox Jewish Congregations, 1950; pres. Rabbinical Council Am., 1980-82, N.Y. Bd. Rabbis, 1976-79; chmn. Israel Commn. Rabbinical Council Am., 1976-78; dean Chaplaincy Sch., N.Y. Bd. Rabbis, 1976-79; Samson R. Hirsch prof. dept. philosophy Yeshiva U., N.Y.C.; rabbi Jewish Ctr. Atlantic Beach, N.Y., 1956-86; Fifth Ave Synagogue, 1986—; pres. Religious Zionists Am., 1991-94. Author: Science and Religion, 1967, The Jewish Idea of Community, 1977, Halakhah and Politics: The Jewish Idea of a State, 1988 (Samuel Belkin Meml. Lit. award 1989), The Jewish Idea of Culture, 1997; editor: Morasha. Recipient award Synagogue Adv. Council United Jewish Appeal, 1975. The Rabbi Dr. Sol Roth Chair in Talmud and Contemporary Halakha established at Yeshiva U., 1989. Home: 30 E 62nd St New York NY 10021-8026 Office: Yeshiva U Dept Philosophy 500 W 185th St New York NY 10033-3201

ROTH, SUSAN KING, design educator; b. Millville, N.J., Nov. 13, 1945; d. Frank N. and Ruth (Ludlam) King; m. Richard L. Roth, Sept. 17, 1973; 1 child, Justin King Roth. BFA, Cooper Union, 1968; MA, Ohio State U., 1988. With advt. prodn. Mayer/Martin, Inc., N.Y.C., 1968-70; dir. graphics N.Y.C. Parks, Recreation and Cultural Affairs Adminstrn., 1970-73; designer Whole Earth Epilog, Sausalito, Calif., 1974-75; asst. art dir. TV Guide mag., Radnor, Pa., 1975-77; design cons. various orgns., Chgo., 1978-80; instr., tchg. assoc. Ohio State U., Columbus, 1985-88, asst. prof., 1988-95, assoc. prof., 1996—, assoc. dean Coll. Arts, 1996—; vis. designer Sch. Art Inst., Chgo., 1980-81, Ohio Wesleyan U., Delaware, 1982-84; co-founder, co-dir. Ctr. for Interdisciplinary Studies, Columbus, 1992—; vis. evaluator Nat. Assn. Schs. Art and Design, Reston, Va., 1994—; mem. faculty adv. com. to chancellor Ohio Bd. Regents, 1994—; cons. Elections Adminstrn., Franklin County Bd. Elections, Columbus, 1995—. Consulting editor Jour. Visual Literacy, 1992—; contbr. articles to profl. jours. Battelle grantee Battelle Endowment for Tech. & Human Affairs, 1993-94. Mem. Assn. Computing Machinery, Graphic Design Edn. Assn., Internat. Visual Literacy Assn., Indsl. Designers Soc. Am. (mem. edn. bd. 1993-95). Home: 3158 Glenrich Pky Columbus OH 43221-2639 Office: Ohio State U 152 Hopkins Hall Columbus OH 43210

ROTH, SUZANNE ALLEN, financial services agent; b. Santa Monica, Calif., May 31, 1963; d. Raymond A. and Ethel Allen; m. Steve Milstein Roth, Dec. 27, 1992. BA, U. Calif., Santa Cruz, 1986; student, Calif. State U., L.A., 1987-93, Art Ctr. Sch. Design, Pasadena, Calif., 1994—. Cert. tchr., Calif.; lic. real estate agt., Calif. Interviewer L.A. Times Newspaper, 1986-88; educator L.A. Unified Sch. Dist., 1987-90; educator Burbank (Calif.) Unified Sch. Dist., 1990-94, vol., 1994—; ptnr. fin. svcs. Roth & Assocs./N.Y. Life, L.A., 1993—. Mem. NEA, Burbank Tchrs. Union. Avocations: painting, illustrating, writing, weight training, old house renovation, wood restoration, light carpentry, landscape design.

ROTH, THOMAS, marketing executive. Grad., Western Mich. U. With Tarkenton and Co., Atlanta; dir. product devel. Wilson Learning Corp., Eden Prairie, Minn., 1981-88, v.p. product mgmt. in global R & D, 1992-94, v.p. product mgmt. and tng. group, 1994—, v.p. strategic implementation group; founder HR Skills Divsn. Nat. Edn. Tng. Group, 1988-92; cons. IBM, AT&T, Ford Motor Co., Gen. Motors, E.I. DuPont, Gen. Electric, Oracle, Dow Chem., Hughes Aircraft, Eli Lily, Colgate-Palmolive, Honeywell, others; spkr. in field. Co-author: Creating the High Performance Team, 1987. Office: Wilson Learning Corp 7500 Flying Cloud Dr Eden Prairie MN 55344-3748

ROTH, THOMAS J., physicist; b. Berwyn, Ill., Apr. 2, 1955; s. Raymond Edward and Elizabeth Ann (Robbins) R. BS, U. Ill., 1977, MS, 1981, PhD, 1986. Mem. tech. staff TRW ElectroOptics Rsch. Ctr., El Segundo, Calif., 1985-88; scientist TRW Group Rsch. Staff, Redondo Beach, Calif., 1988-90, TRW Rsch. Ctr., Redondo Beach, 1990-93; TRW Automotive Electronics Group, 1993—. Author: GaInAsP Alloy Semiconductors, 1982; contbr. to profl. publs. Mem. IEEE, Am. Physics Soc., Ave. A Athletic Assn. (sgt. at arms 1989-90), So. Calif. Crystal Growers (v.p., program chair 1988-92, pres. 1992-96), Sigma Xi. Achievements include patents for phase-locked array of semiconductor lasers using closely-spaced antiguides, vertical-cavity, surface-emitting diode laser. Office: TRW R6/1361 1 Space Park Redondo Beach CA 90278

ROTH, TOBY, former congressman, political consultant; b. Strasburg, N.D., Oct. 10, 1938; s. Kasper and Julia (Roehrich) R.; m. Barbara Fischer, Nov. 28, 1964; children: Toby Jr., Vicky, Barbie. BA, Marquette U., 1961. Mem. 96th-104th Congresses from 8th Wis. dist., Washington, D.C., 1979-97; ptnr. Flippo, Roth & Assocs., Washington, 1997—; mem. banking, fin., urban affairs com., subcoms. fin. instns. and consumer credit, internat. rels. com., chmn. econ. policy, trade coms., Africa. 1st lt. USAR, 1962-69. Named Wis. Legislator of Yr. Wis. Towns Assn., 1978. Mem. VFW (hon.), Optimists (hon.), Kiwanis (hon.). Republican.

ROTH, WILLIAM GEORGE, manufacturing company executive; b. Lamberton, Minn., Oct. 3, 1938; s. Euclair Ford and Kathryn (Kluegel) R.; m. Patricia Elizabeth Gibson, Aug. 27, 1960; children: William, David. B.S.M.E., U. Notre Dame, 1960; MS in Indsl. Adminstrn., Purdue U., 1961. With The Trane Co., LaCrosse, Wis., 1961-85, v.p., gen. mgr., 1973-77, dep. chmn., 1977-78, chmn., chief exec. officer, 1978-85; pres. Am. Standard, Inc., N.Y.C., 1985-87; pres., chief exec. officer Dravo Corp., Pitts., 1987-89, chmn. bd., 1990-93; bd. dirs. Amcast Indsl., Dayton, Svc. Experts Nashurce, Palo Alto. Mem. NAM (bd. dirs. 1978-87). Republican. Roman Catholic. Office: Dravo Corp 1 Oliver Plz Pittsburgh PA 15222-2620

ROTH, WILLIAM STANLEY, hospital foundation executive; b. N.Y.C., Jan. 12, 1929; s. Sam Irving and Louise Caroline (Martin) R.; m. Hazel Adcock, May 6, 1963; children: R. Charles, W. Stanley. AA, Asheville-Biltmore Jr. Coll., 1948; BS, U. N.C., 1950. Dep. regional exec. Nat. council Boy Scouts Am., 1953-65; exec. v.p. Am. Humanics Found., 1965-67; dir. devel. Bethany Med. Ctr., Kansas City, Kans., 1967-74; exec. v.p. Geisinger Med. Ctr. Found., Danville, Pa., 1974-78; found. pres. Baptist Med. Ctrs., Birmingham, Ala., 1978—; sec. Western Med. Systems, Cherokee Cmty. Homes, Cullman Sr. Housing, Dekalb Sr. Housing, Limestone Sr. Housing, Oxford Sr. Housing. Mem.-at-large Nat. council Boy Scouts Am., 1972-86; chmn. NAHD Ednl. Fund, 1980-82; ruling elder John Knox Kirk, Kansas City, Mo., Grove Presbyn. Ch., Danville, Pa. Recipient Silver award United Methodist Ch., 1970, Mid-West Health Congress, 1971; Seymour award for outstanding hosp. devel. officer 1983. Fellow Assn. for Healthcare Philanthropy (life, nat. pres. 1975-76); mem. Nat. Soc. Fund Raising Execs. (pres. Ala. chpt. 1980-82, nat. dir. 1980-84, mem. ethics bd. 1993—, advanced cert. fund raising exec., Outstanding Fund Raising Exec., Ala. chpt. 1983), Mid-Am. Hosp. Devel. Assn. (pres. 1973-74), Mid-West Health Congress (devel. chmn. 1972-74), Am. Soc. for Healthcare Mktg. and Pub. Rels., Ala. Soc. for Sleep Disorders, Ala. Heart Inst., Ala. Assn. Healthcare Philanthropy (pres. 1991-93, chmn. bd. 1993-94), Ala. Planned Giving Coun. (bd. dirs. 1991—, pres. 1994-95), Alpha Phi Omega (nat. pres. 1958-62, dir. 1950—, Nat. Disting. Service award 1962), Delta Upsilon (pres. N.C. Alumni 1963-65). Clubs: Rotary (pres. club 1976-77), Relay House, Summit, Green Valley (bd. govs.), Elks, Order Holy Grail, Order Golden Fleece, Order of The Arrow (Nat. Disting. Service award 1958). Editor Torch and Trefoil, 1960-61. Home: 341 Laredo Dr Birmingham AL 35226-2325 Office: 3500 Blue Lake Dr Ste 101 Birmingham AL 35243-1908

ROTH, WILLIAM V., JR., senator; b. Great Falls, Mont., July 22, 1921; m. Jane K. Richards; children: William V. III, Katharine Kellond. BA, U. Oreg., 1944; MBA, Harvard U., 1947, LLB, 1949. Bar: Del., U.S. Supreme Ct., Calif. Mem. 90th-91st congresses at large from, Del., 1967-71; senator State of Del., 1971—; chmn. senate fin. com., former chmn govt affairs com.; chmn. Del. Rep. State Com., 1961-64; mem. Rep. Nat. Com., 1961-64. Served to capt. AUS, 1943-46. Decorated Bronze Star medal. Mem. ABA, Del. Bar Assn. Episcopalian. Office: US Senate 104 Hart Senate Bldg Washington DC 20510

ROTHBAUM, IRA, retired advertising and marketing executive; b. Phila.; s. Samuel and Charlotte (Gross) R.; m. Eileen Glickfeld, Dec. 26, 1972; children: Stephen Ira, Peggy Ann, John E. A.B. in Journalism, U. N.C., 1947; student, Columbia U., 1944. Copywriter RCA Victor, 1947-49, advt. and sales promotion mgr., 1949-50; divisional sales mgr. RCA Service Co., 1953; instr. Tulane U., 1952; copywriter N.W. Ayer, Phila., 1953-56; account exec., account supr. N.W. Ayer, Detroit, 1956-63; v.p., sr. v.p., mgmt. supr. N.W. Ayer, N.Y.C., 1963-71; sr. v.p., mgmt. supr. SSC & B, 1971-77; asst. to pres. W.B. Doner & Co., Southfield, Mich., 1977-80; pres. Wingfoot Mktg. Co., Boynton Beach, Fla., 1980-83; sr. broker Alan Bush Brokerage Co., Delray Beach, Fla.; v.p. investments Gruntal & Co. Inc., Boca Raton, Fla.; v.p. J.W. Charles Securities, Boca Raton, 1989-94; v.p. investments Stock Depot Inc., Delray Beach, Fla., 1994-96; ret., 1996; adj. prof. Fla. Atlantic U., Boca Raton. Served with USNR, 1943-46, 50-52. Home: 8784 Thames River Dr Boca Raton FL 33433-7844

ROTHBERG, ABRAHAM, author, educator, editor; b. N.Y.C., Jan. 14, 1922; s. Louis and Lottie (Drimmer) R.; m. Esther Conwell, Sept. 30, 1945; 1 son, Lewis Josiah. A.B., Bklyn. Coll., 1942; M.A., U. Iowa, 1947; Ph.D., Columbia U., 1952. Chmn. editorial bd. Stateside (mag.), N.Y.C., 1947-49; instr. English, creative writing Columbia U., N.Y.C., 1948; instr. English, humanities Hofstra Coll., Hempstead, N.Y., 1947-51; prof. English St. John Fisher Coll., 1973-83, chmn. dept. English, 1981-82; disting. writer-in-residence, vis. prof. Wichita State U., 1985; Ford Found. fellow, N.Y.C., 1951-52; editor-in-chief Free Europe Press, N.Y.C., 1952-59; mng. editor George Braziller, Inc., N.Y.C., 1959, New Leader (mag.), N.Y.C., 1960-61; cons. editor New Jewish Ency., 1960-62; writer, editorial cons.; European corr. Nat. Observer, Washington, Manchester (Eng.) Guardian, 1962-63; sr. editor Bantam Books, Inc., N.Y.C., 1966-67; Cons. editor The New Union Prayer Book, N.Y.C., 1975. (Recipient John H. McGinnis Meml. award for short story 1970, John H. McGinnis Meml. award for essay 1973-74, Lit. award Friends of Rochester Library 1980); Author: Abraham, Eyewitness History of World War II, 1962, The Thousand Doors, 1965, The Heirs of Cain, 1966, The Song of David Freed, 1968, The Other Man's Shoes, 1969, The Boy and the Dolphin, 1969, The Sword of the Golem, 1971, Aleksandr Solzhenitsyn: The Major Novels, 1971, The Heirs of Stalin: Dissidence and the Soviet Regime, 1953-1970, 1972, The Stalking Horse, 1972, The Great Waltz, 1978, The Four Corners of the House, 1981; Editor: U.S. Stories, 1949, Flashes in the Night, 1958, Anatomy of a Moral, 1959, A Bar-Mitzvah Companion, 1959, Great Adventure Stories of Jack London, 1967; Contbr. articles, essays, stories, poems to various publs., anthologies, collections. Served with AUS, 1943-45. Home: 340 Pelham Rd Rochester NY 14610-3355

ROTHBERG, GERALD, editor, publisher; b. Bklyn., Oct. 29, 1937; s. Abraham and Pauline Rothberg; m. Glenda Fay Morris, June 18, 1970 (div. 1988); children: Laura, Abigail. B.A., Bklyn. Coll., 1960; postgrad., Dickinson Law Sch., 1962. Spl. projects editor Esquire (mag.), 1963-66; owner, editor, pub., founder Circus (mag.), N.Y.C., 1966—; owner, founder, editor Sci. and Living Tomorrow, 1980—, Who's In, 1981; founder, editor Sports Mirror mag., 1983—, MGF mag., 1985—; Country Mirror mag., 1994—. Author: (novels) Composition 36, 1993, The Six-Hour Song, 1994, Redeeming Esau, 1995. Mem. Periodical and Book Assn. Am. (pres.). Office: Circus Mag 6 W 18th St New York NY 10011-4608

ROTHBERG, JUNE SIMMONDS, retired nursing educator, psychotherapist, psychoanalyst; b. Phila., Sept. 4, 1923; d. David and Rose (Protzel) Simmonds; m. Jacob Rothberg, Sept. 7, 1952; children: Robert, Alan. Diploma in nursing, Lenox Hill Hosp., 1944; BS, N.Y. U., 1950, MA, 1959, PhD (NIH fellow), 1965; Diploma in Psychotherapy and Psychoanalysis, Adelphi U., Inst. for Advanced Psychol. Studies, 1987. USPHS traineeship N.Y. U., 1957-59; sr. public health nurse Bklyn. Vis. Nurse Assn., 1951-53; prin. investigator in nursing, homestead study project Goldwater Hosp. and N.Y. U., 1959-61; instr. N.Y. U., 1964-65, asst. prof., 1965-68, assoc. prof., 1968-69, project dir. grad. program rehab. nursing, 1964-69, prof., 1969-87, prof. emeritus, 1987—; dean Adelphi U., Garden City, N.Y., 1969-85; v.p. acad. adminstrn. Adelphi U., 1985-86; pvt. practice West Hempstead, N.Y., 1993—; pres. David Simmonds Co. Inc., Med. Supply Co., 1982-89; dir., chmn. compensation com. Quality Care, Inc.; cons. to various ednl. and svc. instns.; cons. region 2 Bur. Health Resources Devel., HHS.; speaker on radio and TV; bd. dirs., mem. audit com. Ipco Corp. (formerly Sterling Optical Corp.), 1991. Contbr. articles to profl. jours. Mem. pres's coun. N.Y. U. Sch. Edn., 1973-75; treas. Nurses for Polit. Action, 1971-73; trustee Nurses Coalition for Action in Politics, 1974-76; bd. visitors Duke Med. Ctr., 1970-74; mem. governing bd. Nassau-Suffolk Health Systems Agy., 1976-79; leader People-to-People Internat. med. rehab. del. to People's Republic of China, 1981; mem. com. for the study pain disability and chronic illness behavior Inst. Medicine, 1985-86, com. on ethics in rehab. Hastings Ctr., 1985-87; trustee Paget's Disease Found., 1987-89. Recipient Disting. Alumna award NYU, 1974, recognition award Am. Assn. Colls. Nursing, 1976, Achievers award Ctr. for Bus. and Profl. Women, 1980. Fellow Am. Acad. Nursing (governing coun. 1980-82); mem. Nat. League Nursing (exec. com. coun. of baccalaureate and higher degree programs 1969-73), Am. Nurses Assn. (joint liaison com. 1970-72), Commn. Accreditation of Rehab. Facilities, Am. Congress Rehab. Medicine (pres. 1977-78, chmn. continuing edn. com. 1979-86, 34th Ann. John Stanley Coulter Meml. lectr. 1984, Gold Key award 1984, Edward W. Lowman award 1990), Am. Assn. Colls. Nursing (pres. 1974-76), L.I. Women's Network (pres. 1980-81), Kappa Delta Pi, Sigma Theta Tau, Pi Lambda Theta. June S. Rothberg collection in Nursing Archives, Mugar Meml. Library, Boston U. Home and Office: 8668 Via Giulia Boca Raton FL 33496-1912

ROTHBLATT, DONALD NOAH, urban and regional planner, educator; b. N.Y.C., Apr. 28, 1935; s. Harry and Sophie (Chernofsky) R.; m. Ann S. Vogel, June 16, 1957; children: Joel Michael, Steven Saul. BCE, CUNY, 1957; MS in Urban Planning, Columbia U., 1963; Diploma in Comprehensive Planning, Inst. Social Studies, The Hague, 1964; PhD in City and Regional Planning, Harvard U., 1969. Registered profl. engr. N.Y. Planner N.Y.C. Planning Commn., 1960-62, N.Y. Housing and Redevel. Bd., 1963-66; research fellow Ctr. for Environ. Design Studies, Harvard U., Cambridge, Mass., 1965-71; teaching fellow, instr., then asst. prof. city and regional planning Harvard U., 1967-71; prof. urban and regional planning, chmn. dept. San Jose State U., Calif., 1971—; Lady Davis vis. prof. urban and regional planning Hebrew U., Jerusalem and Tel Aviv U., 1978; vis. scholar Indian Inst. Architects, 1979, Shandong Province, China, 1996; vis. scholar, rsch. assoc. Inst. Govtl. Studies, U. Calif., Berkeley, 1980—; cons. to pvt. industry and govt. agys. Author: Human Needs and Public Housing, 1964, Thailand's Northeast, 1967, Regional Planning: The Appalachian Experience, 1971, Allocation of Resources for Regional Planning, 1972, The Suburban Environment and Women, 1979, Regional-Local Development Policy Making, 1981, Planning the Metropolis: The Multiple Advocacy Approach, 1982, Comparative Suburban Data, 1983, Suburbia: An International Assessment, 1986, Metropolitan Dispute Resolution in Silicon Valley, 1989, Good Practices for the Congestion Management Program, 1994, Activity-Based Travel Survey and Analysis of Responses to Increased Congestion, 1995, An Experiment in Sub-Regional Planning: California's Congestion Management Policy, 1995, Estimating the Origins and Destinations of Transit Passengers from On/Off Counts, 1995, Changes in Property Values Induced by Light Transit, 1996, Models of Statewide Transportation Planning Under ISTEA, 1996; editor: National policy for Urban and Regional Development, 1974, Regional Advocacy Planning: Expanding Air Transport Facilities for the San Jose Metropolitan Area, 1975, Metropolitan-wide Advocacy Planning; Dispersion of Low and Moderate Cost Housing in the San Jose Metropolitan Area, 1976, Multiple Advocacy Planning: Public Surface Transportation in the San Jose Metropolitan Area, 1977, A Multiple Advocacy Approach to Regional Planning: Open Space and Recreational Facilities for the San Jose Metropolitan Area, 1979, Regional Transpotation Planning for the San Jose Metropolitan Area, 1981, Planning for Open Space and Recreational Facilities in the San Jose Metropolitan Area, 1982, Regional Economic Development Planning for the San Jose Metropolitan Area, 1984, Planning for Surface Transportation in the San Jose Metropolitan Area, 1986, Expansion of Air Transportation Facilities in the San Jose Metropolitan Area, 1987, Provision of Economic Development in the San Jose Met. Area, 1988, Metropolitan Governance: American/Canadian Intergovernmental Perspectives, 1993; contbr. numerous articles to profl. jours.; dir.: Pub. TV series Sta. KTEH, 1976. Mem. adv. coun. Bay Area Met. Transp. Commn., 1995—. Served to 1st lt. C.E., U.S. Army, 1957-59. Rsch. fellow John F. Kennedy Sch. Govt. Harvard U., 1967-69; William F. Milton rsch. fellow, 1970-71; faculty rsch. grantee, NSF, 1972-82, Calif. State U., 1977-78; grantee Nat. Inst. Dispute Resolution, 1987-88, Can. Studies Enrichment Program, 1989-90, Can. Studies Rsch. Program, 1992-93, Univ. Rsch. and Tng. Program grantee Calif. Dept. Transp., 1993-97; recipient Innovative Teaching award Calif. State U. and Coll., 1975-79; co-recipient Best of West award Western Ednl. Soc. for Tele-communication, 1976; recipient award Internat. Festival of Films on Architecture and Planning, 1983, Meritorious Performance award San Jose State U., 1986, 88, 90. Mem. Assn. Collegiate Schs. of Planning (pres. 1975-76), Am. Inst. Cert. Planners, Am. Planning Assn., Planners for Equal Opportunity, Internat. Fedn. Housing and Planning, AAUP, Calif. Edn. Com. on Architecture and Landscape, Architecture and Urban and Regional Planning (chmn. 1973-75). Office: San Jose State U Dept Urban & Regional Planning San Jose CA 95192-0185 *My basic view is that we should try to develop ourselves fully and help others do the same, so that we will be able to live in harmony with, and contribute to, our world community.*

ROTHCHILD, HOWARD LESLIE, advertising executive; b. Burlington, Vt., June 14, 1929; s. Daniel and Florence (Agel) R.; m. Sheila Segelman, June 3, 1973; children—Staci, Erik, Jessica. B.S., U. Vt., 1951; M.Litt., U. Pitts., 1952. Account exec. Lando Advt., Inc., Pitts., 1957-64; v.p. Goldman, Shoop & Rothchild, Inc., Pitts., 1964-67, Marc & Co., Inc., Pitts., 1967-72; chmn. bd. Rafshoon Shivers Tolpin, Inc., Atlanta, 1972-81; exec. v.p. Garber, Goodman & Rothchild Advt., Inc., Miami, Fla., 1981-87; pres. The Rothchild Group, Inc., Miami, 1987-89; chmn., pres., chief exec. officer The Rothchild Cos., Inc., Miami, 1989-93; dir. account devel. Gold Coast Advt. Assoc. Inc., Miami, 1994—; instr. U. Pitts. Grad. Sch. Bus., 1964-71. Bd. dirs. Big Bros. Am., Pitts., 1967-71, Lucky Acorns, Miami, 1991—. Served with AUS, 1952-54. Recipient Top Radio Comml. of Yr. award Nat. Retail Mchts. Assn. Mem. Am. Mktg. Assn., Bus./Profl. Advt. Assn., Advt. Fedn. Miami, Fla. Advt. Golf Assn. (founding dir.). Office: Gold Coast Advt Assoc Inc 4141 NW 2nd Ave Miami FL 33127-2843

ROTHEIM, ELEANOR SUE, elementary education specialist; d. Samuel Nathan and Sallie (Madow) R.; divorced; 1 child, Shara Johnson. BS, Mills. Coll. Edn.; Masters, Syracuse U., CAS. Cert. reading specialist, N.Y. Tchr. Cleve. Bd. Edn., Jericho (N.Y.) Sch. Dist., 1969-72; reading specialist Syracuse (N.Y.) City Sch. Dist., 1972—; policy bd. dirs. Syracuse Tchr. Ctr., 1988—, author pamphlet Adult Learner, 1989. Trainer, tutor Literacy Vols. Greater Syracuse, 1982-89. Recipient Svc. award Onondago County Tchr. Assn., 1990. Avocations: biking, walking, hand-crafted clothing business.

ROTHENBERG, ADAM LEIGH, lawyer; b. Chgo., Sept. 9, 1963; s. Philip Burton and Roberta Lynn (Keylin) R.; m. Christie Curry, Sept. 23, 1989; children: Alexa Leigh, Zachary Ryan. Student, Tulane U., 1981-83; BABA, U. Wash., 1987; JD cum laude, Seton Hall U., 1993. Bar: N.J. 1993, U.S. Dist. Ct. N.J. 1993. Law clk. Blume Vazquez Goldfaden Berkowitz & Donnelly, Newark, 1992-93; assoc. Levinson, Axelrod, Wheaton, Grayzel, Caulfield, et al, Edison, N.J., 1993—. Mem. ATLA, N.J. ATLA (bd. govs. 1996-97), Middlesex County Bar Assn., Middlesex County Trial Lawyers, Essex County Bar Assn. Avocations: tennis, golf, sailing. Office: Levinson Axelrod Wheaton Grayzel Caulfield Marcoulus & Dunn 2 Lincoln Ave Edison NJ 08837-3217

ROTHENBERG, ALAN I., lawyer, professional sports association executive; b. Detroit, Apr. 10, 1939; m. Georgina Rothenberg; 3 children. B.A., U. Mich., 1960, J.D., 1963. Bar: Calif. 1964. Assoc. O'Melveny & Myers, L.A., 1963-66; ptnr. Manatt Phelps Rothenberg & Phillips, L.A., 1968-90, Latham & Watkins, L.A., 1990—; instr. sports law U. So. Calif., 1969, 76, 84, Whittier Coll. Law, 1980, 84; pres., gen. counsel L.A. Lakers and L.A. Kings, 1967-79, L.A. Clippers Basketball Team, 1982-89; pres. U.S. Soccer Fedn., Chgo., 1990—; chmn., founder Maj. League Soccer, N.Y.C., 1995. Soccer commr. 1984 Olympic Games; chmn., pres., CEO 1994 World Cup Organizing Com., 1990-94; founder, chmn. Major League Soccer, 1994—; bd. dirs., pres. Constl. Rights Found., 1987-90. Mem. aBA, State Bar Calif. (pres. 1989-90), Los Angeles County Bar Assn., L.A. Bar Assn., Nat. Basketball Assn. (bd. govs. 1971-79, 82-89), N.Am. Soccer League (bd. govs. 1977-80, Major League Soccer mgmt. com. 1994—), Order of Coif. Office: Latham & Watkins 633 W 5th St Ste 4000 Los Angeles CA 90071-2005*

ROTHENBERG, ALBERT, psychiatrist, educator; b. N.Y.C., June 2, 1930; s. Gabriel and Rose (Goldberg) R.; m. Julia C. Johnson, June 28, 1970; children: Michael, Mora, Rina. A.B., Harvard U., 1952; M.D., Tufts U., 1956. Diplomate: Am. Bd. Psychiatry and Neurology. Intern Pa. Hosp., Phila., 1956-57; resident in psychiatry Yale U., West Haven (Conn.) VA Hosp., 1957-58, Grace-New Haven Hosp., 1958-59; resident in psychiatry Yale Psychiat. Inst., New Haven, 1959-60, chief resident, 1960-61; practice medicine specializing in psychiatry New Haven, 1960-61, 1963-75; chief neuropsychiatry Rodriguez U.S. Army Hosp., San Juan, P.R., 1961-63; practice medicine specializing in psychiatry Farmington, Conn., 1975-79, Stockbridge, Mass., 1979-94, Chatham, N.Y., 1994—, Great Barrington, Mass., 1994—; dir. rsch. Austen Riggs Center, Stockbridge, Mass., 1979-94; asst. dir. Yale Psychiat. Inst., 1963-64, sr. staff mem., 1964-83; mem. staff Yale-New Haven Med. Ctr., West Haven VA Hosp., U. Conn. Health Ctr., Farmington; cons., mem. editorial bd. various jours. in psychiatry and psychology; instr. dept. psychiatry Yale U. Sch. Medicine, 1960-61, 63-64, asst. prof., 1964-68, assoc. prof., 1968-74, clin. prof., 1974-84; prof. psychiatry U. Conn. Sch. Medicine, Farmington, 1975-79, dir. residency tng., 1976-78, dir. clin. svcs., 1975-78; prin. investigator Studies in the Creative Process, 1964—; vis. prof. Pa. State U., 1971, adj. prof., 1971-78; vis. prof. dept. Am. studies Yale U., 1974-76; lectr. dept. psychiatry Harvard U. Med. Sch., 1982-86, clin. prof., 1986—; researcher in psychotherapy. Author: (with B. Greenberg) Index of Scientific Writings on Creativity: Creative Men and Women, 1974, Index of Scientific Writings on Creativity: General 1566-1974, 1976; (with C.R. Hausman) The Creativity Question, 1976; The Emerging Goddess: The Creative Process in Art, Science and Other Fields, 1979; The Creative Process of Psychotherapy, 1988; Adolescence: Psychopathology, Normality, and Creativity, 1990; Creativity and Madness: New Findings and Old Stereotypes, 1990; contbr. numerous articles on the creative process, schizophrenia, anorexia nervosa, and psychotherapy to profl. and popular jours. Researcher on creativity in the arts, sci. and tech. Served with M.C. U.S. Army, 1961-63. Recipient Tufts Med. Alumni award 1956, Rsch. Scientist Career Devel. award NIMH 1964, 69, Golestan Found. award 1991, 92; Guggenheim Meml. fellow 1974-75, Ctr. Adv. Study in Behavioral Studies fellow 1986-87, Netherlands Inst. for Adv. Study in Humanities and Social Scis. fellow, 1992-93. Fellow Am. Psychiat. Assn. (life), Am. Coll. Psychoanalysts; mem. AAAS, Mass. Psychiat. Soc., Am. Soc. Aesthetics, Rappaport-Klein Group, Sigma Xi. Democrat. Home: PO Box 236 52 Pine Ridge Rd Canaan NY 12029

ROTHENBERG, ELLIOT CALVIN, lawyer, writer; b. Mpls., Nov. 12, 1939; s. Sam S. and Claire Sylvia (Feller) R.; m. Sally Smayling; children: Sarah, Rebecca, Sam. BA summa cum laude, U. Minn., 1961; JD, Harvard U. (Fulbright fellow), 1964. Bar: Minn. 1966, U.S. Dist. Ct. Minn. 1966, D.C. 1968, U.S. Supreme Ct. 1972, N.Y. 1974, U.S. Ct. Appeals (2d cir.)

1974, U.S. Ct. Appeals (8th cir.) 1975. Assoc. project dir. Brookings Inst., Washington, 1966-67; fgn. svc. officer, legal advisor U.S. Dept. State, Washington, 1968-73; Am. Embassy, Saigon; U.S. Mission to the UN; nat. law dir. Anti-Defamation League, N.Y.C., 1973-74; legal dir. Minn. Pub. Interest Rsch. Group, Mpls., 1974-77; pvt. practice law, Mpls., 1977—; adj. prof. William Mitchell Coll. Law, St. Paul, 1983—; faculty mem. several nat. communications law and First Amendment seminars. State bd. dirs. YMCA Youth in Govt. Program, 1981-84; v.p. Twin Cities chpt. Am. Jewish Com., 1980-84; mem. Minn. House of Reps., 1978-82, asst. floor leader (whip), 1981-82; pres., dir. North Star Legal Found., 1983—; Legal affairs editor Pub. Rsch. Syndicated, 1986—; briefs and oral arguments published in full Landmark Briefs and Arguments of the Supreme Court of the U.S., Vol. 200, 1992; Mem. citizens adv. com. Voyageurs Nat. Park, 1979-81. Fulbright fellow, 1964-65; recipient Legis. Evaluation Assembly Legis. Excellence award, 1980, Vietnam Civilian Service medal U.S Dept. State, 1970, North Star award, U. Minn., 1961. Mem. Am. Bar Assn., Harvard Law Sch. Assn., Minn. Bar Assn., Am. Legion, Mensa, Phi Beta Kappa. Jewish. Contbr. articles to profl. and scholarly jours. and books, newspapers, popular magazines; author: (with Zelman Cowen) Sir John Latham and Other Papers, 1965. Avocations: long distance running, classical music, baseball. Home and Office: 3901 W 25th St Saint Louis Park MN 55416-3803

ROTHENBERG, GUNTHER ERICH, history educator; b. Berlin, July 11, 1923; came to U.S., 1949, naturalized, 1952; s. Erich and Lotte Rothenberg; m. Ruth Gillah Smith, June 19, 1969 (dec. 1992); children: Judith, Laura, Georgia; m. Eleanor Iris Margarete Hancock, Apr. 2, 1995. B.A., U. Ill., 1954, Ph.D., 1958; M.A., U. Chgo., 1956. Asst. prof. history So. Ill. U., 1958-63; assoc. prof. U. N.Mex., 1963-69, prof., 1969-73; prof. mil. history Purdue U., 1973—; rsch. assoc. Monash U., Australia, 1995—; lectr. U.S. Army Command and Gen. Staff Coll., U.S. Army War Coll., USAF Acad., USAF War Coll., U.S. Mil. Acad., USMC Command and Gen. Staff Coll., disting. chair mil. affairs 1992—. Author: The Military Border in Croatia, 1740-1882, 1960, The Austrian Military Border in Croatia, 1522-1747, 1966, The Army of Francis Joseph, 1976, The Art of Warfare in the Age of Napoleon, 1978, The Anatomy of the Israeli Army, 1979, Napoleon's Great Adversaries, 1981; also others. With Brit. Army, 1941-48, USAF, 1949-56. Guggenheim fellow, 1962-63; Fullbright fellow, vis. prof. Royal Mil. Coll., Duntroon, Australia, 1985. Jewish. Home: 210 E Lutz Ave West Lafayette IN 47906-3015 Office: Purdue U Dept History West Lafayette IN 47907

ROTHENBERG, JEROME, author, visual arts and literary educator; b. N.Y.C., Dec. 11, 1931; s. Morris and Estelle (Lichtenstein) R.; m. Diane Brodatz, Dec. 25, 1952; 1 son, Matthew. B.A., CCNY, 1952; M.A., U. Mich., 1953. With Mannes Coll. Music, N.Y.C., 1961-70; vis. prof. U. Calif., San Diego, 1971, 77-84, U. Wis.-Mils., 1974-75, San Diego State U., 1976-77, U. Calif., Riverside, 1980, U. Okla., Norman, 1984; vis. Aerol Arnold prof. English U.So. Calif., 1983; vis. writer in residence SUNY, Albany, 1986, prof. English SUNY, Binghamton, 1986-88; prof. visual arts and lit. U. Calif., San Diego, 1989—, chmn. visual arts, 1990-93; head, creative writing, 1994-95. Poet, freelance writer, 1956—; author: numerous books of poetry and prose including Between, 1967, Technicians of the Sacred, 1968, Poems for the Game of Silence, 1971, Shaking the Pumpkin, 1972, America a Prophecy, 1973, Revolution of the Word, 1974, Poland/1931, 1974, A Big Jewish Book, 1978, A Seneca Journal, 1978, Vienna Blood, 1980, Pre-Faces, 1981, Symposium of the Whole, 1983, That Dada Strain, 1983, New Selected Poems, 1986, Khurbn, 1989, Exiled in the Word, 1989, The Lorca Variations I-VIII, 1990, Apres le jeu de silence, 1991, The Lorca Variations (complete), 1993, Gematria, 1994, An Oracle for Delfi, 1995, Poems for The Millennium, vol. 1, 1995, Seedings, 1996, The Book, Spiritual Instrument, 1996; editor, pub. Hawk's Well Press., N.Y.C., 1958-65, Some/Thing mag., 1966-69, Alcheringa: Ethnopoetics, 1970-76, New Wilderness Letter, 1976-86. Served with AUS, 1953-55. Recipient award in poetry Longview Found., 1960, Am. Book award, 1982, PEN Ctr. USA West award, 1994, PEN Oakland Josephine Miles award, 1994, 96; Wenner-Gren Found. grantee-in-aide for rsch. in Am. Indian poetry, 1968; Guggenheim fellow in creative writing, 1974; NEA poetry grantee, 1976. Mem. P.E.N. Am. Center, New Wilderness Found. Office: care New Directions 80 8th Ave New York NY 10011-5126

ROTHENBERG, JOSEPH HOWARD, federal agency administrator; b. N.Y.C., Dec. 23, 1940; s. Abe Arthur and Nevia Theresa (Vuotto) R.; m. Frances Bernice Albano, Feb. 1, 1964; children: Edward, Joyce, Annette. BS Engring. Sci., SUNY, Farmingdale, 1964; MS Mgmt. Engring., C.W. Post Coll., 1973, MS, 1977; PhD in Engring. (hon.), Stevens Inst. Tech., 1997. Project engr. Grumman Aerospace, Bethpage, N.Y., 1964-78, mgr. solar Max Mission Ops., 1978-81; mgr. ops. and test projects Computer Tech., Assocs., Englewood, Colo., 1981-83; space telescope ops. mgr. NASA, Goddard Space Flight Ctr., Greenbelt, Md., 1983-87, chief, mission ops. div., 1987-89; dep. dir. mission ops. and data systems directorate, 1989-90, assoc. dir. flight projects Hubble Space Telescope, 1990-94; exec. v.p. space systems divsn. CTA Inc., 1994-95; dir. NASA Goddard Space Flight Ctr., 1995—. With USN, 1957-62. Recipient Laurel award Space/Missiles, Aviation Week & Space Tech., 1993, Collier trophy, 1994, Disting. Svc. medal NASA, 1994, Robert H. Goddard Astronautics award Am. Inst. of Aeronautics and Astronautics, 1994, Meritorious Exec. fed. svc. SES, 1995. Mem. AIAA (Robert H. Goddard Astronautics award 1994), Instrument Soc. Am. (pres. L.I. sect. 1968-69). Avocations: sailing, skiing, music. Office: NASA Goddard Space Code # 100 Greenbelt MD 20771

ROTHENBERG, LESLIE STEVEN, lawyer, ethicist; b. Wheeling, W.Va., June 22, 1941; s. Emil and Lucie (Kern) R.; m. Rose-Emily Horkheimer, Dec. 22, 1963; children—Joshua Samuel. B.S., Northwestern U., 1963; M.A., Stanford U., 1964; J.D., UCLA, 1968. Bar: Calif. 1969, U.S. Supreme Ct. 1972. Spl. asst. to pres. U. Calif. and to chancellor UCLA, 1968-69; exec. sec. Los Angeles County Employee Relations Commn., 1969; assoc. firm Kaplan, Livingston, Goodwin, Berkowitz & Selvin, Beverly Hills, Calif., 1969-71; dep. dir. Los Angeles Legal Aid Found., 1971-73; acting prof. law Loyola U., Los Angeles, 1973-77; vis. prof. law U. Calif., Berkeley, 1977-78; pvt. practice, L.A., 1978-84; pres. Leslie Steven Rothenberg A.P.C., Pacific Palisades, Calif., 1984—; adj. asst. prof. medicine UCLA Med. Sch., 1980-87, adj. assoc. prof. medicine, 1987-91, assoc. prof. clin. medicine, 1991—; dir. program in med. ethics UCLA Med. Ctr., 1984—, UCLA Hosp. Enterprise, 1997—; cons. ethics, 1979—; fellow The Hastings Ctr., Briarcliff Manor, N.Y. Author: The Draft and You, 1968; contbr. articles to profl. jours. Bd. govs. U. Judaism, Los Angeles, 1980-88. Woodrow Wilson fellow, 1963-64. Mem. AAAS, ABA, L.A. County Bar Assn. (trustee 1979-80), Bar Assn. San Francisco, State Bar Calif., Am. Soc. Human Genetics, European Soc. Human Genetics, Assn. Jewish Studies, Soc. Christian Ethics, Soc. Values in Higher Edn., Soc. Health and Human Values, Can. Bioethics Soc., Soc. Bioethics Consultation, Assn. Practical and Profl. Ethics, Soc. for Bus. Ethics, European Bus. Ethics Network. Jewish. Office: 16751 Edgar St Pacific Palisades CA 90272-3226

ROTHENBERG, MIRA KOWARSKI, clinical psychologist and psychotherapist; b. Wilno, Poland; came to U.S., 1938; d. Jacob and Rosa (Joffe) Kowarski; m. Tev Goldsman, Dec. 7, 1960 (div. June 1974); 1 child, Akiva. BA, Bklyn. Coll., 1943; MA, Columbia U., 1957, Yeshiva U., 1959; ABD, Yeshiva U., 1962. Lic. psychologist, N.Y. Therapist, tchr.ir. Hawthorne (N.Y.) Cedar Knolls, 1952-53, League Sch., Bklyn., 1953-58; founder, clin. dir. Blueberry Treatment Ctrs., Bklyn., 1958-90; staff psychologist L.I. Coll. Hosp., Bklyn., 1966—; cons. Beachbrook Nursery, Bkyn., 1969-70, San Felipe Del Rio, Santa Fe, 1980—, Children's House Montessori Nursery, Bklyn., 1982-89, Austrlia Dept. Edn., Carynia, New South Wales; adj. prof. L.I. U., Bklyn., 1976-78; internat. speaker in field; worker with psychotic and autistic children, Croatia, 1994, Lithuania, 1994, 95, 96; cons. for movies on foster care, 1990—. Author: Children with Emerald Eyes, 1977, (with others) Pet Oriented Psychotherapy, 1980, The Outsiders, 1989; contbr. to books and articles to profl. jours. Mem. APA, World Fedn. Mental Health, N.Y. State Psychol. Assn., Inter. Soc. Child Abuse and Neglect (Hamburg, Germany), Physicians for Social Responsibility, N.Y. Acad. Scis., Amnest Internat., ACLU, NOW, Anti Defamation League, Yivo, Nat. Register Svc. Providers in Psychology. Avocations: writing, painting, sculpture, dance. Home and Office: 160 State St Brooklyn NY 11201-5610

ROTHENBERG, ROBERT EDWARD, physician, surgeon, author; b. Bklyn., Sept. 27, 1908; s. Simon and Caroline A. (Baer) R.; m. Lillian Lustig, 1933 (dec. 1977); m. Eileen Fein, 1977 (dec. 1987); children: Robert Philip, Lynn Barbara Rothenberg Kay; m. Florence Richman, 1989. A.B., Cornell U., 1929, M.D., 1932. Diplomate Am. Bd. Surgery. Intern Jewish Hosp., Bklyn., 1932-34; attending surgeon Jewish Hosp., 1955-82; postgrad. study Royal Infirmary, Edinburgh, 1934-35; civilian cons. U.S. Army Hosp., Ft. Jay, N.Y., 1960-66; attending surgeon French Polyclinic Med. Sch. and Health Center, N.Y.C., 1964-76; pres., 1973-76, trustee, 1972-76; attending surgeon Cabrini Health Care Center, 1976-86; cons. surgeon Cabrini Med. Ctr., 1986—, dir. surg. research, 1981—; clin. asst. prof. environ. medicine and community health State U. Coll. Medicine, N.Y.C., 1950-60; clin. prof. surgery N.Y. Med. Coll., 1981-86, prof. emeritus, 1986—; pvt. practice, 1935-86; chmn. Med. Group Coun. Health Ins. Plan of Greater N.Y., 1947-64; cons. Office and Profl. Employees Internat. Union (Local 153) Health Plan, 1960-82, United Automobile Workers (Local 259) Health Plan, 1960-86, Sanitationmen's Security Benefit Fund, 1964-83; dir. Surgery Internat. Ladies Garment Workers Union, 1970-85; med. adv. bd. Hotel Assn. and Hotel Workers Health Plan, 1950-60, Hosp. Workers Health Plan, 1970-76; past bd. dirs. Health Ins. Plan of Greater N.Y. Author and/or editor: Group Medicine and Health Insurance in Action, 1949, Understanding Surgery, 1955, New Illustrated Med. Ency., 4 vols., 1959, New Am. Med. Dictionary and Health Manual, 1962, Reoperative Surgery, 1964, Health in Later Years, 1964, Child Care Ency., 12 vols., 1966, Doctor's Premarital Medical Adviser, 1969, The Fast Diet Book, 1970, The Unabridged Medical Encyclopedia, 20 vols., 1973, Our Family Medical Record Book, 1973, The Complete Surgical Guide, 1973, What Every Patient Wants to Know, 1975, The Complete Book of Breast Care, 1975, Disney's Growing Up Healthy, 4 vols., 1975, First Aid—What to Do in an Emergency, 1976, The Plain Language Law Dictionary, 1980; contbr. articles to med. jours. on breast cancer, 1987 and surgical problems in AIDS, 1994. Mem. N.Y. Acad. Scis. Served to lt. col. M.C., AUS, 1942- 45. Recipient Cabrini Gold medal, 1986. Fellow ACS; mem. AMA, Bklyn. Surg. Assn., N.Y. County Med. Soc., Alpha Omega Alpha. Home: 35 Sutton Pl New York NY 10022-2464 also: Monterosso, Camaiore Italy *Truly great ideas are had by a large number of people. Success, however, is limited to the very few who have the ability to carry them out.*

ROTHENBERG, ROBERT PHILIP, public relations counselor; b. N.Y.C., June 5, 1936; s. Robert Edward and Lillian Babette (Lustig) R. BA, Cornell U., 1956; MS, Boston U., 1958. With publicity dept. Columbia Pictures Corp., N.Y.C., 1959-60; asst. to pres., pub. rels. dir. Harry N. Abrams Pub. Co., N.Y.C., 1960-62; press sec. to gubernatorial candidate William R. Anderson Tenn., 1962; with Rowland Co., N.Y.C., 1963-70, v.p., 1965-67, sr. v.p., 1967-70; ptnr., exec. v.p. Robert Marston and Assocs., N.Y.C., 1970-88, sr. exec. v.p., 1978-88, also bd. dirs.; ptnr., pres. Marston and Rothenberg Pub. Affairs, Inc., N.Y.C. and Washington, 1977-88; chmn., pres. Rothenberg Pub. Rels. Comms. Counsel, N.Y.C., 1988—; v.p. Medbook Publs., Inc., 1995—; sr. cons. The Lund Group, Inc. Trustee Mus. of Holography, N.Y.C.; bd. dirs. Found. to Save African Endangered Wildlife; assoc. Nat. Park Found.; counselor Am. Bus. Cancer Rsch. Found., Southport, Conn.; bd. dirs. World Rehab. Fund, N.Y.C.; fellow Met. Mus. of Art, 1990—; pres., chmn., bd. trustees St. Bartholomew's Preservation Found., 1992-95; mem. Blue Hill Troupe, Ltd. With USAFR, 1959-65. Mem. Internat. Soc. Poets, Pride and Alarm Soc., English-Speaking Union. Unitarian. Home and Office: Ste 29B 400 E 54th St Apt 29B New York NY 10022-5169

ROTHENBERGER, DAVID ALBERT, surgeon; b. Sioux Falls, S.D., 1947. MD, Tufts U., 1973. Cert. colon and rectal surgery. Intern St. Paul-Ramsey Med. Ctr., 1973-74, resident gen. surgery, 1974-78; fellow colon rectal surgery U. Minn., Mpls., 1978-79; mem. staff United Hosp., St. Paul; cln. prof. surgery U. Minn., Mpls., chief divsn. colon and rectal surgery; dir. U. Minn. Cancer Ctr., Mpls. Fellow ACS, Am. Soc. Colon and Rectal Surgeons (exec. coun., pres. 1996-97), Am. Surg. Assn., Soc. for Surgery of the Alimentary Tract, Western Surg. Assn. Office: 299 Fort Rd Med Bldg Minneapolis MN 55102-2409

ROTHENBERGER, JACK RENNINGER, clergyman; b. Boyertown, Pa., Oct. 4, 1930; s. Stuart Henry and Beulah (Renninger) R.; m. Jean Delores Schultz, Sept. 8, 1951; children: Susan Marie, Bruce Wayne. BS, Juniata Coll., 1952; MDiv, Hartford Theol. Sem., 1955; STM, Temple U., 1962; D Ministry, Lancaster Theol. Sem., 1977. Ordained to ministry Schwenkfelder Ch., 1955. Pastor Palm and Lansdale (Pa.) Schwenkfelder Ch., 1955-63, 65-66; stated supply, interim pastor Pa. United Ch. of Christ, 1963-69; chaplain, tchr., coach, dir. admissions Perkiomen Sch., Pennsburg, Pa., 1955-56, 62-67, asst. headmaster, headmaster, coach football backfield, basketball, 1967-69; min. Christian edn. Cen. Schwenkfelder Ch., Worcester, Pa., 1969-74, sr. min., 1974-95; ret., 1995; pres. World Christian Endeavor, 1994—, Internat. Christian Endeavor, Columbus, Ohio, 1983-87; v.p. World Christian Endeavor, 1990-94; mem. cabinet and bd. Pa. Coun. Chs., 1957—, sec., 1993—; mem. Pa. Conf. Interch. Coop.; mem. Schwenckfeld Mission Bd., 1957—, Schwenckfelder Bd. Pubs., 1957—, Schwenckfelder Libr. Bd., 1957—, Schwenckfeldian in Exile Soc., 1955—, also others. Author: Casper Schwenckfeld and the Ecumenical Ideal, 1962; editor The Schwenckfeldion mag., 1964-87; contbr. articles to profl. jours. First v.p. Schwenckfeld Manor, Lansdale, 1973—; v.p. Meadowood Total Care Retirement Community, Worcester, Pa., 1983—. Mem. No. Pa. Assn. United Ch. of Christ Ministerium, No. Pa. Ministerium, Methacton Area Ministerium, Montgomery County Sunday Sch. Assn., also others. Republican. Home: 3914 Gate House Ln Skippack PA 19474 Office: World Christian Endeavor 3575 Valley Rd Box 820 Liberty Corner NJ 07938-0820 *I extend the hand of fellowship to all believers in the Living Christ regardless of their specific expression of that faith. In a world of constant rapid change we can find direction through faith in the Living God revealed by Jesus.*

ROTHERHAM, LARRY CHARLES, insurance executive; b. Council Bluffs, Iowa, Oct. 22, 1940; s. Charles Sylvester and Edna Mary (Sylvanus) R.; m. Florene F. Black, May 29, 1965; children: Christopher Charles, Phillip Larry, Kathleen Florene. Student, Creighton U., 1959-61; BSBA, U. Nebr., 1965; postgrad., Am. Coll., Bryn Mawr, Pa., 1985, 87. CPCU, CLU, ARM. Claims rep. and underwriter Safeco Ins. Co., Albuquerque, New Mex., 1965-69; br. mgr. Ohio Casualty Group, Albuquerque, 1969—; assoc. in risk mgmt. Ins. Inst. Am., 1976—. Mem. PTA Collet Park Elem. Sch., Albuquerque, 1963-82, Freedom H.S., Albuquerque, 1982-86; bd. chmn. N.Mex. Property Ins. Program; mem. N.Mex. Workers compensation Appeals Bd. Mem. New Mex. Soc. Chartered Property & Casualty Underwriters (charter mem., pres. 1975-77), New Mex. Soc. Chartered Life Underwriters, New Mex. Ins. Assn. Democrat. Roman Catholic. Avocations: race walking, swimming, hiking, camping. Home: 2112 Gretta St NE Albuquerque NM 87112-3238 Office: Ohio Casualty Group 10400 Academy Rd NE Ste 200 Albuquerque NM 87111-7365

ROTHERMEL, DANIEL KROTT, lawyer, holding company executive; b. West Reading, Pa., Mar. 21, 1938; s. Daniel Grim and Ruth Elizabeth (Krott) R.; m. Sarah Finch, July 9, 1960; children: Anne, Daniel F., K. Melissa. BS, Pa. State U., 1960; JD, Am. U., 1966. Bar: D.C. 1967. Acct. Lukens Steel Co., Coatesville, Pa., 1960-61; pvt. practice Reading, Pa., 1966-68; atty. Carpenter Tech. Corp., Reading, 1968-70, resident counsel, 1970-78, asst. sec., 1972-73, sec., 1973-88, v.p., gen. counsel, sec., 1978-88; pres., chief exec. officer Cumru Assocs. Inc., Reading, Pa., 1989—; bd. dirs. Sovereign Bank, Sovereign Bancorp, Inc. Mem. Inst. Cmty. Affairs, Pa. State U., 1974-78; bd. dirs. Berks County chpt. ARC, 1983-86; mem., chmn. adv. bd. Berks campus Pa. State U., 1982—; ch. lay leader. Lt. USNR, 1961-66. Mem. ABA, D.C. Bar Assn., Am. Soc. Corp. Secs., U.S. C. of C., Pa. C. of C., Reading-Berks C. of C., Rotary. Republican. Lutheran. Home: 20 Glenbrook Dr Reading PA 19607-9645 Office: Cumru Assocs Inc PO Box 6573 Reading PA 19610-0573

ROTHERY, CHET, business executive; b. Washington, Feb. 5, 1955; s. Chester Grogan Sr. and Mary (Tomlinson) R. BA in Mgmt., Nat. Louis U., McLean, Va., 1990. Sys. analyst Technology Applications Inc., Alexandria, Va., 1983-86; user svcs. con. Fin. Techs., Chantilly, Va., 1986-88, mgmt. analyst, 1988-89, sr. account rep., 1989-90, product support mgr., 1990-91, bus. devel. specialist, 1991-92; bus. sys. analyst Cable/Wireless, Inc., Vienna, Va., 1993-95, enterprise project mgr., 1995-96, sr. mgr. bus. improvement, 1996—. Sec. Concord Mews Civic Assn., Arlington, Va., 1988-90, pres., 1990-91. Mem. Soc. for Tech. Comm. (Excellence award 1990, Merit award 1994). Avocations: Japanese gardening, biking. Home: 4013 19th St S Arlington VA 22204-5115 Office: Cable/Wireless Inc 8219 Leesburg Pike Vienna VA 22182-2625

ROTHFELD, MICHAEL B., investment principal; b. N.Y.C., May 19, 1947; m. Ella M. Foshay, May 2, 1970; 2 children. BA, Columbia U., 1969, MS, 1971, MBA, 1971, cert. internatl fellows program, 1971. With Time, Inc., 1971-76; assoc. editor Fortune Time, Inc., N.Y.C., 1971-74; asst. to chmn. bd. dirs., CEO Time Inc., N.Y.C., 1974-76; with Salomon Bros., N.Y.C., 1976-83, v.p., 1979-83; v.p. The First Boston Corp., N.Y.C., 1983-84, mng. dir., 1985-89; gen. ptnr. Bessemer Ptnrs. and Bessemer Holdings, 1989—; chmn. bd. dirs. Graphic Controls Corp., 1995—; bd. dirs. Contour Prodn. Co., Kelley Oil and Gas Corp. Office: Bessemer Ptnrs & Co 630 5th Ave Fl 39 New York NY 10111-0100

ROTHFIELD, LAWRENCE I., microbiology educator; b. N.Y.C., Dec. 30, 1927; s. Joseph and Henrietta (Brown) R.; m. Naomi Fox, Sept. 18, 1953; children: Susan Anne, Lawrence, Jane, John. BA, Cornell U., 1947; MD, NYU, 1951. Intern, then resident Bellevue, Presbyn. hosps., N.Y.C., 1951-53, 55-57; successively instr., clin. asst. prof., asst. prof. NYU Sch. Medicine, 1957-64; from asst. prof. to assoc. prof. Albert Einstein Coll. Medicine, N.Y.C., 1964-68; prof. U. Conn. Sch. Medicine, Farmington, 1968—, chmn. dept. microbiology, 1968-80; mem. molecular biology rev. panel NIH, 1970-75, microbiology and immunology adv. com. Pres.'s Biomed. Rsch. Panel, 1975, molecular biology rev. panel NSF, 1979-83; mem. microbial physiology and genetics rev. panel NIH, 1990-94, chairperson, 1991-93. Author: Structure and Function of Biological Membranes, 1972; mem. editorial bd. Jour. Membrane Biology, 1969-83, Jour. Biol. Chemistry, 1974-80. With M.C. U.S. Army, 1953-55. Mem. Am. Soc. Biol. Chemists, Am. Soc. Microbiology (chmn. microbial physiology div. 1975). Home: 540 Deercliff Rd Avon CT 06001-2859 Office: U Conn Health Center Farmington CT 06032

ROTHFIELD, NAOMI FOX, physician; b. Bklyn., Apr. 5, 1929; d. Morris and Violet (Bloomgarden) Fox; m. Lawrence Rothfield, Sept. 18, 1954; children—Susan, Lawrence, John, Jane. B.A., Bard Coll., 1950; M.D., N.Y. U., 1955. Intern Lenox Hill Hosp., N.Y.C., 1955-56; instr. N.Y. U. Sch. Medicine, 1956-62, asst. prof., 1962-68; assoc. prof. U. Conn. Sch. Medicine, Farmington, 1968-72; prof., chief div. rheumatic diseases U. Conn. Sch. Medicine, 1972—. Contbr. chpts. to books; contbr. articles to med. jours. Mem. Am. Soc. Clin. Investigation, Am. Rheumatism Assn., Assn. Am. Physics. Jewish. Home: 540 Deercliff Rd Avon CT 06001-2859 Office: U Conn Sch Medicine Div of Rheumatic Diseases Farmington CT 06030

ROTHHOLZ, PETER LUTZ, public relations executive; b. Berlin, June 23, 1929; came to U.S., 1945, naturalized, 1947; s. Alfred and Bertha (Isner) R.; m. Paula Trachtman, Sept. 16, 1951; 1 dau., Amy Elisabeth (dec.); m. Barbara Peters Margules, July 4, 1971; stepchildren: David, Thomas. B.A., Queens Coll., 1950; postgrad., N.Y. U., 1956-60; certificates, U. London, 1949, McGill U., 1950. With Lissone-Lindeman U.S., Inc., N.Y.C., 1953-56, KLM Royal Dutch Airlines, N.Y.C., 1956-61; exec. v.p. Simmons Tours, Inc., N.Y.C., 1961-62; pres., prin. Peter Rothholz Assocs., Inc., N.Y.C., 1962—; mem. faculty div. bus. mgmt. Sch. Continuing Edn. N.Y. U., 1969-70; mem. faculty Queens Coll., 1992—; former mem. exec. com. pacific Asia Travel Assn., Caribbean Tourism Orgn. Contbr. articles to various publs. Bd. dirs. Queens Coll. Found., 1973-94, Nat. Coun. on Aging. With U.S. Army, 1951-52. Fellow Inst. Certified Travel Agts; mem. Pub. Relations Soc. Am., Soc. Am. Travel Writers, Queens Mus. (pres. 1977-78, chmn. 1978-80), Queens Coll. Alumni Assn. (pres. 1973-75), Phi Alpha Theta. Club: N.Y. Publicity (past v.p., dir.). Home: 55 Squaw Rd East Hampton NY 11937-4510 Office: Peter Rothholz Assocs Inc 355 Lexington Ave New York NY 10017-6603

ROTHING, FRANK JOHN, government official; b. Chgo., July 4, 1924; s. Frank Joseph and Eva A. (Buhl) R.; m. Carita Reiss Corbett, June 16, 1951; children: Frank John, Reginald, Peter, James, Richard, Joseph, Thomas, Carita Ann. B.S., U. Notre Dame, 1948. C.P.A., U. Ill., 1954. Pub. accountant Arthur Young & Co., Chgo., 1948-55; v.p. Midwest Stock Exchange, 1955-60, v.p., treas., 1960-66, sr. v.p., 1966-71; exec. v.p., sec., dir. Ill. Co., 1971-74; v.p. 1st Nat. Bank Chgo., 1974-75; exec. v.p. Front St. Securities, Inc., 1975-78; mem. Chgo. Office SEC, 1978, ret., 1989; chmn. bd. Chgo. Bd. Options Exchange Clearing Corp.; mem. Chgo. Bd. Trade. Adviser Jr. Achievement Chgo.; bd. dirs. St. Elizabeth's Hosp., Chgo.; mem. citizens bd. U. Chgo.; bd. dirs., mem. exec. bd. North Shore Area Boy Scouts Am.; chmn. bd. trustees St. Mary of Woods Coll., Terre Haute, Ind. Served to 1st lt. USAAF, 1943-45. Decorated D.F.C., Air medal. Mem. VFW, Am. Legion, Am. Inst. Accountants, Ill. Soc. C.P.A.s, Am. Accounting Assn., Newcomen Soc., Navy League U.S. Clubs: Michigan Shores; Bond of Chicago (dir.), Economic, Chgo. Athletic, Notre Dame (dir.), Attic (Chgo.).

ROTHKOPF, ARTHUR J., college president; b. N.Y.C., May 24, 1935; s. Abraham and Sarah (Mehlman) R.; m. Barbara Sarnoff, Dec. 25, 1958; children: Jennifer, Katherine. AB, Lafayette Coll., 1955; JD, Harvard U., 1958. Bar: N.Y. 1959, D.C. 1967. Atty. U.S. Dept. Treasury, N.Y.C., 1958-60, SEC, Washington, 1960-63; assoc. tax legis. counsel U.S. Dept. Treasury, Washington, 1963-66; ptnr. Hogan & Hartson, Washington, 1967-91; gen. counsel U.S. Dept. Transp., Washington, 1991-92, dep. sec., 1992-93; pres. Lafayette Coll., Easton, Pa., 1993—; dir. Ins. Svcs. Office, Inc., N.Y.C., 1993—. Trustee Fed. City Coun., Washington, 1983-91, Lehigh Valley Hosp; dir. Lehigh-Northampton (Pa.) Airport Authority, Assn. Ind. Colls. and Univs. Pa., Easton (Pa.) Econ. Devel. Corp., 1993—, Lehigh Valley Econ. Devel. Corp., 1995—; adv. bd. Nat. Mus. Indsl. History. Mem. Met. Club of Washington, Chevy Chase Club, Harvard Club of N.Y.C. Jewish. Home: 515 College Ave Easton PA 18042 Office: Lafayette Coll 316 Markle Hall Easton PA 18042

ROTHKOPF, DAVID JOCHANAN, federal official; b. Urbana, Ill., Dec. 24, 1955; s. Ernst Zacharias and Carol Louise (Zeman) R.; m. Jane Octavia Prelinger, Dec. 14, 1985; children: Joanna Susan, Laura Madeleine. BA, Columbia U., 1977, postgrad., 1977-78. Press sec. Office of Congressman Stephen J. Solarz, Washington, 1979-80; sr. v.p. Tilley, Marlieb & Alan, Inc., N.Y.C., 1980-82; coord. prodr. TV Series-Omni: The New Frontier, N.Y.C., 1980-82; exec. prodr. PBS Series-Flashpoint, Newark, 1984; v.p. Fin. World Mag., N.Y.C., 1984-85; v.p., pub. spl. pubs. Instnl. Investor, Inc., N.Y.C., 1985-87; chmn., CEO Internat. Media Ptnrs., Inc., N.Y.C., 1987-93; dep. under sec. commerce for internat. trade policy devel. U.S. Dept. Commerce, Washington, 1993-95, acting under sec. commerce for internat. trade, 1995-96; mng. dir. Kissinger Assocs., Inc., N.Y.C. and Washington, 1996—; adj. prof. internat. affairs Columbia U. Sch. of Internat. and Pub. Affairs, 1996—; vis. assoc. Carnegie Endowment for Internat. Peace, 1996—; CEO, chmn., The CEO Insts., N.Y.C., 1987-93. Author: The Common Market, 1978; editor Global Money Mgmt. Forum, 1986-87, Global Capital Markets Forum, 1986-87; editor-in-chief CEO/Internat. Strategies Mag., 1989-93, Emerging Markets Newspapers, 1987-93, World Market Outlook, 1991-93, Nat. Conv. News, 1992. Mem. Coun. Fgn. Rels., Columbia Club. Democrat. Jewish. Office: 350 Park Ave New York NY 10022-6022 also: 1800 K St Washington DC 20007

ROTHLISBERGER, RODNEY JOHN, music educator; b. Bottineau, N.D., May 13, 1940; s. Forrest John and Ellen Rothlisberger; m. Gay Elaine Mohr, Dec. 20, 1975 (div.). BA, St. Olaf Coll., 1962; MA, Eastman Sch. Music, 1967; DMusA, U. Colo., 1978. Organist, choirmaster U.S. Mil. Acad., West Point, N.Y., 1965-67; instr., prof. Bowdoin Coll., Brunswick, Maine, 1967-70; instr. Melbourne (Australia) H.S., 1973-75; prof. Berea (Ky.) Coll., 1976-77; instr. Concordia Coll., Moorhead, Minn., 1979-81, Moorhead Pub. Schs., 1989-95; prof. Moorhead State U., 1995—. Bd. dirs. Red River Boy Choir, Moorhead, 1984—, Arts Coun., Moorhead, 1985-89, Luth. Brotherhood, Moorhead, 1988—; mem. Civic Opera Bd., 1996—. With U.S. Army, 1985-87. Recipient Achievement award Lake Agassiz Arts Coun., 1987. Mem. Am. Choral Dirs. Assn., Music Educators Nat. Conf., Coll. Music Soc., Am. Guild Organists (dean Red River Valley chpt. 1985-87, Minn. state chair 1995—). Presbyterian. Avocation: reading. Home: 1021 River Dr Moorhead MN 56560-3369 Office: Moorhead State U 1104 7th Ave S Moorhead MN 56563-0001

ROTHMAN, BARBARA SCHAEFFER, education director; b. Bklyn., Sept. 29, 1934; d. Samuel and Edythe (Manuta) Schaeffer; m. Bernard Rothman, Aug. 23, 1953; children: Brian, Adam, Helene. BS, SUNY, New Paltz, 1955; MS, Coll. New Rochelle, 1979. Cert. sch. adminstrn., supervision, N.Y. State Dept. Edn. Tchr. N.Y.C. Bd. Edn., 1955-75, with child program, 1975-77, placement officer dist. 7, 8, 1978-80, chpt. 53 supr. dist. 8, 1980-83, supr. pupil personell dist. 8, 1983-85, asst. chairperson Com. of Handicapped dist. 11, 1985-89; educational evaluator N.Y. Bd. Edn., 1977-78; educational dir. Western Queens (N.Y.) Devel. Sch., 1989—; adj. faculty Coll. New Rochelle, N.Y., 1980-85, Lehman Coll., Bronx, N.Y., 1982; mem. pre-sch. task force Bd. Edn., 1991—, Queens regional pre-sch. task force, N.Y.C., 1995—. Chair voter svc. League Women Voters, S.I., N.Y., 1968; neighbor adv. com. Group Home, Larchmont, N.Y., 1985-87; pres. Westchester Symphony Orch., Harrison, N.Y., 1986-88; past pres. sisterhood B'Nai Israel, S.I.; chmn. Handicapped Boy Scouts Am., White Plains, N.Y., 1985; corr. sec. N.Y. City Coalition Children with Special Needs, 1992-96. Avocations: reading, classical music, walking. Home: 7 Bayard St Larchmont NY 10538 Office: 10-24 49th Ave Long Island City NY 11101

ROTHMAN, BERNARD, lawyer; b. N.Y.C., Aug. 11, 1932; s. Harry and Rebecca (Fritz) R.; m. Barbara Joan Schaeffer, Aug. 1953; children: Brian, Adam, Helene. BA cum laude, CCNY, 1953; LLB, NYU, 1959. Bar: N.Y. 1959, U.S Dist. Ct. (ea. and so. dists.) N.Y. 1962, U.S. Ct. Apls. (2d cir.) 1965, U.S. Supreme Ct. 1966, U.S. Tax Ct. 1971. Assoc. Held, Telchin & Held, 1961-62; asst. U.S. atty. U.S. Dept. Justice, 1962-66; assoc. Edward Gettinger & Peter Gettinger, 1966-68; ptnr. Schwartz, Rothman & Abrams, P.C., 1968-78; ptnr. Finkelstein, Bruckman, Wohl, Most & Rothman, LLP, N.Y.C., 1978—; acting judge Village of Larchmont, 1982-88, dep. Village atty., 1974-81, former arbitrator Civil Ct. N.Y.C., family disputes panel Am. Arbitration Assn., guest lectr. domestic rels. and family law on radio and TV, also numerous legal and mental health orgns. Author: Loving and Leaving-Winning at the Business of Divorce, 1991; co-author: Family Law Syracuse Law Rev. of N.Y. Law, 1992, Leaving Home, Family Law Review, 1987; contbr. articles to profl. jours. Mem. exec. bd., past v.p. Westchester Putnam coun. Boy Scouts Am., 1975—; past mem. nat. coun., 1977-81; mem. N.Y. State PEACE Adv. Commn., 1991—. Recipient Silver Beaver award Boy Scouts Am., Wood Badge award; pres. Congregation B'nai Israel, 1961-63, B'nai Brith, Larchmont chpt., 1981-83. Fellow Am. Acad. Matrimonial Lawyers (bd. govs. N.Y. chpt. 1986-87, 91-93), Interdisciplinary Forum on Mental Health and Family Law (co-chair 1986—); mem. ABA (family law sect.), N.Y. State Bar Assn. (exec. com. family law sect. 1982—, co-chmn. com. on mediation and arbitration 1982-88, 93—, com. on legis. 1978-88, com. on child custody 1985-88, com. alternative dispute resolution, peace adv. com.), Assn. of Bar of City of N.Y. (mem. women in the courts com. 1996—), N.Y. State Magistrate Assn., Westchestr Magistrate Assn., N.Y. Road Runners Club, Limousine 6 Track Club. Democrat. Office: Finkelstein Bruckman Wohl Most & Rothman LLP 575 Lexington Ave New York NY 10022-6102

ROTHMAN, DAVID J., history and medical educator; b. N.Y.C., Apr. 30, 1937; s. Murray and Anne (Beier) R.; m. Sheila Miller, June 26, 1960; children: Matthew, Micol. B.A., Columbia U., 1958; M.A., Harvard U., 1959, Ph.D., 1964. Asst. prof. history Columbia U., N.Y.C., 1964-67; assoc. prof. Columbia U., 1967-71, prof., 1971—, Bernard Schoenberg prof. social medicine, dir. Ctr. for Study of Society and Medicine; Fulbright-Hayes prof. Hebrew U., Jerusalem, 1968-69, India, 1982; vis. Pinkerton Prof. Sch. Criminal Justice, State U. N.Y., at Albany, 1973-74; Samuel Paley lectr. Hebrew U., Jerusalem, 1977; Mem. Com. for Study of Incarceration, 1971-74; co-dir. Project on Community Alternatives, 1978-82; chmn. adv. bd. on criminal justice Clark Found., 1978-82; mem. bd. advisors The Project on Death in Am., Open Soc. Inst., 1995—, trustee; mem. bd. trustees Open Soc. Inst., 1996—. Author: Politics and Power, 1966, The Discovery of the Asylum, 1971; co-author: Doing Good, 1978, Conscience and Convenience: The Asylum and its Alternatives in Progressive America, 1980; (with Sheila M. Rothman) The Willowbrook Wars, 1984; Strangers at the Bedside, 1991, Beginings Count: The Technological Imperative in American Health Care, 1997, Beginnings Count: The Technological Imperative in AMerican Health Care, 1997; Editor: The World of the Adams Chronicles, 1976, (with Sheila M. Rothman) On Their Own: The Poor in Modern America, 1972, The Sources of American Social Tradition, 1975, (with Stanton Wheeler) Social History and Social Policy, 1981, (with Norval Morris) The Oxford History of the Prison, 1995, (with Steven Marcus and Stephanie Kiceluk) Medicine and Western Civilization, 1995. Bd. dirs. Mental Health Law Project, 1973-80, 82—. Recipient Albert J. Beveridge prize Am. Hist. Assn., 1971. Mem. Am. Hist. Assn., Orgn. Am. Historians, N.Y. Acad. Medicine, Phi Beta Kappa. Office: Columbia U Coll Physicians and Surgeons Ctr Study Soc and Medicine 630 W 168th St New York NY 10032-3702

ROTHMAN, FRANK, lawyer, motion picture company executive; b. Los Angeles, Dec. 24, 1926; s. Leon and Rose (Gendel) R.; m. Mariana Richardson, Aug. 7, 1985; children: Steven, Robin, Susan. B.A., U. So. Calif., 1949, LL.B., 1951. Bar: Calif. 1952, D.C., U.S. Dist. Ct. (cen. dist.) Calif. 1951. Dep. city atty. City of Los Angeles, 1951-55; mem. law firm Wyman, Bautzer, Rothman, Kuchel & Silbert, Los Angeles, 1956-82; chmn. bd., chief exec. officer MGM-UA Entertainment Co., Culver City, Calif., 1982-86; ptnr. Skadden Arps Slate, L.A., 1986—. Bd. editors U. So. Calif. Law Rev., 1948. Served with USAAF, 1945-46. Fellow Am. Coll. Trial Lawyers; mem. L.A. Bar Assn., Calif. Bar Assn., Univ. Club. Democrat. Home: 10555 Rocca Pl Los Angeles CA 90077-2904 Office: Skadden Arps Slate 300 S Grand Ave Bldg 3400 Los Angeles CA 90071-3109

ROTHMAN, FRANK GEORGE, biology educator, biochemical genetics researcher; b. Budapest, Hungary, Feb. 2, 1930; came to U.S., 1938; s. Stephen and Irene Elizabeth (Manheim) R.; m. Joan Therese Kiernan, Aug.22, 1953; children: Michael, Jean, Stephen, Maria. BA, U. Chgo., 1948, MS, 1951; PhD, Harvard U., 1955. Postdoctoral fellow NSF, U. Wis., MIT, 1956-58, Am. Cancer Soc., MIT, Cambridge, 1958-59; postdoctoral assoc. MIT, Cambridge, 1957-61; asst. prof. Brown U., Providence, 1961-65, assoc. prof., 1965-70, prof., 1970—, dean of biology, 1984-90, provost, 1990-95. Contbr. articles to profl. jours. Served with U.S. Army, 1954-56. Spl. fellow USPHS, U. Sussex, Eng., 1967-68; NSF grantee, 1961-84. Fellow AAAS; mem. Genetics Soc. Am. Office: Brown U Box G-J119 Providence RI 02912

ROTHMAN, HENRY ISAAC, lawyer; b. Rochester, N.Y., Mar. 29, 1943; s. Maurice M. and Golde (Nusbaum) R.; m. Golda R. Shatz, July 3, 1966; children: Alan, Miriam, Cheryl, Suri. BA, Yeshiva U., 1964; JD, Cornell U., 1967. Bar: N.Y. 1967. Trial atty. SEC, N.Y.C., 1967-69; ptnr. Booth, Lipton & Lipton, N.Y.C., 1969-87, Parker, Chapin, Flattau & Klimpl, N.Y.C., 1987—. Bd. dirs. Camp Morasha, Lake Como, Pa., 1982—, vice chmn., 1992—; bd. dirs. Assn. of Jewish Sponsored Camps, Inc., 1986—; bd. dirs. Yeshiva U. High Schs., N.Y.C., 1984—, vice chmn. bd., 1990-91, chmn. bd., 1992-95; v.p. Manhattan Day Sch., N.Y.C., 1985-96, bd. dirs.; assoc. v.p. Orthodox Union, N.Y.C., 1990—. Mem. ABA (com. on fed. regulation of securities), N.Y. State Bar Assn., Assn. of Bar of City of N.Y., Nat. Assn. Hebrew Day Schs., Yeshiva U. Alumni Assn. (pres. 1986-88, hon. pres. 1988-90). Office: Parker Chapin Flattau & Klimpl LLP 1211 Avenue Of The Americas New York NY 10036-8701

ROTHMAN, HOWARD JOEL, lawyer; b. N.Y.C., July 10, 1945; s. Samuel and Avy (Avrutin) R.; m. Joan Andrea Solomon, July 2, 1967; children: Samantha, Rodney. BA, CCNY, 1967; JD, Bklyn. Law Sch., 1971; LLM, NYU, 1972. Bar: N.Y. 1972. From assoc. to ptnr. Marshall, Bratter, Greene, Allison & Tucker, N.Y.C., 1972-82; ptnr. Rosenman & Colin LLP, N.Y.C., 1982-97, Kramer, Levin, Naftalis & Frankel, N.Y.C., 1997—; mem. adv. panel Commr. Fin. of City of N.Y., 1981-83. Author profl. books and articles. Bd. dirs. Alliance Resident Theatres N.Y., 1989-96. Mem. ABA (corp. tax. com. 1977-87, income from real property com. 1980—), Internat. Bar Assn., N.Y. State Bar Assn. (corps. com. 1979-87, partnerships com. 1979—, N.Y.C. tax matters com. 1977—, income from real property com. 1987—), Bur. Nat. Affairs (real estate jour. 1984—, tax mgmt. adv. bd. 1979—), Alliance Resident Theatres N.Y. (bd. dirs. 1989-96), Alliance for Young Artists and Writers (bd. dirs. 1994—), Poetry Soc. Am. (bd. dirs.). Office: Kramer Levin Naftalis & Frankel 575 Madison Ave New York NY 10022-2511

ROTHMAN, MARTIN, finance company executive, accountant; b. N.Y.C., June 26, 1946; s. Seymour and Ethel (Swirson) R.; children: Jason David, Heather Michelle. BBA, Pace U., 1968. CPA, N.Y. Sr. acct. Ernst & Young, N.Y.C., 1968-72; audit mgr. Eisner & Lubin, CPAs, N.Y.C., 1972-79; exec. v.p., treas., bd. dirs. Orix Comml. Alliance Corp., N.Y.C., 1979—. Mem. AICPAs, N.Y. State Soc. CPAs. Avocations: aerobics, weight training, reading, theater, travel. Office: Orix Comml Alliance Corp 300 Lighting Way Secaucus NJ 07094-3622

ROTHMAN, MELVIN L., judge; b. Montreal, Que., Can., Apr. 6, 1930; s. Charles and Nellie (Rosen) R.; m. Joan Elizabeth Present, Aug. 4, 1954; children: Ann Elizabeth, Claire Present, Margot Sneyd. B.A., McGill U., 1951, B.C.L., 1954. Bar: Que. 1954. Practice law Montreal, 1954-71; mem. Phillips, Vineberg, Goodman, Phillips & Rothman; judge Superior Ct., Dist. of Montreal, 1971-83, Ct. Appeal of Que., 1983—. Mem. Jr. Bar of Montreal (pres. 1963-64), Bar of Montreal (council 1964-65), Institut Philippe Pinel (sec., dir. 1965-70). Home: 487 Argyle Ave, Westmount, PQ Canada H3Y 3B3 Office: Que Ct of Appeal, Court House, 10 St Antoine St E, Montreal, PQ Canada

ROTHMAN, MICHAEL JUDAH, lawyer; b. Mpls., June 7, 1962; s. Harvey Michael and Elaine Louise (London) R.; m. Shari Latz, Aug. 1, 1993. BA, Carleton Coll., 1984; JD, U. Minn., 1988. Bar: Minn. 1988, U.S. Dist. Ct. Minn. 1988, Calif. 1993, U.S. Dist. Ct. (ctrl. dist.) Calif. 1993, U.S. Ct. Appeals (9th cir.) 1995, U.S. Supreme Ct. 1995. Law clk. to J. Gary Crippen Minn. Ct. of Appeals, St. Paul, 1988-89; adminstrv. asst. Minn. State Senate, St. Paul, 1989-92; atty. Rubenstein & Perry, L.A., 1993-95, Loeb & Loeb, L.A., 1995-96; assoc. Barger & Wolen, LLP, L.A., 1996—. Vol. atty. F.A.M.E. Ch. and Temple Isaiah Legal Project, L.A., 1994-96. Recipient Best Brief award Regional Internat. Moot Ct. Competition, Colo., 1988. Mem. ABA, Calif. Bar Assn., L.A. County Bar Assn. Democrat. Avocations: golf, running, reading. Office: Barger & Wolen 515 S Flower St Fl 34 Los Angeles CA 90071-2201

ROTHMAN, STEVEN R., lawyer; b. Englewood, N.J., Oct. 14, 1952; divorced; 2 children. BA, Syracuse U., 1974; JD, Washington U., 1977. Pvt. practice law, 1978-93; judge Bergen County's Surrogate's Ct., 1993-96; mem. 105th Congress from 9th N.J. dist., 1997—. Mayor City of Englewood, 1983-89; Dem. nominee for Bergen County Freeholder, 1989; Dem. candidate for U.S. House 9th dist., N.J., 1996. Jewish. Office: US Ho Reps 1607 Longworth Bldg Washington DC 20515

ROTHMAN-DENES, LUCIA BEATRIZ, biology educator; b. Buenos Aires, Feb. 17, 1943; came to U.S., 1967; d. Boris and Carmen (Couto) Rothman; m. Pablo Denes, May 24, 1968; children: Christian Andrew, Anne Elizabeth. Lic. in Chemistry, Sch. Scis., U. Buenos Aires, 1964, PhD in Biochemistry, 1967. Vis. fellow NIH, Bethesda, Md., 1967-70; postdoctoral fellow biophysics U. Chgo., 1970-73, rsch. assoc., 1973-74, from asst. prof. to assoc. prof., 1974-83, prof. molecular genetics and cell biology, 1983—; mem. microbial genetics study sect. NIH, 1980-83, 93-96, chair, 1994-96, genetic basis of disease study sect., 1985-89; mem. Damon Runyon and Walter Winchell Sci. Adv. Com., N.Y.C., 1989-93; mem. biochemistry panel NSF, 1990-92. Contbr. articles to profl. jours. Fellow Am. Acad. Microbiology; mem. AAAS, Am. Soc. Microbiology (divsn. chair 1985, divsn. group II rep. 1990-92, vice chair GMPC 1995—), Am. Soc. Virology (councilor 1987-90), Am. Soc. Biochemistry and Molecular Biology. Office: Univ Chgo 920 E 58th St Chicago IL 60637-1432

ROTHMAN-MARSHALL, GAIL ANN, counseling services administrator; b. Rochester, N.Y., June 25, 1944; d. Herman Tony and Grace Helen (Fortuna) Giancola; m. Michael Frederick Rothman, Feb. 6, 1967 (div. 1977); m. Gerald Francis Marshall, Feb. 26, 1995. BA, SUNY, Albany, 1970; MS, SUNY, Brockport, 1976; PhD, SUNY, Buffalo, 1989. Cert. clin. mental health counselor, cert. fitness profl. Dance and drama instr. Baden St. Settlement, Rochester, N.Y., 1968-69; day care ctr. instr. Action for a Better Community, Rochester, N.Y., 1968-70; sr. residential counselor Rochester Sch. for the Deaf, 1970-74; interpreter Rochester Inst. of Tech., 1974-75, counselor, 1975-79, chairperson of counseling svcs., 1979—, diagnostician learning assessment team, 1987-90; sign and content expert Nat. Tech. Inst. for the Deaf, Rochester, 1983; part-time adj. prof. psychology Coll. Liberal Arts Rochester Inst. Tech., 1990-93, 94—, part-time adj. prof. aerobics dept. phys. edn. and recreation, 1992—; mem. activity faculty Am. Jour. Health Promotion Conf., 1994; presenter comms. workshops, symposiums on learning style, student retention. assessment and outcomes in counseling. Contbr. articles to profl. jours. Program com. co-chmn. Niagara Assn. for Psychol. Type, Rochester, 1986-88; chaperone, vol. Spl. Olympics, Rochester, 1989, 90, tenure com. chmn., 1991-94. Sch. of Visual Comms. grantee, 1986, 89, 93, Ctr. for Student Resources grantee, 1994. Mem. Am. Counseling Assn., Assn. for Psychol. Type, Am. Coll. Pers. Assn., Assn. for Counselor Edn. and Supervision, Am. Mental Health Counselors Assn., Nat. Career Devel. Assn., Aerobic Fitness Assn. Am. Avocations: teaching aerobics, internet, skiing, dancing, crafts. Home: 61 Marquette Dr Rochester NY 14618-5613 Office: Rochester Inst of Tech Johnson Bldg 52 Lomb Memorial Dr Rochester NY 14623-5604

ROTHMANN, BRUCE FRANKLIN, pediatric surgeon; b. Akron, Ohio, July 11, 1924; s. Edwin Franklin Rothmann and Mary Madoline Policy; m. Lola May Secor, June 14, 1947; children: Susan Ann, Pamela Jane, Elizabeth Rothmann Rusnak. Student, Case Western Reserve U., 1942-43, Wesleyan U., 1943-44; MD, NYU, 1948. Diplomate Am. Bd. Surgery. Intern Akron City Hosp., 1948-49, from resident in surgery to chief resident surgeon, 1949-55; from resident pediatric surgeon to chief staff Children's Hosp., Akron, 1953-74; pvt. practice in surgery Akron, 1955, pvt. practice in pediatric surgery, 1968—; clin. instr. Case Western Reserve U., Cleve. 1962-64, asst. clin prof, 1967--, assoc. clin. prof. pediatric surgery, 1983--, asst. surgeon Univ. Hosp., Cleve. 1962--; cons. in pediatric surgery Akron City Hosp.; v.p. devel. Nat. Invention Ctr., Inc. Contbr. med. articles to profl. jours. Dir. Med. Outreach Children Hosp. Med. Ctr. of Akron, 1986; bd. mgmt. Cuyahoga Falls Comty. YMCA, 1957-63; trustee Akron Symphony Orch., 1959-85, Akron Jr. Achievement, 1980—, First Congl. Ch. Akron, 1960-64; mem. adv. bd. Children's Concert Soc., Akron, 1970—; bd. trustees Children's Family Care, 1984-86, Cuyahoga H.S. Found., 1988—; v.p. fin., mem. exec. bd. Gt. Trail coun. Boy Scouts Am.; mem. Nat. Inventors Hall of Fame, Cleve. Inst. Music. With USN, 1942-45, 50-52. Home: 3020 Kent Rd Cuyahoga Falls OH 44224-3044 Office: 330 Locust St Akron OH 44302-1801

ROTHMEIER, STEVEN GEORGE, merchant banker, investment manager; b. Mankato, Minn., Oct. 4, 1946; s. Edwin George and Alice Joan (Johnson) R. BBA, U. Notre Dame, 1968; MBA, U. Chgo., 1972. Corp. fin. analyst Northwest Airlines, Inc., St. Paul, 1973, mgr. econ. analysis, 1973-78, dir. econ. planning, 1978, v.p. fin., treas., 1978-82, exec. v.p., treas., dir., 1982-83, exec. v.p. fin. and adminstrn., treas., dir., 1983, pres., chief operating officer, 1984, pres., chief exec. officer, 1985-86, chmn., chief exec. officer, 1986-89, also bd. dirs.; pres. IAI Capital Group, Mpls., 1989-93; chmn., CEO Great No. Capital, St. Paul, 1993—; bd. dirs. Honeywell Inc., Precision Castparts, E.W. Blanch Holdings Inc., Dept. 56 Inc. Chmn. St. Agnes Found., Channel 53 Cath. TV Minn. Decorated Bronze Star. Mem. Mpls. Club, Minn. Club, Chgo. Club. Republican. Roman Catholic. Clubs: Mpls.; Minn. Office: Great Northern Capital 332 Minnesota St Ste W 1295 Saint Paul MN 55101-1305 *Success is not an accident; it is a habit. Success is the result of desire, dedication, sacrifice, mental toughness, hard work—and prayer. And you are not successful until you can share your success with others.*

ROTHROCK, ROBERT WILLIAM, physician assistant; b. Phila., Apr. 21, 1955; s. Arthur Andrew and Margaret (Pilkington) R.; m. Maria Donna Marinelli, May 10, 1980; children: Matthew Robert, Tara Nicole. AS with honors, Cmty. Coll. Phila., 1979; BS, Hahnemann U., 1982. Cert. physician assts.; cert. pain mgmt. specialist. Respiratory therapist Jefferson U. Hops., Phila., 1979-80; physician asst. Pennsbury Family Med. Ctr., Morrisville, Pa., 1982-83, Pennsbury Orthop. Medicine Assocs., Morrisville, Pa., 1983-97; physician dept. anesthesia U. Pa. Med. Ctr., Phila., 1997—; mem. admissions com. Physician Asst. Program, Hahnemann U., 1985; cons. World Boxing Assn. Edo Aragua, Venezuela, 1990—. Author: Chronic Pain, 1991, 2d edit., 1992; contbg. author: Minor Head Trauma, 1993, Innovations of Pain Management, 1993; contbg. editor Bucks Fortune Mag., 1988-89; peer reviewer Jour. Am. Acad. Physician Assts., 1992—; contbr. articles to profl. jours. Fellow Am. Acad. Physician Assts.; mem. Am. Acad. Pain Mgmt. (site reviewer 1992—), Phila. Pain Soc., Pa. State Soc. Physician Assts., N.J. State Soc. Physician Assts., Pa. State Soc. Physician Assts., Phi Theta Kappa. Avocations: sports, painting, family activities. Home: 2 Creek Rd Sewell NJ 08080-2720 Office: U Pa Health System Dept Pain Medicine 250 King Of Prussia Rd Radnor PA 19087-5220

ROTHS, BEVERLY OWEN, organization executive; b. Kansas City, Kans., Aug. 25, 1935; d. Edward Charles and Josephine Mary (Vogel) Owen; m. Robert L. Roths, Sept. 4, 1954; children: Karen Kay, Daniel Owen, Nancy Jo. AA with honors, Antelope Valley Coll., 1975. Sec. McDonnell Aircraft Co., St. Louis, 1955-58; exec. dir. Florissant (Mo.) Valley C. of C., 1976-86; pres. Poppy Reserve/Mojave Desert Interpretive Assn., Lancaster, Calif., 1989—; pres. Soroptomist Internat., North St. Louis County, 1981-82; sec.-treas. St. Louis County League C. of C., Clayton, 1978. Prodr. Small Bus. Profiles, condr. interviews Storer Cable TV, Florissant, 1983-86. Mem. Florissant City Coun., 1968-72; bd. dirs. Mo. Mcpl. League First Woman, Florissant, 1970-71; co-chair Bicentennial, Florissant, 1985-86, Police Bldg. Bond Issue, Florissant, 1980. Recipient Woman of Achievement award Florissant Bus. and Profl. Women, 1979; Inst. Orgn. Mgmt. scholar C. of C., Jefferson City, Mo., 1980. Mem. Lancaster Woman's Club., Wildflower Preservation Found. (bd. dirs., treas. 1991—), League Calif. State Park Non-Profit Orgns. (bd. dirs., sec. 1994—). Roman Catholic. Avocations: bird watching, gardening, golf, reading, geneaology. Office: PO Box 1408 Lancaster CA 93584-1408

ROTHSCHILD, AMALIE RANDOLPH, filmmaker, producer, director, digital artist, photographer; b. Balt., June 3, 1945; d. Randolph Schamberg and Amalie Getta (Rosenfeld) R. BFA, R.I. Sch. Design, 1967; MFA in Motion Picture Production, NYU, 1969. Spl. effects staff in film and photography Joshua Light Show, Fillmore E. Theatre, NYC, 1969-71; still photographer TWA Airlines Pub. Relations Dept., Village Voice newspaper Rolling Stone magazine, Newsweek magazine, After Dark, N.Y. Daily News, numerous others, 1968-72; co-founder, partner New Day Films, distbn. coop., 1971—; owner, operator Anomaly Films Co., NYC, 1971—; Represented by Beltmann Archives, 1994—; Exhibitions include: Soho Triad Fine Arts Gallery, 1996—; mem., co-founder Assn. of Independent Video and Filmmakers, Inc., NYC, 1974, bd. dirs., 1974-78; instr. in film and TV, N.Y. U. Inst. of Film and TV, 1976-78; cons. in field to various organizations including Youthgrant Program of Nat. Endowment for Humanities, Washington, 1973-76; motion pictures include: Woo Who? May Wilson, 1969; It Happens to Us, 1972; Nana, Mom and Me, 1974; Radioimmunoassay of Renin, Radioimmunoassay of Aldosterone, 1973; Conversations with Willard Van Dyke, 1981; Richard Haas: Work in Progress, 1984; Painting the Town: The Illusionistic Murals of Richard Haas, 1990 (Emily award Am. Film and Video Festival 1990), A Meditation on the Olive, 1996; editor: Doing It Yourself, Handbook on Independent Film Distribution, 1977. Mem. Community Planning Bd. 1, Borough of Manhattan, N.Y.C., 1974-86. Recipient spl. achievement award Mademoiselle mag., 1972; independent filmmaker grant, Am. Film Inst., 1973; film grantee N.Y. State Coun. on the Arts, 1977, 85, 87, Nat. Endowment Arts, 1978, 85, 87, Md. Arts Coun., 1977, Ohio Arts and Humanities Couns., 1985. Mem. Assn. Ind. Video Filmmakers (bd. dirs. 1974-78) Univ. Film and Video Assn., N.Y. Women in Film, Ind. Documentary Assn., Laboratorio Immagine Donna. Democrat. Address: 135 Hudson St New York NY 10013-2102 also: Via delle Mantellate 19, Rome 00165, Italy

ROTHSCHILD, AMALIE ROSENFELD, artist; b. Balt., Jan. 1, 1916; d. Eugene Isaac and Addye (Goldsmith) Rosenfeld; m. Randolph S. Rothschild, Aug. 3, 1936; children: Amalie R., Adrien R. Diploma, Md. Inst. Coll. Art, 1934, BFA (hon.), 1996; student, N.Y. Sch. Fine and Applied Art, 1934. Instr. painting Met. Sch. Art, Balt., 1956-59; lectr. fine arts Goucher Coll., 1960-68. One-woman shows include Balt. Mus. Art, 1971, NAS, Washington, 1975, Kornblatt Gallery, Balt., 1978, 80, travelling retrospective exhbn., 1984, C. Grimaldis Gallery, Balt., 1985, 88, 91, Md. Inst. Coll. Art, 1985, Franz Bader Gallery, Washington, 1989, 91, Artist's Pavillion, Tel Aviv, 1990, Gomez Gallery, Balt., 1993, 95, 97, Art Rsch. and Tech., Lancaster, Pa., 1993; group shows include Jewish Mus., N.Y.C., 1952, Corcoran Gallery Art, Washington, 1958-59, Pub. Art Trust, Washington, 1985, Elements of Style, Md. Inst. Coll. Art, 1986, Internat. Sculpture Ctr. Conf. Exhbn. Sculptors Inc., Phila., 1992, Sculptors Guild N.Y., 1994-95, 96, George Mason U., Fairfax, Va., 1995, Govt. House State of Md., 1997; represented in permanent collections Corcoran Gallery Art, Phillips Collection, Washington, Peale Mus. Balt., Balt. Mus. Art, Honolulu Acad. Arts, Fed. Res. Bank, Richmond, Va., Md. Sci. Ctr., corp. and univ. collections; commns. include archtl. panels Martin Luther King, Jr. Elem. Sch., Balt., 1969, wall hanging Walters Art Gallery, Balt., 1974, plexiglass window wall, Forest Park H.S., Balt., 1981. Chmn. artists com. Balt. Mus. Art, 1956-58, trustee, 1977-83, mem. accessions com., 1980-83; trustee Md. Inst. Coll. Art., 1991—. Recipient Disting. Alumni award Md. Inst. Coll. Art, 1985. Mem. Artists Equity Assn. (bd. dirs. Md. chpt. 1977-83), Sculptors Inc., Internat. Sculpture Ctr., New York Sculptor's Guild. Democrat. Jewish. Address: 2909 Woodvalley Dr Baltimore MD 21208-1915 *The definition of talent as power of mind and body committed to one for use and improvement describes my purpose in life. Late intellectual motivation followed early practical preparation for commercial art. Continuing self-education through multi-disciplinary reading, directing of energy into daily art-related endeavor, expecting integrity of performance in myself and others—these are my criteria for pursuit of excellence and fulfillment.*

ROTHSCHILD, BERYL ELAINE, mayor; m. Edmund W. Rothschild; children: Margaret, Dan. BS in Journalism, Ohio U., 1951. Councilman City of University Heights, Ohio, 1968-78, mayor, 1979—; sec. Regional Coun. of Govts. Former mem. legis. policy com. Ohio Mcpl. League; past mem. exec. bd. N.E. Ohio Areawide Coord. Agy.; former trustee Citizens League Greater Cleve. and Citizens League Rsch. Inst., YWCA (Metro) Cleve., Meridia Suburban Hosp., 1987-90, chmn. Cuyahoga County Nursing Home; mem. cmty. adv. bd. Coop. Human Tissue Network, Case Western Res. U.; former mem. adv. bd. Adult Basic and Literacy Edn.; charter mem., v.p. Ind. Living Experience Achievement Program; mem. adv. com. dept. edn. John Carroll U., 1988-90; past mem. com. on svcs. to the disabled Jewish Cmty. Fedn. Cleve.; mem. spl. needs adv. com. Jewish Cmty. Cor.; mem. advanced program employer adv. coun. Jewish Vocat. Svcs.;mem. learing Disabiliteis Assn. Greater Cleve., Friends of Cleveland Hts.-University Hts. Libr. Sys., Hadassah, Coun. of Jewish Women, NAMAT, Fairmount Temple, Women's Com. of the Cleve. Orch., Cleve. Mus. Art. Recipient Career Woman of Achievement award Cleve. YWCA, 1986, Woman of Achievement Recognition award Greater Cleve. chpt. Hadassah, Recognition cert. Cleveland Heights-University Heights Bd. Edn., 1980-81, City of Peace award State of Israel Bonds, 1984, Kenneth R. Oldman Meml. award (with husband) Cleve. Assn. for Children and Adults with Learning Disabilities, 1988; named one of Outstanding Women of Yr. Greater Cleve. State of Israel Bonds, 1988. Mem. Nat. League of Cities and U.S. Conf. Mayors, Cuyahoga County Mayors and Mgrs. Assn. (sec., exec. bd., legis. com., cable TV com.), Women in Comms. Inc., Alpha Sigma Nu. Office: City of University Heights 2300 Warrensville Center Rd University Heights OH 44118-3825

ROTHSCHILD, DONALD PHILLIP, lawyer, arbitrator; b. Dayton, Ohio, Mar. 31, 1927; s. Leo and Anne (Office) R.; m. Ruth Eckstein, July 7, 1950; children: Nancy Lee, Judy Lynn Hoffman, James Alex. AB, U. Mich., 1950; JD summa cum laude, U. Toledo, 1965; LLM, Harvard U., 1966. Bar: Ohio 1966, D.C. 1970, U.S. Supreme Ct. 1975, R.I. 1989. Teaching fellow Harvard U. Law Sch., Cambridge, Mass., 1965-66; instr. solicitor's office U.S. Dept. Labor, Washington, 1966-67; vis. prof. U. Mich. Law Sch., Ann Arbor, 1976; prof. law George Washington U. Nat. Law Ctr., Washington, 1966-89, emeritus, 1989; prof. law N.Y. Law Sch., 1989-96; dir. Consumer Protection Ctr., 1971—; dir. Inst. Law and Aging, Washington, 1973-89, Ctr. for Community Justice, Washington, 1974-88, Nat. Consumers League, Washington, 1981-87; v.p. Regulatory Alternatives Devel. Corp., Washington, 1982—; cons. Washington Met. Council Govt., 1979-82; mayoral appointee Adv. Com. on Consumer Protection, Washington, 1979-80; chmn. bd. dirs. D.C. Citizens Complaint Ctr., Washington, 1980; counsel Tillinghast, Collins & Graham, Providence, 1989-95, chair human resource group. Co-author: Consumer Protection Text and Materials, 1973; Collective Bargaining and

Labor Arbitration, 1979; Fundamentals of Administrative Practice and Procedure, 1981. Contbr. numerous articles to profl. publs. Mem. Fed. Trade Commn. Adv. Council, Washington, 1970. Recipient Community Service award Television Acad., Washington, 1981. Mem. Nat. Acad. Arbitrators, Fed. Mediation and Conciliation Service, Am. Arbitration Assn., ABA, D.C. Bar Assn., Phi Kappa Phi. Jewish. Office: Shadow Farm Way Unit 4 Wakefield RI 02879-3631

ROTHSCHILD, JOSEPH, political science educator; b. Fulda, Germany, Apr. 5, 1931; came to U.S., 1940, naturalized, 1945; s. Meinhold and Henriette (Loewenstein) R.; m. Ruth Deborah Nachmansohn, July 19, 1959; children: Nina, Gerson. A.B. summa cum laude, Columbia U., 1951, A.M., 1952; D.Phil. (Euretta J. Kellett fellow), Oxford U., 1955. Instr. dept. polit. sci. Columbia, N.Y.C., 1955-58; asst. prof. Columbia, 1958-62, asso. prof., 1962-68, prof., 1968—, Class of 1919 endowed prof., 1978—, chmn. dept., 1971-75, 81-82, 89-91; Vice chmn., mem. exec. com. Am. Profs. for Peace in Mid. East, 1975-90. Author: The Communist Party of Bulgaria, 1959, Introduction to Contemporary Civilization in the West, 3d edit, 1960, Chapters in Western Civilization, 3d edit, 1962, Communist Eastern Europe, 1964, Pilsudski's Coup d'Etat, 1966, East Central Europe Between the Two World Wars, 1974, Ethnopolitics: A Conceptual Framework, 1981 (transl. into Italian 1984, Japanese 1989), Return to Diversity: A Political History of East Central Europe Since World War II, 1989; contbr. articles to profl. jours. Recipient Mark Van Doren Great Tchr. award Columbia Coll., 1991; Social Sci. Rsch. Coun. fellow, 1963-64, J.S. Guggenheim fellow, 1967-68, Am. Coun. Learned Socs. fellow, 1971-72, Chamberlain sr. fellow, 1974, Ford rsch. fellow, summer 1976, NEH fellow, 1978-79, Lehrman Inst. fellow, 1979-80, Ford Found.-Am. Coun. Learned Socs. rsch. fellow, 1985-87, Woodrow Wilson fellow, 1994. Mem. Polit. Sci. Acad., Am. Assn. for Advancement Slavic Studies, Polish Inst. Arts and Scis. in Am., Phi Beta Kappa. Home: 445 Riverside Dr New York NY 10027-6842

ROTHSCHILD, STEVEN JAMES, lawyer; b. Worcester, Mass., Mar. 23, 1944; s. Alfred and Ilse (Blumenfeld) R. B.A., U. Vt., 1965; J.D., Georgetown U., 1968. Bar: D.C. 1968, Del. 1969, N.Y. 1992. Ptnr. Skadden Arps Slate Meagher & Flom, Wilmington; mem. Del. Bd. Bar Examiners, 1979-83; chmn. Del. Citizens Conf. on Adminstrn. of Justice, 1982; mem. Del. Bd. on Profl. Responsibility, 1992—, vice chmn., 1993, chmn., 1994—; vice chmn. rules com. Del. Supreme Ct., 1991-94; chmn. Del. Gov.'s Commn. on Major Comml. Litigation Reform, 1993-94. Bd. dirs. United Way Del., 1978-85, 93—, v.p., 1981-84, chmn. 1994-95; bd. dirs. Milton and Hattie Kutz Home, 1972—, pres., 1982-84; bd. dirs. Del. region NCCJ, 1981-92, Hebrew Immigrant Aid Soc., 1986-91, Jewish Fedn. Del., 1988-91; trustee Del. Art Mus., 1986-92, pres., 1990-92. Mem. ABA, Bar Assn. D.C., Assn. of Bar of City of N.Y., Del. Bar Assn. Office: Skadden Arps Slate Meagher & Flom One Rodney Sq PO Box 636 Wilmington DE 19899

ROTHSTEIN, ASER, radiation biology educator; b. Vancouver, B.C., Can., Apr. 29, 1918; emigrated to U.S., 1940, naturalized, 1955; s. Samuel and Etta (Wiseman) R.; m. Evelyn Paperny, Aug. 18, 1940; children: Sharon Leslie, David Michael, Steven Jay. B.A. in Zoology, U.B.C., 1938; student, U. Calif. at Berkeley, 1938-40; Ph.D., U. Rochester, 1943, D.Sc. (hon.), 1983. With atomic energy project U. Rochester, 1948—, co-dir., 1965—; mem. faculty U. Rochester (Med. Sch.), 1946—, prof. radiation biology, 1959—, co-chmn. dept., 1965—; dir. Rsch. Inst. Hosp. for Sick Children, Toronto, Ont., 1971-87, dir. emeritus, 1987—; prof. med. biophysics U. Toronto Med. Sch., 1972-87, prof. emeritus, 1987—, Univ. prof., 1980; vis. prof. Eidgenossische Technische Hochschule, Zurich, 1977; U.S. del. UNESCO Conf., Paris, France, 1957; NSF sr. postdoctoral fellow U. Bern, Switzerland, 1959-60. Recipient Wightman award Gairdner Found., 1986. Fellow AAAS, Royal Soc. Can. Home: 33 Harbour Sq #2018, Toronto, ON Canada M5J 2G2

ROTHSTEIN, BARBARA JACOBS, federal judge; b. Bklyn., Feb. 3, 1939; d. Solomon and Pauline Jacobs; m. Ted L. Rothstein, Dec. 28, 1968; 1 child, Daniel. B.A., Cornell U., 1960; LL.B., Harvard U., 1966. Bar: Mass. 1966, Wash. 1969, U.S. Ct. Appeals (9th cir.) 1977, U.S. Dist. Ct. (we. dist.) Wash. 1971, U.S. Supreme Ct. 1975. Pvt. practice law Boston, 1966-68; asst. atty. gen. State of Wash., 1968-77; judge Superior Ct., Seattle, 1977-80; judge Fed. Dist. Ct. Western Wash., Seattle, 1980—, chief judge, 1987-94; faculty Law Sch. U. Wash., 1975-77, Hastings Inst. Trial Advocacy, 1977, N.W. Inst. Trial Advocacy, 1979—; mem. state-fed. com. U.S. Jud. Conf., chair subcom. on health reform. Recipient Matrix Table Women of Yr. award Women in Communication, Judge of the Yr. award Fed. Bar Assn., 1989; King County Wash. Women Lawyers Vanguard Honor, 1995. Mem. ABA (jud. sect.), Am. Judicature Soc., Nat. Assn. Women Judges, Fellows of the Am. Bar, Wash. State Bar Assn., U.S. Jud. Conf. (state-fed. com., health reform subcom.), Phi Beta Kappa, Phi Kappa Phi. Office: US Dist Ct 705 US Courthouse 1010 5th Ave Seattle WA 98104-1130

ROTHSTEIN, GERALD ALAN, investment company executive; b. Bklyn., Oct. 18, 1941; s. Manuel and Gertrude (Buxbaum) R.; m. Cynthia Bea Pincus, June 11, 1967; children: Michael Neil, Lori Pamela, Meryl Patricia. BBA, City Coll. N.Y., 1962; MBA, U. Pa., 1965. 1st v.p. Shearson Hammill & Co., N.Y.C., 1966-74, Shearson Hayden Stone, N.Y.C., 1974-75; v.p. William D. Witter, Inc., N.Y.C., 1975-76; v.p. Oppenheimer & Co., N.Y.C., 1976-79, sr. v.p., 1979-83, mng. dir., 1983—; dir. internat. rsch., 1991-95, internat. investment banker, 1995—; bd. dirs. Pathfinder Investment Co. Ltd. (India). Mem. N.Y. Soc. Security Analysts, Inst. Chartered Fin. Analysts, Coun. of the Americas, Internat. Soc. Fin. Analysts. Office: Oppenheimer & Co Inc Oppenheimer Tower World Fin Ctr New York NY 10281

ROTHSTEIN, MORTON, historian, retired educator; b. Omaha, Jan. 8, 1926; s. Joseph Isadore and Rose (Landman) R.; m. Frances Irene Lustig, Nov. 18, 1950; children: Laurence, Eric, David. Student, Bklyn. Coll., 1952-54; Ph.D., Cornell U., 1960; postgrad., London Sch. Econs., 1956-57. Instr. U. Del., 1958-61; asst. prof. U. Wis.-Madison, 1961-65, assoc. prof., 1965-69, prof. history and agrl. econs., 1969-84, chmn. history dept., 1969-72; prof. history U. Calif., Davis, 1984-94; emeritus prof. U. Calif., Davis, 1994—; vis. prof. London Sch. Econs., 1977; mem. acad. adv. bd. Eleutherian Mills-Hagley Found., 1970-74; mem. Wis. Humanities Com., 1978-84, chmn., 1980-82, Calif. Coun. Humanities, 1985-90, chmn. 1988-90. Editor: Explorations in Economic History, 1970-73, Agricultural History, 1984-94; co-editor: Outstanding In His Field: Essays in Honor of Wayne D. Rasmussen, 1993, Quantification in Agrarian History: Essays by American and Soviet Historians, 1994; contbr. articles to profl. jours. Social Sci. Research Council fellow, 1956-57, 67-68; NEH fellow, 1976-77, 83. Mem. Orgn. Am. Historians, Agrl. History Soc. (pres. 1975-76), Bus. History Conf. (pres. 1985-86), Econ. History Assn., Econ. History Soc. (U.K.), So. History Assn., We. History Assn., Calif. Hist. Soc. (trustee 1989-90). Jewish. Home: 3417 Seabright Ave Davis CA 95616-5641 Office: U Calif Dept History Davis CA 95616 *The example of teachers who were thoroughly engaged in research, and generated excitement from it, has informed my own efforts at writing and in the classroom. A professor must have something to profess. Openness and generosity has benefited me, and taught me never to count other people's money, or to fear doing someone a favor.*

ROTHSTEIN, PAUL FREDERICK, lawyer, educator; b. Chgo., June 6, 1938. B.S., Northwestern U., 1958, LL.B., 1961. Bar: Ill. 1962, D.C. 1967, U.S. Supreme Ct. 1975. Instr. U. Mich. Law Sch., 1963; assoc. prof. law U. Tex., 1964-67; mem. Surrey, Karasik, Gould & Greene, Washington, 1967-70; prof. Georgetown U. Law Ctr., Washington, 1970—ABA (chmn. rules of evidence and criminal procedure com., criminal justice sect. 1984—), univs.; spl. counsel U.S. Senate Jud. Com. Subcom. on Criminal Laws and Procedures, 1975-77, U.S. Ho. of Reps. Jud. Com. Subcom. on Criminal Law, 1980; cons. Treasury, 1967-74, HEW, 1970, Commrs. on Uniform State Laws, 1969-75, Nat. Acad. Scis., 1976-77, D.C. Law Revision Commn., 1976-78; speaker, coordinator numerous legal edn. seminars for judges and lawyers, 1970—. Recipient U. Iowa Legal Edn. award 1974, Disting. Pub. Service award Crime Victims Compensation Bd., 1978; other civic and profl. awards; Fulbright scholar, Oxford, Eng., 1962-63. Mem. Fed. Bar Assn. (chmn. fed. rules of evidence com. 1974-77, Disting. Service award 1975 nat. council 1976—, chmn. continuing legal edn. com. 1980), D.C. Bar (continuing legal edn. bd. 1980—), ABA (chmn. rules of evidence and criminal procedure com., criminal justice sect. 1984—), Assn. Am. Law Schs. (sec. evidence sect. 1976, chmn. 1977), Nat. Assn. Criminal Injuries Compensations Bds. (sec. 1977—), Internat. Assn. Criminal Injuries Compensation Bds. Author: Evidence in a Nutshell, 1970, 2d edit., 1981; Understanding the New Federal Rules of Evidence, 1973, 74, 75; Federal Rules of Evidence with Practice Comments and Annotations, 1978, 2d edit., 1981; Cases, Materials and Problems in Evidence, 1986; contbr. articles on evidence and trial to profl. jours.; editor-in-chief Northwestern U. Law Rev., 1960-61. Office: Georgetown U Law Ctr 600 New Jersey Ave NW Washington DC 20001-2075

ROTHSTEIN, RICHARD, public relations executive; b. N.Y., Oct. 22, 1948. BA in Hist., Montclaire State Coll., 1970. Assoc. editor Lebhar-Friedman, 1971-72; editor Harcourt Brace Jovanovitch, 1972-76; sr. editor Med. Econs. Co., 1977-80; A/S Daniel J. Edelman, 1981-83, v.p., 1983-84, sr. v.p., 1984-85, exec. v.p., 1986-87; R & R, mng. dir. Med. Comms., 1987; pres. Ruder Finn & Rotman Med. Mktg. Unit, 1987; pres. Edelman Med. Communications Edelman PR Worldwide, 1991—. Recipient Jesse H. Neal award in Journalism, 1973. Office: Edelman PR Worldwide 1500 Broadway New York NY 10036-4015

ROTHSTEIN, RONALD, professional basketball coach; b. Bronxville, NY, Dec. 27, 1942; m. Olivia Pierorazio; children: David, Dana. Grad., U. R.I., 1964; M degree, CCNY. Asst. coach Upsala Coll., 1974-75; high sch. coach, 1976-79; northeastern regional scout Atlanta Hawks, 1979-82, asst. coach, 1983-86; asst. coach Detroit Pistons, 1986-88, head coach, 1992-93; head coach Miami Heat, 1988-91; scout N.Y. Knicks, 1982-83; asst. coach Cleveland Cavaliers, 1993—. Office: care Cleveland Cavaliers 1 Center Ct Cleveland OH 44115-4001*

ROTHSTEIN, RUTH M., hospital adminstrator. Dir. Cook County Hosp., Chgo.; chief Cook County Bur. of Health Svcs. Office: Cook County Hosp 1835 W Harrison St Chicago IL 60612-3701

ROTHSTEIN, SAMUEL, librarian, educator; b. Moscow, Jan. 12, 1921; arrived in Can., 1922, naturalized, 1929; s. Louis Israel and Rose (Checov) R.; m. Miriam Ruth Teitelbaum, Aug. 26, 1951; children: Linda Rose, Sharon Lee. BA, U. B.C., 1939, MA, 1940; grad. student, U. Calif., Berkeley, 1941-42, U. Calif., Berkeley, 1946-47; BLS, U. Calif., Berkeley, 1947; student, U. Wash., 1942-43; PhD (Carnegie Corp. fellow 1951-54), U. Ill., 1954; DLitt, York U., 1971. Teaching fellow U. Wash., 1942-43; prin. libr. asst. U. Calif., Berkeley, 1947; mem. staff U. B.C. Libr., Vancouver, Can., 1946-51, 54-62; acting univ. libr. U. B.C., Vancouver, Can., 1961-62, prof. libr. sci., 1961-86, prof. emeritus, 1986—, dir. Sch. Librarianship, 1961-70; vis. prof. U. Hawaii, 1969, U. Toronto, 1970, 79, Hebrew U., Jerusalem, 1973; mem. Commn. Nat. Plan Libr. Edn., 1963—; mem. assoc. com. sci. info. Nat. Rsch. Coun. Can., 1962-69; councillor B.C. Med. Libr. Svc., 1971; mem. exec. com. Pacific divsn. Can. Jewish Congress, 1962-69, Internat. House Assn. B.C., 1959-60; mem. Can. Adv. Bd. Sci. and Tech. Info.; mem. cabinet Combined Jewish Appeal of Greater Vancouver, 1992-95; pres. Vancouver Pub. Libr. Trust, 1987-88. Author: The Development of Reference Services, 1955, (with others) Training Professional Librarians for Western Canada, 1957, The University-The Library, 1972, Rothstein on Reference..., 1989; also articles.; co-editor: As We Remember It, 1970. Life mem. bd. dirs. Jewish Cmty. Ctr. of Greater Vancouver, pres., 1972-74; bd. dirs. Jewish Fedn. of Greater Vancouver, 1993—. Recipient ALISE award Assn. Library Info. Sci. Edn., 1987, Beta Phi Mu award ALA, 1988. Mem. Can. Libr. Assn. (hon. life), Assn. Am. Libr. Schs. (pres. 1968-69), Can. Assn. Libr. Schs. (hon. life, pres. 1982-84), ALA (coun. 1963-69, Beta Phi Mu award 1988), B.C. Libr. Assn. (hon. life, pres. 1959-60, Helen Gordon Stewart award 1970), Pacific N.W. Libr. Assn. (pres. 1963-64, hon. life), Can. Libr. Assn. (hon. life, coun. 1958-60, Outstanding Svc. to Librarianship award 1986), Bibliog. Soc. Can. (coun. 1959-63), Can. Assn. Univ. Tchrs. Home: 1416 W 40th Ave, Vancouver, BC Canada

ROTHWARF, ALLEN, electrical engineering educator; b. Phila., Oct. 1, 1935; s. Max and Bessie (Dichter) R.; m. Bernice Cecelia Golansky, June 16, 1957; children: Richard, Jeanne, David. BA in Physics, Temple U., 1957; MS in Physics, U. Pa., 1960, PhD in Physics, 1964. Instr. Rutgers, The State U., Camden, N.J., 1960-62; mem. tech. staff RCA Labs., David Sarnoff Rsch. Ctr., Princeton, N.J., 1964-72; postdoctoral fellow U. Pa., Phila., 1972-73; sr. scientist Inst. Energy Conversion, U. Del., Newark, 1973-79; prof. elec. engring. dept. Drexel U., Phila., 1979—; dir. Ben Franklin Superconductivity Ctr., Phila., 1989-94; cons. RCA Labs., Princeton, 1979-83, Solarex Thin Film Div., Newtown, Pa., 1983—. Contbr. articles to profl. jours.; patentee in field. Recipient Rsch. award Drexel U., 1989. Fellow IEEE; mem. Am. Phys. Soc. Office: Drexel U Elec & Computer Engring Depts Philadelphia PA 19104

ROTHWELL, ROBERT CLARK, agricultural products executive; b. St. Louis, Dec. 7, 1939; s. Fountain and Frances Marie (Bickell) R.; m. Virginia Warren Hubbard, Apr. 18, 1961; children: Sharon Lee, James Clark, Janice Lynn, David Matthews. BSBA, U. Mo., 1967. CPA, Mo. Staff auditor Arthur Andersen & Co., Kansas City, Mo., 1967-71; internal auditor MFA, Inc., Columbia, Mo., 1971-75, mgr. auditing, 1975-79, contr., 1979-81, v.p. fin., 1981-88, treas., 1987—, sr. v.p. fin., 1988—; treas. Agmo Corp., Columbia, Morris Farms, Inc., Columbia, MFA of Okla., Columbia; mem. investment com. MFA Found., Columbia, MFA Employees Retirement Plan, Columbia; advisor U. Mo. Sch. Accountancy, Columbia, 1987-91. Author various presentations on fin. mgmt. Instr. Mo. Inst. Cooperation, Columbia, 1987-91; bd. dirs. Coop. Buyers Assn., Stuttgart, Ark., Inst. Coop. Fin. Officers, Mo. Coun. on Econ. Edn., Mid-Mo. Alzheimer's Assn., 1995—. Mem. AICPA, Mo. Soc. CPAs, Fin. Execs. Inst., Nat. Assn. Accts. for Coops., Nat. Coun. Farmer Coops. Republican. Office: MFA Inc 201 Ray Young Dr Columbia MO 65201-3568

ROTHWELL, TIMOTHY GORDON, pharmaceutical company executive; b. London, Jan. 8, 1951; came to us., 1966; s. Kenneth Gordon Rothwell and Jean Mary (Stedman) Davey; m. Joanne Claire Fleming; children: Tiffany, Heather. BA, Drew U., 1972; JD, Seton Hall U., 1976; LLM, NYU, 1979, MBA, 1983. With Sandoz Pharms., East Hanover, N.J., 1972—, patent atty., 1974-77, patent and trademark counsel, 1980-82, mng. ops. planning and adminstrn., 1982-84, dir. mktg. ops., 1984-85, exec. dir. field ops., 1985-86, v.p. field ops., 1986-87, pres. profl. bus. ops., 1987-88, corp. v.p., chief oper. officer, 1988-89; sr. v.p. sales Squibb, Princeton, N.J., 1989; gen. mgr. Squibb U.S. Pharm. divsn. Bristol-Myers Squibb, 1991; sr. v.p. mktg. and sales Burroughs-Wellcome, 1992; pres., CEO Sandoz Pharm. Corp., 1995; pres. pharm. op. Rhone-Poulenc Rorer Inc., 1996, pres., bd. dirs., 1996—. Mem. N.J. State Bar Assn., N.Y. State Bar Assn., Am. Soc. for Pharmacy Law, Nat. Health Care Quality Coun., Am. Found. for Pharm. Exec. (bd. dirs.), N.J. Patent Law Assn. (pres. 1986). Republican. Episcopalian. Avocations: philately, coaching youth soccer, golf, tennis. Office: Rhone Poulenc Rorer Pharm Co 500 Arcola Rd Collegeville PA 19426-3930

ROTI, THOMAS DAVID, lawyer, food service executive; b. Evanston, Ill., Jan. 20, 1945; s. Sam N. and Theresa S. (Salerno) R.; m. Donna Sumichrast, July 22, 1972; children: Thomas S., Kyle D., Rebecca D., Gregory J. BS, Loyola U., Chgo., 1967, JD cum laude, 1970. Bar: Ill. 1970, U.S. Dist. Ct. (no. dist.) Ill. 1971, U.S. Ct. Appeals (7th cir.) 1971. Sr. law clk. to presiding justice U.S. Dist. Ct. No. Dist. Ill., 1971-72; assoc. Arnstein, Gluck & Lehr, Chgo., 1972-73, Boodell, Sears et al., Chgo., 1973-75; asst. gen. counsel Dominick's Finer Foods, Inc., Northlake, Ill., 1975-77, v.p., gen. counsel, 1977—; mem. lawyers & econs. com. Food Mktg. Inst., Washington, 1987—, legis. com. Ill. Retail Mchts. Assn., Chgo., 1987—. Trustee Joint Civic Com. Italian Ams., Chgo., 1986—; mem. Chgo. Coun. EDU-CARE Scholarship Program, 1988. Maj. U.S. Army, 1967-83. Recipient Am. Jurisprudence award, 1970; Alumni Assn. award Loyola U., 1970. Mem. ABA, Ill. Bar Assn., Chgo. Bar Assn., Am. Corp. Counsel Assn., Chgo. Zool. Soc., Loyola Alumni Assn., Art Inst. Chgo., Phi Alpha Delta, Alpha Sigma Nu. Roman Catholic. Home: 1141 Hunting Palatine IL 60067 Office: Dominick's Finer Foods Inc 333 Northwest Ave Northlake IL 60164-1604

ROTITHOR, HEMANT GOVIND, electrical engineer; b. Patan, India, July 5, 1958; came to U.S., 1985; s. Govind Hari and Suman (Govind) R.; m. Shubhada Hemant, Sept. 1, 1987; children: Sagar, Jaydeep. PhD in Elec. Engring., U. Ky., 1989. Devel. engr. ORG Systems, Baroda, India, 1981-82, Philips India, 1982-85; asst. prof. Worcester (Mass.) Poly. Inst., 1990-95; prin. engr. Digital Equipment Corp., Nashua, N.H., 1995—; mem. steering com. 3d Internat. Symposium on personal, indoor, mobile, radio comm., 1992. Contbr. articles to profl. jours. Grantee Worcester Poly. Inst., 1990, NSF, 1992, 94, 95, Nynex Corp. Mem. IEEE (sr.), Assn. for Computing Machinery, Sigma Xi, Tau Beta Pi, Eta Kappa Nu. Achievements include research in instrumentation measurement, computer architecture and distributed computers, compilers, and performance management. Home: 25 Saint Anthony Dr Hudson NH 03051-5066 Office: Digital Equipment Corp ZK02/3/N30 110 Spit Brook Rd Nashua NH 03062-2711

ROTMAN, CARLOTTA J.H. HILL, physician; b. Chgo., Apr. 8, 1948; d. Clarence Kenneth and Vlasta (Cizek) Hayes; m. Chester James Hill III, June 10, 1967 (div. 1974); m. Carlos Alberto Rotman, July 31, 1980; children: Robin Mercedes. BA magna cum laude, Knox Coll., 1969; MD with honors, U. Ill., 1973. Diplomate Nat. Bd. Med. Examiners, 1974, Am. Bd. Dermatology, 1978. Intern Mayo Sch. Medicine, Rochester, Minn., 1973-74; resident U. Ill., Chgo., 1975-78, asst. prof. clin. dermatology Coll. Medicine, 1978-93, assoc. prof. clin. dermatology Coll. Medicine, 1993—; sen. U. Ill. Senate, Chgo., 1986-91; councilor Chgo. Med. Soc., 1990-96. Contbr. articles to profl. jours. Bd. dirs. Summerfest St. James Cathedral, Chgo., 1986-91, YWCA, Lake Forest, Ill., 1995—; master gardner Chgo. Botanic Garden, Glencoe, Ill., 1994—. Recipient Janet Glascow award Am. Women's Med. Assn., 1973. Mem. AMA, Am. Acad. Dermatology, Herb Soc. Am. (chmn. ways and means No. Ill. unit 1994-96, treas. N. Ill. unit 1996—), Ill. State Med. Assn., Ill. State Dermatologic Soc., Chgo. Med. Soc., Chgo. Dermatologic Soc., Phi Beta Kappa, Alpha Omega Alpha. Episcopalian. Avocations: travel, cooking, gardening, reading. Office: Dept Dermatology 808 S Wood St Chicago IL 60612-7300

ROTMAN, MORRIS BERNARD, public relations consultant; b. Chgo., June 6, 1918; s. Louis and Etta (Harris) R.; m. Sylvia Sugar, Mar. 1, 1944; children: Betty Ruth, Jesse, Richard. Student, Wright Jr. Coll., 1936-37, Northwestern U., 1937-39. Editor Times Neighborhood publs., Chgo., 1938-40; asst. editor City News Bur., 1940-42; mng. editor Scott Field Broadcaster, USAAF, 1942-43; publicity dir. Community and War Fund of Met. Chgo., 1943-45; v.p. William R. Harshe Assocs., 1945-49, pres., 1949-66; chmn. bd., chief exec. officer (name changed to Harshe-Rotman & Druck, Inc.), 1966-81; pres. Ruder Finn & Rotman, Inc. (merger of Harshe-Rotman & Druck and Ruder & Finn), 1982, ret.; founder Morris B. Rotman & Assocs., Chgo., 1989—. Chmn. solicitations pub. rels. div. Community Fund Chgo., 1948-49, spl. events chmn., 1953; chmn. communications div. Jewish Fedn. Chgo., 1965, Combined Jewish Appeal,1 966; life dir. Rehab. Inst. Chgo.; U.S. dir. The Shakespeare Globe Centre (N.Am.) Inc.; trustee Roosevelt U. (emeritus). Recipient Prime Minister Israel medal, 1969. Mem. Pub. Rels. Soc. Am. (past dir.), Chgo. Presidents' Orgn. (pres. 1970-71), Acad. Motion Picture Arts and Scis. (assoc.), Chief Execs. Orgn., Chgo. Press Vets. Assn., Standard Club, Tamarisk Country Club, Headline Club, Desert Rats (chair), Sigma Delta Chi. Home: 3 Columbia Dr Rancho Mirage CA 92270-3149

ROTNEM, DIANE LOUISE, clinical social worker, educator, researcher; b. Rochester, Minn., Jan. 13, 1948; d. Orville Morris and Marjorie Ann (Higgins) Moore; m. Clark Franklin Springgate, Oct. 19, 1991; stepchildren: Elizabeth Avery Springgate, Benjamin Franklin Springgate. BA, U. Minn., 1970; MSW, Washington U., St. Louis, 1973; PhD, Smith Coll., 1989. Diplomate Am. Bd. Examiners in Clin. Social Work; lic. clin. social worker, Conn. Trainee divsn. Indian health USPHS, Phoenix, 1972-73; pediatric rsch. social worker, pediatric social worker Yale-New Haven Hosp., New Haven, 1973-77; clin. instr. med. sch. U. Colo., Denver, 1977-78; asst. clin. prof. Yale Child Study Ctr., New Haven, 1978-84; assoc. in rsch. dept. psychiatry Yale Sch. Medicine, New Haven, 1987-89; psychotherapist in pvt. practice Branford, Conn., 1984-94, Guilford, Conn., 1994—; adj. faculty So. Conn. State U., New Haven, 1993-95; asst. clin. prof. Yale U. Sch. Medicine, New Haven, 1995—; fellow Nat. Ctr. for Clin. Infant programs, Washington, 1983-85; mid-career fellow The Bush Ctr. in Child Devel. & Social Policy Yale U., New Haven, 1987-89. Contbr. numerous articles to profl. jours. Fundraiser Dem. party, Conn. and nationwide, 1990—, Emily's List, 1995—. NIMH tng. fellow, 1971-73. Fellow Am. Orthopsychiatry Assn.; mem. NASW, AAUW, AAUP, Conn. Soc. Clin. Social Work (bd. dirs., co-chair continuing edn. com. 1989-97, pres.-elect 1996-97, pres. 1997-99), Smith Club of New Haven (bd. dirs. 1994—), Nat. Fedn. of Socs. in Clin. Social Work (bd. dirs.). Home: 1320 Little Meadow Rd Guilford CT 06437-1659 Office: 42 Long Hill Rd Guilford CT 06437-1870

ROTT, NICHOLAS, fluid mechanics educator; b. Budapest, Hungary, Oct. 6, 1917; came to U.S. 1951; s. Alexander and Margaret (Pollak) R.; m. Rosanna Saredi, Sept. 30, 1944; children: Paul, Kathy. Diploma in Mechanical engring., Swiss Fed. Inst. Tech., Zurich, 1940; PhD, ETH, Zurich, 1944. Rsch. asst., pvt. dozent Aerodynamics Inst., Zurich, 1944-51; prof. Grad. Sch. Aeronautical Engring. Cornell U., Ithaca, N.Y., 1951-60; prof. UCLA, 1960-67, ETH, Zurich, 1967-83; vis. prof. Stanford (Calif.) U., 1983—. Fellow AIAA, Am. Phys. Soc.; mem. NAE, Acoustical Soc. Am. Home: 1865 Bryant St Palo Alto CA 94301-3710 Office: Stanford U Aero Astro Dept Stanford CA 94305

ROTTER, PAUL TALBOTT, retired insurance executive; b. Parsons, Kans., Feb. 21, 1918; s. J. and LaNora (Talbott) R.; m. Virginia Sutherlin Barksdale, July 17, 1943; children—Carolyn Sutherlin, Diane Talbott. BS summa cum laude, Harvard U., 1937. Asst. mathematician Prudential Ins. Co. of Am., Newark, 1938-46; with Mut. Benefit Life Ins. Co., Newark, 1946—; successively asst. mathematician, asso. mathematician, mathematician Mut. Benefit Life Ins. Co., 1946-59, from v.p. to exec. v.p., 1959-80, ret., 1980. Mem. Madison Bd. Edn., 1958-64, pres., 1959-64; Trustee, mem. budget com. United Campaign of Madison, 1951-55; mem. bd., chmn. advancement com. Robert Treat council Boy Scouts Am., 1959-64. Fellow Soc. Actuaries (bd. govs. 1965-68, gen. chmn. edn. and exam. com. 1963-66, chmn. adv. com. edn. and exam. 1969-72); mem. Brit. Inst. Actuaries (asso.), Am. Acad. Actuaries (v.p. 1968-70, bd. dirs., chmn. edn. and exam. com. 1965-66, chmn. rev. and evaluation com. 1968-74), Asso. Harvard Alumni (regional dir. 1965-69), Actuaries Club N.Y. (pres. 1967-68), Harvard Alumni Assn. (v.p. 1964-66),Am. Lawn Bowls Assn. (pres. SW div.), Phi Beta Kappa Assos., Phi Beta Kappa. Clubs: Harvard N.J. (pres. 1956-57); Harvard (N.Y.C.); Morris County Golf (Convent, N.J.); Joslyn-Lake Hodges Lawn Bowling (pres. 1989-90). Home: 18278 Canfield Pl San Diego CA 92128-1002

ROTTER, STEPHEN A., film editor. Editor: (films) Night Moves, 1975, (with Dede Allen and Jerry Greenberg) The Missouri Breaks, 1976, (with Ronald Roose) The World According to Garp, 1982, (with Glenn Farr, Lisa Fruchtman, Douglas Stewart, and Tom Rolf) The Right Stuff, 1983 (Academy award best film editing 1983), (with Richard P. Cirincone) Target, 1985, Heaven Help Us, 1985, (with Cirincone and William Reynolds) Ishtar, 1987, (with William Scharf) Dirty Rotten Scoundrels, 1988, (with Vivien Hollgrove Gilliam and B.J. Sears) The Unbearable Lightness of Being, 1988, (with Scharf) An Innocent Man, 1989, My Blue Heaven, 1990, (with Robert Reitano) True Colors, 1991, Prelude to a Kiss, 1992, (with Scharf) Rising Sun, 1993, (with Scharf) Cops and Robbersons, 1994. Address: 40 W 86th St Ste 6B New York NY 10024*

ROTTMAN, ELLIS, public information officer; b. Balt., Apr. 5, 1930; s. Abraham Isaac and Sadie (Harris) R.; m. Carol Parker Donovan, May 30, 1965; children—Marcus, Lisa, Jason, Adam. B.S., U. Md., 1952. Assoc. editor Army Times Pub. Co., Washington, 1956-59; editor, dir. pub. relations Am. Fedn. Govt. Employees, AFL-CIO, 1959-65; pub. info. officer U.S. Post Office Dept., 1966-69; editor Manpower mag. Dept. Labor, 1969-75; editor, publs. dir. FDA, Rockville, Md., 1975-78; public info. dir. Labor-Mgmt. Services Adminstrn. Dept. Labor, 1978-84; pub. info. officer Office Sec. of Labor, 1984-94. Served with AUS, 1952-54. Recipient Journalism award Internat. Labor Press Assn., AFL-CIO, 1959, 60, 61, 62, 64; award merit Fed. Editors Assn., 1974, 75, 77, 78. Jewish. Home: 901 N Belgrade Rd Silver Spring MD 20902-3247 Office: 2nd St and Constitution Ave NW Washington DC 20210

ROTUNDA, DONALD THEODORE, public relations consultant; b. Blue Island, Ill., Feb. 14, 1945; s. Nicholas and Frances (Manna) R. B.A., Georgetown U., 1967; M.A., London Sch. Econs., 1968, Ph.D., 1972. Analyst

NASA, Washington, 1972; lectr. in econs. U. D.C., 1973; legis. asst. Ho. of Reps., Washington, 1974-76, economist budget com., 1977; mgmt. analyst Office Mgmt. and Budget, Washington, 1977-81; cons., 1981-82; mgr. editorial svcs. United Technologies Corp., Hartford, Conn., 1982-87, Pepsico, Inc., Purchase, N.Y., 1987-89, Union Carbide Corp., Danbury, Conn., 1989-90; dir. editorial svcs. Martin Marietta, Bethesda, Md., 1990-92; cons. pub. rels., 1992—. Contbr. numerous articles to Washington Post, New Republic, Saturday Rev. Roman Catholic. Home: 4431 Klingle St NW Washington DC 20016-3578

ROTUNDA, RONALD DANIEL, law educator, consultant; b. Blue Island, Ill., Feb. 14, 1945; s. Nicholas and Frances (Manna) R.; m. Marcia Ann Mainland, June 21, 1969; children—Nora, Mark. A.B. magna cum laude, Harvard U., 1967, J.D. magna cum laude, 1970. Bar: N.Y. 1971, U.S. Ct. Appeals (2d cir.) 1971, U.S. Ct. Appeals (D.C. cir.) 1971, U.S. Ct. Appeals (7th cir.) 1990, U.S. Supreme Ct. 1974, Ill. 1975. Law clk. U.S. Ct. Appeals (2d cir.), 1970-71; assoc. Wilmer, Cutler & Pickering, Washington, 1971-73; asst. majority counsel Watergate Com., U.S. Senate, Washington, 1973-74; asst. prof. U. Ill. Coll. Law, Champaign, 1974-77, assoc. prof., 1977-80, prof., 1980-93, Albert E. Jenner, Jr. prof. of law, 1993—; vis. prof. law European U. Inst., Florence, Italy, 1981; mem. profl. responsibility exam. com. Nat. Conf. Bar Examiners, 1980-87; constl. advisor Supreme Nat. Coun. Cambodia, 1993; cons. Supreme Ct. Modova, 1996. Author: (with Morgan) Problems and Materials of Professional Responsibility, 1976, 6th edit., 1996; (with Nowak and Young) Constitutional Law, 1978, (with Nowak) 2d edit., 1983, 3d edit., 1986, 4th edit., 1991, 5th edit., 1995, Modern Constitutional Law: Cases and Materials, 1981, 5th edit., 1997, (with Nowak) Treatise on Constitutional Law, 4 vols., 2d edit., 1992. Fulbright research scholar, Italy, 1981, Venezuela, 1986. Fellow Am. Bar Found. (life), Ill. Bar Found. (life); mem. Am. Law Inst. Roman Catholic. Office: U Ill Coll Law 504 E Pennsylvania Ave Rm 216 Champaign IL 61820-6909

ROTUNNO, GIUSEPPE, cinematographer; b. Rome, Italy, Mar. 19, 1923. Camera operator: (films) Senso, 1954; cinematographer: (films) Pane amore e..., 1955, Tosca, 1956, The Monte Carlo Story, 1957, Le notti bianche, 1957, Anna of Brooklyn, 1958, La Maja desnuda, 1958, La ragazza del palio, 1959, (with Daniel Fapp) On the Beach, 1959, (with Robert Gerardi) La grande guerra, 1959, The Angel Wore Red, 1960, Five Branded Women, 1960, Rocco e i suoi fratelli, 1960, The Best of Enemies, 1962, Boccaccio '70 ("The Job"), 1962, Cronaca familiare, 1962, Le guepard, 1963, I compagni, 1963, Ieri, oggi e domani, 1963, The Bible...In the Beginning, 1966, Lo straniero, 1967, Le streghe, 1967, Anzio, 1968, (with Aldo Graziata and Robert Krasker) Senso, 1968, Candy, 1968, Fellini Satyricon, 1969, The Secret of Santa Vittoria, 1969, Histoires extraordinaires ("Never Bet the Devil Your Head"), 1968, Sunflower, 1969, Carnal Knowledge, 1971, Man of La Mancha, 1972, Roma, 1972, Film d'amore e d'anarchia, 1973, Amarcord, 1974, Il bestione, 1974, Tutto a posto e niente in ordine, 1974, Il Casanova di Federico Fellini, 1976, Sturmtruppen, 1976, Divina Creatura, 1976, The End of the World in Our Usual Bed in a Night Full of Rain, 1978, Prova d'orchestra, 1978, All That Jazz, 1979 (Academy award nomination best cinematography 1979), La Citta delle donne, 1980, Popeye, 1980, (with William Garroni) Rollover, 1981, Bello mio bellezza mia, 1982, Five Days One Summer, 1982, E la nave va, 1983, American Dreamer, 1984, Non ci resta che piangere, 1984, Desiderio, 1984, The Assisi Underground, 1985, Red Sonja, 1985, Hotel Colonial, 1986, Julia and Julia, 1987, Rent-a-Cop, 1988, Haunted Summer, 1988, The Adventures of Baron Munchausen, 1989, Rebus, 1989, Regarding Henry, 1991, Once Upon a Crime, 1992, Wolf, 1994, The Night and the Moment, 1994, Sabrina, 1995, La Sindrome di Stendhal, 1996, Marcello Mastroianni Mi ricordo, si mi ricordo, 1997, (TV movies) The Scarlet and the Black, 1983. Office: The Gersh Agency 232 N Canon Dr Beverly Hills CA 90210-5302 also: ICM care Paul Hook 8942 Wilshire Blvd Beverly Hills CA 90211*

ROTZOLL, KIM BREWER, advertising and communications educator; b. Altoona, Pa., Aug. 21, 1935; s. Fredrick Charles and Anna (Brewer) R.; m. Nancy Benson, Aug. 26, 1961; children: Keith, Kristine, Amanda, Jason. BA in Advt., Pa. State U., 1957, MA in Journalism, 1965, PhD in Sociology, 1971. Account exec. Ketchum, Macleod and Grove, Pitts., 1957-61; instr. advt. Pa. State U., University Park, 1961-71; asst. prof. advt. U. Ill, Urbana, 1971-72, assoc. prof., 1972-78, prof., 1978—, rsch. prof., head advt. dept., 1983-92; dean Coll. Comms., 1992—; lectr. in People's Republic of China, Bahrain. Author, co-author, editor: Is There Any Hope for Advertising, 1986, Advertising in Contemporary Society, 1990, 96, Media Ethics, 1995, 97, The Book of Gossage, 1995, Last Rights: Revisiting Four Theories of the Press, 1995. Named Disting. Advt. Educator of Yr. by Am. Advt. Fedn., 1992. Fellow Am. Acad. Advt. (pres. 1991); mem. Am. Advt. Found., Nat. Advt. Rev. Bd., Alpha Kappa Delta, Phi Kappa Phi. Democrat. Presbyterian. Avocations: reading, films, cycling. Office: U Ill 119 Gregory Hall 810 S Wright St Urbana IL 61801-3611

ROUB, BRYAN R(OGER), financial executive; b. Berea, Ohio, May 1, 1941; s. Bernard Augustus and Pearl Irene (Koeblitz) R.; m. Judith Elaine Penman, June 19, 1965; children: Paul, Bradley, Michael. Student, Ohio Wesleyan U., 1959-62; BS, Ohio State U., 1966; MBA, U. Pa., 1978. Mem. audit staff Ernst & Ernst, Cleve., 1966-70; asst. contr. Midland-Ross, Cleve., 1970-73, contr., 1973-81, v.p., 1977-81, sr. v.p., 1981-82, exec. v.p. fin., 1982-84; sr. v.p. fin. Harris Corp., Melbourne, Fla., 1984-93, sr. v.p., CFO, 1993—; mem. fin. coun. II Machinery and Allied Products Inst., Washington, 1978-84, coun. I, 1984—, vice chmn., 1994-95, chmn., 1996—; mem. conf. bd. coun. of CFO's, 1993-96. Mem. adv. coun. Coll. Adminstrv. Scis., Ohio State U., 1978-81; mem. citizen's adv. coun. Westlake (Ohio) Schs., 1981-83; trustee Alcoholism Svcs. Cleve., 1982-84; mem. devel. bd. St. John's Hosp., 1983-84; pres. Westridge Homeowners' Assn., 1977; dir., treas. Tortoise Island Homeowners' Assn., 1988-90; bd. dirs. Easter Seal Soc. of Brevard County, 1993—. Mem. AICPA, Ohio Soc. CPAs, Fin. Execs. Inst. (treas. N.E. Ohio chpt. 1976-78, bd. dirs. 1980-81, 83-84, v.p. 1981-82, pres. 1982-83, bd. dirs. Orlando chpt. 1984—, v.p. 1985-86, pres. 1986-87, nat. bd. dirs. 1987-90, area v.p. 1990-91, chmn. budget and fin. com. 1988-89, chmn. planning com. 1995—), Fin. Execs. Rsch. Found. (trustee 1994—), Westwood Country Club, Eau Gallie Yacht Club (bd. govs., treas. 1990-92). Home: 556 Lanternback Island Dr Satellite Beach FL 32937-4712 Office: Harris Corp 1025 W NASA Blvd Melbourne FL 32919-0001

ROUBIK, CHARLENE MARY, nursing administrator; b. Chgo., Mar. 12, 1956; d. Walter Francis and Florence Mary (Thomas) Nied; m. Robert Edward Roubik; children: Kristine, Robert, Jessica. BS in Nursing, No. Ill. U., 1978. Registered profl. nurse. Coord. women's health svcs. Des Plaines Valley Health Ctr., Summit, Ill., 1981-83; RN Mercy Hosp., Chgo., 1984-89; RN emergency rm. svcs. Olympia Fields Osteo. Med. Ctr., Chgo., 1989-93, Holy Cross Hosp., Chgo., 1990-92; RN Ingalls Hosp., Harvey, Ill., 1989-93; case mgr. Shay Health Care Svcs., Crestwood, Ill., 1992-96; dir. cmty. rels. Windsor Manor Nursing & Rehab. Ctr., Palos Hills, Ill., 1995—. Sec. Conrady Jr. H.S. PTSA, 1994-95, publicity chair, 1995-96; publicity chair Oak Ridge PTA, 1992-95. Mem. AAUW, Palos Hills Baseball Assn. (sec. 1993-94, pres. 1994-95, past pres. 1995-96, sponsorship chair 1993-94, girls softball coach 1991-93). Roman Catholic.

ROUBOS, GARY LYNN, diversified manufacturing company executive; b. Denver, Nov. 7, 1936; s. Dorr and Lillian Margaret (Coover) R.; m. Terie Joan Anderson, Feb. 20, 1960; children: Lyndel, Leslie. BSChemE with high honors, U. Colo., 1959; MBA with distinction, Harvard U., 1963. With Boise Cascade Corp., 1963-71, Dieterich Standard Corp., Boulder, Colo., 1971-76; exec. v.p., then pres. Dieterich Standard Corp. (co. acquired by Dover Corp. 1975), 1975-76; exec. v.p. Dover Corp., N.Y.C., 1976, pres., 1977-93, chief exec. officer, 1981-94, chmn., 1989—; bd. dirs. Omnicom Group, Inc., N.Y.C., Bell & Howell Co., Skokie, Ill.; treas. Fund, Darien, Conn.; chmn. engring. adv. coun. U. Colo., 990—. 1st lt. C.E., U.S. Army, 1959-61. Mem. Winged Foot Golf Club, Boulder Country Club, Pine alley Golf Club, Econ. Club N.Y. Office: Dover Corp 280 Park Ave New York NY 10017-1216

ROUDANE, CHARLES, metal and plastics products company executive; b. Los Angeles, July 16, 1927; s. Rudolph and Irene (Warner) R.; BSME, Tulane, 1950; m. Orient Fox, Aug. 20, 1948; children: Mark, Matthew. Gen. mgr. Master div. Koehring Co., Chgo., 1955-67; gen. sales mgr. Wilton Corp., Schiller Park, Ill., 1967-70; dir. mktg. Flexonics div. UOP Inc., Bartlett, Ill., 1970-73, v.p., gen. mgr. div., 1973-83; pres., chief exec. officer Resistoflex Co. div. Crane Co., Marion, N.C., 1983-93; chmn., CEO ASM Corp., Chgo., 1993—; dir. Center Indsl. Mktg. Planning, Inc., PowRhouse Products, Inc. Served with AUS, 1945-46. Elected to Inaugural Hall of Fame, Am. Mgmt. Assn., 1978. Mem. Am. Mgmt. Assn. (former trustee, chmn. mktg. council, mem. internat. coun.), Chgo. Pres. Assn., ASME, Newcomen Soc. Gt. Britain. Republican. Presbyterian.

ROUDYBUSH, FRANKLIN, diplomat, educator; b. Washington, Sept. 17, 1906; s. Rumsey Franklin and Frances (Mahon) R.; student U. Vienna, 1925, Ecole National des Langues Orientales Vivantes, Paris, 1926, U. Paris, 1926-28, U. Madrid, 1928, Academie Julian, Paris, 1967; B.Fgn. Svc., 1930; postgrad. Harvard U., 1931; MA, George Washington U., 1944; PhD, U. Strasbourg (France), 1953; m. Alexandra Brown, May 22, 1941. Dean Roudybush Fgn. Svc. Schs., Washington, L.A., Phila., N.Y.C., 1932—. Prof. internat. econ. rels. Southeastern U., Washington, 1938-42; dir. Pan Am. Inst., Washington, 1934, London Econ. Conf., 1934, Internat. Textile Conf., Washington, 1935; editor Affairs, 1934-45; v.p. France Libre, Washington; censor Diplomatic Pouch World War II; head translation sect. for fgn. langs. U.S. Govt., 1940, 42; commodity economist, statistician Dept. State, 1945; editor of the Newsletter of the Fgn. Liquidation Commn. of the Dept. States, 1946, with Fgn. Svc. Inst., Dept. State, 1945-48, Council of Europe, Strasbourg and the Saar, Germany, 1948-54, Saar, 1949, Am. Embassy, Paris, 1954, Pakistan, 1955, Dublin, 1956; consular Acad. Vienna, 1925; mem. Punjab U., Lahore, Pakistan, 1954; mem., broadster Washington Pub. Affairs Forum, 1935-40. Creator: the cultural pouch for cultural attachees, 1957. Recipient prize Julian painting, Paris. Mem. Am. Soc. Internat. Law, Brit. Inst. Internat. and Comparative Law (London), Delta Phi Epsilon. Clubs: Assns. des Amis du Salon d'Automne (Paris); France Amerique; English Speaking Union (London); Nat. Press (Washington); Harvard (Paris), Royal Aberdeen Golf; Miramar Golf (Oporto, Portugal), Yacht (Angiers, France); Pormarnock Golf (Dublin); Les Societe des Artistes Independants Grand Palais (Paris). Author: The Twentieth Century; The Battle of Cultures; Diplomatic Language; Twentieth Century Diplomacy; The Present State of Western Capitalism, 1959; Diplomacy and Art, French Educational System, 1971; The Techniques of International Negotiation, 1979; The Diplomacy of the Cardinal, Duke de Richilieu, 1980, From Calcutta to Chungking, 1982, The Mysteries of Marsailles, 1983, Tea for Two, 1984, The Fromme Family, 1985, Casino Protocol, 1987, Talleyrand - The Diplomat, 1989, The French Government Political Science School, 1989, History of a Family During the XXth Century, 1990, The Flying Dutchman, 1990, Monsieur Fedeaux, 1990, Death in Darjeeling, 1991, The Alsatians, 1991, The Oriental Express to Constantinople and On To Teheran, 1992, The Elegant Facade of Macaó, 1992, Café Royal, 1993, The Roman Holiday, 1992, The Burlington Sisters, 1993, The Strange Fate of Madame Tarleton, 1980, Rendezvous in Basle, 1989, From Naples to Buenos Aires, 1977, Drawn Blinds, 1972, Roudybush's Twentieth Century Diplomacy, 1967. Home: Villa St Honoré, Moledo do Minho, Minho Portugal also: Sauveterre de Rouerque, 12800 Aveyron France

ROUECHE, JOHN EDWARD, II, education educator, leadership program director; b. Statesville, N.C., Sept. 3, 1938; s. John Edward and Mary (Harris) R.; m. Suanne Davis; 1 stepchild, Robin Sue Maca; children by previous marriage: Michelle Renee, John Edward III. BA, Lenoir Rhyne Coll., Hickory, N.C., 1960; MA, Appalachian Coll., Boone, N.C., 1961; PhD, Fla. State U., 1964. Dean Gaston Coll., Gastonia, N.C., 1964-67; assoc. rsch. educator U. Calif., L.A., 1967-69; dir. jr. coll. div. Nat. Lab. Higher Edn., 1968-71, also assoc. prof. edn. Duke U.; prof. edn., dir. c.c. leadership program U. Tex., Austin, 1971—, Sid W. Richardson regents chair, 1987—; mem. chancellor's coun. U. Tex. System, 1990—, U. Tex. Littlefield Soc., 1992—; lectr. Earl Pullias lectr. U. So. Calif., 1992, Coll. Bd. Disting. Lectr. N.Y.C., 1993, Frances Crain Cook Disting. Lectr. U. Tex., 1994; chmn. nat. edn. adv. bd. Great Am. Res. Ins. Co., 1991-95; bd. dirs. Acordia Collegiate Benefits, Inc.; co-chair, Nat. Adv. Bd. for C.C.s, Invest Learning Corp., 1993—; chair nat. adv. com. Kaplan EdnI. Partnerships, 1995—. C.C. editor Jossey-Bass Pubs., 1971-82; editor Creative Teaching Series, Media Systems Corp., 1980-85; mem. editorial bd. C.C. Times, C.C. Jour., 1990-94, others; author 33 books, including Profiles of Excellence in America's Schools, 1986, Access With Excellence, 1987, Shared Vision, 1989, Teaching As Leading, 1990, Under-representation: A Question of Diversity, 1991, Between a Rock and a Hard Place, 1993, The Company We Keep, 1995, Strangers in Their Own Land: Part Time Faculty, 1995, Embracing the Tiger: The Effectiveness Debate and the Community College, 1997, over 100 articles and monographs. Chmn. nat. community coll. adv. bd. Invest Learning Corp.; pres. Doss Sch. PTA, 1974-75; chmn. bd. N.W. Hills United Meth. Ch., 1973-76. Recipient Disting. Svc. award A.M.E. Ch., 1971, Disting. Rsch. award Nat. Coun. Univs. and Colls., 1990, Disting. Rsch. Publ. award, 1990, Outstanding Alumnus award Appalachian State U., 1979, Disting. Grad. award Fla. State U., 1981, Teaching Excellence award U. Tex., 1982, Outstanding Researcher award, 1985, Excellence award for outstanding learned article U.S. Edn. Press Assn., 1983, Disting. Rsch. award Nat. Assn. Devel. Edn., 1984, 86, Disting. Rsch. Publ. award Nat. Coun. Student Devel., 1987, Disting. Rsch. award Nat. Coun. Staff, Program, and Orgn. Devel., B. Lamar Johnson Nat. Leadership award, 1988, Disting. Svc. & Leadership award, CCP, INC., 1993—; Disting Faculty award U. Texas, 1994, Disting. Rsch. award Interassn. Student Devel. Orgns., 1995, Chancellor's Leadership award State of Ala., 1995; named lifetime ambassador for N.C., 1978; Kellogg fellow, 1962-64. Mem. Am. Assn. Community and Jr. Colls. (bd. dirs. 1989-94, Nat. Leadership award 1986, 1994, Disting. Rsch. award coun. colls. and univs. 1990, 94, 96, dist. rsch. sr. scholar award 1994, 96, nat. student devel. inter-assn. rsch. award 1995-96), Am. Assn. Higher Edn., Coun. Univs. and Colls. (past pres., bd. dirs.), Phi Beta Kappa, Phi Delta Kappa. Home: 6804 Edgefield Dr Austin TX 78731-2906 Office: U Tex Austin Coll Education Ste 348 Austin TX 78712

ROUFA, ARNOLD, gynecologist, obstetrician; b. St. Louis, Oct. 30, 1938; s. Maurice I. and Bee (Hoffman) R.; B.S., Tulane U., 1959; M.D., La. State U., 1963; m. Myrna March, July 29, 1973. Diplomate Am. Bd. Quality Assurance Utilization Rev. Physicians. Intern, Kings County Hosp. Center, Bklyn., 1964; resident in ob-gyn Woman's Hosp., St. Lukes Hosp. Center, N.Y.C., 1966-70, asst. attending, 1970-88, sr. attending, 1988—; chief pregnancy counseling service, 1970-77; med. dir. Planned Parenthood N.Y.C., Boro Hall Center, 1974-80, Margaret Sanger Center, 1980-83; asst. dir. Ambulatory Care, Woman's Hosp./St. Luke's-Roosevelt Hosp. Ctr., N.Y.C., 1988—; dir. ambulatory care, ob-gyn. St. Luke's-Roosevelt Hosp. Ctr., 1989—; practice medicine, specializing in ob-gyn, N.Y.C.; author Matthew Bender Pub. Co. Served with U.S. Army, 1963-65. Diplomate Am. Bd. Ob-Gyn. Mem. Am. Coll. Ob-Gyn, N.Y. County Med. Soc., Phi Delta Epsilon. Home: 400 E 56th St New York NY 10022-4147

ROUGEOT, HENRI MAX, medical imaging engineer, physicist; b. Paris, Nov. 22, 1934; arrived in U.S., 1989; s. Henri Felix and Yvette Therese (Ferreira) R.; m. Fanny Astrid Brebion, July 11, 1960; children: Claire, Anne, Pierre, Helene. BSc, Acad. Paris, 1954; degree in math., physics and chemistry, U. Sorbonne, Paris, 1957, M in Physics, 1962; degree in physics of accelerators, Orsay (France) U., 1968. Rsch. engr. Nat. Ctr. Scientific Rsch., Strasbourg, France, 1962-64, Corp. Rsch. Lab., Orsay, 1964-69; project mgr. Thomson-CSF Electron Tube, Grenoble, France, 1969-74; engring. mgr. x-ray II Thomson CSF, Grenoble, 1974-85, tech. dir., 1985-89; program mgr. G.E. Corp. Rsch. & Devel., Schenectady, N.Y., 1989—. Author: Negative Election Affinity, Digital Imaging in Medicine, 1993. With Artillery, 1959-62, Algeria. Recipient grant Nat. Cancer Inst., 1993. Mem. Am. Assn. Physicists in Medicine. Roman Catholic. Achievements include development and promotion of fifth generation high resolution image intensifiers at Thomson-CSF standard in medical industry since 1989; initiation of concept and launching of panel digital radiography image detector at Thomson-CSF and development of a full field digital Mammography system at GE. Home: 79 Celtic Dr, Beaconsfield, PQ Canada H9W 3M6 Office: Gen Elec River Rd Schenectady NY 12309

ROUGIER, GUILLERMO WALTER, paleontologist; b. Buenos Aires, Nov. 6, 1964; came to U.S., 1994; s. Nivel Abelardo and Enid Teodosia (Viollaz) R.; m. Adela Lucía Reale, Sept. 20, 1990. Lic. in Cs. Biológicas, Buenos Aires U., 1989, PhD in Biology, 1993. Technician in vert. paleontology Museo Argentino de Ciencias Naturales Bernardino Rivadavia, Buenos Aires, 1983-88; becario investigación P/A estud. U. Buenos Aires, 1988-89; fellow Consejo Nat. Sci. and Tech. Rsch., Buenos Aires, 1989-94; postdoctoral fellow Consejo Nacional de Investigaciones Cietificas y Tecnologicas, Buenos Aires, 1994-95; Frick rsch. fellow Am. Mus. Nat. History, N.Y.C., 1995—; prof. paleobiology Insan Inst., Buenos Aires, 1989-92; vis. rschr. Deutsches Foschungsgemeinschaft, Germany, 1994. Grantee: Sigma Xi, 1992, NSF, 1995. Mem. AAAS (grant-in-aid 1992), Argentine Paleontol. Assn. (treas. 1990-92). Achievements include discovery of earliest known fossil turtles from South America (210 million years) and the development of a new systematic hypothesis for turtle relationships; research in Mesozoic therian mammals from South and North America, Europe and Asia, with emphasis in the systematic and evolution of these groups. Office: Am Mus Natural History Dept Vertebrate Paleontol Central Park West & 79th St New York NY 10024

ROUGIER-CHAPMAN, ALWYN SPENCER DOUGLAS, furniture manufacturing company executive; b. Ostende, Belgium, Feb. 19, 1939; came to U.S., 1970; s. Douglas Alwyn and Simone (Stiernet) Rougier-C.; m. Christine Hayes, Mar. 14, 1964; children—Andrew Douglas, Duncan Peter. Chartered Acct., City of London Coll., 1963. Chartered acct., Eng. and Wales; C.P.A., Mich. Articled clk. Spain Bros., London, 1958-64; mgr. Deloitte & Co., Brussels, 1964-70; ptnr. Seidman & Seidman, Grand Rapids, Mich., 1970-81; v.p. planning Steelcase Inc., Grand Rapids, Mich., 1981-83, sr. v.p., CFO, 1983—; dir. Meijer, Inc. Pres. French Soc., Grand Rapids, Mich., 1974-75; treas., vice chmn. Opera Grand Rapids, 1981-86, pres., 1987-89; treas. Grand Rapids Symphony, 1991-96; bd. trustees Blodgett Meml. Hosp., 1989—; bd. dirs. Fin. Execs. Inst., Western Mich., 1988-94, pres., 1991-92. Fellow Inst. Chartered Accts. Eng. and Wales; mem. Am. Inst. C.P.A.s (computer exec. com. 1977-81), Mich. Assn. C.P.A.s (auditing standards com. 1973-78). Roman Catholic. Clubs: Cascade Country, Peninsular (Grand Rapids). Avocations: golf; tennis; squash; travel; music (symphony and opera). Home: 2018 San Lu Rae Dr SE Grand Rapids MI 49506-3473 Office: 901 44th St SE Grand Rapids MI 49508-7575

ROUHANA, WILLIAM JOSEPH, JR., business executive; b. Bklyn., June 23, 1952; s. William Joseph and Anna Freida (Stephan) R.; m. Claudia Caruso, Aug. 27, 1972; children: Timothy, Rosemary. BA, Colby Coll., 1972; JD, Georgetown U., 1976. Bar: N.Y. 1977, U.S. Dist. Ct. (so. and ea. dists.) N.Y. 1977. Founding ptnr. Beinhauer, Rouhana & Pike, N.Y.C., 1977-80; sole practice N.Y.C., 1980-81; ptnr. Rouhana and Trinko, P.C., N.Y.C., 1981-85, Baer, Marks & Upham, N.Y.C., 1985-86; pres. WinStar Corp., N.Y.C., 1984-90; chief exec. officer WinStar Ptnrs., N.Y.C., 1989-90, WinStar Oil Ptnrs., N.Y.C., 1990-91; chmn. Manson Internat., L.A., 1986-87; vice chmn. Mgmt. Co. Entertainment Group, Inc., L.A., 1987-90; bd. dirs., chmn., CEO Win Star Comm., Inc., 1989—; bd. dirs. Lancit Media Prodns., Ltd., 1991-94, TII Industries, Inc., 1992—, Found. Emmes, 1991-92; bd. overseers Colby Coll., 1987-90; bd. dirs., chmn. CEO WinStar Cos., Inc., 1990-94; vice chmn. UN Assn., 1996—, bd. govs., 1992—. Adv. bd. Nassau County Dem. Com., Jericho, N.Y., 1984, Bus. Execs. Nat. Security, 1991—, bd. dirs. 1997—. Grantee NSF, 1968, Thomas J. Watson Found., 1972-73. Mem. UN Assn. (bd. dirs. 1992—, vice chmn. 1996—), Phi Beta Kappa. Democrat. Roman Catholic. Office: WinStar Communications Inc 230 Park Ave 27th Fl New York NY 10169-3199

ROUKEMA, MARGARET SCAFATI, congresswoman; b. Newark, N.J., Sept. 19, 1929; d. Claude Thomas and Margaret (D'Alessio) Scafati; m. Richard W. Roukema, Aug. 23, 1951; children—Margaret, Todd (dec.), Gregory. B.A. with honors in History and Polit. Sci, Montclair State Coll., 1951, postgrad. in history and guidance, 1951-53; postgrad. program in city and regional planning, Rutgers U., 1975. Tchr. history, govt., public schs. Livingston and Ridgewood, N.J., 1951-55; mem. 97th-105th Congresses from 5th N.J. dist., Washington, D.C., 1981—; mem. Banking, Fin. Urban Affairs com., subcom. Housing, Community devel., Internat. devel., Fin., Trade, Monetary Policy, Econ. Growth on; mem. Credit formation, Edn. Labor com., subcom. labor mgmt. rels., elementary, sec., vocat. edn., postsecondary edn. tng.; vice pres. Ridgewood Bd. Edn., 1970-73; bd. dirs., co-founder Ridgewood Sr. Citizens Housing Corp.; chairwoman Fin. Inst. and Consumer Credit Sub. Com. U.S. Congress; sponcer Family Med. Leave U.S. Congress. Trustee Spring House, Paramus, N.J.; trustee Leukemia Soc. No. N.J., Family Counseling Service for Ridgewood and Vicinity; mem. Bergen County (N.J.) Republican Com.; NW Bergen County campaign mgr. for gubernatorial candidate Tom Kean, 1977. Mem. Bus. and Profl. Women's Orgn. Clubs: Coll. of Ridgewood, Ridgewood Rep. Office: US Ho of Reps 2469 Rayburn Bldg Washington DC 20515-3005 *I have served in several roles in my life. Wife, mother, teacher, public servant. All are personally rewarding; each affords the opportunity to help others in need and to enrich the lives of those around you. As a member of Congress, I find the most rewards are in the knowledge that I can truly make a difference and improve the lives of thousands of people. The challenges are frequently insurmountable, but the rewards are incalculable.**

ROULAC, STEPHEN E., real estate consultant; b. San Francisco, Aug. 15, 1945; s. Phil Williams and Elizabeth (Young) R.; children: Arthur, Fiona. BA, Pomona Coll., 1967; MBA with distinction, Harvard Grad. Sch. Bus. Adminstrn., 1970; JD, U. Calif., Berkeley, 1976; PhD, Stanford U., 1978. CPA, Hawaii. Asst. constrn. supt., foreman, adminstr. Roulac Constrn. Co., Pasadena, Calif., 1963-66; rsch. asst. Econs. Rsch. Assocs., L.A., 1966-67; assoc. economist Urbanomics Rsch. Assocs., Claremont, Calif., 1967; acquisition auditor Litton Industries Inc., Chgo., Beverly Hills, 1967-68; tax cons. Lybrand, Ross Bros. and Montgomery, L.A., 1968; cons. to constrn. group and corp. planning dept. Owens-Corning Fiberglas Corp., Toledo, 1969-70; CEO Questor Assocs., San Francisco, 1972-83; chmn. nat. mgmt. adv. svcs. Kenneth Leventhal & Co., 1983-84; pres. Stephen E. Roulac & Co., 1985-86; mng. ptnr. Roulac Group of Deloitte Haskins & Sells (Deloitte & Touche), 1987-91; CEO The Roulac Group, Larkspur, Calif., 1992—; strategic fin. econ. and transactions cons. Roulac Capitol Mkt. Strategies, Roulac Capitol Flows; expert witness, preparer econ. analyses for legal matters including civil trial of Irvine Co., Jewell et. al. vs. Bank of Am., Tchrs. vs. Olympia & York, Calif. Legis., Calif. Corps. Dept., Midwest Securities Commrs. Assn., Nat. Assn. Securities Dealers, SEC, Dept. of Labor, HUD; advisor to investment arm of Asian country, Calif. Pub. Employees Retirement System, U.S. Dept. Labor, numerous others; adj. prof. Tex. A&M U., 1986, U. Chgo., 1985, UCLA, 1983-84, Stanford Grad. Sch. Bus., 1970-79, Pacific Coast Banking Sch., 1978, Hastings Coll. Law, 1977-78, U. Calif., Berkeley, 1972-77, Calif. State U., 1970-71, Northeastern U., 1969-70; keynote speaker, instr. continuing edn. sessions, program chmn., corps., orgns. Author: Real Estate Syndications Digest: Principles and Applications, 1972, Case Studies in Property Development, 1973, Syndication Landmarks, 1974, Tax Shelter Sale-Leaseback Financing: The Economic Realities, 1976, Modern Real Estate Investment: An Institutional Approach, 1976, (with Sherman Maisel) Real Estate Investment and Finance, 1976 (1976 Bus. Book of Yr. The Libr. Jour.); editor-in-chief, pub. Calif. Bicyclist, 1988-95, Tex. Bicyclist, 1989-94, Roulac's Strategic Real Estate, 1979-89; columnist Forbes, 1983, 84, 87, 92, 93, Intuition Network, Ctr Real Estate Rsch. Nortwestern U., Nat. Bureau Real Estate Rsch., New Leaders, World 2000, NACORE/ARES Corp. Rsch. Found., Mystery Sch.; mem. editorial adv. bd. Am. Real Estate and Urban Econs. Assn. Jour., 1977-81, Housing Devel. Reporter, 1978-80, Fin. Edn. Jour., 1976-70, Jour. Housing Rsch., 1996—, Jour. Real Estated Edn. and Practice, 1996—, Jour. Real Estate Lit., 1996—, Jour. Property Valuation and Investment, 1992—, Real Estate Workouts and Asset Mgmt., 1992—; assoc. editor Real Estate Rev., 1993—; editor Jour. Real Estate Rsch., 1992—; contbg. editor Real Estate Law Jour., 1973-78, Real Estate Rev., 1973-75; spl. issue editor Calif. Mgmt. Rev., 1976; editor: Real Estate Syndication Digest, 1971-72, Notable Syndications Sourcebook, 1972, Real Estate Securities and Syndication: A Workbook, 1973, Due Diligence in Real Estate Transactions, 1974, Real Estate Venture Analysis, 1974, Real Estate Securities Regulation Sourcebook, 1975, Questor Real Estate Investment Manager Profiles, 1982, Questor Real Estate Securities Yearbook, 1980-85, Retail Giants and Real Estate, 1986, Roulac's Top Real Estate Brokers, 1984-88, (monograph) Ethics in Real Estate; contbr. articles to profl. jours., newspapers; cassettes; frequent appearer on TV shows including MacNeil/Lehrer Newshour, 1986, Cable News Network, 1987, ABC TV, 1987, KCBS Radio, 1986, WABC Radio, Dallas, 1986. Mem. real estate adv. com. to Calif. Commr. Corps., 1973, Calif. Corp. Commr.'s Blue Ribbon Com. on Projections and Track Records, 1973-74; mem. adv. bd. Nat. Bicycle Month, League of Am. Wheelmen, Ctr. for Real Estate Rsch. Kellogg Grad. Sch. Mgmt., Northwestern U. Named Highest Instr. Student Teaching Evaluations, Schs.

Bus. Adminstrn., U. Calif., Berkeley, 1975-76; named to Pomona Coll. Athletic Hall of Fame, 1981; W.T. Grant fellow Harvard U., 1969-70,; George F. Baker scholar Harvard Grad. Sch. Bus. Adminstrn., 1970; Stanford U. Grad. Sch. Bus. fellow, 1970-71. Mem. Strategic Mgmt. Soc., Am. Acad. Mgmt., Am. Fin. Assn., Am. Planning Assn, European Real Estate Soc., Internat. Real Estate Soc., Inst. Mgmt. Cons., ISSSEEM, Soc. Sci. Exploration, Am. Real Estate and Urban Econs. Assn., Intuition Network (bd. dirs.), World Future Soc. (exec. com. and adv. bd. World 2000), Am. Econ. Assn., Am. Real Estate Soc. (pres. 1995-96, award for best paper presented in ann. meeting, 1995, 96), Noetic Soc., Nat. Bur. Real Estate Rsch. (founder, bd. dirs.), Harvard Club N.Y., L.A. Adventures Club. Avocations: arts, antiquarian books, reading, bicycle racing (U.S. team 1990), outdoor activities. Office: The Roulac Group 900 Larkspur Landing Cir Larkspur CA 94939-1757

ROULEAU, REYNALD, bishop; b. St.-Jean-de-Dieu, Que., Can., Nov. 30, 1935. Ordained priest, 1963, bishop, 1987. Bishop Churchill-Hudson Bay, 1987—. Office: Diocese of Churchill-Baie D'Hudson, C P 10, Churchill, MB Canada R0B 0E0

ROULHAC, NELLIE GORDON, retired special education educator; b. Washington, June 5; d. Levi Preston and Agnes Pauline (Lee) Gordon; m. Christopher Maxwell Roulhac, Jr., Aug. 1, 1942; children: Christopher Maxwell III, Yvonne Agnes Roulhac Horton. BS, Cheyney (Pa.) State U., 1944; MA, Columbia U., 1946; EdD, U. Sarasota, Fla., 1978; postgrad., Temple U., U. Pa. Cert. spl. edn. tchr., Pa. Instr. Albany (Ga.) State Coll., 1947-51; tchr. Coatesville (Pa.) sch. sys., 1944-46; special class tchr. Phila. sch. sys., 1957-71, supr. special classes, 1971-84. Author: (books) Seventeen Days of Jimmie, 1981, Work, Play and Commitment: The First Fifty Years Jack and Jill of America, Incorporated, 1989, Jumping Over the Moon, 1994; (booklet) ABCs of Fundraising, 1984. Del. to White House Conf. on Children and Youth, 1955; nat. pres. Jack and Jill of Am., Inc., 1954-58; pres. Jack and Jill of Am. Found., 1975-78, bd. dirs., 1975-78; bd. commns. Mayors Comm. for Women, Phila., 1983-91; trustee Combs Coll. of Music, Phila., 1976-77, Free Libr. Phila., 1986-96; pres., bd. trustees Pennhurst State Sch. and Hosp., Spring City, Pa., 1979-82; trustee United Cerebral Palsy Assn., 1970-74; vol. ARC, Phila. Recipient award Nat. Found. for Infantile Paralysis, 1956, Leadership in Fundraising award, Svc. to Youth award Century Club award YMCA, Memphis, 1953-54, Phila., 1965-69, 1st prize Best Student Tchg. award Cheyney State U., Meritorious Svc. award ARC, Phila., 1954, Continuing Svc. award Jack and Jill of Am., 1974, 78, 88, Cert. of award Phila. Assn. for Retarded Children, 1967, Outstanding Contribution award Pennhurst Ctr., Spring City, 1973-87, Main Line Comm. Phila. Grand Opera Co., Humanitarian Svc. award Liberian Children Rehab. Network, 1995, award for contbn. in field of spl. edn. Phila. Assn. Sch. Adminstrs, citation City of Phila., 1994. Mem. Thirty Clusters (founder), The Links Inc., Karma Club, Nat. Assn. Parliamentarians (N.L. Carter unit), Delta Sigma Theta (Phila. alumnae chpt., nat. sec. 1954-60, chairperson nat. pers. com. 1960-64, Sadie T.M. Alexander award 1988). Avocations: writing, decoupage, crafts, collecting foreign dolls and autographs, travel.

ROULSTON, THOMAS HENRY, investment adviser; b. N.Y.C., Apr. 6, 1933; s. Henry Davies and Marjorie (Heather) R.; m. Lois Mueller, July 31, 1954; children: Scott Davies, Thomas Henry III, Heather Ettinger. BA, Dartmouth, 1955. Vice pres. Gunn, Carey & Roulston (stockbrokers), Cleve., 1960-63; pres. Roulston & Co., Inc., Cleve., 1963-90, chmn., 1990—; vice chmn. Bank Roulston Ltd., Zurich, Switzerland, 1972-76; pres., chmn. Investment Guidance Fund, 1967-80; chmn., dir. Womens Fed. Savs. Bank, 1983-93; chmn. bd. dirs. MJM Industries, 1994—, Am. Stone Industries, 1996—, Defiance, Inc., 1990—, Continental Pharmacy, 1994—, Ramwear, 1994—, Roulston Investment Capital Corp., 1984-95, Roulston Capital Ltd., 1982-93; chmn. Roulston Investment Trust, 1988, Roulston Venture Fund; bd. dirs. City Life Inc., 1985—; dir., chmn. bd. RB Mfg. Co., 1996—. Mem. Ohio Criminal Justice Supervisory Commn., 1970-73; chmn. Adminstrn. of Justice Com., 1968-70; past trustee Soc. for Crippled Children, Hill House, Health Hill Hosp., Cleve. Coun. World Affairs, Choate Rosemary Hall, Lakeview Cemetery Assn.; past trustee, mem. exec. com. Univ. Circle, Inc.; trustee, chmn. Bluecoats Inc., State Troopers; vice chmn. Midtown Corridor, 1981-84; past trustee Cleve. State U. Devel. Found. Capt. USAF, 1955-58. Mem. World Bus. Coun., Chief Execs. Orgn., Union Club, Country Club, Pepper Pike Club, Univ. Club (chmn.), Country Club of the Rockies. Home: 2627 Fairmount Blvd Cleveland Heights OH 44106-3601 Office: 4000 Chester Ave Cleveland OH 44103-3612

ROUMAN, JOHN CHRIST, classics educator; b. Tomahawk, Wis., May 1, 1926; s. Christ and Soteria (Dedes) R. BA in Greek, Carleton Coll., 1950; MA in Greek, Columbia U., 1951; student, Rutgers U., 1951-53, U. Kiel, Germany, 1956-57, U. Minn., Mpls., 1959-60; PhD in Classics, U. Wis., 1965. German tchr. Seton Hall Preparatory Sch., South Orange, N.J., 1954-56; ancient history tchr. Malverne (N.Y.) High Sch., 1957-59; tchg. asst. in ancient history U. Wis., Madison, 1960-61, rsch. asst. in ancient history, 1961-65; rsch. asst. in Greek epigraphy Inst. Advanced Study, Princeton, N.J., 1962-63; asst. prof. Classics U. N.H., Durham, 1965-71, assoc. prof., 1971-91, prof., 1991—, co-chmn. Spanish and Classics depts.; examiner N.H. State Bd. Edn. in Latin and Greek, 1979-80; judge Warren H. Held Jr. Exam-Contests in Latin and Mythology, 1988—; cons. Nat. Classical Greek Examination, 1980; presenter, lectr. in field. Active Colovos Rd. Com., 1981-82. With USN, 1944-46. Fulbright scholar U. Kiel, 1956-57; recipient Disting. Tchg. award U. N.H. Alumni Assn., 1985, Pericles award Am. Hellenic Ednl. Progressive Assn. and Daus. of Penelope, 1993. Mem. Am. Classical League (rep. to TCNE at ann. meeting 1978, mem. fin. com. 1981-82, treas. 1982-83), Am. Philol. Assn. (Nat. Excellence in Teaching Classics award, 1991), Archaeol. Inst. Am., Classical Assn. Can., Classical Assn. New Eng. (mem. exec. com. at-large 1981-84, mem. nominating com. 1983-84, 86-87, pres. 1987-88, Barlow-Beach award 1991, mem. ad hoc com. on elections and appointments), Medieval Acad. Am., Modern Greek Studies Assn., Nat. Assn. Advisors for Health Professions, N.H. Classical Assn. (mem. exec. com. 1965—, chair nominating com. 1986—), Strafford County Greco-Roman Found. (pres. 1978—), Vergilian Soc. Am., Phi Kappa Theta (faculty advisor, 1982—, chmn. nat. bd., 1993—). Office: U NH Dept Spanish and Classics 209G Murkland Hall Durham NH 03824-3596

ROUND, ALICE FAYE BRUCE, school psychologist; b. Ironton, Ohio, July 19, 1934; d. Wade Hamilton and Martha Matilda (Toops) Bruce; children: Leonard Bruce, Christopher Frederick. BA, Asbury Coll., 1956; MS in Sch. Psychology, Miami U., Oxford, Ohio, 1975. Cert. tchr., sch. psychologist, supr., Ohio; cert. tchr., Calif. Tchr. Madison County (Ohio) Schs., 1956-58, Columbus (Ohio) Pub. Schs., 1958, San Diego Pub. Schs., 1958-60, Poway (Calif.) Unified Sch. Dist., 1960-64; substitute tchr. Princeton City Schs., Cin., 1969-75; sch. psychologist, intern Greenhills/Forest Park City Schs., Cin., 1975-76; sch. psychologist Fulton County Schs., Wauseon, Ohio, 1976-77, Sandusky (Ohio) pub. and Cath. schs., 1977-96; tchr. art cmty. group and pvt. lessons, Sandusky, 1962, Springdale, Ohio, 1962-69; mem. Youth Svcs. Bd., Sandusky, 1978-88; bd. dirs., cons. Sandusky Sch. Practical Nursing, 1983-91; presenter suicide prevention seminars for mental health orgns.; speaker at ch., civic and youth orgns., local radio and TV programs; cons. on teen pregnancy to various schs., health depts. Mem. Huron (Ohio) Boosters Club, 1978-92, Vols. in Action, Sandusky, 1987—. Mem. NAACP, NEA, Nat. Sch. Psychologist Assn., Ohio Sch. Psychologist Assn., Maumee Valley Sch. Psychologist Assn., Ohio Edn. Assn., Sandusky Edn. Assn., Phi Delta Kappa (historian 1984-88, Most Innovative Preservation of History award 1988). Home: 821 Seneca Ave Huron OH 44839-1842 Office: Sandusky Bd Edn 407 Decatur St Sandusky OH 44870-2442

ROUNDS, BARBARA LYNN, psychiatrist; b. L.A., Mar. 17, 1934; d. Ralph Arthur and Florene V. (Heyer) Behrend; divorced 1962; children: Steve, Mike, Pamela, Ronald, Thomas. BA, Stanford U., 1964, MD, 1966; postgrad., San Francisco Psychoanalytic, 1973-81. Diplomate Am. Bd. Psychiatry and Neurology; cert. psychoanalyst. Intern New Orleans Pub. Health Svc., 1966-67; resident psychiat. Mendocino State Hosp., 1967-69, U. Calif. Davis, 1969-70; staff psychiatrist U. Calif. Davis Med. Sch., Sacramento, 1970-77, clin. instr., 1970-76; psychiatrist pvt. practice, Sacramento, 1971—; asst. clin. prof. U. Calif. Davis, Sacramento, 1976-84, assoc. clin. prof., 1984—. Mem. Am. Psychiat. Assn., Am. Psychoanalytic Assn., AMA, Cen. Calif. Psychiat. Soc. (pres.-elect 1990-91, pres. 1991-92). Democrat. Home: 8910 Leatham Ave Fair Oaks CA 95628-6506 Office: 1317 H St Sacramento CA 95814-1928

ROUNDS, DONALD EDWIN, retired cell biologist; b. Maywood, Ill., Jan. 17, 1926; s. Howard Gilmore and Dorothy May (Stucker) R.; m. Helen Lorraine Cann, Mar. 16, 1951 (dec. 1986); children: Robin Anne, Wendy Jeanne; m. Janice Mary Price, Oct. 17, 1987. BA, Occidental Coll., 1951; PhD, UCLA, 1958. Research asso. med. br. U. Tex., Galveston, 1958-59; dir. dept. cell biology Pasadena Found. for Med. Research, Calif., 1959-65; research coordinator Pasadena Found. for Med. Research, 1965-72, sr. research investigator, dir. carcinogenesis lab., 1972-82; dir. cell biology and laser labs. Huntington Med. Research Insts., 1982-90; chief scientist Advanced Med. Diagnostics Ltd., 1990-94, dir., cons., 1995—; prof. Loma Linda Med. Sch., 1974—; adj. prof. U. So. Calif. Med. Sch. Contbr. numerous articles to profl. jours., also chpts. books.; Reviewing editor: In Vitro, 1970-83. Served with U.S. Army, 1945-47. Mem. AAAS, Am. Soc. Zoologists, Tissue Culture Assn., Am. Soc. Cell Biologists, Am. Film Assn., Am. Inst. Biol. Scis., Sigma Xi. Home: 3111 NW Norwood Pl Corvallis OR 97330-1150

ROUNDS, DONALD MICHAEL, public relations executive; b. Centralia, Ill., May 9, 1941; s. Donald Merritt and Alice Josephine (Soulsby) R.; m. Alma Genevieve Beyer, Dec. 13, 1975. BS in History, Polit. Sci., Colo. State U., 1963. Police reporter, night city editor The Rocky Mountain News, Denver, 1960-70; mgr. Don M. Rounds Co., Denver, 1970-75; sr. editor Western Oil Reporter, Denver, 1975-80; energy writer The Rocky Mountain News, Denver, 1980-87; sr. media rels. advisor Cyprus Minerals Co., Englewood, Colo., 1987-92, media and community rels. mgr., 1992-93; media and community rels. mgr. Cyprus Amax Minerals Co., Englewood, 1994-95, dir. coms., 1995—; adv. bd Colo. State Minerals, Energy, and Geology (appointed by gov.), 1992—. Contbr. articles to mags. and newspapers. Mem. covenant com. Ken Caryl Ranch Master Assn., Littleton, Colo., 1996—; vol. naturalist Roxborough State Park, Colo., 1997—. Recipient MerComm Mercury Gold award, 1995, MerComm Silver award (Denver Post), 1995, 1996, 1st pl. spl. news series AP, 1987, 1st pl. news sweepstakes, 1987, Margolin award U. Denver Coll. Bus., 1986, Betty McWhorter Commendation of Honor Desk & Derrick Club of Denver, 1987, Journalism award Rocky Mountain Assn. Geologists, 1985, Citizen Svc. award Denver Police Dept., 1969, Pub. Svc. award Englewood Police Dept., 1967. Mem. Nat. Mining Assn. (pub. rels. com.), Soc. Profl. Journalists, Sigma Delta Chi, Denver Press Club (bd. dirs. 1987). Republican. Methodist. Avocations: scuba diving, skiing, hiking, photography. Home: 8220 S San Juan Range Rd Littleton CO 80127-4011 Office: Cyprus Amax Minerals Co 9100 E Mineral Cir Englewood CO 80112-3401

ROUNICK, JACK A., lawyer, company executive; b. Phila., June 5, 1935; s. Philip and Nettie (Brownstein) R.; BBA, U. Mich., 1956; JD, U. Pa., 1959; m. Noreen A. Garrigan, Sept. 4, 1970; children: Ellen, Eric, Amy, Michelle. Bar: Pa. 1960, U.S. Dist. Ct. (ea. dist.) Pa., 1960. Spl. asst. atty. gen., 1963-71; ptnr. Israelit & Rounick, 1960-67, Moss & Rounick, 1968-69, Moss, Rounick & Hurowitz, Norristown, Pa., 1969-72, Moss & Rounick, Norristown, 1972-73; ptnr. Pechner, Dorfman, Wolffe, Rounick and Cabot, Norristown, 1973-87; v.p., gen. counsel Martin Lawrence Ltd. Edits., Inc., 1987-93; dir. Martin Lawrence Ltd. Edits., Inc., 1984—, Deb Shops, Inc., 1974—. Fin. chmn. Pa. Young Rep., 1964-66, treas., 1966-68, chmn., 1968-70. Recipient Boss of Yr. award Montgomery County Legal Secs. Assn., 1970, Cert. of appreciation Pa. Bar Inst., 1980. Fellow Internat. Acad. Matrimonial Lawyers, Am. Acad. Matrimonial Lawyers (pres. Pa. chpt. 1982-84, gov. 1983-85, v.p. 1985-87); mem. ABA (coun. family law sect. 1982-87), Pa. Bar Assn. (past chmn. family law sect., Spl. Achievement award 1979-80), Montgomery Bar Assn., Am. Friends of the Hebrew U. (v.p. 1990-91, bd. dirs. 1987-93, Nat. Coun. Trustees 1987-93, pres. Phila. chpt. 1988-91). Republican. Jewish. Author: Pennsylvania Matrimonial Practice, 6 vols., 1982; editor Pa. Family Lawyer, 1980-87. Office: 516 Swede St Norristown PA 19401-4807

ROUNTREE, ASA, lawyer; b. Birmingham, Ala., Aug. 9, 1927; s. John Asa and Cherokee Jemison (Van de Graaff) R.; m. Elizabeth Rhodes Blue, Aug. 11, 1951; children—Robert B., John A. A.B., U. Ala., 1949; LL.B., Harvard U., 1954. Bar: Ala. 1954, U.S. Dist. Ct. (no. dist.) Ala. 1954, U.S. Ct. Appeals (5th cir.) 1955, N.Y. 1962, U.S. Dist. Ct. (so. dist.) N.Y. 1963, U.S. Ct. Appeals (2d cir.) 1963, U.S. Supreme Ct. 1972. Assoc. Cabaniss & Johnston, Birmingham, Ala., 1954-60, ptnr., 1960-62; assoc. Debevoise & Plimpton, N.Y.C., 1962-63, ptnr., 1963-91; mem. Maynard, Cooper & Gale, P.C., Birmingham, 1991—. Bd. dirs. U. Ala. Law Sch. Found. Served with U.S. Army, 1945-46, to lt., 1951-53. Mem. ABA (chmn. litigation sect. 1980-81), Ala. Bar Assn., N.Y. State Bar Assn., Assn. Bar City N.Y., Am. Law Inst., Am. Coll. Trial Lawyers, Am. Bar Found. Episcopalian. Clubs: River (N.Y.C.); Mountain Brook (Birmingham). Office: Maynard Cooper Gale PC 2400 AmSouth/Harbert Plz 1901 6th Ave N Birmingham AL 35203-2618

ROUNTREE, GEORGE DENTON, health services management consultant; b. Houston, Mar. 14, 1937; s. George Washington and Verda Mae (Wagnon) R. B.S., Lamar U., 1960; M.H.A., Washington U., St. Louis, 1963; postgrad. Grad. Sch. Bus. and Public Health, Harvard U., 1976. Vice pres. Methodist Hosp., Houston, 1963-75; pres. Quadrus Internat. Inc. Tex., Houston, 1977—. Adj. asst. prof. Washington U. Med. Sch., St. Louis, 1978-85; adj. prof. U. Istanbul, Turkey; guest lectr. U. Tex. Health Sci. Ct., Houston, 1983. Contbr. articles to profl. jours. Mem. profl. adv. com. Mental Health Assn. Houston and Harris County; adv. and instl. rep. Boy Scouts Am. Served with USNR, 1956-63. Fellow Am. Coll. Hosp. Adminstrs.; mem. Houston C. of C. (chmn. art com. Ronald McDonald House), Am. Assn. Hosp. Planning, Greater Houston Hosp. Council, Nat. Council Internat. Health, Assn. Univ. Programs in Health Adminstrn. Club: Rotary. Home: 1101 Post Oak Blvd Ste 9B Houston TX 77056-3105 Office: Am Hosp Istanbul, Guzelbahce Sokak Nisantasi, 80220 Istanbul Turkey

ROUNTREE, JANET CARYL, astrophysicist; b. Chgo., Aug. 14, 1937; d. Ernest Alonzo and Frances Careta (Vogel) R.; m. J. Harold Lesh, Apr. 19, 1960 (div. 1971); 1 child, Kathryn Frances; m. Morris L. Aizenman, June 24, 1977. A.B., Cornell U., 1958; postgrad., U. Paris, 1958-60; Ph.D., U. Chgo., 1967. Sci. officer Leiden (Netherlands) Obs., 1968-70; astronomer adjoint Meudon (France) Obs., 1970-71; vis. fellow U. Colo., 1971-72; research astronomer, lectr. astronomy U. Denver, 1972-77, dir. obs. ops., 1974-77; rsch. prof. of elec. and computer engring. U. Ariz., 1994—; NASA-NRC sr. resident research asso. Goddard Space Flight Center, 1977-79; phys. scientist Dept. Air Force, 1979-93; cons., sr. scientist Sci. Applications Internat. Corp., 1993—. English lang. editor, translator: Astronomy and Astrophysics: A European Jour, 1969-71; Contbr. numerous articles to profl. publs.; translator books from French, numerous articles from French and German. Fulbright fellow, 1958-60. Mem. Internat. Astron. Union (commn. mem.), Am. Astron. Soc., Royal Astron. Soc., Fulbright Alumni Assn. (dir. 1978-83, nat. capital area, treas. 1991-93), Phi Beta Kappa, Sigma Xi, Phi Kappa Phi. Achievements include visible and ultraviolet classification systems for early-type stars. Office: PO Box 65285 Tucson AZ 85728-5285

ROUNTREE, JOHN GRIFFIN RICHARDSON, association and retail executive; b. Ocala, Fla., Oct. 31, 1936; s. Otis J. and Harriet (Griffin) R.; 1 child: Robert Ivan Shreve-Rountree. Student graphic arts and advt. Ringling Sch. Art, Sarasota, Fla., 1957. Hon. accademico corrispondento L'Accademia Tiberina, Rome, 1970. Pres., Rountree Printing & Advt. Co., Miami, Fla., 1959-63; asst. exec. v.p., statistician Inst. Shortening & Edible Oils, Washington, 1963-65; asst. exec. v.p. Automotive Trade Assn., Washington, 1965-67; exec. dir. DP&S Inc., Washington, 1968-73; pres., pub. The Hereditry Register of the U.S.A., Washington, 1971-75; pres. St. Johns Printing & Office Supply, Inc., St. Augustine, 1976—; dep. Harbor Master Port St. Augustine, 1982-86; mem. various nat. associations. Served with F.A., U.S. Army, 1958-60. Decorated Grand Cross Magistral Grace, Sovereign Greek Order St. Dennis of Zante; Gran Cruz, Soberana e Imperial Orden de la Corona Azteca; grand officer Sovereign Mil. Order Temple of Jerusalem; Hospitaller Order of St. John of Jerusalem, Knights of Malta; lt. col., aide de camp Gov. Jimmy Carter Staff, Ga., 1971; Gov. George Wallace Staff, Ala. 1972; col. Gov. Edwin Edwards Staff, La., 1972; hon. col., aide de camp Gov. Robert Ray, Iowa, 1972; hon. citizen State Tex., 1973; hon. sec. state State Ind., 1972; hon. Silver State plenipotentiary, Gov. O'Callaghan, Nev., 1973; Disting. Hooser, Gov. Ind., 1973; Hon. citizen W. Va., 1973; recipient 1st place award hard bound volumes Printing Industries Virginias, 1971. Mem. St. Andrews Soc., Royal Soc. St. George, London, Gen. Soc. War 1812, Fla. Soc. (v.p. gen.), Gen. Soc. S.R. (bd. dirs. Washington 1970), Nat. Soc. SAR (librarian gen. nat. soc. 1969-71), St. Johns County C. of C. (com. of 100), Gen. Soc. Colonial Wars (gentleman of council D.C. 1976), Mil. Order Fgn. Wars U.S., Sons. Confederate Vets., Nat. Soc. Sons and Daus. of the Pilgrims, Soc. Descendants of the Colonial Clergy, Order Stars and Bars (1st vice comdr. D.C. 1970), Nat. Huguenot Soc., Order of Lafayette, Hereditary Order Descendants of the Loyalists and Patriots of the Am. Revolution (librarian general 1972), Descendants of Knights of the Garter, Windsor Castle, England, Clan MacArthur Soc., Nat. Soc. Sons of the Am. Colonists, First Families of Ga., Republican. Episcopalian. Clubs: Ponte Vedra (Fla.); St. Augustine Yacht (chmn. bd. 1982, Man of Yr. award 1990); St. George's (London). Lodges: Masons, K.T., 32 Degree Scottish Rite, Nat. Sojourners. Avocations: boating, tennis. Office: St Johns Printing & Office Supply Inc 107 King St Saint Augustine FL 32084-4320

ROUNTREE, PATRICIA ANN, youth organization administrator; b. Rochester, N.Y., Apr. 2, 1942; d. Robert James and Myrtle Margaret (Cuthbertson) R. AA, Cazenovia Coll., 1961; BA, Parsons Coll., 1965. Gen. clk. Eastman Kodak, Rochester, 1961-63; 6th grade tchr. Wayland (N.Y.) Ctrl. Sch., 1965-67; field dir. Seven Lakes Coun. Girl Scouts U.S.A., Phelps, N.Y., 1967-73; program dir. Palm Glades Coun. Girl Scouts U.S.A., Lake Worth, Fla., 1973-76; asst. exec. dir. Seven Lakes Coun. Girl Scouts U.S.A., 1976-86; exec. dir. Mich. Trails Coun. Girl Scouts U.S.A., Grand Rapids, 1986-89; exec. dir. Ctrl. N.Y. Coun. Girl Scouts U.S.A., Syracuse, 1989—. Pres., bd. dirs. Planned Parenthood of Fingerlakes, Geneva, N.Y., 1982-86. Mem. Zonta Internat. Rotary Syracuse. Presbyn. Avocations: needlework, reading, travel. Home: 4 Robinson Dr Baldwinsville NY 13027 Office: Ctrl NY Girl Scout Coun 6724 Thompson Rd # 482 Syracuse NY 13211-2122

ROUPE, JAMES PAUL, accountant; b. Havre de Grace, Md., Apr. 20, 1957; s. Paul Clyde and Shirley Louise (Trivette) R. AA, Harford C.C., Bel Air, Md., 1977; BS, Towson State U., 1979. CPA, Md. Mgmt. asst. Loyola Fed. Savings and Loan, Balt., 1979-81; asst. treas. Legum Chevrolet-Nissan, Balt., 1983-89; contr. Bob Bell Chevrolet/Nissan, Inc., Balt., 1989-92, corp. sec.-treas., 1992—; sr. controller Bob Bell Chevrolet Geo of Bel Air (Md.) Inc., 1991-92, corp. sec.-treas., 1992—; corp. sec.-treas. Bob Bell of Upper Marlboro (Md.), L.C., 1995—. Recipient Bus. Mgmt. Excellence award Nissan Motor Corp., 1990-96. Mem. AICPA, Md. Assn. CPAs, Inst. Mgmt. Accts., Chevrolet Coun. Bus. Acctg. Mgrs., Soc. for Preservation and Encouragement of Barbershop Quartet Singing in Am., Inc. (Dundalk, Md. chpt.). Republican. Baptist. Office: Bob Bell Chevrolet Nissan 7900 Eastern Ave Baltimore MD 21224-2125

ROUS, STEPHEN NORMAN, urologist, educator; b. N.Y.C., Nov. 1, 1931; s. David H. and Luba (Margulies) R.; m. Margot Woolfolk, Nov. 12, 1966; children: Benjamin, David. A.B., Amherst Coll., 1952; M.D., N.Y. Med. Coll., 1956; M.S., U. Minn., 1963. Diplomate: Am. Bd. Urology. Intern Phila. Gen. Hosp., 1956-57, resident, 1959-60; resident Flower-Fifth Ave. and Met. Hosp., N.Y.C., 1957-59, Mayo Clinic, Rochester, Minn., 1960-63; practice medicine specializing in urology San Francisco, 1963-68; assoc. prof. urology N.Y. Med. Coll., N.Y.C., 1968-72; assoc. dean N.Y. Med. Coll., 1970-72; prof. surgery, chief div. urology Mich. State U., East Lansing, 1972-75; prof., chmn. dept. urology Med. U. S.C., Charleston, 1975-88; urologist-in-chief Med. U. S.C. and County hosps., Charleston, 1975-88; editorial dir. Norton Med. Books div. W.W. Norton and Co., 1988-94, editorial cons., 1994—; clin. prof. surgery Uniformed Svcs. U. of Health Scis., Bethesda, Md., 1992—; adj. prof. urology Med. U. S.C., 1988—, adj. prof. surgery Dartmouth Med. Sch., 1988-91, prof. surgery (urology), 1991—; staff urologist Dartmouth-Hitchcock Med. Ctr., 1991—; cons. urologist Saginaw VA Hosp., 1971-75, Charleston VA Hosp., 1975-88; hon. cons. St. Peter's Hosp., London, 1981-82; sr. vis. fellow Inst. Urology, London, 1981-82; mil. cons. in urology USAF Surgeon Gen., 1982-85; chmn. alumni devel. com. Mayo Clinic, 1979-82; hon. staff The Exeter Hosp., N.H., 1988—; mem. nat. bd. visitors N.Y. Med. Coll., 1988—; chief urology VA Med. Ctr., White River Junction, Vt., 1991—. Author: Understanding Urology, 1973, Urology in Primary Care, 1976, Spanish edit., 1978, Russian edit., 1979, Urology: A Core Textbook, 1985, 2d edit., 1996, The Prostate Book, 1988, latest rev. edit., 1995, (with Judge Hiller B. Zobel) Doctors and the Law: Defendants and Expert Witnesses, 1993; editor Urology Ann., 1987-97, Stone Disease: Diagnosis and Management, 1987; mem. editl. bd. Mil. Medicine, 1984-94; contbr. articles to med. jours. Mem. East Lansing (Mich.) Planning Commn., 1974-75; vestryman, jr. warden All Saints Episcopal Ch., East Lansing, 1973-75, lay reader, mem. diocesan com. on continuing edn., 1975-86; vestryman St. Michael's Episc. Ch., 1979-82, Charleston, S.C., chmn. every mem. canvas, 1979-80, chmn. lay readers, 1983-86; mem. fin. com., lay reader Christ Episc. Ch., Exeter, N.H., 1989-91; lector St. Thomas Episc. Ch., Hanover, N.H., 1991—, vestryman, 1992-96, stewardship chmn., 1992-94, jr. warden, 1994-96; mem. selectman's alt. Hampton Falls Planning Bd., 1989-91. Col. USAFR, 1981-85, col. USAR, 1985—. Recipient "A" designator in urology, U.S. Army Surgeon Gen., 1986. Fellow ACS, Am. Acad. Pediatrics; mem. AMA, Soc. Univ. Urologists, Internat. Soc. Urology, Am. Urol. Assn., Nat. Urologic Forum, Soc. Pediatric Urology, Brit. Assn. Urol. Surgeons, German Urol. Assn. (hon.), Mayo Alumni Assn. (v.p. 1979-81, pres. 1983-85), Army and Navy Club (Washington), Lotos Club (N.Y.C.), Sigma Xi, Alpha Omega Alpha (hon.). Republican. Home: 6 Partridge Rd Etna NH 03750-0354 Office: Dartmouth Hitchcock Med Ctr Sect Urology Lebanon NH 03756

ROUSAKIS, JOHN PAUL, former mayor; b. Savannah, Ga., Jan. 14, 1929; s. Paul V. and Antigone (Alexopoulos) R.; m. Elizabeth Lattimore, Oct. 24, 1987; children: Rhonda, Paul, Thea, Tina. B.B.A., U. Ga., 1952. Commr. Chatham County, Ga., 1965-69; vice chmn. Chatham County, 1969-70; mayor of Savannah, 1970-92; ins. broker Savannah, 1956—. Past pres. Nat. League Cities. With AUS, 1953-56. Named Outstanding Young Man of Savannah, Outstanding Young Man of Ga., 1962, Archon Greek Orthodox Ch., 1988, Outstanding City Ofcl., State of Ga.; recipient Tree of Life award Jewish Nat. Fund, 1983, Pres.'s award Nat. League of Cities, 1991. Mem. Ga. Mcpl. Assn. (past pres.), Am. Legion, Ahepa, Masons, (Shriner, Knight Comdr. 32d deg.). Office: 24 E Liberty St Savannah GA 31401

ROUSE, CHRISTOPHER CHAPMAN, III, composer; b. Balt., Feb. 15, 1949; s. Christopher Chapman Jr. and Margery (Harper) R.; m. Ann Jensen, Aug. 28, 1983; children: Jillian, Alexandra, Adrian; 1 stepchild, Angela. MusB, Oberlin Conservatory, 1971; MFA, DMA, Cornell U., 1977; DMus (hon.), Oberlin Coll., 1996. Asst. prof. composition U. Mich., Ann Arbor, 1978-81; asst. prof. composition Eastman Sch. Music, Rochester, N.Y., 1981-85, assoc. prof. composition, 1985-91, prof. composition, 1991—; composer-in-residence Balt. Symphony Orch., 1986-89, Schleswir Holstein Festival, 1989, Helsinki Biennale, 1997, Tanglewood Music Ctr., 1997; faculty Juilliard Sch., 1997—; writer numerous musical subjects; historian rock music. Composer for numerous renowned soloist and ensembles including Yo-Yo Ma, Evelyn Glennie, Emanuel Ax, Dawn Upshaw, Charles Castleman, James VanDemark, Jan de Gaetani, Leslie Guinn, Carol Wincenc, Cho-Liang Lin, William Albright, Soc. New Music, Blackearth Percussion Group; commd. composer Atlanta Symphony, Phila. Orch., N.Y. Philharm., L.A. Philharm., Balt. Symphony, Houston Symphony, London Symphony, Cleve. Orch., Detroit Symphony, St. Louis Symphony, Rochester Philharmonic, Cleve. Quartet, Boston Musica Viva, Aspen Music Festival, Chamber Music Soc. Lincoln Ctr., N.Y. Internat. Festival of Arts, Chamber Music Am., New England Conservatory Music, Nonesuch Records; orchestral works programmed by Berlin, Stockholm, N.Y.C., Buffalo, L.A., Rochester Philharmonics, Orchestre Nat. de France Residentie, Concertgebouw, New Zealand, also Philharmonia Chgo., Boston, St. Louis, Detroit, Balt., Nat. Pitts., Houston, Denver, Milw., Cleve., Minn., Phila., Oakland, Cin., Atlanta, Indpls., Memphis, San Francisco, Dallas Symphony Orchs., also Finnish, Frankfurt, Austrian, and NHK Tokyo Radio Orchs. Recipient awards from Guggenheim Found., League Composers/ISCM, NEA, Rockefeller Found., Am. Music Ctr., Warner Bros. Record Co., Koussevitzky Found., BMI and Pitney Bowes, Friedheim 1st prize Kennedy Ctr., 1988, Pulitzer prize for music, 1993, Acad. award Am. Acad. Arts and

Letters, 1993. Home: 15 Surrey Hill Ln Pittsford NY 14534 Office: Eastman Sch Music 26 Gibbs St Rochester NY 14604-2505

ROUSE, DORIS JANE, physiologist, research administrator; b. Greensboro, N.C., Oct. 3, 1948; d. Welby Corbett and Nadia Elizabeth (Grainger) R.; m. Blake Shaw Wilson, Jan. 6, 1974; children: Nadia Jacqueline, Blair Elizabeth. B.A. in Chemistry, Duke U., 1970, Ph.D. in Physiology and Pharmacology, 1980. Tchr. sci. Peace Corps, Tugbake, Liberia, 1970-71; research scientist Burroughs Wellcome Co., Research Triangle Park, N.C., 1971-76; sr. physiologist Rsch. Triangle Inst., 1976-83, ctr. dir., 1980—, also dir. NASA tech. application team, 1980—; adminstr. ANSI Tech. Adv. Group for Wheelchairs, N.Y.C., 1982-86; adj. asst. prof. Sch. Medicine U. N.C., 1983—; chair Instl. Rev. Bd., Profl. Devel. Award Com., Rsch. Triangle Inst.; mem. adv. bd. Assistive Tech. Rsch. Ctr., 1994—. Mem. adv. bd. Assn. Retarded Citizens, Arlington (Tex.), 1981-88, Western Gerontology Soc., San Francisco, 1982-85; bd. dirs. Simon Found., Chgo. 1983—; mem. spl. rev. com. small bus. applications; Nat. Forum on Tech. and Aging. Recipient Group Achievement award NASA, 1979. Mem. Rehab. Engring. Soc. N.Am. (chmn. wheelchair com. 1981-86), Am. Soc. on Aging, Rehab. Engring. Soc. N.Am., Tech. Transfer Soc., Assn. Fed. Tech. Transfer Execs., Nat. Space Soc. Club: Triangle Dive. Home: 2410 Wrightwood Ave Durham NC 27705-5802 Office: Research Triangle Inst PO Box 12194 Durham NC 27709-2194

ROUSE, IRVING, anthropologist, emeritus educator; b. Rochester, N.Y., Aug. 29, 1913; s. Benjamin Irving and Louise Gillespie (Bohachek) R.; m. Mary Uta Mikami, June 24, 1939; children: Peter, David. BS, Yale U., 1934, PhD, 1938; D in Philosophy and Letters (hon.), Centro de Estudios Avanzados de Puerto Rico y el Caribe, 1990. Asst. anthropology Yale Peabody Museum, 1934-38, asst. curator, 1938-47, assoc. curator, 1947-54, research assoc., 1954-62, curator, 1977-85, emeritus curator, 1985—; instr. anthropology Yale U., 1939-43, asst. prof., 1943-48; assoc. prof. Yale, 1948-54; prof. Yale U., 1954-69, Charles J. MacCurdy prof. anthropology, 1969-84, prof. emeritus, 1984—. Author monographs on archaeology of Fla., Cuba, Haiti, P.R., Venezuela. Recipient Medalla Commemorativa del Vuelo Panamericano pro Faro de Colon Govt. Cuba, 1945, A. Cressy Morrison prize in natural sci. N.Y. Acad. Sci., 1951, Viking fund medal Wenner-Gren Found., 1960, Wilbur Cross medal Yale U., 1992; Guggenheim fellow, 1963-64; fellow Phi Beta Kappa, 1996. Mem. Am. Anthrop. Assn. (pres. 1967-68), Eastern States Archeol. Fedn. (pres. 1946-50), Assn. Field Archaeology (pres. 1977-78), Soc. Am. Archaeology (editor 1946-50, pres. 1952-53), Nat. Acad. Scis., Am. Acad. Arts and Scis., Internat. Assn. Caribbean Archaeology (hon. mem.), Soc. Antiquaries (London). Office: Yale U Dept Anthropology PO Box 208277 New Haven CT 06520-8277

ROUSE, JEFF, Olympic athlete, swimmer. Olympic swimmer Barcelona, Spain, 1992. Recipient 100m Backstroke Silver medal Olympics, Barcelona, 1992, 4*100 Medley Relay Gold Medal Olympics, Barcelona, 1992. World record holder 100m backstroke long course and short course, 1992. Address: care US Swimming Inc One Olympic Plz Colorado Springs CO 80909 Address: 4 Brittany Mdws Atherton CA 94027-4101*

ROUSE, JOHN WILSON, JR., research institute administrator; b. Kansas City, Mo., Dec. 7, 1937; s. John Wilson and Gail Agnes (Palmer) R.; m. Susan Jane Davis, May 3, 1981; 1 son, Jeffrey Scott. A.S., Kansas City Jr. Coll., 1957; B.S., Purdue U., 1959; M.S., U. Kans., 1965, Ph.D., 1968. Registered profl. engr., Mo., Tex. Engr. Bendix Corp., Kansas City, Mo., 1959-64; rsch. coord. Ctr. for Rsch., U. Kans., Lawrence, 1964-68; prof. elec. engring., dir. remote sensing ctr. Tex. A&M U., College Station, 1968-78; Logan prof. engr., chmn. elec. engring. U. Mo., Columbia, 1978-81; dean engring. U. Tex., Arlington, 1981-87; pres. So. Rsch. Inst., Birmingham, Ala., 1987—; mgr. microwave program NASA Hdqrs., Washington, 1975-77; bd. dirs. Protective Life Corp., Ala. Power Co.; chmn. bd. So. Rsch. Techs. Inc. Contbr. articles to profl. jours. Recipient Outstanding Tchr. award Tex. A&M U., 1971; Outstanding Prof. award U. Mo., 1980; Engr. of Yr. Tex. Soc. Profl. Engrs., 1983. Mem. IEEE, Nat. Soc. Profl. Engrs., Am. Soc. Engring. Edn., Internat. Bus. Fellows, Internat. Union Radio Sci., Sigma Xi, Eta Kappa Nu., Tau Beta Pi. Home: 2004 Bridgelake Dr Birmingham AL 35244-1421 Office: Southern Research Institute PO Box 55305 2000 9th Ave S Birmingham AL 35205-2708

ROUSE, RICHARD HUNTER, historian, educator; b. Boston, Aug. 14, 1933; s. Hunter and Dorothee (Hüsmert) R.; m. Mary L. Ames, Sept. 7, 1959; children: Thomas, Andrew, Jonathan. B.A., State U. Iowa, 1955; M.A., U. Chgo., 1957; Ph.D., Cornell U., 1963. Mem. faculty UCLA, 1963—, prof. history, 1975—; assoc. dir. Ctr. Medieval and Renaissance Studies, 1966-67, acting dir., 1967-68; dir. Summer Inst. in Paleography, 1978, chair grad. coun., 1989-90; adv. bd. Hill Monastic Microfilm Libr., St. John's U., Collegeville, Minn., Ambrosiana Microfilm Library, Notre Dame (Ind.) U., Corpus of Brit. Medieval Libr. Catalogues, Brit. Acad. Author: Serial Bibliographies for Medieval Studies, 1969, (with M.A. Rouse) Preachers, Florilegia and Sermons: Studies on the Manipulus Florum of Thomas of Ireland, 1979; (with others) Texts and Transmission, 1983; (with C.W. Dutschke) Medieval and Renaissance Manuscripts in the Claremont Libraries, 1986; (with M.A. Rouse) Cartolai, Illuminators and Printers in Fifteenth-Century Italy, 1988; (with L. Bataillon and B. Guyot) La Production du livre universitaire au moyen age, exemplar et pecia, 1988, (with others) Guide to Medieval and Renaissance Manuscripts in the Huntington Library, 1989, (with M. Ferrari) Medieval and Renaissance Manuscripts at the University of California, Los Angeles, 1991, (with M.A. Rouse and R.A.B. Mynors) Registrum de libris doctorum et auctorum veterum, 1991, (with M.A. Rouse) Authentic Witnesses: Approaches to Medieval Texts and Manuscripts, 1991; co-editor: Viator: Medieval and Renaissance Studies, 1970—; mem. editorial bd. Medieval and renaissance manuscripts in Calif. libraries, Medieval Texts, Toronto; Medieval Texts, Binghamton, Library Quar., 1984-88, Speculum, 1981-85, Revue d'histoire des Textes, 1986—, Cambridge Studies in Paleography and Codicology, 1990—, Catalogue of Medieval and Renaissance Manuscripts in the Beinecke Rare Book and Manuscript Library Yale University, 1984—. Am. Coun. Learned Socs. fellow, 1972-73, fellow All Souls Coll., Oxford, 1978-79, Guggenheim fellow, 1975-76, Rosenbach fellow in bibliogrpahy U. Pa., 1976, NEH fellow, 1981-82, 84-85, 94-96, Inst. for Advanced Studies fellow Jerusalem, 1991; J.R. Lyell reader in bibliogrpahy U. Oxford, 1991-92; vis. fellow Pembroke Coll., U. Oxford, 1992. Fellow Royal Hist. Soc., Medieval Acad. Am.; mem. Medieval Assn. Pacific (councillor 1965-68, pres. 1968-70), Medieval Acad. Am. (councillor 1977-80), Comité international de paléographie (treas. 1985-90), Comité international du vocabulaire des institutions et de la communication intellectuelles au moyen age, 1987—, Societa internazionale per lo studio del medioevo latino, 1988—. Home: 11444 Berwick St Los Angeles CA 90049-3416 Office: Univ Calif Dept History Los Angeles CA 90024

ROUSE, ROBERT MOOREFIELD, mathematician, educator; b. Auburn, N.Y., Aug. 1, 1936; s. Lester Mallory and Margaret (Moore) R.; m. Mary Josephine Sellers, Aug. 3, 1968; 1 child, Meredeth Elizabeth. BEE, Clarkson U., 1958, M in Engring. Sci., 1972; MS, Syracuse U., 1962. Registered profl. engr., N.Y. Envr. Gulf Oil Corp., Phila, Port Arthur, Tex., 1958-61; prof. SUNY, Morrisville, 1964—. 1st. lt. U.S. Army, 1962-63. Mem. IEEE, ASCE, Am. Soc. for Engring. Edn. Republican. Presbyterian. Home: PO Box 963 Oneonta AL 35121-0013 Office: SUNY Math Dept Morrisville NY 13408

ROUSE, ROBERT SUMNER, former college official; b. Northampton, Mass., Sept. 2, 1930; s. Charles Edward and Laura Elisabeth (Rowbotham) R.; m. children: R. Daniel, Roland, James, Katherine; m. Mary Ellen Morgan, Dec. 5, 1992; children: Morgan, Laura; stepchildren: Matthew, James, Joseph. B.S., Yale U., 1951, M.S., 1953, Ph.D. in Chemistry, 1957. Lab. asst., then asst. in instrn. Yale, 1951-56; asst. prof. chemistry Lehigh U., 1956-62; group leader, plastics div. Allied Chems. Corp., 1962-66, tech. supr., 1966-67; prof. chemistry Monmouth U., West Long Branch, N.J., 1967—; chmn. chemistry dept. Monmouth Coll., 1967-73, asso. dean faculty, 1968-73, dean faculty, v.p. acad. affairs, 1973-80, provost and v.p. acad. affairs, 1980-81, chmn. faculty coun., 1990-93; mem. licensure adv. and approval bd. N.J. Dept. Higher Edn., 1973-82, chmn., 1980-81; bd. dirs. Assn. Ind. Colls. and Univs. N.J., 1978-81. Author: (with Robert O. Smith) Energy: Resource, Slave, Pollutant-A Physical Science Text, 1975. Recipient Disting. Tchr. award Monmouth Coll., 1991. Fellow N.Y. Acad. Scis.; mem. Am. Chem. Soc., AAUP, Sigma Xi. Home: 482 Cedar Ave West Long Branch NJ 07764-1806

ROUSE, ROSCOE, JR., librarian, educator; b. Valdosta, Ga., Nov. 26, 1919; s. Roscoe and Minnie Estelle (Corbett) R.; m. Charlie Lou Miller, June 23, 1945; children: Charles Richard, Robin Lou. BA, U. Okla., 1948, MA, 1952; MALS, U. Mich., 1958, PhD, 1962; student (Grolier Soc. scholar), Rutgers U., 1956. Bookkeeper C & S Nat. Bank, Valdosta, Ga., 1937-41; draftsman R.K. Rouse Co. (heating engrs.), Greenville, S.C., 1941-42; student asst. U. Okla. and Rice U., 1947-48; asst. librarian Northeastern State Coll., Tahlequah, Okla., 1948-49; acting librarian, instr. library sci. Northeastern State Coll., 1949-51; circulation librarian Baylor U., 1952-53, acting univ. librarian, 1953-54, univ. librarian, prof., 1954-63, chmn. dept. library sci., 1956-63; dir. libraries State U. N.Y. at Stony Brook, L.I., 1963-67; dean libr. svcs., prof. Okla. State U., Stillwater, 1967-87, univ. libr. historian, 1987-92; chmn. dept. libr. edn. Okla. State U., 1967-74; Vis. prof. U. Okla. Sch. Library Sci., summer 1962, N. Tex. State U., summer 1965; acad. library cons.; mem. AIA-Am. Library Assn. Library Bldg. Awards Jury, 1976; bd. dirs. Fellowship Christian Libr. and Info. Specialists. Author: A History of the Baylor University Library, 1845-1919, 1962; editor: Okla. Librarian, 1951-52; co-author: Organization Charts of Selected Libraries, 1973; A History of the Okla. State U. Library, 1992; contbr. articles, book revs., chpts. to publs. in field. Bd. dirs. Okla. Dept. Librs., 1989-92, chmn., 1990-92. 1st lt. USAAF, 1942-45. Decorated Air medal with 4 oak leaf clusters; recipient citation Okla. State Senate, 1987, Rotary Outstanding Achievement award, 1996; named in 150 Prominent Individuals in Baylor's History. Mem. ALA (life, mem. coun. 1971-72, 76-80, 83-84, 84-88, chmn. libr. orgn. and mgmt. sect. 1973-75, planning and budget assembly 1978-79, coun. com. on coms. 1979-80, bldgs. and equipment sect. exec. bd. 1979-80, chmn. bldgs. for coll. and univ. librs. com. 1983-85, chmn. nominating com. libr. history roundtable 1993-94), Okla. Libr. Assn. (life, pres. 1971-72, ALA coun. rep. 1976-80, 83-84, OLA Disting. Svc. award 1979, Spl. Merit award 1987), S.W. Libr. Assn. (chmn. coll. and univ. div. 1958-60, chmn. scholarship com. 1968-70), Internat. Fedn. Libr. Assns. (standing com. on libr. bldgs. and equipment 1976-88), Assn. Coll. and Rsch. Librs. (chmn. univ. librs. sect. 1969-70, mem. exec. bd. and rep. to ALA Coun., 1971-72), U. Mich. Sch. Libr. Sci. Alumni Soc. (pres. 1979-80, Alumni Recognition award 1988), mem. Alumni Found. Com., 1992—, Payne County Ret. Educators Assn. (v.p., pres. elect 1991-92, pres. 1992-93), Okla. Hist. Soc. (com. on Okla. Higher Edn. mus. 1985—), Beta Phi Mu. Baptist (chmn. bd. deacons 1973). Clubs: Archons of Colophon, Stillwater Rotary (dir. 1978-82, pres. 1980-81). *It is sometimes a hidden influence in our lives which drives us toward a set goal. We ourselves may not recognize the real source of that urge to fulfill a dream. Only after many years was I able to look back and discern the factors in my youth that pushed me toward my goal of attaining a good education. They grew out of the influence that the Great Depression had on my early life. Because of that experience the preparation for a career became my first goal in life, yet the ways and means for achieving it were virtually nonexistent. It was to be, however, and I was fortunate to realize that goal. It causes me to think now that perhaps the degree of determination and endurance one possesses is paced more by adverse condition than by times of comfort and ease.*

ROUSE, ROY DENNIS, retired university dean; b. Andersonville, Ga., Sept. 20, 1920; s. Joseph B. and Janie (Wicker) R.; m. Madge Mathis, Mar. 6, 1946; children—David Benjamin, Sharon. Student, Ga. Southwestern Coll., 1937-39; B.S. in Agr, U. Ga., 1942, M.S., 1947; Ph.D., Purdue U., 1949. Asst. prof. agronomy and soils Auburn (Ala.) U., 1949-50, assoc. prof., 1950-56, prof., 1956-66, assoc. dir., asst. dean Sch. Agr. and Agrl. Expt. Sta., 1966-72, dean, dir., 1972-81, emeritus, 1981—; mem. Com. of Nine, Dept. Agr., 1970-74. Contbr. articles to profl. jours. Pres. Auburn Beautification Coun., 1987-88. Capt. USN, 1942-46, PTO; USNR, 1946-67, ret. Recipient Leadership award Farm-City Com. Ala., 1975, Disting. Svcs. award Catfish Farmers Am., 1976, Disting. Svcs. award Ala. Vocat.-Agrl. Tchrs. Assn., 1976, Man of Yr. in Agr. award Progressive Farmer, 1977, Aeolian award Ga. Southwestern Coll., 1981, Charles W. Summerour award Ala. Soil Fertility Soc., 1987, Conservation medal Nat. Soc. DAR, 1993; named Hon. State Farmer Future Farmers Am., 1976, Man of Yr. Crop Improvement Assn., 1981, Hon. County Agt., 1981; named to Ala. Agrl. Hall of Honor, 1985; R. Dennis Rouse Life Sciences Bldg. named in honor Auburn U., 1993. Fellow Am. Soc. Agronomy, Soil Sci. Soc. Am., Am. Rhododendron Soc. (pres. Chattahoochee chpt. 1993); mem. Am. Assn. Ret. Persons (pres. Lee County chpt. 1989-91), So. Assn. Agrl. Scientists (pres. 1976), Assn. So. Agrl. Expt. Sta. Dirs. (chmn. 1974), Assn. Univs. and Land-Grant Colls (chmn. expt. sta. com. on orgn. and policy 1977), Men's Camellia Club (pres. 1965-66, 82-83), Outing Club, Lions (pres. Auburn 1993-94, Melvin Jones fellow 1994), Sigma Xi, Alpha Zeta, Phi Kappa Phi, Xi Phi Xi. Presbyterian. Home: 827 Salmon St Auburn AL 36830-5930

ROUSE, WILLIAM BRADFORD, systems engineering executive, researcher, educator; b. Fall River, Mass., Jan. 20, 1947; s. Gaylor Louis Rouse and Barbara (Peirce) Rouse Sherman; m. Sandra Howard Kane, Sept. 8, 1968; children: Rebecca Kane, William Howard. B.S.M.E., U. R.I., 1969; S.M., MIT, 1970, Ph.D., 1972. Postdoctoral research assoc. MIT, Cambridge, 1972; asst. prof. Tufts U., Medford, Mass., 1973; prof. U. Ill., Urbana, 1974-81; adj. prof. indsl. and systems engring. Ga. Inst. Tech., Atlanta, 1981—; CEO Enterprise Support Syss., Inc., Norcross, Ga., 1995—. Author/editor 18 books including: Start Where You Are, 1996; also numerous chpts., articles. Recipient O. Hugo Schuck award Am. Automatic Control Council, 1979. Fellow IEEE (Centennial medal 1984), Human Factors Soc.; mem. NAE, Systems, Man and Cybernetics Soc. of IEEE (pres. 1982-83, Norbert Wiener award 1986), Unitarian-Universalist Assn. Home: 2389 Little Brooke Dr Atlanta GA 30338-3187 Office: Enterprise Support Syss 4898 S Old Peachtree Rd Ste 106 Norcross GA 30071-4757

ROUSH, WILLIAM R., chemistry educator. BS in Chemistry, UCLA, 1974; PhD in Chemistry, Harvard U., 1977. Disting. prof. chemistry dept. Ind. U., Bloomington. Recipient Arthur C. Cope Scholar award Am. Chem. Soc., 1994, Alan R. Day award Phila. Organic Chemist's Club, 1992. Office: Indiana U Dept Chemistry Bloomington IN 47405-4000

ROUSS, RUTH, lawyer; b. Des Moines, May 21, 1914; d. Simon Jacob and Dora (Goldin) R.; m. Dennis O'Rourke, Jan. 21, 1940; children: Susan Jerene, Kathleen Frances, Brian Jay, Dennis Robert, Ruth Elizabeth, Dolores Ann. B.A., Drake U., 1934, J.D., 1937. Bar: Iowa bar 1937, U.S. Supreme Ct. bar 1945, Colo. bar 1946, D.C. bar 1971. Legal counsel to Jay N. Darling, Des Moines, 1937-38; atty. Office of Solicitor, Dept. Agr., 1938-45, asst. to solicitor, 1940-45; practice law Colorado Springs, Colo., 1946—; mem. firm Williams & Rouss, 1946-50, individual practice law, 1950-69; of counsel firm Sutton, Shull & O'Rourke, Colorado Springs and Washington, 1969-72; mem. firm Rouss & O'Rourke, Colorado Springs and Washington, 1972—; dir., sec.-treas. ManExec., Inc. Mem. cast chorus, Colo. Opera Festival, 1976, 78; mem., Colorado Springs Chorale, 1976—. Bd. dirs. Human Relations Commn. City Colorado Springs, 1968-73, chmn., 1971-72; bd. dirs., sec. Colorado Springs Community Planning and Research Council, 1972-78; bd. dirs. Logos, Inc., Colorado Springs, 1972-78, sec., 1976-77, v.p., 1977-78; bd. dirs. Colorado Springs Opera Festival, Colorado Springs World Affairs Council, Urban League of Pikes Peak Region; mem. com. protection human rights Penrose Hosp., adv. council Am. Lung Assn. of Colo., Pikes Peak region; dir. Joseph Henry Edmondson Found.; adv. bd. Care Castle Divsn. Pikes Peak Seniors,El Paso County, Colo. Mem. El Paso County (Colo.) Bar Assn., Colo. Bar Assn., D.C. Bar Assn., Am. Law Inst. (life), Internat. Fedn. Women Lawyers, Women's Forum Colo., Phi Beta Kappa. Home: 8 Heather Dr Colorado Springs CO 80906-3114 Office: Rouss & O'Rourke Box 572 231 E Vermijo Ave Colorado Springs CO 80901

ROUSSEAU, EUGENE ELLSWORTH, musician, music educator, consultant; b. Blue Island, Ill., Aug. 23, 1932; s. Joseph E. and Laura M. (Schindler) R.; m. Norma J. Rigel, Aug. 15, 1959; children—Lisa-Marie, Joseph. B of Mus Edn., Chgo. Mus. Coll., 1953; MusM, Northwestern U., 1954; student, Paris Conservatory of Music, 1960-61; PhD, U. Iowa, 1962. Instr. Luther Coll., 1956-59; asst. prof. Cen. Mo. State Coll., 1962-64; prof. music Ind. U., Bloomington, 1964-88, disting. prof. music, 1988—; guest prof. U. Iowa, 1964, Hochschule fur Musik, Vienna, Austria, 1981-82, Ariz. State U., 1984, Prague Conservatory Music, 1985, Showa Coll. Music, 1996, 97, Tokyo Coll. Music, 1997, Paris Conservatory, 1997; tchr. U. Wis.-Ext., 1969—; chief adviser for design and mfg. saxophones Yamaha, 1972—, R & D of saxophone mouthpieces; music arranger; svc. on numerous acad. coms.; tchr. 1st course in saxophone Mozarteum in Salzburg, Austria, 1991—; mem. jury Munich Internat. competitions, 1987, 90, pres. of juries, 1991-92; first saxophonist to perform on Prague Spring Festival, 1993; mem. jury Can. Nat. Music competition, 1994. Worldwide concert saxophonist; Carnegie Hall debut, 1965; author: Marcel Mule: His Life and the Saxophone, 1982, Saxophone High Tones, 1978, Method for Saxophone (2 vols.), 1975; performer 1st solo saxophone recitals, several European cities, 1st Am. solo saxophone performance in Japan, 1984; 1st to record concert saxophone on compact disc (Delos); radio broadcasts in Berlin, Bremen, London, Montreal, Ostrava, Paris, Prague, Toronto, Vienna; saxophone recs. for Deutsche Gramophon, Golden Crest, Coronet, Delos, Liscio, ALM and McGill. Instr., asst. band leader 25th Infantry Div. U.S. Army, 1954-56. Grantee Fulbright Found., 1960-61, Rsch. and Exch. Bd., 1985, NEA, 1986; named hon. prof. music Prague Conservatory, 1993—; recipient Edwin Franko Goldman award ABA, 1995. Mem. N.Am. Saxophone Alliance (pres. 1978-80), Comite Internat. de Saxophone (pres. 1982-85), Coll. Music Soc., Clarinet and Saxophone Soc. (U.K.), Music Tchrs. Nat. Assn. (Tchr. of Yr. award for Ind. 1993), Fulbright Assn. (life), World Saxophone Congress (co-founder 1969). Office: Indiana U Sch Music Bloomington IN 47405

ROUSSEAU, GEORGE SEBASTIAN, eighteenth century studies educator, chamber musician; b. N.Y.C., Feb. 23, 1941; s. Hyman Victoire and Esther (Zacuto) R. B.A., Amherst Coll., 1962; diploma, Am. Sch. Classical Studies, Athens, 1963; M.A., Princeton U., 1964, Ph.D., 1966. Instr. English Harvard U., Cambridge, Mass., 1966-68; asst. prof. UCLA, 1968-70, prof. English, 1970-79, prof. 18th Century studies, 1980-94; Regius prof. English U. Aberdeen, Scotland, 1994—; dir. Thomas Reid Inst. Rsch. in Humanities, Scis., Medicine, 1994—; vis. fellow Magdalen Coll., Oxford, 1993-94; Fulbright vis. prof. U. Lausanne, 1994. Author: (with Marjorie Hope Nicolson) This Long Disease, My Life: Alexander Pope and the Sciences, 1968, The Rape of the Lock: Twentieth-Century Interpretations, 1969, The Augustan Milieu: Essays Presented to Louis A. Landa, 1970, (with Neil Rudenstine) English Poetic Satire: Wyatt to Byron, 1972, (with P.G. Boucé) Tobias Smollett: Bicentennial Essays Presented to L.M. Knapp, 1971, Organic Form: The Life of an Idea, 1972, Goldsmith: The Critical Heritage, 1974, (with Roy Porter) The Ferment of Knowledge: Studies in the Historiography of Science, 1980, The Letters and Papers of Sir John Hill, 1982, Tobias Smollett: Essays of Two Decades, 1982, (with Roy Porter) Sexual Underworlds of the Enlightenment, 1987, Exoticism in the Enlightenment, 1989, The Languages of Psyche: Mind and Body in Enlightenment Thought, 1990, Enlightenment Crossings, Perilous Enlightenment, Enlightenment Borders: Pre- and Post-Modern Discourses, 3 vols., 1991 (with others) Hysteria Beyond Freud, 1993; mem. editorial bd. The Eighteenth Century, 1974—, History of Psychiatry, 1990—; contbr. The Crisis in Modernism: Bergson and the Vitalist Tradition, 1992. Osgood fellow in lit. Princeton U., 1965-66; Am. Council Learned Socs. fellow, 1970; vis. fellow commoner Trinity Coll., Cambridge U., 1982; sr. Fulbright research prof. Sir Thomas Browne Inst., Leiden, Netherlands, 1983; Clark Library prof. U. Calif., 1985-86; sr. research fellow NEH, 1986-87. Mem. Am. Soc. 18th-Century Studies, MLA, History of Sci. Soc., Am. Hist. Assn. (1972), Am. Assn. History of Medicine, Royal Soc. Arts, Royal Soc. Medicine. Home and Office: Taylor Bldg, Univ Aberdeen, Aberdeen AB24 3UB, Scotland

ROUSSEAU, IRENE VICTORIA, artist, sculptor; m. Denis Lawrence Rousseau; children: Douglas, Scott. BA, Hunter Coll., N.Y.C.; MFA, Claremont (Calif.) Grad. Sch., 1969; PhD, N.Y. U., 1977. Tenured prof. William Paterson Coll., Wayne, N.J., 1970-74; invited spkr. Coll. Art Assn./Women Caucus on Art Conf., L.A., 1985, N.J. Ctr. for Visual Arts, Summit, N.J., 1985, Noyes Mus., 1994, Mus. African Art, 1994. Exhbns. include Betty Parsons Gallery, N.Y.C., Claremonte Colls., State Mus. Sci. and Industry, L.A., Morris Mus. Arts and Scis., Morristown, N.J., The Bronx Mus. of Art, Galleri Sci. Agnes, Copenhagen/Roskilde, Denmark, Sculptors 5, Madison, N.J., Edmund Sci. Co., Barrington, N.J., AT&T World Hdqrs., Basking Ridge, N.J., N.J. Ctr. for Visual Arts, The Brotherhood Synagogue Holocaust Meml. Gramercy Pk. (mosaic), N.Y.C., 1986, 1st Internat. Art Biennale, Malta, 1995, painted aluminum wall reliefs Capital Sports, Inc., hdqrs. Sports in Action, Stamford, Conn., 1989, mosaic mural Spiriling Light, Overlook Hosp., Summit, N.J., 1993, Nayes Mus., N.J., 1994; represented in permanent collections Brit. Mus., Met. Mus., Guggenheim Mus., Walker Art Ctr., Nat. Mus. Am. Art, Smithsonian Instn.; commn. of mosaic murals concert hall LaRoche, Switzerland, 1995-96. Recipient seven 1st prize awards for creative work in N.J., ER Squibb and Sons Sculpture award, AIA N.J. Presentation Design award, 1995. Mem. AIA (profl. affiliate N.J., N.Y., chmn. architecture dialogue com. Presentation award 1995), Internat. Sculptors Assn., Am. Abstract Artists (exhbn. chmn. 1978-79, pres. 1979-82), Fine Arts Fedn. (bd. dirs.), Coll. Art Assn., Women's Caucus on Art (conf. spkr.), Phi Delta Kappa. Home: 41 Sunset Dr Summit NJ 07901-2322

ROUSSEL, LEE DENNISON, economist; b. N.Y.C., May 15, 1944; d. Ethan Allen and Frances Isabel (Ferry) Dennison; m. Andre Homo Roussel, Sept. 6, 1980; children: Cecilia Frances, Stephanie Anne. AB, Wellesley Coll., 1966; MA, Northeastern U., 1973. Mgmt. intern U.S. Dept. HEW, 1966-68; with Planning Office Commonwealth of Mass., 1968-70; exec. dir. Gov.'s Commn. Citizen Participation, Boston, 1973; with Boston Area Office U.S. Dept. HUD, 1970-78; fgn. svc. officer USAID, 1978—; with Housing and Urban Devel. Office USAID, Washington and Tunis, 1978-82; chief Housing and Urban Devel. Office for C.Am. USAID, Honduras, 1982-87; asst. dir. Office Housing and Urban Programs USAID, Washington, 1987-91; country rep. for Czech and Slovak Fed. Rep. USAID, 1991-92, country rep. for Czech Rep., 1993-94; min. counselor, U.S. rep. to Devel. Assistance Com. OECD, Paris, 1994—. Episcopalian. Office: USOECD, 19 rue de Franqueville, 75016 Paris France also: OECD/USAID Psc 116 APO AE 09777-5000

ROUSSELOT, PETER FRESE, lawyer; b. N.Y.C., Jan. 7, 1942; s. Louis Marcel and Evelyn Valdez (Hastrup) R.; m. Mary Dumesnil, Cobb, Nov. 22, 1975; children: Laura Andren, Richard Frese, Anne Stewart, Louise Dierks. BA summa cum laude, Yale U., 1963; LLB, Harvard U., 1966. Bar: U.S. Dist. Ct. D.C. 1967, U.S. Ct. Appeals (D.C. cir.) 1967, U.S. Ct. Appeals (3d cir.) 1993, U.S. Supreme Ct. 1970. Assoc. Hogan & Hartson, Washington, 1966-74, ptnr., 1975-94, mem. exec. com., 1986-88; mng. dir. corp. affairs So. Pacific Rail Corp., Washington, 1994—. Asst. to nat. co-chmn. Citizens for Robert F. Kennedy, Washington, 1968; vol. Kerrey for Pres., 1992. Mem. Yale Club Washington, Phi Beta Kappa. Democrat. Episcopalian. Avocations: tennis, hiking, photography. Office: So Pacific Rail Corp Columbia Sq Ste 450 West 55513th St NW Washington DC 20004

ROUSSEY, ROBERT STANLEY, accountant, educator; b. N.Y.C., July 20, 1935; s. George Albert and Estelle (Smegelski) R.; m. Jeanne Archer, May 8, 1965; children: Robert Scott, John Stephen. BS, Fordham U., 1957. CPA, N.Y., Japan. Staff acct. Arthur Andersen & Co., N.Y.C., 1957-63; mgr. Arthur Andersen & Co., N.Y.C. and Tokyo, 1964-69; ptnr. Arthur Andersen & Co., N.Y.C. and Chgo., 1969-92, dir. auditing procedures, 1977-92; prof. acctg. U. So. Calif., L.A., 1992—; adj. prof. auditing Northwestern U. Kellogg Grad. Sch. Mgmt., 1990, 91. Edit. cons. Handbook of Corporate Finance, 1986, Handbook of Financial Markets and Institutions, 1987; mem. edit. bd. Advances in Accounting, 1987—, Jour. Internat. Acctg. Auditing and Taxation, 1991—, Auditing: A Journal of Theory and Practice, 1994—; mem. adv. bd.: Internat. Jour. Auditing; contbr. articles to profl. jours. Treas., bd. dirs. Kenilworth (Ill.) Community House, 1979-81, Troop 13 Boy Scouts Am., Kenilworth, 1978-80, St. Joseph's Ch. Men's Club, Bronxville, N.Y., 1971-73. With U.S. Army, 1958, 61-62. Mem. AICPA (chmn. EDP auditing stds. com. 1978-81, auditing stds. bd. 1986-90, MAS practice stds. and adminstrn. com. 1990-93), Am. Acctg. Assn. (v.p. auditing sect. 1987-90, pubs. com. 1993-96), Info. Systems Audit and Control Assn. (stds. bd. 1986-96, v.p., mem. internat. bd. dirs. 1996—), Ill. State Soc. CPAs, N.Y. State Soc. CPAs, Inst. Internal Auditors (bd. rsch. advisors 1986—), Internat. Fedn. Accts. (internat. auditing practices com. 1990—, chmn. 1995—, EDP audit com. 1980-88), Met. Club (gov. 1977-78), Tokyo-Am. Club (life), Beaver Creek Club, Beta Alpha Psi, Beta Gamma Sigma. Republican. Roman Catholic. Avocations: skiing, sailing, tennis, karate. Office: U So Calif Dept Acctg Los Angeles CA 90089-1421

ROUSUCK, J. WYNN, theater critic; b. Cleve., Mar. 19, 1951; d. Morton I. and Irene Zelda (Winograd) R.; m. James William Cox, Jr., May 8, 1983. BA summa cum laude, Wellesley Coll., 1972; MS, Columbia U., 1974. Assoc. editor, program guide, Sta. WCLV-FM, Cleve., 1972-73; theater and film reviewer Cleve. Press, 1973; gen. assignment arts reporter Balt. Sun, 1974-84, theater critic, 1984—; instr. English Goucher Coll., Towson, Md., 1981; master critic Nat. Critics Inst., Waterford, Conn., 1990—; theater critic Md. Pub. TV., 1986; spkr. in field. Recipient Dog Writers Assn. Am. awards 1977, 79, Md. chpt. 1st Place Arts Reporting award Soc. Profl. Journalists, 1993; NEH journalism fellow U. Mich., 1979-80, fellow Nat. Critics Inst., 1982. Mem. Balt. Bibliophiles (bd. dirs. 1982-83), Octavo Plus, Walters Art Gallery, Balt. Wellesley Club (pres. 1978-79). Jewish. Avocations: rare books, art, dogs. Office: The Baltimore Sun 501 N Calvert St Baltimore MD 21202-3604

ROUTH, DONALD K(ENT), psychology educator; b. Oklahoma City, Mar. 3, 1937; s. Ross Holland and Fay (Campbell) R.; m. Marion Starbird Wendler, Sept. 10, 1960; children—Rebecca Ann (dec.), Laura Diane. B.A., U. Okla., 1962; Ph.D., U. Pitts., 1967. Diplomate Am. Bd. Profl. Psychology; lic. psychologist, Fla. Asst. prof. psychology and pediatrics U. Iowa, Iowa City, 1967-70; prof. U. Iowa, 1977-85; assoc. prof. psychology Bowling Green State U., Ohio, 1970-71; assoc. prof. U. N.C., Chapel Hill, 1971-77; prof. psychology and pediatrics U. Miami, Coral Gables, Fla., 1985—; Chmn. behavioral medicine study sect. NIH, 1983-85. Editor Jour. Pediatric Psychology, 1976-82, Jour. Clin. Child Psychology, 1987-91, Jour. of Abnormal Child Psychology, 1992—; contbr. numerous articles to profl. jours., books. Pres. Eno River Unitarian Universalist Fellowship, 1976-77. Recipient award for disting. contbn. Soc. Pediatric Psychology, 1981, Presidential award, 1988; Fla. Psychol. Assn. Research Psychologist of Yr. award, 1987. Mem. APA (pres. div. child, youth and family services, 1984, pres. div. on mental retardation 1987), Disting. Profl. Contbns. to Clin. Psychology (sect. on clin. child psychology 1989, div. clin. psychology, 1992, Nicholas Hobbs award, div. child youth and family services, 1996). Democrat. Home: 9394 SW 77th Ave Apt F-7 Miami FL 33156 Office: Dept Psychology Univ Miami PO Box 249229 Miami FL 33124-9229

ROUTH, JOSEPH ISAAC, biochemist; b. Logansport, Ind., May 8, 1910; s. William Arthur and Ethel Marie (Etnire) R.; m. Dorothy Francis Hayes, Sept. 4, 1937 (widowed May 1972); children: Joseph Hayes, John Michael; m. Elizabeth Marie Hayes, Dec. 4, 1976 (widowed Feb. 1990). BSChemE, Purdue U., 1933, MS, 1934; PhD, U. Mich., 1937. Diplomate Am. Bd. Clin. Chemistry. Instr. dept. biochemistry U. Iowa, Iowa City, 1937-42, asst. prof., 1942-46, assoc. prof., 1946-51, prof., 1951-78; dir. clin. biochemistry lab. Univ. Hosps., 1952-64; prof. pathology U. Iowa, 1970-78, dir. spl. clin. chem. lab., 1970-78; pres. Am. Bd. Clin. Chemistry, Washington, 1957-73; cons. VA Hosp., Iowa City, 1952-78. Sect. editor Chem. Abstracts, Clin. Chemistry; contbr. articles to profl. jours. Fellow Am. Inst. Chemists; mem. Am. Assn. Clin. Chemists (past pres., award for outstanding efforts in edn. and tng. 1973). Republican. Roman Catholic. Achievements include research in first chemical and nutritional studies on powdered keratins. Home: PO Box 712 Cherokee Vlg AR 72525-0712 Office: Dept Biochemistry Univ Iowa Iowa City IA 52242

ROUTIEN, JOHN BRODERICK, mycologist; b. Mt. Vernon, Ind., Jan. 23, 1913; s. William Evert and Frances Lolita (Broderick) R.; m. Helen Harrison Boyd, Mar. 11, 1944 (dec. 1965); m. Constance C. Connolly, Feb. 22, 1967 (dec. 1996). B.A., DePauw U., 1934; M.A., Northwestern U., 1936; Ph.D., Mich. State Coll., 1939. Instr. botany U. Mo., 1939-42; mycologist Pfizer, Inc., N.Y.C., 1946-77; research adviser Pfizer, Inc., 1974-77. Editorial bd.: Applied Microbiology, 1964-71, Antimicrobial Agts. and Chemotherapy, 1974-77. Recipient Comml. Solvents award in antibiotics, 1950. Mem. Mycol. Soc. Am., Bot. Soc. Am., Soc. Am. Bacteriologists, Soc. Indsl. Microbiology. Research on molds producing new antibiotics, strain improvement of cultures, identification of fungi. Home: 318 Grassy Hill Rd Old Lyme CT 06371-3312 Office: Pfizer Inc Groton CT 06340

ROUTMAN, DANIEL GLENN, marketing and business development professional, lawyer; b. Birmingham, Ala., July 26, 1961; s. Stanley and Joyce R.; m. Elizabeth Horchow, Mar. 9, 1991; 1 child, Regen. BBA, U. Tex., 1983, JD, 1985. Bar: Tex. 1986. Assoc. Liddell, Sapp, Zivley & LaBoon, Austin, 1986-88, Baker & Botts, Dallas, 1989-91; assoc. gen. counsel Perot '92 Campaign/United We Stand Am., Dallas, 1992-94; prin. Wilson Comms., Dallas, 1994-95; dir. comms. C/Net: The Computer Network, San Francisco, 1996; dir. mktg. AudioNet, Dallas, 1996—. Mem. adv. bd. The Family Gateway, Dallas, 1996—; chmn. jr. asscs. Dallas Mus. Art, 1991-92, Friends of the Ctr. for Human Nutrition U. Tex. Southwestern Med. Sch., 1992-96. Home: 5845 Lupton Dr Dallas TX 75225 Office: AudioNet 2929 Elm St Dallas TX 75226-1510

ROUVELAS, EMANUEL LARRY, lawyer; b. Seattle, Sept. 10, 1944; s. Larry E. and Mary (Derezes) R.; m. Marilyn S. Edmunds, Jan. 23, 1967; children: Eleftherios, Mary. BA, U. Wash., 1965; JD, Harvard U., 1968, AMP, 1996. Bar: Ill. 1968, D.C. 1973. Assoc. Kirkland & Ellis, Chgo., 1968-69; counsel U.S. Senate Com. on Commerce, Washington, 1969-73; chief counsel U.S. Senate Mcht. Marine and Fgn. Commerce Subcoms., Washington, 1969-73; chmn., ptnr. Preston, Gates, Ellis & Rouvelas Meeds, Washington, 1974—; advisor to two Presdl. transitions and bi-partisan congl.caucus; bd. dirs. OMI Corp. Trustee Am. Coll. of Greece, 1993—. Office: Preston Gates Ellis Et Al 1735 New York Ave NW Washington DC 20006-5209

ROUW, CARLA SUE ROBERTS, medical nurse; b. Chariton, Iowa, June 5, 1968; d. Glen Marlin and Phyllis Darlene (Allison) Roberts. ADN, Indian Hills C.C., 1988. RN, Iowa. Float med.-surg. LPN; lic. practical nurse med.-surg. float Ottumwa (Iowa) Regional Health Ctr., 1987-88; adolescent and children's charge nurse Laughlin Pavilion, Kirksville, Mo., 1988-89; charge nurse, dir. med. records Monroe Care Ctr., Albia, 1989-91; gen. surgery/urology nurse, office nurse Dr. Edeliro A. Escobar, Fort Madison, Iowa, 1991-96; nursing svc. supr. Homestead Living & Learning Ctr.-Serving Iowans with Autism, Runnells, Iowa, 1996—.

ROUX, MILDRED ANNA, retired secondary school educator; b. New Castle, Pa., June 1, 1914; d. Louis Henri and Frances Amanda (Gillespie) R. BA, Westminster Coll., 1936, MS in Edn., 1951. Tchr. Farrell (Pa.) Sch. Dist., 1939-55; tchr. Latin, English New Castle (Pa.) Sch. Dist., 1956-76; ret., 1976; chmn. sr. high sch. fgn. lang. dept. New Castle Sch. Dist., 1968-76, faculty sponsor sch. fgn. lang. newspapers, 1960-76, 71-76, Jr. Classical League, 1958-76. Mem. Lawrence County Hist. Soc., Am. Classical League, 1958-76. Mem. AAUW (chmn. publicity, chmn. program com. Lawrence County chpt. 1992-96), Am. Assn. Ret. Persons, Nat. Ret. Tchrs. Assn., Pa. Assn. Sch. Retirees (chmn. cmty. participation com. Lawrence County br. 1976-81), Coll. Club New Castle (chmn. sunshine com. 1989-91, mem. social com. 1991-92), Woman's Club New Castle (chmn. pub. affairs com. 1988-90, internat. affairs com. 1990-92, program com. 1990-92, telephone com. 1992-95). Republican. Roman Catholic. Avocations: church choir, reading, civic interests. Home: 6 E Moody Ave New Castle PA 16101-2356

ROVELSTAD, MATHILDE VERNER, library science educator; b. Kempten, Germany, Aug. 12, 1920; came to U.S., 1951, naturalized, 1953; d. George and Therese (Hohl) Hotter; m. Howard Rovelstad, Nov. 23, 1970. Ph.D., U. Tubingen, 1953; M.S. in L.S, Catholic U. Am., 1960. Cataloger Mt. St. Mary's Coll., Los Angeles, 1953; sch. librarian Yoyogi Elem. Sch., Tokyo, 1954-56; mem. faculty Cath. U. Am., 1960-90, prof. library sci., 1975-90, prof. emeritus, 1990—; vis. prof. U. Montreal, 1969. Author: Bibliotheken in den Vereinigten Staaten, 1974; translator Bibliographia, an Inquiry into its Definition and Designations (R. Blum), 1980, Bibliotheken in den Vereinigten Staaten von Amerika und in Kanada, 1988; contbr. articles to profl. jours. Research grantee German Acad. Exch. Svc., 1969, Herzog August Bibliothek Wolfenbüttel, Germany, 1995. Mem. ALA (internat. relations com. 1977-80), Internat. Fedn. Library Assns. and Instns. (standing adv. com. on library schs. 1975-81), Assn. for Library and Info. Sci. Edn. Home: Apt HR T35 719 Maiden Choice Ln Catonsville MD 21228 Office: Cath U Am Sch Libr & Info Sci Washington DC 20064

ROVER, EDWARD FRANK, lawyer; b. N.Y.C., Oct. 4, 1938; s. Frederick James and Wanda (Charkowski) R.; m. Maureen Wyer, June 15, 1968; children: Elizabeth, Emily, William. AB, Fordham U., 1961; JD, Harvard U., 1964. Bar: N.Y. 1964, U.S. Tax Ct. 1968, U.S. Dist. Ct. (so. dist.) N.Y. 1975, U.S. Supreme Ct. 1994. Assoc. White & Case, N.Y.C., 1964-71, ptnr., 1972—; bd. dirs. Cranshaw Corp., N.Y.C., The Brearley Sch., N.Y.C., Harvard-Mahoney Neuroscience Inst., Boston, Waterford Sch., Sandy, Utah, E.N. Dana Inst., N.Y.C., Norton Simon Art Mus., L.A., Rumsey-Carter Found., Geneva, Charles A. Dana Found. Mem. ABA, N.Y. Bar Assn., N.Y. County Lawyers Assn., Assn. Bar City N.Y, Century Assn., Scarsdale Golf Club, Harvard Club. Avocations: sailing, skiing. Home: 1111 Park Ave New York NY 10128-1234 Office: White & Case 1155 Avenue Of The Americas New York NY 10036-2711

ROVERA, GIOVANNI AURELIO, medical educator, scientist; b. Cocconato, Italy, Sept. 23, 1940; came to U.S., naturalized, 1984.; Student, Liceo Classico Valsalice, Torino, Italy, 1955-58; MD summa cum laude, U. Torino, 1964, postgrad., 1965-68. Diplomate Am. Bd. Anatomic Pathology; lic. physician, Italy, Pa. Postdoctoral fellow Fels Rsch. Inst. Temple U. Sch. of Medicine, Phila., 1968-70, resident in anatomic pathology, 1970-72, chief resident in pathology, 1972; asst. prof. pathology Sch. Medicine Temple U., Phila., 1972-75; assoc. prof. Wistar Inst., Phila., 1975-78, prof., 1979—, assoc. dir., 1988-91, dir., 1991—; Wistar Inst. prof. pathology and lab. medicine Sch. Medicine U. Pa., Phila., 1984—; Wistar Inst. prof. pediatrics U. Pa. Sch. of Medicine, Phila., 1987—; mem. promotion coms. U. Pa. Sch. of Medicine, The Wistar Inst., 1979—; chmn. grad. tng. program The Wistar Inst., 1981-91; mem. sci. adv. com. Leukemia Soc. Am., 1983-88, Am. Cancer Soc., 1986-90; mem. ad. hoc sci. adv. com. Nat. Cancer Inst., 1985—; mem. NCI Devel. Diagnostic Working Group, 1996. Editor: (with H. Koprowski) Current Opinion in Immunology: Cancer and Immunology, 1990; assoc. editor Proceedings Soc. Exptl. Biol. Medicine, 1975-78, Jour. Cellular Physiology, 1978—, Leukemia, 1988—, Haematologica Pathology, 1990—; mem. editorial adv. bd. Haematologica, 1989—. Fellow EURATOM, 1965-66, Ministero della Publica Istruzione, 1966-67; scholar Leukemia Soc., 1974-79; recipient Eagles Fly for Leukemia Lifetime Achievement award, 1996. Mem. Coll. of Physicians of Phila. Achievements include development of techniques of monitoring the extent of residual leukemia in B and T lineage malignancies. Home: 933 Wootton Rd Bryn Mawr PA 19010-2227 Office: The Wistar Inst 3601 Spruce St Philadelphia PA 19104-4205

ROVERUD, ELEANOR, pathologist, neuropathologist; b. Spring Grove, Minn., Oct. 24, 1912; d. Henry S. and Sigrid (Bakken) R.; m. Stuart Henry Nam (dec. Nov. 1986); adopted children: Sue, Kay, Becky, Howard, Signe, Sonia, Tom, Ted, Kurt. Diploma, Kahler Sch. Nursing, Rochester, Minn., 1934; BS in Nursing Edn., U. Minn., 1940; MD, Med. Coll. Pa., 1947. Intern Swedish Hosp., Mpls., 1947-48; resident in pathology, resident instr. Sch. of Tropical Medicine U. P.R., San Juan, 1949-52; fellow in Neuropathology Columbia U., Presbyn. Hosp., N.Y.C., 1952-54; neuropathologist Wayne County Gen. Hosp., Eloise, Mich., 1954-59; assoc. prof. Woman's Med. Coll./Med. Coll. Pa., Phila., 1959-61; pathologist Women's Hosp., Phila., 1961-62, St. Anthony Regional Hosp., Carroll, Iowa, 1962-77; cons. in pathology Carroll, Iowa, 1977-87, Spring Grove, 1987—; expert witness forensic cases Carroll County, Iowa, 1962-77. Chmn., v.p., sec. Carroll chpt. ARC, 1968-75. Mem. AMA, Am. Assn. Neuropathologists, Iowa Med. Soc. (life), Carroll County Med. Assn. (sec. 1968-74), Am. Med. Women's Assn., Zumbro Valley Med. Soc., Minn. Med. Assn. Democrat. Lutheran. Office: PO Box 706 Spring Grove MN 55974-0706

ROVETO, CONNIE IDA, financial services executive; b. Montreal, Que., Can.; d. Charles and Angela (Difruscia) R. BA in English Lang. & Lit., U. Toronto, Ont., Can., 1972, BEd, 1973. Cert. officer/dir. Investment Dealers Assn. Can. Mgr. human resources Can. Permanent Trust, Toronto, 1980-81, mgr. orgn. planning, 1981-82, mgr. trust bus. systems, 1982-84, project dir., 1984-85; asst. v.p. Can. Trust, Toronto, 1986; v.p. Cen. Guaranty Trust, Toronto, 1988, Cen. Capital Mgmt. Inc., Toronto, 1986-89; exec. v.p. United Fin. Mgmt. Ltd., Toronto, 1989-93; pres., CEO United Fin. Mgmt. Ltd., 1993-95; also bd. dirs.; COO, sr. v.p. asset mgmt. svcs. Trust Co. of Bank of Montreal, 1996—; bd. dirs. Ont. Film Devel. Corp. Mem. senate U. St. Michael's Coll., Toronto, 1989—, mem. acad. planning com., 1991—; mem. com. health care planning Archdiocese Toronto, 1986-90; bd. dirs. Queen Elizabeth Hosp. Found. Mem. Can. Club of Toronto (bd. dirs. 1994), Investment Funds Inst. Can. Avocations: films, reading, tennis, fitness.

ROVINE, ARTHUR WILLIAM, lawyer; b. Phila., Apr. 29, 1937; s. George Isaac and Rosanna (Lipsitz) R.; m. Phyllis Ellen Hamburger, Apr. 7, 1963; children: Joshua, Deborah. AB, U. Pa., 1958; LLB, Harvard U., 1961; PhD, Columbia U., 1966. Bar: D.C. 1964, N.Y. 1984. Assoc. Curtis, Mallet-Prevost, Colt & Mosle, N.Y.C., 1964-66; asst. prof. Cornell U., Ithaca, N.Y., 1966-72; editor Digest of U.S. Practice in International Law U.S. Dept. State, Washington, 1972-75, asst. legal adviser, 1975-81; agt. U.S. Govt. to Iran-U.S. Claims Tribunal U.S. Dept. State, The Hague, Netherlands, 1981-83; of counsel Baker & McKenzie, N.Y.C., 1983-85, ptnr., 1985—; adj. prof. law Georgetown U., Washington, 1977-81. Author: The First Fifty Years: The Secretary-General in World Politics, 1920-1970, 1970; editor: Digest of U.S. Practice in International Law, 1973, 74; co-editor: The Case Law of the International Court of Justice, 1968, 1972, 1974, 1976; bd. editors Am. Jour. Internat. Law, 1977-87; also articles on internat. law. Mem. panel on settlement of transnat. bus. disputes, N.Y. panel Ctr. for Pub. Resources; chmn. law subcom. of internat. adv. coun. on profl. edn. Coun. on Internat. Ednl. Exch.; mem. Coun. on Fgn. Rels. Mem. ABA (chmn. internat. law sect. 1985-86, del. to Ho. of Dels. 1988-90), Am. Soc. Internat. Law (cert. of merit 1974, exec. coun. 1975-77, 97—), U.S. Coun. for Internat. Bus. (arbitration com.), Am. Arbitration Assn. (panel of arbitrators), Assn. Bar City of N.Y. (coun. on internat. affairs). Home: 150 E 61st St New York NY 10021-8529 Office: Baker & McKenzie 805 3rd Ave New York NY 10022-7513

ROVINSKY, JOSEPH JUDAH, obstetrician, gynecologist; b. Phila., Sept. 4, 1927; s. Israel and Sarah (Blackman) R.; m. Judith S. Levin, June 24, 1964; children: Audrey, John, Jill, Michael, Paul, David. B.A., U. Pa., 1948, M.D., 1952. Diplomate Am. Bd. Ob-Gyn. Intern U. Pa. Hosp., Phila., 1952-53; resident in ob-gyn Mt. Sinai Hosp., N.Y.C., 1953-58; practice medicine specializing in ob-gyn, 1958—; chmn. dept. ob-gyn City Hosp. Center, Elmhurst, N.Y., 1964-74; prof. ob-gyn Mt. Sinai Sch. Medicine, N.Y.C., 1969-74; prof., chmn. dept. ob-gyn Sch. Medicine Health Scis. Center, SUNY, Stony Brook, 1975-79, prof., 1975-89; chmn. dept. ob-gyn L.I. Jewish Med. Center, 1973-92; prof. ob-gyn. Albert Einstein Coll. Medicine, 1989-94; dir. dept. ob/gyn. Sound Shore Med. Ctr. of Westchester, New Rochelle, 1992—; mem. obstetric adv. com. N.Y.C. Dept. Health, 1964-92. Author: Medical, Surgical and Gynecological Complications of Pregnancy, 1961, 2d edit., 1965; editor: Davis' Gynecology and Obstetrics, 1968-73. Served to capt., M.C. USAF, 1964-66. Mem. ACS, Am. Coll. Obstetricians and Gynecologists, Am. Soc. Reproductive Medicine, Am. Uro-Gynecologic Soc., N.Y. Acad. Medicine, N.Y. Obstetrical Soc., N.Y. Gynecol. Assn., Med. Soc. State N.Y. Jewish. Office: Sound Shore Medical Center of Westchester 16 Guion Pl New Rochelle NY 10801-5503

ROVIRA, LUIS DARIO, state supreme court justice; b. San Juan, P.R., Sept. 8, 1923; s. Peter S. and Mae (Morris) R.; m. Lois Ann Thau, June 25, 1966; children—Douglas, Merilyn. B.A., U. Colo., 1948, LL.B., 1950. Bar: Colo. 1950. Chief justice Colo. Supreme Ct., Denver., 1990-95; ret., 1995; mem. Pres.'s Com. on Mental Retardation, 1970-71; chmn. State Health Facilities Council, 1967-76. Bd. dirs Children's Hosp.; trustee Temple Buell Found., Denver Found., Harry S. Truman Scholarship Found. With AUS, 1943-46. Mem. ABA, Colo. Bar Assn., Denver Bar Assn. (pres. 1970-71), Colo. Assn. Retarded Children (pres. 1968-70), Alpha Tau Omega, Phi Alpha Delta. Clubs: Athletic (Denver), Country (Denver). Home: 4810 E 6th Ave Denver CO 80220-5137

ROVIS, CHRISTOPHER PATRICK, clinical social worker, psychotherapist; b. N.Y.C., Dec. 2, 1950; s. Del Patrick and Patricia Joan (Martin) R.; m. Lorraine Theresa LaPanna, July 26, 1985; children: Lauren Christine, Vincent Christopher. BS, George Mason U., 1973; MSW, Va. Commonwealth U., 1975; cert., Cath. U., 1985; PsyD, Newport U., 1988; cert. in family therapy, Family Therapy Inst., 1984. Lic. clin. social worker, Va., Md. D.C.; diplomate Am. Bd. Examiners in Clin. Social Work. Sr. staff psychotherapist N.W. Ctr. for Community Mental Health, Reston, Va., 1976-84; pvt. practice Tysons Corner Psychotherapy Assocs., Vienna, Va., 1982-91, Ctr. Psychotherapy at Tyson's Corner, Vienna, Va., 1991—. Mem. NASW, Acad. Cert. Social Workers, Greater Washington Soc. for Clin. Social Work. Roman Catholic. Avocations: skiing, travel, running, photography, real estate. Home: 3189 Mary Etta Ln Herndon VA 22071-1620 Office: Ctr Psychotherapy at Tysons Corner 8308 Old Courthouse Rd # B Vienna VA 22182-3809

ROVISON, JOHN MICHAEL, JR., chemical engineer; b. North Tonawanda, N.Y., June 15, 1959; s. John Michael and Veronica Marie (Donat) R.; m. Beverly Jean Farinet, Sept. 6, 1986 (div. Oct. 1989); m. Janet Marie Konieczny, Apr. 27, 1991; 1 child, Kevin Michael (dec.). BA in Biology, BSChemE, Washington U., 1982; MS in Cancer Biology, Niagara U., 1986. Physics tchr. North Tonawanda High Sch., 1985; assoc. process engr. Ag Chem. Group FMC Corp., Middleport, N.Y., 1982-83, process engr. Ag Chem. Group, 1983-84, sr. process engr. Ag Chem. Group, 1986-90; sr. process engr. divsn. peroxygen chem. FMC Corp., Buffalo, 1990-91, process group leader divsn. peroxygen chem., 1992-93, prod. area supr. divsn. peroxygen chem., 1993-94, prodn. mgr. PXD, 1994-96, tech. mgr. AOD, 1996—; mem. new products evaluation bd. Chem. Engring. McGraw Hill, 1983-84; tech. cons. Ag Chem. Group FMC Corp., Middleport, 1985. Mem. Resolve through Sharing Parents Group, Williamsville, N.Y., 1992. Mem. Am. Inst. Chem. Engrs., Am. Chem. Soc. Roman Catholic. Achievements include redesigning Furadan Milling Plant to reduce N@ usage, persulfate caking issues and development of mineral peroxides; design and installation of process ventilation system for phosplant; originated mathematical system to study S1 endonuclease activity on plasmids in alcohol environments using hyperchromic shifts; helped lead effort for plant ISO 9002 certification, implemented first self-directed union workforce in FMC; converted potential waste stream into environmental end use product. Home: 1394 Saybrook Ave North Tonawanda NY 14120-2359 Office: FMC Corp Sawyer Ave And River Rd Tonawanda NY 14150

ROVIT, RICHARD LEE, neurological surgeon; b. Boston, Apr. 3, 1924; s. Samuel and Frances (Ehrenberg) R.; m. Barbara Sayre Margolis, Mar. 29, 1953; children: Sandra Amy Golze, Adam John, Hugh Russel. Grad., U. Mich., 1944; MD, Jefferson Med. Coll., 1950; MSc, McGill U., 1961. Diplomate Am. Bd. Neurol. Surgery (dir. vice chmn. 1986-92). Intern in surgery Beth Israel Hosp., Boston, 1950-51; resident, then chief resident Mass. Gen. Hosp., Boston, 1951-58; U.S.P.H. fellow in neurology The Nat. Hosp., London, England, 1956; sr. fellow in neurosurgery Lahey Clinic, Boston, 1957; fellow in neurophysiology and EEG Montreal (Can.) Neurol. Inst., 1958-59; prof. clin. neurosurgery NYU, 1967—; chmn. neurosurgery St. Vincent's Hosp. and Med. Ctr., N.Y.C., 1967-92, past chmn. neurosurgery, 1992—. Editor, author: Trigeminal Neuralgia, 1991; contbr. articles to profl. jours. Lt. USN, 1952-54. Fellow ACS (v.p. 1994-95), Am. Assn. Neurol. Surgeons (v.p. 1980-81); mem. N.Y. Soc. Neurosurgeons (pres. 1974-76, 79-80), Soc. Neurol. Surgeons, Fairview Country Club, Harvard Club of N.Y. Avocations: golf, running. Home: 42 Brite Ave Scarsdale NY 10583 Office: Manhattan Neurosurg 153 W 11th St New York NY 10011-8305

ROVNER, DAVID RICHARD, endocrinology educator; b. Phila., Sept. 20, 1930; s. Arthur and Rae Theresa (Lieb) R.; m. Margaret McCann, Jan. 15, 1987; children: Arthur, Daniel, Gregory, Robert, Paul, Jessica. AB in Chemistry with distinction, Temple U., 1951, MD, 1955. Diplomate Am. Bd. Internal Medicine. Resident, fellow in internal medicine U. Mich., Ann Arbor, 1956-61, from instr. to assoc. prof. endocrinology and metabolism, 1961-71, prof., 1971; prof. medicine, chief endocrinology and metabolism Mich. State U., East Lansing, 1971-96, asst. to dean for tech., 1996—, assoc. chmn. dept. medicine, 1975-77, acting chmn., 1976-77; chmn. dept. medicine Ingham Med. Ctr., Lansing, Mich., 1984-86. Contbr. articles to profl. jours. Pres. PTO, Ann Arbor, 1966-71; pilot Civil Air Patrol, Lansing, 1975-87. Served to capt. USAFR, 1960-70. Fellow ACP (sec., treas., various coms.); mem. Mich. State Med. Soc. (chmn. continuing edn. com.), Am. Diabetes Assn. (pres. Mich. affiliate 1990-92), Am. Heart Assn., Alpha Omega Alpha. Avocations: electronics, computers. Office: Mich State Univ A108 B E-FEE East Lansing MI 48824

ROVNER, ILANA KARA DIAMOND, federal judge; b. Aug. 21, 1938; came to U.S., 1939; d. Stanley and Ronny (Medalje) Diamond; m. Richard Nyles Rovner, Mar. 9, 1963; 1 child, Maxwell Rabson. AB, Bryn Mawr Coll., 1960; postgrad., U. London King's Coll., 1961, Georgetown U., 1961-63; JD, Ill. Inst. Tech., 1966; LittD (hon.), Rosary Coll., 1989, Mundelein Coll., 1989; DHL (hon.), Spertus Coll. of Judaica, 1992. Bar: Ill. 1972, U.S. Dist. Ct. (no. dist.) Ill. 1972, U.S. Ct. Appeals (7th cir.) 1977, U.S. Supreme Ct. 1981, Fed. Trial Bar (no. dist.) Ill. 1982. Jud. clk. U.S. Dist. Ct. (no. dist.) Ill., Chgo., 1972-73; asst. U.S. atty. U.S. Atty.'s Office, Chgo., 1973-77; dep. chief of pub. protection, 1975-76, chief pub. protection, 1976-77; dep. gov., legal counsel Gov. James R. Thompson, Chgo., 1977-84; dist. judge U.S. Dist. Ct. (no. dist.) Ill., Chgo., 1984-92; cir. judge U.S. Ct. Appeals (7th cir.), Chgo., 1992—. Trustee Bryn Mawr Coll., Pa., 1983-89; mem. bd. overseers Ill. Inst. Tech./Kent Coll. Law, 1983—; trustee Ill. Inst. Tech., 1989—; mem. adv. coun. Rush Ctr. for Sports Medicine, Chgo., 1991-96; civil justice reform act adv. com. for the 7th cir., Chgo., 1991-95; bd. vis. No. Ill. U. Coll. Law, 1992-94; vis. com. Northwestern U. Sch. Law, 1993—, U. Chgo. Law Sch., 1993-96, 7th cir. race and gender fairness com., 1993—, U.S. Ct. Appeals (7th cir.) fairness com., 1996—, 7th cir. gender study task force, 1995-96. Recipient Spl. Commendation award U.S. Dept. Justice, 1975, Spl. Achievement award 1976, Ann. Nat. Law and Social Justice Leadership award League to Improve the Cmty., 1975, Ann. Guardian Police award, 1977, Profl. Achievement award Ill. Inst. Tech., 1986, Louis Dembitz Brandeis medal for Disting. Legal Svc. Brandeis U., 1993, 1st Woman award, Valparaiso U. Sch. Law, 1993, ORT Women's Am. Cmty. Svc. award, 1987-88, svc. award Spertus Coll. of Judaica, 1987, Ann. award Chgo. Found. for Women, 1990; named Today's Chgo. Woman of Yr., 1985, Woman of Achievement Chgo. Women's Club, 1986, others; Hebrew Immigrant Aid Soc. Chgo. 85th Anniversary honoree, 1996. Mem. ABA, Fed. Bar Assn. (jud. selection com. Chgo. chpt. 1977-80, treas. Chgo. chpt. 1978-79, sec. Chgo. chpt. 1979-80, 2d v.p. Chgo. chpt. 1980-81, 1st v.p. Chgo. chpt. 1981-82, pres. Chgo. chpt. 1982-83, 2d v.p. 7th cir. 1983-84, v.p. 7th cir. 1984-85), Fed. Judges Assn., Nat. Assn. Women Judges, Women's Bar Assn. Ill. (ann. award 1989, 1st Myra Bradwell Woman of Achievement award 1994), Chgo. Bar Assn. (commendation def. of prisoners com. 1987), Chgo. Coun. Lawyers, Decalogue Soc. of Lawyers (citation of honor 1991, merit award 1997), Kappa Beta Pi, Phi Alpha Delta (hon.). Republican. Jewish. Office: 219 S Dearborn St Ste 2774 Chicago IL 60604-1803

ROVNER, JACK ALAN, lawyer; b. Boston, May 6, 1946; s. Abraham George and Sarah Rebecca (Miller) R.; m. Sheila Marie Boyle, June 24, 1979; children—Joseph Conahan, Edward Witty, Benjamin Flanagan. B.A., Brandeis U., 1968; J.D. cum laude, Boston U., 1976. Bar: Ill. 1976, U.S. Dist. Ct. (no. dist.) Ill. 1976, U.S. Ct. Appeals (7th and 9th cir.) 1979, U.S. Supreme Ct. 1979. Admin. asst. U.S. EPA, Boston, 1971-73; assoc. Kirkland & Ellis, Chgo., 1976-81, ptnr. 1982-93; pvt. practice, Naperville, Ill., 1993-96; ptnr. Michael, Best & Friedrich, Chgo., 1996—. Served to lt. jr. grade USCG, 1968-71. Article editor Boston U. Law Rev., 1974-76. Mem. ABA (litigation sect., antitrust sect., health law sect.), Nat. Health Lawyers Assn., Ill. State Bar Assn., Ill. Assn. Hosp. Attys., White Eagle Golf Club. Office: 77 W Wacker Dr Ste 4300 Chicago IL 60601-1635

ROW, PETER LYMAN, musician, educator. Student, Rabindra Bharati U., Calcutta; BM, Prayag Sangit Samiti, Allahabad, India, 1968; MM, Prayag Sangit Samiti, 1970, DM, 1973. Rsch. assoc. Harvard U., Cambridge, Mass., 1973-74; mgt. devel. program Inst. for Ednl. Mgmt. Harvard U., 1986; educator, provost New Eng. Conservatory Music; lectr. on Indian music nationwide; cons. on Asian music Smithsonian Instn. Performed as sitarist throughout U.S., India; appeared on TV, radio show numerous times. Mem. Soc. Ethnomusicology (former pres. N.E. chpt.). Office: New Eng Conservatory 290 Huntington Ave Boston MA 02115-5018*

ROWAN, CARL THOMAS, columnist; b. Ravenscroft, Tenn., Aug. 11, 1925; s. Thomas David and Johnnie (Bradford) R.; m. Vivien Louise Murphy, Aug. 2, 1950; children: Barbara, Carl Thomas, Geoffrey. Student, Tenn. State U., 1942-43, Washburn U., 1943-44; A.B. in Math, Oberlin Coll., 1947, D.Litt., 1962; M.A. in Journalism, U. Minn., 1948; D.Litt., Simpson Coll., 1957, Hamline U., 1958, Coll. Wooster, 1968, Drexel Inst. Tech., 1969;

L.H.D., Washburn U., 1964, Talladega Coll., 1965, St. Olaf Coll., 1966, Knoxville Coll., 1966, R.I. Coll., 1970, U. Maine, 1971, Am. U., 1980; LL.D., Howard U., 1964, Alfred U., 1964, Temple U., 1964, Atlanta U., 1965, Allegheny Coll., 1966, Colby Coll., 1968, Clark U., 1971; D. Pub. Adminstrn., Morgan State Coll., 1964. Copywriter Mpls. Tribune, 1948-50, staff writer, 1950-61; dep. asst. sec. State for pub. affairs Dept. of State, 1961-63; U.S. ambassador to Finland Helsinki, 1963-64; dir. USIA, Washington, 1964-65; syndicated columnist News Am. Syndicate (formerly Field Syndicate); now panelist Inside Washington, Washington, D.C.; now syndicated columnist King Features, N.Y. Author: South of Freedom, 1953 (named to A.L.A. ann. list best books), The Pitiful and the Proud, 1956 (A.L.A. ann. list best books), Go South to Sorrow, 1957, Wait Till Next Year, 1960, Just Between Us Blacks, 1974, Breaking Barriers: A Memoir, 1991, Dream Makers, Dream Breakers: The World of Justice Thurgood Marshall, 1993. Recipient Sidney Hillman award for best newspaper reporting, 1952; selected one of 10 outstanding young men of Am. U.S. Jr. C. of C., 1954; award for best gen. reporting on segregation cases pending before U.S. Supreme Ct. Sigma Delta Chi, 1954; fgn. corr. medallion for articles on India, 1955; fgn. corr. medallion for articles on S.E. Asia, coverage of Bandung Conf., 1956; Distinguished Achievement award Regents; Distinguished Achievement award U. Minn., 1961; Communications award in Human Relations Anti- Defamation League B'nai B'rith, 1964; Contbns. to Am. Democracy award Roosevelt U., 1964; Nat. Brotherhood award Nat. Conf. Christians and Jews, 1964; Liberty Bell award Howard U., 1965; George Foster Peabody award for TV spl. Race War in Rhodesia, 1978. Address: 3251 Sutton Pl NW # C Washington DC 20016-3507 also: King Features Inc 235 E 45th St New York NY 10017-3305*

ROWAN, GERALD BURDETTE, insurance company executive, lawyer; b. Powersville, Mo., Feb. 9, 1916; s. M. C. and Blanch (Spidle) R.; m. Mary Elizabeth Turner, Dec. 24, 1939; children: Sandra Josephine, Roger Turner. A.B., N.W. Mo. State Coll., 1937; LL.B., Mo. U., 1940. Bar: Mo. bar 1940. Practice in Marble Hill, 1940-49, Cape Girardeau, 1949-59, Kansas City, 1959-81, Eagle Rock, Mo., 1981—; mem. firm Frye & Rowan, 1940-42, 46-49, Oliver & Oliver, 1949-59; with legal dept. Kansas City Life Ins. Co., 1959-76, sr. v.p. tech. services, 1976-81, also dir.; pros. atty., Bollinger County, 1946-49; city atty., Cape Girardeau, 1954-59. Pres. Jackson County unit Am. Cancer Soc., 1963-65, 70-73; chmn. Mo. div. Am. Cancer Soc., 1974-76; mem. Mo. Park Bd., 1965-77. Served with F.A. AUS, 1943-45, MTO. Mem. Mo. Bar Assn. (com. chmn.), World Assn. Lawyers, Assn. Life Ins. Counsel, State City Attys. Assn. (past pres.), Mo. Law Sch. Alumni Assn. (past pres.), Order of Coif, Sigma Tau Gamma. Republican. Methodist. Home: 2835 S Oak Ave Springfield MO 65804

ROWAN, JOHN ROBERT, retired medical center director; b. Joliet, Ill., Aug. 19, 1919; s. Hugh Hamilton and Elizabeth Margaret (Maloney) R.; m. Ruth Elaine Boyle, June 17, 1944; 1 child, Robert J. Student, Butler U., 1952-53, Ind. U., 1953-54. Personnel specialist VA Br. Office 7, Chgo., 1946; personnel officer VA Hosp., Ft. Benjamin Harrison, Ind., 1946-51, Indpls., 1951-56; asst. dir. VA Hosp., 1960-67; asst. mgr. VA Hosp., Iron Mountain, Mich., 1956-60; hosp. adminstrn. specialist VA Central Office, Washington, 1967-69; dir. VA Hosp., Manchester, N.H., 1969-71, Buffalo, 1971-72; dir. VA Med. Center, Lexington, Ky., 1972-88, Montgomery, Ala., 1988-97; dir. VA Med. Dist. 11, 1975-86; ret., 1997. Bd. dirs. Marion County (Ind.) unit Am. Cancer Soc., 1960-67, pres., 1964-66, bd. dirs. Ind. div., 1966-67; bd. dirs. Western N.Y. Regional Med. Program, 1971-72, Eastern Ky. Health Systems Agy., 1976-79, United Way of Bluegrass, 1976-79, 82-85; mem. regional advisory council Ohio Valley Regional Med. Program, 1972-76; mem. State Health Planning Bd., 1982-88; bd. dirs. Hosp. Hospitality House of Lexington, 1981; mem. adv. coun. Cen. Ala. Aging Consortium, 1991; chmn. Montgomery Area Combined Fed. Campaign, 1991. Served in USAAF, 1942-46. Decorated Bronze Star; recipient Meritorious Svc. citations Ind. dept. DAV, 1964, Meritorious Svc. citations Ky. dept. Am. Legion, 1975, Meritorious Svc. citations Ky. dept. VFW, 1976, Meritorious Svc. citations Eastern Ky. U., 1974, Meritorious Svc. citations Ky. dept. DAV 1978, Spl. Recognition award VFW, 1982, cert. of Merit, DAV, 1982; recipient Dedicated Svc. to Vets. award DAV, 1984, Meritorious Svc. to Vets. award, Am. Legion, 1985, Meritorious Svc. award, Chpt. I, Ky. DAV, 1988, VA Performance award, 1990, Joint Fed. Campaign Meritorious Svc. award, 1990, Dedicated Svc. award DAV, 1992, McClusky award Ala. State Nurses Assn., 1993. Fellow Am. Coll. Healthcare Execs.; mem. Am. Hosp. Assn., Ala. Hosp. Assn. (profl. standards and quality assurance com. 1991—), Ctrl. Ala. Hosp. Coun., Ala. Assn. Hosp. Execs., Assn. Mil. Surgeons U.S., Fed. Hosp. Inst. Alumni Assn. Roman Catholic. Home: 2040 Clubview St Montgomery AL 36106-1625 Office: Va Med Ctr 215 Perry Hill Rd Montgomery AL 36109-3725

ROWAN, KEITH PATTERSON, communications executive, consultant; b. Youngstown, Ohio, Aug. 14, 1934; s. James Arthur and Elisabeth (Patterson) R.; m. Elizabeth Guthrie, Dec. 23, 1958; children: Dora E. Rowan Jiles, Keith P. Jr., Michelle D., James G. BS in Indsl. and Labor Rels., Cornell U., 1956; postgrad., London Sch. Econ., 1960-62, NYU, 1962-66; exec. program cert., UCLA, 1978. V.p. acct. exec. Hill & Knowlton, Inc., N.Y.C., 1967-70; v.p. communications Avco Corp., Greenwich, Conn., 1969-72; chmn. and pres. Carte Blanche Corp., L.A., 1973-75; v.p. investor rels. Rockwell Internat. Corp., Pitts., 1976-77; v.p. corp. and fin. rels. Smith Internat., Inc., Newport Beach, Calif., 1977-80; sr. v.p., gen. mgr. Bozell & Jacobs, Inc., N.Y.C., 1981-82, Doyle Dane Bernbach, L.A., 1983-85; sr. v.p. Burson Marsteller, Inc., L.A., 1986-89; pres. Rowan Cons., Inc., L.A., 1989-94; mng. dir. global bus. unit Shandwick/Rogers & Cowan, Inc., Beverly Hills, Calif., 1994—. Bd. dirs. exec. program UCLA, 1980-81, young pres. orgn., 1974-77. Republican. Presbyterian. Avocations: long distance running, cooking, writing. Home: 121 N Almont Dr Apt 104 Beverly Hills CA 90211-1856

ROWAN, RICHARD LAMAR, business management educator; b. Guntersville, Ala., July 10, 1931; s. Leon Virgle and Mae (Williamson) R.; m. Marilyn Walker, Aug. 3, 1963; children: John Richard, Jennifer Walker. A.B., Birmingham-So. Coll., 1953; postgrad., Auburn U., 1956-57; Ph.D., U. N.C., 1961. Instr. Auburn (Ala.) U., 1956-57, U. N.C., Chapel Hill, 1958-59, 60-61; lectr. U. Pa., Phila., 1961-62, asst. prof., 1962-66, assoc. prof. industry, 1966-73, prof. industry, 1973—; dir. indsl. research unit, 1989-91; co-dir. Ctr. for Human Resources, 1991—; visitor to Faculty Econs. and Politics Cambridge (Eng.) U., 1972; pvt. sector advisor U.S. State Dept. Com. on Internat. Investment and Multinational Enterprises, OECD, 1982-89; chmn. Labor Relations Council, 1985—. Author: (with H.R. Northrup) The Negro and Employment Opportunity, 1965, Readings in Labor Economics and Labor Relations, 5th edit., 1984, The Negro in the Steel Industry, 1969, The Negro in the Textile Industry, 1970, (with others) Studies of Negro Employment, 1970, Educating the Employed Disadvantaged for Upgrading, 1972, Collective Bargaining: Survival in the 1970's, 1972, Opening the Skilled Construction Trades to Blacks, 1972, The Impact of Government Manpower Programs, 1975, International Enforcement of Union Standards in Ocean Transport, 1977, The Impact of OSHA, 1978, Multinational Bargaining Attempts: The Record, the Cases, and the Prospects, 1980; (with H.R. Northrup) Employee Relations and Regulations in the 80s, 1982; (with others) Multinational Union Organizations in the Manufacturing Industries, (with D.C. Campbell) The Multinational Enterprises and the OECD Industrial Relations Guidelines, 1984, Trade Union Clout Erodes, But For How Long?, 1985, Employee Relations Trends and Practices in the Textile Industry, 1986; contbr. articles to profl. jours. Mem. personnel com. Del. Valley Settlement Alliance, 1966-68. Served with Transp. Corps U.S. Army, 1953-56. Mem. Indsl. Rels. Rsch. Assn. (sec. Phila. 1964-65), Acad. Internat. Bus., The Penn Club, The Carolina Club. Democrat. Episcopalian. Home: 113 Blackthorn Rd Wallingford PA 19086-6046 Office: U Pa Wharton Sch 3733 Spruce St Philadelphia PA 19104-4108

ROWARK, MAUREEN, fine arts photographer; b. Edinburgh, Midlothian, Scotland, Feb. 28, 1933; came to U.S., 1960, naturalized, 1970; d. Alexander Pennycook and Margaret (Gorman) Prezdpelski; m. Robert Rowark, May 3, 1952 (div. July 1965). 1 child, Mark Steven. Student, Warmington Bus. Coll., Royal Leamington Spa, Eng., 1950-51, Royal Leamington Spa Art Sch.; diploma, Speedwriting Inst., N.Y.C., 1961; AS in Edn., St. Clair County Community Coll., Port Huron, Mich., 1977, AA, 1978. Supr. proof reading Nevin D. Hirst Advt., Ltd., Leeds, Eng., 1952-55; publicity asst. Alvis Aero Engines, Ltd., Coventry, Eng., 1955-57; adminstrv. asst. Port Huron Motor Inn, 1964-66; adminstrv. asst. pub. rels. dept. Geophysics and Computer Svcs., Inc., New Orleans, 1966-68; sales mgr. Holiday Inn, Port Huron, 1968-70; adminstrv. asst. Howard Corp., Port Huron, 1971-73; sales and systems coord. Am. Wood Products, Ann Arbor, Mich., 1973-74; systems coord. Daniels & Zermack Architects, Ann Arbor, 1974; systems coord., cataloger fine arts dept. St. Clair County Community Coll., Port Huron, 1976-79; freelance fine arts photographer Port Huron, 1978—; photographer Patterns mag. front cover, 1978, Erie Sq. Gazette, 1979, Bluewater Area Tourism Bur. brochure, 1989, Port Huron, Can. Legion, Wyo., Ont. Br., 1987, 88—, Grace Episcopal Ch. Mariner's Day, Port Huron, 1987, 92, 93, 94, 95, 96, Homes mag., 1989. One-woman shows at Grace Episcopal Ch., 1995, Port Huron Mus., 1995, St. Clair River Remedial Action Plan, 1995 (Best in Landscape Category), Mich. Waterways Coun. Girl Scouts Exhibit, 1996; exhibited in internat. shows at Ann. Ea. Mich. Internat. Juried Exhbn., yearly 1982-96 (awards of excellence 1982, 83, Best Photography award 1995, 96), St. Clair County C.C., 1983, 86 (award of excellence), Gallery Lambton, Sarina, Ont., Can., 1983-92, 94 (honorable mention), Bluewater Bridge Juried Exhibit, 1988, Kaskilaaksontie Exhibit, Finland, 1991 (Par Excellence award), Swann Gallery, Detroit, 1996, St. Clair (Mich.) Art Gallery, Genesis Gallery, Lexington, Mich., others; represented in permanent exhibit Capac State Bank, 1996, Grace Episcopal Ch., 1995, Port Huron Hosp., 1996; contbr. short stories to mags. Cons., buyer interior decor Grace Episcopal Ch., 1994; active Port Huron Mus., 1985—. Recipient Hon. Mention award Gallery Lambton, Sarnia, 1981; named Best Photographer, Gallery Lambton, Sarnia, 1988; winner 2d and 3d Pl. awards Times Herald Newspaper, 1988. Mem. St. Clair County C.C. Alumni Assn., Phi Theta Kappa, Lambda Mu. Democrat. Episcopalian. Avocations: costumes and interior design, travel, theater, ballroom dancing, gardening. Home and Office: 2005 Riverside Dr Apt 15 Port Huron MI 48060-2677

ROWDEN, MARCUS AUBREY, lawyer, former government official; b. Detroit, Mar. 13, 1928; s. Louis and Gertrude (Lifsitz) Rosenzweig; m. Justine Leslie Bessman, July 21, 1950; children: Gwen, Stephanie. B.A. in Econs, U. Mich., Ann Arbor, 1950, J.D. with distinction, 1953. Bar: Mich. 1953, D.C. 1978. Trial atty. Dept. Justice, 1953-58; legal advisor U.S. Mission to European Communities, 1959-62; solicitor, assoc. gen. counsel, gen. counsel AEC, 1965-74; commr., chmn. U.S. NRC, Washington, 1975-77; 2tnr. Fried, Frank, Harris, Shriver and Jacobson, Washington, 1977—. Served with AUS, 1946-47. Decorated officer Order Legion of Honor Republic of France; Recipient Disting. Service award AEC, 1972. Mem. Am., Fed., Mich., D.C. bar assns., Internat. Nuclear Law Assn., Order of Coif. Home: 7937 Deepwell Dr Bethesda MD 20817-1927 Office: Fried Frank Harris Shriver and Jacobson 1001 Pennsylvania Ave NW Washington DC 20004-2505

ROWDEN, WILLIAM HENRY, naval officer; b. Woodsville, N.H., May 12, 1930; s. Henry Thomas and Kathleen M. (Gochey) R.; m. Sarah Sumner, Apr. 14, 1956; children: Sarah Jane, Thomas Sumner, John William. B.S., U.S. Naval Acad., 1952, U.S. Naval Postgrad. Sch., 1963. Commd. ensign U.S. Navy, 1952, advanced through grades to vice adm., 1980; comdr. cruiser-destroyer group 3 U.S. Navy, San Diego, 1977-79; staff chief naval ops. U.S. Navy, Washington, 1979-81; comdr. 6th Fleet U.S. Navy, 1981-83, comdr. Mil. Sealift Command, 1983-85; comdr. Naval Sea Systems Command U.S. Navy, Washington, 1985-88, ret., 1988; Disting. fellow Ctr. for Naval Analyses, Alexandria, Va., 1988—. Decorated D.S.M., Legion of Merit, Bronze Star. Mem. Naval Inst. Presbyterian. Avocations: walking, sailing. Home: 55 Pinewood Ct Lancaster VA 22503-9739 Office: Ctr for Naval Analyses Alexandria VA 22302

ROWDER, WILLIAM LOUIS, lawyer; b. Chgo., Aug. 21, 1937; s. John Joseph and Theresa Veronica (Major) R.; m. Josephine M. Laurino, Apr. 20, 1940; children: Lauren, Lisa, Jessica, William. BA, DePaul U., 1961, JD, 1965. Bar: Ill. 1965, U.S. Dist. Ct. (no. dist.) Ill. 1967. Atty. Kirkland & Ellis, Chgo., 1965-76; sr. ptnr. estate planning dept. Kirkland & Ellis, 1979-87; mem. Pope, Ballard, Shephard & Fowle, 1976-79; sr. ptnr. estate planning dept. Coffield, Ungaretti, Harris & Slavin, Chgo., 1987-90, of counsel, 1990—; of counsel Ungaretti & Harris, Chgo.; dir. Forest Park Nat. Bank; adj. prof. law DePaul U. Contbr. articles to profl. jours. Village trustee Village of River Forest, 1975-76. Fellow Am. Coll. Trust & Estate Counsel; mem. ABA, Ill. Bar Assn., Chgo. Bar Assn., Chgo. Athletic Club, The Law Club. Office: Ungaretti & Harris 3500 Three 1st National Plz Chicago IL 60602

ROWE, ALLAN DUNCAN, food products executive; b. Corner Brook, Nfld., Can., Feb. 23, 1951. B in Commerce, Dalhousie U., 1974; MBA, U. Western Ont., 1978. V.p. fin. B.F. Goodrich Can. Inc., Kitchener, Ont., 1978-87; chief fin. officer Sobeys Inc., Stellarton, N.S., Can., 1987-96; sr. v.p., chief fin. officer Empire Co. Ltd., Stellarton, N.S., Can., 1996—. Mem. Fin. Execs. Inst. Office: Empire Co Ltd, 115 King St, Stellarton, NS Canada B0K 1S0

ROWE, AUDREY, postal service administrator; b. Albuquerque, June 26, 1958; d. James Franklin Ringold and Geneva Doris (Jennings) Robinson. ASB in Acctg., ICS Ctr. for Degrees, Scranton, Pa., 1988, ASB in Fin., 1989; BSBA, Century U., 1991, MBA, 1995, grad. paralegal studies, 1996. Svc. rep. Mountain and Southwestern Bell Telephone Co., Albuquerque, Houston, 1978-83; clk., carrier U.S. Postal Svc. PS05, Bellaire, Sugar Land, Tex., 1983-86; supr. mails U.S. Postal Svc. EAS15, Sugar Land, 1986-87; officer-in-charge U.S. Postal Svc. EAS 18, Rosharon, Tex., 1987; from supr. mails EAS 15 to gen. supr. mails EAS 17 U.S. Postal Svc., Houston, 1987-89; relief tour supt. U.S. Postal Svc. EAS 21 (Detail Assignment), Houston, 1989; mgr. gen. mail facility U.S. Postal Svc. EAS22 (Detail Assignment), Capitol Heights, Md., 1989-90; mgr. mail processing U.S. Postal Svc. EAS21, Charlottesville, Va., 1990-91; MSC dir. city ops. U.S. Postal Svc. EAS23 (Detail Assignment), Roanoke, Va., 1991; mgr. gen. mail facility U.S. Postal Svc. EAS24, Washington, 1991—; plant mgr. U.S. Postal Svc. EAS25, Dulles, Va., 1992. Mem. NAFE, Am. Soc. Notaries. Avocations: piano, violin, reading. Home: PO Box 220411 Chantilly VA 22022-0411

ROWE, BONNIE GORDON, music company executive; b. Buford, Ga., May 3, 1922; s. Bonnie Gordon and Alma (Poole) R.; m. Mary Wilburta Shidler; 1 child, Sharon Lynn; m. Gloria Lucille Fairfax, Feb. 17, 1962 (div.); 1 child, Susan Rebecca. Student Ga. Evening Coll., 1939-41, U. Wichita, 1948-49, Ga. State Coll., 1949-52. Traffic mgr. Bonanza Air Lines, Las Vegas, 1946-48; music tchr. 1948-52; owner Rowe Accordion Distbg. Co., Rowe Accordion Center, Atlanta, 1952-56, Atlanta Music Pub. Co., 1956—, B. Rowe Music Co., Atlanta, 1957—; pres.-treas. B. Rowe Enterprises, Inc., 1973—. Composer: Accordionique, 1953, Vivolet, 1956, More and More and More, 1964, Dedication, 1964, All I Really See is You, 1965, I Love Only You, 1965, Festival March, 1965, Preludio Reminisci, 1969. Bd. dirs. Sandtown Found., Atlanta. Lt. col. USAAF, World War II, ETO. Decorated Air medals with three oak leaf clusters. Mem. 781st Bomb Squadron Assn. (465th bomb group WWII), Southeastern Accordion Assn. (past pres.), Nat. Assn. Music Mchts., Atlanta Fedn. Musicians (life mem.), Travelers Protective Assn., Atlanta C. of C., Res. Officers Assn., Ret. Officers Assn., Air Force Assn., Internat. Platform Assn., Am. Legion, Sandtown Civitan Club (past pres., lt. gov., past pres. Met. Atlanta Council), Elks (exalted ruler 1987, 88, 89, past pres. past exalted rulers assn., trustee Union City, state organist Ga. Elks Assn.), Dobbins AFB Officers Club, Gamma Delta Phi. Home: 5085 Erin Rd SW Atlanta GA 30331-7810 Office: 6102 Mableton Pkwy Mableton GA 30126-4302

ROWE, CHARLES ALFRED, artist, designer, educator; b. Great Falls, Mont., Feb. 7, 1934; s. Alfred Lewis and Alice Lillian (Ledbetter) R.; m. Eugenia Dean, July 5, 1958; children: Allison Rene, Jon Garner, Dorian Leigh. Student, Mont. State U., 1952-53, So. Meth. U., 1956-57, U. Chgo., 1959-60; BFA, Sch. Art Inst., Chgo., 1960; MFA, Tyler Sch. Art, 1968. Prin. Charles Rowe Advt., Chgo., 1957-60; graphic designer Am. Can Co., Bellwood, Ill., 1960-62, Abrams-Bannister Engraving, Inc., Greenville, S.C., 1962-64; prof. art U. Del., Newark, 1964—. One-man shows include Tyler Sch. Art, Phila, 1968, C.M. Russell Mus., Gt. Falls, 1972-73, 81, 92, Mickelson Gallery, Washington, 1970, 74, Pleiades Gallery, N.Y.C., 1977, 81, Vision of La Herradura, Almuñecar, Spain, 1988, USAF exhbn. Soc. Illustrators, N.Y.C., 1989, 91, West Chester (Pa.) U., 1992, Soc. Illustrators, N.Y.C., 1993; exhibited in group shows at C.M. Russell Mus., 1974, 76, 78, 80, 82-83, Am. Painters in Paris, 1976, Monac-Western Art Exhbt. Spokane, Wash., 1977-78, Easton (Md.) Waterfowl Festival, 1981-82, USAF Nat. Collection, 1989, 91-96; group shows in Artrium Gallery, N.Y.C., 1995, 96, numerous others; represented in permanent collections U. Del., Mont. State Collection, Mont. State U., Del. State Collection, Gt. Falls Pub. Schs., Michael Landon Prodns., Calif., Collection Knissel, Austria, Archives Victoria and Albert Mus., London; artists USAF Nat. Collection, Washington, 1989, 91, NASA Space Mus., 1992, Hauptman and Greenwood Collections, N.Y.C., 1994, Vera Haas, Dallas, Baker, Honolulu; fabric designer Galleon Fabrics, Inc., N.Y.C., Jones of N.Y., Saks Fifth Ave.; designed graphics Mont. State Arts Coun. With inf. U.S. Army, 1954-56. Ctr. for Advanced Study fellow, 1981-82; grantee U. Del., 1964-79, Nat. Endowment for Arts and Humanities, 1972-73, U. Del. Bicentennial, 1976. Mem. AAUP. Home: Chapel Hill 133 Aronimink Dr Newark DE 19711-3802 Office: U Delaware Dept Art Newark DE 19711 *In my paintings and other artforms I strive for perfection, uniqueness, and a special inner beauty, but more than that, I try to create art that has a universal quality. This universality makes an artform communicate beyond a specific locale, continent or a limited time reference. All great works of art have this special element regardless of when they were created.*

ROWE, CHARLES SPURGEON, newspaper publishing and broadcasting executive; b. Fredericksburg, Va., May 28, 1925; s. Josiah Pollard and Genevieve Sinclair (Bailey) R.; divorced; children: Ashley K. Rowe Gould, Charles Spurgeon, Timothy D. AB, Washington and Lee U., 1947, postgrad. Law Sch., 1947-49. Editor, co-pub. Free Lance-Star, Fredericksburg, 1949—, mng. editor, 1949-76; pres. Free Lance-Star Pub. Co. (newspaper and radio stas. WFLS AM-FM, WYSK-FM), Fredericksburg, 1949—; dir. AP, 1976-85, vice chmn., 1983-85, dir. Fredericksburg Savs. & Loan Assn.; trustee Washington and Lee U., 1984-94; former mem. bar news media rels. com. Va. State Bar, 1969-85, co-chmn., 1981-85. Chmn. bd. trustees Cen. Rappahannock Regional Libr., 1969-75; Pulitzer Prize juror, 1982-83, 92-93. Lt. (j.g.) USNR, 1943-46, now capt. Res. ret. Recipient George Mason award, 1974; named Outstanding Young Man of 1958 Fredericksburg Jaycees; named to Va. Communication Hall of Fame, 1989. Mem. A.P. Mng. Editors Assn. (pres. 1969, chmn. regents 1973-75), Am. Soc. Newspaper Editors (dir. 1971-77, 79-84), Newspaper Assn. Am. (dir. 1985-93, chmn. found. 1991-92), So. Newspaper Pubs. Assn. (dir. 1984-87), Va. Press Assn. (dir. 1977-83), World Press Freedom Com. (exec. com.), Soc. Profl. Journalists, Phi Beta Kappa, Omicron Delta Kappa, Phi Delta Phi, Delta Tau Delta. Episcopalian. Clubs: Nat. Press, Fredericksburg Country, Dominion, John's Island. Home: PO Box 754 Fredericksburg VA 22404-0754 Office: The Free Lance-Star 616 Amelia St Fredericksburg VA 22401-3887

ROWE, DAVID JOHN, physics educator; b. Totnes, Devonshire, Eng., Feb. 4, 1936; came to Can., 1968; s. Herbert Tyack and Marguerite Ella (Whitehead) R.; m. Una Mary Dawson, Oct. 4, 1959; children: Mark Jørgen Dawson, Jacqueline Amanda. BA, Cambridge (Eng.) U., 1959; MA, DPhil, Oxford (Eng.) U., 1959-62. Research assoc. U. Rochester, N.Y., 1966-68; assoc. prof. U. Toronto, Ont., Can., 1968-74, prof., 1974—. Author: Nuclear Collective Motion, 1970; editor: Dynamic Properties of Nuclear States, 1972; mem. editorial bd. (jour.) Phys. Rev., 1983-86, Jour. Phys. G., 1988-92, assoc. editor, 1992; contbr. articles to profl. jours. Dir. Mont Tremblant Internat. Summer Sch., 1971. Served to cpl. RAF, 1954-56. Ford Found. fellow, 1962-63, U.K. Atomic Energy Authority fellow, 1963-66, Sloan Found. fellow, 1972-74, Isaac Walton Killam rsch. fellow, 1990-92. Fellow Royal Soc. Can. (Rutherford Meml. medal and prize 1983); mem. Can. Assn. Physicists (chmn. theoretical physics div. 1970-71). Avocations: piano, woodworking, skiing. Office: U Toronto Physics Dept, Toronto, ON Canada M5S 1A7

ROWE, EDWARD LAWRENCE, JR., graphic designer; b. Bridgeport, Conn., Nov. 5, 1940; s. Edward L. Sr. and Elvera Rowe; m. Elayne Bassler, Oct. 24, 1964; children: Heather, Jonathan David. Assoc., U. Bridgeport, 1960, BS, 1963. Graphic designer Lester Beall, Brookfield, Conn., 1965-69; graphic design cons. Stead Young & Rowe, New Milford, Conn., 1969-87, Rowe & Ballantine, Brookfield, Conn., 1987—; design cons. Atlas Corp., Allied Signal, Borden, Caterpillar Tractor Co., Com. for Econ. Devel., Internat. Paper, Martin Marietta, N.Y. Clearing House, Otis Elevator. Design cons. Literacy Vols. N.Y., N.Y.C., 1990, Harlem R.B.I. (Returning Baseball to Inner Cities), N.Y.C., 1993. With U.S. Army, 1963-65. Recipient award Jour. Am. Inst. Graphic Arts, 1967, 68, Indsl. Design Mag., 1969, Packaging Design Mag., 1969, 74, Fin. World merit award, 1978, Design Excellence award, 1991, Mohawk Paper Merit award, 1993, cert. spl. merit 53d Ann. Graphic Arts Exhbn., 1995, cert. of merit award Printing Industries Am. Mem. Conn. Art Dirs. Club. Avocatins: scuba diving, photography, architecture, jazz music. Office: Rowe & Ballantine 8 Galloping Hl Brookfield CT 06804-3611

ROWE, ELIZABETH WEBB, paralegal administrator; b. Canton, Ohio, Dec. 2, 1957; d. Thomas Dudley Webb and Verity Elizabeth (Voight) O'Brien; m. David Lee Rowe, June 21, 1986; children: Schuyler Jourdan, Thomas Prentiss. AB in History, Mt. Holyoke Coll., 1979. Legal asst. Willkie Farr & Gallagher, N.Y.C., 1979-82, legal asst. supr., 1983-88, adminstrv. asst., 1988-89; outreach dir. St. Bartholomew's Ch., 1989-93, dir. comm., 1991-93; paralegal mgr. Patterson, Belknap, Webb & Tyler LLP, N.Y.C., 1993—; legal asst. Cmty. Law Offices, N.Y.C., 1980-82; clerical asst. 17th Precinct Police Detective, N.Y.C., 1981-82. Chair homeless shelter St. Bartholomew's Ch., N.Y.C., 1984-85; vol. Breakfast Feeding Program, 1983-92, mem. Community Ministry Coun., 1986-88, 93-96; mem. N.Y. Jr. League, 1979-94; Pres.'s Coun. Mt. Holyoke Coll., 1988-91; rep. Mt. Holyoke Coll. Alumnae Fund, 1986-89, 94—, class officer, 1989-94; bd. dirs. 509 E 83d St Corp., E 67th St. Owners, Inc., Emma J. Adams Meml. Fund. Recipient Mary Lyon award Mt. Holyoke Coll., 1994. Home: 133 E 80th St Apt 2C New York NY 10021-0332 Office: Patterson Belknap Webb & Tyler LLP 1133 Avenue Of The Americas New York NY 10036-6710

ROWE, ERNEST RAS, education educator, academic administrator; b. Hot Springs, Ark., July 19, 1933; s. Stephen Paul and Emma Leathia (Martin) R.; m. Carla True Dirk, May 27, 1995. BS with distinction, Ariz. State U., 1955, MEd, 1962, EdD, 1965; postgrad., Gonzaga U., 1975, Dublin City U., Ireland, summer 1989. Tchr. Madison Sch. Dist., Phoenix, 1960-61, Garden Grove (Calif.) Unified Sch. Dist., 1964-66; cons. spl. edn. Ariz. Dept. Pub. Instrn., Phoenix, 1966-67; asst. prof. Idaho State U., Pocatello, 1967-70, assoc. prof., 1970-74, prof. edn., 1974-95, interim chmn. dept. edn., summer 1992; adminstrv. intern Cen. Adminstrn., 1982-83, 94-95; vis. prof. edn. Calif. State U., Long Beach, 1965; adv. mem. Idaho Task Force on Higher Edn., 1982-83; gov. apptd. Idaho commr. to Edn. Commn. of the States, 1979-93, rep. to steering com., 1989-93; elected chmn. Idaho State U. Faculty Senate, 1969, 70, 71-72, 86-87. Contbr. articles to profl. jours. Bd. dirs. Bannock Meml. Hosp., 1975-78; mem. Idaho Bd. Medicine pre-litigation panel for malpractice hearings, 1980-95. 1st lt. U.S. Army, 1955-57. Mem. AAUP, Nat. Soc. Study Edn., Am. Inst. Parliamentarians (univ. parliamentarian, gov. N.W. region 1992-94), Rotary (pres. 1981-82), Mason, Phi Delta Kappa, Phi Kappa Phi (pres. 1972-73, 87-88). Episcopalian. Avocations: music, reading, photography, physical fitness. Home: 678 N Poplar Ct Chandler AZ 85226 *Initiative and responsibility are cornerstones of a meaningful personal and professional life. Sadly they are missing in much of contemporary society. Apathy and self-indulgence appear most prominently at the turn of the century.*

ROWE, GEORGE GILES, cardiologist, educator; b. Vulcan, Alta., Can., May 17, 1921; came to U.S., 1923, naturalized, 1929; s. James Giles and Cora (Blotz) R.; m. Patsy Barnett, Sept. 12, 1947; children—George Lee, James Andrew, Jane Ellen. B.A., U. Wis., Madison, 1943, M.D., 1945. Diplomate: Am. Bd. Internal Medicine. Intern Phila. Gen. Hosp., 1945-46; resident U. Wis., 1950-52; instr. in anatomy Washington U., St. Louis, 1948-50; Am. Heart Assn. rsch. fellow cardiovascular rsch. lab. U. Wis., 1952-54, rsch. assoc. in medicine, 1954-55, asst. prof. medicine, 1957-59, assoc. prof., 1959-64, prof., 1964-89, prof. emeritus, 1989—, lab. dir., 1969-76, Markle scholar in med. sci. dept. medicine, 1955-60; vol. research asso. Hamersmith Hosp., London, 1956-57. Contbr. numerous articles on congenital and acquired heart disease to profl. publs.; co-editor: Cardiovascular Nursing, 1968-71. Served with M.C. U.S. Army, 1946-48. Mem. Wis. Heart Assn. (pres. 1969-70), Am. Heart Assn., Assn. Univ. Cardiologists (pres. 1974-75), Central Clin. Research Club (pres. 1968-69), Am. Physiol. Soc., Am. soc. Pharmacology, and Exptl. Therapeutics. Home: 5 Walworth Ct Madison WI 53705-4805 Office: 600 Highland Ave Madison WI 53792-0001

ROWE, HARRISON EDWARD, electrical engineer; b. Chgo., Jan. 29, 1927; s. Edward and Joan (Golden) R.; m. Alicia Jane Steeves, Feb. 10, 1951; children—Amy Rogers, Elizabeth Joanne, Edward Steeves, Alison Pickard. B.S. in Elec. Engring, Mass. Inst. Tech., 1948, M.S., 1950, Sc.D., 1952; M of Engring. (hon.), Stevens Inst. Tech., 1988. Mem. tech. staff Radio Research Lab., Bell Labs., Holmdel, N.J., 1952-84; Anson Wood Burchard prof. elec. engring. Stevens Inst. Tech., Hoboken, N.J., 1984-93, prof. emeritus, 1993—; vis. lectr. U. Calif., Berkeley, 1963, Imperial Coll., U. London, 1968; mem. Def. Sci. Bd. Task Force, 1972-74. Author: Signals and Noise in Communication Systems, 1965; asso. editor: IEEE Trans. on Communication, 1974-76; contbr. articles to profl. jours. Served with USN, 1945-46. Co-recipient Microwave prize, 1972, David Sarnoff award, 1977. Fellow IEEE; mem. Internat. Union Radio Sci., Monmouth Symphony Soc., Navesink Country Club, Sigma Xi, Tau Beta Pi, Eta Kappa Nu. Unitarian. Clubs: Shrewsbury Sailing and Yacht, Appalachian Mountain. Patentee in field. Home: 9 Buttonwood Ln Rumson NJ 07760-1045

ROWE, HERBERT JOSEPH, retired trade association executive; b. Granite City, Ill., Mar. 25, 1924; s. Herbert Bernard and Maude (Klein) R.; m. Ann Muter, Dec. 2, 1950; children: Douglas H., Stephen F., James D., Edith L., Allen. Student, U. Tex., 1942-43, Purdue U., 1943-44; BS in Mgmt.; BS in Mktg., U. Ill., 1948; LittD (hon.), London Inst. for Applied Research, 1975. With Edward Valves, Inc. (subs. Rockwell Mfg. Co.), 1948-50; with Muter Co., Chgo., 1952-71, v.p., 1957-64, pres., 1964-71, treas., 1964-67, chmn. bd., 1965-71, also dir., 1957-71; pres., treas., dir. Wescoil Co., 1964-66, Tri-Axial Corp., 1966-67; v.p., treas. Gen. Magnetic Corp., 1965-67, chmn. bd., 1967-70, dir., 1964-70; chmn. bd., dir; Pemcor, Inc., Westchester, Ill., 1971-75; assoc. adminstr. external affairs NASA, 1975-78; sr. v.p. Electronic Industries Assn., 1978-89; chmn. Famro Corp., 1989-90; pres. Internat. Electronics Fedn., 1989-90; sec.-treas. Englewood Elec. Supply Wis., Inc., 1972-75, Rahr's Inc., 1972-75; pres. Enclave of Naples, Inc., 1992-94, treas., 1994-96; pres. Rowe Corp., 1994—; treas. Quality wholesale Foods of S.W. Fla., 1994-96. Pres. Pokagon Trails coun. Boy Scouts Am., 1964-66, pres. Calumet coun., 1966-68, region 7 exec. com., 1966-72, vice chmn., 1971-72, bd. dirs. East Ctrl. region, 1972-75, mem. nat. program com., 1970-78, 90-94, nat. Cub Scout com., 1970-80, chmn., 1990-94, S.E. regional exec. com., 1975-78, So. regional exec. bd., 1993—, bd. dirs. Nat. Capital Area coun., 1978-90, adv. bd., 1990-94, mem. exec. bd. S.W. Fla. coun., 1992—, mem. nat. exec. com. and exec. bd., 1990-95, nat. adv. bd., 1995—; membership chmn. Nat. Eagle Scouts Assn., 1976-80; corp. campaign chmn. Chgo. Met. Crusade Mercy, 1964-68; chmn. Bd. Edn. Caucus, Flossmoor, Ill., 1962; mem. bd. Flossmoor United Party, 1963-68; mem. U. Ill. Found., 1967—; mem. adv. com. U. Ill. Coll. Commerce and Bus. Adminstrn., 1968-78; bd. dirs. Electronic Industries Found., 1974-94; mem. adv. bd. Air and Space Mus., Smithsonian Inst., 1975-78; active Moorings Presbyn. Ch., Naples, Fla. With USMCR, 1942-46, 50-52. Recipient Silver Beaver award Boy Scouts Am., 1966, Silver Antelope award, 1969, Silver Buffalo award, 1994; NASA team award Bicentennial Expo on Sci. and Tech., Exceptional Svc. medal, 1978, Baden-Powell fellow World Scout Found., 1992. Mem. AIAA, AAAS, Electronic Industries Assn. (hon., bd. dirs. 1967-69, bd. govs. 1969-75, exec. com. parts divsn. 1966-75, vice chmn. parts divsn. 1970-74, chmn. 74-75, bd. dirs. consumer electronics divsn. 1972-75, chmn. world trade com. 1968-70, vice chmn. 1970-73, chmn. membership and scope com. 1972-74, Disting. Svc. award 1989), Am. Loudspeaker Mfrs. Assn. (v.p., dir. 1967-68, pres., bd. dirs. 1968-70), Assn. Electronic Mfrs. (bd. dirs. 1970-73), Nat. Space Club, Nat. Space Inst., Am. Acad. Polit. Social Sci., Am. Soc. Assn. Execs. (vice chmn. internat. sect. 1986-87, chmn. 1987-88), U.S. Naval Inst., Field Mus. Natural History, European Soc. of Assn. Execs., Greater Washington Soc. Assn. Execs., Chgo. Art Inst., Beta Gamma Sigma, Alpha Phi Omega, Sigma Chi (dir. Kappa Kappa corp. 1954-75, sec. 1971-73, pres. 1973-75, Charles J. Kiler award 1975, Grand Consul's citation 1976), Am. Legion, Chaine des Rôtisseurs, L'Ordre Mondial, English Speaking Union (pres. Naples chpt. 1996—), Naples Conservancy. Home: Apt 12 4601 Gulf Shore Blvd N Naples FL 34103-2214

ROWE, JACK FIELD, retired electric utility executive; b. Minn., May 10, 1927; s. William F. and Anna (Stenborg) R.; m. Mary E. Moen, Mar. 26, 1955; 1 dau., Lizette Ann. B.E.E., U. Minn., 1950. Registered profl. engr., Minn., Wis. With Minn. Power and Light Co., Duluth, 1950-89; asst. to pres. Minn. Power and Light Co., 1966-67, v.p., 1967-68, exec. v.p., 1969-74, pres., 1974-84, chief exec. officer, 1978-89, chmn., 1969-93, bd. dirs.; chmn. bd., CEO FiberCore, Inc., Minn. Paper, Inc., So. States Utilities, Universal Telephone, Inc., Topeka Group, Inc., NorLight, Inc.; mem. exec. bd. Nat. Electric Reliability Coun., 1970-73; vice chmn. Mid-Continent Area Reliability Coun., 1970-71, chmn., 1972-73; mem. bus. and econs. adv. bd. U. Minn., Duluth, 1980; bd. dirs. Na Tec, Inc., Houston. Past bd. dirs., v.p. Duluth Jr. C. of C.; mem. exec. bd. Lake Superior coun. Boy Scouts Am., 1967-75, chmn. Explorers, 1968-72; comml. chmn. Duluth United Fund, 1960-61; vice chmn. Duluth United Way, 1975, chmn., 1976, U.S. Savs. Bond chmn., St. Louis County, Minn., 1974-77; chmn. St. Louis County Heritage and Arts Ctr., 1979-81; pres. NE Minn. Devel./Assn., 1981-83; mem. Minn. Bus. Partnership, 1979-88; bd. dirs. Minn. Safety Coun., 1979-85, pres., 1983-84, chmn., 1984-85; bd. dirs. Duluth Downtown Devel. Corp., 1979-81, Duluth Growth Co., 1984-85, Greysolon Mall Corp., 1980-86, Duluth Superior Area Cmty. Found., 1984-86, Duluth Clin. Edn. and Rsch. Found., 1985-86, Benedictine Health Sys., 1985-88; mem. adv. bd. exec. program U. Minn., 1979; adv. coun. Inst. Tech., 1979; mem. Minn. High Tech. Coun., 1982-87. With USNR, 1945-46. Recipient Distinguished Service award Duluth Jr. C. of C., 1960, Outstanding Leadership award in energy conversion scis. N.Y.C. sect. ASME, 1980, Outstanding Achievement award U. Minn. Alumni Assn., 1986, Bronze Chief Exec. Officer of Decade award Fin. World Mag., 1989; named Chief Exec. Officer of Yr., Fin. World mag., 1986, 89; Jack F. Rowe Chair of Engring. named in his honor U. Minn., Duluth, 1986. Mem. NAM (dir. 1975-78), IEEE, Electric Info. Coun. (pres. 1978-82), North Cen. Electric Assn., Duluth C. of C. (pres. 1972-73, exec. com., bd. dirs.), Mpls. Club, Engrs. Club (Duluth), Northland Country Club (Duluth), Quail Creek County Club (Naples), Naples Yacht Club, Kitchi Gammi (Duluth) (dir. 1979-87, pres. 1985-87), Rotary Club (Duluth) (pres. 1974-75), Masons, Shriners, Jesters, Kappa Eta Kappa. Lutheran. Home: 4735 Villa Mare Ln Naples FL 34103-3473

ROWE, JOHN HOWLAND, anthropologist, educator; b. Sorrento, Maine, June 10, 1918; s. Louis Earle and Margaret Talbot (Jackson) R.; m. Barbara Bent Burnett, June 6, 1942; children: Ann Pollard, Lucy Burnett; m. Patricia Jean Lyon, Apr. 24, 1970. A.B., Brown U., 1939, L.H.D. (hon.), 1969; M.A. in Anthropology, Harvard U., 1941, Ph.D. in Latin Am. History and Anthropology, 1947; Litt.D. (hon.), U. Nacional del Cuzco, Peru, 1954; student, U. Paris, France, 1945-46. Field supr. So. Peru, Inst. Andean Research, 1941-42; prof. archaeology dir. Sect. Archaeology U. Nacional del Cuzco, 1942-43; rep. in Colombia, Inst. Social Anthropology, Smithsonian Instn., also tchr. U. del Cauca, Popayán, 1946-48; mem. faculty U. Calif., Berkeley, 1948—, prof. anthropology, 1956-88, prof. emeritus, 1988—, chmn. dept., 1963-67; curator S. Am. archaeology Mus. Anthropology, 1949—; cons. UNESCO, Cuzco, Peru, 1975; sr. fellow Dumbarton Oaks, 1984-90; field rsch. in Maine, 1938, 40, Mass., 1939-41, Fla., 1940, Guambia and Popayan, Colombia, 1946-48, Peru, 1939, 41-43, 46, 54, 58, 59, 61-78, 80-90, 92-96; hon. prof. U. del Cauca, 1947, U. Catolica, Lima, 1996; rsch. prof. Mil. Inst. Basic Rsch. Sci., U. Calif., Berkeley, 1964-65. Author: An Introduction to the Archaeology of Cuzco, 1944, Max Uhle, 1954, Chavin Art, 1962, (with Menzel and Dawson) The Paracas Pottery of Ica, 1964; Editor: (with Patricia Lyon) Nawpa Pacha, 1963—. Served with AUS, 1944-46, ETO. Recipient Diploma de Honor Soc. Cientifica del Cuzco, 1954, Prémio de Honor Concejo Provincial de Ica, Peru, 1958; ofcl. Orden El Sol del Peru, 1968; Diploma de Honor Concejo Provincial del Cuzco, Peru, 1974; Gran Cruz Orden Al Merito por Servicios Distinguidos, Peru, 1981, Medalla de la Ciudad, Municipalidad del Qosqo, Peru, 1993; Guggenheim fellow, 1958. Mem. Archaeol. Inst. Am., Soc. Am. Archaeology, Soc. des Americanistes de Paris, Soc. Antiquaries London, German Archaeol. Inst., Am. Anthropl. Assn., Acad. Nacional de la Historia (Peru), Soc. History Tech., Inst. Andean Studies (pres. 1960—). Home: 1029 Cragmont Ave Berkeley CA 94708-1411

ROWE, JOHN WALLIS, medical school president, hospital administrator; b. Jersey City, June 20, 1944; s. Albert Wallis and Elizabeth (Lynch) R.; m. Valerie Ann DelTufo, Aug. 10, 1968; children: Meredith, Abigail, Rebecca. BS with honors, Canisius Coll., 1966; MD with distinction, U. Rochester, 1970. Diplomate Am. Bd. Internal Medicine, Am. Bd. Nephrology. Resident in internal medicine Harvard Med. Sch., Beth Israel Hosp., Boston, 1970-72; clin. assoc. Nat. Inst. Child Health and Human Devel., Balt., 1972-74; rsch. clin. fellow Harvard Med. Sch., Mass. Gen. Hosp., Boston, 1974-75; from instr. to prof. Harvard Med. Sch., Boston, 1976-88; pres. Mt. Sinai Sch. Medicine and Mt. Sinai Hosp., N.Y.C., 1988—, prof. geriatrics and medicine, 1988—; trustee N.Y. Acad. Medicine, 1989—, Buck Ctr. for Rsch. in Aging, Marin, Calif., 1989—. Editor: Health and Disease in Old Age, 1982, Geriatric Medicine, 1988, Handbook of the Biology of Aging, 1990, Geriatric Neurology, 1991; contbr. articles to jours. in field. Lt. comdr. USPHS, 1972-74. MacArthur Found. grantee, 1985—. Mem. NAS Inst. Med., Gerontol. Soc. Am. (pres. 1988), Am. Fedn. for Aging Rsch. (pres. 1988), N.Y. Yacht Club, Century Assn. Roman Catholic. Avocation: sailing. Home: 300 Central Park W New York NY 10024-1513 Office: Mt Sinai Med Ctr Fifth Ave & 100th St New York NY 10029

ROWE, JOHN WESTEL, retired organic chemist; b. Forest Hills, N.Y., Sept. 3, 1924; s. John Edward and laura Robinson (Willoughby) R.; m. Mary Dorothy Lowens, June 26, 1949; children: Peter Willoughby, William Westel, Michael Delano. B.S., MIT, 1948; M.S., U. Colo., 1952; Sc.D., Swiss Fedn. Inst. Tech., Zurich, 1956. With Forest Products Lab., Forest Service, USDA, 1957-89; project leader Forest Products Lab., Forest Service, USDA, Madison, Wis., 1966-84; also supervisory research chemist Forest Products Lab., Forest Service, USDA; lectr. U. Wis. Editor: Natural Products of Wood Planets, 1989; contbr. articles on wood and natural products chemistry to profl. jours. Active Boy Scouts Am., 1962-74. Served with USN, 1942-44. Recipient Wood Salutes award Wood & Wood Products, 1975. Fellow Internat. Acad. Wood Sci., AAAS, Am. Inst. Chemists; mem. Soc. Econ. Botany, Phytochem. Assn. N.Am., Am. Chem. Soc. (chmn. Wis. sect. 1968, 69, alt. counselor 1976-78), Am. Soc. Pharmacology, Forest Products Research Soc., Internat. Assn. for Biomass Utilization, TAPPI,. Republican. Unitarian. Home: 1001 Tumalo Trl Madison WI 53711-3024

ROWE, JOHN WILLIAM, utility executive; b. Dodgeville, Wis., May 18, 1945; s. William J. and Lola (Rule) R.; m. Jeanne M.; 1 son, William John. BS, U. Wis., 1967, JD, 1970. Bar: Wis. 1970, Ill. 1970, U.S. Supreme Ct. 1979, Pa. 1982. Assoc. Isham, Lincoln & Beale, Chgo., 1970-77, ptnr., 1978-80; counsel to trustee Chgo. Milw. St. Paul & Pacific R.R., Chgo., 1979-80; v.p. law Consol. Rail Corp., Phila., 1980-82, sr. v.p. law, 1982-84; pres., chief exec. officer Cen. Maine Power Co., Augusta, 1984-89; pres., chief exec. officer New Eng. Elec. System, Westboro, Mass., 1989—, also bd. dirs.; bd. dirs. UNUM Corp., Bank of Boston Corp. Trustee Pa. Ballet, 1982-84, Bryant Coll.; chmn. Ft. Western Endowment Fund, 1987-88; co-chmn. Maine Aspirations Compact, 1988; bd. dirs. USS Constitution Mus., Jobs for Mass., Edison Electric Inst., Worcester C. of C., Dana Farber Cancer Inst.; pres. Worcester Mcpl. Rsch. Bur.; trustee Mechanics Hall, Pioneer Inst. Mem. Mass. Bus. Roundtable (chmn.), R.I. Commodores, Order of Coif, Chgo. Club, Worcester Club, Framingham Country Club, Phi Beta Kappa. Home and Office: New England Electric System 25 Research Dr Westborough MA 01582-0001

ROWE, JOSEPH EVERETT, electrical engineering educator, administrator; b. Highland Park, Mich., June 4, 1927; s. Joseph and Lillian May (Osbourne) R.; m. Margaret Anne Prine, Sept. 1, 1950; children: Jonathan Dale, Carol Kay. BSEE, U. Mich., 1951, BS Engring. in Math., 1951, MSEE, 1952, PhD, 1955. Mem. faculty U. Mich., Ann Arbor, 1953-74; prof. elec. engring. U. Mich., 1960-74, dir. electron physics lab., 1958-68, chmn. dept. elec. and computer engring., 1968-74; vice provost, dean engring. Case Western Res. U., Cleve., 1974-76; provost Case Inst. Tech., 1976-78; v.p. tech. Harris Corp., Melbourne, Fla., 1978-81; v.p., gen. mgr. Controls divsn. Harris Corp., 1981-82; exec. v.p. rsch. and def. Gould Inc., 1982, vice chmn., chief tech. officer, 1983-87; sr. v.p., chief technologist Inst. Rsch., Ill. Inst. Tech., Chgo., 1987; v.p. and chief scientist PPG Industries, Inc., Pitts., 1987-92; v.p., dir. Rsch. Inst., U. Dayton, Ohio, 1992-97; cons. to industry; mem. adv. group electron devices Dept. Def., 1966-78, 93—; bd. govs. Rsch. inst. of Ill. Inst. Tech.; chmn. Coalition for Advancement of Indsl. Tech., U. Ill.; mem. indsl. adv. bd. U. Ill. at Chgo.; mem. Army Sci. Bd., 1985-91, 93—. Author: Nonlinear Electron-Wave Interaction Phenomena, 1965, also articles. Fellow AAAS, IEEE (chmn. adminstrv. com. group electron devices 1968-69, editor procs. 1971-73, Harrell V. Nobel award 1994); mem. NAE, Am. Phys. Soc., Am. Soc. Engring. Edn. (Curtis McGraw Rsch. award 1964), Am. Mgmt. Assn. (R&D), Sigma Xi, Phi Kappa Phi, Tau Beta Pi, Eta Kappa Nu. Office: U Dayton 300 College Park Ave Dayton OH 45469-0001

ROWE, KEVIN S., banker; b. Seldom come bye, Nfld., Can., Feb. 14, 1938; m. Valma Jean Rowe, Aug. 28, 1958; children: Todd, Michelle, Natalie, Scott. Student, Curtis Acad., St. Johns, Nfld. With The Bank of N.S., various locations, Can., U.S. and abroad, 1955-70; agt. N.Y.C., 1970-73; area mgr. V.I. and P.R., 1973-77; v.p., gen. mgr. Pacific Regional Office Manila, 1977-83; exec. v.p., gen. mgr. internat. Bank of N.S., Toronto, Ont., Can., 1983-86, exec. v.p. Pacific Region, 1987—; bd. dirs. BNS Internat. (Hong Kong) Ltd., The Bank of Nova Scotia Asia Ltd., The Bank of Nova Scotia Berhad, Solidbank Corp., Poonpipat Fin. & Securities Co. Ltd. Office: Bank of NS, United Ctr 95 Queensway 25th Fl, Hong Kong Hong Kong

ROWE, LISA DAWN, computer programmer/analyst, computer consultant; b. Kenton, Ohio, Feb. 2, 1966; d. Daniel Lee and Frances Elaine (Johnson) Edelblute; m. Jeffrey Mark Rowe, Feb. 13, 1982; children: Anthony David, Samantha Paige Elizabeth. Student, Inst. of Lit., 1988-90, Acad. Ct. Reporting, 1988, Marion Tech. Coll., 1991-92; postgrad., Ohio State U., 1993—. Writer, model Newslife, Marion, Ohio, 1982-83; bookkeeper Nat. Ch. Residences, Columbus, Ohio, 1985, Insty-Prints, Columbus, 1985; asst. editor Columbus Entertainment, 1984-85; book reviewer, writer Columbus Dispatch, 1989-91; writer Consumer News, Delaware, Ohio, 1989-90; computer programmer, supr. Dyserv, Inc., Columbus, 1986-92; bookkeeper, acct., office mgr. Marion Music Ctr., Inc., 1990; computer programmer EBCO Mfg., Columbus, 1992-93; sr. programmer/analyst Borden, Inc., Columbus, 1993-94; computer cons. System X, Columbus, 1994-95, LDA Systems, Dublin, Ohio, 1995-96; v.p. Jones, Mitchell, Rowe & Assoc., Worthington, Ohio, 1996—. Editor newsletter Assn. System Users, 1989-90; contbr. articles and revs. to profl. jours. Mem. NAFE, MADD, DAV (chaplain 1990). Republican. Mormon. Avocations: horseback riding, swimming, camping, fishing, reading. Home: 1150 Toulon Ave Marion OH 43302-6610 Office: Jones Mitchell Rowe & Assoc 599 Scherers Ct Worthington OH 43085-5710

ROWE, MARJORIE DOUGLAS, retired social services administrator; b. Bklyn., July 29, 1912; d. Herbert Lynn and Mary Manson (Hall) Douglas; m. Richard Daniel Rowe, July 29, 1937 (dec.); 1 child, Richard Douglas. AB cum laude, Whitman Coll., 1933; MS in Social Adminstrn., Case Western Res. U., 1936. Caseworker Children's Svcs., Cleve., 1933-36, supr., 1937-39; dir. Adoption Svc. Bur., Cleve., 1940-41; social work supr., psychiat. social work cons. Ea. State Hosp., Medical Lake, Wash., 1962-67; dir. social svcs. Interlake Sch.for Developmentally Disabled, Medical Lake, 1967-74, supt., 1975-82; retired, 1982. Pres. chpt. R.P.E.O., Spokane, Wash., 1949, Spokane Alumnae chpt. Delta Delta Delta, 1955-57; chpt. mem. ARC, Orofino, Idaho, 1941-45, Orofino chpt. chmn., 1945-46; sec. Idaho state chpt. AAUW, 1945-46. Mem. Am. Assn. for Mental Deficiency (region I chmn. 1976-77, social work chmn. 1971-73), NASW (gold card mem.), P.E.O. (pres. Spokane Reciprocity 1950), Acad. Cert. Social Workers, Spokane Women of Rotary (pres. 1960-61), Phi Beta Kappa, Delta Sigma Rho, Mortar Bd. Episcopalian. Avocations: local museum volunteer, traveling, antiques, lake cabin activities. Home: 946 E Thurston Ave Spokane WA 99203-2948

ROWE, MARY P., academic administrator, management educator; b. Chgo., Feb. 18, 1936; married; children: Katherine, Susannah, Timothy. BA in History, Swarthmore Coll., 1957; PhD in Econs., Columbia U., 1971; LLD (hon.), Regis Coll., 1975. With World Council of Chs./Office of UN High Commr. for Refugees, Salzburg and Vienna, Austria, 1957-58; research asst. Nat. Bur. Econ. Research, N.Y.C., 1961; economist planning bd. Office of Gov., V.I., 1962-63; free-lance cons. Nigeria, 1963-66, Boston, 1967-69; cons., sr. economist with Ctr. for Ednl. Policy Research, Harvard U. Harvard U., Cambridge, Mass., 1970, cons., sr. economist with Abt Assocs., 1970; tech. dir. early edn. project Harvard U., 1971-72, cons. economist with Abt Assocs., 1971; dir. Carnegie Corp. Grant Radcliffe Inst., Cambridge, 1972; spl. asst. to pres., ombudsperson MIT, Cambridge, 1973—, adj. prof. Sloan Sch. Mgmt., 1985—; mem. steering com., program on negotiations Harvard U., 1995—. Mem. editorial bd. Negotiation Jour., 1985—, Alternative Dispute Resolution Report, 1987—; contbr. articles to profl. jours. Trustee Cambridge Friends Sch., 1969-75; mem. bd. advisors Brookline Children's Ctr., 1971-76; mem. Cambridge Friends Meeting and Com. on Clearness, 1971-78, New Eng. Concerns Com., 1973—, Mass. Policy Adv. Com. on Child Abuse/Neglect, 1977-79, Mass. State Youth Council, 1978-83; mem. Mass. State Employment and Tng. Council, 1975-83, chair, 1980-83; mem. nat. adv. Com. Black Women's Ednl. Policy and Research Network Project/Wellesley Coll. Ctr. for Research on Women, 1980-83; bd. dirs. Bay State Skills Commn., 1980-81, Wellesley Women's Research Ctr., 1984-87; sec. bd. dirs. Bay State Skills Corp., 1981-90; mem. panel on employment disputes Ctr. for Pub. Resources, 1986—. Recipient Meritorious Civilian Svc. award Dept. of Navy, 1993. Mem. Am. Econs. Assn., Soc. Profls. in Dispute Resolution (chair com. on ombudspersons 1982—, com. law and pub. policy in employment disputes), Calif. Caucus Coll. and Univ. Ombudsmen, Univ. and Coll. Ombudsman Aassn., Corp. Ombudsman Assn. (pres. 1985-87, program on negotiation steering com. 1995—), Disting. Neutral Ctr. for Pub. Resources 1990—). Office: MIT 10-213 77 Massachusetts Ave Cambridge MA 02139

ROWE, MAX L., lawyer, corporate executive, management consultant, judge; b. Dallas City, Ill., Aug. 14, 1921; s. Samuel Guy and Nellie (Moyes) R.; m. Maxine Marilyn Gladson, May 23, 1944; children: Melody Ann (Mrs. Gunn), Susan Elaine, Joyce Lynn, Andrew Blair. Student, Knox Coll., Galesburg, Ill., 1939-40; A.B., U. Ill., 1943, J.D., 1946; M.B.A., U. Chgo., 1952. Bar: Ill. 1947, Ind. 1954, also U.S. Supreme Ct. 1964. Pvt. practice in Aurora and Urbana, 1947; asst. to sec., asst. treas. Elgin Nat. Watch Co., 1948-50; gen. atty., asst. to pres.-treas. Rival Packing Co., 1950- 51; gen. counsel, asst. sec.-treas. Victor Mfg. & Gasket Co., Chgo., 1951-54; sec. Mead Johnson & Co., Evansville, Ind., 1954-55; assoc. counsel Caterpillar Tractor Co., 1955-62; assoc. gen. counsel, sec., asst. treas. Thomas J. Lipton, Inc. and subs., 1962-68; v.p., treas. Seeburg Corp., Chgo., 1968-69; v.p. fin., law and adminstrn. Nightingale Conant Corp., Chgo., 1970-71; pvt. legal practice, also mgmt. cons., 1968—; v.p. law, sec. Ward Foods, Inc., Wilmette, Ill., 1972-76; mem. firm Kirkland & Ellis, Chgo., 1978-87; atty. Ill. Dept. Profl. Regulation, Chgo. and Springfield, 1987-92; adminstrv. law judge State of Ill., 1993—; dir. Ward-Johnston, Inc., Ward Internat., Inc., Superior Potato Chips, Inc., Quinlan Pretzel Co., Honiron-Philippines, Inc.; instr. extension div. U. Ill., 1960-61, eve. div. Fairleigh Dickinson U., 1966-68; leader Am. Mgmt. Assn., other corp. seminars, 1966-87. actor various TV, radio and print commercials, 1992—. Treas. Peoria County (Ill.) Republican Central Com., 1958-62, Rep. precinct committeeman, Peoria County, 1958-62, Bergen County, N.J., 1966-68, del., Rep. Nat. Conv., 1980; elder Presbyterian Ch., 1975—; mem. nat. adv. council SBA, 1976-78; chmn., mem. adv. bd. Ill. Dept. Personnel, 1979-82; mem. Ill. Compensation Rev. Bd., 1984-87; mem. Pres. Reagan's Nat. Commn. for Employment Policy, 1984-88; mem. U. Ill. Found. and Pres.'s Council, 1979—, bd. visitors Coll. of Law, 1993—; dir., mem. exec. com., chmn. Outreach and Devel., World Heritage Mus., 1992—; mem. bd. dirs. Oak Ridge Cemetary, 1994—. Served to 2d lt. AUS, 1943-45. Named Alumni of Month, U. Ill. Coll. Law, 1982; inductee Sr. Illinoisans Hall of Fame, 1995. Mem. Am. Mgmt. Assn., Conf. Bd., Am., Ill, Chgo., Sangamon County bar assns., Am. Soc. Corp. Secs., Phi Gamma Delta. Republican. Clubs: Union League (Chgo.), Execs. (Chgo.). Office: 49 Inverness Rd Springfield IL 62704-3110

ROWE, MELINDA GRACE, public health service officer; b. Decatur, Ala., Aug. 18, 1953; m. Dana Calvin Craig Jr., Jan. 1, 1994. MD, U. Ala., 1978, MPH, 1985, MBA, 1987. Bd. cert. Am. Bd. Pediatrics, Am. Bd. Preventive Medicine. Pediatrics intern U. Ky., Lexington, 1978-79; pediatrics resident Lloyd Nolan Hosp., Fairfield, Ala., 1979-81; physician Columbus (Miss.) Children's Clinic, 1981, pvt. practice, Winfield, Ala., 1982-84; preventive medicine resident U. Ala., Birmingham, 1984-85; asst. state health officer Pub. Health Area III, Pelham, Ala., 1985-95; dir. health Jefferson County Health Dept., Louisville, 1995—; asst. prof. U. Ala., Birmingham, 1988—, U. Louisville, 1995—. Bd. dirs. Cahaba River Soc., Birmingham, 1988-95, UAB Nat. Alumni Soc., 1988-93. Mem. Ky. Med. Assn., Ky. Pub. Health Assn. (bd. dirs.), Ky. Pediatric Soc., Jefferson County Med. Soc., Louisville/Jefferson County Primary Care Assn. (bd. dirs.), Health Ky. (bd. dirs.), Ky. Health Depts. Assn. (v.p.). Methodist. Avocations: walking, travel, music. Office: Jefferson County Health 400 E Gray St PO Box 1704 Louisville KY 40201-1704

ROWE, MICHAEL DUANE, artist; b. Lykens, Pa., Nov. 5, 1947; m. Kathryn Jean Branoff. Student, Art Inst. Pitts., 1971-72. Exhibited in shows at Art Assn. Harrisburg, Pa., 1985, 86, 87, State Mus. Pa., 1986, 87, Doshi Gallery, Harrisburg, 1987, Cheltenham (Pa.) Art Ctr., 1989, 92, Delaplaine Art Ctr., 1989 (1st prize 1989), 90, 91, Immaculata (Pa.) Coll., 1990, U. of the Arts, Phil., 1990, Butler Inst. of Am. Art, Youngstown, Ohio, 1990, 92, Phila. Art Alliance, 1990, Altenative Mus., N.Y.C., 1990, 91, 95, Spaces, Cleve., 1991, Alexandria (La.) Art Mus., 1991, Pa. State U., 1992, Allentown (Pa.) Mus. Art, 1992, Muhlenberg Coll., Allentown, 1992 (award 1992), Michael Stone Gallery, Washington, 1992, Ea. N.Mex. U., 1992, Del. Ctr. for Contemporary Arts, Wilmington, 1993, Laguna Gloria Art Mus., Austin, Tex., 1993, Silvermine Art Guild Exhibit, New Cannan, Conn., 1993, Pa. State U., Univ. Park, 1993, East Tenn. U., Johnson city, 1994, Chrysler Mus., Norfolk, Va., 1994, Davidson (N.C.) Coll. Visual Arts Ctr., 1995; represented in collection So. Alleghenies Mus., Loreto, Pa. Grantee Art Matters, Inc., 1988; Pa. Coun. of the Arts fellow, 1993. Episcopalian. Avocations: running, travelling, reading.

ROWE, PETER A., newspaper columnist; b. Walnut Creek, Calif., Sept. 7, 1955; s. Raymond Alan and Marion (Green) R.; m. Lynn Hanson, Aug. 13, 1977; children: Kyle, Reid, Alec. BA in History, U. Calif., Berkeley, 1977, BA in Journalism, 1977; MSJ, Northwestern U., 1981. Reporter Argus, Fremont, Calif., 1977-80, Va.-Pilot, Norfolk, 1981-84; reporter San Diego Union, 1984-87, asst. features editor, 1987-88, features editor, 1988-92; columnist San Diego Union-Tribune, 1992—. Gannett fellow Northwestern U., 1980-81. Roman Catholic. Office: San Diego Union Tribune PO Box 191 San Diego CA 92112-4106

ROWE, PETER GRIMMOND, architecture educator, researcher; b. Wellington, New Zealand, June 28, 1945; came to U.S., 1969; s. Leslie Grimmond and Dorothy Olive (Perkins) R.; m. Lauretta Vinciarelli, Oct. 18, 1993; 1 child, Anthony. BArch, Melbourne (Australia) U., 1969; MArch in Urban Design, Rice U., 1971; AM (hon.), Harvard U., 1986. Asst. prof. architecture Rice U., Houston, 1973-78, assoc. prof., 1978-85, dir. Sch. Architecture, 1981-85; Raymond Garbe prof. architecture and urban design Grad. Sch. Design, Harvard U., Cambridge, Mass., 1985—, chmn. dept. urban planning and design, 1989-92, dean Grad. Sch. Design, 1992—; program dir. S.W. Ctr. Urban Rsch., Houston, 1974-78; rsch. dir. Rice Ctr., Houston, 1978-81, v.p., 1979-81; prin. Environ. Planning and Design, Houston, 1980-86. Author: Principles for Environmental Management, 1978, Design Thinking, 1987, Making a Middle Landscape, 1991, Modernity and Housing, 1993, Civic Realism, 1997. Mem. Boston Soc. Architects (hon.). Office: Harvard U Grad Sch Design 48 Quincy St Cambridge MA 02138-3000

ROWE, RANDALL KEITH, real estate executive; b. N.Y.C., July 9, 1954; s. Stanley Robert and Jean (Knoche) R.; m. Susan Ayres Utley, May 29, 1982; children: Elizabeth Ayres, Katherine Ayres, Margaret Ayres. BA, Denison U., 1977; MBA, Harvard U., 1979; JD, U. Mich., 1982. Bar: Ill. Atty. Hopkins & Sutter, Chgo., 1982-86; v.p. Goldman, Sachs & Co., Chgo., 1986-89; exec. v.p. Equity Fin. & Mgmt. Co., Chgo., 1989-96; mng. dir., CEO Equity Venture Partners, Inc., Chicago, 1995-96, Transwestern Investment Co., L.L.C., Chgo., 1996—; chmn. Equity Office Properties, Inc., Chgo., 1989-95; pres. CEO Equity Assets Mgmt., Inc., Chgo., 1989-95; co-chmn., CEO Manufactured Home Communities, Inc., Chgo., 1989-95. Trustee Storage Trust Realty, 1994—. Mem. Urban Land Inst., Nat. Realty Com. (sr. vice chmn. 1992-95), Econ. Club Chgo. Avocations: tennis, golf.

Office: Transwestern Investment Co LLC 3 First Nat Plz Ste 4030 Chicago IL 60602

ROWE, RICHARD HOLMES, lawyer; b. Waltham, Mass., Jan. 2, 1937; s. Robert C. Rowe and Roberta (Holmes) Hayes; m. Sylvia C. Barrow, Aug. 23, 1963; children: Elizabeth C., Dorothy H., Christopher H. AB, Bates Coll., 1957; JD, Harvard U., 1964. Bar: D.C. 1965, N.Y. 1980. Atty., exec. SEC, Washington, 1964-69, 70-79; v.p. Shareholders Mgmt. Co., L.A., 1969-70; ptnr. Proskauer Rose Goetz & Mendelsohn, Washington, 1979—. 1st lt. USMCR, 1957-60. Mem. ABA, FBA, D.C. Bar Assn., Assn. Bar City of N.Y. Democrat. Office: Proskauer Rose Goetz & Mendelsohn 1233 20th St NW Ste 800 Washington DC 20036-2377

ROWE, SANDRA MIMS, newspaper editor; b. Charlotte, N.C., May 26, 1948; d. David Lathan and Shirley (Stovall) Mims; m. Gerard Paul Rowe, June 5, 1971; children: Mims Elizabeth, Sarah Stovall. BA, East Carolina U., Greenville, N.C., 1970; postgrad., Harvard U., 1991. Reporter to asst. mng. editor The Ledger-Star, Norfolk, Va., 1971-80, mng. editor, 1980-82; mng. editor The Virginian-Pilot and The Ledger Star, Norfolk, Va., 1982-84, exec. editor, 1984-86, v.p., exec. editor, 1986-93; editor The Oregonian, Portland, 1993—; mem. Pulitzer Prize Bd., 1994—. Bd. visitors James Madison U., Harrisonburg, VA., 1991-95. Named Woman of Yr. Outstanding Profl. Women of Hampton Rds., 1987. Mem. Am. Soc. Newspaper Editors (pres., bd. dirs. 1992—), Va. Press Assn. (bd. dirs. 1985-93). Episcopalian. Office: The Oregonian 1320 SW Broadway Portland OR 97201-3411

ROWE, SHERYL ANN, librarian; b. Stephenville, Tex., Sept. 29, 1946; d. Horace Milton and Letha Faye (Hensley) Hughes; m. Darrell Vanoy Rowe, Nov. 27, 1969; children: Jason Burt, Shelley Jean. BA in English, Tarleton State U., Stephenville, 1967; MS in Libr. Sci., Tex. Women's U., Denton, 1986. Cert. tchr. secondary edn. Tchr. Lake Worth (Tex.) H.S., 1967-69; tchr. Aledo (Tex.) H.S., 1967-73, 78-84, libr., 1984—. Mem. Tex. Libr. Assn., Region XI Librs. Assn. (treas. 1984—). Office: Aledo High School 412 Fm 1187 S Aledo TX 76008-4407

ROWE, STEPHEN COOPER, venture capitalist, entrepreneur; b. Glen Ridge, N.J., Dec. 24, 1951; s. Malcolm James and Audrey Ruth (Christian); m. Anne Mary Maddock, June 7, 1986; children: Lauren Elizabeth, Christopher Malcolm. BA, Harvard Coll., 1975; MBA, U. Calif., Berkeley, 1986. Mgr. Genentech, Inc., San Francisco, 1978-80, mktg. mgr., 1980-82, product mgr., 1982-86; dir. mktg. DAC, Foster City, Calif., 1987-88; founder Cell Genesys, Foster City, 1988-90, Cytotherapeutics, Providence, 1989-91, Endotex, 1993—; prin. Mayfield Fund, Menlo Park, Calif., 1989—, Med Impact, Wellesley, Mass., 1986-93; dir. bus. devel., founder Focal, Inc., Cambridge, Mass., 1993-95; pres., CEO Sontra Med., 1995—; gen. ptnr. Med. Impact Ventures, Wellesley, 1996—. Home: 1 Chatham Cir Wellesley MA 02181-2804 also: Sontra Med 767 C Concord Ave Cambridge MA 02138

ROWE, THOMAS DUDLEY, JR., law educator; b. Richmond, Va., Feb. 26, 1942; s. Thomas Dudley and Georgia Rosamond (Stripp) R. BA, Yale U., 1964; MPhil, Oxford U., Eng., 1967; JD, Harvard U., 1970. Bar: D.C. 1971, N.C. 1976. Law clk. to assoc. justice Potter Stewart U.S. Supreme Ct., 1970-71; asst. counsel adminstrv. practice subcom. U.S. Senate, 1971-73; assoc. Miller, Cassidy, Larroca & Lewin, Washington, 1973-75; assoc. prof. Duke U. Sch. Law, Durham, N.C., 1975-79, prof., 1979-96, Elvin R. Latty prof., 1996—, assoc. dean for rsch., 1981-84, sr. assoc. dean acad. affairs, 1995-96; vis. prof. Georgetown U. Law Ctr., Washington, 1979-80, U. Mich. Law Sch., Ann Arbor, fall 1985, U. Va. Law Sch., Charlottesville, fall 1991; atty. Munger, Tolles & Olson, L.A., 1991; mem. adv. com. on rules of civil procedure U.S. Jud. Conf., 1993—; chmn. adv. com. on rules and procedures U.S. Ct. Appeals (4th cir.), 1994—. Author: (with M. Gerhardt) Constitutional Theory: Arguments and Perspectives, 1993; co-author: (with others) Federal Courts in the 21st Century: Cases and Materials, 1996; contbr. articles to profl. jours. Fellow U.S. Dept. Justice, Washington, 1980-81; Rhodes scholar, 1964-67; recipient Disting. Teaching award Duke Bar Assn., 1985. Mem. ABA, Am. Law Inst. Democrat. Office: Duke U Sch Law Durham NC 27708-0360

ROWE, WILLIAM DAVIS, financial services company executive; b. Hibbing, Minn., June 5, 1937; s. Richard Lawrence and Alicia (Davis) R.; m. Bobbie Grace Childress, Apr. 20, 1963; children—Lisa, William. BA in Psychology, U. Minn, 1959, postgrad. in indsl. relations and bus. adminstrn., 1960; grad. exec. devel. program, Northeastern U., 1975; grad. Advanced Mgmt. Program, Harvard U., 1980. Dir. personnel, adminstrn. EDP Control Data Corp., Mpls., 1964-70; with Comml. Credit Co. subs. Control Data Corp, 1971-84, 85—; sr. v.p. consumer group Balt., 1975-81, sr. v.p. consumer realty services, 1981-83, sr. v.p. consumer banking services, 1983-84; v.p. market devel. Computer Service Co., Control Data Corp., Mpls., 1984; sr. v.p., chief adminstrv. officer Comml. Credit Co., Balt., 1985-87, officer, 1985-87; pres. Enterprise Bank Network Bank Svcs. Co., Atlanta, 1988-91; exec. mng. dir., vice chmn. Foster Ptnrs. Inc., Peat Marwick Alliance Co., 1991—; lectr. in field. Mem. Mayor's Vol. Council of Equal Opportunity, Balt.; trustee St. Paul's Sch. for Girls, Brooklandville, Md., 1981—; bd. dirs. Boy Scouts Am. Served to capt. USMC, 1960-63. Mem. Am. Fin. Services Assn. (bd. dirs. and mem. exec. com. 1980-84, consumer banking adv. com. 1983-84), Am. Mgmt. Assn. (pres.'s roundtable 1976). Republican. Avocations: hunting, skiing, cattle ranching.

ROWE, WILLIAM JOHN, newspaper publishing executive; b. Detroit, Jan. 11, 1936; s. Howard Tiedeman and Thelma Irene (Fox) R.; m. Ellen McCabe, Nov. 28, 1959; children: Peter William, Susan Victoria. BA in Journalism and Advt., Mich. State U., 1958. With Chgo. Tribune, 1958-79; pres., gen. mgr. area publs. Suburban Trib., 1977-79; pres., gen. mgr. Merrill Printing Co., Chgo., 1977-79; pres., CEO Peninsula Times Tribune, Palo Alto, Calif., 1979-84; exec. v.p., COO Times Mirror Nat. Mktg., N.Y.C., 1984-85, pres., CEO, 1985-86; pres., pub., CEO Adv. and Greenwich Time, Stamford, Conn., 1986—. Bd. dirs. United Way, Greenwich, Conn., 1986—. 2d lt. inf. USAR, 1950. Mem. Newspaper Assn. Am., New England Newspaper Assn. (bd. dirs.), Indian Harbor Yacht Club (bd. dirs.), Landmark Club (bd. dirs.). Office: Advocate So Conn Newspapers Box 9307 75 Tresser Blvd Stamford CT 06901-3300*

ROWELL, CHARLES FREDERICK, chemistry educator; b. Lowville, N.Y., May 29, 1935; s. Erwin Charles and Winifred Jane (Manning) R.; m. JoAnn Cowling, June 19, 1955; children: Mark Edward, Jan Ellen. BS, Syracuse U., 1956; MS, Iowa State U., 1959; PhD, Oreg. State U., 1963. From. asst. to assoc. prof. U.S. Naval Postgrad. Sch., Monterey, Calif., 1962-75; field scientist Office Naval Research, Chgo., 1975-76; prof. U.S. Naval Acad., Annapolis, Md., 1976—, chmn. dept. chemistry, 1984-88; scientist Forensic Techs. Internat., Annapolis, 1980—. Mem. AAAS, Am. Chem. Soc. (counselor 1980—, sect. chair 1982-83, nat. sec. membership affairs com. 1988-90, chmn. admissions com. 1989-91, chmn. constitution and bylaws com. 1994-96, local sect. activities com. 1997—), Royal Soc. Chemistry, Sigma Xi (sec. chpt. 1972-73, v.p. 1973-74). Presbyterian. Home: 900 Randell Rd Severna Park MD 21146-4726 Office: US Naval Acad Dept Of Chemistry Annapolis MD 21402

ROWELL, EDWARD MORGAN, retired foreign service officer, lecturer; b. Oakland, Calif., Oct. 13, 1931; s. Edward Joseph and Mary Helen (Mohler) R.; m. Lenora Mary Wood, Aug. 23, 1957; children: Edward Oliver, Karen Elizabeth Schuler, Christopher Douglas. B.A. in Internat. Relations, Yale U., 1953; postgrad., Stanford U., 1964-65, Stanford Bus. Sch., 1970-71. Fgn. service insp. U.S. Govt., Washington, 1971-74; dep. dir., econ. officer Office Iberian Affairs, Washington, 1974-75; dep. dir. Office West European Affairs, Washington, 1975-76, dir., 1977-78; minister-counselor U.S. Embassy, Lisbon, Portugal, 1978-83; dep. asst. sec. Bur. Consular Affairs, Washington, 1983-85; U.S. amb. to Bolivia La Paz, 1985-88; U.S. amb. to Portugal Lisbon, 1988-90; U.S. amb. to Luxemburg, 1990-94; assoc. Global Bus. Access, Ltd., 1994—; bd. dirs. F.Y.I. Inc., Dallas. Treas. Cleveland Park Congl. Ch., Washington, 1984-85; bd. dirs. Luso-Am. Devel. Found., 1988-90; mem. adv. bd. Portuguese-Am. Leadership Coun. of U.S. Cpl. U.S. Army, 1953-55. Recipient Bolivian Condor of the Andes, Grand Cross, 1988, Luxembourg Oaken Crown, Grand Cross, 1994, Superior Honor award, 1983, 91, Presdl. Honor award, 1988, scholar Yale U., 1949, 50, 51, 52; U. Calif. fellow, 1953; Una Chapman Cox Found. grantee, 1984. Mem. Am. Fgn. Svc. Assn. (v.p. 1995—), Stanford U. Alumni Assn., Yale U. Alumni Assn., Arena Stage Assocs., Smithsonian Assocs., The Phillips Collection, Friends of Kennedy Ctr. Avocations: photography, tennis, music. Home: 5414 Newington Rd Bethesda MD 20816-3316

ROWELL, LESTER JOHN, JR., retired insurance company executive; b. Cleve., Apr. 2, 1932; s. Lester John and Francis Laureen (Corbett) R.; m. Patricia Ann Loesch, Jan. 16, 1953 (div. Sept. 1970); children: Deborah, Cynthia, Gregory, Maureen, Diane; m. Carol Ann Jankowski, Sept. 26, 1970. BS, Pa. State U., 1955; grad. Advanced Mgmt. Program, Harvard U. Bus. Sch., 1971. CLU. Second v.p., field mgmt. Mut. Life Ins. Co. N.Y., N.Y.C., 1969-70, v.p. agys., 1970-72, v.p. sales, 1972-78, sr. v.p., 1978-80; exec. v.p. Provident Mut. Life Ins. Co., Phila., 1980-84, pres., 1984-86, pres., chief oper. officer, 1987, pres., chief exec. officer, 1991-93, chmn., pres., chief exec. officer, 1993—. Bd. dirs. Pa. State U., The PMA Group. Capt. USMC, 1953-62. Recipient Alumni award Pa. State U., 1972, Disting. Alumni award Pa. State U., 1988; Alumni Fellow Pa. State U., 1987. Republican.

ROWEN, MARSHALL, radiologist; b. Chgo.; s. Harry and Dorothy (Kasnow) R.; m. Helen Lee Friedman, Apr. 5, 1952; children: Eric, Scott, Mark. AB in Chemistry with highest honors, U. Ill., Urbana, 1951; MD with honors, U. Ill., Chgo., 1954, MS in Internal Medicine, 1954. Diplomate Am. Bd. Radiology. Intern Long Beach (Calif.) VA Hosp., 1955; resident in radiology Los Angeles VA Hosp., 1955-58; practice medicine specializing in radiology Orange, Calif., 1960—; chmn. bd. dirs. Moran, Rowen and Dorsey, Inc., Radiologists, 1969—; asst. radiologist L.A. Children's Hosp., 1958; assoc. radiologist Valley Presbyn. Hosp., Van Nuys, Calif., 1960; dir. dept. radiology St. Joseph Hosp., Orange, 1961—, v.p. staff, 1972; dir. dept. radiology Children's Hosp. Orange County, 1964—, chief staff, 1977-78, v.p., 1978-83, v.p., trustee, 1990-91, 92-95; asst. clin. prof. radiology U. Calif., Irvine, 1967-70, assoc. clin. prof., 1979-72, clin. prof. radiology and pediatrics, 1976-97, pres. clin. faculty assn., 1980-81; trustee Choc. Padrinos; sec. Choco Health Svcs., 1987-89, v.p., 1990-93, trustee, 1995—; trustee Found. Med. Care Orange County, 1972-76, Calif. Commn. Adminstrn. Svcs. Hosp., 1975-79, Profl. Practice Systems, 1990-92, Med. Specialty Mgrs., 1990—, St. Joseph Med. Corp., 1993—; v.p. Found. Med. Care Children's Hosp., 1988-89; v.p., sr. v.p., bd. dirs. St. Joseph Med. Corp. IPA, 1995-97; bd. dirs. Orange Coast Managed Care Svcs., 1995-97, sr. v.p., 1995-97, Paragon Med. Imaging, 1993—, Calif. Managed Imaging, 1994—, Alliance Premier Hosps., 1995-96; chmn. bd. dirs. Children's Healthcare of Calif., 1995-97; corp. mem. Blue Shield Calif., 1995-97; mem. physician's rev. com. Blue Cross Calif., 1996-97. Mem. editorial bd. Western Jour. Medicine; contbr. articles to med. jours. Founder Orange County Performing Arts Ctr., mem. Laguna Art Mus., Laguna Festival of Arts, Opera Pacific, S. Coast Reportory, Am. Ballet Theater, World Affairs Council. Served to capt. M.C., U.S. Army, 1958-60. Recipient Rea sr. med. prize U. Ill, 1953; William Cook scholar U. Ill., 1951, Friend of Children award, 1995, Charley award Children's Hosp., 1996. Fellow Am. Coll. Radiology; mem. AMA, Am. Heart Assn., Soc. Nuclear Medicine (trustee 1961-62), Orange County Radiol. Soc. (pres. 1968-69), Calif. Radiol. Soc. (pres. 1978-79), Radiol. Soc. So. Calif. (pres. 1976), Pacific Coast Pediatric Radiologists Assn. (pres. 1971), Soc. Pediatric Radiology, Calif. Med. Assn. (chmn. sect. on radiology 1978-79), Orange County Med. Assn. (chmn. UCI liaison com. 1976-78), Cardioradiology Soc. So. Calif., Radiol. Soc. N.Am., Am. Roentgen Ray Soc., Am. Coll. Physician Execs., Soc. Chmn. Radiologists Children Hosp., Center Club, Phi Beta Kappa, Phi Eta Sigma, Omega Beta Phi, Alpha Omega Alpha. Office: 1201 W La Veta Ave Orange CA 92868-4213

ROWEN, RUTH HALLE, musicologist, educator; b. N.Y.C., Apr. 5, 1918; d. Louis and Ethel (Fried) Halle; m. Seymour M. Rowen, Oct. 13, 1940; children: Mary Helen Rowen, Louis Halle Rowen. B.A., Barnard Coll., 1939; M.A., Columbia U., 1941, Ph.D., 1948. Mgmt. ednl. dept. Carl Fischer, Inc., N.Y.C., 1954-63; assoc. prof. musicology CUNY, 1967-72, prof., 1972—, mem. doctoral faculty in musicology, 1967—. Author: Early Chamber Music, 1948, reprinted, 1974; (with Adele T. Katz) Hearing-Gateway to Music, 1959, (with William Simon) Jolly Come Sing and Play, 1956, Music Through Sources and Documents, 1979, (with Mary Rowen) Instant Piano, 1979, 80, 83, Symphonic and Chamber Music Score and Parts Bank, 1996; contbr. articles to profl. jours. Mem. ASCAP, Am. Musicol. Soc., Music Library Assn., Coll. Music Soc., Nat. Fedn. Music Clubs (nat. musicianship chmn. 1962-74, nat. young artist auditions com. 1964-74, N.Y. state chmn. Young Artist Auditions 1981, dist. coord. 1983, nat. bd. dirs. 1989—, rep. UN 1991—), N.Y. Fedn. Music Clubs (pres.), Phi Beta Kappa. Home: 115 Central Park W New York NY 10023-4153 *Opportunity grows with each constructive thought.*

ROWLAND, ARTHUR RAY, librarian; b. Hampton, Ga., Jan. 6, 1930; s. Arthur and Jennie (Goodman) R.; m. Jane Thomas July 1, 1955; children: Dell Ruth, Anna Jane. A.B., Mercer U., Macon, Ga., 1951; M. Librarianship, Emory U., 1952. Circulation asst. Ga. State Coll. Library, 1952, circulation librarian, 1952-53; librarian Armstrong Coll., Savannah, Ga., 1954-56; head circulation dept. Auburn U. Library, 1956-58; librarian, asso. prof. library sci. Jacksonville U., 1958-61; librarian, asso. prof. library sci. Augusta Coll., 1961-76, prof., libr., 1976-91, libr. emeritus, 1991—; lectr. libr. edn. U. Ga., 1962-66; trustee Augusta-Richmond County Pub. Libr., 1980-93, pres. bd. trustees, 1983-85, v.p. bd., 1988-91; trustee Augusta Regional Libr., chmn., 1984-85; trustee East Cen. Ga. Regional Libr., 1987-93, chmn., 1988-91; chmn. Gov.'s Conf. on Ga. Librs. and Info. Svcs., 1977; del. White House Conf. on Librs. and Info. Sci., 1979; cons. on libr. mgmt. to Govt. of Indonesia, 1986. Author: Bibliography of the Writings of Georgia History, 1966, A Guide to the Study of Augusta and Richmond County, Georgia, 1967, (with Helen Callahan) Yesterday's Augusta, 1976, (with James E. Dorsey) A Bibliography of the Writings on Georgia History 1900-1970, rev. edit., 1978, (with Marguerite F. Fogleman) Reese Library Genealogical Resources, 1988, supplement, 1990, Goodman Cousins, 1988, Rowland Cousins, 1990, New Guide to the Study of Augusta, 1990, Index to City Directory of Augusta, Georgia, 1841-1879, 1991, More Goodman Cousins, 1993, My Fair Grandmother, 1994, Distant Cousins, The Huguenots Connecting Rowland, Bulloch, de Bourdeaux, DeVeaux and Roosevelt Families of S.C., N.C. and Ga., 1995, The Bessent Family of Georgia, 1995, Reeves Family of Georgia, 1996, Descendants of Wiley Reeves, 1996, Rowland-Huckaby Connections, 1996, Georgia Almanacs, 1996; editor: Reference Services, 1964, Historical Markers of Richmond County, Georgia, rev. edit., 1971, The Catalog and Cataloging, 1969, The Librarian and Reference Service, 1977, Reminiscences of Augusta Marines, 1985; supervising editor (with Heard Robertson) Jour. Archibald Campbell, 1981; contbr. to profl. jours. V.p. Ga. Libr. Assn. Trustees and Friends, 1989-91. With USN, 1948-49. Recipient Nix-Jones award for disting. service Ga. Library Assn., 1981,,Town and Gown award Augusta Coll. Alumni Assn., 1985. Mem. ALA, Am. Assn. State and Local History, Bibliog. Soc. Am., Southeastern Libr. Assn. (hon. life, exec. bd. 1971-72), Ga. Libr. Assn. (hon. life, 2d v.p. 1965-67, 71-73, 1st v.p., pres.-elect 1973-75, pres. 1975-77, chmn. budget com. 1977-79, adv. to pres. 1979-83, 85-92), Ctrl. Savannah River Area Libr. Assn. (past pres., editor union list of serials 1967), Duval County Libr. Assn. (past v.p.), Nat. Geneal. Soc., Ga. Geneal. Soc., N.C. Geneal. Soc., Va. Geneal. Soc., Augusta Geneal. Soc., Richmond County Hist. Soc. (curator 1964-91, pres. 1967-69, founder, editor Richmond County History), Huguenot Soc. S.C., Ga. Hist. Soc. (curator emeritus), Ga. Bapt. Hist. Soc., Nat., Young Men's Libr. Assn. (v.p. 1988-91), Ga. Trusts for Hist. Preservation, Hist. Augusta (trustee emeritus), Soc. Ga. Archivists, Kappa Phi Kappa. Baptist. Address: One Seventh St Ste 1503 Augusta GA 30901

ROWLAND, DAVID JACK, academic administrator; b. Columbus, Ohio, June 17, 1921; s. David Henry and Ethel (Ryan) R.; m. Mary Ellen Stinson, Apr. 8, 1944; children: David Allen, Ryan Stinson, Sue Ellen Rowland Summers. BS, Ohio U., 1949; MA, U. Ala., 1951; LittD (hon.), Athens State Coll., 1967; LLD (hon.), Jacksonville State U., 1969. Pres. Walker Coll., Jasper, Ala., 1956-88, chancellor, 1988-95; interim pres. U. Ala./Walker Coll., 1995-96; bd. dirs. First Nat. Bank, Jasper, first Comml. Bancshares, Birmingham, Ala.; chmn. Ala. ACT Bd., Tuscaloosa, 1968—; real estate developer. Chmn. Jasper Indsl. Bd., 1987—; commr. Ala. Mining commn., Jasper, 1976—; mem. Ala. Employer Guard Res. commn., Birmingham, 1988—; trustee Walker Coll.; chmn. adv. bd. Jasper Salvation Army. Col. U.S. Army, 1942-46, ATO. Decorated Legion of Merit; recipient Silver Beaver award Boy Scouts Am., 1972. Mem. Res. Officers Assn. (pres. Jasper chpt.), Summit Club, Met. Dinner Club, Rotary (pres. Jasper 1967-68, Paul Harris fellow), Masons. Avocations: tree farmer, growing Christmas trees, wildfowl carver. Home: 1000 Valley Rd Jasper AL 35501-4964 Office: Walker Coll Office of President UAB/Walker College Jasper AL 35501

ROWLAND, DOYLE ALFRED, federal judge; b. Northville, Mich., May 22, 1938; s. Doyle Vernal and Georgiana (Britcher) R.; m. Carol Ann Fritz, July 26, 1964; children: Doyle Andrew, Matthew Mark. BS, Ea. Mich. U., 1965; JD, Detroit Coll., 1967. Bar: Mich. 1968, U.S. Dist. Ct. (ea. dist.) Mich. 1968, U.S. Dist. Ct. (we. dist.) Mich. 1984. Asst. city atty. City of Midland, Mich., 1967-69; friend of the ct. Midland County, Mich., 1969-72; ptnr. Whittaker & Rowland, Midland, 1969-77; pros. atty. Midland County, 1977-81; pvt. practice Midland, 1981-84; U.S. magistrate judge Western Dist. Mich., Kalamazoo, 1984—. Mem. Midland County Bar Assn. (pres. 1978-79), Kalamazoo County Bar Assn. Office: US Dist Ct We Dist Mich 410 W Michigan Ave Kalamazoo MI 49007-3746

ROWLAND, ESTHER E(DELMAN), college dean, retired; b. N.Y.C., Apr. 12, 1926; d. Abraham Simon and Ida Sarah (Shifrin) Edelman; m. Lewis P. Rowland, Aug. 31, 1952; children: Andrew, Steven, Judith. B.A., U. Wis., 1946; M.A., Columbia U., 1948, M.Phil., 1984. Instr. in polit. sci. CCNY, 1947-51, Mt. Holyoke Coll., South Hadley, Mass., 1948-49; dir. health professions adv. bd. U. Pa., Phila., 1971-73; adviser to pre-profl. students Barnard Coll., N.Y.C., 1974-79, dean for pre-profl. students, 1980-93, assoc. dean studies, 1989-95; ret., 1995—. Mem. exec. com. Nat. Emergency Civil Liberties Com., N.Y.C., 1975-90; mem. exec. com. Women's Counseling Project, 1981-86. Mem. N.E. Assn. Health Professions Advisers (exec. com. 1973-74), N.E. Assn. Pre Law Advisors (exec. com. 1981-83, 85-86), Neurol. Inst. Aux. Home: 404 Riverside Dr New York NY 10025-1861

ROWLAND, FRANK SHERWOOD, chemistry educator; b. Delaware, Ohio, June 28, 1927; m. Joan Lundberg, 1952; children: Ingrid Drake, Jeffrey Sherwood. AB, Ohio Wesleyan U., 1948; MS, U. Chgo., 1951, PhD, 1952, DSc (hon.), 1989; DSc (hon.), Duke U., 1989, Whittier Coll., 1989, Princeton U., 1990, Haverford Coll., 1992, Clark U., 1996, U. East Anglia, 1996; LLD (hon.), Ohio Wesleyan U., 1989, Simon Fraser U., 1991, U. Calgary, 1997. Instr. chemistry Princeton (N.J.) U., 1952-56; asst. prof. chemistry U. Kans., 1956-58, assoc. prof. chemistry, 1958-63, prof. chemistry, 1963-64; prof. chemistry U. Calif., Irvine, 1964—, dept. chmn., 1964-70, Aldrich prof. chemistry, 1985-89, Bren prof. chemistry, 1989-94, Bren rsch. prof., 1994—; Humboldt sr. scientist, Fed. Republic of Germany, 1981; chmn. Dahlem (Fed. Republic of Germany) Conf. on Changing Atmosphere, 1987; vis. scientist Japan Soc. for Promotion Sci., 1980; co-dir. western region Nat. Inst. Global Environ. Changes, 1989-93; del. Internat. Coun. Sci. Unions, 1993—; fgn. sec. NAS, 1994—; lectr., cons. in field. Contbr. numerous articles to profl. jours. Mem. ozone commn. Internat. Assn. Meteorology and Atmospheric Physics, 1980-88, hon. life mem., 1996, mem. commn. on atmospheric chemistry and global pollution, 1979-91; mem. acid rain peer rev. panel U.S. Office of Sci. and Tech., Exec. Office of White House, 1982-84; mem. vis. com. Max Planck Insts., Heidelberg and Mainz, Fed. Republic Germany, 1982-96; ozone trends panel mem. NASA, 1986-88; chmn. Gordon Conf. Environ. Scis.-Air, 1987; mem. Calif. Coun. Sci. Tech., 1989-95, Exec. Com. Tyler Prize, 1992—. Recipient numerous awards including John Wiley Jones award Rochester Inst. of Tech., 1975, Disting. Faculty Rsch. award U. Calif., Irvine, 1976, Profl. Achievement award U. Chgo., 1977, Billard award N.Y. Acad. Sci., 1977, Tyler World Prize in Environment Achievement, 1983, Global 500 Roll of Honor for Environ. Achievement UN Environment Program, 1988, Dana award for Pioneering Achievements in Health, 1987, Silver medal Royal Inst. Chemistry, U.K., 1989, Wadsworth award N.Y. State Dept. Health, 1989, medal U. Calif., Irvine, 1989, Japan prize in Environ. Sci., 1989, Dickson prize Carnegie-Mellon U., 1991, Albert Einstein prize of World Cultural Coun., 1994, Nobel Prize in Chemistry, 1995, Alumni medal U. Chgo., 1997, Nevada medal, 1997; Guggenheim fellow, 1962, 74. Fellow AAAS (pres. elect 1991, pres. 1992, chmn. bd. dirs. 1993), Am. Phys. Soc. (Leo Szilard award for Physics in Pub. Interest 1979), Am. Geophys. Union (Roger Revelle medal 1994); mem. NAS (bd. environ. studies and toxicology 1986-91, com. on atmospheric chemistry 1987-89, com. atmospheric scis., solar-terrestial com. 1979-83, co-DATA com. 1977-82, sci. com. on problems environment 1986-89, Infinite Voyage film com. 1988-92, Robertson Meml. lectr. 1993, chmn. com. on internat. orgns. and programs 1993—, chmn. office of internat. affairs 1994—, co-chmn. interacad. panel 1995—), Am. Acad. Arts and Scis., Am. Chem. Soc. (chmn. divsn. nuclear sci. and tech. 1973-74, chmn. divsn. phys. chemistry 1974-75, Orange County award 1975, Tolman medal 1976, Zimmerman award 1980, E.F. Smith lectureship 1980, Environ. Sci. and Tech. award 1983, Esselen award 1987, Peter Debye Phys. Chem. award 1993), Am. Meteorological Soc. (hon.), European Acad. Arts, Scis. and Humanities, Phi Beta Kappa. Home: 4807 Dorchester Rd Corona Del Mar CA 92625-2718 Office: U Calif Irvine Dept of Chemistry 571 PS1 Irvine CA 92697-2025

ROWLAND, HOWARD RAY, mass communications educator; b. Eddy County, N.Mex., Sept. 9, 1929; s. Lewis Marion and Ursula Lorene (Hunt) R.; m. Meredith June Lee, Apr. 19, 1951; children: Runay Ilene Smith, Rhonda Lee Fisher. B in Journalism, U. Mo., 1950; MS in Journalism, So. Ill. U., 1959; PhD, Mich. State U., 1969. Feature writer Springfield (Mo.) Newspapers, Inc., 1954; newspaper editor Monett (Mo.) Times, 1954-55; editorial writer So. Ill. U., Carbondale, 1955-59; pub. rels. dir. St. Cloud (Minn.) State U., 1959-86, asst. dean, 1986-87, 88-90; dir. Ctr. for British Studies, Alnwick, Eng., 1987-88, 90-91; adj. prof. Mass Comms., St. Cloud State U., 1986—; cons. Conf. of Campus Ombudsmen, Berkeley, 1971; recorder Seminar on Fund Raising, Washington, 1985; bibliographer Higher Edn. Bibliography Yearbook, 1987. Author: American Students in Alnwick Castle, 1990, St. Cloud State University--125 Years, 1994; editor: Effective Community Relations, 1980; sect. editor: Handbook of Institutional Advancement, 1986; author book revs. Chair All-Am. City Com., St. Cloud, 1973-74. With U.S. Army, 1951-53. NDEA doctoral fellowship Mich. State U., 1967-69; recipient Appreciation award Mayor of St. Cloud, 1974, Disting Svc. award Coun. for Advancement and Support of Edn., 1985. Mem. Soc. of Profl. Journalists (Minn. chpt. pres. 1963-64, dep. dir. 1965-67), Coun. for Advancement and Support of Edn. (dist. 5 chair 1977-79, Leadership award 1979), Rotary Internat., Phi Delta Kappa (Mich. State U. chpt. pres. 1968-69, St. Cloud State Univ. chpt. pres. 1978-79). Presbyterian. Avocations: writing, fishing, travel, photography, antiques. Home: 29467 Kraemer Lake Rd Saint Joseph MN 56374-9646 *Striving to achieve is more rewarding than striving to succeed. Achievement brings personal satisfaction more fulfilling than recognition and compensation.*

ROWLAND, JAMES RICHARD, electrical engineering educator; b. Muldrow, Okla., Jan. 24, 1940; s. Richard Cleveland and Imogene Beatrice (Angel) R.; m. Jonell Condren, Aug. 24, 1963 (dec. May 1991); children: Jennifer Lynn, Angela Janel; m. Mary Anderson, Jan. 2, 1995. BSEE, Okla. State U., 1962; MSEE, Purdue U., 1964, PhD in Elec. Engring., 1966. Registered profl. engr., Okla. Instr. Purdue U., West Lafayette, Ind., 1964-65; from asst. to assoc. prof. Ga. Inst. Tech., Atlanta, 1966-71; from assoc. to full prof. Okla. State U., Stillwater, 1971-85; prof., chmn. dept. elec. and computer engring. U. Kans., Lawrence, 1985-89, prof., 1985—; cons. Lockheed-Ga. Co., Marietta, 1966-71, U.S. Army Missile Command, Huntsville, Ala., 1969-79, Sandia Nat. Labs., Albuquerque, 1979, Puritan-Bennett, Lenexa, Kans., 1992. Author: Linear Control Systems, 1986; mem. editorial adv. bd. Computer and Elec. Engring., 1971—; co-contbr. 50 articles to profl. jours. Fellow IEEE (edn. soc. pres. 1982-83, Centennial medal 1984, edn. soc. Achievement award 1986, edn. conf. award 1988, Region 5 Oustanding Educator award 1995), Am. Soc. Engring. Edn. (dir. grad. div. 1987-89), Eta Kappa Nu (dir. 1989-91). Republican. Methodist. Lodge: Kiwanis. Avocations: golf, gardening. Home: 2424 Free State Ct Lawrence KS 66047-2831 Office: U Kans Dept Elec Engring & Computer Sci 1013 Learned Hall Lawrence KS 66044-7526

ROWLAND, JOHN ARTHUR, lawyer; b. Joliet, Ill., Mar. 6, 1943; s. John Fornof and Grace Ada (Baskerville) R.; m. Lana D. Lee, Sept. 8, 1984; children: Sean B., Keira L. B.A., U. Notre Dame, 1965; J.D., U. San Francisco, 1968. Bar: Calif. 1969, U.S. Dist. Ct. (no. dist.) Calif. 1982. Asst. dist. atty. San Francisco Dist. Atty.'s Office, 1971-81; assoc. Ropers, Majeski, Kohn and Bentley, San Francisco, 1982—, ptnr., 1985—. Pres., South of Market Boys, San Francisco, 1981. Served to capt. U.S. Army, 1969-71, Korea. Recipient Commendation San Francisco Bd. Suprs., 1981,

Merit award Mayor of San Francisco, 1982. Mem. Am. Bd. Trial Advocates. Roman Catholic. Office: 670 Howard St San Francisco CA 94105-3916

ROWLAND, JOHN G., governor, former congressman; b. Waterbury, Conn., May 24, 1957; s. Sherwood L. and Florence (Jackson) R.; m. Deborah Nabhan; children: Kirsten Elizabeth, Robert John, Julianne Marie. B.S. in Bus. Adminstrn., Villanova U., 1979. Former mem. Conn. Ho. of Reps.; mem. 99th-101st Congress from 5th Conn. dist., 1985-91; governor Conn., 1995—; pres. Rowland Assocs. Ambassador, St. Mary's Hosp., Waterbury; bd. dirs. Am. Cancer Soc., Waterbury. Recipient Disting. Service award VFW, Holy Cross Alumni Assn. Republican. Home: 990 Prospect Ave Hartford CT 06105-1102 Office: Off of the Governor Exec Chambers 210 Capitol Ave Hartford CT 06106-1535*

ROWLAND, LAWRENCE SANDERS, history educator; b. St. Paul, May 19, 1942; s. Richard Henry and Elizabeth (Sanders) R.; m. Margot Hunter, Jan. 5, 1974; children: Lawrence S., Katherine Hunter, Margaret Waterhouse. BA, Hamilton Coll., 1964; MA, U. S.C., Columbia, 1971, PhD, 1978. Asst. dir. U. S.C., Beaufort, 1971-77, assoc. dean acad. affairs, 1977-83, assoc. prof. history, 1983-86, prof., 1986—. Author: Window on the Atlantic, 1990, History of Beaufort County, S.C., 1996; author articles on S.C. history. Pres. Beaufort County Hist. Soc., 1975-76, S.C. Hist. Soc., Charleston, 1995-96; chmn. Beaufort County Hist. Preservation Bd., 1993—; trustee Beaufort Coll., 1997—, Beaufort Acad., 1991-93, 95-97; conv. chmn. Beaufort County Rep. Party, 1991, 93; bd. dirs. S.C. Policy Coun. and Ednl. Found., vice chair, 1996-97. Lt. U.S. Navy, 1964-68. Recipient Gov.'s award in the humanities State of S.C., 1993; named Outstanding Tchr., U. S.C. at Beaufort, 1972, 76, 78, 83, 95. Mem. Ga. Hist. Soc., Rotary Club of Beaufort. Republican. Roman Catholic. Avocations: boating, sailing. Office: U SC at Beaufort 801 Carteret St Beaufort SC 29902-4601

ROWLAND, LEWIS PHILLIP, neurologist, medical editor, educator; b. Bklyn., Aug. 3, 1925; s. Henry Alexander and Cecile (Coles) R.; m. Esther Edelman, Aug. 31, 1952; children: Andrew Simon, Steven Samuel, Joy Rosenthal. B.S., Yale U., 1945, M.D., 1948; hon. doctorate, U. Aix-Marseilles, France, 1986, U. Padua, 1996. Diplomate: Am. Bd. Psychiatry and Neurology. Intern New Haven Hosp., 1949-50; asst. resident N.Y. Neurol. Inst., 1950-52, fellow, 1953; clin. assoc. NIH, Bethesda, Md., 1953-54; practice research medicine, specializing in neurology N.Y.C., 1954-67, Phila., 1967-73, N.Y.C., 1973—; asst. neurologist Montefiore Hosp., N.Y.C., 1954-57; vis. fellow Nat. Inst. Med. Research, London, 1956; from asst. prof. to prof. neurology Columbia Coll. Physicians and Surgeons, 1957-67, prof., chmn. dept. neurology, 1973—; prof., chmn. dept. neurology U. Pa., Med. Sch., 1967-73; from asst. neurologist to attending neurologist Presbyn. Hosp., 1957-67; co-dir. Neurol. Clin. Research Center, 1961-67, dir. neurology service, 1973—, pres. med. bd., 1991-94; cons. Harlem Hosp., 1973—; mem. med. adv. bd. Myasthenia Gravis Found., pres., 1971-73; med. adv. bd. Muscular Dystrophy Assocs., Nat. Multiple Sclerosis Soc., Com. to Combat Huntington's Disease; pres. Parkinson's Disease Found., 1979—; mem. tng. grants com. Nat. Inst. Neurol. Diseases and Stroke, NIH, 1971-73, bd. sci. counselors, 1978-83, chmn., 1981-83, nat. adv. council, 1986-90. Editorial bd.; Archives of Neurology, 1968-76, Advances in Neurology, 1969—, Italian Jour. Neurol. Sci., 1979—, Handbook of Clin. Neurology, 1982—, New England Jour. Medicine, 1990—, Medical Letter, 1990-97, Jour. Neurol. Sci., 1991—, Jour. Neuromuscular Disorders, 1991—, Clin. Neurosci., 1995—; editor-in-chief: Neurology, 1977-87. Served with USNR, 1942-44; with USPHS, 1953-54. Mem. Am. Neurol. Assn. (pres. 1980, hon. mem. 1989—), Am. Acad. Neurology (pres.-elect 1987-89, pres. 1989-91), Phila. Neurol. Soc. (pres. 1972), Assn. Research Nervous Mental Disease (pres. 1969, trustee 1976—, v.p. 1980, chmn. bd. trustees 1992—), Assn. Univ. Profs. Neurology (sec. 1971-74, pres. 1978), Am. Acad. Neurol. Edn. and Rsch. Found. (pres. 1996, chair bd. trustees 1997—), Eastern Pa. Multiple Sclerosis Soc. (chmn. med. adv. bd. 1969-73); hon. mem. Neurol. Socs. France, Poland, Can., Europe, Italy, Gt. Britain, Spain, Japan; mem. N.Y.C. Multiple Sclerosis Soc. (chmn. med. adv. bd. 1977-92). Home: 404 Riverside Dr New York NY 10025-1861 Office: Columbia-Presbyn Med Ctr Neurological Inst 710 W 168th St New York NY 10032-2603

ROWLAND, RALPH THOMAS, architect; b. Elizabeth, N.J., Oct. 10, 1920; s. Thomas Aloysius and Anna Frances (McQuaid) R.; m. Bernice Barbara Cannizzo, Sept. 7, 1946; children: Glenn Thomas, Mark Louis, Roy Joseph, Lisa Rowland Majewski. Student, Manhattan Coll., 1937-38, Columbia U., 1945-49. Archtl. field supr., specifier Voorhees Walker Foley & Smith, N.Y.C., 1945-50; specifier, project mgr. Sargent Webster Crenshaw & Folley, Watertown, N.Y., 1951-53; individual archtl. practice Hamden, Conn., 1958-65; field supr. Fletcher Thompson, Inc., Bridgeport, Conn., 1954-56; project mgr. Fletcher Thompson, Inc., 1957, 65-73, asso., 1969-73, v.p., 1973-81, dir. archtl. research, 1981-85, also dir., 1973-93, adv. coun., 1994—; cons. Cheshire, Conn., 1981-97; chmn. Conn. Bldg. Code Standards Com., 1978-82; vice chmn. Conn. State Codes and Standards Com., 1982-86. Editorial chmn.: Conn. Architect Mag., 1966-74; project mgr. design, St. Vincents Med. Center, Bridgeport. Mem. Cheshire Planning Commn., 1966-72, chmn., 1967-68; pres. Hamden C. of C., 1964, New Eng. Bldg. Code Assn., 1989; mem. Cen. Naugatuck Valley Regional Planning Agy., 1966-74, chmn., 1969; mem. Cheshire Democratic Town Com., 1960-70, treas., 1963-69; mem. Conn. Archtl. Sch. Task Force, 1987-88. With USN, 1942-45. Fellow AIA; mem. AIA Conn. (past pres.), AARP (pres. Cheshire chpt. 1995—), Conn. Bldg. Ofcls. Assn., Cheshire C. of C. Roman Catholic. Home and Office: 201 N Rolling Acres Rd Cheshire CT 06410-2119

ROWLAND, ROBERT CHARLES, writer, clinical psychotherapist, researcher; b. Columbus, Ohio, Jan. 18, 1946; s. Charles Albert and Lorene Bernadine (Friedlinghaus) R.; m. Saundra Marie Gardner, Dec. 21, 1968 (div. Mar. 1987); children: Carrie Ann, Marcus Jules Harrad, Heather Renée. BS in Physiol. Psychology, Ohio State U., 1971, MSW, 1981. Cert. marital and family therapist; cert. in drug and alcohol treatment; cert. sex therapist; cert. hypnotist. Respiratory therapist Mt. Carmel Med. Ctr., Columbus, Ohio, 1965-68; adj. prof. Columbus Ctr. Sci. and Industry, Columbus, Ohio, 1968-71; researcher in tetrahydrocannabinol/learning experiments Ohio State U. Rsch. Ctr., 1970-71; secondary tchr. Columbus (Ohio) Pub. Schs., 1971-73; case cons. Bur. Disability Determination, Columbus, 1973-80; clin. social worker Clarke County Out-Patient Mental Health Ctr., Springfield, Ohio, 1979-80, Upham Hall, Ohio State U. Hosps., 1980-81; clin. psychotherapist Psychol. Systems, Inc., Columbus, 1981-84; psychotherapist, cons. Columbus, 1974-87, 94—, Delray Beach, Fla., 1987-93; dir. social svc. and cmty. rels. Apple Creek (Ohio) Devel. Ctr., 1981-82; pres., rsch. dir. Neurosocial Scis. Inst., Delray Beach, 1987-93, Columbus, 1994—. Author: Brain Wars-The End of the Drug Game, 1991; contbr. articles to profl. jours. Advisor Neighbor to Neighbor, Delray Beach, 1991-93. Recipient scholarship grant, Ohio State U. Coll. of Social Work, 1980-81. Mem. AAAS, NASW (chmn. Ohio Pace chpt., lobbyist 1980-81, Excellence award 1981, mem. Fla. chpt.), Archaeol. Soc. Ohio, Archaeol. Soc. Fla., Fla. Freelance Writer's Assn., Union of Concerned Scientists, Palm Beach County Scis. Jour. Club, Alpha Delta Mu. Avocations: rockhounding, scuba diving, tennis, music, chess. Home: 6378 Busch Blvd Apt 386 Columbus OH 43229-1845

ROWLAND, ROBERT E., secondary school principal. Prin. Danville (Ky.) High Sch. Recipient Blue Ribbon award U.S. Dept. Edn., 1990-91. Office: Danville High Sch 203 E Lexington Ave Danville KY 40422-1519*

ROWLAND, THEODORE JUSTIN, physicist, educator; b. Cleve., May 15, 1927; s. Thurston Justin and Lillian (Nesser) R.; m. Janet Claire Millar, June 28, 1952 (div. 1967); children: Theodore Justin, Dawson Ann, Claire Millar; m. Patsy Marie Beard, Aug. 21, 1968. BS, Western Res. U., 1948; MA, Harvard U., 1949, PhD, 1954. Rsch. physicist Union Carbide Metals Co., Niagara Falls, N.Y., 1954-61; prof. phys. metallurgy U. Ill., 1961-92, asst. dean Coll. Engring., acting assoc. dean Grad. Coll., 1990-91, prof. emeritus, 1992—; pres., dir. Materials Cons., Inc.; cons. physicist, 1961—; cons. metallurgist, 1976—. Editor 2 books; author monograph; contbr. articles to profl. jours. Fellow Am. Phys. Soc.; mem. AIME, AAAS, AAUP, Phi Beta Kappa, Sigma Xi. Achievements include initial verification of charge density waves in dilute alloys; original contributions to theory and experiment in nuclear magnetic resonance in metals. Home: 805 Park Lane Dr Champaign IL 61820-7613 Office: U Ill Dept Materials Sci and Engring 1304 W Green St Urbana IL 61801-2920

ROWLANDS, DAVID THOMAS, pathology educator; b. Wilkes-Barre, Pa., Mar. 22, 1930; s. David Thomas and Anna Jule (Morgan) R.; m. Gwendolyn Marie York, Mar. 1, 1958; children: Julie Marie, Carolyn Jane. M.D., U. Pa., 1955. Diplomate: Am. Bd. Pathology, Am. Bd. Allergy and Immunology. Intern Pa. Hosp., Phila., 1955-56; resident Cin. Gen. Hosp., 1956-60; asst. prof. U. Colo., 1962-64, Rockefeller U., 1964-66; assoc. prof. Duke U., Durham, N.C., 1966-70; prof. pathology U. Pa., Phila., 1970-82; chmn. dept. pathology U. Pa., 1973-78, prof. medicine, 1979-82; prof., chmn. dept. pathology U. So. Fla., Tampa, 1982-91; assoc. dean U. So. Fla., 1983-84, prof. pediatrics, 1986-91; med. dir. Lifelink Tissue Bank, 1991-93. Mem. editorial bd.: Am. Jour. Pathology, 1971-81, Developmental and Comparative Immunology, 1977-79. Served with USNR, 1960-62. Recipient Lederle Med. Faculty award U. Colo., 1964, Jacob Ehrenzeller award Pa. Hosp., 1976. Mem. Am. Assn. Pathologists, Internat. Acad. Pathology, Am. Soc. Clin. Pathology, Am. Assn. Immunologists, Coll. Am. Pathologist, Arthur Purdy Stout Soc. Presbyterian. Home: 13804 Cypress Village Cir Tampa FL 33624-4406

ROWLANDS, MARVIN LLOYD, JR., publishing and communications consultant; b. Wellington, Kans., Apr. 30, 1926; s. Marvin Lloyd and Opal Mary (Pilant) R. BS in Journalism, U. Kans., 1950. Wire editor Manhattan (Kans.) Mercury, 1950-51; reporter Leavenworth (Kans.) Times, 1951-56, Topeka (Kans.) Daily Capital, 1956-57, Cin. Times-Star, 1957-58; assoc. editor The Am. Med. News, Chgo., 1958-61, mng. editor, 1961-65, editor, 1965-75; editor-in-chief Modern Healthcare, Chgo., 1975-76; editor Contemporary Surgery and Contemporary Ob/Gyn, N.Y.C., 1976-77; dir. devel. McGraw-Hill Publs. Co., N.Y.C., 1978-84, dir. planning, 1984-85, v.p. planning, 1985-86, v.p. editorial, planning and devel., 1986-88; v.p. editorial McGraw-Hill Fin. Services Co., N.Y.C., 1988-89; sr. v.p. comm. McGraw-Hill Fin. Svcs. Co., N.Y.C., 1989-90; pub., communications cons., N.Y.C., 1990-92, North Chatham, Mass., 1992—. Mem., chmn. bd. dirs. Rush Dance, A Found., Inc., N.Y.C., 1980—. Served with USNR, 1944-46. Mem. Omicron Delta Kappa. Baptist. Home and Office: PO Box 757 52 Spring Hill Rd North Chatham MA 02650

ROWLANDS, ROBERT EDWARD, engineer, educator; b. Trail, B.C., Can., July 7, 1936; s. Edward and Eda May (Randell) R.; m. Mary Roma Ranaghan, Nov. 14, 1959; children: Robert Philip, Edward Hugh. BA. Sc., U. B.C., Vancouver, 1959; MS, U. Ill., 1964, PhD, 1967. Engr. mechanics MacMillan & Bloedel, Powell River, B.C., 1959, Ill. Inst. Tech. Rsch. Inst., Chgo., 1967-74; asst. prof., engring. U. Wis., 1974-76, assoc. prof. engring., 1976-79, prof. engring., 1979—, dir. structural and materials testing lab., 1983-90; vis. scholar People's Republic China, 1985; Clark C. Heritage vis. scientist USDA Forest Products Lab., 1987; vis. scholar Gadjah Mada U., Yogyakarta, Indonesia, 1991; lectr. in field; cons. to rsch. insts., engring. orgns., instrument mfrs., ins. cos., auto, farm-implement, food processing, paper products, foresty, composite, plastics, petroleum and mining industries; expert witness law firms; internat. extensive tech. travel throughout Scandanavia, Europe, U.K., Japan, Spain, Portugal, Australia, China, Slovenia, Singapore, Indonesia and former USSR. Registered profl. engr., Wis. Fellow ASME, Soc. Exptl. Mechanics; mem. Soc. Exptl. Mechanics (mem. papers rev. com. 1967—, mem. editorial com. 1976—, book rev. editor 1976—, chmn. composite com. 1977-79, tech. chmn. 1975, also chmn. various tech. sessions, Hetényi award 1970, 76, fellow 1982, Frocht award 1989), Am. Acad. Mechanics. Author chpt. Handbook of Composite Materials, Handbook of Experimental Mechanics; contbr. over 100 articles to profl. jours. Home: 5401 Russett Rd Madison WI 53711-3564 Office: Dept Mechanical Engring U Wisc 1415 Engineering Dr Madison WI 53706-1607

ROWLENSON, RICHARD CHARLES, lawyer; b. Camden, N.J., Dec. 27, 1949; s. Alton Joseph and Margaret (Mietzelfeld) R.; m. Frances Ambury, July 28, 1979; children: Mary, Anne. BS, Georgetown U., 1971, JD, 1975. Bar: D.C. 1975, U.S. Ct. Appeals (D.C. cir.) 1975, U.S. Supreme Ct. 1979. Atty. Hennessey, Stambler & Siebert, Washington, 1975-87; exec. v.p. Vanguard Cellular Systems Inc., Greensboro, N.C., 1987—. Mem. ABA, Bar Assn. D.C., Greensboro Bar Assn., Fed. Communications Bar Assn., Sherwood Swim and Racquet Club (Greensboro). Office: Vanguard Cellular Systems 2002 Pisgah Church Rd Ste 300 Greensboro NC 27455-3318

ROWLETT, RALPH MORGAN, archaeologist, educator; b. Richmond, Ky., Sept. 11, 1934; s. Robert Kenny and Daisy (Mullikin) R.; m. Elsebet Sander-Jorgensen, Aug. 25, 1963 (div. Jan. 1986); children: Rolf Arvid, Erik Kenneth; m. Elizabeth Helen Dinan, Apr. 21, 1989 (div. Oct. 1995); 1 child, Helen Holly. Student, U. Ky., 1952-53; BA summa cum laude, Marshall U., 1956; postgrad., U. London, 1962-63; PhD, Harvard U., 1968. Instr. anthropology U. Mo., Columbia, 1965-67, asst. prof., 1967-69, assoc. prof., 1969-75, prof., 1975—; postdoctoral fellow Ghent U., 1969. Co-author: Neolithic Levels on the Titelberg, Luxembourg, 1981; anthropology editor Random House Unabridged Dictionary of English, 1980—; editor: Horizons and Styles, 1993, Horizons and Styles in West Eurasiatic Archaeology; developer thermoluminescence dating of flint, 1972; co-developer electron spin resonance dating of flint, 1981. 1st lt. arty., U.S. Army, 1956-58. Decorated officer Legion de Merit (Luxembourg); named Ky. col., 1976; grantee NSF, 1973-75, 76-79, 82-83, Svc. Archeologique de Neuchatel, 1989, British Coun., 1993, Acad. of Romania, 1996. Fellow Am. Anthrop. Assn.; mem. AAAS, Archaeol. Inst. Am., Soc. Am. Archaeology, Prehistory Soc., Societe Prehistorique de Luxembourg, Societe Archeologique Champenoise, English Heritage, Palomino Horse Breeders Assn. Democrat. Mem. Christian Ch. (Disciples of Christ). Home: Hollywell Hill 1197 State Rd WW Fulton MO 65251-9805 Office: Univ Mo Dept Anthropology Columbia MO 65211

ROWLETTE, HENRY ALLEN, JR., social worker; b. Phila., July 8, 1947; s. Henry Allen Sr. and Ophelia Alberta (Kilson) R.; m. Geraldine Lee Stevens, Mar. 1972 (div. Mar. 1986); children: Cessandra N., Deaeon D., Christiene A., Janetta M.; m. Ann Laura Rowe, Mar. 19, 1989. BA, Cheyney State Coll., 1970; MEd, Boston U., 1981; MSW, Temple U., 1988. Cert. sch. social worker, N.J.; ordained minister Bapt. Ch. Cardiac monitor technician Bapt. Med. Ctr., Little Rock, Ark., 1982-83; mental health technician The Horsham Clinic, Ampler, Pa., 1984; psychiat. technician The Lower Bucks Hosp., Bristol, Pa., 1984-90; mental health technician The Helene Fuld Med. Ctr., Trenton, N.J., 1988-90, psychiat. social worker, 1988-92; profl. sch. social worker The Willingboro (N.J.) Sch. Dist., 1990—; dist. crisis intervention team Willingboro Sch. Dist., 1994—; therapist The N.J. State Prison, Trenton, 1996; therapist, short term care unit Rancocas Hosp./The Grad. Hlth System, Willingboro, N.J., 1997; writer, cons. The Amer-I-Can Acad., Trenton, 1995. Mem. NAACP, Trenton, 1990. With U.S. Army, 1971-79. Mem. NASW, Am. Assn. Christian Counselors, Omega Psi Phi (Delta Upsilon chpt.), Phi Delta Kappa (Trenton chpt.). Democrat. Baptist. Avocations: fishing, reading, computer technology/games. Home: 18 Foxchase Dr Burlington NJ 08016

ROWLEY, BEVERLEY DAVIES, medical sociologist; b. Antioch, Calif., July 28, 1941; d. George M. and Eloise (DeWhitt) Davies; m. Richard B. Rowley, Apr. 1, 1966 (div. 1983). BS, Colo. State U., 1963; MA, U. Nev., 1975; PhD, Union Inst., 1983. Social worker Nev. Dept. Pub. Welfare, Reno, 1963-65, Santa Clara County Dept. Welfare, San Jose, Calif., 1965-66; field dir. Sierra Sage Council Camp Fire Girls, Sparks, Nev., 1966-70; program coord. div. health scis. sch. medicine U. Nev., 1976-78, program coord., health analyst office rural health, 1978-84, acting dir. office rural health, 1982-84; exec. asst. to pres. Med. Coll. of Hampton Rds., Norfolk, Va., 1984-87; rsch. mgr. Office Med. Edn. Info. AMA, Chgo., 1987-88, dir. dept. data systems, 1988-91; dir. med. edn. Maricopa Med. Ctr., Phoenix, 1992—; v.p. Med. Edn. and Rsch. Assocs., Inc., Phoenix, Chgo., 1992—; various positions as adj. prof. and lectr. in health scis. U. Nev. Sch. of Medicine, 1972-75; lectr. Dept. of Family and Community Medicine, U. Nev., 1978-84, asst. dir., evaluator Health Careers for Am. Indians Programs, 1978-84; cons. Nev. Statewide Health Survey, 1979-84; interim dir. Health Max, 1985-86; asst. prof. dept. of family and community medicine Med. Coll. of Hampton Rds., Norfolk, Va., 1985-87; v.p., treas. Systems Devel. Assocs., Reno, 1981-84. Editor of five books; contbr. numerous articles to profl. jours; developer three computer systems including AMA-FREIDA. Mem. Am. Sociol. Assn., Nat. Rural Health Assn. (bd. dirs. 1986-88), Assn. Behavioral Sci. and Med. Edn. (pres. 1986), Assn. Am. Med. Colls. (exec. coun. 1993-95), Coun. Acad. Scis. (adminstrv. bd. 1992—), Delta, Delta, Delta. Avocations: hiking, skiing, gardening, sewing, ceramics. Office: Maricopa Med Ctr Dept Acad Affairs 2601 E Roosevelt St Phoenix AZ 85008-4973

ROWLEY, FRANK SELBY, JR., artist; b. N.Y.C., Aug. 2, 1913; s. Frank Selby and Caroline Estelle (Bremmer) R.; m. Dorothy Folger, June 30, 1942. Student, Art Students League, N.Y.C., 1934, Nassau Inst. of Art, Hempstead, N.Y., 1935-38, U. Richmond, Va., 1952. Designer, illustrator Nina Robinson Studio, Hempstead, 1938-41; designer, muralist, 1946-49; tchr. comml. art John Marshall High Sch., Richmond, 1949-57; lectr. various art orgns. 1957—; judge art exhbns., 1957—. Exhibited in group shows at Portraits Inc., N.Y.C., 1959-87, Gallery Mayo, Richmond, Va., 1975—, Va. Mus. of Fine Arts; represented in permanent collections Va. Mus. of Fine Arts, State of Va., City of Richmond, Richmond Meml. Hosp., Va. Fedn. Womens Clubs and numerous pvt. collections. Founder Richmond Concert Band, 1970; music dir., conductor Richmond Pops Band, 1977—; chmn. bd. Richmond Band Assn., 1977—; vol. art tchr. Va. Home, 1989—. Sgt. U.S. Army, 1941-45. Mem. Lions. Avocations: water color painting, music. Home: 8909 Elm Rd Richmond VA 23235-1427

ROWLEY, GEOFFREY HERBERT, management consultant; b. Harrow, Middlesex, Eng., Nov. 10, 1935; s. Herbert and Muriel Jessie (Nicolls) R.; came to U.S., 1962; BA, Bristol U. (Eng.), 1958; Certificate of Indsl. Adminstrn., Glasgow U., 1962; MBA, Harvard U., 1964. Purchasing officer Pirelli Ltd., London, 1958-61; rsch. assoc. Assn. for Internat. Rsch., Inc., Cambridge, Mass., 1964-68, v.p., dir., 1968—, cons. in expatriate compensation, 1964—; lectr. in field, dir. U. Bristol Found., Inc. Served with Royal Navy, 1953-55. Mem. Am. Compensation Assn., Inst. for Human Resources, Brit. Inst. Mgmt. Club: Harvard. Contbr. articles to profl. jours. Home: 11 Berkeley Pl Cambridge MA 02138-3411 Office: care AirInc 1100 Massachusetts Ave Cambridge MA 02138-5241

ROWLEY, GLENN HARRY, lawyer; b. Hyannis, Mass., May 16, 1948; s. Harold Frederick and Olive Nellie (Jones) R.; 1 child, Brewster Westgate. BBA, U. Mass., 1970; JD with cum laude, Western New Eng. Coll., 1980. Bar: Mass. 1980, U.S. Dist. Ct. Mass. 1981, U.S. Tax Ct. 1981; cert. elder law atty. Nat. Elder Law Found./ABA. Staff mem. Cape Cod Planning and Econ. Devel. Commn., Barnstable, Mass., 1975-76; staff, estate planning tax dept. Coopers and Lybrand, Springfield, Mass., 1980-81; legal assoc. Roberts and Farrell, West Chatham, Mass., 1982-84; ptnr. Roberts, Farrell & Rowley, West Chatham, 1984—; cons. Local Citizen Scholarship Trusts, Harwich and Chatham, Mass., 1985—. Contbr.: (weekly news column) The Cape Codder, The Enterprise, The Register, others.; contbr. articles to profl. jours. Founding mem. Brewster (Mass.) Conservation Trust, 1984; past elected mem. Brewster Hist. Dist. Com., 1975; mem. adv. bd. The May Inst., The Cape Cod Writers Ctr., Inc. With USN, 1971-74, Iceland. Recipient Am. Jurisprudence awards Lawyers Co-op. Pub. Co., 1978, 79. Mem. Mass. Bar Assn., Ocean Edge Exec. Club, Profl. Writers of Cape Cod, Cape Cod Estate Planning Coun., Nat. Acad. Elder Law Attys., Phi Delta Phi. Avocations: travel, writing. Home: Annaniases Knoll/Sheep Pond Brewster MA 02631 Office: Roberts Farrell & Rowley The Marketplace 26 George Ryder Rd S West Chatham MA 02669

ROWLEY, JANET DAVISON, physician; b. N.Y.C., Apr. 5, 1925; d. Hurford Henry and Ethel Mary (Ballantyne) Davison; m. Donald A. Rowley, Dec. 18, 1948; children: Donald, David, Robert, Roger. PhB, U. Chgo., 1944, BS, 1946, MD, 1948; DSc (hon.), U. Ariz., 1989, U. Pa., 1989, Knox Coll., 1991, U. So. Calif., 1992, St. Louis U., 1997. Cert. Am. Bd. Med. Genetics. Rsch. asst. U. Chgo., 1949-50; intern Marine Hosp., USPHS, Chgo., 1950-51; attending physician Infant Welfare and Prenatal Clinics Dept. Pub. Health, Montgomery County, Md., 1953-54; rsch. fellow Levinson Found., Cook County Hosp., Chgo., 1955-61; clin. instr. neurology U. Ill., Chgo., 1957-61; USPHS spl. trainee Radiobiology Lab. The Churchill Hosp., Oxford, Eng., 1961-62; rsch. assoc. dept. medicine and Argonne Cancer Rsch. Hosp. U. Chgo., 1962-69, assoc. prof. dept. medicine and Argonne Cancer Rsch. Hosp., 1969-77, prof. dept. medicine and Franklin McLean Meml. Rsch. Inst., 1977-84; Blum-Riese Disting. Svc. prof., dept. medicine and dept. molecular genetics and cell biology, 1984—; mem. Nat. Cancer Adv. Bd., 1979-84; bd. sci. counsellors Nat. Ctr. for Human Genome Rscg., NIH, 1994—, chmn., 1994—; Bernard Cohen Meml. lectr. U. Pa., 1993, Katherine D. McCormick Disting. lectr. Stanford U., 1994, Donald D. Van Slyke lectr. Brookhaven Nat. Lab., 1994, Hilary Koprowski lectr. Thomas Jefferson U., 1994, W. Jack Stuckey Jr. lectr. Tulane Career Ctr., 1996; Presdl. Symposium Am. Soc. Pediatric Hematology/Oncology, 1995; Brit. Jour. of Haematology Plenary lectr. Brit. Soc. Haematology, 1997; Peacock Meml. lectr. in pathology U. Tex. Southwestern Med. Sch., 1997; Casbie lectr. Royal Coll. Physicians and Surgeons Can., 1997. Co-founder, co-editor Genes, Chromosomes and Cancer; mem. editl. bds. Oncology Rsch., Cancer Genetics and Cytogenetics, Internat. Jour. Hematology, Genomics, Internat. Jour. Cancer, Leukemia; past mem. editorial bd. Blood, Cancer Rsch., Hematol. Oncology, Leukemia Rsch.; contbr. chpts. to books., articles to profl. jours. Mem. Bd. Sci. Counsellors, Nat. Inst. Dental Rsch., NIH, 1972-76, chmn., 1974-76; mem. Nat. Cancer Adv. Bd., Nat. Cancer Inst., 1979-84; mem. adv. com. Frederick Cancer Rsch. Facility, 1983-85; chmn. bd. scientific counsellors, Nat. Ctr. for Human Genome Rsch., NIH, 1994—; mem. adv. bd. Leukemia Soc. Am., 1979-84; mem. MIT Corp. vis. com. Dept. Applied Biol. Scis., 1983-86; mem. selection com. scholar award in Biomed. Sci., Lucille P. Markey Charitable Trust, 1984-87; trustee Adler Planetarium, Chgo., 1978—; bd. dirs. Am. Bd. Med. Genetics, 1982-83, Am. Bd. Human Genetics, 1985-88; bd. sci. coms. Meml. Sloan-Kettering Cancer Ctr., 1988-90; nat. adv. com. McDonnell Found. Program for Molecular Medicine in Cancer Rsch., 1988—; adv. com. Ency. Britannica U. Chgo., 1988-96; mem. adv. bd. Howard Hughes Med. Inst., 1989-94; adv. com. for career awards in biomed. scis. Burroughs Wellcome Fund, 1994—. Recipient First Kuwait Cancer prize, 1984, Esther Langer award Ann Langer Cancer Rsch. Found., 1983, A. Cressy Morrison award in natural scis. N.Y. Acad. Scis., 1985, Past State Pres. award Tex. Fedn. Bus. and Profl. Women's Clubs, 1986, Karnofsky award and lecture Am.Soc. Clin. Oncology, 1987, prix Antoine Lacassagne Lique Nationale Francaise Contre le Cancer, 1987, King Faisal Internat. prize in medicine (co-recipient), 1988, Katherine Berkan Judd award Meml. Sloan-Kettering Cancer Ctr., 1989, (co-recipient) Charles Mott prize GM Cancer Rsch. Found., 1989, Steven C. Beering award U. Ind. Med. Sch., 1992, Robert de Villiers award Leukemia Soc. Am., 1993, Kaplan Family prize for cancer rsch. excellence Oncology Soc. Dayton, 1995, Cotlove award and lecture Acad. Clin. Lab. Physicians and Scientists, 1995, Nilsson-Ehle lecture Mendelian Soc. and Royal Physiographic Soc., U. Lund, 1995, The Gairdner Found. award, 1996; medal of honor Basic Sci. Am. Cancer Soc., 1996. Mem. NAS (chmn. sect. 41 1995—), Am. Acad. Arts and Scis., Am. Philos. Soc., Am. Soc. Human Genetics (pres.-elect 1992, pres. 1993, Allen award and lectr. 1991), Genetical Soc. (Gt. Britain), Am. Soc. Hematology (Presdl. Symposium 1982, Dameshek prize 1982, Ham-Wasserman award 1995), Am. Assn. Cancer Rsch. (G.H.A. Clowes Meml. award 1989), Inst. Medicine (coun. 1988-90), Sigma Xi (William Proctor prize for sci. achievement 1989), Alpha Omega Alpha Alumnus. Episcopalian. Home: 5310 S University Ave Chicago IL 60615-5106 Office: U Chgo 5841 S Maryland Ave # 2115 Chicago IL 60637-1463

ROWLEY, PETER TEMPLETON, physician, educator; b. Greenville, Pa., Apr. 29, 1929; s. George Hardy and Susan Mossman (Templeton) R.; m. Carol Stone, Mar. 19, 1967; children: Derek Stone, Jason Templeton. AB magna cum laude, Harvard U., 1951; MD, Columbia U., 1955. Diplomate: Am. Bd. Internal Medicine. Intern med. service N.Y. Hosp.-Cornell Med. Center, 1955-56; clin. assoc. Nat. Inst. Neurol. Disease and Blindness, NIH, 1956-58; asst. resident, then resident Harvard Med. Service, Boston City Hosp.; asst. in medicine Harvard U. Med. Sch. and researcher Thorndike Meml. Lab., 1958-60; hon. research asst. dept. eugenics, biometry and genetics Univ. Coll., U. London, 1960-61; postdoctoral fellow dept. microbiology NYU Sch. Medicine, 1961-63; asst. prof. medicine Stanford U., 1963-70; assoc. prof. medicine pediatrics and genetics U. Rochester, 1970-75, prof. medicine, pediatrics, genetics and microbiology, 1975—, prof. oncology, 1991—, chmn. div. genetics, 1990—; physician, pediatrician Strong Meml. Hosp., 1970—; mem. N.Y. State Exec. and Adv. Coms. on Genetic Disease, 1979—; WHO vis. scholar Inst. Biol. Chemistry, U. Ferrara, Italy, 1970. Editor: (with M. Lipkin Jr.) Genetic Responsibility: On Choosing Our Children's Genes, 1974. With USPHS, 1956-58. Recipient Excellence in Teaching award U. Rochester Class of 1976, 1973; NRC fellow, 1960-63;

Buswell research fellow, 1970-71, 71-72. Fellow ACP, Am. Coll. Genetics; mem. Am. Fedn. Clin. Rsch., Am. Soc. Hematology, Am. Soc. Human Genetics (social issues com. 1980-89, program com. 1993-96). Office: U Rochester Med Sch Div Genetics PO Box 641 601 Elmwood Ave Rochester NY 14642-0001

ROWLEY, ROBERT DEANE, JR., bishop; b. Cumberland, Md., July 6, 1941; s. Robert Deane Sr. and Alice Marquerite (Wilson) W.; m. Nancy Ann Roland, June 27, 1964; children: Karen Gordon Rowley Butler, Robert Deane III. BA, U. Pitts., 1962, LLB, 1965; LLM, George Washington U., 1970; MDiv, Episcopal Sem. of S.W., 1977, DD (hon.), 1989. Ordained deacon Episcopal Ch., 1977; priest, 1978; bishop, 1989. Bar: Pa. 1965, U.S. Supreme Ct. 1970. Dean of students St. Andrew's Priory Sch., Honolulu, 1977-80; canon St. Andrew's Cathedral, Honolulu, 1979-81; rector St. Timothy's Episcopal Ch., Aiea, Hawaii, 1981-83; canon to bishop Diocese of Bethlehem (Pa.), 1983-89; bishop Diocese of Northwestern Pa., Erie, 1989—; pres. 3rd prov., 1993—. Capt. USN, 1966-92. Mem. Erie County Bar Assn., Erie Club, Lake Shore Country Club. Home: 810 Huntington Dr Erie PA 16505-1087 Office: Diocese of Northwestern Pa 145 W 6th St Erie PA 16501-1001

ROWLEY, WILLIAM ROBERT, surgeon; b. Omaha, June 7, 1943; s. Robert Kuhlmeyer and Dorothy Eleanor (Larson) R.; m. Eileen Ruth Murray, Aug. 11, 1968; children: Bill II, Jeff, Jill. BA in Psychology, U. Minn., 1966, MD, 1970. Diplomate Am. Bd. Surgery. Commd. lt. USN, 1972, advanced through grades to rear admiral, 1994; intern U. Calif., San Diego, 1970-71, gen. surgery resident, 1971-72; gen. surgery resident Naval Regional Med. Ctr., Phila., 1973-76; peripheral vascular surgery fellow Naval Regional Med. Ctr., San Diego, 1977-78; staff surgeon Naval Regional Med. Ctr., Phila., 1977; staff vascular surgeon Naval Regional Med. Ctr., San Diego, 1978-85, chmn. dept. surgery, 1985-88, dir. surg. svcs., 1987-88; asst. chief of staff for plans and ops. Naval Med. Command S.W. Region, San Diego, 1988-89; dep. comdr. Nat. Naval Med. Ctr., Bethesda, Md., 1989-91; comdg. officer Naval Hospital, Camp Pendleton, Calif., 1991-93; dep. asst. chief for health care ops. Navy Bur. of Medicine and Surgery, Washington, 1993-94, asst. chief for plans, analysis and evaluation, 1994-95; commdr. Naval Med. Ctr., Portsmouth, Va., 1995—; program dir. vascular surgery fellowship Naval Hosp., San Diego, 1980-85, gen. surgery residency, 1985-89; assoc. prof. surgery Uniformed Svcs. U. for Health Scis., Bethesda, 1985—. Fellow ACS; mem. AMA, Am. Coll. Physician Execs., Am. Coll. Healthcare Execs. Avocations: backpacking, boating. Home: 580 Williamson Dr Portsmouth VA 23704 Office: Naval Med Ctr 620 John Paul Jones Cir Portsmouth VA 23708-2111

ROWLINGSON, JOHN CLYDE, anesthesiologist, educator, physician; b. Syracuse, N.Y., Aug. 3, 1948; s. John Winthrop and Genevieve Estelle (Mahan) R.; m. Rosemary Colette Laney, Oct. 26, 1974 (div. 1992); children: Kristen, Andrew. BS, Allegheny Coll., 1970; MD, SUNY, Buffalo, 1974. Intern Millard Fillmore Hosp., Buffalo, 1974-75; resident in anesthesiology U. Va., Charlottesville, 1975-77; fellow in anesthesia pain mgmt. U. Va. Med. Ctr., 1977-78; asst. prof. anesthesiology U. Va. Sch. Medicine, Charlottesville, 1978-82, assoc. prof., 1982-86, prof., 1986—, tenured prof., 1995—; assoc. dir. Pain Mgmt. Ctr., U. Va. Health Sci. Ctr., 1978-79, dir., 1980—. Author: Regional Anesthesia, 1984; co-editor: Handbook of Critical Care Pain Management, 1993. Nat. Inst. Handicapped Rsch. fellow, 1983-87, Pain fellow 1977-78. Felllow Am. Coll. Anesthesiology; mem. Am. Soc. Anesthesiologists, Am. Soc. Regional Anesthesia (rsch. grantee 1977, pres. 1996-97), Am. Pain Soc., Internat. Assn. Study of Pain, Am. Acad. Pain Medicine (editl. bd. Anesthesia Analg 1996—). Methodist. Avocations: running, tennis, skiing, biking. Home: 1255 Hunters Ridge Ln Earlysville VA 22936-9571 Office: U Va Health Sci Ctr Anesthesiology PO Box 10010 Charlottesville VA 22906-0010

ROWSON, RICHARD CAVANAGH, publisher; b. Hollywood, Calif., Apr. 7, 1926; s. Louis Cavanagh and Mable Louise (Montney) R.; m. Elena Louisa Costabile, Nov. 22, 1952; children: Peter Cavanagh, John Cummings. A.B., U. Calif., Berkeley, 1946; certificate, Sorbonne, 1949; M.I.A., Columbia U., 1950. Trainee Fgn. Policy Assn., 1950; dir. World Affairs Council R.I., 1951-52; with Fgn. Policy Assn., 1951-62, dir. finance and devel., 1960-62; with Radio Free Europe, 1962-69, dir. policy and planning, 1964-69; dir. spl. studies Praeger Pubs., Inc., N.Y.C., 1969-77; pres. Praeger Pubs., Inc., 1975-77, Pergamon Press, 1977-80, R.R. Bowker, 1980; info. and pub. cons., 1981; dir. Duke U. Press, 1981-90, sr. cons. editor, 1990-91; dir. Am. U. Press, 1989-91, cons. acquisitions, 1992-94, cons. pub., dir., 1994—; pub. Woodrow Wilson Ctr. Press, 1992-93; pub. cons., lectr., condr. workshops in field. Contbr. articles to profl. jours. Served to lt. (j.g.) USNR, 1944-47. Mem. Am. Assn. Advancement Slavic Studies, N.Y. Acad. Scis., Soc. for Scholarly Pub., U. Calif. Alumni Assn., Columbia U. Alumni Assn., Pomona Coll. Alumni Assn., Overseas Press Club. Democrat.$Dlubs: Century Assn., Overseas Press (N.Y.C.). Home: 4701 Connecticut Ave NW Washington DC 20008-5630 also: Am U Press Bender Libr 4400 Massachusetts Ave NW Washington DC 20016-8001

ROXIN, EMILIO OSCAR, mathematics educator; b. Buenos Aires, Apr. 6, 1922; came to U.S., 1960; s. Emil Karl and Ullranda Hildegard (Loebel) R.; m. Gudrun D. Kappus, 1962 (div. 1983); children: Ursula R., Walter E. Diploma in engring., U. Buenos Aires, 1947, PhD in Math., 1958. Mem. faculty U. Buenos Aires, 1947-62; researcher Rsch. Inst. Advanced Study, Balt., 1960-64; prof. math. U. R.I., Kingston, 1960-92, prof. emeritus, 1992—; researcher, AEC of Argentina, Buenos Aires, 1956-59. Author: Differential Equations, 1972, Control Theory and its Applications, 1996; contbr. to sci. publs. Mem. Am. Math. Soc., Math. Assn. Am., Soc. Indsl. and Applied Math., Union Math. Argentina, AAAS. Home: 31 Nichols Rd Kingston RI 02881-1803 Office: U RI Dept Math Kingston RI 02881

ROY, CATHERINE ELIZABETH, physical therapist; b. Tucson, Jan. 16, 1948; d. Francis Albert and Dorothy Orme (Thomas) R.; m. Richard M. Johnson, Aug. 31, 1968 (div. 1978); children: Kimberly Anne, Troy Michael. BA in Social Sci. magna cum laude, San Diego State U., 1980; MS in Phys. Therapy, U. So. Calif., 1984. Staff therapist Sharp Meml. Hosp., San Diego, 1984-89, chairperson patient and family edn. com., 1986-87, chairperson sex edn. and counselling com., 1987-89, chairperson adv. bd. for phys. therapy, asst. for edn. program, 1987-89; mgr. rehab. phys. therapy San Diego Rehab. Inst., Alvarado Hosp., 1989-91; dir. therapeutic svcs. VA Med. Ctr., San Diego, 1991—; lectr. patient edn., family edn., peer edn.; mem. curriculum rev. com. U. So. Calif. Phys. Therapy Dept., 1982; bd. dirs. Ctr. for Edn. in Health; writer, reviewer licensure examination items for phys. therapy Profl. Examination Services.. Tennis coach at clinics Rancho Penasquitos Swim and Tennis Club, San Diego, 1980-81; active Polit. Activities Network, 1985; counselor EEO, 1992-95. Mem. Am. Phys. Therapy Assn. (rsch. presenter nat. conf. 1985, del. nat. conf. 1986-94, rep. state conf. 1987-89, 92-94, Mary McMillan student award 1984, mem. exec. bd. San Diego dist. 1985-88, 92-94), AAUW, NAFE, Am. Congress Rehab. Medicine, Phi Beta Kappa, Phi Kappa Phi, Chi Omega. Avocations: tennis, reading, piano, travel, puzzles. Home: 6086 Coleman Creek Rd Medford OR 97501

ROY, CHUNILAL, psychiatrist; b. Digboi, India, Jan. 1, 1935; came to Can., 1967, naturalized, 1975; s. Atikay Bandhu and Nirupama (Devi) R.; m. Elizabeth Ainscow, Apr. 15, 1967; children: Nicholas, Phillip, Charles. MB, BS, Calcutta Med. Coll., India, 1959; diploma in psychol. medicine, Kings Coll., Newcastle-upon-Tyne, Eng., 1963. Intern Middlesborough Gen. Hosp., Eng., 1960-61; jr. hosp. officer St. Luke's Hosp., Middlesborough, Eng., 1961-64, sr. registrar, 1964; sr. hosp. med. officer Parkside Hosp., Macclesfield, Eng., 1964-66; sr. registrar Moorehaven Hosp., Ivybridge, Eng., 1966; reader, head dept. psychiatry Maulana Azad Med. Coll., New Delhi, 1966; sr. med. officer Republic of Ireland, County Louth, 1966; sr. psychiatrist Sask. Dept. Psychiat. Services, Can., 1967-68; regional dir. Swift Current, Can., 1968-71; practice medicine specializing in psychiatry Regina, Sask., Can., 1971-72; founding dir., med. dir. Regional Psychiat. Ctr., Abbotsford, B.C., Can., 1972-82; with dept. psychiatry Vancouver Gen. Hosp., 1987—; cons. to prison adminstrs.; hon. lectr. psychology and clin. prof. dept. psychiatry U. B.C.; ex-officio mem. Nat. Adv. Com. on Health Care of Prisoners in Can.; cons. psychiatrist Vancouver Hosp.; advisor Asian chpt. Psychosomatic Medicine, World Congress of Law and Medicine, New Delhi, 1985. Author: (with D.J. West and F.L. Nichols) Understanding Sexual Attacks, 1978; co-author: Oath of Athens, 1979; ; assoc. editor Internat. Jour. Offender Therapy and Comparative Criminology, 1978—; field editor Jour. of Medicine and Law; corr. editor Internat. Jour. Medicine; mem. bd. Internat. Law Medicine, 1979—; mem. editl. rev. bd. Evaluation, 1977—; contbr. articles to profl. jours. Recipient merit awards Dept. Health, Republic of Ireland, 1966, Can. Penitentiary Svc., 1974, Correctional Svcs. Can., 1983, citation by pres. U. B.C., 1983, Lahenf. Scuagstrand Found. prize, Holland, 1995; knighted by Order of St. John Ecumenical Found., 1993; hon. consul of Burkina Faso, 1997. Fellow Royal Coll. Psychiatry (Can.), Royal Coll. Psychiatry (Eng.), Pacific Rim Coll. Psychiatrists (founder); mem. World Psychiat. Assn. (sec., vice chmn. forensic psychiatry 1983), World Fedn. Mental Health, Internat. Coun. Prison Med. Svcs. (founding sec.-gen. 1977), Can. Med. Assn., Can. Psychiat. Assn., Amnesty Internat., Internat. Acad. Legal Medicine and Social Medicine, Indian Psychiat. Assn. (life), Can. Assn. Profl. Treatment Offenders (founding dir. 1975), Assn. Physicians and Surgeons Who Work in Can. Prisons (founding pres. 1974), Internat. Found. for Tng. in Penitentiary Medicine and Forensic Psychiatry (founding pres. 1980, vice chmn., sec.), World Psychiatry Assn., Australian Acad. Forensic Sci. (corr.), Can. Physicians Interested in South Asia (v.p. 1989, pres. 1990), Internat. Coll. Psychosomatic Medicine (adv. Asian chpt.), Internat. Conf. on Health, Culture and Contemporary Soc. (chief advisor Bombay 1989, v.p. 1989, pres. 1990), Internat. Coun. Penitentiary Medicine (founding sec., bd. dirs.), World Psyciat. Assn. (vice chmn. forensic psychiat. sect. 1989), World Assn. Health, Culture and Environ. (sec.-gen. 1995, award 1995), Order of St. John (knight 1992), Vancouver MultiCultural Soc. (bd. dirs. 1992-93), B.C. Psychiat. Assn. (pres. 1995-96). Home: 2439 Trinity St, Vancouver, BC Canada V5K 1C9 Office: 1417-750 W Broadway, Vancouver, BC Canada V5Z 1J4

ROY, CLARENCE LESLIE, landscape architect; b. Ironwood, Mich., Mar. 6, 1927; s. Theodore Gideon and Myrtle May (Mathews) R.; m. Ruth Serou, Nov. 11, 1959. B.S. in Landscape Architecture, U. Mich., 1951. Landscape architect Lambert Assoc. Cos., Dallas, 1951-59; assoc. Eichstedt-Johnson Assoc., Grosse Pointe, Mich., 1960; prin. Johnson Johnson & Roy/inc., Ann Arbor, Mich., 1961-81, Dallas, 1982-92, ret.; dir. The Smith Group, Detroit, 1979-82. Founder Old West Assn., Ann Arbor, 1966, pres., 1968-73; pres. Ann Arbor Tomorrow, 1978-79. Served with USN, 1945-46. Fellow Am. Soc. Landscape Architects; mem. Am. Planners Assn., U. Mich. Alumni Assn. (bd. dirs. 1976-79), Tau Sigma Delta, Alpha Rho Chi. Home: 4039 Travis St Dallas TX 75204

ROY, DAVID TOD, Chinese literature educator; b. Nanking, China, Apr. 5, 1933; s. Andrew Tod and Margaret (Crutchfield) R.; m. Barbara Jean Chew, Feb. 4, 1967. AB, Harvard U., 1958, AM, 1960, PhD, 1965. Asst. prof. Princeton U., 1963-67; assoc. prof. U. Chgo., 1967-73, prof., 1973—, chmn. com. on Far Eastern Studies, 1968-70, chmn. dept. Far Eastern Langs. and Civilizations, 1972-75. Author: Kuo Mo-jo: The Early Years, 1971; contbr.: How to Read the Chinese Novel, 1990; co-editor: Ancient China: Studies in Early Civilization, 1978; translator: The Plum in the Golden Vase or Chin P'ing Mei, 1993. Served with U.S. Army, 1954-56. Ford Found. fellow, 1958-60, Jr. fellow Harvard Soc. Fellows, 1960-63, fellow Fulbright-Hays Commn., 1967, Chgo. Humanities Inst. fellow, 1994-95; grantee Am. Coun. Learned Socs., 1976-77, NEH, 1983-86, 95-96. Mem. Am. Oriental Soc., Assn. for Asian Studies. Democrat. Club: Quadrangle (Chgo.). Home: 5443 S Cornell Ave Chicago IL 60615-5603 Office: U Chgo 1050 E 59th St Chicago IL 60637-1512

ROY, ELMON HAROLD, minister; b. Russell Springs, Ky., Dec. 17, 1924; s. Leslie C. and Olza (Gosser) R.; m. Retha Adkins; children: Joel, Michael. BA in Theology, So. Missionary Coll., 1953; MA, Belin U., 1958, Spalding U., 1970; PhD in Theology, Pacific We. U., 1966; postgraduate, Andrews Theol. Seminary, 1959; LLD, Coll. St. Thomas, 1982. Ordained to ministry, 1950. Assoc. pastor Bucyrus, Ohio, 1955-56, Akron, Ohio, 1956-57; pastor East Liverpool, Ohio, 1957-60, Coudersport, Pa., 1960-64, Huntsville, Ala., 1964-65, Louisville, Ky., 1965-71; chaplain Pleasant Grove Hosp., Louisville, Ky., 1965-71; pastor Springfield, Ohio, 1975-85, Wooster, Ohio, 1985-88; chaplain Louisville, Ky., 1989—; cons. religious liberty, 1983-88; chaplain Jefferson County Ct. Author: In Remembrance of Redemption, 1996, Courage for Hospital Days 1973, Earth's Coming Events, 1968, Israel's Early Leaders, 1984, Moments of Meditation, 1975, The Word for These Times, 1988, Morning is Coming, 1989, Something to Live By, 1958, Prescription for Personal Peace, 1995, Decisions Determine Destiny, 1994; contbr. numerous articles to mags. Pres. South Oldham Ch. Coun., 1971-72; mem. Ohio conf. bd. edn., 1985-88. With USN, 1943-46. Recipient Outstanding Cmty. Svc. award Pleasant Grove Hosp., Commrs. Commendation award Wayne County, Ohio Senate Commendation award, Gov.'s Outstanding Kentuckian award; decorated six battle stars, knight Sovereign Order of St. John of Jerusalem, Knights of Malta, Hospitallers, comdr. Star of Peace Fedn. des Combattants En Europe, Tenn. Col., Ky. Adm., Croix De Guerre, Cross of Valor, Royal Afghanistan Order of Crown of Amanullah, Order of Polonia Restituta; named hon. citizen of Tenn., hon. sheriff Clark County, Ohio, hon. Ky. Sec. of State, Ky. Amb.; named to Order Ky. Cols. Fellow Philos. Soc. Gt. Britain, Huguenot Soc., Royal Soc. Arts; mem. SAR (chaplain Louisville-Thruston chpt. 1974-75), Am. Acad. Religion, Ky. Hist. Soc., Order Founders and Patriots of Am., East Liverpool Ministerial Assn. (sec., treas. 1960), Coudersport Ministerial Assn. (v.p. 1971-72), Soc. Ky. Pioneers. Address: 2417 W Highway 22 Crestwood KY 40014-9481

ROY, ELSIJANE TRIMBLE, federal judge; b. Lonoke, Ark., Apr. 2, 1916; d. Thomas Clark and Elsie Jane (Walls) Trimble; m. James M. Roy, Nov. 23, 1943; 1 son, James Morrison. JD, U. Ark., Fayetteville, 1939; LLD (hon.), U. Ark., Little Rock, 1978. Bar: Ark. 1939. Atty. Rose, Loughborough, Dobyns & House, Little Rock, 1940-41, Ark. Revenue Dept., Little Rock, 1941-42; mem. firm Reid, Evrard & Roy, Blytheville, Ark., 1945-54, Roy & Roy, Blytheville, 1954-63; law clk. Ark. Supreme Ct., Little Rock, 1963-65; assoc. justice Ark. Supreme Ct., 1975-77; U.S. dist. judge then sr. judge Ea. and We. Dists. Ark., Little Rock, 1977—; judge Pulaski County (Ark.) Cir. Ct., Little Rock, 1966; asst. atty. gen. Ark., Little Rock, 1967; sr. law clk. U.S. Dist. Ct., Little Rock and Ft. Smith, 1967-75; Mem. med. adv. com. U. Ark. Med. Center, 1952-54; Committeewoman Democratic Party 16th Jud. Dist., 1940-42; vice chmn. Ark. Dem. State Com., 1946-48; mem. chmn. com. Ark. Constnl. Commn., 1967-68. Recipient disting. alumnae citation U. Ark., 1978, Gayle Pettus Pontz award, 1986, Brooks Hays Meml. Christian Citizenship award, 1994; named Ark. woman of yr., Bus. and Profl. Women's Club, 1969, 76, outstanding appellate judge, Ark. Trial Lawyers Assn., 1976-77, Delta Theta Phi mem. of yr. 1989; named among top 100 women in Ark. bus., 1995; Paul Harris fellow Rotary Club Little Rock, 1992. Recipient disting. alumnae citation U. Ark., 1978, Gayle Pettus Pontz award, 1986, Brooks Hays Meml. Christian Citizenship award, 1994; named Ark. Woman of Yr., Bus. and Profl. Women's Club, 1969, 76, Outstanding Appellate Judge, Ark. Trial Lawyers Assn., 1976-77, Mem. of Yr., Delta Theta Phi, 1989; named among top 100 women in Ark. bus., 1995, Ark. Bus. Top 100 Women in Ark., 1995; Paul Harris fellow Rotary Little Rock, 1992. Office: US Dist Ct 600 W Capitol Ave Ste 423 Little Rock AR 72201-3326

ROY, J(AMES) STAPLETON, ambassador; b. Nanking, China, June 16, 1935; s. Andrew Tod and Margaret (Crutchfield) R.; m. Elissandra Nicole Fiore, Jan. 27, 1968; children—Andrew, David, Anthony. B.A. magna cum laude, Princeton U., 1956; postgrad., U. Wash., 1964-65, Nat. War Coll., 1974-75. Dep. dir. Office of Soviet Union Affairs Dept. of State, Washington, 1972-74, dep. dir. Office of Chinese Affairs, 1975-78; minister counselor U.S. Embassy, Beijing, Peoples Republic of China, 1978-81, Bangkok, Thailand, 1981-84; U.S. amb. to Singapore, 1984-86; dep. asst. sec. Bur. East Asian and Pacific Affairs Dept. of State, 1986-89, spl. asst. to sec. and exec. sec., 1989-91; U.S. amb. to People's Republic of China Beijing, 1991-95; U.S. amb. to Indonesia, 1995—. Recipient Presdl. Meritorious Service award Pres. of U.S., 1983, 88, 90, Superior Honor award Dept. of State, 1977, 80. Mem. Am. Fgn. Svc. Assn., Phi Beta Kappa. Avocations: swimming; jogging; chess; computers. Office: US Embassy, Jl Medan Merdeka Selatan 5, Jakarta 10110, Indonesia

ROY, KENNETH RUSSELL, educator; b. Hartford, Conn., Mar. 29, 1946; s. Russell George and Irene Mary (Birkowski) R.; BS, Central Conn. State Coll., New Britain, 1968, MS, 1974; 6th yr. degree in profl. edn. U. Conn., 1981, Ph.D., 1985; m. Marisa Anne Russo, Jan. 27, 1968; children: Lisa Marie, Louise Irene. Tchr. sci. Rocky Hill (Conn.) High Sch., 1968-73, N.W. Cath. High Sch., West Hartford, Conn., 1973-74; sci. and math. coord. Bolton (Conn.) High Sch., 1974-78; chmn. scis. Bacon Acad., Colchester, Conn., 1978-81; K-12 dir. sci. and safety Glastonbury (Conn.) Pub. Schs., 1981—; pres. Nat. Safety Cons.; mem. adj. faculty Manchester C.C., 1976-90, Tunxis C.C., 1975-90; instr. U. Conn. Coop. Program, 1974-78; cons./adv. Project Rise, 1978-81; lectr., sci. curriculum cons. various Conn. sch. dists.; nat. dir. Nat. Sci. Suprs. Assn., 1988-91, exec. dir. Leadership Inst. Cen. Conn. State U., New Britain, 1989-91; exec. dir. Nat. Sci. Suprs. Assn., 1992-95; bd. dirs. Lab. Safety Workshop Nat. Ctr., 1995—, Conn. United for Rsch. Excellence, 1995—. Co-editor Conn. Jour. Sci. Edn., 1984-88; editor Sci. Leadership Trend Notes, 1989-91; contbr. articles to profl. jours. Mem. St. Christopher Sch. Bd., 1982-83. Recipient Disting. Educator's and Conn. Educator's awards Milken Family Found., 1989; named Tchr. of Yr., Colchester, 1980; NSF grantee, 1968, staff devel. grantee, 1979, 80, Nat. Sci. Supr. Leadership Conf. grantee, 1980. Mem. ASCD, AAAS, Am. Indsl. Hygiene Assn., Am. Soc. Safety Engrs., Nat. Sci. Tchrs. Assn., Nat. Sci. Suprs. Assn. (pres.-elect 1986-87, pres. 1987-88), Conn. Sci. Tchrs. Assn., Conn. Sci. Suprs. Assn. (pres. 1985-86), Conn. Assn. Profl. Devel., Conn. Assn. Supervision and Curriculum Devel., Glastonbury Adminstrs. and Suprs. Assn., Nat. Ctr. Improvement Sci. Teaching and Learning (mem. adv. bd. 1988-91), Internat. Council Assns. Sci. Edn. (nat. rep. 1987-88, N.Am. region rep. and exec. com. mem. 1989—), Phi Delta Kappa. Roman Catholic. Office: Glastonbury Pub Schs Glastonbury CT 06033

ROY, MELINDA, dancer; b. Lafayette, La.. Student, Sch. Am. Ballet. Mem. corps de ballet N.Y.C. Ballet, 1978—, soloist, 1984, prin., 1989—. Dancer in ballets including The Nutcracker, Symphony in C (third movement), Symphony in Three Movements, Apollo (polyhymnia), Brahms-Schoenberg Quartet (first movement), Who Cares, the rubies sect. of Jewels, Divertimento no. 15, Serenade, Western Symphony (first movement), Chaconne (fast pas de deux), Tschaikovsky suite no. 3 (Scherzo), Stars and Stripes, Tschaikovsky pas de Deux, Walpurgisnacht ballet, Golberg Variations, The Concert, Gershwin Concerto, Fanfare, Interplay, The Four Seasons (spring), The Unanswered Questions, Behind the China Dogs, The Waltz Project, Seven by Five, N.Y.C. Ballet's Balanchine Celebration, 1993; performed in Spain, Italy, Denmark, Eng., France, Germany, China, Japan. Office: NYC Ballet Inc NY State Theater Lincoln Ctr Plz New York NY 10023*

ROY, PATRICK, professional hockey player; b. Quebec City, Que., Can., Oct. 5, 1965. Goaltender Montreal Canadiens, 1984-95, Colo. Avalanche, 1995—; mem. Stanley Cup Championship teams, 1986, 93, 96. Recipient Conn Smythe trophy as playoff MVP, 1986, William M. Jennings trophy 1986-89, 91-92, Trico Goaltender award, 1988-89, 89-90, Georges Vezina trophy, 1988-89, 89-90, 91-92; named to NHL All-Rookie Team, 1985-86, NHL All-Star Second Team, 1987-88, 90-91, NHL All-Star First Team, 1988-89, 89-90, 91-92., Sporting News All-Star Team, 1988-89, 89-90, 91-92. Played in Stanley Cup Championships, 1986, 93. Office: Colo Avalanche 1635 Clay St Denver CO 80204-1743*

ROY, PAUL EMILE, JR., county official; b. Sumter, S.C., Dec. 18, 1942; s. Paul Emile and Harriette Orvilla (Sorenson) R.; m. Patricia Jane Stariha, July 2, 1977; 1 child, Jennifer Jo. AA, Grand Rapids Jr. Coll., 1963; student, Universidad de las Americas, Mexico City, 1963-64, Instituto Mexicano-Norteamericano de Relaciones Culturales, Mexico City, 1964-65; BA, Aquinas Coll., Grand Rapids, 1967; MA, U. Americas Escuela de Graduados, Mexico City, 1968; postgrad., U. Mich., 1977-79; MBA, Calif. Coast U., 1994. Asst. prin., instr. Spanish Muskegon (Mich.) Cath. Cen. High Sch., 1971-75; govt. offcl. County of Muskegon, 1975—, dir. employment and tng. Muskegon/Oceana Consortium, 1975-87, dir. employment and tng., 1988-95, dir. employment and tng. and facilities mgmt., 1995—; mem. Mich. Com. for Devel. of Romance Lang. Performance Objectives; adult edn. adv. com. Muskegon Pub. Schs.; appointee Mich. Youth Employment Coun.; v.p. regional adv. coun. U.S. Dept. Labor, 1981; mem. City of Muskegon Local Devel. Funding Authority, 1988—, Downtown Devel. Authority, 1988—, City of Whitehall (Mich.) Local Devel. Funding Authority, 1988—, Muskegon Econ. Growth Alliance Edn. Com.; cons. U.S. Dept. Labor, Washington, Mich. Dept. Labor, Lansing, Gov.'s Office Manpower, Ind., U. Mich., Ann Arbor, various pvt. cos., non-profit orgns. Campaign chmn. Muskegon County United Way, 1986-88, Pacesetter award, 1987. Mem. Am. Assn. Tchrs. Spanish and Portuguese, Mich. Assn. Tchrs. English as Second Lang., Mich. Assn. Employment and Tng. Dirs. (pres. 1980-81), Mich. Employment and Tng. Inst. (founding bd. dirs. 1980-81), Nat. Assn. Counties (employment steering com.), Nat. Assn. County Employment and Tng. Adminstrs. (nat. bd. dirs. 1979-80, nat. chmn. organizational resources com. 1981). Avocations: golf, travel, reading, theater. Office: Muskegon Cty Dept Employment & Tng 20 W Muskegon Ave Muskegon MI 49440-1317

ROY, RALPH LORD, clergyman; b. St. Albans, Vt., Sept. 30, 1928; s. Howard Allen and Olive Lydia (Corliss) R.; m. Margaret Ellen Finlay, Feb. 12, 1960 (dec.); 1 child, Joyce Victoria. BA, Swarthmore Coll., 1950; MA, Columbia U. and Union, Theol. Seminary, 1952. Ordained to ministry United Meth. Ch. as deacon, 1952, as elder, 1961. Asst. minister Met. Community United. Meth. Ch., N.Y.C., 1957-60; minister Grace United Meth. Ch., N.Y.C., 1960-63, Greene Ave./Knickerbocker United Meth. Ch., Bklyn., 1964-68, Cuyler Warren St. Community Ch., Bklyn., 1968-70, United Meth. Ch., Clinton, Conn., 1970-74, Mary Taylor United Meth. Ch., Milford, Conn., 1974-79, First United Meth. Ch., Meriden, Conn., 1979-94; pastor First United Meth. Ch., Thomaston, Conn., 1994—. Author: Apostles of Discord, 1953, Communism and the Churches, 1960; contbr. articles to profl. jours. Chaplain Meriden (Conn.) Police Dept., 1981-92. *When I consider the magnificence and vastness of the universe, I can be overwhelmed by childlike marvel. That's one key aspect of God's creation. Another is the almost infinite variety, complexity, and beauty of life on our planet, all of it interdependent, making it urgent that we dwell together in harmony, mutual respect and peace.*

ROY, RANJIT KUMAR, mechanical engineer; b. Barisal, E. Bengal, India, Jan. 1, 1947; came to U.S., 1968; s. Rajani and Kumundini (Baral) R.; m. Krishna Majumder, Apr. 25, 1970; children: Purba, Paula. Student, Khulna U., East Bengal, India, 1963; BSME, Regional Engring. Coll., Durgapur, India, 1968; MSME, U. Mo., Rolla, 1970, PhD, 1972. Registered profl. engr., Mich. Sr. engr. Burroughs Corp., Detroit, 1972-76; sr. project engr. GM, Warren, Mich., 1976-79; staff engr. Chevrolet Motors GM, Warren, Mcih., 1979-82, mgr. reliability CPC engring., 1982-87; cons., trainer Nutek Inc., Birmingham, Mich., 1987—; adj. prof. Oakland U., Rochester, Mich., 1976-87. Author: A Primer On The Taguchi Method, 1990; author computer software Qualitek-4, 1991. Pres. Bichitra Inc., Troy, 1980-82. Fellow Am. Soc. Quality Control (sr., v.p. profl. devel. 1987-88); mem. Soc. Automotive Engrs. Democrat. Hindu. Avocations: photography, computer programming, music, chess. Home: 3829 Quarton Rd Bloomfield Hills MI 48302-4059 Office: Nutek Inc Bingham Ctr 30600 Telegraph Rd Ste 2230 Franklin MI 48025-4532

ROY, RAYMOND, bishop; b. Man., Can., May 3, 1919; s. Charles-Borromé e and Zephirina (Milette) R. B.A. in Philosophy and Theology, U. Man., 1942; student, Philos. Sem., Montreal, 1942-43, Major Sem., Montreal, 1943-46, Major Sem. St. Boniface, 1946-47. Ordained priest Roman Catholic Ch. 1947. Asst. pastor, then pastor chs. in Man., 1947-50, 53-66; chaplain St. Boniface (Man.) Hosp., 1950-53; superior Minor Sem., St. Boniface, 1966-69; pastor Cathedral Parish, St. Boniface, 1969-72; ordained bishop, 1972; bishop of St. Paul, Alta., Can., 1972—. Club: K.C. Address: 4410 51st Ave Box 339, Saint Paul, AB Canada T0A 3A0*

ROY, RAYMOND CLYDE, anesthesiologist; b. 1944. PhD in Chemistry, Duke U., 1971; MD, Tulane U., 1974. Resident Hosp. U. Pa.; prof., chair dept. anesthesia & perioperative medicine Med. U. S.C., 1996; prof., chmn. dept. anesthesiology U. Vir. Med. Ctr., Charlottesville, 1996—; dir. Am. Bd. Anesthesiology. Office: U Va Med Ctr Dept Anesthesiology PO Box 10010 Charlottesville VA 22906-0010*

ROY, ROB J., biomedical engineer, anesthesiologist; b. Bklyn., Jan. 2, 1933; m. Carole Ann Webb, Aug. 1, 1959 (div.); children: Robert Bruce, David John, Bruce Glenn; m. Judith Anne Roy, Oct. 6, 1996. BSEE, Cooper

Union, N.Y.C., 1954; MSEE, Columbia U., 1956; DEngSc, Rensselaer Poly. Inst., 1962; MD, Albany (N.Y.) Med. Coll., 1976. Profl. engr., N.Y.; diplomate Am. Bd. Anesthesiology. Prof. elec. engrin. dept. Rensselaer Poly. Inst., Troy, N.Y., 1962, prof. elec. engring. dept., 1980—, head biomed. engring. dept., 1985-94; prof. anesthesiology Albany (N.Y.) Med. Ctr., 1979—. Author: State Variables for Engineers, 1965; author 150 papers in field. Sr. mem. IEEE; mem. Am. Soc. Anesthesiologists, Sigma Xi. Home: 565 Highwood Cir Albany NY 12203 Office: Albany Med Ctr Dept Anesthesiology 47 New Scotland Ave Albany NY 12208-3412

ROY, ROBERT RUSSELL, toxicologist; b. Mpls., Sept. 14, 1957; s. Rudolph Russell and Arlene Charlotte (Miller) R.; m. Barbara Jane Richie, Oct. 10, 1987; children: Andrew, Katherine. BA cum laude, Augsburg Coll., 1980; MS, U. Minn., 1986, PhD, 1989. Bd. cert. in toxicology. Rsch. asst. U. Minn., Mpls., 1986-88; toxicologist, project mgr. Pace Labs., Inc., Mpls., 1989-90; toxicologist Minn. Dept. Health, Mpls., 1990-93, Minn. Regional Poison Ctr., St. Paul, 1990-97; toxicology specialist 3M, St. Paul, 1997—; lectr. U. Minn., Mpls., 1986-90, Midwest Ctr. Occupl. Health and Safety, St. Paul, 1990—, instr., 1989; clin. asst. prof. U. Minn., 1993—; mem. grad. faculty in toxicology U. Minn.; adj. asst. prof. emergency medicine Oreg. Health Sci. U., Portland. Tutor Mpls. Pub. Schs., 1982; vol. U. Minn. Hosps., Mpls., 1983; mem. Waite Pk. Community Coun., Mpls., 1977-80, Mt. Carmel Luth. Ch. Coun., Mpls., 1983-85. Mem. Am. Coll. Toxicology, Soc. Toxicology, Am. Indsl. Hygiene Assn., Minn. Acad. Sci., Sigma Xi, Delta Omega. Home: 6201 Near Mountain Blvd Chanhassen MN 55317-9117 Office: 3M Toxicology Svcs 3M Center Bldg 220-2E-02 Saint Paul MN 55144-1000

ROY, ROBIN JENNIFER, educational fund raiser, marketing professional; b. N.Y.C., June 3, 1953; d. George Robert and Margaret (Snow) R.; m. Michael Katz, July 19, 1986; 1 child, Edward Alexander. AB, Smith Coll., 1975, MA, 1978; MBA, Columbia U., 1988. With Mus. of Fine Arts, Boston, 1979-80, N.Y. State Dept. of Commerce, 1980-81; pub. rel., advt. coord. No. Adirondack Planned Parenthood, Inc., Plattsburg, N.Y., 1981-83; dir. pub. rels., mktg. and devel. Gen. Hosp. of Saranac Lake, N.Y., 1982-84; coord. editorial and mktg. communications svcs. Presbyn. Hosp., N.Y.C., 1985-86; dir. devel. and alumni affairs, Sch. Nursing Columbia U., N.Y.C., 1989-92, dir. devel. Spence Sch., 1992-93, devel. specialist Coll. Physicians & Surgeons, 1993-95, assoc. dean devel. Sch. Pub. Health, 1995—. Adv. bd. Women at Risk, Presbyn. Hosp., N.Y. Mem. Coun. for the Advancement and Support of Edn., Nat. Soc. Fund Raising Execs., Alumnae Assn. of Smith Coll. (class spl. gifts chair 1980-85, class nominating com. 1990, class v.p. 1990-95). Office: Columbia U Sch Pub Health 600 W 168th St New York NY 10032-3702

ROY, ROLAND G., information systems executive; b. Norwich, Conn., Apr. 1, 1953; s. Joseph Paul and Ellenor Mae (Quinn) R. BA in Psychology, U. Conn., 1975, MS in Computer Sci., 1977; MBA in Fin., NYU, 1983. MIS mgr. Pepsico, Purchase, N.Y., 1977-81; pres. Roy-Josephs Assocs., Purdys, N.Y., 1986—; v.p. MIS Fidelity Investments, Boston, 1986—. Chairperson program com. Fed. Hill House, Providence, 1991—. Roman Catholic. Avocations: softball, basketball, jogging, reading, photography.

ROY, RUSTUM, interdisciplinary materials researcher, educator; b. Ranchi, India, July 3, 1924; came to U.S., 1945, naturalized, 1961; s. Narendra Kumar and Rajkumari (Mukherjee) R.; m. Della M. Martin, June 8, 1948; children: Neill, Ronnen, Jeremy. BS, Patna (India) U., 1942; MS, Patna (India) U., India, 1944; Ph.D., Pa. State U., 1948; DSc (hon.), Tokyo Inst. Tech., 1987, Alfred U, 1993. Research asst. Pa. State U., 1948-49, mem. faculty, 1950—, prof. geochemistry, 1957—, prof. solid state, 1968—, chmn. solid state tech. program, 1960-67, chmn. sci. tech. and soc. program, 1977-84, dir., 1984—, dir. materials research lab., 1962-85, Evan Pugh prof., 1981—; sr. sci. officer Nat. Ceramic Lab., India, 1950; mem. com. mineral sci. tech. Nat. Acad. Scis., 1967-69, com. survey materials sci. tech., 1970-74; exec. com. chem. div. NRC, 1967-70, nat. materials adv. bd., 1970-77, mem. com. radioactive waste mgmt., 1974-80, chmn. panel waste solidification, 1976-80; chmn. com. NRC, USSR and Eastern Europe, 1976-81; mem. com. material sci. and engring. NRC, 1986-89; mem. Pa. Gov.'s Sci. Adv. Com.; chmn. materials adv. panel Gov.'s Sci. Adv. Com., 1965; mem. adv. com. on engring. NSF, 1968-72, adv. com. to ethical and human value implications sci. and tech., 1974-76, adv. com. div. materials rsch., 1974-77; Hibbert lectr. U. London, 1979; bd. dirs. Kirkridge, Inc., Bangor, Pa.; cons. to industry; mem. adv. com. Coll. Engring., Stanford U., 1984-86. Author: Honest Sex, 1968, Crystal Chemistry of Non-metallic Materials, 1974, Experimenting with Truth, 1981, Radioactive Waste Disposal, Vol. 1, the Waste Package, 1983, Lost at the Frontier, 1985; also articles.; editor-in-chief: Materials Research Bull, 1966—, Bull. Sci. Tech. and Soc, 1981—. Chmn. bd. Dag Hammarskjold Coll., 1973-75; chmn. ad hoc com. sci., tech. and ch. Nat. Council Chs., 1966-68. Sci. policy fellow Brookings Instn., 1982-83. Fellow Indian Acad. Scis. (hon.); mem. AAAS (chmn. chemistry sect. 1985), NAE, Nat. Rsch. Coun. (internat. sci. lectr. 1991-92), Royal Swedish Acad. Engring. Scis. (fgn.), Indian Nat. Acad. Sci. (fgn.), Engring. Acad. Japan, Fedn. Materials Socs. (Nat. Materials Advancement award 1991), Ceramic Soc. Japan (Centennial award 1991, hon. mem. 1991), Mineral Soc. Am. (award 1957), Fine Ceramics Assn. Japan (Internat. award), Am. Chem. Soc. (Petroleum Rsch. Fund award 1960, Dupont award for Chem. of Materials 1993), Acad. Natural Scis. (chem. sect., elected fgn. mem. 1995), Am. Ceramic Soc. (Sosman lectr. 1975, Orton lectr. 1984, disting. life mem. 1993, Educator of Yr. 1993), Am. Soc. Engring. Educators (Centennial medal 1993, named to Hall of Fame 1993), Materials Rsch. Soc. (founder, pres. 1976). Home: 528 S Pugh St State College PA 16801-5312 Office: 102 Materials Rsch Lab University Park PA 16802 *My major responsibility to the increasingly unified world culture, as a scientist supported largely by the public, is to integrate into its emerging radically pluralist yet globally unifying Religion, the insights from Science and the impact of Technology on the human condition. As a Christian Radical Pluralist, I am committed to presenting to my fellow humans—expecially all non-scientists, from Presidents and CEOs to the person in the street—an accurate picture of the whole truth about my scientific "advances" and those of others—their limited and ambivalent nature and their relatively minor position in the sum total of human concerns.*

ROY, WILLIAM ROBERT, physician, lawyer, former congressman; b. Bloomington, Ill., Feb. 23, 1926; s. Elmer Javan and Edna Blanche (Foley) R.; m. Jane Twining Osterhoudt, Sept. 1947; children: Robin Jo, Randall Jay, Richelle Jane, William Robert, Renee Jan, Rise Javan. B.S., Ill. Wesleyan U., 1946; M.D., Northwestern U., 1949; J.D. with honors, Washburn U., 1970. Mem. 92d-93d congresses from 2d Dist. Kans.; dir. Sentry Ins.; Democratic candidate for U.S. Senate, 1974, 78. Mem. Inst. Medicine of Nat. Acad. Scis. Democrat. Methodist. Home: 6137 SW 38th Ter Topeka KS 66610-1307

ROYAL, DARRELL K., university official, former football coach; b. Hollis, Okla., July 6, 1924; s. Burley Ray and Katy Elizabeth (Harmon) R.; m. Edith Marie Thomason, July 26, 1944; children: Marian (Mrs. Abraham Kazen III) (dec.), Mack, David (dec.). B.S. in Bus, U. Okla., 1950. Former head football coach, then dir. athletics U. Tex., now asst. to univ. pres. Author: Darrell Royal Talks Football, 1963. Named Coach of Yr., Football Coaches Assn., 1963, 70, Tex. Sports Writers, 1961, 63, 69, 70, Southwesterner of Yr., 1961, 62, 63; named to U. Tex. Longhorn Hall of Fame, 1976, Tex. Sports Hall of Fame, 1976, Jim Thorpe Okla. Hall of Fame, 1977, Nat. Football Hall of Fame, 1983, Coach of Decade for 1960's, ABC; recipient Horatio Alger award, 1996; Darrell K. Royal Meml. Football Stadium, U. Tex. named in his honor, 1996. Mem. Delta Upsilon. Presbyterian. Office: SRH2.101 Univ Tex Austin TX 78712

ROYAL, HENRY DUVAL, nuclear medicine physician; b. Norwich, Conn., May 14, 1948. MD, St. Louis U., 1974. Diplomate Am. Bd. Internal Medicine; Am. Bd. Nuclear Medicine. Intern R.I. Hosp., Providence, 1974, resident in internal medicine, 1975-76; resident in nuclear medicine Harvard Med. Sch., Boston, 1977-79; assoc. Barnes Hosp., St. Louis, 1987—, Children's Hosp., St. Louis, 1987—, Jewish Hosp., St. Louis, 1993—; prof. Washington U., St. Louis, 1993—; co-team leader health effects sect. Internat. Atome Energy Agy. Internat. Chernobyl Project, 1990; bd. dirs. Am. Bd. Nuclear Medicine; mem. com. on assessment of CDC radiation studies NRC/NAS, 1993—; mem. sci. com. Nat. Coun. on Radiation Protection and Measurements, 1993—; mem. coun. Nat. Coun. on Radiation Protection, 1996—; adv. com. on environ. hazards VA, 1997—. Contbr. articles to profl. jours. Mem. Soc. Nuclear Medicine, Alpha Omega Alpha. Office: Acad Faculty Mallinkrodt Inst Radiology 510 S Kingshighway Blvd Saint Louis MO 63110-1016

ROYALTY, KENNETH MARVIN, lawyer; b. Cin., Nov. 1, 1940; s. Maurice K. and Frances G. (Budd) R.; div. 1991; children by previous marriages: Ted, Sara. BA, Ohio State U., 1962, JD summa cum laude, 1970. Bar: Ohio 1970. From assoc. to ptnr. Vorys, Sater, Seymour & Pease, Columbus, Ohio, 1970-77, 81—; assoc. regional counsel Prudential Ins. Co. Am., Cin., 1977-81; spl. counsel Ohio Divsn. Securities, Columbus, 1973. Contbr. articles to profl. jours.; presenter in field. Lt. USN, 1962-67, Vietnam. Mem. ABA, Ohio State Bar Assn., Columbus Bar Assn.

ROYBAL-ALLARD, LUCILLE, congresswoman; b. Boyle Heights, Calif., June 12, 1941; d. Edward Roybal; m. Edward T. Allard; 4 children. BA, Calif. State U., L.A. Former mem. Calif. State Assembly; mem. 103rd Congress from 33rd Calif. dist., 1993—; mem. Banking and Fin. Svcs., Budget Com. Office: Ho of Reps 2435 Rayburn Bldg Washington DC 20515-0533

ROYCE, BARRIE SAUNDERS HART, physicist, educator; b. Eng., Jan. 10, 1933; came to U.S., 1957, naturalized, 1978; s. Vincent Pateman Hart and Kathlene (Saunders) R.; m. Dominique J.M. Vallee, May 7, 1964; children: Vincent Rene Hart, Marc Edward Hart. BSc in Physics, King's Coll., U. London, 1954; PhD, U. London, 1957. Rsch. assoc. Carnegie Inst. Tech., 1957-60; rsch. assoc. Princeton U., 1960-61, mem. faculty, 1961—, prof. applied physics and materials scis., 1978—; master of Dean Mathey Coll. Dean Mathey Coll., 1986-94. Editorial adv. bd.: Jour. Photoacoustics, to 1984, Crystal Lattice Defects. Mem. Princeton Borough Zoning Bd. Adjustment, 1980-93, chair, 1993—. Grantee NSF; Grantee Air Force Office Sci. and Rsch.; Grantee Army Rsch. Office. Mem. Am. Phys. Soc., Sigma Xi. Office: Princeton U D416 Duffield Hall (EQ) Princeton NJ 08544

ROYCE, EDWARD R. (ED ROYCE), congressman; b. Los Angeles, Oct. 12, 1951; m. Marie Porter. BA, Calif. State U., Fullerton. Tax mgr. Southwestern Portland Cement Co.; mem. Calif. Senate, 1983-93, 103rd Congress from 39th dist. Calif., 1993—; mem. banking and fin. svcs. com., internat. rels. com.; vice chmn. Public Employment and Retirement Com.; mem. Bus. and Profs. com., Indsl. Rels. com.; legis. author, campaign cochmn. Proposition 15 Crime Victims/Speedy Trial Initiative; author nation's 1st felony stalking law, bill creating Foster Family Home Ins. Fund, legis. creating foster parent recruitment and tng. program; mem. Banking and Fin. Svcs. Com., Internat. Rels. Com. Named Legis. of Yr. Orange County Rep. Com., 1986, Child Adv. of Yr. Calif. Assn. Svc. for Children, 1987. Mem. Anaheim C. of C. Republican. Office: US Ho of Reps 1113 Longworth Ho Office Bldg Washington DC 20515-0539*

ROYCE, PAUL CHADWICK, medical administrator; b. Mpls., July 2, 1928. BA, U. Minn., 1948, MD, 1952; PhD, Case Western Res. U., 1959. Diplomate Am. Bd. of Internal Medicine. Intern U. Chgo. Clinics, 1952-53; fellow NSF Case Western Res. U., Cleve., 1953-54, 56-58, Upjohn fellow, 1958-59; resident internal medicine Bronx Mcpl. Hosp., N.Y., 1959-61; asst. prof. of medicine Albert Einstein Coll. of Med., N.Y.C., 1961-69; sr. staff endocrinologist Guthrie Clinic, Sayre, Pa., 1970-81; assoc. prof. of medicine Hahnemann Med. Sch., Phila., 1973-81; emeritus prof. medicine Med. Coll. Pa./Hahnemann U., 1996—; dean and prof. clin. sci. and physiology Sch. Medicine U. Minn., Duluth, 1981-87; sr. v.p., clin. dir. Monmouth Med. Ctr., Long Branch, N.J., 1987-94; med. dir. The Segal Co. N.Y., 1995—; prin. Royce Assocs., Atlantic Highlands, N.J., 1995—. Producer, host TV prgram Doctors on Call, 1983-87 (Nat. Friends of Pub. Broadcasting Hill award 1987). Lt. USNR, 1954-56. Mem. Harvey Soc., Am. Physiol. Soc., Fedn. Am. Scientists, Physicians for Social Responsibility, Am. Coll. Physician Execs., Sigma Xi, Alpha Omega Alpha. Avocations: skiing, cycling, canoeing. Office: Royce Associates 9 Prospect Rd Atlantic Highlands NJ 07716-1721

ROYCE, RAYMOND WATSON, lawyer, rancher, citrus grower; b. West Palm Beach, Fla., Mar. 5, 1936; s. Wilbur E. and Veda (Watson) R.; m. Catherine L. Setzer, Apr. 21, 1979; children: Raymond, Steven, Nancy, Kathryn, Ryan. BCE, U. Fla., 1958, JD, 1961. Bar: Fla. 1961, U.S. Dist. Ct. (so. dist.) Fla. 1961, U.S. Ct. Appeals (5th cir.) 1961, U.S. Ct. Appeals (11th cir.) 1981. With Scott, Royce, Harris & Bryan P.A., Palm Beach, Fla., 1962-94; pres. Scott, Royce, Harris, Bryan, Barra and Jorgensen, P.A., Palm Beach Gardens, Fla., 1982—. Bd. suprs. No. Palm Beach County Water Control Dist. Mem. Fla. Bar (bd. govs. 1974-78), Fla. Citrus Mut., Fla. Cattleman's Assn., Fla. Blue Key, Phi Delta Phi. Democrat. Presbyterian. Home: 5550 Whirlaway Rd West Palm Beach FL 33418-7735 Office: Scott Royce Harris Bryan Barra and Jorgensen PA 4400 P G A Blvd Ste 800 West Palm Beach FL 33410-6562

ROYCHOUDHURI, CHANDRASEKHAR, physicist; b. Barisal, Bengal, India, Apr. 7, 1942; s. Hiralal and Amiyabala (Sengupta) R.; children: Asim, Onnesha. BS in Physics, Jadavpur U., India, 1963; MS in Physics, Jadavpur U., 1965; PhD in Optics, U. Rochester, 1973. Asst. prof. U. Kalyani, West Bengal, India, 1965-68; sr. scientist Nat. Inst. Astrophysics, Puebla, Mex., 1974-78; sr. staff scientist TRW Inc., Redondo Beach, 1978-86; mgr. laser systems Perkin-Elmer, Danbury, Conn., 1986-89; chief scientist Optics & Applied Tech. Lab. United Technologies Optical Systems, West Palm Beach, Fla., 1990-91; dir. Photonics Rsch. Ctr. U. Conn., Storrs, 1991—. Author: chpt. Optical Shoptesting, 1978; contbr. articles to profl. jours. Fulbright scholar U. Vt., 1968. Fellow Conn. Acad. Sci. and Engring.; mem. IEEE, Optical Soc. Am., Soc. Photo-optical Instrumentation, Am. Phys. Soc. (life). Avocations: hiking, spl. edn. programs for children.

ROYCROFT, EDWARD J., publishing company executive. Sr. v.p. sales Reed Elsevier New Providence, N.J., now rating v.p. Office: Reed Elsevier New Providence 121 Chanlon Rd New Providence NJ 07974-1541*

ROYCROFT, HOWARD FRANCIS, lawyer; b. Balt., Sept. 9, 1930; s. Howard F. and Bessie (Weaver) R.; B.A., U. Md., 1953; LL.B., Georgetown U., 1958; m. Barbara Lee Seal, Mar. 20, 1954; children: Suzanne Carol Roycroft Soderberg, Nancy Lee Roycroft Branigan. Admitted to D.C. bar, 1958, since practiced in Washington; mem. firm Hogan & Hartson, 1958, ptnr., 1965-87, mem. exec. com., 1970-73, counsel, 1987—; dir. United TV, Inc., 1982—, U TV San Francisco, Inc., 1983; mng. ptnr., dir. WIJY, Inc., Hilton Head, S.C.; lectr. Howard U. Sch. Law, 1973-74; guest lectr. U. Tex., 1980; mem. Met. Washington Bd. Trade. Bd. dirs. YMCA Met. Washington, 1974-76. Served to 1st lt. USMC, 1953-55. Mem. ABA, Va. Bar Assn., Fed. Communications Bar Assn., Bar Assn. D.C., Nat. Broadcasters Club, Barristers, Aircraft Owners and Pilots Assn., Nat. Acad. TV Arts and Scis., Broadcast Pioneers, Kappa Alpha, Beta Kappa, Delta Theta Phi. Republican. Methodist. Clubs: Bryce Mountain Ski and Country (dir., pres. 1974-87, 82-87), Mt. Vernon Country, Old Dominion Boat, Washington Tennis Patrons, Army-Navy, Chaine des Rotisseurs Gastronome, Skull Creek Yacht Club. Office: Hogan & Hartson 555 13th St NW Washington DC 20004-1109 also: WIJY 2 Park Ln Hilton Head Island SC 29928-3420

ROYDS, ROBERT BRUCE, physician; b. Harrogate, England, Oct. 3, 1944; came to U.S., 1974; s. John Edmund and Ailsa Dorothea (Williams) R.; m. Marilyn Maria Valerio, Apr. 28, 1948; children: Elizabeth Caroline, Leslie Alexandra. M.B., B.S., U. London, 1967, M.R.C.P., 1970. Sr. house officer Royal Northern Hosp., London, 1968; sr. house officer Luton and Dunstable Hosp., Beds, England, 1968-69; registrar St. Albans City Hosp., Herts, England, 1969-70; research fellow clin. pharmacology dept. St. Bartholomew's Hosp., U. London, London, 1970-72; chief asst., sr. registrar med. professorial unit St. Bartholomew's Hosp., U. London, 1972-74; assoc. dir. Merck, Sharp & Dohme, Inc., Rahway, N.J., 1974-75; sr. research physician Hoffmann-La Roche Inc., Nutley, N.J., 1976-78; v.p. Besselaar Assocs., Princeton, N.J., 1979-82; pres. Theradex Sys., Inc., Princeton, 1982-94, chmn. bd. dirs., 1994—; cons. Ctr. for Rsch. Mothers/Infants Nat. Inst. Child Health & Human Devel., Washington, 1983. Bd. trustees Chapin Sch., Princeton, 1984-89, pres. bd. trustees, 1986-89; pres. Riverside Condominium Assn., Cranford, N.J., 1978-79. Fellow Royal Soc. Medicine; mem. Royal Coll. Physicians, Am. Coll. Clin. Pharmacology Therapeutics, Am. Soc. for Clin. Research (sr. mem.), Am. Soc. Microbiology. Home: 5 Quick Ln Plainsboro NJ 08536-1424

ROYER, ROBERT LEWIS, retired utility company executive; b. Louisville, Jan. 2, 1928; s. Carl Brown and Martha Helen (Garrett) R.; m. Carol Jean Pierce, June 24, 1950; children: Jenifer Lea, Todd Pierce, Robert Douglas. BS in Elec. Engring., Rose Hulman Inst. Tech., 1949. Registered profl. engr., Ky. With Louisville Gas and Electric Co., 1949-91, asst. v.p. ops., 1962-63, asst. v.p., asst. gen. supt., 1963-64, v.p., gen. supt., 1964-69, v.p. ops., 1969-78, exec. v.p., 1978, pres., chief exec. officer, 1978-89; chmn., 1989-91; dir. Louisville Gas and Electric Co., 1972-91, chmn. emeritus, 1991—; dir. LG&E Energy Corp., 1990-91; mem. exec. bd. East Cen. Area Reliability Coun., 1978-89; mem. Ky. Energy Resources Commn., 1975-79; mem. energy task force Gov.'s Econ. Devel. Commn., 1976-79; mem. Ky. Energy Rsch. Bd., 1978-88; v.p. Ind.-Ky. Electric Corp., 1979-89; dir. Ohio Valley Transmission Corp., 1978-90, Ohio Valley Electric Corp., 1979-89, Citizens Fidelity Corp. & Citizens Fidelity Bank and Trust Co., 1976-90. Mem. exec. bd. Old Ky. Home Coun. Boy Scouts Am., v.p. dist. ops., 1970-75, 79-80, 1st v.p., 1981-82, pres., 1982-84, commr., 1975-79, rep. to nat. coun., 1975-84, 95—, mem. regional bd., 1985—, S.E. region area pres., 1988-93; bd. dirs. East End Boys Club, 1975-78, Louisville Indsl. Found., 1980-86, Ky. Coun. Sci. and Tech., 1987-92; trustee Spirit of Louisville Found., 1978-90, J. Graham, Brown Found., 1980—; bd. mgrs. Rose Hulman Inst. Tech., 1979—; bd. dirs. Ky. Derby Mus., 1991-93, Leadership Louisville Found., 1985-91, Alliant Health Sys., 1989-94; mem. Louisville Devel. Com., 1979-83. Served with U.S. Army, 1953-55. Recipient Silver Beaver award Boy Scouts Am., 1975, Disting. Eagle award, 1989, Silver Antelope award, 1990. Mem. IEEE, Execs. Club Louisville (dir. 1980-83), Louisville Automobile Club (dir. 1974-96, treas. 1977-79, v.p. 1979-81, pres. 1981-83, nat. adv. coun. 1982-86), Louisville Area C. of C. (dir. 1978-80), Hurstbourne Country Club, Pendennis Club, Rotary. Methodist. Home and Office: 4014 Norbourne Blvd Louisville KY 40207-3806

ROYHAB, RONALD, journalist, newspaper editor; b. Lorain, Ohio, Oct. 6, 1942; s. Halim Farah and Elizabeth Della (Naiser) R.; m. Roberta Lee Libb, Apr. 20, 1969; children: David Libb, Aaron Nicholas. Student, Lorain County (Ohio) Coll., Kent State U.; postgrad., Am. U., Washington. Reporter Lorain Jour., 1966-69; chief bur. Scripps Howard Ohio Bur., Columbus, 1975-78; reporter spl. assignment Scripps Howard Cin. Post, 1971-72; investigative reporter Scripps Howard Cleve. Press, 1972-75; chief bur. Scripps Howard Ohio Bur., Columbus, 1975-78; asst. mng. editor Scripps Howard News Svc., Washington, 1978-81; mng. editor Scripps Howard El Paso (Tex.) Herald Post, 1981-83; asst. mng. editor Scripps Howard Pitts. Press, 1983-92; assoc. editor Pitts. Post Gazette, 1992-93; mng. editor Toledo Blade, 1993—; bd. dirs. Toledo Blade Co. Bd. dirs. Am. Lebanese Congress. With USAR, 1964-70. Recipient 7 awards for Excellence Cleve. Newspaper Guild, 1972-75; Spl. Sect. awards Pa. Newspaper Pubs. Assn., 1985, 86, 88; fellow Am. Polit. Sci. Assn., 1970-71. Mem. AP Mng. Editors Assn., AP Soc. Ohio (bd. dirs.). Eastern Orthodox. Home: 27262 Fort Meigs Rd Perrysburg OH 43551-1230 Office: Toledo Blade 541 N Superior St Toledo OH 43660-1000

ROYLE, DAVID BRIAN LAYTON, television producer, journalist; b. Claygate, Surrey, England, Jan. 29, 1955; came to U.S., 1974; s. John Hardy Layton and Jessie Monica (Pringle) R.; m. Cornelia Boardman Service; 1 child, William Brian Layton. BA cum laude, U. N.C., 1978; MA, U. Minn., 1983. Journalist Northcliffe Newspapers, Stoke-on-Trent, England, 1979-82; news producer Ctrl. Ind. TV, Birmingham, England, 1982-83; producer Inside Story, N.Y.C., 1984-86; pres. New Atlantic Prodns., N.Y.C., 1986-89, David Royle Prodns., N.Y.C., 1989—; field prodr. Am. Detective in Russia, ABC, L.A., 1992; exec. prodr. Target: Mafia, A&E, CBS, N.Y.C., 1993; prodr. TV Nation, NBC, BBC, N.Y.C., 1994, Wall St. Jour. TV, 1995; pres. Pub. Media Inc., N.Y.C., 1992—; dir. The Russian Archive, N.Y.C., 1992—; sr. prodr. Nat. Geog. TV, Washington, 1996—. TV shows produced include: Rupert Murdoch: Press Baron Who Would Be King, PBS, 1985 (Emmy nomination), Assignment Africa, PBS, 1986 (Emmy nomination), Senator Sam, PBS, 1988 (Ohio State award 1990, Cine Golden Eagle), (series) The Eagle and The Bear, ABC/A&E, 1993 (Cine Golden Eagle), Dr. Frank, PBS, 1994 (Cine Golden Eagle, Regional Emmy award), TV Nation, NBC/BBC, 1994 (Prime Time Emmy award), Emerging Powers: Brazil, PBS/NHK Japan, 1996, Trauma: Life and Death in the E.R., The Learning Channel, 1996. Pres. British Morehead Scholarship Fund, 1993—; gov. Clifton Coll., Bristol, Ga., 1997—. Morehead scholar, 1974-78, scholar Rotary Internat., 1983, N.J. Arts Fellowship, 1995; named Hon. Citizen, Mpls., 1983. Mem. NATAS, Soc. Profl. Journalists, Writers Guild of Am. Avocations: running, sailing, photography, reading. Office: Nat Geog TV 1145 17th St NW Washington DC 20036-4701

ROYSE, MARY KAY, judge; b. Hutchinson, Kans., Oct. 3, 1949; d. J.R. and Patricia Ann (Lamont) R. BS in Edn., Emporia State U., 1970, MA, 1972; JD, Kans. U., 1978. Instr. Miami U., Hamilton, Ohio, 1972-75; assoc. atty. Foulston & Siefkin, Wichita, 1978-82, Law Offices Bryson E. Mills, Wichita, 1982-86; judge Dist. Ct. (18th dist.) Kans., Wichita, 1986-93, Kans. Ct. Appeals, Topeka, 1993—; mem. Kans. Jud. Coun. Com. Pattern Instructions Kans., 1989—. Bd. dirs. Work Option Women, Wichita, 1980, Emporia State U. Alumni Assn., 1982-85, Kans. Dialysis Assn., Wichita, 1986-93. Named Woman Achievement, Women in Communications, Wichita, 1988, Disting. Alumni, Emporia State U., 1990. Mem. ABA, Kans. Bar Assn., Kans. Commn. Bicentenial U.S. Constitution, Kans. Bar Assn. Commn. Status of Women in Profession, Wichita Bar Assn. Avocations: travel, movies, reading.

ROZEBOOM, JOHN A., religious organization administrator. Dir. Christian Ref. Home Missions. Office: Christian Ref Ch in N Am 2850 Kalamazoo Ave SE Grand Rapids MI 49508-1433*

ROZEL, SAMUEL JOSEPH, lawyer; b. Louisville, Apr. 22, 1935; s. Sam and Anna (Sessmer) R.; m. Jeanne Frances Foulkes, July 3, 1965; children: Brooke Jane, John Samuel. BSL, U. Louisville, 1955, LLB, 1957; grad., Advanced Mgmt. Program, Harvard U., 1979. Bar: Ky. 1958, D.C. 1962, Minn. 1968, Ind. 1970, N.Y. 1983. Atty. FTC, Washington, 1962-67; antitrust counsel Honeywell, Inc., Mpls., 1967-69; atty. Magnavox Corp., Ft. Wayne, Ind., 1969-71, gen. counsel, 1971, v.p., 1972-75, sec., 1973-75; v.p. U.S. Philips Corp., N.Y.C., 1975-77, sr. v.p., 1977—; assoc. gen. counsel Philips Electronics N.Am. Corp., N.Y.C., sec. exec. mgmt. com., 1980—; v.p., sec., gen. counsel, dir. Phillips Electronics N.Am. Corp., N.Y.C., 1987-91, sr. v.p., sec., gen. counsel, mem. exec. com. bd. dirs., 1991—; bd. dirs. Philips Electronics N.Am. Corp., Std. Communications Corp. Served to capt. JAGC, AUS, 1957-62. Mem. ABA, Fed. Bar Assn., Ky. Bar Assn., Ind. Bar Assn., N.Y. Bar Assn., Harvard Club (N.Y.C.), Met. Club (Washington). Home: 215 S Bald Hill Rd New Canaan CT 06840-2908 Office: Philips Electronics N Am 125 Park Ave New York NY 10017-5529

ROZELLE, LEE THEODORE, physical chemist; b. Rhinelander, Wis., Mar. 9, 1933; s. Theodore and Alice (Omholt) R.; m. Barbara J. Ingli, June 21, 1955; children—David, Steven, Carolyn, Ann, Kenneth. B.S., U. Wis., 1955, Ph.D., 1960. Rsch. chemist DuPont Corp., Circleville, Ohio, 1960-63; prin. scientist-tech. coord. Honeywell Corp., Mpls., 1963-67; dir. chemistry div. North Star Rsch. Inst., Mpls., 1967-74; v.p. R&D USCI div. C.R. Bard, Billerica, Mass., 1974-77; dir. engring. tech. div. Mellon Inst., Pitts., 1977-78; dir. rsch. and devel. Permutit Co., Monmouth Junction, N.J., 1978-80; v.p. rsch. and devel. Gelman Scis., Inc., Ann Arbor, Mich., 1980-82; v.p. sci. and tech. Culligan Internat. Co., Northbrook, Ill., 1982-87; assoc. dir. rsch. Olin Chems. Rsch. div. Olin Corp., Cheshire, Conn., 1987-92; cons. in water treatment tech., mktg. and mgmt., 1992—; pres., cons. Water Solutions, Inc., 1995—; v.p., mng. ptnr. Puraq Water Systems, Inc., 1996—; cons. in field; mem. Nat. Drinking Water Adv. Council EPA, 1987-90. Contbr. chpts. to books, numerous articles to profl. jours. Bd. dirs. Unitarian Ch., Andover, Mass., 1974-77. NIH fellow, 1958-60; recipient Spl. Hominum award Nat. Sanitation Found., 1988. Fellow Am. Inst. Chemists; mem. AAAS, Am. Chem. Soc., Am. Soc. Artificial Internal Organs, Health Industry Mfrs. Assn. (chmn. spl. activities com.), Water Pollution Control Fedn., Water Quality Assn. (chmn. sci. adv. com., Award of Merit 1989), Am. Water Works Assn., Assn. Met. Water Agencies, Filtration Soc., Pacific Water

Quality Assn. (bd. dirs. 1987-90, Robert Gans award 1988), Am. Soc. Agrl. Engring., Internat. Water Supply Assn., European Membrane Soc., N.Am. Membrane Soc., Asociacion Interamericano De Ingenieria Sanaitaria y Ambiental, Sigma Xi, Eta Phi Alpha, Phi Lambda Upsilon. Home and Office: 626 23rd St N La Crosse WI 54601-3825 *My professional goal has always been to make significant contributions to the well being of our society through science. Goals have been accomplished from contributions to water purification to health care.*

ROZEN, JEROME GEORGE, JR., research entomologist, museum curator and research administrator; b. Evanston, Ill., Mar. 19, 1928; s. Jerome George and Della (Kretchmar) R.; m. Barbara L. Lindner, Dec. 18, 1948; children—Steven George, Kenneth Charles, James Robert. Student, U. Pa., 1946-48; B.A., U. Kans., 1950; Ph.D., U. Calif.-Berkeley, 1955. Entomologist in taxonomy U.S. Dept. Agr., 1956-58; asst. prof. entomology Ohio State U., 1958-60; assoc. curator hymenoptera, dept. entomology Am. Mus. Natural History, N.Y.C., 1960-65, curator hymenoptera, 1965—, chmn. dept. entomology, 1960-71, dep. dir. research, 1972-86; field expdns. in U.S., Europe, Mex., Trinidad, Argentina, Chile, Brazil, Peru, Venezuela, Morocco, Pakistan, Republic of South Africa, Namibia, Israel, Egypt; adj. prof. CUNY, 1968—. Contbr. numerous sci. articles on bees (Apoidea) and beetles (Coleoptera). Fellow AAAS; mem. Am. Inst. Biol. Scis., Entomol. Soc. Am. (editor misc. publs. 1959-60), Soc. Study of Evolution, Soc. Systematic Biology, N.Y. Entomol Soc. (pres. 1964-65), Washington Entomol. Soc., Pacific Coast Entomol. Soc., Kans. Entomol. Soc., Orgn. Biol. Field Stas. (pres. 1990), Internat. Soc. Hymenopterists. Home: 55 Haring St Closter NJ 07624-1709 Office: Am Mus Natural History Central Park West New York NY 10024-5192

ROZMAN, GILBERT FRIEDELL, sociologist, educator; b. Mpls., Feb. 18, 1943; s. David and Celia (Friedell) R.; m. Masha Dwosh, Jan. 25, 1945; children: Thea Dwosh, Noah Dwosh. B.A., Carleton Coll., Northfield, Minn., 1965; Ph.D. (Woodrow Wilson fellow 1965-66), Princeton U., 1971. Mem. faculty Princeton U., 1970—, prof. sociology, 1979—, Musgrave prof. sociology, 1992—, dir. Internat. Studies Program, 1993—; dir. Coun. on Regional Studies, 1993—; mem. com. studies Chinese civilization Am. Council Learned Socs., 1975-80; mem. U.S.-USSR Bi-Nat. Commn. Humanities and Social Scis., 1978-86. Author: Urban Networks in Ch'ing China and Tokugawa Japan, 1973, Urban Networks in Russia, 1750-1800, and Premodern Periodization, 1976, Population and Marketing Settlements in Ch'ing China, 1982, A Mirror for Socialism: Soviet Criticisms of China, 1985, The Chinese Debate About Soviet Socialism 1978-85, 1987, Japan's Response to the Gorbachev Era, 1985-1991: A Rising Superpower Views a Declining One, 1992; co-author: The Modernization of Japan and Russia, 1975; editor: The Modernization of China, 1981, Soviet Studies of Premodern China: Assessments of Recent Scholarship, 1984, Japan in Transition: From Tokugawa to Meiji, 1986, The East Asian Region: Confucian Heritage and Its Modern Adaptation, 1991, Dismantling Communism: Common Causes and Regional Variations, 1992. Guggenheim fellow, 1979-80; grantee NSF, NEH, Social Sci. Rsch. Coun., Nat. Coun. for Soviet and E. European Studies, U.S. Inst. Peace, Woodrow Wilson Internat. Ctr. Mem. Assn. Asian Studies, Am. Sociol. Assn., Am. Assn. Advancement Slavic Studies. Home: 20 Springwood Dr Trenton NJ 08648-1048 Office: Princeton U 2-N-2 Green Hall Princeton NJ 08544

ROZOF, PHYLLIS CLAIRE, lawyer; b. Flint, Mich., Aug. 3, 1948; d. Eugene Robert and Loveta Lucille Greenwood; m. Robert James Rozof, July 17, 1970 (dec. Oct. 1995); children: Nathan, Zachary. AB with high distinction, U. Mich., 1970, JD magna cum laude, 1977. Bar: Mich. 1977, Fla. 1978. Assoc. Honigman Miller Schwartz and Cohn, Detroit, 1977-81, ptnr., 1982—. Mem. Comml. Real Estate Women Detroit (pres. 1992-93). Office: Honigman Miller Schwartz & Cohn 2290 1st National Bldg Detroit MI 48226

ROZZELL, SCOTT ELLIS, lawyer; b. Texarkana, Tex., Apr. 12, 1949; s. George M. and Dora Mae (Boyett) R.; m. Jackie Golden, June 1, 1996; children by previous marriage: Stacey Elizabeth, Kimberly Marie. BA, So. Meth. U., 1971; JD, U. Tex., 1975. Bar: Tex. 1975, U.S. Dist. Ct. (so. dist.) Tex. 1975, U.S. Dist. Ct. (no. dist.) Tex. 1977, U.S. Ct. Appeals (1st, 3d, 9th cirs.) 1977, U.S. Ct. Appeals (5th and D.C. cirs.) 1976. Assoc. Baker & Botts, Houston, 1975-82, ptnr., 1983—. Bd. dirs. Houston Vol. Lawyers, 1984-86, 91-93, Manned Space Flight Edn. Found., Inc., 1997—; vice chair Cancer Counseling Inc., Houston, 1991-92; mem. devel. bd. U. Tex. Houston Health Sci. Ctr., 1994—. Fellow Tex. Bar Found. (sustaining life), Houston Bar Found. (sustaining life, bd. dirs. 1991-93, chair 1993), Am. Bar Found.; mem. ABA, State Bar Tex. (bd. dirs. 1997—), Houston Bar Assn. (bd. dirs. 1991-95, pres. 1996—), Fed. Energy Bar Assn., Houston Young Lawyers Assn. (bd. dirs. 1978-82, pres. 1983-84), Plaza Club (bd. dirs. 1995—). Republican. Presbyterian. Avocation: flying vintage airplanes. Home: 2740 Barbara Ln Houston TX 77005 Office: Baker & Botts 3000 One Shell Plz 910 Louisiana St Houston TX 77002-4916

RUANE, JOSEPH WILLIAM, sociology educator; b. Lansdowne, Pa., Feb. 23, 1933; s. Joseph William and F. Viola (Davis) R.; m. Nancy Di Pasquale, Nov. 25, 1971; 1 child, Krista. Student St. Joseph's U., 1951-53, 68-69, B.A. in Philosophy, St. Charles Sem., 1958; M.A. in Sociology, Temple U., 1971; Ph.D. in Sociology, U. Del., 1978. Ordained priest Roman Catholic Ch., 1962. Asst. pastor, priest Archdiocese, Phila., 1962-68; tchr. social studies Sch. Dist. of Phila., 1968-71; asst. prof. sociology Phila. Coll. Pharmacy and Sci., 1971-77, assoc. prof., 1977—; mem. adj. faculty Gt. Lakes Colls. Assn., Phila., 1983-90; interim chmn. dept. humanities and social scis. Phila. Coll. Pharmacy and Sci., 1984-86, chair dept. social science, 1989-96; dir. West Phila. Mental Health Consortium, 1985-86, Health Svcs. Group, Inc., 1986—, vice chair 1987—; dir. West Phila. C. of C., 1993—, ARC, West Phila., 1990—; dir., exec. com., chmn. urban com. West Phila. Partnership, 1975—. Contbr. articles to profl. jours. Co-editor, prin. author Pub. Edn. Platform of W. Wilson Goode, 1983. Founding dir. West Phila. Community Fed. Credit Union, 1980-88, pres., 1982-88; bd. dirs. University City Clean, Phila., 1981-87, Friends of Clark Park, Phila., 1982-86; dir. Green to Green, 1995—, Spruce Hill Cmty. Assn., 1995. Decorated Legion of Honor Chapel of Four Chaplains, 1967; Lilly fellow, 1980. Mem. Am. Acad. Polit. and Social Scis., Am. Sociol. Assn., Eastern Sociol. Soc., Pa. Sociol. Soc. (chmn. long range planning com. 1982-86, pres. 1989-90, exec. com. 1987—), Global Edn. Assocs., Fedn. Christian Ministries (v.p. Middle Atlantic 181-84, pres. 1988-92, chmn. bd. dirs. 1992-96), Corps of Res. Priests U.S. (regional coordinator 1984—), AAUP, Sigma Xi. Democrat. Clubs: Vesper (Phila); Westwood (Split Rock, Pa.). Avocations: basketball; attending theatre; travel. Home: 4226 Regent Sq Philadelphia PA 19104-4439 Office: Phila Coll Pharmacy and Sci 43d and Kingsessing Mall Philadelphia PA 19104

RUBANO, RICHARD FRANK, civil engineer; b. N.Y.C., Mar. 10, 1946; s. Emil and Bessie Ann (Goldberg) R.; m. Jane M. Biamonte, June 5, 1975 (dec. 1987); children: David C., Kimberly A.; m. Phyllis E. Sneider, Feb. 17, 1996; children: Jonathan Spisto, Andrea Spisto. BSE, CUNY, 1969; MSCE, Columbia U., 1976. Lic. profl. engr. N.Y., Tex., Fla., Ill., Mass. Structural engr. Burns & Roe Inc., Paramus, N.J., 1976-81; mech. engr. Stone & Webster Inc., N.Y.C., 1981-83; nuclear engr. cons. N.Y.C., 1983-86; auditor constrn. N.Y.C. Dept. Constrn., 1986-88; sr. engr., resident engr. Ammann & Whitney Inc., N.Y.C., 1988-92; sr. resident engr. Goodkind & O'Dea, Rutherford, N.J., 1993—, A & H Engrs., P.C., N.Y.C., 1993-95; supr. quality control and engring. UR Bahn Assocs., N.Y.C., 1995-96; owner Rubano Constrn. Corp., 1996—; cons. Columbia U. Alumni Assn., N.Y.C., 1976—; guest speaker Deans Day Columbia, 1977.; resident engr. rehab. Triborough Bridge, N.Y.C. Performer blues jazz group, N.Y.C.; contbr. articles to profl. jours. Jazz workshop Local Evening Program, Roslyn, N.Y., 1991; performer Comty. Big Band, Bitter End, N.Y.C., various choruses. Fellow ASCE; mem. NSPE, N.Y. Soc. Profl. Engrs. (sec. L.I. chpt. 1988-94). Achievements include work on Olmstead Terrace Restoration of U.S. Capitol, reconstruction of several blocks in Queens, N.Y., high pressure gas pipeline constrn. in N.Y., Mass., Rubano Constrn. Corp., Women's Business Enterprise. Office: Rubano Construction Corp 41 Heitz Pl Hicksville NY 11801-3103

RUBANYI, GABOR MICHAEL, medical research company executive; b. Budapest, Hungary, Jan. 7, 1947; arrived in U.S., 1982; s. Paul and Agnes (Hofmann) R.; m. Edith Linda Zoltan, May 5, 1973; children: Thomas and Dora. MD, Semmelweis Med. Sch., Budapest, 1971; PhD, Nat. Acad. Scis., Budapest, 1980. Med. diplomate. Asst. prof. dept. physiology Semmelweis Med. U., Budapest, 1971-76, assoc. prof. dept. physiology, 1976-82; vis. prof. dept. physiology U. Cin., 1982-83; assoc. cons. dept. physiology Mayo Clinic, Rochester, Minn., 1983-86; dir. dept. pharmacology Berlex Labs., Cedar Knolls, N.J., 1986-90; head inst. Schering AG, Berlin, 1990-92; dir. vascular rsch. Berlex Bioscis., Richmond, Calif., 1992—. Editor: EDRF and EDCF, 1989, Cardiovascular Significance of Endothelium-Derived Vasoactive Factors, 1990, Endothelin, 1991, others; founder and editor-in-chief Endothelium, 1993—. Grantee NIH, 1988, AHA, 1989. Avocations: tennis, classical music, books, bridge, traveling. Home: 2426 Heritage Oaks Dr Alamo CA 94507-1445 Office: Berlex Bioscis 15049 San Pablo Ave Richmond CA 94806-1834

RUBARDT, PETER CRAIG, conductor, educator; b. Oakland, Calif., Aug. 7, 1958; s. Kenneth and Betty (Maspero) R.; m. Hedi Salanki; 1 child, Daniel. BA, U. Calif., Berkeley, 1981; M of Music, SUNY, Stony Brook, 1984; student, Hochschule fur Musik, Vienna, 1984-86; D Mus. Arts, Julliard Sch., 1989. Prof., conductor SUNY, Purchase, 1989-90, Rutgers U., New Brunswick, N.J., 1991-96; resident conductor N.J. Symphony, Newark, 1990-93; assoc. conductor Syracuse (N.Y.) Symphony, 1993-97; music dir., condr. Greater Pensacola (Fla.) Symphony Orch., 1997—; guest conductor various orchs. Condr. rec. Bach Concerti, 1988. Fullbright fellow USIA, 1984-86; Bruno Walter scholar, Julliard Sch., 1986-88. Mem. Am. Symphony Orch. League, Condrs. Guild. Democrat. Office: Syracuse Symphony Orch 411 Montgomery St Syracuse NY 13202-2930

RUBBERT, PAUL EDWARD, engineering executive; b. Mpls., Feb. 18, 1937; s. Adolf Christian and Esther Ruth Rubbert; m. Mary Parpart, Oct. 6, 1958 (div. 1985); children: Mark, David, Stephen; m. Rita Monica Saiia, Oct. 7, 1989. BS with high distinction, U. Minn., 1958, MS in Aero. Engring., 1960; PhD in Aerodyn., MIT, 1965. Rsch. engr. The Boeing Co., Seattle, 1960-62, 65-72, unit chief aerodyns rsch., comml. airplane group, 1972—; cons. NASA, 1989—, aeronautics adv. com., aerospace rsch. and tech. subcoms.; corp. vis. com. MIT, 1990—; served on various coms. Nat. Rsch. Coun. Panel; aerodyns. cons. GM; speaker in field. Contbr. articles to profl. jours. Recipient Arch T. Colwell Merit award Soc. Automotive Engrs., 1968, Wright Brothers Lectureship in Aeronautics Am. Inst. of Aeronautics and Astronautics, 1994. Fellow AIAA (Outstanding Tech. Mgmt. award Pacific Northwest sect., disting. lectr., assoc. editor jour., past mem. fellow selection com., dir., chmn. various workshops and coms.); mem. NAE. Achievements include three patents in field. Office: Boeing Comml Airplane Group MS 67-UC PO Box 3707 Seattle WA 98124-2207 Home: 20131 SE 23rd Pl Issaquah WA 98029-9642

RUBELL, BONNIE LEVINE, occupational therapist; b. Bklyn., Aug. 6, 1957; d. Seymour and Gladys Levine; m. Paul Rubell, June 3, 1990. BS in Occupational Therapy, NYU, 1979. Staff occupational therapist Main Campus Vocat. Workshop United Cerebral Palsy, Bklyn., 1980-83; sr. occupational therapist N.Y.C. Bd. Edn. Office Related and Contractual Svcs., 1983-86, supr. occupational therapy, 1986-87; sr. staff occupational therapist United Cerebral Palsy Treatment and Rehab. Ctr., Roosevelt, N.Y., 1987-89; master profl. occupational therapist The Sch. for Lang. and Communication Devel., North Bellmore, N.Y., 1987-92; staff occupational therapist Nassau Bd. Coop. Ednl. Svcs., The Lewis Ames Sch., 1992—; cons. On Your Mark program Staten Island Jewish Community Ctrs., 1984-85. Author: Big Strokes for Little Folks, 1995. Mem. Assn. Occupational Therapists Am., N.Y. Met. and L.I. Dists. Occupational Therapy Assn.

RUBELLO, DAVID JEROME, artist; b. Detroit, Sept. 3, 1935; s. Ludovico and Girolama (Trupiano) R.; m. Mary Anne Keithan, Oct. 14, 1978. BFA, Am. Acad. Art, Rome, 1961; MFA, U. Mich., 1972; cert., Acad. Fine Art, Copenhagen, 1966. Lect. art U. Mich., Ann Arbor, 1973-74; asst. prof. art Pa. State U., University Park, 1974-80; assoc. prof. art Towson (Md.) State U., 1980-81; assoc. prof. U. Mich., Ann Arbor, 1988-90. One man shows include Cade Gallery, Royal Oak, Mich., 1987; exhibited in group shows at Detroit Inst. Art, 1987, GMB Gallery Internat., Bloomfield Hills, Mich., 1991, Kresge Art Inst., 1989, Kalamazoo Art Inst., 1990, 91, Photo Nat. 2, Ella Sharp Mus., Jackson, Mich., BBAA, Birmingham, Mich., Arts Coun., Traverse City, Mich., 1995-96, Patrimonio Invitational Wayne State U., Detroit, 1996, Ann. Celebrate Mich. Artists P.C. Art Ctr., Rochester, 1994, 95, 96; exhibited Null Dimension, Fulda, Germany, 1988, Systematica Constructive Art, Madrid, 1989, B4 Pub. Invitational, London, 1990, Archive 90s, Amsterdam and London, Konkrete Miniatures Invitational, Amsterdam, 1991; gallery affiliation: Halsted, Birmingham, Mich.

RUBEN, ALAN MILES, law educator; b. Phila., May 13, 1931; s. Maurice Robert and Ruth (Blatt) R.; m. Betty Jane Willis, May 23, 1965. AB, U. Pa., 1953, MA, 1956, JD, 1956. Bar: Pa. 1957, Ohio 1972. Law clk. Supreme Ct. Pa., 1956-58; pvt. practice Phila., 1958-65; assoc. counsel Aetna Life & Casualty Co., Hartford, Conn., 1965-69; corp. counsel Lubrizol Corp., Cleve., 1969-70; prof. Cleve.-Marshall Coll. Law, Cleve. State U., 1970—; adv. prof. law Fudan U., Shanghai, People's Republic of China, 1993—; dep. to city solicitor Phila., 1958-61; dep. atty. gen. State of Pa., 1961-65; spl. counsel to U.S. Senate Subcom. on Nat. Stockpile, 1962; commentator Higher Edn. Issues Sta. WCLV-FM, Cleve., 1975-87; mem. nat. panel labor arbitrators Nat. Acad. Arbitrators, Fed. Mediation and Conciliation Svc. and Am. Arbitration Assn., Ohio State Employment Rels. Bd.; lectr. law U. Conn. Law Sch., 1968; vis. prof. law FuDan U., Shanghai, Peoples Republic of China, 1988-89; cons. Shanghai Law Office for Fgn. Economy and Trade, Peoples Republic of China, 1991—. Author: The Constitutionality of Basic Protection for the Automobile Accident Victim, 1968, Unauthorized Insurance: The Regulation of the Unregulated, 1968, Arbitration in Public Employee Labor Disputes: Myth, Shibboleth and Reality, 1971, Illicit Sex of Campus: Federal Remedies for Employment Discrimination, 1971, Model Public Employees Labor Relations Act, 1972, Sentencing the Corporate Criminal, 1972, Modern Corporation Law, supp. edit., 1978, An American Lawyer's Observations on the Inauguration of the Shanghai Stock Exchange, 1989, Ohio Limited Partnership Law, 1992—, Practice Guides, Ohio Limited Liability Company, Law, 1995—; co-editor: How Arbitration Works, 1997; contbr.: With an Eye to Tomorrow: The Future Outlook of the Life Insurance Industry, 1968, The Urban Transportation Crisis: The Philadelphia Plan, 1961, Philadelphia's Union Shop Contract, 1961, The Administrative Agency Law: Reform of Adjudicative Procedure and the Revised Model Act, 1963, The Computer in Court: Computer Simulation and the robinson Patman Act, 1964, State Ltd. Partnership Laws, 1993. Bd. dirs. U.S. Olympic Com., 1968-73; chmn. U.S. Olympic Fencing Sport Com., 1969-73; pres. U.S. Fencing Assn., 1968-73; capt. U.S. Pan-Am. Fencing Team, 1971, U.S. Olympic Fencing Team, 1972; bd. dirs. Legal Aid Soc. Cleve., 1973-77. Winner Internat. Inst. Edn. Internat. Debate Championship, 1953; recipient Harrison Tweed Bowl and Am. Law Inst. prizes Nat. Moot Ct. Competition, 1955; named Guggenheim scholar, 1949-53, Fulbright scholar FuDan U., Shanghai, 1993-94. Mem. ABA, Ohio Bar Assn. (corp. law and profl. responsibility com.), Cleve. Bar Assn. (Securities Law Inst.), Assn. Am. Law Schs. (chmn. sect. law and edn. 1976-78), Internat. Indsl. Rels. Rsch. Assn., Internat. Soc. Labor Law, AAUP (pres. Ohio conf. 1974-75), Phi Beta Kappa, Pi Gamma Mu. Home: 9925 Lake Shore Blvd Bratenahl OH 44108-1052 Office: Cleve State U 18th St And Euclid Ave Cleveland OH 44115

RUBEN, BRENT DAVID, communication educator; b. Cedar Rapids, Iowa, Oct. 17, 1944; s. Nate and Ruth (Subotnik) R. m. Jann M., Oct. 3, 1967; children, Robbi Lynn, Marc David. BA in Psychology and Advt., U. Iowa, 1966, MA in Mass Communication Rsch., 1968, PhD in Communication, 1970. Instr. to asst. prof. mass communication U. Iowa, 1969-71; asst. to assoc. prof. communication Rutgers U., New Brunswick, N.J., 1971-80, chmn. dept., 1980-84, prof., 1980-87, mem. exec. com. faculty profl. studies, 1981-82, mem. exec. com. PhD program in info. and libr. studies, 1981-83; fellow Rutgers Coll., New Brunswick, N.J., 1982—; dir. PhD program Sch. Communication, Inf. and Libr. Studies Rutgers U., New Brunswick, N.J., 1984-93; exec. dir. univ. program for organizational quality and comm. improvement, 1993—; mem. Inst. for Health, Health Policy and Aging Rsch. Rutgers U., New Brunswick, N.J., 1986—, 1986—, Disting. prof. communication, 1987—; co-project dir. adv. bd. Nat. Survey Pub. Perceptions of Digestive Health and Disease and Louis Harris & Assocs., 1982-84; chmn. steering com. nat. digestive disease edn. program, NIH, 1983-84; sr. cons. grants Fund for Improvement Post-Secondary Edn., 1984-86; mem. nat. digestive diseases adv. bd. HHS, 1982-84; spl. cons. Can. Royal Commn. on Conditions Fgn. Svc., 1980-81; mem. Malcolm Baldrige Nat. Quality Awards Examination Com., 1994—; judge Quality N.J. Awards, 1996—; chmn. conf. bd. Higher Edn. Nat. Quality Coun., 1995-96; invited lectr. Yale U., W.Va. U. Med. Sch., Wayne State U., Tex., Pitts. U., Duquesne U., Drake U., James Madison U., Columbia-Free State Health System, NIH, others; cons. Johnson & Johnson, Ford, Humana Hosp.-Sunrise, N.J. Bell, Bell Can., AT&T, Can. Agy. Internat. Devel., U.S. AID, Merck Sharpe & Dohme, Morristown Meml. Hosp., Cathedral Health Care Systems, York Rehab. Hosp. Chilton Meml. Hosp. Author: Quality in Higher Education., 1995, (with Richard W.Budd) Human Communication Handbook: Simulations and Games, Vol. 1, 1975, (with John Y. Kim) General Systems and Human Communication Theory, 1975, Human Communication Handbook: Simulations and Games, Vol. 2, 1978, (with Budd) Beyond Media: New Approaches to Mass Communication, 1979, Vol. 2, 2d rev. edit., 1988, Communication and Human Behavior, 1984, 2d rev. edit., 1988, 3d rev. edit., 1992,(with Lea Stewart Aklyn-Bacon) 4th rev. edit., 1997, Non-Verbal Codes: Appearance, Action, Space and Time, 1985 (Japanese adaptation 1984, 95), The Bottom Line: A Patient Relations Training Program, 1985, 2d rev. edit, 1988, (with Hunt) Mass Communication: Producers and Consumers, 1993, Communicating with Patients, 1992, (with Nurit Guttman) Caregiver-Patient Communication: Readings, 1993; author, editor: (with Budd) Approaches to Human Communication, 1972; (with John Kim) General Systems Theory and Human Communication, 1975; Communication Yearbook 1, 1977 (also founding editor), Communication Yearbook 2, 1978, Interdisciplinary Approaches to Human Communication, 1979, Information and Behavior, Vol. 1, 1985, Vol. 2, 1988, (with Leah Lievrouw) Vol. 3, 1990, Vol. 4 (with Jorge Schement), 1993, Quality in Higher Education, 1995; cons. editor: Hayden Communication and Human Behavior Series, 1978-78; Ablex, Communication: The Human Context Series, 1986—; mem. editl. bd. Internat. and Intercultural Communication Annual, 1980-86, Jour. Communication Therapy, 1982-86, Society, 1983-86, Communication Quar., 1979—; rev. editor Behavioral Sci., 1974-77; cons. editor Internat. Jour. Intercultural Rels., 1983—; reviewer Jour. Am. Soc. Info. Sci.; contbr. numerous articles, book revs., essays, conf. papers to profl. jours., chpts. to books. Mem. Franklin County, (N.J.) Twp. Human Rels. Commn., 1973-75; spl. cons. Ctr. for Disease Control, N.J. Collegiate Consortium for Health in Edn., 1981-82, chair Univ. Community Affairs and Outreach Com., 1992-93, Univ. Sen. Com. Rutgers and the Pub., 1992-93. Recipient Disting. Svc. award Coalition Digestive Disease Orgns., 1984; grantee , project co-dir. Nat. Assn. Broadcasters, 1970, U.S. Office Edn., 1970, Rutgers U., 1973-74, 74-75. Mem. Internat. Communication Assn. (chair pubs. com., conf. site selection com.), Ea. Communication Assn. (pubs. com., adv. bd.), Speech Communication Assn., Am. Soc. Info. Sci., Am. Hosp. Assn., Am. Soc. Patient Representation and Consumer Affairs, Am. Soc. Health Edn. and Tng., Assn. Libr. and Info. Sci Educators (rsch. com. 1988-89), Kappa Tau Alpha, Alpha Kappa Psi. Office: Univ Office of Quality & Comm Improvement 4 Huntington St New Brunswick NJ 08901-1071

RUBEN, GARY A., marketing and communications consultant; b. Cochem, Germany, Jan. 1, 1924; came to U.S., 1939, naturalized, 1943; s. Jules and Erna (Hirsch) R.; m. Irene Jehle, Aug. 12, 1962; 1 child, Monique L. Student, Acad. Comml. Art, Indpls., 1940-41. With advt. dept. Indpls. News, 1940-41; advt. mgr. Greater Indpls. Amusement Corp., 1941-42; pres. Ruben Advt. Agy., Indpls., 1948-68; chmn. bd. Ruben, Montgomery & Assos., 1968-76; pres. Prestige Program Sales Inc., 1973-76, Gary A. Ruben Inc. (advt. and mktg. cons.), Indpls., 1976—; past lectr. advt. and bd. fellows Northwood Inst.; past pres. Nat. Fedn. Advt. Agys., 1971; bd. dirs. Connor Prairie Settlement, Noblesville, Ind., Acordia Sr. Benefits Corp. Hon. trustee Indpls. Children's Mus. With Combat Engrs. AUS, 1943-46. Paul Harris fellow Rotary Internat. Home: 7370-D Lions Head Dr Indianapolis IN 46260 Office: 931 E 86th St Ste 206 Indianapolis IN 46240-1852 *It was years ago, in the late 30's in Vienna, that the cry "Lebensraum" echoed across yet another land. And, a family, judged comfortable by most standards, scattered to the four winds, leaving behind all things material, but salvaging the will to survive and to commence once again in a new land. To a boy in his teens and still dressed in European-style short pants upon arrival in this country, the emotion, the sights, the sounds, and the smells were overwhelming and exciting to say the least. . .so began another chapter in my life. In the ensuing years, I learned the true meaning of individual freedom. And while the echoes of Vienna have become dim, that dim sound will continue to remind me that all worthwhile things in life are earned—not given, and even in adversity, there is opportunity.*

RUBEN, IDA GASS, state senator; b. Washington, Jan. 7, 1929; d. Sol and Sonia E. (Darman) Gass; m. L. Leonard Ruben, Aug. 29, 1948; children: Garry, Michael, Scott, Stephen. Del. Md. Ho. of Dels., Annapolis, 1974-86; mem. Md. Senate, Annapolis, 1986—, majority whip, 1995—; chair Montgomery County House Delegation, 1981-86, Montgomery County Senate Delegation, 1987—; mem. house econ. matters com., 1974-85, house ways and means com., 1985-86, legis. policy com., 1991—, senate budget and taxation com., joint budget and audit com., 1991—, exec. nominations com., 1991—, joint protocol com., 1991—, chair subcom. on pub. safety, transp., econ. devel. and natural resources, 1995—, mem. joint com. on spending affordability, 1995—, mem. capital budget subcom., 1995—; mem. Gov.'s Motor Carrier Task Force, 1989—; conv. chair Nat. Order Women Legislators, 1980. Chair Women Legislators Caucus Md., 1982-84; trustee Adventist Health Care Mid-Atlantic, Takoma Park, Md.; bd. dirs. Ctrs. for Handicapped, Silver Spring, Md.; former internat. v.p. B'nai Brith Women. Recipient Cert. of Appreciation Ctrs. for Handicapped, 1987, Meritorious Svc. award Safety and Survival, 1989, Cover Those Trucks award AAA Potomac, 1989, Leadership Laurel award Safety First Club Md., 1989, Woman of Valor award B'nai B'rith Women, 1991, Pub. Affairs award Planned Parenthood Md., 1992, ESOL support recognition Montgomery County Pub. Schs., 1992, Appreciation award Fraternal Order Police, 1992, John Dewey award Montgomery County Fedn. Tchrs., 1992, Appreciation award ARC of Md., 1992, Safety Leader award Advocates for Hwy. and Auto Safety, 1993, Disting. Svc. award Gov.'s Commn. Employment of People with Disabilities, 1993, award Faculty Guild U. Md. for support of faculty and univ., 1993, Sincere Appreciation award for commitment to Md.'s youth Md. Underage Drinking Prevention Coalition, 1994, Faithful Svc. to citizens of Montgomery County award Montgomery County Assn. of Realtors, 1994; named Most Effective Pub. Ofcl. by residents of Silver Spring, 1990, One of 100 Most Powerful Women in Washington Metro Area by Washingtonian Mag., 1994, Legislator of Yr. award Nat. Commn. Against Drunk Driving, 1995, Legislator of Yr. award Montgomery County Med. Soc., 1995, Carmen S. Turner Achievement in Cmty. Svc. award Montgomery County Dept. Transp., 1995; inducted into Washington, Md., Del., Pa. Svc. Sta. Assn. Hall of Fame, 1994. Mem. Coun. State Govts. (com. on suggested legislation), Hadassah. Democrat. Jewish. Home: 11 Schindler Ct Silver Spring MD 20903-1329 Office: Md State Senate 204 James Senate Off Bldg 110 College Ave Annapolis MD 21401-8012

RUBEN, LAWRENCE, real estate developer, building company executive, lawyer; b. Bklyn., Sept. 28, 1926; s. Irving and Minnie (Sruelif) R.; m. Selma Belfer, Dec. 20, 1952; children: Richard Gordon, Lenore Denise, Rochelle Gail Ruben Kivell. BA, NYU, 1949; LLB, Bklyn. Law Sch., 1951. Bar: N.Y. 1952. Gen. practice law N.Y.C., 1952-53; pres. Ru-Min Constrn. Co., N.Y.C., 1953-54; exec. v.p. Belco Petroleum Corp., N.Y.C., 1954-64, dir., 1954-85; v.p. Fundamental Bldg. Corp., 1952—; pres. Randall Devel. Co., Aragon Devel. Corp., Lawrence Ruben Co., Inc.; ptnr. Lexington Madison Co., Tower Plaza Assocs., Devonshire Assocs., Boylston Ptnrs., Devonshire Constrn. Co. Inc., Lawrence Assocs.; pres. Washington Mgmt. Corp.; mem. adv. bd. NYU Real Estate Inst. Chmn. N.Y. Builders and Realtors Fellowship Fund; trustee Nat. Jewish Ctr. for Immunology and Respiratory Medicine, Denver; patron Albert Einstein Coll. Medicine; sponsor Grad. Sch. Sci.; bd. dirs. Cardoza Sch. Law at Yeshiva U.; chmn. United Jewish Appeal, Scarsdale, N.Y., 1974-75. With AUS, 1945-46. Mem. ABA. Clubs: Fenway Golf, Boca Rio Golf. Office: 600 Madison Ave New York NY 10022-1615

RUBEN, LEONARD, retired art educator; b. St. Paul, June 3, 1921; s. Theodore and Elizabeth (Hauchman) R.; m. Sue Levey; children: James M., Elizabeth A., Nancy L., Thomas C. Diploma with hon., Pratt Inst., 1948, BFA, 1952; MA, Columbia Tchrs. Coll., 1961; PhD, NYU, 1970. Designer

L.W. Frolich, N.Y.C., 1949-52; art dir. Young & Rubicam, N.Y.C., 1952-60; art group head North Advt., N.Y.C., 1960-62; instr. Columbia U. Tchrs. Coll., N.Y.C., 1962-63; assoc. creative dir. Compton Advt., N.Y.C., 1962-64; v.p. assoc. creative dir. J.M. Mathes, N.Y.C., 1964-68; exec. creative dir. Lake Spiro Shurman, Memphis, 1968-69; asst. prof. art Northeast La. U., Monroe, 1969-71; asst. prof. art U. Tex., Austin, 1971-74, assoc. prof., 1974-79, prof. art, 1979-82, F.J. Heyne Centennial Prof. in Communication, 1983-87; design cons. B.B. Martin Pub. Co., Austin, 1978; creative dir. Heart Assn., Austin, 1973. Precinct chmn. Dems., Lake Travis, Tex., 1979; chmn. advt. com. Austin Community Coll., 1980-84. 1st lt. U.S. Army, 1940-46, ETO, PTO. Decorated Bronze Arrowhead, Presdl. Unit emblem; recipient numerous awards including Advt. Appreciation award City of Houston, 1980, Thomas McCartin Tchg. Excellence award, 1983, Founders Day award NYU, 1971; Leo Burnet Creative Excellence Endowment, 1986, Frank Rizzo Meml. Creative grant Tracy-Locke, 1986. Mem. 27th Infantry Div. Assn., 105th (226th) Field Arty Assn., Dallas Soc. Visual Communication. Jewish. Home: 1102A Locust Ave Charlottesville VA 22901-4034

RUBEN, ROBERT JOEL, physician, educator; b. N.Y.C., Aug. 2, 1933; s. Julian Carl and Sadie (Weiss) R.; children—Ann, Emily, Karin, Arthur. A.B., Princeton U., 1955; M.D., Johns Hopkins U., 1959. Intern Johns Hopkins Hosp., Balt., 1959-60; resident Johns Hopkins Hosp., 1960-64, dir. neurophysiology lab., div. otolaryngology, 1958-64; practice specializing in pediatric otorhinolaryngology N.Y.C., 1964—; asst. prof. otorhinolaryngology N.Y. U. Sch. Medicine, 1966-68; mem. staff hosps. Montefiore Med. Ctr., Bronx Med. Hosp. Ctr., N. Cen. Bronx Hosp., Montefiore Med.; prof., chmn. Montefiore Med. Ctr., Bronx Mcpl. Hosp. Ctr., N. Cen. Bronx, Bronx, N.Y., 1979—; prof. pediatrics Albert Einstein Coll. Medicine, Bronx, 1983—; assoc. prof. otorhinolaryngology Albert Einstein Coll. Medicine, N.Y.C., 1968-70, prof., chmn. dept. otolaryngology, 1970—; prof. pediatrics Albert Einstein Coll. Medicine and Montefiore Med. Ctr., 1983—; chmn. Nat. Com. for Rsch. and Neurol. and Communicative Disorders, pres., 1982-84; bd. dirs. Am. Bd. Otolaryngology-Head and Neck Surgery, 1989—; chmn. ENT devices com. FDA, 1993-96. Editor-in-chief: Internat. Jour. Pediatric Otorhinolaryngology, 1979—. Bd. dirs. N.Y. League Hard of Hearing, 1969-75, 76-85. Served to surgeon USPHS, 1964-66. Recipient Rsch. award Am. Acad. Ophthalmology and Otolaryngology, 1962, Edmund Prince Fowler award Am. Rhinological-Laryngological-Otological Assn., 1973, Gold medal Best Didactic Film, IX World Congress Otorhinolaryngology, 1977, Pres.'s award Am. Acad. Otolaryngology-Head and Neck Surgery, 1992, Johns Hopkins U. Soc. of Scholars, 1993, George E. Schambaugh Otology prize, 1996. Fellow ACS, N.Y. Acad. Medicine; mem. AMA, Am. Assn. Anatomists, Audiology Study Group N.Y. (pres. 1964-66), Acoustical Soc. Am., Am. Acad. Ophthalmology and Otolaryngology, Soc. Univ. Otolaryngologists, Am. Otol. Soc. (sec.-treas. rsch. fund 1979—), Soc. for Ear, Nose and Throat Advances in Children (pres. 1973), Assn. for Rsch. in Otolaryngology (pres. 1985-86), Am. Acad. Pediat. (chmn. otol. bronchoesphology 1983-85), Am. Soc. Pediat. Otolaryngology (historian 1986-95), Am. Soc. Pediat. Otolaryngologists (historian 1986-93, pres.-elect 1993-94, pres. 1994-95), Nat. Inst. Deafness and Other Comm. Disorders (adv. coun. 1989-93), Am. Laryngol. Soc. Home: 1025 Fifth Ave Apt 12C S New York NY 10028-0134 Office: Montefiore Med Ctr 111 E 210th St Bronx NY 10467-2401

RUBEN, ROBERT JOSEPH, lawyer; b. N.Y.C., Apr. 9, 1923; s. Ira Herbert and Kathleen Marie (Murphy) R.; m. Audrey H. Zweig, Nov. 20, 1949; children: Pamela Joan, James Bradford. B.S., Columbia U., 1943; M.A., Harvard U., 1948; LL.B., Fordham U., 1953. Bar: N.Y. 1954. Exec. trainee Chase Nat. Bank, N.Y.C., 1948-49; economist, 1949-53; assoc. Milbank, Tweed, Hope & Hadley, N.Y.C., 1953-55; assoc., then ptnr. Shea & Gould, N.Y.C., 1955-90; sec. Gen. Battery Corp., Reading, Pa., 1963-73, Fiat Metal Mfg. Co., Inc., Plainview, N.Y., 1961-64, Filtors, Inc., East Northport, N.Y., 1961-64, Trans-Industries, Inc., 1969—; asst. sec. Elgin Nat. Industries, 1975-88; asst. judge City Ct., Rye, N.Y., 1977-90; arbitrator Nat. Assn. Securities Dealers, 1990—, Pacific Stock Exch., 1992—, Am. Arbitration Assn., 1990—, N.Y. Stock Exch., 1994—. Trustee Rye Hist. Soc.; bd. dirs. Carver Center, Port Chester, N.Y., 1972-90. Served with AUS, 1943-46. Decorated Combat Inf. medal. Mem. ABA, N.Y. State Bar Assn., Assn. Bar of City of N.Y., Am. Arbitration Assn., Harvard Club (N.Y.C.), Harvard-Radcliffe Club So. Calif., Columbia U. Club So. Calif., Beta Gamma Sigma, Zeta Beta Tau. Home: 21285 Amora Mission Viejo CA 92692-4930

RUBEN, WILLIAM SAMUEL, marketing consultant; b. N.Y.C., June 23, 1927; s. Nathaniel Benjamin and Bertha Teresa (Stein) R.; children: Michaele, Marc. B.B.A., Syracuse U., 1950. Exec. trainee, buyer Dey Bros., Syracuse, N.Y., 1950-54; staff asst.-sr. v.p. Allied Stores Corp., N.Y.C., 1954-58; with Jordan Marsch-Fla., Miami, 1958—; gen. mdse. mgr. Jordan Marsch-Fla., 1962-64, mng. dir., 1964-66, pres., 1966-79, chmn. bd., 1979-83; pres. Bonwit Teller, N.Y.C., 1983-89, William Ruben, Inc., N.Y.C., 1989—; bd. dirs. Carnival Cruise Lines Inc. Pres. United Way of Dade County, 1979; mem. stategic planning com. United Way Am.; chmn. Dade County Co-ordinating Council, 1979—; mem. Gov.'s Revitalization Bd., 1980—; bd. dirs. Fla. Philharm., 1980-81; bd. overseers Parsons Sch. of Design, 1986—; chmn. Nat. Found. for Advancement in the Arts, 1983-88; bd. dirs. Theatre for a New Audience, Concordia Chamber Symphony. Served with USMCR, 1945-46. Recipient Silver medallion NCCJ, 1978, Humanitarian award Nat. B'nai B'rith, 1980, Outstanding Citizen award Dade County B'nai B'rith, 1979, Parsons Fashion award, 1983. Mem. Fla. Retail Fedn., Greater Miami C. of C. (v.p. 1979—). Jewish. Clubs: Standard, Sky, Jockey, New World Center. Office: William Ruben Inc 40 E 88th St New York NY 10128-1176

RUBENFELD, STANLEY IRWIN, lawyer; b. N.Y.C., Dec. 7, 1930; s. George and Mildred (Rose) R.; m. Caryl P. Ellner, June 8, 1952; children: Leslie Ann, Lise Susan, Kenneth Michael. B.A., Columbia U., 1952, J.D., 1956. Bar: N.Y. 1956. Practice law N.Y.C., 1956-65, 68—, 1965-68; assoc. Shearman & Sterling, 1956-65; ptnr. Shearman & Sterling, Paris, 1965-68; ptnr. Shearman & Sterling, N.Y.C., 1968-93, of counsel, 1994—crw; mediator U.S. Fed. Ct. Editor-in-chief Columbia Law Rev., 1955-56; contbr. articles to profl. jours. Bd. dirs., past pres. Port Washington (N.Y.) Comty. Chest; former bd. dirs. Residents for a More Beautiful Port Washington. Lt. (j.g.) USNR, 1952-54. Stone scholar, 1951-52, 54-55, 55-56; Rockefeller Found. grantee, 1955. Mem. ABA, N.Y. State Bar Assn. (past chmn. fgn. activities com., reorgn. corp.), Assn. Bar City N.Y. (tax com., past chmn. com. on recruitment lawyers), Nat. Assn. Law Placement (past bd. dirs., exec. com.), Columbia U. Law Sch. Alumni Assn. (bd. visitors, adviser past bd. dirs.), Columbia Coll. Alumni Assn., Tax Club (past chmn.), Phi Delta Phi, Tau Epsilon Phi (past pres.). Home: 41 Longview Rd Port Washington NY 11050-3039 Office: Citicorp Ctr 153 E 53rd St New York NY 10022-4611

RUBENS, LINDA MARCIA, home health services administrator; d. Harry and Ruth Slutzah; m. Robert A. Rubens; children: Scott, Mark. AS, Fla. Jr. Coll., Jacksonville. Lic. nursing home adminstr. RN U. Hosp. of Jacksonville, 1976-82; dir. nursing Mandarin Manor Nursing Home and Retirement Village, 1982-85, asst. adminstr., 1985-87; dir. nursing P.H.E.O. Med. Ctr., 1987-88; dir. clin. and profl. svcs. Kimberly Quality Care, 1988-90, br. mgr., 1990-93; adminstr. Health Care Mgmt. Cons., Jacksonville, 1993—; exec. dir. Mount Carmel Gardens Retirement Cmty., 1995—; part-time Dept. Labor, Office of Worker's Compensation, 1992—. Past mem. Gerontol. Search Team for Cathedral Found.; past treas. Mayor's Orgn. for Vol. Effort, past bd. dirs.; chairperson State-Wide Human Rights Advocacy Com., State of Fla., 1996—, chairperson consumer rels. subcom., 1990—; apptd. to Dist. IV Ombudsman Com., 1982-90, Dist. IV Human Rights Advocacy Com., 1989-90; bd. dir.s Mt. Carmel Retirement Cmty., State Mental Health Planning Coun. Mem. Rehab. Nurses Assn., Dirs. of Nursing Assn. (sec. long term care). Home: 13116 Mandarin Rd Jacksonville FL 32223-1748

RUBENS, PHILIP, communications educator, technical writer; b. Washington, Jan. 13, 1943; s. Maurice and Anna Mae (Kindilien) R.; m. Brenda Knowles, May 4, 1969; children: Theresa Marie Norman, Alesia Lauree Chavez. BA, U. Tex., Arlington, 1970; MA, U. Tex., 1972; PhD, No. Ill. U., 1976. Instr. Braniff Airways, Santiago, Chile, 1966-67; teaching asst. U. Tex. at Arlington, 1970-71, No. Ill. U., DeKalb, 1972-74; asst. prof. William Rainey Harper Coll., Chgo., 1975-76; assoc. prof. Mich. Tech. U., Houghton, 1976-80; prof. visual & tech. comm. Rensselaer Poly. Inst., Troy, N.Y., 1980—; tech. writer Washington Gas Light Co.; dir. comm. Braniff Airways, LTV Aerospace, Gas Dynamics Lab., City of Arlington; sr. rsch. assoc. TechWriting Affiliates, Inc.; cons. in field including Software Group, 1984, N.Y. Edn. Assn., 1981-84, IBM Corp., 1984, 85, 87, TechWriting Affiliates Inc., 1985, 86, 88—, Short Bros., Inc., Belfast, Ireland, 1985, Info. Assocs., 1985, DuPont Corp., 1985, Bell Labs., 1985, U. Leeds, 1986, High Tech., Inc., Tokyo, 1987. Editor: (book) Science and Technical Writing: A Manual of Style, 1993; mem. editorial bd. Mohawk Monitor, 1980—, Roxbury Press, 1986, Iowa Jour. Bus. and Tech. Comm., 1987—, Computers and Composition, 1987—, MIT Press, 1988—. Mem. Smithsonian Inst., Washington, 1976—; faculty advisor Keweenaw Chpt. Soc. for Tech. Comm., 1976-80; mem. Sierra Club, 1980—; dept. rep. Hudson-Mohawk Consortium, 1980-81; sustaining mem. No. Ill. U. Exec. Alumni Assn., 1980—; chair, membership com. Mohawk Chpt. Soc. for Tech. Comm., 1980-81, vice chair, 1981-82; exec. alumni U. Tex. at Arlington, 1981—; mem. Saratoga Sailing Club, 1981—, Saratoga Performing Arts Ctr., 1981—; mem. Westport (Conn.) Hist. Soc., 1985—. Recipient Chgo. Poetry Soc. Award for Outstanding Religious Poetry, Award for Outstanding Children's Poetry, Award for Most Outstanding Poem for Yr., 1975, Writer's Key for Outstanding Writing Ability, Sigma Tau Delta, 1976, Chpt. Achievement award Soc. for Tech. Comm., 1979, Outstanding Article award, 1982, Tchr. of Excellence award N.Y. State English Coun., 1984, Award of Merit for Softbridge Online Tutorial, 1986; MIT Sloan Sch. Mgmt. Rsch. fellow, 1990, Soc. for Tech. Comm. fellow, 1992. Mem. AAAS (edn. com. 1982—, MLA, Am. Bus. Comm. Assn. (chair undergrad. studies com. 1977), Coun. for Programs in Tech. and Sci. Comm. (charter mem., judge CPTSC Logo Competition 1982), IEEE Profl. Comm. Soc. (edn. com. 1986, co-program chair of 1989 conf.), Midwest MLA, Nat. Coun. Tchrs. English (mem. tech. writing com. 1976—), Popular Culture Assn., Sci. Fiction Rsch. Assn., Sci. Writing Educators Group, Soc. for Tech. Comm. (judge internat. audio-visual competition 1985— and others. Home: 303 Bebington Dr Cary NC 27513-1750 Office: Rensselaer Poly Inst Sage Labs Troy NY 12180

RUBENS, SIDNEY MICHEL, physicist, technical advisor; b. Spokane, Wash., Mar. 21, 1910; s. Max Zvoln and Jennie Golda (Rubinovich) R.; m. Julienne Rose Fridner, May 11, 1944; 1 dau., Deborah Janet. BS, U. Wash., 1934, PhD, 1939. Instr. U. So. Calif., 1939-40; research assoc. UCLA, 1940-41; physicist Naval Ordnance Lab., Washington, 1941-46; physicist Engring. Research Assos., St. Paul, 1946-52; mgr. physics Univac div. Sperry Rand, St. Paul, 1958-61, dir. research, 1961-66, staff scientist, 1969-71, dir. spl. projects, 1971-75; cons., 1975-81; technical advisor Vertimag Systems Corp., 1981—, Advanced Research Corp., 1986—; lectr. U. Pa., 1960-61; mem. adv. subcom. on instrumentation and data processing NASA, 1967-69, panel on computer tech. Nat. Acad. Sci., 1969. Hon. fellow U. Minn., 1977—. Fellow IEEE (magnetic soc. info. storage award 1987); mem. AAAS, N.Y. Acad. Sci., Am. Phys. Soc., Am. Geophys. Union, Acad. Applied Sci., Minn. Acad. Sci., Am. Optical Soc., Phi Beta Kappa, Sigma Xi, Pi Mu Epsilon. Patentee in magnetic material and devices. Author: Amplifier and Memory Devices, 1965. Contbr. articles to profl. jours. Home: 1007 Sibley Hwy Apt 506 Saint Paul MN 55118-3616 Office: Advanced Rsch Corp 815 14th Ave SE Minneapolis MN 55414-1515

RUBENSTEIN, ALBERT HAROLD, industrial engineering and management sciences educator; b. Phila., Nov. 11, 1923; s. Leo and Jean (Kaplan) R.; m. Hildette Grossman, Sept. 11, 1949; children—Michael Stephen, Lisa Joan. B.S. magna cum laude in Indsl. Engring. (Sr. prize econs.), Lehigh U., 1949; M.S. in Indsl. Engring, Columbia, 1950, Ph.D. in Indsl. Engring. and Mgmt, 1954; DEng (hon.), Lehigh U., 1993. Asst. to pres. Perry Equipment Corp., 1940-43; research assoc. Columbia U., 1950-53; asst. prof. indsl. mgmt. MIT, 1954-59; prof. indsl. engring. and mgmt. scis. Northwestern U., 1959—, Walter P. Murphy prof., 1986—, dir. Ctr. for Info. Tech., 1986—; pres. Internat. Applied Sci. and Tech. Assos., 1977—; vis. prof. U. Calif., Berkeley; pres. Sr. Strategy Group, 1995—; cons. to govt. and industry. Dir. Narragansett Capital Corp. Author books and articles in field. Served with inf. AUS, World War II. Decorated Purple Heart, Combat Inf. badge.; Recipient Lincoln Arc Welding Found. prize paper, 1948, Pioneer in Innovation Mgmt. award Ctr. Innovation Mgmt., 1992; Omicron Delta Kappa annual fellow, 1949-50; Fulbright research fellow, 1955. Fellow IEEE (editor trans. 1959—, Engring. Mgr. of Yr. award 1992), Soc. Applied Anthropology; sr. mem. Inst. Mgmt. Scis. (dir. studies for coll. on research and devel. 1960—, v.p. research and edn. 1966-68). Home: 2348 Ridge Ave Evanston IL 60201-2600

RUBENSTEIN, ARTHUR HAROLD, physician, educator; b. Johannesburg, South Africa, Dec. 28, 1937; came to U.S., 1967; s. Montague and Isabel (Nathanson) R.; m. Denise Hack, Aug. 19, 1962; children: Jeffrey Lawrence, Errol Charles. MB, BChir, U. Witwatersrand, 1960. Diplomate Am. Bd. Internal Medicine. Intern, then resident Johannesburg Gen. Hosp., 1961, 63-65, 66-67; fellow in endocrinology Postgrad. Med. Sch., London, 1965-66; fellow in medicine U. Chgo., 1967-68, from asst. prof. to assoc. prof., 1968-74, prof., 1974—, Lowell T. Coggeshall prof. med. sci., 1981—, assoc. chmn. dept. medicine, 1975-81, chmn., 1981—, dir. Diabetes Rsch. and Tng. Ctr., 1986-91; attending physician Mitchell Hosp., U. Chgo., 1968—; mem. study sect. NIH, 1973-77, Hadassah Med. Adv. Bd., 1986-95, adv. council Nat. Inst. Arthritis, Metabolism and Digestive Diseases, 1978-80; chmn. Nat. Diabetes Adv. Bd., 1982, mem., 1981-83. Mem. editorial bd. Diabetes, 1973-77, Endocrinology, 1973-77, Jour. Clin. Investigation, 1976-81, Am. Jour. Medicine, 1978-81, Diabetologia, 1982-86, Diabetes Medicine, 1987-91, Annals of Internal Medicine, 1991—, Medicine, 1992—; contbr. articles to profl. jours. Mem. Gov.'s Sci. Adv. Coun. State of Ill., 1989-96. Recipient David Rumbough Meml. award Juvenile Diabetes Found., 1978. Master ACP (John Phillips Meml. award 1995); fellow South African Coll. Physicians, Royal Coll. Physicians (London); mem. Am. Soc. for Clin. Investigation, Am. Diabetes Assn. (Eli Lilly award 1973, Banting medal 1983, Solomon Berson Meml. lectr. 1985), Brit. Diabetes Assn. (Banting lectr. 1987), Endocrine Soc., Am. Fedn. Clin. Rsch., Ctrl. Soc. Clin. Rsch. (v.p. 1988, pres. 1989), Assn. Am. Physicians (treas. 1984-89, councillor 1989-94, v.p. 1994-95, pres. 1995-96), Am. Bd. Internal Medicine (bd. govs. 1985-93, exec. com. 1990-93, chmn. 1992-93), Residency Rev. Com., Am. Acad. Arts and Scis., Inst. Medicine (coun. 1991-96), Assn. Profs. Medicine (councillor 1991-94, v.p. 1994-95, pres. 1995-96, Robert Williams award 1997). Home: 5517 S Kimbark Ave Chicago IL 60637-1618 Office: U Chgo Dept of Medicine 5841 S Maryland Ave Chicago IL 60637-1463

RUBENSTEIN, BERNARD, orchestra conductor; b. Springfield, Mo., Oct. 30, 1937; s. Milton and Evelyn Marion (Friedman) R.; m. Ann Warren Little, Aug. 28, 1961; children: Tanya, Stefan Alexei. B.Mus. with distinction, Eastman Sch. Music, U. Rochester, 1958; M.Mus., Yale U., 1961. Assoc. prof. conducting, dir. orch. orgns. Northwestern U., Evanston, Ill., 1968-80. Asst. condr. R.I. Philharm. Orch., 1961-62; condr. music dir. Santa Fe Symphony Orch., 1962-64; condr. Greenwood Chamber Orch., Cummington, Mass., 1968-79; asst. condr. Stuttgart Opera, 1966-68; condr., music dir. Music for Youth, Milw., 1970-80; assoc. condr. Cin. Symphony Orch., 1980-86; music dir. Tulsa Philharm., 1984-96, condr. laureate, 1996—, condr. laureate, 1996—; music dir. San Juan Symphony, 1997—; guest condr. numerous orchs. including Milw. Symphony Orch., St. Paul Chamber Orch., Guadalajara Symphony Orch., Berlin Radio Orch., Frankfurt Radio Orch., Grant Park Orch., Chgo., die reihe, Vienna, Austrian Radio Orch., Eastman Philharm., Halle Symphony Orch., E. Ger., Warsaw Philharm., St. Louis Little Symphony, W. German Radio Orch., Palazzo Pitti Orch. Florence, Italy, Frankfurt Opera, Tonkuenstler Orch., Vienna, S.W. German Radio Orch., Baden-Baden, Jerusalem Symphony, Anchorage, Hamilton, Ont., Hartford Conn., L.A. Chamber Orch., Austin (Tex.) Symphony, Am. Composers Orch. N.Y.C. Winner internat. conducting competition Serate Musicale Fiorentine, 1965; Fulbright scholar, 1964-66; recipient Charles Ditson award Yale U., 1961, Martha Baird Rockefeller award, 1966-68. Mem. Am. Symphony Orch. League, Condrs. Guild. Office: 1070 Governor Dempsey Dr Santa Fe NM 87501-1078

RUBENSTEIN, DAVID H., media manufacturing executive; b. Bklyn.; s. Maxwell and Rella (Leventhol) R. BA, Hofstra U., 1977. Rec. engr. A&R Rec., N.Y.C., 1977-78; nat. sales mgr. AgFg - Gevgent, Teterboro, N.J., 1978-84; exec. v.p. Technicolor, Inc., Newbury Park, Calif., 1984-85, Custom Duplication, Inglewood, Calif., 1986-91; pres. Cinram U.S. Holdings, Richmond, Ind., 1992—. Avocation: private pilot. Office: Cinram Inc 1600 Rich Rd Richmond IN 47374-1435

RUBENSTEIN, EDWARD, physician, educator; b. Cin., Dec. 5, 1924; s. Louis and Nettie R.; m. Nancy Ellen Millman, June 20, 1954; children: John, William, James. MD, U. Cin., 1947. House staff Cin. Gen. Hosp., 1947-50; fellow May Inst., Cin., 1950; sr. asst. resident Ward Med. Service, Barnes Hosp., St. Louis, 1953-54; chief of medicine San Mateo County Hosp., Calif., 1960-70; assoc. dean postgrad. med. edn., prof. medicine Stanford (Calif.) U., 1971—, emeritus, active; mem. faculty Stanford Photon Research Lab.; affiliated faculty mem. Stanford Synchortron Radiation Lab., 1971—; mem. maj. materials facilities com. Nat. Research Council, 1984-85, Nat. Steering Com. 6 GeV Electron Storage Ring., 1986—. Author: (textbook) Intensive Medical Care; editor-in-chief: (textbook) Sci. Am. Medicine, 1978-94; editor: Synchotron Radiation Handbook, 1988, vol. 4, 1991; editor Synchotron Radiation in the Biosciences, Molecular Medicine; mem. editorial adv. bd. Sci. Am., Inc., 1991-94. Served with USAF, 1950-52. Recipient Kaiser award for outstanding and innovative contbns. to med. edn., 1989, Albion Walter Hewlett Award, 1993. Fellow AAAS, Royal Soc. Medicine; mem. APS, ACP (master), Inst. Medicine, Calif. Acad. Medicine, Western Assn. Physicians, Soc. Photo-Optical Engrs., Am. Clin. and Climatol. Assn., Alpha Omega Alpha. Research on synchrotron radiation. Office: Stanford Medical Center Dept of Medicine Stanford CA 94305

RUBENSTEIN, HOWARD JOSEPH, public relations executive; b. N.Y.C., Feb. 3, 1932; s. Samuel and Ada (Sall) R.; m. Amy Forman, Dec. 17, 1959; children: Roni, Richard, Steven. A.B., U. Pa., 1953; student law, Harvard, 1953; LL.B. (Dean's scholar), St. Johns Sch. Law, 1959, LLD (hon.), 1990. Bar: N.Y. State bar 1960. Pres. Rubenstein Assocs., Inc. pub. rels. cons., N.Y.C., 1954—; asst. counsel judiciary com. U.S. Ho. of Reps., 1960; cons. U.S. Fgn. Claims Commn., 1961-62; cons. joint legis. com. child care needs N.Y., 1965-66; adviser SBA,, 1965-66. Mem. Gov.'s Com. on Sale of World Trade Ctr., 1981, Mayor's Com. on Holocaust Commemoration, 1981—, N.Y. State Task Force on Energy Conservation, Dept. Housing, 1981-83, Mayor's Coun. Econ. Bus. Advisors, 1991-93; co-chmn. Holocaust Commn., 1993—; v.p. Jewish Cmty. Rels. Coun., 1988-94, advisor, 1995—; past dir. Brownsville Boys Club; bd. dirs. Provide Addict Care Today, Police Athletic League, N.Y. chpt. March of Dimes; mem. U.S. Internat. Coun., 1977-81, Commn. on Status of Women, 1982-89, N.Y.C. Commn. Operation Welcom Home, 1991-92; trustee Ctrl. Park Conservancy; mem. Mayor's Bus. Adv. Coun., 1996—; advisor N.Y. Commn. on Status of Women, 1995—; comm. advisor Gov.'s Com. Jerusalem 3000, 1996—. Mem. Assn. Better N.Y. (mem. exec. com. 1972—), Phi Beta Kappa, Beta Sigma Rho. Jewish (dir. congregation). Home: 993 Fifth Ave New York NY 10028-0105 Office: Rubenstein Assoc Inc 1345 Avenue Of The Americas New York NY 10105-0302

RUBENSTEIN, JEROME MAX, lawyer; b. St. Louis, Feb. 16, 1927; s. Jacob J. and Anne (Frankel) R.; m. Judith Hope Grand, July 31, 1954; children—Edward J., Emily Rubenstein Muslin, Daniel H. A.B., Harvard U., 1950, LL.B., 1955. Bar: Mo. 1956, U.S. Dist. Ct. (ea. dist.) Mo. 1956, U.S. Ct. Appeals (8th cir.) 1956. Mem. English lit. faculty U. So. Philippines, Cebu, 1950-51; law clk U.S. Dist. Ct., St. Louis, 1955-56; assoc. Lewis, Rice, Tucker, Allen & Chubb, St. Louis, 1956-64; assoc. Grand, Peper & Martin, St. Louis, 1964-65, ptnr., 1965-66; jr. ptnr. Bryan, Cave, McPheeters & McRoberts, St. Louis, 1966-67, sr. ptnr., 1968—; dir. Commerce Bank of St. Louis, N.A. Bd. dirs. Independence Ctr., St. Louis, 1985-88, The Arts and Edn. Coun. Greater St. Louis, 1991—. Served with USN, 1945-46. Bd. dirs. Independence Ctr., St. Louis, 1985. Served with USN, 1945-46. Mem. ABA, Mo. Bar Assn., St. Louis Bar Assn., Mo. Athletic Club, Harvard Club of St. Louis (pres. 1982-83, bd. dirs. 1983-90). Jewish. Avocations: jogging; tennis. Home: 7394 Westmoreland Dr Saint Louis MO 63130-4240 Office: Bryan Cave 1 Metropolitan Sq Saint Louis MO 63102-2733

RUBENSTEIN, JOSHUA SETH, lawyer; b. Bklyn., Aug. 5, 1954; s. Seth and Elaine (Freedman) R.; m. Marta Johnson: children: Mary-Jane, Kenan, Rebecca, Marlena. BA magna cum laude, Columbia U., 1976, JD, 1979. Bar: N.Y. 1980, N.J. 1980, U.S. Dist. Ct. (ea. dist.) N.Y. 1980, U.S. Dist. Ct. (so. dist.) N.Y. 1980, U.S. Dist. Ct. N.J. 1980, U.S. Tax Ct. 1986. Assoc. Fried, Frank, Harris, Shriver & Jacobson, N.Y.C., 1979-82; assoc. Rosenman & Colin LLP, N.Y.C., 1982-88, ptnr., 1988—; mgmt. com. Rosenman & Colin, N.Y.C., 1994—, chmn. trusts & Estates dept., 1995—; adv. bd. TE/DEC Systems, Inc., Jour. N.Y. Taxation; lectr. in field; adv. com. on surrogate's cts. Office of Ct. Adminstrn., 1997—; adv. coun. Columbia Law Sch. Trusts, Wills and Estate Planning, 1997—. Contbr. articles to legal publs. Pres. Brasch Farms Civic Assn., Middletown, N.J., 1982-84, 340 E. 74th St. Owners Corp., 1990-91; dir., sec. Irvington Inst. Med. Rsch., 1991, treas., 1991-92, sec., 1992-93, co-pres., 1993-94, pres., 1994—; chmn. estates and trust splty. group, chmn. splty. group; task force, mem. exec. com. lawyers divsn. United Jewish Appeal-Fedn., 1989—; mem. legis. com., devel. com., bd. governance com., Madeleine Borg com., chmn., mem. exec. com., 1994—; trustee Jewish Bd. Family and Children's Svcs., 1991—. Recipient James H. Fogelson award Lawyer's divsn. United Jewish Appeal-Fedn., 1993; named to Best Lawyers in N.Y., N.Y. Mag. Fellow Am. Coll. Trusts and Estate Counsel (state laws com.), N.Y. State Bar Found.; mem. ABA (real property and probate sect.), Internat. Acad. Estate and Trust Law (academician 1997—), Practising Law Inst. (estate adv. com., lectr. 1984—, Hadassah estate planning seminar faculty and adv. bd. 1993—), N.Y. State Bar Assn. (trust and estate law sect., lect. 1984—, vice chmn. legis. com. 1988, chmn. 1988-91, co-chmn. ad hoc com. to rev. proposals of EPTL adv. com. of N.Y. State 1991—, mem.-at-large exec. com. 1992-95, liaison to legis. policy com. 1995—, Pres.'s Pro Bono Svc. award 1991, Exec. Com. award, 1992, 95, 96, treas. 1997), N.J. Bar Assn. adv. com. rels. with legis. and exec. brs., real property and probate sect.), Assn. of Bar of City of N.Y, Phi Beta Kappa. Democrat. Jewish. Office: Rosenman & Colin 575 Madison Ave New York NY 10022-2511

RUBENSTEIN, LEONARD SAMUEL, communications executive, ceramist, painter, sculptor, photographer; b. Rochester, N.Y., Sept. 22, 1918; s. Jacob S. and Zelda H. (Gordon) R.; m. (dec. 1983); children: Carolinda, Eric, Harley. BFA cum laude, Alfred U., 1939; student Case Western Res. U., 1938; postgrad. U. Rochester, 1940-41. Creative dir. Henry Hempstead Advt. Agy., Chgo., 1949-55; v.p., exec. art dir. Clinton E. Frank Advt. Agy., Chgo., 1955-63; v.p., nat. creative dir. Foster & Kleiser divsn. Metromedia, Inc., L.A., 1967-73, v.p. corp. creative cons., Metromedia, Inc., L.A., 1973-88; guest lectr. U. Chgo.; instr. Columbia Coll., Chgo.; past. pres. Art Dirs. Club Chgo. (spl. citation); instr. Fashion Inst., L.A.; lectr. in field. Mem. Soc. Typog. Arts (past dir.), Am. Ceramic Soc. (design chpt.), Am. Craft Coun., Inst. Outdoor Advt. (mem. past plans bd.), L.A. County Mus. Art, Mus. Contemporary Art of L.A. (charter), Palos Verdes (Calif.) Art Ctr., B'nai B'rith, Phi Epsilon Pi. Author: (with Charles Hardison) Outdoor Advertising; contbr. articles to profl. publs.; one-man show at Calif. Mus. Sci. and Industry, 1970; two-person exhibition of porcelains, Palos Verdes Art Ctr., 1987; participant nat. and regional group shows; creator concept for Smithsonian exhibition Images of China: East and West, 1982; writer-prodr. (ednl. video) Paul Soldner, Thoughts on Creativity, 1989, (video documentary) High-Tech/Low-Tech: The Science and Art of Ceramics, 1994; porcelains in permanent collections. Home and Office: 30616 Ganado Dr Rancho Palos Verdes CA 90275 *Personal philosophy: I have a disdain for the trendy, the superficial and the transient.*

RUBENSTEIN, RICHARD LOWELL, theologian, educator; b. N.Y.C., Jan. 8, 1924; s. Jesse George and Sara (Fine) R.; m. Betty Rogers Alschuler, Aug. 21, 1966; children by previous marriage: Aaron, Nathaniel (dec.), Hannah Rachel, Jeremy. Student, Hebrew Union Coll., Cin., 1942-45; AB, U. Cin., 1946; MHL rabbi, Jewish Theol. Sem., N.Y.C., 1952; DHL (honoris causa), Jewish Theol. Sem., 1987; STM, Harvard U., 1955, PhD, 1960. Rabbi in Brockton, Mass., 1952-54, Natick, Mass., 1954-56; chaplain to Jewish students Harvard U., 1956-68; univ. chaplain to Jewish students U. Pitts. and Carnegie Inst. Tech., 1958-70; adj. prof. humanities U. Pitts., 1969-70; prof. religion Fla. State U., Tallahassee, 1970-77; Disting. prof. religion Fla. State U., 1977-81, Robert O. Lawton Disting. prof. religion, 1981-95; prof. emeritus religion Fla. State U., $D, 1995—; co-dir. Inst. for Humanities Fla. State U., 1980-95; pres. Washington Inst. for Values in Pub. Policy, 1982-95; Edgar M. Bronfman vis. prof. U. Va., 1985; adv. bd. Washington Times, 1982-91, chmn. editl. adv. bd., 1991—; exec. adv. bd. The World and I mag., 1986—; exec. com. Internat. Jour. of the Unity of Scis., 1987-95; mem. presiding coun. Internat. Religious Fedn. for World Peace, 1991—; chmn. bd. trustees U. Bridgeport, 1994. Author: After Auschwitz: Radical Theology and Contemporary Judaism, 1966, The Religious

Imagination, 1968 (Portico d'Ottavia lit. prize for Italian transl. 1977), Morality and Eros, 1970, My Brother Paul, 1972, Power Struggle: An Autobiographical Confession, 1974, The Cunning of History, 1975, The Age of Triage, 1983, (with John K. Roth) Approaches to Auschwitz, 1986, After Auschwitz: History, Theology and Contemporary Judaism, Johns Hopkins U. Press, 1992; editor: Modernization: The Humanist Response to Its Promise and Problems, 1982, Spirit Matters: The Worldwide Impact of Religion on Contemporary Politics, 1987, The Dissolving Alliance: The United States and the Future of the NATO Alliance, 1987, In Depth: A Journal of Values in Public Policy, 1991-94; regular columnist Sekai Nippo, Tokyo, 1987-94. Trustee Greater Bridgeport Regional Bus. Coun., 1996—; vice chmn. acad. divsn. United Way of Ea. Fairfield County, Conn., 1997—; trustee Bridgeport Pub. Edn. Fund, 1997—. Recipient Portico d' Ottavia lit. prize Rome, 1977; John Phillips fellow Phillips Exeter Acad., 1970; postdoctoral fellow Soc. Religion in Higher Edn.; Nat. Humanities Inst. fellow Yale U., 1976-77; Rockefeller Found. fellow Aspen Inst. for Humanistic Studies, 1979. Mem. Rabbinical Assembly Am., Am. Acad. Religion, Soc. Sci. Study Religion, Profs. World Peace Acad. (exec. com. 1980—, pres. 1981-82), Internat. House of Japan, Conn. Acad. Arts and Scis., Harvard Club (N.Y.C.), Cosmos Club, Rotary. Office: Univ Bridgeport Office of Pres Bridgeport CT 06601

RUBENSTEIN, STANLEY ELLIS, public relations consultant; b. Balt., July 25, 1930; s. Albert B. and Lee (Goodman) R.; m. Ruth Anne Zinder, Feb. 8, 1953; children: Deborah C., Steven M., Michael L., Kenneth J., Andrew L. BA, U. Md., 1953. Writer, researcher Bozell & Jacobs, Inc., N.Y.C., 1953-54; reporter Jour. of Commerce, N.Y.C., 1954-56; writer, account exec. Ruder & Finn, Inc., N.Y.C., 1956-60; founder, prin. Rubenstein, Wolfson & Co., Inc., N.Y.C., 1960-91; pub. rels. cons. S. E. Rubenstein, N.Y.C., 1991—. Mem. Bd. Edn. Gt. Neck (N.Y.) Pub. Sch., 1968-74, pres. 3 yrs. Served with USN, 1948-49. Mem. Pub. Relations Soc. Am., N.Y. Fin. Writers Assn. (assoc.). Jewish. Clubs: Nat. Press; World Trade (N.Y.C.). Avocations: photography, travel. Home: 51 Colgate Rd Great Neck NY 11023-1519 Office: 150 E 58th St Fl 33 New York NY 10155-0099

RUBENSTEIN, STEVEN PAUL, newspaper columnist; b. L.A., Oct. 31, 1951; s. Victor Gerald and Florence (Fox) R.; m. Caroline Moira Grannan, Jan. 1, 1989; children: William Laurence, Anna Katherine. BA, U. Calif., Berkeley, 1977. Reporter L.A. Herald Examiner, 1974-76; reporter San Francisco Chronicle, 1976-81, columnist, 1981—. Office: San Francisco Chronicle 901 Mission St San Francisco CA 94103-2905

RUBEO, BRUNO, production designer. Art dir.: (films) Spring Fever, 1983; prodn. designer: (films) Platoon, 1986, Salvador, 1986, Walker, 1987, Talk Radio, 1988, Blood Red, 1988, Born on the Fourth of July, 1989, Driving Miss Daisy, 1989 (Academy award nomination best art direction 1989), (with Stuart Wurtzel) Old Gringo, 1989, Kindergarten Cop, 1990, Sommersby, 1992, (with Marek Dobrowolski) Blood In Blood Out, 1993, The Client, 1994, Dolores Claiborne, 1995. Office: Sandra Marsh Mgt 9150 Wilshire Blvd Ste 220 Beverly Hills CA 90212-3429*

RUBERG, ROBERT LIONEL, surgery educator; b. Phila., July 22, 1941; s. Norman and Yetta (Wolfman) R.; m. Cynthia Lief, June 26, 1966; children: Frederick, Mark, Joshua. BA, Haverford (Pa.) Coll., 1963; MD, Harvard U., 1967. Diplomate Am. Bd. Surgery, Am. Bd. Plastic Surgery. Instr. surgery U. Pa., Phila., 1972-75; asst. prof. Ohio State U., Columbus, 1975-81, assoc. prof., 1981-88, prof., 1988—; bd. dirs. Am. Bd. Plastic Surgery, 1991—, vice-chair, 1996—; chmn. curriculum com. Coll. Medicine, Ohio State U., 1984—; chief plastic surgery Ohio State U. Hosps., 1985—. Plastic Surgery Ednl. Found. research grantee, 1976, 78. Fellow ACS; mem. Am. Assn. Plastic Surgeons, Assn. Acad. Chairmen of Plastic Surgery (sec.-treas. 1990-93, pres. 1994-95). Avocations: basketball, bicycling. Home: 100 Walnut Woods Ct Gahanna OH 43230-6200 Office: Ohio State U Hosps 410 W 10th Ave # 809 Columbus OH 43210-1240

RUBIN, A. LOUIS, advertising executive; b. Paterson, N.J., Jan. 15, 1954; m. Jeanne Stark, Jan. 21, 1978; 1 child, Matthew. BA, Clark U., 1976; MEd, Harvard U., 1977. Project dir. Benton & Bowles, N.Y.C., 1977-79; account exec. Dancer Fitzgerald Sample, N.Y.C., 1979-81; product mgr. Gen. Foods, White Plains, N.Y., 1981-84; account supr. Scali McCabe Sloves, N.Y.C., 1984-85; v.p., mgmt. dir. FCB/Leberkatz Ptnrs., N.Y.C., 1985-88; sr. v.p., mgmt. dir. Scali McCabe Sloves, N.Y.C., 1988-92; exec. v.p. Y & R Inc., LD & P, N.Y.C., 1992-96; exec. v.p., dir. mktg. planning Doremus, N.Y.C., 1996—. Home: 15 Whig Rd Scarsdale NY 10583-3013

RUBIN, ALAN A., pharmaceutical and biotechnology consultant; b. N.Y.C., July 10, 1926; s. Harry and Gertrude R.; m. Helen M. Feinstein; children: Jeffrey, Ronald, Howard. B.S., NYU, 1950, M.S., 1953, Ph.D., 1959. Pharmacologist Schering Corp., Bloomfield, N.J., 1954-64; dir. pharmacology Endo Labs., Garden City, N.Y., 1964-70, v.p. research, 1970-74; dir. research DuPont Pharms., Wilmington, Del., 1974-82, dir. sci. info. and tech., 1982-87; dir. licensing tech. DuPont Merck Pharms., Wilmington, Del., 1987-91; cons. ARA Assocs., Rockland, Del., 1991—; bd. dirs. Lexington Scis., 1996—. Editor: Search for New Drugs, 1972, New Drugs: Discovery and Development, 1978; contbr. articles to profl. jours. Served with U.S. Army, 1944-46. Mem. AAAS, Am. Soc. Pharmacology and Exptl. Therapeutics, Soc. Exptl. and Biol. Medicine, Am. Heart Assn. Home: 207 Hitching Post Dr Wilmington DE 19803-1914 Office: ARA Assoc PO Box 244 Rockland DE 19732-0244

RUBIN, ALAN J., environmental engineer, chemist; b. Yonkers, N.Y., Mar. 20, 1934; s. Jerome and Lydia R.; m. Ann Kopyt, June 17, 1962; 1 dau., Sara. B.S. in Civil Engring, U. Miami (Fla.), 1959; M.S. in San. Engring, U. N.C., Chapel Hill, 1962, Ph.D. in Environ. Chemistry, 1966. Civil engr. FAA, Ft. Worth, 1959-60; asst. prof. U. Cin., 1965-68; prof. civil engring. Ohio State U., Columbus, 1968-91, prof. emeritus, 1991—; with U.S. Geol. Survey, Columbus, 1991-93; vis. prof. Technion, Haifa, 1984. Editor 4 books on environ. chemistry; contbr. articles profl. jours. Served with AUS, 1953-55. Mem. Am. Water Works Assn., Water Pollution Control Fedn., Internat. Assn. Water Pollution Research. Achievements include research on giardia cysts, metal ion chemistry, flotation techniques, disinfection, flocculation, coagulation, adsorption, and other physical-chemical treatment processes. Home: 1438 Sherbrooke Pl Columbus OH 43209-3113 Office: Ohio State Univ Dept of Civil Engring Columbus OH 43210-1058

RUBIN, ALBERT LOUIS, physician, educator; b. Memphis, May 9, 1927; s. Malcolm M. and Sarah Anne (Bryan) R.; m. Carolyn M. Diehl, Sept. 28, 1953; 1 child, Marc. Student, Williams College, 1944-45, MIT, 1945-46; MD, Cornell U., 1950. Diplomate Am. Bd. Internal Medicine. Intern Bellevue Hosp., N.Y.C., 1950-51, resident internal medicine, 1951-54, fellow nephrology, 1954-55; physician-in-charge Bellevue Hosp., 1953-61; established investigator Am. Heart Assn., N.Y.C., 1958-63; dir. Rogosin Labs., Cornell U. Med. Coll., N.Y.C., 1963—, The Rogosin Kidney Ctr., N.Y.C., 1971—, The Rogosin Inst., N.Y.C., 1983—; prof. biochemistry, surgery, medicine Cornell U. Med. Coll., N.Y.C., 1969—; surgeon The N.Y. Hosp., N.Y.C., 1969—; mem. com. on sci. and tech. aspects of processing materials in space NRC, N.Y.C.; dir. affiliations and patient referrals N.Y. Hosp.-Cornell Med. Ctr., 1977-80; bd. dirs., bd. incorporators neuroscis. rsch. program MIT. Author: Physical Diagnosis: A Textbook and Workbook in Methods of Clinical Examination, 1972, Humoral Aspects of Transplantation, 1976, Manual of Clinical Nephrology, 1980; cons. editor Am. Jour. Medicine; med. editl. cons. Time mag., 1983-94. With USN, 1944-45. Recipient Hoeing award Nat. Kidney Found., 1982. Mem. ACP, AAAS, Am. Soc. for Artificial Internal Organs, Transplantation Soc., Sigma XI. Home: 220 Allison Ct Englewood NJ 07631-4301 Office: The Rogosin Inst 505 E 70th St # 230 New York NY 10021-4872

RUBIN, ALLAN MAIER, physician, surgeon; b. Bavaria, Germany, Aug. 4, 1947; s. Benjamin Rubin and Ida Spiegle; children: Alanna T., Marissa D., Sarina D.; m. Jean Tellander, Mar. 5, 1989. BS, McGill U., Montreal, Que., Can., 1968, MS, 1970; PhD, MD, U. Toronto, Ont., Can., 1979. Diplomate Am. Bd. Otolaryngology. Demonstrator neuroanatomy U. Toronto, 1971-73, resident, 1979-84; investigator Toronto Gen. Hosp., 1976-78; fellow otolaryngology Toronto East Gen. Hosp., 1985; asst. prof. dept. otolaryngology Creighton U., Omaha, 1986-87; assoc. prof. dept. surgery Med. Coll. Ohio, Toledo, 1987-88, chmn., prof. dept. otolaryngology, 1988—; mem. resident edn. com. Blue Cross N.W. Ohio, Toledo, 1992-93, HMO/Toledo Health Plan, 1989-93; pres. Acad. Senate Med. Coll. Ohio, Toledo, 1991-92; chmn. search for urology chair Med. Coll. Ohio, 1991-92, presdl. search com., 1991-93. Mem. internat. editl. adv. bd. Jour. Otolaryngology, 1991—, editl. rev. bd. Am. Jour. Otolaryngology, 1989-94. Rsch. grantee Biomed. Rsch. Support Grant, 1984, NIH, 1986, 87. Fellow ACS, Royal Soc. Medicine, Am. Neurotology Soc., Am. Acad. Otolaryngology-Head and Neck Surgery (subcom. on equilibrium 1988—, subcom. on med. aspects of noise, editl. rev. bd. 1993—); mem. Soc. Univ. Otolarygologists (resident edn. com., membership com.), Barany Soc., Triological Soc., Sigma Xi, Alpha Omega Alpha (v.p. Delta of Ohio chpt. 1996—, chmn. search com. for orthopaedic surgery chmn.). Achievements include management and treatment of vestibular dysfunction and dizziness in children; correlation and transcranial doppler (TCD) and brain single photon emission computed tomography (SPECT) in patients with dizziness. Office: Med Coll Ohio 3000 Arlington Ave Toledo OH 43614-2595

RUBIN, ARNOLD JESSE, aeronautical engineer; b. Bklyn., Sept. 30, 1924; s. Jack and Birdie (Reiss) R.; B. Aero. Engring., N.Y.U., 1949; postgrad., U. Va., 1950, Poly. Inst. Bklyn., 1960-62; m. Gloria Form, June 19, 1949 (dec. Sept. 1994); children—Jacqueline Sue Rubin Grob, Mitchell Myles. Aero. research scientist Langley Research Center, NASA, Hampton, Va., 1949-51; with Fairchild Republic Co., Fairchild Industries, Inc., Farmingdale, N.Y., 1951-87, prin. aerodyn. engr., 1979-82, chief aerodyns., T-46A, 1982-87. Served with USAAF, 1943-45. Fellow AIAA (assoc.); mem. Soc. Flight Test Engrs., N.Y.U. Alumni Assn. Club: Huron. Home: 106 Sprucewood Dr Levittown NY 11756-3837

RUBIN, BARRY MITCHEL, foreign policy analyst, writer; b. Washington, Jan. 28, 1950; s. David and Helen Victoria (Segal) R.; m. Judith Colp; 1 child, Gavriella. BA, Richmond Coll., 1972; MA, Rutgers U., 1974; PhD, Georgetown U., 1978. Sr. fellow CSIS, Washington, 1978-85, Washington Inst. Near East Policy, Washington, 1988-91; congl. fellow Coun. Fgn. Rels., Washington, 1985-86; fellow Johns Hopkins SAIS, Washington, 1986-93, prof., 1986-93; sr. fellow Hebrew U. Harry S. Truman Inst., 1989—, U. Haifa Jewish-Arab Ctr., 1993—, Bar-Ilan U. BESA Ctr., 1994—; sr. resident scholar BESA Ctr., 1996—; adj. prof. Johns Hopkins SAIS, Washington, 1986-93, dir. SAIS project polit. study terrorism; mem. fgn. policy staff U.S. Senate, 1985-86; prof. Hebrew U., 1994-95. Author: Paved with Good Intentions, 1980, The Arab States and the Palestine Conflict, 1982, Secrets of State, 1985, Modern Dictators, 1987, Istanbul Intrigues, 1989, Islamic Fundamentalists in Egyptian Politics, 1991, Cauldron of Turmoil, 1992, Resolution Until Victory?: The Politics of the PLO, 1994, Assimilation and its Discontents, 1995; editor: (with others) The Human Rights Reader, 1979, The Israel-Arab Reader, 1984, 95, Central American Crisis Reader, 1987, The Politics of Terrorism, 3 vols., Iraq's Road to War, 1994; editor Middle East Rev. Internat. Affairs. Internat. affairs fellow Coun. on Fgn. Rels., 1984-85, Fulbright fellow, 1990-91; grantee U.S. Inst. of Peace, 1989-91, Davis Inst., 1994; Harry Guggenheim fellow, 1990. Mem. Assn. Israel Studies (v.p. 1984-89). Address: Haim ve-Elisha 16, Tel Aviv Israel 64288

RUBIN, BERNARD, pharmacologist, biomedical writer, consultant; b. N.Y.C., Feb. 15, 1919; s. Charles and Ann (Slutskin) R.; m. Betty R. Schindler, June 15, 1945; children: Stefi Gail, Robert Henry. BA, Bklyn. Coll., 1939; PhD, Yale U., 1951. Rsch. asst. various orgns., N.Y., 1940-48; rsch. pharmacologist E.R. Squibb & Sons, Inc., New Brunswick, N.J., 1951-65; group leader, pharmacology E.R. Squibb & Sons, Inc., Princeton, N.J., 1965-84; cons., licensing Bristol-Myers Squibb Co., Princeton, 1984-97. Contbr. over 100 rsch. articles to profl. jours., 1948-85. With U.S. Army, 1942-43. Recipient A.E.C. pre-doctoral fellowship, Washington, 1949-50. Achievements include rsch. on novel antihypertensive captopril (an inhibitor of converting enzyme of angiotensin), on bioassays applicable to rauwolfia and reserpine-like compounds, on the first effective (orally) antitubercular drug isoniazid. Home: 2 Pin Oak Dr Trenton NJ 08648-3134

RUBIN, BRUCE ALAN, lawyer; b. Pitts., Sept. 12, 1951; s. Stanley and Elaine (Roth) R.; m. Suzanne Kay Boss, Aug. 23, 1975; children: Daniel, Jay. BA, Yale U., 1973; JD, Stanford U., 1976. Bar: Oreg. 1976, U.S. Dist. Ct. Oreg. 1976, U.S. Ct. Appeals (9th cir.) 1976. Atty. Miller, Nash, Wiener, Hager & Carlsen, Portland, 1976—; bd. dirs. Classroom Law Project, Portland, 1990-94. Author: Wrongful Discharge in Oregon, 1988. Mem. ABA (com. on corp. counsel, subcom. chair), Oreg. State Bar (disciplinary coun. 1990—), Multnomah Bar Assn. (ct. liaison com.). Avocation: competitive long distance running. Office: Miller Nash Wiener Hager & Carlsen 111 SW 5th Ave Portland OR 97204-3604

RUBIN, BRUCE JOEL, screenwriter, director, producer; b. Detroit, Mar. 10, 1943; s. Jim and Sondra R.; m. Blanche Mallins; children: Joshua, Ari. Student, Wayne State U., 1960-62; grad. film sch., NYU, 1965. Former asst. film editor NBC News; mem. film dept. Whitney Mus., assoc. curator. Screenwriter: (with Robert Statzel and Phillip Frank Messina) Brainstorm, 1983, Deadly Friend, 1986, Ghost, 1990 (Academy award best original screenplay 1990), Jacob's Ladder, 1990; writer, dir., prodr. My Life, 1993. Office: care Geoffrey Sanford 1015 Gayley Ave Fl 3 Los Angeles CA 90024-3424*

RUBIN, BRUCE STUART, public relations executive; b. Miami, Fla., June 28, 1947; s. Earl Myron and Claire (Malbin) R.; m. Cheryl Joy Cunningham, Aug. 1, 1980. BA in Journalism, U. Miami, 1969. Reporter The Miami News, 1969; v.p. Ronald Levitt Assocs., Inc., Coral Gables, Fla., 1970-75; pres. Bruce Rubin & Assocs., Miami, 1975-94; chmn. bd. Rubin Barney & Birger, Inc., Miami, 1994—; chmn. Counselors Acad., 1987. Recipient Exec. Achievement in Pub. Rels. award O'Dwyer's Directory of Pub. Rels. Execs., 1991, 94. Mem. Pub. Rels. Soc. Am. (accredited, pres. Miami chpt., counselor of pub. rels. 1978). Home: 8065 SW 86 Ter Miami FL 33143 Office: 255 Alhambra Cir Ste 500 Miami FL 33134-7404

RUBIN, CHANDA, professional tennis player; b. Lafayette, La., Feb. 18, 1976; d. Edward and Bernadette Rubin. Grad., Episcopal Sch. Acadiana, 1993. Mem. USTA Jr. Devel. Team, 1989, USTA Nat. Team, 1990; prof. tennis player, 1991—; player 20 tournaments and Fed. Cup with 43 wins, 19 losses, 1995, named to Olympic Team, Atlanta,1996,. Recipient 3 U.S. Jr. Titles, 12 Singles, 1988, 14 Singles, 1989, 16 Indoor Doubles, 1989; winner U.S. nat. title and Rolex Orange Bowl 12s crown, 1988, 14 Nat., 1989, 16 Indoor Doubles, 1989, U.S. Tennis Assn. Challenge of Midland Mich. Office: USTA 70 W Red Oak Ln White Plains NY 10604-3602*

RUBIN, CHARLES ELLIOTT, lawyer, sports agent; b. Kansas City, Mo., May 28, 1947; s. Irving C. and Anna Lee (Strauss) R.; m. Linda Jean Nichols, Aug. 6, 1973; children: Aaron Matthew, Joanne Michelle. BSBA, U. Mo., 1969, JD, 1972. Bar: Mo. 1973, U.S. Dist. Ct. (we. dist.) Mo. 1973, U.S. Tax Ct. 1974, U.S. Ct. Appeals (8th cir.) 1974, U.S. Supreme Ct. 1976. Ptnr. Pummil & Rubin, Kansas City, 1973—; chmn. Assured Mgmt. Co., Westwood, Kans., 1990—. Mem. Kansas City Bd. Zoning Adjustment, 1981-84; bd. dirs. New Reform Temple, Kansas City, 1985—, Menorah Med. Ctr., Kansas City, 1987—, Children's Mercy Hosp., Kansas City, 1988—. Mem. ABA, Kansas City Bar Assn., Am. Judicature Assn., Oakwood Country Club (bd. dirs.), Shadow Glen Club. Avocations: outdoor activities, golf, scuba diving. Office: Assured Mgmt Co 1901 W 47th Pl Ste 200 Shawnee Mission KS 66205-1834

RUBIN, DAVID LEE, French literature educator, critic, editor, publisher; b. Indpls., Sept. 30, 1939; s. Ira Bertram and Jeanne Iva (Gamso) R.; m. Carolyn Dettman, June 12, 1965; 1 child, Timothy Craig. BA, U. Tenn., 1962; cert., U. Paris, 1963; MA, U. Ill., 1964, PhD, 1967. Instr. French U. Ill., Urbana, 1966-67; asst. prof. U. Chgo., 1967-69; asst. prof. U. Va., Charlottesville, 1969-74, assoc. prof., 1974-82, prof. French, 1982—; seminar dir. Folger Inst., 1989; founder Rookwood Press, 1992—; cons. Can. Coun., Etudes littéraires françaises, NEH, numerous univ. presses; lectr., spkr. in field. Author: Higher Hidden Order, 1972, The Knot of Artifice, 1981, A Pact with Silence, 1991; editor: The Selected Poetry and Prose of John T. Napier, 1972, La poèsie française du premier 17e siècle, 1986, Sun King, 1991; co-editor: La Cohèrence Intèrieure, 1977, Convergences, 1989, The Ladder of High Designs, 1991, The Fulbright Difference, 1993; founding editor Continuum, 1989-93, EMF; Studies in Early Modern France, 1994, EMF Monographs, 1994; mem. editl. bd. Purdue Monographs, 1975—, Oeuvres et Critiques, 1976—, French Rev., 1986-94; Am. corr. Cahiers Maynard, 1973—, Cahiers Tristan L'Hermite, 1989; contbr. articles to profl. jours., chpts. to books. U.S. State Dept. Fulbright fellow, 1962-63, Woodrow Wilson Found. fellow, 1963-64, Guggenheim Found. fellow, 1980-81. Mem. MLA, ACLU, Farmington Club, Boar's Head Club, Phi Beta Kappa. Avocations: reading, travel, fitness. Home: 520 Rookwood Pl Charlottesville VA 22903-4734 Office: U Va French Dept 302 Cabell Hall Charlottesville VA 22903

RUBIN, DONALD BRUCE, statistician, educator, research company executive; b. Washington, Dec. 22, 1943; s. Allan A. and Harriet (Schainis) R.; m. Kathryn M. Kazarow; children: Scott Wilk, Paul Stuart. AB magna cum laude, Princeton U., 1965; MS, Harvard U., 1966, PhD, 1970. Rsch. statistician Ednl. Testing Svc., Princeton, N.J., 1971-75, chmn. stats., 1975-79, sr. statis. advisor, 1979-81; pres. Datametrics Rsch. Inc., Waban, Mass., 1981—; prof. U. Chgo., 1982-84; prof. Harvard U., Cambridge, Mass., 1984—, chmn. stats., 1985-94. Author: Handling Nonresponse in Sample Surveys by Multiple Imputation, 1980, Multiple Imputation for Nonresponse in Surveys, 1987; author: (with others) Incomplete Data in Sample Surveys (Vol. 2): Theory and Bibliography, 1983; co-author: (with R.J.A. Little) Statistical Analysis With Missing Data, 1987, (with A. Gelman, J. Carlin. H. Stern) Bayasian Data Analysis, 1995; co-editor: (with P.W. Holland) Test Equating, 1982; contbr. over 200 articles to profl. jours. Recipient Parzen prize for statis. innovation, 1996; Woodrow Wilson Grad. fellow, 1965; NSF Grad. fellow, 1965, 68, John Simon Guggenheim fellow, 1977-78. Fellow AAAS (chmn. stats. 1992), Am. Statis. Assn. (editor jour. 1980-82, dir. 1980-82, statistician of yr. Boston chpt. 1995, S.S. Wilks medal 1995), Inst. Math. Stats. (coun. mem. 1990-92); mem. NAS (com. on nat. stats. 1989-92, mem. panel on confidentiality data 1989-92, panel on bilingual edn. 1990-92, working group on statis. analysis of com. on basic rsch. in behavioral and social scis. 1985-86, panel statis. in 21st century 1995, other coms.), AAAS, Am. Acad. Arts and Sci., Biometric Soc., Internat. Assn. Survey Statisticians, Internat. Statis. Inst., Psychometric Soc., Royal Statis. Soc. Office: Harvard U Dept Statistics Cambridge MA 02138

RUBIN, EMANUEL, pathologist, educator; b. N.Y.C., Dec. 5, 1928; s. Jacob and Sophie R.; m. Barbara Kurn, Mar. 27, 1955 (div. 1985); children: Raphael, Jonathan, Daniel, Rebecca; m. Linda A. Haegele, Oct. 13, 1985; children: Ariel, Ethan. B.S., Villanova U., 1950; M.D., Harvard U., 1954. Intern Boston City Hosp., 1954-55; resident Children's Hosp. of Phila., 1957-58; research fellow in pathology Mt. Sinai Hosp., N.Y.C., 1958-62, asst. attending pathologist, 1962-64, assoc. attending pathologist, 1964-68; attending pathologist, dir. hosp. pathology services Mt. Sinai Hosp., 1968-72, pathologist-in-chief, 1972-76; dir. labs. Hahnemann Hosp., Phila., 1977-86; physician-in-chief pathology Thomas Jefferson U. Hosp., 1986—; prof. pathology Mr. Sinai Sch. Medicine, CUNY, 1966-72, Irene Heinz and John LaPorte Givien prof. pathology, chmn. dept., 1972-76; prof., chmn. dept. pathology and lab. medicine Hahnemann U. Sch. Medicine, Phila., 1977-86; Gonzalo Aponte prof. pathology, chmn. dept. pathology and cell biology Thomas Jefferson U. Coll. Medicine, Phila., 1986-94, chmn. dept. pathology, anatomy and cell biology, 1994—; adj. prof. biochemistry and biophysics U. Pa. Sch. Medicine, Phila., 1977-88. Author: (with J.L. Farber) Pathology, 1988, 94; (with K.W. Miller and S.H. Roth) Cellular and Molecular Mechanisms of Alcohol and Anesthetics, 1991; editor-in-chief Lab. Investigation, 1982-96; pathology editor: Fedn. Proc., 1982-86, J Stud Alc, 1982-94. Served with USN, 1955-57. Mem. ACP, Am. Soc. Investigative Pathology, Internat. Acad. Pathology, U.S.-Can. Acad. Pathology, Am. Soc. Biol. Chemists and Molecular Biology, Am. Assn. Study of Liver Diseases, Am. Gastroent. Assn., Internat. Assn. Study of the Liver, Am. Coll. Toxicology. Home: 1505 Monk Rd Gladwyne PA 19035-1316 Office: 1020 Locust St Philadelphia PA 19107-6731

RUBIN, E(RWIN) LEONARD, lawyer; b. Chgo., Jan. 11, 1933; s. Samuel and Frances Birdie (Rabin) R.; m. Stephanie Siegel, Mar. 4, 1961 (div. Dec. 1981); children: Matthew, Suzanne; m. Audrey Gay Holzer, May 8, 1983; children: Margot, Bette. Student, U. Ill., Urbana, 1948-51; AB, U. Miami, 1956, JD, 1959. s. N.Y. 1960, Ill. 1962, U.S. Dist. Ct. (no. dist.) Ill. 1962, U.S. Ct. Appeals (7th cir.) 1990. Assoc. Hays, St. John A&H, N.Y.C., 1960-62, Devoe, Shadur, Mikva & P., Chgo., 1962-65; gen. counsel Playboy Enterprises, Inc., Chgo., 1965-78; ptnr. E. Leonard Rubin Law Offices, Chgo., 1978-81, Epton, Mullin & Druth Ltd., Chgo., 1981-86, Brinks, Hofer, Gilson & Lione, Chgo., 1986-96, Gordon & Glickson, Chgo., 1996—; adj. prof. U. Ill., John Marshall Law Sch. Pres. Lawyers for Creative Arts, Chgo., 1983-85; chmn. bd. dirs. Mus. Holography; bd. dirs. Wisdom Bridge Theatre, Chgo., 1983-85. Cpl. U.S. Army, 1953-5, ETO. Mem. ABA, Ill. Bar Assn., Chgo. Bar Assn. (bd. mgrs. 1983-85, chmn. various coms., dir. Christmas Spirits Satire Show 1965—), Union Internat. Des Avocats (v.p. intellectual property commn.), Copyright Soc. Am. (trustee, pres. midwest chpt.). Jewish. Home: 270 Sunset Dr Northfield IL 60093-1047 Office: Gordon & Glickson PC 444 N Michigan Ave Ste 3600 Chicago IL 60611-3957

RUBIN, GERALD MAYER, molecular biologist, biochemistry educator; b. Boston, Mar. 31, 1950; s. Benjamin H. and Edith (Weisberg) R.; m. Lynn S. Mastalir, May 7, 1978; 1 child, Alan F. B.S., MIT, 1971; Ph.D., Cambridge U., Eng., 1974. Helen Hay Whitney Found. fellow Stanford U. Sch. Medicine, Calif., 1974-76; asst. prof. biol. chemistry Sidney Farber Cancer Inst.-Harvard U. Med. Sch., Boston, 1977-80; staff mem. Carnegie Instn. of Washington, Balt., 1980-83; John D. MacArthur prof. genetics U. Calif., Berkeley, 1983—; investigator Howard Hughes Med. Inst., 1987—. Recipient Young Scientist award Passano Found., 1983, U.S. Steel Found. award Nat. Acad. Scis., 1985, Eli Lilly award in biochemistry Am. Chem. Soc., 1985, Genetics Soc. Am. medal, 1986. Mem. Nat. Acad. Scis. Office: U Calif Dept MCB 539 LSA Bldg Berkeley CA 94720-3200

RUBIN, GERROLD ROBERT, advertising executive; b. Evanston, Ill., Mar. 31, 1940; s. Bennie George and Anita (Perich) R.; m. Barbara Ann Nieman, Sept. 5, 1962; children: John, Ann. B.S. in Radio, TV, Film, Northwestern U., 1962. Account exec. Leo Burnett Advt., Chgo., 1962-67; account supr. Leo Burnett Advt., Toronto, Ont., 1967-68, Needham, Harper Steers, Chgo., 1968-73; account dir. Needham, Harper Steers, Los Angeles, 1973-78; mgmt. rep. Needham, Harper & Steers, Chgo., 1978-81; pres. Needham, Harper & Steers, Los Angeles, 1981—. Bd. dirs. Country Music Assn., Nashville, 1983—. Presbyterian. Office: Rubin Postaer & Assocs 1333 2nd St Santa Monica CA 90401-1100

RUBIN, GUSTAV, orthopedic surgeon, consultant, researcher; b. N.Y.C., May 19, 1913; s. William and Rose (Strongin) R.; m. Mildred Synthia Holtzer, July 4, 1946 (dec. Dec. 1964); m. Esther Rosenberg Partnow, July 23, 1965; 1 stepchild, Michael Partnow. B.S., NYU, 1934; M.D., SUNY-Downstate Med. Ctr., 1939. Diplomate Am. Bd. Orthopedic Surgery. Intern Maimonides Hosp., Bklyn., 1939-41; resident in orthopedics Hosp. for Joint Diseases, N.Y.C., 1941-42, 1946; practice medicine specializing in orthopedics Bklyn., 1947-56; from orthopedic surgeon to dir. clinic VA Clinic, Bklyn., 1956-70; chief Spl. Prosthetic Clinic VA Prosthetics Ctr., N.Y.C., 1970-85, dir. spl. team for amputations, mobility, prosthetics/orthotics, 1985-87, mem. chief med. dir. adv. group on prosthetics services, rehab. research and devel., 1985-87, orthopedic cons., 1970-87, ret., 1987; pvt. practice N.Y.C., 1987—; med. advisor prosthetic rsch. com. N.Y. State DAV, 1970—; lectr. prosthetics NYU, 1972-89; clin. prof. orthopedics N.Y. Coll. Podiatric Medicine, 1980—; orthopedic cons. Internat. Ctr. for the Disabled, N.Y.C., 1987—. Contbr. book chpts., articles to profl. jours.; contbr. article on amputations Ency. for Disability and Rehab., 1995. Capt. U.S. Army, 1943-46. Recipient Nat. Comdrs. award DAV, 1968, Amvets award for outstanding service, 1969, award for Service to Veterans Allied Veterans Meml. Com., 1970, Eastern Paralyzed Veterans Assn. award, 1977, award for Service to Israeli Wounded Israeli Govt. Dept. Rehab., 1981, Cert. of Merit, Nat. Amputation Found., 1972, Olin E. Teague award VA, 1984, Physician of Yr. award Pres.'s Commn. on Employment of People with Disabilities, 1984. Fellow Am. Acad. Orthopedic Surgeons, ACS, Am. Acad. Neurol. and Orthopedic Surgeons; mem. Alumni Assn. Hosp. Joint Disease, Sigma Xi. Jewish. Avocations: sculpting; oil painting. Home: PO Box 572 15 Circle Dr Moorestown NJ 08057 Office: 304 E 24th St New York NY 10010-4019

RUBIN, HARRIS B., psychology educator; b. Jersey City, May 12, 1932; s. Eli L. and Doris R.; m. Angela Battaglia, June 11, 1960; children: Amy L., Chad A., Thea F., Garth A. B.A. in Psychology, So. Ill. U., 1959; Ph.D., U. Chgo., 1965. Research scientist behavior research lab. Anna State Hosp., Ill., 1965-72; asst. prof. rehab. inst. So. Ill. U., Carbondale, 1966-71, assoc. prof. behavioral sci. Sch. Medicine and Rehab. Inst., 1972-78, prof., 1978-95, interim asst. dean student affairs, 1994-96, prof. emeritus, 1996—; cons. Ill. Dept. Corrections, Ill. Dept. Mental Health. Bd. editors Jour. Applied Behavior Analysis, 1972-75, Jour. Exptl. Analysis of Behavior, 1973-75, The Behavior Analyst, 1986-90; adv. editor various jours.; contbr. articles to profl. jours. Mem. Carbondale Human Relations Com., 1968-73, chmn., 1969-72. Served with U.S. Army, 1952-54. Fellow APA, Am. Psychol. Soc., Am. Assn. Applied and Preventive Psychology; mem. Assn. Behavior Analysis, Midwest Psychol. Assn., Behavior Analysis Soc. Ill. (pres. 1989-90). Office: So Ill U Sch Medicine Carbondale IL 62901

RUBIN, HARRY MEYER, entertainment industry executive; b. N.Y.C., Dec. 21, 1952; s. Martin J. and Helene Rubin; m. Cathy Hemery, May 26, 1990; children: Gabriella, James. B.A., Stanford U., 1974; M.B.A., Harvard U., 1976. Investment banker Wertheim & Co., Inc., N.Y.C., 1976-77; fin. mgr. Am. Airlines, Inc., N.Y.C., 1977-79; dir. fin. planning-entertainment, electronics groups RCA Corp., N.Y.C., 1979-81; CFO RCA Videodiscs, RCA Home Video, RCA Cable RCA Entertainment Group, N.Y.C.; v.p. strategic planning RCA Corp.; group fin. exec. RCA entertainment ops. RCA Corp., N.Y.C., 1981-86; gen. mgr. Home Video Gen. Electric Co., 1986-87; v.p., gen. mgr. home video ops. NBC, Inc., 1988-93; exec. v.p. GT Interactive Software Corp., 1994—; dir., co-head exec. com. RCA/Columbia Pictures Worldwide Video; founding ptnr. Samuel Adams Beer; founding dir. Arts & Entertainment Network. Mem. Phi Beta Kappa, 22 Club. Avocations: travel, foreign languages. Home: 784 Park Ave New York NY 10021-3553

RUBIN, HERBERT, lawyer; b. Lisbon, Conn., June 4, 1918; s. Simon and Rose (Berko) R.; m. Rose Luttan, July 6, 1941; children: Barbara, Caroline, Donald. AB, CCNY, 1938; JD, NYU, 1942. Bar: N.Y. 1942, U.S. Dist. Ct. (so. and ea. dists.) N.Y. 1951, U.S. Supreme Ct. 1956, U.S. Ct. Appeals (2d, 3d, 4th, 6th, 9th, 10th, D.C. cirs.). Assoc., Newman & Bisco, 1942; mem. faculty N.Y. U. Law Sch., 1946-50, 57-62; prof. creditors' rightsRutgers U. Law Sch., 1949-57; pvt. practice, 1946-47, 50-56; ptnr. Atkin & Rubin, 1948-50; ptnr. Sereni, Herzfeld & Rubin, and successor, Herzfeld & Rubin, N.Y.C., 1956—, sr. ptnr., 1968—; instr. mil. law, 1944-46; prof. constl. law LIU, 1963-68; trustee L.I. Jewish Hosp. Editor-in chief NYU Law Rev., 1940-41; bd. editors N.Y. Law Jour., 1971—; contbr. articles to profl. jours. Mem. N.Y. State Banking Bd., 1975-85, N.Y. State Jud. Selection Com., 1975-83, Sen. Moynihan's Jud. Selection Com., 1977—, Mayor's Jud. Selection Com., 1982—. Served to 1st lt. Signal Corps, AUS, 1942-46. Recipient awards NCCJ, 1967, United Jewish Appeal, 1968, 97, Israel Bonds, 1973, NYU Law Assn. award, 1987, Judge Weinfeld award, 1992. Fellow Am. Bar Found.; mem. ABA (mem. coun. N.Y. State), N.Y. State Bar Assn., Queens County Bar Assn. (pres. 1970), Assn. Bar City of N.Y., Fed. Bar Council, ABA. Mem. Liberal Party. Jewish. Clubs: City Downtown, World Trade Ctr., Woodmere (N.Y.C.). 53 jours. Office: Herzfeld & Rubin 40 Wall St New York NY 10005-2301

RUBIN, IRVING, pharmaceutical editor; b. N.Y.C., Apr. 7, 1916; s. Julius and Sadie (Seidman) R.; m. Florence Podolsky, Mar. 12, 1949; children: Joanne, Saul Robert. PhG, Bklyn. Coll. Pharmacy, 1936; BA, Bklyn. Evening Coll., 1948; PharmD (hon.), Mass. Coll. Pharmacy, 1973; DSc (hon.), Union U., 1986; DHL (hon.), L.I. U., 1986; DSc (hon.), St. John's U., 1989. With retail pharmacies N.Y.C., 1933-38; assoc. editor, then mng. editor Pharmacy, Am. Druggist mag.; editorial dir. Blue Price Book, 1938-60; editor, v.p., publ. dir. Pharmacy Times (and predecessors), Port Washington, N.Y., 1960-86; pub. Pharmacy Times (and predecessors), Port Washington, 1984, editor-in-chief, pub., 1987, editor-at-large, 1988-93; pharmacy cons. Resident and Staff Physician mag., 1978—; mem. consumer interest/health edn. panel U.S. Pharmacopeial Conv., Inc., 1991-95; mem. dean's adv. bd. steering com. Coll. Pharmacy and Allied Health Professions, St. John's U. Author: The Pharmacy Graduate's Career Guide, 1970; editor Wellcome Trends in Pharmacy, 1990-93; editor-in-chief emeritus Pharmacy Times, 1994—; chmn. editl. adv. bd. Glaxo Wellcome Trends in Pharmacy, 1996—; interprofl. editor: Glaxo Wellcome Trends in Nursing, 1997—. Trustee Arnold and Marie Schwartz Coll. Pharmacy, Bklyn.; del. leader People to People Internat., People's Republic China, 1988, USSR, 1990, Great Britain and Ireland, 1992; also addressed about 150 mems. of the Supreme Soviet in the Kremlin about the Chernobyl disaster, 1990. With AUS, 1941-46, ETO. Decorated Bronze Star; recipient Alumni Achievement award Alumni Assn. Bklyn. Coll. Pharmacy, 1963, Editorial Achievement award Alpha Zeta Omega, 1968, Am. Cancer Soc., 1964, Gold medal Nicholas S. Gesoalde Pharm. Econ. Research Found., 1972, J. Leon Lascoff award Am. Coll. Apothecaries, 1977, Presdl. citation ADA, 1982, Disting. Journalism award Pharm. Soc. State N.Y., 1984, Citation Merit, Nat. Assn. Chain Drug Stores, 1986, Spl. Journalism award Nat. Assn. Chain Drug Stores, 1987; named Man of Yr. Pharmacy, B'nai B'rith, 1973, Man of Yr., Empire State Pharm. Soc., 1985; established Irving Rubin scholarship Arnold and Marie Schwartz Coll. of Pharmacy and Health Scis., L.I. U., 1988. Fellow N.Y. Acad. Pharmacy; mem. Am. Coll. Pharmacists (hon. life), Am. Inst. History of Pharmacy (coun. 1982-88), Nat. Assn. Retail Druggists (award 1987), Am. Pharm. Assn. (pres. N.Y. chpt. 1955-56, ho. of dels., Remington Honor medal 1986), NARD Found. (John W. Dargavel Outstanding Svc. medal 1995), Am. Soc. Health System Pharmacists, Am. Found. for Pharm. Edn. (exec. com., bd. dirs. 1988—), Okla. Pharm. Assn. (hon.), Alumni Assn. Bklyn. Coll. Pharmacy (prs. 1946-48), Alpha Zeta Omega, Rho Pi Phi, Delta Sigma Theta, Rho Chi, Kappa Psi, Phi Delta Chi (hon.), Phi Lambda Sigma (hon., Nat. Leadership award 1993, award for Comprehensive Svc. to State of N.Y. 1996). Jewish. Home: 39 Ruxton Rd Great Neck NY 11023-1514 Office: Irv Rubin Assocs 39 Ruxton Rd Great Neck NY 11023-1514

RUBIN, JACOB CARL, mechanical research engineer; b. N.Y.C., Nov. 22, 1926; s. Abraham and Bessie (Tockman) R.; m. Nancy Jean Weinstein, Aug. 2, 1952; children: Sara Lee, Jeffrey Daniel. BSME, CUNY, 1945; MMechE, NYU, 1947; MS of Applied Statistics, Rochester (N.Y.) Inst. Tech., 1969, MSEE, 1971, MS in Imaging Sci., 1975. Registered profl. engr., N.Y., D.C. Design group leader MacDonnell Aircraft Corp., St. Louis, 1955-56; mem. research staff U. Mich., Ann Arbor, 1956-57; staff engr. IBM, Vestal, N.Y., 1957-58; engr. advance design GE, Johnson City, N.Y., 1958-60; program engr. GE, Phila., 1960-62; mgr. standards engring. Martin-Marietta Corp., Balt., 1962-63; mgr. product design dept. Am. Car & Foundry Co., Rockville, Md., 1963-64; cons. reliability NASA, Greenbelt, Md., 1964-65; project engr. Eastman Kodak Co., Rochester, 1965-75, sr. rsch. assoc., 1975-90; staff mech. engr. Med. Lab. Automation, Inc., Pleasantville, N.Y., 1990-91; prin. engr. instrument div. Dresser Industries, Stratford, Conn., 1992; sr. mech. engr. Materials Rsch. Corp., Congers, N.Y., 1993; sr. mech. design engr. Electronics Retailing Sys. Inc., Wilton, Conn., 1993-94; mfg. engr. Contact Sys. Inc., Danbury, Conn., 1995; sr. mech. engr. Barnes engring. divsn. EDO Corp., Shelton, Conn., 1995-96; mech. engr. Screen Tech, Oakville, Conn., 1996—; course dir. Ctr. Profl. Advancement, East Brunswick, N.J., 1975—; adj. faculty Rochester Inst. Tech., 1965-90; assoc. prof. mech. engring. Bridgeport Engring. Inst., 1991-94; assoc. prof. mech. engring. Fairfield U., 1994—. Patentee artificial kidney, piezo-electric generator. Pres. Grove Place Neighborhood Assn., Rochester, 1984. Mem. NSPE (life), N.Y. State Soc. Profl. Engrs. Republican. Jewish. Avocations: teaching Sunday sch., music appreciation, theater, travel. Home: 161B Heritage Vlg Southbury CT 06488-1433 Office: Premier Microwave Corp 33 New Broad St Port Chester NY 10573

RUBIN, JEAN ESTELLE, mathematics educator; b. Bklyn., Oct. 29, 1926; d. Leonard Lewis and Phyllis Irma (Mann) Hirsh; m. Herman Rubin, Mar. 23, 1952; children: Arthur Leonard, Leonore Anne Rubin Findsen. B.S., Queens Coll., 1948; M.A., Columbia U., 1949; Ph.D., Stanford U., 1955. Instr. Queens Coll., 1949-51, Stanford U., 1953-55; lectr. U. Oreg., 1955-59; asst. prof. Mich. State U., 1960-67; asso. prof. math. Purdue U., West Lafayette, Ind., 1968-75; prof. Purdue U., 1975—. Author: Set Theory for the Mathematician, 1967, Mathematical Logic: Applications and Theory, 1990; co-author: (with H. Rubin) Equivalents of the Axiom of Choice, 1963, Equivalents of the Axiom of Choice II, 1985. Vol. West Lafayette Libr., 1981—; bd. dirs. Lafayette Symphony Orch., Inc., 1987-93, Friends of West Lafayette Libr., 1993—. Mem. Am. Math. Soc., Assn. Symbolic Logic, Math. Assn. Am. (vis. lectr. 1976-86), Purdue Staff Aero Club Inc. (bd. dirs. 1975-90). Home: 1214 Sunset Ln West Lafayette IN 47906-2429 Office: Purdue U Math Dept Lafayette IN 47907-1395

RUBIN, JEFFREY REED, vascular surgeon; b. Chgo., Sept. 19, 1952; s. Marvin Joseph and Francine Faith (Miller) R.; m. Janis Lynn James; children: Ryan, Kimberly, Lindsey. BS, Tulane U., New Orleans, 1974; MD, Northwestern U., Chgo., 1978. Chief vascular surgeon Case Western Reserve U., Cleve., 1985-93; chmn. dept. surgery, prof. surgery Northeastern Ohio U. Coll. Medicine, Youngstown, 1993—; bd. mem. Pridecare Ins. Co., Youngstown; mem. com. Soc. Clin. Vascular Soc.; past pres. Cleve. Vascular Soc.; pres. Peripheral Vascular Soc. Editor: Vascular Surgery, Annals Vascular Surgery; contbr. chpts. to books. Republican. Jewish. Avocations: fly fishing, golf. Office: Western Reserve Healthcare 500 Gypsy Ln Youngstown OH 44504-1315

RUBIN, JOEL EDWARD, consulting company executive; b. Cleve., Sept. 5, 1928; s. Morris and Pearl (Jacobs) R.; m. Lucille Schutmaat, Dec. 18, 1953; children: Brian G., Jennifer L., Rebecca R. BS, Case Inst. of Tech., 1949; MFA, Yale U., 1951; PhD, Stanford U., 1960. Exec. v.p. Kliegl Bros. Lighting, N.Y.C., 1954-85; prin. cons. Joel E. Rubin & Assocs., N.Y.C., 1985—; sr. advisor theater planning, mng. dir. Artec Cons., Inc., N.Y.C., 1993—. Co-author: Theatrical Lighting Practice 1954; author: Technological Development of Stage Lighting 1960. Member Coll. of Fellows of Am. Theatre, John F. Kennedy Ctr. for the Performing Arts, Washington. Recipient Golden Triaga, Prague Quadrennial, 1987, Zlatou medal, 1991, 1st time award Bus. Com. for the Arts, Forbes Mag., 1987, Founders' award U.S. Inst. for Theatre Tech., 1972, 79, U.S. Inst. Tech. Nat. award, 1990, USITT lifetime hon. membership award, 1996, Spl. citation, 1996. Fellow Am. Theatre Assn. (v.p. 1961-63), U.S. Inst. of Theatre Technology (pres. 1963-64); mem. Am. Nat. Theatre Acad. (bd. dirs. 1971-75), Internat. Theatre Inst. of the U.S. (bd. dirs. 1975-79), Nat. Coun. of Arts and Govt. (bd. dirs. 1975-79), Internat. Orgn. Theatre Architects and Scenographers (U.S. chmn., rep. 1968—, pres. 1971-79, Gold medal award 1996), Illuminating Engring. Soc. Avocations: collecting books, stage design, Lincolniana. Home: 24 Edgewood Ave Hastings On Hudson NY 10706-2024 Office: Artec Cons 114 W 26th St New York NY 10001-6812

RUBIN, KARL COOPER, mathematics educator; b. Urbana, Ill., Jan. 27, 1956; s. Robert J. and Vera (Cooper) R. AB, Princeton U., 1976; MA, Harvard U., 1977, PhD, 1981. Instr. Princeton (N.J.) U., 1982-83; mem. Inst. Advanced Study, Princeton, 1983-84; prof. Columbia U., N.Y.C., 1988-89; asst. prof. math. Ohio State U., Columbus, 1984-87, prof., 1987-97; prof. math. Stanford (Calif.) U., 1997—. Contbr. articles to Inventiones Math. Recipient Presdl. Young Investigator award NSF, 1988; NSF postdoctoral fellow, 1981, Sloan fellow, 1985, Guggenheim fellow, 1994. Mem. Am. Math. Soc. (recipient Cole Prize, 1992), Phi Beta Kappa. Achievements include rsch. on elliptic curves, Tate-Shafarevich groups, Birch and Swinnerton-Dyer conjecture, Iwasawa theory and p-adic L-functions. Office: Stanford U Dept Math Stanford CA 94305-2125

RUBIN, KENNETH ALLEN, lawyer; b. Rockville Centre, N.Y., Nov. 24, 1947; s. Albert Alton and Marion (Osterweis) R.; m. Susan Kurman, Sept. 14, 1980; children: Jennifer, Kelly. BS, Cornell U., 1969, MS, 1971, JD, 1973. Bar: D.C. 1974, N.Y. 1974, U.S. Ct. Appeals (D.C. crct.) 1974, U.S. Ct. Appeals (5th crct. 1975, U.S. Ct. Appeals (4th, 9th and 10th crct.) 1976, U.S. Ct. Appeals (3d, 8th and 11th crcts.) 1986, U.S. Supreme Ct. 1992. Trial atty. Dept. Justice, Washington, 1973-74; sr. ptnr. Morgan, Lewis & Bockius, Washington, 1974—; adj. prof. USDA Grad. Sch., Washington, 1977-85, U. Ala., Huntsville, 1978-91, Antioch U., Washington, 1978; lectr. Cornell U., Ithaca, N.Y., 1979—. Author: What the Business Executive Needs To Know about U.S. Environmental Laws and Liabilities, 1991. Mem. adv. com. Cornell Ctr. for Environment. Mem. ABA, Am. Water Works Assn., Swiss Club Washington, Cornell Club Washington. Office: Morgan Lewis & Bockius 1800 M St NW Washington DC 20036-5802

RUBIN, LAWRENCE GILBERT, physicist, laboratory manager; b. Bklyn., Sept. 17, 1925; s. Harry E. and Ruth (Feirberg) R.; m. Florence Ruth Kagan, Feb. 11, 1951; children: Michael G., Richard D., Jeffrey N. Student, Cooper Union, N.Y.C., 1943, 46-47; B.S. in Physics, U. Chgo., 1949; M.A. in Physics, Columbia U., 1950. Staff mem., physicist research div. Raytheon Co., Waltham, Mass., 1950-64; group leader Nat. Magnet Lab., MIT, Cambridge, Mass., 1964-78, divsn. head high magnetic field facility, 1978-93; advisor to high magnetic field facility, 1994-95; vis. scientist MIT, 1996—; mem. NAS adv. panel Nat. Bur. Standards, 1976-82, 85-90; bd. dirs. Lake Shore Cryotronics, Inc., Columbus, Ohio; gen. chmn. 6th Internat. Temperature Symposium, Washington, 1982, 7th Internat. Temperature Symposium, Toronto, Ont., Can., 1992—; chmn. adv. com. Physics Today Buyers' Guide; part time staff Am. Physical Soc. Tutorial program. Mem. editorial bd. Rev. Sci. Instruments, 1968-70, 79-81; assoc. editor Ency. Scientific Instrumentation, 1995—; contbr. articles to physics jours. With U.S. Army, 1943-46, ETO. Fellow IEEE (life), Am. Phys. Soc. (organizer and 1st chmn. instrument and measurement sci. group 1985); mem. Instrument Soc. Am. (sr.), Am. Vacuum Soc. Jewish. Home: 1504 Centre St Newton Centre MA 02159-2447 Office: MIT Bldg NW14 1209 170 Albany St Cambridge MA 02139-4208

RUBIN, LOUIS DECIMUS, JR., English language and literature educator, writer, publisher; b. Charleston, S.C., Nov. 19, 1923; s. Louis Decimus and Janet (Weinstein) R.; m. Eva M. Redfield, June 2, 1951; children: Robert Alden, William Louis. Student, Coll. of Charleston, 1940-42, LittD (hon.), 1989; AB, U. Richmond, 1946, LittD (hon.), 1972; MA, Johns Hopkins U., 1949, PhD, 1954; LittD (hon.), Clemson U., 1986, U. of the South, 1991; U. N.C. at Asheville, 1993, U. N.C., Chapel Hill, 1995. Instr. Johns Hopkins U.; editor Hopkins Rev., 1950-54; fellow criticism Sewanee Rev., 1953-54; exec. sec. Am. Studies Assn., asst. prof. Am. civilization U. Pa., 1954-56; assoc. editor Richmond (Va.) News Leader, 1956-57; assoc. prof. English Hollins Coll., 1957-60, prof., chmn. dept., 1960-67; prof. English U. N.C., 1967-73, Univ. Disting. prof., 1973-89, prof. emeritus, 1989—; editor Hollins Critic, 1963-68; vis. prof. history La. State U., 1957; Fulbright lectr. U. Aix-Marseille, 1960; lectr. Breadloaf Writer's Conf., 1961; vis. prof. U. N.C., 1965, Harvard U., 1969; lectr. Am. studies seminars Kyoto (Japan) U., 1979; pub., editl. dir. Algonquin Books Chapel Hill, 1982-91. Author: Thomas Wolfe: The Weather of His Youth, 1955, No Place on Earth, 1959, The Golden Weather, 1961, The Faraway Country, 1963, The Teller in the Tale, 1967, The Curious Death of the Novel, 1967, George W. Cable, 1969, The Writer in the South, 1972, William Elliott Shoots A Bear, 1975, Virginia: A History, 1977, The Wary Fugitives, 1978, Surfaces of a Diamond, 1981, A Gallery of Southerners, 1982, The Even-Tempered Angler, 1983, The Edge of the Swamp, 1989, The Algonquin Literary Quiz Book, 1990, The Mockingbird in the Gum Tree, 1991, Small Craft Advisory, 1991, The Heat of the Sun, 1995, Babe Ruth's Ghost, 1996; editor: South Renascence, 1953, The Lasting South, 1957, Teach the Freeman: R.B. Hayes and the Slater Fund for Negro Education, 1959, The Idea of an American Novel, 1961, South: Modern Southern Literature in Its Cultural Setting, 1961, Bibliographical Guide to the Study of Southern Literature, 1969, The Comic Imagination in American Literature, 1973, The Literary South, 1978, The American South, 1980, The History of Southern Literature, 1985, An Apple for My Teacher, 1987, A Writer's Companion, 1995; co-editor: So. Lit. Jour., 1968-89; contbr. articles to periodicals. Served with AUS, 1943-46. Guggenheim fellow, 1958-59, fellow Am. Coun. Learned Socs., 1964. Fellow So. Writers (chancellor 1991-93); mem. Soc. Study So. Lit. (pres. 1975-76), Phi Beta Kappa. Address: 702 Gimghoul Rd Chapel Hill NC 27514-3811

RUBIN, MELVIN LYNNE, ophthalmologist, educator; b. San Francisco, May 10, 1932; s. Morris and May (Gelman) R.; m. Lorna Isen, June 21, 1953; children: Gabrielle, Daniel, Michael. AA, U. Calif., Berkeley, 1951, BS, 1953; MD, U. Calif., San Francisco, 1957; MS, State U. Iowa, 1961. Diplomate Am. Bd. Ophthalmology (bd. dirs. 1977-83, chmn. 1984). Intern U. Calif. Hosp., San Francisco, 1957-58; resident in ophthalmology State U. Iowa, 1958-61; attending surgeon Georgetown U., Washington, 1961-63; asst. prof. surgery U. Fla. Med. Sch., Gainesville, 1963-66; assoc. prof. ophthalmology U. Fla. Med. Sch., 1966-67, prof. ophthalmology, 1967—, chmn. dept. ophthalmology, 1978-95; eminent scholar U. Fla. Med. Sch., Gainesville, 1989-97, eminent scholar emeritus, 1997; research cons. Dawson Corp.; ophthalmology cons. VA Hosp., Gainesville. Author: Studies in Physiological Optics, 1965, Fundamentals of Visual Science, 1969, Optics for Clinicians, 1971, 2d edit., 1974, 25th ann. edit., 1995, The Fine Art of Prescribing Glasses, 1978, 2d edit., 1991; editor: Dictionary of Eye Terminology, 1984, 3d edit., 1996, Eye Care Notes, 1989; mem. editorial bd. Survey Ophthalmology; contbr. more than 100 articles to profl. jours. Co-founder Gainesville Assn. Creative Arts, Citizens for Pub. Schs., Inc., ProArteMusica Gainesville, Inc., 1969, pres., 1971-73; mem. Thomas Ctr. Adv. Bd. for the Arts, 1978-84, nat. sci. adv. bd. Helen Keller Eye Rsch. Found., 1989—; bd. dirs. Hippodrome State Theater, 1981-87; bd. trustees U. Fla. Performing ARts Ctr., 1995—, Friends of Photography Ansel Adams Ctr., 1991—. With USPHS, 1961-63. Recipient Best Med. Book for 1978 award Am. Med. Writers Assn., 1979, Shaler Richardson award for svc. to medicine Fla. Soc. Ophthalmology, 1995; M.L. Rubin Ann. Lectureship established in his honor by Fla. Soc. of Ophthalmology, 1993. Fellow ACS, Am. Acad. Ophthalmology (sec., dir. 1978-92, pres. 1988, Sr. Honor award 1987. Guest of Honor 1992), Found. Am. Acad. Ophthalmology (bd. trustees, 1988-95, chmn., 1992-94), Joint Commn. on Allied Health Pers. in Ophthalmology (Statesman of Yr. award 1987); mem. Assn. Rsch. in Vision and Ophthalmology (trustee 1973-78, pres. 1979), Retina Soc., Macula Soc., Club Jules Gonin, N.Y. Acad. Sci., Fla. Soc. Ophthalmology, Am. Ophthal. Soc., Pan Am. Soc. Ophthalmology, Ophthalmic Photographers Soc., Alachua County Med. Soc., Fla. Med. Assn., AMA (editorial bd. Archives of Ophthalmology 1975-85), Sigma Xi, Alpha Omega Alpha., Phi Kappa Phi. Office: U Fla Med Ctr PO Box 100284 Gainesville FL 32610-0284

RUBIN, MICHAEL, lawyer; b. Boston, July 19, 1952; m. Andrea L. Peterson, May 29, 1983; children: Peter, Eric, Emily. AB, Brandeis U., 1973; JD, Georgetown U., 1977. Bar: Calif. 1978, U.S. Dist. Ct. (no. dist.) Calif. 1978, U.S. Ct. Appeals (9th cir.) 1978, U.S. Ct. Appeals (5th, 7th, 10th cirs.) 1982, U.S. Supreme Ct. 1984, U.S. Ct. Appeals (D.C. cir.) 1984, U.S. Ct. Appeals (11th cir.) 1987. Teaching fellow Law Sch. Stanford (Calif.) U., 1977-78; law clerk to Hon. Charles B. Renfrew U.S. Dist. Ct. (no. dist.) Calif., San Francisco, 1978-79; law clerk to Hon. James R. Browning U.S. Ct. Appeals (9th cir.), San Francisco, 1979-80; law clerk to Hon. William J. Brennan, Jr. U.S. Supreme Ct., Washington, 1980-81; assoc. Altshuler & Berzon, San Francisco, 1981-85, ptnr., 1985-89; ptnr. Altshuler, Berzon, Nussbaum, Berzon & Rubin, San Francisco, 1989—. Office: Altshuler Berzon Nussbaum Berzon & Rubin 177 Post St Ste 300 San Francisco CA 94108-4700

RUBIN, NORMAN JULIUS, public relations consultant; b. New Haven, May 22, 1923; s. Louis and Ida (Levine) R. BA, Yale U., 1948. City hall-police reporter Meriden (Conn.) Record, 1948-50; assoc. editor Meriden Jour., 1950-53; reporter news bur. Yale U., New Haven, 1953-55, asst. dir. news bur., 1955-58; dir. pub. rels. New York Tb Health Assn., N.Y.C., 1958-61; pub. affairs assoc. Western Electric Co., N.Y.C., 1961-64, asst. mgr. pub. affairs, 1964-80, asst. mgr. cmty. rels., 1980-86, mgr. com. rels., 1980-86; columnist N.Y. Newsday, N.Y.C., 1986-95; freelance writer, metro area non-profit orgns. N.Y.C., 1995—; sec. Western Electric Fund, N.Y.C., 1974-80. With inf., U.S. Army, 1943-46, ETO. Recipient Media award United Way N.Y.C., 1995; cited for successfully promoting N.Y.C.'s non-profit sector by Nonprofit Coord. Com. N.Y., 1992. Mem. Pub. Rels. Soc. Am. (accredited mem.), Yale Club, Grads. Club. Avocations: squash tennis, ballet. Home and Office: 115 E 9th St Apt 14E New York NY 10003-5414

RUBIN, PATRICIA, internist; b. Apr. 27, 1962. MD, Wright State U., 1988. Cert. internal medicine. Resident in internal medicine U. Cin., 1988-91; fellow in cardiology U. Hosp., Cleve., 1991; rsch. fellow in cardiology U. Wash. Sch. Medicine, Seattle, 1993—. Recipient Clinician Scientist award Am. Heart Assn., 1995-96. Mem. ACP, AMA, ACC. Office: Cardiology One Box 8086 1330 Marcy Dr NW Ste 200 Kent OH 44708*

RUBIN, RICHARD ALLAN, lawyer; b. N.Y.C., June 19, 1942; s. Louis Max and Ruth Ann (Goldman) R.; m. Susan Deborah Levitt, June 18, 1966; children: Karen, Jill. BS, Queens Coll., 1964; JD, Bklyn. Law Sch., 1967; LLM, NYU, 1968. Bar: N.Y. 1967. Assoc. Schwartz and Frank, N.Y.C., 1968-69, Javits and Javits, N.Y.C., 1969-71; ptnr. Wolf Haldenstein Adler Freeman Herz & Frank, N.Y.C., 1972-76, Parker Chapin Flattau & Klimpl, N.Y.C., 1977—; lectr. Am. Mgmt. Assn., N.Y. Bar Assn. Mem. ABA. Office: Parker Chapin Flattau & Klimpl 1211 Avenue Of The Americas New York NY 10036-8701

RUBIN, RICK, record producer; b. Long Beach, N.Y., Mar. 10, 1963; s. Mickey and Linda (Tomberg) R. BFA, NYU, 1985. Owner, founding pres. DEF JAM Recordings, N.Y.C., 1984-88, Am. (formerly DEF Am.) Recordings, L.A., 1988—; producer recordings including: L.L. Cool J. Radio, 1985 (Gold), Beastie Boys License to Kill, 1986 (4x Platinum), Run DMC Raising Hell, 1986 (4x Platinum), The Cult Electric, 1987 (Gold), Slayer: South of Heaven, 1988, sound track Less Than Zero, 1988 (Gold), Andrew Dice Clay, 1989 (Gold), Red Hot Chili Peppers Blood Sugar Sex Magic; exec. producer recordings Public Enemy It Take A Nation, 1988 (Platinum); dir., co-producer movie Tougher than Leather, 1987. Named Hot Producer of Yr. Rolling Stone Mag., 1988; recipient Joel Weber award New Music Seminar, 1990. *

RUBIN, ROBERT E., federal official; b. N.Y.C., Aug. 29, 1938; s. Alexander and Sylvia (Seiderman) R.; m. Judith Leah Oxenberg, Mar. 27, 1963; children: James Samuel, Philip Matthew. AB summa cum laude, Harvard U., 1960; postgrad., London Sch. Econs., 1960-61; LLB, Yale U., 1964. Bar: N.Y. 1965. Assoc. Cleary, Gottlieb, Steen & Hamilton, N.Y.C., 1964-66; assoc. Goldman Sachs & Co., N.Y.C., 1966-70, ptnr., 1971, mem. mgmt. com., 1980, vice chmn., co-chief oper. officer, 1987-90, co-sr. ptnr., co-chmn., 1990-93; asst. to Pres. Clinton for econ. policy The White House, Washington, 1993-95, lead nat. econ. coun. Exec. Office of Pres., 1993-95; sec. U.S. Dept. of the Treasury, Washington, 1995—; ptnr., bd. dirs. N.Y.C. Partnership, Inc., 1991-93; mem. Pres.'s Adv. Com. for Trade Negotiations, Washington, 1980-82, mem. adv. com. on tender offers SEC, Washington, 1983, Gov.'s Commn. on Trade Competitiveness, 1987, regulatory adv. com. N.Y. Stock Exch., 1988-90, adv. com. internat. capital markets Fed. Res. Bank N.Y., 1989-93; mem. Securities and Exch. Commn. Market Oversight and Fin. Svcs. Adv. Com., 1991-93; Gov.'s Adv. Panel on Fin. Svcs., 1988-89; bd. dirs. Ctr. for Nat. Policy, 1982-93, vice chmn., 1984; trustee Sta. WNET-TV, 1985-93; mem., trustee Carnegie Corp. of N.Y., 1990-93; mem. Mayor's Coun. Econ. Advisors, 1990, Gov.'s Coun. on Fiscal and Econ. Priorities, 1990-92. Trustee Am. Ballet Theatre Found., Inc., N.Y.C., 1969-93, Collegiate Sch., 1978-84; mem. bd. overseers' com. to visit econs. dept. Harvard U., 1981-87, com. on univ. resources, 1987-92; mem. fin. com. N.Y. campaign Mondale for Pres., 1983-84; mem. investment adv. coun. N.Y.C. Pension Fund, 1980-89; chmn. Dem. Congl. Dinner, Washington, 1982; Dems. for the 80s, 1985-89, Dems. for the 90s, 1989-90; chmn. N.Y.C. host com. 1992 Dem. Conv., 1989-92; mem. Commn. Nat. Elections. Recipient award Nat. Assn. of Christians and Jews, N.Y.C., 1977, Disting. Leadership in Govt. award Columbia Bus. Sch., 1996, Euromoney Mag. award Fin. Min. Yr., 1966. Mem. Phi Beta Kappa, Harvard Club (N.Y.C.), Century Country Club (Purchase, N.Y.). Jewish. Office: Dept of Treasury Office of the Sec 1500 Pennsylvania Ave NW Washington DC 20220-0001

RUBIN, ROBERT JOSEPH, physician, health care consultant; b. Bklyn., Feb. 7, 1946; s. B. Norman and Suzanne (Fried) R.; m. Fran Auerbach, June 14, 1970; children: Elyse Beth, David Jon. AB, Williams Coll., 1966; MD, Cornell U., 1970. Diplomate Am. Bd. Internal Medicine. Intern New England Med. Ctr. Hosps., Boston, 1970-71, resident, 1971-72, 74-76; epidemic intelligence officer, respiratory disease and spl. pathogens, divsn. viral diseases Ctr. for Disease Control, 1972-74; asst. dean govt. affairs Tufts U., 1979-84, assoc. prof. medicine, 1981-84; chief renal divsn. Lemuel Shattuck Hosp., Boston, 1979-81; asst. sec. planning and evaluation U.S. HHS, Washington, 1981-84; clin. assoc. prof. Georgetown U., Washington, 1984-95, clin. prof., 1995—; exec. v.p. ICF, Inc., 1984-88; pres. Health and Scis. Internat., 1988-92, Lewin ICF Inc., 1992, Lewin-VHI, Inc., 1992-96, Lewin Group, 1996—. Contbr. articles to profl. jours. With USPHS, 1972-74. Robert Wood Johnson Health Policy fellow, 1977. Mem. ACP, AMA, Am. Soc. Nephrology, Internat. Soc. Nephrology, Am. Fedn. Clin. Rsch., Mass. Med. Soc., Kenwood Club, Potomac Club, Williams Club, Phi Beta Kappa. Republican. Jewish. Office: 9302 Lee Hwy Ste 500 Fairfax VA 22031-1214

RUBIN, ROBERT SAMUEL, investment banker; b. Boston, Sept. 22, 1931; s. Jesse Abraham and Rose (Solomon) R.; m. Martha Lucy Adams, Dec. 15, 1956; children: Rebecca, David, James, Nathaniel. BA, Yale U., 1953; MBA, Harvard Coll., 1955. With Lehman Bros., 1958-70, ptnr., 1967-70; mng. dir., bd. dirs. Lehman Bros. Kuhn Loeb, Inc., N.Y.C., 1970-84; mng. dir. Smith Barney, Inc., N.Y.C., 1989—. Trustee Bklyn. Hosp.; chmn. Bklyn. Mus.; treas. N.Y. Mcpl. Arts Soc.; bd. dirs. St. Ann's Sch. 2nd lt. AUS, 1955-58. Home: 218 Columbia Hts Brooklyn NY 11201-2105 Office: Smith Barney Inc 390 Greenwich St New York NY 10013-2309

RUBIN, ROBERT SAMUEL, lawyer; b. Cin., Apr. 25, 1954; s. Carl B. and Gloria (Weiland) R.; m. Virginia K. Carson, May 14, 1983; children: John C., Claire W., Elizabeth K. LLB, U. Wales, Aberystwyth, Eng., 1976; JD, U. Cin., 1979. Bar: Ohio 1979, U.S. Dist. Ct. (so. dist.) Ohio 1979. Assoc. Brown, Cummins & Brown, Cin., 1979-82; assoc. Porter, Wright, Morris & Arthur, Cin., 1982-88, partner, 1988-92; ptnr. Cohen Todd Kite & Stanford, Cin., 1992—; mem. arbitration rules com. U.S. Dist. Ct. (so. dist.) Ohio 1984, fed. mediation panel, 1990—. Mem. Ohio Bar Assn. (banking law subcom.), Cin. Bar Assn., U. Cin. Coll. Law Alumni Assn. (trustee 1988-90), Univ. Club. Home: 2210 Bedford Ter Cincinnati OH 45208-2604 Office: Cohen Todd Kite & Stanford 525 Vine St Ste 16 Cincinnati OH 45202-3121

RUBIN, ROBERT TERRY, physician, researcher; b. Los Angeles, Aug. 26, 1936; s. Joseph Salem and Lorraine Grace (Baum) R.; m. Lynne Esther Mathews, Mar. 10, 1962 (div. Dec. 1980); children: Deborah, Sharon, Rachel; m. Ada Joan Mickas, Jan. 18, 1985. AB, UCLA, 1958; MD, U. Calif., San Francisco, 1961; PhD, U. So. Calif., Los Angeles, 1977. Diplomate Am. Bd. Psychiatry and Neurology. Asst. prof. psychiatry UCLA, 1965-71, prof. psychiatry, 1972—; prof. Pa. State U., Hershey, 1972-93; Blue Cross of Western Pa. prof. neurosci., prof. psychiatry, dir. neurosci. rsch. ctr. Allegheny campus Med. Coll. Pa., Hahnemann Sch. Medicine, Allegheny U. Health Scis., Pitts., 1992—; cons. Naval Health Rsch. Ctr., San Diego, 1969-70; mem. Brain Rsch. Inst. UCLA, 1969—; trustee Kinsey Inst. Sex Rsch., Ind. U., 1986-90. Contbr. articles to profl. jours. With USNR, 1967-69. Recipient Rsch. Sci. Devel. awards NIMH, 1972-77, Rsch. Scientist award, 1982, 87, 93. Fellow AAAS, Am. Psychiat. Assn., Am. Coll. Psychiatrists; mem. World Psychiat. Assn. (sec. sect. biol. psychiatry 1983-88, chmn. sect. biol. psychiatry 1988-93), Internat. Soc. Psychoneuroendocrinology (pres. 1984-87). Avocations: masters' swimming, bagpiping. Office: Allegheny Gen Hosp Neurosci Rsch Ctr 320 E North Ave Pittsburgh PA 15212-4756

RUBIN, SAMUEL HAROLD, physician, consultant; b. N.Y.C., July 24, 1916; s. Joseph and Esther (Goldfarb) R.; m. Audrey Arndt, Nov. 20, 1943; children: James E., David A. A.B., Brown U., 1938; M.D., St. Louis U., 1943; M.S., U. Chgo., 1957; DSc (hon.), N.Y. Med. Coll., 1997. Diplomate: Am. Bd. Internal Medicine. Intern Jewish Hosp., St. Louis, 1943-44; resident St. Louis U. Group Hosp., 1944-45, St. Mary's Hosp., Kansas City, Mo., 1945-46; practice medicine Asbury Park, N.J., 1948-61; vol. faculty mem. N.Y. Med. Coll., 1948-61, assoc. prof. dept. medicine, 1962-65, prof., 1965—, dir. Inst. Human Values in Med. Ethics, 1984-86; chief med. service N.Y. Med. Coll.-Met. Hosp. Center, 1966-71, assoc. dean, 1971-72, exec. dean, 1972-74, dean, v.p. acad. affairs, 1975, provost, dean, 1977-83, provost, dean emeritus, 1983—, cons., 1983—; mem. bd. trustees St. Clares' Hosp., N.Y.C., 1985—, N.Y. Med. Coll., 1988-94. Contbr. articles to med. jours. With M.C. AUS, 1946-48. NIH program dir. grantee, 1966-71. Fellow A.C.P.; mem. N.Y. Acad. Sci. Home: 425E Heritage Hills Dr Somers NY 10589-1912

RUBIN, SANDRA MENDELSOHN, artist; b. Santa Monica, Calif., Nov. 7, 1947; d. Murry and Freda (Atliss) Mendelsohn; m. Stephen Edward Rubin, Aug. 6, 1966. BA, UCLA, 1976, MFA, 1979. Instr. Art Ctr. Coll. Design, Pasadena, Calif., 1980, UCLA, 1981. One-woman exhbns. include L.A. County Mus. Art, 1985, Fischer Fine Arts, London, 1985, Claude Bernard Gallery, N.Y.C., 1987, L.A. Louver Gallery, L.A., 1992; group exhbns. include L.A. County Mus. Artm 1977, 82, 83, L.A. Mcpl. Art Gallery, 1977, 83, 93, L.A. Contemporary Exhbns., 1978, L.A. Inst. Contemporary Arts, 1978, Newport Harbor Art Mus., Newport Beach, Calif., 1981, Odyssia Gallery, N.Y.C., 1981, Nagoya (Japan) City Mus., 1982, Long Beach (Calif.) Mus. Art, 1982, Brooke Alexander Gallery, N.Y.C., 1982, Laguna Beach (Calif.) Mus. Art, 1982, Jan Baum Gallery, L.A., 1984, San Francisco Mus. Art, 1986, Claude Bernard Gallery, 1986, Struve Gallery, Chgo., 1987, Boise (Idaho) Mus., 1988, Judy Youen's Gallery, London, 1988, Tatistscheff Gallery, Inc., Santa Monica, Calif., 1989, Tortue Gallery, Santa Monica, 1990, Contemporary Arts Forum, Santa Barbara, Calif., 1990, San Diego Mus. Art, 1991, Fresno (Calif.) Met. Mus., 1992, Jack Rutberg Fine Arts, L.A., 1993. Recipient Young Talent Purchase award L.A. County Mus. Art, 1980; Artist's Fellowship grant NEA, 1981, 91. Avocations: gardening, exercise, reading, singing.

RUBIN, SEYMOUR JEFFREY, judge, lawyer, educator; b. Chgo., Apr. 6, 1914; s. Sol and Sadie (Bloom) R.; m. Janet Beck, Mar. 26, 1943. BA, U. Mich., 1935; LLB magna cum laude, Harvard U., 1938, LLM, 1939. Bar: Ill. 1939, D.C. 1941. Mem. U.S. Reparations Del., 1945, Inter-Am. Conf. on Problems of War and Peace, 1945; chief U.S. Delegation on Post-War Problems, Portugal, Spain, Sweden, 1946; asst. legal adviser econ. affairs Dept. State, 1946-48; legal adviser U.S. dels. to organizing confs. GATT, 1947-48; practiced law Washington, 1948-61; mem. Spl. Presdl. Mission to Bolivia, 1961; personal rep. Pres. to Bolivia wih rank of spl. ambassador, 1962; gen. counsel ICA and AID, 1961-62; U.S. rep. Devel. Assistance Com., 1962-64; U.S. rep. to spl. com. UN Security Council, 1964-65; counsel Surrey, Karasik & Morse, 1964-75; U.S. rep. UN Commn. on Internat. Trade Law, 1967-69; prof. law sch. Am. U., Washington, 1973-85, prof. emeritus, 1985—; exec. v.p. Am. Soc. Internat. Law, 1975-85; mem. Inter Am. Juridical Commn., 1974-94, chmn., 1988; U.S. rep. UN Commn. on Transnat. Corps., 1975-87; hon. mem. Inter Am. Juridical Commn., 1995—; mem. U.S. del. UNCTAD Tech. Transfer Conf., 1978; mem. panel of conciliators Internat. Centre for Settlement of Investment Disputes, 1981—; prof. emeritus in residence Am. Univ. Law Sch., Washington, 1988—; judge adminstrv. tribunal Inter-Am. Devel. Bd., 1994—; cons. U.S. Dept. State, Brookings Instn., 1948-49; chief U.S. del. negotiating Marshall Plan Agreements, 1951-52; dep. adminstr. Mut. Def. Assistance Control Act, 1952-53; pub. mem. Commn. on Internat. Rules of Jud. Procedure, 1961-62; adj. prof. Georgetown U. Law Ctr., Washington, 1964-72; lectr. Sloan Sch. Bus. Adminstrn., MIT, Cambridge, 1969; pres. InterAm. Legal Svcs. Assn., 1980-82; sr. cons. Am. Soc. Internat. Law; lectr. in field various univs. worldwide, 1949—; chmn. Bellagio Trade Conf., 1985, Symposium on U.S.-European Cmty. Trade Issues, Boston, 1987; chmn. U.S. Govt. Constitution Com. on Dem. Instns., 1987—; cons. legal issues of trade and investment. Author: Private Foreign Investment, 1956, The Conscience of the Rich Nations - The Common Aid Effort and the Development Assistance Committee, 1966, (with others) The International Corporation, 1970, Global Companies, 1975, Emerging Standards for Internat. Trade and Investment, 1983, Managing Trade Relations in the 1980s, 1984; editor, contbr.: Foreign Development Lending—Legal Aspects, 1971, Environment and Trade, 1981; editor: Avoidance and Settlement of International Trade Disputes, 1986; contbr. (with others) articles in field to profl. jours. Mem. bd. Inst. Internat. Law, Consumers for World Trade. Recipient Sesquicentennial award U. Mich., 1967, Grand Silver medal Austria, 1967, Cert. of Honor from U.S. Dept. State, 1994. Mem. Am. Soc. Internat. Law (sr. advisor), Internat. Law Assn., Washington Inst. Fgn. Affairs, ABA, Coun. Fgn. Affairs, Am. Law Inst., InterAm. Bar Assn. (trustee), Soc. Internat. Devel., Washington Fgn. Law Soc. (bd. dirs.). Democrat. Home: 1675 35th St NW Washington DC 20007-2335 Office: American Univ Law School 4801 Massachusetts Ave NW Washington DC 20016-8180

RUBIN, STANLEY CREAMER, producer; b. N.Y.C., Oct. 8, 1917; s. Michael Isaac and Anne (Creamer) R.; m. Elizabeth Margaret von Gerkan (actress Kathleen Hughes), July 25, 1954; children: John, Chris, Angela, Michael. Student, UCLA, 1933-37. Writer Universal Studios, Universal City, Calif., 1940-42, Columbia Pictures, Los Angeles, 1946-47; writer, producer NBC-TV, Burbank, Calif., 1948-49; theatrical film producer various studios, 1949-55, Rastar Prodns., Columbia Pictures, 1988-91; TV producer CBS-TV, Los Angeles, 1956-59, Universal Studios, Universal City, 1960-63, 20th Century-Fox, Los Angeles, 1967-71, MGM Studios, Culver City, Calif., 1972-77; pres. TBA Prodns., Los Angeles, 1978—. Producer theatrical films including The Narrow Margin, 1950, My Pal Gus, 1950, Destination Gobi, 1951, River of No Return, 1952, Promise Her Anything, 1966, The President's Analyst, 1967, Revenge, 1989; co-producer White Hunter, Black Heart, 1990; TV prodns. include G.E. Theatre, 1959-63, Ghost and Mrs. Muir, 1968-69, Bracken's World, 1969-71; writer, producer TV film The Diamond Necklace, 1948 (Emmy award 1949); producer TV films including Babe, 1975 (Hollywood Fgn. Press Golden Globe award, Christopher medal), And Your Name is Jonah, 1978 (Christopher medal 1979), The Story of Satchel Paige, 1980 (Image award 1981); exec. producer TV prodn. Escape from Iran: The Canadian Caper, 1981. Producer spl. programming Dem. Nat. Conv., San Francisco, 1984, Columbia Pictures and Rastar Prodns., 1988-91. 1st lt. USAAF, 1942-46. Mem. Writers Guild Am. (dir. 1941-42), Producers Guild Am. (bd. dirs. 1968-74, pres. 1974-79, v.p. 1987-94, bd. dirs. 1994—), Acad. Motion Picture Arts and Scis., Acad. TV Arts and Scis. (bd. govs. 1971, 73), Phi Beta Kappa. Home and Office: 8818 Rising Glen Pl Los Angeles CA 90069-1222 *I'm still too young to sum up my life, but here's a thought in progress: Stay curious.*

RUBIN, STANLEY GERALD, aerospace engineering educator; b. Bklyn., May 11, 1938; s. Harry Jack and Cele (Sake) R.; m. Carol Ruth Kalvin, Sept. 29, 1963; children—Stephany, Elizabeth, Barbara. B.Ae.E., Poly Inst. Bklyn., 1959; Ph.D., Cornell U., 1963. Asst. prof. to prof. dept. aerospace engring. Poly. Inst. N.Y., Farmingdale, 1964-79, Assoc. dir. aerodynamic labs., 1977-79; prof. aerospace engring. and engring. mechanics U. Cin., 1979—, head dept., 1979-89, dir. NASA Univ. Space Engring. Ctr. on Health Monitoring Space Propulsion Systems, U. Cin., 1988-91; cons. Aerospace Corp., NASA AAC/ARTS, Allison (GM), others; mem. adv. com. Inst. for Computational Methods in Propulsion, NASA; keynote spkr. 9th Internat. Conf. Numerical Methods in Fluid Mechanics, Saclay, France. Editor-in-chief Internat. Jour. Computers and Fluids, 1978—; contbr. articles to profl. jours. and Ann. Rev. Fluid Mechanics, 1992. NSF fellow, 1963-64; grantee Office Naval Research, 1978-88, AFOSR 1968-92, NASA, 1973—, others. Fellow AIAA (assoc.), ASME; mem. Am. Soc. Engring. Edn., Sigma Xi, Sigma Gamma Tau, Tau Beta Pi. Home: U Cin PO Box 210070 761 Baldwin Hall Cincinnati OH 45221-0070 Office: U Cin ML 070 761 Baldwin Hall Cincinnati OH 45221

RUBIN, STEPHEN CURTIS, gynecologic oncologist, educator; b. Phila., May 24, 1951; s. Alan and Helen (Metz) R.; m. Anne Loughran, May 30, 1985; children: Michael, Elisabeth. BS, Franklin & Marshall U., 1972; MD, U. Pa., 1976. Diplomate Am. Bd. Ob-Gyn., Nat. Bd. Med. Examiners. Intern in ob.-gyn. Hosp. of Univ. of Pa., Phila., 1976-77, residency in ob.-gyn., 1977-80, fellow in gynecologic oncology, 1980-82; asst. prof. of ob-gyn Med. Coll. of Pa., Phila., 1982-85, dir. surg. gynecology, 1982-85, chief gynecol. oncology, 1984-85; asst. mem. gynecol. staff Meml. Sloan-Kettering Hosp., N.Y.C., 1985-90, assoc. mem., 1990-93; asst. prof. ob-gyn Cornell U. Med. Coll., N.Y.C., 1985-90, assoc. prof., 1990-93; prof. ob-gyn, dir. gynecologic oncology U. Pa., Phila., 1993—. Editor: Ovarian Cancer, Cervical Cancer, Chemotherapy of Gynecologic Cancer; contbr. over 150 articles to profl. publs. Recipient Career Devel. award Am. Cancer Soc., 1987, Boyer award Meml. Sloan-Kettering; Nat. Cancer Inst. grantee, 1991, 96. Mem. ACS, Am. Coll. Ob-Gyn., Am. Soc. Clin. Oncology, Soc. Gynecol. Oncologists (Pres.'s award 1993), Soc. Gynecologic Investigation, Soc. Pelvic Surgeons, Gynecol. Cancer Found. (Karin Smith award 1996). Office: U Pa Med Ctr 3400 Spruce St Philadelphia PA 19104

RUBIN, STEPHEN EDWARD, editor, journalist; b. N.Y.C., Nov. 10, 1941; s. Irving and Evelyn (Halprin) R. B.A., NYU, 1965; M.S., Boston U., 1966. Editor UPI, N.Y.C., 1966-69; freelance writer N.Y.C., 1969-82; founder, dir. Writers Bloc, N.Y.C., 1976-82; editor Vanity Fair Mag., N.Y.C., 1982-83; exec. editor Bantam Books, N.Y.C., 1984-85, v.p., editorial dir., 1985-88, sr. v.p., editor-in-chief adult fiction and non-fiction, 1987-88, sr. v.p., pub., editor-in-chief adult fiction and non-fiction, 1988-90; pres., pub. Doubleday divsn. Bantam Doubleday Dell Pub. Group, N.Y.C., 1990-95; chmn., CEO Bantam Doubleday Dell Internat. Divsn., London, 1995—. Author: The New Met in Profile, 1974. Avocations: listening to musical performances, collecting records, tapes and cds, reading, exercising. Office: Bantam Doubleday Dell 1540 Broadway New York NY 10036-4039

RUBIN, STUART HARVEY, computer science educator, researcher; b. N.Y.C., Mar. 18, 1954; s. Jack and Rhoda Rochelle (Lentz) R. BS, U. R.I., 1975; MS in Indsl. and Systems Engring., Ohio U., 1977; MS, Rutgers U., 1980; PhD, Lehigh U., 1988. Lectr. U. Cin., 1977-78; electronic engr. U.S. Army Rsch. Labs., Ft. Monmouth, N.J., 1980-83; assoc. prof. computer sci. Ctrl. Mich. U., Mt. Pleasant, 1988—, assoc. prof., 1996—, founder, dir. Ctr. for Intelligent Systems, 1990—; tech. cons. RCA, Princeton, N.J., 1982-83, Babcock and Wilcox Corp., Alliance, Ohio, 1990, Booz-Allen and Hamilton, Inc., San Diego, 1990-91, Adept Tech., San Jose, Calif., 1990-91; mem. rsch. coun. Scripps Clin.; cons. USAF, 1995. Contbr. articles to profl. jours.; inventor in field. Agt. United Fund Isabella County, Mt. Pleasant, 1988; supporting coach Mich. Spl. Olympics, Mt. Pleasant, 1990; event capt. San Diego Regional Sci. Olympic Competition, 1990, 92; judge 37th, 38th, 39th, 40th, 41st, 42nd & 43d Ann. Greater San Diego Sci. and Engring. Fair, 1991-97. Recipient Am. Chem. Soc. award, 1972, U.S. Govt. Cert. of Merit, Washington, 1987, Letter of Appreciation, Gen. Charles C. McDonald, 1990; grantee NSF, Office Naval Tech., State of Mich., others, 1988—. Mem. IEEE, Am. Assn. Artificial Intelligence, Am. Soc. Engring. Edn. (ONT postdoctoral fellow 1990-93), N.Y. Acad. Scis., Internat. Assn. Knowledge Engrs., Assn. for Computer Machinery. Avocations: boating, skiing, hiking and nature. Home: 1604 Canterbury Trl Apt E Mount Pleasant MI 48858-4067 Office: Ctrl Mich U Dept Computer Sci Pearce Hall Mount Pleasant MI 48859

RUBIN, THEODORE ISAAC, psychiatrist; b. Bklyn., Apr. 11, 1923; s. Nathan and Esther (Marcus) R.; m. Eleanor Katz, June 16, 1946; children: Jeffrey, Trudy, Eugene. B.A., Bklyn. Coll., 1946; M.D., U. Lausanne, Switzerland, 1951; grad., Am. Inst. Psychoanalysis, 1964. Resident psychiatrist Los Angeles VA Hosp., 1953, Rockland (N.Y.) State Hosp., 1954, Bklyn. State Hosp., 1955, Kings County (N.Y.) Hosp., 1956; chief psychiatrist Women's House of Detention, N.Y.C., 1957; mem. faculty Downstate Med. Sch., N.Y. State U., 1957-59; pvt. practice N.Y.C., 1956—; tng. and supervising psychoanalyst Am. Inst. for Psychoanalysis of Karen Horney Clinic and Ctr.; mem. faculty Am. Inst. Psychoanalytic Psychoanalysis, 1962—; pres. emeritus bd. trustees Am. Inst. Psychoanalysis. Author: Jordi, 1960, Lisa and David, 1961, Sweet Daddy, 1963, In The Life, 1964, Platzo and the Mexican Pony Rider, 1965, The Thin Book by a Formerly Fat Psychiatrist, 1966, The 29th Summer, 1966, Cat, 1966, Coming Out, 1967, The Winner's Note Book, 1967, The Angry Book, 1969, Forever Thin, 1970, Emergency Room Diary, 1972, Doctor Rubin Please Make Me Happy, 1974, Shrink, 1974, Compassion and Self-Hate, An Alternative to Despair, 1975, Love Me, Love My Fool, 1976, Reflections in a Goldfish Tank, 1977, Alive and Fat and Thinning in America, 1978, Reconciliations, 1980, Through My Own Eyes, 1982, One to One, Understanding Personal Relationships, 1983, Not to Worry, The American Family Book of Mental Health, 1984, Overcoming Indecisiveness, 1985, Lisa and David, The Story Continues, 1986, Miracle at Bellevue, 1986, Real Love, 1990, Child Potential, 1990, Anti-Semitism: A Disease of the Mind, 1990, Little Ralphie and The Creature, 1997; mem. editorial bd. Am. Jour. Psychoanalysis; also articles, columns. Served as officer USNR, World War II. Recipient Adolf Meyer award Assn. Improvement Mental Health, 1963. Fellow Am. Acad. Psychoanalysis; mem. N.Y. County Med. Soc., Am. Psychiat. Assn., Assn. Advancement Psychoanalysis, Authors Guild, Contemporary Authors. Office: 219 E 62nd St New York NY 10021-7685

RUBIN, VERA COOPER, research astronomer; b. Phila., July 23, 1928; d. Philip and Rose (Applebaum) Cooper; m. Robert J. Rubin, June 25, 1948; children: David M., Judith S. Young, Karl C., Allan M. BA, Vassar Coll., 1948; MA, Cornell U., 1951; PhD, Georgetown U., 1954; DSc (hon.), Creighton U., 1978, Harvard U., 1988, Yale U., 1990, Williams Coll., 1993, U. Mich., 1996. Research assoc. to asst. prof. Georgetown U., Washington, 1955-65; physicist U. Calif.-LaJolla, 1963-64; astronomer Carnegie Inst., Washington, 1965—; Chancellor's Disting. prof. U. Calif., Berkeley, 1981; vis. com. Harvard Coll. Obs., Cambridge, Mass., 1976-82, 92—, Space Telescope Sci. Inst., 1990-92; Beatrice Tinsley vis. prof. U. Tex., 1988; Commonwealth lectr. U. Mass., 1991, Yunker lectr. Oreg. State U., 1991, Bernhard vis. fellow Williams Coll., 1993, Oort vis. prof. U. Leiden, The Netherlands, 1995; lectr. in field, U.S., Chile, Russia, Armenia, India, Japan, China, Europe; trustee Associated Univs., Inc., 1993—. Assoc. editor: Astrophys. Jour. Letters, 1977-82; editorial bd.: Sci. Mag., 1979-87; contbr. numerous articles sci. jours.; assoc. editor: Astron. Jour., 1972-77. Pres.'s Disting. Visitor, Vassar Coll., 1987. Recipient U.S. medal of Sci., 1993, Gold medal Royal Astron. Soc. London, 1996, Weizmann Women and Sci. award, 1996; President's disting. visitor Vassar Coll., 1987; mem. President's Commn. To Select U.S. Nat. Medal Sci. Awardees; named Henry Norris Russell lectr. Am. Astron. Soc., 1994, Nat. Sci. Bd., 1996. Mem. NAS (space sci. bd. 1974-77, chmn. sect. on astronomy 1992-95), Am. Astron. Soc. (coun. 1977-80, Russell prize lectr. 1994), Internat. Astron. Union (pres. Commn. on Galaxies 1982-85), Pontifical Acad. Scis., Assn. Univ. Rsch. in Astronomy (trustee 1973-76, 94-96), Am. Philos. Soc., AAAS, Commn. Nat. Med. Sci., Phi Beta Kappa (scholar 1982-83). Democrat. Jewish. *As an observational astronomer, it is my aim to obtain data of highest quality in order to answer questions concerning the universe in which we live. In spite of our enormous ignorance, each day offers exciting opportunities to learn a little more. This is the real joy of doing science.*

RUBIN, WILLIAM, editor; b. N.Y.C., Jan. 10, 1928; s. Herman and Molly (Goodman) R.; m. Claire Levine, Aug. 30, 1953; children: Deborah E., Joan S., Howard I. BA, Bklyn. Coll., 1953. Tech. editor Drug Trade News, N.Y.C., 1952-63; dir. pub. info. Nat. Vitamin Found., N.Y.C., 1958-61; editorial dir. FDC Reports & Drug Rsch. Reports, Washington, 1963-64; proprietor Sci. Reports and Projects, Bethesda, MD., 1964-67; editor Internat. Med. News Group, Rockville, Md., 1967-91; editorial cons., 1992—. Editor Clin. Psychiatry News, Family Practice News, Internal Medicine News, Ob-Gyn. News, Pediatric News, Skin & Allergy News, Internat. Med. News Group. Adminstr. Washington chpt. Am. Suicide Found.; chmn. Md. State Adv. Coun. on Arthritis and Related Diseases; bd. dirs. Reginald Lourie Ctr. for Infants and Young Children; mem. spkrs' bur. Met. Washington chpt. Arthritis Found.; libr. adv. bd. Montgomery County, Md. With USAAF, 1946-47. Mem. Nat. Assn. Sci. Writers (life), Am. Med. Writers Assn., N.Y. Acad. Scis., Nat. Press Club. Avocations: book accumulating, reading history, woodworking. Office: 6808 Greyswood Rd Bethesda MD 20817-1541

RUBIN, ZICK, psychology educator, lawyer, writer; b. N.Y.C., Apr. 29, 1944; s. Eli and Adena (Lipschitz) R.; m. Carol Moses, June 21, 1969; children—Elihu James, Noam Moses. BA, Yale U., 1965; PhD, U. Mich., 1969; JD, Harvard U., 1988. Bar: Mass., 1988. Asst. to assoc. prof. Harvard U., Cambridge, Mass., 1969-76; Louis and Frances Salvage prof. social psychology Brandeis U., Waltham, Mass., 1976-89, adj. prof. psychology, 1989—; law clk. chief judge U.S. Ct. Appeals (1st cir.), 1988-89; assoc. Palmer & Dodge, Boston, 1990-93, counsel, 1994—; chmn. com. behavioral scis. Yale U. Coun., New Haven, 1981-86; mem. adv. bd. Palmer & Dodge Agy., 1994—. Author: Liking and Loving, 1973, Children's Friendships, 1980; co-author: Psychology, 1993; editor: Doing Unto Others, 1974, Relationships and Development, 1986; contbg. editor: Psychology Today, 1980-85; editorial bd.: Harvard Law Rev., 1986-88. Recipient Socio-Psychol. prize AAAS, 1969, Nat. Media award Am. Psychol. Found., 1980; grantee NSF, NIMH, Ford Found., Social Sci. Research Council, Found. Child Devel. Mem. ABA, Mass. Bar Assn., Boston Bar Assn., Am. Psychology-Law Soc., Authors Guild, Text and Acad. Authors Assn. (mem. coun. 1994-95), Soc. Exptl. Social Psychology, Phi Beta Kappa. Jewish. Club: Elihu (New Haven).

RUBINE, ROBERT SAMUEL, lawyer; b. Rockaway, N.Y., Feb. 28, 1947; s. George and Beatrice (Simon) R.; m. Marilyn Goldberg Rubine, Aug. 15, 1970; children: Seth B., Marisa H. BA, Queens Coll., 1968; JD, Syracuse U., 1971. Bar: N.Y. 1972, Fla. 1975; U.S. Dist. Ct. (ea. and so. dists.) N.Y., 1976; U.S. Supreme Ct. 1976. Trial atty. Legal Aid Soc. Nassau County, Mineola, N.Y., 1971-77; atty. Reifman and Rubine, Jericho, N.Y., 1977-79; ptnr. Stein, Rubine and Stein, Mineola, 1979-94, Rubine and Rubine, Mineola, 1995—; adj. prof. C.W. Post Coll., Greenvale, N.Y., 1979-82. Author: (chpt.) Criminal and Civil Investigation Handbook, 1981. Pres. Legal Aid Soc. Nassau County, 1994—; dir. Legal Aid Soc., Nassau County, 1989—. Mem. ATLA, N.Y. State Bar Assn., N.Y. State Assn. Criminal Def. Lawyers, N.Y. State Defenders Assn., Nassau County Bar Assn. Avocation: golf. Home: 5 Woodland Rd Oyster Bay NY 11771 Office: Rubine and Rubine Attys at Law PLLC 114 Old Country Rd Mineola NY 11501-4410

RUBINFIEN, LEO H., photographer, filmmaker; b. Chgo., Aug. 16, 1953. Student, Reed Coll.; BFA, Calif. Inst. Arts, 1974; MFA, Yale U., 1976. Instr. in photography Swarthmore Coll., 1977, Sch. Visual Arts, N.Y.C., 1978-87; assoc. prof. art Fordham U., 1981-87; represented by Robert Mann Gallery, N.Y.C.; vis. lectr. Cooper Union, 1982. One man shows include Gastelli Gallery, N.Y., 1981, Fraenkel Gallery, San Francisco, 1982, 86, Robert Mann Gallery, N.Y.C., Met. Mus. Art, N.Y.C., 1992, Seibu Art Forum, Tokyo, 1993, Cleve. Mus. Art, 1994, Seattle Art Mus., 1994, Robert Mann Gallery, N.Y.C.; exhibited in group shows at Internat. Ctr. Photography, N.Y., 1981, Inst. Contemporary Arts, London, 1981, San Francisco Mus. Modern Art, 1981, George Eastman House, Rochester, N.Y., 1981, Corcoran Gallery, Washington, 1981, Mus. Modern Art, N.Y., 1984; dir., co-author (film) The Money Juggler, 1988, My Bed in the Leaves, 1990; author: (books) A Map of the East, 1992, 10 Takeoffs 5 Landings, 1994, (essays) A Love-Hate Relations, Artforum, 1978. Fellow Guggenheim Found., 1982-83, Asian Cult Coun., 1984. Home: 1 Furnace Dock Rd Croton On Hudson NY 10520-1406

RUBINO, JOHN ANTHONY, management and human resources consultant; b. Port Chester, N.Y., Nov. 22, 1956; s. Angelo J. and Ann (Posillipo) R.; m. Cynthia C. Corica, Nov. 9, 1980; 1 child, Sean Anthony. BA in Psychology magna cum laude, Wagner Coll., 1978; MBA with distinction, Pace U., 1985. Cert. compensation profl. Convention svc. mgr. Waldorf-Astoria Hotel, N.Y.C., 1978-80; compensation analyst County of Westchester, White Plains, N.Y., 1980-82; sr. compensation analyst Anaconda-Ericsson, Inc., Greenwich, Conn., 1982-83; compensation mgr. ASEA, Inc., White Plains, N.Y., 1983-84, Sterling Drug, Inc., N.Y.C., 1984-87; dir. exec. compensation The Equitable Life Insur. Co., N.Y.C., 1987-93; sr. mgr. human resources cons. Ernst & Young, N.Y.C., 1993-96; pres. Rubino Cons. Svcs., Pound Ridge, N.Y., 1996—. Author: Developing Compensation Programs, 1990, Communicating Compensation Programs, 1992; contbr. articles to profl. jours. Mem. Am. Compensation Assn. (instr., course leader, guest speaker 1988—), Am. Mgmt. Assn. (instr., course leader, guest speaker 1988—), Soc. for Human resource Mgmt. Avocations: performing renaissance music, writing poetry, golf. Home: 29 Conant Valley Rd Pound Ridge NY 10576-1815 Office: Rubino Cons Svcs 29 Conant Valley Rd Pound Ridge NY 10576-1815 Office: Ernst & Young 277 Park Ave New York NY 10172

RUBINO, VICTOR JOSEPH, law institute executive; b. N.Y.C., Dec. 25, 1940; s. Joseph V. and Olympia (Gayda) R.; 1 child, Victor Gayda. BA in Govt., Cornell U., 1962, LLB, 1965. Bar: N.Y. 1965, U.S. Dist. Ct. (so. dist.) N.Y. 1969. Staff atty. Westchester Legal Svcs., White Plains, N.Y., 1968-71; assoc. Squadron Ellenoff Plesent & Lehrer, N.Y.C., 1971; treas., program officer Council on Legal Edn., N.Y.C., 1971-79; assoc. dir. Practising Law Inst., N.Y.C., 1979-83, exec. dir., 1983—. Democratic candidate for N.Y. State Assembly, 1970; chmn. Rye (N.Y.) Human Rights Commn., 1975-76. Served to capt. U.S. Army, 1966-68. Mem. ABA, Assn. Bar City N.Y. Office: Practising Law Inst 810 7th Ave New York NY 10019-5818

RUBINOFF, IRA, biologist, research administrator, conservationist; b. N.Y.C., Dec. 21, 1938; s. Jacob and Bessie (Rose) R.; m. Roberta Wolff, Mar. 19, 1961; 1 son, Jason; m. Anabella Guardia, Feb. 10, 1978; children: Andres, Ana. B.S., Queens Coll., 1959; A.M., Harvard U., 1960, Ph.D., 1963. Biologist, asst. dir. marine biology Smithsonian Tropical Research Inst., Balboa, Republic of Panama, 1964-70; asst. dir. sci. Smithsonian Tropical Research Inst., 1970-73, dir., 1973—; assoc. in ichthyology Harvard U., 1965—; courtesy prof. Fla. State U., Tallahassee, 1976—; mem. sci. adv. bd. Gorgas Meml. Inst., 1964-88; trustee Rare Animal Relief Effort, 1976-85; bd. dirs. Charles Darwin Found. for Galapagos Islands, 1977—; chmn. bd. fellowships and grants Smithsonian Instn., 1978-79; vis. fellow Wolfson Coll., Oxford (Eng.) U., 1980-81; vis. scientist Mus. Comparative Biology-Harvard U., 1987-88. Author Strategy for Preservation of Moist Tropical

Forests; contbr. articles to profl. jours. Vice chmn. bd. dirs. Panama Canal Coll., 1989-93; bd. dirs. Internat. Sch. Panama, 1983-85, 90-93, Fundacion Natura, sec., bd. dirs., 1991—; bd. dirs. Earthwatch, 1995—, City of Knowledge, 1996—; hon. dir. Instituto Latino Americano de Estudios Avanzados. Awarded Order of Vasco Nunez de Balboa of Republic of Panama. Fellow Linnean Soc. (London), AAAS, Am. Acad. Arts & Scis.; mem. Am. Soc. Naturalists, Soc. Study of Evolution, N.Y. Acad. Scis., Ancon Panama (bd. dirs.). Club: Cosmos (Washington). Home: Box 2072, Balboa Panama Office: Smithsonian Tropical Rsch Inst Unit 948 APO AA 34002-9948

RUBINOFF, ROBERTA WOLFF, government administrator; b. N.Y.C., Aug. 26, 1939; d. Leon and Leah (Landauer) W.; m. Ira Rubinoff, 1961 (div. 1975); 1 child, Jason. BS, Queens Coll., 1959; Masters of Environ. Mgmt., Duke U., 1981. Biologist Smithsonian Tropical Rsch. Inst., Balboa, Canal Zone, 1966-75, marine sci. coord., 1975-79; asst. dir. Office Fellowships and Grants Smithsonian Instn., Washington, 1980-84, acting dir. Office Fellowships and Grants, 1984-85, dir. Office Fellowships and Grants, 1985—. Mem. AAAS, Am. Soc. Zoologists, Am. Inst. Biol. Sci. Office: Smithsonian Instn Office Fellowships & Grants 955 Lenfant Plz SW Ste 7000 Washington DC 20024-2119

RUBINOVITZ, SAMUEL, diversified manufacturing company executive; b. Boston, Dec. 26, 1929; s. Benjamin Ephraim and Pauline (Kaufman) R.; m. Phyllis Ann Silverstein; children: David Jay, Robert Neal. BS, MIT, 1951, MS, 1952. Sales engr. Clevite Transistor Products, Waltham, Mass., 1954-63; sales mgr. EG&G Inc., Wellesley, Mass., 1963-72, div. mgr., 1972-79, v.p., 1979-86, sr. v.p., 1986-89, exec. v.p., 1989-94; ret.; bd. dirs. KLA Instruments, Inc., Santa Clara, Calif., Richardson Electronics Ltd., Chgo., Kronos Inc., Waltham, Temptronic Corp., Newton, Mass., LTX Corp., Westwood, Mass. Served to 1st lt. USAF, 1952-54. Democrat. Jewish.

RUBINS, ALEX, physical education educator; b. Cleve., Feb. 26, 1926; s. Harry and Nellie (Cutler) R.; m. Betty Buller, May 19, 1946; children: Ira Marc, Jan Merl, Brett Cory. BS in Phys. Edn. and Math., Case Western Res. U., 1949, MA in Ednl. Adminstrn., 1950, PhD in Ednl. Adminstrn., 1971. Tchr. math., athletic dir. Cleve. Pub. Schs., 1950-58, tchr. math. and adult edn., 1966; prof. phys. and health edn. and math. Cuyahoga Community Coll., Cleve., 1966—; pres. Keystone Mortgage Corp. and CCC Ins. Agy. Cleve., 1958-63; broker Realty Mortgage Svc., 1958-63; regional mgr. World Book Ency., 1963-66; football and basketball ofcl., 1946; adminstr. religious sch. Fairmount Temple, Cleve., 1978-91; tchr. Sunday sch. Park Synagogue, 1991; dir. Red Wing Day Camp, summers 1950--58; visitor, evaluator community colls., Calif., 1978. Author: Programmed Learning Activities for Fencing, 1973. Tchr. religious sch. Park Synagogue, Heights Temple, Community Temple, Cleve., 1946-78; coach Little League Baseball, Cleveland Heights, Ohio, 1962-67; tchr. Cleve. Soc. for Blind, 1971—, County Jail, Cleve., 1981-85; reader Cleve. Soc. for Blind, 1971—; pub. speaker to community orgns., 1967—; lectr. Coun. Gardans Retirement Home, Cleve., 1985—; program dir. Elders Hostel, 1980—; div. head Jewish Welfare Fund, Cleve., 1970—. Master sgt. AUS, 1944-46, CBI. Named Advisor of Yr., Cuyahoga Community Coll., 1971; named to Founders wall as ofcl. Basketball Hall of Fame, 1974. Mem. AAUP, AAHPER and Dance, Midwest Alliance Health, Phys. Edn., Recreation and Dance, Ohio Assn. Health, Phys. Edn., Recreation and Dance (bd. dirs. 1980-85, Mentoring award 1990), Internat. Assn. Approved Basketball Ofcls., Ohio High Sch. Athletic Assn., Ohio Assn. 2-Yr. Colls. (past pres., bd. dirs.), Greater Cleve. Football Ofcls. Assn. (pres., bd. dirs., Outstanding Football Ofcl. award 1985), Jewish War Vets., B'nai B'rith. Avocations: bridge, crossword puzzles, jogging, writing pooetry, sketching. Home: 1112 Rutherford Rd Cleveland OH 44112-3654 Office: Cuyahoga Community Coll 2900 Community College Ave Cleveland OH 44115-3123

RUBINSTEIN, ALVIN ZACHARY, political science educator, author; b. Bklyn., Apr. 23, 1927; s. Max and Sylvia (Stone) R.; m. Frankie Kimmelman, Nov. 12, 1960. BBA, CCNY, 1949; MA, U. Pa., 1950, PhD, 1954. Mem. faculty U. Pa., 1957—, prof. polit. sci., 1966—; vis. lectr. Queen Coll., 1959; vis. prof. U. Calif. at Santa Barbara, summer, 1968, Am. U., Cairo, 1971, Lehigh U., spring, 1973, U. Va., spring 1977, 80; chmn. grad. program internat. relations U. Pa., 1966-70; dir. Anspach Inst. Diplomacy and Fgn. Affairs, 1968-70; cons. Inst. Def. Analysis, 1966-70, Inst. for Fgn. Policy Analysis, 1976-81; vis. assoc. Russian Research Center, Harvard, 1956-57. Author: Communist Political Systems, 1966, (with P. Berton) Soviet Writings on Southeast Asia, 1968, The Soviets in International Organizations, 1964, The Foreign Policy of the Soviet Union, 3rd edit., 1972, Yugoslavia and the Nonaligned World, 1970; co-author: Russian Foreign Policy: From Empire to Nation-State, 1997; editor: Soviet and Chinese Influence in the Third World, 1975, Red Star on the Nile: The Soviet-Egyptian Influence Relationship Since the June War, 1977, The Great Game: Rivalry in the Persian Gulf and South Asia, 1983, The Arab-Israeli Conflict: Perspectives, 2nd edit., 1991, Moscow's Third World Strategy, 1988 (Marshall Shulman prize Am. Assn. Slavic Studies 1989); co-editor: Soviet and American Policies in the United Nations: A Twenty-Five Year Perspective, 1971, Soviet Foreign Policy Toward Western Europe, 1978, Soviet Foreign Policy Since World War II: Imperial and Global, 4th edit., 1992, Soviet Policy Toward Turkey, Iran and Afghanistan, 1982, Anti-Americanism in the Third World, 1985, Perestroika at the Crossroads, 1991, Russia and America: From Rivalry to Reconciliation, 1993, America's National Interest in a Post Cold War World, 1994, Regional Power Rivalries in the New Eurasia, 1995; book rev. editor Current History, 1959-69, mem. bd. editors, 1968—; mem. editl. bd. Studies in Comparative Communism, 1973-89, ORBIS, 1974, Soviet Union, 1974-80. Mem. bd. advisors Naval War Coll., 1983-85. Lt. USNR, 1954-56. Ford Found. fellow, 1956-57; Rockefeller Found. grantee, 1961-62; Guggenheim fellow, 1965-66; grantee Am. Philos. Soc., 1958, 59, 68, 73; NSF travel grant, 1970-71; Barra Found. research grant, 1970-71; resident scholar Bellagio Study and Conf. Center, Rockefeller Found., Italy, 1974; Earhart Found. research grantee, 1974; Joint Com. on Soviet Studies of Am. Council Learned Socs. and Social Sci. Research Council grantee, 1975; vis. fellow Clare Hall, Cambridge (Eng.) U., 1974-75; NATO research fellow, 1977; Earhart Found. research grantee, 1979, 81; sr. fellow Fgn. Policy Research Inst., 1981—; sr. assoc. St. Anthony's Coll., Oxford U., spring 1985. Home: The Mermont Apt 503 Bryn Mawr PA 19010 Office: Univ Pa Dept Polit Sci SH 217 Philadelphia PA 19104-6215

RUBINSTEIN, ARYE, pediatrician, microbiology and immunology educator; b. Tel Aviv, Oct. 2; came to U.S., 1971; s. Reuven and Kathe (Samson) R.; m. Orna Eisenstein, Dec. 7, 1965 (div. 1982); children: Ran, Yair, Avner, Noam; m. Charline Nezri, Dec. 27, 1983; children: Reuven, Rena, Rachel. MD, U. Berne, Switzerland, 1962. Diplomate Am. Bd. Pediatrics; bd. cert. in pediatrics, Israel, Switzerland; Am. Bd. Allergy and Immunology cert. in allergy and immunology. Intern, pediatrics resident, fellow U. Tel Aviv, 1962-67; rsch. assoc. divsn. immunology Med. Sch. Harvard Coll., 1971-73; dir. divsn. immunology and bone marrow transplantation U. Berne, 1969-71; asst. prof. cell biology Albert Einstein Coll. Medicine, Bronx, 1973-80, asst. prof. pediatrics, 1973-77, assoc. prof., 1977-82, assoc. prof. microbiology and immunology, 1981-85, prof. pediatrics, 1982—, prof. microbiology and immunology, 1985—; dir. divsn. clin. allergy and immunology Albert Einstein Coll. Medicine, dir. tng. program for allergy and immunology; dir. divsn. clin. allergy and immunology Montefiore Med. Ctr.; attending pediatrician Bronx Mcpl. Med. Ctr., Hosp. Albert Einstein Coll. Medicine; mem. study sect. on AIDS rsch. NIH. Mem. editl. bd. Annals of Allergy; reviewer New England Jour. Medicine, Jour. for Clin. Investigation, Jour. Pediatrics; contbr. over 175 articles to profl. publs. Lt. armed svcs., Israel, 1955-57. Recipient Lifetime award in Immunology, Humanitarian award DIFFA, Birch Svcs. for Children, Annual award U.S. Asst. Sec. of Health for excellence in AIDS rsch. and treatment, 1990, Bela Shick award for Pediatric Rsch., 1993, Ackerman award for Sci. and Humanity, 1995; AIDS Rsch. Program grantee NIH, Bronx. Fellow Am. Acad. Allergy and Immunology, Am. Coll. Allergy & Immunology; mem. N.Y. Acad. Scis., Soc. Pediatric Rsch., The Harvey Soc., Am. Coll. Allergy, Clin. Immunology Soc., Clin. Immunology Soc. Office: Albert Einstein Coll Medicine 1300 Morris Park Ave Bronx NY 10461-1926

RUBINSTEIN, EVA (ANNA), photographer; b. Buenos Aires, Argentina, 1933; d. Arthur and Aniela (Mlynarska) R.; m. William Sloane Coffin Jr., 1956 (div. 1968); children: Amy, Alexander (dec.), David. Ballet tng., Paris, N.Y.C., Calif., 1938-53; student, Scripps Coll., 1950-51, UCLA, 1952-53; student in photography, Lisette Model, 1969, Jim Hughes, 1971, Ken Heyman, 1970, Diane Arbus, 1971. lectr. numerous workshops, seminars, confs.; instr. photo seminars Lodz Film Sch., Poland, 1986, 86-87. Dancer, actress: off-Broadway and Broadway, including original prodn. The Diary of Anne Frank, 1955-56; European dance tour, 1955; one-person shows of photographs include Underground Gallery, N.Y.C., 1972, Dayton Art Inst., Ohio, 1973, Arles Festival, France, 1975, Canon Photo Gallery, Amsterdam, 1975, Neikrug Gallery, N.Y.C., 1975, 79, 81, 82, 85, La Photogalerie, Paris, 1975, Friends of Photography, Carmel, Calif., 1975, Galerie 5.6, Ghent, Belgium, 1976, Gallery Trochenpresse, Berlin, 1977, Frumkin Gallery, Chgo., 1977, Galeria Sinisca, Rome, 1979, Hermitage Found. Mus., Norfolk, Va., 1982, Photographers Gallery, London, 1983, Galerie Forum Labo, Arles, France, 1983, Galerie Nicephore, Lyon, France, 1983, Image Gallery, Madrid, 1984, Muzeum Sztuki, Lodz, Poland, 1984, Il Diaframma/Canon Gallery, Milan, 1984, A.R.P.A. Gallery, Bordeaux, 1984, Chateau d'Eau, Toulouse, France, 1985, Galerie Demi-Teinte, Paris, 1985, Associated Artist Photographers galleries in Warsaw, Krakow, Lodz, Katowice and Gdansk, Poland, 1985-86, Foto/Medium/Art Gallery, Wroclaw, Poland, 1986, Visions Gallery, San Francisco, 1986, Canon Galerie, Paris, 1986, Salone Internat. SICOF, Milan, 1987, St. Krzysztof Gallery, Lodz, 1987, L'Image Fixe, Lyon, 1988, Artotheque, Grenoble, 1988, Neikrug Photographica, N.Y.C., 1989, Heuser Art Ctr. Gallery, Bradley U., Peoria, Ill., 1989, 3-os Encontros da Imagem, Braga, Portugal, 1989, Bibliotheque Nat. Galerie Colbert, Paris, 1989, Galerie Picto-Bastille, Paris, 1989-90, Portfolio Gallery, London, 1990, Vaison-La-Romaine, France, 1990, Hist. Mus. of City of Lodz, 1990, Galerie Artem, Quimper, France, 1993, Galerie F.N.A.C. Etoile, Paris, 1994, other F.N.A.C. galleries (France, Belgium, Spain), 1994-97, Galerie Augustus, Berlin, 1995, L'Imagerie, Lannion, France, 1995, Zacheta Gallery, Warsaw, 1996, Salon of Modern Art B.W.A., Bydgoszcz, Poland, 1997, Galleries of Polish Insts., Sofia, Bulgaria, Berlin, Moscow, Bratislava, Slovakia, I. Beszkova Gallery, Plewen, Bulgaria, 1997, Hungarian Mus. Photographic Art, Budapest, 1997; group shows include, Internat. Salon, Krakow, Poland, 1971, Delgado Mus., New Orleans, 1972, Neikrug Gallery, 1972, 73, 75, Salone Internationale, Milan, Italy, 1973, Photo-OVO, Montreal, Que., Can., 1974, Nat. Portrait Gallery, London, 1976, Hera Gallery, R.I., 1977, Musee National d'Art Moderne Georges Pompidou, Paris, 1977, Centre Culturel de l'ouest Aquitain, Bordeaux, France, 1978, Fotografiska Museet, Stockholm, 1978, Nat. Arts Club, N.Y.C., 1979, Chrysler Mus., Norfolk, 1979, Maine Photog. Gallery, 1981, Floating Found. Photography, N.Y.C., 1970, 71, 72, 73, 79, 82, Ffoto Gallery, Cardiff, Wales, 1983, Musée d'Art Moderne de la Ville de Paris, 1987-88, Boca Raton (Fla.) Mus., 1989, Galerie PICTO Bastille, Paris, 1989, Galerie Arena, Arles, 1989-90, Settimana della Fotografia, Palermo, 1990, Festival de l'Image, Le Mans, France, 1993, Quimper (France), 1995, Galerie Camera Obscura, Paris, 1996; represented: in permanent collections Library of Congress, Washington, Met. Mus. Art, N.Y.C., Bibliotheque Nationale, Paris, Musee Reattu, Arles, France, Kalamazoo Inst. Arts, Israel Mus., Jerusalem, Fotografiska Museet, Stockholm, Muzeum Sztuki, Lodz, Poland, Histo Mus. of City of Lodz, others; author 2 monographs, 2 ltd. edit. portfolios with introductions by John Vachon and André Kertész; contbr. photographs in various books, mags., profl. jours. *Making photographs is my way of exploring the questions that keep me alive by ever leading to further questions.*

RUBINSTEIN, FREDERIC ARMAND, lawyer; b. Antwerp, Belgium, Apr. 20, 1931; came to U.S., 1942; s. Samuel N. and Steffa (Warrenreich) R.; m. Susan August, Dec. 24, 1968; 1 child, Nicolas Eric August Rubinstein. BA, Cornell U., 1953, JD, 1955. Bar: N.Y. 1955. Assoc. Law Offices of I. Robert Feinberg, N.Y.C., 1955-60; assoc. Guggenheimer & Untermyer, N.Y.C., 1960-65, ptnr., 1965-85; ptnr. Kelley Drye & Warren LLP, N.Y.C., 1985—. Vice chmn. zoning & planning com. Local Community Bd. # 6, N.Y.C., 1980-86. Mem. ABA (bus. law sect., emerging growth ventures subcom., chmn. 1988-96), Cornell Club of N.Y. Office: Kelley Drye & Warren LLP 101 Park Ave New York NY 10178

RUBINSTEIN, MOSHE FAJWEL, engineering educator; b. Miechow, Poland, Aug. 13, 1930; came to U.S., 1950, naturalized, 1965; s. Shlomo and Sarah (Rosen) R.; m. Zafrira Gorstein, Feb. 3, 1953; children—Iris, Dorit. B.S., UCLA, 1954, M.S., 1957, Ph.D., 1961. Designer Murray Erick Assos. (engrs. and architects), Los Angeles, 1954-56; structural designer Victor Gruen Assos., Los Angeles, 1956-61; asst. prof. U. Calif. at Los Angeles, 1961-64, asso. prof. dept. engring., 1964-69, prof., 1969—, chmn. engring. systems dept., 1970-75, program dir. modern engring. for execs. program, 1965-70; cons. Pacific Power & Light Co., Portland, Oreg., Northrop Corp., U.S. Army, NASA Research Center, Langley, Tex. Instruments Co., Hughes Space System Div., U.S. Army Sci. Adv. Com., Kaiser Aluminum and Chem. Corp., IBM Corp., TRW. Author: (with W.C. Hurty) Dynamics of Structures, 1964 (Yugoslavian transl. 1973), Matrix Computer Analysis of Structures, 1966 (Japanese transl. 1974), Structural Systems, Statics Dynamics and Stability, 1970 (Japanese transl. 1979), Patterns of Problem Solving, 1975, (with K. Pfeiffer) Concepts in Problem Solving, 1980, Tools for Thinking and Problem Solving, 1986; IEEE Press Videotapes; Models for People Driven Quality, 1991, Quality through Innovation, 1991, Creativity for Ongoing Total Quality, 1993, Relentless Improvement, 1993, (with I.R. Firstenberg) Patterns of Problem Solving, 2d edit., 1995. Recipient Disting. Tchr. award UCLA Acad. Senate, 1964, Western Electric Fund award Am. Soc. Engring. Edn., 1965, Disting. Tchr. trophy Engring. Student Soc., UCLA, 1966; Sussman prof. for disting. visitor Technion-Israel Inst. Tech., 1967-68; named Outstanding Faculty Mem., UCLA Engring. Alumni award, 1979, Outstanding UCLA Civil Engring. Alumni award, 1990, Outstanding Faculty Mem., State of Calif. Command Coll., 1987, 88, 89, 94, 95; Fulbright-Hays fellow, Yugoslavia and Eng., 1975-76. Mem. ASCE, Am. Soc. Engring. Edn., Seismol. Soc. Am., Sigma Xi, Tau Beta Phi. Research in use of computers in structural systems, analysis and synthesis; problem solving and decision theory. Home: 10488 Charing Cross Rd Los Angeles CA 90024-2646 Office: UCLA Sch Engring and Applied Sci Los Angeles CA 90024

RUBINSTEIN, PHYLLIS M., lawyer. BA in English, Pa. State U., 1966; JD, Temple U., 1977. Bar: Pa. 1977, D.C. 1980, Va. 1982. Jud. clk. to Hon. Israel Packel Phila. Supreme Ct., 1977-78; with Samuel B. Hornstein & Assocs., Doylestown, Pa., 1978-79; adj. instr. Inst. Paralegal Tng., Phila., 1979; counsel Hunton & Williams, Richmond, Va., 1981-95; dir. Mezzullo & McCandlish, Richmond, 1995—; speaker in field. Mem. condominium adv. bd. Commonwealth of Va.; former mem. exec. bd. Comml. Real Estate Women; former bd. dirs. B'Nai B'rith Youth Orgn., Beth Sholom Home Ctrl. Va. Mem. ABA (coun., real property, probate and trust law sect. 1993—, former chair com. ethics and professionalism, task force on Applying Fed. Legis. to Congress, mem. standing com. on membership of real property, probate and trust law sect., former vice chair com. on significant decisions of real property, probate and trust law sect., former mem. real estate fin. com.), Va. Bar Assn., Va. State Bar, Met. Richmond Women's Bar Assn. Home: 1905 Oakway Dr Richmond VA 23233-3513

RUBINSTEIN, ROBERT LAWRENCE, anthropologist, gerontologist; b. Bklyn., Jan. 3, 1951; s. Jack Rubinstein and Enid Farley; m. Susan Hersker, Feb. 13, 1980; children: Lily, Gabriel. BA, Case Western Res. U., 1972; MA, Bryn Mawr Coll., 1974, PhD, 1978. Rsch. anthropologist Polisher Rsch. Inst. of the Phila. Geriatric Ctr., 1981-89, asst. dir. rsch., 1989-91, assoc. dir. rsch., 1991-92, dir. rsch., 1992—. Author: Singular Paths: Old Men Living Alone, 1986, Elders Living Alone, 1992. NIH grantee. Fellow Gerontol. Soc. Am.; mem. Am. Anthrop. Assn. Achievments include research on old age and aging, older men, childless elders, home environments of older people. Office: Polisher Rsch Inst Phila Geriatric Ctr 5301 Old York Rd Philadelphia PA 19141-2912

RUBINSTEIN, SIDNEY JACOB, orthopedic technologist; b. Boston, July 4, 1936; s. Harry and Shirley (Block) R.; m. Sheila Ruby Goldstein, Sept. 1, 1955 (div. 1974); children: Ronda, Barry, Terry, Debra, Neysa; m. Margaret Catherine Burns, Nov. 19, 1976; 1 stepchild, Jerry Hiltonen. Cert., Dimock Ctr., Boston, 1971. Cert. Nat. Bd. of Cert. of Orthopaedic Technologists. Chief orthopaedic technologist Beverly (Mass.) Hosp., 1971-82; orthopaedic technologist Beverly Orthopaedic Assoc., 1982—; owner Orthotics Lab., Danvers, Mass., 1993—. Mem. Nat. Assn. Orthopaedic Technologists (pres. 1992-96), Can. Soc. Orthopaedic Technologists, Venezuela Soc. Orthopaedic Technologists, New Eng. Soc. Orthopaedic Technologists (pres. 1988-92). Democrat. Jewish. Avocations: music, traveling, theater, literature. Office: Orthotics Lab 74 Elm St Danvers MA 01923-2838

RUBIO, SUZANNE SARAH, ballet dancer; b. Montreal, Que.. Grad., Nat. Ballet Sch., Toronto, Ont., 1983. Mem. corps de ballet Royal Winnipeg Ballet, Man., 1985-90, soloist, 1990-94, prin. dancer, 1994—; invited guest artist Dance in Canada Gala, Calgary, Alta., 1989. Stage appearances include (musicals) Kismet, 1984, Mame, 1985, (film) The Big Top, Flamenco at 5:15; prin. roles in The Nutcracker, Rodeo, Swan Lake, The Dream, The Sleeping Beauty, Romeo and Juliet, Tarantella, Ballo Della Regina, Allegro Brillante, Piano Variations III, 5 Tangos, Four Last Songs, others. Recipient Can. Coun. Arts grant, 1984, 2nd prize Helsinki Internat. Ballet Competition, 1991. Mem. Can. Actors Equity Assn., Alliance Can. Cinema, TV & Radio Artists. Office: Royal Winnipeg Ballet, 380 Graham Ave, Winnipeg, MB Canada R3C 4K2*

RUBLE, RANDALL TUCKER, theologian, educator, academic administrator; b. Greenville, Va., Apr. 15, 1932; s. William Cecil and Carrie Mae (Connor) R.; m. Martha L. Grant, Sept. 6, 1958; children: John, Jeffrey, Ellen. A.B., Erskine Coll., 1958, B.D., 1961; Th.M., Princeton Theol. Sem., 1962; Ph.D., U. Edinburgh, 1964. Prof. Hebrew and Old Testament Erskine Sem., Due West, S.C., 1965—, v.p., dean, 1976—; supply pastor Abbeville (S.C.) Assoc. Ref. Presbyn. Ch., 1967—; chmn. N.Am. and Carribean area World Alliance of Reformed Chs., 1979-80. Author: The Ten Commandents For Our Day, 1971; contbr. articles to jours., mags. Mem. Town Council, Due West, 1972-75; chmn. Christian Prison Ministries, 1987—. Served with USAF, 1951-55. Mem. Sob. Bibl. Lit., Brit. Old Testament Soc., Nat. Assn. Profs. of Hebrew, S.C. Acad. Religion, Atlanta Theol. Assn. (pres. 1990—). Presbyterian. Home and Office: PO Box 172 Due West SC 29639-0172

RUBLE, RONALD MERLIN, humanities and theater communications educator; b. Mansfield, Ohio, July 4, 1940; s. Eldred Roy and Dessie Cedelia (Shaw) Briner; m. Nancy Kay Dillon, Aug. 29, 1970 (div. Apr. 1976); children: Eric Douglas, Kristofer Philip. BA, Otterbein Coll., 1962; MA, Bowling Green State U., 1966, PhD, 1975. Site coord. Arts Unltd. Firelands Coll. of Bowling Green U., Huron, Ohio, 1989-92, instr. speech and theater, 1970-75, program dir. speech and theater, 1970—, asst. prof. speech and theater, 1976-79, chmn. dept. humanities, 1976-80, assoc. prof. humanities and theater, 1979—, tchg. artist Arts Unltd., 1987-89; bus. mgr., play dir. Huron Playhouse Bowling Green U., 1966-78; artistic dir. Caryl Crane Children's Theatre, Huron, 1990—; co-chmn. Arts in the Parks Festival, North Ctrl. Ohio Arts Coun., Sandusky, 1976-78, v.p. bd. dirs., 1977-78; theater cons. Caryl Crane Children's Theatre, Sandusky, 1984-90. Dir. play The Gingerbread lady, 1978 (1st place N.W. region Ohio Cmty. Theatre Assn. 1978); contbr. poems, short story to profl. publs; playwright. Unit commr. Erie dist. of Firelands coun. Boy Scouts Am., Huron, 1984-87, mem. troop rev. bd., 1985—, merit badge counselor Firelands dist. Heart of Ohio coun., Vermilion, Ohio, 1984—; elder 1st Presbyn. Ch., Huron, 1988-90, 95—. Recipient Outstanding Educator in Arts award Ohio Ho. of Reps., 1975, Outstanding Young Man of Am. award Nat. Jaycees, 1977, Outstanding Cmty. Svc. award Huron C. of C., 1983, 84, 85, Outstanding Leader award Firelands Area Coun. Boy Scouts Am., 1988, Scouter's Key award, 1987, Scouter of the Yr. award Troop 31, 1985. Mem. Am. Theatre in Higher Edn., Am. Alliance Theatre Edn., Am. Assn. Univ. Prof., Drama League, Ohio Theatre Alliance, Am. Film Inst., Children's Theatre Assn., Ohio Humanities Coun., Internat. Soc. of Poets, Nat. Authors Registry, Poets Guild. Avocations: creative writing, concerts, plays, yardwork. Home: 729 Taylor Ave Huron OH 44839-2522 Office: Bowling Green State U Firelands Coll 901 Rye Beach Rd Huron OH 44839-9791

RUBLEY, CAROLE A., state legislator; b. Bethel, Conn., Jan. 18, 1939; d. George B. and Evelyn M. (Maloney) Drumm; m. C. Ronald Rubley, Aug. 25, 1962; children: Lauren M. Rubley Simpson, Stephen R., Kristin A. BA in Biology, Albertus Magnus Coll., 1960; MS in Environ. Health, West Chester U., 1988. Tchr. biology Danbury (Conn.) High Sch., 1960-62, Waltham (Mass.) High Sch., 1962-63; real estate salesperson Henderson-Dewey, Wayne, Pa., 1976-81; solid waste coord. Chester County Health Dept., West Chester, Pa., 1981-88; environ. cons. Environ. Resources Mgmt., Exton, Pa., 1988-92; mem. Pa. Ho. Reps., Valley Forge, 1992—; mem. environ. resources, energy, consumer affairs, finance and urban affairs coms. House of Reps. Author: (with others) Leading Pennsylvania into 21st Century, 1990. Chmn. Ea. Chester County Regional Planning Commn., 1976-85; vice chmn. planning commn. Tredyffrin Twp., Berwyn, Pa., 1976-86, mem. bd. suprs., 1987-92; bd. dirs. Pa. Resources Coun., exec. v.p., 1988-92. Mem. LWV (pres. Upper Main Line chpt. 1976-78, Involved Voter of Yr. award 1993), Pa. Environ. Coun., Green Valleys Assn., Open Land Conservancy. Republican. Roman Catholic. Avocations: aerobics, tennis, hiking, reading, traveling. Home: 621 Vassar Rd Wayne PA 19087-5312

RUBNITZ, MYRON ETHAN, pathologist, educator; b. Omaha, Mar. 2, 1924; s. Abraham Srol and Esther Molly (Jonich) R.; m. Susan Belle Block, Feb. 9, 1952; children: Mary Ly Rubnitz Roffe, Peter, Thomas (dec.), Robert. BSc, U. Nebr., 1945; MD, U. Nebr., Omaha, 1947. Diplomate Am. Bd. Pathology. Intern Mt. Sinai Hosp., Cleve., 1947-48; fellow Mt. Sinai Hosp., N.Y.C., 1948-49; resident in pathology Michael Reese Hosp., Chgo., 1949-51; pathologist VA Hosp., Hines, Ill., 1953-56, chief labs., 1956-93, cons., 1993—; assoc. prof. pathology Loyola U. Med. Sch., Maywood, Ill., 1963-70, prof., 1970—; adj. prof. Ill. State U., Normal, 1979—, Coll. St. Francis, Joliet, Ill., 1989—, Ea. Ill. U. Charleston, 1991—, Western Ill. U., Macomb, 1991—; adj. assoc. prof. No. Ill. U., DeKalb, 1979-92; clin. instr. Augustana Coll., Rock Island, Ill., 1991—. Chmn. candidates com. Village Caucus, Winnteka, Ill., 1969-70; bd. dirs. Chgo. Commons Assn., 1968—; mem. New Trier High Sch. Caucus, Winnetka, 1972-74. With AUS, 1943-46, PTO; 1st lt. M.C., U.S. Army, 1951-53. Fellow Am. Soc. Clin. Pathologists, Coll. Am. Pathologists; mem. Internat. Acad. Pathology, Assn. VA Pathologists (pres. 1982-84), Chgo. Pathology Soc., Lake Shore Country Club (Glencoe, Ill.), North Shore Racquet Club, Mich. Shores Club (Wilmette, Ill.). Republican. Jewish. Avocations: electronics, tennis, travel.

RUBOTTOM, DONALD JULIAN, management consultant; b. Tulsa, Sept. 29, 1926; s. George William and Nellie Dorcas (Core) R.; m. Wanda Mae Stockton, Apr. 29, 1951; children: Rinda Louise, Joy Lynn, Donald Jay, Jill Anna. BS in Fin., Okla. State U., 1951; postgrad., Tulsa U. Chartered fin. analyst; cert. mgmt. cons. V.p., trust officer 1st Nat. Bank & Trust Co., Tulsa, 1955-56; exec. v.p., trust officer, dir. F&M Bank & Trust Co., Tulsa, 1966-68; pres. Rubottom, Dudash & Assocs., Tulsa, 1968—; tchr. Boston Ave. United Meth. Ch., Tulsa, 1962—. With U.S. Army, 1945-46. Mem. Inst. Mgmt. Cons., Nat. Assn. Bus. Economists, CFA Inst., Okla. Soc. Fin. Analysts, S.W. Regional Assn., Small Bus. Investments Cos. (pres. 1979), Tulsa Knife and Fork Club (pres. 1985-86), Tulsa So. Tennis Club, Rotary (pres. 1988-89, dist. gov. 1993-94). Avocations: tennis, skiing, gardening. Home: 2450 E 47th Pl Tulsa OK 74105-5112 Office: Rubottom Dudash & Assocs Inc 4870 S Lewis Ave Ste 180 Tulsa OK 74105-5172

RUBOTTOM, ROY RICHARD, JR., retired diplomat and educator, consultant; b. Brownwood, Tex., Feb. 13, 1912; s. Roy Richard and Jennie Eleanor (Watkins) R.; m. Billy Ruth Young, Dec. 23, 1938; children: Eleanor Ann Rubottom Odden, Frank, John. BS, So. Meth. U., 1932, MA, 1933; postgrad., U. Tex.; LLD, Southwestern Coll., Winfield, Kans., 1968, Cen. Meth. Coll., Fayette, Mo., 1985. Asst. dean student life U. Tex., 1937-41; apptd. fgn. service officer, 1947; sec. of embassy and consul Bogota, Colombia, 1947-49; officer-in-charge Mex. affairs State Dept., 1950, dep. dir. Middle Am. Affairs, 1951, dir., 1952-53; 1st sec. embassy Madrid, 1953, counselor of embassy, 1954, dir. U.S. Ops. Mission, 1954-56; asst. sec. of state for inter-Am. affairs, 1957-60, U.S. Ambassador to Argentina, 1960-62; advisor Naval War Coll., Newport, R.I., 1962-64; v.p. So. Meth. U., Dallas, 1964-71, prof. polit. sci. emeritus, 1975—; dir. Ctr. of Ibero-Am. Civilization, 1975-77; pres. U. Americas, Puebla, Mex., 1971-73; dir. Office Internat. Affairs, Dallas, 1985-87. Co-author: Spain and the U.S. Since W.W. II, 1984. Active Scouting U.S.A. Served with USNR, 1941-46. Recipient Silver Beaver award Boy Scouts Am., 1975, Inter-Am. award Boy Scouts Am., Silver Buffalo, 1993. Mem. Lambda Chi Alpha, Pi Sigma Alpha. Methodist. Lodge: Rotary. Office: 3429 University Blvd Dallas TX 75205-1833

RUBRIGHT, JAMES ALFRED, oil and gas company executive; b. Phila., Dec. 17, 1946; s. James Alfred and Helen Lucille (Evans) R.; children: Noah Michael, Benjamin James, Jaime Anne, Nathaniel Drew, James McCurdy; m. Mary Elizabeth Angelich, Dec. 30, 1988. BA, Yale U., 1969; JD, U. Va., 1972. Bar: Ga. 1972. Ptnr. King & Spalding, Atlanta, 1972-94; sr. v.p., gen. counsel Sonat Inc., Birmingham, 1994—. Mem. ABA. Office: Sonat Inc 1900 5th Ave N Birmingham AL 35203-2610 also: Sonat Inc PO Box 2563 Birmingham AL 35202-2563

RUBRIGHT, ROYAL CUSHING, lawyer; b. Denver, Nov. 27, 1909; s. John Compton and Marie (Popovich) R.; m. Dorothy Kelley, Jan. 4, 1985; 1 child, Lynnell. BA, LLB, U. Colo., 1932, LLM, 1933. Bar: Colo. 1933. Pvt. practice law Denver, 1933-40; ptnr. Fairfield & Woods, P.C., Denver, 1940-90; ret., 1990; part-time instr. law U. Denver; spl. lectr. law U. Colo. Recipient William Lee Knous award U. Colo. Law Sch. Mem. ABA, Colo. Bar Assn. (mem. award deserving sect.), Denver Bar Assn. (pres., award of merit), City Club, Rotary, Masons, Pi Kappa Alpha. Home: 7877 E Mississippi Ave Apt 601 Denver CO 80231-2035

RUBY, CHARLES LEROY, law educator, lawyer, civic leader; b. Carthage, Ind., Dec. 28, 1900; s. Edgar Valentine and Mary Emma (Butler) R.; certificate Ball State U., 1921-22; AB, Cen. Normal Coll., 1924, LLB, 1926, BS, 1931, BPE, 1932; MA, Stanford, 1929; JD, Pacific Coll. of Law, 1931; PhD, Olympic U., 1933; m. Rachael Elizabeth Martindale, Aug. 30, 1925; children: Phyllis Arline (Mrs. Norman Braskat), Charles L., Martin Dale. Prin., Pine Village (Ind.) High Sch., 1923-25; Glenwood (Ind.) Pub. Schs., 1925-26; tchr. El Centro (Calif.) Pub. Sch., 1926-27, Fresno Cen. (Calif.) Union High Sch., 1927-29; prof. law Fullerton Coll., 1929-66; prof. edn. Armstrong Coll., summer 1935, Cen. Normal Coll., summers 1929-33; admitted to Ind. bar, 1926, U.S. Supreme Ct. bar, 1970; pres. Ret. Service Vol. Program, North Orange County, Calif., 1973-76, 83-84; dir. North Orange County Vol. Bur., Fullerton Sr. Citizens Task Force. Life trustee, co-founder Continuing Learning Experiences program Calif. State U., Fullerton, hon. chmn. fund com. Gerontology Bldg; founder, dir. Fullerton Pub. Forum, 1929-39; founder Elks Nat. Found.; co-founder, benefactor Gerontology Ctr. Calif. State U., Fullerton; pres. Fullerton Rotary, 1939-40, hon. mem., 1983—; mem. U.S. Assay Commn., 1968—; mem. Orange County Dem. Cen. Com., 1962-78; bd. dirs. Fullerton Sr. Multi-purpose Ctr., 1981—; bd. dirs. Orange County Sr. Citizens Adv. Council; mem. pres.'s com. Calif. State U., Fullerton. Recipient Medal of Merit, Am. Numis. Assn., 1954, Spl. Commendation Calif. State Assembly, 1966, 88, Calif. State Senate, 1978, 86, Commendation Ind. Sec. of State, 1984, Commendation Bd. Suprs. Orange County, 1985, Commendation Fullerton City Council, 1986, 88, Commendation Orange County Bd. Supervisors, 1986, Commendation Calif. State Senate, 1986, Commendation Exec. Com. Pres. Calif. State U., Fullerton, 1986, Commendation Calif. gov., 1988; Charles L. and Rachael E. Ruby Gerontology Ctr. named in his and late wife's honor, Calif. State U., Fullerton. Fellow Ind. Bar Found.; mem. Pres. Assocs. Calif. State U. Fullerton, Fullerton Coll. Assocs. (named Spl. Retiree of Yr. 1986, Commendation 1986), Calif. (life, pres. So. sect. 1962-63, treas. 1964-65, pres. 1960-61, dir. 1956-65), pres. Fullerton Secondary Tchrs. Assn., Orange County Tchrs. Assn. (pres. 1953-55), Fullerton Coll. (pres. 1958-60) Tchrs. Assn., NEA (life), Ind. Bar Assn., Stanford U. Law Soc., Calif. State Council Edn., Am. Numismatic Assn. (gov. 1951-53, life adv. bd.), Ind. Bar Assn. (hon. life, Golden Career award 1983), Calif. Bus. Educators Assn. (hon. life), Calif. Assn. Univ. Profs., Pacific S.W. Bus. Law Assn. (pres. 1969-70, life), Numismatic Assn. So. Calif. (life, pres. 1961), Calif. Numis. Assn., Indpls. Coin Club (hon. life), Los Angeles Coin Club (hon. life), U.S. Supreme Ct. Hist. Soc., Calif. Town Hall, North Orange County Mus. Assn. (life, benefactor dir.), Stanford U. Alumni Assn. (life), Old Timers Assay Commn. (life), Fullerton Archeology (hon. life, benefactor dir.). Methodist. Clubs: Elks, Fullerton Coll. Vets. (hon. life). Contbr. articles in field to profl. jours. Home: 308 Marwood Ave Fullerton CA 92832-1139

RUBY, MICHAEL, magazine executive. Editor U.S. News and World Report, Washington, now contbg. editor.

RUBY, RALPH, JR., vocational business educator; b. Newburgh, N.Y., Apr. 11, 1944; m. Dorothy Nelle Privette; children: Laconya Dannet, Ralph III, Vanessa Rae. AAS, Orange County C.C., 1968; BS, U. Tenn., Knoxville, 1969, MS in Bus. Edn., 1972; EdD, U. Mo., Columbia, 1975. Cert. tchr., adminstr., N.Y. Tchr. keyboarding, bus. law Valley Cen. High Sch., Montgomery, N.Y., 1969-76, chair bus. dept., 1974-75; asst. prof. vocat. bus. edn. U. Ark., Fayetteville, 1976-79; from asst. prof. to prof. bus. edn., coord. vocat. bus. edn. Ark. State U., State University, 1979—; mem. ednl. adv. com. 26th Congl. Dist., N.Y.; vis. prof. McGill U., Montreal, Que., Can., 1977; acctg. author Gregg divsn. McGraw-Hill Book Co., 1978—; presenter workshops, tngs. programs. Author: Rough Draft Typing Practice, 1980, Target Type!: Improving Speed and Accuracy, 1987, Word Processing and Editing Techniques, 1988, Real Life Keyboarding Applications: (Word Processor, Data Base, Spreadsheet), 1990, Top Row Target Type, 1991, Starship Speller, 1991, Number Pad Tutor, 1991, Lotus in Your Classroom, 1991, WordPerfect in Your Classroom, 1992, Microsoft Works in Your Classroom, 1993, The Big Board Stock Market (simulation), 1993, PageMaker in Your Classroom, 1993, MS-DOS Made Easy, 1993, WordPerfect for Desktop Publications, 1993, Microsoft Windows in Your Classroom, 1994, Mystery at Laser Age Hardware, 1994, The Class Works, 1994, WordPerfect in Your Classroom Using the MacIntosh, 1994, PageMaker in Your Classroom for Windows, 1996, WordPerfect for Desktop Publishing, 1996, Quattro Pro in Your Classroom, 1996, Espionage at International Electronics, 1996, Microsoft Works for Windows in Your Classroom, 1996, Ami Pro For Windows in Your Classroom, 1996, System 7 in Your Classroom, 1997, Excel in Your Classroom, 1997; editor Jour. Edn. for Bus., 1980—, also others. Mem. Am. Vocat. Assn. (life), Nat. Bus. Edn. Assn., So. Bus. Edn. Assn., Nat. Assn. Tchr. Edn. for Bus. and Office Edn. (life), Delta Pi Epsilon, Kappa Delta Pi, Phi Delta Kappa (life). Office: Ark State Univ Coll Business State University AR 72467

RUBY, RUSSELL (GLENN), lawyer; b. Albany, Mo., Nov. 19, 1911; s. Gordon Romeo and Minnie (Hazelrigg) R.; m. Elizabeth Bradford Popkin, Feb. 11, 1939 (dec. Aug. 1967); children: Michael Gordon, Adrienne Elizabeth, Glenn Russell; m. Dorothea King, 1972 (dec. Dec. 1991). Student, Palmer Coll., 1929-31; B.J., U. Mo., 1933; LL.B., Tulsa U., 1939. Bar: Okla. 1939, U.S. Dist. Ct. (ea. dist.) Okla. 1941, U.S. Supreme Ct. 1957. Pvt. practice, Muskogee, 1939—; spl. agt. FBI, 1942-47; pres. Mandire Corp., 1974—. Mem. Okla. Ho. of Reps., 1955-66; mem. Muskogee City Coun., 1968-72, 76-88, vice mayor, 1968-72, dep. mayor, 1976-83, 84-88, mayor, 1983-84; chmn. Muskogee City-County Port Authority, 1974-76; mem. Muskogee Met. Planning Commn., 1968-72, 76-88, chmn., 1978-79; mem. small cities adv. com. Nat. League Cities, 1980-84; trustee Okla. Mcpl. Pension Fund, 1980-84; bd. dirs. Muskogee Community Concert Assn., Kate Frank Manor, Family Guidance Center; chmn. bd. trustees Muskogee Pub. Libr., 1986-88. Named Outstanding Older Oklahoman Eastern Okla. Devel. Dist., 1984. Mem. ABA, Okla. Bar Assn. (50 Yr. plaque 1989), Muskogee Bar Assn. (past pres., 50 Yr. plaque 1989), Assn. Fed. Attys., Soc. Former Agts. FBI, SAR, Masons, Shriners (potentate 1970), Jesters, Elks. Democrat. Episcopalian. Address: 4500 Girard St Muskogee OK 74401-1543

RUCH, CHARLES P., academic administrator; b. Longbranch, N.J., Mar. 25, 1938; s. Claud C. and Marcella (Pierce) R.; m. Sally Joan Brandenburg, June 18, 1960; children: Cheryl, Charles, Christopher, Cathleen. BA, Coll. of Wooster, 1959; MA, Northwestern U., 1960, PhD, 1966. Counselor, tchr. Evanston (Ill.) Twp. High Sch., 1960-66; asst. prof. U. Pitts., 1966-70, assoc. prof., dept. chmn., 1970-74; assoc. dean sch. edn. Va. Commonwealth U., Richmond, 1974-76, dean sch. edn., 1976-85, interim provost, v.p., 1985-86, provost, v.p., 1986-93; pres. Boise (Idaho) State U., 1993—; cons. various univs., govtl. agys., ednl. founds. Author or co-author over 50 articles, revs., tech. reports. Mem. Am. Psychol. Assn., Am. Ednl. Research Assn., Phi Delta Kappa. Office: Boise State U 1910 University Dr Boise ID 83725-0001

RUCH, MARCELLA JOYCE, educator, biographer; b. Brutus, Mich., Sept. 20, 1937; d. Virgil Murray and Grace Milbry (Collier) Wallace; m. Robert Kirkman McMain, Aug. 29, 1956 (div. Aug. 1970); children: Melodie Froom, Kirk McMain, Nancy Hedges, Elizabeth Curran; m. Peter Jerome Ruch, Dec. 22, 1973; children: David, Dan, Michael and Justin Moore Ruch. BS, Western Mich. U., 1964; MA, U. Colo., Colorado Springs, 1973; PhD, U. Colo., Boulder, 1980. Cert. tchr., prin., counselor, Colo. Tchr. Colorado Springs Pub. Schs., 1964-69; supr. child care El Paso County Social Svcs., Colorado Springs, 1970-73; exec. dir. Antlers Day Care Ctr., Colorado Springs, 1973-77, Green Shade Schs., Colorado Springs, 1977-81, Pueblo (Colo.) Toddler Ctr., 1981-83; tchr. Penrose (Colo.) Elem. Sch., 1983-86; adminstrv. intern Cottonwood Elem. Sch., Denver, 1986-87; elem. prin. Simla (Colo.) Pub. Schs., 1987-89; tchr. Colorado Springs Pub. Schs., 1989—; mem. adv. bd. for early childhood edn. Pikes Peak C.C., Colorado Springs, 1970-75; child care specialist Cmty. Agencies Working Together, Colorado Springs, 1970-75. Founder Green Shade Schs., 1977; campaign chair United Way, Canon City, Colo., 1983-84, pres., 1984-85; chair adult coun. St. Paul's United Meth. Ch., 1994—. Mem. Delta Kappa Gamma (v.p. membership 1994-96), Phi Delta Kappa. Methodist. Avocations: gardening, hiking, reading, camping. Home: 2444 Virgo Dr Colorado Springs CO 80906 Office: Lincoln Elem Sch 2727 N Cascade Ave Colorado Springs CO 80907-6210

RUCH, WILLIAM VAUGHN, writer, educator, consultant; b. Allentown, Pa., Sept. 29, 1937; s. Weston H. and Dorothy D. (Daubert) R. BA, Moravian Coll., 1959; MA in Comm., Syracuse U., 1969; MBA, Fairleigh Dickinson U., 1972; PhD, Rensselaer Poly. Inst., 1980; JD, Western State U. Coll. Law, 1983. Reporter Call-Chronicle Newspapers, Allentown, Pa., 1959-60; tchr. English conversation Jonan Sr. High Sch., Matsuyama, Japan, 1960-62; asst. editor Dixie News, Am. Can Co., Easton, Pa., 1964-65; fin. editor Pa. Power & Light Co., Allentown, 1967-69, advt. asst., 1966-67, sales promotion writer, 1965-66; tech. writer, editor Space Tech. Ctr., GE Co., King of Prussia, Pa., 1969; asst. editor Bell System Tech. Jour., Bell Telephone Labs., Murray Hill, N.J., 1969-71; field rep. N.W. Ayer & Son, Inc., N.Y.C., 1972-73; asst. prof. bus. communication Fairleigh Dickinson U., Madison, N.J., 1974-75, Bloomsburg (Pa.) State Coll., 1975-76; lectr. Sch. Bus. and Pub. Adminstrn., Calif. State U., Sacramento, 1977-79; asst. prof. bus. communication Coll. Bus. Adminstrn., San Diego (Calif.) State U., 1979-84; lectr. European div. U. Md., 1984-85; prof. mgmt. Monmouth Coll., West Long Br., N.J., 1985-88; cons. Corp. Communication, 1988-91; pres., owner WVR Assocs., 1991—; founder, exec. dir. Internat. Inst. of Corp. Communication, 1992—; adj. prof. orgnl. commn., N.Y.U., 1993—. Author: Corporate Communications: A Comparison of Japanese and American Practices, 1984, Business Reports: Written and Oral, 1988, International Handbook of Corporate Communication, 1989, Business Communication, 1990, The Manager's Complete Handbook of Communication, 1992, Business Reporting in the Information Age, 1994, (novels) Effective Business Reports, 1995, Infinity/Affinity, 1994, It Takes Great Strive, 1996. Named Outstanding Prof. of Yr. San Diego State U., 1983. Mem. Acad. Mgmt., Assn. for Bus. Communication, Internat. Assn. Bus. Communicators, Internat. Platform Assn. Republican. Mem. United Ch. of Christ. Home: PO Box 517 Rockaway NJ 07866-0517

RUCKELSHAUS, WILLIAM DOYLE, investment group executive; b. Indpls., July 24, 1932; s. John K. and Marion (Doyle) R.; m. Jill Elizabeth Strickland, May 11, 1962; children: Catherine Kiley, Mary Hughes, Jennifer Lea, William Justice, Robin Elizabeth. B.A. cum laude, Princeton U., 1957; LL.B., Harvard U., 1960. Bar: Ind. 1960. Atty. Ruckelshaus, Bobbitt & O'Connor, Indpls., 1960-68; dep. atty.-gen. Ind., 1960-65, chief counsel office atty.-gen. Ind., 1963-65; minority atty. Ind. Senate, 1965-67; mem. Ind. Ho. of Reps., 1967-69, majority leader, 1967-69; asst. atty.-gen. charge civil div. Dept. Justice, 1969-70; adminstr. EPA, Washington, 1970-73; acting dir. FBI, 1973; dep. atty. gen. U.S., 1973; mem. firm Ruckelshaus, Beveridge, Fairbanks & Diamond, Washington, 1974-76; sr. v.p. law and corp. affairs Weyerhaeuser Co., Tacoma, 1975-85; adminstr. EPA, Washington, 1983-85; pres. William D. Ruckelshaus Assocs., 1985-88; mem. firm Perkins Coie, Seattle, 1985-88; chmn. bd. Browning-Ferris Industries, Inc., Houston, 1988-95; founder, prin. Madrona Investment Group, LLC, 1996—; also bd. dirs.; bd. dirs. Cummins Engine Co., Monsanto Co., Nordstrom, Inc., Weyerhaeuser Co., Inc., Gargoyles, Inc. Rep. nominee for U.S. Senate, Ind., 1968. With AUS, 1953-55. Mem. Fed. Bar Assn., Ind. Bar Assn., D.C. Bar Assn., Indpls. Bar Assn. Office: Madrone Investment Group LLC 1000 2nd Ave Ste 3700 Seattle WA 98104-1053

RUCKENSTEIN, ELI, chemical engineering educator; b. Botosani, Romania, Aug. 13, 1925; came to U.S., 1969; m. Velina Rothstein, May 15, 1948; children: Andrei, Lelia. BSChemE, Poly. Inst., Bucharest, Romania, 1949, PhD in Chem. Engring., 1967; doctor honoris causa, Tech. U. Bucharest, 1993. Prof. Poly. Inst., Bucharest, 1949-69; vis. prof. U. London, 1969; NSF sr. scientist Clarkson Coll. Tech., Potsdam, N.Y., 1969-70; prof. U. Del., Newark, 1970-73; prof. SUNY, Buffalo, 1973-81, disting. prof., 1981—; vis. Humbolt prof. Bayreuth U., Fed. Republic Germany, 1986; Gulf vis. prof. Carnegie Mellon U., Pitts., 1988-89; disting. lectr. U. Waterloo, 1985, U. Mo., 1983; Fair Meml. lectr. U. Okla., 1987, Colburn Symposium lectr. U. Del., 1988, Van Winkle lectr. U. Tex., 1989. Contbr. articles, papers to profl. jours. Recipient Nat. award Romanian Dept. Edn., 1958, 64, Teaching award, 1961, George Spacu award Romanian Acad. Sci., 1963, Sr. Humbolt award Alexander von Humbolt Found., 1985, Creativity award NSF, 1985. Mem. NAE, AIChE (Alpha Chi Sigma award 1977, Walker award 1988), Am. Chem. Soc. (Kendall award 1986, Jacob F. Schoellkopf medal 1991, Langmuir Disting. Lectr. award 1994, E.V. Murphree award 1996). Office: SUNY Dept Chem Engring Buffalo NY 14260

RUCKER, DENNIS MORTON ARTHUR, telecommunications executive; b. Bloomington, Ind., Sept. 23, 1949; s. Arthur Morton and A. Ileen (Tiemeyer) R.; m. Barbara Rose Daniels, Mar. 1, 1986. BSEE, BS in Speech and English, Purdue U., 1972, MSEE, 1983. Staff assoc. engr. C&P Telephone Co. of Md., Balt., 1973-74; asst. plant engr. Ind. Telephone Corp., Seymour, 1974-76; transmissions and radio planning engr. United Telephone Co. of Ohio, Mansfield, 1976-78, network mgr., 1978-79, gen. mgr. rates and tariffs, 1979-82; dir. cellular engr. Western Union Corp., Upper Saddle River, N.J., 1982-84; dir. planning Ameritech Mobile Communications Inc., Schaumburg, Ill., 1984-90; sr. dir. sci. and tech. Ameritech Mobile Communications Inc., Hoffman Estates, Ill., 1990-93; dir. engring. and personal comms. U.S. Cellular Corp, Chgo., 1993—; owner D&B Media Prodns., 1997—; bd. dirs. Ga. Rural Svc. Area # 12 Partnership. Author: Balancing Wireless Systems, 1995; contbr. articles to profl. jours. Recipient awards for rsch. in optical comms. U.S. Army, USAF, and Nat. Aero. & Space Adminstrn. Mem. IEEE, Cellular Telecom. Industry Assn. (Industry Svc. award 1990, chmn. advanced radio techs. subcom. 1986-89, tech. com. 1985-93, mem. CDMA devel. group 1993—, mem. radio spectrum adv. group 1997—), Nat. Spectrum Mgrs. Assn., Telecom. Industry Assn. (sec. tech. rev. com. 45.5 1992-93), Rutgers U. Wireless Info Network Lab (bd. industry advisors), Internat. Engring. Consortium (overseers coun. 1993—). Roman Catholic. Avocation: photography. Office: US Cellular Corp 8410 W Bryn Mawr Ave Ste 700 Chicago IL 60631-3463

RUCKER, KENNETH LAMAR, public administrator, educator; b. Atlanta, July 16, 1961; s. Jack Lamar and Priscilla Anne (Anderson) R.; m. Kerri Lynn Hairston; 1 child, Kenneth Lamar II. BSBA, Brenau U., 1991; MPA in Pub. Mgmt., Ga. State U., 1993; postgrad., U. Ga., 1993—. Cert. peace officer, supr., Ga.; cert. supply corps, Navy Supply Corps Sch., 1997. Law enforcement officer Met. Atlanta Rapid Transit Authority, 1984-93; sch. resource officer Fulton County Bd. Edn., Atlanta, 1993-95; field facilitator Cmtys. in Schs. of Ga., Inc., Atlanta, 1995—, field facilitator Cross Roads program, 1995—; bd. dirs. Benefactors of Edn., Inc., Atlanta; cons. pub. security Fulton County Bd. Edn., Atlanta, 1993-95; supply corps officer Navy Supply Corps Sch. USNR, Athens, 1997. Sunday sch. tchr. Simpson St. Ch. of Christ, Atlanta, 1991—; youth motivator Atlanta Pub. Schs., 1988—; bd. dirs. Benefactors Edn., Inc., 1996—. Commd. officer Supply Corps, USNR, 1995—. Doctoral fellow U. Ga. Mem. Am. Soc. Pub. Adminstrn., Nat. Orgn. Black Law Enforcement Execs., Conf. on Minority Transp. Ofcls., Nat. Forum Black Pub. Adminstrs., Internat. Platform Assn., Benefactors of Edn., Inc. (bd. dirs. 1996—), Brenau U. Alumni Club, Ga. State U. Alumni Club, U.S. Naval Inst., Naval Res. Assn., Res. Officer's Assn., Pi Alpha Alpha, Pi Sigma Alpha, Omicron Delta Kappa (cir. pres. 1992-93). Avocations: computer tech., reading, photography, classical music, fitness. Home: 1823 Tiger Flowers Dr NW Atlanta GA 30314-1833 Office: Cmtys in Schs of Ga Inc 1252 W Peachtree St NW Ste 43D Atlanta GA 30309-3406

RUCKER, THOMAS DOUGLAS, purchasing executive; b. Ottumwa, Iowa, Aug. 30, 1926; s. Everett Henry and Harriett Mary (Evans) R.; A.B., Loyola U., 1951; postgrad. St. Patrick's Coll., 1950-52; m. Rita Mary Rommelfanger, Apr. 18, 1953; children—David, Theresa, Martin, Paul. Asst. purchasing agt. Radio TV Supply, Los Angeles, 1952-53; buyer Consol. Western Steel div. U.S. Steel, Commerce, Calif., 1953-64, S.W. Welding & Mfg. Co., Alhambra, Calif., 1964-70; dir. purchasing Sr. Engring. (formerly Southwestern Engring.), Commerce, Calif., 1970-87, ret. Served with USAAF, 1945-46. Home: 330 W Central Ave Brea CA 92821-3029 Office: Sr Engring 5701 S Eastern Ave Ste 300 Los Angeles CA 90040-2934

RUCKERT, RITA E., elementary education educator; b. Monett, Mo., Feb. 15, 1947; d. Wesley Swearengin and Eva Anna Harriet (Spradling) R. BS in Edn., U. Mo., 1969. Cert. tchr., Mo. Jr. high sch. tchr. Milw. (Wis.) Pub. Schs., 1969-70; high sch. tchr. Houston (Mo.) Schs., 1970-79, elem. tchr., 1979-95; volleyball ofcl. Mo. State High Sch. Activities Assn., Columbia, 1980-93, volleyball rules interpreter, 1983-93. Election judge Tex. County Clk.'s Office, Houston, 1987-95; mem. Houston (Mo.) Pk. Bd., 1988-92, pres., 1991-92. Recipient Fitness Ctr. grant Wells Fargo Bank, Calif., 1990; named Volleyball Outstanding Ofcl., Nat. Fedn. Interscholastic Ofcls. Assn., 1991. Mem. NEA (v.p. 1994-95, pres.-elect 1995-96, pres. 1996-97), AAHPERD, Mo. Assn. Health, Phys. Edn., Recreation and Dance (Dist. Elem. Phys. Educator of Yr. 1990, quality phys. edn. com. 1991-93), Optimist Internat., Delta Kappa Gamma. Republican. Avocations: stained glass, cross-stitch, reading, gardening. Home: 505 Hawthorn St Houston MO 65483-1721 Office: Houston Elem Sch 423 W Pine St Houston MO 65483-1147

RUCKMAN, MARK WARREN, physicist; b. Rolla, Mo., Dec. 26, 1954; s. Homer Leslie and Audrey (Warren) R. BS in Physics, Pa. State U., 1977; PhD in Physics, Rensselaer Polytechnic Inst., 1984. Asst. physicist Brookhaven Nat. Lab., Upton, N.Y., 1985-87, assoc. physicist, 1987-91, physicist, 1991-93, physics assoc. I, 1993—. Contbr. articles to profl. jours. Mem. Am. Phys. Soc., Am. Vacuum Soc., Am. Chem. Soc., Materials Rsch. Soc., Phi Beta Kappa, Phi Kappa Phi. Republican. Baptist. Office: Brookhaven Nat Lab 20 Pa Ave Upton NY 11973

RUCKMAN, ROGER NORRIS, pediatric cardiologist; b. Washington, Dec. 15, 1944; s. Norris Elliott and Eugenia (Campbell) R.; m. Kathleen Anne Smith; children: Robert, Karen, Stephen, Jonathan. BA in Chemistry, Williams Coll., Williamstown, Mass., 1966; MD, U. Va., 1970. Intern Peter Bent Brigham Hosp., 1970-71; resident Med. Ctr. Hosp. of Vermont, 1973-75; fellow in cardiology Children's Hosp., Boston, 1975-77; asst. prof. pediatrics U. Nebr., Omaha, 1977-79; asst. prof. pediatrics George Washington U., Washington, 1980-82, assoc. prof. pediatrics, 1982-90, prof. pediatrics, 1990—; pediatric cardiologist Children's Hosp. Nat. Med. Ctr., Washington, 1980—, chmn. cardiology, 1986-89. Contbr. articles to profl. jours. Served to capt. U.S. Army, 1971-73. Recipient Disting. Service award, Am.-Korea Found., 1972; NIH grantee, 1982—. Fellow Am. Acad. Pediatrics, Am. Coll. Cardiology; mem. Am. Heart Assn., Teratology Soc., Soc. Pediatric Research, Columbia Country Club (Chevy Chase, Md.). Republican. Presbyterian. Avocations: tennis, golf. Office: CNMC Dept Cardiology 111 Michigan Ave NW Washington DC 20010-2916

RUDAN, VINCENT THADDEUS, nursing administrator; b. N.Y.C., June 19, 1955; s. Vincent and Elvira (Palma) R. BSN, SUNY, Stony Brook, 1977; MA, NYU, 1979; postgrad., Villanova U., 1984-85, Columbia U., 1987—. RN, N.Y., N.J.; CNAA. Staff nurse N.Y. Hosp., N.Y.C., 1977-79; asst. dir. nursing Downstate Med. Ctr., Bklyn., 1979-80; instr. Rutgers U., Newark, N.J., 1980-83; asst. dir. nursing Manhattan Eye, Ear & Throat Hosp., N.Y.C., 1983-84, assoc. dir nursing, 1984-94, dir. nursing/patient care svcs., 1994—. Mem. ANA, Am. Orgn. Nurse Execs., Sigma Theta Tau, Kappa Delta Pi. Avocations: tennis, jogging, reading, travel. Office: Manhattan Eye Ear Throat Hosp 210 E 64th St New York NY 10021-7480

RUDAWSKI, JOSEPH GEORGE, educational administrator; b. Nanticoke, Pa., Feb. 22, 1942; s. Nicholas Rudawski and Pauline Zelek; m. Regina Marie Jamiolkowski, Aug. 19, 1967; children: Joseph, Tamra, Valerie, Jeanne. BA, King's Coll., Wilkes-Barre, Pa., 1963; MS in Counseling Psychology, U. Scranton, 1967; postgrad., East Stroudsburg State Coll., summer 1981, Pa. State U., summer 1988. Cert. tchr. math. and English, Pa.; instrnl. II cert. secondary sch. guidance counselor, Pa. Counselor, caseworker Kis-Lyn Indsl. Sch. for Boys, Drums, Pa., 1963-64, adminstrv. caseworker, 1964; math. and psychology instr. MMI Prep. Sch., Freeland, Pa., 1964-67, math. and psychology instr., guidance dir., 1967-71, psychology instr., guidance dir., dean students and faculty, 1971-73, guidance dir., pres., 1973—; guidance counselor Luzerne Intermediate Unit, Kingston, Pa., 1974-84; rep. Bd. of Coll. Bd., 1976—, Bd. Coll. Scholarship Svc., Pa. Assn. Ind. Schs., 1973—; rep. Nat. Assn. Ind. Schs., 1982—, pres., 1986; rep. Mid. States Assn. Colls. and Secondary Schs., 1970—, vice-chmn. evaluating com., 1991. Dir. Freeland YMCA, 1973—, pres. bd. dirs. 1981-83, chmn. budget com., mem. bldg. com., 1984—, svc. award 1983; bd. dirs. United Way, 1975-86; bd. v.p., chmn. coms. Hazleton-St. Joseph Med. Ctr., 1984-92, chmn. nuclear task force com., 1992; comml. div. chmn. United Way Campaign, Hazleton, 1985-86; facilitator edn. program Leadership Hazleton, 1986—; mem. Freeland Indsl. Corp., 1981—; vice-chmn. Sophia G. Coxe Charitable Trust, 1987—; mem. adv. bd. WOLF-TV, 1988—; bd. mem. Luth. Welfare Svc., 1991-93, chmn. resource devel. com., 1992—; bd. dirs. Luth. Welfare Svc. Found., 1993—. Recipient Appreciation award Ea. Pa. chpt. Arthritis Found., 1983, Svc. award YMCA, Freeland, 1983, Cmty. award VFW, Freeland, 1988, Declaration of Achievement Pa. Senate, Harrisburg, 1988; named Citizen of Yr. Freeland Sons of Erin, 1996. Mem. Pers. and Guidance Assn., Pa. Sch. Counselors Assn., Luzerne County Counselors Assn. (pres. 1975-76, Outstanding Svc. award 1976), Freeland Rotary Club Pres. 1976-77, 96—). Office: MMI Prep Sch 154 Centre St Freeland PA 18224-2117

RUDBACH, JON ANTHONY, biotechnical company executive; b. Long Beach, Calif., Sept. 23, 1937; s. John Alexander and Lola (Whitcomb) R.; m. Inge Clye Steincke, July 4, 1959; children: Lucy Trine, Karl Kristian. BA, U. Calif., Berkeley, 1959; MS, U. Mich., 1961, PhD, 1964; MBA, Lake Forest Coll., 1986. Rsch. scientist Rocky Mountain Lab., Hamilton, Mont., 1964-70; prof. microbiology U. Mont., Missoula, 1970-77; mgr. exploratory rsch. Abbott Labs., North Chicago, Ill., 1977-79; dir. Stella Duncan Meml. Rsch. Inst., Missoula, 1979-82; head infectious disease rsch. Abbott Labs., Missoula, 1982-85; v.p. rsch. and devel. Ribi Immunochem Rsch., Inc., Hamilton, 1985-95; pres. TRI, Ltd., Hamilton, 1995—. Contbr. articles to profl. jours.; author 2 books; patentee in field. Mem. Bitteroot Community Bd., Hamilton, 1988—. USPHS grantee, 1970-79, fellow, 1964-66. Mem. Am. Assn. Immunologists, Am. Soc. Microbiology, Soc. for Exptl. Biology and Medicine, Soc. for Biol. Therapy, Lions (local pres. 1993-94, bd. dirs. 1987—). Republican. Congregationalist. Avocations: skiing, fishing, hunting, hiking, band. Home: 243 Hilltop Dr Hamilton MT 59840-9317 Office: TRI Ltd PO Box 527 Hamilton MT 59840

RUDCZYNSKI, ANDREW B., academic administrator, medical researcher; b. Nottingham, England, Sept. 7, 1947; came to U.S., 1951; s. Richard B. and Krystyna Z. (Stachlewska) R.; m. Andrea Skalny, Oct. 16, 1976 (div. Oct. 1990); children: Christina, Thomas. BSc in Biology/Biochemistry, McGill U., 1969; PhD in Immunology, Syracuse U., 1974; MBA in Adminstrn., So. Ill. U., 1984. Prin. investigator scrub typhus project divsn. Rickettsiology U.S. Army Med. Rsch. Infectious Diseases, Ft. Detrick, Md., 1974-76; rsch. assoc. dept. Biology Mich. Cancer Found., Detroit, 1976-77, rsch. scientist dept. Immunology, unit chef immunology unit Breast Cancer Prognostic Study, 1977-80; asst. dir. Office Rsch. and Grants U. Md. Ea. Shore, Princess Anne, 1980-83; extramural assoc. Office Extramural Rsch. and Tng., Office of Dir. NIH, 1981-82; asst. dir. Office Rsch. & Sponsored Programs Rutgers U., Piscataway, N.J., 1983-84, dir., 1984—, asst. v.p. rsch. adminstrn., 1985-93, assoc. v.p. rsch. policy and adminstrn., 1993—; field reader strengthening devel. instns. program U.S. Dept. Edn., 1990; mem. Chancellor's task force instrn. and rsch. infrastructure support N.J. Dept. Higher Edn., 1992. Contbr. articles, abstracts to profl. jours. Capt. U.S. Army Med. Svc. Corps, 1974-76. Recipient traineeship award NSF, 1969-71; predoctoral fellow NIH, 1973-74. Mem. AAAS, Nat. Coun. Univ. Rsch. Adminstrs. (profl. devel. com. 1988-90, region II program com. 1989-90, chmn. region II 1990-92, nat. program com. 1994-95), Coun. Govtl. Rels.

(fed. mgmt. devel. com. 1989-90), Soc. Rsch. Adminstrs., Assn. Univ. Tech. Mgrs., Beta Gamma Sigma, Sigma Xi. Roman Catholic. Home: 2 Carina Dr Milltown NJ 08850-1640 Office: Rutgers U Office Rsch/Sponsored Programs Adminstrv Svcs Bldg 123 Annex II PO Box 1179 Piscataway NJ 08855-1179

RUDD, ELDON, retired congressman, political consultant; b. Camp Verde, Ariz.; m. Ann Merritt. B.A., Ariz. State U., 1947; J.D., U. Ariz., 1950. Bar: Ariz. 1949, U.S. Supreme Ct. 1953. Pvt. practice Tucson, 1950; spl. agt.-diplomatic assignment principally Latin Am. FBI, 1950-70; mem. Maricopa County (Ariz.) Bd. Suprs., 1972-76; bd. dirs. Ariz.-Mex. Commn., 1972-92; with U.S.-Mex. Interparliamentary Com., 1976-84; mem. 95th-99th Congresses from 4th Dist. Ariz., 1976-87; of counsel Shimmel, Hill, Bishop & Gruender, P.C., Phoenix, 1987-93; pres. Eldon Rudd Consultancy, Scottsdale, Ariz., 1993—; bd. dirs. Salt River Project, 1988—; chmn. Phoenix chpt. Soc. Former Spl. Agts. FBI, 1995-96. Author: World Communism-Threat to Freedom, 1987. Mem. numerous pub. svc. orgns., including energy and water, mil. and internat. affairs. Fighter pilot USMCR, 1942-46. Mem. Fed. Bar Assn. (chpt. pres. 1976), Ariz. Bar Assn., Maricopa County Bar Assn., Scottsdale Bar Assn., Paradise Valley Country Club (bd. dirs. 1989-92), Phi Delta Phi, Blue Key. Republican. Roman Catholic. Home: PO Box 873 Scottsdale AZ 85252-0873 Office: 6909 E Main St Scottsdale AZ 85251-4311

RUDD, NICHOLAS, marketing communications company executive; b. N.Y.C., Mar. 18, 1943; s. Emmanuel and Lucie Lia Rudd; children: Alexis Henry, Kenneth Charles. B.A., Columbia U., 1964, M.B.A., 1967. Mem. pub. relations staff Ford Motor Co., N.Y.C., 1964-65; account mgr. Young & Rubicam Inc., N.Y.C., 1968-75, v.p., mgmt. supr., 1975-80, sr. v.p. mgmt. svcs., 1980-90, chief info. officer, 1990-95; chief knowledge officer Wunderman Cato Johnson, N.Y.C., 1996—; cons. Nat. Neurofibromatosis Found., Inc., 1981—; bd. dirs. Vol. Cons. Group, Inc., N.Y.C., 1987—. Bd. dirs. Nat. Choral Coun., chmn., 1993-95, Veritas Therapeutic Cmty. Found. Mem. Beta Gamma Sigma. Office: Wunderman Cato Johnson 675 Avenue Of The Americas New York NY 10010-5100

RUDD, PETER, physician, medical educator; b. N.Y.C., Feb. 15, 1945; s. Emmanuel and Lucie Lia (Weinberg) R.; m. Rebecca Cabrera, Feb. 10, 1975 (div. Sept. 1979); children: Christopher R., Natasha S.; m. Susan L. ernhard, June 26, 1993. BA magna cum laude, Amherst Coll., 1966; MD, Case Western Res. U., 1970. Diplomate Am. Bd. Internal Medicine, Nat. Bd. Med. Examiners. Intern Stanford U. Hosp., 19770-71, resident, 1973-75; staff physician Rodrigo Tenonez Clinic, Delano, Calif., 1971-73; clin. scholar McGill U., Montreal, 1975-76; asst. prof. U. Chgo., 1976-77; asst. prof. Stanford U., 1977-84, assoc. prof., 1984-94, prof., 1994—; chief divsn. gen. internal medicine, chief sect. ambulatory care tchg., dir. primary care svcs. Stanford U. Hosp. Mem. editl. bd. Ambulatory Medicine letter, Modern Medicine; contbr. articles to profl. jours. W.K. Kellogg Found. fellow, 1977, Andrew W. Mellon Found. fellow, 1977-79, 80-81. Fellow ACP; mem. Am. Fedn. Clin. Rsch., Soc. Gen. Internal Medicine, Am. Soc. for Clin. Pharmacology and Therapeutics, Am. Heart Assn., Physicians for Social Responsibility, Soc. for Med. Decision-Making, Am. Soc. Hypertension, Physicians for a Nat. Health Program, Phi Beta Kappa. Office: Stanford U Med Ctr Rm X-216 MSOB MC5475 Stanford CA 94305-5475

RUDD, RICKY, professional race car driver; b. Sept. 12, 1956; m. Linda Rudd; 1 child, Landon. Profl. race car driver NASCAR, 1975—, team owner, driver, 1993—. Named Winston Cup Rookie of Yr., 1977; won Riverside, 1983, Winston Cup, AC-Delco 400, 1996; 9th in NASCAR standings, 1995. Office: c/o NASCAR PO Box 2875 Daytona Beach FL 32120-2875

RUDDER, CATHERINE ESTELLE, political science association administrator; b. Atlanta, Dec. 16; d. James M. and Virginia Rudder. BA, Emory U., 1969; MA, Ohio State U., 1972, PhD, 1973. Asst. prof. U. Ga., Athens, 1973-77; chief staff to Rep. W. Fowler, Jr. U.S. House Reps., Washington, 1978-81, assoc. dir., 1983-87; exec. dir. Am. Polit. Sci. Assn., Washington, 1987—. Office: Am Polit Scis Assn 1527 New Hampshire Ave NW Washington DC 20036-1206

RUDDY, FRANK S., lawyer, former ambassador; b. N.Y.C., Sept. 15, 1937; s. Francis Stephen and Teresa (O'Neil) R.; m. Kateri Mary O'Neill, Aug. 29, 1964; children—Neil, David, Stephen. A.B., Holy Cross Coll., 1959; M.A., NYU, 1962, LL.M., 1967; LL.B., Loyola U., New Orleans, 1965; Ph.D., Cambridge U., Eng., 1969. Bar: D.C., N.Y., Tex., U.S. Supreme Ct. Faculty Cambridge U., 1967-69; asst. gen. counsel USIA, Washington, 1969-72; sr. atty. Office of Telecommunication Policy, White House, Washington, 1972-73; dep. gen. counsel Exxon Corp., Houston, 1973-74, counsel, 1974-81; asst. adminstr. AID (with rank asst. sec. state) Dept. State, Washington, 1981-84; U.S. ambassador to Equatorial Guinea, 1984-88; gen. counsel U.S. Dept. Energy, Washington, 1988-89; v.p. Sierra Blanc Devel. Corp., Washington, 1989-92; prin. Law Offices of Frank Ruddy, Washington, 1992-94; vis. scholar Johns Hopkins Sch. Advanced Internat. Studies, 1990-96; dep. chmn. UN Referendum for Western Sahara, 1994, Johnston, Rivlin & Foley, Washington, D.C., 1995—. Author: International Law in the Enlightenment, 1975; editor: American International Law Cases (series), 1972—; editor in chief Internat. Lawyer, 1978-83; contbr. articles to legal jours. Bd. dirs. African Devel. Found., Washington, 1983-84. Served with USMCR, 1956-61. Mem. ABA (chmn. treaty compliance sect. 1991-93), Am. Soc. Internat. Law, Internat. Law Assn., Hague Acad. Internat. Law Alumni Assn., Oxford and Cambridge Club (London), Conservative Club, Internat. Club, Dacor House. Republican. Roman Catholic. Home: 5600 Western Ave Chevy Chase MD 20815-3406 Office: Johnston Rivlin & Foley 12th Fl 1627 K St NW Fl 12 Washington DC 20006-1702

RUDE, BRIAN DAVID, state legislator; b. Viroqua, Wis., Aug. 25, 1955; s. Raymond and Conelee (Johnson) R.; m. Karen Thulin; children: Erik, Nels. BA magna cum laude, Luther Coll., 1977; MA, U. Wis., Madison, 1994. Mem. Wis. Assembly, Madison, 1982-84; mem. Wis. Senate, Madison, 1984—, asst. minority leader, 1989-93, 96—; pres. Wis. State Sen., 1993-96; with corp. communications The Trane Co., La Crosse, Wis., 1981-85. Bd. advisers Nat. Trust Historic Preservation, 1990—. Mem. Lions, Sons of Norway, Norwegian-Am. Hist. Assn. (trustee). Republican. Lutheran. Avocations: reading, gardening, traveling, fishing. Home: 307 Babcock St PO Box 367 Coon Valley WI 54623-0367 Office: Wis State Senate State Capitol Rm 239-S PO Box 7882 Madison WI 53703

RUDEE, MERVYN LEA, engineering educator, researcher; b. Palo Alto, Calif., Oct. 4, 1935; s. Mervyn C. and Hannah (Mathews) R.; m. Elizabeth Eager, June 20, 1958; children: Elizabeth Diane, David Benjamin. BS, Stanford U., 1958, MS, 1962, PhD, 1965. Asst. prof. materials sci. Rice U., Houston, 1964-68, assoc. prof., 1968-72, prof. materials sci., 1972-74; prof. U. Calif. San Diego, La Jolla, 1974—, founding provost Warren Coll., 1974-82, founding dean Sch. Engring., 1982-93, coord. grad. program on materials sci., 1994—; interim dean engring. U. Calif., Riverside, 1995-97; vis. scholar Corpus Christi Coll., Cambridge, Eng., 1971-72; CFO, prin. Univ. Planning Assocs., Inc.; vis. scientist IBM Thomas J. Watson Rsch. Ctr., Yorktown Heights, N.Y., 1987. Pres., bd. trustees Mus. Photographic Art, San Diego, 1995-96. Lt. (j.g.) USN, 1958-61. Guggenheim fellow, 1971-72. Fellow AAAS; mem. Microscopy Soc. Am., Materials Rsch. Soc., Am. Physics Soc., Tex. Soc. Electron Microscopy (hon., pres. 1966), Sigma Xi, Tau Beta Pi. Home: 1745 Kearsarge Rd La Jolla CA 92037-3829 Office: Univ Calif San Diego Dept Elec & Cptr Engring La Jolla CA 92093-0407

RUDEL, JULIUS, conductor; b. Vienna, Austria, Mar. 6, 1921; came to U.S., 1938, naturalized, 1944; s. Jakob and Josephine (Sonnenblum) R.; m. Rita Gillis, June 24, 1942 (dec. May 1984); children: Joan, Madeleine, Anthony Jason. Student, Acad. Music, Vienna; diploma in conducting, Mannes Coll. Music, 1942; diploma hon. doctorates, U. Vt., 1961, U. Mich., 1971; doctorates hon. causa, Pace Coll., Manhattan Coll., 1994, Mannes Coll. Music, 1994, Manhattanville Coll., 1994, Manhattan Sch. Music, 1996. With N.Y. City Opera, 1943-79, debut, 1944, gen. dir., 1957-79, 3rd St. Music Sch. Settlement, 1945-52, mus. dir. Chautauqua Opera Assn., 1958-59, Caramoor Festival, Katonah, N.Y., 1964-76, Cin. May Festival, 1971-72, Kennedy Ctr. Performing Arts, 1971-75; music advisor Wolf Trap Farm Pk., 1971, Phila. Opera, 1978-81; condr. Spoleto (Italy) Festival, 1962-63; music dir. Buffalo Philarm. Orch., 1979-85, debut as condr. Met. Opera, 1978, San Francisco Opera, 1979, Vienna State Opera, 1976, Royal Opera, Covent Garden, 1984, Rome Opera, 1987, Opera de la Bastille, 1992, Teatro Colon, Buenos Aires, 1992, Royal Danish Opera, Copenhagen, 1993, L.A. Opera, 1995; dir. prodn.: Kiss Me Kate, Vienna Volksoper Opera, 1956; guest condr. Chgo. Symphony, Phila. Orch., N.Y. Philharm., Boston Symphony, Detroit Symphony, Israel Philharm., Paris Opera, Munich Opera, Hamburg State Opera, Vienna State Opera, other symphonic, operatic orgns. in U.S. and Europe. Decorated Croix du Chevalier in arts and letters France; recipient gold medal Nat. Arts Club, 1958, citation Nat. Assn. Am. Composers and Conductors, 1958, citation Nat. Fedn. Music Clubs, 1959, Ditson award Columbia, 1959, Page One award in music Newspaper Guild, 1959, hon. insignia for arts and sci. Govt. of Austria, 1961, Handel medal for music City N.Y., 1965, citation Nat. Assn. Negro Musicians, 1965, citation Nat. Opera Assn., 1971, comdr.'s Cross German Order Merit, 1967, hon. lt. Israeli Army, 1969, Julius Rudel award for young condrs., Pan Am./Pan African award for humanism, 1981, Peabody award, 1985. Office: c/o Shuman Assocs 120 W 58th St Apt 8D New York NY 10019-2126

RUDELIUS, WILLIAM, marketing educator; b. Rockford, Ill., Sept. 2, 1931; s. Carl William and Clarissa Euclid (Davis) R.; m. Jacqueline Urch Dunham, July 3, 1954; children: Robert, Jeanne, Katherine, Kristi. B.S. in Mech. Engring., U. Wis., 1953; M.B.A., U. Pa., 1959, Ph.D. in Econs., 1964. Program engr., missile and space vehicle dept. Gen. Electric Co., Phila., 1956-57, 59-61; sr. research economist North Star Research Inst., Mpls., 1964-66; lectr. U. Minn., Mpls., 1961-64; asst. prof. mktg. Coll. Bus. Adminstrn. U. Minn., 1964, assoc. prof., 1966-72, prof., 1972—. Co-author: (with W. Bruce Erickson) An Introduction to Contemporary Business, 1973, rev. 4th edit., 1985, (with Eric N. Berkowitz, Roger A. Kerin and Steven W. Hartley) Marketing, 1986, rev. 5th edit., 1997, (with Krzysztof Przybytowski, Roger A. Kerin and Steven W. Hartley) Marketing na Przykładach, 1994; contbr. articles to profl. jours. Served with USAF, 1954-55. Home: 1425 Alpine Pass Minneapolis MN 55416-3560 Office: Carlson Sch Mgmt U Minn 271 19th Ave S Minneapolis MN 55455-0430

RUDELL, MILTON WESLEY, aerospace engineer; b. Rice Lake, Wis., July 9, 1920; s. George C. and Edna (Bjoraa) R.; m. Doris Lorraine Shella, Nov. 30, 1941; children: Helen, Geoffrey, Lynn, Deborah, Leah, Andrea, Kessea, Eric, Erin. B in Aerospace Engring., U. Minn., 1946. Registered profl. engr. Chief tool engr. Boeing Airplane Co., Wichita, Kans. and Seattle, 1941-43, stateside and overseas field engr., 1943-45; chief fueling systems engr. N.W. Airlines, Mpls., 1946-50; pres. Rumoco Co., Frederic, Wis., 1950-68; registrar ECPI-Nat. IBM computer sch., Mpls., 1968-69; pres. Life Engring. Co., Milw. and Frederic, Wis., 1969—. Designer original med. surg. suture tape, 1951; designer 1st match-book cover with strike plate on rear side for safety, 1942; pioneered high-speed underwing fueling systems for comml. aircraft and 1st hydrant ground fueling systems for comml. aircraft; co-author Ops. & Maintenance Manual for B-29 aircraft, 1943. Founder Frederic Found. for Advanced Edn. Recipient WWII Aeronautical Engring. Citation from Pres. Eisenhower, 1944. Mem. Exptl. Aircraft Assn., Wis. Aviation Hall of Fame, Northwestern Wis. Mycol. Soc. (charter). Lutheran. Home and Office: 501 Wisconsin Ave N Frederic WI 54837-0400 *We shall pass through this world but once. Any good therefore that we can do or any kindness that we can show to any human being, let us do it now. Let us not defer nor neglect it, for we shall not pass this way again.*

RUDENSTINE, NEIL LEON, academic administrator, educator; b. Ossining, N.Y., Jan. 21, 1935; s. Harry and Mae (Esperito) R.; m. Angelica Zander, Aug. 27, 1960; children: Antonia Margaret, Nicholas David, Sonya. B.A., Princeton U., 1956; B.A. (Rhodes Scholar), Oxford U., 1959, M.A., 1963; Ph.D., Harvard U., 1964. Instr. dept. English Harvard U., Cambridge, Mass., 1964-66; asst. prof. Harvard U., 1966-68; assoc. prof. English Princeton (N.J.) U., 1968-73, prof. English, 1973-88, dean of students, 1968-72, dean of Coll., 1972-77, provost, 1977-88, provost emeritus, 1988—; exec. v.p. Andrew W. Mellon Found., N.Y.C., 1988-91; pres. Harvard U., Cambridge, Mass., 1991—, prof. English, 1991—. Author: Sidney's Poetic Development, 1967, (with George Rousseau) English Poetic Satire, 1972, (with William Bowen) In Pursuit of the PhD, 1992. Served to 1st lt. arty. AUS, 1959-60. Hon. fellow New Coll./Oxford U., Emmanuel Coll./Cambridge U., 1991. Fellow Am. Acad. Arts and Scis.; mem. Am. Philos. Soc., Coun. on Fgn. Rels., Com. for Econ. Devel. Office: Harvard U Office of Pres Massachusetts Hall Cambridge MA 02138

RUDER, DAVID STURTEVANT, lawyer, educator, government official; b. Wausau, Wis., May 25, 1929; s. George Louis and Josephine (Sturtevant) R.; m. Susan M. Small; children: Victoria Chesley, Julia Larson, David Sturtevant II, John Coulter; m stepchildren: Elizabeth Frankel, Rebecca Wilkinson. BA cum laude, Williams Coll., 1951; JD with honors, U. Wis., 1957. Bar: Wis. 1957, Ill. 1962. Of counsel Schiff Hardin & Waite, Chgo., 1971-76; assoc. Quarles & Brady, Milw., 1957-61; asst. prof. law Northwestern U., Chgo., 1961-63, assoc. prof., 1963-65, prof., 1965—, assoc. dean Law Sch., 1965-66, dean Law Sch., 1977-85; chmn. Securities and Exch. Commn., Washington, 1987-89; ptnr. Baker & McKenzie, Chgo., 1990-94, sr. counsel, 1994—; cons. Am. Law Inst. Fed. Securities Code; planning dir. Corp. Counsel Inst., 1962-66, 76-77, com. mem., 1962-87, 90—; cons. Ray Garrett Jr. Corp. and Securities Law Inst., 1980-87, 90—; vis. lectr. U. de Liege, 1967; vis. prof. law U. Pa., Phila., 1971; faculty Salzburg Seminar, 1976; mem. legal adv. com. bd. dirs. N.Y. Stock Exch., 1978-82; mem. com. profl. responsibility Ill. Supreme Ct., 1978-87; adv. bd. Securities Regulation Inst., 1978—, chmn., 1994-97; bd. govs. Nat. Assn. Securities Dealers, 1990-93, chmn. Legal Adv. Bd., 1993-96, Arbitration Policy Task Force, 1994—; trustee Fin. Acctg. Found., 1996—. Editor-in-chief: Williams Coll. Record, 1950-51, U. Wis. Law Rev, 1957; editor: Proc. Corp. Counsel Inst, 1962-66; contbr. articles to legal periodicals. 1st lt. AUS, 1951-54. Fellow Am. Bar Found.; mem., com. chmn. ABA (coun. sect. corp. banking and bus. law 1970-74), Chgo. Bar Assn., Wis. Bar Assn., Am. Law Inst., Order of Coif, Comml. Club of Chgo., Econ. Club of Chgo., Gargoyle Soc., Phi Beta Kappa, Phi Delta Pi, Zeta Psi. Home: 325 Orchard Ln Highland Park IL 60035-1939 Office: Northwestern U Sch Law 357 E Chicago Ave Chicago IL 60611-3008 also: Baker & McKenzie One Prudential Pla 130 E Randolph St Chicago IL 60601-6207

RUDER, MELVIN HARVEY, retired newspaper editor; b. Manning, N.D., Jan. 19, 1915; s. Moris M. and Rebecca (Friedman) R.; m. Ruth Bergan, Feb. 10, 1950; 1 dau., Patricia E. Morton. B.A., U. N.D., 1937, M.A., 1941; grad. student, Northwestern U., 1940. Asst. prof. journalism U. N.D., 1940; indsl. relations specialist Westinghouse Electric Co., Sharon, Pa., 1940-41; pub. relations with Am. Machine & Foundry Co., N.Y.C., 1946; founder, editor Hungry Horse News, Columbia Falls, Mont., 1946-78; editor emeritus Hungry Horse News, 1978—. Chmn. adv. coun. Flathead Nat. Forest, Dist. 6 Sch. Bd., 1967-70; pres. Buffalo Hill Terr. Resident Coun., 1997. Served to lt. (s.g.) USNR, 1942-45. Recipient Pulitzer prize for gen. local reporting, 1965. Mem. Mont. Press Assn. (pres. 1957), Flathead Associated C. of C. (pres. 1971), Glacier Natural History Assn. (pres. 1983). Home: Buffalo Hill Terr 40 Claremont Kalispell MT 59901

RUDER, WILLIAM, public relations executive; b. N.Y.C., Oct. 17, 1921; s. Jacob L. and Rose (Rosenberg) R.; m. Betty Cott, May 23, 1980; children—Robin Ann, Abby, Brian, Michal Ellen, Eric. B.S.S., City Coll., N.Y., 1942. With Samuel Goldwyn Prodns., 1946-48; pres. Ruder & Finn, Inc., N.Y.C., 1948-80, William Ruder Inc., 1981—; asst. sec. commerce, 1961-62; Tobe lectr. Harvard Grad. Sch. Bus., 1962; mem. grad. adv. bd. City Coll. N.Y., Baruch Sch. Bus., N.Y.C.; cons. State Dept.; bd. dirs. W.P. Carey & Co., Inc. Author: The Businessman's Guide to Washington. Bd. dirs. Bus. Com. for Arts, Jewish Bd. Guardians, Chamber Music Soc. Lincoln Ctr., Fund for Peace, Project Return Found.; exec. com. United Way Am.; trustee, chmn. Manhattanville Coll., Purchase, N.Y., 1974-75; bd. overseers Wharton Sch. U. Pa.; mem. pres.'s coun. Meml. Sloan-Kettering Cancer Ctr.; chmn. bd. ACCESS. Capt. USAAF, 1941-45. Mem. UN Assn. U.S.A. (nat. policy panel dir.). Home: 430 E 86th St New York NY 10028-6441 Office: Ruder Finn Inc 301 E 57th St New York NY 10022-2900

RUDERMAN, ARMAND PETER, health economics educator, consultant, volunteer; b. N.Y.C., Nov. 19, 1923; s. Louis and Lillian (Prigohzy) R.; m. Alice Helen Holton, June 17, 1948; children: Ann, Mary, William, John. SB, Harvard U., 1943; MA, 1946, PhD, 1947; MBA, U. Chgo., 1944. Instr. econs. various U.S. univs., 1946-50; statistician, economist ILO, Pan.-Am. Health Orgn., WHO, 1950-67; chmn. sci. working group on social and econ. aspects of tropical disease research WHO/TDR, 1979-83; prof. health adminstrn. U. Toronto, Ont., Can., 1967-75; founding dean adminstrv. studies Dalhousie U., N.S., Can., 1975-80, prof. health adminstrn., 1981-89, prof. emeritus, 1989—; vis. prof. Nat. U. Singapore, 1982-83; cons. in field. Contbr. articles to profl. jours. and books. Bd. dirs. Northwood Home Care, 1987-89, Northwestern Gen. Hosp., Toronto, 1991-96; mem. Etobicoke Bd. Health, 1991-95; mem. cmty. adv. com. Toronto Hosp., 1992-95; mem. regional 3 exec. com. Ont. Hosp. Assn., 1994-96. Mem. Can. Pub. Health Assn., Royal Econ. Soc.

RUDERMAN, ROBERT, internist, hematologist; b. Bklyn., Aug. 1, 1938; s. Israel Irving and Rebecca (Kochman) R.; m. Elaine Savatsky, June 9, 1962; children—Mindy Lisa, Marchelle Ann. BS cum laude in Chemistry Bklyn. Coll., 1959; MD, SUNY-Syracuse, 1963. Diplomate Am. Bd. Internal Medicine. Intern Syracuse Med. Ctr. Hosp., N.Y., 1963-64; resident Kings County Hosp. Ctr., Bklyn., 1964-65, V.A. Hosp., Washington, 1967-69; fellow hematology, 1969-70; practice medicine specializing in internal medicine-hematology College Park, Md., 1970-84, Riverdale, 1984—; chief, div. hematology-oncology Med. Ctr. of Prince George Gen. Hosp., Cheverly, Md, 1974-86; v.p. Prince George Found. Med. Care, Landover, Md., 1981-84, pres. 1984-87; chmn. utilization rev. dept. Leland Meml. Hosp., Riverdale, Md., 1986-93; pres. Nat. Frozen Blood Svcs., Inc., 1986-87; med. dir. utilization mgmt. Dr.'s Community Hosp., Lanham, Md., 1992-94, treas., 1993-95. Mem. steering com. ARC (Prince George chpt.) Hyattsville, Md., 1983-87, 94; bd. dirs. Mishkan Torah Synagogue, Greenbelt, Md., 1980; Capt., AUS, 1965-67. Army Commendation medal; recipient Gubernatorial citation State of Md., 1990, Exec. citation Prince George's County, 1990, Citation Senate of State of Md., 1990; N.Y. State Regents scholar, 1955. Mem. Prince George County Med. Soc. (bd. dirs. 1984, treas. 1986, sec. 1987, pres. elect 1988, pres. 1989-90), Med. Surg. Faculty Md., Am. Physician Fellowship, Am. Soc. Internal Med., D.C. Soc. Internal Medicine, Jaycees, Upsilon Lambda Phi (nat. sec. 1956-58, reg. pres. 1955-56). Democrat. Jewish. Club: Prospect Bay Yacht (commodore 1986-87, past-commodore 1988). Office: 6510 Kenilworth Ave Riverdale MD 20737-1339

RUDIBAUGH, MELINDA CAMPBELL, mathematics educator; b. Indiana, Pa., Feb. 25, 1948; d. Steele Evans and Kathryn Norine (Grater) C.; m. Jerry Rudibaugh, Dec. 5, 1970; children: Amy, Evan. BS in Edn., Indiana (Pa.) U., 1970; M Natural Sci., Arizona State U., 1981, postgrad.; postgrad., No. Arizona U., Ariz. State U. Tchr. sci., math. Western Christian High, Phoenix, Ariz., 1979-80, Phoenix Hebrew Sch., 1980-81; instr. math. Arizona State U., Tempe, 1980-84, Maricopa C.C., Phoenix, 1981-89, Chandler-Gilbert C.C., Chandler, Ariz., 1989—; instr. Ottawa U. Vol. March of Dimes, 1988—, Am. Cancer Soc., 1989—; advisor Phi Theta Kappa, Chandler-Gilbert C.C., 1993. 2d lt. USAF, 1970-71. Mem. ASCD, Nat. Coun. Tchrs. Math., Math. Assn. Am., Am. Math. Assn. Two-Yr. Colls., Am. Assn. Higher Edn., Ariz. Assn. Supervision and Curriculum Devel., Phi Delta Kappa, Phi Kappa Phi. Republican. Avocations: jogging, hiking, camping. Home: 10417 S 46th Way Phoenix AZ 85044-1112 Office: Chandler Gilbert C C 2626 E Pecos Rd Chandler AZ 85225-2413

RUDIGER, LANCE WADE, secondary school educator; b. Bklyn., Mar. 27, 1948; s. H.F. and Muriel Marie (Staudermann) R.; 1 child, Heidi. BS in Chemistry, SUNY, Albany, 1976; MEd, St. Lawrence U., 1982. Cert. sci. tchr., N.Y. Tchr. chemistry Potsdam High Schs., 1982—, sci. dept. chair, 1992-97; adj. prof. Empire Coll., Albany, 1986—; adj. prof. Canton (N.Y.) Coll. Tech., Mater Dei Coll., Ogdensburg, N.Y.; tchr. Inst. Chem. Edn.-Sci. demonstration; bd. dirs., treas. St. Lawrence Valley Tchrs. Learning Ctr., Canton; sci. coord. Upward Bound St. LAwrence U.; mem. program com., bd. dirs. N.Y. State Computers & Tech. in Edn. Co-author: Chemistry Environment, 1990. Bd. dirs. March of Dimes N.Y. State, Syracuse. Recipient Newmast award NASA, 1987, Dreyfus Master Tchr. award, 1989; grantee Am. Chem Soc., Woodrow Wilson Found., Binghamtom U. Step Program, St. Lawrence Valley Tchrs. Ctr., 1991, 92, 94, Sweetwater Found., Miami U. (Ohio), 1995, Johns Hopkins Space Grant Consortium, Wright Ctr. for Aerospace and Space Engring., Reynolds Metals Excellence in Edn., 1990, 91-93, 94. Mem. Nat. Sci. Tchrs. Assn. (local leader), Nat. Radio Astronomy Obs. (assoc.), Am. Astron. Soc. (tchr. resource agent 1996), Sci. Tchrs. Assn. N.Y. State (bd. dirs. 1990-95, chmn. sect. 1992-95, presenter at convs. 1988-94), Canton Club, Lions (past pres. Waddington, N.Y., Pres.'s award, bd. dirs. Canton), Potsdam Kiwanis (charter, bd. dirs. 1989-91), Phi Delta Kappa (rsch. dir.). Home: 54 Court St Canton NY 13617-0251 Office: Potsdam High School Leroy St Potsdam NY 13676

RUDIN, ANNE NOTO, former mayor, nurse; b. Passaic, N.J., Jan. 27, 1924; m. Edward Rudin, June 6, 1948; 4 children. BS in Edn., Temple U., 1945, RN, 1946; MPA, U. So. Calif., 1983; LLD (hon.), Golden Gate U., 1990. RN, Calif. Mem. faculty Temple U. Sch. Nursing, Phila., 1946-48; mem. nursing faculty Mt. Zion Hosp., San Francisco, 1948-49; mem. Sacramento City Council, 1971-83; mayor City of Sacramento, 1983-92; ind. pub. policy cons. Pres. LWV, Riverside, 1957, Sacramento, 1961, Calif., 1969-71, Calif. Elected Women's Assn., 1973—; trustee Golden Gate U., 1993-96; mem. adv. bd. U. So. Calif., Army Depot Reuse Commn., 1992-94; bd. dirs. Sacramento Theatre Co., Sacramento Symphony, 1993-96, Calif. Common Cause, 1993-96, Japan Soc. No. Calif., Sacramento Edn. Found.; v.p. Sacramento Traditional Jazz Soc. Found. Recipient Women in Govt. award U.S. Jaycee Women, 1984, Woman of Distinction award Sacramento Area Soroptimist Clubs, 1985, Civic Contbn. award LWV Sacramento, 1989, Woman of Courage award Sacramento History Ctr., 1989, Peacemaker of Yr. award Sacramento Mediation Ctr., 1992, Regional Pride award Sacramento Mag., 1993, Humanitarian award Japanese Am. Citizen's League, 1993, Outstanding Pub. Svc. award Am. Soc. Pub. Adminstrn., 1994; named Girl Scouts Am. Role model, 1989.

RUDIN, SCOTT, film and theatre producer; b. N.Y.C., July 14, 1958. Prodn. asst., asst. to theatre prodrs. Kermit Bloomgarden and Robert Whitehead; casting dir. motion pictures and theatre, prodr. with Edgar Scherick, exec. v.p. prodn. 20th Century Fox, 1984-86, pres. prodn., 1986-87; founder Scott Rudin Prodns., 1990—. Prodr.: (films) He Makes Me Feel Like Dancing, 1982 (Outstanding Children's Program Emmy award 1982, Feature Documentary Acad. award 1982), Mrs. Soffel, 1984, Flatliners, 1990, Pacific Heights, 1990, Regarding Henry, 1991, Little Man Tate, 1991, The Addams Family, 1991, White Sands, 1992, Sister Act, 1992, Jennifer Eight, 1992, Life With Mikey, 1993, The Firm, 1993, Searching for Bobby Fischer, 1993, Sister Act 2, 1993, Addams Family Values, 1993, I.Q., 1994, Nobody's Fool, 1994, Sabrina, 1995, Clueless, 1995, Up Close and Personal, 1996, Ransom, 1996, Marvin's Room, 1996; (theatre) Passion, 1994 (Best Musical Tony award 1994). Office: Paramount Pictures DeMille 200 5555 Melrose Ave Los Angeles CA 90038-3112*

RUDING, HERMAN ONNO, banker, former Dutch government official; b. Aug. 15, 1939; m. Renee V.M. Hekking; 2 children. MA in Econs., Netherlands Sch. Econs. (Erasmus U.), 1964, PhD in Econs. cum laude, 1969. Head div. internat. monetary affairs Treas. Gen. of Ministry of Fin., The Hague, Netherlands, 1965-70; joint gen. mgr. Amsterdam-Rotterdam Bank N.V., Amsterdam, 1971-76; exec. dir. IMF, Washington, 1977-80; bd. mng. dirs. Amsterdam-Rotterdam Bank N.V., 1981-82; minister of fin. Netherlands, The Hague, 1982-89; chmn. Netherlands Christian Fedn. Employers, The Hague, 1990-92; vice chmn., bd. dirs. Citicorp, N.Y.C., 1992—. Contbr. articles to profl. jours. Bd. dirs. Foster Parents Plan Internat., 1981-82, Mt. Sinai Hosp., N.Y.C. Mem. Christian Democratic Alliance, Com. Monetary Union of Europe, Trilateral Commn. Office: Citibank 399 Park Ave New York NY 10022

RUDINS, LEONIDS (LEE RUDINS), retired chemical company executive, financial executive; b. Linava, Latvia, Dec. 15, 1928; came to U.S., 1949; s. Leonids and Aleksandra (Zimins) R.; m. Galina Zakidalski, July 24, 1960; 1 child, Andrew. BS in Commerce, Rider Coll., 1953; MBA, Seton Hall U., 1967, cert. of internat. bus., 1968. Acct. Johnson & Johnson, New Brunswick, N.J., 1957-58; mgr. budget and cost LePage's, Johnson & Johnson, Gloucester, Mass., 1958-60; plant contr. Permacel, Johnson & Johnson, Decatur, Ill., 1960-62; asst. contr. Permacel, Johnson & Johnson, New Brunswick, 1962-63, treas., contr., 1963-70; div. contr. Titanium Pigments,

NL Industries, Inc., Sayreville, N.J., 1970-71, group contr., 1971-76; dir. fin. and adminstrn. NL Pigments-U.S., NL Industries, Inc., Sayreville, N.J., 1976-77; dir. fin. and planning NL Pigments-Worldwide, NL Industries, Inc., Sayreville, N.J., 1977-79; v.p. fin., chief fin. officer NL Chemicals, Inc., Hightstown, N.J., 1979-89; pres. Internat. Bus. Mgmt. Assocs., Inc., Princeton, 1990-91; bd. dirs. Robertson-CECO Corp., Boston, Benton-Chemie, GmbH, Nordenham, Germany, Abbey Chems., Ltd., Livingston, Eng., Enenco, Inc., Memphis. Solicitor, budget com. mem., United Fund, New Brunswick, 1962-69; bd. dirs. St. Vladimir Russian Cath. Soc., 1992—. With U.S. Army, 1953-56, Korea. Mem. Nat. Assn. Accts., Fin. Exec. Inst., Forsgate Club, Battleground Club. Republican. Greek/Russian Orthodox. Avocations: golf, stamp collecting, hiking. Home: 28 Tamarack Dr Englishtown NJ 07726-2734

RUDLEY, LLOYD DAVE, psychiatrist; b. Phila., Aug. 7, 1955; s. John Frank and Ida (Rthmann) R. BA summa cum laude, U. Pa., 1977; MD, Hahnemann U., 1981. Diplomate Am. Bd. Psychiatry and Neurology. Resident in psychiatry Med. Coll. Pa., Phila., 1981-85; pvt. practice Phila., 1985—, Elmer, N.J., 1986—; staff psychiatrist N.E. Cmty. Mental Health Ctr., Phila., 1985-87, Counseling Program N.J., Marlton, 1987-88; attending psychiatrist Hosp. U. Pa., Phila., 1985—; attending psychiatrist Inst. of Pa. Hosp., Phila. Psychiat. Ctr.; cons. psychiatrist Horizon Ho, Phila, 1989—; mem. med. adv. bd. Juvenile Diabetes Found., Phila., 1986—. Mem. jr. com. Scheie Eye Inst., Phila., 1985—. Mem. AMA, Am. Psychiat. Assn., Pa. Psychiat. Soc., Pa. Med. Soc., Philadelphia County Med. Soc. (mental health subcom. 1988—, Janssen clin. scholar 1994), Phi Beta Kappa. Republican. Avocation: collecting maps. Office: Inst of Pa Hosp 111 N 49th St Philadelphia PA 19139-2718

RUDLIN, DAVID ALAN, lawyer; b. Richmond, Va., Nov. 4, 1947; s. Herbert and Dorothy Jean (Durham) R.; m. Judith Bond Faulkner, Oct. 4, 1975; 1 child, Sara Elizabeth. BA with high distinction, U. Va., 1969, JD with honors, 1973. Bar: Va. 1973, U.S. Dist. Ct. (ea. dist.) Va. 1975, U.S. Ct. Appeals (4th cir.) 1975, U.S. Ct. Appeals (10th cir.) 1980, U.S. Ct. Appeals (2d cir.) 1983, U.S. Supreme Ct. 1979. Assoc. gen. counsel U.S. Commn. on Orgn. of Govt. for Conduct of Fgn. Policy, Washington, 1973-75; assoc. Hunton & Williams, Richmond, 1975-82, ptnr., 1982—; adj. faculty William and Mary Coll., Marshall-Wythe Sch. Law, Williamsburg, Va., 1982—, U. Richmond, 1993—; faculty mem. Boulder and S.E. Regional programs Nat. Inst. Trial Advocacy; vis. lectr. U. Va. Sch. Law, Charlottesville, 1980—; mem. Va. Mediation Panel, Am. Arbitration Assn., 1996—; mem. dispute resolution svcs. adv. coun. Supreme Ct. Va. Bd. dirs., ex officio mem. Cystic Fibrosis Found., Richmond; alumni Metro Leadership Richmond, 1988-89; mem. bd. editorial advisors The Environmental Counselor, Chesterland, Ohio, 1989—, The Toxics Law Reporter, Washington, 1988—; bd. dirs., apt. special adv., adv. com. Richmond Juvenile and Domestic Rels. Ct., 1990-94. Author: (book chpts.) Toxic Torts: Litigation Of Hazardous Substances Cases, 1983, 2nd edit., 1992, Federal Litigation Guide, 1989, Corporate Counselor's Guide To Environmental Law, 1989, Sanctions: Rule 11 and Other Powers, 1992; contbr. articles to profl. jours. and mags, chpts. to books. Mem. ABA (chmn. litigation sect. environ. litigation com. 1985-88, co-chmn. litigation sect. liaison with jud. com. 1988-91, vice-chmn. toxic and hazardous substances and environ. law com. tort and ins. practice sect., 1988-91, co-liaison to standing com. on environ. law from environ. litigation com. litigation section, 1988-92, dir. divsn. IV litigation sect. 1991-95, litigation sect. co-chair programs subcom. first amendment & media litigation com. 1993—, mem. litigation sect. task force on specialization 1994—, mem. litigation sect. task force on justice sys. 1994—, litigation sect. liaison to ABA jud. adminstrn. divsn. task force on reduction of litigation cost and delay 1995—, chair litigation sect. 1997 ann. meeting Washington 1995—), Am. Arbitration Assn. (Va. mediation panel 1996—), Va. Bar Assn. (chair joint com. on alternative dispute resolution with Va. State Bar 1991—), Va. Trial Lawyers Assn., Richmond Bar Assn. (chmn. membership com. 1988-91, mem. judiciary com. 1991-94, mem. continuing legal edn. com. 1994—), Va. Assn. Def. Attys., Ctr. Pub. Resources (products liability com. 1988—, judge Ann. Awards in Alternative Dispute Resolution 1990—). Office: Hunton & Williams Riverfront Pla E Tower 951 E Byrd St Richmond VA 23219-4040

RUDMAN, HERBERT CHARLES, education educator; b. N.Y.C., July 29, 1923; s. Abraham and Celia (Factor) R.; m. Florence Bromberg, Sept. 25, 1943; 1 child, Jane Ann (Mrs. Robert Schumacher). B.S., Bradley U., 1947; M.S., U. Ill., 1950, Ed.D., 1954. Tchr., asst. to prin. Peoria (Ill.) Bd. Edn., 1946-51; instr. U. Ill., 1951-53; chmn. dept. elementary edn. U.S.C., 1954-56; prof. adminstrn. and higher edn. Mich. State U., East Lansing, 1956-83, prof. ednl. measurement, evaluation and research design, 1983-93, prof. emeritus, 1993—; admissions testing cons. Nat. U. Sci. and Tech., Pakistan, 1992; chmn. tchr. testing tech. adv. coun. State of Mich., 1989-91. Author: (with Truman Kelly, Richard Madden and Eric Gardner) Stanford Achievement Tests, 1964, (with Richard Featherstone) Urban Schooling, 1968, (with Donald J. Leu) Preparation Programs for School Administrators, 1968, (with Frederick King, Herbert Epperly) Concepts in Social Science, 1970, School and State in the USSR, 1967, (with others) Stanford Achievement Tests, 1973, (with Frederick King) Understanding People, 1977, Understanding Communities, 1977, Understanding Regions, 1978, Understanding Our Country, 1979, Understanding Our World, 1979, tests for At Your Best, 1977, Toward Your Future, 1977, Balance In Your Life, 1977; (with others): Stanford Achievement Tests, 1982; editor: Measurement in Education, 1979-82; guest editor: Bull. Nat. Secondary Sch. Prins., 1986; contbr. articles to profl. jours. Assoc. bd. trustees Bradley U., 1992—. With USAAF, 1942-46. Recipient Outstanding Leadership award Mich. Assn. Elem. Prins., 1972, Disting. Alumnus award Bradley U., 1988, U. Ill. Coll. Edn. Alumni Assn., 1996; resolution for contbns. to ednl. measurement Mich. Senate, 1980; named Outstanding Prof. of Yr., Mich. State U. Alumni Assn., 1980; Ford Found. fellow USSR, 1958; head U.S. dep. to USSR for U.S. State Dept., 1963-64. Office: Mich State U Coll Edn 463 Erickson Hall East Lansing MI 48824-1034 *I have, all of my life, valued integrity and truth above all else. Without these two values all relationships—professional and personal—mean little. While I have valued excellence in professional conduct and commitment to professional goals, I have rarely lost perspective concerning my commitment to family and community. While honors, such as this one, are appreciated and valued by me, the greatest honor is that of watching our daughter grow into a fine young woman who, in turn, has developed many of the same values in her professional and personal life, and who now passes them on to her son and daughter.*

RUDMAN, JOAN ELEANOR, artist, educator; b. Owensburg, Ind., Oct. 7, 1927; d. William Hobart and Elizabeth Joaquin (Edington) Combs; m. William Rudman, June 9, 1951; children: Mary Beth, Pamela Ann. BA, Mich. State U., 1949, MA, 1951. tchr. Arlington Jr. and High Sch., Poughkeepsie, N.Y., Rippowam High Sch., Stamford, Conn., North Branch Club, West Dover, Vt., Greenwich (Conn.) Art Soc.; lectr., demonstrator Round Hill Community House, Greenwich; artist-in-residence So. Vt. Art Ctr., Manchester; arts reporter to 42 newspapers, N.Y., N.J. and Conn.; jurist of selection Hudson Valley Art Assn., 1971—; selection and awards jurist 2d Bergen County Mus. Open Mems. Juried Awards-Allied Artist, N.Y.; dir. Watercolor Workshops, Greenwich; liaison to Metro. Mus. Catharine Lorillard Wolfe Art Club; watercolor lectr. and demonstrator tri-state area. One-woman shows include Burning Tree Country Club, Greenwich, Town and Country Club, Hartford, Conn., U. Conn., Stamford, Conn. Valley Art Gallery, New Milford, So. Vt. Art Ctr., Manchester, The Nathaniel Witherall Gallery, Greenwich, Burke Rehab. Ctr., White Plains, N.Y.; exhibited in group shows at Wadsworth Antheneum, 1970, Mus. of Am. Art, New Britain, Conn., So. Vt. Art Ctr., Manchester, 1980-81, Nature Ctr., Westport, Conn., 1979-80, Mus. Fine Arts, Springfield, Mass., 1977, Wadsworth Antheneum, 1970, Mus. Am. Art, New Britain, Conn., Nat. Arts Club Open Show, 1969, 78, 79, 81, 82, Salmagundi Club, N.Y.C., 1978, 79, 80, 82, Am. Watercolor Soc., N.Y.C., 1974, 77, 82, Nat. Acad. Design, 1986, 94; represented in permanent collection Kresge Mus., East Lansing, Mich., numerous others; contbr. chpts. to books. Active North Stamford Cong. Ch. Recipient Nat. Art League awards, 1969, 71, 72, 73, Art Soc. Old Greenwich award, 1989, 94, Windsor Newton award, 1982, YWCA Greenwich Contemporary Women's Art Exhibit award, 1985, Best in Show award Art Soc. Old Greenwich, 1991, 1st Prize Graphics award Art Soc. Old Greenwich, 1994, 2nd Prize award Watercolor. Mem. Am. Watercolor Soc. (bd. dirs., asst. editor newsletter), Acad. Artists, Inc., Hoosier Salon (awards 1975, 76), Am. Artists Profl. League (50th Nat. Exhbn. award 1978), Hudson Valley Art Assn. (bd. dirs., publ. rels. editor, awards 1970, 80-90), Conn. Watercolor Soc. (award 1978), Conn. Artists 33, Whiskey Painters Am. (award 1978), Conn. Women Artists, Catharine Lorillard Wolfe Art Club (awards 1989, 90, chmn. 1989-90, co-chair 1994), Pen and Brush (award 1977-78), Nat. League Am. Pen Women (awards 1967, 69, 76-87), Nat. Press Club, Round Hill Community Guild (art dir.), New Canaan - Am. Assn. Univ. Women, Columbia U. Alumni Club (hon.), Nat. Soc. Daus. Am. Revolution (mem. Stamford chpt., historian), Mich. State Alumni Club, Delta Phi Delta (hon.), Phi Kappa Phi (hon.), Alpha Xi Delta. Republican. Home: 274 Quarry Rd Stamford CT 06903-5004

RUDMAN, MARK, poet, educator; b. N.Y.C., Dec. 11, 1948; s. Charles Kenneth and Marjorie Louise (Levy) R.; m. Madelaine Bates, Dec. 28, 1977; 1 child, Samuel. BA, New Sch. Social Rsch., 1971; MFA, Columbia U., 1974. With Tchrs. and Writers Collaborative, 1971-72, Poetry in the Schs. Program, 1974-80; adj. lectr. Queens Coll., CUNY, Flushing, 1980-81; poet-in-residence, assoc. prof. York Coll., CUNY, Jamaica, 1984-88; adj. prof., asst. dir. grad. creative writing program NYU, 1986—; adj. prof. creative writing sch. gen. studies Columbia U., 1988—, adj. prof. sch. of the arts, 1992; writer-in-residence U. Hawaii, Manoa, 1978, Wabash Coll., 1979, SUNY, Buffalo, 1979; lectr. Parsons Sch. Design, 1983; poet in residence SUNY, Purchase, 1991; lectr. in field. Author: Robert Lowell: An Introduction to Poetry, 1983, The Mystery in the Garden, 1985, The Ruin Revived, 1986, Literature and the Visual Arts, 1990, Diverse Voices: Essays on Poetry, 1993, Rider, 1994 (Cir. award Nat. Book Critics Cir. 1995), Realm of Unknowing: Meditatations on Art, Suicide, Uncertainty, and Other Transformations, 1995 (poems) IN the Neighboring Cell, 1982, By Contraries and Other Poems, 1970-84, Selected and New, The Nowhere Steps, 1990, The Millennium Hotel, 1996; translator (with Bohdan Boychuk) Square of Angels: The Selected Poems of Bohdan Antonych, 1977, Orchard Lamps (Ivan Drach), 1978, My Sister--Life (Boris Pasternak), 1983, rev. edit., 1993, The Sublime Malady (Boris Pasternak), 1983; editor and co-translator: Memories of Love: The Selected Poems of Bohdan Boychuk, 1981; editor: Secret Destinations: Writers on Travel, 1986; poetry and criticism editor Pequod, 1975—, editor-in-chief, 1984—; contbr. poems, tranls. of poems and essays to anthologies and profl. jours. Recipient Acad. Am. Poets award, 1971, Hackney award Birmingham Arts Festival, 1972, Max Hayward award Columbia U. Translation Ctr., 1985, Editor's award N.Y. Coun. Arts, 1986; Internat. P.E.N. fellow, 1976-77, Yaddo fellow, 1977, 83, Coordinating Coun. for Literary Mags. fellow, 1981-82, Ingram Merrill fellow, 1983-84, N.Y. Found. Arts fellow, 1988, fellow in poetry NEA, 1994, Guggenheim fellow in poetry, 1996—. Mem. Internat. P.E.N., Poetry Soc. Am. (mem. bd. govs. 1984-88), Nat. Book Critics Circle. Office: 817 W End Ave New York NY 10025 also: New York Univ Dept of English New York NY 10003

RUDMAN, MICHAEL P., publishing executive; b. N.Y.C., 1950. Grad., U. Mich., 1972, NYU, 1975. Pres., chief exec. officer Nat. Learning Corp., Syosset, N.Y., also dir.; pres., chief exec. officer, dir., Delaney Books Inc., Frank Merriwell, Inc. Mem. Assn. Am. Pubs., Nat. Assn. Corp. Dirs., Nat. Assn. Coll. Stores. Office: Nat Learning Corp 212 Michael Dr Syosset NY 11791-5305

RUDMAN, SOLOMON KAL, magazine publisher; b. Phila., Mar. 6, 1930; s. Benjamin and Lena (Holtzman) R.; m. Lucille Steinhauer, June 29, 1958; 1 child, Mitchell. BS in Edn., U. Pa., 1951; MS in Edn., Temple U., 1957. Chmn. dept. spl. edn. Franklin D. Roosevelt Sch., Bristol Twp., Pa., 1960-68; pub. premier record/ radio trade Fri. Morning Quarterback, Cherry Hill, Pa., 1968—; bd. dirs. Variety Club, NARAS; co-host Merv Griffin TV Show, 1981-82; music expert Today Show, 1981-82, Tomorrow Show, 1981-82, Tom Snyder TV Show; creator-sponsor high sch. jazz piano competition, Phila. and suburbs of Pa., with Univ. of the Arts, Phila.; sponsor-host Phila. Franklin Inst. of Sci. and Fels Planetarium mobile sci. programs, top-level entertainment shows to most Phila.-N.J. Sr. Citizens' homes, children's and vets. hosps.; co-host, talent booker Easter Seals Telethon; mem. Phila. bd. dirs. NARAS; sponsor 47 scholarships for h.s. jazz musicians 2-week summer workshop at Univ. of the Arts; sponsor, creator 1st ann. classical piano competition Temple U. Pub.: (mag.) MQB (Modern QB) for Modern Rock Music; prodr. CD's of advance hists N.Am. radio stas.; launched 3d mag. MQB for alternative music radio. Bd. dirs. Phila. Broadcast Pioneers; sponsor carillon blls Ave. of Arts, Phila. Recipient Lifetime Achievement award in music Phila. Music Conf., Lifetime Music Achievement award Delaware Valley Music Poll. Mem. Phila. Music Alliance (bd. dirs.), Nat. Arthritis Found. (bd. dirs.), NARAS (bd. dirs.), Masons. Office: Friday Morning Quarterback 1930 Marlton Pike E Cherry Hill NJ 08003-2150

RUDMAN, WARREN BRUCE, former senator, lawyer, think tank executive; b. Boston, May 18, 1930; s. Edward G. and Theresa (Levenson) R.; m. Shirley Wahl, July 9, 1952; children: Laura, Alan, Debra. B.S., Syracuse (N.Y.) U., 1952; LL.B., Boston Coll., 1960. Bar: N.H. 1960, D.C. Mem. firm Rudman & Gormley, Nashua, N.H., 1960-69; counsel to Gov. Walter Peterson, Concord, N.H., 1970; atty. gen. State of N.H., Concord, 1970-76; mem. firm. Sheehan Phinney Bass & Green, 1976-80; U.S. Senator from N.H., 1981-92; co-founder Concord Coalition, 1992—; ptnr. Paul, Weiss, Rifkind, Wharton & Garrison, N.Y.C., Washington, 1993—; deputy chmn. Fed. Reserve Bank of Boston. 1993, mem. bd. dirs. Chubb Corp., 1993—, Raytheon Corp., 1993—, Dreyfus Corp., 1993—. Founder, chmn. bd. trustees Daniel Webster Jr. Coll., 1965—, trustees Boston Coll., Aspen Inst., Valley Forge, Mil Acad.; chmn., founder New Eng. Aero. Inst., v. chmn. Pres. Fgn. Intelligence adv. bd.; sr. adv. com. Inst. of Politics John F. Kennedy Sch. Capt. AUS, 1952-54, Korea. Decorated Bronze Star, Combat Inf. Badge. Mem. Am. Legion. Republican. Office: Paul Weiss Rifkind Wharton & Garrison 1615 L St NW Ste 1300 Washington DC 20036-5626*

RUDMANN, SALLY VANDER LINDEN, medical technology educator; b. Rochester, N.Y., Sept. 10, 1942; d. Egbert W. and Mildred M. (Schrader) Vander Linden; m. Ronald J. Rudmann, June 4, 1964 (div.); children: Daniel G., Stephen M.; m. James G. Barlow, Mar. 31, 1980. BA, Russell Sage Coll., 1964; MS, Wright State U., 1980; PhD, Ohio State U., 1986. Lic. med. technologist, Calif.; registered med. technologist; cert. Nat. Agy. Med. Lab. Pers.; CPR instr., ARC. Intern in med. tech. South bay Hosp., Redondo Beach, Calif., 1965-66; med. technologist Green Meml. Hosp., Xenia, Ohio, 1968-72; med. technologist Community Blood Ctr., Dayton, Ohio, 1974-75, intern, 1975-76; tech. supr. Greene Meml. Hosp., Xenia, 1976-78; tech. dir. Brown Labs., Columbus, Ohio, 1979-82; med. technologist Drs. Hosp. North, Columbus, Ohio, 1982-84; instr med. tech. Ohio State U., Columbus, Ohio, 1984-87, from asst. prof. to assoc. prof. med. tech., 1987—, dir. med. tech., 1987—; lect. and cons. in field. Editor: Textbook of Blood Banking and Transfusion Medicine, 1994; cons. MacMillan Pub. Co., 1984; editl. assoc. procs., editl. rev. Modern Blood Banking and Transfusion Practice, 1987, 88; cons. editor Clin. Lab. Sci., 1987—, editor-in-chief, 1988; profl. adv. panel Med. Lab. Observer, Lab. Med., 1989-90; contbr. numerous articles to profl. jours. Mem. Am. Assn. Blood Banks (abstract rev. com., inspector inspection and accreditation program, sci. and tech. workshop com.), Am. Soc. Clin. Lab. Sci. (planning com. region IV 1985), Am. Soc. Clin. Pathologists (R&D com., cons., lic. specialist in blood banking), Am. Soc. Allied Health Professions, Ohio Soc. Allied Health Professions, Ohio Soc. Med. Tech., Ohio Assn. BLood Banks (chairperson awards com. 1990-92, mem. award com. 1982—), Dayton Area Blood Bankers (pres. 1976), Phi Kappa Phi. Avocations: hiking, fitness, photography. Office: Ohio State U Med Tech Divsn 1583 Perry St Columbus OH 43210-1234

RUDNER, SARA, dancer, choreographer; b. Bklyn., Feb. 16, 1944; d. Henry Nathaniel and Jeannette (Smolensky) R.; 1 child, Eli Rudner Marschner. AB in Russian Studies, Barnard Coll., 1964. Dancer Sansardo Dance Co., N.Y.C., 1964-65, Am. Dance Co. at Lincoln Ctr., N.Y.C., 1965, Shakespeare Festival Touring Children's Show, N.Y.C., 1966; featured dancer Twyla Tharp Dance Found., N.Y.C., 1966-85; artistic dir., dancer 18th St. Dance Found., N.Y.C., 1977—; guest dancer Joffrey Ballet, N.Y.C., 1973, Pilobolus Dance Theatre, N.Y.C., 1975, Lar Lubovitch Dance Co., N.Y.C., 1975-76; guest lectr., choreographer grad. dance dept. UCLA, 1975; tchr. master workshop NYU Theater Program, 1988, 89, 90. Choreographer: Palm Trees and Flamingoes, 1980, Dancing for an Hour or So, 1981, Minute by Minute, 1982, Eight Solos, 1991, Heartbeats, Inside Out, 1993 (with Jennifer Tipton and Dana Reitz) Necessary Weather, 1994, with Rona Pondick and Robert Feintuch and Jennifer Tipton) Mine, 1996, Alley Theater—The Greeks part 1 and II, 1997. Grantee Creative Artists Pub. Svc. Program, N.Y., 1975-76, N.Y. State Coun. on Arts, 1975-78, Nat. Endowment for Arts, 1979-81, 91-92, 94-97; Guggenheim fellow, 1981-82; recipient N.Y. Dance and Performance award, 1984.

RUDNEY, HARRY, biochemist, educator; b. Toronto, Ont., Can., Apr. 14, 1918; came to U.S., 1948, naturalized, 1956; s. Joshua and Dina (Gorback) R.; m. Bernice Dina Snider, June 25, 1946; children—Joel David, Paul Robert. B.A., U. Toronto, 1947, M.A., 1948; Ph.D., Western Res. U., 1952. Faculty Western Res. U., Cleve., 1952-67; prof. biochemistry Western Res. U., 1965-67; prof., dir. dept. biochemistry and molecular biology U. Cin. Coll. Medicine, 1967-89, Andrew Carnegie Found. prof. biol. chemistry, 1967-89, prof. emeritus, 1989—; vis. prof. Case Inst. Tech., Cleve., 1965-66; mem. rsch. adv. panel N.E. Ohio Heart Assn., 1966-67; mem. panel metabolic biology NSF, 1968-71; rsch. career award com. NIH, 1969-73; mem. biochemistry test com. Nat. Bd. Med. Examiners, 1974-77; co-chair Instnl. Rev. Bd., U. Cinn. Med. Ctr., 1994—, interim chair dept. ph armacology, 1994-97. Mem. editorial bd. Archives of Biochemistry and Biophysics, 1965-89, Jour. Biol. Chemistry, 1975-80; contbr. articles profl. jours. Recipient USPHS Research Career award, 1963-67; Am. Cancer Soc. scholar, 1954-56; NSF Sr. Research fellow U. Amsterdam, Netherlands, 1957. Mem. Am. Soc. Biol. Chemists, Am. Chem. Soc., Am. Soc. Microbiology, Biochem. Soc. (Eng.), Sigma Xi. Home: 4040 Winding Way Cincinnati OH 45229-1919

RUDNICK, ELLEN AVA, health care executive; b. New Haven; d. Harold and C. Vivian (Soybel) R.; children from previous marriage: Sarah, Noah; m. Paul W. Earle. BA, Vassar Coll., 1972; MBA, U. Chgo., 1973. Sr. fin. analyst Quaker Oats, Chgo., 1973-75; various positions Baxter Internat., Deerfield, Ill., 1975-80, dir. planning, 1980-83, corp. v.p., 1985-1990; pres. Baxter Mgmt. Svcs., Deerfield, 1983-1990, HCIA, Balt., 1990-92, CEO Advs., Northbrook, Ill., 1992—; prin., chmn. Pacific Biometrics, Irvine, Calif., 1993—. Chief crusader Met. Chgo. United Way, 1982-85; pres. coun. Nat. Coll. Edn., Evanston, Ill., 1983—; cir. of friends Chgo. YMCA, 1985-89; bd. dirs. Highland Park Hosp., 1990—, NCCI. Mem. Chgo. Network, Econs. Club Chgo. (officer, bd. dirs.). Office: CEO Advs 255 Revere Dr Ste 111 Northbrook IL 60062-1595

RUDNICK, IRENE KRUGMAN, lawyer, former state legislator, educator; b. Columbia, S.C., Dec. 27, 1929; d. Jack and Jean (Getter) Krugman; AB cum laude, U. S.C., 1949, JD, 1952; m. Harold Rudnick, Nov. 7, 1954; children: Morris, Helen Gail. Admitted to S.C. bar, 1952; individual practice law, Aiken, S.C., 1952—, now ptnr. Rudnick & Rudnick; instr. bus. law, criminal law U. S.C., Aiken, 1962—; tchr. Warrenville Elem. Sch., 1965-70; supt. edn. Aiken County, 1970-72; mem. S.C. Ho. of Reps., 1972-78, 80-84, 86-94; pres. Adath Yeshurun Synagogue; active Aiken County Dem. Party, S.C. Dem. Party, Network Aiken; hon. mem. Aiken Able-Disabled. Recipient Citizen of Yr. award, 1976-77, Bus. and Profl. Women's Career Woman of Yr., 1978, 94, Aiken County Friend of Edn. award, 1985, 93, Outstanding Legis. award Disabled Vets., 1991, Citizen of the Yr. award Planned Parenthood, 1994, Sertoma Svc. to Mankind award, 1996. Mem. NEA, S.C. Tchrs. Assn., Aiken County Tchrs. Assn., Am. Bar Assn., Aiken County Bar Assn., Nat. Order Women Legislators, AAUW, Network Aiken, Aiken Able-Disabled (hon.), Alpha Delta Kappa. Jewish. Clubs: Order Eastern Star, Hadassah, Am. Legion Aux. Office: PO Box 544 135 Pendleton NW Aiken SC 29801

RUDNICK, PAUL DAVID, lawyer; b. Chgo., May 15, 1940; s. Harry Louis and Cele (Gordon) R.; m. Hope Korshak, June 13, 1963; children: William A., Carolyn. BS, Tulane U., 1962; JD cum laude, Northwestern U., 1965. Bar: Ill. 1965, Colo. 1994, U.S. Dist. Ct. (no. dist.) Ill. Assoc. Schiff, Hardin & Waite, Chgo., 1965-66; ptnr. Rudnick & Wolfe, Chgo., 1966—. Editor Northwestern U. Law Rev., 1964-65; co-editor, author: Illinois Real Estate Forms, 1989. Mem. Am. Coll. Real Estate Lawyers, Internat. Found. Employee Benefits, Tavern Club, Order of Coif. Avocations: skiing, music. Office: Rudnick & Wolfe 203 N La Salle St Ste 1800 Chicago IL 60601-1225

RUDNICK, REBECCA SOPHIE, lawyer, educator; b. Bakersfield, Calif., Nov. 26, 1952; d. Oscar and Sophie Mary (Loven) R.; m. Robert Anthoine, Dec. 2, 1990. BA, Willamette U., Salem, Oreg., 1974; JD, U. Tex., 1978; LLM, NYU, 1984. Bar: Tex. 1978, La. 1979, N.Y. 1980, Calif. 1980. Law clk. to Hon. Charles Schwartz, Jr. U.S. Dist. Ct., New Orleans, 1978-79; assoc. Winthrop, Stimson, Putnam & Roberts, N.Y.C., 1979-85; spl. counsel N.Y. Legis. Tax Study Commn., N.Y.C., 1983-84; asst. prof. law Ind. U., Bloomington, 1985-90; assoc. prof. of law Ind. U. Sch. of Law, Bloomington, 1990-94; assoc. prof. law London Law Consortium, Eng., 1994; vis. assoc. prof. law U. Conn., Hartford, 1984-85; vis. asst. prof. law U. Tex., Austin, 1988; vis. assoc. prof. law U. N.C., Chapel Hill, 1991, Boston U., 1994-95, U. Pa., Phila., 1995-96; prof.-in-residence, IRS, 1991-92; vis. scholar NSW, Australia, 1994, U. Sydney, Australia, 1994; vis. prof. law Seattle U., 1996—. Contbr. articles to various profl. jours. and publs. Dir., gen. counsel Project GreenHope: Svcs. for Women, N.Y.C., 1980-83; advisor, tech. asst. Internat. Monetary Fund, Washington, 1994. Mem. ABA (tax sect. 1982—, sec. tax sect. passthrough entities task force 1986-88, subcom. chairs for incorps. and CLE/important devel. tax sect., 1989—, corp. tax com. 1989—, tax sect. task force on integration 1990—), Am. Assn. Law Schs. (editor tax sect. newsletter 1987—), Assn. Bar of City of N.Y. (admiralty com. 1982-85), Internat. Fiscal Assn., Internat. Bar Assn. Office: Seattle U Sch Law 950 Broadway Tacoma WA 98402-4405

RUDO, MILTON, retired manufacturing company executive, consultant; b. Balt., Jan. 17, 1919; s. Saul E. and Bertha (Berkowitz) R.m. Roslind Mandel, Mar. 27, 1943; children: Stephanie Ellen, Neil Dennis. BA, Johns Hopkins U., 1940; AMP, Harvard U., 1964. With Brunswick Corp., Skokie, Ill., 1940-84, beginning as sales rep., Balt., successively br. mgr., Pitts., billiard mdse. mgr., Chgo., bowling and billiard products mdse. mgr., Chgo., sales v.p. Ea. region, Harrisburg, Pa., div. sales v.p., gen. sales mgr., Chgo., mktg. v.p., Chgo., pres. Bowling div., corp. v.p., Chgo., pres. Bowling div., Chgo., 1966-74, group v.p. recreation bus., 1974-84, ret., 1984, cons. to chief exec. officer, 1984-87; dir., cons. to chief exec., Donlen Leasing Corp, Skokie, Ill., 1986-90. Pres. Nat. Bowling Hall of Fame and Mus., 1979. Capt. AUS, 1942-45, ETO. Recipient ann. award N.Y. Mktg. Club, 1960, Industry Service award, 1973; named to Bowling Hall of Fame, 1984. Mem. Nat. Bowling Council (pres. 1972), Briarwood Country Club, Hamlet Country Club (Delray Beach, Fla.). Home (summer): 1777 Balsam Rd Highland Park IL 60035-4343

RUDOFF, SHELDON, lawyer, former religious organization executive; b. Bklyn., May 29, 1933; s. Raphael and Goldie (Gorelick) R.; m. Hedda Muller, Nov. 22, 1964; children: Shaindy, Sara, Simone. BA cum laude, Yeshiva Coll., 1954; JSD cum laude, NYU, 1958; ordination, RIETS, 1957. Bar: N.Y. 1958, U.S. Dist. Ct. (so. and ea. dists.) N.Y. 1958, U.S. Supreme Ct. 1978. Ptnr. Shatzkin, Cooper & Rudoff, N.Y.C., 1970-84, Goodkind, Labaton, Rudoff & Sucharow, N.Y.C., 1984—; hon. pres. Union Orthodox Jewish Congregation Am., 1990-94, 1994—. V.p. Yeshiva Coll. Alumni, N.Y.C., 1962-64; pres. Young Israel West Side, N.Y.C., 1969-72; sec. Orthodox Union, 1972-76, v.p., 1976-78, sr. v.p., 1978-84, chmn. bd., 1984-90, pres. 1990—, mem. exec. com. World Zionist Orgn.; bd. dirs. Am. Zionist Movement; trustee United Israel Appeal, Fedn. Jewish Philanthropies, 1980-91, United Jewish Appeal, Ctrl. Claims Conf. Recipient Pres.'s award Orthodox Union, N.Y.C., 1972, Nat. Leadership award Nat. Conf. Synagogue Youth, N.Y.C., 1974, Kesser Shem Tov award Ortohdox Union, 1995. Mem. ABA, N.Y. State Bar Assn., N.Y. City Bar Assn. (transp. com. 1976—). Home: 110 Riverside Dr New York NY 10024-3715 Office: Goodkind Labaton Rudoff & Sucharow 100 Park Ave New York NY 10017-5516

RUDOLPH, ABRAHAM MORRIS, physician, educator; b. Johannesburg, Republic of South Africa, Feb. 3, 1924; s. Chone and Sarah (Feinstein) R.; m. Rhona Sax, Nov. 2, 1949; children: Linda, Colin, Jeffrey. M.B.B.Ch. summa cum laude, U. Witwatersrand, Johannesburg, 1946, M.D., 1951; D (hon.), Rene Descartes U., Paris, 1996. Instr. Harvard Med. Sch., 1955-57, assoc. pediatrics, 1957-60; assoc. cardiologist in charge cardiopulmonary lab. Children's Hosp., Boston, 1955-60; dir. pediatric cardiology Albert Einstein Coll. Medicine, 1960-66; prof. pediatrics, assoc. prof. physiology Albert Einstein Coll. Medicine, N.Y.C., 1962-66; vis. pediatrician Bronx Mcpl. Hosp. Ctr., N.Y.C., 1960-66; prof. pediatrics U. Calif., San Francisco, 1966—, prof. physiology, 1974-88, Neider prof. pediatric cardiology, prof. ob-gyn and reproductive scis., 1974-94, chmn. dept. pediatrics, 1987-91, prof. pediatrics emeritus, 1994—; practice medicine, specializing in pediatric cardiology San Francisco.; mem. cardiovascular study sect. NIH, 1961-65, mem. nat. adv. heart council, 1968-72; established investigator Am. Heart Assn., 1958-62; career scientist Health Research Council, City N.Y., 1962-66; Harvey lectr., Oxford, Eng., 1984; inaugural lectr. 1st Nat. Congress Italian Soc. Perinatal Medicine, 1985. Mem. editorial bd. Pediatrics, 1964-70; assoc. editor Circulation Research, 1965-70; mem. editorial bd. Circulation, 1966-74, 83—; Am. Assoc. editor Pediatric Research, 1970-77; contbr. articles profl. jours. Recipient Merit award Nat. Heart, Lung and Blood Inst., 1986, Arvo Yllpo medal Helsinki U., Finland, 1987, Jonxis medal Children's Hosp. Groningen, 1993. Fellow Royal Coll. Physicians (Edinburgh), Royal Coll. Physicians (London); mem. NAS Inst. Medicine, Am. Acad. Pediatrics (E. Mead Johnson award for research in pediatrics 1964, Borden award 1979, past chmn. sect. on cardiology, Lifetime Med. Edn. award 1992, Joseph St. Geme leadership award Pediatrics 1993), Am. Phys. Soc., Soc. for Clin. Investigation, Soc. for Pediatric Research (coun. 1961-64), Am. Pediatric Soc. (coun. 1985-92, v.p. 1992-93, pres. 1993-94), Am. Heart Assn. (Rsch. Achievement award 1991). Office: U Calif Cardiovascular Rsch Inst Calif Rm 1403 Hse San Francisco CA 94143

RUDOLPH, ANDREW HENRY, dermatologist, educator; b. Detroit, Jan. 30, 1943; s. John J. and Mary M. (Mizesko) R.; children: Kristen Ann, Kevin Andrew. MD cum laude, U. Mich., 1966. Diplomate Am. Bd. Dermatology. Intern, Univ. Hosp., U. Mich. Med. Center, Ann Arbor, 1966-67, resident dept. dermatology, 1967-70; practice medicine specializing in dermatology, 1972—; asst. prof. dermatology Baylor Coll. Medicine, Houston, 1972-75, assoc. prof., 1975-83, clin. prof., 1983—; chief dermatology svc. VA Hosp., Houston, 1977-82; mem. staff Meth. Hosp., Tex. Children's Hosp., St. Luke's Episcopal Hosp. Served as surgeon USPHS, 1970-72. Regent's scholar U. Mich., 1966. Fellow Am. Acad. Dermatology; mem. Am. Dermatol. Assn., AMA, So. Med. Assn., Tex. Med. Assn., Harris County Med. Soc., Houston Dermatol. Soc. (past pres.), Tex. Dermatol. Soc., Assn. Mil. Dermatologists, Internat. Soc. Tropical Dermatology, Royal Soc. Health, Royal Soc. Medicine, Dermatology Found., Skin Cancer Found., Am. Venereal Disease Assn. (past pres.), Assn. Mil. Surgeons U.S., Am. Soc. for Dermatol. Surgery, Soc. for Investigative Dermatology, S. Central Dermatologic Congress, Mich. Alumni Assn. (life), Alpha Omega Alpha, Phi Kappa Phi, Phi Rho Sigma, Theta Xi. Mem. editorial bd. Jour. of Sexually Transmitted Diseases, 1977-85. Contbr. to med. jours., periodicals and textbooks. Office: 6560 Fannin St Ste 724 Houston TX 77030-2725

RUDOLPH, CHARLES HERMAN, computer software development executive; b. Balt., Mar. 14, 1953; s. Charles Henry and Margaret Theresa (McCarron) R.; m. Terri Gay; children: Kristin Margaret, Charles William. B.S. summa cum laude, King's Coll., 1975. Asst. mgr. product mktg. Datapoint Corp., San Antonio, 1977-78, mgr. systems planning, 1978-79, mgr. software devel., 1979-82, dir. software devel., 1982-84; sr. dir. Custom Systems, San Antonio, 1984-85; dir. engring. Digital Communications Assocs., Atlanta, 1985-88; v.p. mktg. Crosstalk Communications, Roswell, Ga., 1988-89, v.p., 1989-90; pres. Pacific Data Producers, San Diego, 1990-93; v.p. Peregrine Sys. Inc., San Diego, Calif., 1994—. Republican. Lutheran. Home: 13814 Lake Poway Rd Poway CA 92064-2278 Office: Peregrine Sys Inc 12670 High Bluff Dr San Diego CA 92130-2013

RUDOLPH, FREDERICK, history educator; b. Balt., June 19, 1920; s. Charles Frederick and Jennie Hill (Swope) R.; m. Dorothy Dannenbaum, June 18, 1949; children: Marta R. MacDonald, Lisa R. Cushman. B.A., Williams Coll., 1942, Litt.D., 1985; M.A., Yale U., 1949, Ph.D., 1953; LHD, U. Rochester, 1994. Instr. history Williams Coll., 1946-47; asst. instr. Yale, 1949-50; mem. faculty Williams Coll., 1951—, prof., 1961—, Mark Hopkins prof. history, 1964-82, emeritus, 1982—, chmn. Am. civilization program, 1971-80; Williams Coll. marshal, 1978-87; vis. lectr. history and edn. Harvard U., 1960, 61; vis. prof. Sch. Edn., U. Calif.-Berkeley, 1983; mem. commn. plans and objectives Am. Council Edn., 1963-66; mem. study group on postsecondary edn. Nat. Inst. Edn., 1980-83; mem. com. on baccalaureate degrees Assn. Am. Colls., 1981-85; vis. assoc. Ctr. Studies in Higher Edn., U. Calif.-Berkeley, 1983. Author: Mark Hopkins and the Log, 1956, rev. edit. 1996, The American College and University: A History, 1962, rev. edit., 1990, Curriculum: A History of the American Undergraduate Course of Study Since 1636, 1977, rev. edit., 1993; editor: Essays on Education in the Early Republic, 1965, Perspectives: A Williams Anthology, 1983; exec. editor: Change, 1980-84, cons. editor, 1985-92. Founding mem. Berkshire County Hist. Soc., 1962, v.p., 1962-66, pres., 1966-68, bd. dirs., 1974-76; trustee Hancock-Shaker Cmty. Inc., 1974-91, Wyoming Sem., 1976-79, Bennington Mus., 1985-95; bd. dirs. Armand Hammer United World Coll. Am. West, 1993—. Capt. AUS, 1942-46. Guggenheim fellow, 1958-59, 68-69; recipient Frederic W. Ness award Assn. Am. Colls., 1980, Rogerson cup Williams Coll., 1982, Disting. Svc. award Wyo. Seminary, 1986. Mem. Nat. Acad. Edn., Mass. Hist. Soc., Am. Hist. Assn., Am. Studies Assn., Orgn. Am. Historians, AAUP, Phi Beta Kappa. Democrat. Home: 234 Ide Rd Williamstown MA 01267-2800

RUDOLPH, FREDERICK BYRON, biochemistry educator; b. St. Joseph, Mo., Oct. 17, 1944; s. John Max and Maxine Leah (Wood) R.; m. Glenda M. Myers, June 18, 1971; children: Anna Dorine, William K. BS in Chemistry, U. Mo., Rolla, 1966; PhD in Biochemistry, Iowa State U., 1971. Prof. biochemistry Rice U., Houston, 1972—; chair biochemistry and cell biology, 1995—, dir. Lab. for Biochem. and Genetic Engring., 1986—, exec. dir. Inst. Bioscience and Bioengineering, 1993—; cons. World Book, Chgo., 1972—; mem. biochemistry study sect. NIH, Bethesda, Md., 1983-87; bd. dirs. S.W. Assn. Biotech. Cos., Houston, 1990-93. Contbr. over 160 articles to profl. jours. including Jour. Biol. Chemistry, Biochemistry, Transplantation, Exptl. Hematology, Jour. Parenteral and Enteral Nutrition, Jour. Molecular Biology, Applied and Environ. Microbiology, Life Scis., Archives Biochem. Biophysics, Critical Care Medicine, Archives Surgery, Sci.; also chots. to books. Recipient Disting. Alumnus award Iowa State U., 1980. Mem. Am. Chem. Soc., Am. Soc. for Biochemistry and Molecular Biology. Achievements include research on dietary requirements for immune function, new techniques for protein purification, new methods for kinetic analysis of enzymes, structure and function of various enzymes. Office: Rice U Dept Biochemistry and Cell Biology MS 140 6100 Main St Houston TX 77005-1827

RUDOLPH, GILBERT LAWRENCE, lawyer; b. L.A., Aug. 23, 1946; s. Martin Muttel and Marion (Perlman) R.; Susan Ilene Fellenbaum, Sept. 18, 1983; children: Samara Lisa, Felicia Beth. BA, Ariz. State U., 1967; postgrad., Am. U., Washington, 1967-69; JD, U. Cin., 1973. Bar: D.C. 1973, U.S. Dist. Ct. D.C. 1974, U.S. Ct. Appeals (D.C. cir.) 1974, Ariz. 1975, U.S. Dist. Ct. Ariz. 1975, Calif. 1979. Assoc. Streich, Lang, Weeks & Cardon, P.A., Phoenix, 1975-78; ptnr. Gilbert L. Rudolph, P.C., Phoenix, 1978-87; sr. mem. O'Connor, Cavanagh, Anderson, Killingsworth & Beshears, P.A., Phoenix, 1987—; lectr. on lending issues. Bd. dirs. Make-A-Wish Found. of Am., 1984-89, Aid to Adoption of Spl. Kids, Ariz., 1995—. Mem. ABA (com. on consumer fin. svcs. bus. law sect. 1981—, com. on comml. fin. svcs. 1989—, mem. com. on uniform comml. code 1992—), Conf. on Consumer Fin. Lqaw (governing com. 1986—), Ariz. Consumer Fin. Assn. (regulatory counsel 1996—), Mortgage Attys. Consortium (pres., bd. dirs. 1996—). Republican. Jewish. Office: O'Connor Cavanagh Anderson Killingsworth & Beshears PA 1 E Camelback Rd Ste 1100 Phoenix AZ 85012-1656

RUDOLPH, JEFFREY N., museum director. Exec. dir. California Museum of Science and Industry, Los Angles, Calif. Office: Calif Mus Sci & Industry 700 State Dr Los Angeles CA 90037-1237*

RUDOLPH, LAVERE CHRISTIAN, library director; b. Jasper, Ind., Dec. 24, 1921; s. Joseph Frank and Rose (Stradtner) R. A.B., DePauw U., 1948; B.D., Louisville Presbyn. Sem., 1951; Ph.D., Yale, 1958; student, U. Zurich, Switzerland, 1960; M.L.S., Ind. U., 1968. Ordained to Ministry Presbyn. Ch., 1950; pastor in Ind. and Conn., 1950-54; mem. faculty Louisville Presbyn. Sem., 1954-69, prof. ch. history, 1960-69; lectr. history U. Louisville, 1965-69; rare books bibliographer Van Pelt Library U. Pa.; head tech. services Lilly Library, Ind. U., 1970-78, curator of books, 1978-86, librarian emeritus, 1987—. Author: Hoosier Zion, 1963 (Thomas Kuch award Ind. U. Writers Conf. 1964), Story of the Church, 1966, Francis Asbury, 1966, Indiana Letters, 1979, Religion in Indiana, 1986, Hoosier Faiths, 1995. Served to capt. USAAF, 1940-46. Mem. Am. Soc. Ch. History, ALA, Assn. Coll. and Research Libraries, Presbyn. Hist. Soc., Phi Beta Kappa. Democrat. Home: 1509 E Dunstan Dr Bloomington IN 47401-8607 Office: Ind U Library Bloomington IN 47405

RUDOLPH, MALCOLM ROME, investment banker; b. Balt., Sept. 22, 1924; s. Louis and Sara E. (Rome) R.; m. Zita Herzmark, July 1, 1956 (div. 1979); children: Madelon R. II, Margot R.; m. Barbara J. Girson, 1979. AB, Harvard U., 1947; postgrad., Grenoble U., France, 1948, Hayden Stone Mgmt. Sch., 1965. With div. internat. confs. U.S. Dept. State, Paris, 1949; registered rep. trainee Orvis Bros. & Co., N.Y.C., 1949, rep., asst. mgr., acting mgr., 1950-64; mgr. Hayden Stone Inc., Washington, 1964-68, ptnr., 1968-69; chmn. bd. Donatelli, Rudolph & Schoen Inc., Washington, 1970-74; chmn. bd. Multi-Nat. Fin. Group, Inc., Washington, 1974-79, pres., 1979-86; chmn. Multi-Nat. Precious Metals Corp., 1974-75; chmn. bd. Multi-Nat. Money Mgmt. Co. Inc., 1974-79, pres., 1979—; pres. Rudolph & Schoen Inc., 1975-85; sr. v.p., dir. Laidlaw Adams & Peck Inc., 1975-79; pres. Laidlaw Resources Inc., 1976-95, Sutton Energy, Inc., 1976-90, DeRand Resources Corp., 1979-88; sr. v.p., dir. DeRand Corp. Am., 1979-88; chmn. bd. Arlington Energy Corp., 1980-88; mem. Phila.-Balt.-Washington Stock Exch., 1972-75; pres. Rome Resources Corp., 1982—. Investment Bankers and Cons.; assoc. mem. Pitts., Boston, Montreal stock exchs., 1972-75; allied mem. N.Y. Stock Exch., 1975-79. Mem. Presdl. Inaugural Com., 1960, 64; mem. select com. Palm Beach County Coop Ext. Svc., 1993, U. Fla. Inst. Food and Agrl. Scis. ext. 2000 Select Com.; treas. and dir. Friends of the Mounts Bot. Garden, West Palm Beach, 1994; v.p., dir. Hort. Soc. South Fla., 1994. Mem. Assn. Investment Brokers Met. Washington (v.p. 1965-66, pres. 1967), Bond Club Washington, Ohio Oil and Gas Assn., Ind. Oil and Gas Assn. W.Va., Ind. Petroleum Assn. Am., Southeastern Ohio Oil and Gas Assn., Washignton Met. Bd. Trade, Internat. Assn. Fin. Planners, Internat. Club of Washington, Hasty-Pudding Inst. 1770, Harvard Club of Washington (asst. treas. 1957-60, treas. 1960-64, exec. com. 1957-67), Harvard Club Palm Beaches, Nat. Aviation Club, Club Colette (Palm Beach), Palm Beach Yacht Club, Poinsiana Club (Palm Beach). Home: 1333 N Lake Way Palm Beach FL 33480-3109

RUDOLPH, ROBERT NORMAN, secondary school educator, adult education educator; b. Ft. Worth, Nov. 2, 1956; s. Robert John and Lenabel (Thurman) R.; m. Cynthia Ann Williams, Oct. 20, 1979; 1 child, Renee Megan Rudolph. BSE, Millersville U., 1978, MEd in Tech. Edn., 1983, supervisory cert., 1992. Cert. profl. tchr., program specialist, Pa. Project engr. Frankel Engring., Reading, Pa., 1978; tech. edn. tchr. Cumberland Valley Sch. Dist., Mechanicsburg, 1978—, chmn. tech. edn. dept., 1993—, adult edn. tchr., 1979—; carpenter R.G. Lunger Industries, Mechanicsburg, Pa., 1979-82; landscape designer Country Market Nursery, Mechanicsburg, 1983-90; advisor Tech. Student Assn., Mechanicsburg, 1991—, Am. Tech. Honor Soc., 1996—; cons. Calif. (Pa.) U. Dept. Industry and Tech., 1990; evaluator Mid. Atlantic States Accrediting Assn. for Secondary Schs., 1995. Creator display of calligraphy at Am. Indsl. Arts Assn. conv., 1979. Recipient Certs. of Merit Indsl. Arts Assn. of Pa., 1985, Tech. Edn. Assn. Pa., 1996, Nevin Andre Meml. award for outstanding jour. article Tech. Edn. Assn. Pa., 1996. Mem. NEA, Future Farmers Am. (hon.), Internat. Tech. Edn. Assn., Nat. Air and Space Mus., Soc. Mfg. Engrs., Robotics Internat., Tech. Edn. Assn. of Pa. (supr.'s coun.), Pa. Nurseryman Assn. (accredited nurseryman), Epsilon Pi Tau. Avocation: reading, triathlons. Office: Cumberland Valley High Sch 6746 Carlisle Pike Mechanicsburg PA 17055-1711

RUDOLPH, WALLACE MORTON, law educator; b. Chgo., Sept. 11, 1930; s. Norman Charles and Bertha (Margolin) R.; m. Janet L. Gordon, Feb. 14, 1964; children: Alexey, Rebecca, Sarah. B.A., U. Chgo., 1950, J.D., 1953. Bar: Ill. 1953, U.S. Ct. Mil. Appeals 1954, U.S. Supreme Ct. 1954, Nebr. 1962, Wash. 1978, also others. Research assoc. Ford Found., 1953-54, Ford Found. (Project in Law and Behavior Sci.), 1954-55; instr. U. Chgo. Law Sch., 1959; assoc. firm Antonow & Fink, Chgo., 1960-61; asst. prof. law U. Nebr., Lincoln, 1961-63; assoc. prof. U. Nebr., 1963-64, prof., 1965-76; prof. U. Puget Sound Sch. Law, 1976-94, dean, 1976-80; prof. Sch. of Law Seattle U., 1994—; vis. prof. law U. Wis., 1980-81, U. Ill., 1984; chair excellence in law Memphis State U. Law Sch., 1991; mem. Commrs. Uniform State Law, 1973-77; judge Ct. Indsl. Rels., Nebr., 1975-77; mem. Wash. Jud. Coun. and COm. II, 1976-80, Pub. Employment Rels. Commn., Wash., 1977—. Author: Handbook for Correctional Law; contbr. articles to profl. jours.; author: Model Criminal Procedure Code, 1975, Model Sentencing and Corrections Act, 1978, Amicus Curiae Brief, Wash. State Supreme Ct, 1979. Bd. dirs. LIMIT, 1992-94, Nebr. chpt. ACLU, 1965-72; mem. Nebr. Dem. Contact Com., 1973-74, 75-76; chmn. Firt Congl. Dist. Dem. Party, 1975-76; mem. exec. com. Unitarian Ch., Lincoln, 1965-67. Served with JAGC, U.S. Army, 1954-57. Mem. AAUP, Soc. Criminology, ABA Am. Law Inst., Am. Arbitration Assn. Office: U Orlando Sch Law 6441 E Colonial Dr Orlando FL 32807-3650

RUDSTEIN, DAVID STEWART, law educator; b. Leeds, Eng., Sept. 27, 1946. B.S., U. Ill., 1968, LL.M., 1975; J.D., Northwestern U., 1971. Bar: Ill. 1971, U.S. Supreme Ct. 1977. Teaching asst. U. Ill. Coll. Law, 1971-72; law clk. to Justice Walter V. Schaefer Supreme Ct. Ill., Chgo., 1972-73; asst. prof. law Ill. Inst. Tech.-Chgo. Kent Coll., 1973-76, assoc. prof., 1976-79, prof., 1979—, assoc. dean, 1983-87. Author: (with C.P. Erlinder and D. Thomas) Criminal Constitutional Law, 1990. Mem. ABA, Chgo. Council Lawyers, Order of Coif. Office: Ill Inst Tech-Chgo 565 W Adams St Chicago IL 60661-3601

RU DUSKY, BASIL MICHAEL, cardiologist; b. Wilkes-Barre, Pa., July 27, 1933; s. Michael and Anne RuD.; m. Bernadine RuDusky, 1957; children: Daryl, Bryan. B.A., Va. Mil. Inst., 1955; M.D., U. Pitts., 1959. Diplomate Am. Bd. Forensic Medicine. Intern, Martin Army Hosp., Ft. Benning, Ga., 1959-60; resident Youngstown (Ohio) Hosp. Assn., 1962-63, Temple U. Hosp., 1963-66; practice medicine specializing in internal medicine, cardiovascular medicine and forensic medicine, Wilkes-Barre, Pa., 1966—; mem. staff Mercy Hosp., 1966—, chief of medicine, 1966-70, dir. ICU and CCU, 1966-70, dir. phonocardiography lab., 1966-70; dir. N.E. Cardiovascular Clinic and Research Inst.; mem. staff Wilkes-Barre Gen. Hosp.; cons. cardiology Armed Forces Examining Service; sr. cons. Social Security Adminstrn., HEW; sr. cons. physician Met. Ins. Co. Am., Liberty Mut. Ins. Co., Aetna Ins. Co.; cons. internal medicine and cardiology Retreat State Hosp.; dir. Northeast Cardiovascular Clinic and Research Inst.; clin. instr. medicine Temple U., 1966-70. Served to capt. M.C., U.S. Army, 1959-62. Diplomate Am. Bd. Internal Medicine, Am. Bd. Forensic Medicine, Am. Bd. Forensic Examiners (fellow). Fellow ACP, Am. Coll. Angiology (bd. govs. Eastern Pa.), Am. Coll. Chest Physicians, Am. Coll. Cardiology; mem. Am. Soc. Internal Medicine, AMA, Am. Coll. Occupl. and Environ. Medicine, Nat. Rehab. Assn., N.Y. Acad. Scis., Am. Geriatrics Soc., Assn. Mil. Surgeons U.S., Pan-Am. Med. Assn., Amateur Fencers League Am. Home: 7 Pine Tree Rd Wilkes Barre PA 18707-1707 Office: Bicentennial Bldg 15 Public Sq Wilkes Barre PA 18701-1702

RUDY, DAVID ROBERT, physician, educator; b. Columbus, Ohio, Oct. 19, 1934; s. Robert Sale and Lois May (Arthur) R.; m. Rose Mary Sims; children by previous marriages: Douglas D., Steven W., Katharine L. Rudy Hoffer, Hunter A. Elam. BSc, Ohio State U., 1956, MD, 1960, MPH Med. Coll. Wis., 1995. Intern, Northwestern Meml. Hosp., Chgo., 1960-61; resident in internal medicine Ohio State U. Hosp., 1963-64; resident in pediatrics Children's Hosp., Columbus, Ohio, 1964; practice medicine specializing in family practice, Columbus, 1964-75; dir. Family Practice Center and residency program Riverside Meth. Hosp., Columbus, 1975-85; dir. Family Practice Ctr. and residency Monsour Med. Ctr., Jeannette, Pa., 1985-88; dir. Family Practice Ctr. and residency Bon Secours Hosp., Grosse Pointe, Mich., 1988-91; prof., dept. chmn. Finch U. Health Scis., Chgo. Med. Sch., 1991-95, 97—; prof., Pomerene chair family medicine Ohio State U., 1995-97; former clin. assoc. prof. Ohio State U., Penn. State U., Wayne State U. Dept. Family Medicine. Editor, contbr. (textbook) Family Medicine for the House Office; contbr. articles to profl. jours. Served as capt., flight surgeon, M.C., USAF, 1961-63; col. Ohio Air N.G. Recipient USAF Commendation medal. Diplomate Am. Bd. Family Practice (charter). Fellow Am. Acad. Family Physicians; mem. AMA, Ohio State Med. Assn. Republican. Office: Chgo Med Sch Thomas E Rardin Family Practice Ctr 3333 Green Bay Rd North Chicago IL 60064-3037 also: 540 Ambria Dr Mundelein IL 60060

RUDY, FRANK R., pathologist; b. Harrisburg, Pa., Jan. 23, 1949; s. Burton B. and Blanch T. (Rhoads) R.; m. Debra R. Bromberg, Dec. 27, 1970; children: Allison, Nicole. BA, Franklin & Marshall Coll., 1970; MD, U. Pitts., 1974. From assoc. pathologist to chmn. lab. Polyclinic Hosp., Harrisburg, 1979-95; chmn. Pinnacle Health Lab., Harrisburg, 1996—; pres. Pathology Assocs. Ctrl. Pa., Harrisburg, 1997—. Author: Uropathology, 1989, Principles and Practices of Surgical Pathology; contbr. articles to profl. jours. Fellow Coll. Am. Pathology, Am. Soc. Clin. Pathologists; mem. Internat. Acad. Pathology, Am. Pathology Found., U.S. Acad. Pathology, Canadian Acad. Pathology. Avocation: scuba diving. Office: Polyclinic Hosp 2601 N 3rd St Harrisburg PA 17110-2004

RUDY, JAMES FRANCIS XAVIER, lawyer; b. N.Y.C., Feb. 1, 1954; s. Bertrand Robert and Margaret Eleanor (Campiglia) R.; m. Mary Elizabeth Haas, Aug. 17, 1978; children: Lauren Elizabeth, James F.X. Jr. BA, U. Ariz., 1976; JD, Fordham U., 1979. Bar: N.Y. 1980, N.J. 1981, U.S. Dist. Ct. (so. dist.) N.Y. 1980, U.S. Dist. Ct. N.J. 1981, U.S. Supreme Ct. 1985. Assoc. Briger & Assocs., N.Y.C., 1979-81, Katzenbach, Gildea & Rudner, Trenton, N.J., 1981-85; ptnr. Katzenbach, Gildea & Rudner, Lawrenceville, N.J., 1985-93; ptnr. Fox, Rothschild, O'Brien & Frankel, Lawrenceville, 1993—, chmn. health law group, 1994—; twp. atty. Ewing Twp., N.J., 1992-93, atty. Rent Control Bd., 1992-93, atty. Ethical Stds. Bd., 1992-93, atty. Condemnation Bd., 1992-93. Author: University of San Francisco Law Review, 1991. Legal counsel Ewing Rep. Club, 1991-93; mem. Washington Twp. Planning Bd., Robbinsville, N.J., 1993—; wrestling coach Washington Twp. Recreation, Robbinsville, 1993—; dist. committeeperson Ewing Twp. Rep. Com., Ewing, 1990-92. Mem. Nat. Health Lawyers Assn., Assn. of Bar City of N.Y., N.J. State Bar Assn. , Mercer County C. of C. (bus. com. 1993—), Ewing Twp. Kiwanis Club (dir. 1994-95), Phi Beta Kappa. Republican. Roman Catholic. Avocations: golf, home improvement, gardening, wrestling, rollerblading. Home: 8 Barto Way Robbinsville NJ 08691-2422 Office: Fox Rothschild OBrien & Frankel 997 Lenox Dr Lawrenceville NJ 08648-2317

RUDY, LESTER HOWARD, psychiatrist; b. Chgo., Mar. 6, 1918; s. Sol and Mildred (Weinzimmer) R.; m. Ruth Jean Schmidt, Nov. 25, 1950; 1 dau., Sharon Ruth. B.S., U. Ill., 1939, M.D., 1941; M.S. in Hosp. Adminstrn, Northwestern U., 1957. Diplomate: Am. Bd. Psychiatry and Neurology (exec. dir. 1972-86). Intern Cedars of Lebanon Hosp., Los Angeles, 1941-42; resident in psychiatry VA Hosp., Downey, Ill., 1946-48; staff psychiatrist VA Hosp., 1948-52, chief service, 1952-54; supt. Galesburg (Ill.) State Research Hosp., 1954-58; practice medicine specializing in psychiatry Chgo.; supt. Ill. State Psychiat. Inst., Chgo., 1958-61; dir. Ill. State Psychiat. Inst., 1961—, Ill. Mental Health Insts., Chgo., 1967-75; prof. psychiatry U. Ill. Coll. Medicine, 1971-88, emeritus, 1988—, head dept. psychiatry, 1975-88, pres. hosp. staff, 1979-80; dir. U. Ill. Hosp., 1981-82; sr. med. dir. Health Care Compare, 1988—; Chmn. research rev. com. mental health services NIMH, 1972-73; AMA commr. Joint Commn. on Accreditation of Hosps., 1967-75; sr. cons. VA; cons. adv. bd. Chgo., Police Dept.; lectr. dept. psychiatry and neurology Loyola U., 1968-75; mem. Ill. Gov.'s Com. Competency to Stand Trial, 1968; cons. psychiatry Blue Cross/Blue Shield of Ill., 1996—, Cir. Ct. of Winnebago County (Ill.), 1995—. Contbr. articles to profl. jours. Served to col. AUS, 1942-46. Decorated Bronze Star with two oak leaf clusters. Fellow Am. Psychiat. Assn. (chmn. ethics com. 1963, Simon Bolivar award 1985), Am. Coll. Psychiatrists (charter, Bowis award 1979); mem. Am. Acad. Psychoanalysis (sci. asso.), Ill. Psychiat. Soc. (pres. 1962-63), U. Ill. Med. Alumni Assn. (ann. outstanding achievement award 1980). Home: 6343 Collingswood Ct Rockford IL 61103-8961 Office: 912 S Wood St Chicago IL 60612-7325

RUDY, LINDA MAE, secondary school educator; b. York, Maine, Mar. 26, 1948; d. Maynard Everett and Frances Irene (Cross) Fuller; m. Jacob William Rudy, Sept. 27, 1980. BS, U. So. Maine, 1971, postgrad., 1978-81; postgrad., George Washington U., 1983-86. Cert. tchr., Md. Math tchr. Cape Elizabeth (Maine) Middle Sch., 1971-78, Meml. Jr. High Sch., South Portland, Maine, 1978-79, York (Maine) High Sch., 1979-81; math tchr. LaPlata (Md.) High Sch., 1983—, chmn. Md. student assistance program, 1988-94; math tchr. Md. Tomorrow Program, LaPlata, 1988, Certificate of Appreciation, 1988. Co-author: (teaching program) Challenging Choices, 1989. Mem. Cobb Island Citizens Assn., 1983—; treas. Cobb Island Bapt. Ch., 1989-94. Recipient Certificate of Recognition, Charles County Bd. Edn., LaPlata, 1988, Certificate of Appreciation, 1990, Certificate of Instructional Leadership, Md. State Dept. of Edn., Annapolis, Md., 1989. Mem. NEA, Nat. Coun. Tchrs. Math., Edn. Assn. Charles County (bldg. rep. 1988-89), Md. State Tchrs. Assn., Md. Coun. Tchrs. Math. Baptist. Avocations: needlework, sailing, aerobics. Home: 12048 Neale Sound Dr Cobb Island MD 20625

RUDY, RAYMOND BRUCE, JR., retired food company executive; b. L.A., Apr. 24, 1931; s. Raymond Bruce and Wrena Margaret (Higgins) R.; m. Kathleen Vermeulen; children: Bruce Calvin, Alice M.R. Price, Barbara R. Frith. BS, UCLA, 1953; MBA, Xavier U., Cin., 1960. Brand mgr. Procter & Gamble, Cin., 1956-62; product mgr. Hunt-Wesson Foods, Fullerton, Calif., 1962-63; group v.p. Gen. Foods Corp., White Plains, N.Y., 1963-79; pres. Oroweat Foods Co. subs. Continental Grain Co., N.Y.C., 1979-83; chmn., pres. Arnold Foods Co., Inc., Greenwich, Conn., 1984-86; pres. Affiliates of Best Foods subs. CPC Internat., Englewood Cliffs, N.J., 1987-89; ret., 1989; chmn., CEO, New Hampton, Inc., 1993-94; dep. chmn. Snapple Natural Beverages, Inc., 1992-94; mng. dir. J.W. Childs Assoc., 1995—; chmn. Personal Care Group, Inc., 1996—; bd. dirs. Bros. Gourmet Coffees, Inc., Widmer Brothers Brewing, Inc., Personal Care Group, Inc.; advisor Desai Capital Mgmt., Inc., Kirshenbaum Bond & Ptnrs., Advt. With U.S. Army, 1954-56. Mem. Greenwich Country Club, Dorset Field Club. Congregational.

RUDY, RUTH CORMAN, former state legislator; b. Millheim, Pa., Jan. 3, 1938; d. Orvis E. and Mabel Jan (Stover) Corman; m. C. Guy Rudy, Nov. 21, 1956; children: Douglas G., Donita Rudy Koval, Dianna F. Degree in x-ray tech. Carnegie Inst., 1956; student Pa. State U., 1968-71. Clk. of cts. County of Centre (Pa.), Bellefonte, 1976-82; rep. Pa. Gen. Assembly, Harrisburg, 1982-96. Mem. Dem. Nat. Com., 1980—, chair women's caucus, 1989-91; past pres. Pa. Fedn. Dem. Women, Harrisburg; pres. Nat. Fedn. Dem. Women, 1987-89; mem. exec. com. Dem. Nat. Com., 1987-89, chmn. women's caucus, 1989-91; candidate U.S. Congress, 5th Dist., 1995-96; rep. Nat. Dem. Inst. for Internat. Affairs, Centre Hall, Pa., 1997—. Named Woman of Yr., Pa. Fedn. Dem. Women, 1982. Methodist. Granted U.S. Patent on hair spray face shield 1995. Office: Nat Dem Inst Internat Affairs Rd # 1, Box 570 Centre Hall PA 16828

RUDY, WILLIS, historian; b. N.Y.C., Jan. 25, 1920; s. Philip and Rose (Handman) R; B.S.S., CCNY, 1939; M.A., Columbia U., 1940, Ph.D., 1948; m. Dorothy L. Richardson, Jan. 31, 1948; children: Dee Dee, Willis Philip, Willa. Instr. Coll. City N.Y., 1939-49; instr., lectr. Harvard U., 1949-53, 57-58; prof. Mass. State Coll., Worcester, 1953-63; prof. history Fairleigh Dickinson U., Teaneck, N.J., 1963-82, prof. emeritus, 1982—; mem. editorial bd. Fairleigh Dickinson U. Press, 1966-77. Mem. Orgn. Am. Historians, Phi Beta Kappa. Author: The College of the City of New York, A History, 1847-1947, 1949; 1976; The American Liberal Arts College Curriculum, 1960; Higher Education in Transition, 1958, 68, 76, 97; Schools in an Age of Mass Culture, 1965; The Universities of Europe: a History, 1984; Total War and Twentieth Century Higher Learning, 1991, The Campus and a Nation in Crisis: From the Revolution to Vietnam, 1996. Home: 161 W Clinton Ave Tenafly NJ 07670-1916 Office: Fairleigh Dickinson U Dept Of Hist Teaneck NJ 07666 *As a teacher, my greatest reward has been to see people get involved in the sheer joy of learning new things and seeking answers to the big questions that life proposes. As a writer, my enduring satisfaction has come from the opportunity to explore the seemingly chaotic events on human history in the hope of finding a meaningful and instructive pattern.*

RUDZKI, EUGENIUSZ MACIEJ, chemical engineer, consultant; b. Warsaw, Poland, Feb. 24, 1914; came to U.S., 1955.; s. Aleksander and

Wanda (Łukaszewicz) R.; m. Fiorina Maria Di Vito, Feb. 23, 1952; children: Robert Alexander, Marcella Wanda Rudzki Meddick. Diploma with honors, Warsaw (Poland) Poly. Inst., 1937; Chem. Engr., The Polish U. Coll., London, 1951. Project devel. and field engr. Chance Bros. Ltd., Eng., 1951-54; head instr. chem. engring. dept. U. Toronto, Can., 1954-55; rsch. engr. T.C. Wheaton Co., N.J., 1955-56; rsch. engr. Bethlehem (Pa.) Steel Corp., 1956-61, supr. rsch. dept., 1961-82, ret., 1982; cons. Am. Flame Rsch. com., 1982—. Patentee in field, U.S., Eng., Can., Belgium; contbr. articles to profl. jours. Active The Polish Inst. Arts and Scis., N.Y.C., 1975, The Kosciuszko Found., N.Y.C., 1977; polit. prisoner Gulag Abis forced labor camp, Peczora, USSR, 1940-41. Maj. 2d Polish Army Corp. Gen. Anders, 1942-46. Decorated the Virtuti Militari Order, The Cross of Valor with Bar, The Silver Order of Merit with Swords. Fellow Inst. Energy London, Coun. Engring. Insts. London (chartered engr.); mem. AIME, AIChE, Combustion Inst., Polish Vets. WWII, Assn. Vets. of 2nd Polish Army Corp. Roman Catholic. Avocations: gardening, reading, travel.

RUEBHAUSEN, OSCAR MELICK, lawyer; b. N.Y.C., Aug. 28, 1912; s. Oscar and Eleonora J. (Melick) R.; m. Zelia Krumbhaar Peet, Oct. 31, 1942. AB summa cum laude, Dartmouth Coll., 1934; LLB cum laude, Yale U., 1937. Bar: N.Y. 1938, U.S. Supreme Ct., 1945. Assoc. Debevoise, Stevenson, Plimpton & Page, N.Y.C., 1937-42, Lend-Lease Adminstrn., Washington, 1942-44; gen. counsel Office Sci. Rsch. and Devel., Washington, 1944-46; ptnr. Debevoise and Plimpton, 1946-84, presiding ptnr., 1972-81, of counsel, 1984-87; counselor to ednl. instn., 1988—. Editor: Pension and Retirement Policies in Colleges and Universities, 1990; contbr. articles to profl. jours. Chmn. Commn. on Coll. Retirement, 1984-93; spl. adviser atomic energy to gov. N.Y. State, 1959; vice chmn. N.Y. State adv. com. on atomic energy, 1959-62; chmn. N.Y. State Gov.'s Task Force on protection from radioactive fallout, 1959; mem. Pres.'s Task Force on Sci. Policy, 1969-70, Pres.'s Sci. Adv. Com. Panel on Chems. and Health, 1970-72, Commn. on Critical Choices for Am., 1973-77, adv. com. Carnegie Commn. on Sci., Tech. and Govt., 1988-93; chmn. UN Day, N.Y. State, 1962, chmn. Spl. N.Y. Com. on Ins. Holding Cos., 1967-68; mem. U.S. govt. panel on Privacy and Behavioral Rsch., 1965-66; mem. presdl. panel Chronic Renal Disease, 1966-67; sec., dir. Fund Peaceful Atomic Devel., Inc., 1954-72; dir. Carrie Chapman Catt Meml. Fund, 1948-58; chmn. bd. Bennington Coll., 1957-61, 62-67; trustee Hudson Inst., Inc., 1961-71; trustee Russell Sage Found., chmn. bd., 1965-80; vice-chmn. N.Y.C. Univ. Constrn. Fund, 1966-69; mem. Coun. on Fgn. Rels., nat. com. on U.S.-China rels., Rockefeller U. Coun.; bd. dirs. Greenwall Found., 1956-95, chmn., 1982-91, chmn. emeritus, 1991—; bd. dirs. Scripps Clinic and Rsch. Found, 1983-89. Recipient U.S. Presdl. Cert. of Merit, 1948. Mem. ABA, N.Y. State Bar Assn., Yale Law Sch. Assn. (exec. com. and pres. 1960-62, chmn. 1962-64), Assn. of Bar of City of N.Y. (pres. 1980-82, pres. and bd. dirs. fund 1980-82), Order of Coif, Phi Beta Kappa, Sigma Phi Epsilon, Sigma Xi (hon.). Clubs: Century (N.Y.C.), River (N.Y.C.); Rancho Santa Fe Assn. (Calif.); Rockefeller Ctr.(N.Y.C.). Home: 450 E 52nd St New York NY 10022-6448

RUECK, JON MICHAEL, manufacturing executive; b. Riley, Kans., Oct. 23, 1940; s. G.M. Karl and Esther Margaret (Jones) R.; m. Connie Lee Dick Rueck, Apr. 14, 1962; children: Michael Jon, Robin Renee. BS in Nuclear Engring., Kans. State U., 1964, MS in Mech. Engring., 1971. Registered profl. engr., KS, Ohio. Radiation safety trainee Argonne Nat. Lab., Lemont, Ill., 1962; tech. sales trainee Owens-Corning Fiberglas Corp., Granville, Ohio, 1964-65; tech. sales Owens-Corning Fiberglas Corp., Mpls., 1965-66; customer svc. engr. Owens-Corning Fiberglas Corp., Granville, Ohio, 1966-67; environ. engr. Owens-Corning Fiberglas Corp., Toledo, 1971-75; dir. plant ops. Leila Y. Post Montgomery Hosp., Battle Creek, Mich., 1975; environ. engr. Thompson Dehydrating Co., Topeka, 1976, Kans. Dept. Health Environ., Topeka, 1976-77; v.p. Hosp. Instrument Svc. Co., Silver Lake, Kans., 1977-80; supr. air pollution source monitoring Kans. Dept. of Health and Environ., 1979-85; chmn. Rueck Assocs., Silver Lake, Kans., 1985—; pres. Computer Et Cetera, Silver Lake, 1995—; cons. to Nat. Coun. Examiners for Engring. and Surveying, 1993—. Co-author: Environmental Engineering Examination Guide & Handbook, 1996. Res. police officer St. Mary's (Kans.) Police Dept., 1981-86; cert. lay spkr. Kans. East Conf., United Meth. Ch., 1979—, vol. coord. Topeka dist. disaster response, 1993, coord. Kans. East Conf. United Meth. Disaster Relief, 1994—; merit badge counselor Boy Scouts Am., Silver Lake, 1988—; del. candidate for Robertson for Pres., Shawnee County, Kans., 1988; coord. Kans. Interfaith Disaster Recovery, 1993. Mem. Am. Acad. Environ. Engrs. (diplomate, chmn. admissions com. Annapolis, Md. 1986-90, state rep. Kans. 1990—), Midwest Air and Waste Mgmt. Assn. (officer 1987-90), Kaw Valley Bicycle Touring Club (Topeka), Lions. Republican. United Methodist. Avocations: bicycling, vocalist, amateur radio, computers. Home: 617 Walnut St Silver Lake KS 66539-9467 Office: Rueck Assocs 617 Walnut St Silver Lake KS 66539-9467

RUECKER, MARTHA ENGELS, retired special education educator; b. South Gate, Calif., Sept. 22, 1931; d. Eugene and Minna (Wilhelm) Engels; m. Geert Frank Ruecker, Aug. 10, 1959 (div. 1964); 1 child, Ann. MusB, U. So. Calif., 1954, Calif. tchr. credential, 1955. Tchr. educationally handicapped Downey (Calif.) Unified Schs., 1964-92. Recipient award for work with mentally gifted Johns Hopkins U., 1992; South Gate Kiwanis scholar U. So. Calif., 1949-54. Mem. NEA (life), Los Angeles County Art Mus. Republican. Methodist. Avocations: interior design, gardening, music, travel. Home: PO Box 630 Downey CA 90241-0630

RUECKERT, FREDERIC, plastic surgeon; b. Boston, Oct. 24, 1921; s. Frederic and Elizabeth (Howe) R.; m. Joan Dodge, May 31, 1947; children: Nancy Lee, Patricia, William Dodge, Carolyn. AB, Hamilton Coll., 1945; MD, Columbia U., 1947. Diplomate Am. Bd. Plastic Surgery, Nat. Bd. Med. Examiners; lic. physician, N.Y., N.H. Intern internal medicine Bellevue Hosp., N.Y.C., 1947-48; resident gen. surgery Am. U. Hosp., Beirut, 1948-50; fellow surg. pathology Columbia-Presbyn. Hosp., N.Y.C., 1950-51; resident gen. surgery Dartmouth-Hitchcock Med. Ctr., Hanover, N.H., 1953-54, staff surgeon, 1956-86; resident plastic surgery, teaching fellow plastic surgery U. Pitts. Med. Ctr., 1954-56; mem. faculty Dartmouth Med. Sch., Hanover, 1956—, prof. plastic surgery, 1974-86, prof. plastic surgery emeritus, 1986—; cons. VA Hosp., White River Junction, Vt., 1956—. Contbr. articles to profl. jours., chpts. to books. Mem. Sch. Bd. Edn., Hanover, N.H., 1964-67; bd. trustees Northfield (Mass.) Mt. Hermon Sch., 1969-71, 80-90. Capt. USAF, 1951-53. Recipient Lamplighter award Northfield Mt. Herman Sch., 1991. Mem. AMA, ACS, Am. Assn. Plastic Surgeons, Am. Assn. Med. Colls., Am. Soc. Plastic and Reconstructive Surgeons (bd. dirs. 1980-83, 84-86), Plastic Surgery Ednl. Found. (pres. 1985-86), Plastic Surgeons Assn. Am. (pres. 1984-85), Internat. Confederation Plastic, Reconstructive and Aesthetic Surgeons, Am. Soc. Aesthetic Plastic Surgeons, New Eng. Surg. Soc., Northeastern Soc. Plastic Surgeons, New Eng. Soc. Plastic and Reconstructive Surgeons (pres. 1969-71), N.H. State Med. Soc., Grafton County Med. Soc. (pres. 1974-75), Univ. Club (N.Y.C.). Republican. Presbyterian. Avocations: swimming, tennis, skiing, photography, wood carving. Home: 18 Berrill Farms Ln Hanover NH 03755-3213

RUECKERT, ROLAND RUDYARD, virologist, educator; b. Rhinelander, Wis., Nov. 24, 1931; s. George Leonard and Monica Amelia (Seiberlich) R.; m. Ruth Helen Ullrich, Sept. 5, 1959; 1 child, Wanda Lynne. BS in Chemistry, U. Wis., 1953, PhD in Oncology, 1960. Fellow Max Planck Inst. for Biochemistry, Munich, 1960-61, Tübingen, Fed. Republic Germany, 1961-62; asst. rsch. virologist virus lab. U. Calif., Berkeley, 1962-65; asst. prof. biophysics lab. U. Wis., Madison, 1965-69; assoc. prof. biophysics lab. U. Wis., 1969-73; prof. Inst. for Molecular Virology, Madison, 1973-85; dist. rsch. prof. Inst. for Molecular Virology, 1985—. Mem. virology study sect. NIH, Bethesda, Md., 1981-85; pres. Am. Soc. Virology, 1989-90. With U.S. Army, 1953-55. Recipient William D. Stovall award U. Wis., 1953, Marie Christine Kohler award U. Wis., 1959, Rsch. Career Devel. award, 1966, Faculty rsch. award Am. Cancer Soc., 1972; named Hilldale Disting. prof. 1988. Achievements include research in dodecahedral model for picornavirus structure and assembly, molecular biology of picornaviruses (polio 8 common cold), structure 8 biology of small insect viruses, mechanism of neutralization by antibodies and antivirals. Home: 2234 W Lawn Ave Madison WI 53711-1952 Office: U Wis Inst Molecular Biology 1525 Linden Dr Madison WI 53706-1534

RUECKERT, RONALD FRANK, engineering executive; b. Shawano, Wis., Aug. 19, 1947; s. Frank William and Meta Marie (Karstedt) R.; m. Annette Marion Mulay; children: Douglas, Stacy, Nicholas, Amanda. BSEE, Devry Inst. Tech., 1967. Calibration technician Lockheed Missiles & Space Co., Sunnyvale, Calif., 1967-70; sr. test technician Burroughs Bus. Machines, Mission Niejo, Calif., 1970-71; sr. technician Telex Direct Access Divsn., Santa Clara, Calif., 1971-73; staff engr. Storage Tech., Louisville, Colo., 1973-76, Memorex, Santa Clara, 1976-78; program mgr. Priam, Inc., San Jose, Calif., 1978-82, Seagate Tech., Scotts Valley, Calif., 1991-93, Mini Scribe, Longmont, Colo., 1982-91; dir. engring. Maxtor, Longmont, Colo., 1993—. Avocations: skiing, fishing, woodworking, electronics tinkering. Home: 2621 Danbury Dr Longmont CO 80503

RUEDENBERG, KLAUS, theoretical chemist, educator; b. Bielefeld, Germany, Aug. 25, 1920; came to U.S., 1948, naturalized, 1955; s. Otto and Meta (Wertheimer) R.; m. Veronika Kutter, Apr. 8, 1948; children: Lucia Meta, Ursula Hedwig, Annette Veronika, Emanuel Klaus. Student, Montana Coll., Zugerberg, Switzerland, 1938-39; licence es Scis., U. Fribourg, Switzerland, 1944; postgrad., U. Chgo., 1948-50; PhD, U. Zurich, Switzerland, 1950; PhD (hon.), U. Basel, Switzerland, 1975, U. Bielefeld, Germany, 1991, U. Siegen, Germany, 1994. Research assoc. physics U. Chgo., 1950-55; asst. prof. chemistry, physics Iowa State U., Ames, 1955-60; assoc. prof. Iowa State U., 1960-62, prof., 1964-78, disting. prof. in sci. and humanities, 1978-91, disting. prof. emeritus, 1991—, sr. chemist Ames Lab., U.S. Dept. Energy, 1964-91, assoc., 1991—; prof. chemistry Johns Hopkins, Balt., 1962-64; vis. prof. U. Naples, Italy, 1961, Fed. Inst. Tech., Zurich, 1966-67, Wash State U. at Pullman, 1970, U. Calif. at Santa Cruz, 1973, U. Bonn (Germany), 1974, Monash U. and CSIRO, Clayton, Victoria, Australia, 1982, U. Kaiserlautern, Germany, 1987; lectr. univs., rsch. instns. and sci. symposia, 1953—. Author articles in field; assoc. editor: Jour. Chem. Physics, 1964-67, Internat. Jour. Quantum Chemistry; Chem. Physics Letters, 1967-81, Lecture Notes in Chemistry, 1976—, Advances in Quantum Chemistry, 1987—; editor-in-chief Theoretica Chimica Acta, 1985-97; hon. editor Theoretical Chemistry Accounts, 1997—. Co-founder Octagon Center for the Arts, Ames, 1966, treas., 1966-71, also bd. dirs. Guggenheim fellow, 1966-67; Fulbright sr. scholar, 1982. Fellow AAAS, Am. Phys. Soc., Am. Inst. Chemists, Internat. Acad. for Quantum Molecular Scis.; mem. AAUP, Am. Chem. Soc. (Midwest award 1982), Sigma Xi, Phi Lambda Upsilon. Home: 2834 Ross Rd Ames IA 50014-4030 Office: Dept Chemistry Iowa State Univ Ames IA 50011

RUEGER, LAUREN JOHN, retired physicist, consultant; b. Archbold, Ohio, Dec. 30, 1921; s. Edwin Z. and Hazel Lulu (Fisher) R.; m. Florence Marian Scott, July 30, 1944; children: Carol, Beth, Lauren A., Mary. BS in Engring. Physics, Ohio State U., 1943, MS in Physics, 1947. Advanced tech. planner Johns Hopkins U. Applied Physics Lab., Laurel, Md., 1953-88; project leader Nat. Bur. Standards, Washington, 1948-52; research assoc. Battelle Meml. Inst., Columbus, Ohio, 1946-48; staff MIT Radiation Lab., 1943-45; U.S. del. Internat. Radio Cons. Com., Geneva, 1978, 80, 81, 83, 85, 88; tech. program com. Frequency Control Symposium, Phila., 1976-78, 84-88; com. co-chmn. Internat. Time and Frequency Symposium, Helsinki, Finland, 1978; exec. com. Conf. on Precision Electromagnetic Measurements, Delft, Holland, 1984, Braunschweig, Fed. Republic of Germany, 1980, Tsukuba, Japan, 1988; cons. in precision frequency measurements Rueger Enterprises, Silver Spring, Md., 1989—. Patentee in field. Fellow IEEE; mem. Am. Phys. Soc., Photog. Soc. Am. Avocation: photography. Home: 1415 Glenallan Ave Silver Spring MD 20902-1360

RUEGG, DONALD GEORGE, retired railway company executive; b. LaJunta, Colo., Sept. 11, 1924; s. George Albert and Cecilia Corrine (Decker) R.; m. Ruth Carson, June 27, 1946 (dec. 1963); m. Mary Ann Eichelberger, June 24, 1964. B.A., Dartmouth Coll., 1947; M.B.A., U. Chgo., 1972. Stenographer Atchison, Topeka & Santa Fe Ry. Co., Pueblo, Colo., 1942-51; supr., trainmaster Atchison, Topeka & Santa Fe Ry. Co., various locations, 1951-68; asst. to v.p. info. systems Atchison, Topeka & Santa Fe Ry. Co., Topeka, 1968-69; asst. to v.p. ops. Atchison Topeka & Santa Fe Ry. Co., Chgo., 1969-72; gen. mgr. Atchison Topeka & Santa Fe Ry. Co., Los Angeles, 1972-73; asst. v.p. ops. Atchison, Topeka & Santa Fe Ry. Co., Chgo., 1973-78, v.p. ops., 1978-83, exec. v.p., 1983-86. Served with USN, 1943-46. Republican. Roman Catholic.

RUEGGER, PHILIP T., III, lawyer; b. Plainfield, N.J., Oct. 14, 1949; s. Philip T. Jr. and Gloria Marie (McLaughlin) R.; m. Rebecca Lee Huffman, Aug. 3, 1974; children: Sarah, Britt, Michael. AB, Dartmouth Coll., 1971; JD, U. Va., 1974. Bar: N.Y. 1975. Assoc. Simpson Thacher & Bartlett, N.Y.C., 1974-81, ptnr., 1981—. Chmn. Rye Edn. Fund, Inc. Mem. Assn. of Bar City N.Y., Phi Beta Kappa. Clubs: Manursing Island (Rye, N.Y.), Apawamis (Rye). Avocation: sports. Home: 275 Grace Church St Rye NY 10580-4201 Office: Simpson Thacher & Bartlett 425 Lexington Ave New York NY 10017-3903

RUEHL, MERCEDES, actress; b. Queens, N.Y.. BA in English, Coll. of New Rochelle; studied acting with Uta Hagen, Tad Danielewski. Appearances include (theatre) Vanities, 1977-78, Billy Irish, 1980, Much Ado About Nothing, Misalliance, Androcles and the Lion, Tartuffe, Medea, 1980-82, Three Sisters, 1982-83, The Day They Shot John Lennon, 1982-83, Flirtation, 1983, June Moon, 1983-84, Monday After the Miracle, 1983-84, Coming of Age in Soho, 1985, The Marriage of Bette and Boo, 1985, I'm Not Rappaport, 1985 (Obie Award), American Notes, 1988, Other People's Money, 1989, Lost in Yonkers, 1991 (Tony award, 1991, Drama Desk award, 1991, Outer Critics Circle award 1991), The Shadow Box, 1994 (Tony nominee - Featured Actress in a Play, 1995), The Rose Tattoo, 1995, (film) The Warriors, 1979, Four Friends, 1981, Heartburn, 1986, 84 Charing Cross Road, 1987, Leader of the Band, 1987, The Secret of My Success, 1987, Radio Days, 1987, Big, 1988, Married to the Mob, 1988, Slaves of New York, 1989, Crazy People, 1990, Another You, 1991, The Fisher King, 1991 (Academy award Best Supporting Actress 1991), Lost in Yonkers, 1993, Last Action Hero, 1993, Roseanna's Grave, 1996, (TV movie) Indictment: The McMartin Trial, 1995, (TV series) Frazier, 1996. Recipient Nat. Film Critics Circle award, 1988, Clarence Derwent award, 1989.

RUEHLE, DIANNE MARIE, retired elementary education educator; b. Detroit, Aug. 14, 1943; d. Richard Francis and Luella Mary (Kopp) R. BS, Ea. Mich. U., 1966, MA, 1971, adminstrv. cert., 1990, renewed adminstrv. cert., 1995. Cert. tchr., adminstr., Mich. Tchr. Cherry Hill Sch. Dist., Inkster, Mich., 1966-85; tchr. elem. sch. Wayne-Westland (Mich.) Community Schs., 1985-95; dist. com. Pub. Act 25 for State of Mich., Westland, 1990-93, chair bldg., 1991-95. Improvement Instrn. grantee Wayne Westland Found., 1992-94. Mem. ASCD, NEA, Mich. Edn. Assn. Avocations: reading, golf, photography, travel. Home: 3935 County Rd 612 Lewiston MI 49756

RUELLAN, ANDREE, artist; b. N.Y.C., Apr. 6, 1905; d. André and Louise (Lambert) R.; m. John W. Taylor, May 28, 1929. Student, Art Students League, 1920-22; art schs., France and Italy. guest instr. Pa. State Coll., summer 1957. One-man shows include Paris, 1925, Weyhe Galleries, N.Y.C., 1928, 31, Maynard Walker Galleries, 1937, 40, Kraushaar Galleries, 1945, 52, 56, 63, 80-81, Phila. Art Alliance, 1955, S.I. Mus., 1958, nat. exhbns., Carnegie Inst., Whitney Mus., Art Inst. Chgo., Corcoran Gallery, Internat. Expn., San Francisco, Artists for Victory Exhbn., N.Y.C., other cities U.S.; retrospective exhbns., Storm King Art Ctr., Mountainville, N.Y., 1966, Lehigh U., 1965, Woodstock Artists Assn., 1977, Ga. Mus. of Art, 1993, Hyde Collection, Glens Falls, N.Y., 1993, Gibbs Mus of Art, Charleston, S.C., 1993, Prints Gallery at Parkbest, Kingston, N.Y., 1995; drawing retrospective Kaushaar Galleries, 1990, 93, Ga. Mus. Art, Athens, 1993, The Hyde Collection, Glen Falls, N.Y., 1993, Gibbs Mus. Art, Charleston, S.C., 1993, Butler Inst., 1996, Grolier Club, 1996-97; executed murals in Emporia, Va., Lawrenceville, Ga.; represented in permanent collections at Met. Mus. Art, Whitney Mus. Am. Art, N.Y.C., Fogg Mus., Harvard U., Phila. Mus., Storm King Art Ctr., William Rockhill Nelson Mus., Kansas City, Mo., Duncan Phillips Gallery, Washington, Springfield Mus., Norton Gallery, Art Mus., New Britain, Conn., Libr. of Congress, Ency. Brit., IBM Collections, Art Inst., Zanesville, Ohio, U. Ga., S.I. Mus., Butler Inst., Pa. State U., Lehigh U., Columbia (S.C.) Mus. Art, The Whatcom Mus., Washington, Springville (Utah) Mus. Art, S.C. State Mus., Wichita Art Mus., drawing retrospective Butler Inst. Am. Art, 1996; also numerous pvt. collections. Recipient 3d prize for painting Charleston Worcester Mus. Biennial, Jan. 1938; 1,000 grant in arts Am. Acad. and Inst. Arts and Letters, 1945; Pennell medal Pa. Acad., 1945; medal of Honor and purchase Pepsi-Cola Paintings of Year, 1948; Dawson Meml. medal Pa. Acad., 1950; Purchase award N.Y. State Fair, 1951; Drawing award Ball State Tchrs. Coll.; Guggenheim fellow, 1950-51; recipient Kuniyoshi award, 1994. Mem. Woodstock Artists Assn. (Sally Jacobs award 1981), Art Students League (life), Nat. Mus. Women in Arts. Home: RR 2 Box 154 Shady NY 12409-9510

RUEPPEL, MELVIN LESLIE, environmental research director and educator; b. Rolla, Mo., Sept. 18, 1945; married; three children. BS, U. Mo., 1966; PhD in Chemistry, U. Calif., Berkeley, 1970. NIH fellow biochemistry Cornell U., Ithaca, N.Y., 1970-71; sr. rsch. chemist metab. Monsanto Co., 1971-75, group leader, 1975-77, rsch. mgr. environ. process, 1977-80, rsch. dir. synthesis, 1980-82, rsch. dir. process technology, 1982-85, tech. adv. patent litigation, 1982-86, dir. plant protection, 1985-86, dir. herbicide technology, 1986-89, dir. global product devel., 1989-90, dir. technology Roundup Divsn., 1991-93; dir. Ctr. Environ. Sci. and Technology & Lab. Trace Subs. U. Mo., Rolla, 1993—; prin. Rueppel Consulting, 1993—. Mem. AAAS, Am. Chem. Soc., Am. Mgmt. Assn., Weed Sci. Soc., Internat. Union Pure and Applied Chemicals, Sigma Xi. Office: U of Missouri Rolla 1870 Miner Cir Rolla MO 65409-0001 Office: 1904 Grassy Ridge Rd Saint Louis MO 63122-3539*

RUESCHEMEYER, DIETRICH, sociology educator; b. Berlin, Aug. 28, 1930; came to U.S., 1966; s. Philipp and Eufemia (Ross) R.; m. Marilyn R. Schattner, June 14, 1962; children: Julia Yael, Simone Margalit. Degree, U. Cologne, 1953, PhD in Sociology, 1958; postgrad., Columbia U., U. Chgo., U. Calif. Berkeley, 1960-61. Postdoctoral fellow Rockefeller Found., 1960-61; asst. prof. Dartmouth Coll., Hanover, N.H., 1962-63; from asst. prof. to assoc. prof. U. Toronto, 1963-66; assoc. prof. Brown U., Providence, R.I., 1966-71, prof. sociology, 1971—, Asa Messer Prof., 1995—; vis. assoc. prof. Hebrew U. of Jerusalem, 1969, vis. fellow, 1990; dir. Ctr. Comparative Study of Devel., Brown U., 1989—; mem. selection com. Berlin program for Advanced German and European Studies, 1986-91; mem. rsch. planning com. on states and social structures Social Sci. Rsch. Coun., N.Y., 1983-90, now Working Group on States and Social Structures, Russell Sage Found., 1990—; acad. vis. Nuffield Coll., Oxford, 1979, Wolfson Coll., Oxford, 1982. Author: Lawyers and Their Society, 1973, German edit., 1976, Power and the Division of Labour, 1986, (with others) Capitalist Development and Democracy (Outstanding Book award Am. Sociological Assn. 1991-92); editor, co-editor: Das Interview: Formen, Technik, Auswertung, 2d edit., 1957, Beitrage zur soziologischen Theorie, 1964, Bringing the State Back In, 1985, States Vs. Markets in the World System, 1985, State and Market in Development: Synergy or Rivalry?, 1992, States, Social Knowledge, and the Origins of Modern Social Policies; cons. editor Am. Jour. Sociology, 1977-79, Geschichte und Gesellschaft: Zeitschrift fuer historische Sozialwissenschaft, 1975—; assoc. editor Sociological Forum, 1985-92; mem. editorial bd. Am. Bar Found. Rsch. Jour., 1987, now Law and Social Inquiry, 1991-94, Sociological Theory, 1980-83; editor Working Papers on Comparative Development, 1983—; contbr. articles to profl. jours., book chpts.; presenter papers in field; speaker in field. Rsch. fellow Can. Coun., 1966; Faculty fellow Ford Found., 1968-69; Inst. Advanced Study Berlin fellow, 1987-88, Swedish Collegium for Advanced Study in the Social Scis. fellow Uppsala, 1992; recipient Torgny T. Segerstedt Professorship of Swedish Coun. for Studies in Higher Edn., 1992, Fgn. Franqui Chair of Belgium Free U. Brussels, 1987. Mem. Am. Sociol. Assn., Internat. Sociol. Assn., Am. Polit. Sci. Assn. Home: 60 Oriole Ave Providence RI 02906-5528 Office: Brown U Dept Sociology 79 Waterman St Providence RI 02912-9079

RUESINK, ALBERT WILLIAM, biologist, plant sciences educator; b. Adrian, Mich., Apr. 16, 1940; s. Lloyd William and Alberta May (Foltz) R.; m. Kathleen Joy Cramer, June 8, 1963; children: Jennifer Li, Adriana Eleanor. B.A., U. Mich., 1962; M.A., Harvard U., 1965, Ph.D., 1966. Postdoctoral fellow Swiss Fed. Inst. Tech., Zurich, 1966-67; prof. biology Ind. U., Bloomington, 1967—. Recipient Amoco Teaching award Ind. U., 1980. Mem. AAUP (pres. chpt. 1978-79, 90-91), Am. Soc. Plant Physiologists, Bot. Soc. Am. Democrat. Mem. United Ch. of Christ. Home: 2605 E 5th St Bloomington IN 47408-4286 Office: Ind U Dept Biology Bloomington IN 47405

RUFA, ROBERT HENRY, writer, editor, photographer, artist; b. Bklyn., Jan. 11, 1943; s. Joseph Simon and Alma (Weinbrecht) R.; m. Barbara LeeJohnson, June 25, 1971 (div. Oct. 1980); 1 child, Eric; m. Donnita Butler Dicus, June 27, 1990 (div. Aug. 1994). Grad. high sch. Tech. editor Tele-Signal Corp., Woodbury, N.Y., 1968; assoc. editor Tobacco Leaf mag., Rockville Centre, N.Y., 1969; mem. staff Travel mag., Floral Park, N.Y., 1969-76; mng. editor Travel mag., 1973-74, editor, 1975-76; artist, writer, photographer, 1976—; mng. editor The Pinehurst Outlook, 1977-78, 88; columnist Moore County Citizen News-Record, 1987-88; columnist The Pilot, 1988—, feature writer, 1990-93; feature writer Stringer News and Observer, Raleigh, 1990-91; dir. publs. Asheville-Buncombe Discovery, Asheville, N.C., 1991-92; arts & features editor Green Line/Mountain Xpress, Asheville, N.C., 1992-95. With USAF, 1961-65. Home: 59 Watauga St Apt 8 Asheville NC 28801-1048

RUFEH, FIROOZ, high technology company executive; b. Isfahan, Iran, Feb. 15, 1937; s. Eberhim and Marian R. Rufeh; m. Heide Marie Haseruck, June 12, 1965; children: Bejan Renard, Jiela Mariam. BS in Chemistry, Cornell U., 1959; MS in Nuclear Engring., U. Calif., Berkeley, 1963. Rsch. scientist Thermo Electron Corp., Waltham, Mass., 1963-67, mgr. rsch. dept., 1967-75, dir. energy conservation and rsch., 1975-79, pres. R & D, new bus. div., 1979-84, group exec., 1984-86, v.p., 1986—; CEO, pres., bd. dirs. Thermotrex Corp., San Diego, 1995—; bd. dirs. Thermo Lase Corp., Thermo Trex Med. Corp., Inc. Office: Thermo Trex Corp 10455 Pacific Center Ct San Diego CA 92121-4339

RUFENACHT, ROGER ALLEN, accounting educator; b. Waldron, Mich., Dec. 17, 1933; s. Alphus Leroy and Frieda (Aschliman) R.; m. Carol Carnahan, June 13, 1965; children: Jeffrey, Jonathan. BS, Mich. State U., 1959, MS, 1965. Cert. tchr., Fla. Tchr. Madison High Sch., Adrian, Mich., 1959-61; bus. edn. instr. Charlotte High Sch., Rochester, N.Y., 1961-62; bus. edn. instr. Edgewater High Sch., Orlando, Fla., 1962-68, chmn. bus. dept., 1965-68; instr. in acctg. Orlando Vo Tech. Ctr. (formerly Orlando Vocat. Sch.), 1968-94, chmn. bus. dept., 1980-85; ret., 1994. Bd. dirs., v.p. Winter Park Jaycees, 1963-68; asst. coach, scorekeeper N.W. Little League; chmn. adv. com. local PTA, 1973-83; pres. Bandboosters 1985-86; cub scout den leader, com. chmn., mem. dist. com., mem. coms. Boy Scouts Am.; adminstrv. bd. local Meth. Ch., 1965—. Recipient Scouters Tng. award, Fifteen Yr. Vet. award Boy Scouts Am., 1996. Mem. NEA, Am. Vocat. Assn., Fla. Vocat. Assn. (registration com. ann. conf., pres.'s reception planning com.), Orange County Classroom Tchrs. Assn. (bd. dirs., bldg. rep.), Orange County Credit Union (rep.), Orange County Vocat. Assn. (bd. dirs., Pres.'s award 1988-89, Outstanding Vocat. Educator Bus. Edn. award 1988-89), Fla. Bus. Edn. Assn. (chmn., mem. various coms.), Orange County Bus. Edn. Assn. (pres. 1968, 76, chmn., mem. various coms.). Republican. Avocations: reading, gardening, golf, swimming. Home: 9510 Bear Lake Rd Apopka FL 32703-1917

RUFF, LORRAINE MARIE, public relations executive; b. Washington, Feb. 13, 1947; d. William Stanley and Jeanne Ann (Murray) Charlton; m. R. Eugene Ruff, July 17, 1968; 1 child, David Michael. BS in Liberal Arts, Oreg. State U., 1976. Reporter The Oregonian, Corvallis, Oreg., 1976-79, Union-Bull., Walla Walla, Wash., 1979-80; dir. pub. rels. Strategic Mktg., Corvallis, 1980-82; gen. mgr. Campaigns Northwest, Corvallis, 1982-84; account supr. Arthur D. Little, Inc., Cambridge, Mass., 1985-87, mgr. corp. ID, 1988-89; dir. biotechnology New Eng. Hill and Knowlton, Waltham, Mass., 1989, v.p., dir. biotechnology, 1990, sr. v.p., mng. dir. internat. biotechnology practice, 1990-91, sr. v.p., gen. mgr., 1991-93; sr. v.p., mng. dir. divsn. biosci. comm. Stoorza, Ziegaus & Metzger, San Diego, 1993-94, dir. life scis. practice, 1993-94; owner Charlton Ruff Comm., Puyallup, Wash., 1994—; founder Chronos Molecular Sys., Vancouver, B.C., Can., 1996—; owner, founder Milestones-The Critical Thinking Co., Seattle, 1997—; mem. bd. dirs. Coll. Liberal Arts Devel. Coun., Oreg. State U. Bd. dirs. Wash. State Biotech. & Biomed Assn., Oreg. State U. Coll. Liberal Arts Devel.

Coun. Mem. Pub. Rels. Soc. Am., Nat. Investor Rels. Inst., Oreg. Biotech. Assn., Wash. State Biotech. and Biomed. Assn. (bd. dirs.), B.C. Biotech. Alliance, Coll. Club Seattle, Rotary (univ. dist. chpt.). Republican. Avocations: collecting antique ivories, international cuisine, gardening, writing. Office: Milestones 12124 138th Ave E Puyallup WA 98374-4536

RUFF, ROBERT LOUIS, neurologist, physiology researcher; b. Bklyn., Dec. 16, 1950; s. John Joseph and Rhoda (Alpert) R.; m. Louise Seymour Acheson, Apr. 26, 1980. BS summa cum laude, Cooper Union, 1971; MD summa cum laude, U. Wash., 1976, PhD in Physiology, 1976. Diplomate Am. Bd. Neurology and Psychiatry. Asst. neurologist N.Y. Hosp., Cornell Med. Sch., N.Y.C., 1977-80; asst. prof. physiology and medicine U. Wash., Seattle, 1980-84; assoc. prof. neurology Case Western Res. Med. Sch., Cleve., 1984-92, prof. neurology and neuroscis., 1993—, residency dir., neurology dept., 1994—, vice chair neurology dept., 1995—; chief dept. neurology Cleve. VA Med. Ctr., 1984—; adv. Child Devel. and Mental Retardation Ctr., Seattle, 1980-84, Burien Devel. Disability Ctr., Wash., 1982-84; mem. med. adv. bd. Muscular Dystrophy Assn., Seattle, 1984, NE Ohio chpt. Multiple Sclerosis Soc., 1986—; mem. adv. bd. for Neurology Dept. Vets. Affairs, 1989—; chmn. med. adv. bd. N.E. Ohio chpt. Myasthenia Gravis Found., 1987—, bd. trustees, 1993—, nat. med. adv. bd., 1988—, grant and fellowship com., 1990—. Assoc. editor: Neurology, 1994-96; ad hoc reviewer various profl. and sci. jours.; mem. editl. bd. Neurology, 1996—; contbr. articles to profl. jours. and chpts. to books. Nat. bd. dirs. Myasthenia Gravis Found., 1994—. Recipient Tchr. Investigator award NIH; NSF fellow, 1971; NIH grantee, Muscular Dystrophy Assn. grantee, Dept. Vets. Affair grantee; N.Y. State Regents med. scholar, 1971. Fellow Am. Heart Assn. (stroke coun.), Am. Acad. Neurology (scientific issues com., legis. action com.); mem. AMA, Am. Physics Soc., Neurosci. Soc., Biophys. Soc., Am. Neurol. Assn., N.Y. Acad. Sci., Am. Geriatrics Soc., Sigma Pi Sigma (v.p. 1970-71), Alpha Omega Alpha (v.p. 1975-76). Home: 2572 Stratford Rd Cleveland OH 44118-4063 Office: VA Med Ctr 10701 East Blvd Ste 127W Cleveland OH 44106-1702

RUFFER, DAVID GRAY, museum director, former college president; b. Archbold, Ohio, Aug. 25, 1937; s. Lawrence A. and Florence A. (Newcomer) R.; m. Marilyn Elaine Taylor, Aug. 23, 1958; children: Rochelle Lynne, Robyn Lynne, David Geoffrey. B.S., Defiance Coll., 1959; M.A., Bowling Green State U., 1960; Ph.D., U. Okla., 1964. Spl. instr. U. Okla., 1963-64; asst. prof. biology Defiance Coll., 1964-68, asso. prof., 1968-73, faculty dean, 1969-73; provost Elmira (N.Y.) Coll., 1973-78; pres. Albright Coll., Reading, Pa., 1978-91, U. Tampa, Fla., 1991-94; exec. dir. Dayton (Ohio) Soc. Natural History, 1995—. Author: Exploring and Understanding Mammals, 1971; contbr. articles to profl. jours. NSF grantee, 1965, 67; Ohio Biol. Survey grantee, 1968-69. Fellow AAAS; mem. Am. Assn. Higher Edn., Animal Behavior Soc., Am. Soc. Mammalogists, Sigma Xi. Methodist. Club: Rotary. Home: 3700 Wales Dr Dayton OH 45405-1847 Office: Dayton Mus Natural History 2600 Deweese Pkwy Dayton OH 45414-5400

RUFFING, ANNE ELIZABETH, artist; b. Bklyn.; d. John Paul and Ruth Elizabeth (Price) Frampton; m. George W. Ruffing, Mar. 29, 1967; 1 dau., Elizabeth Anne. B.S., Cornell U., 1964; postgrad., Drexel Inst. Tech., 1966. One-woman exhbns. include, IBM, 1966, Hall of Fame, Goshen, N.Y., 1971, group exhbns. include, Internat. Women's Arts Festival, World Trade Center, N.Y.C., 1975-76, Berkshire Mus., Pittsfield, Mass., 1965, 76, Cooperstown (N.Y.) Mus., 1969; represented in permanent collections, Met. Mus. Art, Bklyn. Mus., Library of Congress, Harvard U., Smithsonian Instn., N.Y. Hist. Soc. Johnston Hist. Mus., Atwater Kent Mus., Albany Inst. History and Art, Whitney Mus. Am. Art, Boston Public Library. Recipient 1st place Eric Sloane award, 1974; Internat. Women's Year award Internat. Women's Art Festival, 1976. Address: PO Box 125 Bloomington NY 12411-0125

RUFFNER, CHARLES LOUIS, lawyer; b. Cin., Nov. 7, 1936; s. Joseph H. and Edith (Solomon) R.; m. Mary Ann Kaufman, Jan. 30, 1966 (div. 1993); children: Robin Sue, David Robert; m. Nanette Diemer, Feb. 26, 1995. BSBA in Acctg., U. Fla., 1958; JD cum laude, U. Miami, 1964. Bar: Fla. 1964, U.S. Dist. Ct. (so. and mid. dists.) Fla. 1964, U.S. Ct. Appeals (5th cir.) 1964, U.S. Ct. Appeals (11th cir.) 1984, U.S. Claims Ct. 1966, U.S. Tax Ct. 1966, U.S. Supreme Ct. 1968. Cert. in taxation. Trial atty. tax div. Dept. Justice, Washington, 1964-67; pres. Forrest, Ruffner, Traum & Hagen, P.A., Miami, Fla., 1967-78; pres. Ruffner, Hagen & Rifkin, P.A., Miami, 1978-81; tax ptnr. Myers, Kenin, Levinson, Ruffner, Frank & Richards, Miami, 1982-84; pres. Charles L. Ruffner, P.A., 1984—; lectr. Fla. Internat. U., Miami. Author: A Practical Approach to Professional Corporations and Associations, 4 edits., 1970, (column) Tax Talk, Miami Law Rev.; editor: Miami Law Rev., 1963-64; contbr. numerous articles on taxation to law jours. Mem. ABA, Fed. Bar Assn., Fla. Bar (exec. council tax sect. 1967-92, 95—, amicus curiae in test case of validity profl. corps.), Dade County Bar Assn., South Fla. Tax Litigation Assn. (chmn. 1986—), Phi Alpha Delta, Phi Kappa Phi. Office: Courvoisier Centre II 601 Brickell Key Dr Ste 507 Miami FL 33131-2652

RUFFNER, FREDERICK G., JR., book publisher; b. Akron, Ohio, Aug. 6, 1926; s. Frederick G. and Olive Mae (Taylor) R.; m. Mary Ann Evans, Oct. 8, 1954; children: Frederic G. III, Peter Evans. B.S., Ohio State U., 1950. Advt. mgr. Jim Robbins Co., Royal Oak, Mich., 1950-52; research mgr. Gen. Detroit Corp., 1953-54; pres. Gale Research Co., Detroit, 1954-87, Omnigraphics, Inc., 1987—. Editor: Ency. of Assns, 1956-68, Code Names Dictionary, 1963, Acronyms and Initialisms Dictionary, 1965, Allusions Dictionary, 1985; pub. Gold Coast Mag., 1992—; patentee in field. Bd. dirs. Friends of Detroit Pub. Libr., pres., 1975-76; mem. exec. bd. Detroit coun. Boy Scouts Am., 1974—, v.p., 1976-82; pres. Coun. for Fla. Librs., 1979—; trustee Bon Secours Hosp., Grosse Pointe, Mich., 1980-81; v.p. Etruscan Found., Florence, Italy, 1980—; pres. Mich. Ctr. for the Book, 1990, Literary Landmarks Assn., Gold Coast Jazz Soc., Ft. Lauderdale, 1992—; bd. dirs. Ohio State U. Found., Bonnet House, Ft. Lauderdale, 1992. 1st lt. AUS, 1944-46. Decorated Bronze Star, Combat Inf. award; recipient Centennial award Ohio State U., 1970, Benjamin Creativity award Assn. Am. Pubs., 1985, Career medal Ohioana Libr. Assn., 1988, Lifetime Achievement award Am. Libr. Trustees Assn., 1992; named to Entrepreneurs Hall of Fame, Nova U. Mem. Am. Antiquarian Soc., ALA (hon. life), Am. Mgmt. Assn., Am. Assn. Mus., Detroit Hist. Soc., Am. Hist. Print Collectors Soc., Bibliog. Soc. Am., Sierra Club, Pres. Assn., Audubon Soc., Am. Name Soc., Early Am. Industries Assn., Ephemera Soc., Johnny Appleseed Soc., Navy League, Newcomen Soc., Cen. Bus. Dist. Assn. Detroit (vice-chmn. 1985-87), Jazz Forum (Grosse Pointe Farms, Mich., pres. 1989—), Nat. Trust Hist. Preservation, Fairfield Heritage Soc., Archives Am. Art, Pvt. Librs. Assn., Friend Ft. Lauderdale Pub. Libr. (pres. 1974-78), Phileas Soc. (pres. 1985—), Ohio State U. Club (pres. Detroit club 1958, nat. chmn. Ohio State U. campaighn, 1985-88), Masons, Shriners, Book Club, Detroit Athletic Club, Econ. Club, Prismatic Club (pres. 1990), Fontenada Soc. (pres. 1990-91), Detroit Club, Country Club Detroit, Ocean Reef Club, Grosse Pointe Yacht Club, Coral Ridge Yacht Club, Lauderdale Yacht Club, Princeton Club, Salmagundi Club, Grolier Club, Century Assn., Marco Polo Club, Faculty Club Ohio State U., Old Club, Tau Kappa Epsilon. Republican. Presbyterian. Home: 221 Lewiston Rd Grosse Pointe Farms MI 48236-3519 also: 1000 Flamingo Isle Dr Fort Lauderdale FL 33301-2670 Office: Omnigraphics Inc 2500 Penobscot Bldg Detroit MI 48226 also: 901 E Las Olas Blvd Fort Lauderdale FL 33301-2320

RUFFOLO, MARILYN CLAIRE, primary education educator; b. Harvey, Ill., Aug. 2, 1952; d. Carmen Anthony and Helen Elaine (Welch) R. AA with high honors, Thornton C.C., 1972; BS in Edn. with high honors, Ill. State U., 1974; MEd, Nat.-Louis U., 1990. Cert. K-9, Ill. Tchr. kindergarten Primary Acad. Ctr., Markham, Ill., 1976-91, tchr. K-3, 1991—. Ill. State scholar, 1969. Mem. Ill. Edn. Assn. (assn. rep. 1976-88), Kappa Delta Pi, Phi Theta Kappa. Republican. Avocations: music, travel. Home: 2522 183rd St Homewood IL 60430-3037 Office: Prairie-Hills Prim Acad Ctr 3055 W 163rd St Markham IL 60426-5626

RUFFOLO, PAUL GREGORY, police officer, educator; b. Chgo., Feb. 4, 1952; s. Dante William and Anne Marie (Paese) R.; m. Janet Louise Anderson, July 8, 1978; 1 child, Annemarie. BA, U. Ill., Chgo., 1973; grad. Traffic Inst., Northwestern U., 1986, postgrad., 1993; MA in Edn. and Human Resources Devel., U. Ill., 1994, doctoral studies, 1995—. Cert. tchr. and law enforcement officer, Ill. Singer, musician night club, Las Vegas, Nev., 1974; tchr. Chgo. Pub. Schs., 1976; officer Naperville (Ill.) Police Dept., 1978-86, sgt., 1986-94; comdr. Woodridge Police Dept., 1994-95; internat. lectr., police cons., 1995—; police instr. Chgo. City-Wide Colls., 1990—, Chgo. Police Acad., 1990—; lectr. Office Internat. Criminal Justice, Chgo., 1990—; talk show host Sta. WHBC-TV, Willowbrook, Ill., 1990—, Sta. WMRO, Aurora, Ill., 1990; team mem. Profl. Occult Response Team, Wheaton, Ill., 1990—; guest lectr., cons. South African Police Dept. Govt. South Africa, 1994; dir. Internat. Affairs; tng. specialist on gangs and counter-terrorism Ill. State Crime Commn. Columnist Chicagoland newspaper, 1990; contbr. articles to profl. publs. Mem. choir St. Michael's Ch., Orland Park, Ill., 1978—; prodr., dir. Summerfest Rock and Roll Show, Orland Park, 1984. Named Most Contbg. Speaker, Internat. Police Inst., Cologne, Germany, 1991; recipient Presdl. Comsn. award 1992. Mem. Internat. Assn. Chiefs Police, Internat. Police Assn., Ill. Police Assn., DuPage County Police Assn., Fraternal Order Police, Am. Fedn. Musicians, Am. Bartending Sch. Republican. Avocations: reading, music, teaching, debating, cars. Home: 7233 Oneill Rd Downers Grove IL 60516-3771

RUGABER, WALTER FEUCHT, JR., newspaper executive; b. Macon, Ga., Nov. 29, 1938; s. Walter Feucht and Edith Almeda (Maynard) R.; m. Sally Sanford, Oct. 6, 1962; children—Leslie, Christopher, Mark. B.S., Northwestern U., 1960. Corr., editor N.Y. Times, 1965-78; v.p., exec. editor Greensboro Daily News & Record, N.C., 1978-82; pres., pub. The Roanoke Times, Va., 1982—; pres. Landmark Pub. Group; mem. Pulitzer Prize Bd. Bd. dirs. United Way of Roanoke Valley, 1982-88, Roanoke Symphony Soc., 1985—, pres., 1986-88; trustee Hollins Coll. Mem. Am. Newspaper Pubs. Assn., Am. Soc. Newspaper Editors, So. Newspaper Pubs. Assn. Office: Times World Corp PO Box 2491 201-209 W Campbell Ave Roanoke VA 24010

RUGALA, KAREN FRANCIS (KAREN FRANCIS), television producer, painter; b. Memphis, Apr. 27, 1950; d. Ben Porter Francis and Marguerite K. Higginbotham; children: Sarah Helfinstein, Ben Helfinstein. BA in Communication Arts, Rhodes Coll., 1971; MA, U. Mo., 1973. Cert. tchr., Tenn. Secondary sch. tchr. Memphis City Schs., 1971-72; speech tchr. U. Ga., Athens, 1973-75; dir. computer systems installations Planning Rsch. Corp., McLean, Va., 1976-78; dir. account mgmt. TDX Systems, Cable & Wireless, Vienna, Va., 1978-80; cons. telecommunications MCI, Washington, 1985-87; producer Fairfax Cable Access, Merrifield, Va., 1991—; owner Art Promotions, McLean, 1989—. Exhibited paintings in numerous group and one-woman shows including Clark & Co. Gallery, Washington, 1994, McLean Project for Arts, 1992, Hospice of No. Va. Auction Gala, 1992, Capitol Hill Art League, Washington, 1995, Mus. Contemporary Art, Washington, 1996, many others; paintings represented in numerous pvt. collections. Active Family AIDS Housing Found., 1992, Hospice No. Va., 1991, 92, Friends of Vietnam Vets. Meml., 1992; founding bd. mem. Jobs for Homeless People, 1988-90. Avocations: tennis, bridge, skiing. Office: Art Promotions PO Box 3104 Mc Lean VA 22103-3104

RUGE, DANIEL AUGUST, retired neurosurgeon, educator; b. Murdock, Nebr., May 13, 1917; s. August Daniel and Mary Louise R.; m. Greta Piper, June 12, 1942; children: Charlotte, Thomas. B.A., N. Central Coll., Naperville, Ill., 1939, Sc.D., 1971; M.D., Northwestern U., 1945, Ph.D., 1961. Intern Wesley Meml. Hosp., Chgo., 1945-46; resident Wesley Meml. Hosp., 1949-50, Passavant Meml. Hosp., Chgo., 1946-49, VA Hosp., Hines, Ill., 1950-52; practice medicine specializing in neurosurgery Chgo., 1952-76; prof. surgery Northwestern U., Chgo., 1973-76; professorial lectr. George Washington U., Washington, 1976-86, ret., 1986; dep. dir. spinal cord injury service VA Central Office, Washington, 1976-80; dir. VA Central Office, 1980-81, 85-86, ret., 1986; physician to pres. U.S., White House, 1981-85. Author: Spinal Cord Injuries, 1969, Spinal Disorders: Diagnosis and Treatment, 1977; editor: Jour. Am. Paraplegia Soc., 1976-88. Trustee North Cen. Coll., 1960—, chmn. bd., 1974-77. Lt comdr. USN, 1954-56. Recipient Service award Northwestern U., 1966, Merit award Northwestern U., 1983; Outstanding Alumnus award N. Central Coll., 1978, Meritorious Service award VA, 1986. Fellow A.C.S.; mem. AMA, Am. Assn. Neurol. Surgeons, Central Surg. Assn., James IV Assn. Surgeons. Republican. Presbyterian. Home: 240 S High St Denver CO 80209-2628

RUGER, WILLIAM BATTERMAN, firearms manufacturing company executive; b. Bklyn., June 21, 1916; s. Adolph and May R.; m. Mary Thompson, Aug. 26, 1938 (dec.); children: William Batterman, Carolyn Amalie Ruger Vogel, James Thompson (dec.). Student, U. N.C. Firearms design engr. U.S. Armory, Springfield, Mass., 1939-40; machine gun designer Auto Ordnance Corp., Hartford, Conn., World War II; founder, pres. Ruger Corp. (hand tool mfrs.), Southport, Conn., 1946-48; co-founder, 1948; since pres., chmn. bd., treas. Sturm, Ruger & Co., Inc., Southport; v.p. Sporting Arms and Ammunition Inst., 1978—; past bd. dirs. Nat. Shooting Sports Found. Author, editor; patentee in field. Trustee Salisbury (Conn.) Sch., 1970-75, Naval War Coll. Found., Buffalo Bill Hist. Ctr. Recipient Nat. Leadership award Hunting Hall of Fame, 1979; named Handgunner of Year Am. Handgunner Found., 1975. Mem. NRA (past bd. dirs.), Blue Mountain Forest Assn., Vintage Sports Car Club Am., Auburn-Cord-Duesenberg, Rolls Royce Owners Club, Rolls Royce Silver Ghost Assn., Am. Bugatti Club, Bugatti Owners' Club, Vet. Motor Club, Stutz Club, Ferrari Club Am., Campfire Club, Pequot Yacht Club, N.Y. Yacht Club, Boone and Crockett Club, Cat Cay Club, Clambake Club, Delta Kappa Epsilon. Lutheran. Office: Sturm Ruger & Co Inc 411 Sunapee St Newport NH 03773-1490

RUGGE, HENRY FERDINAND, medical products executive; b. South San Francisco, Oct. 28, 1936; s. Hugo Heinrich and Marie Mathilde (Breiholz) R.; m. Sue Callow, Dec. 29, 1967. BS in Physics, U. Calif., Berkeley, 1958, PhD in Physics, 1963. Sr. physicist Physics Internat. Co., San Leandro, 1963-68; dir. adminstrn. and fin. Arkon Sci. Labs., Berkeley, Calif., 1969-71; v.p. Norse Systems, Inc., Hayward, Calif., 1972-74; v.p. Rasor Assocs., Inc., Sunnyvale, Calif., 1974-81, v.p., gen. mgr., 1983-87, exec. v.p. fin., 1988-89, pres., chief exec. officer, 1990—; chmn. UltraVision, Inc., Calgary, Alta., Can., 1993—, also bd. dirs., 1993—; pres., CEO Mission Med., Inc., Fremont, Calif., 1997—; pres. Berlinscan, Inc., Sunnyvale, 1981-82; cons. The Rugge Group, Berkeley, 1987-90; bd. dirs. Rasor Assocs., Inc., Space Power Inc., Analatom, Inc. Patentee in area med. devices. U. Calif. scholar, 1954-58. Mem. Am. Heart Assn., Berkeley Bicycle (treas. 1983-84), Phi Beta Kappa. Avocations: bicycle racing, wine, food. Home: 46 Hiller Dr Oakland CA 94618-2302 Office: Rasor Assocs Inc 5670 Stewart Ave Fremont CA 94538-3174

RUGGE, HUGO ROBERT, physicist; b. South San Francisco, Calif., Nov. 7, 1935; s. Hugo Heinrich and Marie (Breiholz) R.; m. Coral Loy Irish, Dec. 28, 1969; children—Leslie Anne, Robert David. A.B., U. Calif.-Berkeley, 1957, Ph.D., 1962. Research physicist Lawrence Berkeley Lab., 1961-62; mem. tech. staff Aerospace Corp., Los Angeles, 1962-68, dept. head, 1968-79, prin. dir., 1979-81, lab. dir., 1981-89, v.p. lab. ops., 1989-91, v.p. tech. ops., 1991—. mem. mission systems panel AGARD/NATO. Contbr. numerous articles on space sci. and astrophysics to profl. jours. Fellow Am. Phys. Soc.; mem. Am. Astron. Soc., Am. Geophys. Union, Internat. Astron. Union, Phi Beta Kappa, Sigma Xi.

RUGGIERO, LAURENCE JOSEPH, museum director; b. Paterson, N.J., Mar. 25, 1948; s. Salvatore Joseph and Grace Marie (Williams) R.; m. Virginia Frances Fornaci, Mar. 7, 1970; 1 child, John Laurence. BA, U. Pa., 1969, MA, 1979, PhD, 1975; MBA, Boston U., 1978. Asst. prof. history of architecture U. Ill., Chgo., 1973-77; fin. analyst Met. Mus. Art, N.Y.C., 1979-80, asst. to pres., 1980-81; exec. dir. Oakland (Calif.) Mus. Assocs., 1981-85; dir. John and Mable Ringling Mus., Sarasota, Fla., 1985-92; assoc. dir. Charles Hosmer Morse Mus. Am. Art, Winter Park, Fla., 1992—, dir., 1995—; adj. prof. Ringling Sch. Art and Design, Sarasota, 1986-92. Kress Found. fellow, 1971-73. Mem. Fla. Art Mus. Dirs. Assn. (treas. 1987-92), Coll. Art Assn. Am., Am. Assn. Mus., Il Cenacolo (San Francisco). Office: 445 Park Ave N Winter Park FL 32789-3212

RUGGIERO, MATTHEW JOHN, bassoonist; b. Phila., Sept. 18, 1932; s. Pompeo and Theresa (Ciampa) R.; m. Nancy Cirillo, Apr. 2, 1961; children: Eleanor, Claudia, Lisa. Diploma, Curtis Inst. Music, 1957; AA, Harvard U., 1982, BA cum laude, 1984, MA, 1987; PhD, Boston U., 1993. Second bassoonist Nat. Symphony Orch., Washington, 1957-60; asst. prin. bassoonist Boston Symphony Orch., 1961-89; prin. bassoonist Boston Pops Orch., 1974-89; ret., 1989; mem. faculty Boston U., 1963—, New Eng. Conservatory Music, 1963—. Served with U.S. Army, 1954-57. Boston U. Profs. Program scholar and fellow, 1989.

RUGGLES, BARBARA ANN, elementary education educator; b. Chgo., Mar. 19, 1943; d. Ernest Leonard and Nigel Marie Hvale; 1 child, David M. BS in Edn., Kans. U., 1965; MA in Social Scis., Gov.'s State U., 1984. Tchr. Sch. Dist. 163, Park Forest, Ill.; bd. dirs. Employee's Fed. Credit Union. Legis. Adv. Coun. State Ill. 80th House Dist. Mem. ASCD, Devel. Am. Women in Sci., Nat. Women's History Project, Intermediate Svc. Ctr. #4 (governing bd.), Am. Fedn. Tchrs. Local 604 (v.p.), Tchrs. Fedn. Park Forest (pres.), Am. Fedn. Tchrs. Edn. Rsch. and Dissemination (local site coord.). Home: 21426 Hillside Rd Frankfort IL 60423-9195

RUGGLES, RUDY LAMONT, JR., investment banker, consultant; b. Evanston, Ill., Nov. 11, 1938; s. Rudy Lamont and Ruth (Cain) R.; m. Cecelia Ann Consorte, July 20, 1974; children—Rudy, Christopher, Daniel, Andrew. B.A., Harvard U., 1960, M.B.A., 1966. Sr. assoc. physicist IBM Labs., Poughkeepsie, N.Y., 1960-64; corp. planning cons. corp. hdqrs. IBM, Armonk, N.Y., 1966-71; sr. mem. profl. staff Hudson Inst., Croton-on-Hudson, N.Y., 1971-75; pres. Hudson Inst., 1975-79, also dir.; prin. Cresap, McCormick & Paget, Inc., 1979-82; ptnr. The Phila. Mgmt. Cons. Group, Inc., 1982—; mng. dir. New China Group, Inc., 1982—. Chmn. residential solicitation United Fund, Pound Ridge, N.Y., 1969; mem. parents com. St. Paul's Sch., Concord, N.H.; dir. Danbury Hosp. and Danbury Hosp. Devel. Fund, Conn., 1978—, also mem. med. affairs com.; chmn. fin. com. Pound Ridge Community Ch., 1969-70; bd. dirs. Harry Frank Guggenheim Found., 1982—; bd. visitors Sch. Langs. and Linguistics Georgetown U.; trustee New Canaan Country Sch. With C.E., U.S. Army, 1962. Fellow Explorers Club; mem. Hudson Inst. (hon.), N. Am. Soc. Corp. Planning (dir. 1966-72), Sci. Rsch. Soc. Am. (hon.), Internat. Inst. Strategic Studies, Ends of the Earth (hon.), U.S.-China Bus. Coun., Harvard Club of N.Y.C., Silver Spring Country Club.

RUGH, WILLIAM ARTHUR, diplomat; b. N.Y.C., May 10, 1936; s. Roberts and Harriette (Sheldon) R.; m. Andrea Scott Bear, July 12, 1958; children—David William, Douglas Edward, Nicholas Alexander. Student, Hamburg U., Germany, 1958-59; B.A., Oberlin Coll., 1958; M.A., Johns Hopkins U., 1961; Ph.D., Columbia U., 1967. Near East policy dir. USIA, Washington, 1971-72, dep. asst. dir., 1973-76; pub. affairs counsellor U.S. Embassy, Cairo, 1976-81; dep. chief of mission U.S. Embassy, Damascus, Syria, 1981-84; amb. U.S. Embassy, Sanaa, Yemen, 1984-87; diplomat in residence Fletcher Sch. Tufts U., Medford, Mass., 1987-89; dir. Near East, North Africa, South Asia divs. USIA, Washington, 1989-92; U.S. amb. to United Arab Emirates, Abu Dhabi, 1992-95; pres. America-Mideast Edn. and Tng. Svcs., Inc., Washington, 1995—. Author: Riyadh, a History, 1969; The Arab Press; 1979, 87; also contbr. articles and chpts. to books. Coun. on Fgn. Rels. fellow, 1972-73; recipient Presdl. award U.S. Pres., 1983. Mem. Middle East Inst., Middle East Studies Assn. Office: Amideast 1730 M St NW Ste 1100 Washington DC 20036-4500*

RUHLMAN, HERMAN C(LOYD), JR., manufacturing company executive; b. Warren, Pa., Jan. 17, 1949; s. Herman Cloyd and Virginia Lee (Wimer) R.; B.S. in Indsl. Tech., California (Pa.) State Coll., 1974; divorced; children—Brian, Jason, Chad; m. Lorraine; stepchildren: Bethany, Michelle, Randy. Gen. mgr. Rand Machine Products, Inc., Falconer, N.Y., 1974-80, pres., chmn. bd. dirs., 1980—; pres. Spartan Tool Co., Gerry, N.Y., 1986—. Active local Boy Scouts Am. Served with USAF, 1968-72. Mem. Epsilon Pi Tau. Republican. Home: PO Box 284 15 Annis St Frewsburg NY 14738 Office: PO Box 72 Allen St Extension Falconer NY 14733

RUHLMAN, TERRELL LOUIS, business executive; b. Warren, Pa., Nov. 13, 1926; s. Ross L. and Gertrude R.; m. Phyllis E., Jan. 15, 1951; children: Robyn Ruhlman Dempsey, Randall L., Heather Ruhlman Martin, Mark A. BS, Pa. State U., 1949; JD, George Washington U., 1954; postgrad., Duquesne U. Grad. Bus. Sch., 1966-68. Bar: D.C. bar. Patent counsel Joy Mfg. Co., Pitts., 1954-59; gen. counsel Joy Mfg. Co., 1959-62, asst. to pres., 1962-69; v.p. oilfield ops. Joy Mfg. Co., Houston, 1969-73; gen. mgr. Reed Tool Co., Houston, 1973-74; pres., COO Reed Tool Co., 1974-76, dir., 1975-76; v.p., dir. Baker Internat. Corp., 1975-76, pres. mining group, 1976; pres., CEO, dir. Ansul Co., Marinette, Wis., 1976-80; pres. Wormald Americas, Inc., Scottsdale, Ariz., 1980-88; chmn., CEO Cade Industries, Inc., Scottsdale, 1988—, also bd. dirs.; chmn., bd. dirs. Environ. Engring. Concepts Inc. With USAF. Served with USAF. Home: 9710 E La Posada Cir Scottsdale AZ 85255-3716 Office: 8711 E Pinnacle Peak Rd # 114 Scottsdale AZ 85255-3517

RUHRUP, CLIFTON BROWN, sales executive; b. Jacksonville, Fla., Nov. 9, 1916; s. Ernest Alfred and Elizabeth L. (Garrett) R. Student, U. Okla., 1934-35, Oklahoma City U., 1946-48; cert. sales mgmt., U. Okla., 1962. From intern trainee to asst. sales mgr. Dolese Bros. Co., Oklahoma City, 1950-54, gen. sales mgr. aggregate div., 1955-61, gen. sales mgr. aggregate and prestress div., 1966—, asst. sec., 1971—. Chmn. bd. dirs. Cen. YMCA, Oklahoma City, 1973-78, named Outstanding Vol. of Yr., 1978, fellow mem., 1978—; bd. dirs. Better Bus. Bur., 1992—; mem. assoc. bd. Associated Bd. Contractors Okla. S/Sgt. USAAF, 1943-46, PTO. Mem. Oklahoma City C. of C., Toastmasters (pres. 1968), Rotary (editor newspaper 1972-76, contbg. editor 1988—, Paul Harris fellow), Phi Eta Sigma. Republican. Mem. First Christian Ch. Avocations: photography, fishing, travel, real estate. Office: Dolese Bros Co 20 NW 13th St Oklahoma City OK 73103-4806 *Success in life does not come because you wish for it; success in life comes because you want and work for it.*

RUI, HALLGEIR, cancer researcher; b. Rissa, Norway, Dec. 13, 1961; came to U.S., 1989; s. Tarald Martin and Gerd (Neverlien) R. MD, U. Oslo, 1987, PhD in Pathology, 1988. Lic. med. doctor, Norway. Clin. resident in surgery and internal medicine Notodden (Norway) Hosp., 1987-89; postdoctoral fellow U. South Fla., Tampa, 1989-91; scientist Nat. Cancer Inst., Frederick, Md., 1991-95; asst. prof. Uniformed Svcs. U. Health Scis. Sch. Medicine, Bethesda, Md., 1995—. Contbr. over 70 articles to profl. jours. Norwegian Sci. Coun. fellow, 1983-87, Fulbright fellow, 1989, Fogarty fellow, 1989-95. Mem. AAAS, N.Y. Acad. Scis., Endocrine Soc., Norwegian Med. Assn. Achievements include cloning of rat Jak2 tyrosine kinase and demonstrating that prolactin activates Jak-Stat and Shc-Ras signaling pathways. Avocations: skiing, running, hiking.

RUINA, JACK PHILIP, electrical engineer, educator; b. Rypin, Poland, Aug. 19, 1923; came to U.S., 1927; naturalized, 1932; s. Michael and Nechuma (Warshaw) R.; m. Edith Elster, Oct. 26, 1947; children: Ellen, Andrew, Rachel. BEE, CCNY, 1944; MEE, Poly. Inst. Bklyn., 1949, DEE, 1951. Rsch. fellow Microwave Rsch. Inst., Poly. Inst. Bklyn., 1948-50; from instr. to assoc. prof. elec. engring. Brown U., 1950-54; rsch. assoc. prof. coordinated sci. lab. U. Ill., 1954-59, rsch. prof., prof. elec. engring., 1959-63; prof. elec. engring. MIT, 1963—, v.p. for spl. labs., 1966-70; U.S. observer Antarctica, 1964; on leave to U.S. Govt., 1959-63, pres. Inst. Def. Analysis, 1964-66; dep. for rsch. to asst. sec. air force, 1959-60; asst. dir. for def. rsch. and engring. Office Sec. Def., 1960-61; dir. Advanced Rsch. Projects Agy., Dept. Def., 1961-63; mem. panel Presdl. Sci. Adv. Commn., 1963-72, sci. adv. bd. USAF, 1964-67, adv. bd. and panels for Dept. Def., HEW, Dept. Transp., ACDA, Office Tech. Assessment, NSF, NSC, 1963—; mem. gen. adv. com. ACDA, 1969-74; sr. cons. Office Sci. and Tech. Policy, The White House, 1977-80; chmn. com. on environ. decision making NAS, 1974-77; bd. dirs. Mitre Corp. Recipient Fleming award, 1962, Disting. Alumnus award Poly. Inst. Bklyn., 1970, One Hundred and Twenty Fifth Anniversary medal CCNY, 1973. Fellow IEEE, AAAS, Am. Acad. Arts and Scis.; mem. Inst. Strategic Studies, Coun. on Fgn. Rels., Internat. Sci. Radio Union, Sigma Xi. Home: 130 Mount Auburn St Apt 409 Cambridge MA 02138-5779 Office: MIT Dept Elec Engring 292 Main St Cambridge MA 02142-1014

RUIZ, EDUARDO ANTONIO, psychology and sociology educator; b. Rio Piedras, P.R., Jan. 21, 1953; came to U.S., 1988; s. Emiliano H. and Pura C. (Rodriguez) Ruiz; m. Maria N. Reyes, Dec. 21, 1976. BA in Psychology, U. P.R., 1976, MA in Psychology, 1979. Psychology instr. Cath. U. of P.R., Ponce, 1979-88; prevention specialist The Psychol. Ctr., Lawrence, Mass.,

1988-91; program coord. Family Svc. Assn., Lawrence, 1991-93; asst. prof. No. Essex C.C., Haverhill, Mass., 1993—, chmn. behavioral scis., 1994—. Author (children's booklet) The Large Clawed Caribbean Fiddler Crab, 1989, The Flight of the Butterflies, 1989. Mem. G. Lawrence Teen Pregnancy Coalition. Recipient Commrs. award Mass. Dept. of Mental Health, 1992. Mem. Puerto Rican Psychol. Assn. (v.p. 1980-82, pres. legis. affairs 1980-82), Soc. for Neurosci., Animal Behavior Soc., Psi Beta. Roman Catholic. Avocations: scuba diving, downhill skiing, sailing, computers, photography. Office: No Essex Community Coll Dept Behavioral Scis Haverhill MA 01830

RUIZ, RAMON EDUARDO, history educator; b. La Jolla, Calif., Sept. 9, 1921; s. Ramon and Dolores (Urueta) R.; m. Natalia Marrujo, Oct. 14, 1944; children—Olivia, Maura. BA, San Diego State Coll., 1947; MA, Claremont Grad. Sch., 1948; PhD, U. Calif., Berkeley, 1954. Asst. prof. U. Oreg., Eugene, 1955-57, So. Meth. U., Dallas, 1957-58; prof. Smith Coll., Northampton, Mass., 1958-69; prof. Lat. Am. history U. Calif. at San Diego, 1969-91; prof. emeritus, 1991—; chmn. dept. history U. Calif. at San Diego, 1971-76, div. humanities, 1972-74; mem. project grant com. NEH, 1972-73, 75-77, dir. public programs div., 1979-80; vis. prof. Facultad de Economia, Univ. de Nuevo Leon, Mexico, 1965-66, Coll. de Sonora, Mexico, summer 1983, Pomona Coll., 1983-84, Coll. de Michoacan, Mexico, summer 1986, 87, Univ. Nacional Autonoma de Mexico, fall 1992; scholar-in-residence Colegio de la Frontero Norte, Mexico, 1994-96; MacArthur Found. nominator, 1981-82; mem. project grant com. Ford Found. Author: Cuba: The Making of A Revolution, 1968 (One of Best History Books, Book World Washington Post 1968), Mexico: The Challenge of Poverty and Illiteracy, 1963, An American in Maximillians's Mexico, 1865-1866, 1959; (with James D. Atwater) Out From Under; Benito Juarez and Mexico's Struggle for Independence, 1969; (with John Tebbel) South by Southwest: The Mexican-American and His Heritage, 1969, Interpreting Latin American History, 1970, Labor and the Ambivalent Revolutionaries: Mexico, 1911-23, 1975, The Mexican War: Was it Manifest Destiny?, 1963, The Great Rebellion: Mexico, 1905-1924, 1980 (Hubert C. Herring prize), The People of Sonora and Yanqui Capitalists, 1988, Triumphs and Tragedy: A History of the Mexican People, 1992 (named One of Five Best History Books 1991-92, L.A. Times, Gold Medal award Commonwealth Club San Francisco 1993); (with Olivia Teresa Ruiz) Reflexiones Sobre la Identidad de los Pueblos, 1996. Served to lt. USAAF, 1943-46. William Harrison Mills traveling fellow in internat. relations, 1950; John Hay Whitney Found. fellow, 1950; Fulbright fellow Mex., 1965-66; fellow Ctr. for Advanced Study in Behavioral Scis., 1984-85, Ena H. Thompson lectureship, Pomona Coll., 1995;recipient Am. Philos. Soc. grant in aid, 1959. Mem. Am. Hist. Assn. (Beveridge prize com. 1974-76), Conf. Latin Am. History, Chicano-Latino Faculty Assn. U. Calif. (pres. 1989-91), Phi Beta Kappa, Sigma Delta Pi. Home: PO Box 1775 Rancho Santa Fe CA 92067-1775

RUIZ, VANESSA, judge; b. San Jaun, P.R., Mar. 22, 1950; D. Fernando and Irma (Bosch) Ruiz-Suria; m. Eduardo Elejalde, Feb. 11, 1972 (div. Jan. 1982); children: Natalia, Alexia; m. David E. Birenbaum, Oct. 22, 1983; stepchildren: Tracy, Matthew. BA, Wellesley Coll., 1972; JD, Georgetown U., 1975. Bar: D.C. 1972, U.S. Supreme Ct. 1981. Assoc. Fried, Frank, Harris, Shrives & Kampelman, Washington, 1975-83; sr. mgr., counsel Sears World Trade Inc., Washington, 1983-94; assoc. judge D.C. Ct. of Appeals, 1994—; speaker in field. Mem. ABA, Inter-Am. Bar Assn. Office: 500 Indiana Ave NW Ste 6 Washington DC 20001-2131 also: Pepper Hamilton & Scheetz 1300 19th St NW Washington DC 20036-1609*

RUIZ, VICKI LYNN, history educator; b. Atlanta, May 21, 1955; d. Robert Paul and Erminia Pablita (Ruiz) Mercer; m. Jerry Joseph Ruiz, Sept. 1, 1979 (div. Jan. 1990); children: Miguel, Daniel; m. Victor Becerra, Aug. 14, 1992. AS in Social Studies, Gulf Coast Community Coll., 1975; BA in Social Sci., Fla. State, 1977; MA in History, Stanford U., 1978, PhD in History, 1982. Asst. prof. U. Tex., El Paso, 1982-85; asst. prof. U. Calif., Davis, 1985-87, assoc. prof., 1987-92; Andrew W. Mellon prof. Claremont (Calif.) Grad. Sch., 1992-95, chmn. history dept., 1993-95; prof. history Ariz. State U., Tempe, 1995—; dir. Inst. of Oral History, U. Tex., El Paso, 1983-85, minority undergrad. rsch. program U. Calif., Davis, 1988-92. Author: Cannery Women, Cannery Lives, 1987, From Out of the Shadows, 1997; co-editor: Women on U.S.-Mexican Border, 1987, Western Women, 1988, Unequal Sisters, 1990, 2d edit., 1994. Mem. Calif. Coun. for Humanities, 1990-94, vice chmn., 1991-93. Fellow Univ. Calif. Davis Humanities Inst., 1990-91, Am. Coun. of Learned Socs., 1986, Danforth Found., 1977. Mem. Orgn. Am. Historians (chmn. com. on status of minority history 1989-91, nominating com. 1987-88, exec. bd. 1995—), Immigration History Soc. (exec. bd. 1989-91), Am. Studies Assn. (nominating bd. 1992-94), Western History (nominating bd. 1993-95). Democrat. Roman Catholic. Avocations: walking, needlework. Office: Ariz State U History Dept Tempe AZ 85287

RUIZ-PETRICH, ELENA, biophysicist; b. Mendoza, Argentina, Nov. 19, 1933; widowed. MD, U. Cuyo, 1959, DSc (hon.), 1976. Sr. instr. physiololy, Faculty Medicine U. Cuyo, 1959-63; gellow Argentina Nat. Coun. Sci. and Technol. Investment, 1960-62; fellow heart electrophysiology U. So. Calif., 1963-65; fellow Can. Heart Found., 1969-70, rsch. scholar, 1971-75; from asst. prof. to assoc. prof. U. Sherbrooke, Chemin Stokes, Que., Can., 1968-77, chmn. dept. biophysics, 1978-84, prof. biophysics, 1977—, chmn. dept. physiol. biophysics, 1987—. Grantee Argentina Nat. Coun. Sci. and Technology, 1966-67, Med. Rsch. Coun. Ottawa, 1967-71, Que Heart Found., 1969-73. Mem. Internat. Soc. Heart Rsch., Can. Physiol. Soc., Am. Physiol. Soc. Office: Electrophysiology Rsch Group, Sherbrooke U / Faculte de med, Sherbrooke, PQ Canada J1H 5N4 Office: Univ Sherbrooke Faculty Med, Dept Physiol & Biophys, Chemin Stokes, PQ Canada J1H 5N4

RUIZ SACRISTÁN, CARLOS, Mexican government official; b. Mexico City, Oct. 27, 1949. BA in Bus. Adminstrn., Anahuac U., 1972; MA in Fin., Northwestern U., Chgo., 1974. From chief of currency exch. to mgr. internat. ops. Bank of Mex., 1974-86; dir. Commn. on Exch. Rate Risk Ins., 1986-88; gen. dir. pub. credit Secretarian of Fin. and Pub. Credit, 1988-92, dep. sec. expenditures, 1992-94; dir. Gen. Mex. Petroleum "Pemex", 1994; sec. comm. and transport Govt. Mex., 1994—. Office: Xola esq Av Universidad, Cuerpo c 1er piso, 03028 Mexico City Mexico

RUKEYSER, LOUIS RICHARD, economic commentator; b. N.Y.C., Jan. 30, 1933; s. Merryle Stanley and Berenice Helene (Simon) R.; m. Alexandra Gill, Mar. 3, 1962; children: Beverley Jane, Susan Athena, Stacy Alexandra. AB, Princeton U., 1954; LittD (hon.), N.H. Coll., 1975; LLD (hon.), Moravian Coll., 1978, Mercy Coll., 1984, Am. U., 1991; DBA (hon.), Southeastern Mass. U., 1979; LHD (hon.), Loyola Coll., 1982, Johns Hopkins U., 1986, Western Md. Coll., 1992; D in Fin. (hon.), Roger Williams U., 1997. Reporter Balt. Sun newspapers, 1954-65; chief polit. corr. Evening Sun, 1957-59; chief London bur. The Sun, 1959-63, chief Asian corr., 1963-65; sr. corr., commentator ABC News, 1965-73, Paris corr., 1965-66, chief London bur., 1966-68, econ. editor, commentator, 1968-73; host Wall St. Week With Louis Rukeyser PBS-TV, 1970—; nationally syndicated econ. columnist McNaught Syndicate, 1976-86, Tribune Media Services, 1986-93; frequent lectr. Author: How to Make Money in Wall Street, 1974, 2d edit., 1976 (Literary Guild selection 1974, 76), What's Ahead for the Economy: The Challenge and the Chance, 1983, 2d edit., 1985 (Literary Guild selection 1984), Louis Rukeyser's Business Almanac, 1988, 2d edit., 1991; editor-in-chief monthly newsletters, Louis Rukeyser's Wall Street, 1992—, Louis Rukeyser's Mutual Funds, 1994—. With U.S. Army, 1954-56. Recipient Overseas Press Club award, 1963, Overseas Press Club citation, 1964, G.M. Loeb award U. Conn., 1972, Janus award for excellence in fin. news programming, 1975, George Washington Honor medal Freedoms Found., 1972, 78, N.Y. Fin. Writers Assn. award, 1980, Free Enterprise Man of the Yr. award Tex. A&M U. Ctr. for Edn. and Research in Free Enterprise, 1987, Women's Econ. Round Table award, 1990. Office: 586 Round Hill Rd Greenwich CT 06831-2724

RUKEYSER, M. S., JR., television consultant, writer; b. N.Y.C., Apr. 15, 1931; s. Merryle Stanley and Berenice (Simon) R.; children: Jill Victoria, Patricia Bern; m. Susan Gardinor Chopin, Mar. 10, 1997. Student, U. Va., 1948-52. Reporter Albany (N.Y.) Times-Union, 1949, Internat. News Service, N.Y.C., 1951; TV publicist Young & Rubicam, Inc., N.Y.C., 1952-57; with NBC, 1958-80, 81-88; dir. news info. NBC, Washington, 1962; v.p. press and publicity NBC, N.Y.C., 1963-72; v.p. corp. info. NBC, 1972-74, v.p. pub. info., 1974-77, exec. v.p. pub. info., 1977-80, 81-84, exec. v.p. corp. communications, 1984-88; v.p. comm. Newsweek Inc., 1980-81; sr. v.p. GTG Entertainment, N.Y.C., 1988-90; pres. Rukeyser Communications, N.Y.C., 1990—; sr. fellow Freedom Forum Media Ctr., 1991-92. Author: (with Grant Tinker) Tinker in Television: From General Sarnoff to General Electric, 1994. Mem. adv. coun. Ctr. for Media in the Pub. Interest. Served with U.S. Army, 1953-54. Home and Office: 5872 NW 25th Terr Boca Raton FL 33496-2830

RUKEYSER, ROBERT JAMES, manufacturing executive; b. New Rochelle, N.Y., June 26, 1942; s. Merryle Stanley and Berenice Helene (Simon) R.; m. Leah A. Spiro, July 26, 1964; children: David Bern, Peter Lloyd. BA, Cornell U., 1964; MBA with distinction, N.Y.U., 1969. Mcpl. services analyst Dun & Bradstreet, N.Y.C., 1964-65; bond analyst Standard & Poors, N.Y.C., 1965-66; mktg. rep. data processing div. IBM, N.Y.C., 1967-72, regional mktg. staff, 1973-74, mktg. mgr., 1974-76; corp. mgr. internal communications IBM, Armonk, N.Y., 1976-79; mgr. communication ops. IBM, Franklin Lakes, N.J., 1979-81; pub. affairs dir., asst. to chmn. Am. Brands, Inc., N.Y.C., 1981-83, v.p. pub. affairs, asst. to chmn., 1983-85; v.p. office products Am. Brands, Inc., Old Greenwich, Conn., 1986-87, v.p. ops., 1987-89, sr. v.p. corp. affairs, 1990—; bd. dirs. Am. Brands Internat. Co., JBB Worldwide, Inc., Acushnet Co., MasterBrand Industries, Acco World Corp. Bd. dirs., mem. fin. and devel. com. The Hole in the Wall Gang Camp.; bd. dirs. Stamford Ctr. for Arts. Mem. Bus. Products Industry Assn. Office: Am Brands Inc 1700 E Putnam Ave Old Greenwich CT 06870-1321

RUKEYSER, WILLIAM SIMON, journalist; b. N.Y.C., June 8, 1939; s. Merryle Stanley and Berenice (Simon) R.; m. Elisabeth Mary Garnett, Nov. 21, 1963; children: Lisa Rukeyser Burn, James William. A.B., Princeton U., 1961; student, Christ's Coll., Cambridge (Eng.) U., 1962-63. Copyreader Wall St. Jour., 1961-62; staff reporter Wall St. Jour., Europe, 1963-67; assoc. editor Fortune mag., 1967-71, mem. bd. editors, 1971-72; mng. editor Money mag., N.Y.C., 1972-80, Fortune mag., 1980-86; dir. internat. bus. devel. Time Inc., 1986-88; editor in chief, exec. v.p. Whittle Communications, Knoxville, Tenn., 1988-91; chmn., CEO, Whittle Books, Knoxville, 1991-94; pres. William Rukeyser, Inc., Knoxville, 1994—; contbg. editor CNN, 1995—; commentator Good Morning America, ABC-TV, 1978-85, CBS Radio Stas. News Svc., 1979-86; bd. dirs. Computational Systems, Inc., Tri-Media Comm., Inc. Mem. jud. com. Union County (N.J.) Med. Soc., 1977-80; co-chair capital campaign Nat. Mental Health Assn., 1984-85; dir., mem. exec. com. Knoxville Symphony Orch.; mem. liaison com. U. Tenn. Med. Ctr.; mem. adv. coun. U. Tenn. Coll. Bus. Adminstrn.; dir. Bijou Theatre Ctr., Knoxville. Office: 2101 First Tennessee Plz Knoxville TN 37929

RULAND, RICHARD EUGENE, English and American literature educator, critic, literary historian; b. Detroit, May 1, 1932; s. Eugene John and Irene (Janette) R.; m. Mary Ann Monaghan; children: Joseph, Michael, Paul, Susan; m. Birgit Noll. BA, Assumption Coll. U. Western Ont., Can., 1953; MA, U. Detroit, 1955; PhD, U. Mich., 1960. Instr., then asst. prof. English and Am. studies Yale U., New Haven, 1960-67, Morse rsch. fellow, 1966-67; prof. English and Am. lit. Washington U., St. Louis, 1967—, chmn. dept. English, 1969-74; chmn. comparative lit. program, 1993-94; vis. Bruern prof. Am. lit. Leeds (Eng.) U., 1964-65; vis. Fulbright prof. U. Groningen, The Netherlands, 1975, Sch. of English and Am. Studies U. East Anglia, Eng., 1978-79; vis. disting. prof. Am. lit. Coll. of William and Mary, 1980-81. Author: The Rediscovery of American Literature: Premises of Critical Taste, 1900-1940, 1967, America in Modern European Literature: From Image to Metaphor, 1976, (with Malcolm Bradbury) From Puritanism to Postmodernism: A History of American Literature, 1991 (paperback 1992), translation into Czech and Hungarian, 1997; editor: Walden: A Collection of Critical Essays, 1967, The Native Muse: Theories of American Literature, Vol. I, 1972, 76, A Storied Land: Theories of American Literature, Vol. II, 1976; contbr. articles to profl. jours. Guggenheim Rsch. fellow, 1982-83. Mem. Assn. Depts. English (pres. 1974). Avocation: jazz musician. Office: Washington U Dept English Saint Louis MO 63130

RULAU, RUSSELL, numismatic consultant; b. Chgo., Sept. 21, 1926; s. Alphonse and Ruth (Thorsen) R.; student U. Wis., 1946-48; m. Hazel Darlene Grizzell, Feb. 1, 1968; children by previous marriage: Lance Eric, Carla Rae, Russell A.W., Marsha June, Scott Quentin, Roberta Ann, Kyle Christopher, Yvonne Marie; 1 step-dau., Sharon Maria Dennis. With U.S. Army, 1944-1950, master sgt. USAF, 1950-62; resigned active duty, 1962; asst. editor Coin World newspaper, Sidney, Ohio, 1962-74, editor World Coins mag., 1964-74, Numis. Scrapbook mag., 1968-74; editorial coordinator How to Order Fgn. Coins guidebook, 1966-74; editor in chief World Coin News newspaper, 1974-84, Bank Note Reporter, 1983-84; fgn. editor Numis. News newspaper, 1974-77; cons. editor Standard Catalog of World Paper Money, 1975-83; contbg. editor Standard Catalog of World Coins, 1974-81; pres. House of Rulau, 1984—, Alpha Enterprises Inc., 1989—; v.p. Keogh-Rulau Galleries, Dallas, 1984-85, Pobjoy Mint Ltd., Iola, Wis., 1985-97, cons., 1997—; U.S. agent Christie's Pty. Ltd, 1992-95. Recipient Clemy Literary award 1993, Smedley Lifetime Achievement award, 1994, Numismatic Ambassador award, 1995; elector Numismatic Hall of Fame, 1995—. Mem. U.S. Assay Commn., 1973. Sec., Numismatic Terms Standardization Com., 1966-74; vice-chmn. Waupaca County Republican party, 1977-79, 1988-89, chmn., 1979-82; chmn. county chairmen, 3d vice chmn. Wis. Rep. Party, 1981-83; del. Rep. Nat. Conv., 1980; exec. com. 6th Wis. Dist. Rep. Com., 1984-87 . Fellow Royal Numis. Soc., Am. Numis. Soc. (assoc.); mem. Token and Medal Soc. (editor 1962-63, gold cataloging medals 1982, 83, 92), Am. Numis. Assn. (Merit medal 1995), Canadian, S. African numis. assns., Mont. Hist. Soc., Am. Vecturist Assn., Numis. Lit. Guild (dir. 1974-78, editor 1984-86, best specialized book awards 1985, 89, 92, 94), VFW (post commdr. 1985-89, 96—), Am. Legion. Lutheran. Author: (with George Fuld) Spiel Marken, 1962-65, American Game Counters, 1972; World Mint Marks, 1966; Modern World Mint Marks, 1970; (with J. U. Rixen and Frovin Sieg) Seddelkatalog Slesvig Plebiscit Zone I og II, 1970; Numismatics of Old Alabama, 1971-73; Hard Times Tokens, 1980; Early American Tokens, 1981; U.S. Merchant Tokens 1845-1860, 1982; U.S. Trade Tokens 1866-1889, 1983, Tokens of the Gay Nineties, 1987, Discovering America: The Coin Collecting Connection, 1989, Latin American Tokens, 1992; (with George Fuld) Medallic Portraits of Washington, 1985, Standard Catalog of U.S. Tokens 1700-1900, 1994; contbr. numis. articles to profl. jours. Home: N7747 County J Iola WI 54945 Office: Pobjoy Mint USA Ltd PO Box 153 Iola WI 54945-0153

RULE, CHARLES FREDERICK (RICK RULE), lawyer; b. Nashville, Apr. 28, 1955; s. Frederick Charles and Mary Elizabeth (Malone) R.; m. Ellen Friedland, May 13, 1976. BA, Vanderbilt U., 1978; JD, U. Chgo., 1981. Bar: U.S. Ct. Appeals. (D.C. cir.) 1983. Law clk. U.S. Ct. Appeals (fed. cir.), Washington, 1981-82; spl. asst. to asst. atty. gen. Antitrust div. Dept. Justice, Washington, 1982-83, dep. asst. atty. gen. policy planning, 1984-85, acting asst. atty. gen., then dep. asst. atty. gen. regulatory affairs, 1985-86, asst. atty. gen., 1986-89; ptnr. Covington & Burling, Washington, 1989—; legal, econ. analyst Lexecon, Inc., Chgo., 1979-80. Mem. Bar of D.C. Ct. Appeals, Phi Beta Kappa, Phi Eta Sigma. Republican. Presbyterian. Office: Covington & Burling PO Box 7566 Rm 915B 1200 Pennsylvania Ave NW Washington DC 20004-2411

RULE, JOHN CORWIN, history educator; b. Evanston, Ill., Mar. 2, 1929; s. Corwin V. and Elaine (Simons) R. A.B., Stanford U., 1951, M.A., 1952; M.A., Harvard U., 1955, Ph.D., 1958. Tutor and fellow Harvard U., Cambridge, Mass., 1956-58; instr. Northeastern U., Boston, 1955-56; from instr. to prof. history Ohio State U., Columbus, 1958—; vis. asst. prof. Western Res. U., Cleve., 1961; vis. prof. Johns Hopkins U., Balt., 1968. Editor and contbg. author: Louis XIV and the Craft of Kingship, 1970; editor: Louis XIV, 1974, Letters from the Hague and Utrecht, 1711-1712, 1979, The Reign of Louis XIV, 1990. Folger Shakespeare Library fellow, 1968., 1970; Huntington Library fellow, 1978; Am. Council Learned Socs. fellow, 1981. Fellow Royal Hist. Soc. (London); mem. Soc. for French Hist. Studies (sec. 1963-70, assoc. editor jour. 1975-86, co-pres. 1989-91), Signet Soc., Crichton Club. Democrat. Home: 118 E Beck St Columbus OH 43206-1110 Office: Dept History Ohio State U 230 W 17th Ave Columbus OH 43210-1361

RULIFSON, JOHNS FREDERICK, computer company executive, computer scientist; b. Bellefontaine, Ohio, Aug. 20, 1941; s. Erwin Charles and Virginia Helen (Johns) R.; m. Janet Irving, June 8, 1963; children: Eric Johns, Ingrid Catharine. BS in Math., U. Wash., 1966; PhD in Computer Sci., Stanford U., 1973. Mathematician SRI, Internat., Menlo Park, Calif., 1966-73; scientist Xerox Rsch., Palo Alto, Calif., 1973-80; mgr. ROLM, Santa Clara, Calif., 1980-85; scientist Syntelligence, Sunnyvale, Calif., 1985-87; exec. Sun Microsystems, Mountain View, Calif., 1987—. Fellow Assn. for Computing Machinery (System Software award 1990); mem. IEEE. Avocation: photography. Home: 3785 El Centro Ave Palo Alto CA 94306-2642 Office: Sun Microsystems 2550 Garcia Ave Mountain View CA 94043-1109

RULIS, RAYMOND JOSEPH, manufacturing company executive, consultant; b. New Britain, Conn., June 2, 1924; s. James Alexander and Eva (Ragauskas) R.; m. Thelma Pelchat, June 16, 1949; children: Elaine, Jeffery, Catherine, Elizabeth, Amy, Daniel, Jean. BSME, U. Conn., 1949; postgrad., U. Conn., Ohio State U., Northeastern U., 1949-58; student, Fed. Exec. Inst., Charlottesville, Va., 1976. Devel. engr. Hamilton Standard, U.T.C., Windsorlocks, Conn., 1951-55; mgr. fuel controls Lycoming Textron, Stratford, Conn., 1955-59; mgr. controls and accessories GE, Lynn, Mass., 1959-62; successively program mgr. sert spacecraft, chief spacecraft engr., chief launch vehicle engr., chief engring design, program mgr. QCSEE program NASA Lewis Rsch. Ctr., Cleve., 1962-81; v.p. rsch. and. devel. Textron Turbocomponents Group, Walled Lake, Mich., 1981-92; cons., 1992—; cons. Joint FAA/NASA Civil Aero Rsch. Document Study, 1972, Cruise Missile PRogram, 1977-78, C-17 Aircraft Source Selection Bd., 1978, Tri-Svcs. Propulsion Group, 1976-78; chmn. Conf. on Short Haul Systems, NASA, 1976; mem. exec. coun. Aerospace Industries Tech. Coun., 1988-89. Contbr. articles to profl. jours.; patentee in field. Chmn. Boy Scouts Am. Fund Drives, Cleve., 1976-78; mem. Coun. on World Affairs, Cleve., 1976-81. Mem. Am. Helicopter Soc. (chmn. tech. session 1970), AIAA (chmn. tech. session 1965), Detroit Engring Soc., KC. Roman Catholic. Avocation: golf. Office: RJR Cons 9 Outpost Ln Hilton Head Island SC 29928-3820

RULISON, JOSEPH RICHARD, investment advisor; b. Syracuse, N.Y., May 14, 1956; s. Laurence M. and Catherine (Fox) R.; m. Karen Richards, Sept. 6, 1980; children: Elizabeth, Mallorie, Morgan, Abigail. BA, St. John Fisher Coll., 1978. Mgr. area sales, corp. travel Nat. Car Rental Systems, Inc., Rochester, N.Y., 1978-82; account exec. Prudential-Bache Securities, Rochester, 1982-84; investment exec. Tucker Anthony & R.L. Day, Inc., Rochester, 1984-89; ptnr., ex v.p. Marsh Capital Mgmt., Rochester, 1989-96; pres., CEO Rulison & Co., Inc., 1996—; mem. instnl. coun. NASDAQ. Pres. bd. dirs. Geva Theatre, pres., chmn. bd. trustees; investment advisor Nat. Braille Assn.; treas. Monroe County Rep. Com., County Monroe Indsl. Devel. Agy., Monroe County Greater Outdoor Sports Facility-Frontier Field; past councilman Brighton Town Bd.; past mem. Town of Brighton Planning Bd., Master Plan Com., Archtl. Rev. Bd.; bd. dirs. Rochester Gen. Hosp. Found., Rochester Community Baseball, Camp Good Days and Spl. Times. Roman Catholic. Avocations: politics, theatre, art, wine. Home: 1166 Clover St Rochester NY 14610-3368 Office: Rulison & Co Inc 2300 Chase Sq Rochester NY 14604-1922

RUMACK, BARRY H., physician, toxicologist, pediatrician; b. Chgo., Nov. 1, 1942; s. Alvin Eugene and Shirley (Kazan) R.; m. Carol Masters, June 10, 1964; children—Becky, Marc. B.S., in Microbiology, U. Chgo., 1964; M.D., U. Wis., 1968. Diplomate Nat. Bd. Med. Examiners, Am. Bd. Pediatrics, Am. Bd. Med. Toxicology (v.p.). Intern U. Colo., 1968-69, resident in pediatrics, 1971-72; fellow U. Colo. Med. Ctr., 1972-73; clin. assoc. Regional Poisoning Treatment Ctr., Royal Infirmary of Edinburgh, Scotland, 1973; assoc. prof. pediatrics U. Colo. Sch. Medicine, 1978-86, prof., 1986-92, dir. drug assay lab., 1975-77, Rocky Mountain Poison Ctr., 1974-92; pres., CEO Micromedex Inc., 1974—; chmn. pharmacy and therapeutics com., 1976-80; cons. Nat. Clearinghouse Poison Control Ctrs., 1975-91. Editor: (with A.R. Temple) Management of the Acutely Poisoned Patients, 1977; (with E. Salzman) Mushroom Poisoning, 1978; (with M.J. Bayer) Poisoning and Overdose, 1982; (with M.J. Bayer and L. Wanke) Toxicologic Emergencies: A Manual of Diagnosis and Management, 1984; contbr. chpts. to books, articles to profl. jours.; author abstracts. Active hazardous substances com. State of Colo., 1974-88; mem. adv. panel on toxicology U.S. Pharmacopeia, 1975-80; mem. Gov.'s Tech. Rev. com. on Rocky Mountain Arsenal, 1975; mem. adv. com. toxicology info. Nat. Library of Medicine, 1976-79; active Colo. State Bd. of Health, 1977-81; chmn. Internat. Congress of Clin. Toxicology, Colo., 1982; com. to advise Red Cross, 1984-91. Fellow Am. Acad. Clin. Toxicology (mem. edn. com. 1976-79, bd. dirs. 1978-81), Am. Acad. Pediatrics (com. on accidents and poisoning 1977-82, com. on drugs 1983-91); mem. Am. Assn. Poison Control Ctrs. (com. on standards 1974-79, bd. dirs. 1975-79, pres. 1982-84, v.p. 1980-82), Western Soc. Pediatric Research, Soc. Pediatric Research, Soc. Toxicology, Am. Coll. Emergency Medicine, N. Am. Mycological Assn. (toxicology com. 1975-79). Quaker. Office: Micromedex Inc 6200 S Syracuse Way Englewood CO 80111 Address: 33 Silver Fox Cir Littleton CO 80121-2129

RUMBAUGH, CHARLES EARL, lawyer, arbitrator/mediator; b. San Bernardino, Calif., Mar. 11, 1943; s. Max Elden and Gertrude Maude (Gulker) R.; m. Christina Carol Pinder, Mar. 2, 1968; children: Eckwood, Cynthia, Aaron, Heather. BS, UCLA, 1966; JD, Calif. Western Sch. Law, 1971; cert. in Advanced Mgmt., U. So. Calif., 1993. Bar: Calif. 1972, U.S. Dist. Ct. (cen. dist.) Calif. 1972, U.S. Ct. Appeals (9th cir.) 1972. Engr. Westinghouse Electric Corp., Balt., 1966-68; legal counsel Calif. Dept. of Corps., L.A., 1971-77; legal counsel Hughes Aircraft Co., L.A., 1977-84, asst. to corp. dir. contracts, 1984-89, asst. to corp. v.p. contracts, 1989-95; corp. dir. contracts/pricing Lear Astronics Corp., 1995-97; arbitrator, mediator, 1997—; arbitrator/mediator, 1997—, comml., franchise, securities, real estate and constrn. panels Am. Arbitration Assn., L.A., 1989—; mem. arbitration and mediation panels Franchise Arbitration and Mediation, Inc., 1994—, Arbitration and Mediation Internat., 1994—, Ctr. for Conflict Resolution, L.A., 1990—, Nat. Assn. Security Dealers, L.A. County Superior Ct., 1993; spkr. to profl. and trade assns. Mem. editl. bd. Nat. Contract Mgmt. Jour.; contbr. articles to profl. jours. Counselor Boy Scouts Am., L.A., 1976—; mem. City of Palos Verdes Estates (Calif.) Citizen's Planning Com., 1986-90; judge pro tem Los Angeles County Superior Ct., L.A., 1991—. Fellow Nat. Contract Mgmt. Assn. (founder, chmn. alt. dispute resolution com., cert. profl. contracts mgr., nat. bd. advisors, nat. v.p. southwestern region 1993-95, nat. dir. 1992-93, pres. L.A./South Bay chpt. 1991-92, Outstanding Fellow award 1994); mem. ABA (alt. dispute resolution sect., forum on franchising, forum on constrn. industry), Nat. Security Indsl. Assn. (vice-chmn. west coast legal subcom. 1994—), Fed. Bar Assn. (pres. Beverly Hills chpt. 1992-93), State Bar Calif. (franchise law com. 1992-95, Wiley W. Manual award 1992), LA County Bar Assn., South Bay Bar Assn., Soc. Profls. in Dispute Resolution (co-chmn. internat. sector), Aerospace Industries Assn. (chmn. procurement techniques com. 1987-88, 93-94), Christian Legal Soc. Avocations: camping, skiing, jogging, equestrian. Office: PO Box 2636 Rolling Hills CA 90274-8636

RUMBAUGH, MAX ELDEN, JR., professional society administrator; b. Ada, Okla., Dec. 11, 1937; s. Max E. and Gertrude (Gulker) R.; m. Joan E. Brockway; children: Maria Rumbaugh Gross, Max E. III. BS in Engring., U.S. Mil. Acad., 1960; MS in Engring. Scis., Purdue U., 1965, MBA, 1972. Instr. Purdue U., West Lafayette, Ind., 1964-65; corp. officer Midwest Applied Sci. Corp., West Lafayette, 1965-72; chief engr. advanced tech. Schwitzer div. Wallace-Murray Corp., Indpls., 1972-77, dir. research, 1977-81; mgr. engring. activities div. Soc. Automotive Engrs., Warrendale, Pa., 1981-84, v.p., asst. gen. mgr., 1984-86, exec. v.p., 1986—; pres. Performance Rev. Inst., 1991—; pres. Soc. Rsch. Adminstrs. Internat., 1973-74; chmn. Ind. sect. Soc. Automotive Engrs., 1978-79; bd. dirs., exec. com. Am. Nat. Standards Inst., N.Y.C., 1986—; bd. dirs. Intelligent Transp. Soc. of Am., 1992—. Author mag. column Focus, 1986—. Bd. dirs. Jr. Achievement Western Pa., Pitts., 1986-97, YMCA, North Hills, Pitts., 1985-94. 1st lt. U.S. Army, 1960-63,. Mem. ASME, Coun. Engring. and Sci. Soc. Execs. (bd. dirs. 1990—, sec. 1993-94, v.p. 1994-95, pres. 1995-96), Rotary (bd. dirs. 1982-84, 93—, v.p. 1994-95, pres. 1995-96). Avocations: skiing, photography. Home: 2274 Wood Acre Ct Pittsburgh PA 15237-1524 Office: Soc of Automotive Engrs Inc 400 Commonwealth Dr Warrendale PA 15086-7511

RUMBAUGH, MELVIN DALE, geneticist, agronomist; b. Pella, Iowa, Sept. 13, 1929; s. Herbert Robert and Lena (Schakel) R.; m. Annabelle Eis,

July 5, 1953; children: Alan Lee, Rosemary Ann, David James, Steven Thomas. BS, Cen. Coll., Pella, 1951; MS, U. Nebr., 1953, PhD, 1958. Prof. agronomy Colo. State U., Ft. Collins, 1958; prof. plant sci. S.D. State U., Brookings, 1959-77; rsch. scientist USDA-Agrl. Rsch. Svc., Logan, Utah, 1977-92; pvt. cons. Humboldt, Nebr., 1993—; participant plant germplasm collection Can., China, Bolivia, Peru, Ecuador, USSR, Morocco, Pakistan, Spain, Romania; exch. scientist People's Republic of China, 1987, 90, 91; mem. joint U.S.-Russian expdn. to inventory and collect legumes in Caucasus Mountains Nat. Park, 1995. Contbr. 250 articles to profl. jours., chpts. to books, sci. papers; inventor superior methods to genetically improve rangeland plant species; authority plant growth on saline soils. Cpl. U.S. Army, 1953-55. Fellow Am. Soc. Agronomy, Crop Sci. Soc. Am.; mem. Soc. Range Mgmt. Republican. Avocations: genealogy, history, fishing. Home: RR 3 Box 125 Humboldt NE 68376-9352

RUMBOUGH, STANLEY MADDOX, JR., industrialist; b. N.Y.C., Apr. 25, 1920; s. Stanley Maddox and Elizabeth (Colgate) R.; m. Nedenia Hutton, Mar. 23, 1946 (div. 1966); children: Stanley H., David P. (dec.), Nedenia Colgate; m. Margaretha Wagstrom, Dec. 21, 1967 (div. 1990); m. Janna Herlow, Mar. 8, 1990. A.B., Yale U., 1942; postgrad. in bus. adminstrn., NYU, 1947-51. Vice pres., dir. Willis Air Service, Teterboro, N.J., 1946-47; v.p., dir. White Metal Mfg. Co., Hoboken, N.J., 1945-61; pres. White Metal Mfg. Co., 1960-61; pres., dir. Metal Container Corp., 1950-59, Am. Totalisator, Balt., 1956-58; chmn. bd. Extrusion Devel. Corp., 1959-61; co-founder, chmn. bd. Elec. Engring. Ltd., 1960-69; chmn. bd. Wallace Clark & Co., 1962-69; co-founder, dir. Trinidad Flour Mills, 1961-72, Jamaica Flour Mills, 1963-66; dir. Telemedia Inc., 1980-89; dir. Dart Industries, 1961-80, ABT Family of Funds, 1983-95; bd. dirs. Internat. Flavors and Fragrances, CUC Internat., Inc.; spl. asst. to sec. Dept. Commerce, 1953; spl. asst. White House charge exec. br. liaison, 1953-55. Chmn. U.S. Com. for UN, 1957-58; co-founder Citizens for Eisenhower, 1951; vice chmn. Citizens for Eisenhower-Nixon Com., 1952; trustee Young Pres. Found., 1957-70, pres., 1962-65; bd. dirs. N.Y. World's Fair Corp., 1961-70, Nat. Conf. on Citizenship, 1973—, Population Resource Ctr., 1978-92, Planned Parenthood of Palm Beach Area, 1979-95, Planned Parenthood Fedn. Am., 1981-84, Kravis Ctr. Performing Arts, Palm Beach Civic Assn.; trustee Libr. for Presdl. Papers, 1966-70, Internat. House, 1959—, Fgn. Policy Assn., 1961-70, Am. Health Found., 1972-76. Capt. USMCR, 1942-46. Decorated Air medal (8), D.F.C. (2). Mem. Chief Execs. Orgn., World Pres.'s Orgn., Def. Orientation Conf. Assn., Racquet and Tennis Club, Internat. Lawn Tennis Club, Maidstone Club, Seminole Club, Bath and Tennis Club, Everglades Club, Nat. Golf Links Am. Club, Zeta Psi. Republican. Home: 655 Island Dr Palm Beach FL 33480-6121 Office: 280 Sunset Ave Palm Beach FL 33480-3815

RUMER, RALPH RAYMOND, JR., civil engineer, educator; b. Ocean City, N.J., June 22, 1931; s. Ralph Raymond and Anna (Hibbard) R.; m. Shirley Louise Haynes, Nov. 30, 1953 (dec. 1995); children: Sherri, Sue, Sandra, Sarah; m. Sallie Anne Wallace Kornegay, 1997. BS. in Civil Engring, Duke U., 1953; M.S., Rutgers U., 1959; Sc.D. (ASCE research fellow), M.I.T., 1962. Lic. prof. engr., N.Y. With Lukens Steel Co., Coatesville, Pa., 1953-54; instr. dept. civil engring. Rutgers U., New Brunswick, N.J., 1956-59; civil engr. U.S. Dept. Agr., New Brunswick, summer 1957-59; research asst. Hydrodynamics lab. M.I.T., Boston, 1961-62; asst. prof. dept. civil engring. M.I.T., 1962-63; assoc. prof. dept. civil engring. SUNY, Buffalo, 1963-69; prof. SUNY, 1969-76, 78—, acting head, 1966-67, chmn., 1967-73, 84-87; dir. SUNY (Gt. Lakes Program), 1986-90, acting provost engring. and applied scis., 1974-75; prof., chmn. dept. civil engring. U. Del., Newark, 1976-78; dir. N.Y. Ctr. Hazardous Waste Mgmt., 1987-95; tech. cons. to govt. and industry in hydraulics, water resources and environ. engring.; mem. water resources rsch. com. Nat. Acad. Sci., 1985-86; mem. water mgmt. adv. com. N.Y. State Dept. Environ. Conservation, 1988-93; chmn. sci. adv. com. EPA regions 1 & 2 Hazardous Substance Rsch. Ctr., N.J. Inst. Tech., 1989—; mem. sci. adv. com. Gulf Coast States Hazardous Substance Rsch. Ctr., Lamar U., Tex., 1991—. Contbr. research articles in field to profl. jours. Served with U.S. Army, 1954-56. Recipient Educator of Yr. award Erie-Niagara chpt. N.Y. State Soc. Profl. Engrs., 1989, Excellence award N.Y. State/United Univ. Professions, 1990; Ford fellow, 1962-63; sr. rsch. fellow Calif. Inst. Tech., 1970-71. Fellow ASCE (dir. Buffalo sect., pres. Buffalo sect. 1984-85); mem. Internat. Assn., Hydraulic Rsch., Am. Geophys. Union, Internat. Assn. Gt. Lakes Rsch., Sigma Xi, Tau Beta Pi, Chi Epsilon. Home: 821 Eggert Rd Buffalo NY 14226-4135

RUMLER, DIANA GALE, geriatrics nurse; b. Manchester, Tenn., Feb. 23, 1943; d. Donald Yale and Thelma Irene (Beach) Miller; m. Herschel Hinkle, Aug. 1961 (div. Jan. 1978); children: David, John, Jody Hinkle West; m. Lester Rumler, Jr. (div. June 1984). AA in Nursing, Ind. U.-Purdue U., Indpls., 1974; BS in Pub. Health-Journalism-Psychology, Ball State U., Muncie, 1983. RN; cert. ACLS, BLS. Psychiat. nurse Meth. Hosp., Indpls., 1974-78; women's infant and children's coord. Cmty. & Family Svcs. Inc., Portland, Ind., 1978-81, Ball Meml. Hosp., Muncie, Ind., 1981-84; pub. health nurse Health & Rehab. Svcs., Ft. Lauderdale, Fla., 1984; med.-surg. nurse Holy Cross Hosp., Ft. Lauderdale, 1985; pre-op/post-op nurse VA Med. Ctr., Nashville, 1986-89; nurse vascular, orthopedics, intensive care, telemetry, tchg VA Med. Ctr., Tucson, 1990—; WIC advocate hearings/radio show, Ind., 1978-81; health vol. outreach clinic St. Mary's Hosp., Tucson, 1993-94; vol. Hospice Family Care, Tucson. Contbr. articles to profl. jours. Mem. Nurses of Vet. Affairs, Am. Fedn. Govt. Employees, Ladies' Hermitage Assn. Democrat. Roman Catholic. Avocations: ceramics, crossstitch, health club activities, travel. Home: PO Box 17764 Tucson AZ 85731-7764 Office: VA Med Ctr S 6th Ave Tucson AZ 85723

RUMLER, ROBERT HOKE, agricultural consultant, retired association executive; b. Chambersburg, Pa., Apr. 4, 1915; s. Daniel Webster and Jennie (Sellers) R.; m. Frances Jeannette Montgomery, June 7, 1939 (dec. 1983); children: Craig M., Karen A. Loden; m. Hazel Miller-Karper, Aug. 23, 1986. B.S., Pa. State U., 1936. Asst. county agt. U. Mo., 1936-37; county agrl. agt. Pa. State U., 1937-45; asst. mgr., editor agrl. promotion div. E. I. duPont de Nemours & Co., Inc., Wilmington, Del., 1945-48; asst. exec. sec. Holstein-Friesian Assn. Am., 1948-53, 53-75, exec. sec., chief exec. officer, 1975-81, exec. chmn., 1981-82, chmn. emeritus, 1982—; pres. Holstein-Friesian Svcs., Inc., 1968-81; agribus. cons., 1982—; hon. mem. Holstein-Friesian de Mex. (C.A.); bd. dirs., chmn. Vt. Nat. Bank, Vt. Fin. Svcs., Inc., 1957-88; mem. U.S./USSR Joint Com. Agrl. Cooperation; past chmn. U.S. Agrl. Export Devel. Coun., FAS-USDA; mem. coordinating group Nat. Coop. Dairy Herd Improvement program USDA, 1964-80; mem. agrl. policy adv. com. USTR/USDA Multilateral Trade Negotiations, 1973-87, mem. agrl. tech. adv. com., 1987-95. Contbg. editorial writer Holstein World. Trustee Ea. States Expn., trustee emeritus, 1993—; trustee Assoc. Industries Vt.; past bd. dirs. Internat. Stockmans Ednl. Found.; chmn. adv. bd. Pa. State U., Mont Alto, 1990-94; bd. advisors Pa. State U., Harrisburg. Recipient Disting. award Nat. Dairy Herd Improvement Assn., 1974, Disting. Svc. award Nat. Agrl. Mktg. Orgn., 1977, Cert. of Appreciation, USDA, 1982, Disting. Svc. award Holstein Assn., 1985; named Dist. Alumnus Pa. State U., 1978, Dairy Industry Man of Yr., 1979, Headliner-of-Yr. Livestock Publs. Coun., 1995, Internat. Person of Yr. World Dairy Expo, 1996, 1st Disting. Alumnus AZ Fraternity Penn State, 1996; named to Internat. Livestock Hall of Fame, 1987; Robert H. Rumler scholar. Fellow Agr. Adventures; mem. Purebred Dairy Cattle Assn. (dir., exec. com.), Nat. Soc. Livestock Record Assns. (past pres., dir., Disting. Svcs. award 1981), Am. Dairy Sci. Assn. (Disting. Svc. award 1977), Agri-Bus. Found. (All-Time Gt. award 1981), Nat. Dairy Shrine (Dairy Hall of Fame 1976), N.E. Master Farmers Assn. (hon. master farmer), U.S. Animal Health Assn., Kiwanis, Masons, Elks, Alpha Zeta, Gamma Sigma Delta. Mem. United Ch. of Christ. Home: 937 Wallace Ave Chambersburg PA 17201-3884 Office: PO Box 945 Chambersburg PA 17201-0945

RUMMAGE, STEPHEN MICHAEL, lawyer; b. Massillon, Ohio, Dec. 27, 1955; s. Robert Everett and Kathleen Patricia (Newman) R.; m. Elizabeth Anne Seivert, Mar. 24, 1979; children: Everett Martin, Carter Kevin. BA in History and English, Stanford U., 1977; JD, U. Calif., Berkeley, 1980. Bar: Wash. 1980, U.S. Dist. Ct. (we. dist.) 1980, U.S. Ct. Appeals (9th cir.) 1983, U.S. Supreme Ct. 1985. Assoc. Davis, Wright et al, Seattle, 1980-85; ptnr. Davis Wright Tremaine, Seattle, 1986—. Co-author: Employer's Guide to Strike Planning and Prevention, 1985. Mem. Wash. Athletic Club. Democrat. Roman Catholic. Office: Davis Wright Tremaine 1501 4th Ave Ste 2600 Seattle WA 98101-1662

RUMMAN, WADI (SALIBA RUMMAN), civil engineer; b. Beit-Jala, Palestine, Sept. 7, 1926; came to U.S., 1948, naturalized, 1959; s. Saliba Y. and Miladeh (Nasrallah) R.; m. Doris E. Reed, Sept. 6, 1955; children—Mary Elaine, Linda Jean. B.S.E., U. Mich., 1949, M.S.E., 1953, Ph.D., 1959. Field engr. Finkbeiner Pettis and Strout, Toledo, 1949; structural engr. Vogt, Ivers, Seaman and Assos., Cin., 1950-51, Giffels and Vallet, Inc., Detroit, 1951-52; instr. U. Mich., 1952-59, asst. prof. civil engring., 1959-64, assoc. prof., 1964-75, prof., 1975-88, prof. emeritus, 1988—; cons. on design of reinforced concrete chimneys and other tower structures to industry and other agys. Author: Engineering, 1974, 3d edit., 1991. Fellow Am. Concrete Inst.; mem. ASCE (life), Am. Soc. Engring. Edn. (life), Internat. Assn. Bridge and Structural Engring., Sigma Xi, Chi Epsilon, Phi Kappa Phi. Home: 709 Woodhill Dr Saline MI 48176-1708 Office: U Mich Dept Civil Engring Ann Arbor MI 48109

RUMMEL, HAROLD EDWIN, real estate development executive; b. Youngstown, Ohio, Oct. 4, 1940; s. Harold Edward and Florence Louise (Hill) R.; children: Timothy B., Jonathan S., Briana. BS, U. Fla., 1963. Writer, editor various newspapers, Fla., 1958-70; polit. campaign mgr. various state campaigns, Tallahassee, Fla., 1971-79; sr. v.p. Fla. Fed. Sav. Bank, St. Petersburg, 1979-86; pres., chief exec. officer Rummel Cos., St. Petersburg, Fla., Mobile, Ala., 1986—. Active in civic and polit. orgns. Democrat. Home: 1682 Oceanview Dr Tierra Verde FL 33715-2500 Office: Rummel Cos 5401 Central Ave Saint Petersburg FL 33710-8049

RUMMEL, ROBERT WILAND, aeronautical engineer, author; b. Dakota, Ill., Aug. 4, 1915; s. William Howard and Dora (Ely) R.; m. Marjorie B. Cox, Sept. 30, 1939; children—Linda Kay, Sharon Lee, Marjorie Susan, Robert Wiland, Diana Beth. Diploma aeronautical engring., Curtiss Wright Tech. Inst. Aeros., 1935. Stress analyst Hughes Aircraft Co., Burbank, Calif., 1935-36, Lockheed Aircraft Corp., Burbank, 1936; draftsman Aero Engring. Corp., Long Beach, Calif., 1936, Nat. Aircraft Co., Alhambra, Calif., 1936-37; chief engr. Rearwin A/C & Engines, Inc., Kansas City, Kans., 1937-42; chief design engr. Commonwealth A/C, Inc., Kansas City, Kans., 1942-43; v.p. engring. Trans World Airlines, Inc., Kansas City, Mo., 1943-59; v.p. planning and research Trans World Airlines, Inc., 1959-69, v.p. tech. devel., 1969-78; pres. Robert W. Rummel Assos., Inc., Mesa, Ariz., 1978-87; aerospace cons., 1987—; commnr. Presdl. Commn. Space Shuttle Challenger Accident, 1986; chmn. nat. rsch. coun. Aero Space Engring. Bd. Fellow Inst. Aero. Scis., Soc. Automotive Engrs.; mem. NAE, Masons (32 deg.), Shriners. Home and Office: 1189 Leisure Word Mesa AZ 85206

RUMMERFIELD, BENJAMIN FRANKLIN, geophysicist; b. Denver, May 25, 1917; s. Lawrence L. and Helen A. (Roper) R.; Engr. Geology, Colo. Sch. Mines, 1940; grad. Harvard U. Advanced Mgmt. Program, 1947, Aspen Inst. Humanistic Studies, 1958, Indsl. Coll. Armed Forces, 1963; m. Mary Merchant, Feb. 16, 1979; children: Ann S., Michael J., Benjamin F., Mary Susan, Sonya, Karim. Asst. mgr. Seismograph Service Corp., Mexico City, 1947-50, Venezuela and Colombia, 1945-47; exec. v.p. U.S. and Can. ops. Century Geophys. Corp., Tulsa, 1950-60, also dir.; pres. GeoData Corp., Tulsa, 1960—, Gulf Coast GeoData, Houston, 1962—; dir. Permian Exploration, Custom Data Services; cons. Petróleos Mexicanos. Bd. dirs. YMCA, Tulsa, 1955—, pres., 1956-59. Recipient Outstanding Service award YMCA, Tulsa, 1958, 63, Disting. Achievement medal Colo. Sch. Mines, 1978, hon. mention for painting Philbrook Art Mus., 1961. Mem. Tulsa Geol. Soc., Colo. Sch. Mines Alumni Assn. (pres. 1953), Asociación Mexicana de Geólogos Petróleos, Am. Assn. Petroleum Geologists, Soc. Exploration Geophysicists (life, nat. v.p. 1958), Sigma Gamma Epsilon. Clubs: Tulsa, Harvard (Tulsa). Contbr. numerous articles to profl. jours. Home: 6787 Timberlane Rd Tulsa OK 74136-4518 Office: care GeoData Corp 211 S Cheyenne Ave Tulsa OK 74103-3009

RUMP, KENDALL E., air transportation executive; b. Valparaiso, Ind., Sept. 15, 1960; s. Erwin E. and D. Jean (Folkening) R. BSBA, Ball State U., 1982. Sales rep. CF Airfreight, Richmond, Va., 1982-83; account mgr. CF Airfreight, Norfolk, Va., 1984-85; terminal mgr. CF Airfreight, Saginaw, Mich., 1985-86; v.p., co-owner CCX Express Svcs., Inc., Richmond, 1987-91; exec. v.p. CCX Express Svcs., Inc., Norfolk, 1991-94, pres., 1993-96; pres., co-owner KRB Couriers, Inc., Norfolk, 1994-96; pres. Express Cargo Svcs., Inc., Norfolk, 1996—; advisor com. Dulles Washington Airport Task Force, 1992-93. Recipient Top 75 Alumni award Ball State U., 1994. Mem. Nat. Air Freight Trucking Alliance, Washington Air Cargo Assn., Balt.-Washington Air Cargo Assn., Hampton Rds. Air Cargo Assn. (1st v.p. 1991, pres. 1992, bd. dirs. 1993, Past Pres. award 1992), Air and Expedited Motor Carrier Assn., Dulles Airport Broker's Assn., Richmond Export-Import Club, Hampton Rds. Traffic Club (fund raiser, program chair joy fund 1992-93, advisor 1993), Richmond Traffic Club, Delta Nu Alpha (sec. 1984). Office: CCX Express Svcs Inc PO Box 14309 Norfolk VA 23518-0309

RUMPEL, PETER LOYD, architect, educator, artist; b. Hamilton, Ont., Can., Mar. 25, 1939; s. George Hilburn and Reine (Loyd) R.; children: Hillary, Reine. B.Arch., U. Fla., 1961. Registered architect. Architect Clements, Rumpel, Assocs., Jacksonville, Fla., 1976-84; architect Clements, Rumpel, Goodwin, d'Avi, Jacksonville, 1984—; CRG Archs./Planners, Inc., 1992; assoc. prof. U. Fla., Gainesville, 1984-92; adj. prof. U. Fla., 1982-84; disting. lectr. 1984-92. Prin. works include Fla. Jr. Coll. Jacksonville-N. Campus (honor award Fla. Assn. AIA 1979, merit award Jacksonville chpt. AIA 1972), River Garden Hebrew Home for Aged (Modern Nursing Home of Month award 1971, hon. mention Fla. Assn. AIA 1971, merit award Jacksonville chpt. AIA 1972), Fla. Christian Home Apts. (award merit Fla. Assn. AIA 1973, merit award Jacksonville chpt. AIA 1974, 4th ann. award Outstanding Concrete Structure in Fla. 1974), St. Mary's Episcopal Ch. Renovation (honor award Jacksonville chpt. AIA 1974, award merit Fla. Assn. AIA 1974), Rumpel Residence (first award Jacksonville chpt. Am. Plywood Assn. 1974, honor award Jacksonville chpt. AIA 1974, award merit AIA Homes for Better Living Program 1975), Higginson Residence (merit award Jacksonville chpt. AIA 1974), Sawgrass Harbor Condominiums (award merit Jacksonville chpt. AIA 1975), Sawgrass Golf Club (citation Jacksonville chpt. AIA 1975), Jacksonville Jewish Ctr. (honor award Fla. Assn. AIA 1976, citation Jacksonville chpt. AIA 1977), U. N. Fla. Lab.-Office Bldg. (merit award Jacksonville chpt. AIA 1977), Fla. Jr. Coll., S. Campus, Phase II (honor award Jacksonville chpt. AIA 1977), Drew Bldg. Renovation (merit award Jacksonville chpt. AIA 1978), Mayport Jr. High Sch. (merit award Jacksonville chpt. AIA 1978, award merit Fla. Assn. AIA 1978, First Ann. Gov.'s Design award 1981), T.R.E.E.O. U. Fla. (honor award Jacksonville chpt. AIA 1979, honor award Fla. Assn. AIA 1979), Officer's Conf. Ctr., Camp Keystone (merit award Jacksonville chpt. AIA 1980), St. James Community Life Ctr. (honor award Jacksonville chpt. AIA 1981), U. N. Fla., student activity ctr. (honor award Jacksonville chpt. AIA 1982, award excellence Fla. Assn. AIA 1982), Unenlisted Personnel Housing (award merit ASID 1983), Hurley Manor Elderly Housing (award excellence Jacksonville chpt. AIA 1984), Arlington By the River (honor award Jacksonville chpt. AIA 1984, award excellence Jacksonville chpt. AIA 1984), 120-Bed Nursing Home Care Unit (honor award Jacksonville chpt. AIA 1984, award excellence Concrete Inst. Fla. 1984), Fla. A&M U. Sch. Architecture Bldg. (honor award Jacksonville chpt. AIA 1985), Drew Bldg. (design recognition award Jacksonville area C. of C. 1984, preservation award City of Jacksonville and Jacksonville Hist. Landmarks Com. 1985), Cypress Village Apts. (award for excellence Jacksonville chpt. AIA 1991), Drew Bldg. Renovation (Merit award Jacksonville chpt. AIA. 1989), Bachelor Enlisted Quarters and Enlisted Men's Dining Facility (Significant Concrete Structure Fla. First Coast chpt. ACI 1994), Additions and remodeling Pine Forest Elem. Sch. (award for excellence Jacksonville chpt. AIA 1995). Pres. Jacksonville Community Design Ctr.; mem. Jacksonville Hist. Landmarks Com., 1981-84. Served with USMC. Recipient first award nat. competition to design new sch. architecture at Fla. A&M U., 1980, Dist. Alumni award U. Fla., 1995. Fellow AIA (honor award Fla. chpt. 1981, John Dyal award Jacksonville chpt. 1985). Democrat. Episcopalian. Home: 133 Marine St Saint Augustine FL 32084-5003 Office: CRG Architects Planners Inc 2111 Corporate Square Blvd Jacksonville FL 32216-1919

RUMPF, JOHN LOUIS, civil engineer, consultant; b. Phila., Feb. 21, 1921; s. Harry L. and Emma S. R.; m. Grace Willis, Apr. 1, 1944 (dec.); children—Jonathan, Christopher; m. Patricia E. Burkitt, June 20, 1970. B.S.C.E., Drexel U., 1943; M.S.C.E., U. Pa., 1954; Ph.D. in Civil Engring. (NSF fellow), Lehigh U., 1960. Structural engr. Belmont Iron Works, Phila., 1946; instr. Drexel U., 1947-50, asst. prof. civil engring., 1950-54, assoc. prof., 1954-56, prof., head dept. civil engring., 1960-69; research instr. Fritz Engring. Lab., Lehigh U., 1956-60; dean Coll. Engring. and Architecture Temple U., Phila., 1969-76; v.p. acad. affairs Temple U., 1976-82, exec. v.p., 1982-84, prof. civil engring., 1984-86; cons. engr. for bldg. and bridge design and investigations, 1947—. Author: Plastic Design of Braced Multistory Steel Frames, 1968; contbg. author Structural Steel Design, 1974. Mem. Lower Moreland Twp. (Pa.) Zoning Bd., 1953-56; mem. Lower Moreland Twp. Sch. Dist. Authority, 1962-70; bd. dirs. Abington Meml. Hosp. (Pa.), 1982-88. Served to capt. C.E. U.S. Army, 1943-46. Decorated Army Commendation medal.; Named Engr. of Yr. Tech. Socs. of Delaware Valley, 1975. Fellow ASCE; mem. Am. Soc. Engring. Edn., Nat. Soc. Profl. Engrs., Research Council for Structural Connections, Am. Concrete Inst., Sigma Xi, Tau Beta Pi, Phi Kappa Phi, Chi Epsilon. Club: Engrs. of Phila. (George Washington medal 1979). Research, publs. on structural connections and members, 1956-69. Home: 1213 Red Rambler Rd Jenkintown PA 19046-2916 Office: Temple U Coll Engring Philadelphia PA 19122

RUMSEY, VICTOR HENRY, electrical engineering educator emeritus; b. Devizes, Eng., Nov. 22, 1919; s. Albert Victor and Susan Mary (Norman) R.; m. Doris Herring, Apr. 2, 1942; children: John David, Peter Alan, Catherine Anne. B.A., Cambridge U., 1941, D.Sc. in Physics, 1972; D.Eng., Tohoku U., Japan, 1962. With U.K. Sci. Civil Service, 1941-48; asst. to asso. prof. Ohio State U., 1948-54; prof. U. Ill., 1954-57, U. Calif., Berkeley, 1957-66; prof. elec. engring. and computer scis. U. Calif., San Diego, 1966-87, prof. emeritus, 1987—; dept. chmn. U. Calif., 1977-81. Author 1 book in field; contbr. articles to profl. jours. Guggenheim fellow.; recipient George Sinclair award Ohio State U., 1982. Fellow IEEE (Morris Liebman prize), Union Radio Scientifique Internationale, Internat. Astron. Union; mem. Nat. Acad. Engring. Patentee in field. Home: PO Box 400 Occidental CA 95465-0400

RUMSFELD, DONALD HENRY, former government official, corporate executive; b. Chgo., July 9, 1932; s. George Donald and Jeannette (Husted) R.; m. Joyce Pierson, Dec. 27, 1954; 3 children. A.B., Princeton U., 1954; hon. degree, De Paul U. Coll. Commerce, Ill. Coll., Lake Forest Coll., Park Coll., Tuskegee Inst., Nat. Coll. Edn., Bryant Coll., Claremont (Calif.) Grad. Sch., Ill. Wesleyan U., Rand Grad. Sch. Adminstrv. asst. U.S. Ho. of Reps., 1957-59; with A.G. Becker & Co., Chgo., 1960-62; mem. 88th-91st Congresses from 13th Ill. dist., Pres. Richard Nixon's Cabinet, 1969-73; dir. OEO, asst. to pres., 1969-70; counsellor to Pres., dir. econ. stabilization program, 1971-72; U.S. ambassador and permanent rep. to NATO, 1973-74; White House chief of staff for Pres. Gerald Ford, 1974-75; sec. Dept. Def., 1975-77; pres., chief exec. officer, then chmn. G.D. Searle & Co., Skokie, Ill., 1977-85; spl. envoy of Pres. Ronald Reagan to Mid. East, 1983-84; sr. advisor William Blair & Co., Chgo., 1985-90; chmn., chief exec. officer General Instrument Corp., Chgo., 1990-93; chmn. bd. dirs. Gilead Scis., Inc., Foster City, Calif., 1997—; bd. dirs. ABB AB, Gulfstream Aerospace Corp., Kellogg Co. Metricom, Sears, Roebuck & Co., Tribune Co.; bd. trustees RAND Corp., 1977—; chmn. bd. trustees RAND Corp. Naval Aviator USN, 1954-57. Recipient Presdl. Medal of Freedom, 1977, George Catlett Marshall award, Woodrow Wilson award, Dwight David Eisenhower medal. Office: 400 N Michigan Ave Ste 405 Chicago IL 60611-4129

RUND, DOUGLAS ANDREW, emergency physician; b. Columbus, Ohio, July 20, 1945; s. Carl Andrew and Caroline Amelia (Row) R.; m. Sue E Padavana, 1980; children: Carie, Emily, Ashley. BA, Yale U., 1967; MD, Stanford U., 1971. Lic. physician, Ohio; Diplomate Nat. Bd. Med. Examiners, Am. Bd. Family Practice, Am. Bd. Emergency Medicine (pres., 1995—). Intern in medicine U. Calif., San Francisco-Moffett Hosp., 1971-72; resident in gen. surgery Stanford U., 1972-74; Robert Wood Johnson Found. clin. scholar in medicine Stanford U., 1974-76; med. dir. Mid-Peninsula Health Svc., Palo Alto, Calif., 1975-76; clin. instr. dept. medicine and preventive medicine Stanford U. Med. Sch., 1975-76; assoc. prof., dir. div. emergency medicine Ohio State Coll. Medicine, 1982-87; dir. emergency medicine residency program, assoc. prof. dept. family medicine, 1976-87, prof., chmn. dept. preventive medicine, 1988-90, prof., chmn. dept. emergency medicine, 1990—, prof., interim chmn. dept. family medicine, 1994-95; attending staff Ohio State U. Hosps., 1976—; med. dir. CSCC, Emergency Med. Svcs. Dept.; pres. Internat. Rsch. Inst. Emergency Medicine; med. dir. Internat. Soc. for Emergency Med. Svcs.; sr. rsch. fellow NATO: Health and Med. Aspects of Disaster Preparedness, 1985-87; bd. dirs. ABEM, 1988-97, sr. editor in tng. exam., 1989—; mem. Residency Rev. Com. for Emergency Medicine, 1997—; on profl. leave epidemiology and injury control, U. Edinburgh, Scotland, 1987. Fellow Am. Coll. Emergency Physicians (task force on substance abuse and injury control); Mem. Nat. Inst. on Alcohol Abuse and Alcoholism, IAAA, Assn. Acad. Chairs Emergency Medicine (pres. 1992-93), Soc. Acad. Emergency Medicine (chmn. internat. com. 1991—), Columbus Medical Forum (pres. 1993), Alpha Omega Alpha. Author: Triage, 1981; Essentials of Emergency Medicine, 1982, 2nd edit., 1986; Emergency Radiology, 1982; Emergency Psychiatry, 1983; Environmental Emergencies, 1985; editor: Emergency Medicine Ann., 1983, 84; Emergency Medicine Survey, Annals of Emergency Medicine; editor-in-chief Ohio State Series on Emergency Medicine, Emergency Medicine Observer, 1986-87; guest editor Annals of Emergency Medicine Symposium, 1986; mem. editorial bd. Physician, Sports Medicine, Emergency Med. Svcs.; contbr. chpt. to Family Medicine Principles and Practice, 1978, 2d edit., 1983; contbr. articles to profl. jours. Office: Ohio State U 473 W 12th Ave Columbus OH 43210-1252

RUNDELL, ORVIS HERMAN, JR., psychologist; b. Oklahoma City, June 16, 1940; s. Orvis Herman and Virginia Reid (George) R.; BS, U. Okla., 1962, MS, 1972, PhD, 1976; m. Jane Shannon Brians, June 25, 1966; children: Leslie Jane, Anne Reid. Lab. mgr. Okla. Center Alcohol and Drug-Related Studies, Oklahoma City, 1969-76, staff scientist, 1974—; asst. prof. psychiatry and behavioral scis. U. Okla. Health Sci. Center, 1976—; dir. clin. physiology and sleep disorders ctr. Columbia Presbyterian Hosp., Oklahoma City, 1982—; clin. dir. Diagnostic Sleep Ctr. of Dallas, 1989-93; ptnr. Sleep Medicine Assocs., 1994—; dir. Columbia Sleep Ptnrs. Program, 1996—; cons. in field; mem. instl. rev. bd. U. Okla. Health Sci. Ctr., 1989—. Bd. dirs. Hist. Preservation, Inc., Oklahoma City, 1978-90. Served with USAR, 1963-69. Grantee Nat. Inst. Drug Abuse, Nat. Inst. Alcohol Abuse and Alcoholism, Kerr Found. Fellow Am. Sleep Disorders Assn.; mem. Am. Psychol. Assn., N.Y. Acad. Scis., Psi Chi, Phi Gamma Delta. Author articles, papers in field, chpts. in books; asst. editor Alcohol Tech. Reports, 1976—; cons. editor Psychophysiology, 1974—. Home: 431 NW 20th St Oklahoma City OK 73103-1918 Office: 700 NE 13th St Oklahoma City OK 73104-5004

RUNDGREN, TODD, musician, record producer; b. Upper Darby, Pa., June 22, 1948; 3 children. Solo artist, 1970—; mem. mus. groups Nazz, 1967-69, Utopia, 1973— ; record producer for numerous mus. groups including Badfinger, Paul Butterfield, Grand Funk, Hall & Oates, New York Dolls, The Band, Patti Smith, The Tubes, The Pursuit of Happiness, XTC; numerous recs. and compositions including Can We Still be Friends, Hello, It's Me, Up Against It, 1989; albums include Another Life, 1975, (with The Nazz) Nazz, 1968, Nazz Nazz, 1969, Nazz III, 1970, (with Utopia) Todd Rundgren's Utopia, 1974, Oops! Wrong Planet, 1987, Adventures in Utopia, 1980, Deface the Music, 1980, Swing to the Right, 1982, Utopia, 1982, Anthology, 1989; solo albums include Runt, 1970, Something/Anything, 1972, Initiation, 1975, Faithful, 1976, Hermit of the Mink Hollow, 1978, Back to the Bars, 1978, Healing, 1981, A Capella, 1985, Nearly Human, 1989, -2nd Wind, 1991, No World Order, 1993, The Best of Todd Rundgren, 1994; composer TV mus. scores Crime Story, Pee-wee's Playhouse, theatre musical score Up Against It, 1990. Office: Rhino Records 10635 Santa Monica Blvd Los Angeles CA 90025-8300*

RUNDIO, JOAN PETERS (JO RUNDIO), public administrator; b. Dearborn, Mich., Mar. 17, 1941; d. Joe and Donna (Sells) Peters; m. Florian (Pug) Frank Rundio Jr., Sept. 8., 1971; children: Jeffrey Daniel, David Eric. Diploma, Bronson Meth. Sch. Nursing, 1962; BA, U. Redlands, 1978; MPA, U. South Ala., 1987. RN Mich., 1962. Emergency nurse Bronson Meth. Hosp., Kalamazoo, 1962-63, The Queen's Med. Ctr., Honolulu, 1963-65; orthopaedic nurse The Honolulu Med. Group, 1965-72; sch. nurse Corpus Christi (Tex.) Sch. Dist., 1979-81; pub. health nurse Tri-County Health Dept., Traverse City, Mich., 1983-85; adminstrv. intern City of Troy

(Mich.), 1987-88; acring econ. devel. dir. City of Traverse City, 1988-89; mgr. personal health svcs. Tri-County Health Dept., Traverse City, 1989; asst. city mgr. City of Traverse City, 1990—. V.p. Women's Econ. Devel. Orgn., Traverse City, 1993-95, mem., 1984—; mem. Traverse City Planning Commn., 1995—; rep. Traverse City Schs. Adv. Com., 1982-85, 88-89; mem. bd. trustees Nat. Cherry Festival, 1996—. Recipient James H. Boyd award U. South Ala., Mobile, 1987. Mem. NOW (founding mem. Meridian, MIss. chpt. 1973), Michigan City. Mgmt. Assn. (bd. dirs. 1996—), Internat. City Mgmt. Assn., Cherryland Humane Soc., Pi Sigma Alpha. Avocations: travel, reading, canoeing, cross-country skiing. Office: City of Traverse City 400 Boardman Ave Traverse City MI 49684-2542

RUNDIO, LOUIS MICHAEL, JR., lawyer; b. Chgo., Sept. 13, 1943; s. Louis Michael Sr. and Germaine Matilda (Pasternack) R.; m. Ann Marie Bartlett, July 10, 1971; children: Matthew, Melissa. BS in Physics, Loyola U., Chgo., 1965, JD, 1972. Bar: Ill. 1972, U.S. Dist. Ct. (no. dist.) Ill. 1972, U.S. Ct. Appeals (7th cir.) 1974, U.S. Dist. Ct. (ea. dist.) Mich. 1983. Assoc. McDermott, Will & Emery, Chgo., 1972-77, ptnr., 1978—. Served to 1st lt. U.S. Army, 1965-68, Vietnam. Mem. ABA, Chgo. Bar Assn. Home: 676 Skye Ln Barrington IL 60010-5506 Office: McDermott Will & Emery 227 W Monroe St Chicago IL 60606-5016

RUNDQUIST, HOWARD IRVING, investment banker; b. Winona, Minn., Mar. 21, 1929; s. Howard Wadsworth and Delilah Jeanette (Erickson) R.; m. Nancy Evelyn Hood, July 30, 1980; children: Sarah Louise, Beth Anne, Peter Hood, Susan Jenniffer, Rebecca Jane. AB, Gustavus Adolphus Coll., 1951; MBA, Harvard U., 1958. Mem. staff MIT Lincoln Lab., Lexington, Mass., 1954-56, 58-60; sr. v.p. Aubrey G. Lanston Co. Inc., N.Y.C., 1960-92; ret., 1992. Investment advisor bd. pensions Evang. Luth. Ch. in Am., 1992—. Lt. USNR, 1951-54. Mem. Webhanet Golf Club, Edgcomb Tennis Club (Kennebunk, Maine). Republican. Lutheran.

RUNG, RICHARD ALLEN, lawyer, retired air force officer, retired educator; b. Rome, N.Y., Dec. 16, 1929; s. George Stuart and Ruth Marie (Henderberg) R.; m. Yolande Moalli, June 15, 1957; children: Michael, Bruce, Colette. B.A. summa cum laude, St. Michael's Coll., 1957; J.D., Syracuse U., 1960. Bar: N.Y. 1961. Law partner Lawler & Rung, DeWitt, N.Y., 1960-61; law assoc. J. F. Ferlo Law Office, Rome, N.Y., 1961-63; commd. 2d lt. USAF, 1952, advanced through grades to col., 1979; USAF fighter pilot, 1952-55; USAF fighter pilot and flight comdr. La., Spain, Vietnam, N.Y., 1963-74; USAF flight safety evaluator and cons. Norton AFB, Calif., 1974-79; prof. aerospace studies, Air Force ROTC detachment comdr. U. Ill., Champaign-Urbana, 1979-82; commandant AFJROTC Pompano Beach High Sch., (Fla.), 1982-85, Northeast High Sch., (Fla.), 1985-92. Decorated Legion of Merit, DFC, Air medal with 7 oak leaf clusters; recipient award Aerospace Safety Hall Fame, 1979, Disting. Svc. award Am. Vets., 1980, Citation Am. Legion, 1984, Citizenship medal SAR, 1989, Citation Air Force Assn. Fla., 1990, Eagle Scout. Mem. Delta Epsilon Sigma, Sigma Nu, Phi Delta Phi. Roman Catholic. Home: 2672 Emerald Way N Deerfield Beach FL 33442-8640 *The human being, a magnificent creation, remains obscure if the element of motivation lies dormant. The human will is the key to personal achievement. Discipline is the remedy for what besets many of our American institutions, including our public schools, our criminal justice system, our transportation system, the professions, industry and government. Discipline is simply making good laws and rules and enforcing them. Without discipline, our institutions are fostering dysfunction.*

RUNGE, BARBARA KAY, lawyer, arbitrator, mediator; b. Houston, July 15, 1949; d. William A. and Martha Ellen (Boynton) R.; m. W.R. Howard, May 26, 1979. BA in govt., Tex. Tech. U., Lubbock, 1971; JD, Tex. Tech. Sch. of Law, Lubbock, 1974. Bar: Tex. 1974, U.S. Supreme Ct. 1986. Owner, operator Law Offices of Barbara K. Runge, Houston, 1975—; pres., bd. trustees Tex. Tech. Sch. of Law, 1993—; v.p. Tex. chpt. Am. Acad. of Matrimonial Lawyers, 1995— (fellow 1992). Contbr. articles to profl. jours. Life fellow Tex. Bar Found., Austin, Tex., 1981. Fellow Houston Bar Found. (past pres. Family Law Section); mem. ABA, Tex. Bar Assn., Assn. of Woman Attorneys (past pres.), Charter 100 of Houston (v.p. social 1996—). Presbyterian. Avocations: art, travel, swimming, beachcombing. Office: Law Ofcs of B K Runge 5615 Kirby Dr Ste 920 Houston TX 77005-2447

RUNGE, DE LYLE PAUL, retired library director, consultant; b. Madison, Wis., Feb. 3, 1918; s. Charles Delial and Josephine Ida Clara (Niebuhr) R.; m. Ethelyn Fay Green, Sept. 26, 1943; children: Richard Rene, Willa Dee, Robert Roy. BA in Commerce, U. Wis., 1940, BSLS, 1943. Dir. pub. rels., coord. ref. svcs. Grand Rapids (Mich.) Pub. Libr., 1946-53; libr. dir. St. Petersburg (Fla.) Pub. Libr., 1953-82; cons. on libr. bldgs., 1964—; mem. Fla. State Libr. Adv. Coun., 1973-82. With AUS, 1943-46, ETO, lt. col. USAR. Mem. ALA, Fla. Libr. Assn. (pres. 1968-69, exec. bd. 1969-70), Southeastern Libr. Assn., ASPA, Am. Philatelic Soc., St. Petersburg Stamp Club, Kiwanis, Beta Phi Mu. Home: 4520 Cortez Way S Saint Petersburg FL 33712-4029

RUNGE, DONALD EDWARD, food wholesale company executive; b. Milw., Mar. 20, 1938; s. Adam and Helen Teresa (Voss) R.; divorced; children: Roland, Richard, Lori. Grad., Spencerian Coll., Milw., 1960. Fin. v.p. Milw. Cheese Co., Waukesha, Wis., 1962-69; dir. Farm House Foods Corp., Milw., 1966-89, pres., 1966-89, chief exec. officer, treas., 1984-89, chmn., pres., 1985-89; chmn., chief exec. officer Retailing Corp. Am., Milw., 1982-89; chief exec. officer, treas. Drug Systems Inc., Milw., 1984-89; chmn. Drug Systems Inc. (now Retailing Corp. of Am.), Milw., 1985-89; pres. TDC, 1987-89; chmn., pres. Runge Industries, Gen. Growth, Inc., 1989—; bd. dirs. Convenient Food Mart, CasaBlanca Industries, Inc., City of Industry, Calif.; sec. The Diana Corp., Milw., 1985-86, treas. 1986—, pres. 1987-96; chmn. Economy Dry Goods Co. Inc.; treas. Fairbanks Farms Inc. Adventist. *I believe there is very little in life that cannot be accomplished if a person truly wants to attain the goal.*

RUNGE, KAY KRETSCHMAR, library director; b. Davenport, Iowa, Dec. 9, 1946; d. Alfred Edwin and Ina (Paul) Kretschmar; m. Peter S. Runge Sr., Aug. 17, 1968; children: Peter Jr., Katherine. BS in History Edn., Iowa State U., 1969; MLS, U. Iowa, 1970. Pub. service librarian Anoka County Library, Blaine, Minn., 1971-72; cataloger Augustana Coll., Rock Island, Ill., 1972-74; dir. Scott County Library System, Eldridge, Iowa, 1974-85, Davenport (Iowa) Pub. Libr., 1985—. Bd. dirs. River Ctr. for Performing Arts, Davenport, 1983—; chmn. bd. dirs. Am. Inst. Commerce, 1989—; v.p. Quad-Cities Conv. and Visitors Bur., 1997—, Quad-Cities Grad. Study Ctr., 1992—, Downtown Davenport Devel. Corp., 1992—, Hall of Honor Bd. Davenport Ctrl. H.S., 1992-95, Brenton Bank, 1996—; mem. steering com. Quad-Cities Visions for the Future, 1987-91, Iowa Humanities Bd., 1994-97; bd. govs. Iowa State U. Found., 1991—. Recipient Svc. Key award Iowa State U. Alumni Assn., 1979. Mem. ALA (chmn. library adminstrs. and mgrs. div., fundraising section 1988), Iowa Library Assn. (pres. 1983), Pub. Library Assn. (bd. dirs. 1990-96), Iowa Edn. Media Assn. (Intellectual Freedom award 1984), Alpha Delta Pi (alumni state pres. 1978). Lutheran. Office: Davenport Pub Libr 321 N Main St Davenport IA 52801-1409

RUNGE, PATRICK RICHARD, lawyer; b. Iowa City, Iowa, Oct. 25, 1969; s. Richard Gary and Sally Louise (Cozzolino) R.; m. Kimberly Marie Hansen, Mar. 16, 1996. BSBA in Econs., U. Nebr., Omaha, 1991; JD, Creighton U., 1994. Bar: Nebr. 1994, U.S. Dist. Ct. Nebr. 1994. Prodn. editor U.N.O. Gateway, Omaha, 1990-91; graphic designer Omaha (Nebr.) Pub. Power Dist., 1991-97; intern U.S. Dist. Ct., Omaha, 1993; rsch. asst. Creighton U., Omaha, 1993; sr. cert. law student Creighton Legal Clinic, Omaha, 1994; atty. Runge Law Office, Omaha, 1994-95, Runge & Chase, Omaha, 1995—; pub. defender Winnebago Tribe, 1996—. Disting. scholar Omaha (Nebr.) World-Herald, 1987-91; Merit scholar Creighton Law Sch., Omaha, 1991-94. Democrat. Roman Catholic. Home: 7710 Howard St Apt 7 Omaha NE 68114-5446 Office: Runge & Chase 1941 S 42nd St Ste 218 Omaha NE 68105-2946

RUNGE, PAUL EDWARD, baseball umpire, realtor; b. St. Catherine's, Ont., Can., Oct. 20, 1940; came to U.S., 1947; s. Edward Paul and Viola Irene (Meek) R.; m. Anastasia Mouzas, Oct. 17, 1965; children: Brian Edward, Reneé Dyann. Student, San Diego City Coll., 1959-61; BA in Edn. and Bus., Ariz. State U., 1964. Lic. real estate broker. Umpire Nat. League of Profl. Baseball. Mem. Helenic Cultural Soc. Baseball scholar Ariz. State U., 1961; named Umpire of Yr. by Harry Wendelsted Sch. of Umpiring, 1993; inducted Hall of Fame San Diego H.S., 1991. Mem. Major League Umpires Assn. Union (pres., v.p., bd. dirs.), San Diego Bd. Realtors, Ariz. State U. Alumni Assn., Phi Delta Theta. Republican. Mem. New Apostolic Ch. Umpire All-Star games, San Diego, Houston, Pitts., 1978, 86, 94, Championship Series, 1977, 81, 82, 85, 88, 90, World Series, 1979, 84, 89, 93. Home: 649 Calle De La Sierra El Cajon CA 92019-1243 Office: Major League Umpires Assoc 1735 Market St Ste 3420 Philadelphia PA 19103-7501

RUNK, CARL, head coach men's lacrosse. Grad., U. Ariz., 1962, MA in Phys. Edn., 1964. Coach Towson State U., 1968—. Recipient Francis L. "Babe" Kraus Meml. award, Coll. Divsn. Coach of Yr. Office: Towson State U Dept Athletics 8000 York Rd Baltimore MD 21252-0001

RUNKLE, MARTIN DAVEY, library director; b. Cin., Oct. 18, 1937; s. Newton and Ilo (Neal) R.; m. Nancy Force, Aug. 7, 1965; children: Seth, Elizabeth. BA, Muskingum Coll., 1959; MA, U. Pitts., 1964, U. Chgo., 1973. Library systems analyst U. Chgo., 1970-75, head cataloging librarian, 1975-79, asst. dir. tech. services, 1979-80, dir. library, 1980—; sr. lectr. grad. library sch. U. Chgo., 1977-90. Fulbright grantee, 1965. Mem. ALA, Univ. Club Chgo. Office: U Chgo 1100 E 57th St Chicago IL 60637-1502

RUNNALLS, (OLIVER) JOHN (CLYVE), nuclear engineering educator; b. Barrie Island, Ont., Can., June 26, 1924; s. John Lawrence and Ethel May (Arnold) R.; m. Vivian Constance Stowe, Sept. 13, 1947; children: David John, Catherine Ruth. B.A.Sc., U. Toronto, 1948, M.A.Sc., 1949, Ph.D., 1951. Registered profl. engr., Ont. Research and devel. scientist Atomic Energy of Can., Ltd., Chalk River, Ont. and Paris, 1951-71; sr. adviser uranium and nuclear energy Energy, Mines and Resources Can., Ottawa, Ont., 1971-79; prof. energy studies U. Toronto, 1979-89, chmn. Ctr. Nuclear Engring., 1983-89; prof. emeritus nuclear engring. and energy studies, 1989—; chmn. bd. Inst. Hydrogen Systems, 1983-89; pres. O.J.C. Runnalls & Assocs., Ltd.; bd. dirs. Rio Narcea Gold Mines Ltd., Toronto. Contbr. articles to profl. jours.; patentee in field. Decorated Queen's Silver Jubilee medal, 1977; recipient B.T.A. Bell Commemorative medal Can. Mining Jour., 1979, Ian F. McRae award Can. Nuclear Assn., 1980. Fellow Royal Soc. Can., Can. Acad. Engring.; mem. Assn. Profl. Engrs., Can. Nuclear Assn. (bd. dirs., past chmn.), Can. Nuclear Soc. Home and Office: 170 Lytton Blvd, Toronto, ON Canada M4R 1L4

RUNNELLS, DONALD DEMAR, geochemist, consultant; b. Eureka, Utah, Dec. 30, 1936; s. Raymond DeMar and Cleo Cecil (Beckstead) R.; m. Erika Anna Bahe, Sept. 3, 1958; children: Timothy, Suzanne. BS with high honors, U. Utah, 1958; MA, Harvard U., 1960, PhD, 1963. Rsch. geochemist Shell Devel. Co., Houston and Miami, 1963-67; asst. prof. U. Calif.-Santa Barbara, 1967-69; assoc. prof. geochemistry U. Colo., Boulder, 1969-75, prof., 1975-92, chair dept. geol. sci., 1990-92; v.p. Shepherd Miller, Inc., Ft. Collins, Colo., 1993—. cons. geochemistry to cos., and govt. agys. Mem. water sci. and tech. bd. NRC/NAS, 1989-92. Contbr. articles to profl. pubs. NSF fellow, 1958-62. Fellow Geol. Soc. Am.; mem. Am. Chem. Soc., Assn. Exploration Geologists (pres. 1990-91), Geochemical Soc., Assn. Ground Water Scientists and Engrs. Home: 8032 Allott Ave Fort Collins CO 80525-4269 Office: Shepherd Miller Inc 3801 Automation Way Fort Collins CO 80525-3434

RUNNICLES, DONALD, conductor; b. Edinburgh, Scotland, Nov. 16, 1954. Student, Edinburgh U., Cambridge U., London Opera Ctr. Repetiteur Mannheim, Germany, Nat. theatre, from 1980, Kapellmeister, from 1984; prin. condr. Hanover, from 1987; numerous appearances with Hamburg Staatsoper; former gen. music dir. Stadtische Buhnen, Freiburg/Breisgau; mus. dir. San Francisco Opera, 1992—; appearances with Met. Opera include Lulu, 1988, The Flying Dutchman, 1990, The Magic Flute; condr. Vienna Staatsoper, 1990-91; debut at Glyndebourne with Don Giovanni, 1991, Salzburg Festival with Don Giovanni, 1996, also numerous symphonic engagements; condr. London Symphony Orch., Orch. de Paris, Israel Philharm., Rotterdam Philharm., Seattle Symphony, Pitts. Symphony, Chgo. Symphony, St. Louis Symphony, San Francisco Symphony, Cleve. Orch., New World Symphony, Bavarian Radio Symphony Orch., 2 complete ring cycles with Wiener Staatsoper; rec. Hansel and Gretel (Humperdinck), Gluck's Orphée with San Francisco Opera Orch., 1995, Tannhäuser-Bayreuth Festspick, 1995, Harvey Milk with San Francisco Opera, 1996; opened Edinburgh Festival, 1994, 96. Office: San Francisco Opera War Meml Opera House, 301 Van Ness Ave San Francisco CA 94102 also: Stadtische Buhnen, Bertoldstr 46, W-7800 Freiburg/Breisgau Germany

RUNNING, NELS, air force officer; b. Missoula, Mont.. BS, USAF Acad., 1964; postgrad., George Washington U., 1978-79. Commn. 2d lt. USAF, 1964, advanced through grades to maj. gen., 1992; pilot F4E, left wing position, ops. officer USAF Thunderbirds, 1973-74; comdr. 26th tactical fighter aggressor squadron USAF, Clark AB, The Philippines, 1980-81; dep. comdr. ops., vice comdr. 8th tactical fighter wing USAF, Kunsan AB, Korea, 1981-82; chief ho. liaison officer Office of Sec. USAF, Washington, 1982-84; dir. inspection, hdqs. Pacific Air Forces USAF, Hickam AFB, Hawaii, 1984-85; comdr. 8th tactical fighter wing USAF, Kunsan AB, Korea, 1985-86; dep. dir. internat. programs, hdqs. USAF, Washington, 1986-88, dep. dir. internat. negotiations The Joint Staff, 1988-90; dir. plans, policy, doctrine, simulations and analysis U.S. Spl. Ops. Command, MacDill AFB, Fla., 1990-92; dep. chief of staff UN Command, Seoul, Korea, 1992-95; vice comdr. 12th Air Force and Air Force Component U.S. So. Command, Davis-Monthan AFB, Ariz., 1995-97; ret., 1997. Mem. Air Force Assn., Air Force Acad. Alumni Assn. (bd. dirs. 1971-75), Korean Am. Friendship Assn. (dir. 1994-95), Order of Daedalians, Red River Valley Fighter Pilots Assn. Avocations: racquetball, skiing, running, hunting, golf. Office: Ste 218 2915 S 12th Air Force Dr Tucson AZ 85713-5816

RUNNION, HOWARD J., JR., banker; b. Hot Spring, N.C., May 23, 1930; s. Howard Jackson and Blanche Mae (Elam) R.; m. Betty Ann Bishop, June 30, 1951; children: Debra Joy Sizemore, Jill Marie Glenn. BS, U. N.C., 1952. Various postions Wachovia Bank and Trust Co.-Wachovia Corp., Winston-Salem, N.C., 1952—; ret. vice chmn., former dir. Depository Trust Co., N.Y.C., 1985-95; chmn. bd. PSA Treasury Com, 1984-85; ret. exec. v.p. First Wachovia Corp.; bd. dirs. Cardinal Bancshares, Lexington, Ky.; dir. T.R.I.F.I.D. Inc., St. Louis, Security First Network Bank, Pinville, Ky. Chmn. bd. trustees Coll. Found. Raleigh, 1978—. Mem. Res. City Bankers Assn., Pub. Securities Assn. (dir. 1976-79, 84-85). Republican. Presbyterian. Clubs: Forsyth Country, Roaring Gap. Lodge: Elk. Avocation: golf. Home: 3521 York Rd Winston Salem NC 27104-1346 Office: 1st Wachovia Corp PO Box 3099 Winston Salem NC 27102-3099

RUNQUIST, LISA A., lawyer; b. Mpls., Sept. 22, 1952; d. Ralf E. and Violet R. BA, Hamline U., 1973; JD, U. Minn., 1976. Bar: Minn. 1977, Calif. 1978, U.S. Dist. Ct. (ctrl. dist.) Calif. 1985, U.S. Supreme Ct. 1995. Assoc. Caldwell & Toms, L.A., 1978-82; ptnr. Runquist & Flagg, L.A., 1982-85; pvt. practice Runquist & Assocs., L.A., 1985—; mem. adv. bd. Exempt Orgn. Tax Rev., 1990—, Calif. State U. L.A. Continuing Edn. Acctg. and Tax Program, 1995—. Mem. editorial bd. ABA Bus. Law Today, 1995—; contbr. articles to profl. jours. Mem. ABA (bus. law sect. coun. 1995—, com. on nonprofit corps. 1986—, chair 1991-95, subcom. current devels. in nonprofit corp. law 1989—, chair 1989-91, subcom. rels. orgns. 1989—, chair 1987-91, subcom. legal guidebook for dirs. 1986—, subcom. model nonprofit corp. act, partnerships and unincorp. bus. orgns. com. 1987—, state regulation of securities com. 1988—, tax law sect. exempt orgns. com. 1987—, subcom. religious orgns. 1989—, co-chair 1995—), Calif. Bar Assn. (bus. law sect., nonprofit and unincorp. orgns. com. 1985-92, 93-96, chair 1989-91), Christian Legal Soc., Ctr. Law and Religious Freedom, Christian Mgmt. Assn. (dir. 1983-89). Office: 10821 Huston St North Hollywood CA 91601-4613

RUNSER, DIANNE STRONG, music educator, music director; b. Atlanta, Jan. 30, 1953; d. Daniel Kline and Mary Anne (Logan) Strong; m. Frederic William Runser, June 24, 1978; children: Heather Dianne, Megan Danielle. B in Music Edn. cum laude, W. Va. Wesleyan Coll., 1974; M in Music Edn., Duquesne Univ., 1977. Cert. tchr. vocal and instrumental grades K-12, Pa. Tchr. vocal music K-12 Edgewood (Pa.) Sch. Dist., 1974-78; pvt. practice Trafford, Pa., 1978—; substitute tchr. Penn-Trafford Sch. Dist., Penn. Twp., Pa., 1978-94; dir. music Monroeville (Pa.) Cmty. Chorus, 1984—, 1st United Meth. Ch., Irwin, Pa., 1986—; music tchr. Level Green Pres. Pre-Sch., Trafford, 1989—; plays organ for weddings; accompanist soloists and ensembles, Pitts. Co-author: Strong Family History Update, Vol. IV, 1995. Bd. dirs., corr. sec. Strong Family Association Am., Inc., 1977—, charter and life mem. Mem. Music Educators Nat. Conf., Fedn. Music Clubs, Pa. Music Educators Assn., Order Ea. Star (Pa. Grand Chpt. Worthy Matron 1981-82, Dist. Deputy Grand Matron 1984-85, Grand Choir Dir. 1987-88, Grand Choir Accompanist 1983, 84, 86, 94, 95, 96, 97), Mortarboard, Sigma Alpha Iota, Zeta Tau Alpha. Avocations: geneology, needlework, reading, computers. Home: 201 Maple Dr Trafford PA 15085 Office: 1st United Meth Ch 310 Oak St Irwin PA 15642-3558

RUNTE, ROSEANN, academic administrator; b. Kingston, N.Y., Jan. 31, 1948; arrived in Can., 1971, naturalized, 1983; d. Robert B. and Anna Loretta (Schorkopf) O'Reilly; m. Hans-Rainer Runte, Aug. 9, 1969. BA summa cum laude, SUNY-New Paltz, 1968; MA, U. Kans., 1969, PhD, 1974, DLitt (hon.), Acadia U., 1989, Meml. U., 1990, U. de Vest Timisoară, 1996. Lectr. Bethany Coll., W.Va., 1970-71; lectr. adult studies St. Mary's U., Halifax, N.S., Can., 1971-72; from lectr. to assoc. prof. Dalhousie U., Halifax, 1972-83, asst. dean, 1980-82, chmn. dept. French, 1980-83; pres. Universite Sainte-Anne, Pointe-de-l'Eglise, N.S., Can., 1983-88; prin. Glendon Coll., Toronto, 1988-94; pres.,Victoria U., 1994—. Author: Brumes bleues, 1982; Faux-Soleils, 1984, Birmanie Blues, 1993; editor: Studies in 18th Century Culture, vols. VII, VIII, IX, 1977, 78, 79; co-editor: Man and Nature, 1982, Le Development regional, 1986, 87, From Orality to Literature/de L'Oralite á la littérature, 1991, Lectures canadiennes, 1993, Visions of Beauty, 1994; rev. editor French Rev., 1988-94; editor Lit. Rsch., 1994—; co-translator Local Development, 1987. Bd. dirs. Assn. Med. Svcs., 1989-92; adv. bd. Nat. Libr., 1984-91; v.p. Can. Commn. for UNESCO, 1991-92, pres., 1992-96; vice chair exec. bd. Found. for Internat. Tng., 1994—, 95—, chair exec. bd. Found. for Inst. Tng., 1995—; chair Gottschalk Prize Com., 1994; chairwoman publs. com. Hannah Found, 1989-92; vice-chair bd. Gardiner Mus., 1994—; internat. adv. bd. Expo. 2000, 1995—, mem. Royal Coll. Physcian and Surugeons, 1996, Decorated Ordre du Mérite; recipient Prix Fr. Coppée French Acad., 1989; Regents scholar SUNY-New Paltz, 1965; NDEA Title IV grantee U. Kans., Lawrence, 1968; Acad. Palmes, 1986. Fellow Soc. Study Values in Edn.; mem. Internat. Soc. 18th Century Studies (assoc. treas. 1983-87), Internat. Assn. of Comparative Lit. (treas. 1985-91, sec. 1991-94), Can. Fedn. Humanities (pres. 1982-84), Atlantic Soc. 18th Century Studies (pres. 1972-76), Canadian Soc. 18th Century Studies (pres. 1975-76), Soc. for Study Higher Edn. (bd. dirs. 1988-90), Found., Knights of Malta (grande dame 1991—), Delta Kappa Gamma, Phi Delta Kappa, Club of Rome. Home: 44 Charles St W # 3803, Toronto, ON Canada M4Y 1R8 Office: 73 Queen's Park Crescent, Toronto, ON Canada M5S 1K7

RUNYAN, JOHN WILLIAM, JR., medical educator; b. Memphis, Jan. 23, 1924; s. John William and Lottie (Roberts) R.; m. Barbara Ruth Zerbe, July 16, 1949; children: John William III, Scott Baylor, Keith Roberts. A.B., Washington and Lee U., 1945; M.D., Johns Hopkins, 1947. Diplomate: Am. Bd. Internal Medicine (examiner 1967-72). Intern Johns Hopkins Hosp., 1947-48; asst. to chief resident medicine Albany (N.Y.) Hosp., 1948-50; research fellow Harvard Med. Sch., 1950-53, also Thorndike Meml. Lab., Boston City Hosp.; instr., then asso. prof. medicine Albany Med. Coll., 1953-60; mem. faculty U. Tenn. Med. Sch., 1960—, prof. medicine, 1964—, chief sect. endocrinology, 1963-72, dir. div. health care scis., chmn. dept. community medicine, 1972-87, prof., chmn. preventive medicine, 1987-94, Univ. Disting. prof., 1988—; assoc. med. dir. Family Care Healthplan, 1994—; chief med. svc. John Gaston Hosp., Memphis, 1965-72; cons. endocrinology Memphias VA Hosp., 1962—, USPHS, 1962-70; chmn. Nat. Heart, Blood, Lung Inst. com. on Diabetes and Hypertension, 1985-87; chmn. Generalist and Curriculum Reform Task Force U. of Tenn., 1992-94. Author: Primary Care Guide, 1975, Problem Oriented Primary Care, 1982. Served with AUS, 1951-53. Commonwealth Fund fellow, 1950; recipient John D. Rockefeller III Public Service award in health, 1977; Upjohn award, 1981. Fellow ACP (Rosenthal award 1980, Laureate award Tenn. chpt. 1991, abetes master 1993); mem. AMA, Am. Fedn. Clin. Rsch., Am. Diabetes Assn. (Outstanding Physician Educator in Diabetes 1981), Tenn. Med. Soc., Memphis Med. Soc., Tenn. Diabetes Soc. (pres. 1968-69). Home: 5496 S Angela Ln Memphis TN 38120-2208

RUNYAN, TIMOTHY JACK, historian, educator; b. Gary, Ind., Aug. 9, 1941; s. Jack Elmore and Mavis Lydia (Lewis) R.; m. Laurie Ann Blackmore, July 25, 1964; children: Christopher T., Michael A. BS, Capital U., 1963; MA, U. Md., 1965; postgrad., U. Md. fellow, U. London, 1967-69; PhD, U. Md., 1972. Instr. U. Md., College Park, 1969; instr. Cleve. State U., 1969-71, asst. prof., 1971-74, assoc. prof., 1974-87, prof. dept. history, 1987—, asst. dean Coll. Arts and Scis., 1976-79, dir. classical and medieval studies, 1978-86, chmn. dept. art, 1981-82, chmn. dept. modern langs., 1982-86; chmn. dept. history, 1991-94; vis. prof. Oberlin (Ohio) Coll., 1989; vis. prof., dir. Program in Maritime History and Nautical Archaeology East Carolina U., N.C., 1994-96; editor Am. Neptune, Jour. of Maritime History, Peabody Essex Mus., Salem, Mass., 1990-95. Author: European Naval and Maritime History, 300-1500, 1985; editor: Ships, Seafaring and Society, 1987 (John Lyman Book award 1988), To Die Gallantly: The Battle of the Atlantic, 1994; contbr. articles to scholarly publs. Mgr. Cleve. Commn. on Higher Edn., 1976-79; pres. Gt. Lakes Mus. Sci., Tech. and Environment, Cleve., 1987-91, vice chair bd. trustees, 1991-94; gov.'s appointee to Ohio 1992 Commn., Columbus, 1989-92. Grantee Am. Philos. Soc., 1973, 76; recipient Award of Achievement for Mus. N. Ohio Live, 1991. Fellow Royal Hist. Soc. (London); mem. Internat. Commn. Maritime History (exec. coun. 1985—, treas. 1990-95, v.p. 1995—), N.Am. Soc. Oceanic History (pres. 1980-84), Nat. Maritime Alliance Bd. (treas. 1992—), Nat. Maritime Hist. Soc. (adv bd. 1989—), Gt. Lakes Hist. Soc. (pres. 1985-95), Medieval Acad. Am. (nominating com. 1985-87, chair 1990-91), Midwest Medieval Hist. Conf. (pres. 1981-82), Assn. Gt. Lakes Maritime History (v.p. 1984-87). Episcopalian. Avocations: sports, travel. Home: 2597 Dartmoor Rd Cleveland OH 44118-4233 Office: Cleve State U E 22d and Euclid Ave Cleveland OH 44115

RUNYON, KEITH LESLIE, lawyer, newspaper editor; b. Louisville, Oct. 3, 1950; s. Leslie Thomas and Marjorie Fillmore (Fisher) R.; M. Amelia Payne Sweets, Dec. 29, 1979; children; Amelia Brown Payne, Keith Leslie Jr. Student, U. London, 1971; BA cum laude, U. Louisville, 1972, JD, 1982. Staff writer Courier-Jour., Louisville, 1972-77, staff atty., 1984-86; staff atty., assoc. editor Louisville Times and Courier Jour., 1977-86, forum editor, 1986-90; editorial page editor, 1990-92, editor opinion pages, 1992-96, opinion editor, 1996—; moderator Ky. Author Forum, 1996—. Nat. bd. dirs. English-Speaking Union U.S., N.Y., 1976-79, pres. Ky. br., Louisville, 1986-87, U. Louisville Alumni Assn., 1987-93; mem. exec. com. Louisville com. on fgn. rels., 1985-87, Leadership Louisville, 1990-91; clk. Session Calvin Presbyn. Ch., Louisville, 1986-88. Recipient William E. Leidt award The Episc. Ch. of U.S., 1975, Roy Howard award (shared) Scripps Howard Journalists Nat. for Pub. Svc., 1976; named Alumnus of Yr., U. Louisville, 1991, disting. alumnus U. Louisville Sch. Law, 1996; Ctr. Fgn. Journalists fellow, 1993, Bingham fellow, 1995-96. Mem. ABA, Ky. Bar Assn., Louisville Bar Assn., Nat. Conf. Edit. Writers (editor The masthead, 1994-96), Soc. Profl. Jours. (Outstanding Editl. Writing award, 1983, 84, 85. Home: Nitta Yuma Harrods Creek KY 40027 Office: Courier-Jour and Louisville Times Co 525 W Broadway Louisville KY 40202-2206

RUNYON, MARVIN TRAVIS, postmaster general; b. Ft. Worth, Sept. 16, 1924; s. Marvin T. and Lora Lee (Whittington) R.; children: Marvin, Elizabeth Anne, Paul, James. BS in Mgmt. Engring., Tex. A&M U., 1948. Staff mem. mfg. engring. areas assembly plants Ford Motor Co., 1943-60, asst., plant mgr. various assembly plants, 1960-70; mgr. assembly engring. automotive assembly div. gen. office Ford Motor Co., Dearborn, Mich., 1970-72; gen. mgr. automotive assembly div. Ford Motor Co., 1972-73, v.p. body and assembly ops., 1973-77, v.p. powertrain and chassis ops., 1977-78, v.p. body and assembly ops., 1979-80; pres., chief exec. officer Nissan Motor Mfg. Corp. U.S.A., Smyrna, Tenn., 1980-87; chmn. bd. TVA, Knoxville, Tenn., 1988-92; postmaster gen. U.S. Postal Svc., Washington, 1992—; mem. at large Nuclear Power Oversight Com., 1991-92. Bd. dirs. United Way Knoxville, 1988-92, mem. campaign adv. com. 1990; bd. dirs. Downtown

Orgn., Knoxville, 1988-92, Tenn. Tech. Found., 1982, NCCJ, 1985-88, Nashville-Davidson County unit Am. Cancer Soc., 1986-88, United Way Rutherford County, 1986-89, Cumberland Mus., Nashville, 1986; participant Leadership Nashville Assn., 1982—, pres., 1986, Leadership Knoxville, 1989, Leadership Memphis, 1990-91; hon. chmn. Clinic Bowl, Nashville, 1986; mem. devel. adv. bd. Ctr. for Internat. Bus. Studies Tex. A&M U., 1987, mem. coll. bus. adminstrv. devel. coun., 1984-87; mem. outreach com. Knoxville Bicentennial '91 Coord. Coun.; mem. adv. bd. Inroads/Nashville, Inc., 1983—; mem. devel. adv. bd. Nashville State Tech. Inst., 1987; chmn. corp. adv. com. Middle Tenn. Regional Minority Purchasing Coun., 1982-83; mem. gov.'s adv. bd. to S.E./U.S. Japan Assn., 1981; gen. campaign chmn. United Way Nashville and Middle Tenn., 1985-86, trustee, 1984-86; trustee Automotive Hall of Fame, 1985—; chmn. Tenn. Minority Bus. Opportunity Fair, 1987-89, 1992 Trade Fair, Midsouth Minority Purchasing Coun., 1991-92;, Sr. Ptnrs. Bd. for May 1992 World Congress of Indsl. Devel. Rsch. Coun., 1991-92; bd. dir. Memphis in May Internat. Festival Inc., 1991-92, Met. Nashville Pub. Edn. Found., 1991-92; mem. U. Tenn. Devel. Coun., 1990—, Nucleus Fund Com. and Internat. Programs Resource Devel. Com., Tex. A&M U. Named Outstanding Man of Year Soc. Advanced Mgmt., 1968, Pres. slot on 1985 Model Yr. Automotive News All-Star Team, Automotive News; recipient Mgr. of Yr. award Avco Aerostructures chpt. Nat. Mgmt. Assn., 1985, CEO of Yr., Advantage mag., 1985, Disting. Service citation Automotive Hall of Fame, 1986, Salesman of Yr., Nashville chpt. Sales and Mktg. Exec. Club, 1985, award Tenn.-Japan Friends in Commerce, 1989; hon. gen. com. Internat. Fedn. Automotive Engring. Socs. 1988 Congress; recipient Human Rels. award NCCJ Nashville chpt., 1990, Spl. Recognition award Minority Bus. Devel. Agy., 1990, Gold Knight of Mgmt. award Nat. Mgmt. Assn., 1992, Exec. of Yr. award Nat. Mgmt. Assn., 1992, Adv. Mail Mktg. Assns. J. Edward Day award, 1993. Mem. Soc. Automotive Engrs., Engring. Soc. Detroit, Nashville Area C. of C. (bd. govs. 1983-85), Knoxville C. of C. (bd. dirs. 1988-92), Memphis C. of C. (bd. dirs. 1990-92), Tenn. Assn. Bus. (bd. dirs.), Soc. Internat. Bus Fellows, Belle Meade Country Club (Nashville). Episcopalian. Office: US Postal Svc Office of Postmaster Gen 475 Lenfant Plz SW Washington DC 20260-0004

RUOFF, ARTHUR LOUIS, physicist, educator; b. Ft. Wayne, Ind., Sept. 17, 1930; s. Louis A. and Wilma (Rall) R.; m. Enid Frances Seaton, Jan. 24, 1954; children—William Louis, Stephen Arthur, Rodney Scott, Jeffrey Kevin, Kenneth James. B.S., Purdue U., 1952; Ph.D., U. Utah, 1955. Asst. prof. materials sci. and engring. Cornell U., 1955-58, asso. prof., 1958-65, prof., 1965—, Class of 1912 prof. engring., 1978—, chmn. dept. materials sci. and engring., 1978-88, dir. Cornell ceramics program, 1987—. Author: Introduction to Materials Science, 1972, Materials Science, 1973, Introductory Materials Science, 1973, Concepts of Packaged Courses, 1973. Pres. Ithaca (N.Y.) Youth Hockey, 1972-73. Named Engr. of Distinction Engrs. Joint Coun., 1970; recipient Bridgman award Internat. Assn. Advancement of High Pressure Sci. and Tech., 1993. Fellow Am. Phys. Soc., Böehmlische Physicalische Soc.; mem. N.Y. Acad. Scis., Assn. Internat. Pour L'Avancement De La Recherche Et De La Technologie Aux Hautes Pressions (pres. 1995—). Office: Materials Sci and Engring Bard Hall Cornell U Ithaca NY 14853

RUOFF, CYNTHIA OSOWIEC, foreign language educator; b. Chgo., Mar. 1, 1943; d. Stephen R. and Estelle (Wozniak) O.; m. Gary Edward Ruoff, June 5, 1965; children: Gary S., Laura A. AB, Loyola U., 1965; MA, Western Mich. U., 1973; PhD in French Lang. and Lit., Mich. State U., 1992. Tchr. Kalamazoo (Mic.) Pub. Schs., 1965-68; instr. Western Mich. U., Kalamazoo, 1980—; nat. and internat. spkr. in field. Contbr. articles to profl. jours. Mem. MLA, N.Am. Soc. Seventeenth-Century French Lit., Am. Assn. Tchrs. of French, Mich. Fgn. Lang. Assn., Internat. Soc. Phenomenology and Lit., L'Alliance Française, Soc. Interdisciplinary French Seventeenth-Century Studies, Phi Sigma Iota, Pi Delta Phi. Avocations: piano, skiing. Office: Dept Fgn Langs & Lit Western Mich Univ Kalamazoo MI 49008 *Reach beyond intelligence and reason by experiencing the beauty, harmony, grandeur, and mystery of the cosmos..to achieve a higher understanding and truth.*

RUOHO, ARNOLD EINO, pharmacology educator; b. Thunder Bay, Ont., Can., Nov. 26, 1941; s. Eino Armas and Toini Helen (Kuusisto) R.; m. Marjorie Denise Anderson, Aug. 21, 1965; children—David, Daniel, Jonathon. B.S. in Pharmacy, U. Toronto, Ont., Can., 1964; Ph.D. in Physiol. Chemistry, U. Wis.-Madison, 1970. Helen Hay Whitney postdoctoral fellow U. Calif.-San Diego, 1971-74; asst. prof. pharmacology U Wis.-Madison, 1974-80, assoc. prof., 1980-84, prof., 1984—, acting chair dept. pharmacology Med. Sch., 1994-95, chair, 1995—; cons. NIH, Bethesda, Md., 1984—. Contbr. articles to profl. jours., chpts. to books. Den leader local council Boy Scouts Am., Madison, 1975-77, mem. at large, 1979—; hockey coach, 1983—. Grantee March of Dimes, 1975-78, Pharm. Mfrs., 1975-76, NIH, 1975—. Mem. AAAS. Lutheran.

RUOTSALA, JAMES ALFRED, historian, writer; b. Juneau, Alaska, Feb. 17, 1934; s. Bert Alfred and Eva (Karppi) E.; m. Janet Ann Whelan, July 31, 1987; stepchildren: Theresa Cowden, Douglas Whelan, Peggy MacInnis, Michael Whelan, Bruce Whelan. Student, U. Md., 1960-61, Basic Officers Sch., Maxwell AFB, 1964, Air U., Maxwell AFB, 1985; AA, U. Alaska, Kenai, 1990. Asst. div. mgr. Macmillan Pub. Co., 1964-80; mgr. Denny's Restaurants, 1980-82; dir. mktg. and sales Air Alaska, 1982-89; state security supr., lt. Knightwatch Security, Juneau, Alaska, 1990-96; ret., 1996; archival dir. Alaska Aviation Heritage Mus., 1987-90. Author: Lockheed Vegas in Southeast Alaska, 1980, We Stand Ready, 1986, Eielson, Father of Alaskan Aviation, 1986, Pilots of the Panhandle, The Early Years 1920-1935, 1997; Alaska's Aviation Heritage Air Alaska newspaper; contbr. articles to profl. jours. Journalist 1st cl. USN, 1951-56; sgt. U.S. Army, 1958-64; 1st sgt. USAR, 1983-94; ret. USAR, 1994; lt. col. ASDF, 1985—. Decorated Korean Svc. medal with 2 combat stars, Korean Presdl. unit citation, UN Svc. medal, Nat. Def. Svc. medal, Vietnam Svc. medal, Meritorious Svc. medal with 2 oak leaf clusters, Army Commendation medal with 4 oak leaf clusters; recipient USAF Brewer Aerospace award, Grover Leoning award, Paul E. Garber award, 1984-85, State of Alaska Gov.'s Cert. Appreciation, 1983, Mayor's Pub. Svc. award, Anchorage, 1985, Commendation from Gov. of Alaska, 1993, 94, 18th Session Alaska Legis. Cert. Recognition, 1993, 94. Mem. VFW (sr. vice comdr. 1995, post quartermaster 1996-97), Res. Officers Assn. (pub. affairs officer 1985—), U.S. Naval Inst., Aviation and Space Writers Assn., Am. Aviation Hist. Soc., Am. Legion (historian), Pioneers of Alaska (sec. 1988, v.p. 1989, pres. 1990, Igloo 33, treas. 1994-95, Igloo 6, Cert. Appreciation 1988). Lutheran. Home: 2723 John St Juneau AK 99801-2020

RUPAUL (ANDRE CHARLES), model, singer; b. New Orleans. on-air reporter Manhattan Cable, England. Albums include RuPaul is Star Booty, Supermodel of the World; formed groups RuPaul and the U-Hauls, Wee Wee Pole; appearances include (TV) The Am. Music Show, (TV movie) A Mother's Prayer, 1995, (films) Crooklyn, 1994, Wigstock: The Movie, 1995, To Wong Foo, Thanks for Everything! Julie Newmar, 1995, Smoke, 1995, Red Ribon Blues, 1995, The Brady Bunch Movie, 1995, Blue in the Face, 1995, A Very brady Sequel, 1996, Fled, 1996, (video) B-52's Love Shack. Office: C/O Tommy Boy Records 902 Broadway Fl 13 New York NY 10010-6002 also: Randy Barbato World of Wonder 1157 N Highland Ave 1st Fl Los Angeles CA 90038*

RUPERT, DANIEL LEO, elementary education consultant; b. Waynoka, Okla., Nov. 12, 1953; s. Robert Anthony and Georgia Yvonne (Lewis) R.; m. Emily Carol Lummus, June 12, 1977; 1 child, Joshua Daniel. AA, Miss. County C.C., 1979; BA in Social Psychology, Park Coll., 1981; MDiv, New Orleans Bapt. Theol. Sem., 1985; EdS, Miss. State U., Starkville, 1991. Chaplain East Miss. State Hosp., Meridian, 1985-87; dir. of rsch. Am. Family Assn., Tupelo, Miss., 1988-89; cons. Rupert & Assocs., Tupelo, 1989-93; guidance counselor Okolona (Miss.) Elem. Sch., 1993-94, guidance counselor, asst. prin., chpt. 1 coord., 1994-96, prin., 1996—; computer cons. Lee County Schs., Tupelo, 1990. Author: Selected Poems by Author, 1990; co-author: (state core objectives) Health Education Core Objectives for the State of Mississippi, 1991. Prt-time pastor Koinonia Bapt. Mission, Mooreville, Miss., 1992-96; mem. Christian Bus. Men's Com., Tupelo, 1989-94. With USAF, 1976-82; capt. USAFR, 1983-91, ret., 1995. Mem. ASCD, Am. Assn. Christian Counselors, United Am. Karate Assn., Christian Martial Arts Instrs. Assn. (bd. dirs.), Miss. Counseling Assn. (bd. dirs.), Miss. Spiritual, Ethical and Religious Values in Counseling (pres.), Tupelo Martial Arts Acad., Luncheon Civitan Club, Chi Sigma Iota. Republican. Southern Baptist. Avocations: Karate, writing, singing, playing guitar, spending time with family. Home: 1931 E Main St PO Box 495 Tupelo MS 38802 Office: 1933 E Main St Tupelo MS 38801

RUPERT, DONALD WILLIAM, lawyer; b. Clearfield, Pa., Oct. 15, 1946; s. Donald Lee and Dorothy Mae (Bonsall) R.; m. Patricia A. Rupert, June 21, 1969. BS in Chemistry, Miami U., Ohio, 1968; JD, Washburn U., Topeka, 1976. Bar: Tex. 1976, Ill. 1978, U.S. Ct. Appeals (Fed. cir.) 1978, U.S. Dist. Ct. (so. dist.) Tex. 1977, U.S. Ct. Appeals (7th cir.) 1981, U.S. Dist. Ct. (no. dist.) Ill. 1979, U.S. Supreme Ct., 1992. Assoc. Arnold, White & Durkee, Houston, 1976-78, Kirkland & Ellis, Chgo., 1978-83, ptnr., 1983-86; ptnr. Neuman, Williams, Anderson & Olson, Chgo., 1986-90; founding ptnr. Roper & Quigg, 1990-93; ptnr. Keck, Mahin & Cate, Chgo., 1993-96; ptnr. Mayer, Brown & Platt, Chgo., 1996—; cons. USAF, Dayton, Ohio, 1974-81. Contbr. articles to profl. jours. Served to capt. USAF, 1968-74. Miami U. Undergrad. Rsch. fellow, 1967, Grad. Rsch. fellow, 1968. Mem. ABA, Am. Intellectual Property Law Assn., Tex. Bar Assn., Phi Kappa Phi. Democrat. Presbyterian. Home: 2519 Park Pl Evanston IL 60201-1315 Office: Mayer, Brown & Platt 190 S La Salle St Chicago IL 60603-3410

RUPERT, ELIZABETH ANASTASIA, retired university dean; b. Emlenton, Pa., July 12, 1918; d. John Hamilton and Eva Blanche (Elliott) R. Diploma, Altoona Sch. Commerce, 1936; BS in Edn., Clarion State Coll., 1959; MSLS, Syracuse U., 1962; PhD, U. Pitts., 1970. Sec. Quaker State Oil Refining Corp., 1939-56; tchr., libr. Oil City Area Schs., 1959-61; libr. Venango campus Clarion (Pa.) U., 1961-62; prof. Coll. Libr. Sci. Clarion (Pa.) U., Clarion, 1962-70; dean Sch. Libr. Sci., Coll. Libr. Sci. Clarion (Pa.) U., 1971-85; prof. emeritus, 1994; interim pres. Clarion U., spring 1977; acct. William Rupert Mortuary, Inc., 1948-88. Author: Pennsylvania Practicum Program for School Librarians: An Appraisal, 1970; mem. ad hoc edit. com. Pa. Media Guidelines, Pa. Dept. Edn., 1976, author (with others) Encylopedia of Library and Information Science, 1984. Bd. dirs. Knox Pub. Libr.; mem. Abscurf Sec. Ch. Orgns.; active Knox Civic Club. Recipient Disting. Faculty award Clarion U. Alumni Assn., 1976, Disting. Alumni award, 1987. Mem. ALA, Zonta Internat. (Women of Achievement award 1987), Beta Phi Mu, Pi Gamma Mu. Republican. Home: PO Box H Knox PA 16232-0608

RUPERT, (LYNN) HOOVER, minister; b. Madison, N.J., Nov. 3, 1917; s. Lynn Hoover and Hazel L. (Linabary) R.; m. Hazel Pearl Senti, June 22, 1941; children—Susan (Mrs. Max Unland), Elizabeth (Mrs. Warren W. Wright). A.B., Baker U., 1938; A.M., Boston U., 1940, M.Div. cum laude, 1941; student (summers), Garrett Bibl. Inst. and Northwestern U., 1942, Union Theol. Sem., 1943; D.D., Adrian Coll., 1952, Baker U., 1966; L.H.D., Milliken U., 1974. Ordained to ministry Methodist Ch., 1940; asst. pastor First Meth. Ch., Baldwin, Kans., 1936-38, St. Mark's Meth. Ch., Brookline, Mass., 1938-41; pastor Thayer-St. Paul, Kans., 1941-43, First Ch., Olathe, Kans., 1943-45; dir. youth dept. Gen. Bd. Edn. Meth. Ch., Nashville, 1945-50; pastor 1st Meth. Ch., Jackson, Mich., 1950-59; pastor 1st United Meth. Ch., Ann Arbor, Mich., 1959-72, Kalamazoo, 1972-83; faculty dept. religion Fla. So. Coll., Lakeland, 1983-89; adj. faculty Wesley Theol. Sem., Washington, 1989-93; dean Mich. Meth. Pastors Sch., 1959-65; mem. Jud. Council United Meth. Ch., 1968-88 , sec., 1976-88, sec. emeritus, 1988. Author: Prayer Poems on the Prayer Perfect, 1943, Christ Above All (editor), 1948, Youth and Evangelism, 1948, Youth and Stewardship, rev. edit., 1960, Your Life Counts (editor), 1950, What Methodists Believe, rev. edit., 1959, John Wesley and People Called Methodists, 1953, I Belong, 1954, And Jesus Said, 1960, Enjoy Your Teen-Ager, 1962, A Sense of What is Vital, 1964, The Church in Renewal, 1965, My People are Your People, 1968, Where is thy Sting?, Christian Perspectives on Death, 1969, What's Good About God?, 1975 God Will See You Through, 1976, An Instrument of Thy Peace, 1982, The High Cost of Being Human, 1986, Why Didn't Noah Swat Both Mosquitoes, 1993, Up to Your Armpits in Alligators, 1996; writer, syndicated weekly mag. column Accent on Living; newspaper feature Talking to Teens; other publs., periodicals, and newspapers. Trustee Bronson Hosp., 1972-88, Adrian Coll., Asbury Meth. Village, 1996—; pres., bd. dirs. Youth for Understanding, 1970-83, Ann Arbor United Fund, YMCA-YWCA. Recipient Distinguished Alumnus award Boston U., 1969; Lucinda Bidwell Beebe fellow Boston U., 1941. Mem. World Meth. Council, Nat. Council Chs., Mark Twain Soc., Nat. Forensic League, Pi Kappa Delta, Alpha Psi Omega. Lodges: Mason, Rotary (Paul Harris fellow 1983). Home: 403 Russell Ave Gaithersburg MD 20877-2811

RUPERT, JOHN EDWARD, retired savings and loan executive, business and civic affairs consultant; b. Cleve., Oct. 19, 1927; s. Edward J. and Emma (Levegood) R.; m. Virginia Carlson, Oct. 27, 1951; children: Kristen, Karen Rupert Keating, David. B.A., Cornell U., 1949, LL.B., 1951; certificate, Grad. Sch. Savs. & Loan, Ind. U., 1958. With Broadview Savs. & Loan Co., Cleve., 1953-86; v.p. Broadview Savs. & Loan Co., 1964-74, mng. officer, 1965-86, pres., chief exec. officer, 1974-86, chmn., 1979-86. Mem. Cleve. Real Estate Bd., 1955-86; mem. Lakewood (Ohio) Bd. Edn., 1971-77, pres., 1975-77; v.p., trustee Lakewood Hosp., 1966-71; trustee exec. com. of Cleve. Zool. Soc., pres., 1987-92, chmn., 1992—; trustee Cleve. Orch., WVIZ Ednl. TV; mem. Greater Cleve. Literacy Coalition, 1991—; mem. Cornell U. Coun., 1971—, pres., 1977; trustee Med. Ctr. Corp., 1987-96, chair, 1990-96; trustee Internat. Ctr. for Preservation of Wild Animals, 1991—. With USAF, 1951-53. Mem. Cleve. Interfaith Housing Corp. (pres. 1971—), Inst. Fin. Edn. (pres. 1970), Cleve. Real Property Inventory (pres. 1976—), Ohio Motorists Assn., Delta Kappa Epsilon, Phi Delta Phi, Sphinx Head Soc. Clubs: Cleve. Yachting, Cornell (Cleve.) (trustee); Cornell (N.Y.C.). Home and Office: 18129 W Clifton Rd Cleveland OH 44107-1037

RUPP, FRANK A., III, association executive; b. Syracuse, N.Y., Sept. 29, 1947; s. Frank A. Jr. and Marilyn June (Hammerle) R.; m. Cynthia Marie Montague, Oct. 8, 1993; twins: Peter and Colin; children from previous marriage: Frank A. IV, Jason W. BS, Rutgers U., 1970, postgrad., 1970-72. Environ. engr. City of Raleigh, N.C., 1972-75, State of Ill., Chgo., 1975-85; mng. dir. Chgo. Historic Races, 1985-87; pres. Sportscar Vintage Racing Assn., Charleston, S.C., 1988-89, 91—, Racing Ventures, Charleston, 1989-90. Avocations: vintage car racing, wooden boats, electronics. Office: Sportscar Vintage Racing PO Box 489 N Atlantic Wharf Charleston SC 29402

RUPP, GEORGE ERIK, academic administrator; b. Summit, N.J., Sept. 22, 1942; s. Gustav Wilhelm and Erika (Braunoehler) R.; m. Nancy Katherine Farrar, Aug. 22, 1964; children: Katherine Heather, Stephanie Karin. Student, Ludwig Maximilians U., Munich, Germany, 1962-63; A.B., Princeton U., 1964; B.D., Yale U., 1967; postgrad., U. Sri Lanka, Peradeniya, 1969-70; PhD, Harvard U., 1972. Ordained to ministry Presbyn. Ch. U.S.A., 1971; faculty fellow in religion, vice chancellor Johnston College, U. Redlands, Redlands, Calif., 1971-74; asst. prof. Harvard Divinity School, Harvard U., Cambridge, Mass., 1974-76, assoc. prof., 1976-77, prof., dean, 1979-85; prof., dean acad. affairs U. Wis., Green Bay, 1977-79; prof., pres. Rice U., Houston, Tex., 1985-93, Columbia U., N.Y.C., 1993—; bd. dirs. Com. for Econ. Devel., Freedom Forum Media Studies Ctr., Martel Found., N.Y. Partnership. Author: Christologies and Cultures: Toward a Typology of Religious Worldviews, 1974, Culture Protestantism: German Liberal Theology at the Turn of the Twentieth Century, 1977, Beyond Existentialism and Zen: Religion in a Pluralistic World, 1979, Commitment and Community, 1989; contbr. articles to profl. jours. Bd. dirs. Amigos de las Americas, Am. Assembly, Assn. Am. Univs., Cathedrals Ch. St. John Divine, Commn. on Ind. Colls. and Univs., Coun. on Alcohol and Substance Abuse, Inst. Internat. Edn., Nat. Assn. Ind. Colls. and Univs., The Presbyn. Hosp., YMCA of Am. Danforth Grad. fellow, 1964-71. Mem. AAAS, Am. Acad. Religion, Soc. for Values in Higher Edn. Office: Columbia Univ 202 Low Libr New York NY 10027

RUPP, MARK EDMUND, medical educator. BSChemE, U. Tex., 1981; MD, Baylor Coll. Medicine, 1984. Diplomate Am. Bd. Internal Medicine, Am. Bd. Infectious Diseases. Postdoctoral fellow dept. microbiology and immunology Baylor Coll. Medicine, Houston, 1985; intern in internal medicine Med. Coll. Va./Va. Commonwealth U., Richmond, 1985-86, resident in internal medicine, 1986-88, infectious disease fellow, 1988-91, instr. internal medicine, 1991-92; asst. prof. dept. medicine and med. microbiology Sch. Medicine Creighton U., Omaha, 1992—; asst. prof. dept. internal medicine U. Nebr. Med. Ctr., Omaha, 1992—, asst. prof. dept. pathology and microbiology, 1993—; attending physician McGuire Vets Affairs Med. Ctr., Richmond, 1991-92, St. Joseph's Hosp., Omaha, 1992—, Omaha Vets Affairs Med. Ctr.; spkr. in field; instr. physical diagnosis Med. Coll. Va., Va. Commonwealth U., 1991, U. Nebr. Med. Ctr., 1993; guest, invited lectr. univs., confs., med. socs., med. schs. Contbr. book chpts., abstracts, articles to profl. jours.; patentee. Recipient Young Investigators award Nat. Found. Infectious Diseases, 1993, Nat. Rsch. Svc. award NIH, 1991; Am. Heart Assn. grantee, 1993, 95, 96, Rsch. Project grantee, So. Med. Assn., 1991, Collaborative Rsch. grantee NATO, 1993. Fellow ACP; mem. Infectious Diseases Soc. Am., Am. Soc. Microbiology, Soc. Healthcare Epidemiology of Am. Office: U Nebraska Med Ctr Dept Internal Med 600 S 42nd St Omaha NE 68198-1002

RUPP, RALPH RUSSELL, audiologist, educator, author; b. Saginaw, Mich., Apr. 12, 1929; s. Martin Carl and Veronica Marie (Riethmeier) R. B.A., U. Mich., 1951, M.A., 1952; Ph.D., Wayne State U., 1964. Speech and hearing cons. Detroit Pub. Schs., 1955-60; exec. dir. Detroit Hearing and Speech Center, 1960-62; assoc. in audiology Henry Ford Hosp., Detroit, 1962-65; prof. audiology U. Mich., Ann Arbor, 1965-89; coordinator audiology Eastern Mich. U., 1985-93; cons. St. Joseph Mercy Hosp., Ann Arbor, Ann Arbor VA Hosp., Mott Children's Health Ctr., Flint, Mich., Pontiac (Mich.) Gen. Hosp., U. Mich. Health Svcs.; pres. Detroit Hearing Ctr., 1966. Author: (with James Maurer) Hearing and Aging: Tactics for Intervention, 1979, (with Kenneth Stockdell) Speech Protocols in Audiology, 1980; contbr. articles to profl. jours. Served with Med. Service Corps, U.S. Army, 1953-55. Named Disting. Alumnus, Saginaw High Sch., 1981, Outstanding Grad., Wayne State U. Fellow Am. Speech, Lang. and Hearing Assn. (Editor's award); mem. Acad. Rehab. Audiology (past editor Jour.), Mich. Speech and Hearing Assn. (pres. 1954, Disting. Service award, past editor Jour, honor award). Home: 1395 Laurel View Dr Ann Arbor MI 48105-9412

RUPP, SHERON ADELINE, photographer, educator; b. Mansfield, Ohio, Jan. 14, 1943; d. Warren Edmund Rupp and Frances Adeline (Hanson) Christian. BA in Sociology and Psychology, Denison U., 1965; MFA in Photography, U. Mass., 1982. Teaching asst. in photography Hampshire Coll., Amherst, Mass., 1981; instr. photography Northfield (Mass.) Mt. Hermon Sch., 1982-83, U. Mass., Amherst, 1984, Holyoke (Mass.) Community Coll., 1986, 87-88; vis. asst. prof. photography Hampshire Coll., 1985, 87; vis. lectr. photography Amherst (Mass.) Coll., 1994; guest artist, lectr. Boston Mus. Sch., Portland (Maine) Sch. Art, NYU, U. Mass., Deerfield (Mass.) Acad., Hartford Sch. Art/U. Hartford-Conn., Springfield Mus. Fine Arts, Mass., Bard Coll, N.Y., Mass. Coll. Art, Boston, others. Exhibited in one-person shows at Tisch Sch. Arts NYU, 1987, Portland Sch. Art, 1989, Hart Gallery, Northampton, Mass., 1992, O.K. Harris Gallery, N.Y.C., 1992; exhibited in group shows at Zone Art Ctr., N.Y.C., 1987, Mus. Modern Art, N.Y.C., 1991, Springfield Mus. Fine Art, 1993, U. Mass., Amherst, 1993, Dirs. Guild, L.A., 1994, Manchester (N.H.) Inst. Arts and Scis., 1995, Weber State U., Utah, 1995, Grand Ctrl. Terminal, N.Y.C., 1995, Photographic Resource Ctr. 3d Biennial, Boston, 1995; represented in collections at Mus. Modern Art, N.Y.C., Fogg Art Mus. at Harvard U., Mus. Fine Arts, Boston, Rose Art Mus. Brandeis U., Mead Art Mus. Amherst Coll., Smith Coll. Mus. Art, Danforth Mus. Art, Springfield Tech. C.C. Found., Carpenter Ctr. for Visual Arts Harvard U. Bd. dirs. Zone Art Ctr., 1987-94. Recipient Mass. Fellowship award in photography Artist Found., 1984, 87; visual artist fellow Nat. Endowment for the Arts, 1986, 94, Guggenheim fellow, 1990. Avocations: gardening, bicycling, writing. Home and Office: 100 Chestnut St Northampton MA 01060-1407

RUPP, WILLIAM JOHN, architect; b. Phila., Aug. 25, 1927; s. Frank Julius and Sara Viola (Hibbs) R.; m. Gwendolyn O'Rourke, May 10, 1956; children: Susan Hibbs, Molly O'Rourke, Jason Franz. B.Arch., U. Fla., 1953. Draftsman Paul Rudolph, Architect, Sarasota, Fla., 1953-55; pvt. practice architecture Sarasota and Naples, Fla., 1956-67; asso. Morris Ketchum, Jr. & Assos., Architects, N.Y.C., 1968-72; mem. firm Callister, Payne & Bischoff (architects and community planners), Amherst, Mass., 1972-75; pvt. practice architecture and planning, 1975—; vis. lectr. U. Mass., 1976-78, asst. prof., 1978-84, assoc. prof., 1984-91, prof., 1991-95, prof. emeritus, 1995—. Author: (with A.W. Friedmann) Construction Materials for Interior Designers, 1989; contbr. articles to jours. With AUS, 1945-46, 2d lt., 1953. Recipient Archtl. Record award for Housing Design, 1960; Progressive Architecture Design award, 1961. Corp. mem. AIA (N.Y. chpt. 1st award for House Design 1964). Home: 128 Dry Hill Rd Montague MA 01351-9555 Office: U of Mass Fine Arts Center Amherst MA 01003

RUPPEL, GEORGE ROBERT, accountant; b. N.Y.C., Jan. 6, 1911; s. George W. and Cornelia (Klein) R.; m. Eleanor Holton, Apr. 4, 1941; children—Sandra, Shirley, Lorraine. Grad., St. John's U., 1933. C.P.A., N.Y. State. Chief accountant Am. Agrl. Chem. Co., 1930-36; financial supr. Am. Water Works & Electric Co., 1936-44; v.p., treas., dir. MBS, Inc., 1944-57; v.p., treas. RKO Gen., Inc., 1957-60; treas. Visual Drama, Inc., 1957-60; v.p. finance, dir. Hwy. Trailer Industries, Inc.; v.p., treas. Clinton Engines Corp., 1960-63; pres. Tomahawk Enterprises, Inc., 1963-94, Gehar Co., 1963—; financial cons. Treas. RKO Teleradio Found., 1957-60. Mem. Tax Execs. Inst. (past pres., dir. N.Y. chpt.), Fin. Execs. Inst., N.Y. State Soc. CPAs, Inst. of Mgmt. Accts., Nat. Tax Assn. Address: Country Club Appts 301 Tam Shanter Blvd Williamsburg VA 23185

RUPPEL, HOWARD JAMES, JR., sociologist, sexologist, educator; b. Orange, N.J., July 22, 1941; s. Howard J. and Lillian M. (Wordley) R.; m. Barbara Margaret Wiedemann, June 3, 1967. BA, St. Joseph's Coll., Ind., 1963; MA, No. Ill. U., 1968; postgrad. U. Iowa, 1968-76; EdD Inst. for Advanced Study of Human Sexualty, San Francisco, Ca., 1993; PhD 1994. Diplomate Am. Bd. Sexology. Instr. social sci. St. Francis High Sch., Wheaton, Ill., 1963-65, debate coach, 1963-65; instr. sociology St. Dominic Coll., St. Charles, Ill., 1966-67; instr. sociology Cornell Coll., Mt. Vernon, Iowa, 1969-70, asst. prof., 1970-72, lectr., 1972-73; rsch. dir. Social Sci. Rsch. Assos., Cedar Rapids, Iowa, 1973-80; founder, co-dir. Center for Sexual Growth and Devel., Mt. Vernon, 1980-95; instr. Sch. Social Work, U. Iowa, 1976-78, adj. asst. prof., 1979-81, adj. assoc. prof., 1981-96, prof., 1997—; prof. Inst. Advanced Study of Human Sexuality, 1996—; exec. dir. Soc. for Sci. Study of Sexuality, 1988—, Found. for the Sci. Study of Sexuality, 1989—; cons. Iowa Dept. Social Svcs., Families Inc., West Branch, A&E Network (Biography); bd. dirs. The Human Outreach and Achievement Inst., Boston, 1988-90, Inst. Advanced Study Human Sexuality, 1995—; NSF fellow, 1968. Cert. sexologist Am. Coll. Sexologists. Mem. Am. Sociol. Assn., Nat. Coun. Family Rels., Iowa Coun. Family Rels. (sec. 1983-84, treas. 1985), Changing Family Conf. (bd. dirs. 1983-87), Soc. Sci. Study of Sex Inc. (bd. dirs. 1983-88, pres. Midcontinent Region, 1984-85, treas. 1986-88, chmn. membership com. 1983-85, chmn. exhibits com. 1983-88, ann. meeting chmn. 1986), Am. Assn. Sex Educators, Counselors and Therapists (exec. dir. 1996—, cert. sex educator), Harry Benjamin Internat. Gender Dysphoria Assn., Coun. Assns. for Sexual Sci., Health and Edn. (del.), Inst. for the Advanced Study of Human Sexuality Alumni Assn., Alpha Kappa Delta, Alpha Sigma Lambda (hon.). Democrat. Co-editor: Sexuality and the Family Life Span, 1983; assoc. editor: Annual Review of Sex Research, 1992, 93, 94, 95, 96, 97; contbr. articles on complex orgns., marriage and the family, sexual attitudes and behavior, childhood and preadolescent sexuality, methodology and child care theory to profl. publs. Home: 608 5th Ave N Mount Vernon IA 52314-1107 Office: 103 A Ave S Ste 2-b Mount Vernon IA 52314-1400

RUPPERT, JOHN LAWRENCE, lawyer; b. Chgo., Oct. 7, 1953; s. Merle Arvin and Loretta Marie (Ford) R.; m. Katharine Marie Tarbox, June 5, 1976. BA, Northwestern U., 1975; JD, U. Denver, 1978; LLM in Taxation, NYU, 1979. Bar: Colo. 1978, U.S. Dist. Ct. Colo. 1978, Ill. 1979, U.S. Tax Ct. 1981. Assoc. Kirkland & Ellis, Denver, 1979-84, ptnr., 1984-88; ptnr. Ballard, Spahr, Andrews & Ingersoll, Denver, 1988-96; shareholder Brownstein Hyatt Farber & Strickland, P.C., Denver, 1996—; lectr. U. Denver Coll. Law, fall 1984-92; adj. prof. law grad. tax program, 1993-94; sec. Capital Assocs., Inc., 1989-96, acting gen. counsel, 1989-90; sec. and spl. counsel to the bd. dirs. Bros. Gourmet Coffees, Inc., 1995—; asst. sec. Renaissance Cosmetics, Inc., 1996—. Contbr. articles to profl. jours. Mem. ABA, Colo. Bar Assn. (mem. exec. coun. tax sect. 1985-89), Denver Bar

Assn., Equipment Leasing Assn. Am. Office: Brownstein Hyatt et al 410 17th St Fl 22 Denver CO 80202-4402

RUPPERT, MARY FRANCES, management consultant, school counselor; b. Flushing, N.Y., May 14; d. Raymond Edward and Mary Josephine (Reilly) R.; m. Donald Francis O'Brien (div.); children: Donald Francis O'Brien III, Kevin Raymond O'Brien; m. Patrick J. Falzone, July 31, 1993. BA in English, Loyola Coll.; MS in Psychology, Counseling, Queens Coll., 1965. Counselor Plainview (N.Y.)-Old Bethpage Schs., 1965—; trainer, cons. stress mgmt., time mgmt., comm., pres. Productivity Programs, Huntington, N.Y., 1975—. Contbr. articles in field; author audiotapes on stress mgmt., 1975—; appearances radio and TV. Mem. ASTD (pres. 1988, chmn. bd. dirs. 1989-95), AAUW, N.Y. State Counselors Assn., Nassau Counselors Assn., Huntington Camera Club (treas. 1996—). Avocations: photography (awards), tennis, golf, reading, wine tasting. Office: 20 Richard Ln Huntington NY 11743-2354

RUPPERT, PAUL RICHARD, telecommunications executive; b. Cleve., Aug. 30, 1958; s. Richard Arthur and Pierrette (Bougneteau) R.; m. Barbara Ann Mock, Jan. 30, 1988; 1 child, Jacob Paul. AB, Washington U., St. Louis, 1982; MPA, Harvard U., 1989. Legis. asst. Senator John C. Danforth, Washington, 1983-85; elections dir. Nat. Conservative Polit. Action Com., Washington, 1985; dep. campaign mgr. Congressman Tom Kindness for Senate, Columbus, Ohio, 1986; campaign mgr. McIntee for Congress, Waterloo, Iowa, 1986; dir. govtl. affairs Computer Dealers & Lessors Assn., Washington, 1987; chief of staff Office Fed. Contract Compliance, U.S. Dept. Labor, Washington, 1988; legis. officer to Sec. Jack Kemp U.S. Dept. HUD, Washington, 1990-93; dep. exec. dir. Rep. Govs. Assn., Rep. Nat. Com., 1993-94; pres. The Lodestar Group, 1994-97; dir. strategic programs Pacific Bell Mobile Svcs., San Francisco, Calif., 1997—; dir. strategic programs, bus. devel. and mktg. Pacific Bell Mobile Svcs., Pleasanton, Calif., 1997—; mem. Rep. Congl. Leadership Coun., Washington, 1987; dep. exec. dir. Rep. Govs. Assn., 1992-94; bd. dirs. John Paul Mitchell Systems, Beverly Hills, Calif. Contbr. articles to profl. publs. Dep. site coord. Bicentennial Presdl. Inaugural, Washington, 1988; mem. Mass. coalition devel. com. Bush-Quayle campaign, Boston, 1988; media com. Kemper PGA Open, TPC Avenel, Potomac, Md., 1991—; dep. regional polit. dir. Phil Gramm for Pres., 1996; chmn. media com. The Pres.'s Cup, 1996, Robert Trent Jones Internat.; Kemp advance team leader Dole-Kemp, 1996. Named among outstanding young men of Am., 1996. Mem. Am. Coun. Young Polit. Leaders, Kennedy Sch. Alumni Assn. (exec. coun. 1991), Washington U. Alumni Assn. (exec. coun. 1984-86), Capitol Hill Club, Harvard Club Boston, Harvard Club Washington (exec. com., membership com. 1990—), The Phoenix Forum (charter), Profl. Ski Instrs. Am. Episcopalian. Avocations: Alpine skiing, golf, bicycle touring, reading. Office: Pacific Bell Mobile Svcs 4420 Rosewood Dr Bldg 2 Pleasanton CA 94588-3082

RUPPRECHT, CAROL SCHREIER, comparative literature educator, dream researcher; b. Stafford Springs, Conn., June 30, 1939; d. William Joseph and Caroline Brown (Comstock) Schreier; divorced; children: Jody Francine, Whitney Glenn; m. Richard P. Suttmeier, May 8, 1987. BS, U. Va., 1962; MA, Yale U., 1963, M in Philosophy, 1973, PhD, 1977. Teaching fellow Yale U., 1973; asst. prof. Kirkland Coll., Clinton, N.Y., 1974-78; asst. prof. Hamilton, Coll., Clinton, 1978-81, assoc. dean, 1981-82, assoc. prof. comparative lit., 1982-89; prof., 1989—, chmn. dept., 1984-89; lectr. Switzerland, Israel, The Netherlands, Ireland, People's Republic China, Eng., Japan. Author, editor: The Dream and the Text: Essays on Literature and Language, 1993; co-editor and author: Feminist Archetypal Theory, 1985; sr. editor, cons. editor Dreaming; contbr. articles to profl. jours., chpts. to books. NEH fellow Dartmouth Dante Inst., 1986. Founding mem. Assn. for Study Dreams, 1983, Conn. Assn. Jungian Psychology, 1981. Merrill fellow Bunting Inst., 1970-72. Mem. MLA, Am. Comparative Lit. Assn., Shakespeare Soc., Assn. Study of Dreams (pres., v.p. bd. dirs., mem. editorial bd.), Conn. Assn. for Jungian Psychology (bd. dirs.). Avocations: sports; wilderness activities. Address: 198 College Hill Rd Clinton NY 13323-1218

RUPPRECHT, NANCY ELLEN, historian, educator; b. Coeur d'Alene, Idaho, Sept. 23, 1948; d. George John and Nancy Berneeda (Baird) R. BA with honors, U. Mo., 1967, MA, 1969; PhD, U. Mich., 1982. Acad. dir. pilot program U. Mich., Ann Arbor, 1971-73, lectr. in women studies, 1973-75; vis. lectr. history U. Mo., St. Louis, 1976-77; vis. instr. of history Wash. U., St. Louis, 1977-79, Grinnell (Iowa) Coll., 1979-81; asst. prof. Oakland U., Rochester, Mich., 1981-83; asst. prof. of history Mid. Tenn. State U., Murfreesboro, 1985-91, assoc. prof., 1991—; dir. women's studies program Middle Tenn. State U., 1988—, publicity dir. women's history month, 1989-92, mem. faculty senate, 1992-95. Contbr. articles to profl. jours. Mem. AAUP (chpt. v.p. 1988-89, pres. 1989-93), AAUW, NOW, Am. Hist. Assn., S.E. Women's Studies Assn., So. Hist. Assn. (chair nominating com. European divsn. 1996—), So. Humanities Assn., Holocaust Studies Assn., Mid. Tenn. Women's Studies Assn., German Studies Assn., Women in Higher Edn. in Tenn., Concerned Faculty and Adminstrv. Women (chpt. v.p. 1993-95, chpt. pres. 1995-96), Assn. of Faculty and Adminstrv. Women (chpt. pres. 1995—). Home: 1106 Jones Blvd Murfreesboro TN 37129-2310 Office: Middle Tenn State U 275 Peck Hall Murfreesboro TN 37132-0001

RUSAW, SALLY ELLEN, librarian; b. Potsdam, N.Y., Apr. 24, 1939; d. Ralph Clinton and Marion Ellen (Jenack) R. BS in Edn., Potsdam Coll., 1964; MLS, SUNY, Albany, 1975. Cert. libr. media specialist, pub. libr., permanent tchr. N-6, N.Y. Tchr. grade 7th-9th Diocese of Ogdensburg, N.Y., 1960-74, cons. office edn., 1975-78; assoc. libr. Mater Dei Coll., Ogdensburg, 1974-89, head libr., 1989—. Vol. Ogdensburg Correctional Facility, 1982, Riverview Correctional Facility, Ogdensburg, 1987—; lector, Eucharistic min. Rite for Christian Initiation of Adults catechist St. Mary's Cathedral; vol. Ogdensburg Cath. Ctrl. Sch., sch. bd., 1995—. Named Vol. of Yr. Ogdensburg Correctional Facility, 1985, Outstanding Vol. Riverview Correctional Facility, 1991; Nat. Def. Edn. Act grantee, 1965. Mem. ALA, N.Y. Libr. Assn., North Country 3Rs Coun., North Country Ref. and Rsch. Resources Coun. (trustee 1994—). Roman Catholic. Avocations: music, reading, berrying, outdoor activities, swimming. Office: Mater Dei Coll Augsbury Meml Libr Ogdensburg NY 13669-9669

RUSCH, PAMELA JEAN, middle school educator; b. Berwyn, Ill., Mar. 1, 1949; d. James M. and Arlene A. (Meyer) Sanders; m. Steven Paul Rusch, Dec. 23, 1973; children: Matthew, Christiana. BFA with honors, U. Denver, 1971; MA, Lesley Coll., Cambridge, Mass., 1983. Art tchr. Jefferson County Pub. Schs., Lakewood, Colo., 1971—; area coord. Lesley Coll. Outreach Program, Denver, 1981-84; cons. Standard Based Edn., Jefferson County, 1993—; writing team mem. Jefferson County Art Stds., 1995—; cons. Middle Sch. Resource Team, 1990—. Author curricula. Mem. ASCD, Nat. Mid. Sch. Assn., Colo. Art Edn. Assn. Lutheran. Avocations: flower arranging, skiing, water sports, painting, travel. Home: 7746 Orion St Arvada CO 80007

RUSCH, THOMAS WILLIAM, manufacturing executive; b. Alliance, Nebr., Oct. 3, 1946; s. Oscar William and Gwen Falerne (Middleswart) R.; m. Gloria Ann Sutton, June 20, 1968 (div. Oct. 1979); children: Alicia Catherine, Colin William; m. Lynn Biebighauser, Jan. 17, 1981. BEE, U. of Minn., 1968, MSEE, 1970, PhD, 1973; MS in Mgmt. of Tech., U. Minn., 1993. Sr. physicist cen. rsch. 3M Co., St. Paul, 1973-77, rsch. specialist cen. rsch., 1977-79; project scientist phys. electronics div. Perkin Elmer Corp., Eden Prairie, Minn., 1979-83, sr. project scientist phys. electronics div., 1983-85, lab mgr. phys. electronics div., 1985-87, product mgr. phys. electronics div., 1987-88, sr. product mgr. phys. electronics div., 1988-93; v.p. product devel. Chorus Corp., St. Paul, 1993-94; pres. Creekside Techs. Corp., Plymouth, Minn., 1994—. Editor: X-rays in Materials Analysis, 1986; co-author: Oscillatory Ion Yields, 1977; patentee in field. Recipient IR100 award for transfer vessel Rsch. and Devel. mag., 1981, IR100 award for energy analyser, 1985. Office: 2405 Annapolis Ln N Plymouth MN 55441-3636

RUSCH, WILLIAM GRAHAM, religious organization administrator; b. Buffalo, Dec. 23, 1937; s. William Godfrey and Hope (French) R.; m. Thora Joan Ellefsen, Sept. 2, 1967. BA, SUNY, Buffalo, 1959, MA in Classical Langs., 1960; MDiv, Luth. Theol. Sem., Phila., 1963; PhD, Oxford (Eng.) U., 1965; DD (hon.), Yale U., 1995. Ordained to ministry Evang. Luth. Ch., 1966. Assoc. pastor Evang. Luth. Ch. of the Holy Trinity, N.Y.C., 1966-68; asst. prof., chmn. dept. classical langs. Augsburg Coll., Mpls., 1968-71; assoc. exec. dir. div. Theol. Studies Luth. Coun. in the USA, 1971-78; adj. prof. The Gen. Theol. Sem., N.Y.C., 1978-82, 95; exec. dir., asst. to Bishop Evang. Luth. Ch. in Am., Chgo., 1987-96; dir. Commn. on Faith and Order Nat. Coun. of Chs. of Christ USA, N.Y.C., 1996—; vis. lectr. Waterloo Luth. Theol. Sem., 1969; adj. prof. theology Fordham U., N.Y.C., 1984-86; mem. cen. com. World Coun. Chs., 1991—, mem. standing com. faith and order commn., 1991—. Author: The Trinitarian Controversy, Ecumenism: A Movement Toward Church Unity; contbr. articles to profl. jours. Samuel Trexler fellow of N.Y. Synod Luth. Ch. in Am., 1964, 65. Mem. Am. Acad. Religion, Am. Soc. Christian Ethics, Am. Soc. Ch. History, Internat. Assn. Coptic Studies. Avocations: book collecting, chess, tennis. Office: Nat Coun of Chs of Christ USA 475 Riverside Dr New York NY 10115-0122

RUSCHA, EDWARD, artist; b. Omaha, Dec. 16, 1937; m. Danna Knego, 1967; children: Edward Joseph. Studied at, Chouinard Art Inst., Los Angeles, 1956-60. Numerous vis. artist positions including UCLA, 1969-70. Author: Twentysix Gasoline Stations, 1962, Various Small Fires, 1964, Some Los Angeles Apartments, 1965, The Sunset Strip, 1966, Thirtyfour Parking Lots, 1967, Royal Road Test, 1967, Business Cards, 1968, Nine Swimming Pools, 1968, Crackers, 1969, Real Estate Opportunities, 1970, Records, 1971, A Few Palm Trees, 1971, Colored People, 1972, Hard Light, 1978; noted for numerous graphite, gunpowder and pastel drawings, over 200 limited-edit. prints; producer, dir.: films Premium, 1970, Miracle, 1974; works include (paintings) Standard Station, Amarillo, Tex., 1963; Annie, 1963, Smash, 1963, Electric, 1964, (mural) Miami-Dade Pub. Library, Fla., 1985; one-man exhbns. include Minn. Inst. Arts, 1972, Nigel Greenwood Ltd., London, 1970, 73, 80, Leo Castelli Gallery, N.Y.C., (10 shows) 1973—, Albright-Knox Art Gallery, Buffalo, 1976, Stedelijk Mus., Amsterdam, 1976, Ft. Worth Art Mus., 1977, San Francisco Mus. Modern Art, 1982, Whitney Mus. Am. Art, 1982, Vancouver Art Gallery, 1982, Contemporary Arts Mus., Houston, 1983, Los Angeles County Mus. Art, 1983, James Corcoran Gallery, Los Angeles, 1985, also others; exhibited in group shows at 64th Whitney Biennial, 1987, Centre Pompidou, Paris, 1989, Mus. Boymans—van Beuningen, Rotterdam, The Netherlands, 1990, Ghislaine Hussenot, Paris, 1990, Fundacio Caixa, Barcelona, Spain, 1990, Serpentine Gallery, London, 1990, Mus. Contemporary Art, L.A., 1990-91, Robert Miller Gallery, N.Y.C., 1992, Thaddaeus Ropac, Salzburg, Austria, 1992; represented in permanent collections including Mus. Modern Art, Los Angeles County Mus. Art, Whitney Mus., Hirshhorn, Washington, Miami-Dade Pub. Libr., Denver Pub. Libr., also others. Guggenheim fellow; Nat. Endowment Arts grantee. Office: care Leo Castelli 420 W Broadway New York NY 10012-3764

RUSCHE, HERMAN FREDERICK, gastroenterologist; b. Evansville, Ind., Oct. 20, 1935; s. Herman Frederick and Eleanor Clementine (Schu) R.; m. Dorisann Branen, July 24, 1965; children: Kristin Marie, Herman Frederick, Michael Branen, Karen Elizabeth. BS in Optometry, Ind. U., 1957, MO in Optometry, 1958, MD, 1963. Bd. cert. Rotating intern Phila. Gen. Hosp., 1963-64; resident in internal medicine Mayo Clinic, Rochester, Minn., 1964, 67; resident in internal medicine Ind. U. Med. Ctr., Indpls., 1967-89, fellow in gastroenterology, 1969-71; pvt. practice, founder Gastroenterology Assoc., Evansville, 1971—; pres., bd. dirs. Vanderburgh County Med. Soc., Evansville. Capt. U.S. Army M.C., 1965-66. Fellow Am. Coll. Gastroenterology; mem. Am. Soc. Gastrointestinal Endoscopy. Avocations: travel, photography, music, gardening. Office: Gastroenterology Assocs # 110 W 801 Saint Marys Dr Evansville IN 47714-0511

RUSH, ANDREW WILSON, artist; b. Detroit, Sept. 24, 1931; s. Harvey Ditman and Mary Louise (Stalker) R.; m. Jean Cochran, Apr., 1957; children: Benjamin, Samuel, Joseph, Margaret; m. Ann Woodin, Oct., 1978. B.F.A. with honors, U. Ill., 1953; M.F.A., U. Iowa, 1958. Asso. prof. art U. Ariz., 1959-69; co-dir. Rockefeller Found. Indian Arts Project, 1960-64; vis. artist, artist-in-residence Ohio State U., 1970, U. Ark., 1972, Colo. Coll., 1973-74; resident mem. Rancho Linda Vista, Community of the Arts, Oracle, Ariz., 1969—. One-man shows include Carlin Galleries, Ft. Worth, 1973, Graphics Gallery, Tucson, 1972, 75, Tucson Art Inst., 1984, Cruzitas Gallery, San Antonio, 1996; exhibited in group shows at World's Fair, N.Y.C., 1964, USIS exhbns., Europe, Latin Am., 1960-65; represented in permanent collections Libr. of Congress, Uffizzi Mus., Dallas Mus., Ft. Worth Mus., Seattle Mus., Free Libr., Phila.; illustrator: Andrew Rush on Oliver Wendell Holmes, 1973, Rule of Two (Ann Woodin), 1984, Voice Crying in the Wilderness (Edward Abbey), 1990, Ask Marilyn, 1992. Served with USMC, 1953-55. Fulbright grantee, 1958-59. Address: Rancho Linda Vista O M Star Rte 2360 Oracle AZ 85623

RUSH, BENJAMIN MCGRAW, surgeon; b. Vaughn, Miss., Nov. 1, 1925; s. Benjamin C. and Celia Perry (McGraw) R.; m. Doris Jean (dec. 1977); children: Celia, Benjamin, Jill; m. Mary Jane, Dec. 30, 1981; children: Donna, Deborah. BS, U. Miss., 1949, MD cert., 1949; MD, La. State U. Medicine, 1951. Diplomate Am. Bd. Surgery, Am. Bd. Colon and Rectal Surgery. Intern Shreveport (La.) Charity Hosp., 1951-52; fellow surgery Ochsner Clinic, New Orleans, 1954-59; Colo-Rectal fellow Ochsner Clinic, 1957-58; resident E.A. Conway Meml. Hosp., Monroe, 1958-59; pvt. practice Union, Miss., 1952-54; acting med. dir. E.A. Conway Meml. Hosp., New Orleans, 1959; instr. surgery Tulane U. Sch. Medicine, New Orleans, 1958-59; pvt. practice Lake Charles, La., 1959-65; clin. asst. prof. surgery Monroe Clinic, 1965-72, La. State U. Med. Ctr., Shreveport, 1973-79; preceptor U. S. Dakota Med. Sch., 1977, La. State U. Med. Sch., 1977-80; pvt. practice Coushatta, La., 1972-89; clin. assoc. prof. surgery La. State U. Med. Ctr., Shreveport, 1979-89, vice chmn. and prof. of surgery, 1989—; clin. prof., 1994—. Contbr. numerous articles to med. jours.; author numerous poems. mem. U.S. Infantry, 1943-46. Named Honored Prof. La. State U. Med. Ctr. Sr. Class 1979, Poet Laureate, 1995; recipient Purple Heart, Bronze Star. Fellow Am. Coll. Colon-Rectal Surgeons; mem. AMA, Am. Coll. Surgeons, Assn. Am. Med. Colls. (dean's del. 1989), Soc. Am. Gastrointestinal Endoscopic Surgeons, So. Med. Soc., La. State Med. Soc. (del.), Surgical Assn. La., Wis. Surgical Soc.,LSU Shreveport Surgical Soc., Sabine Parish Med. Soc., John. C. McDonald Undergrad. Surg. Soc. (originator, sec. 1977—), Assn. Program Dirs. in Surgery, Assn. Surg. Edn. Office: LSU Med Ctr Dept Surgery 1501 Kings Hwy Shreveport LA 71103-4228

RUSH, BOBBY L., congressman; b. Ga., Nov. 23, 1946; m. Carolyn Rush; 5 children. BA in Polit. Sci., Roosevelt U., 1974; MA in Polit. Sci., U. Ill., 1992. Fin. planner Sanmar Fin. Planning Corp.; assoc. dean Daniel Hale Williams U.; ins. agent Prudential Ins. Co.; city alderman Chgo., 1984-93; democratic committeeman Chgo. 2nd ward, 1984, 88, Central Ill., 1990; dep. chmn. Ill. Democratic Party, 1990; mem. 103rd-105th Congresses from 1st Ill. Dist., 1993—; chmn. Environ. Protection, Energy and Pub. Utilities com., Budget and Govt. Operations com., Capitol Devel. com., Hist. Landmark Preservation Com.; mem. Commerce com. Former mem. Student Non-Violent Coordinating com.; founder Ill. Black Panther Party; past coord. Free Breakfast for Children, Free Med. Clinic. With US Army, 1963-68. Recipient Ill. Enterprise Zone award Dept. Commerce and Community, Operation PUSH Outstanding Young Man award, Henry Booth House Outstanding Community Svc. award, Outstanding Bus. and Profl. Achievement award South End Jaycees, Chgo. Black United Communities Disting. Polit. Leadership award. Office: US Ho of Reps 131 Cannon Ho Office Bldg Washington DC 20515-1301*

RUSH, DAVID, medical investigator, epidemiologist; b. N.Y.C., May 3, 1934; s. Samuel Hersh and Fannie (Dubin) R.; m. Catharine Ireland Dawson, June 24, 1957; children: Naomi Rush Olson, Hannah M., Leah D. BA cum laude, Harvard U., 1955, MD, 1959. Diplomate Am. Bd. Pediatrics. Resident in medicine U. Ill. Hosp., Chgo., 1959-61; resident in pediatrics Children's Hosp., Boston, 1963-65; registrar in pediatrics St. Mary's Hosp. Med. Sch., London, 1964-65; rsch. fellow, Harvard U. Med. Sch., Boston, 1965-66; asst. prof. preventive medicine and pediatrics, U. Rochester (N.Y.), 1967-69; asst. prof. pub. health (epidemiology) and pediatrics Columbia U., N.Y.C., also dir. prenatal project, 1969-76, assoc. prof., 1976-82; prof. pediatrics, social medicine and ob-gyn Albert Einstein Coll. Medicine, Bronx, N.Y., 1983-88; dir. epidemiology program USDA, Human Nutrition Research Ctr. on Aging, 1988-96, prof. nutrition, community health, pediatrics Tufts U., Boston, 1988—; mem. human devel. and aging study sect. NIH, USPHS, 1982-86; prin. investigator nat. evaluation of spl. supplemental food program for women, infants and children U.S. Dept. Agr., 1981-86. Author: Diet in Pregnancy, 1980, Dead Reckoning, 1992; assoc. editor Medicine and Global Survival; mem. editorial bd. Am. Jour. Pub. Health; contbr. articles to profl. jours. Trustee, chmn. health services com. Children's Aid Soc., N.Y.C., 1971-86. Served as surgeon USPHS, 1961-63; capt. Res. Recipient career investigator award N.Y.C. Health Research Council, 1977; sr. internat. fellow Fogarty Ctr., NIH, USPHS, U. Bristol, Eng., 1977-78, U. Paris, 1984-85; research grantee Nat. Inst. Child and Human Devel., NIH, 1979-86. Fellow Am. Pub. Health Assn. (governing council 1976-79); mem. Soc. for Epidemiologic Research (pres. 1980-81), Soc. for Pediatric Research, Internat. Epidemiologic. Assn., Am. Epidemiol. Soc., Am. Pediatric Soc., Perinatal Research Soc., Am. Inst. of Nutrition, Am. Soc. Clin. Nutrition, Am. Coll. of Epidemiology. Office: Human Nutrition Rsch Ctr 711 Washington St Boston MA 02111-1524

RUSH, DOMENICA MARIE, health facilities administrator; b. Gallup, N.Mex., Apr. 10, 1937; d. Bernardo G. and Guadalupe (Milan) Iorio; m. W. E. Rush, Jan. 5, 1967. Diploma, Regina Sch. Nursing, Albuquerque, 1958. RN N.Mex.; lic. nursing home adminstr. Charge nurse, house supr. St. Joseph Hosp., Albuquerque, 1958-63; dir. nursing Cibola Hosp., Grants, 1960-64; supr. operating room, dir. med. seminars Carrie Tingley Crippled Children's Hosp., Truth or Consequences, N.Mex., 1964-73; adminstr. Sierra Vista Hosp., Truth or Consequences, 1974-88, pres., 1980-89; clin. nursing mgr. U. N.Mex. Hosp., 1989-90; adminstr. Nor-Lea Hosp., Lovington, N.Mex., 1990-94; with regional ops. divsn. Presbyn. Healthcare Svcs., Albuquerque, 1994—, regional ops., 1994—; adminstr. Sierra Vista Hosp., Truth or Consequences, N.Mex., 1995—; bd. dirs. N.Mex. Blue Cross/Blue Shield, 1977-88, chmn. hosp. relations com., 1983-85, exec. com. 1983—; bd. dirs. Region II Emergency Med. Svcs. Originating bd. SW Mental Health Ctr., Sierra County, N.Mex., 1975; chmn. Sierra County Personnel Bd., 1983—. Named Lea County Outstanding Woman, N.Mex. Commn. on Status of Women; Woman of Yr. for Lea County, N.Mex., 1993. Mem. Am. Coll. Health Care Adminstrs., Sierra County C. of C. (bd. dirs. 1972, 75-76, svc. award 1973, Businesswoman of the Yr. 1973-74), N.Mex. Hosp. Assn. (bd. dirs., sec.-treas., pres.-elect, com. chmn., 1977-88, pres. 1980-81, exec. com., 1980-83, 84-85, recipient meritorius svc. award 1988), N.Mex. So. Hosp. Coun. (sec. 1980-81, pres. 1981-82), Am. Hosp. Assn. (N.Mex. del. 1984-88, regional adv. bd. 1984-88). Republican. Roman Catholic. Avocations: raising thoroughbred horses, cooking. Home: 1100 N Riverside Truth Or Consequences NM 87901 Office: 800 E 9th Ave Truth Or Consequences NM 87901-1954

RUSH, FLETCHER GREY, JR., lawyer; b. Orlando, Fla., Dec. 28, 1917; s. Fletcher Grey and Elizabeth (Knox) R.; m. Lena Mae Willis, June 6, 1942; children: Patricia Rush White, Richard Fletcher. BSBA, JD with honors, U. Fla., 1942; LLD (hon.), Fla. So. Coll., 1975. Bar: Fla. 1942. Practice in Orlando, 1946—; pres. firm Rush, Marshall, Reber & Jones, P.A., 1957-91, of counsel, 1991—; Trustee Lawyers Title Guaranty Fund, 1953-65, chmn. bd., 1962-63, gen. counsel, 1968-90; v.p., dir., gen. counsel Orlando Fed. Savs. & Loan Assn., 1955-75; dir. Trust Co. Fla., 1974-82; mem. jud. nominating council Supreme Ct. Fla., 1972-73, jud. nominating commn., 1983-87. Contbr. articles to legal jours. Mem. Orlando Municipal Planning Bd., 1961-63; mem. Orlando Loch Haven Park Bd., 1973-81, vice chmn., 1978-81; bd. regents State Fla. Colls. and Univs., 1965; trustee Coll. Orlando, 1960-71, Fla. House, Inc., Washington, 1974-76, Fla. Supreme Ct. Hist. Soc., 1988-91; mem. president's council U. Fla., 1970—; v.p., exec. com. U. Fla. Found., 1973-75, bd. dirs., 1971-75; bd. dirs. Inst. for Study of Trial, Central Fla. U., 1978-80; mem. president's council Nat. Meth. Found., 1977-82. Served as officer F.A. AUS, 1942-46, ETO. Recipient Distinguished Service award Stetson U., 1967; Outstanding Alumnus award John Marshall Bar Assn. U. Fla. Coll. Law, 1971; Distinguished Alumnus award U. Fla., 1976. Fellow Am. Bar Found., Fla. Bar Found.; mem. ABA (ho. of dels. 1967-85, adv. bd. jour. 1968-71, chmn. standing com. on legislation 1973-75, on lawyers title guaranty funds 1979-83), Orange County (Fla.) Bar Assn. (pres. 1960-61), Fla. Bar (bd. govs. 1959-67, pres. 1966-67), Am. Judicature Soc. (dir. 1968—, exec. com. 1972, treas. 1973-75, v.p. 1975-77, pres. 1977-79), U. Fla. Law Center Assn. (trustee, exec. com., chmn. bd. trustees 1973-75), Blue Key (pres. Fla. 1941), Phi Kappa Phi, Alpha Tau Omega, Phi Delta Phi. Republican. Methodist (chmn. ch. adminstrv. bd. 1961-63, 75-76, trustee 1968-74, 77-80, trustee Fla. Conf., 1973-76). Clubs: Country, Univ. (Orlando) Orange County Old Timers (pres. 1986-87). Lodge: Kiwanis (pres. North Orlando club 1954). Home: 1105 Edgewater Dr Orlando FL 32804-6311 Office: Rush Marshall Reber & Jones Magnolia Pl 5th Fl 109 E Church St Orlando FL 32801

RUSH, GEOFFREY, actor; married; 2 children. Appeared in plays Wrong Side of The Moon, 1971, Lock Up Your Daughters, 1972, Assault With a Deadly Weapon, 1972, Twelfth Night, 1972, 83, 84, Ruling Class, 1972, You're a Good Man Charlie Brown, 1972, Puss in Boots, 1972, Juno and the Paycock, 1973, Expresso Bongo, 1973, National Health, 1973, The Imaginary Invalid, 1973, Suddenly at Home, 1973, Aladdin, 1973, Hamlet on Ice, 1973, Godspell, 1974, The Rivals, 1974, The Philanthropist, 1974, Present Laughter, 1974, Jack and The Beanstalk, 1975-77, King Lear, 1978, Point of Departure, 1978, Clowneroonies, 1978, Waiting for Godot, 1979, On Our Selection, 1979, Teeth and Smiles, 1980, Revenger's Tragedy, 1981, No End of Blame, 1981, You Can't Take It With You, 1981, A Midsummer Night's Dream, 1982, 83, Mother Courage, 1982, Silver Lining, 1982, The Prince of Homburg, 1982, Royal Show, 1983, Blood Wedding, 1983, Netherwood, 1983, 84, The Marriage of Figaro, 1983, Pal Joey, 1983, The Blind Giant is Dancing, 1983, Sunrise, 1983, Benefactors, 1986, On Parliament Hill, 1987, Shepherd on The Rocks, 1987, The Winter's Tale, 1987, Tristram Shandy-Gent, 1988, King Lear, 1988, Les Enfants du Paradis, 1988, The Importance of Being Earnest, 1988, 90-91, 92, Troilus & Cressida, 1989, The Diary of a Madman, 1989, 90, 92, (Variety Club award for Stage Actor of Yr. 1989, Sydney Theatre Critics Circle award for Most Outstanding Performance 1989, Victorian Green Room award for Best Actor 1990), Marat/Sade, 1990, The Comedy of Errors, 1990, The Government Inspector, 1991, Uncle Vanya, 1992, The Dutch Courtesan, 1993, Oleanna, 1993, Hamlet, 1994, 95, films Hoodwink, 1980, Starstruck, 1981, Twelfth Night, 1985, On Our Selection, 1994, Five Easy Pizzas, 1994, Children of The Revolution, 1995, Shine, 1996 (Oscar award for Best Actor 1996), TV series Consumer Capers, 1979-81, Menotti, 1980-81, The Burning Piano, 1992, Mercury, 1996; dir. plays Clowneroonies, 1978-80, Animal Acts, 1984-86, Teen-Ages, 1984-86, Carols-By-Lazerlight, 1984-86, Definitely Not The Last, 1984-86, Unreal, 1984-86, The Small Poppies, 1984-86, Carols-By-Lazerlight, 1984-86, The 1985 Scandals, 1986, Pearls Before Swine, 1986, Pell Mell, 1986, 87, 88, The Merry Wives of Windsor, 1987, The Popular Mechanicals, 1987, 88, 92, Les Enfants du Paradis, 1989, The Wolf's Banquet, 1989, Popular Mechanicals 2, 1992, Aristophane's Frogs, 1992; co-translator The Government Inspector, 1991; writer (with George Whaley) TV film Clowning Around, 1992, (with John Clarke) play Aristophane's Frogs, 1992. *

RUSH, HERMAN E., television executive; b. Phila., June 20, 1929; s. Eugene and Bella (Sacks) R.; m. Joan Silberman, Mar. 18, 1951; children: James Harrison, Mandie Susan. BBA, Temple U., 1950. With Ofcl. Films, 1951-57; owner Flamingo Films, 1957-60; with Creative Mgmt. Assos., N.Y.C., 1960-71; pres. TV divsn. Creative Mgmt. Assos., 1964-71, exec. v.p. parent co., dir., 1964-71; ind. prodr., 1971-75; prodr. Wolper Orgn., 1975-76; pres. Herman Rush Assos., Inc. (Rush-Flaherty Agy. subs.), 1977-78, Marble Arch TV, Los Angeles, 1979-80, Columbia Pictures TV, Burbank, Calif., 1980-87; chmn., CEO, Coca-Cola Telecom., 1987-88, Rush Assocs., Inc., Burbank, 1988—, Katz/Rush Entertainment, Beverly Hills, Calif., 1990-96, New Tech Entertainment, LLC, Beverly Hills, 1996—; chmn. Entertainment Industries Coun.; pres., chmn. Royal Animated Art, Inc. Trustee Sugar Ray Robinson Youth Found., 1967-75; pres. Retarded Infant Services, N.Y.C., 1957-63; bd. dirs. U.S. Marshall's Service Found., Just Say No Found.; conferee White House Conf. for a Drug Free America, 1987, 88. Mem. Acad. TV Arts and Scis., Hollywood Radio and TV Soc., Producers Caucus. Clubs: Friars, Filmex. Office: Katz/Rush Entertainment 345 N Maple Dr Ste 235 Beverly Hills CA 90210-3827

RUSH, NORMAN, author; b. San Francisco, Oct. 24, 1933; s. Roger and Leslie (Chessé) R.; m. Elsa Scheidt, July 10, 1955; children: Jason, Liza. BA, Swarthmore Coll., 1956. Dealer antiquarian books, 1960-78; instr. English, history Rockland C.C., Suffern, N.Y., 1973-78; co-dir. Peace Corps, Botswana, 1978-83; freelance writer, 1983—. Author: Whites, 1986, Mating, 1991 (Nat. Book award for fiction 1991, Internat. Fiction prize Irish

Times and Aer Lingus 1992). Mem. lit. com. War Resisters League, N.Y.C., 1985—; bd. dirs. A.J. Muste Inst., N.Y.C., 1988-92; sec. Rockland County, N.Y. chpt. Amnesty Internat., 1990—. Recipient Rosenthal award Nat. Acad. and Inst. Arts and Letters, 1987, Nat. Book award for fiction, 1991, internat. fiction prize Aer Lingus/Irish Times, 1992; fellow Nat. Endowment for Arts, 1986, Guggenheim fellow, 1987, Bellagio residency fellow Rockeller Found., 1990. Mem. PEN Am. Ctr.

RUSH, RICHARD HENRY, financial executive, writer, lecturer; b. N.Y.C., Mar. 6, 1915; s. Henry Frederick and Bessie (Vreeland) R.; m. Julia Ann Halloran, Aug. 15, 1956; 1 dau., Sallie Haywood. B.A. summa cum laude, Dartmouth Coll., 1937, M.C.S., 1938; M.B.A., Harvard U., 1941, D.C.S. (Littauer fellow), 1942. Dir. aviation U.S. Bur. Fgn. and Domestic Commerce, 1945-46; chief economist, chmn. planning com. All Am. Aviation (U.S. Air), 1943-45; dir. aircraft div. Nat. Security Resources Bd., 1948-51; Washington rep. to J. Paul Getty, 1951-52; partner Rush & Halloran (finance and ins.), 1953-58; pres., chmn. bd. N.Am. Acceptance Corp., Atlanta, also Washington, 1956-59; owner Richard H. Rush Enterprises, Greenwich, Conn., also Washington, 1953-73; prof., chmn. dept. finance and investments Sch. Bus. Adminstrn., Am. U., Washington, 1967-70, 77-79. Author: 12 books, including Art as an Investment, 1961, A Strategy of Investing for Higher Return, 1962, The Techniques of Becoming Wealthy, 1963, Antiques as an Investment, 1968, The Wrecking Operation: Phase One, 1972, Investments You Can Live With and Enjoy, 1976, Techniques of Becoming Wealthy, 1977, Automobiles as an Investment, 1982, Selling Collectibles, 1982, Collecting Classic Cars for Profit and Capital Gain, 1984; contbr. over 700 articles to newspapers, mags. and profl. jours.; editor series of books on starting businesses for U.S. Dept. Commerce; contbg. editor Wall St. Transcript, 1971—, Art/Antiques Investment Report, 1972—. Trustee, mem. exec. com. Finch Coll., 1968-72. Mem. Am. Mktg. Assn. (chmn. nat. com.), Am. Econ. Assn., Am. Statis. Assn., Internat. Platform Assn., AAUP, Harvard Club (N.Y.C.), BocaWest Club (Boca Raton), Royal Palm Yacht Club (Ft. Myers), Phi Beta Kappa, Phi Kappa Phi, Omicron Delta Kappa. Episcopalian.

RUSH, RICHARD P., chamber of commerce executive; b. Chgo., Apr. 2, 1945; s. Frederick William and Virginia (Predmore) R.; m. Jennifer Amy Mosetick, Dec. 18, 1965; children: Jennette Marie, Dawn Essence, Adam Justin. BS in Communications, So. Ill. U., 1968. Cert. chamber exec. Entertainment editor Life Printing & Pub. Co., Berwyn, Ill., 1970-71; dir. nat. advtg. Fred Harvey, Inc., Brisbane, Calif., 1971-72; assoc. pub. Hudson Home Publs., Los Altos, Calif., 1972-73; asst. mgr. membership San Francisco C. of C., 1973-74; exec. v.p. San Rafael (Calif.) C. of C., 1974-77; dir. small bus. dept. Calif. C. of C., Sacramento, 1977-81; regional mgr. U.S. C. of C., Dallas, 1981-86; pres., chief exec. officer Okla. State C. of C. and Industry, Oklahoma City, 1986—; cons. Zimbabwe Nat. C. of C., Harare, 1985; vice chmn. Coun. State Cs of C., Washington, 1986—; bd. mem. Am. C. of C. Execs., Alexandria, Va., 1988—, mem. ChamberNet, 1990—; mem. Okla. 2000, Oklahoma City, 1986—; mem. exec. com. Okla. Coun. on Econ. Edn., 1986—; bd. mem. Okla. Good Rds. and Sts. Assn., 1988—; chmn. state C. of C. task force U.S. C. of C., 1988—; mem. Okla. Congl. Econ. Devel. Task Force, 1988—. Contbr. numerous articles to profl. jours. Bd. mem. Okla. Alliance Against Drugs, Oklahoma City, 1989—; charter class mem. Leadership Okla., Oklahoma City, 1987-88; mem. interagy. coun. Okla. Futures, Oklahoma City, 1989; mem. exec. com. S.W. Ctr. for Human Rels. Studies, Norman, Okla., 1988—; mem. adv. bd. Keep Okla. Beautiful, 1988; mem. adv. com. Okla. Ctr. for Advancement of Sci. and Tech., 1989—. With U.S. Army, 1968-70. Decorated Bronze Star; recipient William E. Hammond award Calif. Assn. Chamber Execs., 1975; named resource person White House Conf. on Small Bus., 1980, adv. bd. mem. Ctr. for Internat. Trade Devel., 1988-90, del. head Gov.'s Internat. Team, 1988; Okla. State C. of C. and Industry named 1st accredited State C. of C. in nation while under his leadership by U.S. C. of C., 1990. Baha'i'. Avocations: parenting, pub. speaking, bowling, bridge, photography. Office: Okla State C of C Industry 330 NE 10th St Oklahoma City OK 73104-3220*

RUSH, RICHARD R., academic administrator. Pres. Mankato (Minn.) U. Office: Mankato State U South Rd And Ellis Ave Mankato MN 56001

RUSH, WILLIAM JOHN, newspaper executive; b. Alliance, Ohio, Nov. 11, 1936; s. Serle Emmons and Doris Esther (Crider) R.; BA in Journalism, Ohio State U., 1958; m. Ruth Ann Lee, Feb. 29, 1972; children—Kayci, Wendy, Nathan, Jenny, Molly. Mgr., The Madison Press, London, Ohio, 1960-62; adv. mgr. Times Pub. Co., New Milford, Conn., 1962-65; asst. to pub. N.Adams (Mass.) Transcript, 1965-69; asst. to pub. Horvitz Newspapers, 1969-70; gen. mgr. Lake City (Ohio) News-Herald, 1970-72; v.p./gen. mgr. Times Record, Troy, N.Y., 1972-82; assoc. pub., v.p. Times Record and News Jour., Mansfield, Ohio, 1982-86; pub. Warren (Ohio) Tribune-Chronicle, 1986-89, Lorain (Ohio) Morning Jour., 1989-90; pub., chief exec. New Haven (Conn.) Register, 1990—; v.p. Jour. Register Co., 1995—. Bd. dirs. Long Wharf Theater, Conn. Policy and Econ. Coun., Inc., Regional Leadership Coun., United Way; bd. govs. U. New Haven. Mem. Conn. Daily Newspaper Assn. (v.p.), Nat. Co. Mil. Historians, Gateway C. C. Found., Habitat for Humanity, Pine Orchard Yacht and Country Club, Quinnipiac Club, Ohio State U. Alumni Assn., Hon. Order of Ky. Cols., Masons, Shriners, Elks, Theta Chi. Episcopalian. Office: New Haven Register Inc Long Wharf 40 Sargent Dr New Haven CT 06511-6111

RUSHER, WILLIAM ALLEN, writer, commentator; b. Chgo., July 19, 1923; s. Evan Singleton and Verna (Self) R. AB, Princeton, 1943; JD, Harvard U., 1948; DLit (hon.), Nathaniel Hawthorne Coll., 1973. Bar: N.Y. bar 1949. Assoc. Shearman & Sterling & Wright, N.Y.C., 1948-56; spl. counsel fin. com. N.Y. Senate, 1955; assoc. counsel internal security subcom. U.S. Senate, 1956-57; pub., v.p. Nat. Review mag., N.Y.C., 1957-88, also bd. dirs.; Disting. fellow The Claremont Inst, 1989—; mem. Adv. Task Force on Civil Disorders, 1972. Author: Special Counsel, 1968, (with Mark Hatfield and Arlie Schardt) Amnesty?, 1973, The Making of the New Majority Party, 1975, How to Win Arguments, 1981, The Rise of the Right, 1984, The Coming Battle for the Media, 1988; editor: The Ambiguous Legacy of the Enlightenment, 1995; columnist Universal Press Syndicate, 1973-82, Newspaper Enterprise Assn., 1982—; played role of Advocate in TV program The Advocates, 1970-73. Bd. dirs. Media Rsch. Ctr., Washington, Nat. Rev. Bd., 1990—; bd. advisors Ashbrook Ctr., Ashland, Ohio; past vice chmn. Am. Conservative Union; past trustee Pacific Legal Found., Sacramento; trustee, treas. Wilbur Found., Santa Barbara. Served as 2d lt. to capt., USAAF, 1943-45, India-Burma Theater. Recipient Disting. Citizen award NYU Sch. Law, 1973. Mem. ABA, U. Club (N.Y.C. and San Francisco), Met. Club (Washington). Anglican. Home and Office: 850 Powell St San Francisco CA 94108-2051

RUSHFELT, GERALD LLOYD, magistrate judge; b. Kansas City, Kans., Aug. 4, 1929; s. Henry Lawrence and Marie Ernestine (Heinrich) R.; m. Joy Marie Jungferman, May 28, 1960. AA, Graceland Coll., 1949; BA, U. Kans., 1953, LLB, 1958. Bar: Kans. 1958, U.S. Dist. Ct. Kans. 1958, U.S. Ct. Appeals (10th cir.) 1969. From assoc. to ptnr. Sullivant and Smith and successor firms, Kans. City, Overland Park, Kans., 1958-75; sr. ptnr. Rushfelt, Mueller, Lamar and Druten and successors, Overland Park, 1975-85; U.S. magistrate judge U.S. Dist. Ct. Kans., Kansas City, 1985—; mcpl. judge pro tem City of Leawood (Kans.) 1977-85; critique instr. U. Kans. Law Sch., Lawrence, 1981-92. Active Roeland Park (Kans.) City Council, 1964-69. With U.S. Army, 1953-55. Fellow Am. Coll. Trial Lawyers, Internat. Soc. Barristers; mem. ABA, Kans. Bar Assn., Johnson County Bar Assn. (pres. 1986-87), Am. Bd. Trial Advocates. Democrat. Mem. Reorganized Ch. of Jesus Christ of Latter-day Saints. Avocations: swimming, baseball, philately. Office: US Ct House 500 State Ave Rm 219 Kansas City KS 66101-2400

RUSHING, JANE GILMORE, writer; b. Pyron, Tex., Nov. 15, 1925; d. Clyde Preston and Mabel Irene (Adams) Gilmore; m. James Arthur Rushing, Nov. 29, 1956; 1 son, James Arthur. BA, Tex. Tech U., 1944, MA, 1945, PhD, 1957. Reporter Abilene (Tex.) Reporter-News, 1946-47; tchr. Tex. high schs., 1947-54; instr. U. Tenn., 1957-59; instr. to asst. prof. Tex. Tech U., intermittently, 1959-68. Author: Walnut Grove, 1964, Against the Moon, 1968, Tamzen, 1972, Mary Dove, 1974, The Raincrow, 1977, Covenant of Grace, 1982, Winds of Blame, 1983, Starting from Pyron, 1992; co-author (with Kline A. Nall) Evolution of a University, Texas Tech's First Fifty Years, 1975. Vassie James Hill fellow of AAUW, 1956-57; recipient Emily Clark Balch prize, 1961; LeBaron R. Barker, Jr., Fiction award, 1975; Tex. Lit. award for fiction, 1984. Mem. Tex. Inst. Letters. Methodist. Home: 3809 39th St Lubbock TX 79413-2521

RUSHING, PHILIP DALE, retired social worker; b. Carbondale, Ill., Mar. 15, 1932; S. Paul and Beulah Myrl (Benton) R.; m. Linda North, July 5, 1958 (div. July 1964); 1 child, Lisa Ann Rushing Burrow; m. Rosalie Anne Sturm, Aug. 20, 1966. BA, So. Ill. U., 1958; MSW, Washington U., St. Louis, 1960. Bd. cert. diplomate, ACSW; lic. social worker, Ill. Child welfare worker Ill. Dept. Pub. Welfare, Salem, E. St. Louis, 1958-60; child welfare supr. Ill. Dept. Pub. Welfare, E. St. Louis, 1960-63; field rep. Nat. Assn. for Retarded Children, Dallas, Denver, 1963-65; dir. social svcs. A.L. Bowen Children's Ctr., Harrisburg, Ill., 1965-68; asst. zone dir. for mentally retarded Ill. Dept. of Mental Health, Harrisburg, 1968-74; regional coord. for devel. disabilities Ill. Dept. of Mental Health & Dev. Disabilities, Marion, 1974-83; social work adminstr. Choate Mental Health & Devel. Ctr., Anna, Ill., 1983-95; ret., 1995; adj. asst. prof. So. Ill. U. Rehab. Inst., Carbondale, Ill., 1968-78. Bd. cert. diplomate ACSW; lic. clin. social worker. Bd. deacons First Presbyn. Ch., Harrisburg, 1974-77, bd. trustees, 1978-80, bd. elders, 1980-83, 96—. With USN, 1951-55, Korea. Fellow Am. Assn. on Mental Retardation (life, chmn. social work divsn. Ill. chpt. 1973-74); mem. NASW (chmn. East St. Louis br. 1962). Home: 6542 Highway 13 W Harrisburg IL 62946-4142

RUSHMER, ESTELLA VIRGINIA DIX (DIXIE RUSHMER), artist; b. Sullivan, Ind., Oct. 17, 1919; d. William Porter Jessop and Roxie Gertrude (Johnson) Dix; m. Robert Frazer Rushmer, Apr. 5, 1942; children: Donald Scott, Anne, Elizabeth. BS, Purdue U., 1940. cert. am. Dietetic Assn. docent Wash. State Burke Mus., 1963-78. Author, artist: Whidbey Island Sketchbook, 1985; one-woman shows include Good Years Gallery, Edmonds, Wash., 1975, 75, 77, Stillwater Gallery, Seattle, 1979, Artists Gallery Northwest, 1979, 82, 83, Stonington Gallery, Seattle, 1985, Port Angeles (Wash.) Fine Arts Ctr., 1988; group shows include Bellevue (Wash.) Art Mus., 1979, 82, 84, 86-90, Peter Kirk Gallery, Kirkland, Wash., 1985-90, Frye Mus., Seattle, 1979, Frederick and Nelson Gallery, Seattle, 1980, 82, Fremont Fine Art Gallery, Seattle, 1987, Black Swan Gallery, Seattle, 1989, Portico Gallery, Kobe, Japan, 1987, Meguro Mus., Tokyo, Japan, 1987, Columbia Art Ctr., Vancouver, Wash., 1990, Nat. Watercolor Soc. Show, Muckenthaler Cultural Ctr., Fullerton, Calif., 1990; represented in permanent collections at Rainier Bank, Samotomo Bank, Alpac Corp., Honeywell, Seattle; represented in pvt. collections. Pres. U. Wash. Med. Sch. Aux., Seattle, 1948; leader Girl Scouts U.S.A., Lake Forest Park, Wash., 1958-63. Mem. Northwest Watercolor Soc., U. Wash. Auxiliary, U. Wash. Med. Auxiliary, U. Wash. Retiree Assn., Women Painters of Wash. Avocations: gardening, travel, reading, genealogy, grandparenting. Home: 10901 176 Circle NE # 3526 Redmond WA 98052

RUSHNELL, SQUIRE DERRICK, television executive; b. Adams Center, N.Y., Oct. 31, 1938; s. Reginald Grant and Erica Mifanwy Redwood Sedgemore (Squire) R.; m. Jinny Schreckinger, Feb. 29, 1980; 1 child, Squire Grant Sedgemore; children by previous marriage: Robin Tracy, Hilary Adair. Ed., Syracuse U., 1956-60. Disc jockey Stas. WOLF, WHEN and WFBL, Syracuse, N.Y., 1958-61, Sta. WTRL, Bradenton, B, 1961-62; exec. prodr. Sta. WBZ AM-TV, Boston, 1962-67; program dir. KYW News-Radio, Phila., 1968; exec. prodr. Kennedy & Co. Sta. WLS-TV, Chgo., 1969-71, program dir., 1971-73; v.p. programs ABC-owned TV stas., N.Y.C., 1973-74; v.p. children's TV ABC Entertainment Network, N.Y.C., 1974-78; v.p. Good Morning Am. and children's programs ABC-TV Network, N.Y.C., 1978-81, v.p. long range planning and children's TV, 1981-87; v.p. late night and children's TV ABC Entertainment, N.Y.C., 1987-89; pres. Rushnell Comm. & Pub., Inc., 1990-96; pres., CEO Nostalgia TV Network, 1996—. Author: The Kingdom Chums Greatest Stories, 1986, Coincidence: Everyday Miracles, 1998; co-author: Broadcast Programming, 1981, Broadcast/Cable Programming, 1985, rev. edit., 1989, 93. Recipient Emmy awards, 1975-88, TV Critics Circle award, 1976, all for outstanding children's TV programming, Am. Children's TV Festival award, 1985, 87. Mem. NATAS, Nat. Acad. Arts and Scis., Internat. Radio and TV Soc., Action for Children's TV (award for outstanding children's TV programming). Office: Nostalgia TV 650 Massachusetts Ave NW Washington DC 20001

RUSHTON, BRIAN MANDEL, chemical company executive; b. Sale, Cheshire, Eng., Nov. 16, 1933; came to U.S., 1957; s. Ronald Henry and Edith (Slater) Riley; m. Jean Wrigley, Apr. 1, 1958; children: Jacqueline, Lisa, Amy. A.R.I.C. in Chemistry, U. Salford, Eng., 1957; M.S. in Phys. Organic Chemistry, U. Minn., 1959; Ph.D. in Phys. Organic Chemistry, U. Leicester, Eng., 1963; postgrad. Sr. Exec. program, MIT, 1972. Prodn. mgr. trainee 3M Co. U.K., 1959-60; sr. research chemist Petrolite Corp., 1963-65, group leader, 1965-66; sect. mgr. Ashland Chem. Co., 1966-69; corp. research mgr. Hooker Chem. Corp. subs. Occidental Petroleum, 1969-72, dir. polymer and plastics research and devel., 1972-74, v.p. research and devel. chem. and plastics div., 1974-75; pres. Celanese Research Corp., 1975-80; corp. v.p. tech. Celanese Corp.; also pres. Celanese Research Corp., 1980-81; v.p. research and devel. Air Products & Chem., Inc., Allentown, Pa., 1981-92, sr. v.p. rsch. and devel., 1992-94; pres., mem. exec. com., bd. dirs. Indsl. Rsch. Inst., 1990-94, chmn. plans and policies com., 1988-90; bd. dirs. Mallinckrodt, Inc., Petrolite Corp., Inc.; mem. chem. vis. com. Lehigh U., 1992-96; mem. exec. master sci.-in-engring. adv. coun. of U. Pa., 1992-94. Contbr. articles to profl. jours.; patentee in field. Mem. life scis., vis. com. Lehigh U., chmn. surface sci. vis. com., 1983-86; bd. dirs. WLVT Channel 39, Bethlehem, Pa., 1992-95; trustee Summit YMCA, N.J., 1976-79; mem. nat. materials bd. NRC, 1980-84. Mem. Coun. Chem. Rsch. (dir., treas.), Am. Chem. Soc. (pres.-elect 1994, pres. 1995), Soc. Chem. Industry, Saucon Valley Country Club. Episcopalian. Home: 3366 Bingen Rd Bethlehem PA 18015-5715

RUSHTON, WILLIAM JAMES, III, insurance company executive; b. Birmingham, Ala., Apr. 23, 1929; s. William James and Elizabeth (Perry) R.; m. LaVona Price, Aug. 19, 1955; children: William James IV, Deakins Ford, Tunstall Perry. B.A. magna cum laude, Princeton U., 1951; LL.D. (hon.), Birmingham So. Coll., 1981. Asso. actuary Protective Life Ins. Co., Birmingham, Ala., 1954-59; dir. Protective Life Ins. Co., 1956—, agt., 1959-62, v.p., 1962-63, agy. v.p., 1963-67, pres., from 1967, pres., chief exec. officer, 1969-82, chmn., 1982—; pres. Protective Life Corp., Birmingham, 1981-82, CEO, chmn., 1982-92, chmn., 1992-94, chmn. emeritus, 1994—; dir. Ala. Power Co., The Southern Co., Amsouth Bank N.A., Amsouth Bancorp. Trustee So. Rsch. Inst., Children's Hosp., Birmingham So. Coll., Highland Day Sch.; mem., deacon 1 st Presbyn. Ch., Birmingham, chmn. bd. deacons, 1960—; chmn. United Way campaign, 1977, pres., 1986, life mem., 1993; chmn. Leadership Birmingham, United Appeal, Indsl. Health Coun.; mem. adv. com. Meyer Found., Greater Birmingham Found. (chmn.). Capt. arty., U.S. Army, Korea. Decorated Bronze Star; named to Ala. Acad. of Honors, 1979; recipient Disting. Eagle Scout award Boy Scouts Am., 1980, Brotherhood award NCCJ, 1990. Fellow Soc. Actuaries; mem. Am. Council Life Ins. (dir.), Am. Life Conv. (state v.p. 1975), Am. Life Ins. Assn. (Ala. v.p. 1975), Health Ins. Assn. Am. (dir. from 1982), Million Dollar Round Table, Birmingham C. of C. (dir.). Clubs: Rotary (bd. dirs. 1973-74, treas. 1978-79, pres. 1988-89), Mountain Brook Country, Redstone. Office: Protective Life Corp 2801 Highway 280 S Birmingham AL 35223-2407

RUSINKO, FRANK, JR., fuels and materials scientist; b. Nanticoke, Pa., Oct. 12, 1930; s. Frank Sr. and Eva (Ruduski) R.; m. Lucy Geryak, June 1, 1957; children: Nancy, Lawrence. BS, Pa. State U., 1952, MS, 1954, PhD, 1958. Vice-pres., tech. dir. Airco Carbon, St. Mary's, Pa., 1959-76; pres. Electrotools Inc., Broadview, Ill., 1976-89, Intech EDM Electrotools, Broadview, Ill., 1989-91; sr. scientist, dir. Carbon Rsch. Ctr. Pa. State U., University Park, 1991—; dir. Anthracite Inst., dir. coop. program in coal rsch. Carbon Rsch. Ctr., Pa. State U., University Park, 1991—; bd. dirs., bd. chmn. transor Filter USA, Elk Grove Village, Ill., C-Cor Electronics State Coll., Pa.; cons. in field., 1996—. Contbr. articles to profl. jours. Mem. Hinsdale (Ill.) Plan Commn., 1986; mem. Region Campaign Pa. State U., 1989; pres. Sch. Bd. Edn., St. Marys, Pa., 1965-76. Fellow Pa. State Alumni Assn. (indsl. cons.); mem. Am. Chem. Soc., Am. Carbon Soc., N.Y. Acad. Sci., Sigma Xi. Orthodox. Home: 2392 Pine Hurst Dr State College PA 16803-3385 Office: Pa State U Carbon Rsch Ctr C204 Coal Utilization Lab University Park PA 16802

RUSKAI, MARY BETH, mathematics researcher, educator; b. Cleve., Feb. 26, 1944; d. Michael J. and Evelyn (Gortz) R. BS, Notre Dame Coll., Cleve., 1965; MA, PhD, U. Wis., 1969. Battelle fellow in theoretical physics U. Geneva, 1969-71; rsch. assoc. in math. MIT, Cambridge, Mass., 1971-72; rsch. assoc. in physics U. Alta., Edmonton, Can., 1972-73; asst. prof. math. U. Oreg., Eugene, 1973-76; asst. prof. U. Lowell, Mass., 1977-82, assoc. prof., 1982-86, prof. dept. math., 1986—, pres. faculty senate, 1990-91; sci. scholar Bunting Inst., Cambridge, Mass., 1983-85; vis. prof. Rockefeller U., N.Y.C., 1980-81, U. Vienna, Austria, 1981, Rome, 1988, Ga. Tech., Atlanta, 1997; faculty rsch. assoc. Naval Surface Warfare Ctr., Silver Springs, Md., 1986; vis. prof. math. U. Mich., Ann Arbor, 1991-92; vis. mem. Courant Inst. Math. Sci., NYU, 1988-89; cons. Bell Labs., Murray Hill, N.J., 1972, 83, 88-89; conf. dir. NSF/CBMS Conf. on Wavelets, 1990; Flora Stone Mather vis. prof. Case Western Res. U., Cleve., 1995. Editor-in-chief Wavelets and Their Applications, 1990-92; mem. editorial bd. Notices of Am. Math. Soc., 1994—; mem. editorial adv. bd. Internat. Jour. Quantum Chemistry, 1996—; contbr. articles to profl. jours. NSF predoctoral fellow, 1965-69; recipient NSF Career Advancement award, 1988-89. Fellow AAAS (symposium organizer 1991, 94, nominating com. math. sect. 1991-94); mem. Internat. Assn. Math. Physicists, Am. Math. Soc. (reviewer, session chmn., com. 1987—, com. chmn.), Math. Assn. Am. (com.), Am. Phys. Soc. (reviewer), Assn. Women in Math., Assn. Women in Sci. (pres. New Eng. chpt. 1986-87), Appalachian Mountain Club (Boston; winter leader 1979—), Sigma Xi. Office: U Lowell Dept Math 1 University Ave Lowell MA 01854-2827

RUSKIN, JOSEPH RICHARD, actor, director; b. Haverhill, Mass., Apr. 14, 1924; s. Ely and Betty Edith (Chaimson) Schlafman; m. Barbara Greene; 1 child, Alicia. Grad., Carnegie Inst. Tech., 1949. Founder Rochester (N.Y.) Arena Theatre, 1949-52. Actor N.Y. stage plays, 1952-58, Theatre Group, UCLA, Mark Taper Forum, 1959—, (films) Fall of Legs Diamond, 1959, Magnificent Seven, 1960, Escape from Zahrein, 1963, Robin and the Seven Hoods, 1965, Prizzi's Honor, 1985, Longshot, 1987, Indecent Proposal, 1992, regular appearances various TV programs, 1952—; dir. Houston Alley, 1965-69; freelance dir., 1969—. Served with USNR, 1943-46. Mem. AFTRA, SAG (nat. bd. dirs.), Actors Equity Assn. (nat. coun.). Home: 1326 Devon Ave Los Angeles CA 90024-5346

RUSMISEL, STEPHEN R., lawyer; b. N.Y.C., Jan. 27, 1946; s. R. Raymond and Esther Florence (Kutz) R.; m. Beirne Donaldson, Sept. 6, 1980 (div. Jan. 1984); 1 child, Margo Alexander; m. Melissa J. MacLeod, Aug. 24, 1985 (div. Oct. 1996); children: Benjamin William, Eric Scot Kunze, Erin Lea Kunze. AB, Yale U., 1968; JD, U. Va., 1971. Bar: N.Y. 1972, U.S. Ct. Appeals (2d cir.) 1974, U.S. Dist. Ct. (so. dist.) N.Y. 1975. Assoc. Winthrop, Stimson, Putnam & Roberts, N.Y.C., 1971-80, ptnr., 1980—. Aux. officer Bedminster Twp. (N.J.) Police, 1976—. Mem. Practicing Law Inst., Am. Arbitration Assn. (arbitrator 1976—), Far Hills Polo Club (Annandale, N.J.), Ausable Club (St. Huberts, N.Y.), Essex Hunt Club (Peapack, N.J.), Phi Delta Phi. Republican. Avocations: polo, flying, carpentry, gardening, poetry. Home: Shadowline Farm Bedminster NJ 07921 Office: Winthrop Stimson Putnam & Roberts One Battery Park Plz New York NY 10004-1490

RUSNAK, MICHAEL, bishop; b. Beaverdale, Pa., Aug. 21, 1921; arrived in Can., 1951; s. Andrew and Maria (Sotak) R. Student, Slovak U. Bratislava, Oberište. Ordained priest Slovak Cath. Byzantine Rite Ch., 1949, joined Redemptorist Fathers, 1949. Founder Maria publ., 1953; dean Slovak parishes Byzantine Rite, Ukrainian Eparchy Toronto, Can., 1957; apptd. titular bishop Diocese of Cernik, 1964; apptd. apostolic visitator for Slovak Caths. of Byzantine Rite in Can., 1964, consecrated bishop, 1965; named eparch Diocese of Sts. Cyril and Methodius, Slovak Byzantine Cath. Eparchy in N.Am., Can., 1980. Address: Slovak Cath Ch in Can, 223 Carlton Rd, Unionville, ON Canada L3R 2L8*

RUSOFF, IRVING ISADORE, industrial food scientist, consultant; b. Newark, Jan. 29, 1915; s. Max and Rachel (Dodin) R.; m. Perle Greenspan, Sept. 12, 1941 (dec. Nov. 1986); children: Susan, Arnold; m. Lillian Louise Skora, Sept. 6, 1987. BS, U. Fla., 1937, MS, 1939; PhD, U. Minn., 1943. Dairy chemistry instr. U. Fla., Gainesville, 1939-40; Nat. Def. Coun. fellow U. Minn., Mpls., 1944-46; head of nutritional rsch. Standard Brands, Inc., N.Y.C., 1946-47; head of nutrition, fats and oils Gen. Foods Corp., Hoboken and Tarrytown, N.Y., 1947-62; mgr. rsch. DCA Food Industries, N.Y.C., 1962-63; dir. nutritional biochemistry Beech Nut Life Savers, N.Y.C., 1963-66; dir. basic studies Nabisco, Inc., Fairlawn, N.J., 1966-76; sr. scientist Nabisco Brands, Inc., East Hanover, N.J., 1976-85; cons. Brick, N.J., 1985—; membership chmn. indslo. liaison panel NRC, Washington, 1979-83; liaison chmn. of IFT, Nat. Inventors Hall of Fame, Akron, Ohio, 1980-95; chmn. Gordon Rsch. Conf. on Food and Nutrition, 1981-82; rep. Grocery Mfrs. Assn.; mem. tech. com. for Nabisco, 1975-82; rep. to nutrition com. Biscuit and Crackers Mfrs. Assn., 1978-82. Contbr. articles to profl. jours.; patentee in field. Pres. Park Ridge (N.J.) Bd. Health, 1968. Nat. Found. for Infantile Paralysis fellow, 1943. Fellow Inst. Food Technologists (chmn. 1979-80); mem. Am. Assn. of Cereal Chemists (Charles N. Frey award 1984), Am. Chem. Soc., Am. Inst. Nutrition, Am. Oil Chemists Soc. (assoc. editor 1960-62), N.Y. Acad. Scis., Sigma Xi, Phi Tau Sigma. Jewish. Avocations: photography, magic, gardening. Home: 65 Central Blvd Brick NJ 08724-2451

RUSS, JOANNA, author; b. N.Y.C., Feb. 22, 1937; d. Evarett and Bertha (Zinner) R. B.A. in English with high honors, Cornell U., 1957; M.F.A. in Playwriting and Dramatic Lit, Yale U., 1960. Lectr. in English Cornell U., 1967-70, asst. prof., 1970-72; asst. prof. English, Harpur Coll., State U. N.Y. at Binghamton, 1972-75, U. Colo., 1975-77; asso. prof. English, U. Wash., 1977-90, prof., 1984-90. Author: Picnic on Paradise, 1968, And Chaos Died, 1970, The Female Man, 1975, We Who Are About To, 1977, Kittatinny: A Tale of Magic, 1978, The Two of Them, 1978, On Strike Against God, 1980, The Adventures of Alyx, 1983, The Zanzibar Cat, 1983, How To Suppress Women's Writing, 1983, Extra (Ordinary) People, 1984, Magic Mommas, Trembling Sisters, Puritans and Perverts: Feminist Essays, 1985, The Hidden Side of the Moon, 1987, To Write Like a Woman, 1995, (nonfiction) What Are We Fighting For, 1997; also numerous short stories. Mem. Sci. Fiction Writers Am. (Nebula award for best short story 1972, Hugo award for best novella 1983). Address: 8961 E Lester St Tucson AZ 85715-5568

RUSSEL, RICHARD ALLEN, telecommunications consultant, aerospace engineer, nuclear engineer, electrical engineer, retired naval officer; b. Shreveport, La., Jan. 24, 1958; s. Robert Lee and Gloria Jeanette (Gile) R.; m. Kathryn Joy Koehler, Dec. 30, 1983; children: Richard Allen Russel Jr., Kammie Joyce Jeanette, Jonathan Mark, Katie Jacqueline Keala, Stephen Sungmin. BSEE, U. N.Mex., 1980; Engrs. Degree in Aeros. and Astronautics, Naval Postgrad. Sch., Monterey, Calif., 1994, MSc in Astron. Engring., 1994. Commd. ensign, nuclear submarine officer USN, 1980, advanced through grades to lt. comdr., 1990; main propulsion analyst USS Puffer, Pearl Harbor, Hawaii, 1981-85; antisubmarine analyst, nuclear engr., comdr. 3d fleet USN, Pearl Harbor, 1985-87; combat systems officer USS TAUTUG, Pearl Harbor, 1987-89; navigator, ops. officer USS Indpls., Pearl Harbor, 1989-92; UHF/EHF satellite navy rep. PEO-SCS USN, El Segundo, Calif., 1994-96; project mgr. for spacecraft comms. Booz-Allen and Hamilton, Inc., San Diego, 1996—. Contbr. articles to profl. jours. Sch. bd. mem. Our Savior Luth. Sch., Aiea, Hawaii, 1986; den leader webelos Boy Scouts Am., 1995—. Fellow Inst. for the Advancement of Engring.; assoc. fellow AIAA (vice-chair edn. L.A. sect. 1991—, dep. dir. edn. region VI 1994—); mem. Space Nuclear Thermal Propulsion, Eta Kappa Nu. Republican. Lutheran. Achievements include design of predictive control system for thermoacoustic refrigerator, 3D laser range and orientation measuring system, navy satellite/computer secure communications systems; asynchronous transfer mode (ATM) networks; satellite and ground system design on CYBERSTAR, EHF Power Satellite, Global Broadcase Service, Navy UHF Follow-On Satellite, GEOSTAT Follow-On satellite. Home: 7405 Andasol St San Diego CA 92126-1014

RUSSELL, ALAN HAROLD, computer specialist, educator; b. Waterbury, Conn., Aug. 15, 1948; s. Vernon Harold and Sylvia Louise (Pierpont) R.; m.

Donna Ruth Van De Car, July 17, 1971; children: Christopher, Kimberly. BS in Computer Sci., Mich. State U., 1969, MS in Computer Sci., MBA, 1971; PhD, Kennedy Western U., 1988. Cert. computer profl. V.p. Toar Assocs., East Lansing, Mich., 1970-71; systems analyst Uniroyal, Inc., Oxford, Conn., 1971-72, Olin Corp., New Haven, 1972-75, Air Products and Chems., Allentown, Pa., 1975-80; systems assurance mgr. Air Products and Chems., Allentown, 1980-85, info. tech. specialist, 1985—; instr. Allentown (Pa.) Coll., 1980—; commr. Computer Sci. Accreditation Commn., N.Y.C., 1985-91. Vice chmn. Lehigh Christian Acad., Allentown, 1991-94; chmn. bd. Lehigh Valley Christian High Sch., Allentown, 1992—. Mem. IEEE, IEEE Computer Soc. (cert. of appreciation 1990), Assn. for computing Machinery (recognition of svc. award 1985), Am. Sci. Affiliation, Computer Profls. for Social Responsibility. Avocations: teaching, reading. Home: 6601 Crown Ln Zionsville PA 18092-2327 Office: Air Products & Chems Inc 7201 Hamilton Blvd Allentown PA 18195-1526

RUSSELL, ALLAN DAVID, lawyer; b. Cleve., May 6, 1924; s. Allan MacGillivray and Marvel (Codling) R.; m. Lois Anne Robinson, June 12, 1947; children: Lisa Anne, Robinson David, Martha Leslie. B.A., Yale U., 1945, LL.B., 1951. Bar: N.Y. 1952, Conn. 1956, Mass. 1969, U.S. Supreme Ct. 1977. Atty. Sylvania Electric Products, Inc., N.Y.C., 1951-56; div. counsel Sylvania Electric Products, Inc., Batavia, N.Y., 1956-65; sr. counsel Sylvania Electric Products, Inc., 1965-71; sec., sr. counsel GTE Sylvania Inc., Stamford, Conn., 1971-76; asst. gen. counsel GTE Service Corp., 1976-80, v.p., assoc. gen. counsel staff, 1980-83; sole practice law Redding, Conn., 1983—; sec., dir. mktg. subs. Sylvania Entertainment Products Corp., 1961-67; sec. Wilbur B. Driver Co. Dist. leader Rep. Party, New Canaan, Conn., 1955-56; sec. bd. dirs. Youth Found., Inc., 19812-83, bd. dirs., 1985—; mem. planning commn., Redding, Conn., 1987-89; mem. Redding Bd. Ethics, 1990-96, chmn., 1992-96; warden Christ Ch. Parish, Redding, 1987-89; bd. dirs. Mark Twain Libr., 1988-94, v.p., 1988-89, pres., 1990-92. With USAAF, 1943-46. Mem. SAR, Assn. of Bar of City of N.Y., Conn. Bar Assn. (exec. com. corp. counsel sect. 1986-90), Am. Soc. Corp. Secs., St. Nicholas Soc., Collie Club Am. Found., Inc. (v.p., dir. 1986-89, pres. 1989-90), Soc. Colonial Wars, Yale Alumni Assn. (sec. local chpt. 1953-56), Yale Club of Danbury (pres. 1990—), Phi Delta Phi. Home: 9 Little River Ln Redding CT 06896-2018

RUSSELL, ALLEN STEVENSON, retired aluminum company executive; b. Bedford, Pa., May 27, 1915; s. Arthur Stainton and Ruth (Stevenson) R.; m. Judith Pauline Sexauer, Apr. 5, 1941. B.S., Pa. State U., 1936, M.S., 1937, Ph.D., 1941. With Aluminum Co. Am., 1940-82, assoc. dir. research, 1973-74; v.p. Alcoa, Pa., 1974-78; v.p. sci. and tech. Pitts., 1978-81, v.p., chief scientist, 1981-82; adj. prof. U. Pitts., 1981-86. Contbr. articles to profl. jours. Named IR-100 Scientist of Yr., 1979; Pa. State U. alumni fellow, 1980; K.J. Bayer medalist, 1981; recipient chem. Pioneer award Am. Inst. Chemists, 1983. Fellow Am. Soc. Metals (Gold medal 1982), AIME (James Douglas gold medal 1987), Am. Inst. Chemists; mem. NAE (coun. 1978-84), Am. Chem. Soc., Sigma Xi. Republican. Presbyterian. Patentee in field. Home: 9 N Calibogue Cay Rd Sea Pines Plantation Hilton Head Island SC 29928

RUSSELL, ANDREW GEORGE ALEXANDER, author, naturalist; b. Lethbridge, Alta., Can., Dec. 8, 1915; s. Harold George and Lorenda Scarlett (McTavish) R.; m. Anna Kathleen Riggall, Nov. 1, 1936; children: Richard, Charles, John, Gordon, Anne. Grad. high sch., Lethbridge; LLD (hon.), U. Lethbridge, 1978, U. Calgary, Alta., 1978. Rocky Mountain guide, author, photographer, cinematographer, Alta., 1936—, rancher, lectr., 1936—. Author: Grizzy Country, 1964, Trails of a Wilderness Wanderer, 1971, Horns in the High Country, 1973, The High West, 1974, The Rockies, 1975, Wild Animals, 1977, Men of the Saddle, 1978, Alpine Canada, 1979, Memoirs of a Mountain Man, 1984, Life of a River, 1987, The Canadian Cowboy, 1993; contbr. articles to mags.; columnist; prodr. 3 feature films; writer radio scripts. Liberal candidate for Parliament, 1972. Decorated Order of Can.; recipient commemorative medal Confedn. of Can., 1992. Mem. Explorers Club. Avocations: fly fishing, target shooting, corresponding. Office: Box 68, Waterton Lakes Park, AB Canada T0K 2M0

RUSSELL, ANDREW MILO, music educator; b. Fredericksburg, Tex., July 16, 1948; s. Daniel Louden and Evelyn Sarah (Allen) R.; m. Sharon Anne Shelburne, June 2, 1968 (div. June 1994); children: Emily Christine, Andrea Layne, Dana Leslie. MusB, U. Houston, 1974; performance cert., Ind. U., 1974; MusM, Ind. U., Bloomington, 1975. Asst. prof. Baylor U., Waco, Tex., 1975-79; assoc. prof. U. Tex., Arlington, 1979—; cons. Tex. Commn. on Arts, Austin, 1985—. Performer numerous concerts, recitals nationwide, 1968—. E-5 with U.S. Army, 1971-74. Mem. Internat. Trombone Assn. (Emory B. Remington award), Am. Fedn. Musicians, Tex. Music Educators Assn., Chgo. Chamber Brass. Democrat. Baptist. Home: 1213 Scott Dr Hurst TX 76053-4223 Office: U Tex PO Box 19105 Arlington TX 76019

RUSSELL, ANGELA VETA, state legislator, social worker; b. Crow Agency, Mont., Aug. 25, 1943; d. William A. and Josephine (Pease) R. BA, U. Mont., 1965; MSW, Tulane U., 1974. Lic. social worker, Mont. Field rep. United Scholar Svc., Denver, 1965-67; child welfare worker Yellowstone County Pub. Welfare, Billings, Mont., 1968-72; counselor Rocky Mt. Coll., Billings, Mont., 1972-73; com. organizer Crow Tribe Office of Coal Rsch., Crow Agency, Mont., 1975-76; cons. pvt. practice, Lodge Grass, Mont., 1976-77; project dir. Denver U. Social Rsch., 1977-78; med. social worker USPHS, Crow Agency, 1978-85; psychotherapist, cons. pvt. practice, Billings, 1985-95; bd. mem. Rocky Mountain Coll., Billings. Editor Hist. Crow Calender, 1978—. State adv. com. U.S. Civil Rights Commn. Rocky Mt. Region, Denver, 1976-83; trustee Lodge Grass Schs., 1981-84; rep. Mont. Ho. of Reps., Helena, 1987-94; chmn. Mt. Rhodes Scholar Com., Missoula, Mont., 1990-94, Nat. Assn. Native Am. Legis., Denver, 1991-94; mem. adv. bd. Mont. Initiative for Abatement of Mortality in Infants, Helena, Mont., 1991-97; cmty. organizer Crow Healthy Mothers/Healthy Babies, Apsaalooke Com. for the Arts. Named to Salute to Women, YWCA, Billings, 1990; named Mont. Social Worker of Yr., 1993. Mem. NASW, Nat. Assn. Indian Social Workers (treas. 1986-88), Indian Law Resource Ctr. (bd. dirs. 1992—). Democrat. Baptist. Avocations: walking, reading, sewing, beading. Home: PO Box 333 Lodge Grass MT 59050-0333 Office: PO Box 551 Hardin MT 59034-0551

RUSSELL, ATTIE YVONNE, academic administrator, dean, pediatrics educator; b. Washington, Aug. 10, 1923; d. George and Kathleen L. (Milliner) Werner; m. Rex Hillier, Apr. 19, 1954 (dec.); m. Henry J. Russell, 1960 (div. 1971); children: Richard Russell, Margaret Jane Russell-Harde; m. Harry F. Camper, Sept. 2, 1984. BS, Am. U., 1944; PhD, State U. Iowa, 1952; MD, U. Chgo., 1958. Intern Phila. Gen. Hosp., 1958-59; resident in pediatrics Bronx (N.Y.) Mcpl. Hosp., 1960-61, Del. Hosp., Wilmington, 1962-63; dir. maternal and child health, crippled children's svcs. Del. State Bd. Health, Dover, 1963-68; asst. dean community health affairs, assoc. prof. pediatrics U. Cin. Coll. Medicine, 1968-71; clin. assoc. prof. pediatrics Med. Coll. Pa., Phila., 1966-68, 71-74; dep. dir. div. pub. health State of Del., Dover, 1971-74; dir. Santa Clara Valley Med. Ctr., San Jose, Calif., 1974-79; assoc. dean, clin. prof. pediatrics, family medicine Stanford (Calif.) U. Sch. Medicine, 1974-79; dir. USPHS Hosp., Boston, 1979-81, Balt. City Hosps., 1981-82; asst. v.p. community affairs, prof. pediatrics U. Tex. Med. Br., Galveston, 1982-87, asst. v.p. student affairs, dean students, prof. pediatrics, 1987-92, clin. prof. pediatrics, 1992—; reviewer Coun. for Internat. Exchange of Scholars, Washington, 1987-94; dir. III Symposium on Health and Human Svcs. in the U.S.-Mex., Brownsville, 1988; mem. sci. coun. Am. Fedn. for Aging Rsch., Inc., 1983-86. Contbr. articles and abstracts to profl. jours. Mem. budget com. United Way, Galveston, 1982-84; mem. Mayor's Adv. Com. for Sr. Citizens and Handicapped Persons for the City of Galveston, 1983-85; bd. dirs. Galveston County Coordinated Community Clinics, 1983-87; bd. advisors Galveston Hist. Found., 1983-88; mem. Com. for Coop. Action Planning, 1983-88, Houston-Galveston Health Promotion Consortium, 1983-88, Injury Control Prevention (Houston), 1984-89, aging programs adv. com. Houston-Galveston Area Coun., 1985-92. Recipient Disting. Alumni award Am. U., 1984. Fellow Am. Acad. Pediatrics, Am. Pub. Health Assn.; mem. AMA, Am. Coll. Preventive Medicine, Soc. for Adolescent Medicine, Am. Physiol. Soc., Am. Fedn. for Aging Rsch., Am. Geriatrics Soc., Mass. State Med. Soc., Galveston Med. Soc., Tex. Med. Assn., Tex. Pediatric Soc., Galveston C. of C. (legis. com. 1983-88), Order of Eastern Star, Sigma Xi, Alpha Omega Alpha.

RUSSELL, BILL, former professional basketball team executive, former professional basketball player; b. Monroe, La., Feb. 12, 1934. Grad., San Francisco State Coll., 1956. Player, NBA Boston Celtics Profl. Basketball Club, 1956-69, coach, 1966-69; sportscaster ABC-TV, 1969-80, CBS-TV, 1980-83; coach NBA Seattle Supersonics, 1973-77; coach NBA Sacramento Kings, 1987-88, v.p. basketball ops., then exec. v.p., 1988-89; mem. U.S. Olympic Basketball Team (Gold medal), 1956. Appeared in: TV series Cowboy in Africa; also commls.; co-host: The Superstars, ABC-TV, 1978-79; Author: Second Wind: Memoirs of an Opinionated Man, 1979. Inducted into Basketball Hall of Fame, 1974; mem. 11 NBA championship teams. Office: c/o Retired Players Assn 30 Kennedy Plz Providence RI 02903-2329*

RUSSELL, BYRON EDWARD, physical therapy educator; b. Louisiana, Mo., Apr. 27, 1949; s. John Franklin and Nellie Mae (Bryant) R.; m. Anna Jean Talkington, Mar. 25, 1972 (div. Dec. 19, 1979); children: Brad Michael, Audrey Lynn; m. Roberta Louise Snover, May 22, 1982. BS in Microbiology, Colo. State U., 1975; BS in Phys. Therapy, Tex. Tech. Health Sci. Ctr., 1988; MHS in Phys. Therapy, U. Indpls., 1994. Staff therapist Lubbock (Tex.) Gen. Hosp., 1988-89, S.W. Gen. Hosp., San Antonio, 1989-90; dir. phys. therapy Brady/Green Health Ctr., San Antonio, 1990-92; asst. prof. phys. therapy U. Tex. Health Sci. Ctr., San Antonio, 1992-95, Hardin-Simmons U., Abilene, Tex., 1995—; item writer Profl. Exam Svc., N.Y.C., 1996—; editor PT Series, Del-Mar Pubs., 1993-94. Editl. bd. Indsl. Rehab. Jour., 1996. Capt. USAR, 1989—. Mem. Am. Phys. Therapy Assn., Tex. Phys. Therapy Assn. (vice chair ctrl. dist.), Am. Coll. Sports Medicine, Sigma Xi. Baptist. Avocations: golf, hiking, fishing, horseback riding. Office: Hardin-Simmons University Box 16065 Abilene TX 79698-6065

RUSSELL, C. EDWARD, JR., lawyer; b. Portsmouth, Va., Aug. 19, 1942. BA, Hampden-Sydney Coll., 1964; LLB, Washington & Lee U., 1967. Bar: Va. 1967. Law clk. to Hon. John A. MacKenzie U.S. Dist. Ct. (ea. dist.) Va., 1967-68; atty. Kaufman & Canoles, Norfolk. Mem. ABA (bus. law sect., real property, probate and trust law sect.), Va. State Bar (bus. law sect., real property sect., health law sect.), Va. Bar Assn. (bus. law sect., real estate sect., chmn. young lawyers sect. 1977), Omicron Delta Kappa, Phi Alpha Delta. Office: Kaufman & Canoles One Commercial Place PO Box 3037 Norfolk VA 23514-3037

RUSSELL, CAROL ANN, personnel service company executive; b. Detroit, Dec. 14, 1943; d. Billy and Iris Koud; m. Victor Rojas (div.). BA in English, CUNY-Hunter Coll., 1993. Registered employment cons. Various positions in temp. help cos. N.Y.C., 1964-74; v.p. Wollborg-Michelson, San Francisco, 1974-82; co-owner, pres. Russell Staffing Resources, Inc., San Francisco and Sonoma, 1983—; media guest, spkr., workshop and seminar leader in field; host/cmty. prodr. Job Net program for TCI Cable T.V. Pub. Checkpoint Newsletter; contbr. articles to profl. pubs. Named to the Inc. 500, 1989, 90. Mem. Am. Women in Radio and TV, Soc. to Preserve and Encourage Radio Drama Variety and Comedy, No. Calif. Human Resources Coun., Soc. Human Resource Mgmt., Calif. Assn. Pers. Cons. (pres. Golden State chpt. 1984-85), Calif. Assn. Temp. Svcs., Bay Area Pers. Assn. (pres. 1983-84), Pers. Assn. Sonoma County, Profl. Resume Writers Am., Am. Jewish Congress. Office: Russell Staffing Resources Inc 351 California St Fl 8 San Francisco CA 94104-2412

RUSSELL, CHARLES F., newspaper publishing executive. V.p. technology The Wall Street Journal, N.Y.C. Office: Wall Street Journal 200 Liberty St New York NY 10281-1003*

RUSSELL, CHARLES ROBERTS, chemical engineer; b. Spokane, Wash., July 13, 1914; s. Marvin Alvin and Dessie Corselia (Price) R.; m. Dolores Kopriva, May 17, 1943; children—Ann E., John C., David F., Thomas R. B.S. in Chem. Engring, Wash. State U., 1936; Ph.D. in Chem. Engring. (Procter and Gamble Co. fellow 1940-41), U. Wis., 1941. Egr. div. reactor devel. AEC, Washington, 1950-56; engr. Gen. Motors Tech. Center, Warren, Mich. and Santa Barbara, Calif., 1956-68; assoc. dean engring. Calif. Poly. State U., San Luis Obispo, 1968-73; prof. mech. engring. Calif. Poly. State U., 1973-80; mem. nuclear standards bd. Am. Nat. Standards Inst., 1956-78; cons., 1980—; sec. adv. com. reactor safeguards AEC, 1950-55. Author: Reactor Safeguards, 1962, Elements of Energy Conversion, 1967, Energy Sources, Ency. Britannica. Served with USNR, 1944-46. Mem. Am. Chem. Soc. Republican. Roman Catholic. Club: Channel City (Santa Barbara). Home and Office: 3071 Marilyn Way Santa Barbara CA 93105-2040

RUSSELL, CHARLOTTE SANANES, biochemistry educator, researcher; b. N.Y.C., Jan. 4, 1927; d. Joseph and Marguerite (Saltiel) Sananes; m. Joseph Brooke Russell, Dec. 20, 1947; children: James Robert, Joshua Sananes. BA, Bklyn. Coll., 1946; MA, Columbia U., 1947, PhD, 1951. Asst. prof. biochemistry CCNY, N.Y.C., 1958-68, assoc. prof., 1968-72, prof., 1972—; peer reviewer NSF, NIH; ad hoc reviewer sci. jours. including Jour. Bacteriology, Biochemistry. Contbr. articles to profl. jours. Mem. AAAS, AAUP, AAUW (internat. fellowship panel 1986-89), Am. Soc. Biochemistry and Molecular Biology, Am. Chem. Soc., Amnesty Internat., Urgent Action Network, Sigma Xi. Office: CCNY Dept Chemistry 138th St & Convent Ave New York NY 10031

RUSSELL, CLIFFORD SPRINGER, economics and public policy educator; b. Holyoke, Mass., Feb. 11, 1938; s. Kenneth Clifford and Helen Alwilda (Springer) R.; m. Louise Pancoast Bennett, Feb. 3, 1965 (div. June 1985); m. Susan Vanston Reid, Sept. 7, 1985; stepchildren: Timothy Taylor Greene, Elizabeth Claussen Greene. BA, Dartmouth Coll., 1960; PhD, Harvard U., 1968. Sr. rsch. assoc. Resources for the Future, Washington, 1968-70, fellow, 1970-73, sr. fellow, 1973-85, div. dir., 1981-85; prof. econs. and pub. policy Vanderbilt U., Nashville, 1986—, dir. Vanderbilt Inst. for Pub. Policy Studies, 1986—; Valfrid Paulsson vis. prof. environ. econs. Beider Inst., Royal Swedish Acad. Scis., Stockholm, 1996-97. Author: Drought and Water Supply: Implications of the Massachusetts Experience for Municipal Planning, 1970, Residuals Management in Industry: A Case Study of Petroleum Refining, 1973, Steel Production: Processes, Products and Residuals, 1976, Environment Quality Management: An Application to the Lower Delaware Valley, 1976, Freshwater Recreational Fishing: The National Benefits of Water Pollution Control, 1982, Enforcing Pollution Control Laws, 1986; contbr. articles to profl. jours. Trustee, treas. Environ. Def. Fund, N.Y.C., and Washington, 1973-85; mem. Tenn. Gov.'s Energy Adv. Bd., Nashville, 1989-94; trustee Tenn. Environ. Coun., Nashville, 1989-96; pres. 1992-95. Lt. USN, 1960-63. Mem. Assn. Environ. and Resource Econs. (bd. dirs. 1983-85, chmn. workshop com., pres. 1993-94). Avocations: tennis, fly fishing, sailing, boat building. Home: 1222 Cliffee Dr Brentwood TN 37027-4105 Office: Vanderbilt Inst Pub Policy Studies 1207 18th Ave S Nashville TN 37212-2807

RUSSELL, CYNTHIA PINCUS, social worker, educator; b. N.Y.C., May 30, 1935. BA magna cum laude, Radcliffe Coll., 1957; MSW, Columbia U., 1959; postgrad., Hebrew U., Jerusalem, 1974-75; PhD, Union Rsch. Inst., 1978. Med. social worker Neurol. Inst.-Columbia-Presbyn. Med. Ctr., N.Y.C., 1958; caseworker Edwin Gould found. for Children, N.Y.C., 1958-61; med. social worker Yale-New Haven Hosp., 1961; instr. Yale Child Study Ctr., Psychiat Social Work in the Child Guidance Clinic, 1961-62; rsch. asst. Yale child Study Ctr. Nursery Sch., 1962-65; psychiat. social worker, rsch. asst. Regional Ctr. for Mental Retardation U. Conn. Sch. Social Work, 1966; psychiat. social worker Clifford Beers Guild Guidance Clinic, New Haven, 1966; dir. Info. and Counseling Svc. for Women, New Haven, 1969-77; asst. clin. prof. dept. psychiatry Yale U., New Haven, 1969—; mem. dept. student counseling Hebrew U., Jerusalem, 1974-75; pvt. practice New Haven and Stratford, Conn., 1977—; lectr. Albertus Magnus Coll., 1975; supr. social work and counseling U. Bridgeport, So. Conn. State U., 1975-77; psychosynthesis trainer Temenos Inst., Westport, 1987, N.Y. Inst., 1988, Amherst Synthesis Ctr., 1988—; founder Conn. Inst. for Pschosynthesis, 1990; adj. prof. Union Doctoral Program, 1990; presenter in field. Editor: Psychosynthesis Lifeline, 1984—; contbr. articles to profl. jours. Mem. Mayor's Com. on voluntarism, 1975-76, Regional Manpower Coun. New Haven, 1975-76, New Haven YWCA Women in Leadership, 1977-78, 89-91; pres. Except Cancer Patients, 1990-91, health profl. trainer, 1995; bd. dirs. Connection for Health, 1990; nat. adv. bd. Vital Active Life After Trauma, Cambridge, Mass., 1990. Mem. NASW, Acad. Cert. Social Workers (diplomate),. Home: PO Box 3833 Woodbridge CT 06525-0833 also: 2225 Main St Stratford CT 06497-5920

RUSSELL, DAN M., JR., federal judge; b. Magee, Miss., Mar. 15, 1913; s. Dan M. and Beulah (Watkins) R.; m. Dorothy Tudury, Dec. 27, 1942; children—Ronald Truett, Dorothy Dale, Richard Brian. B.A., U. Miss., 1935, LL.B., 1937. Bar: Miss. bar 1937. Practice in Gulfport and Bay St. Louis, Miss.; U.S. judge So. Dist. Miss., 1965—; now sr. judge. Lt. comdr. U.S. Naval Intelligence, 1941-45. Mem. Miss. Bar Assn., Hancock County Bar Assn. (v.p. 1964-65), Hancock & Harrison Counties Bar Assn., Bay St. Louis Rotary Club (hon.), Gulfport Rotary Club (hon.), Am. Inns Ct. (hon. Russell-Blass-Walker chpt.), Federalist Soc. (adv. bd. Miss. chpt.), Hancock County C. of C. (pres. 1946), Tau Kappa Alpha, Scribblers. Club: Rotarian (pres. Bay St. Louis, Miss. 1946). Office: US Dist Ct PO Box 1930 Gulfport MS 39502-1930

RUSSELL, DAVID E., judge; b. Chicago Heights, Ill., Mar. 19, 1935; s. Robert W. and Nellie Russell; m. Denise A. Hurst, Apr. 1, 1968 (div. 1978); children: Dirk, Kent, Laura, Rachel; m. Sandra M. Niemeyer, Oct. 31, 1982. BS in Acctg., U. Calif., Berkeley, 1957, LLB, 1960. Bar: Calif. 1961, U.S. Dist. Ct. (no. dist.) Calif. 1961, U.S. Tax Ct. 1967; CPA, Calif. Staff acct. Lybrand, Ross Bros. & Montgomery, San Francisco, 1960-64; assoc. Robert C. Burnstein, Esquire, Oakland, Calif., 1964-65; ptnr. Russell & Humphreys, Sacramento, 1965; ptnr. Russell, Humphreys & Estabrook, Sacramento, 1966-70, prin., 1971-73; shareholder Russell, Jarvis, Estabrook & Dashiell, Sacramento, 1974-86; bankruptcy judge U.S. Bankruptcy Ct. for Ea. Dist. Calif., Sacramento, 1986—. Office: US Bankruptcy Ct 650 Capitol Mall Rm 8308 Sacramento CA 95814

RUSSELL, DAVID EMERSON, mechanical engineer, consultant; b. Jacksonville, Fla., Dec. 20, 1922; s. David Herbert and Wilhelmina (Ash) R.; B.Mech. Engring., U. Fla., 1948; postgrad. Oxford (Eng.) U. Mech. engr. United Fruit Co., N.Y.C., 1948-50, U.S. Army C.E., Jacksonville, 1950-54, Aramco, Saudi Arabia, 1954-55; v.p. Beiswenger Hoch and Assocs., Inc., Jacksonville, 1955-57; owner, operator David E. Russell and Assos., cons. engrs., Jacksonville, 1957—. Chmn. Jacksonville Water Quality Control Bd., 1969-73; bd. dirs. Jacksonville Hist. Soc., 1981-82; mem. Jacksonville Bicentennial Commn., 1973-79. Served to 2d lt. AUS, 1943-46. Recipient Outstanding Service award City of Jacksonville, 1974. Registered profl. engr., Fla., Ga. Mem. ASME (chmn. N.E. Fla. 1967-68), Nat. Soc. Profl. Engrs., ASHRAE, Fla. Engring. Soc. Episcopalian. Club: University (Jacksonville). Contbr. articles to profl. jours.; holder of 5 U.S. patents. Avocations: world travel, boating, classical music. Home: 4720 Timuquana Rd Jacksonville FL 32210-8231 Office: 110 Riverside Ave Jacksonville FL 32202-4906

RUSSELL, DAVID L., federal judge; b. Sapulpa, Okla., July 7, 1942; s. Lynn and Florence E. (Brown) R.; m. Dana J. Wilson, Apr. 16, 1971; 1 child, Sarah Elizabeth. BS, Okla. Bapt. U., 1963; J.D., Okla. U., 1965. Bar: Okla. 1965. Asst. atty. gen. State of Okla., Oklahoma City, 1968-69, legal adviser to gov., 1969-70; legal adviser Senator Dewey Bartlett, Washington, 1973-75; U.S. atty. for Western dist. Okla. Dept. Justice, 1975-77, 81-82; ptnr. Benefield & Russell, Oklahoma City, 1977-81; chief judge U.S. Dist. Ct. (we. dist.) Okla., Oklahoma City, 1982—. Lt. comdr. JAGC, USN, 1965-68. Selected Outstanding Fed. Ct. Trial judge Okla. Trial Lawyers Assn., 1988. Mem. Okla. Bar Assn., Fed. Bar Assn. (pres. Oklahoma City chpt. 1981). Republican. Methodist. Office: US Dist Ct 3309 US Courthouse 200 NW 4th St Oklahoma City OK 73102-3026

RUSSELL, DAVID WILLIAMS, lawyer; b. Lockport, N.Y., Apr. 5, 1945; s. David Lawson and Jean Graves (Williams) R.; AB, Dartmouth Coll., 1967, MBA, 1969; JD cum laude, Northwestern U., 1976; m. Frances Yung Chung Chen, May 23, 1970; children: Bayard Chen, Ming Rennick. Bar: Ill. 1976, Ind. 1983. English tchr. Talledega (Ala.) Coll., summer 1967; math. tchr. Lyndon Inst., Lyndonville, Vt., 1967-68; instr. econs. Royalton Coll., South Royalton, Vt., part-time 1968-69; asst. to pres. for planning Tougaloo (Miss.) Coll., 1969-71, bus. mgr., 1971-73; mgr. will and trust rev. project Continental Ill. Nat. Bank & Trust Co. Chgo., summer 1974; law clk. Montgomery, McCracken, Walker & Rhoads, Phila., summer 1975; with Winston & Strawn, Chgo., 1976-83; ptnr. Klineman, Rose, Wolf & Wallack, Indpls., 1983-87, Johnson, Smith, Pence, Densborn, Wright & Heath, 1987—; cons. Alfred P. Sloan Found., 1972-73; dir. Forum for Internat. Profl. Svcs., 1985—, sec., 1985-88, pres. 1988-89; U.S. Dept. Justice del. to U.S. China Joint Session on Trade, Investment & Econ. Law, Beijing, 1987; leader Ind. Products Trade Fair, Kawachinagano, Japan, 1996; lectr. internat. Law, Gov's Ind. Trade Mission to Japan, 1986, bus. law Ind. Continuing Legal Edn. Forum, 1986-96, chmn., 1987, 89, 91; adj. prof. internat. bus. law Ind. U., 1993—; bd. dirs. Ind. ASEAN Coun., Inc., 1988—; nat. selection com. Woodrow Wilson Found. Adminstrv. Fellowship Program, 1973-76; vol. Lawyers for Creative Arts, Chgo., 1977-83; dir. World Trade Club of Ind., 1987-93, v.p., 1987-91, pres., 1991-92; dir. Ind. Swiss Found., 1991—; dir. Ind. Soviet Trade Consortium, 1991—, sec., 1991-92; v.p., bd. dirs. Ind. Sister Cities, 1988—; dir. Internat. Ctr. Indpls., 1988-92, v.p. 1988-89; Ind. dist. enrollment dir. Dartmouth Coll., 1990—; bd. dirs. Indpls. Sister Cities, 1992—, Carmel Sister Cities, 1993—, v.p. 1995-96, pres., 1997—; v.p. gen. coun. Lawrence Durrell Soc., 1993—; mem. bd. advisors Ctr. for Internat. Bus. Edn. and Rsch. Krannert Grad. Sch. Mgmt. Purdue U., 1995—; dir., v.p., gen. coun. Global Crossroads Found., Inc., 1995—. Woodrow Wilson Found. Adminstrv. fellow, 1969-72. Mem. ABA, ACLU, Ill. Bar Assn., Ind. Bar Assn. (vice chmn. internat. law section, 1988-90, chmn. 1990-92), Indpls. Bar Assn., Dartmouth Lawyers Assn., Indpls. Assn. Chinese Ams., Chinese Music Soc., Dartmouth Club of Ind. (sec. 1986-87, pres. 1987-88), Zeta Psi. Presbyterian. Home: 10926 Lakeview Dr Carmel IN 46033-3937 Office: Johnson Smith Pence Densborn Wright & Heath 1800 NBD Tower One Indiana Sq Indianapolis IN 46204

RUSSELL, DONALD STUART, federal judge; b. Lafayette Springs, Miss., Feb. 22, 1906; s. Jesse and Lula (Russell) R.; m. Virginia Utsey, June 15, 1929; children: Donald, Mildred, Scott, John. AB, U. S.C., 1925, LLB, 1928; postgrad., U. Mich., 1929; LLD (hon.), Wofford Coll., Lander Coll., The Citadel, U.S.C., Emory U., Clemson U., C.W. Post Coll. Bar: S.C. 1928. Pvt. practice law Spartanburg, 1930-42, 1938-42, 47-51, 57-63; with Nicholls, Wyche & Byrnes, Nicholls, Wyche & Russell, and Nicholls & Russell, 1930-42; mem. Price Adjustment Bd., War Dept., Washington, 1942; asst. to dir. econ. stabilization, 1942, asst. to dir. war mobilization, 1943; dep. dir. Office War Mobilization Reconversion, 1945; asst. sec. state, 1945-47; pres. U. S.C., 1951-57; gov. S.C., 1963-65, mem. U.S. Senate from S.C., 1965-66, U.S. Dist. Ct. judge, 1967-71; judge U.S. Ct. Appeals, Spartanburg, S.C., 1971—. Mem. Wriston Com. on Reorgn. Fgn. Service, 1954; trustee emeritus Emory U., Atlanta, Converse Coll., Spartanburg, S.C., Benedict Coll., Columbia, S.C. Served as maj. AUS, 1944, SHAEF, France. Mem. ABA, Am. Law Inst., S.C. Bar Assn., Spartanburg County Bar Assn., Phi Beta Kappa. Methodist. Office: US Ct Appeals 4th Ct PO Box 1985 Spartanburg SC 29304-1985

RUSSELL, DOUGLAS CAMPBELL, cardiologist; b. Oxford, Eng., July 26, 1945; came to U.S., 1989; s. David Syme and Marion Hamilton (Campbell) R.; m. Mercedes Dumas, Nov. 16, 1975; 1 child, Georgina Mercedes. BA with 1st class honors, Cambridge U., 1966, MB, BChir, 1969, MD, 1981; PhD, Edinburgh (Scotland) U., 1979. House officer Charing Cross Hosp. Med. Sch., London, 1970-71, sr. house officer, 1971-73; sr. house officer Hammersmith Hosp., London, 1973; registrar cardiology London Chest Hosp., 1973-75; rsch. asst. Med. Rsch. Coun. Edinburgh U., 1975-77, Brit. Heart Found. fellow, 1977-79, lectr. medicine, 1979-83, sr. lectr., sr. rsch. fellow cardiovascular rsch. unit, 1983-89; prof. medicine, chief cardiology U. Va. Sch. Medicine, Salem (Va.) VA Med. Ctr., Roanoke, 1989—; cons. cardiologist Royal Infirmary Edinburgh, 1983-89. Contbr. articles to med. jours. Rsch. grantee British Heart Found., Chest Heart and Stroke Assn., Thyssen Found., Scottish Home & Health, Pharm. Cos., 1976-89; John French Meml. lectr. Arterosclerosis Discussion Grop, Oxford, 1979. Fellow Am. Coll. Cardiology, Royal Coll. Physicians; mem. British Cardiac Soc., British Soc. Cardiovascular Rsch. (treas. 1984-87), Internat. Soc. Heart Rsch., British Med. Assn. Baptist. Avocation: orchid culture. Home: 6315 Spring Run Dr Roanoke VA 24018-5417 Office: U Va Dept Cardiology Salem VA 24157

RUSSELL, ELBERT WINSLOW, neuropsychologist; b. Las Vegas, N.Mex., June 4, 1929; s. Josiah Cox and Ruth Annice (Winslow) R.; children from previous marriage: Gwendolyn Marie Harvey, Franklin Winslow, Kirsten Nash, Jonathan Nash; m. Sally Lynn Kolitz, Apr. 2, 1989. BA, Earlham Coll., Richmond, Ind., 1951; MA, U. Ill., 1953; MS, Pa. State U., 1958; PhD, U. Kans., 1968. Clin. psychologist Warnersville (Pa.) State Hosp., 1959-61; clin. neuropsychologist VA Med. Ctr., Cin., 1968-71; dir. neuropsychology lab. VA Med. Ctr., Miami, Fla., 1971-89, rsch. psychologist, 1989—; adj. prof. Nova U., Ft. Lauderdale, 1980-87, U. Miami Med. Sch., 1980-94, U. Miami, 1979—. Author: (with C. Neuringer and G. Goldstein) Assessment of Brain Damage, 1970; (with R.I. Starkey) Halstead Russell Neuropsychology Evaluation System (manual and computer program), 1993; contbr. articles to profl. jours. Fellow APA, Am. Psychol. Soc., Nat. Acad. Neuropsychology; mem. Sigma Xi. Democrat. Soc. of Friends. Home: 6091 SW 79th St Miami FL 33143-5030 Office: 6262 Sunset Dr Ste 228 Miami FL 33143-4843

RUSSELL, EUGENE ROBERT, SR., engineering educator, administrator; b. Cromwell, Conn., Aug. 24, 1932; s. Arland William and Annie Margaret (LeBlanc) R.; m. Mary Lou Conner, June 29, 1957; children: Theresa, Janice, Eugene Jr., Anna, Ruth, Julie, Susan, Paul, Carol, Cecilia. BSCE, U. Mo., Rolla, 1958; MS in Civil Engring., Iowa State U., 1965; PhD, Purdue U., West Lafayette, Ind., 1974. Registered profl. engr., Iowa, Ind. Asst. bridge engr. State of Calif. Pub. Works, Sacramento, 1958-62; asst. area constrn. engr. Iowa Hwy. Commn., Grinnell, 1962-63; rsch. asst. soils Iowa State U., Ames, 1963-65; asst. prof. Ind. Inst. Tech., Ft. Wayne, 1965-69; rsch. assoc. Purdue U., West Lafayette, 1969-74; assoc. prof. Kans. State U., Manhattan, 1974-80, prof. civil engring., 1980—, dir. Ctr. for Transp. Rsch. and Tng., 1990—, assoc. dir. Mid-Am. Transp. Ctr., 1995—. Contbr. more than 60 articles to profl. jours. With USN, 1951-53. Fellow ASCE (br. pres.); mem. Inst. Transp. Engrs., Am. R.R. Engring. Assn., Transp. Rsch. Bd. (univ. rep.), Transp. Rsch. Forum, Am. Soc. Engring. Edn., Nat. Assn. County Engrs., Am. Pub. Works Assn., Sigma Xi, Chi Epsilon. Home: 3424 Dickens Ave Manhattan KS 66503-2413 Office: Kansas State Univ Dept Civil Engring Seaton Hall Manhattan KS 66506-2905

RUSSELL, FRANCIA, ballet director, educator; b. Los Angeles, Jan. 10, 1938; d. W. Frank and Marion (Whitney) R.; m. Kent Stowell, Nov. 19, 1965; children: Christopher, Darren, Ethan. Studies with, George Balanchine, Vera Volkova, Felia Doubrouska, Antonina Tumkovsky, Benjamin Harkarvy; student, NYU, Columbia U. Dancer, soloist N.Y.C. Ballet, 1956-62, ballet mistress, 1965-70; dancer Ballets USA/Jerome Robbins, N.Y.C., 1962; tchr. ballet Sch. Am. Ballet, N.Y.C., 1963-64; co-dir. Frankfurt (Fed. Republic Germany) Opera Ballet, 1976-77; dir., co-artistic dir. Pacific N.W. Ballet, Seattle, 1977—; dir. Pacific N.W. Ballet Sch., Seattle; affiliate prof. of dance U. Wash. Dir. staging over 100 George Balanchine ballet prodns. throughout world, including the Soviet Union and People's Republic of China, 1964—. Named Woman of Achievement, Matrix Table, Women in Comm., Seattle, 1987, Gov.'s Arts award, 1989, Dance Mag. award, 1996. Mem. Internat. Women's Forum. Home: 2833 Broadway E Seattle WA 98102-3935 Office: Pacific NW Ballet 301 Mercer St Seattle WA 98109-4600

RUSSELL, FRANK ELI, newspaper publishing executive; b. Kokomo, Ind., Dec. 6, 1920; s. Frank E. and Maude (Wiggins) R.; children: Linda Carole Russell Atkins, Richard Lee, Frank E. III, Rita Jane Russell Eagle, Julie Beth Russell Smith; m. Nancy M. Shover, Oct. 5, 1991. AB, Evansville Coll., 1942; JD, Ind. U., 1951; LLD (hon.), U. Evansville, 1985; HHD (hon.), Franklin Coll., 1989. Bar: Ind. 1951; CPA, Ind. Ptnr. George S. Olive & Co., Indpls., 1947-53; exec. v.p. Spickelmier Industries, Inc., Indpls., 1953-59; bus. mgr. Indpls. Star & News, 1959-77; v.p., gen. mgr. New Ctrl. Newspapers, Inc., Indpls., 1977-79, pres., 1979-95, chmn., bd. dirs., 1996—; pres. Ctrl. Newsprint, also bd. dirs.; pres. Bradley Paper Co., also bd. dirs.; sec.-treas., bd. dirs. Phoenix Newspapers Inc., Indpls., Newspapers, Inc., Muncie Newspapers, Inc., Ctrl. Newspapers Found., Indpls.; past chmn. adv. bd. Met. Indpls. TV Assn., Inc.; trustee retirement trust Ctrl. Newspapers, Inc.; bd. dirs. Newspaper Advt. Bur.; chmn. retirement com. Hoosier State Press. Bd. dirs. Ariz. Cmty. Found., 1992—, Eiteljorg Mus., 1994—. Recipient Life Salvation award Salvation Army, 1989, Disting. Alumni award Ind. U. Sch. Law, 1989, Life Trustee award U. Evansville, 1991. Mem. ABA, AICPA, Ind. Bar. Assn., Indpls. Bar Assn. (past bd. dirs., past treas.), Ind. Assn. CPAs (past dir.), Tax Execs. Inst. (past pres.), Ind. Assn. Credit Mgmt. (dir., v.p.), Inst. Newspaper Controllers and Fin. Officers (dir., past pres.), Ind. Acad. Ind. Assn. Colls., Midwest Pension Conf. (Ind. chpt.), Newspaper Advt. Bur. (bd. dirs.), Salvation Army (life mem. award), Order of Coif, Phi Delta Phi, Sigma Alpha Epsilon. Methodist. Clubs: Indpls. Athletic, Columbia, Meridian Hills Country, Skyline. Lodges: Masons, Shriners. Office: Ctrl Newspapers Inc 135 N Pennsylvania St Ste 1200 Indianapolis IN 46204-2487

RUSSELL, FRED MCFERRIN, journalist, author, lawyer; b. Nashville, Aug. 27, 1906; s. John E. and Mabel Lee (McFerrin) R.; m. Katherine Wyche Early, Nov. 2, 1933; children: Katherine (Mrs. Earl Beasley), Ellen (Mrs. Robert Sadler), Lee (Mrs. John Brown, Carolyn Russell. Student, Vanderbilt U., 1923-27. Bar: Tenn. 1928. Atty. Real Estate Title Co., 1928; reporter Nashville Banner, 1929, sports editor, 1930-69, sports dir., 1969-87, v.p., 1955—; chmn. honors ct. Nat. Football Found. and Hall of Fame, 1967-92; So. chmn. Heisman Trophy Com., 1946-92. Author: 50 Years of Vanderbilt Football, 1938, I'll Go Quietly, 1944, I'll Try Anything Twice, 1945, Funny Thing About Sport, 1948, Bury Me in an Old Press Box, 1957, Big Bowl Football, 1963; contbr. to mags. including Saturday Evening Post, 1939-63. A founder Harpeth Hall Sch., 1951, trustee, 1951-55; nat. pres. Vanderbilt Alumni Assn., 1960-61; dir. Children's Regional Med. Center, 1970-72. Recipient Nat. Headliners award, 1936; Grantland Rice award for sports writing, 1955; Jake Wade award, 1966; Coll. Football Centennial award, 1969; writing award Golf Writers Assn. Am., 1972; award for disting. journalism U.S. Olympic Com., 1976; Disting. Am. award Nat. Football Found. and Hall of Fame, 1980; Amos Alonzo Stagg award Am. Football Coaches Assn., 1981; award Nat. Turf Writers Assn., 1983; Red Smith award AP Sports Editors, 1984; named to Tenn. Sports Hall of Fame, 1974, Nat. Sportscasters and Sportswriters Hall of Fame, 1988. Mem. Football Writers Assn. Am. (pres. 1960-61), Sigma Delta Chi, Kappa Sigma (nat. man of yr. 1983), Omicron Delta Kappa. Methodist. Clubs: Belle Meade Country, Univ. Lodges: Masons (33 degree), Shriners. Office: Nashville Banner 1100 Broad St Nashville TN 37203 *There is a close affinity between sport and humor, and a sportswriter can provide a good measure of entertainment just by putting into print some of the humor he sees and hears along the way.*

RUSSELL, FREDERICK WILLIAM, Canadian provincial official; b. St. John's, Nfld., Can., Sept. 10, 1923; s. Herbert J. and Jean (Campbell) R.; m. Margaret M. Cross, June 15, 1946; children: Douglas, Janice, James, Peter. Student, Prince of Wales Coll., St. John's, Dalhousie U., Halifax, N.S., Can.; LLD (hon.), Meml. U. Nfld., St. John's, 1976. Pres. Blue Peter Steamships, St. John's, 1949-72, Terra Nova Motors Ltd., St. John's, 1962-79, Gen. Industries, St. John's, 1980-88, Delta Holdings Ltd., St. John's, 1980-88, Fremar Investments Ltd., St. John's, 1980-91; lt. gov. Province of Nfld., St. John's, 1991-97; mem. Royal Trust Adv. Bd., St. John's, 1980-91. Mem. Nfld. Labour Rels. Bd., St. John's 1953-89; chmn. United Ch. Sch. Bd., St. John's, 1958-67; chmn. bd. regents Meml. U. Nfld., 1974-82; bd. dirs. Atlantic Can. Opportunities Agy., Moncton, N.B., Can., 1986-91. Decorated Order of Can.; knight of justice Order of St. John; recipient Can. Forces Decoration, 1995; apptd. HCol of 5 Wing Goose Bay, Nfld., 9 Wing Gander, Nfld., 1995. Mem. Rotary (bd. dirs. St. John's). Mem. United Ch. of Canada. Avocations: skiing, boating, salmon fishing. Home: Ste 303, 156 Portugal Cove Rd, Saint Johns, NF Canada A1B 4H9

RUSSELL, GEORGE ALLEN, composer, theoritician, author, conductor; b. Cin., June 23, 1923; s. Joseph and Bessie (Sledge) R.; 1 son, Jock Millgardh; m. Alice Norbury, Aug. 4, 1981. Grad. h.s.; ed. in pupil composition, Stephan Volpe, 1949. Apptd. mem. faculty New England Conservatory Music, 1969; also tchr. in Sweden, Norway, Finland, U.K., Italy, Austria, Germany, France and Japan; mem. panel Nat. Endowment of Arts, 1975-76. Composer (with Dizzy Gillespie); 1st composition featuring jazz and Latin influences Cubana-Be, Cubana Bop; presented Carnegie Hall, 1947; performed John F. Kennedy's People to People Music Festival, Washington, 1962, Philharmonic Hall, Lincoln Center, 1963, tours of Europe with Newport Jazz Festival, 1964, jazz orchestras 1970—; performed original compostions with large and small European ensembles for radio, TV and new music socs., in Scandinavia, Italy, Sweden, W.Ger., also other parts Europe, 1964-70; Carnegie Hall performance, 1975; participant 1st White House Jazz Festival, 1978; recs. for RCA Records, Decca, Prestige, Capitol, Atlantic, Columbia, Contemporary, Blue Note, Soul Note, numerous others.; commd. composer maj. jazz work, Brandeis U., 1957, Norwegian TV; other commns. include original music for ballet Othello, 1967, Norwegian Cultural Fund, 1st choral work Listen to the Silence, 1971, Columbia Recs., Living Time for big band featuring Bill Evans, 1975, Swedish Radio for orch., 1977, 81, 83, Mass. Council on the Arts, 1983, Boston Musica Viva, 1987, work for orch. New Eng. Presentors, 1988, work for Relache New Music Ensemble, 1989; sponsor Am. Music Week, 1985, 86; artist-in-residence Glasgow Internat. Festival, 1990, Ezz-thetics with Don Ellis, Dave Baker, et al, N.Y. Big Band, New York, N.Y., Electronic Sonata for Souls Loved By Nature, The Essence of George Russell; tours of U.K., Europe, Japan with George Russell Living Time Orch., 1986-97; co-commn. Swedish Concert Inst. and Brit. Coun., 1995; recordings Label Bleu, 1989, 96; seminars: Paris Conservatoire Nat. Superier, Royal Coll. Music, Stockholm, Huddersfield Contemporary Music Festival, Guildhall, others, 1986-96. Recipient Outstanding Composer award Metronome mag., 1958, New Star Composer award Downbeat mag., 1961, Nat. Endowment of the Arts award, 1969, 76, 80, 81, Jazz Masters fellow, 1989; recipient Nat. Music award Am. Music Conf., 1976, numerous awards for recs.; Guggenheim fellow, 1969, 72; Nat. Endowment for Arts grantee, 1979; MacArthur Found. fellow, 1989. Mem. Internat. Soc. Contemporary Music, Norwegian Soc. New Music, Am. Fedn. Musicians. Address: care Concept 1770 Massachusetts Ave Ste 182 Cambridge MA 02140-2808

RUSSELL, GLEN ALLAN, chemist, educator; b. Johnsonville, N.Y., Aug. 23, 1925; s. John Allen and Marion (Cottrell) R.; m. Martha Ellen Havill, June 6, 1953; children: Susan Ann, June Ellen. B.S., Rensselaer Poly Inst., 1947, M.S., 1948; Ph.D., Purdue U., 1951. Research assoc. Gen. Electric Research Lab., Schenectady, 1951-58; assoc. prof. Iowa State U., Ames, 1958-61, prof., 1961—, disting. prof. scis. and humanities, 1972—; vis. prof. Chemistry Rsch. Promotion Ctr., Taiwan, 1994, Korean Soc. Advanced Sci., 1993, U. Grenoble, France, 1985; mem. adv. panel Petroleum Research Fund, 1964-67; vis. prof. U. Würzburg, Fed. Republic Germany, 1966; Reilly lectr. U. Notre Dame, 1966. Edit. adv. bd. Jour. Organic Chem., 1985-89. Recipient Iowa Gov.'s medal for sci. achievement, 1988; Guggenheim fellow Centre d'Etude Nucleaires de Grenoble, France, 1972; Alfred P. Sloan Found. fellow, 1959-63; Fulbright-Hayes lectr., 1966. Fellow AAAS, Japan Soc. for Promotion of Sci.; mem. Am. Chem. Soc. (award in petroleum chemistry 1965, Iowa medal 1971, Midwest award 1974, James Flack Norris award 1983, mem. editorial adv. bd. Jour. Am. Chem. Soc. 1966-76), AAUP, Chem. Soc. (London). Research, numerous publs. on directive effects in aliphatic substitutions occurring via free radicals, photochlorination, oxidation, bromination, solvent effects, application of E.S.R. spectroscopy to problems of structure and conformation, mechanism of autoxidation of organic substances in basic solution. Home: 1014 Murray Dr Ames IA 50010-5151 Office: Iowa State U Dept Chemistry Ames IA 50011

RUSSELL, H. DIANE, museum curator, educator; b. Kansas City, Mo., Apr. 8, 1936; d. Harry Fay Russell and Georgia Mae (Canfield) Haeberle. AB, Vassar Coll., 1958; PhD, Johns Hopkins U., 1970; postgrad., Inst. for Advanced Study, Princeton, N.J., 1980-81. Mus. curator Nat. Gallery Art, Washington, 1964-90, curator of Old Master Prints, 1990—; professorial lectr. The Am. U., Washington, 1966-82, adj. prof. Art History, 1982—. Author: Rare Etchings of G.B. and G.D. Tiepolo, 1972, Jacques Callot, 1975, Claude Lorrain, 1982 (Barr award 1984), EVA/AVE: Woman in Renaissance and Baroque Prints, 1990. Woodrow Wilson Foun. fellow, 1958-59; Univ. fellow, Johns Hopkins U., 1961-63; Kress Found. fellow, 1973; Nat. Endowment for Arts fellow, 1980-81. Mem. Coll. Art Assn., Renaissance Soc. Am., Print Coun. Am., Vassar Club. Avocations: gardening, walking, poodles. Office: Nat Gallery Art 4th & Constitution Ave NW Washington DC 20565-0001

RUSSELL, HAROLD LOUIS, lawyer; b. Abingdon, Va., July 1, 1916; s. Harold L. and Bess N. (Kinzel) R.; m. Katherine C. (Thompson) May 19, 1939; 1 child, Katherine T. Russell Prophet; m. Mildred Baggett Roach, Sept. 5, 1970. AB, Hendrix Coll., 1937; JD, Columbia U., 1940. Bar: N.Y. 1941, Ga. 1942, U.S. Ct. Appeals (1st, 2d, 3d, 5th, 11th and D.C. cirs.), U.S. Supreme Ct. 1950, D.C. 1972. Assoc. Gambrell & Russell and predecessors, Atlanta and N.Y.C., 1941-47, ptnr., 1947-84; ptnr. Smith, Gambrell & Russell, 1984—. Bd. dirs. Atlanta Fed. Defender Program, 1973-80, pres. 1978-79; bd. visitors, Columbia Law Sch., 1959—; mem. council Adminstrv. Conf. of U.S., 1968-76; bd. legal advisers Southeastern Legal Found., 1976—. Recipient Alumni Fedn. medal Columbia U., 1965; Disting. Alumnus award, Hendrix Coll., 1969. Fellow Am. Coll. Trial Lawyers, Am. Bar Found.; mem. ABA (past chmn. pub. utilities law sect., past chmn. spl. com. on legal service procedure, past chmn. adminstrv. law sect., ho. of dels. 1983-96), D.C. Bar Assn., Fed. Bar Assn., Atlanta Bar Assn., Atlanta Lawyers Club, Assn. Bar City of N.Y., Columbia Law Sch. Assn. (nat. pres. 1973-75), Atlanta C. of C., Phi Delta Phi. Democrat. Clubs: Capital City, Piedmont Driving. Home: 3999 Parian Ridge Rd NW Atlanta GA 30327-3029 Office: Smith Gambrell & Russell 3100 Promenade II 1230 Peachtree St NE Atlanta GA 30309-3575

RUSSELL, HARRIET SHAW, social worker; b. Detroit, Apr. 12, 1952; d. Louis Thomas and Lureleen (Hughes) Shaw; m. Donald Edward Russell, June 27, 1980; children: Lachante Tyree, Krystal Lanae. BS, Mich. State U., 1974; AB, Detroit Bus. Inst., 1976; BA in Pub. Adminstrn., Mercy Coll. Detroit, 1988; MSW, Wayne State U., 1992. Factory employee Gen. Motors Corp., Lansing, Mich., 1973; student supr. tour guides State of Mich., Lansing, 1974; mgr. Ky. Fried Chicken, Detroit, 1974-75; unemployment claims examiner State of Mich. Dept. Labor, Detroit, 1975-77, asst. payment worker, 1977-84, social svcs. specialist, 1984-90; ind. contractor Detroit Compact pres. Victory Enterprises, 1991; sch. social worker Detroit Bd. of Edn., 1992—; moderator Michigan Opportunity Skills and Tng. Program, 1985-86. Vol. Mich. Cancer Soc., East Lansing, 1970-72, Big Sisters/Big Bros., Lansing, 1972-73; elected rep. Mich. Coun. Social Svcs. Workers; speaker Triumphant Bapt. Ch., Detroit, 1976-80; chief union steward Mich. Employees Assn., Lincoln Park, 1982-83; leader Girl Scouts U.S.; area capt. Life Worker Project Program. Recipient Outstanding Work Performance Merit award Mich. Dept. Social Services, 1979, Unsung Hero award Neighborhood Found., 1995; grad. profl. scholar, 1990-91, Dean's scholar, 1991-92; elected to Wayne State Sch. Social Work Bd., 1992—. Mem. NAFE, Am. Soc. Profl. and Exec. Women, Assn. Internat. Platform Speakers, Mich. Coun. Social Svcs. Workers, Nat. Fedn. Bus. and Profl. Women's Clubs, Inc. U.S.A. (elected del. to China), Nat. Assn. Black Social Workers, Wayne State U. Social Work Alumni Assn. (bd. dirs. 1992—), Delta Sigma Theta. Democrat. Baptist. Office: PO Box 361 Lincoln Park MI 48146-0361

RUSSELL, HENRY GEORGE, structural engineer; b. Tewkesbury, Eng., June 12, 1941; came to U.S., 1968. BE, Sheffield U., Eng., 1962, PhD, 1965. Registered structural engr., Ill.; registered profl. engr., Wash., Minn. Rsch. fellow Bldg. Rsch., Eng., 1965-68; structural engr. Constrn. Tech. Labs., Inc. (formerly Portland Cement Assn.), Skokie, Ill., 1968-74, mgr., 1974-79, dir., 1979-88, pres., 1989-91, v.p. 1991-94; v.p. Henry G. Russell, Inc., Glenview, Ill., 1994-95. Contbr. articles to profl. jours. Named one Those Who Made Marks in 1992, Engring. News Record. Fellow Am. Concrete Inst. (Delmar L. Bloem award 1986, Wason medal 1992, Anderson award 1994); mem. Prestressed Concrete Inst. (Martin P. Korn award 1980). Office: 720 Coronet Rd Glenview IL 60025-4457

RUSSELL, HORACE ORLANDO, dean of chapel, theology educator; b. Clarendon, Jamaica, Nov. 3, 1929; Came to the U.S., 1988; s. Cleveland Augustus and Rowena Nerissa (Gordon) R.; m. Beryl Joyce Redman, Aug. 31, 1957; children: Elisabeth Jennifer, Jonathan Paul Carey, Heather Dawn Marie. BD, Calabar Theological Coll., London, 1954; BA, St. Catherine Coll., Oxford, 1957; PhD, Regent's Park Coll., Oxford, 1972. Ordained Baptist min. Febr. 10, 1958. Prof. church history United Theol. Coll. W.I., U. W.I., Jamaica, 1958-76, pres., 1972-76; sr. pastor Jamaica Bapt. Union, 1976-89; dean of chapel, prof. hist. theology Ea. Bapt. Theol. Sem., Phila., 1989—; mem. faith and order commn. World Coun. of Chs., Geneva, Switzerland, 1968-90, world assoc. of Christian commn., London, 1969—; v.p. Jamaica Baptist Union, 1980. Author: (books) Five Words of Love, 1982, The Baptist Witness, 1983, Foundations and Anticipations-The Baptist Story in Jamaica 1783-1892, 1993; founder, editor: (jour.) Carribean Jour. of Religious Studies, 1966. Mem. nat. commn. on unemployment Govt. of Jamaica, 1969, mem. pub. svc. commn., 1980-88, mem. nat. commn. on drug abuse, 1984-89, chair nat. heritage commn., 1988-89, mem. cultural devel. commn. 1987-88. Recipient Jamaica Prime Minister's medal Jamaican Govt., 1984, Marcus Garvey medal Marcus Garvey Internat., 1984, Jamaica Council of Churches award Churches of Jamaica, 1986. Mem. Am. Soc. of Ch. History, West Indies Group of Univ. Tchrs., Soc. for the Study of Black Religion, Hist. Soc. of Great Britain, Univ. Lodge English Masons (chaplain 1970), Oxford Soc. Baptist. Avocations: photography, creative writing. Home and Office: Ea Baptist Theological Seminary 6 Lancaster Ave Wynnewood PA 19096

RUSSELL, JAMES ALVIN, JR., college administrator; b. Lawrenceville, Va., Dec. 25, 1917; s. Dr. James Alvin and Nellie M. (Pratt) R.; m. Lottye J. Washington, Dec. 25, 1943; children: Charlotte Justyne, James Alvin III. BA, Oberlin Coll., 1940; BS, Bradley U., 1941, MS, 1950, spl. insts.; EdD, U. Md., 1967; spl. insts., Wayne U., U. Mich., U. Ill., NSF. Prof., dir. div. engring., also prof. edn. div. grad. studies Hampton Inst., 1950-71; pres. St. Paul's Coll., Lawrenceville, 1971-81; dir. instructional programs and student services Va. C.C. System, 1981-82; chmn. div. profl. studies W.Va. State Coll., 1982-86, acting pres., 1986-87, exec. asst. to pres., 1987-88; pres. So. W.Va. C.C., 1988-89, ret., 1989. Pres. Peninsula Council Human Relations, 1961-65. United Negro Coll. Fund fellow, 1966-67. Mem. IEEE, Am. Soc. Engring. Edn., Am. Assn. Univ. Adminstrs., Am. Vocat. Assn., Am. Tech. Edn. Assn., Nat. Assn. Indsl. Tech., Am. Assn. for Higher Edn., Nat. Assn. for Equal Opportunity in Edn., Brunswick C. of C., Sigma Pi Phi, Alpha Kappa Mu, Iota Lambda Sigma, Omega Psi Phi. Home: 811 Grandview Dr Dunbar WV 25064-1175

RUSSELL, JAMES BRIAN, broadcast executive; b. Hartford, Conn., Jan. 30, 1946; s. Seymour and Marian (Kamins) R.; m. Kathleen Anne Schardt, Dec. 28, 1968; children: Theodore, Jennifer, Kimberly. BA in Journalism, Am. U., 1968; postgrad., U. Pa., Stanford U. News dir. Sta. WPIK-AM, Arlington, Va., 1965-66; editor, anchorman Sta. WAVA-AM/FM, Washington, 1966-68; editor, corr. UPI, Washington, Cambodia and, Vietnam, 1968-71; from reporter to exec. prodr. All Things Considered Nat. Pub. Radio, Washington, 1971-78; sta. dir., sr. v.p. programming Stas. KTCA/KTCA-TV, Mpls./St. Paul, 1978-88; v.p. nat. prodns., exec. prodr. Marketplace U. So. Calif., L.A., 1988-97; v.p. USC Radio Worldwide Prodns., L.A., 1997—; mem. media leader's forum La. State U.; cons. Corp. Pub. Broadcasting, Nat. Endowment Arts, Sta. WNET-TV, N.Y.C., Sta. WGBH-TV, Boston, Nat. Pub. Radio, Am. Pub. Radio, Pub. Radio Internat., Am. Documentary Consortium, The Learning Channel, The Pacific Rim Consortium, Internat. Pub. TV Conf., Audible Words Corp. Columnist pub. broadcasting's Current newspaper. Mem. prison visitor program AMICUS, St. Paul, 1984-85. Postgrad. fellow U. Mich.; recipient Nat. Headliner award 1972, 74, Ohio State award, 1973, 75, duPont Columbia awards Columbia U., 1979, 81, Peabody award, Nat. TV Emmy award Acad. TV Arts and Scis., 1989. Home: 3820 Gundry Ave Long Beach CA 90807-4227 Office: Marketplace U So Calif Radio 3716 S Hope St Los Angeles CA 90007-4344

RUSSELL, JAMES FRANKLIN, lawyer; b. Memphis, Mar. 21, 1945; s. Frank Hall and Helen (Brunson) R.; m. Marilyn Land, June 1, 1968 (div. May 1976); children: Mary Helen, Myles Edward; m. Linda Hatcher, July 9, 1977; 1 child, Maggie Abele. BA, Rhodes Coll., 1967; JD, Memphis State U., 1970. Bar: Tenn. 1971, U.S. Dist. Ct. (we. dist.) Tenn. 1971, U.S. Ct. Appeals (6th cir.) 1971, U.S. Dist. Ct. (no. dist.) Miss. 1976, U.S. Ct. Appeals (5th cir.) 1977, U.S. Ct. Appeals (8th cir.) 1987. Assoc. Nelson, Norvell, Wilson, McRae, Ivy & Sevier, Memphis, 1971-75; ptnr. Stanton, Russell & Challen, Memphis, 1975-78, Russell, Price, Weatherford & Warlick, Memphis, 1978-82, Price, Vance & Criss, Memphis, 1982-85, Apperson, Crump, Duzane & Maxwell, Memphis, 1985-97, 1985-97; cir. ct. judge Divsn. II 30th Jud. Dist., 1997—. V.p. mid-south chpt. Am. Red Cross, Memphis, 1992-94; treas. Epilepsy Found. West Tenn., Memphis, 1992-94. Mem. ABA, Nat. Assn. R.R. Trial Counsel, Internat. Assn. Def. Counsel, Tenn. Bar Assn., Tenn. Def. Lawyers Assn., Memphis Bar Assn. (pres. 1992). Episcopalian. Avocations: golf, snow skiing. Home: 1045 Reed Hooker Rd North Eads TN 38028 Office: Apperson Crump Duzane and Maxwell 2110 One Commerce Sq Memphis TN 38103

RUSSELL, JAMES WEBSTER, JR., newspaper editor, columnist; b. Shreveport, La., Nov. 30, 1921; s. James Webster and Aline (Faulk) R.; m. Jean Buck, June 29, 1949; children: Nancy Russell Dearr, Eileen Russell Goure. B.A., La. State U., 1942. Fla. mgr. Internat. News Service, 1946-51; bur. chief UPI, Tallahassee, 1951-52; regional editor U.P.I., Atlanta, 1953-57; asst. city editor Miami (Fla.) Herald, 1957-58, bus.-fin. editor, 1958-74, fin.-econ. columnist, 1974—; guest lectr. U. Miami, Fla. Internat. U., Miami-Dade Community Coll., La. State U. Contbr. articles to: Fla. Trend, Times of London, N.Y. Times, Gentlemen's Quar. Trustee Fla. So. Coll. Served with USAAF, 1942-45. Recipient Eagle award Invest-in-Am. Nat. Council, 1976; Decorated Air medal with eleven oak leaf clusters. Mem. Soc. Am. Bus. Writers, Lambda Chi Alpha, Sigma Delta Chi. Republican. Methodist (chmn. ch. council on ministries 1971-72). Home: 4800 SW 64th Ct Miami FL 33155-6133 Office: 1 Herald Plz Miami FL 33132-1609

RUSSELL, JEFFREY BURTON, historian, educator; b. Fresno, Calif., Aug. 1, 1934; s. Lewis Henry and Ieda Velma (Ogborn) R.; m. Diana Emily Mansfield, June 30, 1956; children: Jennifer, Mark, William, Penelope. A.B., U. Calif., Berkeley, 1955, A.M., 1957; Ph.D., Emory U., 1960. Asst. prof. U. N.Mex., Albuquerque, 1960-61; jr. fellow Soc. of Fellows, Harvard U., Cambridge, Mass., 1961-62; mem. faculty U. Calif., Riverside, 1962-75; prof. dept. history U. Calif., 1969-75, assoc. dean grad. div., 1967-72; dir. Medieval Inst.; Michael P. Grace prof. medieval studies U. Notre Dame, South Bend, Ind., 1975-77; dean grad. studies Calif. State U., Sacramento, 1977-79; prof. history U. Calif., Santa Barbara, 1979—, prof. religious studies, 1994—. Author: Dissent and Reform in the Early Middle Ages, 1965, Medieval Civilization, 1968, A History of Medieval Christianity: Prophecy and Order, 1968, Religious Dissent in the Middle Ages, 1971, Witchcraft in the Middle Ages, 1972, The Devil: Perceptions of Evil from Antiquity to Primitive Christianity, 1977, A History of Witchcraft: Sorcerers, Heretics, and Pagans, 1980, Medieval Heresies: a Bibliography, 1981, Satan: The Early Christian Tradition, 1981, Lucifer: The Devil in the Middle Ages, 1984, Mephistopheles: The Devil in the Modern World, 1986, The Prince of Darkness, 1988, Ruga in Aevis, 1990, Inventing the Flat Earth: Columbus and the Historians, 1991, Dissent and Order in the Middle Ages, 1992, A History of Heaven: The Singing Silence, 1997; contbr. articles in field to profl. jours. Fulbright fellow, 1959-60; Am. Council Learned Socs. grantee, 1965, 70; Social Sci. Research Council grantee, 1968; Guggenheim fellow, 1968-69; Nat. Endowment for Humanities sr. fellow, 1972-73. Fellow Medieval Acad. Am.; mem. Medieval Assn. of Pacific, Am. Soc. Ch. History, Am. Acad. Religion, Sierra Club. Home: 4796 Calle Camarada Santa Barbara CA 93110-2053 Office: U Calif Dept History Santa Barbara CA 93106

RUSSELL, JERRY LEWIS, public relations counselor, political consultant; b. Little Rock, July 21, 1933; s. Jerry Lewis and Frances (Lieb) R.; m. Alice Anne Cason, Feb. 14, 1969; children—Leigh Anne, Andrew J. III, Christopher R.; children by previous marriage—Jerry Lewis III, Susan Frances. B.A. in Journalism, U. Ark., 1958; postgrad. in history U. Central Ark., 1978-82. Pub. relations dir. Little Rock C. of C., 1958; editor, pub. The Visitor, Little Rock, 1959-60; sec.-mgr. Ark. Press Assn., Little Rock, 1960-61; account exec. Brandon Agy., Little Rock, 1961-65; founder, pres. Guide Advt. (now part of River City Enterprises), also River City Pubs., Little Rock 1965-70, 72—; pres. River City Enterprises, 1974—; dir. pub. relations services S.M. Brooks Agy., Little Rock, 1970-72; founder, pres. Campaign Cons., 1974—; pub., editor Grass Roots Campaigning newsletter, 1979—. With AUS, 1953-56. Mem. Ark. Advt. Fedn. (pres. 1967-68), Pub. Relations Soc. Am. (pres. Ark. chpt. 1974), Am. Assn. Polit. Cons., Orgn. Am. Historians, Co. Mil. Historians, Western Hist. Assn., Custer Battlefield Hist. and Mus. Assn. (bd. dirs. 1988-93), Custer Battlefield Preservation Com. (bd. dirs. 1989-94), Ft. Laramie Hist. Assn., Council on Am.'s Mil. Past (state dir. 1979—), So. Hist. Soc., Little Big Horn Assos., Ark. Hist. Soc., Civil War Round Table Ark. (charter pres. 1964-65), Civil War Round Table Assos. (founder 1968, nat. chmn.), Order Indian Wars (founder 1979, nat. chmn.), Circus Fans Assn. Am. (pres. Little Rock chpt. 1981-83), Westerners Internat. (charter pres. Little Rock Corral 1974—), Confederate Hist. Inst. (founder 1979, nat. chmn.), Soc. Civil War Historians (founder 1984, exec. dir.), Ft. Phil Kearny Bozeman Trail Assn. (bd. dirs. 1985-95), Friends of Ft. Davis. Home: 9 Lefever Ln Little Rock AR 72227-3303

RUSSELL, JOHN FRANCIS, retired librarian; b. Mt. Carmel, Ind., Apr. 30, 1929; s. David Freeman and Bertha (Major) R.; B.A., DePauw U., 1951; postgrad. Ind. U., 1951-52; M.A., Johns Hopkins U., 1954; student Cath. U. Am., summer 1955; M.S., Grad. Sch. Library Sci. Drexel U., 1977; m. Edith Raymond Hyde, June 27, 1953; 1 dau., Anne Marie. Tchr. English, Park Sch. Balt., 1954-75, chmn. dept., 1957-75; tchr. speech, dir. Ira Aldridge Players Morgan State Coll., fall 1965-66; tchr. drama Loyola Coll., 1964, 66. Pres. Tchrs.' Assn. Ind. Sch. Balt. Area, 1960-62, advisory bd., 1966-67, chmn. com. on English, 1966-68; exec. com. Assn. Ind. Md. Sch., 1967-68. Dir., costumer Johns Hopkins U. Playshop, 1963-64; lectr. Lecture Group, Woman's Club Roland Park, others, 1964—. Bd. dirs. Balt. area council World Federalists U.S.A., 1961-67, vice chmn., 1964-67, nat. exec. council, 1963-65; bd. dirs. Center Stage, 1964-77; dir. Blvd. Players, pres., 1960-67; dir. Pasadena Little Theatre, v.p., 1979-83, pres., 1983-85, 2d v.p., 1990—; dir. Center Stage Players, New Image Theatre, Theatre Network of Houston, U.S.A. Theatre, Actors Conservatory Tex., v.p., 1990-91; bd. dirs. Unicorn Sch. Acting, 1996—; adv. com. Am. H.S. Theatre Festival, 1975; mem. adminstrv. bd. St. Mark's United Meth. Ch., 1957-67, Towson United Meth. Ch., 1967-77, First United Meth. Ch., 1980-89; adminstrv. coun., vice-chmn. Glenbrook United Meth. Ch., 1997—; sec. Festival Angels, 1982—(outstanding svc. award 1991); community vol. svcs. com., ARC, 1985-90; comprehensive volunteerism adv. com., Sheltering Arms, 1986-89. Recipient Nat. Citation of Merit Am. Shakespeare Festival, 1961; Critics Choice award Houston Post, 1984; certs. of appreciation Sheltering Arms, 1986-89, cer. of recognition, 1988. Mem. Am. Assn. Cmty. Theatre, Harris County Heritage Soc., Am. Film Inst., Nat. Film Soc., Drama League, Am. Theatre Assn. (v.p. Mid-Atlantic dist. 1967-68, pres. 1968-69, nat. dir. 1970-73, Mid-Atlantic chpt. award for achievement and contbn. to theatre 1973), Secondary Sch. Theatre Assn. (v.p. devel. 1974-75), Tex. Non-Profit Theatre, Nat. (bd. dirs. 1969), Md. (pres. 1969-70) Coun. Tchrs. English, Capital Area Media Educators Orgn. (exec. com. 1970-73, screening chmn. 1971-73), ALA, Tex. Libr. Assn. (audiovisual chmn. conv. planning com. 1981), Council Info. and Referral Svcs. (newsletter editor 1984-86), Tex. Alliance Info. and Referral Svcs. (conv. speaker 1981, 83, 84, 85), Alliance of Info. and Referral Svcs. (conv. speaker 1985), Houston Public Library Staff Assn. (pres. 1981-82), Literacy Vols. Am. (sec. Houston 1984-87, adv. bd. 1989-91, 95-96, bd. dirs. 1992-95, chmn. program com. 1991-93), Reading, Edn. and Devel. Coun. (recruitment chmn., exec. com. 1984-86), Cultural Arts Coun. of Houston/ Harris County, Park Pl. Civic Club (exemplary svc. award 1991), Phi Beta Kappa, Phi Eta Sigma, Beta Phi Mu. Editor: The Secondary School Theatre, 1972-74. Home: 7817 Grove Ridge Dr Houston TX 77061-1405

RUSSELL, JOHN ST. CLAIR, JR., lawyer; b. Albany, N.Y., Mar. 21, 1917; s. John St. Clair and Hazel (Barbiers) R.; m. Betty Kixmiller, Sept. 12, 1941; children: Patricia Russell, John St. Clair III (dec.), David K. AB cum laude, Dartmouth Coll., 1938; LLB, Yale U., 1941. Bar: N.Y. 1942, D.C. 1965. Mem. Hale Russell & Gray (and predecessors), N.Y.C., 1948-85; mem. Winthrop, Stimson, Putnam & Roberts, N.Y.C., 1985-90, sr. counsel, ret. ptnr., 1991—. Mem. Irvington (N.Y.) Zoning Bd. Appeals, 1955-89; chmn. Raoul Wallenberg Com. of U.S., 1985-90; exec. trustee Am.-Scandinavian Found.; mem. alumni coun. Dartmouth Coll., 1994—. Maj. USMCR, OSS, 1942-46. Decorated Order of Vasa Sweden; recipient medal of merit Swedish Red Cross. Mem. ABA, Assn. Bar City N.Y., Dartmouth Club, Phi Beta Kappa, Phi Sigma Kappa. Office: Winthrop Stimson Putnam and Roberts One Battery Park Pla New York NY 10004-1490

RUSSELL, JOSEPH WILLIAM, regional planner, emergency planner; b. Ware, Mass., Sept. 22, 1947; s. Joseph Stanley Urban and Phyllis (Merrill) Chalue. BA in English, Am. Internat. Coll., 1972, MA in English and Comm., 1973; MA in Archaeology, U. Mass., 1992. Project coord., transp. planner Pioneer Valley Planning Commn., West Springfield, Mass., 1978-81; site supr. Valley Opportunity Coun., Chicopee, Mass., 1981-82; program dir. New Eng. Farm Worker's Coun., Springfield, Mass., 1982-84; laborer divsn. watershed mgmt. Met. Dist. Commn., Belchertown, Mass., 1985-86; adminstrv. asst. II Divsn. Watershed Mgmt., Met. Dist. Commn., Belchertown, Mass., 1986-91, mgmt. analyst, 1991-93, regional planner II, 1993-94, regional planner III, 1994—; adj. instr. Mass. Emergency Mgmt. Agy., 1994—. Author: The Quabbin Valley: Then and Now, 1985, Vestiges of the Lost Valley: Buildings and Bells from the Quabbin, 1986, A Place Called Quabbin, 1987, A Quabbin Chronicle 1938-1988, 1988, The Archaeology of the Swift River Valley: Recent Developments, 1994, DWM Emergency Document Training and Testing Program, 1995, Quabbin Section Right-to-Know Program, Quabbin Section New Employee Orientation Program, 1988; co-author: Emergency Action Plan, Quabbin Reservoir, 1992, Emergency Action Plan, Wachusett Reservoir, 1993, Emergency Action Plan Sudbury Reservoir, 1995; founder, first editor The Quabbin Chronicle. Chmn. Joint Transp. Com., Pioneer Valley Planning Commn., 1981, rep. Town of Palmer, 1981, mem. exec. com. 1982; rep. Town of Palmer, Joint Transp. Com.; mem. Palmer Planning Bd., 1982, chmn., 1983; mem. Palmer Lic. Commn., 1986, vice chmn., 1988; apptd. notary public Commonwealth of Mass., 1989. Mem. Mass. Archeol. Soc. (treas. Norwottuck chpt.), Assn. State Dam Safety Ofcls., Mass. Orgn. State Engrs. and Scientists (dir. 1997—), Conf. on New Eng. Archaeology, Pewter Collectors Club of Am., Greenwich Ch. Found. Inc. (past pres.), Friends of Quabbin, Inc. (past pres.), Vernon Lodge, Newton Lodge, Melha Temple (noble 1993—). Avocations: antique American pewter collecting, baseball memorabilia, Confederate states memorabilia, mineral collecting. Home: 26 Nipmuck St Apt 12 Palmer MA 01069-2238 Office: Commonwealth of Mass Met Dist Commn. Quabbin Reservoir Belchertown MA 01007

RUSSELL, JOSETTE RENEE, industrial engineer; b. Defiance, Ohio, June 14, 1964; d. Eugene Alvin and Carole Josette (Galusha) R. BS in Indsl. Engring., GMI Engring. and Mgmt. Inst., 1988. Electronics engr. aero. systems div. USAF, Wright Patterson AFB, Ohio, 1985-90; process engr. Masland Industries, Carlisle, Pa., 1990-91, prodn. supr., 1991-92, prodn. tech. dir., 1992-93; mgr. quality McCord Winn Textron, Cookeville, Tenn., Cookeville, 1993; tech. sales rep. Deezee Chem. Co., Camden, N.J., 1994; dyehouse tech. cons. Downs Carpet Co., Willow Grove, Pa., 1995; mgr. mfg. Holley Performance Products, Bowling Green, Ky., 1995—. Appeared on cover of Woman Engr. Mag., 1988. Mem. Mensa, Sweet Adelines Internat. Republican. Avocations: Mickey Mouse memorabilia, composing, arranging, reading. Home: 5000 Plano Rd Bowling Green KY 42104 Office: Holley Performance Products PO Box 10360 1801 Russellville Rd Bowling Green KY 42102

RUSSELL, JOYCE ANNE ROGERS, librarian; b. Chgo., Nov. 6, 1920; d. Truman Allen and Mary Louise (Hoelzle) Rogers; m. John VanCleve Russell, Dec. 24, 1942; children: Malcolm David, John VanCleve. Student, Adelphi Coll., 1937; B.S. in Chemistry, U. Ky., 1942; M.L.S., Rosary Coll., 1967; postgrad., Rutgers U., 1970-71. Research chemist Sherwin Williams Paint Co., Chgo., 1942-45; reference librarian Chicago Heights (Ill.) Pub. Library, 1959-61; librarian Victor Chem. Works, Chicago Heights, 1961-62; lit. chemist Velsicol Chem. Corp., Chgo., 1964-67; chemistry librarian U. Fla., Gainesville, 1967-69; interim assoc. prof. U. Fla., 1967-69; librarian Thiokol Chem. Corp., Trenton, N.J., 1969-73; supr. library operations E.R. Squibb Co., Princeton, N.J., 1973-80, sr. research info scientist, 1980-91; mem. library adv. commn. Mercer Community Coll., 1979—; adv. asso. Rutgers U. Grad. Sch. Library and Info. Scis., 1978—. Editor: Bibliofile, 1967-69; contbr. articles to profl. jours. Mem. PTA, 1950-66; den mother Cub Scouts, 1952-59. Mem. Spl. Libraries Assn. (sec., dir., v.p., pres. Princeton-Trenton 1971, 75-80), Am. Chem. Soc. (bus. mgr., sec., dir. Trenton sect. 1969-78), AAUW, Mortar Board, Beta Phi Mu, Sigma Pi Sigma, Chi Delta Phi, Pi Sigma Alpha. Home: 1189 Parkside Ave Trenton NJ 08618-2625

RUSSELL, JOYCE M., lawyer, apparel executive; b. Green County, Ky., Oct. 23, 1946; d. Woodson and Sybil (Milby) R.; m. Arnold H. Haberkorn, Apr. 7, 1977. BA, Western Ky. U., 1968; JD, U. Ky., 1972. Bar: Ky. Supreme Ct. 1972. Assoc. Harlin, Parker, Lucas and English, Bowling Green, Ky., 1972-74; ptnr. Cole, Harned & Broderick, Bowling Green, 1974-75; corp. counsel Fruit of the Loom, Bowling Green, 1975-80, v.p., gen. counsel, 1980-93, sr. v.p., gen. counsel, 1993—. Pres., bd. dirs. Pub. Theatre Ky. Mem. ABA, Am. Corp. Counsel, Internat. Trademark Assn., Ky. Bar Assn., Bowling Green Bar Assn. Republican. Avocations: reading, gardening. Office: Fruit of the Loom PO Box 90015 1 Fruit of the Loom Dr Bowling Green KY 42102

RUSSELL, JOYCE WEBER, principal; b. Detroit, Feb. 21, 1948; d. Ronald Robert and Eleanor Treva (Burns) Weber; m. James Edward Russell, Mar. 25, 1970; 1 child, Jennifer Eileen. AA, Palm Beach C.C., Lake Worth, Fla., 1968; BA, Fla. Atlantic U., 1970, MA, 1975. Cert. tchr., prin. Tchr. Palm Beach County Sch. Bd., West Palm Beach, Fla., 1970-79, staff devel. specialist, 1979-84; asst. prin. Allamanda Elem., 1984-88; prin. Addison Mizner Elem., Boca Raton, Fla., 1988-90, South Olive Elem., West Palm Beach, 1990-95; adminstr. Safe Schs. AFTER Sch. Programs, Sch. Police, 1995-96; coord. Internat. Student Support/Multicultural Awareness, 1996-97. Chair Vision 2000 Good Shepherd Meth. Ch., West Palm Beach, 1990-97, chancel choir, pastor parrish com.; mem. Leadership Palm Beach County, 1990-97; vol. funding distbn. United Way Palm Beach County. Mem. ASCD, Palm Beach County Adminstr. Assn., Forum Club (bd. dirs.), Phi Delta Kappa. Avocations: water sports, genealogy, writing poetry, designing curriculum and writing summaries of educational research. Office: Sch Bd Palm County Ste 1010B 3330 Forest Hill Blvd West Palm Beach FL 33406-5869

RUSSELL, KENNETH CALVIN, metallurgical engineer, educator; b. Greeley, Colo., Feb. 4, 1936; s. Doyle James and Jennie Frances (Smith) R.; m. Charlotte Louise Wolf, Apr. 13, 1963 (div. 1978); children: David Allan, Doyle John. Met.E., Colo. Sch. Mines, 1959; Ph.D., Carnegie Inst. Tec., 1963. Engr. Westinghouse Research and Devel. Center, 1959-61; NSF postdoctoral fellow Physics Inst., U. Oslo, 1963-64; asst. prof. metallurgy M.I.T., Cambridge, 1964-69; assoc. prof. M.I.T., 1969-78, prof. metallurgy, 1978—, prof. nuclear engring., 1979—. Contbr. articles to profl. publs, Served as 2d lt. U.S. Army, 1959-60. DuPont fellow, 1961-62; NSF grad. fellow, 1962-63. Mem. AIME, Am. Phys. Soc., Am. Soc. for Metals. Office: MIT Rm 8-411 Cambridge MA 02139

RUSSELL, LILLIAN, medical, surgical nurse; b. N.Y.C., Feb. 21, 1942; d. Joserelle Russell; 1 child, Evan Gregory. AAS, N.Y.C. Community Coll., 1973; BS, St. Xavier Coll., Chgo., 1986; MS, Spertus Coll. of Judaica, Chgo., 1989. Staff/charge nurse Beth Israel Med. Ctr., N.Y.C., 1973-76; charge nurse Roosevelt Hosp., N.Y.C., 1977-78; staff/charge nurse U. Ill. Hosp., Chgo., 1979-90; asst. adminstrv. coord. Bethany Hosp., Chgo., 1990-91; adminstv. nurse I Mile Square Health Ctr. & U. Ill. Hosp., Chgo., 1991-95; asst. dir. nursing Mile Square Health Ctr., Chgo., 1995—; mem. instnl. rev. com. Bethany Hosp., 1987—; adj. asst. prof. Trinity Christian Coll., Palos Heights, Ill., 1996—. Mem. Great Cities Com., Chgo., 1994—. Mem. ANA, NAFE, AAUW, Ill. Nurses Assn., Res. Officers Assn. Home: 1342 N Oakley Blvd Chicago IL 60622-3048 *Everyone is born a genius. Some are recognized and nurtured to greatness; some are ignored and the genius withers and fades. The rest of us are fortunate to have a teacher or mentor who finds our special genius and makes it shine so everyone we encounter sees it too.*

RUSSELL, LOUISE BENNETT, economist, educator; b. Exeter, N.H., May 12, 1942; d. Frederick Dewey and Esther (Smith) B.; m. Robert Hardy Cosgriff, May 3, 1987; 1 child, Benjamin Smith Cosgriff. BA, U. Mich., 1964; PhD, Harvard U., 1971. Economist Social Security Adminstrn., Washington, 1968-71, Nat. Commn. on State Workmen's Compensation Laws, Washington, 1971-72, Dept. Labor, Washington, 1972-73; sr. economist Nat. Planning Assn., Washington, 1973-75; sr. fellow Brookings Instn., Washington, 1975-87; rsch. prof. Inst. for Health, Health Care Policy and Aging Rsch. Rutgers U., New Brunswick, N.J., 1987—, prof. econs., 1987—; chmn. health care policy divsn. Rutgers U., 1988—; mem. tech. bd. Milbank Fund, 1993-95. Author: Technology in Hospitals, 1979, The Baby Boom Generation and the Economy, 1982, Is Prevention Better Than Cure, 1986, Evaluating Preventive Care: Report on a Workshop, 1987, Medicare's New Hospital Payment System: Is It Working, 1989, Educated Guesses: Making Policy About Medical Screening Tests, 1994, (with MR Gold, JE Siegel and MC Weinstein) Cost-Effectiveness in Health and Medicine, 1996; also numerous articles. Mem. U.S. Preventive Svcs. Task Force, 1984-88; co-chair Panel on Cost Effectiveness in Health and Medicine DHHS, ODPHP, 1993-96. Mem. Inst. Medicine of NAS (com. to study future pub. health 1986-87, bd. on health scis. policy 1989-91, com. on clin. practice guidelines 1990-91, com. on setting priorities for practice guidelines 1994). Office: Rutgers U Inst for Health Care Policy 30 College Ave New Brunswick NJ 08901-1245

RUSSELL, LYNN DARNELL, mechanical engineer, educator; b. Pontotoc, Miss., Nov. 1, 1937; s. Clyde Austin and Clytee Lora (Faulkner) R.; m. Elaine Lowery, June 16, 1963; children—Kathy, Brent, Mark, Jeffrey. B.S., Miss. State U., 1960, M.S., 1961; Ph.D., Rice U., 1966. Profl. engr. Ala., Miss., Tenn. Engr. NASA Marshall Space Flight Ctr., Johnson Spacecraft Ctr., 1961-64; research scientist Lockheed, Huntsville, Ala., 1966-67; mem. tech. staff TRW, Huntsville, 1967-69; dean engring. U. Tenn.-Chattanooga, 1969-79; prof. mech. engring. Miss. State U., 1979-87, dean Coll. Engring., U. Ala., Huntsville, 1987—; energy cons. Recipient numerous fellowships and grants. Mem. Chattanooga Engrs. Club (pres. 1975); pres. Tenn. Soc. Profl. Engrs., 1978-79. Mem. ASME, Nat. Soc. Profl. Engrs., Ala. Soc. Profl. Engrs., Am. Soc. Engring. Edn., Internat. Solar Energy Soc., Sigma Xi, Pi Tau Sigma (past pres. Miss. chpt.). Contbr. articles to profl. jours. Office: U Ala 300 Sparkman Dr NW Huntsville AL 35805-1912

RUSSELL, MARGARET JONES (PEG RUSSELL), secondary school educator, retired writer; b. Durham, N.C., Apr. 25, 1938; d. Roderic O. and Margaret (Moore) Jones; m. Michael Morgan Russell; children: Lauren Skinner, Carol Martin, Seth Russell, Jay Russell. BA, Muskingum Coll., 1961. Ordained deacon Presbyn. Ch., 1970. Tchr. Sarasota (Fla.) County Sch. Bd., 1962-97; tchr. Sarasota H.S., 1982-96, ret., 1997; sponsor literary mag. Quest, 1988—. Editor: (newsletter) The Mainsail, 1992-95; contbr. poems to profl. pubs. ARC vol. Sarasota Meml. Hosp., 1966-83, aux. vol., 1994—; reader Fla. Studio Theatre, Sarasota, 1980—. Sarasota Herald Tribune scholar, 1993; Fla. Writing Project fellow, 1990. Mem. Nat. Coun. Tchrs. English, Fla. Coun. Tchrs. English, Fla. Freelance Writers, Light Verse Workshop (co-chair 1995), Sarasota Fiction Writers, Meadows Country Club, Alpha Gamma Delta. Republican. Presbyterian. Home: 1150 Willis Ave Sarasota FL 34232-2148

RUSSELL, MARJORIE ROSE, manufacturing company executive; b. Welcome, Minn., Sept. 3, 1925; d. Emil Frederick and Ella Magdalene (Sothman) Wohlenhaus; m. Kenneth Kollmann Russell, Sept. 15, 1947 (div. May 1973); children: Jennie Rose, Richard Lowell, Laura Eloise, James Wesley. Student, Northwestern Sch., Mpls., 1944-45, St. Paul Bible Inst., 1946-47. Cook U. Minn., Mpls., 1943-45; maintenance person U. Farm Campus/N.W. Schs., St. Paul, 1945-46; clk. Kresge Corp., Mpls., 1945; cook, waitress, mgr. Union City Mission Bible Camp, Mpls., 1944-47; caterer for v.p. Gt. No. R.R., St. Paul, 1947; custodian Old Soldiers Home, St. Paul, 1946; nurse Sister Elizabeth Kenney Polio Hosp., St. Paul, 1946; seamstress Hirsch, Weis, White Stag, Pendleton, Mayfair, Portland, Oreg., 1960-72; owner, operator, contract mgr., creative designer The Brass Needle, Portland, 1972—; contractor Forrester's Sanderson Safety, Scotsco, Nero & Assocs., Gara Gear, Portland, 1972—, Columbia Sportswear; tchr. Indo Chinese Cultural Ctr., Portland, 1982; mfr. of protective chaps and vests for the Pacific Northwest hogging industry. Designer, producer Kisn Bridal Fair, 1969; composer: He Liveth in Me, 1968; prodr. Safety Chaps for Loggers. Sec. Model Cities Com., Portland, 1969; com. mem. Neighborhood Black Christmas Parade, Portland, 1970; custume designer Local Miss Jr. Black Beauty Contest, Portland, 1973; nominating com. Nat. Contract Mgmt. Assn., Portland, 1978; mem. nominating com. Multi-Cultural Sr. Adv. Com., 1988-91. Mem. NAFE, Urban League, Urban League Guild (historian 1991-92), Am. Assn. Ret. Persons, Nat. Contract Mgmt. Assn. Democrat. Mem. United Ch. of Christ. Avocations: music, swimming, painting, gardening, arts. Home and Office: The Brass Needle 2809 NE 12th Ave Portland OR 97212-3219

RUSSELL, MARK, comedian; b. Buffalo, Aug. 23, 1932; s. Marcus Joseph and Marie Elizabeth (Perry) Ruslander; m. Alison Kaplan, Dec. 17, 1978; children: Monica, John, Matthew. Student, George Washington U., 1952; LittD, Union Coll., 1987; LHD, Canisius Coll., 1988; LHD (hon.), Goucher Coll., 1990. lectr., public speaker. Polit. comedian, featured performer Shoreham Hotel, Washington, 1961-81; prin. Mark Russell Comedy Spls., Pub. Broadcasting Svc., 1975—; host Mark Russell's England, PBS-TV, 1988, Mark Russell's Irish Fling, 1993, Mark Russell's Great Ala. Trek, 1994, Mark Russell's Tour de France, 1995, Mark Russell's Viva Italia, 1996; co-host NBC's Real People, 1979-84; regular contbr. Good Morning Am., ABC-TV, Inside Politics Weekend, CNN; author: Presenting Mark Russell, 1980; syndicated columnist via L.A. Times Syndicate, 1975. Served with USMC, 1953-56. Recipient Mark Twain award Internat. Platform Assn., 1980, 86, 4th Ann. Lucy award Shea's Buffalo, 1992, Nat. Humor Treasure award Nat. Humor Conf., 1995, SOAR St. Elizabeth Ann Seton award Washington, 1995, Washingtonian of the Yr. Washingtonian Mag., 1996. Mem. AFTRA, Am. Fedn. Musicians. Home and Office: PO Box 9904 Washington DC 20016

RUSSELL, MARY WENDELL VANDER POEL, non-profit organization executive, interior; b. N.Y.C., Feb. 6, 1919; d. William Halsted and Blanche Pauline (Billings) Vander Poel; m. George Montagu Miller, Apr. 5, 1940 (div. 1974); children: Wendell Miller Steavenson, Gretchen Miller Elkus; m. Sinclair Hatch, May 14, 1977 (dec. July 1989); m. William F. Russell, June 24, 1995 (dec. Apr. 1996). Pres. Miller Richard, Inc., Interior Decorators, Glen Head, N.Y., 1972—; bd. dirs. Eye Bank Sight Restoration, N.Y.C., 1975—, pres., 1980-88, hon. chair, 1988—; bd. dirs. Manhattan Eye Ear and Throat Hosp., N.Y.C., 1966-92, v.p., 1978-90; sec. Cold Spring Harbor Lab., N.Y., 1985-89, 92—, bd. dirs., 1985-90; chair DNA Learning Ctr., 1991—; bd. dirs. Cold Spring Harbor Lab, 1991—, sec., 1992—. V.p. North Country Garden Club, Nassau County, N.Y., 1979-81, 1983-85; dir. Planned Parenthood Nassau County, Mineola, N.Y., 1982-84, Hutton House C.W.Post Coll.,Greenvale, N.Y., 1982—; chair Hutton House, 1992-94. Recipient Disting. Trustee award United Hosp. Fund, 1992. Mem. Colony Club (N.Y.C.), Church Club (N.Y.C.), Piping Rock Club (Long Island), Order St. John Jerusalem (N.Y.C.). Republican. Episcopalian. Home: Mill River Rd # 330 Oyster Bay NY 11771-2733

RUSSELL, MICHAEL JAMES, lawyer; b. Northampton, Mass., May 19, 1958; s. John Michael and Celia Russell. Cert. in German, U. Vienna, 1979; BA summa cum laude, Gettysburg Coll., 1980; MA, JD, Vanderbilt U., 1984. Bar: Pa. 1984, D.C. 1985. Rsch. asst. Vanderbilt U., Nashville, 1982-84; legal intern U.S. State Dept., Washington, 1982; law clk. Stewart, Estes & Donnell, Nashville, 1983; atty. U.S. Dept. Agr., Washington, 1984-85; majority counsel subcom. on juvenile justice senate judiciary com. U.S. Senate, Washington, 1985-86, minority gen. counsel subcom. on constn., 1987, legis. dir. to Senator Arlen Specter, 1987-90; senate staff mem. Congrl. Crime Caucus, 1987-90; dep. dir. Nat. Inst. Justice U.S. Dept. Justice, Washington, 1990-93, acting dir., 1993-94; pres. Russell & Assocs., Washington, 1994-96; sr. pub. safety advisor Corp. Nat. Svc., Washington, 1994-96; dep. chief of staff to Senator Ben Nighthorse Campbell, 1996—. Editorial staff Vanderbilt Jour. Transnat. Law, Nashville, 1982-83, contbr., 1983, rsch. editor, 1983-84 (editor award 1984). Mem. senate staff club, 1985-90, Bush/Quayle Campaign's Crime Adv. Com., 1988, Friends of the Nat. Parks at Gettysburg, Pa., 1989—; bd. fellows Gettysburg Coll., 1990—; vol. Nat. Constrn. Ctr., Phila., 1990; mem. Bush/Quayle Adminstrn. S.E.S. Assn., 1990-92; Eisenhower Leadership Prize Dinner Com., Eisenhower World Affairs Inst., 1992, 93, mem. com. to celebrate bicentennial of constn., Northampton, Mass., 1987; mem. Bush/Quayle Alumni Assn., 1993—. Recipient Voluntary Svc. award VA, Northampton, 1978, Trustees award Forbes Libr., Northampton, 1989, cert. of appreciation Correctional Edn. Assn., 1991, Phi Alpha Delta, 1989, Fed. Bur. Alcohol, Tobacco and Firearms, 1989, Gettysburg Coll. Career Svcs. Office, 1992, Young Alumni Achievement award Gettysburg Coll., 1992, Wasserstein Fellowship Harvard Law Sch. Office of Pub. Interest Adv., 1995-96. Mem. ABA, Am. Soc. Internat. Law, Pa. Soc. of Washington, Phi Beta Kappa, Psi Chi (jr. award 1979). Avocations: racquetball, politics, volunteer svc. Office: Office Senator Ben Nighthorse Campbell 380 Russell Senate Office Bldg Washington DC 20510

RUSSELL, NEDRA JOAN BIBBY, secondary school educator; b. May, Tex., Mar. 19, 1942; d. Samuel Ross Bibby and Velva (Osburn) Bibby Bowden; m. James L. Russell, Aug. 27, 1960; children: Pettye Russell Arrington, Jamie Len Russell Trammell, Joan Lee Russell Dela Rosa. BS, Howard Payne U., 1967; postgrad., Hardin Simmons U., summer 1968; MA in Teaching, Angelo State U., 1976; vocat. office cert., North Tex. State U., 1986. Cert. tchr. secondary gen., bus., provisional lang./learning disabilities, Tex. Tchr. bus. and vocat. courses to at-risk students Coleman (Tex.) Ind. Sch. Dist. Alternative H.S., 1967—; instr. keyboarding technique Brain Damaged Children Conf., Angelo State U. and San Angelo Sch. Sys.; participant profl. workshops and confs., including State Vocat. Office Conf., 1985—, Trade and Indsl. Arts State Conf., 1990, Tex. Commn. on Ednl. Tech. Conf., summer 1992. Named Bus. Tchr. of Yr. for Dist. XV, 1993. Mem. NEA, ASCD, Tex. Bus. Edn. Assn. (dist. chmn. 1977, state historian 1980-81, mem. ednl. adv. com. to dist. 15 rep.), Tex. State Tchrs. Assn. (treas. Coleman County unit, dist. del., membership chairperson), Nat. Bus. Edn. Assn., Vocat. Office Edn. Assn., Tex. Computer Edn. Assn., Mountain-Plains Bus. Edn. Assn. Home: RR 2 Box 199 Coleman TX 76834-9518 Office: CAP High Sch RR 1 Box 43 Talpa TX 76882-9608

RUSSELL, NEWTON REQUA, retired state senator; b. L.A., June 25, 1927; s. John Henry and Amy (Requa) R.; m. Diane Henderson, Feb. 12, 1953; children: Stephen, Sharon, Julia. BS, U. So. Calif., 1951; postgrad. UCLA, Georgetown U. Spl. agt. Northwestern Mut. Life Ins. Co., Calif., 1954-64; mem. Calif. State Assembly, 1964-74, Calif. Senate, 1974-96; ret., 1996; vice-chmn. com. on energy, utilities and comm., mem. com. on local govt., mem. com. on fin. and investment, internat. trade, mem. com. on transp., com. ins., joint com. on rules, select com. on Calif.'s wine industry, mem. Com. on Legis. Ethics, Joint Oversight Com. on Lowering the Cost of Electric Svcs, chmn. senate select com. mediation. Mem. Rep. State Central Com. Served with USN, 1945-46. Recipient Outstanding Legislator award Calif. Rep. Assembly, 1968, 76, 81, Mayor's commendation City of Burbank, 1978, Disting. Service award County Suprs. Assn. Calif., 1980, Nat. Rep. Legislator of Yr., 1981, Legislator of Yr. award Los Angeles County Fedn. Rep. Women, 1982, Legislator of Yr. award Calif. Credit Union League, 1983, Paul Harris Fellow award Rotary Found. Rotary Internat., numerous honors from cmty. orgns. and instns. Mem. Rotary Internat., Am. Legion, Delta Tau Delta, Alpha Kappa Phi. Mem. Church on the Way. Office: Office of State Senate 401 N Brand Blvd Ste 424 Glendale CA 91203-2307

RUSSELL, PAMELA REDFORD, writer, film documentarian; b. Long Beach, Calif., June 11, 1950; d. George Martin and Helen Glyn (Brewen) R.; m. Robert John Colleary, 1984; children: Caitlin, Maggie, Tess. Student, UCLA, 1970-74. Field prodr. Santa Fe Comm., L.A., 1983-84; exec. prodr. Guiding Star Prodns., L.A., 1994—. Author: The Woman Who Loved John Wilkes Booth, 1978, Wild Flowers, 1982, (screenplay) Am American Woman, 1993; writer for Mary Tyler Moore Show, 1974, Touched By An Angel, 1997, also 14 scripts for Sears and Mut. Radio Theater, 1980-81, (TV show) Touched by An Angel, 1997. Mem. Nat. Trust for Hist. Preservation, Civil War Trust., Pacific Grove Heritage Soc. Mem. Authors Guild, Writers Guild Am. West. Avocation: historic preservation. Office: Parradign # 2500 10100 Santa Monica Blvd Los Angeles CA 90067-4003

RUSSELL, PAUL EDGAR, electrical engineering educator; b. Roswell, N.Mex., Oct. 10, 1924; s. Rueben Matthias and Mary (Parsons) R.; m. Lorna Margaret Clayshulte, Aug. 29, 1943; children: Carol Potter, Janice Russell Cook, Gregory. BSEE, N.Mex. State U., 1946, BSME, 1947; MSEE, U. Wis., 1950, PhDEE, 1951. Registered elec. engr., Ariz., Minn., S.C. From instr. to asst. prof. elec. engring. U. Wis., Madison, 1947-52; sr. engr., design specialist Gen. Dynamics Corp., San Diego, 1952-54; from prof. to chmn. elec. engring. dept. U. Ariz., Tucson, 1954-63; dean engring. Kans. State U., Manhattan, 1963-67; prof. Ariz. State U., Tempe, 1967-90; dir.

engring. Ariz. State U. West, Phoenix, 1985-88; dir. Sch. Constrn. and Tech. Ariz. State U., Tempe, 1988-90; cons. in field, 1954—; programs evaluator, mem. engring. commn. Accreditation Bd. for Engring. and Tech., N.Y.C., 1968-81. Contbr. articles to jours. and chpts. to books. Served as sgt. U.S. Army, 1944-46. Recipient Disting. Service award N.Mex. State U., 1965. Fellow IEEE (life, chmn. Ariz. sect. 1960), Accreditation Bd. Engring. and Tech.; mem. Am. Soc. Engring. Educators. Home: 5902 E Caballo Ln Paradise Valley AZ 85253

RUSSELL, PAUL FREDERICK, lawyer; b. Kansas City, Mo., Feb. 3, 1948; s. Walter Edward and Dorothy Marie (Sickels) R.; m. Kerry Diann Anderson, June 2, 1973; children: Philip, Erin, Shannon, Kelsey, Scott. BA, Northwestern, 1970; JD, U. Mich., 1973. Bar: Ill. 1973, U.S. Dist. Ct. (no. dist.) Ill. 1973. Assoc. Vedder, Price, Kaufman & Kammholz, Chgo., 1973-79, ptnr., 1980—. Mem. ABA, Chgo. Bar Assn., Ill. State Bar Assn., Midwest Benefits Coun., University Club (Chgo.), Mich. Shores Club. Office: Vedder Price Kaufman & Kammholz 222 N La Salle St Chicago IL 60601-1002

RUSSELL, PAUL SNOWDEN, surgeon, educator; b. Chgo., Jan. 22, 1925; s. Paul Snowden and Carroll (Mason) R.; m. Allene Lummis, Sept. 24, 1952; children—Katherine Swift, Paul Snowden, Allene, Laura Rice. Student, Groton (Mass.) Sch., 1939-41; Ph.B., U. Chgo., 1944, B.S., 1945, M.D., 1947; M.A. (hon.), Harvard U., 1962. Diplomate: Am. Bd. Surgery, Am. Bd. Thoracic Surgery. From surg. intern. to resident Mass. Gen. Hosp., 1948-56, asst. surgery, 1957-60, chief gen. surg. services, 1962-69, vis. surgeon, 1969—, chief transplantation unit, 1969-90, chmn. com. on research, 1973-76; postdoctoral fellow USPHS, 1954-55; successively teaching fellow, instr., clin. asso. surgery Harvard Med. Sch., 1956-60, John Homans prof. surgery, 1962—; asso. prof. surgery Columbia Coll. Phys. and Surg., 1960-62; asso. attending surgeon Presbyn. Hosp., N.Y.C., 1960-62; assoc. vis. surgeon Francis Delafield Hosp., N.Y.C., 1960-62, 74-94; mem. com. tissue transplantation NRC-Nat. Acad. Scis., 1963-71, com. trauma, 1963-68; ad hoc com. to study clin. investigation and edn. in USN, 1971-73; allergy and immunology study sect. USPHS, 1963-65, chmn. allergy and immunology study sect. B, 1965-67; mem. transplantation and immunology com. Nat. Inst. Allergy and Infectious Diseases, 1967-69, chmn., 1970; mem. com. on cancer immunotherapy Nat. Cancer Inst., 1974-79. Contbr. papers in field.; Editorial bd.: Archives Surgery, 1963-72, Surgery, 1963-71, Transplantation, 1965-79, Annals of Surgery, 1966—, Transplantation Procs, 1966—, Jour. Immunology, 1977-80. Trustee Pine Manor Coll., Chestnut Hill, Mass., 1963-76, Groton Sch., 1964-79; bd. dirs. Boston Fulbright Com., 1968, pres., 1980—; bd. governing trustees Jackson Lab.; bd. trustees Worcester Found. for Biomed. Rsch. With USAF, 1951-53. Fellow ACS, Royal Soc. Medicine; mem. AAAS, Am. Acad. Arts and Scis., Assn. Immunologists, N.Y. Acad. Scis., Mass. Med. Soc., New Eng. Surg. Soc., Boston Surg. Soc. (pres. 1994), Soc. Univ. Surgeons, Soc. Exptl. Biology and Medicine, Halsted Soc., Whipple Soc., Internat. Soc. Surgery, Am. Surg. Assn., Transplantation Soc. (pres. 1970), Polish Acad. Sci. (fgn.), Sigma Xi. Home: 32 Lawrence Rd Chestnut Hill MA 02167-1230 Office: Dept Surgery Mass Gen Hosp Boston MA 02114

RUSSELL, PEGGY TAYLOR, soprano, educator; b. Newton, N.C., Apr. 5, 1927; d. William G. and Sue B. (Cordell) Taylor; Mus.B. in Voice, Salem Coll., 1948; Mus.M., Columbia U., 1950; postgrad. U. N.C., Greensboro, 1977; student Am. Inst. Mus. Studies, Austria, 1972, 78; student of Clifford Bair, Nell Starr, Salem Coll., Winston-Salem, N.C., Edgar Schofield, Chloe Owen, N.Y.C.; student opera-dramatics Boris Goldovsky, Southwestern Opera Inst., Ande Andersen, Max Lehner, Graz, Austria; m. John B. Russell, Feb. 23, 1952; children: John Spotswood, Susan Bryce. Mem. faculty dept. voice Guilford Coll., Greensboro, 1952-53, Greensboro Coll., 1971-72; pvt. tchr. voice, Greensboro, 1963—; co-founder, v.p. sales, mktg. Russell Textiles, Inc., 1988; vis. instr. in voice U. N.C., Chapel Hill, 1973-77; founding artistic dir., gen. mgr. Young Artists Opera Theatre, Greensboro, 1983; staged and produced 18 operatic prodns., 1983-91; guest lectr. opera workshop U. N.C., Greensboro, 1990-91; lectr. opera Friends of Weymouth, So. Pines, N.C., 1994; lectr. on music history and opera, High Point, N.C., Center for Creative Leadership, Greensboro, 1979-80, First Presbyn. Ch., 1982; debut in light opera as Gretchen in The Red Mill, Winston-Salem Opera Assn., 1947; debuts include: Rosalinda in Die Fledermaus, Piedmont Festival Opera Assn., 1949, Lola in Cavalleria Rusticana, Greensboro Opera Assn., 1951, Violetta in La Traviata, Greensboro Opera Assn., 1953, Fiordiligi in Cosi fan tutte, Piedmont Opera Co., 1956; appeared as Marguerite in Faust, Brevard Music Center Resident Opera Co., 1967, First Lady in The Magic Flute, Am. Inst. Mus. Studies, Graz, Austria, 1972; mem. Greensboro Oratorio Soc., 1955-59, soprano soloist in The Messiah, 1952, 58, The Creation, 1955, Solomon, 1958; soprano soloist Presbyterian Ch. of the Covenant, Greensboro, 1958-71; guest appearances Sta. WFMY-TV, Greensboro, 1958-62; soprano soloist with Greensboro Symphony Orch., 1964, 80, Eastern Music Festival Orch. 1965, Greensboro Civic Orch., 1980; soloist in numerous recitals including: Wesleyan Coll., 1964, Roanoke Symphony Guild, 1967, Am. Inst. Mus. Studies, Austria, 1972, 78, U. N.C., Chapel Hill, 1974, 75, 76, 77, N.C. Mus. of Art, 1978; recital, masterclass Mars Hill Coll., 1981. Bd. dirs. Music Theater Assocs., Greensboro Friends of Music, N.C. Lyric Opera; judge Charlotte Opera Guild Auditions, 1994. Mem. Friendship Force of Guilford County, Holland, 1985, No. Germany, 1987. scholarship grantee N.C. Arts Council and Nat. Endowment for the Arts, 1991. Mem. Nat. Opera Assn. (chmn. regional opera cos. com. 1985-91, judge vocal competition auditions 1991, 92, 94, chmn. trustees Cofield Endowment 1991), Central Opera Service, Nat. Assn. Tchrs. of Singing (state gov. 1976-82, coordinator Regional Artist Contest 1982-84), N.C. Fedn. Music Clubs (dir. 1956-58), Music Educators Nat. Conf., Greensboro Music Tchrs. Assn. (pres. 1966-67), Symphony Guild (dir. 1977-78), Broadway Theater League (chmn. 1961-63), Atlanta Opera Guild, Civic Music Assn. (chmn. 1963-64), English Speaking Union (bd. dirs. Greensboro chpt., chmn. Shakespeare competition 1995), N.C. Symphony Soc., Piedmont Triad Coun. Internat. Vis. (Appreciation award Nat. Coun. Internat. Visitors 1994), Greensboro Preservation Soc., Guilford County Planning/Devel. Office (Forecast 2015 Com.). Presbyterian. Clubs: Sherwood Swim and Racquet, The Greensboro City. Home: 3012 W Cornwallis Dr Greensboro NC 27408-6730

RUSSELL, RICHARD DONCASTER, geophysicist, educator, geoscientist; b. Toronto, Ont., Can., Feb. 27, 1929; s. Richard Douglas and Ada Gwennola (Doncaster) R.; m. Virginia Ann Reid Clippingdale, Aug. 11, 1951; children: Linda Jean, Morna Ann, Mary Joyce. BA, U. Toronto, 1951, MA, 1952, PhD, 1954. Asst. prof. physics U. Toronto, 1956-58, prof., 1962-63; asso. prof. physics U. B.C., Vancouver, 1958-62; prof. geophysics U. B.C., 1963-91, prof. emeritus, 1991—, head dept. geophysics, 1968-72, head dept. geophysics and astronomy, 1972-79, bd. govs., 1978-81, assoc. dean sci., 1980-83, assoc. v.p. acad., 1983-86; sec.-gen. Inter-Union Commn. on Geodynamics, 1976-80; profl. geoscientist. Author textbooks.; Contbr. articles to profl. jours. Fellow Royal Soc. Can.; mem. Am. Geophys. Union, Can. Geophys. Union (J. Tuzo Wilson medal 1992). Home: 226-4955 River Rd, Delta, BC Canada V4K 4V9 Office: Dept Earth and Ocean Scis, U BC, Vancouver, BC Canada V6T 1Z4

RUSSELL, RICHARD OLNEY, JR., cardiologist, educator; b. Birmingham, Ala., July 9, 1932; s. Richard Olney and Louise (Taylor) R.; m. Phyllis Hutchinson, June 15, 1963; children: Scott Richard, Katherine Hutchinson, Meredith Cooper, Stephen Wilbon. A.B., Vanderbilt U., 1953, M.D., 1956. Diplomate Am. Bd. Internal Medicine, Am. Bd. Cardiovascular Disease. Intern Peter Bent Brigham Hosp., Boston, 1956-57; resident Peter Bent Brigham Hosp., 1959-60, 63-64; fellow in cardiology Med. Coll. Ala., Birmingham, 1960-62; instr. Med. Coll. Ala., 1962-63; instr. medicine U. Ala., Birmingham, 1964-65; asst. prof. U. Ala., 1965-70, assoc. prof., 1970-73, prof., 1973-81, clin. prof., 1981—; practice medicine specializing in cardiology Birmingham, 1981—; Mem. Jefferson County Bd. Health, 1977-81, chmn., 1979. Author: (with Charles Edward Rackley) Hemodynamic Monitoring in a Coronary Intensive Care Unit, 1974, 2d rev. and enlarged edit., 1981, Coronary Artery Disease: Recognition and Management, 1979, (with others) Radiographic Anatomy of the Coronary Arteries: An Atlas, 1976, Acute Ischemic Syndromes in American College of Cardiology Self Assessment Program, 1993; mem. editorial bd. Circulation, 1976-80, Am. Jour. Cardiology, 1977-82, Heart and Lung, 1978-83, Chest, 1978-83, Ala. Jour. Med. Scis, 1977-80, Jour. Am. Coll. Cardiology, 1987-90; contbr. articles to profl. jours. Distbn. com. Greater Birmingham Found., 1984-90; exec. bd. Birmingham area coun. Boy Scouts Am., 1987—, v.p., 1990-96, coun. commr., 1996—, vice chmn. Vulcan dist., 1988-89, chmn., 1989-91, bd. dirs. S.E. region, 1990-92, bd. dirs. southern region, 1992—; bd. dirs. Ctrl. Ala. United Way, 1988-92; mem. Newcomen Soc., 1988—; chmn. exec. com. Birmingham Bapt. Med. Ctr., Montclair, 1995. Decorated Commendation medal; recipient Dist. Award of Merit, Boy Scouts Am., 1991, Silver Beaver award, 1990; NIH rsch. fellow, 1966-67. Fellow ACP, Am. Coll. Cardiology (bd. govs. 1979-81, trustee 1984-85, 89-94, ann. sci. session program chmn. 1994); mem. Am. Heart Assn. (pres. Ala. affiliate 1975-76, v.p. so. region 1986-87), Am. Coll. Chest Physicians (bd. regents 1985-91), Am. Fedn. Clin. Rsch., Am. Bd. Cardiovascular Disease, So. Soc. Clin. Investigation, Jefferson County Med. Soc. (v.p. 1982, pres. 1984), Birmingham Cardiovascular Soc. (pres. 1981), Med. Assn. State Ala. (speaker house counselors dels. 1989-94), Leadership Birmingham, Kiwanis (Birmingham sec. 1984-85, pres. 1994-95), Phi Beta Kappa, Alpha Omega Alpha, Omicron Delta Kappa. Home: 4408 Kennesaw Dr Birmingham AL 35213-1826 Office: Ala Heart Inst 880 Montclair Rd 1st Fl Birmingham AL 35213

RUSSELL, RICHARD R., chemicals executive. CEO Gen. Chem. Group, Hampton, N.H. Office: General Chemical Group Liberty Ln Hampton NH 03842*

RUSSELL, ROBERT GILMORE, lawyer; b. Detroit, May 22, 1928; s. William Gilmore and Esther Marion (Redmond) R.; m. Martha Jones, July 9, 1955; children: Robin Russell Millstein, Julie Russell Smith. AB, U. Mich., 1951, JD, 1953. Bar: Mich. 1954. Atty. Kerr, Russell & Weber (and predecessors), Detroit, 1953—; ptnr. Kerr, Russell & Weber (and predecessors), 1959-93, of counsel, 1994—; instr. Wayne State U. Law Sch., 1954-60. Assoc. editor Mich. Law Rev., 1952-53. Fellow Am. Coll. Trial Lawyers, Am. Bar Found. (sustaining life), Mich. Bar Found. (charter); mem. ABA, ABOTA (advocate, charter mem. Mich. chpt.), Mich. Bar assn. (chair negligence coun. 1988-89), Detroit Bar Assn. (dir. 1977—, pres. 1981-82), Am. Judicature Soc., Am. Arbitration Assn., Internat. Assn. Def. Counsel, Assn. Def. Trial Counsel Detroit (pres. 1973-74), U.S. Supreme Ct. Hist. Soc., Mich. Supreme Ct. Hist. Soc., Nat. Conf. State Trial Cts. (mem. lawyers com.), Def. Rsch. Inst. Barristers, Order of Coif, Mimes, Theta Xi, Phi Delta Phi, Phi Eta Sigma, Thomas Cooley Club. Home: 879 Sunningdale Dr Grosse Pointe Woods MI 48236-1629 Office: Kerr Russell & Weber 500 Woodward Ave Detroit MI 48226-3423

RUSSELL, ROBERT HILTON, Romance languages and literature educator; b. Oak Park, Ill., Dec. 26, 1927; s. Melvin Alvord and Gladys (Hilton) R.; m. June Adele Thayer, Oct. 27, 1956. A.B., Knox Coll., 1949; A.M., Harvard U., 1950, Ph.D., 1963; A.M., Dartmouth Coll., 1968. Instr. Romance langs. and lits. Dartmouth Coll., 1957-61, asst. prof., 1961-63, assoc. prof., 1963-67, prof., 1967-91, prof. emeritus, 1991—; vis. prof. Spanish, U. San Diego, 1989, 90, 91, Knox Coll., 1993; guest lectr. Trinity Coll., Dublin, 1967, U. Salamanca, 1977, U. Leeds, 1978, Oxford U., 1978, U. P.R., 1987. Author: The Christ Figure in Misericordia, 1968; translator: Our Friend Manso, 1987. Corporate mem. United Ch. Bd. Homeland Ministries, 1963-69; N.H. del. Gen. Synod, United Ch. Christ, 1973, 75; corporator Internat. Inst. in Spain. Mem. MLA, Asociación Internacional de Hispanistas, Asociación Internacional de Galdosistas, Phi Beta Kappa. Democrat. Home: 14 Allen St Hanover NH 03755-2005 Office: 6072 Dartmouth Hall Hanover NH 03755-3511

RUSSELL, SUSAN WEBB, elementary and middle school education educator; b. Richmond, Va., Feb. 18, 1948; d. William Camper and Isabel McLeod (Smith) Webb; m. Russell Christian Proctor, III, Dec. 30, 1972 (div. 1981); 1 child, Alexander Christian Proctor; m. Walter William Russell, III, July 16, 1988; stepchildren: Walter William IV, Brian Earl. AB in English, Fine Arts, and Edn., Randolph-Macon Woman's Coll., 1970. Cert. tchr., Va. Customer svc. rep. Xerox Corp., Richmond, 1970-72; tchr. English grades 7, 8, 9 Am. Internat. Sch., Lagos, Nigeria, West Africa, 1973-75; group travel counselor Dynasty World Travel, Richmond, 1980-81; sec. to dir. athletics and receptionist The Collegiate Schs., Richmond, 1982-84, tchr. English and reading grades 6, 7, 9, 1984-88, tchr. word processing grade 5, 1984-86; tchr. social studies Norfolk (Va.) Acad., 1988-91, tchr. English and reading, 1991—; forensics coach Norfolk Acad., 1991—, 6th grad. chmn. 1995—. Editor Bulldog News, 1988-90; advisor Bullpup News, 1990-95. Mem. Norfolk Reading Coun., Va. Beach Reading Coun. Methodist. Avocations: travel, collecting art, theatre, music, movies. Office: Norfolk Acad 1585 Wesleyan Dr Norfolk VA 23502-5512

RUSSELL, THEODORE EMERY, diplomat; b. Madras, India, Nov. 21, 1936; s. Paul Farr and Phyllis Hope (Additon) R.; m. Sara Mather (Stedman) Russell, Sept. 3, 1960; children: Douglas Richmond Russell, Richard Mather Russell. BA, Yale U., 1958; MA, Fletcher Sch. Law & Diplomacy, 1960, MALD, 1961; sr. tng., Nat. War Coll., 1980-81. Fgn. svc. officer Dept. State, Italy, Czechoslovakia, Washington, 1963-80; dep. office dir. (EUR/RPE) Dept. State, Washington, 1981-83; dep. chief mission Dept. State, Copenhagen, 1983-87, Prague, Czechoslovakia, 1988-91; dep. asst. adminstr. for internat. activities EPA, Washington, 1992-93; ambassador to Slovak Republic Bratislava, Slovakia, 1993-96; dep. comdt. internat. affairs Army War Coll., Carlisle, Pa., 1996—. Councillor Atlantic Coun.; mem. Army-Navy Club, Fgn. Svc. Assn., Nat. War Coll. Alumni Assn. Avocations: hiking, fishing, history, numismatics, philately. Home and Office: 3 Garrison Ln Carlisle PA 17013

RUSSELL, THERESA LYNN, actress; b. San Diego, Mar. 20, 1957; d. Jerry Russell Paup and Carole (Mall) Platt; m. Nicholas Jack Roeg, Feb. 12, 1986; children: Statten Jack, Maximilian Nicolas Sextus. Appeared in films including The Last Tycoon, 1976, Straight Time, 1977, Blind Ambition, 1978, Bad Timing, 1980, Eureka, 1981, Razor's Edge, 1983, Insignificance, 1984, Aria, 1984, Black Widow, 1985 (Nat. Assn. Theater Owners award 1985), Track 29, 1986 (Newcomer of Yr. award), Physical Evidence, 1987, Impulse, 1988, Cold Heaven, 1989 (Best Actress award Viareggio Film Festival 1991), Whore, 1990, Kafka, 1990, Thicker Than Water, 1992, Flight of the Dove, 1994, The Trade Off, 1994, (narrator) Being Human, 1994, Grotesque, 1995, The Proposition, 1995; TV movies Blind Ambition, 1979, Women's Guide to Adultery, 1993, Hotel Paradise, 1995, When You Meet a Stranger, 1996; BBC radio play Double Indemnity, 1993.

RUSSELL, THOMAS, British government official; b. Melrose, Scotland, May 27, 1920; s. Thomas and Margaret Thomson (Wilkie) R.; m. Andrée Irma Désfossés, Jan. 2, 1951 (dec. May 1989). MA, St. Andrews U., Scotland, 1941; diploma in anthropology, Cambridge (Eng.) U., 1947. Dist. commr. Colonial Adminstrv. Svc., Solomon Islands, 1948-51, 54-56; asst. sec. Western Pacific high commn. Colonial Adminstrv. Svc., 1951-54; adminstrv. officer on secondment to col. Office, London, 1956-57; dep. fin. sec. Western Pacific high commn. Colonial Adminstrv. Svc., Solomon Islands, 1956-65, fin. sec., 1965-70, chief sec., 1970-74; gov. Cayman Islands, 1974-81; Cayman Islands govt. rep. U.K., 1982—. Capt. Brit. armed forces, 1940-46, North Africa and Italy, prisoner of war, Germany. Named Comdr. of Order of Brit. Empire, The Queen of England, 1970, Companion of the Order of St. Michael and St. George, The Queen of England, 1980. Fellow Royal Anthropol. Inst. (hon.); mem. Commonwealth Parliamentary Assn. (pres. Cayman Islands br. 1974-81, hon.), Brit. Commonwealth Ex-Svcs. League (mem. coun. 1982—, chmn. welfare com. 1993—), Pacific Islands Soc. (mem. coun. 1989—, past chmn.), Dependent Territories Assn. (chmn. 1997—), Caledonian Club, Royal Commonwealth Soc. Mem. Ch. of Scotland. Avocations: archaeology, anthropology. Home: 6 Eldon Dr Frensham Rd, Farnham GU10 3JE, England Office: Cayman Islands Govt Office, 6 Arlington St, London SW1A 1RE, England

RUSSELL, THOMAS J., critical care supervisor; b. Meriden, Conn., July 30, 1954; s. Joseph George and Anna M. (Rusczek) R. BS in Immunology, Kans. State U., 1977; BS in Microbiology, U. New Haven, 1981; MS, Yale U., 1984; cert. EMT-P, Norwalk Community Coll. Instr. in biology U. New Haven, West Haven, Conn., So. Conn. State U., New Haven; PALS instr, ACLS instr., PHTLS instr. Yale U.; ops. supr. New Eng. Ambulance, Shelton, Conn., New Haven Ambulance; instr. EMS, Conn.; EMS coord. Bradley Meml. Hosp., Southington, Conn.; mem. pre-hosp. pediatric task force State of Conn. Mem. Nat. Assn. EMT's, Nat. Paramedic Assn., N.Y. Acad. Scis., Nat. Acad. Scis., Am. Soc. Microbiology, Am. Soc. Immunology, Conn. Soc. Paramedics, Conn. CISD Team, Conn. EMS-C Com., Conn. Spl. Olympics World Games Med. Team Leader, Phi Beta Kappa, Tau Kappa Epsilon (Teke of Yr.), Beta Beta Beta. Home: 129 Tuttle Rd Durham CT 06422-2208

RUSSELL, THOMAS WILLIAM FRASER, chemical engineering educator; b. Moose Jaw, Saskatchewan, Can., Aug. 5, 1934; s. Thomas D. and Evelyn May (Fraser) R.; m. Shirley A. Aldrich, Aug. 1956; children: Bruce, Brian, Carey. BS, U. Alberta, Edmonton, Can., 1956, MS, 1958; PhD, U. Del., 1964. Registered profl. engr., Del. Asst. prof. U. Del., 1964-67, assoc. prof., 1967-70, prof., 1970-81, assoc. dean, 1974-77, acting dean, 1978-79, dir. Inst. of Energy Conversion, 1979-95, Allan P. Colburn prof., 1981—, chmn. chem. engring. dept., 1986-91; cons. E.I. duPont de Nemours & Co., Inc., Wilmington, Del., 1968—. Author 2 books; contbr. articles to profl. jours., patentee in field. Mem. NAE, Am. Inst. Chem. Engring. (Thomas H. Chilton award 1988, Chem. Engring. Practice award 1987), Am. Chem. Soc., Am. Soc. Engring. Edn. (3M Lecture award chem. engring. divsn. 1984). Avocations: wind surfing, hiking, skiing. Home: 46 Darien Rd Newark DE 19711-2024 Office: U Del Inst Energy Conversion Wyoming Rd Newark DE 19716-3820

RUSSELL, WILLIAM ALEXANDER, JR., environmental scientist; b. Havre de Grace, Md., Nov. 12, 1946; s. William Alexander Sr. and Margaret Adams Webster (Scott) R.; m. Nancy Dion Stacey, Jan. 4, 1965 (div. June 1971); 1 child, Angela Dion; m. Lynne Allison Ertle, July 10, 1971; children: Sara Lynne, Brent William. AA, Harford Community Coll., 1973; BS, Towson State U., 1983, MA, 1991; grad., Army Mgmt. Staff Coll., 1991. Cert. EMT level III firefighter. Environ. coord. U.S. Army Aberdeen Proving Ground (Md.), 1976-81; environmental protection specialist Hdqrs. Dept. Army Nat. Guard Bur., Washington, 1981-85, U.S. Army Environ. Hygiene Agy., Aberdeen Proving Ground, 1985-94, U.S. Army Ctr. Health Promotion & Preventive Medicine, Aberdeen Proving Ground, 1995—; cons. U.S.A. Ctr. Health Promotion Preventive Medicine, 1997. Contbr. tech. papers. Bd. dirs. Md. Ornithol. Soc., Balt., 1982-92, Harford Glen Found., Bel Air, Md., 1989-92; chmn. Harford County Environ. Adv. Bd., Bel Air, 1985-96; vol., asst. chief, dir., others Aberdeen (Md.) Fire Dept., 1962—; asst. scout master Boy Scouts Am., 1989-91, troop com. chmn., 1992-96, mem. Order of the Arrow Advisor, 1996—. Mem. Nat. Assn. Environ. Profls., Nat. Wildlife Fedn. (life), Nat. Audubon Soc., Md. Conservation Fedn. (charter), Raptor Rsch. Found., Nature Conservancy, Internat. Geographical Honor Soc. Democrat. Avocations: birding, hiking, environ. conservation. Home: 703 Beards Hill Aberdeen MD 21001-1776

RUSSELL, WILLIAM FLETCHER, III, opera company director; b. Denver, Aug. 31, 1950; S. William Fletcher Jr. and Ruth Talcott (Kenyon) R. MusB, U. Colo., 1973; MBA, UCLA, 1981. Singer various opera cos. including N.Y. Met. Opera, 1956-78; asst. bus. mgr. San Francisco Opera Co., 1980-84; mng. dir. The Washington Opera, 1984-87, L.A. Music Ctr. Opera, 1987-88; gen. dir. Anchorage Opera Co., 1988-92, Opera/Columbus, Ohio, 1991—; cons. NEA, Washington, 1984—; dramatic coach Anchorage Opera Co., 1988-92. Actor: (TV film) Disappearance of Aimee, 1976, (film) Duchess and Dirtwater Fox, 1977; assoc. prodr.: (TV operas) La Gioconda, 1979, Samson et Dalila, 1982, Pavarotti in Concert, 1983 (Emmy award 1983), Aida, 1984; prodr.: (TV opera) Goya, 1986 (Emmy award 1987). Mem. Anchorage East Rotary. Avocation: ski jouring. Home: 1779 N Galena Rd Sunbury OH 43074-9588 Office: Opera/Columbus 177 E Naghten St Columbus OH 43215-2613*

RUSSELL, WILLIAM JOSEPH, educational association administrator; b. Boston, Sept. 23, 1941; s. Stanley Whiteside and Helen Rita R.; m. Frances Marie Chapdelaine, June 25, 1967; 1 son, Scott David. B.S., Boston Coll., 1963; M.Ed., Northeastern U., 1966; Ph.D., U. Calif., Berkeley, 1971. Head math. dept. Oceana, Pacifica, Calif., 1966-71; asst. for fed. and profl. affairs Am. Ednl. Research Assn., Washington, 1971-73; dep. exec. officer Am. Ednl. Research Assn., 1973-74, exec. officer, 1974—; adv. bd. Edn. Resource Info. Center Ednl. Testing Center, Princeton, N.J., 1975-87; exec. officer Nat. Council on Measurement in Edn., Internat. Assn. Computing in Edn., 1987-89. Editor: Ednl. Researcher, 1979-90. Mem. Am. Ednl. Research Assn., Phi Delta Kappa. Roman Catholic. Home: 1443 Creekside Ct Vienna VA 22182-1701 Office: AERA 1230 17th St NW Washington DC 20036-3003

RUSSELL, WILLIAM STEVEN, finance executive; b. Evanston, Ill., Aug. 5, 1948; s. John W. and Lillian H. Russell; m. Susan M. Hanson, Aug. 20, 1972. BS, So. Ill. U., 1970. CPA, Ill. Sr. staff auditor Arthur Andersen & Co., Chgo., 1972-76; acctg. mgr., controller, asst. sec. and treas. Lawter Internat., Inc., Northbrook, Ill., 1976-86, treas., sec., 1986-87, v.p. fin., treas. and sec., 1987-96, pvt. investigator, 1996—. Served with U.S. Army, 1970-72. Mem. Am. Inst. CPA's, Beta Alpha Psi, Beta Gamma Sigma. Roman Catholic. Home and Office: 2690 Edgewood Ct Deerfield IL 60015-1906

RUSSELL-HUNTER, GUS W(ILLIAM) D(EVIGNE), zoology educator, research biologist, writer; b. Rutherglen, Scotland, May 3, 1926; came to U.S., 1963, naturalized, 1968; s. Robert R. and Gwladys (Dew) R-H.; m. Myra Porter Chapman, Mar. 22, 1951 (dec. 1989); 1 child, Peregrine D. BSc with honors, U. Glasgow, 1946, PhD, 1953, DSc, 1961. Sci. officer Bisra, Brit. Admiralty, Millport, Scotland, 1946-48; asst. lectr U. Glasgow, Scotland, 1948-51, univ. lectr. in zoology, 1951-63; examiner in biology Pharm. Soc. Gt. Britain, Edinburgh, 1957-63; chmn. dept. invertebrate zoology Marine Biol. Lab., Woods Hole, Mass., 1964-68, trustee, 1967-75, 77-87, trustee emeritus, 1989—; prof. zoology Syracuse (N.Y.) U., 1963-90, emeritus prof., 1990—, continuing rsch. fellow in biology, 1990—; cons. editor McGraw-Hill Encys., 1977—; bd. dirs. Upstate Freshwater Inst., Syracuse, 1981—. Author: Biology of Lower Invertebrates, 1967, Biology of Higher Invertebrates, 1968, Aquatic Productivity, 1970, A Life of Invertebrates, 1979, The Mollusca: Ecology, 1983; mng. editor: Biol. Bull. Woods Hole, Mass., 1968-80; contbr. over 120 articles to sci. jours. William Wasserstrom award Syracuse U., 1988; Carnegie and Browne fellow, 1954; rsch. grantee NIH, 1964-70, NSF, 1971-81, U.S. Army C.E., 1985-87; confirmed Scottish armiger, 1967. Fellow AAAS, Linnean Soc. London, Royal Soc. Edinburgh, Inst. Biology U.K.; mem. AAUP, Ecol. Soc. Am., Soc. Internat. Limnology, Am. Malacological Union, Malacological Soc. London, Soc. Sys. Biol. Avocations: book collecting, small boat sailing, model railroading, painting (oils and acrylics). Home: 711 Howard St Easton MD 21601-3934 Office: Syracuse U 026C Lyman Hall Syracuse NY 13244 *Having a sufficiency of books around one results in more than mere contentment. Many of us who come from a more literate pre-electronic civilization cannot imagine - if we exclude only the counterchanging transports of sex - any bliss superior to that of living surrounded by books.*

RUSSELL-WOOD, ANTHONY JOHN R., history educator; b. Corbridge-on-Tyne, Northumberland, Eng., Oct. 11, 1939; came to U.S., 1971; s. James and Ethel Kate (Roberts) R.-W.; m. Hannelore Elisabeth Schmidt, May 19, 1972; children: Christopher James Owen, Karsten Anthony Alexander. Diploma in Portuguese studies, Lisbon U., Portugal, 1960; BA with honors, Oxford (Eng.) U., 1963, MA, DPhil., 1967. Lectr. Portuguese lang. and lit. Oxford U., 1963-64; rsch. fellow St. Antony's Coll., Oxford, 1967-70; vis. assoc. prof. Johns Hopkins U., Balt., 1971-72, assoc. prof., 1972-76, prof., 1976—, chmn. dept. history, 1984-90, 96—, chmn. dept. Hispanic and Italian studies, 1996—; chmn. Albert Beveridge award and the Dunning prize coms., 1986-87; mem. U.S. Commn. Maritime History, 1977—. Author: Manuel Francisco Lisboa: A Craftsman of the Golden Age of Brazil, 1968, Fidalgos and Philanthropists: The Santa Casa da Misericordia of Bahia, 1550-1755, 1968, The Black Man in Slavery and Freedom in Colonial Brazil, 1982; Society and Government in Colonial Brazil, 1500-1822, 1992; A World on the Move: The Portuguese in Africa, Asia and America 1415-1808, 1992; co-author: From Colony to Nation: Essays on the Independence of Brazil, 1975; general editor: An Expanding World: The European Impact on World History, 1450-1800, 1995—; mem. editorial com. L.Am. Studies, Tsukuba, Japan, 1989—. Chmn. CLAH Columbus Quincentennial Com., 1987-90, Md. State Humanities Coun., 1980-82; mem. Md. Heritage Com., 1982-85, Balt. County Commn. Arts and Scis., 1982-84. Recipient Bolton Meml. prize Conf. Latin Am. Hist., 1969, Whitaker prize Middle-Atlantic Coun. Latin Am. Studies, 1983, Dom João de Castro prize Portuguese Nat. Commn. for Commemoration of Discoveries, 1993; decorated comendador Order of Prince Henry (Portugal), 1996. Fellow Royal Geog. Soc. (life), Instituto Historico e Geografica da Bahia (corr.); mem. Brazilian Studies Assn., Forum on European Expansion and Global Interaction, Latin Am.

Studies Assn., Conf. on Latin Am. History, European Acad. Scis. and Arts (Vienna, elected mem.). Avocations: squash, hiking, cycling. Home: 113 Belmore Rd Lutherville Timonium MD 21093-6111 Office: Johns Hopkins Univ Dept Of History Baltimore MD 21218

RUSSERT, TIMOTHY JOHN, broadcast journalist, executive; b. Buffalo, N.Y., May 7, 1950; m. Maureen Orth; 1 child, Luke. BA, John Carroll U., 1972; JD, Cleve. State U., 1976; LHD (hon.), Canisius Coll., Marist Coll., D'Youville Coll.; LLD (hon.), Albany Law Sch. Bar: N.Y., D.C. Spl. counsel, then chief of staff U.S. Senator Daniel Patrick Moynihan, 1977-82; counselor N.Y. Gov. Mario M. Cuomo, 1983-84; with NBC News, 1984—; moderator Meet the Press, 1991—; anchor The Tim Russert Show CNBC, 1994—; sr. v.p., Washington bureau chief NBC News; nat. polit. analyst Today program and NBC Nightly News with Tom Brokaw; supr. NBC News Today program live broadcasts from Rome, 1985; overseer prodn. prime time spl. A Day in the Life of President Bush, 1990, A Day in the Life of President Clinton, 1993; has covered 8 U.S./Russian Summits, Geneva, Malta, Washington, Moscow, Vancouver; lectr. at more than 30 univs. Recipient Alumni Spl. Achievement award Cleve.-Marshall Coll. Law, Pres.'s medal Trocaire Coll., Dean's award Cleve.-Marshall Coll. Law, John Peter Zenger award N.Y. State Bar Assn., 1992, Disting. Grad. award Nat. Cath. Educator's Assn., 1995, Spl. Achievement Alumni medal John Carroll U. Fellow Commn. European Communities. Office: NBC News Meet the Press 4001 Nebraska Ave NW Washington DC 20016-2733

RUSSETT, BRUCE MARTIN, political science educator; b. North Adams, Mass., Jan. 26, 1935; s. Raymond Edgar and Ruth Marian (Martin) R.; m. Cynthia Margaret Eagle, June 18, 1960; children: Margaret Ellen, Mark David, Lucia Elizabeth, Daniel Alden. BA magna cum laude, Williams Coll., 1956; diploma in econs., Cambridge (Eng.) U., 1957; MA, Yale U., 1958, PhD, 1961. Instr. MIT, Cambridge, 1961-62; asst. prof., then assoc. prof. Yale U., New Haven, 1961-68, prof., 1968—, Dean Acheson prof. internat. rels. and polit. sci., 1985—, chair dept. polit. sci., 1990-96, dir. UN studies, 1993—; vis. prof. Columbia U., 1965, U. Mich., 1965-66, U. Libre Brussels, 1969-70, U. N.C., 1979-80, Richardson Inst., London, 1973-74, Netherlands Inst. Advanced Study, 1984, Tel Aviv U., 1989, U. Tokyo, 1996; prin. cons. pastoral letter on peace Nat. Conf. Cath. Bishops, Washington, 1981-83; co-dir., secretariat ind. working group Future of the UN, 1993—. Author: World Handbook of Political and Social Indicators, 1964, What Price Vigilance?, 1970 (Kammerer award Am. Polit. Sci. Assn. 1971), Interest and Ideology (with E. Hanson), 1975, Controlling the Sword, 1990, Grasping the Democratic Peace, 1993, The Once and Future Security Council, 1997, others; editor: Jour. Conflict Resolution, 1972—; contbr. articles to profl. jours. Grantee NSF, 1964, 65, 69, 77, 79, 85, 88, 89, 90, 95, Ford Found., 1993, 94, John and Catherine MacArthur Found., 1988; Fulbright-Hayes fellow, Belgium and Israel, 1969, 89; John Simon Guggenheim Found. fellow, 1969, 77; German Marshall Fund fellow, 1977. Fellow Am. Acad. Arts and Scis.; mem. AAUP, Am. Polit. Sci. Assn. (coun. 1984-86), Internat. Studies Assn. (pres. 1983-84), Peace Sci. Soc. Internat. (pres. 1977-79), Internat. Polit. Sci. Assn. (chair N.Am. adv. coun. 1977-80), Fedn. Am. Scientists. Avocations: tennis, classical music, hiking. Home: 70 Martin Ter Hamden CT 06517-2333 Office: Yale U Dept Polit Sci PO Box 208301 New Haven CT 06520-8301

RUSSI, JOHN JOSEPH, priest, educational administrator; b. San Francisco, Oct. 27, 1939; s. Frank John and Catherine Mary (Carroll) R. BA, Chaminade U., 1962; STL, U. Fribourg, Switzerland, 1967; MA, U. San Francisco, 1978; PhD, Kennedy We. U., 1993. Cert. secondary tchr., jr. coll. tchr., marriage, family, child counselor, Calif. Tchr. St. Louis Sch., Honolulu, 1961-62, pres., 1988—; tchr. Riordan High Sch., San Francisco, 1962-63; tchr., counselor, prin., pres. Archbishop Mitty High Sch., San Jose, Calif., 1967-88; pres. St. Louis Sch., 1988—; regent Archbishop Mitty High Sch., 1990—, Chaminade U., Honolulu, 1988—; bd. dirs. St. Anthony Sch., Wailuku, Hawaii, 1989—. Bd. dirs. Kukui Gardens, Honolulu, 1988. Mem. Waialae Country Club, Elks Club. Democrat. Roman Catholic. Home: 3140 Waialae Ave Honolulu HI 96816-1510 Office: St Louis Sch 3142 Waialae Ave Honolulu HI 96816-1510

RUSSIANO, JOHN See MILES, JACK

RUSSIN, JONATHAN, lawyer, consultant; b. Wilkes-Barre, Pa., Oct. 30, 1937; s. Jacob S. and Anne (Wartella) R.; m. Antoinette Stackpole, Oct. 6, 1962; children: Alexander, Andrew, Benjamin, Jacob. BA, Yale U., 1959, LLB., 1963. Bar: D.C. 1963. Guide interpreter Am. Nat. Exhibit, Moscow, 1959; rsch. asst. Law Faculty, U. East Africa, Dar es Salaam, Tanganyika, 1961-62; regional legal adviser for Caribbean, AID, 1967-69; ptnr. Kirkwood, Kaplan, Russin & Vecchi, Santo Domingo, Dominican Republic, 1969-74, Washington, 1974-78; ptnr. Kaplan Russin & Vecchi, Madrid, 1978-81, Washington, 1981-92; ptnr. Russin & Vecchi, 1992—; cons. on financing worker's housing in less developed countries of Latin Am., 1991; Washington rep. for Moscow Patriarchate of Russian Orthodox Ch.; convener adv. coun. Inst. for European, Russian and Eurasian Studies, George Washington U.; mem. adv. bd. Caribbean Am. Directory; trustee St. Nicholas Cathedral, Washington, St. Vladimir's Orthodox Theol. Sem., Crestwood, N.Y., 1985-93; legal adviser Orthodox Ch. in Am.; bd. dirs. Delphi Rsch. Assocs., Washington; Dominican Am. Cultural Inst., Santo Domingo, Dominican Republic, 1988-92, Nat. Coun. Internat. Visitors, Washington, 1987-93, Fund for Democracy and Devel., Washington, 1993—, MUCIA Global Edn. Group, Inc. Recipient Order of St. Vladimir, Moscow Patriarchate, Russian Orthodox Ch., 1991. Mem. ABA, L.Am. Studies Assn., Caribbean Studies Assn., Inter-Am. Bar Assn., Yale Club N.Y., Yale Club Washington. Republican. Contbr. articles to profl. jours. Office: 815 Connecticut Ave NW Ste 650 Washington DC 20006-4004

RUSSIN, ROBERT ISAIAH, sculptor, educator; b. N.Y.C., Aug. 26, 1914; s. Uriel and Olga (Winnett) R.; m. Adele Mutchnick, May 21, 1937; children: Joseph Mark, Lincoln David, Uriel Robin. BA, CCNY, 1933, MS, 1935; postgrad. (Inst. fellow), Beaux Arts Inst. Design, 1935-36. Tchr. sculpture Copper Union Art Inst., N.Y.C., 1944-47; prof. art U. Wyo., Laramie, 1947-86; prof., artist-in-residence U. Wyo., 1976-85, Disting. prof. emeritus, 1985—. One-man shows Tucson Fine Arts Ctr., 1966, Colorado Springs (Colo.) Fine Arts Ctr., 1967, Palm Springs (Calif.) Desert Mus., Chas. G. Bowers Meml. Mus., Judah L. Magnes Meml. Mus., Berkeley, Calif.; retrospective one-man exhbn. Nat. Gallery Modern Art, Santo Domingo, Dominican Republic, 1976, Tubac Ctr. of the Arts, Ariz., 1987, Old Town Gallery-Park City, Ut., Riggins Gallery, Scottsdale, Ariz., 1989, Fine Arts Mus., U. Wyo., 1991; sculpture commns. include 2 8-foot metal figures, Evanston (Ill.) Post Office, 1939, three life-size carved figures, Conshohocken (Pa.) Post Office, 1940, Benjamin Franklin Monument, U. Wyo., 1957, Bust of Lincoln, Lincoln Mus., Washington, (now in Gettysburg Mus.), 1959, Lincoln Monument atop summit Lincoln Hwy., (now U.S. Interstate 80), Wyo, 1959, monumental bas-relief bronze Cheyenne (Wyo.) Fed. Bldg, 1966, two carved wood walls, Denver Fed. Bldg., 1966, monumental fountain, City of Hope Med. Ctr., Los Angeles, 1966-67, statue, Brookhaven (N.Y.) Nat. Lab., 1968, life-size bronze sculpture fountain, Pomona Coll., 1969, monumental bronze sculpture Prometheus Natrona County (Wyo.) Pub. Library, 1974, Man and Energy, Casper (Wyo.) C. of C., 1974, 12-foot marble carving Menorah Med. Ctr., Kansas City, Mo., 1975, Einstein and Gershwin medals Magnes Meml. Mus, Berkeley, Nat. Mus. Art, Santo Domingo, Dominican Republic, 1975, monumental fountain, Galleria d'Arte Moderna, Santo Domingo, 1977, Duarte Monument, Santo Domingo, 1977, 30 foot steel and water fountain monument City Hall, Casper, 1980, marble and bronze monument, Lincoln Centre, Dallas, 1982, acrylic steel and bronze monument, Herschler State Office Bldg., Cheyenne, 1984, marble monument, U. Wyo., Laramie, 1985, portrait head Charles Bluhdorn, chmn. Gulf & Western, 1975, portrait bust Pres. J. Balaguer of Dominican Republic, 1975, portrait head G. Wilson Knight, Shakespearean actor and scholar, 1975, 2 12-foot bronze figures The Greeting and the Gift for Bicentennial Commn., Cheyenne, 1976, monumental marble head of Juan Pablo Duarte liberator Dominican Republic, Santo Domingo, 1976, marble sculpture Trio, U. Wyo., 1985, Isaac B. Singer medal for Magnes Mus., 1983, monumental Holocaust figure Tucson Jewish Community Ctr., 1989, granite monument Chthodynamis, Dept. Energy Bldg., Washington, 1992, bust Hon. Milward Simpson, 1993, bust James Forest U. Wyo., 1993, bronze statue Univ. Med. Ctr., Tuscon, Head, Gov. Stanley Hathway, Cheyenne, Wy, 1995; contbr. articles to profl. jours.Head, Pres. Franklin D. Roosevelt, Rotunda (pres.hosp. Bethsda, Md.). Recipient awards sec. fine arts U.S. Treasury, 1939, 40, Lincoln medal U.S. Congress, 1959, Alfred G.B. Steel award Pa. Acad. Fine Arts, 1961, medal of Order of Duarte Sanchez y Mella, Dominican Republic, 1977; Ford Found. fellow, 1953. Mem. Nat. Sculpture Conf. (exec. bd.), Sculptors Guild, Nat. Sculpture Soc., AIA, AAUP, Coll. Art Internat. Inst. Arts and Letters, Phi Beta Kappa (hon.). Home: 61 N Fork Rd Centennial WY 82055 also: 1160 Placita Salubre Green Valley AZ 85614

RUSSMAN, THOMAS ANTHONY, philosophy educator; b. Pitts., June 20, 1944; s. Joseph Anthony and Mary Virginia (LaGuardia) R. BA, St. Fidelis Coll., 1967; MA in Philosophy, Cath. U. of Am., 1971; M of Theology, Capuchin Coll., 1971; PhD, Princeton U., 1976. Asst. prof. Cath. U. Am., Washington, 1976-83; assoc. prof. U. St. Thomas, Houston, 1983-90, dept. chmn., dir. PhD and MA programs, 1987—, dir. Ctr. for Thomistic Studies, 1987—, prof., 1990—; fin. cons., portfolio mgr. St. Augustine Province of Capuchin Order, Pitts., 1986—; bd. dirs. San Antonio Law Ctr., 1995—. Author: Prospectus for Triumph of Realism, 1987; editor: Thomistic Papers V, 1990, Thomistic Papers VI, 1994, Studies in Thomistic Theology, 1996; contbr. articles to profl. jours. Mem. Am. Philos. Assn., Am. Cath. Philos. Assn. (treas. 1977-83, v.p. 1997—), Metaphys. Soc. Avocations: performing arts, hiking, canoeing, Bridge, trail riding. Office: U St Thomas 3800 Montrose Blvd Houston TX 77006-4626

RUSSO, ALEXANDER PETER, artist, educator; b. Atlantic City, June 11, 1922; s. Peter Joseph and Lillian Mary (Soma) R.; 1 child, Eugenie. Student, Pratt Inst., 1940-42, Swarthmore Coll., 1946-47; S.S., Bard Coll., 1947; B.F.A. (Breevort-Eickenmeyer fellow), Columbia U., 1952; postgrad., Acad. Fine Arts, Rome, 1952-54, Inst. Advanced Fine Arts, 1977-79. Instr. New Orleans Acad. Art, 1948-49; asst. prof. art U. Buffalo, 1955-58; instr. in graphic design Parsons Sch. Design, 1958-60; chmn. dept. drawing and painting Corcoran Sch. Art, 1961-70, chmn. faculty, acting dean, 1967-70; lectr., thesis adv. George Washington U., 1961-70; prof. Hood Coll., Frederick, Md., 1970-90, prof. emeritus, 1990—, chmn. dept. art, 1970-87; vis. guest prof. art Instituto Allende, San Miguel de Allende, Mexico, 1993-94; panelist Md. State Coun. Arts, Balt., 1981-82; reviewer art programs Md. State Bd. Edn., 1981—; guest art critic Southampton Press, N.Y., 1989, 91; cons. in field. One-man shows include Corcoran Gallery Art, Washington, 1946, 64, Chiurazzi Gallery, Rome, 1953, Cavallino Gallery, Venice, Italy, 1954, U. So. Ill., 1955, Frank Rehn Gallery, N.Y.C., periodic exhbns., 1954-74, Phoenix II Gallery, Washington, 1983, Ingber Gallery, N.Y.C., 1983, Washington Gallery Art, 1963, Franz Bader Gallery, Washington, 1967, Internat. Monetary Fund, Washington, 1968, 79, Agra Gallery, Washington, 1971, Benson Gallery, Bridgehampton, L.I., 1976, Phoenix Fine Arts, Frederick, 1981, Benton Gallery, Southampton, N.Y., 1985, 86, 88, 90, 91, Arlene Bujese Gallery, East Hampton, N.Y., 1994, 95, 97, Hood Coll., Frederick, Md., 1991, Western Md. Coll., Westminster, 1991, Bell Gallery, Seattle, 1991, 92, Gettysburg (Pa.) Coll., 1989; group exhbns. include Salon de la Marne, Paris, 1945, Met. Mus. Art, N.Y.C., 1948, Bordighera Internat., Italy, 1953-54 (hon. mention), Mus. Modern Art, Madrid, 1953, Sala di Esposizione delle Biblioteca Americano, Rome, 1953, Whitney Mus. Am. Art, N.Y.C., 1960, Mus. Modern Art, N.Y.C., 1969, Guild Hall, East Hampton, N.Y., 1976, East Hampton Avant-Garde, A Salute to the Signa Gallery, 1990, NAS, Washington, 1984, Bell Gallery, Seattle, 1990, Illustrator's Club, N.Y.C., 1991, Armory Exhbn., N.Y.C., 1991, Instituto Alleude, San Niguel de Allende, Mex., 1994, Josh Kligerman Gallery, San Miguel de Allende, Mex., 1994; represented in permanent collections Albright-Know Gallery, Buffalo, Columbia U., N.Y.C., Delgado Mus. Art, New Orleans, Corcoran Gallery Art, Fiat Automobile Co., Rome, Nat. Collection Smithsonian Inst., Washington, Fed. Ins. Deposit Corp., Washington, Gettysburg Coll. of Pa.; author: Profiles on Women Artists, 1985, The Challenge of Drawing, 1986, (poetry) Vignettes, 1996. Served with USNR, 1942-46. Fellow Guggenheim Found., 1947-48, 49-50,Edward McDowell Found., 1956, Hood Coll. Hodson teaching fellow, 1983; Fulbright grantee for painting and research, Rome, 1952-54, U.S.-Indo Subcommn. on Edn. and Culture grantee, India, 1984. Office: PO Box 1377 Wainscott NY 11975-1377 also: Arlene Bujese Gallery 66 Newtown Ln East Hampton NY 11937 *Success is an equivocal matter. "Outward success", no doubt, is meaningful and necessary to most people in terms of fulfilling goals or for some similar reason. "Interior success" is more difficult to achieve, for it means the labor of a developing soul, and, more often than not, the relinquishing of what most would consider to be "material success." Whatever I have achieved in the way of outward or material success, therefore, is but a minute reflection of that which I would wish to achieve on the spiritual level. There is a long way to go.*

RUSSO, ANTHONY JOSEPH, public relations professional; b. N.Y.C., Oct. 23, 1953; s. Lucio and Tina (Iarossi) R. BA cum laude, Alfred U., 1974; MA, Columbia U., 1975; PhD, Claremont Grad. Sch., 1982. Asst. to chmn. Mocatta Metals, N.Y.C., 1982-83; account exec. Gavin Anderson and Co., N.Y.C., 1983-85; sr. account exec. Adams and Reinhart, N.Y.C., 1985; dir. corp. rels. Geto and DeMilly, N.Y.C., 1985-86; v.p. Cameron Assocs., N.Y.C., 1986-88; CEO Noonan/Russo Communications, N.Y.C., 1988—; chmn. Noonan/Russo Ltd., London, 1995—. Mem. Am. Psychol. Assn., Pub. Rels. Soc. Am., Psi Chi. Democrat. Office: Noonan/Russo Comm 220 5th Ave New York NY 10001-7708 also: Noonan/Russo Ltd, 3 Olaf St, London W11 4BE, England

RUSSO, ANTHONY SEBASTIAN, telecommunications executive; b. Woodbury, N.J., Sept. 9, 1947; s. Anthony Joseph and Rose (Leonardi) R.; m. Carmen Sanchez, July 1970; children: A. Scott, Thomas Allen, Darryl Alexander. BS, Belknap Coll., 1969. Sales and system engr. IBM, Balt., Washington, 1969-78; regional staff IBM, Washington, 1978-80; mgr. data and teleconferencing svc. SBS, McLean, Va., 1980-82; mktg. mgr. Va., 1982-83, dir. shared network products, 1983-86; v.p. mktg. and sales Lightnet, Rockville, Md., 1986-87; pres. CEI, Rockville, 1987-88; v.p. mktg. and sales TCom Systems, Washington, 1988-89; dir. data mktg. MCI, Washington, 1990-95, v.p. global mktg., 1995—. Sgt. U.S. Army, 1969-71. Mem. IEEE, KC, Train Collectors Assn. Roman Catholic. Avocation: model trains. Home: 16200 Whitehaven Rd Silver Spring MD 20906-1128 Office: MCI 1650 Tysons Blvd Mc Lean VA 22102-3915

RUSSO, GILBERTO, engineering educator; b. Rome, Aug. 23, 1954; s. Guido and Maria (Mazzoni) R. Laurea, Poly. Inst. Turin, Italy, 1975; ScD, MIT, 1980; MD, U. Chgo. Pritaker Sch. of Medicine. Pres. Studio Russo, Inc. Engring. Cons., Turin, 1970; asst. prof. Poly. Inst. Turin, 1975-80; lectr. MIT, Cambridge, Mass., 1985-91; dr. dept. plastic and reconstructive surgery U. Chgo., 1992-95; mem. dept. surgery U. Calif., San Francisco, 1995—; mem. designer selection bd. State of Mass., Boston, 1989. Contbr. articles to profl. pubs., chpts. to books. Pres. Dante Alisheri Soc., Cambridge, 1986-88; treas. MIT/Poly. Alumni Assn., Turin, 1970. Fulbright fellow, 1978. Fellow Nat. Coun. Engring. Examiners; mem. Mass. Soc. Profl. Engrs. (v.p. 1991—), Tau Beta Pi (chpt. advisor 1985, Eminent Engr. 1985). Achievements include patents in solar energy collectors, development of computer aided therodynamics, computer methods for engineering, optimization of non-steady-state systems, compressible fluid flow with heat transfer, thermal dynamics models, diagnostics and surgical repair of electric/burn injuries. Office: U Chgo Dept Plastic-Reconstrv Surg Chicago IL 60637 also: U Calif Dept Surgery Rm S-343 Box 0470 513 Parnassus Ave San Francisco CA 94143

RUSSO, GREGORY THOMAS, lawyer; b. Bellerose, N.Y., Dec. 19, 1949; s. Albert Thomas and Geraldine Ann (Norton) R.; m. Helen Mary Shannon, Dec. 29, 1973; children: Deirdre Leslie, Nicholas Shannon, Barbara Celeste. AB, Georgetown U., 1971; JD, Cath. U. Am., 1974. Bar: N.Y. 1975, D.C. 1978, U.S. Supreme Ct. 1979. Sr. counsel, v.p. corp. staff, corp. sec. Merrill Lynch & Co., Inc., N.Y.C., 1974—. Capt. USAR, 1975. Mem. ABA. Republican. Roman Catholic. Avocation: golf. Office: Merrill Lynch & Co Inc 100 Church St New York NY 10007-2601

RUSSO, IRMA HAYDEE ALVAREZ DE, pathologist; b. San Rafael, Mendoza, Argentina, Feb. 28, 1942; came to U. S., 1972; d. Jose Maria and Maria Carmen (Martinez) de Alvarez; m. Jose Russo, Feb. 8, 1969; 1 child, Patricia Alexandra. BA, Escuela Normal MTSM de Balcarce, 1959; MD, U. Nat. of Cuyo, Mendoza, 1970. Diplomate Am. Bd. Pathology. Intern Sch. of Medicine Hosps., Argentina, 1969-70; resident in pathology Wayne State U. Sch. Medicine, Detroit, 1976-80; rsch. asst. and instr. Inst. of Histology and Embryology Sch. Medicine U. Nat. of Cuyo, 1963-71, assoc. prof. histology Faculty of Phys., Chem. and Math. Scis., 1970-72; rsch. assoc. Inst. for Molecular and Cellular Evolution, U. Miami, Fla., 1972-73; rsch. assoc. exptl. pathology lab. div. biol. scis., Mich. Cancer Found., Detroit, 1973-75, rsch. scientist, 1975-76, vis. rsch. scientist, 1976-82, asst. mem., pathologist, 1982-89, assoc. rsch. mem., 1989-91, co-dir. pathology reference lab., 1982-86, chief exptl. pathology lab., 1989-91; co-dir. Mich. Cancer Found. Lab. Svcs., 1986-91; mem. Fox Chase Cancer Ctr., 1991—, dir. anatomic pathology Am. Oncologic Hosp. Dept. Pathology, 1991-92; dir. Lab. Svcs., 1992-94; chief molecular endocrinology sect. Breast Cancer Rsch. Lab. Fox Chase Cancer Ctr., 1994—; chief resident physician dept. pathology Wayne State U. Sch. Medicine, 1978-80, asst. prof., 1980-82; mem. staff Harper-Grace Hosps., Detroit, 1980-82; adj. prof. Pathology and Cell Biology Jefferson Sch. of Medicine/Thomas Jefferson Univ., 1992—; mem. endocrinology panel peer rev. com. breast cancer rsch. program U.S. Army R&D Command, 1994, 95, 96; ad-hoc mem. biochem. endocrinology study sect. NIH, DHHS, 1994, metabolic pathology study sect., 1996—; mem. European Commn. on Cancer Prevention, 1994—; mem. bd. scientific counselor, sec. of health & human svcs. Nat. Toxicology Program Bd., 1994—; mem. Internat. Life Scis. Inst.-Risk Sc. Inst. Mammary Working Group, 1992—; pres., founder League of Women Against Cancer, Rydal, Pa., 1994—. Rockefeller grantee, 1972-73; Nat. Cancer Inst. grantee, 1978-81, 84-87, 1994—; Am. Cancer Soc. grantee 1988-89, 91-94, U.S. Army Med. R&D Command grant, 1994—; Recipient Shannon award Nat. Cancer Inst./NHHSS, 1992-94. guest lectr. dept. obstetrics Sch. Medicine U. Nat. of Cuyo, 1965-71. Mem. AAAS, Nat. Cancer Inst. (breast cancer working group, breast cancer program 1984-88), Nat. Alliance Breast Cancer Orgns. (med. adv. bd. N.Y.C. chpt. 1986—), Eastern Coop. Oncology Group, 1992—, Coll. Am. Pathologists, Am. Soc. Clin. Pathologists, Am. Assn. for Cancer Research, Mich. Soc. Pathologists, Am. Assn. Clin. Chemistry, Electron Microscopy Soc. Am., Internat. Coll. Physicians and Surgeons, Women in Cancer Rsch., The Endocrine Soc, Internat. Assn. Against Cancer, Mich. Electron Microscopy Forum, Sigma Xi. Roman Catholic. Contbr. numerous articles on pathology to profl. jours. Office: Fox Chase Cancer Ctr 7701 Burholme Ave Philadelphia PA 19111-2412

RUSSO, JOSE, pathologist; b. Mendoza, Argentina, Mar. 24, 1942; came to U.S., 1971; s. Felipe and Teresa (Pagano) R.; m. Irma Haydee, Feb. 8, 1969; 1 child, Patricia Alexandra. BS, Agustin Alvarez Nat. Coll., 1959; MD, U. Nat. Cuyo, 1967. Instr. Inst. Gen. and Exptl. Pathology Med. Sch., Mendoza, 1961-66; asst. prof. Inst. Histology and Embryology, 1967-71; Rockefeller Found. postdoctoral fellow Inst. Molecular and Cellular Evolution U. Miami, 1971-73; chief exptl. pathology lab. Mich. Cancer Found., Detroit, 1973-81; assoc. clin. prof. pathology Wayne State U., Detroit, 1979-91, chmn. dept. pathology, 1981-91; chmn. dept. pathology, sr. mem. Fox Chase Cancer Ctr., Phila., 1991-94, sr. mem., dir. Breast Cancer Rsch. Lab., 1994—; mem. Mich. Cancer Found., 1982-91; adj. prof. pathology Jefferson Sch. Medicine, Univ. Penn. Sch. Medicine, Phila. Author: Tumor Diagnosis by Electron Microscopy, vol. 1, 1986, vol. 2, 1988, vol. 3, 1990, Immunocytochemistry in Tumor Diagnosis, 1985; contbr. over 200 articles to profl. jours. USPHS grantee, 1978, 80, 84, 88, 90, 93, 94, 95, grantee Am. Cancer Soc., 1982; NRC Argentina fellow, 1967-71. Mem. Am. Assn. Cancer Rsch., Am. Soc. Cell Biology, Soc. Exptl. Biology and Medicine, Tissue Culture Assn., Am. Soc. Clin. Pathology, Internat. Acad. Pathology, Am. Coll. Pathology, Sigma Xi. Roman Catholic.

RUSSO, KATHLEEN MARIE, art educator; b. Worcester, Mass., Jan. 14, 1947; d. Cornelius Joseph and Miriam Nancy (Bradford) Lucey; m. Don Albert Russo, Apr. 12, 1969 (div. Apr. 1988). BA, U. Miami, Coral Gables, Fla., 1968, MA, 1971; PhD, Fla. State U., 1976. Prof. art history Fla. Atlantic U., Boca Raton, 1976—, chair art dept., 1988—. Co-author: Encyclopedia of Architects, 1982, Eros in the Mind's Eye, 1985, International Dictionary of Art and Artists, 1990, The Symbolism of Vanitas in the Arts, Literature and Music, 1992, Dictionary of Art, 1996. Summer fellow Nat. Endowment for the Humanities, 1979, 83. Mem. Am. Soc. Archtl. Historians, S.E. Soc. Archtl. Historians (Fla. rep. 1985-92), Coll. Art Assn., Am. Soc. 18th Century Studies, Am. Assn. Italian Studies, Phi Kappa Phi. Home: 925 Iris Dr Delray Beach FL 33483-4810 Office: Fla Atlantic U Art Dept Boca Raton FL 33431

RUSSO, MICHAEL ARNOLD, sales manager; b. Bklyn., Feb. 15, 1959; s. Bernard Russo and Eve (Sutkin) Miller; m. Meryl Lisa Kasner, Aug. 27, 1989. BBA, Emory U., 1980. CPA. Acct. Habif, Arogeti & Wynne, Atlanta, 1980-81, Georgia Power Co., Atlanta, 1981-82; sales Northwestern Mutual Life, Atlanta, 1982-84; cons. Adizes Inst., Los Angeles, 1984-85; sales mgr. Qintex Entertainment, Los Angeles, N.Y.C., 1985-87; v.p. Northeast sales ITC Distribution, N.Y.C., 1989—. Mem. Nat. Assn. TV Programming Execs., Ind. TV Assn., Internat. Radio & TV Soc. Jewish. Home: 1 Astor Pl # 44 New York NY 10003-6930

RUSSO, PEGGY ANNE, English language educator; b. Sturgis, Mich., Sept. 7, 1940; d. Dale Miller and Virginia (Rifenburg) B.; m. Jerry Russo (dec.); children: Daniel Carleton, Christopher Sanford. AA with honors, Jackson C.C., 1967; BA in English Lang. and Lit., U. Mich., 1972, MA in English Lang. and Lit., 1979, PhD in English Lang. and Lit., 1988. Teaching asst. English dept. U. Mich., Ann Arbor, 1979-83; lectr. Pa. State U., University Park, 1985-88; asst. prof. English Pa. State U., Mont Alto, 1988—; part-time instr. Jackson (Mich.) C.C., 1979; adj. instr. Wayne C.C., Detroit, 1979-83; adj. lectr. U. Mich., 1984-85; participant workshops in field; presenter in field. Sr. editor: The Adelphi Theater Calendar, Part II, 1993; asst. editor RaJah, 1981-83; contbr. articles to profl. jours. Recipient Avery Hopwood award in drama U. Mich., 1979; Roy W. Cowden Meml. fellow U. Mich., 1983, Rackham Thesis grantee, 1982, Dorothy Guies McGuigan scholar, 1983; Cranbrook Writers Conf. scholar Cranbrook Acad., 1979, 80. Mem. MLA, Am. Soc. Theatre Rsch., Internat. Fedn. Theatre Rsch., Pa. Coll. English Assn., Shakespeare Assn. Am. Office: Pa State U Dept English Mont Alto PA 17237

RUSSO, ROY LAWRENCE, electronic design automation engineer, retired; b. Kelayres, Pa., Nov. 6, 1935; s. Peter John and Mary (Fudge) R.; m. Elizabeth Jean Tautkus, Dec. 26, 1959; children: Mark, Keith, Aileen, Linda. B.S.E.E., Pa. State U., 1957, M.S.E.E., 1959, Ph.D.E.E., 1964. Asst. prof. elec. engring. Pa. State U., University Park, 1964-65; mgr., staff mem. IBM Research, Yorktown Heights, N.Y., 1965-77, mem. research staff, 1983-85; mgr. design automation lab. IBM Research, 1985-94; sr. engr. Gen. Tech. div. IBM, Hopewell Junction, 1977-81; mgr. strategy Gen. Tech. div. IBM, 1981-82; cons. prof. elec. engring Stanford U., 1982-83; retired, 1994. Editor-in-chief IEEE Computer Soc., 1983-85; co-inventor ink jet printer correction system. Treas. St. Patrick's Ch., Yorktown Heights, 1975-77. Recipient Invention Achievement award IBM, 1978, Outstanding Contbn. award IBM, 1968, 89, Outstanding Writing award Pa. State U., 1967. Fellow IEEE (dir. computer disvn. 1989); mem. IEEE Computer Soc. (pres. 1986-87, Svc. award, Centennial medal 1984, Richard E. Merwin award 1992), Eta Kappa Nu.

RUSSO, ROY R., lawyer; b. Utica, N.Y., July 26, 1936; s. Chester F. and Helen L. (Gacek) R.; m. Ann M. Obernesser, Sept. 19, 1959; children: Andrew F., Susan Elizabeth. BA, Columbia U., 1956; LLB cum laude, Syracuse U., 1959. Bar: N.Y. 1959, D.C. 1967, U.S. Supreme Ct. 1969. Pvt. practice law, Washington, 1959—; atty. FCC, Washington, 1959-66; ptnr. Cohn and Marks, Washington, 1966—; spl. counsel Nat. Cath. Conf. for Interracial Justice, Washington, 1984—. Mem. editl. adv. com. The Communications Act: A Legislative History of the Major Amendments 1934-96; mem. adv. bd. Pike and Fischer Comms. Regulation. Founding chmn. Commn. on Social Ministry, Richmond (Va.) Diocese, 1970-74; v.p., bd. dirs. St. Mary's Housing Corp., Annandale and Manassas, Va., 1971—; pres., bd. dirs. Caths. for Housing, Inc., 1979-84, Cath. Charities, Arlington (Va.) Diocese, 1980-84. With USAF, 1960-61. Recipient Alumni medal Alumni Fedn. Columbia U., 1994. Mem. ABA, Fed. Communications Bar Assn. (co-chair mass media practice com. 1988-91, nominations com. 1991-92), Computer Law Assn., Internat. Inst. Communications, John Jay Assocs., Soc. Columbia Grads., Columbia U. Club of Washington (sr. v.p. 1989-91, pres. 1991-95), Order of Coif, Phi Alpha Delta. Democrat. Club: Columbia Coll. (Washington) (mem. steering com. 1985—, chmn. Deans' Day program 1988—). Home: 6528 Bowie Dr Springfield VA 22150-1309 Office: Cohn & Marks 1333 New Hampshire Ave NW Washington DC 20036-1511

RUSSO, THOMAS ANTHONY, lawyer; b. N.Y.C., Nov. 6, 1943; s. Lucio F. and Tina (Iarossi) R.; m. Nancy Felipe, June 18, 1966 (div. 1974); m. Janice Davis, June 10, 1977 (div. 1979); m. Marcy C. Applebaum, June 16, 1985; children: Morgan Danielle and Alexa Anne (twins), Tyler James. BA, Fordham U., 1965; MBA, Cornell U., 1969, JD, 1969. Bar: N.Y., 1970, U.S. Ct. Appeals (2d cir.) 1970, U.S. Dist. Ct. (so. and ea. dists.) N.Y. 1971, U.S. Ct. Appeals (7th cir.) 1982. Staff atty. SEC, Washington, 1969-71; assoc. Cadwalader, Wickersham & Taft, N.Y.C., 1971-75; dir. div. trading and markets Commodity Futures Trading Commn., Washington, 1975-77; ptnr. Cadwalader, Wickersham & Taft, N.Y.C., 1977-92; mgmt. com., 1984-92; mng. dir., mem. op. com. Lehman Bros., N.Y.C., 1993—; bd. dirs. Futures Industry Inst., Rev. Securities and Commodities Regulation, N.Y.C. Author: Regulation of the Commodities Futures and Options Markets; co-author: Regulation of Brokers, Dealers and Securities Markets, Supplement Markets; editorial bd. mem. Internat. Jour. Regulatory Law and Practice; practitioner bd. advisors Stanford Jour. of Law.; mem. editl. bd. Futures and Derivatives Law Report. Mem. ABA (mem. futures regulations, exec. coun., adv. com. on fed. regulation of securities, past co-chmn. derivative instruments subcom. of com. on fed. regulation), Assn. of Bar of City of N.Y. (chmn. internat. law sub com. of the com. on commodities regulation 1984-85, chmn. com. commodities regulations 1981-82), D.C. Bar Assn. Office: Lehman Bros Inc 10th Fl 200 Vesey St Fl 10 New York NY 10281-1009

RUSSO, THOMAS JOSEPH, hospitality and consumer durables industry executive; b. Stamford, Conn., Sept. 15, 1941; s. Thomas and Ann (Petrozzi) R.; m. Wendy Fenwick, May 2, 1964; children: Michelle, Matthew. BS, Fordham U., 1963; postgrad., Chewton Pl., Bristol, Eng., 1980; D of Bus. Adminstrn. in Hospitality Mgmt. honoris causa, Johnson and Wales U., 1990. Div. gen. mgr. Howard Johnson Co., Wilmington, Del., 1974-76; v.p. Howard Johnson Co., Braintree, Mass., 1976-78, group v.p., 1978-80, sr. v.p., 1980-82, exec. v.p., 1982-83, pres., 1983-85; pres., chief exec. officer Ponderosa Steakhouse div., 1984-87; group chmn., CEO Hanson Industries Housewares Group, Framingham, Mass., 1987-94; chmn., CEO, pres. Miami Subs Corp., Ft. Lauderdale, Fla., 1994—; bd. dirs. Summit Family Restaunts, Inc., The Ground Round Inc., Legal Sea Foods, Inc. Trustee Framingham Union Hosp., 1981—. Mem. Nat. Restaurant Assn. (bd. dirs. 1982-83), Mass. Restaurant Assn., Del. Restaurant Assn. (bd. dirs. 1974-76), Rotary. Roman Catholic. Home: 2650 Edgewater Dr Fort Lauderdale FL 33332 Office: Miami Subs Corp 6300 NW 31st Ave Fort Lauderdale FL 33309-1633

RUSSONIELLO, JOSEPH PASCAL, lawyer; b. Jersey City, Oct. 12, 1941; s. Sabin G. and Justine B. (Terraciano) R.; m. Moira F. Ward, Aug. 29, 1969. B in Social Sci., Fairfield U., 1963; JD, NYU, 1966. Bar: N.J. 1967, Calif. 1969. Spl. agt. FBI, Washington, 1966-67; dep. dist. atty. City and County San Francisco (Calif.) Dist. Atty. Offices, 1969-75; assoc. Cooley Godward Castro Huddleson & Tatum, San Francisco, 1975-78; U.S. atty. U.S. Dept. Justice (no. dist.) Calif., San Francisco, 1982-90; ptnr. Cooley Godward L.L.P., San Francisco, 1978-82, 90—; pres., bd. dirs. San Francisco (Calif.) Law Sch., 1984—; analyst KTVU-Ch. 2, Oakland, Calif., 1994—. Pres. Northgate Cottages, Napa, Calif., 1988—; chmn. Catholics for Truth and Justice, San Francisco, 1991—; v.p. Mid-Pacific region Nat. Italian Am. Fedn. Recipient Man of Yr. award NIAF, 1986; named Alumni of Yr.-Pub. Sector, NYU Law Sch., 1991. Fellow Am. Coll. Trial Lawyers; mem. Am. bd. Trial Lawyers (adv.), McFetridge Inn of Ct. (barrister). Republican. Avocations: tennis, reading, playing the saxophone. Home: 2850 Jackson St San Francisco CA 94115 Office: Cooley Godward LLP 1 Maritime Plz San Francisco CA 94111-3404

RUST, EDWARD BARRY, JR., insurance company executive, lawyer; b. Chgo., Aug. 3, 1950; s. Edward Barry Sr. and Harriett B. (Fuller) R.; m. Sally Buckler, Feb. 28, 1976; 1 child, Edward Barry III. Student, Lawrence U., 1968-69; BS, Ill. Wesleyan U., 1972; JD, MBA, So. Meth. U., 1975. Bar: Tex. 1975, Ill. 1976. Mgmt. trainee State Farm Ins. Cos., Dallas, 1975-76; atty. State Farm Ins. Cos., Bloomington, 1976, sr. atty., 1976-78, asst. v.p., 1978-81, v.p., 1981-83, exec. v.p., 1983-85, chmn., 1987—; pres., CEO State Farm Life Ins. Cos., Bloomington, 1985—; now also pres., CEO, chmn. State Farm Mutual Auto Ins. Co.; pres. and bd. dirs. State Farm Investment Mgmt. Corp., State Farm Internat. Services, Inc., State Farm Cos. Found.; chmn. State Farm Mut. Automobile Ins. Co., 1987; bd. dirs. exec. and investment coms. State Farm Annuity and Life Ins. Co., State Farm Mut. Automobile Ins. Co., State Farm Life Ins. Co., State Farm Fire and Casualty, State Farm Gen. Trustee Ill. Wesleyan U., 1985—; mem. adv. coun. Grad. Sch. Bus. Stanford U., 1987-94; mem. bus. adv. coun. Coll. Commerce and Bus. Adminstrn. U. Ill. Mem. Am. Enterprise Inst., Bus. Roundtable, Tex. State Bar Assn., Ill. Bar Assn., Am. Inst. Property and Liability Underwriters (trustee 1986—), Ins. Inst. Am. (trustee 1986—). Office: State Farm Ins Cos 1 State Farm Plz Bloomington IL 61710-0001

RUST, FRANCES O'CONNELL, education educator; b. Laguna Beach, Calif., Oct. 10, 1944; d. Walter Francis and Pauline Peyton (Forney) O'Connell; m. Langbourne Williams Rust, June 4, 1966; children: Edgar Forney Rust, Susanne Lancaster Rust. BA in English Lit., Manhattanville Coll., 1966, MA in Teaching, 1970; MEd, Columbia U., 1982, EdD, 1984. Asst. tchr. Bede Sch., Englewood, N.J., 1966-67; tchr., trainer, supr. Am. Montessori Soc., Fairleigh Dickinson U., Tenafly, N.J., 1967-68; tchr. Acorn Sch., N.Y.C., 1967-68; lectr. in edn. Briarcliff Coll., Briarcliff, N.Y., 1968-70; founder, dir., head tchr. Hudson Community Sch., Briarcliff, 1970-71; dir., head tchr. Woodland Sch., Chappaqua, N.Y., 1975-81; assoc. dir., asst. prof. preservice program Tchr.'s Coll. Columbia U., N.Y.C., 1983-85; assoc. prof., dir. dept. edn. Manhattanville Coll., Purchase, N.Y., 1985-89; assoc. prof., chair dept. of curriculum and teaching Hofstra U., Hempstead, N.Y., 1989-91; assoc. prof., coord. undergraduate early childhood/elem. edn. NYU, 1991—; mem. editorial bd. Ency. of Early Childhood, 1988-92; mem. adv. bd. Great Potential Westchester, Purchase, 1989; cons. on early childhood Metro Ctr. of NYU, N.Y.C., 1986—, New Rochelle (N.Y.) Pub. Schs., 1989-90. Author: Changing Teaching; Changing Schools: Bringing Early Childhood into Public Education, 1993; editor: Care & Education of Young Children, 1989. Chair Region 2 Resource Team of Episcopal Diocese of N.Y., Westchester County, 1980-88; bd. dirs. alumni coun. Columbia U. Tchr.'s Coll., N.Y.C., 1987-97; pres., 1994-97; bd. dirs. Westchester County Jr. Achievement, 1988-89. Mem. Am. Ednl. Rsch. Assn. (pres. instrnl. supervision SIG 1995—, Nat. Soc. for Study of Edn., Assn. for Supervision and Curriculum Devel., Nat. Assn. for Edn. of Young Children, Soc. for Rsch. in Child Devel. Democrat. Episcopalian. Avocations: sailing, running. Home: 96 Round Hill Dr Briarcliff Manor NY 10510-1929 Office: NYU Dept of Teaching and Learning 239 Greene St New York NY 10003-6674

RUST, JOHN LAURENCE, heavy equipment sales/service company executive; b. Normal, Ill., June 23, 1925; married. Student, Ill. Wesleyan U., 1943; BA, U.S. Mil. Acad., West Point, N.Y., 1949. Enlisted U.S. Army, 1943, advanced through grades to capt., 1954; resigned from active duty Ill. Army N.G., 1954; owner, mgr. Chevrolet dealership, Bloomington, Ill., 1954-60; pres. Rust Tractor Co., Albuquerque, 1960—. Campaign chmn. United Cmty. Fund, Albuquerque, 1965, pres., 1967-68; bd. regents N.Mex. Mil. Inst., Roswell, 1962-74; vice chmn. Presbyn. Healthcare Svcs., Albuquerque, 1968-82, chmn., 1982-95; pres. U. N.Mex. Found., Inc., 1980-86. Col. USAR, ret. Home: 3550 Tucson Ct NW Albuquerque NM 87120-1124 Office: Rust Tractor Co 4000 Osuna Rd NE Albuquerque NM 87109-4423

RUST, ROBERT WARREN, retired lawyer; b. Jamaica, N.Y., Aug. 16, 1928; s. Adolf Harry and Helen Margaret (Dauth) R.; m. Mary Ruth Duncan, Jan. 28, 1953 (dec. Aug. 1981); children: Benjamin, Lani, Debra, Bonnie, Randall, Wendy; m. Theresa Maria Nagymihaly, Dec. 18, 1982; 1 stepchild, Brandon. Student, St. Lawrence U., 1946-48; JD, U. Miami, Coral Gables, Fla., 1954; postgrad., Naval War Coll., 1975. Bar: Fla. 1954, U.S. Supreme Ct. 1960. Police officer City of Miami (Fla.) Police Dept., 1953-54; asst. auditor First Nat. Bank, Miami, 1954-56; assoc. Smathers, Thompson & Dyer, Miami, 1956-57; asst. U.S. atty. Dept. of Justice, Miami, 1957-61; assoc. Shutts & Bowen, Miami, 1961-63; asst. county solicitor Palm Beach County, West Palm Beach, Fla., 1963-66; state rep. Fla. Legislature, Palm Beach, Fla., Martin County, Fla., 1966-68; chief counsel House Crime Com., Tallahassee, Fla., 1968-69; U.S. atty. So. Dist. Fla., Miami, 1969-77; ptnr. Rust & Rust, Miami, 1977-89; ret., 1989,, 1989. Col. USMCR, 1947-80, Ret. Recipient award of merit for assisting in preventing assassination Pres. of U.S., Sec. of Treasury and Chief U.S. Secret Svc., 1964, Outstanding Legislator award St. Petersburg Times, 1967, Fla. lodge Fraternal Order Police, 1967. Mem. NRA, Fla. Bar, Navy League, Marine Corps Res. Officers Assn. (pres. West Palm Beach chpt. 1964-65), Am. Legion, Mil. Order World Wars, Res. Officers Assn., Key Biscayne Yacht Club, Capitol Hill Club, Coconut Grove Sailing Club, Rotary. Republican. Presbyterian. Avocations: sailing, shooting, skiing, dog sledding. Office: 1700 S Bayshore Ln Apt 2A Miami FL 33133-4041 Home: PO Box 7339 0251 Gold Nugget Dr Breckenridge CO 80424

RUST, WILLIAM JAMES, retired steel company executive; b. Newark, Mar. 21, 1929; s. William G. and Anna (Glavin) R.; m. Adele M. Laubner, July 29, 1950; 1 dau., Rita Marie. B.S. in Math. magna cum laude, Boston Coll., 1953; M.B.A. with high distinction, Harvard, 1955. With Nat. Cash Register Co., 1955-68, dir. distbn. and material, 1964-68; v.p., treas. Indian Head, Inc., 1968-72, v.p. planning and fin., 1972-77; v.p. fin. Nat. Steel Co., Pitts., 1977-84, ret., 1984. Pres. Social Health Agy., Dayton, Ohio, 1966-68; chmn. United Fund campaigns, Dayton, 1962-68; Bd. dirs. Good Samaritan Hosp., 1965-68. Served with USAAF, 1946-49. Mem. Nat. Assn. Accountants (bd. dirs. Dayton 1960-63), Fin. Execs. Inst. Clubs: Duquesne, Fox Chapel Golf. Home: 117 Haverford Rd Pittsburgh PA 15238-1639

RUSTIN, DOWSE BRADWELL, III, credit union executive; b. Charleston, S.C., Sept. 14, 1950; s. Dowse Bradwell, Jr. and Mary Bill Rustin; m. Ruth Ann Johnson, June 26,1976; children: Dowse Bradwell IV, Sarah Caroline. BS, Coll. of Charleston, 1975; postgrad., U. N.C., 1982. Internal auditor Wachovia Bank & Trust Co. N.A., Winston-Salem, N.C., 1975; retail loan officer, banking officer Wachovia Bank & Trust Co. N.A., Eden, N.C., 1978-81; city office mgr., asst. v.p. Wachovia Bank & Trust Co. N.A., Graham, N.C., 1981-85; pres. Charleston Area Fed. Credit Union, S.C., 1985—; bd. dirs. S.C. Credit Union League, Columbia, 1992-97, treas. bd. dirs., 1994, 2d vice chmn., 1995; mem. supervisory com. Carolina Corp. Credit Union, Columbia, 1991-92; treas. Charleston Area Chpt. Credit Unions, 1990-93, pres., 1994; faculty mem. S.C. Credit Union Lending Sch., Columbia, 1989—; regional spkr. on banking, econs. and disaster recovery planning. Mem. exec. bd. Coll. of Charleston Alumni Assn., 1992; mem. allocations bd. Trident United Way, Charleston, 1991-92. Served with USNR, 1968-74. Mem. S.C. Credit Union Mgmt. Assn., Charleston Trident C. of C. (speakers bur. 1987—), Masons (master mason), Charleston Rod and Reel Club (pres. 1991-92). Republican. Methodist. Avocations: golf, gardening, vintage automobiles. Office: Charleston Area Fed Credit Union 1845 Sam Rittenberg Blvd Charleston SC 29407-4870

RUSTIN, RUDOLPH BYRD, III, physician; b. Charleston, S.C., May 14, 1957; s. Rudolph Byrd and Mary Pringle (Herrin) R.; m. Sandra Lee Talbott, Nov. 28, 1985; children: Jonathan, Jeffrey. BS in Chemistry cum laude, Hampden Sydney Coll., 1979; MD, Med. U. S.C., 1983. Diplomate Am. Bd. Surgery, Am. Bd. Colon and Rectal Surgery; lic. physician, S.C. Intern Cleve. Clinic Found., 1983-84, resident, 1984-88, chief resident gen. surgery, 1987-88, fellow, 1988-89; private practice colon rectal surgery Charleston, 1989—; clin. assoc. surgery Med. U. S.C., Charleston, 1989—; active staff Roper Hosp., Charleston, St. Francis Xavier Hosp., Trident Med. Ctr.; courtesy staff Baker Hosp., N. Charleston, AMI East Cooper Community Hosp., Mt. Pleasant, S.C.; clin. assoc. Charleston Meml. Hosp.; presenter in field. Fellow ACS, Am. Soc. Colon Rectal Surgeons, Southeastern Surgical Congress; mem. Med. Soc. S.C., S.C. State Med. Assn., S.C. Med. Assn. (del.), So. Med. Assn., Charleston County Med. Soc., Phi Beta Kappa. Office: 125 Doughty St Ste 770 Charleston SC 29403-5731

RUSZKIEWICZ, CAROLYN MAE, newspaper editor; b. Tucson, Nov. 10, 1946; d. Robert Frank and Charlotte Ruth (Hadley) Knapton; m. Joseph Charles Ruszkiewicz, July 11, 1969. BA, Calif. State U., Long Beach, 1971, MA, 1973. Reporter Long Beach (Calif.) Press-Telegram, 1968-85, consumer editor, 1985-86, lifestyle editor, 1986-89, regional news editor, 1989-91, city editor, 1991-95, asst. mng. editor, 1995—. Avocations: swimming, walking, reading. Office: Long Beach Press-Telegram 604 Pine Ave Long Beach CA 90844-0003

RUTECKI, GREGORY WILLIAM, physician, educator; b. Chgo., Nov. 27, 1948; s. William John and Alice J. (Jankowski) R.; m. Janis Louise Howenstine, July 15, 1976; children: Jared, John. BS, DePaul U., 1970; MD cum laude, U. Ill., 1974. Diplomate Am. Bd. Internal Medicine, Am. Bd. Nephrology. Resident Ohio State U., Columbus, 1974-78; rsch. assoc. U. Minn., Mpls., 1978-80; asst. prof. medicine Northeastern Ohio U. Coll. Medicine, Rootstown, Ohio, 1982-86; assoc. prof. medicine Northeastern Ohio U. Coll. Medicine, Rootstown, 1986-97, prof. medicine, 1997—, master tchr., 1996; assoc. program dir. Internal Medicine Residency Affiliated Hosps., Canton, Ohio, 1992—; master tchr. Northeastern Ohio U. Coll. Medicine, 1996—). Contbr. articles to profl. jours., chpts. to books. Bd. trustees Ky. Christian Coll., 1992—; bd. dirs. Juvenile Diabetes Found., 1992—; elder Jackson Christian Ch., 1988—. Fellow ACP; mem. Am. Soc. Nephrology, Christian Med. Soc., Am. Acad. Med. Ethics, Alpha Omega Alpha (councillor 1993-96). Avocations: black belt, judo.

RUTENBERG-ROSENBERG, SHARON LESLIE, retired journalist; b. Chgo., May 23, 1951; d. Arthur and Bernice (Berman) Rutenberg; m. Michael J. Rosenberg, Feb. 3, 1980; children: David Kaifel and Jonathan Reuben (twins), Emily Mara. Student, Harvard U., 1972; B.A., Northwestern U., 1973, M.S.J., 1975; cert. student pilot. Reporter-photographer Lerner Home Newspapers, Chgo., 1973-74; corr. Medill News Service, Washington, 1975; reporter-newsperson, sci. writer UPI, Chgo., 1975-84; ret., 1984. Interviewer: exclusives White House chief of staff, nation's only mother and son on death row; others. Vol. Chgo.-Read Mental Health Ctr. Recipient Peter Lisagor award for exemplary journalism in features category, 1980, 81; Golden Key Nat. Adv. Bd. of Children's Oncology Service Inc., 1981; Media awards for wire service feature stories, 1983, 84, wire service news stories, 1983, 84, all from Chgo. Hosp. Pub. Relations Soc. Mem. Profl. Assn. Diving Instrs., Nat. Assn. Underwater Instrs., Hon. Order Ky. Cols., Hadassah, Sigma Delta Chi, Sigma Delta Tau. Home: 745 Marion Ave Highland Park IL 60035-5123

RUTES, WALTER ALAN, architect; b. N.Y.C., Sept. 21, 1928; s. Jack and Sarah (Ogur) R.; m. Helene Darville, Apr. 2, 1952; children: Daniel J., Linda Lee. B.Arch. (Sands Meml. medal 1950), Cornell U., 1950; fellow city planning, MIT, 1951; postgrad., Harvard U. Grad. Sch. Design, 1978. Cert. Nat. Council Archtl. Registration Bds. Assoc. ptnr. Skidmore, Owings & Merrill, N.Y.C., 1951-72; v.p. John Carl Warnecke & Assocs., N.Y.C., 1972-74; staff v.p. Intercontinental Hotels Corp., N.Y.C., 1974-80; dir. architecture Holiday Inns, Inc., Memphis, 1980-83; dir. design The Sheraton Corp., Boston, 1983-85; chmn 9 Tek Ltd. Hotel Cons., 1985—; chmn. adv. bd. Hult Fellowships for Constrn. Industry, 1968-75, Architects and Engrs. Com. New Bldg. Code, 1968; mem. zoning adv. com. N.Y.C. Planning Commn., 1970; lectr. in field, 1968—; mem. steering com. UNESCO Council Tall Bldgs. and Urban Habitat, 1980—; vis. prof. Cornell-Essec Grad. Program; vis. prof. Nova U. Author: Hotel Planning and Design, New Trends in Resort Design and Development; (software system) SHAPE, Megatrends and Marketecture; contbr. articles to profl. jours.; prin. works include Lincoln Center Library for Performing Arts, N.Y.C., 1967, Am. Republic Ins. Co. Nat. Hdqrs., Des Moines, 1967, HUD Apts., Jersey City, 1972, Merrill Lynch Bldg., N.Y.C., 1973, Tour Fiat, Paris, 1974, Aid Assn. for Luths. Nat. Hdqrs., Appleton, Wis., 1976, Semiramis Intercontinental Hotel, Cairo, 1985, Intercontinental, Jeddah, 1983, Embassy Suites Internat., 1985, Universal City Hotel Complex, L.A., 1986, TechWorld Conv. Hotel, Washington, 1986, Sheraton Fairplex Conv. Ctr., L.A., 1992, Orlando Conv. Ctr. Hotel, 1993, Winter Olympiad Media Complex, Norway, 1993, Ephesus Resort Complex, Turkey, 1986, Royal Christiania Hotel, Oslo, Norway, 1991, EuroFrance Leisure Park Complex, Cannes, 1993, Kuna Hills Multi Resort, Guam, 1994. Recipient Platinum Circle award Hotel Design Industry, 1988. Fellow AIA; mem. Ethical Culture Soc. Office: 8501 N 84th Pl Scottsdale AZ 85258-2419 also: 25 Richbell Rd White Plains NY 10605-4110

RUTFORD, ROBERT HOXIE, geoscience educator; b. Duluth, Minn., Jan. 26, 1933; s. Skuli and Ruth (Hoxie) R.; m. Marjorie Ann, June 19, 1954; children: Gregory, Kristian, Barbara. BA, U. Minn., 1954, MA, 1963, PhD, 1969; DSc (hon.), St Petersburg State Tech U., Russia, 1994. Football and track coach Hamline U., 1958-62; rsch. fellow U. Minn., 1963-66; asst. prof. geology U. S.D., 1967-70, assoc. prof., 1970-72, chmn. dept. geology, 1968-72, chmn. dept. physics, 1971-72; dir. Ross Ice Shelf Project U. Nebr., Lincoln, 1972-75; dir. divsn. Polar Programs NSF, Washington, 1975-77; vice chancellor for research and grad. studies, prof. geology U. Nebr., 1977-82, interim chancellor, 1980-81; pres. U. Tex., Dallas, 1982-94, Excellence in Edn. Found. prof. of geoscis., 1984-94; U.S. del. to Sci. Com. on Antarctic Rsch., 1986—, v.p., 1996—; chmn. NRC Polar Rsch. Bd., 1991-95. Mem. editl. bd. Issues in Sci. and Tech., 1991-94. Trustee Baylor Coll. Dentistry, 1989-96. 1st lt. U.S. Army, 1954-56. Recipient Antarctic Svc. medal, 1964, Disting. Svc. award NSF, 1977, Ernie Gunderson award for svc. to amateur athletics S.D. AAU, 1972, Outstanding Achievement award U. Minn., 1993, "M" Club Lifetime Achievement award, 1995. Fellow Geol. Soc. Am.; mem. Antarctican Soc. (pres. 1988-90), Arctic Inst. N.Am., Explorers Club, Am. Polar Soc., Philos. Soc. Tex., St. Petersburg Acad. Engring. (Russia), Cosmos Club, Sigma Xi. Lutheran. Home: 1882 Quail Ln Richardson TX 75080-3456 Office: Univ Tex Dallas Geosciences Program Richardson TX 75083-0688

RUTGERS, KATHARINE PHILLIPS (MRS. FREDERIK LODEWIJK RUTGERS), dancer; b. Butler, Pa., Sept. 2, 1910; d. Thomas Wharton and Alma (Sherman) Phillips; m. Frederik Lodewijk Rutgers, Feb. 2, 1942; children: Alma, Corinne Tolles. Diploma Briarcliff Coll., 1928; student L'Hermiage, Versailles, France, 1929-30; pupil ballet Vera Trefilova, Paris, Carl Raimund, Vienna, Varga Troyanoff, Budapest; pupil modern dance with Iris Barbura, Bucharest Ballet, Vincenzo Celli, N.Y.C., Igor Schwezoff, N.Y.C., Jean Yazvinsky, N.Y.C. Performed dance concerts Bucharest, 1937-40, U.S., 1941—; repertoire includes patriotic, dramatic, poetical dances, religious interpretations; dance therapist St. Barnabas Hosp., N.Y.C., 1965-70; author numerous pamphlets on dance, verses for choreographies. Chmn. ethnol. dance dept. Bruce Mus. Assocs., Greenwich, Conn., 1970—. Bd. dirs. Bruce Mus. Recipient citation for promoting culture with dance programs Nat. Fedn. Music Clubs, 1973. Mem. DAR, Conn. Fedn. Music Clubs (chmn. dance dept. 1965-66), Nat. League Am. Pen Women (local pres. 1973-78), Alliance Francaise, Mayflower Soc., Colonial Dames Am., Federated Music Club N.Y.C. (dir., dance chmn.), Met. Farm and Garden Club (dir.), Indian Harbor Club. Home: 9 Riversville Rd Greenwich CT 06831-3666

RUTH, ALPHEUS LANDIS, dairy farmer; b. Souderton, Pa., Sept. 6, 1915; s. Henry M. and Mary (Landis) R.; m. Miriam D. Rittenhouse, Sept. 26, 1936; children: Esther R., Mary Ellen, Samuel, Joseph, Phoebe. Student, pub. schs. Sunday sch. supt. Oley Mennonite Sunday Sch., Fleetwood, Pa., 1954-64; dir. Lehigh Valley Coop., Allentown, Pa., 1969—; lay minister Oley Mennonite Ch., 1977—; dir. Berks Lehigh Fed. Land Bank Bd., 1960—; diary farmer; treas. Hope Christian Ctr., South Bronx, N.Y., 1975—; pres. Lehigh Valley Farmers, Lansdale, Pa., 1978—; chmn. bd. Atlantic Processing, Inc., Allentown, Pa., 1978—; sales exec. Prudential Rittenhouse Realty Group, Harleysville, Pa.; mem. North Penn. Bd. of Realtors, 1992—. Active N.E. Dairy Coord. Com., 1985—, Berks County Farm Land Preservation Task Force, 1986-92; pres. Dock Woods Residence Coun. Named to Pa. Holstein Hall of Fame, 1989. Mem. Nat. Holsten Club, Pa. Holstein Club, Nat. Holstein Assn., Berks County Soil Conservation, Pa. Farmer Assn. Republican. Office: Prudential Rittenhouse 418 Main St Harleysville PA 19438-2350

RUTH, BETTY MUSE, school system administrator; b. Florence, Ala., Oct. 24, 1943; d. Paul and Mary Lucille (Gresham) Muse; m. Thomas Gary Ruth, Dec. 17, 1965 (div. Sept. 1979); 1 child, Thomas Paul; m. Charles Larry Oliver, Jr., Mar. 10, 1990. BSBA, Athens State Coll., 1982; MBA, U. N.Ala., 1986. Sec., bookkeeper Anderson News Co., Florence, 1963-65; acct. receivable bookkeeper McConnell AFB, Wichita, Kans., 1967-68; legal sec. Reynolds Law Firm, Selmer, Tenn., 1973-74; subs. tchr. Athens (Ala.) City Schs., 1974-78, dir. RSVP, 1978—; del. White House Conf. on Aging, 1995; mem. Nat. Coun. on Aging, 1985—. Active United Way, Athens, 1990-94; sec. Gov.'s Commn. Nat. and Comty. Svc., Ala, 1994; vice chair Tenn. Valley Exhibit Commn., Ala., 1984—; past pres. Athens-Limestone County Beautification Bd., 1991-94; People-to-People internat. del. to People's Republic of China, 1994. Named outstanding project dir. Action, Atlanta, 1985, outstanding woman of Ala., 1989. Mem. NEA, Ala. Edn. Assn., Nat. Assn. RSVP Dirs. (v.p., treas., del. 1985—, svc. award 1993), Region IV Assn. RSVP dirs. (pres., v.p., treas. 1979—, svc. award 1989), Ala. Assn. RSVP Dirs. (v.p., sec., treas. 1978—, Citizens award 1991), Athens State Coll. Alumni Assn. (bd. dirs. 1993—). Mem. Ch. of Christ. Avocations: reading, traveling, volunteerism. Home: 15705 Kings Dr Athens AL 35611-5667 Office: PO Box 852 Athens AL 35612-0852

RUTH, BRYCE CLINTON, JR., lawyer; b. Greenwood, Miss., Dec. 19, 1948; s. Bryce Clinton and Kathryn (Arant) R.; m. Martha M. Ruth; children: Lauren Elizabeth, Bryce Clinton III. BS, Delta State U., 1970; JD, Memphis State U., 1979. Bar: Tenn., 1979, U.S. Dist. Ct. (mid. dist.) Tenn. 1979, U.S. Ct. Mil. Appeals 1991, U.S. Ct. Appeals (6th cir.), 1994. Criminal investigation spl. agt. IRS, Memphis and Nashville, 1971-82; asst. dist. atty. Dist. Atty. Office, Gallatin, Tenn., 1982-89; asst. pub. defender Pub. Defender's Office, Gallatin, 1989-90; pvt. practice White House, Tenn., 1989—; judge City of Cross Plains, Tenn., 1992—; juvenile ct. referee judge Robertson County, Tenn., 1995—; mem. dist. investigating com. dist. VI Tenn. Bd. Law Examiners, 1989—; mem. child enforcement steering com. Asst. Dist. Atty. Office, 1983-84, chmn. legis. subcom., 1985; lectr. in field. Chmn. fin. com. White House First United Meth. Ch., 1983-88, trustee, 1988-90, chmn., 1990; trustee Vol. State Coll. Found., 1993—; bd. dirs. Crime Stoppers of Sumner County, 1989-94; bd. dirs. White House Youth Soccer, 1992-93, coach, 1987-91; bd. dirs. Sumner County CASA, 1992-93; coach Jr. Pro Football, 1980-85; video cameraman for football team White House H.S., 1991—; mem. Leadership Sumner, 1989; bd. dirs. White House Men's Club, 1981-83, 85-88, v.p., 1984, 88, pres., 1985. Maj. USAR, JAGC, 1983—. Recipient Disting. Expert award for pistol marksmanship U.S. Treasury, Disting. Svc. award City of White House. Mem. NRA, Tenn. Bar Assn. (del. 1993—), Sumner County Bar Assn. (chmn. domestic rels. com. 1984-85), White House Area C. of C. (bd. dirs. 1990-95, pres. 1993-94). Avocations: scuba diving, skiing, golf, hunting, pistol shooting. Office: 3210 Hwy 31W PO Box 68 White House TN 37188

RUTH, CAROL A., public relations executive; b. N.Y.C., June 19, 1942; d. Edward McDonald and Dorothea (Beauman) Smith. BBA, CUNY, 1979. Sr. v.p. Hill and Knowlton, Inc., N.Y.C., 1968-86; pres., chief exec. officer Dewe Rogerson, Inc., N.Y.C., 1986—, also bd. dirs.; Dewe Rogerson Group, London; exec. dir. Dewe Rogerson Asia; pres., CEO Dewe Rogerson, Inc., N.Y.C. Recipient Woman Achievers award YWCA of N.Y. 1985, bd. dirs. 1991—. Mem. Nat. Investors Rels. Inst. (bd. dirs. 1981-85, chmn. bd. 1984-85). Office: Dewe Rogerson Inc 850 3rd Ave New York NY 10022-6222*

RUTH, DANIEL JOHN, journalist; b. Akron, Ohio, Sept. 16, 1949; s. John Edgar and Ruth (Motz) R.; m. Barbara Verde, July 10, 1980 (div. June 1988); m. Angela Pecoulas, July 31, 1992. BA in Polit. Sci., Gannon U., 1972. Reporter, critic Tampa (Fla.) Tribune, 1973-81; v.p., pub. Group W Satellite Com., Stamford, Conn., 1981-84; reporter, critic, columnist Chgo. Sun-Times, 1984-91; editor The Big Guava Mag., Tampa, Fla., 1991-92; columnist Tampa (Fla.) Tribune, 1992—; critic Sta. WMAQ, Chgo., 1988-91; tchr. Columbia Coll., Chgo., 1988-90. Pres. Hillsborough County (Fla.) Suicide and Crisis Ctr., Tampa, 1979-80. Recipient 1st place in commentary Fla. chpt. Sigma Delta Chi, 1980, Peter Lisagor award Chgo. chpt., 1985. Roman Catholic. Home: 10706 N Rome Ave Tampa FL 33612-6577

RUTH, EDWARD B., principal; b. Lancaster, Pa., Aug. 23, 1943; s. Edward B. and Jeanne L. (Schaeffer) R.; m. Betsy A. Lorenz, Aug. 28, 1965; 1 child, Heather L. BS in Biology, Lebanon Valley Coll., Annville, Pa., 1965; MEd, Millersville (Pa.) U., 1970; cert. secondary prin., Temple U., 1990. Cert. secondary prin., secondary tchr. gen. sci., biology. Sci. tchr. Milton Hershey (Pa.) Sch., 1965-87, mid. sch. asst. prin., 1987-92, mid. sch. prin., 1992—, asst. athletic dir., 1983-87; recreation supr., Milton Hershey Sch.; mgr. Palmyra Swimming Pool, summers; mem. evaluation team Pa. Assn. Pvt. Acad. Schs., 1991; mem. planning com. Pa. Commonwealth Partnership, F&M Coll., Lancaster, Pa., 1987; mem. biol. safety and recombinant DNA com. Hershey Med. Ctr., 1987—; mem. union negotiations team Milton Hershey Sch., 1994—; judge regional and state meetings Pa. Jr. Acad. Sci.,

Capital Area Sci. and Engring. Fairs, Pa. Coll. Energy Debates. Author, editor: Energy Teaching Units Energy Concepts, 1982; tech. writer Harrisburg Energy Edn. Adv. Coun.; author: (flow chart) Summary: Modern Interpretation of the Central Dogma (Watson & Crick's DNA Model), 1983; reviewer pre-publ. articles, books, audio-visual materials Am. Biology Tchr. Mem. camping program com. Keystone Area Boy Scouts, Harrisburg, Pa., 1994; chmn. Derry Twp. Environ. Adv. Coun., Hershey, Pa., 1993-94. Mem. Nat. Assn. Biology Tchrs. (Outstanding Pa. Biology Tchr. 1984), Nat. Assn. Secondary Sch. Prins., Pa. Assn. Secondary Sch. Prins., Nat. Eagle Scout Assn., Lancaster County Conservancy. Avocation: distance running. Home: 356 William Dr Hershey PA 17033-1859 Office: Milton Hershey Sch PO Box 830 Hershey PA 17033-0830

RUTH, JAMES PERRY, financial planning executive; b. Washington, Feb. 27, 1946; s. Robert Walker and Virginia Null Ruth; m. Kathleen McHugh, Aug. 10, 1968; children: Heather Lynn, Michael James. BS in Bus. and Public Adminstrn., U. Md., 1970; postgrad. Am. Coll., Bryn Mawr, Pa., 1971-83; CLU, CFP, chartered fin. cons. agt., Northwestern Mutual Life Ins. Co., Washington, 1967-74; gen. agt. Indpls. Life, Rockville, Md., 1974-82; partner Fox, Ruth & Middledorf, Rockville, 1975-82; mgr. Mfrs. Fin. Svcs., Rosslyn, Va., 1982-84; pres. Potomac Fin. Group, 1984—. Past pres. Jelleff Boys' Club; past pres. Montgomery County Police Boys' and Girls' Club; bd. dirs. Boys' Clubs Greater Washington. Named Outstanding Young Man Am., U.S. Jaycees, 1979. Mem. Nat. Assn. Life Underwriters, Nat. Assn. Securities Dealers, Suburban Md. Life Underwriters Assn. (past pres.; H.L. Meyer Meml. award 1980), Internat. Assn. Fin. Planning, Suburban Md. Estate Planning Coun. (past pres.), Million Dollar Round Table, Md. State Life Underwriters Assn. (pres. 1995-96). Lutheran. Contbr. articles to profl. publs; quoted in N.Y. Times, U.S. News and World Report, USA Today, others. Home: 7920 Warfield Rd Gaithersburg MD 20882-4409 Office: Ste 420 18310 Montgomery Village Ave Gaithersburg MD 20879-3551

RUTH, THOMAS GRISWOLD, history educator; b. Benton Harbor, Mich., Nov. 7, 1940; s. John Griswold and Ruth Margery (Hopkins) R. BA, U. Mich., 1963; MA, U. Tex., 1968. Instr. Am.-Nicaraguan Sch., Managua, 1965-67; instr. history (Ind. Found. Teaching Endowment) The Hill Sch., Pottstown, Pa., 1968—. Mem. Assn. Am. Historians, Sloan Club (London). Avocations: travel, coin collecting, ancient map collecting. Home and Office: The Hill Sch Pottstown PA 19464

RUTHCHILD, GERALDINE QUIETLAKE, training and development consultant, writer, poet; d. Nathan and Ruth (Feldman) Stein; m. Neil Wolinsky, Dec. 31, 1993; 1 child, Nathaniel Gideon Wolinsky. BA summa cum laude, Queens Coll., 1977; MA in Am. Lit., Johns Hopkins U., 1980, PhD in Am. Lit., 1983. Asst. prof. Albion (Mich.) Coll., 1982-84; assoc. Investor Access Corp., N.Y.C., 1984-85; program dir. Exec. Enterprises, Inc., N.Y.C., 1985-86; pres. Ruthchild Assocs., N.Y.C., 1987-90, Exemplar, N.Y.C., 1991-95, Examplar, Ltd., N.Y.C., 1995—; cons. J.P. Morgan & Co., Inc., Bankers Trust Co., Koch Industries, Inc., Chase Manhattan Bank N.A., Merrill Lynch, Koch Industries, Inc., NatWest Bank, U.S.A., Citibank N.A., Robert Morris Assocs., Goldman, Sachs & Co., Dean Witter Reynolds, Inc., also others, 1987—. Contbr. articles, poems to profl. and lit. jours. Vol. handicapped children N.Y. Foundling Hosp., N.Y.C., 1988-90, Fgn. Visitors Desk, Met. Mus. Art, N.Y.C., 1989—. Hopkins fellow Johns Hopkins U., 1979-80, Andrew Mellon Found. fellow, 1980-81, 81-82. Mem. ASTD, Assn. Bank Trainers and Cons., Internat. Soc. Philos. Enquiry, Phi Beta Kappa. Avocations: foreign languages, needlework, house plants. Office: Exemplar 501 E 87th St Fl 12 New York NY 10128-7665

RUTHERFOORD, REBECCA HUDSON, computer science educator; b. Elkhart, Ind., Feb. 24, 1948; d. Charles Melvin Hudson and Eunice Klaire (Lund) Edmonds; m. James Kincanon Rutherfoord, Aug. 31, 1968; children: James Kincanon Jr., Charles Penn. BS, Ind. State U., 1971, MS, 1972, EdD, 1975; MS in Computer Sci., So. Poly State U., Marietta, Ga., 1995. Cert. data processor. Staff asst. Ind. State U., Terre Haute, 1969-71; vocal music tchr. S.W. Parke Schs., Rockville, Ind., 1971-73; fellowship asst. Ind. State U., Terre Haute, 1974-75; vocal music tchr. Slidell (La.) H.S., 1977-78; programmer, analyst La. State U., Baton Rouge, 1978-79, dir. computer rehab. program, 1979-80; programmer, analyst Hanes Corp., Atlanta, 1980-81; asst. prof. Devry Inst., Atlanta, 1981-83; acting dept. chair So. Poly. State U., Marietta, Ga., 1989-92, prof. computer sci., 1983—, computer sci. grad. program coord., 1996—, asst. to pres., 1997—; asst. to pres., cons. The Assocs. Group, Inc., Roswell, Ga., 1986-88, Crawford Comm., Atlanta, 1987; adj. prof. Cobb County Bd. Edn., Marietta, 1985-87, Joseph T. Walker Sch., Marietta, 1985-86; vis. prof. Leicester (U.K.) Poly., 1990. Choir dir. St. Peter and Paul Episcopal Ch., Marietta, 1981-85, choir mem., 1992—; Christian edn. dir. St. Francis Episcopal Ch., Denham Springs, La., 1978-80; choir mem. St. David's Episcopal Ch., Roswell, 1985-92; bd. dirs., mem. Cherokee Cmty. Habitat for Humanity, 1994—. Mem. Data Processing Mgmt. Assn., Assn. Computing Machinery, Sigma Alpha Iota. Republican. Avocations: boating, reading. Office: So Poly State Univ 1100 S Marietta Pky Marietta GA 30060-2855

RUTHERFORD, JIM, professional sports team executive; b. 1948; m. Heidi Rutherford; 1 child, Andrea. Goal tender Detroit Red Wings, Pitts., Toronto, L.A. profl. hockey teams, 1969-82; dir. hockey ops Compuware Sports Corp., 1982-94; gen. mgr. Windsor (Ont.) Spitfires, 1984-88, head coach, 1986-87; dir. hockey ops. Detroit Ambassadors, 1989-91, coach, dir. hockey ops., 1991-92; coach, dir. hockey ops. Detroit Jr. Red Wings (formerly Ambassadors), 1992-94; COO KTR Hockey Ltd. Partnership, Hartford, Conn., 1984—; pres., gen. mgr., chief operating officer Hartford Whalers, 1994—; mem. Team Can. hockey world championships Vienna, 1977, Moscow, 1979; Red Wings' player rep. 5 seasons. Recipient Exec. of Yr. award Ont. Hockey League, Can. Hockey League, 1993, Ont. Hockey League, 1994. Achievements include directing Windsor Spitfires to 1988 Meml. Cup finals, leading Detroit Ambassadors to first-ever playoff in 1992, winning Emms Divsn. championship with Jr. Red Wings in 1994, bringing 1st Am.-based Ont. Hockey League franchise to Detroit, 1989, securing Nat. Hockey League approval of KTR purchase of Hartford Whalers from Conn. Devel. Authority, 1994. Office: Hartford Whalers 242 Trumbull St Hartford CT 06103-1212*

RUTHERFORD, JOHN SHERMAN, III (JOHNNY RUTHERFORD), professional race car driver; b. Coffeyville, Kans., Mar. 12, 1938; s. John Sherman and Mary Henrietta (Brooks) R.; m. Betty Rose Hoyer, July 7, 1963; children: John Sherman, Angela Ann. Student, Tex. Christian U., 1956. Profl. race car driver, 1959-94, ret., 1994, driver super-modified race cars, sprint cars, stock cars, midgets, sports cars, Indy cars, Trans-Am cars and formula 5000; mem. Indy Car Racing Inc.; appointed spl. events coord. Indy Racing League, 1995—; pace car driver for Championship Auto Racing Teams, 1992-95; lectr. in field. Host: TV show The Racers; race commentator TV show, NBC, ESPN, CBS, ABC; appeared in numerous TV commercials; art work included in traveling exhbn. Art and Athletes; TV and radio pub. services messages for Nat. Safety Council, Calif. Hwy. Patrol, U.S. Marines, Muscular Dystrophy Assn., Cystic Fibrosis Assn., Boy Scouts, Camp Fire, Shriner's Hosp., Tex. Soc. to Prevent Blindness, Air N.G. Hon. state chmn. Am. Cancer Soc., Tex., Tarrant County Soc. to Prevent Blindness, Emergency Medicine Found., Ft. Worth Kidney Assn., Ft. Worth Burn Ctr.; Ind. chmn. Am. Heart Assn. Named Ft. Worth Newsmaker of Yr., 1974, Driver of Yr. Sport Mag., 1976, Driver of Yr. Auto Race Writers and Broadcasters Am., 1974, 80, Olsonite Driver of Yr., 1980, Corvette Challenge's Sportsman of Yr., 1988, Motorsports amb., 1993; recipient Jim Clark award, 1969, Extra Mile award, 1973, Mim Malloy award, 1974, Eddie Sachs award, 1975, Louie Meyer award, 1992; chosen for Internat. Race of Champions, 1974, 76, 77, 78, 79, 84, chosen Fast Masters, 1993; elected to Tex. Sports Hall of Fame, 1981, Indy 500 Hall of Fame, 1987, Boys Clubs Am.'s Celebrity Hall of Fame, 1987, Tex. Auto Racing Hall of Fame, 1988, Nat. Sprint Car Hall of Fame, 1995, Internat. Motorsports Hall of Fame, 1996, Motorsports Hall of Fame, 1996. Mem. Fedn. Internat. Automobile, Internat. Motors Sports Assn., Exptl. Aircraft Assn., Warbirds of Am., Confederate Air Force, Internat. Aerobatic Club, League Auto Racing (exec., bd. dirs.), Championship Drivers Assn. (bd. dirs.), Nat. Rifle Assn., Air Force Assn., Air Power Coun., Blue Angels Assn., Ft. Worth Boat Club, Shady Oaks Country Club, Lions. Winner 27 championship car races; winner Indianapolis 500, 1974, 76, 80, second place, 1975; set new world's record for stock cars, Daytona Beach, Fla., 1963; set record at Indpls. 500, 1973; at Mich. Internat. Raceway, 1984; U.S. Auto Club Nat. Sprint Car champion, 1965; Nat. Driving champion USAC and CART, 1980; oldest driver (48) to win a 500 mile Indy Car Race, 1986. *I am a firm believer in the fact that a person can do anything in this world he or she wants to as long as you have desire. People have to set goals, things to achieve. No one ever remembers who finished second. Luck is where preparation meets opportunity.*

RUTHERFORD, PAUL HARDING, physicist; b. Shipley, Yorkshire, Eng., Jan. 22, 1938; came to U.S., 1965, naturalized, 1976; s. Joseph William and Annie (Harding) R.; m. Audrey Jones Irvine, Oct. 31, 1959; children—Andrea Christine, Julia Irvine. B.A., Cambridge (Eng.) U., 1959, M.A., 1963, Ph.D., 1963. Research asso. Princeton (N.J.) U. Plasma Physics Lab., 1962-63, mem. research staff, 1965-68, research physicist, 1968-71, sr. research physicist, 1971—, head theoretical div., 1972-80, dep. asso. dir. for research, 1978-80, asso. dir. research, 1980-95; chair tech. adv. com. Internat. Thermonuclear Exptl. Reactor, 1992—; research asso. U.K. Atomic Energy Authority Culham (Berkshire, Eng.) Lab., 1963-65; lectr. astrophys. scis. Princeton U. Co-author: (with R.J. Goldston) Introduction to Plasma Physics, 1995; mem. bd. assoc. editors Physics of Fluids, 1973-75; mem. editl. bd. Nuclear Fusion, 1980—. Recipient E.O. Lawrence award U.S. Dept. Energy, 1983. Fellow Am. Phys. Soc. Home: 10 Burr Dr Princeton NJ 08540-1950 Office: Plasma Physics Lab PO Box 451 Princeton NJ 08543

RUTHERFORD, ROBERT BARRY, surgeon; b. Edmonton, Alta., Can., July 29, 1931; s. Robert Lyon and Kathleen Emily (Gunn) R.; m. Beulah Kay Folk, Aug. 20, 1955; children: Robert Scott, Lori Jayne, Holly Anne, Trudy Kaye, Jay Wilson. BA in Biology, Johns Hopkins U., 1952, MD, 1956. Surgeon U. Colo. Health Sci. Ctr., Denver; emeritus prof. surgery U. Colo., Denver, 1996—. Editor: (texts) Management of Trauma, 1968, 4 edits., Vascular Surgery, 1978, 4 edits., An Atlas of Vascular Surgery, 1993; editor quar. rev. Seminars in Vascular Surgery; sr. editor Jour. Vascular Surgery. Mem. Internat. Soc. for Cardiovascular Surgery, Phi Beta Kappa, Alpha Omega Alpha. Republican. Unitarian. Avocations: skiing, biking, wind surfing, sailing. Office: 0146 Spring Beauty Dr Box 23159 Silverthorne CO 80498

RUTHERFORD, THOMAS TRUXTUN, II, state senator, lawyer; b. Columbus, Ohio, Mar. 3, 1947; s. James William and Elizabeth Whiting (Colby) R.; m. Linda Sue Rogers, Aug. 28, 1965 (div.); 1 child, Jeremy Todd. BBA, U. N.Mex., 1970, JD, 1982. Page, reading clk. N.Mex. State Legislature, 1960-65; mem. N.Mex. Atty. Gen. Environ. Adv. Commn., 1972; radio broadcaster Sta. KOB Radio and TV, 1963-72; mem. N.Mex. Senate, Albuquerque, 1972-96, majority whip, 1978-88, chmn. rules com., 1988—, chmn. econ. devel. and new tech. interim com., mem. sci. and new tech. oversight com., majority fl. leader; pres. Rutherford & Assocs., Albuquerque, 1978-83; pvt. practice, Albuquerque, 1983—; commr. chair Bernalillo County Commn., 1996; former bd. dirs. Union Savs. Bank, Albuquerque; past pres. Albuquerque Cable TV adv. bd.; mem. Southwest Regional Energy Council, N.Mex. Gov.'s Commn. on Public Broadcasting; bd. dirs., v.p. Rocky Mountain Corp. for Pub. Broadcasting; mem. Am. Coun. Young Polit. Leaders, del. mission to Hungary, Austria, Greece, 1983; mem. Fgn. Trade Adv. Com. Bd. Econ. Devel. and Tourism; trade del. to People's Republic of China, 1985. N.Mex. Broadcasting Assn. scholar, 1970. Home: 1910 Ridgecrest SE Albuquerque NM 87108-1267 also: PO Box 1610 Albuquerque NM 87103-1610

RUTHERFORD, VICKY LYNN, special education educator; b. Florence, S.C., Sept. 12, 1947. BS, Hampton U., 1969, MA, 1971; PhD, Mich. State U., 1991. Cert. tchr. French, spl. edn., reading specialist, Va., tchr. spl. edn., S.C. Social worker day care Hampton (Va.) Dept. Social Svc., 1970-72; reading therapist, asst. dir., dir. Bayberry Reading Clinic, Hampton, 1973-77; tchr. reading, English, counselor York County Schs., Yorktown, Va., 1977-85; staff advisor, asst. to course coord. Mich. State U., East Lansing, 1985-90; tchr. autism Florence (S.C.) Dist. 1 Sch. Sys., 1992-96, tchr. emotionally impaired, 1996—. Instrnl. designer: Addiction Severity Index #1, 1987, #2, 1988, Managing a Diverse Workforce, 1990; designer, trainer: Project Teach, 1991; designer, developer: (video) Camp Takona Summer Experience, 1992. Bass guitarist, Sun. sch. sec., youth worker, Sun. sch. supt. Progressive Ch. of Jesus, Florence, 1992—. Fellow Mich. Dept. Edn., 1987-89. Mem. Internat. Reading Assn. Office: Briggs Elem Sch 1012 Congaree Dr Florence SC 29501-5768

RUTHERFORD, WILLIAM DRAKE, investment executive, lawyer; b. Marshalltown, Iowa, Jan. 14, 1939; s. William Donald and Lois Esther (Drake) R.; m. Janice W. Rutherford, Feb. 4, 1965 (div. Mar. 1982); children: Wayne Donald, Melissa Drake; m. Karen Anderegg, Jan. 2, 1994. BS, U. Oreg., 1961; LLB, Harvard U., 1964. Bar: Oreg. 1964, U.S. Dist. Ct. Oreg. 1966. Assoc. Maguire, Kester & Cosgrave, Portland, Oreg., 1966-69; house counsel May & Co., Portland, 1969-70, pvt. practice, 1970-71; pvt. practice McMinnville, Oreg., 1971-84; mem. Oreg. Ho. of Reps., Salem, 1977-84; state treas. State of Oreg., Salem, 1984-87; chmn. Oreg. Investment Coun., Salem, 1986-87; exec. v.p., dir. U.S. and Australia ops. ABD Internat. Mgmt. Corp., N.Y.C., 1987-88, pres., chief exec. officer, bd. dirs., 1988-89; pres., bd. dirs. Societé Gen. Touche Remnant, 1990-93; dir. spl. projects Metallgesellschaft Corp., N.Y.C., 1994-95; mng. dir. Macadam Capital Ptnrs., Portland, 1995-96; CEO Fiberboard Asbestos Compensation Trust, Portland, 1996—; bd. dirs. Metro One Telecomms. Bd. dirs. Portland Opera Assn. 1st lt. U.S. Army, 1964-66. Recipient Contbn. to Individual Freedom award ACLU, 1981. Mem. Internat. Bar Assn., Nat. Assn. State Treas. (exec. v.p. 1985, 86, pres. western region 1985, 86), Nat. Assn. State Auditors, Comptr. and Treas. (exec. com. 1987). Republican. Home and Office: 6978 SW Foxfield Ct Portland OR 97225-6054

RUTHVEN, DOUGLAS MORRIS, chemical engineering educator; b. Ernakulum, India, Oct. 9, 1938; arrived in Can., 1966; s. Joseph Morris and Beryl (Mackay) R.; m. Patricia Evelyn Goodwin, July 20, 1968; 1 child, Fiona Beryl. BA, U. Cambridge, Eng., 1960, MA, 1963, PhD, 1966, ScD, 1988. Design engr. Davy Power Gas Corp., Stockton-on-Tees, Eng., 1961-63; asst. prof. dept. chem. engring. U. N.B., Fredericton, Can., 1966-72, assoc. prof., 1973-74, prof., 1975-95; prof., chair chem. engring. U. Maine, Orono, 1995—. Author: Principles of Adsorption and Adsorption Processes, 1984; co-author: Diffusion in Zeolites, 1992, Pressures Swing Adsorption, 1994; contbr. numerous articles to profl. jours. Recipient Max Planck rsch. prize, 1993. Fellow Royal Soc. Can.; mem. Am. Inst. Chem. Engrs. Avocation: Scottish country dancing. Home: 2650 Bennoch Rd Old Town ME 04468 Office: Univ Maine Dept Chem Engring Orono ME 04469

RUTISHAUSER, URS STEPHEN, cell biologist; b. Pasadena, Feb. 27, 1946; s. Hans and Elsa (Riese) R.; m. Stephanie Waddey, June 23, 1990; children: Justin, Emily, Stephen. ScB, Brown U., 1967; PhD, Rockefeller U., 1973. Asst. to assoc. prof. cell biology Rockefeller U., N.Y.C., 1973-83; prof. cell biology Case Western Res. U., Cleve., 1983—. Assoc. editor Jour. Neurosci., 1990—, European Jour. of Cell Biology, 1991—; contbr. over 100 articles to profl. jours. NIH grantee, 1975—; McKnight scholar, 1979-82; Jane Coffin Childs fellow, 1973-74. Mem. AAAS, Am. Soc. Cell Biology, Soc. for Neurosci., Soc. for Developmental Biology. Achievements include co-discovery of first cell adhesion molecule (CAM). Office: Case Western Res Univ Sch Medicine 2109 Adelbert Rd Cleveland OH 44106-2624

RUTKIN, SEYMOUR, architect; b. Weehawken, N.J., Oct. 22, 1927; s. Herman Irving and Dora (Oltarsh) R. B.S. in Architecture, Ill. Inst. Tech., 1949; certificate arts and architecture, Cooper Union. Apprentice with R.M. Schindler (architect), L.A. One-man show projected designs, Peter Cooper Gallery, N.Y.C., 1957; presented new shell designs and theories, World Conf., San Francisco, 1962, Internat. Congress Internat. Assn. Shell & Space Structures, Mexico City, 1967, Internat. Colloquim, Madrid, 1969; group juried art show, East Islip (N.Y.) Arts Coun., 1984, exhibited, 1985-90 (honorable mention water colors); two-person architecture show of new designs Storefront for Art and Architecture Gallery, N.Y.C., 1985; new prototype design advanced concrete shell residence construction, 1995-96; prin. works include schs., hotel, 42 story office bldg., hosp., shell bldg. design and constrn., dormitories, residential, and interiors; patentee in field; contbr. articles to profl. jours. Schweinburg scholar Cooper Union; recipient Art in Am.-New Talent USA award, 1959. Address: 445 E 65th St New York NY 10021-6912

RUTKOFF, ALAN STUART, lawyer; b. Chgo., May 31, 1952; s. Roy and Harriet (Ruskin) R.; m. Mally Zoberman, Dec. 22, 1974; children: Aaron Samuel, Jordana Michal, Robert Nathaniel. BA with high distinction, U. Mich., 1973; JD magna cum laude, Northwestern U., 1976. Bar: Ill. 1976, U.S. Dist. Ct. (no. dist.) Ill. 1976, U.S. Ct. Appeals (7th cir.) 1977, U.S. Ct. Appeals (3d cir.) 1978, U.S. Supreme Ct. 1981, U.S. Ct. Appeals (5th cir.) 1983, U.S. Ct. Appeals (8th cir.) 1990, U.S. Dist. Ct. (we. dist.) Wis. 1996. Assoc. Altheimer & Gray, Chgo., 1976-80; ptnr. Kastel & Rutkoff, Chgo., 1980-83, Holleb & Coff Ltd., Chgo., 1983-84, McDermott, Will & Emery, Chgo., 1984—. Mem. ABA, Chgo. Bar Assn., Order of Coif. Home: 801 Timberhill Rd Highland Park IL 60035-5148 Office: McDermott Will & Emery 227 W Monroe St Chicago IL 60606-5016

RUTKOWSKI, JAMES ANTHONY, state legislator; b. Milw., Apr. 6, 1942. BS in Bus., Marquette U., 1964, JD, 1966. Former instr. Marquette U., Milw.; asst. instr. U. Wis., Milw.; state legis. State of Wis., Madison, 1970. With USAR, 1966-72. Recipient Clean 16 award, 1982, 88, 90, 94, Wis. Man of Achievement award, 1976. Mem. KC, Greendale Jaycee Roosters. Home: 4550 S 117th St Greenfield WI 53228-2451 Office: State Capitol 216 North PO Box 8953 Madison WI 53708

RUTLEDGE, CHARLES OZWIN, pharmacology educator; b. Topeka, Oct. 1, 1937; s. Charles Ozwin and Alta (Seaman) R.; m. Jane Ellen Crow, Aug. 13, 1961; children: David Ozwin, Susan Harriett, Elizabeth Jane, Karen Ann. BS in Pharmacy, U. Kans., 1959, MS in Pharmacology, 1961; PhD in Pharmacology, Harvard U., 1966. NATO postdoctoral fellow Gothenburg U., Sweden, 1966-67; asst. prof. U. Colo. Med. Ctr., Denver, 1967-74, assoc. prof., 1974-75; prof., chmn. dept. pharmacology U. Kans., Lawrence, 1975-87; dean, prof. pharmacology Purdue U., West Lafayette, Ind., 1987—. Contbr. articles on neuropharmacology to profl. jours. Grantee: NIH, 1970, Kans. Heart Assn., 1978. Mem. Am. Soc. Pharmacology and Exptl. Therapeutics (councillor 1982-84, sec.-treas. 1990-93, pres. 1996-97), Am. Assn. Coll. Pharmacy (chmn. biol. scis. sect. 1983-84, chmn. council of faculties 1986-87, chmn. coun. deans, 1993-94, comm. implement change pharm. edn. 1989-92, pres. 1996-97), Soc. for Neurosci., Am. Pharm. Assn. AAAS. Avocations: gardening; skiing. Home: 40 Brynteg Est West Lafayette IN 47906-5643 Office: Purdue U Office of Dean Sch Pharmacy 1330 R Heine Pharm Bldg West Lafayette IN 47907-1330

RUTLEDGE, ELLIOTT MOYE, soil scientist, educator; b. Gallatin, Tenn., Mar. 26, 1935; s. Elliott Moye and Emma Sugg (McKoin) R.; m. Barbara Bolton Green, Sept. 14, 1957; children: Malinda Sugg Rutledge Kirchner, Elliott Moye III. BS, Tenn. Tech., 1958; MS, U. Ark., 1963; PhD, Ohio State U., 1969. Soil sci.-trainee Soil Conservation Svc., Summerville, Tenn., 1957, Cookville, Tenn., 1958; rsch. asst. U. Ark., Fayetteville, 1958-62, asst. prof. agronomy, 1969-73, assoc. prof., 1973-77, prof., 1977—; asst. agronomy Ohio State U., Columbus, 1962-68. Tour leader Friends of Pleistocene, 1990. Fellow Am. Soc. Agronomy (bd. dirs. 1992-95), Soil Sci. Am. (divsn. chmn. 1984-85, bd. dirs. 1992-95); mem. Soil and Water Conservation Soc., Internat. Soil Sci. Soc., Ark. Soc. Profl. Soil Classifiers, Rotary. Democrat. Presbyterian. Avocations: travel, history, riding, current events. Home: 1507 Rolling Hills Dr Fayetteville AR 72703-3625 Office: U Ark at Fayetteville Agronomy Dept Plant Sci 115 Fayetteville AR 72701

RUTLEDGE, IVAN CATE, retired legal educator, arbitrator; b. White Pine, Tenn., Dec. 24, 1915; s. Wiley Blount and Tamsey (Cate) R.; children: Ann, Thomas Carroll. BA, Carson-Newman Coll., 1934; MA, Duke U., 1940, LLB, 1946; LLM, Columbia U., 1952. Bar: Ga. 1946, Wash. 1951, Ohio 1966. Asst. prof. law Mercer U., Macon, Ga., 1946-47; from asst. prof. to prof. law U. Wash., Seattle, 1947-54; prof. law Ind. U., Bloomington, 1954-63; prof. law Ohio State U., Columbus, 1963-79, dean, 1965-70; Walter F. George prof. law Mercer U., Macon, 1979—, prof. emeritus, 1986—. Home: 3188 Vista Cir Macon GA 31204-1960

RUTLEDGE, JOHN WILLIAM, former watch company executive; b. Eureka, Calif., Mar. 12, 1923; s. William Eugene and Ellen Agnes (Jordan) R.; m. Mary Jo McKinley, Nov. 23, 1951; children: Ellen, John William, Amy. B.S., Northwestern U., 1943; M.B.A., Harvard U., 1947; MA. in Archaeology, Yale U., 1985. Tchr. Charlestown State Penitentiary, Boston, 1946-47; salesman Lahey Fargo & Co., 1947-48; asst. controller Lehigh Coal & Navigation Co., 1948-54; sr. v.p., dir. Xerox Corp., Stamford, Conn., 1954-71; sr. v.p. home furnishings group, dir. Magnavox Co., N.Y.C., 1971-73; pres., dir. Bulova Watch Co., N.Y.C., 1973-79; dir. Nat. Telecommunications and Tech., Network Controls, Nat. Aviation & Tech. Corp., Orion Capital Corp. Served to lt. USNR. Mem. Sigma Alpha Epsilon. Clubs: Harvard (N.Y.C.), N.Y. Athletic (N.Y.C.). Home: 127 Dunning Rd New Canaan CT 06840-4011 also: 893 S County Rd Palm Beach FL 33480-4908

RUTMAN, MARK CHARLES, public relations executive; b. N.Y.C., Sept. 3, 1930; s. Nathan and Sarah Barbara (Korman) R.; m. Geraldine N. Leitner, Jan. 31, 1954; children: Lee, Lisa, Neil. B.A., NYU, 1952; M.S. in Journalism, Columbia U., 1953. Account exec., then v.p., gen. mgr. Affiliated Public Relations Agy., N.Y.C., 1956-60; pres., owner Nat. Public Relations Counsel, N.Y.C., 1960-78; exec. v.p. Grey & Davis Inc., N.Y.C., 1978; pres. Grey & Davis Inc., 1979-84; chmn. Grey Com Inc., 1984-85; sr. assoc. Fred Rosen Assocs., Inc., 1985-90; mng. dir. LH&H Pub. Rels., N.Y.C., 1990—. Served with Ordnance Corps AUS, 1953-55. Recipient Freedoms Found. medal, 1955. Jewish. Club: Overseas Press (N.Y.C.). Home: 9 Crossway Scarsdale NY 10583-7136 Office: 545 Madison Ave New York NY 10022-4219

RUTMAN, ROBERT JESSE, biochemist, educator; b. Kingston, N.Y., June 23, 1919; s. Leon and Anne (Porringer) R.; B.S., Pa. State U., 1940; postgrad. U. Idaho, 1942, U. Calif., Berkeley, Ph.D., 1950; M.S., U. Pa., 1975; m. Geraldine Burwell, Jan. 1971; children—Rose, Randy, Steven, Brian, David, Ellen. Mem. teaching rsch. staffs Jefferson U., Phila., 1950-53; rsch. assoc. chemistry dept. U. Pa., 1954-60, assoc. prof., 1961-68, prof. biochemistry and molecular biology Sch. Vet. Medicine, 1968-87, prof. emeritus, 1987—, chmn. dept. biochemistry, 1976-80; vis. prof. U. Ibadan (Nigeria), 1974; coord. U. Pa.-U. Ibadan Exch. Agreement; expert witness on carcinogenesis; cons. on environ. contamination. Mem. nat. steering com. Am. Found. Negro Affairs, also co-chmn. sci. and tech. div.; pres. C.W. Henry Home and Sch. Assn., 1960; pres. Phila. Citizens Com. on Pub. Edn., 1963; campaign fin. mgr. Mayoralty Campaign, Phila., 1978; bd. dirs. S.E. Pa. region Leukemia Soc., Southeastern Pa. Anti-Drug Symposium; chmn. bd. Ile-Ife Ctr. for Humanities, Parkside Human Svcs., Inc., corp. sec.; v.p. Phila. region Martin Luther King Jr. Ctr., Pa. State Commn. Martin Luther King Celebration; bd. dirs. Earth Regeneration Soc., adv. bd. dirs., Univ. Conversion Project; chmn. bd. dir. WACI-TV Channel 62, Atlantic City, N.J., chair Del. Valley Rain Forest Action Group, 1995—; chair conf. com. Nat. Black Leadership Initiative on Cancer; bd. dirs. Nat. Conf. Christians/Jews. Served to capt. C.E., AUS, 1944-48, PTO. USPHS grantee, 1960-82. Mem. AAAS, AAUP, Am. Soc. Biol. Chemistry, Am. Chem. Soc., Am. Assn. Cancer Rsch., Phila. Cancer Club, Vet. Oncology Soc., Am. Assn. Vet. Educators, Phila. Biochemists Club (pres.), U.S. Fedn. Sci. Scholars (exec. bd.), World Fedn. Sci. Workers (exec. com.). Office: 3900 Ford Rd Apt PH-P Philadelphia PA 19131

RUTSALA, VERN A., poet, English language educator, writer; b. Feb. 5, 1934; s. Ray Edwin and Virginia Mae (Brady) R.; m. Joan Merle Colby, Apr. 6, 1957; children: Matthew, David, Kirsten. BA, Reed Coll., 1956; MFA, U. Iowa, 1960. Instr. Lewis and Clark Coll., Portland, 1961-64, asst. prof., 1964-69, assoc. prof., 1969-76, prof., 1976—; vis. prof. U. Minn., Mpls., 1968-69, Bowling Green (Ohio) State U., 1970; writer-in-residence U. Idaho, Moscow, 1988, Redlands (Calif.) U., 1979; chair English dept. Lewis and Clark, Portland, 1986-89. Author: The Window, 1964, Laments, 1975, The Journey Begins, 1976, Paragraphs, 1978, Walking Home from the Icehouse, 1981, Backtracking, 1985, Ruined Cities, 1987, Selected Poems, 1991, Little-Known Sports, 1994. With U.S. Army, 1956-58. GUggenheim Found. fellow, 1982-83, NEA fellow, 1975, 79, Masters fellow Oreg. Arts Commn., 1990; recipient Carolyn Kizer prize Western Oreg. State Coll., 1988, N.W. Poets prize N.W. Rev., 1975, Hazel Hall award Oreg. Inst. Lit. Arts, 1992, Juniper prize U. Mass. Press, 1993, Duncan Lawrie prize Arvon Found., 1994. Mem. AAUP, AWP, PEN, Poetry Soc. Am. Avocations: drawing, painting, watching the ocean, sports. Office: Lewis and Clark Coll Dept English Portland OR 97212

RUTSTEIN, STANLEY HAROLD, apparel retailing company executive; b. Wilkes-Barre, Pa., July 1, 1941; s. Sydney D. and Bessie H. (Cohen) R.; m. Jo Ella Rutstein; children—Wendy Sue, Michael Scott, Lynne Elizabeth. Student, Wilkes Coll., 1959-61; grad., Advanced Mgmt. Program, Harvard U., 1975. Buyer Barbara Lynn Stores, Inc., N.Y.C., 1961-63; buyer, then mdsg. mgr. Casual Corner div. U.S. Shoe Corp., Enfield, Conn., 1963-71; pres. Casual Corner div. U.S. Shoe Corp., 1971-76; pres., cons., dir. U.S. Shoe Corp., Cin., 1976-79; pres. Commonwealth Trading, Inc., Stoughton, Mass., 1979-85, Chadwick's of Boston Ltd., 1983-85; cons. Commonwealth Trading, Inc., 1985—; pres. Trim Trends, Inc., Boston, 1986-87, chmn., 1987-91; chmn., chief exec. officer, pres. Narragansett Clothing Co., Tiverton, R.I., 1987-90, also bd. dirs.; bd. dirs. Reynolds Bros. Inc., 1989-95; pres., chief exec. officer S/J Designs Inc.;, 1989—; pres., chief exec. officer DBA, Northeast Knitters; bd. dirs. The Icing, Inc., Sycamore Shops, Inc. Bd. dirs. Ptnrs. for Disabled Youth, 1992. Mem. Young Pres. Orgn. Home: 18 Charles River Sq Boston MA 02114-3266 Office: 560 Harrison Ave Boston MA 02118-2436

RUTTAN, VERNON WESLEY, agricultural economist; b. Alden, Mich., Aug. 16, 1924; s. Ward W. and Marjorie Ann (Chaney) R.; m. Marilyn M. Barone, July 30, 1945; children: Lia Marie, Christopher, Alison Elaine, Lore Megan. BA, Yale U., 1948; MA, U. Chgo., 1950, PhD, 1952; LLD (hon.), Rutgers U., 1978; D Agrl. Sci. ((hon.), U. Kiel, Germany, 1986, Purdue U., 1991. Economist TVA, 1951-54; prof. agrl. econs. Purdue U., 1954-63; staff economist President's Council Econ. Advisers, 1961-63; economist Rockefeller Found., 1963-65; head dept. agrl. econs. U. Minn., St. Paul, 1965-70, Regent's prof., 1986—; pres. Agrl. Devel. Council, N.Y.C., 1973-77. Author: (with Y. Hayami) Agricultural Development: An International Perspective, 1971, 85, Agricultural Research Policy, 1982, Aid and Development, 1989, Agriculture, Environment and Health, 1994, U.S. Development Assistance Policy, 1996. Recipient Alexander von Humboldt award, 1985. Fellow AAAS, Am. Acad. Arts and Scis., Am. Agrl. Econs. Assn. (pres. 1971-72, Publ. award 1956, 57, 62, 66, 67, 71, 79, 85); mem. NAS. Home: 2381 Commonwealth Ave Saint Paul MN 55108-1605 Office: Dept Applied Econs U Minn Saint Paul MN 55108

RUTTENBERG, CHARLES BYRON, lawyer; b. Reading, Pa., Nov. 16, 1922; s. Abraham David and Mollie Belle (Rabinowitz) R.; m. Arden Honore Suk, July 29, 1955; children—Victoria Arden, Valerie Honore, Alexandra Anne. B.A., U. Va., 1946; LL.B., U. Pa., 1949. Bar: D.C. With Covington & Burling, Washington; gen. counsel NSF, Washington, Nat. Found. Arts and Humanities, Washington, 1949-69; ptnr. Arent, Fox, Kintner, Plotkin & Kahn, Washington, 1969—; chmn. Legis. Bur., mem. exec. com., bd. dirs., gen. counsel Greater Washington Bd. of Trade, 1983-92. Co-chmn. U. Pa. Law Sch. Alumni Fund, Washington, 1983-91, chmn. lawyers com. D.C. Commn. on Arts, 1972-75; gen. counsel People to People Music Program, Washington, 1970-91; trustee, gen. counsel Wolf Trap Found. Performing Arts, Vienna, Va., 1981-91, Nat. Inst. Music Theatre, Washington, 1969-90; bd. dirs. Washington Area Lawyers for Arts, 1984-95, Greater Washington Rsch. Ctr., Washington, 1980-95; trustee U. D.C., 1990-94; bd. dirs., v.p. Cosmos Club Hist. Preservation Found., 1987—. With USAAF, 1942-46, capt. USAFR, 1946-55. Recipient Outstanding Service awards U.S. Govt., 1967, 68. Mem. ABA, U. Pa. Law Alumni Assn. (pres. 1967-71, bd. dirs. 1967-78), Arts Internat. (gen. counsel), Phi Beta Kappa. Clubs: Cosmos, St. Alban's, Mitchell Law, Washington Athletic (bd. govs. 1969-74). Home: 4735 Butterworth Pl NW Washington DC 20016-4459 Office: Arent Fox Kintner Plotkin & Kahn 1050 Connecticut Ave NW Washington DC 20036

RUTTENBERG, FRANK Z., lawyer; b. San Antonio, June 4, 1954. BBA, U. Tex., 1976; JD, St. Mary's U., 1979; LLM in Taxation, NYU, 1982. Bar: Tex. 1979. Lawyer Wells Pinckney & McHugh, P.C., San Antonio. Office: Wells Pinckney & McHugh One Alamo Ctr 106 S Saint Marys St Ste 800 San Antonio TX 78205-3692

RUTTENBERG, HAROLD JOSEPH, manufacturing executive; b. St. Paul, May 22, 1914; s. Charles H. and Fannie R. (Weinstein) R.; m. Katherine Monori, Sept. 23, 1936; children: Charles L. (dec.), James E., Edward F., Ellen Ruttenberg Rabin. B.A., U. Pitts., 1935. Research dir. United Steelworkers Am., 1936-46; asst. dir. steel div. WPB, 1942-44; exec. v.p. Portsmouth Steel Co., Ohio, 1946-49; pres. Harkit Corp., Pitts., 1949-51; pres., chmn. bd. Stardrill-Keystone Co., Beaver Falls, Pa., 1951-59; mng. dir. Humanation Assos., Pitts., 1959-64; chmn. bd., pres. United Steel & Wire Co., Battle Creek, Mich., 1964-68; chmn. Rehovoth Instruments Co., Israel, 1968-78; chmn. bd., pres. AVM Corp. (name changed to Am. Locker Group Inc. 1985), Pitts., from 1973, now chmn. bd., chief exec. officer, treas.; chmn., treas. Rollform of Jamestown (N.Y.), Inc. Author: (with C.S. Golden) Dynamics of Industrial Democracy, 1942, Self-Developing America, 1960. Democrat. Jewish. Home: 307 S Dithridge St Apt 814 Pittsburgh PA 15213-3519 Office: 300 S Craig St Pittsburgh PA 15213-3707

RUTTENBERG, STANLEY HARVEY, economist; b. St. Paul, Mar. 19, 1917; s. Charles and Fannie (Weinstein) R.; m. Gertrude Bernstein, Nov. 28, 1940; children: Joel, Ruth, Charles. Student, Massanutten Mil. Acad., Woodstock, Va., 1929-33; B.S., U. Pitts., 1937. Asst. to dir. Hull House, Chgo., 1938-39; with CIO, 1937-55; organizer and field rep. in Ohio Valley CIO, Cin., 1937-38; assoc. dir. research CIO, Washington, 1939-48; dir. dept. edn. and research CIO, 1948-55; dir. dept. research AFL-CIO, 1955-62; spl. asst. to sec. of labor, 1963-65, manpower adminstr., 1965-69, asst. sec. labor, manpower adminstr., 1966-69; pres. Stanley H. Ruttenberg Assos. Inc., 1969-82; chmn. bd. RFK & A, Inc., 1982—; bd. dirs. Nat. Planning Assn.; dir. Nat. Bur. Econ. Res., 1940-41, 48-62; exec. com. U.S. nat. commn. UNESCO, 1948-53, vice chmn., 1952; spl. adviser to (Am. del. 4th and 5th Internat. Confs.), 1949, 50; del. to Internat. Labor Orgn. Conf., Geneva, 1952; dir. Resources for the Future, Inc., 1952-79; pub. mem. Fgn. Service Selection Bd., 1950; mem. Presdl. Price Adv. Com., 1979-80. Author: (with Jocelyn Gutchess) Manpower Challenge of the 1970s: Institutions and Social Change, 1970, The Federal-State Employment Service: A Critique, 1970. Served as 1st lt. AUS, 1943-46, PTO. Mem. Am. Econ. Assn., Am. Statis. Assn., Indsl. Relations Research Assn. (exec. bd. 1953). Home: 6310 Maiden Ln Bethesda MD 20817-5610 Office: 1211 Connecticut Ave NW Washington DC 20036

RUTTER, ELIZABETH JANE, consulting firm executive; b. Lansing, Mich., June 27, 1955; d. Robert Emmett and Anna Lou (Edwards) Martin; m. David Bruce Rutter, June 25, 1988; children: Robert Corey Myers, Jacob Martin Myers, Laura June Rutter. Student, Harrisburg Area C.C., Pa., 1975-76, U. Mo., 1990-91, Stephens Coll., 1995—. Exec. sec. Timeter Instrument, Inc., Lancaster, Pa., 1983-85; editorial asst. U. Extension, Columbia, Mo., 1985-88; grants/contracts specialist U. Mo. Office of Sponsored Programs, Columbia, Mo., 1988-91; pres. Grants Link, Inc., Columbia, Mo., 1991—; mem. Econ. Devel. Com. Ashland (Mo.) C. of C., 1991-93; mem Columbia (Mo.) C. of C., 1991—; chair Adminstrn. Commn. Sacred Heart Cath. Ch., Columbia, Mo., 1996; officer Exec. Bd. Advent Enterprises, Inc., Columbia, Mo., 1992-95. Editor: Corporate Funders Operating in Missouri, 1992, 3d edit., 1996, The Funding Connection Newsletter, 1994, Right on The Money Newsletter, 1994, Corporate Funders Operating in Texas, 1996, Corporate Funders Operating in Illinois, 1996. Named Small Svc. Bus. of Yr. Columbia C. of C., 1994, Vol. of Yr., Advent Enterprises, Inc., 1997. Mem. Nat. Soc. Fund Raising Execs. (chair ctrl. Mo. chpt. 1996). Roman Catholic. Avocations: reading, fishing, camping, children's sports. Office: Grants Link Inc 5650A S Sinclair Rd Columbia MO 65203

RUTTER, FRANCES TOMPSON, publisher; b. Arlington, Mass., Apr. 12, 1920; d. Harold F. and Mildred F. (Wheeler) Tompson; m. John H. Ottemiller, Mar. 24, 1943; children: Joan Tompson, John Tompson; m. William D. Rutter, Oct. 26, 1970. AB magna cum laude, Pembroke Coll., Brown U., 1941; postgrad., Mt. Holyoke Coll., 1942-43. Res. book librarian Brown U., 1941-42; annotator ship's papers John Carter Brown Library, Providence, 1943-44; librarian Sci. Service, Washington, 1944-45; ptnr. Shoe String Press, Hamden, Conn., 1952-58; sec., treas. Shoe String Press, Inc., 1958-68, pres., treas., 1968-80, also bd. dirs.; sec.-treas., dir. Tompson-Malone, Inc., book mfrs., 1967-80; pres., treas., dir. Tompson & Rutter, Inc., 1980-89. V.p. class 1941 Pembroke Coll., 1967-73, 76—, pres., 1973-76, head class agt., 1979-85, bequests and trust chmn., 1979-90, 40th reunion gift com., 1980, co-chair 50th reunion gift com., 1990-91, 55th reunion gift com., 1995-96; spl. projects adv. panel N.H. Commn. on Arts, 1980-84; mem. natural resources com. Grantham, 1980; mem. Grantham Planning Bd., 1981-87, sec., 1981-83, chmn., 1985-87; chmn. Grantham Recycling Com., 1988-89, Grantham Hist. Soc., 1992-96, Habitat for Humanity-Kearsarge/Sunapee chpt., 1989-94; mem. Diocesan Altar Guild Bd., 1990-93, sec., 1991-92; vol. Mary Hitchcock Meml. Hosp. Aux., 1991—; mem. vestry St. Paul's Episc. Ch., 1997—; assoc. Holy Cross Monastery, West Park, N.Y. Mem. Friends of Fernald Libr. of Colby-Sawyer Coll., ACLU (life), LWV (editor newsletter 1987-89), Assoc. Alumni Brown U. (bd. dirs. 1981-83), Nicholas Brown Soc., Pembroke Ctr. Assocs. (coun. 1984-86), Soc. for Preservation N.H. Forests, Episcopal Peace Fellowship, Phi Beta Kappa. Episcopalian. Home: 19 The Gardens White River Junction VT 05001-3344

RUTTER, JEREMY BENTHAM, archaeologist, educator; b. Boston, Mass., June 23, 1946; s. Peter and Nancy Kendall (Comstock) R.; m. Sarah Robbins Herndon, Jan. 31, 1970; children: Benjamin Ryerson, Nicholas Kendall. BA Classics with honors, Haverford Coll., 1967; PhD Classical Archaeology, U. Pa., 1974; MA, Dartmouth Coll., 1993. Vis. asst. prof. dept. classics UCLA, 1975-76, from asst. prof. to prof. dept. classics, 1976—, chmn. dept. classics, 1992—; participant excavations West Germany, 1966, Italy, 1968-69, Greece, 1972, 73-74, 75, 77, 78, 80-81, 84-86, 88-89, 91—. Author: Lerna III: The Pottery of Lerna IV, 1995; excavation com. Am. Sch. Classical Studies at Athens; contbr. numerous articles, reviews to profl. jours. With U.S. Army, 1969-71, Vietnam. Woodrow Wilson fellow, 1967-68; NDEA fellow U. Pa., 1968-69, 71-73; Olivia James Traveling fellow Archeol. Inst. Am., 1974-75; NEH rsch. grantee, 1979-81; travel grantee Am. Coun. Learned Socs., 1982; sr. faculty grantee, 1985-86, 91-92. Mem. Archaeol. Inst. Am. (numerous coms.), Classical Assn. New England, Phi Beta Kappa. Home: 47 Eagle Rdg Lebanon NH 03766-1900 Office: Dept Classics Dartmouth College Hanover NH 03755

RUTTER, MARSHALL ANTHONY, lawyer; b. Pottstown, Pa., Oct. 18, 1931; s. Carroll Lennox and Dorothy (Tagert) R.; m. Winifred Hitz, June 6, 1953 (div. 1970); m. Virginia Ann Hardy, Jan. 30, 1971 (div. 1992); children: Deborah Frances, Gregory Russell, Theodore Thomas; m. Terry Susan Knowles, Dec. 19, 1992. BA, Amherst (Mass.) Coll., 1954; JD, U. Pa., 1959. Bar: Calif 1960. Assoc. O'Melveny & Myers, Los Angeles, 1959-64; assoc. Flint & MacKay, Los Angeles, 1964-67, ptnr., 1967-72; ptnr. Rutter, Hobbs & Davidoff, Los Angeles, 1973—. Gov. The Music Ctr. of L.A. County, 1978-86, 89-92; dir. Music Ctr. Operating Co., 1992-96; bd. dirs. Chorus Am., Phila., 1987-96, pres., 1993-95; bd. dirs., pres. L.A. Master Chorale Assn., 1963-92, chmn. 1992-96; vestryman All Saints Ch., Beverly Hills, Calif., 1983-86, 88-90; bd. dirs. Music Ctr. Operating Co., 1992-96. Mem. ABA, Assn. Bus. Trial Lawyers (bd. dirs. 1980-82), L.A. County Bar Assn., Beverly Hills Bar Assn., Century City Bar Assn., English-Speaking Union (various offices L.A. chpt. 1963-91), L.A. Jr. C. of C. (bd. dirs. 1964-67). Democrat. Episcopalian. Avocations: classical and choral music, tennis, golf. Home: 1045 S Orange Grove Blvd # 10 Pasadena CA 91105 Office: Rutter Hobbs & Davidoff Ste 2700 1900 Avenue Of The Stars Los Angeles CA 90067-4508

RUTTER, MICHAEL LLEWELLYN, child psychiatry educator; b. Brummanna, Lebanon, Aug. 15, 1933; s. Llewellyn Charles and Winifred Olive (Barber) R.; m. Marjorie Heys, Dec. 27, 1958; children: Sheila Carol, Stephen Michael, Christine Ann. MBChB, U. Birmingham, 1955; DPM, U. London, 1961; MD with honors, U. Birmingham, 1963; degree (hon.) U. Leiden, 1985, Catholic U., 1990, U. Birmingham, 1990, U. Edinburgh, 1990, U. Chgo., 1993, U. Minn., 1993, U. Ghent, 1994, U. Jyvaskyla, 1996. Various tng. positions in pediatrics, neurology and internal medicine, 1955-58; registrar then sr. registrar Maudsley Hosp., London, 1958-62; mem. sci. staff MRC Social Psychiatry Research Unit, London, 1962-65; sr. lectr., then reader U. London Inst. Psychiatry, 1966-73, prof. child psychiatry, 1973—, hon. dir. MRC Child Psychiatry unit, 1984—, Social Genetic and Devel. Psychiatry Rsch. Ctr., 1994; Nuffield med. travelling fellow, Albert Einstein Coll. Medicine, N.Y.C., 1961-62; fellow Ctr. for Advanced Study in Behavioral Scis., Stanford, Calif., 1979-80. Author: Helping Troubled Children, 1975; Maternal Deprivation Reassessed, 2nd edit. 1981; (with Henri Giller) Juvenile Delinquency: Trends & Perspectives, 1983, (with Marjorie Rutter) Developing Minds: Challenge and Continuity Accross the Lifespan, 1993; co-editor: Child and Adolescent Psychiatry: Modern Approaches, 3d edit., 1994, Stress, Risk and Resilience In Children and Adolescents: Processes, Mechanisms and Interventions, 1994, Psychosocial Disorders in Young People: Time Trends & Their Causes, 1995; Autism: A Reappraisal of Concepts and Treatment, 1978, Development Through Life: A Handbook For Clinicians, 1994; editor: Scientific Foundations of Developmental Psychiatry, 1980, Developmental Neuropsychiatry, 1983. Belding travelling scholar, 1963; Goulstonian lectr., Royal Coll. Physicians, 1973; Am. Assn. Mental Deficiency rsch. award, 1975; Rock Carling fellow, 1979; Salmon lectr. N.Y. Acad. Medicine, 1979; C. Anderson Aldrich award Am. Acad. Pediatrics, 1981; Adolf Meyer ward lectr. APA, 1985, Disting. Sci. Contbn. award APA, 1995, Castilla del Pino prize for achievement in psychiatry, Spain, 1995; Royal Soc. fellow, 1987. Fellow Royal Soc. Medicine (London, hon.), Royal Coll. Paediatrics and Child Health (hon. founding fellow 1996); mem. AAAS (fgn. hon.), U.S. Nat. Acad. Edn. (fgn. assoc.), Brit. Paediatric Assn. (hon.), Assn. Child Psychology and Psychiatry (chmn. 1973-74), Brit. Psychol. Soc. (hon. fellow), Am. Acad. Child Psychiatry (hon. membership), NAS (fgn. assoc. Inst. Medicine), Soc. Research in Adolescence (John P. Hill award for excellence in theory devel. and rsch. 1992), Soc. Rsch Child Devel. (pres.-elect 1997), Inst. Child Health (London, hon. fellow 1996), Internat. Acad. Rsch. in Learning Disabilities, Academia Europaea (founding mem.), Soc. for Rsch. in Child Devel. (pres.-elect 1997). Home: 190 Court Ln, London SE21 7ED, England Office: Inst Psychiatry, DeCrespigny Park, London SE5 8AF, England

RUTTER, NATHANIEL WESTLUND, geologist, educator; b. Omaha, Nov. 22, 1932; s. John Elliot and Karleen (Ludden) R.; m. Mary Marie Munson, Sept. 11, 1961; children: Todd, Christopher. B.S., Tufts U., 1955; M.S., U. Alaska, 1962; Ph.D., U. Alta., 1965. Geologist Venezuelan Atlantic Refining Co., 1955-58; research scientist Geol. Survey Can., Calgary, Alta., 1965-74; head urban projects sect Geol. Survey Can., Ottawa, Ont., 1974; environ. advisor Nat. Energy Bd., Ottawa, 1974-75; assoc. prof. dept. geology U. Alta., Edmonton, 1975-77, 77-80, prof., chmn. dept., 1980-89, 77-97; pres. Can. nat. com. Internat. Geol. Correlation Program, UNESCO, 1996-97; prof. dept. atmospheric scis. U. Alta. (Can.), Edmonton, 1997—; pres. Internat. Union Quaternary Rsch. Congress, 1982-87; mem. Internat. Geosphere-Biosphere Program: A Study of Global Change, 1988-94; mem. rsch. com. Can. Global Change Program, 1992-94; chmn. global change com. INUQA, 1991-95; hon. prof. Chinese Acad. Sci., Beijing, 1994—; nat. lectr. Sigma Xi, 1995-97; mem. scientific bd. Internat. Union of Geol. Scis.-UNESCO, 1997—. Contbr. numerous articles to profl. jours.; assoc. editor Arctic, Geosci. Can. Quaternary Rsch.; mem. editorial bd. Quaternary Sci. Revs.; editor in chief Quaternary Internat. Grantee Natural Scis. and Engring. Research Council of Can.; grantee Energy, Mines and Resources. Fellow Royal Soc. Can.; mem. Assn. Profl. Engrs., Geologists and Geophysicists of Alta., Internat. Union Quaternary Research (v.p. 1982-87, pres. 1987-91), Can. Quaternary Assn. (v.p. 1981-82, Johnston medal 1997), Geol. Soc. Am. (mgmt. bd. dirs. quaternary geol. and geomorphology div. 1982-84). Clubs: Explorer's, Cosmos. Home: Rural Route 3, Stony Plain, AB Canada T7Z 1X3 Office: Dept Earth & Atmospheric Scis, U Alta, Edmonton, AB Canada T6G 2E3

RUTTINGER, GEORGE DAVID, lawyer; b. Detroit, Jan. 17, 1948; s. George Jacob and Margaret Mary (Smith) R.; m. Camille Ann Larson, Oct. 4, 1975; children: Joseph Charles, David Hayes, Philip George. AB with high distinction and honors, U. Mich., 1970, JD magna cum laude, 1973. Bar: Calif. 1975, D.C. 1975, U.S. Dist. Ct. D.C. 1975, U.S. Dist. Ct. Md. 1987, U.S. Ct. Appeals (D.C. and 4th cirs.) 1984, U.S. Ct. Appeals (1st cir.) 1988, U.S. Supreme Ct. 1984, U.S. Ct. Appeals (6th cir.) 1996. Law clk. to Hon. Malcolm R. Wilkey U.S. Ct. Appeals, Washington, 1973-74; assoc. Latham & Watkins, L.A., 1974; assoc. Crowell & Moring (formerly Jones, Day, Reavis & Pogue), Washington, 1975-79, ptnr., 1980—. Author: (with others) Containing Legal Costs: ADR Strategies for Corporations, Law Firms and Government, 1988; contbr. articles to profl. jours. Office: Crowell & Moring 1001 Pennsylvania Ave NW Washington DC 20004-2505

RUTZ, RICHARD FREDERICK, physicist, researcher; b. Alton, Ill., Feb. 9, 1919; s. Erwin William and Esther Norma (Brooks) R.; m. Mary Lamsom Lambert, June 10, 1945; children—Frederick R., Carl R., William L. BA, Shurtleff Coll., Alton, Ill., 1941; MS, State U. Iowa, 1947. Staff mem. Sandia Corp., Albuquerque, 1948-51; mem. staff, mgr. IBM T.J. Watson Sr. Rsch. Ctr., Yorktown Heights, N.Y., 1951-87. Contbr. articles to profl. jours.; patentee numerous semicond. devices. With U.S. Maritime Svc., 1941-42, USAAF, 1942-46. Fellow IEEE; mem. Am. Phys. Soc. Home: 9 Burgundy Ct Grand Junction CO 81503

RUTZICK, MARK CHARLES, lawyer; b. St. Paul, Sept. 6, 1948; s. Max Arthur and Bertha (Ward) R.; children from a previous marriage: Elizabeth Leslie, Karen Deborah; m. Cynthia Lombardi Jan. 16, 1994. B.A., U. Mich., 1970; J.D., Harvard U., 1973. Bar: N.Y. 1974, U.S. Supreme Ct. 1977, U.S. Ct. Appeals (9th cir.) 1982, Oreg. 1984, Wash. 1987. Spl. asst. corp. counsel N.Y.C. Housing Adminstrn., 1973-75; assoc. Alexander Hammond P.C., N.Y.C., 1975-76; asst. atty. gen. N.Y. State Atty. Gen., N.Y.C., 1976-78; atty. Dept. Justice, Washington, 1978-82, spl. litigation counsel, 1982-83, atty.-in-charge field office, Portland, Oreg., 1983-86; counsel Preston, Thorgrimson, Shidler, Gates & Ellis, Portland, 1986-87, ptnr. 1988-94; shareholder Mark C. Rutzick Law Firm, P.C., 1994-96; ptnr. LeBoeuf, Lamb, Greene & MacRae, L.L.P., Portland, 1996—. Mem. ABA, Oreg. State Bar Assn., Wash. State Bar Assn. Home: 3450 SW Downsview Ter Portland OR 97221-3173 Office: Koin Ctr 500 Pioneer Tower 222 SW Columbia St Ste 1600 Portland OR 97201-6616

RUUD, CLAYTON OLAF, engineering educator; b. Glasgow, Mont., July 31, 1934; s. Asle and Myrtle (Bleken) R.; children: Kelley Astrid, Kirsten Anne; m. Paula Kay Mannino, Feb. 24, 1990. BS in Metallurgy, Wash. State U., 1957; MS in Matl. Sci., San Jose State U., 1967; PhD in Materials Sci., U. Denver, 1970. Registered profl. engr., Calif., Colo. Asst. remelt metallurgist Kaiser Aluminum & Chem. Corp., Trentwood, Wash., 1957-58; devel. engr. Boeing Airplane Co., Seattle, 1958-60; mfg. rsch. engr. Lockheed Missiles & Space Corp., Sunnyvale, Calif., 1960-63; rsch. engr. FMC Corp., San Jose, 1963-67; sr. rsch. scientist U. Denver, 1967-79; prof. indsl. engring. Pa. State U., University Park, 1979—; cons. in field; bd. dirs. Denver X-Ray Inst. Inc., Altoona, Pa. Editor series of books: Advances in X-Ray Analysis, Vol. 12-22, 1970-80, Nondestructive Character of Materials, Vol. 1-6, 1983—; editor X-Ray Spectrometry, 1975-87; editl. com. Nondestructive Testing and Evaluation, 1991—. Mem., chmn. Nat. Acad. Sci. Safe Drinking Water Com., Washington, 1976-78. Recipient IR 100 award, 1983, Gov.'s New Product Award, Pa. Soc. Profl. Engrs., 1988. Mem. ASM Internat. (chmn. Resid. Stress Conf. 1989-91), Internat. Ctr. for Diffraction Data, Soc. Mfg. Engrs., Metall. Soc. of AIME. Achievements include patent on Method for Determining Internal Stresses in Polycrystalline Solids; patent on Stress-Unstressed Standard for X-Ray Stress Analysis; invention of a Fiber Optic Based Position Sensitive Scintillation X-Ray Detector; invention of an instrument for simultaneous stress and phase composition measurement; development of an X-ray diffraction instrument for manufacturing process quality control; founder, developer, and co-director of Pa. State U. quality and manufacturing management masters degree. Office: Pa State U 207 Hammond Bldg University Park PA 16802-1401

RUUD, MILLARD HARRINGTON, former legal association administrator, retired educator; b. Ostrander, Minn., Jan. 7, 1917; s. Mentor L. and Helma M. (Olson) R.; m. Barbara W. Dailey, Aug. 28, 1943; children: Stephen D., Christopher O., Michael L. B.S. in Law, U. Minn., 1942, LL.B., 1947; LL.D., Georgetown U., 1980, U. Pacific, 1981, New Eng. Sch. Law, 1981, Southwestern U., 1983, Widener U., 1987, John Marshall Law Sch., 1987. Bar: Minn. 1947, Tex. 1956. Asst. prof. law U. Kans., Lawrence, 1947-48; assoc. prof. U. Tex., Austin, 1948-52, prof., 1952-78, 80-83, prof. emeritus, 1983—; asst. exec. dir. Tex. Legis. Council, 1950-52; exec. dir. Assn. Am. Law Schs., Washington, 1973-80, 83-87; mem. Tex. Commn. Uniform State Laws, 1967—; cons. legal edn. Am. Bar Assn., 1968-73; chmn. Law Sch. Admission Council, 1966-69, Council on Legal Edn. Opportunity, 1968. Bd. visitors U. Miami, 1980-94, McGeorge Sch. Law, U. of Pacific, 1985-92, U. Minn., 1994—. Recipient Disting. Grad. award U. Minn., 1980. Mem. ABA (Robert J. Kutak award for disting. svc. to legal edn. and profession 1988), Tex. Bar Assn., Am. Law Inst., Order of Coif (nat. sec.-treas. 1981-83). Club: Cosmos. Home: 3416 Foothill Ter Austin TX 78731-5836 Office: U Tex Sch Law 727 E 26th St Austin TX 78705-3224

RUVANE, JOHN AUSTIN, pharmaceutical industry consultant; b. Jersey City, N.J., Nov. 27, 1935; s. Joseph Jerome and Anne Agnes (Sullivan) R.; m. Anne Patricia Beebe, Apr. 13, 1957; children: Anne Julie, Kathleen Kearney Vrabel, Molly Vaughn Kamensky, Alice Regan, John Austin, Susan Sullivan D'Avanzo. A.B. in Econs., Princeton U, 1957; postgrad., NYU, 1958-60. Salesman Ayerst Co., N.Y.C., 1960-65; asst. to v.p. McCann-Erickson Co., N.Y.C., 1965-70; pres., chief exec. officer J.R. Druid-Ruvane-Leverte, N.Y.C., 1970-83; chmn., bd. dirs. Bozell & Jacobs Co., N.Y.C., 1983-85; pres. JARCOM Inc., N.Y.C., 1985—; bd. dirs. Pharm. Advt. Coun., N.Y.C., 1974-86, pres., 1983; mem. adv. coun. Health Care Expo, N.Y.C., 1984-88. Contbr. articles to profl. jours., newsletter. mem. fin. coun. St. Rose of Lima Parish Coun., Short Hills, N.J., 1974-76; chmn., interviewer Princeton Schs. & Scholarship Commn., Short Hills; jazz pianist, choral singer Univ. Glee Club N.Y.C.; pres., bd. dirs. Buck Hill Lot and Cottage Assn., Buck Hills Falls, Pa., 1988-94. Recipient numerous advt. awards. Mem. Pharm. Advt. Council (pres. 1983), Med. Advt. Agy. Assn. Republican. Roman Catholic. Clubs: Princeton (N.Y.C.); Canoe Brook Country (committeeman 1980-87, Summit, N.J.), Buck Hill Golf Club. Avocations: music; golf. Home: PO Box 275 64 Hemlock Ln Buck Hill Falls PA 18323 Office: Jarcom Inc 304 Park Ave S New York NY 10010-5339

RUWE, ROBERT P., federal judge; b. 1941. Grad., Xavier U., 1963; JD, No. Ky. U., 1970. Chief counsel IRS Dept. Treasury, 1970-87; judge U.S. Tax Ct., Washington, 1987—. Office: US Tax Ct 400 2nd St NW Washington DC 20217-0001*

RUXIN, PAUL THEODORE, lawyer; b. Cleve., Apr. 14, 1943; s. Charles and Olyn Judith (Koller) R.; m. Joanne Camy, May 25, 1965; children: Marc J., Sarah. BA, Amherst Coll., 1965; LLB, U. Va., 1968. Bar: Ill. 1968, Ohio 1977, U.S. Dist. Ct. (no. dist.) Ill. 1968, U.S. Ct. Appeals D.C. 1972. Assoc. Isham, Lincoln & Beale, Chgo., 1968-73, ptnr., 1974-77; ptnr., chmn. energy utilities sect. Jones, Day, Reavis & Pogue, Cleve., 1977—. Mem. Hudson Archtl. and Hist. Bd. Rev., 1981-91; exec. bd. Greater Cleve. Boy Scouts Am., 1978-90; bd. dirs. ARC Cleveland Chpt., 1991—. Mem. ABA, Ohio State Bar Assn. (pub. utilities sect.), Bar Assn. Greater Cleve., Fed. Energy Bar Assn. (com. chmn. 1981), Chgo. Bar Assn., Western Res. Hist. Soc. (collections com. Chgo. chpt.), Club at Soc. Ctr., Rowfant Club, Chgo. Club. Office: Jones Day Reavis & Pogue 77 W Wacker Dr Chicago IL 60601 also: 901 Lakeside Ave Cleveland OH 44114

RUYTER, NANCY LEE CHALFA, dance educator; b. Phila., May 23, 1933; d. Andrew Benedict Chalfa and Lois Elizabeth (Strode) McClary; m. Ralph Markson (div.); m. Hans C. Ruyter, Dec. 7, 1968. BA in History, U. Calif., Riverside, 1964; PhD in History, Claremont Grad. Sch., 1970. Tchr. theater dept. Pomona Coll., 1965-72; instr. dance program U. Calif., Riverside, 1972-76, acting chair dance program, 1974-75; instr. dance dept. UCLA, 1976; instr. phys. edn. dept. Orange Coast Coll., 1976-77; asst. prof. dept. phys. edn. and dance Tufts U., 1977-78; asst. prof. phys. edn. dept. Calif. State U., Northridge, 1978-82; asst. prof., then assoc. prof. dance dept. U. Calif., Irvine, 1982—, assoc. dean Sch. Fine Arts, 1984-88, 95-96, chair dept. dance, 1989-91; presenter in field. Appeared with Jasna Planina Folk Ensemble, 1972-77, 78-79, Di Falco and Co., 1955-57; choreographer, dir. numerous coll. dance prodns.; contbr. articles, revs. to profl. publs.; author: Reformers and Visionaries: The Americanization of the Art of Dance, 1979. Mem. Am. Soc. Theatre Rsch., Bulgarian Studies Assn., Congress on Rsch. in Dance (bd. dirs. 1977-80, pres. 1981-85), Folk Dance Fedn., Internat. Fedn. Theatre Rsch., Soc. Dance Rsch., Soc. Ethnomusicology, Soc. Dance History Scholars (steering com. 1980-81), Spanish Dance Soc., Theatre Libr. Assn. Office: U Calif-Irvine Dept Dance Irvine CA 92697

RYALL, JO-ELLYN M., psychiatrist; b. Newark, May 25, 1949; d. Joseph P. and Tekla (Paraszczuk) R.; BA in Chemistry with gen. honors, Douglass Coll., Rutgers U., 1971; MD, Washington U., St. Louis, 1975. Diplomate Am. Bd. Psychiatry and Neurology. Resident in psychiatry Washington U.,

1975-78, psychiatrist Student Health, 1980-84, clin. instr. psychiatry, 1978-83, clin. asst. prof. psychiatry, 1983—; inpatient supr. Malcolm Bliss Mental Health Ctr., St. Louis, 1978-80, psychiatrist outpatient clinic, 1980-82; pvt. practice medicine specializing in psychiatry, St. Louis, 1980—. Bd. dirs. Women's Self Help Ctr., St. Louis, 1980-83. Fellow APA, Soc. (pres. Ea. Mo. Dist. Br. 1983-85, sect. coun. AMA 1986—, dep. rep. to assembly 1994—); mem. AMA (alt. del. Mo. 1988-90, 93-94, del. 1995—), Am. Med. Women's Assn. (pres. St. Louis Dist. br. 1981-82, 92, regional gov. VIII 1986-89, spkr. house of dels., 1993-96), St. Louis Met. Med. Soc. (del. to state conv. 1981-86, 93—, councilor 1985-87, v.p. 1989), Mo. State Med. Assn. (vice speaker ho. of dels. 1986-89, speaker 1989-92), Manic Depressive Assn. St. Louis (chmn. bd. dirs. 1985-89), Washington U. Faculty Club. Office: 9216 Clayton Rd Saint Louis MO 63124-1560

RYALS, CLYDE DE LOACHE, humanities educator; b. Atlanta, Dec. 19, 1928; s. Chester A. and Ruth C. (de Loache) R.; m. Hildegard Thun Scheffey Ellerkmann, Sept. 4, 1971. A.B., Emory U., 1947, M.A., 1949; Ph.D., U. Pa., 1957. Instr. U. Md., 1956-57; instr. U. Pa., Phila., 1957-60; asst. prof. U. Pa., 1960-64, assoc. prof., 1964-69, prof. English, 1969-73, grad. chmn. dept. English, 1969-72; prof. English Duke U., Durham, N.C., 1973—, chmn. dept., 1979-82; exec. dir. Carlyle Letters Project, 1980—; mem. Christian Gauss Award Com., 1989-91. Author: Theme and Symbol in Tennyson's Poetry to 1850, 1964, From the Great Deep, 1967, Browning's Later Poetry, 1871-1889, 1975, Becoming Browning: The Poems and Plays of Robert Browning, 1833-46, 1983, A World of Possibilities: Romantic Irony in Victorian Literature, 1990, The Life of Robert Browning: A Critical Biography, 1993, paperback edit. 1996; editor: Tennyson's Poems, Chiefly Lyrical, 1966, Mrs. Humphry Ward's Robert Elsmere, 1967, Nineteenth-Century Literary Perspectives, 1974, The Collected Letters of Thomas and Jane Welsh Carlyle, 1980—; mem. editl. bd.: Victorian Poetry, 1964—, South Atlantic Quar., 1975-87, Nineteenth Century Lit., 1986-96, Studies in Browning and His Circle, 1987—, Jour. Narrative Lit., 1986-90, South Atlantic Rev., 1988-90, The Carlyle Ann., 1989-93, Carlyle Studies Ann. 1993—, Victorian Literature and Culture, 1991—; contbr. articles to profl. jours. Guggenheim fellow, 1972-73; fellow Beinecke Libr., Yale U., 1994; recipient Pa. Tchg. award 1964. Mem. MLA, Am. Soc. for Aesthetics, Century Assn. N.Y., Chi Phi. Democrat. Episcopalian. Home: 1620 University Dr Durham NC 27707-1629

RYAN, ALLAN ANDREW, JR., lawyer, author, lecturer; b. Cambridge, Mass., July 3, 1945; s. Allan Andrew and Anne (Conway) R.; m. Nancy Foote, June 30, 1978; children: Elisabeth, Andrew. AB, Dartmouth Coll., 1966; JD magna cum laude, U. Minn., 1970. Bar: D.C. 1972, Mass. 1985. Law clk. to assoc. justice Byron R. White U.S. Supreme Ct., 1970-71; assoc. Williams, Connolly & Califano, Washington, 1974-77; asst. to Solicitor Gen. U.S., Washington, 1977-80; dir. office of spl. investigations, Dept. Justice, Washington, 1980-83, spl. asst. to atty. gen., 1983; pvt. practice law, 1983-85; with office of gen. counsel, Harvard U., 1985—; presenting counsel Internat. Commn. Inquiry on Kurt Waldheim, London, 1988; adj. prof. Law Sch., Boston Coll., 1989—. Author: Quiet Neighbors: Prosecuting Nazi War Criminals in America, 1984. pres., editor-in-chief: Minn. Law Rev., 1969-70. Mem. adv. bd. holocaust and human rights rsch. project Boston Coll. Law Sch., 1984—; bd. dirs. Facing History and Ourselves Nat. Found., 1985-92; mem. exec. com. New Eng. region Anti-Defamation League, 1990—. Capt. USMC, 1971-74. Recipient Internat. Human Rights award B'nai B'rith, 1986. Mem. ABA, Boston Bar Assn. Office: Harvard U Office Gen Counsel 1350 Massachusetts Ave Ste 980 Cambridge MA 02138-3846

RYAN, ALLAN JAMES, publishing executive, editor; b. Bklyn., Dec. 9, 1915; s. Lorne McDonnell and Valerie (Britton) R.; m. Agnes Louise Nelson, July 4, 1942; children: Brendan Michael, James Allan, Robert Edward. BA, Yale U., 1936; MD, Columbia U., 1940; D in Sports Sci., U.S. Sports Acad., 1983. Diplomate Am. Bd. Gen. Surgery. Intern in gen. surgery Kings County Hosp., Bklyn., 1940-42, research fellow surgery, 1942-43; asst. resident surgery Grace New Haven (Conn.) Hosp., 1943-45; chief resident surgery Long Island (N.Y.) Coll. Hosp., Bklyn., 1945-46; attending surgeon Meriden (Conn.) Hosp., 1947-1965; assoc. prof. U. Wis., Madison, 1965-70; prof. U. Wis., 1970-76; editor-in-chief Postgrad. Medicine, Mpls., 1976-79, The Physician & Sports Medicine, Mpls., 1973-85; dir. Sports Medicine Enterprise, Edina, Minn., 1985-95; editor-in-chief Fitness in Bus. mag., 1986-90; athletic teams physician U. Wis., Madison, 1965-76. Author: Medical Care of Athlete, 1962, Guide to Running, 1980; co-author: The Healthy Dancer's Complete Guide to Health Care, 1989; editor: Sports Medicine, 1974, Dance Medicine, 1986; co-editor: Sports Medicine, 2d edit., 1989, The Healthy Dancer, 1989. Mem. Commn. Mil. Accidents, Washington, 1964-69; med. examiner City of Meriden, 1947-65; trustee U.S. Sports Academy, Mobile, 1985-87; mem. Minn. Gov.'s Coun. on Phys. Fitness and Sports, 1986—. Recipient Silver Medal award City of Paris, 1983, Nat. Phys. Fitness Leadership award Jr. C. of C., 1971. Fellow Am. Coll. Sports Medicine (pres. 1963—), Am. Orthopaedic Soc. Sports Medicine (assoc.); mem. Am. Alliance Health, Phys. Edn. Recreation and Dance, Council Phys. Fitness and Sports (cons., pres. 1960—), AMA (commn. on med. aspects of athletics), Internat. Fedn. Sports Medicine (sec. gen. 1980-86), Phi Beta Kappa, Sigma Xi. Republican. Roman Catholic. Avocations: racing bicycles, attending veterans classification. Office: 5800 Jeff Pl Edina MN 55436-1938

RYAN, ARTHUR FREDERICK, insurance company executive; b. Bklyn., Sept. 14, 1942; s. Arthur Vincent and Gertrude (Wingert) R.; m. Patricia Elizabeth Kelly; children: Arthur, Kelly Ann, Kevin, Kathleen. BA in Math., Providence Coll., 1963. Area mgr. Data Corp., Washington, 1965-72; project mgr. Chase Manhattan Corp. and Bank, N.Y.C., 1972-73, 2d v.p., 1973-74, v.p., 1974-75, from 1978, former ops. exec., from 1978, former exec. v.p., from 1982, former vice-chmn., then pres., chief operating officer, 1990-94; chmn., CEO Prudential Ins. Co. Am., Newark, N.J., 1994—; mem. policy and planning com.; bd. dirs., chmn. audit com. Depository Trust Co.; past mem. exec. com., Cedel (European Depository); past chmn. steering com., program mgr. CHIPS Same Day Settlement, N.Y. Clearing House. Past bd. dirs. Urban Acad. N.Y.C. Lt. U.S. Army, 1963-65. Mem. Am. Bankers Assn. (vice chmn. ops. and automation div. and govt. rels. coun., past chmn. internat. ops. com.). Home: 144 The Helm East Islip NY 11730-2918 Office: Prudential Ins Co Am 751 Broad St Newark NJ 07102-3777*

RYAN, BARBARA DIANE, management information systems director; b. Phila., Nov. 3, 1950; d. Joseph Wayne and Elsie Elaine (Schafer) Hart; m. Dennis M. Ryan, Mar. 20, 1976; 1 child, Christine Susan. BA in Math., Eastern Coll., St. Davids, Pa., 1972. Computer programmer H. F. Michel, King of Prussia, Pa., 1972-73, L. P. Muller, King of Prussia, 1973-77, Hajoca Corp., Ardmore, Pa., 1977-78; MIS dir. Hajoca Corp., Ardmore, 1978—; pvt. practice installing, setting up and tng. for home personal computers, 1991—. Vol. chmn. publicity com. Trinity Luth. Ch., 1985-87, supt. Sunday sch., 1986-88, vol. Sunday sch. tchr., 1988-91, chmn. staff support Cong. Coun. 1988-91, v.p. Congl. Coun., 1991-92, sec. Congl. Coun., 1992-94, chmn. Evangelism, 1992-94, mem. 1995-96, co-chmn. fall holiday bazaar, 1994, fin. rec. sec., 1995—, intern com. mem., 1996—; mem. Haverford Band & Orch. Parents, 1994—, treas., 1994—, Haverford Parent's Assn. of Women's Sports, 1994—; mem. prom com. Haverford PTO, 1996—. Mem. Llanerch Civic Assn., Coll. Alumni Assn. Republican. Avocations: cooking, gardening, traveling, walking on the beach. Office: Hajoca Corp 127 Coulter Ave Ardmore PA 19003-2410

RYAN, CARL RAY, electrical engineer; b. Gateway, Ark., Mar. 3, 1938; s. Clarence and Stella (Schnitzer) R.; m. Arline Walker; children: Carline, Julie. BSEE, U. Ark., 1962; MSEE, Iowa State U., 1963; PhD in Elec. Engring., U. Mo.-Rolla, 1969, profl. degree Elec. Engring., 1994. Instr. U. Mo.-Rolla, 1968-69; sr. engr. Govt. Electronics Group, Motorola Inc., Scottsdale, Ariz., 1969-72, mem. tech. staff, 1972-76, sr. mem. tech. staff, chief engr., 1979-89, v.p. tech. staff, 1989-90, dir. communication systems tech., 1990—; prof. Mich. Tech. U., 1976-79; adj. prof. Ariz. State U., Tempe, 1980-89; panel mem. Internat. Solid States Circuits Conf., Phila., 1977; session chmn. Future Space Communications Tech. Workshop, Pasadena, Calif., 1980; external advisor Mich. Technol. U. Contbr. articles to profl. jours.; patentee in field. Assoc. Motorola Sci. Adv. Bd. Served with USAF, 1956-60. Fellow IEEE (communications tech., solid state circuits, accreditation com., Dan Nobel fellow, chmn. Phoenix chpt. 1981-82, program chmn. 1989, gen. chmn. Phoenix Conf. on computers and communication 1988).

RYAN, CHARLOTTE MURIEL, oncology nurse; b. Beedeville, Ark., Sept. 2, 1939; d. Eugene Sanford and Edith Elizabeth (Goforth) Breckenridge; children: Russell Kent, Cary Randall, Molly Renee. BSN cum laude, Calif. State U., Fresno, 1991, MSN, 1997. OCN cert. nurse. Psychiat. technician Porterville (Calif.) State Hosp., 1959-67; tchr. developmentally disabled Ariz. Tng. Ctr., Coolidge, 1967-71; Montessori tchr. Tucson, 1972-77; tchr. developmentally disabled Heartland Opportunity Ctr., Madera, Calif., 1977-79; med. office mgr. office of orthopedic surgeon, Madera, 1979-83, office mgr., x-ray technician, 1983-87; staff nurse in oncology St. Agnes Med. Ctr., Fresno, 1991—; instr. nursing dept. Calif. State U., Fresno, 1992, 93, 95. Treas. Hospice of Madera County, 1990-92, bd. dirs., 1992; peer counselor Calif. State U., Fresno, 1989-91; pres. bd. dirs. Easter Seals Soc., Madera, 1981. Mem. Oncology Nursing Soc., Nightingale Soc., Golden Key, Sigma Theta Tau (chair pub. com., editor MUNEWS newsletter 1994-95). Republican. Avocations: reading, improving quality of life for cancer patients. Home: 4544 N Barton Ave Fresno CA 93726-2621 Office: Saint Agnes Med Ctr 1303 E Herndon Ave Fresno CA 93720-3309

RYAN, CLARENCE AUGUSTINE, JR., biochemistry educator; b. Butte, Mont., Sept. 29, 1931; s. Clarence A. Sr. and Agnes L. (Duckham) R.; m. Patricia Louise Meunier, Feb. 8, 1936; children: Jamie Arlette, Steven Michael (dec.), Janice Marie, Joseph Patrick (dec.). BA in Chemistry, Carroll Coll., 1953; MS in Chemistry, Mont. State U., 1956, PhD in Chemistry, 1959. Postdoctoral fellow in biochemistry Oreg. State U., Corvallis, 1959-61, U.S. Western Regional Lab., Albany, Calif., 1961-63; chemist U.S. Western Regional Lab., Berkeley, Calif., 1963-64; asst. prof. biochemistry Wash. State U., Pullman, 1964-68, assoc. prof., 1968-72, prof., 1972—, Charlotte Y. Martin disting. prof., 1991—, chmn. dept. agrl. chemistry, 1977-80, fellow Inst. Biol. Chemistry, 1980—; faculty athletics rep. to PAC-10 & NCAA Wash. State U., 1991-94, 96-97; vis. scientist dept. biochemistry U. Wash., 1981, Harvard U. Med. Sch., 1982, Bert and Natalie Vallee vis. prof., 1997; res. adv. bd. Kemin Industries, Des Moines, 1981—, Plant Genetics, Davis, Calif., 1987-89; research adv. bd. Frito-Lay, Inc., Dallas, 1982, Plant Genetic Engring. Lab., N.M. State U., Las Cruces, 1986-89, Noble Found., 1996—; mem. NRC rev. bd. Plant Gene Exptl. Ctr., Albany, Calif., 1990-93; mgr. biol. stress program USDA Competitve Grants Program, Washington, 1983-84; former mem. adv. panels for H. McKnight Found., Internat. Potato Ctr., Lima, Peru, Internat. Ctr. Genetic Engring. and Biotech., New Delhi, Internat. Ctr. Tropical Agr., Cali, Columbia, Internat. Tropical Agr., Ibandan, Africa; mem. grant rev. panels NSF, USDA, DOE, NIH; co-organizer Internat. Telecommunications Symposium on Plant Biotech.; mem. adv. bd. Bert and Natalie Vallee Found., Harvard Med. Sch., 1997—. Mem. edit. bd. several biochem. and plant physiology jours.; contbr. articles to profl. publs., chpts. to books; co-editor 2 books. Grantee USDA, NSF, NIH, Rockefeller Found., McKnight Found.; recipient Merck award for grad. rsch. Mont. State U., 1959, career devel. awards NIH, 1964-74, Alumni Achievement award Carroll Coll., 1986, Pres.'s Faculty Excellence award in rsch. Wash. State U., 1986; named to Carroll Coll. Alumni Hall of Fame, 1981, Carroll Coll. Basketball Hall of Fame, 1982; non-resident fellow Noble Found., 1996—. Mem. AAAS, Nat. Acad. Scis. (elected 1986), Am. Chem. Soc. (Kenneth A. Spencer award 1992), Am. Soc. Plant Physiologists (Steven Hales Prize 1992), Am. Soc. Exptl. Biology, Biochem. Soc., Internat. Soc. Chem. Ecology (Silverstein-Simione award 1997), Internat. Soc. Plant Molecular Biology (bd. dirs.), Phytochem. Soc. N.Am., Nat. U. Continuing Assn. (Creative Programming award 1991), Phi Kappa Phi (Recognition award 1976, selected 1 of 100 centennial disting. alumni Mont. State U. 1993). Democrat. Avocations: fishing, basketball, golf. Office: Wash State Univ Inst Biol Chemistry Pullman WA 99164

RYAN, CORNELIUS O'BRIEN, lawyer; b. Abilene, Tex., Oct. 15, 1917; s. William Cornelius and Joanna Genevieve (Morris) R.; m. Mary Anne Kelley, Mar. 24, 1942; children: Elisabeth Ryan Goldstein, Robert C., Carl E., William E., Joseph W., Mary Louise Ryan Ray. BA, Rice U., 1937; LLB, So. Meth. U., 1940. Bar: Tex. 1940. Mem. firm Kelley & Ryan, Houston, 1951-97, 1951-97; pres., dir. The Burkitt Found., 1997—; v.p., gen. counsel Tex. United Corp., 1982-88. Bd. dirs. Am. Irish Found., 1977-90, hon. life trustee, 1990—. Lt. USNR, 1942-46. Decorated knight grand cross Order Holy Sepulchre Knight of Malta. Mem. Am., Houston bar assns., Tex. State Bar, Am. Judicature Soc., Phi Beta Kappa, Phi Delta Theta, Phi Alpha Delta. Republican. Roman Catholic. Clubs: Houston (Houston), Serra (Houston). Home: 3107 Newcastle Dr Houston TX 77027-5507 Office: 5311 Kirby Dr Ste 102 Houston TX 77005-1315

RYAN, DANIEL JOHN, university administrator; b. Buffalo, June 5, 1960; s. Michael E. and Joan F. (Walther) R.; m. Sandra Suffoleto, Aug. 19, 1989. BA in Pol. Sci., Canisius Coll., Buffalo, 1982, MS in Edn., 1992; PhD in Edn., SUNY, Buffalo, 1997. Fin. cons. First Albany Corp., Buffalo, 1982-84; confidential investigator County of Erie, Buffalo, 1984-87; econ. mkt. analyst City of Buffalo, Buffalo, 1987-90; asst. dir. career planning Canisius Coll., Buffalo, 1990—, asst. to dean students svcs.; lectr. Buffalo and Erie County Pub. Libr., Buffalo, 1990—. Pres. Univ. Dist. N. Buffalo Civic Assn., Buffalo, 1990-91; v.p. Kiwanis Club of N. Buffalo, 1987-88; vice chmn. City of Buffalo rep. Com., 1989-91, sec. 1993—; chmn. Delaware Ward Rep. Com., 1985-91. Mem. Nat. Assn. Student Personnel Admininstrn.(region II Outstanding New Profl.), N. Buffalo Community Devel. Corp., Assn. for Higher Edn. and Disabilities. Republican. Avocations: reading, raquetball.

RYAN, DANIEL LEO, bishop; b. Mankato, Minn., Sept. 28, 1930; s. Leonard Bennett and Irene Ruth (Larson) R. BA, Ill. Benedictine Coll., 1952; JCL, Pontificia Università Lateranense, Rome, 1960. Ordained priest Roman Cath. Ch., 1956, consecrated bishop, 1981. Parish priest Roman Cath. Diocese, Joliet, Ill, 1956-82, chancellor, 1965-78, vicar gen., 1977-79, aux. bishop, 1981-84; bishop Roman Cath. Diocese, Springfield, Ill., 1984—. Office: Diocese of Springfield PO Box 3187 1615 W Washington Springfield IL 62708-3187

RYAN, DAVID ALAN, computer specialist; b. Cin., Nov. 13, 1961; s. James Patrick and Virginia Ann (Stewart) R. BS, Wright State U., 1983; MS, Tex. A&M U., 1988. Statistician U.S. Bur. of Census, Washington, 1988-92, computer specialist, 1992—. Vol. math. modeling Soil Conservation Svc., Washington, 1991—; date modeling vol. Washington Opera, 1992—; data entry/programming vol. Opera Am., Washington, 1990-91; hist. rschr. Gasby's Tavern Mus., Alexandria, Va., 1991—; mem. Bravo! for the Washington Opera, 1991-95. Recipient Vol. Svc. award Soil Conservation Svc., 1992, 93. Mem. Am. Statis. Assn., Capitol PC Users Group, Ballston-Va. Square Civic Assn. (exec. com. 1995—, sec. 1996—). Avocations: classical music, ethnomusicology, history, geography, travel. Office: Bur of Census/CES Ste 211 Washington Plz II Washington DC 20233-6300

RYAN, DAVID THOMAS, lawyer; b. Torrington, Conn., Apr. 18, 1939; s. Edward John and Margaret (Murphy) R.; m. Dale Anderson, Aug. 21, 1965; children: Rachael Anderson, Conor Anne. BS, U. Md., 1961; LLB, Georgetown U., 1965. Bar: Conn. 1966, U.S. Dist. Ct. Conn. 1967, U.S. Ct. Appeals (2d cir.) 1969, U.S. Ct. Appeals (fed. cir.) 1982, U.S. Claims Ct. 1983, U.S. Supreme Ct. 1992. Ptnr. Cooney, Scully & Dowling, Hartford, Conn., 1966-77, Robinson & Cole, Hartford, 1977—. Fellow Am. Coll. Trial Lawyers; mem. Am. Bd. Trial Advs. Home: 126 Westerly Ter Hartford CT 06105-1117 Office: Robinson & Cole 1 Commercial Plz Hartford CT 06103-3599

RYAN, DEBBIE, university athletic coach. B.Phys. Edn., Ursinus Coll., 1975; M.Phys. Edn., U. Va., 1977. Asst. basketball and field hockey coach U. Va., Charlottesville, 1975-77, head women's basketball coach, 1977—; lectr. in field; adv. coach Nike; head coach U.S. Jr. Nat. Team, 1988, Jr. World Championship Team, 1989; mem. U.S.A. Basketball Women's Games Com. for 189-92 quadrennium; dir. West team U.S. Olympic festival, Chapel Hill, N.C., 1987 (gold medal). Author: Virginia Defense, Virginia Summer Development Program, Women's Basketball Drills-Conditioning. Recipient ACC Coach of the Yr. award, 19884, 86, 87, 91, 93, 95; named Outstanding Woman of the Yr. Va. Women's Forum, 1991, Converse Dist. III Coach of the Yr., 1985-86, Nat. Coach of the Yr., Shreveport Jour., 1986, Natsmith Coach of the Yr., Atlanta Tipoff club, 1991. Avocations: fishing, golf. Office: University of Virginia University Hall PO Box 3785 Charlottesville VA 22903*

RYAN, DESMOND, film critic; b. London, May 30, 1943; came to U.S., 1967; s. Christopher and Evelyn (Daley) R.; m. Patricia Mazer, Jan. 27, 1967; 1 child, Christopher. B.A. with honors, New Coll., Oxford U., Eng., 1965, M.A., 1968. Reporter Phila. Inquirer, 1969-74, film critic, 1974—, columnist mag., 1975-82. Author: (novels) Helix, 1979, Deadlines, 1984 (Athanaeum award 1984); (video capsule revs.) Guide to 3000 Movies, 1985. Office: Phila Inquirer 400 N Broad St Philadelphia PA 19130-4015*

RYAN, EARL M., public affairs analyst; b. Detroit, Oct. 23, 1942; s. Thomas M. and Margaret L. (Halsey) R.; m. Jo Ellen Junod, July 3, 1965; children: Andrew M., Jeffrey A. BA in Polit. Sci., U. Mich., 1964; MA in Polit. Sci., Wayne State U., 1968. Dir. rsch. Detroit Urban League, 1965-67; resch. assoc. Citizens Rsch. Coun. Mich., Lansing, 1967-70; budget analyst Dept. Social Svcs., Lansing, 1970-71; dir. rsch. Health Impact Project, Lansing, 1971, Office of Program Effectiveness Rev., Lansing, 1971-74, Legis. Program Effectiveness Rev., Lansing, 1974-77, Citizens Rch. Coun. Mich., Detroit, 1977-84; pres. Pub. Affairs Rsch. Coun. La., Baton Rouge, 1984-87, Ind. Fiscal Policy Inst., Indpls., 1987-94, Citizens Rsch. Coun. Mich., Farmington Hills, 1994—; polit. analyst Sta. WWL-TV, New Orleans, 1986; mem. blue ribbon panel Indpls. Bus. Jour., 1992-94. Recipient disting. achievement award grad. program pub. adminstrn. Wayne State U., Detroit, 1991. Mem. Govtl. Rsch. Assn. (pres. 1985-86, Disting. rsch. award 1977), Govtl. Fin. Officers Assn. Avocations: photography, Anthony Trollope novels. Home: 40292 Woodside Dr N Northville MI 48167-3431 Office: Citizens Rsch Coun Mich 38200 W Ten Mile Rd Ste 200 Farmington Hills MI 48335-2806

RYAN, EDWARD W., economics educator; b. Plainfield, N.J., Aug. 23, 1932; s. Edward A. and Helen R. (Shannon) R.; m. Georgian Hurley, Dec. 17, 1966; children: Sarah, Jennifer. BS, U. Pa., 1955; MA, Duke U., 1957. Lectr. Fordham U., N.Y.C., 1956-57; instr. Iona Coll., New Rochelle, N.Y., 1958-60; prof. econs. Manhattanville Coll., Purchase, N.Y., 1958—; dir. Econ. Freedom Inst. Author: In the Words of Adam Smith: The First Consumer Advocate, 1990. Mem. Am. Econ. Assn., Indsl. Rels. Rsch. Assn., Pub. Choice Assn., Econ. History Assn. Roman Catholic. Home: 25 Jefferson Rd Scarsdale NY 10583-6411 Office: Manhattanville College 2900 Purchase St Purchase NY 10577-2103

RYAN, ELLEN BOUCHARD, psychology educator, gerontologist; b. Holyoke, Mass., Jan. 11, 1947; emigrated to Can., 1982; d. Raoul Rosario and Etiennette Marie (Morin) Bouchard; m. Patrick J. Ryan, July 12, 1969; children: Lorraine Yvette, Dennis Patrick, Kevin Myles. BA, MA, Brown U., 1968; PhD, U. Mich., 1970. Asst. prof. psychology U. Notre Dame, 1970-76, assoc. prof., 1976-81, prof., 1981-82, chmn. dept., 1978-82; prof. psychiatry McMaster U., Hamilton, Ont., Can., 1982—, dir. Office Gerontol. Studies, 1985-95. Editor: Attitudes Toward Language Variation, 1982, Language Communication and The Elderly, 1986, Intergenerational Communication, 1994, Language Attitudes, 1994, Communication, Aging and Health, 1996. Grantee NICHD, 1972-75, NSF, 1976-79, Nat. Inst. Edn., 1979-82, Natural Scis. and Engring. Rsch., 1983-89, Gerontol. Rsch. Coun. of Ont., 1983-85, Ont. Ministry Health, 1986-89, Soc. Sci. and Humanities Rsch. Coun., 1986—. Fellow APA, Gerontol. Soc. Am., Can. Psychol. Assn.; mem. Internat. Comm. Assn., Can. Assn. Gerontology. Roman Catholic. Home: 346 Brookview Ct, Ancaster, ON Canada L9G 4C2 Office: McMaster U Dept Psychiatry, 1200 Main St W, Hamilton, ON Canada L8N 3Z5

RYAN, FREDERICK JOSEPH, JR., lawyer, public official; b. Tampa, Fla., Apr. 12, 1955; s. Frederick Joseph and Cordelia Beth (Hartman) R.; m. Genevieve Ann McSweeney, Dec. 28, 1985; children: Genevieve Madeline, Madeline Elizabeth. BA, U. So. Calif., 1977, JD, 1980. Bar: Calif. 1980, D.C. 1986. Assoc. Hill, Farrer and Burrill, Los Angeles, 1980-82; dep. dir. then dir. presdl. appointments and scheduling The White House, Washington, 1982-87, dir. pvt. sector initiatives, 1985-87, asst. to the Pres., 1987-89; chief of staff Office of Ronald Reagan, L.A., 1989-95; vice chmn. Allbritton Comm. Co., Washington, 1995—; bd. cons. Riggs Bank Washington, 1995—; mem. staff Reagan-Bush Campaign, Los Angeles, 1980; dir. Internat. Conf. on Pvt. Sector Initiatives, Paris, 1986, Italian-Am. Conf. on Pvt. Sector Initiatives, 1987, Brit.-Am. Conf. on Pvt. Sector Initiatives, 1988; bd. dirs. Riggs Bank Europe Ltd., London. Author (column) Legal Briefs, 1980-82; editor: Ronald Reagan: The Wisdom and Humor of the Great Communicator, 1995. Chmn. Monterey Park (Calif.) Cmty. Rels. Commn., 1977-78; bd. dirs. Ford's Theater, Washington, Town Hall of Calif., L.A., Nancy Reagan Found.; trustee Ronald Reagan Presdl. Found.; mem. bd. advisors Ronald Reagan Inst. for Emergency Medicine, George Washington U. Med. Ctr. Recipient Presdl. Commendation for pvt. sector initiatives Pres. Ronald Reagan, 1986, Medal of Arts and Letters, Govt. of France, 1986, Golden Ambrosiana medal of Milan, Italy, 1987, The Lion of Venice medal, Italy, 1987, comdr. Order of Merit of Republic of Italy, 1992, comdr. Ouissam Alaouite of Morocco, 1995. Mem. ABA, Jonathan Club (L.A.), Metro. Club (Washington). Presbyterian. Avocations: Karate, tennis, skiing. Office: Allbritton Comm Co 808 17th St NW Washington DC 20006-3910

RYAN, GEORGE H., state government official, pharmacist; b. Maquoketa, Iowa, Feb. 24, 1934; s. Thomas J. and Jeanette (Bowman) R.; m. Lura Lynn Lowe, June 10, 1956; children: Nancy, Lynda, Julie, Joanne, Jeanette, George. BS in Pharmacy, Ferris State Coll., Big Rapids, Mich. Mem. Ill. Ho. of Reps., 1973-82, minority leader, 1977-80, speaker, 1981-82; lt. gov. State of Ill., 1983-91, sec. of state, 1991—. Mem. Kankakee County Bd., 1966-72, chmn., 1971-72; chmn. Ill. Literacy Coun., 1991—. With U.S. Army, Korea. Recipient Humphrey award Am. Pharm. Assn., 1980, Top award Ill. chpt. DARE, 1989, Govt. Leadership award Nat. Commn. Against Drunk Driving and MADD Govt. Leader Against Drunk Driving award, 1994-95, City Club of Chgo. Man of Yr. award, 1995. Mem. Am. Pharm. Assn., Ill. Pharm. Assn., One Hundred Club, Masons (33d degree). Republican. Methodist. Lodges: Elks, Moose, Shriners.

RYAN, GEORGE WILLIAM, manufacturing executive; b. Sinking Springs, Ohio, Oct. 13, 1939; s. Winson Mark and Mary Edith (Smalley) R.; 1 child: Gina Kristin. Student, Wilmington Coll., 1962. Process engr. B.F. Goodrich Co., Marietta, Ohio, 1962-66; product dev. mgr. Chrysler Corp., Sandusky, Ohio, 1966-70; asst. tech. mgr. Inmont Corp., Toledo, Ohio, 1970-72; tech. mgr. Occidental Petroleum, Burlington, N.J., 1973; owner Ryan Devel. Corp., Peebles, 1973-88; prin. Straight Fork Valley Ranch, Ohio, 1986—; cons. Hooker Chem. Corp., Burlington, N.J., 1973. Bd. dirs., pres. Missionary Evang. Ch. of Christ. Mem. Soc. Plastic Engrs., Senatorial Trust (Washington), Peebles Ind. Inc. (sec., treas., bd. dirs., 1984-88). Republican.

RYAN, GERALD ANTHONY, financial adviser, venture capitalist; b. Milw., Oct. 24, 1935; s. Gerald Edward and Frances (Dierksmeier) R.; m. Carole Lesley Schuster, May 19, 1956; children: Karen P., Kevin M., Kimberly F., Kendra A., Keith A. B.S.M.E., MIT, 1957. Engr., Johnson Controls, Buffalo, 1958-61; mgr. Johnson Controls, Erie, Pa., 1961-73; pres. TEI Corp., Erie, 1973-75; chmn., CEO Erie Bus. Mgmt. Corp., 1975—; chmn., CEO Skinner Engine Co., 1986—; pres. Ryco Holding Ltd., 1986—; chmn. bd. Automated Indsl. Sys., Fairview, Pa., 1981—, Spectrum Control, Inc., Erie, 1990—, Personal Svc. Corp., 1974-82, Rent-Way, Inc., 1981—, Wolf Pub. Co., Kauai, Hawaii, 1987—. Mem. Kahkwa Club. Republican. Roman Catholic. Home: 10 Peninsula Dr Erie PA 16505 Office: EBMC PO Box 6242 Erie PA 16512-6242

RYAN, GERARD SPENCER, inn executive; b. N.Y.C., June 10, 1926; s. Gerard Aloysius and Helen (Kirwan) R.; m. Barbara Battle, May 3, 1952; children—Jerry, Catherine, Janet, Mary Ellen, Barbara, Elizabeth, David, Peter. B.A., Georgetown U., 1950. Dir. fund raising Georgetown U., 1950-51; sales rep. McGraw Hill Pub. Co., Chgo., 1951-53; mgr. Pitts. Chem. Engring. Dist., 1953-68; sales mgr. Power Mag., N.Y.C., 1968-73; SLS mgr. Elec. Constrn. and Maintenance and Elec. Wholesaling mags., N.Y.C., 1973-74; pub. Elec. Constrn. and Maintenance and Elec. Wholesaling mags., 1974-85; propr. Arrowhead Inn, Durham, N.C., 1985—. Pres. South Hills Assn. Racial Equality, Pitts., 1966-68, Debra, Montclair, N.J., 1981-83. Served with USN, 1944-46. Mem. N.C. Bed and Breakfast Assn. (past pres.).

Democrat. Roman Catholic. Home and Office: Arrowhead Inn 106 Mason Rd Durham NC 27712-9201

RYAN, HALFORD ROSS, speech educator; b. Anderson, Ind., Dec. 29, 1943. AB, Wabash Coll., 1966; MA, U. Ill., 1968, PhD, 1972. Prof. Washington and Lee U., Lexington, Va., 1970—. Author: FDR's Rhetorical Presidency, 1988, Harry Emerson Fosdick, 1989, Henry Ward Beecher, 1990, Classical Communication for the Contemporary Communicator, 1992, Harry S. Truman, 1993; editor: Oratorial Encounters, 1988, Inaugural Addresses of Twentieth-Century American Presidents, 1993, U.S. Presidents as Orators, 1995; also articles. Recipient awards Eleanor Roosevelt Inst., 1979, Herbert Hoover Inst., 1986, Maurice Mednick Found., 1991; Rockefeller Theol. fellow, 1967. Mem. Speech Communication Assn. Office: Washington and Lee U Robinson Hall Lexington VA 24450

RYAN, HOWARD CHRIS, retired state supreme court justice; b. Tonica, Ill., June 17, 1916; s. John F. and Sarah (Egger) R.; m. Helen Cizek, Oct. 16, 1943; children: John F., Elizabeth Ellen, Howard Chris. B.A., U. Ill., 1940, LL.B., J.D., 1942; LL.D. (hon.), John Marshall Law Sch., 1978. Bar: Ill. 1942. Practice in Decatur, 1946-47, Peru, 1947-57; asst. state's atty. LaSalle County, 1952-54, county judge, 1954-57, circuit judge, 1957-68; chief judge, 1964-68; judge appellate ct. 3d Jud. Dist. Ill., 1968-70; justice Ill. Supreme Ct., 1970-90, chief justice, 1981-84; of counsel Peterson & Ross, Chgo., 1990-93. Served with USAAF, 1942-45. Mem. ABA, Ill. Bar Assn., LaSalle County Bar Assn., Am. Legion, Masons, Elks, Odd Fellows, Phi Alpha Delta. Republican. Methodist. Home: PO Box 397 Tonica IL 61370-0397

RYAN, IONE JEAN ALOHILANI, retired educator, counselor; b. Honolulu, Oct. 18, 1926; d. William Alexander and Lilia (Nainoa) Rathburn; m. Edward Parsons Ryan, June 23, 1962 (dec.); children: Ralph M., Lilia K. BEd, U. Hawaii, 1948; MS in Pub. Health, U. Minn., 1950; EdD, Stanford U., 1960. Lic. marital and family therapist, N.C. Tchr. W.R. Farrington High Sch., Honolulu, 1948; instr. to asst. prof. U. Hawaii, Honolulu, 1950-66; assoc. prof. to prof. East Carolina U., Greenville, 1966-90; prof. emerita East Carolina U., Greenville, N.C., 1990—; adv. com. Eastern Regional Tng. Program, Greenville, N.C., 1975-80; cons. Title III Grant, Lenoir Community Coll., Kinston, N.C., 1981; adult svcs. adv. com. Pitt County Mental Health, Greenville, N.C., 1976-78. Contbr. articles to profl. publs. Recipient first scholarship Honolulu C. of C., 1948-50. Mem. APA.

RYAN, J. BRUCE, health care management consulting executive; b. Southbridge, Mass., Mar. 28, 1944; s. Charles J. and Doris (Olney) R.; m. Sarah E. Pattison, Aug. 16, 1993. BSBA in Fin., U. Mass., 1972, MSBA, 1975; MA in Econs., U. Wash., 1976. Regional v.p. Amherst Assocs. Inc., Atlanta, 1976-85; exec. v.p. Jennings Ryan & Kolb, Inc., Atlanta, 1985—; mem. managed care adv. bd. St. Anthony Pub.; bd. advs. Managed Care Contest Negotiation. Mem. editl. rev. bd. Healthcare Fin. Mgmt., Managed Care Reimbursment Advisory; contbr. articles to profl. jours. With U.S. Army, 1968-70. Mem. Healthcare Fin. Mgmt. Assn. (Helen M. Yerger/L. Van Seawell best article award 1990), Soc. for Healthcare Planning & Mktg., Fin. Mgmt. Assn., Am. Assn. Physician-Hosp. Orgns. Avocation: sailing. Home: 1060 Kentucky Ave NE Atlanta GA 30306-3534 Office: Jennings Ryan & Kolb Inc 17 Executive Park Dr NE Ste 500 Atlanta GA 30329-2222

RYAN, J. RICHARD, lawyer; b. N.Y.C., Oct. 23, 1929; s. Peter Leon and Mary Martha (Franklin) R.; m. Diana Louise Gambarelli, Nov. 6, 1954 (dec. Feb. 1988); children: Christopher, Claudia; m. Joan Frances Revelle, Jan. 21, 1995. BA, Georgetown U., 1951, JD, Fordham U., 1954. Bar: N.Y. 1956, U.S. Dist. Ct. (so. dist.) N.Y., 1957, U.S. Supreme Ct., 1987. Assoc. Engel, Judge, Miller, Sterling & Reddy, N.Y.C., 1956-63, ptnr., 1963-66; ptnr. Kantor, Shaw & Ryan, N.Y.C., 1966-71; ptnr. Ryan & Silberberg, N.Y.C., 1971-84, Ryan & Fogerty, 1984-88, Ryan, Botway, Reddy and Mesrop, 1988-90; sole practice, 1990—. Bd. dirs. Guiding Eyes for the Blind, Inc., pres., 1973-77, Am. Health Capital Ins. Co.; trustee Cooper Inst. for Advanced Studies in Medicine and Humanities. Mem. Bar Assn. City N.Y. (Young Lawyers Com. 1957-60), N.Y. State Bar Assn., ABA, The Soc. of the Friendly Sons of St. Patrick, Copyright Soc. Candidate for mayor, Pelham, N.Y., 1963. Served with AUS, 1954-56. Clubs: Pelham Country (past pres.), Union League, Winged Foot Golf Club. Office: 516 5th Ave New York NY 10036-7501

RYAN, JACK, physician, retired hospital corporation executive; b. Benton Harbor, Mich., Aug. 26, 1925; s. Leonard Joseph and Beulah (Southworth) R.; m. Lois Patricia Patterson; children: Michele, Kevin, Timothy, Sarah, Daniel. AB, Western Mich. U., 1948; postgrad., U. Mich. Law Sch., 1949-50, Emory U., 1950-51; MD, Wayne State U., 1955. Intern St. Luke's Hosp., Saginaw, Mich., 1955-56; pres. Meml. Med. Ctr., Warren, Mich., 1956-77; v.p. med. affairs Detroit-Macomb Hosps. Corp., 1976-77, pres. and chief exec. officer, 1977-96; ret., 1996; assoc. prof. medicine Wayne State U., Detroit, 1974—; bd. chmn. Mich. Hosp. Ins. Co., 1990—. Recipient Disting. Alumnus award Wayne State U. Med. Sch., 1974, Wayne State U., 1979, Western Mich. U., 1989, Disting. Key award Mich. Hosp. Assn., 1986, Tree of Life award Jewish Nat. Fund, 1996. Fellow Am. Coll. Family Physicians, Am. Coll. Physician Execs., Detroit Acad. Medicine; mem. Internat. Health Econs. and Mgmt. Inst. (charter), Econ. Club Detroit, Detroit Athletic Club, Renaissance Club, Red Run Club. Avocations: Civil War, history, golf, tennis. Home: 175 Hendrie Blvd Royal Oak MI 48067-2412

RYAN, JAMES, insurance company executive; b. Pittsburgh, Pa., Jan. 21, 1937; s. Martin Charles and Lucy Elizabeth (Misklow) r.; m. Marlene Sullivan Ryan, Jan. 27, 1973. BA, U. Pitts., U. Louisville. Cert. ins. wholesaler. Chmn. Market Finders Ins. Corp., Louisville, 1972—; com. chmn. Am. Assn. Mng. Gen. Agts., 1988-89; pres. Ky. Lloyd's Agts. Assn., 1985—; bd. dirs. Nat. Assn. Profl. Surplus Lines Office, Inc., 1983-86; pres. Ky. Surplus Lines Assn., Louisville, 1988-89; mem. adv. coun. Essex Ins. Co., 1991-93. Pub. in Best Rev., 1995. Mem. Ky. Thoroughbred Owners & Breeders, Inc., Hon. Order of Blue Goose Internat., Kosair Shrine Temple, Hon. Order of Ky. Col. Named Adv. Coun. Colony Ins. Co., Glen Allen, Va., 1991-93, Hamilton Ins. Co., 1993, Cardinal Ins. Co., 1991-93. Mem. Profl. Ins. Agts., Ind. Ins. Agts. Assn., Am. Assn. Mng. Gen. Agts. (cert., chmn. adv. com. 1991-92, bd. dirs. 1994-96, v.p. zone 2 1995-96, pres.-elect 1996-97, pres. 1997—), Nat. Assn. Profl. Surplus Lines Offices (chmn. legis. com. 1988-89, Published Best Rev. 1995), Am. Assn. of Gen. Agts. Republican. Roman Catholic. Avocations: breeding and racing Thoroughbred horses, golf.

RYAN, JAMES E., attorney general; married; 5 children. BA in Polit. Sci., Ill. Benedictine Coll., 1968; JD, Ill. Inst. Tech., 1971. Bar: Ill. 1971. Asst. state's atty. criminal divsn. DuPage County State's Atty.'s Office, 1971-74, 1st. asst. state's atty., 1974-76; founder Ryan & Darrah; state's atty. DuPage County State's Atty.'s Office, 1984-94; atty. gen. State of Ill., 1994—. Recipient numerous awards from various orgns. including Nat. Assn. Counties, Alliance Against Intoxicated Motorists. Republican. Office: Office of Atty General 500 S 2nd St Springfield IL 62701-1705

RYAN, JAMES EDWIN, industrial arts educator; b. Pittsburg, Kans., Oct. 21, 1919; s. James Joseph and Eva May (Bates) R.; m. Carol Floella Nowell, June 15, 1941; 1 child, Carol Jean. B.S., Kans. State Coll., 1940; M.A., Calif. State Coll., Long Beach, 1954; Ed.D., UCLA, 1964. High sch. tchr. Mo. and Kans., 1940-43; journeyman printer Long Beach (Calif.) Ind. Press-Telegram, 1947-54; mem. faculty Calif. State U., Long Beach, 1954-83; prof. indsl. arts Calif. State U., 1964-83, prof. emeritus, 1983—, chmn. acad. senate, 1976-78; mem. acad. senate Calif. State Univs. and Colls., 1979-83; mem. graphic arts adv. com. Downey (Calif.) City Schs., 1966-83, Golden West Coll., 1970-83; mem. visitation team accreditation council Calif. Assn. Schs. Cosmetology, 1965-83; judge tech. exhibits Gt. Western Exposition, Los Angeles, 1962-83; cons. in field. Contbr. articles to profl. jours. Served with AUS, 1943-46. Mem. Soc. History Tech., Am. Indsl. Arts Assn., Assn. Calif. State Univ. Profs. (past officer), Am. Coun. Indsl. Arts Tchr. Educators, Calif. Indsl. Edn. Assn. (life), Congress Faculty Assn. (v.p. 1976-79, treas. 1979-81), Calif. Colls. Univ. Faculty Assn. (chpt. pres. 1977-79), Calif. State U. Long Beach Emeritus and Ret. Faculty Assn. (pres. 1988-89, 92-93), Calif. State U. Emeritus and Ret. Faculty Assn. (v.p. 1992—), Epsilon Pi Tau (Laureate citation 1960), Phi Kappa Phi, Phi Delta Kappa. Home: 13952 Falmouth Walk Westminster CA 92683-3432

RYAN, JAMES FRANKLIN, retail executive; b. London, Ont., Can., July 21, 1948; s. Patrick and Helen Anne (Wenechuk) R.; m. Dora Lee Ballan, Mar. 17, 1979 ; children: Christine, Carol. BS, U. Western Ont., London, 1970; MBA, York U., Toronto, Ont., 1972. Various mgmt. positions Shell Can. Ltd., Toronto, 1972-84; mgr. retail Shell Can. Ltd., Calgary, 1984-85; dir. mktg. svcs. Petro-Can., Inc., Toronto, 1985-86; pres. Pyne Mgmt., Inc., Toronto, 1986-88, Can. Tire Petroleum, Toronto, 1988-92; sr. v.p. dealer rels. Can. Tire Corp., Toronto, 1992—. also: 28 Weatherstone Ct, Niagara-on-the-Lake, ON Canada L0S 1J0 Office: Can Tire Corp, 2180 Yonge St, Toronto, ON Canada M4S 2B9

RYAN, JAMES GILBERT, historian, educator, writer; b. Wilmington, Del., Jan. 31, 1947; s. James A. and Audrey May (Davis) Urian; m. Anita Louise Noble, Jan. 20, 1973 (div. Sept. 1978). BA, U. Del., 1970, MA, 1973; MA, U. Notre Dame, 1975, PhD, 1981. Vis. instr. dept. history Purdue U., 1976, 77, 78; lectr. dept. history Pa. State U., Delaware County campus, 1978-79; instr. dept. history U. Notre Dame, summers 1979-80; adj. asst. prof. dept. history Ind. U. at South Bend, 1980-81; adj. asst. prof. dept. polit. sci. Temple U., 1982-84, 85-87; adj. asst. prof. dept. history and politics Drexel U., Phila., 1982-85, 85-87, vis. asst. prof. dept. history and politics, 1985; vis. asst. prof. dept. polit. sci. Muhlenberg Coll., Allentown, Pa., 1987-90; asst. prof. history dept. gen. acad. Tex. A&M U., Galveston, 1990-96; assoc. prof. Tex. A & M U., Galveston, 1996—; faculty senate Tex. A&M U., 1997—; vis. researcher Russian Ctr. for Preservation and Study of Documents of Recent History, Moscow, 1993; presenter in field. Author: Earl Browder: The Failure of American Communism, 1997; contbr. chpt. to book and articles to profl. jours. Grantee Muhlenberg Coll., 1988, 90, Tex. A&M U., 1990, 91, 92, 93, 95, 96, 97. Mem. NEA, Am. Hist. Assn., Orgn. Am. Historians, Historians of Am. Communism (ctrl. com. mem. 1995—), Southwestern Hist. Assn., Tex. Faculty Assn. Democrat. Avocations: weightlifting, skiing. Home: 7302 Heards Ln Apt 313 Galveston TX 77551-1152 Office: Tex A & M Univ Dept Gen Acad PO Box 1675 Galveston TX 77553-1675

RYAN, JAMES HERBERT, security and retail services company executive; b. Petersburg, Va., Feb. 1, 1931; s. Richard Hillsdon and Mary Orgain (Mann) R.; BS, U.S. Mil. Acad., 1955; MA, U. Pa., 1962; MS, George Washington U., 1972; grad. Program for Mgmt. Devel. Harvard U., 1972; PhD, Walden U., 1984; m. Patricia Louise Abbott, June 7, 1955; 1 child, Pamela Louise. Commd. 2nd lt. U.S. Army, 1955, advanced through grades to lt. col., 1968, ret., 1972; gen. mgr. U.S. ops. Ryan Enterprises, Washington, 1970-73; pres. Ford Enterprises, Ltd., Mt. Rainier, Md., 1973-87; pres. James H. Ryan Assocs., Inc., Petersburg, Va., 1987-97. Advisor to Sec. of Army, 1975, chief of naval material, 1980-82; mem. Pres.'s Pvt. Sector Survey on Cost Control (Grace Commn.), 1982; bd. govs. USO, 1977-86; pres. Hist. Petersburg Found., 1991-93; vestryman St. Paul's Episcopal Ch., 1994-96. Decorated Legion of Merit, Soldiers medal, Bronze Star, Air medal, Vietnamese Gallantry Cross. Mem. Am. Mgmt. Assn., Nat. Retail Federation, Am. Soc. Indsl. Security, Internat. Assn. Profl. Security Cons. (pres. 1993-95), Ret. Officers Assn., West Point Soc. Ctrl. Va., Rotary Club of Petersburg (pres. 1993-94). Episcopalian. Home: 1666 Westover Ave Petersburg VA 23805-2820 Office: Ryan Security Mgmt Consulting 520 Grove Ave PO Box 2126 Petersburg VA 23804

RYAN, JAMES JOSEPH, lawyer; b. Cin., June 17, 1929; s. Robert J. and Marian (Hoffman) R.; m. Mary A. Noonan, Nov. 25, 1954; children: Kevin, Timothy, Nora, Daniel. AB, Xavier U., 1951, JD, U. Cin., 1954. Bar: Ohio 1954. Teaching assoc. Northwestern U., Chgo., 1954-55; ptnr. Dolle, O'Donnell & Cash, Cin., 1958-71, Taft, Stettinius & Hollister, Cin., 1971—; lectr. U. Cin. Coll. Law, 1960-65. Chmn. Health Planning Assn. Ohio River Valley, Cin., 1978-85; bd. dirs. Hamilton County Bd. of Mentally Retarded, 1968-80; trustee Resident Home for Mentally Retarded, 1980—, St. Francis-St. George Hosp. Devel. Coun., 1989—. Mem. ABA, Ohio Bar Assn., Cin. Bar Assn. Republican. Roman Catholic. Clubs: Queen City, Western Hill. Avocations: reading, sports. Home: 5316 Cleves Warsaw Pike Cincinnati OH 45238-3602 Office: 1800 Star Bank Ctr 425 Walnut St Cincinnati OH 45202

RYAN, JAMES LEO, federal judge; b. Detroit, Mich., Nov. 19, 1932; s. Leo Francis and Irene Agnes R.; m. Mary Elizabeth Rogers, Oct. 12, 1957; children: Daniel P., James R., Colleen M. Hansen, Kathleen A. LL.B., U. Detroit, 1956, BA, 1992; LL.D. (hon.), Madonna Coll., 1976, Detroit Coll. Law, 1978, Thomas M. Cooley Law Sch., Lansing, Mich., 1986, U. Detroit Sch. Law, 1986. Justice of peace Redford Twp., Mich., 1963-66; cir. judge 3d Jud. Circuit Mich., 1966-75; justice Mich. Supreme Ct., 1975-86; judge U.S. Ct. Appeals (6th cir.), 1986—; faculty U. Detroit Sch. Law, Nat. Jud. Coll., Reno, Am. Acad. Jud. Edn., Washington, Thos M.Cooley Law Sch. Contbr. article to legal jour. Served with JAGC, USNR, 1957-60; to capt. JAGC, mil. judge Res., 1960-92, ret., 1992. Mem. Naval Res. Lawyers Assn., Nat. Conf. Appellate Ct. Judges, Fed. Judges Assn., State Bar Mich., Fed. Bar Assn., KC. Office: US Ct Appeals US Courthouse 231 W Lafayette Blvd Detroit MI 48226-2720*

RYAN, JAMES WALTER, physician, medical researcher; b. Amarillo, Tex., June 8, 1935; s. Lee W. and Emma E. (Haddox) R.; children: James P.A., Alexandra L.E., Amy J.S. A.B. in Polit. Sci., Dartmouth Coll., 1957; M.D., Cornell U., 1961; D.Phil., Oxford U. (Eng.), 1967. Diplomate: Nat. Bd. Med. Examiners. Intern, Montreal (Que.) Gen. Hosp., McGill U., Can., 1961-62; asst. resident in medicine Montreal (Que.) Gen. Hosp., McGill U., 1962-63; USPHS research asso. NIMH, NIH, 1963-65; guest investigator Rockefeller U., N.Y.C., 1967-68; asst. prof. biochemistry Rockefeller U., 1968; asso. prof. medicine U. Miami (Fla.) Sch. Medicine, 1968-79, prof. medicine, 1979-95; prof. anesthesiology, pharmacology and toxicology Med. Coll. Ga., Augusta, 1995—; sr. scientist Papanicolaou Cancer Rsch. Inst., Miami, 1972-77; hon. med. officer to Regius prof. medicine Oxford U., 1965-67; vis. prof. Clin. Rsch. Inst. Montreal, 1974; mem. vis. faculty thoracic disease divsn., dept. internal medicine Mayo Clinic, 1974; cons. Apotex, Inc., Toronto. Contbr. numerous articles on biochem. research and pathology to sci. jours.; patentee in field. Rockefeller Found. travel awardee, 1962; William Waldorf Astor travelling fellow, 1966; USPHS spl. fellow, 1967-68; Pfizer travelling fellow, 1972; recipient Louis and Artur Luciano award for research of circulatory diseases McGill U., 1984-85. Fellow Am. Inst. Chemists; mem. Am. Chem. Soc., Biochem. Soc., Am. Soc. Biol. Chemists, Am. Heart Assn. (mem. council cardiopulmonary diseases 1972—, Council for High Blood Pressure Research 1976—), Microcirculatory Soc., So. Soc. Clin. Investigation, AAAS, N.Y. Acad. Scis., Sigma Xi. Baptist. Club: United Oxford and Cambridge U. (London). Home: 3047 Lake Forest Dr Augusta GA 30909-3027 Office: Med Coll Ga Vascular Biology Ctr Augusta GA 30912

RYAN, JERRY WILLIAM, lawyer; b. Highland Park, Mich., Mar. 18, 1928; s. Jeremiah Ryan and Irene (Evans) R. BA, U. Mich., 1949, JD, 1952; postgrad., Inst. Universitaire des Hautes Etudes Internat., Geneva, Switzerland, 1954, 55. Bar: Mich. 1952, N.Y. 1958, D.C. 1966. Field atty. VA, Detroit, 1953-54; sr. atty. Pan Am. World Airways Inc., N.Y.C., 1956-66; ptnr. Pogue & Neal, Washington, 1966-67, Jones, Day, Reavis & Pogue and predecessor firm Reavis, Pogue, Neal & Rose, Washington, 1967-79, Crowell & Moring, Washington, 1979—; arbitrator U.S. and internat. arbitrations; speaker Inst. Continuing Edn., U. Mich., 1989-90. Capt. USAF, 1952-53. Mem. ABA (speaker 1985), Assn. of Bar of City of N.Y., Sky Club (N.Y.C.), Metropolitan Club (washington). Office: Crowell & Moring 1001 Pennsylvania Ave NW Washington DC 20004-2505

RYAN, JOHN DUNCAN, lawyer; b. Portland, Oreg., Dec. 20, 1920; s. Thomas Gough and Virgian Abigail (Hadley) R.; m. Florence A. Ryan, Jan. 30, 1970 (dec. 1987); m. Virginia Kane Wilson, June 15, 1996. BS, Fordham U., 1943; JD, Lewis & Clark Coll., Portland, 1950. Bar: Oreg. 1950. Private practice Portland, 1950—; adj. instr. Northwestern Sch. Law Lewis & Clark Coll., 1953-70. Author: (poems) Expressions, 1993, Expressions II, 1995. Sgt. Air Corps, U.S. Army, 1942-46, ETO. Recipient St. Thomas More award Catholic Lawyers for Social Justice, 1993. Mem. ABA (Oreg. delegate 1985-93, chmn. spl. com. on law & literacy 1991-93), Am. Coll. Trial Lawyers, Am. Trial Lawyers Assn., Oreg. State Bar (bd. govs. 1963-67), Oreg. Trial Lawyers Assn. (Trial Lawyer of Yr. 1993), Multnomah Bar Assn., Washington County Bar Assn. Home and Office: 1760 SW 90th Ave Portland OR 97225-6509 Home: 5826 S W Riverpoint Ln Portland OR 97201

RYAN, JOHN EDWARD, federal judge; b. Boston, Jan. 22, 1941; s. Howard Frederick and Mary (Burke) R.; m. Terri Reynolds; children: Valerie, Jennifer, Keely. BSEE, U.S. Naval Acad., 1963; LLB, Georgetown U., 1972; MS, Pacific Christian U., 1979. Assoc. Hale and Dorr, Boston, 1972-76, C.F. Braun, Alhambra, Calif., 1976-77; gen. counsel Altec Corp., Anaheim, Calif., 1977-79; v.p., sr. atty. Oak Industries, San Diego, 1979-82; sr. v.p. Oak Media, San Diego, 1982-84; ptnr. Dale and Lloyd, La Jolla, Calif., 1984-85, Jennings, Engstrand and Henrikson, San Diego, 1985-86; bankruptcy judge U.S. Bankruptcy Ct., Santa Ana, Calif., 1986—; ex officio dir. Orange County Bankruptcy Forum; exec. com. 9th Cir. conf. With USN, 1963-69. Fellow Am. Coll. Bankruptcy; mem. Mass. Bar Assn., Calif. Bar Assn., Orange County Bar Assn., Bankruptcy Judges Assn. Republican. Roman Catholic. Avocations: tennis, camping, basketball. Home: 3155 Summit Dr Escondido CA 92025-7529 Office: US Bankruptcy Ct PO Box 12600 Santa Ana CA 92712-2600

RYAN, JOHN FRANKLIN, multinational company executive; b. Huntington, W.Va., Apr. 10, 1925; s. Oscar F. and Mamie J. (Tyler) R.; m. Renee B. Bourn, June 17, 1948; children—Carolyn, Linda, Elizabeth. Student, Emory and Henry Coll., 1943-44; B.S., Marshall U., 1948. Data processing sales mgr. IBM, Phila., 1958-60; dir. worldwide integrated data systems ITT, Washington, 1960-62, dept. dir., 1962-72, dir. corp. relations, 1972-87, v.p., 1981-87; cons., 1987—. Mem. Bus.-Govt. Relations Council, pres. 1978; bd. dirs. Pub. Affairs Council. Served with USNR, 1943-45. Clubs: Carlton (pres. 1982), Burning Tree. Home: 8447 Portland Pl Mc Lean VA 22102-1707

RYAN, JOHN M., lawyer; b. Glen Ridge, N.J., May 18, 1936. AB, Dartmouth Coll., 1958; LLB, U. Va., 1963. Bar: Va. 1964. Lectr. at law Marshall-Wythe Sch. Law Coll. William and Mary, 1976-86; ptnr. Vandeventer, Black, Meredith & Martin, Norfolk, Va.; gen. counsel Va. Internat. Terminals, Inc. Trustee John Marshall Found.; bd. dirs. Va. Symphony. Fellow Am. Coll. Trial Lawyers, Va. Law Found.; mem. ABA (labor rels., litigation sect.), Southea. Admiralty Law Inst., Va. Bar Assn. (pres. 1988), Maritime Law Assn. of U.S., Norfolk-Portsmouth Bar Assn., Va. State Bar, Nat. Conf. Bar Pres., So. Conf. Bar Pres. Office: Vandeventer Black Meredith & Martin 500 World Trade Ctr Norfolk VA 23510-1617

RYAN, JOHN MICHAEL, landscape architect; b. Chgo., Sept. 27, 1946; s. Terrance Joseph and Norma (Morris) R.; m. Victoria Jean Wheetley, June 26, 1986; children: Micheline Giannasi-Mennecke, Tony Giannasi, Nick Giannasi, Andrew Morris Jennings, Melissa Contance Victoria, Cameron Michael Montgomery. B in Landscape Architecture, U. Ill., 1969. Registered landscape architect, Ill., Mich., Ariz.; cert. CLARB. Assoc. landscape architect Carl Garnder & Assocs., Inc., Chgo., 1969-71; sr. landscape architect Collaborative Rsch. & Planning, Chgo., 1971-73; v.p. Michael L. Ives & Assocs., Inc., Downers Grove, Ill., 1973-84; pres. Ives/Ryan Group, Inc., Naperville, 1984—. Prin. works include renovation of Old Orchard Shopping Ctr., Skokie, Ill., Lake Katherine Nature Preserve, Palos Heights, Ill., Crystal Tree Residential Golf Course Cmty., Orland Park, Ill., Corporetum Office Campus, Lisle, Ill. Bldg. com. mem. Wheaton Evangelical Free Ch., 1995—. Crew chief search and rescue USCG Aux., 1980—. Recipient Nat. Landscape award Am. Assn. Nurserymen, 1988, 92, Key award in landscape arch. Home Bldrs. Assn. Greater Chgo., 1981, 84, 90. Mem. Am. Soc. Landscape Archs. (Merit award 1991, 94, 96), Ill. Landscape Contractors Assn. (Gold award 1991, 96, Silver award 1986, 90, 93, Merit award 1988, 91), Chgo. Hort. Soc., Perennial Plant Assn. (Nat. Honor award 1993), Morton Arboretum. Avocations: competitive volleyball, golf, gardening, travel. *My life is committed to raising my dear children as best I can in a loving christian atmosphere, which I believe to be my true purpose for being here. As a professional landscape architect, if I can enhance or imporve the environment for my children and their children, I have made a worthwhile professional contribution to my perceived purpose in life.*

RYAN, JOHN WILLIAM, retired university president; b. Chgo., Aug. 12, 1929; s. Leonard John and Maxine (Mitchell) R.; m. D. Patricia Goodday, Mar. 20, 1949; children: Kathleen Elynne Ryan Acker, Kevin Dennis Mitchell, Kerrick Charles Casey. BA, U. Utah, 1951; MA, Ind. U., 1958, PhD, 1959, LLD (hon.), 1988; LLD (hon.), U. Notre Dame, 1978, Oakland City Coll., 1981, St. Joseph Coll., 1981, Hanover Coll., 1982, DePauw U., 1983, U. Ma., 1983, Manchester Coll., 1983, U. Evansville, 1985, Wabash Coll., 1986, Ind. U., 1988; DLitt (hon.), U. St. Thomas, 1977; D Pub. Adminstrn., Nat. Inst. Devel. Adminstrn., Thailand, 1991; LLD (hon.), U. Md., 1994. Rsch. analyst Ky. Dept. Revenue, Frankfort, 1954-55; vis. rsch. prof. U. Thammasat, Bangkok, Thailand, 1955-57; asst. dir. Inst. Tng. for Pub. Svc. Ind. U., 1957-58; successively asst. prof., assoc. prof. polit. sci., assoc. dir., Bur. Govt. U. Wis., 1958-62; exec. asst. to pres., sec. of univ. U. Mass., Amherst, 1962-63; chancellor U. Mass., Boston, 1965-68; v.p. acad. affairs Ariz. State U., 1963-65; v.p., chancellor regional campuses Ind. U., Bloomington, 1968-71, pres., 1971-87, prof. polit. sci., 1968-95, prof. pub. and environ. affairs, 1981-95, prof. emeritus, 1995—; cons. AID, 1991-92; chancellor SUNY, Albany; cons. AID, 1991-92; interim pres. Fla. Atlantic U., 1989, U. Md., Balt., 1994; bd. dirs. Ind. U. Found., chmn. 1972-87; chmn. Nat. Adv. Bd. on Internat. Edn. Programs, 1985-89; interim chancellor SUNY System, 1996-97. Contbr. articles to profl. jours. Bd. govs. Pub. Broadcasting Svc., 1973-82; bd. visitors Air U., 1974-81; chmn. Air Force Inst. Tech Subcom., 1976-81; mem. univ. adv. com. Am. Coun. Life Ins.; bd. dirs. Corp. Community Coun., 1976; mem. nat. adv. coun. Pan Am. Games, 1985; mem. adv. bd. Assocs. for Religious and Intellectual Life, 1984—; active United Way Ind. Centennial Commn. Mem. Am. Soc. Pub. Adminstrn. (pres. Ind. chpt. 1969-70, nat. chpt. 1972-73, nat. coun. from 1970, Ind. Soc. Chgo. (non-resident v.p. from 1976, Am. Polit. Sci. Assn., Assn. Asian Studies, Am. Coun. Edn., Am. Judicature Soc., Assn. Am. Univs. (exec. com. from 1978, chmn. com. on coms. 1984, health edn. com. from 1978, chmn. 1981-82), Ind. Soc. N.Y.C., Ind. Soc. Washington, Nat. Acad. Public Adminstrn., Ind. Acad., Explorers Club, Adelphia (hon.), Circumnavigators Club (N.Y.C.), Columbia Club (Indpls.), Skyline Club, Cosmos Club (Washington), St. Botolph (Boston), K.C, Elks, Phi Kappa Phi, Phi Alpha Theta, Pi Sigma Alpha, Beta Gamma Sigma, Kappa Sigma (worthy grand master 1985-87). Office: Ind U Spea # 316 Bloomington IN 47405

RYAN, JOHN WILLIAM, association executive; b. Manchester, N.H., Sept. 16, 1937; s. William Charles and Mary Ann (Marcoux) R.; m. Carol Jean Battaglia, Sept. 17, 1960; children: James, Kathleen, John, Michael. A.B., St. Anselm Coll., 1959; M.A., Niagara U., 1960; Ph.D., St. John's U., 1965. Asst. prof. history Gannon U., Erie, Pa., 1965-66; edn. specialist, div. grad. programs U.S. Office Edn., Washington, 1966-68; regional coordinator, grad. acad. programs U.S. Office Edn., 1968-70; dir. univ. programs Univ. Assocs., Inc., Washington, 1970-72; asst. to pres., sec. Council of Grad. Schs. in U.S., Washington, 1972-80; exec. v.p. Renewables Research Inst., Annandale, Va., 1980-81; exec. dir. Worcester (Mass.) Consortium Higher Edn., 1981-89, N.H. Coll. and Univ. Coun., Manchester, 1989-93; cons.; exec. dir. Mass. Vet. Med. Assn., Marlborough, Mass., 1995—. Contbr. articles to profl. jours. Office: 169 Lakeside Ave Marlborough MA 01752-4556

RYAN, JOSEPH, lawyer; b. Seattle, Feb. 11, 1942; s. John Joseph and Jane (Wing) R.; m. Mary Katherine Gavin, Aug. 10, 1963; children: Michael Gavin, Kathleen Ann, Jennifer Jo. BA, U. Washington, 1964; JD, Columbia U., 1967. Bar: Calif. 1968, N.Y. 1983, D.C. 1983. Ptnr. O'Melveny & Myers, Los Angeles, 1976-94; exec. v.p., gen. counsel Marriott Internat., Inc., Washington, 1994—; sr. v.p., gen. counsel, bd. dirs. Ritz-Carlton Hotel Co., LLC, Atlanta, 1996—; tchr., lectr. N.Y. Law Jour. Author: Stating Your Case--How To Interview for a Job as a Lawyer, 1982, Take or Pay Contracts: Alive and Well in California, vol. 192, 1987, Current Investment Banking Activities in the United States, vol. 2, #15 M&A Report, 1988; coauthor (with Lorin Fife) The Urban Lawyer, 1987; contbr. articles to law publs. Bd. dirs. Pasadena Playhouse, L.A., 1981-92, Planetary Soc., Pasadena, 1981, Westridge Sch., L.A., 1982-91, Natural History Mus. Los Angeles County, 1988-93. Capt. U.S. Army, 1968-70. Mem. ABA, N.Y. Bar Assn., D.C. Bar Assn., Calif. Bar Assn., Nat. Assn. Bond Lawyers (legis. com.). Republican. Roman Catholic. Avocations: running, biking, camping, hunting and fishing, boating. Home: 10836 Alloway Dr Potomac

MD 20854-1503 Office: Marriott Internat Inc Dept 52/923 Marriott Dr Washington DC 20058

RYAN, JOSEPH W., JR., lawyer; b. Phila., June 24, 1948; s. Joseph W. Sr. and Marie R. (Hilgrube) R.; m. Mary Pat Law, Sept. 11, 1971; children: Caitlin, Joseph W. III. BA, St. Joseph's U., Phila., 1970; MA, Villanova U., 1971; JD, U. Va., 1978. Bar: Ohio 1978, U.S. Supreme Ct. 1982. Ptnr. Porter, Wright, Morris & Arthur, Columbus, Ohio, 1978—; lectr. Sch. Dentistry Ohio State U., Columbus, 1982-89, Continuing Legal Edn. Inst., 1984—. Author: Use of Demonstrative Evidence, 1985; assoc. editor Litigation News, 1986—. Trustee Columbus Zool. Assn., 1980-90; bd. dirs. Columbus Speech and Hearing Ctr., 1988, pres., 1995-96. Mem. ABA, Ohio State Bar Assn., Columbus Bar Assn., Internat. Assn. Def. Counsel, Am. Arbitration Assn. (panel of arbitrators). Republican. Roman Catholic. Office: Porter Wright Morris & Arthur 41 S High St Ste 30 Columbus OH 43215-6113

RYAN, JUDITH LYNDAL, German language and literature educator; b. Sydney, Australia, Apr. 6, 1943; came to U.S., 1967; d. William Matthew and Kathleen (Ferris) O'Neil; m. Lawrence Ryan, Feb. 24, 1964 (div. 1985); children: Antony Lawrence, Vanessa Lyndal; m. Lawrence A. Joseph, Sept. 26, 1986. B.A. with honors, U. Sydney, 1964; Dr. Phil., U. Munster, Westfalia, W. Ger., 1970. Research student U. Sydney, 1965; instr., asst. prof. then assoc. prof. German Smith Coll., Northampton, Mass., 1967-79; prof. German German Smith Coll., 1979—, Doris Silbert prof. humanities, 1982-85; prof. German and comparative lit. Harvard U., Cambridge, 1985-90, Robert K. & Dale J. Weary prof. German and comparative lit., 1990—, chmn. dept. comparative lit., 1988-93, chair dept. Germanic langs. and lits., 1993-96; vis. assoc. prof. Brown U., Providence, 1978-79. Author: Umschlag und Verwandlung, 1972, The Uncompleted Past, 1983 (Basilius award 1983), The Vanishing Subject, 1991; mem. editorial bd. German Quar., 1983-90; mem. adv. bd. German Studies Rev., 1983-87, PMLA, 1984-87. NEH fellow, 1978; Humboldt-Stiftung grantee, 1970-71. Mem. MLA (del. 1973-75, 77-79, programs com. 1980-83, exec. coun. 1987-90, nominating com. 1994-95, editorial bd. Texts and Translations Series, 1991-94), AAUP (pres. Smith Coll. chpt. 1982-83). Office: Harvard U Dept German Cambridge MA 02138

RYAN, JUDITH W., geriatrics nurse, adult nurse practitioner, educator, researcher; b. Waterbury, Conn., Dec. 8, 1943; d. James Patrick Ryan and Edna (Swanson) Billings. BS, U. Conn., 1965; MS, Boston U., 1967; PhD, U. Md., 1984. RN, Md., Conn.; cert. adult nurse practitioner ANA. Instr. U. Conn., Storrs, 1967-69; asst. prof. Ind. U., Purdue U., Indpls., 1969-73; asst. prof. U. Md., Balt., 1973-82, dir. nursing and health care dept. family medicine, supportive care project, 1985-87, asst. prof. sch. nursing, 1987-95; asst. prof. Coll. Notre Dame, Balt., 1982-83; clin. dir. EverCare, Linthicum, Md., 1995—; dir. primary care adult nurse practitioner cert. program U. Md., 1976-82; arbitrator Health Claims Arbitration Program, Md., 1976—; bd. mem. Md. Bd. Nursing, Balt., 1991—, pres., 1993-96; bd. trustees Md. Nurses Assn. Polit. Action Com., Balt., treas., 1989-91. Contbr. articles to profl. jours. Named Distinguished Practitioner Nursing, Nat. Acad. Practice, 1984—. Mem. Md. Nurses Assn. (2d v.p. 1986-88), Md. Gerontol. Assn., Nat. Conf. Gerontol. Nurse Practitioner, Nurse Practitioner Assn. Md., Sigma Theta Tau, Phi Kappa Phi. Home: 622 Lucia Ave Baltimore MD 21229-4516 Office: 849 International Dr # 125 Linthicum Heights MD 21090-2229

RYAN, JULIE MAE, optometrist, educator, researcher; b. Des Moines, Sept. 3, 1951; d. Albert Boyd and A. Gretchen (Manderscheid) Berg; m. Patrick D. Ryan, June 27, 1976. AA, Southwestern C.C., Creston, Iowa, 1971; BS in Visual Sci., Ill. Coll. Optometry, Chgo., 1975, OD, 1975; MS, Calif. State U., Fullerton, 1986. Diplomate Am. Acad. Optometry. Pvt. practice assoc. Champaign, Ill., 1976-77; instr. So. Calif. Coll. Optometry, Fullerton, 1977-81, asst. prof., 1981-86, assoc. prof., 1986—, chief pediatric vision svcs., 1986-88; co-owner, ptnr. Irvine (Calif.) Optometric Group, 1988—; bd. dirs. Irvine Child Devel. Ctr., 1991-93. Contbr. chpt. to book, articles to profl. jours. Named to Outstanding Young Women of Am., 1979. Fellow Am. Acad. Optometry (vice chair binocular vision and perception sect. 1986-88, coord. written exam. 1991-96), Coll. Optometrists in Vision Devel.; mem. Am. Optometric Assn. (primary care com. 1988-90, long range planning com. 1990-92, mem. membership com. 1992-94, mem. binocular vision com. 1994—), Orton Dyslexia Soc. (bd. dirs. 1994-96), Orange County Optometric Soc. (trustee 1995-96). Home: 5510 Avenida Del Tren Yorba Linda CA 92887-4901 Office: Irvine Optometric Group 4950 Barranca Pkwy Ste 310 Irvine CA 92604-4631

RYAN, KENNETH JOHN, physician, educator; b. N.Y.C., Aug. 26, 1926; s. Joseph M. R.; m. Marion Elizabeth Kinney, June 8, 1948; children: Alison Leigh, Kenneth John, Christopher Elliot. Student, Northwestern U., 1946-48; MD, Harvard U., 1952. Diplomate Am. Bd. Ob-Gyn. Intern, then resident internal medicine Mass. Gen. Hosp., Boston, also Columbia-Presbyn. Med. Center, N.Y.C., 1952-54, 56-57; resident in ob-gyn. Boston Lying-in Hosp., also Free Hosp. for Women, Brookline, Mass., 1957-60; prof. ob-gyn., dir. dept. Med. Sch. Western Res. U., 1961-70; prof. reproductive biology, dept. ob-gyn. U. Calif. San Diego, La Jolla, 1970-73; chief of staff Boston Hosp. for Women, 1973-80; chmn. dept. ob-gyn. Brigham Women's Hosp., Boston, 1980-93; instr. ob-gyn. Harvard U., also dir. Fearing Rsch. Lab., 1960-61, Kate Macy Ladd prof., chmn. dept. ob-gyn. Med. Sch., 1973-93, dir. Lab. Human Reprodn. and Reproductive Biology, 1974-93, Disting. prof., 1993-96, prof. emeritus, 1996—; chief staff Boston Hosp. for Women, 1973-80; chmn. dept. ob-gyn. Brigham Women's Hosp., Boston, 1980-93; now chmn. ethic com. Chmn. Nat. Commn. for Protection of Human Subjects Biomed. and Behavioral Rsch., 1974-78. Recipient Schering award Harvard Med. Sch., 1951, Soma Weis award, 1952, Bordon award, 1952; Ernst Oppenheimer award, 1964; Max Weinstein award, 1970; fellow Mass. Gen. Hosp., 1954-56. Fellow Am. Cancer Soc.; mem. ACOG, Am. Soc. Biol. Chemists, Endocrine Soc., Soc. Gynecol. Investigation, Am. Gynecol. Soc., Am. Soc. Clin. Investigation, Mass. Med. Soc., Alpha Omega Alpha. Office: Brigham & Women's Hosp PBB Edmin 4 75 Francis St Boston MA 02115-6110

RYAN, KEVIN WILLIAM, research virologist, educator; b. Fort Dodge, Iowa, Dec. 8, 1952; s. Joseph Michael Ryan and Etoile Evelyn Werth; m. Mary Ellen Lyman, June 1, 1974; children: Matthew Lyman, Mark Joseph. BS, U. Iowa, 1978; PhD, U. Mich., 1984. Staff fellow Nat. Inst. of Allergy and Infectious Diseases/NIH, Bethesda, Md., 1984-86; rsch. asst. dept. virology and molecular biology St. Jude Children's Rsch. Hosp., Memphis, 1986-89, asst. mem., 1989—; asst. prof. pathology U. Tenn. Coll. Medicine, Memphis, 1994—. Contbr. articles to profl. jours., chpts. to tech. manuals. Predoctoral fellow Mich. Cancer Rsch. Inst., U. Mich., Ann Arbor, 1982; prin. investigator grantee Nat. Inst. Allergy and Infectious Diseases, 1992—. Mem. AAAS, Am. Soc. for Virology (co-chair pub. affairs com. 1995-96), Am. Soc. Microbiology, Soc. Gen. Microbiology, Radiol. Soc. N.Am., Sigma Xi. Roman Catholic. Avocations: golf, chess. Office: St Jude Children Rsch Hosp Children Rsch Hosp 332 N Lauderdale St Memphis TN 38105-2729

RYAN, LEO VINCENT, business educator; b. Waukon, Iowa, Apr. 6, 1927; s. John Joseph and Mary Irene (O'Brien) R. BS, Marquette U., 1949; MBA, DePaul U., 1954; PhD, St. Louis U., 1958; postgrad., Catholic U. Am., 1951-52, Bradley U., 1952-54, Northwestern U., 1950; LLD, Seton Hall U., 1988; DHL, Ill. Benedictine U., 1997. Joined Order Clerics of St. Viator, Roman Cath. Ch., 1950. Mem. faculty Marquette U., Milw., 1957-65; dir. continuing edn. summer sessions, coord. evening divs. Marquette U., 1959-65, prof. indsl. mgmt., 1964; prof. and chmn. dept. mgmt. Loyola U., Chgo., 1965-66; adj. prof. mgmt. Loyola U., 1967-69; dep. dir. Peace Corps, Lagos, Nigeria, 1966-67; dir. Western Nigeria Peace Corps, Ibadan, 1967-68; asst. superior gen. and treas. gen. Clerics of St. Viator, Rome, 1968-69; dir. edn. Am. province Clerics of St. Viator, Arlington Heights, Ill., 1969-74; pres. St. Viator High Sch., 1972-74; dean, prof. mgmt. Coll. Bus. Adminstrn. U. Notre Dame, Ind., 1975-80; dean Coll. Commerce DePaul U., 1980-88, prof. mgmt. Coll. Commerce, 1980—, Wicklander prof. profl. ethics, 1993-94; dir. Peace Corps tng. programs Marquette U., 1962-65; adj. prof. human devel. St. Mary's Coll., Winona, Minn., 1972-74; mem. sch. bd. Archdiocese Chgo., 1972-75, vice chmn., 1973-75, mem. nat. edn. com. U.S. Cath. Conf., 1971-75, mem. exec. com., 1973-75; mem. nat. adv. bd. Benedictine Sisters of Nauvoo, 1973-83; mem. nat. adv. coun. SBA, 1982-85, vice chmn. minority bus., 1982-85, exec. com. Chgo. chpt., 1982-84; vis. prof. U. Ife, Ibadan, 1967-68; mem. adv. bd. 1st Bank-Milw., 1991-93, chmn. trust audit com., 1980-85, chmn. audit and examination com., 1985-90, mem. bus. adv. coun., 1991-93; bd. dirs. Vilter Mfg. Co., external dir. Vilter ESOP, Filbert Corp., Vilter Internat. (now Vilter Export Corp.), Henricksen & Co., Inc.; mem. fin. commn. Clerics of St. Viator, 1978—, mem. provincial chpt., 1985—; cons. Pontifical Commn. on Justice and Peace, 1968-70; vis. prof. Helsinki Sch. Econs., Mikkeli, Finland, 1990, 91, 94, 96, 97, Poznan (Poland) Sch. Mgmt., 1991, 92, 93; coord. Polish Am. summer program in econs. Acad. Econs., Poznan, 1991; Fulbright prof. Adam Mickiewicz U., Poland, 1993, 94, 95; co-chair bus. and profl. com. Archdiocese of Chgo. Sesquetennial Com. Out Reach Divsn. Ctrl. Planning Group, 1993-94. Mem. editl. bd. Internat. Jour. Value Based Mgmt., European Bus. Jour., Bus. Ethics Quar. Mem. Pres.'s Com. on Employment Handicapped, 1959-65, Wis. Gov.'s Com. on Employment Handicapped, 1959-65, Wis. Gov.'s Com. on UN, 1961-64, Burnham Park Planning Commn., 1982-88; bd. dirs. Ctr. Pastoral Liturgy U. Notre Dame, 1976-79, Lake Forest Grad. Sch. Mgmt., 1989-91; trustee St. Mary of Woods Coll., 1978-81; regent Seton Hall U., 1981-87, mem. acad. affairs com., 1981-87, chmn., 1983-87; trustee Cath. Theol. Union, U. Chgo., 1992-95, Divine Word Coll., 1997—; dir. Ctr. for Enterprise Devel., 1992-95; fellow St. Edmonds Coll. Cambridge U., 1992; mem. Cath. Commn. Intellectual and Cultural Affairs, 1992—, Cath. Campaign for Am., 1994—; bd. dirs. Internat. Bus. Ethics Inst., Am. Grad. Sch. Internat. Mgmt., 1995—, Assn. Profl. Ethics, 1995-96; mem. adv. coun. Mgmt. Edn. in Poland, U. Md., College Park, 1995—. Recipient Freedom award Berlin Commn., 1961, chieftancy title Asoju Atoaja of Oshogbo Oba Adenle I, Yorubaland, Nigeria, 1967, B'nai B'rith Interfaith award, Milw., 1963, Disting. Alumnus award Marquette U., 1974, DePaul U., 1976, Tchr. of Yr. award Beta Alpha Psi, 1980, Centennial Alumni Achievement award Marquette U., 1981, Boland Meml. Disting. Alumni award, St. Louis, 1989, Disting. Alumni and Bicentennial awards Jesuit Bus. Schs., 1989, Pres.' award St. Vinton H.S., 1992, Medal of Merit Adam Mickiewicz U., 1995, Excellence in Teaching award DePaul U., 1995; Brother Leo V. Ryan award created in his honor Cath. Bus. Edn. Assn., 1962; Ryan Scholars in Mgmt. established in his honor DePaul U., 1989, Outstanding Svc. award, 1991-93, Commerce Alumni award of merit, 1997; Ryan Scholarship established in his honor St. Vinton High Sch., 1992, Lion award, 1997; named Man of Yr. Jr. C. of C., Milw., 1959, Marquette U. Bus. Adminstrn. Alumni Man of Yr., 1974, Tchr. of Yr. U. Notre Dame, 1980; Milw. Bd. Realtors traveling fellow, 1964, Nat. Assn. Purchasing Agts. faculty fellow, 1958, German Am. Acad. Exch. Coun. fellow, summer 1983, Presdl. fellow Am. Grad. Sch. Internat. Mgmt., 1989, vis. scholar, 1995, Malone fellow in Islamic studies, 1990, fellow Kosciuszko Found. Adam Mickiewicz U., 1990; scholar-in-residence Mgmt. Sch. Imperial Coll. Sci. and Tech. U. London, 1988; vis. scholar U. Calif., Berkeley, spring 1989; USIA Acad. Specialists grantee (3), Poland, 1991, 92, 93; fellow St. Edmund's Coll. Cambridge U., 1992; named vis. rsch. fellow Von Hugel Inst., 1992-93; scholar-in-residence Am. Grad. Sch. Internat. Mgmt., 1995; guest scholar Kellogg Inst. Internat. Studies U. Notre Dame, 1997. Mem. Cath. Bus. Edn. Assn. (nat. pres. 1960-62, nat. exec. bd. 1960-64), Assn. Sch. Bus. Ofcls. (nat. com. chmn. 1965-67), Am. Assembly Collegiate Schs. Bus. (com. internat. affairs 1977-84, chmn. 1981-84, bd. dirs. 1981-87, program chmn. 1979-80, exec. com., chmn. projects/svc. mgmt. com. 1984-86), Am. Fgn. Svc. Assn., Am. Assn. Profl. Ethics (bd. dirs. 1996—), Allamakee County Hist. Soc. (charter life), Acad. Internat. Bus., Acad. Mgmt. (social issues div., chmn. membership com. 1990-91), Ancient Order of Hibernians, Nat. Returned Peace Corps Assn., Atomic Vets. Assn., August Derleth Soc., Chgo. Area Return Peace Corps Vols., Econ. Club Chgo., Chgo. Coun. Fgn. Rels., Coun. Fgn. Rels. (Chgo. com.), European Found. Mgmt. Edn., European Bus. Ethics Network, Soc. Bus. Ethics (mem. exec. com. 1991—, pres. 1993-94, adv. bd. 1995—), Assn. Social Econs. (life), Assn. Christian Economists, Inst. Global Ethics, Inst. Internat. Ethics (adv. bd.), Dubuque County Hist. Soc., Iowa Hist. Soc., Iowa Postal History Soc., Fulbright Assn. (life), Internat. Assn. for Bus. and Soc. (founder), Internat. Soc. for Bus., Econs. and Ethics (charter), Internat. Trade and Fin. Assn. (founder, bd. dirs. 1989-92, 96—, v.p. membership 1991-92, 96—), Internat. Learned Soc. Praxiology, Polish Inst. Arts and Scis. in Am., Milw. Press Club (hon.), USS Mt. McKinley Reunion Assn. (hon. chaplain AGC-7 1989-96, Disting. Svc. award 1991, 96), Alpha Sigma Nu, Alpha Kappa Psi (bd. dirs. found. 1985-91, vice chmn. 1987-91, chmn. scholarship com. 1987-91, chmn. devel. com. 1987, mem. exec. com. 1990-91, Bronze Disting. Svc. award 1949, Silver Disting. Svc. award 1958), Beta Alpha Psi, Beta Gamma Sigma (co-chair 75th Anniversary com. Ill., faculty advisor DePaul chpt. 1986-92), Delta Mu Delta, Pi Gamma Mu, Tau Kappa Epsilon.

RYAN, LEONARD EAMES, administrative law judge; b. Albion, N.Y., July 8, 1930; s. Bernard and Harriet Earle (Fitts) R.; m. Ann Allen, June 18, 1973; 1 child, Thomas Eames Allen-Ryan. Grad., Kent Sch., 1948; AB, U. Pa., 1954; JD, NYU, 1962. Bar: D.C. 1963, N.Y. 1963, U.S. Ct. Appeals (D.C. cir.) 1963, U.S. Dist. Ct. (so. and ea. dists.) N.Y. 1965, U.S. Ct. Appeals (2nd cir.) 1966, U.S. Supreme Ct. 1967. Reporter Upper Darby (Pa.) News, 1954; newsman AP, Pitts., Phila., Harrisburg, N.Y.C., 1955-62; reporter, spl. writer on law N.Y. Times, 1962-63; info. adviser corp. hdqrs. IBM, N.Y.C., 1963; trial atty. firm Perrell, Nielsen & Stephens, N.Y.C., 1964-66; trial atty. civil rights div. Dept. Justice, Washington, 1966-68; asst. to dir. bus. affairs CBS News, N.Y.C., 1968; program officer Office Govt. and Law, Ford Found., N.Y.C., 1968-74; pvt. practice law, cons. pub. affairs, N.Y.C., 1974-91; v.p., sec. W. P. Carey & Co., Inc., Investment Bankers, N.Y.C., 1976-81; apptd. U.S. adminstrv. law judge Office of Hearings and Appeals, San Rafael, Calif., June 1991; adminstrv. law judge Office of Hearings and Appeals, Phila., N.Y.C., 1993-94, 94—; impartial hearing officer Edn. for All Handicapped Children Act of 1975, 1976-91; per diem adminstrv. law judge N.Y. State Agys., 1976-91; arbitrator Small Claims Ct., N.Y.C., 1974-84; bd. dirs. Community Action for Legal Svcs. Inc., N.Y.C., 1971-77, vice-chmn., 1975-77; co-chmn. Citizens Com. to Save Legal Svcs., N.Y.C., 1975-76; bd. dirs. Lower East Side Svc. Ctr., N.Y.C., 1977-89. Author: (with Bernard Ryan Jr.) So You Want to Go Into Journalism, 1963; contbr. articles to profl. jours. Served with USAR, 1950-57. Mem. Am. Judicature Soc., Assn. of Bar of City of N.Y., N.Y. State Bar Assn., St. Elmo Club (Phila.), Heights Casino (Bklyn.). Home: 32 Orange St Brooklyn NY 11201-1634

RYAN, LOUIS FARTHING, lawyer; b. Richmond, Va., Mar. 18, 1947; s. Louis Anthony and Catherine Louise (Farthing) R.; m. Prudence Elwell Hartshorn, Sept. 5, 1970. BSE, Princeton U., 1969; JD, U. Va., 1973. Bar: Va. 1973. Mgmt. cons. Arthur Andersen & Co., Boston, 1969-70; assoc. firm Kaufman and Canoles, Norfolk, Va., 1973-77; sec. Landmark Communications, Inc., Norfolk, 1977-85, v.p., gen. counsel, 1985-88, exec. v.p., gen. counsel, 1988-95, exec. v.p. fin., gen. counsel, 1995—; sec. TeleCable Corp., Norfolk, 1984-85, v.p., gen. counsel, 1985-88., exec. v.p., gen. counsel, 1988-95. Bd. dirs. Feldman Chamber Music Soc., 1975-77, Jr. Achievement Tidewater, 1979-81, adv. coun., 1986—; bd. dirs., exec. com. Va. Symphony, 1979-89, pres., 1983-84; vol. United Way, 1975-88, chmn. campaign Norfolk divsn., 1988; mem. Norfolk Harborfest Com., 1979; mem. allocation com. Bus. Consortium for Arts Support, South Hampton Roads, 1987—; chmn. auction Sta. WHRO-Pub. TV, 1987; bd. dirs., exec. com. Planning Coun., Norfolk, Va., 1988-93; bd. dirs. Leadership Hampton Rds., 1990—, chmn. budget com., 1993, chmn. bd., 1993-95, chmn. nominating com., 1997; mem. exec. adv. coun. Coll. Bus. and Pub. Adminstrn., Old Dominion U., 1990—; mem. exec. steering com. Hampton Roads Black Achiever Program, 1990-92, mem. Forward Hampton Roads, 1990-91; mem. memberships com. Chrysler Mus., 1991, com. 101 of Future of Hampton Roads, Inc., 1992—; bd. dirs. Norfolk Assembly, 1991-95, Norfolk Festevents, 1994—. Mem. ABA, Va. Bar Assn., Va. State Bar (chmn. bus. law sect. 1980-81), Norfolk-Portsmouth Bar Assn., Am. Newspaper Pubs. Assn. (legal affairs com. 1986—), Hampton Roads C. of C. (bd. dirs. 1989-94, Norfolk divsn. 1990—, treas. 1994), Town Point Club, Norfolk Yacht and Country Club, Country Club Va. Episcopalian. Office: Landmark Communications Inc 150 W Brambleton Ave Norfolk VA 23510-2018

RYAN, MARK ANTHONY, architect; b. Council Bluffs, Iowa, Sept. 6, 1964; s. Paul Elmer and Darreline Kay (Wyland) R.; m. Shelli Ann Hagerbaumer, Sept. 26, 1992. BA in Architecture with distinction, Iowa State U., 1987. Registered profl. architect, Wis. Project architect U.S. Army Corps. of Engrs., Omaha, 1987-90, architect, security engr., 1990-91, environ. project mgr., 1991-96; owner, architect Ryan Designs, Omaha, 1987—; project mgr. Bovis Constrn. Corp., Omaha, 1997—; owner The Ryan Co., Omaha, 1994-96; bd. adv. Fitness Plus, Council Bluffs, Iowa, 1990-92; expert witness for pvt. attys., Iowa and Nebr., 1991—. Chmn. City Devel. Commn., Council Bluffs, 1992; bd. trustees San. and Improvement Dist. No. 142, Douglas County, Nebr., 1995-96. State of Iowa scholar, 1982. Mem. AIA (sec. S.W. Iowa sect. 1991, treas. 1992, v.p. 1993, pres. 1994-96), Soc. Am. Mil. Engrs., Nat. Trust for Hist. Preservation, Golden Key, Phi Kappa Phi, Tau Sigma Delta. Avocations: archl. restoration, biking, freshwater aquatics. Home: 9030 Raven Oaks Dr Omaha NE 68152-1759 Office: Bovis Constrn Co 940 Woodmen Tower 1700 Farnam St Omaha NE 68102-2002

RYAN, MARLEIGH GRAYER, Japanese language educator; b. N.Y.C., May 1, 1930; d. Harry and Betty (Hurwick) Grayer; m. Edward Ryan, June 4, 1950; 1 child, David Patrick. B.A., NYU, 1951; M.A., Columbia U., 1956, Ph.D., 1965; Cert., East Asian Inst., 1956; postgrad., Kyoto U., 1958-59. Research assoc. Columbia U., N.Y.C., 1960-61, lectr. Japanese, 1961-65, asst. prof., 1965-70, assoc. prof., 1970-72; vis. asst. prof. Yale U ., New Haven, 1966-67; assoc. prof. U. Iowa, Iowa City, 1972-75, prof., 1975-81, chmn. dept., 1972-81; prof. Japanese SUNY, New Paltz, 1981—, dean liberal arts and scis., 1981-90; vice chmn. seminar on modern Japan, Columbia U., 1984-85, chmn., 1985-86; co-chmn. N.Y. State Conf. on Asian Studies, 1986, editor, 1993—, mem. exec. com., 1993-96, sec., 1993—. Co-author: (with Herschel Webb) Research in Japanese Sources, 1965; author: Japan's First Modern Novel, 1967, The Development of Realism in the Fiction of Tsubouchi Shoyo, 1975; assoc. editor: Jour. Assn. Tchrs. Japanese, 1962-71, editor, 1971-75. East Asian Inst. fellow Columbia U., 1955; Ford Found. fellow, 1958-60; Japan Found. fellow, 1973, Woodrow Wilson Ctr. Internat. Scholars fellow, 1988-89; recipient Van. Am. Disting. Book award Columbia, 1968. Mem. MLA (sec. com. on teaching Japanese Lang. 1962-68, mem. del. assembly 1979-87, mem. exec. com. div. Asian lit. 1981-86), Assn. Tchrs. Japanese (exec. com. 1969-72, 74-77), Assn. Asian Studies (bd. dirs. 1975-78, coun. of confs., 1993-96), Midwest Conf. Asian Studies (pres. 1980-81). Office: SUNY Ft # 414 New Paltz NY 12561 *Studying the most difficult language in the world has taught me patience and tact. One learns what it is to sit completely still at the Japanese No theatre and absorb wondrous sights and sounds in an atmosphere of absolute peace. Discovering the stillness in movement is perhaps the most important lesson we in the West can derive from our Asian experience.*

RYAN, MARY A., diplomat; b. New York, N.Y., Oct. 1, 1940. B.A., St. John's Univ., 1963, M.A., 1965. With Foreign Service, Dept. of State, 1966—; consular and adminstrv. officer Naples, Italy, 1966-69; personnel officer Am. Embassy, Tegucigalpa, Honduras, 1970-71; consular officer Am. Consulate Gen., Monterrey, Mexico, 1971-73; adminstrv. officer Bur. of African Affairs, Dept. of State, Washington, 1973-75, post mgmt. officer, 1975-77; career devel. officer Bur. of Personnel, Dept. of State, 1977-80; adminstrv. counselor Abidjan, Ivory Coast, 1980-81, Khartoum, Sudan, 1981-82; inspector, Office of Insp. Gen. Dept. of State, Washington, 1982-83, exec. dir. Bur. of European and Can. Affairs, 1983-85, exec. asst. to Under Sec. of State for Mgmt., 1985-88; ambassador to Swaziland, 1988-90; dep. asst. sec. Bur. of Consular Affairs, Washington, 1990; dir. Kuwait task force, 1990-91, ops. dir. UN spl. commn. on elimination of Iraqi weapons, 1991; dep. asst. sec. Bur. European & Can. Affairs, Washington, 1991-93; asst. sec. Bur. of Consular Affairs, Washington, 1993—. Office: Dept State Bureau of Consular Affairs 2201 C St NW Washington DC 20520-0001*

RYAN, MARY CATHERINE, pediatrician; b. N.Y.C., Mar. 22, 1938; d. Thomas Michael and Catherine (Scullin) McLaughlin; m. Enda Kieran Ryan, Feb. 8, 1969; children: Denise Marie, Kathleen May. BS in Chemistry, St. John's U., Bklyn., 1959; MD, NYU, 1963; MPH, George Washington U., 1996. Diplomate Am. Bd. Pediatrics. Cons. Hampton health dept. Va. State Dept. Health, 1969-71; med. coord. N.Y.C. Bur. Handicapped, 1971-72; asst. prof. pediatrics L.I. Coll. Hosp., Bklyn., 1972-73; pub. health clinician Fairfax County Health Dept., Fairfax, Va., 1973—; pvt. contractor pediatrics PHP Healthcare Corp., Fairfax, 1987-93. Tchr. religious edn. St. Thomas à Becket Ch., Reston, Va., 1978-81. Maj. M.C., U.S. Army, 1969. Fellow Am. Acad. Pediatrics; mem. AMA, Med. Soc. Va., No. Va. Pediatric Soc., Fairfax County Med. Soc., Soc. Devel. Pediatrics. Avocation: gardening. Home: 1423 Aldenham Ln Reston VA 22090-3903 Office: Fairfax County Health Dept 1850 Cameron Glen Dr Ste 100 Reston VA 20190-3310

RYAN, MARY NELL H., training consultant; b. Milw., Oct. 17, 1956; d. Robert Healey and Elizabeth Anne (Schulte) R.; 1 child, Katharine Scarlett. BA, Marquette U., 1979; MS, U. Wis., Milw., 1991. Tchr. St. Francis Borgia Sch., Cedarburg, Wis., 1979-81; dir. pub. rels. Aerobics West Club, N.Y.C., 1981; unit head, team leader Northwestern Mut. Life Ins. Co., Milw., 1982-84, asst. supr., 1984-86, tng. coord., 1986-87, mgr. tng., 1987-92; tng. cons., pres. Workplace Learning, Inc., Milw., 1992—; cons. Aetna Life and Casualty Co., Hartford, Conn., 1988, Robertson-Ryan & Co., Milw., 1989, Blue Cross/Blue Shield United of Wis., Northwestern Mut. Life Ins. Co., CMI Group, Inc., Aurora Health Care, Literacy Svcs. Wis., Executrain, Inc., Milw. First in Quality, Wis. Quality Network, United Wis. Svcs., Inc., Ameritech, Milw. Art Mus., Blood Ctr. Southeastern Wis., Meretz, Inc., Radiology Assocs. Wis., Deluxe Data, Inc., Hewlett-Packard Users Group of Wis., Miller Brewing Co.; guest lectr. U. Wis., Milw., 1989, Milw. Area Tech. Coll., 1990, Marquette U., 1990; speaker confs., developer/trainer workshops. Mem. exec. com. Lakefront Festival Arts, Milw., 1985—, vol. com. chair, silent auction chair; exec. fundraiser United Performing Arts Fund, Milw., 1986; com. chmn. Jr. League Milw., 1983-87; fundraiser YMCA Ptnr. Youth, Milw. 1987-88; tutorHead Start Read with Me program, 1993—. Recipient gold medal Life Communicators Assn., 1987. Mem. ASTD (bd. dirs. Wis. chpt., membership com. 1989-90, chmn. Train Am.'s Workforce and comty. svcs. 1992-94), Milw. Mgmt. Support Orgn. (bd. dirs. 1988), Wis. Ins. Club (spkr.), InRoads (bd. dirs. Wis. chpt.), Phi Kappa Phi. Avocations: reading, tennis, swimming, theatre, travel. Office: Workplace Learning Inc 1426 W Westport Cir Mequon WI 53092-5753

RYAN, MEG, actress; b. Fairfield, Conn., Nov. 19, 1961; m. Dennis Quaid, 1991; 1 child, Jack Henry. Student, NYU. Appearences include (TV) One of the Boys, 1982, As The World Turns, 1982-84, Wild Side, 1985, (films) Rich and Famous, 1981, Amityville 3-D, 1983, Top Gun, 1986, Armed and Dangerous, 1986, Innerspace, 1987, Promised Land, 1987, D.O.A., 1988, The Presidio, 1988, When Harry Met Sally, 1989, Joe Versus the Volcano, 1990, The Doors, 1991, Prelude to a Kiss, 1992, Sleepless in Seattle, 1993, Flesh and Bone, 1993, When a Man Loves a Woman, 1994, Restoration, 1994, I.Q., 1994, French Kiss, 1995, Two for the Road, 1996, Courage Under Fire, 1996, Addicted to Love, 1996; owner Prufrock Pictures movie prodn. co. Recipient Golden Apple award Hollywood Women's Press Club, 1989. Office: care ICM 8942 Wilshire Blvd Beverly Hills CA 90211-1934

RYAN, MICHAEL BEECHER, lawyer, former government official; b. Chgo., Aug. 20, 1936; s. Walter Joseph and Mary Agnes (Beecher) R.; m. Maria Chantal Wiesman, June 1, 1963; children—Mary, Catherine, Matthew. B.S. in Labor Relations, Manhattan Coll., 1957; J.D., U. Notre Dame, 1964. Bar: N.Y. 1964, Ill. 1991. With NLRB, 1964-91; sr. trial atty. NLRB, Peoria, Ill. region, 1968-74, dep. officer in charge, 1974-78, regional atty., 1978-91; exec. v.p. NLRB Union, 1968-69, pres., 1969-71; mem. Peoria Planning Commn., 1977-89, chmn., 1979-89; sole practice Peoria; adj. prof. labor relations Bradley U., 1972-74. Mem. Tri-County Land Use Adv. Com., 1978-82; Pres. Catholic Interracial Council Peoria, 1971-72, North Sterling Homeowners Assn., 1973-77. Served with AUS, 1958-61, Korea. Mem. Regional Attys. Guild (chmn. 1982-88), Wedgewood Country Club. Roman Catholic. Home: 3438 W Villa Rdg Apt A Peoria IL 61604-1739 also: E-9 Plantation Hale Kapaa Kauai HI 96746

RYAN, MICHAEL LEE, lawyer; b. N.Y.C., Feb. 23, 1951; s. William Francis and Helen (Lee) R.; m. Julia A. Smith, Dec. 1, 1979; children: Matthew, Rachel. BA, Harvard U., 1973; JD, NYU, 1978. Bar: N.Y. 1979, Mass. 1980. Sr. editor E.P Dutton, N.Y.C., 1974-77; assoc. Cleary, Gottlieb, Steen & Hamilton, N.Y.C., 1978-80, 83-86, ptnr., 1986—; assoc. Ropes & Gray, Boston, 1980-82. Articles editor NYU Law Rev., 1977-78. Dir. Pub. Interest Law Found. NYU. Named Urban Fellow Office of Mayor, N.Y.C. 1973. Mem. Order of Coif.

RYAN, MILES FRANCIS, III, lawyer; b. Washington, July 31, 1963; s. Miles Francis Jr. and Vernance Dolores (Beste) R. AB cum laude, Harvard

U., 1986; JD, Columbia U., 1990. Bar: Pa. 1991, U.S. Ct. Fed. Claims 1995, U.S. Tax Ct. 1995, U.S. Ct. Appeals for Armed Forces 1995, U.S. Ct. Vets. Appeals 1995, U.S. Supreme Ct. 1995. Staff mem. U.S. Senator William Proxmire, Washington, 1980, 82, 83; intern U.S. Senator Tom Harkin, Washington, 1989; law clerk U.S. Dept. Commerce Office of Gen. Counsel's Honors Program, Washington, 1990-91, atty.-advisor, 1991-92; atty.-advisor U.S. Dept. Commerce Office Gen. Counsel's Office of Chief Counsel for Econ. Affairs, Washington, 1992-96; mem. U.S. Dept. Commerce Office of Gen. Counsel's Law Libr. Com., Washington, 1992, 93; key worker U.S. Dept. Commerce's Combined Fed. Campaign, Washington, 1992, 93. Mem. Harvard-Radcliffe Dem. Club, Cambridge, Mass., 1983-86; vol. Joe Kennedy for Congress Campaign, Cambridge, 1986, Don Mooers for Congress Campaign, Wheaton, Md., 1996; at-large mem., treas. Columbia U. Law Sch. Student Senate, N.Y.C., 1987-90, 89-90. Jaffin Pub. Interest and Student Funded Fellowship grantee Columbia U. Sch. Law, 1989, John Harvard scholar Harvard U., 1983-86; recipient Gold Medal award U.S. Dept. Commerce, 1995. Mem. ABA, FBA (D.C. chpt., bd. dirs., alt. nat. del., elected sec., nat. coun. del., nat. membership com., younger lawyers divsn. bd. dirs.), Columbia U. Law Sch. Alumni Assn., Columbia U. Club, Harvard U. Club Washington, KC (local coun. co-comty. activities dir. 1982). Democrat. Roman Catholic. Avocations: reading historical, political and current affairs books and articles, attending public policy and historical lectures, visiting museums, attending the theater and concerts, travel. Home: 12502 Two Farm Dr Silver Spring MD 20904-2931

RYAN, NOEL, librarian, consultant; b. St. John, N.B., Canada, May 27, 1925; s. Fergus James and Evelyn Grace (Hayes) R.; m. Doreen Lillian Allison, Dec. 19, 1950; children: Colin Allison, Karen Jennifer. B.A., Sir George Williams U., Montreal, 1964; M.L.S., McGill U., 1967; M.B.A., Northland U., Toronto, 1983. Vice-pres. Temco Electric Mfg. Co., Montreal, 1949-57; owner, operator photo finishing co. Local Photo, Montreal, 1957-67; chief librarian Dorval (Que.) Pub. Library, 1967-69, Brampton (Ont.) Pub. Library, 1969-71, Mississauga (Ont). Libr. Sys., 1971-87; bldg. projects mgr. Noel Ryan Auditorium Libr. Missauga Ctrl., 1987-89. Joint author: Juxtapoised, 1974. Served with Can. Army, 1944-46, ETO. Mem. Toronto Black Watch Assn. Avocations: painting, making pots, writing poetry. Home and Office: 55 Falconer Dr Apt 35, Mississauga, ON Canada L5N 1B3

RYAN, NOLAN, former professional baseball player; b. Refugio, Tex., Jan. 31, 1947; s. Lynn Nolan and Martha (Hancock) R.; m. Ruth Elsie Holdruff, June 26, 1967. Student, Alvin (Tex.) Jr. Coll., 1966-69. Pitcher N.Y. Mets, N.Y.C., 1966-71, Calif. Angels, 1972-79, Houston Astros, 1980-88, Texas Rangers, 1989-93; mem. Am. League All-Star Team, 1972, 73, 75, 79, Nat. League All-Star Team, 1981, 85. Author: (with Steve Jacobson) Nolan Ryan: Strike-Out King, 1975, (with Bill Libby) Nolan Ryan: The Other Game, 1977, (with Joe Torre) Pitching and Hitting, 1977, (with Harvey Frommer) Throwing Heat: The Autobiography of Nolan Ryan, 1988, (with Tom House) Nolan Ryan's Pitcher's Bible, 1991, (with Jerry Jenkins) Miracle Man: Nolan Ryan, The Autobiography, 1992, (with others) Kings of Hill, 1992. Served with AUS, 1967. Named Sporting News AL pitcher of yr., 1977. Holds over 50 Major League records including most seasons pitched (27), most strikeouts (5,714) and most no-hit games (7). Address: care Texas Rangers Arlington Stadium PO Box 1111 Arlington TX 76004*

RYAN, PATRICK ANDREW, educator; b. Washington, June 15, 1968; s. Miles Francis Jr. and Vernance Dolores (Beste) R. Student, Harvard U., 1985, U. London, 1989-90; BA in English Lit. summa cum laude, U. Pa., 1991; MA in English Lit., U. Va., 1994. Cert. catechist Archdiocese of Washington. Study abroad adviser Office Internat. Programs U. Pa., Phila., 1990-91; seminar leader summer enrichment program U. Va., Charlottesville, 1993-94; lang. arts and religion tchr. St. Bartholomew Sch., Bethesda, Md., 1994—; mem. secondary sch. com. U. Pa., 1996—. Mem. Phi Beta Kappa, Phi Beta Delta. Democrat. Roman Catholic. Avocations: reading, creative writing, travel. Home: 12502 Two Farm Dr Silver Spring MD 20904

RYAN, PATRICK G., insurance company executive; b. Milw., May 15, 1937; m. Shirley Welsh, Apr. 16, 1966; children: Patrick Jr., Robert J., Corbett M. BS, Northwestern U., 1959. Sales agt. Penn Mut., 1959-64; Pat Ryan & Assocs. Penn Mut., Chgo., 1964-71; chmn., pres. Ryan Ins. Group Inc., Chgo., 1971-82; pres., chief exec. officer Combined Internat. Corp. (now Aon Corp.), Northbrook, Ill., 1982—, bd. dirs., 1982—; chmn., pres., chief exec. officer Aon Corp., Chgo., 1990—; bd. dirs. First Chgo., NBD Corp., Chgo. Trustee Rush-Presbyterian-St. Luke's Med. Ctr., Chgo., chmn. bd. trustees; trustee Northwestern U., Field Mus. Natural History, Chgo. Office: Aon Corp 123 N Wacker Dr Ste 30 Chicago IL 60606-1700*

RYAN, PATRICK M., prosecutor; m. Barbara K. Heinen; children: Michael, Jason, Megan. BA, U. Okla., 1967, JD, 1969. Bar: Okla., U.S. Dist. Ct. (we. and ea. dists.) Okla., U.S. Ct. Appeals (10th cir.), U.S. Ct. Mil. Appeals, U.S. Supreme Ct. Ptnr. Crowe & Dunlevy, Oklahoma City, 1974-81; pres., dir. Ryan, Geister & Whaley, Oklahoma City, 1982-95; U.S. atty. for western dist. Okla. Office of U.S. Atty., Oklahoma City, 1995—. Editor Okla. Law Rev. Trustee World Neighbors, 1994-97; active St. John the Bapt. Cath. Ch., Edmond, Okla. Served JAGC, USAF, 1969-74. Recipient Leadership award Okla. County Bar Assn., 1989. Fellow Okla. Bar Found. (v.p. 1978, 80), Am. Coll. Trial Lawyers (mem. Okla. state com. 1990—); mem. ABA, Okla. Bar Assn. (pv. bd. govs. 1990-93, mem. young lawyers sect.), Order of Coif. Office: US Atty Office Western Dist 210 Park Ave Ste 400 Oklahoma City OK 73102-5602

RYAN, PATRICK MICHAEL, lawyer; b. Chgo., May 26, 1944; s. Edward Michael and Kathleen Teresa (Crimmins) R.; m. Holly Ann Daleske, Aug. 31, 1968; children: Rebecca Eileen, Brendan Patrick, Abigail Christine, Lucas Christopher. BA, St. Mary's Coll., Winona, Minn., 1966; JD, Marquette U., 1969. Bar: Wis. 1969. Law clk. Wis. Supreme Ct., Madison, 1969-70; ptnr. Quarles & Brady, Milw., 1970—; dir. and officer several pvt. bus. corps. Mem. ABA, Wis. Bar Assn., Milw. Bar Assn., University Club. Avocations: reading, sports. Home: 363 Huntington Dr Cedarburg WI 53012-9507 Office: Quarles & Brady 411 E Wisconsin Ave Milwaukee WI 53202-4409

RYAN, RANDEL EDWARD, JR., airline pilot; b. N.Y.C., Jan. 11, 1940; s. Randel Edward and Ann Augusta (Horwath) R.; m. Pamela Michael Wiley, May 12, 1962; children: Katherine, Gregory. BS in Sci., Trinity Coll., 1961. Quality control supr. Ideal Toy Corp., Jamaica, N.Y., 1961-62; airline pilot United Airlines, San Francisco, 1967—. Editor: The Lowdown, 1980-83. Pres., Highlands Community Assn., San Mateo, Calif., 1975; chmn. Com. to Re-elect County Supr., San Mateo, 1976; mediator San Mateo County, 1986-95; arbitrator Better Bus. Bureau, 1988-95; rep. Highlands Community Assn., San Mateo, 1970-86; coach Little League and Babe Ruth Baseball, San Mateo, 1979-83. Served to capt. USAF, 1962-68. Recipient Vandor award San Mateo PTA, 1976, awards of merit United Airlines, San Francisco, 1975, 79. Mem. Air Line Pilots Assn. (chmn. speakers panel 1983-86, community rels com. 1983-86, bd. dirs. 1986-89, 91-93, chmn. coun. 34 1991-93, vice-chmn. 1986-89, editor newspaper The Bayliner 1984-86, mem. contract study com. 1984-86, vice-chmn. MEC grievance com. 1989-91, chmn. MEC grievance rev. 1993—, mem. nat. hearing bd. 1994—).Democrat. Club: Midtown Tennis (Chgo.). Home: 175 N Harbor Dr Apt 5402 Chicago IL 60601-7353 Office: United Airlines O Hare Internat Airport Chicago IL 60601

RYAN, RAYMOND D., retired steel company executive, insurance and marketing firm executive; b. Big Timber, Mont., Feb. 7, 1922; s. Robert Allen and Elsie (Beery) R.; m. Eunice Dale Burnett, Jan. 17, 1943; children: Raymond Brant, Brenda Ruth, Ronald Dale. BA, U. Mont., 1948, JD (hon.), 1970; LLM, NYU, 1949. Bar: Mont. 1948. Various fin. officer positions U.S. Steel and subsidiaries in U.S. and Venezuela, 1949-75; v.p., treas. U.S. Steel, 1975-83; pres. The Evergreen Group Inc., Stamford, Conn., 1984-94, chmn., 1995-96; chmn. Evergreen Benefits Inc., 1996—. With mil. police AUS, 1943-45, ETO. Mem. ABA, Duquesne Club (Pitts.), Allegheny County Club (Sewickley), Met. Club (N.Y.C.), Phi Sigma Kappa, Phi Delta Phi. Office: 301 Tresser Blvd Stamford CT 06901-3239 *Although luck and ambition are the basis of many apparently successful careers, true success comes from hard work, ethical relationships, dedication, and a willingness to accept responsibility.*

RYAN, REGINA CLAIRE (MRS. PAUL DEUTSCHMAN), editor, book packager, literary agent; b. N.Y.C., June 19, 1938; d. Edward F.X. and Kathryn Regina (Gallagher) R.; m. Paul Deutschman, Apr. 11, 1970. B.A., Trinity Coll., 1960; postgrad., New Sch. for Social Research, 1960-61, N.Y. U. Film Sch., 1961, N.Y. U. Grad. Sch. English, 1962-63. Copywriter trainee, sec. J. Walter Thompson Co., N.Y.C., 1960-64; asst. to mng. editor Alfred A. Knopf, Inc., N.Y.C., 1964-67; editor Alfred A. Knopf, Inc., 1967-75, editor-in-chief, v.p. Gen. Books div. Macmillan Pub. Co., N.Y.C., 1975-76; pres. Regina Ryan Pub. Enterprises, Inc., N.Y.C., 1976—. Co-author: Janice LaRouche's Strategies for Women at Work, 1984, 1987. Active Larchmont-Mamaroneck Young Reps., 1960-64; campaign worker, speech writer mayoralty campaign, Larchmont, 1962, 64; mem. Manhattan Women's Polit. Caucus, 1972-74; mem. com. Jimmy Carter Presdl. Campaign; mem., chmn. Sherman Dem. Town Com., 1985-86; mem. Jewish Cmty. Ctr. for Sherman; Justice of the Peace, Sherman Ct., 1986-96. Mem. PEN Am. Ctr., Women's Forum (bd. dirs. 1976-77, co-chair issues com. 1990-92), Am. Book Prodrs.' Assn. (pres. 1985-86, dir. 1985-88, 93-96), Women's Media Group, Nat. Women's Health Network, Nat. Abortion Rights Action League, Internat. Women's Com. on Human Rights, Planned Parenthood of Conn., The Mad Gardeners. Democrat. Home and Office: 251 Central Park W New York NY 10024-4134 also: 3 Coburn Rd W Sherman CT 06784-2218

RYAN, ROBERT, consulting company executive; b. Columbus, Ohio, July 25, 1922; s. Howard L. and Jannie Gertrude (McComis) R.; m. Esther Lee Moore, Mar. 15, 1947; children: Phillip Craig, Lynda Joyce, Lois Jean. BS in Indsl. Engring, Ohio State U., 1947. Registered profl. engr., Ohio, Ind. Maintenance foreman Internat. Harvester Co., Richmond, Ind., 1947-52; prin. welding engr. Battelle Meml. Inst., Columbus, 1952-55; dir. engring. Columbia Gas System, Columbus, 1955-67; sr. v.p. Columbia Gas System, Pitts., 1967-73; sr. v.p., dir. Columbia Gas Cos. in Pa., W.Va., Md., N.Y., 1973-75; dir. Columbia Gas Distbn. Cos., N.Y., Md., Ky., Ohio, W.Va., Va., Ohio Energy and Resource Devel. Agy., 1975-76, Ohio Dept. Energy, 1977-80; mem. Gov.'s Cabinet; pres. Robert S. Ryan & Assocs., 1981—; chmn. bd. dirs. Resource Gen. Corp., Columbus, 1995-96. Contbr. articles profl. jours. Served to capt. U.S. Army, 1943-46, Japan. Recipient Disting. Alumnus award Ohio State U. Coll. Engring., 1970. Mem. NSPE, Am. Gas Assn., Pa. Gas Assn. (pres. 1974), Capital Club (Columbus). Republican. Methodist. Avocation: golf. Home: 6566 Plesenton Dr S Columbus OH 43085-2931 Office: Robert S Ryan & Assocs 6566 Plesenton Dr S Columbus OH 43085-2931

RYAN, ROBERT COLLINS, lawyer; b. Evanston, Ill., Sept. 15, 1953; s. Donald Thomas and Patricia J. (Collins) R.; m. Joanne Kay Holata, Nov. 5, 1983. BA in Econs., BS in Indsl. Engring. with high honors, U. Ill., 1976; JD, Northwestern U., 1979. Bar: Ill. 1979, U.S. Dist. Ct. (no. dist.) Ill. 1980, U.S. Ct. Appeals (Fed. cir.) 1982, U.S. Supreme Ct. 1984. Assoc., Allegretti, Newitt, Witcoff & McAndrews, Ltd., Chgo., 1979-83, ptnr. 1983-88; founding ptnr. McAndrews, Held & Malloy, Ltd., Chgo., 1988-96, of counsel, 1996—; gen. intellectual property and licensing counsel, exec. v.p. StarGuide Digital Networks, Inc., Reno, 1996—; lectr. engring. law Northwestern U. Tech. Inst., Evanston, Ill., 1981-85, adj. prof. engring. law, 1985-90; lectr. patent law and appellate practice John Marshall Law Sch., 1991-93, adj. prof. patent law and appellate advocacy, 1993—; mem. alumni bd. mech. and indsl. engring. dept. U. Ill., Urbana, 1996—. Exec. editor Northwestern Jour. Internat. Law & Bus., 1978-79; contbr. articles to profl. jours. Bd. dirs. Washoe Assn. Retarded Citizens, Reno. Recipient Mech. and Indsl. Engring. Dept. Outstanding Alumnus award U. Ill., 1997; James scholar U. Ill., 1976. Mem. ABA, Fed. Cir. Bar Assn., Intellectual Property Law Assn. Chgo., Licensing Execs. Soc., Tau Beta Pi, Phi Eta Sigma, Alpha Pi Mu, Phi Kappa Phi. Home: 95 Rimfire Cir Reno NV 89509 Office: StarGuide Digital Networks 300 E 2nd St Ste 1510 Reno NV 89501-1584

RYAN, STEPHEN COLLISTER, funeral director; b. Salina, Kans., Jan. 10, 1942; s. Kenneth Richard and Janys (Collister) R.; m. Lynne Katheryn Slease, June 18, 1966; children: Scott Richard, Carrie Anne. BS in Bus. Adminstrn., U. Kans., 1964; Cert. in Mortuary Sci., Kans. U. Med. Ctr., 1965. Cert. funeral svc. practitioner; lic. funeral dir. and embalmer. Sec.-treas. Ryan Mortuary, Inc., Salina, 1969-80, pres., COO, 1980—. Contbr. articles to profl. jours. Mem., chmn. City Planning Commn., Salina, 1981-85; mem. Salina City Commn., 1985-93, 95, mayor, 1987-88, 91-92; chmn. Govt. Bldg. Authority, Salina, 1990-91, 92-93; mem. Kans. State Bd. Mortuary Arts, 1996—. Capt. USAF, 1965-69. Mem. Nat. Selected Morticians (bd. dirs. 1993-96, pres. 1995-96), Nat. Funeral Dirs. Assn. (Spl. Recognition award 1991), Kans. Funeral Dirs. Assn. (bd. dirs. 1984-92, pres. 1990-91), Kans. State Bd. Mortuary Arts, Morticians of the S.W. (Kans. Funeral Dir. of Yr. 1991), Salina Area C. of C. (bd. dirs. 1982-84, 94—, vice chair 1984-85, sec./treas. 1994-95, chmn. 1996-97), Lions, Masons (Knight Comdrs. Ct. of Honor, 32 KCCH), Shriners, Phi Gamma Delta. Republican. Lutheran. Avocations: golf, nautilus exercise. Home: 2313 Melrose Ln Salina KS 67401-3546 Office: Ryan Mortuary Inc 137 N 8th St Salina KS 67401-2605

RYAN, STEPHEN J., academic dean. AB, Providence Coll., 1961; MD, Johns Hopkins U., 1965. Intern Bellevue Hosp., N.Y.C., 1965-66; resident Wilmer Inst. Ophthalmology Johns Hopkins U., Balt., 1966-69, chief resident, 1969-70; fellow Armed Force Inst. Pathology, Washington, 1970-71; instr. ophthalmology Johns Hopkins U., Balt., 1970-71, asst. prof., 1971-72, assoc. prof., 1972-74; prof., chmn. dept. ophthalmology L.A. County-U. So. Calif. Med. Ctr., 1974-95; prof. dept. ophthalmology, 1974—; acting head ophthalmology divsn. dept. surgery Children's Hosp., L.A., 1975-77; med. dir. Doheny Eye Inst., L.A., 1977-86, chief of staff, 1985-88; dean U. So. Calif. Sch. Medicine, L.A., 1991—; mem. adv. panel Calif. Med. Assn., 1975—. Editor: (with M.D. Andrews) A Survey of Ophthalmology--Manual for Medical Students, 1970, (with R.E. Smith) Selected Topics on the Eye in Systemic Disease, 1974, (with Dawson and Little) Retinal Diseases, 1985, (with others) Retina, 1989; assoc. editor: Ophthalmol. Surgery, 1974-85; mem. editl. bd. Am. Jour. Ophthalmology, 1981—, Internat. Ophthalmology, 1982—, Retina, 1983—, Graefes Archives, 1984—; contbr. articles to med. jours. Recipient cert. of merit AMA, 1971; Louis B. Mayer Scholar award Rsch. to Prevent Blindness, 1973; Rear Adm. William Campbell Chambliss USN award, 1982. Mem. Wilmer Ophthal. Inst. Residents Assn., Am. Acad. Ophthalmology and Otolaryngology (award of Merit 1975), Am. Ophthal. Soc., Pan-Am. Assn. Ophthalmology, Assn. Univ. Profs. of Ophthalmology, L.A. Soc. Ophthalmology, AMA, Calif. Med. Assn., L.A. County Med. Assn., Pacific Coast Oto-Ophthal. Soc., L.A. Acad. Medicine, Pan Am. Assn. Microsurgery, Macula Soc., Retina Soc., Nat. Eye Care Project, Rsch. Study Club, Jules Gonin Club, Soc. Scholars of Johns Hopkins U. (life). Office: U So Calif Sch Medicine 840 W 34th St # 403 Los Angeles CA 90007-3501

RYAN, STEPHEN JOSEPH, JR., ophthalmology educator, university dean; b. Honolulu, Mar. 20, 1940; s. S.J. and Mildred Elizabeth (Farrer) F.; m. Anne Christine Mullady, Sept. 25, 1965; 1 dau., Patricia Anne. A.B., Providence Coll., 1961; M.D., Johns Hopkins U., 1965. Intern Bellevue Hosp., N.Y.C., 1965-66; resident Wilmer Inst. Ophthalmology, Johns Hopkins Hosp., Balt., 1966-69, chief resident, 1969-70; fellow Armed Force Inst. Pathology, Washington, 1970-71; instr. ophthalmology Johns Hopkins U., Balt., 1970-71, asst. prof., 1971-72, assoc. prof., 1972-74; prof., chmn. dept. ophthalmology Los Angeles County-U. So. Calif. Med. Ctr., L.A., 1974-95, prof. dept. ophthalmology, 1974—; acting head ophthalmology div., dept. surgery Children's Hosp., L.A., 1975-77; med. dir. Doheny Eye Inst. (formerly Estelle Doheny Eye Found.), L.A., 1977-86; chief of staff Doheny Eye Hosp., L.A., 1985-88; dean U. So. Calif. Sch. Medicine, L.A., 1991—; mem. advisory panel Calif. Med. Assn., 1975—. Editor: (with M.D. Andrews) A Survey of Ophthalmology--Manual for Medical Students, 1970, (with R.E. Smith) Selected Topics on the Eye in Systemic Disease, 1974, (with Dawson and Little) Retinal Diseases, 1985, (with others) Retina, 1989; assoc. editor: Ophthalmol. Surgery, 1974-85; mem. editorial bd. Am. Jour. Ophthalmology, 1981—, Internat. Ophthalmology, 1982—, Retina, 1983—, Graefes Archives, 1984—; contbr. articles to med. jours. Recipient cert. of merit AMA, 1971; Louis B. Mayer Scholar award Research to Prevent Blindness, 1973; Rear Adm. William Campbell Chambliss USN award, 1982. Mem. Wilmer Ophthal. Inst. Residents Assn., Am. Acad. Ophthalmology and Otolaryngology (award of Merit 1975), Am. Ophthal. Soc., Pan-Am. Assn. Ophthalmology, Assn. Univ. Profs. of Ophthalmology, L.A. Soc. Ophthalmology, AMA, Calif. Med. Assn., Los Angeles County Med. Assn., Pacific Coast Oto-Ophthal. Soc., L.A. Acad. Medicine, Pan Am. Assn. Microsurgery, Macula Soc, Retina Soc., Nat. Eye Care Project, Rsch. Study Club, Jules Gonin Club, Soc. Scholars of Johns Hopkins U. (life). Office: U So Calif Sch of Medicine 1450 San Pablo St Los Angeles CA 90033-4615

RYAN, STEPHEN MICHAEL, JR., professional hockey team executive; m. Marie Ryan; 1 child. BS, Fordham U., 1964. Br. mgr., sales mgr. Maxwell House divsn. Gen Foods Corp., 1965-72; sr. mgr. Marriott Corp., 1972-75, Am. Brands Corp., 1975-77; v.p., chief mktg. officer Paddington Corp., 1978-81; v.p. mktg. and pub. rels. NHL Enterprises, 1981-86, pres. CEO, 1986-95; pres., COO Pitts. Sports Assocs. Holding Co., 1995—; dir. Hockey Hall of Fame Entertainment Complex, 1990. Creator The NHL TV Awards: A Celebration of Excellence; establisher NHL All-Star Weekend, 1990. Mem. USO World Bd., Washington; nat. bd. dirs. Boys Home, St. Louis; mem. Bus. Coun. for UN and Cardinals's Com. of Laity; past trustee Dominican Coll., Blauvelt, N.Y., chmn. devel. and pub. rels. com. Office: Pitts Penguins Civic Arena Gate No 9 Pittsburgh PA 15219*

RYAN, SUZANNE IRENE, nursing educator; b. Yonkers, N.Y., Mar. 13, 1939; d. Edward Vincent and Winifred E. (Goemann) R. BA in Biology, Mt. St. Agnes Coll., Balt., 1962; BSN, Columbia U., 1967, MA in Nursing Svc., 1973, MEd in Nursing Edn., 1975; MS in Oncology, San Jose (Calif.) State Coll. U., 1982. RN, N.Y.; cert. AIDS educator, N.Y. Prof. nursing Molloy Coll., Rockville Centre, N.Y., 1970—, co-dir. health svcs., dir. ednl. programs, 1987-94, dir. health svcs., 1994—, health educator, 1992—, co-dir. mobile health van, adminstr. health edn., 1992—; pres., CEO SIR Enterprises, Inc., 1982—; photographer Molloy Coll. Pubs., 1991—; photographic dir. Bali-Art, Inc., 1992—; mem. N.Y. State AIDS Coun., 1987—, L.I. Alcohol Consortium, 1987—; educator Nassau County Dept. Sr. Citizens Health, 1991—; photographer-in-residence Molloy Coll., 1992—; lectr. on landscape, wildlife and flower photography, L.I., N.H., Can., 1993—. Represented in permanent collections in photographic galleries in Carmel, Calif., Laconia, Wolfboro and Moultonboro, N.H., 1963—; one-woman shows include Mollay Coll., Rockville Ctr. Library; photographer 4 books on Monterey Peninulsa, New Eng. and N.H.; writer, editor Health News Letter Molloy Coll., 1990—. Health educator Nassau County Dept. of Sr. Citizens Outreach Program, Molloy Coll., AIDS educator, 1991—; adminstr., chief AIDS counselor Interaction AIDS Counseling, Babylon, N.Y., 1992—; lic. AIDS educator N.Y. Metro Area; chairperson of grants com. in higher edn. Nassau U. USPHS fellow, 1962, Nat. Cancer Inst. fellow, 1981-82. Mem. AAUP, AAUW, Nat. Congress Oncology Nurses, N.Y. State Fedn. Health Educators, Inc., Nurses Assn. Counties L.I. Dist. 14, N.Y. State Nurses Assn., World Wildlife Orgn., Audubon Soc., Internat. Ctr. Photography, Nature Conservancy, Sierra Club, Sigma Theta Tau (Epsilon Kappa chpt., rsch. grantee 1985, 87), Zeta Epsilon Gamma. Roman Catholic. Avocation: writing, photography. Home: 16 Walker St Malverne NY 11565-1829

RYAN, SYLVESTER D., bishop; b. Catalina Island, Calif., Sept. 3, 1930. Grad., St. John's Sem., Camarillo, Calif. Ordained priest Roman Cath. Ch., 1957, titular bishop of Remesiana. Aux. bishop L.A., 1990-92; bishop Monterey, Calif., 1992—. Office: Chancery Office PO Box 2048 580 Fremont St Monterey CA 93942*

RYAN, TERESA WEAVER, obstetrical and clinical nurse specialist; b. Dallas, July 18, 1956; d. J.E. and Mary (Davis) Weaver; m. Patrick Hallaron Ryan, Apr. 7, 1991. BS, Troy State U., 1983; BSN, Tex. Christian U., 1987; MSN, U. South Ala., 1994; postgrad., La. State U. RN, Fla.; cert. maternal-newborn nurse ANCC. Intelligence analyst USN, Dallas, 1983-87; enlisted USAF, 1987, advanced through grades to capt. (obstetrical nurse), 1987—; childbirth educator USAF, 1988—. Mem. NOW, Assn. Women's Health, Obstetrical and Neonatal Nurses, Nat. Humane Soc. Educators, People for the Ethical Treatment of Animals, Sigma Theta Tau (sec. 1987—, rsch. grant 1987), Phi Kappa Phi. Roman Catholic. Avocations: aerobics, nursing history, gourmet cooking, animal welfare. Home: 35 Imperial Woods Dr Harahan LA 70123

RYAN, TERRY, professional sports team executive; m. Karilyn Ryan; children: Tim, Kathleen. Diploma in Phys. Edn., U. Wis., 1979. Scouting dir. Minn. Twins, 1986-91; profl. scout N.Y. Mets, 1980-86; profl. baseball player Minn. Twins, 1972-76, v.p. player personnel, 1991-94, v.p., gen. mgr., 1994—. Office: Minnesota Twins 501 Chicago Ave Minneapolis MN 55415-1517

RYAN, THOMAS F., lawyer; b. Detroit, Nov. 4, 1943. BS, Ferris State U., 1965; JD magna cum laude, Wayne State U., 1971. Bar: Ill. 1972, U.S. Supreme Ct. 1978. Ptnr. Sidley & Austin, Chgo.; mem. adv. com. cir. rules 7th Fed Ct. Appeals. 1st lt. U.S. Army, 1966-68. Fellow Am. Coll. Trial Lawyers; mem. Chgo. Bar Assn. (mem. jud. evaluation com.), 7th Cir. Bar Assn. (bd. govs. 1986-89, 2nd v.p. 1990-91, pres. 1991-92). Office: Sidley & Austin 1 First Natl Plz Chicago IL 60603-2003

RYAN, TIMOTHY CHRISTOPHER, anchor, reporter; b. Albany, N.Y., Mar. 7, 1955; s. Donald H. and Maureen (Fitzsimmons) R.; m. Beth Hunt, Oct. 7, 1984; children: Meghan, Patrick. BS in Mass Comm. with honors, Ariz. State U., 1976. Anchor, reporter Sta. KPNX-TV, Phoenix, 1977-81; reporter Sta. KTRK-TV, Houston, 1981-83, Sta. WLS-TV, Chgo., 1983-89; reporter Sta. KDFW-TV, Dallas, 1989-94, anchor, reporter, 1995—; news dir. Sta. KSTU-TV, Salt Lake City, 1994-95. Recipient Chgo. Emmy award, 1988. Mem. Radio-TV News Dir. Assn. (Edward R. Murrow award 1995). Office: Sta KDFW-TV 400 N Griffin St Dallas TX 75202-1905

RYAN, TOM KREUSCH, cartoonist; b. Anderson, Ind., June 6, 1926; s. Francis Gavin and Mary Katherine (Kreusch) Ryan Smith; m. Joanne Faulkner, Dec. 19, 1947; children—Linda, Tim, Dan, Diane. Student, U. Notre Dame, 1945, U. Cin., 1946-47. Artist Del. Engraving Co., Muncie, Ind., 1950-54, Robinson Agy., Muncie, 1954-60; free-lance artist, 1960-65. Author: Best of Tumbleweeds, 1993; syndicated cartoonist Tumbleweeds, Lew Little Syndicate, 1965-82; pub. 20 paperback book compilations of strips, 1970-87; created Tumbleweeds Gulch, a sect. MGM Grand Theme Park, Las Vegas. Named Hon. Old Master Purdue U., 1978. Mem. Nat. Cartoonists Soc. (Outstanding Cartoonist cert. 1970, 80), Graphic Artists Guild. Roman Catholic.

RYAN, WILLIAM FRANCIS, priest; b. Renfrew, Ont., Can., Apr. 4, 1925; s. William Patrick Ryan and Helen Mary Doneg. BA, Montreal U., 1951; MA in Labor Rels., St. Louis U., 1953; postgrad., Heythrop Coll., Oxon, Eng.; STL, St. Albert Coll., Louvain, 1958; PhD in Econs., Harvard U., 1964. Ordained priest Roman Catholic Ch., 1957. Asst. prof. econs. Loyola Coll., Montreal, Que., Can., 1963-65; nat. dir. Social Justice Office Can. Conf. Cath. Bishops, Ottawa, Ont., 1964-70, gen. sec., 1984-90; founding dir. Ctr. of Concern, Washington, 1970-78; nat. supr. Jesuit Order, Toronto, Ont., Can., 1978-84; chancellor Sch. Theology Regis Coll., Toronto, 1978-84; vis. sr. rsch. fellow Can. Inst. for Internat. Peace and Security, Ottawa, 1990-91; chair on Cath. social thought St. Paul U., Ottawa, 1991-92; dir. Jesuit Project on Ethics in Politics, Ottawa, 1992—; exec. sec. Inter-religious Peace Colloquium, Washington, 1975-78; bd. dirs. Roncalli Internat. Found., Montreal, 1979-83, North/South Inst., Ottawa, 1979-91; spl. advisor to Internat. Devel. Rsch. Ctr., Ottawa, 1993—; lectr. in field. Author: The Clergy and Economic Growth in Quebec, 1966, Culture, Spirituality and Economic Development—Opening a Dialogue, 1995; co-author: Religious as Contemplatives in the 80's, 1984; translator: The Primacy of Charity in Moral Theology, 1961; contbr. articles to profl. jours. Mem. Am. Econs. Assn. Avocations: hiking; skiing. Office: 169 Sunnyside Ave, Ottawa, ON Canada K1S 0R2

RYAN, WILLIAM JOSEPH, communications company executive; b. Nyack, N.Y., Apr. 14, 1932; s. William Joseph and Elizabeth (Langley) R.; m. Jane Householder, June 27, 1970; children: Ashley Allison, William Joseph, III. BA, U. Notre Dame, 1954. TV producer Jules Power Prodn., Chgo., 1954-56; pres., gen. mgr. Radio Naples, Naples, Fla., 1956-70; gen. mgr. Radio Naples (Fla.) div. Palmer Broadcasting, 1970-73; v.p., cable-radio Palmer Broadcasting, Fla. and Calif., 1973-80; v.p. cable Palmer Communications, Naples, 1980-82; pres. Palmer Communications, Inc., Des Moines, 1982-84, pres., chief exec. officer, 1984-95; pres. CEO Palmer Wireless Inc., 1995—; bd. dirs. Norwest Bank, Des Moines, C&S Bank, Ft.

Myers, Fla., Naples Cmty. Hosp. State committeeman Rep. Com., Collier County, Fla., 1970-72; pres. Navy League, Naples, local chpt. Am. Cancer Soc.; chmn. Collier County Econ. Devel. Coun.; bd. dirs. Philharm. Ctr. Arts, Naples Philharm.; chmn. Collier County Econ. Devel. Coun. Recipient Walter Kaitz award Nat. Cable TV Assn. Mem. Cable Advt. Bur. (founding chmn., bd. dirs.), Econ. Develop. Coun. (chmn.), So. Cable Assn. (pres.), Fla. Cable Assn. (pres.), Fla. Assn. Broadcasters (pres.), Cable TV Pioneers, Broadcast Pioneers, Cable TV Adminstrn. and Mktg. Soc. (Grand Tammy award 1981), Cellular Telephone Industry Assn. (bd. dirs.), Naples C. of C. (pres.), Royal Poinciana Club, Bay Colony Club. Office: Palmer Wireless Inc 12800 University Dr Ste 500 Fort Myers FL 33907-5337

RYAN, WILLIAM MATTHEW, state legislator, safety educator; b. Great Falls, Mont., June 28, 1955; s. William Duncan and Jeanette Rosette (Merrill) R.; m. Elaine Louise Brastrup, Jan. 19, 1974; children: Jennifer, Kelli, Katie. Grad., Great Falls. Cert. journeyman, lineman. Meter reader Mont. Power Co., Great Falls, 1973, head meter reader, 1974, dispatcher, 1975, groundman, 1976-79, apprentice, 1979-82, lineman, 1982—; mem. Ho. of Reps. Mont. State Legislature, Helena, 1993—; instr. Mont. Power Apprentice Program, 1982—. Recipient Medal of Valor State of Mont., 1995. Mem. NAACP, Internat. Brotherhood Elec. Workers (local 44, unit v.p. 1984—, officer exam bd. 1988—, sec. Joint Apprenticeship Tng. Com. 1988—), Rocky Mountain Coord. Assn., Russell Country Sportsman, Walleyes Unlimited. Democrat. Roman Catholic. Avocations: rose gardening, fishing, hunting, youth coach. Home: 8 18th Ave S Great Falls MT 59405-4113 Office: Montana Electric Coop Assoc 501 Bay Dr Po Box 59403 Great Falls MT 59404-2880

RYANS, REGINALD VERNON, music education educator; b. Easton, Md., Oct. 12, 1955; s. Alfred Sr. and Alfreda Elizabeth (Thomas) R. AA, Chesapeake Coll., 1975; BS, Morgan State U., 1980; postgrad., Liberty U., Faith Biblical Theol. Inst. Cert. tchr., Md. Tchr. music Balt. City Pub. Schs., 1980-82; minister of music Faith Unity Fellowship Ch., Millington, Md., 1987—; guest musician various chs., Queen Anne's County, Md., 1970—; European tour to Switzerland, Belgium, France, Germany, The Whosoever Will Choir of Balt., Md., 1995. Mng. editor (news publ.) In Touch, 1992. Mem. NAACP. Recipient Svc. award St. James Male Chorus, 1990, Cert. of Appreciation Faith Unity Fellowship Ministries, 1992; Oradined elder Faith Unity Ministries, 1992; scholar Raskob Found., 1975, Md. State Senate. Avocations: photography, traveling. Home: 121 Rustic Acres Ln Queenstown MD 21658-1270

RYBAK, JAMES PATRICK, engineering educator; b. Cleve., Mar. 16, 1941; s. John Anthony and Irene Marcella (Kovar) R.; m. Linda Louise Watkins, Oct. 12, 1968. BSEE, Case Western Res. U., 1963; MS, U. N.Mex., 1965; PhD, Colo. State U., 1970. Registered profl. engr., Colo. Mem. tech. staff Sandia Nat. Labs., Albuquerque, 1963-66; rsch. asst., NDEA fellow Colo. State U., Ft. Collins, 1966-70, postdoctoral fellow, 1970-72; prof. engring. and math. Mesa State Coll., Grand Junction, Colo., 1972—, asst. v.p. acad. affairs, 1986-88, v.p. acad. affairs, 1988—. Contbr. articles to profl. publs. including IEEE Transactions, Engring. Edn., Popular Electronics, Elektrosvyaz (Russia), Radio (Russia). Mem. adv. bd. Grand Mesa Youth Svcs., Grand Junction, 1986-88; bd. dirs. Hilltop Rehab. Hosp., Grand Junction, 1989-93, Salvation Army, Grand Junction, 1993—. NEDA fellow, 1968-70, THEMIS fellow, 1970-72. Mem. IEEE, Am. Soc. Engring. Edn. (vice chmn. Rocky Mountain sect. 1974-75, chmn. 1975-76). Avocation: amateur radio. Home: 314 Quail Dr Grand Junction CO 81503 Office: Mesa State Coll 1175 Texas Ave Grand Junction CO 81501-7605

RYBCZYK, EDWARD JOSEPH, university director, consultant; b. Middletown, Conn., June 27, 1947; s. Anthony John and Marion (Davis) R.; m. Janice Marie Capasso, Aug. 22, 1970; children: Kurt Anthony, Adam Edward. BS, Ctrl. Conn. State U., 1969; MS, U. Bridgeport, 1974, EdD, 1987. Tchr. Bridgeport (Conn.) Bd. Edn., 1969-74, Shelton (Conn.) Bd. Edn., 1974-79; tng. supr. Emhart Corp., Ansonia, Conn., 1979-83, Atlantic Richfield co., Ansonia, Conn., 1983-84; orgn. devel. specialist Textron Lycoming, Stratford, Conn., 1984-88; dir. personnel Danbury Printing & Litho, Danbury, Conn., 1988-90; exec. dir. Inst. Idls. and Engring. Tech. Ctrl. Conn. U., New Britain, 1990—; adj. prof. U. Bridgeport (Conn.), 1987-88, U. New Haven (Conn.), 1988-92, Ctrl. Conn. State U., New Britain, 1992—. Contbr. articles to profl. jours. Indystry empolyer rep. Conn. State Apprenticeship Coun., Wethersfield, 1979—. Mem. Am. Soc. Tng. and Devel., Rotary Internat. Avocations: computer hobbies, sports. Home: 72 Counselor Dr Naugatuck CT 06770-3174 Office: Ctrl Conn State U Inst Indsl and Engring Tech 185 Main St New Britain CT 06051-2296

RYBCZYNSKI, WITOLD MARIAN, architect, educator, writer; b. Edinburgh, Scotland, Mar. 1, 1943; emigrated to Can., 1953; s. Witold Kasimir and Anna Jadwiga (Hofman) R.; m. Shirley Hallam, Nov. 15, 1974. Diploma, Loyola Coll., Montreal, 1960; B.Arch., McGill U., 1966, M.Arch., 1972. Pvt. practice architecture Montreal, 1970-82; research assoc. McGill U., Montreal, 1972-75, asst. prof. architecture, 1975-80, assoc. prof., 1980-86, prof., 1986-93; Meyerson prof. of Urbanism U. Pa., 1994—; cons. UN, Manila, 1976, Internat. Devel. Research Ctr., Ottawa, 1977, Banco de Mex., 1979-80. Author: Paper Heroes: A Review of Appropriate Technology, 1980, Taming the Tiger: The Struggle to Control Technology, 1983, Home: A Short History of an Idea, 1986, The Most Beautiful House in the World, 1989, Waiting for the Weekend, 1991, Looking Around: A Journey Through Architecture, 1992, A Place for Art, 1993, City Life, 1995; contbg. editor: Saturday Night, 1990—; adv. bd. Encyclopedia Americana; editor Wharton Real Estate Rev., 1996—. Recipient QSPELL lit. prize for nonfiction, 1988, 89, Prix Paul-Henri Lapointe, 1988, Progressive Architecture Design award, 1991, Alfred Jurzykowski Found. award, 1993, Athanaeum Lit. prize, 1997; Ballard Real Estate scholar, 1994-95. Fellow AIA (hon.); mem. Authors Guild, Congress for a New Urbanism. Home: 230 Rex Ave Philadelphia PA 19118-3719 Office: Grad Sch Fine Arts U Pa 215 Meyerson Hall Philadelphia PA 19104

RYCE, DONALD THEODORE, lawyer; b. New Orleans, Dec. 15, 1943; s. Donald Theodore and Martha (Herndon) R.; m. Claudine Dianne Walker, July 8, 1984; children: Ted, Martha, Jimmy. BA, U. Fla., 1966, JD, 1968. Bar: Fla. 1968, U.S. Dist. Ct. (so. dist.) Fla. 1972, U.S. Ct. Appeals (5th and 11th cirs.) 1973; approved arbitrator Broward County Sheriff's Office. Jud. law clk. Fla. Dist. Ct. Appeals (4th cir.), West Palm Beach, 1968-70; ptnr. Hogg, Allen, Ryce, Norton & Blue, Miami, Fla., 1970-89; pvt. practice Miami, 1989-96; ptnr. Hogg, Ryce & Hudson, Miami, 1997—; co-chmn. liaison com. labor and employment sect. NLRB, Fla., 1990—, mem. publs. com., 1990—, exec. coun. labor and employment sect. Active Fla. Police Chiefs Edn. Rsch. Found.; dir. Jimmy Ryce Ctr. for Victims of Predatory Abduction, Internat. Ctr. Search and Recovery of Missing Children. Named to Policeman Hall of Fame, 1996; recipient Leadership award Fla. Police Chiefs Edn. Rsch. Found., 1993. Mem. ABA, Microcomputer Edn. for Employment of the Disabled (bus. adv. coun.), Winter Haven C. of C. (Cmty. Leadership award 1994), Miami Beach C. of C., Bankers Club, Grand Knight of Order of Michael the Archangel, Rotary. Episcopalian. Avocations: tennis, gourmet cooking. Home: Ste 1036 1506 Seacoast Towers Miami Beach FL 33140 Office: 5151 Collins Ave Apt 1036 Miami FL 33140-2716

RYCHETSKY, STEVE, civil and environmental engineer, consultant; b. Phoenix, Oct. 9, 1951; s. Edward and Maria (Zabroni) R.; m. Dawna Marie Strunk, June 10, 1972 (div. Oct. 1985); children: Brian, Melissa; m. Michaele Ann Turner, Dec. 28, 1986; children: Mike, Kristi, Jaye, Karly. AA in Engring., Oreg. Inst. Tech., 1972, BTech, 1976. Registered profl. civil engr., Oreg., Calif. Mgr. sales engring. Varcopruden, Turlock, Calif., 1976-79, AMCA Internat., Winston-Salem, N.C., 1979-82; civil engr. USDA Natural Resources Conservation Svc., Klamath Falls, Oreg., 1983-85; tech. advisor USDA Soil Conservation Service, Klamath Falls, Oreg., 1983-88; civil engr., tech. advisor USDA Natural Resources Conservation Svc., Tillamook, Oreg., 1985—; private cons. engr. Tillamook, Oreg., 1985—. Active vol. cons. svcs. for environ. handicapped and children projects; bd. dirs. Tillamook Anglers, Inc., 1990-94. Democrat. Roman Catholic. Avocation: outdoor activities. Home: PO Box 1457 Redmond OR 97756 Office: Rychetsky Turner & Assocs Inc PO Box 1457 Redmond OR 97756

RYCHLAK, JOSEPH FRANK, psychology educator, theoretician; b. Cudahy, Wis., Dec. 17, 1928; s. Joseph Walter and Helen Mary (Bieniek) R.; m. Lenora Pearl Smith, June 16, 1956; children: Ronald, Stephanie. B.S., U. Wis., 1953; M.A., Ohio State U., 1954, Ph.D., 1957. Diplomate Am. Bd. Examiners in Profl. Psychology. Asst. prof. psychology Fla. State U., Tallahassee, 1957-58, Washington State U., Pullman, 1958-61; assoc. prof., then prof. psychology St. Louis U., 1961-69; prof. psychology Purdue U., West Lafayette, Ind., 1969-83, interim dept. head, 1979-80; prof. Loyola U. Chgo., 1983—, Maude C. Clarke prof. humanistic psychology, 1983—; dir. Human Relations Ctr., Pullman, Wash., 1958-61; research cons. AT&T, 1957-82. Author: The Psychology of Rigorous Humanism, 1977, 2d edit., 1988, Discovering Free Will and Personal Responsibility, 1979, A Philosophy of Science for Personality Theory, 2d edit., 1981, Personality and Life Style of Young Male Managers, 1982, (with N. Cameron) Personality Development and Psychopathology, 2d edit., 1985, Artificial Intelligence and Human Reason: A Teleological Critique, 1991; assoc. editor Psychotherapy: Theory, Research and Practice, 1965-76, Jour. Mind and Behavior, 1985-94, Logical Learning Theory: A Human Teleology and Its Empirical Support, 1994, In Defense of Human Consciousness, 1996. With USAF, 1946-49. Named Outstanding Contbr. to Human Understanding, Internat. Assn. Social Psychiatry, 1971. Fellow Am. Psychol. Assn. (div. 24 pres. 1977-78, 86-87), Am. Psychol. Soc.; mem. Soc. Personality Assessment, Phi Beta Kappa. Roman Catholic. Home: 916 Michigan Ave Apt 2 Evanston IL 60202-1463 Office: Loyola U Chgo Dept Psychology 6525 N Sheridan Rd Chicago IL 60626-5311 *From my father I learned to have a sense of purpose, work hard, and assume responsibility. From my mother I learned not to take myself too seriously, and to realize that my achievements are never entirely up to me.*

RYCKMAN, DEVERE WELLINGTON, consulting environmental engineer; b. South Boardman, Mich., May 27, 1924; s. Seymour Willard and LaVerne Eliza (Jenkins) R.; m. Betty Jane Rendall, May 28, 1949; children—Mark, Jill, Stewart. Student, U. Maine at Orono, 1941-43; BS in Civil Engring, Rensselaer Poly. Inst., 1944; MS in Civil Engring, Mich. State U., 1949; ScD, MIT, 1956. Diplomate: Am. Acad. Environ. Engrs. Cons. san. engr. Frank R. Theroux & Assos., East Lansing, Mich., 1946-53; environ. engr., research asst. Mass. Inst. Tech., 1953-56; A.P. Greensfelder prof. environ. engring. Washington U., St. Louis, 1956-69; founder, pres. Ryckman/Edgerley/Tomlinson & Assocs., St. Louis, 1956-75; pres., dir. Reta/Nolte & Assocs., San Francisco, 1974-76; founder, mem. bd. dirs. D.W. Ryckman & Assocs., St. Louis, 1975—; also Ryckman's Emergency Action and Cons. Team (REACT); asst. prof. Mich. State U., 1946-53; vis. prof. U. Hawaii, Honolulu, 1962-63; pres., dir. Environ. Triple S Co., St. Louis, 1969-75. Contbr. articles to profl. jours. Mem., dir. Mo. Gov.'s Sci. Adv. Bd., 1959-66; mem. Washington Arch. and Engrs. Pub. Affairs Conf., 1969-75; founder grad. program environ. engring. Washington U.; mem. adv. bd. Salvation Army, 1987—; bd. dirs. Ctr. for Biology, Washington U., 1964-70, Arts and Edn. Fund, St. Louis, 1970-75; chmn. Salvation Army Bequest & Endowment Fund, 1991—; mem. U.S. EPA Rsch. Rev. Bd. With USNR, 1944-46, capt. USPHS Res., 1946—. Mem. ASCE (Profl. Recognition award 1991), MIT Alumni (dir. leadership fund 1970-74), Am. Water Works Assn. (Man of Yr. 1965), Engrs. Club St. Louis (award of merit 1970, Hon. Mem. award 1993), Cons. Engring. Coun. U.S. (Grand Conceptor award for excellence in design 1969), Cons. Engrs. Coun. Mo. (dir. 1971-75, pres. 1973-75), Nat. Soc. Profl. Engrs., Air Pollution Control Assn., Water Environment Fedn., Assn. Environ. Engring. Profls., William Greenleaf Eliot Soc., Washington U. Mo. Athletic Club, Masons, Shriners, Rotary (mem. program and membership coms.), Sigma Xi, Tau Beta Pi, Chi Epsilon, Lambda Chi Alpha. Republican. Congregationalist (chmn. exec. com., bd. deacons, bd. Christian edn. 1960-72, chmn. stewardship campaign 1992-93). Clubs: Washington U. Century, Masons, Shriners, Rotary (mem. program and membership coms.). Patentee in field. Address: 1733 S Vandeventer Ave Saint Louis MO 63110-2223

RYCROFT, DONALD CAHILL, insurance executive; b. Chgo., Jan. 3, 1938; s. Ernest C. and Helen C. (Cahill) R.; m. Sabina Bielawski; children—Deborah, Laura, Taylor, Elliot. B.S., Northwestern U., 1960. Chartered financial analyst. Sales rep. Penn Mut. Life Ins. Co., Chgo., 1960-62; investment analyst Continental Assurance Co., Chgo., 1962-67; asst. treas. Continental Assurance Co., 1967-70, treas., 1970-75, v.p., dir. investments, 1973—; also chmn. com. for separate account B; asst. treas. Continental Casualty Co., 1967—; v.p., dir. in investments, 1973—; treas. Valley Forge Life Ins. Co., 1970-75; pres., dir. CNA Income Shares Inc.; sr. v.p., treas. Continental Assurance and Continental Casualty Co., Chgo., 1993—. Alumni adviser Phi Delta Theta, Northwestern U., 1965-70. Served with U.S. Army, 1961. Mem. Transp. Securities Club of Chgo. (past pres.), Investment Analysts Soc. Chgo., Sunset Ridge Country Club (Winnetka, Ill.). Home: 1133 Taylorsport Ln Winnetka IL 60093-1543 Office: Continental Assurance Co CNA Plz Chicago IL 60685

RYCUS, MITCHELL JULIAN, urban planning educator, urban security and energy planning consultant; b. Detroit, June 20, 1932; s. Samuel Israel and Esther (Mitnick) R.; m. Carole Ann Lepofsky, Aug. 31, 1958; children: Lisa Karen Rycus Mikalonis, Peter Todd. BS in Math., U. Mich., 1958, MS in Math., 1961, MS in Physics, 1965, PhD in Urban and Regional Planning, 1976. Asst. rsch. scientist radiation lab. U. Mich., Ann Arbor, 1958-61, pvt. cons. extension gaming svc., 1972-77, rsch. assoc. Mental Health Rsch. Inst., 1977-80; asst. prof. Coll. Architecture and Urban Planning, Ann Arbor, 1980-83; assoc. prof. U. Mich., Ann Arbor, 1983-86; chmn. Coll. Architecture and Urban Planning, Ann Arbor, 1986-92; prof. Coll. Architecture and Urban Planning, 1989—; co-dir. Studies in Urban Security Group U. Mich., Ann Arbor, 1985—; mathematician Bendix Corp. & Rocketdyne, Ann Arbor, 1961-62; group scientist Conductron Corp., Ann Arbor, 1962-70; project assoc. Mich. State C. of C., Lansing, 1970-72; cons. Community Systems Found., Ann Arbor, 1985—. Contbr. rsch. reports, articles. Advisor assessment com. United Way of Washtenaw County, Ann Arbor, 1988-89. With USN, 1950-54. Recipient Faculty Recognition award U. Mich., 1982-83. Mem. AAAS, Am. Planning Assn. Democrat. Jewish. Avocation: computer applications to planning. Office: U Mich Coll Architecture & Urban Planning Ann Arbor MI 48109-2069

RYDELL, AMNELL ROY, artist, landscape architect; b. Mpls., Sept. 17, 1915; s. John S. and Josephine Henrietta (King) R.; m. Frances Cooksey, Jan. 24, 1942. BFA, U. So. Calif., 1937; postgrad., Atelier 17, Paris, 1938, U. Calif., Berkeley, 1939-40, U. Calif., Santa Cruz, 1988. Instr. engring. Douglas Aircraft, El Segundo, Calif., 1940-46; ind. artist, designer San Francisco, 1946-48; ind. artist, designer Santa Cruz, 1948—, ind. landscape architect, 1958-91. Author, cons.: Low Maintenance Gardening, 1974; restoration design Sesnon House Garden Cabrillo Coll., 1995. Pres. Santa Cruz Hist. Soc., 1978-79, Rural Bonny Doon Assn., 1955-56, Santa Cruz Orgn. for Progress and Euthenics, 1977-78; mem. vision bd. City of Santa Cruz, 1991-92; mem. task force Ctr. for Art and History, 1986-94; bd. dirs. Santa Cruz Hist. Trust, 1978-94, Art Mus. Santa Cruz County, 1982-94; donor advisor Roy and Frances Rydell Visual Arts Fund, Greater Santa Cruz County Cmty. Found.; archivist pers. hist. archives, spl. collections Libr. U. Calif., Santa Cruz. Recipient Eloise Pickard Smith award, 1997. Mem. Am. Soc. Landscape Architects (emeritus), William James Assn. (vice chair bd. 1979-95, chair 1995-96), Art Forum (chair 1983-90), Art League (Disting. Artist 1996, Eloise Pickard Smith award 1997), Friends of Sesnon Gallery U. Calif., Santa Cruz. Avocation: gardening. Home: 201 Pine Flat Rd Santa Cruz CA 95060-9708

RYDELL, MARK, film director, producer, actor; b. N.Y.C., Mar. 23, 1934; s. Sidney and Evelyn R.; children: Christopher, Amy, Alexander. Student, NYU, The Julliard Sch. Bd. dirs. Actors Studio. Actor TV series As the World Turns, play Seagulls Over Sorrento, Moonbirds, Handful of Fire, films Crime in the Streets, The Long Goodbye, Havana, Punchline; dir. motion pictures The Fox, 1968, The Reivers, 1970; producer, dir.: motion pictures The Cowboys, 1972, Cinderella Liberty, 1974; prodn. dir. Intersection, 1993; dir. motion pictures Harry and Walter Go to N.Y., 1976, The Rose, 1979, On Golden Pond, 1980 (nominated for Acad. award for best dir.), The River, 1984, For the Boys, 1991, Crime of the Century, 1996; producer: The Man in the Moon, 1991. Mem. Dirs. Guild Am. Office: Concourse Prodns 171 Pier Ave Ste 354 Santa Monica CA 90405-5363 also: ICM 8942 Wilshire Blvd Beverly Hills CA 90211-1934

RYDEN, JOHN GRAHAM, publishing executive; b. N.Y.C., Dec. 19, 1939; s. Albert Graham and Margaret Keating (Bastable) R.; m. Barbara Dee Kelly, June 19, 1962; children: Linda, Patricia. A.B., Harvard U., 1961. Sales rep. McGraw-Hill Book Co., 1965-68; editor coll. dept. Harper & Row, 1968-71, editor in chief coll. dept., 1971-74; editor in chief, asst. dir. U. Chgo. Press, 1974-78, assoc. dir., 1978-79; dir. Yale U. Press, New Haven, 1979—; chmn. bd. trustees Yale Univ. Press, London, 1981—; mem. adminstr. bd. The Papers of Benjamin Franklin, 1979—; chmn. adv. bd. Beacon Press, 1983—. Mem. editl. bd. Public Historian, 1980-86, Scholarly Publishing, 1992-95, The Yale Editions of the Private Papers of James Boswell, 1993—; adv. bd. The Yale Review, 1992—. Trustee Orch. New Eng., 1980—, pres., 1983-86, chmn., 1995—; bd. dirs. Fund for Free Expression, 1990-96; mem. Helsinki Watch Com., 1992-96. With USNR, 1962-65. Berkeley Coll. fellow Yale U. Mem. Assn. Am. Publs. (bd. dirs. 1990-94), Assn. Am. U. Presses (bd. dirs. 1980-83, 87-90, pres. 1988-89), Conn. Acad. Arts and Scis., Internat. Assn. Scholarly Pubs., Grads. Club, New Haven Lawn Club, Hasty Pudding Club (Cambridge, Mass.), Yale Club (N.Y.C.), Century Assn. (N.Y.C.). Office: Yale Univ Press PO Box 209040 New Haven CT 06520-9040 also: Yale U Press 302 Temple St New Haven CT 06511-6601

RYDER, GENE ED, retired United States Air Force training administrator; b. Canyon, Tex., Sept. 19, 1932; s. Johnny Allen and Rilda (New) R.; m. Mary Louise Wilson, Feb. 16, 1958; children: Carlyn, Katherine, Anita, Valerie. BA in Govt. cum laude, St. Mary's U., 1965; MEd, Our Lady of the Lake U., 1968; PhD in Adminstrn., The Union Inst., 1979. Instr. USAF, Scott, Keesler & Lackland AFB, 1958-65; tng. specialist USAF, Lackland AFB, Tex., 1965-69, tng. evaluator, 1969-72, curriculum coord., 1972-75, supr. curriculum devel., 1975-78, supr. tng. evaluation, 1978-83, tng. advisor, 1983-92; chief tng. policy USAF, Randolph AFB, Tex., 1992-95; ret., 1995; chmn. affiliated schs. adv. panel C.C. of Air Force, Maxwell AFB, Ala., 1984-88; co-chmn. USAF Tng. and Instrnl. Sys. Career Program, Randolph AFB, 1992-95; apptd. to Tex. State Bd. Profl. Counselors, 1995—. Author: Basics of Sunday School Leadership: A Guide for Lay Leaders, 1982. Dir. edn. Calvary Hills Bapt. Ch., San Antonio, 1981-94; coord. state scripture Gideons Internat., Nashville, 1991-94; elected mem. Tex. State Rep. Exec. Com., 1994—. With USAF, 1953-56. Mem. Phi Delta Kappa. Home: 1502 Copperfield Rd San Antonio TX 78251-3324

RYDER, GEORGIA ATKINS, university dean, educator; b. Newport News, Va., Jan. 30, 1924; d. Benjamin Franklin and Mary Lou (Carter) Atkins; m. Noah Francis Ryder, Sept. 16, 1947; children: Olive Diana, Malcolm Eliot, Aleta Renee. BS, Hampton (Va.) Inst., 1944; MusM, U. Mich., 1946; PhD, NYU, 1970. Resource music tchr., Alexandria, Va., 1945-48; faculty music dept. Norfolk State U., 1948—, prof., 1970—, head dept., 1969-79, dean Sch. Arts and Letters, 1979-86. Contbr. articles to profl. jours, contbr. chpts. to books. Trustee Va. Symphony, Va. Wesleyan Coll.; bd. dirs. Black Music Rsch. Ctr., Columbia Coll., Chgo., Nat. Assn. Negro Musicians, Southeastern Va. Arts Assn.; mem. advisory com. Norfolk chpt. Young Audiences, Va. Coalition for Mus. Edn., Virginians for the Arts. Grantee So. Fellowship Fund, 1967-69, Consortium Rsch. Tng., 1973; recipient Norfolk Com. Improvement Edn. award, 1974, People's Acad. of Arts award, 1985, City of Norfolk award, 1989, Nat. Assn. Negro Musicians award, 1989, NCCJ award, 1990, Va. Laureate in Music award, 1992, Cultural Alliance award Greater Hampton Roads, 1992, Disting Alumni award Hampton U., 1993, Norfolk State U. Alumni. award, 1994, Maude Ellen Coats Armstrong Found. award, 1995. Mem. Music Educators Nat. Conf., Coll. Music Soc., Intercoll. Music Assn., Va. Music Educators Assn., Delta Sigma Theta.

RYDER, HENRY C(LAY), lawyer; b. Lafayette, Ind., Feb. 18, 1928; s. Raymond Robert and Mina Elizabeth (Arnold) R.; m. Ann Sater Clay, Nov. 29, 1952 (dec.); children: David C., Sarah Paige Hugon, Anne M.; m. Velma Iris Dean, Aug. 27, 1976. BS, Purdue U., 1948; LLB, U. Mich., 1951. Bar: Mich. 1951, Ind. 1952, U.S. Dist. Ct. (so. dist.) Ind. 1953, U.S. Ct. Appeals (7th cir.) 1957, U.S. Supreme Ct. 1981. Assoc. Buschmann, Krieg, DeVault & Alexander, Indpls., 1953-57, ptnr., 1957-60; ptnr. Roberts & Ryder and successor firms, Indpls., 1960-86, of counsel, 1996—; ptnr. Barnes & Thornburg (merger), Indpls., 1987-95, of counsel, 1996—; bd. dirs. Peoples Bank and Trust Co., Indpls., 1985—. Pres. Ind. State Symphony Soc. Inc., 1979-82, bd. dirs., 1972-91, trustee, 1991—, chmn., 1997—; chmn. United Way of Greater Indpls., 1984; vice chmn. Greater Indpls. Progress Com., 1979-86, chmn., 1987-89, mem. exec. com., 1979—; trustee Purdue U., 1983-89, Hanover Coll., 1979, chmn., 1988—; bd. dirs. Hist. Landmark Found. of Ind., 1985-96, chmn., 1992-95; bd. dirs. Purdue Rsch. Found., 1992—; hon. v.p. Ind. Soc. Chgo. Lt. U.S. Army, 1951-53. 'ecipient Jefferson award Indpls. Star, 1983, Whistler award Greater Indpls. Progress Com., 1989; named Man of Yr., B'nai B'rith Soc., 1984. Fellow Am. Bar Found., Ind. Bar Found.; mem. ABA, Ind. Bar Assn., Indpls. Bar Assn., Purdue U. Alumni Assn. (pres. 1975-77, Alumni Svc. award 1982, Citizenship award 1989), Ind. C. of C. (bd. dirs. 1991-94), Ind. Acad., Lawyers Club (pres. Indpls. 1966), Sagamore of the Wabash, U.S. Automobile Club (sec., bd. dirs., Pres.'s award 1989), USAC Properties (sec., bd. dirs.), Columbia Club (bd. dirs. 1987-90, sec. 1988, pres. Found. 1990-95, Benjamin Harrison award 1983), Kiwanis (pres. Indpls. 1983, Civic award 1981). Republican. Presbyterian. Office: Barnes & Thornburg 1313 Merchants Bank Bldg 11 S Meridian St Indianapolis IN 46204-3506

RYDER, JACK MCBRIDE, educational consultant; b. Newport, Ky., Dec. 2, 1928; s. Amon McBride Ryder and Esther Mabel (Harris) Ryder Rachford; m. Roberta Joyce Hayward, Mar. 17, 1951 (div. 1964); children: Joyce Ann (dec.), Constance Lynn, Judith Louise, John McBride; m. Lila Joan Baker, Oct. 2, 1964; 1 child, Suzanne Carol. BS in Biology, Mich State U., East Lansing, 1952; MA in Sch. Adminstrn., Mich State U., 1955, PhD in Ednl. Adminstrn., 1962; LLD (hon.), Saginaw Valley State U., 1992. Tchr. Anglo-Am. Schs., Athens, Greece, 1952-54; supt. of schs. Brady Community Schs., Oakley, Mich., 1955-57, Cassopolis (Mich.) Pub. Schs., 1957-61; assoc. instr. Coll. Edn. Mich. State U., East Lansing, 1961-62; asst. to dean univ. extension adminstrn. Purdue U., W. Lafayette, Ind., 1962-63; interim dir. (on loan) Ind. Vocat. Tech. Coll., Indpls., 1964-65; dir., dean and dir. Purdue U., Indpls., 1963-69; vice chancellor, dean for adminstrv. affairs Indiana U. and Purdue U., Indpls., 1969-74; prof. edn., pres. Saginaw Valley State U., University Center, Mich., 1974-89, prof. edn., 1989-92; pres. J&L Assoc. Internat. Edni. Cons., 1992—; bd. dirs. Saginaw Citizens Bank; chmn. Valley Libr. Consortium, Saginaw, 1981-89, Saginaw Valley R&D Corp., Univ. Ctr., 1982-89; vis. prof., cons. Fedn. Universitaire ET PolyTechnique, De Lille, France, 1989. Mem. Saginaw Area Growth Alliance, 1989; bd. dirs. Saginaw Future, 1989, St. Luke's Healthcare Assn., Saginaw, 1981-89; mem. Leadership Bay County, Bay City, Mich., 1988; bd. dirs., 1st vice chmn. Saginaw Valley State U. Found., 1974-89; pres. emeritus Saginaw Valley State U. Bd. Control, 1992. Recipient Albert Community Svc. award Saginaw Area C. of C., 1989, Disting. Contbr. of Svc. award Delta Coll., Bay City, 1989, Leadership and Svc. award Saginaw Valley State U., 1989, Saginaw Valley State U. Found., 1989; Ryder Ctr. for Health and Phys. Edn. named in honor of him and his wife Saginaw Valley State U.; Paul Harris fellow Rotary Internat., 1988. Mem. Am. Assn. State Colls. and Univs. (Disting. Leadership award 1988), President's Coun. State Univs. (chmn. 1984-86, Leadership and Svc. award 1989), Internat. Torch Club (bd. dirs. Chgo. 1988-89), Phi Delta Kappa. Avocations: fishing, spectator sports, gardening, walking, tennis.

RYDER, THOMAS MICHAEL, newspaper editor; b. East Chicago, Ind., May 17, 1934; s. Thomas Henry and Margaret (Lauber) R.; m. George-Anne Richmond, Sept. 22, 1962. B.S. in Journalism, Marquette U., 1956. Reporter Daily Dispatch, Moline, Ill., 1956-60; reporter The Press, Evansville, Ind., 1960-62, Tri-state editor, 1962-64, asst. city editor, 1964-69, city editor, 1969-83; editor The Sunday Courier & Press, Evansville, 1983-86; asst. mng. editor Evansville Courier, 1986—; adj. prof. Ind. State U., Evansville, 1984. Contbr. articles to mags. Served with U.S. Army, 1967-69. Mem. Stamp Club (pres. 1966). Roman Catholic. Club: Meml. Patrons (pres. 1983). Office: The Courier 300 E Walnut St Evansville IN 47713-1938

RYDER, WINONA (WINONA LAURA HOROWITZ), actress; b. Winona, Minn., Oct. 29, 1971; d. Michael and Cynthia (Istas) Horowitz. Films include: Lucas, 1986, Square Dance, 1987, 1969, 1988, Beetlejuice, 1988, Great Balls of Fire, 1989, Heathers, 1989, Edward Scissorhands, 1990, Mermaids, 1990, Welcome Home, Roxy Carmichael, 1990, Night On Earth,

1992, Bram Stoker's Dracula, 1992, Age of Innocence, 1993 (Golden Globe for Best Supporting Actress, 1994, Academy award nominee, Best Supporting Actress, 1993), The House of the Spirits, 1994, Reality Bites, 1994, Little Women, 1994 (Acad. Awd. nom., Best Actress), Boys, 1995, How to Make An American Quilt, 1995, Looking for Richard, 1995, The Crucible, 1996, Boys, 1996. Office: care Carole Obie Arts Entertainment 9460 Wilshire Blvd Fl 7 Beverly Hills CA 90212

RYDHOLM, RALPH WILLIAMS, advertising agency executive; b. Chgo., June 1, 1937; s. Thor Gabriel and Vivian Constance (Williams) R.; m. Jo Anne Beechler, Oct. 5, 1963; children: Kristin, Erik, Julia. B.A., Northwestern U., 1958, postgrad. in bus. adminstrn, 1958-59; postgrad. Advanced Mgmt. Program, Harvard U., 1982. Acct. trainee, copywriter Young & Rubicam Advt., Chgo., 1960-63; copywriter Post-Keyes-Gardner Advt., Chgo., 1963, E. H. Weiss Advt., Chgo., 1963-65; copy group head BBDO Advt., Chgo., 1965-66; with J. Walter Thompson Advt., Chgo., 1966-86; creative dir., v.p. J. Walter Thompson Advt., 1969-76, exec. creative dir., 1976-86, sr. v.p., 1972-80, exec. v.p., dir., 1980-86; exec. v.p., chief creative officer, dir. Ted Bates Worldwide, N.Y.C., 1986-87; mng. ptnr., chmn. mgmt. com., chief creative officer, chmn., CEO EURO RSCG Tatham Advt., Chgo., 1987—; bd. dirs., ops. com., chmn. creative com., vice chmn., 1996, chmn., 1997; 4A's, guest spkr. Ad Age Workshop, 1969, 77, 86, Adweek Seminar, 1993; keynote spkr. Stephen B. Kelly Awards, 1993; dir. Euro RSCG, USA. Mem. assoc. bd. Newberry Libr. Assn.; Scandinavian-Am. Coun. With USAFR, 1959-65. Recipient Clio awards, Internat. Broadcast award, Lion awards, Cannes Film Festival, Addy awards; named one of Top 100 Creative Ad People Ad Daily, 1972, Advt. Exec. of Yr. Adweek, 1991, Best Man in Advt. McCalls and Adweek, 1992, Creative Leader Wall St. Jour., 1994. Mem. ASCAP, Chgo. Advt. Fedn., Saddle and Cycle Club, Econ. Club Chgo. (bd. dirs.), Northwestern Club Chgo., Harvard Club Chgo., Harvard Club Boston, Exec.'s Club Chgo., Tavern Club, Carlton Club, Chikaming Country Club (Mich.), Dunes Club (Mich.), Internat. Club, Phi Delta Theta. Office: EURO RSCG Tatham 980 N Michigan Ave Chicago IL 60611-4501

RYDSTROM, CARLTON LIONEL, chemist, paint and coating consultant; b. Indpls., Dec. 4, 1928; s. Carlton Lionel and Sara Ann (McNeese) R.; m. Kathleen O'Leary, Oct. 21, 1954 (dec.); children: Carlton L. III, Michael, Mary (dec.), Leslie, Patricia, Timothy, Molly. BS in Polymer Chemistry, N.D. State U., 1951; MS in Phys. Chemistry, U. Puerto Rico, Rio, Piedras, 1953. Chemist Am. Marietta Co., Kankakee, Ill., 1951-52; chemist, plant mgr. Chinamel Paints, Hato Rey, Puerto Rico, 1952-53; tech. mgr. Midwest Synthetics (Valspar), Rockford, Ill., 1953-55; mng. ptnr. Norcote Co., St. Petersburg, Fla., 1955-71; pres. C.M. Industries, Inc., St. Petersburg, 1971-74, Tuf-top/Norcote Coatings, Inc., St. Petersburg, 1974-80; owner Rydstrom Lab., Inc., St. Petersburg, 1980—; bd. dirs. Stacote Finishes, Ltd., W.I.; cons. Sch. Bds. State of Fla., 1981—, paint and adhesive industries. Pres. parish coun. St. Jude Cath. Cathedral Parish, 1977-78, 78-79, 97—, St. Vincent de Paul Pinellas Dist., St. Petersburg, 1988-91; nat. secretariat Cursillo Movement, Roman Cath. Ch., Dallas, 1985-88; dir. Cursillo Movement, Diocese of St. Petersburg, 1995—; dir. St. Vincent de Paul Food Ctr., St. Petersburg, 1988—; chmn. Waterfront Planning Com., St. Petersburg, 1959; mem. bd. dirs. St. Petersburg Cath. H.S., 1977-80. Fellow N.Y. Acad. Sci., Am. Inst. Chemists; mem. Nat. Assn. Corrosion Engrs., Soc. Coatings Tech. (chmn./pres. 1958-59, Disting. Svc. award 1975), Fla. Paint and Coating Assn. (treas., dir. 1959-75), St. Vincent dePaul Soc. (Top Hat award 1991), Jr. C. of C. (DSA 1960). Republican. Roman Catholic. Avocations: golf, gardening, travel, public speaking, working with needy. Home and Office: 6300 25th Ave N Saint Petersburg FL 33710-4128

RYDZ, JOHN S., educator; b. Milw., May 7, 1925; s. John M. and Victoria A. (Kosse) R.; m. Clare L. Steinke, May 18, 1946; children: John A., Karen E. BS in Physics, MIT, 1952; MS in Physics, U. Pa., 1956; postgrad., Case Western Res. U., 1965-70. Mem. staff of sr. exec. v.p. RCA, N.Y.C., 1952-61; exec. v.p. Nuclear Corp. Am. (NUCOR), Phoenix, 1961-63; dir. research Adressograph/Multigraph, Cleve., 1963-65; v.p. Diebold Inc., Canton, Ohio, 1965-70; v.p., chief tech. officer The Singer Co., N.Y.C., 1970-80; corp. v.p. Emhart Corp., Farmington, Conn., 1980-89; pres. Music Memories Inc., Avon, Conn., 1989—; vis. prof. U. Conn., 1988—; mem. engring. adv. com. NSF, Washington, 1986—. Author: Managing Innovation and Common Sense Manufacturing Management, 1986; contbr. articles to profl. jours.; patentee in field. Mem. MIT Lab. for Mfg. and Productivity, Cambridge, Mass., 1975—, U. Hartford Engring. Exec. Council, West Hartford, Conn., 1982—, Worcester (Mass.) Poly. Inst. Mech. Engring. Adv. Com., 1980—; chmn. engring adv. com. U. Conn., Storrs, 1986—. Served with USN, 1943-46, WWII. Mem. Soc. Mfg. Engrs., IEEE, Indsl. Research Inst. Avocations: astronomy, swimming.

RYDZEL, JAMES A., lawyer; b. Worcester, Mass., Nov. 13, 1946; s. Joseph S. and Shirley F. Rydzel; m. Mary C. Chandler; 1 child, Molly. BA, St. Louis U., 1968; JD, Duke U., 1971. Bar: Ohio, 1972, Fla. 1975, U.S. Dist. Ct. (no. dist.) Ohio, U.S. Dist. Ct. (ea. dist.) Mich., U.S. Ct. Appeals (2d, 3d, 4th and 6th cirs.). Ptnr. Jones, Day, Reavis & Pogue, Cleve., 1972—; adj. prof. law Case Western Res. U. Bd. dirs. New Orgn. Visual Arts, 1990, Greater Cleve. Growth Assn., Citizens League. Mem. ABA (litigation labor and employment law com.), Ohio State Bar Assn., Fla. Bar Assn., Def. Rsch. Inst. Office: Jones Day Reavis & Pogue 901 Lakeside Ave E Cleveland OH 44114-1116

RYERSON, PAUL SOMMER, lawyer; b. Newark, Oct. 2, 1946; s. Robert Paul and Audrey Mae (Sommer) R.; m. Susan Jean Duckrow, Aug. 7, 1971 (div. Apr. 1995); children: James Sommer, Jill Carin. BA, Wesleyan U., 1968; JD, Columbia U., 1971. Bar: N.Y. 1972, D.C. 1972, U.S. Ct. Appeals (D.C. cir.) 1973, U.S. Dist. Ct. D.C. 1973, U.S. Supreme Ct. 1976, U.S. Ct. Appeals (5th cir.) 1979, U.S. Ct. Appeals (4th cir.) 1980. Law clk. to judge Jack B. Weinstein U.S. Dist. Ct. ea. dist. N.Y., 1971-72; assoc. Arnold & Porter, Washington, 1972-79, ptnr., 1980-89; ptnr. Jones, Day, Reavis & Pogue, Washington, 1989—. Contbr. articles to profl. publs. Mem. ABA, D.C. Bar Assn. Home: 4903 Edgemoor Ln Bethesda MD 20814 Office: Jones Day Reavis & Pogue 1450 G St NW Washington DC 20005-2001

RYERSON, W. NEWTON, association executive; b. N.Y.C., Sept. 29, 1902; s. William Newton and Martha (Taft) R.; m. Jean Hamilton, May 15, 1936 (dec. Sept. 1973); children: Timothy (dec.), Amy Ryerson Borer, Marjorie, William N.; m. Henriette Keil, July 13, 1974 (dec. Nov. 1992). BS in Engring., Yale U., 1925. Cadet engr. to pers. supr. Phila. Gas Works Co., 1927-44; various positions Sun Oil Co., Phila., 1944-67; dir. placement Vt. Tech. Coll., Randolph Center, Vt., 1967-82; exec. dir. Randolph C. of C., 1983-91; bd. mem. Green Mountain Econ. Devel. Corp., 1986-90; vis. instr. Pa. State U., University Park, 1962-68. V.p. Swarthmore (Pa.) Sch. Bd., 1956-62; chmn. troop Boy Scouts Am., Swarthmore, 1952-55; mem. Rep. Com., Swarthmore, 1951-55; jr. warden Trinity Ch. Vestry, Swarthmore, 1953-56. Named Randolph Bus. Exec. of Yr., 1988. Mem. Appalachian Mountain Club, Tau Alpha Pi. Episcopalian. Home: RR 1 Box 594 Randolph Center VT 05061-9743

RYGIEWICZ, PAUL THADDEUS, plant ecologist; b. Chgo., Feb. 19, 1952; s. Sigismund Thaddeus and Regina (Korpalski) R. BS in Forestry, U. Ill., 1974; MS in Wood Sci., U. Calif., Berkeley, 1976; PhD in Forest Resources, U. Wash., 1983. Research wood technologist ITT Rayonier, Inc., Shelton, Wash., 1977; research assoc. Centre National de Recherches Forestières, Nancy, France, 1983-84; research soil microbiologist U. Calif., Berkeley, 1984-85; rsch. ecologist, global climate change project leader EPA, Corvallis, Oreg., 1985—; asst. prof. dept. forest sci. Oreg. State U., 1987—. Contbr. articles to profl. jours.; rsch. on reforestation of tropical forests in Brazil, global climate changes on forests. Vol. Big Bros. of Am., Urbana, Ill., 1972-74. Fellow Regents U. Calif., Berkeley, 1973-74, Weyerhaeuser U. Calif., Berkeley, 1978-79, Inst. Nat. de la Recherche Agronomique, France, 1983-84, French Ministry of Fgn. Affairs, 1983-84. Mem. Ecol. Soc. Am., Soil Ecology Soc., Forestry Club, Sigma Xi, Gamma Sigma Delta, Xi Sigma Pi (officer 1973-74). Avocations: bicycling, skiing, mountain climbing, camping, hiking. Office: EPA 200 SW 35th St Corvallis OR 97333-4902

RYKER, CHARLES EDWIN, former aerospace company executive; b. Baxter Springs, Kans., Mar. 17, 1920; s. Herbert Earl and Nellie (Sims) R.; m. Evelyn Maude Fairchild, July 28, 1943; children: Patricia Evelyn, Charles Franklyn. Student, San Diego State Coll., 1937-38; B.S. cum laude, U. So. Calif., 1947. C.P.A., Calif. Sr. accountant Arthur Andersen & Co., Los Angeles, 1947-49; auditor Airquipment Co., Burbank, Calif., 1949-50; accounting mgr. Hughes Aircraft Co., Culver City, Calif., 1950-52; with N.Am. Aviation, Inc., Los Angeles, 1952-67; v.p., controller Los Angeles airplane div. N.Am. Aviation, Inc., 1959-62, asst. corp. controller, asst. corp. treas., 1962-67; controller Rockwell Internat. Corp. (merger N.Am. Aviation, Inc. and Rockwell-Standard Corp.), 1967-73, staff v.p. controller's office Western region, 1973-75, v.p., controller, 1975-81, v.p. corp. fin.-major programs, 1981-84; fin. cons., 1984-86. Served to lt. USNR, 1941-45, PTO. Mem. Fin. Execs. Inst., Am. Inst. C.P.A.'s, Calif. Soc. C.P.A.'s, Nat. Assn. Accountants, Beta Gamma Sigma, Beta Alpha Psi, Phi Kappa Phi, Chi Phi. Home: 248 Rocky Point Rd Palos Verdes Peninsula CA 90274-2622

RYKER, NORMAN J., JR., retired manufacturing company executive; b. Tacoma, Dec. 25, 1926; s. Norman Jenkins and Adelia Gustine (Macomber) R.; m. Kathleen Marie Crawford, June 20, 1947 (div. 1983); children: Jeanne Ryker Flores, Christina, Vickie Ryker Risley, Norman Jenkins, Kathy; m. Judith Kay Schneider, Dec. 18, 1983. B.S., U. Calif.-Berkeley, 1949, M.S., 1951; postgrad. Advanced Mgmt. Program, Harvard U., 1973. Asst. chief engr. space divsn. Rockwell Internat., Downey, Calif., 1962-68, v.p. rsch. engring. and testing, 1968-70, v.p. rsch. and engring. graphic systems group, 1970-74, v.p., gen. mgr. Webb divsn., 1974, v.p., gen mgr. transp. and equipment divsn., 1974-76; pres. Rocketdyne divsn. Rockwell Internat., Canoga Park, Calif., 1976-83; sr. v.p. aerospace and indsl. group Pneumo Corp., Boston, 1983-84, exec. v.p., COO, 1984-85; pres., CEO Pneumo Corp. subs. IC Industries, 1985-86, Pneumo Abex Corp., 1986-88; vice chmn., CEO Cross & Trecker Corp., 1989-91; lectr. in field. Contbr. articles to profl. jours. Served with U.S. Army, 1944-46. Recipient cert. of appreciation NASA, 1969, merit award, 1979, Disting. Pub. Svc. medal, 1981, Silver Knight award Nat. Mgmt. Assn., 1979, Tech. Mgmt. award Calif. Soc. Profl. Engrs., 1979. Fellow Inst. Advancement Engring., AIAA; mem. ASCE, Am. Astronautical Soc., Nat. Mgmt. Assn., Instn. Prodn. Engrs. (elected companion). Republican. Address: 100 West Rd Ste 300 Towson MD 21204

RYKWERT, JOSEPH, architecture and art history educator; b. Warsaw, Poland, Apr. 5, 1926; arrived in Eng., 1939; s. Szymon Mieczyslaw and Elizabeth (Melup) R.; m. Anne-Marie Sandersley, Feb. 14, 1972; 1 child from previous marriage, Simon Sebastian; 1 stepchild, Marina Joanna Engel. Student, Archtl. Assn., London, 1944-47; MA, U. Cambridge, London; PhD, Royal Coll. Art, London, 1970; MA (hon.), U. Pa., 1988; DSc (hon.), U. Edinburgh, Scotland, 1995. Libr., tutor Royal Coll. Art, 1960-67; prof. art, chmn. dept. U. Essex, Colchester, Eng., 1967-81; Slade prof. fine arts U. Cambridge, 1980, reader in architecture, 1981-87; Paul Philippe Cret prof. architecture, prof. art history U. Pa., Phila., 1988—, also chmn. PhD program in architecture; Andrew Mellon prof. Cooper Union, N.Y.C., 1977; George Lurcy prof. Columbia U., N.Y.C., 1986; commr. Venice (Italy) Biennale, 1974-77; mem. jury Parc de la Villette Competition, Paris, 1982, Wolf Found. Prize, Jerusalem, 1983; trustee Cubitt Trust, London, 1986—; sr. scholar Getty Ctr. for History Art and Humanities, 1992, 93; co-editor catalogue, curator Alberti Exhbn., Mantua, Italy, 1994. Author: The Golden House, 1947, The Idea of a Town, 1963, 76, 88, Church Building, 1966, On Adam's House in Paradise, 1972, 82, The First Moderns, 1980, 84, The Necessity of Artifice, 1982, (with Anne-Marie Rykwert) The Brothers Adam, 1985; editl. transl.: One the Art of Building (L.B. Alberti), 1989, 91, The Dancing Column, 1996; editor Res. jour., Peabody Mus., Cambridge, Mass., 1979—. Mem. steering com. UNESCO Conf. on Urbanism, 1989—. Decorated Chevalier des Arts et des Lettres, Govt. of France, 1985; recipient Alfred Jurzykowski Found. award, 1990, Accademia di San Luca, 1993. Mem. Coll. Art Assn., Comite Internat. des Critiques d'Arch. (pres.), Savile Club (London). Office: U Pa Dept Architecture 210 S 34th St 207 Meyerson Hall Philadelphia PA 19104-6311

RYLAND, DAVID RONALD, lawyer; b. Ashland, Ohio, Mar. 22, 1945; s. Willis A. and Lois Eleanor (Landis) R.; m. Rita Ann Cooney, Jan. 20, 1973. BA, Coll. of Wooster, 1967; JD, Columbia U., 1970. Bar: Calif. 1970. Assoc. U. of Calif., Berkeley, 1970-71; from assoc. to ptnr. Severson, Werson, Berke & Melchior, San Francisco, 1971-82; ptnr. Sheppard, Mullin, Richter & Hampton, San Francisco, 1982—. V.p., bd. dirs. Homeward Bound of Marin; trustee St. Paul's Episcopal Sch. Home: 3 Edgewater Rd Belvedere CA 94920-2315 Office: Sheppard Mullin Richter & Hampton 4 Embarcadero Ctr Ste 1700 San Francisco CA 94111-4158

RYLANDER, HENRY GRADY, JR., mechanical engineering educator; b. Pearsall, Tex., Aug. 23, 1921; married; 4 children. B.S., U. Tex., 1943, M.S., 1952; Ph.D. in Mech. Engring., Ga. Inst. Tech., 1965. Design engr. Steam Div., Aviation Gas Turbine Div., Westinghouse Elec. Corp., 1943-47; from asst. to assoc. prof. mech. engring. U. Tex., Austin, 1947-68, research scientist, 1950, prof. mech. engring., 1968—, Joe J. King prof. engring., 1980—; cons. engr. TRACOR, Inc., 1964-69; founding dir. Ctr. for Electromechanics, U. Tex., 1977-85, chmn., mech. engring. dept., 1976-86. Named Disting. Grad. Coll. Engring., U. Tex., Austin, 1989. Fellow ASME (Leonardo da Vinci award 1985); mem. ASME. Office: U Tex Coll Engring Austin TX 78712

RYLANT, CYNTHIA, author; b. Hopewell, Va., June 6, 1954; d. John Tune and Leatrel (Rylant) Smith; 1 child, Nathaniel. BA, Morris Harvey Coll., 1975; MA, Marshall U., 1976; MLS, Kent State U., 1982. English instr. Marshall U., Huntington, W.Va., 1979-80, U. Akron, Ohio, 1983-84; children's libr. Akron (Ohio) Pub. Libr., 1983; part-time lectr. Northeast Ohio Univs. Coll. Medicine, Rootstown, Ohio, 1991—. Author: (picture books) When I Was Young in the Mountains, 1982 (Caldecott Honor book 1983, English Speaking Union Book-Across-the-Sea Amb. of Honor award 1984, Am. Book award nomination 1983), Miss Maggie, 1983, This Year's Garden, 1984, The Relatives Came, 1985 (Horn Book Honor book 1985, Children's Book of Yr. Child Study Assn. Am. 1985, Caldecott Honor Book 1986), Night in the Country, 1986, Birthday Presents, 1987, All I See, 1988, Mr. Grigg's Work, 1989, An Angel for Solomon Singer, 1992, The Everyday Town, 1993, The Everyday School, 1993, The Everyday House, 1993, The Everyday Garden, 1993, The Everyday Children, 1993, The Everyday Pets, 1993, Mr. Putter and Tabby Pour the Tea, 1994, Mr. Putter and Tabby Walk the Dog, 1994, The Old Woman Who Named Things, 1994, The Blue Hill Meadows and the Much Loved Dog, 1994, Gooseberry Park, 1995, A Story of E.B. White, 1996, A Story of Margaret Wise, 1996; (Henry and Mudge series) Henry and Mudge: The First Book of Their Adventures, 1987, Henry and Mudge in Puddle Trouble, 1987, Henry and Mudge in the Green Time, 1987, Henry and Mudge Under the Yellow Moon, 1987, Henry and Mudge in the Sparkle Days, 1988, Henry and Mudge and the Forever Sea, 1989, Henry and Mudge Get the Cold Shivers, 1989, Henry and Mudge and the Happy Cat, 1990, Henry and Mudge and the Bedtime Thumps, 1991, Henry and Mudge Take the Big Test, 1991, Henry and Mudge and the Long Weekend, 1992, Henry and Mudge and the Wild Wind, 1993, Henry and Mudge and the Careful Cousin, 1994, Henry and Mudge and the Best Day Ever, 1995; (poetry) Waiting to Waltz ... a Childhood, 1984 (Nat. Coun. for Social Studies Best Book 1984), Soda Jerk, 1990, Something Permanent, 1994; (novels) A Blue-Eyed Daisy, 1985 (Children's Book of Yr. Child Study Assn. Am. 1985), A Fine White Dust, 1986 (Newbery Honor Book 1987), A Kindness, 1988; (stories) Every Living Thing, 1985, Children of Christmas: Stories for the Season, 1987, A Couple of Kooks: And Other Stories About Love, 1990; (autobiography) But I'll Be Back Again: An Album, 1989, Best Wishes, 1992; (other) Appalachia: The Voices of Sleeping Birds, 1991 (Boston Globe/Horn Book Honor book for nonfiction 1991), Missing May, 1992 (John Newbery medal 1992), I Have Seen Castles, 1993, The Dreamer, 1993. Office: Simon & Schuster Children's 1230 Avenue of the Americas New York NY 10020*

RYLE, JOSEPH DONALD, public relations executive; b. Stamford, Conn., Aug. 19, 1910; s. Joseph P. and Vivian (Sander) R. B.S., NYU, 1933. With pub. relations dept. Joseph D. Ryle, N.Y.C., 1933-41; dir. pub. relations Am. Overseas Airlines, London, 1946-50, Am. Airlines, N.Y.C., 1950-52; exec. v.p. Fedn. Ry. Progress, Washington, 1953-55, vice chmn., 1955—; pres. Nat. Transit Ads., 1955-57; exec. v.p. pub. relations Thomas J. Deegan Jr., Inc., now dir.; pub. relations cons., N.Y.C.; promotion cons. Met. Mus. Art. Exec. dir. Gov.'s Com. for the Centennial of Thoroughbred Racing at Saratoga; v.p., bd. dirs. East Side Settlement House; adv. com. Am. Folk Art Mus.; chmn. emeritus Winter Antiques Show; trustee Hancock (Mass.) Shaker Village; bd. dirs. Isabel O'Neil Sch., N.Y.C. Served with USAAF, 1942-45; dep. to Gen. H. H. Arnold, pub. relations. Decorated Legion of Merit. Mem. Air Transport Assn. (past chmn. pub. relations com.), Newcomen Soc., Irish Georgian Soc. (bd. dirs.). Clubs: Nat. Press (Washington), Army Navy (Washington); Overseas Press (N.Y.C.), Wings (N.Y.C.); Squadron A; Reading Room (Saratoga, N.Y.). Home: 455 E 51st St New York NY 10022-6474 also: The Academy Remsenburg NY 11960

RYLES, GERALD FAY, private investor, business executive; b. Walla Walla, Wash., Apr. 3, 1936; s. L. F. and Janie Geraldine (Bassett) R.; m. Ann Jane Birkenmeyer, June 12, 1959; children—Grant, Mark, Kelly. B.A., U. Wash., 1958; M.B.A., Harvard U., 1962. With Gen. Foods Corp., White Plains, N.Y., 1962-65, Purex Corp., Ltd., Lakewood, Calif., 1966-68; cons. McKinsey & Co., Inc., Los Angeles, 1968-71; with Fibreboard Corp., San Francisco, 1971-79, v.p., 1973-75, group v.p., 1975-79; with Consol. Fibres, Inc., San Francisco, 1979-88, exec. v.p., 1979-81, pres., dir., 1981-86, chief exec. officer, 1986-88; cons. Orinda, Calif., 1988-90; with Interchecks Inc., 1990-92, pres., CEO, 1990-92; bus. exec., pvt. investor, 1992-94; chmn. bd., CEO Microserv, Inc., Kirkland, Wash., 1994—; bd. dirs. Morning Sun, Inc., Tacoma, Sitewerks Inc., Seattle. Mem. adv. com. entrepreneur and innovation program U. Wash. Bus. Sch. Served to capt. U.S. Army, 1958-66. Mem. Harvard Bus. Sch. Assn., Univ. Wash. Alumni Assn., World Trade Club (San Francisco), Wash. Athletic Club. Republican. Episcopalian. Home: 2625 90th Ave NE Bellevue WA 98004-1601

RYLL, FRANK MAYNARD, JR., professional society administrator; b. St. Petersburg, Fla., Jan. 22, 1942; s. Frank Maynard and Laura Marjorie (Howarth) R.; m. Patti Sue Craig, Mar. 2, 1984; children: Christopher E. Gibson, Rebekah H. Gibson. BA, Fla. State U., 1964. Office mgr. So. Bell Telephone, Miami Beach, Fla., 1966-67; account exec. Francis I. DuPont & Co., St. Petersburg, 1967-68, Merril Lynch, St. Petersburg, 1969-74; mgr. news and info., exec. dir. Sarasota (Fla.) County C. of C., 1974-76; dir. fin. Greater Greenville (S.C.) C. of C., 1976-77, mgt. govt. affairs, 1977-78, gen. mgr., 1978-80; staff v.p. govt. affairs Fla. C. of C., Tallahassee, 1980-83; pres. Fla. C. of C., 1983—, treas., 1994—. Exec. com. Greenville chpt. ARC, 1979; active Tallavana Community Ch. Served with U.S. Army, 1965-69, Vietnam. Mem. Am. C. of C. Execs. (bd. dirs.), U.S. C. of C. (bd. dirs.), Coun. State Chambers (chmn.), Fla. State U. Alumni Assn. (v.p. 1982-85), Pi Kappa Phi. Republican. Avocation: tennis. Office: Fla C of C 136 S Bronough St Tallahassee FL 32301-7706*

RYMAN, ROBERT TRACY, artist; b. Nashville, May 30, 1930; s. William Tracy and Nora (Boston) R.; m. Lucy Lippard, 1961 (div. 1966); children: Ethan, Ryman; m. Merrill Wagner, Jan. 31, 1969; children: William Tracy, George Corydon. Exhibited one man shows: Paul Bianchini Gallery, 1967, Solomon R. Guggenheim Mus., N.Y.C., 1972, Kunsthalle, Basel, Switzerland, 1975, Palais des Beaux-Arts, Brussels, 1974, Stedelijk Mus., Amsterdam, Netherlands, 1974, Whitechapel Gallery, London, 1977, Centre Pompidou, Paris, 1981, Sidney Janis Gallery, N.Y.C., 1981, Kunsthalle, Dusseldorf, Germay, 1982, Bonnier Gallery, N.Y.C., 1983, Daniel Weinberg Gallery, L.A., 1983, Galerie Maeght LeLong, Paris, 1984, Rhona Hoffman Gallery, Chgo., 1985, Leo Castelli Gallery, N.Y.C., 1986, Galerie Maeght LeLong, N.Y.C., 1986, Pace Gallery, N.Y.C., 1990, DIA Art Found., N.Y.C., 1988-89, Konrad Fischer Gallery, Dusseldorf, Fed. Republic Germany, 1987, Pace Gallery, N.Y., Tate Gallery, London, MMA, N.Y., San Francisco Mus. Modern Art, Walker Arts Ctr., Mpls.; group shows: Biennal Whitney Mus. Am. Art, N.Y.C., 1977, Stedelijk Mus., Amsterdam, 1978, Art of the 70's, Venice Bernnale, Italy, 1980, Haus der Kunst, Munich, 1981, Stedelijk Mus., Amsterdam, 1983, Whitney Mus. Am. Art, 1983, Skowhegan Sch. of Painting and Sculpture Medal, 1987, Whitney Biennal Exhbn, 1987; Mus. Modern Art, N.Y.C., 1985, Carnegie International, 1985; represented permanent collections: Mus. Modern Art, N.Y.C., Milw. Art Center, Stedelijk Mus., Amsterdam, Whitney Mus. Am. Art, pvt. collections; apptd. commr. City of N.Y. Art Commn. Mem. AAAL, Mcpl. Art Soc. N.Y. (bd. dirs. 1991—). Home: 17 W 16th St New York NY 10011-6301 Studio: 637 Greenwich St New York NY 10014-3306 *There is never a question of what to paint, but only how to paint. The "how" of painting is the image, the end product.*

RYMAN, RUTH (STACIE) MARIE, primary education educator; b. Moline, Ill., July 22, 1952; d. Henry Joseph and Gladys Julia (Campbell) DeKeyzer; m. Phillip DeForrest Ryman, Aug. 14, 1976; children: Michelle, Daniel, Jennifer. BA, Augustana Coll., 1974; MA, U. Denver, 1988. Cert. tchr. Resource tchr. Notre Dame Sch., Denver, 1986-91, 2nd grade tchr., 1991—; cons. Notre Dame Sch., Denver, 1991—. mem. Nat. Cath. Edn. Assn., Nat. Coun. Tchrs. Math. Office: Notre Dame Sch 2165 S Zenobia St Denver CO 80219-5058

RYMAR, JULIAN W., manufacturing company executive; b. Grand Rapids, Mich., June 29, 1919; student Grand Rapids Jr. Coll., 1937-39, U. Mich., 1939-41, Am. Sch. Dramatic Arts, 1946-47, Wayne U., 1948-52, Rockhurst Coll., 1952-53; Naval War Coll., 1954-58; m. Margaret Macon Van Brunt, Dec. 11, 1954; children: Margaret Gibson, Gracen Macon, Ann Mackall. Entered USN as aviation cadet, 1942, advanced through grades to capt., 1964; chmn. bd., chief exec. officer, dir. Grace Co., Belton, Mo., 1955-90; chmn. bd. dirs. Shock & Vibration Research, Inc., 1956-66; chmn. bd., CEO Bedtime Story Fashions; bd. dirs. Am. Bank & Trust; comdg. officer Naval Air Res. Squadron, 1957-60, staff air bn. comdr., 1960-64. Mem. Kansas City Hist. Soc.; bd. dirs. Bros. of Mercy, St. Lukes Hosp.; adv. bd. dirs. St. Joseph Hosp.; trustee Missouri Valley Coll., 1969-74; pres. Rymar Found. Active Sch. Am. Rsch., Inst. Am. Arts, Mus. N.Mex. Found., Spanish Colonial Art Soc. Mem. Mil. Order World Wars, Navy League U.S. (pres. 1959-60, dir. 1960-70), Rockhill Homes Assn. (v.p.) Friends of Art (pres., chmn. bd. govs. 1969-70, exec. bd. 1971-74), Soc. of Fellows of Nelson Gallery Found. (exec. bd. 1972-77), Soc. Profl. Journalists, Press Club, Univ. of Mich. Club, Arts Club of Washington, Sch. of Am. Rsch., Santa Fe Symphony, Inst. Am. Indian Art, Mus. NMex. Found., Mus. Indian Arts & Culture, Mus. Internat. Folk Art, Mus. Fine Arts, Spanish Colonial Arts Soc., Quiet Birdman Club, Sigma Delta Chi. Episcopalian (dir., lay reader, lay chalice, vestryman, jr. warden, sr. warden, diocesan fin. bd., parish investment bd.).

RYMER, PAMELA ANN, federal judge; b. Knoxville, Tenn., Jan. 6, 1941. AB, Vassar Coll., 1961; LLB, Stanford U., 1964; LLD (hon.), Pepperdine U., 1988. Bar: Calif. 1966, U.S. Ct. Appeals (9th cir.) 1966, U.S. Ct. Appeals (10th cir.), U.S. Supreme Ct. V.p. Rus Walton & Assoc., Los Altos, Calif., 1965-66; Assoc. Lillick McHose & Charles, L.A., 1966-72, ptnr., 1973-75; ptnr. Toy and Rymer, L.A., 1975-83; judge U.S. Dist. Ct. (cen. dist.) Calif., L.A., 1983-89, U.S. Ct. Appeals (9th cir.), L.A., 1989—; faculty The Nat. Jud. Coll., 1986-88; mem. com. summer ednl. programs Fed. Jud. Ctr., 1987-88; chair exec. com. 9th Cir. Jud. Conf., 1990; mem. com. criminal law Jud. Conf. U.S., 1988-93, Ad Hoc com. gender-based violence, 1991-94, fed.-state jurisdiction com., 1993—. Mem. editorial bd. The Judges' jour., 1989-91; contbr. articles to profl. jours. and newsletters. Mem. Calif. Postsecondary Edn. Commn., 1974-84, chmn., 1980-84; mem. L.A. Olympic Citizens Adv. Commn.; bd. visitors Stanford U. Law Sch., 1986—, chair, 1993-96, exec. com.; bd. visitors Pepperdine U. Law Sch., 1987—; mem. Edn. Commn. of States Task Force on State Policy and Ind. Higher Edn., 1987-89; bd. dirs. Constnl. Rights Found., 1985; Jud. Conf. U.S. Com. Fed.-State Jurisdiction, 1993, Com. Criminal Law, 1988-93, ad hoc com. gender based violence, 1991-94; chair exec. com. 9th cir. jud. conf., 1990-94. Recipient Outstanding Trial Jurist award L.A. County Bar Assn., 1988. Mem. ABA (task force on civil justice reform 1991—), State Bar Calif. (antitrust and trade regulation sect., exec. com. 1990-92), L.A. County Bar Assn. (chmn. antitrust sect. 1981-82), Assn. of Bus. Trial Lawyers (bd. govs. 1990-92), Stanford Alumni Assn., Stanford Law Soc. Calif., Vassar Club So. Calif. (past pres.). Office: US Ct Appeals 9th Cir US Court of Appeals Bldg 125 S Grand Ave Box 91510 Pasadena CA 91109-1510*

RYMER, RANDAL EUGENE, chemical engineer; b. Youngstown, Ohio, Jan. 19, 1964; s. Rodney Eugene Rymer and Carol Jean (Sandusky-Rymer) Stahl; m. Amy Sue Williams, Sept. 13, 1986; children: Ashley Mae, Rachel Irene. B of Engring., Youngstown State U., 1986. Chem. loss prevention cons. IRI, Cleve., 1986-90; supr. dist. loss prevention IRI, Chgo., 1990-92, account cons., 1992-94; sr. engr. Starr Tech. Risks Agy., Chgo., 1994—.

Mem. PTA, Aurora, Ill., 1993—; USA Bowling cert. instr., coach Young Am. Bowling Alliance, Youngstown and Naperville, Ill., 1985-86, 94—. Recipient Dow Rsch. award Dow Chem. Co., 1986. Mem. AIChE, Soc. of Fire Protection Engrs., Nat. Fire Protection Assn., Am. Bowling Congress (league pres., treas. 1981—). Republican. Presbyterian. Achievements include rsch. in adsorptive seperation of carbon monoxide/nitrogren for groundwork in alterative fuel development with carbon monoxide and hydrogren or replacing oxygen with compressed air. Home: 3150 Compton Rd Aurora IL 60504-4205 Office: Starr Tech Risks Agy Inc Ste 1000 500 W Madison Chicago IL 60661-2511

RYMER, S. BRADFORD, JR., retired appliance manufacturing company executive; b. Cleveland, Tenn., May 30, 1915; s. S. Bradford and Clara Ladosky (Gee) R.; m. Anne Roddye Caudle, Nov. 7, 1942; children: Anita Elise, S. Bradford III. Grad., Fishburne Mil. Sch., 1933; BS in Indsl. Mgmt, Ga. Inst. Tech., 1937; D of Bus. Adminstration (hon.), Tenn. Wesleyan Coll. Indsl. engr. Dixie Foundry Co., Inc., Cleveland, Tenn., 1937-40, sec.-treas., dir. prodn., 1940-50; pres. Dixie Foundry Co., Inc. (name changed to Magic Chef Inc. 1961), Cleveland, Tenn., 1950-61; pres., chmn. Magic Chef Inc., Cleveland, 1961-87; chmn. Magic Chef Inc. div. Maytag Corp., Cleveland, 1986-87, ret., 1987; past chmn. Dixie-Narco, Inc., Ranson, W. Va.; forum dir. Munford Co.; former dir. Provident Life and Accident Ins. Co., Citizens & So. Nat. Bank, Atlanta. Past pres. Cleveland Asso. Industries; past trustee Tenn. Wesleyan Coll., Ga. Tech. Found.; past bd. dirs. Bradley County Meml. Hosp., Allied Arts of Chattanooga; past nat. dir. Jr. Achievement; trustee Fishburne Mil. Sch.; trustee Hiwassee Coll., John Templeton Found., 1993—. War Tng. Svc. flight instr. World War II. Recipient Palm Beach Atlantic Colleges Am. Free Enterprise medal. Mem. Am. Gas Assn. (past exec. com., dir.), NAM (past dir.), Chief Execs. Orgn. (pres. 1971, dir.), Gas Appliance Mfrs. Assn. (pres. 1965), Young Pres. Orgn. (past dir., area v.p., chmn. Rebel chpt.), Ga. Tech. Nat. Alumni Assn. (past trustee), Toastmasters (bd. dirs. 1992—), Phi Gamma Delta. Methodist (past chmn. bd. trustees). Home: 28 Stonedge 100 Scenic Hwy Lookout Mountain TN 37350-1267 also: 1326 Lake Worth Ln Lost Tree Village North Palm Beach FL 33408 *No man is a success unto himself; for his success has been wrought with the help and talents of many associates.*

RYMER, WILLIAM ZEV, research scientist, administrator; b. Melbourne, Victoria, Australia, June 3, 1939; came to U.S., 1971; s. Jacob and Luba Rymer; m. Helena Bardas, Apr. 10, 1961 (div. 1975); children: Michael Morris, Melissa Anne; m. Linda Marie Faller, Sept. 5, 1977; 1 child, Daniel Jacob. MBBS, Melbourne U., 1962; PhD, Monash U., Victoria, 1971. Resident med. officer dept. medicine Monash U., Victoria, 1964-66; Fogarty internat. fellow NIH, Bethesda, Md., 1971-74; rsch. assoc. Johns Hopkins U. Med. Sch., Balt., 1975-76; asst. prof. SUNY, Syracuse, 1976-78; asst. prof. Northwestern U., Chgo., 1978-81, assoc. prof., 1981-87, prof., 1987—; rsch. dir. Rehab. Inst. Chgo., 1989—. Contbr. articles to profl. jours. Grantee NIH, VA, Dept. of Def., Nat. Inst. Disability Rehab. Rsch., pvt. founds. Fellow Royal Australian Coll. Physicians; mem. Soc. Neurosci., Am. Soc. Biomechanics. Democrat. Avocations: tennis, racquetball. Office: Rehab Inst Chgo 345 E Superior St Chicago IL 60611-3015

RYN, CLAES GÖSTA, political science educator, author, research institute administrator; b. Norrköping, Sweden, June 12, 1943; permanent resident of U.S., 1979; s. Gösta Karl and Cecilia Edit (Blom) R.; m. Marianne Carin Tedhagen, Aug. 30, 1969; children: Charlotte, Viveka, Elisabet. Fil.kand. (MA), Uppsala (Sweden) U., 1967, postgrad., 1969-71; postgrad., Syracuse U., 1968-69; PhD, La. State U., 1974. Asst. prof. politics Cath. U. Am., Washington, 1974-78, assoc. prof. politics, 1978-82, prof. politics, 1982—; asst. dean Sch. Arts and Scis., Catholic U. Am., Washington, 1977-79; chmn. dept. politics Catholic U. Am., Washington, 1979-85; vis. assoc. prof. U. Va., Charlottesville, 1981; co-founder, chmn. Nat. Humanities Inst., Washington, 1984—; referee, evaluator NEH, Dept. Edn., USIA, others; dir. numerous scholarly confs. and lecture series; mem. Richard M. Weaver fellowship selection com., 1980—; faculty sponsor Earhart Found., 1989—; mem. awards com. Ingersoll Prizes, 1990; mem. Salvatori doctoral fellowship selection com. Intercollegiate Studies Inst., 1990—. Author: (with Bertil Häggman) Nykonservatismen i USA, 1971, Democracy and the Ethical Life, 1978, 2nd expanded edit., 1990, Will, Imagination and Reason, 1986, 2nd expanded edit., 1997, Individualism och Gemenskap, 1986, The New Jacobinism, 1991; editor: Humanitas, 1992—; co-editor (with George Panichas), author (with others): Irving Babbitt in Our Time, 1986; editor, author introduction for other volumes; contbr. numerous articles to profl. jours. and collective vols.; mem. editl. adv. bd. Modern Age, 1981—; editl. advisor Marknadsekonomisk Tidskrift, Sweden, 1986-92; mem. editl. bd. This World, 1992—; editl. columnist Svenska Dagbladet, Sweden, 1996—. Mem. vestry St. Francis Episcopal Ch., Potomac, Md., 1986-88. Served with Swedish Army, Royal Life Company, 1963, Signal Corps, 1967-68. Rsch. fellow various orgns., including Earhart Found., 1980-81, 87-88, Wilbur Found., 1980-81, 90, 93-94; recipient award King of Sweden, 1983; named Outstanding Grad. Prof., Cath. U. Am., 1992. Episcopalian. Home: 10008 Crestleigh Ln Potomac MD 20854-1820 Office: Cath Univ Am Dept Politics Washington DC 20064

RYNEAR, NINA COX, retired registered nurse, author, artist; b. Cochranville, Pa., July 11, 1916; d. Fredrick Allen and Nina Natalie (Drane) Cox; m. Charles Spencer Rynear, Aug. 22, 1934 (dec. May 1941); children: Charles Joseph, Stanley Spencer. RN, Coatesville Hosp. Sch. Nursing, 1945; BS in Nursing Edn., U. Pa., 1954. Interviewer Nat. Opinion Rsch. Ctr., U. Denver, Colo., 1942-47; sch. nurse West Goshen Elem. Sch., West Chester, Pa., 1946-47; pub. health nurse Pa. Dept. Health Bur. Pub. Health Nursing, Harrisburg, 1947-51; staff nurse V.A. Hosp., Coatesville, Pa., 1951-54; staff nurse, asst. head nurse V.A. Hosp., Menlo Park, Calif., 1954-56; asst. chief nursing svc. Palo Alto and Menlo Park VA Hosps., Palo Alto, Menlo Park, Calif., 1956-76; self employed Reno, Nev., 1976—. Author: (poems, musical compositions) Old Glory and the U.S.A., 1989, Mister Snowman, 1988, Dawn Shadow of Lenape, 1988; (poem and song compilation) This Side of Forever, 1990; (musical compositions) Blessed Are Those Who Listen, What Can I Leave, The Hobo's Promise; (childrens' stories) Wilyum of Orange 1st, Lady Harley and Pepper, 1995; contbr. sonnets to Newsletter of N.Am. Acad. Esoteric Studies; paintings represented in numerous pvt. collections. Pres. Chester County Pub. Health Nurses Assn., 1950. Staff nurse Cadet Corps, 1944-45. Mem. VFW Aux. (patriotic instr. 1989-90, chmn. safety div. Silver State #3396 chpt. 1990-91), New Century Rebekah Lodge #244. Methodist. Home and Office: 3476 Harbor Beach Dr Lake Wales FL 33853-8059

RYNEARSON, PATRICIA HEAVISIDE, elementary school educator; b. Balt., Dec. 19, 1951; d. William and Evelyn (Davis) Heaviside; m. Leo E. Rynearson, Jr., Aug. 6, 1977; children: Courtney, Cliff. BS, U. Del., 1973; MA, U. N. Mex., 1979. Cert. tchr. multiple subjects and reading, Calif. Tchr. Lavaland Sch., Albuquerque, N. Mex., 1977-78, Santo Domingo Sch., Albuquerque, 1978-79, Chapparal Sch., Albuquerque, 1979-80, Liberty Sch., Buckeye, Ariz., 1980-86, Royal Palm Sch., Phoenix, 1986-87, Juniper Sch., Fontana, Calif., 1987-89, Almeria Middle Sch., Fontana, 1989-90, Redwood Sch., Fontana, 1990—; mem. planning com. Environ. EXPO Calif. State Univ., San Bernardino, Calif., 1995-96. Named Inland Empire Environ. Educator of Yr., Calif. State U., San Bernardino, 1996, Conservation Tchr. of Yr., Inland Empire West Resource Conservation Dist., 1997; recipient Eleanor Roosevelt Tchg. fellowship AAUW, 1996. Home: 2233 Drummond St Riverside CA 92506-1533 Office: Redwood Elem Sch 8570 Redwood Ave Fontana CA 92335-3117

RYNEARSON, W. JOHN, foundation administrator; b. Grosse Point, Mich., Oct. 10, 1948; s. William J. and Anna Lee (Hutto) R.; m. Justine M. Pointer, Aug. 28, 1971; children: Jill, Amy, Julie. Cert. in French, Sorbonne U., Paris, 1967; BA in Mktg., Jacksonville U., 1970, MA in Teaching, 1973. Instr. Duval County Schs., Jacksonville, Fla., 1970-73, Fla. Jr. Coll., Jacksonville, 1973-74; territory mgr. Burroughs Corp., Jacksonville, 1974-76; Mideast, Far East sales administr. Coleman Co., Wichita, Kans., 1976-77; Asia sales mgr. Coleman Co., Wichita, 1977-79, Asia, Europe mktg. mgr., 1979-82; v.p. mktg. O'Brien Co. div. Coleman Co., Seattle, 1982-84; pres., gen. mgr. Knight Internat., Seattle, 1984-85; exec. v.p., found. sec., bd. dirs. Civitan Internat., Birmingham, 1985—; com. chmn. Shoreline Community Coll. Internat. Studies, Seattle, 1984-85. Author: Yankee Traveler, 1986. Sunday sch. tchr., dir. youth program Emmanual Bapt. Ch., Jacksonville, 1975-76; bd. dirs., missions bd. Faith Chapel, Wichita, 1976-82, bd. mgr., 1976-82, Redmond (Redmond) Assembly of God, 1982-85. Mem. Am. Soc. Assn. Execs. (cert. assn. exec. 1991), Am. Mktg. Assn. Republican. Pentacostal. Lodges: Civitan. Avocations: sailing, snow skiing. Home: 3404 Field Stone Ln Birmingham AL 35242-3936 Office: Civitan Internat 1 Civitan Pl Birmingham AL 35213-1983

RYNKIEWICZ, STEPHEN MICHAEL, journalist; b. Sheboygan, Wis., Oct. 20, 1955; s. Walter Paul and Ruth Catherine (Van Hercke) R.; m. Brenda Gail Russell, Sept. 27, 1986. BA, U. Wis., 1976. Various staff assignments Chgo. Sun-Times, 1979—, real estate editor, 1990—; pres. Ill. Freedom of Info. Coun., 1991-93. Pres. Chgo. Headline Club, 1991-92. Mem. Soc. Profl. Journalists (regional dir. 1992-95, sec. treas. 1995-96, diversity chair 1996—), Sigma Delta Chi Found. (bd. dirs. 1995-96). Office: Chicago Sun-Times 401 N Wabash Ave Chicago IL 60611-5642

RYNN, NATHAN, physics educator, consultant; b. N.Y.C., Dec. 2, 1923; s. Meyer and Rose (Wolkerwiczer) Rynkowsky; m. Glenda Brown, June 24, 1989; children by previous marriage: Jonathan, Margaret, David. BSEE, CCNY, 1944; MS, U. Ill., 1947; PhD, Stanford U., 1956. Rsch. engr., RCA Labs., Princeton, 1947-52; rsch. asst. Stanford U., 1952-56, rsch. assoc., 1958; mem. tech. staff Ramo-Woolridge, L.A., 1956-57; supr. Huggins Labs., Menlo Park, Calif., 1957-58; rsch. staff physicist Princeton U., 1958-65; prof. physics U. Calif.-Irvine, 1965-94, prof. physics emeritus, rsch. prof. physics, 1994—; vis. prof. Ecole Polytechnique Fed. of Lausanne, Switzerland, 1984-90, Ecole Polytechnique, Paris, and other European univs. and labs., 1973-80; indsl. sci. advisor/cons., 1964—; com. mem. Plasma Sci. Com. Nat. Rsch. Coun. Contbr. articles and revs. to profl. jours. Founder and leader plasma physics research facility. With USN, 1944-46. Grantee NSF, U.S. Dept. Energy, Air Force Geophys. Lab.; Fulbright sr. fellow, 1978. Fellow Am. Phys. Soc., IEEE, AAAS; mem. Am. Geophys. Union, Sigma Xi. Office: U Calif Dept Physics and Astronomy Irvine CA 92697-4575

RYPIEN, DAVID VINCENT, welding engineer; b. Youngstown, Ohio, July 31, 1956; s. Vincent Mark and Anna Marie (Carr) R. BS, Walsh Coll., 1983; MS, Ohio State U., 1985, PhD, 1990. Registered profl. engr., Ohio, Tex. Instr. Stark Tech. Coll., Canton, 1978-79; analyst Timken Co., Canton, 1979-83; rschr. Ohio State U., Columbus, 1983-85, instr., 1985-90; scientist Shell Oil Co., Houston, 1990-93; mgr. tng. Am. Bureau Shipping, 1993—; judge Ohio Acad. Sci., Columbus, 1983-90. Author: (with others) Nondestructive Characteristics, 1987; contbr. articles to profl. jours. Bd. dirs. AGA-NDE Supervisory, Washington, 1990-92, CNDE Iowa State U., Ames, 1990-92; scientist Houston Children Mus., 1992. Lt. USN, 1991—. Acoustics scholarship NATO, 1985. Mem. Am. Nondestructive (lectr. 1987), Am. Welding Soc. (lectr. 1989), Sigma Xi (rsch. mem. 1986). Roman Catholic. Achievements include research in ultrasonic evaluation of cast aluminum, nonlinear acoustics evaluation of adhesive bonded joints, electromagnetic induced ultrasonic velocity changes to evaluate ferromagnetic materials, failure analysis and nondestructive evaluation of large metallic structures. Office: Am Bureau Shipping 16855 Northchase Dr Houston TX 77060-6008

RYPIEN, MARK ROBERT, professional football player; b. Calgary, Alta., Can., Oct. 2, 1962. Student, Wash. State U. Quarterback Washington Redskins, 1987-94, Cleve. Browns, 1994-97, Phila. Eagles, 1997—. Named to Pro Bowl team, 1989, 91; recipient Most Valuable Player award Superbowl, 1992. Office: Phila Eagles 3501 S Broad St Philadelphia PA 19148*

RYSANEK, LEONIE, soprano; b. Vienna, Austria, Nov. 14, 1926; d. Peter and Josefine (Hoeberth) R.; m. Ernst-Ludwig Gausmann, Dec. 23, 1968. Student, Vienna Conservatory, 1947-49. First singing engagements include Bayreuth, (Sieglinde-Die Walkure), 1951, San Francisco Opera, (Senta-Der Fliegende Hollaender), 1956, Met. Opera, (Lady Macbeth), 1959; now appears in world's foremost opera houses, N.Y.C., Vienna, Milan, San Francisco, London, Paris, (Chrysothemis-Elektra 1973), Berlin, (Gioconda 1974), Munich, Hamburg, Budapest, Moscow, (Parsifal 1975), and festivals of Salzburg, (Kaiserin-Die Frau Ohne Schatten 1974), Bayreuth, Orange, (Salome 1974), Sieglinde-Die Walkuere, 1975, Aix en Provende, Athens, (Medea 1973), Edinburgh recordings for RCA Victor, Deutsche Grammophon, London Records, EMI and Phillips, Kundry, Parsifal (Stuttgart 1978), Kammersangerin of Austria and Bavaria, Kostelnicka, Jenufa, Australian Opera, 1985, Vienna, 1986, San Francisco, 1986, N.Y. Carnegie Hall, 1988; only artist to sing three major roles in opera Elektra on videocassette; debut Spain, Sieglinde in Die Walküre, Kostelnicka in Janufa, Carnegie Hall, 1988, Liceo, Barcelona, Spain, 1989, Kabanicha in Katya Kabanova, Paris and L.A., 1988, Klytaemnesha in Elektra, Marseille, France, 1989, Orange, 1991, Met. Opera, N.Y.C., 1992, 95-96, Old Countess, Queen of Spades, Barcelona, 1992, San Francisco, 1994, S.Am. Teatro Color, Buenos Aires, 1995, Rio de Janeiro, 1996, Operate Farewell Salzburg Festival, Elektra, 1996; Met. Farewell, 1996. Recipient Chappel Gold medal of singing London; Silver Rose Vienna Philharmonic; Austrian Gold Cross 1st class for arts and scis.; San Francisco medal. Hon. mem. Vienna Staatsoper. Office: Merle Hubbard Mgmt 133 W 71st St Apt 8A New York NY 10023-3881

RYSER, HUGUES JEAN-PAUL, pharmacologist, medical educator, cell biologist; b. Chaux-de-Fonds, Switzerland, June 11, 1926; came to U.S., 1958, naturalized, 1972; s. Ernest Jacob and Marthe Alice (Zimmermann) R.; m. Carol Leigh Pierson, June 10, 1961; children: Marc Alain, Jeannine, Eve. M.D., U. Berne, Switzerland, 1953, Dr. Med., 1955. Instr. pharmacology Harvard U. Med. Sch., Boston, 1960-62; assoc. in pharmacology Harvard U. Med. Sch., 1962-64, asst. prof. pharmacology, 1964-69; assoc. prof. cell biology and pharmacology U. Md. Med. Sch., Balt., 1969-70; prof. U. Md. Med. Sch., 1970-72; prof. pathology and pharmacology Sch. Medicine, Boston U., 1972—, prof. biochemistry, 1981—; prof. pub. health Sch. Pub. Health, Boston U., 1980—. Contbr. numerous articles to sci. jours. Bd. dirs. Am. Cancer Soc., Mass. div., 1983—. Recipient Lederle Med. Faculty award, 1964-67; Nat. Cancer Inst. Rsch. Career Devel. awardee, 1968-69, grantee, 1972—; NIH rsch. grantee, 1961-69, Am. Cancer Soc. Instl. Rsch. Group grantee, 1975—. Fellow AAAS; mem. Am. Assn. Cancer Rsch., Am. Soc. Cell Biology, Am. Soc. Exptl. Pharmacology and Therapeutics. Home: 503 Annursnac Hill Rd Concord MA 01742-5414 Office: Boston U 80 E Concord St Boston MA 02118-2307 *My purpose as an educator is to engage in the creative process of making important knowledge exciting. As a scientist, I am driven by curiosity and derive pleasure from being at the cutting edge of a field, however narrow it may be.*

RYSKAMP, BRUCE E., publishing executive; b. Grand Rapids, Mich., 1941. AB, Calvin Coll., 1962; MBA, Mich. State U., 1964. With R. H. Donnelly Corp., 1964-82; with Zondervan Pub. House Zondervan Corp., Grand Rapids, 1983—, v.p. book and bible pub. Zondervan Pub. House, 1986-93; pres., CEO Zondervan Corp., 1993—. Office: Zondervan Pub House 5300 Patterson Ave SE Grand Rapids MI 49512-9659

RYSKAMP, CHARLES ANDREW, museum executive, educator; b. East Grand Rapids, Mich., Oct. 21, 1928; s. Henry Jacob and Flora (DeGraaf) R. A.B., Calvin Coll., 1950; M.A., Yale U., 1951, Ph.D., 1956; postgrad., Pembroke Coll., Cambridge U., 1953-54; Litt.D., Trinity Coll., Hartford, 1975; L.H.D., Union Coll., 1977. Nathan Hale fellow Yale U., 1954-55; instr. English Princeton U., 1955-59, asst. prof., 1959-63, assoc. prof., 1963-69; curator English and Am. lit. Univ. Library, 1967-69, prof., 1969—; Procter & Gamble faculty fellow, 1958-59; jr. fellow Council of Humanities, 1960-61, John E. Annan preceptor, 1961-64; dir. Pierpont Morgan Library, N.Y.C., 1969-87, Frick Collection, N.Y.C., 1987—; mem. adv. bd. Skowhegan Sch. Painting and Sculpture, Private Papers of James Boswell, Yale U. Author: William Cowper of the Inner Temple, Esq, 1959, William Blake, Engraver, 1969; editor: (with F.A. Pottle) Boswell: The Ominous Years, 1963, The Cast-Away, 1963, Wilde and the Nineties, 1966, William Blake: The Pickering Manuscript, 1972, (with J. King) The Letters and Prose Writings of William Cowper, vol. I, 1979, vol. II, 1981, vol. III, 1982, Vol. IV, 1984, Vol. V, 1986, (with R. Wendorf) The Works of William Collins, 1979, (with J. Baird) The Poetical Works of William Cowper, vol. I, 1980, vols. II-III, 1995, (with J. King) William Cowper: Selected Letters, 1989, Report to the Fellows of the Pierpont Morgan Library, vols. 16-21, 1969-89. Trustee, mem. exec. com. Mus. Broadcasting, 1977-87; trustee Andrew W. Mellon Found., John Simon Guggenheim Meml. Found., Corning Mus. Glass (hon. trustee), Amon Carter Mus.; mem. adv. coun. art mus. Princeton U.; mem. vis. com. dept. paintings conservation Met. Mus. Art; patron William Blake Trust; mem. bd. mgrs. Lewis Walpole Libr., Yale U.; bd. dirs., v.p. Gerard B. Lambert Found.; v.p. Frederick R. Koch Found.; hon. felllow Pierpont Morgan Libr. Decorated Order St. John of Jerusalem, comdr. Order Orange Nassau, The Netherlands, officer Order Leopold II, Belgium, comdr. Order of Falcon, Iceland; recipient Peter Stuyvesant award Dutch Am. West-India Co., 1987, Gold medal Holland Soc., 1991. Mem. Am. Acad. Arts and Scis., Am. Philosphical Soc., Museums Coun. N.Y.C. (past v.p.), Keats-Shelley Assn. Am. (past v.p.), Master Drawings Assn. (pres.), Met. Opera Assn. (bd. advisors), Drawing Soc. (nat. com.), Bibliog. Soc. Am., Acad. Am., Acad. Am. Poets, Am. Antiquarian Soc., Assn. Art Mus. Dirs. (past pres.), N.Y. Geneal. and Biog. Soc. (spl. corr.), Cowper Soc., Assn. Internationale de Bibliophilie (com. of Honor), Found. French Mus. (adv. bd.), Royal Soc. Arts (London), Wordsworth Rydel Mount Trust, Pilgrims, Grolier Club, Century Assn., Lotos Club (N.Y.C.), Elizabethan Club (New Haven), Roxburghe Club (London). Office: Inst for Advanced Study Princeton NJ 08540

RYSKAMP, KENNETH LEE, federal judge; b. 1932; m. Karyl Sonja Ryskamp; 1 child, Cara Leigh. AB, Calvin Coll., 1955; JD, U. Miami, 1956. Bar: Fla. 1956, Mich. 1957, U.S. Supreme Ct. 1970. Law clk. to presiding judge Fla. Ct. Appeals 3d Dist., 1957-59; pvt. practice law Miami, Fla., 1959-61; ptnr. Goodwin, Ryskamp, Welcher & Carrier, Miami, 1961-84; mng. ptnr. Squire, Sanders & Dempsey, Miami, 1984-86; judge U.S. Dist. Ct. (so. dist.) Fla., Miami, 1986—. Office: US Dist Ct 701 Clematis St Rm 416 West Palm Beach FL 33401-5112*

RYU, KYOO-HAI LEE, physiologist; b. Seoul, Republic of Korea, Sept. 5, 1948; came to U.S., 1972; d. Hee Soon and Jung Ock Lee; m. David Tai-Hyung Ryu, May 13, 1978; children: Eugenia, Christina, John. BS, Yonsei U., Seoul, 1971; PhD, U. Minn., 1981. Postdoctoral fellow U. Minn., Mpls., 1980-81, staff scientist, 1981-82; sr. rsch. assoc. Wright State U., Dayton, Ohio, 1985-91; adminstr. Ohio Ctr. of Cosmetic Surgery, Bellefontaine, Ohio, 1991—. Mem. Am. Physiol. Soc., Biophys. Soc., Soc. Gen. Physiologists. Home: 15 Bexley Ave Springfield OH 45503-1103

SA, JULIE, restaurant chain owner, former mayor; b. Korea, Dec. 15, 1950; came to U.S., 1973, naturalized, 1982; married. Degree in Polit. Sci., Dong-A U., Korea. Owner restaurant chain; councilwoman City of Fullerton, Calif., 1992-94, 96—, mayor, 1994-95; rep. bd. Orange County Sanitation Dists.; rep. to Tri-City Park Authority, City of Fullerton. Mem. Fullerton C. of C., Orange County Korean C. of C., Orange County Chinese C. of C. Office: Office of City Council 303 W Commonwealth Ave Fullerton CA 92632*

SA, LUIZ AUGUSTO DISCHER, physicist; b. Lages, Brazil, Sept. 28, 1944; came to U.S., 1983; s. Catulo J.C. and Maria (Discher) S. MSc in Physics, Carnegie Mellon U., 1969; PhD in Elec. Engring., Stanford U., 1989. Asst. prof. Cath. U. of Rio, Rio de Janeiro, 1969-72, Fed. U. of Rio, Rio de Janeiro, 1973-83; post-doctoral scholar Stanford (Calif.) U., 1990-91, rsch. scientist, 1991—; rsch. scientist SOI/MDI project The MDI instrument is on board the SOHO spacecraft launched by NASA, 1995. Contbr. articles to Jour. of Applied Physics, Jour. Geophys. Rsch., Proc. of 4th SOHO Workshop on Helioseismology, ESA, 1995. Recipient of Recognition award NASA, 1994. Mem. Am. Astronomical Soc., Am. Geophysical Union, Sigma Xi. Roman Catholic. Achievements include research in non-linear plasma physics, naturally occuring plasmas, large scale flows on the sun. Office: CSSA HEPL Annex A207 Stanford CA 94305

SAAD, THEODORE SHAFICK, retired microwave company executive; b. Boston, Sept. 13, 1920; s. Wadie Assad and Mary (Shalhoub) S.; m. Afeefi Abdelnour, May 5, 1943; children: Karen Jeanne, Janet Elaine. BSEE, MIT, 1941. Engr. Sylvania Electric Products, Danvers, Mass., 1941-42; rsch. assoc. radiation lab. Radiation Lab. MIT, Cambridge, 1942-45; sr. engr. Submarine Signal Co., Boston, 1945-49; v.p., chief engr. Microwave Devel. Labs., Waltham, Mass., 1949-53; engring. specialist Sylvania Electric Products, Woburn, Mass., 1953-55; pres., chmn. Sage Labs. Inc., Natick, Mass., 1955-93; ret., 1993; cons. Horizon House Microwave, Norwood, Mass., 1958—. Editor: Microwave Engineers Handbook, 1971, Historical Perspectives of Microwave Technology, 1984; patentee in microwavetech. and passive components fields. Fellow IEEE (life; Richard M. Emberson award 1996), AAAS; mem. Microwave Soc. of IEEE (hon. life; nat. lectr. 1972, Disting. Svc. award 1983, Centennial medal 1984, Career award 1992). Avocations: photography, reading, travel, music. Home: 52 Doublet Hill Rd Weston MA 02193-2331

SAADA, ADEL SELIM, civil engineer, educator; b. Heliopolis, Egypt, Oct. 24, 1934; came to U.S., 1959, naturalized, 1965; s. Selim N. and Marie (Chahyne) S.; m. Nancy Helen Hernan, June 5, 1960; children: Christiane Mona, Richard Adel. Ingénieur des Arts et Manufactures, École Centrale, Paris, 1958; M.S., U. Grenoble, France, 1959; Ph.D. in Civil Engring, Princeton U., 1961. Registered profl. engr., Ohio. Engr. Société Dumez, Paris, 1959; research assoc. dept. civil engring. Princeton (N.J.) U., 1961-62; asst. prof. civil engring. Case Western Reserve U., Cleve., 1962-67; asso. prof. Case Western Reserve U., 1967-72, prof., 1973—, chmn. dept. civil engring., 1978—, Frank H. Neff prof. civil engring., chmn. dept., 1987; R.J. Carroll Meml. lectr. Johns Hopkins U., 1990; cons., lectr. soil testing and properties Waterways Expt. Sta. (C.E.), Vicksburg, Miss., 1974-79; cons. to various firms, 1962—. Author: Elasticity Theory and Applications, 1974, 2d edit., 1993; contbr. numerous articles on soil mechanics and foundation engring. to profl. jours. Recipient Telford Prize Instn. of Civil Engrs., U.K., 1995. Fellow ASCE (Civil Engr. of Yr. Cleve. sect. 1992); mem. Internat. Soc. Soil Mechanics, ASTM, One Two One Athletic Club. Inventor pneumatic analog computer and loading frame. Home: 3342 Braemar Rd Cleveland OH 44120-3332 Office: Case Western Res U Dept Civil Engring Case Sch Engring Cleveland OH 44106

SAADEH, CONSTANTINE KHALIL, internist, health facility administrator, educator; b. Beirut, Sept. 6, 1957; came to U.S., 1982; s. Khalil Constantine and Angel Janet (Iskendarian) S.; m. Vivian Camille Novni, June 28, 1988 (div. Apr. 1993); 1 child, Charles; m. M. Celeste Gaylor, 1996; 2 children: Charles, McKenzie. BS in Biology-Chemistry, Am. U. Beirut, 1978, MD, 1982. Diplomate Nat. Bd. Med. Examiners, Am. Bd. Internal Medicine, Am. Bd. Allergy and Immunology, Am. Bd. Internal Medicine, Am. Bd. Rheumatology, Am. Bd. Geriatrics, Am. Acad. Pain Mgmt. Intern dept. of medicine U. Miami, Jackson Meml. Hosp., Fla., 1982-83, resident dept. of medicine, 1983-85; fellow in clin. immunology Baylor Coll. of Medicine, Houston, 1985-87; fellow in rheumatology U. Colo. Health Sci. Ctr., Denver, 1987-88, instr. dept. internal medicine, 1988-89; acting chief med. svc. VA Med. Ctr., Amarillo, Tex., 1989, med. svc. staff physician, 1989—; asst. prof. dept. internal medicine Tex. Tech U. Health Scis. Ctr., Amarillo, 1989-91, assoc. prof. internal medicine and pediatrics, dir., 1991—, regional chair internal medicine, dir. residency program, 1992—, assoc. prof. dept. microbiology and immunology, 1992—; mem. grad. med. edn. com. Tex. Tech. U. Health Sci. Ctr.; mem. pharmacy and therapeutics com. N.W. Tex. Hosp.; mem. pharmacy and therapeutics com., R&D com. VA Med. Ctr., faculty appointments com., MPIP com. Tex. Tech. U., program dir., chmn. residency evaluation com., 1992—; lectr. in field. Contbr. articles to profl. jours. Fellow ACP, Am. Acad. Allergy and Immunology, Am. Coll. Rheumatology; mem. AMA, So. Med. Assn. (chmn. rheumatology sect. 1996-97). Home: 7100 Canterbury Amarillo TX 79109 Office: Tex Tech U Health Scis Ctr 1400 Wallace Blvd Amarillo TX 79106-1708

SAADEH, PETER BOUTROS, physiatrist, educator; b. Beirut, Aug. 8, 1930; came to U.S., 1975; s. Beshara B. and Edma A. Saadeh; m. Genevieve L. Verbrugghen, Apr. 27, 1968; children: Pierre, Kris. BA, Coll. de Sagesse, Beirut, 19s49; MD, St. Joseph French U., Beirut, 1957. Diplomate Am. Bd. Phys. Medicine and Rehab. Intern Elizabeth (N.J.) Gen. Hosp., 1957-58; resident in neurology Montefiore Hosp., Bronx, N.Y., 1958-60; resident in phys. medicine and rehab. NYU Hosp., N.Y.C., 1960-62; assoc. Am. U. Hosp., Beirut, 1962-75; pvt. practice, N.Y.C., 1978—; asst. clin. prof. NYU, N.Y.C. Contbr. articles to med. jours. Mem. AMA, Am. Acad. Phys. Medicine and Rehab., Am. Assn. Electrodiagnostic Medicine, Assn. Acad. Physiatrists, Am. Coll. Occpl. and Environ. Medicine, Am. Assn. Electrodiagnostic Medicine, N.Y. Soc. Phys. Medicine Rehab. (pres. 1989-90), N.Y. Acad. Medicine. Republican. Office: 5 World Trade Ctr Ste 367B New York NY 10048

SAAL, HOWARD MAX, clinical geneticist, pediatrician, educator; b. N.Y.C., Aug. 20, 1951; s. Josef and Ester (Morgenstern) S.; m. Cara Tina Schweitzer, May 3, 1987; 1 child, Rebecca. BS, U. Mass., Amherst, 1973, MS, 1975; MD, Wayne State U., 1979. Intern pediatrics U. Conn. Med. Ctr., 1979-80; resident pediatrics U. Conn. Health Ctr., 1980-82; fellow med. genetics U. Wash. Sch. Medicine, 1982-84; dir. cytogenetics U. Conn. Health Ctr., Farmington, 1984-87; vice chmn. med. genetics Children's Nat. Med. Ctr., Washington, 1987-93; head clin. genetics Children's Nat. Med. Ctr., Cin., 1993—; asst. prof. pediats. George Washington U., Washington, 1987-93, assoc. prof. pediats., 1993; assoc. prof. clin. pediats. U. Cin. Sch. Medicine, 1993—. Contbr. articles to profl. jours. Mem. med. adv. com. Nat. Neurofibromatosis Found., N.Y.C., 1987—; mem. health profl. adv. com. March of Dimes, Arlington, Va., 1991-93; bd. dirs. Capital Area March of Dines, 1993. Tng. grantee NIH, 1979-82. Fellow Am. Acad. Pediats., Am. Coll. Med. Genetics; mem. Am. Soc. Human Genetics, Soc. Craniofacial Genetics (sec.-treas. 1990-96). Avocation: photography. Home: 3715 Monets Ln Cincinnati OH 45241-3847 Office: Childrens Hosp Med Ctr 3333 Burnet Ave Cincinnati OH 45229-3026

SAALFELD, FRED ERICH, naval researcher; b. Joplin, Mo., Apr. 9, 1935; s. Eric Arthur and Milla (Kessler) S.; m. Elizabeth Renner, Nov. 22, 1958; 1 child, Fred E. Jr. (dec.). BS cum laude, So. East Mo. State U., 1957; MS in Phys. Chemistry, Iowa State U., 1959, PhD in Phys. Chem., 1961. Instr. Iowa State U., Ames, 1961-62; chemist Naval Rsch. Lab, Washington, 1962-63, head mass spectrometry sect., 1963-74, head physical chm. br., 1974-76, supt. chem. divsn., 1976-82; chief scientist Office Naval Rsch., London, 1979-80; dir. rsch. Office Naval Rsch., Arlington, Va., 1982-87, dir., 1987-93, dep. chief naval rsch., tech. dir., 1993—. Author more than 500 publications, reports, presentations on applications of mass spectrometry to fields of combustion, laser, environ. analysis. Recipient Disting. Rank awards U.S. Pres., Washington, 1989, 96, Meritorious Rank award U.S. Pres., Washington, 1986, Robert Conrad award Sec. USN, Washington, 1988; named Fed. Exec. of Yr., Fed. Exec. Inst., Washington, 1991. Fellow AAAS; mem. Am. Chem. Soc. (councilor 1973-89), Am. Soc. Mass Spectrometry (sec. 1970-74), Combustion Inst., Chem. Soc. Washington (pres. 1972). Achievements include provision for science base for life support systems used in all U.S. submarines; development of educational programs used by USN for scientist training. Avocations: history, woodworking, sports. Office: Office of Naval Rsch 800 N Quincy St Arlington VA 22203-1906

SAAR, ALISON, sculptor; b. L.A., Feb. 5, 1956. BA, Scripps Coll., 1978; MFA, Otis Art Inst., 1981. One-woman shows include Bellevue (Wash.) Art Mus., 1992, Neuberger Mus., Purchase, N.Y., 1992, Cleve. Ctr. Contemporary Art, 1992, High Mus., Atlanta, 1993, Hirshhorn Mus., Washington, 1993, Freedman Gallery, Allbright Coll. Ctr. Arts, Reading, Pa., 1993, Va. Mus. Fine Arts, 1994, Otis Art Inst. Jan Baum Gallery, L.A., 1993, Laguna Gloria Art Mus., Austin, 1993, Whitney Mus. Am. Art, 1993, Clar Humanities Mus., Scipps Coll., Pomona, Calif., 1994, Denver Art Mus., 1994, Columbus Mus. Art, 1994, Jan Baum Gallery, L.A., 1994, San Francisco Cmty. Arts, Hines Internat. Ltd., L.A., 1994; commd. bronze gates Metro Transit Authority, N.Y., 1990-91; exhibited works at Met. Mus. Art, N.Y., 1987, Whitney Mus. Am. Art, N.Y., 1988, Met. Mus. Art, N.Y., 1988, Aldrich Mus., 1991. Recipient awards Nat. Endowment Arts, 1985, 88, John Solomon Guggenheim award, 1989. Office: c/o Jan Baum Gallery 170 S La Brea Ave Los Angeles CA 90036-2910*

SAAR, BETYE (IRENE SAAR), artist; b. L.A., July 30, 1926; d. Jefferson Maze and Beatrice Lillian (Parson) Brown; m. Richard W. Saar, Sept. 16, 1952 (div. 1968); children: Lesley Irene, Alison Marie, Tracye Ann. BA, UCLA, 1949. Instr. art Calif. State U., Hayward, 1971, Northridge, 1973-74; instr. art Otis Art Inst., L.A., 1976-83; lectr., free-lance designer for films, 1970-75—; costume designer Inner City Cultural Ctr., Napa Valley Theatre Co., 1968-73. One-woman exhbns. include Monique Knowlton, N.Y.C., 1976, 81, Calif. State U. Gallery, L.A., 1972, Whitney Mus. Art, N.Y.C., 1975, Jan Baum, L.A., 1977, 79, 81, Maneville Art Gallery, U. Calif., San Diego, 1979, Quay Gallery, San Francisco, 1982, Mus. Contemporary Art, L.A., 1984, Pa. Acad. Art, Phila., 1987, MIT, Cambridge, Mass., 1987, Calif. State U., Fullerton, 1988, also galleries in Manila, Kuala Lumpur, Malaysia, Taichung, Taiwan, 1988, Aukland and Wellington, New Zealand, 1988, 89, Montgomery Art Gallery Pomona Coll., 1991, U. Hartford (Conn.) Art Gallery, 1992, Fresno (Calif.) Art Mus., 1993, U. Ctrl. Fla. Art Gallery, Orlando, 1994, Santa Monica (Calif.) Mus. Art, 1994, Salina (Kans.) Art Ctr., 1995, Davidson (N.C.) Coll., 1995, de Saisset Mus., Santa Clara, Calif., 1996, Pa. State U., University Park, 1996, Ctr. Women and Their Work, Austin, Tex., 1996, Joslyn Art Mus., Omaha, 1996, Tacoma Art Mus., 1997; two-woman exhbns. San Francisco Mus. Modern Art, 1977, Wight Gallery, UCLA, 1990; group exhbns. include Small Environments, Univ. Galleries, So. Ill. U., 1972, 20th Century Black Am. Art, San Jose (Calif.) Mus., 1976, San Francisco Mus. Modern Art, 1977, Smithsonian Instn., Africus Johannasberg Biennale, South Africa, 1995; touring exhbn. with daughter Alison Saar, 1990—, Netherlands Textile Mus., Tilburg, 1993, Mus. Applied Arts, Helsinki, Finland, 1993, Ctr. for Arts at Yerba Buena Gardens, San Francisco, 1993, Mus. Modern Art, Sao Paulo, 1994, Wilfredo Law Ctr., Havana, Cuba, 1994. NEA grantee, 1974, 84, James Van Der Zee grantee, 1992; J. Paul Getty fellow, 1990, Guggenheim Found. fellow, 1991. Mem. L.A. Inst. Contemporary Art. Democrat.

SAARI, DONALD GENE, mathematician; b. Ironwood, Mich., Mar. 9, 1940; s. Gene August and Martha Mary (Jackson) S.; m. Lillian Joy Kalinen, June 11, 1966; children: Katri, Anneli. BS, Mich. Tech. U., 1962; PhD, Purdue U., 1967, DSc (hon.), 1989. Research astronomer Yale U., New Haven, 1967-68; prof. dept. math. Northwestern U., Evanston, Ill., 1968—, prof. econs., 1988—, Pancoe prof. math., 1995—, chmn. dept., 1981-84; prof. U. Nanjing (China), 1995; cons. Nat. Bur. Standards, Gaithersburg, Md., 1979-86, Commn. 9, Internat. Astron. Union, 1985-91. Assoc. editor Jour. Econ. Behavior and Orgn., 1988-94, Celestial Mechanics and Dynamical Astronomy. 1989-95, Econ. Theory, 1990—. Recipient Duncan Black award, Pub. Choice Soc., 1991, Chauvenet prize Mathematical Assn. of Am., 1995; Guggenheim fellow, 1988-89. Mem. Am. Math. Soc., Math. Assn. Am. (Chauvenet prize 1995), Am. Astron. Soc., Soc. Indsl. and Applied Math. (editor jour. 1981-88), Econometric Soc. Office: Dept Math Northwestern U Evanston IL 60208-2730

SAARI, JOHN WILLIAM, JR., lawyer; b. Jersey City, Oct. 12, 1937; s. John William Sr. and Ina Marie (Bain) S.; m. Susan Jo Olson, Aug. 27, 1967 (div. June 1971); m. Marjorie Ann Palm, Nov. 16, 1973. Student, Duke U., 1955-58, U. N.C., 1962-63; JD with honors, Ill. Inst. Tech., Chgo., 1972. Bar: Ill. 1972, U.S. Dist. Ct. (no. dist.) Ill. 1972, Wis. 1980, U.S. Dist. Ct. (ea. and we. dists.) Wis. 1980, U.S. Ct. Appeals (7th cir.) 1972. Assoc. Yates, Goff, Gustafson & Been, Chgo., 1972-76, Hubbard, Hubbard, O'Brien & Hall, Chgo., 1976-78; atty. Ill. Bell Telephone Co., Chgo., 1978-79; assoc. Cirilli Law Office, Rhinelander, Wis., 1979-83; pvt. practice Rhinelander, 1983-90; ptnr. Rodd, Mouw, Saari & Krueger, Rhinelander, 1990—. Bd. dirs. Northwoods United Way, 1980-88, pres., 1983-84. With U.S. Army, 1958-61, ETO. Mem. ABA, Ill. Bar Assn., Wis. Bar Assn., Oneida-Vilas-Forest Bar Assn. (pres. 1996—), Lions (pres. Sugarcamp 1983-84). Avocations: hunting, fishing, baseball, reading, golf. Home: 7279 Arbutus Dr Eagle River WI 54521-9249 Office: Rodd Mouw Saari & Krueger 8A W Davenport St Rhinelander WI 54501-3467

SAARI, JOY ANN, family nurse practitioner, geriatrics medical and surgical nurse; b. Chippewa Falls, Wis., July 14, 1953; d. Harry R. and Hilda R. (Christianson) Harwood; m. Allan A. Saari, Dec. 31, 1973 (dec.); children: Christopher, Erik. BSN summa cum laude, U. Wis., Eau Claire, 1978; postgrad., Blue Ridge Community Coll., Verona, Va., 1987; MSN, FNP, George Mason U., 1995; MSN. RN, Mich., Wis., Va.; FNP, Va.; cert. BLS instr., ACLS. Staff nurse Portage View Hosp., Hancock, Mich., 1979-80; evening supr., asst. dir. nursing Chippewa Manor, Chippewa Falls, 1980-86; staff nurse Bridgewater (Va.) Home, Inc., 1986-90; p.m. charge nurse Medicalodge Leavenworth, Kans., 1990-91; outdoor edn. nurse Montgomery County (Md.) Schs., 1991-93; FNP Leesburg/Sterling Family Practice, 1995—. Capt. USAR Nurse Corps. Mem. Am. Acad. Nurse Practitioners, Nat. League of Nursing, No. Va. Nurse Practitioner Assn., Res. Officer Assn., Am. Legion Aux., Phi Kappa Phi.

SAAVEDRA, CHARLES JAMES, banker; b. Denver, Nov. 2, 1941; s. Charles James and Evangeline Cecilia (Aragon) S.; m. Ann Helen Taylor, 1967; children: Michael, Kevin, Sarah. BSBA, Regis U., Denver, 1963; postgrad. U. Calif., San Francisco, 1964-66. Vice-pres., Western States Bankcard Assn., San Francisco, 1969-77; dir. info. systems World Airways, Inc., Oakland, Calif., 1977-79; v.p. computer services First Nationwide Bank, San Francisco, 1979-83; sr. v.p. Wells Fargo Bank, San Francisco, 1983-92; sr. v.p. Union Bank of Calif., San Francisco, 1992—; instr. Programming & Systems Inst., San Francisco, 1968-69; lectr. Am. Mgmt. Assn., 1984—; pres. Right Direction Project of Contra Costa County; bd. dirs. No. Calif. Family Ctr. With USNR, 1963-64. Mem. Data Processing Mgrs. Assn. (bd. dirs., chmn. program com. 1981), Am. Nat. Standards Inst., Am. Bankers Assn., San Francisco Jaycees, Alpha Delta Gamma. Clubs: Commonwealth of Calif., Lake Lakewood Assn. Home: 210 Lakewood Rd Walnut Creek CA 94598-4826 Office: Union Bank Calif 350 California St San Francisco CA 94104

SABANAS-WELLS, ALVINA OLGA, orthopedic surgeon; b. Riga, Latvia, Lithuania, July 30, 1914; d. Adomas and Olga (Dagilyte) Pipyne; m. Juozas Sabanas, Aug. 20, 1939 (dec. Mar. 1968); 1 child, Algis (dec.); m. Alfonse F. Wells, Dec. 31, 1977 (dec. 1990). MD, U. Vytautas The Great, Kaunas, Lithuania, 1939; MS in Orthopaedic Surgery, U. Minn., 1955. Diplomate Am. Bd. Orthopaedic Surgery. Intern Univ. Clinics, Kaunas, 1939-40; resident orthopaedic surgery and trauma Red Cross Trauma Hosp., Kaunas, 1940-44; orthopaedic and trauma fellow Unfall Krankenhous, Vienna, Austria, 1943-44; intern Jackson Park Hosp., Chgo., 1947-48; fellow in orthopaedic surgery Mayo Clinic, Rochester, Minn., 1952-55; assoc. orthopaedic surgery Northwestern U., 1956-72; asst. prof. orthopaedic surgery Rush Med. Sch., 1973-76; pvt. practice orthopaedic surgery Sun City, Ariz., 1976-89; pres. cattle ranch corp. Contbr. articles to profl. jours. Fellow ACS; mem. Am. Acad. Orthopaedic Surgery, Physicians Club Sun City, Mayo Alumni Assn. Mem. U. Minn. Alumni Assn., Ruth Jackson Orthopedic Soc. Republican. Mem. Evang. Reformed Ch. Avocations: art, antiques, environment. Home: 3101 Skipworth Dr Las Vegas NV 89107-3241

SABAROFF, ROSE EPSTEIN, retired education educator; b. Cleve., Sept. 4, 1918; d. Hyman Israel and Bertha (Glaser) Epstein; m. Bernard Joseph Sabaroff, Dec. 28, 1940; children: Ronald Asher, Katya Nina. B.A., U. Ariz., 1941; M.A., San Francisco State U., 1954; Ed.D., Stanford U., 1957. Tchr. Presidio Hill Elem. Sch., San Francisco, 1951-55; asst. prof. edn. Oreg. State U., Corvallis, 1958-61; asst. dir., then dir. elem. edn. Harvard Grad. Sch. Edn., Cambridge, Mass., 1961-66; prof. edn., head elem. edn., head reading program Va. Poly. Inst. and State U., Blacksburg, 1967-82; dir. Grad. Edn. Ctr. Calif. Luth. Coll., North Hollywood, 1982-84; reading specialist How to Learn, Inc., West Los Angeles, Calif., 1983-88. Author: (with Hanna, Davies, Farrar) Geography in the Teaching of Social Studies, 1966, (with Mary Ann Hanna) The Open Classroom, 1974, Teaching Reading with a Linguistic Approach, 1980, Developing Linguistic Awareness, 1981; contbr. articles to profl. jours. Recipient Disting. Research award Va. Edn. Research Assn., 1977; Phi Delta Kappa grantee, 1980. Mem. AAUP, Internat. Reading Assn., NEA, Va. Edn. Assn., Va. Coll. Reading Educators (pres. 1976-77), Va. Reading Assn., Phi Delta Kappa, Pi Lambda Theta, Gamma Theta Upsilon. Democrat. Jewish. Conducted 15 month study abroad comparing ednl. systems in 4 European countries with differing social-econ. systems. Home: 23826 Villena Mission Viejo CA 92692-1818

SABAT, ROBERT HARTMAN, magazine editor; b. Newark, Aug. 28, 1957; s. Charles and Marilyn Ruth (Hartman) S.; m. Jessica Schilling Fine, Oct. 15, 1989; children: Nathaniel, Olivia. BA, Brandeis U., 1980. Mng. editor Penthouse mag., N.Y.C., 1986-91, Connoisseur mag., N.Y.C., 1991-92, Lear's mag., N.Y.C., 1992-94, Interview mag., N.Y.C., 1994-95, Smart Money mag., N.Y.C., 1995—. Mem. Am. Soc. Mag. Editors. Office: Smart Money 1790 Broadway New York NY 10019-1412

SABATELLA, ELIZABETH MARIA, clinical therapist, educator, mental health facility administrator; b. Mineola, N.Y., Nov. 9, 1940; d. D. F. and Blanche M. (Schmetzle) S; 1 child, Kevin Woog. BS, SUNY, Brockport, 1961; MA, SUNY, Stony Brook, 1971, MSW, 1983. Lic. social worker, N.Y., N.Mex., tchr., N.Y., N.Mex.; registered clin. social worker, Calif. Tchr. physical edn. Comseqogue Sch. Dist., Port Jefferson, N.Y., 1968-73, 84-87, 88-91; clin. therapist Cibola Counseling Svcs., Grants, N.Mex., 1991-95, regional dir., 1993-95; clin. therapist Family Growth Counseling Ctr., Encinitos, Calif., 1995-96; clin. social worker Family Advocacy, San Diego, 1995—; therapist for abused children Farmingville Mental Health Clinic; therapist for adolescents Comsewogue Sch. Dist.; therapist for alcoholics Lighthouse Ctr.; mem. Family Systems Network for Continuing Edn., Calif., Colo., 1978-80; mem. biofeedback and mediation com. McLean Hosp., Boston, 1978; mem. therapeutic touch team East and West Ctr., N.Y.C., 1980-84, sexual abuse treatment coord., 1992-95. Art and photographs exhibited at group show N.Mex. Art League, 1991; contbr. poetry and children's story to various publs. Recipient Editor's Choice award and Best New Poet award Nat. Libr. Poetry, 1988, Merit award and Place Winner for Poetry, Iliad Press, 1993. Mem. NASW, N.Y. State United Tchrs., Writers Assn., Sierra Club. Avocations: travel, cycling, jazzercise, dance, photography. Home: 3852 Jewell St Apt L 208 San Diego CA 92109-6417

SABATINI, DAVID DOMINGO, cell biologist, biochemist; b. Bolivar, Argentina, May 10, 1931; came to U.S., 1961; m. Zulema Lena Sabatini, 1960; children: Bernardo L., David M. MD, U. Litoral, Rosario, Argentina, 1954; PhD in Cell Biology, Rockefeller U., 1966. Instr., lectr., assoc. prof. cell biology Inst. Gen. Anatomy and Embryology, U. Buenos Aires, 1957-60; dir. admissions Sch. Medicine U. Buenos Aires, 1957-60; Rockefeller Found. fellow Sch. Medicine Yale U., 1961; rsch. assoc. cell biol. lab Rockefeller U., N.Y.C., 1961-63, from asst. prof. to assoc. prof. cell biology, 1966-72; prof., chmn. dept. cell biology Sch. Medicine NYU, 1972-74, Frederick L. Ehrman prof., chmn. dept. cell biol. Sch. Med., 1975—, dir. MD-PhD program, 1987—; Wendell Griffith Meml. lectr. St. Louis U., 1977; Mary Peterman Meml. lectr. Meml.-Sloan Kettering Inst., N.Y., 1977; 25th Robert J. Terry lectr. Wash. U., 1978; 3d ann. Keith R. Porter lectr. cell biology, 1994; vis. prof. Coll. France, Paris, 1986, George Washington U., 1986; 7th Ann. Kenneth F. Naidorff Meml. lectr. Columbia U., 1989; fellow Nat. Acad. Medicine, Argentina, 1956; UNESCO fellow Biophysics Inst., Rio de Janeiro, 1957; Pfizer traveling fellow, 1972; mem. molecular biology study sect. NIH, 1973-77, chmn., 1976-77; mem. bd. basic biology Nat. Rsch. Coun., 1986-89. Editor Jour. Cell Biology, 1971—, Jour. Cellular Biochemistry, 1980-84, Molecular & Cellular Biology, 1980-82, Procs. NAS USA, 1985—, Biol. Cell, 1986—, Current Opinions Cell Biology, 1990—; mem. editl. bd. Procs. NAS, 1993-96. Mem. sci. adv. com. Irma T. Hirshcl Charitable Trust, 1979-85; bd. dirs. Pub. Health Rsch. Inst., 1980-88; bd. sci. dirs. Jane Coffin Childs Meml. Fund, 1980-86, Nat. Inst. Diabetes Digest Kidney Disease, 1982-86; sci. adv. com. Robert Wood Johnson Found. Minority Med. Faculty Devel. Program, 1987—, Human Frontier Sci. Program, 1991—, chair molecular grants, 1994—; mem. sci. rev. com. Pew Internat. Fellows Program, 1990—, med. adv. bd., 1989-93, internat. program, 1994—; mem. sci. adv. com. Inst. d'Embryologie Cellular Mol., Coll. France, 1994—;, Ctr. Adv. Biotech. and Medicine, 1996—; mem. Alfred P. Sloan Jr. award selection com. GM Cancer Rsch. Found., 1996—. Recipient Samuel Roberts Noble Rsch. Recognition award, 1980. Fellow AAAS, Am. Acad. Microbiology, N.Y. Acad. Sci.; mem. NAS (chmn. cell and devel. biology sect. 1994-96), Am. Soc. Cell Biology (pres. 1978-79, coun. mem. 1974-77, E. B. Wilson award 1986), Harvey Soc. (v.p. 1985-86, pres. 1986-87), Argentine Med. Assn. (hon.), French Acad. Sci. (fgn. assoc., Charles Leopold Mayer prize 1988), Am. Soc. Biol. Chemistry, Am. Soc. Microbiology, N.Y. Soc. Electron Microbiology ((pres. 1971), Am. Assn. Anatomy (chair cell biology, neurobiology, exec. coun. 1992—).

SABATINI, GABRIELA, retired tennis player; b. Buenos Aires, May 16, 1970; d. Osvaldo and Beatriz S. Winner French Jr. Open, 1984, Italian Jr. Open, 1984, Japan Open, 1985, Tokyo Open, 1987, Brighton Open, 1987, Italian Open, 1988, 1989, 1991, 1992, Virginia Slims Championship, 1988, 94, U.S. Open, 1990; Silver medalist in Tennis, 1988 Summer Olympics. Office: care Womens Tennis Assn 133 First St NE Saint Petersburg FL 33701*

SABATINI, LAWRENCE, bishop; b. Chgo., May 15, 1930; s. Dominic and Ada (Piloi) S. Ph.L., Gregorian U., Rome, 1953, S.T.L., 1957, J.C.D., 1960; M.S. in Edn., Iona Coll., 1968. Ordained priest, Roman Catholic Ch., 1957, bishop, 1978. Prof. canon law St. Charles Sem., S.I., N.Y., 1960-71; pastor St. Stephen's Parish, North Vancouver, B.C., Canada, 1970-78; provincial superior Missionaries of St. Charles, Oak Park, Ill., 1978; aux. bishop Archdiocese Vancouver, B.C., Can., 1978-82; bishop Diocese Kamloops, B.C., Can., 1982—; procurator, adviser Matrimonial Tribunal, N.Y.C., 1964-71; founder, dir. RAP Youth Counseling Service, S.I., N.Y., 1969-71; vice ofcl. Regional Matrimonial tribunal of Diocese Kamloops, 1978-82; chmn. Kamloops Cath. Pub. Schs., 1982—. Named Man of Yr. Confratellanza Italo-Canadese, 1979. Mem. Can. Canon Law Soc., Canon Law Soc. Am., Can. Conf. Cath. Bishops. Office: Diocese of Kamloops, 635A Tranquille Rd, Kamloops, BC Canada V2B 3H5*

SABATINI, NELSON JOHN, government official; b. Rochester, N.Y., Jan. 20, 1940; s. John R. and Ida M. (Ceconi) S.; m. Marilyn Jean Gromala, Jan. 19, 1963; children—John Nelson, Michael Christopher. Student, Lewis Coll., Lockport, Ill., 1958-62; B.A. in Psychology, George Washington U., 1971, postgrad. Claims rep. Social Security Adminstrn., Chgo., 1962-65; various positions Social Security Adminstrn., Balt., 1965-79, dep. dir. disability programs, 1979-81, exec. asst. to commr., 1981-82, assoc. commr., 1982—, dep. commr., 1983-88; dep. sec. health and mental hygiene State of Md., 1988, sec. health and mental hygiene, 1991—; v.p. U. Md. Med. System, 1995—. Named Disting. Marylander of Yr. 1993; recipient Sec.'s cert. HHS, 1975; Commr.'s citation Social Security Adminstrn., 1977, 81; Presdl. Merit Rank award Pres. of U.S., 1984. Roman Catholic. Avocations: sailing; tennis. *

SABATINI, WILLIAM QUINN, architect; b. Pitts.; s. William L. and Lydia M. (Contento) S.; m. Carol Anne Christoffel, Feb. 26, 1972; children: Quinn, Jay, Jillian. BA, Franklin & Marshall Coll., 1971; MArch, U. N.Mex., 1978. Registered arch., N.Mex., Nev.; cert. Nat. Coun. Archtl. Registration Bds. Intern Jess Holmes, Arch., Albuquerque, 1974-78; project mgr. Jack Miller & Assocs., Las Vegas, 1978-81; sr. design arch. HNTB, Kansas City, Mo., 1981-84; prin. Holmes Sabatini Assocs. Arch., Albuquerque, 1984—. Prin. works include Ctrl. Campus Bookstore U. N.Mex. (Merit award N.Mex. Soc. Archs. 1977), Luna County Courthouse, Deming, N.Mex. (Honor award N.Mex. Hist. Preservation Soc. 1978), James R. Dickinson Libr. U. Nev., Las Vegas (Merit award AIA 1981, Honor award Nev. Soc. Arch. 1981), Reno Conv. Ctr. (Merit award Nev. Soc. Archs. 1983), Corp. Hdqs. Nev. Power Co., Las Vegas (Honor award Nev. Soc. Archs. 1983), YMCA, Las Vegas (Honor award Nev. Soc. Archs. 1983), Sanctuary Remodel St. Johns United Meth. Ch., Albuquerque (Best Interiors award N.Mex. Bus. Jour. 1986), The Presidio Office Bldg., Albuquerque (Best Bldgs. award and Best Interiors award N.Mex. Bus. Jour. 1987, Project of Yr. award Assoc. Gen. Contractors N.Mex. 1987), Suarez Residence, Albuquerque (Merit award N.Mex. Soc. Am. 1988), Fire Sta. Number 13 and Fire Marshall's Office, Albuquerque (Merit award Albuquerque Conservation Soc. 1987, Best Bldgs. award N.Mex. Bus. Jour. 1988), Santa Fe Imaging Ctr. (Citation of Excellence, Modern Health Care Mag., AIA com. on healthcare 1989, Best Bldgs. award N.Mex. Bus. Jour. 1989), Health Scis. Bldg. U. N.Mex. (Best Bldgs. award N.Mex. Bus. Jour. 1989), U.S. Port of Entry, Columbus, N.Mex. (Best Bldgs. award N.Mex. Bus. Jour. 1989, Honor award N.Mex. Soc. Archs. 1990, GSA Design award U.S. Gen. Svcs. Adminstrn. 1990), Student Svcs. Bldg., Albuquerque TVI (Best Bldgs. award N.Mex. Bus. Jour. 1989, Merit award Albuquerque Conservation Soc. 1990), Expansion and Renovation Albuquerque Conv. Ctr. (Best Bldgs. award N.Mex. Bus. Jour. 1990), Lovelace Multi-Specialty Clinic Facility, Albuquerque (Merit award N.Mex. Soc. Archs. 1991), Pete's Playground U. N.Mex. Hosp. (Honor award N.Mex. Soc. Archs. 1992, Best Bldgs. Spl. award N.Mex. Bus. Jour. 1993), Nursing Unit Remodel U. N.Mex. Hosp. (Excellence award Am. Soc. Interior Designers 1992), 3.5 Meter Telescope Kirtland AFB, N.Mex. (Honor award AIA 1993). Bd. dirs. Albuquerque Chamber Orch., 1988, Hospice Rio Grande, 1992—; mem. adv. bd. Balloon Mus., 1989—; v.p., mem. adv. bd. St. Pius High Sch., 1993—. With USAR, 1971-78. Mem. AIA (bd. dirs. Albuquerque chpt. 1986-87). Roman Catholic. Office: Holmes Sabatini Assocs Archs West Courtyard 202 Central Ave SE Albuquerque NM 87102*

SABATO, LARRY JOSEPH, political science educator; b. Norfolk, Va., Aug. 7, 1952; s. N.J. and Margaret F. (Simmons) S. BA, U. Va., 1974; postgrad. Princeton U., 1974-75; DPhil, Oxford U., 1977. Lectr. politics New Coll., Oxford U., 1977-78; Robert Kent Gooch prof. Govt. and Foreign Affairs, U. Va., Charlottesville, 1978—; guest scholar Brookings Instn., 1980; Thomas Jefferson vis. prof. Downing Coll., Cambridge U., 1982; Danforth fellow, 1975; Kellogg fellow, 1983; Rhodes scholar. Mem. Am. Polit. Sci. Assn., Phi Beta Kappa. Author: The Rise of Political Consultants: New Ways of Winning Elections, 1981, Goodbye to Goodtime Charlie: The American Governorship Transformed, 1983, PAC Power: Inside the World of Political Action Committees, 1984, The Party's Just Begun: Shaping Political Parties for America's Future, 1988, Feeding Frenzy: How Attack Journalism Has Transformed American Politics, 1991, American Government: Roots and Reform, 1992, Dirty Little Secrets: The Persistence of Corruption in American Politics, 1996, Toward the Millennium: The Elections of 1996. Office: U Va Dept Govt 240 Cabell Charlottesville VA 22901

SABAT-RIVERS, GEORGINA, Latin American literature educator; b. Santiago, Oriente, Cuba; came to U.S., 1962; d. José and Balbina (Mercadé) Sabat; m. Armando A. Guernica (div.); children: Armando A., Antonio J., Rodolfo M., Georgina M.; m. Elias L. Rivers, Sept. 19, 1969. MA in Romance Langs., Johns Hopkins U., 1967, PhD in Romance Langs., 1969. Instr. U. Oriente, Santiago de Cuba, 1956-61; asst. prof. Georgetown Visitation Coll., Washington, 1962-63; asst. prof. Western Md. Coll., Westminster, 1963-69, assoc. prof., 1969-73, prof., 1973-78, chair dept., 1974-78; assoc. prof. SUNY, Stony Brook, 1978-86, prof., 1986—, chair dept., 1981-84; vis. prof. U. Calif., Irvine, 1989, U. Iowa, Iowa City, 1994, UNAM, Mexico City. Author: El Sueño de Sor Juana Inés de la Cruz: tradiciones literarias y originalidad, 1976, Sor Juana Inés de la Cruz Inundación castálida, 1982, Literatura Femenina conventual: Sor Marcela de San Félix Hija de Lope, 1992, others; mem. editl. bd. Colonial L.Am. Rev., 1990—, Calíope, others; contbr. articles to profl. jours. Fellow NEH, 1984-85, Fulbright, 1987; Soviet Union Internat. Rsch. and Exch. Bd. grantee, 1986, Summer seminar grantee NEH, 1995. Fellow Am. Philos. Soc.; mem. MLA (del. 1988-93), AAUW, Inst. Internat. Revista Iberoamericana Lit. (editl. bd. 1987-90).

SABBAGHA, RUDY E., obstetrician, gynecologist, educator; b. Tel Aviv, Oct. 29, 1931; s. Elias C. and Sonia B. S.; m. Asma E. Sahyouny, Oct. 5, 1957; children: Elias, Randa. BA, MD, Am. U., Beirut. Sr. physician Tapline, Saudi Arabia, 1958-64, ob-gyn specialist, 1969-70; teaching fellow U. Pitts., 1965-68; asst. prof. ob-gyn, 1970-75; prof. Northwestern U., Chgo., 1975—; obstetrician, gynecologist Prentice Women's Hosp., Chgo. Author: Ultrasound-High Risk Obstetrics, 1979; editor: Ultrasound Applied to Obstetrics and Gynecology, 1980, 2d edit., 1987; contbr. articles to profl. jours. Fellow Am. Coll. Obstetricians and Gynecologists; mem. Soc. Gynecol. Investigation, Am. Gynecol. and Obstet. Soc., Central Assn. Obstetricians and Gynecologists, Assn. Profs. Ob-Gyn, Am. Inst. Ultrasound in Medicine. Research on diagnostic ultrasound, obstetrics and gynecology. Office: 680 N Lake Shore Dr Chicago IL 60611-4402*

SABBY, LELAND, state legislator; m. Ina M. Peterson, Aug. 27, 1950; 4 children. BA, Luther Coll., 1943; postgrad., U. Notre Dame, 1943, Harvard U., 1943; MA, U. No. Colo., 1953; postgrad., U. Ill., U. N.D., Stanford U., Denver U. Tchr., 1947-85; rep. Dist. 24 N.D. Ho. of Reps., 1995—, mem. judiciary and govt. and vet. affairs coms., 1985. Active Our Saviors Luth. Ch. Recipient Presdl. Award for Excellence in Teaching Math. N.D. Coun. of Tchrs. of Math., 1985. Mem. Kiwanis. Home: 1133 6th Ave NE Valley City ND 58072-2342

SABEL, BRADLEY KENT, lawyer; b. Charleston, Ill., Oct. 6, 1948; s. Walter Bernard and Charlotte (Ahlstrom) S.; m. Nancy Jean Parker, Apr. 4, 1984. B.A., Vanderbilt U., 1970; J.D., Cornell U., 1975; M.S. in Bus. Policy, Columbia U., 1983. Bar: N.Y. 1976. Atty. Fed. Reserve Bank of

N.Y., N.Y.C., 1975-80; asst. counsel Fed. Reserve Bank of N.Y., 1980, sec., asst. counsel, 1981-85, assoc. counsel, 1985-87, counsel, 1988-93, counsel, v.p., 1993-94; counsel Shearman & Sterling, N.Y.C., 1994-97, ptnr., 1997—. Contbr. numerous articles to profl. jours. Bd. dirs., treas. N.Y. Chamber Orch., N.Y.C., 1985-87; Served with U.S. Army, 1970-72. Home: 2 Midland Gdns Apt 4E Bronxville NY 10708-4727 Office: Shearman & Sterling 599 Lexington Ave New York NY 10022-6030

SABERHAGEN, BRET WILLIAM, professional baseball player; b. Chicago Heights, Ill., Apr. 13, 1964; s. Bob Saberhagen; m. Janeane Saberhagen; children—Drew, William. Pitcher Kansas City Royals, 1982-91, N.Y. Mets, 1991—, Colorado Rockies, Denver, 1995-96, Boston Red Sox, 1996—. Recipient Cy Young award Baseball Writers' Assn. Am., 1985, 89, Gold Glove award, 1989; named Am. League Pitcher of the Year Sporting News, 1985, 89; pitched no-hit game, 1991; mem. All-Star team, 1987, 90, named AL Comeback Player of the Year, 1987; named to The Sporting News Am. League All-Star Team, 1985, 89. Office: Boston Red Sox 4 Yawkey Way Boston MA 02215*

SABERS, RICHARD WAYNE, state supreme court justice; b. Salem, S.D., Feb. 12, 1938; s. Emil William and Elrena Veronica (Godfrey) S.; m. Colleen D. Kelley, Aug. 28, 1965; children: Steven Richard, Susan Michelle, Michael Kelley. BA in English, St. John's U., Collegeville, Minn., 1960; JD, U. S.D., 1966. Bar: S.D. 1966, U.S. Dist. Ct. S.D. 1966, U.S. Ct. Appeals (8th cir.) 1983. From assoc. to ptnr. Moore, Rasmussen, Sabers & Kading, Sioux Falls, S.D., 1966-86; justice Supreme Ct. S.D., Pierre and Sioux Falls, 1986—. Mem. editorial bd. U. S.D. Law Rev., 1965-66. State rep. March of Dimes, Bismarck, N.D., 1963; bd. dirs. St. Joseph Cathedral, Sioux Falls, 1971-86; trustee, bd. dirs. O'Gorman Found., Sioux Falls, 1978-86; active sch. bd. O'Gorman High Sch., Sioux Falls, 1985-86. Lt. U.S. Army, 1960-63. Named Outstanding Young Religious Leader, Jaycees, Sioux Falls, 1971. Mem. ABA, S.D. Bar Assn., Inst. Jud. Adminstrn., St. John's Alumni Assn. (pres. Sioux Falls chpt. 1975-91). Republican. Roman Catholic. Avocations: tennis, skiing, sailing, sports. Home: 1409 E Cedar Ln Sioux Falls SD 57103-4514 Office: SD Supreme Ct 500 E Capitol Ave Pierre SD 57501-5070*

SABERSKY, ROLF HEINRICH, mechanical engineer; b. Berlin, Germany, Oct. 20, 1920; came to U.S., 1938, naturalized, 1944; s. Fritz and Berta (Eisner) S.; m. Bettina Sofie Schuster, June 16, 1946; children—Carol, Sandra. B.S., Calif. Inst. Tech., 1942, M.S., 1943, Ph.D., 1949. Devel. engr. Aerojet Gen. Co., 1943-46, regular cons., 1949-70; asst. prof. Calif. Inst. Tech., Pasadena, 1949-55, asso. prof., 1955-61, prof. mech. engring., 1961-88, prof. emeritus, 1988—; cons. various indsl. orgns. Author: Engineering Thermodynamics, 1957, Fluid Flow, 3d edit., 1989; contbr. articles to profl. jours. Fellow ASME (Heat Transfer Meml. award 1977, 50th anniversary award Heat Transfer Div 1988); mem. Sigma Xi, Tau Beta Pi. Home: 1060 Fallen Leaf Rd Arcadia CA 91006-1903 Office: Div Engring and Applied Sci Calif Inst Tech Pasadena CA 91125

SABEY, J(OHN) WAYNE, academic administrator, consultant; b. Murray, Utah, Dec. 10, 1939; s. Alfred John and Bertha (Lind) S.; m. Marie Bringhurst, Sept. 10, 1964; children: Clark Wayne, Colleen, Carolyn, Natasha Lynne. BA in Asian Studies, Brigham Young U., 1964, MA in Asian History, 1965; PhD in East Asian History, U. Mich., 1972. Teaching asst. Brigham Young U., Provo, 1964-65, rsch. asst., 1965, adj. prof. history, 1988-89; rsch. asst. U. Mich., Ann Arbor, 1966; from instr. to asst. prof. history U. Utah, Salt Lake City, 1970-80; v.p. Western Am. Lang. Inst., Salt Lake City, 1980-84, dir., 1984-86, pres., 1986—; exec. v.p. Pacific Rim Bus. Coords., Salt Lake City, 1993—, also bd. dirs., 1993—; dir. Japan Ops. E'OLA Products, Inc., St. George, Utah, 1996—; assoc. dir. exch. program between U. Utah and Nagoya Broadcasting Network of Japan, 1973-79; lectr. in field, Superior award in extemporaneous speaking, 1956. Author essay, contbr. articles to ency. Chmn. bd. trustees Western Am. Lang. Inst., 1986—, sec. to bd. trustees, 1980-86; chmn. bd. trustees Found. for Internat. Understanding, 1982—; mem. internat. adv. coun. Salt Lake C.C., 1988-94; mem. bd. advisors Consortium for Internat. Edn., 1972-77. Horace H. Rackham Sch. grad. studies fellow, 1969-70, Fulbright-Hays rsch. fellow (Japan), 1968-69, U.S. Nat. Def. fgn. lang. fellow, 1965-68. Mem. Assn. for Asian Studies (gen. chairperson, chairperson local arrangements western conf. 1970-72), Phi Kappa Phi. Avocations: piano, hiking, basketball, stamp collecting, tennis. Home: 8710 Oakwood Park Cir Sandy UT 84094

SABHARWAL, RANJIT SINGH, mathematician; b. Dhudial, India, Dec. 11, 1925; came to U.S., 1958, naturalized, 1981; s. Krishan Ch and Devti (An) S.; m. Pritam Kaur Chadha, Mar. 5, 1948; children—Rajinderpal, Amarjit, Jasbir. B.A. with honors, Punjab U., 1944, M.A., 1948; M.A. U. Calif, Berkeley, 1962; Ph.D., Wash. State U., 1966. Lectr. math. Khalsa Coll., Bombay, India, 1951-58; teaching asst. U. Calif., Berkeley, 1958-62; instr. math. Portland (Oreg.) State U., 1962-62, Wash. State U., 1963-66; asst. prof. Kans. State U., 1966-68; mem. faculty Calif. State Hayward, 1968—, prof. math., 1974—. Author papers on non-Desarguesian planes. Mem. Am. Math. Soc., Math. Assn. Am., Sigma Xi. Address: 27892 Adobe Ct Hayward CA 94542-2102

SABIN, WILLIAM ALBERT, editor; b. Paterson, N.J., May 29, 1931; s. David and Esther (Goodman) S.; m. Marie Frances Noonan, May 31, 1958; children—Margaret, John, Katherine, Christopher, James. B.A. in English, Yale Coll., 1952; M.A. in English, Yale U., 1956. Pub. bus. and office edn. McGraw Hill Book Co., N.Y.C., 1973-78, editor in chief bus. books, 1979-86, pub. bus. books, 1987-90. Author: The Gregg Reference Manual, 8th edit., 1996; co-author: College English: Grammar and Style, 1967. Served as cpl. U.S. Army, 1952-54, ETO. Home: 38 Afterglow Way Montclair NJ 07042-1712

SABINE, GORDON ARTHUR, educator, writer; b. Brockton, Mass., Feb. 10, 1917; s. Charles Arthur and Esther (Carey) S.; m. Lois Eleanor Freiburg, June 26, 1941 (div. 1973); children: Ellen Jean, Gordon Arthur, Robert Allan, Roger Malcolm; m. Patricia Lundblade Williams, May 15, 1980; children: Patricia Glyn Williams Rhodes, John Paul, Nina Lynn Williams Keenan, Janet Anne Williams Maxim. A.B., U. Wis., 1939, M.A., 1941; Ph.D., U. Minn., 1949. Reporter, Lynchburg (Va.) News, 1931-35; reporter, copy editor Wis. State Jour., 1939-42; corr. UP, 1946-47; grad. asst. journalism U. Wis., 1939-41; instr., later asst. prof. journalism U. Kans., 1945-47; lectr. journalism U. Minn., 1947-48; asst. prof. U. Oreg., 1948-50, assoc. prof., 1950-52, prof. journalism, 1952-55, dean Sch. Journalism, 1950-55; prof. communication arts, dean Coll. Communication Arts, Mich. State U., East Lansing, 1955-60; prof. Coll. Communication Arts, Mich. State U., 1955-72, v.p. spl. projects, 1960-71; spl. asst. to pres. Ill. State U., 1971-72; dir. Sch. Journalism, U. Iowa, 1972-75; prof. journalism Va. Poly. Inst. and State U., 1975-84; prof. journalism Ariz. State U., 1985, spl. asst. to univ. libr. dean, 1986-93; dir. Nat. Project in Agrl. Communication, 1960-62, GI Project MEMO, 1969-70; prof.-in-residence Time, Inc., 1951; Bd. dirs. Oregon Newspaper Pubs. Assn., 1950-55. Contbr. articles to nat. mags. and newspapers, 1938—; writer syndicated newspaper column Youthpoll America, 1976-77, Books That Made the Difference project Ctr. for the Book, Libr. of Congress, 1980-81; author: When You Listen, This Is What You Can Hear, 1971, How Students Rate Their Schools and Teachers, 1971, Teachers Tell It like It Is, Like It Should Be, 1972, The Folks in the Newsroom, 1977, Broadcasting in Virginia: Benchmark '79, 1980; (with Patricia L. Sabine) Books That Made the Difference: What People Told Us, 1983, Monsignor Donohoe, 1988; (with Donald Riggs) Libraries in the '90s: What the Leaders Expect, 1988, Tom Chauncey, A Memoir, 1989, Rabbi Plotkin, A Memoir, 1992, G. Homer, A Biography of Arizona State University President G. Homer Durham, 1992, Culver Bill Nelson, 1992, Phyllis B. Steckler and the Oryx Press, 1993, "... a damn beautiful butterfly": The Memoir of the Rev. William Lee Burkhardt, 1993, Nan Pyle: Payson's Unhappy Millionaire, 1993, Father Jack: Physician to the Soul, 1993, The Memoir of a Book: The Norton Reader of Expository Prose, 1993; prodr. The Evolution of a Dream, 1996. Mem. Gov.'s Commn. on Employment of Handicapped, 1958-59; mem. rsch. com. Am. Coun. Edn. for Journalism, 1951-53; founder (with Patricia L. Sabine) FRIENDS of the AZ Talking Book Libr., 1995. 1st lt. AUS, 1942-45, Iceland. Carnegie Corp. fellow, 1953; FAE-NAEB scholar TV, 1954; sr. postdoctoral research fellow Am. Coll. Testing Program, 1970-71. Mem. Assn. Edn. in Journalism, Assn. Accredited Schs. and Depts. Journalism (pres. 1954-55), Am. Polit. Sci. Assn., Sigma Delta Chi (nat. research com. 1949-51), Omicron Delta Kappa. Home: 2625 E Southern Ave C-102 Tempe AZ 85282

SABINO, CATHERINE ANN, magazine editor; b. N.Y.C., May 6, 1952; d. Joseph A. and Frances (Phelan) S. AB, Barnard Coll., 1973. Beauty editor, editor-at-large Harper's Bazaar, Italia, Men's Bazaar, 1976-79; beauty editor Seventeen mag. Triangle Comms., 1979-83; N.Y. editor Linea Italiana Mondadori, 1983-85; N.Y. editor Moda RAI, 1985-86; editor in chief Worldstyle The Aegis Venture Group, 1987-88; editor in chief In Fashion Murdoch Mags., 1988-89; editor mag. devel. European Home, 1989-91; cons. Hachette Mags., 1992; editor in chief Woman's Day Beauty Hachette Mags., 1993; editor in chief, group editor N.Y. Times Custom Pub., 1993—. Author: Italian Style, 1985, Italian Country, 1988. Mem. Am. Soc. Mag. Editors, Barnard-Columbia Club N.Y. (dir. at large 1991-93), Yale Club. Office: NY Times Custom Pub 122 E 42nd St New York NY 10168-0002

SABINSON, HARVEY BARNETT, cultural organiztion administrator; b. N.Y.C., Oct. 24, 1924; s. Samuel and Sarah Sabinson; m. Sarah S. Sabinson, Aug. 15, 1944; children: Eric, Allen. BS, Queens Coll., 1947. Freelance publicist N.Y., 1946-73; dir. spl. projects League Am. Theatres & Prodrs., N.Y.C., 1976-82, exec. dir., 1982-95; vis. prof. theatre adminstrn. Yale U. Sch. of Drama, New Haven, 1966-70. Author: Darling, You Were Wonderful, 1977. Recipient Lifetime Achievement award United Jewish Appeal Fedn., 1990, Lifetime Achievement Tony award, 1995, Theatre Hall of Fame Founder's award, 1996. Mem. Actor's Fund of Am. (trustee 1990—), Broadway Assn. (bd. dirs. 1977—), Theater Devel. Fund (bd. dirs. 1992-96), Berkshire Theatre Festival (trustee 1995—), Mayor's Midtown Citizens Com. Avocation: theatre.

SABINSON, MARA BETH, theatre educator, director, actress; b. N.Y.C., Mar. 1, 1946; d. Lee S. and Belle M. (Lindenauer) S.; m. John David Bergman, Sept. 6, 1987. BA, U. Calif., Berkeley, 1968; acting studies with Joseph Chaikin, Herbert Berghoff, Carl Weber, directing studies with Aaron Frankel, Jan Kott, Augusto Boal, voice and singing studies with Kristin Linklater and Mark Zeller. Mem. faculty Dell'Arte Sch. of Mime and Comedy, Blue Lake, Calif., 1978-81; acting coach N.Y.C., 1982-84; assoc. prof. drama/film studies, dir. theatre, dept. chair Dartmouth Coll., Hanover, N.H., 1984—; tchr. numerous workshops and programs including Mark Taper Forum, L.A., Stanford U., U. Calif. Berkeley, Santa Cruz and Irvine, San Jose State U., Calif. State U. at Hayward, San Francisco State U., Laney Coll., U. San Francisco, Studiejamfrandet, Stockholm, Humboldt State U., Geese Theatre Co., Berkshire Theatre Festival; vis. faculty Calif. State Coll. of the Redwoods, 1980, Dell'Arte Sch. Phys. Theatre, 1990; extensive adminstrn. and prodn. experience. Co-author: (plays) Profiles in Porridge, 1972, Clowns, 1973, Ever Since Felix Moved to New Zealand, 1974, Phenoxy Follies, 1979, Intrigue at Ah-Pah, 1979, Whiteman Meets Bigfoot, 1980, The Gump Show, 1985, The Fall and Rise of Roger Gump, 1987; dir. plays including Space Bondage, 1979, Italian Detectives, 1981, Judy's Floating Head, 1984-85, Female Transport, 1987, Hurlyburly, 1987, The Normal Heart, 1988, Lone Star, 1989, The Taming of the Shrew, 1989, Cloud 9, 1990, Evita, 1992, Red Noses, 1993, Mountain Language, 1994, Modern Noh Plays, 1995, Romeo and Juliet, 1996, numerous others; stage appearances include The Fool of the World, 1972, Human Rites, 1975, And Still I Rise, 1976, Intrigue at Ah-Pah, 1979-80, Heartbreak House, 1985, Aunt Dan and Lemon, 1986, The Good Woman of Szechwan, 1988, A Streetcar Named Desire, 1989, In the Jungle of Cities, 1991, God, 1991, Mother Courage, 1996, numerous others; TV appearances on Sid Caesar's Show of Shows, 1956, The Immigrants, 1979, September Song: An American Autumn, 1987; film appearances include The Projectionist, 1975, History Book: Part I, 1975, Family Plot, 1976, The Killer Elite, 1976, The Reunion, 1976, Shaping Things, 1977, The Great Weirton Steel, 1984; also radio appearances, commls., theatrical adaptations, interviews, play readings; editorial contbr. various publs.; contbr. photographs and articles to numerous jours. and publs. Grantee Nat. Endowment for the Arts, Calif. State Arts Coun., Berkeley City Arts Coun., Rosenberg Found.; recipient Bay Area Critics' Circle award, Critic's Choice/Best Bets citations, Lila Wallace/Reader's Digest Found. Arts Ptnrs. award, 1990, Marion and Jasper Whiting Found. fellowship, 1993. Home: RR 2 Box 312 Cornish NH 03745-9720 Office: Dartmouth Coll Dept Drama Hanover NH 03755

SABISTON, DAVID COSTON, JR., surgeon, educator; b. Onslow County, N.C., Oct. 4, 1924; s. David Coston and Marie (Jackson) S.; m. Agnes Foy Barden, Sept. 24, 1955; children: Anne Sabiston Leggett, Agnes Sabiston Butler, Sarah Coston. BS, U. N.C., 1944; MD, Johns Hopkins U., 1947; DSc (hon.), U. Madrid. Diplomate: Am. Bd. Surgery (chmn. 1971-72). Successively intern, asst. resident, chief resident surgery Johns Hopkins Hosp., 1947-53; successively asst. prof., assoc. prof., prof. surgery Johns Hopkins Med. Sch., 1955-64, Howard Hughes investigator, 1955-61; Fulbright research scholar U. Oxford, Eng., 1960; research assoc. Hosp. Sick Children, U. London, Eng., 1961; James B. Duke prof. surgery, chmn. dept. Duke Med. Sch., 1964-94; chief of staff Duke U. Med. Ctr., Durham, N.C., 1994-96, dir. internat. programs, 1996—; chmn. Accreditation Council for Grad. Med. Edn., 1985-86. Editor: Textbook of Surgery, Essentials of Surgery, Atlas of General Surgery, Atlas of Cardiothoracic Surgery, A Review of Surgery; co-editor: Gibbon's Surgery of the Chest, Companion Handbook to Textbook of Surgery; chmn. editl. bd. Annals of Surgery; mem. editl. bd. Annals Clin. Rsch., ISI Atlas of Sci.: The Classics of Surgery Libr., Surgery, Gynecology and Obsetrics, Jour. Applied Cardiology, Jour. Cardiac Surgery, World Jour. Surgery, Jour. Served to capt., M.C. AUS, 1953-55. Recipient Career Rsch. award NIH, 1962-64, N.C. award in Sci., 1978, Disting. Achievement award Am. Heart Assn. Sci. Coun., 1983 Michael E. DeBakey award for Outstanding Achievement, 1984, Significant Sigma Chi award, 1987, Coll. medalist Am. Coll. Chest Physicians, 1987, Disting. Tchr. award Alpha Omega Alpha, 1992; named Disting. Physician, U.S. VA, 1995. Mem. ACS (chmn. bd. govs. 1974-75, regent 1975-82, chmn. bd. regents 1982-84, pres. 1985-86), NAS Inst. Medicine, Am. Surg. Assn. (pres. 1977-78), So. Surg. Assn. (sec. 1969-73, pres. 1973-74), Am. Assn. Thoracic Surgery (pres. 1984-85), Soc. Clin. Surgery, Internat. Soc. Cardiovascular Surgery, Soc. Vascular Surgery (v.p. 1967-68), Soc. Univ. Surgeons (pres. 1968-69), Halsted Soc., Surg. Biology Club II, Soc. Thoracic Surgery, Soc. Surgery Alimentary Tract, Johns Hopkins U. Soc. Scholars, Soc. Surg. Chairmen (pres. 1974-76), Soc. Thoracic Surgeons Great Britain and Ireland, Soc. Internat. De Chirurgie, James IV Assn. Surgeons (bd. dirs. U.S. chpt.), Ill. Surg. Soc. (hon.), Phila. Acad. Surgery (hon.), Royal Coll. Surgeons Edinburgh (hon., editl. bd. jour.), Royal Coll. Surgeons Eng. (hon.), Asociación de Cirugía del Litoral (Argentina) (hon.), Royal Coll. Physicians and Surgeons Can. (hon.), Royal Coll. Surgeons Ireland (hon.), Royal Australasian Coll. Surgeons (hon.), German Surgical Soc. (hon.), Colombian Surg. Soc. (hon.), Brazilian Coll. Surgeons (hon.), Japanese Coll. Surgeons (hon.), French Surg. Assn. (hon.), Surg. Congress Assn. Espanola de Cirujanos (hon.), Philippine Coll. Surgeons (hon.), Phi Beta Kappa, Alpha Omega Alpha. Clubs: Cosmos (Washington), Hope Valley Country Club (Durham), Univ. Club (Durham), University Club (Durham). Home: 1528 Pinecrest Rd Durham NC 27705-5817 Office: Duke U Med Ctr PO Box 2600 MSRB Durham NC 27710

SABL, JOHN J., lawyer; b. L.A., June 16, 1951. AB with distinction, Stanford U., 1973, JD, 1976. Bar: Calif. 1976, Ill. 1977. Ptnr. Sidley & Austin, Chgo. editorial bd. Stanford U. Law Review, 1974-75, assoc. mng. editor, 1975-76. Mem. Chgo. Bar Assn. (chmn. securities law com. 1985-86), Legal Club Chgo. Office: Sidley & Austin 1 First Natl Plz Chicago IL 60603-2003

SABLE, BARBARA KINSEY, former music educator; b. Astoria, L.I., N.Y., Oct. 6, 1927; d. Albert and Verna Rowe Kinsey; B.A., Coll. Wooster, 1949; M.A., Tchrs. Coll. Columbia U., N.Y.C., 1950; D.Mus., U. Ind., 1966; m. Arthur J. Sable, Nov. 3, 1973. Office mgr., music dir. sta. WCAX, Burlington, Vt., 1954; instr. Cottey Coll., 1959-60; asst. prof. N.E. Mo. State U., Kirksville, 1962-64; asst. prof. U. Calif., Santa Barbara, 1964-69; prof. music U. Colo., Boulder, 1969—, prof. emeritus, 1992—. Author: The Vocal Sound, 1982; contbr. poetry to literary jours. Mem. Nat. Assn. Tchrs. Singing (past state gov., asso. editor bull.), AAUP, Colo. State Music Tchrs. Assn. Democrat. Avocation: poetry. Home: 3430 Ash Ave Boulder CO 80303-3432 Office: U Colo Coll Music Campus Box 301 Boulder CO 80309

SABLE, ROBERT ALLEN, gastroenterologist; b. Bklyn., June 21, 1948; s. Benjamin and Sara (Dickstein) S.; m. Valerie P. Kubie Kopelman, July 1, 1969 (div. Mar. 1982); 1 child, Jesse; m. Ellen Sue Finer, May 29, 1982; children: Scott, Eric. BS, MIT, 1969; MD, Albert Einstein U., 1973. Bd. cert. in internal medicine, gastroenterology and geriatrics Am. Bd. Internal Medicine. Staff physician N.Y. Telephone Co. Mid Manhattan Med. Dept., N.Y.C., 1978-81; physician Riverdale Gastroenterology Cons., Bronx, N.Y., 1981—; chief gastroenterology St. Barnabas Hosp., Bronx, 1982—, pres. med. bd., 1985-90. Contbr. articles, reports, revs. to profl. jours. Fellow ACP, Am. Coll. Gastroenterology; mem. AMA, Am. Gastroenterologic Assn., Am. Soc. for Gastrointestinal Endoscopy. Avocations: philately, numismatics. Office: Riverdale Gastroenterol Con 3765 Riverdale Ave Bronx NY 10463-1845

SABLIK, MARTIN JOHN, research physicist; b. Bklyn., Oct. 21, 1939; s. Martin C. and Elsie M. (Fuzia) S.; m. Beverly Ann Shively, Nov. 26, 1965; children: Jeanne, Karen, Marjorie, Larry. BA in Physics, Cornell U., 1960; MS in Physics, U. Ky., 1965; PhD, Fordham U., 1972. Jr. engr. The Martin Co., Orlando, Fla., 1962-63; half-time instr. U. Ky., Lexington, 1963-65; rsch. assoc. Fairleigh Dickinson U., Teaneck, N.J., 1965-67, instr. physics, 1967-1972, asst. prof., 1972-76, assoc. prof., 1976-80; sr. rsch. scientist Southwest Rsch. Inst., San Antonio, 1980-87, staff scientist, 1987—; local chmn. Intermag. Conf., San Antonio, 1995. Mem. editorial bd. Nondestructive Testing and Evaluation, 1989—; mem. adv. bd. Conf. on Properties and Applications of Magnetic Materials, 1990—, Workshop on Advances in Measurement Techniques and Instrumentation for Magnetic Properties Determination, 1994, Magnetic Materials, Measurements and Modeling Symposium, 1996, exec. bd. topical group on magnetism and its applications, 1996-97; contbr. articles to profl. jours.; referee, patentee in field. Recipient Imagineer award Mind Sci. Found., 1989. Mem. IEEE, Am. Phys. Soc., Am. Geophys. Union, Am. Soc. Nondestructive Testing (chmn. So. Tex. sect. 1983-84), Am. Assn. Physics Tchrs. Roman Catholic. Office: SW Rsch Inst PO Box 28510 San Antonio TX 78228-0510

SABLOFF, JEREMY ARAC, archaeologist; b. N.Y.C., Apr. 16, 1944; s. Louis and Helen (Arac) S.; m. Paula Lynne Weinberg, May 26, 1968; children: Joshua, Saralinda. A.B., U. Pa., 1964; M.A., Ph.D., Harvard U., 1969. Asst. prof., asso. prof. Harvard U., Cambridge, Mass., 1969-76; asso. prof. anthropology U. Utah, Salt Lake City, 1976-77; curator anthropology Utah Mus. Natural History, Salt Lake City, 1976-77; prof. anthropology U. N.Mex., Albuquerque, 1978-86; chmn. dept. U. N.Mex., 1980-83; Univ. prof. anthropology and the history and philosphy of sci. U. Pitts., 1986-94, chmn. dept. anthropology, 1990-92; Charles K. Williams II dir. U. Mus., U. Mus. Term prof. anthropology, curator Mesoamerican archaeology U. Pa., Phila., 1994—; sr. fellow for Pre-Columbian Studies, Dumbarton Oaks, 1986-92, chmn. 1989-92. Author: (with G.R. Willey) A History of American Archaeology, 1974, 2d edit., 1980, 3d edit., 1993, Excavations at Seibal: Ceramics, 1975, (with C.C. Lamberg-Karlovsky) Ancient Civilizations: The Near East and Mesoamerica, 1979, 2nd edit., 1995, (with D. A. Freidel) Cozumel: Late Maya Settlement Patterns, 1984, The Cities of Ancient Mexico, 1989, rev. edit., 1997, The New Archaeology and the Ancient Maya, 1990, (with G. Tourtellot) The Ancient Maya City of Sayil: The Mapping of a Puuc Region Center, 1991; editor(with C.C. Lamberg-Karlovsky) The Rise and Fall of Civilizations, 1974, (with C.C. Lamberg-Karlovsky) Ancient Civilization and Trade, 1975, (with W.L. Rathje) A Study of Changing Pre-Columbian Commercial Systems, 1975, American Antiquity, 1977-81, (with G.R. Willey) Scientific American Readings in Pre-Columbian Archaeology, 1980, Simulations in Archaeology, 1981, Supplement to the Handbook of Middle American Indians: Archaeology, 1981, Archaeology: Myth and Reality: A Scientific American Reader, 1982, Analyses of Fine Paste Ceramics, 1982, (with D. Meltzer and D. Fowler) American Archaeology: Past and Future, 1986, (with E.W. Andrews V) Late Lowland Maya Civilization: Classic to Postclassic, 1986, (with J.S. Henderson) Lowland Maya Civilization in the Eighth Century A.D., 1993. Nat. Geog. Soc. grantee, 1972-74; NSF grantee, 1983-88; NEH grantee, 1990-91. Fellow Am. Anthrop. Assn., AAAS (sec. H. chair 1994-95), Royal Anthrop. Inst., Soc. Antiquaries London; mem. Nat. Acad. Sci., Am. Phil. Soc., Soc. Am. Archaeology (pres. 1989-91), Internat. Soc., Comparative Study of Civilizations, Sigma Xi. Office: U Pa Mus Archaeology and Anthropology 33d and Spruce Sts Philadelphia PA 19104-6324

SABO, MARTIN OLAV, congressman; b. Crosby, N.D., Feb. 28, 1938; s. Bjorn O. and Klara (Haga) S.; m. Sylvia Ann Lee, June 30, 1963; children: Karin, Julie. BA cum laude, Augsburg Coll., Mpls., 1959; postgrad., U. Minn., 1961-62. Mem. Minn. Ho. of Reps. from 57B Dist., 1960-78, minority leader Dem.-Farmer-Labor party, 1969-72, speaker, 1973-78; mem. 96th to 105th U.S. Congresses from 5th Minn. Dist., 1979—; chmn. Dem. Study Group 96th to 101st Congresses; dep. majority whip 96th to 103rd Congresses, mem. appropriations com.; mem. permanent select com. on intelligence 102d Congress; chmn. Ho. Budget Com. 103d Congress; ranking minority house budget com. 104th Congress; ranking minority transp. subcom. com. appropriations 105th Congress; former mem. Nat. Adv. Commn. on Intergovtl. Rels.; past pres. Nat. Legis. Conf.; bd. regents Augsburg Coll. Mgr., player Dem. Congl. Baseball Team, 1987—. Recipient Disting. Alumni citation Augsburg Coll., Arms Control Leadership award Employees Union, Local 113, SEIU, AFL-CIO; named One of 200 Rising Young Leaders in Am. Time mag., 1974; Man of Yr. Mpls. Jr. C. of C., 1973-74, One of Ten Outstanding Young Men of Yr. Minn. Jr. C. of C., 1974; inducted Scandinavian Am. Hall of Fame, 1994. Mem. Nat. Conf. State Legis. Leaders (past pres.). Office: 2336 Rayburn Bldg Ofc B Washington DC 20515-2305

SABO, RICHARD STEVEN, electrical company executive; b. Walkertown, Pa., Jan. 1, 1934; s. Alex S. and Elizabeth (Haluska) S.; m. Gail P. Digon, Feb. 15, 1954; children: Gailyn J., Richard A., Kerry S., Dale A. BS in Edn., California (Pa.) U., 1955; MS in Edn., Edinboro (Pa.) U., 1965. Tchr. Northwestern Sch. Dist., Albion, Pa., 1955-65; prodn. technician The Lincoln Electric Co., Cleve., 1965-66, staff asst. mktg., 1966-70, mgr. pub. rels., 1971-86, asst. to chmn., 1986-96, dir. cop. comms. and investor rels.; also exec. dir. James F. Lincoln Arc Welding Found. Editor: The Procedure Handbook of Arc Welding, 1994, 10 other books on arc welding; contbr. numerous articles to profl. jours. Chmn. Area Recreation Bd., Chesterland, Ohio, 1970, West Geauga Boosters, Chesterland, 1973-77; mem., bd. dirs. Profit Sharing Coun. Am., 1991—. Recipient Svc. award Future Farmers Am., 1970—, Svc. award U.S. Skill Olympics, 1980, Lakeland Community Coll. award, 1990, Ohio State U. Hon. Welding Engring. Alumni award, 1990, Calif. U. (Pa.) medallion of Distinction, 1990, Internat. Bus. Exec. of Yr. Internat. Acad. of Bus. Disciplines, 1997. Mem. Am. Welding Soc. (vice chmn. edn. and fin. com., mem. fin. com. 1988—, speaker, various awards, Plummer lectr. 1992), Am. Soc. for Engring. Edn., Am. Inst. Steel Cons. (mem. edn. com. 1986—), Steel Plate Fabricators Assn. (past chmn. promotions com., mem. bd. dirs.s profit sharing coun. 1991—), California U. Alumni Assn. (trustee 1983—). Republican. Presbyterian. Lodge: Masons. Avocations: golf, hunting, fishing, classical music. Office: The Lincoln Electric Co 22801 Saint Clair Ave Cleveland OH 44117-2524

SABO, RONALD WILLIAM, lawyer, financial consultant; b. Pottstown, Pa., Oct. 13, 1944; s. William Sabo and Margaret (Dutchman) S.; 1 child by previous marriage, Richard. BBA cum laude, U. Miami, 1966, JD cum laude, 1969. Bar: Fla. 1969, Calif. 1972, U.S. Tax Ct. 1985. Research atty. Fla. Ct. Appeals (3d dist.), Miami, 1969; asst. atty. gen. State of Fla., Tallahassee, 1970-71; asst. counsel Ventura County, Calif., 1972-73, spl. asst. dist. atty., 1979-84; dir. research Nat. Legal Data Ctr., Thousand Oaks, Calif., 1974-78; pvt. practice Lompoc and Cambria, Calif., 1985—; lectr. FBI Nat. Acad., Quantico, Va., 1974; cons. Battelle Meml. Ins., Seattle, 1975, Rand Corp., Santa Monica, Calif., 1976-78,; cons. rules com. Calif. Senate. Mem. ABA, Calif. Bar Assn. (disciplinary examiner). Republican. Methodist Episcopalian. Avocations: sailing, cooking. Home: 508 Newport Dr Lompoc CA 93436-6320

SABOL, STEVE, film company executive. Cinematographer to pres. NFL Films, Inc., 1964—. Films include: Semi Tough, Paper Lion, Brian's Song, Black Sunday, others; host: (TV) NFL Films Presents (longest running syndicated sports series in TV history). Recipient 23 Emmys for sports writing, 65 Emmys for NFL Films; former All-Rocky Mountain Conf.

Running Back. Office: NFL Films Inc 330 Fellowship Rd Mount Laurel NJ 08054-1201

SABOSIK, PATRICIA ELIZABETH, publisher, editor; b. Newark, Aug. 25, 1949; d. George Aloysius and Elizabeth Ann (Simko) S.; m. Kenneth Donald Gursky, Apr. 21, 1972 (div. 1980). BA in English, Kean Coll. N.J., 1976; MBA in Mktg., Seton Hall U., 1984; cert. advanced study in fin., Fairfield U., 1989. Proofreader Baker & Taylor, Somerville, N.J., 1969-71, database coordinator, 1971-74, prodn. editor, 1974-77, publs. mgr., editor, 1977-82; dir. mktg. services H.W. Wilson Pub. Co., Bronx, N.Y., 1982-84; editor, pub. Choice mag. Am. Library Assn., Middletown, Conn., 1984-94; project dir. Books for Coll. Librs. Am. Library Assn., Middletown, 1985-88, project dir. Guide to Ref. Books, 1988-94; v.p. electronic text Booklink Technologies, Wilmington, Mass., 1994-95; v.p. Linked Media, Navi Soft Divsn. Am. Online, Inc., Needham, Mass., 1994-96; editor-in-chief Whole Internet Catalog, GNN an Am. Online, Inc. Co., 1995-96; dir, product mrktg. Am. Online, Inc., 1997—; membership chmn. Serials Industry Systems Adv. Com., 1983-89, vice chmn., 1985-86, newsletter editor, 1986-87. Contbr. articles to profl. jours. Party rep. Twp. Com. Cranford, N.J., 1977-79; hon. bd. advisors U. Conn. Women's Ctr., 1989-91; mem. Conn. Women's Edn. and Legal Fund; nat. bd. dirs. Literacy Vols. of Am., 1992-94, also chair pub. and mktg. com. Mem. ALA (coms., editorial bd. Choice), AAUW, Assn. Coll. and Rsch. Librs. (publs. com.), Soc. for Scholarly Pub. (membership com., editor newsletter 1988-91, budget and fin. com. 1990-92, sec.-treas. 1994—, bd. dirs. 1994—), Appalachian Mountain Club, Women's Outdoors Club (newsletter editor 1984-86, regional rep. 1986-87). Republican. Roman Catholic. Office: Am Online Inc 22070 Broderick Dr Sterling VA 20166-9323

SABOT, RICHARD HENRY, economics educator, researcher, consultant; b. N.Y.C., Feb. 16, 1944; s. Arnold G. and Victoria (Gomberg) S.; m. Judith A. Plunkett, Sept. 9, 1969; children: Diana, Christopher, Oliver, Julia. BA, U. Pa., 1966, Oxford U., 1968; MA, Oxford U., 1970, DPhil, 1973. Rsch. officer Inst. Econs. and Stats. Oxford (Eng.) U., 1972-74; rsch. economist World Bank, Washington, 1974-84; John J. Gibson prof. econs. Williams Coll., Williamstown, Mass., 1984—; chmn., co-founder Tripod Inc., 1992—; econ. advisor Office of the Exec. Vice Pres., Interam. Devel. Bank, Washington, 1994—; sr. rsch. fellow Internat. Food Policy Rsch. Inst., Washington, 1987-92; sr. rsch. fellow policy rsch. dept. World Bank, 1992—; cons. OECD Devel. Ctr., Paris, 1971-74, Internat. Inst. Applied Sys. Analysis, Vienna, Austria, 1982-83, Harvard Inst. Internat. Devel., Cambridge, Mass., 1985-88, World Bank, 1985—. Author: Economic Development and Urban Migration, 1979, Education Productivity and Inequality, 1990, The East Asian Miracle, 1993, Making Schools Work, 1995; editor: Migration and the Labor Market in Developing Countries, 1982, Unfair Advantage, 1991, Opportunity Foregone: Education in Brazil, 1996; contbr. numerous articles to scholarly jours. Mem. Nat. Panel on the Econ. of Ednl. Reform, Pew Found., 1991-95; trustee Nat. Child Rsch. Ctr., Washington, 1978-81; mem. nat. bd. Fund for Improvement Post-Secondary Edn., Washington, 1987-91. Rsch. grantee Ford Found., Mellon Found., Rockefeller Found., MacArthur Found., World Bank; Fulbright fellow, Thouron fellow, Danforth fellow. Mem. Am. Econ. Assn., Royal Econ.l Soc., United Oxford and Cambridge U. Club (London), Williams Club (N.Y.C.), Mt. Greylook Ski Club (bd. dirs. 1984-85). Avocations: hiking, yoga, cross country skiing, swimming. Home: Birch Hollow Oblong Rd Williamstown MA 01267 Office: Williams Coll Fernald House Williamstown MA 01267

SABRA, STEVEN PETER, lawyer; b. Fall River, Mass., Dec. 1, 1951; s. Peter B. and Eliza J. Sabra; m. Bernadette L. Brown, Sept. 24, 1977. BA in Polit. Sci., Fairfield U., 1973; JD, Duquesne U., 1976. Bar: Mass. 1977, U.S. Dist. Ct. Mass. 1977, U.S. Supreme Ct. 1985. Assoc. Law Offices of Richard N. LaSalle, Fall River, Mass., 1977-80; owner Law Offices of Steven P. Sabra, Somerset, Mass., 1980-87, Sabra Law Offices, Somerset, 1987-93, Law Offices Sabra & Aspden. P.A., Somerset, 1993—; arbitrator accident claims Am. Arbitration Assn., Boston, 1988—; mem. hearing com. Bd. of Bar Overseers, Mass., 1988-93; mem. Southeastern Regional Com. of Jud. Nominating Coun., 1995—; corporator Fall River Five Cents Savs. Bank, 1987—. Chmn., pres. Fall River Port Authority/Fall River Line Pier, Inc., 1992-95. Mem. ABA, ATLA, Mass. Bar Assn., Mass. Acad. Trial Attys., Bristol County Bar Assn. (pres. 1994-95), Fall River Bar Assn. (pres. 1985-87), Mass. Bar Found. Avocation: sports. Office: Law Offices Sabra & Aspden 1026 County St Somerset MA 02726-5138

SABSAY, DAVID, library consultant; b. Waltham, Mass., Sept. 12, 1931; s. Wiegard Isaac and Ruth (Weinstein) S.; m. Helen Glenna Tolliver, Sept. 24,1 966. AB, Harvard U., 1953; BLS, U. Calif., Berkeley, 1955. Circulation dept. supr. Richmond (Calif.) Pub. Library, 1955-56; city libr. Santa Rosa (Calif.) Pub. Library, 1956-65; dir. Sonoma County Library, Santa Rosa, 1965-92; libr. cons., 1992—; coordinator North Bay Coop. Library System, Santa Rosa, 1960-64; cons. in field, Sebastopol, Calif., 1968—. Contbr. articles to profl. jours. Commendation, Calif. Assn. Library Trustees and Commrs., 1984. Mem. Calif. Library Assn. (pres. 1971, cert. appreciation 1971, 80), ALA. Club: Harvard (San Francisco). Home and Office: 667 Montgomery Rd Sebastopol CA 95472-3020

SABSHIN, MELVIN, psychiatrist, educator, medical association administrator; b. N.Y.C., Oct. 28, 1925; s. Zalman and Sonia (Barnhard) S.; m. Edith Goldfarb, June 12, 1955; 1 child, James K. BS, U. Fla., Gainesville, 1944; MD, Tulane U., New Orleans, 1948. Diplomate Am. Bd. Psychiatry and Neurology. Assoc. dir. Michael Reese Hosp. Psychosomatic and Psychiat. Inst., Chgo., 1953-61; prof., head dept. psychiatry U. Ill. Coll. Medicine, Chgo., 1961-74; med. dir. Am. Psychiat. Assn., Washington, 1974—. Author Depression, 1960, Psychiatric Ideology, 1961; Normality, 1978; Normality and Life Cycle, 1984. Served with U.S. Army, 1944. Recipient Bowen award Am. Coll. Psychiatrists, 1978, Disting. Psychiatrist award, 1985. Mem. Am. Coll. Psychiatrists (pres. 1974-75). Home: 2801 New Mexico Ave NW Washington DC 20007-3921 Office: Am Psychiat Assn 1400 K St NW Washington DC 20005-2403

SABY, JOHN SANFORD, physicist; b. Ithaca, N.Y., Mar. 21, 1921; s. Rasmus S. and Maude Emily (Sanford) S.; m. Mary Elizabeth Long, June 9, 1945; children: Arthur D., Thomas S., Joseph A., Jean E. B.A., Gettysburg (Pa.) Coll., 1942, Sc.D. (hon.), 1969; M.S., Pa. State U., 1944, Ph.D., 1947. Lab. instr. Gettysburg Coll., 1940-42; instr. Cornell U., 1947-50; with Gen. Electric Co., 1951-82; mgr. semicondr./solid state Gen. Electric Co., Syracuse, N.Y., 1954-56; mgr. lamp phenomena research Gen. Electric Co., Cleve., 1956-82; cons., 1982—; mem. vis. com. biol. and phys. scis. Case Western Res. U., chmn., 1969. Co-author: Principles of Transistor Circuits, 1953. Fellow IEEE (past com. officer); mem. Am. Phys. Soc., Cleve. Assn. Research Dirs. (pres. 1963-64), Am. Watchmakers Inst., Nat. Assn. Watch and Clock Collectors, Phi Beta Kappa, Sigma Xi, Phi Kappa Phi, Phi Sigma Kappa. Patentee in field. Home: 8 Tamarac Ter Hendersonville NC 28791-9770

SACCHET, EDWARD M., foreign service officer; b. Bklyn., Sept. 28, 1936; m. Elizabeth Priore. BA in Internat. Affairs, George Washington U., 1958; postgrad., Sch. Advanced Internat. Studies, Johns Hopkins U., Bologna, Italy, 1958-59; MA in Internat. Affairs, Sch. Advanced Internat. Studies, Johns Hopkins U., 1960; postgrad., U. Oslo, Norway, 1959. Labor economist U.S. Dept. of Labor, Washington, 1961-63; mem. U.S. Fgn. Service-Dept. of State, Washington, 1963—; internat. economist White House Office of Spl. Trade Rep., Washington and Geneva, 1964-67; sec., econ. comml. officer Am. Embassy, Tananarive, Madagascar, 1967-69; consul, econ. comml. officer Am. Consulate Gen., Naples, Italy, 1969-72; 1st sec., fin. economist Am. Embassy, Rome, Italy, 1972-75; congl. fellow U.S. House of Reps and U.S. Senate, 1975-76; econ. officer Bur. Econ. and Bus. Affairs-U.S. Dept. State, 1976-78; career devel. and assignments officer Bur. of Personnel-U.S. Dept. State, 1978-80; consul gen. Am. Consulate Gen., Marseille, France, 1980-84; Pearson fellow, spl. advisor to Gov. of Fla. for Internat. Issues Tallahassee, 1984-85; fgn. svc. inspector Office Inspector Gen. Fgn. Svc.-U.S. Dept. State, Washington, 1985-87; U.S. consul gen. Am. Consulate Gen., Martinique, French W. Indies, 1987-88; spl. asst. Office Exec. Dir., Bur. Econ. and Bus. Affairs-Dept. State, 1987; acting ambassador U.S. Embassy, Antigua, W.I., 1988; cons. Bur. Adminstrn., info. mgmt. system and diplomatic security U.S. Dept. State, 1989-95; dir. state dept. br. U.S. Archives, College Park, Md., 1996—; lectr. in field. George Washington U. scholar, 1954-58, Johns Hopkins Sch. Internat. Studies scholar, Washington and Bologna, Italy, 1958-60; State Dept. fellow, 1980, Pearson fellow Office of Gov. Fla., 1984, Congl. fellow Am. Polit. Sci. Assn., 1980. Mem. Am. Fgn. Svc. Assn., Johns Hopkins U. Alumni Assn., Army-Navy Club of Washington. Home: 118 Monroe St Apt 907 Rockville MD 20850-2513 also: 13167 La Lique Ct Palm Bch Gdns FL 33410-1417

SACCO, JOHN MICHAEL, accountant; b. N.Y.C., Oct. 17, 1952; s. Anthony Carmine and Angelina (Pellegrino) S. BS, St. John's U., 1974. CPA, N.Y. Staff acct. Price Waterhouse & Co., N.Y.C., 1974-75; semi-sr. acct. Seidman & Seidman, CPAs, White Plains, N.Y., 1976-77; sr. acct. Diamond Internat. Corp., N.Y.C., 1977-79, Burns Internat. Security Services, Inc., Briarcliff Manor, N.Y., 1979-81; acctg. mgr. Burns Integrated Systems, Inc., Briarcliff Manor, N.Y., 1981-83; pvt. practice acctg. White Plains, N.Y., 1978—. Mem. AICPA, N.Y. Soc. CPAs. Republican. Roman Catholic. Home: 9 Tanglewood Rd Pleasantville NY 10570-2529 Office: 925 Westchester Ave White Plains NY 10604-3507

SACERDOTE, MANUEL RICARDO, banker; b. Buenos Aires, Feb. 20, 1943; s. Ricardo Edmundo and Ana Maria (Devoto) S.; m. Nora Alejandrina Mascarenhas, Aug. 24, 1966; children: Juan Martín, Diego Raul, Andrea María, Matías. E.E., U. Buenos Aires, 1966; M.B.A., Harvard U., 1968. Treas., Chrysler Argentina, Buenos Aires, 1969-71; gen. mgr. Sasín S.A., Buenos Aires, 1971-74; pres. Banco de Boston, Buenos Aires, 1974—; pres. Bank of Boston Found., Buenos Aires; chmn. Previnter Pension Co., Buenos Aires; pres. La Continental Ins. Co., Buenos Aires, Pfizer S.A., Buenos Aires, Swift Armour S.A., Buenos Aires. Mem. Argentine Bankers Assn. (bd. dirs. 1976—, vice chmn. 1989—, chmn. 1987-89), Argentine Bus. Coun., Latin Am. Found. Econ. Research (bd. dirs. 1983—). Clubs: Martindale, Belgrano Athletic, Harvard of Argentina (pres. 1979-80). Avocations: tennis, swimming, reading. Office: First Nat Bank of Boston, Florida 99, Buenos Aires 1005, Argentina

SACERDOTE, PETER M., investment banker; b. Turin, Italy, Oct. 15, 1937; came to U.S., 1940; s. Giorgio S. and Luciana (Levi) S.; m. Bonnie Lee Johnson, June 18, 1967; children: Alisa, Alexander, Laurence. B.E.E., Cornell U., 1960; M.B.A., Harvard U., 1964. Assoc. investment banking div. Goldman, Sachs & Co., N.Y.C., 1964-69, v.p. investment banking div., 1969-73, gen. ptnr., 1973-90, ltd. ptnr., 1990—; bd. dirs. AMF Corp., Richmond, Va., Qualcomm, Inc., San Diego, Franklin Resource, San Mateo, Calif.; in charge Pvt. Fin. Dept., 1974-80, The Corp. Fin. Dept., 1980-87, Merch Bank, 1987-90; chmn. Committments, Credit and Investment Cons., 1987-90, GS Capital Partnership; adj. prof. Columbia Grad. Sch. Bus., 1984-86; nat. chmn. HBSFD, Milton (Mass.) Acad. Trustee Day Sch., N.Y.C., 1980—; chmn. Alumni Bd. Harvard Bus. Sch., 1990; bd. visitors Fuqua Sch. Duke U., 1990; bd. overseers Cornell Med. Coll. Served to lt. (j.g.) USNR, 1960-62. Mem. Harvard Club N.Y.C., River Club N.Y.C., Downtown Assn., Nantucket Yacht Club, Stanwich Golf Club, Country Club of the Rockies, Sankaty Head Golf Club (Siasconset, Mass.). Office: Goldman Sachs & Co 85 Broad St New York NY 10004-2434

SACHA, ROBERT FRANK, osteopathic physician, allergist; b. East Chicago, Ind., Nov. 29, 1946; b. S. Frank John and Ann Theresa Sacha; m. Linda T. Le Page, 1988; children: Joshua Jude, Josiah Gerard, Anastasia Levon, Jonah Bradley. BS, Purdue U., 1969; DO, Chgo. Coll. Osteo. Medicine, 1975. Diplomate Am. Bd. Pediatrics, Am. Bd. Allergy and Immunology. Pharmacist, asst. mgr. Walgreens Drug Store East Chicago, Ind., 1969-75; intern David Grant Med. Ctr., San Francisco, 1975-76, resident in pediatrics, 1976-78; fellow in allergy and immunology Wilford Hall Med. Ctr., 1978-80; staff pediatrician, allergist Scott AFB (Ill.), 1980-83; practice medicine specializing in allergy and immunology Cape Girardeau, Mo., 1983—; assoc. clin. instr. St. Louis U., 1980—; clin. instr. Purdue U., 1971-72, Pepperdine U., 1975-76, U. Tex.-San Antonio, 1978-80, assoc. clin. instr. So. Ill. U. Pres., Parent Tchrs. League. Maj. M.C., USAF, 1975-83, comdr., USNR. Fellow Am. Coll. Allergy, Am. Coll. Chest Physicians, Am. Acad. Pediatrics, Am. Acad. Allergy-Immunology, Am. Assn. Cert. Allergists; mem. AMA, Am. Acad. Allergy, Assn. Mil. Allergists, ACP, Am. Coll. Emergency Physicians, Mil. Surgeons and Physicians. Republican. Lutheran.

SACHAR, DAVID BERNARD, gastroenterologist, medical educator; b. Urbana, Ill., Mar. 2, 1940; s. Abram Leon and Thelma (Horwitz) S.; m. Joanna Maud Belford Silver, Aug. 29, 1961; children: Mark Benson, Kenneth Hulbert Belford (dec.). AB magna cum laude, Harvard U., 1959, MD cum laude, 1963. Diplomate Bd. Gastroenterology Am. Bd. Internal Medicine. Intern medicine Beth Israel Hosp., Boston, 1963-65, resident, 1967-68; asst. chief clin. rsch. Pakistan-SEATO Cholera Rsch. Lab., Dhaka, Bangladesh, 1965-67; resident in gastroenterology Mt. Sinai Hosp., N.Y.C., 1968-70; from instr. to prof. medicine Mt. Sinai Sch. Medicine, CUNY, N.Y.C., 1970-92, 1st Burrill B. Crohn prof. medicine, 1992—; dir. div. gastroenterology Mt. Sinai Hosp., N.Y.C., 1983—, vice chmn. dept. medicine, 1992—; co-chmn. work group on inflammatory bowel disease NIH, 1973-75; expert adv. panel on gastroenterology and nutrition U.S. Pharmacopeial Conf., 1980-85; chmn. rsch. devel. com. Nat. Found. for Ileitis and Colitis, 1984-89; co-founder, sec.-treas. Burrill B. Crohn Rsch. Found., N.Y.C., 1984—; K.H. Koster meml. lectr. Danish Soc. of Gastroenterology, 1992; Internat. State of the Art lectr. Brit. Soc. Gastroenterology, 1995 and Falk Symposium, Germany, 1996; 20th Annual Norman Tanner Meml. lectr. St. George's Hosp. Med. Sch., London, 1997; mem. Gastroenterology Leadership Coun. Task Force on Fellowship Curriculum, 1994. Author over 130 articles and chpts. on natural history and treatment of inflammatory bowel disease; editor 7 books and monographs on gastroenterology. Trustee Bangladesh Coun. of the Asia Soc., N.Y.C., 1972-75, Bd. Edn., Englewood Cliffs, N.J., 1973-75. Sr. surgeon, comdr. USPHS,1965-67. Recipient Jacobi medallion for Disting. Achievement, Mt. Sinai Alumni Assn., 1994, Alexander Richman Commemorative award for humanism in medicine, 1996, Norman Tanner medal St. George's Hosp. Med. Sch., 1997, Gold Headed Cane award, 1997. Fellow ACP, Am. Coll. Gastroenterolotgy (program dirs. com. 1991—, Henry Baker Presdl. lectr. 1989); mem. Am. Gastroent. Assn. (chmn. subcom. on cert. 1987, 1st chmn. clin. tchg. project 1984-90, nominating com., chmn. Immunology-Microbiology-Inflammatory Disorders sect. 1995, Disting. Educator award 1996), Crohn's and Colitis Found. Am. (grants rev. com. and coun. 1990-94, Disting. Svc. award 1991, N.Y. Govs. medal 1992, chmn. clin. rsch. subcom. Disease Classification and Measurement 1994), Internat. Orgtn. for Study of Inflammatory Bowel Disease (1st Am. elected chmn. 1989-92), Phi Beta Kappa, Alpha Omega Alpha. Achievements include co-development of oral rehydration therapy for diarrhea; development of resources and standards for clinical teaching in gastroenterology. Office: Mt Sinai Med Ctr One Gustave L Levy Pl New York NY 10029

SACHDEV, MOHINDAR SINGH, engineering educator; b. Amritsar, Punjab, India, Apr. 1, 1928; naturalized Can. citizen; s. Khushal Singh and Kishen Kour (Chawla) S.; m. Joginder Kour, Feb. 4, 1951; children—Narinder P., Mandhir, Sukhbir, Sukhvinder. B.Sc., Benares Hindu U., Varanasi, India, 1950; M.Sc., Panjab U., Chandigarh, India, 1965, U. Sask., 1967; Ph.D., U. Sask., 1969; DSc, U. Sask, 1994. Registered profl. engr., Sask.; chartered engr. U.K. Asst. engr. Pub. Works Dept., Amritsar, India, 1950-59; exec. engr. Pub. Works Dept., Nangal, India, 1960-61; assoc. prof. Punjab Engring. Coll., Chandigarh, India, 1961-65; supt. engr. State Electricity Bd., Patiala, India, 1968-69; asst. to assoc. prof. U. Sask., Saskatoon, 1969-76; prof. U. Sask., 1976-95, prof. emeritus, 1995—, head elec. engring. dept., 1988-93; pres. Sachdev Engring. Assocs. (Can.) Ltd., 1996—; cons., lectr. in field; chmn. Can. subcom. Internat. Electrotech. Commn., 1975-85, mem. 1985-90; mem. grant selection com. Nat. Sci. and Rsch. Coun. Can., 1991-94, chmn., 1993-94. Coordinator/author: (IEEE Course text) Computer Relaying, 1979, Microprocessor Relays and Protection Systems, 1988, Advancements in Microprocessor Based Protection and Communication, 1997. Instr. def. driving courses Can. Safety Council, Ottawa, Ont., 1973-84; bd. dirs. Sask. Safety Council, 1976-81, chmn. traffic div., 1979-80. Recipient Cert. of Appreciation, Punjab State Electricity Bd., India, 1962; Sci. Research Council sr. vis. fellow, U.K., 1980. Fellow IEEE (chmn. western Can. coun. 1984-86, awards com. 1989-91, Outstanding Engring. Educator award IEEE Can. 1994), Instn. Engrs. India, Instn. Elec. Engrs. (U.K.), Engring. Inst. Can.; mem. Can. Elec. Assn. (vice chmn. power sys. planning and operation sect. 1989-92, chmn. 1993-96). Sikh. Office: Dept Elec Engring, 57 Campus Dr, Saskatoon, SK Canada S7N 5A9

SACHDEV, VED PARKASH, neurosurgeon; b. Mitranwali, India, Feb. 22, 1932; came to the U.S., 1969; s. Girdhari Lal and Amar Kaur Sachdev; m. Ranjit Kaur Sachdev, Apr. 17, 1970; children: Ulka, Rivka. MB BS, Govt. Med. Coll., Amritsar, Panjab, India, 1955. Diplomate Am. Bd. Neurosurgery. Asst. prof. neurosurgery Med. Inst., Chandigarh, India, 1964-69; intern St. Josephs Hosp., Lorain, Ohio, 1969-70; resident in neurosurgery Mt. Sinai Med. Ctr., N.Y.C., 1970-73, from asst. to assoc. clin. prof. dept. neurosurgery, 1974-88, clin. prof. dept. neurosurgery, 1988—; vice chmn. dept. neurosurgery Mt. Sinai Med. Ctr., N.Y.C., 1988-92. Author chpts. in 7 med. books. Surgeon lt., Indian Navy, 1957-60. Fellow ACS, Royal Coll. Surgeons Eng. (diplomate laryngology and otology). Avocation: music. Home: 128 Moorland Dr Scarsdale NY 10583-1937 Office: Mt Sinai Med Ctr Dept Neurosurgery 1148 5th Ave New York NY 10128

SACHER, BARTON STUART, lawyer; b. Birmingham, Ala., Apr. 9, 1948; s. Martin R. and Inez (Zuckerman) S.; 1 child, Joseph Alan; m. Susan Angela Anton, Sept. 30, 1976. BS, U. Ala., 1970, JD, 1973. Law clk. to judge S. Pointer U.S. Dist. Ct., Birmingham, 1973-74; assoc. Berkkowitz, Lefkowitz & Patrick, Birmingham, 1974-77; atty. investigations, trial counsel SEC, Washington, 1977-79; chief of investigations and enforcement SEC, Atlanta Region, 1979-85; ptnr. Tew, Jorden, Schulte & Beasley, Miami, 1986-90; pres., dir., ptnr. Hornsby, Sacher, Zelman, Stanton, Paul & Beiley, P.A., Miami, 1990—. Vice chmn. bd. dirs. Atlanta Fantasy Fair Inc., 1982—; v.p., trustee Temple Israel of Greater Miami, Inc.; v.p., dir. Alex Muss H.S., Israel; regional dir. ADL, Nat. Fin. Com., Dem. Party, Dem. Leadership Coun. Mem. ABA, Fed. Bar Assn., Fla. Bar Assn., D.C. Bar Assn., Ala. State Bar Assn., Greater Miami C. of C. (trustee), Grove Isle Club, Brickell Club. Jewish. Office: Hornsby Sacher Zelman Stanton Paul & Beiley PA 1401 Brickell Ave Fl 7 Miami FL 33131-3506

SACHER, STEVEN JAY, lawyer; b. Cleve., Jan. 28, 1942; s. Albert N. and Cecil P. (Chessin) S.; m. Colleen Marie Gibbons, Nov. 28, 1970; children—Alexander Jerome, Barry Elizabeth, William Paul. B.S., U. Wis., 1964; J.D., U. Chgo., 1967. Bar: D.C. 1968. Assoc. solicitor Employee Retirement Income Security Act U.S. Dept. Labor, Washington, 1974-77; spl. counsel com. on labor and human resources U.S. Senate, Washington, 1977-79, gen. counsel, 1980-81; ptnr. Pepper, Hamilton & Scheetz, Washington, 1982-88; shareholder Johnson & Wortley, Washington, 1988-94; ptnr. Kilpatrick Stockton LLP, Washington, 1994—; adj. prof. law Georgetown U. Law Ctr., 1977; co-chair sr. editors Employee Benefits Law and Annual Supplements, Bur. Nat. Affairs, Washington, 1991—. Mem. adv. bd. BNA Pension and Benefits Reporter; mem. editorial bd. Benefits Law Jour., Jour. Pension Planning and Compliance, Jour. Taxation of Employee Benefits. Founding mem. ERISA Roundtable, Washington. Mem. ABA (mgmt. co-chmn. com. on employee benefits, sect. on labor and employment law 1988-91, chmn. prohibited trans. subcom., com. on employee benefits, sect. on taxation 1986-91), Fed. Bar Assn., D.C. Bar Assn. Office: Kilpatrick Stockton LLP 700 13th St NW Ste 800 Washington DC 20005-3960

SACHS, ALAN ARTHUR, lawyer, corporate executive; b. Bklyn., Feb. 7, 1947; s. Herman and Clara Ethel (Treinkman) S.; m. Marilyn Neda Mushlin, May 19, 1974; children: David Henry, Stephen Edward. B.A., Columbia U., 1967; J.D., Harvard U., 1970. Bar: N.Y. 1971, U.S. Dist. Ct. (ea. and so. dists.) N.Y. 1972, U.S. Ct. Appeals (2d cir.) 1973, U.S. Dist. Ct. (no. dist.) N.Y. 1977, Wis. 1983, Mo. 1989. Law clk. to judge U.S. Dist. Ct. (ea. dist.) N.Y., 1970-71; assoc. Cleary, Gottlieb, Steen & Hamilton, N.Y.C., 1971-79, Paskus, Gordon & Hyman, N.Y.C., 1979-81; sec., gen. counsel The Trane Co., LaCrosse, Wis., 1981-85; exec. v.p., gen. counsel, sec. Edison Bros. Stores Inc., St. Louis, 1985—, also bd. dirs. Mem. ABA, Am. Soc. Corp. Secs. Office: Edison Bros Stores Inc 501 N Broadway Saint Louis MO 63102-2102

SACHS, DAVID, lawyer; b. N.Y.C., Aug. 4, 1933; s. Morris and Fannie R. (Kaplan) S.; m. Frumet P. Lome, July 7, 1957; children: Diane R., Daniel L., Francine E. BS, U. Pa., 1954; JD, Harvard U., 1957. Bar: N.Y. 1958, U.S. Tax Ct. 1959, U.S. Ct. Fed. Claims 1960, U.S. Ct. Appeals (2d cir.) 1960, U.S. Supreme Ct. 1967. Assoc. White & Case, N.Y.C., 1957-68, ptnr., 1968-88, ret. ptnr., 1988—. Fellow Am Coll. Tax Counsel, N.Y. Bar Found.; mem. N.Y. Bar Assn. (chmn. tax sect. 1980), N.Y.C. Bar Assn. (chmn. com. on taxation 1986-89, mem. coun. on taxation 1990-96). Office: White & Case 1155 Avenue Of The Americas New York NY 10036-2711

SACHS, HOWARD F(REDERIC), federal judge; b. Kansas City, Mo., Sept. 13, 1925; s. Alex F. and Rose (Lyon) S.; m. Susanne Wilson, 1960; children: Alex Wilson, Adam Phinney. B.A. summa cum laude, Williams Coll., 1947; J.D., Harvard U., 1950. Bar: Mo. 1950. Law clk. U.S. Dist. Ct., Kansas City, Mo., 1950-51; pvt. practice law Phineas Rosenberg, Kansas City, 1951-56; with Spencer, Fane, Britt & Browne, 1956-79; U.S. dist. judge Western Dist. Mo., Kansas City, 1979—, chief dist. judge, 1990-92, now sr. judge. Contbr. articles to various publs.; contbr. chpt. to Mid-America's Promise, 1982. Mem. Kansas City Commn. Human Rels., 1967-73; chmn. Jewish Community Rels. Bur., 1968-71, Kansas City chpt. Am. Jewish Com., 1963-65; mem. exec. com. Nat. Jewish Community Rels. Adv. Coun., 1968-71; pres. Urban League Kansas City, 1957-58, Kansas City chpt. Am. Jewish Congress, 1974-77; co-chmn. Kansas City chpt. NCCJ, 1958-60; mem. Kansas City Sch. Dist. Desegregation Task Force, 1976-77; pres. Jackson County Young Democrats, 1959-60; treas. Kennedy-Johnson Club, Jackson County, 1960. Served with USNR, 1944-46. Mem. ABA, Mo. Bar, Kansas City Bar Assn., Am. Judicature Soc., Lawyers Assn. Kansas City, Dist. Judges Assn. (8th cir., pres. 1992-94), Phi Beta Kappa. Office: US Dist Ct US Courthouse 811 Grand Ave Rm 716 Kansas City MO 64106-1909

SACHS, JOHN PETER, carbon company executive; b. Duesseldorf, Germany, 1926; married. BAChemE, Ill. Inst. Tech., 1948, MAChemE, 1950, PhDChemE, 1952. Various mgmt. positions in research and devel., engring. and ops. Union Carbide Corp., 1951-66; v.p. ops. then group v.p. Great Lakes Carbon Corp., N.Y.C., 1966-78; pres., chief exec. officer Gt. Lakes Carbon Corp., N.Y.C., 1978-86, now bd. dirs.; chmn. bd., dir. Gen. Refractories Co., 1978-85; ptnr. J.P. Sachs Assocs., Mgmt. Cons., New Canaan, Conn., 1987—. Trustee Fairfield U., 1978-92; bd. dirs. Kneissl-Dachstein 1992—, Peridot, 1989—. Mem. Am. Inst. Chem. Engrs. (pres. 1985). Home and Office: JP Sachs Assocs 67 Dunning Rd New Canaan CT 06840-4009

SACHS, LLOYD ROBERT, entertainment critic, writer; b. Flushing, N.Y., Dec. 3, 1950; s. Sidney Howard Sachs and Eleanor Sachs Brown. BA in English, Marietta Coll., 1972; MSJ, Northwestern U., 1974. Reporter, critic Variety, Chgo., 1975-76; pop culture columnist The Reader, Chgo., 1976-80; pop music reviewer USA Today, Washington, 1983-84; entertainment critic Chgo. Sun-Times, 1984—; vis. lectr. in journalism U. Ill., Chgo., 1983. Trustee The Ragdale Found., Lake Forest, Ill., 1985—; vol. The Peace Mus., Chgo., 1984—. Grantee Ill. Arts Coun., Chgo., 1985. Democrat. Jewish. Office: Chgo Sun-Times Inc 401 N Wabash Ave Chicago IL 60611-5642*

SACHS, MARILYN STICKLE, author, lecturer, editor; b. N.Y.C., Dec. 18, 1927; d. Samuel and Anna (Smith) Stickle; m. Morris Sachs, Jan. 26, 1947; children: Anne, Paul. BA, Hunter Coll., 1949; MSLS, Columbia U., 1953. Children's libr. Bklyn. Pub. Libr., 1949-60, San Francisco Pub. Libr., 1961-67. Author: Amy Moves In, 1964, Laura's Luck, 1965, Amy and Laura, 1966, Veronica Ganz, 1968, Peter and Veronica, 1969, Marv, 1970, The Bears' House, 1971 (Austrian Children's Book prize 1977, Recognition of Merit award George C. Stone Ctr. for Children's Books 1989), The Truth About Mary Rose, 1973 (Silver Slate Pencil award 1974), A Pocket Full of Seeds, 1973 (Jane Addams Children's Book Honor award 1974), Matt's Mitt, 1975, Dorrie's Book, 1975 (Silver State Pencil award 1977, Garden State Children's Book award 1978), A December Tale, 1976, A Secret Friends, 1978, A Summer's Lease, 1979, Bus Ride, 1980, Class Pictures, 1980, Fleet Footed Florence, 1981, Hello...Wrong Number, 1981, Call Me Ruth, 1982 (Assn. Jewish Librs. award 1983), Beach Towels, 1982, Fourteen, 1983, The Fat Girl, 1984, Thunderbird, 1985, Underdog, 1985 (Christopher 1986), Baby Sister 1986, Almost Fifteen, 1987, Fran Ellen's House, 1987 (award Bay Area Book Reviewers Assn. 1988, Recognition of Merit award George C. Stone Ctr. for Children's Books 1989), Just Like A Friend, 1989, At the Sound of the Beep, 1990, Circles, 1991, What My Sister Remembered, 1992, Thirteen, 1993, Ghosts in the Family, 1995, Another Day, 1997; co-editor:

(with Ann Durell) Big Book for Peace, 1990 (Calif. Children's Book award 1991, Jane Addams Children's Book prize 1991); reviewer books N.Y. Times, San Francisco Chronicle, 1970—. Mem. PEN, ACLU, SANE-Freeze, Sierra Club, Authors' Guild, Soc. Children's Bookwriters. Democrat. Jewish. Avocations: reading, hiking, baseball. Home: 733-31st Ave San Francisco CA 94121

SACHS, MURRAY B., audiologist, educator. BS, MIT, 1962, MS, 1964, PhD in Elec. Engring., 1966. From asst. prof. to assoc. prof. biomed. engring. Johns Hopkins U., Balt., 1970-80, dir. Ctr. Hearing Sci., 1986-91, Massey prof., dir. dept. biomed. engring., 1991—; mem. com. communication and control Internat. Union Pure and Applied Biophysics, 1975-80; mem. communication disease panel and basic sci. task force Nat. Inst. Neurol. and Communicative Disorders and Stroke NIH, 1977-78, chmn. communicative disease rev. com., 1977-79, ad hoc adv. com., 1979-86, sci. program adv. com., 1984-86; prof. biomed. engring. Johns Hopkins U., 1980—, prof. neurosci., 1981—, prof. otolaryngology-head and neck surgery, 1982-85. Mem. Inst. Medicine-Nat. Acad. Sci., Sigma Xi. Office: Johns Hopkins U Sch Medicine 720 Rutland Ave Baltimore MD 21205-2109*

SACHS, ROBERT GREEN, physicist, educator, laboratory administrator; b. Hagerstown, Md., May 4, 1916; s. Harry Maurice and Anna (Green) S.; m. Selma Solomon, Aug. 28, 1941; m. Jean K. Woolf, Dec. 17, 1950; children: Rebecca, Jennifer, Jeffrey, Judith, Joel; m. Carolyn L. Wolf, Aug. 21, 1968; stepchildren: Thomas Wolf, Jacqueline Wolf, Katherine Wolf. Ph.D., Johns Hopkins U., 1939; D.Sc. (hon.), Purdue U., 1967, U. Ill., 1977, Elmhurst Coll., 1987. Research fellow George Washington U., 1939-41; instr. physics Purdue U., 1941-43; on leave as lectr., research fellow U. Calif. at Berkeley, 1941; sect. chief Ballistic Rsch. Lab., Aberdeen Proving Ground, Md., 1943-46; dir. theoretical physics divsn. Argonne (Ill.) Nat. Lab., Ill., 1946-47; asso. prof. physics U. Wis., 1947-48, prof., 1948-64; assoc. dir. Argonne Nat. Lab., 1964-68, dir., 1973-79; prof. physics U. Chgo., 1964-86, prof. emeritus, 1986—; dir. Enrico Fermi Inst., 1968-73, 83-86; Higgins vis. prof. Princeton U., 1955-56; vis. prof. U. Paris, 1959-60, Tohoku U., Japan, 1974; cons. Ballistic Research Labs., 1945-59, Argonne Nat. Lab., 1947-50, 60-64; cons. radiation lab. U. Calif. at Berkeley, 1955-59; adv. panel physics NSF, 1958-61; mem. physics survey com., chmn. elem. particle physics panel Nat. Acad. Scis., 1969-72; high energy physics adv. panel div. research AEC, 1966-69; mem. steering com. (Sci. and Tech., A Five Year Outlook), 1979; mem. DOE task force on energy rsch. priorities, 1991-93. Author: Nuclear Theory, 1953, The Physics of Time Reversal, 1987; chief editor: High Energy Nuclear Physics, 1957; editor: National Energy Issues: How Do We Decide, 1980, The Nuclear Chain Reaction--Forty Years Later, 1984. Recipient Disting. Svc. to Engring. citation U. Wis., 1977; Guggenheim fellow, 1959-60. Fellow Am. Phys. Soc. (coun. 1968-71, regional sec. Cen. States 1964-69), Am. Acad. Arts and Scis. (v.p. Midwest Ctr. 1980-83); mem. NAS (chmn. physics sect. 1977-80, chmn. Class I Math. and Phys. Scis. 1980-83), AAAS (v.p., chmn. physics sect. 1970-71), Am. Inst. Physics (mem. gov. bd. 1969-71), Phi Beta Kappa, Sigma Xi. Achievements include reseach in theoretical particle, nuclear and solid state physics, terminal ballistics, nuclear power reactors. Office: U Chicago Enrico Fermi Inst Enrico Fermi Inst 5640 S Ellis Ave Chicago IL 60637-1433

SACHS, SAMUEL, II, museum director; b. N.Y.C., Nov. 30, 1935; s. James Henry and Margery (Fay) S.; m. Susan McAllen (div.); children: Katherine, Eleanor; m. Jerre S. Hollander (div.); 1 child, Alexander; m. Elizabeth M. Gordon; 1 child, Hadley Elizabeth. BA cum laude, Harvard U., 1957; MA, NYU Inst. Fine Arts, 1962. With Mpls. Inst. Arts, 1958-60; asst. dir. U. Mich. Mus. of Art, Ann Arbor, 1963-64; chief curator Mpls. Inst. Arts, 1964-73, dir., 1973-85; dir. Detroit Inst. Arts, 1985—. Bd. dirs. Ctr. for Creative Studies, Detroit, Univ. Liggett Sch., Grosse Pointe. Decorated knight 1st class Order North Star (Sweden); Order of Dannebrog (Denmark). Mem. Am. Assn. Museums, Coll. Art Assn., Assn. Art Mus. Dirs. Clubs: Detroit, Century Assn, Harvard, Grosse Pointe. Home: 19344 Cumberland Way Detroit MI 48203-1456 Office: Detroit Inst Arts 5200 Woodward Ave Detroit MI 48202-4008

SACHS, STEPHEN HOWARD, lawyer; b. Balt., Jan. 31, 1934; s. Leon and Shirley (Blum) S.; m. Sheila Kleinman, Sept. 4, 1960; children: Elisabeth Leon. BA, Haverford Coll., 1954; postgrad., New Coll., Oxford, Eng., 1954-55; LLB, Yale U., 1960. Bar: Md. 1960, D.C. 1988, U.S. Supreme Ct. 1965. Law clk. U.S. Ct. Appeals, Washington, 1960-61; asst. U.S. atty. Dist. of Md., 1961-64, U.S. atty., 1967-70; pvt. practice law Balt., 1970-78; atty. gen. State of Md., Balt., 1979-87; with firm Wilmer, Cutler & Pickering, Washington, 1987—. Served with U.S. Army, 1955-57. Fulbright scholar, 1954-55. Fellow Am. Coll. Trial Lawyers; mem. ABA, Md. Bar Assn., Balt. Bar Assn., Fed. Bar Assn., Nat. Urban Coalition and Lawyers Com. for Civil Rights Under the Law. Democrat. Jewish. Home: 5 Roland Mews Baltimore MD 21210-1560 Office: Wilmer Cutler & Pickering 2445 M St NW Washington DC 20037-1435

SACHTLER, WOLFGANG MAX HUGO, chemistry educator; b. Delitzsch, Germany, Nov. 8, 1924; came to U.S., 1983; s. Gottfried Hugo and Johanna Elisabeth (Bollmann) S.; m. Anne-Lore Luise Adrian, Dec. 9, 1953; children: Johann Wolfgang Adriaan, Heike Kathleen Julia, Yvonne Rhea Valeska. Diplomchemiker, Tech. U., Braunschweig, Ger., 1949; Dr.rer.nat. (Ph.D), 1952. Research chemist Kon-Shell Lab., Amsterdam, Netherlands, 1952-71, dept. head, 1972-83; extraordinary prof. chemistry U. Leiden, Netherlands, 1963-83; V.N. Ipatieff prof. Northwestern U., Evanston, Ill., 1983-96; chmn. Gordon Research Conf. Catalysis, N.H., 1985; Rideal lectr. Faraday div. Royal Soc. Chemistry, 1981; F. Gault lectr., 1991. Mem. editl. bd. Jour. Catalysis, 1976-88, Applied Catalysis, 1983-87, Catalysis Letters, 1987—, Advances in Catalysis, 1987—, Catalysis Reviews, 1997—; contbr. numerous articles to sci. jours. Recipient Deutsche Gesellschaft Mineraloel und Kohle Kolleg, 1991. Fellow AAAS; mem. Royal Netherlands Acad. Scis., Internat. Congress Catalysis (pres. coun. 1992-96), Royal Dutch Chem. Soc. (hon. mem. catalysis divsn.), Am. Chem. Soc. (E.V. Murphee award 1987, Petroleum Chemistry award 1992), Catalysis Soc. N.Am. (Robert L. Burwell award 1985, E. Houdry award 1993). Home: 2141 Ridge Ave Apt 2D Evanston IL 60201-2788 Office: Northwestern U Sheridan Rd Evanston IL 60208-0002

SACK, BURTON MARSHALL, restaurant company executive; b. Melrose, Mass., Dec. 13, 1937; s. Samuel and Bertha (Gersin) S.; m. Susan Lightbown, June 9, 1963 (dec.); children: Brian, David, Scott; m. Gail Summerfield, June 17, 1990. B.S., Cornell U., 1961; P.M.D., Harvard Bus. Sch., 1967. With Howard Johnson's, 1951-83, successively dishwasher, counter-man, cook, and asst. mgr., to 1955, advt. asst., 1961, asst. dir. mktg., 1961-62, dir. public relations, 1962-67, gen. mgr. fast food service div., 1967-70; gen. mgr. Ground Round Restaurant div., 1970-73, v.p. splty. restaurants, 1973-76, group v.p. corp. devel., 1976-81, sr. v.p. corp. devel., 1981-83; pres. Exeter Hospitality Group, Boston, 1983-87, Pub Ventures of New Eng., Braintree, Mass., 1984-94; exec. v.p. Applebees Internat., Inc., 1994—; lectr. Cornell U., Wharton Sch. Bus. U. Pa., Cape Cod C.C., Babson Coll. With USMC, 1955-58. Mem. Nat. Restaurant Assn. (past chpt. pres., dir., bd. dirs.), Nat. Assn. Corp. Real Estate Execs., Broadcasting Execs. of New Eng. (past dir.), Mass. Restaurant Assn. (past 1st v.p., mem. bd. dirs.), Cornell Soc. Hotelmen (past pres. New Eng. chpt., past nat. pres.). Home: 415 L'Ambiance Dr PH-D Longboat Key FL 34228 Office: Applebee's Internat Inc 4551 W 107th St Shawnee Mission KS 66207-4024

SACK, EDGAR ALBERT, electronics company executive; b. Pitts., Jan. 31, 1930; s. Edgar Albert and Margaret Valentine (Engelmohr) S.; m. Eugenia Ferris, June 7, 1952; children: Elaine Kimberley, Richard Warren. B.S., Carnegie-Mellon U., 1951, M.S., 1952, Ph.D., 1954. Dept. mgr. Westinghouse Research Lab., Pitts., 1960-63; engring. mgr. Westinghouse Microelectronics, Balt., 1963-65; operations mgr. Westinghouse Microelectronics, 1965-67, div. mgr., 1967-69; div. v.p. Gen. Instrument Corp., Hicksville, N.Y., 1969-73; group v.p. Gen. Instrument Corp., 1973-77, sr. v.p., 1977-84; pres., chief exec. officer Zilog Inc., Campbell, Calif., 1984—, also chmn. bd. dirs.; vis. com. elec. engring. dept. Carnegie-Mellon U., 1969-74; bd. dirs. Catalyst Semiconductor, Inc.; mem. indsl. adv. council SUNY, Stony Brook, 1979-83; mem. Adv. Com. on Solid State Electronics for Poly. Inst. Tech., 1981-83. Author: Forward Controllership Business Management System, 1989, 2nd edit., 1993. Mem. Action Com. Long Island, 1982-84. Recipient 2nd Ann. Hammerschlag Disting. Lectr. award Carnegie Mellon U., 1995. Fellow IEEE, Poly. Inst. Tech.; mem. Semicondr. Industry Assn. (dir. 1982-85); mem. Carnegie Mellon Alumni Assn. (Merit award 1981), Eta Kappa Nu (Outstanding Young Elec. Engr. 1959), Huntington Yacht Club (vice comdr. 1977), Tau Beta Pi (finalist San Francisco Entrepreneur of Yr. award 1991), Phi Kappa Phi. Patentee in field. Home: 21412 Sarahills Ct Saratoga CA 95070-4814 Office: Zilog Inc 210 E Hacienda Ave Campbell CA 95008-6617

SACK, GEORGE HENRY, JR., molecular geneticist; b. Balt., Apr. 17, 1943; s. George Henry and Sophia Ann (Philippi) S. BA, Johns Hopkins U., 1965, MD, 1968, PhD, 1974. Diplomate Am. Bd. Med. Examiners, Md. Bd. Med. Genetics. Intern Johns Hopkins Hosp., Balt., 1968-69, asst. resident, 1969-70, fellow genetics, 1975-76; rsch. fellow Johns Hopkins Sch. Medicine, Balt., 1970-73; asst. prof. dept. medicine Johns Hopkins U., Balt., 1976-84, assoc. prof. dept. medicine and biological chemistry, 1984—; molecular biologist Kennedy Inst., Balt., 1982-93. Contbr. articles to profl. jours. Maj. USAR, 1973-75. Andrew W. Mellon scholar Johns Hopkins U., 1976, Kennedy Found. scholar, 1982. Fellow Am. Coll. Med. Genetics; mem. AMA, AAAS, Am. Soc. Human Genetics, Phi Beta Kappa. Office: Johns Hopkins Hosp Blalock 1008 600 N Wolfe St Baltimore MD 21205-2110

SACK, JAMES MCDONALD, JR., radio and television producer, marketing executive; b. London, Ky., Oct. 11, 1948; s. James McDonald and Ruth Elmore (Bryant) S.; m. Cheryl S. Gremaux, July 13, 1969 (div. June 1974); 1 child, Graehm McDonald. BA in History, Ind. U., 1975, MS in Telecommunications, 1976. Coordinator Latin Am. Ednl. Ctr., Ft. Wayne, Ind., 1979-81, Mayor's Office, Ft. Wayne, 1981-83; producer WMEE-WQHK Radio, Ft. Wayne, 1983-85; owner, operator Festival Mgmt. and Devel., Ft. Wayne, 1984—; owner Lily Co., Fort Wayne, 1991-95; region sales mgr. Plan Mgmt., Ft. Wayne, Ind., 1995-96; v.p. communications, mktg. United Way of Allen County, Ft. Wayne, Ind., 1989—; owner The Sack Co., 1992; owner The Lily Co.; pub. affairs prodr. WBYR, Ft. Wayne. Producer radio documentary, 1985 (First Place award Ind. Broadcasters Assn., 1985), producer WFWA-PBS Eye on the Arts, 1987-89. Founder, pres. Germanfest of Ft. Wayne, 1981-92; pres. cable TV program adv. coun. City of Ft. Wayne; founder Ft. Wayne-Gera (Germany) Sister City Affilation; commr. Ind. Hoosier Celebration, 1988; dir. Ind. Highland Games, 1992, cons., 1993—; market dir. Germanfest of Ft. Wayne, 1996—. Named Ky. Col., 1991. Mem. German Heritage Soc. (founder, bd. dirs. 1986—), Ind. German Heritage Soc. (founder, bd. dirs. 1986-92, Gov.'s Commendation award 1983), N.Am. Sängerbund (sec. 1985-86), Männerchor Club (Ft. Wayne), Ft. Wayne Sport Club (sec. 1985-86, trustee 1987-89). Lutheran. Avocations: canoeing, flying, politics, linguistics. Home and Office: 2502 S Harrison St Fort Wayne IN 46807-1318

SACK, ROBERT DAVID, lawyer; b. Phila., Oct. 4, 1939; s. Eugene J. and Sylvia I. (Rivlin) S.; div.; children: Deborah Gail, Suzanne Michelle, David Rivlin; m. Anne K. Hilker, 1989. B.A., U. Rochester, 1960; LL.B., Columbia U., 1963. Bar: N.Y. 1963. Law clk. to judge Fed. Dist. Ct., Dist. of N.J., 1963-64; assoc. Patterson, Belknap & Webb, N.Y.C., 1964-70; ptnr. Patterson, Belknap, Webb & Tyler, N.Y.C., 1970-74, 74-86, Gibson, Dunn & Crutcher, N.Y.C., 1986—; sr. assoc. spl. counsel U.S. Ho. of Reps. Impeachment Inquiry, 1974; lectr. Practising Law Inst., 1973—; mem. adv. bd. Media Law Reporter. Author: Libel, Slander and Related Problems, 1980, 2nd edit., 1994, CD-Rom edit., 1995, N.Y.C. Commission on Public Information and Communication, 1995; mem. adv. bd. Media Law Reporter BNA; contbr. articles to legal jours. Chmn. bd. dirs. Nat. Council on Crime and Delinquency, 1982-83; trustee Columbia seminars on media and society Columbia U. Sch. Journalism, 1985-92; v.p., dir. William F. Kerby and Robert S. Potter Fund. Mem. ABA (bd. govs. forum com. on communications law 1980-88), N.Y. State Bar Assn., Assn. Bar City N.Y. (chmn. communications law com. 1986-89). Office: Gibson Dunn & Crutcher 200 Park Ave Fl 47 New York NY 10166-4799

SACK, SYLVAN HANAN, lawyer; b. Phila., Dec. 26, 1932; s. Isidore F. and Mollye (Bellmore) S.; m. Ellen L. Foreman, Aug. 13, 1972; children: Reuben H., Sara I. M.S. in Bus. Adminstrn, Pa. State U., 1956; J.D., U. Balt., 1964. Bar: Md. 1964, U.S. Tax Ct. 1967, U.S. Supreme Ct. 1970; C.P.A., Md. Pvt. practice Balt., 1967—; assoc. counsel Safety First Club of Md., 1975-78, spl. counsel, 1979—; gov. Md. chpt. Retinitis Pigmentosa Found., 1974-75. Contbr. articles to profl. jours. Chmn. Indsl. Toxicology NIOSH Function, 1977, Occupational Disease Forum, 1979, OSHA and Diseases in Workplace Seminar, 1981. Mem. Fed. Bar Assn. (gov. chpt. 1968—, chmn. bd. govs. 1969-70, chmn. environ. law program 1984), ABA (chmn. subcom. sect. taxation 1972-75), Md. Bar Assn., Assn. Trial Lawyers Am.; mem. Md. Trial Lawyers Assn. (lectr. toxic torts 1983 conv.). Home: 27 Brightside Ave Baltimore MD 21208-4802 Office: 2404 Saint Paul St Baltimore MD 21218-5118

SACKEIM, HAROLD, psychologist; b. Hackensack, N.J., July 13, 1951; s. Alexander and Ruth (Frymer) S.; m. Donna Zucchi, Oct. 9, 1977. BA, Columbia U., 1972; BA, MA, Oxford (Eng.) U., 1974; PhD, U. Pa., 1977. Asst. prof. psychology Columbia U., N.Y.C., 1977-79, lectr. psychiatry Coll. Physicians and Surgeons, 1980-87; asst. prof. psychology N.Y.U., N.Y.C., 1979-81, assoc. prof., 1981-87; assoc. prof. dept. psychiatry Columbia U., N.Y.C., 1987-90, prof. dept. psychiatry, 1990—, chief dept. biol. psychiatry, 1991—; assoc. attending psychologist N.Y. State Psychiat. Inst., N.Y.C., 1980—, rsch. sci. and dep. chief dept. biol. psychiatry, 1980-91, chief dept. biol. psychiatry, 1991—; cons. WNET, 1978, 85; pvt. practice psychology, N.Y.C., 1977—; established investigator award Nat. Alliance for Rsch. in Schizophrenia and Depression. NIMH grantee, 1981—, NYU Rsch. Challenge Fund grantee, 1981-82, McGraw-Hill grantee, 1979-80, NIA grantee, 1985—; recipient Rsch. Excellence award N.Y. Office Mental Health, 1995. Fellow Am. Psychiat. Assn. (hon.); mem. AAAS, APA, Am. Coll. Neuropsychopharmacology (Joel Elkes Internat. award 1994), Am. Psychopathol. Assn., Internat. Neuropsychol. Soc., Soc. Biol. Psychiatry. Assoc. editor Jour. Social and Clin. Psychology, 1982-87; cons. editor jour. Imagination, Cognition and Personality, 1981—, Convulsive Therapy, 1985—, Neuropsychiatry, Neuropsychol. and Behavior Neurology, 1987—; contbr. numerous articles to profl. jours. Office: Columbia U Dept Psychiatry 722 W 168th St # 72 New York NY 10032-2603

SACKETT, DIANNE MARIE, city treasurer, accountant; b. Oil City, Pa., Dec. 29, 1956; d. Clarence Benjamin and Donna Jean (Grosteffon) Knight; m. Mark Douglas Sackett, May 26, 1984; children: Jason Michael, Cory James. BBA, Ea. Mich. U., 1979, MBA, 1986. Cert. mcpl. fin. adminstr. Accounts payable supr. Sarns, Inc., Ann Arbor, Mich., 1979-81; cost acct. Simplex Products Divsn., Adrian, Mich., 1981-83, gen. acctg. supr., 1983-88; city treas. City of Tecumseh, Mich., 1991—. Mem. Mich. Mcpl. Treas.' Assn., Mich. Mcpl. Fin. Officers Assn., Mcpl. Treas.' Assn. of the U.S. and Can. Pentecostal. Office: 309 E Chicago Blvd Tecumseh MI 49286-1550

SACKETT, JOSEPH FREDERIC, radiologist, educator, administrator; b. Cleve., Jan. 16, 1940; s. George Leslie and Cora Lenore (Hurst) S.; children: Joseph Frederic, Samson Occom, Penelope Cora. B.A., Dartmouth Coll., 1962; M.D., Tulane U., 1966. Diplomate Am. Bd. Radiology. Intern Mary Hitchcock Meml. Hosp., Hanover, N.H., 1966-67; resident Dartmouth Coll.-Hitchcock Hosp., Hanover, 1969-72; fellow in neuroradiology Ulleval Hosp., Oslo, 1972-73, N.Y. Hosp.-Cornell U., N.Y.C., 1973-74; asst. prof. radiology U. Wis.-Madison, 1974-78, assoc. prof., 1978-81, chmn. dept., prof., 1981—; vis. prof. U. Nebr.-Omaha, 1977, Dartmouth Med. Sch., 1977, 82, U. Calif.-San Francisco, 1977, Med. Coll. Wis., Milw., 1977, Cleve. Clinic, 1978, Case Western Res. Sch. Medicine, 1978, UCLA, 1978, U. Kans., 1979, U. Cin., 1979, Rutgers Med. Sch., New Brunswick, N.J., 1979, Cornell U. Med. Ctr., 1980, U. Louisville, 1981, others; lectr. in field. Author: New Techniques in Myelography, 1979; editor: Digital Subtraction Angiography, 1981; contbr. numerous articles to profl. jours. Served to capt. M.C., U.S. Army, 1967-69, Vietnam. Fellow Am. Coll. Radiology; mem. Assn. Univ. Radiologists (fin. chmn. 1984—), Radiol. Soc. N.Am., Am. Soc. Neuroradiology, Rotary Internat. Republican. Avocations: sailing; yacht racing. Home: 3100 Lake Mendota Dr Madison WI 53705-1481 Office: Clin Sci Ctr 600 Highland Ave Madison WI 53792-0001*

SACKETT, ROSS DEFOREST, publisher; b. Chgo., Mar. 26, 1930; s. DeForest and Margaret (Ross) S.; m. Marvyda Wild, Sept. 1, 1951; children: David, Scott, Cynthia, Amy, Stuart. BA, Lawrence Coll., 1951. Editor in chief Charles Merrill Books, Inc., Columbus, Ohio, 1959-61; gen. mgr., v.p., exec. v.p., dir. Holt, Rinehart & Winston, N.Y.C., 1961-67, pres., dir., 1967-70, chmn. bd., 1970-72; pres. CBS Edn. Pub. Group, 1970-72, Ency. Brit. Ednl. Corp., 1972-76; chmn. Crescent Park Press, Angeles Toy Corp., Childs/Play, Inc.; chmn. bd. Big Toys Inc.; pres., chmn. bd. Kompan Holdings; dir. Ency. Brit. Corp., Kompan, Inc.; former dir. CBS. Trustee Highscope Ednl. Rsch. Found. Mem. Assn. Am. Pubs. (chmn.), Civil War Round Table, Delta Tau Delta, Eta Sigma Phi. Episcopalian. Office: PO Box 448 Eureka Springs AR 72632-0448

SACKETT, SUSAN DEANNA, film and television production associate, writer; b. N.Y.C., Dec. 18, 1943; adopted d. Maxwell and Gertrude Selma (Kugel) S. B.A. in Edn., U. Fla., 1964, M.Ed., 1965. Tchr. Dade County Schs., Miami, Fla., 1966-68, L.A. City Schs., 1968-69; asst. publicist, comml. coordinator NBC-TV, Burbank, Calif., 1970-73; asst. to creator of Star Trek Gene Roddenberry, 1974-91; prodn. assoc. Star Trek: The Next Generation TV Series, 1987-91; writer Star Trek: The Next Generation, 1990-91; lectr. and guest speaker STAR TREK convs. in U.S., Eng., Australia, 1974-93. Author and editor: Letters to Star Trek, 1977; co-author: Star Trek Speaks, 1979; The Making of Star Trek-The Motion Picture, 1979; You Can Be a Game Show Contestant and Win, 1982, Say Goodnight Gracie, 1986; author: The Hollywood Reporter Book of Box Office Hits, 1990, 2nd edit., 96, Prime Time Hits, 1993, Hollywood Sings, 1995. Mem. ACLU, Writers Guild Am., Am. Humanist Assn., Mensa, Sierra Club. Democrat.

SACKHEIM, ROBERT LEWIS, aerospace engineer, educator; b. N.Y.C., N.Y., May 16, 1937; s. A. Frederick and Lillian L. (Emmer) S.; m. Babette Freund, Jan. 12, 1964; children: Karen Holly, Andrew Frederick. B-SChemE, U. Va., 1959; MSChemE, Columbia U., 1961; postgrad., UCLA, 1966-72. Project engr. Comsat Corp., El Segundo, Calif., 1969-72; project mgr. TRW, Redondo Beach, Calif., 1964-69, sect. head, 1972-76, dept. mgr., 1976-81, mgr. new bus., 1981-86, lab. mgr., 1986-90, dep. ctr. dir., 1990-93, ctr. dir., 1993—; instr. UCLA engring. ext., 1986; mem. adv. bds. NASA, Washington, 1989—; mem. peer rev. bd. various univs. and govtl. agys., 1990—; mem. Nat. Rsch. Coun./Aeronautics and Space Engring. Bd., 1994—; guest lectr. various univs. and AIAA short courses. Author: Space Mission Analysis and Design, 1991, Space Propulsion Analysis and Design, 1995; contbr. over 90 articles to profl. jours., confs. Mem. adv. bd. L.A. Bd. Edn., 1990-92; fund raiser March of Dimes, L.A., 1970-90, YMCA, San Pedro, Calif., 1974-86. Capt. USAF, 1960-63. Recipient Group Achievement award NASA, 1970, 78, 86. Fellow AIAA (chmn. com. 1980-83, chmn. L.A. sect. 1997, J.H. Wyld Propulsion award 1992, Shuttle Flag award 1984). Achievements include 6 patents for spacecraft propulsion systems, devices and components. Office: TRW Space & Elects Group Bldg 01/RM 2010 1 Space Park Blvd Rm 2010 Redondo Beach CA 90278-1001

SACKIN, CLAIRE, social work educator; b. N.Y.C., Oct. 1, 1925; d. Harry and Diana (Mednick) Gershfeld; m. Milton Sackin, Feb. 4, 1955; children: William, Daniel, David. BA, Hunter Coll., 1946; MEd, U. Pitts., 1968, MSW, 1972, PhD, 1976. Tenured tchr. jr. high sch. Bronx, N.Y., 1947-57; rsch. asst. U. Pitts., 1973, instr. dept. urban mgmt., 1974; rsch. assoc. U. Pitts. Sch. of Social Work, 1975-76, Health & Welfare Planning Assn., 1974; prof. social work, dir. social work program St. Francis Coll., Loretto, Pa., 1976—; registered trainer alcoholism specialists cert. program; mem. adv. bd. Cedar Manor Treatment Ctr., Cresson, Pa., 1994-95; mem. Pa. Gov.'s Coun. Alcoholism, 1980, Nat. Assn. People with AIDS; presenter in field. Contbr. articles to jours. Mem. NASW (social action com. Pa. chpt. 1983-85, mem. Del. Assembly 1984, eastern regional coalition liaison 1984), Coun. on Social Work Edn., Alpha Delta Mu (nat. bd. dirs.). Avocations: reading, crossword puzzles, opera, gardening, travel. Home: 531 Sandrae Dr Pittsburgh PA 15243-1727 Office: St Francis Coll Loretto PA 15940

SACKLOW, STEWART IRWIN, advertising executive; b. Albany, N.Y., July 29, 1942; s. Jacob David and Freda Ruth (Pearlman) S.; A.A.S., N.Y.C. C.C., 1962; BS, Western Mich. U., 1965; m. Harriette Lynn Cooperman, July 2, 1967; 1 son, Ian Marc. Asst. dist. office Humble Oil & Refining Co., Inc., Albany, 1963-65; dir. advt. and sales promotion Albany Pub. Markets div. Weiss Foods, 1965-68; Golub Corp., v.p. and dir. advt. Price Chopper Discount Foods, Schenectady, 1968-78; pres., creative dir. Wolkcas Advt., Inc., 1978-93, pres., CEO, 1993-95; pres., creative dir. Wolkcas Comms. Group, 1995—; exec. dir. Ski the Catskills, 1982-84; pres. Broadcast Creations, 1985—; pres. Testimonials, Inc., 1991-93. Mem. Dist. Atty.'s readiness team; active Albany County Cerebral Palsy Telethons, 1966-68; mem. fund drive com. Sta. WMHT-TV ednl. TV, 1967-74; bd. dirs. N.E. Cystic Fibrosis Found., Video Spirit; bd. dirs., mem. exec. com. Upstate Leukemia Assn.; mem. bd. Gov. Clinton council Boy Scouts Am., leader, Voorheesville, N.Y.; chmn. N.Y. State Arbor Day Com., 1990—; pres. Takundewide Home Owners Assn., 1991-92; key market coord. Partnership Drug Free Am.; coord. Drug Free N.Y. State; bd. dirs. Daughter of Sarah Found.; instr. skindiving program YMCA. Recipient certificate merit Nat. Research Bur., 1966, Freedoms Found., 1966, Amsterdam Recorder, 1968, Retail Advt. Conf., 1969, 70, Woman's Day Mag., 1971, 72, 73, 74, 75, 76; Grand Nat. award Am. Dairy Assn., 1969, Hunt Wesson Foods, 1970; recipient 4 1st place awards Am. Advt. Fedn., 1972, Crystal Prism award, 1973; Effie award Am. Mgmt. Assn., 1972; Silver medal award Am. Advt. Fed., 1973, Addy award, 1973, 74, 75; award excellence Retail Advt. Conf., 1971; Best 15 Internat. Ads award Internat. Newspaper Advt. Execs., 1972, Gold Leaf award Internat. Arborist Soc., 1993. Mem. Ad Club N.Y. (bd. dirs. 1974-79, 93-94, pres. 1976-77), Am. Advt. Fedn. (bd. govs. 1975), Profl. Pub. Rels. Coun. Albany Execs. Assn. Mem. B'nai B'rith (bd. dir. housing 1992-93), N.Y. Art Dirs. Club, Capital Dist. Creative Club, Mohawk Antique Auto Club, Albany Yacht Club, Schenectady Racquet Club, KP. Home: 716 St Marks Ln Niskayuna NY 12309-4843

SACKNER, MARVIN ARTHUR, physician; b. Phila., Feb. 16, 1932; s. Albert B. and Goldie Mildred (Haber) S.; m. Ruth Karsch, June 24, 1956; children: Sara, Deborah, Jonathan. BS, Temple U., 1953; MD, Jefferson Med. Coll., 1957. Diplomate Am. Bd. Internal Medicine. Intern Phila. Gen. Hosp., 1957-58, med. resident, 1958-61; ACP rsch. fellow U. Pa., Phila., 1961-64; chief pulmonary disease Mt. Sinai Hosp., Miami Beach, Fla., 1964-74, dir. med. svcs., 1974-91; dir. med. svcs. emeritus Mt. Sinai Hosp., Fla., 1992—; prof. medicine U. Miami, Fla., 1973—; gov., chmn. pulmonary disease exam. bd. Am. Bd. Internal Medicine, 1977-80; chief exec. officer Non-Invasive Monitoring Systems, Inc., Miami Beach, Fla., 1986—. Author: Scleroderma, 1966; editor: Diagnostic Techniques in Pulmonary Disease, Parts I and II, 1980; mem. editorial bd. Fla. Med. Assn., 1974, Am. Rev. Respiratory Physiology, 1976-80, Jour. Applied Physiology, 1976-80, Annals Internal Medicine, 1979; patentee in field; contbr. articles to profl. jours. Pres. Art in Pub. Places, Inc., 1975-78; co-dir. Ruth and Marvin Sackner Archive of Concrete and Visual Poetry, 1979—; bd. dirs. Ctr. for Book Art, N.Y.C., 1987-93; mem. libr. com. Mus. Modern Art, N.Y.C., 1990-94. NEA grantee, 1977-78, Nat. Heart, Lung and Blood Inst. grantee, 1966—, others. Fellow ACP, Am. Coll. Chest Physicians; mem. Am. Thoracic Soc. (pres.1980), Am. Physiol. Soc., Grolier Club N.Y.C. Jewish. Office: 1840 West Ave Miami FL 33139-1432

SACKS, ARTHUR BRUCE, environmental and liberal arts educator; b. N.Y.C., Apr. 21, 1946; s. Fred and Lillian Pearl (Levy) S.; m. Normandy Roden, May 17, 1987; children: Rachel, Erica. BA, Bklyn. Coll., 1967; MA, U. Wis., 1968, PhD, 1975. Teaching asst. dept. English, U. Wis., Madison, 1968-72, asst. to assoc. dean for student acad. affairs, 1972-76, lectr. dept. English, 1975, sr. lectr. Inst. for Environ. Studies, 1976-90, coord. acad. programs, 1976-78, asst. to dir., asst. dir., then assoc. dir., 1983-85, acting dir., then dir., 1985-90, assoc. mem. dept. urban and regional planning, 1985-93, adminstr. acad. programs, 1978-85; sr. spl. asst. to dean grad. sch. U. Wis., 1990-93; assoc. mem. Russian and East European studies U. Wis., Madison, 1992-93, acting dir. internat. faculty and staff svcs., 1993; dir., prof. liberal arts and internat. studies Colo. Sch. Mines, Golden, 1993—; mem. adj. faculty Ohio State U., Columbus, 1992-94; prof. environ. sci. Internat. U., Moscow, 1992—. Bd. dirs. Friends of Waisman Ctr. on Mental Retardation and Human Devel., 1991-93; mem. Emergency Med. Svcs. Commn., 1992-93. Recipient blue ribbon for poetry Am. Assn. Interpretive Naturalists, 1983. Mem. AAAS, Am. Assn. Higher Edn., N.Am. Assn. Environ. Edn. (adv. group internat. rels. com. 1991-94, rep. to jour. 1988—, nominating com. 1989-90, pres. 1984-85, pres.-elect 1983-84, sec. 1982-83, exec. com. 1982-86, chmn. devel. com. 1986-94, liaison to Friends of the UN

Environ. Programme, chmn. participation World Decade of the Environ., 1982-92, bd. dirs., 1980-84, chmn. environ. studies sect. 1980-82, program com. confs., publs. com. 1978-83, chmn. 1981-83, polit. strategies com. 1982-83, sec.-treas. environ. studies sect. 1978-80, chmn. com. on establishing jour. environ. studies 1978, mem. spl. task force on mission, membership and orgnl. structure 1977-78, mem. planning group nat. com. environ. edn. rsch. 1979-80), Internat. Soc. Environ. Edn., World Conservation Union, Russian Acad. Edn. (fgn.). Office: Colo Sch Mines 301 Stratton Hall Golden CO 80401

SACKS, DAVID G., retired distilling company executive, lawyer; b. N.Y.C., Jan. 6, 1924; s. Irving and Jeannette (Greenhoot) S.; children: Jonathan E., Deborah A., Judith A., Joshua M. A.B., Columbia U., 1944, LL.B., 1948. Ptnr. Simpson Thacher & Bartlett, N.Y.C., 1961-67, sr. ptnr., 1967-76, counsel, 1981-83; chief adminstrv. officer Lehman Bros., Inc., N.Y.C., 1976-81; exec. v.p. fin. adminstrn. The Seagram Co. Ltd., Montreal, Que., Can., 1983-86, pres., chief operating officer, 1986-89, also bd. dirs.; exec. v.p. fin. adminstrn. Joseph E. Seagram & Sons, N.Y.C., 1983-86, pres., chief operating officer, 1986-89; vice chmn. The Seagram Co. Ltd. and Joseph E. Seagram & Sons, Inc., Montreal and N.Y.C., 1989-91. Pres. United Jewish Appeal, Fedn. Jewish Philanthropies, N.Y.C., 1989-92. Cpl. USAAF, 1943-46. Office: 375 Park Ave Bsmt 4 New York NY 10152-0099

SACKS, HERBERT SIMEON, psychiatrist, educator, consultant; b. N.Y.C., Nov. 29, 1926; s. Maxwell Lawrence and Anne (Edelstein) S.; m. Helen Margery Levin, Dec. 26, 1948; children—Eric Livingston, Katharine Bird, Douglas Lowell, Russell Avery. A.B. magna cum laude, Dickinson Coll., 1948; M.D., Cornell U., 1952. Diplomate Am. Bd. Psychiatry and Neurology and subspecialty Child and Adolescent Psychiatry. Clin. assoc. Western New Eng. Psychoanalytic Inst., New Haven, 1955-63; intern in pediatrics Yale-New Haven Med. Ctr., 1952-53; jr. asst. resident in psychiatry Yale Psychiat. Inst., 1953-54; sr. asst. resident in psychiatry, USPHS fellow Yale-New Haven Med. Ctr., psychiat. out patient dept., 1954-55; USPHS fellow in child psychiatry Yale U. Child Study Ctr., 1955-57; clin. dir. Mid-Fairfield Child Guidance Ctr., Norwalk, Conn., 1957-59; cons. Expt. in Internat. Living, Putney, Vt., 1962-69; sr. cons. U.S. Peace Corps, Washington, 1962-69; cons. AID, U.S. Dept. State, Office of Sahel, West Africa, 1974-84, Neurosci. Consultation Group, Grosse Point Farms, Mich., 1984-94; clin. prof. child and adolescent psychiatry Child Study Ctr., Yale U. Sch. Medicine, New Haven; co-investigator, co-dir. Senegal River pilot health research program, New Haven and West Africa, 1976-78, co-investigator, co-dir. health sector, design team Senegal River integrated devel. project, 1981-83; vis. lectr. Yale Coll., 1969-71; mem. com. reviewers Dept. Commerce Nat. Bur. Standards, Inst. for Computer Scis. and Tech., Washington, 1975-77; mem. exec. com. Nat. Commn. on Confidentiality of Health Records, 1975-80. Author: Hurdles: The Admissions Dilemma in American Higher Education, 1978; contbg. author chpts. in books, articles on confidentiality, juvenile justice, higher edn., issues of youth in transition, other topics; author monographs. Mem. Conn. Juvenile Justice Commn., Hartford, 1975-80; bd. advisors Dickinson Coll., Carlisle, Pa., 1980-85. Served to lt. (j.g.) U.S. Navy, 1944-46; PTO. Fellow AMA, ACPO, Am. Psychiat. Assn. (trustee 1988-94, v.p. 1994-96, pres. 1997—), Am. Acad. Child and Adolescent Psychiatry, Am. Orthopsychiat. Assn., Am. Coll. Psychiatrists; mem. Conn. Psychiat. Soc. (pres. 1976-77), Conn. Coun. Child and Adolescent Psychiatrists (pres. 1972-73), World Fedn. for Mental Health, Phi Beta Kappa. Avocations: farming, photography, fishing, lawn bowling. Home: 110 Laurel Rd New Haven CT 06515-2426 Office: 260 Riverside Ave Westport CT 06880-4804 also: Yale U Child Study Ctr PO Box 207900 New Haven CT 06520

SACKS, IRA STEPHEN, lawyer; b. N.Y.C., Dec. 6, 1948; s. Marvin Leonard and Mildred (Finkelstein) S.; children: Jennifer, Allison, Gillian. BS, MIT, 1970; JD, Georgetown U., 1974. Bar: N.Y. 1975, U.S. Dist. Ct. (so. and ea. dists.) N.Y. 1975, U.S. Ct. Appeals (2d cir.) 1975, U.S. Ct. Appeals (3d cir.) 1984, U.S. Supreme Ct. 1985, U.S. Ct. Appeals (9th cir.) 1986, U.S. Ct. Appeals (11th cir.) 1987, U.S. Ct. Appeals (D.C. and fed. cirs.) 1993. Assoc. Kaye, Scholer, Fierman, Hays & Handler, N.Y.C., 1974-82, ptnr., 1983-87; ptnr. Fried, Frank, Harris, Shriver & Jacobson, N.Y.C., 1988—. Contbr. articles to profl. jours. NSF fellow, 1970. Mem. ABA, Supreme Ct. Hist. Soc., N.Y. State Bar Assn., Assn. of Bar of City of N.Y. Democrat. Jewish. Avocations: tennis, skiing, softball. Home: 105 Old Colony Rd Hartsdale NY 10530-9999 Office: Fried Frank Harris Shriver & Jacobson 1 New York Plz Fl 24 New York NY 10004-1901

SACKS, OLIVER WOLF, neurologist, writer; b. London, July 9, 1933; Came to U.S., 1960; s. Samuel and Muriel Elsie (Landau) S. BA, U. Oxford, 1954; MA, BM, BCh, Middlesex Hosp., London, 1958; DHL (hon.), Georgetown U., 1990, Coll. Staten Island, CUNY, 1991; DS (hon.), Tufts U., 1991, N.Y. Med. Coll., 1991. Intern in medicine, surgery and neurology Middlesex Hosp., 1958-60; rotating intern Mt. Zion Hosp., San Francisco, 1961-62; resident in neurology UCLA, 1962-65; I.D. fellow in neuropathology and neurochemistry Albert Einstein Coll. Medicine, N.Y.C., 1965-66, instr. neurology, 1966-75, asst. prof., 1975-78, assoc. prof., 1978-85, clin. prof. neurology, 1985—; cons., speaker, lectr. in field; hon. lectureships in field. Author: Migraine, 1970, Awakenings, 1973, rev. paperback edit., 1990 (Hawthornden prize 1975), A Leg To Stand On, 1984, The Man Who Mistook His Wife for a Hat, 1985, Seeing Voices: A Journey into the World of the Deaf, 1989, An Anthropologist on Mars, 1995, The Island of the Color Blind, 1996. Recipient Felix Mart-Ibanez book award MD mag., 1987, Oskar Pfister award APA, 1988, Harold D. Vursell Meml. award Am. Acad. and Inst. Arts and Letters, 1989, Odd Fellows book award, 1990, Scriptor award U. So. Calif., 1991, profl. support award Nat. Headache Found., 1991; open scholar in biology Queen's Coll., Oxford U., 1950, Theodoe Williams scholar in anatomy, 1953, med. rsch. scholar, 1954; Guggenheim fellow, 1989. Mem. Am. Acad. Neurology (presdl. citation 1991), Am. Acad. Arts & Letters, N.Y. State Med. Soc., N.Y. Inst for the Humanities, Alpha Omega Alpha. Office: 2 Horatio St Apt 3G New York NY 10014-1638

SACKS, PATRICIA ANN, librarian, consultant; b. Allentown, Pa., Nov. 6, 1939; d. Lloyd Alva and Dorothy Estelle (Stoneback) Stahl; m. Kenneth LeRoy Sacks, June 27, 1959. A.B., Cedar Crest Coll., 1959; M.S. in L.S., Drexel U., 1965. News reporter Call-Chronicle, Allentown, 1956-59, 1961-63; reference librarian Cedar Crest Coll., Allentown, 1964-66, head librarian, 1966-73; dir. libraries Muhlenberg and Cedar Crest Colls., Allentown, 1973-94; dir. libr. svcs. Cedar Crest Coll., 1994; sr. fellow Lehigh Valley Assn. Ind. Colls., 1994—. del. On Line Computer Library Ctr. Users Council, Columbus, Ohio, 1977-84; cons. colls./health care orgns., libr. orgns. 1981—. Author: (with Whildin Sara Lou) Preparing for Accreditation: A Handbook for Academic Librarians, 1993; mem. editorial bd. Jour. Acad. Librarianship, 1982-84. Trustee Cedar Crest Coll., 1985-89. Mem. United Way Lehigh Valley Coms., 1993—; bd. dirs. John and Dorothy Morgan Cancer Ctr., 1994—. Named Outstanding Acad. Woman, Lehigh Valley Assn. for Acad. Women, 1984, Muhlenberg Coll. Outstanding Adminstr., 1987, Alumni Tricorn award Muhlenberg Coll., 1989, Alumnae Achievement award Cedar Crest Coll., 1994. Mem. ALA (chmn. copyright com. 1985-87), Assn. Coll. and Research Libraries (chmn. standards and accreditation com. 1976-78, 81-84), Lehigh Valley Assn. Ind. Colls. (chmn. librarians sect. 1967-81, 88-92), AAUW, LWV Lehigh Valley Conservancy, Appalachian Mountain Club, Phi Alpha Theta, Phi Kappa Phi, Beta Phi Mu. Democrat. Home: 2997 Fairfield Dr Allentown PA 18103-5413 Office: Lehigh Valley Assn Ind Colls 119 W Greenwich St Bethlehem PA 18018-2307

SACKS, TEMI J., public relations executive; b. Phila.; d. Jule and Adeline (Levin) S. BA, Temple U. Pubs. editor Del. Valley Regional Planning Commn., Phila.; comms. assoc. Fedn. Jewish Agys., Phila.; pres. T. J. Sacks Pub. Relations, Phila.; exec. v.p., mng. dir. healthcare div. Lobsenz-Stevens Inc., N.Y.C.; sr. v.p., dir. nat. healthcare practice Shandwick, N.Y.C.; guest lectr. Temple U. Sch. Communications. Mem. Healthcare Businesswomen's Assn., Pharm. Advt. Coun., Women Execs. in Pub. Rels. Avocations: skiing, Americana antiques, jewelry design. Home: 142 W End Ave New York NY 10023-6103 Office: 235 Park Ave S New York NY 10003-1405

SACKSTEDER, FREDERICK HENRY, former foreign service officer; b. N.Y.C., July 12, 1924; s. Frederick H. and Denise (Dorin) S.; m. Evelyn M. Blickensderfer, Oct. 14, 1977; children by previous marriage: Frederick Henry, III, Timothy W. B.A., Amherst Coll., 1947; postgrad., Sch. Advanced Internat. Studies, Washington, 1947. Asst. to exec. v.p. Internat. Standard Electric Corp., N.Y.C., 1948-49; joined U.S. Fgn. Service, 1950; Kreis resident officer U.S. High Commn. for Germany, 1950-52; vice consul, consul, sec. Am. embassy, Lyon, France, 1952-55, Madrid, 1959-61, Barcelona, Spain, 1962-65, Tunis, Tunisia, 1967-69; internat. relations officer Dept. State, 1955-59; 65-67; mem. U.S. Mission to UN, 1969-72, Internat. Boundary and Water Com., El Paso, Tex., 1972-75; consul gen. Hermosillo, Sonora, Mexico, 1975-79; bd. examiners Fgn. Service, Dept. State, 1979-81, expert cons. Bur. Personnel, 1981-86; mem. U.S. del. to UN Gen. Assembly, N.Y.C., 1969-71. Mem. UN Trusteeship Coun., 1970-71, U.S. rep., 1971; pres. El Paso chpt. UN Assn., 1973-75. Lt. (j.g.) USNR, 1943-46. Mem. Fgn. Service Assn., Diplomatic and Consular Officers Ret., Council Fgn. Relations (chmn. Charlottesville com.). Lodge: Rotary (local club pres. 1988-89). Home: The Westchester 4000 Cathedral Ave NW # 344-b Washington DC 20016-5249

SACKTON, FRANK JOSEPH, public affairs educator; b. Chgo., Aug. 11, 1912; m. June Dorothy Raymond, Sept. 21, 1940. Student, Northwestern U., 1936, Yale, 1946, U. Md., 1951-52; BS, U. Md., 1970; grad., Army Inf. Sch., 1941, Command and Gen. Staff Coll., 1942, Armed Forces Staff Coll., 1949, Nat. War Coll., 1954; MPA, Ariz. State U., 1976, DHL (hon.), 1996. Mem. 131st Inf. Regt., Ill. N.G., 1929-40; commd. 2d lt. U.S. Army, 1934, advanced through grades to lt. gen., 1967; brigade plans and ops. officer (33d Inf. Div.), 1941, PTO, 1943-45; div. signal officer, 1942-43, div. intelligence officer, 1944, div. plans and ops. officer, 1945; sec. to gen. staff for Gen. MacArthur Tokyo, 1947-48; bn. comdr. 30th Inf. Regt., 1949-50; mem. spl. staff Dept. Army, 1951; plans and ops. officer Joint Task Force 132, PTO, 1952; comdr. Joint Task Force 7, Marshall Islands, 1953; mem. gen. staff Dept. Army, 1954-55; with Office Sec. Def., 1956; comdr. 18th Inf. Regt., 1957-58; chief staff 1st Inf. Div., 1959; chief army Mil. Mission to Turkey, 1960-62; comdr. XIV Army Corps, 1963; dep. dir. plans Joint Chiefs Staff, 1964-66; army general staff mil. ops., 1966-67, comptroller of the army, 1967-70, ret., 1970; spl. asst. for fed./state relations Gov. Ariz., 1971-75; chmn. Ariz. Programming and Coordinating Com. for Fed. Programs, 1971-75; lectr. Am. Grad. Sch. Internat. Mgmt., 1973-77; vis. asst. prof., lectr. public affairs Ariz. State U., Tempe, 1976-78; founding dean Ariz. State U. Coll. Public Programs, 1979-80; prof. public affairs Ariz. State U., 1980—, finance educator, v.p. bus. affairs, 1981-83, dep. dir. intercollegiate athletics, 1984-85, dir. strategic planning, 1987-88. Contbr. articles to public affairs and mil. jours. Mem. Ariz. Steering Com. for Restoration of the State Capitol, 1974-75, Ariz. State Personnel Bd., 1978-83, Ariz. Regulatory Coun., 1981-93. Decorated D.S.M., Silver Star, also Legion of Merit with 4 oak leaf clusters, Bronze Star with 2 oak leaf clusters, Air medal, Army Commendation medal with 1 oak leaf cluster, Combat Inf. badge. Mem. Ariz. Acad. Public Adminstrn., Pi Alpha Alpha (pres. chpt. 1976-82). Clubs: Army-Navy (Washington); Arizona (Phoenix). Home: 12000 N 90th St Apt 3072 Scottsdale AZ 85260-8635 Office: Ariz State U Sch Pub Affairs Tempe AZ 85287-0603

SADAO, SHOJI, architect; b. Los Angeles, Jan. 2, 1927; s. Riichi and Otatsu (Kodama) S.; m. Tsuneko Sawada, Apr. 8, 1972. B.Arch., Cornell U., 1954; Fulbright scholar, Waseda U., Tokyo, 1956-57. Designer Geodesics, Inc., Raleigh, N.C., 1954-56; job capt. Edison Price, Inc., N.Y.C., 1959-64; v.p. Fuller & Sadao (P.C.), Long Island City, N.Y., 1965—; assoc. prof. archtl. design Sch. Architecture and Environ. Design, SUNY, Buffalo, 1976-77. Works include Dymaxion World Map, 1954; co-designer works include, U.S. Pavilion at Montreal Expo 67. Trustee and exec. dir. Isamu Noguchi Found., Long Island City, N.Y., 1989—. With AUS, 1945-49. Mem. Japan Soc., Yamashita Sekkei Archs. and Engrs. (U.S. rep. 1989—), The Century Assn. Address: Fuller & Sadao 32-37 Vernon Blvd Long Island City NY 11106-4926

SADDLEMYER, ANN (ELEANOR SADDLEMYER), educator, critic, theater historian; b. Prince Albert, Sask., Can., Nov. 28, 1932; d. Orrin Angus and Elsie Sarah (Ellis) S. BA, U. Sask., 1953, DLitt, 1991; MA, Queen's U., 1956, LLD (hon.), 1977; PhD, U. London, 1961; DLitt (hon.), U. Victoria, 1989, McGill U., 1989, Windsor U., 1990. Lectr. Victoria (B.C.) Coll., 1956-57, instr., 1960-62, asst. prof., 1962-65; assoc. prof. U. Victoria, 1965-68, prof. English, 1968-71; prof. English Victoria Coll. U. Toronto, 1971-95; prof., dir. Grad. Ctr. for Study of Drama, U. Toronto, 1972-77, 85-86; prof. emerita Grad Ctr. for Study of Drama, U. Toronto, 1995—; sr. fellow Massey Coll., 1975-88, master, 1988-95, master emerita, 1995—; Berg prof. NYU, 1975. Dir. Theatre Plus, 1972-84; dir. Colin Smythe Pubs.; author: (with Robin Skelton) The World of W.B. Yeats, 1965, In Defence of Lady Gregory, Playwright, 1966, Synge and Modern Comedy, 1968, J.M. Synge Plays Books One and Two, 1968, Lady Gregory Plays, 4 vols., 1970, Letters to Molly: Synge to Maire O'Neill, 1971, Letters from Synge to W.B. Yeats and Lady Gregory, 1971, Collected Letters of John Millington Synge, Vol. 1, 1983, vol. II, 1984, Theatre Business, The Correspondence of the First Abbey Theatre Directors, 1982, (with Colin Smythe) Lady Gregory Fifty Years After, 1987, Early Stages: Theatre in Ontario, 1980-1914, 1990; (with Richard Plant) Later Stages: Theatre in Ontario, 1914-1970s, 1997; co-editor Theatre History in Canada, 1980-86; editorial bds. Modern Drama, 1972-82, English Studies in Can., 1973-83, Themes in Drama, 1974—, Shaw Rev., 1977—, Research in the Humanities, 1976-90; Irish Univ. Rev., 1970—, Yeats Ann., 1982-86; Studies in Contemporary Irish Lit., 1986—; contbr. articles to profl. jours. Recipient Brit. Acad. Rose Mary Crawshay award, 1986, Disting. Svc. award Province of Ont., 1985, U. Toronto Alumni award of excellence, 1991; named Disting. Dau. of Pa., 1992, Woman of Distinction in Letters, Toronto, YWCA, 1994; Officer of Order of Can., 1995; Can. Coun. scholar, 1958-59, fellow, 1968, Guggenheim fellow, 1968, 77, sr. rsch. fellow Connaught, 1985. Fellow Royal Soc. Can., Royal Soc. Arts; mem. Internat. Assn. Study Anglo-Irish Lit. (chmn. 1973-76), Assn. Can. Theatre Rsch. (pres. 1976-77), Can. Assn. Irish Studies, Assn. Can. Univ. Tchrs. English, Can. Assn. Univ. Tchrs., Assn. Can. and Que. Lit. Home: 10876 Madrona Dr, Sidney, BC Canada V8L 5NR

SADDLER, DONALD EDWARD, choreographer, dancer; b. Van Nuys, Calif., Jan. 24, 1920; s. Elmer Edward and Mary Elizabeth (Roberts) S. Student, Los Angeles City Coll., 1939; dance pupil of, Carmalita Maracci, Anton Dolin, Anthony Tudor, Madame Anderson Ivantzova. Mem. Ballet Theatre, N.Y.C., 1940-43, 46-47; asst. dir., then artistic dir. Harkness Ballet, N.Y.C., 1964-70; exec. v.p. Rebekah Harkness Found., 1967-69; mem. exec. bd. Internat. Ballet Corp., 1979; prodr. N.Y. Dance Festival, Delacorte Theatre; guest artist Valerie Bettis Co. Stage appearances include Grand Canyon Suite, 1937, High Button Shoes, 1947, Dance Me A Song, 1950, Bless You All, 1950, The Song of Norway, 1951, Winesburg, Ohio, 1958, The Golden Round, 1960, The Castle Period, 1961, Happy Birthday, Mr. Abbot!, 1987, (with the Ballet Theatre, N.Y.C.) Bluebeard, Billy the Kid, Swan Lake, Aurora's Wedding, Les patineurs, Lilac Garden, Gala Performance, Romeo and Juliet, Peter and the Wolf, (television) Holiday Hotel, 1950; choreographer: (theatre) Blue Mountain Ballads, 1948, Wish Your Were Here, 1952, Wonderful Town, 1952 (Tony award for choreography 1953), 55, John Murray Anderson's Almanac, 1953, Tobia la Candida Spia, 1954 (Maschera d'Argento 1954), La patrona di raddio di luna, 1955, Shangri-La, 1956, Buona notte Bettina, 1956, L'adorabile Giulio, 1957, Winesburg, Ohio, 1958, This Property is Condemned, 1958, Un trapezio per Lisistrata, 1958, When in Rome, 1959, Un manderino per Teo, 1959, Dreams of Glory, 1961, Milk and Honey, 1961, Sophie, 1963, Morning Sun, 1963, To Broadway, With Love, 1964, No, No, Nanette, 1971 (Tony award for choreography 1971, Drama Desk award for choreography 1971), 73, Much Ado About Nothing, 1972 (Tony award nomination for choreography 1973), Fanfare Gala, 1973, Good News, 1973, Tricks, 1973, The Merry Wives of Windsor, 1974, Miss Moffat, 1974, A Midsummer Night's Dream, 1975, A Doll's House, 1975, A Gala Tribute to Joshua Logan, 1975, Rodgers and Hart, 1975, The Robber Bridegroom, 1975, 1976, Koshare, 1976, Vaudeville, 1976, Dear Friends and Gentle Hearts, 1976, Icedancing, 1978, The Grand Tour, 1979, A Long Way to Boston, 1979, Happy New Year, 1980, Hey Look Me Over!, 1981, Pardon, Monsieur Moliere, 1982, On Your Toes, 1983 (Tony award nomination for choreography 1983), The Loves of Anatol, 1985, The Golden Land, 1985, Broadway, 1987, The Student Prince, 1987, Teddy and Alice, 1987, My Fair Lady, 1993, The Boys from Syracuse, Aida, La Perichole, The Merry Widow, Tropicana, (tours) We Take This Town, 1962, Knickerbocker Holiday, 1971, No, No, Nanette, 1971-73, Good News, 1973-74, Hellzapoppin', 1976-77, On Your Toes, 1984, (films) April in Paris, 1952, By the Light of the Silvery Moon, 1953, Young at Heart, 1954, The Main Attraction, 1963, The Happy Hooker, 1975, Radio Days, 1987, (television) Holiday Hotel, 1950, The Perry Como Show, 1950, Canozionissima, 1959-60, Bell Telephone Hour, 1961-64, Much Ado About Nothing, 1973, Tony award broadcasts, 1973, 75-78, 83, Verna: U.S.O. Girl, 1978; dir., choreographer: (theatre) Wonderful Town, 1955, (tour) Oh, Kay!, 1978, A Celebration for Sir Anton Dolin, 1984, 100 Years of Performing Arts at the Metropolitan, 1984, Kiss Me Kate, 1989, American Ballet Theatre's Fortieth Anniversary, Tribute to Lucille Lortel, Tribute to Richard Rodgers, Merman-Martin Gala, Tribute to Cy Coleman, An Evening with Kurt Weill, Jo Sullivan in Concert, Tribute to George Abbott, Tribute to Lerner and Loewe, Stratford Shakespeare Festival Gala, American Guild of Musical Artists 100th Anniversary Gala, (operas) Bitter Sweet, Weiner Blut, Abduction fron the Seraglio, Washington Opera Follies; dir.: (theatre) Berlin to Broadway with Kurt Weill, 1972, George Abbott...A Celebration, 1976, Life with Father, 1982, I Hear Music...of Frank Loesser and Friends, 1984, State Fair Music Hall, Dallas, 1957, 59, Carousel Theatre, Framingham, Mass., 1958, Stratford Shakespeare Festival, 1979; prodr.: (theatre) The Sol Hurok Birthday Gala, 1973, The 30th Anniversary of City Center Theatre, 1975, (with Martin Feinstein) The Pre-Inaugural Ballet-Opera Gala, 1981, The Dance Collection Gala, 1972, The 35th Anniversary of the American Ballet Theatre, 1975, The Cynthia Gregory Gala. Recipient Dance Mag. award, 1984. Address: Coleman-Rosenberg 155 E 55th St Apt 5D New York NY 10022-4039*

SADDLER, GEORGE FLOYD, government economic adviser; b. Memphis, Sept. 27, 1925; s. Henry Rutherford and Ludorn Myrtle (Woods) S.; m. Pauline Evelyn McKissack, Jan. 3, 1944 (dec. Aug. 1988); children: Paula Frederica, Paulette Yvonne. BS, NYU, 1950; postgrad. Northwestern U., Chgo., 1954, U. Chgo., 1961-62. Supr. acctg. dept. Aldens, Inc., Chgo., 1950-57; sr. acct. City of Chgo., 1957-65; internat. adminstrn. officer U.S. Dept. State, Washington, 1965-68; chief budget sect. UN, N.Y.C., 1968-74; dir. fin. UN Devel. Program, N.Y.C., 1974-78; minister-counselor U.S. Mission to UN, N.Y.C., 1978-81; asst. dir. gen. UNESCO, Paris, 1981-86; sr. econ. adviser U.S. Mission to UN, N.Y.C., 1986-89; sr. advisor, cons. UN Orgns., 1989-96; pres. Assn. Former Internat. Civil Servants in N.Y., 1994—, Riverdale chpt. of the UN Assn. of the U.S. Served as cpl. U.S. Army, 1944-46.

SADE (HELEN FOLASADE ADU), singer, songwriter; b. Ibadan, Nigeria, 1959; d. Adebisi Adu and Anne. BA, St. Martin's Coll. of Art, London, 1979. Mem. band Sade; recording artist Epic, A Division of Sony Music, N.Y.C. Albums include Diamond Life, 1984, Promise, 1985, Stronger Than Pride, 1988, Love Deluxe, 1992, Cherish the Day, 1993, The Best of Sade, 1994, Sweetback, 1997; singles include Smooth Operator, 1984. Recipient Grammy award Best New Artist, 1986, Best R&B duo or group performance for "No Ordinary Love", 1994. Office: Epic Records 550 Madison Ave New York NY 10019*

SADE, DONALD STONE, anthropology educator; b. Charleston, W.Va., July 17, 1937; s. Samuel and Charlotte Tracy (Stone) S.; m. Bonita Diane Chepko, Dec. 24, 1971 (div. Feb. 1994); children: Irony Cuervo del Norte, Omen Ondatra; m. Kerry L. Knox, Nov. 24, 1994. Grad., N.Y. State Ranger Sch., 1957; student, Hamilton Coll., 1957-60; A.B., U. Calif., Berkeley, 1963, Ph.D., 1966. Instr. anthropology Northwestern U., Evanston, Ill., 1965-66; asst. prof. Northwestern U., 1966-70, asso. prof., 1970-75, prof., 1975-95; scientist-in-charge Cayo Santiago, U. P.R., 1970-77; founder, pres. North Country Inst. for Natural Philosophy, Inc., Mexico, N.Y., 1980—. Sr. author: Basic Demographic Observations on Free-Ranging Rhesus Monkeys, 3 vols., 1985; editor: The North Country Naturalist, Vol. 1, 1987. NSF grantee, 1967—. Mem. AAAS, Am. Assn. Phys. Anthropologists, Am. Soc. Mammalogists, Animal Behavior Soc. Office: North Country Inst for Natural Philosophy Inc 18 Emery Rd Mexico NY 13114-3311 *I have never given undue heed to the opinions of others regarding my work or character.*

SADEGH, ALI M., mechanical engineering educator, researcher, consultant; b. Tehran, Iran, Sept. 1, 1950; came to U.S., 1974; s. Saleh S. Mir-Mohamad-Sadegh and Asam Lotfi; m. Guita Miremadi, July 10, 1980; children: Mietra, Cameron, Mona, Jasmin, David. BS in Mech. Engring., Arya-Mehr U. Tech., Tehran, 1972; MS in Mech. Engring., Mich. State U., 1975, PhD in Mechanics, 1978; postdoctoral, U. Mich., 1979. Registered profl. engr., Mich.; cert. mfg. engr. Design engr. Nat. Radio engring. sect., Tehran, 1972-74; rsch. and teaching asst. Mich. State U., East Lansing, 1975-78; postdoctoral scholar U. Mich., Ann Arbor, 1978-79; asst. prof. Arya-Mehr U. Tech., 1979-81; vis. asst. prof. Mich. State U., 1981-82; asst. prof. CUNY, N.Y.C., 1982-87, assoc. prof., 1987-91, prof., 1991—, chmn. dept. mech. engring., 1992-96, tchr. courses in solid mechanics, design and CAD/CAM; cons. Devel. Iranian Heavy Industries, Tehran, 1979-81; tech. cons. AC Rochester Gen. Motors Co., 1986-92; cons. to numerous industries, 1988—; expert witness, 1990—. Contbr. some 80 articles to profl. and sci. jours., 43 tech. reports, also presentations to nat. and internat. confs.; holder 3 U.S. patents. Recipient 32 rsch. awards NSF, AT&T Found., PSC-CUNY, others. Fellow ASME (Best Paper award 1992, Melville medal 1993), Soc. Mfg. Engrs. (chmn. chpt. 320); mem. Am. Acad. Mechanics, Biomed. Engrs. Soc., Sigma Xi. Avocations: tennis, swimming, soccer. Home: 33 Greenway Ct Closter NJ 07624-2201 Office: CUNY Dept Mech Engring 140th St and Convent Ave New York NY 10031

SADEGHI-NEJAD, ABDOLLAH, pediatrician, educator; b. Meshed, Iran, Apr. 29, 1938; s. Abdolhossein and Azizeh (Jabbari) S.-N.; m. Marion M. Marquardt, Jan. 26, 1974; children; Nathan R., Adrienne R. BA, Beloit Coll., 1960; MS in Pathology, U. Chgo., 1964, MD, 1964. Diplomate Am. Bd. Pediatrics. Intern then resident U. Chgo., 1964-67; fellow pediatric endocrinology New Eng. Med. Ctr., Boston, 1967-69, U. Calif., San Francisco, 1969-70; from asst. prof. to prof. pediatrics Tufts U., Boston, 1970—; chief pediatric endocrinology and metabolism divsn. New Eng. Med. Ctr., Boston, 1989—. Author and co-author books and articles. Mem. town meeting Town of Brookline, Mass., 1987—, mem. adv. com., 1993—; founder, mem. Friends of Lost Pond. Fellow Am. Acad. Pediatrics; mem. Am. Pediatric Soc., Am. Diabetes Assn., Endocrine Soc., European Soc. Pediatric Rsch., Lawson Wilkins Pediat. Endocrine Soc., Soc. Pediat. Rsch. Office: New Eng Med Ctr 750 Washington St Boston MA 02111-1526

SADER, CAROL HOPE, former state legislator; b. Bklyn., July 19, 1935; d. Nathan and Mollie (Farkas) Shimkin; m. Harold M. Sader, June 9, 1957; children: Neil, Randi Sader Friedlander, Elisa. BA, Barnard Coll., Columbia U., 1957. Sch. tchr. Bd. Edn., Morris, Conn., 1957-58; legal editor W. H. Anderson Co., Cin., 1974-78; freelance legal editor Shawnee Mission, Kans., 1978-87; mem. Kans. Ho. of Reps., 1987-94; chair Ho. Pub. Health and Welfare Com., 1991-92; chair Joint Ho. and Senate Com. on Health Care Decisions for the 90's, 1992; vice chair Ho. Econ. Devel. Com., 1991-92; policy chair Ho. Dem. Caucus, 1993-94; appointee Kans. judicial qualifications commn. Kans. Supreme Ct., 1995—. Dem. candidate for Kans. Lt. Gov., 1994; chmn. bd. trustees Johns County C.C., Overland Park, Kans., 1984-86, trustee Johnson County Cmty. Coll., 1981-86; pres. League of Women Voters, Johnson County, 1983-85; State of Kans. League of Women Voters Bd, 1986-87; bd. dirs. United Cmty. Svcs. of Johnson County Shawnee Mission, 1984-92, Jewish Vocat. Svc. Bd., 1983-92; chmn. Kans. State Holocaust Commn., 1991-94; pres. Mainstream Coalition of Johnson County, 1995-97. Recipient Trustee award Assn. of Women in Jr. and C.C., 1985, awards Kans. Pub. Transit Assn., 1990, AARP, 1992, Assn. Kans. Theater, 1992, Nat. Coun. Jewish Women, 1992, Kans. Assn. Osteo. Medicine, 1992, Kans. Chiropractic Assn., 1992, United Com. Svcs. Johnson County, 1992, Disting. Pub. Svcs. award Johnson County, 1993, Hallpac Kans. Pub. Svc. award Hallmark Cards, Inc., 1993. Mem. Coun. Women Legislators, Phi Delta Kappa. Democrat. Avocations: lakehouse, theatre, travel, granparenting. Home: 8612 Linden Dr Shawnee Mission KS 66207-1807

SADIK, MARVIN SHERWOOD, art consultant, former museum director; b. Springfield, Mass., June 27, 1932; s. Harry Benjamin and Florence (Askinas) S. A.B. magna cum laude, Harvard U., 1954, A.M., 1960; D.F.A. (hon.), Bowdoin Coll., Brunswick, Maine, 1978. Curatorial asst. Worcester (Mass.) Art Mus., 1955-57; curator Mus. Art Bowdoin Coll., 1961-64, dir., 1964-67; dir. Mus. Art U. Conn. at Storrs, 1967-69, Nat. Portrait Gallery, Washington, 1969-81; cons. Am. and European art, 1981—; mem. bd.

visitors Edmund S. Muskie Sch. Pub. Svcs.; bd. overseers Strawbery Banke, Portsmouth, N.H. Author: Colonial and Federal Portraits at Bowdoin College, 1966, The Drawings of Hyman Bloom, 1968, The Paintings of Charles Hawthorne, 1968, Christian Gullager: Portrait Painter to Federal America, 1976; co-author: American Portrait Drawings, 1980. Decorated knight Order Dannebrog Denmark; recipient Maine State Art award, 1975, gold medal for exceptional svc. Smithsonian Instn., 1981; Harris fellow, 1957-61; Barr fellow, 1957-61. Fellow Pierpont Morgan Library; mem. Am. Antiquarian Soc., Colonial Soc. Mass. (corr.). Clubs: Century Assn, Grolier. Home: PO Box 6360 Scarborough ME 04070-6360

SADLER, DAVID GARY, management executive; b. Iowa City, Mar. 14, 1939; s. Edward Anthony and Elsie June (Sherman) S.; m. Karen Sadler. Student, St. Ambrose Coll., 1957-59; BS in Indsl. Adminstrn. and Prodn., Kent State U., 1961. Various mgmt. positions Ford Motor Co., Lorain, Ohio, 1962-67, Sperry-New Holland, Lebanon, Ohio, 1967-71; mgr. mfg. Allis Chalmer, Springfield, Ill., 1971-72; dir. mfg. Purolator, Inc., Fayetteville, N.C., 1972-73; v.p. mfg. farm equipment and ops. truck div. White Motor Co., Eastlake, Ohio and Chgo., 1973-78; corp. v.p. mfg. Massey Ferguson Ltd., Toronto, Ont., Can., 1978-80; corp. v.p. mfg. Internat. Harvester, Chgo., 1980-81, sr. v.p. ops. staff, 1981-82, v.p. bus. devel., 1982, pres. diversified group, 1982-83, pres. internat. group, 1983-85; pres. AMI, Inc., Chgo., 1985-86; vice chmn., chief exec. officer Savin Corp., Stamford, Conn., 1986, chmn., chief exec. officer, 1986-89, also bd. dirs.; pres. Asset Mgmt. Internat., Westport, Conn., 1989-95; chmn., CEO, Rowe Internat., Grand Rapids, Mich., 1995—, also bd. dirs. Bd. dirs. greater Chgo. Safety Coun., 1981-84; mem. adb. bd. Hellmond Assocs. Opportunity Fund II. Roman Catholic. Home: 751 Bradford Farms Ln NE Grand Rapids MI 49546-1188 Office: Rowe International 1500 Union Ave SE Grand Rapids MI 49507-1830

SADLER, GRAHAM HYDRICK, library administrator; b. Sikeston, Mo., Aug. 17, 1931; s. Philip Landis and Montie Pearl (Hydrick) S.; m. Betty A. Grugett, Nov. 22, 1950; children—Graham Hydrick, Lee, Susan, Harrison. B.S., S.E. Mo. State Coll., 1952; M.L.S., Emory U., 1957. Asst. libr. S.E. Mo. State Coll., Cape Girardeau, 1954-61; adminstrv. libr. Kinderhook Regional Libr., Lebanon, Mo., 1961-66; dir. Fort Lewis Coll. Libr., Durango, Colo., 1966-67; assoc. prof. librarianship Kans. State Tchrs. Coll., Emporia, 1967-69; asst. libr., dir. community svc. Denver Pub. Libr., 1970-77; dir. County of Henrico Pub. Libr., Richmond, Va., 1978-94, ret., 1994; mem. adv. com. Office of Library Service to Disadvantaged, 1978-91. Mem. ALA (membership com. 1989-92).

SADLER, LUTHER FULLER, JR., lawyer; b. Jacksonville, Fla., Apr. 10, 1942; s. Luther Fuller and Jane Grey (Lloyd) S.; children: Catherine Winchester, Anna Stephenson Lloyd. BA, Yale U., 1964, LLB, 1967. Bar: Fla. 1967. Ptnr. Mahoney, Hadlow, Chambers & Adams, Jacksonville, 1967-81, Commander, Legler, Werber, Dawes, Sadler & Howell, Jacksonville, 1982-91, Foley & Lardner, Jacksonville, 1991—; gen. counsel Jacksonville C. of C., 1987. Trustee Jacksonville Mus. of Contemporary Art, 1984-94, Episcopal Child Care and Devel. Ctrs., Inc., 1990-94. Lt. USNR, 1967-73. Mem. ABA, Fla. Bar Assn. (chmn. corp. banking and bus. law sect. 1979-80), Timuquana Country Club. Episcopalian. Office: Foley & Lardner PO Box 240 200 N Laura St Jacksonville FL 32202-3528

SADLER, ROBERT LIVINGSTON, banker; b. Beloit, Kans., Dec. 19, 1935; s. D.M. and Retha (Livingston) S.; m. E. Elllen Lewis, July 14, 1957; children: Diane, Julia. AB, Baker U., 1958; MBA, Ind. U., 1959; student, Stonier Grad. Sch. Banking, Rutgers U., 1970. Dir. alumni relations Baker U., Baldwin, Kans., 1957-58; indsl. engr. Colgate-Palmolive Co., N.Y.C., 1958-60, pers. mgr., 1961-64, product mgr., 1964-65; v.p. pers. and adminstrv. svcs. Old Kent Bank & Trust Co., Grand Rapids, Mich., 1965-72, exec. v.p., 1972-86; exec. v.p. Old Kent Fin. Corp., Grand Rapids, 1972-89, vice chmn., 1989—; pres. Old Kent Bank, Grand Rapids, 1994-95, pres., CEO, 1995—. Pres. Grand Rapids Jr. Achievement, 1976; pres. United Way Kent County, 1982; chmn. Grand Rapids Found., 1987; Davenport Coll. Bus., Grand Rapids. Mem. Am. Bankers Assn. (chmn. communications council 1980—, dir. 1982-83), Sigma Iota Epsilon, Delta Mu Delta. Republican. Methodist. Clubs: Cascade Country (dir. 1978-80); University (Grand Rapids). Office: Old Kent Fin Corp 1 Vandenburg Ctr NW Grand Rapids MI 49503-2406

SADLER, SALLIE INGLIS, psychotherapist; b. Phila., Nov. 16, 1941; d. H. Barton Off and Janet (Miller) Nelson; m. William A. Sadler, Jr., Apr. 23, 1977; children: Bill, Lisa, Nelson, Ashley, Kirsten. BA, Rollins Coll., Winter Park, Fla., 1964; MSW with high acad. achievement, Rutgers U., 1979; postgrad., Pa. State U., 1986-89. Cert. social worker. Caseworker II, dir. group work Family and Children's Svc. West Essex, Caldwell, N.J., 1979-81; dir. Single Parent Ctr. West Essex, Montclair, N.J., 1981-85; pvt. practice Upper Montclair, N.J., 1981-85; chief clin. svcs. Family Svc. Ctr., U.S. Naval Air Base, Alameda, Calif., 1990-95; sr. psychiat. social worker dept. psychiatry Kaiser Permanente Med. Ctr., San Francisco, 1995—; oral license examiner Calif. Bd. Behavioral Sci. Examiners; adj. instr. div. social scis. Bloomfield (N.J.) Coll., 1979-81, N.J. Inst. Tech., 1984-85; instr. psychology dept. Lock Haven (Pa.) U., 1985-90. Mem. NASW, APA, Assn. Women Faculty in Higher Edn. Avocations: skiing, sailing, aerobics, cooking.

SADLER, THEODORE R., JR., thoracic and cardiovascular surgeon; b. St. Louis, Mar. 26, 1930; s. Theodore R. and Nellie R. (Guffey) S.; m. Roberta Cary Moody, Nov. 26, 1953; children: Michael, Patrick, Susan, Daniel, Shelley. AB, U. Mo., 1951, BS in Medicine, 1954; MD, Washington U., 1956. Diplomate Am. Bd. Thoracic and Cardiovascular Surgery. Commd. U.S. Army, 1956, advanced through grades to brig. gen., 1990; chief of surgery Noble Army Hosp., Ft. McClellans, Ala., 1964-66; comdr. 3d Surgery Hosp., Vietnam, 1966-67; chief thoracic surgery Fitzsimmons Army Hosp., Denver, 1968-71; resigned U.S. Army, 1971, with Res., 1971-82; comdr. 181st Thoracic Detachment, 1971-73, 5502d U.S. Army Hosp. Augmentation Fitzsimmons Army Hosp., Denver, 1974-77; brig. gen. 2d Hosp. Ctr., Hamilton AFB, Calif., 1977-81; ret. Res. U.S. Army, 1990; rotating intern Walter Reed Hosp., Washington, 1956-57; resident in gen. surgery Brooke Gen. Hosp., San Antonio, 1958-61, resident thoracic and cardiovascular surgery, 1964-66; practice medicine specializing in thoracic and cardiovascular surgery St. Joseph's Hosp. and Presbyn. Hosp., Denver, 1971-88; comdr. 147th U.S. Army Hosp. Colo. N.G., 1987-90; mem. staff St. Mary' Hosp., Grand Junction, 1988—, Community Hosp., Hilltop Rehab. Hosp., 1989—; ret.; cons. to surgeon gen. Fitzsimmons Army Hosp., 1983—, VA Hosp., Grand Junction, 1989—; past pres. bd. dirs. St. Joseph's Hosp. Contbr. articles to profl. jours. Vice chmn. Bd. of Health and Hosps., 1982-88; mem. Commn. Mental Health, Denver, 1985-88. Fellow ACS, Am. Coll. Chest Physicians; mem. Soc. Thoracic Surgeons, Western Thoracic Assn., AMA, Colo. Med. Soc. (pres.-elect 1986, bd. dirs., house speaker, pres. 1987-88), Denver Med. Soc. (bd. dirs., past pres.), Mesa County Med. Soc. (bd. dirs. 1989—), Rocky Mounty Individual Physicians Assn. (bd. dirs. 1990—). Republican. Presbyterian. Clubs: Denver Athletic, Bookcliff Country, Metropolitan. Avocations: golf, sports, stamp collecting. Home: 2680 Kimberly Dr Grand Junction CO 81506-1850 Office: 425 Patterson Rd Ste 506 Grand Junction CO 81506-1910

SADLOCK, RICHARD ALAN, lawyer; b. Paterson, N.J., Aug. 26, 1961; s. George Edward and Joan Theresa (Godleski) S.; m. Patricia Ellen Roth, Sept. 27, 1986; children: Joshua David, Tessa. BA, Gettysburg Coll., 1983; JD cum laude, Vt. Law Sch., 1986. Bar: Pa. 1986, U.S. Dist. Ct. (mid. dist.) Pa. 1987, U.S. Ct. Appeals (3rd cir.) 1991, U.S. Dist. Ct. (ea. dist.) Pa. 1993. Assoc. Angino & Rovner, P.C., Harrisburg, Pa., 1986—; mediator U.S. Dist. Ct. Middle Dist. Pa. Mem. Pa. Bar Assn., Dauphin County Bar Assn., Assn. Trial Lawyers Am., Pa. Trial Lawyers Assn. (speaker 1989—), Am. Arbitration Assn. (arbitrator). Roman Catholic. Avocations: tennis, golf, reading, weight lifting. Office: Angino & Rovner PC 4503 N Front St Harrisburg PA 17110-1708

SADOCK, BENJAMIN JAMES, psychiatrist, educator; b. N.Y.C., Dec. 22, 1933; s. Samuel William and Gertrude S.; m. Virginia Alcott, Oct. 20, 1963; children: James William, Victoria Anne. A.B., Union Coll., 1955; M.D., N.Y. Med. Coll., 1959. Rotating intern Albany (N.Y.) Hosp., 1959-60; resident Bellevue Psychiat. Hosp., N.Y.C., 1960-63; instr. psychiatry Southwestern Med. Sch., Dallas, 1964-65, N.Y. Med. Coll., N.Y.C., 1965-67; asst. prof. N.Y. Med. Coll., 1967-71, assoc. prof., 1972-74, prof., 1975-80, dir. student health psychiatry, 1980—; prof. psychiatry NYU Sch Medicine, 1981—, vice chmn. dept. psychiatry, 1984—; attending physician Lenox Hill Hosp.; attending psychiatrist Tisch Univ. Hosp. of NYU Med. Ctr., Bellevue Hosp.; cons. psychiatrist Franklin Delano Roosevelt VA Hosp., 1970-78, U.S. Dept. State, 1980-81, P.R. Inst. Psychiatry, 1976-80; examiner Am. Bd. Psychiatry and Neurology, 1970—; mem. conf. on recert. Am. Bd. Med. Spltys.-Am. Psychiat. Assn., 1974; mem. Commn. on Continuing Edn. in Psychiatry, NIMH-Am. Psychiat. Assn., 1974-75. Co-author: Comprehensive Group Psychotherapy, 1971, 3d edit., 1993, Synopsis of Psychiatry, 1972, 4th edit., 1985, 5th edit., 1989, 6th edit., 1991, 7th edit., 1994, The Sexual Experience, 1976, Study Guide Modern Synopsis of Psychiatry, 1983, 2d edit., 1985, 3d edit., 1989, 4th edit., 1991, 5th edit., 1994, Comprehensive Textbook of Psychiatry, 5th edit., 1988, 6th edit., 1995, Pocket Handbook of Clinical Psychiatry, 1991, 2d edit., 1995, Comprehensive Glossary of Psychiatry and Psychology, 1991, Pocket Handbook of Drug Treatment in Psychiatry, 1992, 2d edit., 1995, Pocket Handbook of Psychiatric Emergency Medicine, 1993, Pocket Handbook of Primary Care Psychiatry, 1996; contbr. articles on psychiat. edn., individual and group psychotherapy, diagnosis and treatment psychiat. and sexual disorders to med. jours.; contbr. to Ency. Americana. Fellow Am. Psychiat. Assn. (treas. N.Y. County dist. br. 1973-76, mem. conf. on psychiatry and med. edn. 1967), N.Y. Acad. Medicine, A.C.P.; mem. AMA, Med. Soc. County and State N.Y., N.Y. Acad. Scis., Am. Group Psychotherapy Assn., World Psychiat. Assn., Royal Soc. Medicine (London), Psychiat. Soc. N.Y. Med. Coll. (founder, pres. 1975-79), N.Y. Med. Coll. Alumni Assn. (gov. 1965-90), NYU-Bellevue Psychiat. Soc. (pres. 1981—), Alpha Omega Alpha. Office: 4 E 89th St New York NY 10128-0636 also: NYU Med Ctr 550 1st Ave New York NY 10016-6481

SADOFF, ROBERT LESLIE, psychiatrist; b. Mpls., Feb. 8, 1936; s. Max and Rose C. (Karroll) S.; m. Joan A. Handleman, June 21, 1959; children—Debra, David, Julie, Sherry. B.A., U. Minn., 1956, B.S., 1957, M.D., 1959; M.S., UCLA, 1963. Intern Los Angeles VA Hosp., 1959-60; resident UCLA, 1960-63; asst. prof. psychiatry Temple U., Phila., 1966-72; clin. prof. psychiatry U. Pa., Phila., 1972—; lectr. in law Villanova U., 1972-85. Author: (with Marvin Lewis) Psychic Injuries, 1975; Forensic Psychiatry, 1975, 2d edit., 1988; Legal Issues in the Care of Psychiatric Patients, 1982, Violence and Responsibility, 1988; (with Robert I. Simon) Psychiatric Malpractice, 1992; editor: Psychiatric Clinics of North America, 1984. Bd. dirs. Joseph T. Peters Inst., Phila., 1980-92 . Served to capt. U.S. Army, 1963-65. Recipient Earl Bond award U. Pa., 1979, VIIth Annual Nathaniel Winkelman award Phila. Psychiat. Ctr., 1988, Manfred Guttmacher award Am. Psychiat. Assn., 1992. Fellow Am. Psychiat. Assn., Am. Coll. Psychiatrists, Am. Coll. Legal Medicine; mem. AMA, Am. Acad. Psychiatry and Law (pres. 1971-73), Internat. Soc. for Philos. Enquiry (mentor 1987—), Am. Red Magen David for Israel (nat. pres. 1987—), Internat. Acad. Law and Mental Health (bd. dirs. 1989—, Philippe Pinel award 1995) . Avocation: collecting antique books in law and medicine. Office: Benjamin Fox Pavilion Ste 326 Jenkintown PA 19046

SADOSKI, MARK CHRISTIAN, education educator; b. Bristol, Conn., June 2, 1945; s. Waldmyr John Sadoski and Ruth Elaine (Gustafson) Kantorski; m. Carol Ann Bove, June 28, 1969; 1 child, Thomas Christian. BS, So. Conn. State U., 1968, MS, 1973; PhD, U. Conn., 1981. Cert. reading, English, social studies tchr. Tchr., reading cons. Milford (Conn.) Pub. Schs., 1968-81; assoc. faculty So. Conn. State U., New Haven, 1978-81; prof. edn. Tex. A&M Univ., College Station, 1981—. Mem. editl. bd. Reading Reasearch Quarterly, 1989—, Jour. Reading Behavior, 1990-95, Reading Psychology, 1990—, Jour. Literacy Rsch., 1995—; contbr. over 60 articles to profl. jours. Accident prevention counselor S.W. region FAA, 1989-91. Recipient Disting. Alumnus award So. Conn. State U., 1994. Mem. Internat. Reading Assn. (outstanding dissertation award com. 1983-85, finalist Outstanding Dissertation award 1982), Nat. Reading Conf., Am. Ednl. Rsch. Assn. (outstanding book award com. 1994—), Soc. for Sci. Study of Reading (chair pubs. com. 1996—). Avocations: reading, cinema. Office: Tex A&M Univ Dept EDCI College Station TX 77843

SADOULET, BERNARD, astrophysicist, educator; b. Nice, France, Apr. 23, 1944; s. Maurice and Genevieve (Berard) S.; m. Elisabeth M.L. Chaine, Apr. 27, 1967; children: Loic, Helene, Samuel. Lic. in Physics., U. Paris, 1965; diploma, Ecole Polytechnique, Paris, 1965; Diploma in Theoretical Physics, U. Orsay, France, 1966, PhD in Phys. Scis., 1971. Fellow CERN, Berkeley, Calif., 1966-73; physicist, then sr. physicist CERN, France, 1976-84; postdoctoral fellow Lawrence Berkeley (Calif.) Nat. Lab., 1973-76; mem. faculty U. Calif., Berkeley, 1984—, prof. physics, 1985—, dir. Ctr. Particle Astrophysics, 1988—; mem. commn. astrophysics Internat. Union Pure and Applied Physics, 1991—; vis. com. Max Planck Inst., Heidelberg, Germany, 1991—, Fermilab, 1992—, Lawrence Livermore Nat. Lab., 1992—; mem. program initiation com. NAS, 1992; internat. adv. com. various profl. confs. Contbr. to Sky and Telescope, The Early Universe Observable from Diffuse Backgrounds, other profl. publs. Fellow Am. Phys. Soc., U.S. Nat. Res. Coun. (com. on astronomy & astrophysics 1992). Achievements include work on the problem of the dark matter which constitutes more than 90% of the mass of the universe; devel. of a high-pressure gas scintillation drift chamber; search for WIMPs using cryogenic detectors of phonons and ionization. Office: Univ Calif Berkeley Ctr Particle Astrophysics 301 Le Conte Hall Berkeley CA 94720

SADOVE, STEPHEN IRVING, consumer products company executive; b. Washington, July 25, 1951; s. A. Robert and Harriet (Tenenbaum) S.; m. Sandra Rozenberg, Feb. 24, 1982; children: Stacy, David, Laurie. BA, Hamilton Coll., 1973; MBA, Harvard U., 1975. Asst. product mgr. Gen. Foods Corp.-Desserts Div., White Plains, N.Y., 1975-76; assoc. product mgr. Gen. Foods Corp.-Desserts Div., White Plains, 1976-77, product mgr., 1977-80, group product mgr., 1980-82, category mgr., 1982-84; mktg. mgr. Gen. Foods Corp.-Meals Div., White Plains, 1984-86, bus. unit mgr., 1986-88, v.p., gen. mgr., 1988-89; exec. v.p., gen. mgr. Gen. Foods Corp.-Desserts Div., White Plains, 1989-91; pres. Clairol, Inc., 1991-96, Bristol-Meyers Squibb Beauty Care, Stamford, Conn., 1996—; alumni coun. Hamilton Coll., Clinton, N.Y.; bd. dirs. Saks Holdings. Bd. trustees Coun. for Arts in Westchester, White Plains, 1990—; bd. trustees Caramoor, Hazelden. Avocations: tennis, golf, reading, arts. Home: 6 Crest Ct Armonk NY 10504-2901 Office: Clairol Inc 1 Blachley Rd Stamford CT 06922-0002

SADOW, HARVEY S., health care company executive; b. N.Y.C., Oct. 6, 1922; s. Nat. and Frances Donna (Saveth) S.; m. Sylvia June Riber, Dec. 22, 1944 (div. 1966); children: Harvey Jr., Suzanne Gail, Todd Forrest, Gay Summer; m. Jacqueline Lucille Clavel, Jan. 24, 1969 (div. 1993); 1 adopted child, Daniel Jean marie; m. Mary Morrissey McSwiggan, July 13, 1995. BS, Va. Mil. Inst., Lexington, 1947; MS, U. Kans., 1949; PhD, U. Conn., 1953. Intelligence officer CIA, Washington, 1951-53; assoc. dir. rsch. Lakeside Labs., Inc., Milw., 1953-56; med. rsch. cons. Milw., 1956; dir. clin. rsch. U.S. Vitamin & Pharm. Corp., N.Y.C., 1957-64, v.p. rsch. and devel., 1964-68; sr. v.p. scientific affairs USV Pharm./Revlon Corp., N.Y.C., 1969-71; pres., CEO Boehringer Ingelheim, Ltd. (named changed to Boehringer Ingelheim Pharms., Inc. 1984), Ridgefield, Conn., 1971-88; pres., CEO Boehringer Ingelheim Corp., Ridgefield, 1984-88, chmn. bd., 1988-90; chmn. bd. Roxane Labs., Inc., Columbus, Ohio, 1981-88, Boehringer Ingelheim Animal Health, Inc., St. Joseph, Mo., 1981-88, Henley Co., N.Y.C., 1986-88, U. Conn. Rsch. and Devel. Corp., Storrs, 1984-87; bd. dirs. Cortex Pharms., Inc., Irvine, Calif., 1989—, chmn. bd., 1991—; bd. dirs. Cholestech Corp., Hayward, Calif., chmn. bd. 1992—; bd. dirs. Anika Rsch. Corp., Houghton Pharm., Inc., Penederm Corp.; mem. adv. bd. Salk Inst. Biotechnology-Indsl. Assocs., Inc., La Jolla, 1988-90; chmn. bd. dirs. Acacia Bioscis. Inc., 1996—. Co-author: Oral Treatment of Diabetes, 1967; author, co-author 23 papers on intermediary metabolism, diabetes, obesity and cardiovascular disease., 1963-72. Bd. dirs. Pharm. Mfrs. Assn., 1983-90; chmn. Pharm. Mfrs. Assn. Found., 1988-90; bd. dirs. Conn. Bd. Higher Edn., Hartford, 1977-83, Govs. Tech. Adv. Bd., Hartford, 1984-87; mem. Conn. Commn. on Bus. Opportunity, Def. Diversification and Indsl. Policy, 1991-93; mem. bd. visitors Va. Mil. Inst., Lexington, 1987—, pres. bd., 1991-95; chmn. bd. Comm. Law Enforcement Found., Hartford, 1981-86, 92—, U. Conn. Found., Storrs, 1984-87; chmn., pres.' coun. Am. Lung Assn., N.Y.C., 1986-87, York Sch., Monterey, Calif., 1988-89; trustee Conn. Coll., Groton, 1991-96, ALdrich Mus. Contemporary Art, Ridgefield, Conn., 1991—. Decorated Disting. Svc. Cross, Fed. Republic of Germany, 1987; recipient Univ. medal U. Conn., 1987, Recognition award Nat. Hypertension Assn., 1990, Humanitarian award Am. Lung Assn. Conn., 1993, Disting. Svc. award Conn. Innovations, Inc., 1996. Mem. Am. Soc. for Clin. Pharmacology and Therapeutics, Am. Fedn. for Clin. Rsch., Am. Diabetes Assn., Danbury C. of C. (Abraham Ribicoff Community Svc. award City of Danbury 1987, bd. dirs. 1978-81), Union League (N.Y.C.), Landmark Club (Stamford, Conn.), Masons, Sigma Xi, Sigma Pi Sigma, Phi Lambda Upsilon. Avocations: art collecting, photography, music, writing, golfing. Home and Office: 120-36 Prospect St Ridgefield CT 06877-4648

SADOWAY, DONALD ROBERT, materials science educator; b. Toronto, Mar. 7, 1950; s. Donald Anthony and Irene Mary (Romanko) S.; m. Sandra Lynn Mary Babij, Sept. 8, 1973 (div. Sept. 1996); children: Steven, Laryssa, Andrew; m. Anne Marie Mayes, Jan. 4, 1997. BASc, U. Toronto, 1972, MASc, 1973, PhD, 1977. Cert. in chem. metallurgy. Asst. prof. materials engring. MIT, Cambridge, 1978-82, assoc. prof., 1982-92, prof. materials chemistry, 1992—; MacVicar faculty fellow MIT, 1995—. Contbr. over 80 articles on electro and phys. chemistry to profl. jours.; patentee in field, U.S., Can., and Europe. Recipient Grad. Student Coun. Teaching award MIT, 1982, 84, 87, 88, 93, Prof. T.B. King Meml. award dept. materials sci. and engring. undergrad. students MIT, 1986; NATO postdoctoral fellow Nat. Rsch. Coun. Can., 1977; AT&T Faculty Fellow in Indsl. Ecology, 1993-95, MacVicar Faculty fellow, 1995—. Mem. AAAS, Minerals, Metals and Materials Soc., Electrochem. Soc., Internat. Soc. Electrochemistry. Home: 75 Trapelo Rd Waltham MA 02154-6303 Office: MIT # 8-109 77 Massachusetts Ave Cambridge MA 02139-4301

SADOWSKI, CAROL JOHNSON, artist; b. Chgo., Mar. 20, 1929; d. Carl Valdamar Johnson and Elizabeth Hilma (Booth) Johnson-Chellberg; m. Edmund Sadowski, July 9, 1949; children: Lynn Carol Mahoney, Christie Sadowski Cortez. AAS, Wright-Ill. Coll., 1949. Tchr. art Malverne (N.Y.) H.S., 1968-69; artist Valley Stream, N.Y., 1968-76, Hollywood, Fla., 1976—; guest speaker Mus. Art Ft. Lauderdale, Fla., 1991, others; TV appearances on WCGB, Gainesville, WSVN, Miami, Storer and Hollywood Cable. One-woman shows include Mus. Fla. History, 1984-85, 87, Hist. Mus. South Fla., Miami, 1986, Thomas Ctr. Arts, Gainesville, Gla., 1985, 87, Hist. Mus. South Fla., Miami, 1986, Thomas Ctr. Arts, Gainesville, Gla., 1985, 87, Elliott Mus., Stuart, Fla., 1987, Hemingway Mus. & Home, Key West, Fla., 1986, Mus. Fla. History, Tallahassee, 1985, 87, Alliance Francaise de Miami, 1995; commd. painting St. Agustin Antigua Found., St. Augustine, Fla., 1985, Atlantic Bank, Ft. Lauderdale, Fla., Bonnet House Fla. Trust, Ft. Lauderdale, Tropical Art Gallery, Naples, Fla., 1981-83, Tequesta (Fla.) Art Gallery, 1985-89, Gingerbread Square Gallery, Key West, 1990—, Wally Findlay Galleries, Inc., Palm Beach, 1996—, Key West Graphics, Tamarac. Recipient Hemingway medal Ernest Hemingway Mus., Cuba, 1990, appreciation award City of Hollywood. Mem. Internat. Platform Assn., Broward Art Guild, Fla. Hist. Assn., Ernest Hemingway Soc., Chopin Found., Am. Inst. for Polish Culture, Alliance Francaise de Miami, Women in the Arts Nat. Mus. (charter mem.). Avocations: travel, hiking, biking, swimming, reading. Home and Studio: 1480 Sheridan St Apt B-17 Hollywood FL 33020-2295 *I try to do my best at what I love to do, not for money or fame, but for self satisfaction.*

SADOWSKI, JOHN STANLEY, utility executive; b. Maspeth, N.Y., Oct. 29, 1948; s. John Thomas and Mary Ann (Roman) S.; m. Jessica, May 21, 1977; children: Daniel John, Christopher Brendan. BBA, Hofstra U., 1976; MBA with distinction, N.Y. Inst. Tech., 1979. Acctg. asst. Consol. Edison Co. N.Y., N.Y.C., 1973-76, staff acct., 1976, analyst forecasting and econ. analysis, 1976-77, supr. acctg. and stats., 1977-78; mgr. gas supply N.J. Natural Gas Co., Asbury Park, 1978-82; mgr. gas supply planning and regulatory affairs UGI Corp., 1982-85; dir. mktg. HNG/North Gas Mktg., Inc., Malvern, Pa., 1985; account exec. HNG/Internorth Gas Mktg., Inc., Malvern, 1985-86; dir. Eastern region Enron Gas Mktg., Malvern, 1986-87, dir. planning and analysis, Houston, 1987-88, gen. mgr. ea. div. sales, 1988-89, gen. mgr. spl. projects, 1989-90; mng. dir. Enron Gas Liquids Internat.-LNG Ventures, 1990-91, dir. bus. devel., 1991-92; dir. mktg. devel., O & R Energy Inc., 1993, v.p. mktg., 1994—; prof. bus. mgmt. Kutztown State U.; sr. v.p. mktg. Norstar Energy, 1994-95. With U.S. Army, 1969-73. Roman Catholic. Lodge: K.C.

SADRUDDIN, MOE, oil company executive, consultant; b. Hyderabad, India, Mar. 3, 1943; came to U.S., 1964; m. Azmath Oureshi, 1964; 3 children. BSME, Osmania U., Hyderabad, 1964; MS in Indsl. Engring., NYU, 1966; MBA, Columbia U., 1970. Cons. project engr. Ford, Bacon & Davis, N.Y.C., 1966; staff indsl. engr. J.C. Penney, N.Y.C., 1966-68; sr. cons. Drake, Sheahan, Stewart & Dougall, N.Y.C., 1968-70, Beech-Nut Inc. subs. Squibb Corp., N.Y.C., 1970-72; founder, pres. Azmath Constrn. Co., Englewood, N.J., 1972-77; crude oil cons., fgn. govt. rep., 1977—; pres. A-One Petroleum Co., Fullerton, Calif., 1985—; govt. advisor Puerto Rico, 1980-82, Dominica, 1983-84, St. Vincent, 1981-82, Kenya, 1983-84, Belize 1984-85, Costa Rica 1983-86, Paraguay 1984-87. Chmn. Azhar Found., 1989—; bldg. 6 charitable hosps. in India; mem. L.A. World Affairs Coun. Mem. Internat. Platform Assn. Address: A-One Petroleum Co 2656 Camino Del Sol Fullerton CA 92833-4806 *Personal philosophy: I learned from a young age that acquisition of knowledge, developing honesty and integrity and service to humanity in the form of charity, love and struggle to help the poor and needy, are the main foundation stones of a successful life. I believe that acquisition of wealth is only a means to an end and not an end in itself. With accumulation of wealth, one has to care for the underprivileged and try to improve their lot.*

SADUN, ALBERTO CARLO, astrophysicist, physics educator; b. Atlanta, Apr. 28, 1955; s. Elvio Herbert and Lina (Ottolenghi) S.; m. Erica Liebman. BS in Physics, Mass. Inst. Tech., 1977; PhD in Physics, MIT, 1984. Asst. prof. Agnes Scott Coll., Decatur, Ga., 1984-90, assoc. prof., 1990—, dir. Bradley Obs., 1984—; adj. prof. Ga. State U., Atlanta, 1986—; rsch. affiliate NASA/Caltech Jet Propulsion Lab., Pasadena, Calif., 1988-90, summer faculty fellow, 1987, 88. Contbr. articles to Nature, Astrophys. Jour., Astron. Jour., Publ. Aston. Soc. of the Pacific, Astrophys. Letters and Communications. Mem. Am. Jewish Com., Atlanta, 1984—. Fellow Royal Astron. Soc.; mem. Internat. Astron. Union, Am. Astron. Soc., N.Y. Acad. Scis. Achievements include relocation of Agnes Scott College's telescope to Hard Labor Creek Observatory. Home: 4739 Springfield Dr Dunwoody GA 30338 Office: Agnes Scott Coll 141 E College Ave Decatur GA 30030-3770

SADUN, ALFREDO ARRIGO, neuro-ophthalmologist, scientist, educator; b. New Orleans, Oct. 23, 1950; s. Elvio H. and Lina (Ottoleghi) S.; m. Debra Leigh Rice, Mar. 18, 1978; children: Rebecca Eli, Elvio Aaron, Benjamin Maxwell. BS, MIT, 1972; PhD, Albert Einstein Med. Sch., Bronx, N.Y., 1976, MD, 1978. Intern Huntington Meml. Hosp. U. So. Calif., Pasadena, 1978-79; resident Harvard U. Med. Sch., Boston, 1979-82, HEED Found. fellow in neuro-ophthalmology Mass. Eye and Ear Inst., 1982-83, instr. ophthalmology, 1983, asst. prof. ophthalmology, 1984; dir. residential tng. U. So. Calif. Dept. Ophthalmology, L.A., 1984-85, 90—; asst. prof. ophthalmology and neurosurgery U. So. Calif., L.A., 1984-87, assoc. prof., 1987-90; full prof. U. So. Calif., 1990—, mem. internal review bd.; prin. investigator Howe Lab. Harvard U., Boston, 1981-84, E. Doheny Eye Inst., L.A., 1984—; examiner Am. Bd. Ophthalmology; mem. internal rev. bd. U. So. Calif.; mem. sci. exec. bd. K. Rasmussen Found.; mem. sci. adv. bd. Internat. Found. for Optic Nerve Diseases. Author: Optics for Opthalmologists, 1988, New Methods of Sensory Visual Testing, 1989; contbr. articles to profl. jours. and chpts. to books. James Adams scholar, 1990-91; recipient Pecan D. award, 1988-92, Rsch. to Prevent Blindness Sr. Investigator award, 1996-97, Rsch. to Prevent Blindness Sr. Investigator award, 1996. Fellow Am. Acad. Ophthalmology Neuro-Ophthalmologists; mem. NIH (Med. Scientists Tng. award 1972-78), Am. Assn. Anatomists, Assn. Univ. Prof. Ophthalmology (assoc.), Am. Bd. Ophthalmology (rep. to residency rev. com. 1994—), Soc. to Prevent Blindness, Nat. Eye Inst. (New Investigator Rsch. award 1983-86, rsch. grants 1988-91, 93—), Soc. Neuroscis., Assn. Rsch. in Vision and Ophthalmology, N.Am. Neuro-Ophthal. Soc. (chmn. membership com. 1990—, v.p. 1994—). Avocation: writing. Home: 2478 Adair St San Marino CA 91108-2610 Office: U So Calif E Doheny Eye Inst 1450 San Pablo St Los Angeles CA 90033-4615

SAEED, MOHAMMED, Islamic historian, eqyptologist, educator; b. El Paso, Tex., Aug. 15, 1948; s. Willard Wood and Grace Margaret (Weddle)

W.; m. Jeanne Burger, Apr. 2, 1970 (div. 1979); children: Grace Ann, Annabelle Jane; m. Katleen M. D'Annette, Dec. 12, 1992. Student, Fullerton Coll., 1973-76; AA, Wichita State U., 1983, BS, 1983; MA, Emporia State U., 1989; student, Am. U., Cairo, Egypt. Rschr. Lawrence (Kans.) Islamic Student Assn., 1989-92, Islamic Studies Student Assn., Lawrence, 1992—; dir. Islamic Rsch. Ctr.; pres., owner MIS Export and Import. Author: The Jayhawk Nazi, 1983, Perceptions: Vietnam Veterans, 1989, Allah, The Glorious Quran and the Muslim Family, 1995; contbr. articles to profl. jours. Mem. DAV, World Wildlife Fund, Nat. Parks and Conservation Assn., Blinded Veterans Assn., Nat. Wildlife Fedn., Nat. Audubon Soc., Hist. Preservation Soc., Emporia State Alumni Assn., Greenpeace, Amnesty Internat., Disabled Am. Blind Vets., Archeol. Inst. Am., Egypt Exploration Soc. Moslem. Avocations: travel, Middle Eastern cooking, model trains, reading, classical music. Home and Office: Apt 106 3751 SW Park South Ct Topeka KS 66609-2112

SAEKS, ALLEN IRVING, lawyer; b. Bemidji, Minn., July 14, 1932; m. Linda J. Levin; 1 child, Adam Charles. BS in Law, U. Minn., 1954, JD, 1956. Bar: Minn. 1956, U.S. Dist. Ct. Minn. 1956, U.S. Ct. Appeals (8th cir.) 1957, U.S. Ct. Appeals (fed. cir.) 1959, U.S. Supreme Ct. 1959; cert. civil trial specialist. Asst. U.S. atty. Dept. Justice, St. Paul, 1956-57; assoc. Leonard Street & Deinard, Mpls., 1960-63, ptnr., 1964-96; adj. prof. law U. Minn. Law Sch., 1960-65; chmn. Lawyer Trust Account Bd., Interest on Lawyers Trust Accounts, 1984-87; chmn. Fund for the Legal Aid Soc., 1997—. Chmn. Property Tax Com., 1986-87; bd. dirs. Citizens League, Mpls., 1984-87; pres. Jewish Cmty. Rels. Coun. of Minn. and the Dakotas, 1994-96. Served to 1st lt. JAGC, U.S. Army, 1957-60. Recipient City of Mpls. award, 1996. Fellow Am. Bar Found. (life); mem. Fund for the Legal Aid Soc. (chmn. 1997—, Law Day Testimonial award 1996), Hennepin County Bar Assn. (pres. 1983-84), ABA (commn. on interest on lawyers trust accts. 1990-93), Minn. State Bar Assn. (cert. trial specialist 1988), Order of Coif, Phi Delta Phi. Office: Leonard Street and Deinard 150 S 5th St Ste 2300 Minneapolis MN 55402-4223

SAEKS, RICHARD EPHRAIM, engineering executive; b. Chgo., Nov. 30, 1941; s. Morris G. and Elsie E. S. B.S., Northwestern U., 1964; M.S., Colo. State U., 1965; Ph.D., Cornell U., 1967. Elec. engr. Warwick Mfg. Co., Niles, Ill., 1961-63; asst. prof. dept. elec. engring. U. Notre Dame, 1967-71, asso. prof., 1971-73; asso. prof. depts. elec. engring., math. Tex. Tech U., Lubbock, 1973-77; prof. Tex. Tech U., 1977-79, Paul Whitfield Horn prof. elec. engring., math. computer sci, 1979-83; prof., chmn. elec. engring. Ariz. State U., 1983-88; dean Armour Coll. Engring. Ill. Inst. Tech., 1988-91, Motorola prof., 1991-92; v.p. engring. Accurate Automation Corp., 1992—; cons. Research Triangle Inst., 1978-80, Marcel Dekker Inc., 1978-80. Author: Generalized Networks, 1972, Resolution Space Operators and Systems, 1973, Interconnected Dynamical Systems, 1981, System Theory: A Hilbert Space Approach, 1982; contbr. articles to profl. jours.; Editor: Large-Scale Dynamical Systems, 1976, Rational Fault Analysis, 1977, The World of Large Scale Systems, 1982. Recipient Disting. Faculty Research award Tex. Tech U., 1978. Fellow IEEE, AIAA (assoc.).

SAENGER, EUGENE LANGE, radiology educator, laboratory director; b. Cin., Mar. 5, 1917; s. Eugene and Therese (Lange) S.; m. Sue Reis, June 18, 1941 (dec.); children: Katherine Saenger Soodek (dec.), Eugene Lange. A.B., Harvard U., 1938; M.D., U. Cin., 1942. Diplomate: Am. Bd. Radiology, Am. Bd. Nuclear Medicine. Intern Cin. Gen. Hosp., 1942-43, resident in radiology, 1943-46; asst. prof., then assoc. prof. radiology U. Cin. Med. Ctr., 1949-62, prof., vice chmn. dept., 1962-87, prof. radiology emeritus, 1987—; radiation therapist Children's Hosp., Cin., 1947-87; dir. E.L. Saenger Radioisotope Lab., U. Cin., 1950-87; cons. AEC and NRC, 1962-88, to med. liaison EPA, 1968—; dir. Nat. Coun. Radiation Protection, 1967—; mem. Internat. Com. on Radiation Protection, 1977-84. Author: Medical Aspects of Radiation Accidents: A Handbook for Physicians, Health Physicists and Industrial Hygienists, 1963. Trustee Cin. Community Chest and Council, 1964-70. Served to maj. M.C. U.S. Army, 1953-55. Mem. Soc. Med. Decision Making (pres., co-founder 1979-80), Nat. Coun. Radiation Protection (hon. mem.), Queen City Club, Literary Club (Cin.), Cosmos Club (Washington), Optimists Club. Jewish. Home: 9160 Given Rd Cincinnati OH 45243-1148 Office: Eugene L Saenger Radioisotope Lab U Cin Hosp ML 569 Cincinnati OH 45267-0569

SAENGER, THEODORE JEROME, telephone company executive; b. Pomona, Calif., July 28, 1928; s. Carl Louis and Anna Magdalene (Mangold) S.; m. Catherine MacDonald, 1949 (dec.); children: Lynne Anne, Jeffrey Joseph, Tracey Susan, Brian Louis; m. Gayle Inez Johnson, Oct. 19, 1963. B.S., U. Calif.-Berkeley, 1951. With Pacific Telephone & Telegraph (now Pacific Bell), 1952—, v.p., 1974-77, pres., chief operating officer, 1977-84, pres., chief exec. officer, 1984—, also dir.; vice chmn., dir. parent co. Pacific Telesis Group, San Francisco, 1984—. Trustee San Francisco Theol. Sem., Drew Med. Found.; mem. adv. bd. U. Calif. Bus. Sch.; div. chmn. United Way, Los Angeles, 1980-81. Served with U.S. Army, 1946-47. Mem. Phi Beta Kappa, Theta Chi. Republican. Presbyterian. Club: California, Pacific Union. Office: Pacific Telesis Group 140 New Montgomery St San Francisco CA 94105-3705

SAENZ, MICHAEL, college president; b. Laredo, Tex., Oct. 25, 1925; s. C. A. and Pola R. Saenz; B.S. with honors in Accounting, Tex. Christian U., 1949, M.Ed., 1952; Ph.D. in Econs., U. Pa., 1961; m. Nancy Elizabeth King; children—Michael King, Cynthia Elizabeth. Dep. collector IRS, Ft. Worth, Dallas, 1949-52; adminstr. United Christian Missionary Soc., Bayamon, P.R., 1954-57, 59-65, exec. sec., Indpls., 1965-71; acad. dean Laredo Jr. Coll., 1971-74; pres. N.W. campus Tarrant County Jr. Coll., 1975—; founder Nat. Comm. Coll. Hispanic coun., 1985, bd. dirs. 1985— (pres. 1989-91); founder, co-dir. Nat. Hispanic Leadership Inst., 1989—; trustee Tex. Christian U., Brite Div. Sch., 1973—. Bd. dirs. Civic Ballet of Laredo (Tex.), Ft. Worth chpt. NCCJ, Juliette Fowler Homes, Dallas; chmn. Aztec Dist., dir. Gulf Coast council Boy Scouts Am., 1971-75; gov. Career Devel. Center, Arlington, Tex.; chmn. Laredo's Bicentennial Com., 1973-76; trustee, bd. dirs. United Way Ft. Worth, 1979—; mem., vice moderator gen. bd. Christian Ch. (Disciples of Christ), 1991-93. Mem. Am. Assn. Cmty. Colls.(bd. dirs., 1991-94), Commn. Internat. Edn. Am. Coun. Edn, Tex. Jr. Coll. Tchrs. Assn., Tex. Assn. Jr. Coll. Instructional Adminstrs., Am. Acad. Polit. and Social Scis., Urban Ministries in Higher Edn, Civic Music Assn. Laredo, N. Ft. Worth C. of C. (dir. 1978—). Lodge: Rotary (North Ft. Worth). Home: 4427 Tamworth Rd Fort Worth TX 76116-8127 Office: Tarrant County Jr Coll NW Capmus 4801 Marine Pkwy Fort Worth TX 76179*

SAETA, PHILIP MAX, judge; b. L.A., Feb. 21, 1931; s. Maurice and Elizabeth (Jacobs) S.; m. Joanne Edith Hixson, Aug. 28, 1954; children: David, Peter, Sandra. AB, Stanford U., 1953, LLB, 1957. Bar: Calif. 1958, U.S. Dist. Ct. (cen. dist.) Calif. Assoc., ptnr. Beardsley, Hufstedler & Kemble, L.A., 1964-75; judge Mcpl. Ct., L.A., 1964-75; judge L.A. County Superior Ct., L.A., 1975-91, ret., 1991; pvt. judge, 1991—. With U.S. Army, 1953-55. Mem. ABA, Calif. Judges Assn. (Jefferson award 1987), L.A. County Bar Assn. Democrat. Jewish. Avocation: music. Home and Office: 2036 Oak St South Pasadena CA 91030-4954

SAFADI-PSYLLOS, GINA MONI, administrative assistant, business owner; b. Astoria, N.Y., Nov. 21, 1966; d. Juan Safadi and Lourdes Jannette (Navarette-Zavala) Achury; m. Peter John Psyllos, Nov. 15, 1992. BA, Marymount Manhattan Coll., 1988; Art Adminstrn. Cert., NYU, 1996; BS, U. of the State of N.Y., Albany, 1997. Computer lab. asst. Marymount Manhattan Coll., N.Y.C., 1986-88; adminstrv. aide NYU, N.Y.C., 1988-90; adminstrv. asst. BBDO, N.Y.C., 1990-97; owner, art dealer SPace Art Corp., Auberndale, N.Y., 1996—; mgr. The Bank Restaurant, Hampton Bays, N.Y., 1997—; pub. chair dance dept. Marymount Manhattan Coll., 1987-88; artist, newsletter Streetlife Serenade, 1996. Chairperson St. Vincent Ferrer H.S. Class of '84 Reunion Com., N.Y.C., 1993-94; vol. Nassau County Mus. of Art, Roslyn, N.Y., 1997. Mem. NAFE, Nat. Assn. of Fine Artists, Am. Assn. of Mus. Roman Catholic. Avocations: contemporary and animation art collecting, travel. Home: 40-26-171 St Flushing NY 11358

SAFAN, CRAIG ALAN, film composer; b. L.A., Dec. 17, 1948; s. Eugene Leroy and Betty Lou (Torchin) S.; m. Linda Sue McClelland, Aug. 27, 1978; children: Alec, Kira. BA, Brandeis U., 1970. Film composer, 1973—. Composer film scores The Great Texas Dynamite Chase, 1976, The Bad News Bears in Breaking Training, 1977, Corvette Summer, 1978, Good Guys Wear Black, 1978, The Great Smokey Roadblock, 1978, Roller Boogie, 1979, Fade to Black, 1980, Die Laughing, 1980, T.A.G.: The Assassination Game, 1982, Nightmares, 1983, Angel, 1984, The Last Starfighter, 1984, The Legend of Billie Jean, 1985, Remo Williams: The Adventure Begins, 1985, Warning Sign, 1985, Lady Beware, 1987, The Stranger, 1987, Stand and Deliver, 1988, A Nightmare on Elm Street IV: The Dream Master, 1988, Money for Nothing, 1993, Major Payne, 1995, Mr. Wrong, 1995, TV scores Cheers, 1983-94, Life Goes On, 1990-94, Hope and Gloria, 1995. Fellow Watson Found., 1970-71. Mem. NARAS, ASCAP (award for Cheers 1987-93), Acad. Motion Picture Arts and Scis. (exec. music com. 1987-95). Avocation: collecting American sheet music. Office: Film Music Asso 6525 W Sunset Blvd Hollywood CA 90028-7212*

SAFARS, BERTA See FISZER-SZAFARZ, BERTA

SAFDIE, MOSHE, architect; b. Haifa, Israel, July 14, 1938; s. Leon and Rachael Esses; m. Nina Nusynowicz, Sept. 6, 1959 (div. 1981); children: Taal, Oren; m. Michal Ronnen, June 7, 1981; children: Carmelle, Yasmin. BArch, McGill U., 1961; LLD (hon.), 1982; DSc (hon.), Laval U., 1988; DFA (hon.), U. Victoria, 1989. With H.P.D. Van Ginkel (architect), Montreal, Que., Can., 1961-62, then Louis I. Kahn, Phila., 1962-63; assoc. David, Barrott and Boulva, Montreal, 1964; pvt. practice Montreal, 1964—, Jerusalem, 1970—; pvt. practice (prin. office) Boston, 1978—; pvt. practice Harvard U. Grad. Sch. Design, Toronto, 1985—; Ian Woodner Studio prof. architecture and urban design Harvard U. Grad. Sch. Design, 1984-89. Prin. works include Tomb of Yitzhak Rabin, Jerusalem, Skirball Mus. and Cultural Ctr., L.A., Ford Ctr. for Performing Arts, Vancouver, B.C., Can., Libr. Sq., Vancouver, Ottawa City Hall, Ont., Rosovsky Harvard-Radcliffe Hillel, Cambridge, Mass., Elwyn Rehab. Ctr., Tel Aviv, Neve Ofer Ctr., Tel Aviv, Harvard Bus. Sch. Morgan Hall and '59 Chapel, Cambridge, Esplanade Apts., Cambridge, Musee des Beaux Arts, Montreal, Nat. Gallery Can., Ottawa, Colegio Hebreo Maguen David, Mexico City, Musee de la Civilisation, Que., Cambridge Ctr., Ardmore Habitat Apts., Singapore, Kibbutz Idmit (Israel) Housing, Callahan Residence, Birmingham, Ala., Hebrew Union Coll., Jerusalem, Yad Vashem Transport and Children's Meml., Jerusalem, Hosh Dist. Restoration, Jerusalem, Coldspring New Town, Balt., Block 38 Housing, Jerusalem, Yeshiva Porat Yosef, Jerusalem, Habitat '67, Montreal. Recipient Massey medal in architecture, Lt. Gov. Can. gold medal, urban design concept award HUD, 1980, internat. design award in urban design Am. Soc. Interior Designers, 1980, Prix d'Excellence in architecture Que. Order Architects, 1988, Gov. Gen.'s medal for architecture, 1992, Richard J. Neutra award, 1993, RAIC Gold medal Royal Architectural Inst. of Canada, 1995. Fellow Royal Inst. Architects Can. (Gold Medal 1995), Order of Can., AIA, Order Architects Province Que., Ont. Assn. Architects. Office: 100 Properzi Way Somerville MA 02143-3740 also: Ste 301, 165 Avenue Rd, Toronto, ON Canada M5R 3S4 also: 4 Ha'emek St 7 Shlomo, Hamelech Jerusalem 94182, Israel

SAFE, KENNETH SHAW, JR., fiduciary firm executive; b. Providence, Oct. 13, 1929; s. Kenneth Shaw and Louise (King) S.; m. Elizabeth Kelley, Dec. 20, 1952; children: Hope, Elizabeth, Kenneth, Thorn and Edith (triplets). AB, Harvard U., 1951. Intelligence officer CIA, Washington, 1954-56; with trust dept. Old Colony Trust Co., Bank of Boston, 1956-59; registered rep. Tucker, Anthony & R.L. Day, Boston, 1959-68; ptnr. Welch & Forbes, Boston, 1968—, mng. ptnr., 1983—. Pres. Travelers Aid Soc. Boston, 1956-82, Cmty. Workshops, Inc., Boston, 1968-72; asst. treas. Wellesley (Mass.) Coll., 1970-80; trustee Georgiana Goddard Eaton Meml. Trust, Boston, 1975—, G. Howland Shaw Found., Boston, 1977—; treas. Woods Hole (Mass.) Oceanographic Inst., 1981-92, Mass. Soc. Cin.; bd. dirs. Beverly Land Co., Providence, 1982—; trustee R.I. Hosp., Providence; trustee Boys and Girls Camps, Inc., Boston; bd. dirs. Boston Port and Seaman's Aid Soc. With CIC, U.S. Army, 1952-54. Mem. Boston Security Analysts Soc., Somerset Club, Duxbury Yacht Club, Marshall St. Hist. Soc., Mason, Country Club. Republican. Episcopalian. Avocations: sailing, skiing, hunting, snorkeling. Home: 207 King Caesar Rd Duxbury MA 02332-3912 Office: Welch & Forbes 45 School St Boston MA 02108-3204

SAFER, JAY GERALD, lawyer; b. Jacksonville, Fla., Oct. 11, 1946; s. Moe B. and Rubye (Lipsitz) S.; m. Annette Fashing, Nov. 26, 1970; children: Michelle Laurie, Ellie Renee. BA, Vanderbilt U., 1968; JD, Columbia U., 1971. Bar: N.Y. 1972, U.S. Dist. Ct. (so. and ea. dists.) N.Y. 1973, U.S. Dist. Ct. Conn. 1984, U.S. Ct. Appeals (2d cir.) 1974, U.S. Supreme Ct. 1992. Assoc. Paul, Weiss, Rifkind, Wharton & Garrison, N.Y.C., 1971-75, Hardee, Barovick, Konecky & Braun, N.Y.C., 1975, LeBoeuf, Lamb, Leiby & MacRae, N.Y.C., 1975-80; ptnr. LeBoeuf, Lamb, Greene & MacRae, L.L.P., N.Y.C., 1980—. Contbr. articles to profl. jours. Served to capt. U.S. Army, 1972. Harlan Fiske Stone scholar, Columbia U., 1971. Mem. ABA, N.Y. State Bar Assn., Assn. Bar City N.Y. Office: LeBoeuf Lamb Greene and MacRae LLP 125 W 55th St New York NY 10019-5369

SAFER, JOHN, artist, lecturer; b. Washington, Sept. 6, 1922; s. John M. and Rebecca (Herzmark) S.; m. Joy Scott; children: Janine Whitney, Thomas. AB, George Washington U., 1947; LLB, Harvard, 1949. chmn. NationsBank/D.C., 1980-92; chmn. exec. com. Fin. Gen. Bankshares, 1977-80. Represented in permanent collections at Balt. Mus. Art, Corocoran Gallery Art, Nat. Air and Space Mus., Washington Tennis Ctr., Washington High Mus. Art, Atlanta, Milw. Mus. Art, Harvard Law Sch., Harvard Bus. Sch., Phila. Mus. Art, San Francisco Mus. Art, Duke U. Med. Ctr., Georgetown U., George Washington U., Williams Coll., Scripps Rsch. Inst., Mus. Fine Arts, Caracas, Venezuela, Royal Collection, Amman, Jordan, Royal Collection, Madrid, Am. Hosp., Paris, Embassy of U.S., London, Nassau, Beijing Royal Collection, Amman; pub. sculpture includes World Series of Golf Trophy, Timepiece (World's Largest Clock - Guiness Book of Records), Christa McAuliffe Meml., Bowie, Md. Served as 1st lt. USAAF, 1942-46. Clubs: Cosmos, Burning Tree, Harvard, Woodmont (Washington); Harvard (N.Y.); Lyford Cay (Nassau); Mid-Ocean (Bermuda); Linville Ridge (N.C.). Office: 3 Bethesda Metro Ctr Bethesda MD 20814-5330

SAFER, MORLEY, journalist; b. Toronto, Ont., Can., Nov. 8, 1931; came to U.S., 1964; s. Max and Anna (Cohn) S. Student, U. Western Ont., 1952. With Reuters, London, Eng., 1955; corr., producer Canadian Broadcasting Corp., 1955-60, writer, London corr., 1961-64; corr., producer BBC, 1961; Vietnam corr. CBS, 1964-71; co-host 60 Minutes news program CBS-TV, 1971—; writer-corr. news documentary The Second Battle of Britain, 1976. Author: Flashbacks: On Returning to Vietnam, 1990. Recipient Polk award L.I.U., 1965, Overseas Press Club award, 1965, 66, Sigma Delta Chi award, 1965, Peabody award, 1965, Paul White award Radio and TV, News Dirs. Assn., 1966, 4 Emmy awards, 1981, 82, 3 Emmy awards, 1985, George Foster Peabody award, 1983, 3 prestigious awards, George Foster Peabody, Alfred I. duPont-Columbia U., Emmy for "Lenell Geter's in Jail", 60 Min. broadcast, 1984. Fellow Royal Coll. Bloviation (Edinburgh). Office: care CBS News 60 Minutes 555 W 57th St New York NY 10019-2925*

SAFERITE, LINDA LEE, library director; b. Santa Barbara, Calif., Mar. 25, 1947; d. Elwyn C. and Polly (Frazer) S.; m. Andre Doyon, July 16, 1985. BA, Calif. State U., Chico, 1969; MS in Library Sci., U. So. Calif., 1970; cert. in Indsl. Relations, UCLA, 1976; MBA, Pepperdine U., 1979. Librarian-in-charge, reference librarian Los Angeles County Pub. Libr. System, 1970-73, regional reference librarian, 1973-75, sr. librarian-in-charge, 1975-78, regional adminstr., 1978-80; libr. dir. Scottsdale (Ariz.) Pub. Libr. System, 1980-93, Fort Collins (Colo.) Pub. Libr., 1993-96; exec. dir. Tulsa (Okla.) City County Libr., 1996—; task force del. White House Conf. on Libr. and Info. Svcs., 1992—, rep. Region V, 1992-94. Bd. dirs. Scottsdale-Paradise Valley YMCA, 1981-86, Ariz. Libr. Friends, 1990-92; bd. dirs. AMIGOS, 1990, chmn., 1992-93; mem. Class 5, Scottsdale Leavership, 1991. Recipient Cert. Recognition for efforts in civil rights Ariz. Atty. Gen.'s Office, 1985, Libr. award Ariz. Libr. Friends, 1988, Women of Distinction award for Edn., 1989, State Project of Yr. award, 1995, Ariz. Disting. Svc. award, 1993; named State Libr. of Yr., 1990. Mem. ALA, Ariz. State Libr. Assn. (pres. 1987-88), Ariz. Women's Town Hall AlumniAssn., Met. Bus. and Profl. Women (Scottsdale, pres. 1986-87), Soroptimist (pres. 1981-83). Republican. Avocations: mountain jaunts, reading, ballroom dancing, photography. Office: Tulsa City County Libr 400 Civic Ctr Tulsa OK 74103-3857

SAFFELS, DALE EMERSON, federal judge; b. Moline, Kans., Aug. 13, 1921; s. Edwin Clayton and Lillian May (Cook) S.; m. Margaret Elaine Nieman, Apr. 2, 1976; children by previous marriage: Suzanne Saffels Gravitt, Deborah Saffels Godowns, James B.; stepchildren: Lynda Cowger Harris, Christopher Cowger. AB, Emporia State U., 1947; JD cum laude, LLB cum laude, Washburn U., 1949. Bar: Kans. 1949. Pvt. practice law Garden City, Kans., 1949-71, Topeka, 1971-75, Wichita, Kans., 1975-79; U.S. dist. judge Dist. of Kans., Topeka, 1979—; county atty. Finney County, Kans., 1951-55; chmn. bd. Fed. Home Loan Bank Topeka, 1978-79; mem. Jud. Conf. Com. on Fin. Disclosure, 1993—. Mem. bd. govs. Sch. Law Washburn U., 1973-85; pres. Kans. Dem. Club, 1957; Dem. nominee Gov. of Kans., 1962; mem. Kans. Ho. of Reps., 1955-63, minority leader, 1961-63; mem. Kans. Corp. Commn., 1967-75, chmn., 1968-75; mem. Kans. Legis. Coun., 1957-63; Kans. rep. Interstate Oil Compact Commn., 1967-75, 1st vice chmn., 1971-72; pres. Midwest Assn. Regulatory Commn., 1972-73, Midwest Assn. R.R. and Utilities Commrs., 1972-73; trustee Emporia State U. Endowment Assn.; bd. dirs. Nat. Assn. Regulatory Utility Commrs., 1972-75. Maj. Signal Corps U.S. Army, 1942-46. Fellow Am. Bar Found., Kans. Bar Found.; mem. ABA, Kans. Bar Assn., Wichita Bar assn., Am. Judicature Soc., Delta Theta Phi. Lutheran. Office: US Dist Ct 420 Federal Bldg 444 SE Quincy St Topeka KS 66683

SAFFER, ALFRED, retired chemical company executive; b. N.Y.C., Dec. 3, 1918; s. Louis and Ruth (Mirkis) S.; m. Ruth Lillian Rudow, Jan. 31, 1942 (dec. Dec. 1983); children: Anita Carolyn Horowitz, Martin Kenneth; m. Doris Barbara Graubard, June 18, 1985. AB in Chemistry, NYU, 1939, MS in Chemistry, 1941, PhD, 1943. Research chemist Princeton (N.J.) U., 1943-46; sr. research assoc. Firestone Tire and Rubber Co., Akron, Ohio, 1946-48; dir. research Sci. Design Co., Inc., N.Y.C., 1948-57, v.p. mfg.; pres. Catalyst Devel. Corp., Little Ferry, N.J., 1957-69; exec. v.p. Halcon Internat., Inc., N.Y.C., 1963-69; vice chmn. ret. Halcon SD Group, Inc., N.Y.C., 1978-81; exec. v.p. Oxirane Corp, Princeton, 1969-76; pres. Oxirane Internat., Princeton, 1976-78; bd. dirs. Norwood Venture Co., N.Y.C. Contbr. articles to profl. jours.; patentee in field. Trustee Internat. Ctr. for Disabled, N.Y.C., 1978—; assoc. trustee North Shore U. Hosp., Manhasset, N.Y., 1981—; active instl. rev. bd. Boca Raton (Fla.) Community Hosp., 1992—. Fellow Am. Inst. Chemists (Chem. Pioneer award, 1982); mem. Nat. Acad. Engring., Am. Chem. Soc., Soc. Chem. Industry. Clubs: Glen Oaks (Old Westbury, N.Y.); Delaire Country (Delray Beach, Fla.). Avocation: golf. Home: 16629 Ironwood Dr Delray Beach FL 33445-7050

SAFFER, AMY BETH, foreign language educator; b. N.Y.C., Apr. 19, 1950; d. William and Evelyn (Yankowitz) S. BA, Fairleigh Dickinson U., 1972, MA, 1983; postgrad., Jersey City State Coll., 1983-84. Cert. tchr. Spanish K-12, N.J. Tchr. Madison (N.J.) High Sch., 1973, Livingston (N.J.) High Sch., 1973—; mem. faculty and dist. coms. Livingston Sch. Dist., 1975—; advisor to class of 1977, Livingston High Sch., 1975-77, chair mid. states subcom., 1990. Inducted Livingston H.S. Alumni Hall of Fame, 1993. Mem. NEA, Am. Assn. Tchrs. of Spanish and Portuguese, N.J. Edn. Assn., Fgn. Lang. Educators of N.J., Livingston Edn. Assn. (negotiations rep. 1980—), Essex County Edn. Assn. Office: Livingston High Sch Livingston NJ 07039

SAFFERMAN, ROBERT SAMUEL, microbiologist; b. Bronx, N.Y., Dec. 19, 1932; s. Irving and Rose (Schuler) S.; m. Jewel S. Reisman, June 7, 1958; children—Karen M., Sharon L., Steven I. B.S., Bklyn. Coll., 1955; Ph.D., Rutgers U., 1960. With USPHS, Cin., 1959-64; with Dept. Interior, Cin., 1964-70, U.S. EPA, Cin., 1970—; chief virology sect. Environ. Monitoring and Support Lab. EPA, Cin., 1974-88, chief virology br. Environ. Monitoring Systems Lab., 1988-94; chief virology and parasitology br. Environ. Monitoring Sys. Lab., Cin., 1994-95; chief biohazard assessment rsch. br. Nat. Exposure Rsch. Lab., 1995—; mem. Internat. Com. on Taxonomy of Viruses. Recipient Spl. Service award San. Engring. Ctr., USPHS, 1963; Gans medal Soc. Water Treatment and Examination, Eng., 1970; named Fed. Employee of Yr., Cin., 1974. Fellow Am. Acad. Microbiology; mem. ASTM, Am. Soc. Microbiology, Phycological Soc. Am., Sigma Xi. Home: 1669 Locksley Dr Cincinnati OH 45230-2220 Office: 26 Martin Luther King Dr W Cincinnati OH 45220-2242

SAFFIOTTI, UMBERTO, pathologist; b. Milan, Jan. 22, 1928; came to U.S., 1960, naturalized, 1966; s. Francesco Umberto and Maddalena (Valenzano) S.; m. Paola Amman, June 21, 1958; children: Luisa M., Maria Francesca. MD cum laude, U. Milan, 1951, splty. diploma occupational medicine cum laude, 1957. Intern Inst. Pathol. Anatomy U. Milan, 1951-52, asst. to chmn. occupational medicine, chief lab. pathology, Inst. Occupational Medicine, 1956-60, fellow Inst. Gen. Pathology, 1957-60; rsch. asst. oncology, rsch. assoc. Chgo. Med. Sch., 1952-55, from asst. prof. to prof. oncology, 1960-68; mem. staff Nat. Cancer Inst., NIH, Bethesda, Md., 1968—, assoc. dir. carcinogenesis, 1968-76, chief lab. exptl. pathology, 1974—, acting head Registry of Exptl. Cancers, 1988—; mem. pathology B study sect., NIH, 1964-68; mem. various adv. coms. govt. agys.; mem. cancer prevention com. Internat. Union Against Cancer, 1959-66, panel on carcinogenicity, 1963-66; chmn. ad hoc com. evaluation low levels environ. carcinogens HEW, 1969-70. Co-editor books; contbr. articles to profl. jours. Bd. dirs. Rachel Carson Trust, 1976-79. Recipient Career Devel. award NIH, 1965-68, Superior Svc. Honor award HEW, 1971, Pub. Interest Sci. award Environ. Def. Fund, 1977, Spl. Recognition award USPHS, 1980. Fellow NYAS; mem. AAAS, Am. Assn. Cancer Rsch. (pres. Chgo. chpt. 1966-67), Am. Soc. Investigative Pathology, Internat. Commn. Occupational Health, Soc. Occupational and Environ. Health (councillor 1972-76, v.p. 1976-78, pres. 1978-82), Soc. Toxicology, Sigma Xi. Democrat. Home: 5114 Wissioming Rd Bethesda MD 20816-2259 Office: NIH Nat Cancer Inst Lab Exptl Pathology Bldg 41 Bethesda MD 20892-5055

SAFFIR, HERBERT SEYMOUR, structural engineer, consultant; b. N.Y.C., Mar. 29, 1917; s. A.L. and Gertrude (Samuels) S.; m. Sarah Young, May 9, 1941; children: Richard Young, Barbara Joan. BS in Civil Engring. cum laude, Ga. Inst. Tech., 1940. Registered profl. engr., Fla., N.Y., Tex., P.R., Miss. Civil engr. TVA, Chattanooga, 1940, NACA, Langley Field, Va., 1940-41; structural engr. Ebasco Services, N.Y.C., 1941-43, York & Sawyer & Fred Severud, N.Y.C., 1945; engr. Waddell & Hardesty, Cons. Engrs., N.Y.C., 1945-47; asst. county engr. Dade County, Miami, Fla., 1947-59; cons. engr. Herbert S. Saffir, Coral Gables, Fla., 1959—; adj. prof. civil engring. Coll. Engring., U. Miami, 1964—; adviser civil engring. Fla. Internat. U., 1975-80; cons. on bldg. codes Govt. Bahamas; cons. on engring. in housing to UN; mem., chmn. Met. Dade County Unsafe Structures Bd., 1977-92; mem. Bldg. Code Evaluation Task Force after Hurricane Andrew; mem. Am. Nat. Stds. Inst. Commn. Bldg. Design Loads, Nat. Adv. Group on Glass Design, Dade County Bldg. Code Com. 1993—; mem. U. Miami/Coral Gables Community Rels. Com., 1993—; cons. to govt. and industry, condr. seminars, Australia; reviewer for NSF; mem. bd. adjustment Coral Gables, 1994—. Author: Housing Construction in Hurricane Prone Areas, 1971, Nature and Extent of Damage by Hurricane Camille, 1972, Evaluation of Structural Damage Caused by Hurricanes, 1993; contbg. author: Wind Effects on Structures, 1976; editor: Wind Engr., 1986-92; editor Manual of Wind Damage Investigation; contbr. articles to profl. jours.; designer Saffir/Simpson hurricane scale. With N.Y. Guard, 1942-43, AUS, 1943-44. Recipient Outstanding Service award Fla. Profl. Engrs., 1954, Pub. Service award Nat. Weather Service, 1975, Disting. Service award Nat. Hurricane Conf., 1987; named Miami Engr. of Year, 1978, 94, Gov.'s Design award, 1986, Gov. Gilchrist award for Profl. Excellence, 1988, Albert H. Friedman Community Svc. award, 1992; named to Ga. Tech. Engring. Hall of Fame, 1995. Fellow ASCE (past pres., sec., aerodynamics com. 1983—, mem. mitigation of wind damage com. 1985—, chmn. com. on damage investigation 1989—, mem. com. A7 on design loads for bldgs. 1972—), Fla. Engring. Soc. (award for outstanding tech. achievement 1973, Cmty. Svc. award 1980); mem. Soc. Am. Mil. Engrs., Am. Concrete Inst., ASTM (mem. com. performance bldg. constrn.), Prestressed Concrete Inst., Internat. Assn. for Bridge and Structural Engring., Colegio de Ingenieros P.R., Am. Meterol. Soc., Am. Arbitration Assn., Wind Engring. Rsch. Coun. (past bd. dirs., Svc. award 1990), Coral Gables C. of C. (bd. dirs., past pres., past chmn.), Tau Beta Pi, Chi Epsilon (hon.). Club: Country of Coral Gables. Home: 4818 Alhambra Cir Coral Gables FL 33146-1615 Office: 350 Sevilla Ave Ste 210 Coral Gables FL 33134-6617

SAFFIR, LEONARD, public relations executive; b. N.Y.C., Apr. 19, 1930; s. Abraham and Gertrude (Samuels) S.; m. Patricia Roemer (div. 1980); children: Andrew, Michelle; m. Wendy McConaughy (div. 1992); 1 child, Samantha; m. Eleanor Unger, 1997. Student, Syracuse U., 1948-51. Editor, bur. chief Internat. News Service, Dallas, Tokyo, 1953-58; producer Eng., Australia, Asia, 1958-60; ptnr. Haft, Saffir, Siegel Polit. Pub. Relations & Advt., N.Y.C., 1960-64; cons. Ferdinand Marcos, 1964; pub. Latin Am. Times, N.Y.C., 1965; exec. v.p. Franchises Internat., N.Y.C., 1965-69; chief of staff to Senator James Buckley U.S. Senate, Washington, 1970-76; pub., editor The Trib, N.Y.C., 1977-78, The Sun, Bridgehampton, N.Y., 1978-84; exec. v.p. Porter/Novelli, N.Y.C., 1984-90; pres. Jay DeBow & Ptnrs., Boca Raton, Fla., 1990—. Author: Power Public Relations. Chmn. Marchi for Mayor, N.Y.C., 1973, Buckley for Senator, N.Y., 1976. Served as sgt. USMC, 1951-53. Recipient Silver Anvil and Big Apple awards Pub. Rels. Soc. Am., Mayor's award City of N.Y., others. Mem. Overseas Press Club (pres. 1988-89). Home: 11181 Boca Woods Ln Boca Raton FL 33428-1840

SAFFMAN, PHILIP G., mathematician; b. Leeds, Eng., Mar. 19, 1931; s. Sam Ralph and Sarah (Rebecca) S.; m. Ruth Arion, Sept. 2, 1954; children—Louise J., Mark E., Emma E. B.A., Trinity Coll., Cambridge U., 1953; M.A., Cambridge U., 1956, Ph.D., 1956. Asst. lectr. applied math. Cambridge U., 1958-60; reader in applied math. Kings Coll., London U., 1960-64; prof. fluid mechanics Calif. Inst. Tech., Pasadena, 1964-69; prof. applied math. Calif. Inst. Tech., 1969-95, Theodore von Kármán prof. applied math. and aeros., 1995—. Contbr. articles to profl. jours. Trinity Coll. fellow, 1955-59; recipient Otto Laporte award, Am. Physical Soc., 1994, Fluid Dynamics Award, Am. Inst. Aeronautics and Astronautics, 1995. Fellow Am. Acad. Arts and Scis., Royal Soc. London. Office: 217-50 Firestone Calif Inst Tech Pasadena CA 91125

SAFFRAN, BERNARD, economist, educator; b. Bklyn., May 13, 1936; s. Isidore and Goldie (Bleeker) S.; m. Eleanor Meyerowitz, Aug. 23, 1959; children: Jenny, Linnea (dec.). BA, CCNY, 1956; PhD, U. Minn., 1963. Asst. prof. econs. U. Calif., Berkeley, 1961-67; assoc. prof. Swarthmore Coll., Pa., 1967-73, prof., 1973—, Franklin and Betty Barr prof. econs., 1989, chmn. dept. econs., 1976-83; sr. staff economist Coun. Econ. Advisors, Washington, 1971-72; vis. lectr. London Sch. Econs., 1979-80, CED Rsch. Adv. bd., 1992-96. Assoc. editor Jour. Econ. Perspectives, 1987—. Home: 201 Garrett Ave Swarthmore PA 19081-1433 Office: Swarthmore Coll Dept Econs Swarthmore PA 19081

SAFFRAN, KALMAN, engineering consulting company executive, entrepreneur; b. Boston, Dec. 28, 1947; s. Max and Marion (Patick) S. B.A., Northeastern U., 1971; postgrad. MIT, 1971-72. Lic. real estate broker, Mass. Mgr. systems MIT, 1972-76; corp. cons. United Brands Co., Boston, 1977-78; chief exec. officer Monitrex Corp., Boston, 1977-82; pres. Kalman Saffran Assocs., Inc., Newton, Mass., 1978—; bd. advisors Blackstone Bank and Trust Col, Boston; mem. network implementation panel U.S. Energy Research and Devel. Adminstrn., Washington, 1975-76; mem. computer com. MIT Lab. for Nuclear Sci., 1975-76. Mem. Data Processing Mgmt. Assn., Assn. Computing Machinery, Soc. for Info. Mgmt., IEEE, Mensa. Republican. Jewish. Home: 1564 Commonwealth Ave Newton MA 02165-2806 Office: Kalman Saffran Assocs Inc 1841 Commonwealth Ave Newton MA 02166-2725

SAFFRAN, MURRAY, biochemist; b. Montreal, Oct. 30, 1924; s. Isidore Irving and Rebecca Reva (Elimelech) S.; m. Judith Cohen, June 8, 1947; children—Michael David, Wilma Anne, Arthur Martin, Richard Eli. B.Sc., McGill U., 1945, M.Sc., 1946, Ph.D., 1949. Mem. faculty depts. psychiatry and biochemistry McGill U., Montreal, 1948-69; prof. McGill U., 1966-69; prof. biochemistry Med. Coll. Ohio, Toledo, 1969—, chmn. dept., 1969-80, asst. dean Med. Edn., 1992—; Dozor vis. prof. biochemistry Ben Gurion U., Israel, 1981; vis. prof. Inst. Biochemistry, Armenian Acad. Scis., Yerevan, 1988, U. Automon, Guadalajara, 1991-94. Mem. editl. bd. Biochem. Edn., Med. Biochemistry Question Bank, Drug Delivery; contbr. articles to profl. jours. Recipient Ayerst-Squibb award Endocrine Soc., 1968. Fellow AAAS, Ohio Acad. Sci.; mem. Am. Soc. Biochemistry and Molecular Biology, Endocrine Soc., Internat. Brain Rsch. Orgn., Alpha Omega Alpha. Home: 2331 Hempstead Rd Toledo OH 43606-2447 Office: Med Coll Ohio PO Box 10008 Toledo OH 43699

SAFIAN, GAIL ROBYN, public relations executive; b. Bklyn., Dec. 12, 1947; d. Jack I. and Harriet S.; m. Jay Mark Eisenberg, Jan. 6, 1979; children: Julia, Eric. BA, SUNY, Albany, 1968; MBA, NYU, 1982. Reporter Albany (N.Y.)-Knickerbocker News/Times-Union, 1969, Athens (Ohio) Messenger, 1969-71; pub. relations asst. Mountainside Hosp., Montclair, N.J., 1971-74; dir. pub. relations Riverside Hosp., Boonton, N.J., 1974-78; consumer affairs coordinator Johnson & Johnson Personal Products Div., Milltown, N.J., 1978-79; v.p., group mgr. Harshe Rotman & Druck, N.Y.C., 1979-82; exec. v.p., dir. Health Care Div. Ruder Finn & Rotman, N.Y.C., 1982-84; v.p., mgr. client services Burson-Marsteller, N.Y.C., 1984-86; v.p., group mgr. health care Cohn & Wolfe, N.Y.C., 1986-90; exec. v.p., gen. mgr. MCS, Summit, N.J., 1990-94; pres. Safian Comm. Inc., Maplewood, N.J., 1994—. Mem. devel. com. Cancer Care, N.Y.C., 1985—. Recipient MacEachern award Am. Hosp. Assn., 1974, Communications Award Internat. Assn. Bus. Communicators, 1976, Creativity in Pub. Rels. award Inside PR, 1992, 93. Mem. Healthcare Businesswomen's Assn. (mem. bd. dirs.), N.Y. Acad. Scis., Women in Comm. (Clarion award 1974). Jewish. Home: 31 Hickory Dr Maplewood NJ 07040-2107 Office: Safian Comm Inc 31 Hickory Dr Maplewood NJ 07040-2107

SAFIAN, KEITH FRANKLIN, hospital administrator; b. Bklyn., June 22, 1950; s. Jack I. and Harriet S. (Cohen) S.; m. Ellen Rita Babat, May 18, 1974; children: Elizabeth Anne, Alexander William. BS in EE and Indsl. Engring., SUNY, Buffalo, 1972; MBA, U. Pa., 1974. Asst. dir. Kings County Hosp. Ctr., Bklyn., 1974-76; asst. adminstr. NYU Med. Ctr., N.Y.C., 1977-80, assoc. adminstr., 1981-84, sr. assoc. adminstr., 1984-85; adminstr. St. John's Episcopal Hosp., Far Rockaway, N.Y., 1985-89; pres., CEO Phelps Meml. Hosp. Ctr., North Tarrytown, N.Y., 1989—. Bd. dirs. Addabbo Family Health Ctr., Arverne, N.Y., 1987-89, Rockaway Devel. and Revitalization Corp., Far Rockaway, 1988-89; bd. dirs. The ExcelCare Sys., Bronxville, N.Y., 1993—, chmn. 1995—; chmn. No. Met. Hosp. Assn., Newburgh, N.Y., 1996. Fellow Am. Coll. Healthcare Execs.; mem. Hosp. Adminstrs. Club of N.Y., Health Assn. N.Y. State (trustee 1996—). Home: 16 Brokaw Ln Great Neck NY 11023 Office: Phelps Memorial Hosp 701 N Broadway Sleepy Hollow NY 10591-1020

SAFIOL, GEORGE E., electronics company executive; b. Bklyn., Apr. 23, 1932; s. Charles and Effie (Patika) S.; m. Demetra Karambelas, July 12, 1958; children: Olympia Safiol Twomey, Peter, Christina. BS in Engring., NYU, 1954; postgrad. Sch. Engring., Columbia U., 1954-55. V.p., gen. mgr. No. Am. Telecom, ITT, Memphis, 1957-69; exec. v.p., chief operating officer Sycor, Inc., Ann Arbor, Mich., 1969-70; v.p. investments Heizer Co., Chgo., 1970-71; sr. v.p. Gen. Instrument Corp., Chicopee, Mass., 1971-77; pres., chief exec. officer Am. Biltrite, Cambridge, Mass., 1977-83; various sr. exec. positions Gen. Instrument Corp., N.Y.C., 1984-87, chief operating offficer, pres., 1987-91, also dir.; pvt. practice mgmt. cons., 1983-84. Served to 1st lt. U.S. Army, 1955-57. Mem. Alpha Omega. Republican. Greek Orthodox. Club: Metropolitan (N.Y.C.). Avocations: racquetball, golf, reading. Home: 64 Juniper Rd Weston MA 02493-1358

SAFIRE, WILLIAM, journalist, author; b. N.Y.C., Dec. 17, 1929; s. Oliver C. and Ida (Panish) S.; m. Helene Belmar Julius, Dec. 16, 1962; children: Mark Lindsey, Annabel Victoria. Student, Syracuse U., 1947-49. Reporter N.Y. Herald Tribune Syndicate, 1949-51; corr. WNBC-WNBT, Europe and Middle East, 1951; radio-TV producer WNBC, N.Y.C., 1954-55; v.p. Tex McCrary, Inc., 1955-60; pres. Safire Pub. Relations, Inc., 1960-68; spl. asst. to Pres. Nixon, Washington, 1969-73; columnist N.Y. Times, Washington, 1973—. Author: The Relations Explosion, 1963, Plunging into Politics, 1964, Safire's Political Dictionary, 1968, rev. edit., 1972-78, Before the Fall, 1975, Full Disclosure, 1977, Safire's Washington, 1980, On Language, 1980, What's the Good Word?, 1982, (with Leonard Safir) Good Advice on Writing, 1982, I Stand Corrected, 1984, Take My Word for It, 1986, Freedom, 1987, You Could Look It Up, 1988, Words of Wisdom, 1989, (with Leonard Safir) Leadership, 1990, Language Maven Strikes Again, 1990, Fumblerules, 1990, Coming to Terms, 1991, The First Dissident, 1992, Lend Me Your Ears, 1992, Good Advice on Writing, 1992, Quoth the Maven, 1993, Safire's New Political Dictionary, 1993, In Love with Norma Loquendi, 1994, Sleeper Spy, 1995. Served with AUS, 1952-54. Recipient Pulitzer prize for Disting. Commentary, 1978. Mem. Pulitzer Bd. Republican. Office: NY Times 1627 I St NW Washington DC 20006-4007

SAFLEY, JAMES ROBERT, lawyer; b. Cedar Rapids, Iowa, Sept. 19, 1943; s. Robert Starr and Jean (Engelman) S.; m. Dianne Lee McInnis; children: Anne Michele, Jamie Leigh. BA, U. Iowa, 1965; JD, Duke U., 1968. Bar: Minn. 1968, U.S. Ct. Appeals (4th, 6th, 8th, 9th and 11th cirs.), U.S. Supreme Ct. Law clk. U.S. Dist. Ct. Minn., Mpls., 1968-69; assoc. Robins, Kaplan, Miller & Ciresi, Mpls., 1969-74, ptnr., 1974—. Mem. adv. coun. Women's Intercollegiate Athletics, U. Minn., 1988-94; mem. Minn. Fed. Bar Assn. Commn. on ADR, 1995—. Mem. ABA, Minn. State Bar Assn. (antitrust sect. chmn. 1985-87), Hennepin County Bar Assn., Phi Beta Kappa. Office: Robins Kaplan Miller & Ciresi 2800 LaSalle Pla 800 Lasalle Ave Minneapolis MN 55402-2006

SAFONOV, MICHAEL GEORGE, electrical engineering educator, consultant; b. Pasadena, Calif., Nov. 1, 1948; s. George Michael and Ruth Garnet (Ware) S.; m. Nancy Kelshaw Schorn, Aug. 31, 1968 (div. Oct. 1983); 1 child, Alexander; m. Janet Sunderland, Feb. 25, 1985; 1 child, Peter. BSEE, MSEE, MIT, 1971, EE, 1976, PhDEE, 1977. Electronic engr. Air Force Cambridge Rsch. Lab., Hanscom AFB, Mass., 1968-71; rsch. asst. MIT, Cambridge, 1975-77; prof. elec. engring. U. So. Calif., L.A., 1977—, assoc. chmn. dept., 1989-93; vis. scholar Cambridge (Eng.) U., 1983-84, Imperial Coll., London, 1987, Calif. Inst. Tech., Pasadena, 1990-91; cons. Honeywell Systems and Rsch. Ctr., Mpls., 1978-83, Space Systems div. TRW, Redondo Beach, Calif., 1984, Northrop Aircraft, Hawthorne, Calif., 1985-91, also numerous others. Author: Stability and Robustness of Multivariable Feedback Systems (hon. mention Phi Beta Kappa 1981); co-author: (book and software) Robust-Control Toolbox, 1988; assoc. editor IEEE Trans. on Automatic Control, 1985-87, Internat. Jour. Robust and Nonlinear Control, 1989-93, Sys. and Control Letters, 1995—. Awards com. chair Am. Automatic Control Coun., 1993-95. Lt. (j.g.) USNR, 1972-75. Rsch. grantee Air Force Office Sci. Rsch., 1978—, NSF, 1982-84. Fellow IEEE; mem. AIAA (sr.), Common Cause. Republican. Office: U So Calif Dept EE-Systems MC-2563 3740 Mcclintock Ave # 310 Los Angeles CA 90007-4012 *Consider first only the very simplest problem--but strive for a representation of the simplest problem that generalizes easily.*

SAFRAN, CLAIRE, writer, editor; b. N.Y.C.; d. Simon and Flora (R) S.; m. John Milton Williams, June 8, 1958; 1 son, Scott Edward. B.A. in English cum laude, Bklyn. Coll., 1951. News editor Photo Dealer mag., 1951-53; assoc. editor TV Radio Mirror, 1954-58; mng. editor Photoplay mag., 1958-61; editor TV Radio Mirror, 1961-65, IN mag., 1965-67; assoc. editor Family Weekly mag., 1967-68; editor Coronet mag., 1968-71; contbg. editor Redbook, 1974-77; exec. editor, 1977-78, contbg. editor, 1979-81; roving editor Reader's Digest, 1983-88; contbg. editor Woman's Day, 1988-91. Author: New Ways to Lower Your Blood Pressure, 1984, Secret Exodus, 1987; contbr. to maj. nat. mags., 1972—. Recipient Media award Am. Psychol. Found., 1977; finalist Penney-Missouri Mag. Awards, 1977, Merit award in journalism Religious Pub. Rels. Coun., 1978, hon. mention journalism awards Am. Acad. Pediatrics, 1979, 1st pl. nat. editorials Odyssey Inst. Media Awards, 1979, 80, 86, Matrix award Women in Comm., 1982, 83, 84, William Harvey award, 1984, 91, Journalism award Am. Acad. Family Physicians, 1984, Investigative Journalism citation Deadline Club, 1993, Cert. of Merit Cmty. Action Network, 1995, PASS award Nat. Coun. on Crime and Delinquency, 1996. Mem. Am. Soc. Journalists and Authors (Outstanding Mag. Article award 1984, pres. 1996-98). Home: 53 Evergreen Ave Westport CT 06880-2563

SAFRAN, EDWARD MYRON, financial service company executive; b. Boston, Oct. 9, 1937; s. Morris and Sophie (Radin) S.; m. Harriet Reva Podolsky, Jan. 15, 1966; children: Steven, Rebecca. BS in Metall., MIT, 1959; MBA, Harvard U., 1961. Pres. Suncrest Corp., Worcester, Mass., 1962-65; exec. asst. Am. Metal Climax, N.Y.C., 1966; sr. auditor Gen. Electric Co., Lynn, Mass., 1966-68; fin. analyst Polaroid Corp., Cambridge, Mass., 1968-70, mgr. banking and investments, 1970-84, asst. treas., 1984-87; pres. Merganser Capital Mgmt. Corp., Cambridge, 1984—; chmn. Direct Fed. Credit Union, Needham, Mass., 1986—. Gleason Works fellow Harvard U., 1959-60. Mem. Harvard Club of Boston, Bond Analysts Soc. of Boston. Home: 37 Barney Hill Rd Wayland MA 01778-3601 Office: Merganser Capital Mgmt Corp One Cambridge Ctr Cambridge MA 02142

SAFRAN, LINDA JACQUELINE, fundraising consultant; b. Buffalo, Oct. 1, 1946; d. Nathaniel and Dorothy Louise (Luce) S.; m. Eliel G. Redstone, 1967 (div., 1970); m. James K. Smolev (div. 1983); children: Jennifer Smolev, Melanie Smolev. BA, U. Mich., 1968; mgmt. cert., Goucher Coll., 1983. Cert. Fundraising Exec., Nat. Soc. Fundraising Execs. Program dir., dir. libr. devel. Johns Hopkins U., Balt., 1984-90; assoc. dir. resource devel. Enterprise Edn., Columbia, Md., 1990-92; v.p. devel. and pub. rels. Childrens Hosp., Balt., 1993-94; pres. Devel. Collaborative, Balt., 1994—; bd. dirs., membership chair Chesapeake Planned Giving Coun., Balt., 1994—. Vol. Peace Corps, Brazil, 1968-70; chair 125th Anniversary Brown Meml. Park Ave Presbyn. Ch., Balt., 1995; mem. Balt. Presbytery Planned Giving Com. Mem. Nat. Soc. Fundraising Execs. (cert. fundraising exec.), U. Mich. Alumni Assn. (bd. dirs. 1989-92), Md. Assn. Non-Profit Orgns. Task Force on Ethics, Johns Hopkins Club, Hamilton St. Club. Democrat. Avocations: genealogy, oral history, vexilology. Office: Devel Collaborative 221 Ridgemede Rd Baltimore MD 21210-2942

SAFT, STUART MARK, lawyer; b. N.Y.C., Feb. 17, 1947; s. Stanley and Dorothy (Ligerman) S.; m. Stephanie C. Optekman, June 6, 1970; children: Bradley S., Gordon D. BA, Hofstra U., 1968; JD, Columbia U., 1971. Bar: N.Y. 1972, Fla. 1975, U.S. Dist. Ct. (so. dist.) N.Y. 1975, U.S. Supreme Ct. 1990. Asst. gen. counsel Joseph Bancroft & Son Co., N.Y.C., 1972-74; ptnr. Brauner, Baron, Rosenzwerz, Kligler & Sparber, N.Y.C., 1974-81, Powsner, Saft & Powsner, N.Y.C., 1981-84, Goldschmidt & Saft, N.Y.C., 1984-88; Wolf Haldenstein Adler Freeman & Herz, N.Y.C., 1988—; chmn., bd. dirs. Coun. of N.Y. Coops., N.Y.C., 1981—; bd. dirs. Pvt. Industry Coun. of N.Y.C., Am. Women's Econ. Devel. Corp.; adj. asst. prof. NYU, Real Estate Inst. Author: Commercial Real Estate Forms, 3 vols., 1987, Commercial Real Estate Transactions, 1989, Commercial Real Estate Workouts, 1991, Real Estate Development: Strategies for a Changing Market, 1990, Commercial Real Estate Leasing, 1992, Real Estate Investor's Survival Guide, 1992, Commercial Real Estate Financing, 1993, Commercial Real Estate Forms, 2d edit., 5 vols., 1994, Commercial Real Estate Transactions, 2d edit., 1995, Commercial Real Estate Workouts, 2d edit., 1996; contbg. editor: The Real Estate Finance Jour., 1989—; contbr. articles to profl. jours. Served to capt. USAR, 1968-76. Mem. ABA, N.Y. Bar Assn., Fla. Bar Assn. Office: Wolf Haldenstein Adler Freeman & Herz 270 Madison Ave New York NY 10016-0601

SAGALKIN, SANFORD, lawyer; b. N.Y.C., June 24, 1942; s. Nathan and Blanche (Hoffner) S.; m. Monda E. Fifield, Aug. 25, 1969; children: Nicholas, Amy. BA, Queens Coll., 1964; LLB, Columbia U., 1967. Bar: N.Y. 1967, Alaska 1969, D.C. 1980, Md., 1986. Staff atty. N.Y. Mental Health Info. Service, N.Y.C., 1967-69; mem. firm Faulkner, Banfield, Doogan, Gross and Holmes, Juneau, Alaska, 1969-74; firm Ely, Guess & Rudd, Juneau, 1974-75; asst. atty. gen. Atty. Gen.'s Office, State of Alaska, 1975-77; dep. asst. atty. gen. Dept. Justice, Washington, 1977-80; mem. firm Ely, Guess & Rudd, Washington, 1980-82; pvt. practice Sharpsburg, Md., 1982-86; assoc. gen. counsel CIA, Washington, 1986—. Mem. Juneau Parks and Recreation Com., 1972-74; bd. dirs. Defenders of Wildlife, 1986-90. Mem. Alaska Bar Assn., D.C. Bar Assn., Md. Bar Assn. Democrat. Jewish. Office: CIA Washington DC 20505

SAGAMI, KIM, dancer; b. Inglewood, Calif.. Scholarship student, The Joffrey Ballet Sch. Dancer Am. Ballet Theatre II, N.Y.C., 1981-82, Garden State Ballet, 1982, The Joffrey Ballet, N.Y.C., 1983—. Office: The Joffrey Ballet 434 6th Ave New York NY 10011-8411*

SAGAN, HANS, mathematician, educator, author; b. Vienna, Austria, Feb. 15, 1928; came to U.S., 1954, naturalized, 1960; s. Hans and Josefa (Seif) S.; m. Ingeborg Ulbrich, Mar. 20, 1954; 1 child, Ingrid. Ph.D. in Math., U. Vienna, 1950. Asst. prof. U. Tech., Vienna, 1950-54; asst. prof. Mont. State U., Bozeman, 1954-57; assoc. prof. U. Idaho, Moscow, 1957-61, prof., head dept., 1961-63; prof. N.C. State U., Raleigh, 1963-94, prof. emeritus, 1994—; vis. prof. U. Tech., Munich, 1964, U. Vienna, 1972, 95; vis. lectr. Math. Assn. Am., 1963-73, 77—; assoc. editor Math. Mag., 1963-73; mem. sci. adv. bd. Monatshefte für Mathematik, 1994—. Co-author: Die Laplace Transformation and Ihre Anwendung, 1953; author: Boundary and Eigenvalue Problems in Mathematical Physics, 1961, Integral and Differential Calculus-an Intuitive Approach, 1962, Introduction to the Calculus of Variations, 1969, Advanced Calculus, 1974, Beat the Odds, 1980, Calculus-Accompanied on the Apple, 1984, Space-Filling Curves, 1994; co-author: Ten Easy Pieces, 1980; also articles in field. Recipient Outstanding Faculty award U. Idaho, 1959-60; Poteat award N.C. Acad. Sci., 1966. Mem. Math. Assn. Am., AAUP, Oesterreichische Mathematische Gesellschaft, Sigma Xi. Avocations: swimming; sailing; horseback riding; fishing.

SAGAN, JOHN, former automobile company executive; b. Youngstown, Ohio, Mar. 9, 1921; s. John and Mary (Jubinsky) S.; m. Margaret Pickett, July 24, 1948; children: John, Linda, Scott. B.A. in Econs, Ohio Wesleyan U., 1948; M.A., U. Ill., 1949, Ph.D., 1951; Fellow, Ohio Wesleyan U., 1946-48; scholar, fellow research, U. Ill., 1948-51. Various positions Ford Motor Co., Dearborn, Mich., 1951-66; v.p., treas. Ford Motor Co., 1966-86; pres. John Sagan Assocs., Dearborn, 1986—; bd. dirs. Telident Corp., Chartwell Corp., SBCM Derivatives Products, Ltd. Trustee Ohio Wesleyan U., 1964—, Com. Econ. Devel. U.S.A., Oakwood Hosp., Dearborn, Mich., YMCA Found., Detroit Fund for Henry Ford Hosp. Served with USNR, 1943-46. Mem. Am. Econ. Assn., Phi Beta Kappa, Phi Kappa Phi, Delta Sigma Rho. Home and Office: 22149 Long Blvd Dearborn MI 48124-1104

SAGAN, STANLEY DANIEL, career officer, retired; b. Niagara Falls, N.Y., Jan. 6, 1916; s. Stanley and Kathryn Sagan; m. Eleanor Stella Krzesimowski, Apr. 19, 1941; children: Lawrence S., Deborah E. BA, U. Dayton, 1944. Lic. aircraft pilot. Designer aircraft U.S. War Dept., Dayton, Ohio, 1942-45; instr. U. Dayton, 1946-47, U. Detroit, 1947-48; commd. 1st lt. USAF, Dayton, 1950; advanced through grades to lt. col. USAF, 1971; rsch. and devel. officer USAF, Dayton, 1948-51; spl. staff officer USAF, 1951-55; tech. cons. USAF, San Antonio, 1961-71; ret. USAF, 1971; tchr., bus. mgr. Antonian H.S., San Antonio, 1971-74; aircraft designer Saga Corp., San Antonio, 1974-77; staff com. vocat. edn., Target 90 of San Antonio, 1982-88. Author: Dithyramb, 1996; author of poems; inventor in field. Vol. Rep. party, San Antonio, 1987-88. Recipient cert. of merit San Antonio Archdiocese, 1987, cert. of svc. U.S. Dept. Air Force, 1971. Mem. Soc. of Automotive Engrs., San Antonio Ret. Officers Assn. (v.p., legis. liaison officer 1980-91, bd. dirs. 1996—, Pres.'s award 1986), Mil. Order of World Wars (comdr. 1983-84, nat. officer, chmn. law and order com. 1992-94), Tex. Tchrs. State Assn., Am. Legion (cert. appreciation 1987, adjutant 1977). Roman Catholic. Avocations: travel, photography, linguistics.

SAGANSKY, JEFF, broadcast executive. BA, Harvard U., MBA. Fin. analyst CBS-TV, 1976-77; mgr. film programs NBC-TV, 1977, dir. dramatic devel. entertainment div., 1978, sr. v.p. series programming, 1982-85; v.p. devel. David Gerber Co., 1979-82; pres. prodn., then pres. Tri-Star Pictures Inc., 1985-90; pres. CBS Entertainment Divsn., 1990-94; exec. v.p. Sony U.S., 1994-96; co-pres. Sony Pictures Entertainment, N.Y.C., 1996—; exec. v.p. Sony Pictures Entertainment, Culver City, Calif., 1996—. Office: Sony Pictures Entertainment Co Thalberg Bldg Rm 3407 10202 W Washington Blvd Culver City CA 90232*

SAGAWA, SHIRLEY SACHI, lawyer; b. Rochester, N.Y., Aug. 25, 1961; d. Hidetaka H. and Patricia (Ford) S.; m. Gregory A. Baer; children: Jackson Ford Baer, Matthew Sagawa Baer. AB, Smith Coll., 1983; MSc, London Sch. Econs., 1984; JD, Harvard U., 1987. Bar: Md. 1988. Chief counsel youth policy, labor and human resources com. U.S. Senate, Washington, 1987-91; sr. counsel and dir. family and youth policy Nat. Women's Law Ctr., Washington, 1991-93; spl. asst. to Pres. Clinton for domestic policy, 1993; exec. dir., mng. dir., exec. v.p. Corp. for Nat. and Comty. Svc., Washington, 1993-97; exec. dir. Forum of Ednl. Orgn. Leaders, Washington, 1997—. Mem. exec. bd. Orgn. for Pan-Asian Am. Women, Washington, 1987-89; mem. Women of Color Leadership Coun., 1991-92; vice chair, bd. dirs. Nat. Community Svc. Commn., 1991-93; trustee Am. Folklife Ctr., Libr. Congress, 1996-97; commr. Head Start Fellowships Commn., 1996—; bd. dirs. My Sister's Place, 1996—. Recipient Philip V. McGance award Coun. for Advancement of Citizenship, 1991, cert. of recognition Nat. Coun. Jewish Women, 1989, Alexandrine medal Coll. St. Catherine, St. Paul, 1995; Harry S. Truman scholar, 1981; Smith Coll. Alumnae Assn. fellow, 1983, AAUW fellow, 1986. Mem. Md. Bar Assn. Democrat. Episcopalian. Office: #310 1001 Connecticut Ave NW Ste 310 Washington DC 20036-5530

SAGAWA, YONEO, horticulturist, educator; b. Olaa, Hawaii, Oct. 11, 1926; s. Chikatada and Mume (Kuno) S.; m. Masayo Yamamoto, May 24, 1962 (dec. Apr. 1988); children: Penelope Toshiko, Irene Teruko. AB, Washington U., St. Louis, 1950, MS, 1952; PhD, U. Conn., 1956. Postdoctoral research assoc. biology Brookhaven Nat. Lab., Upton, N.Y., 1955-57; guest in biology Brookhaven Nat. Lab., 1958; asst. prof., then assoc. prof. U. Fla., 1957-64; dir. undergrad. sci. ednl. research participation program NSF, 1964; cons. biosatellite project NASA, 1966-67; prof. horticulture U. Hawaii, 1964—; dir. Lyon Arboretum, 1967-91; assoc. dir. Hawaiian Sci. Fair, 1966-67, dir., 1967-68; research assoc. in biology U. Calif., Berkeley, 1970-71; rsch. assoc. Bishop Mus., Honolulu, 1992—, Botanical Rsch. Inst. of Tex., 1993—, Hawaii Tropical Botanical Garden, 1995—; external assessor U. Pertanian, Malaysia, 1994—; mem. Internat. Orchid Commn. on Classification, Nomenclature and Registration; fellow Inst. voor Toepassing van Atoomenergie in de Landbouw, U. Agr., Wageningen, The Netherlands, 1979-80; mem. sci. adv. bd. Nat. Tropical Bot. Garden, Kauai, Hawaii, bd. dirs., rsch. affiliate; councilor Las Cruces Bot. Garden, Costa Rica; cons. FAO, Singapore, 1971, USAID-Agribusiness Assistance Program, Vols. in Overseas Cooperative Assistance, UN Devel. Program-UN Internat. Short Term Advisory Resources; dir. Hawaii Tropical Bot. Garden. Editor: Hawaii Orchid Jour., 1972—, Pacific Orchid Soc. Bull., 1966-71; mem. editl. bd.: Allertonia, 1976; contbr. numerous articles to profl. jours. Trustee Friends of Honolulu Bot. Gardens, 1973—. Recipient Disting. Svc. award South Fla. Orchid Soc., 1968, Cert. of Achievement Garden Club Am., 1995, Gold award Hawaii Orchid Growers Assn., 1996; grantee Am. Orchid Soc., Atomic Energy Commn., NIH, HEW, Inst. Mus. Svcs., Stanley Smith Hort. Trust, Honolulu Orchid Soc. Fellow Am. Orchid Soc. (hon. life); mem. AAAS, Internat. Assn. Hort. Sci., Am. Assn. Hort. Sci., Am. Inst. for Biol. Scis., Bot. Soc. Am., Hawn Bot. Soc. (past v.p.), Internat. Assn. Plant Tissue Culture, Internat. Palm Soc., Am. Anthurium Soc. (hon. life), Pacific Orchid Soc. (trustee 1994), Kaimuki Orchid Soc. (hon. life), Honolulu Orchid Soc. (hon., life), Lyon Arboretum Assn. (trustee 1974-91), Garden Club Honolulu (hon., life), Aloha Bonsai Club, Sigma Xi, Gamma Sigma Delta, Phi Kappa Phi (past pres., v.p., councillor U. Hawaii chpt.). Democrat. Office: U Hawaii Horticulture Rm 102 3190 Maile Way Honolulu HI 96822-2232

SAGE, ANDREW GREGG CURTIN, II, corporate investor, manager; b. Bryn Mawr, Pa., Mar. 11, 1926; s. Henry W. and Eleanor (Purviance) S.; m. Sara Wakefield, Sept. 29, 1956; children: Andrew Gregg Curtin III, Sally. Mem. staff DeCoppet & Doremus (odd lot stock house), N.Y.C., 1946-47, Sage & Co., N.Y. Stock Exchange Specialists, N.Y.C., 1947-48; assoc. Lehman Bros., N.Y.C., 1948-60; gen. partner Lehman Bros., 1960-68, pres., 1970-73, vice chmn., 1973-77, mng. dir., 1977-82; mng. dir. Lehman Bros. Kuhn Loeb, Inc., 1977-82; mng. dir. Shearson Lehman Bros., Inc., 1982-87, sr. cons., 1987-90; pres., CEO, dir. Robertson CECO Corp., Boston, 1992-93, chmn. bd. dirs., 1994—; bd. dirs. Fluid Conditioning Products, Lititz, Pa., Tom's Foods, Computervision Corp., Am. Superconductor Corp.; pres., treas. Sage Land Devel. Co.; pres., dir. Sage Capital Corp. Served with USAAF, 1944-46. Home: PO Box 937 Wilson WY 83014-0937

SAGE, ANDREW PATRICK, JR., systems information and software engineering educator; b. Charleston, S.C., Aug. 27, 1933; s. Andrew Patrick and Pearl Louise (Britt) S.; m. LaVerne Galhouse, Mar. 3, 1962; children: Theresa Annette, Karen Margaret, Philip Andrew. BS in Elec. Enging, The Citadel, 1955; SM, MIT, 1956; PhD, Purdue U., 1960; DEng (hon.), U. Waterloo, Can., 1987, Dalhousie U., Halifax, Nova Scotia, Can., 1997. Registered profl. engr., Tex. Instr. elec. engring. Purdue U., 1956-60; assoc. prof. U. Ariz., 1960-63; mem. tech. staff Aerospace Corp., Los Angeles, 1963-64; prof. elec. engring. and nuclear engring. scis. U. Fla., 1964-67; prof., dir. Info. and Control Scis. Center, So. Methodist U., Dallas, 1967-74; head elec. engring. dept. So. Meth. U., 1973-74; Quarles prof. engring. sci. and systems U. Va., Charlottesville, 1974-84; chmn. dept. chem. engring. U. Va., 1974-75, chmn. dept. engring. sci. and systems, 1977-84, assoc. dean, 1974-80; First Am. Bank prof. info. tech. George Mason U., Fairfax, Va., 1984—, assoc. v.p. for acad. affairs, 1984-85; dean Sch. Info. Tech. and Engring. George Mason U., 1985-96, univ. prof., founding dean emeritus, 1996—; cons. Martin Marietta, Collins Radio, Atlantic Richfield, Tex. Instruments, LTV Aerospace, Battelle Meml. Inst., TRW Sys., NSF, Inst. Def. Analyses, Planning Rsch. Corp., MITRE, Engring. Rsch. Assocs., Software Productivity Consortium; gen. chmn. Internat. Conf. on Sys., Man and Cybernetics, 1974, 87; mem. spl. program panel on sys. sci. NATO, 1981-82; trustee, cons. Ctr. Naval Analysis, 1990-94. Author: Optimum Systems Control, 1968, 2d edit., 1977, Estimation Theory with Applications to Communications and Control, 1971, System Identification, 1971, An Introduction to Probability and Stochastic Processes, 1973, Methodology for Large Scale Systems, 1977, Systems Engineering: Methodology and Applications, 1977, Linear Systems Control, 1978, Economic Systems Analysis, 1983, System Design for Human Interaction, 1987, Information Processing in Systems and Organizations, 1990, Introduction to Computer Systems Analysis, Design, and Applications, 1989, Software Systems Engineering, 1990, Decision Support Systems Engineering, 1991, Systems Engineering, 1992, Systems Management for Information Technology and Software Engineering, 1995; assoc. editor IEEE Transactions on Systems Sci. and Cybernetics, 1968-72; editor: IEEE Transactions on Systems, Man and Cybernetics, 1972—; assoc. editor: Automatica, 1968-81; editor, 1981-96; mem. editl. bd. Systems Engring, 1968-72, IEEE Spectrum, 1972-73, Computers and Elec. Engring., 1972-94, Jour. Interdisciplinary Modeling and Simulation, 1976-80, Internat. Jour. Intelligent Sys., 1986—, Orgn. Sci.-94, 1990; editor Elsevier North Holland textbook series in sys. sci. and engring., 1970-88, John Wiley textbook series on sys. engring., 1989—; co-editor-in-chief Jour. Large Scale Sys.: Theory and Applications, 1978-88, Info. and Decision Technologies, 1988-94, Info. and Sys. Engring., 1995—, Sys. Engring., 1996—; contbr. articles on computer sci. and sys. engring. to profl. jours. Recipient Norbert Wiener award, 1980, Joseph G. Wohl career award, 1991, Superior Pub. Svc. award Sec. of the Navy, 1994; Case Centennial scholar, 1980, Award Washington Soc. of Engrs., 1996. Fellow IEEE (life, M. Barry Carlton award 1970, Centennial medal 1984, Outstanding Contbn. award 1986, Donald G. Fink prize 1994), AAAS (chmn. sect. M 1990), IEEE Sys. Soc.; mem. Man and Cybernetics Soc. (pres. 1984-85, Inst. Mgmt. Scis., Internat. Fedn. Automatic Control (Outstanding Svc. award), Am. Soc. Engring. Edn. (Frederick Emmonds Terman award 1970, Centennial cert. for exceptional contbn. 1993), Washington Soc. Engrs. (award 1996), Inst. for Mgmt. Sci. and Ops. Rsch., Sigma Xi, Eta Kappa Nu, Tau Beta Pi. Home: 8011 Woodland Hills Ln Fairfax VA 22039-2433 Office: George Mason U Sch Info Tech Fairfax VA 22030-4444

SAGER, CLIFFORD J(ULIUS), psychiatrist, educator; b. N.Y.C.; s. Max and Lena (Lipman) S.; m. Anne Scheinman; children by previous marriage: Barbara L., Philip T., Rebecca J., Anthony F. BS, Pa. State U., 1937; MD, NYU, 1941; cert. in psychoanalysis, N.Y. Med. Coll., 1949. Diplomate: Am. Bd. Psychiatry and Neurology. Rotating intern Montefiore Hosp., N.Y.C., 1941-42; resident in psychiatry Bellevue Hosp., N.Y.C., 1942, 46-48; practice medicine specializing in psychiatry N.Y.C. and East Hampton, N.Y., 1946—; dir. therapeutic services, assoc. dean, dir. tng. Postgrad. Ctr. Mental Health, 1948-60; vis. psychiatrist, med. bd. Flower and Fifth Ave Hosp., 1960-71, Met. Hosp., 1960-71; dir. psychiat. tng. and edn. N.Y. Med. Coll., 1960-71; attending psychiatrist Bird S. Coler Hosp., 1960-71; clin. dir. N.Y. Med. Coll., 1960-63, assoc. prof. psychiatry, 1960-65, prof., 1966-71, dir. partial hosp. programs and family treatment and study unit, 1964-71; clin. prof. psychiatry Mt. Sinai Sch. Medicine, 1971-80; assoc. dir. psychiatry Beth Israel Hosp. for Family and Mental Therapy; chief of psychiatry Gov.'s Hosp., 1970-74; dir. family therapy Mt. Sinai Sch. Medicine, 1974-80; clin. prof. psychiatry N.Y. Hosp.-Cornell Univ. Med. Ctr., 1980—; attending psychiatrist N.Y. Hosp.-Payne Whitney Clinic, 1980—; dir. marital and family clinic N.Y. Hosp., 1991—; attending psychiatrist Mt. Sinai Hosp., 1971-80; chief behavioral scis. Gouverneur Hosp.; chief family treatment unit Beth Israel Med. Ctr., 1970-74, assoc. dir. psychiatry family and group therapy, 1971-74; psychiat. dir. Jewish Family Svc., 1974-77; dir. family psychiatry Jewish Bd. Family and Childrens Svcs., 1978-90; dir. Remarried Consultation Svc., 1976-90; dir. Tng. and Sex Therapy Clinic, 1974-90; founder The Relationship Inst., N.Y.C., 1990—; psychiat. dir. Employee Consultation and Corp. Health Programs, 1980—; faculty , supr. Contemporary Ctr. Advanced Psychoanalytic Studies; chief neuropsychiatry 42d and 312th Gen. Hosp. Author: Marriage Contracts and Couple Therapy, 1976, Intimate Partners, 1979, Treating the Remarried Family, 1983; 5 other books; mem. editorial bd. Am. Jour. Orthopsychiatry, 1960-69, Internat. Jour. Group Psychotherapy, 1968—, Family Process, 1969-92, Divorce and Remarriage, 1977—, Comprehensive Rev. Jour. Family and Marriage, 1978—; cons. Sexual Medicine, 1974-82; co-editor, founder Jour. Sex and Marital Therapy, 1974—; mem. editorial bd.: Jour. Marriage and Family Counseling, 1977—, Internat. Jour. Family Counseling, 1977—; author or contbr. over 88 sci. articles to jours. Capt. M.C. AUS, 1942-46, chief neuropsychiatry 42d and 312th Gen. Hosp. Recipient Am. Family Therapy Assn. award for Outstanding Contribution to Family Therapy 1983, Assn. Marriage and Family Therapists award for Outstanding Contributions to the field of Marital and Family Therapy, 1984. Fellow Am. Psychiat. Assn. (life), Am. Orthopsychiat. Assn. (life), Acad. Psychoanalysis (charter), Am. Group Psychotherapy Assn. (pres. 1968-70, dir. 1962-74), Soc. Med. Psychoanalysts (pres. 1960-61, dir. 1958-62), Am. Assn. Marital and Famiy Therapists; mem. AMA, Am. Soc. Advancement Psychotherapy (dir. 1954-67), N.Y. Soc. Clin. Psychiatry, Soc. for Sex Therapy and Rsch. (pres. 1976-77, bd. dirs. 1953-58) PAIRS Found. (bd. dirs. 1985—). Office: 65 E 76th St New York NY 10021-1844 also: 33 Breeze Hill Rd East Hampton NY 11937-4505

SAGER, DONALD JACK, publisher, former librarian; b. Milw., Mar. 3, 1938; s. Alfred Herman and Sophia (Sagan) S.; m. Sarah Ann Long, May 23, 1987; children: Geoffrey, Andrew. BS, U. Wis., Milw., 1963; MSLS, U. Wis., 1964. Sr. documentalist AC Electronics divsn. GM, Milw., 1958-63; teaching asst. U. Wis., Madison, 1963-64; dir. Kingston (N.Y.) Pub. Libr., 1964-66, Elyria (Ohio) Pub. Libr., 1966-71, Mobile Pub. Libr., 1971-75, Pub. Libr. Columbus and Franklin County, Ohio, 1975-78; commr. Chgo. Pub. Libr., 1978-81; dir. Elmhurst Pub. Libr., Ill., 1982-83, Milw. Pub. Libr., 1983-91; pub. Highsmith Press, Ft. Atkinson, Wis., 1991—; sec. Online Computer Libr. Ctr., 1977-78, disting. vis. scholar, 1982; chmn. mus. com. PLA Pub. Libr., 1989-91, history com., 1993-95, chmn. investment com., 1985-89, chmn. PLA nat. conf. com., 1986-88; bd. dirs. Coun. Wis. Librs., 1982-91, Urban Librs. Coun., 1985-93, sec., 1991-93; adj. faculty U. Wis., Milw., 1984-91; cons. in field. Author: Reference: A Programmed Instruction, 1970, Binders, Books and Budgets, 1971, Participatory Management, 1981, The American Public Library, 1982, Public Library Administrators Planning Guide to Automation, 1983, Managing the Public Library, 1984, 2d rev. edit., 1989, Small Libraries, 1992, 2d rev. edit., 1996; co-editor: Urban Library Management Trends, 1989; contbg. editor: Public Libraries, 1990—; contbr. articles to profls. publs. Bd. dirs. Goethe House, 1985-91; pres. Milw. Civic Alliance, 1990-91; chmn. Milw. United Way Campaign, 1984; pres. Milw. Westown Assn., 1987-90. With inf. AUS, 1956-58. Mem. ALA (coun. mem. 1995—, policy monitoring com., awards com.), Pub. Libr. Assn. (bd. dirs., v.p., pres.-elect, pres. 1982-83), Ill. Libr. Assn., Chgo. Book Clinic, Wis. Libr. Assn., Wis. Libr. Assn. Found. (chmn. 1986-88), Libr. Adminstrn. Assn. Wis. (chmn. 1987-88), Exch. Club Milw. (pres. 1988-89). Home: 590 Wilmot Rd Deerfield IL 60015-3955 Office: Highsmith Press 5527W Highway 106 Fort Atkinson WI 53538

SAGER, PHILIP TRAVIS, academic physician, cardiac electrophysiologist; b. N.Y.C., Jan. 23, 1956; s. Clifford Julius nad Ruth (Levy) S. BS in Chemistry and Biology, MIT, Cambridge, Mass., 1977; MD, Yale U., New Haven, Conn., 1982, resident, cardiology fellow, 1982-88. Diplomate Am. Bd. Internal Medicine, Am. Bd. Cardiology, AM. Bd. Cardiac Electrophysiology. Asst. prof. medicine Sch. Medicine, U. So. Calif., L.A., 1988-90, asst. dir. electrophysiology, 1988-90, dir. Pacemaker Ctr., 1988-90; asst. prof. medicine Sch. Medicine, UCLA, 1990-96, assoc. prof. of medicine, 1996—; dir. cardiac electrophysiology West L.A. VA Med. Ctr., 1990-96; mem. cardiology adv. com. VA Adminstrn., Washington, 1990-94; cons. electrophysiology ACGME, Chgo., 1995—; vis. prof. Kern Med. Ctr., Bakersfield, Calif., 1991, 94, U. Iowa Sch. Medicine, 1994, Northwestern U. Sch. Medicine, 1994, Yale U. Sch. Medicine, 1995, U. Calif., San Francisco, 1996; invited lectr. Contbr. chpts. to books, numerous rsch. articles to profl. jours. of innovative rsch.; reviewer many scientific jours. Recipient many rsch. grants, including Am. Heart Assn., 1996. Fellow Am. Heart Assn. (coun. on clin. cardiology 1997—), Am. Coll. Cardiology, Am. Coll. Physicians; mem. Am. Fedn. Clin. Rsch., Nat. Assn. Pacing and Electrophysiology (program dirs. com. 1992—, govt. com. 1994—, assoc. chair program dirs. com. 1997—), Phi Beta Kappa, Alpha Omega Alpha. Avocations: bicycling, scuba diving, reading history, movies. Office: W LA VAMC-UCLA Dept 111E 11301 Wilshire Blvd Dept 111E Los Angeles CA 90073-1003

SAGER, RODERICK COOPER, retired life insurance company executive; b. Washington, May 25, 1923; s. Theron Parker and Rebecca (Ward) S.; m. Ruth Regina Ross, Sept. 2, 1947; children: Lawrence Cooper, Jonathan Ward, Timothy Charles. A.B., Syracuse U., 1948, J.D., 1950. Bar: N.Y. 1951, U.S. Supreme Ct. 1958; C.L.U., 1969; chartered fin. cons. Assoc. Mackenzie, Smith, Lewis, Michell and Hughes, Syracuse, 1950-62; gen. counsel Farmers and Traders Life Ins. Co., Syracuse, 1962-66, v.p., gen. counsel, 1966-69, sr. v.p., gen. counsel, 1969-74, exec. v.p., gen. counsel, 1974-79, pres., chief exec. officer, 1979-89, also bd. dirs., ret., 1989; chmn. Life Ins. Council, N.Y., 1984. Trustee Jamesville-DeWitt Cen. Sch. Dist., 1956-69, Onondaga Community Coll., 1971-75; bd. dirs. N.Y. State Tchrs. Retirement System, 1977-92, Onondaga Indsl. Devel. Corp., 1984-89, Lit. Vols. of Greater Syracuse, Inc., 1990-91; trustee Rescue Mission Alliance, Syracuse, 1980—, pres., 1985-86. 1st lt. U.S. Army, 1943-46, 51-52. Mem. Onondaga County Bar Assn., Assn. Life Ins. Counsel. Clubs: Century (Syracuse); Onondaga Golf and Country (Fayetteville, N.Y.). Lodge: Rotary. Home: 3 Wynnridge Rd Fayetteville NY 13066-2532

SAGER, THOMAS WILLIAM, statistics research administrator. BA, U. Iowa, 1968, MS, 1971, PhD in Stats., 1973. Asst. prof. stats. Stanford U., 1973-78; vis. asst. prof. math. and bus. U. Tex., Austin, 1978-79, asst. prof., 1979-82, assoc. prof. stats., 1982-93, prof. stats., 1993—. Mem. Inst. Math. Stats., Am. Statis. Assn., Sigma Xi. Office: U Tex Ctr Statis Sci Ctr Statis Scis GSB5.176 & CBA 5.202 Austin TX 78712

SAGER, WILLIAM F., retired chemistry educator; b. Glencoe, Ill., Jan. 22, 1918; s. Fred Anson and Alta (Stansbury) S.; m. Marilyn Olga Williams, Dec. 26, 1941; children: Karen Louise Sager Dickinson, Judith Lynn SagerPeyton), Kathryn Gwen Sager Potts. B.S. in Chemistry, George Washington U., 1939, M.A. in Organic Chemistry, 1941; Ph.D. in Organic Chemistry, Harvard U., 1948. Research chemist The Texas Co., 1941-45; prof. chemistry George Washington U., 1948-65; prof. chemistry U. Ill.-Chgo., 1965-86, prof. emeritus, 1986—, chmn., 1965-80; cons. to govt. and industry, 1952—. Recipient Disting. Service award U. Ill. Alumni Assn.; Guggenheim fellow, 1954-55. Mem. Am. Chem. Soc., Sigma Xi, Alpha Chi Sigma. Home: 1552 John Anderson Dr Ormond Beach FL 32176-3567 Office: Dept Chemistry U Ill-Chicago Chicago IL 60680

SAGERHOLM, JAMES ALVIN, retired naval officer; b. Uniontown, Pa., Dec. 23, 1927; s. Frithiof Norris and Margaret Blocher S.; m. Margaret Ann Herrlich, June 7, 1952; children—Lisa Marie, Ann Denise, Jeannine Louise, Mark Christian. B.S., U.S. Naval Acad., 1952. Commd. ensign U.S. Navy, 1952, advanced through grades to vice admiral, navigator USS Seadragon, 1965, exec. officer blue crew USS Mariano G. Vallejo, 1966-67, commanding officer gold crew USS Kamehameha, 1968-71, head gen. purpose warfare forces group Office of Chief Naval Ops., 1971, dep. exec. dir. Chief Naval Ops. Exec. Panel, 1972, exec. sec. Chief Naval Ops. Exec. Bd., 1973; comdr. Naval Intelligence Support Ctr. U.S. Navy, Washington, 1974-75; dep. dir. naval intelligence Chief Naval Ops. U.S. Navy, 1975-76, comdr. South Atlantic Force, U.S. Atlantic Fleet, 1976-78, dir. Office of Program Appraisal, Office of Sec. Navy, 1978-81; chief naval edn. and tng. U.S. Navy, Pensacola, Fla., 1983-85; exec. dir. Pres. Fgn. Intelligence Adv. Bd. White House, Washington, 1981-82; ret., 1985; chmn. bd. dirs. Piedmont Environ. Coun., 1987-89; v.p. for nat. affairs Gen. George C. Marshall Home Found., 1990-91. Decorated D.S.M., Legion of Merit, Meritorious Service medal. Mem. Naval Submarine League, U.S. Naval Inst., Civil War Soc., K.C. Roman Catholic. Avocations: golf; tennis; Civil War enthusiast. Home: 414 Rockfleet Rd Unit 102 Lutherville MD 21093

SAGETT, JAN JEFFREY, lawyer, former government official; b. Chgo., Dec. 12, 1943; s. Leonard Henry and Carolyn (Zilberman) S.; BS with honors, U. Ill.-Urbana, 1965; JD, U. Chgo., 1968. Bar: Ill. 1969, D.C. 1969, U.S. Supreme Ct. 1972; CPA, Ill. Assoc., McDermott, Will, and Emery, Chgo., 1968-69; spl. asst. to dir. Office of Minority Bus. Enterprise, Washington, 1969; spl. counsel, asst. gen. counsel Office Econ. Opportunity, Washington, 1969-73; legis. counsel Small Bus. Adminstrn., Washington, 1973-74; dep. assoc. commr., legal counsel Social Security Adminstrn., Washington, 1974-81; asst. gen. counsel, asst. treas. Edison Electric Inst., Washington, 1981-94; v.p., mem. trust mgmt. com. First Nat. Bank Md., Balt., 1995-97, FMB Trust Co., Balt., 1997—; treas., mem. exec. com., bd. dirs., chmn. audit com. U.S. Energy Assn., 1991-93; mem. bd. dirs Dreyfus Edison Electric Index Fund, 1992-94, mem. industry adv. bd., 1991-94. Contbg. author: Federal Regulatory Process: Agency Practices and Procedures, 1981-84. Ill. State scholar, 1961-65; selected for Sr. Mgrs. in Govt. program Harvard U., 1978. Mem. ABA (taxation sect., employee benefits com.), Washington Met. Area Corp. Counsel Assn., Am. Corp. Counsel Assn., Beta Gamma Sigma, Phi Eta Sigma, Pi Lambda Phi (exec. council 1963-64), Phi Kappa Phi, Beta Alpha Psi. Jewish. Office: First Nat Bank Md 25 S Charles St Baltimore MD 21201-3330

SAGHIR, ADEL JAMIL, artist, painter, sculptor; b. Beirut, Lebanon, May 27, 1930; came to U.S., 1973; s. Jamil Khalil and Aisha Rachid (Mirii) S.; m. Jindriska Antonin Moucka, Aug. 24, 1968; children: Jamil, Ryan. BA, Am. U., Beirut, 1968, diploma in tchg., 1973; MFA, Pratt Inst., 1975; postgrad., NYU, 1976-79. Asst. prof. Fine Arts Inst., Lebanese U., Beirut, 1963-73; lectr. Am. Beirut U. Coll., 1972-73; adj. prof. Western Conn. State U., Danbury, 1988—; instr. sculpture, mural painting, art history Silvermine Sch. Art, New Canaan, Conn., 1989—. Artist various murals and tapestries. Recipient 4th prize Alexandria Biennale, Egyptian Govt., 1963, 1st prize silk tapestries Nat. Contest Lebanon, 1965, 1st prize major sculpture monuments, 1966, 1st prize City Ctr. Sculpture Contest, 1969; Fine Arts scholar, Germany, Munic Acad., 1958-60; Fulbright-Hayes fellow NYU, N.Y.C., 1973-79. Mem. Internat. Soc. Advancement of Living Traditions in Art, Washington Pl. Artists Assn. (pres. 1977-80), Lebanese Artists Assn. (v.p. 1964-73). Avocations: gardening, fishing, upland hunting. Home: 20 Newfane Rd New Fairfield CT 06812-4721 Office: Western Conn State U 181 White St Danbury CT 06810

SAGMEISTER, EDWARD FRANK, business owner, hospitality industry executive, civic official, retired consultant, fund raiser, career officer; b. N.Y.C., Dec. 10, 1939; s. Frank and Anna (Unger) S.; m. Anne Marie Ducker, Aug. 18, 1962; children: Cynthia Anne, Laura Marie, Cheryl Suzanne, Eric Edward. BS, U. San Francisco, 1962; MBA, Syracuse U., 1968; postgrad., Air Command and Staff Coll., 1977, Air War Coll., 1981. Commd. 2d lt. USAF, 1963, advanced through grades to lt. col., pers. officer, 1963, aide-de-camp, 1965; dir. pers. sys. Alaskan Air Command, 1968; sys. design program analysis officer HQ USAF, The Pentagon, 1971; spl. asst. sec. Air Force Pers. Coun., USAF, 1975; dir. pers. programs and assignments HQUSAF Europe, 1979; Air Force dep. asst. inspector gen., 1982; ret. USAF, 1984; dir. devel. Am. Cancer Soc., Riverside, Calif., 1984-87; cons. Redlands, Calif., 1987-92; chmn. of bd., pres., CEO Hospitality Pub and Grub, Inc., San Bernardino, Calif., 1992—; instr. Am. Internat. U., L.A., 1987; program dir. Am. Radio Network, L.A., 1987; ptnr., owner Midway Med. Ctr., San Bernardino, 1990-91. Foreman pro-tem San Bernardino County Grand Jury, 1990-91; mem. Redlands 2000 Com., 1988; campaign cabinet mem. Arrowhead United Way, San Bernardino, 1986-87, loaned exec., 1985; exec. dir. Crafton hills Coll. Found., Yucaipa, Calif., 1988; vol. San Bernardino County Dept. Probation, 1985-88; mem. Redlands Cmty., Chorus, 1988-90; vice-chmn., charter mem. Redlands Human Rels. Commn., 1994—, chmn., 1996; mem. Redlands Youth Accountability Bd., San Bernardino County, 1994—, treas. 1996; mem. supt.'s human rels. adv. com., Redlands Unified Sch. Dist., 1996—. Mem. San Bernardino C. of C., Redlands C. of C., Ret. Officers Assn., Nat. Soc. Fundraising Execs., (dir., charter mem. Inland Empire chpt. 1987-88), Empire Singers (v.p. 1987). Republican. Roman Catholic. Avocations: travel, music, singing, tennis, reading. Home: 503 Sunnyside Ave Redlands CA 92373-5629 Office: Hospitality Pub and Grub Inc 1987 Diners Ct San Bernardino CA 92408-3330

SAGNESS, RICHARD LEE, education educator, former academic dean; b. Rock Rapids, Iowa, Jan. 9, 1937; s. David Harold and Joyce Morrow (Carlson) S.; m. Donna Jayne Lanxon, Feb. 18, 1956; children: Debbi Van Vooren, Becky Hardy, Beth Sagness Higbee. BA, U. No. Iowa, 1961; MS, Emporia State U., 1965; PhD, Ohio State U., 1970; grad. Inst. for Higher Edn. Mgmt., Harvard U., 1977. Tchr. biology Cen. High Sch., Sioux City, Iowa, 1961-66; lectr. biology Emporia (Kans.) State U., 1966-67; info. analyst Ohio State U., 1967-70; asst. prof. sci. edn. U. S.D., Vermillion, 1970-72, assoc. prof., 1972-75, coord. sci. edn., 1970-75; prof. sci. edn., assoc. dean Sch. Edn. U. S.D., Vermillion, 1975-79; prof. edn. Coll. Edn. Idaho State U., Pocatello, 1979—, dean Coll. Edn., 1979-89, dir. clin. experiences and student svcs., 1993—; past mem. Idaho Profl. Stds. Commn.; faculty rep. to bd. dirs. Idaho State U. Found., 1992—; mem. Idaho Sch.-to-Work Collaborative Team, 1994—. Contbr. articles to profl. jours. Bd. dirs. Vermillion Devel. Corp., 1974-78, pres., 1976-77; bd. dirs. Pocatello United Fund, 1976-79, 82-83, v.p., 1982-83, pres., 1985-86. With U.S. Army, 1955-57. Mem. Idaho Assn. Colls. Tchr. Edn. (pres. 1984-88), Am. Assn. Colls. of Tchr. Edn. (rep., chairperson govtl. rels. com. 1988-89, bd. dirs. 1988-92), Pocatello C. of C. (bd. dirs. 1983-89, pres. 1987-88), Tchr. Edn. Coun. State Colls. and Univs. (exec. coun. 1988-90), N.W. Assn. Schs. and Colls. (commn. on schs. 1995—, bd. trustees 1997—), Rotary (bd. dirs. local club 1988-89, team leader study exch. team to Sweden 1991, pres.-elect 1997—), Masons, Order Eastern Star (past patron), Phi Delta Kappa (past pres.). Office: Idaho State Univ PO Box 8059 Pocatello ID 83209-8059

SAHA, BADAL CHANDRA, biochemist; b. Jamurki, Tangail, Bangladesh, July 1, 1949; came to U.S., 1984, naturalized; s. Kalachand and Milan (Deshmukhya) S.; m. Sarabi Roychowdhury, June 7, 1976; children: Susmita, Saroj. BS with honors, Dhaka U., Bangladesh, 1969, MS, 1970; MS, Kyushu U., Fukuoka, Japan, 1981, PhD, 1984. Biochemist Dhaka (Bangladesh) Med. Coll. Hosp., 1972-73; rsch. scholar Dhaka U., 1973-74; lectr. Bangladesh Agrl. U., Mymensingh, 1974-75, asst. prof., 1975-79; rsch. assoc. U. Md., College Park, 1984-85, Mich. State U., East Lansing, 1985-86; rsch. scientist Mich. Biotech. Inst., Lansing, 1986-92; vis. scientist, rsch. chemist USDA Agrl. Rsch. Svc., Peoria, Ill., 1992—; asst. adj. prof. Mich. State U., East Lansing, 1988-92. Author: Clostridia, 1989, Biocatalysis, 1990, (with others) Mixed Cultures in Biotechnology, 1991; mem. editl. bd. Jour. Indsl. Microbiology and Biotech.; contbr. more than 50 articles to profl. jours. including Trends in Biotech., Biochem. Jour., Applied Environ. Microbiology, others. Recipient UNESCO fellowship Japanese Nat. Commn. for UNESCO, 1977-78, Rsch. scholarship Japanese Govt., 1979-84, Grad. scholarship Dhaka U., 1969-70, Dhaka Bd. scholarships, 1962-69. Mem. AAAS, Am. Chem. Soc., Am. Soc. for Microbiology, Soc. for Indsl. Microbiology, Japan Soc. for Biosci., Biotech. and Agrochemistry. Hindu. Achievements include patent in field. Home: 1519 W Queens Court Rd Peoria IL 61614 Office: USDA-ARS Nat Ctr. for Agrl Utilization Rsch 1815 N University St Peoria IL 61604-3902

SAHAI, HARDEO, medical statistics educator; b. Bahraich, India, Jan. 10, 1942; m. Lillian Sahai, Dec. 28, 1973; 3 children. BS in Math., Stats. and Physics, Lucknow U., India, 1962; MS in Math., Banaras U., Varanasi, India, 1964; MS in Math. Stats., U. Chgo., 1968; PhD in Stats., U. Ky., 1971. Lectr. in math. and stats. Banaras U., Varanasi, India, 1964-65; asst. stats. officer Durgapur Steel Plant, Durgapur West Bengal, India, 1965; statistician Rsch. and Planning div. Blue Cross Assn., Chgo., 1966; statis. programmer Cleft Palate Ctr., U. Ill., 1967, Chgo. Health Rsch. Found., 1968; mgmt. scientist Mgmt. Systems Devel. Dept. Burroughs Corp., Detroit, 1971-72; from asst. prof. to prof. dept. math. U. P.R., Mayaguez, 1972-82; vis. research prof. Dept. Stats. and Applied Math. Fed. U. of Ceara, Brazil, 1978-79; sr. research statistician Travenol Labs., Inc., Round Lake, Ill., 1982-83; chief statistician U.S. Army Hqrs., Ft. Sheridan, Ill., 1983-84; sr. math. statistician U.S. Bur. of Census Dept. of Commerce, Washington, 1984-85; sr. ops. rsch. analyst Def. Logistics Agy. Dept. Def., Chgo., 1985-86; prof. Dept. Biostats. and Epidemiology U. P.R. Med. Scis., San Juan, 1986—; cons. P.R. Univ Cons., P.R. Driving Safety Evaluation Project, Water Resources Rsch. Inst., Travenol Labs., Campo Rico, P.R., U.S. Bur. Census, Washington, Lawrence Livermore Nat. Lab., Calif., others; vis. prof. U. Granada, Spain, U. Veracruzana, Mex., U. Nacional de Colombia; vis. prof. U. Nacional de Trujillo, Peru, 1993-94, hon. prof. dept. stats., 1994—; adj. prof. dept. math. U. P.R. Natural Scis. Faculty, 1995—. Author: Statistics and Probability: Learning Module, 1984; author: (with Jose Berrios) A Dictionary of Statistical Scientific and Technical Terms: English-Spanish and Spanish-English, 1981, (with Wilfredo Martinez) Statistical Tables and Formulas for the Biological Social and Physical Sciences, 1996, (with Anwer Khurshid) Statistics in Epidemiology: Methods, Techniques and Applications, 1996, (with Satish C. Misra and Michael Graham) Quotations on Probability and Statistics with Illustrations, 1997, (with Mohammad I. Ageel) The Analysis of Variance: Fixed, Random and Mixed Models, 1997, (with Wilfredo Martnez) Statistical Glossary: English-Spanish, 1997, (with Hector W. Colon) Statistics Vocabulary for Health Professionals, 1997, (with Mario M. Ojeda) Distribuciones Centrales Y No Centrales de t, x2 y F, 1997, (with Mario M. Ojeda) A Glossary of Computer and Management Terms: English/Spanish, 1997, (with Anwer Khurshid) A Pocket Dictionary of Statistics, 1997; mem. editl. bd. Sociedad Colombiana de Matematicas, P.R. Health Scis. Jour.; contbr. editor Current Index to Stats.; reviewer Collegiate Microcomputer, Comm. in Statistics, Indian Jour. Stats., Jour. Royal Statis. Soc. (series D, The Statistician), New Zealand Statistician, Biometrics, Can. Jour. Stats., Technometrics, Problems, Resources and Issues in Math. Undergrad. Studies; contbr. more than 100 articles and papers to profl. and sci. jours., numerous articles to tech. mags. Active Dept. Consumer Affairs Svcs. Commonwealth of P.R., San Juan, Dept. Anti-Addiction Svcs., Commonwealth of P.R., San Juan., Inst. of AIDS, Municipality of San Juan, VA Med. Ctr. of San Juan, Caribbean Primate Rsch. Ctr., Ctr. Addiction Studies Caribbean Ctrl. U. Recipient Dept. Army Cert. Achievement award, 1984, U. Ky. Outstanding Alumnus award, 1993, medal of honor U. Granada, 1994, plaque of honor U. Nacional de Trujillo, 1994; fellow Coun. Sci. and Indsl. Rsch., 1964-65, U. Chgo., 1965-68, Harvard U., 1979, Fulbright Found., 1982; U.P. Bd. Merit scholar, 1957-59, Govt. India Merit scholar, 1959-64; grantee NSF, 1974-77, NIMH, 1987-90, 91—, NIDA, 1991—. Fellow AAAS, Am. Coll. Epidemiology, Inst. Statisticians (charter statistician), Inst. Math. and Its Applications (charter mathematician), N.Y. Acad. Scis., Royal Statis. Soc.; mem. Internat. Statis. Inst., Internat. Assn. Tchg. Stats., Soc. Epidemiol. Rsch., Inst. Math. Stats., Bernouilli Soc. for Math. Stats. and Probabillity, Internat. Biometric Soc., Am. Soc. for Quality Control, Am. Stats. Assn., Japan Statis. Soc., Can. Statis. Soc., Inter-Am. Statis. Inst., Internat. Assn. Statis. Computing, Sch. Sci. and Math. Assn., Sigma Xi. Avocations: religious studies, philosophy, reading, gardening. Home: K-5-B Terrace Calle Dr Gaudier Texidor Mayaguez PR 00680-1149

SAHAI, YOGESHWAR, engineering educator; b. Moradabad, India, Feb. 26, 1945; came to U.S., 1982; s. Someshwar and Shakuntla Sahai; m. Usha Saxena, June 2, 1971; children: Smita, Vivek. BE, U. Roorkee, India, 1968; ME, U. Roorkee, 1973; PhD and DIC, U. London, 1979. Lecturer U. Roorkee, Roorkee, India, 1968-75; researcher U. London, London, Eng., 1975-79; rsch. assoc. McGill U., Montreal, Can., 1979-82; asst. prof. Ohio State U., Columbus, Ohio, 1983-86; assoc. prof. Ohio State U., Columbus, 1986-88; I.S.S. prof. Iron and Steel Soc. prof., Columbus, 1988—; cons. various metal and materials cos., 1982—. Author over 100 tech. papers, 3 tech. books. Recipient P.T.D. award, Iron and Steel Soc., 1988, 90, Mars G. Fontana award, Ohio State U., 1986, extractive metallurgy sci. award, Metallurgical Soc. of AIME, 1984; Stanley Elmore fellow, Inst. Mining and Metallurgy, Eng., 1975-78; Thomson Meml. gold medal, U. Roorkee, 1968. Home: 877 Highview Dr Columbus OH 43235-1232 Office: Ohio State U Dept MSE 2041 N College Rd Columbus OH 43210-1124

SAHATJIAN, MANIK, nurse, psychologist; b. Tabris, Iran, July 24, 1921; came to U.S., 1951; d. Dicran and Shushanig (Der-Galustian) Mnatzaganian; m. George Sahatjian, Jan. 21, 1954; children: Robert, Edwin. Nursing Cert., Am. Mission Hosps.-Boston U., 1954; BA in Psychology, San Jose State U., 1974, MA in Psychology, 1979. RN, Calif., Mass. Head nurse Am. Mission

Hosp., Tabris, 1945-46; charge nurse Banke-Melli Hosp., Tehran, 1946-51; vis. nurse Vis. Nurse Assn., Oakland, Calif., 1956-57; research asst. Stanford U., 1979-81, Palo Alto (Calif.) Med. Research Found., 1981-84; documentation supr. Bethesda Convalescent Ctr., Los Gatos, Calif., 1985-86; sr. outreach worker City of Fremont (Calif.) Human Svcs., 1987-90, case mgr., 1990—; guest rsch. asst. NASA Ames Lab., Mountain View, Calif., summers 1978, 79. Author (with others) psychol. research reports. Fulbright scholar, 1951; Iran Found. scholar, 1953. Mem. AAUW, Western Psychol. Assn. Democrat. Mem. St. Andrew Armenian Church. Avocations: oil painting, classic dance. Home: 339 Starlite Way Fremont CA 94539-7642

SAHATJIAN, RONALD ALEXANDER, science foundation executive; b. Cambridge, Mass., Oct. 1, 1942; s. Vartan and Roxy (Abrahamian) S.; m. Jean Khachadoorian, July 15, 1966; 1 child, Jennifer. BS in Chemistry, Tufts U., 1964; MS in Chemistry, U. Mass., 1968, PhD in Chemistry, 1969. Scientist color photographic rsch. lab. Polaroid Corp., Cambridge, 1971-73, sr. scientist color photogrphic rsch. lab., 1973-75, sr. rsch. group leader photographic/optical materials, 1976-79, program mgr. polacolor transparency projects, 1979-81, mgr. applications rsch. lab., 1980-84; dir. R & D Chem. Fabrics Corp., Merrimack, N.H., 1984-87; v.p. corp. tech. Boston Sci. Corp., Watertown, Mass., 1987—; mem. adv. bd. Franklin Inst., Boston, 1989—. Contbr. articles to Jour. Polymer Sci., Macromolecules, Radiology. Fellow Am. Inst. Chemists; mem. ASTM, Radiol. Soc. N.Am., Watertown C. of C. (bd. dirs. 1991—). Achievements include 58 U.S. and internat. patents. Home: 29 Saddle Club Rd Lexington MA 02173-2121 Office: Boston Sci Corp 1 Boston Scientific Pl Natick MA 01760-1536

SAHID, JOSEPH ROBERT, lawyer; b. Paterson, N.J., Feb. 14, 1944; s. Joseph James and Helen (Vitale) S.; children: Annunziata, Joseph. BS, Rutgers U., 1965; LLB, U. Va., 1968. Bar: N.Y. 1973, U.S. Dist. Ct. N.Y., U.S. Ct. Appeals (2d and 3d cirs.), U.S. Supreme Ct. Staff mem. Nat. Commn. on Causes and Prevention of Violence, Washington, 1968-69; cons. Pres.'s Commn. on Campus Unrest, Washington, 1970; assoc. Cravath, Swaine & Moore, N.Y.C., 1972-77, ptnr., 1977-93, cons., 1994—; ptnr. Barrack, Rodos & Bacine, N.Y.C., 1994-96; pvt. practice N.Y.C., 1996—. Author: Rights in Concord, 1969; co-author: Law and Order Reconsidered, 1969; contbr. articles to profl. jours. Lt. USCG, 1968-72. Office: 18 E 50th St 7th Fl New York NY 10022

SAHLER, CHRISTY LEE, real estate manager; b. Bangor, Maine, Dec. 16, 1962; d. James Howard and Diane Alma (Sandstrom) Sahler; divorced; 1 child, Tahler Diane. BS in Computer Sci., U.S. Naval Acad., 1985. Mdse. mgr. Lenscrafters, Cin., 1990-91, sr. acct., 1991-93; gen. mgr. LaSalle Ptnrs. Asset Mgmt., Chgo., 1994—. Lt. USN, 1985-90. Republican. Lutheran. Avocations: golf, volleyball, reading. Office: LaSalle Ptnrs Asset Mgmt 30 N Lasalle St Ste 3220 Chicago IL 60602-2506

SAHLI, NANCY ANN, retired federal agency administrator, consultant; b. Beaver Falls, Pa., Jan. 4, 1946; d. John Rankin and Betty Melville (McClane) S. AB, Vassar Coll., 1967; MA, U. Pa., 1971, PhD, 1974. Rsch. asst. Drexel U., Phila., 1969-74; archivist Nat. Hist. Publs. and Records Commn., Washington, 1975-81, 83-84, archives cons., 1981-84, archives specialist, 1984-87, dir. records program, 1987-95, program dir., 1991-96, acting exec. dir., 1994-95, ret., 1996; cons. Princeton Theol. Sem., N.J., 1981-82, Vassar Coll., Poughkeepsie, N.Y., 1981-82, Smithsonian Instn., Washington, 1983, Libr. of Congress, 1997. Author: Elizabeth Blackwell, 1982, Women and Sexuality, 1984, MARC for Archives and Manuscripts, 1985 (Coker prize 1986); editor Directory of Archives and Mss. Repos., 1978. NEH grantee, 1981-83; AAUW fellow, 1973-74; recipient Commendable Svc. award GSA, 1978, GSA citation, 1979, 81, Archivist's Achievement award, 1994, 95, 96. Fellow Soc. Am. Archivists (cons. 1983-84); mem. Assn. Documentary Editing, Orgn. Am. Historians (life), Sierra Club (life), Appalachian Trail Conf. Democrat. Buddhist. Avocations: gardening, hiking, traveling. Home: 9 Indian Spring Dr Silver Spring MD 20901-3016

SAHLSTROM, E(LMER) B(ERNARD), retired lawyer; b. Seattle, Feb. 25, 1918; s. August Waldimer and Alma Carolyn (Ostrom) S.; m. Phyllis May Horstman, June 18, 1946; children: Gary Bernard, Cheryl Linn Sahlstrom Monohan, Gregory Lane. B.S., U. Oreg., 1945, J.D., 1947. Bar: Oreg. 1947, U.S. Dist. Ct. Oreg. 1948, U.S. Dist. Ct. Hawaii, 1961, U.S. Ct. Appeals (9th cir.), 1950, U.S. Supreme Ct. 1977; CPA, Oreg. Acct. Haskins & Sells, N.Y.C., 1941-44; mem. Thompson & Sahlstrom, Eugene, Oreg., 1947-57, Sahlstrom, Lombard, Starr & Vinson, and predecessor, Eugene, 1957-76, Sahlstrom & Lombard, Eugene, 1976-78; sole practice Eugene, 1978-80; ptnr. Sahlstrom & Dugdale, Eugene, 1980—. Bd. visitors U. Oreg. Law Sch., 1977-79, 92—. Mem. ATLA (1st v.p. western regional conf. 1954, 4th v.p. conf. 1956, dir. 1955-56, v.p. Oreg. chpt. 1970-71, pres. So. Oreg. chpt. 1972-74), ABA, Oreg. State Bar (com. taxations, unauthorized practice of law, procedure and practice, CLE, coun. on ct. procedures), Am. Judicature Soc., Assn. Attys. and CPA's, U. Oreg. Sch. Law Alumni Assn. (bd. dirs., pres.), C. of C., Country Club, Town Club (dir. 1970-71, pres. 1978) (Eugene), Multnomah Club (Portland), Elks, Sister Theodore Marie Soc., Order of the Antelope, Order of the Buggy Ride, Phi Alpha Delta, Beta Alpha Psi. Home: 715 Fairoaks Dr Eugene OR 97401-2392

SAHR, MORRIS GALLUP, financial planner; b. Schenectady, Nov. 28, 1928; s. Nathan and Esther (Gallup) S.; m. Sarah Diane Eisenberg, Dec. 23, 1956; children: Evelyn, David, Janet. AB, U. Oreg., 1951, MA, 1953; PhD, Calif. Open U., Oakland, 1978. CFP. Pres. Deposit Mgmt. Svc., Inc., Palmyra, Va., 1978—. Co-author: Your Book of Financial Planning, 1983, Encyclopedia of Financial Planning, 1984, The Financial Planner, 1986, Financial Planning Can Make You Rich, 1987. Chmn. Fairfax County Planning Commn., 1964-68; del. White House Conf. on Aging, 1980, U.S. Congl. Adv. Bd., 1984-87; bd. dirs. Fairfax Indsl. Devel. Authority, 1985-96; adjudicator Am. Arbitration Assn. Recipient award Danforth Found.; named 1 of Top 200 Planners in U.S., Money Mag.; hon. fellow Kennedy Libr., 1985; Paul Harris fellow, 1989. Mem. Internat. Assn. Fin. Planning (founder, 1st pres. Metro Washington chpt.), Inst. Cert. Fin. Planners (nat. govt. affairs com.), Am. Assn. Practicing Fin. Planners (past pres.), Rotary (pres. Fairfax 1984-85), Sr. Leadership Coun. Charlottesville. Home and Office: DMS Inc 61 Wildwood Dr Palmyra VA 22963

SAHS, MAJORIE JANE, art educator; b. Altadena, Calif., Aug. 27, 1926; d. Grayson Michael and Janie Belle (Aaron) McCarty; m. Eugene Otto Sahs, July 21, 1949; children: Victoria, Stephen, Jeffry. Student, Art Ctr. of L.A., 1943-45, Emerson Coll., Boston, 1945; BA, Sacramento State U., 1970; MA in Art Edn., Calif. State U., Sacramento, 1972, postgrad., 1973-79. Cert. secondary tchr., Calif. Tchr. art Sacramento County Schs., 1971-80; cons. Whole Brain Learning Modes, Sacramento, 1980-84; tng. specialist Art Media, Sacramento, Calif., 1983—; instr. Found. for Continuing Med. Edn., Calif., 1985; presenter Nat. Art Edn. Conf., Chgo., 1992, 93, Asian Pacific Conf. on Arts Edn., Franklin, Australia, Internat. Conf., Montreal, Can., 1993; cons., lectr. in field; judge U.S. Treas., 1994, 95, 96, 97, Dept. of Calif. Student Art. Prodr., writer guide and video Gesture Painting Through T'ai Chi, 1992; editor, pub. Calif.'s state newspaper for art edn., 1987-90; editor: Crocker Mus. Docent Guide, 1990; mem. editl. bd. Jour. for Nat. Art Edn. Assn., 1990—; editor: (newsletter) U.S. Soc. for Edn. Through Art, 1994-97; designer of ltd. edits. scarves and cards for Nat. Breast Cancer Rsch. Fund, Exploration Inspiration '95; works publ. in The Best in Silk Painting, 1997. Del. Calif. Arts Leadership Symposium for Arts Edn., 1979, Legis. Coalition Through The Arts, Calif., 1989, 95; judge Calif. State Fair Art Show, 1989, 95, Fed. Treasury Poster Contest, 1994, 95, 96, 97; organizer and host art show and fundraiser for women candidates, 1992. Recipient Patriotic Svc. award Fed. Treasury Dept., 1996, 97, State award of Merit. Mem. Internat. Assn. Edn. through Art, U.S. Soc. Edn. through Art (editor newsletter 1994-97), Nat. Art Edn. Assn. (mem. editl. bd. jour. 1990—, Nat. Outstanding Newspaper Editor award 1988, 89), Calif. Art Edn. Assn. (mem. state coun., mem. area coun., editor state paper, State Award of Merit), Calif. Children's Homes Soc. (pres. Camellia chpt. 1990-91), Asian Pacific Arts Educators Assn., Creative Arts League Sacramento, Emerson Coll. Alumni, Art Ctr. L.A. Alumni. Avocations: creating art pieces, textile clothing design, writing, designing jewelry, designing greeting cards. Home and Office: 1836 Walnut Ave Carmichael CA 95608-5417

SAIBLE, STEPHANIE, magazine editor; b. Mobile, Ala., Sept. 11, 1954; d. Lewis J. Slaff and Phoebe-Jane (Berse) Deats; m. Mark Saible, May 31, 1981 (div. 1983). Student, Va. Commonwealth U., 1972-75. Editorial asst. Woman's World Magazine, Englewood, N.J., 1980-81, service copywriter, 1981-83, assoc. articles editor, 1983-84, articles editor, 1984-85, sr. editor features dept., 1985-86, sr. editor services dept., 1986, now editor-in-chief. Contbr. articles to Woman's World, Modern Bride, New Body, Celebrity Beauty, Trim & Fit. Named Wonder Woman of the Yr., Bus. Jour. N.J., 1986. Mem. Women in Communications. Office: Woman's World Mag 270 Sylvan Ave Englewd Clfs NJ 07632-2521*

SAID, KAMAL E., accounting educator; b. Cairo, Egypt, May 26, 1937; came to U.S., 1965; s. Mohamed A. and Ehsan (Yasin) S.; m. Sally Sneed, Dec. 22, 1967 (div. 1979); children: Jamal E., Karim E.; m. Maria A. Gruner, Aug. 11, 1984; 1 child, Noelle Rianne. B in Comm., Ain-Shams U., Cairo, 1957; MBA, U. Tex., 1967, PhD, 1971. CPA, Tex., La. Asst. prof. U. Houston, 1971-75, assoc. prof., 1975-76, assoc. prof. acctg., 1978-83; Fulbright prof. U. Khartoum, Sudan, 1976-78; chmn. acctg. dept. King Saud U., Saudi Arabia, 1984-88; prof. acctg. U. Southwestern La., Lafayette, 1988-92; prof. Coll. of Indsl. Mgmt., U. Petroleum & Minerals, Dhahran, Saudi Arabia, 1992—; cons. Nat. Coun. Higher Edn., Khartoum, 1976-78, European Econ. Community, Khartoum, 1977; external examiner U. Calcutta, India, 1978-79. Author: Auditing: Theory and Practice, 1989, Modern Advanced Accounting, 1989, Accounting Information Systems, 1988, Intermediate Accounting, I and II, 1987, The Voice of Music, Inc. Practice Set, 1986, Naggie and Sons, Inc. Practice Set, 1986, Gasseem Sporting Goods, Inc. Practice Set, 1986, Cost Accounting I and II, 1985, Managerial Accounting, 1984, Implementation of Long-Range Plans Through Current Operating Budgets, 1978, A Budgeting Model for Institutions of Higher Education, 1974, others. U. Houston grantee, 1974, 75, 78. Mem. Am. Acctg. Assn. (rschr. 1973-75), Inst. Internal Auditors, Phi Beta Delta, Delta Sigma Pi, Beta Gamma Sigma, Beta Alpha Psi. Avocations: Arabian horse shows, horse-back riding, swimming, racquetball.

SAIDMAN, GARY K., lawyer; b. Washington, July 29, 1952; s. Harry and Rose K. (Kruger) S.; m. Suzan R. Kinbar, Mar. 25, 1984; children: Benjamin A., David M. BS, SUNY, Stony Brook, 1974; JD, Emory U., 1978. Bar: Ga. 1978, D.C. 1983, U.S. Dist. Ct. (no. dist.) Ga. 1978, U.S. Ct. Appeals (5th cir.) 1978, U.S. Ct. Appeals (11th cir.) 1981. Assoc. Seward & Kissel, Atlanta, 1978-80; assoc. Kilpatrick & Cody, Atlanta, 1980-86, ptnr., 1986—. Mem. Lawyers Club Atlanta, Ga. State Bar Assn. (chmn. Computer Law Section 1987-88). Office: Kilpatrick & Cody 1100 Peachtree St NE Ste 2800 Atlanta GA 30309-4528

SAIER, MILTON H, JR., biology educator; b. Palo Alto, Calif., July 30, 1941; s. Milton H. and Lucelia (Bates) S.; m. Jeanne K. Woodhams; children: Hans H., Anila J., Amanda L. BS, U. Calif., Berkeley, 1964, PhD, 1968. Prof. biology U. Calif., Berkeley, 1959-68, Johns Hopkins U., Balt., 1968-72, U. Calif., San Diego, 1972—; cons. Merck, Eli Lilly. Author 4 books; contbr. 400 sci. articles to profl. jours. U.S. Pub. Health Svc. grantee NIH. Mem. Am. Soc. Microbiology, Am. Soc. Biochemistry and Molecular Biology. Avocations: music, tennis, ping pong, swimming, hiking. Home: 666 Quail Gardens Dr Encinitas CA 92024-2715 Office: U Calif San Diego Dept Bio 0116 La Jolla CA 92093-0116

SAIFER, MARK GARY PIERCE, pharmaceutical executive; b. Phila., Sept. 16, 1938; s. Albert and Sylvia (Jolles) S.; m. Phyllis Lynne Trommer, Jan. 28, 1961 (dec.); children: Scott David, Alandria Gail; m. Merry R. Sherman, June 26, 1994. AB, U. Pa., 1960; PhD, U. Calif., Berkeley, 1966. Acting asst. prof. zoology U. Calif., Berkeley, 1966, postdoctoral fellow, 1967-68; sr. cancer research scientist Roswell Park Meml. Inst., Buffalo, 1968-70; lab. dir. Diagnostic Data Inc., Palo Alto, Calif., 1970-78; v.p. DDI Pharms., Inc., Mountain View, Calif., 1978-94, Oxis Internat., Inc., 1994-95; sci. dir. Mountain View Pharms., Inc., Menlo Park, Calif., 1996—. Patentee in field. Mem. AAAS (life), Am. Assn. Pharm. Scientists, Parenteral Drug Assn. Home: 1114 Royal Ln San Carlos CA 94070-4277 Office: Mountain View Pharms Inc 3475-S Edison Way Menlo Park CA 94025

SAIGO, ROY HIROFUMI, university chancellor; b. Aug. 6, 1940. BA, U. Calif., Davis, 1962; PhD, Oreg. State U., 1969. Mem. faculty U. Wis., Eau Claire, 1967-84; intern acad. affairs U. Wis. Sys., Madison, 1976-77, dir. rsch. projects, summer 1976; asst. to dean Coll. Arts and Scis. U. Wis., Eau Claire, 1976-80; asst. dean, 1981-84; dean Coll. Natural Scis. U. No. Iowa, Cedar Falls, 1984-90; provost, v.p. acad. and student affairs Southeastern La. U., Hammond, 1990-94; chancellor Auburn U., Montgomery, Ala., 1994—; bd. dirs. Colonial Bank. Bd. dirs. Children's Trust Fund, Ala. Shakespeare Festival, Montgomery Mus. Fine Arts, Com. of 100; mem. alumni bd. Auburn U., Montgomery; mem. med. bd. Columbia East; named to AGR Hall of Fame, Phi chpt., 1996. Recipient Charles E. Bessey award Bot. Soc. Am., svc. and contbn. award Am. Inst. Biol. Scis., Disting. Alumni award U. Calif., Davis, 1994. Fellow AAAS (life); mem. Am. Assn. Higher Edn., Montgomery C. of C. (bd. dirs.), Phi Delta Kappa. Office: Auburn U 7300 University Dr Montgomery AL 36117-3531

SAIKEVYCH, IRENE A., pathologist; b. Perth Amboy, N.J., Oct. 16, 1950; d. Victor C. and Maria (Shomber) S.; divorced; 1 child, Natalie S. White. BA in Chemistry, U. Ill., 1972; MD, Northwestern, 1976. Diplomate Am. Bd. Med. Genetics; cert. pathologist. Resident Northwestern U., Honolulu, 1976-81; fellow in cytogenetics U. Hawaii, Honolulu, 1982-84, dir. cytogenetics rsch. lab., 1985-92, asst. prof. to assoc. prof. Dept. Pathology, 1982-92; med. dir. clin. cytogenetics Dept. Pathology St. Francis Hosp., Honolulu, 1988-92; staff pathologist Presbyn. Hosp., Charlotte, N.C., 1993—, dir. genetic svcs., 1993—. Contbr. numerous articles to profl. jours. Fellow Am. Coll. Med. Genetics (founder); mem. AAAS, AMA, Coll. Am. Pathologists (cytogenetics resource com. 1987—), Am. Soc. Human Genetics, Am. Soc. Hematology. Avocations: classical music, hiking, dancing, painting, reading. Office: Presbyn Path Grp Presbyn Hosp Path Lab Med 200 Hawthorne Ln Charlotte NC 28204-2515

SAIKI, PATRICIA (MRS. STANLEY MITSUO SAIKI), former federal agency administrator, former congresswoman; b. Hilo, Hawaii, May 28, 1930; d. Kazuo and Shizue (Inoue) Fukuda; m. Stanley Mitsuo Saiki, June 19, 1954; children: Stanley Mitsuo, Sandra Saiki Williams, Margaret C., Stuart K., Laura H. BA, U. Hawaii, 1952. Tchr. U.S. history Punahou Sch., Kaimuki Intermediate Sch., Kalani High Sch., Honolulu, 1952-64; sec. Rep. Party Hawaii, Honolulu, 1964-66, vice chmn., 1966-68, 82-83, chmn., 1983-85; rsch. asst. Hawaii State Senate, 1966-68; mem. Hawaii Ho. of Reps., 1968-74, Hawaii State Senate, 1974-82, 100th-101st Congresses from 1st Hawaii dist., Washington, 1987-91; adminstr. SBA, Washington, 1991-93; mem. Pres.'s Adv. Coun. on Status of Women, 1969-76; mem. Nat. Commn. Internat. Women's Yr., 1969-70; commr. We. Interstate Commn. on Higher Edn.; fellow Eagleton Inst., Rutgers U., 1970; fellow Inst. of Politics, Kennedy Sch. Govt., Harvard U., 1993; bd. dirs. Bank of Am.-Hawaii, Landmark Systems Corp., Internat. Asset Recovery Corp. Mem. Kapiolano Hosp. Aux.; sec. Hawaii Rep. Com., 1964-66, vice chmn., 1966-68, chmn., 1983-85; del. Hawaii Constl. Conv., 1968; alt. del. Rep. Nat. Conv., 1968, del., 1984, Rep. nominee for lt. gov. Hawaii, 1982, for U.S. Senate, 1990, for. gov. Hawaii, 1990; mem. Fedn. Rep. Women; trustee Hawaii Pacific Coll.; past bd. govs. Boys and Girls Clubs Hawaii; mem. adv. coun. ARC; bd. dirs. Nat. Fund for Improvement of Post-Secondary Edn., 1982-85; past bd. dirs. Straub Med. Rsch. Found., Honolulu, Hawaii's Visitors Bur., Honolulu, Edn. Commn. of States, Honolulu, Hawaii Visitors Bur., 1983-85; trustee U. Hawaii Found., 1984-86, Hawaii Pacific Coll., Honolulu. Episcopalian. Avocation: golf. Home: 784 Elepaio St Honolulu HI 96816-4710

SAIMAN, MARTIN S., lawyer; b. N.Y.C., Jan. 27, 1932; s. Adolph and Mary (Kaplan) S.; m. Rita C. Chernick, Apr. 10, 1955; children: Lisa, Richard, Gwen. A.B., Columbia Coll., 1953; LL.B., Columbia U., 1955. Bar: N.Y. 1956. Ptnr. Kaye, Scholer, Fierman, Hays & Handler, N.Y.C., 1971-94, spl. counsel firm, 1995. Bd. dirs. Smalley Found., 1966—; trustee Lower East Side Tenement Mus., 1996—. Office: Kaye Scholer Fierman Hays & Handler 425 Park Ave New York NY 10022-3506

SAIN, CHARLES HASKELL, civil engineer, surveyor; b. New Market, Ala., Jan. 20, 1923; s. Will Oris and Clayta (Speck) S.; m. Marie Myers, Aug. 8, 1942; children: Charles R., Elizabeth Lester Stockdale, Ann Marie Hays. BSCE, U. Fla., 1949. Registered profl. engr., Ala., Ariz., Colo., Conn., Fla., Ga., Ill., Ind., Iowa, Kans., Ky., La., Minn., Miss., N.J., N.Y., N.C., Okla., Pa., S.C., S.D., Tenn., Vt., Va., W.Va., Wis. V.p. engring. Moss-Thornton Co., Inc., Leeds, Ala., 1946-59; gen. mgr. Vecellio & Grogan, Beckley, W.Va., 1960-64; v.p. engring. A.E. Burgess Co., Inc., Birmingham, Ala., 1964-67; pres. Charles H. Sain Assocs., Birmingham, 1968-89, Sain South Engring., Birmingham, 1978-89; CEO, chmn. bd. dirs. Sain Assocs., Inc., Birmingham, 1989—; bd. visitors civil engring. dept. Coll. Engring. U. Ala., Birmingham; lectr. Auburn U., 1971, 72. Author: (with others) Standard Handbook for Civil Engineers, 1968, 4th edit., 1996; contbr. articles to profl. jours. Bd. dirs. State of Ala. Toll Bridge Authority, 1970-74; city engr. City of Vestavia Hilla, Ala., 1976-88, City of Homewood, Ala., 1976-80; vice chmn., bd. dirs. Ala. Bapt. Retirement Ctrs., Montgomery, 1986-93; mem. Vestavia Hills, Ala. Bd. Zoning Adjustment, 1986-90; vice chmn. Jefferson County Bd. Zoning Adjustment, 1986—; mem. Vestavia Hills Bapt. Ch., 1991—, deacon. Lt. U.S. Army, 1944-46. Mem. NSPE, ASCE (program chmn. Ala. chpt. 1966, equipment maintenance com. 1958-78, Life Achievement award), Am. Soc. Mil. Engrs., Internat. Platform Assn., Internat. Coun. Shopping Ctrs. (water quality com., environ. site assessment com., lectr.), Birmingham C. of C. (environ. ethicc com., lectr.), Tau Beta Phi, Sigma Tau. Avocations: golf, reading. Office: Sain Assocs Inc 244 W Valley Ave Ste 200 Birmingham AL 35209-3616

SAIN, MICHAEL KENT, electrical engineering educator; b. St. Louis, Mar. 22, 1937; s. Charles George and Marie Estelle (Ritch) S.; m. Frances Elizabeth Bettin, Aug. 24, 1963; children: Patrick, Mary, John, Barbara, Elizabeth. BSEE, St. Louis U., 1959, MSEE, 1962; PhD, U. Ill., 1965. Engr. Sandia Corp., Albuquerque, 1958-61, Vickers Electric Corp., St. Louis, 1962; instr. U. Ill., Urbana, 1962-63; asst. prof. U. Notre Dame (Ind.), 1965-68, assoc. prof., 1968-72, prof., 1972-82, Frank M. Freimann prof. elec. engring., 1982—; vis. scientist U. Toronto, Ont., Can., 1972-73; disting. vis. prof. Ohio State U., Columbus, 1987; cons. Allied-Bendix Aerospace, South Bend, Ind., 1976—, Deere & Co., Moline, Ill., 1981, 82, Garrett Corp., Phoenix, 1984, GM, Warren, Mich., 1984-94; plenary spkr. IEEE Conf. on Decision and Control, 1990. Author: Introduction to Algebraic System Theory, 1981; editor: Alternatives for Linear Multivariable Control, 1978; hon. editor: Ency. of Systems and Control, 1987; editor jour. IEEE Trans. on Automatic Control, 1979-83; contbr. 275 articles to profl. jours., books and refereed proc. Grantee Army Rsch. Office, NSF, Ames Rsch. Ctr., Lewis Rsch. Ctr. NASA, Office Naval Rsch., Air Force Office Sci. Rsch., Law Enforcement Assistance Adminstrn., Clark-Hurth Components. Fellow IEEE (prize papers com. 1992-96, chair 1994-96, awards bd. 1994-96); mem. Control Sys. Soc. IEEE (bd. govs. 1978-84, Disting. Mem. award 1983, Centennial medal 1984, Axelby prize chair 1991-96, awards com. chair 1993-96), Circuits and Sys. Soc. IEEE (co-chair internat. symposium on circuits and sys. 1990, newsletter editor 1990-96, v.p. adminstrn. 1992-93, v.p. tech. activities 1994-95), Soc. Indsl. and Applied Math. Republican. Roman Catholic. Avocations: photography, swimming, jogging. Office: U Notre Dame Dept Elec Engring 275 Fitzpatrick Hl Engrng Notre Dame IN 46556-5637*

SAINE, BETTY BOSTON, elementary school educator; b. Newton, N.C., Dec. 1, 1932; d. Glenn and Carrie Queen Boston; m. Thomas Paul Saine, Aug. 3, 1968; 1 child, Carrie Ann. BA, Lenoir Rhyne Coll., 1956. Tchr. grade 4 High Point (N.C.) City Schs., 1956-59, Charlotte City Schs./Charlotte-Mecklenburg Schs., 1959-66; art tchr. grades 1-8 Newton-Conover City Schs., 1966-67; tchr. grade 4 Charlotte-Mecklenburg Schs., 1967-68; tchr. grade 6 Lincolnton (N.C.) City Schs., 1968-70; tchr. grades 5 and 6 Lincolnton City Schs./Lincoln County Schs., 1972-90; ret. Historian, publicity chair beautification com. Sunflower Garden Club, Lincolnton, 1976-87. Mem. Alpha Delta Kappa (various offices and coms.). Methodist. Avocations: painting, creative embroidery, horticulture, calligraphy, children's books. Home: 2492 Pickwick Pl Lincolnton NC 28092-7748

SAINER, ARTHUR, writer, theater educator; b. N.Y.C., Sept. 12, 1924; s. Louis and Sadie (Roth) S.; m. Maryjane Treloar, Apr. 18, 1981; children: Douglas M., Stephanie M., Jane M., Ross M. B.A., Washington Sq. Coll., N.Y.C., 1946; M.A., Columbia U., 1948. Tchr. Bennington Coll., Vt., 1967-69, Adelphi U., Garden City, N.Y., 1974-75, S.I. Community Coll., 1974-75; faculty Wesleyan U., Middletown, Conn., 1977-80, Hunter Coll., N.Y.C., 1980-81; assoc. prof. theatre Middlebury Coll., Vt., 1981-83; theater faculty New Sch. for Social Rsch., N.Y.C., 1985—, Sarah Lawrence Coll., Bronxville, N.Y., 1990—; play dir. Boat Sun Cavern Middlebury Coll., Vt., 1983; drama critic Village Voice, N.Y.C., 1961—; play dir. Lord Tom Goldsmith at Theatre for New City, N.Y.C., 1979, Witnesses at Open Space, N.Y.C., 1977, Poor Man Rich Man, Theatre for the New City, 1992. Editor: Village Voice, 1962; author: (plays) The Celebration Reclaimed, 1993-95, Images of the Coming Dead, 1980, After the Baal-Shem Tov, 1979, Carol in Winter Sunlight, 1977, The Children's Army Is Late, 1974, The Burning Out of '82, 1983, Cruising Angel, 1984, Sunday Childhood Journeys to Nobody at Home (Berman award), 1984, Jews and Christians in the End Zone, 1987, (criticisms), The New Radical Theatre Notebook, 1975, 97, The Sleepwalker and the Assassin, 1964, Zero Dances, 1997; reporter: Nat. Endowment for Arts, Washington, 1979-82. Panelist Vt. Council on the Arts, Montpelier, 1982, 83; panelist N.Y. State Council on the Arts, 1976-78. Ford Found. grantee, 1979, 80; recipient grant Office for Advanced Drama Research, U. Minn., 1967, award for Grab Your Hat John Golden Found., 1946. Address: 462 First St Brooklyn NY 11215 *From a work of mine in progress: Francis: But finally, who is going to do my work? No one is going to do it. Lev: Each will do his work. But in the end only God's work amounts to anything. Francis: And does that make you happy? Lev: It makes me useful.*

SAINI, GULSHAN RAI, soil physicist, agricultural hydrologist; b. Hoshiarpur, India, Oct. 1, 1924; s. Ram Saran and Parmeshri Devi (Bhondi) S.; B.Sc., Panjab U., 1945, M.Sc., 1956; Ph.D., Ohio State U., 1960; Soil & Water Conservation cert. USDA Tng. Ctr., 1959. m. Veena Chaudhri, Jan. 14, 1950; 1 child, Vikas. Rsch. asst. Govt. Agrl. Coll., Ludhiana, India, 1945-57; rsch. assoc. Ohio State U., Columbus, 1957-60; asst. prof. Punjab Agrl. U., Ludhiana, India, 1960-61; rsch. scientist Can. Dept. Agr., Fredericton, N.B., 1962-84; adj. prof. Faculty of Forestry, U. N.B., Fredericton, 1968-76; founding bd. dirs. U. Human Rights Group, Inc.; vis. prof. Rutgers U., 1984-85; mem. hydrology subcom. Atlantic Provinces Inter-Univ. Com. on Scis., 1966-76, Atlantic Provinces Soil & Water Engring. Com., 1972-82; mem. Restore Olmsted's Waterway Coalition, 1986—, treas. 1990-93, chair 1994-96; CSO tech. adv. com. Commonwealth of Mass., 1995—; chmn. Saini Found. for Edn. & Human Progress. Fellow Internat. Inst. Land Reclamation and Improvement, 1960; Mem. Indian Sci. Congress Assn. (life), Profl. Inst. Pub. Svc. Can. (nat. v.p. 1980, 81, chmn. Atlantic regional coun. 1978, 79), Union Concerned Scientists, Fredericton Rotary Club (dir. internat. svc. 1967-68), Third world Scholars, Consortium, Treas., 1995—; mem. exec. com. Coalition for a Strong United Nations. Contbr. articles to profl. jours. Home: 24 Brook St Brookline MA 02146-6914

SAINSBURY OF PRESTON CANDOVER, LORD (JOHN DAVAN SAINSBURY), food retailer executive, art patron; b. London, Nov. 2, 1927; m. Anya Linden, 1963. Student, Oxford U., fellow (hon.), 1982; LittD (hon.), South Bank, 1992; LLD (hon.), Bristol, 1993. Vice chmn. J. Sainsbury PLC, 1967-69, chmn., 1969-92; pres. J. Sainsbury plc, 1992—; also bd. dirs. J. Sainsbury PLC. Bd. dirs. Royal Opera House, Covent Garden, Eng., 1969-85, chmn., 1987-97; bd. dirs. Royal Opera House Trust, 1974-84, 84—, The Economist, 1972-80, chmn. Coun. Friends of Covent Garden, 1969-81, Benesh Inst. Choreology, 1986-87; gov. Royal Ballet Sch., 1965-76, 1995—; joint hon. treas. European Movement, 1972-75, pres., 1975-89; trustee Nat. Gallery, 1976-83, Westminster Abbey Trust, 1977-83, Tate Gallery, 1982-83, Rhodes Trust, 1984—; mem. Nat. Com. for Electoral Reform, 1976-85; chmn. bd. trustees Dulwich Picture Gallery, 1994—. Named Hon. Bencher Inner Temple, 1985. Fellow Inst. Grocery Distbrs., Royal Inst. Brit. Archs. (hon.); mem. Coun. Retail Consortium, Garrick Club, Contemporary Arts Soc. (v.p. 1984—), Brit. Retail Consortium (pres. 1993-97). Office: J Sainsbury PLC, care Stamford House Stamford St, SE1 9LL London England

SAINT, CROSBIE EDGERTON, retired army officer; b. West Point, N.Y., Sept. 29, 1936; s. Frederick Gilman and Jean (Crosbie) Saint Malevich; m. Virginia Fisher Carnahan, Aug. 3, 1961; children: Frederick Gilman II, Mary Elizabeth. B.S., U.S. Mil. Acad., 1958; M.A., Am. U., 1973. Commd. 2d lt. U.S. Army, 1958, advanced through grades to gen.; comdr. 1st Squadron, 1st Cav., Vietnam, 1970; exec. to chief of staff U.S. Army, Washington; comdr. 11th Armored Cav. Regt., Fulda, Germany, 1976-78, 7th Army Tng. Command, Grafenwohr, Germany, 1979-81; dept. comdt. Command and Gen. Staff Coll., Ft. Leavenworth, Kans., 1981-83; comdr. 1st Armored Div., Ansbach, Germany, 1983-85; comdr. 3d Corps and Ft. Hood Tex., 1985-88; comdr. in chief U.S. Army Europe, Heidelberg, Germany, 1988-92; ret. U.S. Army, 1992; v.p. Europe Mil. Profl. Resources, Inc.; ind. cons. Decorated DSM with two oak leaf clusters, DFC, Air medal with V device, Legion of Honor (France), German Armed Forces Gt. Cross of Merit with star, Vietnamese Cross of Gallantry. Mem. Assn. U.S. Army, Armor Assn. Address: 1116 N Pitt St Alexandria VA 22314-1455

SAINT, EVA MARIE, actress; b. Newark, July 4, 1924; d. John Merle and Eva Marie (Rice) S.; m. Jeffrey Hayden, Oct. 28, 1951; children: Darrell, Laurette. BA, DFA, Bowling Green State U., 1946; student, Actors Studio, after 1950. Appeared in various radio and TV dramatic shows, N.Y.C., 1947—; theater roles include The Trip to Bountiful, 1953 (Outer Circle Critics award, N.Y. Drama Critics award, 1953), The Rainmaker, 1953, Winesburg, Ohio, 1970, The Lincoln Mask, 1972, Summer and Smoke, 1973, Desire Under the Elms, 1974, The Fatal Weakness, 1976, Candida, 1977, Mr. Roberts, First Monday in October, 1979, Duet for One 1982-83, The Country Girl, 1986 (L.A. Dramalogue award 1986), Death of a Salesman, 1994, Love Letters, 1994, On the Divide, 1994-97; appeared in films On the Waterfront, 1954 (Acad. Award for best supporting actress, 1955), Raintree County, 1957, That Certain Feeling, 1956, A Hatful of Rain, 1957, North by Northwest, 1959, Exodus, 1961, All Fall Down, 1962, 36 Hours, 1963, The Sandpiper, 1964, The Russians are Coming, The Russians Are Coming!, 1965, Grand Prix, 1966, The Stalking Moon, 1969, Loving, 1970, Cancel My Reservation, 1972, Nothing in Common, 1986, Marietta In Ecstacy, 1995; TV dramas The Macahans, 1976 (Emmy nom.), the Fatal Weakness, 1976, Taxi!!, 1978 (Emmy nom.), A Christmas to Remember, 1978, When Hell Was in Session, 1980, the Curse of King Tut's Tomb, The Best Little Girl in the World, 1981, Splendor in the Grass, 1981, Love Leads the Way, 1983, Jane Doe, 1983, Fatal Vision, 1984, The Last Days of Patton, 1986, A Year in the Life, 1986, Breaking Home Times, 1987, I'll Be Home for Christmas, 1988, Voyage of Terror: The Achille Lauro Affair, 1990, People Like Us, 1990 (Emmy award, 1990), Palomino, 1991, Kiss of the Killer, ABC, 1992, My Antonia, 1994, After Jimmy, 1996, Killing Me Softly, 1997, documentary Primary Colors: The Story of Corita, 1991, Children In America's Schools, 1997.

ST. AMAND, PIERRE, geophysicist; b. Tacoma, Wash., Feb. 4, 1920; s. Cyrias Z. and Mable (Berg) St. A.; m. Marie Pöss, Dec. 5, 1945; children: Gene, Barbara, Denali, David. BS in Physics, U. Alaska, 1948; MS in Geophysics, Calif. Inst. Tech., 1951, PhD in Geophysics and Geology, 1953; Dr. honoris causa, U. De Los Altos, Tepatitlan, Mex., 1992. Asst. dir. Geophys. Lab., U. Alaska, also head ionospheric and seismologic investigations, 1946-49; physicist U.S. Naval Ordnance Test Sta., China Lake, Calif., 1950-54; head optics br. U.S. Naval Ordnance Test Sta., 1955-58; head earth and planetary sci. div. U.S. Ordnance Test Sta., 1961-78, now cons. to tech. dir., head spl. projects office, 1978-88; fgn. service with ICA as prof. geol. and geophys. Sch. Earth Scis., U. Chile, 1958-60; originator theory rotational displacement Pacific Ocean Basin; pres. Saint-Amand Sci. Services; adj. prof. McKay Sch. Mines, U. Nev., U. N.D.; v.p., dir. Covillea Corp.; v.p., dir. tech. Muetal Corp.; cons. World Bank, Calif. Div. Water Resources, Am. Potash & Chem. Co., OAS; mem. U.S. Army airways communications system, Alaska and Can., 1942-46; cons. Mexican, Chilean, Argentine, Philipines, Can. govts.; mem. Calif. Gov.'s Com. Geol. Hazards; mem. com. magnetic instruments Internat. Union Geodesy and Geophys., 1954-59, Disaster Preparation Commn. for Los Angeles; charter mem. Sr. Exec. Service. Adv. bd. GeoScience News; contbr. 100 articles to scientific jours. Chmn. bd. dirs. Ridgecrest Comty. Hosp.; chmn. bd. dirs. Indian Wells Valley Airport Dist.; dir. Indian Wells Valley Water Dist.; v.p. bd. dirs. Kern County Acad. Decathlon. Decorated knight Mark Twain, Mark Twain Jour.; recipient cert. of merit OSRD, 1945, cert. of merit USAAF, 1946, letter of commendation USAAF, 1948, Spl. award Philippine Air Force, 1969, Diploma de Honor Sociedad Geologica de Chile, Disting. Civilian Svc. medal USN, 1968, L.T.E. Thompson medal, 1973, Thunderbird award Weather Modification Assn., 1974, Disting. Pub. Svc. award Fed. Exec. Inst., 1976, Meritorious Svc. medal USN, 1988, Disting. Alumnus award U. Alaska, 1990; Fulbright rsch. fellow France, 1954-55. Fellow AAAS, Geol. Soc. Am., Earthquake Engr. Rsch. Inst.; mem. Am. Geophys. Union, Weather Modification Assn., Am. Seismol. Soc., Sister Cities (Ridgecrest-Tepatitlan) Assn. (pres.), Rotary (past pres., Paul Harris fellow), Footprinters Internat. (mem. grand bd., pres.), Sigma Xi. Achievements include patents in photometric instrument, weather and ordnance devices, pvt. pilot multi-engine-instruments. Home: 1748 W Las Flores Ave Ridgecrest CA 93555-8635

SAINT-AMAND, PIERRE NEMOURS, humanities educator; b. Port-Au-Prince, Haiti, Feb. 22, 1957; came to U.S., 1978; s. Nemours and Carmen (Clerveaux) Saint-A. BA, U. Montreal, 1978; MA, Johns Hopkins U., 1980, PhD, 1981. Asst. prof. Yale U., New Haven, 1981-82, Stanford (Calif.) U., 1982-86; assoc. prof. Brown U., Providence, 1986-90, prof., 1990—; Francis Wayland prof. Brown U., Providence, R.I., 1996—; vis. prof. Harvard U., Cambridge, Mass., 1992. Author: Diderot, Le Labyrinthe de La Relation, 1984, Seduire Ou La Passion des Lumieres, 1986, Les Lois de L'Hostilite, 1992, The Libertine's Progress, 1994, The Laws of Hostility, 1996; editor: Diderot, 1984, Le Roman an Dix-huitième siecle, 1987, Autonomy in the Age of the Enlightenment, 1993. Fellow Stanford Humanities Ctr., 1985-86, John Simon Guggenheim Meml. Found., 1989. Office: Brown U Box 1961 French Dept Providence RI 02912

ST. ANTOINE, THEODORE JOSEPH, law educator, arbitrator; b. St. Albans, Vt., May 29, 1929; s. Arthur Joseph and Mary Beatrice (Callery) S.; m. Elizabeth Lloyd Frier, Jan. 2, 1960; children: Arthur, Claire, Paul, Sara. AB, Fordham Coll., 1951; JD U. Mich., 1954; postgrad. (Fulbright grantee), U. London, 1957-58. Bar: Mich. 1954, Ohio 1954, D.C. 1959. Assoc., Squire, Sanders & Dempsey, Cleve., 1954; assoc., ptnr. Woll, Mayer & St. Antoine, Washington, D.C., 1958-65; assoc. prof. law U. Mich. Law Sch., Ann Arbor, 1965-69, prof. 1969—; Degan prof. 1981—; dean, 1971-78; pres. Nat. Resource Ctr. for Consumers of Legal Svcs., 1974-78; mem. Pub. Rev. Bd., UAW, 1973—; chmn. UAW-GM Legal Svcs. Plan, 1983-95; Mich. Gov.'s spl. counselor on workers' compensation, 1983-85; reporter Uniform Law Commrs., 1987-92; life mem. Clare Hall, Cambridge (Eng.) U. 1st lt. JAGC, U.S. Army, 1955-57. Mem. ABA (past sec. labor law sect., coun. 1984-92), Am. Bar Found., State Bar Mich. (past chmn. labor rels. law sect.), Nat. Acad. Arbitrators (bd. govs. 1985-88, v.p. 1994-96), Internat. Soc. Labor Law and Social Security (U.S. br. exec. bd. 1983—, vice chmn. 1989-95), Indsl. Rels. Rsch. Assn., Order of Coif (life). Democrat. Roman Catholic. Author (with R. Smith, L. Merrifield and C. Craver) Labor Relations Law: Cases and Materials, 4th edit., 1968, 9th edit., 1994; contbr. articles to profl. jours. Home: 1421 Roxbury Rd Ann Arbor MI 48104-4047 Office: U Mich Law Sch 625 S State St Ann Arbor MI 48109-1215

ST. AUBYN, RONALD ANTHONY, pediatrics nurse; b. Vineland, N.J., Nov. 30, 1954; s. Richard Francis and Rita Margaret (DeFeo) St. A. BSN, Northwestern State U., Natchitoches, La., 1980. RN, La. High-risk infant homecare nurse Physicians Prescription Svcs., Shreveport, La., 1982-86; nursing dir., neonatal cons. Quality Care, Inc., Shreveport, 1985-86; poison info. specialist La. Poison Control Ctr., Shreveport, 1987; pediatric clin. supr. La. State U. Med. Ctr., Shreveport, 1988-92, pediatric edn. nurse, 1993—. Mem. ANA, La. State Nursing Assn., Soc. of Pediatric Nurses of La., Krewe Club of Aesclepius, Royalty Club, Beta Beta Beta. Home: 865 Sewanee Pl Shreveport LA 71105-2245

ST. CLAIR, CARL, conductor, music director. Music dir. Pacific Symphony Orch., Santa Ana, Calif., 1990—. Office: Pacific Symphony Orch 1231 E Dyer Rd Santa Ana CA 92705-5606

ST. CLAIR, DONALD DAVID, lawyer; b. Hammond, Ind., Dec. 30, 1932; s. Victor Peter and Wanda (Rubinska) Small; m. Sergine Anne Oliver, June 6, 1970 (dec. June 1974); m. Beverly Joyce Tipton, Dec. 28, 1987. BS, Ind. U., 1955, MS, 1963, EdD, 1967; JD, U. Toledo, 1992. Bar: Ohio 1992, U.S. Dist. Ct. (no. dist.) Ohio 1993, U.S. Supreme Ct., 1996. Assoc. prof. Coll. Edn. Western Ky. U., Bowling Green, 1967-68; assoc. prof. U. Toledo, 1968-77, prof., 1977-92; atty., ptnr. Garand, Bollinger, & St. Clair, Oregon, Ohio, 1992-97; pvt. practice, Toledo, 1997—; bd. dirs. Toledo Mental Health Ctr., 1977-79; mem. Ohio Coun. Mental Health Ctrs., Columbus, 1978-79; dir. honors programs U. Toledo. Author: (poetry) Daymarks and Beacons, 1983; contbr. numerous articles to profl. jours. Organizer Students Toledo Organized for Peace, 1970-71; mem. Lucas County Dem. Party, 1990—. With U.S. Army, 1955-57. Mem. ABA, AAU (nat. bd. dirs. 1973-74), Ohio Bar Assn., Toledo Bar Assn., Ohio Acad. Trial Lawyers, Toledo Power Squadron (comdg. officer 1981), Bay View Yacht Club, Masons (32 degree), Shriners, Ancient Order Friars, Phi Alpha Delta. Home: 3353 Christie Blvd Toledo OH 43606-2862 Office: 5415 Monroe St Toledo OH 43623-2877

ST. CLAIR, HAL KAY, electrical engineer; b. Los Angeles, Oct. 11, 1925; s. Millard T. and Ruth (McGrew) St. C.; m. Jane Creely, June 24, 1949; children: Gregory, Russell, Elizabeth. Student, U. So. Calif., 1943-44; BS, U. Calif.-Berkeley, 1946, MS, 1948. Research engr. Marchant Calculators, Emeryville, Calif., 1948-52; project engr. RCA, Camden, N.J., 1953-54; program mgr. IBM, San Jose, Calif., 1954-69; tech. staff IBM, Boca Raton, Fla., 1969-72, mgr. input/output devel., 1972-75, mgr. gen. lab. devel., 1975-81, mgr. small comml. systems engring., 1981-83; ergonomics adviser div. hdqrs. staff IBM, White Plains, N.Y., 1983-85, devel. edn. mgr., 1986-88, ret., 1988; instr. U. Calif. Extension Div., 1951-52; tech. adv. U.S. Nat. Com. Internat. Electrotechnical Commn., 1967-69. Mem. Republican Central Com. of Calif., 1962-66. Served to lt. (j.g.) USNR, 1943-46. Mem. IEEE, SAR, Mensa, Phi Beta Kappa, Sigma Xi, Tau Beta Pi, Eta Kappa Nu. Home: 17137 Bernardo Oaks Dr San Diego CA 92128-2104

ST. CLAIR, JAMES DRAPER, lawyer; b. Akron, Ohio, Apr. 14, 1920; s. Clinton Draper and Margaret Joanna (Glenn) St. C.; m. Asenath Nestle, Nov. 25, 1944; children: Margaret Nestle, David Scott, Thomas Bruce. Student, Augustana Coll., 1938-39; AB, U. Ill., 1941; LLB, Harvard U., 1947; LLD, Gettysburg Coll., 1975, New Eng. Sch. Law, 1975, Emerson Coll., 1993. Bar: Mass. Assoc. Hale & Dorr, Boston, 1947-52; jr. ptnr. Hale & Dorr, 1952-56, sr. ptnr., 1956-95; spl. counsel to Pres. Richard Nixon, 1974; lectr. Harvard Law Sch.; asst. counsel to Army, Army-McCarthy Hearings, 1954; co-mng. trustee Amelia Peabody Found., 1985—. Author: (with others) Assignments in Trial Practice, 1960. Mem. Town Meeting, Wellesley, Mass., 1963-73; gen. counsel United Fund, 1966; mem. Town of Wellesley Adv. Com., 1966-69; mem. steering com. Lawyers Com. for Civil Rights Under Law, 1968-73; mem. adv. com. Mass. Jud. Conf. Com. on Criminal Rules Project, 1972-73; Trustee, bd. dirs. Walker Home for Children, 1951-73, 75-95; pres. Horizons for Youth, 1981-94, chmn. bd., 1994—; bd. dirs. The Met in Boston, The Boston Opera Assn.; mem. New Eng. Bapt. Health Care Corp., 1991—; chair mgmt. rev. com. Boston Police Dept., 1991-92; mem. Corporation Mass. Gen. Hosp., 1992—. Served to lt. USNR, 1942-45. Mem. ABA (council of litigation sect. 1974—), Boston Bar Assn. (council), Am. Law Inst., Am. Coll. Trial Lawyers, Practising Law Inst. (nat. adv. council 1967-73), New Eng. Law Inst. (adv. council 1970-71), Order of Coif. Republican. Conglist. Clubs: Brae Burn Country, Eastward Ho Country. Office: Hale & Dorr 60 State St Boston MA 02109-1800

ST. CLAIR, JAMES WILLIAM, lawyer; b. Charleston, W.Va., Apr. 1, 1935; s. James William and Daisy Catherine (Litz) St. C.; m. Doria Diana Arrington, Aug. 10, 1956; children: Patricia A. St. Clair Deford, Laura J. St. Clair Johnson, J. William, Samual A. AB in History, U. Va., 1957, LLB, 1960. Bar: Va. 1960, W.Va. 1960, U.S. Dist. Ct. (no. and so. dists.) W.Va. 1960, U.S. Ct. Appeals 1965, U.S. Supreme Ct. 1970. Ptnr. Marshall Harghbarer & St. Clair, Huntington, W.Va., 1960-70, Marshall & St. Clair, Huntington, 1970-80, Marshall, St. Clair & Levine, Huntington, 1980-89, St. Clair & Levine, Huntington, 1989—; bd. dirs. 1st Huntington Nat. Bank; dir., officer Huntington Realty Corp., Gen. Allied Oil and Gas Corp., Frankfurt, Germany, Town and Country Shopping Ctr., Inc., Huntington. Pres., bd. mem. Cabell Wayne Hist. Soc., Huntington, 1970—, Greater Huntington Pk. Bd., 1973—. 1st lt. U.S. Army, 1957-62. Mem. ABA (law practice mgmt. sect., bd. mem. 1985-91, specialist to Ukraine, Kazakhstan & Kyrgyzstan). Democrat. Presbyn. Avocations: lawn and gardening. Home: 1805 Mccoy Rd Huntington WV 25701-4823 Office: St Clair & Levine 717 6th Ave Huntington WV 25701-2105

ST. CLAIR, JESSE WALTON, JR., retired savings and loan executive; b. Phila., Jan. 15, 1930; s. Jesse Walton and Susan Elizabeth (Leath) St. C.; m. Elizabeth Anne Bartlett, Oct. 6, 1951; children: Jesse Walton III, Susan Elizabeth, Bruce Bartlett, Anne Leath. BA, Coll. of William and Mary, 1951; MBA, U. Pa., 1958; postgrad., Harvard U., 1968. Trainee Fed. Res. Bank, Phila., 1955-57; with Girard Trust Bank, Phila., 1957-78; asst. treas. Girard Trust Bank, 1960-64, asst. v.p., 1964-67, v.p., 1967-70, sr. v.p., 1970-75, exec. v.p., 1976-78; pres., chief exec. officer First Nat. Bank of Allentown (Pa.), 1978-82; chmn., chief exec. officer Wilmington Savs. Fund Soc., 1982-90, ret., 1990. Trustee emeritus endowment fund Coll. William and Mary; dir. Del. Am. Ins. Co.; mem. exec. bd. Delmarva coun. Boy Scouts Am.; trustee Wesley Coll.; treas. St. Paul's United Meth. Ch. With USN, 1951-55. Mem. Wilmington Country Club, Theta Delta Chi. Republican. Methodist. Home: 4011 Springfield Ln Greenville Wilmington DE 19807

ST. CLAIR, MICHAEL, art dealer; b. Bradford, Pa., May 28, 1912. Student, Kans. City Art Inst., Colo. Springs Fine Arts Ctr. Instr. Okla. Art Ctr. Sch., Oklahoma City; dir. Babcock Galleries, N.Y.C., 1959—. Named Vanderslice scholar Kansas City Art Inst. Mem. Art Dealers Assn. Am. (founding mem. 1962), Architecture & Am. Art Drawing Soc. Office: Babcock Galleries 724 5th Ave New York NY 10019-4106

ST. CLAIR, THOMAS MCBRYAR, mining and manufacturing company executive; b. Wilkinsburg, Pa., Sept. 26, 1935; s. Fred C. and Dorothy (Renner) St. C.; m. Sarah K. Stewart, Aug. 1, 1959; children—Janet, Susan, Carol. AB, Allegheny Coll., 1957; MS, MIT, 1958; grad. advanced mgmt. program, Harvard U. With Koppers Co., Inc., Pitts., 1958-88, asst. to gen. mgr. engring. and constrn. div., 1966-69, comptroller, asst. treas., 1969-78, pres. Engineered Metal Products Group, 1978-83, v.p., asst. to chmn., 1983-84, v.p., treas., chief fin. officer, 1984-88; sr. v.p., chief fin. officer Phelps Dodge Corp., Phoenix, 1989—; bd. dirs. Nortrust of Ariz. Bd. dirs., treas. Herberger Theater Ctr., Phoenix; trustee Allegheny Coll. Mem. Fin. Execs. Inst., Duquesne Club (Pitts.), Univ. Club (Pitts. and Phoenix). Presbyterian. Office: Phelps Dodge Corp 2600 N Central Ave Phoenix AZ 85004-3050

ST. CLAIRE, FRANK ARTHUR, lawyer; b. Charlotte, N.C., June 16, 1949. BS, MIT, 1972; JD, NYU, 1975. Bar: Tex. 1975, U.S. Dist. Ct. (no. dist.) Tex. 1985; bd. cert. in comml. real estate law. Assoc. James H. Wallenstein, Dallas, 1975-78; v.p. Wallenstein & St. Claire, Dallas, 1978-81; pres. Frank A. St. Claire, P.C., Dallas, 1981-84; ptnr. St. Claire & Case, P.C., Dallas, 1984-88, pres., 1988-93; chmn. bd. Sunbelt Empire Title Co., Dallas, 1983-88; pres. St. Claire & Assocs., Dallas, 1993—; chmn. real estate section Godwin & Carlton, P.C., Dallas, 1994-96; ptnr. bus. and fin. divsn. Strasburger & Price, L.L.P., Dallas, 1996—. Author: Texas Condominium Law, 1986; contbr. articles to profl. jours. Ofcl. del. Dallas to Baltic Legal Conf., Riga, Latvia, 1990. Mem. ABA, Tex. Bar Assn. (study of uniform condominium act com., legis. liaison com. 1981-85, vice chmn. 1981-82, chmn. 1982-85, chmn. condominium and coop. housing com. 1985-89, title ins. com., mem. coun. real estate, probate and trust coun. 1991-95, treas. 1996—), Dallas Bar Assn., Cmty. Assn. Inst. (bd. dirs. Dallas-Ft. Worth chpt. 1984-85, 87-89, pres.-elect 1989-90), Real Estate Fin. Exec. Assn. (asst. sec. 1996—), Real Estate Coun., Am. Coll. Real Estate Lawyers (planning com. 1990—, chmn. practice tech. com. 1993-96, mem. common interest ownership com. 1986—, alternative dispute resolution com. 1993-95), Tex. Coll. Real Estate Attys. (chmn. projects com. 1991-92, bd. dirs. 1994—). Episcopalian. Office: Nations Bank Plz Ste 4300 901 Main St Dallas TX 75202

ST. CYR, JOHN ALBERT, II, cardiovascular and thoracic surgeon; b. Mpls., Nov. 26, 1949; s. John Albert and Myrtle Lavira (Jensen) St. C.; m. Mary Helen Malinoski, Oct. 29, 1977. BA summa cum laude, U. Minn., 1973, BS, 1975, MS, 1977, MD, 1980, PhD, 1988. Teaching asst. dept. biochemistry U. Minn., Mpls., 1973, rsch. asst. dept. surgery, 1977-78, intern surgery dept. surgery, 1980-81, resident surgery, 1981-88, cardiovascular rsch. fellow dept. surgery, 1983-86, with dept. surgery, 1991-92; rsch. assoc. fellow Cardiovasular Pathology, United Hosp., St. Paul, 1987-88; cardiovascular surg. resident U. Colo., Dept. Cardiovascular Surgery, Denver, 1988-91; med. advisor Organetics, Ltd., Mpls., 1992, med. dir., 1992; med. advisor Aor Tech., Inc., St. Paul, 1992; bd. dirs. Minn. Acad. Sci.; pres. Virotech, Inc., 1993-94; ind. rsch., 1992—; dir. R&D Medcorp Internat., 1996, Jacqmar, Inc., 1996—; med. dir. IHI, 1996. Contbr. more than 70 articles to profl. jours. Recipient NIH Rsch./Fellowship award, 1983-86, Grant in Aid Rsch. award Minn. Heart Assn., 1983-85, Med. Student Rsch. award Minn. Med. Found., 1980, Acad. Excellence award Merck Found., 1980. Mem. AAAS, ACS, AMA, Assn. Acad. Surgeons, Soc. Thoracic Surgeons, Am. Physiol. Soc., Am. Fedn. and Clin. Rsch., N.Y. Acad. Scis., Phi Kappa Phi. Republican. Achievements include patent in field with subsequent clin. studies.

ST. GEORGE, JUDITH ALEXANDER, author; b. Westfield, N.J., Feb. 26, 1931; d. John Heald and Edna (Perkins) Alexander; m. David St. George, June 5, 1954; children: Peter, James, Philip, Sarah Anne. BA, Smith Coll., 1952. Author: Turncoat Winter, Rebel Spring, 1970, The Girl with Spunk, 1975, By George, Bloomers!, 1976, The Chinese Puzzle of Shag Island, 1976, The Shad Are Running, 1977, The Shadow of the Shaman, 1977, The Halo Wind, 1978, The Halloween Pumpkin Smasher, 1978, Mystery at St. Martin's, 1979, The Amazing Voyage of the New Orleans, 1980, Haunted, 1980, Call Me Margo, 1981, The Mysterious Girl in the Garden, 1981, The Brooklyn Bridge: They Said It Couldn't Be Built, 1982 (Am. Book award), Do You See What I See?, 1982, In The Shadow of the Bear, 1983, What's Happening to My Junior Year?, 1983, Who's Scared? Not Me!, 1984, The Mount Rushmore, 1985 (Christopher award), Panama Canal: Gateway to the World, 1989 (Golden Kite award), The White House, 1990, Mason and Dixon's Line of Fire, 1991, Dear Dr. Bell...Your Friend Helen Keller, 1992, Crazy Horse, 1994, To See With the Heart: The Life of Sitting Bull, 1996, Betsy Ross: Patriot of Philadelphia, 1997, Sacagawea, 1997; (from filmscript) A View to a Kill, 1985; (from screenscript) Tales of the Gold Monkey, 1983. Mem. adv. coun. on children's lit. Rutgers U., 1977-94; chmn. ednl. com. Bklyn. Bridge Centennial Commn., 1981-83. Mem. Soc. Children's Book Writers, Author's Guild. Episcopalian. Avocations: tennis, hiking, travel. Home: 8 Binney Rd Old Lyme CT 06371-1445

ST. GEORGE, NICHOLAS JAMES, lawyer, manufactured housing company executive; b. Waltham, Mass., Feb. 11, 1939; s. Louis and Rose (Argonti) St. G.; B.A. in Econs., Coll. William and Mary, 1960, J.D., 1965; children: Blane Stephen, Nicholas John; m. Eugenia Metzger, July 25, 1987. Trainee, Gen. Electric Co., Schenectady, 1960; admitted to Va. bar, 1965; trust rep. Va. Nat. Bank, Norfolk, 1965-66; group v.p.-in-charge investment banking dept. Ferguson Enterprises, Newport News, Va., 1977-78; pres., chief exec. officer Oakwood Homes Corp., Greensboro, N.C., 1979—, also dir.; dir. Am. Bankers Ins. Group, First Union Nat. Bank Greensboro, Legg Mason, Inc.; dir. Manufactured Housing Inst.; trustee Marshall-Wythe Sch. Law Coll. William and Mary. Office: Oakwood Homes Corp PO Box 27081 Greensboro NC 27425-7081

ST. GEORGE, WILLIAM ROSS, lawyer, retired naval officer, consultant; b. Southport, N.C., Nov. 19, 1924; s. William B. and Ila (Ross) St. G.; m. Emma Louise Bridger, June 10, 1950; children—Victoria Butler, William Ross, Susan Bridger. B.S., U.S. Naval Acad., 1946; J.D., George Washington U., 1953. Bar: D.C. 1953, U.S. Supreme Ct. 1964, Calif. 1980. Commd. ensign U.S. Navy, 1946, advanced through grades to vice adm., 1973; comdg. officer U.S.S. Josephus Daniels, 1969-70; comdr. Cruiser-Destroyer Flotilla 11, also comdr. Cruiser-Destroyer Flotilla 3, 1973; dep. and chief staff to comdr.-in-chief U.S. Pacific Fleet, 1973-76; comdr. Naval Surface Force, U.S. Pacific Fleet, 1976-79, ret., 1979; sole practice San Diego, 1980—. Decorated D.S.M. with oak leaf cluster, Legion of Merit, Bronze Star. Presbyterian. Home: 862 San Antonio Pl San Diego CA 92106-3057 Office: PO Box 6932 1110 Rosecrans St Fl 2D San Diego CA 92106-2630

ST. GERMAIN, FERNAND JOSEPH, congressman; b. Blackstone, Mass.; s. Andrew Joseph and Pearl (Talaby) St Germain; m. Rachel O'Neill, Aug. 20, 1953; children: Laurene, Lisette. Ph.B. in Social Sci, Providence Coll., 1948, LL.D., 1965; LL.B., Boston U., 1955; J.S.D. (hon.), Suffolk U., 1976; D.C.L. (hon.), Our Lady of Providence Sem., 1968; D.B.A. (hon.), Bryant Coll., 1981; D.Public Service (hon.), Roger Williams Coll., 1981; LL.B., Brown U., 1985. Bar: R.I. 1956, Fed. 1957, U.S. Supreme Ct. 1983. Mem. R.I. Ho. of Reps., 1952-60; mem. 87th to 100th Congresses from 1st R.I. Dist., 1961-1989, chmn. house com. on banking fin. and urban affairs, 1980-88. Served with AUS, 1949-52. Recipient Silver Shingle award for disting. public service Boston U. Sch. Law Alumni Assn., 1981, Alumni award disting. pub. service Boston U. Sch. Law, 1982. Mem. ABA, R.I., Bar Assn. Fed. Bar Assn., alumni assns. Our Lady of Providence Sem., Providence Coll., Boston U. Law Sch., Am. Legion. Office: 7601 Lewinsville Rd Ste 205 Mc Lean VA 22102-2815

ST. GOAR, HERBERT, food corporation executive; b. Hamburg, Germany, Apr. 7, 1916; came to U.S., 1938, naturalized, 1943; s. Otto and Thekla St.G.; m. Maria Karsch, Sept. 3, 1954; children: Edward, Elisabeth. Student schs., Hamburg, Germany; LL.B., Chattanooga Coll. Law, 1943. With Internat. Harvester Co., Hamburg, Germany, 1936-38; with Dixie Saving Stores, Inc., Chattanooga, 1938—; pres. Dixie Saving Stores, Inc., 1969—, chief exec. officer, 1969—. Bd. dirs. Chattanooga Opera Assn., Jr. C. of C., 1945-54; mem. Hamilton County Juvenile Ct. Commn. Served with Intelligence Sect., U.S. Army, World War II. Decorated Bronze Star, Legion of Merit.; Named Disting. Citizen Chattanooga, 1979. Mem. Southeastern Food Coop. Assn. (past pres.), Tenn. Wholesale Grocers Assn. (bd. dirs. 1988-91), Retailer-Owned Food Distrbrs. Assn. (bd. dirs. 1988—), NGA Retailer-Owned Exec. Coun., Asparagus Club. Home: 1502 Hixson Pike Chattanooga TN 37405-2431 Office: PO Box 1637 Chattanooga TN 37401-1637

SAINT-JACQUES, BERNARD, linguistics educator; b. Montreal, Que., Can., Apr. 26, 1928; s. Albert and Germaine (Lefebvre) Saint-J.; m. Marguerite Fauquenoy. M.A., Sophia U., Tokyo, 1962; M.S., Georgetown U., 1964; Doctorat es Lettres and Scis. Humaines, Paris U., 1975. Asst. prof. linguistics U. B.C., Vancouver, 1967-69; assoc. prof. U. B.C., 1969-78, prof., 1978-90, prof. emeritus, 1991—; prof. Aichi U., Japan, 1990—; mem. U.S. Citizen Amb. Program. Author: Structural Analysis of Modern Japanese, 1971, Aspects sociolinguistiques du bilinguisme canadien, 1976, Language and Ethnic Relations, 1979, Japanese Studies in Canada, 1985, Studies in Language and Culture, 1995. Leave fellow Can. Council, 1974; profl. fellow Japan Found., 1981; research fellow French Govt., 1982, Ohira Programme, Japan, 1983. Fellow Royal Soc. Can. Acad.; mem. Sociolinguistic Assn. (co-editor), Linguistic Soc. Am., Can. Soc. Asian Studies, Can. Linguistics Assn. Office: U BC, Dept Linguistics, Vancouver, BC Canada V6T 1Z1 also: Aichi ShuKutoKu U., Katahira NagaKute, NagaKute-cho Aichi-gun Aichi 480-11, Japan

SAINT-JACQUES, MADELEINE, advertising agency executive; b. Montreal, Can., June 27, 1935; d. Henri and Marie-Jeanne (Ostiguy) S.J. BA, U. Montreal, 1972. Writer, producer Saint-Jacques Vallée Young & Rubicam Inc., Montreal, 1955-70, creative dir., 1970-77, exec. v.p., mng. dir., 1977-90, pres., 1990-94, chmn. bd. dirs., 1995; bd. dirs. Télé Métropole Inc., Ultramar Diamond Shamrock Corp., Les Reseaux Premier Choix, Inc.; bd. govs. Inno-Centre Québec; v.p. Soc. d'édition de la revue Forces, La Corp. des Célébrations du 350e anniversaire de Montréal, 1989-93; adv. bd. Guarant Trust, 1979-84. Bd. dirs. Internat. Mag. Mgmt., 1980-92. 1st v.p. Children's Broadcast Inst., 1972-77; grievance com. L'Union des Artistes, 1976-78; gen. v.p. comm. divsn. Centraide campaign, 1980, v.p. bd. dirs. 1983-87; v.p. Coun. Arts Montreal Urban Community, 1979-89; co-pres. Com. Econ. Promotion Montreal, 1981-82; bd. govs. McGill U. 1986-90; bd. dirs. Terry Fox Humanitarian Award Program, St. Mary's Hosp. Found., Can. Mental Health Assn., 1975-79, Soc. Devel. Industries and Culture of Comm. (SDICC), 1979-82, Via Rail Can. Inc., 1977-82, Soc. Devel. Montreal, 1982-88, Found. Films of World Festival, Montreal, 1990-92. Recipient advt. award Assn. Can. Advertisers, 1975, 76, Gold award, 1977, award distinction Faculty commerce and adminstrn. Concordia U., 1992, mgmt. achievement award Mgmt. Undergrad. Soc. McGill U., 1993. Mem. Can. Club Montréal (bd. dirs., pres. 1993—, pres. centennial yr. 1987), Club St.-Denis, Forest and Stream, Publicité Club Montreal (pres. 1972-73). Roman Catholic. Avocations: skiing, tennis, golf. Office: Saint Jacques Vallée Young & Rubicam Inc, 1600 René-Lévesque Ste 1200, Montreal, PQ Canada H3H 1P9

ST. JAMES, LYN, business owner, professional race car driver; b. Willoughby, Ohio, Mar. 13, 1947; d. Alfred W. and Maxine W. (Rawson) Cornwall; m. John Raymond Carusso, Dec. 7, 1970 (div. 1979); m. Roger Lessman, Feb. 27, 1993; 1 stepchild, Lindsay. Cert. in piano, St. Louis Inst. Music, 1967. Sec. Cleve. dist. sales office U.S. Steel Corp., 1967-69, Mike Roth Sales Corp., Euclid, Ohio, 1969-70; co-owner, v.p. Dynasales Fla., Hollywood, 1970-79; owner, pres. Autodyne, Ft. Lauderdale, Fla., 1974-91, Lyn St. James Enterprises, Inc., Daytona Beach, Fla., 1979—; profl. race car driver, 1979—; ranked 11th Indpls. 500, 1992; race car driver Ford Motor Co., Dearborn, Mich., 1981—, spokesperson, cons., 1981—; media spokesperson JC Penney, 1992—. Author: Lyn St. James Car Owner's Manual, 1989; contbg. editor automotive articles Seventeen mag., 1987—, Cosmopolitan mag., 1989-90. Bd. trustees Women's Sports Found., N.Y.C., 1988—. Recipient Rookie of the Year, AutoWeek Magazine, 1984, Woman of Yr. award McCalls mag., 1986, Leadership award Girl Scouts U.S., 1988, Rookie of Yr. at the Indy 500, 1992, Touchstone award Girls Inc. Indpls., 1995; first woman since Janet Guthrie to qualify for the Indpls. 500. Mem. Internat. Motorsports Assn., Sports Car Club of Am. Republican. Avocation: tennis.Only woman winner in the Internat. Motor Sports Assn.'s Camel GTO series; holder of 31 auto racing speed records; first woman to win a professional road race driving solo; first woman to drive over 200 mph on an oval track. Office: Lyn St James Enterprises Ste 100 2570 W International Speedway Blvd Daytona Beach FL 32114-7103

ST. JEAN, GUY, electric power industry executive; b. Montreal, Que., Can., Oct. 8, 1941; s. Jean-Paul and Marie Marthe (Vandemeulebroecke) St. J. BSc in Math. and Physics, Sir George Williams U., Montreal, 1964; MSc in Physics, U. Que., Varennes, 1977; postgrad., Internat. Mgmt. Inst., Geneva. Analyst spl. tests Hydro-Que., Montreal, 1965-67, analyst self-synchronization large generators, 1967-69; researcher Electricité de France, Paris, 1969-70; researcher Hydro-Que., Varennes, 1970-83, program mgr., 1975-83, mgr. switchgear rsch., 1983-86, mgr. power apparatus rsch., 1986—; lectr. grad. course Ecole Poly. Montreal, 1977-84, thesis dir., 1978-88; mem. Can. com. Internat. Electrotech. Commn., Ottawa, Ont., Can., 1985—, chmn. coms. 17 and 37, 1985—; Can. rep. Internat. Commn. Electric Rsch., 1982—; mem. Conf. Bd. Can., 1991—. Author: Power System Recoverry Voltages, 1987; also over 50 articles; patentee synthetic test cir., cir. for protecting device, surge arrester, U.S. Recipient prize paper award IEEE Power Engring. Soc., 1986, 87, R&D 100 award R&D mag., 1990. Fellow IEEE (technol. editor Can. Rev. 1988-91); mem. Can. Standard Assn. (chmn. 1985—). Avocations: skiing, windsurfing, sailing and officiating regattas. Home: 560 St-Laurent Apt 122, Longueuil, PQ Canada J4H 3X3 Office: Hydro-Quebec, Apparatus Rsch Dept PO Box 1000, Varennes, PQ Canada J0L 2P0 *The pursuit of truth will set you free, even if you never catch up to it.*

ST. JEAN, JOSEPH, JR., micropaleontologist, educator; b. Tacoma, July 24, 1923; s. Joseph Leger and Ruby Pearl (Burg) St. J.; m. Elena Mikhailovna Melnikova, Sept. 22, 1971. B.S., Coll. Puget Sound, 1949; M.A., Ind. U., 1953, Ph.D., 1956. Field asst., party chief Ind. Geol. Survey, summers 1950-53; instr. Kans. State U., Manhattan, 1951-52; instr., asst. prof. Trinity Coll., Hartford, Conn., 1955-57; faculty U. N.C., Chapel Hill, 1957-90; prof. geology U. N.C., 1966-90, gen. coll. advisor, 1979-90, ret., 1990; peer reviewer NSF, 1966—, profl. jours., 1960—. 2d violinist, Durham (N.C.) Symphony Orch., 1977-84; Contbr. sects. to McGraw-Hill Ency. Sci. and Tech; papers to paleontol., biol. jours. Served as Q.M. USNR, 1942-45. Grantee Geol. Soc. Am., 1956-58; Grantee AEC, 1958-60; Grantee NSF, 1960-62; Grantee U. N.C. Faculty Research Council, 1960-62; Grantee Soc. Sigma Xi, 1954-56. Mem. Paleontol. Soc., Soc. Econ. Paleontologists and Mineralogists, Carolina Geol. Soc., Paleontol. Rsch. Instn., N.C. Acad. Scis., Paleontol. Assn. London, Sigma Xi. Home: 1212 Hillsborough Rd Chapel Hill NC 27516-8712 Office: U NC Dept Geology CB #3315 Mitchell Hall Chapel Hill NC 27599-3315

ST. JOHN, ADRIAN, II, retired army officer; b. Ft. Leavenworth, Kans., Nov. 16, 1921; s. Adrian and Marie (McMahon) St John; m. Petronella Elizabeth Durham, Jan. 19, 1943; children: Adrian III, Brian. BS, U.S. Mil. Acad., 1943; MA, U. Va., 1951; MPA, Am. U., 1981; postgrad., Army War Coll., 1960, U. Hawaii, 1963, Am. U., 1977-82. Commd. 2d lt. U.S. Army, 1943, advanced through grades to maj. gen., 1969, co. comdg. officer 15th Cav., 1943-45; intelligence staff officer U.S. Army, Berlin, 1945-47; China desk officer gen. staff U.S. Army, Washington, 1951-53; bn. comdg. officer 3d Bn., 31st Inf. Regt. U.S. Army, Korea, 1954, comdr. 73d Tank Bn., 1955; mem. faculty Command and Gen. Staff Coll., Ft. Leavenworth, 1956-59; faculty adviser Iranian Def. Coll., 1959; S.E. Asia plans officer G3, U.S. Army-Pacific, 1960-64; long range plans br. Strategic Div., Orgn. Joint Chiefs of Staff, Washington, 1964-66; chief Surface P & O Div. J3, US-MACV, Vietnam, 1966-67; comdg. officer 14th Armored Cav. Regt., Europe, 1967-69; asst. div. comdr. 4th Armored Div., Europe, 1969-70; chief Strategic Plans and Policy Div. J5, Orgn. Joint Chiefs of Staff, Washington, 1970-71; dir. plans gen. staff U.S. Army, Washington, 1971-72; comdg. gen. 1st Armored Div., Europe, 1972-74; vice dir. joint staff Joint Chiefs of Staff, 1974-76; ret., 1976; mem. adv. council on internat. security affairs Republican Nat. Com., 1977-80; del. Va. State Rep. Conv., 1980, 81; sr. mil. adv. U.S. Negotiating Del. Mut. Balanced Force Reductions, Vienna, 1982-88; Joint Chiefs of Staff rep. U.S. Del. Conventional Stability Talks, Vienna, 1987-88, negotiations on Conventional Armed Forces, Europe, 1989-92; del., presenter Congress Arms Control Mid. East, Delphi, Greece, 1994; U.S. del. World Helicopter Championships, Moscow, 1994; chmn. operational working group internat. conf. on arms control in Mid. East, Jordan, 1994; mem. advance party OSCE to prepare for elections, Bosnia, 1997; presenter plaques signed by Sec. of Def. to Australian authorities in 6 cities during ceremonies commemorating VJ Day, 1995. Co-chmn. orchestral benefit ball Austrian Embassy, 1993, 94; U.S. del. World Helicopter Championships, Oreg., 1996. Decorated D.S.M. with oak leaf cluster, Silver Star, Legion of Merit with 3 oak leaf clusters, Bronze Star with V device, Joint Svc. Commendation medal, Army Commendation medal with oak leaf cluster, Joint Meritorious Unit award, French Croix de Guerre with silver star, Vietnamese Gallantry Cross with palm; recipient European Comdr. in Chief's Individual Project partnership award, 1968, Presdl. award Disting. Citizen, 1993, Dept. State Superior honor award, 1989, 91, Sec. of Def. medal for disting. pub. svc., 1992. Mem. Am. Security Coun., Am. Fgn. Affairs Coun., Heritage Found., World Affairs Coun. Roman Catholic. Home: # 118 9110 Belvoir Woods Pkwy Fort Belvoir VA 22060-2716 Office: Pentagon Bldg Washington DC 20301 *There are no limits to the heights man can reach so long as he cares not who gets the credit.*

ST. JOHN, BILL DEAN, diversified equipment and services company executive; b. Wewoka, Okla., 1931. BBA, So. Meth. U., 1952. Asst. treas. Seaboard Oil Co., 1954-58; auditor Alford Merony & Co., 1958-60; v.p. fin. Can. Refractories Ltd., 1968; with Dresser Industries Inc., Dallas, 1960—; treas. Ideco div. Dresser Industries, Dallas, 1961-63; fin. contr. Dresser Industries Inc., Dallas, 1970-73, staff v.p. fin. svcs., 1975-76, v.p. acctg., 1976-80; exec. v.p. adminstrn. Dresser Industries, Inc., Dallas, 1980-92, vice chmn., 1992—, CFO, 1993—; Allendale Ins. So. adv. bd., 1995—. With U.S. Army, 1952-54. Mem. AICPA, Mfrs.' Alliance for Productivity and Innovation (fin. coun.), The Conf. Bd. (chief adminstrv. officers coun.), Allendale Ins. So. Adv. Bd. Office: Dresser Industries Inc PO Box 718 2001 Ross Ave Dallas TX 75221-0718

ST. JOHN, BOB, journalist, columnist, author; b. Canton, Okla., Jan. 10, 1937. Sportswriter, sports columnist, until 1978; gen. columnist Dallas Morning News, 1978—. Author: On Down the Road, 1977, Landry: The Man Inside, 1978, Tex, 1988, The Landry Legend, 1990, Sketches, 1981, While The Music Lasts, 1989, South Padre: The Island and Its People, Heart of a Lion, 1991, others; co-author: Staubach: First and Lifetime With Sam Blair, 1974; over 150 radio, TV intenviews. Recipient Disting. Alumni award U. North Tex., 1986, two 1st place awards Pro Football Writers Assn. Am., over 40 awards for newspaper writing; named to North Tex. U. Journalism Hall of Honor, 1986. Office: The Dallas Morning News Communications Ctr PO Box 655237 Dallas TX 75265-5237

ST. JOHN, CHARLES VIRGIL, retired pharmaceutical company executive; b. Bryan, Ohio, Dec. 18, 1922; s. Clyde W. and Elsie (Kintner) St. J.; m. Ruth Ilene Wilson, Oct. 27, 1946; children: Janet Sue St. John Amy, Debra Ann St. John Mishler. AB, Manchester Coll., 1943; MS, Purdue U., 1946. Asst. gen. mgr., dir. ops. Eli Lilly and Co., Clinton, Ind., 1971-75; gen. mgr. Eli Lilly and Co., Lafayette, Ind., 1975-77, v.p. prodn. ops. divsn., 1977-89; bd. dirs. Bank One of Lafayette, Lafayette Life Ins. Co., Lafayette Cmty. Found., Bioanalytical Sys., Inc., West Lafayette, Ind. Past pres. bd. dirs. United Way Greater Lafayette and Tippecanoe County; bd. trustees Lafayette Symphony Found.; past chmn. lay adv. coun. St. Elizabeth Hosp.; mem. pres.'s coun. Purdue U.; trustee Manchester (Ind.) Coll.; bd. dirs. Lafayette Cmty. Found., Jr. Achievement of Greater Lafayette. Recipient Elizabethan award, St. Elizabeth Hosp., Lafayette, 1985; named Cmty. Hero Olympic Torch Bearer, 1996. Mem. Am. Chem. Soc., Purdue Rsch. Found., Greater Lafayette C. of C. (past bd. dirs., Grand Marquis de Lafayette award Cmty. Svc. 1996), Lafayette Country Club, Rotary. Republican. Methodist. Home: 321 Overlook Dr West Lafayette IN 47906-1249

ST. JOHN, HENRY SEWELL, JR., utility company executive; b. Birmingham, Ala., Aug. 18, 1938; s. H. Sewell and Carrie M. (Bond) St. J.; student David Lipscomb Coll., 1956-58, U. Tenn., 1958-59, U. Ala., 1962-64; m. J. Ann Morris, Mar. 7, 1959; children: Sherri Ann, Brian Lee, Teresa Lynn, Cynthia Faye. Engring. aide Ala. Power Co., Enterprise, 1960-62, Birmingham, 1962-66; asst. chief engr. Riviera Utilities, Foley, 1966-71, sec.-treas., gen. mgr., 1971—. Deacon, Foley Ch. of Christ, 1975-82, elder, 1983—; active Am. Cancer Soc., chmn. bd. Baldwin County unit, 1977; bd. dirs. AGAPE of Mobile, 1977-80; treas. Christian Care Ctr., Inc., 1981—; bd. dirs. South Baldwin Civic Chorus, pres., 1979-82 . Mem. IEEE., South Ala. Power Distbrs. Assn. (chmn. 1973-74), Ala. Consumer-Owned Power Distbrs. Assn. (chmn. 1974-75, 82-83, vice-chmn. 1981, sec.-treas. 1980), S.E. Electric Reliability Coun. (assoc.), Mcpl. Electric Utility Assn. Ala. (exec. com., dir. 1971—), Ala. Mcpl. Electric Authority (bd. dir. 1981—, vice chmn. 1981-82, chmn. 1983—), Electric Cities Ala. (bd. dirs., exec. com. 1989—), United Mcpl. Distbrs. Group (bd. dirs. 1972—), Am. Pub. Power Assn. (cable communications com.), Pub. Gas. Assn. Ala. (bd. dirs. 1987-88), South Baldwin C. of C. (pres. 1974, dir. 1972-75, 81-90, 92-95). Clubs: Foley Quarterback (sec.-treas. 1984-85); Gulf Shores Golf (dir. 1974-75), Classic Chevy, Internat. (life mem.), Azalea City Classic Chevy (bd. dirs., exec. com. 1989—), v.p. 1991-92, 96—), Chevrolet Nomad Assn. (bd. dirs. 1992—, v.p. 1993—). Rotarian. Home: PO Box 1817 Foley AL 36536-1817 Office: PO Box 2050 Foley AL 36536-2050

ST. JOHN, JOHN, food company executive; b. Battle Creek, Mich., Aug. 8, 1921; s. Raymond Martin and Hazel (Eastman) St. J.; m. Lorraine Margaret McCarthy, Feb. 27, 1943; 1 dau., Shannon Elaine. B.A., Mich. State U., 1943. With Minute Maid Co. (and predecessors), 1949—, fin. v.p., 1963-65, pres., 1965-69; v.p. finance and ops. Citrus Central, Inc., Orlando, Fla., 1969-71; exec. v.p. Citrus Central, Inc., 1971-87, mgmt. cons., 1987—; dir., chmn. Farm Credit Capital Corp., Kansas City, Mo., 1985-87; bd. dirs., chmn. Fed. Farm Credit Banks Funding Corp., N.Y., 1983-88; asset mgr. Treasure Coast Citrus, Inc., Ft. Pierce, Fla., 1989—. Past pres., bd. dirs. Central Fla. unit Am. Cancer Soc. Served with USAAF, 1943-46. Mem. Country Club of Orlando, Racquet Club (Winter Park, Fla.), Univ. Club (Lansing, Mich.). Episcopalian. Home: 910 Pace Ave Maitland FL 32751-5768 Office: 1920 Boothe Cir Ste 200 Longwood FL 32750-6774

ST. JOHN, KATHERINE IVA, artistic director, dance educator; b. St. Paul, Nov. 18, 1948; d. Arthur E. and Lillian Faye (Teetsell) Tester; m. Curtis St. John (div.). BA, U. Utah, 1989; MA, Brigham Young U., 1994, U. Utah, 1994; postgrad., U. Calif., Riverside. Instr. U. Utah, Salt Lake City, 1989-94; dir. Ea. Arts, Salt Lake City, 1989—; artistic dir. Internat. Dance Theatre, Salt Lake City, 1993—. Author, choreographer: Radif E Raos; author: Afghan Dance: A Cultural and Historical Study; contbr. articles to profl. publs. Vol. Salt Lake Ethnic Arts Coun.; bd. chair Assn. Students Univ. Utah, 1992; speaker Utah Humanities Coun. Grantee Utah Arts Coun., Salt Lake City Arts Coun. Mem. Internat. Orgn. of Folk Arts, Mid. East Studies Assn., Soc. Ethnomusicology, Congress on Rsch. in Dance, Dance and the Child Internat., Phi Kappa Phi. Home: PO Box 526362 Salt Lake City UT 84152-6362 Office: Eastern Arts Ethnic Dance Co PO Box 526362 Salt Lake City UT 84152-6362

ST. JOHN, MARIA ANN, nurse anesthetist; b. Rochester, Pa., Dec. 15, 1953; d. James Edward and Evelyn Marie (Sayers) St. J.; m. Paul David Dworsky, Aug. 19, 1978 (div. Dec. 13, 1991); children: Lauren Marie Dworsky, Michael David Dworsky. BSN, U. Pitts., 1975; cert. reg. nurse anesthetist, U. Health Ctr. Pitts. Sch. Anesthesia for Nurses, 1984. RN Pa.; adv. reg. nurse practitioner Fla.; cert. reg. nurse anesthetist. Nurse Presbyn. U. Hosp., Pitts., 1975-77, VA Hosp., Pitts., 1977-82; nurse anesthetist Anesthesia Assocs. of Hollywood, Fla., 1984-87, North Hills Anesthesia Assocs., Pitts., 1987—. Vol. tchr. art history, fundraiser St. Alexis Sch., Wexford, Pa., 1991—, recording sec. PT6 Bd., 1996-, 97, v.p. PT6 Bd., 1997—. Recipient scholarship March of Dimes, Beaver County, Pa., 1971. Mem. Am. Assn. Nurse Anesthetists, Pa. Assn. Nurse Anesthetists, Cranberry Twp. Athletic Assn., D.A.R. Republican. Roman Catholic. Avocations: playing piano, reading, traveling, school volunteering. Home: 436 Anna Marie Dr Cranberry Township PA 16066

ST. JOHN, RICHARD See HARRIS, RICHARD

ST. LOUIS, PAUL MICHAEL, foreign language educator; b. Vernon, Conn., Aug. 30, 1946; s. Wilfred Henry and Alice Agnes (Brennan) St. L. Spl. cert. Jr. Yr. Abroad program, U. Louvain, Belgium, 1967; BA, Boston Coll., 1968; MA, Trinity Coll., 1975. Cert. tchr. secondary French, Conn. Tchr. French East Hartford (Conn.) H.S., 1968-96, head dept. fgn. lang., 1984-85; retired, 1996; advisor to French club East Hartford H.S., 1969-85, jr. class advisor, 1985, 87, 89-90, 92, sr. class advisor, 1986, 88, 90-92, bus. mgr. grades 9-12, 1993—. Vis. com. New England Assn. Schs. and Colls., Milford, Conn., 1980, steering com. for sch. evaluation, 1978, 88. Mem. NEA, Am. Coun. Tchg. of Fgn. Lang., Conn. Edn. Assn., Conn. Coun. Lang. Tchrs. (treas. bd. dirs. 1992—, chairperson registration fall conf. 1989—, co-chairperson fall conf. 1991, cons. poetry recitation contest 1992—), Am. Assn. Tchrs. of French (cons. regional conf. 1990), Mass. Fgn. Lang. Assn., East Hartford Edn. Assn. Avocation: computer technology. Home and office: 275 Cedar Swamp Rd Monson MA 01057-9303

ST. MARIE, SATENIG, writer; b. Brockton, Mass., June 2, 1927; d. Harry and Mary K. Sahjian; m. Gerald L. St. Marie, Dec. 26, 1959. B.S., Simmons Coll., Boston, 1949; M.A., Columbia U., 1959; LL.D. (hon.), N.D. State U., 1976. Extension home economist U. Mass. Extension Service, 1949-52, U. Conn. Extension Service, 1953-56; with J.C. Penney Co., Inc., 1959-87, mgr. endl. and consumer relations, 1967-73, dir. consumer affairs, 1973-87, div. v.p., 1974-87; dir. Nat. Reins. Co.; mem. U.S. Metric Bd. Author: Homes Are For People, 1973, Romantic Victorian Weddings: Then and Now, 1992; pub. J.C. Penney Consumer Edn. Services, 1981-87; lifestyles editor: Victorian Homes Mag., 1987—. Mem. Am. Home Econs. Assn. (past pres.), Antiques Dealers Assn. Am. (exec. dir. 1987—). Office: PO Box 335 Greens Farms CT 06436-0335

ST. MARY, EDWARD SYLVESTER, direct mail marketing company executive; b. Campbellsport, Wis., May 31, 1941; s. Raymond O. and Freida (Beisbier) St. Mary; m. Patricia Dyer, Aug. 5, 1961; children—Todd M., Brian D. B.S. in Bus. Adminstrn, Drake U., Des Moines, 1963. CPA, Wis., Minn. With Gen. Electric Co., 1963-72, mgr. sales analysis and planning, 1972; asst. contr., then contr. and treas. Fingerhut Corp., Minnetonka, Minn., 1972-75; v.p. fin. Fingerhut Corp., Minnetonka, Minn., 1975-80, sr. v.p. adminstrn., CFO, 1981-87; CFO, Hanover (Pa.) House, 1988-90; prin. SEC Cons. Group, Maple Grove, Minn., 1991—; bd. dirs. HomServ Co. Mem. AICPA, Nat. Acctg. Assn., Minn. Soc. CPA's. Roman Catholic. Home and Office: 13831 Tonbridge Ct Bonita Springs FL 34135

ST-ONGE, DENIS ALDERIC, geologist, research scientist; b. Ste-Agathe, Man., Can., May 11, 1929; s. Adolphe and Jeanne M. (Ritchot) St-O.; m. Jeanne Marie Behaegel, Jan. 7, 1955; children—Marc R., Nicole J.M. B.A., Coll. St-Boniface, 1951; Lic. Sci., U. Louvain, Belgium, 1957, D.Sc., 1962; D.Sc. honoris causa, U. Man., 1990. Research scientist Geol. Survey, Ottawa, Ont., Can., 1958-68, sect. head, 1982-85; chief sub. div. Quaternary Geology, 1985-87, dir. terrain scis. div., 1987-91, sci. advisor Polar Continental Shelf Project, 1991-97; prof. geography U. Ottawa, 1968-82, chmn. geography, 1974-77, vice dean grad. studies, 1977-80; scientist emeritus Geol. Survey Can., 1997—. Author: Geomorphologie Ellef-Ringnes Island, 1965, Quaternary Geology, Inman River Region, N.W.T. Canada, 1995; contbr. articles to profl. jours. Pres. Ont. Francophone PTA, 1967-69. Recipient Medal Queen Elizabeth II, 1989, medal of Honor U. Liege, Belgium, 1980, medal A. Cailleux, 1991, medal Can. 125, 1992, medal Royal Scottish Geog. Soc., 1994; officer Order of Can., 1996. Fellow Geol. Assn. Can. (pres. 1984-85), Royal Can. Geog. Soc. (bd. dirs. 1980-92, pres. 1992—), Arctic Inst. N.Am.; mem. Can. Assn. Geographers (pres. 1979-80), Can. Quaternary Assn., Assn. Quebecoise pour l'etude du Quaternaire (hon.), Internat. Union Quaternary Rsch. (hon. life), Can. Geosci. Coun. (pres. 1996-97). Avocations: swimming; skiing; photography. Home: 1115 Sherman Dr, Ottawa, ON Canada K2C 2M3 Office: Polar Continental Shelf Project, 615 Booth St, Ottawa, ON Canada K1A 0E9

ST. PIERRE, CHERYL ANN, art educator; b. Buffalo, Apr. 26, 1945; d. Guy Thomas and Madeline (Duncan) St. P. BS in Art Edn., SUNY, Buffalo, 1967, MS in Art Edn., 1970; MA in Italian, Middlebury Coll., 1976; PhD in Humanities, NYU, 1992. K-12 art tchr. Kenmore-Town of Tonawanda (N.Y.) Union Free Sch. Dist., 1967—; cooperating tchr. for art student tchrs. SUNY, Buffalo, 1972—; advisor on original multi-media prodn. N.Y. State Coun. for Arts, Tonawanda, 1990—; coord., tchr. Parents As Reading Ptnrs. Artwork, Tonawanda, 1990—; grad. asst. NYU, N.Y.C., 1987-88. Illustrator jour. Italian Americana, 1971-81; designer greeting cards for State of N.Y. and Maine, Am. Lung Assn., 1978-79. Earthwatch vol. Identity through Native Costume, Macedonia, 1995. Mem. ASCD, AAUW, Internat. Mentor Assn., N.Y. State United Tchrs., Nat. Art Edn. Assn., N.Y. State Tchrs. Assn., Am. Fedn. Tchrs., Kenmore Tchrs.' Assn., Alpha Delta Kappa. Avocations: travel, photography, film studies, animal rights, reading. Home: 3881 N Bailey Ave Buffalo NY 14226-3202

ST. PIERRE, GEORGE ROLAND, JR., materials science and engineering administrator, educator; b. Cambridge, Mass., June 2, 1930; s. George Rol and Rose Ann (Levesque) St. P.; m. Roberta Ann Hansen, July 20, 1956; children: Anne Renee, Jeanne Louise, John David, Thomas George; m. Mary Elizabeth Adams, Dec. 11, 1976. BS, MIT, 1951, ScD, 1954. Rsch. metallurgist Inland Steel Co., 1954-56; mem. faculty Ohio State U., 1956—, prof. metall. engring., 1957-88, assoc. dean Grad. Sch., 1964-66, chmn. Metall. Engring., 1983-88, chmn. mining engring., 1985-92; dir. Ohio Mineral Rsch. Inst., 1984-92, prof., chmn. material sci. and engring., 1988-92, Presdl. prof., 1988-92, chmn., presdl. prof. emeritus, 1992—; chief scientist Materials Directorate, Wright-Patterson AFB, 1995-96; cons. in field, 1957—; vis. prof. U. Newcastle, NSW, Australia, 1975; mem. adv. com. materials sci. MIT, 1990-97; mem. adv. bd. Argonne Nat. Lab., 1994—. Editor: Physical Chemistry of Process Metallurgy, Vols. 7 and 8, 1961, Advances in Transport Processes in Metallurgical Systems, 1992, Transactions Iron and Steel Soc., 1994—; contbr. articles to profl. jours. Bd. dirs. Edward Orton Jr. Ceramic Found., 1989-92. With USAF, 1956-57. Recipient Milton (Mass.) Sci. prize, 1947; MacQuigg award, 1971; Alumni Disting. Tchr. award, 1978; named Disting. scholar Ohio State U., 1988, Presdl. prof. Ohio State U., 1988. Fellow Minerals, Metals & Materials Soc., AIME (bd. dirs. 1988-91, 93-96, Educator award 1996), Am. Soc. Materials Internat. (Bradley Stoughton Outstanding Tchr. award 1961, Gold medal 1987); mem. Am. Inst. Mining Metall. and Petroleum Engrs. (Mineral Industry Edn. award 1987), Iron and Steel Soc. (Elliott lectr. 1994), Am. Contract Bridge League (silver life master), Faculty Club (pres. 1990-92), Sigma Xi. Home: 4495 Carriage Hill Ln Columbus OH 43220-3801 Office: Ohio State U Dept Materials Sci/Engring 2041 N College Rd Columbus OH 43210-1124

SAINT-PIERRE, GUY, engineering executive; b. Windsor Mills, Que., Can., Aug. 3, 1934; s. Arm and Alice (Perra) Saint-P.; m. Francine Garneau, May 4, 1957; children—Marc, Guylaine, Nathalie. B in Applied Sci. in Civil Engring, Laval U., 1957; diploma, Imperial Coll., London, 1958; MSc, U. London, 1959; LLD (hon.), Concordia U., 1992; hon. degree, le Coll. militaire Royal de Saint-Jean, 1993; DSc (hon.), Laval U., 1992; hon. degree Applied Sci., Sherbrooke, 1994; DSe (hon.), Montreal U. Registrar, Corp. Engrs. Que., 1964-66. Dir. Irnes Inc., 1966-67; v.p. Acres Que., 1967-70; minister of edn. Govt. Que., 1970-72, of industry and commerce, 1972-76; asst. to pres. John Labatt Ltd., Montreal, 1977-80; sr. v.p. John Labatt Ltd.; pres., chief operating officer Ogilvie Mills Ltd., Montreal, 1977-80; pres., chief exec. officer, bd. dirs. The SNC-Lavalin Group Inc., 1989-96; chmn. bd. The SNC-Lavalin Group, Inc., 1996—; dir. GM of Can., Royal Bank, BCE Inc., Alcan Aluminum; chmn. Bus. Coun. Nat. Issues, 1995—. Gov. Conseil de Patronat de Que. Served as officer C.E. Can. Army, 1959-64. Decorated officer Order of Can.; named Canada's CEO of Yr., 1994, Canada's Internat. Exec. of Yr., 1996; recipient Sir John Medal, 1993; Engring. Inst. of Can. Mem. Engring. Inst. Can., Can. Mfrs. Assn. (chmn. bd., pres. 1987), Order Engrs. Que., Coun. Can. Unity (v.p.), Mil. and Hospitalier Order St. Lazarus Jerusalem, Met. Montreal C. of C., Can. Club Montreal (adv. com.), Mt. Royal Club, Mt. Bruno Club, Forest and Streams Club, Hermitage Club. Liberal. Roman Catholic. Office: SNC-Lavalin Group Inc, 455 Boul René-Lèvesque O, Montreal, PQ Canada H2Z 1Z3

SAINT-PIERRE, JACQUES, statistics educator, consultant; b. Trois Rivières, Que., Can., Aug. 30, 1920; s. Oscar and Lucie (Landreville) St. P.; m. Marguerite Lachaine, July 15, 1947; children: Marc, Guy, Andre, Louis, Francois, Mireille. B.S., U. Montreal, 1948, M.S., 1951; Ph.D., U. N.C., 1954. Mem. faculty U. Montreal, 1947—, prof. stats., 1960-83, prof. emeritus, 1983—, dir. computing center, 1964-71, v.p. planning, 1971-82; cons. statistician, 1954—. Contbr. articles to profl. jours. Mem. Canadian Assn. Univ. Tchrs. (pres. 1965-66). Home: 4949 Earnscliffe, Montreal, PQ Canada H3X 2P4 Office: U Montreal, Box 6128, Montreal, PQ Canada H3C 3J7

ST-PIERRE, JEAN-CLAUDE, federal government official; b. St-Jean-sur-Richeleau, Que., Can., Aug. 21, 1942; s. Georges and Marie-Jeanne (Roy) St-P.; m. Louise Larivière, Aug. 24, 1963; children: Guy, Benoit. BSc, Laval (Quebec, Que.) U., 1964, MS, 1967; PhD, Cornell U., 1970. Rsch. scientist Agr. Can., Ste-Foy, Que., 1970-80; spl. advisor Agr. Can., Ottawa, Ont., 1980-81, program analyst, 1981-82, dir. rsch. program svc., 1982-84; dir. rsch. sta. Agr. Can., Lennoxville, Que., 1984-88; dir. gen. rsch. br. Agr. and Agri-Food Can., Ottawa, 1988—, dir. gen. rsch. coordination, 1995-96; dir. gen. min. tech. br. Nat. Res. Can., Ottawa, 1996—; pres. Que. Crop Coun., Ste-Foy, 1979-81; v.p. Que. Agrl. Rsch. Coun., Quebec City, 1984-89. Assoc. editor Can. Jour. Plant Sci., 1977-83; contbr. articles to sci. jours. Campaign chair United Way, Sherbrooke, Que., 1987; bd. dirs. Can. Soc. Agronomy, 1974-79. Que. Agrl. Rsch. Coun. scholar, 1964-70. Mem. Assn. Rsch. Mgrs., Assn. Pub. Svcs. Execs., Que. Order Agrologists. Home: 3 Des Genevriers, Hull, PQ Canada J9A 2P2 Office: Agr and Agri-Food Can, 930 Carling Ave, Ottawa, ON Canada K1A 0C5

SAINT-PIERRE, MICHAEL R., financial services executive; b. Montreal, Dec. 30, 1944; s. Roger and Francoise (Lagagé) S.; m. Nicole Pimparé, Apr. 15, 1968; children: Charles-Philippe, Nicolas. BSc in Agronomy, Laval U., Quebec City, 1966; DSA in Adminstrn., U. Montreal, 1970. Analyst Can. Devel. Bank, Montreal, 1970-75; asst. regional mgr. Can. Devel. Bank, Quebec City, 1975-76; asst. gen. mgr. Soquia, Quebec City, 1976-86; pres., gen. mgr. Régie des Assurance Agricoles, Lévis, Que., 1986-88; pres. Societé de Financement Agricole, Sainte-Foy, Que., 1988—. Recipient Prix d'Excellence de L'Administration Publique, Ecole Nationale D'Administration Publique, Sainte-Foy, 1995. Office: Societe de Financement Agricole, 1020 rte de l'Eglise, Sainte Foy, PQ Canada G1V 4P2

ST. PIERRE, RONALD LESLIE, anatomy educator, university administrator; b. Dayton, Ohio, Feb. 2, 1938; s. Leslie Frank and Ruth Eleanor (Rhoten) St.P.; m. Joyce A. Guilford, Apr. 1, 1961; children: Michele Christine, David Bryan. B.S., Ohio U., 1961; M.Sc., Ohio State U., 1962, Ph.D., 1965. Instr. anatomy Ohio State U., Columbus, 1965-67; asst. prof. Ohio State U., 1967-69, assoc. prof., 1969-72, prof., 1972—, chmn. dept. anatomy, 1972-81, assoc. v.p. health scis., 1981-83, assoc. v.p. health scis. and acad. affairs, 1983, assoc. dean coll. medicine, 1987-96; vice dean coll. of medicine, 1996—; assoc. dir. Cancer Research Center, 1974-78; vis. research assoc. Duke U., 1966-67; cons. Battelle Meml. Inst., Columbus. Contbr. articles to profl. jours. Chmn. Ohio Gov.'s Com. on Employment of Handicapped, 1970-78; mem. state exec. com. Presdl. Commn. Employment of Handicapped, 1970-78, chmn., 1971-72; mem. planning and adv. council White House Conf. on Handicapped Individuals, 1975-78; mem. Columbus Mayor's Com. on Internat. Yr. of Disabled. Recipient Lederle Med. Faculty award, 1968-71; prize for basic research South Atlantic Assn. Obstetricians and

Gynecologists, 1968; Outstanding Individual award Ohio Rehab. Assn., 1969; Gov.'s award for community service, 1973. Mem. Am. Assn. Anatomists, Am. Assn. Immunologists, Soc. Exptl. Biology and Medicine, Sigma Xi (pres. Ohio State chpt. 1979-80). Republican. Presbyterian. Home: 8586 Buttonbush Ln Westerville OH 43082-8675 Office: Ohio State U 218 Meiling Hall 370 W 9th Ave Columbus OH 43210-1238

SAISSELIN, REMY GILBERT, fine arts educator; b. Moutier, Bern, Switzerland, Aug. 17, 1925; came to U.S., 1938, naturalized, 1944; s. Paul A. and Jeanne (Nydegger) S.; m. Nicole M. Fischer, May 31, 1955; children: Anne, Juliet, Peter. B.A., Queens Coll., 1951; M.A., U. Wis-Madison, 1952; M.A. in French, U. Wis.-Madison, 1953, Ph.D, 1957. Asst. prof. French Western Res. U., Cleve., 1956-59; asst. curator publs. Cleve. Mus. Art, 1959-65; prof. French lit. U. Rochester (N.Y.), 1965-70, prof. fine arts, 1970-87; prof. humanities Hobart & William Smith Coll., 1987-90. Asst. editor: Jour. Aesthetics and Art Criticism, 1959-62; author: Taste in Eighteenth Centruy France, 1965, Rule of Reason and Rues of the Heart, 1970, Literary Enterprise in XVIII Century France, 1979, The Bourgeois and the Bibelot, 1984, The Enlightenment Against the Baroque, 1992. Served with U.S. Army, 1944-46. Guggenheim fellow, 1972-73. Mem. Phi Beta Kappa. Home: 117 Westland Ave Rochester NY 14618-1044

SAITO, SHUZO, electrical engineering educator; b. Nagoya, Aichi, Japan, Jan. 12, 1924; s. Sukesaburo and Masa Saito; m. Yoko Nakane, Mar. 26, 1953; children: Jun'ichiro, Ken'jiro. BSEE, Nagoya U., 1948, MSEE, 1953, PhD, 1962. Mem. tech. staff Elec. Com. Lab. NT&T, Tokyo, 1953-64, chief rsch. sect., 1964-75, dir. rsch. dept., 1975-79; prof. speech sci. U. Tokyo, 1979-84; prof. elec. engring. Kogakuin U., 1984-92; prof. info. sci. Hokkaido Info. U., 1992—; mem. tech. staff Japanese Patent Agy., Tokyo, 1963; tech. specialist Japanese Ministry Transp., Tokyo, 1982. Author: Fundamental Speech Signal Processing, 1979; contbr. articles to profl. publs.; inventor PARCOR speech synthesis. Recipient Meritorious award Min. Sci. & Tech., Japan, 1977, promotion award Asahi Newspaper Co., 1981. Fellow IEEE (chmn. acoustics, speech and signal processing Tokyo chpt. 1986-88, chmn. tech. program com. internat. conf. on acoustics, speech and signal processing 1986), Acoustical Soc. Am.; mem. Audio and Visual Rsch. Group (hon., pres. 1985-88), Inst. Elec. and Comm. Engrs. Japan (adviser speech rsch. com. and pattern recognition com. 1983, paper award 1970, 71, 79, achievement award 1973), Acoustical Soc. Japan (exec. coun. 1969-83, Sato paper award 1972, meritorious award 1994). Avocations: golf, photography. Home: 1-1-3-38-704 Atsubetsu Chuo, Atsubetsu-ku, Sapporo 004, Japan Office: Hokkaido Info U, Nishinopporo 59-2, Ebetsu Hokkaido 069, Japan

SAITO-FURUKAWA, JANET CHIYO, primary school educator; b. L.A., June 29, 1951; d. Shin and Nobuko Ann (Seki) Saito; m. Neil Yasuhiko Furukawa, June 30, 1990. BS, U. So. Calif., 1973; MA, Mt. St. Mary's Coll., L.A., 1990. Cert. elem. tchr. K-8, adminstrn. 1st tier, lang. devel. specialist, Calif. Tchr. grades four through six Rosemont Elem. Sch., L.A., 1973-80, psychomotor specialist, 1979-80; tchr. mid. sch. lang. arts Virgil, Parkman Mid. Schs., L.A./Woodland Hills, Calif., 1980-87, 87-90, dept. chairperson, 1974-77, 80-84, 1989-90; drama tchr. Virgil Mid. Sch., L.A., 1980-81, dance tchr., 1984-87; mid. sch. advisor L.A. Unified Sch. Dist., Encino, Calif., 1990-91; practitioner facilitator L.A. Unified Sch. Dist., Encino, 1990-97; young authors chairperson Parkman Mid. Sch., Woodland Hills, 1988-90; multicultural performance educator, Great Leap, L.A., 1988-93; mentor tchr. L.A. Unified Sch. dist., 1980-90; trainer dist. standards project, 1996—; presenter/cons. in field. Tchr./leader Psychomotor Grant, 1979; writer Level II Teamin' and Theme-in, 1994. Recipient Nancy McHugh English award English Coun. L.A., Woodland Hills, 1987, 88, 91, Outstanding Reading and Lang. Tchr. award L.A. Reading Assn., Woodland Hills, 1991, Apple award L.A. Mayor's Office, 1990, Tchr. of the Month award Phi Delta Kappa, San Fernando, Calif., 1989. Mem. ASCD, Nat. Mid. Schs. Assn. (presenter), Nat. Coun. Tchrs. Math., Calif. Sci. Tchrs. Assn., Nat. Coun. Tchrs. English, The Learning Collaborative. Lutheran. Avocations: volleyball, fishing, reading, skiing. Office: Practitioner Ctr LA Unified Sch Dist 3010 Estara Ave Los Angeles CA 90065-2205

SAIZAN, PAULA THERESA, oil company executive; b. New Orleans, Sept. 12, 1947; d. Paul Morine and Hattie Mae (Hayes) Saizan; m. George H. Smith, May 26, 1973 (div. July 1976). BS in Acctg. summa cum laude, Xavier U., 1969. CPA, Tex.; notary pub. Systems engr. IBM, New Orleans, 1969-71; acct., then sr. acct. Shell Oil Co., Houston, Tex., 1971-76, sr. fin. analyst, 1976-77, fin. rep., 1977-79, corp. auditor, 1979-81, treasury rep., 1981-82, sr. treasury rep., 1982-86; asst. treas. Shell Credit Inc., Shell Leasing Co., Shell Fin. Co. 1986-88, sr. pub. affairs rep., 1988-89, sr. staff pub. affairs rep., 1990-91, program mgr., 1991-96, sr. program mgr., 1996—. Bd. dirs. Houston Downtown Mgmt. Dist., Greater Houston Conv. and Visitors Bur. (treas.), St. Joseph Hosp. Found., United Negro Coll. Fund, Associated Cath. Charities, Houston, Galveston; mem. adv. coun. U.S. SBA region VI, Houston; acctg. dept. adv. bd. Tex. So. U.; del. White House Conf. on small bus., 1995. Mem. AICPA, NAACP, Tex. Soc. CPAs, Leadership Houston, Greater Inwood Partnership, LWV of Houston, Xavier U. Alumni Assn., Nat. Assn. Black Accts., Nat. Coun. Negro Women, Inc., Nat. Political Congress Black Women, Alpha Kappa Alpha, Phi Gamma Nu, Kappa Gamma Pi. Roman Catholic. Home: 5426 Long Creek Ln Houston TX 77088-4407 Office: Shell Oil Co PO Box 2463 Houston TX 77252-2463

SAJAK, PAT, television game show host; b. Chgo., Oct. 26, 1947; m. Lesly Brown, Dec. 31, 1990. Newscaster WEDC-Radio, Chicago, IL; disk jockey WNBS-Radio, Murray, KY; staff announcer, public affairs program host, weatherman WSM-TV, Nashville, TN; weatherman, host The Sunday Show, 1977-81; host Wheel of Fortune, 1981—, The Pat Sajak Show, 1989-90. film appearances include: Airplane II: The Sequel, 1982, Jack Paar is Alive and Well, 1987; NBC television specials, host, The Thanksgiving Day Parade, The Rose Parade. Served with U.S. Army, Vietnam. *

SAKAI, AKIYOSHI, urban redevelopment consultant; b. Oguchi, Aichi, Japan, Jan. 1, 1930; s. Hisayoshi and Asako S.; m. Toshiko A. Sakai, Dec. 8, 1956; children: Seiji, Tatsuto. BS, Gitu Agrl. Coll., 1951. Microbiologist Fujisawa Pharm. Co., Ltd., Nagoya, Japan, 1951-59; pres. Takaha Archtl. Engring. Co., Ltd., Nagoya, 1960-73; chmn. Urban Dynamics Inst. Takaha Co. Ltd., Tokyo, 1974—, Toshikagaku Engring. Co., Ltd., Tokyo, 1986—. Author: Shigaichi Saikaihatsu, 1974. Trustee Regional Bus. Devel. Inst., 1994—. Mem. City Planning Assn. Japan, Urban Renewal Coord. Assn. Japan (trustee 1996—). Avocations: new thinking for intelligent creative process by subdivision and digitization. Office: Urban Dynamics Inst Takaha, 1-3-2 Nishiazabu Minato, Tokyo 106, Japan

SAKAI, HIROKO, trading company executive; b. Nishiharu, Aichi-ken, Japan, Jan. 9, 1939; came to U.S., 1956; d. Kichiya and Saki (Shiraishi) S. BA, Wellesley Coll., 1963; MA, Columbia U., 1967, PhD, 1972. Journalist Asahi Evening News, Tokyo, 1963-65; escort interpreter Dept. State, Washington, 1967-68; econ. analyst Port Authority N.Y. and N.J., N.Y.C., 1968-69; sr. cons. Harbridge House, Inc., Boston, 1970-84, Quantum Sci. Corp., White Plains, N.Y., 1984-87; corp. planner ITOCHU Internat. Inc., N.Y.C., N.Y., 1988-92; dir. bus. devel. ITOCHU Internat. Inc., N.Y.C., 1993-94, dir. venture and investment, 1995—. Interpreter Govt. Mass., Boston, 1974. Wellesley Coll. fellow, 1960-63, Columbia U. fellow, 1965-68; Columbia U. grantee, 1969. Mem. Regional Sci. Assn., Assn. Am. Geographers. Buddhist. Avocations: piano, oil painting, tennis. Home: 235 E 51st St Apt 5C New York NY 10022-6523 Office: ITOCHU Internat Inc 335 Madison Ave New York NY 10017-4605

SAKAI, YOSHIRO, chemistry educator; b. Nagasaki, Japan, Dec. 28, 1935; s. Tsuyoshi and Rei (Ikeno) S.; m. Mutsuko Abe, Oct. 18, 1964; children: Hideaki, Masako. BS, Kyushu U., Fukuoka, Japan, 1958, ScD, 1970. Research fellow Govt. Indsl. Research Inst., Nagoya, Japan, 1958-68; assoc. prof. Ehime U., Matsuyama, Japan, 1968-74, prof. chemistry, 1974—. Mem. Chem. Soc. Japan, Soc. Polymer Sci., Electrochem. Soc. Japan, Japan Assn. Chem. Sensors (pres. 1995—). Avocations: traveling, reading. Home: 225-4 Shin-ishite, Matsuyama 790, Ehime Japan Office: Ehime Univ, Bunkyo-cho Matsuyama, Ehime Japan

SAKAMOTO, RYUICHI, composer. Score include (films) Merry Christmas, Mr. Lawrence, 1983, (with David Byrne and Cong Su) The Last Emperor, 1987 (Academy award best original score 1987), The Handmaid's Tale, 1990, The Sheltering Sky, 1990, Tacones Lejanos, 1991, Emily Bronte's Wuthering Heights, 1992, Little Buddha, 1993, (TV miniseries) Wild Palms, 1993. Office: Creative Artists Agency 9830 Wilshire Blvd Beverly Hills CA 90212-1804*

SAKELLARIOS, GERTRUDE EDITH, retired office nurse; b. Lowell, Mass., Mar. 14, 1929; d. William V. and Eileen E. (Hale) Yoachimciuk; m. Angelos D. Sakellarios, Dec. 30, 1966. Diploma, Lowell Gen. Hosp., 1949; student, Boston U., 1949-53, Boston Coll./St. Josephs Hosp., Lowell, 1951. Gen. duty med.-surg. nurse Lowell Gen. Hosp., 1949-50, operating room nurse, 1950-52; office nurse gen. practitioner's office, Lowell, 1952-83. Home: 124 Cashin St Lowell MA 01851-2004

SAKIC, JOSEPH STEVE, professional hockey player; b. Burnaby, B.C., Canada, July 7, 1969. Capt. Quebec Nordiques, 1991-95; with Colo. Avalanche, 1995—. Won WHL East Most Valuable Player Trophy, 1986-87, WHL Stewart (Butch) Paul Meml. Trophy, 1986-87, Four Broncos Meml. Trophy, 1987-88, Bob Clarke Trophy, 1987-88, Conn Smythe Trophy NHL, 1996; named to WHL All-Star Second Team, 1986-87, Can. Hockey League Player of Yr., 1987-88, WHL Player of Yr., 1987-88; played in NHL All-Star Game, 1990-94, 96. Office: c/o Colo Avalanche 1635 Clay St Denver CO 80204-1743

SAKIEWICZ, NICK, professional sports team executive; b. Passaic, N.J.; m. Isabel Sakiewicz; 1 child, Nick, Jr. Grad., U. New Haven. Soccer player F.C. Nantes, French 1st Divsn., 1982, N.Y. Arrows, Major Indoor Soccer League, 1983, F.C. Belenenses, Portuguese 1st Divsn., 1984; sales mgr. TIF Instruments, Miami, Fla., 1985-90; zone mgr. Agy. Svcs., Inc., Atlanta, 1990; dir. sales Agy. Svcs., Inc., Tampa, Fla.; v.p. sales & mktg. Agy. Svcs., Inc., Balt.; asst. coach, goalkeeper coach Coll. Boca Raton (Fla.), 1987; goalkeeper coach Southeast Region, Olympic Devel. Program, 1985-89, Fla. Youth Soccer Assn., 1985-89; dir., then v.p. Providian Bancorp, San Francisco, 1995; past v.p. corp. sales Major League Soccer; pres., gen. mgr. Tampa Bay Mutiny, Major League Soccer, 1996—. Office: Tampa Bay Mutiny Ste 1004 1408 N Westshore Blvd Tampa FL 33607-4512

SAKIN, LARRY ALBERT, shop owner; b. Tucson, Feb. 24, 1960; s. Larry and Doris W. (Glenn) S. AA, Pima C.C., 1984; BS in Bus. Adminstrn., Kennedy We. U., Thousand Oaks, Calif., 1995. Owner Awareness Music Prodn., Tucson, 1979-82; sales rep. Alphagraphics Inc., Tucson, 1984-85; owner Kept in the Dark Records, Tucson, 1986—; ptnr. PDQ Records and Tapes, Tucson, 1988-95; co-chairperson Simon Peter Inc., Tucson, 1979; co-founder, dir. Retail Employers Against Censorship, Tucson, 1991-94. Author: "Networks": A Resource Manual for Viral Illness Patients, 1994. Mem. urgent action network Amnesty Internat., Tucson, 1993—; co-founder, chair United Fedn. Viral Illness Orgns., 1989-93; mem. Citizens Transp. Adv. Coun., 1994. Recipient Roger Baldwin Medal of Liberty nominee ACLU, 1992. Democrat. Avocations: reading, travel, tennis, walking, biking. Office: Kept in the Dark Records 332 Bleecker St # K 138 New York NY 10014-2980

SAKITA, BUNJI, physicist, educator; b. Inami, Toyama-ken, Japan, June 6, 1930; came to U.S., 1956; s. Eiichi and Fumi (Morimatsu) S.; children—Mariko, Taro. B.S., Kanazawa U., 1953; M.S., Nagoya U., 1956; Ph.D., U. Rochester, 1959. Research asso. U. Wis., Madison, 1959-62; asst. prof. U. Wis., 1963-64, prof., 1966-70; assoc. physicist Argonne (Ill.) Nat. Lab., 1964-66; distinguished prof. City Coll. CUNY, N.Y.C., 1970—; vis. prof. IHES, Bures-sur-Yvette, France, 1970-71, Ecole Normale Superieur, Paris, 1979-80, 88, U. Tokyo, 1987. Recipient Nishina prize, 1974; Guggenheim fellow, 1970-71, Japan Soc. Promotion Sci. fellow, 1975, 80, 87, 95. Fellow Am. Phys. Soc. Home: 5 Horizon Rd Apt 2406 Fort Lee NJ 07024-6646 Office: CUNY City College Convent Ave at 138th St New York NY 10031

SAKKAL, SAAD, endocrinologist, geriatrician; b. Aleppo, Syria, Nov. 5, 1947; came to U.S., 1972; s. Mohamed Loutfy and Durie (Khatib) S.; m. Maysa Mounla, 1981; children: Luna, Mohammed. PCB, Damascus U., Syria, 1966; MD, Damascus Med. Sch., Syria, 1972. Diplomate Am. Bd. Internal Medicine, Am. Bd. Endocrinology and Metabolism, Am. Bd. Geriatrics, Am. Bd. Med. Mgmt. Intern Luth. Med. Ctr., Bklyn., 1972-73; resident internal medicine St. Joseph's Hosp. Med. Ctr., Paterson, N.J., 1973-74, Phila. Gen. Hosp., 1974-75; chief resident internal medicine Conemaugh Valley Meml. Hosp., Johnstown, Pa., 1975-76; fellow in endocrinology and metabolism George Washington U. Med. Ctr., Washington, 1976-78, asst. in medicine, 1979-80; guest worker NIH NICHD, Bethesda, Md., 1979-81; med. dir. Metabolic Care Ctr., Greenville, Pa., 1982—; acting dir. endocrinology and metabolism Youngstown (Ohio) Hosp. Assn., 1984-86; asst. clin. prof. medicine Northeastern Ohio U. Coll. Medicine, Rootstown, 1984; med. dir. Regional Diabetes Ctr., Greenville, 1991—; pres. med. staff Greenville Regional Hosp., Horizon Hosp. Sys., 1993-94; rep. Managed Care Leader, Horizon Hosp. Sys., 1984—; sec.-treas. Physicians Orgn. for Mercer County, Pa., 1993—; bd. dirs. Pa. Physicians Healthcare Plan, 1994—. Contbr. articles to profl. jours. Trustee Mahoning, Shenango Area Health Edn. Network, Youngstown, 1985-90; pres. Mercer County Med. Soc., 1991. Recipient Govt. award for Best Med. Student, Damascus Med. Sch., 1966-72, The Eudowood award Am. Coll. Chest Physicians, 1976, AMA Physicians Recognition award AMA, 1975-93. Fellow ACP, Am. Coll. Internat. Physicians, Am. Coll. Endocrinology; mem. The Endocrine Soc., Soc. for Clin. Densitometry, Islamic Med. Assn., Assn. Insulin Pump Therapists. Muslim. Office: Metabolic Care Ctr 81 N Main St Greenville PA 16125-1781

SAKS, GENE, theater and film director, actor; b. N.Y.C.. Began career as an actor off-Broadway at Provincetown Playhouse and the Cherry Lane Theatre; played in: Auden's Dog Beneath the Skin, E.E. Cummings' Him, Molière's The Bourgeois Gentilhomme; appeared on Broadway in Mr. Roberts, South Pacific, Middle of the Night, The Tenth Man, A Shot in the Dark, Love and Libel, A Thousand Clowns; debut as dir. on Broadway Enter Laughing, 1963; dir. stage plays Nobody Loves an Albatross, 1964, Half a Sixpense, 1964, Generation, 1965, Mame, 1960, Same Time, Next Year, 1975, California Suite, 1972, I Love My Wife (best dir. of Musical award Drama Desk, Tony), 1967, Brighton Beach Memoirs (best dir. award, Tony), 1983, Biloxi Blues (best dir. of play award, Tony), 1985, The Odd Couple (female version), 1985, Broadway Bound, 1986, A Month of Sundays, 1987, Rumors, 1988, Lost in Yonkers, 1991, Jake's Women, 1992; dir. films Barefoot in the Park, The Odd Couple, Cactus Flower, Last of the Red Hot Lovers, Mame, Brighton Beach Memoirs, A Fine Romance; dir. TV movie Bye, Bye Birdie, 1995; appeared in films including a Thousand Clowns, Prisoner of Second Aveneue, Lovesick, The One and Only, The Goodbye People, 1986, Nobody's Fool, 1994, TQ, 1994. Recipient George Abbott award for lifetime achievement in the theatre, 1990; elected to Theatre Hall of Fame, 1991. *

SAKS, MICHAEL JAY, law educator; b. Phila., Mar. 8, 1947; s. Harold and Bella (Pall) S.; m. Roselle Wissler, May 18, 1986. BS in Psychology, BA in English, Pa. State U., 1969; MA in Social Psychology, Ohio State U., 1972, PhD in Social Psychology, 1975; MSL in Law, Yale U., 1983. Prof. psychology Boston Coll., Chestnut Hill, Mass., 1973-88; sr. staff assoc. Nat. Ctr. for State Cts., Williamsburg, Va., 1978-80; vis. prof. law Georgetown U. Law Ctr., Washington, 1985-86; prof. law U. Iowa, Iowa City, 1986—; disting. vis. prof. law grad. program for judges U. Va., Charlottesville, 1981, 83, 85, 87, 89; cons. Office of Tech. Assessment, U.S. Congress, Washington, numerous law firms; mem. adv. com. law and social sci. NSF. Editor-in-chief Law & Human Behavior, 1985-87; co-editor: Modern Scientific Evidence: The Law & Science of Expert Testimony; mem. editorial bd. Jour. Personality and Social Psychology, Law & Society Rev., Law & Human Behavior, Law & Policy, Applied Social Psychology Annual, Social Behaviour: An Internat. Jour. Applied Social Psychology, Ethics and Behavior; contbr. articles to profl. jours. Chair bd. Cen. Ohio chpt. Ohio Civil Liberties Union, Columbus, 1972-73; bd. dirs. Civil Liberties Union Mass., Boston, 1984-86, Iowa City Area Sci. Ctr.; mem. subcom. on organ and tissue transplants Mass. Legis., Boston, 1975. U. Iowa Faculty scholar, 1990-93. Fellow Am. Psychol. Assn. (Disting. Contbn. award 1987), Am. Psychology Law Soc. (pres. 1988-89), Soc. for the Psychol. Study of Social Issues (bd. dirs.); mem. Law & Soc. Assn., Assn. Am. Law Schs. (chair sect. law and social scis. 1997), Law Sch. Admissions Coun. (chair grants subcommittee). Office: U Iowa Coll Law Iowa City IA 52242

SAKS, STEPHEN HOWARD, accountant; b. Phila., May 16, 1941; s. Samuel and Edythe (Edelman) S.; m. Ruth Workman, Dec. 22, 1963; children: Amy Meryl, Brian Eric, Joshua Marc. BS in Econs., U. Pa., 1962. CPA, Pa. Staff acct. to ptnr. Peat, Marwick, Mitchell & Co., Phila., 1962-78; ptnr. Laventhol & Horwath, Phila., 1978-91; chief fin. officer Northeastern Health Sys., Phila., 1991—, Neumann Med. Ctr., Phila., 1992—. Bd. dirs. Jewish Family and Children's Agy, Phila,. 1979-88; treas. Jewish Employment and Vocat. Svc., Phila., 1984-88; chmn. bd. overseers Gratz Coll., Melrose Pk., Pa., 1987-90; pres. Beth Sholom Men's Club, Elkins Pk., Pa., 1987-90. Mem. AICPA, Pa. Inst. CPAs, Healthcare Fin. Mgmt. Assn. (advanced). Democrat. Avocations: community activities, travel. Home: 1110 Gypsy Ln Oreland PA 19075-2508 Office: Northeastern Health System 2346 E Allegheny Ave Philadelphia PA 19134-4434

SAKSEN, LOUIS CARL, hospital administrator, architect; b. Washington, Dec. 30, 1946; s. Louis Karl and Sara Flower (Farr) S.; m. Elizabeth Helen Wilson, June 24, 1972; children: Alexander, Katie, Micheal. BArch, Cath. U. Am., 1969; MArch, Va. Poly. Inst. and State U., 1974; MS in Psychology, Old Dominion U., 1975. Registered architect, Va., Calif., NCARB. Mgr. planning, instl. rsch. and planning Va. Commonwealth U., Richmond, 1975-78, dir. facilities planning and constrn., 1978-81, asst. v.p. facilities mgmt. div., 1981-85; dep. v.p. health scis. facilities Columbia U., N.Y.C., 1986-88; v.p. for facilities Presbyn. Hosp. in the City of N.Y., 1988-90, sr. v.p., gen. mgr. facilities and svcs., 1990-91; assoc. hosp. dir., environ. and support svcs. Stanford (Calif.) Hosp., 1991—. Pres. parish coun. St. Peters Roman Cath. Ch., 1981-82; mem. Mayor's Com. on Handicapped, 1984; chmn. property com. ARC, 1982; chmn. ops. com. Port of Richmond Commn., 1983-84; mem. adv. bd. Hosp. Hospitality House, 1984-85; mem. Bd. Recreation, Essex Fells, N.J., 1988-92; mem. Archtl. Rev. Com., Half Moon Bay, Calif., 1992-95; bd. mem. Coastside Youth Hockey, 1996—, Wilkinson Sch., 1996—. With USN, 1971-74. Recipient Letters of Appreciation, Supreme Allied Comdr. Atlantic; Letter of Commendation from comdr. U.S. Naval Communication Sta., Londonderry, No. Ireland, 1972; winner design competition for urban park Smithsonian Inst., Washington, 1968; named to Outstanding Young Mem. of Am., 1981. Mem. AIA (chpt. pres. 1982), Assn. Univ. Architects, Assn. Phys. Plant Admisntrs., Am. Hosp. Assn., Univ. Hosp. Consortium, Rotary Internat. Republican. Roman Catholic. Avocations: fishing, tennis, hunting, camping, photography. Office: Stanford U Hosp 300 Pasteur Dr Palo Alto CA 94304-2203

SAKUTA, MANABU, neurologist, educator; b. Ichikawa, Japan, Oct. 31, 1947; s. Jun and Shizuko (Tsuji) S.; m. Yuko Fukushi, June 17, 1973; children: Akiko, Junko, Ken-Ichi. MD, U. Tokyo, 1973, PhD, 1978; MS in Neurology, U. Minn., 1981. Med. diplomate. Diplomat Japanese Bd. Neurology, Japanese Bd. Internal Medicine. Asst. Dept. Neurology U. Tokyo, Japan, 1980; rsch. fellow Dept. Neurology U. Minn., Mpls., 1980-81, asst. prof., 1981-82; head Dept. Neurology Japanese Red Cross Med. Ctr., Tokyo, 1982—; prof. Japanese Red Cross Women's Coll. Sch. Nursing, Tokyo, 1983-85, instr. 1986-88; lectr. dept. neurology, U. Tokyo, 1984—, dept. medicine U. Kobe, 1990—; cons. Nakayama Hosp., Ichikawa, Japan, 1980—. Contbr. articles to profl. jours. Fellow Royal Soc. Medicine (London); mem. AAAS, N.Y. Acad. Sci., Japanese Soc. Internal Medicine (pres. Kanto br. 1992), Japanese Soc. Neurology (mem. coun., 1985—, mem. coun. Kanto Br., 1984—, pres. Kanto Br. 1984, mem. editorial bd. 1988—), Japanese Soc. Diabetology, Japanese Soc. Electroencephalography and Electromyography, Japanese Soc. Autonomic Nervous System (mem. coun.), Clinical Neurology Club, Chevalier Club (pres. internat. com. 1995—), U. Minn. Alumni Club, Tetsumon Club. Democrat. Buddhist. Office: Japanese Red Cross Med Ctr, 4-1-22 Hiroo Shibuya-ku, Tokyo 150, Japan

SAKUTA, MASAAKI, engineering educator, consultant; b. Kagoshima, Japan, Feb. 16, 1929; s. Masanori and Haruko (Oozato) S.; m. Akiko Shimomura, Nov. 4, 1956; children: Shigeru, Mitsuru. B of Engring., Tokyo Inst. Tech., 1952; postgrad, MIT, 1959-60; DEng, Tokyo Inst. Tech., 1966. Cert. oceanic architect, architect-engr., Japan. Rschr. Taisei Constrn. Co. Ltd., Tokyo, 1956-58, chief rschr., 1960-69; mng. dir. Fuyo Ocean Devel. and Engring. Co. Ltd., Tokyo, 1969-77; advisor Taisei Corp. Co. Ltd., Tokyo, 1978-79; prof. Nihon U., Tokyo, 1977—; councilor Archtl. Inst. Japan, Tokyo, 1975-76, dir., 1989-91; vice dean Coll. Sci. and Tech., Nihon U., 1978-94; vice chmn., life mem. Pacific Congress on Marine Sci. and Tech., Japan, 1990—. Author: Transportation in Ocean Space, 1975, Construction Method of Marine Structures, 1976, Introduction of Ocean Development, 1977; patentee in field of Marine structure system with soft-touched basement. Mem. Visualization Soc. Japan, Inc. (pres. 1991-92, Merit award 1992), Rotary (sr., charter). Mem. Liberal Dem. Party. Buddhist. Avocations: hiking, tennis, table tennis, painting, reading. Home: 39-723 2-2 chome Jingumae, Shibuya-ku Tokyo 150, Japan Office: Coll Sci & Tech Funabashi Campus, 7-24 Narashinodai, Funabashi Chiba 274, Japan

SALA, LUIS FRANCISCO, surgeon, educator; b. N.Y.C., Dec. 13, 1919; s. Luis and Josefina (Goenaga) S.; m. Judith Colon, June 5, 1943; children: Luis E., Francisco A., Jorge P., Jose M. B.S. cum laude, Georgetown U., 1939, M.D., 1943; M.Sc. in Surgery, U. Pa., 1951. Diplomate: Am. Bd. Surgery. Intern, resident Presbyn. Hosp., San Juan, P.R., 1943-45; resident Presbyn. Hosp., 1944-45; chief resident Grad. Hosp. U. Pa., 1947-51, instr. surgery, 1950-51; clin. asst. surgery Med. Coll. Pa.; practice medicine, specializing in surgery Ponce, P.R., 1951-91; chmn. dept. surgery Damas Hosp., Ponce, 1955-88; prof. surgery U. P.R. Sch. Medicine, 1968-88; pres., dean, prof. surgery Ponce Sch. of Medicine, 1988-94; del. P.R. Med. Assn., 1960-93, pres., 1965-66; apptd. mem. Med. Examining Bd. by Gov. of P.R., 1995. Author: Consideraciones Basicas para la Acreditacion de Hospitales, 1978; contbr. chpts. to books, articles to profl. jours. Active Boy Scouts Am., 1955-74; pres. adv. com. to pres. Cath. U. P.R., 1963-72; bd. dirs. Boys Home of Ponce, 1966-76; bd. regents Amigos Museo de Arte de Ponce, 1968-73, Cath. U., 1972-93; pres. bd. regents Ponce Med. Sch. Found., 1980-92. Served with M.C. U.S. Army, 1945-47. Recipient Silver Beaver award, 1965, Acad. Médica, Dto. Sur, 1st. Dr. Luis F. Sasa medal, 1995; named lt. P.R. Equestrian Order of Holy Sepulchre of Jerusalem, 1982—. Fellow ACS (gov. for P.R. 1965-74, Disting. Svc. award 1989), Internat. Soc. Surgery, P.R. Med. Assn. (so. dist., Dr. Pila medal for disting. svc. 1991), Indsl. Med. Coun. of SIF (apptd. pres. by Gov. of P.R. 1993-95), P.R. Mfrs. Assn. (Profl. of Yr. in area of svcs. 1994), C. of C. (Profl. of Yr. 1990), State Med. Examining Bd. (appt. by Gov. of P.R. 1995—). Republican. Roman Catholic. Home: 6 Almena Alhambra Ponce PR 00731 Office: 43 Calle Concordia Ponce PR 00731-4984

SALAAM, RASHAAN, professional football player; b. San Diego, Oct. 8, 1974; s. Teddy Washington and Dolores Shelly Salaam. Attended, U. Colo., 1992-94. Running back Chgo. Bears, 1995—; mem. Aloha Bowl, 1992. Recipient Heisman trophy, 1994, Doak Walker award, 1994, Walter Camp Player of Yr. trophy, 1994; named to AP All-Am. Team, 1994. Avocations: rap music, sega. Office: Chgo Bears Halas Hall 250 N Washington Rd Lake Forest IL 60045-2459*

SALACUSE, JESWALD WILLIAM, lawyer, educator; b. Niagara Falls, N.Y., Jan. 28, 1938; s. William L. and Bessie B. (Buzzelli) S.; m. Donna Booth, Oct. 1, 1966; children: William, Maria. Diploma U. Paris, 1959; AB, Hamilton Coll., 1960; JD, Harvard U., 1963. Bar: N.Y. 1965, Tex. 1980. Lectr. in law Ahmadu Bello U., Nigeria, 1963-65; assoc. Conboy, Hewitt, O'Brien & Boardman, N.Y.C., 1965-67; assoc. dir. African Law Ctr., Columbia U., 1967-68; prof., dir. Research Ctr., Nat. Sch. Adminstrn., Zaire, 1968-71; Middle East regional advisor on law and devel. Ford Found., Beirut, 1971-74, rep. in Sudan, 1974-77; vis. prof. U. Khartoum (Sudan), 1974-77; vis. scholar Harvard Law Sch., 1977-78; prof. law So. Meth U., Dallas, 1978-80, dean, prof. law, 1980-86; dean, prof. internat. law The Fletcher Sch. Law and Diplomacy Tufts U., Medford, Mass., 1986-94; Henry J. Braker prof. comml. law Fletcher Sch. Law and Diplomacy Tufts U., 1994—; fellow Inst. Advanced Legal Studies, U. London, 1995; vis. prof. Ecole Nat. des Ponts et Chaussées, Paris, 1990—, Instituto de Empressa, U. Bristol, Madrid, 1995—, Sch. Oriental and African Studies U. London, 1995;

cons. Ford Found., 1978-82, 93, U.S. Dept. State, 1978-80, U.N. Ctr. on Transnat. Corps., 1988—, Harvard Inst. Internat. Devel., 1990—, Asia Found., 1992, Harvard Law Sch./World Bank Laos Project, 1991-93; with Sri Lanka fin. sector project ISTI/USAID, 1993-94; lectr. Georgetown U. Internat. Law Inst., 1978-94, Universidad Panamericana, Mexico City, 1981; chmn. com. on Middle Eastern law Social Sci. Research Council, 1978-84; chmn. Coun. Internat. Exchange of Scholars, 1987-91; bd. dirs. Boston World Affairs Coun., 1988-95, Emerging Markets Income Funds. I & II, Inc., Global Ptnrs. Income Fund, Inc., Salomon Brothers Worldwide Income Fund, Inc., The Asia Tigers Fund, Inc., The India Fund. Inc., Emerging Markets Floating Rate Fund, Inc., Mcpl. Advantage Fund, Inc., Salomon Bros. High Income Fund; trustee Southwestern Legal Found., 1992—, Am. U. of Paris, 1993-97; pres. Internat. Third World Legal Studies Assn., 1987-91; chmn. Inst. Transnat. Arbitration, 1991-93; pres. Assn. Profl. Schs. Internat. Affairs, 1988-89. Author: (with Kasunmu) Nigerian Family Law, 1966, An Introduction to Law in French-Speaking Africa, vol. I, 1969, vol. II, 1976, (with Steng) International Business Planning, 1982; Making Global Deals-Negotiating in the International Marketplace, 1991, The Art of Advice, 1994; contbr. articles to profl. jours. Mem. ABA, Dallas Bar Found. (trustee 1983-86), Coun. on Fgn. Rels., Am. Law Inst., Am. Soc. Internat. Law, Cosmos Club (Washington). Home: 220 Stone Root Ln Concord MA 01742-4755 Office: Tufts U Fletcher Sch Law & Diplomacy Medford MA 02155

SALAH, JOSEPH ELIAS, research scientist, educator; b. Jerusalem, Feb. 27, 1944; came to U.S., 1961; s. Elias and Souraya (Nesnas) S.; m. Marie Shintani, Jan. 30, 1965; 1 child, Anthony. BSEE, U. Ill., 1965, MSEE, 1966; PhD, MIT, 1972. Staff mem. Lincoln Lab., MIT, Lexington, 1966-76, group leader, 1977-83; sr. lectr. dept. earth, atmospheric and planetary scis. MIT, Cambridge, 1983—, prin. rsch. scientist, 1983—; dir. Haystack Obs. MIT, Westford, 1983—; mem. adv. com. for astron. scis. NSF, Washington, 1985-88, mem. steering com. Coupling, Energetics and Dynamics of Atmospheric Regions, 1987-90; mem. com. on solar terrestrial rsch. NRC-NAS, Washington, 1986-89. Contbr. articles on physics of earth's upper atmosphere and ionosphere to sci. jours. Mem. Am. Geophys. Union, Am. Astron. Soc., Am. Meteorol. Soc., Internat. Union Radio and Sci., Internat. Assn. for Geomagnetism and Aeronomy. Office: MIT Haystack Obs RR 40 Westford MA 01886

SALAH, SAGID, retired nuclear engineer; b. Seoul, Sept. 2, 1932; came to U.S., 1954; s. Galim and Faiza (Sultan) Salahutdin; m. Ravile Almakay, Apr. 2, 1966; children: Shamil, Kamil, Safiye. BChemE, U. Fla., 1958, MS in Nuclear Engring., 1960, PhD in Nuclear Engring., 1964. Nuclear engr. AEC, Bethesda, Md., 1964-66; sr. design engr. Westinghouse Astronuclear Lab., Large, Pa., 1966-70; sr. sys. engr. Westinghouse Nuclear Energy Sys., Pitts., 1970-73; mem. sys. safety engring. staff U.S. Nuclear Regulatory Commn., Bethesda, 1973-93; ret., 1993; nuclear engring. cons. Oak Ridge (Tenn.) Inst. Nuclear Studies, 1963, 64; instr. U. Md., College Park, 1973-76. Contbr. articles to Nuclear Sci. and Engring. Youth coach Nat. Capital Soccer League, Vienna, Va., 1975-85. Mem. Am. Nuclear Soc. (emeritus, reviewer trans. papers 1972), Sigma Tau. Moslem. Achievements include measurements of neutron energy spectra in heterogeneous media using differential and integral methods, neutron energy spectra measurements and analysis in intermediate spectra reactors, three-dimensional transient analysis of boron dilution in PWR reactors. Avocations: astronomy, neurology, financial analysis, tennis, swimming. Home: 9302 Kilport Ct Vienna VA 22182

SALAMA, C. ANDRE TEWFIK, electrical engineering educator; b. Heliopolis, Egypt, Sept. 27, 1938; arrived in Can., 1957; s. Tewfik and Sarine (Bigio) S.; m. Rhoda R. Kurtz, Dec. 19, 1974. BASc with honours, U. B.C., Vancouver, Can., 1961, MASc, 1963, PhD, 1966. Registered profl. engr., Ont. Mem. sci. staff Bell No. Rsch., Ottawa, Ont., Can., 1966-67; asst. prof. elec. engring. U. Toronto, Ont., 1967-70, assoc. prof., 1970-77, prof., 1977-92, univ. prof., 1992—; chmn., bd. dirs. Can. Microelectronics Corp., Kingston, Ont., 1984—; program leader, bd. dirs. Micronet, Toronto, 1990—. Mem. editorial bd. Solid State Electronics, 1982—; contbr. over 200 articles to sci. jours. Recipient Izaak Walton Killam Meml. prize, 1994; Info. Tech. Assn. Can. and Natural Scis. and Engring. Rsch. Coun. fellow U. Toronto, 1989-90. Fellow IEEE (assoc. editor Trans. on Cirs. and Systems 1987-89); mem. Electrochem. Soc., Assn. Profl. Engrs. Ont. Avocations: swimming, sailing, scuba diving, horseback riding, reading. Office: U Toronto, Dept Elec Engring, Toronto, ON Canada M5S 1A4

SALAMAN, MAUREEN KENNEDY, nutritionist; b. Glendale, Calif., Apr. 4, 1936; d. Ted and Elena (Peters) Kennedy; 1 child, Sean. West Coast Report, Sta. WMCA-AM, N.Y.C., 1980—; hostess Maximize Your Life with Maureen Kennedy Salaman; pres. Nat. Health Fedn., Monrovia, Calif., 1982—; cons., lectr., rschr. on cancer rsch. and metabolic medicine, nutrition; freedom of choice lobbyist. Author: Foods That Heal, Nutrition: The Cancer Answer, 1983, The Diet Bible, The Light at the End of the Refrigerator, Health Freedom News, 1982-85, Nutrition: The Cancer Answer II, 1995. Contbr. articles to profl. jours.; hostess TV show Maureen Salaman's Maximize Your Life. Developer nutrition programs for radio and TV. Office: Nat Health Fedn PO Box 688 Monrovia CA 91017-0688 also: Maureen Kennedy Salaman Inc 1259 El Camino Real Ste 1500 Menlo Park CA 94025-4227

SALAMON, LESTER MILTON, political science educator; b. Pitts., Jan. 11, 1943; s. Victor William Salamon and Helen (Sanders) Weiss; m. Lynda Anne Brown, June 27, 1965; children: Noah, Matthew. BA in Econs. and Pub. Policy, Princeton U., 1964; PhD in Govt., Harvard U., 1971. Instr. dept. polit. sci. Tougaloo (Miss.) Coll., 1966-67; asst. prof. Vanderbilt U., Nashville, 1970-73; assoc. prof. policy scis. and polit. sci. Duke U., Durham, N.C., 1973-80, dir. Ctr. for Urban and Regional Devel., 1977-80; dep. assoc. dir. U.S. Office Mgmt. and Budget, Washington, 1977-79; dir. Ctr. for Governance and Mgmt. Rsch., Urban Inst., Washington, 1980-86; prof., dir. Inst. for Policy Studies, Johns Hopkins U., Balt., 1987—. Author: America's Nonprofit Sector: A Primer, 1992, The Emerging Sector: Nonprofit Organizations in Comparative Perspective, 1994, Partners in Public Service: Government Nonprofit Relations in the Modern Welfare State, 1995, Defining the Nonprofit Sector: A Cross-National Analysis, International Guide to Nonprofit Law; editor: The Tools of Government Action, 1989, Human Capital and America's Future, 1991; mem. editl. bd. Adminstrn. and Soc., 1985—, Voluntas, 1988—, Nonprofit and Voluntary Sector Quar., 1990—. Mem. Balt. City Planning Commn., 1987-95. Recipient Laverne Burchfield award Am. Soc. Pub. Adminstrn., 1977, Disting. Book award Assn. of Rschrs. on Nonprofit Orgns. and Vol. Action. Mem. Internat. Soc. Third Sector Rsch. (vice chmn. 1991—), Nat. Acad. Pub. Adminstrn. Avocations: tennis, swimming, carpentry. Home: 903 Lynch Dr Arnold MD 21012 Office: Johns Hopkins U Inst Policy Studies 3400 N Charles St Baltimore MD 21218-2608

SALAMON, LINDA BRADLEY, university administrator, English literature educator; b. Elmira, N.Y., Nov. 20, 1941; d. Grant Ellsworth and Evelyn E. (Ward) Bradley; divorced; children: Michael Lawrence, Timothy Martin. B.A., Radcliffe Coll., 1963; M.A., Bryn Mawr Coll., 1964, Ph.D., 1971; Advanced Mgmt. Cert., Harvard U. Bus. Sch., 1978; D.H.L., St. Louis Coll. Pharmacy, 1993. Lectr., adj. asst. prof. Eng. Dartmouth Coll., Hanover, N.H., 1967-72; mem. faculty lit. Bennington Coll., Vt., 1974-75; dean students Wells Coll., Aurora, N.Y., 1975-77; exec. asst. to pres. U. Pa., Phila., 1977-79; assoc. prof. English Washington U., St. Louis, 1979-88, prof., 1988-92, dean Coll. Arts and Scis., 1979-92; prof. English, dean Columbia Sch. Arts and Scis. George Washington U., Washington, 1992—, interim v.p. for acad. affairs, 1995-96; mem. faculty Bryn Mawr Summer Inst. for Women, 1979—. Author, co-editor: Nicholas Hilliard's Art of Limning, 1983; co-author: Integrity in the College Curriculum, 1985; contbr. numerous articles to literary and ednl. jours. Bd. dirs. Assn. Am. Colls., vice chmn., 1985, chmn., 1986; bd. dirs. Greater St. Louis council Girl Scouts U.S.A.; trustee Coll. Bd., St. Louis Coll. Pharmacy. Fellow Radcliffe Coll. Bunting Inst., 1973-74; Am. Philos. Soc. Penrose grantee, 1974; fellow Folger Shakespeare Library, 1986, NEH Montaigne Inst., 1988. Mem. MLA, Cosmos Club, Phi Beta Kappa. Office: George Washington U Dept of Eng Rome Hall 760 80122 St NW Washington DC 20052

SALAMON, MIKLOS DEZSO GYORGY, mining engineer, educator; b. Balkany, Hungary, May 20, 1933; came to U.S., 1986; s. Miklos and Sarolta (Obetko) S.; m. Agota Maria Meszaros, July 11, 1953; children: Miklos, Gabor. Diploma in Engring., Polytech U., Sopron, Hungary, 1956; PhD, U. Durham, Newcastle, England, 1962; doctorem honoris causa, U. Miskolc, Hungary, 1990. Research asst. dept. mining engring. U. Durham, 1959-63; dir. research Coal Mining Research Controlling Council, Johannesburg, South Africa, 1963-66; dir. collieries research lab Chamber of Mines of South Africa, Johannesburg, 1966-74, dir. gen. research org., 1974-86; disting. prof. Colo. Sch. Mines, Golden, 1986—, dir. Colo. Mining and Mineral Resources Rsch. Inst., 1990-94; pres. Salamon Cons. Inc., Golden, 1995—; 22d Sir Julius Wernher Meml. lectr., 1988; hon. prof. U. Witwatersrand, Johannesburg, 1979-86; vis. prof. U. Minn., Mpls., 1981, U. Tex., Austin, 1982, U. NSW, Sydney, Australia, 1990, 91-96; mem. Presdl. Commn. of Inquiry into Safety and Health in South African Mining Industry, 1994-95. Co-author: Rock Mechanics Applied to the Study of Rockbursts, 1966, Rock Mechanics in Coal Mining, 1976; contbr. articles to profl. jours. Mem. Pres.'s Sci. Adv. Council, Cape Town, South Africa, 1984-86, Nat. Sci. Priorities Com., Pretoria, South Africa, 1984-86. Recipient Nat. award Assn. Scis. and Tech. Socs., South Africa, 1971. Fellow South African Inst. Mining and Metallurgy (hon. life, v.p. 1974-76, pres. 1976-77, gold medal 1964, 85, Stokes award 1986, silver medal 1991), Inst. Mining and Metallurgy (London); mem. AIME, Internat. Soc. Rock Mechanics. Roman Catholic. Office: Colo Sch of Mines Dept Of Mining Engring Golden CO 80401

SALAMON, MYRON BEN, physicist, educator; b. Pitts., June 4, 1939; s. Victor William and Helen (Sanders) S.; m. Sonya Maxine Blank, June 12, 1960; children—David, Aaron. B.S., Carnegie-Mellon U., 1961; Ph.D., U. Calif., Berkeley, 1966. Asst. prof. physics U. Ill., Urbana, 1966-72, assoc. prof., 1972-74, prof., 1974—, program dir. materials research lab., 1984-91; vis. scientist U. Tokyo, 1966, 71, Tech. U. Munich, Fed. Republic Germany, 1974-75; cons. NSF; Disting. Vis. Prof. Tsukuba (Japan) U., 1995-96. Editor: Physics of Superionic Conductors, 1979; co-editor: Modulated Structures, 1979; divisional assoc. editor: Phys. Rev. Letters, 1992-96; contbr. sci. papers to profl. jours. Recipient Alexander von Humboldt Sr. U.S. Scientist award, 1974-75; NSF coop. fellow, 1964-66; postdoctoral fellow, 1966; A.P. Sloan fellow, 1972-73; Berndt Matthias scholar Los Alamos Nat. Lab., 1995-96; visiting scientist CNRS and Inst. Laue-Langevin Grenoble, France, 1981-82. Fellow Am. Phys. Soc. Office: U Ill Dept Physics 1110 W Green St Urbana IL 61801-3003

SALAMON, RENAY, real estate broker; b. N.Y.C., May 13, 1948; d. Solomon and Mollie (Friedman) Langman; m. Maier Salamon, Aug. 10, 1968; children: Mollie, Jean, Leah, Sharon, Eugene. BA, Hunter Coll., 1969. Licensed real estate borker, N.J. Mgr. office Customode Designs Inc., N.Y.C., 1966-68; co-owner Salamon Dairy Farms, Three Bridges, N.J., 1968-86; assoc. realtor Max. D. Shuman Realty Inc., Flemington, N.J., 1983-85; pres., chief exec. officer Liberty Hill Realty Inc., Flemington, N.J., 1985—; cons. Illva Saronna Inc. (Illva Group), Edison, N.J. 1985—; real estate devel. joint venture with M.R.F.S. Realty Inc. (Illva Group), 1986—. Mem. Readington twp. Environ. Commn., Whitehouse Sta., N.J., 1978-87, N.J. Assn. Environ. Commrs., Trenton, 1978—; fundraiser Rutgers Prep. Sch., Somerset, N.J., 1984-95; bd. dirs. Hunterdon County YMCA, 1987-95. Named N.J. Broker Record, Forbes Inc., N.Y.C. 1987. Mem. Nat. Assn. Realtors, N.J. Assn. Realtors, Hunterdon County Bd. Realtors (mem. chair 1986), Realtor's Land Inst. Republican. Jewish. Office: Liberty Hill Realty Inc 415 Us Highway 202 Flemington NJ 08822-6021

SALAMONE, JOSEPH CHARLES, polymer chemistry educator; b. Bklyn., Dec. 27, 1939; s. Joseph John and Angela (Barbagallo) S.; children: Robert, Alicia, Christopher. BS in Chemistry, Hofstra U., 1961; PhD in Chemistry, Poly. Inst. N.Y., 1967. NIH postdoctoral fellow U. Liverpool, Eng., 1966-67; rsch. assoc., Horace H. Rackham postdoctoral fellow U. Mich., Ann Arbor, 1967-70, adminstrv. sec., 1968-70; asst. prof., then assoc. prof. chemistry U. Mass., Lowell, 1970-76, prof., 1976-90, prof. emeritus, 1990—, dean Coll Sci., 1978-84, Disting. Rsch. fellow, 1984-90, chmn. dept. chemistry, 1975-78; pres. Optimers Inc., Lowell, 1985—; bd. dirs. Rochal Industries, Inc., Boca Raton, Fla.; cons. editor CRC Press, Inc., Boca Raton, 1992—. Mem. editl. bd. Polymer, 1976-94, Jour. Macromolecular Sci.-Chemistry, 1985—, Progress of Polymer Sci., 1987—, ChemTech, 1995—; adv. bd. Jour. Polymer Sci., 1974—; editor-in-chief Polymeric Materials Ency., 1993—; contbr. more than 160 articles to profl. jours. Recipient Disting Alumnus award, Poly. Inst. N.Y., 1984. Mem. Am. Chem. Soc. (chmn. div. polymer chemistry 1982), Soc. Plastics Engrs., Polymer Sci., Am. Acad. Ophthalmology (assoc.), Pacific Polymer Fedn. (sec., treas. 1988-90, dep. v.p. 1991-92, v.p., 1993, pres. 1994-95). Office: U Mass Dept Chemistry 1 University Ave Lowell MA 01854-2827

SALAND, LINDA CAROL, anatomy educator, researcher; b. N.Y.C., Oct. 24, 1942; d. Charles and Esther (Weingarten) Gewirtz; m. Joel S. Saland, Aug. 16, 1964; children—Kenneth, Jeffrey. B.S., CCNY, 1963, Ph.D. in Biology, 1968; M.A. in Zoology, Columbia U., 1965. Research assoc. dept. anatomy Columbia U. Coll. Physicians and Surgeons, N.Y.C., 1968-69; sr. research assoc. dept. anatomy Sch. Medicine, U. N.Mex., Albuquerque, 1971-78, asst. prof. anatomy, 1978-83, assoc. prof., 1983-89, prof., 1989—, prof. dept. neurosci., 1997—. Ad hoc reviewer NIH study sect., 1994, 95, site visit team. Mem. editorial bd. Anat. Record, 1980—; contbr. articles to profl. jours. Predoctoral fellow NDEA, 1966-68; research grantee Nat. Inst. on Drug Abuse, 1979-83, NIH Minority Biomed. Research Support Program, 1980—; NIH research grantee, 1986-95. Mem. AAAS, Am. Assn. Anatomists, Soc. for Neurosci., Women in Neuroscience (chair steering comm. 1991-93), Am. Soc. Cell Biology, Sigma Xi. Office: U NMex Sch Medicine Dept Neurosci Basic Med Sci Bldg Albuquerque NM 87131

SALANS, CARL FREDRIC, lawyer; b. Chicago Heights, Ill., Mar. 13, 1933; s. Leon and Jean (Rudnick) S.; m. Edith Motel, Sept. 26, 1956; children: Eric Lee, Marc Robert, Christopher John. A.B., Harvard, 1954; B.A., Trinity Coll., Cambridge (Eng.) U., 1956, LL.B., 1958, M.A., 1962; J.D., U. Chgo., 1957. Bar: Ill. 1958, D.C. 1973, U.S. Supreme Ct. 1972, admitted in France as avocat, 1972. With State Dept., 1959-72, dep. legal adviser, 1966-72; practice law Paris, 1972—; legal adviser U.S. del. Vietnam Peace Talks, Paris, 1968-71; assoc. prof. law George Washington U., 1965-66; lectr. on internat. comml. arbitration Inst. Internat. Bus. Law and Practice, Internat. C. of C., Paris, France; arbitrator internat. cases; arbitrator U.S.-Iran Claims Tribunal, The Hague. Mem. ABA (chmn. com. East-West trade and investment 1975-82), Am. Soc. Internat. Law, Am. Arbitration Assn. (panel arbitrators), Am. C. of C. in France (bd. dirs. 1977-87, chmn. laws and pub. affairs com. 1980-85). Home: 18 Ave Raphael, 75016 Paris France Office: Salans Hertzfeld & Heilbronn, 9 Rue Boissy d'Anglas, 75008 Paris France

SALANS, LESTER BARRY, physician, scientist, educator; b. Chicago Heights, Ill., Jan. 25, 1936; s. Leon K. and Jean (Rudnick) S.; m. Lois Audrey Kapp, Dec. 21, 1958; children: Laurence Eliot, Andrea Eileen. B.A., U. Mich., 1957; M.D. with honors, U. Ill., 1961. Internal medicine intern Stanford U. Med. Ctr., 1961, resident, 1962-64; USPHS postdoctoral and spl. fellow Rockefeller U., 1964-67, asst. prof., 1967-68, adj. prof., 1984—; asst. prof. medicine Dartmouth Coll., 1968-70, assoc. prof., 1970-77, adj. prof., 1978-79; assoc. dir. diabetes, endocrinology, metabolism, also chief lab. cellular metabolism and obesity Nat. Inst. Arthritis, Metabolism and Digestive Diseases, NIH, Bethesda, 1976-81; dir. Nat. Inst. Arthritis, Diabetes, Digestive and Kidney Diseases, NIH, 1981-84; v.p., head preclin. rsch. Sandoz Rsch. Inst., 1985-92, v.p. scientific and acad. affairs, 1993—; dean Mt. Sinai Sch. Medicine, 1984, prof. internal medicine, 1984-85, clin. prof. medicine, 1987—; adj. prof. Rockefeller U., 1985—; vis. prof. U. Geneva, Switzerland, 1974-75. Contbr. articles on insulin, diabetes mellitus, obesity to profl. jours., textbooks. Recipient NIH Research Career Devel. award, 1972-76, NIH Dirs. award, 1980, Juvenile Diabetes Fedn Pub. Service award, 1979. Fellow ACP; mem. AAAS, Am. Soc. Clin. Investigation, Am. Fed. Clin. Rsch., Am. Diabetes Soc., Am. Diabetes Assn. (Charles H. Best award 1985), Endocrine Soc., Assn. Am. Physicians, Am. Soc. Clin. Nutrition. Office: Sandoz Rsch Inst 59 State Route 10 East Hanover NJ 07936-1005

SALANT, ARI, medical advertising writer; b. Bronx, N.Y., July 6, 1942; s. Samuel and Lillian (Gersow) Saland.; m. Anne Lam, July 17, 1986. BA in English with spl. honors cum laude, CCNY, 1963; MA, Columbia U., 1966, MPhil, 1973. Instr. English Touro Coll., Bklyn. Coll., Manhattan Coll., N.Y.C., 1967-80; mng. editor N.Y. Theater Voice, N.Y.C., 1981-84; assoc. editor Women's Am. Orgn. for Rehab. Through Tng. Reporter, N.Y.C., 1985-88; libr. Klemtner Advt., N.Y.C., 1990-91; dir. Ari Salant Tech. Rsch. Assocs., N.Y.C., 1991—; freelance writer Klemtner Advt., Robert A. Becker Advt., Falk Comms., N.Y.C., Integrated Comms., Parsippany, N.J., Creative Coun., Flemington, N.J. Contbr. articles to profl. jours. Mem. Am. Med. Writers Assn., N.Y. Acad. Sci., Phi Beta Kappa. Jewish. Avocations: writing, reading, computing. Home and Office: Ari Salant Tech Rsch Assocs 334 W 85th St New York NY 10024

SALANT, NATHAN NATHANIEL, athletic conference commissioner; b. Bronx, N.Y., June 25, 1955; s. Benjamin B. and Marilyn (Balterman) S. BA cum laude, SUNY, Albany, 1976; JD, Boston U., 1979. Bar: N.J. 1981. Asst. athletic dir. SUNY, Albany, 1979-80, St. Francis Coll., Bklyn., 1981-85; spl. asst. athletic dir. Adelphi U., Garden City, N.Y., 1985-88; commr. Mid. Atlantic States Collegiate Athletic Conf., Chester, Pa., 1988-92; adj. prof. English Widener U., Chester, 1988-92; commr. Gulf South Conf., Birmingham, Ala., 1992—; mem. men's com. on coms. NCAA, 1993-96, mem. D-II men's basketball south ctrl. regional adv. com., 1995-96, south regional adv. com., 1996—. Author: This Date in New York Yankees History, 1979, 81, 83, Superstars, Stars and Just Plain Heroes, 1982. Head coach Rockland (N.Y.) OTB Pirates Am. Legion Baseball Team, 1974-76, 77—. Named Coach of Yr., Rockland County Big League, 1979-81, 83, 85-86, 87, 89, N.Y. State Am. Legion, 1987, 89-94. Avocations: writing, collecting sports memorabilia, stamps and coins. Home: 174 Woodmere Creek Ln Birmingham AL 35226-3561 Office: Gulf South Conf 4 Office Park Cir Ste 218 Birmingham AL 35223-2538

SALANT, WALTER S., economist; b. N.Y.C., Oct. 24, 1911; s. Aaron Bennett and Josephine Adele (Scheider) S.; m. Edna Goldstein, Jan. 25, 1939; children—Michael Alan, Stephen Walter. B.S., Harvard, 1933; A.M., Grad. Sch. Pub. Adminstrn., 1937-38, Ph.D., 1962; postgrad., Cambridge U., Eng., 1933-34. Research, statistics Treasury Dept., 1934-36; research Wall St. firm, 1936; asst. econs. Harvard, 1938; research SEC, 1938-39; mem. sr. staff indsl. econ. div. Office of Sec. Dept. Commerce, 1939-40; head economist research div. OPA (and predecessor agencies), 1940-45; econ. adviser to Econ. Stblzn. Dir., 1945-46, Price Decontrol Bd., 1946; economist Council Econ. Advisers, Exec. Office Pres., 1946-52; cons. econ. and finance div. NATO, 1952-53; vis. prof. Stanford, 1954, 69; sr. fellow Brookings Instn., 1954-76, emeritus, 1977—; cons. to sec. of treasury, 1961—, mem. U.S. econ. survey team to, Indonesia, 1961; cons. AID, 1963-66. Author: (with B.N. Vaccara) Import Liberalization and Employment, 1961, (with others) Indonesia: Perspectives and Proposals for U.S. Economic Aid, 1963, The U.S. Balance of Payments in 1968, 1963, International Monetary Arrangements: The Problem of Choice, 1967, Maintaining and Restoring Balance in International Payments, 1966, International Mobility and Movement of Capital, 1972, European Monetary Unification and Its Meaning for the United States, 1973, Worldwide Inflation: Theory and Recent Experience, 1977, also The Effects of Increases in Imports on Domestic Employment: A Clarification of Concepts, 1978; bd. editors: (with others) Am. Econ. Rev, 1956-58; contbr. (with others) articles to econs. jours. Mem. Univ.-Nat. Bur. Com. Econ. Research, 1956—, mem. exec. com., 1962-74, vice chmn., 1967-74. Mem. Am. Econ. Assn., Royal Econ. Soc., Phi Beta Kappa. Clubs: Cosmos (Washington), Harvard (Washington). Home: 2101 Connecticut Ave NW Washington DC 20008-1728

SALATHE, JOHN, JR., manufacturing company executive; b. Montreal, Que., Can., Sept. 25, 1928; s. John and Ida (Schenk) S.; m. Harriet Edith Styles; children: Linda Paul, Craig. BSME, San Jose State U., 1950. Gen. mgr. Indsl. Steel Tank & Body Co., Berkeley, Calif., 1958-62; project mgr. Pacific Foundry div. PACCAR Inc., Renton, Wash., 1962-66, prodn. mgr., 1966-70, asst. gen. mgr., 1970-71, gen. mgr., 1971-79; asst. v.p. PACCAR Inc., Bellevue, Wash., 1979-81, v.p., 1981-90; ret., 1991. Bd. dirs. Jr. Achievement, Seattle, 1979-85; mem. adv. bd. Seattle Pacific U., 1985—. Sloan fellow Stanford U., 1970. Mem. Soc. Mfg. Engrs. (sr.), Am. Soc. Quality Control (sr.). Avocations: gardening, boating, reading.

SALATICH, JOHN SMYTH, cardiologist; b. New Orleans, Nov. 28, 1926; s. Peter B. and Gladys (Malter) S.; BS cum laude, Loyola U., New Orleans, 1946; MD, La. State U., 1950; m. Patricia L. Mattison, Sept. 26, 1959; children: John Smyth, Elizabeth, Allison, Stephanie. Intern Charity Hosp., New Orleans, 1950-51, resident, 1951-54; practice medicine, specializing in cardiology and internal medicine, New Orleans, 1954-92, Gen. Internal Med. Clinic Tulane Med. Sch., 1992—; dir. EKG dept. Southeastern La. Hosp., Mandeville, La.; prof. clin. medicine La. State U., 1994; mem. staff Touro Infirmary, St. Charles Gen. Hosp.; chmn. dept. medicine Hotel Dieu, 1974-86 pres., New Orleans Emergency Room Corp., Physician Supplemental Services; adv. bd. Bank La., 1960-89; mem. Pres.'s Coun. Loyola U., 1990-92. Bd. dirs. La. Regional Med. Program, 1972. Served to capt. M.C., AUS, 1954-56; Korea. Decorated Medallion of Greek Army. Diplomate Am. Bd. Internal Medicine. Fellow Am. Coll. Chest Physicians, ACP; mem. Am. Heart Assn., La. Heart Assn., New Orleans Acad. Internal Medicine, La. Soc. Internal Medicine, AMA, La. Med. Soc., Orleans Parish Med. Soc., Theta Beta, Alpha Sigma Nu, Delta Epsilon Sigma. Club: New Orleans Country. Contbr. articles to profl. and bus. jours. Home: 433 Country Club Dr New Orleans LA 70124-1038 Office: Nola 70112 144 Elk Pl Ste 1100 New Orleans LA 70112-2636

SALATKA, CHARLES ALEXANDER, archbishop; b. Grand Rapids, Mich., Feb. 26, 1918; s. Charles and Mary (Balun) S. Student, St. Joseph's Sem., Grand Rapids, 1932-38; M.A., Cath. U. Am., 1941; J.C.L., Inst. Civil and Canon Law, Rome, 1948. Instr. St. Joseph's Sem., Grand Rapids, Mich., 1945; ordained priest Roman Catholic Ch., 1945; assigned chancery office Diocese of Grand Rapids, 1948-54, vice chancellor, 1954-61; aux. bishop, 1961, vicar gen., 1961, consecrated bishop, 1962; pastor St. James Parish, Grand Rapids, 1962-68; titular bishop of Cariana and aux. bishop of Grand Rapids, 1962-68; bishop of Marquette, 1968-77; archbishop of Okla. City, 1977-92; ret., 1992. Mem. Canon Law Soc. Am. *

SALAVERRIA, HELENA CLARA, educator; b. San Francisco, May 19, 1923; d. Blas Saturnino and Eugenia Irene (Loyarte) S. AB, U. Calif., Berkeley, 1945, secondary teaching cert., 1946; MA, Stanford U., 1962. High sch. tchr., 1946-57; asst. prof. Luther Coll., Decorah, Iowa, 1959-60; prof. Spanish, Bakersfield (Calif.) Coll., 1961-84, chmn. dept., 1973-80. Vol., Hearst Castle; mem. srs. adv. group edn. Cuesta Coll. Community Svcs. Mem. AAUW (edn. com.), NEA, Calif. Fgn. Lang. Tchrs. Assn. (dir. 1976-77), Kern County Fgn. Lang. Tchrs. Assn. (pres. 1975-77), Union Concerned Scientists, Natural Resources Def. Coun., Calif. Tchrs. Assn. (chpt. sec. 1951-52), Yolo County Coun. Retarded, Soc. Basque Studies in Am., RSVP, Amnesty Internat., Common Cause, Sierra Club, Prytanean Alumnae, U. Women of Cambria, U. Calif. Alumni Assn., Stanford U. Alumni Assn., Friends of the Carbria Libr. Democrat. Presbyterian. Address: PO Box 63 Cambria CA 93428-0063

SALAZAR, RAMIRO S., library administrator; b. Del Rio, Tex., Mar. 3, 1954; s. Jesus and Juanita (Suarez) S.; m. Cynthia Castillo, Dec. 19, 1976 (div. 1990); children: Ramiro Orlando, Selinda Yvette. BA, Tex. A&I U., 1978; MLS, Tex. Woman's U., 1979. Asst. libr. dir. Val Verde County Libr., Del Rio, 1975-76; libr. Robert J. Kleberg Libr., Kingsville, Tex., 1977-78; libr. dir. Eagle Pass (Tex.) Pub. Libr., 1980-84; dir. Main Libr. San Antonio Pub. Libr., 1984-90; dir. librs. El Paso Pub. Libr., 1991-93, Dallas Pub. Libr., 1993—; chmn. Tex. State Libr. Planning Task Force, 1991-92; active Tex. Women's U. Sch. Libr. and Info. Studies Adv. Bd., 1993—, Alliance for Higher Edn. Libr. Dirs. Coun., 1993—; trustee AMIGOS Bibliographic Coun.; bd. advs. U. N. Tex. Sch. Lib. and Info. Scis., 1993, Booker T. Washington H.S. of Performing and Visual Arts, 1995-96. Chair customer svc. steering com. City of Dallas, 1993—; chair coupon book/resident privilege card task force City of Dallas, 1995-96; active home instrn. program for presch. children Nat. Coun. Jewish Women, 1996—. Recipient H.W. Wilson Staff Devel. award jury, 1995-96. Mem. ALA, Coun., 1996-2000 (mem. nominations com. 1997—), Libr. Adminstrn. and Mgmt. Assn. (bldg. and equipment sect., arch. for pub. libr. com. 1993-95, cultural diversity com. 1995—, pres.'s programs com. 1996—), Tex. Mcpl. League (resolutions com. 1995—), Tex. Mcpl. Libr. Dirs. Assn. (Libr. Dir. of the Yr. 1996), Pub. Libr. Adminstrs. North Tex., Reforma (exec. bd. dirs.), Tex. Libr. Assn.

(chmn. pubs. com. 1992-93, legis. com. 1993-95, ad hoc com. value of pub. librs. 1995—, awards com. 1995—), Jaycees. Democrat. Roman Catholic. Home: PO Box 15031 Dallas TX 75201-0031 Office: Dallas Pub Libr 1515 Young St Dallas TX 75201-5411

SALAZAR-CARRILLO, JORGE, economics educator; b. Havana, Cuba, Jan. 17, 1938; came to U.S., 1960; s. Jose Salazar and Ana Maria Carrillo; m. Maria Eugenia Winthrop, Aug. 30, 1959; children: Jorge, Manning, Mario, Maria Eugenia. BBA, U. Miami, 1958; MA in Econs., U. Calif., Berkeley, 1964, cert. in econ. planning, 1964, PhD in Econs., 1967. Sr. fellow, non-resident staff mem. Brookings Instn., Washington, 1965—; dir., mission chief UN, Rio de Janeiro, Brazil, 1974-80; prof. econs. Fla. Internat. U., Miami, 1980—, chmn. dept. econs., 1980-89; dir. Ctr. Econ. Rsch. & Edn.; mem. coun. econ. advisors State of Fla.; advisor U.S. Info. Agy., advisor, contbg. editor Library of Congress, Washington, 1972—; chmn. program com. Hispanic Profs. of Econs. and Bus.; cons. econs. Agy. for Internat. Devel., Washington, 1979—; council mem. Internat. Assn. Housing, Vienna, 1981—; exec. bd. Cuban Am. Nat. Council, Miami, 1982—; bd. dirs., pres. Fla. chpt. Insts. of Econ. and Social Rsch. of Caribbean Basin, Dominican Republic and Costa Rica, 1983—, U.S.-Chile Council, Miami, 1984—, Fla.-Brazil Inst. Co-author: Trade, Debt and Growth in Latin America, 1984; Prices for Estimation in Cuba, 1985; The Foreign Debt and Latin America, 1983; External Debt and Strategy of Development in Latin America, 1985; The Brazilian Economy in the Eighties, 1987, Foreign Investment, Debt and Growth in Latin America, 1988; World Comparisons of Incomes, Prices, and Product, 1988, Comparisons of Prices and Real Products in Latin America, 1990, The Latin American Debt, 1992; author: Wage Structure in Latin America, 1982, Oil and Development of Venezuela During the Twentieth Century, 1994. Fellow Brit. Council, London, 1960, Georgetown U., Washington, 1961-62, OAS, Washington, 1962-64, Brookings Instn., Washington, 1964-65. Mem. Am. Econ. Assn., Internat. Assn. Research in Income and Wealth, Econometric Soc. Latin Am., N.Am. Econs. and Fin. Assn., Nat. Assn. Cuban Am. Educators (treas. exec. com.), Internat. Assn. Energy Economists (pres. Fla. chpt.), Nat. Assn. Forensic Economists, Assn. for Study Cuban Economy (exec. com., dir. Cuban banking study group), Latin Am. Studies Assn., Knights of Malta. Roman Catholic. Home: 1105 Almeria Coral Gables FL 33134 Office: Fla Internat U Tamiami Campus DM 347 Miami FL 33199

SALBAING, PIERRE ALCEE, retired chemical company executive; b. Lectoure, France, May 8, 1914; emigrated to Can., 1946, naturalized, 1968; s. Jean and Sylvia (LaForgue) S.; m. Genevieve Nehlil, July 18, 1942; children: Michel, Christian, Francois, Patrick. B.A., Caen (France) U., 1931; Engring. Degree, Ecole Polytechnique, Paris, 1937; Naval Architecture Degree, Ecole Genie Maritime, Paris, 1939. With N.Am. dept. Air Liquide, Montreal, Que., Can., 1946-91, asst. gen. mgr., 1957-58, gen. mgr., 1958-60; exec. v.p. Canadian Liquid Air Ltd., Montreal, 1960-62, pres., 1962-82, chmn. bd., 1982-91; vice chmn. bd. Liquid Air Corp N.Am., San Francisco, 1984-91. Served to lt. comdr. French Navy, 1939-46. Decorated Legion of Honour., Nat. Order of Merit. Mem. Montreal Amateur Athletic Assn.

SALCH, STEVEN CHARLES, lawyer; b. Palm Beach, Fla., Oct. 25, 1943; s. Charles Henry and Helen Louise (Alverson) S.; m. Mary Ann Prim, Oct. 7, 1967; children—Susan Elizabeth, Stuart Trenton. B.B.A., So. Meth. U., 1965, J.D., 1968. Bar: Tex. 1968, U.S. Tax Ct. 1969, U.S. Dist. Ct. (so. dist.) Tex. 1969, U.S. Dist. Ct. (ea. dist.) Tex. 1972, U.S. Ct. Appeals (5th cir.) 1969, U.S. Ct. Appeals (fed. cir.) 1982, U.S. Ct. Fed. Claims, 1982. Assoc. Fulbright & Jaworski, Houston, 1968-71, participating assoc., 1971-75, ptnr., 1975—. Co-author: Tax Practice Before the IRS, 1994; contbr. articles to legal jours. Pres. Tealwood Owners Assn., 1982-83, Meml. High Sch. PTA, 1985-86; mem. Tex. PTA (Hon. Life Member award 1986). Mem. ABA (coun. dir. 1985-88, vice chair tax sect. 1988-91, chair elect 1995-96, chair 1996—), State Bar Tex., Houston Bar Assn., Am. Law Inst., Nat. Tax Assn., Am. Coll. Tax Counsel, Internat. Fiscal Assn., Harris County Heritage Soc., Galveston Hist. Found., Smithsonian Assocs., Colonial Williamsburg Found., Am. Bar Found., Southwestern Legal Found., Houston Bar Found., Order of Coif, Beta Alpha Psi, Phi Eta Sigma, Phi Delta Phi. Presbyterian. Clubs: Lakeside Country, Houston Center, Governor's, Galveston Coun try, Yacht, Pelican of Galveston, Galveston Artillery. Home: 342 Tamerlaine Dr Houston TX 77024-6147 Office: Fulbright & Jaworski 51st Fl 1301 Mckinney St Fl 51 Houston TX 77010-3031 *Set goals for yourself. Unless you know where you are and where you want to be in life, you will not be able to map a plan to accomplish your goals.*

SALCUDEAN, MARTHA EVA, mechanical engineer, educator; b. Cluj, Romania, Feb. 26, 1934; emigrated to Can., 1976, naturalized, 1979; d. Edmund and Sarolta (Hirsch) Abel. B.Eng., U. Cluj, 1956; postgrad., 1962; PhD, U. Brasov (Romania), 1969; PhD (hon.), U. Ottawa, 1992; m. George Salcudean, May 28, 1955; 1 child, Septimiu E. (Tim). Mech. engr. Armatura, Cluj, 1956-63; sr. rsch. officer Nat. Rsch. Inst. Metallurgy, Bucharest, 1963-75; part-time lectr. Inst. Poly., Bucharest, 1967-75; sessional lectr. U. Ottawa (Ont., Can.), 1976-77, asst. prof., 1977-79, assoc. prof., 1979-81, prof., 1981-85; prof., head dept. mech. engring. U. B.C., 1985-93, assoc. v.p. rsch., 1993-96, acting v.p. rsch. pro-tem, 1995, Weyerhaeuser Indsl. Rsch. chair computational fluid dynamics, 1996—; mem. grant selection com. for mech. engring. Natural Scis. and Engring. Rsch. Coun. Can.; mem. Nat. Adv. Panel to Min. Sci. and Tech. on advanced indsl. materials, Can., 1990; mem. governing coun. Nat. Rsch. Coun.; mem. defense science adv. bd. Dept. Nat. Defense. Recipient Gold medal B.C. Sci. Coun., Killam Rsch. prize U. B.C. Rsch. Coun. Can. grantee, 1978—, Commemorative medal 125th anniversary Can. Confederation, 1993, Julian C. Smith medal Engring. Inst. Can., 1994-95, Meritorious Achievement award Assn. Profl. Engrs. & Geoscientists B.C., 1996. Fellow CSME, Can. Acad. Engring., Royal Soc. Can.; mem. ASME, Assn. Profl. Engrs. Ont. Contbr. numerous articles to profl. jours. Home: 1938 Western Pkwy, Vancouver, BC Canada V6T 1W5

SALDICH, ROBERT JOSEPH, electronics company executive; b. N.Y.C., June 7, 1933; s. Alexander and Bertha (Kasakove) S.; m. Anne Rawley, July 21, 1963 (div. Nov. 1979); 1 child, Alan; m. Virginia Vaughan, Sept. 4, 1983; stepchildren: Tad Thomas, Stan Thomas, Melinda Thomas, Margaret Thomas Dudley. BSChemE, Rice U., 1956; MBA, Harvard U., 1961. Mfg. mgr. Procter & Gamble Mfg. Co., Dallas, Kansas City, Kans., 1956-59; rsch. asst. Harvard Bus. Sch., Boston, 1961-62; asst. to pres. Kaiser Aluminum & Chem. Corp., Oakland, Calif., 1962-64; mgr. fin. and pers., then gen. mgr. various divsns. Raychem Corp., Menlo Park, Calif., 1964-83, with office of pres., 1983-87, pres. Raynet Corp. subs., 1987-88, sr. v.p. telecomms. and tech., 1988-90; pres., CEO Raychem Corp., Menlo Park, 1990-95; ret. Raynet Corp. subs. Raychem Corp., 1995. Chair mfg. com. adv. bd. Leavy Sch. Bus. and Administrn., Santa Clara U. Mem. Calif. Roundtable (dir. Bay Area Coun.), San Francisco Com. on Fgn. Rels. Jewish. Avocations: sailing, skiing. Office: 635 Bryant St Palo Alto CA 94301-2502

SALE, GEORGE EDGAR, physician; b. Missoula, Mont., Apr. 18, 1941; s. George Goble and Ruth Edna (Polleys) S.; m. Joan M. Sutliff, 1989; children: George Gregory Colby, Teo Marie Jonsson. AB, Harvard U., 1963; MD, Stanford U., 1968. Intern U. Oreg., Portland, 1968-69; sr. asst. surgeon USPHS, Albuquerque, 1969-71; resident in pathology U. Wash., Seattle, 1971-75, instr. pathology, 1975-78, asst. prof., 1978-81, assoc. prof., 1981-88, prof., 1988—; asst. mem. faculty, dept. oncology Hutchinson Cancer Ctr., Seattle, 1975-88, assoc. mem., 1988-91, mem., 1991—. Author, editor: Pathology of Bone Marrow Transplantation, 1984, Pathology of Transplantation, 1990. Mem. AAAS, Internat. Acad. Pathology, Coll. Am. Pathologists, Am. Assn. Investigative Pathologists, Physicians for Social Responsibility. Home: 12146 Sunrise Dr NE Bainbridge Island WA 98110-4304 Office: Fred Hutchinson Cancer Rsh Ctr 1100 Fairview Ave N Seattle WA 98109-4433

SALE, (JOHN) KIRKPATRICK, writer; b. Ithaca, N.Y., June 27, 1937; s. William M. Jr. and Helen (Stearns) S.; m. Faith Apfelbaum Sale, June 17, 1962; children: Rebekah Zoe, Kalista Jennings. BA, Cornell U., 1958. Editor The New Leader, N.Y.C., 1959-61; corr. Chgo. Tribune, San Francisco Chronicle, 1961-62; lectr. U. Ghana, Accra, 1963-65; editor N.Y. Times mag., N.Y.C., 1965-68, The Nation, N.Y.C., 1981-82; ind. scholar and writer, 1968—; bd. dirs. PEN Am. Ctr. N.Y.C., The Learning Alliance, N.Y.C. Author: The Land and People of Ghana, 1963, SDS: The Rise of the Students for a Democratic Society..., 1973, Power Shift: The Rise of the Southern Rim and Its Challenge to the Eastern Establishment, 1975, Human Scale, 1980, Dwellers in the Land: The Bioregional Vision, 1985, The Conquest of Paradise: Christopher Columbus and the Columbian Legacy, 1990, The Green Revolution: The American Environmental Movement, 1962-92, 1993, Rebels Against the Future: The Luddites and Their War on the Industrial Revolution: Lessons for the Computer Age, 1995; contbg. editor The Nation; contbr. articles to profl. jours. Bd. dirs. EF Schumacher Soc., Great Barrington, Mass., 1981—; co-dir. Hudson Bioregional Coun., N.Y.C., 1985—. Home: 113 W 11th St New York NY 10011-8325

SALE, LLEWELLYN, III, lawyer; b. St. Louis, May 19, 1942; s. Llewellyn Jr. and Kathleen (Rice) S.; m. Cynthia Jean Bricker, Aug. 17, 1968 (div. Apr. 1995); children: Allyson J., Eryn E. AB cum laude, Yale U., 1964; LLB cum laude, Harvard U., 1967. Bar: Mo. 1967, U.S. Dist. Ct. (ea. dist.) Mo. 1967, U.S. Tax Ct. 1982, U.S. Ct. Claims 1985. From assoc. to ptnr. to mng. ptnr. Husch & Eppenberger, St. Louis, 1967-88; ptnr. Bryan Cave, St. Louis, 1988—. Bd. dirs. Washington U. Child Guidance Clinic, St. Louis, 1978-80, Mental Health Assn. St. Louis, 1988-89. Mem. ABA, Bar Assn. Met. St. Louis (chmn. law econs. subcom. 1982), Media Club, Noonday Club. Avocations: spectator sports, jogging. Office: Bryan Cave 211 N Broadway Ste 3600 Saint Louis MO 63102-2733

SALE, MERRITT, classicist, comparatist, educator; b. New Haven, Nov. 27, 1929; s. William Merritt and Helen (Stearns) S.; m. Marilyn Mills, June 13, 1953 (div. Oct. 1967); children: Elizabeth, David; m. Anne Perkins, May 18, 1991. B.A., Cornell U., 1951, M.A., 1954, Ph.D., 1958. Engr. U.S. Metals Co., Carteret, N.J., 1951-52; instr. in classics Yale U., New Haven, 1957-58; asst. prof., assoc. prof. Washington U., St. Louis, 1958-75, chmn. classics dept., 1961-69, prof. classics and comparative lit., 1975—, chmn. comparative lit. dept., 1981-90. Author: Sophocles' Electra: Commentary with Introduction and Translation, 1970, Existentialism and Euripides, 1977, Homer and the Roland, 1993, The Government of Troy, 1995. Recipient Founder's Day award for Excellence in Teaching Washington U., 1978. Mem. Am. Philol. Assn., London Inst. for Classical Studies. Home: 2342 Albion Pl Saint Louis MO 63104-2524

SALE, TOM S., III, economist, educator; b. Haynesville, La., July 27, 1942; s. Thomas and Mary Belle (Fagg) S.; divorced; children: Jennifer Elizabeth, Sarah Elaine. BA, Tulane U., 1964; MA, Duke U., 1965; PhD, La. State U., 1972. Mem. faculty La. Tech. U., Ruston, 1965—, prof. econs., 1975—, head dept. econs. and fin., 1974-86, 90-95, dir. grad. studies Coll. Adminstrn and Bus., 1988-89. Chartered fin. analyst. Mem. Am. Econs. Assn., So. Econs. Assns., Southwestern Fin. Assn. (pres. 1985-86), Am. Fin. Assn., Inst. Chartered Fin. Analysts (exam. com. 1983-92, curriculum com. 1993—), SW Fedn. Adminstrv. Disciplines (v.p. 1988-89, pres. 1989-90), Dallas Assn. Fin. Analysts, Omicron Delta Kappa, Omicron Delta Epsilon. Episcopalian. Contbr. articles to profl. jours. Home: PO Box 1365 Ruston LA 71273-1365 Office: La Tech U Ruston LA 71272

SALEH, BAHAA E. A., electrical engineering educator; b. Cairo, Sept. 30, 1944; came to U.S., 1977; BS, Cairo U., 1966; PhD, Johns Hopkins U., 1971. Lectr. Johns Hopkins U., Balt., 1969-71; asst. prof. U. Santa Catarina, Brazil, 1971-74; rsch. assoc. Max Planck Inst., Göttingen, Germany, 1974-76; asst. prof. elec. engring. U. Wis., Madison, 1977-79, assoc. prof., 1979-81, prof., 1981-94, chmn. dept. elec. and computer engring., 1990-94; prof., chmn. dept. elec. and computer engring Boston U., 1994—. Author: Photoelectron Statistics, 1978, Fundamentals of Photonics, 1991; also over 200 articles on optics and image processing. Romnes faculty fellow U. Wis., 1981, Guggenheim fellow, 1984. Fellow IEEE, Optical Soc. Am. (editor-in-chief jour.); mem. Phi Beta Kappa, Sigma Xi. Office: 44 Cummington St Boston MA 02215-2407

SALEH, FARIDA YOUSRY, chemistry educator; b. Cairo, Egypt, June 17, 1939; came to U.S., 1968; d. Michael Yousry and Fakiha Yousef (Badawy) Wassif; m. Hosny Gabra Saleh, Oct. 8, 1959; children: Magda, Nagwa. BS, Ain Shams U., 1959; MS, Alexandrial U., Egypt, 1967; PhD, U. Tex., 1976. Postdoctoral rsch. assoc. Tex. A&M U., College Station, 1977-78; rsch. scientist II U. North Tex., Denton, 1978-83, asst. prof. chemistry, 1980-83, assoc. prof., 1985-94, prof., 1994—; cons. Stanford Rsch. Inst., Menlo Park, Calif., 1983-84, Allied Chems. Co., Hackettstown, N.J., 1985-86, Am. Chrome Chems., Corpus Christi, Tex., 1988-89, USEPA Rev. Panel, Washington, 1986—. Contbg. author book chpts. in field; contbr. more than 60 articles to profl. jours. Recipient Svc. award U.S. EPA, Washington, 1993; recipient numerous grants in field. Mem. Am. Chem. Soc., Internat. Union of Pure and Applied Chemistry, Internat. Humic Substances Soc., Assn. Women in Sci. Avocations: music, swimming, tennis. Home: 1314 Valley Pkwy Lewisville TX 75067 Office: Univ North Tex Corner Mulberry & Ave B Denton TX 76203

SALEM, GEORGE RICHARD, lawyer; b. Jacksonville, Fla., Dec. 24, 1953; s. Kamel Abraham and Margaret Virginia (Bateh) S.; m. Rhonda M. Ziadeh, June 28, 1980; children: James George, Jihan Camille, Laila Suad. BA, Emory U., 1975, JD, 1977; LLM, Georgetown U., 1984. Bar: Ga. 1978, Fla. 1979, D.C. 1981. Ptnr. Thompson, Mann & Hutson, Washington, 1977-85; dep. solicitor U.S. Dept. Labor, Washington, 1985-86, solicitor of labor, 1986-89; ptnr. Akin, Gump, Strauss, Hauer & Feld, Washington, 1990—; bd. dirs. Overseas Pvt. Investment Corp. Contbr. articles to profl. jours. Nat. exec. dir. ethnic voters div. Reagan Bus '84; bd. dirs. United Palestinian Appeal, Inc., 1981-85, 86—, Arab Am. Inst., Jan.-Mar., 1985, Dec. 1986—; chmn. Arab Am. Leadership Coun., 1990—; mem. Am. Arab Anti-Discrimination Com., Interagy. Coordinating Coun.; chmn. Arab-Ams. for Bush-Quayle '88, '92. Recipient Ellis Island Medal of Honor, 1992. Mem. ABA (labor and employment law sect.), Ga. Bar Assn. (labor rels. div.), fla. Bar Assn. (labor rels. div.), D.C. Bar Assn. (labor rels. div.), Nat. Assn. Arab Ams. (bd. dirs. 1987, pres. 1992—), Am. Ramallah Club (pres. D.C. chpt. 1984, Wash. rep. 1982-84), Am. Ramallah Fedn. (chmn. human rights com., Washington rep. 1982-84), Arab Am. Rep. Fedn. (chmn. 1985), Assn. Am. Arab Univ. Grads., Century Club Nat. Rep. Heritage Groups Coun., Delta Theta Phi, Omicron Delta Kappa. Mem. Eastern Orthodox Christian Ch. Office: Akin Gump Hauer & Feld Ste 210 1333 New Hampshire Ave NW Washington DC 20036-1533

SALEMBIER, VALERIE BIRNBAUM, publishing executive; b. Teaneck, N.J., July 2, 1945; d. Jack and Sara (Gordon) Birnbaum; m. David J. Salembier, June 23, 1968 (div. 1980); m. Paul J. Block, Dec. 9, 1990. B.A., Coll. of New Rochelle, 1973. Merchandising mgr. Life Internat., Time, Inc., N.Y.C., 1964-69; merchandising copywriter Newsweek, Inc., N.Y.C., 1970; promotion prodn. mgr. Newsweek, Inc., 1971, adv. sales rep., 1972-76; advt. dir. Ms. Mag., N.Y.C., 1976-79, assoc. pub., 1979-81; pub. Inside Sports Mag., N.Y.C., 1982; v.p., pub. 13-30 Corp., N.Y.C., 1983; sr. v.p. advt. USA Today, 1983-88; pub. TV Guide, Radnor, PA, 1988-89; pres. N.Y. Post, N.Y.C., 1989-90; pub. Family Circle Mag., N.Y.C., 1991-93; v.p. advt. The N.Y. Times, 1993-94; pres. Quest Mag., 1995-96; v.p. mag. devel. Meigher Comms., 1995-96; pub. Esquire Mag., 1996—; lectr. in field. Author: Rotisserie League Baseball, 1982; contbr. articles to mags. Former trustee Coll. of New Rochelle; trustee, exec. com. N.Y.C. Police Found.; trustee N.Y.C. Sports Devel. Corp., Ctrl. Synagogue; pres., bd. dirs. Nat. Alliance Breast Cancer Orgns., BOX (Beneficial Orgn. to Aid Ex-Fighters). Mem. C200, Women in Comm., Womens Forum, Nat. Coun. Jewish Women. Home: 1075 Park Ave New York NY 10128-1003 Office: Esquire 250 W 55th St New York NY 10019-5201

SALENTINE, THOMAS JAMES, pharmaceutical company executive; b. Milw., Aug. 8, 1939; s. James Edward and Loretta Marie (Burg) S.; m. Susan Anne Sisk, Apr. 16, 1966; children: Anne Elizabeth, Thomas James Jr. BS in Acctg., Marquette U., Milw., 1961. CPA, Ind., Wis. Sr. audit mgr. Price Waterhouse, Milw., 1961-74; dir. corp. acctg. Ward Foods Inc., Wilmette, Ill., 1974-78; corp. contr. Johnson Controls Inc., Milw., 1984-85; v.p., contr. Stokely Van Camp Inc., Indpls., 1978-87; exec. v.p., chief fin. officer Bindley Western Industries Inc., Indpls., 1987—, also bd. dirs. Chmn. com. United Way, Indpls., 1989-90. Lt. USN, 1962-65. Mem. AICPA, Fin. Execs. Inst. Republican. Roman Catholic. Home: 13540 Brentwood Ln Carmel IN 46033-9488 Office: Bindley Western Industries 10333 N Meridian St Ste 300 Indianapolis IN 46290-1074

SALERNO, THOMAS JAMES, lawyer; b. Jersey City, Aug. 30, 1957; s. Thomas E. and Imelda (Gyurik) S.; m. Tricia Joan Neary, Feb. 14, 1982; children: Alissa Lee, Lauren Mae, Thomas James Jr., Laina Hope. BA summa cum laude, Rutgers U., 1979; JD cum laude, U. Notre Dame, 1982. Bar: Ariz. 1982, U.S. Dist. Ct. Ariz. 1982, U.S. Ct. Appeals (9th cir.) 1982. Ptnr. Streich Lang, Phoenix, Ariz., 1982-94, Meyer, Hendricks, Victor, Osborn & Maledon, Phoenix, 1994-95, Squire, Sanders & Dempsey, Phoenix, 1995—; lectr. Profl. Edn. Sys., Inc., Eau Claire, Wis., 1984—, Robert Morris Assn., Phoenix, 1984—, Comml. Law League of Am., 1986—, Am. Law Inst.-ABA, 1990—, Nat. Conf. Bankruptcy Judges, 1991—, Continuing Legal Edn. Satellite Network, 1991; adj. prof. London Inst. Internat. Bus. and Comml. Law, Inns of Ct. Sch. Law, Gray's Inn, London, 1994—; adj. prof. Salzburg (Austria) U., 1995, 96. Co-author: Bankruptcy Litigation and Practice: A Practitioner's Guide, 1988, 2d edit., 1995, Arizona's New Exemption Statute, 1983, Bankruptcy Law and Procedure: A Fundamental Guide for Law Office Professionals, 1989, Troubled Construction Loans: Law and Practice, 1990, In and Outs of Foreclosure, 1989, Advanced Chapter 11 Banktuptcy Practice, 1990, 2d edit., 1996, Norton Bankruptcy Law and Practice, 1993, Chapter 11 Theory and Practice: A Guide to Reorganizations, 1994. Mem. Vol. Legal Svcs. Program. Mem. ABA (bankruptcy com., lectr. 1990—, mem. working group prepackaged plans bus. bankruptcy com. 1991), ATLA, Am. Bankruptcy Bd. of Certification (bd. dirs. 1994—), Ariz. State Bar Assn. (chmn. bankruptcy sect. 1988-90, co-chmn. bankruptcy sect. of continuing legal edn. com. 1988-89, mem. bankruptcy adv. commn. 1992-96), Am. Bankruptcy Inst. (editor jour. 1991—, bd. dirs. 1993—, mem. bd. dir. 1993—), Comml. Law League, Phi Beta Kappa, Pi Sigma Alpha. Avocations: tennis, golf, travel. Home: 5714 E Claire Dr Scottsdale AZ 85254 Office: Squire Sanders & Dempsey 40 N Central Ave Ste 2700 Phoenix AZ 85004-4424

SALERNO-SONNENBERG, NADJA, violinist; b. Rome, Jan. 10, 1961; came to U.S., 1969; d. Josephine Salerno-Sonnenberg. Grad., Curtis Inst. Music, 1975, Juilliard Sch., 1982. Profl. debut with Phila. Orch., 1971; appearances include Am. Symphony Orch., Balt., Chgo., Cin., Detroit, Houston, Indpls., Milw., Montreal, N.J., Pitts. symphonys, Cleve., L.A. Chamber, Phila., Minn. orchs., New Orleans, N.Y., L.A. philharms.; festival appearances include Mostly Mozart Festival, Ravinia, Blossom, Meadow Brook, Gt. Woods, Caramoor, Aspen, Hollywood Bowl; internat. orchestral appearances include Vienna, Munich, Stuttgart, Frankfurt, Geneva, Rotterdam, Lisbon, Tokyo; featured on 60 Minutes, CBS, CBS Sunday Morning, NBC Nat. News, PBS Live from Lindoln Ctr., Charlie Rose Show; numerous appearances on The Tonight Show with Johnny Carson; rec. artist Angel, 1987—, Nonesuch, 1996. Recipient 1st prize Naumburg Violin Competition, N.Y.C., 1981; Avery Fisher Career grantee., N.Y.C., 1983. Mem. AFTRA, Screen Actors Guild. Office: care M L Falcone Pub Rels 155 W 68th St Ste 114 New York NY 10023-5808

SALES, A. R., financial executive; b. Holguin, Oriente, Cuba, Sept. 20, 1948; came to U.S., 1961; s. Angel Alberto and Adeina Rosa (Paneque) S.; m. Barbara Cornell Felix, Aug. 26, 1972; children: Ashley Lynden, Alison Lane. BS, Ind. U., 1972, MBA, 1977. Mgmt. trainee Lincoln Nat. Bank, Ft. Wayne, Ind., 1972-73; asst. v.p. Am. Fletcher Nat. Bank, Indpls., 1973-77; treasury mgr. The Upjohn Co., Kalamazoo, 1977-82, v.p., treas., 1985-90; asst. treas. Midland-Ross Corp., Cleve., 1982-85; treas. Arvin Industries, Inc., Columbus, Ind., 1990—. Bd. dirs. C. Brown Speech and Hearing Ctr., Kalamazoo, 1987-90, treas., 1989; bd. dirs. Columbus Econ. Devel. Bd., Columbus Regional Hosp. Found., Bartholomew Co. United Way, chmn. 1997—; adv. bd. Ind. U.-Purdue U., Columbus. Mem. Fin. Execs. Inst., Nat. Assn. Corp. Treas., Beta Gamma Sigma. United Methodist. Avocations: tennis, golf, art. Office: Arvin Industries PO Box 3000 Columbus IN 47202-3000

SALES, EUGENIO DE ARAUJO CARDINAL, archbishop; b. Acari, Brazil, Nov. 8, 1920; s. Celso Dantas and Josefa de A. Sales; student Seminary Fortaleza City. Ordained priest Roman Cath. Ch., 1943, consecrated bishop, 1954, elevated to cardinal, 1969; Sede Plena apostolic adminstr., Natal, 1962, Salvador, 1964; archbishop, Sao Salvador, 1968-71, Rio de Janeiro, 1971—; mem. Coun. of Cardinals and Bishops in the State Sec.-2d Sect. Mem. Congregations, for Divine Cult, clergy, Evangelization, Oriental Chs., Couns. for Social Communication. Editor: The Pastors Voice. Address: Gloria 446, 20241-150 Rio de Janeiro Brazil

SALES, JAMES BOHUS, lawyer; b. Weimar, Tex., Aug. 24, 1934; s. Henry B. and Agnes Mary (Pesek) S.; m. Beuna M. Vornsand, June 3, 1956; children: Mark Keith, Debra Lynn, Travis James. BS, U. Tex., 1956, LLB with honors, 1960. Bar: Tex. 1960. Practiced in Houston, 1960—; sr. ptnr. firm, head litigation dept., mem. exec. com. Fulbright & Jaworski, 1960—; pres. State Bar of Tex., 1988-89. Author: Products Liability in Texas, 1985; co-author: Texas Torts and Remedies, 5 vols., 1986; assoc. editor Tex. Law Rev., 1960; editl. bd. Def. Law Jour.; contbr. articles to profl. jours. Trustee South Tex. Coll. Law, 1982-88, 90—, A.A. White Dispute Resolution Ctr., 1991-94; bd. dirs. Tex. Resource Ctr., 1990-97, Tex. Bar Hist. Found., 1990-96. 1st lt. USMCR, 1956-58. Named among Best Lawyers in Am., 1989-96. Fellow Internat. Acad. Trial Lawyers, Am. Coll. Trial Lawyers (state chmn. 1993-96), Am. Bd. Trial Advocates, Am. Bar Found. (sustaining life, state chmn. 1993—), Tex. Bar Found. (trustee 1991-95, vice-chmn. 1992-93, chmn. 1993-94, chair adv. bd. for planned giving 1994-97, sustaining life mem.), Houston Bar Found. (sustaining life, chmn. bd. 1982-83); mem. ABA (ho. of dels. 1984—, mem. Commn. on IOLTA 1995—), Internat. Assn. Def. Counsel, Nat. Conf. Bar Pres. (coun. 1989-92), So. Conf. Bar Pres., Def. Rsch. Inst., So. Tex. Coll. Trial Advocacy (dir. 1983-87), Fed. Bar Assn., State Bar Tex. (pres. 1988-89, bd. dirs. 1983-87, chmn. bd. 1985-86), Tex. Assn. Def. Counsel (v.p. 1977-79, 83-84), Tex. Law Rev. Assn. (bd. dirs. 1996—), Houston Bar Assn. (officer, bd. dirs. 1970-79, pres.-elect 1979-80, pres. 1980-81), Gulf Coast Legal Found. (bd. dirs. 1982-85), Bar Assn. 5th Fed. Cir., The Forum, Westlake Club (bd. govs. 1980-85), Inns of Ct. (bd. dirs. 1981-84), Ramada-Tejas, Order of Coif. Roman Catholic. Home: 10803 Oak Creek St Houston TX 77024-3016 Office: Fulbright & Jaworski 1301 Mckinney St Houston TX 77010-3031

SALESSES, JOHN JOSEPH, university executive; b. Providence, Feb. 13, 1933; s. William Edward and Alice Marie (McConnell) S.; m. Dolores Ann Serbst, Nov. 27, 1954; children: John J., Robert G., Gregory M., Beth Ann. AB, Providence Coll., 1954; MA, U. R.I., 1960, PhD, 1979. Instr. Coll. Steubenville, Ohio, 1960-62; asst. prof. English R.I. Coll., Providence, 1962-79, assoc. prof. English, 1979—, chmn. dept. English, 1976-79, asst. v.p., dean, 1979-90, v.p., 1990—; adj. faculty U.S. Naval War Coll., Newport, R.I., 1963-73; mem. Dept. Def. Res. Forces Policy Bd., Washington, 1985-88. Mem. bd. visitors Maine Corps U., Quantico, Va. Maj. gen. USMCR, 1954-88. Decorated Disting. Svc. medal; recipient Disting. Svc. award R.I. Coll., 1985; inducted into R.I. Heritage Hall of Fame, 1997. Mem. N.E. MLA, Internat. Soc. for Eighteenth Century Studies, Am. Soc. for Eighteenth Century Studies, Res. Officers Assn., Marine Corps Res. Officers Assn., Renaissance Soc. Am., Barrington Yacht Club (R.I.), Newport Arty. Co. (master gunner) Waneumetonomy Golf Club (R.I.). Roman Catholic. Avocations: running, golf, sailing. Home: 63 Rhode Island Ave Newport RI 02840 Office: RI Coll 600 Mt Pleasant Ave Providence RI 02908-1924

SALEWSKI, RUBY MARIE GRAF, nursing educator; b. Vernon, Tex., Feb. 22, 1932; d. Albert Carl and Olga Emma (Mertink) Graf; children: Stephen, Elizabeth, Matthew, Rebecca, Deborah. Diploma in nursing, Meth. Hosp. Sch. Nursing, Dallas, 1952; BSN, U. Tex., Galveston, 1956; postgrad., U. Tex., Austin, 1979-82, 87, St. Louis U., 1960-61; MEd in Nursing, U. Minn., 1967, postgrad., 1982. Lic. nurse, Minn., Tex. Mem. nursing faculty U. Tex., Galveston, 1956-59, Luth. Hosp., St. Louis, 1959-60, Anoka-Ramsey Community Coll., Coon Rapids, Minn., 1968-69; faculty pre-nursing advisor U. Minn., Mpls., 1970, 72, 73-74; mem. nursing faculty Austin (Minn.) C.C., 1975-76; mem. faculty Rochester (Minn) C.C., 1976-90, coord. continuing edn. in nursing, 1981-82; asst. prof. Tex. Tech U. Health Scis. Ctr. Sch. Nursing, Lubbock, 1991-95, U. Tex. Coll. Nursing and Health Scis., El Paso, 1995—; staff nurse St. John's Hosp., Springfield, Ill.; staff and charge nurse Dist. 1 Hosp., Faribault, Minn., U. Tex. Med. Br. Hosps., Galveston, Meth. Hosp., Dallas, Meml. Hosp., Springfield, Seton Hosp., Austin Tx., St. Mary's Hosp., Rochester. Bd. dirs., coord. Family Edn. Ctr., 1985;; vol. Contact Ministries, 1984-89; mem. organized caring and sharing ministry Good Shepherd Luth. Ch., 1990; parish nurse Hope Luth. Ch., Lubbock, 1991-92. Mem. ANA, LWV (bd. dirs. local chpt. 1985-88), NEA, Minn. Nurses Assn. (govtl. affairs com. 1987-89, chmn. dist. 13 1988), Nat. League for Nursing, Minn. League for Nursing (v.p. 1985-87, founding com. mem. educators coun.), Adlerian Soc., Sigma Theta Tau, Pi Lambda Theta. Home: 1601 McRae Apt H-6 El Paso TX 79925

SALGADO, LISSETTE, dancer; b. Hialeah, Fla.. Dancer Miami (Fla.) Dance Theater Co., 1980-86, Joffrey II Dancers, N.Y.C., 1986-88, The Joffrey Ballet, N.Y.C., 1988—. Office: Canada Royal Winnipeg Ballet, 380 Graham Ave, Winnipeg, MB Canada R3C 4K2*

SALGANICOFF, LEON, pharmacology educator; b. Buenos Aires, Sept. 11, 1924; came to U.S., 1964; s. Marcos Salganicoff and Ana Rosa Zelicson; m. Matilde Saffier, Dec. 11, 1957; children, Alina, Marcos. MSc in Pharmacy, U. Buenos Aires, 1948, DSc in Biochemistry, 1955. Instr. U. Buenos Aires, 1947-49; chief clin. pathologist Hosp. Mil. Cen., Buenos Aires, 1955-59; chief lab. Conicet, Buenos Aires, 1959-64; rsch. asst. Nat. Coun. Investigation, Buenos Aires, 1959-64; rsch. fellow Johnson Found., U. Pa., Phila., 1965-68, Nat. Multiple Sclerosis Soc., 1968-71; assoc. prof. pharmacology Temple U., Phila., 1972-84, sect. leader, 1971—, prof. pharmacology Med. Sch., 1976-95, prof. emeritus, 1995—; vis. prof. U. Rome la Sapienza, 1976—, NATO vis. prof., 1992; dir. rsch. Barnett Found. for Mitochondrial Diseases. Grantee NIH, 1984-87; recipient W.W. Smith Charitable Trust award, 1992. Mem. AAAS, Fedn. Am. Socs. Exptl. Biology, Sigma Xi. Avocation: piano music. Home: 556 N 23rd St Philadelphia PA 19130-3117 Office: Temple U Sch Medicine 3400 N Broad St Philadelphia PA 19140-5104

SALHANI, CLAUDE, photojournalist; b. Cairo, Mar. 25, 1952; s. I. and Edith (Rogalska) S.; m. Cynthia Nuckolls, Dec. 1985; children: Justin Olivier, Isabelle Faustine. Certificate of Edn., U. London, 1969. Freelance war and roving corr. Sygma, 1970-81; dep. news pictures editor for Europe, Africa and Mid. East, Reuters, 1984-91; pres., gen. mgr. U.S. operation Sipa Press, N.Y.C., 1991-92; chief Mid. East photog. corr. UPI, Beirut, 1981-84; chief photographer for Europe, UPI, Brussels, 1983-84; mng. editor UPI NewsPictures, UPI, Washington, 1992—; asst. prof. photojournalism Beirut U. Coll., 1982-83; mem. adv. coun. Am. News Svc. Co-author: Lebanon, Days of Tragedy, 2 vols., Bravado & Trepidation, A Journalist's Guide to the Middle East-Black September to Desert Storm; photographs on covers Time, Newsweek, also others. Recipient Pulitzer prize nomination for picture of crying U.S. Marine after Beirut barracks bombing. Office: UPI World Hdqs 1510 H St NW Washington DC 20005-1008

SALHANY, LUCILLE S., broadcast executive. Formerly with Paramount Pictures; pres. Paramount Domestic Television, from 1985; chmn. Twentieth Television, a unit of Fox Inc., 1991-92, Fox Broadcasting Co., Beverly Hills, Calif., 1993-94; pres. United ParamountNetwork, 1994—. Office: United Paramount Network 11800 Wilshire Blvd Los Angeles CA 90025-6602*

SALIBA, JACOB, manufacturing executive; b. East Broughton, Que., Can., June 10, 1913; s. Said and Nazira (David) S.; m. Adla Mudarri, May 31, 1942; children: John, Thomas, Barbara. BS, Boston U., 1941. Sr. supervising engr. Thompson and Lichtner Co., Boston, 1944-49; pres. Kingston Dress Co., Boston, 1949-51, Indsl. & Mgmt. Assocs., Inc., Boston, 1951-54, Maine Dress Co., Cornish, 1948-61; exec. v.p., mem. exec. com. Cortland Corp., Inc. (formerly Brockway Motor Co., Inc.), N.Y.C., 1954-59; exec. v.p. Sawyer-Tower, Inc., Boston, 1955-56, pres., 1956-59; v.p. Farrington Mfg. Co.; exec. v.p. Farrington Packaging Corp., 1959-61, Farrington Instruments Corp.; pres. N.E. Industries, Inc., from 1961, also bd. dirs.; pres. Fanny Farmer Candy Shops, Inc., 1963-66, W.F. Schrafft & Sons Corp., 1967-68; pres. frozen foods div. W.R. Grace & Co., 1966-68; pres. Katy Industries, Inc., Elgin, Ill., 1969-88, chmn., CEO, 1988-94; bd. dirs. Schon & Cie, Emerging Germany Fund, NYSE, Syratech Corp., NYSE, Katy Industries, NYSE; spl. cons. Air Material Commmand, USAF, Dayton, Ohio, 1942-43; cons. to chief air staff USAF, 1952-54; co-chmn. Air Force Spare Study Group, 1953. Mem. corp. Mass. Gen. Hosp., Mus. Sci. Mem. Union League Club, Bridgton Club, Highlands Country Club, Palm Beach Yacht Club. Methodist. Office: Katy Industries Inc 6300 S Syracuse Way Englewood CO 80111-6720

SALIBA, PHILIP E., archbishop; b. Abou-Mizan, Lebanon, 1931; came to U.S., 1956, naturalized, 1961; s. Elias Abdallah and Salema (Saliba) S. B.A., Wayne State U., 1959; M.Div., D.D., St. Vladimir's Sem., N.Y., 1964; DHL, Wayne State U., 1986. Became sub-deacon Antiochian Orthodox Christian Ch. N.Am., 1945-49, ordained deacon, 1949-59, priest, 1959-66, consecrated archbishop, 1966, now primate; chmn. Standing Conf. Am.-Middle Eastern Christian and Moslem Leaders; chmn. Orthodox Christian Edn. Commn.; vice chmn. Standing Conf. Canonical Orthodox Bishops in Ams. Vice-chmn. St. Vladimir's Orthodox Theol. Sem. Address: 358 Mountain Rd Englewood NJ 07631-3727

SALIBELLO, COSMO, optometrist, medical products executive; b. N.Y.C., Sept. 21, 1943; s. Joseph and Maria (Patalano) S.; m. Jane Susan Wilde Crawford, July 1, 1984. B Mgmt. Engring., Rensselaer Poly. Inst., 1965; BA in Biology summa cum laude, Ctrl. Wash. U., 1979; B Visual Sci., Pacific U., Forest Grove, Oreg., 1981, OD, 1983. Lic. optometrist, Oreg., Wash. Mgmt. devel. assoc. Bendix Corp., Elmira, N.Y., 1965-66; dep. aircrew tng. mgr. Grumman Aerospace, Tehran, Iran, 1974-76; pvt. practice Salem, Oreg., 1983-91; pres., chmn. Applied Vision Concepts, Inc., Portland, Oreg., 1991-93; v.p. tech. PRIO Corp., Lake Oswego, Oreg., 1993—, also bd. dirs.; cons. on VDT workplace, Salem, 1983-91; mem. bd. optometry advisors Pacific U., 1986-93; founder PRIO Corp. Contbr. articles to profl. jours.; inventor VDT prescription sys.; nat. spkr. on issues of computer eye strain. Pres. Laurel West Homeowners Assn., Forest Grove, 1979-82. Lt. comdr. USN, 1966-74, Vietnam. Fellow Am. Acad. Optometry; mem. Am. Optometric Assn., Human Factors and Ergonomics Soc., Oreg. Optometric Assn., Portland Met. Optometric Soc. Avocations: music, model airplanes, bicycle touring. Office: PRIO Corp 4000 Kruse Way Pl Ste 2-355 Lake Oswego OR 97035-2545

SALIGMAN, HARVEY, consumer products and services company executive; b. Phila., July 18, 1938; s. Martin and Lillian (Zitin) S.; m. Linda Powell, Nov. 25, 1979; children: Martin, Lilli Ann, Todd Michael, Adam Andrew, Brian Matthew. BS, Phila. Coll. Textiles and Sci., 1960. With Queen Casuals, Inc., Phila., 1960-88; v.p. Queen Casuals, Inc., 1966-68, pres., chief exec. officer, 1968-81, chmn., 1981-88; pres., chief operating officer Interco Inc., St. Louis, 1981-83, chief exec. officer, 1983-85; chief exec. officer Interco Inc., 1985-89, chmn., 1989-90; bd. dirs. Merc. Bank, Union Electric. Trustee Washington U., St. Louis. Mem. St. Louis Club, Masons. Office: 10 S Brentwood Bvld Ste 408 Saint Louis MO 63105-1694

SALINAS, CARLOS FRANCISCO, dentist, educator; b. Iquique, Chile, Apr. 9, 1941; came to U.S., 1972; s. Carlos F. and Victoria (Cerda) S.; m. Maria Asunción Córdova, 1963; children: Carlos Miguel, Claudio Andres, Maria Asunción. BS, U. Chile, Santiago, 1958; DDS, U. Chile, 1963; DMD, Med. U. S.C., 1985. Cert. Fla., 1982, Tenn., 1982, S.C., 1985. Dentist Nat. Health Svc., Viña del Mar, Chile, 1963-65; pvt. practice Viña del Mar, 1963-72; fellow in medicine/genetics Johns Hopkins U., Balt., 1972-74; faculty mem. Med. Univ. S.C., Charleston, 1974-88, assoc. prof., 1988-94, prof., 1994—, dir. divsn. craniofacial genetics, 1981—; dir. craniofacial anomalies and cleft lip palate ctr. Med. U. S.C., Charleston, 1995—; faculty mem. U. Chile, Valparaiso, 1965-74; dentist Dental Ctrl. Clinic for Chilean Navy, Valparaiso, 1964-66; vis. scientist U. Montreal, 1974; internat. cons. Inter-american Coll. Physicians and Surgeons, Ptnrs. of Ams., WHO/Pan Am. Health Orgn. Editor: Genetica Craniofacial, 1979, Craniofacial Anomalies: New Perspectives, 1982, (with R.J. Jorgenson) Dentistry in the Interdisciplinary Treatment of Genetic Diseases, 1980, (with K.S. Brown) Craniofacial Mesenchyme In Morphogensis and Malformations, 1984, (with J.M. Opitz) Recent Advances in Ectodermal Dysplasias, 1988; contbr. articles to profl. jours. Bd. dirs. Ptnrs. Am. (award 1992), East Cooper Cmty. Outreach, S.C. World Trade Ctr., Charleston; chmn. bd. S.C. Hispanic Coalition, 1994—; founder Circulo Hispanoamericano de Charleston, pres. 1978-96; hon. consul of Chile, 1978—. Fogarty Internat. Rsch. fellow; grantee NIH, 1972-74, HEW, 1979-80, 80-81, 81-82, 82-83, 83-84, Dept. Health and Human Svcs., 1983-84, 84-85, March of Dimes Birth Defects Found., 1984-85, S.C. State Health and Human Svcs. Fin. Commn., 1989—. Mem. AAAS, Soc. Craniofacial Genetics (pres. 1985, 92, chmn. membership com. 1993-94), Iberoam. Soc. Human Genetics of N.Am. (v.p. 1992-94, pres. 1994—), Am. Assn. Dental Schs., Am. Soc. Human Genetics, Am. Cleft Palate and Craniofacial Anomalies Assn., Internat. Assn. for Dental Rsch., Am. Assn. for Dental Rsch., Interam. Coll. Physicians and Surgeons (bd. dirs. chpt. faculty and rschrs. 1994—), Incontinentia Pigmenti Found. (sci. adv. coun. 1995—), Med. Assn. P.R. (hon.), Peruvian Soc. Human Genetics (hon.), Med. Soc. Western Dist. P.R. (hon.). Home: 948 Equestrian Dr Mount Pleasant SC 29464-3608 Office: Med Univ SC 171 Ashley Ave Charleston SC 29425-0001

SALINGER, JEROME DAVID, author; b. N.Y.C., Jan. 1, 1919; s. Sol and Miriam (Jillich) S.; m. Claire Douglas, 1953 (div. 1967); children: Margaret Ann, Matthew. Student, Valley Forge Mil. Acad., Columbia U. Author: Catcher in the Rye, 1951, Nine Stories, 1953, Franny and Zooey, 1961, Raise High the Roof Beam, Carpenters; and Seymour: An Introduction, 1963, Hapworth 16, 1924, 1997; contbr. stories to New Yorker mag. Sgt. AUS, 1942-46. Address: care Harold Ober Assocs 425 Madison Ave New York NY 10017-1110*

SALINGER, PIERRE EMIL GEORGE, journalist; b. San Francisco, June 14, 1925; s. Herbert and Jehanne (Bietry) S.; m. Renee Laboure, Jan. 1, 1947; children: Marc (dec.), Suzanne (dec.), Stephen; m. Nancy Brook Joy, June 28, 1957; m. Nicole Helene Gillmann, June 18, 1965 (div. June 1988); 1 son, Gregory; m. Nicole Beauvillain de Menthon, June 17, 1989. BS, U. San Francisco, 1947. Reporter, night city editor San Francisco Chronicle, 1946-55; guest lectr. journalism Mills Coll., 1950-55; West Coast editor, contbg. editor Collier's mag., 1955-56; investigator select com. to investigate improper activities in labor or mgmt. field U.S. Senate, 1957-59; press sec. U.S. Senator Kennedy, 1959-60, Pres. Kennedy, 1961-63, Pres. Johnson, 1963-64; U.S. Senator from Calif., 1964; v.p. Nat. Gen. Corp., 1965; v.p. internat. affairs Continental Airlines, Inc. and Continental Air Services, Inc. (subsidiary), 1965-68; pres. Gramco Devel. Corp., 1968—; dep. chmn. Gramco (U.K.) Ltd., 1970-71; sr. v.p. AMROP Inc., 1969; L'Express, Paris, 1973-78; contbg. corr. ABC for Europe, 1977—, Paris bur. chief, 1979-87, sr. editor, 1988-90; sr. editor ABC News, 1988-93; vice chmn. Burson Marsteller, Washington, 1993-96; ind. pub. rels. profl., 1996—. Author: With Kennedy, 1966, On Instructions of My Government; editor A Tribute to John F. Kennedy, 1964, A Tribute to Robert F. Kennedy, 1968, Je Suis un Americain, 1975, La France et le Nouveau Monde, 1976, America Held Hostage-The Secret Negotiations, 1981, The Dossier, 1984, Mortal Games, 1988, Secret Dossier--The Hidden Agenda Behind the Gulf Crisis, 1991, PS-A Memoir, 1995. Press officer Calif. Stevenson for Pres. Campaign, 1952, Richard Graves for Gov. Calif. Campaign, 1954; trustee Robert F. Kennedy Meml. Found.; chmn. bd. trustees Am. U. in Paris, 1978-88, hon. chmn., 1988—. With USNR, World War II. Decorated officer Legion of Honor (France); recipient Ellis Island Medal of Honor, 1992. Mem. Nat. Press Club.

SALISBURY, ALICIA LAING, state senator; b. N.Y.C., Sept. 20, 1939; d. Herbert Farnsworth and Augusta Belle (Marshall) Laing; m. John Eagan Salisbury, June 23, 1962; children: John Eagan Jr., Margaret Salisbury La Rue. Student Sweet Briar Coll., 1957-60; BA, Kans. U., 1961. Mem. Kans. Senate, 1985—, v.p., chmn. commerce com., telecomm. strategic planning com.; vice chmn. ways and means com., mem. legis. post audit com., mem. joint com. on econ. devel. (mem. orgn. and calendar rules comm.). Elected mem. State Bd. Edn., Topeka, 1981-85, Kans.; past pres. Jr. League of Topeka; trustee Leadership Kans., 1982-89; bd. dirs. Topeka Community Found., 1983—, Topeka Pub. Sch. Found., 1985-89, Capitol Area Pla. Authority, 1989—, Kans. Inc., 1996—, Mid-Am. Mfg. Tech. Ctr., 1994-96, mem. workers' compensation fund oversight com., 1993—, mem. Kids Count steering com., mem. Stormont-Vail Hosp. Aux.; mem. adv. commn. Juvenile Offenders Program, Kans., 1985-95; mem. adv. bd. Topeka State Hosp., Kans. Action for Children, 1982—, Kans. Ins. Edn. Found., 1984-95, Youth Center at Topeka, 1987—; steering com. One Stop Career Ctr., Interstate Cooperation Com. Coun. State Govts.; mem. Nat. Fedn. Rep. Women; past bd. mem. United Way Greater Topeka, ARC, Family Service and Guidance, Topeka, Shawnee County Mental Health Assn., Florence Crittenton Services, Topeka, Topeka City Commn. Govtl. Adv. Com. Mem. Nat. Conf. State Legislators (exec. com.), Nat. Rep. Legislators' Assn. (Nat. Rep. Legislator of Yr. 1993, Bus. Guardian award 1990, Outstanding Individual Legis. Achievement award 1989), Shawnee County Rep. Women, Kappa Kappa Gamma; recipient Woman of Year award Topeka Panhellenic Coun., 1997. Episcopalian. Avocations: tennis; downhill skiing; water sports; horseback riding; gardening. Office: Kans State Senate State Capital Topeka KS 66612

SALISBURY, DALLAS L., research institute administrator. BA in Fin., U. Wash., 1970; MBA in Pub. Policy and Adminstrn., Syracuse U., 1973. With Pension and Welfare Benefits Adminstrn. of U.S. Dept. Labor, 1975-76, Pension Benefit Guaranty Corp., 1977-78, U.S. Dept. Justice, 1074, Wash. State Legislature, 1971-72; with Employee Benefit Rsch. Inst., Washington, 1978—, pres., CEO, mem. bd. trustees; chmn., CEO Am. Savs. Edn. Coun., Washington; bd. dirs. Nat. Acad. Social Ins., The Health Project; mem. adv. bd. Nat. Acad. on Aging; lectr. in field; cons. in field. Mem. editl. adv. bd. Employee Benefit News, Benefits Quar., Employee Benefits Jour., Healthplan: The Mag. of Trends, Insights and Best Practices; contbr. articles to profl. jours. Mem. ERISA adv. coun. Sec. of Labor. Fellow Nat. Acad. Human Resources. Office: Employee Benefit Research Inst 2121 K St NW Ste 600 Washington DC 20037-1801

SALISBURY, EUGENE W., lawyer, justice; b. Blasdell, N.Y., Mar. 20, 1933; s. W. Dean and Mary I. (Burns) S.; m. Joanne M. Salisbury, July 14, 1950; children: Mark, Ellen, Susan, David, Scott. BA in History and Govt. cum laude, U. Buffalo, 1959, JD cum laude, 1968. Bar: N.Y. 1960, D.C. 1973, U.S. Dist. Ct. (we. and no. dists.) 1961, U.S. Ct. Appeals (2d cir.) 1970, U.S. Ct. Appeals (D.C. cir.) 1973, U.S. Supreme Ct. 1973. Ptnr. Lipsitz, Green, Fahringer, Roll, Salisbury and Cambria, Buffalo, 1960—; justice Village of Blasdell, 1961—; lectr. N.Y. Office Ct. Adminstrn., N.Y.C., 1961—; mem. N.Y. State Commn. on Jud. Conduct, 1989—. Author: Manual for N.Y. Courts, 1973, Forms for N.Y. Courts, 1977. Capt. U.S. Army, 1948-54, Korea. Decorated Bronze Star, Purple Heart. Mem. ABA (del. spl. ct. sect. 1988—), D.C. Bar Assn., Erie County Bar Assn., N.Y. State Bar Assn., World Judges Assn., N.Y. State Magistrates Assn. (pres. 1973, Man of Yr. 1974), N.Y. State Jud. Conf., Upstate N.Y. Labor Adv. Council, 1995—. Office: Lipsitz Green Fahringer Roll Salisbury and Cambria 42 Delaware Ave Ste 300 Buffalo NY 14202-3901

SALISBURY, FRANK BOYER, plant physiologist, educator; b. Provo, Utah, Aug. 3, 1926; s. Frank M. and Catherine (Boyer) S.; m. Lois Marilyn Olson, Sept. 1, 1949; children: Frank Clark, Steven Scott, Michael James, Cynthia Kay, Phillip Boyer (dec.), Rebecca Lynn, Blake Charles; m. Mary Thorpe Robinson, June 28, 1991. BS, U. Utah, 1951, MA, 1952; PhD, Calif. Inst. Tech., 1955. Asst. prof. botany Pomona Coll., Claremont, Calif., 1954-55; faculty Colo. State U., Ft. Collins, 1955-66; prof. plant physiology Colo. State U., 1961-66; plant physiologist Expt. Sta., 1961-66; prof. plant physiology Utah State U., Logan, 1966-97, disting. prof. Agr., 1987-97, prof. emeritus, 1997—, head dept. plant sci., 1966-70; tech. rep. plant physiology AEC, Germantown, Md., 1973-74; vis. prof. U. Innsbruck, Austria; Lady Davis fellow Hebrew U. Jerusalem, 1983; mem. aerospace medicine adv. com. NASA, 1988-93, life scis. adv. com., 1986-88, chmn. NASA Controlled Ecol. Life Support System Discipline Working Group, 1989—. Author: The Flowering Process, 1963, Truth by Reason and by Revelation, 1965, The Biology of Flowering, 1971, The Utah UFO Display, 1974, The Creation, 1976; co-author: (with R.V. Parke) Vascular Plants, Form and Function, 2d edit., 1970, (with C. Ross) Plant Physiology, 1969, 4th edit., 1992; (with W. Jensen) Botany: An Ecological Approach, 1972, Botany, 2d edit., 1984, (with others) Biology, 1977; editor Jour. Plant Physiology, Ams. and the Pacific Rim, 1989-96; editor, contbr.: Units, Symbols, and Terminology for Plant Physiology, 1996. Trustee Colo. State U. Rsch. Found., 1959-62; leader People to People bot. del. to Republic South Africa, 1984, Peoples Republic China, 1988, Soviet Union, 1990. NSF sr. postdoctoral fellow Germany and Austria, 1962-63. Fellow AAAS; mem. Am. Soc. for Gravitational and Space Biology (Founders award 1994), Am. Soc. Plant Physiologists (editorial bd. 1967-92), Utah Acad. Sci., Arts and Letters, Am. Inst. Biol. Scis. (governing bd. 1976-79), Bot. Soc. Am. (Merit award), Sigma Xi, Phi Kappa Phi. Mem. LDS Ch. Office: Utah State U Dept Plants Soils and Biometeorology Logan UT 84322-4820 *This is an extremely exciting time to live! Science has provided marvelous insight into the cosmos, the earth, and the nature of life. The fact that mankind exists and can contemplate it all cries out that it has purpose and direction. My life is full to overflowing because God's revelation of Himself adds the final capstone to this beautiful structure.*

SALISBURY, JUDITH MURIEL, marketing consultant; b. Plainfield, N.J., Aug. 5, 1940; d. James Donald and Gladys Maybelle (Scull) S.; m. Leonard Gordon Hartsoe, July 9, 1966 (div. 1982); 1 child, Allison Lynn Hartsoe. BA in English, Vassar Coll., 1962; MA, Ind. U. Pa., 1972. Cert. paralegal; lic. real estate broker, Pa.; cert. secondary sch. tchr., N.J., Pa. Tchr. Greater Johnstown (Pa.) Pub. Schs., 1967-68, Altoona (Pa.) Area Pub. Schs., 1968-71; instr. Pa. State U., Altoona, 1970-72, C.C. Allegheny County, Pitts., 1973-84; realtor Greater Pitts. Bd. Realtors, 1973-91; instr. La Roche Coll., Pitts., 1974-75; cons. Salisbury Mktg. Assocs., Evans City, Pa., 1991—; mktg. mgr. TRI-V, Inc., 1994—; staff writer Butler (Pa.) Eagle, 1993-94; sales rep. Future Electronics Corp., Westborough, Mass., 1984-87. Vol. Peace Corps, Sierra Leone, West Africa, 1962-64, Butler County Literacy, 1991-94, Neighborhood Legal Svc., Butler, 1993, Butler County Hospice, 1990-94; telephone bank coord. Campaign for State Rep., Butler County, 1992; active pub. rels. LWV, Butler County, 1990-91, AAUW, Pa., 1990-91. Recipient Andron Epiphanon award Greater Pitts. Bd. Realtors, 1975-77, Pa. Gov.'s award Pennserve, 1991; named Top 25 Realtors North Suburban Multi-List, 1974. Mem. Internat. Toastmasters (v.p. pub. rels. 1993-94), West. Pa. Press Club, Returned Peace Corps Vols. Episcopalian. Avocations: genealogy research, history, needlework, poetry. Office: 121 Needle Point Rd Evans City PA 16033-7625

SALISBURY, MARGARET MARY, retired elementary school educator; b. LaGrange, Tex., Oct. 23, 1932; d. Charles Frederick and Hedwig Mary (Fajkus) Meyer; m. Harrison Bryan Salisbury, Jan. 8, 1955; children: Elaine, Kathleen, David, Stephen, Mark, Margaret II. BA, Our Lady of the Lake, San Antonio, 1954; MA, U. Tex., San Antonio, 1975. Lic. elem., secondary edn., English and sch. adminstrn. Tchr. h.s. St. Joseph's Sch. for Girls, El Paso, Tex., 1954-55; tchr. 1st grade St. Patricks Cathedral Sch., El Paso, 1955; tchr. 2nd grade S.W. Ind. Sch. Dist., San Antonio, 1971-74, tchr. 6th grade, 1974-75, supr. testing, reading, 1975-81, 82-86, prin. jr. h.s., 1981-82, dir. alternative sch., 1986-87, tchr. 3rd grade, 1987-96, ret., 1996; pres. Cooperating Tchr./Student Tchr. U. at Tex., San Antonio, 1986-87. Mem. AAUW (chairperson pub. policy com. 1995-97—), Internat. Reading Assn., Tex. State Reading Assn., Alamo Reading Coun., Reading Improvement, Pres. Club, San Antonio Ret. Tchrs. Assn. Republican. Roman Catholic. Avocations: gardening, reading, travel, photography. Home: 126 Meadow Trail Dr San Antonio TX 78227-1639

SALISBURY, NANCY, convent director. Head Convent of Sacred Heart, N.Y.C. Office: Convent of the Sacred Heart 1 E 91st St New York NY 10128-0605*

SALISBURY, ROBERT HOLT, political science educator; b. Elmhurst, Ill., Apr. 29, 1930; s. Robert Holt and Beulah (Hammer) S.; m. Rose Marie Cipriani, June 19, 1953; children: Susan Marie, Robert Holt, Matthew Gary. A.B., Washington and Lee U., 1951; M.A., U. Ill., 1952, Ph.D., 1955. Mem. faculty Washington U., St. Louis, 1955-65; prof. Washington U., 1965-97, prof. emeritus, 1997—, chmn. dept. polit. sci., 1966-73, 86-92, dir. Center for Study Pub. Affairs, 1974-77, Sidney W. Souers prof. govt., 1982-97; vis. prof. SUNY, Buffalo, 1965, So. Ill. U., Edwardsville, 1975; affiliated scholar Am. Bar Found., 1981-95; cons. U.S. Conf. Mayors, 1965, Hartford (Conn.) C. of C., 1964, NSF, 1973. Author: Interest Groups Politics in America, 1970, Governing America, 1973, Citizen Participation in the Public Schools, 1980, Interests and Institutions, 1992, The Hollow Core, 1993; contbr. articles to profl. jours. Mem. St. Louis County Charter Commn., 1967, Gov.'s Commn. on Local Govt., 1968-69. Guggenheim fellow, 1990; Rockefeller Ctr. scholar, 1990. Mem. Mo. Polit. Sci. Assn. (pres. 1964-65), Am. Polit. Sci. Assn. (exec. council 1969-71, v.p. 1980-81), Midwest Polit. Sci. Assn. (pres. 1977-78), Pi Sigma Alpha. Democrat. Methodist. Home: 709 S Skinker Saint Louis MO 63105 Office: Washington U Dept Polit Sci Saint Louis MO 63130

SALISBURY, TAMARA PAULA, foundation executive; b. N.Y.C., Dec. 14, 1927; d. Paul Terrance and Nadine (Korolkova) Voloshin; m. Franklin Cary Salisbury, Jan. 22, 1955; children: Franklin Jr., John, Elizabeth, Elaine, Claire. BA, Coll. Notre Dame, 1948; postgrad., Am. U., George Washington U. Chemist depts. pathology and chemotherapy NIH Cancer Inst., Bethesda, Md., 1946-52; asst. to chief of Chemistry Br. Office of Naval Rsch., Bethesda, 1953-55; v.p., COO Nat. Found. Cancer Rsch., Bethesda, 1973—. Mem. Assn. Internat. Cancer Rsch., 1995. Decorated d'Officier De L'Ordre De Leopold II; outstanding contbns. award Internat. Soc. Quantum Biology, 1983, award of appreciation Beth Israel Hosp., Harvard Med. Sch., Brigham & Women's Hosp., 1993. Mem. AAAS, Am. Chem. Soc., N.Y. Acad. Scis., Inst. Phys. and Chem. Biology (fgn.), Krebforschung Internat., Nat. Liberal Club. Home: 10811 Alloway Dr Potomac MD 20854-1504 Office: Nat Found Cancer Rsch 7315 Wisconsin Ave Ste 500W Bethesda MD 20814-3206

SALIT, GARY, lawyer. Sr. v.p., gen. counsel, sec. Bell Howell Co., Skokie, Ill. Office: Bell & Howell Company 5215 Old Orchard Rd Skokie IL 60077-1035*

SALITERMAN, RICHARD ARLEN, lawyer, educator; b. Mpls., Aug. 3, 1946; s. Leonard Slitz and Dorothy (Sloan) S.; m. Laura Shrager, June 15, 1975; 1 child, Robert Warren. BA summa cum laude, U. Minn., 1968; JD, Columbia U., 1971; LLM, NYU, 1974. Bar: Minn. 1972, D.C. 1974. Mem. legal staff U.S. Senate Subcom. on Antitrust and Monopoly, 1971-72; acting dir., dep. dir. Compliance and Enforcement div. Fed. Energy Office, N.Y.C., 1974; mil. atty. Presdl. Clemency Bd., White House, Washington, 1975; sr. ptnr. Saliterman & Siefferman, Mpls., 1975—; adj. prof. law Hamline U., 1976-81. Chmn. Hennepin County Bar Jour., 1985-87; trustee, sec. Hopkins Edn. Found.; pres. twin cities coun. Navy League U.S., 1997—.

SALJINSKA-MARKOVIC, OLIVERA T., oncology researcher, educator; b. Skopje, Macedonia, Oct. 27, 1938; d. Trajko and Radmila Saljinska; m. Nenad Markovic, July 9, 1961; children: Svetomir, Mila. MD, Med. Faculty, Skopje, 1962; PhD, Med. Faculty, Belgrade, 1977; Specialist Med. Biochemistry, U. Kiril and Metodij, Skopje, 1969. Asst. prof. Med. Faculty, Skopje, 1964-79, assoc. prof., 1979-84; dir. clin. lab. U. Children's Hosp., Skopje, 1974-84; sr. rsch. assoc. Pa. State U., State College, 1984-85; sr. fellow U. Pa., Phila., 1985-88; prof. U. Belgrade, 1988-93; adj. prof. Med. Coll. of Pa., 1993-95; vis. scientist NIAMDN, NIH, Bethesda, 1976-77; vis. scientist ATCC, Rockville, Md., 1995-96; dir. BioSciCon, Md., 1996—; primarius Univ. Children's Hosp., Skopje, 1983-86; head lab. for rsch. and devel., Clin. Ctr., Belgrade, 1990-93; mem. exam. com., State of Macedonia, 1980-90. Author: Quantitative Cytoch of Enzymes, 1986; contbr. articles to profl. jours., publs. Postdoctoral intern rsch. fellowship Fogarty Internat. Ctr., NIH, Bethesda, 1971-73; recipient several rsch. grants NIH, Pharm. Co., 1984-95. Mem. Histochem. Soc., Am. Assn. Clin. Chem., N.Y. Acad. Scis., Am. Assn. Cell Biology. Achievements include inosinic acid dehydrogenase assay patent; patent pending tissue injury protective agt.; new concept for the reversal of multidrug resistance of cancer cells to antineoplast; novel methods for cancer diagnosis and treatment. Home: Apt 602 259 Congressional Ln Rockville MD 20852 Office: BioSciCon Inc Rockville MD 20852

SALKIN, PATRICIA E., law educator; b. Suffern, N.Y., Aug. 18, 1964; d. Stuart David and Sheila Diane (Gustin) S.; m. Howard F. Gross, Aug. 17, 1986. BA, SUNY, Albany, 1985; JD, Albany Law Sch., 1988. Bar: N.J. 1988, N.Y. 1989. Asst. counsel N.Y. State Office of Rural Affairs, Albany, 1988-90; asst. dir. Govt. Law Ctr., Albany, 1990-91, acting dir., 1992, dir., 1992—; mem. adj. faculty Renssalaer Poly. Inst., Troy, N.Y., 1990-93, Albany Law Sch., 1992—, SUNY, Albany, 1993—. Editor: Everything You Wanted to Know About Zoning, 2d edit. 1993; contbr. articles to profl. jours, chpts. to books. Active Albany Civic Forum, 1992-96, cmty. devel. coun. Ctr. for Econ. Growth, 1992-95; bd. dirs. Albany-Tula Alliance, 1992-94, Homeless and Travelers Aid Soc. of Capital Dist., 1992—, N.Y. Planning

Fedn., 1995—, Capital Leadership Program, 1996. Recipient Pres.'s award for Outstanding Alumni Svc., SUNY, Albany, 1990, Tribute to Women award YMCA, Albany, 1994, Outstanding Young Alumni award Albany Law Sch., 1996. Mem. ABA (co-chair state adminstrv. law com. 1993—, chair govt. ops. com. 1992—, editor state and local news, state and local govt. law sect.), Am. Planning Assn. (reporter Land Use Law & Zoning Digest 1992—), N.Y. State Bar Assn. (mem. exec. com. mcpl. law sect. 1993—), Capital Dist. Women's Bar Assn., SUNY Albany Alumni Assn. (bd. dirs., pres. 1994-97). Office: Albany Law Sch Govt Law Ctr 80 New Scotland Ave Albany NY 12208-3434

SALKIND, ALVIN J., electrochemical engineer, educator; b. N.Y.C., June 12, 1927; s. Samuel M. and Florence (Zins) S.; m. Marion Ruth Koenig, Nov. 7, 1965; children: Susanne, James. B.Ch.E., Poly. Inst. N.Y., 1949, M.Ch.E., 1952, D.Ch.E., 1958; postgrad. and mgmt. courses, Pa. State U., 1965, Harvard U., 1976. Registered profl. engr., N.Y., N.J. Chem. engr. U.S. Electric Mfg. Co., N.Y.C., 1952-54; sr. scientist Sonotone Corp., Elmsford, N.Y., 1954-56; research assoc. Poly. Inst. N.Y., 1956-58, adj. prof. chem. engring., 1960-70; with ESB-Ray OVAC Co., Yardley, Pa., 1958-79; dir. tech. ESB-Ray OVAC Co., 1971-72, v.p. tech., 1972-79; pres. ESB Tech. Co., 1978-79; prof., chief bioengring. div., dept. surgery UMDNJ-Robert Wood Johnson Med. Sch., Piscataway, N.J., 1970—, vis. prof. chem. enging., 1979-85; prof. biomed. engring. and chem. and biochem. engring Rutgers U., Piscataway, 1985—, dir. Bur. Engring. Rsch., assoc. dean Coll. Engring., 1989—; vis. prof. and exec. officer Case Ctr. for Electrochem. Sci., 1981-82; bd. dirs., cons. various cos., rsch. instns. and govt. orgns. Author: (with S.U. Falk) Alkaline Storage Batteries, 1969, (with Herbert T. Silverman and Irving F. Miller) Electrochemical Bioscience and Bioengineering, 1973; editor: (with E. Yeager) Techniques of Electrochemistry, 1971, vol. 2, 1973, vol. 3, 1978, History of Battery Technology, 1987, (with F. McLarnon and V. Bogatzky) Rechargeable Zinc Electrodes, 1996; contbr. articles to profl. jours. Served with USNR, 1945-46. Recipient Alumnus citation Poly. Inst. N.Y., 1975, award Internat. Tech. Exch. Soc., 1992; Case Centennial scholar Case-Western Res. U., 1980. Fellow Acad. Medicine of N.J., Am. Coll. Cardiology, AAAS; mem. Electrochem. Soc. (past chmn. new tech. com., past chmn. battery div.), Assn. Advancement Med. Instrumentation, Indsl. Research Inst. (emeritus 1979), Internat. Soc. Electrochemistry, N.Y. Acad. Scis., Sigma Xi, Phi Lambda Upsilon. Home: 51 Adams Dr Princeton NJ 08540-5401 Office: Rutgers U Coll Engring PO Box 909 Piscataway NJ 08855-0909 also Office: UMDNJ-Robert Wood Johnson Med Sch 675 Moes Ln Piscataway NJ 08854-5635

SALKIND, MICHAEL JAY, technology administrator; b. N.Y.C, Oct. 1, 1938; s. Milton and Esther (Jaffe) S.; m. Miriam E. Schwartz, Aug. 16, 1959 (div. 1979); children: Michael Jay, Elizabeth Jane, Jonathan Hillson, Joshua Isaac; m. Carol T. Gill, Dec. 23, 1990. B in Metall. Engring., Rensselaer Polytech. Inst., 1959, PhD, 1962. Chief advanced metallurgy United Techs. Rsch. Labs., East Hartford, 1964-68; chief structures and materials Sikorsky Aircraft div. United Techs. Corp., 1968-75; dir. product devel. Avco Systems div., 1975-76; mgr. structures NASA, 1976-80; dir. aerospace scis. Air Force Office of Sci. Rsch., 1980-89; pres. Ohio Aerospace Inst., 1990—; adj. faculty metallurgy Trinity Coll., Hartford; adj. faculty aerospace U. Md., 1982-85; adj. faculty materials Johns Hopkins U., 1985-89. Cons. editor Internat. Jour. Fibre Sci. and Tech.; editor Applications Composite Materials, 1973; contbr. to profl. jours. and textbooks. Evaluator Accreditation Bd. Engring. and Tech., 1989—; mem. Daniel Guggenheim Medal Bd. Awards, 1984-90; mem. Spirit of St. Louis Medal Bd., 1984-89. Capt. AUS, 1962-64. Fellow AAAS, AIAA (assoc.), ASM Internat.; mem. ASME (Disting. lectr. 1989-93), ASTM (chmn. com. D-30 on high modulous fibers and their composites 1968-74), Am. Helicopter Soc., AIME, Brit. Inst. Metals, Rsch. Soc. Am., Plansee Soc., Cosmos Club, Union Club, Leadership Cleve., Sigma Xi, Alpha Sigma Mu. Office: Ohio Aerospace Inst 22800 Cedar Point Rd Cleveland OH 44142-1012

SALLAH, MAJEED (JIM SALLAH), real estate developer; b. Boston, Aug. 5, 1920; s. Herbert K. and Rose (Karem) S. Student, Gloucester (Mass.) pub. schs.; m. Aline C. Powers, Apr. 10, 1970; children: Christopher M., Melissa Rose. Pres., dir. Glo-Bit Fish Co., Gloucester, 1947-48, Live-Pak of Ohio, Inc., 1947-51, Cape Ann Glass Co., Inc., Gloucester, 1950-72, Cape Ann Realty Corp., Gloucester, 1961—, Marias Restaurant, Gloucester, 1960—; pres., treas., dir. Gloucester Hot-Top Constrn. Co., Gloucester, 1967-75; pres., bd. dirs. SGF Corp., Gloucester, 1983-85, SALFAD, Inc. Rossford, Ohio; pres. treas. Points East, Inc.; trustee Christopher Investment Trust; bd. dirs. Lutsal, Inc.; bd. dirs., ptnr. Barsal, Inc., Toledo, Ohio, Hamsal, Inc., Toledo. Pres. Lebanese-Am. Bus. Men's Club; treas. Lebanese-Maronite Soc. With U.S. Army, 1942-45. Decorated Bronze Star. Mem. Gloucester Assocs., Cape Ann Investment Corp., Am. Legion, Amvets, Gloucester Fraternity Assn., Order Ky. Cols. (hon.), Lions, Elks, Moose. Roman Catholic. Home and Office: PO Box 78 56 Hilltop Rd Gloucester MA 01931-0078

SALLAN, STEPHEN E., pediatrician; b. Detroit. MD, Wayne State U., 1967. Cert. pediat. Intern Boston Fleating Hosp., 1967-68; resident in pediatrics Children's Hosp., Phila., 1968-69, Hosp. Sick Children, London, 1969-70; fellow in pediatric oncology Children's Hosp. Med. Ctr./Harvard U., Boston, 1973-75; mem. med. staff Dana Farber Cancer Inst., Boston, chief of staff, 1975—; prof. pediatrics Harvard Med. Sch., Boston. Mem. AMA, AACR, ASCO, ASH, SPR. Office: Dana Farber Cancer Inst 44 Binney St Boston MA 02115-6013

SALLANI, MARION DAVIS (MRS. WERNER SALLANI), social work administrator, therapist; b. Derby, Conn., Oct. 9, 1918; d. John Wood and Myrtle Stowe (Humphrey) Pease; m. Paul Davis, Oct. 15, 1938; children: Linda Davis Looney, Robert, Richard. BA in Psychology, U. Bridgeport, 1964; MSW, U. Conn., 1969. Cert. Ind. social worker, Conn.; cert. hypnotherapist, past life therapist. Caseworker dept. welfare State of Conn., Bridgeport, 1964-65, social worker dept. protective svcs., 1965-67, supr. protective svcs. unit, 1969-73, sr. psychiat. social worker, 1973-75, supervisory psychiat. social worker, 1975-78; dir. psychiat. social workers Greater Bridgeport Community Mental Health Ctr., 1973-82, chmn. housing com., 1974-78, mem. accreditation com., 1974-78, chmn., 1978-81, chief psychiat. social work, 1978-82; pvt. practice psychiatric social worker, 1982-91; owner Winning Combinations, 1983-86. Contbg. author: The Courage to Grow Old. Mem. profl. adv. com. Vis. Nurses Assn., 1987-91; mem. Sr. Citizens Needs Assessment Com., 1987-89; sec., co-chair by-laws com. Washington Sr. Citizens Ctr. Coun., 1987-89; vice-chair Washington Srs. Coun., 1987-88; mem. profl. adv. bd. Rainbow Nursery Sch., 1989-91; mem. evangelism com. Gt. Hill United Meth. Ch., 1994—, mem. worship com., 1995—, coord. prayer chair, 1995—, communion steward, 1995—. Editor: A Witness to God's Love in Our Lives, 1994; co-editor: Washington Sr. Ctr. News, 1987-89. Mem. Nat. Assn. Social Workers (diplomate, registered clin. social worker, mem. exec. com. 1974-75, editorial com. 1975-77), Am. Assn. Marriage Family Counsellors (assoc. 1978-80), Logos World Univ. Bd. (chair curriculum com. 1986-88), Huxley Inst. Biosocial Rsch. (v.p., bd. dirs. 1978-81), Conn. Assn. Human Svcs., Mental Health Svcs. Coordinating Com. (rec. sec., exec. com. 1975-82, corr. sec. 1978-82), Assn. for Rsch. and Enlightenment (rep. study group 1963-79, 84-92, N.E. region core group 1991-94, Conn. study group coord. 1994-95), Conn. Assn. Rsch. and Enlightenment (sec. 1986-88, v.p. 1987-88, chair Conn. coun. 1989-91, editorial com. 1989-91), Assn. for Past Life Rsch. and Therapy (accreditation 1988), Soc. for Clin. and Exptl. Hypnosis, Internat. Soc. Hypnosis, Nat. Guild Hypnotists (cert. 1988), LWV (bd. dirs. 1981-91, pres. 1986-88, chair agrl. study com. 1986-88, co-chmn. mem. com. 1988-91), Acad. of Certified Social Workers. Home: 264B Heritage Vlg Southbury CT 06488-1736

SALLER, RICHARD PAUL, classics educator; b. Ft. Bragg, N.C., Oct. 18, 1952; s. George E. and Arthea E. (North) S.; m. Carol Joann Fisher, Jan. 12, 1974; children: John E., Benjamin T. BA in Greek and History, U. Ill., 1974; PHD in Classics, U. Cambridge, Eng., 1978. Asst. prof. Swarthmore (Pa.) Coll., 1979-84; assoc. prof. U. Chgo., 1984-89, prof., 1990—; dean of social scis., 1994—. Author: Personal Patronage, 1982, Patriarchy, Property and Death in the Roman Family, 1994; co-editor: Economy and Society in Ancient Greece, 1981; co-author: Roman Empire, 1987; editor Classical Philology, 1991-93. Rsch. fellow Jesus Coll., U. Cambridge, 1978-79; Ctr. for Adv. Study fellow, Stanford U., 1986-87; Trinity Coll., U. Cambridge fellow commoner, 1991. Mem. Am. Philol. Assn., Am. Hist. Assn. Office: U Chgo Dept History 1126 E 59th St Chicago IL 60637-1539

SALLEY, JOHN JONES, university administrator, oral pathologist; b. Richmond, Va., Oct. 29, 1926; s. Thomas Raysor and Kathryn (Josey) S.; m. Jean Gordon Cunningham, Dec. 21, 1950; children: Katharine Gordon, John Jones, Martha Cunningham. DDS, Med. Coll. Va., 1951; PhD, U. Rochester, 1954; DSc, Boston U., 1975. Research fellow U. Rochester, 1951-54; from instr. to prof., chmn. dept. oral pathology Med. Coll. Va., 1954-63, prof. emeritus, 1991—; prof. pathology, dean Sch. Dentistry U. Md., 1963-74, dean emeritus Sch. Dentistry, 1977—, ret., 1991; v.p. research and grad. affairs Va. Commonwealth U., Richmond, 1974-85; acting pres. Va. Ctr. for Innovative Tech., 1985, v.p., 1985-87; cons. div. research grants NIH, 1962-66; cons. U.S. Naval Dental Sch., Bethesda, Md., 1966-75; spl. cons. Nat. Inst. Dental Research, NIH, 1957-64; cons. USPHS Hosp., Balt., 1963-74, U.S. Naval Hosp., Portsmouth, Va., VA Hosp., Balt., 1964-74; dental health div. USPHS; mem. Md. Adv. Council Comprehensive Health Planning, 1968-74, Nat. Health Council, 1970-71; pres. Am. Assn. Dental Schs., 1971-72, Conf. So. Grad. Schs., 1983-84; sr. program cons. Robert Wood Johnson Found., 1978-84; mem. career devel. rev. com. VA, 1974-78; mem. com. health care resources in VA, NRC, 1974-77; cons. WHO, 1969-75; mem. Va. Gov.'s Task Force Sci. and Tech., 1982-83, sci. advisor to Gov. of Va., 1984-86; mem. research com. Va. State Council Higher Edn., 1974-84; chmn. task force Council Grad. Schs. in U.S., 1979-82. Contbr. articles in field; editorial rev. bd.: Jour. Dental Edn, 1974-78. Bd. dirs. Md. divsn. Am. Cancer Soc., 1963-70, Am. Fund Dental Health, Nat. Found. Dentistry for the Handicapped, 1986, pres., 1992-94; mem. adv. bd. Va. Inst. for Devel. Disabilities, 1987-91; bd. trustees Middlesex County Pub. Libr., 1994-98, pres., 1995-97. With USAAF, 1944-46. Recipient Outstanding Civilian Service medal Dept. Army, 1961, Disting. Citizenship award State Md., 1974. Fellow AAAS, Am. Coll. Dentists; mem. ADA, Nat. Conf. Univ. Research Adminstrs., Am. Acad. Oral Pathology, Internat. Assn. Dental Research (Novice award 1953), Internat. Med. Informatics Assn. (chmn. working group 1989-92), Sigma Xi, Sigma Zeta, Omicron Kappa Upsilon. Episcopalian (vestryman). Home and Office: PO Box 838 Urbanna VA 23175-0838

SALMAN, ROBERT RONALD, lawyer; b. N.Y., Dec. 26, 1939; s. Samuel L. and Lillian Gertrude (Sincoff) S.; m. Reva Carol Rappaport, June 16, 1963; children: Elyse D. Spiewak, Suzanne A. BA magna cum laude, Columbia Coll., 1961, LLB cum laude, 1964. Bar: N.Y. 1965, U.S. Supreme Ct. 1974, U.S. Ct. Appeals (2nd cir.) 1967, U.S. Ct. Appeals (3rd cir.) 1993, U.S. Ct. Appeals (11th cir.) 1985, U.S. Ct. Appeals (9th cir.) 1979, U.S. Dist. Ct. so. dist., ea. dist.) N.Y. 1969. Assoc. Proskauer, Rose, Goetz & Mendelsohn, N.Y.C., 1964-67; asst. corp. counsel Law Dept. N.Y., N.Y.C., 1967-69; assoc. Phillips, Nizer, N.Y.C., 1969-73; ptnr. Phillips, Nizer, Benjamin, Krim & Ballon, N.Y.C., 1973-87, Reavis & McGrath, N.Y.C., 1987-88, Carter, Ledyard & Milburn, N.Y.C., 1988-94, Phillips & Salman, N.Y.C., 1994-97, Phillips Salman & Stein, N.Y.C., 1997—; adj. prof. Seton Hall Law Sch., Newark, N.J., 1995—. Contbr. articles to profl. jours. Pres., founder The Assn. for A Better N.J. Inc., 1991—; pres. Marlboro Jewish Ctr., 1982-84. Recipient NEGEV Builder award Israel Bonds, 1980, Award of Honor UJA Fedn., 1981. Mem. N.Y. State Bar Assn., ABA. Avocations: charitable and communal work, baseball, reading, writing. Office: 111 Broadway New York NY 10006-1901

SALMANS, CHARLES GARDINER, banker; b. Washington, Apr. 23, 1945; s. Marion K. and Agnes A. (Gardiner) S.; m. Robin Elizabeth Wakeman, June 8, 1986; children: Jonathan, Peter, Charles II. BS, Northwestern U., 1967; MBA in Fin., Columbia U., 1970. Account supr. Burson-Marsteller, N.Y.C., 1970-74; v.p. Bankers Trust Co., N.Y.C., 1974-84; sr. v.p., divsn. head Chem. Bank, N.Y.C., 1984-96; global bank mng. dir. Chase Manhattan Bank (merger with Chem. Bank 1996), N.Y.C., 1996-97; sr. v.p., head of corp. comm. and investor rels. Quick & Reilly, Inc., N.Y.C., 1997—; mem. editl. adv. bd. Grad. Sch. of Bus., Columbia U., N.Y.C., 1984—; chmn. bus. adv. com. Guggenheim Mus., N.Y.C., 1994—. Home: 6 Red Rose Cir Darien CT 06820-4928 Office: Quick and Reilly Inc 26 Broadway New York NY 10004-1703

SALMELA, DAVID DANIEL, architect; b. Wadena, Minn., Mar. 28, 1945; s. Laurie Fredrich and Lempi Christin (Matti) S.; m. Gladys Elaine Hanka, June 23, 1967; children: Cory, Chad, Tia, Kai, Brit. Grad. high sch., Sebeka, Minn. Registered profl. architect, Minn., Wis. Draftsman McKenzie Hague & Gilles, Mpls., 1965-66, A.G. McKee, Hibbing, Minn., 1966, ABI Contracting, Virginia, Minn., 1966-69, Archtl. Resources, Hibbing, 1969-70; designer, arch. Damberg Scott Peck & Booker, Virginia, 1970-89; arch. Mulfinger Susanka, Duluth, Minn., 1989-90; prin. Salmela Fospick Ltd., Duluth, 1990-94, Salmela, Arch., Duluth, 1994—. Recipient Minn. Masonry Inst. award, 1987, citation Am. Wood Coun., 1994. Mem. AIA (Honor award Minn. br. 1985, 87, 90, 92, 93, 94, 95, 96, Honor award Western Rek Cedar Coun./AIA 1994). Office: Architect 852 Grandview Ave Duluth MN 55812-1170

SALMOIRAGHI, GIAN CARLO, physiologist, educator; b. Gorla Minore, Italy, Sept. 19, 1924; came to U.S., 1952, naturalized, 1958; s. Giuseppe Carlo and Dina (Rinetti) S.; m. Eva Tchoukourlieva, Dec. 5, 1970; 1 child, George Charles. MD, U. Rome, 1948; PhD, McGill U., 1959; DSc (hon.), Hahnemann U., 1995. Sr. med. officer Internat. Refugee Orgn., Naples, Italy, 1949-52; research fellow Cleve. Clinic Found., 1952-55; lectr. dept. physiology McGill U., Montreal, Que., Can., 1956-58; from neurophysiologist to dir., div. spl. mental health research NIMH, Washington, 1959-73; assoc. commr. research N.Y. State Dept. Mental Hygiene, Albany, 1973-77; assoc. dir. for research Nat. Inst. Alcohol Abuse, HHS, Bethesda, Md., 1977-84; prof. neurology and physiology Hahnemann U., Phila., 1984-85, vice provost for research affairs, 1984-85, chmn. dept. physiology, asst. v.p sci. affairs, 1986-94; clin. prof. psychiatry George Washington U., 1966-73. Contbr. articles to profl. jours. Recipient Superior Service award HEW, 1970. Fellow Am. Coll. Neuropsychopharmacology; mem. AAAS, Am. Physiol. Soc., Am. Soc. Pharmacology and Exptl. Therapeutics, Internat. Brain Research Orgn., Internat. Soc. Psychoneuroendocrinology, Am. Psychiat. Assn., Soc. Neurosci., Royal Soc. Medicine, Soc. Biol. Psychiat., Assn. Research Neurol. and Mental Disease, Research Soc. Alcoholism, Assn. Chmn. Dept. Physiology, Sci. Research Soc., Sigma Xi. Club: Cosmos (Washington). Home: 8216 Hamilton Spring Ct Bethesda MD 20817-2714

SALMON, EDWARD LLOYD, JR., bishop; b. Jan. 30, 1934; s. Edward Lloyd Sr. and Helen Bernice (Burley) S.; m. Louise Hack, 1972; children: Catherine, Edward III. BA, U. of the South, 1956; BD, Va. Theol. Seminary, 1960. Ordained to deaconate Episc. Ch., 1960, to priesthood, 1961. Vicar St. Andrew's Ch., Rogers, Ark.; rector St. Andrew's Ch., Rogers, 1963-68; vicar St. James Ch., Eureka Springs, Ark., St. Thomas Ch., Springdale, Grace Ch., Siloam Springs; assoc. St. Paul's Ch., Fayetteville, 1968, rector, 1968-78; rector Ch. St. Michael and St. George, St. Louis, 1978-90; elected bishop Diocese S.C., 1990—; chmn. bd. dirs. Speak, Inc., The Anglican Digest; trustee Univ. of South, Nashotah House Seminary, Voorhees Coll., Denmark, S.C.;pres. Kanuga Confs., Inc.; chmn. Anglican Inst. Office: PO Box 20127 Charleston SC 29413-0127

SALMON, JOHN HEARSEY MCMILLAN, historian, educator; b. Thames, New Zealand, Dec. 2, 1925; came to U.S., 1969; s. John Hearsey and Elizabeth (McMillan) S. M.A., U. New Zealand, 1951; M.Litt., Cambridge (Eng.) U., 1957; Litt.D., Victoria U., 1970. Prof. history U. New S. Wales, Sydney, Australia, 1960-65; prof. history, dean humanities U. Waikato, New Zealand, 1965-69; Marjorie Walter Goodhart prof. history Bryn Mawr Coll., 1969-91, prof. emeritus, 1991—. Author: The French Religious Wars in English Political Thought, 1959, A History of Goldmining in New Zealand, 1963, Cardinal de Retz, 1969, Society in Crisis - France in The 16th Century, 1975, Renaissance and Revolt: Essays in the Intellectual and Social History of Early Modern France, 1987; editor: The French Wars of Religion, 1967; co-editor: Francogallia by François Hotman, 1972; contbr. to hist. jours. Fellow Royal Hist. Soc. Home: 1853 County Line Rd Villanova PA 19085-1729 Office: Bryn Mawr Coll Bryn Mawr PA 19010

SALMON, JOSEPH THADDEUS, lawyer; b. Auburn, Ala., Nov. 13, 1927; s. William Davis and Helen (Bowman) S.; m. Mabel Marie Groves, July 7, 1951; children: Joseph Thaddeus Jr., Bruce Groves. B.S., Auburn U., 1949; J.D., U. Ala., 1951. Bar: Ala. 1951. Practice in Montgomery, 1953-93; sec., gen. counsel Alfa Mut. Ins. Co., Alfa Mut. Fire Ins. Co., Alfa Mut. Gen. Ins. Co., Alfa Corp., Alfa Ins. Corp., Alfa Gen. Ins. Corp., Alfa Life Ins. Co.; ret., 1993. Served with USNR, 1946-47; to 1st lt. USAF, 1951-53. Mem. Internat. Assn. Def. Counsel, Ala. Def. Lawyers Assn., Montgomery County Bar Assn., Phi Alpha Delta, Kappa Sigma. Episcopalian. Home: 2731 Lansdowne Dr Montgomery AL 36111-1741

SALMON, MATT, congressman; b. Salt Lake City, Jan. 21, 1958; s. Robert James and Gloria (Aagard) S.; m. Nancy Huish, June, 1979; children: Lara, Jacob, Katie, Matthew. BA in English Lit., Ariz. State U., 1981; MA in Pub. Adminstrn., Brigham Young U., 1986. Mgr. pub. affairs U.S. West, Phoenix, 1988-94; mem. Ariz. Senate, Mesa, 1990-94; congressman, Ariz. U.S. House of Reps., Washington, D.C., 1995—, 1995—. Bd. dirs. Mesa United Way, 1990—, Ariz. Sci. Mus., 1992—. Recipient Outstanding Svc. award Ariz. Citizens with Disabilities, 1991, Excellence in Govt. award Tempe Ctr. for Handicapped, 1992; named Outstanding Young Phoenician, Phelps Dodge/Phoenix Jaycees, 1990, Outstanding Legislator, Mesa United Way, 1991. Republican. Mormon. Avocations: tennis, racquetball, cycling. Office: 105th Congress Cannon 115 House Office Bldg Washington DC 20515

SALMON, MERLYN LEIGH, laboratory executive; b. Macksville, Kans., June 24, 1924; s. Kenneth Elbert and Inez Melba (Prose) S.; student U. Kans., 1943-44; BS, U. Denver, 1951, MS, 1952; m. Flora Charlotte Sievers, Mar. 20, 1948; children: Charla Lee, Merlyn Leigh. Rsch. engr. Denver Rsch. Inst., U. Denver, 1951-56; owner-operator Fluo-X-Spec Lab., Denver, 1956-92; ret. 1992; cons. in field. With AUS, 1943-45, 45-47. Mem. Am. Chem. Soc., Am. Soc. Metals, Sigma Xi, Tau Beta Pi, Phi Lambda Upsilon. Omicron Delta Kappa. Democrat. Contbr. articles to profl. jours. Address: 718 Sherman St Denver CO 80203

SALMON, SYDNEY ELIAS, medical educator, director; b. S.I., N.Y., May 8, 1936; m. Joan; children: Howard, Julia, Laura, Stewart, Russell. BA cum laude, U. Ariz., 1958; MD, Washington U., St. Louis, 1962. Intern, then resident in medicine Strong Meml. Hosp., Rochester, N.Y., 1962-64; rsch. fellow in immunology dept. pediats. Harvard U. Med. Sch., Boston, 1965-66; rsch. fellow dept. medicine Medicine and Cancer Rsch. Inst. U. Calif., San Francisco, 1966-68, asst. prof. medicine dept. medicine, 1968-72; assoc. prof. medicine U. Ariz., Tucson, 1972-74, head sect. hematology and oncology, 1972-81, prof. medicine, 1974-89, founding dir. Ariz. Cancer Ctr., 1976—, regents prof. medicine, 1989—; NIH spl. fellow Cancer Rsch. Inst., U. Calif., San Francisco, 1966-68, rsch. assoc., 1968-72; mem. nat. cancer adv. bd. Nat. Cancer Inst., 1990—; founding sci. Selectide Corp., 1990; mem. sci. adv. bds. Amplimed Corp., SUGEN Corp.; bd. dirs. Synergen Devel. Corp., Repligen Devel. Corp. Editor: Cloning of Human Tumor Cells, Human Tumor Cloning, Adjuvant Therapies of Cancer, 1982, Clinics of Haematology, 1982; mem. adv. bd. Cancer Treatment Reports, 1979-82; mem. editl. bd. Stell Cells, Jour. Clin. Oncology; patentee in field; contbr. articles to profl. jours. Surgeon USPHS, 1964-66. Recipient Lectureship award Gold Headed Cane Soc., 1979, Alumni Achievement award U. Ariz., 1986. Mem. AAAS, Am. Soc. Hematology, Am. Soc. Clin. Investigation, Am. Soc. Clin. Oncology (pres. 1984-85), Am. Cancer Soc. (bd. dirs. Ariz. divsn.), Leukemia Soc. Am., Am. Assn. Cancer Rsch., Assn. Am. Cancer Insts. (pres. 1988-89). Office: U Ariz Cancer Ctr 1515 N Campbell Ave Tucson AZ 85724-0001*

SALMON, TIMOTHY JAMES, professional baseball player; b. Long Beach, Calif., Aug. 24, 1968. Outfielder Calif. Angels, Anaheim, 1992—. Named Minor League Player of Yr. The Sporting News, 1992, Am. League Rookie of Yr., 1993, Pacific Coast League MVP, 1992, Am. League Rookie of Yr. Baseball Writer's Assn. of Am., 1993. Office: Calif Angels 2000 E Gene Autry Way Anaheim CA 92806-6100

SALMON, VINCENT, acoustical consultant; b. Kingston, Jamaica, Jan. 21, 1912; came to U.S., 1914; s. Albert James and Ethlin (Baruch) S.; m. Madeline L. Giuffra, June 11, 1937 (dec. 1977); children—Margaret Elizabeth, Jean Louise. B.A., Temple U., 1934, M.A., 1936; Ph.D., MIT, 1938. Registered profl. engr., Calif. Physicist research and devel. Jensen Mfg. Co., Chgo., 1939-49; mgr. sonics sect. Stanford Research Inst., Menlo Park, Calif., 1949-65; staff scientist SRI Internat., Menlo Park, Calif., 1965-94; acoustical cons., Chgo., 1946-49, Menlo Park, 1949-71, 76—; dir. Acoustical Svcs., v.p., sec. Indsl. Helath, Inc., 1971-76; cons. prof. dept. aeronautics and astronautics Stanford U., Calif., 1977-95. Contbr. articles to profl. jours.; inventor new family of horns, 1942, 46. Pres. Palo Alto Sr. Housing Project, Calif., 1966; v.p. Stebbins Found. for Community Facilities, San Francisco, 1966; pres. Planned Parenthood Assn. of Santa Clara County, 1967, Sr. Coordinating Council of Palo Alto, 1971. Recipient Disting. Alumnus award Temple U., Phila., 1964. Fellow Acoustical Soc. Am. (pres. 1970-71, Biennial award 1946, Silver Medal in engring. acoustics 84), Audio Engring. Soc. (life charter, western v.p. 1958-59); mem. Chgo. Audio and Acoustical Group (founder, pres. 1948), Inst. Noise Control Engring. (pres. 1974-75), Nat. Council of Acoustical Cons. (pres. 1969-71). Democrat. Unitarian. Club: Stanford Faculty. Avocations: chamber music; photography; automobile technology. Home: 765 Hobart St Menlo Park CA 94025-5705

SALMON, WILLIAM COOPER, mechanical engineer, engineering academy executive; b. N.Y.C., Sept. 3, 1935; s. Chenery and Mary (Cooper) S.; m. Josephine Stone, Sept. 16, 1967; children—William Cooper, Mary Bradford, Pauline Alexandra. S.B. in Mech. Engring., MIT, 1957, S.M. in Mech. Engring., 1958, Mech. Engr., 1959, S.M. in Mgmt. Sci., 1969. Registered profl. engr., Mass. Research and teaching asst. MIT, Cambridge, 1957-59; sr. engr. Microtech, Cambridge, 1959-60; 1st lt. U.S. Army Ord. C., Aberdeen, Md., 1960; asst. sci. advisor U.S. Dept. State, Washington, 1961-74, sr. advisor for sci. and tech., 1978-86; counselor for sci. and tech. Am. embassy, Paris, 1974-78; exec. officer Nat. Acad. Engring., Washington, 1986—. Recipient Superior Honor award Dept. State, 1984, Meritorious Svc. award Pres. U.S., 1984, Kenneth A. Roe award AAES, 1996; Sloan fellow MIT, 1969. Fellow ASME; mem. NSPE, Am. Soc. Engring. Edn., Cosmos Club, Masons. Episcopalian. Office: Nat Acad Engring 2101 Constitution Ave NW Washington DC 20418-0007

SALMONSON, MARTY LEE, stockbroker, consulting engineer; b. Wellsville, N.Y., Sept. 23, 1946; s. John William and Alice May (Olson) S.; Gail White, Sept. 17, 1971; children: René, Marci. AS in Engring. Sci., SUNY, Alfred, 1970; postgrad., SUNY, Buffalo, 1971; BS in Sci. and Bus. Mgmt., Empire State Coll., 1979. Engr. Dresser-Rand, Olean, N.Y., 1974-90, Petro-Marine, Gretna, La., 1990-91; stockbroker Franklin Lord, Scottsdale, Ariz., 1992, Charles Schwab, Phoenix, Ariz., 1993—; cons. engr., Phoenix, 1994—. With U.S. Army, 1967-69, Vietnam. Mem. NSPE, ASME, VFW, Moose, Elks. Episcopalian. Achievements include development of state of the art programs for centrifugal compressors. Home: PO Box 26601 Phoenix AZ 85068

SALO, ANN SEXTON DISTLER, lawyer; b. Indpls., Sept. 2, 1947; d. Harry W. and Ann (Malloy) Distler; m. Donald R. Salo, June 3, 1972 (div. Feb. 1983); 1 child, Eric V. Salo; m. Phillip G. Clark, May 5, 1990; children: Ann Potter Clark, Philip Gray Clark. BA, Purdue U., 1969; JD, George Washington U., 1972; LLM in Taxation, Emory U., 1976. Bar: Ga. 1973, U.S. Dist. Ct. (no. dist.) Ga. 1974. Assoc. Hansell & Post, Atlanta, 1972-78, mng. ptnr., 1978-89; ptnr. Grenwald and Salo, Atlanta, 1989-92, Long, Aldridge & Norman, Atlanta, 1992-95, Salo & Walker, Atlanta, 1995—; adj. prof. law Emory U., 1983-86; mem. fin. planning adv. bd. Warren Gorham & Lamont, 1988—. Author: Estate Planning, 1988. Bd. dirs. Auditory Edn. Ctr., Atlanta, 1987-93; pres. Planned Parenthood of Atlanta, 1984-86; pres. Atlanta Humane Soc., 1990-93. Fellow Am. Coll. Trust and Estate Counsel; mem. Atlanta Estate Planning Coun., Atlanta Tax Forum. Office: Salo & Walker 3023 Maple Dr NE Atlanta GA 30305-2621

SALO, HARRY A., health care executive; b. Rahway, N.J., Jan. 27, 1944; s. E. Arthur and Nina (Hill) S.; m. Karen Waugh, Sept. 7, 1964 (div. 1972); 1 child, Jannine; m. Carol Ann Vath, Mar. 17, 1973; children: Jessica, Adam. BA, Cornell U., 1967; MA, Barry U., 1974; postgrad., Columbia U., 1974, NYU, 1974-75. Tchr. Miami (Fla.) Country Day Sch., 1967-69, Fairfield (Conn.) Country Day Sch., 1968-74; MA Barry U., 1969; dir. admissions Fairfield (Conn.) Country Day Sch., 1972-74; adminstr. med. Pers. Pool, Cin., 1975-77; v.p. Salo Inc., Cin., 1977-79; v.p., founder T.S.O.

Mgmt. Corp., Media, Pa., 1979-84, pres., 1984-90, chmn., 1990—; chmn. bd. dirs. Ind. Franchise Assn., San Francisco; mem. Owners Adv. Coun., Ft. Lauderdale, Fla., 1981-82, chmn., 1993—. Bd. dirs. Women Against Rape, Delaware County, Pa., 1985-88; mem. leadership group, exec. dir.'s adv. coun. Amnesty Internat., N.Y.C., 1989—; fundraiser Berkshire Sch., Sheffield, Mass., 1990; vol. Oxfam Am., N.Y.C., 1991—. Recipient L.E. Dettman Founders award Pers. Pool Am., 1981, Raymond Herrighes Mgmt. award, 1986. Office: TSO Mgmt Corp 113 N Olive St Media PA 19063-2809

SALOMAN, MARK ANDREW, lawyer; b. North Brunswick, N.J., Sept. 12, 1967; s. Josef Goldner and Susan (Lind) S.; m. Laurie Jill Greenwald, Mar. 14, 1993. BA in Am. Studies summa cum laude, Brandeis U., 1989; JD, U. Pa., 1992. Bar: N.J. 1992, U.S. Dist. Ct. N.J. 1992, N.Y. 1993, Pa. 1994, U.S. Ct. Appeals (3d cir.) 1995. Jud. law clk. Superior Ct. N.J., New Brunswick, 1992-93; assoc. Gebhardt & Kiefer, Clinton, N.J., 1993-96, Norris, McLaughlin & Marcus, Somerville, N.J., 1996-97, Grota, Glassman & Hoffman, Roseland, N.J., 1997—. Mem. Hunterdon County Bar Assn. Republican. Jewish. Avocations: alpine skiing, cross training. Home: 178 Locust Ln Basking Ridge NJ 07920-3178 Office: Grotta Glassman et al 75 Livingston Ave Roseland NJ 07068-3701

SALOMON, DARRELL JOSEPH, lawyer; b. San Francisco, Feb. 16, 1939; s. Joseph and Rosalie Rita (Pool) S.; m. Christine Mariscal, Apr. 25, 1992; 1 child, Camilla Lind. Student Georgetown U., 1957-59; BS, U. San Francisco, 1964, JD, 1966. Bar: Calif. 1970, U.S. Dist. Ct. (ctrl. and no. dists.) Calif. 1970, U.S. Supreme Ct. 1971. Assoc., Offices of Joseph L. Alioto, San Francisco, 1970, 73., 1972; dep. city atty. City of San Francisco, 1972; assoc. Salomon & Costello, 1981; ptnr. Hill, Farrer & Burrill, L.A., 1984-87, Arter & Hadden, L.A., 1987-94; assoc. Keck, Mahin & Cate, San Francisco, 1994-96; chmn. Commerce Law Group A Profl. Corp., 1996—; lectr. law Santa Clara U. Mem. Human Rights Commn. City and County of San Francisco, 1975, mem., past pres. Civil Svc. Commn., San Francisco, 1976-84; trustee San Francisco War Meml. and Performing Arts Ctr., 1984-88; bd. dirs. L.A. Symphony Master Chorale, 1985-87, Marin Symphony Assn., 1995—. D'alton-Power scholar Georgetown U., 1957; recipient Disting. Svc. citation United Negro Coll. Fund, 1975. Mem. ABA, Calif. Trial Lawyers Assn. (bd. govs. 1977), Soc. Calif. Pioneers, L.A. Bar Assn., Chit Chat Club, San Francisco Lawyers Club. Office: Commerce Law Group 744 Montgomery St Fl 4 San Francisco CA 94111-2104

SALOMON, MIKAEL, cinematographer, director; b. Copenhagen, Denmark, Feb. 24, 1945. Cinematographer, Zelly and Me, 1988, Torch Song Trilogy, 1988, The Abyss, 1989 (Oscar nomination), Always, 1989, Stealing Heaven, 1989, Arachnophobia, 1990, Backdraft, 1991, Far and Away, 1992; TV, The Man Who Broke 1,000 Chaines, 1987 (ACE award); dir.: (films) A Far Off Place, 1993, (television) Space Rangers, 1993.. Office: Am Soc Cinematographers N Orange Dr Hollywood CA 90028*

SALOMON, ROGER BLAINE, English language educator; b. Providence, Feb. 26, 1928; s. Henry and Lucia Angell (Capewell) S.; m. Elizabeth Helen Lowenstein, June 14, 1950; children—Pamela, Wendy. B.A., Harvard, 1950; M.A., U. Calif. at Berkeley, 1951, Ph.D., 1957. Instr. Mills Coll., Oakland, Calif., 1955-57; instr., then asst. prof. Yale U., New Haven, 1957-66; mem. faculty Case Western Res. U., Cleve., 1966—, prof. English, 1969—, Oviatt prof. English, 1990, chmn. dept., 1974-80, now part-time prof. English, 1994—; Mem. adv. screening com. Am. lit. Sr. Fulbright-Hayes Program, 1973-76, chmn., 1975; mem. grants-in-aid selection com. Am. Council Learned Socs., 1976-78. Author: Twain and the Image of History, 1961, Desperate Storytelling: Post-Romantic Elaborations of the Mock-Heroic Mode, 1987. Served to 1st lt. USAF, 1952-53. Morse fellow, 1960-61; Guggenheim fellow, 1972-73. Mem. AAUP, MLA. Home: 2830 Coventry Rd Cleveland OH 44120-2231 Office: Case Western Reserve U Dept English Cleveland OH 44106

SALONER, GARTH, management educator; b. Johannesburg, South Africa, Jan. 18, 1955; came to U.S. 1978; s. Max and Rachel (Aronowitz) S.; m. Marlene Shoolman, Dec. 26, 1978; children: Amber, Romy, Kim. BCom, U. Witwatersrand, S. Africa, 1976; MBA, U. Witwatersrand, 1977; MS in Statistics, Stanford U., 1981, MA in Econs., PhD, 1982. Asst. lectr. U. Witwatersrand, 1977-78; asst. prof. econs. MIT, Cambridge, 1982-86, assoc. prof. econs. and mgmt., 1986-89, prof., 1990; vis. assoc. prof. bus. adminstrn. Harvard Bus. Sch., Boston, 1989-90; vis. asst. prof. Stanford (Calif.) U., 1986-87, prof. strategic mgmt. and econs. Grad. Sch. Bus., 1990—, Robert A Magowan prof., 1993—, dir. rsch. and curriculum devel., 1993-96, assoc. dean for acad. affairs, 1994-96; bd. dirs. Brilliant Digital Entertainment; rsch. assoc. Nat. Bur. Econ. Rsch., 1991—; bd. dirs. Quick Response Svcs. Inc., 1993—. Assoc. editor Rand Jour. Econs., 1986-88, co-editor, 1988-95; assoc. editor Internat. Jour. Indsl. Orgn., 1988-95, Econs. of Innovation and New Tech., 1988-95, Strategic Mgmt. Jour., 1991-94; contbr. articles to profl. jours. Nat. fellow, Hoover Inst., 1986-87, Sloan fellow, 1987-89; grantee, NSF, 1982, 85, 88. Mem. Am. Econ. Assn., Acad. Mgmt. Jewish. Avocations: bicycling, photography. Home: 4151 Amaranta Ave Palo Alto CA 94306-3903 Office: Stanford U Grad Sch Bus Stanford CA 94305

SALONGA, LEA, actress, singer; b. Manila, Feb. 22, 1971; d. Feliciano Genuino and Maria Ligaya (Imutan) S. Attended, Ateneo De Manila U., 1988-89. Actress, singer The King and I, Manila, 1978, Annie, Manila, 1980, The Rose Tattoo, Manila, 1980, The Bad Seed, Manila, 1981, The Goodbye Girl, Manila, 1982, Paper Moon, Manila, 1983, The Fantasticks, Manila, 1988, Miss Saigon, London, 1989-90 (Outstanding Performance by Actress in Musical Olivier award 1990), Broadway, 1991-92 (Best Actress in Musical Tony award 1991, Best Actress in Musical Drama Desk award 1991, Best Actress in Musical Outer Critics Circle award 1991, Outstanding Debut Theatre World award 1991), Les Miserables, Broadway, 1993, My Fair Lady, Manila, 1994, Into the Woods, Singapore, 1994, Les Miserables, London, 1996, 3rd nat. tour, 1996, also The Sound of Music, Manila, Fiddler on the Roof, Manila, Cat on a Hot Tin Roof; Philippine films include Bakit Labis Kitang Mahal?, Dear Diary, Pik Pak Boom, Captain Barbell, Ninja Kids, Like Father, Like Son, Tropang Bulilit; Philippine TV: (host) Kulit Bulilit, Love Lea, Naku, Ha!, Sunday Special, Iba Ito!, That's Entertainment!, This is It!, (co-host) Patok Na Patok!; opening act for Stevie Wonder, Menudo; concerts: The Filipinos of Miss Saigon, A Miss Called Lea, Lea Salonga in Concert, L.A., San Francisco, Les Miserables 10th Anniversary Concert, London, 1995; recs. include Small Voice, 1981 (gold record), Lea, Happy Children's Club, Christmas Album, We are the World, (debut album) Lea Salonga, 1993, Miss Saigon original London cast rec. (gold record), The King and I, Aladdin, 1992 (singing voice Princess Jasmine, motion picture soundtrack), Les Miserables 10th Anniversary Concert Album, 1996, Royal Couyabyab: The Silver Album, 1996, The Little Tramp; TV films include: Redwood Curtain, 1995. Recipient AWIT award outstanding svc. Philippings Recording Industry, 1993, ASEAN Industry award performing arts, 1992, Ten Outstanding Young Men award outstanding debut, 1991, AWIT award outstanding performer, 1990, Presdl. Award of Merit Pres. Aquino, 1990, Laurence Olivier award best actress musical, 1990, Cecil award best recording by a child, 1984, Tinig award one of 10 outstanding singers, 1983, 94, 92, ALIW award best child performer, 1980, 81, 82; named Outstanding Manilan by Govt. City of Manila, 1990. Mem. AFTRA, Actors' Equity Assn., Screen Actors' Guild. Roman Catholic. Avocations: music, reading, collecting raised-trunk elephants, collecting swatches, working on computers. Office: c/o Jeff Hunter 1325 Avenue Of The Americas New York NY 10019-6026

SALONY, JOHN, III, banker; b. N.Y.C., July 12, 1947; s. John and Anne (Sokol) S.; m. Betty Charlene McDonald, Aug. 17, 1973; children: John IV, Jason R. BA, Jersey State Coll., 1971; cert. in Adminstrn., U. Md., 1993. Budget analyst Maher Terminals, N.Y.C., 1969-71; sales officer Provident Bank, Jersey City, N.J., 1971-73, Md. Nat. Bank, Balt., 1973-77; v.p. Fidelity Fed. Savs., Balt., 1977-78; prin. Bus. Cons. Group, Eldersburg, Md., 1978-83; sr. v.p. ops., sales and adminstrn. Reisterstown (Md.) Fed. Bank, 1983—; pres. Time Fin. Svcs., Inc., Reisterstown, 1983—; pres. Reisterstown/Ownings Mills, 1989-90;advisor U.S. Small Bus. Adminstrn., Balt., 1977—. active pub. speaker, contbr. articles to profl. jours. Chmn. bd. Carroll C.C., Westminster, Md., 1982-88; mem. jud. nominating comm. State Md., Annapolis, 1988-94; treas. Cystic Fibrosis Fedn., Md., 1977; pres. Houses, Inc., Md., 1994; baseball commr. Reisterstown Recreation, 1991; co-founder Champion Nat. Handicapped Baseball League; founding pres. Carroll C.C. Found., 1994-96; founder Small Bus. Found. USA, 1995, Appalachian Found. USA, 1995. Co. cmdr. Md. State Guard, 1987-93. Recipient Balt. is Best award, 1979; Senate citation Md. Senate, 1990; Assembly citation Md. House, 1990; Gov.'s citationMd., 1990. Mem. KC. Democrat. Roman Catholic. Avocations: Bonsai, fly fishing, orienteering, book collecting.

SALOOM, JOSEPH A., III, diplomat; b. Urbana, Ill., Apr. 8, 1948; s. Joseph A. and Barbara (Bombard) S.; m. Anne Elizabeth Mayer, Jan. 22, 1972; children: Elizabeth, Shahin, Ilyas. BA in Econs., Georgetown U., 1970; MS, MIT, 1973. Joined Fgn. Svc.; comml. officer U.S. Consulate Gen., Dusseldorf, Germany, 1974-76; econ. officer Am. Embassy, Rabat, Morocco, 1976-78; fin. economist Am. Embassy, Jidda, Saudi Arabia, 1978-80; econ. counselor Am. Embassy, Kinshasa, Zaire, 1983-87; dep. chief mission Am. Embassy, Niamey, Niger, 1987-90; U.S. amb. to Guinea Am. Embassy, Conakry, Guinea, 1993-96; transp. economist Dept. State, Washington, 1980-83, dir. office monetary affairs, 1990-91, dep. asst. sec., 1991-93, dir. econ. policy African-Affairs bureau, 1996—. Office: African-Affairs Bur US Dept State Washington DC 20521*

SALOOM, KALISTE JOSEPH, JR., lawyer, retired judge; b. Lafayette, La., May 15, 1918; s. Kaliste and Asma Ann (Boustany) S.; m. Yvonne Adelle Nassar, Oct. 19, 1958; children: Kaliste III, Douglas James, Leanne Isabelle, Gregory John. BA with high distinction, U. Southwestern La., 1939; JD, Tulane U., 1942. Bar: La. 1942. Atty. City of Lafayette (La.), 1948-52; judge City and Juvenile Ct., Lafayette, 1952-93, ret., 1993; judge pro tempore La. Ct. Appeal 3d Cir., 1992; of counsel Saloom & Saloom, Lafayette, La., 1993—; tech. adviser Jud. Adminstrn. of Traffic Cts.; mem. jud. coun. La. Supreme Ct., 1960-64; bd. dirs. Nat. Ctr. for State Cts., Williamsburg, Va., 1978-84, adv. coun., 1984—, mem. assocs. com., 1986— (Disting. Svc. award Trial Judge on State Level 1988); mem. Nat. Hwy. Traffic Safety Adminstrn. Adv. Com., U.S. Dept. Transp., 1977-80, Nat. Com. on Uniform Traffic Laws, 1986; expert panel Drunk Driving Protection Act U.S. Congress, 1989-91. With U.S. Army, 1942-45. mem. editorial bd. Tulane Law Rev., 1941; contbr. articles to profl. jours. Recipient Civic Cup, City of Lafayette, 1965, Pub. Svc. award U.S. Dept. Transp., 1980, Disting. Jurist award Miss. State U. Pre-Law Soc., 1987, Disting. Svc. award Nat. Ctr. for State Cts., 1988, Disting. La. Jurist award La. State Bar Found., 1992. Mem. ABA (Benjamin Flaschner award 1981, vice chair JAD com. on traffic ct. program 1989-97), Am. Judges Assn. (William H. Burnett award 1982), Nat. Coun. Juvenile Ct. Judges, La. City Judges Assn. (past pres.), La. Juvenile Ct. Judges Assn. (past pres.), Am. Judicature Soc. (panel drafting La. children's code 1989-91), Order of Coif, Equestrian Order of Holy Sepulchre (knight comdr.), Oakbourne Country Club, Rotary (Paul Harris fellow), KC. Democrat. Roman Catholic. Home: 502 Marguerite Blvd Lafayette LA 70503-3138 Office: 211 W Main St Lafayette LA 70501-6843

SALOP, STEVEN CHARLES, economics educator; b. Reading, Pa., Dec. 23, 1946; s. Saul Harold and Byrd (Kalish) S.; m. Judith Rebecca Gelman, Mar. 14, 1982; children: Aviva, Ezra, Joshua. BA summa cum laude, U. Pa., 1968; M Phil, Yale U., 1971, PhD, 1972. Economist Fed. Res. Bd., Washington, 1972-77, CAB, Washington, 1977-78; economist FTC, Washington, 1978-79, asst. dir., 1979-80, assoc. dir., 1980-81; prof. econs and law Georgetown U. Law Ctr., Washington, 1981—; spl. cons., bd. dirs. Charles River Assocs., Boston, 1987—. Editor: Strategic Competition, 1982. Bd. dirs. Lowell Sch., 1989-95. Mem. Am. Econ. Assn., Phi Beta Kappa. Jewish. Office: Georgetown U Law Ctr 600 New Jersey Ave NW Washington DC 20001-2075

SALPETER, EDWIN ERNEST, physical sciences educator; b. Vienna, Austria, Dec. 3, 1924; came to U.S., 1949, naturalized, 1953; s. Jakob L. and Frieder (Horn) S.; m. Miriam Mark, June 11, 1950; children—Judy Gail, Shelley Ruth. M.S., Sydney U., 1946; Ph.D., Birmingham (Eng.) U., 1948; DSc, U. Chgo., 1969, Case-Western Reserve U., 1970, U. Sydney, 1994, U. New South Wales, Sydney, 1996. Research fellow Birmingham U., 1948-49; faculty Cornell U., Ithaca, N.Y., 1949—; now J.G. White prof. phys. scis. Cornell U.; mem. U.S. Nat. Sci. Bd., 1979-85. Author: Quantum Mechanics, 1957, 77; mem. editorial bd. Astrophys. Jour, 1966-69; assoc. editor Rev. Modern Physics, 1971—; contbr. articles to profl. jours. Mem. AURA bd., 1970-72. Recipient Gold medal Royal Astron. Soc., 1973, J.R. Oppenheimer Meml. prize U. Miami, 1974, C. Bruce medal Astron. Soc. Pacific, 1987, A. Devaucouleurs medal, 1992, Dirac Meml. medal U. New South Wales, 1996. Mem. NAS, Am. Astron. Soc. (v.p. 1971-73), Am. Philos. Soc., Am. Acad. Arts and Scis., The Royal Soc. (fgn.), Australian Acad. Sci., Deutsche Akademie Leopoldina. Home: 116 Westbourne Ln Ithaca NY 14850-2414 Office: Cornell U 612 Space Science Bldg Ithaca NY 14853-6801

SALSBERG, ARTHUR PHILIP, publishing company executive; b. Bklyn., Aug. 28, 1929; s. Solomon William and Rae (Miller) S.; m. Rhoda Gelb, Sept. 11, 1960; children: Charles Martin, Solomon William. BBA, CCNY, 1951. Mng. editor Ojibway Press, N.Y.C., 1957-64; advt. and promotion mgr. RCA Corp., Harrison, N.J., 1965-67; editor N.Am. Pub. Co., Phila., 1967-70; v.p., gen. mgr. Lawyers World, Inc., Phila., 1970-72; editorial dir. Ziff-Davis Pub. Co., N.Y.C., 1973-83; editor, assoc. pub. CQ Communications, Inc., Hicksville, N.Y., 1984—; mag. and newspaper pub. cons.; electronics instr.; local campaign publicist, speech writer for town mayor, town coun., libr. bd., sch. bd. Author: Complete Book of Video Games, 1977, Collier's Ency. Yearbook, 1977, 78, 79, 80, 81, 82, First Book of Modern Electronics Fun Projects, 1986, Second Book of Modern Electronics Fun Projects, 1986; editor: Audio Mag, 1967-70, Lawyers World, 1970-72, Popular Electronics, 1973-83, Comm. Handbook, 1973-83, Stereo Directory, 1973-83, Tape Recorder Directory, 1973-83, Citizens Band Handbook, 1976-83, Invitation to Electronics, 1972-83, Modern Electronics, 1984-91, Computer Craft, 1992-93, MicroComputer Jour., 1994-96; assoc. pub.: Amateur Radio Equipment Buyers Guide, 1988, 89, 90, 91, 92, Amateur Radio Antenna Buyers Guide, 1989, 90, 91-92. Publicity chmn. Nassau coun. Boy Scouts Am., 1975; mem. adv. com. Bramson OR Tech. Inst., 1975. With AUS, 1951-53, Korea. Recipient Indsl. Mktg. Mag. award, 1959. Home: 7844A Lexington Club Blvd Delray Beach FL 33446-3401

SALSBURY, STEPHEN MATTHEW, historian, educator; b. Oakland, Calif., Oct. 12, 1931; s. Ralph Thomas and Roma Enola (Connor) S. AB, Occidental Coll., 1953; AM, Harvard U., 1957, PhD, 1961; PhD (hon.), St. Petersburg State U., 1995. Research assoc. Harvard Sch. Bus. Adminstrn., 1961-62; asst. prof. history U. Del., Newark, 1963-68; assoc. prof. U. Del., 1968-70, prof., 1970-77, chmn. history dept., 1974-77; prof. econ. history U. Sydney, Australia, 1977—; also head dept., dean Faculty Econs. U. Sydney, 1980-88, prof., dean Faculty Econs., 1989-90—; vis. asst. prof. Johns Hopkins, 1967-68; vis. scholar La Trobe U., Melbourne, Australia, 1974; Hunter Baillie fellow St. Andrew's Coll., Sydney; vis. prof. history U. Calif., Berkeley, 1987-88; hon. curator Harvard U. Libr., 1989—; dir. Australian-Russia Bus. Coun., 1996—. Author: The State, The Investor and the Railroad, 1967, (with Alfred D. Chandler, Jr.) Pierre S. duPont and the Making of the Modern Corporation, 1971, Essays on the History of the American West, 1975, No Way to Run a Railroad: The Untold Story of the Penn Central Crisis, 1982, (with Kay Sweeney) The Bull, The Bear and the Kangaroo: The History of the Sydney Stock Exchange, 1988, (with Kay Sweeney) Sydney Stockbrokers: Biographies of the Members of the Sydney Stock Exchange 1871-1987, 1992; assoc. editor: American National Biography, 1992—. Mem. adv. bd. Eleutherian-Mills-Hagley Found., 1975-78, Bus. History Rev., 1981-85. Served with USAF, 1955-57, 62-63. Mem. Am. Hist. Assn., Econ. History Assn. (chmn. com. research 1976-77), Econ. History Assn. Australia and N.Z., Orgn. Am. Historians, Agrl. History Soc., Hist. Soc. Del., AAUP, Assn. Evolutionary Econs., Phi Beta Kappa, Alpha Tau Omega. Congregationalist. Club: Am. Nat. (Sydney), Rotary (Sydney), Union Club (Sydney). Home: 28 Wahroonga Ave, Wahroonga NSW, Australia Office: U Sydney, Dean Faculty Econs, Sydney NSW 2006, Australia

SALTEN, DAVID GEORGE, county agency administrator, academic administrator; b. N.Y.C., Aug. 23, 1913; s. Max Elias and Gertrude (Brauer) S.; m. Frances Claire Brown (div. 1983); children: Phoebe, Cynthia, Melissa; m. Adrienne O'Brien, 1989. ScB, Washington Sq. Coll., N.Y.C., 1933; AM, Columbia U., 1939; PhD, NYU, 1944; LLD (hon.), Lynn U., 1976; L.H.D., Nova U., Ft. Lauderdale, Fla., 1983; Sc.D. (hon.), N.Y. Inst. Tech., 1984; LHD (hon.), Hofstra U., 1996. Registered psychologist, N.Y. Chemist Almay Cosmetics, 1934-35, City of New York, 1938-40; tchr., chem. dept., high sch. prin. N.Y.C. Bd. Edn., 1940-50; assoc. prof. Hunter Coll. Grad. Program, 1947-63; supt. of schs. City of Long Beach, N.Y., 1950-62, City of New Rochelle, N.Y., 1962-65; exec. v.p. Fedn. of Jewish Philanthropies, N.Y.C., 1965-69; exec. v.p., provost N.Y. Inst. Tech., Old Westbury, 1969-90; chmn. Nassau County Indsl. Devel. Agy., Mineola, N.Y., 1985—; exec. dir. Nassau County Tax Relief Commn., 1990-93; mem. White House Conf. on Edn., 1955, White House Conf. on Youth, 1960; U.S. resource person on edn. World Mental Health Congress, Paris, 1961; mem. Bd. Edn., Hawthorne, Cedar Knolls, N.Y., 1963-65; mem. adv. council Columbia U. Sch. of Social Work, 1967-69; chmn. adv. council NYU Sch. Edn., 1963-65; chmn. adv. council to Select Com. on Higher Edn. N.Y. Legislature, 1971-73. Author: Mathematics: A Basic Course, 1957. Editor instructional software. Contbr. articles on edn. and ednl. adminstrn. to profl. publs. Vice chmn. N.Y. State Mental Health Council, Albany, 1965-72; pres. N.Y. State Citizens Council, 1957, Nat. Council on Aging, Washington, 1975-77; chmn. Nassau County Local Devel. Agy., 1982—. Nassau County Local Devel. Corp., N.Y., 1982—, pres., 1992—; chmn. Nassau County Cultural Devel. Bd., 1980—; bd. dirs. NAACP Legal Def. Fund, 1964-74; chmn. bd. trustees The Hewlett Sch., 1991—. Recipient citation U.S. Navy, 1947, Mental Health Assn., Nassau County, N.Y., 1955, Long Beach Edn. Assn., N.Y., 1962, Council of City of New Rochelle, N.Y., 1965, Council of Town of Islip, N.Y., 1982. Fellow AAAS, Am. Orthopsychiat. Assn.; mem. Princeton Club (N.Y.C.). Avocations: opera, ballet, international travel, photography. Office: Nassau County Indsl Devel Agy 400 County Seat Dr Mineola NY 11501-4825

SALTER, DAVID WYATT, secondary school educator; b. Augusta, Ga., Aug. 10, 1950; s. Wyatt Jackson and Annie Lee (Coleman) S.; m. Dorothy Mikell Fishburne, Aug. 11, 1973; 1 child, Caroline Elizabeth. BS, U. S.C., 1973, MEd, 1977, postgrad., 1982-92; postgrad., Clemson U., 1985. Cert. tchr., S.C. Tchr. biology Aiken (S.C.) High Sch., 1973—, chair dept. biology, 1985—; curriculum assoc. for h.s. sci., Sch. Dist. of Aiken County, 1994—, adult edn. tchr., 1976-85; bd. dirs. S.C. Jr. Acad. Sci., 1984—; mem. adult edn. curriculum com. S.D. Dept. Edn., 1984; mem. state textbook com., 1989, 92. Organist Warrenville (S.C.) United Meth. Ch., 1963-91, 93—; speaker Prayer Breakfast for High Sch. Srs. St. John's United Meth. Ch., Aiken, 1984; mem. ednl. adv. com. Aiken County Human Rels. Commn., 1993-95. Recipient Svc. award to S.C. Jr. Acad. Sci., 1994; named Outstanding Tchr. in Math. and Sci., Am. Nuclear Soc. Savannah River Sect., 1991-92, Midlands Sci. Tchr. of Yr., U. S.C. chpt. Sigma Xi, 1994, S.C. Acad. Sci. award Excellence in Sci. or Math. Teaching, 1995. Mem. NEA, Nat. Biology Tchrs. Assn., S.C. Edn. Assn., Aiken County Edn. Assn., S.C. Acad. Sci., S.C. Assn. Biology Tchrs. (2d v.p. 1993-94, 1st v.p. 1994-95, pres. 1996-97), S.C. Suprs. Assn., S.C. Sci. Coun., Nat. Sci. Tchrs. Assn., Am. Guild Organists (sub-dean Augusta chpt. 1993-94, dean Augusta chpt. 1994-96), Phi Delta Kappa. Methodist. Avocations: piano and organ music, fishing, travel. Home: PO Box 904 52 Sunnyside Ln Aiken SC 29803-9420 Office: Aiken High Sch 449 Rutland Dr Aiken SC 29801-4011

SALTER, EDWIN CARROLL, physician; b. Oklahoma City, Jan. 19, 1927; s. Leslie Ernest and Maud (Carroll) S.; m. Ellen Gertrude Malone, June 30, 1962; children—Mary Susanna, David Patrick. B.A., DePauw U., 1947; M.D., Northwestern U., 1951. Intern Cook County Hosp., Chgo., 1951-53; resident in pediatrics Children's Meml. Hosp., Chgo., 1956-58, Cook County Hosp., Chgo., 1956-58; practice medicine specializing in pediatrics Lake Forest, Ill., 1958—; attending physician Lake Forest Hosp., 1958—, pres. med. staff, 1981-82; attending physician Children's Meml. Hosp., Chgo.; clin. faculty mem. dept. pediatrics Northwestern U. Med. Sch. Served to capt. M.C., U.S. Army, 1954-56. Mem. AMA, Ill. State Med. Soc., Lake County Med. Soc. (pres. 1984), Phi Beta Kappa. Republican. Methodist. Home: 19 N Maywood Rd Lake Forest IL 60045-3233 Office: 900 N Westmoreland Rd Ste 110 Lake Forest IL 60045-1688

SALTER, KEVIN THORNTON, lawyer; b. N.Y.C., Oct. 21, 1947; s. Hershel Fletcher and Elizabeth (Thornton) S.; m. Eleanor Raftery, Aug. 28, 1982. BA, Iona Coll., 1973; JD, St. John's U., 1977. Bar: N.Y. 1978, U.S. Dist. Ct. (so. and ea. dists.) N.Y., 1978. Atty. Nat. Coun. on Compensation Ins., N.Y.C., 1978-80; coun. James G. Barron, N.Y.C., 1980-81; assoc. St. Regis Paper Co./ Champion Internat., N.Y.C. and Stamford, Conn., 1981-88; sr. ptnr. Kroll & Tract, N.Y.C., 1988-94; ptnr. Peterson & Ross, N.Y.C., 1994—; bd. dirs. Alliance Assurance Co. Am. Inc., N.Y.C., Sea Ins. Co. Am. Inc., N.Y.C., Sun Ins. Office Am. Inc., N.Y.C., London Assurance Co. Am. Inc., N.Y.C., Marine Indemnity Ins. Co. Am., Merc. and Gen. Reins Co. Am., Morristown, N.J., Fortress Ins. Co. Am., N.Y.C., Fiduciary Ins. Co. Am., N.Y.C., Realm Nat. Ins. Co., N.Y.C. With U.S. Army, 1967-69. Mem. ABA, N.Y. State Bar Assn., Brit. Ins. Law Assn. Office: Peterson & Ross 33 Whitehall St Fl 27 New York NY 10004-2112

SALTER, LANORA JEANETTE, corporate financial officer; b. Omaha, Nebr., June 7, 1964; d. Phillip Ray Sr. and Charlene (Sanford) Hinton; m. Howard Douglas Salter, Mar. 26, 1964; children: Ryan Douglas, Erin Jeanette, Evan Tainter. AS, Chattohochee Valley C.C., 1988; diploma, Am. Inst. Banking, 1988; BS, Spring Hill Coll., 1995. Office mgr. Zales, Mobile, Ala., 1983-85; customer svc. rep. Columbus (Ga.) Bank & Trust, 1985-88; adminstrv. asst. First Atlanta Bank, Augusta, Ga., 1988-90; customer svc. specialist Am. South Bank, Mobile, 1990-92; v.p. finance adminstrn. Performance Rehab. Assocs., Inc., Fairhope, Ala., 1992—; treas. bd. dirs. AIB, 1989-90. tutor Am. Literacy Coun., 1994. Republican. Episcopalian. Avocations: biking, sailing. Office: Performance Rehab Assoc Inc PO Box 1100 Point Clear AL 36564

SALTER, LEO GUILFORD, mental health services professional; b. Atlanta, Nov. 12, 1937; s. Robert Franklin and Era Mae (Mask) S.; m. Evelyn Sue Clements. BA, Ga. State U., 1962; MEd, U. Ga., 1966; PhD, U. So. Miss., 1972. Lic. clin. psychologist, Fla.. Exec. dir. Human Resources Ctr., Daytona Beach, Fla., 1975-80; asst. dir. ACT Corp., Daytona Beach, 1980-85, dir. psychology svcs., 1986-91; pres. Behavioral Health Svcs., Daytona Beach, 1988—; adj. prof. Stetson U., Deland, Fla., 1980-91; clin. cons. West Volusia Meml. Hosp., Deland, 1988—; bd. dirs. ARCC Corp., Daytona Beach. Author: Labor Research Project, 1968. Del. Fla. State Dem. Conv., Hollywood, 1984; mem. Dem. Exec. Com., Volusia County, 1991. With USN, 1958-62. Recipient Excellence in Crime and Drug Intervention award ARP, Daytona Beach, 1987, Spl. Commendation award Nat. Coun. Cmty. Mental Health, Washington, 1980, Outstanding Svc. award Dist. Mental Health Bd., Volusia County, 1978, Outstanding Vol. Svc. award State of Fla., 1978, Spl. Commendation award Fla. Coun. for Cmty. Mental Health, 1993, Clinician of Yr. award ACT Corp., 1995. Mem. APA, Fla. Psychol. Assn. Avocations: breeding and tng. race horses, writing, music. Home: 1980 Reynolds Rd De Leon Springs FL 32130-3262 Office: ACT Corp 1220 Willis Ave Daytona Beach FL 32114-2810

SALTER, LESTER HERBERT, lawyer; b. Waterbury, Conn., Apr. 26, 1918; s. Nathan M. and Eva G. (Levy) S.; m. Nina P. Scheftel, Sept. 15, 1951; 1 child, Ellen Lee. BS in Econs, U. Pa., 1940, LLB, 1948. Bar: R.I. 1948. Trial atty. Office of Chief Counsel, IRS, Newark and Boston, 1949-53; pvt. practice Providence, 1953-57; partner Salter & McGowan, Providence, 1957-70, Salter, McGowan, Arcaro & Swartz, 1970-74; pres. Salter, McGowan, Swartz & Holden, Inc., Providence, 1974-95, Salter, McGowan & Swartz, Inc., Providence, 1995-97, Salter, McGowan, Swartz & Sylvia, Inc., 1997—; lectr. Northeastern U., 1955-56; chmn. U. R.I. Fed. Tax Inst., 1972-77; chmn. disciplinary bd. Supreme Ct., R.I., 1975-81; mem. R.I. Adv. Commn. Jud. Appts., 1978-82, ethics adv. panel Supreme Ct., R.I., 1987-92. Assoc. editor: R.I. Bar Jour, 1961-68. Served with F.A. AUS, 1941-46. Decorated Bronze Star. Fellow Am. Bar Found.; mem. ABA (ho. of dels. 1987—), R.I. Bar Assn. (pres. 1986-87), New Eng. Bar Assn. (v.p. 1995-96, pres. 1996-97), Am. Judicature Soc., Am. Law Inst. Home: 75 Blackstone Blvd Providence RI 02906-5413 Office: 321 S Main St Providence RI 02903-7108

SALTER, LINDA LEE, security officer; b. Garden City, Mich., Oct. 10, 1953; d. Bertram Edward Salter and Gertrude Theresa (Barnes) Ashby; children: Korina Reshell Irene Miller, Terry Wayne Tomlin II. Student, Henry Ford C.C., 1990. Security supr. Guardsmark, Memphis, 1979-86; security officer Detroit Newspapers, 1986—; emergency first aid specialist ARC, Dearborn, Mich., 1993—. Pres. Downriver/Monroe County Women Involved in Wings, South Rockwood, Mich., 1991—; mem. Mich. Lupus Found., 1995—, Monroe County Humane Soc., 1993—, Ladies Aux., 9363,

1971—; reunion class tchr. Carlson H.S., Gibraltar, Mich., 1971; ch. treas. South Rockwood United Meth. Ch.; mem. United Meth. Women. Mem. NOW, Woman's Bowling Assn., Woodhaven Moose, Huron Eagles. Methodist. Avocations: reading, travel, horses, sports, gardening. Home: 19544 S Glen Blvd Trenton MI 48183-4901 Office: Detroit Newspapers 615 W Lafayette Blvd Detroit MI 48226-3124

SALTER, MARY JO, poet; b. Grand Rapids, Aug. 15, 1954; d. Albert Gregory and Lormina (Paradise) S.; m. Brad Leithauser, 1980; children: Emily Salter, Hilary Garner. BA cum laude, Harvard U., 1976; MA, Cambridge U., 1978. Instr. Harvard U., 1978-79; instr. English conversation Japan, 1980-83; lectr. English Mount Holyoke Coll., S. Hadley, 1984—, apptd. Emily Dickinson lectr. in humanities, 1995—; staff editor Atlantic Monthly, 1978-80; poet-in-residence Robert Frost Place, 1981; poetry editor The New Republic, 1992-95. Author: Henry Purcell in Japan, 1985, Unfinished Painting, 1989 (Lamont prize in poetry 1988), The Moon Comes Home, 1989, Sunday Skaters: Poems, 1994 (Nat. Book Critics Circle award nomination 1994); contbr. to periodicals including New Yorker, New Republic, Kenyon Rev. Recipient Discovery prize Nation, 1983; Nat. Endowment for Arts fellow, 1983-84, Guggenheim fellow, 1993. Mem. Internat. P.E.N. Office: care Alfred A Knopf Inc 201 E 50th St New York NY 10022-7703

SALTER, ROBERT MUNDHENK, JR., physicist, consultant; b. Morgantown, W. Va., Apr. 24, 1920; s. Robert Mundhenk and Sara Opal (Godfrey) S.; m. Darlene Jeanette Oliva, Jan. 21, 1977; children by previous marriage: Robert Mundhenk III, Wendy Lou Salter Reynolds, Gary Coddington. BME, Ohio State U., 1941; MA, UCLA, 1957, PhD, 1965. Research engr. Gen. Motors Research Labs., Detroit, 1941-42; research engr. Aerophysics Lab. N.Am. Aviation, Los Angeles, 1946-48; project dir. USAF satellite devel. Rand Corp., Santa Monica, Calif., 1948-54, phys. scientist, 1965-82; project dir. USAF WS-117L satellite devel. Lockheed Aircraft, Palo Alto, Calif., 1954-59; founder, pres. Quantatron, Inc., Pioneer Laser Co., Santa Monica, 1960-62; sci. cons. to various industries, 1962—; chief exec. officer Xerad, Inc., Santa Monica, 1973—. Patentee in field. Founding dir. U.S. chpt. Elsa Wild Animal Appeal, 1968. Lt. USN, 1942-46. Recipient Space Pioneer medal Dept. Def., 1985. Mem. Sigma Xi, Sigma Pi Sigma, Tau Beta Pi. Republican. Presbyterian. Club: Riviera Country. Achievements include design and constrn. of Giga-bit optical CD/rom; and an invention of variable-geometry, moving spike supersonic aircraft diffuser. Home and Office: 3277 Peacock Ln Machipongo VA 23405 *My professional goal has been to apply and focus knowledge of new and emerging technologies in the development of large and complex systems to benefit both U.S. defense and the public sector. Examples are the early Air Force Discoverer/Corona and Midas "Spy" satellite programs forerunners to NASA and Planatran, a future ultra high speed subway system magnetically levitated and propelled in evacuated tubeways.*

SALTMAN, STUART IVAN, lawyer; b. Holyoke, Mass., Mar. 16, 1940; s. Abraham and Sidel Esther (Schultz) S.; m. Sandra Lee, Sept. 19, 1964; children: Jason, Michael, Laura. BS in Polit. Sci., U. Mass., 1961; JD, Case Western Res. U., 1964. Bar: Mass. 1965, Ohio 1965, Pa. 1975. Assoc. gen. counsel Internat. Chem. Workers, Akron, Ohio, 1965; assoc. Metzenbaum, Gaines, Krupansky, Finley & Stern, Cleve., 1965-67; staff U.S. Dept. Labor, Cleve., 1967-69; staff NLRB, Cleve., 1969-70; regional atty. EEOC, Cleve., Phila. and Washington, 1970-75; chief labor counsel Westinghouse Electric Corp., Pitts., 1975-88, chmn. labor law sect. Grigsby, Gaca & Davies, Pitts., 1988-90; asst. gen. counsel Asea Brown Boveri Power T & D Inc., Windsor, Conn., 1990—. Recipient Excellence Hon. award in labor law Case Western Res. U. 1965. Mem. ABA, Allegheny County Bar Assn. (chmn. 1986-88). Club: Masons (Holyoke). Home: 23 Ivy Ln Windsor CT 06095-4736 Office: 2000 Day Hill Rd Windsor CT 06095

SALTZ, HOWARD JOEL, newspaper editor; b. Bronx, N.Y., Apr. 11, 1960; s. Fred Raymond and Sheila Lois (Goldberg) S. BA in Liberal Arts, SUNY, Stony Brook, 1983. Reporter Greenwich Time So. Conn. Newspapers, divsn. Times Mirror, 1983-85; with Garden State Newspapers, divsn. MediaNews Group, 1985—; with N.J. Advance, Garden State Newspapers div. MediaNews Group, Dover, 1985-87, editor, 1987-88; editor Hamilton (Ohio) Jour.-News Garden State Newspapers div. MediaNews Group, 1988-89, editor Fremont (Calif.) Argus, 1989-91, editor Johnstown (Pa.) Tribune-Democrat, 1991-96; dep. bus. editor Denver Post, 1996—; mem. adv. com. dept. journalism Ohlone Coll., Fremont, Calif., 1990-91. Bd. dirs. YMCA of Fremont-Newark, Calif., 1990-91, Johnstown Area Heritage Assn., 1991-93. Mem. Greater Johnstown C. of C. (bd. dirs. 1991-96), Soc. Profl. Journalists (bd. dirs. Northern Calif. chpt. 1990-91). Avocations: skiing, travel. Office: Denver Post Bus News 1560 Broadway Denver CO 80202-6000

SALTZ, RALPH, corporate lawyer; b. May 31, 1948; s. Peter and Eve (Bass) S.; m. Linda Bergman, Mar. 15, 1970; children: Erica, Alan. BA, Queens Coll., 1969; JD, St. John's U., 1972. Bar: N.Y. 1973, N.J. 1975. Atty. The Port Authority of N.Y. and N.J., N.Y.C., 1972-76, The Great Atlantic and Pacific Tea Co., Montvale, N.J., 1976-77; asst. real estate counsel Supermarkets Gen. Corp., Woodbridge, N.J., 1977-82, Toys 'R' Us, Inc., Rochelle Park, N.J., 1982-84; v.p., house counsel, sec. Jamesway Corp., Secaucus, N.J., 1984-94; v.p., gen. counsel Rickel Home Ctrs., Inc., South Plainfield, N.J., 1994—. Mem. ABA. Democrat. Office: Rickel Home Ctrs Inc 200 Helen St South Plainfield NJ 07080-3817

SALTZBERG, EUGENE ERNEST, physician, educator; b. Chgo., Feb. 2, 1947; s. Samuel and Florence (Weiner) S.; m. Roberta Rice, Apr. 28, 1984; children: Noah Edward, Evan Hale, Paige Erica. BA in Psychology cum laude, U. Ill., 1968; MD, Chgo. Med. Sch. U. Health Scis., 1972. Diplomate Am. Bd. Emergency Medicine, Am. Bd. Med. Examiners. Resident Children's Meml. Hosp., Chgo., 1974; health officer Pitkin County, Aspen, Colo., 1975-79; clin. instr. dept. medicine Northwestern U., Chgo., 1981—; chief of staff Condell Med. Ctr., Libertyville, Ill., 1996-97; med. dir. The Lambs Farm, Libertyville, 1986—; asst. clin. prof. U. Health Svcs. Chgo. Med. Sch., 1988—. Fellow Am. Coll. Emergency Physicians; mem. Univ. Assn. for Emergency Medicine, Soc. for Critical Care Medicine, Physicians for Social Responsibility, Am. Coll. Physicians. Jewish. Avocations: golf. Home: 620 Euclid Ct Highland Park IL 60035-1271

SALTZBURG, STEPHEN ALLAN, law educator, consultant; b. Phila., Sept. 10, 1945; s. Jack Leonard and Mildrid (Osgood) Adelman; m. Susan Lee, March 10, 1990; children: Mark Winston, Lisa Marie, Diane Elizabeth, David Lee Musselhl. AB, Dickinson Coll., 1967; JD, U. Pa., 1970. Bar: Calif. 1971, D.C. 1972, Va. 1976. Law clk. U.S. Dist. Ct. (no. dist.) Calif., San Francisco, 1970-71, U.S. Supreme Ct., 1971-72; asst. prof. law sch. U. Va., Charlottesville, 1972-74, assoc. prof., 1974-77, prof., 1977-87, Class of 1962 chairholder, 1987-90; Howrey prof. trial advocacy, litigation and profl. responsibility George Washington U. Nat. Law Ctr., Washington, 1990—; reporter Alaska Rules of Evidence, 1976-77, Alaska Civil Jury Instrns., 1979-81, Adv. Com. on Rules of Criminal Procedure, 1984-89, Va. Rules on Evidence, 1984-85, Civil Justice Act Adv. Group, U.S. Dist. Ct. D.C., 1992-93, chmn., 1994—; dep. asst. atty. gen. criminal divsn. U.S. Dept. Justice, 1988-89; mem. adv. com. on Fed. Rules of Criminal Procedure, 1989-95, on Fed. Rules of Evidence, 1992-95; mediator dispute resolution program U.S. Ct. Appeals, 1993—. Author: American Criminal Procedure, 5th edit., 1996, Criminal Law: Cases and Materials, 1994, Evidence: The Objection Method, 1997, Federal Rules of Evidence Manual, 6th edit., 1994, A Modern Approach to Evidence, 2d edit., 1991, Evidence in America, 1987, Military Rules of Evidence Manual, 3d edit., 1991, Basic Criminal Procedure, 1994, Military Evidentiary Foundations, 1994. Mem. ABA (chmn. com. on trial advocacy criminal justice sect. 1992-96, co-chair task force on civil trial stds. litigation sect. 1996—), Am. Law Inst. Office: George Washington U Nat Law Ctr 720 20th St NW Washington DC 20006-4306

SALTZER, JEROME HOWARD, computer science educator; b. Nampa, Idaho, Oct. 9, 1939; s. Joseph and Helene (Scheuermann) S.; m. Marlys Anne Hughes, June 16, 1961; children—Rebecca, Sarah, Mark. B.S., MIT, 1961, M.S., 1963, Sc.D., 1966. Faculty dept. elec. engring. and computer sci. MIT, Cambridge, Mass., 1966—, now prof. emeritus and sr. lectr.; tech. dir. Project Athena, Cambridge, Mass., 1984-88; cons. Chem. Abstracts Svc., 1968-88, IBM Corp., 1970-84. Mem. Mayor's Cable Adv. Bd., Newton, Mass., 1984—. Fellow AAAS, IEEE; mem. NRC (computer sci. and telecom. bd. 1991-93), Assn. for Computing Machinery (mem. com. on computers and pub. policy 1984—), Eta Kappa Nu, Tau Beta Pi. Home: 54 Gammons Rd Newton MA 02168-1216 Office: MIT Lab Computer Sci 545 Technology Sq Cambridge MA 02139-3539

SALTZMAN, BARRY, meteorologist, educator; b. N.Y.C., Feb. 26, 1931; s. Benjamin and Bertha (Burmil) S.; m. Sheila Eisenberg, June 10, 1962; children—Matthew David, Jennifer Ann. B.S., CCNY, 1952; S.M., Mass. Inst. Tech., 1954, Ph.D., 1957; M.A. (hon.), Yale, 1968. Research staff meteorologist MIT, 1957-61; sr. research scientist Travelers Research Center, Inc., Hartford, Conn., 1961-66, research fellow, 1966-68; prof. geophysics Yale U., 1968—, chmn. dept. geology and geophysics, 1988-91. Editor: Selected Papers on the Theory of Thermal Convection, 1962, Advances in Geophysics, 1977—; asso. editor Jour. Geophys. Research, 1971-74; mem. editorial bd. Climate Dynamics, 1986—, ATMOSFERA, 1987—; co-editor Milankovitch and Climate, 1984; contbr. articles to profl. publs. Fellow AAAS, Am. Meteorol. Soc.; mem. Conn. Acad. Sci. and Engring., Am. Geophys. Union, Acad. Scis. Lisbon (hon. fgn.), European Geophys. Soc., Phi Beta Kappa, Sigma Xi. Home: 9 Forest Glen Dr Woodbridge CT 06525-1420 Office: Yale U Dept Geology and Geophysics PO Box 208109 New Haven CT 06520-8109

SALTZMAN, BARRY, actor; b. Chgo., Nov. 1, 1961; s. Bernard William and Cynthia Iris (Gordon) S. BA in Theatre and Drama, Ind. U., 1983. Appeared in theatrical prodns. Rosencrantz and Guilderstern Are Dead, Stage Left Theatre, Chgo., 1984, Chaos Doesn't Run the Whole Show, City Lit Theatre, Chgo., 1986, On the Verge, Body Politic Theatre, Chgo., 1986, The Skin of Our Teeth, Baliwick Repertory, 1987, The Magic Barrel and Other Stories, Nat. Jewish Theatre, Skokie, Ill., 1988, The Little Prince, Children's Classical Theatre Co., Chgo., 1990, Broadway Bound, Briar Street Theatre, Chgo., 1991, Owners, Buffalo Theatre Ensemble, Glen Ellyn, Ill., 1992, The Miser, The Liar, Green Stockings, Festival Theatre, Wis., 1992, Julius Caesar, Next Theatre, Evanston, Ill., 1992, The Real Live Brady Bunch (nat. tour), 1993, Beachwood Palace Jubilee, L.A., 1994-95, Theft, Hudson Theatre, L.A., 1994, The Smell of Ennui, Theater/Theatre, L.A., 1995, The Big Time Jubilee, Acme Theatre, L.A., 1995-96, numerous others; on camera performances include Bradymania, ABC, 1993, others. Adminstr., fundraiser The Hunger Project, 1986-88; fundraiser Youth at Risk, 1988, AIDS Walk Chgo., 1990; group discussion leader, fundraiser Stop AIDS Chgo., 1987-90; various adminstrv. and enrollment roles Werner Erhard and Assocs., Chgo., 1986-90; mem. Human Rights Campaign Fund, 1990-94. Recipient Medallion for Acting Excellence, Amoco Cos./Am. Coll. Theatre Festival, Kennedy Ctr., Washington, 1982. Mem. AFTRA. Home: 319 S Cloverdale Ave #204 Los Angeles CA 90036

SALTZMAN, BENJAMIN NATHAN, retired state health administrator, physician; b. Ansonia, Conn., Apr. 24, 1914; s. Joseph N. and Frances (Levine) S.; m. Ruth Elizabeth Bohan, Dec. 19, 1941 (dec. May 1994); children: Sue Ann, John Joseph, Mark Stephen. B.A., U. Oreg., 1935, M.A., 1936, M.D., 1940; D.Sc., U. Ark., 1989. Diplomate Am. Bd. Family Practice. Intern, then resident Gorgas Hosp., Ancon, Panama, 1940-42; gen. practice medicine Saltzman Clinic, Mountain Home, Ark., Panama Canal Zone, 1946-74; prof. family and community medicine U. Ark. for Med. Scis., Little Rock, 1974-81; prof. emeritus U. Ark. for Med. Scis., 1981—; dir. Ark. Dept. Health, Little Rock, 1981-87; med. dir. Pulaski County unit Ark Dept. Health, Little Rock, 1987-91. Mem. editorial bd. Jour. Ark. Med. Soc., 1989—; contbr. articles to profl. publs. Alderman Mountain Home City Coun., 1947-55; pres. Ark. Brotherhood NCCJ, 1986-88; sr. bd. pres. Florence Crittendon Home Svcs., Ark., 1986-89; v.p. Ark. 4H Found., 1988-89, pres., 1989—; vice chmn. bd. dirs. Ark. Aging Found., 1996—. Capt. AUS, 1942-46, lt. col. USAFR, ret. 1973. Recipient Ark. Man of Yr. award Ark. Democrat, 1975, Will Ross award Am. Lung Assn., 1979; Tom T. Ross award Ark. Pub. Health Assn., 1975, Outstanding Achievement award 1975; Ark. Human Rels. award NCCJ, Ark., 1980, Disting. Leadership award Am. Rural Health Assn., 1985; named Arkansan of Yr., Ark. Gerontol. Soc., 1987. Fellow Am. Acad. Family Physicians (chmn. rural health and mental health com. 1956-71), Am. Coll. Preventive Medicine, AMA (chmn. council on rural health 1966-69, 50 yr. club); mem. Ark. Acad. Family Physicians (life mem., pres. 1955-56), Ark. Med. Soc. (life, pres. 1974-75, 50 yr. club), Gerontologic Soc. (life, Arkansan of the Yr. 1987), Mountain Home C. of C. (pres. 1955-68), Am. Lung Assn. (Ark. rep. to bd. 1964-75, pres. bd. Ark. div. 1957-63, hon. life mem. 1991), Am. Cancer Soc. (pres. bd. Ark. div. 1983, hon. life mem. 1991), Sigma Xi. Lodges: Rotary Internat. (bd. dirs. 1961-63, trustee Rotary Internat. Found. 1965-67, bd. dirs. internat. chpt., Rotary Found Citation for Meritorious Svc. 1982-83, Disting. Svc. award 1988-89), Masons (33 degree), Elks (state pres. 1956-59). Avocation: lapidary work. Home: PO Box 823 Mountain Home AR 72653-0823

SALTZMAN, CHARLES MCKINLEY, educational consultant; b. N.Y.C., Apr. 6, 1937; s. Charles Eskridge Saltzman and Gertrude (Lamont) Saltzman Rockwood; m. Cornelia Metz Biddle, Sept. 3, 1965; children: Cornelia Biddle Saltzman Tierney, Charles Eskridge. AB, Harvard Coll., 1959, MA in Teaching, 1962. Cert. prin. and supr., La. Tchr., coach, dorm head St. Albans Sch., Washington, 1962-66, 67-73; tchr., coach Athenian Sch., Danville, Calif., 1966-67; headmaster Hannah More Acad., Reisterstown, Md., 1973-74, Metairie (La.) Park Country Day Sch., 1974-81, Madeira Sch., McLean, Va., 1981-88; cons. Ind. Ednl. Svcs., Princeton, N.J., 1988-95; adj. instr. Gettysburg (Pa.) Coll., 1988—; dir. Upper Adams Sch. Dist., Biglerville, Pa., 1991-95, 96-97; cons. Search Assocs., 1996—. Capt. U.S. Army, 1959-61. Mem. Country Day Sch. Headmasters Assn. Episcopalian. Avocations: farming, gardening, tennis. Home and Office: 622 Chestnut Hill Rd Aspers PA 17304-9746

SALTZMAN, ELLEN S., mediator; b. Bklyn., Apr. 6, 1946; d. Joseph and Hilda (Lazar) Estrin; m. Stuart Saltzman, June 25, 1966; children: Todd, Michael. BA in Sociology, L.I. U., 1967; JD, CUNY, 1993. Bar: Pa. 1993, N.J. 1994. Fin. cons. Cigna Fin. Svcs., Syosset, N.Y., 1983-84; pension cons. Pension Svcs. Corp., Port Washington, N.Y., 1984-86, Consulting Actuaries Internat., Inc., N.Y.C., 1986-89; mktg. mgr. New Eng. Life Ins. Co., N.Y.C., 1986-89; atty. Vaccaro & Prisco, Hauppauge, N.Y., 1993-95; arbitrator, mediator pvt. practice, 1996—. Mem. task force Women on the Job, Port Washington, N.Y., 1989—, bd. dirs., 1994—; bd. dirs., chair pub. affairs com. L.I. region March of Dimes, 1994—; mem. N.Y. State legis. com. March of Dimes. Recipient Women of Distinction award March of Dimes, 1994, Spl. Congl. cert., 1994, Nassau County Exec. citation, 1994, Suffolk County Exec. citation, 1994; named to Town of North Hempstead's Women's Roll of Honor, 1995. Mem. Am. Acad. Family Mediators, Nat. Women's Polit. Caucus, L.I. Ctr. for Bus. and Profl. Women (pres. 1992-94). Home: 28 Driftwood Dr Port Washington NY 11050-1717

SALTZMAN, IRENE CAMERON, perfume manufacturing executive, art gallery owner; b. Cocoa, Fla., Mar. 23, 1927; d. Argyle Bruce and Marie T. (Neel) Cameron; m. Herman Saltzman, Mar. 23, 1946 (dec. May 1986); children: Martin Howard (dec.), Arlene Norma Hanly. Owner Irene Perfume and Cosmetics Lab., Jacksonville, Fla., 1972—, Irene Gallery of Art, Jacksonville, 1973—. Mem. Cummer Gallery of Art, Jacksonville, 1972—, Jacksonville Gallery of Art, 1972—; mem. Jacksonville and Beaches Conv. and Vis. Bur. Mem. Aircraft Owners and Pilots Assn., USAF Assn., Jacksonville C. of C. (mem. downtown coun.), U.S. C. of C., Ret. Judge Advocates Assn. of USAF (hon.), First Coast Women in Internat. Trade, Cosmetic, Toiletry and Fragrance Assn., Jacksonville Navy Flying Club, Ponte Vedra Club. Democrat. Episcopalian. Avocations: aviation, painting, traveling, swimming, golf. Home: 2701 Ocean Dr S Jacksonville FL 32250-5946

SALTZMAN, JOSEPH, journalist, producer, educator; b. L.A., Oct. 28, 1939; s. Morris and Ruth (Weiss) S.; m. Barbara Dale Epstein, July 1, 1962; children: Michael Stephen Ulysses, David Charles Laertes. BA, U. So. Calif., 1961; MS, Columbia U., 1962. Freelance writer, reporter, prodr., 1960—; reporter Valley Times Today, L.A., 1962-64; editor Pacific Palisades Palisadian Post, 1964; sr. writer-prodr. CBS-KNXT TV, L.A., 1964-74; freelance broadcast cons. L.A., 1974—; prof. journalism UCLA, 1974—, assoc. dir. Sch. Journalism, 11995—; sr. prodr. investigative unit Entertainment Tonight, 1983; prof. journalism U. So. Calif., L.A., 1974—; supervising producer Feeling Fine Prodns., L.A., 1984-92; assoc. dir. Sch. Journalism U. So. Calif., L.A., 1996—. Documentaries include Black on Black, 1968, The Unhappy Hunting Ground, 1971, The Junior High School, 1971, The Very Personal Death of Elizabeth Schell-Holt-Hartford, 1972, Rape, 1972, Why Me?, 1974; spl. producer: Entertainment Tonight, 1983; supervising producer med. films, video, audio, 1984-93; assoc. mass media editor, columnist USA Today, 1983—; syndicated columnist: King Features Syndicate, 1983-92; contbg. editor Emmy Mag., 1986—, Roberts Reviewing Svc., 1964—; others. Recipient AP certificates of excellence and merit, 1968, 72, 73, 74, 75, Edward R. Murrow awards for distinguished achievements in broadcast journalism, 1969, 72, Alfred I. duPont-Columbia U. award in broadcast journalism, 1973-74, Silver Gavel award Am. Bar Assn., 1973, Ohio State award Am. Exhbn. Ednl. Radio-Television Programs and Inst. for Edn. by Radio-TV Telecom. Ctr., 1974, Broadcast Media awards San Francisco State U., 1974, 75, Media award for excellence in comm. Am. Cancer Soc., 1976, Disting. Alumni award U. So. Calif., 1992; Seymour Berkson fellow, 1961; Robert E. Sherwood fellow, 1962; alt. Pulitzer traveling fellow, 1962-63. Mem. NATAS (regional Emmy awards 1965, 68, 74, 75), Radio-TV News Assn. (Golden Mike awards 1969, 71, 73, 75), Writers Guild Am., Greater Los Angeles Press Club (awards 1968, 74, 75), Columbia U., U. So. Calif. alumni assns., Skull and Dagger, Blue Key, Phi Beta Kappa, Sigma Delta Chi, Pi Sigma Alpha, Alpha Epsilon Rho. Home: 2116 Via Estudillo Palos Verdes Peninsula CA 90274-1931 Office: U So Calif Sch Journalism Univ Park Los Angeles CA 90007

SALTZMAN, PHILIP, television writer, producer; b. Sonora, Mexico, Sept. 19, 1928; came to U.S., 1929, naturalized, 1948; s. Louis and Vanya (Liberman) S.; m. Caroline Veiller, Jan. 24, 1960; children: Jennifer, Daniel, Anthony. BA, UCLA, 1951, MA, 1953. Free lance writer, 1958-68; pres. Woodruff Prodns., Inc. Writer: TV shows Alcoa Goodyear Theater, 1959, Richard Diamond, 1959, Rifleman, 1961, Perry Mason, 1964, Dr. Kildare, 1964, Fugitive, 1964, Twelve O'Clock High, 1966; producer, writer: TV shows Felony Squad, 1966-69, F.B.I, 1969-73, Barnaby Jones, 1973-77; producer, writer, creator Intertect, 1973; producer: TV movie The FBI vs. Alvin Karpis, 1974, Attack on Terror: The FBI vs. the KKK in Mississippi, 1975, Brinks: The Great Robbery, 1976; co-writer: feature film The Swiss Conspiracy, 1975; creator-writer-producer TV movie Crossfire, 1975; exec. producer: TV shows Barnaby Jones, 1978-80, Escapade, 1978, Colorado C-I, 1978, A Man Called Sloane, 1979, The Aliens Are Coming, 1979, Freebie and the Bean, 1980; producer: TV shows Bare Essence, 1982; supervising producer-writer Partners in Crime, 1984; producer-writer Crazy Like a Fox, 1985; producer, co-writer TV movie That Secret Sunday, 1986; exec. supervising producer The New Perry Mason movies, 1987-88; exec. supervising producer, writer Jake and The Fatman, 1987-88; supervising producer Columbo, 1989-90; creator-writer The Caller, 1991. Mem. dean's coun. Coll. Letters and Sci., UCLA, Friends of English, UCLA. Mem. Writers Guild Am., West, Caucus for Writers, Producers, Dirs., Acad. TV Arts and Scis., PEN Ctr. USA West.

SALTZMAN, ROBERT PAUL, insurance company executive; b. Chgo., Oct. 25, 1942; s. Al and Viola (Grossman) S.; m. Diane Maureen Schulman, Apr. 10, 1964; children: Amy, Adam, Suzanne. BA in Math., Northwestern U., 1964. Mgr. Continental Casualty Co., Chgo., 1964-69; sr. v.p. Colonial Penn Group, Phila., 1969-83; pres., CEO Sun Life Ins. of Am. and Anchor Nat. Life Ins. Co., 1985-93; exec. v.p. mktg. Kaufman & Broad (now Broad, Inc.), L.A., 1987-93; pres., CEO Jackson Nat. Life Ins. Co., Lansing, Mich., 1994—. Office: Jackson Nat Life Ins Co 5901 Executive Dr Lansing MI 48911-5333

SALTZMAN, WILLIAM, painter, sculptor, designer; b. Mpls., July 9, 1916. B.S., U. Minn. Asst. dir. U. Minn. Art Gallery, 1946-48; resident artist, also dir. Rochester (Minn.) Art Ctr., 1948-64; vis. prof. art U. Nebr., Lincoln, 1964; vis. prof. art Macalester Coll., St. Paul, 1967-68, assoc. prof. art, 1969-74, prof. art, 1974-83, emeritus, 1983—. One-man shows include St. Olaf Coll., Minn., Rochester Art Ctr., 1948-58, Ctrl. Luth. Ch., Mpls., 1983, Philbrook Art Ctr., Tulsa, Macalester Coll., 1982, Douglas-Baker Gallery, Mpls., 1995, Dorothy Berge Gallery, Stillwater, Minn., 1995, also others; group exhbns. include Calif. Palace Legion of Honor, 1945, St. Paul Art Gallery, 1946, 54, 57, Chgo. Art Inst., 1947, Carnegie Inst., 1952, numerous others; spl. invitational showing nat. conf. Stained Glass Assn. Am., 1980, Artbanque Gallery, Mpls., 1989, S.K. Gallery, Mpls., 1990; major watercolor show Premier Gallery, Mpls., 1991-92, Am. Contemporary Artist Premier Gallery, Mpls., 1992; major works include mural Mayo Clinic Bldg., Rochester, Minn., 1953, stained glass Midwest Fed. Bldg., 1968, glass mobile 1st Bank, Crystal, Minn., 1986, copper relief Nationality Cultural Ctr., Internat. Inst., St. Paul, mixed relief sculpture Bryan Mem. Hosp., Lincoln, Nebr., low relief sculpture Temple of Aaron, 1995, numerous other sculptures and stained glass in various corps., chs., pvt. residence, 1994; designer sets and costumes Minn. Opera prodn. The Abduction from the Seraglio (Mozart), 1979. Recipient awards from Mpls. Inst. Art, 1936, Minn. State Fair, 1937, 40, Walker Art Ctr. 1949, 51, Guild for Religious Architecture, 1973, AIA, 1973; honor award for stained glass Interfaith Forum on Religion, Art, and Architecture, 1981, 92; Ford Found. grantee. Mem. Nat. Soc. Mural Painters. Home and Studio: 5916 Walnut Dr Edina MN 55436-1750

SALUJA, SUNDAR S., international engineering consultant; b. Wasu, Punjab, India, June 23, 1927; came to U.S., 1981; s. Wadhaya Mal and Gur Devi (Bagga) S.; m. Kamla S. Grover Saluja, Oct. 12, 1953; children: Bhupinder, Urvashi, Dipender. AISM, Indian Sch. of Mines, Dhanbad, India, 1950; postgrad. diploma, U. Sheffield, United Kingdom, 1955; MS, U. Ill., 1961; PhD, U. Wis., 1963. Cert. mine surveyor and mine mgr., India. Mine engr., surveyor Mining Industry, 1950-53, mine mgr., 1953-57; prof. of coal mining Banaras Hindu U., Varanasi, India, 1957-66, head dept of mining engring., 1966-71, prin. coll. mining & met., 1966-68, dean faculty of engring. & tech., 1968-71, dir. inst. tech., 1971-81; prof. mining engring. U. N.D., Grand Forks, 1982-96, prof. emeritus, 1997—; mem. Univ. Grants, Commn. India, 1976-79; pres. assn. engring., sci. sect. Indian Sci. Congress, 1980. Co-author: Handbook on Mechanical Properties of Rocks, vol. 1, 1974, translated in Japanese, 1989. Mem. state adv. com. U.S. Commn. on Civil Rights, 1993-95; founder, pres. Gt. Plains Forum, Grand Forks, N.D., 1985—, ROUSE Found. For Reclamation of Our Spiritual Environ.; advisor N.D. State Pub. Svc. Commn., 1983-84. Grad. fellowship, Colombo Plan, 1954-55, fellowship in Engring., Nuffield Found., 1959, Commonwealth U. Tchrs. Exch., Australia, 1960, TCM fellowship, U.S Ag. for Int. Devel., 1961; recipient Dr. Rajendra Pasad Meml. Gold medal Inst. of Engrs., Calcutta, India, 1978. Mem. AAUP, Mining, Geol. & Met. Inst. of India (coun. mem. 1966-69), Am. Soc. Engring. Edn., Am. Soc. Mining Met. & Exploration, Indian Sci. Congress Assn. (pres. engring. 1979-80). Achievements include pioneer rsch. on roof bolting (1954-66), blasting mechanics (1961-71), mining of thick coal seams (1964-71), airlift pumping (1976-78), Nat. Reconstruction Corps. (1972), architect of engr. clinic c prototype dev. centres (1963-78), Indian Energy Policy (1979-81), World Energy Policy (1982—), leadership role in saving the $ 3.8 billion coal gasification plant in N.D. (1984-86), rsch. in environ. of human mind to improve the quality of life and its impact on soc. (1992—). Avocations: photography, travelling and study of different cultures. Home: 885 Russett Drive Sunnyvale CA 94086 Office: 467F Costa Mesa Terrace Sunnyvale CA 94086

SALVADOR, RICHARD ANTHONY, pharmaceutical company executive; b. Albany, N.Y., May 19, 1927; s. Domenico and Irma Ida Salvador; m. Carole Snarski, Sept. 17, 1966; children: Barbara, Diana. BS in Chemistry-Biology, Siena Coll., 1951; AM in Pharmacology, Boston U., 1953; PhD in Pharmacology, George Washington U., 1956. Rsch. fellow Boston U. Sch. Medicine, 1951-53, George Washington U. Sch. Medicine, Washington, 1953-57; postdoctoral fellow NIH, Bethesda, Md., 1957-58; rsch. instr. Sch. U. Wash. U., St. Louis, 1958-60; sr. pharmacologist Burroughs Wellcome & Co., Tuckahoe, N.Y., 1960-69; group chief biochem. nutrition Hoffmann-La Roche Inc., Nutley, N.J., 1970-73, sect. head pharmacology, 1973-75, asst. dir. pharmacology, 1975-79, dir. exptl. therapeutics, 1979-83, asst. v.p. exptl. therapeutics, 1983-85, v.p. preclin. devel., 1985-94, v.p. internat. preclin. devel., 1984-96; ret.; sci. advisor Crummy, Del Deo, Dolan, Griffinger & Vecchlone, 1997—. With U.S. Army, 1945-47. Mem. AAAS, Am. Assn. Pharmaceutics Scientists, Am. Soc. Pharmacology and Exptl. Therapeutics, Am. Soc. Clin. Pharmacology and Therapeutics, N.Y. Acad. Sci. Office: Hoffmann-La Roche Inc One Riverfront Plz Newark NJ 07102-5497

SALVADORI, MARIO, mathematical physicist, structural engineer; b. Rome, Italy, Mar. 19, 1907; came to U.S., 1939; s. Riccardo and Ermelinda (Alatri) S.; m. Giuseppina Tagliacozzo, July 30, 1935 (div. June 1975); 1 child, Vieri R.; m. Carol B. Salvadori, Apr. 5, 1975. DCE, U. Rome, 1930, D of Math. Physics, 1933; DSc, Columbia U., 1977; D of Fine Letters, New Sch. for Social Rsch., 1990; LHD, Lehman Coll., 1994. Prof. U. Rome (Italy) Sch. Engring., 1932-38, Columbia U., N.Y.C., 1940-90; chmn. Weidlinger Assocs., N.Y.C., 1957-90, hon. chmn, 1991—; founder, chmn. Salvadori Ednl. Ctr. on Built Environment, 1975-91, hon. chmn., 1993—. Author of 25 books; contbr. articles to profl. jours. Recipient more than 20 awards from univs., engring. and archtl. socs. and ednl. assns., 1970-95. Fellow ASME, Am. Concrete Inst.; mem. ASCE (hon.), AIA (hon.). Democrat. Achievements include research in applied mathematics and engineering structures; 27 new routes and 3 virgin peaks climbed in the Eastern Alps. Home: 2 Beekman Pl New York NY 10022-8058 Office: Weidlinger Assocs 375 Hudson St New York NY 10014-3658

SALVANESCHI, LUIGI, real estate and development executive, business educator; b. Casale, Italy, 1929; came to U.S., 1959; s. Ernesto and Carolina (Bassignana) S.; m. Lenore M. Rickels, Aug. 20, 1958; 1 child, Margherita Lina. Classical Maturity, Valsalice, Torino, Italy, 1950; PhD, Vatican U., Rome, 1958; cert. in real estate, UCLA, 1965. Restaurant mgr. McDonalds Co., Chgo., 1959-61; restaurant mgr. and supr. McDonalds Co., Los Angeles, 1961-63, real estate mgr., 1964-68; v.p. real estate McDonalds Co., Oakbrook, Ill., 1969-83; sr. v.p. real estate and constrn. Kentucky Fried Chicken, Louisville, 1983-88; pres., COO, dir. Blockbuster Entertainment, Ft. Lauderdale, Fla., 1988-91; dir. First American Railways Inc., 1995-96; disting. adj. prof. Barry Univ., 1991—; adj. prof. Sch. Bus. U. Louisville, 1987; dir. Fla. Fun-Train subs. First Am. Rwys., Hollywood, Fla. Author: Location, Location, Location, Renaissance 2000: Liberal Arts Essentials for Tomorrow's Leaders. Served as 2d lt. in Italian Infantry, 1945-46. Recipient Outstanding Italo-Am. award Italian Am. Fedn., 1991; named Colonel of the Commonwealth of Ky., 1984. Mem. Nat. Assn. Real Estate Execs. (co-founder, bd. dirs.). Roman Catholic. Avocations: reading classics in Latin and Greek, mountain hiking. Office: Barry Univ Sch of Bus 11300 NE 2nd Ave Miami FL 33161-6628

SALVATIERRA, OSCAR, JR., physician; b. Phoenix, Apr. 15, 1935; s. Oscar and Josefine S.; m. Pamela Moss; children: Mark, Lisa Marie. B.S., Georgetown U., 1957; M.D., U. So. Calif., 1961. Intern, resident in surgery and urology U. So. Calif.-Los Angeles County Med. Center, 1961-66; practice medicine Pomona, Calif., 1968-72; chief staff Casa Colina Hosp., 1972; post doctoral fellow in transplantation U. Calif.-San Francisco, 1972-73, asst. prof. surgery and urology, 1973-75, assoc. prof., 1975-81, prof., 1981-91, chmn. transplant service, 1974-91; attending surgeon and urologist Moffitt Hosp., 1973—; exec. dir. Pacific Transplant Inst., 1991-94; prof. surgery/pediatrics, dir. pediat. renal transplantation Stanford U. Med. Ctr., 1994—, attending surgeon urologist and pediat.; attending surgeon urologist and pediat. Packard Children's Hosp., Stanford; mem. study sect. NIH, 1981-85, nat. adv. bd., 1986-92, chmn. NIH Nat. Adv. Bd., 1990-92. Contbr. over 220 articles and chpts. to med. lit.; mem. editorial bd. Transplantation and Immunology, 1984—, Transplantation, 1987—, Transplantation Procs., 1990—; assoc. editor Am. Jour. Kidney Diseases, 1987-89. Mem. nat. bd. advisors Agent Orange Class Assistance Program, 1988-96. Served with M.C., U.S. Army, Vietnam, 1966-68. Decorated Army Commendation medal; recipient Chancellor's award for pub. service U. Calif., 1986, Commendation resolution Calif. State Legislature, 1990; NIH grantee, 1974-76, 80-83, 88-90; USPHS grantee, 1986-89. Fellow ACS (bd. govs. 1986-92); mem. Am. Surg. Assn., Am. Soc. Transplant Surgeons (bd. dirs. 1977-85, pres. 1983-84, chmn. adv. com. on issues 1984-87), Soc. Univ. Surgeons, Soc. Univ. Urologists, N.Y. Acad. Scis., Am. Soc. Nephrology, Internat. Transplantation Soc. (bd. dirs. 1984—, pres.-elect 1996—), Soc. Pediatric Urology, Am. Urol. Assn., Nat. Kidney Found., Renal Physicians Assn. (bd. dirs. 1984-87), Pacific Coast Surg. Assn., San Francisco Surg. Soc., United Network Organ Sharing (bd. dirs. 1984-88, pres. 1985-86), Internat. Soc. for Organ Sharing (bd. dirs. 1991—, pres. 1993-95), Am. Soc. for Minority Health and Transplant Profls. (pres. 1992-94), Nafziger Surg. Soc. Office: Stanford U Med Ctr 703 Welch Rd Ste H-2 Palo Alto CA 94304-1710

SALVATORELLI, JOSEPH J., engineer, consultant; b. Phila., Oct. 22, 1924; s. Luigi and Agnes (D'Amario) S.; m. Dolores A. Biello, Aug. 11, 1946; 1 son, Joel Girard. Diploma in Civil Engring., Drexel U., 1954, B.S.C.E., 1956. Registered profl. engr. N.J., Pa., Md., Va., Del., N.Y., Nebr.; lic. sewage/water treatment plant operator; registered land surveyor; With Albright & Friel, Inc., Phila., 1946-71, ptnr., 1959-71, v.p., 1962-71, also dir.; sr. assoc. Taylor Wiseman Taylor, Mt. Laurel, N.J., 1971-75, v.p., ptnr., 1975-85; ret.; cons. in field, 1986—; mem. research adv. council P.S.E.G. Research Corp., 1986-89. Contbr. to profl. publs. Pres. Assn. Island House Unit Owners, 1974-76, 79-84; pres. Island House Condominium Assn., Margate, N.J., 1976-77. Served as sgt. U.S. Army, 1943-46, PTO. Recipient Alumni Achievement award Drexel U., 1959, named Alumnus of Yr., 1976. Mem. Am. Acad. Eviron. Engrs. (diplomate, life, cert. environ. inspector), Nat. Soc. Profl. Engrs. (life), Franklin Inst. (supporting mem.), Pa. Water Environ. Assn. (life, pres. 1971-72; High Hat award 1975, Hazeltine award 1980), Water Environ. Fedn. (life, dir. 1973-76; Arthur Sidney Bedell award 1973, Service award 76), Eastern Pa. Water Pollution Control Operators Assn. (life, Service award 1973, Bolenius-Wiest Clean Streams award 1983), ASCE (life, dir. Phila. sect., chmn. san. engring. div. 1968-69), Am. Water Works Assn. (life), N.J. Water Environment Assn. (life), Pa. Mcpl. Authorities Assn., N.J. Assn. Environ. Authorities (dir. 1972-74, hon. life), Environ. Assessment Assn., Alpha Sigma Lambda (ETA chpt.). Roman Catholic. Lodge: Yeadon Kiwanis (sec. 1968-70, pres. 1972, dir.) (Pa.). Current work: Consultant in environmental engineering, engineering management, forensic engineering. Subspecialties: Civil engineering; Environmental engineering.

SALVATORI, VINCENT LOUIS, corporate executive; b. Phila., Apr. 22, 1932; s. Louis and Lydia (Tofani) S.; m. Carol Hope Rissmiller, 1989; children: Leslie Ann, Robert Louis, Sandra Ann, Stephanie Marie. Diploma, Temple U., 1954; BSEE, Pa. State U., 1958. Dept. head Radiation Systems, Inc., McLean, Va., 1966-68; founder, v.p. Quest Rsch. Corp., McLean, Va., 1968-80; exec. v.p. QuesTech, Inc., McLean, Va., 1980-88; pres., CEO, QuesTech, Inc., Falls Church, Va., 1988-91, chmn., CEO, 1991—, also bd. dirs.; bd. dirs. QuesTech Svc. Co., QuesTech Pkg., Inc.; chmn. Dynamic Engring., Inc. Author: Investigations into Microwave Multipath Interferometer, 1959,Investigation of Luxembourg Effect Utilizing Cubic Function Solid State Devices, 1960, Factors Influencing Communications with Satellites, 1959. Pres. PTA, Springhill Sch., Fairfax County, Va., 1973. Sgt. USAF, 1948-52. Mem. IEEE, AAAS, Assn. for Corp. Growth (D.C. chpt.), Am. Def. Preparedness Assn., Armed Forces Comm. and Electronics Assn., Am. Mgmt. Assn., Security Affairs Support Assn., Annapolis Yacht Club. Office: QuesTech Inc 7600W Leesburg Pike Falls Church VA 22043-2004

SALVENDY, GAVRIEL, industrial engineer; b. Budapest, Hungary, Sept. 30, 1938; came to U.S., 1968; s. Paul and Katarina (Brown) S.; m. Catherine Vivien Dees, Apr. 1, 1966; children: Laura Dorit, Kevin David. MSc in Engring. Prodn, U. Birmingham, Eng., 1966, PhD, 1968; Doctorate (hon.), Academia Sinica, 1995; degree, Chinese Acad. Scis., 1995. Asst. prof. indsl. engring. SUNY, Buffalo, 1968-71; mem. faculty Purdue U., 1971—, prof. indsl. engring., chmn. human factors program, 1977, Fulbright distinguished prof., 1979-80, 81-82, NEC prof. indsl. engring., 1984—; chmn. Internat. Commn. on Human Aspects in Computing, Switzerland, 1986-91. Co-author: Prediction and Development of Industrial Work Performance, 1973, Human Aspects of Computer Aided Design, 1987; sr. editor: Machine-Pacing and Occupational Stress, 1981, Social, Ergonomic and Stress Aspects of Work with Computers, 1987, Designing and Using Human-Computer Interfaces and Knowledge Based Systems, 1989; editor: Handbook of Industrial Engineering, 1982, 2d edit., 1992, Human Computer Interaction, 1984, Handbook of Human Factors, 1987, Cognitive Engineering in the Design of Human Computer Interaction and Expert Systems, 1987; founding editor: Internat. Jour. on Human-Computer Interaction, Internat. Jour. Human Factors in Mfg., Internat. Jour. of Cognitive Ergonomics; co-editor: Work with Computers: Organizational Management, Stress and Health Aspects, 1989, Human Computer Interaction: Software and Hardware Interfaces, 1993, Human-Computer Interaction: Applications and Case Studies, 1993, Design of Work and Development of Personnel in Advanced Manufacturing, 1994, Organization and Management of Advanced Manufacturing, 1994, Advanceds in Applied Ergonomics, 1996, Handbook of Human Factors and Ergonomics, 2d edit., 1997; contbr. articles to profl. jours., chpts. to books. Pres. Lafayette Jewish Sunday Sch., 1980-81. Recipient Mikhail Vasilievich Lomonosov medal USSR Acad. Sci., 1991. Fellow APA, Inst. Indsl. Engrs. (sr., Phil Carroll award 1973), Human Factors and Ergonomics Soc. (past officer), Ergonomics Soc. (hon., life mem.); mem. NAE. Office: Purdue U Sch Indsl Engring West Lafayette IN 47907

SALYER, KENNETH E., surgeon; b. Kansas City, Kans., Aug. 18, 1936; s. Everett A. and Laurene S.; m. Luci Lara-Salyer; children: Kenneth E. Jr., Leigh Green-Salyer. BS, U. Mo., 1958; MD, U. Kans., 1962. Intern Parkland Meml. Hosp., Dallas, 1962-63; resident in gen. surgery Parkland Meml. Hosp., 1963-67; fellow in surgery U. Tex. SW Sch. Med., Dallas, 1965-67; founder, dir. residency tng. program U. Tex. SW Sch. Med., 1969-78; prof. surgery, chair plastic surgery $, 1969-78; resident in plastic surgery U. Kans. Sch. Med., Kansas City, 1967-69; founder, dir. Internat. Craniofacial Inst., Dallas, 1986—; editl. bd. mem. Annals of Plastic Surgery, 1977-79, Jour. of Speech and Hearing Disorders (editl. cons.) 1982, Tex. Medicine (editl. cons.) 1981-85, Jour. of Craniofacial Surgery, 1990—, Italian Jour. Craniomaxillofacial Surgery, 1990—, Argentinian Jour. Plastic Surgery (internat. consultative coun. 1995—). Author: Techniques in Aesthetic Craniofacial Surgery, 1989, Cleft Lip and Palate Treatment Center: A Booklet for Parents, 1994, (with J. Bardach) Surgical Techniques in Cleft Lip and Palate, 1987, 2d edit. 1991, (with others) The Atlas of Craniomaxillofacial Surgery, 1982; editor: Symposium on Plastic Surgery in the Orbital Region, 1976; author various book chpts. Recipient Nat. Inst. Health award public health svc., sr. clin. traineeship Cancer Control Program 1967-69, Plastic Surgery Resident Program Participation award 2nd place 1967-69, scholar. competition (hon. mention) Edn. Found. Am. Soc. Plastic and Reconstructive Surgeons, 1972, Rsch. Grant award Ednl. Found. Am. Soc. Plastic and Reconstructive Surgeons 1975-76, Hektoen Gold medal for original investigation "Spectrum of Rsch. and Clin. Mgmt. of Craniofacial Anomalies" exhibit at AMA, San Francisco 1977, selected hon. mem. Japanese Soc. Craniofacial Surgery 1993, selected chmn. med. adv. bd. Children's Craniofacial Assn. 1993; grantee Internat. NIH Microvascular Surg. Rsch. 1969, Vets. Admin. Hosp. Maxillofacial Rsch. 1972-78, Sid Richardson Found. med. rsch. 1975-76, Gen. Electric Found. for Craniofacial Deformities 1985-87; recipient various awards for videos. Mem. AMA (mem. various coms.), Am. Acad. Pediat. (exec. com. section on plastic surgery, founding mem., sec.-treas. 1987-90, chmn. 1991—), Am. Assn. of Pediat. Plastic Surgery (founding mem., chmn. 1991—), Am. Assn. Plastic Surgery (mem. various coms.), Am. Burn Assn., Am. Cleft Palate Assn. (mem. various coms.), Am. Coll. Surgeons, Am. Soc. for Aesthetic Plastic Surgery, Am. Soc. Maxiofacial Surgery (mem. various coms.), Am. Soc. Plastic and Reconstructive Surgery (mem. various coms.), Am. Soc. for Reconstructive Microsurgery, Argentine Soc. of Plastic Surgery, Children's Craniofacial Assn. (chmn. med. adv. bd.), Chirugio Soc., Craniofacial Biology Group, Dallas County Med. Soc., Dallas Soc. Plastic Surgery, Euro. Assn. for Craniomaxillofacial Surgery, Internat. Coll. Surgeons, Internat. Confederation for Plastic Reconstructive Surgery (founding mem.), Internat. Craniofacial Club, Internat. Craniofacial Travel Club, Internat. Soc. Clin. Plastic Surgery, Internat. Soc. Cranofacial Surgery (hon. mem.), Lipoplasty Soc. of N.A., Inc., McKorkle Soc., Pan-Pacific Surg. Assn., Physicians Art Assn., Plastic Surgery Rsch. Coun., Soc. for Biomaterials, Soc. Craniofacial Genetics, Soc. Head and Neck Surgery, So. Med. Assn., Southwestern Med. Found., Tex. Soc. Plastic Surgery (mem. various coms., pres.-elect 1982-83, pres. 1983-84), Tex. State Med. Assn., Wound Healing Soc. Avocations: skiing, running, travel. Office: Internat Cranio Inst 7777 Forest Ln Ste C717 Dallas TX 75230-2518

SALYER, STEPHEN LEE, broadcast executive; b. Lexington, Ky., July 20, 1950; s. Ralph Conley Salyer and Margaret (Greenlee) Miles; m. Martha Ingels Ruddy, Apr. 21, 1985; children: Samuel Wilmot, Duncan Davis, Clara Josephine. BA, Davidson Coll., 1972; MPA, Harvard U., 1975. Pres. Citizens' Com. on Population and the Am. Future, Washington, 1972-73; cons. to John D. Rockefeller 3d Rockefeller Family Assocs., N.Y.C., 1973-75; assoc. pub. issues program Population Coun., N.Y.C., 1977-79; asst. to the pres. Ednl. Broadcasting Corp., Sta. WNET TV, N.Y.C., 1975-76, v.p. corp. affairs, 1979-80, v.p. program devel. and mktg., 1981-82, sr. v.p. edn. divsn., 1982-86, sr. v.p. mktg. and comm., 1986-88; pres., CEO Pub. Radio Internat., Mpls., 1988—, also bd. dirs.; bd. dirs. Minn. Meeting; mem. nat. adv. com. Save the Children, 1991—, Nat. Peace Found., 1991—. Co-author: (with James J. Bausch) Toward Safe, Convenient and Effective Contraceptives, 1978. Fellow Japan Soc. U.S.-Japan Leadership, 1996; mem. Nat. Commn. on Population Growth and the Am. Future, Washington, 1970-72. Mem. Harvard Club (N.Y.C.), Mpls. Club., Japan Soc. Avocations: tennis, reading. Home: 1801 Irving Ave S Minneapolis MN 55403-2822 Office: Pub Radio Internat 100 N 6th St Ste 900 A Minneapolis MN 55403-1516

SALZBERG, BRIAN MATTHEW, neuroscience and physiology educator; b. N.Y.C., Sept. 4, 1942; s. Saul and Betty Bernice (Jacobs) S. BS, Yale U., 1963; PhD, Harvard U., 1971. Woodrow Wilson fellow in physics Harvard U., Cambridge, Mass., 1963-64, rsch. asst. in high energy physics, 1964-71; rsch. assoc. physiology Yale Med. Sch., New Haven, 1971-75; asst. prof. physiology U. Pa. Sch. Dental Medicine, Phila., 1975-80; assoc. prof. physiology U. Pa., Phila., 1980-82; prof. physiology U. Pa. Sch. Medicine, Phila., 1982-92, prof. neurosci. and physiology, 1992—; Arthur Rosenblueth vis. prof. CINVESTAV, Mexico City, 1987. Contbr. over 100 sci. articles on neurophysiology and biophysics to profl. jours. Trustee Marine Biol. Lab., Woods Hole, Mass., 1980-84, 87-95. Guest fellow Royal Soc., Cambridge U., 1991, fellow Japan Soc. for Promotion of Sci., Tokyo, 1989, STEPS fellow Marine Biol. Lab., 1977, 78; recipient Marine Biol. Lab. award, 1981. Fellow Am. Phys. Soc., AAAS; mem. Biophys. Soc. (exec. bd. 1987-90), Soc. Gen. Physioloists (coun. 1986-88), Phi Beta Kappa, Sigma Xi. Achievements include co-discovery of voltage-sensitive merocyanine, styryl, oxonol and cyanine dyes; application of optical methods to cell physiology and neuroscience. Avocation: marathon runner. Home: 4632 Spruce St Philadelphia PA 19139-4540 Office: U Pa Physiology Dept 234 Stemmler Hall Philadelphia PA 19104-6074

SALZBERG, EMMETT RUSSELL, new product developer; b. N.Y.C., Aug. 15, 1924; s. Herman and Freda (Russell) S.; m. Ilene Roslyn Greenhut, Oct. 29, 1960; children: Shelby Russell, Laurie Russell. Grad., Bronx High Sch. of Sci., 1941; student, Columbia U., CCNY. Pres. Dixey Tapes Corp., Stratford, Conn., 1969-85; sr. product mgr. Tuck Tape, New Rochelle, N.Y., 1986-88; pres. Dixey Tapes Corp., Stratford, 1993—; cons. Tape div. Shuford Mills, Hickory, N.C., 1990-92. Patentee telephone answering equipment. Mem. Trumbull Yr.-Round. Edn. Feasibility Study Com.; bd. dirs. Trumbull Librs., 1997. Served with U.S. Army, 1943-45, PTO. Mem. Mensa (pres. So. Conn. chpt. 1996), Inventors Assn. Conn. (co-founder, past mem. exec. bd.). Democrat. Jewish. Avocations: target shooting, photography. Home: 37 Partridge Ln Trumbull CT 06611-4919 Office: Dixey Tapes Corp 959 Main St Stratford CT 06497-7400

SALZER, JOHN MICHAEL, technical and management consultant; b. Vienna, Austria, Sept. 12, 1917; came to U.S., 1940; s. Siegfried and Rose (Deutsch) S.; m. Eva R. Arvay, Mar. 26, 1944; children: Arleen, Ronald, Myra, Gary. BSEE, Case Inst. Tech., 1947, MSEE, 1948; ScDEE, MIT, 1951. Instr. in mechanics and electronics Case Inst. Tech., Cleve., 1947-48; rsch. assoc. Electronic Computer Lab., MIT, Cambridge, Mass., 1948-51; mem. tech. staff Hughes Aircraft Co., El Segundo, Calif., group mgr., 1951-54; asst. dir rsch. lab. Maganvox Co., L.A., 1954-59, dir. systems, 1959; dir. Intellectronics Labs. TRW Inc., 1959-62, spl. asst. to exec. v.p. corp. planning, 1962-63; v.p. tech. and planning Librascope div. Singer Co. Inc., 1963-69; pres. Salzer Tech. Enterprises Inc., tech. and mgmt. cons., Santa Monica, Calif., 1968—. Author: Evolutionary Design of Complex Systems, 1961, Sampled-Data Theory, 1961. Fellow IEEE, Inst. Advancement Engring; mem. Internat. Soc. Hybrid Microelectronics, Semicondr. Equipment and Materials Inst., Sigma Xi, Tau Beta Pi, Eta Kappa Nu. Office: Salzer Tech Enterprises Inc 909 Berkeley St Santa Monica CA 90403-2307

SALZER, LOUIS WILLIAM, chemist; b. Cleve., Sept. 3, 1918; s. Louis and Anna (Froelich) S.; m. Shirley R. Robinson, July 2, 1956. BS in Edn., Kent State U., 1940, postgrad., 1941. Chemist/mass spectromopist Standard Oil Co. Ohio, Cleve., 1944-54; tng. engr. mass spectrometry Consol. Electrodynamics, Pasadena, 1954-58; prof. chemistry Fenn Coll., Cleve., 1956-59; devel. scientist B.F. Goodrich Co., Avon Lake, Ohio, 1959-75; on line analytical process instrumentation specialist B.F. Goodrich Co., U.S., Can., France, Italy, Wales, Japan, 1963-72, Venezuela, 1982; cons on line analytical instrumentation/mass spectrometry Dunedin, Fla., 1975—; tng. engr. mass spectrometer atomic energy establishment, India, 1958. Mem. ACS, Instrument Soc. Am. Republican. Lutheran. *Personal philosophy: In my formative years I believed in researching every aspect of the analytical instrumentation and related fields. I felt that there were many attainable challenges in the profession. Through these efforts many innovations in analytical instruments were made. These results were achieved by close cooperation with my fellow scientists from many branches of the scientific community.*

SALZINGER, MARK ALAN, editor, violinist; b. Cleve., Nov. 20, 1965; s. Carl Benjamin and Margriet Regina Salzinger. BA in Econs. with honors, U. Chgo., 1988; MBA, Cornell U., 1992. Economist U.S. Dept. of Labor, Washington, 1988-89; rschr./writer KCI Comm., Alexandria, Va., 1989-90; investment assoc. J & W Seligman, N.Y.C., 1992-94; sr. analyst Citicorp, N.Y.C., 1994-95; mng. editor Fin. Svcs. Assocs., Alexandria, 1995-96, exec. editor, 1996—; violinist Arlington (Va.) Symphony, 1988-90, 95-97, Fairfax (Va.) Symphony, 1988-90. Intern Voinovich for Senate, Cleve., 1987. Republican. Avocations: violin playing, fantasy football, baseball and basketball, exercise. Home: 820 Bashford Ln Alexandria VA 22314 Office: Financial Services Assocs 1750 Old Meadow Rd Mc Lean VA 22102-4304

SALZMAN, ARTHUR GEORGE, architect; b. Chgo., June 20, 1929; s. Russell Harvey Salzman and Mildred Olive (Olsen) Erickson; m. Joan Marie Larson, Aug. 16, 1952; children: Lisa Jo Salzman Braucher, David Ralph. BS in Archtl. Engring., U. Ill., 1952; MArch, Ill. Inst. Tech., 1960. Registered architect, Ill., Mich., Nat. Coun. Archtl. Registration Bds. Architect Skidmore, Owings & Merrill, Chgo., 1960, Mies van der Rohe, Arch., Chgo., 1960-69; assoc. The Office of Mies Van Der Rohe, Chgo., 1969-81; v.p. FCL Assocs., Chgo., 1981-86; ex. v.p. Lohan Assocs., Chgo., 1986-91; pvt. practice architecture Evanston, Ill., 1992—; mem. Bldg. Code Restructuring Com., City of Chgo., 1994-96; Bldg. Code Electronic Version Com., City of Chgo., 1997. Mem. Chgo. Com. on High Rise Bldgs.; bd. dirs. Savoy Aires, Evanston, 1985-88, 90-93, pres. 1992-93; v.p. Chgo. area Unitarian-Universalist Coun., Chgo., 1974-76. Cpl. U.S. Army, 1952-54. Mem. AIA (bd. dirs. Chgo. chpt. 1992-96, sec. 1994-96), Constrn. Specifications Inst., Bldg. Ofcls. and Code Adminstrs. Internat. (profl.), Coun. on Tall Bldgs. and Urban Habitat (alt. del. AIA Ill. coun. 1997—), The American Assn. for Wind Engring., Precast-Prestressed Concrete Inst., Cliff Dwellers Club. Avocations: community theater, choral singing, sailing. Home: 1018 Greenwood St Evanston IL 60201-4212 Office: 1603 Orrington Ave Ste 1060 Evanston IL 60201-5000

SALZMAN, DAVID ELLIOT, entertainment industry executive; b. Bklyn., Dec. 1, 1943; s. Benjamin and Rose Harriet (Touby) S.; m. Sonia Camelia Gonsalves, Oct. 19, 1968; children: Daniel Mark, Andrea Jessica, Adam Gabriel. B.A., Bklyn. Coll., 1965; M.A., Wayne State U., 1967. Dir. TV ops. Wayne State U., 1966-67; producer Lou Gordon Program, 1967-70; program mgr. Sta. WKBD-TV, Detroit, 1970-71; program mgr. Sta. KDKA-TV, Pitts., 1971-72, gen. mgr., 1973-75; program mgr. Sta. KYW-TV, Phila., 1972-73; chmn. bd. Group W Prodns., N.Y.C and Los Angeles, 1975—; founder, pres. United Software Assocs., 1980-81; creator News Info. Weekly Service, 1981; exec. v.p. Telepictures Corp., 1980-84, vice chmn., 1984; pres. Lorimar Telepictures Corp. (merger Telepictures and Lorimar, Inc.), 1985-90, Lorimar TV, 1986-90; creator Newscope: Nat. TV News Cooperative, 1983; pres., CEO David Salzman Entertainment, Burbank, Calif., 1990-93; co-CEO Quincy Jones-David Salzman Entertainment (QDE), 1993—; exec. prodr. Jenny Jones Show, 1991—; exec. prodr. Mad-TV, In the House, 68th Ann. Acad. awards; co-owner QD7 Interactive, 1994; bd. dirs. Premiere Radio, 1994, 7th Level; guest lectr. at schs.; bd. govs. Films of Coll. and Univ. Students. Contbr. articles to Variety and numerous communications trade publs. Bd. dirs. Pitts. Civic Light Opera, Am. Blood Bank, Pitts., Hebrew Inst., Jewish Community Ctr., Harrison, N.Y., Temple Etz Chaim, USC Sch. Cinema-TV, Emory U. Ctr. for Leadership, Emory Bus. Sch., Bklyn. Coll. Found. Recipient award Detroit chpt. Am. Women in Radio and TV, 1969, award Golden Quill, 1971, award Golden Gavel, 1971, local Emmy award, 1972, award AP, 1974, Gold medal Broadcast Promotion Assn., 1983, Lifetime Achievement award Bklyn. Coll., 1990, Disting. Alumnus award, Golden Plate award Am. Acad. Achievement, 1995; BPME Gold medal San Francisco Film Festival, 1984, N.Y., 1985, Chgo., 1986, Tree of Life award Jewish Nat. Fund, 1988. Mem. Acad. TV Arts and Scis., Nat. Assn. TV Program Execs., Radio-TV News Dirs. Assn., Am. Mgmt. Assn., Am. Film Inst., Brooklyn Coll. Found. Office: QDE Entertainment 3800 Barham Blvd Ste 503 Los Angeles CA 90068-1042 *"Courage is the first of human qualities because it is the quality which guarantees all the others."**

SALZMAN, EDWIN WILLIAM, surgery educator; b. St. Louis, Dec. 11, 1928; s. J. Marvin and Sophie (Brook) S.; m. Nancy Lurie Salzman, Nov. 27, 1954; children: Andrew, David, James. AB, Washington U., St. Louis, 1950, MD, 1953; MA (hon.), Harvard U., 1969. Resident in surgery Mass. Gen. Hosp., Boston, 1953-61, asst. surgeon, 1961-66; instr. in med. sci. Harvard Med. Sch., Boston, 1961-62, asst. prof. surgery, 1967-69, assoc. prof. surgery, 1969-72, prof. surgery, 1972—; assoc. dir. surgery Beth Israel Hosp., Boston, 1966-82. Author books; dep. editor New Eng. Jour. Medicine, 1981-94; contbr. numerous articles to profl. jours. Capt. USAF, 1954-56. Vis. scholar Corpus Christi Coll., Cambridge, Eng., 1976-77; recipient Disting. Achievement award Am. Heart Assn., 1986. Mem. Am. Soc. Clin. Investigations, Am. Soc. Hematology, Am. Surg. Assn., Internat. Soc. Thrombosis and Haemostasis (Disting. Career award 1991), Internat. Cardiovascular Soc., Soc. Vascular Surgery, Am. Coll. Surgeons, New Eng. Surg. Soc. Jewish. Office: Beth Israel Hosp 330 Brookline Ave Boston MA 02215-5400

SALZMAN, ERIC, composer, writer; b. N.Y.C., Sept. 8, 1933; s. Samuel and Frances (Klenett) S.; m. Lorna Jackson, Dec. 24, 1955; children: Eva, Stephanie. BA in Music with honors, Columbia U., 1954; MFA, Princeton U., 1956. Music critic N.Y. Times, N.Y.C., 1958-62; dir. music Sta. WBAI-FM, N.Y.C., 1962-64, 68-72; music critic N.Y. Herald Tribune, N.Y.C., 1964-67; asst. prof. Queens Coll. CUNY, Queens, 1967-68; artistic dir. Quog Music Theater, N.Y.C., 1970-80; co-founder, artistic dir. Am. Music Theater Festival, Phila., 1981-94; founder, co-artistic dir. MusicTheater/N.Y., 1994—; mem. guest faculty NYU, Yale U., Banff Ctr. for Arts, Can., Conservatoire Nationale, Lyon, France; organizer ann. conf. Small Scale Opera and Music Theatre, Brussels, 1992, Antwerp, Belgium, 1983, Colmar, 1994; founder, artistic dir. Electric Ear, Electric Circus, N.Y.C., 1967-68, New Image of Sound, Hunter Coll., N.Y.C., 1968-71, Free Music Store, N.Y.C., 1978-82. Principal works include: (compositions) String Quartet, 1955, Sonata for Flute and Piano, 1956, Night Dance for Orch., 1957, Whitman Songs for Voice and Piano, 1955-57, Cummings Set for Voice and Piano, 1958, Partita for Violin, 1958, Inventions for Orch., 1957, In Praise of the Owl and the Cuckoo for Soprano, Guitar, Violin, and Viola, 1963, Foxes and Hedgehogs, Verses and Cantos for 4 Voices, two Instrumental Groups with Sound Sys., 1964, Queens Collage An Acad. Festival Overture for Tape, 1966, Larynx Music Verses for Soprano, Guitar, and 4 track Tape, 1966, Helix, 1971, Fantasy on Lazarus, 1974, Accord, 1975, Variations on Sacred Harp Tunes, 1982, and numerous others, (radio opera) Voices, 1971, (mime-dance prodn.) The Peloponnesian War, 1967, (multimedia participatory work) Feedback 1968, The Nude Paper Sermon, 1969, (multimedia environ. work) Can Man Survive?, 1968, (media poem) Ecolog, 1982, (musical theater prodn.) Saying Something, 1972, Biograffiti, 1972, Lazarus, 1973, (with Michael Stahl) The Conjuror, 1974, Sahl, 1976, Noah, 1978, The Passion of Simple Simon, 1979, Boxes, 1982 (Seagram Prodn. award), (opera buffa) Civilization and its Discontents, 1980 (Prix Italia award Assn European Broadcasters), (with Ned Jackson) Big Jim and the Small-time Investors, 1996, (with Valeria Vasilevski) The Last Words of Dutch Schultz, 1996, (with Michel Rostain) Prières, 1997; (media and live performance piece) Toward a New American Opera, 1985, (adaptations) Strike Up the Band, 1984, Love Life, 1990, The Silent Twins, 1992; prodr., dir. (with Theresa Stratas) The Unknown Kurt Weill, (with Joel Gray and N.Y.C. Opera) Silverlake, Civilization and its Discontents, The Tango Project (Record of Yr. award Stereo Rev.), Two to Tango, The Palm Court, The Waltz Project, Moore's Irish Melodies, A Portrait Album, Notebooks of Anna Magdalena Bach, An Old-Fashioned Christmas, Revelation in the Courthouse Park, Casino Paradise; recs. include Civilization and its Discontents, Wiretap, The Nude Paper Sermon, Noah, Accord; author: 20th Century Music: An Introduction, 1967, 3d edit., 1989, translated into Spanish, Portuguese, Hungarian, and Japanese; editor Musical Quar., 1984-91; contbg. editor, critic Stereo Rev., N.Y.C., 1970—; contbr. N.Y. Times, New York Herald-Tribune, N.Y. Mag., others. Fulbright scholar St. Cecilia Acad., 1956-58, Darmstadt Ferienkurse, 1957; recipient Armstrong, Prix Italia radio awards. Mem. Linnaean Soc. (mem. coun.), South Fork Nat. History Soc. (mem. coun.). Avocations: natural history, ornithology. Home: 29 Middagh St Brooklyn NY 11201-1339

SALZMAN, MARILYN B. WOLFSON, service company executive; b. Chgo., Dec. 25, 1943; d. Joseph and Sera (Krol) Wolfson; 1 son, Lawrence Todd. Student, U. Ill., Barat Coll., Lake Forest, Ill., U. Calif., Irvine. Adminstrv. project asst. Sci. Research Assocs., Chgo., 1964-70; reporter Suburban Trib of Chgo. Tribune, 1979-80; pres. MWS Assocs., Los Angeles and Fullerton, Calif., 1980—; exec. adminstrv. dir. Crystal Tips of No. Ill., Inc., 1980-83; dir. adminstrn. Ice Dispensers, Inc., 1981-83, Sani-Serv of Ill., Inc., 1981-83; adminstrv. and organizational cons. 1140 Corp., 1980-83; adminstrv. dir. Iceman's Ico Co., Inc., 1980-83; founder, moderator DWC Workshops, 1984; dir. data processing Florence Crittenton Svs., Orange County, 1984-86, dir. MIS, 1986-88, dir. support svcs., 1988-92, bd. dirs. devel. & cmty. svcs., ways and means com., 1991—, fin. com., found. com., bd. devel. com., ann. meeting com., 1995—, dir. adminstrn. & contract compliance, 1992-94, dir. devel. & cmty. svcs., 1994—; pres. MWS Prodns., L.A. and Fullerton, Calif., 1990—; exec. producer (TV series) The State of the Child, 1990-91; panelist computers in residential treatment Child Welfare League Am. Biennial Conf. Workshop, 1986; presenter outcomes and svc. evaluation North Am. Out-of-Home Care Conf., 1991, families & children in residential treatment Calif. State U. Child Devel. Conf., Fullerton, 1994, advancing your message Child Welfare League of Am. Nat. Conf., 1995; comm. & Pub. Rels. for Profl., Child Welfare League Am. Nat. Conf., 1996, 97. Active Friends of Fullerton Library; panelist Child Welfare League Am., Bienniel Conf. Workshop; chmn. govtl., pub. affairs coms. Orange County Assn. of Children's Svcs.; mem. steering com. Orange County UN Assn. Yr. of Family, 1993-95; mem. com. Internat. Yr. of the Family Exhibit & Celebration, Bowers Mus., 1994; mem. planning com. Orange County Summit for Children, 1994—, chair outreach com., 1996—; mem. exec. com. Anne Frank Orange County Organizing Com., 1994—; mem. adv. com. Child Devel. & Family Life Dept., Fullerton Coll., 1994; mem. bd. mgrs. N. Orange County Family YMCA, 1995—, chmn. child care adv. com., 1995-96, mem. sr. care adv. com., exec. dir. selection com., 1996, mem. program com., 1996—; facilitator Orange County Together, 1994—. Mem. Calif. Assn. Svcs. for Children (rsch. and evaluation com. 1993—, pub. rels. com. 1996—), Soroptimist Internat. of Fullerton (TAP chmn. 1995—, v.p. 1996, pres. elect, 1997), Mgmt. Forum, Fullerton C. of C. (indsl. com. 1994-96, local govt. com. 1995—), Nat. Soc. Fund Raising Execs. (Orange County chpt. 1996—). Contbr. articles to newspapers and indsl. jours.

SALZMAN, RICHARD WILLIAM, artists' representative; b. Los Angeles, Nov. 22, 1958; s. Paul and Anne (Meyersburg) S.; student public schs., Los Angeles. Stockboy, Marathon Clothing, Los Angeles, 1976-77, salesman, 1977, sales and mgmt. trainee, 1977-78, br. mgr., San Francisco, 1978-80, San Diego, 1980-82; artist rep., 1982—; owner Salzman Internat., San Francisco; dir. Therapy Springs Presents. Tchr. freelance bus. practices San Diego City Coll. Contbr. illustrations Communication Arts mag., 1992, Graphic Arts of the World. Recipient 2 Gold medals N.Y. Soc. Illustrators. Mem. Union of Concerned Scientists, Green Peace, Environ. Def. Fund, Coalition for Non-Nuclear World, Communicating Arts Group San Diego (2 Gold awards 1989), Internat. Assn. Bus. Communicators, Soc. Photographers and Artists Reps., Am. Inst. Graphic Arts (founder, v.p. San Diego chpt., mem. nat. task force), Graphic Artist Guild, Western Art Dirs. Club, San Francisco Creative Alliance. Democrat. Home: 716 Sanchez St San Francisco CA 94114-2929 Office: Salzman Internat 716 Sanchez St San Francisco CA 94114-2929

SALZMAN, ROBERT JAY, accountant; b. Bklyn., Dec. 7, 1941; s. Irving and Sydelle (Feingold) S.; m. Constance A. Freeman, Sept. 16, 1990. BA, Allegheny Coll., Meadville, Pa., 1962; MBA, U. Pa., 1965; JD, N.Y. Law Sch., 1972. Bar: N.Y. 1973; CPA, N.Y. Acct. N.Y.C., 1965—; pvt. practice Robert J. Salzman, CPA, P.C., N.Y.C., 1970—. Home: 10 East End Ave New York NY 10021 also: 82 Sycamore Dr East Hampton NY 11937-1482 also: 2801 NE 183rd St North Miami Beach FL 33160 Office: 845 3rd Ave New York NY 10022-6601

SALZSTEIN, RICHARD ALAN, biomedical engineer, researcher; b. Elkins Park, Pa., Sept. 16, 1959; s. Eli and Lorraine (Reese) S.; m. Sharon Lazar; children: Hillary, Lauren. BS in Engring., U. Pa., 1981, MS in Engring., 1982, PhD in Bioengring., 1985. Rsch. fellow U. Pa., Phila., 1981-85; rsch. scientist Hercules, Inc., Wilmington, Del., 1986—. Mem. Soc. for Biomaterials, Orthopaedic Rsch. Soc., Tau Beta Pi. Recipient Kappa Delta award Bioelectrical Repair & Growth Soc., 1985; NSF fellow, 1981-85. Avocations: racquetball, skiing. Office: Hercules Inc Rsch Ctr 500 Hercules Rd Wilmington DE 19808-1513

SAM, DAVID, federal judge; b. Hobart, Ind., Aug. 12, 1933; s. Andrew and Flora (Toma) S.; m. Betty Jean Brennan, Feb. 1, 1957; children: Betty Jean, David Dwight, Daniel Scott, Tamara Lynn, Pamela Rae, Daryl Paul, Angie, Sheyla. BS, Brigham Young U., 1957; JD, Utah U., 1960. Bar: Utah 1960, U.S. Dist. Ct. Utah 1966. Sole practice and ptnr. Duchesne, Utah, 1963-76; dist. judge State of Utah, 1976-85; judge U.S. Dist. Ct. Utah, Salt Lake City, 1985—; atty. City of Duchesne, 1963-72; Duchesne County atty., 1966-72; commr. Duchesne, 1972-74; mem. adv. com. Codes of Conduct of Jud. Conf. U.S., 1987-91, Jud. Coun. of 10th Cir., 1991-93; mem. U.S. Del. to Romania, Aug. 1991. Chmn. Jud. Nomination Com. for Cir. Ct. Judge, Provo, Utah, 1983; bd. dirs. Water Resources, Salt Lake City, 1973-76. Served to capt. JAGC, USAF, 1961-63. Mem. Utah Bar Assn., Am. Judicature Soc., Supreme Ct. Hist. Soc., Am. Inns of Ct. VII (counselor 1986-89), A. Sherman Christensen Am. Inn of Ct. I (counselor 1989—), Utah Jud. Conf. (chmn. 1982), Utah Dist. Judges Assn. (pres. 1982-83), Order of Coif (hon. Brigham Young U. chpt.). Mem. LDS Ch. Avocations: beekeeping, reading, sports, cooking chinese food. Office: US Dist Ct 148 US Courthouse 350 S Main St Salt Lake City UT 84101-2106

SAM, DAVID FIIFI, political economist, educator; b. Winneba, Ghana, Sept. 9, 1957; came to U.S., 1975; s. Alfred Sam and Christiana Impraim; m. Juliana Sam, Jan. 3, 1987; children: Michelle Ann Tabirwaa, David Charles Impraim. BA, Ill. State U., 1981; MBA, Northwestern U., 1987; M.A.L.D., Tufts U., 1984, PhD, 1990. Tchg. asst. in polit. sci. Tufts U., Medford, Mass., 1982-84, adminstr. Fletcher Sch., 1983-84; fin. asst. Arthur Andersen & Co., Chgo., 1984-86; assoc. dir. City Colls. of Chgo., 1986-88; asst. prof., coord. Coll. of DuPage, Glen Ellyn, Ill., 1988-90; dean natural and social scis. Mott C.C., Flint, Mich., 1990-92, acting exec. v.p., 1992-93; v.p., prof. Harrisburg (Pa.) Area C.C., 1993-96; dean, prof. social sci. U. Akron, 1996—; cons. internat. bus. and edn., 1989—. Co-editor: International Business: Designing Effective Programs for Community Colleges, 1988. Bd. dirs. Flint Internat. Inst., 1992-93, Am. Coun. Internat./Intercultural Edn., 1994—, Ill. Consortium for Internat. Studies and Programs, 1987-90. Recipient Martin Luther King Svc. award Ill. State U., 1981. Avocations: reading, travel, sports. Home: 2085 Applegrove St NW North Canton OH 44720-6205 Office: U Akron Akron OH 44325-6001

SAM, JOSEPH, retired university dean; b. Gary, Ind., Aug. 15, 1923; s. Andrew and Flora (Toma) S.; m. Frances Adickes, Sept. 11, 1945; children—Sherrie, Joseph A., Suzanne F. Student, Drake U., 1942-43; B.S., U. S.C., 1948; Ph.D., Kans. U., 1951. Sr. research chemist McNeil Labs., Phila., 1951-54; research group leader Bristol Labs., Syracuse, N.Y., 1955-57; sr. scientist E.I. duPont de Nemours & Co., Inc., 1957-59; faculty U. Miss., 1959-86, prof. pharm. chemistry, 1961-68, chmn. dept., 1963-68, dir. univ. research, 1968-81, asso. vice chancellor research, 1981-86; dean U. Miss. (Grad. Sch.), 1968-86; Fulbright lectr. Cairo U., 1965-66. Mem. Am. Pharm. Assn. (found. research achievement award in pharm. and medicinal chemistry 1968), Sigma Xi, Rho Chi, Phi Lambda Upsilon, Phi Kappa Phi. Home: PO Box 351 University MS 38677-0351

SAMALIN, EDWIN, lawyer, educator; b. N.Y.C., Sept. 19, 1935; s. Harry Louis and Sydell (Fisher) S.; children: David Seth, Andrew Evan, Jonathan Daniel. B.S., U. R.I., 1957; J.D., N.Y. Law Sch., 1962. Bar: N.Y. 1963, U.S. Supreme Ct. 1976. Tax atty. Electric Bond & Share Co., N.Y.C., 1963; ptnr. Samalin & Sklaver, Yorktown Heights, N.Y., 1969-78; pvt. practice law, Yorktown Heights, 1963-69, 78-84; mng. ptnr. Yorktown Office Park Assocs., Yorktown Heights, 1971—; pres. Samalin & Bock, P.C., Yorktown Heights, 1984—; adj. faculty Mercy Coll., Dobbs Ferry, N.Y., 1974-92; commodity cons. Murlas Commodities, Yorktown Heights, 1982-85; ptnr. Patterson (N.Y.) Realty Assn., 1983—; pres. Sammark Realty Corp., Westchester, N.Y., 1984—, Old Smoke House Realty Corp., 1987—, Atty.'s Asset Mgmt. Corp., Registered Investment Advisors, 1992—; Dem. candidate for County Legislature, 1973. Capt. U.S. Army, 1957-59. Mem. N.Y. State Bar Assn., Westchester County Bar Assn. (dir., former chair atty. client dispute com.), Yorktown Bar Assn. (pres. 1982, Man of Yr. 1983), Am. Arbitration Assn. (arbitrator 1974—), Phi Delta Phi. Home: 951A Heritage Hills Dr Somers NY 10589-1913 Office: Samalin & Bock PC 2000 Maple Hill St Yorktown Heights NY 10598-4122

SAMANIEGO, PAMELA SUSAN, organization administrator; b. San Mateo, Calif., Nov. 29, 1952; d. Armando C. and Harriott Susan (Croot) S. Student, UCLA, 1972, Los Angeles Valley Coll., 1970-72. Asst. new accts. supr. Beverly Hills Fed. Savings, 1970-72; asst. controller Bio-Science Enterprises, Van Nuys, Calif., 1972-74; adminstr. asst. Avery/Tirce Prodns., Hollywood, Calif., 1974-78; sr. estimator N. Lee Lacy and Assocs., Hollywood, 1978-81; head of prodn. Film Consortium, Hollywood, 1981-82; exec. producer EUE/Screen Gems Ltd., Burbank, Calif., 1982-88; advt. agency dir. Barrett & Assocs., Las Vegas, Nev., 1988-90; exec. producer Laguna/Take One, Las Vegas, 1990-93; dir. Sta. KXLY-4 ABC, Spokane, Wash., 1993-94; dir. advt. and mktg. Appaloosa Horse Club, Moscow, Idaho, 1994—. Author: Millimeter & Backstage, 1982-88. Emergency room vol. San Mateo (Calif.) County Hosp., 1968-70; Sunday sch. tchr. Hillsdale Meth. Ch., San Mateo, 1968-70; vol. worker Hillsdale Meth. Ch. Outreach, San Francisco, 1967-70. Recipient CLIO award CLIO Awards, Inc., 1985, ADDY award Las Vegas Advt. Fedn., 1988. Mem. Dirs. Guild Am. (2nd asst. dir. 1987-88), Assn. Ind. Comml. Producers, Am. Horse Show Assn., Internat. Arabian Horse Assn., AHASFV (sec. 1978-79), AHASC (sec. 1978-88). Democrat. Methodist. Avocations: breed and show Arabian horses. Home: 323 E First St Moscow ID 83843 Office: Appaloosa Horse Club 5070 Highway 8 W Moscow ID 83843-4000

SAMANIEGO BREACH, NORMA, Mexican government official; b. Mexico City, Feb. 24, 1944; married; 1 child. BA in Econ., Autonomous U., Mexico City, 1966; MA in Economic Planning, Inst. Social Studies, The Hague, The Netherlands, 1970. Planning analyst Secretariat of the Presidency Govt. of Mex., 1967-69, dep. dir. rsch. on revenue distbn. and salary Secretariat of, 1974-75, dep. dir. econ. rsch. Nat. Commn. on Minimum Wages, 1975-76, sr. analyst planning Secretariat of Edn., 1977-78; advisor for svcs. Mex. Inst. Social Security, 1978-82, tech. dir. Nat. Commn. on Minimum Wages, 1982-88, pres. Nat. Commn. on Minimum Wages, 1988-90, undersec. "B" Secretariat of Labor and Social Assistance, 1991-94, comptroller gen., 1995—. Author several works on labor market in Mex. Mem. Instl. Revolutionary Party. Office: Embassy of Mexico 1911 Pennsylvania Ave NW Washington DC 20006-3403*

SAMANOWITZ, RONALD ARTHUR, lawyer; b. N.Y.C., June 1, 1944; s. Sam and Thelma (Levin) S.; m. Ann Frieda Weisman, Dec. 18, 1971; 1 child, Samuel. BBA, CUNY, 1965; JD, Bklyn. Law Sch., 1967. Bar: N.Y. 1968, U.S. Dist. Ct. (ea. and so. dists.) N.Y. 1974, U.S. Supreme Ct. 1991. Ptnr. Krakower, Samanowitz & Goldman, N.Y.C., 1968-86, Resnicoff, Samanowitz, Endzweig & Brawer, Great Neck, N.Y., 1986-90, Samanowitz & Endzweig, Great Neck, N.Y., 1990—. Pres. Greater Fresh Meadows Civic Assn., Flushing, N.Y., 1984-85, award for Civic Svc. 1985, Flower Hill Civic Assn., 1992. Mem. N.Y. State Trial Lawyers Assn. (gov. L.I. divsn.), Brandeis Lawyers Assn. (sec. 1985—), Queens Bar Assn. (family law com.), Nassau Bar Assn. (plaintiff roundtable 1988—), Great Neck Lawyers Assn. (past pres., chmn. bd.). Avocation: marathon running. Office: Samanowitz & Endzweig 98 Cuttermill Rd Great Neck NY 11021-3006

SAMARTINI, JAMES ROGERS, retired appliance company executive; b. Cleve., Apr. 13, 1935; s. Leonard Henry and Grace Rogers (Tully) S.; m. Irene Ann Kurnava, Sept. 16, 1961 (dec. June 1994); m. Julia S. Rubin, Sept. 8, 1996; children: David L., James F., Patrick R. AB, Dartmouth Coll., 1957; MBA, Harvard U., 1961. Fin. supr. Ford Motor Co., Dearborn, Mich., 1966-72; v.p. fin. and adminstrn. Thonet Industries Inc., York, Pa., 1972-74; from asst. controller to v.p., CFO Mead Corp., Dayton, 1974-91; exec. v.p., chief adminstrv. officer Whirlpool Corp., Benton Harbor, Mich., 1991-95; ret., 1995; bd. dirs. Peoples State Bank, St. Joseph, Mich. Chmn. bd. trustees Whirlpool Found., 1993-95; trustee Dayton Opera Assn., 1977-86, pres., 1985-86; mem. adv. bd. Salvation Army; bd. dirs. Epilepsy Assn. Western Ohio, 1986, S.W. Mich. Symphony Orch., 1991-93. Mem. Fin. Execs. Inst. (dir. 1983-86). Home: Apt 702 3133 Connecticut Ave NW Washington DC 20008

SAMBASIVAM, EZHILARASAN, computer science and mathematics educator; b. Edaiyur, Tamil Nadu, India, Apr. 7, 1956; came to U.S., 1987; s. Sambasivam Kuppusamy and Valliyammal (Loganathan) S.; m. Vijayalakshmi Ramachandran, July 9, 1989; children: Richard Cecil, Joshua David. BS, Madras (India) U., 1976; MS, Mysore (India) U., 1978; PhD, Moscow State U., 1986; MS, Western Mich. U., 1990. Rsch. asst. Indian Inst. Tech., Delhi, 1979-81; instr. Indian Inst. Tech., Bombay, 1981-82; rschr. Moscow State U., 1983-87; instr. Western Mich. U., Kalamazoo, 1987-88, grad. asst., 1988-90; assoc. prof. computer sci. and math. Mo. Western State Coll., St. Joseph, 1990-95, coord. computer sci., 1991-95; assoc. prof. computer sci. Azusa (Calif.) Pacific U., 1996—, acting chmn. computer sci., 1996-97, chmn. computer sci., 1997—. Contbr. articles to profl. jours. Merit scholar Nat. Coun. India, 1976-78, rsch. fellow, 1978-81; fellow Govt. of India, 1982-86; scholar Western Mich. U., 1989, Coun. of Chairpersons award, 1992. Mem. Assn. Computing Machinery (dir. Scholastic programming contest 1990—), Upsilon Pi Epsilon, Kappa Mu Epsilon. Avocations: travel, swimming, tennis, chess, racquetball. Home: 520 Claraday # 4 Glendora CA 91740 Office: Azusa Pacific U Computer Sci Dept Azusa CA 91702-7000 Office: Azusa Pacific U Computer Sci Dept 901 E Alosta Ave Azusa CA 91702-2701

SAMBI, MARGARET ANN, curator; b. Uniontown, Pa., Apr. 28, 1945; d. Thomas Joseph and Helen Adrienne (Reagan) Meehan; m. Walter John Sambi, Dec. 15, 1973; children: Elizabeth A., Tiffany R. BA in Art History, U. Cin., 1971, MA in Art History, 1973. Cert. in non-profit orgn. mgmt. and volunteer adminstrn. Archtl. historian Miami Purchase Assn., Cin., 1974-76; lectr. fine arts U. Cin., 1975-87; dir. Summerfair, Inc., Cin., 1987-89; asst. curator mus. edn. Cin. Art Mus., 1989-91; curator mus. edn. Contemporary Arts Ctr., Cin., 1991—; mem. nat. adv. com. Save Our Sculpture, Smithsonian Inst., Nat. Mus. Am. Art, 1991-95, edn. adv. com. Cin. Arts Assn., 1994-95; chair off-site mus. visits Ohio Art Edn. Assn., 1994-95; provider adv. com. Assn. Advancement of Arts Edn., 1994-95. Author: Joyce J. Scott: Dream Weaver, 1994. Trustee, bd. dirs. A Day in Eden, Inc., Cin., 1991; mem. nominating com. Greater Cin. Beautiful, Inc., 1991-93. Mem. Am. Assn. Muss., Nat. Art Edn. Assn., Mid-West Mus. Assn., Mus. Edn. Roundtable. Avocations: needlework, bookmaking, painting. Home: 3945 Clifton Ave Cincinnati OH 45220-1145 Office: Contemporary Arts Ctr 115 E 5th St Cincinnati OH 45202-3902

SAMBURG, A. GENE, security company executive; b. Indpls., Apr. 25, 1941; s. A. George and Hermine (Wittgenstein) S.; m. Lorrie Silverman, June 26, 1966; children: Kimberly Jill, Thomas Blair. BEE, Cornell U., 1964; OPM, Harvard U., 1985. Engr. Westinghouse Corp., 1964-72; founder, pres. and CEO Kastle Systems, Inc., 1972—; adv. on bus. programs Cornell U.; spl. lectr. for numerous profl. and ednl. courses in field. Patentee in field. Mem. IEEE, ASME, CPP, Am. Soc. Indsl. Security, Woodmont Country Club, City Club (Washington), Tower Club (McLean, Va.). Home: 1206 Stable Gate Ct Mc Lean VA 22102 Office: Kastle Systems Inc 1501 Wilson Blvd Arlington VA 22209-2403

SAMEK, MICHAEL JOHANN, corporation executive; b. Vienna, Austria, Feb. 26, 1920; came to U.S., 1939; s. Berthold and Leontine (Bruell) S.; m. Edith Raymond, Apr. 1948 (div. 1961); m. Stacy Graham, Dec. 20, 1964 (div. 1974). B.S., Vienna, 1938; postgrad., Columbia U., 1949-51. Pres. Computech Inc., N.Y.C., 1956-60; v.p. Data Systems ITT, Paramus, N.J., 1961-64; mgr. dir. internat. Auerbach Corp., Europe and U.S., 1964-69; v.p. Celanese Corp., N.Y.C., 1969-83; pres. Primary Care Software Inc., Riverhead, N.Y., 1987—; chmn. Am. Mgmt. Assn. Info. Systems and Tech. Council, 1960-83; chmn. adv. com. on data processing City of N.Y., 1963—. Served to lt. col. USAF, 1941-45, ETO. Mem. AAAS, AIAA, Assn. Computing Machinery, N.Y. Acad. Scis.

SAMEROFF, ARNOLD JOSHUA, developmental psychologist, educator, research scientist; b. N.Y.C., Apr. 20, 1937; s. Stanley and Zeena (Shapiro) S.; m. Susan C. McDonough, Jan. 2, 1982; children: Shira, Rebecca, Crista, Andrew. BS, U. Mich., 1961; PhD, Yale U., 1965; MA (hon.), Brown U., 1987. Asst. prof. psychology, pediatrics and psychiatry U. Rochester, 1967-70, assoc. prof., 1970-73, prof., 1973-78, dir. developmental psychology tng. program, 1975-78; prof. psychology U. Ill., Chgo., 1978-86, assoc. dir. Inst. for Study Developmental Disabilities, 1978-86; assoc. dir., dir. rsch. Ill. Inst. for Developmental Disabilities, Ill. Dept. Mental Health and Developmental Disabilities, 1978-86; prof. psychiatry and human behavior Brown U., Providence, 1986-92; dir. Developmental Psychopathology Rsch. Ctr., Bradley Hosp., East Providence, 1986-92; prof. psychology, rsch. scientist Ctr. for Human Growth and Devel., U. Mich., Ann Arbor, 1992—, dir. devel., psychopathology and mental health program, 1995—; vis. prof. psychology Birkbeck Coll., U. London, 1974-75; vis. scientist Ctr. for Interdisciplinary Rsch., U. Bielefeld, Fed. Republic Germany, 1977-78; W.T. Grant Found. lectr. Soc. for Behavioral Pediatrics, 1984; dir. Summer Inst. on Human Devel. and Psychopathology, Ctr. for Advanced Study in Behavioral Scis., Stanford, Calif., 1989; mem. small grants adv. com. NIH, 1977-81, behavioral scis. assessment panel, 1987-88; mem. organizational planning com. Internat. Conf. for Infant Studies, 1980-84. Editor: (with R.N. Emde) Relationship Disturbances in Early Childhood: A Developmental Approach, 1989, (with F. Kessel and M. Bornstein) Contemporary Constructions of the Child: Essays in Honor of William Kessen, 1991, (with M. Haith) The Five to Seven Year Shift, 1996; also monographs; mem. editl. bds. Devel. and Psychopathology, 1988-94, Jour. Devel. and Behavioral Pediatrics, 1989-93, Jour. Family Psychology, 1990-91, others. Mem. social and behavioral scis. rsch. adv. com. March of Dimes Birth Defects Found., 1977-94, rsch. adv. com. Little City Found., 1986-88; bd. dirs. Zero to Three: Nat. Ctr. for Infants Toddlers and Families, 1986—; mem. program on successful adolescent devel. among youth in high-risk settings John D. and Catherine T. MacArthur Found., 1986-95, network on early childhood transitions, 1989-92. Recipient rsch. scientist award NIMH, 1994—; GE fellow Yale U., 1961; NIMH predoctoral rsch. fellow Yale U., 1962, NIMH postdoctoral rsch. fellow, 1965-67, Ctr. for Advanced Study in Behavioral Scis. fellow Stanford U., 1984-85. Fellow AAAS, Am. Acad. Mental Retardation, Am. Psychol. Soc., Devel. Psychology and Mental Retardation divsn. Am. Psychol. Assn. (mem. program com. devel. psychology divsn. 1978-90, chair 1979, mem. coun. 1980-83, mem.-at-large exec. com. 1985-88, pres. devel. psychology divsn. 1995-96); mem. AAUP, Soc. for Rsch. in Child Devel. (com. on summer insts. and study groups 1985-88), World Assn. Infant Mental Health, Internat. Soc. for Infant Studies, Soc. for Rsch. on Adolescence.

SAMET, ANDREW, government official; b. Boston, June 29, 1957; s. Theodore S. and Elaine S. (Sloane) S.; m. Kennari S. Sargent, May 10, 1986; children: Daniel Jeremy, Hanna Gabrielle. BA, Carleton Univ., 1978; MA, Carleton U., Ottawa, Ont., Can., 1981; JD, Georgetown U., 1983. Bar: D.C. Assoc. Chapman, Duff and Paul, Washington, 1983-85, Mudge Rose Guthrie Alexander & Ferdon, Washington, 1985-87; legis. counsel. Senator Daniel P. Moynihan, Washington, 1987-89, legis. dir., 1989-93; assoc. dep. under sec. for internat. affairs Dept. Labor, Washington, 1993—. Editor: Human Rights Law and Reagan Adminstration, 1984, The U.S.-Israel Free Trade Area Agreement, 1989; contbr. articles to profl. jours. Democrat. Jewish. Office: Dept of Labor Internat Labor Affairs 200 Constitution Ave NW Washington DC 20210-0001

SAMET, DEAN HENRY, safety engineer; b. Elgin, Ill., Mar. 22, 1947; s. Henry Ralph and Ardella Mary (Schiebel) S.; m. Karen Rae Meyer, Feb. 11, 1979; children: Chris, Lisa, Sean. AAS, Elgin C.C., 1972; BS in Engring. Tech., So. Ill. U., 1974. Cert. healthcare safety profl. Internat. Healthcare Safety Profl. Cert. Bd. Project engr. McBro Planning & Devel. Co., Grand Island, Nebr., 1974-78; field constrn. engr. Arabian Am. Oil Co., Dhahran, Saudi Arabia, 1978-79; project engr. McCarthy Co., Jeddah, Saudi Arabia, 1979-81; sr. project engr. Univ. Mech., Riyadh, Saudi Arabia, 1981-82; staff engr. Joint Commn., Chgo., 1983-85; chief mech. cons. engr. Architects Collaborative, Baghdad, Iraq, 1985; codes and stds. engr. King Faisal Specialist Hosp., Riyadh, 1985-89; assoc. dir. Joint Commn., Oakbrook Terrace, Ill., 1989—; mem. architecture for health com. AIA, Washington, 1983-85. Co-author: Plant, Technology and Safety Management Handbook, 1985, The 1996 KIPS Survey Guide, 1996. Staff sgt. USAF, 1966-69. Mem. Am. Soc. Hosp. Engring., Nat. Fire Protection Assn., Tenn. Squires Assn. Avocation: playing guitar. Office: Joint Commn 1 Renaissance Blvd Oakbrook Terrace IL 60181-4294

SAMET, JACK I., lawyer; b. N.Y.C., Aug. 6, 1940; s. William and Tillie (Katz) S.; m. Helen Ray, Feb. 12, 1967; 1 son, Peter Lawrence. BA, Columbia U., 1961; JD, Harvard U., 1964. Bar: N.Y. 1964, Calif. 1973. Assoc. Whitman & Ransom, N.Y.C., 1966-69, Hall, Casey, Dickler & Howley, N.Y.C., 1969-73; ptnr. Ball, Hunt, Hart, Brown & Baerwitz, L.A., 1973-81, Buchalter, Nemer, Fields & Younger, L.A., 1981-94, Baker & Hostetler, L.A., 1994—; arbitrator Nat. Assn. Securities Dealers, L.A., 1976—, mem. policy com., 1997—; speaker, panelist Calif. Continuing Edn. of Bar, 1988. Mem. ABA, Sports Club/L.A. Avocations: exercise, reading. Home: 2741 Aqua Verde Cir Los Angeles CA 90077-1502 Office: Baker & Hostetler 600 Wilshire Blvd Fl 12 Los Angeles CA 90017-3212

SAMET, JONATHAN MICHAEL, epidemiologist, educator; b. Va., Mar. 26, 1948. AB in Chemistry and Physics, Harvard Coll., 1966; MD, U. Rochester, 1970; MS in Epidemiology, Harvard Sch. Pub Health, 1977. Diplomate Am. Bd. of Internal Medicine, Nat. Bd. Med. Examiners. Intern in medicine U. Ky. Med. Ctr., Lexington, 1970-71; asst. resident in medicine U. N.Mex. Affiliated Hosps., Albuquerque, 1973-74, sr. resident, 1974-75; rsch. fellow in clin. epidemiology Channing lab. Harvard Med. Sch., Boston, 1975-78, rsch. assoc. in medicine, 1978-83; epidemiologist Cancer Rsch. and Treatment Ctr. U. N.Mex., Albuquerque, 1980—, asst. prof. medicine, 1978-82, assoc. prof. medicine, 1982-88, assoc. prof. family, cmty., and emergency medicine, 1985-88, prof. family, cmty., and emergency medicine, 1986-94, prof. medicine, 1988-94, clin. prof. medicine, 1994—; prof., chmn. dept. epidemiology The Johns Hopkins U., Balt., 1994—, co-dir. risk scis. and pub. policy inst., 1995—; chief pulmonary divsn. U. N.Mex. Hosp., Albuquerque, 1985-94, chief pulmonary and critical care divsn. dept. medicine, 1986-94; mem. indoor air quality and total human exposure com., sci. adv. bd. U.S. EPA, 1987—; chmn. biol. effects of ionizing radiation VI com. Nat. Rsch. Coun., 1994—. Editor pro tem Am. Jour. of Epidemiology, 1991-92, editor, 1992—; assoc. editor Tobacco Control: An Internat. Jour., 1991—; editor Epidemiologic Revs., 1994—. With U.S. Army, 1971-73. Recipient Clinton P. Anderson award Am. Lung Assn. N.Mex., 1988, Surgeon Gen.'s medallion, 1990, Award for Excellence in Environ. Health Rsch. The Lovelace Inst., 1996. Fellow AAAS, Am. Coll. Epidemiology; mem. Soc. for Epidemiologic Rsch. (pres.-elect 1988-89, pres. 1989-90, exec. com. 1988-91), Am. Thoracic Soc. (long range planning com. environ. and occupational health assembly 1992—, program com. behavioral scis. sect. 1994-95), N.Mex. Thoracic Soc. (sec.-treas. 1982-83, v.p. 1983-84, pres. 1984-85), Internat. Epidemiol. Assn., Internat. Soc. of Indoor Air Quality and Climate, Md. Thoracic Soc., Alpha Omega Alpha, Delta Omega Alpha. Office: Dept Epidemiology The Johns Hopkins U 615 N Wolfe St Ste 6030 Baltimore MD 21205-2103

SAMET, KENNETH ALAN, hospital administrator; b. Bklyn., Mar. 17, 1958; married. BA, Old Dominion U., 1990; MA, U. Mich., 1982. Adminstrv. intern Mt. Vernon Hosp., Fairfax, Va., 1981; adminstrv. resident Washington Hosp. Ctr., 1982-83, pres., 1991—; asst. to pres. Washington Health Care Corp., 1983-85, dir. system devel., 1985-86; v.p. system devel. Medlantic Health Care Group, Washington, 1986-88, exec. v.p. systems, bus. devel., 1988-91; pres. Medlantic Enterprises, Washington, 1988-91. Mem. D.C. Hosp. Assn., Md. Hosp. Assn., Va. Hosp. Assn. (bd. dirs.). Home: 9041 Holly Leaf Ln Bethesda MD 20817-2657 Office: Washington Hosp Ctr 110 Irving St NW Rm 2a2 Washington DC 20010-2931

SAMFORD, THOMAS DRAKE, III, lawyer; b. Opelika, Ala., Mar. 4, 1934; s. Thomas Drake and Aileen (Maxwell) S., Jr.; m. Jacqueline Screws, June 7, 1955; children: Thomas Drake IV, Jacquelyn, Robert Maxwell, Richard Drake. A.B. magna cum laude, Princeton U., 1955; J.D., U. Ala., 1961. Bar: Ala. 1961. Owner firm Samford & Samford, 1961-88; judge Mcpl. Ct., Opelika, 1961-88; mem. Ala. Permanent Jud. Commn., 1979-83; gen. counsel Auburn U., 1965-95, gen. counsel emeritus, 1995—; lectr. Ala. Law Inst., 1969, Am. Judicature Soc., 1969—. Editor-in-chief: Ala. Law Rev, 1960-61. Dir., bd. trustees Opelika Comty. Chest, 1965-68, pres., 1966-67; bd. dirs. U. Ala. Law Sch. Found., Jr. Achievement Chattahoochee-Lee; elder Presbyn. ch., 1974-94, Meth. ch., 1994—. Recipient John G. Buchanan prize politics, 1955, Jaycee Disting. Svc. award, 1996; Farrah, Order Jurisprudence U. Ala., 1956; named one of four Outstanding Young Men in Ala. Jr. C. of C., 1967. Mem. ABA, Lee County Bar Assn. (pres. 1965), Ala. State Bar, U. Ala. Nat. Alumni Assn. (pres. 1966-67), Opelika C. of C. (dir. 1967, pres. 1968), Phi Beta Kappa, Alpha Tau Omega, Phi Delta Phi, Omicron Delta Kappa. Lodge: Kiwanis (bd. dirs. 1966-67, pres. 1969-70). Home: PO Box 550 Opelika AL 36803-0550 Office: Auburn Univ Off Gen Counsel 101 Samford Ave Auburn AL 36830-7415

SAMFORD, YETTA GLENN, JR., lawyer; b. Opelika, Ala., June 8, 1923; s. Yetta Glenn and Mary Elizabeth (Denson) S.; m. Mary Austill, Sept. 6, 1949; children: Mary Austill Lott, Katherine Park Alford, Yetta Glenn III (dec.). BS, Ala. Poly. Inst., 1947; LLB, U. Ala., 1949, LLD (hon.), 1995. Bar: Ala. 1949, U.S. Dist. Ct. (mid. dist.) Ala. 1950, U.S. Ct. Appeals (5th cir.) 1961, U.S. Ct. Appeals (11th cir.) 1981. Since practiced in Opelika; ptnr. Samford, Denson, Horsley, Pettey & Martin (and predecessors), 1949—; mem. Ala. Senate from Lee and Russell counties, 1958-62; mem. State of Ala. Bd. of Corrections, 1969-75; mem. adv. bd. State Docks, 1987—. Trustee U. Mobile, 1963-92, life trustee, 1992—, trustee U. Ala., 1972-93, trustee emeritus, 1993—. Mem. Ala. Law Inst. Council (exec. com.), Ala. Acad. of Honor, Phi Delta Phi, Omicron Delta Kappa, Alpha Tau Omega. Republican. Baptist. Lodge: Masons. Home: 615 Terracewood Dr Opelika AL 36801-3850 Office: Samford Denson Horsley Pettey & Martin PO Box 2345 Opelika AL 36803-2345

SAMII, ABDOL HOSSEIN, physician, educator; b. Rasht, Iran, June 20, 1930; came to U.S., 1947; s. Mehdi Ebtehaj and Zahra (Mojdehi-Akbar) S.; m. Shahla Khosrowshahi; children: Ali, Golnaz. Student, Stanford U., 1947-49; BA, UCLA, 1950, MA, 1952; MD, Cornell U., 1956. Intern N.Y. Hosp., N.Y.C., 1956, asst. in medicine, 1956-58; asst. in physiology Cornell U. Med. Sch., N.Y.C., 1958-59; resident and sr. resident N.Y. Hosp., Peter Bent Brigham Hosp. and Mass. Gen. Hosp., Boston, 1959-61; adj. prof. medicine Cornell U. Med. Sch., 1973-79, prof. clin. medicine, 1979—; rsch. fellow Harvard U., Boston, 1959-60; prof. medicine Nat. Univ. Iran, Tehran, 1963-68; med. dir. Pars Hosp., Tehran, 1968-73; dir. div. medicine N.Y. Hosp.-Cornell Med. Coll., White Plains, 1979—; chancellor Reza Shah Kabir Grad. Univ., Tehran, 1973-78; cons. med. rsch. WHO, Geneva, 1973-79; v.p. Imperial Acad. Sci., Tehran, 1974-78. Gen. editor: International Textbook of Medicine, 1981; author, editor: Medical Clinics of North America, 1983, Textbook of Diagnostic Medicine, 1987. Dep. minister, Ministry of Health, Tehran, 1963-65; minister, Ministry Sci. and Higher Edn., Tehran, 1973-75. Fellow Rockefeller Found., Helen Hay Whitney Found. Fellow Royal Soc. of Medicine; mem. N.Y. Acad. Medicine, Harvey Soc., Internat. Soc. Nephrology, Am. Fed. Clin. Rsch. Avocations: music, antiques. Office: NY Hosp CMC WD 21 Bloomingdale Rd White Plains NY 10605-1504 also: 14 E 63d St New York NY 10021

SAMIOS, NICHOLAS PETER, physicist; b. N.Y.C., Mar. 15, 1932; s. Peter and Niki (Vatick) S.; m. Mary Linakis, Jan. 12, 1958; children: Peter, Gregory, Alexandra. AB, Columbia U., 1953, PhD, 1957. Instr. physics Columbia U., N.Y.C., 1956-59; asst. physicist Brookhaven Nat. Lab., Upton, N.Y., 1959-62, assoc. physicist, 1962-64, physicist, 1964-68, sr. physicist, 1968—, group leader, 1965-75, chmn. dept. physics, 1975-81, dep. dir. for high energy and nuclear physics, 1981, dir., 1982—; adj. prof. Stevens Inst. Tech., 1969-75, Columbia U., 1970—. Contbr. articles in field to profl. jours. Bd. dirs. Stony Brook Found., 1989, L.I. Assn., 1989. Recipient E.O. Lawrence Meml. award, 1980, award in physics and math. scis. N.Y. Acad. Scis., 1980; named AUI Disting. Scientist, 1992, W.K.H. Panofsky prize, 1993. Fellow Am. Phys. Soc. (chmn. divsn. of particles and fields 1975-76, chmn. PEP exptl. program com. 1976-78); mem. Internat. Ctr. Future Acceleration, Akademia Athenon (corr.). Achievements include being an expert in field of high energy particle and nuclear physics. Office: Brookhaven Nat Lab Office of Dir Upton NY 11973

SAMMAN, GEORGE, obstetrician, gynecologist; b. Syria, Dec. 12, 1946; came to U.S., 1971; naturalized, 1982; s. Nicolaki and Antoinette (Charaoui) S.; M.D., Damascus U., 1971; m. Husn Massouh, July 4, 1971; children—Fadi, Luna Miriam. Intern, Washington Hosp. Center, 1971-72, resident in ob-gyn., 1972-75, mem. hosp. staff, 1975—, vice chmn. dept. gynecology, 1980, teaching faculty, 1985-88; practice medicine specializing in ob-gyn, Washington, 1975—, Fairfax, Va., 1980—; mem. staff Providence Hosp., 1975—, Columbia Hosp. for Women. Recipient Best Teaching award Washington Hosp. Ctr., 1985, 88. Diplomate Am. Bd. Ob-Gyn. Fellow Am. Coll. Obstetricians and Gynecologists, Am. Fertility Assn.; mem. Med. Soc. D.C. (maternal health com. 1978-80). Melkite Catholic. Home: 10400 Bit & Spur Ln Potomac MD 20854 Office: 2021 K St NW Washington DC 20006-1003

SAMMAN, JUAN M., prosthodontist; b. Damascus, Syria, Nov. 4, 1953; s. Moukhtar and Souha S; m. Angela Mignone, Oct. 3, 1983 (div. July, 1989). BS, Am. U., Beirut, 1976; DDS, NYU, 1981; MSc, London U., 1983. Hon. clin. asst. to the Dental Hosp. Univ. Coll. Hosp., London, 1983; scientific rschr. NYU, N.Y.C., 1984-87, clin. asst. prof., 1987-93; pvt. practice Manhattan, N.Y., 1988—; assoc. N.Y. Dental Implant Restorative and Cosmetic Dentistry Ctr., 1985-87, Sam Weber, DDS, 1987-88; lectr. NYU. Contbr. articles to profl. publs. Fellow Brit. Soc. for Study of Prosthetic Dentistry; mem. Internat. Assn. Dental Rsch., European Prosthodontic Assn., Acad. Osseointegration, Am. Dental Assn., Internat. Coll. Prosthodontists. Avocations: music, painting, travel. Office: 200 Central Park S New York NY 10019-1415

SAMMARCO, PAUL WILLIAM, ecologist; b. Hackensack, N.J., Oct. 18, 1948; s. Giacomo and Esther (Galanti) S.; m. Jean Sogioka, May 29, 1971; children: Mimi Cecile, Dustin Paul, Jack Isao. BA, Syracuse U., 1970, postgrad., 1970-71; cert. Marine Biology Lab., Woods Hole, Mass., 1971, Fairleigh Dickinson U. W.I. Lab., U.S. V.I., 1972; PhD, SUNY-Stony Brook, 1977. Teaching asst. Syracuse (N.Y.) U., 1970-71, Discovery Bay Marine Lab., SUNY-Stony Brook Overseas Acad. Program, Jamaica, 1974, SUNY-Stony Brook, 1971-77; asst. prof. Clarkson U., Potsdam, N.Y., 1977-79; vis. asst. prof. tropical ecology, in St. Croix, V.I., SUNY-Potsdam, 1979; sr. rsch. scientist Australian Inst. Marine Sci., Townsville, Queensland, 1979-89, coord. Shelf Seas Rsch. Program 1985-86; dir. environ. rsch. of Resource Assessment Commn. Prime Minister's commn. on natural resources, Canberra, Australia, 1989-91; exec. dir. La. Univs. Marine Consortium, Chauvin, 1991-95, prof., 1995—; dir. inter-univ. seminar program Assn. Colls. St. Lawrence Valley, Potsdam, 1977-79; adj. prof. La. State U., U. So. La., U. New Orleans, Nicholls State U. Composer ballads, sacred music; former mem. Australian Chamber Choir, Wesley Choir, Canberra; editor (with M.L. Heron) The Bio-Physics of Marine Larval Dispersal, 1994; contbr. numerous articles to profl. jours.; editorial advisor Marine Ecology Progress Series, 1985-93; co-editor Proceedings Inaugural Great Barrier Conf., 1983, Proceedings 6th Internat. Coral Reef Symposium, 1988, Proceedings 8th Internat. Coral Reef Symposium. Recipient Internat. Sci. Exch. award, 1988-89. Mem. chancel choir First United Meth. Ch., Houma, La. Mem. Australian Marine Scis. Assn. (keynote speaker 1981, counselor 1984-89, chmn., organizer nat. conf. 1987, chmn. Australia Acad. Sci. Boden Conf. 1990), Internat. Soc. Reef Studies, Australian Coral Reef Soc., Australasian Performing Rights Assn., Sigma Xi. Democrat. Methodist. Home: 1350 Tunnel Blvd 17 C Houma LA 70360 Office: La Univs Marine Consortium 8124 Highway 56 Chauvin LA 70344-2110

SAMMOND, JOHN STOWELL, lawyer; b. Milw., Dec. 27, 1928; s. C. Frederic and Marie (Freitag) S.; m. Cynthia Miller, Feb. 13, 1951 (dec. Dec. 1992); m. Diana Denholm, July 1995; children: Frederic, Christopher, Nicholas, Timothy. BA, Yale U., 1950; SJD, Harvard U., 1955. Bar: Wis. 1955, Fla. 1969, D.C. 1972, Fla. Supreme Ct. as Cir. Ct. mediator, 1990. Assoc. predecessor firm to Quarles & Brady, Milw., 1955-60; ptnr. Quarles & Brady (and predecessor firms), Milw., 1961—, Quarles & Brady, West Palm Beach, Fla., 1969—; bd. dirs. Medalist Industries Inc., Milw., Associated Commerce Bank, Milw., Tropical Plant Rentals Inc., Riverwoods, Ill., Kelley Co. Inc., Milw., others. Bd. dirs., officer Univ. Sch., Milw., Lakeside Children's Ctr., Milw., Palm Beach Habilitation Ctr., Lake Worth, Fla.; sr. warden Christ Episcopal Ch., Whitefish Bay, Wis. Maj. USMCR, 1948-63. Mem. ABA, Wis. Bar Assn., Milw. Bar Assn., Fla. Bar Assn., Palm Beach County Bar Assn., D.C. Bar Assn., Bath and Tennis Club (Palm Beach), Everglades Club (Palm Beach), Milw. Country Club, Milw. Club, Governor's Club (Palm Beach). Republican. Office: Quarles & Brady PO Box 3188 West Palm Beach FL 33402-3188 also: Quarles & Brady 411 E Wisconsin Ave Milwaukee WI 53202-4409

SAMMONS, ELAINE D., corporate executive. Chmn. Sammons Enterprises, Inc., Dallas. Office: Sammons Enterprises Inc 300 Crescent Ct Ste 700 Dallas TX 75201-7849*

SAMMONS, JEFFREY LEONARD, foreign language educator; b. Cleve., Nov. 9, 1936; s. Harold Leonard and Therese (Herrmann) S.; m. Kathryn Josephine Stella, July 1958 (div. 1962); children: Rebecca Kathryn; m. Christa Ann Smith, Oct. 20, 1967; children: Charles Leonard, Harold Hawthorne, Benjamin Gardner. BA, Yale U., 1958, PhD, 1962. Instr., asst. prof. Brown U., Providence, 1961-64; asst. prof. German, Yale U., 1964-67, assoc. prof., 1967-69, prof., 1969—, Leavenworth prof. German, 1979—; mem. editl. bd. Arbitrium, Munich, 1980-87, Mich. Germanic Studies, 1985—. Author: Heinrich Heine: The Elusive Poet, 1969; Six Essays on the Young German Novel, 1972; Literary Sociology and Practical Criticism, 1977; Heinrich Heine: A Modern Biography, 1979, Wilhelm Raabe: The Fiction of the Alternative Community, 1987, The Shifting Fortunes of Wilhelm Raabe, 1992. Guggenheim fellow, 1972-73; Am. Council Learned Socs. fellow, 1977-78, travel grantee, 1983; Duke August Library, Wolfenbuttel Ger. adoptive stipend, 1983. Mem. MLA, Am. Assn. Tchrs. German, Lessing Soc., Goethe Soc. N.Am., Conn. Acad. Arts and Scis., Heinrich-Heine Gesellschaft. Home: 211 Highland St New Haven CT 06511-2001 Office: Yale U Dept German PO Box 208210 New Haven CT 06520-8210

SAMO, AMANDO, bishop; b. Moch Island, Federated States of Micronesia, Aug. 16, 1948; s. Benito and Esiper Samo. BA in Psychology, Chaminade U., 1973; diploma in religious edn., EAPI, Manila, Philippines, 1982. Ordained priest Roman Cath. Ch. Parish priest Cath. Ch., Truk, Federated States of Micronesia, 1977-87; bishop Diocese of the Carolines and Marshalls, Truk, 1987—; founder, bd. dirs. Marriage Encounter-Carolines-Marshalls, Truk, 1982-88; dir. ch. leadership tng. programs, Truk, 1986—; mem. Bishop's Conf. Oceania, 1988, pontificial commn. Cor Unum, Rome, 1995. Chmn. Bishop's commn. justice and devel., 1995. Home: PO Box 250 Chuuk FM 96942-0250 Office: Diocese Caroline Is PO Box 250 Chuuk FM 96942*

SAMOJLIK, EUGENIUSZ, medical educator, retired researcher; b. Kuchmy-Bialystok, Poland, Aug. 20, 1933; s. Michael and Anastazia S.; m. Anna Morozewicz, Apr. 10, 1965; children: Dorothy, Michael. BS in Biomedicine, U. Warsaw, 1958, PhD in Reproductive Endocrinology, 1964. Rsch. asst. Maternity Inst. Dept. Pharmacology, Warsaw, 1958-62, sr. asst., 1962-66; asst. prof., chief reproductive pharmacology & toxicology Inst. Pharmacy Dept. Pharmacology, Warsaw, 1966-70; assoc. prof., chief hormone rsch. lab. Med. Acad. Dept. Clin. Endocrinology, Warsaw, 1970-73; staff researcher II Syntex, Inc. Rsch. Divsn., Palo Alto, Calif., 1974-75; asst. prof. physiology, dir. radioimmunoassay lab. Milton S. Hershey (Pa.) Med. Ctr., Divsn. Endocrinology, 1975-80; staff endocrinologist VA Med. Ctr. Dept. Medicine, Sect. Endocrinology, East Orange, N.J., 1980-82; dir. endocrine lab. Newark Beth Israel Med. Ctr., Dept. Medicine, 1982-92; assoc. prof. medicine U. Medicine & Dentistry-N.J. Med. Sch., Newark, 1982—; chief endocrine lab. dept. Labs. NBIMC, 1994-96; vis. researcher UCLA Sch. Medicine, Torrance, Calif., 1973; vis. scientist Nat. Inst. Child Health Human Devel., Reproductive Br., Bethesda, Md., 1973-74; lectr. in field. Mem. internat. adv. bd. Jour. Assisted Reproductive Tech. and Andrology, mem. editorial bd., 1996; contbr. articles to profl. jours. Grantee WHO, 1973-74, Ciba-Geigy, 1982-83, Nat. Cancer Inst., 1983-86, 85-88; tng. program fellow Worcester Found. Experimental Biology, Shrewsbury, Mass., 1967-69. Mem. AAAS, Am. Soc. Andrology, Am. Assn. Clin. Chemistry, Nat. Acad. Clin. Biochemistry, Acad. Medicine N.J., Endorcine Soc. Home: 73 Sykes Ave Livingston NJ 07039-1318

SAMOUR, CARLOS MIGUEL, chemist. BA in Chemistry, Am. U. Beirut, 1942, MA, 1944; MS in Organic Chemistry, MIT, 1947; PhD, Boston U., 1950. Postdoctoral rsch. fellow Boston U., 1950-52; rsch. chemist The Kendall Co., 1952-57, dir. Theodore Clark Lab., 1957-73, dir. Lexington Rsch. Lab., 1973-81; pres. Samour Assocs., 1981-84; chmn., scientific dir. MacroChem Corp., Lexington, Mass., 1982—; section chmn. Internat. Union Pure and Applied Chemistry, U. Mass., Amherst, 1982; session chmn. Biomaterials, Sardinia, Italy, 1988, internat. conf. MIT, 1982, tech. advisor; pres., chmn. Augusta Epilepsy Rsch. Found., Washington, 1989—; advisor univs. and med. ctrs. Contbr. numerous articles to profl. jours. Mem. Am. Chem. Soc. (cert. merit 1981, adminstr. Kendall award 1964-83), Am. Assn. Pharm. Scis., Controlled Release Soc. Achievements include over 50 U.S. patents and over 200 foreign patents; research in the fields of polymer chemistry, bio-materials, pharmaceuticals, dental materials and transdermal drug delivery systems. Office: Macrochem Corp 110 Hartwell Ave Lexington MA 02173-3134

SAMPAS, DOROTHY M., government official; b. Washington, Aug. 24, 1933; d. Lawrence and Anna Cornelia (Henkel) Myers; m. James George Sampas, Dec. 8, 1962; children: George, Lawrence James. AB, U. Mich., 1955; postgrad., U. Paris, 1955-56; PhD, Georgetown U., 1970; cert., Nat. War Coll., Washington, 1987, Naval Post Grad. Sch., 1993. With Bur. Pub. Affairs Dept. State, Washington, 1958-60, analyst Bur. of Adminstrn., 1973-75, div. chief, dep. chief Office of Position and Pay Mgmt., 1979-83, div. chief Office of Mgmt., 1983-84, dir. Office of Mgmt., 1984-86; vice consul Am. Consulate Gen., Hamburg, Fed. Republic Germany, 1960-62; cons. Trans Century Corp., Washington, 1972; gen. svcs. officer Am. Embassy, Brussels, 1975-79; embassy minister-counselor Am. Embassy, Beijing, 1987-90; minister-counselor U.S. Mission to UN, N.Y.C., 1991-94; Am. ambassador to Islamic Republic of Mauritania, 1994—. Presbyterian. Home: 4715 Trent Ct Chevy Chase MD 20815-5516 Office: Am Embassy Nouakchott Dept State Washington DC 20521-2430 also: Am Embassy, Boite Postale 222, Nouakchott Mauritania

SAMPER, JOSEPH PHILLIP, retired photographic products company executive; b. Salt Lake City, Aug. 13, 1934; s. Juan M. and Harriet (Howell) S.; married; children: Joaquin P., Christopher F. With Eastman Kodak Co., Rochester, N.Y., 1961—; asst. to gen. mgr. mktg. div. Eastman Kodak Co. (U.S. and Can. photog. div.), 1976-77; asst. v.p., asst. gen. mgr. mktg. div. Eastman Kodak Co. (U.S. and Can. photographic div.), 1977-79; v.p., gen. mgr. mktg. div. Eastman Kodak Co., 1979—, exec. v.p., gen. mgr. photographic div., 1983-86, vice chmn., exec. officer, 1986-90; chief exec. officer, pres. Kinder-Care Learning Ctrs., Inc., 1991-92; pres., CEO Sun Microsystems Computer Co., 1994-95; chmn., CEO Cray Rsch., Inc., Eagan, Minn., 1995-96; chmn., CEO, pres. Quadlex, Inc., Fremont, Calif., 1996—; bd. dirs. Armstrong World Industries, Inc., Lancaster, Pa., Interpub. Group, N.Y.C., Sylvan Learning Systems, Inc., Columbia, Md., Ingram Micro, Inc., Santa Ana, Calif. With USNR, 1952-56. Recipient Alfred Knight award Am. Grad. Sch. Internat. Mgmt., 1961, Barton Kyle Young award, 1961; Sloan fellow, MIT, 1972-73. Roman Catholic.

SAMPINO, ANTHONY F., physician, obstetrician and gynecologist; b. Bklyn., Jan. 13, 1965; s. Frank Paul-Joseph and Lillian Katherine (Cucinotta) S. D Osteopathic Medicine, N.Y. Coll. Osteopathic Medicine, 1991. Rotating intern St. Barnabas Hosp., Bronx, N.Y., 1991-92; resident ob-gyn. St. Vincents Med. Ctr. of Richmond, Staten Island, N.Y., 1992-96; with dept. ob-gyn. Good Samaritan Hosp., West Islip, N.Y., 1996—; pvt. practice Comprehensive Ob-Gyn of L.I., Massapequa Park, N.Y., 1997—; adj. clin. instr. N.Y. Coll. Osteo. Medicine, 1996—. Fellow Am. Coll. Ob-Gyn. (jr., sect. chmn. 1992-94); mem. AMA, Am. Osteo. Assn., Am. Assn. Gynecologic Laparoscopists (Outstanding Resident in Gyn. Endoscopy 1996), Med. Soc. State of N.Y., L.I. Soc. Osteo. Physicians & Surgeons, Richmond County Med. Soc., Suffolk County Med. Soc. Avocation: scuba diving. Home: 69 Wildwood Dr Dix Hills NY 11746

SAMPLE, ALTHEA MERRITT, secondary education educator, conductor; b. Miami, Fla., Apr. 6, 1937; d. Otis and Alma (Carter) S. BS in Music Edn., Fla. A&M, 1960; Master in Music Edn., U. Miami, 1971. Tchr. elem. music edn. Dade County, Miami, Fla., 1960-65, dir. jr. h.s. orch., 1965-84, dir. orch. sr. h.s., 1984—; dir. orch. Miami Northwestern Performing Arts Ctr., 1984—; clin. tchr. internship program U. Miami, 1988-90; clinician Broward County Orch. Evaluation, 1986, 87; participant workshops in field, 1965—. Coord. North Area Festival, 1988; conducted Supt.'s Honors Orch., 1988, 92, South Area Festival Orch., 1989, tribute Dr. George Bornoff Concert, 1994, Gov. Fla. Inaugural Concert, 1991; performed Nat. Educator Reception, 1993; sponsor Miami Herald Silver Knight Award winners, 1988, 90, 92. Recipient Black Music Achievement award, 1992, Outstanding Educator award U.S. Rep. Dante Fussell, 1992, Area III Tchr. of Yr., Dade County, 1992. Mem. United Tchrs. Dade, Fla. Orch. Assn., Fla. Music Educators, Dade Music Educators, Nat. Alliance Educators, Eta Phi Beta. Democrat. Episcopalian. Avocations: reading, playing flute, violin, organ, tennis. Home: 15720 E Bunche Park Dr Opa Locka FL 33054-2020

SAMPLE, BETTE JEANE, elementary educator; b. Long Beach, Calif., Oct. 20, 1943; d. Dennis Lynn and Norma Dorothy (Ladner) Hart; m. Ronald Charles Sample, Oct. 7, 1967; children: Jennifer Lynne Sample Amend, Leah Anne. BS, Augustana Coll., Sioux Falls, S.D., 1966; MA in Edn., U. Wyo., 1994. Tchr. Whittier Elem. Sch., Colorado Springs, Colo., 1966-67, North Park Elem. Sch., Columbia Heights, Minn., 1967-68; tchr. Gertrude Burns Elem. Sch., Newcastle, Wyo., 1976-88, 2d grade tchr., 1989-90, 1st grade tchr., 1990-96; instr. Ea. Wyo. Coll., Torrington, 1987-96; tchr. English Newcastle Mid. Sch., 1988-89. Grantee Ency. Brittanica, 1991. Mem. NEA, Wyo. Edn. Assn. (Tchr. of Yr. 1991), Newcastle Edn. Assn. Democrat. Lutheran. Home: PO Box 537 Newcastle WY 82701-0537 Office: Prin Kitty Moats K-8 Sch 116 Casper Ave Newcastle WY 82701-2705

SAMPLE, FREDERICK PALMER, former college president; b. Columbia, Pa., May 22, 1930; s. William Walter and Erna Rebecca (Roye) S.; m. Mary Jane Drager, Aug. 19, 1951; children: Jeffrey Lynn, Roger Lee. AB, Lebanon Valley Coll., 1952; MEd, Western Md. Coll., 1956; DEd, Pa. State U., 1968; D in Pedagogy, Albright Coll., 1968. Tchr. Annville (Pa.) High Sch., 1952-53; tchr. Red Lion Area (Pa.) High Sch., 1953-57, prin., 1957-59, supervising prin., 1959-64; supt. Manheim Twp. Sch. Dist., Neffsville, Pa., 1964-68; pres. Lebanon Valley Coll., Annville, Pa., 1968-83; supt. Bellefonte (Pa.) Area Sch. Dist., 1987-92; ednl. cons.; adminstr. Bucknell U., 1985-87. Mem. Phi Delta Kappa. Republican. Home: PO Box 92 Eagles Mere PA 17731-0092 *Despite failures, difficulties, and disappointments I have tried to find the honorable, responsible, productive, true, and humane solutions to problems and make decisions for progress.*

SAMPLE, JOSEPH SCANLON, foundation executive; b. Chgo., Mar. 15, 1923; s. John Glen and Helen (Scanlon) S.; m. Patricia M. Law, Dec. 22, 1942 (div.); children: Michael Scanlon, David Forrest, Patrick Glen; m. Miriam Tyler Willing, Nov. 19, 1965. B.A., Yale U., 1947. Trainee, media analyst, media dir. Dancer-Fitzgerald-Sample, Inc., advt. agy., Chgo., 1947-50; v.p., media dir. Dancer-Fitzgerald-Sample, Inc., advt. agy., 1952-53; pres. Mont. Television Network KTVQ, Billings, KXLF-AM-TV, Butte, Mont., KRTV, Great Falls, Mont., KPAX-TV, Missoula, Mont., 1955-84. Pres. Greater Mont. Found., 1986—; chmn. Wheeler Ctr. Mont State U., 1988—. Served with AUS, 1943-46. With U.S. Army, 1950-52. Mem. Rotary, Yellowstone Country Club, Port Royal Club, Hole in The Wall Golf Club, Hilands Golf Club, Naples Yacht Club. Home: 606 Highland Park Dr Billings MT 59102-1909 Office: 14 N 24th St Billings MT 59101-2422

SAMPLE, NATHANIEL WELSHIRE, architect; b. Phila., Apr. 3, 1918; s. Nathaniel Welshire Jr. and Evelyn Aldrich (Hope) S.; m. Virginia Bogert, May 19, 1945; children: Peter, Gregory, Deborah, Phoebe, Joan. BA, Dartmouth Coll., 1940; BArch, Ill. Inst. Tech., 1946. Registered architect, Wis. Archtl. designer Shaw Naess & Murphey, Chgo., 1946-47; designer Weiler, Strang & Assocs., Madison, Wis., 1947-51; project mgr. Weiler, Strang & Assocs., Madison, 1951-58, ptnr., 1958-62; ptnr. Sample & Mullins, Madison, 1962-67, Sample & Potter, Inc., Madison, 1967-84; v.p. Design for Tomorrow, Madison, 1956; pres. Dane County U.N. Assn., Madison, 1965-67; archtl. cons. Mass., N.Y., Ill., 1987—. Prin. works include Sch. Design, a Columbus elem. sch., 1953 (honor award), residence of Shorewood Hills, Wis., 1955 (honor award), Chilren's Treatment Ctr., Madison, 1959, Chgo. Pub. Libr. (1st pl. award nat. competition 1970), design for restoration of historic Stoner House, Madison, 1991 (Preservation award Dane County). Mem. Dane County Regional Plan Commn., 1981-86, Urban Design Commn., Madison, 1990—; bd. dirs. Madison Downtown Sr. Ctr., 1988—. Lt. (j.g.) USNR, 1942-46, PTO. Fellow AIA; mem. Wis. Soc. Architects (chmn. jury housing for homeless competition 1990, Golden award 1992). Democrat. Mem. Soc. of Friends. Avocations: sports, grandchildren, citizenship. Address: 1105 Rutledge St Madison WI 53703-3825

SAMPLE, STEVEN BROWNING, university executive; b. St. Louis, Nov. 29, 1940; s. Howard and Dorothy (Cunningham) S.; m. Kathryn Brunkow, Jan. 28, 1961; children: Michelle Sample Smith, Melissa Ann. BS, U. Ill., 1962, MS, 1963; DHULL (hon.), Canisius Coll., 1989; PhD, U. Ill., 1965; LLD (hon.), U. Sheffield, Eng., 1991; EdD (hon.), Purdue U., 1994; DHL (hon.), Hebrew Union Coll., 1994; DL (hon.), U. Nebr., 1995. Sr. scientist Melpar Inc., Falls Church, Va., 1965-66; assoc. prof. elec. engring. Purdue U., Lafayette, Ind., 1966-73; dep. dir. Ill. Bd. Higher Edn., Springfield, 1971-74; exec. v.p. acad. affairs, dean Grad. Coll., prof. elec. eng. U. Nebr., Lincoln, 1974-82; prof. elec. and computer engring. SUNY, Buffalo, 1982-91, pres., 1982-91; pres. U. So. Calif., L.A., 1991—, prof. elec. engring., 1991—; bd. dirs. Ind., First Interstate Bancorp, L.A., Presley Cos., Newport Beach, Calif., Western Atlas Inc., Beverly Hills, Calif.; vice chmn., bd. dirs. Western N.Y. Tech. Devel. Ctr., Buffalo, 1982-91; chmn. bd. dirs. Calspan-UB Rsch. Ctr., Inc., Buffalo, 1983-91; mem. Calif. Coun. Sci. and Tech., Irvine, Calif.; cons. in field. Contbr. articles to profl. jours.; patentee in field. Timpanist St. Louis Philharm. Orch., 1955-58; chmn. Western N.Y. Regional Econ. Devel. Coun., 1984-91; trustee U. at Buffalo Found., 1982-91, Studio Arena Theatre, Buffalo, 1983-91, Western N.Y. Pub. Broadcasting Assn., 1985-91; bd. dirs. Buffalo Philharm. Orch., 1982-91, Regenstrief Med. Found., Indpls., 1982—, Rsch. Found. SUNY, 1987-91; chmn. Gov.'s Conf. on Sci. and Engring. Edn., Rsch. and Devel., 1989-91; chair Calif. Bus.-Higher Edn. Forum; bd. dirs. L.A. chpt. World Affairs Coun., Hughes Galaxy Inst. Edn., L.A., 1991-94, Rebuild L.A. Com., L.A. Annenberg Metro Project, Coalition of 100 Club of L.A.; trustee L.A. Ednl. Alliance for Restructuring Now. Recipient Disting. Alumnus award Dept. Elec. Engring. U. Ill., 1980, citation award Buffalo Coun. on World Affairs, 1986, Engr. of Yr. award N.Y. State Soc. Profl. Engrs., 1985, Alumni Honor award Coll. Engring., U. Ill., 1985, Outstanding Elec. Engr. award Purdue U., 1993, Humanitarian award Nat. Conf. Christians and Jews, L.A., 1994, Hollzer Meml. award Jewish Fedn. Coun. Greater L.A., 1994; Sloan Found. fellow, 1962-63, NSF grad. fellow, 1963-65, Am. Coun. Edn. fellow Purdue U., 1970-71, NSF. Mem. AAU (chmn. com. on postdoctoral edn. 1994—), IEEE (Outstanding Paper award 1976), Nat. Assn. State Univs. and Land-Grant Colls. (ednl. telecommunications com., 1982-83, chmn. coun. of pres. 1985-86, edn. and tech. com. 1986-87, exec. com. 1987-89), Coun. on Fgn. Rels., Sigma Xi. Episcopalian. Home: 1550 Oak Grove Ave San Marino CA 91108-1108 Office: U So Calif Office of the Pres University Park ADM 110 Los Angeles CA 90089-0012

SAMPLES, MARTINA, nursing home administrator; b. Phila., Nov. 20, 1942; d. Martin Rulon and Mallette Mary (Holden) Sembach; m. Billy Irwin Samples, May 13, 1987; children: Lauren, Lynne, Michael, Andrew, Toni, Christopher, Roberta, John. AA, Daytona Beach Community Coll., 1978. LPN; lic. nursing home adminstr., Tex. Adminstr. Purple Hills Manor/Gray Enterprises, Bandera, Tex., 1985-86, Comanche View-Nat. Heritage, Ft. Stockton, Tex., 1986-87, Louis Pasteur Care Ctr./Camlu Care Ctrs., San Antonio, 1987-88, Castle Hills Manor/Campbell-White Assocs., San Antonio, 1988-89, Briarclifff Health Care Ctr., Greenville, Tex., 1989-91; mgr. physician orders dept. Cullum Industries Page Drug Nursing Home

Svcs., 1992-96; prin. Samples & Assocs., San Antonio, 1992—; adminstr. Our Lady of the Lake Retirement Ctr., McCullough Hail Nursing Ctr., San Antonio, 1996—; sr. long term care cons. Medicare/Medicaid reimbursement, tchr. seminars to long-term care adminstrs.; adj. faculty St. Phillips Coll., San Antonio, 1992—. Mem. NAFE, Tex. Health Care Assn., Tex. Assn. for Homes Svcs. for Aging, Am. Legion, Order Eastern Star, VFW, Nat. Assn. of Miniature Enthusiasts. Republican. Methodist. Avocations: crochet, reading, miniaturist and collector. Home: 860 Dougherty St Prescott AZ 86301

SAMPLINER, LINDA HODES, psychologist, consultant; b. Cleve., Sept. 25, 1945; d. Walter J. and Caroline Jean (Klein) Hodes; m. Richard Evan Sampliner, July 31, 1966; children: Robert David, Steven Jay. BS, Western Res. U., Cleve., 1967; EdM, Boston U., 1972, EdD, 1975. Lic. psychologist, Ariz; cert. grief counselor, cons. in clin. hypnosis. Counselor The Family Life Ctr., Columbia, Md., 1976-80; psychologist Psychology & Rehab. Assocs., Tucson, 1981-85; pvt. practice Tucson, 1985—; cons., psychologist div. econ. security Child and Family Svcs., Tucson, 1985—; psychologist Sonora Behavioral Health Assn., 1994—; cons. SHARE, Tucson, 1985—; trainer comm. skills for police Balt. County Dept. Mental Health, 1975-80, drub abuse adminstrn. trainer for counselors, 1975-80. Bd. dirs. Adapt Inc., Tucson, 1985-93, pres., 1990-91; bd. dirs. Mental Health Resources, 1993-95; bd. dirs. Tucson Symphony Soc., 1984-89, v.p., 1987-89; pres. bd. dirs. Tucson Mus. of Art League, 1985-86; mem. adv. bd. dept. art U. Ariz., 1993—. Mem. APA, Assn. Death Edn. and Counseling, Ariz. Psychol. Assn., So. Ariz. Psychol. Assn. Avocations: hiking, entertaining, bicycling. Office: Sonora Behavioral Health Network 2001 W Orange Grove Rd Ste 410 Tucson AZ 85704-1141

SAMPRAS, PETE, tennis player; b. Washington, Aug. 12, 1971; s. Sam and Georgia Sampras. mem. U.S. Davis Cup team., named to Olympic Team Atlanta, 1996. chairman ATP Tour Charities program, 1992. Winner tournaments including Phila., 1990, Manchester, 1990, U.S. Open, 1990, 1993, Grand Slam Cup, 1990, L.A., 1991, Indpls., 1991, Lyon, 1991, IBM/ATP Tour World Championship-Frankfurt, 1991, 94, U.S. Pro Indoor, 1992, Lipton Internat., 1993, Wimbledon, 1993, 94, 95, Australian Open, 1994, Italian Open, 1994; ranked # 1 during 1993, 94 season, finalist Australian Open, 1995. 1st male to win the U.S Open, Wimbledon, and the Australian Open in succession, mem. U.S. Davis Cup Team, 1991, became only the fourth player to finish as No. 1three (or more) consecutive years, 1st player to surpass $5 million in a season,all-time leader in career earnings, named ATP Tour Player of the Year, 1993-94, Jim Thorpe Tennis Player, 1993. Office: ATP Tour 201 ATP Tour Blvd Ponte Vedra FL 32082*

SAMPSON, DAPHNE RAE, library director; b. Milw., Aug. 11, 1943; d. Gerald Joseph and Helene Virginia Babbitt; m. Charles Sargent Sampson, Oct. 23, 1971. BA, U. Wis., 1965, MLS, 1966. Reference libr. Def. Intelligence Agy., Washington, 1966-68; sr. reference libr. U.S. Dept. of State, Washington, 1968-78, Exec. Office of the Pres., Washington, 1978-80; chief readers' svcs. Fed. Trade Commn., Washington, 1980-81; chief readers' svcs. U.S. Dept. of Justice, Washington, 1981-84, asst. dir. libr. staff, 1984-86, dep. dir. libr. staff, 1986, acting dir. libr. staff, 1986-87, dir. libr. staff, 1987—, sr. exec. svc., 1995—. Active Berkshire Civic Assn., Alexandria, Va., 1976—. Mem. Am. Assn. Law Librs., Law Librs. Soc. of Washington, Fed. Libr. and Info. Ctr. Com. (bd. mem. 1992). Home: 5838 Wyomissing Ct Alexandria VA 22303-1634 Office: US Dept of Justice Libr Rm 5317 10th & Pennsylvania Ave NW Washington DC 20530

SAMPSON, EARLDINE ROBISON, education educator; b. Russell, Iowa, June 18, 1923; d. Lawrence Earl and Mildred Mona (Judy) Robison; m. Wesley Claude Sampson, Nov. 25, 1953; children: Ann Elizabeth, Lisa Ellen. Diploma, Iowa State Tchrs. Coll., 1943, BA, 1950; MS in Edn., Drake U., 1954; postgrad., No. Ill. U., Iowa State U., 1965-66, 74. Cert. tchr., guidance counselor, Iowa. Tchr. elem. sch. various pub. sch. sys., 1943-48; cons. speech and hearing Iowa Dept. Pub. Instrn., Des Moines, 1950-52; speech therapist Des Moines Pub. Schs., 1952-54, 55; lectr. spl. edn. No. Ill. U., DeKalb, 1964-65; tchr. of homebound Cedar Falls (Iowa) Pub. Schs., 1967-68; asst. prof. edn. U. No. Iowa, Cedar Falls, 1968; asst. prof., counselor Wartburg Coll., Waverly, Iowa, 1968-70; instr. elem. edn., then head of advising elem. edn. Iowa State U., Ames, 1972-82; field supr. elem. edn. U. Toledo, 1988, 89; ind. cons. Sylvania, Ohio, 1989—; cons. Des Moines Speech and Hearing Ctr., 1958-59, bd. dirs., 1962, 63; cons. Sartori Hosp., Cedar Falls, 1967-69; bd. dirs. Story County Mental Health Ctr., Ames, 1972-74. NDEA fellow, 1965. Mem. AAUW, Univ. Women's Club, Zeta Phi Eta. Methodist. Avocations: public speaking on preservation of prose and poetry, reading, music, photography. Home: 4047 Newcastle Dr Sylvania OH 43560-3450 *My creed is based on the words of Edwin Markham: "There is a destiny that makes us brothers; none goes his way alone. All that we send into the lives of others comes back into our own. Just reward came from a former student who stated "I have never known you to compromise your principles".*

SAMPSON, EDWARD COOLIDGE, humanities educator; b. Ithaca, N.Y., Dec. 20, 1920; s. Martin W. and Julia (Pattison) S.; m. Frances P. Hanford, Oct. 26, 1946 (div. 1968); children: Susan S. Wilt, Edward H.; m. Cynthia R. Clark, 1968. BA, Cornell U., 1942, PhD, 1957; MA, Columbia U., 1949. Instr. Hofstra Coll., Hempstead, N.Y., 1946-49; teaching fellow Cornell U., Ithaca, 1949-52; with faculty Clarkson Coll. Tech., Potsdam, N.Y., 1952-69, assoc. prof. humanities, 1957-61, prof., 1961-69; prof. SUNY, Oneonta, 1969-82, ret., 1982. Author: E.B. White, 1974, Afterword, The House of the Seven Gables, 1961, E.B. White: Dictionary of Literary Biography, 1982. Capt. USAAF, 1942-46. Decorated Bronze Star medal; Fulbright prof. U. Panjab, 1959-60. Fellow Am. Coun. Learned Studies; mem. MLA. Home: 89 Hemlock Dr Killingworth CT 06419-2225

SAMPSON, FRANKLIN DELANO, minister; b. Houston, Jan. 31, 1947; s. Harry Burney and Annie Belle (Lenzia) S.; m. Fannie Marie Iles, Mar. 12, 1972; children: De Anza Michelle, Franklin Delano, Jr., Frederick Dwayne. BA, U. Houston, 1970; D of Ministries (hon.), Mt. Hope Bible Coll., 1978. Ordained to ministry Nat. Bapt. Conv., 1969. Pastor Friendship Missionary Bapt. Ch., Houston, 1972—; moderator Unity Missionary Bapt. Gen. Assn., Houston, 1985—; chmn. Minister's Conf. of Missionary Bapt. Gen. Conv., Dallas, 1987—, Commn. on Orthodoxy of Nat. Bapt. Conv. of Am., Inc., Shreveport, La., 1987—; chief exec. officer Visions of Faith Ministries, Inc., Houston, 1985—. Mem. Bapt. Mins. Assn. of Houston and Vicinity (v.p. 1990—), Unity Missionary Bapt. Gen. Assn. (Houston, moderator 1985-93), Masons. Democrat. Home: 12947 Wincrest Ct Cypress TX 77429-2001 Office: Friendship Missionary Bapt Ch 4812 Bennington St Houston TX 77016-7003

SAMPSON, JOHN DAVID, lawyer; b. Lackawanna, N.Y., Feb. 20, 1955; s. Hugh Albert Sampson and May (Davidson) Sampson Henderson; m. Carol Jasen, July 29, 1978; children: Rachel Henderson, Matthew David. BA, Canisius Coll., Buffalo, 1977; JD, Union U., Albany, N.Y., 1982. Bar: N.Y. 1983, U.S. Dist. Ct. (we. dist.) N.Y. 1983, U.S. Dist. Ct. (no. dist.) N.Y. 1996. Assoc. Damon & Morey, Buffalo, 1982-87, Lippes Silverstein Mathias & Wexler, Buffalo, 1987-88; ptnr. Walsh & Sampson, P.C., Buffalo, 1988-93, Jasen, Jasen & Sampson P.C., Buffalo, 1993—. Dir. Edu Kids Early Childhood Ctrs., Inc., Orchard Park, N.Y., 1994—. Mem. ABA, N.Y. State Bar Assn., Erie County Bar Assn., Def. Rsch. Inst., Rotary of East Aurora (dir. 1993-97, pres. 1995-96). Wesleyan Methodist. Avocations: golf, cycling, skiing. Home: 44 Elmwood Ave East Aurora NY 14052-2610 Office: Jasen Jasen & Sampson PC # 620 3556 Lake Shore Rd Ste 620 Buffalo NY 14219-1400

SAMPSON, JOHN EUGENE, consulting company executive; b. Lincoln, Nebr., Feb. 25, 1941; s. Delbert John and Mary Etta (Dodrill) S.; m. Mary Margaret Treanor, Aug. 14, 1965; children—J. Mark, Sharon. A.B. with distinction, Nebr. Wesleyan U., 1963; M.B.A., Ind. U., 1964. Mgmt. asst., exec. trainee Office Sec. Def., Washington, 1963-64; mem. staff Com. Econ. Devel., Washington, 1964-69; coordinator environ. planning Gen. Mills Inc., Mpls., 1969-72, mgr. devel. planning, 1972-74; dir. corp. planning Central Soya Co. Inc., Ft. Wayne, Ind., 1974-76, v.p. corp. planning, 1976-80, v.p. corp. planning and devel., 1980-82, v.p. corp. devel., corp. sec., 1982-84; v.p. corp. planning and devel. Internat. Multifoods, Inc., 1984-96; pres. Sampson Assocs., Edina, Minn., 1994—. Mem. bd. govs. Nebr. Wesleyan U., 1974-80; chmn. bd. trustees St. Joseph United Meth. Ch., Ft. Wayne, 1984; bd. dirs., treas. North Ind. United Meth. Found., 1981-84; lay mem. North Ind. Ann. Conf. United Meth. Ch., 1980-84; bd. dirs. Anthony Wayne coun. Boy Scouts Am., 1984; lay mem. Minn. Ann. Conf. United Meth. Church, 1985-91, 97—; chmn. conf. bd. devel. Minn. United Meth. Conf., 1986-91; chmn. bd. trustees Hennepin Ave. United Meth. Ch., Mpls., 1990-92, chair adminstrv. coun., 1993-95, lay leader, 1995—. Mem. Ind. U. Sch. Bus. Alumni Assn. (pres. 1984-85), Interlachen Country Club. Home: 6612 Gleason Ter Edina MN 55439-1131 Office: Sampson Assocs 5200 Willson Rd Edina MN 55424-1332

SAMPSON, RICHARD THOMAS, lawyer; b. Kingsport, Tenn., Aug. 16, 1944; s. Thomas L. and Vera Odene (Keel) S.; m. Carolyn Bland Thomas, Sept. 26, 1973 (div.); m. Myra Lynn, June 14, 1979; children: Ronnie Lynn, Carrie Ann, Richard Thomas II, Virginia Lynn, Carleton Leland. AB, U. Md., 1967; JD with honors, 1971. Bar: Md. 1972, U.S. Ct. Appeals (4th cir.) 1977, U.S. Ct. Appeals (D.C. cir.) 1982, D.C. 1984, U.S. Ct. Appeals (6th cir.) 1982, U.S. Ct. Appeals (fed. cir.) 1990, U.S. Ct. Appeals (1st, 2d, 3d, 5th, 9th cirs.), U.S. Supreme Ct. 1993. Mgmt. auditor U.S. Acctg. Office, Washington, 1967-70; assoc. Semmes, Bowen & Semmes, Balt., 1972-78; ptnr. Semmes, Bowen & Semmes, Washington, 1978—. Editor: EEO Practice Guide/Trial Manual, 1979. Fellow Coll. Labor and Employment Lawyers; mem. ABA, Fed. Bar Assn. (gen. counsel chmn. com., chmn. labor com. 1980—, Robert J. Rosenthal award 1980, disting. service award 1982, leadership award 1988), Kiwanis. Office: Semmes Bowen & Semmes 250 W Pratt St Baltimore MD 21201-2423

SAMPSON, ROBERT NEIL, natural resources consultant; b. Spokane, Wash., Nov. 29, 1938; s. Robert Jay and Juanita Cleone (Hickman) S.; m. Jeanne Louise Stokes, June 7, 1960; children—Robert W., Eric S., Christopher B., Heidi L. B.S. in Agr., U. Idaho, 1960; M.Public Adminstrn., Harvard U., 1974. Soil conservationist Soil Conservation Service, Burley, Idaho, 1960-61; work unit conservationist Soil Conservation Service, Orofino, Idaho, 1962-65; agronomist Soil Conservation Service, Idaho Falls, Idaho, 1967-68; info. specialist Soil Conservation Service, Boise, 1968-70, area conservationist, 1970-72; land use specialist Soil Conservation Service, Washington, 1974-77; dir. environ. services div. Soil Conservation Service, 1977; land use program mgr. Idaho Planning and Community Affairs Agy., Boise, 1972-73; exec. v.p. Nat. Assn. Conservation Dists., Washington, 1978-84, Am. Forestry Assn., Washington, 1984-95; sr. fellow Am. Forests, Washington, 1995—; pres. The Sampson Group, Inc., 1996—; instr. soils and land use Boise State U., 1972; dir. Am. Land Forum, Washington, 1978-88. Author: Farmland or Wasteland: A Time To Choose, 1981, For Love of the Land, 1985; contbr. articles to profl. and popular publs. Pres. Orofino Golf Assn., 1966, Clearwater County Search and Rescue Unit, 1966-67; chmn. Nat. Commn. on Wildfire Disasters, 1992-94. Recipient President's citation Soil Conservation Soc. Am., 1978; named Boise Fed. Civil Servant of Year Boise Fed. Bus. Assn., 1972. Fellow Soil and Water Conservation Soc. (Hugh Hammond Bennett award 1992); mem. Soc. Am. Foresters, Am. Soc. Assn. Execs. Presbyterian.

SAMPSON, RONALD A., advertising executive; b. Charlottesville, Va., Nov. 13, 1933; s. Percy Thomas Sampson and Lucile (Mills) Martin; m. Norvelle Ann Johnson, Aug. 8, 1959; children: David Alan, Cheryl Ann. BS in Commerce, DePaul U., 1956. Advt. sales rep. Ebony Mag., Chgo., 1959-63; merchandising rep. Foote, Cone & Belding Advt., Chgo., 1963-66; account mgr. Tatham, Laird & Kudner Advt., Chgo., 1966-78; account mgr., exec. v.p. Burrell, Advt., Chgo., 1978-81; advt. agy. account mgr., sr. v.p. Darcy McManus Masius, Chgo., 1981-88, Burrell Comm. Group, Chgo., 1990—; mem. diversity com. Am. Advt. Fedn., 1996—. Bd. dirs. Cmty. Renewal Soc., Chgo., 1969-94; deacon Chgo. United, 1992-94; co-chair Protestants for Common Good, 1996—. With U.S. Army, 1956-58. Home: 6175 S Oglesby Ave Chicago IL 60602 Office: Burrell Comm Group 20 N Michigan Ave Chicago IL 60602-4811

SAMPSON, RONALD GARY, lawyer; b. Haverhill, Mass., Apr. 8, 1942; s. Courtney Howard and Irene Velma (Sweetser) S. AB, Yale U., 1963; MA, Cambridge U., Eng., 1967; JD, Harvard U., 1968. Bar: Mass. 1969. Asst. prof., asst. dean sch. law U. Conn., 1968-69; assoc. Goodwin, Procter and Hoar, Boston, 1969-75; gen. counsel The Boston Co., 1975-93. Trustee Longy Sch. Music, Cambridge, Mass., 1973—, pres., 1986-91; trustee Kneisel Hall Chamber Music Sch., 1994—; dir. Early Music Am., 1992—. Mem. Harvard Music Assn. (bd. dirs. 1982-94, pres. 1991-94), St. Botolph Club (v.p., treas. and gov. 1994—), Longwood Cricket Club, Badminton and Tennis Club.

SAMPSON, SAMUEL FRANKLIN, sociology educator; b. Malden, Mass., Sept. 22, 1934; s. Samuel Daniel and Margaret Louise (Grimes) S.; m. Patricia Katherine Driscoll, Apr. 8, 1972. B.A., U. Okla., 1960, M.A., 1961; Ph.D., Cornell U., 1968. Asst. prof. dept. sociology SUNY, Binghamton, 1965-66; research assoc. dept. sociology Cornell U., Ithaca, N.Y., 1966-67; lectr., chmn. bd. tutors and advs. Harvard U., Cambridge, Mass., 1967-72; assoc. prof. dept. urban studies and planning MIT, Cambridge, 1971-72; prof. sociology U. Vt., Burlington, 1972—, chmn. dept. sociology, 1972-76, 90-96; research and policy cons. Public & Community Agys. and Orgns., 1969—. Gen. editor: Bobbs-Merrill Studies in Sociology, 1970-77; contbr. articles to profl. jours. Served with USAF, 1954-58. Mem. AAUP, AAAS, Internat. Sociol. Assn., Am. Sociol. Assn., Am. Acad. Arts and Scis., Ea. Sociol. Soc., Soc. Study Social Problems, New Eng. Sociol. Assn., Soc. Sci. Study Religion, Internat. Soc. Sociology of Knowledge. Home: 215 S Cove Rd Burlington VT 05401-5445 Office: Univ Vt Dept Sociology 31 S Prospect St Burlington VT 05405-1704

SAMPSON, STEVE, professional soccer coach; b. Salt Lake City, Jan. 19, 1957. Graduate, San Jose State U.; MEd, Stanford U. Soccer coach Foothill Cmty. Coll., Los Altos Hills, Calif.; asst. soccer coach U. Calif., L.A., 1982-85; soccer coach Santa Clara (Calif.) U., 1985-90; asst. coach U.S. Nat. Soccer Team, Chgo., 1993-1995, head coach, 1995—; mem. organizing com. World Cup USA 1990-91, co-chmn. U.S. Soccer Coaching com. 1990-91, v.p. competition mgmt. 1994. Named Nat. Coach of the Yr., 1989; earned All-America honors, Foothill Cmty. Coll., 1976. Office: US Soccer 1801 S Prairie Ave Chicago IL 60616-1319*

SAMPSON, SUSAN J., marketing communications consultant, writer; b. St. Louis, Sept. 22, 1939; d. Robert Mantheny Sampson and Lee Quinn Fischbach; m. William Craig Borneman, May 20, 1960 (div. Apr. 1972); children: Katherine Lee Borneman, William Craig Borneman. BA in English Lit., U. Cin., 1969. Writer/photographer WKRC-TV, Cin., 1972-73, art dir., 1973-74; mgr. sta. advt. and promotion WDAF-TV, Kansas City, Mo., 1974-78; creative svcs. dir. WBZ-TV, Boston, 1978-79; supr. comml. prodn. Procter & Gamble Co., Cin., 1979-83, supervising producer Search for Tomorrow, 1983-85, project mgr. corp. comms., 1985-91, exec. producer corp. comms., 1991-95; pres. Insight Comms., Covington, Ky., 1995—. Exec. producer video news mag. P&G This Quarter , 1991-95; author numerous mag. articles. Recipient numerous advt. awards. Mem. Women in Comms. Avocations: art, photography. Home: 312 Garrard St Covington KY 41011-1761

SAMPSON, WESLEY CLAUDE, auditor; b. Terril, Iowa, Mar. 30, 1929; s. Truman Lester and Pauline Marie (Prichard) S.; m. Earldine Robison, Nov. 25, 1953; children: Ann Elizabeth, Lisa Ellen. B in Comml. Sci., Drake U., 1950; MBA, U. Minn., 1964; PhD, U. Mo., 1985. CPA, Iowa, Ohio; cert. data processor; cert. tchr., Iowa. Mgr. A.G. Kiesling, CPA, Des Moines, 1953-56; asst. gen. mgr. Grand River Mutual Telephone Co., Princeton, Mo., 1956-57; mgmt. cons. Des Moines, 1957-59; instr. Rockford (Ill.) Sch. Bus., 1959-60; head tax and data processing dept. Farmers Grain Dealers Assn., Des Moines, 1960-62; dir. fin. svcs. dept. Batten and Assocs., Inc., Des Moines and Mpls., 1962-64; instr. accountancy No. Ill. U., DeKalb, 1964-66; asst. prof. acctg. and data processing U. No. Iowa, Cedar Falls, 1966-70; v.p., trust officer Nevada (Iowa) Nat. Bank, 1970-71; instr. acctg. and data processing Des Moines Area C.C., Ankeny, 1972-75; chief internal auditor Iowa State U., Ames, 1975-76; asst. prof. accountancy U. Mo., Kansas City, Kans., 1979-83; vis. assoc. prof. U. Wis., La Crosse, 1985-87; assoc. prof. acctg. U. Toledo, 1987-94; owner Matrix Auditor, Sylvania, Ohio, 1994—; owner Ctrl. Iowa Computer Svc. Co., Ames, 1970—; speaker in field. Author and designer software for telephone and grain industry; reviewer: Auditing, 1988, Financial Statement Analysis, 1990, EDP Auditing, 1992; contbr. articles to profl. jours.; patentee in field. Auditor United Campus Christian Fellowship, No. Ill. U., DeKalb, 1965, U. Toledo Found., 1991, U. Toledo Campus Fellowship, 1992, Epworth United Meth. Ch., Toledo, 1990-91, mem. fin. com., 1990-91; treas. Congrl. Ch., Cedar Falls, Iowa, 1968-70; mem. faculty senate U. Toledo, 1994. Price Waterhouse Found. scholar, 1977, Peat, Marwick, Mitchell Found. scholar, 1978. Mem. Iowa Soc. CPAs, Ohio Soc CPAs, Inst. Internal Auditors (pres. Toledo chpt. 1996-97), New Enterprise Forum, Info. Sys. Audit and Control Assn. Methodist. Avocations: music, history. Home: 4047 Newcastle Dr Sylvania OH 43560-3450

SAMPSON, WILLIAM ROTH, lawyer; b. Teaneck, N.J., Dec. 11, 1946; s. James and Amelia (Roth) S.; 1 child, Lara; m. Drucilla Jean Mort, Apr. 23, 1988. BA with honors in History, U. Kans., 1968, JD, 1971. Bar: Kans. 1971, U.S. Dist. Ct. Kans. 1971, U.S. Ct. Appeals (10th cir.) 1982, U.S. Ct. Claims 1985, U.S. Ct. Appeals (8th cir.) 1992. Assoc. Turner & Balloun, Gt. Bend, Kans., 1971; ptnr. Foulston & Siefkin, Wichita, Kans., 1975-86, Shook, Hardy & Bacon, Overland Park, Kans., 1987—; presenter legal edn. seminars and confs.; adj. prof. advanced litig. U. Kans., 1994; mem. faculty trial tactics inst. Emory U. Sch. Law, 1994, 95, 96, 97; lectr. area law schs. Author: Kansas Trial Handbook, 1997; mem. Kans. Law Rev., 1969-71, editor, 1970-71; contbr. articles to legal jours. Chmn. stewardship com. Univ. Friends Ch., Wichita, 1984-86; bd. dirs. Friends U. Retirement Corp., Wichita, 1985-87; chmn. capital fund drives Trinity Luth. Ch., Lawrence, Kans., 1990-93, mem. ch. coun., 1990-92; bd. dirs. Lied Ctr. of Kans., 1994-97. Lt. USNR, 1971-75. Fellow Kans. Bar Assn. (chmn. Kans. coll. advocacy 1986, long-range planning, CLE com. 1987-88); mem. ABA, Douglas County Bar Assn., Johnson County Bar Assn. (bench-bar com. 1989-96, Boss of Yr. award 1990), Wichita Bar Assn. (bd. dirs. 1985-86), Am. Bd. Trial Advs. (pres. Kans. chpt. 1990-91, nat. bd. mem. 1990-91), Internat. Assn. Def. Coun. (faculty mem. trial acad. 1994), Def. Rsch. Inst. (Kans. chmn. 1990—, Exceptional Performance Citation 1990, Outstanding State Rep. 1991, 92, 94), Kans. Assn. Def. Counsel (pres. 1989-90, legis. coun. 1991, 93, William H. Kahrs Disting. Achievement award 1994), Kans. U. Law Soc. (bd. govs. 1993-96), Am. Inn Ct. (Judge Hugh Means chpt., Master of Bench), Alvamar Country Club, Order of Coif, Delta Sigma Rho, Phi Alpha Theta, Omicron Delta Kappa. Republican. Lutheran. Avocations: jogging, golf, snow skiing, travel, reading. Office: Shook Hardy & Bacon 9401 Indian Creek Pky Overland Park KS 66210-2005

SAMS, JAMES FARID, real estate development company executive; b. Bay City, Mich., Apr. 21, 1932; s. James and Adele Sams; m. Betty Suham Hamady, Aug. 17, 1957; children: James Karl, Alicia Diane, Victoria Saab. BA, Northwestern U., 1954; JD, U. Mich., 1957; LLM, Harvard U., 1959. Com. counsel ABA spl. com. World Peace/Law, Washington, 1960-63; ptnr. Reeves, Harrison, Sams & Revercomb, Washington, 1964-69, Brown & Sams, Washington, 1969-71, Kirkwood, Kaplan, Russin, Vecchi & Sams, Beirut, 1971-74; owner, prin. Am. Devel. Services Corp., Washington, 1978—; former chmn. bd. DASI, Inc., Washington, 1974-90; dir. Bristol Compressors, Inc., 1983-86, Nat. Bank Wash., 1986-91; rep. U.S. State Dept. Ams. Abroad, Washington, 1965; del. UN Com. on Internat. Trade Law, N.Y.C., 1970. Contbr. articles to profl. jours. Co-founder, dir. Am. Near East Refugee Aid, Washington, 1968-92; mem. adv. bd. Ctr. for Study of Global South, Am. U., Washington, 1983—; mem. visitors com. U. Mich. Law Sch.; mem. exec. com. Am. Task Force for Lebanon, Washington. Served to lt. U.S. Army, 1957-58. Mem. ABA, Bar Assn. of Washington, Am. Soc. Internat. Law, Nat. Assn. Arab Ams. (pres. 1981, chmn. 1983). Avocations: skiing, sports. Home: 8907 Fernwood Rd Bethesda MD 20817-3015 Office: Am Devel Svcs Corp 5454 Wisconsin Ave Ste 1260 Bethesda MD 20815-6901

SAMS, JOHN ROLAND, retired mission executive, missionary; b. Whatcheer, Iowa, Nov. 1, 1922; s. Bert Willian and and Vesta Leora (Wilkins) S.; m. Frances Elizabeth McCluney, July 3, 1924; children: Phyllis Jean, Georgia Ann, Bert Franklin. BS, Iowa State U., 1949; MA, Drake U., 1952; student, Hartford Sem., 1952-54; MA, Chapman Coll., 1972; HHD (hon.), Philippine Christian U., Manila. Tchr. Paullina (Iowa) Pub. Schs., 1949-51; missionary Christian Ch. (Disciples of Christ), Thailand, 1954-67, Philippines, 1968-71; v.p. Am. Leprosy Missions, N.Y.C., 1972-76; exec. v.p. Am. Leprosy Missions, Bloomfield, N.J., 1976-84; pres. Am. Leprosy Missions, Elmwood Park, N.J., 1984-89. Served with USAAF, 1942-46. Mem. United Ch. of Christ. Avocations: travel, reading.

SAMS, W(ILEY) MITCHELL, JR., dermatologist; b. Ann Arbor, Mich., Apr. 15, 1933; s. Wiley Mitchell and Elizabeth (Hastings) S.; m. Marion Ruth Yount, June 7, 1959; children—Robert, Margery, Hunter. B.S., U. Mich., 1955; M.D., Emory U., 1959. Intern Emory U. Hosp., Atlanta, 1959-60; resident in dermatology Duke U., Durham, N.C., 1960-64; clin. asst. prof. U. Calif., San Francisco, 1964-66; asst., asso. prof. Mayo Grad. Sch. Medicine, Mpls., 1966-72; prof., chmn. dept. dermatology U. Colo., Denver, 1972-76; prof. dermatology U. N.C. Sch. Medicine, Chapel Hill, 1976-80; prof., chmn. dept. dermatology U. Ala., Birmingham, 1981—. Served to capt. M.C. U.S. Army, 1964-66. NIH research fellow, 1962-64; grantee, 1972. Mem. Am. Acad. Dermatology, Soc. Investigative Dermatology, Am. Dermatol. Assn., So. Med. Assn. Office: U Ala University Sta Dept Dermatology Kracke Bldg Rm 101 Birmingham AL 35294

SAMSON, ALLEN LAWRENCE, bank executive; b. Milw., Nov. 16, 1939; s. Harry E. and Rose (Landau) S.; m. Vicki Faye Boxer, July 3, 1977; children: Daniel, Rachel; children from previous marriage: Nancy, David. BS, U. Wis., 1962, LLB, 1965. Bar: Wis. 1965. Asst. dist. atty. Milw. County Dist. Attys. Office, 1965-67, dep. dist. atty., 1968-70; assoc. Samson & Nash, Milw., 1967-68; ptnr. Samson, Friebert, Sutton and Finerty, Milw., 1970-73; v.p., sec. Am. Med. Svcs., Inc., Milw., 1973-83, exec. v.p., chief exec. officer, 1983-86, chmn., chief exec. officer, 1986-90; cons. nursing homes Samson Med. Mgmt. Co., Milw., 1990-93; pres. Liberty Bank, Milw., 1993—; pub. mem. nursing home study Wis. Legis. Bur., 1988-89; mem. bd. visitors U. Wis. Law Sch., 1992—; mem. health policy adv. coun. Med. Coll. Wis., 1992-96. Trustee Milw. Ballet, 1982-89, Milw. Art Mus., 1985-95, pres. bd. trustees, 1992-95; bd. dirs. Milw. Symphony Orch., 1995—, treas.; bd. dirs. Wis. Womens Bus. Initiative, War Meml. Corp., 1993-95, Nat. Found. for Jewish Culture, 1996—, Jewish Fedn., 1985—, Milw. Jewish Home, 1992—, Jewish Cmty. Ctr., 1985-96; gen. chmn. Wis. Israel Bond Campaign, 1993, chmn., 1996—. Recipient Kaplan prize for econ. devel. Govt. of Israel, 1986, United Way Fleur de Lys award, 1996. Avocations: tennis, skiing, golf. Office: Liberty Bank 815 N Water St Milwaukee WI 53202-3526 : Liberty Bank 815 N Water St Milwaukee WI 53202-3526

SAMSON, ALVIN, former distributing company executive, consultant; b. N.Y.C., May 2, 1917; s. Morris and Jennie (Buitekant) S.; m. Ann Carol Furmansky, Aug. 15, 1942; children: Leslie Joan, Marla Adriane. Br. mgr. U.S. Hardware and Paper Co., 1947-51; mdse. mgr. U.S. Servateria, 1951-57; dir. purchasing U.S. Consumer Products, Los Angeles, 1959-64; v.p. ops. U.S. Consumer Products, 1964-66, pres., 1966-72; pres. U.S. Consumer Products, San Diego, Bakersfield, Las Vegas, Phoenix, 1966-72, Zelman Co., Los Angeles, San Francisco and Las Vegas, 1968-72, Triple A Corp., Los Angeles, 1966-72, U.S. Consumer Products-Wesco Mdse., Los Angeles, 1972-74; v.p. APL Corp., N.Y.C., 1967-74; pres. USCP-WESCO, 1974-85; cons. A. Samson Cons., Beverly Hills, 1985-92; retired, 1992. Active USCG Aux., 1981—, divsn. capt., 1992—. With USAAF, 1942-45. Named Man of Year Housewares Club So. Calif., 1965. Mem. Housewares Club So. Calif. (pres. 1957, bd. govs. 1955-56), Nat. Assn. Service Merchandisers (dir. 1982-85).

SAMSON, CHARLES HAROLD, JR. (CAR SAMSON), retired engineering educator, consultant; b. Portsmouth, Ohio, July 12, 1924; s. Charles Harold and Gertrude (Morris) S.; m. Ruth Aileen Baumbach, Sept. 12, 1947; children: Peggy Aileen, Charles Harold III. B.S., U. Notre Dame, 1947, M.S., 1948; Ph.D., U. Mo., 1953. Registered profl. engr., Tex., Ind. Asst. field rep. Loebl, Schlossman and Bennett (architects and engrs.), Chgo., 1948-49; structures engr. Convair Aircraft, Fort Worth, 1951-52; sr. structures engr. Convair Aircraft, 1952-53, project aerodynamics engr., 1956-58, project structures engr., 1958-60; asst. prof. civil engring. U. Notre Dame, 1953-56; office engr. Wilbur H. Gartner & Assocs., South Bend, Ind., 1954; grad. lectr. civil engring. So. Meth. U., Dallas, 1952-53, 56-60; prof.

structural engring. and mechanics, depts. aerospace and civil engring. Tex. A&M U., College Station, 1960-64, prof. civil engring., 1964-94; prof. emeritus Tex. A&M, College Station, 1994—; head dept. Tex. A&M U., College Station, 1964-79, assoc. head dept., 1989-92, construction area engring. leader, dir. ctr. construction edn., 1992-93; rsch. engr. Tex. Transp. Inst., Tex. A&M U., 1960-62, head structural research dept., 1962-65, acting pres., 1980-81, v.p. planning, 1981-82; pres. S.W. Athletic Conf., 1979-81; v.p. Nat. Collegiate Athletic Assn., 1981-83, mem. council, 1983-85; cons. systems engring. and quality mgmt. Contbr. articles to profl. jours. Served to ensign USNR, 1943-46. Fellow ASCE (life), Nat. Inst. Engring. Mgmt. and Systems (pres. 1989-90); mem. Am. Soc. Engring. Mgmt., Am. Soc. Engring. Edn., Nat. Soc. Profl. Engrs. (past v.p., chmn. profl. engrs. in edn., pres. 1987-88), Tex. Soc. Profl. Engrs. (past nat. dir., pres. 1973-74), Nat. Assn. Parliamentarians, Internat. Soc. Systems Sci., Order of the Engr. (chmn., bd. govs. 1989-91), Am. Soc. Quality Control, Internat. Coun. on Systems Engring., Nat. Inst. Engring. Ethics, Sigma Xi, Sigma Gamma Tau, Tau Beta Pi, Phi Kappa Phi, Chi Epsilon. Home: 810 Dogwood Ln Bryan TX 77802-1144

SAMSON, FREDERICK EUGENE, JR., neuroscientist, educator; b. Medford, Mass., Aug. 16, 1918; s. Frederick Eugene and Annie Bell (Pratt) S.; m. Camila Albert; children Cecile Samson Folkerts, Julie Samson Thompson, Renée. DO, Mass. Coll. Osteopathy, 1940; PhD, U. Chgo., 1952. Asst. prof. U. Kans., Lawrence, 1952-57, prof. physiology, 1962-73, chmn., prof. dept. physiology and cell biology, 1968-73; prof. physiology U. Kans. Med. Ctr., Kansas City, 1973-89, prof. emeritus, 1989—; dir. Ralph L. Smith Rsch. Ctr. U. Kans., Kansas City, 1973-89; staff scientist neuroscis. rsch. program MIT, Cambridge, Mass., 1968-82, cons., 1982-91; vis. prof. neurobiology U. Catolica de Chile, Santiago, 1972; prof. Inst. de Investigaciones Citologicas, Valenica, Spain, 1981-89; hon. lectr. Mid-Am. State Univs. Assn., 1987. Editor: (with George Adelman) The Neurosciences: Paths of Discovery, II, 1992, (with Merrill Tarr) Oxygen Free Radicals in Tissue Damage, 1993; contbr. articles to profl. publs. Scientist, U.S.A., Spain Friendship Treaty, Madrid and Valencia, 1981. Staff sgt. U.S. Army, 1941-45, PTO. Recipient Rsch. Recognition award U. Kans. Med. Ctr., Kansas City, 1984; Van Liere fellow U. Chgo., 1948; Rawson fellow U. Chgo., 1949-51; USPHS fellow MIT, 1965. Fellow AAAS; mem. Am. Soc. Neurochemistry (chmn. program com. 1980), Am. Soc. Cell Biology (local host com. 1984), Am. Physiol. Soc. (emeritus 1990), Soc. Neurosci. (program com. 1972-73), The Oxygen Soc., N.Y. Acad. Sci., U. Chgo. Kansas City Club (chmn. alumni fund bd. 1975-82, pres. 1979-81), Sigma Xi (regional lectr. 1974-75, pres. Kansas City chpt. 1977-78, pres. neurosci. chpt. 1978). Avocation: hand balancing. Home: 171 Lakeshore Dr S Lake Quivira KS 66106-9516 Office: U Kans Med Ctr Ralph L Smith Rsch Ctr Bldg 37 Kansas City KS 66160

SAMSON, GORDON EDGAR, educator, consultant; b. Waterville, Que., Can., Oct. 25, 1923; came to U.S., 1952; s. Edgar John Knox and Ethel May (Holyon) S. BSc, Bishop's U., 1942, MEd, 1948; PhD, U. Chgo., 1955. Cert. tchr. h.s., 1943. Tchr., prin. various sch. sys. Que., 1943-52; rsch. asst. U. Chgo., 1952-54; exec. asst. Ednl. Policies Commn., NEA, Washington, 1954-57; chmn. dept. edn. Fenn Coll., Cleve., 1957-65; assoc. prof. Cleve. State U., 1965-85, acting dean, 1965-67; vis. scholar Brock U., St. Catharines, Ont., summer 1986, 87, external examiner, 1988. Contbr. articles to profl. jours. Mem. NEA (life), Am. Ednl. Rsch. Assn., Nat. Soc. for Study of Edn., Phi Delta Kappa. Avocations: genealogy, reading. Home: 2636 Haddam Rd Cleveland OH 44120-1532

SAMSON, LINDA FORREST, nursing educator and administrator; b. Miami, Dec. 7, 1949; d. Alvin S. and Grace (Kanner) Forrest; m. Mark I. Samson, Jan. 29, 1972; children: Amy, Josh. BSN, Emory U., 1972, MN, 1973; PhD, U. Pa., 1989. RN, Fla., Ga., N.J., Pa. Nursing instr. Ga. State U., Atlanta, 1974-78; neonatal intensive care nurse Northside Hosp., Atlanta, 1976-78; perinatal clin. specialist Our Lady of Lourdes Med. Ctr., Camden, N.J., 1978-82, per diem staff nurse, ICU nursery, labor and delivery, 1982-88; asst. prof., nursing Kennesaw Coll., Marietta, Ga., 1988-89; asst. prof. Clayton State Coll., Morrow, Ga., 1989-92; head baccalaureate nursing dept. Clayton Coll. and State U., Morrow, Ga., 1991-94; acting dean Sch. Health Scis. Clayton State Coll., Morrow, Ga., 1991-94; dean Sch. Health Scis., 1994—; adj. faculty Gloucester County Coll., 1981-83; adj. clin. preceptor U. Pa. Sch. Nursing, 1981-83, lectr. in perinatal nursing, 1983-88; nursing dir. So. N.J. Perinatal Coop., 1982-84; researcher and lectr. in field. Mem. editorial rev. bds.; contbr. chpts. to textbooks, articles to profl. jours. Bd. dirs., chmn. profl. adv. com. South Jersey chpt. March of Dimes, 1980-85. Named Nurse of Yr. N.J. State Nurses Assn., 1985; recipient Network Edn. grant N.J. State Dept. Health, 1982-84, numerous grants for rsch., 1983-89, Outstanding Svc. award March of Dimes, 1983, Disting. Leadership award March of Dimes, 1984. Mem. ANA (cert. advanced nursing adminstrn., RNC high risk perinatal nursing), AACN (program com. 1987-88, rsch. com. 1988-89, project devel. task force 1989, strategic planning com. 1989, bd. dirs. 1987-90, bd. dirs. certification corp. 1987-90, chair neonatal and pediatric appeal panels 1992), Am. Orgn. Nurse Execs. (planning com. 1994-95), Nat. Assn. Neonatal Nurses (pub. policy and legis. com. 1994-96), Assn. Women's Health, Obstetrics and Neonatal Nurses, Nat. Perinatal Assn. (program planning com. 1983-85, resolutions com. 1984-88, stds. devel. com. spl. interest group task force 1985-88, bd. dirs. 1985-89, chmn. resolutions com. 1988, fin. com. 1989, pub. health policy com.), Ga. Nurses Assn., Ga. Perinatal Assn. N.J. (pres. 1982-86), Sigma Theta Tau. Home: 2915 Four Oaks Dr Atlanta GA 30360-1744 Office: Clayton State Coll Sch Health Scis PO Box 285 Morrow GA 30260-0285

SAMSON, PERRY J., environmental scientist, educator; b. Binghamton, N.Y., May 18, 1950; s. Perry C. and Ann I. Samson; children: Karis, Carla. BS, SUNY, Albany, 1972, MS, 1974; PhD, U. Wis., 1979. Rsch. sci. N.Y. State Dept. Environ. Conservation, Albany, 1973-79; asst. prof. U. Mich., Ann Arbor, 1979-85, assoc. prof., 1985-89, prof., 1989—, Arthur Thureau prof., 1995—; vis. scientist Nat. Ctr. Atmospheric Rsch., Boulder, Colo., 1985-86, Univ. Corp. Atmospheric Rsch., Boulder, 1994—. Author chpts. to books; contbr. articles to profl. jours. Mem. Am. Geophys. Union, Air and Waste Mgmt. Assn. (mem. TT-3 meteorol com., mem. TE-5 visibility com.). Office: U Mich 1539 Space Rsch Bldg Ann Arbor MI 48109-2143

SAMSON, RICHARD MAX, investments and real estate executive; b. Milw., June 13, 1946; s. Harry E. and Rose (Landau) S.; m. Nancy K. Pinter; children: Gina Shoshana, Alayna Tamar; (stepson) Christopher P. BA, U. Wis., 1968. Dir., owner The Puppet Co., Jerusalem, 1972-73; pres. Century Hall, Inc., Milw., 1974-75; dir. purchasing Am. Med. Svcs., Inc., Milw., 1973-74, v.p., 1974-82, exec. v.p., 1982-86, pres., 1986-90; pres. Samson Investments, Milw., 1990—; bd. dirs. Liberty Bank, Milw.; sec. Super Sitters, Mequon, Wis., 1987—. Pres. bd. Theatre X, Milw., 1982, Holton Youth Ctr., Milw., 1994, Children's Outing Assn., 1996, Jewish Found. for Econ. Opportunity, 1996—; v.p. bd. ArtReach, Milw., 1987; bd. dirs. Bnai Or Religious Fellowship, 1988-93, Milw. Jewish Coun., 1992-94; mem. funding bd. Wis. Cmty. Fund, 1989-93. Recipient Humanitarian Peace award Ecumenical Refugee Coun., 1989. Mem. Ams. for Peace Now (bd. dirs. 1990—). Avocations: chess, comic collecting, puppetry. Office: Samson Investments 100A E Pleasant St Milwaukee WI 53212-3961

SAMSOT, ROBERT LOUIS, newspaper editor, consultant; b. New Orleans, July 20, 1943; s. Robert Desposito and Mary Helen (Dohan) S.; m. A. Michael Newton, June 9, 1965; children: Kathleen Anderson Samsot English, Robert Dohan. BA in Journalism, U. N.C., Chapel Hill, 1965; cert. in Bus. Adminstrn., Rockhurst Coll., 1982. Reporter Rocky Mountain News, Denver, 1965-67, The Comml. Appeal, Memphis, 1967-72; reporter, editor Newsday, L.I., N.Y., 1972-80; Gannett profl.-in-residence U. Kans., Lawrence, 1980-81; met. editor The Kansas City (Mo.) Times, 1981-84; city editor The Plain Dealer, Cleve., 1984-87; lifestyle editor, dep. editor N.J., dep. editor nat. The Phila. Inquirer, 1987—; cons. W.K. Kellogg Nat. Fellowship, Battle Creek, Mich., 1984-93; freelance writer, 1965—. Youth soccer coach Northport, N.Y., 1976-80, dir., 1979-80, Shaker Heights, Ohio, 1984-87, Swarthmore (Pa.) Recreation Assn., 1987-88; coach Johnson County (Kans.) Soccer League, 1983-84, U. Kans. Women's Soccer Club, 1980-81; bd. dirs. Suffolk County Heart Assn., L.I., 1974-75. Mem. Nat. Assn. Hispanic Journalists. Democrat. Roman Catholic. Avocations: travel, fishing, outdoor sports. Home: 610 Strath Haven Ave Swarthmore PA 19081-2307 Office: The Phila Inquirer 400 N Broad St Philadelphia PA 19130-4015

SAMTER, MAX, physician, educator; b. Berlin, Germany, Mar. 3, 1908; came to U.S., 1937; s. Paul and Claire (Rawicz) S.; m. Virginia Svarz Ackerman, Oct. 17, 1947; 1 dau., Virginia Claire. Student, U. Freiburg, Germany, 1926, U. Innsbruck, Austria, 1928; M.D., U. Berlin, 1933. Diplomate: Am. Bd. Internal Medicine (past chmn. bd. allergy), Am. Bd. Allergy and Immunology. Intern, Medizinische Universitätsklinik der Charité, Berlin, 1931-32, resident internal medicine, 1932-33; practice medicine Berlin-Karow, Germany, 1933-37; resident internal medicine & hematology Johns Hopkins Hosp., 1937-39; resident anatomy U. Pa. Sch. Medicine, 1939-43; research asso. dept. biochemistry U. Ill., Chgo., 1946-47, from instr. to full prof. dept. medicine, 1948-69, prof. medicine Coll. Medicine (formerly Abraham Lincoln Sch. Medicine), 1969—, assoc. dean for clin. affairs, 1974-75; vis. scholar, immunology Weizmann Inst. of Sci.; chief staff U. Ill. Hosp., 1974-75; dir. inst. allergy & clin. immunology Grant Hosp., Chgo., 1975-83, sr. cons., 1983-93; rsch. sci. otolaryngology, head & neck surg. U. Ill. Coll. Med., Chgo., 1994—; prof. dept. otolaryngology U. Ill. Hosp., 1994-96; clin. prof. otorhinolaryngology Loyola U. Med. Ctr., Chgo., 1996—; cons. in allergy U.S. VA, 1962—. Editor: American Lectures in Allergy, 1950, (with Oren C. Durham) Regional Allergy, 1954, (with Harry L. Alexander) Immunological Diseases, 1965, 71, 78, 88, Excerpts from Classics in Allergy, 1969, rev. edit. (with Sheldon G. Cohen), 1992; (with Charles W. Parker) Hypersensitivity to Drugs, 1972; also articles in field. Served to capt. M.C. AUS, 1943-46, ETO. Recipient Disting. Faculty award U. Ill. Coll. Med. 1987. Fellow ACP; mem. AMA, Am. Acad. Allergy (past pres.), Internat. Assn. Allergology and Clin. Immunology (past pres., Disting. Svc. award 1991), German Soc. Allergology and Clin. Immunology (hon.), Phila. Coll. Physicians (hon.), Interasma (hon.), Sigma Xi, Alpha Omega Alpha. Home: 645 Sheridan Rd Evanston IL 60202-2533

SAMUEL, GEORGE, healthcare information company executive; b. Tiruvalla, Kerala, India, May 25, 1958; came to U.S., 1980; s. VC and Elizabeth (Mammen) S. BS, Kerala U., 1979; AAS, Lehigh Coll., 1980; MBA, So. Calif. U., 1995. Programmer, analyst Knowledge Data Systems, San Antonio, 1982-85, tech. mgr., 1985-87; dir. mgmt. info. system Knowledge Data Systems, Cin., 1987-88; v.p., acct. mgr. Knowledge Data Systems, Detroit, 1988-89; v.p., acct. mgr. Knowledge Data Systems, Larkspur, Calif., 1989-91, v.p., rsch. & devel. products div., 1991-93; pres., CEO Healthcare Media Enterprises Inc., Petaluma, Calif., 1993—. Vol. Project Open Hand, Oakland, Calif., 1992—, Big Bros. and Sisters. Mem. Am. Mgmt. Assn., Toastmasters Internat. Avocations: tennis, skiing, car racing. Office: Healthcare Media Enterprises Inc 1301 Redwood Way Ste 200 Petaluma CA 94954-1136

SAMUEL, GERHARD, orchestra conductor, composer; b. Bonn, Germany, Apr. 20, 1924; came to U.S., 1939, naturalized, 1943; s. Arthur and Hilde (Behr) S. Student violin with Samuel Belov, chamber music with Jacques Gordon; B.Mus. cum laude, Eastman Sch. Music, 1945; choral conducting with Hermann Genhart, conducting with Paul White and Howard Hanson, 1945; student of Serge Koussevitsky, Tanglewood, Mass., 1945-47; student, also Boris Goldowsky; student of Paul Hindemith (scholarship), Yale U., Mus.M. (Haupt prize), 1947; Ph.D. (hon.), Calif. Coll. Arts and Crafts. Fulbright grantee for study in Europe, 1949; exec. com. San Francisco Composers Forum, 1959-62; mem. composers workshop San Francisco Conservatory Music, 1960; prof. music Calif. Inst. Arts, to 1976; condr. Contemporary Ensemble Concert Series, U. Cin. Coll.-Conservatory of Music, 1976—; lectr. in field; guest condr. Oakland (Calif.) Ballet Co. Condr.: Ballet Ballads, Music Box Theatre, Broadway, 1947-48, concerts Am. contemporary music, Paris, 1948-49, Accademia Chigiana (1st prize), Siena, Italy, 1949, Ballets Concertants, Mpls., 1950-59, Collegium Musicum, Mpls., 1952-59, Mpls. Civic Opera Co., 1954-59, Grand Teton Music Festival, 1992, German premiere Hans Rott's Symphony in E with Sudwestfunk Orch., 1993; assoc. condr. Mpls. Symphony Orch., 1949-59, L.A. Philharm., 1970-74; mus. dir. Grand Marais (Minn.) Music Festival, 1957-59, Minn. Centennial Music Festival, 1958, Oakland (Calif.) Symphony Orch., 1959-71; mus. dir., condr. San Francisco Ballet, 1961-70, Oakland Chamber Orch., 1963-69, Ojai (Calif.) Festival, 1970-71, Cin. Philharm. Orch., 1976—, Pacific N.W. Ballet Co., 1982-83, Cin. Chamber Orch., 1983-91; dir. orch. activities Coll. Conservatory of Music, Cin., 1976—; founder, condr., Cabrillo Music Festival, 1962-68, West Coast New Music Ensemble, 1968-70; artistic dir., L.A. Philharmonic Docents; guest condr. Am. Symphony, Lincoln Ctr., N.Y.C., 1964, Denver Symphony, 1965, San Francisco Spring Opera, 1965, 66, Am. Symphony Orch., 1965, Winnipeg (Can.) Symphony, 1967, Rochester Philharm. Orch., 1973, Ives-Schoenberg Festival, Washington, 1974, Fresno Philharm., San Francisco Symphony, Vancouver Opera Orch., ann. European, Far Eastern and S.Am. concert tours.; condr. concerts on TV with Opera Co. of Phila., youth orchs.; composer numerous works including Twelve on Death and No, In Memoriam D.Q., What of My Music, Into Flight From ..., Looking at Orpheus Looking, On A Dream, Requiem for Survivors, Fortieth Day, Beyond McBean, Au Revoir to Lady R., The Relativity of Icarus, Three Hymns to Apollo, Dirge for John Cage, Left Over Mirrors, Music for Four; commd. major orchs., prominent artists; invited participant Lincoln Ctr.'s Mozart Bicentennial Celebration, premiere of Outcries and Consolations, L.A., 1990, Concerto for alto sax and orch., 1996, Five Chinese Love Songs for tenor and orch., 1996, Dramatic Duo for two violins, 1996, Oh Yeah Disagreement for steel drums and orch., 1997; condr. and recs. (world premieres) Charles Ives (Larry Austin) Universe Symphony, Schubert's opera Der Graf von Gleichen, 1993—, (CD recs.) ; recs. String Quartets, Transformations, 1996, Nocturne on an Impossible Dream, 1996; concert tour of China, Beijing and Shenyang Orchs. (Am. music) In Search of Words, The Butterfly, and Two Moods. Mem. adv. panel State Dept. Cultural Exchange; mem. music council Young Musicians Found. Recipient Nat. Endowment for Arts Composition award, 1974-75, Composer's Showcase N.Y. award, 1976, 77, 78, Post-Corbett award, 1987, Meet the Composer award, 1990, George Rieveschl prize U. Cin., 1992, Alice M. Ditson award Columbia U., 1994; Rockefeller Found. grantee. Mem. ASCAP (ann. award 1970—), Cin. Composers Guild, Nat. Assn. Composers. Home: 619 5th Ave W # 203 Seattle WA 98119 Office: Coll Conservatory Music Cincinnati OH 45221-0077

SAMUEL, HOWARD DAVID, union official; b. N.Y.C., Nov. 16, 1924; s. Ralph E. and Florence (Weingarten) S.; m. Ruth H. Zamkin, Apr. 15, 1948; children: Robert H., Donald F., William H. BA, Dartmouth Coll., 1948. Various positions Amalgamated Clothing and Textile Workers (formerly Amalgamated Clothing Workers Am.), N.Y.C., 1949-60; asst. pres. Amalgamated Clothing and Textile Workers (formerly Amalgamated Clothing Workers Am.), 1960-64, v.p., 1966-77; dep. under sec. Bur. Internat. Labor Affairs Dept. Labor, Washington, 1977-79; pres. Indsl. Union Dept. AFL-CIO, Washington, 1979-92; v.p. New Sch. for Social Rsch., N.Y.C., 1964-65, Econ. Strategy Inst., 1992—; vice chmn. N.Y. Urban Coalition, 1968-74; mem. governing bd. Common Cause, 1971-77; sec. Nat. Com. Full Employment, 1975-77, sec.-treas., 1977-89; mem. Pres.'s Commn. on Indsl. Competitiveness, 1983-85; sr. fellow Coun. on Competitiveness, 1993—, sr. chmn., 1986-92; mem. U.S. Dept. Labor Task Force on Econ. Adjustment, and Worker Dislocation, 1985-87; mem. vis. com. advanced tech. Nat. Inst. Stds. and Tech., 1995—; mem. adv. com. Export-Import Bank. Author: (with Stephen K. Bailey) Congress at Work, 1952; Government in America, 1957; Editor: Toward a Better America, 1968. Mem. Nat. Manpower Adv. Com., 1969-74; mem. Commn. Population Growth and the Am. Future, 1970-72; mem. Def. Mfg. Bd., 1988-89, Def. Sci. Bd., 1989-92; chmn. White Plains Dem. Com., 1960-64; vice-chmn. Westchester County com., 1957-70, alt. del. nat. conv., 1964; mem. Nat. Dem. Charter Revision Com., 1972-73; exec. dir. Nat. Labor Com. McGovern-Shriver, 1972; del. Dem. Conv. on Party Orgn. and Policy, Kansas City, 1974, Nat. Dem. Conv., 1976; trustee Carnegie Corp., 1971-77, Joint Coun. Econ. Edn., 1971-77; bd. dirs. ACLU, 1966-68; trustee Brookings Instn.; overseer RAND Inst. for Civil Justice, 1987-93. With AUS, 1943-46. Mem. Coun. on Fgn. Rels., Phi Beta Kappa. Office: Coun on Competitiveness 1401 H St NW Washington DC 20005-2110

SAMUEL, PAUL, cardiologist; b. Janoshaza, Hungary, Feb. 17, 1927; came to U.S., 1954, naturalized, 1960; s. Adolf and Magda (Zollner) S.; m. Gabriella R. Zeichner, Mar. 27, 1954; children: Robert Mark, Adrienne Jill. Baccalaureat, Kemeny Zsigmond Gymnasium, Budapest, 1945; MD, U. Paris, 1953. Intern Queens Hosp. Ctr., N.Y.C., 1954-55; resident L.I. Jewish Med. Ctr., New Hyde Park, N.Y., 1959-61; adj. prof. Rockefeller U., N.Y.C., 1971-81; adj. prof. medicine Cornell U., N.Y.C., 1979—; clin. prof. medicine Albert Einstein Coll. Medicine, Bronx, 1981—; dir. Arteriosclerosis Rsch. Lab., L.I. Jewish-Hillside Med. Ctr., New Hyde Park, 1962—; chmn. N.Y. Lipid Rsch. Club, Rockefeller U., 1977-78. Contbr. articles to profl. jours. Pres. Am. Heart Assn., Nassau County, 1980. Fellow Am. Coll. Cardiology; mem. Am. Heart Assn. (fellow coun. on arteriosclerosis, Disting. Achievement award 1975), Am. Fedn. Clin. Rsch., Harvey Soc., ACP. Home: 25 Nassau Dr Great Neck NY 11021-2163 Office: LI Jewish Med Ctr 1554 Northern Blvd Manhasset NY 11030-3006 also: 110-20 71st Rd Forest Hills NY 11375

SAMUEL, RALPH DAVID, lawyer; b. Augusta, Ga., May 8, 1945; s. Ralph and Louise Elizabeth (Wurreschke) S.; m. Lynn Christel Malmgren, June 12, 1971; children: Lynn Britt, Ralph Erik. AB, Dartmouth Coll., 1967; JD, Dickinson Sch. of Law, 1972. Bar: Pa. 1972, U.S. Dist. Ct. (ea. dist.) Pa. 1972, U.S. Ct. Appeals (3d cir.) 1973, U.S. Supreme Ct. 1976. Law clk. to hon. judge John P. Fullam U.S. Dist. Ct. (ea. dist.) Pa., Phila., 1972-74; assoc. MacCoy, Evans & Lewis, Phila., 1974-76; ptnr. Samuel and Ballard, P.C., Phila., 1976—; established Samuel Poetry Fellow Dartmouth Coll., Hanover, N.H., 1994. Contbr. articles to profl. jours. Trustee The George Sch., Newtown, Pa., 1983-90; chmn. bd. dirs. Stapeley in Germantown, 1985-90; chmn. budget com. Phila. Yearly Meeting of Friends, 1991-93; bd. dirs., mem. fin. com. Phila. Ranger Corps., 1992-94; pres. Cedar Park Neighbors, Phila., 1975-78, West Mt. Airy Neighbors, Phila., 1981-82. Mem. Pa. Soc., Athenaeum of Phila., Germantown Cricket Club, Sunday Breakfast Club. Mem. Soc. of Friends. Avocations: music, writing, squash, tennis. Office: Samuel and Ballard PC 225 S 15th St Fl 1700 Philadelphia PA 19102-3917

SAMUEL, ROBERT THOMPSON, optometrist; b. Kansas City, Mo., June 27, 1944; s. Manlius Thompson and Helen Evelyn (Syverson) S. B.A., William Jewel Coll., 1966; postgrad. U. Mo.-Kansas City, 1967, M.S. U. Mo., 1968; D. Optometry, U. Tenn.-Memphis, 1971. Cert. optometrist, Mo. Buyer Recco, Inc., Kansas City, Mo., 1963-67; histology lab. instr. William Jewell Coll., Liberty, Mo., 1965-66; pvt. practice optometry Gladstone, Mo., 1972—; panel Dr. Ford Motor Co., Claycomo, Mo., 1985—, Union Pacific R.R., Kansas City, 1985—, TWA Airlines, 1990, Union Carbide, 1990. Publicity coord. Rep. Party, Kansas City, Mo., 1975-76; chmn. Save Your Vision Week, Kansas City, 1977; mem. Theatre League of Kansas City, 1976—, Kansas City Mus., 1986—, Friends of Art, 1985, Friends of Mo. Town 1855, 1980—. Recipient Outstanding Young Men of Am. award Jaycees, 1978, Good Citizens award DAR, 1962. Mem. Am. Optometric Assn., Mo. Optometric Assn., Optometric Soc. Greater Kansas City, Heart of Am. Contact Lens Congress, Am. Acad. Sports Vision, Vol. Optometric Svcs. for Humanity, Smithsonian Assocs, Kappa Alpha Order (treas. 1966). Republican. Lutheran. Lodge: Lions (exec. bd. dirs. Lions Eye Clinic 1974-84, bd. dirs. Lions Eye Clinic 1982—, Outstanding Svc. award 1973, 74, editor Lions Optometric Ctr. Quar., 1974-84). Avocations: photography, music, piano, swimming, travel. Home: 6325 N Monroe Ave Kansas City MO 64119-1923 Office: 2700 NE Kendallwood Pkwy Kansas City MO 64119-2032

SAMUELI, HENRY, electrical engineering educator; b. Buffalo, Sept. 20, 1954; s. Aron and Sala (Traubman) S.; m. Susan Faye Eisenberg, Aug. 22, 1982; children: Leslie Pamela, Jillian Meryl, Erin Sydney. BS, UCLA, 1975, MS, 1976, PhD, 1980. Staff engr. TRW Inc., Redondo Beach, Calif., 1980-83, section mgr., 1983-85; asst. prof. UCLA, 1985-90, assoc. prof., 1990-94, prof., 1994—; cons. TRW, Inc., Redondo Beach, 1985-89; chief scientist PairGain Techs., Inc., Tustin, Calif., 1989-94; v.p. R & D Broadcom Corp., Irvine, Calif., 1991—. Mem. IEEE, Sigma Xi, Tau Beta Pi. Republican. Jewish. Avocations: skiing, basketball. Office: Broadcom Corp 16251 Laguna Canyon Rd Irvine CA 92618-3603 also: UCLA Electrical Engring Dept 56-125B Engring IV Los Angeles CA 90095-1594

SAMUELS, ABRAM, stage equipment manufacturing company executive; b. Allentown, Pa., Sept. 15, 1920; s. Irving and Ann (Friedman) S.; m. Harriet Ann Goodman, Sept. 1, 1945; children: Margaret A. Samuels Berger, Katherine E., Sally R. Samuels Slifkin, John A., Dorothy M. Samuels Lampl, Caroline J. Samuels Bagli. B.S., Lehigh U., 1942; auditor philosophy, Princeton U., 1962-65. Pres. Automatic Devices Co., Allentown, 1946-75, chmn. exec. com., 1987-92; chmn. bd. Automatic Devices Co., 1975-87, 93—; chmn. bd. Mchts. Bank, 1981-85, chmn. exec. com., 1985-91; past guest lectr. Cedar Crest Coll., 1969-71, 84, Muhlenberg Coll., 1977-82, 92. Author: Where the Colleges Rank, 1973. Pres. Samuels Family Found., 1959—; past pres. Pa. Soc. for Crippled Children and Adults, 1957-58; past pres., hon. bd. dirs. Lehigh County Crippled Children's Soc., 1949-51; past pres. Lehigh County Humane Soc., 1960-64, Cedar Crest Coll. Assocs., 1968-70; bd. dirs. Allentown Hosp., 1977-88, chmn. bd., 1987; vice chmn. Allentown Hosp.-Lehigh Valley Hosp. Ctr., 1988; pres. Lehigh County Hist. Soc., 1976-78; past bd. dirs. Nat. Soc. for Crippled Children and Adults, Pa. Mental Health Assn., Merchants Bank, 1965-91, Lehigh County Indsl. Devel. Corp., Pa. Stage Co., 1983-84, Health East, Inc., 1985-91, Nightingale Awards of Pa., 1989-91; trustee St. Augustine's Coll., 1970-77, 92-95, Allentown YWCA, 1977-83, Cedar Crest Coll., 1996—; bd. dirs. Fund to Benefit Children and Youth of Lehigh Valley Inc., 1992—. With AUS, 1942-46. Recipient Benjamin Rush award Lehigh County Med. Soc., 1954, Allentown Human Relations award, 1979; named Outstanding Young Man of Year Jr. C. of C., 1954. Mem. Hon. First Defenders, C. of C. (past v.p. 1960), Pa. German Soc., Am. Soc. Psychical Rsch. (trustee 1985-91, treas. 1990), Princeton Club (N.Y.C.), Rotary (pres. Allentown club 1955-56, dist. gov. 1964-65). Republican. Office: 2121 S 12th St Allentown PA 18103-4751

SAMUELS, CYNTHIA KALISH, communications executive; b. Pitts., May 21, 1946; d. Emerson and Jeanne (Kalish) S.; m. Richard Norman Atkins, Sept. 12, 1971; children: Joshua Whitney Samuels Atkins, Daniel Jonathan Samuels Atkins. BA, Smith Coll., 1968. Press aide McCarthy for Pres. Campaign, Washington, 1968; assoc. prodr. Newsroom program Sta. KQED, San Francisco, 1972-73; with CBS News, 1973-80, rschr., Washington, 1969-71, documentary rschr., N.Y.C., 1973-74, asst. fgn. editor, 1973-76, asst. N.Y. bur. chief, 1976-80; writer, field prodr. Today program NBC News, N.Y.C., 1980-84, polit. prodr. Today program, 1984-89; polit. and planning prodr., 1988-89; sr. prodr. Main Street program NBC News, N.Y.C., 1987; founding exec. prodr. Channel One Program, 1989-92; exec. v.p. Whittle Comms., N.Y.C., 1989-94; internet cons., developer TV and multimedia prodn. exec., 1994—; pres., CEO Cobblestone Prodns.: Online and On TV, 1996—. Author: It's A Free Country!: A Young Person's Guide to Politics and Elections, 1988; editor Excite, 1995-96; contbg. editor Women's Wire, 1996—; prodr. 3d Ann. Childrens Interactive Media Festival, 1996; contbr. book revs. to N.Y. Times Book Rev., Washington Post Book World; children's book editor Amazon.com, 1997—. Recipient Emmy award No. Calif. Acad. TV Arts and Scis., 1974, Columbia DuPont citation, 1975, Media Access award Calif. Office of Handicapped, 1991, Silver award Nat. Mental Health Assn., 2 Bronze awards Nat. Assn. Edn. in Film and TV, 1993. Mem. Women in Tech., Internat. Interactive Comms. Soc. Office: 502 Schueren Rd Malibu CA 90265-3046

SAMUELS, DONALD L., lawyer; b. Washington, May 8, 1961; s. Jack Donald Samuels and Francis Diane (Katcher) Yeoman; m. Linda Marie Tveidt, Aug. 17, 1986. AB, Brown U., 1983; JD, Columbia U., 1986. Bar: Calif. 1986, U.S. Dist. Ct. (cen., no., ea. and so. dists.) Calif. 1988, U.S. Ct. Appeals (9th cir.) 1989, Calif. 1996, U.S. Ct. Appeals (7th cir.) 1996, U.S. Dist. Ct. Colo. 1997, U.S. Ct. Appeals (10th cir.) 1997. Law clk. L.A., 1986-87; assoc. Sidley & Austin, L.A., 1987-94, ptnr., 1994-95; ptnr. Samuels & Samuels, L.A., 1995—. Mem. ABA, Los Angeles County Bar Assn., Phi Beta Kappa. Home: 2011 S Canfield Ave Los Angeles CA 90034-1110 Office: Samuels & Samuels 2029 Century Park E Ste 2718 Los Angeles CA 90067-3013

SAMUELS, JOHN STOCKWELL, III, mining company executive, financier; b. Galveston, Tex., Sept. 15, 1933; s. John Stockwell and Helen Yvonne (Poole) S.; children: Evelyn Kathleen, John Stockwell, Ainlay Leontine, Peter Ashton Hayes. AB, Tex. A&M U., 1954, SM, 1954; JD, Harvard U., 1960. Bar: N.Y. 1961. Assoc. Chadbourne, Parke, Whiteside & Wolff, N.Y.C., 1960-73; pres. Internat. Carbon & Minerals, N.Y.C., 1973-78,

Carbomin Group, Inc., N.Y.C., 1978—; chmn. bd. United Energy Ltd., Manama, Bahrain, 1987-93; pres. U.S. Reduction Inc., 1996—; chmn. bd. J.S. Samuels & Co. Bd. dirs. City Center Music and Drama, Inc., N.Y.C.; chmn. bd. dirs. N.Y.C. Ballet, N.Y.C. Opera, 1976-81, Lincoln Ctr. Theatre, N.Y.C., 1979-81, Lincoln Ctr., N.Y.C. With U.S. Army, 1954-57. Mem. Inst. Petroleum, Century Assn., Southampton Bathing Corp. Democrat. Episcopalian.

SAMUELS, LESLIE B., lawyer; b. St. Louis, Nov. 10, 1942; s. Joseph E. and Dorothy J. (Bernstein) S.; m. Judith B. Thorn, June 19, 1966 (div. Aug. 1976); children: Colin T., Polly B.; m. Augusta H. Gross, Nov. 8, 1980. BS in Econs., U. Pa., 1963; LLB magna cum laude, Harvard U., 1966; postgrad., London Sch. Econs., 1966-67. Bar: N.Y., U.S. Dist. Ct. (so. dist.) N.Y., U.S. Tax Ct., U.S. Supreme Ct.; CPA. Tax analyst Gulf Oil Co., London, 1967-68; assoc. Cleary, Gottlieb, Steen & Hamilton, N.Y.C., 1968-75, ptnr., 1975-93, 96—; asst. sec. for tax policy U.S. Dept. Treasury, Washington, 1993-96; vice-chair com. fiscal affairs OECD, 1994-96; mem. Pres.'s Com. on the Arts and the Humanities, Washington, 1994-96. Editor Law Rev.; contbr. articles to profl. jours. Dir. Lower Manhattan Cultural Coun., N.Y.C., 1981-93; active Carter-Mondale Transition Planning Group, Washington, 1976-77. Fulbright fellow London Sch. Econs., 1966-67. Mem. N.Y. State Bar Assn., Assn. of Bar of City of N.Y., Harvard Club (N.Y.C.). Democrat. Office: Cleary Gottlieb Steern & Hamilton One Liberty Plaza New York NY 10006

SAMUELS, REUBEN, engineering consultant; b. Suffern, N.Y., Jan. 11, 1926; s. M.S. and Ida Samuels; m. Diane Joyce Limenfeld, Sept. 16, 1948; children: Julie Ellen, Adam Henry. Student, MIT, 1943-44; BSCE, Dartmouth Coll., 1946; MSCE, Harvard U., 1948, postgrad., 1951-54. Registered profl. engr., N.Y., N.J., Conn., Va., Pa., D.C., Md., Mass.; lic. arbitrator. Found. engr. Mueser, Rutledge, Wentworth & Johnston, 1948-50; v.p., chief engr. Thomas Crimmins Contracting Co., 1950-82, vice chmn., 1982-86, chmn., 1986-90; pres. Crimmins, Samuels & Assocs., 1980-90, Crimmins Constructors, Inc., 1987-90; v.p. Tishman Constrn. Corp., 1990-91; prin. engrng. cons. Parsons Brinckerhoff, N.Y.C., 1991—; arbitrator Am. Arbitration Assn.; mem. Soil Mechanics and Found. Group Bldg. Code Com., N.Y.; past overseer Thayer Sch. Engrng.-Dartmouth Coll.; mem. geotech. bd. NAS, 1991-94; mem. geologic site investigation subcom., mem. parent, past chmn. U.S. Nat. Com. on Tunnelling Tech./NAS. Co-author: Construction Rock Work Guide, 1960's. Past. pres. Paramus Bd. Edn., Bergen County Fedn. Sch. Bds. Ensign CEC, USNR, 1943-47. Recipient Outstanding Achievement in Constrn. award, 1988. Fellow ASCE (nat. com. on deep founds.); mem. ASTM, Am. Concrete Inst., Boston Soc. Civil Engrs., Dartmouth Engrng. Soc. (past pres.), Harvard Engrng. Soc. (past pres.), Nat. Acad. Engrng., The Moles (past pres.), Sigma Xi. Avocations: gardening, reading. Office: Parsons Brinckerhoff Inc 195 Harwood Pl Paramus NJ 07652-4605 Office: Parsons Brinckerhoff 1 Penn Plz New York NY 10119

SAMUELS, RICHARD JOEL, political science educator; b. N.Y.C., Nov. 2, 1951; s. Sidney and Rita (Cohen) S.; m. Debra G., June 11, 1972; children: Bradley M., Alexander J. AB, Colgate U., 1973; MA, Tufts U., 1974; PhD, MIT, 1980. Asst. prof. MIT, Cambridge, Mass., 1980-83, assoc. prof., 1983-87, prof., 1987—, head dept. polit. sci., 1992-97; mem. Coun. Fgn. Rels., N.Y.C., 1985—, vice chmn. com. on Japan, 1988—; founding dir. MIT Japan Program, 1981—. Author: Politics of Regional Policy in Japan, 1983, Business of Japanese State, 1987 (Ohira prize 1988), Rich Nation, Strong Army, 1994 (Hall prize 1996, Arisawa prize, 1996); editor: Political Generations and Political Developments, 1977, Political Culture of Foreign Area Studies, 1993. Mem. Am. Polit. Sci. Assn., Assn. Asian Studies. Office: MIT Dept Polit Sci E53-473 Cambridge MA 02142

SAMUELS, SIMON J., finance, insurance company executive. Various positions Barclays Bank PLC, 1973-77; with S.G. Warburg & Co., London, 1978-79; ptnr. Samuels & Co., 1991, also chmn. bd. dirs., 1991; bd. dirs., mgmt. com. various pvt., pub. cos. Fellow Inst. Dirs.; mem. Chartered Inst. Bankers (assoc.). Office: Templar Internat Mgmt Ltd 4894 W Lone Mountain Rd # 124 Las Vegas NV 89130-2239

SAMUELS, WILLIAM MASON, physiology association executive; b. Dover, Ohio, Jan. 17, 1929; s. William Mason and Anne Frieda (Fankhauser) S.; m. Joanne Gorenflo, Oct. 2, 1971; children: Robert Lee, Ann Frances. A.B., U. Ky., 1951; postgrad., Georgetown U., 1952. Mng. editor for Ind., Courier-Jour. & Times, Louisville, 1955-65; dir. office of v.p. U. Ky. Med. Center, Lexington, 1965-70; exec. dir. Am. Soc. Allied Health Professions, Washington, 1970-78, Am. Assn. Blood Banks, Washington, 1978-80, Nat. Soc. Med. Research Washington, 1980-84, Am. Physiol. Soc., Bethesda, Md., 1984-92; retired, 1992—. Contbr. articles to profl. jours. Mem. secretariat Nat. Commn. Health Certifying Agys.; v.p. Coalition Health Funding; cons. to fed. agys.; vol. Habitat for Humanity, Boca Raton. With USAF, 1951-53, USAFR, 1954-76, lt. col. ret. Named Ky. Man of Yr. Sigma Phi Epsilon, 1968. Mem. Am. Soc. Assn. Execs., Am. Optometric Assn. (mem. coun. on edn., coun. on optometric clin. care), Health Staff Soc., Washington Soc. Assn. Execs., Pinehurst (N.C.) Country Club, Lions. Presbyterian. Home: 3190 Leewood Ter # L-101 Boca Raton FL 33431-6548 Home (summer): 11700 Happy Choice Ln North Potomac MD 20878-2453

SAMUELSEN, ROY, bass-baritone; b. Moss, Norway, June 12, 1933; came to U.S., 1950, naturalized, 1954; s. Ragnar Andreas and Margaret Olivia (Evensen) S.; m. Mary Lou Thorne, May 25, 1955; children—Eric Roy, Robert Ragnar, Rolf Harold. B.S. in Music Edn, Brigham Young U., 1961; Mus.M. in Performance, Ind. U., 1963; diploma, Acad. of West, Santa Barbara, Calif., 1960; student voice, Joseph Heuler, Lotte Lehmann, Victor Fuchs, Frank St. Leger, Paul Matthen Charles Kullman. Sheet metal worker Utah, 1951-61. Performed with, Norwegian Opera Co., guest soloist, Norwegian Singing Soc. Am. convs., also with, Am. orchs., prof. music, Ind. U. Opera Theatre, Bloomington, 1963—, rec. artist., (regional winner Met. Opera Auditions, 1960, San Francisco Opera Auditions 1961). Served with Mil. Police U.S. Army, 1953-55. Recipient Lotte Lehmann award Acad. of West, 1960. Mem. AAUP, Nat. Assn. Tchrs. of Singing, Am. Guild Mus. Artists. Democrat. Mormon. Home: 3615 S Oakridge Dr Bloomington IN 47401-8931 Office: Ind U Bloomington IN 47401 *My success in life is a direct reflection upon the standards set by my parents during my early life and by trying to live according to the teachings of my adopted church. These influences, along with my wife's total devotion, have encouraged me and continue to encourage me in my private and professional life.*

SAMUELSON, BILLIE MARGARET, artist; b. Long Beach, Calif., Apr. 11, 1927; d. William Christian and Gladys Margaret (Caffrey) Newendorp; m. Fritz Eric Samuelson, Aug. 12, 1950 (div. 1985); children: Craig Eric, Clark Alan, Dana Scott. Student, Long Beach City Coll., 1945-46. Pvt. art tchr. Wycokoff/Allendale, N.J., 1985—; workshop instr. Jane Law Studio, Long Beach Island, N.J., 1990—. Exhibited in solo show at Ridgewood (N.J.) Art Inst., 1985, West Wing Gallery, 1991; group shows include Craig Gallery, Ridgewood, 1979, Charisma Gallery, Englewood, N.J., 1981-83, Custom Gallery, Waldwick, N.J., 1985, Wyckoff (N.J.) Gallery, 1987-90, West Wing Gallery, Ringwood State Park, N.J., 1991, Union Camp Corp., 1992, Eisenhauer Gallery, Block Island, R.I., 1996—. Recipient 1st in State N.J. Womens Clubs, 1978-80, Watercolor award N.J. Painters and Sculptors, 1981. Mem. DAR, Community Arts Assn. (pres. 1978-79), Am. Artists Profl. League (bd. dirs. 1985-87, watercolor prize 1992), Ringwood Manor Arts Assn. (sr. profl.), Catherine Lorillard Wolfe Art Club (cash award 1993), Salute to Women in the Arts, Art Ctr. Watercolor Affiliates, Nat. Mus. of Women in the Arts. Avocations: bridge, travel, museums, theatre, reading. Home: 1-3 Chestnut Pl Waldwick NJ 07463-1125

SAMUELSON, DERRICK WILLIAM, lawyer; b. Mpls., July 24, 1929; s. Oscar W. and Ruth (Hill) S.; m. Diana L. Webster, Aug. 10, 1957; children: David W., Deirdre W. B.S., U.S. Mil. Acad., 1951; LL.B., Harvard U., 1957. Bar: N.Y. 1958. Assoc. firm Lowenstein, Pitcher, Hotchkiss, Amann & Parr, N.Y.C., 1957-60; staff atty. internat. div. Warner-Lambert Pharm. Co., Morris Plains, N.J., 1960-63; counsel internat. div. Olin Mathieson Chem. Corp., N.Y.C., 1964-65; v.p., gen. counsel ITT World Communications Inc., N.Y.C., 1965-70, ITT Asia Pacific, Inc., N.Y.C., 1970-81; sr. counsel ITT Corp., N.Y.C., 1981-87, asst. gen. counsel, asst. sec., 1987-92; of counsel Mulvaney, Kahan & Barry, San Diego, 1993—; mem. panel arbitrators Asia Pacific Ctr., 1995—; mem. panel neutrals Am. Arbitration Assn., 1995—; mem. bd. arbitrators Nat. Assn. Securities Dealers, Inc., 1996—. Pres. Am-Indonesian C. of C., 1976-79, Smoke Rise Club, 1976-77, 88-89; chmn. Am. ASEAN Trade Coun., Inc., 1978-92. With U.S. Army, 1951-54. Home: 2940 Via Asoleado Alpine CA 91901-3182 Office: First Nat Bank Bldg 401 W A St San Diego CA 92101-7901

SAMUELSON, JOAN, professional runner; b. Cape Elizabeth, Maine, May 16, 1957; d. André and Nancy Benoit; m. Scott Samuelson; children: Abigail, Anders. Student, Bowdoin Coll., N.C. State U. Long-distance coach Boston U.; runner; bd. dirs. Gulf of Maine Aquarium, Found. for Advancement Edn., Internat. Amateur Athletic Fedn. Coun.; active Maine Lung Found., Natural Resources Coun. Main, Alzheimer's Found., Multiple Sclerosis Soc., Spl. Olympics. Recipient Gold medal Olympic Games, 1984 (set world record); won Boston Marathon, 1983 (set world record). Office: Edwin P Whittemore 114A Massachusetts Ave Arlington MA 02174

SAMUELSON, KENNETH LEE, lawyer; b. Natrona Heights, Pa., Aug. 22, 1946; s. Sam and Frances Bernice (Robbins) S.; m. Marlene Ina Rabinowitz, Jan. 1, 1980; children: Heather, Cheryl. BA magna cum laude, U. Pitts., 1968; JD, U. Mich., 1971. Bar: Md. 1972, D.C. 1980, U.S. Dist. Ct. (trial bar) Md. 1984. Assoc. Weinberg & Green, Balt., 1971-73, Dickerson, Nice, Sokol & Horn, Balt., 1973; asst. atty. gen. State of Md., 1973-77; pvt. practice Balt., 1978; ptnr. Linowes and Blocher, Silver Spring (Md.), Washington, 1979-93, Semmes, Bowen & Semmes, Washington and Balt., 1993-95; Wilkes, Artis, Hedrick & Lane, Chartered, Washington and Md., 1995—. Author in field. Bd. dirs. D.C. Assn. for Retarded Citizens, Inc., 1986—. Mem. ABA (chmn. com. sect. real property, probate and trust law 1993—, moderator programs comml. leases 1987, 88, 89, 90, 91, 92, 94, 96, 97), Am. Coll. Real Estate Lawyers, D.C. Bar (mem. comml. real estate com., chmn. legal opinions project and spkr. programs on real estate 1987, 89, 90), Md. State Bar Assn. (real property, planning and zoning sect., chmn. environ. subcom. legal opinions project 1987-89, litigation sect. 1982-84, chmn. comml. trans. com.), Md. Inst. Continuing Profl. Edn. Lawyers (spkr. on article 9 of Uniform Comml. Code, opinion letters, environ. considerations in real estate transactions, easements, enforcement of liens easements, and leasing to profls. 1981, 83, 88, 89, 91, 94), Am. Arbitration Assn. (arbitrator and mediator), Washington D.C. Assn of Realtors, Inc. (moderator program on comml. leasing 1992, program on letters of intent 1996), Apt. and Office Bldg. Assn. Met. Washington (moderator of programs and spkr. 1989, 92), East Coast Builders Conf. (moderator program on Asian financing 1990), Internat. Coun. Shopping Ctrs. (organized, co-faculty program "univ." 1988, NAFTA 1992, condemnations 1994), Montgomery County Bar Assn. (mem. jud. selections com. 1988-90), Phi Beta Kappa, Lambda Alpha. Office: Wilkes Artis Hedrick & Lane 1666 K St NW Ste 1100 Washington DC 20006-2803

SAMUELSON, MARVIN LEE, veterinarian; b. Oketo, Kans., July 25, 1931; s. Eben R. and Mabel M. (Brown) S.; m. Rubye Rittgers, Aug. 26, 1995; children by previous marriage: Valorie, Vonna, Melanie, John, Jennifer. BS, Kans. State U., 1956, DVM, 1956. Staff veterinarian Carthage (Mo.) Vet. Svcs., 1956, San Pedro (Calif.) Animal Hosp., 1958-61; ptnr., mgr. Clarmar Animal Hosp., Torrance, Calif., 1961-63; owner, dir. South Shore Pet Clinic, San Pedro, Calif., 1963-73; assoc. prof. Coll. Vet. Medicine Kans. State U., Manhattan, 1973-87; dir. Vet. Tchg. Hosp. Tex. A&M U., College Station, 1987-91, asst. to dean pub. programs Coll. Vet. Medicine, 1991-92; dir. Animal Dermatology and Allergy Assocs., Topeka, 1992—. Contbr. book chpts. to vet. textbooks, articles to profl. jours. Mem. Jaycees, San Pedro, 1958-61; pres. Lions Club, 1963-64; v.p. San Pedro C. of C., 1972; precinct committeeman Wildcat Twp., Manhattan, 1985-87. 1st lt. U.S. Army, 1956-58. Recipient Bustad award for Companion Animal Vet. of Yr., 1996. Mem. AVMA (mem. edn. com. vet. fgn. grads. 1994—), Am. Acad. Vet. Dermatology (sec.-treas. 1986-91), Acad. Vet. Allergy (bd. dirs. 1983-91), Am. Assn. Vet. Clinicians (pres. 1990-91), Tex. Vet. Med. Assn., Kans. Vet. Med. Assn. (Kans. Vet. of Yr. 1992), Kans. Bd. Vet. Examiners (pres.), Calif. Vet. Med. Assn., So. Calif. Vet. Med. Assn. (pres. 1972), Soc. for Internat. Vet. Symposium (pres.-elect 1991), Alpha Zeta. Republican. Methodist. Avocation: farming. Office: Animal Dermat Allrgy Assocs 11520 SW 57th St Topeka KS 66610-9647

SAMUELSON, NORMA GRACIELA, architectural illustrator, artist; b. Mar del Plata, Argentina, May 29, 1957; came to U.S., 1979; d. Jose and Elsa Florinda (Camaras) Nunez; m. Jeffrey Thomas Samuelson, Oct. 9, 1982; 1 child, Taylor Sebastian. Student, Conservatory Mendelssohn, Mar del Plata, 1970-76; MFA, Superior Sch. Visual Arts, Mar del Plata, 1976. Tchr. art Domingo F. Sarmiento, Mar del Plata, 1976; graphic artist Atelier Marzoratti Munoz, Mar del Plata, 1976-79; archtl. illustrator Szabo Inc., Irvine, Calif., 1981-84; owner, archtl. illustrator Norma Samuelson Illustrations, Mission Viejo, Calif., 1985—. Illustrator: Centennial of Immigration Law, 1975 (2d nat. award), Historical Buildings in Los Angeles, 1995 (ltd. edits.); art work published in Best of Colored Pencil III. Mem. Color Pencil Soc. Am., Mus. Contemporary Art L.A., Knickerbocker Artists N.Y. (assoc.). Avocations: playing piano, painting and drawing, foreign travel, French art and language. Home: 26862 Via Corta San Juan Capistrano CA 92675 Office: 27001 La Paz Rd Ste 406-b Mission Viejo CA 92691-5502

SAMUELSON, PAUL ANTHONY, economics educator; b. Gary, Ind., May 15, 1915; s. Frank and Ella (Lipton) S.; m. Marion E. Crawford, July 2, 1938 (dec.); children: Jane Kendall, Margaret Wray, William Frank, Robert James, John Crawford, Paul Reid.; m. Risha Eckaus, 1981; stepdaughter, Susan Miller. BA, U. Chgo., 1935; MA, Harvard U., 1936, PhD (David A. Wells prize 1941), 1941; LLD (hon.), U. Chgo., Oberlin Coll., 1961, Boston Coll., 1964, Ind. U., 1966, U. Mich., 1967, Claremont Grad. Sch., 1967, Seton Hall U., 1971, U. N.H., 1971, Keio U., 1971, Widener Coll., 1982, Cath. U. at Riva Aguero U., Lima, Peru, 1980, Harvard, 1972, Gustavus Adolphus Coll., 1974, U. So. Calif., 1975, U. Pa., 1976, U. Rochester, 1976, Emmanuel Coll., 1977, Stonehill Coll., 1978, Indiana U. of Pa., 1993; DLitt (hon.), Ripon Coll., 1962, No. Mich. U., 1973, Valparaiso U., 1987, Columbia U, 1988; LHD (hon.), Williams Coll., 1971; DSc (hon.), U. Mass., 1972, U. R.I., 1972, Tufts U., 1988, East Anglia U., Norwich, Eng., 1966; D (hon.), U. Catholique de Louvain, Belgium, 1976, City U., London, 1980, New U. Lisbon, 1985, Univ. Nat. de Educacion a Distancia, Madrid, 1989, Univ. Politecnica de Valencia, Spain, 1991. Prof. econs. MIT, 1940-65, inst. prof., 1966, prof. emeritus, 1986; mem. staff Radiation Lab., 1944-45; prof. internat. econ. relations Fletcher Sch. Law and Diplomacy, 1945; cons. Nat. Resources Planning Bd., 1941-43, WPB, 1945, U.S. Treasury, 1945-52, 61-74, Bur. Budget, 1952, RAND Corp., 1948-75, Fed. Res. Bd., 1965—; council Econ. Advisers, 1960-68; econ. adviser to Pres. Kennedy; sr. adviser Brookings Panel on Econ. Activity; mem. spl. commn. on social scis. NSF, 1967-68; cons. Congl. Budget Office, Federal Reserve Bd., 1965—; Gordon Y Billard Fellow MIT, Boston, 1986—; vis. prof of polit. econ. Ctr. Japan-U.S. Bus. and Econ. Studies, NYU, 1987—; Stamp Meml. lectr., London, 1961, Wicksell lectr., Stockholm, 1962, Franklin lectr., Detroit, 1962; Carnegie Found. reflective year, 1965-66; John von Neumann lectr. U. Wis., 1971; Gerhard Colm Meml. lectr. New Sch. for Social Research, N.Y.C., 1971; Sulzbacher Meml. lectr. Columbia Law Sch., N.Y.C., 1974; J. Willard Gibbs lectr. Am. Math. Soc., San Francisco, 1974; John Diebold lectr. Harvard, 1976; Alice E. Blurneuf lectr. Boston Coll., 1981, Horowitz lectr. Jerusalem and Tel Aviv, 1984, Marschak Meml. lectr. UCLA, 1984, Tennenbaum lectr. Ga. Inst. Tech., 1985, Julis Steinberg Meml. lectr. Wharton Sch., 1986, Godkin lectr. Harvard, 1986, Woodward lectr. U. British Columbia, 1987; lectr. Harvard 350 Symposium, Harvard U., 1986, Olin lectr. U. Va., 1989, Commemorative lectr. Stonehill Coll., 1990, Lionel Robbins Meml. lectr. Claremont Coll., 1991; mem. nat. advisory com. Inst. for Rsch. on Poverty. Author: Foundations of Economic Analysis, 1947, enlarged edit., 1983, Economics, 1948-95, Readings in Economics, 1955-73, (with R. Dorfman and R.M. Solow) Linear Programming and Economic Analysis, 1958, Collected Scientific Papers, 5 vols., 1966, 72, 78, 86; co-author numerous other books; contbr. numerous articles to profl. jours.; columnist Newsweek, 1966-81; assoc. editor Jour. Pub. Econs., Jour. Internat. Econs., Jour. Fin. Econs., Jour. Nonlinear Analysis; adv. bd. Challenge Mag.; editl. bd. Procs. Nat. Acad. Scis. Chmn. Pres.'s Task Force Maintaining Am. Prosperity, 1964; mem. Nat. Task Force on Econ. Edn., 1960-61; econ. adviser to Pres. John F. Kennedy, 1959-63; mem. adv. bd. Nat. Commn. Money and Credit, 1958-60. Hon. fellow London Sch. Econs. and Polit. Sci. Guggenheim fellow, 1948-49; Ford Found. Research fellow, 1958-59; recipient David A. Wells prize Harvard U., 1941, John Bates Clark medal Am. Econ. Assn., 1947, Alfred Nobel Meml. prize , 1970, medal of Honor U. Evansville, Ill., 1970, Albert Einstein Commemorative award, 1971, Alumni medal U. Chgo., 1983, Britannica award, 1989, Gold Scanno prize, Naples, Italy, 1990; Paul A. Samuelson Professorship established in his name, MIT, 1991; recipient Nat. Medal of Sci., Washington, 1996. Fellow Brit. Acad. (corr.), Am. Philos. Soc., Econometric Soc. (v.p. 1950, pres. 1951), Am. Econ. Assn. (hon.; pres. 1961); mem. AAAS, Com. Econ. Devel. (commn. on nat. goals, research adv. bd. 1959-60), Internat. Econ. Assn. (pres. 1966-68, hon. pres.), Nat. Acad. Scis., Leibniz-Akademie der Wissenschaften und der Literatur (corr. mem. 1987—) Nat. Assn. of Investment Clubs (Disting. Svc. award in Investment Edn. 1974), Club of Econ. and Mgmt. (medal, hon. Valencia, Spain 1990), Phi Beta Kappa, Omicron Delta Epsilon (trustee). Home: 94 Somerset St Belmont MA 02178-2010 Office: MIT Dept Econs E52 # 383C Cambridge MA 02139

SAMUELSON, RITA MICHELLE, speech language pathologist; b. Chgo., July 15, 1954; d. Mike Dabetic and Rita Lorraine (Stasny) Dabertin; m. K. Alan Samuelson, May 7, 1977; children: Amber Michelle, April Claire. BS, Ind. U., 1976, MA in Teaching, 1977. Speech lang. therapist East Maine Dist. 63, Des Plaines, Ill., 1977-80, Cmty. Cons. Dist. 59, Elk Grove, Ill., 1980-83, Fenton High Sch. Dist. 100, Bensenville, Ill., 1988-93, Addison (Ill.) Dist. 4, 1993-94, Elgin (Ill.) Dist. U-46, 1994—. Author: Sound Strategist, 1989, The Birthday Party Adventure, 1991, The Lizard Princess Adventure, 1991; contbr. chpt.: Yuletide Reverie, 1993. Mem. Am. Speech Lang. Hearing Assn., DuPage County Speech Hearing Lang. Assn. (v.p. bd. dirs. 1995—), Ill. Speech Lang. Hearing Assn., Villagers Club Bloomingdale, Writer's Workshop of Bloomingdale (steering com. rep.). Roman Catholic. Avocations: singing in church choir, lectr. in children and humor, doll collecting, antiquing. Home: 156 Longridge Dr Bloomingdale IL 60108-1416 Office: Oakhill Elementary Sch 502 S Oltendorf Rd Streamwood IL 60107-1575

SAMUELSON, ROBERT JACOB, journalist; b. N.Y.C., Dec. 23, 1945; s. Abraham and Joan (Kahn) S.; m. Judith Herr, July 10, 1983; children: Ruth, Michael, John. AB in Govt., Harvard U., 1967. Reporter Washington Post, 1969-73; free-lance writer Washington, 1973-76; reporter, columnist National Jour. mag., Washington, 1976-84; columnist Newsweek, Washington, 1984—; columnist Washington Post, 1977—. Author: The Good Life and Its Discontents: The American Dream in the Age of Entitlement 1945-1995, 1996.

SANBORN, ANNA LUCILLE, pension and insurance consultant; b. Bklyn., Mar. 29, 1924; d. Peter Francis and Matilda M. (Stumpp) Galligen; B.A., Bklyn. Coll., 1945; 1 son, Dean Sanborn. Head dept. benefit and estate planning Union Central Life Ins. Co., N.Y.C., 1949-51; adminstr. employee benefits Seaboard Oil Co., N.Y.C., 1952-56; with Frank J. Walters Assocs., Inc., N.Y.C., 1957—, pres., 1970—. Bd. dirs. Archdiocesan Service Corp. Mem. Am. Acad. Actuaries, Republican. Roman Catholic. Home: 58-11 Seabury St Elmhurst NY 11373-4825 Office: Frank J Walters Assocs 58-13 Seabury St Flushing NY 11373-4825

SANBORN, DAVID, alto saxophonist; b. St. Louis, MO, 1945. Student, Northwestern Univ., Univ. of Iowa. Ind. jazz saxophonist, 1975—. Rec. artist: (with James Taylor) How Sweet It Is, (with David Bowie) Young Americans, (with Gil Evans) Priestess, (with Bob James) Double Vision, (solo albums) Taking Off, 1975, Sanborn, 1976, Promise Me the Moon, 1977, Heart to Heart, 1978, Hideaway, 1980, Voyeur, 1981, Grammy awd., 1981), As We Speak, 1982, Backstreet, 1983, Straight to the Heart, 1984, Close Up, 1988 (Grammy awd., 1989), Upfront, 1992, Hearsay, 1994, Pearls, 1995, Songs From the Night Before, 1996; music for film: Lethal Weapon 2, 1989; host and co-producer of "The Jazz Show," NBC-Radio; TV appearances: host of Night Music, 1988-89, regular guest on Late Night with David Letterman, 1982-94. Office: Warner Bros Records 3300 Warner Blvd Burbank CA 91505-4632

SANBORN, GEORGE FREEMAN, JR., genealogist; b. Laconia, N.H., Jan. 18, 1944; s. George Freeman and Charlotte (Dearborn) S.; m. Melinde Laura Lutz, Mar. 30, 1984; children: Ruth Alice, Lowell Freeman. AB, Boston U., 1967; AM, U. Ill., 1968; MEd, U. N.H., 1981. French tchr. Souris (P.E.I., Can.) Regional H.S., 1968-69; French and occupational studies tchr. Massey-Vanier H.S., Cowansville, Que., Can., 1969-70; French and English tchr. Kings Coll. Sch., Windsor, N.S., Can., 1970-71; translator, revisor Province of N.B., Fredericton, 1971-73; sr. govt. revisor Province of Ont., Toronto, 1973-75; French and Spanish tchr. Tilton (N.H.) Sch., 1978-80; living unit coord. Laconia (N.H.) State Sch., 1982-83; ref. libr. New Eng. Hist. Geneal. Soc., Boston, 1983-85, acquisitions libr. and tech. svcs. dir., 1985-95, publs. asst., 1996—. Editor The N.H. Geneal. Record, 1990-93; compiler Vital Records of Hampton, N.H., 1992, 97; contbr. articles to profl. jours. Fellow Am. Soc. Genealogists; mem. Soc. of the Cin. in the State of N.H., Soc. of Mayflower Descendants in the State of N.H., New Eng. Hist. Geneal. Soc., P.E.I. Geneal. Soc., N.H. Soc. Genealogists (pres. 1988-95), Geneal. Soc. Vt. (chair publs. com. 1992-96). Democrat. Presbyterian. Avocations: gardening, bantam raising, Scottish Gaelic language, P.E.I. history, antique glass and china. Home: 24 Thornton St Derry NH 03038-1628 Office: New Eng Hist Geneal Soc Libr 99 Newbury St Boston MA 02116-3007

SANBRAILO, JOHN A., mission director; b. San Francisco, July 26, 1943; s. John and Ann (Schonfeld) S.; m. Cecilia Del Pozo, Jan. 12, 1974. B in Econs., U. Calif., Berkeley, 1965; M in Econs., San Francisco State U., 1969; MPA, Harvard U., 1976. Vol. U.S. Peace Corps., Sucre State, Venezuela, 1965-68; credit union and coop. extension agt. U.S. Peace Corps., Washington; internat. devel. intern US AID, Washington, 1969-70; chief project devel. Nicaragua, project devel. officer Ecuador US AID, 1970-75; dir. policy planning and budgeting, chief fin. officer Latin Am. and Caribbean Bur. US AID, Washington, 1976-79; dir. US AID Mission, Quito, Ecuador, 1979-82, 93-96, Lima, Peru, 1983-86, Tegucigalpa, Honduras, 1987-91, San Salvador, El Salvador, 1991-93; career minister US Sr. Fgn. Svc. Decorated Honduran Cong., 1991, Govt. Peru, 1984, 86, Govt. Ecuador, 1982, 96. Address: 9216 Talisman Dr Vienna VA 22182

SANCAKTAR, EROL, engineering educator; b. Ankara, Turkey, July 13, 1952; came to U.S., 1974; s. Mehmet Ali and Ulker Mualla (Elveren) S.; m. Teresa Sue Sancaktar, Feb. 16, 1979; children: Orhan Ali, Errol Alan. BS in Mech. Engrng., Robert Coll., Istanbul, Turkey, 1974; MS in Mech. Engrng., Va. Poly. Inst. and State U., 1975, PhD, 1979. Teaching asst. Robert Coll., Istanbul, 1972-74; instr. Va. Poly. Inst. and State U., Blacksburg, Va., 1977-78; visiting scholar Kendall Co., Boston, 1985-86; assoc. prof. Clarkson U., Potsdam, N.Y., 1984-95; prof. U. Akron (Ohio), 1996—; cons. to the UN Devel. Programme, 1987, ALCOA, 1990-91, U.S. Army Benet Labs., 1991. Mem. editl. adv. bd. Jour. Adhesion Sci. Tech., 1993—; assoc. tech. editor Transactions of the ASME, Jour. of Mech. Design, 1995—; contbr. articles to profl. jours.; patentee in field. Recipient various rsch. grants awarded by NSF, NASA, U.S. Army, N.Y., Grumman Corp., Kendall Co., GE, IBM. Mem. ASME (assoc. tech. editor transactions of ASME Jour. of Mech. Design 1995—, editor Reliability, Stress Analysis and Failure Prevention: Aspects of Composite and Active Materials, Issues in Fastening & Joining, Composite & Smart Structures, Numerical & FEA Methods, Risk Minimization, elected mem. RSAFP tech. steering com.). Home: 465 Evergreen Dr Tallmadge OH 44278-1356 Office: Univ Akron Dept Polymer Engrng Akron OH 44325-0301

SANCAR, AZIZ, research biochemist. MD, Istanbul Med. Sch., 1969; PhD in Molecular Biology, U. Tex., Dallas, 1977. Assoc. prof. biochemistry U. N.C., Chapel Hill, 1982—. Office: University of N Carolina School of Medicine Dept of Biochem & Biophysics Chapel Hill NC 27599

SANCETTA, CONSTANCE ANTONINA, oceanographer; b. Richmond, Va., Apr. 17, 1949; d. Anthony Louis and Joyce Louise (Kellogg) S. BA, Brown U., 1971, MSc, 1973; PhD, Oreg. State U., 1976. Rsch. assoc. Stanford (Calif.) U., 1977-78; assoc. rsch. scientist Columbia U., N.Y.C., 1979-84, rsch. scientist, 1985-87, sr. rsch. scientist, 1988-94; assoc. program mgr. divsn. ocean sci. NSF, Washington, 1992—; mem. adv. com. divsn. ocean sci. NSF, 1981-86, 89-92. Editl. bd. Marine Micropaleontology, Oceanography, 1983—; contbr. articles to profl. jours. Fellow AAAS, Geol.

Soc. Am.; mem. Am. Quaternary Soc. (councilor 1988-90), Am. Geophys. Union (sec. ocean sci. sect. 1988-90), Oceanography Soc. (councilor 1989-93), Paleontol. Rsch. Instn. (trustee 1991-92). Home: 1637 Irvin St Vienna VA 22182-2119 Office: NSF Assoc Prog Mgr Divsn Ocean Sci 4201 Wilson Blvd Rm 725 Arlington VA 22230-0001

SANCHEZ, DAVID ALAN, mathematics educator; b. San Francisco, Jan. 13, 1933; m. Joan Patricia Thomas, Dec. 28, 1957; children: Bruce, Christina. BS, U. N.Mex., 1955; MS, U. Mich., 1960, PhD, 1964. Instr. U. Chgo., 1963-65; from asst. to assoc. to full prof. UCLA, 1966-77, assoc. dean grad. sch., 1972-73; prof. U. N.Mex., Albuquerque, 1977-86, chmn. dept. math., 1983-86; v.p., provost Lehigh U., Bethlehem, 1986-90; asst. dir. math. and phys. scis. NSF, Washington, 1990-92; dep. assoc. dir. rsch. and edn. Los Alamos (N.Mex.) Nat. Lab., 1992-93; vice chancellor acad. affairs Tex. A&M Sys., College Station, 1993-95; prof. math. Tex. A&M U., College Station, 1996—. Author books; contbr. articles to profl. jours. Served as 1st lt. USMC, 1956-59. Mem. Am. Math. Soc., Math. Assn. Am. Avocations: fishing, bridge. Office: Tex A & M U Dept Math College Station TX 77843-3368

SÁNCHEZ, FRANK PEREZ, elementary education educator; b. Artesia, N.Mex., June 25, 1957; s. Dolores R. and Delia R. (Perez) S.; m. Angi Lynn Rowland, Sept. 24, 1977; children: Jessica Lynn, Joshua Andrew, Jeremy Franklin; 1 foster child, Tiffiny Maree Robinson. AA, N.Mex. State U., Carlsbad, 1989; BS, Ea. N.Mex. U., Portales, 1991. Cert. tchr., N.Mex. Adult basic edn. tchr. N.Mex. State U., Carlsbad, 1991-92; tchr. math., social studies Artesia (N.Mex.) Pub. Schs., 1992—. Roman Catholic. Avocations: camping, guitar, sports, woodworking. Home: PO Box 103 Loco Hills NM 88255-0103

SANCHEZ, GILBERT, retired academic administrator, microbiologist, researcher; b. Belen, N.Mex., May 7, 1938; s. Macedonio C. and Josephine H. Sanchez; m. Lorena T. Tabet, Aug. 26, 1961; children—Elizabeth, Phillip, Katherine. B.S. in Biology, N.Mex. State U., 1961; Ph.D. in Microbiology, U. Kans., 1967. Research asst. U. Kans., Lawrence, 1963-67; research assoc., postdoctoral fellow Rice U., Houston, 1967-68; prof. N.Mex. Inst. Tech., Socorro, 1968-79; dean grad. studies Eastern N.Mex. U., Portales, 1979-83; v.p. acad. affairs U. So. Colo., Pueblo, 1983-85; pres. N.Mex. Highlands U., Las Vegas, 1985-95; cons. NIH, NSF, Solvex Corp., Albuquerque, 1979-83; bd. dirs. Fed. Res. Bank, Denver. Contbr. numerous articles to profl. jours. Patentee in field. Pres. Socorro Sch. Bd., 1974-79, Presbyn. Hosp. Bd., Socorro, 1977-79. Research grantee Dept. Army, 1976-79, N.Mex. Dept. Energy, 1979-83, NSF, 1979. Mem. Am. Soc. Microbiology, Am. Soc. Indsl. Microbiology, AAAS, Am. Assn. Univs. and Colls. (bd. dirs. 1988-90), Hispanic Assn. Univs. and Colls. (pres. 1986-89). Roman Catholic. Lodge: Rotary. Avocations: auto mechanics; welding; woodworking; golf.

SANCHEZ, ISAAC CORNELIUS, chemical engineer, educator; b. San Antonio, Aug. 11, 1941; s. Isaac Jr. and Marce (Aguilar) S.; m. Karen Patricia Horton, Aug. 7, 1976; children: Matthew, Timothy. BS with honors, St. Mary's U., 1963; PhD, U. Del., 1969. Postdoctoral Nat. Bureau Standards, Gaithersburg, Md., 1969-71; assoc. scientist Xerox Corp., Webster, N.Y., 1971-72; asst. prof. U. Mass., Amherst, 1972-77; rsch. chemist Nat. Bureau Standards, Gaithersburg, 1977-86; fellow Alcoa, Pitts., 1986-88; prof. U. Tex., Austin, 1988—; H.A. disting vis. prof. U. Akron (Ohio), 1995. Mem. editorial bd. Jour. Polymer Sci., 1986-92, Polymer, 1987—; contbr. over 90 articles to profl. jours. Bd. dirs. Tex. Alliance for Minorities in Engrng., Austin, Tex., 1989-91. Lt. USN, 1963-67. Recipient Cullen Trust Endowed professorship in engrng U. Tex., 1992, Bronze medal U.S. Dept. Commerce, 1980, Silver medal, 1983, E.U. Condon award Nat. Bur. Standards, 1983. Fellow Am. Phys. Soc.; mem. AAAS, AICE, Am. Chem. Soc., Nat. Acad. Engrng., Materials Rsch. Soc., Soc. Plastics Engrs. (Internat. Rsch. award 1996). Avocations: golf, tennis, birding. Office: Univ Tex Chem Engring Dept Austin TX 78712

SANCHEZ, JAVIER ALBERTO, industrial engineer; b. San Cristobal, Tachira, Venezuela, Apr. 13, 1960; came to U.S., 1977; s. Leonidas and Ana Mireya (Albornoz) S. AA, Butler County C.C., El Dorado, Kans., 1979; BS in Indls. Engrng., Wichita State U., 1982, MS in Engrng. Mgmt., 1985. Indsl. cons. Ferronikel, C.A., Caracas, Venezuela, 1977-83; project mgr. Trabajos Viales, C.A., Caracas, Venezuela, 1980; applications engr. Major, Inc., Wichita, Kans., 1983; mfg. engr. L.S. Industries, Inc., Wichita, 1983-86; plant mgr. World Wide Mfg., Inc., Miami, Fla., 1986-88; prodn. mgr. Capitol Hardware Mfg. Co., Chgo., 1988-91; product mgr. Ready Metal Mfg.Co., Chgo., 1991-92; engrng. tech. resources and materials mgr. Taurus Internat. Mfg. Inc., Miami, 1992-95; materials mgr. Marino Tech., Inc., Miami, 1996; area mgr. South Fla. Mfg. Tech. Ctr., Miami, 1996—; sr. cons. Ferronikel, C.A., Caracas, 1983—, mgr. internat. ops., 1988—. Recipient scholarship award Venezuelan Govt., 1977, Mariscal Ayacucho award, 1980. Mem. Soc. Mfg. Engrs., Inst. Indsl. Engrs. (sr.), Soc. Safety Engrs., Nat. Safety Coun., Am. Prodn. and Inventory Control Soc., Soc. Plastic Engrs., Nat. Assn. Purchasing Mgmt, Assn. Facility Engrs. Roman Catholic. Achievements include development of applications of world class manufacturing techniques in tube fabricating, sheet metal operations and firearms production; cost estimating techniques for metal fabricators; design and manufacturing of retail store fixtures and racks; worldwide engineering and technical resources for firearms manufacturing and for international businesses; materials management techniques, procurement and negotiating fabrication methods for bulk packaging manufacturing, outsourcing, networking, outreach programs, operational assessments, performance benchmarking, safety and environmental engineering, ISO-9000, QS=9000 implementation, continuous flow, cellular manufacturing. Home: 8357 W Flagler St Ste 308 Miami FL 33144-2072 Office: So Fla Mfg Tech Ctr 11380 NW 27th Ave Miami FL 33167-3418

SANCHEZ, LEONEDES MONARRIZE WORTHINGTON (DUKE DE LEONEDES), fashion designer; b. Flagstaff, Ariz., Mar. 15, 1951; s. Rafael Leonedes and Margaret (Monarrize) S. BS, No. Ariz. U., 1974; studied, Fashion Inst. Tech., N.Y.C., 1974-75; AA, Fashion Inst. D&M, L.A., 1975; lic., La Ecole de la Chambre Syndical de la Couture Parisian, Paris, 1976-78. Lic. in designing. Contract designer/asst. to head designer House of Bonnet, Paris, 1976—; dress designer-in-residence Flagstaff, 1978—; mem. faculty No. Ariz. U., Flagstaff, 1978-80; designer Ambiance, Inc., L.A., 1985—; designer Interiors by Leonedes subs. Studio of Leonedes Couturier, Ariz., 1977, Calif., 1978, London, Paris, 1978, Rome, 1987, Milan, Spain, 1989; designer Liturgical Vesture subs. Studio of Leonedes Couturier; CEO Leonedes Internat.; designer El Casillo de Nuevo Espana, Santa Fe, N.Mex.; owner, CEO, designer Leonedes Internat., Ltd., London, Milan, Paris, Spain, Ambian Ariz, Calif., Appolonian Costuming, Ariz., London, Milan, Paris, El Castillo de Leonedes, Sevilla, Spain, Villa Apollonian de Leonedes, Mykonos, Greece; cns. House of Bonnet, Paris, 1976—, Bob Mackie, Studio City, Calif., 1974-75; CEO, designer artistical dir., Leonedes internat. Bd. dirs. Roman Cath. Social Svcs., 1985-86, Northland Crisis Nursery, 1985—; bd. dirs., chmn. Pine Country Transit, 1986-88; pres. Chicanos for Edn.; active master's swim program ARC, Ariz., 1979—; eucharistic min., mem. art and environ. com., designer liturgical vesture St. Pius X Cath. Ch.; vol. art tchr., instr. St. Mary's Regional Sch., Flagstaff, 1987-90, vol. art dir.; mem. Flagstaff Parks and Recreation Commn., 1994-96, citizens' adv. com. master plan, 1994-96; mem. cmty. bd. adv. com. Flagstaff Unified Sch. Dist., 1995; active Duke de Leonedes Found. de Nuevo Espana, Santa Fe, Duke de Leonedes Found. de Neuvo Espana, Santa Fe. Decorated Duke de Leonedes (Spain), 1994; recipient Camellian Design award 1988, Atlanta. Mem. AAU (life, chairperson swimming Ariz. 1995, vice chairperson physique, mem. citizen adv. bd. parks and recreation), Am. Film Inst., Am. Assn. Hist. Preservation, Costume Soc., Am. Nat. Physique Com., Internat. Consortium Fashion Designers, Nat. Cath. Edn. Assn., La Legion de Honour de la Mode Parisienne, Social Register Assn., Phi Alpha Theta (historian 1972-73, pres. 1973-74), Pi Kappa Delta (pres. 1972-73, historian 1973-74). Republican. Avocations: body building, swimming. Office: El Castillo de Leonedes, Seville Spain Also: El Castillo de Nuevo Espana, Santa Fe Greece

SANCHEZ, LORETTA, congresswoman; b. Anaheim, Calif., Jan. 7, 1960. BA, Chapman U., 1982; MBA, Am. U., 1984. With Orange County Transp. Authority, 1984-87, Fieldman Rolapp & Assocs., 1987-90; strategic mgmt. cons. Booz Allen & Hamilton, 1993—; owner, operator AMIGA Advisors Inc., 1993—; mem. 105th Congress from 46th Calif. dist., 1997—. Mem. Anaheim Rotary Club. Democrat. Office: 116 Cannon Washington DC 20007-7803*

SANCHEZ, MARY ANNE, secondary school educator; b. Galesburg, Ill., Aug. 4, 1939; d. Stephen Mingare and M. Margaret Kennedy; m. J. Manuel Sanchez, Dec. 26, 1980. BS in Edn., Western Ill. U., 1961; MA, Ill. State U., 1970. Tchr. Montgomery County Bd. Edn., Chevy Chase, Md., Hillsborough County Bd. Edn., Tampa, Fla.; tchr. Stanford, Ill., Titusville, Fla. Mem. Nat. Coun. for Social Studies, Fla. Coun. for Social Studies, Adult Edn. Assn. Home: 2715 W Ivy St Tampa FL 33607-1922

SANCHEZ, MIGUEL RAMON, dermatologist, educator; b. Havana, Cuba, May 5, 1950; came to the U.S., 1962; s. Rodolfo and Maria Sanchez. BS, CCNY, 1971; MD, Albert Einstein Coll. Medicine, 1974. Instr. Montefiore Dept. Family Medicine, Bronx, N.Y., 1978-79; sr. med. specialist Kingsborough Psychiat. Ctr., Bklyn., 1979-80; med. dir. Ten Communities Health Ctr., Tulare, Calif., 1980-82; assoc. prof. clin. dermatology NYU, N.Y.C., 1982-83; assoc. dir. Dept. Dermatology Bellevue Hosp. Ctr, N.Y.C., 1983—; mem. Tulare County Mental Health Bd., 1980-81; mem. med. bd. Bellevue Hosp., 1990—. Contbr. articles to profl. jours. and chpts. to books; editor: (software) Derm-Rx, 1986-90, (book) Dermatology Educational Review Manual, 1993. Bd. dirs. Community Health Project, N.Y.C., 1993; mem. patient care com. community bd. Bellevue Hosp., 1990-93; co-founder, pres. Assn. Latino Faculty and Students. Recipient Testimonial of Appreciation So. Tulare County, 1981, 1st Place award Scientific Forum N.Y. Acad. Dermatology, 1985. Mem. Am. Acad. Dermatology, Acad. for Advancement Sci., Dermatologic Found. Democrat. Roman Catholic. Achievements include development of clinics for tropical dermatology, HIV skin disease, disorders of keratinization, connective tissue disease, and photothera py; research in infectious diseases, dermatopharmacology and cutaneous manifestation of HIV infection. Office: NYU Dept Dermatology 562 1st Ave New York NY 10016-6402

SANCHEZ, RAFAEL CAMILO, physician; b. Tampa, Fla., July 18, 1919; s. Francisco and Catalina (Mateo) S.; children: Stephen Francis, John Thomas, David Lear. B.S., Loyola U., New Orleans, 1940; M.D., La. State U., 1950. Diplomate: Am. Bd. Family Practice (bd. dirs. 1976-79, assoc. exec. dir. 1979-84). Intern U.S. Marine Hosp., New Orleans, 1950-51; gen. practice medicine New Orleans, 1951-72; med. educator, dir. continuing med. edn. La. State U., 1963-77, prof. family medicine, 1979-84; prof. family medicine East Carolina U. Sch. Medicine, Greenville, 1984-90, prof. emeritus, 1990—; dir. family practice residency program Charity Hosp. of Bogalusa, La., 1977-79; dir. Continuing Med. Edn.; med. dir. Nat. Med. Info. Network. Served with AUS, 1940-46. Recipient Recognition award Soc. of Tchrs. of Medicine, 1987, Willard M. Duff award Accreditation Coun. for Continuing Med. Edn. Fellow AMA, Am. Acad. Family Physicians (Thomas W. Johnson award 1978, Presdl. award 1983, Pres.'s award 1989); mem. Network for Continuing Med. Edn. (med. dir.), Nat. Med. Info. Network of Lippincott-Raven Healthcare (med. dir.), Alpha Omega Alpha. Democrat. Roman Catholic. Office: PO Box 20035 Greenville NC 27858-0035

SANCHEZ, RICK, newscaster; b. Guanabacoa, Havana, Cuba, July 31, 1958; arrived in U.S., 1960; s. Francisco and Adela Ventura (Reinaldo) Fernandez; m. Suzanne Karen Kent, June 17, 1989; children: Richard Lamar, Robert Francisco. Student, Miami Dade c.C., Miami, Fla., 1977, Moorhead (Minn.) State U., 1978-80, U. Minn., 1980-82. Reporter KCMT-TV, Alexandria, Minn., 1981; writer WCCO-TV, Mpls., 1982; reporter/anchor WCKT-TV, Miami, 1982-86; anchor/reporter KHDU-TV, Houston, 1986-88, WSVN-TV, Miami, 1988—. Prodr./reporter documentary: When I Left Cuba, 1983 (Emmy 1984), The Last Contras, 1991 (Emmy 1992). Spokesperson Habitat for Humanity, Dade and Broward Counties, 1993—, D.A.R.E., 1991-92, Spl. Olympics, 1989-91. Recipient Best Coverage for Hurricane Andrew award Fla. Assn. Broadcasters, 1994; named Fla.'s Best Newscaster, O.T.I., 1990, Best Anchorman, Miami New Times, 1993, Fla.'s Best Reporter, Exito Mag., 1995. Mem. Nat. Assn. TV Arts and Scis. Roman Catholic. Avocations: golf, baseball, softball, boating. Office: WSVN-TV 1401 79th Street Cswy Miami FL 33141-4104

SANCHEZ, ROBERT FRANCIS, journalist; b. Bradenton, Fla., Jan. 1, 1938; s. Robert and Frances Alice (Thompson) S. B.S. in English Edn., Fla. State U., 1959, M.S., 1962, postgrad., 1971-74. Mem. faculty Fla. State U., Tallahassee, 1962-67; mem. faculty Fla. A&M U., Tallahassee, 1968-71; writer, editor Tallahassee Democrat, 1965-74; editorial writer Miami Herald, 1974—. Co-recipient Pulitzer Prize, 1983. Mem. Phi Delta Kappa, Sigma Delta Chi. Republican. Methodist. Home: 7000 Miller Rd Miami FL 33155-5615 Office: Miami Herald 1 Herald Plz Miami FL 33132-1609

SANCHEZ, VICTORIA WAGNER, science educator; b. Milw., Apr. 11, 1934; d. Arthur William and Lorraine Marguerite (Kocovsky) Wagner; m. Rozier Edmond Sanchez, June 23, 1956; children: Mary Elizabeth, Carol Anne, Robert Edmond, Catherine Marie, Linda Therese. BS cum laude, Mt. Mary Coll., 1955; MS, Marquette U., 1957; postgrad., U. N.Mex., 1979-86, U. Del., 1990. Cert. secondary tchr., N.Mex. Chemist Nat. Bur. Standards, Washington, 1958-60; tchr., chmn. sci. dept. Albuquerque Pub. Schs., 1979-94; chmn. pub. info. area conv. Nat. Sci. Tchrs. Assn., 1984, mem. sci. rev. com. Albuquerque Pub. Schs., 1985-86, 92-93, dedication of N.W. Regional Sci. Fair, 1994, Gov.'s Summit on Edn., 1991, 92, Gov.'s Steering Com. Systemic Change in Math. and Sci. Edn. Bd. dirs. Encino House, Albuquerque, 1976-92, treas., 1977-79; leader Albuquerque troop Girl Scouts U.S., 1966-77. Named Outstanding Sci. Tchr., NW Regional Sci. Fair, Albuquerque, 1983, 88, 90; recipient St. George's award N.Mex. Cath. Scouting Com., 1978, Focus on Excellence award ASCD, Albuquerque, 1985, 89, Presdl. awards for excellence in sci. and math., 1989. Mem. AAUW (officer Albuquerque br. 1976-77, N.Mex. divsn. 1977-78), NSTA, N.Mex. Sci. Tchrs. Assn. (treas. 1988-90), Albuquerque Sci. Tchrs. Assn. (treas. 1984-85, v.p., pres.-elect 1986-87, pres. 1987-88, Svc. to Sci. award 1994), N.Mex. Acad. Sci., Am. Coun. on Edn. (math. and sci. edn. nat. com. 1990-92), DuPont Honors Workshop for Tchrs., Albuquerque Rose Soc. (sec. 1962-63). Democrat. Roman Catholic. Avocations: reading, fishing, hiking, needlecraft, camping. Home: 7612 Palo Duro Ave NE Albuquerque NM 87110-2315

SAND, LEONARD B., federal judge; b. N.Y.C., May 24, 1928. B.S., NYU, 1947; LL.B., Harvard, 1951. Bar: N.Y. 1953, U.S. Supreme Ct. 1956, D.C. 1969. Clk. to dist. ct. judge N.Y., 1952-53; asst. U.S. atty. So. Dist. N.Y., 1953-54; asst. to U.S. Solictor Gen., 1956-59; mem. firm Robinson, Silverman, Pearce, Aronsohn Sand and Berman, N.Y.C., 1960-78; judge U.S. Dist. Ct. So. Dist. N.Y., 1978—; adj. prof. law NYU. Note editor: Harvard Law Rev, 1950-51. Del. N.Y. State Constl. Conv., 1967; v.p., treas. Legal Aid Soc. Fellow Am. Coll. Trial Lawyers; mem. ABA, Assn. Bar City N.Y. (v.p.), N.Y. State Bar Assn., Fed. Bar Coun. Office: US Dist Ct US Courthouse 500 Pearl St New York NY 10007-1316

SAND, THOMAS CHARLES, lawyer; b. Portland, Oreg., June 4, 1952; s. Harold Eugene and Marian Anette (Thomas) S.; m. Rhonda Diane Laycoe, June 15, 1974; children: Kendall, Taylor, Justin. Student, Centro des Artes y Lenguas, Cuernavaca, Mex., 1972; BA in English, U. Oreg., 1974; JD, Lewis and Clark Coll., 1977. Bar: Oreg. 1977, U.S. Dist. Ct. Oreg. 1977, U.S. Ct. Appeals (9th cir.) 1984. Assoc. Miller, Nash, Wiener, Hager & Carlsen, Portland, 1977-84, ptnr., 1984—; mem. Oreg. State Bar Com. on Professionalism, 1989, chmn., 1990; dir. young lawyers divsn. Multnomah County Bar Assn., 1980; spl. asst. atty. gen. Wasco County 1983 Gen. Election; speaker in field. Contbr. articles to legal jours. and procs. Mem. U.S. Dist. Ct. of Oreg. Hist. Soc., 1990—; bd. dirs. Portland Area coun. Camp Fire, Inc., 1978-90,pres., 1984-86; bd. dirs. Oreg. Indoor Invitational Track Meet, Inc., 1982-84. Recipient Boss of the Yr. award Portland Legal Secs. Assn., 1989. Mem. ABA (securities litigation com., subcom. on broker-dealer litigation), Oreg. Bar Assn., Multnomah Bar Assn. (bd. dirs. task force on structure and orgn. 1989, chmn. com. on professionalism 1988, nominating com. 1986, participating atty. in N.E. legal clin. Vol Lawyers project, award of merit for svc. to profession 1988), Securities Industry Assn. (compliance and legal divsn.), Northwestern Sch. of Law, Lewis and Clark Coll. Alumni Assn. (bd. dirs. 1992), Valley Comm. Presbyterian Ch., Multnomah Athletic Club, Portland Golf Club. Avocations: golf, guitar, camping, river rafting, children's sports. Office: Miller Nash Wiener Hager & Carlsen 111 SW 5th Ave Ste 3500 Portland OR 97204-3638

SANDAHL, BONNIE BEARDSLEY, pediatric nurse practitioner, clinical nurse specialist, nurse manager; b. Washington, Jan. 17, 1939; d. Erwin Leonard and Carol Myrtle (Collis) B.; m. Glen Emil Sandahl, Aug 17, 1963; children: Cara Lynne, Cory Glen. BSN, U. Wash., 1962, MN, 1974, cert. pediatric nurse practitioner, 1972. Dir. Wash. State Joint Practice Commn., Seattle, 1974-76; instr. pediatric nurse practitioner program U. Wash., Seattle, 1976, course coord. quality assurance, 1977-78; pediatric nurse practitioner/health coord. Snohomish County Head Start, Everett, Wash., 1975-77; clin. nurse educator (specialist), nurse manager Harborview Med. Ctr., Seattle, 1978-97, dir. child abuse prevention project, 1986-97; mgr. Children's Ctr., Providence Health Sys. Northwest, 1997—; spkr. legis. focus on children, 1987; clin. assoc. Dept. of Pediatrics, U. Wash. Sch. medicine, 1987—, clin. faculty Sch. Nursing, nurse mgr. Providence Gen. Children's Ctr., Everett, 1997—. Mem. Task Force on Pharmacotherapeutic Courses, Wash. State Bd. Nursing, 1985-86; Puget Sound Health Sys. Agy., 1975-88, pres., 1980-82; mem. child devel. project adv. bd. Mukilteo Sch. Dist., 1984-85; mem. parenting adv. com. Edmonds Sch. Dist., 1985—; chmn. hospice-home health task force Snohomish County Hospice Program, Everett, 1984-85, bd. dirs. hospice, 1985-87, adv. com. 1986-88; mem. Wash. State Health Coordinating, Coun., 1977-82, chmn. nursing home bed projection methodology task force, 1986-87; mem., interim chair Nat. Coun. Health Planning and Devel., HHS, 1980-87; mem. adv. com. on uncompensated care Wash. State Legislature, 1983-84; mem. Joint Select Com., Tech. Adv. Com. on Managed Health Care Sys., 1984-85. Pres., Alderwood Manor Cmty. Coun., 1983-85; treas. Wash. St. Women's Polit. Caucus, 1983-84; mem. com. to examine changes in Wash. State Criminal Sex Law, 1987; appointee county needs assessment com. Snohomish County Govt. United Way, 1989, 94; chair human svcs. adv. coun. Snohomish County Human Svcs. Dept., chair adv. com., 1992-96; gubernatorial appointee Western Form Health Svcs. Adv. Com. for Wash. State, 1995—. Recipient Golden Acorn award Seattle-King County PTA, 1973, Katherine Rickey Vol. Participation award, 1987. Mem. Am. Nurses Assn. (chmn. pediatric nurse practitioner subcom. Com. Examiners Maternal-Child Nursing Practice, 1986-92, chair Com. Examiners Maternal-Child Nursing Practice 1988-90), Wash. State Nurses Assn. (hon. leadership award 1981, chair healthcare reform task force 1992—), King County Nurses Assn. (Nurse of Yr. 1985, 1st v.p. 1992—, pres. 1996—), Wash. State Soc. Pediatrics, Sigma Theta Tau. Methodist. Home: 1814 201st Pl SW Lynnwood WA 98036-7060 Office: Providence Children's Ctr Everett WA 98204

SANDALOW, TERRANCE, law educator; b. Chgo., Sept. 8, 1934; s. Nathan and Evelyn (Hoffing) S.; m. Ina Davis, Sept. 4, 1955; children: David Blake, Marc Alan, Judith Ann. AB, U. Chgo., 1954, JD, 1957. Bar: Ill. 1958, Mich. 1978. Law clk. to judge Sterry R. Waterman U.S. Ct. Appeals (2d cir.), 1957-58; law clk. to justice Potter Stewart U.S. Supreme Ct., Washington, 1958-59; assoc. Ross, McGowan & O'Keefe, Chgo., 1959-61; assoc. prof. law U. Minn., Mpls., 1961-64, prof., 1964-66; prof. law U. Mich., Ann Arbor, 1966—, dean Law Sch., 1978-87, Edson R. Sunderland prof. law, 1987—. Author: (with F.I. Michelman) Government in Urban Areas, 1970, (with E. Stein) Courts and Free Markets, 1982; contbr. to legal jours., periodicals. Mem. Mpls. Commn. Human Relations, 1965-66. Fellow Ctr. Advanced Study in Behavioral Scis., 1972-73; recipient U. Chgo. Alumni Profl. Achievement award. Fellow Am. Acad. Arts Scis.; mem. Order of Coif, Phi Beta Kappa (hon.). Office: U Mich Law Sch 409 Hutchins Hall Ann Arbor MI 48109-1215

SANDBANK, HENRY, photographer, film director; b. Burg, Germany, Mar. 20, 1932; came to U.S., 1939, naturalized, 1950; s. Sylvan and Bella (Spatz) S.; m. Judith Lebow, July 4, 1952; children: Kenneth, Laura, Lisa, David. Ed. pub. schs. Partner Beach & Sandbank, Syracuse, N.Y., 1960-63; sr. ptnr. Sandbank & Ptnrs., N.Y.C., 1963-88; pres., film dir. Sandbank Films Co., Inc., N.Y.C., 1972—; dir. Vantage Films, 1979—; sr. ptnr. Sandbank Kamen & Ptnrs., 1992-94; lectr. Syracuse U., 1972, Mus. Modern Art, 1994, for Eastman Kodak, Tokyo, 1994; cons. Fashion Inst. Tech., 1974-80. Recipient Gold Medal awards Art Dirs. and Copywriters Show, Gold medal Film Festival of the Americas, several Clio and Andy awards, Cannes Festival award, Gold medal for film documentary Houston Internat. Film Festival 1980). Served to sgt. AUS, 1952-54, Korea. Mem. Am. Soc. Mag. Photographers (chmn. exec. com. 1978-79, Outstanding Achievement award 1981), Soc. Photographers in Communications (trustee 1974-81, 2d v.p. 1975-76, 1st v.p. 1977, chmn. exec. com. 1979). Home: 24 Nutmeg Dr Greenwich CT 06831-3211 Office: 140 Old Saw Mill River Rd Hawthorne NY 10532-1515

SANDBERG, IRWIN WALTER, electrical and computer engineering educator; b. N.Y.C., Jan. 23, 1934; s. Ben and Estelle (Hornick) S.; m. Barbara A. Zimmerman, June 15, 1958; 1 dau. Heidi L. Student, CCNY, 1951-53; B.E.E., Poly. Inst. Bklyn., 1955, M.E.E., 1956, D.E.E., 1958. Tech. aid Bell Telephone Labs., Inc., Murray Hill, N.J., summer 1954, mem. tech. staff, 1958-67, head systems theory research dept., 1967-72, mem. math. and statis. research ctr., 1972-86; prof. elec. and computer engring. U. Tex., Austin, 1986—; now holder Cockrell Family Regents Chair in Engrng. U. Tex.; engr. Wheeler Labs., Great Neck, N.Y., summer 1955; vis. prof. U. Calif.-Berkeley, 1965; U.S. del. Union Radio Scientifique Internationale, Munich, Germany, 1966; U.S. nat. inst. rep. Advanced Study Inst. on Network and Signal Theory, NATO, Bournemouth, Eng., 1972; lectr. study inst. NATO (Knokke), Belgium, 1966, Copenhagen, 1970; disting. invited spkr. Asilomar Conf., 1973-74; main lectr. European Conf. on Circuit Theory and Design, The Hague, 1981; advisor Inst. Electronics, Info. and Comm. Engrs., Tokyo; advisor Am. Men and Women of Sci., 1993. Patentee (in field). Recipient Best Paper award Asilomar Conf., 1970, Achievement award IEEE Circuits and Systems Soc., 1986, Classic Paper citation ISI press, 1984, Outstanding Alumnus award Poly. U., 1993. Fellow IEEE (adminstrv. com. group circuit theory 1969-70, vice chmn. group circuit theory 1971-72, Centennial medal), AAAS; mem. NAE, Soc. for Indsl. and Applied Math., Eta Kappa Nu, Sigma Xi, Tau Beta Pi. Home: 8505 Hickory Creek Dr Austin TX 78735-1527 Office: Univ Tex Dept Elec Comp Engr Austin TX 78712

SANDBERG, JOHN STEVEN, lawyer; b. Mpls., Sept. 1, 1948; s. Donald and Margery Susan (Knudsen) S.; m. Cynthia A. Tucker, July 17, 1982; children: Jennifer, Adam, Luke, Abigail. AB with honors, U. Mo., Columbia, 1970, JD cum laude, 1972. Bar: Mo., Ill., U.S. Ct. Appeals (7th and 8th cirs.), U.S. Dist. Ct. (ea. and we. dists.) Mo., U.S. Dist. Ct. (so. and ctrl. dists.) Ill., U.S. Dist. Ct. (we. dist.) Ky. Ptnr. Coburn, Croft & Putzell, St. Louis, 1972-79, Sandberg, Phoenix & von Gontard, St. Louis, 1979—. Author (books) Damages Deskbook, 1988, Missouri Product Liability Law, 1988. Pres. SAFE KIDS, St. Louis, 1989—. Office: Sandberg Phoenix & von Gontard 1 City Ctr Fl 15 Saint Louis MO 63101-1883

SANDBERG, RYNE, professional baseball player; b. Spokane, Wash., Sept. 19, 1959; s. Derwent and Elizabeth S.; m. Cindy White; children: Lindsey, Justin. Profl. baseball player Phila. Phillies, 1981, Chgo. Cubs, 1982-94. Recipient Gold Glove, 2d base, Nat. League, 1983-91; named Nat. League Most Valuable Player, 1984; Sporting News Player of Yr., 1984; Nat. League Home Run Leader, 1990; mem. Nat. League All-Star Team, 1984-93. Office: care Chgo Cubs Wrigley Field 1060 W Addison St Chicago IL 60613-4305

SANDBURG, HELGA, author; b. Maywood, Ill., Nov. 24, 1918; d. Carl and Lilian (Steichen) S.; m. George Crile, Jr., Nov. 9, 1963; children by previous marriage: John Carl Steichen, Paula Steichen Polega. Student, Mich. State Coll., 1939-40, U. Chgo., 1940. Dairy goat breeder, also personal sec. to father, 1944-51; sec. manuscripts div., also for keeper of collections Library of Congress, 1952-56; adminstrv. asst. for papers of Woodrow Wilson, 1958-59; writer, lectr., 1957—. Author: (novels) The Wheel of Earth, 1958, Measure My Love, 1959, The Owl's Roost, 1962, The Wizard's Child, 1967; (non-fiction) Sweet Music, A Book of Family Reminiscence and Song, 1963; (with George Crile, Jr.) Above and Below, 1969; (poetry) The Unicorns, 1965; To A New Husband, 1970, The Age of the Flower, 1994; (young adult novels) Blueberry, 1963; Gingerbread, 1964; (juveniles) Joel and the Wild Goose, 1963; Bo and the Old Donkey, 1965, Anna and the Baby Buzzard, 1970; Children and Lovers: 15 Stories by Helga Sandburg, 1976; (biography) A Great and Glorious Romance: The Story of Carl Sandburg and Lilian Steichen, 1978; "...Where Love Begins", 1989; (with Diane Leslie)

Joel and The Wild Goose, Contempory Musical Fantasy, 1991, also numerous short stories; rep. in collections.; contbr.short stories, poems, articles to popular mags. including Seventeen. Recipient Va. Quar. Rev. prize for best short story, 1959, Borestone Mountain poetry award, 1962, Poetry award Chgo. Tribune, 1970; 2d prize 7th Ann. Kans. Poetry Contest, Florence Roberts Head Ohioana Book award, 1990; grantee Finnish Am. Soc. and Svenska Inst., 1961. Mem. Authors Guild, Poetry Soc., Am. Milk Goat Record Assn., Am.-Scandinavian Found., Nat. Nubian Club, Coun. Save the Dunes, Am. Luxembourg Soc., Acad. Am. Poets. Address: 2060 Kent Rd Cleveland OH 44106-3339

SANDDAL, NELS DODGE, foundation executive, consultant; b. Salt Lake City, Feb. 17, 1949; s. James Wesley and Charlotte Jean (Ewer) S.; m. Brenda Kay Lille Griffin, Sept. 27, 1970 (div. June 1990); m. Theresa Louise Knipe, Oct. 12, 1992; 1 child, Jami. BA in English, Carroll Coll., 1966-70; MS in Psychology, Mont. State U., 1996. In-svc. trainer Boulder (Mont.) River Sch. and Hosp., 1974-75; group home mgr. REACH, Inc., Bozeman, Mont., 1975-76; community home trainer Devel. Disabilities Tng. Inst., Helena, Mont., 1976-77; tng. coord. emergency med. svcs. bureau State Dept. Health and Environ. Scis., Helena, 1977-82; cons., lead staff Nat. Coun. State Emergency Med. Svcs. Tng. Coords., Inc., Lexington, Ky., 1981-86; account exec., lead staff Nat. Assn. Emergency Med. Techs., Clinton, Miss., 1986-87; pres., CEO Assn. Mgmt. and Cons., Inc., Boulder, 1983-89; writer, prodr., dir. North Country Media Group, Great Falls, Mont., 1990-91; chief conf. planner S.O.S. Conf. Planning Consortium, Great Falls, 1991-92; exec. dir. Critical Illness & Trauma Found., Bozeman, Mont., 1986-91; pres., CEO Critical Illness & Trauma Found., Bozeman, 1991—; season course leader Nat. Outdoor Leadership Sch., Lander, Wyo., 1966-74; mem. exec. com. Nat. Coun. State EMS Tng. Coords., 1977-82, chmn., Lexington, Ky., 1979-81; mem. adv. com. pediatric emergency med. svcs. tng. project Children's Hosp. Nat. Med. Ctr., Washington, 1985-88, pediatrics emergency instr., 1986-90; mem. grant peer rev. com. divsn. injury epidemiology Ctrs. for Disease Control, Atlanta, 1986-87; cons. Emergency Med. Svcs. Bureau, Helena, 1977, Devel. Disabilities Tng. Inst., Helena, 1977-78; mem. injury prevention profls. New Eng. Network to Prevent Childhood Injuries, Newton, Mass., 1988-95; mem. core faculty devel. trauma sys. tng. program U.S. Dept. Transp., Washington, 1989—, tech. assistance team mem. EMS, 1991-93; EMS instr. and program coord. Great Falls Vocat. Tng. Ctr., 1991-93; rsch. asst. inst. for cmty. studies U. Mo., Kansas City, 1983-95; pres. exec. com. Intermountain Regional EMS Children Coord. Coun., Salt Lake City, 1994—. Editor and tech. cons.: Workbook for Prehospital Care and Crisis Interventions, 4th edit., 1992, 5th edit., 1993, Instructor Resource Manual for Prehospital Care and Crisis Intervention, 4th edit., 1992, Workbook for First Responder, 1990; contbg. editor Jour. of Prehospital Care, 1984-85, The EMT Jour., 1980-81; editl. cons. Am. Acad. Orthopaedic Surgeons, 1980-81; contbr. numerous articles to profl. jours.; video prodr. and presenter in field. Mem. Park County DUI Task Force, Livingston, 1993-96; inaugural coord. Mont. Safe Kids Coalition, Big Timber, 1988-90; adv. com. Nat. Significance Project for Respite Care, 1977-78; mem. basic life support com. of Mont., Mont. Heart Assn., 1977-82. Recipient Golden award for humanity ARC, 1976, 500 Hour award, 1976, Outstanding Svc. award Nat. Coun. State EMS Tng. Coords., 1979, Leadership award, 1981, Charter Membership award, 1984, J.D. Farrington award for excellence Nat. Assn. Emergency Med. Technicians, 1981, Jeffrey S. Harris award, 1985, Outstanding Svc. award Am. Heart Assn., 1982, Appreciation cert. for paramedic emergency care U.S. Dept. Transp., 1984. Mem. Nat. Registry EMTs (20 yr. recognition), Mont. Bd. Med. Examiners. Democrat. Avocations: mountaineering, hiking, sailing, golf, skiing. Home: 20 Arrowhead Trail Bozeman MT 59718 Office: Critical Illness Trauma Found 300 N Willson Ave Ste 3002 Bozeman MT 59715-3551

SANDE, THEODORE ANTON, architect, educator, foundation executive; b. New London, Conn., Nov. 21, 1933; s. Lars Anton and Viola (Edgcomb) S.; m. Solveig Inga-Maj Imselius, Aug. 6, 1960; children: Susanne Ingrid, Lars Michael. BSc in Architecture, R.I. Sch. Design, 1956; MArch, Yale U., 1961; PhD, U. Pa., 1972; grad. Cultural Instns. Mgmt. Program, Mus. Collaborative, 1983; postgrad., Attingham (Eng.) Summer Sch., 1980. Vis. prof. history of architecture Rensselaer Poly. Inst., fall 1973-74, U. Pa., 1976-77; adj. prof. Am. studies and history Case-Western Res. U., 1981—; vis. lectr. in historic preservation Cleve. State U., summer 1994; lectr. art Williams Coll., 1972-75; attended teleconfs. non-profit orgn. mgmt. Drucker Found., 1992. Designer, Arkitekt, Hakon Ahlberg, SAR, Arkitekt, Stockholm, 1960, designer, Washburn, Luther & Rowley, Architects, Attleboro, Mass., 1961-62, Barker & Turoff, Architects, Providence, 1962-63, jr. partner, Turoff Assocs., Architects, 1964-67, partner, Turoff & Sande, Architects, Providence, 1968-70, prin., Ted Sande, Architect, Cranston, R.I., 1970, Cleve., 1993—; author: Industrial Archaeology: A New Look at the American Heritage, 2d edit, 1978; contbg. author: Guidebook to Philadelphia Architecture, 1974; editor: New England Textile Mill Survey, 1971; co-editor: Historic Preservation of Engineering Works, 1981; contbr. articles to profl. jours.; two-man show drawings, Providence Art Club, 1970. Dir. profl. svcs. office hist. properties Nat. Trust Hist. Preservation, Washington, 1975-77, dir. planning and devel., 1977-78, acting v.p. office hist. properties, 1978-79, v.p., 1979-80; mem. Old Georgetown Bd. Nat. Commn. Fine Arts, 1979-81; exec. dir. Western Res. Hist. Soc., Cleve., 1981-93, exec. dir. emeritus, 1993—; cons. architecture Mus. and Hist. Soc. Mgmt., Historic Preservation and Archtl. Hist., 1993—; co-chmn. Conf. Indsl. Archeology, Smithsonian Instn., 1971; active Shaker Heights Landmark Commn., 1982-84, Cleve. Landmarks Commn., 1985—, Leadership Cleve. Class 86/87, Ohio Gov.'s Commn. on the Bicentennials the NW Ordinance and U.S. Const., 1986-89, Cleve. Bicentennial Commn., 1992-94; trustee Univ. Circl Inc., 1981-93, Lakeview Cemetery Found., 1985—, Nat. Rock and Roll Mus. and Hall Fame, mem. exec. blgd. com., 1993-95, instnl. rep. Cleve. Arts Consortium, 1987-93; pres. Cleve. Restoration Soc., 1994—; mem. historic properties and collections com. Stan Hywet Hall and Gardens, Akron, Ohio, 1996—. Mem. AIA (architect mem., com. hist. resources 1972-74), SAR, Soc. Indsl. Archeology (co-founder, 1st pres. 1971-72, dir. 1973-76, project supr. handbook on adaptive use of indsl. bldgs., gen. chmn. 15th ann. conf.), Soc. Archtl. Historians (preservation com. 1972-74), Internat. Com. for Conservation of Indsl. Heritage (chmn. bd. dirs. 1978-81), Ohio Mus. Assn. (trustee 1982-87), Am. Assn. Mus., Rowfant Club (coun. fellowes), Philos. Club Cleve. (past pres.). Episcopalian. Home: 13415 Shaker Blvd Cleveland OH 44120-1548

SANDEFER, G(EORGE) LARRY, lawyer; b. Washington, Mar. 2, 1950; s. George Hall and Mary Gray (Babers) S. BS, Auburn U., 1972; JD, U. Fla., 1978. Bar: Fla. 1978, U.S. Dist. Ct. (mid. dist.) Fla. 1978, U.S. Ct. Appeals (5th and 11th cirs.) 1981, U.S. Supreme Ct. 1982; cert. in criminal trial law Fla. Bar. Asst. atty., criminal divsn., lead trial atty. State of Fla., Clearwater, 1977-86; sole practice Clearwater, 1986-88, 90—; assoc. Kimpton, Burke and White, P.A., 1988-90. Mem. Indian Rocks Civic Assn.; city commr. Indian Rocks Beach. 1st lt. USAF, 1973-75. Mem. ATLA, Pinellas County Trial Lawyers Assn., Fla. Assn. Criminal Def. Attys., Colo. Bar Assn., Kiwanis. Avocations: tennis, skiing, boating.

SANDEFUR, JAMES TANDY, mathematics educator; b. Madison, Ind., Apr. 25, 1947; s. James Tandy and Evelyn (Gayle) S.; m. Mary Elizabeth Epes, Sept. 6, 1969 (div. 1982); m. Helen Moriarty, Apr. 14, 1984; 1 child, Scott David. BA, Vanderbilt U., 1969; MA, U. Denver, 1971; PhD, Tulane U., 1974. Prof. math. Georgetown U., Washington, 1974—; vis. assoc. prof. Ctr. for Applied Math., Cornell U., Ithaca, N.Y., 1981-82; vis. prof. U. Iowa, Iowa City, 1988-89; math. cons. It's Academic TV show, Altman Prodns., Washington, 1985—; prin. investigator, dir. math. modelling workshop NSF, Washington, 1988-91; visitor Freudenthal Inst., Utrecht, The Netherlands, 1996; cons. Cerebellum Corp. Author: Discrete Dynamical Systems: Theory and Applications, 1990, Discrete Dynamical Modeling, 1993; adv. bd. to Annenberg/CPB math. and sci. project's Guide to Math and Science Reform; contbr. articles to math. jours. Program dir. in Instrl. Materials Devel. for Div. of Materials, Devel., Rsch. and Informal Sci. Edn.; directorate for Edn. and Human Resources NSF. NSF grantee, prin. investigator Tchr. Leadership Inst., 1993—. Mem. Math. Assn. Am. (former chmn. minicourse com.), Nat. Faculty, Nat. Coun. Tchrs. Math. (adv. panel Yearbook Discrete Math.), Am. Contract Bridge League (chpt. bd. dirs. 1983-85, Life Master). Democrat. Avocations: bridge, tennis, skiing. Office: Georgetown U Dept Math Washington DC 20057

SANDELL, RICHARD ARNOLD, international trade executive, economist; b. Buenos Aires, Argentina, Oct. 22, 1937; s. Kurd Wolfcang and Isolde Mary (Josevich) S.; m. Phyllis H. Levinson, July 6, 1968; children: Laurie Alyssa, Karyn Joy, Sylvie Jennine. BA in Social Sci., U. Buenos Aires, 1957, JD, 1959; MS in Econs., U. San Marcos, 1960; LLM in Internat. Law, NYU, 1962; Ph.D., Columbia U., 1972, M.B.A., 1977. Dir. bus. planning Guerrero Merc. Internat. Ltd., Buenos Aires, 1954-62; gen. mgr. Acquatronic Universal, Inc., 1965-68; corp. v.p. indsl. econs. Mgmt. Analyst Group, Ins., Van Nuys, Calif., 1968-70; pres., CEO A.I.M. Internat. Corp., Alameda, Calif., 1970-76; pres., CEO, dir. Aurag Internat. Corp. and Aura Tech. Corp., Scarsdale, N.Y., 1979—; bd. dirs. FerroCement Internat. Ltd. of Panama, Consorcio Pesquero Marmesa of Guayaquil, Ecuador, INTEX S.A., Buenos Aires, Export Marketeers Ltd., Auckland, N.Z., Aledo Transnat. Trading Corp., Panama, Geneva, Oakland, Calif., dir. Nexus Corp., Santa Rosa, Calif., Guanabara Mining Co., Rio De Janeiro, Brazil, Primax Electronics Ltd., Aimore Internat. Corp., Stockton, Calif., Premisa, S.A., Venezuela; former cons. U.S. Dept. State, govts. Ecuador, Nicaragua, Guyana, Zaire, Fiji, El Salvador, N.Z., Ghana, currently cons. to Taiwan, Chile, Venezuela, Brazil, 1972—; cons. Nat. Security Coun. during Desert Shield and Desert Storm Campaign, 1990-91; cons. on privatization Govt. Argentina; adj. prof. bus. adminstrn. Elbert Covell Coll. and Coll. Pacific at U. Pacific, 1972-77; adj. prof. internat. bus., mgmt. U. Am. States, Miami, Fla., 1977-79, prof. internat. trade and tech., chair bus. enterprise, 1987—; adj. prof. internat. bus., mgmt. U. Francisco Marroquin, Guatemala City, 1977-79; dir. Grad. Inst. Free Enterprise Studies, prof. internat. bus., govt. Mercy Coll. and L.I.U., Dobbs Ferry, N.Y., 1980-83; prof. internat. fin. and bus., chair bus. enterprise Ramapo Coll. of N.J., Mahwah, 1983-87. Author: The Politics of Marketing in Latin America, 1970, Private Investment in the Andean Block - A Study in Conflicts, 1970, Santa Cruz - Crossroads of Heaven and Hell, 1971, U.S.-Latin America - a Time for Reciprocity, 1972, Use of Consultants - How Valuable an Investment, 1972, The Role of U.S. Multinational Corporation, 1972, Summary of Controls on the International Movement of Capital, 1973, The Effects of Rising Energy Costs on LDC Development, 1974, Trade in the Andean Common Market, 1975, U.S. Private Investment - Its Future Role in Interamerican Development, 1976, Tourism in Latin America - Cornerstone of Development, 1976, Administration of Human Resources - Its Effectiveness in the Modern Organization, 1977, A System Called Capitalism, 1977, Marketing Plague - The Regulators, 1978; Prescription for Survival - Can Free Enterprise Make It?, 1979, The Intellectual Defense of Free Enterprise, 1980, Freedom at Bay - Government Controls in the Economy, 1982, American Values: the Economy, the Polity, the Society, 1986, The Debt Bomb: In the Shadow of Depression, 1987, Finance and Stress: The Market Crash of '87, 1988, Investment in Eastern Europe: Good Politics, Bad Finance! 1989, Socialism: The Accomplishment of a Nightmare, 1990, The House That Lenin Built: The Crash of the USSR, 1991, Special Interests: The Politics of Privilege, 1991, North American Free Trade Area: Road to Prosperity, 1992, The Watermelon Syndrome: Green Outside, Red Inside!, 1992, Highway to World Freedom: The Information Superhighway, 1993, To Clinton's Hammer...Does Gore Add the Sickle?, 1994, Marabunta's Passage: The Legacy of Socialism, 1995, Latin America Growth: A Changing Landscape, 1996; editor Interam. Econ. Journal, Univ. Am. States. Advisor Explorer post Alameda coun. Boy Scouts Am., 1969-71, post com. chmn., 1971-75; bd. dirs. San Francisco-Bay area coun. Girls Scouts U.S.A., 1975-80, v.p., 1978-80; trustee Amigos de las Americas, Houston, 1975-80, U. Am. States, Santiago, 1976-80, Am. Rsch. Inst. for Social Environments, Alameda, 1975-82, Princeton Fund, 1976-82, Found. for Free Ent., 1983-87, Aura Tech. Found., 1987—, Electro-Bio-Scis., 1987-89, Am.-Pacific Found., 1989—; mem. Am. Rsch. Inst. for Soc. and Economy, Washington, 1990—, The Maldon Inst. Found., Washington, 1991-95. With U.S. Army, 1962-65. Decorated Bronze Star; decorated Purple Heart; recipient medal Sagitario Found., 1962, Silver Condor award U. Andina, 1969, Kenneth Chilton Meml. award, 1972. Life fellow AAAS; mem. N.Y. Acad. Scis., Am. Numis. Assn., Inst. Mgmt. Cons. (dir., v.p. Latin Am. 1975-80), Am. Econs. Assn., Internat. Inst. Economists, Interam. Soc. Polit. Economists (trustee 1971-81, v.p. 1988-90, pres. 1991-96), Inst. Mgmt. Sci., Internat. Execs. Assn., Fgn. Policy Assn., 2d Amendment Found., Am. Security Coun., Am. Soc. Internat. Execs., N.Am. Corp. Planning Assn., Soc. Internat. Trade Planning (dir. 1989—), Am. Sociol. Assn., Am. Psychol. Assn., Nat. Rifle Assn., Am. Radio Relay League (dir. 1990-96), Soc. for Internat. Tech. Assessment, Mensa, many others. Clubs: Commonwealth (San Francisco, chmn. sect. Latin Am. 1969-75); Oakland World Trade. Lodge: Rotary. Office: PO Box 1367 Scarsdale NY 10583-9367 *Struggling for the preservation of individual freedom is the most noble cause to which I can address my life's endeavor.*

SANDELL, WILLIAM, production designer. Art dir.: (films) Fast Charlie...the Moonbeam Rider, 1979; prodn. designer: (films) The Pack, 1977, The Clones, 1977, Piranha, 1978, The Promise, 1979, Serial, 1980, Blood Beach, 1981, (with Joe Aubel) Dead and Buried, 1981, Airplane II: The Sequel, 1982, Young Lust, 1982, The Wild Life, 1984, St. Elmo's Fire, 1985, Robocop, 1987, Big Business, 1988, Total Recall, 1990, Nothing But Trouble, 1991, Newsies, 1992, Hocus Pocus, 1993, The Flintstones, 1994. Home: 1429 W Valley Hart Dr Burbank CA 91506

SANDENAW, THOMAS ARTHUR, JR., lawyer; b. Harlowton, Mont., Mar. 17, 1936; s. Thomas A. Sr. S.; m. Colleen A. Andrews, June 3, 1956 (div. May 1981); children: Cheryl Lea, Kevin K., Dana Scott; m. Deborah Rose Hammel, Sept. 26, 1981. BS, Mont. State U., 1958; JD, U. N.Mex., 1967. Bar: N.Mex. 1967, U.S. Dist. Ct. N.Mex. 1968, U.S. Ct. Appeals (10th cir.) 1968, U.S. Dist. Ct. N.Mex., 1996. Atty. Wilkinson, Durrett & Conway, Alamogordo, N.Mex., 1968-69, Spence & Sandenaw, Alamogordo, N.Mex., 1969-71, Shipley, Durrett, Conway & Sandenaw, Alamogordo, N.Mex., 1971-77; judge 12th jud. dist. Lincoln and Otero Counties, Alamogordo, N.Mex., 1978-79; atty. Overstreet & Sandenaw, Alamogordo, N.Mex., 1979-82; ptnr. Weinbrenner, Richards, Paulowsky, Sandenaw & Ramirez, Las Cruces, N.Mex., 1982-92; pvt. practice Las Cruces, N.Mex., 1992—. Dir. St. Lukes Health Care, Las Cruces, 1992, Mesilla Valley Hospice, Las Cruces, 1992—. Mem. ABA (econs. of law practice, litigation), Am. Bd. Trial Advocates, Am. Bd. Profl. Liability Attys. (diplomat 1993—), Nat. Bd. Trial Advocacy (cert. civil trial practice 1989), State Bar N.Mex. (chmn. pub. rels. com. 1967-68, bd. mem. family law sect. 1983-86, chmn. trial practice sect. 1987-88, bd. dirs. 1990—), N.Mex. Def. Lawyers Assn. (sec. 1984-85, v.p. 1985-86, pres. 1987-88, bd. dirs. 1983—, chmn. Amicus Curie com. 1991—), N.Mex. Sr. Lawyers Div., N.Mex. Bench and Bar Com., Dona Ana County Bar Assn., Assn. Def. Trial Attorneys (exec. coun. 1996—), Rotary (past pres. Rio Grande chpt.; barrister Am. Inn of Courts. Republican. Lutheran. Avocations: skiing, sailing, woodworking. Office: Law Office of TA Sandenaw 2951 N Roadrunner Pkwy # A Las Cruces NM 88011-0814

SANDER, DONALD HENRY, soil scientist, researcher; b. Creston, Nebr., Apr. 21, 1933; s. Paul L. and Mable O. (Wendt) S.; m. Harriet Ora Palmateer, Dec. 27, 1953; children: Ben, Joan. BS, U. Nebr., 1954, MS in Agronomy, 1958, PhD in Agronomy, 1967. Soil scientist, researcher USDA Forest Svc., Lincoln, Nebr., 1958-64; asst. prof. agronomy, soil fertility specialist Kans. State U., Manhattan, 1964-67; prof. agronomy U. Nebr., Lincoln, 1967—. Contbr. over 40 articles to jours. including Soil Sci. Soc. Am. Jour. 1st lt. U.S. Army, 1954-56, Korea. Recipient USDA Superior Svc. award, 1987, Soil Sci. Applied Rsch. award, 1989, Great Plains Leadership award, Denver, 1990,. Fellow Am. Soc. Agronomy (Agronomic Achievement award 1985), Soil Sci. Soc. Am.; mem. Gama Sigma Delta, Sigma Xi. Republican. Presbyterian. Avocation: woodworking. Home: 6548 Darlington Ct Lincoln NE 68510-2362 Office: Univ Nebr Dept Agronomy Lincoln NE 68583

SANDER, FRANK ERNEST ARNOLD, law educator; b. Stuttgart, Germany, July 22, 1927; came to U.S., 1940, naturalized, 1946; s. Rudolf and Alice (Epstein) S.; m. Emily Bishop Jones, Apr. 26, 1958; children: Alison Bishop, Thomas Harvey, Ernest Ridgway Sander. AB in Math. magna cum laude, Harvard U., 1949, LLB magna cum laude, 1952. Bar: Mass. 1952, U.S. Supreme Ct 1952. Law clk. to Chief Judge Magruder U.S. Ct. Appeals, 1952-53; law clk. to Justice Frankfurter, U.S. Supreme Ct., 1953-54; atty. tax divsn. Dept. Justice, 1954-56; with firm Hill & Barlow, Boston, 1956-59; mem. faculty Harvard Law Sch., 1959—, prof. law, 1962—, Bussey prof., 1981—, assoc. dean, 1987—; spl. fields fed. taxation, family law, welfare law, dispute resolution; chmn. Council on Role of Cts.; mem. panels Am. Arbitration Assn., Fed. Mediation and Conciliation Service; chmn. Council on Legal Edn. Opportunity, 1968-70; cons. Dept. Treasury, 1968; treas. Harvard Law Rev., 1951-52; vice chair dispute resolution standing com. Mass. Supreme Jud. Ct., 1994—. Author: (with Westfall and McIntyre) Readings in Federal Taxation, 2d edit., 1983, (with Foote and Levy) Cases and Materials on Family Law, 3d edit., 1985, (with Gutman) Tax Aspects of Divorce and Separation, 4th edit., 1985, (with Goldberg and Rogers) Dispute Resolution, 2d edit., 1992. Mem. tax mission Internat. Program Taxation to Republic of Colombia, 1959; mem. com. on civil and polit. rights President's Commn. on Status of Women, 1962-63; trustee Buckingham Browne and Nichols Sch., 1969-75; chmn. Mass. Welfare Adv. Bd., 1975-79. With AUS, 1945-46. Recipient Whitney North Seymour medal Am. Arbitration Assn., 1988, spl. award for disting. svc. to dispute resolution Ctr. for Pub. Resources, 1990. Mem. ABA (chmn. standing com. dispute resolution 1986-89, Kutak medal 1993), Boston Bar Assn., Phi Beta Kappa. Home: 74 Buckingham St Cambridge MA 02138-2229 Office: Harvard U Sch of Law Cambridge MA 02138

SANDERCOX, ROBERT ALLEN, college official, clergyman; b. Akron, Ohio, May 20, 1932; s. Monroe J. and Elverda (Arnold) S.; m. Nancy Lee Wertz, Sept. 13, 1958; children—Alison Grace, Megan Louise, Robert Philip. B.A., Bethany Coll., W. Va., 1954; M.Div., Yale U., 1957; postgrad., U. Buffalo, W.Va. U.; LittD, Bethany Coll., 1989. Ordained to ministry Christian Ch. (Disciples of Christ). Asst. minister Park Ave Christian Ch., N.Y.C., 1954-57; asst. provost Bethany Coll., 1957-60, v.p., dean students, 1960-75, v.p., dir. devel., 1975-79, interim pres., 1979-80, v.p., provost for coll. advancement, 1980-89, sr. v.p., 1989-95, cons. to the pres., 1995—. Trustee Christian Ch. Disciples of Christ in W.Va., Parkersburg, 1984-88; chmn. Brooke County Landmarks Commn., 1988—, Brooke County Mus. Bd., 1995. Recipient Alumni Disting. Service award Bethany Coll., 1982. Mem. Coun. for Advancement and Support Edn., Duquesne Club (Pitts.), Order of Symposiarch, Rotary, Kiwanis (pres. 1967), Alpha Sigma Phi (nat. treas. 1982-84, v.p. 1984-86, grad. sr. pres. 1986-88, bd. dirs., trustee Ednl. Found. 1982-95, chmn. Ednl. Found. 1994-95, Delta Beta Xi svc. award 1960). Democrat. Home: Highland Hearth Bethany WV 26032 Office: Bethany Coll. Milsop Ctr Bethany WV 26032

SANDERLIN, TERRY KEITH, counselor; b. Ashland, Oreg., Aug. 5, 1950; s. Calvin Carney and Myrtle Estell (Cope) S.; m. Theresa Emma Garcia, Jan. 19, 1969 (div. Feb. 1976); 1 child, Sean Eric; m. Margaret Lillian Lutz, Dec. 26, 1987. B in Bus., U. N.Mex., 1982, M in Counseling, 1983, EdD, 1993. Lic. clin. mental health, N.Mex.; cert. hypnotherapist Internat. Assn. Counselors and Therapists. Unit supr. Bernalillo County Juvenile Detention Ctr., Albuquerque, 1978-80; counselor Independence Halfway House, Albuquerque, 1980-81; mental health worker Bernalillo County Mental Health Ctr., Albuquerque, 1981-82; probation parole officer N.Mex. Probation/Parole, Albuquerque, 1982-87; dist. supr. N.Mex. Probation/Parole, Gallup, 1987-88; vocat. counselor Internat. Rehab. Assn., Albuquerque, 1989-91; counseling psychologist VA, Albuquerque, 1991—; owner, dir. Counseling and Tng. Specialist, Albuquerque, 1988—; counselor Albuquerque (N.Mex.) Counseling Specialist, 1983-86; guest lectr. sociology dept. U. N.Mex., Albuquerque, 1992; presenter 5th Annual S.W. Substance Abuse Conf., Albuquerque, 1992; presenter N.Mex. Corrections Dept., Santa Fe, 1993. Author: (video tapes) Breathing Free & Good, 1991, Understanding Adolescent Satanism, 1991, (manual) Social Skills and Anger Management, 1993. Vol. counselor Adult Misdemeanor Probation, Albuquerque, 1974-76; panel mem. Cmty. Corrections Selection Panel, Albuquerque, 1987-90. With U.S. Army, 1969-72, Vietnam. Recipient Outstanding Citizenship, Albuquerque Police Dept., 1974; N.Mex. Dept. Pub. Safety rsch. grantee, 1995. Mem. ACA, Am. Corrections Assn., Am. Legion. Democrat. Avocations: scuba diving, martial arts, target shooting, hiking, boating. Office: Counseling & Tng Specialist 8016 Zuni Rd SE Ste G Albuquerque NM 87108-3277

SANDERS, AARON PERRY, radiation biophysics educator; b. Phoenix, Jan. 12, 1924; s. DeWitt and Ruth (Perry) S.; m. Betty Mae Gelein, Aug. 11, 1944 (div.); children: Merle Sanders Ireland, Julie Sanders Jacome, James DeWitt; m. Georgia Anne Bullock, Nov. 26, 1972 (div.); 1 dau., Kai Marie. B.S., U. Tex., El Paso, 1950; M.S. (AEC fellow), U. Rochester, 1952; Ph.D., U. N.C., 1964. Diplomate: Am. Bd. Health Physics. Baggage clk., ticket agt. Greyhound Bus Lines, Phoenix, 1942; dispatcher, ticket agt. Greyhound Bus Lines, El Paso, Tex., 1946-50; asso. health physicist Brookhaven Nat. Lab., Upton, N.Y., 1951-53; instr. physics, radiol. safety officer N.C. State Coll., 1953; instr. radiology Duke Med. Center, Durham, N.C., 1953-56; dir. radiosotope lab. Duke Med. Center, 1953-65; asso. in radiology Duke Med. Ctr., 1956-57, asst. prof., 1957-64, assoc. prof., 1964-65, assoc. prof., dir. div. radiobiology, 1965-70, prof., dir. div. radiobiology, 1970-83, prof. emeritus, 1983—; chmn. Biomed. Physics Dept. King Faisal Specialist Hosp., Riyadh, Saudi Arabia, 1984-86; Fulbright sr. lectr. radiol. physics, Argentina, 1958-59; cons. N.C. Bd. Health, 1961-76; mem. N.C. Radiation Protection Commn., 1976-83, chmn., 1978-79. Contbr. articles to profl. jours. Served with USNR, 1942-45. Mem. AAAS, Am. Assn. Physicists in Medicine, AAUP, Soc. Exptl. Biology and Medicine, Health Physics Soc., Soc. Nuclear Medicine, Biophys. Soc., Radiation Research Soc., Undersea Med Soc., Sigma Xi, Sigma Pi Sigma. Address: 155 W Brown Rd # 262 Mesa AZ 85201 *Each individual has an obligation to himself and society to pursue an education to his maximum capability. This capability should then be used in his career in an effort to contribute to society as much, or more, than he receives. In work and personal relations you must never deny a man the dignity of his work by ridicule or denigration, and you must never use people.*

SANDERS, ADRIAN LIONEL, educational consultant; b. Paragould, Ark., Aug. 3, 1938; s. Herbert Charles and Florence Theresa (Becherer) S.; m. Molly Jean Zecher, Dec. 20, 1961. AA, Bakersfield Coll., 1959; BA, San Francisco State U., 1961; MA, San Jose State U., 1967. 7th grade tchr. Sharp Park Sch., Pacifica, Calif., 1961-62; 5th grade tchr. Mowry Sch., Fremont, Calif., 1962-64; sci. tchr. Blacow Sch., Fremont, Calif., 1964-76; 5th grade tchr. Warm Springs Sch., Fremont, 1977-87, 5th grade gifted and talented edn. tchr., 1987-94; edn. cons., 1994—. Mem. History Mus. of San Jose, 1980—, Nat. Geog. Soc., Washington, 1976—, Alzheimer's Family Relief Program, Rockville, Md., 1986; vol. 7 km. Race for Alzheimer's Disease Willow Glen Founders Day, San Jose, 1988-92. Named Outstanding Young Educator, Jr. C. of C., Fremont, Calif., 1965. Mem. Smithsonian Assocs., U.S. Golf Assn. Avocations: photography, travelling, visiting presidents' birthplaces, collecting license plates, collecting matchbooks worldwide. Home and Office: 15791 Rica Vista Way San Jose CA 95127-2735

SANDERS, ALEXANDER MULLINGS, JR., judge; b. Columbia, S.C., Sept. 29, 1938; s. Alexander Mullings Sr. and Henrietta Courtrier (Thomas) S.; m. Zoe Caroline Dutrow; 1 child, Zoe Caroline. BS, U. S.C., 1960, LLB, 1962; LLM, U. Va., 1990. Bar: S.C. 1962, U.S. Dist. Ct. S.C. 1962, U.S. Supreme Ct. 1975, U.S. Ct. Appeals (4th cir.) 1976. Sr. ptnr. Sanders & Quackenbush, Columbia, 1974-83; of counsel Adams & Quackenbush, Columbia, 1983; chief judge S.C. Ct. Appeals, Columbia, 1983-92; pres. Coll. Charleston, S.C., 1992—; adj. faculty U. S.C., Columbia, 1965-92, Harvard U. Law Sch., Cambridge, Mass., 1983-97. Mem. S.C. Ho. Reps., Columbia, 1966-74, S.C. Senate, Columbia, 1976-83. Served with USAR, 1956. Mem. ABA, S.C. Bar Assn. Office: Coll of Charleston Off of Pres Charleston SC 29424

SANDERS, AUGUSTA SWANN, retired nurse; b. Alexandria, La., July 22, 1932; d. James and Elizabeth (Thompson) Swann; m. James Robert Sanders, Jan. 12, 1962 (div. 1969). Student, Morgan State U., 1956. Pub. health nurse USPHS, Washington, 1963-64; mental health counselor Los Angeles County Sheriff's Dept., 1972-79; program coordinator Los Angeles County Dept. Mental Health, 1979-88; program dir. L.A. County Dept. Health Svcs., 1989-92; ret., 1992; apptd. by Calif. Gov. Jerry Brown to 11th Dist. Bd. Med. Quality Assurance, 1979-85; health cons., legal, 1994—; motivational spkr. Mem. Assemblyman Mike Roo's Commn. on Women's Issues, 1981-86, Senator Diane Watson's Commn. on Health Issues, 1979-85; chmn. Commn. Sex. Equity Los Angeles Unified Sch. Dist., 1984-90; pres. Victor Valley Bus. and Profl. Women Adminstrn.; mem. edn. com. Victor Valley African Am. C. of C. Named Woman of Yr., Crenshaw-Latijera Local Orgn., 1988, Wilshire Local Orgn., 1990, Victor Valley Local Orgn., 1994. Mem. NAFE, L.A. County Employees Assn. (v.p. 1971-72), So. Calif. Black

Nurses Assn. (founding mem.), Internat. Fedn. Bus. and Profl. Women (pres. L.A. Sunset dist. 1988-89, dist. officer 1982-89, Calif. v.p. membership and mktg. 1995-96), Internat. Assn. Chemical Dependency Nurses (treas. 1990-92), Victor Valley Bus. and Profl. Women (pres. 1997—), High Desert LWV (founder), High Desert Intercoun. of Women's Orgns., Am. C. of C. (adminstrn.-ednl. chmn.), Chi Eta Phi. Democrat. Methodist. Avocations: travelling, crocheting, movies, concerts, plays.

SANDERS, BARBARA BOYLES, health services director; b. Charleston, Miss., May 4, 1950; d. Marion Enoch and Bettye Sue (Wright) Boyles; m. James Norton Sanders, June 15, 1974 (div. July 1977). BA in History, Miss. Coll., 1970; MA in History, Delta State U., 1975; postgrad., U. So. Miss., 1974-77. History tchr. McCluer H.S., Jackson, Miss., 1972-74, Laurel (Miss.) Pub. Schs., 1974-77; dir. field svcs. Am. Heart Assn., Little Rock, 1977-81; v.p. Boyles Enterprises, Inc., Jackson, 1981-84; exec. dir. Nat. Multiple Sclerosis Soc., Jackson, 1984-93; nat. exec.-dir. Nat. Assn. EMTS, Clinton, Miss., 1994—; cons. in adminstrn. and devel., Jackson, 1993—; mem. editl. adv. bd. Ed League Cons., Naples, 1996—; adv. bd. Preserve Sight, Jackson, 1993—; adv. bd. ALS Assn., Jackson, 1994—. Sunday sch. tchr. New Covenant Ch., Ridgeland, Miss., 1994—. Mem. Am. Soc. Assn. Execs. Republican. Avocations: reading, travel, hist. rsch. Home: 17 Club Oaks Cir Pearl MS 39208-6614 Office: Nat Assn EMTs 102 W Leake St Clinton MS 39056-4252

SANDERS, BARBARA HEEB, writer, consultant; b. Harrisburg, Ark., May 15, 1938; d. Raymond and Irene (Rice) Heeb; m. Carmack Wilson Sanders, July 6, 1956; children: Gregory Wilson, Stephanie. BS in Edn., Ark. State U., 1963; postgrad., Lyon Coll., 1972-73, 74, East Tex. State U., 1979. Cert. secondary edn. Asst. Poinsett County Tax Assessor's Office, Harrisburg, 1956; sec., clk. Jackson Life Ins. Co., Memphis, 1956-57; owner Heeb, Heeb and Sanders Farms, Harrisburg, 1962-74; cashier Entergy Corp., Harrisburg, 1963; tchr. Harrisburg Pub. Schs., 1963-66; owner, dir. Ozark Attractions, Inc., Mountain View, Ark., 1976-69; owner Sanders Ranch, Timbo, Ark., 1976-87; dir. tchr. workshops East Tex. State U., Mountain View, 1973-84; freelance writer, cons. Harrisburg, 1987—; owner, bd. dirs. Battle Music Inc., Timbo; advisor, cons. Gov. Bill Clinton, Little Rock, 1981—; cons. Chaplin-Martinov Prodns., Woodland Hills, Calif., 1982—; music dir. Crowley's Ridge Folk Festival, 1972-73; performer numerous festivals and schs.; Poinsett County Motion Picture and Film Commn., 1992—. Feature writer The Modern News, 1990—; editor poetry; performer record albums, 1973, 78; contbr. articles to profl. jours. Member Gov.'s Task Force on Edn., Little Rock, 1973-74, Ark. State Libr. Bd., Little Rock, 1988-97, Friends of the Libr. of Craighead County, 1989—; del. Dem. Party State Conv., Little Rock and Hot Springs, Ark., 1978-82; mem. adv. com. H.P. Maddox Sr. Ednl. Found./Ark. Community Found., Inc., 1989—; county coord. U.S. Senator Dale Bumpers, Washington, 1973-74, Gov. Bill Clinton, Little Rock, 1981—; bd. dirs. Folk Music Hall of Fame, Mountain View, 1973; justice of the peace County of Poinsett, 1989-91; mem. Poinsett County Ednl. Planning Com., Harrisburg, 1975, Poinsett County Fair Bd. Assn., 1972-74, N.E. Ark. Forum on Early Childhood Edn., Little Rock, 1974, Poinsett County Farm Bur., 1963—, rice promotion com., 1969; active vol. fund drive Heart Fund, Harrisburg, 1964, Am. Cancer Soc., Harrisburg, 1971, 72, Cystic Fibrosis Rsch. Found., 1970, 71, local chair, 1972; mem. state adv. com. Keep Ark. Beautiful Commn., 1989—; Ark. planner Statue of Liberty Centennial, N.Y.C., 1986; mem. Poinsett County Dem. Women's Club, corr. sec., 1979-81, mem. ways and means com., 1982, mem. state planning com. for nat. meeting, 1986; active local campaign orgns. Mem. Vocat. Bus. Edn. (chmn. adv. coun. 1984—), White House Conf. on Libr. and Info. Svcs. (task force), Rackensack Folklore Soc., Lower Miss. Delta Devel. Commn. (adv. mem.), Harrisburg Garden Club, The Am. Philatelist Soc., Delta Kappa Gamma (hon. mem.). Mem. Ch. of Christ. Home: 409 E Griffin St Harrisburg AR 72432-2805

SANDERS, BARRY, football player; b. Wichita, July 16, 1968; s. William and Shirley Sanders. Student, Okla. State U., 1986-89. With Detroit Lions, 1989—. Recipient Heisman Trophy award, 1988; named Sporting News Coll. Football Player of Yr., 1988, NFL Rookie of Yr., 1990; named to Sporting News Coll. All-Am. team, 1987, 88, All-Pro team, 1989-91, 93, Pro Bowl, 1989-96. Led NFL in rushing, 1990, 94. Office: Detroit Lions 1200 Featherstone Rd Pontiac MI 48342-1938*

SANDERS, BERNARD (BERNIE SANDERS), congressman; b. Bklyn., Sept. 8, 1941; s. Eli and Dorothy (Glassberg) S.; m. Jane O'Meara, 1988; children: Levi, Heather, Carina, David. B.A., U. Chgo., 1964. Freelance writer, carpenter, youth counselor, 1964-76; with Govt. Vt., 1965-66; dir. Am. People's Hist. Soc., Burlington, Vt., 1976-81; mayor of Burlington, 1981-89; mem. U.S. Ho. of Reps. from Vt., 102nd-105th Congresses from Vt., 1991—, mem. progressive caucus, mem. com. on banking and fin. svcs., com. on govt. reform and oversignt. Chmn. Vt. Liberty Union Party, 1975-76, candidate for gov., 1972, 76, 86, U.S. Senate, 1971, 74. Mem. Vt. League Cities and Towns. Jewish. Author filmstrips and articles on social, hist. and polit. subjects. Office: US Ho of Reps 2202 Rayburn Bldg Washington DC 20515-4501

SANDERS, BRICE SIDNEY, bishop; b. Nashville, Oct. 15, 1930; s. Walter Richard and Agnes Mortimer (Jones) S.; m. Nancy Elizabeth Robinson, Aug. 22, 1953; children—Richard Evan, Robert Wesley, Lynne Elizabeth. B.A., Vanderbilt U., 1952; M.S.T., Episcopal Div. Sch., Cambridge, Mass., 1955; D.D. (hon.), Va. Theol. Sem., 1980, U. South, Sewanee, Tenn., 1984. Ordained to ministry. Rector St. James Ch., Union City, Tenn., 1955-58, Good Shepherd Ch., Knoxville, 1958-61, Eastern Shore Chapel, Virginia Beach, Va., 1961-70; assoc. dean Va. Theol. Sem., Alexandria, 1970-75; dean St. Andrews Cathedral, Jackson, Miss., 1975-79; bishop Diocese of East Carolina, Kingston, N.C., 1979—. Home: 2112 Sparre Dr Kinston NC 28501-1926 Office: Diocese of E Carolina PO Box 1336 Kinston NC 28503-1336*

SANDERS, CHARLES ADDISON, physician; b. Dallas, Feb. 10, 1932; s. Harold Barefoot and May Elizabeth (Forrester) S.; m. Elizabeth Ann Chipman, Mar. 6, 1956; children: Elizabeth, Charles Addison, Carlyn, Christopher. MD, U. Tex., 1955. Intern, asst. resident Boston City Hosp., 1955-57, chief resident, 1957-58; clin. and rsch. fellow in medicine Mass. Gen. Hosp., Boston, 1958-60; chief cardiac catheterization lab. Mass. Gen. Hosp., 1962-72, gen. dir., 1972-81, physician, 1973-81, program dir. myocardial infarction rsch. unit, 1967-72; exec. v.p. E.R. Squibb and Sons, 1981-84; exec. v.p. Squibb Corp., 1984-88, vice chmn., 1988-89; chief exec. officer Glaxo Inc., Research Triangle Park, N.C., 1989-94, chmn., 1992-95; assoc. prof. medicine Harvard U. Med. Sch., 1969-80, prof., 1980-83; candidate U.S. Senate, 1996; bd. dirs. Mt. Sinai Med. Ctr., N.Y.C.; chmn. Commonwealth Fund N.Y.C., Nat. Found. for Biomedical Rsch.; mem. Inst. Medicine. Mem. editorial bd. New Eng. Jour. Medicine, 1969-72. Chmn. Project Hope; bd. trustees U.N.C., Chapel Hill; mem. Pres. Coun. Advisors on Sci. and Tech. Capt. USAF, 1960-62. Mem. ACP, Am. Heart Assn., Mass. Med. Soc. Office: 100 Europa Dr Ste 170 Chapel Hill NC 27514-2310

SANDERS, CHARLES FRANKLIN, management and engineering consultant; b. Louisville, Dec. 22, 1931; s. Charles Franklin and Maragret Rhea (Timmons) S.; m. Marie Audrey Galuppo, Dec. 29, 1956; children: Karen Lynn, Craig Joseph, Keith Franklin. B.Chem. Engring., U. Louisville, 1954, M.Chem. Engring., 1958; Ph.D., U. So. Calif., 1970. Research engr. Exxon Research and Engring. Co., Linden, N.J., 1955-62; asst. prof. engring. Calif. State U., Northridge, 1962-68, assoc. prof., 1968-71, prof., 1971-82, chmn. dept., 1969-72, dean Sch. Engring. and Computer Sci., 1972-81; pres., chief exec. officer, dir. Rusco Industries, Los Angeles, 1981-82; exec. v.p. Energy Systems Assocs., Tustin, Calif, 1982-89; exec. v.p. Energeo, San Francisco, 1989-95, also bd. dirs.; v.p. tech. Smith-Bellingham Capital, San Francisco, 1989-91; bd. dirs. Clean-Air Technology, Inc., Kailua-Kona, Hawaii. Bd. dirs. San Fernando Valley Child Guidance Clinic, 1979-81. Served to 1st lt. U.S. Army, 1956-57. NSF fellow, 1965-67. Mem. AIChE, NSPE, Calif. Soc. Profl. Engrs., Am. Soc. for Engring. Edn. Republican.

SANDERS, DAVID P., lawyer; b. Chgo., Sept. 24, 1949. BA with distinction, U. Wis., 1971; JD, Georgetown U., 1974. Bar: Ill. 1974, U.S. Ct. Appeals (7th and 4th cirs.) 1974, U.S. Dist. Ct. (no. dist. trial bar) Ill. 1974. Ptnr. Jenner & Block, Chgo.; adj. prof. trial advocacy Northwestern U., Chgo., 1981-91. Editor Am. Criminal Law Rev., 1974. Mem. ABA, Chgo. Coun. Lawyers (chmn. fed. jud. evaluation com. 1989—, mem. def. counsel sect. libel def. resource ctr.). Office: Jenner & Block One IBM Plz Chicago IL 60611

SANDERS, DEION LUWYNN, baseball and football player; b. Ft. Myers, Fla., Aug. 9, 1967. Student, Fla. State U. Baseball player N.Y. Yankees, 1988-90, Atlanta Braves, 1991-94, Cin. Reds, 1994, 97; football player Atlanta Falcons, 1989-94, San Francisco 49ers, 1994, Dallas Cowboys, 1995—. Named to Sporting News Coll. All-Am. football team, 1986-88, Sporting News NFL All-Pro Football Team, 1991, 92, 94, Pro Bowl team, 1991-94; recipient Jim Thorpe award, 1988. NFL kickoff return leader, 1992, Nat. League Triples Leader, 1992; mem. Championship team Super Bowl XXIX, 1994, Super Bowl XXX, 1995. Address: Cincinnati Reds 100 Cinergy Field Cincinnati OH 45202*

SANDERS, FRANKLIN D., insurance company executive; b. Newton, Mass., Apr. 24, 1935; s. Franklin and Ethel Shriner (Dulaney) S.; m. Jane Gray Collier, June 18, 1960; children—Cynthia, Franklin D., Nancy, Carolyn. A.B., Amherst Coll., 1957; M.B.A., Harvard U., 1959. With 1st Boston Corp., N.Y.C., 1960-86, mng. dir., 1976-86; pres. Aegis Ins. Services Inc., Jersey City, 1986—; treas., bd. dirs. Assoc. Electric & Gas Ins. Services, Ltd., Hamilton, Bermuda. Chmn. Republican Exec. Com., Bernardsville, N.J., 1965-72, Bernardsville Zoning Bd. of Adjustment, 1966—. Episcopalian. Clubs: Down Town, Harvard (N.Y.C.); Somerset Hills Country (Bernardsville), Mid-Ocean (Bermuda). Avocations: sailing, skiing, golf. Home: RR 2 34 Post Kunhardt Rd Bernardsville NJ 07924-1522 Office: Aegis Ins Svcs Inc 10 Exchange Pl Jersey City NJ 07302

SANDERS, FRED JOSEPH, aerospace company executive; b. Tulsa, June 18, 1928; s. Charles Frederick and Mary Ethel (White) S.; m. Marceline Frances Shaw, May 19, 1951; 1 son, Fred William. A.A., Spartan Coll., 1947; M.S.M.E., St. Louis U., 1961. Design engr. McDonnell Aircraft Co., St. Louis, 1947-66; program mgr. Skylab Program, McDonnell Douglas, Huntington Beach, Calif., 1967-74; dir. product devel. McDonnell Douglas, Huntington Beach, 1975-76, v.p., 1977-84; v.p., gen. mgr. McDonnell Douglas Astronautics Co., St. Louis, 1985-88, ret., 1988. Served as cpl. U.S. Army, 1954-56. Recipient Public Service award NASA, 1974. Asso. fellow AIAA. Roman Catholic. Home: 4 Broadview Farm Rd Saint Louis MO 63141-8501

SANDERS, GERALD HOLLIE, communications educator; b. Mt. Vernon, Tex., Dec. 10, 1924; s. Elmer Hugh and Velma Mae (Hollowell) S.; m. Mary Dean Crew, July 18, 1947; children: Michael Dwaine, Rose Ann, Susan Kathleen, Randall Wayne. BA, Southeastern Okla. U., 1947; MA, Tex. Tech U., 1969; PhD, U. Minn., 1974. Program dir. Sta. WEWO, Laurenburg, N.C., 1947-49; sports dir. Sta. KFYO, Lubbock, Tex., 1949-50; gen. mgr. Sta. KLVT, Levelland, Tex., 1950-51, 53-54; sports dir. Sta. KCUL, Ft. Worth, 1954-55; asst. mgr. Sta. KDAV, Lubbock, 1955-57; mgr. Sta. KCBD, Lubbock, 1957-58; owner Sta. KSEL, Lubbock, 1958-67, Sta. KBUY, Amarillo, Tex., Sta. KERB, Kermit, Tex., Sta. KBEK, Elk City, Okla., Sta. KZZN, Littlefield, Tex.; lectr. communications The Coll. of Wooster, Ohio, 1967-68, asst. prof., 1968-75, assoc. prof., 1975-81, chmn. dept. communication, 1974-81; chmn. dept. communication Miami U., Oxford, Ohio, 1981-92, prof. emeritus comm., 1992—; disting. lectr. Jinan U., Zhong Shan U., Fudan U., Nanjing U., Beijing U., China, 1989; cons. in field, Oxford, 1982—; polit. and trial cons., 1996—. Author: Introduction to Contemporary Academic Debate, 1983; also articles. Active Political Campaigns. Served to col. USMC, 1943-46, PTO, 1951-53, Korea. Recipient Disting. Svc. award Delta Sigma Rho-Tau Kappa Alpha, 1991, Am. Forensic Assn., 1991. Mem. Am. Forensic Assn. (pres. 1978-82), Speech Communication Assn., Speech Communication Assn. of Ohio (pres. 1976-77), Disting. Svc. award 1978), Am. Inst. Parliamentarians, Soc. Trial Cons. Presbyterian. Avocations: sports, political campaigns. Home: 200 Country Club Dr Oxford OH 45056-9050 Office: Advocacy Unltd PO Box 457 Oxford OH 45056

SANDERS, GILBERT OTIS, health and addiction psychologist, consultant, educator, motivational speaker; b. Oklahoma City, Aug. 7, 1945; s. Richard Allen and Evelyn Wilmoth (Barker) S.; m. Lidia Julia Grados-Ventura; children: Lisa Dawn Sanders-Coker, Miligros R. AS, Murray State Coll, 1965; BA, Okla. State U., 1967, U. State of N.Y.; MS, Troy State U., 1970; EdD, U. Tulsa, 1974; postdoctoral studies St. Louis U., Am. Tech. U.; grad. U.S. Army Command and Gen. Staff Coll., Ft. Leavenworth, Kas., 1979. Diplomate Am. Bd. Med. Pschotherapist, Am. Bd. Forensic Examiners, Am. Bd. Forensic Medicine, Am. Bd. Disability Cons., Am. Bd. Forensic Counselors. Dir. edn. Am. Humane Edn. Soc., Boston, 1975; chmn. dept. computer sci., dir. Individual Learning and Counseling Ctr., asst. prof. pschology and law enforcement Calumet Coll., Whiting, Ind., 1975-78; rsch. psychologist U.S. Army Rsch. Inst., Ft. Hood, Tex., 1978-79; pvt. practice counseling, Killen, Tex., 1978-79; psychologist U.S. Army Tng. and Doctrine Command Sys. Analysis Activity, White Sands Missile Range, N.Mex., 1979-80; project dir. psychologist Applied Sci. Assocs., Ft. Sill, Okla., 1980-81; pvt. practice counseling, Lake St. Louis, 1981-83; assoc. prof. Pittsburg State U., Kans., 1983-85; pres. Applied Behavioral Rsch. Assocs. (formerly Southwestern Behavioral Rsch.), Oklahoma City, 1985-94; pvt. practice counseling Christian Family Counseling Ctr., Lawton, Okla., 1986-87; psychologist, systems analyst U.S Army Field Artillery Sch.-Directorate of Combat Devels., Ft. Sill, Okla., 1987; psychologist U.S. Army Operational Test and Evaluation Agy., Washington, 1988-89; psychologist, drug abuse program dir. Fed. Bur. of Prisons-Fed. Correctional Inst. El Reno, Okla., 1989-91; psychologist, clin. dir. drug abuse program U.S. Penitentiary, Leavenworth, Kans., 1991-95; pvt. practice psychologist MacArthur Med. and Psychotherapy, Inc. and Acad. Christian Counseling Okla., Oklahoma City, 1992—; adj. prof. bus. and psychology Columbia Coll.-Buder Campus, St. Louis, 1982-84; adj. prof. U.S. Army Command Staff and Gen. Coll., 1983-89, Columbia Pacific U., 1984—, Greenwich U., 1990—, U. Alaska S.E., 1995—. Editor: Evaluation for a Manual Backup System for TACFIRE (ARI), 1978, Training/Humane Factors Implications--Copperhead Operational Test II Livefire Phase, 1979, TRADOC Training Effectiveness Analysis Handbook, 1980, Cost and Training Effectiveness Analysis/TEA 8-80/ Patroit Air Defense Missile System, 1980, Cost and Training Analysis/ Infantry Fighting Vehicle (Bradley), 1980, Human Factors Implications for the Howitzer Improvement Program, 1989, The Drug Education Handbook, 1995, Therapist Handbook for Drug Treatment, 1996; author research reports. Recipient Kavanough Found. Community Builder award, 1967; named Hon. Col. Okla. Gov. Staff, 1972, Hon. Amb., 1974. Mem. APA, ACA, Am. Assn. Marriage and Family Therapists, Am. Mental Health Counselors Assn., Res. Officers Assn., Commd. Officers Assn., U.S. Pub. Health Svc., Pi Kappa Phi, Alpha Phi Omega. Home: 5404 NW 65th St Oklahoma City OK 73132-7747 Office: Mac Arthur Med Inst 7317 N Macarthur Blvd Oklahoma City OK 73132-5727

SANDERS, HAROLD BAREFOOT, JR., federal judge; b. Dallas, Tex., Feb. 5, 1925; s. Harold Barefoot and May Elizabeth (Forrester) S.; m. Jan Scurlock, June 6, 1952; children—Janet Lea, Martha Kay, Mary Frances, Harold Barefoot III. BA, U. Tex., 1949, LLB, 1950. Bar: Tex. bar 1950. U.S. atty. No. Dist. Tex., 1961-65; asst. dep. atty. gen. U.S., 1965-66; asst. atty. gen., 1966-67; legis. counsel to President U.S., 1967-69; partner firm Clark, West, Keller, Sanders & Butler, Dallas, 1969-79; U.S. dist. judge for No. Dist. Tex., Dallas, 1979—, chief judge, 1989-95. Mem. Tex. Ho. of Reps., 1952-58; Dem. nominee U.S. Senate, 1972. Lt. (j.g.) USNR, World War II. Mem. ABA (chmn. nat. conf. fed. trial judges 1988-89), Fed. Bar Assn. (Disting. Svc. award Dallas 1964), Dallas Bar Assn., State Bar Tex. (jud. conf. U.S. 1989-92, jud. panel on multidistrict litigation 1992—), Blue Key, Phi Delta Phi, Phi Delta Theta. Methodist. Office: US Courthouse 1100 Commerce St Ste 15 Dallas TX 75242-1596

SANDERS, HOWARD, investment company executive; b. Phila., June 30, 1941; s. Louis and Freda (Liss) S.; m. Dale Rosenberg, Dec. 15, 1963; children: Lee Michael, Kimberly Joy. BS in Acctg., Temple U., 1962; M in Acctg., Ohio State U., 1963. CPA. Acct., Price, Waterhouse & Co., Phila., 1962-65; asst. prof. acctg. Temple U., 1965-72; v.p. Revere Fund, Inc., Phila., 1966-76; pres. Revere Mgmt. Co., Inc., Phila., 1966-72; chmn. bd. Ladies Center of Nebr., Inc., 1976—, Volk Footwear and Findings Co., 1977-78, Mister Plywood Enterprises, Inc., 1970-82; pres. Sanders Fin. Mgmt., Inc., Fort Lauderdale, 1972—; chmn. bd. Am. Carpet Backing Distbg. Inc., 1978-80, Polis-Sanders Real Estate Corp., 1981—; exec. chmn. Humedco Corp., 1995—. Contbg. author: How to Start a Mutual Fund, 1970. Mem. adv. bd. Phila. Assn. for Retarded Children, 1970-72; chmn. bd. Women's Med. Center of Providence, Inc., 1977—, Women's Med. Center of North Jersey, Inc., 1977-82, Women's Med. Center of Atlanta, Inc., 1977—, Cherry Hill Women's Center, Inc., 1978—, Metairie Women's Center of New Orleans, Inc., 1980-84, Hartford Gynecol. Center, 1980—. Kaiser Aluminum and Chem. Co. fellow, 1962-63. Mem. Am. Inst. C.P.A.s, Pa. Inst. C.P.A.s (award for paper 1961), Phila. Jaycees (dir. 1966), Nat. Assn. Accts., B'rith Shalom Assn., Beta Gamma Sigma, Beta Alpha Psi, Tau Epsilon Phi. Home and Office: 410 Sea Turtle Ter Fort Lauderdale FL 33324-2814 *My life has been guided by careful attention to words which are rapidly disappearing from the "Dictionary of American Life". I have concentrated on integrity, prudence, brevity, clarity, ego control and true friendship. In all dealings I insist upon mutual benefit, taking great effort to assure that the opposite party receives a slightly larger gain. My goal is total value received for all. I attempt to mix my love for life and humor in all my relationships.*

SANDERS, IRWIN TAYLOR, sociology educator; b. Millersburg, Ky., Jan. 17, 1909; s. Robert Stuart and Lucy (Taylor) S.; m. Margaret Rydberg, June 23, 1934; children: Gerda S. (Groff), Robert Stuart. Student, Tenn. Mil. Inst., 1920-25; A.B., Washington and Lee U., 1929; student, Theol. Sem., Princeton, 1932-33; Ph.D., Cornell U., 1938; D.Pedagogy (hon.), R.I. Coll., 1981; Litt.D. (hon.), Washington and Lee U., 1981. Instr. American Coll., Sofia, Bulgaria, 1929-32; dean American Coll., 1934-37; asst. prof. sociology Ala. Coll., 1938-40; successively asst. prof., asso. prof., prof., head dept. sociology, distinguished univ. prof. U. Ky., 1940-56; lectr. sociology Harvard Sch. Pub. Health, 1958-62; chmn. dept. sociology and anthropology Boston U., 1960-63, 69-72, prof. sociology, 1972-77, Univ. lectr., 1973-74, also co-dir. community sociology tng. program; research dir. Assos. Internat. Research, Inc., Cambridge, Mass., 1956-60; asso. dir. Internat. Tng. and Research Program, Ford Found., 1962-66; v.p. Edn. and World Affairs, 1967-69; social science analyst Bur. Agrl. Econ., U.S. Dept. Agr., summer 1943; sr. social scientist Bur. Agrl. Econ., U.S. Dept. Agr. (Office Fgn. Agrl. Relations), 1943; social sci. Bur. Agrl. Econ., U.S. Dept. Agr. (Extension Service), summer 1944; agrl. attaché Am. Embassy, Belgrade, Yugoslavia, 1945-46; research assoc. Harvard, 1952-53; cons. rural welfare division FAO. Author: Balkan Village, 1949, The Community, 1958, 3d rev. edit., 1975, Rainbow in the Rock, People of Rural Greece, 1962, Rural Society, 1977; co-author: Alabama Rural Communities, 1940, Sociological Foundations of Education, 1942, Kentucky: Designs for Her Future, 1944, Farmers of the World, 1945, Making Good Communities Better, 1950, Bridges to Understanding: International Programs at U.S. Colleges and Universities, 1970; Editor: Societies Around the World, 1953, Collectivization of Agriculture in Eastern Europe, 1958, The Professional School and World Affairs, 1968; series editor: Social Movements: Past and Present, 1980-95. Bd. dirs. Am. Farm Sch., Thessaloniki, Greece, Sofia Am. Schs., Inc., Assn. for Study Southeastern Europe, Bucharest, Rumania. Decorated Royal Order of Phoenix Greece). Mem. Am. Sociol. Soc. (disting. cmty. sect. award 1983), Eastern Sociol. Soc., So. Sociol. Soc. (pres. 1955-56), Rural Sociol. Soc. (pres. 1956-57, Disting. Rural Sociologist 1993), New Eng. Sociological Assn. (Apple award 1993), Am. Assn. Advancement Slavic Studies, Bulgarian-Am. Studies Assn. (hon. pres.), Modern Greek Studies Assn. (council), Am. Assn. for S.E. European Studies (pres. 1980), Société European de Culture (Venice), Rumanian Studies Soc. (council), Bulgarian Acad. Scis. (fgn. mem.), Am. Assn. for Promotion Bulgarian Culture (hon. pres.), Cornell Club (N.Y.), Phi Beta Kappa, Omicron Delta Kappa, Kappa Phi Kappa, Delta Sigma Rho, Delta Upsilon. Democrat. Presbyterian. Home: 400 School St Wellesley MA 02181-4715 Office: 96 Cummington St Boston MA 02215-2407

SANDERS, JACK FORD, physician; b. St. Louis, Mich., July 16, 1918; s. Ford and Viva (Marvin) S.; m. Gretchen A. Jellema, Feb. 2, 1945; children: Karen Jean, Vicki Leigh, Mary Beth, Donald Curtis, Wendy Lynn. B.S. summa cum laude, Alma Coll., Mich., 1939; M.D., U. Mich., 1945; LL.D., Northwood U. Diplomate Am. Bd. Internal Medicine; cert. flight instr. aircraft and instruments, airplane single and multi-engine land and sea; flight safety counselor FAA; CAP check pilot; sr. aviation med. examiner. Intern Henry Ford Hosp., 1945-46, resident in internal medicine, 1947-50; practice medicine specializing in internal medicine Alma, Mich.; sr. attending physician internal medicine Butterworth Hosp., Blodgett Hosp., Grand Rapids, Mich.; cons. St. Mary's Hosp., Grand Rapids, Ferguson-Droste-Ferguson Hosp.; med. dir. Mich. Masonic Hosp., Alma, 1960-77; med. dir. rehab. div., chmn. dept. medicine, chief staff Gratiot Community Hosp.; chmn. dept. medicine Tri-County Hosp., Edmore, Mich.; clin. assoc. prof. medicine Coll. Human Medicine, Mich. State U.; mem. Com. on Aging, Gov's Adv. Coun. on Heart Disease, Cancer and Stroke; del White Ho. Conf. on Aging; bd. dirs. Mich. Masonic Home and Hosp.; chmn. bd. Cen. Mich. Wendy's, Inc.; sec., treas. Gratiot Aviation, Inc. Contbr. articles to profl. jours. Chmn. bd. govs. Mich.; bd. dirs. Northwood U., Gratiot Cmty. Airport Bd. Instr. ACTS, U.S. Air Corps and lt. (j.g.) M.C., USNR, WWII. Fellow ACP, Am. Geriatrics Soc.; mem. AMA, Mich. State Med. Soc., Gratiot Med. Soc., Kent Med. Soc., Gratiot-Isabella-Clare County Med. Soc. (pres. 1965), Am. Diabetes Assn., Am. Heart Assn., Am. Multiple Sclerosis Soc., Mich. Crippled Children and Adults Soc., East Ctrl. Mich. Health Svc. Assn., Mason (33d degree), Rotary, Phi Sigma Pi (hon.). Home: 250 Purdy Dr Alma MI 48801-2174 Office: Mich Masonic Hosp Alma MI 48801-2174

SANDERS, JACK THOMAS, religious studies educator; b. Grand Prairie, Tex., Feb. 28, 1935; s. Eula Thomas and Mildred Madge (Parish) S.; m. M. Patricia Chism, Aug. 9, 1959 (dec. Oct. 1973); 1 son, Collin Thomas; m. Susan Elizabeth Plass, Mar. 3, 1979. B.A., Tex. Wesleyan Coll., 1956; M.Div., Emory U., 1960; Ph.D., Claremont Grad. Sch., 1963; postgrad., Eberhard-Karls U., Tuebingen, Germany, 1963-64. Asst. prof. Emory U., Atlanta, 1964-67, Garrett Theol Sem., Evanston, Ill., 1967-68, McCormick Theol. Sem., Chgo., 1968-69; assoc. prof. U. Oreg., Eugene, 1969-75, prof., 1975—, head dept. religious studies, 1973-80, 85-90. Author: The New Testament Christological Hymns, 1971, Ethics in the New Testament, 1975, 2d edit., 1986, Ben Sira and Demotic Wisdom, 1983, The Jews in Luke-Acts, 1987, Schismatics, Sectarians, Dissidents, Deviants: The First One Hundred Years of Jewish-Christian Relations, 1993; editor: Gospel Origins and Christian Beginnings, 1990, Gnosticism and the Early Christian World, 1990; mem. edit. bd. Jour. Bibl. Lit., 1977-83. Mem. policy bd. Dept. Higher Edn. Nat. Council Chs., N.Y.C., 1971-73. NDEA grad. study fellow, 1960-63; Fulbright Commn. fellow, 1963-64; Am. Council Learned Socs. travel grantee, 1981; NEH fellow, 1983-84. Mem. AAUP (chpt. pres. 1981-82), Studiorum Novi Testamenti Soc., World Union Jewish Studies, Assn. for Jewish Studies, Soc. Bibl. Lit. (regional sec. 1969-76, sabbatical rsch. award 1976-77), Archeol. Inst. Am. (chpt. pres. 1988-89), Soc. for Sci. Study of Religion, Assn. for Sociology Religion. Democrat. Home: 2555 Birch Ln Eugene OR 97403-2191 Office: U Oregon Dept Religious Studies Eugene OR 97403

SANDERS, JACQUELYN SEEVAK, psychologist, educator; b. Boston, Apr. 26, 1931; d. Edward Ezral and Dora (Zoken) Seevak; 1 son, Seth. BA, Radcliffe Coll., 1952; MA, U. Chgo., 1964; PhD, UCLA, 1972. Counselor, asst. prin. Orthogenic Sch., Chgo., 1952-65; research assoc. UCLA, 1965-68; cons. Osawatomie State Hosp. (Kans.), 1965-68; asst. prof. Ctr. for Early Edn., L.A., 1969-72; assoc. dir. Sonia Shankman Orthogenic Sch., U. Chgo., 1972-73, dir., 1973-93, dir. emeritus, 1993—; curriculum cons. day care ctrs. L.A. Dept. Social Welfare, 1970-72; instr. Calif. State Coll., L.A., 1972; lectr. dept. edn. U. Chgo., 1972-80, sr. lectr., 1980-93, clin. assoc. prof. dept. psychiatry, 1990-93, emeritus, 1993—; instr. edn. program Inst. Psychoanalysis, Chgo., 1979-82; reading cons. Foreman High Sch., Chgo. Author: Greenhouse for the Mind, 1989; editor: (with Barry L. Childress) Psychoanalytic Approaches to the Very Troubled Child: Therapeutic Practice Innovations in Residential & Educational Settings, 1989, Severly Disturbed Children and the Parental Alliance, 1992, (with Jerome M. Goldsmith) Milieu Therapy: Significant Issues and Innovative Applications, 1993; contbr. articles to profl. jours. Mem. vis. com. univ. sch. rels. U. Chgo. UCLA Univ. fellow, 1966-68; Radcliffe Coll. Scholar, 1948-52; recipient Alumna award Girls' Latin Sch., Boston, Bettelheim award Am. Assn. Children's Residential Ctrs. Mem. Assn. Children's Residential Ctrs. (past pres.), Quadrangle Club, Radcliffe Club (Chgo., sec/treas. 1986-87, pres. 1987-89), Harvard Club (Chgo., bd. dirs. 1986—). Home: 5842 S Stony Island Ave Apt 2G Chicago IL 60637-2033

SANDERS, JAMES ALVIN, minister, biblical studies educator; b. Memphis, Nov. 28, 1927; s. Robert E. and Sue (Black) S.; m. Dora Cargille, June 30, 1951; 1 son, Robin David. BA magna cum laude, Vanderbilt U., 1948, BD with honors, 1951; student, U. Paris, 1950-51; PhD, Hebrew Union Coll., 1955; DLitt, Acadia U., 1973; STD, U. Glasgow, 1975; DHL, Coe Coll., 1988, Hebrew Union Coll., 1988, Hastings Coll., 1996. Ordained teacher Presbyn. Ch., 1955; instr. French Vanderbilt U., 1948-49; faculty Colgate Rochester Div. Sch., 1954-65, assoc. prof., 1957-60, Joseph B. Hoyt prof. O.T. interpretation, 1960-65; prof. O.T. Union Theol. Sem., N.Y.C., 1965-70, Auburn prof. Bibl. studies, 1970-77; adj. prof. Columbia, N.Y.C., 1966-77; prof. Bibl. studies Sch. Theology and Grad. Sch., Claremont, Calif., 1977-97; vis. prof. Union Theol. Seminary and Columbia U., 1997-98; ann. prof. Jerusalem Sch. of Am. Schs. Oreintal Rsch., 1961-62; fellow Ecumenical Isnt., Jerusalem, 1972-73, 85; Ayer lectr., 1971, 79, Shaffer lectr., 1972, Fondren lectr., 1975, Currie lectr., 1976, McFadin lectr., 1979, Colwell lectr., 1979; guest lectr. U. Fribourg, Switzerland, 1981, 90, Hebrew Union Coll., 1982, 88, Oral Roberts U., 1982, Tulsa U., 1982, Ind. U., 1982, Coe Coll., 1983, Garrett Sem., 1984, Pepperdine U., 1985, Western Sem., 1985, Bethany Sem., 1986; lectr. Union Sem. Sesquicentennial, 1987, U. Wis., 1987, U. Chgo., 1987; Gray lectr. Duke U., 1988; guest lectr. Notre Dame U., Georgetown U., Tex. Christian U., 1989, Alexander Robertson lectr. U. Glasgow, 1990-91, Gustavson lectr. United Theol. sem., 1991; assoc. program lectr. Smithsonian, 1990, Am. Bible Soc. Sesquicentennial, 1991, U. N.Mex., 1992, 94, Am. Interfaith Inst., 1992, Georgetown U., 1992; Lily Rosmen lectr. Skirball Mus., 1992; vis. prof. U. N.Mex., 1992, Southwestern U., 1992, Calif. Luth. U., 1992, 94, Willamette U., 19923, Peter Craigie lectr. U. Calgary, 1993, U. So. Ariz., 1993; Samuel Iwry lectr. John Hopkins U., 1993; lectr. San Diego State U., 1994, Creighton U., 1995, The Mercantile Libr., N.Y.C., 1995, U. Heidelberg, Germany, 1995, U. Mich., 1995; session chair, Internat. Congress for Fiftieth Anniversary of Dead Sea Scrolls, Jerusalem, 1997; Womack lectr. The Methodist Coll., 1996; Purcell lectr. Barton Coll., 1997; mem. internt. O.T. text critical com. United Bible Socs., 1969—; exec. officer Ancient Bibl. Manuscript Ctr. for Preservation and Rsch., 1977-80, pres., 1980—. Author: Suffering as Devine Discipline in the Old Testament and Post-Biblical Judaism, 1955, The Old Testament in the Cross, 1961, The Psalms Scroll of Qumran Cave 11, 1965, The Dead Sea Psalms Scroll, 1967, Near Eastern Archaeology in the Twentieth Century, 1970, Torah and Canon, 1972, 74, Identité de la Bible, 1975, God Has a Story Too, 1979, Canon and Community, 1984, From Sacred Story to Sacred Text, 1987, Luke and Scripture, 1993; editor: Paul and the Scriptures of Israel, 1993; contbr. over 250 articles to profl. jours.; mem. editorial bd. Jour. Bibl. Lit., 1970-76, Jour. for Study Judaism, Bibl. Theology Bull., Interpretation, 1973-78, New Rev. Standard Version Bible Com. Trustee Am. Schs. Oriental Research. Fulbright grantee, 1950-51, Lilly Endowment grantee, 1981, NEH grantee, 1980, 91-92; Lefkowitz and Rabinowitz interfaith fellow, 1951-53, Rockefeller fellow, 1953-54, 85, Guggenheim fellow, 1961-62, 72-73, Human Scis. Rsch. fellow, 1989. Mem. Soc. Bibl. Lit. and Exegesis (pres. 1977-78), Phi Beta Kappa, Phi Sigma Iota, Theta Chi Beta. Home: PO Box 593 Claremont CA 91711-0593 Office: Ancient Bible Manuscript Ctr PO Box 670 Claremont CA 91711-0670

SANDERS, JAMES GRADY, biogeochemist; b. Norfolk, Va., June 10, 1951; s. Allen Buford and Maple Seretha (Myers) S.; m. Carmen Lee Nance, Aug. 19, 1972. BS in Zoology, Duke U., 1973; MS in Marine Scis., U. N.C., 1975, PhD in Marine Scis., 1978. Postdoctoral investigator Woods Hole (Mass.) Oceanographic Instn., 1978-80; vis. scientist Chesapeake Biol. Lab. U. Md., Solomons, 1980-81; asst. curator Benedict (Md.) Estuarine Rsch. Lab. Md. Estuarine Rsch. Ctr., Acad. Natural Scis., Benedict, 1981-85, assoc. curator Benedict (Md.) Estuarine Rsch. Lab., 1985-89, curator Benedict (Md.) Estuarine Rsch. Lab., 1989—, dir. Benedict (Md.) Estuarine Rsch. Lab., 1983—; cons. EPA Sweden, Stockholm, 1985-90; mem. Md. Sea Grant Adv. Com., College Park, 1983-90, Environ. Commn., Calvert City, Md., 1981-88; mem. environ. biology panel Office R & D EPA, Washington, 1986-95; regional rep. Coastal Resources Adv. Commn., Md., 1983-86. Assoc. editor Estuaries, 1996—; contbr. more than 60 articles to sci. jours. Grantee NOAA, 1981—, EPA, 1983—. Mem. AAAS, Am. Geophys. Union, Am. Soc. Limnology and Oceanography, Soc. for Environ. Toxicology and Chemistry, Estuarine Rsch. Fedn. (treas. 1993—). Achievements include first identification of relationships between algal growth and chemical transformations of arsenic in aquatic systems. Office: Acad Natural Scis Estuarine Rsch Ctr 10545 Mackall Rd Saint Leonard MD 20685-2433

SANDERS, JAY WILLIAM, audiology educator; b. Balt., July 26, 1924; s. Jay Will and Mary Magdalene (Fisher) S.; m. Mary Elizabeth St. John, Aug. 27, 1950; children—Mary Jean, John Jay, Elizabeth Ann. A.A., Louisburg Coll., 1948; B.A., U. N.C., 1950; M.A., Columbia U., 1951; Ph.D., U. Mo., 1957; postgrad. (spl. fellow), Northwestern U., 1962-64. Instr. speech U. Mo., Columbia, 1952-57; from asst. prof. to assoc. prof. Trenton (N.J.) State Coll., 1957-62; asst. prof. audiology Vanderbilt U. Sch. Medicine, Nashville, 1964-65, assoc. prof., 1965-71, prof., 1971-87, prof. emeritus, 1987—; chmn. Tenn. State Bd. Examiners for Speech Pathology and Audiology, 1973-79. Contbr. chpts. to textbooks, articles to profl. jours. Served with U.S. Navy, 1942-45. Recipient various awards; Nat. Inst. Neurol. Diseases and Blindness spl. fellow, 1962-64. Fellow Am. Speech and Hearing Assn.; mem. Am. Acad. Audiology, Tenn. Speech-Lang.-Hearing Assn., Phi Beta Kappa. Home: 5518 Vanderbilt Rd Old Hickory TN 37138-1133 Office: Wilkerson Hearing & Speech Ctr 1114 19th Ave S Nashville TN 37212-2110

SANDERS, JIMMY DEVON, public administration and health services educator; b. Montgomery, Ala., Nov. 6, 1945; s. Harold Wright Sanders and Elsie M. (Huett) Harris; m. Linda Ruth Sweatt, Mar. 25, 1966; children: Richard Devon, Robert Pearson. B Gen. Studies, U. Nebr., Omaha, 1968; MPA, U. Okla., 1973, U. So. Calif., 1988; D Pub. Adminstrn., U. So. Calif., 1989. Commd. officer USAF, 1964, advanced through grades to lt. col., 1985, various health svc. adminstrv. positions, 1964-83; dir. base med. svcs. USAF, San Vito dei Normanni, Italy, 1980-83; sr. health policy analyst Dept. Def., Washington, 1983-88; ret., 1988; assoc. prof. mgmt. and health-care mgmt. Marymount U., Arlington, Va., 1988-91; dir. Atlantic region Troy State U., Norfolk, Va., 1991-94; dir. Fla. region Troy State U., Ft. Walton Beach, 1995-96, assoc. prof. pub. adminstrn., 1996—; health care cons. various hosps. and cities, 1987—, Ret. Officers Assn., Arlington, 1988-90. Fellow Am. Coll. Health Care Execs.; mem. Assn. Mgmt./Internat. Assn. Mgmt. (pres. 1996—). Republican. Lutheran. Avocations: walking, reading, golf. Home: RR 1 Box 342E Montgomery AL 36105-9762 Office: Troy State U PO Box 2829 Fort Walton Beach FL 32549

SANDERS, JOHN LASSITER, retired academic administrator; b. Four Oaks, N.C., June 30, 1927; s. David Hardy and Louie Jane (Lassiter) S.; m. Ann Beal, Aug. 14, 1954; children—Tracy Elizabeth Sanders Justus, Jane Nesbit, William Hardy. A.B., U. N.C., 1950, J.D., 1954. Bar: N.C. 1955. Law clk. to judge U.S. Ct. Appeals, 1954-55; pvt. practice Raleigh, N.C., 1955-56; mem. faculty Inst. Govt., U. N.C., Chapel Hill, 1956-94, dir., 1962-73, 79-92, v.p. planning at univ., 1973-78. Served with USNR, 1945-46. Recipient N.C. award State of N.C., 1996. Mem. N.C. Bar Assn. Democrat. Baptist. Home: 1107 Sourwood Dr Chapel Hill NC 27514-4914 Office: U NC Inst Govt Cb 3330 Knapp Bldg Chapel Hill NC 27514

SANDERS, KEITH PAGE, journalism educator; b. Ashland, Ohio, Sept. 25, 1938; s. Merwin Morse and Phyllis Pearl (Snyder) S.; m. Jane Carmel Adams, June 11, 1966; children: Paige Ann, Kevin Scott. BS in Journalism, Bowling Green State U., 1960; MS in Journalism, Ohio U., 1964; PhD in Mass. Comm., U. Iowa, 1967. Sports editor Ashland (Ohio) Times Gazette, 1960-61, Dover (Ohio) Daily Reporter, 1961-62; instr. journalism Bowling Green (Ohio) State U., 1963-64, U. Iowa, Iowa City, 1965-67; prof. journalism U. Mo., Columbia, 1967—, assoc. dean grad. studies Sch. Journalism, 1986-87, 90-91; exec. dir. Kappa Tau Alpha, Columbia, 1991—; cons. in field. Contbr. articles to profl. jours. including Journalism Quar., Mass Media Rev., Jour. Broadcasting, Electronic Jour. of Comm.; assoc. editor Mass Comm. Rev., 1981-92, editl. bd., 1972—; editl. bd. Journalism Monographs, 1973-80. Named O.O. McIntyre Disting. Prof., U. Mo., 1993; recipient Award for Outstanding Achievement U. Mo. Alumni Assn., 1986. Mem. Internat. Soc. for Sci. Study of Subjectivity (treas. 1990-95), Assn. for Edn. in Journalism/Mass. Comm. (Trayes Prof. of the Yr. 1987), Soc. of Profl. Journalists, Kappa Tau Alpha, Omicron Delta Kappa. Avocations: bowling, golf, fishing. Home: 6551 N Creasy Springs Rd Columbia MO 65202-8093 Office: Univ of Missouri Sch Journalism Columbia MO 65211

SANDERS, KEITH R., university chancellor; b. Benton, Ill., July 31, 1939; m. Carol Dial, 1961; 1 child, Mark Andrew. BS, So. Ill. U., 1961, MS, 1962; PhD in Communication, U. Pitts., 1968. Asst. prof. speech George Washington U., Washington, 1962-66; instr. So. Ill. U., Carbondale, 1967-68, asst. prof., 1969-72, assoc. prof., 1972-77, prof. speech communications, 1977-89, officer govtl. rels. So. Ill. U. System, 1980-83, prof., dean Coll. Communication and Fine Arts, 1983-89; chancellor U. Wis., Stevens Point, 1989-95; sr. v.p., COO U. Wis. System, 1995—. Author: (with Lynda Kaid and Robert Hirsch) Political Campaign Communication, 1974; co-editor, contbr.: (with Dan Nimmo) The Handbook of Political Communication, 1981; (with Dan Nimmo and Lynda Kaid) Political Communication Yearbook, 1985; (with Dan Nimmo and Lynda Kaid) New Perspectives on Political Advertising, 1986, (with Lynda Kaid and Jacques Gestle) Mediated Politics in Two Cultures, 1991; founder, editor Polit. Communication Rev., 1974-90; cons. editor Human Communication Rsch., 1976-79, Cen. States Speech Jour., 1979-80; contbg. editor: Communication Yearbook III and IV, 1978-80. Pres. Ill. Arts Alliance, Ill. Arts Alliance Found., 1987-88. Am. Coun. on Edn. fellow, 1980-81; honored by Ill. Gen. Assembly, 1983; recipient Alumni Achievement award for Svc. SIV-C Alumni Assn., 1996. Mem. So. Ill. U. Alumni Assn. (pres. 1977-78). Home: 7318 Southern Oak Pl Madison WI 53719-5085 Office: U Wis 1730 Van Hise Hall 1220 Linden Dr Madison WI 53706

SANDERS, LAWRENCE, author; b. Bklyn., 1920. BA, Wabash Coll., 1940. Staff mem. Macy's Dept. Store, N.Y.C., 1940-43; novelist, 1969—. Author: The Anderson Tapes, 1970 (Edgar award best 1st mystery novel Mystery Writers Am. 1970), The Pleasures of Helen, 1971, Love Songs, 1972, The First Deadly Sin, 1973, The Tomorrow File, 1975, The Tangent Objective, 1976, The Marlow Chronicles, 1977, The Second Deadly Sin, 1977, The Tangent Factor, 1978, The Sixth Commandment, 1978, The Tenth Commandment, 1980, The Third Deadly Sin, 1981, The Case of Lucy Bending, 1982, The Seduction of Peter S., 1983, The Passion of Molly T., 1984, The Fourth Deadly Sin, 1985, The Loves of Harry Dancer, 1986, The Eighth Commandment, 1986, Tales of the Wolf, 1986, The Dream Lover, 1987, Caper, 1987, The Timothy Files, 1987, Timothy's Game, 1988, Capital Crimes, 1989, Stolen Blessings, 1989, Sullivan's Sting, 1990, The Seventh Commandment, 1992, McNally's Luck, 1992, McNally's Secret, 1992, McNally's Risk, 1993, Private Pleasures, 1993, The Great Coaster Ride, 1993, McNally's Caper, 1994, McNally's Trail, 1995McNally's Puzzle, McNally's Gamble, 1997; (as Mark Upton) Dark Summer, 1979. Served as sgt. USMC, 1943-46. Office: care Putnam Publishing Group 200 Madison Ave New York NY 10016-3903*

SANDERS, MARLENE, anchor, journalism educator; b. Cleve., Jan. 10, 1931; d. Mac and Evelyn (Menitoff) Sanders; m. Jerome Toobin, May 27, 1958 (dec. Jan. 1984); children: Jeff, Mark. Student, Ohio State U., 1948-49. Writer, prodr. Sta. WNEW-TV, N.Y.C., 1955-60, P.M. program Westinghouse Broadcasting Co., N.Y.C., 1961-62; asst. dir. news and public affairs Sta. WNEW, N.Y.C., 1962-64; anchor, news program ABC News, N.Y.C., 1964-68, corr., 1968-72, documentary prodr., writer, anchor, 1972-76, v.p., dir. TV documentaries, 1976-78; corr. CBS News, N.Y.C., 1978-87; host Currents Sta. WNET-TV, N.Y.C., 1987-88; host Met. Week in Review, 1988-90; host Thirteen Live Sta. WNET-TV, 1990-91; prof. dept. journalism NYU, N.Y.C., 1991-93; adj. prof. journalism, adminstr. Columbia U. Grad. Sch. Journalism, N.Y.C., 1994-95; adj. prof. journalism NYU, 1996; profl.-in-residence Freedom Forum Media Ctr.; freelance journalist. Co-author: Waiting for Prime Time: The Women of Television News, 1988. Recipient award N.Y. State Broadcasters Assn., 1976, award Nat. Press Club, 1976, Emmy awards, 1980, 81, others. Mem. Am. Women in Radio and TV (Woman of Yr. award 1975, Silver Satellite award 1977), Women in Comm. (past pres.), Soc. Profl. Journalists.

SANDERS, PAUL HAMPTON, lawyer, retired educator, arbitrator/mediator; b. Sherman, Tex., Feb. 26, 1909; s. Jewell Richard and Louisa Jane (Gaskill) S.; m. Pauline Cameron, Feb. 23, 1935. A.B., Austin Coll., 1931, LL.D., 1960; J.D., Duke U., 1934. Bar: Tex. 1934, Ga. 1944, N.C. 1946, Tenn. 1951. Practiced with Leo Brewer, San Antonio, 1934; asst. to dir. of nat. bar program Am. Bar Assn., Chgo., 1934-36; asst. prof. law Duke U., 1936-40, assoc. prof. law, 1940-45, prof. law, from 1946; practiced with firm of Wilson and Sanders, Atlanta, 1946-47; vis. prof. law Sch. Jurisprudence, U. Calif. at Berkeley, 1947-48; prof. law Vanderbilt U., 1948-74, prof. emeritus, 1974—, past lectr. Sch. Medicine, adj. prof. mgmt. Grad. Sch. Mgmt.; regional atty. U.S. Dept. of Labor, 1951-53; prin. mediation officer Nat. War Labor Bd., Washington, 1942; regional atty., hdqrs. Nat. War Labor Bd., Atlanta, 1942-44, regional vice chmn., 1944; regional atty. Nat. Wage Stblzn. Bd., Atlanta, 1946; past lectr. Nashville Sch. Social Work; cons. Fed. Civil Rights Commn., 1958-61; dir. Race Relations Law Reporter, 1955-59; apptd. mem. bd. inquiry, labor disputes in atomic energy installations, Oak Ridge, also Ky.; pub. mem., chmn. Industry Com. on Minimum Wages, Puerto Rico, 1950, 56-58, 60-61, 63, 67, 69, 71, 73, 75, 77; apptd. mem. various Presdl. emergency boards to consider labor disputes. Assoc. editor: Law and Contemporary Problems, 1937-46; editor symposia on Unauthorized Practice of Law, The Wage and Hour Law, Governmental Tort Liability, Alcoholic Beverage Control, Combating the Loan Shark, Labor in Wartime and Labor Dispute Settlement, all in Duke Univ., 1938-46; contbr. articles to profl. jours. Indsl. relations specialist, 12th Naval Dist. 1944-46, San Francisco; lt. USNR, 1945-53. Mem. ABA (council mem., sec. labor relations sect. 1949-52), Am. Law Inst. (life), Nat. Acad. Arbitrators (past mem., past bd. govs., regional chmn. Southeastern states 1968-74), Am. Arbitration Assn. (labor panel), Nat. Conf. Jud. Councils, Soc. Profls. in Dispute Resolution, Scholarship Soc. S., Order of Coif, Pi Gamma Mu, Phi Delta Phi. Democrat. Baptist (vice chmn. Christian Life Commn., So. Bapt. Conv. 1953-59). Club: University (Nashville). Home: 115 Woodmont Blvd Apt 320 Nashville TN 37205-2269 *My primary interests as a law teacher and arbitrator have centered in systematic study of the processes of dispute settlement and conflict resolution, particularly in the labor relations field. This reflects a conviction that building "community" is the essence of civilization and that there needs to be individual and group commitment to understanding and utilizing the arts of peaceful accomodation. Social conflict is as inevitable as change. All too frequently, however, we show that we have not learned to distinguish, and maintain the proper balance, between the productive and counterproductive aspects of such conflict.*

SANDERS, REGINALD LAVERNE (REGGIE SANDERS), professional baseball player; b. Florence, S.C., Dec. 1, 1967. Student, Spartanburg Meth. Coll., S.C. Outfield Cin. Reds, 1991—. Named Midwest League Most Valuable Player, 1990; selected to N.L. All-Star Team, 1995. Office: Cin Reds 100 Cinergy Fld Cincinnati OH 45202-3543*

SANDERS, RICHARD HENRY, lawyer; b. Chgo., Apr. 10, 1944; s. Walter J. and Marian (Snyder) Sikorski; m. Sharon A. Marciniak, July 8, 1967 (div. Oct. 1979); 1 child, Douglas Bennett. BS, Loyola U., Chgo., 1967; JD, Northwestern U., 1969. Bar: Ill. 1969, Ind. 1990, D.C. 1990, U.S. Dist. Ct. (no. dist.) Ill. 1970, U.S. Dist. Ct. (no. and so. dists.) Ind. 1990, U.S. Ct. Appeals (7th cir.) 1990, U.S. Supreme Ct. 1990. Assoc. Vedder, Price, Kaufman & Kammholz, Chgo., 1969-76, ptnr., 1976—, mem. exec. com., 1991-93, health law area leader, 1989-91, 93-95; adj. prof. Sch. of Law Northwestern U., 1994—. Mem. adv. coun. campaign com. Greater Chgo. divsn. March of Dimes, 1993—. Mem. ABA, Ill. Bar Assn. (chmn. health sect. 1989-90), Chgo. Bar Assn., Ind. Bar Assn., D.C. Bar Assn., Am. Acad. Health Attys., Cath. Health Attys., Ill. Assn. Health Attys., Univ. Club, Evanston Golf Club (Skokie). Avocations: skiing, diving, photography, golf. Office: Vedder Price Kaufman & Kammholz 222 N La Salle St Chicago IL 60601-1002

SANDERS, RICHARD KINARD, actor; b. Harrisburg, Pa., Aug. 23, 1940; s. Henry Irvine and Thelma S. BFA, Carnegie Inst. Tech., 1962; postgrad. (Fulbright scholar), London Acad. Music and Dramatic Art, 1962-63. pres. Blood Star, Inc. Mem. various acting cos., Front St., Memphis, Champlain Shakespeare Festival, Vt., Center Stage, Balt., N.Y. Shakespeare Festival, N.Y.C., Chelsea Theater Center, N.Y.C., Mark Taper Forum, Los Angeles, Arena Stage, Washington; appeared on: (Broadway) Raisin; (TV series) Les Nessman on WKRP in Cincinnati and The New WKRP in Cincinnati, Paul Sycamore in You Can't Take It With You, Mr. Beanley in Spenser; writer of many episodes of WKRP and other situation comedies; writer NBC movie Max and Sam; numerous TV and film appearances. Vol. Peace Corps, Northeastern Brazil, 1966-69. Recipient Buckeye Newshawk award, 1974-79, Silver Sow award, 1979. Mem. Writers Guild Am., Screen Actors Guild, AFTRA, Actors Equity Assn. Office: PO Box 1644 Woodinville WA 98072-1644

SANDERS, RICHARD LOUIS, executive editor; b. Rockville Centre, N.Y., July 14, 1949; s. Louis Chadrone and Grace Marie (Clarke) S.; m. Laurie Anne Miroff, July 24, 1970. BFA in Film, NYU, 1976. Sr. editor Us mag., N.Y.C., 1978-83, exec. editor, 1983-85; sr. editor People mag., N.Y.C., 1985-91; gen. editor Entertainment Weekly, N.Y.C., 1991-92, assistant mng. editor, 1993-95, exec. editor, 1995—. Office: Entertainment Weekly 1675 Broadway New York NY 10019-5820

SANDERS, ROBERT MARTIN, commodity trader; b. Amsterdam, The Netherlands, Feb. 8, 1928; came to U.S., 1941, naturalized, 1949; s. Hugo Benjamin and Jean (van der Linden) S.; m. Ingrid Vera Borchardt, Apr. 12, 1959 (dec. Jan. 1993); children: Mark Robert, Steven George. BA, Queens Coll., 1948; MS, Columbia U., 1950; postgrad., New Sch. Social Research, 1953-61. Research asst. The Netherlands Govt., 1948-50; with fgn. acctg. dept. Colgate-Palmolive-Peet, 1950; with A.C. Israel Commodity Co., Inc., N.Y.C., 1952-71, asst. mgr. rubber dept., 1963-67, mgr. rubber dept., 1967-71, asst. v.p., 1967-70, v.p., 1970-71; v.p. ACLI Internat., Inc., 1971-81; pres. A.C. Israel Rubber Co. div., 1971-76, ACLI Rubber Co., 1976-81; v.p. ACLI Commodity Services, Inc., 1975-81; dir. ACLI (Malaysia), Kuala Lumpur, 1975-81; pres. Clinton Internat., Inc., 1982—; mem. N.Y. Cocoa Exchange, 1975-78; U.S. rep. Internat. Natural Rubber Orgn., 1982-96. Bd. dirs. Family Resources, 1983—. With AUS, 1950-52. Mem. Internat. Rubber Assn. (pro-tem. com. 1970-71, mgmt. com. 1971-81, dep. chmn. 1974-77), Am.-Indonesian C. of C. (bd. dirs. 1974-80, v.p. 1979-80), Am. Importers Assn. (bd. dirs. 1975-77), Rubber Trade Assn. N.Y. Inc. (bd. dirs. 1970-74, 76-79, 81, v.p. 1971-72, 73-74, pres. 1972, 78-79). Home: 310 Clinton Ave Dobbs Ferry NY 10522-3023 Office: Clinton Internat Inc PO Box 438 Dobbs Ferry NY 10522-0438

SANDERS, RUSSELL EDWARD, protective services official; b. Louisville, Oct. 6, 1949; s. Robert George Sr. and Jean Francis (Stevens) S.; m. Mary Ann Miller, Feb. 12, 1972; children: Scott, Jason. BA in Psychology, U. Louisville, 1976, MEd in Pers. Svcs., 1980, MS in Community Devel., 1987. Firefighter Louisville Fire Dept., 1967-74, sgt., 1974-77, capt., 1977-81, dist. chief, 1986-95; regional mgr. Nat. Fire Protection Assn., Louisville, 1995—; adj. instr. Nat. Fire Acad., Emmitsburg, Md., 1985-86; instr. Western Oreg. State Coll., Monmouth, 1984; cons. numerous locations; tchr. Jefferson County Pub./Cath. Sch. Systems, Louisville, 1976-80; bd. dirs. Gov's. Commn. on Pers. Standards, Frankfort, Ky. Contbr. numerous articles to profl. publs. Tennis coach St. Barnabas Cath. Sch., Louisville, 1985-86; baseball coach Hikes Point Optimist, Louisville, 1988; bd. dirs. Ky. Cmty. Vol. Fire Prevention Program, Louisville, 1986—, Stage One Childrens Theater. Sgt. U.S. Army, 1969-71. Recipient People to watch award Louisville mag., 1988, Dean's Citation/Outstanding Svc. award U. Louisville, 1988; Fed. Emergency Mgr. Agy. fellow Harvard U., 1987. Mem. Nat. Inst. Bldg. Scis. (bd. dirs.), Metro Fire Chiefs Assn. (sec. 1988-89, chmn. 1990-91), Soc. Exec. Fire Officers, Internat. Soc. Fire Svc. Instrs., U. Louisville Alumni Assn. (pres.-elect, sec. Outstanding Alumni award 1987), Commanding Officers Club. Democrat. Roman Catholic. Avocations: jogging, motorcycling. Office: Nat Fire Protection Assn 3257 Beals Branch Dr Louisville KY 40206-3060

SANDERS, SHARON RAYE (SHARRI SANDERS), telecommunications executive, educator; b. Dayton, Ohio, Aug. 25, 1942; d. Robert J. Rapa and Mildred B. Wallace; m. Robert Meredith Sanders, Dec. 28, 1961; children: Robert E., Kenneth B. (dec.). Tchr. cert., U. Tex., 1989, 90. Various positions Rockwell Internat, Bastian-Blessing, others, Mich. and Ill., 1960-79; adminstrv. asst. Tex. Tech. Sch. Medicine, Lubbock, 1980, Thermex Energy Corp., Dallas, 1980-81; exec. asst. Bonser-Philhower Sales, Richardson, Tex., 1982; owner, operator SRS Bus. Svc. Secretarial/Printing, Kaufman, Tex., 1982-89; tchr. Kaufman H.S., 1989-92; prin. ptnr. MetCom of East Tex., Chandler, Tex., 1993—. Author: What's Cooking?, 1988; contbr. poetry to anthologies; contbg. writer Kaufman Herald, 1988-89, The Secretary mag., 1990. Pres. PTA, Allegan, Mich., 1973, sec., 1974; sec. ladies aux. Forest Grove Property Owners Assn., 1993-94; bd. dirs. Forest Grove Property Owners Assn., 1994-96. Recipient Engraved Appreciation award Student Body/Graphic Arts, Kaufman H.S., 1992, 20th Century award for Achievement in Edn., 1994. Mem. NAFE, Nat. League Am. Pen Women (2d place writing contest award 1988), Tex. Printing Instrs. Assn. (sec. 1992), Kaufman C. of C. (bd. dirs. 1983-86), Chandler Lioness Club (co-first v.p., 1995-96). Avocations: oil painting, writing, quilting. Office: MetCom of East Tex PO Box 1590 Chandler TX 75758-1590

SANDERS, STEVE, singer; b. Richland, Ga., Sept. 17; s. Herbert and Lorraine Sanders; m. Janet Sanders (div.); 4 children. Mem. Oak Ridge Boys, 1987—, rhythm guitar, now singer. Albums include Heartbeat, 1987, Monongahela, 1988, Unstoppable, 1991, The Long Haul, 1992, Back to Back, 1994; songs written include Live in Love, 1982; appeared in Broadway prodn. The Yearling; appeared in film Hurry Sundown, 1967; TV appearances include Gunsmoke, Noon Wine. Avocations: scuba diving, fishing. Office: The Oak Ridge Boys 329 Rockland Rd Hendersonville TN 37075-3423*

SANDERS, STEVEN GILL, telecommunications executive; b. Chgo., Aug. 23, 1936; s. Raymond E. and Mildred (Gostow) S.; m. Gretchen Griffith, Jan. 15, 1959 (div. 1985); children: Steven Gill, Meghan Griffith; m. Nancy Lee Wolf, Sept. 23, 1989. BS, MIT, 1958; postgrad., Rutgers U., 1960-61; PhD, U. S.C., 1965. Instr. mechanics U. S.C., Columbia, 1964-65; asst. prof. So. Ill. U., Edwardsville, 1965-67, assoc. prof., 1969-75, prof. physics, 1975-79, chmn. physics faculty, 1967-71; resident rsch. assoc. Agronne (Ill.) Nat. Lab., 1971-72; pres., gen. mgr. No. Ark. Tel. Co., Flippin, 1977—, Nova Systems, Flippin, 1981-92. Contbr. articles on physics to sci. publs. Fellow NSF, 1971. Mem. AAAS, IEEE (sr.), Am. Phys. Soc., U.S. Tel. Assn. (new svcs. and tech. issues subcom. 1991-92, Supercom program com. 1993-94), Ark. Tel. Assn. (pres. 1992, bd. dirs. 1985—), Western Rural Tel. Assn. (bd. dirs. 1993—, chmn. Western Alliance Universal svc. com. 1994—), Ark. C. of C. (bd. dirs. 1989-94), Sigma Xi. Home: 220 N Cardinal Dr Mountain Home AR 72653-3754 Office: No Ark Tel Co 301 E Main St Flippin AR 72634

SANDERS, SUMMER, Olympic athlete; b. 1972; d. Bob and Barbara S. Gold medalist, 200m Butterfly Barcelona Olympic Games, 1992, Silver medalist, 200m Individual Medley, 1992, Bronze medalist, 400m Individual Medley, 1992. Host (game show for children): Figure It Out, Nickelodeon, 1997—; broadcaster (WNBA) Lifetime TV, 1997—. Office: US Swimming Inc One Olympic Plz Colorado Springs CO 80909-5724 also: care Nickelodeon/Figure It Out 1515 Broadway 38th Flr New York NY 10036 also: Lifetime Television 309 W 49th St New York NY 10019*

SANDERS, WALLACE WOLFRED, JR., civil engineer; b. Louisville, June 24, 1933; s. Wallace Wolfred and Mary Jane (Brownfield) S.; m. Julia B. Howard, June 9, 1956; children—Linda, David. B.C.E., U. Louisville, 1955; M.S., U. Ill., Urbana, 1957, Ph.D., 1960; M.Engring., U. Louisville, 1973. Research asst., then research assoc. U. Ill., 1955-60, asst. prof., 1960-64; mem. faculty Iowa State U., Ames, 1964—; prof. civil engring. Iowa State U., 1970—, assoc. dir. engring. research, 1980-91, assoc. dean research, 1988-91, interim asst. vice provost for research and advanced studies, 1991-92; cons. to govt. and industry. Contbr. numerous papers to profl. jours. Bd. dirs. Northcrest Retirement Cmty., Ames, 1976-82, 92—, pres., 1987-91, 96—. Mem. ASCE (R.C. Reese research prize 1978), Am. Welding Soc. (Adams Meml. membership award 1971), Am. Ry. Engring. Assn., Am. Soc. Engring. Edn. Baptist. Home: 1809 Maxwell Ave Ames IA 50010-5539 Office: Iowa State U 374 Town Engring Bldg Ames IA 50011

SANDERS, WALTER JEREMIAH, III, electronics company executive; b. Chgo., Sept. 12, 1936. BEE, U. Ill., 1958. Design engr. Douglas Aircraft Co., Santa Monica, Calif., 1958-59; applications engr. Motorola, Inc., Phoenix, 1959-60; sales engr. Motorola, Inc., 1960-61; with Fairchild Camera & Instrument Co., 1961-69; dir. mktg. Fairchild Camera & Instrument Co., Mountain View, Calif., 1961-68, group dir. mktg. worldwide, 1968-69; pres. Advanced Micro Devices Inc., Sunnyvale, Calif., until 1987, chmn. bd., chief exec. officer, 1969—; dir. Donaldson, Lufkin & Jenrette. Mem. Semicondr. Industry Assn. (co-founder, dir.), Santa Clara County Mfg. Group (co-founder, dir.). Office: Advanced Micro Devices Inc PO Box 3453 One AMD Pl Sunnyvale CA 94086-3453*

SANDERS, WAYNE R., manufacturing executive; b. Chgo., July 6, 1947; s. Ralph G. and Bernice F. (Swanson) S.; m. Kathleen E. Lessard, Aug. 22, 1970; children: Tracy, Amy, Megan. BCE, Ill. Inst. Tech., 1969; MBA, Marquette U., 1972. Fin. analyst Ford Motor Co., Dearborn, Mich., 1972-75; sr. fin. analyst Kimberly-Clark Corp., Neenah, Wis., 1975, dir. bus. planning internat., 1976-80, dir. bus. planning U.S. consumer bus., 1980-81; v.p. strategic planning Kimberly-Clark of Can., Toronto, Ont., 1981-82, pres., 1982-85; sr. v.p. Kimberly-Clark Corp., Dallas, 1986; pres. infant care sector Kimberly-Clark Corp., Neenah, Wis., from 1987; former pres. personal care div. Kimberly-Clark Corp., pres., chief oper. officer world consumer, nonwovens and svc. and indsl. ops., 1990—; pres., CEO Kimberly-Clark Corp., Dallas, 1990-91, chmn., CEO, 1992—, chmn. bd., CEO, 1992—. Elected mem. Neenah Sch. Bd., 1980-81; nat. trustee Boys and Girls Clubs Am., 1994; trustee Marquette U., Milw. Roman Catholic. *

SANDERS, WILLIAM EUGENE, marketing executive; b. Asheboro, N.C., Nov. 16, 1933; s. Arthur Ira and Picola (Loftin) S.; m. Velna Elizabeth Sumner, June 8, 1957; children: William Eugene Jr., George Herbert Sumner. AB in Polit. Sci., U. N.C., 1956, postgrad. in Law, 1956-57. Marketing rep. Encyclopaedia Britannica, Greensboro, N.C., 1957-60, Am. Pubs., Chgo., 1960-66; pres. S&W Distbrs., Inc., Greensboro, 1966—. Little league coach Civitans, Greensboro, 1967-68. With U.S. Army Res., 1957-63. Named Hon. Amb. Dept. of Labor, Ky., 1976, Ky. Col., 1976, Hon. Mem. La. Lt. Gov. Staff, 1984; recipient Cert. Appreciation Jefferson Davis Parish Libr., Jennings, La., 1986, Top Sales award Am. Media. Corp., 1996, Marshall Cavendish Top Prodn. award, 1990-91, Mktg. award Am. Media, 1995. Mem. State Libr. Assns. Va., W.Va., La., Gen. Alumni Assn. (co-chairman Greensboro chpt. 1979-80), Chi Phi. Democrat. Presbyterian. Avocations: billiards, golf, fishing. Office: S&W Distbrs Inc 1600H E Wendover Ave Greensboro NC 27405-6837 *As a youth, someone told me that it cost not one pennymore to be nice in your dealing with otherr individuals. I have followed this advice.*

SANDERS, W(ILLIAM) EUGENE, JR., physician, educator; b. Frederick, Md., June 25, 1934; s. W(illiam) Eugene and E. Gertrude (Wilburn) S.; m. Christine Culp, Feb. 22, 1974. A.B., Cornell U., 1956, M.D., 1960. Diplomate: Am. Bd. Internal Medicine. Intern Johns Hopkins Hosp., Balt., 1960-61; resident Johns Hopkins Hosp., 1961-62; instr. medicine Emory U. Sch. Medicine, Atlanta, 1962-64; chief med. resident, instr. U. Fla. Coll. Medicine, Gainesville, 1964-65; asst. prof. medicine and microbiology U. Fla. Coll. Medicine, 1965-69, asso. prof., 1969-72; prof., chmn. dept. med. microbiology, prof. medicine Creighton U. Sch. Medicine, Omaha, 1972-95; cons.-in-research Fla. Dept. Health and Rehab. Services, 1966—. Editor: Am. Jour. Epidemiology, 1974-95; contbr. sci. articles to profl. jours. Served as med. officer USPHS, 1962-64. Recipient NIH Research Career Devel. award, 1968-72; John and Mary R. Markle scholar in acad. medicine, 1968-73. Mem. Am. Soc. for Microbiology, Infectious Diseases Soc. Am., Soc. for Epidemiol. Research, Am. Lung Assn., Thoracic Soc., N.Y. Acad. Scis., Phi Beta Kappa, Sigma Xi, Phi Kappa Phi. Achievements include patent on enocin antibiotic and RBE limonene and perrilyl alcohol. Home: RR 2 Fremont NE 68025-9802 Office: Creighton U Sch Medicine Dept Med Microbio Omaha NE 68178 *Each day provides more challenges and more opportunities than the preceding. No individual can possibly cope with each of these in any given day. Success depends upon establishing priorities and maintaining them. Fight only those battles and pursue with fervor only those opportunities that improve both one's self and one's fellow man.*

SANDERS, WILLIAM GEORGE, public relations executive; b. Sacramento, Jan. 11, 1932; s. Samuel S. and Alice M. (Trow) S.; m. Teresa Helsel, Oct. 20, 1979. Student, Contra Costa Jr. Coll., 1950-51; B.A. in Journalism, U. Oreg., 1957; postgrad. cinema dept., U. So. Calif., 1962. Reporter Roseburg (Oreg.) News-Rev., 1957; group advt. mgr. Montgomery Ward & Co., Oakland, Calif., 1957-61; advt. public relations dir. Jacuzzi Research, Inc., Berkeley, Calif., 1964-65; asst. v.p. corp. communications Airborne Freight Corp., San Mateo, Calif., 1966-67; sr. editor Motor Trend Mag., Hollywood, Calif., 1967-71; exec. v.p., assoc. pub. Four Wheeler Mag., Canoga Park, Calif., 1971-87; pres. William Sanders & Assocs., Sepulveda, Calif., 1987—; sr. editor Off Road Mag., 1988—. Editor: automotive sect. World Year Book, 1970, 71. Served with Signal Corps U.S. Army, 1952-54, Korea. Decorated U.S. Korean Svc. medal W/1 Bronze Svc. star, U.N. Svc. medal, Nat. Def. Svc. medal, Singman Rhee citation Korea. Mem. Calif. Assn. Four Wheel Dr. Clubs, Specialty Equipment Mfrs. Assn., Am. Automotive Writers and Broadcasters Assn., Chi Psi. Winner Baja 1000 Off Rd. Race for prodn. 4 wheel dr. class, 1973, 4th Pl. Baja 1000, 1979.

SANDERS, WILLIAM HUGGINS, lawyer, rancher; b. Springfield, Mo., Nov. 24, 1922; s. J.W. and Helen Pipkin (Huggins) S.; m. Nancy Jane Crane, Dec. 24, 1943; children—Christopher, Cynthia, William Huggins, Dan Crane. A.B., U. Chgo., 1945. Bar: Mo. bar. Ptnr. Blackwell, Sanders, Matheny, Weary & Lombardi, Kansas City, 1953—. Recipient Lon O. Hocker Meml. Trial Lawyers award Mo. Bar Found., 1957. Club: University (Kansas City, Mo.); Lane Recreation Assn. Office: Blackwell Sanders Matheny Weary & Lombardi 2300 Main St Kansas City MO 64108-2416

SANDERS, WILLIAM JOHN, research scientist; b. Detroit, July 10, 1940; s. John William and Charlotte Barbara (Linsday) Steele; m. Gary Roberts, Sept. 12, 1961; children: Scott David, Susan Deborah. BS, U. Mich., 1962; MSEE, U. Calif., Berkeley, 1964. Sr. rsch. scientist Stanford (Calif.) U., 1967—; pres. Sanders Data Systems, 1991—; pres. Computers in Cardiology, 1990-93. Inventor cardiac probe; contbr. articles to profl. jours. Mem. IEEE Computer Soc., Assn. Computing Machinery. Avocations: bicycling, wind surfing. Home: 3980 Bibbits Dr Palo Alto CA 94303-4531 Office: Stanford U Med Ctr Cardiovasc Medicine Stanford CA 94305

SANDERS, WILLIAM MICHAEL, emergency physician; b. New Britain, Conn., Dec. 27, 1953; s. William Alfred and Marie Teresa (Fox) S.; m. Louise Krawiec, June 16, 1979; children: Kimberly, William J., Meghan. BA in Chemistry, Coll. of the Holy Cross, Worcester, Mass., 1976; MD, U. Conn., 1980. Bd. cert. in emergency medicine and internal medicine. Resident in internal medicine Albany (N.Y.) Med. Ctr., 1980-83; staff physician dept. emergency medicine St. Francis Hosp. and Med. Ctr., Hartford, Conn., 1983-91, assoc. dir. dept. emergency medicine, 1991-95, interim dir. dept. emergency medicine, 1995-96, chmn./dir. dept. emergency medicine, 1996—. Mem. AMA, Am. Coll. Emergency Physicians, Am. Coll. Physician Execs. Office: St Francis Hosp and Med Ctr 114 Woodland St Hartford CT 06105-1200

SANDERSON, ARTHUR CLARK, engineering educator; b. Providence, Oct. 23, 1946; s. Robert Leroy and Julia Ayer (Oldham) S.; m. Susan Rita Walsh, Aug. 14, 1971; children: Angeline Mirada, Andrew McWain. BS, Brown U., 1968; MS, Carnegie-Mellon U., 1970, PhD, 1972. Rsch. engr. Westinghouse Electric Corp., Pitts., 1968-70; vis. rsch. scientist Delft (The Netherlands) U. Tech., 1972-73; prof. Carnegie-Mellon U., Pitts., 1973-87, co-dir. robotics inst., 1981-87; rsch. dir. Philips Rsch. Labs., Briarcliff Manor, N.Y., 1985-87; prof., dept. chmn. Rensselaer Poly. Inst., Troy, N.Y., 1987—; vis. prof. Univ. Iberoamericana, Mexico City, 1975-77. Contbr. over 180 chpts. to books, articles to profl. jours. Fellow AAAS, IEEE (pres. robotics and automation soc. 1989, 90); mem. AIAA (mem. space automation and robotics tech. com.), Am. Assn. Artificial Intelligence, Soc. Mfg. Engrs. Home: 523 Hancock Rd Williamstown MA 01267-3011 Office: Rensselaer Poly Inst 110 8th St Troy NY 12180-3522

SANDERSON, CATHY ANN, histotechnician, researcher; b. Key West, Fla., Apr. 12, 1954; d. Robert Gary and Cheri Dae (Colin) S.; 1 child, Nichole Renee. Grad. h.s., Phoenix, Ariz., 1972. Histology trainee St. Luke's Medical Ctr., Phoenix, 1972-73, histotechnician, 1973-83; histotechnician/rsch. Harrington Arthritis Rsch. Ctr., Phoenix, 1983-87, Emory U., Atlanta, 1987-88, VA Medical Ctr, Salt Lake City, 1988—; founder, chair hard tissue com. Nat. Soc. Histotech., Bowie, Md., 1989—, editor, 1992—, vet. indsl. rsch. com., 1989—, health and safety com., 1988—, mem. ednl. com., 1989-91; owner Wasatch Histo Cons., 1988—. Mem. editl. bd. Jour. Histotechnology, 1993—; contbr. articles to numerous profl. jours. Organizer Neighborhood Watch, West Valley City, Utah, 1993—. Named Histotechnologist of Yr., Nat. Soc. Histotechnology, 1992; recipient Hacker Instruments; Membership Incentive award, 1991-92, Superior Performance award, 1989-92, 95-96, William J. Hacker award, 1988, Rsch. Technician of Yr. award, 1989. Mem. Nat. Wildlife Fedn., Nat. Arbor Day Found., Utah Soc. Histotechnology, Am. Assn. Lab Animal Sci. (bd. dirs. 1989-91), The Cousteau Soc., Inc., Nat. Soc. Histotechnology. Achievements include development of Sandersons Rapid Bone Stain and staining protocol for mineralized bone which differentiates mineralized bone from soft tissue and non-mineralized bone. Office: VA Medical Ctr 500 Foothill Dr # 151F Salt Lake City UT 84148-0001

SANDERSON, DAVID ALAN, training and development administrator; b. Kenton, Ohio, Apr. 17, 1951; s. George H. and Betty Lou (Kelly) S.; m. Carla Lynn Schwyn, Aug. 7, 1976; children: Rachel Ann, Jessica Lynn. BS, Bowling Green State U., 1973, MEd, 1975, postgrad. Tng. coord. Cummins Engine Co., Fostoria, Ohio, 1976-78; tng. mgr. Cummins Engine Co., Fostoria, 1978-82, Doehler-Jarvis Co., Toledo, 1982-87; tng. and devel. mgr. Gen. Mills, Inc., Toledo, 1987—; ptnr., co-founder Applied Technetronics, Cygnet, Ohio, 1987—; owner Sanderson Stables, Cygnet, 1982—; adv. bd. Owens C. C., 1982—, adj. prof., instr. statis. process control, 1991—; mem. edn. adv. com. Ohio Edison Indsl. Ctr.; mem. trades subcom. State of Ohio Apprenticeship Coun. Author: Basic. S.P.C., 1986, Basic Video, 1981, The Apprenticeship System: How It Works, 1996. Councilman Village of Cygnet, 1989; mem. Cygnet Centennial com., 1989; mem. U.S. Equestrian Team. Mem. ASTD, Assn. for Quality and Participation, U.S. Apprenticeship Assn., Internat. Voc. and Tech. Assn., Assn. Jr. Colls. and Vocat. Schs. Assn. Performance and Instrn. Democrat. Methodist. Avocations: computers, cars, horses, woodworking, finance. Home: PO Box 146 46 Washington St Cygnet OH 43413 Office: Gen Mills Inc 1250 W Laskey Rd Toledo OH 43612-2909

SANDERSON, DAVID R., physician; b. South Bend, Ind., Dec. 26, 1933; s. Robert Burns and Alpha (Rodenberger) S.; divorced, 1978; children: David, Kathryn, Robert, Lisa; m. Evelyn Louise Klunder, Sept. 20, 1980. BA, Northwestern U., 1955, MD, 1958. Cons. in medicine Mayo Clinic, Rochester, Minn., 1965-87, chmn. dept. Thoracic Disease, 1977-87; cons. in medicine Mayo Clinic Scottsdale, Ariz., 1987-96, chmn. dept. internal medicine, 1988-96, vice chmn. bd. govs., 1987-94; assoc. dir. Mayo Lung Project, Nat. Cancer Inst., Rochester. Contbr. articles to profl. jours. Recipient Noble award, Mayo Found., Rochester, "Significant Sig" award, Sigma Chi Fraternity, Ill., 1989, Chevalier Jackson award, Am. Bronchoesophagologic Assn., Fla., 1990. Fellow ACP, Am. Coll. Chest Physicians (gov. for Minn. 1981-87); mem. Am. Bronchoesophagologic Assn., World Assn. for Bronchology, Internat. Bronchoesophagologic Assn., Internat. Assn. Study of Lung Cancer, AMA. Presbyterian. Home: 10676 E Bella Vista Dr Scottsdale AZ 85258-6086 Office: Mayo Clinic Scottsdale 13400 E Shea Blvd Scottsdale AZ 85259-5404

SANDERSON, DENNIS CARL, theater director, educator; b. Akron, Ohio, Jan. 20, 1935; s. Carl A. Sanderson and Gladys M. (Minter) Sanderson Buchmiller; m. Carol Ann Heitzman, May 13, 1961; children: Dennis Douglas, Diana Dawn. MA, Kent State U., 1963; PhD, Mich. State U., 1973. Dir. theatre Newberry (S.C.) Coll., 1963-73, Francis Marion U., Florence, S.C., 1973—; chmn. div. humanities Newberry Coll., 1971-73; chair, prof. dept. fine arts and mass comm. Francis Marion U., 1985—, C.B. and Marlene Askins prof. art; chmn. Art's Alive Spring Arts festival, Florence, 1985-95; cons. in field. Dir. plays including Grease, 1981, Children of a Lesser God, 1983, Hedda Gabler, 1984, The Comedy of Errors, 1985, The Rimers of Eldritch, 1986, Royal Gambit, 1988, South Pacific, 1988, Our Town, 1989, Working, 1990; scenic designer plays Bell, Book, & Candle, 1985, The Foreigner, 1987, South Pacific, 1990, Godspell, 1994. Pres. Dem. Com. Precinct 14, Florence, 1980-90. Luth. Ch. Am. fellow, 1966; faculty grantee Newberry Coll., 1970. Mem. Nat. Assn. Schs. of Theatre, Southeastern Theatre Assn., Am. Theatre in Higher Edn., S.C. Theatre Assn. (bd. dirs. 1988), Rotary (bd. dirs. 1987-90), Lions Internat. (bd. dirs. 1995—), Sierra Club, Alpha Psi Omega, Phi Delta Theta (treas. 1960-61). Democrat. Lutheran. Avocations: coaching basketball and baseball, wood carving, research. Office: Francis Marion U PO Box 100547 Florence SC 29501-0547

SANDERSON, DOUGLAS JAY, lawyer; b. Boston, Apr. 21, 1953; s. Warren and Edith S. Sanderson; m. Audrey S. Goldstein, June 6, 1982; children: Scott M.G., Phoebe H.G. BA, Trinity Coll., Hartford, Conn., 1974; JD, George Washington U., 1977. Bar: Va. 1977, D.C. 1978, U.S. Dist. Ct. (ea. dist.) Va. 1978, U.S. Ct. Appeals (4th cir.) 1978. Assoc. Bettius, Rosenberger & Carter, P.C., Fairfax, Va., 1977-82; ptnr. Bettius & Sanderson, P.C. and predecessor firms, Fairfax, 1982-86; prin. Miles & Stockbridge P.C., Fairfax, 1986-95; br. head Miles & Stockbridge, Fairfax, 1989-91; co-owner McCandlish & Lillard, P.C., Fairfax, 1995—; trustee Cambridge Ctr. Behavioral Studies, Cambridge, 1981-90. Editor: Consumer Protection Reporting Svc., 1976-77. Bd. dirs. Legal Svcs. No. Va., Inc., 1991—, pres., 1993-95. Mem. ABA, Va. Bar Assn., Fairfax Bar Assn., Ctrl. Fairfax C. of C. (bd. dirs. 1988-93). Avocations: sports, reading. Office: McCandlish & Lillard 11350 Random Hills Rd Ste 500 Fairfax VA 22030-6044

SANDERSON, EDWARD FRENCH, state official; b. Evanston, Ill., June 25, 1947; s. Edward Gatewood and Barbara (French) S.; m. Carol Clo; children: David, Sarah, Katherine. BA, Wesleyan U., 1969; MA, Brown U., 1974. Exec. dir. Providence Hist. Dist. Commn., 1975-80; dep. dir. R.I. Hist. Preservation Commn., Providence, 1980-84, exec. dir., 1984—; sec. Nat. Conf. of State, Washington, 1989-91, dir., 1985-91; bd. dirs. R.I. Hist. Soc., Providence, 1987-93; commr. Blackstone Valley Nat. Heritage Corridor, Washington, 1988—. Author: Providence, R.I., 1986 (Downing Prize 1987). Office: RI Hist Preservation Commn Old State House 150 Benefit St Providence RI 02903-1209

SANDERSON, FRED HUGO, economist; b. Germany, Apr. 15, 1914; came to U.S., 1937, naturalized, 1944; s. Siegfried and Maria (Schulze) S.; m. Elisabeth Doepfer, Jan. 3, 1938. Lic.Sc.Econ., U. Geneva, Switzerland, 1935; A.M., Harvard U., 1942, Ph.D., 1943. Research asst. Dept. Agr., 1938-42; research asso. com. on research in social scis. Harvard U., 1938-43, teaching fellow, 1942-43; economist OSS, 1943-45; chief Central European econ. sect. div. research for Western Europe Dept. of State, 1946-48, chief Western European econ. br., 1948-52, chief regional econ. staff, 1952-55, asst. chief div., 1955-57, chief div. of research Western Europe, 1957-58; alt. U.S. rep. European Payments Union, 1958-59; dir. finance div. U.S. Mission to OEEC, Paris, 1959-62; chief foodstuffs div. Dept. State, 1963-67; dir. Office Food Policy and Programs, 1967-69, adviser internat. finance, 1970; detailed to Pres.'s Commn. on Internat. Trade and Investment Policy, 1970-71; mem. planning and coordination staff State Dept., 1971-73; fgn. service officer, 1955-73; sr. fellow Brookings Instn., Washington, 1974-83, Resources for Future, Washington, 1983-92, Nat. Ctr. for Food and Agrl. Policy, Washington, 1992—; on leave under Rockefeller Pub. Svc. award to study econ. effects of European coal and steel cmty., 1956-57; cons. to econ. adviser OMGUS, Berlin, 1948; detailed to Pres.'s Materials Policy Commn., 1951; professorial lectr. Sch. Advanced Internat. Studies Johns Hopkins U., 1973-94. Author: Methods of Crop Forecasting, 1954 (David A. Wells prize), Japan's Food Prospects and Policies, 1978, (with S. Roy) Food Trends and Prospects in India, 1979; contbg. author: Resources for Freedom, Vol. III, 1952, The Struggle for Democracy in Germany (G. Almond, editor), 1949, Strains in International Finance and Trade, 1974, The Great Food Fumble, 1975, U.S. Farm Policy in Perspective, 1983, World Food Prospects to the Year 2000, 1984, Agriculture and International Trade, 1988, The GATT Agreement on Agriculture, 1994, Agriculture and Multilateralism, 1994; co-author/editor: Agricultural Protectionism in the Industrialized World, 1990. Mem. Am. Econ. Assn., Am. Agrl. Econ. Assn. Home: 5017 Westport Rd Chevy Chase MD 20815-3714 Office: Nat Ctr for Food and Agrl Policy Washington DC 20036

SANDERSON, GLEN CHARLES, science director; b. Wayne County, Mo., Jan. 21, 1923; married; 2 children. BS, U. Mo., 1947, MA, 1949; PhD, U. Ill., 1961. Game biologist Iowa State Conservation Commn., 1949-55, Ill. Dept. Conservation, 1955-60; game biologist Ill. Nat. History Survey, Champaign, 1955-60, assoc. wildlife specialist, 1960-63, wildlife specialist, acting head wildlife rsch., 1963-64, head sect. wildlife rsch., 1964-90, prin. scientist emeritus, dir., 1990—; prof. U. Ill., 1965—; adj. rsch. prof. So. Ill. U., 1964, adj. prof. 1964-84. Editor Jour. Wildlife Mgmt., 1971-72. Recipient Oak Leaf award Nature Conservancy, 1975. Mem. AAAS, Am. Soc. Mammal, Am. Inst. Biol. Sci., Wildlife Soc. (Aldo Leopold Meml. award 1992). Achievements include research in population dynamics of wild animals, especially furbearers, physiological factors of reproductive and survival rates, and lead poisoning in waterfowl. Office: Ill Natural History Survey Ctr Wildlife Ecology 711 S State St Champaign IL 61820-5114

SANDERSON, HOLLADAY WORTH, domestic violence advocate; b. Raleigh, May 17, 1950; d. Hal Venable Jr. and Mary Simmons (Andrews) W.; m. Glen Wessel Potter, Apr. 15, 1978 (div. Sept. 1980); m. Stanley McNaughton Sanderson, July 2, 1984. AB in Music & French, U. N.C., 1972; MMEd, East Carolina U., 1975; cert. advanced acctg./data processing, Kinman Bus. U., 1985. Orch. tchr. New Hanover County Schs., Wilmington, N.C., 1972-74, 75-78, Fairfax (Va.) County Schs., 1978-80, 86-89, Missoula (Mont.) Elem. Sch. Dist., 1983-84; musician, music tchr. Coeur d'Alene, Idaho, 1980-83, 84-86, 1989-91; adj. music faculty, violin, viola, chamber music North Idaho Coll., Coeur d'Alene, 1980-83, 84-86; organist, choir dir. St. Luke's Episcopal ch., Coeur d'Alene, 1980-83, 84-86, St. Luke's Episcopal Ch., Coeur d'Alene, 1989-95; gen. mgr., artistic dir. Coeur d'Alene Summer Theatre, Coeur d'Alene, 1991-92; bookkeeper, adminstrv. asst. Women's Ctr., Coeur d'Alene, 1993-95, exec. dir., 1995—. Sec. Idaho Coalition Against Sexual and Domestic Violence, 1995—; sec.-treas. North Idaho Coalition on Domestic Violence, 1995—; mem. Vestry of St. Luke's Episcopal Ch., 1995-97, chair audit com., 1992-95, lay reader, chalice bearer, 1992—, parliamentarian, 1996, sr. warden, 1997; orch. dir. Pend Oreille Chamber Orch., Sandpoint, Idaho, 1994-95, North Idaho Symphony, 1991, Coeur d'Alene Summer Theatre, 1982-85; cert. QPR suicide prevention gatekeeper instr. Greentree Behavioral Ctr., Spokane, 1996—; mem. Nat. Coalition Against Domestic Violence, Washington State Coalition Against Domestic Violence. Mem. Coeur d'Alene Sunrise Rotary. Democrat. Avocations: reading, cross-stitch, feminist theology. Home: 504 N 15th St Coeur D Alene ID 83814 Office: Womens Ctr 2201 N Government Way Ste E Coeur D Alene ID 83814-3658

SANDERSON, JAMES RICHARD, naval officer, planning and investment company consultant; b. Selma, Calif., Dec. 27, 1925; s. Charles Maxwell and Edith (Wente) S.; m. Betty Lee Bradley, Sept. 19, 1947. Student, U. Calif.-Berkeley, 1943-44, U. Wash., 1944, U. Willamette, 1944-45; grad., USNR Midshipman Sch. at Columbia U., 1945, Nat. War Coll., 1966; student, Gen. Line Sch., Monterey, Calif., 1953, Sr. Officers Ship Material Mgmt. Course, Idaho Falls, Idaho, 1979; B.A. in Internat. Affairs, George Washington U., 1968. Served as enlisted man U.S. Naval Res., 1943-45; commd. ensign USN, 1946, advanced through grades to vice adm., 1980; gunnery officer U.S.S. Mansfield, 1946-47, U.S.S. Bausell, 1947-48; flight trainee Naval Air Sta., Pensacola, Fla., 1949, Corpus Christi, Tex., 1950; served in Attack Squadron 195, Alameda, Calif., 1950-52; flight instr. Naval Air Sta., Pensacola, 1953-55; served in Attack Squadron 16, 1955-57; air ops. officer on staff Comdr. Carrier Div. Four, U.S.S. Forrestal, 1957-60; ops. officer Attack Squadron 43, Naval Air Sta., Oceana, Va., 1960-62; comdg. officer Attack Squadron 76, 1962-63; comdr. Attack Carrier Air Wing Three in U.S.S. Saratoga, 1963-65; spl. support plans officer, Pacific Area Strategic Plans and Policy Div., Office of Chief of Naval Ops., Washington, 1966-67; exec. asst. and sr. aide to dep. chief. naval ops., 1967-69; comdg. officer U.S.S. Ranier, 1969-70; dep. chief of staff for ops. and plans U.S. Sixth Fleet, 1970-71; comdg. officer U.S.S. Saratoga, 1971-73; dep. comdr. Naval Striking and Support Forces, So. Europe, Naples, Italy, 1973-76; vice dir. ops. Joint Chiefs of Staff, Washington, 1976-77; asst. dep. chief naval ops. for plans, policy and ops., 1977-79; comdr. Task Force Sixty, U.S. 6th Fleet, 1979-80, Carrier Group Two, 1979-80, Battle Force Sixth Fleet, 1979-80, Carrier Striking Force So. Region, 1979-80; dep. and chief staff, comdr. in chief Atlantic/U.S. Atlantic Fleet, Norfolk, Va., 1980-83; ret., 1983; exec. cons. Exec. Planning & Investment Co., Inc., Virginia Beach, Va., 1983-85; sr. v.p. for corp. ops. Computer Dynamics, Inc., 1984-86; asst. to pres. Eastern Computers, Inc., 1986—; cons., prin. Exec. Planning and Investment Co., Inc., 1986-94; sr. fellow joint and combined warfare course Armed Forces Staff Coll., 1994—. Decorated D.S.M., Legion of Merit with 3 gold stars, D.F.C., Meritorious Service medal, Air medal with 4 gold stars, Navy Commendation medal with combat distinguishing device. Mem. U. Calif. Alumni Assn., George Washington U. Alumni Assn., Nat. War Coll. Alumni Assn., Naval Acad. Athletic Assn., Assn. Naval Aviation, Tailhook Assn., Smithsonian Assn., Nat. Eagle Scout Assn. (regent, Disting. Eagle Scout award 1994), Nat. Skeet Shooting Assn., Eye Found., Nat. Assn. Investment Clubs, Nat. Wildlife Assn., Army Navy Country Club (Arlington, Va.), Masons (33d degree), Masons, Shriners, KT, Sojourners, Order of Daedalians. Club: Army Navy Country (Arlington, Va.). Lodges: Masons (33 degree), Shriners, Knight Templer, Sojourners. Office: Eastern Computers Inc 596 Lynnhaven Pky Virginia Beach VA 23452-7303

SANDERSON, JEROME ALAN, survey statistician, accountant; b. Nashville, Nov. 18, 1945; s. Bernard and Anna Sanderson; m. Rhona J. Flehinger, Oct. 5, 1990. BSBA, U. Tenn., 1968; MS in Tech. of Mgmt., Am. U., 1974. CPA, Md. Survey statistician Bur. of Census, Washington, 1968-80, U.S. Dept. Energy-Energy Info. Adminstrn., Washington, 1980—; chief minerals & metals sect. Bur. of Census Fgn. Trade Divsn., Washington, 1977-80. Mem. Hexagon, Inc., Washington, 1984—, Camelot Community Neighborhood Watch, Annandale, Va., 1993—. Mem. Greater Washington Soc. of CPAs, Md. Assn. CPAs, Alpha Epsilon Pi. Avocations: amateur radio, philately. Home: 3806 King Arthur Rd Annandale VA 22003-1323 Office: US Dept Energy 950 Lenfant Plz SW Washington DC 20024-2123

SANDESON, WILLIAM SEYMOUR, cartoonist; b. Mound City, Ill., Dec. 16, 1913; s. William Stephen and Jessie Mae (Mertz) S.; m. Ione Wear, June 4, 1938 (dec. 1975); 1 son, William Scott; m. Ruth Cress, Dec. 31, 1978. Student, Chgo. Acad. Fine Arts, 1931-32. Free-lance cartoonist for nat. mags., 1932-37; editorial cartoonist New Orleans Item-Tribune, 1937-41; cartoonist, picture editor and art dir. St. Louis Star-Times, 1941-51; editorial cartoonist Ft. Wayne (Ind.) News-Sentinel, 1951-82; ret., 1982. Drew daily cartoon feature for, Star-Times, Sketching Up With the News. Recipient Honor medal Freedoms Found., 1952, 53, 56, George Washington Honor medal, 1954, 55, 57, 58, 59, 60, Disting. Service award, 1961-72, cartoon award, 1982;, Ind. Sch. Bell award, 1967, Disting. Service awards, 1971-76, prin. cartoon award, 1977, cartoon award, 1978; co-recipient Pulitzer prize for gen. local reporting, 1982. Mem. Nat. Cartoonist Soc., Assn. Am. Editorial Cartoonists. Congregationalist. Club: Fort Wayne Press (pres. 1965). Home: 119 W Sherwood Ter Fort Wayne IN 46807-2846 Office: Fort Wayne News Sentinel Fort Wayne IN 46802 *Until I'm listed in WHO WAS WHO, I intend to dip my brush in a mixture of self-improvement, stubbornness, and sincere thoughtfulness of my fellow American.*

SANDFORD, JUANITA DADISMAN, sociologist, educator, writer; b. Wichita, Kans., June 20, 1926; d. Carl Orville and Mabel Bernice (Stearman) Dadisman; m. Herman Prestridge Sandford, Dec. 22, 1946; children: Susan Jane, Linda Ann, Mary Kaye. BA, Baylor U., 1947, MA, 1948; LLD (hon.), Hendrix Coll., 1991. Instr. sociology Wayland Bapt. Coll., Plainview, Tex., 1948-49, Ft. Smith (Ark.) Jr. coll., 1959; instr. sociology Ouachita Bapt. U., Arkadelphia, Ark., 1960-68, adj. prof., 1996—; asst. prof. sociology Henderson State U., Arkadelphia, Ark., 1968-89, coord. women's studies, 1975-89; ret., 1989; adj. tchr. Ouachita Bapt. U., 1996—; chmn. bd. Coll. Cmty. Action, Inc., 1974-78; cons. human rels. Ark. Tech. Assistance & Consultative Ctr., 1964-78; mem. Gov. Ark. Commn. on Status of Women, 1975-80, Atty. Gen. Consumer Adv. Bd., 1977-79. Author: I Didn't Get a Lot Done Today, 1974, Poverty in the Land of Opportunity, 1978, Sunbonnet Sue: The Crone, 1996; contbg. author Women & Religion: Images of Women in the Bible, 1977, Arkansas: State in Transition, 1981, Arkadelphia: 2000 AD, 1982. Bd. dirs. Ctrl. Ark. Devel. Coun., 1975-80, Ark. Hunger Project, 1983-86, Ark. Advs. for Children and Families, 1986-89. Recipient Ark. Woman of Achievement award Ark. Womens Polit. Caucus, 1975. Mem. NOW, Ark. Sociolog. & Anthropolog. Assn. (pres. 1991-92), Inst. Noetic Sci. Avocations: quilting, flower gardening. Home: 959 N 8th St Arkadelphia AR 71923-3201

SANDITEN, EDGAR RICHARD, investment company executive; b. Okmulgee, Okla., Feb. 1, 1920; s. Herman and Anna (Sanditen) S.; m. Isabel

Raffkind, Jan. 26, 1945; children: Linda Caryl, Judith Marie, Ellen Jane, Michael Jay. Student, Western Mil. Acad., 1934-37; B.S. in Bus., Okla. U., 1941. With Otasco, Inc., Tulsa, 1941-87, pres., 1974-77, chmn., chief exec. officer, 1977-83, chmn. employees retirement trust, 1983-87; prin., chmn. Sanditen Investments, Ltd., Tulsa, 1987—; bd. dirs. Bank of Okla. Trust Co.; fin. advisor Bank of Okla., 1978-84. Chmn. United Jewish Appeal, Tulsa, 1959; mem. bd. dirs. Jewish Fedn., Tulsa, 1960-62 (Honor award 1960), YMCA, 1966-95, Am. Cancer Soc., 1978-80, Tulsa Met. Ministry, 1977-78, Simon Estes Ednl. Found., 1982—, March of Dimes, 1983—; mem. adv. com. Jr. League, 1977—, Girl Scouts U.S.A., 1987—; chmn. Tulsa Charity Horse Show, 1969-71, 80-84; bd. dirs. Tulsa Opera, 1979—, v.p., 1989 (Champion Fundraiser, 1989-96); bd. dirs. Tulsa Ballet Theatre (Dimedici award 1989), Tulsa Econ. Devel. Commn., 1970-84, Tulsa Philharmonic, 1990—, Tulsa Hist. Soc., 1995—; bd. dirs. Temple Israel Found., 1968-70, chmn., 1979-80; mem. B'nai Emunah Synagogue; pres. Temple Israel, 1968-70; trustee Children's Med. Ctr., 1983—; bd. dirs. St. John Med. Ctr., 1973-82, chmn., 1979-81; bd. dirs. St. John Found., 1983-89, chmn., 1983-85; bd. dirs. Tulsa Jewish Retirement and Health Care Ctr., 1986—, Tulsa Ctr. for Homeless, 1991—, Fenster Mus., 1986—, NCCJ, 1983—, pres., 1985-87; mem. adv. bd. dirs. U. Okla. Coll. Bus. Adminstrn., 1986-91; hon. chmn. Ronald McDonald House, 1991. Served with USAAF, 1943-46. Recipient Nat. Humanitarian award Nat. Jewish Hosp., 1987, Brotherhood award NCCJ, 1991, Alfred Aaronson Cmty. Rels. award, 1993; named Boss of Yr., Am. Bus. Women's Assn., 1976; named to Okla. Hall of Fame, 1996. Mem. Tulsa Jr. C. of C. (honor award 1943), Okla. C. of C. (bd. dirs. 1978-87), Tulsa C. of C. (bd. dirs. 1977-83, v.p. 1978-79), Quarter Century Club Automotive Industry, So. Hills Country Club (bd. dirs. 1990-96, fin. chmn., exec. com., v.p. 1992, pres. 1995), Summit Club (bd. dirs. 1971-77). Office: Sanditen Investments Ltd 3314 E 51st St Ste 207K Tulsa OK 74135-3527

SAND LEE, INGER, artist; b. Sauda, Norway, Apr. 8, 1938; came to U.S., 1960; d. Inge Sigvald and Johanne Elise (Hamre) Sand; m. Charles Allen Lee, Aug. 28, 1981. Cert. in decorative art, N.Y. Sch. Interior Design, 1968; BFA, Marymount Manhattan Coll./N.Y. Sch. Interior Design, 1980; cert. completion, Art Students League, 1993; postgrad., Nat. Acad. Design, 1993-94. One-woman shows include Art 54, N.Y.C., 1988, Pyramid Gallery, N.Y.C., 1990, Exhbn. Space, N.Y.C., 1991, Denise Bibro Fine Art, N.Y.C., 1993, 95; selected exhbns. include Lincoln Ctr., N.Y.C., 1988, Avery Fisher Hall, N.Y.C., 1988, Mus. Atheism and Realism, Lviv, USSR, 1990, Lever House, N.Y.C., 1991, Nat. Acad. Mus., N.Y.C., 1994; group exhbns. include Pyramid Gallery, N.Y.C., 1989, 90, 91, Ariel Gallery, N.Y.C., 1991, Broome Street Gallery, N.Y.C., 1992, 93, Ward-Nasse Gallery, N.Y.C., 1992, Hudson Guild Art Gallery, N.Y.C., 1992, Denise Bibro Fine Art, N.Y.C., 1992, 94, 95, 97, Frank Bustamante Gallery, N.Y.C., 1993, Southern Alleghenies Mus. Art, Loretto, Pa., 1994, Edward William Gallery, 1996, Knoxville (Tenn.) Opera Guild, 1996, Fairleigh Dickinson U., 1996; represented in numerous permanent pvt. and pub. collections. Recipient Alumni award N.Y. Sch. Interior Design, 1979; merit scholar Art Student's League, 1991. Mem. Archtl. League N.Y.

SANDLER, BERNICE RESNICK, women's rights specialist; b. N.Y.C., Mar. 3, 1928; d. Abraham Hyman and Ivy (Ernst) Resnick; children: Deborah Jo, Emily Maud. BA cum laude, Bklyn. Coll., 1948; MA, CCNY, 1950; EdD, U. Md., 1969; LLD (hon.), Bloomfield Coll., 1973, Hood Coll., 1974, R.I. Coll., 1980, Colby-Sawyer Coll., 1984; LHD (hon.), Grand Valley State Coll., 1974; Dr. Pub. Service (hon.), North Adams State Coll., 1985; LLD (hon.), Goucher Coll., 1991; LHD (hon.), Plymouth State Coll., 1992, Wittenberg U., 1993. Research asst., nursery sch. tchr., employment counselor, adult edn. instr., sec.; psychologist HEW, 1970; tchr. psychology Mt. Vernon Coll., 1970; head Action Com. for Fed. Contract Compliance, Women's Equity Action League, 1970-71; edn. specialist U.S. Ho. Reps., Washington, 1970; dep. dir. Womens Action program, HEW, Washington, 1971; dir. project on status and edn. of women Assn. Am. Colls., Washington, 1971-91; sr. assoc. Ctr. for Women Policy Studies, 1991-94; sr. scholar in residence Nat. Assn. Women in Edn., Washington, 1994—; cons., 1991—; expert witness, 1990—; writer, 1971—; vis. lectr. U. Md., 1968-69; adv. bd. Women's Equity Action League Ednl. and Legal Def. Fund, 1980—, trustee, 1974-80, Women's Equity Action League, 1971-78; adv. com. Math./Sci. Network, 1979, Wider Opportunities for Women, 1978-85, Women's Legal Def. Fund, 1978-84; Nat. Coun. for Alternative Work Patterns Inc., 1978-85, Women's Hdqs. State Nat. Bank for Women's Appointments, 1977-78, and others. Mem. adv. bd. Jour. Reprints Documents Affecting Women, 1976-78, Women's Rights Law Reporter, 1970-80; editor: (newsletters) On Campus With Women, 1971-91, About Women on Campus, 1991—; contbr. articles to profl. jours. Mem. bd. overseers Wellesley Coll. Ctr. for Rsch. on Women, 1975-87; bd. dirs. Ctr. for Women's Policy Studies, 1972-75; mem. exec. com. Inst. for Ednl. Leadership, 1982-87, mem. program adv. com., 1987-88, chair bd. dirs., 1981, chair adv. com., 1975-81; mem. affirmative action com., task force on family, nat. affairs commn. Am. Jewish Com., 1978, bd. dirs. D.C. chpt.; tech. adv. com. Nat. Jewish Family Ctr., 1980-89; adv. coun. Ednl. Devel. Ctr., 1980-85; adv. bd. Urban Inst., 1981-85, Women Employed Inst., 1981-84, Ex-New Yorkers for N.Y., 1978-79; mem. adv. com. Arthur and Elizabeth Schlesinger Libr. History of Women in Am., 1981-85; nat. adv. com. Shelter Rsch. Inst., Calif., 1980-82; chair adv. panel project on self-evaluation Am. Insts. for Rsch., 1980-82; bd. dirs. Equality Ctr., 1983, Evaluation and Tng. Inst., Calif., 1980, Inst. for Studies in Equality, 1975-77. Recipient Athena award Intercollegiate Assn. Women Students, 1974, Elizabeth Boyer award Women's Equity Action League, 1976, Rockefeller Pub. Svc. award Princeton U., 1976, Women Educators award for activism, 1987, Anna Roe award Harvard U., 1988, Readers Choice honors Washington Woman Mag., 1987, Woman of Distinction award Nat. Assn. Women in Edn.., 1991, Georgina Smith award AAUP, 1992, Woman of Achievement Turner Broadcasting System, 1994; named one of 100 Most Powerful Women Washingtonian Mag., 1982, one of the nation's 100 Most Important Women, Ladies Home Jour., 1988. Mem. Assn. for Women in Sci. Found. (bd. dirs. 1977—), Am. Soc. Profl. and Exec. Women (adv. bd. 1980). Avocations: birding, music, swimming, hiking. Office: Nat Assn Women in Edn 1350 Connecticut Ave NW Ste 850 Washington DC 20036-1733

SANDLER, GERALD HOWARD, computer science educator, company executive; b. N.Y.C., Sept. 17, 1934; s. Irving and Sally S.; m. Ann Sandler; children: Eric, Steven. BS, CUNY, 1956, MS, 1957. With Grumman Aerospace, 1963-83; past pres. Grumman Data Systems & Svcs., Bethpage, N.Y., 1983-95; pres. GHS Enterprises, 1995—; prof. computer sci. Poly. U., Farmingdale, N.Y., 1995—. Author: System Engineering, 1963. Home: 46 Bonnie Dr Westbury NY 11590-2804

SANDLER, HERBERT M., savings and loan association executive; b. N.Y.C., Nov. 16, 1931; s. William B. and Hilda (Schattan) S.; m. Marion Osher, Mar. 26, 1961. BSS, CCNY, 1951; JD, Columbia U., 1954. Bar: N.Y. 1956. Asst. counsel Waterfront Commn. N.Y. Harbor, 1956-59; partner firm Sandler & Sandler, N.Y.C., 1960-62; pres., dir., mem. exec. com. Golden West Savs. & Loan Assn. and Golden West Fin. Corp., Oakland, Calif., 1963-75; chmn. bd., co-chief exec. officer, dir., mem. exec. com. World Savs. & Loan Assn. and Golden West Fin. Corp., Oakland, 1975—; charter mem. Thrift Instns. Adv. Coun., to Fed. Res. Bd., 1980-81; former chmn. Legis. and Regulation Com. Calif. Savs. and Loan League; former mem. bd. dirs. Fed. Home Loan Bank, San Francisco. Pres., trustee Calif. Neighborhood Services Found.; chmn. Urban Housing Inst.; mem. policy adv. bd. Ctr. for Real Estate and Urban Econs. U. Calif., Berkeley. With U.S. Army, 1954-56. Office: Golden W Fin Corp 1901 Harrison St Oakland CA 94612-3574*

SANDLER, IRVING HARRY, art critic, art historian; b. N.Y.C., July 22, 1925; s. Harry and Anna (Robin) S.; m. Lucy Freeman, Sept. 4, 1958; 1 child, Catherine Harriet. BA, Temple U., 1948; MA, U. Pa., 1950; PhD, NYU, 1976. Instr. in art history NYU, 1960-71; prof. art history SUNY, Purchase, 1971—; art critic N.Y. Post, N.Y.C., 1960-65. Author: The Triumph of American Painting: A History of Abstract Expressionism, 1970, The New York School: Painters and Sculptors of the Fifties, 1978, Alex Katz, 1979, Al Held, 1984, American Art of the 1960s, 1988; editor (with Amy Newman) Defining Modern Art: Selected Writings of Alfred H. Barr Jr., 1986, Mark di Suvero at Storm King Art Ctr., 1996, Art of Postmodern Era: From Late 1960s to Early 1990s, 1996. John Simon Guggenheim fellow, 1965; Nat. Endowment for Arts fellow, 1977. Mem. Coll. Art Assn., Internat. Assn. Art Critics. Home: 100 Bleecker St New York NY 10012-2202 Office: SUNY at Purchase Dept Visual Arts 735 Anderson Hill Rd Purchase NY 10577-1445

SANDLER, JENNY, dancer; b. N.Y.C.. Scholarship student, The Joffrey Ballet Sch. Dancer Joffrey II Dancers, N.Y.C., 1988-90, The Joffrey Ballet, N.Y.C., 1990—. Featured in mag. Mirabella, Aug., 1994. Home: 25 E 9th St #7A New York NY 10003 Office: Joffrey Ballet School 434 6th Ave New York NY 10011-8411*

SANDLER, LUCY FREEMAN, art history educator; b. N.Y.C., June 7, 1930; d. Otto and Frances (Glass) Freeman; m. Irving Sandler, Sept. 4, 1958; 1 child, Catherine Harriet. B.A., Queens Coll., 1951; M.A., Columbia U., 1957; Ph.D., NYU, 1964. Asst. prof. NYU, 1964-70, assoc. prof., 1970-75, prof. fine arts, 1975-86, Helen Gould Sheppard prof. art history, 1986—, chmn. dept., 1975-89; editorial cons. Viator, UCLA, 1983—. Author: The Peterborough Psalter in Brussels, 1974, The Psalter of Robert De Lisle in the British Library, 1983, Gothic Manuscripts 1285-1385, 1986, 'Omne Bonum': A Fourteenth-Century Encyclopedia of Universal Knowledge, 1996; editor: Essays in Memory of Karl Lehmann, 1964, Art the Ape of Nature: Studies in Honor of H.W. Janson, 1981, Monograph Series, 1970-75, 86-89, Gesta, 1991-94; asst. editor Art Bull., 1964-67, mem. editl. bd., 1994; mem. editl. bd. Jour. Jewish Art, 1978, Speculum, 1994. Trustee Godwin-Ternbach Mus., Queens Coll., 1982-94. NEH fellow, 1967-68, 77; fellow Pierpont Morgan Library; Guggenheim fellow, 1988-89. Fellow Soc. Antiquaries (London); mem. AAUP, Coll. Art Assn. (pres. 1981-84), Medieval Acad. Am., Internat. Ctr. Medieval Art (adv. bd., bd. dirs. 1976-80, 84-87, 89-92, 95—). Home: 100 Bleecker St Apt 30A New York NY 10012-2207 Office: NYU Dept Fine Arts New York NY 10003

SANDLER, MARION OSHER, savings and loan association executive; b. Biddeford, Maine, Oct. 17, 1930; d. Samuel and Leah (Lowe) Osher; m. Herbert M. Sandler, Mar. 26, 1961. BA, Wellesley Coll., 1952; postgrad., Harvard U.-Radcliffe Coll., 1953; MBA, NYU, 1958; LLD (hon.), Golden Gate U., 1987. Asst. buyer Bloomingdale's (dept. store), N.Y.C., 1953-55; security analyst Dominick & Dominick, N.Y.C., 1955-61; sr. fin. analyst Oppenheimer & Co., N.Y.C., 1961-63; sr. v.p., dir. Golden West Fin. Corp. and World Savs. & Loan Assn., Oakland, Calif., 1963-75, vice chmn. bd. dirs., CEO, mem. exec. com., dir., 1975-80, pres., co- chief exec. officer, dir., mem. exec. com., 1980-93, chmn. bd. dirs., CEO, mem. exec. com., 1993—; pres., chmn. bd. dirs., CEO Atlas Assets, Inc., Oakland, 1987—, Atlas Advisers, Inc., Oakland, 1987—, Atlas Securities, Inc., Oakland, 1987—; mem. adv. com. Fed. Nat. Mortgage Assn., 1983-84. Mem. Pres.'s Mgmt. Improvement Coun., 1980, Thrift Insts. Adv. Coun. to Fed. Res. Bd., 1989-91, v.p., 1990, pres., 1991; mem. policy adv. bd. Ctr. for Real Estate and Urban Econs. U. Calif., Berkeley, 1981—, mem. exec. com. policy adv. bd., 1985—; mem. ad hoc com. to rev. Schs. Bus. Adminstrn. U. Calif., 1984-85; vice chmn. industry adv. com. Fed. Savs. and Loan Ins. Corp., 1987-88, Ins. Corp., 1987-88; bd. overseers NYU Schs. Bus., 1987-89; mem. Glass Ceiling Commn., 1992-93. Mem. Phi Beta Kappa, Beta Gamma Sigma. Office: Golden W Fin Corp 1901 Harrison St Oakland CA 94612-3574*

SANDLER, ROBERT MICHAEL, insurance company executive, actuary; b. N.Y.C., Apr. 20, 1942; s. Albert and Ruth (Marcus) S.; m. Annette L. Marchese, Aug. 18, 1963; children—David, Glenn. B.A. in Math., Hofstra U., 1963. Various actuarial positions Met. Life, N.Y.C., 1963-68; various actuarial positions Am. Internat., N.Y.C., 1968-80; v.p., casualty actuary American Internat. Group, Inc., N.Y.C., 1980-84, sr. v.p., sr. actuary, sr. claims officer, 1984-95, exec. v.p., 1995—, dir. various subs. Mem. Casualty Acturial Soc. (assoc.), Am. Acad. Actuaries, Internat. Actuarial Assn., Am. Internat. Underwriters (chmn. 1994—). Republican. Home: 3 Crestwood Dr Bridgewater NJ 08807-2209 Office: Am Internat Group 70 Pine St New York NY 10270-0002

SANDLER, ROSS, law educator; b. Milw., Jan. 31, 1939; s. Theodore T. and Laurette (Simons) S.; m. Alice R. Mintzer, Sept. 15, 1968; children: Josephine, Jenny, Dorothy. AB, Dartmouth Coll., 1961; LLB, NYU, 1965. Bar: N.Y. 1965, Fla. 1965. Assoc. atty. Cahill Gordon Reindel & Ohl, N.Y.C., 1965-68; asst. U.S. atty. So. Dist. N.Y., 1968-72; assoc. atty. Trubin Sillcocks Edelman & Knapp, N.Y.C., 1972-75; sr. staff atty. Natural Resources Def. Coun., N.Y.C., 1975-81, 83-86; spl. advisor to mayor City of N.Y., 1981-82; exec. dir. Hudson River Found., N.Y.C., 1983-86; commr. N.Y.C. Dept. Transp., 1986-90; ptnr. Jones Day Reavis & Pogue, N.Y.C., 1991-93; law prof. N.Y. Law Sch., 1993—, dir. Ctr. for N.Y.C. law, 1993—; mem. N.Y.C. Procurement Policy Bd., 1994—; vis. lectr. Yale Law Sch., New Haven, 1977; adj. prof. law NYU Law Sch., 1976-94; chair, mem. N.Y.C. Taxi and Limousine Commn., 1980-90. Co-author: A New Direction in Transit, 1978; columnist Environ. Mag., 1976-80; editor: (jour.) City Law; contbr. book chpt., op-ed columns, articles to profl. jours.; lectr. environ. law, spkr. confs. Trustee Woods Hole (Mass.) Rsch. Ctr., 1983—; mem. exec. com. Hudson River Found., 1986-96; mem. adv. coun. Ctr. Biodiversity and Conservation Am. Mus. Nat. History, 1996—. Recipient Pub. Interest award NYU Law Alumni, 1987, Louis J. Lefkowitz award Fordham Law Sch. Urban Law Jour., 1989. Mem. City Club of N.Y. (chair 1992-93, trustee). Office: NY Law Sch 57 Worth St New York NY 10013-2926

SANDLER, STANLEY IRVING, chemical engineering educator; b. N.Y.C., June 10, 1940; s. Murray C. and Celia M. (Kamenetsky) S.; m. Judith Katherine Ungar, June 17, 1962; children: Catherine Julietta, Joel Abraham, Michael Howard. BChemE, CCNY, 1962; PhD, U. Minn., 1966. NSF postdoctoral fellow Inst. Molecular Physics, U. Md., College Park, 1966-67; successively asst. prof., assoc. prof., prof. dept. chem. engring. U. Del., Newark, 1967-82, H.B. du Pont prof., 1982—, chmn. dept., 1982-86, dir. Ctr. for Molecular and Engring. Thermodynamics, 1992—, interim dean Coll. of Engring., 1992; vis. prof. Imperial Coll., London, 1973-74, U. Nat. del Sur, Bahia Blanca, Argentina, 1985, Tech. U., Berlin, 1981, 88-89, U. Queensland, Brisbane, Australia, 1989, 96, U. Calif., Berkeley, 1995; cons. maj. oil and chem. cos. Author: Chemical and Engineering Thermodynamics, 1977, 2d rev. edit., 1989; editor: Fluid Properties and Phase Equilibria, 1977, Chemical Engineering Education in a Changing Environment, 1989, Kinetic and Thermodynamic Lumping of Multicomponent Mixtures, 1991, Models for Thermodynamic and Phase Equilibria Calculations, 1993; mem. adv. bd. Jour. Chem. Engring. Data, Chem. Engring. Edn., Indsl. Engring. Chem. Rsch., Indian Chem. Engr., Engring. Sci. and Tech. (Malaysia); also numerous articles. Mem. adv. bd. chem. engring. La. State U., Carnegie-Mellon U. Recipient U.S. sr. Scientist award Alexander von Humboldt Found., 1988, Francis Alison award U. Del., 1993, Ashton Cary award Ga. Tech. U., 1994, Phillips Lecture award Okla. State U., 1993. Mem. AIChE (jour. adv. bd., Profl. Progress award 1984, Warren K. Lewis award 1996), U.S. Nat. Acad. Engring., Am. Chem. Soc. (award Del. sect. 1989), Am. Soc. Engring. Edn. (lectr. chem. engring. div. 1988), Cosmos Club (Washington). Jewish. Avocations: jogging, philately. Home: 202 Sypherd Dr Newark DE 19711-3627 Office: U Del Dept Chem Engring Newark DE 19716

SANDLER, SUMNER GERALD, medical educator; b. Lawrence, Mass., Jan. 13, 1935; s. Maurice Lewis and Dorothy Gretchen (Alman) S.; m. Katherine Cushing Rosenberg, May 9, 1969; children: Lisah, David, Jonathan, Joel. AB, Princeton U., 1957; MD, NYU, 1962. Diplomate Am. Bd. Internal Medicine, Am. Bd. Pathology (blood banking). Intern NYU-Bellevue Hosp. Ctr., N.Y.C., 1962-63, assoc. med. resident, 1963-64; clin. assoc. NCI, NIH, 1964-66; hematology fellow NYU-Bellevue Hosp. Ctr., N.Y.C., 1966-68; clin. assoc. NIH, 1964-66; teaching asst. NYU Sch. Medicine, N.Y.C., 1966-67; instr. medicine Georgetown U., Washington, 1968-72, asst. prof. medicine, 1970-72, prof. medicine and pathology, 1991—; sr. lectr. Hebrew U.-Hadassah Med. Ctr., Jerusalem, 1972-78, assoc. prof. medicine, 1977-78; assoc. dir. blood svcs. nat. hdqs. ARC, Washington, 1978-84, assoc. v.p., 1984-90, med. dir., 1989-90, chief med. officer, 1990-91; med. dir. Nat. Reference Lab., ARC, Rockville, Md., 1978-95; sr. lectr. Hebrew U. Sch. Medicine Hebrew U. Hadassah Sch. Medicine, Jerusalem, 1977-78; head blood bank, Hadassah U. Hosp., Jerusalem, 1972-78; profl. lectr. dept. medicine, George Washington U. Sch. Medicine, Washington, 1988-91, others. Editor: Immunobiology of the Erythrocyte, 1980, Autologous Transfusion, 1983, Advances in Immunobiology, 1984; mem. editl. bd. Haematologia, 1990—, Transfusion, 1982—, Immunohematology, 1995—. Lt. Comdr. USPHS, 1964-66; capt. med. corps. reserve, Israel Def. Forces, 1976-81; bd. mgrs. Adas Israel Congregation, Washington, 1986-92. Recipient Vicenniel medal Georgetown U., Washington, 1989. Fellow Am. Coll. Physicians, Coll. Am. Pathologists; mem. Internat. Soc. Blood Transfusion (hon., counsellor 1986-91, v.p. 1991-94, Svc. award 1990), Am. Assn. Blood Banks, Leukemia Soc. Am. (med. adv. bd. 1970-72, D.C. chpt. chmn. 1971-72, bd. dirs. 1970-72), Israel Soc. Hematology and Blood Transfusion (exec. com. 1976), Am. Soc. Hematology, others. Jewish. Avocation: Torah Bible study. Home: 5808 Ogden Ct Bethesda MD 20816-1263 Office: Georgetown U Med Ctr 3800 Reservoir Rd NW Washington DC 20007-2113

SANDLER, THOMAS R., accountant; b. Mt. Kisco, N.Y., Dec. 16, 1946; s. Louis and Susan (Rosen) S.; m. Alison G. Corneau, Aug. 26, 1972; children—Justin C., Shawn A. B.S. summa cum laude, Ithaca Coll., 1968; M.S., SUNY-Binghamton, 1972. C.P.A., N.Y., Colo. 1982. Asst. acct. KPMG Peat Marwick, White Plains, N.Y., 1972; mgr. KPMG Peat Marwick, Phoenix, 1975; sr. mgr. KPMG Peat Marwick, N.Y.C., 1978; ptnr. KPMG Peat Marwick, Denver, 1981-92; ptnr. in-charge corp. recovery svcs. KPMG Peat Marwick, N.Y.C., 1993-94; mng. ptnr. BDO Seidman, Denver, 1994-95; CFO, treas., sec. Samsonite Corp., Denver, 1995—. Contbr. articles to profl. jours. Past trustee, past pres. Colo. Children's Chorale; treas., past pres., gov., mem. exec. com., committeeman Colo. Golf Assn.; committeeman U.S. Golf Assn. bd. dirs. Pacific Coast GOlf Assn. Served with USMC, 1968-70. Mem. Colo. Soc. C.P.A.s (chmn. real estate and govt. acctg. com.), Am. Inst. C.P.A.s. Clubs: Columbine Country (Littleton, Colo.); Whippoorwill Country (Armonk N.Y.); Bear Creek Golf. Home: 896 Anaconda Ct Castle Rock CO 80104 Office: Samsonite Corp South Tower 11200 E 45th Ave Denver CO 80239-3018

SANDLIN, MAX ALLEN, JR., congressman; b. Texarkana, Ark., Sept. 29, 1952; s. Max Allen and Margie Beth (Barnett) S.; m. Leslie Ann Howell; children: Hillary, Max III, Emily. BA, Baylor U., 1975, JD, 1978. Bar: Tex. Assoc. Huffman & Palmer, Inc., Marshall, Tex., 1978-82; ptnr. Sandlin & Buckner, Marshall, 1982—; judge Country of Harrison, Marshall, 1986-89; county ct. judge Country of Harrison, 1989—; v.p., gen. counsel Howol & Sandlin, Inc., 1990—; mem. 105th Congress from 1st Tex dist., 1997—; mem. exec. com. Tex. Supreme Ct. Jud. Edn. Com., Austin, 1987—; bd. dirs. Security State Bank, Elysian Fields, Tex., East Tex. Legal Svcs., Nacogdoches; bd. dirs., treas. East Tex. Housing & Fin. Corp., Marshall, 1990—. Chairman Harrison County Dem. Party, Marshall, 1982-88; mem. exec. com. Marshall-Harrison County Industries, Marshall, 1986-89; founder, sponsor, mem. Michelson-Reves Mus. Art; post supr. Boy Scouts Am., 1982-86; mgr. Marshall Youth Baseball, 1980. Recipient Appreciation award Tex. Dept. Human Resourcs, 1985. Mem. Harrison County Bar Assn. (pres. 1982-84), Baylor U. Alumni Assn. (bd. dirs.), Marshall Symphony Soc. (bd. dirs. 1988-90), Marshall Rotary. Baptist. Avocations: politics, racquetball, golf, baseball, classical cars. Home: 500 Miller Dr Marshall TX 75670-4634 Office: 214 Cannon Washington DC 20515-4301

SANDLOW, LESLIE JORDAN, physician, educator; b. Chgo., Jan. 7, 1934; s. Harry H. and Rose (Ehrlich) S.; m. Joanne J. Fleischer, June 16, 1957; children; Jay, Bruce, Lisa. BS, U. Ill., 1956; MD, Chgo. Med. Sch., 1960. Intern Michael Reese Hosp. and Med. Ctr., Chgo., 1961, med. resident, rsch. fellow gastrointestinal rsch., 1961-64, physician-in-charge clin. gastroenterology lab., 1963-74, asst. attending physician, 1964-67, assoc. attending physician, 1967-72, vice chmn. divsn. gastroenterology, dir. ambulatory medicine, 1968, dir. ambulatory care, 1969-76, attending physician, 1972—, assoc. med. dir., 1972-73; clin. asst. Chgo. Med. Sch., 1963-68, clin. instr., 1966; asst. prof. dept. medicine Pritzker Sch. Medicine, U. Chgo., 1973-76, assoc. prof., 1976-85, prof., 1985-90; prof. clin. medicine and med. edn. U. Ill. Coll. Medicine, Chgo., 1990-91, prof. medicine and med. edn., 1992—, sr. assoc. dean for grad. and continuing med. edn., 1993—, head dept. med. edn., 1993—, sr. assoc. dean for med. edn., 1994—; dep. v.p. profl. affairs Michael Reese Hosp. and Med. Ctr., 1973-78, dir. Office Ednl. Affairs, 1976-81, assoc. v.p. acad. affairs, 1978-82, dir. quality assurance program, 1981-91, v.p. planning, 1982-83, v.p. profl. affairs and planning, 1983-88, dir. divsn. internal medicine, 1986-93, v.p. profl. and acad. affairs, 1988-91, med. dirs. acad. and med. affairs, 1992-94; med. dir. Michael Reese Health Plan, Inc., 1972-74, interim exec. dir., 1976-77; cons. gastroenterologist Ill. Ctrl. Hosp., 1978-80; vis. prof. Pontifica U. Catolica Rio Grande do Sul, Brazil, 1978, U. Fed. Espirito Santo, Brazil, 1978, Nordic Fedn. for Med. Understanding, Akureyri, Iceland, 1978, Seoul Nat. U. Sch. Medicine, 1981, Coll. Physicians and Surgsons, Kharachi, Pakistan, 1994, U. Tex., Ft. Worth, 1977, U. Ariz., Tucson, 1977, Loyola U. Med. Sch., Maywood, Ill., 1979; cons. in field; coord. Health Scis. Librs. in Ill.; mem. Midwest Med. Libr. Network; mem. subcom. on delivery of ambulatory med. care Inst. Medicine Chgo.; mem. cmty. resources task force Interinstnl. Cardiovascular Ctr.; chmn. steering group Ill. Regional Med. Program; past co-chmn. curriculum com. U. Chgo. Reviewer Rsch. in Med. Edn./Assn. Am. Med. Colls., 1985—, Acad. Medicine/Assn. Am. Med. Colls., 1989; contbr. numerous articles to profl. publs. Mem. Skokie (Ill.) Bd. Health, 1973-85, chmn., 1976-85; bd. dirs. Group Health Assn. Am., 1976-78, Portes Ctr., 1980—; bd. dirs. Good Health Program Skokie Valley Hosp., 1978-80; bd. dirs., exec. com. Rsch. and Edn. Found. of Michael Reese Hosp. Med. Staff, 1992—. Recipient numerous grants, including NIH, 1988, Michael Reese Hosp. Found., 1994-95, Chgo. Cmty. Trust, 1994-95. Fellow Am. Coll. Gastroenterology; mem. N.Y. Acad. Scis., Inst. Medicine, Assn. Am. Med. Colls., Am. Coll. Physician Execs. (co-chair resource mgmt. com. of quality assurance forum), Soc. Dirs. Med. Coll. Continuing Med. Edn., Soc. Dir. Rsch. in Med. Edn. Home: 2314 N Lincoln Park W Chicago IL 60614-3454 Office: U Ill Coll Medicine Med Edn MC 784 1819 W Polk St Chicago IL 60612-7331

SANDMAN, IRVIN W(ILLIS), lawyer; b. Seattle, Mar. 19, 1954. BA summa cum laude, U. Wash., 1976; JD, UCLA, 1980. Bar: U.S. Dist. Ct. (we. and ea. dists.) Wash. 1980. Prin. Graham & Dunn, Seattle, 1980—. Staff mem. UCLA Law Review. Mem. ABA (subcom. chmn. hospitality law com. 1996—), Wash. State Bar Assn. (chmn. creditor/debtor sect. 1988-90, editor newsletter 1984—, speaker continuing legal edn.). Office: Graham & Dunn 1420 5th Ave Fl 33 Seattle WA 98101-2333

SANDMAN, PETER M., risk communication consultant; b. N.Y.C., Apr. 18, 1945; s. Howard Edwin and Gertrude Leah (Orgel) S.; m. Susan Marie Goertzel, June 18, 1967 (div. 1975); m. Jody Sue Lanard, June 10, 1990; children: Alison, Jennifer; 1 stepchild, James Sachs. BA in Psychology, Princeton U., 1967; MA in Comm., Stanford U., 1968, PhD, 1971. Reporter Toronto (Ont.) Star, Can., 1966; stringer Time, 1966-67; instr. comm. Stanford (Calif.) U., 1968-70; instr. journalism Calif. State Coll., Hayward, 1970; sr. editor The Magazine, 1970; asst. prof. Ohio State U., Columbus, 1971-72; asst. prof. natural resources, journalism U. Mich., Ann Arbor, 1972-75, assoc. prof. natural resources, 1975-77; assoc. prof. comm., coord. Cook Coll. comm. program Rutgers U., New Brunswick, N.J., 1977-83, prof. journalism, 1983-94, prof. dept. human ecology, 1992-94; adj. prof., 1994—; adj. prof. TV, radio Ithaca (N.Y.) Coll., 1976, grad. program in pub. health Rutgers U., 1986—, dept. environ. and cmty. medicine Robert Wood Johnson Med. Sch., Rutgers U., 1987—; adv. com. environ./occupl. health info. program 1984-89; founder, dir. environ. comm. rsch. program N.J. Agrl. Exptl. Sta., Rutgers U., 1986-92; vis. scholar urban and environ. policy Tufts U., Medford, Mass., 1990-91; rsch. prof. George Perkins Marsh Inst., Clark U.; comm. coun. Environ. Def. Fund, 1985—; bd. advisors grad. program in tech. and sci. comm. Drexel U., Phila., 1988—; cons. on comm. ACP, 1976-79, The Cousteau Soc., 1977-79, Pres. Com. on the Accident at Three Mile Island; specialist in comm. coop. ext. svc. U.S. Dept. Agr., 1977-86; cons. risk commn. office policy analysis EPA, 1986-88; exec. com. Sci. Writing Educators Group, 1978-81; cons. ARCO Chem., Boise Cascade, Chevron, Ciba-Geigy, Consumers Power, Dow, Du Pont, Johnson and Johnson, Johnson Wax, Procter and Gamble, Union Carbide, others. Cons. editor Random House, 1982-89, McGraw-Hill, 1989-94, Holt, Rinehart and Winston, 1978-81; contbg. editor Apt. Life, 1971-75; freelance writer, 1966—; editl. bd. Pub. Rels. Rsch. Ann., 1981-91, Jour. Pub. Rels. Rsch., 1991-94; editl. adv. bd. Environ. and Behavior, 1976-86; contbr. articles to profl. jours. Bd. dirs. N.J. Environ. Lobby, 1984-90, Nuclear Dialogue Project, 1985-90, pres. 1986-90; pub. info. com. N.J. chpt., Am. Cancer Soc., 1981-86, vice-chmn., 1983-86; comm. coord. N.J. Campaign for a Nuclear Weapons Freeze, 1982-85; socioeconomic subcom., com. on biotechnology agr. divsn. Nat. Assn. State Univs. and Land Grant Colls., 1988-90; bd. advisors Environ. Scientists for Global Survival, 1988-91; sci. review panel, radium/radon adv. bd. N.J. Dept. Environ. Protection, 1987-88; com. to survey the health effects mustard gas and lewisite Inst. Medicine, NAS, 1992.

Mem. AAUP, ACLU (bd. dirs. N.J. chpt. 1984-87), Environ. Def. Fund, Nat. Assn. Profl. Environ. Communicators, Sci. Writing Educators Group, Soc. for Risk Analysis, Soc. Environ. Journalists, Internat. Assn. Pub. Participation Practitioners, Sigma Delta Chi. Home: 54 Gray Cliff Rd Newton Center MA 02159-2017

SANDMEL, BEN, journalist, musician; b. Nashville, June 8, 1952; s. Samuel and Frances (Fox) S. BA in Folklore, Ind. U., 1976. Fieldwork researcher La. Folklife Program, 1984—; drummer Hackberry Ramblers; presenter, writer La. Folklife Festival; programming cons. New Orleans Jazz and Heritage Festival, Folk Masters Concert Series, Wolf Trap, Vienna, Va.; pres. Hot Biscuits Rec. Co. Author record liner notes for more than 75 albums, music criticism for Atlantic Monthly, Rolling Stone; prodr.: (albums) Drinkin' and Stinkin' (Boogie Bill Webb), Cincinnati Stomp (Big Joe Duskin), Cajun Boogie (Hackberry Ramblers), Deep Water (Hackberry Ramblers); contbr. travel articles to Esquire. Mem. NARAS, Am. Folklore Soc., Press Club of New Orleans (Critical Rev. of Yr. award 1984, 91). Home: 221 Metairie Ct Metairie LA 70001

SANDMEYER, E. E., toxicologist, consultant; b. Winterthur, Zurich, Switzerland, Aug. 9, 1929; came to U.S., 1955; d. Fritz Henry and Aline (Schoch) S. BSChemE, Technikum, Winterthur, 1951; MS in Organic Chemistry, Ohio State U., 1960, PhD in Biochemistry, 1965. Cert. civil svc. chemist II, Nev., biochemist II, Pa., clin. lab. dir. Ctrs. for Disease Control. Head corp. toxicology Gulf Oil Corp., Pitts., 1971-75; div. head organic analysis Barringer Labs., Denver, 1986-88; pres., toxicologist, owner Transcontec, Inc., Kelseyville, Calif., 1976—; Contbg. author: Patty's Industrial Hygiene and Toxicology, 1981, A Guide to General Toxicology, 1983. Mem. AAAS, Am. Chem. Soc., Soc. Environ. Health, Sigma Xi, Sigma Delta Epsilon. Office: Transcontec Inc 7305 Live Oak Dr Kelseyville CA 95451-9677

SANDMEYER, ROBERT LEE, university dean, economist; b. Evansville, Ind., June 12, 1929; s. Orville G. Sandmeyer and Elizabeth Chandler; m. Loretta Mae Jacobs, Aug. 5, 1950; children: Karen, Bridgit, Barbara, Robert C. B.A., Ft. Hays State U., 1956; M.S., Okla. State U., 1958, Ph.D., 1962. Instr. Ft. Hays (Kans.) State U., 1957-58; instr. Iowa State U., 1958-59; asst. prof. econs. Ariz. State U., 1961-62; asst. prof. Okla. State U., 1962-65, assoc. prof., 1965-70, prof., dean Coll. Bus. Adminstrn., 1977-94, dean emeritus Coll. Bus. Adminstrn., 1994—; econ. adv. Ariz. Gov.'s Tax Study Com., 1961-62; adv. Okla. Gov.'s Com. on Mental Health, 1963; bd. dirs. Reading & Bates Corp.; adviser to Coll. Bus. and Econs., United Arab Emirates U., 1994—. Contbr. articles to profl. publs. With USN, 1947-51. Mem. So. Econ. Assn., Phi Kappa Phi, Beta Gamma Sigma. Democrat. Roman Catholic. Home: Oklahoma State U 1906 Iba Dr Stillwater OK 74074

SANDOR, GEORGE NASON, mechanical engineer, educator; b. Budapest, Hungary, Feb. 24, 1912; came to U.S., 1938, naturalized, 1949; s. Alexander S. and Maria (Adler) S.; m. Magda Breiner, Dec. 5, 1964; stepchildren: Stephen Gergely, Judith Patricia Gergely (Mrs. J. Peter Vernon). Diploma in Mech. Engring, Poly. U. Budapest, 1934; D. Eng. Sci., Columbia U., 1959; D (hon.), Budapest Technol. U., 1986. Registered profl. engr., Fla., N.J., N.Y., N.C., cert. of qualification Nat. Council Engring. Examiners. Asst. to chief engr. Hungarian Rubber Co., Budapest, 1935-36; mfg. dept. head Hungarian Rubber Co., 1936-38; design engr. Babcock Printing Press Corp., New London, Conn., 1939-44; v.p., chief engr. H.W. Faeber Corp., N.Y.C., 1944-46; chief engr. Time Inc. Graphic Arts Research Labs., Springdale, Conn., 1946-61, Huck Co., Inc., N.Y.C., 1961; assoc. prof. mech. engring. Yale, 1961-66; prof. mech. engring. Rennselaer Poly. Inst., Troy, N.Y., 1966-67; Alcoa Found. prof. mech. design, chmn. machines and structures div. Rennselaer Poly. Inst., 1967-75; rsch. prof. mech. engring. U. Fla., Gainesville, 1976-89, rsch. prof. emeritus, 1989—; dir. mech. engring. design and rotordynamics labs. U. Fla., 1979-87; instr. engring. U. Conn. Extension, New London and Norwich, 1940-44; lectr. mech. engring. Columbia U., N.Y.C., 1961-62; dir. Huck Design Corp., Huck Co., Inc., Montvale, N.J., 1964-70; cons. engr., printing equipment and automatic machinery, mech. engring. design, 1961—; cons. NSF Departmental and Instl. Devel. Program, 1970-72; cons. nat. materials adv. bd. Nat. Acad. Scis., 1974; cons. Xerox Corp., Burroughs Corp., Govt. Products div. Pratt & Whitney Aircraft Co., Time Inc., also others, 1961-92; prin. investigator, co-investigator NSF, U.S. Army Research Office and NASA sponsored research at Yale U.; dir. and co-dir. NSF, U.S. Army Research Office and NASA sponsored research at Rensselaer Poly. Inst. and; U. Fla. at Gainesville; chief U.S.A. del. to Internat. Fedn. for Theory Machines and Mechanisms, 1969-75; cons. for materials conservation through design Office Tech. Assessment, Congress U.S., 1977. Author: (with others) Mechanical Design and Systems Handbook, 1964, 2d edit., 1985, Linkage Design Handbook, 1977, Mechanism Design-Analysis and Synthesis, vol. 1, 1984, 2d edit., 1991, Advanced Mechanism Design, Analysis and Synthesis, vol. 2, 1984; mem. editorial bd. Jour. Mechanism, 1966-72, Machine and Mechanism Theory, 1972—, Robotica, 1982—; contbr. articles to profl. jours. Recipient Outstanding Achievement awrd Northctrl. sect. Fla. Engring. Soc., 1983; Fla. Blue Key Leadership award for disting. faculty mem. U. Fla., 1985; elected hon. mem. Internat. Fedn. for Theory Machines and Mechanisms, 1987, Hungarian Acad. Scis., Budapest, 1993. Fellow ASME (life, Machine Design award 1975, mechanisms com. award 1980, hon. mem. 1991); mem. NSPE, Am. Soc. Engring. Edn. (Ralph Coats Roe award 1985), N.Y. Acad. Scis., Am. Acad. Mechanics, Hungarian Acad. Scis. (hon. mem. 1993), Flying Engrs. Internat., Sigma Xi, Tau Beta Pi, Pi Tau Sigma. Achievements include patent for rotary-linear actuator for robotic manipulators, and 5 others. Home: 136 Broadview Acres Highlands NC 28741-9454 *Find out what is expected of you and try to fulfill those expectations to the best of your ability.*

SANDOR, GYORGY, pianist; b. Budapest, Hungary; came to U.S., 1938, naturalized, 1943; s. Ignac and Zsenka (Czipszer) S.; 1 child, Michael. Student, Liszt Ferenc Conservatory, Budapest, 1927-33; studied piano with, Bela Bartok; composition with, Zoltan Kodaly. Mem. piano faculty Juilliard Sch., 1982—. Made concert debut, Budapest, 1931; toured, Europe, 1931-38, Am. debut Carnegie Hall, N.Y.C., 1939, touring throughout U.S., Mexico, Can., W.I., North Africa, C.Am., S.Am., Europe, Australia, Far East; rec. with N.Y. Philharm. and Phila. orchs., also solo rec. (Grand Prix du Disque for rec. entire piano repertory of Bela Bartok's works 1964); rec. entire solo piano repertory of Prokofiev, 1967, Kodály, 1973; author: On Piano Playing, 1981; world premiers include Bartok's 3d Piano Concerto, Ormandy and Phila. Orch., 1946, Dance Suite, Carnegie Hall, 1945, Concerto for Orch., piano version by Bartok, 1990, Sony Classical, Vox Candide Turnabout, Columbia Records, Trio, Phillips Records; compact discs include entire solo piano repertory by Bartok and Prokofieff.

SANDOR, RICHARD LAURENCE, financial company executive; b. N.Y.C., Sept. 7, 1941; s. Randolph Henry and Luba (Mirner) S.; m. Ellen Ruth Simon, June 27, 1963; children: Julie, Penya. B.A., CCNY, 1962; Ph.D., U. Minn., 1967. Asst. prof. applied econs. U. Calif, Berkeley, 1966-72; v.p., chief economist Chgo. Bd. Trade, 1972-75; v.p. ContiCommodity Services, Chgo., 1975-82; dir. ContiFin div. ContiCommodity Services, Chgo., 1975-82; sr. v.p. instl. fin. futures Drexel Burnham Lambert, Inc., Chgo., 1982-90; pres., CEO Indosuez Internat. Capital Markets, Chgo., 1990-93; chmn. Indosuez Carr Futures, 1990-91; mem. Chgo. Bd. Trade, 1975—, bd. dirs., vice chmn., 2d vice chmn., 1996—; exec. mng. dir. Kidder, Peabody Inc., N.Y.C., 1991-93; pres., CEO Centre Fin. Products Ltd., 1993— ; mem. Index and Option Market, 1983—, bd. dirs. Chgo. Mercantile Exch., Internat. Ctr. Photography, N.Y.C., First Fed. Savs. & Loan Assn. of Chgo., Sch. Art Inst. Chgo.; vis. scholar Northwestern U., 1972-74; Martin C. Remer vis. Disting. prof. fin. Grad. Sch. Mgmt., 1974-75; cons. agribus. orgns., securities firms, banks, fgn. exchs., govts., 1969—; mem. faculty NYU, 1964; mem. faculty U. Minn., 1863-67; mem. faculty Stanford U., 1969; disting. adj. prof. Grad. Sch. Bus. Columbia U., 1993; expert advisor UNCTAD; guest lectr. various univs. Contbr. articles to profl. journs., chpts. of books and handbooks. Vice chmn. bd. govs. Sch. of Art Inst. of Chgo.; bd. dirs. Lincoln Park Zool. Soc., 1985—. Summer faculty fellow U. Calif.; NSF grantee. Mem. Am. Econ. Assn., Econometric Soc., Am. Fin. Assn., Am. Agrl. Econs. Assn. Club: Union League of Chgo. Home: 1301 N Astor St Chicago IL 60610-2186 Office: One Chase Manhattan Plz 42nd fl New York NY 10005

SANDORFY, CAMILLE, chemistry educator; b. Budapest, Hungary, Dec. 9, 1920; emigrated to Can., 1951, naturalized, 1957; s. Kamill and Paula (Fenyes) S.; m. Rolande Cayla, Aug. 24, 1971. B.Sc., U. Szeged, Hungary, 1943, Ph.D., 1946; D.Sc., Sorbonne, U. Paris, 1949; PhD (hon.), U. Moncton, N.B., Can., 1986, U. Szeged, Hungary, 1988. Attache de recherches Centre National de la Recherche Scientifique, Paris, France, 1947-51; postdoctoral fellow Nat. Research Council of Can., 1951-53; asst. prof. chemistry U. Montreal, Que., Can., 1954-56; assoc. prof. U. Montreal, 1956-59, prof., 1959—; vis. prof. U. Paris, 1968, 74, univs. in Naples, Italy, 1969, Rio de Janeiro, Brazil, 1970, 82, Lille, France, 1987. Author: Les Spectres Electroniques en Chimie Theorique, 1959, Electronic Spectra and Quantum Chemistry, 1964; (with R. Daudel) Semi-empirical Wave-Mechanical Calculations on Polyatomic Molecules, 1971. Recipient Prix Marie-Victorin Que., 1982, medal Chem. Inst. Can., 1983, Sci. prize of Que., 1964, Herzberg medal, 1980, Killam meml. scholar, 1978, Compagnon de Lavoisier (Que.), 1992, Heyrovsky gold medal Czech Acad. Sci., 1993; decorated Officer of Order of Can., 1995, Chevalier, Ordre du Quebec, 1995. Fellow Royal Soc. Can., Internat. Acad. Quantum Molecular Sci., Hungarian Acad. Sci. Rsch. over 250 publs. in chemistry. Address: 5050 Roslyn, Montreal, PQ Canada H3W 2L2

SANDOVAL, ARTURO ALONZO, art educator, artist; b. Espanola/Cordova, N.Mex., Feb. 1, 1942; s. Lorenzo Sandoval and Cecilia Eulalia (Archuleta) Harrison; (div. Sept. 1982); 1 child, Avalon Valentine Galaglorial. Student, U. Portland, 1959; BA, Calif. State Coll., L.A., 1964, MA, 1969; MFA, Cranbrook Acad. Art, Bloomfield Hills, Mich., 1971. Designer, illustrator Western Lighting Corp., L.A., 1964-66; advt. designer, adult edn. instr. spl. svcs. USN, Yokosuka, Japan, 1966; interior designasst. Walter B. Broderick & Assocs., La Mesa, Calif., 1967; asst. prof. art dept. U. Ky., Lexington, 1974-76, assoc. prof., 1976-86, full prof., 1986—, dir. art dept. Barnhart Gallery, 1976—, curator, 1979—; teaching asst. Calif. State Coll., L.A., 1969, Cranbrook Acad. Art, Bloomfield Hills, 1969-71; fiber art demonstrator Mus. Art, Grand Rapids, Mich., 1970; batik and tie-dye demonstrator Gwynn's Fabric Shop, Birmingham, Mich., 1970; instr. Calif. State Coll., L.A., 1970, So. Ill. U., Carbondale, 1971, Edwardsville, 1971, 72, asst. prof., 1971-73; presenter various lectures and workshops throughout the U.S., 1973—; juror Mo.Women Festival Arts, St. Louis, So. Ill. U., East St. Louis, 1974, Paramount Arts Assn., Ashland, Ky., 1975, Ind. Weavers Guild, Indpls., 1979, Fed. Corrections Inst., Lexington, 1979, Hawaii Craftsman Hui and Art Dept. U. Hawaii, Manoa, Honolulu, 1982, art dept. Va. Intermont Coll., Bristol, 1982, Arrowmont Sch. Arts and Crafts, Gatlinburg, Tenn., 1984, Ctr. Contemporary Art, U. Ky., Lexington, 1984, Guild Greater Cin.,Carnegie Art Ctr., Covington, Ky., 1989, S.C. Arts Commn., Charleston, 1990, Adams Art Gallery, Dunkirk, N.Y., 1994; visual arts cons. Ky. Arts Commn., Frankfort, 1977; curator Visual Arts Ctr. Alaska, Anchorage, 1982, Ky. Art and Crafts Found., Inc., Louisville, 1985 ; mem. artist adv. panel Ky. Art and Crafts Found., Louisville, 1986, 87, 92, 93, 94; visual arts cons. Arts Midwest, 1987; artistic advisor Ky. Guild Mktg. Bd., Berea, 1988, 91, 92, 93; bd. mem. Ky. Guild Mktg. Bd., 1992, Am. Craft Coun., N.Y.C.; vis. artist/critic Allen R. Hite Inst., U. Louisville, 1992; vis. artist Coll. Human Environ. Scis., U. Ky., Lexington, 1993; vis. artist/ lectr. fiber dept. Cranbrook Acad. Art, Bloomfield Hills, Mich., 1994. Exhibited in group shows at Yeiser Art Ctr., Paducah/Paramount Arts Ctr., Ashland/S.E. Cmty. Coll., Cumberland, 1994, Textile Arts Centre, Chgo., 1994, Winnipeg (Man., Can.) Art Gallery, 1994, Riffe Gallery, Ohio Arts Coun., Columbus, 1994, Royal Hiberian Acad., Gallagher Gallery, Dublin, Ireland, Cooper Gallery, Barnsley, South Yorks, Gt. Britain, Shipley Art Gallery,Gateshead, Gt. Britain, 1994, Grand Rapids (Mich.) Art Mus., 1994, Whatcom Mus. History and Art, Bellingham, Wash., The Rockwell Mus., Corning, N.Y., Mus. Art, Washington State U., Pullman,The Hyde Collection, Glen Falls, N.Y., 1994, U. Art Galleries, U. S.D., Vermillion, 1994, Barnhart Gallery, U. Ky., Lexington, 1994, Sawtooth Ctr. Visual Art, 1994, Santa Fe Gallery, Santa Fe Cmty. Coll., Gainesville, Fla., 1994, Liberty Gallery, Louisville, 1994, Asahi Shimbun Gallery, Tokyo, Takashimaya Gallery, Osaka, 1994, Minn. Mus. Art, Landmark Ctr., St. Paul, 1994, S.C. State Mus., Columbia, 1994, Galbreath Gallery, Lexington, 1994, others; represented in permanent collections at Wabash Coll., Crawfordsville, Ind., Greenville County Mus. Art, Greenville, S.C., Mus. Modern Art, N.Y.C., St. Mary's Coll., Notre Dame, Ind., Coll. St. Rose, Albany, N.Y., Bowling Green (Ohio) StateU., U. Notre Dame, Transylvania U., Lexington, U. Ky. Mus. Art, Lexington, Mid-Am. Rare Coin Auction Galleries, Lexington, Henry Luce Found., N.Y.C., Lexington Ctrl. Libr., others. Recipient Alexandra Korsakoff Galston Meml. prize St. Louis Artist's Guild, 1971, Mus. Merit award Mus. Arts and Scis., Evansville, 1972, Creative Rsch. Grant So. Ill. U.-Edwardsville Rsch. Found., 1972, Craftsman fellowship Nat. Endowment for Arts, Washington, 1973, Friend of Mus. award Mus. Arts and Scis., Evansville, 1973, Clay Eugene Jordan ann. bequest prize for crafts St. Louis Artist's Guild, 1973, Teaching Improvement grant U. Ky. Rsch. Found., 1974, Travel grant U. Ky. Rsch. Found., 1977, Judges Choice award Berea (Ky.) Coll., 1978, Handweaver's Guild Am. award, 1978, Fiber award LeMoyne Art Found., Tallahassee, 1981, Elise Strout Merit award Mus. Arts and Scis., Evansville, 1981, Handweavers Guild Am. award, 1983, Martha Ryan Merit award Mus. Arts and Scis., Evansville, 1984, Best of Show award Gayle Willson Galleries, Southampton, 1984, Juror's merit award Brenau Coll., Gainesville, Ga., 1985, Installation Grant Ind. Arts Commn., Ft. Wayne, 1985, All Smith fellowship Ky. Arts Coun., Frankfort, 1987, Merit award Renwick Gallery, Tuscaloosa, Ala., 1988, Merit award Mus. Arts and Scis., Evansville, 1989, Design Grant, Arts and Cultural Coun. for O.A. Singletary Ctr. for Arts, Lexington, 1990, Visual Arts fellowship Nat. Endowment for Arts, Washington, 1992, Hon. award Ky. Crafts Mktg. Bd., Frankfort, 1994; vis. artist grantee NEA, 1996. Mem. Lexington Fiber Guild Inc., Louisville Visual Arts Assn., Ky. Art and Craft Found., Inc., Ky. Guild Artists and Crafstmen, Am. Craft Coun., Craft Alliance, St. Louis, Mo., Whatcom Mus., Bellingham, Wash., Friends of U. Ky. Mus. Art. Home: PO Box 25153 Lexington KY 40524-5153 Office: U Ky Dept Art 207 Fine Arts Bldg Lexington KY 40506-0022

SANDOVAL IÑIGUEZ, JUAN CARDINAL, archbishop; b. Yahualica, Mar. 28, 1933. Archbishop of Guadalajara Mexico; created and proclaimed cardinal, 1994. Office: Arzobispado Guadalajara, Arzobispado Liceo 17 Apdo 1-331, 44100 Guadalajara Jal, Mexico*

SANDQUIST, GARY MARLIN, engineering educator, researcher, consultant, author; b. Salt Lake City, Apr. 19, 1936; s. Donald August Sandquist and Lillian (Evaline) Dunn; m. Kristine Powell, Jan. 17, 1992; children from previous marriage: Titia, Julia, Taunia, Cynthia, Carl; stepchildren: David, Michael, Scott, Diane, Jeff. BSME, U. Utah, 1960, PhD in Mech. Engring., 1964, MBA, 1995; MS in Engring. Sci., U. Calif., Berkeley, 1961; postdoctoral fellow MIT, 1969-70. Registered profl. engr., Utah, N.Y., Minn., Calif.; cert. health physicist, cert. quality auditor. Staff mem. Los Alamos (N.Mex.) Sci. Lab., 1966; rsch. prof. surgery Med. Sch., U. Utah, Salt Lake City, 1974—, prof., dir. nuc. engring., mech. engring. dept., 1975—, acting chmn. dept., 1984-85; expert in nuclear sci. Internat. Atomic Energy Agy., UN, 1980—; chief sci. Rogers and Assocs. Engring. Corp., Salt Lake City, 1980—; vis. sci. MIT, Cambridge, Mass., 1960-70; advisor rocket design Hercules, Inc., Bachus, Utah, 1962; sr. nuc. engr. Idaho Nat. Engring. Lab., Idaho Falls, Idaho, 1963-65; cons. various cos.; cons. nuclear sci. State of Utah, 1982—; speaker for Nuclear Energy Inst., 1990—. Author: Geothermal Energy, 1973; Introduction to System Science, 1985. Comdr. USNR, 1954-56, Korea. Recipient Glen Murphy award in nuclear engring. Am. Soc. Engring. Edn., 1984. Fellow ASME, Am. Nuclear Soc.; mem. Am. Soc. Quality Control (sr.), Am. Health Physics Soc., Alpha Nu Sigma of Am. Nuclear Soc., Sigma Xi, Tau Beta Pi, Pi Tau Sigma. Republican. Mormon. Home: 2564 Neffs Cir Salt Lake City UT 84109-4055 Office: U Utah 2116 Merrill Engring Bldg Salt Lake City UT 84112

SANDRICH, JAY H., television director; b. L.A., Feb. 24, 1932; s. Mark R. and Freda (Wirtschafter) S.; m. Nina Kramer, Feb. 11, 1952 (div.); children: Eric, Tony, Wendy; m. Linda Green Silverstein, Oct. 4, 1984. BA, UCLA, 1953. Producer (TV show) Get Smart, 1965; dir. (TV shows) He and She, 1967, Mary Tyler Moore Show, 1970-88, Soap, 1977-79, Cosby Show, 1984-92; dir. (films) Seems Like Old Times, 1980, For Richer, For Poorer (HBO), 1992, Neil Simon's London Suite (NBC), 1996. Served to 1st lt. Signal Corps U.S. Army, 1952-55. Mem. Dirs. Guild Am. (award 1975, 85, 86), TV Acad. Arts and Scis. (Emmy award 1971, 73, 85, 86).

SANDRIDGE, WILLIAM PENDLETON, JR., lawyer; b. Winston-Salem, N.C., Jan. 27, 1934; s. William Pendleton and Kathryn (Mosby) S.; m. Jane Carolyn Yeager, Dec. 10, 1966; children: Jane, William. AB, U. N.C., 1956; LLB, U. Va., 1961. Bar: N.C. 1961. Ptnr. Womble Carlyle Sandridge & Rice, Winston-Salem, 1962—. Chmn., bd. dirs. Horizons Residential Care Ctr., 1980, Food Bank N.W. N.C., Inc., 1988-89, Data Max Corp., 1996. Mem. ABA. Office: Womble Carlyle Sandridge & Rice PO Drawer 84 1600 BB&T Plz Winston Salem NC 27102

SANDROK, RICHARD WILLIAM, lawyer; b. Evergreen Park, Ill., July 8, 1943; s. Edward George and Gertrude Jeanette (Van Stright) S.; m. Rebecca Fittz, June 9, 1973; children: Richard William Jr., Alexander Edward, Philip Robert, Erika Joy. BA, Wheaton (Ill.) Coll., 1965; JD, U. Ill., 1968. Bar: Ill. 1968, U.S. Dist. Ct. (no. dist.) Ill. 1971. Assoc. Hinshaw Culbertson Moelmann Hoban & Fuller, Chgo. and Wheaton, 1971-75; ptnr. Hinshaw Culbertson Moelmann Hoban & Fuller, Wheaton, 1976-89, Lisle, Ill., 1989—. Reviewer: Legal Checklists. Capt. U.S. Army, 1969-71. Mem. ABA, Ill. Bar Assn., Chgo. Bar Assn., Am. Arbitration Assn. (arbitrator), DuPage County Bar Assn. (chmn. med./legal com. 1978-79), Assn. Def. Trial Attys., Def. Rsch. Inst. Home: 818 Revere Rd Glen Ellyn IL 60137-5537 Office: Hinshaw & Culbertson 4343 Commerce Ct Ste 415 Lisle IL 60532-3617

SANDRY, KARLA KAY FOREMAN, industrial engineering educator; b. Davenport, Iowa, Apr. 2, 1961; d. Donald Glen and Greta Geniveve (VanderMaten) Foreman; m. William James Sandry, Oct. 12, 1985; children: Zachary Quinn, Skyler David. BS in Indsl. Engring., Iowa State U., 1983; MBA, U. Iowa, 1992. Quality control supr., indsl. engr. Baxter Travenol Labs, Hays, Kans., 1983-84; indsl. engr. HQ Amccom, Rock Island, Ill., 1984-86; mgmt. engr. St. Lukes Hosp., Davenport, 1986-90; adj. instr. engring. St. Ambrose U., Davenport, 1990—; chair space allocations St. Luke's Hosp., Davenport, 1987-90; pres. employee rels. coun. HQ Amccom, Rock Island, 1986, chair savings bonds, 1985; speaker in field. Vol., past counselor Fellowship Christian Athletes Ctrl. H.S., Davenport, 1984-87, vol., adult chpt., 1988-90; counselor Explorer Scout Troop, Davenport, 1984-85; leader, counselor ch. youth group, 1985-89; v.p. Crisis Pregnancy Ctr., 1996—, co-chmn. walkathon, 1996, pres. ch. choir, 1992, 95-96, orch. ch., 1994—, fin. com. 1997, dream team, 1996, security com. 1996—, prayer com., 1995, 97—, bd. dirs. Mem. Inst. Indsl. Engrs. (sr. mem.), Healthcare Info. & Mgmt. Systems Soc. (recognition & comms. com. 1988), Soc. for Health Systems (founding mem.), Found. for Christian Living, Iowa State U. Alumni Assn., U. Iowa Alumni Assn.; Positive Thinkers Club. Avocations: vocalist, tennis, golf, violinist, playing with sons.

SANDS, DONALD EDGAR, chemistry educator; b. Leominster, Mass., Feb. 25, 1929; s. George and Emily (Parker) S.; m. Elizabeth Stoll, July 28, 1956; children: Carolyn Looff, Stephen Robert. BS in Chemistry, Worcester Poly. Inst., 1951; PhD in Phys. Chemistry, Cornell U., 1955. Sr. chemist Lawrence Livermore (Calif.) Lab., 1956-62; asst. prof. chemistry U. Ky., Lexington, 1962-65, assoc. prof., 1965-68, prof., 1968—, dir. gen. chemistry, 1974-75, assoc. dean arts and scis., 1975-81, acting dean, 1978, 80-81, assoc. v.p., 1981-82, assoc. vice chancellor, 1982-84, vice chancellor acad. affairs, 1984-89; sect. head sci. and engring. edn. dept. NSF, 1989-91; mem. staff dept. chemistry U. Ky., Lexington, 1991—, chmn. dept. chem., 1993-97, acting dean arts & scis., 1997—. Author: Introduction to Crystallography, 1969, Vectors and Tensors in Crystallography, 1982. Mem. Am. Chem. Soc. (chmn. Lexington 1972), Am. Crystallographic Assn., AAAS, N.Y. Acad. Scis., Sigma Xi (chmn. Lexington 1975), Omicron Delta Kappa. Democrat. Avocations: reading, hiking, music, art. Home: 335 Cassidy Ave Lexington KY 40502-2559 Office: U Ky Dept Chemistry Lexington KY 40506

SANDS, EDITH SYLVIA ABELOFF (MRS. ABRAHAM M. SANDS), retired finance educator, author; b. Bklyn.; d. Louis and Jennie (Goldstein) Abeloff; m. Abraham M. Sands, June 5, 1932; children: Stephanie Lou Sands Fersko, John Eliot. B.A., Adelphi Coll., 1932; M.B.A., Baruch Sch. Bus. Adminstrn., CCNY, 1956; Ph.D., NYU, 1961; cert. fin. planner, Adelphi U., 1985. Asst. prof. L.I. U., Bklyn., 1961-65, asso. prof., 1965-69, prof., 1969-81, prof. fin. emeritus, 1980—, chmn. dept. finance, 1962-72; prof. fin., cons. Touro Coll., N.Y.C., 1980-96, prof. fin. emeritus, 1996—, chmn. dept. fin.; participant in person-to-person citizen ambassador program, China, 1987. Author: How to Select Executive Personnel, 1963; contbr. articles to profl. jours.; editor jour. industry studies for investment decisions. Corr. sec. Welfare Council Bklyn. Cancer Com., 1956-58; mem. council Friends of Adelphi Coll. Library, 1955-60; pres. Foster Care Aux., 1959-61; bd. dirs. Nat. Council Jewish Women, 1935-38; mem. community com. Bklyn. Mus., 1950-52; mem. women's aux. Prospect Heights Hosp., 1954-56, Bklyn. Eye and Ear Hosp., 1950-53; mem. asso. bd. Jewish Child Care Assn., 1959-61; chmn. bd. dirs. Friends Bklyn. Center Libraries, L.I. U. Recipient Alumni Achievement award Baruch Alumni Assn., CCNY, 1969; L.I. U. Alumni Assn. award of appreciation, 1978. Mem. AAUW, AAUP, Nat. Assn. Pers. Fin. Advs., Am. Econ. Assn., Met. Econ. Assn., Fedn. Woman Shareholders (exec. com.), Econ. History Assn., Am. Fin. Assn., Acad. Mgmt., Assn. Investment Mgmt. and Rsch., Soc. Advancement Mgmt., Am. Mgmt. Assn., N.Y. Soc. Security Analysts (Vol. of Yr. award 1990-91), Am. Statis. Assn., Fin. Mgmt. Assn., met. Econs. Assn., Inst. Cert. Fin. Planners, Internat. Assn. for fin. Planning (registered/lic. fin. planner, registered investment adviser), Acad. Fin. Svcs., City Coll. Alumni Assn., NYU Grad. Sch. Bus. Adminstrn. Alumni Assn. (dir. 1968-85, treas. 1975-77), Adelphi Coll. Alumnae Assn. (chpt. pres. 1957-59), Nat. N.Y. assns. bus. economists, Prospect Park Alliance, Parkslope Civic Coun., Money Marketeers NYU (dir. 1973-75), Women's City Club, City Coll. Club, The Exec. Forum of NYU (v.p. 1973-75), Money Marketeers, Exec. Forum, NYU Club, Princeton in N.Y. (guest mem.), Beta Gamma Sigma Alumni N.Y. (pres. 1967-70), Beta Gamma Sigma (nat. exec. com. 1972-76), Phi Sigma Sigma (chpt. archon 1931-32). Home: 874 Carroll St Brooklyn NY 11215-1702

SANDS, FRANK MELVILLE, investment manager; b. Kansas City, Mo., Sept. 5, 1938; s. Melville Reynolds Sands and Louise (Eviston) Olmstead; m. Marjorie Kay Root, July 20, 1963; children: Frank M. Jr., Katharine I., Laura E. BA, Dickinson Coll., 1960; MBA, U. Va., 1963. CFA. Security analyst Loomis Sayles & Co., Boston, 1969-72; sr. v.p., dir. David L. Babson & Co., Inc., Boston, 1972-83, Eppler, Guerin & Turner, Inc., Dallas, 1983-86; chief investment officer Folger Nolan Fleming Douglas, Inc., Washington, 1986-92; pres. Sands Capital Mgmt., Arlington, Va., 1992—. Treas., bd. dirs. Arlington Hosp. Found., 1987-93; mem. bd. trustees Arlington Community Found., 1994—; mem. bd. dirs. The Bank of Northern Va., 1995—. 1st lt. U.S. Army, 1960-61. Mem. Washington Soc. Investment Analysts, Inc. Office: Sands Capital Mgmt Inc 1100 N Glebe Rd Arlington VA 22201-4798

SANDS, I. JAY, corporate executive, business, marketing and real estate consultant, lecturer, realtor, analyst; b. N.Y.C.. B.A., NYU; J.D., Columbia U. Bar: N.Y., U.S. Supreme Ct. Mng. partner Korvette Bldg. Assocs., N.Y.C.; mng. dir., founder, chmn. bd. dirs., sec. First Republic Corp. Am.; chief exec. officer, sec. First Republic Corp., N.Y.; gen. partner Velvex Mid-City Parking Center, N.Y.C., Manhattan Parking Assocs.; dir., chmn. First Republic Underwriters, Inc.; pres., dir. Waltham Mgmt. Inc., Mass.; partner Cypress Parking Assocs., Cypress Plaza Shopping, Pompano Beach, Fla.; partner Sheraton Hotel Randolph House Co., Syracuse, N.Y.; partner Beau Rivage Hotel Co., Bal Harbour, Fla., Gulf Assocs., Fla., Sahara Motel Assocs., Miami Beach, Fla.; chmn. Waltham (Mass.) Engring. & Research Co.; gen. partner Allstate Ins. Bldg. Co., N.Y.C., Fairfax Bldg. Assocs., Kansas City, Mo., Engring. Bldg. Assocs., Chgo., Manhattan Parking Co., Williamsbridge Assocs., N.Y.C., First Republic Funding Life Ins. Agy., N.Y.C.; gen. partner Chateau Motel Atlantic Co., Miami Beach; gen. partner Syracuse-Randolph House Hotel, N.Y.C., Marchwood Realty Co., Phila., Video Film Center Assocs., N.Y.C., Hempstead Real Estate Enterprises, N.Y.C., Imperial Sq. Assocs., N.Y.C., DeMille Theatre Co., N.Y.C., Ohio Indsl. Assocs., Cleve., Pelham Park Assocs., Phila., Peoria (Ill.) Parking Assocs.; chmn., dir. Triple P Parking Corp., Peoria, Ill., Square Mgmt. Corp., N.Y.C., Park Circle Apts., Inc., N.Y.C., Holme Circle Apts., Inc., Phila.; pres., dir., sec. F.S. Mgmt. Corp., N.Y.C.; founder, chmn. exec. com., sec., dir. Imperial Sq. Mgmt. Corp., Hempstead, N.Y.; chmn. bd., chmn. exec. com., sec., dir. Nat. Med. Industries, Inc., Health Insts. Leasing Corp., Am. Med. Computer Corp.; pres. Med. Contract Supply Corp., City Capital Corp., N.J., Claredon Co., N.Y.C.; vis. lectr., adj. prof. ethics, law, class actions NYU, New Sch. for Social Research, U. Fla.; gen. agt. Northeastern Life Ins. Co., Patriot Life Ins. Co., Citizens Life Ins. Co.; expert witness in corp. and securities litigations. Past trustee Baldwin Sch., N.Y.C.; hon. trustee Pres. Harry S. Truman Libr. Served with AUS. Harlan Fiske Stone fellow Columbia U., 1975; named Man of Yr., Real Estate Weekly. Mem. Nat. Real Estate Club, N.Y. Real Estate Bd., Columbia U. Law Sch. Alumni Assn. (class chmn. 1978). Clubs: Shriners, Masons (32 deg.).

SANDS, MARVIN, wine company executive; b. Cleve., Jan. 28, 1924; s. Mack E. and Sally (Kipnis) S.; m. Marilyn Alpert, May 30, 1947; children: Laurie, Richard, Robert. BSBA, U. N.C., 1946. Chmn., dir. Canandaigua Wine Co., Inc., N.Y., 1945—; pres., dir. Tenner Bros., Inc., Patrick N.C., 1965—, Roberts Trading Corp., Canandaigua, 1959—; v.p., dir. Bisceglia Bros. Wine Co., Madera, Calif., 1975—. Pres. F.F. Thompson Health System, Inc., 1990—; past pres., dir. F.F. Thompson Hosp., Canandaigua, 1970—, Finger Lakes Area Hosp. Corp., Geneva, N.Y., 1980—; trustee YMCA, Canandaigua. Served with USN, 1943-46. Mem. Nat. Wine Assn. (treas., dir.), N.Y. State Finger Lakes Wine Growers Assn. (past pres., bd. dirs. 1979—), Assn. Am. Vintners (bd. dirs.). Office: Canandaigua Wine Co Inc 116 Buffalo St Canandaigua NY 14424-1012*

SANDS, MATTHEW LINZEE, physicist, educator; b. Oxford, Mass., Oct. 20, 1919; m. Freya Kidner, 1978; children: Michael, Richard, Michelle. B.A., Clark U., 1940; M.A., Rice Inst., 1941; Ph.D., MIT, 1948. Physicist U.S. Naval Ordnance Lab., 1941-43, Los Alamos Sci. Lab., 1943-46; research asso., then asst. prof. physics Mass. Inst. Tech., 1946-50; sr. research fellow, asso. prof., prof. physics Calif. Inst. Tech., 1950-63; prof., dep. dir. Linear Accelerator Center, Stanford, 1963-69; prof. physics U. Calif.-Santa Cruz, 1969-85, prof. emeritus, 1985—, fellow Kresge Coll.; vice chancellor for sci., 1969-72; pres. Sands-Kidner Assocs., Inc., 1986-90; vis. prof. U. Paris-Sud, spring 1976; mem. Commn. Coll. Physics, 1960-66, chmn., 1964-66; cons. Office Sci. and Tech., ACDA, Inst. Def. Analyses, 1962-67; mem. Pugwash Conf. Sci. and World Affairs, 1960-63; cons. on accelerator physics, 1975-93. Author: (with W.C. Elmore) Electronics-Experimental Techniques, 1948, (with R.P. Feynman and R.B. Leighton) The Feynman Lectures on Physics, 3 vols, 1965, (with others) Physical Science Today, 1973; also articles.; Mem. editorial bd.: Il Nuovo Cimento, 1972-85. Fulbright scholar Italy, 1952-53. Fellow Am. Phys. Soc.; mem. Am. Assn. Physics Tchrs. (Disting. Service award 1972), Fedn. Am. Scientists, AAAS. Spl. research electronic instrumentation for nuclear physics, cosmic rays, accelerators, high-energy physics, sci. edn., sci. and public affairs, electron storage rings. Home: 160 Michael Ln Santa Cruz CA 95060-1704

SANDS, ROBERT O., lawyer; b. Glennville, Ga., Dec. 28, 1953. BS with honor, Ga. Inst. Tech., 1975; JD, U. Ga., 1978. Bar: Ga. 1978. Mem. Ogletree, Deakins, Nash, Smoak & Stewart, Atlanta and Greenville, S.C. Editorial bd. Ga. Law Rev., 1976-78. Mem. ABA, State Bar Ga., Atlanta Bar Assn. Address: Ogletree Deakins et al 1201 W Peachtree St NW Atlanta GA 30309-3400

SANDS, ROBERTA ALYSE, real estate investor; b. N.Y.C., Oct. 7, 1937; d. Harry and Irene (Mytelka) S. BEd, U. Miami, 1960; postgrad., U. Oslo, 1960. Cert. secondary educator biology, Mass. Phys. edn. instr. Key Biscayne and Ludlam Elem. Sch., Miami, 1961-63; sci. tchr. Plantation (Fla.) Mid. Sch., 1969-71, Rickards Middle Sch., Ft. Lauderdale, Fla., 1972-76; founder U. Miami Diabetes Rsch. Inst., 1989. Author: Biology on the Secondary Level, 1970. Vol. Douglas Garden Retirement Home, Miami, 1988-92, Mus. of Art, Ft. Lauderdale, 1988-92, Imperial Point Hosp., Ft. Lauderdale, 1981-83. Mem. AAUW (rec. sec. 1988-92, cultural chair 1993-94, legis. chair Ft. Lauderdale br. 1994-95, women's issue chair Ft. Lauderdale 1994—, edn. chair Pompano Beach br. 1994-96, Recognition of Significant Svc. award 1983). Avocations: oil painting, golf, embroidery, travel. Home: Apt 8S 4250 Galt Ocean Dr Fort Lauderdale FL 33308-6138

SANDS, SHARON LOUISE, graphic design executive, art publisher, artist; b. Jacksonville, Fla., July 4, 1944; d. Clifford Harding Sands and Ruby May (Ray) MacDonald; m. Jonathan Michael Langford, Feb. 14, 1988. BFA, Cen. Washington U., 1968; postgrad, UCLA, 1968. Art dir. East West Network, Inc., L.A., 1973-78, Daisy Pub., L.A., 1978; prodn. dir. L.A. mag., 1979-80; owner, creative dir. Carmel Graphic Design, Carmel Valley, Calif., 1981-85; creative dir., v.p. The Video Sch. House, Monterey, Calif., 1985-88; graphic designer ConAgra, ConAgra, Nebr., 1988; owner, creative dir. Esprit de Fleurs, Ltd., Carmel, Calif., 1988—; lectr. Pub. Expo, L.A., 1979, panelist Women in Mgmt., L.A., 1979; redesign of local newspaper, Carmel, Calif., 1982. Contbr. articles to profl. mags. Designer corp. ID for Carmel Valey C. of C., 1981, 90. Recipient 7 design awards Soc. Pub. Designers, 1977, 78, Maggie award, L.A., 1977, 5 design awards The Ad Club of Monterey Peninsula, 1983, 85, 87, Design awards Print Mag. N.Y., 1986, Desi awards, N.Y., 1986, 88. Mem. NAFE, Soc. for Prevention of Cruelty to Animals, Greenpeace. Democrat. Avocations: publishing art, oil painting, cactus growing, interior decorating. Home and Office: 15489 Via La Gitana Carmel Valley CA 93924-9669

SANDS, W. LOUIS, federal judge; b. 1949. BA, Mercer U., 1971, JD, 1974. Chief legal asst. to dist. atty. Macon Jud. Cir., 1974, asst. dist. atty., 1975-78; asst. U.S. atty. U.S. Dist. Ct. (mid. dist.) Ga., 1978-87; with Mathis, Sands, Jordan & Adams, Macon, 1987-91; judge superior ct. Macon Jud. Cir., 1991-93; dist. judge U.S. Dist. Ct. (mid. dist.) Ga., Albany, 1994—; ptnr. Investors Ltd., 1984-91; mem. task force substance abuse Ga. Supreme Ct., 1991—, mem. com. gender equality, 1993—; bd. dirs. Bank Corp. Ga./1st South Bank, N.A. Organist/min. music, officer Steward Chapel AME Ch., 1976—; active Cmty. Found. Ga., Inc.; mem. 30th anniversary planning com. Mercer U., mem. bd. visitors Walter F. George sch. law, 1994—; v.p. Ga. Commn. Family Violence, 1992—; bd. dirs. Macon Symphony, 1992—. 2d lt. Signal Corps, U.S. Army, 1971, res. Acad. scholar Mercer U.; grad. Leadership Macon, 1985, Leadership Ga., 1986. Mem. ABA, Am. Judicature Soc., State Bar Ga. (mem. bench and bar com. 1991—), Macon Bar Assn. (pres. 1991-92), Coun. Superior Ct. Judges (mem. bench and bar com. 1991—), Walter F. George Sch. Law Alumni Assn. (bd. dirs.), Scabbard and Blade Mil. Honor Soc., Alpha Phi Alpha, Sigma Pi Phi, Homosophian Club. Office: US Dist Ct PO Box 1705 Albany GA 31702-1705

SANDSON, JOHN I., physician, educator, retired university dean; b. Jeannette, Pa., Sept. 20, 1927; s. Abraham and Dora (Whitman) S.; m. Hannah E. Ney, June 17, 1957; children: Jennifer, Thomas. BS, St. Vincent Coll., Latrobe, Pa., 1949; MD, Washington U., St. Louis, 1953. Diplomate Am. Bd. Internal Medicine. Resident in internal medicine Columbia-Presbyn. Med. Ctr., N.Y.C., 1953-56; chief resident Bronx (N.Y.) Mcpl. Hosp. Ctr., 1956-57; from instr. to prof. medicine Albert Einstein Coll. Medicine, Bronx, 1957-74, from asst. to assoc. dean, 1969-74; med. dir. Hosp. Albert Einstein Coll. Medicine, Bronx, 1969-74; prof. medicine Boston U., 1974—, dean Sch. Medicine, 1974-88, dean emeritus, 1988—; mem. Mass. Health Coordinating Com., Boston, 1984-87. Mem. pub. com. New Eng. Jour. Medicine, 1977-89, advisor, 1990—. Trustee Univ. Hosp., Boston, 1974-88, Louis E. Wolfson Found., Boston, 1984—, Whitaker Health Sci. Fund, Cambridge, Mass., 1977-91; pres. Mass. chpt. Arthritis Found., 1990-91, chmn., 1991-93. Served with U.S. Army, 1946-47. Recipient Doris Carr award Health Planning Council, 1981, Maimonides award Anti-Defamation League, 1986, Mayor's award for Disting. Svc. to Boston City Hosp., 1991. Fellow Am. Rheumatism Assn. (founding); mem. AMA, AAAS (study group project on liberal edn. in sci. 1987-90), Am. Soc. for Clin. Investigation, Assn. Am. Physicians, Mass. Med. Soc., Mass. Soc. Med. Rsch. (pres. Waltham 1987-91, chmn.-elect 1991, chmn. 1993—), Alzheimer's Disease and Related Diseases Assn. (bd. dirs. 1989-91), Alpha Omega Alpha, Saint Botolph Club (Boston). Avocation: gardening. Office: Boston U Sch of Medicine Office of the Dean Emeritus 80 E Concord St Boston MA 02118-2307

SANDSTEAD, HAROLD HILTON, medical educator; b. Omaha, May 25, 1932; s. Harold Russel and Lula Florence (Hilton) S.; m. Kathryn Gordon Brownlee, June 6, 1959 (dec. May 13, 1989); m. Victoria Regan Liddle, Feb. 14, 1990 (div. Oct. 1993); children: Eleanor McDonald, James Brownlee, William Harold. BA, Ohio Wesleyan U., 1954; MD, Vanderbilt U., 1958. Diplomate Am. Bd. Internal Medicine, Am. Bd. Nutrition. Intern, asst. resident in internal medicine Barnes Hosp. Washington U., St. Louis, 1958-60; asst. resident in pathology Vanderbilt Hosp., Nashville, 1960-61; asst. surgeon USPHS U.S. NAMRU 3, Cairo, Egypt, 1961-63; asst. resident in internal medicine Thayer VA Hosp. Vanderbilt, Nashville, 1963-64; chief resident in internal medicine Vanderbilt Hosp., Nashville, 1964-65; instr. internal medicine, asst. prof. biochemistry Med. Sch. Vanderbilt U., Nashville, 1965-70, asst. prof. internal medicine, assoc. prof. nutrition, 1970-71; dir. USDA-ARS Human Nutrition Rsch. Ctr., Grand Forks, N.D., 1971-84; adj. prof. biochemistry and internal medicine Sch. Medicine U. N.D., Grand Forks, 1971-84; dir. USDA-ARS Human Nutrition Rsch. Ctr. on Aging, Boston, 1984-85; prof. nutrition Tufts U., Medford, Mass., 1984-85; prof. preventive medicine and community health U. Tex. Med. Br., Galveston, 1985—; chmn. preventive medicine and community health Med. Br. U. Tex., Galveston, 1985-90, prof. internal medicine, human biol. chemistry & genetics, 1986—; cons. NAS, NRC, NIH, WHO, USDA; Joseph Goldberger vis. prof. AMA, 1976, Ellen Swallow Richards Meml. lectr., 1984; W.O. Atwater lectr. USDA, 1984; Sam E. and Mary F. Roberts lectr., 1985, Raymond Ewell Meml. lectr., 1985; Welcome prof. in basic sci. Fedn. Am. Socs. Exptl. Biology, 1988. Contbr. articles to profl. jours. Recipient Future Leader award Nutrition Found., 1968-70, Hull Gold medal AMA, 1970. Fellow ACP; mem. Am. Soc. Nutrition Scis. (Mead Johson award 1972), Cen. Soc. Clin. Rsch., Am. Soc. Clin. Nutrition (various office including pres.), So. Soc. Clin. Investigation, Alpha Omega Alpha. Avocations: gardening, fishing, reading. Office: U Tex Med Br Ewing Bldg Galveston TX 77555-1109

SANDSTROM, DALE VERNON, state supreme court judge; b. Grand Forks, N.D., Mar. 9, 1950; s. Ellis Vernon and Hilde Geneva (Williams) S.; m. Gail Hagerty, Mar. 27, 1993; children: Carrie, Anne; 1 stepchild, Jack. BA, N.D. State U., 1972; JD, U. N.D., 1975. Bar: N.D. 1975, U.S. Dist. Ct. N.D. 1975, U.S. Ct. Appeals (8th cir.) 1976. Asst. atty. gen., chief consumer fraud and antitrust div. State of N.D., Bismarck, 1975-81, securities commr., 1981-83, pub. svc. commr., 1983-92, pres. commn., 1987-91, justice Supreme Ct., 1992—; chair N.D. Commn. on Cameras in the Courtroom, 1993—, Joint Procedure Com., 1996—; mem. exec. com. N.D. Jud. Conf., 1995—; mem. Gov.'s Com. on Security and Privacy, Bismarck, 1975-76, Gov.'s Com. on Refugees, Bismarck, 1976; chmn. Gov's Com. on Comml. Air Transp., Bismarck, 1983-84. Mem. platform com. N.D. Reps., 1972, 76, exec. com., 1972-73, 85-88, dist. chmn., 1981-82; former chmn. bd. deacons Luth. Ch.; mem. ch. coun., exec. com., chmn. legal and constl. rev. com. Evang. Luth Ch. Am., 1993—. Mem. ABA, N.D. Bar Assn., Big Muddy Bar Assn., Nat. Assn. Regulatory Utility Commrs. (electricity com.), N.A. Assn. Securities Adminstrs., Order of De Molay (grand master 1994-95, mem. Internat. Supreme coun., Legion of Honor award), Nat. Eagle Scouts Assn., Shriners, Elks, Eagles, Masons (chmn. grand youth com. 1979-87, Youth Leadership award 1986). Office: State ND Supreme Court Bismarck ND 58505

SANDSTROM, SVEN, federal agency administrator. BA, U. Stockholm; MBA, Stockholm Sch. Econs.; DSc in Civil Engring., Royal Inst. Tech., Stockholm. Cons. Sweden, 1966-68; rsch. asoc. MIT and Harvard Bus. Sch., 1969-72; with World Bank, Washington, 1972—, dir. South African dept., 1987-90, dir. office of pres., 1990-91, mng. dir., also chair policy rev. com., 1991—. Office: IBRD World Bank 1818 H St NW Washington DC 20433-0001*

SANDT, JOHN JOSEPH, psychiatrist, educator; b. N.Y.C., June 29, 1925; s. John Jacob and Victoria Theodora Sandt; m. Mary Cummings Evans, Sept. 14, 1946; children: Christine, Karen, John K., Kurt, Colin, Carol; m. Mary W. Griswold, July 10, 1992. BA, Vanderbilt U., 1948; MA, Yale U., 1951; MD, Vanderbilt U., 1957. Instr. English Vanderbilt U., Nashville, 1951-52, Syracuse (N.Y.) U. Coll., 1960-61; intern SUNY Upstate Med. Ctr., Syracuse, 1957-58, resident, 1958-61; instr. psychiatry Southwestern Med. Sch., Dallas, 1961-63; chief psychiatry VA Med. Ctr., Dallas, 1961-63; chief outpatient clinic Dept. Mental Health, Springfield, Mass., 1963-66; asst. prof. psychiatry U. Rochester (N.Y.) Med. Sch., 1966-75, clin. assoc. prof. psychiatry, 1975—; chief psychiatry Clifton Springs (N.Y.), 1985-88, VA Med. Ctr., Bath, N.Y., 1988-96; pvt. practice Hammondsport, N.Y., 1996—; cons. psychiatry VA Med. Ctr., Northampton, Mass., 1965-66, Springfield Coll., 1964-66, Brockport (N.Y.) State Coll., 1966-75, Fairport (N.Y.) Bapt. Home, 1966-88; asst. dir. ind. study program U. Rochester Med. Sch., 1971-75. Author: Clinical Supervision of Psychiatric Resident, 1972; contbr. articles on psychiat. consultation and treatment to profl. jours. Vestryman All Saints Episcopal Ch., South Hadley, Mass., 1963-66. With USNR 1944-46, PTO. Nathaniel Currier fellow Yale Grad. Sch., 1948-49. Mem. AAAS, Am. Psychiat. Assn.

SANDWEISS, MARTHA A., museum director, author, American studies educator; b. St. Louis, Mar. 29, 1954; d. Jerome Wesley and Marilyn Joy (Glik) S. BA magna cum laude, Radcliffe Coll., 1975; MA in History, Yale U., 1977, MPhil in History, 1981, PhD, 1985. Smithsonian-Nat. Endowment Humanities fellow, Nat. Portrait Gallery, Washington, 1975-76; curator photographs Amon Carter Mus., Ft. Worth, 1979-86, adj. curator photographs, 1987-89; dir. Mead Art Mus. Amherst Coll., 1989-97, adj. assoc. prof. of fine arts and Am. studies, 1989-94, assoc. prof. Am. studies, 1994-97, assoc. prof. Am. studies and history, 1997—. Author: Carlotta Corpron: Designer with Light, 1980, Masterworks of American Photography, 1982, Laura Gilpin: An Enduring Grace, 1986, (catalogue) Pictures from an Expedition: Early Views of the American West, 1979; co-author: Eyewitness to War: Prints and Daguerreotypes of th Mexican War, 1989; editor: Historic Texas: A Photographic Portrait, 1986, Contemporary Texas: A Photographic Portrait, 1986, Denizens of the Desert, 1988, Photography in Nineteenth Century America, 1991; co-editor: Oxford History of the American West, 1994. Fellow Ctr. for Am. Art and Material Culture, Yale U., 1977-79, NEH, 1988, Am. Coun. Learned Socs., 1996-97. Office: Amherst Coll Am Studies Dept Mead Art Mus Amherst MA 01002

SANDWELL, KRISTIN ANN, special education educator; b. Topeka, Kans., Jan. 13, 1955; d. Edwin C. and E. Maxine (Nelson) Henry; children: Dustin Grimm, Chris Creek, Brandon Grimm. AA, Hutchinson (Kans.) C.C., 1986; BS, McPherson (Kans.) Coll., 1989; MEd, Wichita State U., 1992. Cert. tchr. elem., gifted. Math/parenting tchr. Flint Hills Job Corps Ctr., Manhattan, Kans., 1992; gifted facilitator Unified Sch. Dist. 353, Wellington, Kans., 1993-94, Unified Sch. Dist. 260, Derby, Kans., 1995—; head injury counselor, life skills trainer Three Rivers Ind. Living Ctr., Wamego, Kans., 1992. Epiphany Festival prodr. Trinity Luth. Ch., McPherson, 1991, 93; CASA organizer McPherson Coll., 1988-89; vol. Coun. on Violence Against Persons, McPherson, 1990-92. Mem. ASCD, Kans. Gifted, Talented, Creative Assn., Derby Educator Assn., NEA, Kans. Edn. Assn. Avocations: reading, travel, working with disability issues. Office: Derby Middle Sch 801 E Madison Ave Derby KS 67037-2241

SANDY, LEWIS GORDON, physician, foundation administrator; b. Detroit, July 18, 1958; s. William Haskell and Marjorie Mindel (Mazor) S.; m. Kathleen Anne Morgan, June 17, 1984; children: Matthew, Natalie, Jonah. BS, U. Mich., 1979, MD, 1982; MBA, Stanford U., 1988. Diplomate Am. Bd. Internal Medicine, Nat. Bd. Med. Examiners. Intern Beth Israel Hosp., Boston, 1982-83, resident, 1983-85; Robert Wood Johnson clin. scholar U. Calif., San Francisco, 1985-86, clin. fellow in medicine, 1986-88; instr. Harvard Med. Sch., 1988-91; assoc. chief internal medicine Harvard Community Health Plan, Boston, 1988-89, dir. Health Ctr., 1989-91; v.p. Robert Wood Johnson Found., Princeton, N.J., 1991-96, exec. v.p., 1997—; clin. asst. prof. medicine U. Medicine and Dentistry N.J./Robert Wood Johnson Med. Sch., 1991—; cons. Kaiser Found. Health Plan, Oakland, Calif., 1987-88. Fellow ACP; mem. APHA, AMA, Am. Coll. Physician Execs., Soc. Gen. Internal Medicine, Alpha Omega Alpha. Office: Robert Wood Johnson Found PO Box 2316 Princeton NJ 08543-2316

SANDY, ROBERT EDWARD, JR., lawyer; b. Libertyville, Ill., Feb. 16, 1943; s. Robert Edward and Elizabeth Ann (Carroll) S.; m. Joan Mary Phillips, Apr. 19, 1969; children: Mary Rosanne Phillips-Sandy, John Robert Phillips-Sandy. AB, Harvard U., 1965; JD, U. Chgo., 1968. Bar: Mass. 1969, Maine 1972, U.S. Dist. Ct. Mass. 1970, U.S. Dist. Ct. Maine 1972, U.S. Ct. Appeals (1st cir.) 1994, U.S. Supreme Ct. 1980. Atty. Boston Redevel. Authority, 1969-72; ptnr. Sandy and Sandy, Waterville, Maine, 1972-83, Sherman and Sandy, Waterville, 1983-87; sr. ptnr. Sherman & Sandy, Waterville, 1987—. Mem. Waterville Bar Assn., Maine Bar Assn., Maine Trial Lawyers Assn., ABA. Avocations: boating, skiing, community theater. Home: Greenwood Park Waterville ME 04901 Office: Sherman & Sandy 74 Silver St Waterville ME 04901-6524

SANDY, STEPHEN, writer, educator; b. Mpls., Aug. 2, 1934; s. Alan Francis and Evelyn Brown (Martin) S.; AB, Yale U., 1955; AM, Harvard U., 1958, PhD, 1963; m. Virginia Scoville, 1969; children: Nathaniel Merrill, Clare Scoville. Instr., Harvard U., 1963-67; vis. prof. U. Toyko, 1967-68; asst. prof. Brown U., Providence, 1968-69; mem. faculty Bennington (Vt.) Coll., 1969—; McGee prof. of writing Davidson (N.C.) Coll., 1994; lectr. U. R.I., 1969; prof. Harvard U. Summer Sch., 1986, 87, 88; poetry workshop dir. Chautauqua Instn., 1975, 77, Johnson (Vt.) State Coll., 1976, 77, Bennington Coll., summers 1978-80, 1989, Bennington Writing Seminars Program, 1994-96, Wesleyan Writers Conf., 1981; councillor for English, Harvard Grad. Soc. Coun., 1969-74. With U.S. Army, 1955-57. Dexter fellow, 1961; Yaddo fellow, 1963-68, 76, 93, 97; Huber Found. grantee, 1973; Vt. Coun. Arts grantee, 1974; recipient Fulbright postdoctoral award, 1967-68; invited poetry fellow Breadloaf Writers Conf., 1968; nominee for Pulitzer prize, 1971. Fellow Ingram Merrill Found., 1985, MacDowell Colony fellow, 1986, 93, Blue Mt. Ctr. fellow, 1985, 88, creative writing fellow Nat. Endowment for the Arts, 1988, Vt. Coun. on Arts fellow, 1988—; mem. Readers Digest Fellowship Disting. Writers Yaddo, Signet Soc., Elizabethan Club. Author: Stresses in the Peaceable Kingdom, 1967, Roofs, 1971, End of the Picaro, 1977, The Hawthorne Effect, 1980, The Raveling of the Novel: Studies in Romantic Fiction from Walpole to Scott, 1980, Riding to Greylock, 1983, To a Mantis, 1987, Man in the Open Air, 1988, The Epoch, 1990, Thanksgiving Over the Water, 1992; translator Seneca's Hercules Oetaeus, 1995, Vale of Academe A Prose Poem for Bernard Malamud, 1996, Marrow Spoon, 1997. Home: W St Box 524 North Bennington VT 05257 Office: Bennington Coll Bennington VT 05201

SANDY, WILLIAM HASKELL, training and communications systems executive; b. N.Y.C., Apr. 28, 1929; s. Fred and Rose S.; AB, U. Md., 1950, JD, 1953; postgrad. Advanced Mgmt. Program, Harvard Bus. Sch., 1970-71; m. Marjorie Mazor, June 15, 1952; children: Alan, Lewis, Barbara. Admitted to Md. bar, 1953; planner-writer, account exec., account supr. Jam Handy Orgn., Detroit, 1953-64, v.p., 1964-69, sr. v.p., 1969-71; pres. Sandy Corp., Troy, Mich., 1971-88; chmn., 1988-96. Author: Forging the Productivity Partnership, 1990. Bd. govs. Northwood Inst., 1976-80; bd. dirs. Cranbrook Sci. Inst., Met. Ctr. High Tech., 1993; pres. Graphic Arts Coun., 1992-93; trustee Detroit Inst. Arts, 1992-93; v.p. nat. exec. coun. Harvard Bus. Sch., 1985-89; mem. Bloomfield Hills Zoning Bd., Walsh Coll. Leader-in-Residence, Pres.'s Adv. Coun.; mayor City of Bloomfield Hills; mem. Troy Downtown Devel. Authority; Inst. for Humanities trustee U. Mich. Mem. Am. Mktg. Assn. (pres. Detroit chpt. 1975), Nat. Found. Am. Mktg. Assn. (bd. dirs.), Am. Soc. Tng. and Devel., S.E. Mich. BBB (bd. dirs.), Adcraft Club, Nat. Assn. Ednl. Broadcasters, Harvard Bus. Sch. Club (pres. Detroit club 1983-85), The Hundred Club. Home: 596 Rudgate Rd Bloomfield Hills MI 48304-3355 Office: 535 Sanctuary Dr Longboat Key FL 34228

SANETO, RUSSELL PATRICK, pediatrician, neurobiologist; b. Burbank, Calif., Oct. 10, 1950; s. Arthur and Mitzi (Seddon) S.; m. Kathleen D. Saneto. BS with honors, San Diego State U., 1972, MS, 1975; PhD, U. Tex. Med. Br., 1981; DO U. Osteo. Medicine and Surgery, 1994. Teaching asst. San Diego State U. 1969-75; substitute tchr. Salt Lake City Sch. Dist., 1975; teaching and rsch. asst. U. Tex. Med. Br., 1976-77, NIH predoctoral fellow, 1977-81, postdoctoral fellow, 1981; Jeanne B. Kempner postdoctoral fellow UCLA, 1981-82, NIH postdoctoral fellow, 1982-87; asst. prof. Oreg. Regional Primate Rsch. Ctr. div. Neurosci., Beaverton, 1987-89; asst. prof. dept. cell biology and anatomy Oreg. Health Scis. U., Portland, 1988-90, U. Osteo. Medicine & Surgery, 1991-94, Cleve. Clinic, 1994—; lectr. rsch. methods Grad. Sch., 1982; vis. scholar in ethics So. Baptist Theol. Sem., Louisville, 1981. Contbr. articles to profl. jours. Recipient Merit award Nat. March of Dimes, 1978; named one of Outstanding Young Men in Am., 1979, 81, one of Men of Significance, 1985. Mem. AAAS, Am. Acad. Pediats., Bread for World, Save the Whales, Sierra Club, Am. Soc. Human Genetics, Winter Confs. Brain Rsch., Neuroscis. Study Program, N.Y. Acad. Scis., Am. Soc. Neurochem., Soc. Neurosci., Am. Soc. Neurochemistry, Soc. Neurosci., World Runners Club, Sigma Sigma Phi. Democrat. Mem. Evangelical Free Ch.

SANETTI, STEPHEN LOUIS, lawyer; b. Flushing, N.Y., June 25, 1949; s. Alfred Julius Sanetti and Yolanda Marie (DiGioia) Boyes; m. Carole Leighton Koller, Sept. 21, 1974; children: Christopher Edward, Dana Harrison. B.A. in History with honors, Va. Mil. Inst., 1971; J.D., Washington and Lee U., 1974. Bar: Conn. 1975, U.S. Ct. Mil. Appeals 1975, U.S. Dist. Ct. Conn. 1978, U.S. Ct. Appeals (2d cir.) 1979, U.S. Supreme Ct. 1980. Litigation atty. Marsh, Day & Calhoun, Bridgeport, Conn., 1978-80; gen. counsel Sturm, Ruger & Co., Southport, Conn., 1980—; v.p. Sturm, Ruger & Co., 1993—; dir. Product Liability Adv. Coun. Tech. advisor Assn. Firearm and Toolmark Examiners; chmn. legis. & legal affairs com. Sporting Arms & Ammunition Mfrs. Inst. Served to capt., chief criminal law 1st Cavalry Div. Staff Judge Advocate, U.S. Army, 1975-78. Mem. Am. Acad Forensic Sci., Def. Rsch. Inst. Republican. Roman Catholic. Office: Sturm Ruger & Co Inc 1 Lacey Pl Southport CT 06490-1241

SANFELICI, ARTHUR H(UGO), editor, writer; b. Haledon, N.J., May 23, 1934; s. Hugo and Anna (Schilder) S.; m. Betty Louise Van Riper, Aug. 10, 1957; children: Brian Arthur, Amy Elizabeth, Gary Hugh, Bruce Richard. Attended, Lehigh U., 1952-55. Assoc. editor Flying Mag., N.Y.C., 1961-64; mng. editor Am. Aviation Mag., Washington, 1964-68; dist. sales mgr. Gates Learjet Co., N.Y.C., 1969-71; exec. editor Airport World Mag., Westport, Conn., 1971-74; spl. project editor Aircraft Owners & Pilots Assn., Washington, 1974-75, mng. editor Pilot mag., 1975-79, editor AOPA Newsletter, AOPAirport Report, Gen. Aviation Nat. Report, 1979-88; pub. cons., 1989-90; sr. editor Flight Safety Found., Washington, 1989-92; editor S-Cubed divsn. Maxwell Labs., Alexandria, Va., 1992-95; comms. dir. Helicopter Assn. Internat., Alexandria, 1996-97; editor Shooting Sports USA, 1997—. Editor, compiler: Yesterday's Wings; Editor Aviation History Mag., Leesburg, Va., 1990—. Served with USAF, 1955-60. Mem. Nat. Aeronautic Assn., Washington Ind. Writers, Aero Club of Washington, Soc. Aerospace Comms. Home: 5 Oak Shade Rd Sterling VA 20164-1163

SANFELIPPO, PETER MICHAEL, cardiac, thoracic and vascular surgeon; b. Milw., Nov. 1, 1938; s. Michael L. and Genevieve M. (Gagliano) S.; m. Cecelia Monica Reuss, May 25, 1968. MD, Marquette U., Milw., 1965; MS in Surgery, U. Minn., 1976. Diplomate Am. Bd. Surgery, Am. Bd. Thoracic Surgery, Am. Bd. Gen. Vascular Surgery. Intern Sacred Heart Hosp., Spokane, Wash., 1965-66; gen. surgery fellow Mayo Grad. Sch. Medicine, Rochester, Minn., 1966, 69-73; residency in thoracic surgery USAF Med. Ctr., Lackland AFB, Tex., 1973-75; thoracic surgeon USAF Med. Corps, various locations, 1966-78; pvt. practice cardiac, thoracic and vascular surgery Ohio Heart & Thoracic Surgery Ctr., Columbus, 1978-91; prof. cardiothoacic and vascular surgery U. Tex. Health Ctr., Tyler, Tex., 1991—. Contbr. articles to profl. jours. Lt. col. USAF, 1966-78. Decorated Air Force Commendation medal. Fellow ACS, Am. Coll. Cardiology, Am. Coll. Angiology, Am. Coll. Chest Physicians; mem. AMA. Avocations: scouting, camping, photography, gardening.

SANFILIPPO, ALFRED PAUL, pathologist, educator; b. Racine, Wis., Aug. 30, 1949; s. Paul Joseph and Therese (Rhode) S.; m. Janet Lee Thompson, 1973; children: Lisa, Joseph. Student, Max Planck Inst. Exptl. Med., Gottingen, Germany, 1966-68, U. Pa., 1969-70; BA and MS in Physics, U. Pa., 1970; postgrad., Duke U., 1972-75, PhD in Immunology, 1975, MD, 1976. Diplomate Am. Bd. Pathology; lic. physician N.C., Md. Postdoctoral rschr. divsn. tumor virology dept. surgery, 1976-79; intern in anatomic pathology Duke U. Hosp., 1976-77, resident in anatomic and clin. pathology, 1977-79; asst. prof. pathology and exptl. surgery, lectr. immunology Duke U., Durham, 1979-84, from assoc. prof. to prof. pathology, 1984-93, from assoc. prof. to prof. exptl. surgery, 1985-93, prof. immunology, 1990-93; attending pathologist Duke U. and Durham VA Hosps., 1979-93; staff mem. Duke Surg. Pvt. Diagnostic Clinic, 1979-93; dir. Transplantation Lab. Durham VA Hosp., 1979-93; dir. immunopathology Duke U. Med. Ctr., 1982-93, exec. com. dept. pathology, 1989-91; pathologist-in-chief Johns Hopkins Hosp., Balt., 1993—; Baxley prof., dir. dept. pathology Johns Hopkins U., Balt., 1993—; adj. prof. pathology and immunology Duke U.,

1993—, clin. rsch. unit sci. adv. com., 1988-91, at-large rep. basic sci. faculty steering com., 1989-91, dir. interdisciplinary program in transplantation, 1991-93; mem. Duke Comprehensive Cancer Ctr., 1979-93; chmn. comprehensive transplant ctr. planning com. Johns Hopkins Med. Instns., 1993—, mem. physician coun. for Atlantic Alliance, 1994—; med. bd. Johns Hopkins Hosp., 1993—, strategic planning work group, 1993—, quality assessment and improvement coun., 1994—, re-engring. steering com., 1994—; Osler prof., dir. medicine search com. Johns Hopkins U. Sch. Medicine, 1994—, DeVelbiss fund com., 1994—, Clayton fund com., 1993—, Shelley vis. prof. com., 1993—, faculty compensation com., 1993—, bd. dirs. clin. practice assn., 1993—; mem. orgn. student reps. Assn. Am. Med. Colls., 1973-75; sec. Carolina Organ Procurement Agy., 1987-89, exec. com., 1987-93, v.p., 1989-91, pres., 1991-93; com. med. student affairs N.C. Med. Soc., 1972-76, del. Durham County, 1974; cons. Battelle Human Affairs Rsch. Ctrs., Seattle, 1985-93, NSF of Switzerland, 1992-93, also numerous U.S. govt. adv. coms.; speaker and presenter in field. Guest editor: Human Immunology, Vol. 14, 1987; mem. editl. bd. Transplantation, 1985—, Pathobiology, 1989—, Transplantation Now (Japan) 1989—, Pathology, Rsch. and Practice, 1990—, Human Immunology, 1992—, Lab. Investigation, 1993—, Xeno, 1994—; reviewer Am. Jour. Kidney Diseases, Am. Jour. Ophthalmology, Am. Jour. Pathology, Hepatology, Jour. of AMA, Jour. Am. Soc. Nephrology, Jour. Clin. Investigation, Jour. Leukocyte Biology, Kidney Internat., others; contbr. numerous articles to profl. jours. Recipient Kermit G. Osserman award Myasthenia Gravis Found., 1976, Wiley D. Forbus award N.C. Soc. Pathologists, 1979, Reach for Sight Physician Investigator award, 1990; NIH predoctoral fellow Duke U., 1970-76, fellow in exptl. pathology Duke U., 1978-79; numerous rsch. grants. Fellow Coll. Am. Pathologists, Am. Soc. Clin. Pathologists (coun. on edn. and rsch. 1994—); mem. AMA (Physician Recognition award 1979-84), Am. Assn. Immunologists, Am. Soc. Investigative Pathology, U.S.-Can. Acad. Pathology, Southeastern Organ Procurement Found. (sci. projects and publs. com. 1980—, organ preservation com. 1981-83, exec. com. 1992—, sec. 1992-93, treas. 1993-94, v.p. 1994-95, bd. dirs. med. svcs. 1992—, pres. med. svcs. 1994-95), Transplantation Soc., Am. Soc. Histocompatibility and Immunogenetics (chmn. clin. affairs com. 1987-90, chmn. cornea transplant standards subcom. 1985-86), Assn. for Rsch. in Vision and Ophthalmology, Am. Soc. Transplant Physicians (pres.-elect 1984-85, pres. 1985-86, chmn. sci. studies com. 1991-92), Am. Soc. Nephrology, N.C. Kidney Coun. (rep. histocompatibility 1981-92), Md. Soc. Pathologists, Assn. Pathology Chmn. (rep. 1993—om. grad. med. edn. 1994—), Alpha Omega Alpha. Office: Johns Hopkins Med Insts Dept Pathology 415 600 N Wolfe St Baltimore MD 21205-2110

SANFILIPPO, JON WALTER, lawyer; b. Milw., Nov. 10, 1950; s. Joseph Salvator and Jeanne Catherine (Lisinski) S.; m. Pamela Joy Jaeger, July 8, 1972; children: Kerri, Jessica, Jennifer. AS, U. Wis., West Bend, 1972; BS, U. Wis., Milw., 1974, MS, 1978; JD, Marquette U., 1988. Bar: Wis. 1988, U.S. Dist. Ct. (ea. dist.) Wis. 1988, U.S. Dist. Ct. (we. dist.) Wis. 1989, U.S. Ct. Appeals (7th cir.) 1988, U.S. Supreme Ct. 1994; cert. elem. tchr., ednl. adminstr., Wis. Collection agt. West Bend Co., 1970-72; educator, athletic dir., coach St. Francis Cabrini, West Bend, 1974-77; clk. of cir. ct. Washington County, West Bend, 1976-89; ptnr. Schowalter, Edwards & Sanfilippo, S.C., West Bend, 1989-94; sch. prin.K-8 Campbellsport (Wis.) Sch. Dist., 1994-95; chief dep. clk. Cir. Ct. Milw. County, Milw., 1995—; judo tchr. City of West Bend, 1967—; phys. edn. instr., judo coach U. Wis., West Bend, 1992—. Author: Judo for the Physical Educator, 1981, Proper Falling for Education Classes, 1981. Mem. sch. bd. West Bend Sch. Dist., 1979-80; dist. chmn. Wis. Clk. of Cts. Assn., 1976-79, mem. exec. com., 1976-82, mem. legis. com., 1982-84. Recipient cert. study internat. and Chinese law East Chinese Inst. Politics & Law, Willamette U. Law Sch., Shanghai, People's Republic China, 1988, Black Belt 6th Degree U.S. Judo Assn., 1995, Black Belt 3d Degree Universal Tae Kwon Do Assn., 1988. Mem. ABA, Wis. Bar Assn. (bench/bar com. 1986-88), Milw. Bar Assn. (cts. com. 1995—), Washington County Bar Assn., U. Wis.-Washington County Found. Inc. (bd. dirs. 1993-94), Assn. Wis. Sch. Adminstrs., Rotary (bd. dirs. West Bend Sunrise Club 1990-91, Paul Harris fellow). Roman Catholic. Avocations: Tai Kwon Do, Tai Chi, Judo, photography, model railroading. Office: Milw County Ct House Rm 104 901 N 9th St Ste 104 Milwaukee WI 53233-1425

SANFILIPPO, JOSEPH SALVATORE, physician, reproductive endocrinologist, educator; b. Bklyn., Feb. 28, 1948; s. Joseph Philip and Elena Teresa (Canepa) S.; m. Patricia M. Cantwell, June 21, 1974; children: Angela, Andrea, Luke. BS, St. John's U., N.Y.C., 1969; MD, Chgo. Med. Sch., 1973. Diplomate Am. Bd. Ob-Gyn., spl. qualification in reproductive endocrinology. Intern Milwaukee County Gen. Hosp.; resident in ob-gyn. SUNY Upstate Med. Ctr., Syracuse; instr. dept. ob-gyn. U. Louisville Sch. Medicine, 1977-79, asst. prof., 1979-83, assoc. prof., 1983-89, prof., 1989—, dir. div. reproductive endocrinology, 1993—; pres. med. staff Alliant Health System/Norton Hosp. and Alliant Med. Pavilion, Louisville, 1994—; dir. gynecology Kosair-Children's Hosp., Louisville, 1979—. Editor: Operative Gynecologic Endoscopy, 1988, 2d edit., 1996, Pediatric and Adolescent Gynecology, 1994; editor-in-chief Jour. Pediatric Adolescent Gynecology, 1989—. Mem. parish coun. Holy Trinity Roman Cath. Ch., Louisville, 1988-92; mem. prin.'s adv. coun. Sacred Heart Acad., Louisville, 1993-94. Named Disting. Alumnus, Chgo. Med. Sch., 1990. Fellow Am. Soc. for Reproductive Medicine (bd. dirs.), N.Am. Soc. for Pediatric Adolescent Gynecology (founding mem.); mem. Am. Coll. Ob-Gyn. (tech. bull. com., chair prolog-gynecology), Am. Bd. Ob-gyn. (bd. examiner), Alpha Omega Alpha. Avocations: jogging, boating, fishing, ham radio. Home: 5505 Apache Rd Louisville KY 40207-1613 Office: U Louisville Sch Medicine Dept Ob-Gyn ACB Bldg 550 S Jackson St Louisville KY 40202-1622

SANFORD, BRUCE WILLIAM, lawyer; b. Massena, N.Y., Aug. 5, 1945; s. Doris (Suhrland) Sanford; m. Marilou Green, May 17, 1980; children: Ashley Anne, Barrett William. BA, Hamilton Coll., 1967; JD, NYU, 1970. Bar: N.Y. 1970, Ohio 1971, D.C. 1981, Md. 1985. Staff reporter Wall St. Jour., 1966-67; assoc. Baker and Hostetler, Washington, 1971-79, ptnr., 1979—. Author: Sanford's Synopsis Law of Libel and Privacy, rev. edit., 1991, Libel and Privacy, 2nd edit., 1991. Trustee Nat. Symphony Orch. Assn.; bd. dirs. Thomas Jefferson 1st Amendment Ctr., U. Va., Charlottesville. Mem. ABA (governing bd., forum com. on communication law, chmn. defamation torts com. 1985-86). Office: Baker & Hostetler 1050 Connecticut Ave NW Washington DC 20036

SANFORD, CHARLES STEADMAN, JR., banker; b. Savannah, Ga., Oct. 8, 1936; s. Charles Steadman and Ann (Lawrence) S.; m. Mary McRitchie, June 19, 1959; children: Ann Whitney, Charles Steadman III. BA, U. Ga., 1958; MBA, U. Pa., 1960. V.p. nat. div., relationship mgr. Bankers Trust Co., N.Y.C., 1961-68, 1st v.p., asst. to head resources mgmt., 1969-71, sr. v.p., 1973, head resources mgmt., from 1972, exec. v.p., 1974, pres., 1983-86, dep. chmn., from 1986, chmn., chief exec. officer, 1987-96; ret., 1996; mem. mgmt. com. Bankers Trust Co., N.Y.C., 1979-96, CEO, 1996—; chmn. N.Y. Clearing House Com., 1987-88; bd. dirs. J.C. Penney Co., Mobil Corp. Mem. Bus. Roundtable; bd. overseers Wharton Sch., U. Pa. With arty. U.S. Army, 1958-59. Mem. Coun. Fgn. Rels. Office: Bankers Trust NY Corp 130 Liberty St New York NY 10006-1105*

SANFORD, DAVID BOYER, writer, editor; b. Denver, Mar. 4, 1943; s. Filmore Bowyer and Alice Irene (Peterson) S. B.A. with honors, U. Denver, 1964; M.S. in Journalism with honors, Columbia U., 1965. With New Republic mag., Washington, 1965-76; mng. editor New Republic mag., 1970-76, Politics Today (formerly Skeptic), Santa Barbara, Calif., 1976-78; contbg. editor Politics Today (formerly Skeptic), 1978-79; editorial writer Los Angeles Herald Examiner, 1978-79; mng. editor Harper's mag., N.Y.C., 1979-80; editor Wall St. Jour. mag., 1980-81; sr. spl. writer Wall Street Jour., 1981—; syndicated columnist, 1970-71; commentator Can. Broadcasting Corp., 1967-76; judge Heywood Broun award Newspaper Guild, 1971; mem. print screening com. Champion-Tuck awards, 1985, 86, Judge Wuxtry award, 1990. Author: Who Put the Con in Consumer?, 1972, Me and Ralph, 1976; editor, co-author: Hot War on the Consumer, 1970. Recipient Sackett Law prize Columbia, 1965, Eckenberg prize, 1965, Gold award N.Y. Art Dirs. Club, 1977, Wuxtry award for disting. achievement in headline writing Internat. Soc. for Gen. Semantics, 1989, Pulitzer prize, 1997; Centennial scholar, 1960-64; N.Y. Newspaper Guild fellow, 1964-65. Mem. Phi Beta Kappa, Omicron Delta Kappa. Democrat. Home: 118 Prospect Park W Brooklyn NY 11215-4270

SANFORD, DAVID HAWLEY, philosophy educator; b. Detroit, Dec. 13, 1937; s. Hawley Seager and Alice Katherine (Brown) S.; m. Anne Irene Zeleney, July 10, 1965; children: Daria Margaret, Katherine Eugenia. Student, Oberlin Coll., 1955-57; B.A., Wayne State U., 1960; Ph.D., Cornell U., 1966. Instr., asst. prof. philosophy Dartmouth Coll., Hanover, N.H., 1963-70; assoc. prof. Duke U., Durham, N.C., 1970-78; prof. Duke U., 1978—, chmn. dept., 1986-89; vis. faculty U. Oreg., U. Mich., Dalhousie U. Author: If P, then Q: Conditionals and the Foundations of Reasoning, 1989, paperback edit., 1992; contbr. articles to profl. jours. Samuel S. Fells fellow, 1962-63, NEH fellow, 1974-75, 82-83, 89-90, Nat. Humanities Ctr. fellow, 1989-90. Mem. Am. Philos. Assn. (exec. com. Eastern div. 1979-81), N.C. Philos. Soc. (pres. 1983-85), Soc. for Philosophy and Psychology, Phi Beta Kappa. Home: 2227 Cranford Rd Durham NC 27706-2507 Office: Duke Univ Dept Philosophy Box 90743 Durham NC 27708

SANFORD, JAMES KENNETH, public relations executive; b. Clyde, N.C., Jan. 23, 1932; s. James Edward S. and Bernice (Crawford) Peebles; m. Alice Pearl Reavis, Sept. 22, 1957; children: Timothy, Scott, Jeannette. AA, Mars Hill (N.C.) Coll., 1952; AB, U. N.C., 1954, MA, 1958. Pub. rels. officer Asheville (N.C.) United Appeal, 1954; reporter, copy editor Winston-Salem (N.C.) Jour., 1957-59, asst. state editor, 1959-61, news editor, 1961-63, editorial writer, 1963-64; dir. pub. info. and publs. U. N.C., Charlotte, 1964-94; pub. rels. cons. Charlotte, N.C., 1994—; cons. Commn. on Future of Mars Hill Coll., 1990-91, City of Charlotte, 1991. Author: Charlotte and UNC Charlotte: Growing Up Together, 1996; co-author: Fifty Favored Years, 1972; contbr. numerous articles to mag. and newspapers. Active attractions com. Charlotte Conv. and Visitors Bur., 1994—, Internat. House Bd., 1995—, adv. com. Sta. WTVI Pub. TV, Charlotte, 1986-94; chmn. bd. deacons local ch., 1994-95. With U.S. Army, 1954-56. Elected to N.C. Pub. Rels. Hall of Fame, 1995; recipient Alumnus by Choice award U. N.C. at Charlotte, 1996. Fellow Pub. Rels. Soc. Am. (chmn. S.E. dist. 1991); mem. Coll. News Assn. Carolinas (Lewis Gaston award 1982), Charlotte Pub. Rels. Soc. (pres. 1974, Infinity award 1986), Coun. for Advancement and Support Edn. (asst. dist. chmn. 1975-76), Phi Kappa Phi. Baptist. Avocations: writing, hiking, photography. Home and Office: 1216 Braeburn Rd Charlotte NC 28211-4769

SANFORD, KATHERINE KOONTZ, cancer researcher; b. Chgo., July 19, 1915; d. William James and Alta Rachel (Koontz) S.; m. Charles Fleming Richards Mifflin, Dec. 11, 1971. BA, Wellesley Coll., 1937; MA, Brown U., 1939, PhD, 1942; DSc (hon.), Med. Coll. Pa., 1974, Cath. U. Am., 1988. Teaching asst. Brown U., Providence, 1937-39, rsch. asst., 1939-41; instr. biology Western coll., Oxford, Ohio, 1941-42, Allegheny Coll., Meadville, Pa., 1942-43; asst. dir. Johns Hopkins Nursing Sch., Balt., 1943-47; rsch. biologist Nat. Cancer Inst. NIH, Bethesda, Md., 1947-74; head cell physiology and oncogenesis sect. Lab. Biochemistry, Bethesda, 1974-77; chief in vitro carcinogenesis sect. Nat. Cancer Inst. NIH, Bethesda, 1979-95. Contbr. 150 articles to profl. jours. Ross Harrison fellow, 1954. Mem. Phi Beta Kappa, Sigma Xi. Home: 101 Stuart Dr Dover DE 19901-5817 Office: Nat Cancer Inst In Vitro Carcinogenesis Bethesda MD 20892

SANFORD, LEROY LEONARD, rancher; b. Sanford Ranch, Wyo., June 24, 1934; s. Claude Leonard and Herminnie May (Brockmeyer) S.; m. Barbara Jo Shackleford, June 15, 1965 (dec. Oct. 1965); stepchildren: Christina Pedley, Marlena McCollum, Diana Sumners; 1 foster child, Catherine Frost. Cert. satellite geodecy, Johns Hopkins U., 1971; cert. astron. geodecy, U.S. Geol. Survey-Branch R & D, 1971. Cert. Geodesic Surveyor. Rancher Sanford Ranch, Douglas, Wyo., 1952-57; topographer, photogrametrist U.S. Geol. Survey-Topog. Divsn.-Hdqs., Denver, 1957-81; rancher Sanford Ranch, Douglas, 1981—; speaker various schs. and community orgns. Congl. Svc. medal U.S. Congress, 1972. Mem. NRA (patron), Am. Solar Energy Soc., Antarctican Soc., Wyo. Farm Bur. Republican. Avocation: photography. Home: 400 Windy Ridge Rd Douglas WY 82633-0145 *Early on I ran across this saying; author unknown to me, "Why is there never enough time to do it right, but always enough time to do it over?" I feel that anyone's time spent"doing it over" is wasted unless it is to do something better in light of new knowledge. Anything I build now will last longer than me and I want it to survive until the next technological leap forward.*

SANFORD, MARSHALL (MARK SANFORD), congressman; b. Ft. Lauderdale, Fla., May 28, 1960; m. Jenny Sullivan; 3 children. BA, Furman U., 1983; MBA, U. Va., 1988. With Goldman Sachs, 1988, CRC Realty, 1988-89; prin. Southeastern Ptnrs., 1989—, Norton & Sanford, 1993—; mem. 104th Congress from 1st Dist. S.C., 1995—. Republican. Office: US Ho of Reps Washington DC 20515

SANFORD, RICHARD D., computer company executive; b. 1944. With Arthur Andersen Co., N.Y.C., 1968-77; exec. v.p. Commodore Internat. Ltd., 1977-81; chmn., CEO, former pres. Intelligent Electronics Inc., Exton, Pa., 1982—. With USMC, 1964-68. Office: Intelligent Electronics Inc 411 Eagleview Blvd Exton PA 19341-1117*

SANFORD, SARAH J., healthcare executive; b. Seattle, July 20, 1949; d. Jerome G. and Mary L. (Laughlin) S. BS in Nursing, U. Wash., 1972, MA in Nursing, 1977. Cert. in advanced nursing adminstrn. Critical care staff nurse Valley Gen. Hosp., Renton, Wash., 1972-75, Evergreen Gen. Hosp., Kirkland, Wash., 1975-76; instr. nursing Seattle Pacific U., 1977-79; with Overlake Hosp. Med. Ctr., Bellevue, Wash., 1979-88, critical care coord., 1979-80, dir. acute care nursing, 1980-82, assoc. adminstr., 1982-83, sr. v.p. patient care, 1983-88; exec. dir. AACN, Aliso Viejo, Calif., 1988-90, CEO, 1990—; bd. dirs. Partnership for Organ Donation, Boston, Am. Soc. of Assn. Execs. Found., Washington. Co-editor: Standards for Nursing Care of the Critically Ill, 1989; contbr. articles to books and jours. Fellow Am. Acad. Nursing; mem. AACN (pres. 1984-85, bd. dirs. 1981-83), ANA, Soc. for Critical Care Medicine, Am. Orgn. Nurse Execs., Sigma Theta Tau. Office: AACN 101 Columbia Aliso Viejo CA 92656-1491

SANFORD, TERRY, lawyer, educator, former United States Senator, former governor, former university president; b. Laurinburg, N.C., Aug. 20, 1917; s. Cecil and Elizabeth (Martin) S.; m. Margaret Rose Knight, July 4, 1942; children: Elizabeth Knight, Terry. AB, U. N.C., 1939, JD, 1946; 30 hon. degrees from colls. and univs. Bar: N.C. 1946, D.C. 1979. Asst. dir. Inst. Govt., U. N.C., 1940-41, 46-48; spl. agt. FBI, 1941-42; pvt. practice Fayetteville, 1948-60; ptnr. Sanford, Adams, McCullough & Beard, Raleigh, N.C. and Washington, 1965-86; gov. State of N.C., 1961-65; pres. Duke U., Durham, N.C., 1969-85, prof. pub. policy, 1992—; mem. U.S. Senate 99th-102d Congresses from N.C., 1986-93; ptnr. The Sanford-Holhouser Law Firm, PLLC, Raleigh, 1993—; prof. of practice, public policy Duke U., 1992—; pub. gov. Am. Stock Exchange, 1977-83; dir. Study of Am. States, Duke U., 1965-68; mem. Carnegie Commn. Ednl. TV, 1964-67; pres. Urban Am., Inc., 1968-69; chmn. ITT Internat. Fellowship Com., 1974-86, Am. Coun. Young Polit. Leaders, 1976-86; pres. U.S. Del. Inter-Parliamentary Union, 1988-90. Author: But What About the People?, 1966, Storm Over the States, 1967, A Danger of Democracy, 1981, Outlive Your Enemies, 1996. Sec.-treas. N.C. Port Authority, 1950-53; mem. N.C. Senate, 1953-54; pres. N.C. Young Dem. Clubs, 1949-50; del. Nat. Dem. Conv., 1956, 60, 64, 68, 72, 84, 88, 92; chmn. Nat. Dem. Charter Commn., 1972-74; mem. governing bd. Nat. Com. for Citizens in Edn., Am. Art Alliance; trustee Am. Council Learned Socs., 1970-73, Nat. Humanities Center, 1978-86, Meth. Coll., 1958-94, chmn., 1958-68, Howard U., 1968-86; chmn. N.C. Mus. Art, 1993—; bd. dirs. Children's TV Workshop, 1967-71, Council on Founds., 1971-76, N.C. Outward Bound, 1981-88; chmn. bd. trustees U. N.C., 1961-65; chmn. So. Regional Edn. Bd., 1961-63, Sta. ACSN (The Learning Channel), 1980-86, Assn. Am. Univs., 1980-81, Nat. Civic League, 1985-86. Served to 1st lt. AUS, 1942-46. Mem. ABA, Am. Acad. Polit. and Social Sci., Coun. Fgn. Rels., Am. Judicature Soc., Nat. Acad. Pub. Adminstrn., AAAS, Phi Beta Kappa. Methodist. Office: Sanford-Holhouser Law Firm 234 Fayetteville Street Mall Raleigh NC 27601-1370

SANFORD, WILBUR LEE, elementary education educator; b. Lexington, Ky., Aug. 2, 1935; s. Lloyd Daniel and Catherine (Kirtley) S.; m. Dorothy Moore; children: James, Venessa. BA, Ky. State Coll., 1958; MA in Adminstrn., Xavier U., 1969, cert. elem. counselor, 1973. Cert. elem. counselor, Ohio; cert. elem. tchr. and prin., Ohio. Elem. tchr. North Coll. Hill (Ohio) Sch., 1960-65, Cin. Pub. Schs., 1965-73, St. Joseph Elem. Sch., Cin., 1993—; adminstrv. intern Cin. Pub. Schs., 1983-85, asst. prin., 1975-80, elem. prin., 1980-92; cons. PTA, Cin., 1989-92, GED program, Cin., 1990-91; prin./instrnl. leader Windsor Sch. Meritorious Achievement, Cin., 1985-86; dir. After Sch. Evening Tutorial, Cin., 1988-92. Leader 4-H Club, Cin., 1991-92, Boy Scouts Am., Cin., 1985-89; mem. Walnut Hills Victory Community Coun., Cin., 1985-89, Avondale Community Coun., Cin., 1990-92; mem. Sinai Temple. Recipient Notable Recognition award Youth Crime Intervention, Cin., 1991, Community Svc. award So. Bapt. Ch., Cin., 1991, Outstanding Svc. award Cincinnatians Active to Support Edn., 1989. Mem. Ohio Assn. Elem. Sch. Adminstrs. (Exemplary Svc. award 1987), Cin. Assn. Adminstrs. and Suprs., Cin. Assn. Elem. Prins. Democrat. Methodist. Avocations: music, reading, dancing, gardening, traveling. Home: 6748 Stoll Ln Cincinnati OH 45236-4039 Office: St Joseph Elem Sch 745 Ezzard Charles Dr Cincinnati OH 45203-1410

SANGER, HERBERT SHELTON, JR., lawyer, former government official; b. Oak Hill, W.Va., Aug. 6, 1936; s. Herbert Shelton and Ethel Dean (Layne) S.; m. Rita Adele Baumgartner, Aug. 20, 1958; children: Charles, Carole, Warren, George. A.B. in English and Polit. Sci, Concord Coll., Athens, W.Va., 1958; LL.B., W.Va. U., Morgantown, 1961. Bar: W.Va. 1961, U.S. Supreme Ct. 1976, U.S. Ct. Appeals 5th and 6th cirs. 1973, 10th cir. 1978, 11th cir. 1981, 4th cir. 1982, U.S. Dist. Ct. (ea. dist.) Tenn. 1987, Tenn. 1988. Lifetime del. 6th Cir. Jud. Conf.; staff atty. Office of Gen. Counsel, TVA, Knoxville, 1961-69, asst. gen. counsel power, 1969-72; assoc. gen. counsel litigation and power Office of Gen. Counsel, TVA, 1972-73, dep. gen. counsel, 1973-75, gen. counsel, 1975-86; ptnr. Wagner, Myers & Sanger, P.C., Knoxville, 1986—; asst. prof. law U. Tenn.; Arthur B. Hodges prof. law W.Va. U.; chmn. bd. dirs. TVA Retirement System, 1975-86, Paribas Concorde Trust, Ltd., Regal Cinemas, Inc. Bd. dirs. East Tenn. Found., Knoxville Symphony Soc. Recipient Lawyers Coop award, 1961, Lawyers Title Ins. Co. award, 1961. Mem. ABA, Fed. Bar Assn., W.Va. Bar Assn., Tenn. Bar Assn., Am. Corp. Counsel Assn. (bd. dirs. 1982-87), Internat. Nuclear Law Assn., Knoxville Symphony Soc. (bd. dirs.). Baptist. Home: 5100 Malibu Dr Knoxville TN 37918-4513 Office: Wagner Myers & Sanger PC PO Box 1308 1801 Plaza Tower Knoxville TN 37901-1308

SANGER, STEPHEN W., consumer products company executive; b. 1945. With General Mills, Inc., Mpls., 1974—; v.p., gen. mgr. Northstar Divsn. General Mills, Inc., 1983, v.p., gen. mgr. new bus. devel., 1986, pres. Yoplait USA, 1986, pres. Big G Divsn., 1988, sr. v.p., 1989, vice chmn. bd., 1992—, pres., 1993-96, CEO, 1996—; bd. dirs. Donaldson Co., Inc., Mpls. Treas. Guthrie Theatre Found., Mpls. Office: Gen Mills Inc One General Mills Blvd Minneapolis MN 55426-1347

SAN GIACOMO, LAURA, actress. Appeared in films Vital Signs, 1990, Pretty Woman, 1990, Quigley Down Under, 1990, Once Around, 1991, The Other Woman, 1993, Nina Takes A Lover, 1993, The Stand, 1994, Stuart Saves His Family, 1995, Eat Your Heart Out, 1997. Office: More Medavoy Mgmt 7920 Sunset Blvd Ste 401 Los Angeles CA 90046*

SANGIULIANO, BARBARA ANN, tax manager; b. Bronx, N.Y., Dec. 28, 1959; d. Patrick John and Mildred (Soell) Gallo; m. John Warren Sangiuliano, Aug. 28, 1982. BA, Muhlenberg Coll., 1982; MST, Seton Hall U., 1989, JD, 1997. CPA, N.J.; CMA. Sr. tax mgr. KPMG Peat Marwick, Short Hills, N.J., 1988-92; sr. tax analyst Allied Signal, Morristown, N.J., 1992-93; tax mgr. AT&T, Morristown, 1993-96, Lucent Techs., Morristown, 1996—. Mem. N.J. Soc. CPAs (sec. Union County chpt.), AICPA, Inst. Mgmt. Accts., Mensa, Omicron Delta Epsilon, Phi Sigma Iota. Republican. Roman Catholic. Avocations: reading, bicycling. Home: 340 William St Scotch Plains NJ 07076-1430 Office: Lucent Techs Inc 412 Mount Kemble Ave Morristown NJ 07960-6654

SANGMEISTER, GEORGE EDWARD, lawyer, consultant, former congressman; b. Joliet, Ill., Feb. 16, 1931; s. George Conrad and Rose Engaborg (Johnson) S.; m. Doris Marie Hinspeter, Dec. 1, 1951; children: George Kurt, Kimberley Ann. BA, Elmhurst Coll., 1957; LLB, John Marshall Law Sch., 1960, JD, 1970. Bar: Ill. 1960. Ptnr. McKeown, Fitzgerald, Zollner, Buck, Sangmeister & Hutchison, 1969-89; justice of peace, 1961-63; states atty. Will County, 1964-68; mem. Ill. Ho. of Reps., 1972-76, Ill. Senate, 1977-87, 101st-103rd Congresses from 4th (now 11th) Dist. Ill., 1989-95; ret., 1995; cons. McKeown, Fitzgerald, Zollner, Buck, Hutchison, Ruttle and Assocs., 1990—. Chmn. Frankfort Twp. unit Am. Cancer Soc., Will County Emergency Housing Devel. Corp.; past trustee Will County Family Svc. Agy.; past bd. dirs. Joliet Jr. Coll. Found., Joliet Will County Ctr. for Econ. Devel., Silver Cross Found., Silver Cross Hosp. With inf. AUS, 1951-53. Mem. ABA, Ill. Bar Assn., Assn. Trial Lawyers Am., Am. Legion, Frankfort (past pres.), Mokena C. of C., Old Timers Baseball Assn., Lions. Home: 20735 Wolf Rd Mokena IL 60448-8927*

SANGREE, WALTER HINCHMAN, social anthropologist, educator; b. N.Y.C., June 15, 1926; s. Carl Micheal and Constance (LaBoiteaux) S.; m. Mary Lucinda Shaw, June 14, 1952 (div. Jan. 1986); children: Margaretta Elizabeth, Mary Cora; m. Ilse Michaelis, Dec. 31, 1988. A.B., Haverford Coll., 1950; M.A., Wesleyan U., 1952; Ph.D., U. Chgo., 1959. Asst. prof. anthropology U. Rochester, N.Y., 1957-64; assoc. prof. U. Rochester, 1964-73, prof., 1973-95, prof. emeritus, 1995—, chmn. dept. anthropology, 1974-77, acting chmn. dept., 1990; vis. scholar dept. anthropology Harvard U., 1979-80; vis. scholar Ctr. for Population Studies, Harvard U., 1986-87. Author: Age, Prayer & Politics in Tiriki, Kenya, 1966; contbr. articles to profl. jours. Co-clk. Rochester Friends Meeting, 1977-79. Fulbright scholar U.K. and Kenya, 1954-56; NSF research fellow Nigeria, 1963-65. Mem. AAAS, Am. Anthrop. Assn., Internat. African Inst., Royal Anthropol. Soc. Gt. Britain and Ireland, Sigma Xi. Democrat. Mem. Soc. of Friends. Home: PO Box 1290 65 Meadow View Dr Nantucket MA 02554 Office: U Rochester Dept Anthropology Rochester NY 14627

SANI, ROBERT LEROY, chemical engineering educator; b. Antioch, Calif., Apr. 20, 1935; m. Martha Jo Marr, May 28, 1966; children: Cynthia Kay, Elizabeth Ann, Jeffrey Paul. B.S., U. Calif.-Berkeley, 1958, M.S., 1960; Ph.D., U. Minn., 1963. Postdoctoral researcher dept. math Rensselaer Poly. Inst., Troy, N.Y., 1963-64; asst. prof. U. Ill., Urbana, 1964-70, assoc. prof., 1970-76; prof. chem. engring. U. Colo., Boulder, 1976—; co-dir. Ctr. for Low-g Fluid Mechanics and Transport Phenomena, U. Colo., Boulder, 1986-89, dir., 1989—; assoc. prof. French Ministry Edn., 1982, 84, 86, 92, 94, 95; cons. Lawrence Livermore Nat. Lab., Calif., 1974—. Contbr numerous chpts. to profl. publs.; mem. editorial bd. Internat. Jour. Numerical Methods in Fluids, 1981—, Revue Européenne des Éléments Finis, 1990—. Guggenheim fellow, 1970. Mem. AIChE, Soc. for Applied and Indsl. Math., World User Assn. in Applied Computational Fluid Dynamics (bd. dirs.). Democrat. Office: U Colo Dept Chem Engring Campus Box 424 Boulder CO 80309

SANKOVICH, JOSEPH BERNARD, cemetery management consultant; b. Johnstown, Pa., Feb. 6, 1944; s. Joseph George and Helen Mary (Kasprzyk) S. Student, St. Francis Sem., 1964-68; BA, St. Francis Coll., 1966; postgrad., St. John Provincial Sem., 1968-69; MA, U. Detroit, 1973. Cert. cemetery exec., cath. cemetery exec., profl. cons. Assoc. pastor St. Mary's Ch., Nanty Glo, Pa., 1970-71, Sacred Heart Ch., Dearborn, Mich., 1971-74; dir. Mt. Kelly Cemetery, Dearborn, 1972-84; admissions counselor U. Detroit, 1974-81; dir. religious edn. St. James Ch., Ferndale, Mich., 1981-84; exec. Diocesan Cemetery Cons., Wyoming, Pa., 1984-86; dir. cemeteries Archdiocese of Seattle, 1986-91; mgmt. cons., owner Joseph B. Sankovich & Assocs., Edmonds, Wash., 1991—; cons. Archdiocese St. Paul and Mpls., 1990—, Diocese San Diego, 1991—, Archdiocese Santa Fe, 1991—, Diocese Tucson, 1991—, Diocese Toledo, 1992—, Diocese Saginaw, 1992—, Archdiocese Edmonton, Alta., Can., 1993—, Diocese Monterrey, 1993—, Diocese Fresno, Calif., 1994—, Archdiocese Anchorage, 1995, Diocese Gaylord, Mich., 1996; interim dir. cemeteries Diocese Saginaw, 1995-96; mem. Task Force on Cremation of Bishops Com. on Liturgy Nat. Conf. Cath. Bishops, 1990-92; instr. A. Cemetery Assn. Univ. Ops./Maintenance, 1994. Author, editor: Directory of Western Catholic Cemeteries, 1992, 94; author mgmt. assessments, sales programs, market analyses, 1986—; contbr. articles to profl. jours. Trustee St. Patrick's Cathedral Archdiocese N.Y., 1997. Mem. Internat. Cemetery and Funeral Assn., Nat. Cath. Cemetery Conf., Wash. Interment Assn. (bd. dirs. 1990-91), Cath. Cemeteries of the West (founder 1987, governancy com. 1987-90). Avocations: travel, reading.

Address: Joseph B Sankovich & Assocs 9216 240th St SW Edmonds WA 98020-5600

SANKOVITZ, JAMES LEO, development director, lobbyist; b. St. Paul, July 3, 1934; s. John L. and Mabel A. (Hanrahan) S.; m. Margaret E. Mathews, Aug. 3, 1957; children: Richard, Therese, Patrick, Margaret, Katherine. BS in Journalism, Marquette U., 1956; MA in Speech, U. Denver, 1963. Dir. pub. rels. Coll. of St. Mary of the Wasatch, Salt Lake City, 1956-57; dir. pub. info. Colo. Sch. of Mines, Golden, 1957-63; assoc. dir. devel. Marquette U., Milw., 1963-66, dir. alumni fund, 1966-67, dir. alumni rels., 1967-69, asst. v.p. univ. rels., 1969-70, v.p. univ. rels., 1970-78, v.p. govtl. rels., 1978-86, v.p. govtl. and community affairs, 1986-97. Contbr. articles to profl. jours. Founding dir. Univ. Nat. Bank, Milw., 1971-74; bd. dirs. St. Coletta Sch., Jefferson, Wis., 1970-76, 86-93, chair, 1974-76. Mem. Nat. Assn. for Ind. Colls. and Univs. (bd. dirs. Washington 1986-90), Disting. Svc. award 1986), Assn. Jesuit Colls. and Univs. (fed. affairs cons. Washington 1974-90), Assn. Cath. Colls. and Univs. (fed. affairs cons. Washington 1974-85, Blue Key, Alpha Sigma Nu. Roman Catholic. Avocations: woodworking, reading. Home: 4057 N Prospect Ave Milwaukee WI 53211-2121 Office: Marquette U 1324 W Wisconsin Ave Milwaukee WI 53233-2220

SANKS, CHARLES RANDOLPH, JR., clergyman, psychotherapist; b. Yonkers, N.Y., Feb. 14, 1928; s. Charles Randolph and Myrtle Elizabeth (Bunn) S.; m. Jacquelyn Gibson, Nov. 11, 1949; children: Charlene Cynthia Saunders, Valeri Ann. BA cum laude, Stetson U., 1956; BDiv, Southeastern Sem., 1960; ThM, Union Sem., 1961; postgrad., U. Salamanca, Spain, 1975; DMinistry, Wesley Theol. Sem., 1977. Ordained to ministry Baptist Ch., 1957. Minister Judson Meml. Bapt. Ch., Fayetteville, N.C., 1957-60; interim minister First Bapt. Ch. of South Miami, Fla., 1961-62, Sunset Heights Bapt. Ch., Hialeah, Fla., 1962; sr. minister Starling Ave. Bapt. Ch., Martinsville, Va., 1963-69; assoc. pastor 1st Bapt. Ch., Washington, 1969-82, minister to Pres. U.S., 1976-80; developer ministry to community foster-care patients, 1975; dir. Pastoral Counseling Ctr. Greater Marlboro, Md., 1982-87; sr. counselor Washington Pastoral Counseling Svc., 1982-95; dir. clin. mgmt. Washington Pastoral Counseling Svc., 1988-91; ptnr. Pastoral Psychotherapy Assocs., Washington, 1984-91; fellow Am. Assn. Pastoral Counselors, 1984—; trainer Journeyman Program, Fgn. Mission Bd., So. Bapt. Convention, 1968; mem. exec. com. D.C. Bapt. Conv., 1971-77; leader, speaker in liturgics and worship N.C. Bapt. Conv. Conf., 1972, 75; cons. Pastoral Psychotherapy Assocs., Washington, 1981-84; lectr. on worship and liturgics So. Bapt. Theol. Sem., Louisville, 1978; lectr. Stetson U., Deland, Fla., 1978, So. Ecumenical Conf., Atlanta, 1978. Bd. dirs. Uplift House, Washington, 1970-73, Day Care Ctr., Martinsville, Va., 1963-69, Big Brother Orgn. and Sheltered Workshop, Martinsville, Va., 1963-69. Served to cpl. USMC, 1946-49. Fellow Interpreters' House, Lake Junaluska, N.C., 1968-79; guest Oxford U., Eng., 1981. Mem. Am. Digestive Disease Soc. (bd. dirs. 1979-87). Democrat. Baptist. Avocations; travel; horseback riding; music; art. Home: 3087 Oak Chase Dr Roswell GA 30075-5457

SANKS, ROBERT LELAND, environmental engineer, emeritus educator; b. Pomona, Calif., Feb. 19, 1916; s. John B. and Nellie G. (Church) S.; m. Mary Louise Clement, May 16, 1946 (dec. Oct. 1994); children: Margaret Nadine, John Clement. Registered profl. engr., Mont. Draftsman City of La Habra Calif., 1940; asst. engr. Alex Morrison cons. engr., Fullerton, Calif., 1941; jr. engr. U.S. Army Engrs., Los Angeles, 1941-42; asst. research engr. dept. civil engring. U. Calif.-Berkeley, 1942-45; structural engr. The Austin Co., Oakland, Calif., 1945-46; instr. dept. civil engring. U. Utah, Salt Lake city, 1946-49; asst. prof. U. Utah, Salt Lake City, 1949-55, assoc. prof., 1955-58; structural engr. The Lang Co., Salt Lake City, 1950; instrument man Patti McDonald Co., Anchorage, 1951; checker Western Steel Co., Salt Lake City, 1952; structural engr. Moran, Proctor, Meuser and Rutledge, N.Y.C., 1953, F.C. Torkelson Co., Salt Lake City, 1955; soils engr. R.L. Sloane & Assocs., Salt Lake City, 1956; prof., chmn. dept. civil engring. Gonzaga U., Spokane, Wash., 1958-61; prof. dept. civil engring.-engring. mechanics Mont. State U., Bozeman, 1966-82, prof. emeritus, 1982—; vis. prof. U. Tex.-Austin, 1974-75; part-time sr. engr. Christian, Spring, Sielbach & Assoc., Billings, Mont., 1974-82; cons. engr., 1945—; lectr. at pumping sta. design workshops, 1988—; assoc. specialist San. Engring. Research Lab., 1963-65, research engr., 1966. Author: Statically Indeterminate Structural Analysis, 1961; co-author: (with Takashi Assano) Land Treatment and Disposal of Municipal and Industrial Wastewaters, 1976, Water Treatment Plant Design for the Practicing Engineer, 1978; editor-in-chief: Pumping Station Design, 1989 (award Excellence profl. & scholarly pub. div. Assn. Am. Pubs. 1989); contbr. articles on civil engring. to profl. publs. Named to Wall of Fame, Fullerton High Sch., 1987; NSF fellow, 1961-63. Fellow ASCE (chmn. local qualifications com. intermountain sect. 1950-56, pres. intermountain sect. 1957-58); mem. Am. Water Works Assn. (life, pres. Mont. sect. 1981-82, George Warren Fuller award), Mont. Water Environ. Fedn., Assn. Environ. Engring. Profs., Rotary, Sigma Xi, Chi Epsilon. Home: 411 W Dickerson St Bozeman MT 59715-4538 Office: Mont State U Dept Civil Engring Bozeman MT 59717

SAN MARTIN, ROBERT L., federal official. MME, PhDME, U. Fla. Prof. mech. engring. N.Mex. State U.; past dir. N.Mex. Solar Energy Inst., N.Mex. Energy Inst.; dep. asst. sec. renewable energy, solar energy, field ops. Office Conservation and Renewable Energy, Washington, 1978-89; dep. asst. sec. utility techs. Office Energy Efficiency and Renewable Energy (formerly Office Conservation and Renewable Energy), Washington, 1990-95; acting asst. sec. Office Energy Efficiency and Renewable Energy, 1993-95; chief scientist Office Energy Efficiency and Renewable Energy, Washington, 1995—; past chariperson Renewable Energy Working Party Internat. Energy Agy. Mem. ASME (former chair solar divsn.), Am. Solar Energy Soc. (past bd. dirs.). Office: US Dept Energy Energy Efficiency & Renewable Energy 1000 Independence Ave SW Washington DC 20585-0001*

SAN MIGUEL, MANUEL, painter, historian, composer, poet; b. Guayama, P.R., Sept. 29, 1930; s. Manuel and Luisa (Griffo) San M.; m. Sandra Bonilla, July 12, 1969; children: Manuel, Ana. Educated, U. P.R., 1947-51, U. Pa., 1966-68, Arts Students League, N.Y.C., 1968-69. Historian, San Juan Nat. Historic Site, Nat. Park Svc., 1953-63; exec. sec. Acad. Arts and Scis., San Juan, 1963-64; founder of mus. and study collection El Morro Castle San Juan Nat. Hist. Site (U.S. Recipient Commendable Svc. award, 1964, citation for commendable svc. in field of hist. rsch. and interpretation, 1964); painter, writer, musician, 1964—; cons. in field. Exhibited in U. P.R., 1958, 62, Ateneo de P.R., 1962, Pan-Am. Union, Washington, 1963, Bienal Mexico, 1972, Bienal Rio de Janeiro, 1976, Orange County Schs. Mus. Art, Orlando, Fla., 1992, Mus. Modern Art, Paris, 1994, and numerous other nat. and internat. exhbns.; contbr. monographs on historical work in San Juan Nat. Historic Site to U.S. Nat. Archives, Washington; contbr. poetry to anthologies including Anthology of Latin American Poets, vol. III, 1987; rec. artist popular music of P.R. Capt. U.S. Army, 1951-53, Korea. Decorated Bronze Star with valor clasp and oakleaf cluster, Purple Heart, Combat Infantryman Badge, others; recipient citation Nat. Park Svc., 1964, Lifetime Achievement award in cultural arts Govt. of Puerto Rico and Spanish Heritage Found., 1996; named One of Ten Outstanding Hispanic Men, Orlando, Fla., 1991. Mem. VFW (life), Disabled Am. Vets. (life), Am. Legion, Acad. Arts and Scis., Ateneo de P.R. (bd. govs. 1959-60), Am. Biog. Inst. (bd. advisors, life mem. bd. govs.), Am. Philatelic Soc. (postal commemorative soc.), Inst. Puerto Rican Culture (cons.), Puerto Rican Philatelic Assn., Internat. Platform Assn., Lions (Lion of Yr. 1962-63). Achievements include documentary research in the restoration of Castillo San Marcos, St. Augustine, Fla., Castillo San Felipe de Barajas, Colombia, South Am., and restoration of San Juan fortifications and city walls. Home: 1214 Howell Creek Dr Winter Springs FL 32708-4516

SAN MIGUEL, SANDRA BONILLA, social worker; b. Santurce, P.R., May 23, 1944; d. Isidoro and Flora (Carrero) Bonilla; m. Manuel San Miguel, July 12, 1969. BA, St. Joseph's Coll., 1966; MS in Social Work, Columbia U., 1970. Case worker Dept. Labor, Migration Div., N.Y.C., 1966-68; clin. social worker N.Y.C. Housing Authority, N.Y.C., 1968-69, Children's Aid Soc., N.Y.C., 1969-71; sr. social worker Traveler's Aid Soc., San Juan, P.R., 1971-74; coord., supr. Dept. Addiction Control Svcs., San Juan, P.R., 1974-77; substance abuse div. dir. Seminole County Mental Health Ctr., Altamonte Springs, Fla., 1978-81; cons. pvt. practice Hispanic Cons. Svcs., Winter Springs, Fla., 1982—; adj. prof. Seminole Community Coll., Lake Mary, Fla., 1986-90; sch. social worker I Seminole County Pub. Schs., Sanford, Fla., 1986-91, lead sch. social worker, 1991—; mem. pres.'s minority adv. coun. U. Ctrl. Fla., 1982—, vice chair, 1982-86, chair, 1986-90; mem. bd. regents EEO adv. com. State U. Sys. Fla., 1985-89; bd. dirs. Seminole Cmty. Mental Health Ctr., 1986-94, 95—, v.p., 1988-90, pres., 1990-91; adv. bd. Nat. Devereaux Found. Ctrl. Fla., 1993—, women's adv. bd. South Seminloe Hosp., Fla., 1994—, v.p.; mem. Fla. Consortium on Tchr. Edn. for Am. Minorities, 1990—; mem. local com. Hispanic Info. and Telecomms. Network, 1990; mem. Seminole County (Fla.) Juvenile Justice Coun., 1993—; mem. statewide student svcs. adv. com. Dept. Edn. Fla., 1993-96, student svcs. adv. group, 1996—. Recipient Pres.'s Outstanding Svc. award UCF, 1991, Ponce de Leon Hispanic Com. award, 1992, Svc. Recognition Plaque Seminole Cmty. Mental Health Ctr., 1991, Oustanding Contribution to Student Svcs. Cert. Fla. Dept. Edn., 1995. Mem. NASW (appt. nat. sch. social work credential com. 1996—), Fla. Assn. Sch. Social Workers (co-founder minority caucus 1988, columnist quar. newsletter Minority Corner 1988-92, bd. dirs. 1989—, sec. 1990-92, v.p. 1992-93, pres. 1993-94, Leadership Plaque 1994), Sch. Social Work Assn. Am., Fla. Assn. Student Svcs. Adminstrs., Collegiate Social Workers P.R., Columbia U. Alumni Assn., St. Joseph's Coll. Alumni Assn. Home: 1214 Howell Creek Dr Winter Springs FL 32708-4516 Office: Seminole County Pub Schs 1401 S Magnolia Ave Sanford FL 32771-3400

SANNA, RICHARD JEFFREY, lawyer; b. N.Y.C., July 20, 1949; s. Francis and Ann (Bryant) S.; m. Rosemarie A. Lagnena, Nov. 21, 1971; children: John, Kristin, Michele, Elisabeth. BA, St. Johns U., Jamaica, N.Y., 1971; JD, Del. Law Sch., 1975. Bar: N.Y. 1977, U.S. Dist. Ct. (so. dist.) N.Y. 1978, U.S. Dist. Ct. (ea. dist.) N.Y. 1979, U.S. Ct. Appeals (2d cir.) 1979, U.S. Supreme Ct. 1980. Assoc. McKay, King, Castricone & Piazza, Queens, N.Y., 1978-80; sr. ptnr. Sarisohn, Sarisohn, Thierman, Carner & LeBow, Commack, N.Y., 1980-82; ptnr. Migliore, Sanna & Infranco P.C., Commack, 1982-85; sole practice Hauppauge and Commack, N.Y., 1985; sr. counsel Eagle Funding, Natl., Jericho, N.Y., 1990—. mem. adv. council St. Martins of Tours Ch., Bethpage, N.Y., 1983—; atty. Bethpage Civic Assn., 1985—. Mem. N.Y. State Bar Assn., Suffolk County Bar Assn. (chmn. fee dispute com. 1984-86, recipient I.U.J.H. F.D. Roosevelt award for meritorious svc. AFL-CIO, 1992), Assn. Trial Lawyers Am., N.Y. Trial Lawyers Assn., Columbian Lawyers Assn. Republican. Roman Catholic. Lodge: K.C. Home: 91 Sycamore Ave Bethpage NY 11714-2226

SANNEH, LAMIN, religion educator; married; 2 children. MA in Arabic and Islamic Studies, U. Birmingham, Eng., 1968; postgrad., Near East Sch. Theology, Beirut, 1968-69; PhD in African Islamic History, U. London, 1974. Resident tutor Ctr. for Study of Islam and Christianity, Ibadan, Nigeria, 1969-71; vis. scholar U. Sierra Leone, Freetown, 1974-75; lectr. U. Ghana, Legon, 1975-78, U. Aberdeen, Scotland, 1978-81; asst. prof., then assoc. prof. history of religion Harvard U., Cambridge, Mass., 1981-89; prof., chmn. Coun. on African Studies Yale U., New Haven, 1989—; cons. World Coun. Chs., 1974-79, The Africans TV series, PBS, 1986, Program on Christian-Muslim Rels. in Africa, 1988—, Prof. Lamin Sanneh Found., Banjul, The Gambia; instr. San Francisco Theol. Sem., San Anselmo, Calif., 1987, Iliff Sch. Theology, Denver, 1988, Disting. Staley Christian lectr. Mennonite Brethern Bible Coll., Winnipeg, Can., 1988; lectr. Princeton (N.J.) Theol. Sem., 1988; gest lectr. Haverford (Pa.) Coll., 1988; Mars lectr. Northwestern U., 1988, Spriggs lectr. Protestant Episcopal Theol. Sem., Alexandria, Va., 1990; Cullum lectr. Augusta Coll., U. Ga., 1990; mem. Clare Hall, Cambridge (Eng.) U., 1995; participant various acad. confs. Author: West African Christianity: The Religious Impact, 1983, Translating the Message: The Missionary Impact on Culture, 1989, The Jakhanke Muslim Clerics: A Religious and Historical Study of Islam in Senegambia (c. 1250-1905), 1990, Encountering the West: Christianity and the Global Cultural Process, 1993, The Crown and the Turban, 1996, Piety and Power: Muslims and Christians in West Africa, 1996; also articles; co-editor Jour. Religion in Africa, 1979-84; mem. adv. bd. Studies in Interreligious Dialogue; editor-at-large The Christian Century; contbg. editor Internat. Bull. Missionary Rsch. Decorated comdr. de l'Ordre Nat. du Lion (Senegal); recipient award Theol. Edn. Fund, 1971-74, award U. London, 1972, Carnegie Truste of Univs. of Scotland, 1980. Mem. Am. Theol. Soc., African Theologians (exec. com.), Royal African Soc. Home: 47 Morris St Hamden CT 06517-3426 Office: Yale U Div Sch 409 Prospect St New Haven CT 06511-2167

SANNER, JOHN HARPER, retired pharmacologist; b. Anamosa, Iowa, Apr. 29, 1931; s. Lee Michael and Helen (Grace) S.; m. Marilyn Joan Eichorst, Dec. 28, 1958; children: Linda Leigh Costanzo, Steven Bradley. BS, U. Iowa, 1954, MS, 1961, PhD, 1964. Rsch. investigator G.D. Searle & Co., Skokie, Ill., 1963-69, sr. rsch. investigator, 1969-75, rsch. fellow, 1975-86, ret., 1986—; mem. Deerfield (Ill.) Cable and Telecom. Commn. Conducted pioneering rsch. in prostaglandin antogonists; contbr. articles to profl. jours. Mem. Deerfield (Ill.) Cable and Telecomm. Commn. 1st lt. USAFR, 1955-57. Mem. Am. Soc. for Pharmacology and Exptl. Therapeutics (ret.), Ill. Videomakers Assn., Wedding and Event Videographers Assn. Internat., Deerfield C. of C. Republican. Avocations: video photography and production. Office: Sanner Video Svc PO Box 199 Deerfield IL 60015

SANNER, ROYCE NORMAN, lawyer; b. Lancaster, Minn., Mar. 9, 1931; s. Oscar N. and Clara (Hermanson) S.; m. Janice L. Sterne, Dec. 27, 1972; children—Michelle Joy, Craig Allen. BS, Moorhead State U., 1953; LLB cum laude, U. Minn., 1961. Bar: Minn. 1961, U.S. Dist. Ct. Minn. 1961, U.S. Supreme Ct. 1981. Tchr. English Karlstad (Minn.) High Sch., 1955-57; counsel IDS Life Ins. Co., Mpls., 1961-68; v.p., gen. counsel IDS Life Ins. Co., 1969-72, exec. v.p., gen. counsel, 1972-77; dir. corp. devel. Investors Diversified Svcs., Inc., Mpls., 1968-69; v.p., gen. counsel Investors Diversified Svcs., Inc., 1975-78; v.p. Investors Diversified Svcs., Inc. (Benefit Plans Svc. Group), 1978-80, v.p., gen. counsel, 1980-82; v.p. law Northwestern Nat. Life Ins. Co., Mpls., 1982-83, sr. v.p., gen. counsel, sec., 1983-96; sr. v.p., gen. counsel, sec. ReliaStar Fin. Corp. (formerly known as NWNL Cos., Inc.), Mpls., 1988-96; of counsel Maslon Edelman Borman & Brand, Mpls., 1996—; bd. dirs. Fairview Univ. Ctr., chmn. bd. dirs. Friendship Ventures, Inc., Fairview Hosp. and Healthcare Svcs. Served with U.S. Army, 1953-55. Mem. ABA, Am. Soc. Corp. Secs., Minn. Bar Assn., Hennepin County Bar Assn., Fed. Bar Assn., Assn. of Life Ins. Counsel, Minn. Corp. Counsel Assn., Mpls. Club, Rotary. Home: 4811 Westminster Rd Minnetonka MN 55345-3723 Office: Maslon Edelman Borman & Brand 3300 Norwest Ctr 90 S 7th St Minneapolis MN 55402-3903

SANNUTI, PEDDAPULLAIAH, electrical engineering educator; b. Rajupalem, Andhra-Pradesh, India, Apr. 2, 1941; came to U.S., 1965; m. 1965; children: Aruna, Arun. PhD, U. Ill., Urbana, 1968. Asst. prof. dept. elec. and computer engring. Rutgers U., Piscataway, N.J., 1968-71, assoc. prof., 1971-76, prof., 1976—. Fellow IEEE. Office: Rutgers Univ Dept Elec & Computer Engring Piscataway NJ 08855-0909

SANNWALD, WILLIAM WALTER, librarian; b. Chgo., Sept. 12, 1940; s. William Frederick and Irene Virginia (Stanish) S.; children: Sara Ann, William Howard. B.A., Beloit Coll., 1963; M.A.L.S., Rosary Coll., River Forest, Ill., 1966; M.B.A., Loyola U., Chgo., 1974. Mktg. mgr. Xerox Univ. Microfilms, 1972-75; assoc. dir. Detroit Public Library, 1975-77; dir. Ventura (Calif.) County Library, 1977-79; city libr. San Diego Public Libr., 1979—; vis. instr. mktg. San Diego State U. Author: Checklist of Library Building Design Considerations, 3d edit., 1997; chairperson editorial adv. bd. Pub. Librs. Pres. Met. Libraries Sect., 1989. Recipient Outstanding Prof. award and Outstanding Mktg. Prof. award, 1985; Award of Merit AIA San Diego chpt., 1988, Irving Gill award for Architecture and Mgmt., 1995. Mem. ALA, Online Computer Libr. Ctr. (mem. users coun. 1996), Calif. Library Authority for Systems and Services (pres. congress of mems. 1980), Calif. Library Assn., Libr. Admintrn. and Mgmt. Assn. (pres. 1995—). Roman Catholic. Home: 3538 Paseo Salamoner La Mesa CA 91941-7329 Office: San Diego Pub Libr 820 E St San Diego CA 92101-6416

SANO, EMILY JOY, museum director; b. Santa Ana, Calif., Feb. 17, 1942; d. Masao and Lois Kikue (Inokuchi) S. BA, Ind. U., 1967; MA, Columbia U., 1970, MPhil, 1976, PhD, 1983. Lectr. Oriental Art Vassar Coll., Poughkeepsie, N.Y., 1974-79; curator Asian Art, asst. dir. programs Kimbell Art Mus., Ft. Worth, 1979-89; dep. dir. collections and exhbns. Dallas Mus. Art, 1989-92; dep. dir., chief curator Asian Art Mus., San Francisco, 1993-95, dir., 1995—. Author: Great Age of Japanese Buddhist Sculpture, 1982; editor: The Blood of Kings, 1986, Weavers, Merchants and Kings, 1984, Painters of the Great Ming, 1993. Active Assn. Art Mus. Dirs.; vis. com. Harvard U. Art Mus. Woodrow Wilson Fellow, 1966-67; grantee Carnegie, 1963-64, Fulbright-Hays, 1977-78. Office: Asian Art Mus Golden Gate Park San Francisco CA 94118

SANO, ROY I., bishop. Ordained to ministry United Meth. Ch., later consecrated bishop; appointed Bishop Rocky Mountain Conf., United Meth. Ch., Denver. Office: PO Box 6006 Pasadena CA 91102-6006*

SANSBURY, BLAKE EDWARD, product development engineer; b. Louisville, Jan. 6, 1957; s. Edward R. and Marilyn M. (Blake) S.; m. Amy S. Zeldin, June 12, 1994. BS in mech. engring., U. Louisville, 1982. Cert. mfg. tech., 1985. Intern mfg. engring. TubeTurns, Inc., Louisville, 1980-82; tooling engr. Square D Co., Oxford, Ohio, 1982-85; engring. mgr. Dayton-Walther Corp., Dayton, Ohio, 1985-87; process engr. U.S. Precision Lens, Inc. (divsn. Corning, Inc.), Cin., 1987-89; sr. product devel. engr. U.S. Precision Lens, Inc., Cin., 1989—. Author: (manual) Curve-Master, 1989, (handbook) O-Ring Coupler Guidelines for Design, 1992. Asst. scoutmaster Boys Scouts Am., eagle scout, 1974. Mem. Nat. Mgmt. Assn. (Outstanding New Mem. award 1984), Am. Mgmt. Assn., Machining Tech. Assn., Soc. Plastics Engrs., Soc. Mfg. Engrs., Sigma Phi Epsilon (pres. 1981-82). Achievements include U.S. patent for focus adjustment assembly for projection TV. Home: 901 Old Orchard Rd Cincinnati OH 45230 Office: US Precision Lens Inc 3997 Mcmann Rd Cincinnati OH 45245-2307

SANSBURY, OLIN BENNETT, JR., symphony orchestra executive; b. Florence, S.C., Dec. 10, 1937; s. Olin Bennett and Gladys Ruth (Snipes) S.; m. Helen Cecile Hyman, Aug. 24, 1963; 1 child, Olin Bennett, III. B.A. in History, Wofford Coll., 1959; Ph.D. in Internat. Studies, U. S.C., 1972. Reporter, editorial writer WBTW-TV, Florence, 1963-64, 1966-67; asst. dir. student affairs U. S.C., Florence, 1969-70; dean students, Francis Marion Coll. USC, Columbia, 1970-71; asst. vice provost, asst. prof. govt. and internat. studies U. S.C., Spartanburg, 1971-73, chancellor, assoc. prof. govt. and internat. studies, 1973-93; chancellor emeritus, 1993—. Bd. dirs. S.C. Coun. Econ. Edn., 1977-94, S.C. Coun. for the Humanities, 1986-96, Am. Coun. Edn. Commn. Govtl. Rels., 1991-93; rep. Pres.' Commn. Divsn. II NCAA, 1991-93; founding com. bd. regents Leadership, Spartanburg, 1980-85. With U.S. Army, 1960-63. H.B. Earhart fellow, 1965-66, 69. Mem. Am. Assn. State Colls. and Univs. (bd. dirs. 1989-92).

SANSEVERINO, RAYMOND ANTHONY, lawyer; b. Bklyn., Feb. 16, 1947; s. Raphael and Alice Ann (Camerano) S.; m. Karen Marie Mooney, Aug. 24, 1968 (dec. 1980); children: Deirdre Ann, Stacy Lee; m. Victoria Vent, June 6, 1982 (div. 1995). AB in English Lit., Franklin & Marshall Coll., 1968; JD cum laude, Fordham U., 1972. Bar: N.Y. 1973, U.S. Dist. Ct. (so. dist. and ea. dist.) N.Y. 1973, U.S. Ct. Appeals (2d cir.) 1974, U.S. Supreme Ct. 1986. Assoc. Rogers & Wells, N.Y.C., 1972-75, Corbin & Gordon, N.Y.C., 1975-77; ptnr. Corbin Silverman & Sanseverino, N.Y.C., 1978—, mng. ptnr., 1985—. Contbr. articles to profl. jours.; articles editor Fordham Law Rev., 1971-72. Recipient West Pub. Co. prize, 1972. Mem. ABA, Assn. Bar City of N.Y., N.Y. State Bar Assn., Twin Oaks Swim and Tennis Club (bd. dirs. 1981—, pres. 1993—). Republican. Roman Catholic. Office: Corbin Silverman & Sanseverino 805 3rd Ave New York NY 10022-7513

SANSOM, ANDREW, federal agency administrator; b. Hawthorne, Nev., Oct. 10, 1945; s. Ernest Samuel and Imo Leone (Heacock) S.; m. Nona Wood, Dec. 30, 1966; children: Andrew Wood, April Claire. BS cum laude, Tex. Tech. U., 1968. Environ. coord. White House Conf. Youth, Washington; spl. asst. Office Sec. Interior, Washington; dir. conservation edn. Fed. Agy. Adminstrn., Washington, 1974-76; dep. dir. Energy Inst. U. Houston, 1976-80; v.p. devel. Old River Co.; exec. dir. Tex. Nature Conservancy; coord. land acquisition and mgmt. Tex. Parks and Wildlife, Austin, exec. dir., 1991—. Author: Texas Lost, 1995; contbr. articles to Tex. Monthly mag., The Tex. Observer, Houston City Mag., Politics Today, Tex. Hwys., Tex. Parks and Wildlife. Commr. Brazoria County Parks Bd.; founder Cradle Tex. Conservancy; trustee Tex. Hist. Found., Bat Conservation Internat.; del. Rep. Nat. Conv., 1980; chmn. State Senate campaign Buster Brown; county chmn. George Bush campaign; co-chmn. Gov. Clements Brazoria county campaign; appt. Gov.'s Task Force on Flooding and Flood Control, 1981. Recipient Conservationist of Yr. Sportsmans Clubs Tex., Conservation award Chevron, 1990, Cornelius Amory Pugsley medal Nat. Parks Found., 1993. Chuck Yaeger award Nat. Fish and Wildlife Found., 1995. Office: Tex Parks & Wildlife Dept 4200 Smith School Rd Austin TX 78744-3218

SANSONE, PAUL J., automotive executive; b. 1955. CEO Sansone Auto Network, Avenel, N.J., 1980—. Home: 100 Route 1 Avenel NJ 07001-1630*

SANSTEAD, WAYNE GODFREY, state superintendent, former lieutenant governor; b. Hot Springs, Ark., Apr. 16, 1935; s. Godfrey A. and Clara (Buen) S.; m. Mary Jane Bober, June 16, 1957; children: Timothy, Jonathan. B.A. in Speech and Polit. Sci, St. Olaf Coll., 1957; M.A. in Pub. Address, Northwestern U., 1966; Ed.D., U. N.D., 1974. Tchr. Luverne, Minn., 1959-60; dir. forensics Minot (N.D.) High Sch., 1960-71, tchr. social sci., 1960-78; mem. N.D. Ho. of Reps., 1965-70, 83-85, N.D. Senate, 1971-73; lt. gov. N.D. Bismarck, 1973-81; supt. pub. instrn. N.D., Bismarck, 1985—. Served with AUS, 1957-59. Recipient Disting. Alumnus award St. Olaf Coll., 1991; named Outstanding Freshman Senator A.P., 1971, Outstanding Young Educator, N.D. Jr. C. of C., 1967, Outstanding Young Man, Minot Jr. C. of C., 1964; Coe Family Found. scholar, 1963, Eagleton scholar Rutgers U., 1969. Mem. N.D. Edn. Assn., NEA (legis. com. 1969—), Central States Speech Assn., Am. Forensic Assn., Jr. C. of C., Sons of Norway. Democrat. Lutheran (chmn. Western N.D. research and social action com. 1962-68). Clubs: Elk, Toastmaster. Home: 1120 Columbia Dr Bismarck ND 58504-6514 Office: Dept Pub Instrn 600 E Boulevard Ave Bismarck ND 58505-0660*

SANSWEET, STEPHEN JAY, journalist, author, marketing executive; b. Phila., June 14, 1945; s. Jack Morris and Fannie (Axelrod) S. BS, Temple U., 1966. Reporter Phila. Inquirer, 1966-69; reporter Wall Street Jour., Phila., 1969-71, Montreal, Que, Can., 1971-73; reporter Wall Street Jour., L.A., 1973-84, dep. bur. chief, 1984-87, bur. chief, 1987-96; dir. speciality mktg. Lucasfilm Ltd., San Rafael, Calif., 1996—; sr. editor Star Wars Galaxy Mag., 1996—; lectr. bus. journalism U. So. Calif., L.A., 1984-87. Author: The Punishment Cure, 1976, Science Fiction Toys and Models, 1981, Star Wars: From Concept to Screen to Collectible, 1992, Tomart's Guide to Worldwide Star Wars Collectibles, 1994, The Quotable Star Wars, 1996; cons. editor: Star Wars Galaxy, 1993, 2d series, 1994, 3d series, 1995; editor: Star Wars Trilogy Spl. Edn. card sets, 1997. Recipient award for best fire story Phila. Fire Dept., 1968, Pub. Svc.-Team Mem. award Sigma Delta Chi, 1977; finalist Loeb award, 1990. Mem. Soc. Profl. Journalists. Avocation: collecting toys and movie memorabilia. Office: Lucasfilm Ltd PO Box 2009 San Rafael CA 94912-2009

SANT, JOHN TALBOT, lawyer; b. Ann Arbor, Mich., Oct. 7, 1932; s. John Francis and Josephine (Williams) S.; m. Almira Steedman Baldwin, Jan. 31, 1959; children: John Talbot Jr., Richard Baldwin, Frank Williams. AB, Princeton U., 1954; LLB, Harvard U., 1957. Bar: Mo. 1957. Assoc. Thompson, Mitchell, Douglas & Neill, St. Louis, 1958-60; atty. McDonnell Aircraft Co., St. Louis, 1960-61, asst. sec., 1961-62, sec., 1962-67; sec. McDonnell Douglas Corp., St. Louis, 1967-76, asst. gen. counsel, 1969-74, corp. v.p. legal, 1974-75, corp. v.p., gen. counsel, 1975-88, bd. dirs. 1978-82, sr. v.p., gen. counsel, 1988-91; ptnr. Bryan Cave, 1991-96, of counsel, 1997. Vestry of St. Michael and St. George, St. Louis, 1979-82, 87-90, 93-95; bd. dirs. Grace Hill Neighborhood Svcs. Inc., St. Louis, 1987-93; pres. Grace Hill Settlement House, 1996—; mem. transition task force Supt. Elect of St. Louis Pub. Schs., 1996. Mem. ABA (pub. contracts sec., coun. 1987-91), Am. Law Inst., Mo. Bar. Assn., St. Louis Bar Assn. Home: 9 Ridgewood St Saint Louis MO 63124-1849 Office: Bryan Cave 1 Metropolitan Sq Saint Louis MO 63102-2733

SANTA, DONALD F., JR., federal agency administrator; m. Karen Santa; children: Madelyn, Evan. AB, Duke U., 1980; JD, Columbia U., 1983. Assoc. atty. Andrews & Kurth, Washington, 1983-85, Van Nes, Feldman, Sutcliffe & Curtis, P.C., Washington, 1985-89; counsel U.S. Senate com. on Energy and Natural Resources; mem. Fed. Energy Regulatory Commn., 1993—. Co-author: (with Patricia J. Beneke) Federal Natural Gas Policy and the Energy Policy Act of 1992, 1993, (with Clifford S. Sikora) Open Access and Transition Costs: Will the Electric Industry Track the Natural Gas Industry Restructuring?, 1994; contbr. articles to law jours. Mem. Nat. Assn. Regulatory Utilities Commrs. (com. on gas). Office: Fed Energy Regulatory Commn 888 1st St NE Rm 11C Washington DC 20426-0001

SANTACANA, GUIDO E., physiology educator; b. Placetas, Las Villa, Cuba, Dec. 25, 1952; came to U.S., 1964; s. Guido and Concepcion (Sanchez) S.; m. Maria E. Laffitte, May 27, 1978; 1 child, Guido E. BS, Coll. Agrl. and Mech. Arts, Mayaguez, P.R., 1975; PhD, Med. Sci. Campus, San Juan, P.R., 1982. From instr. to asst. prof. dept. nat. sci. Sacred Heart U., Santurce, P.R., 1976-84; instr. dept. physiology S.J.B. Sch. Med., Hato Rey, P.R., 1981-83; from asst. prof. dept. physiology to dir. grad. program U. Central del Caribe Sch. Medicine, Bayamon, P.R., P.R., 1984-95; chmn. dept. physiology Ponce Sch. Medicine, 1995-97; with U. Puerto Rico Sch. Medicine, San Juan, 1997—. Contbr. articles to sci. jours. Recipient Sci. award Bausch & Lomb, San Juan, P.R., 1971, Rsch. Ctr. for Minority Instns. rsch. grant NIH, Bayamon, P.R., 1986—, Minority Access to Rsch. Careers Program faculty fellowship NIH, San Juan, 1979-82. Mem. AAVSO Assn. (Boston), Am. Physiol. Soc. (Porter physiology devel. grants com.), Am. Assn. Chmn. Depts. Physiology, Soc. Exptl. Biology and Medicine, Alpha Omega Alpha. Roman Catholic. Avocations: amateur radio, astronomy.

SANTA-COLOMA, BERNARDO, secondary school educator, counselor; b. N.Y.C., May 31, 1934; s. Bernardo Santa-Coloma Sr. and Belma Remotti; m. Sofia A. Santa-Coloma, Dec. 22, 1981; children: Ananda, Anita. BA in Humanistic Psychology, U. Calif., Santa Cruz, 1973; MA in Integral Counseling Psychology, Calif. Inst. Integral Studies, San Francisco, 1976; MEd in Secondary Edn., U. Nev., Las Vegas, 1979; 3 level cert., Feuerstein's Instrumental, Enrichment Program; postgrad., U. Sarasota and U. Houston. Cert. secondary edn. tchr. ESl, history, English, Tex.; cert. guidance counselor Tex. Edn. Assn., lic. marriage and family therapist, Tex.; nat. cert. counselor. Mem. tchr. corps., vol. VISTA, Las Vegas, Nev., 1976-79; family counselor, English tutor Diocese of Matamoros and Valle Hermoso Tamps, Mexico, Cath. Family Svcs. and Vol. Ednl. and Social Svcs., Amarillo, Tex., 1980-82; grad. asst. Pan Am. U., Brownsville, Tex.; at-risk program, low-level reading instr. Brownsville Ind. Sch. Dist., 1984-94; basic skills instr. James Pace High Sch., Brownsville; counselor and psychotherapist Family Effectiveness and Devel. Program, Kids in Crisis Teenage Crisis Hotline, La Casa Esperanza Home for Boys; basic adult reading instr. Southmost Coll.; ESL, lang. arts tchr. Alternative Ctr.; tchr., pvt. practice counselor, Brownsville Ind. Sch. Dist. Family Ctrs., 1994—. Contbr. articles to profl. jours. in U.S. and Mex. including Integracion Integral, Journey in Matamoros. Vol. VISTA, 1976-79, VISTA Tchr. Corps, Las Vegas, Peace Corps, Thailand, 1979, Vol. Edn./Soc. Svc., Tex., Mex., 1980-82. With USN, 1952-56, medic neuropsychiatric wards San Diego and Guam. Recipient scholarship U. Calif.-Santa Cruz, 1971-73, U. Nev. tchr. corps, 1977-79; named grad. asst. Calif. Inst. Integral Studies, 1974-76. Home: PO Box 3941 Brownsville TX 78523-3941 also: Country Club 2009 Madero Dr Brownsville TX 78521-1734 *Waking up is really the seed of perfection, of personal and transpersonal realization - involution precedes evolution! To be is to do and to do IS. In the final analysis, final judgment, what shall we - yes, you and I contribute to our fellowman, to posterity? - we often die before giving birth to ourselves - truly to be reborn is not easy; we create, instead, an intense paradox, toward life, toward our destiny.*

SANTA MARIA, PHILIP JOSEPH, III, lawyer; b. Ft. Lauderdale, Fla., Oct. 10, 1945; s. Philip Joseph Jr. and Margaret Elizabeth (Hillard) S.; m. Gail Suzanne Claussen, Aug. 23, 1969; children: Todd, Carly. AB, Gettysburg (Pa.) Coll., 1967; JD, Am. U., 1970. Bar: Md. 1970, U.S. Ct. Mil. Appeals 1971, U.S. Supreme Ct. 1975, D.C. 1976, Calif. 1976, U.S. Dist. Ct. Md. 1977, U.S. Ct. Appeals (4th cir.) 1977. Assoc. Simpson & Simpson, Rockville, Md., 1974-75; sole practice Gaithersburg, Md., 1975-79; ptnr. Haight, Rosfeld, Noble & Santa Maria, Gaithersburg, 1980-81, Santa Maria & Weiss, Chartered, Gaithersburg, 1981—. Mem. editorial bd. Am. U. Law Rev., 1969; author pamphlet What To Do. Mem. Standby Selective Service Local Bd. 69, Montgomery County, Md., 1981-83, Standby Selective Service Bd. of Appeals, Md., 1983-92, Met. Wash. YMCA Trustee's Coun., 1990-93. Served to capt. USAF, 1970-74. Named one of Outstanding Young Men in Am., 1971. Mem. ABA, Calif. Bar Assn., D.C. Bar Assn., Montgomery County Bar Assn., Md. Trial Lawyers Assn. Clubs: Montgomery Soccer, Inc. (league commr. 1985); Gaithersburg Tennis Assn. (pres. 1976); Snowbird Youth Ski (Md.) (pres. 1975-76). Home: 10319 Royal Woods Ct Gaithersburg MD 20879-1027 Office: Santa Maria & Weiss Chartered 18522 Office Park Dr Gaithersburg MD 20879-2500

SANTANA, CARLOS, guitarist; b. Autlan de Navarro, Mexico, July 20, 1947. prin. Guts and Grace Records, 1993. Played guitar in Tijuana nightclubs; recorded with Mike Bloomfield and Al Kooper's Super Session; founder, guitarist: rock band Santana, 1966—; appeared at Woodstock Festival, 1969; rec. artist, Columbia Records, 1969—; albums include: Santana, 1968, Abraxas, 1970, Santana III, 1972, Caravanserai, 1972, Welcome, 1973, Greatest Hits, 1974, Barboletta, 1974, Lotus, 1975, Amigos, 1976, Festival, 1977, Moonflower, 1977, Inner Secrets, 1979, Marathon, 1979, Swing of Delight, 1980, Zebop, 1981, Shango, 1982, Havana Moon, 1983, Beyond Appearances, 1985, Freedom, 1987, Viva Santana!, 1988, Doin' It, 1990, Spirits Dancing In the Flesh, 1990, Milagro, 1992, Brothers, 1994, Sacred Fire: Live in South America, 1995; solo albums include Devadip Carlos-Oneness: Silver Dreams, Golden Reality, 1979, Blues for Salvador, 1987; world-wide concert tours with Santana Band; performed and recorded with Buddy Miles, Herbie Hancock, McCoy Tyner, John McLaughlin, Jose Feliciano, Wayne Shorter and Alice Coltrane, Aretha Franklin, Olatunji . Recipient Gold Medal award, 1977, Grammy award, 1989, Century award Billboard Mag., 1996. Office: Santana Mgmt PO Box 10348 San Rafael CA 94912-0348 *Keep an open heart, focus on the positive, be true to your innermost feelings, but most of all make time to visit the Lord within.*

SANTANA, ROBERT RAFAEL, lawyer; b. Bklyn., Apr. 22, 1961; s. Carlos Roberto and Hilda Eva (Cabrera) S.; children: Robert Jr., Alexis. BBA, Fordham U., 1985; JD, NYU, 1990. Bar: N.Y. 1992, U.S. Dist. Ct. (ea. dist.) 1992, U.S. Dist. Ct. (so. dist.) 1993. Police officer N.Y.C. Police Dept., 1981-93, sgt., 1993—; assoc. Morales & Silva, P.C., N.Y.C., 1992-94, ptnr., 1995-96; ptnr. Morales & Assocs., 1996-97. Mem. ABA, N.Y. State Bar Assn., N.Y. County Lawyers Assn., Puerto Rican Bar Assn., Hispanic Nat. Bar Assn. Democrat. Roman Catholic. Avocations: basketball, football, baseball, travel, reading. Office: Ste 617 11 Park Pl Rm 617 New York NY 10007-2801

SANTANGELO, MARIO VINCENT, dental association executive, educator; b. Youngstown, Ohio, Oct. 5, 1931; s. Anthony and Maria (Zarlenga) S.; student U. Pitts., 1949-51; D.D.S., Loyola U. (Chgo.), 1955, M.S., 1960. Instr. Loyola U., Chgo., 1957-60, asst. prof., 1960-66, chmn. dpt. radiology, 1962-70, dir. dental aux. utilization program, 1963-70, assoc. prof., 1966-70, chmn. dept. oral diagnosis, 1967-70, asst. dean, 1969-70; practice dentistry, Chgo., 1960-70; cons. Cert. Bd. Am. Dental Assts. Assn., 1967-76, VA Research Hosp., 1969-75, Chgo. Civil Service Commn., 1967-75; counselor Chgo. Dental Assts. Assn., 1966-69; mem. dental student tng. adv. com. Div. Dental Health USPHS, Dept. Health, Edn. and Welfare, 1969-71; cons. dental edn. rev. com. NIH, 1971-72; cons. USPHS, HEW, Region IV, Atlanta, 1973-76, Region V, Chgo., 1973-77; mem. Commn. on Dental Edn. and Practice, Fedn. Dentaire Internationale, 1984-92. Bd. visitors Sch. Dental Medicine, Washington U., St. Louis, 1974-76. Served to capt. USAF, 1955-57. Recipient Dr. Harry Strusser Meml. award NYU Coll. Dentistry, 1985. Fellow Am. Coll. Dentists; mem. AMA (mem. edn. work group 1982-86), Assembly Specialized Accrediting Bodies (council on postsecondary accreditation 1981-92, award of Merit 1992), Am. Assn. Dental Schs., Odontographic Soc. Chgo. (life), Am. (asst. sec. council dental edn. 1971-81, acting sec. 1981-82, sec. 1982-90, dir., 1990-92, asst. sec. commn. on dental accreditation 1975-81, acting sec. 1981-82, sec. 1982-90, dir., 1990-92, acting sec. commn. on continuing dental edn. 1981-82, sec. 1982-85), Ill., Chgo. Dental Assns. (life), Am. Acad. Oral Pathology, Am. Acad. Dental Radiology, Canadian Dental Assn. (commission on dental accreditation award of merit 1992), Am. Acad. Oral Medicine, Am. Assn. Dental Examiners (hon. 1993), Omicron Kappa Upsilon (pres. 1967-68), Blue Key, Xi Psi Phi. Contbr. articles to profl. jours. Home: 1440 N Lake Shore Dr Chicago IL 60610

SANTANIELLO, ANGELO GARY, retired state supreme court justice; b. New London, Conn., May 28, 1924; s. Samuel C. and Katie Santaniello; m. Catherine A. Driscoll, June 1948 (dec.); children—Samuel Gary, Lisa Mary; m. Catherine M. Cooper, Sept. 27, 1968; 1 child, Maria Roberta. B.A., Coll. Holy Cross, 1945; JD, Georgetown U., 1950. Bar: Conn. 1950, U.S. Dist. Ct. Conn. Sole practice, New London, 1950-53; sr. ptnr. Santaniello & Satti, 1953-61, Santaniello Satti Wilensky & Schwartz, 1962-65; judge Conn. Cir. Ct., 1966-71, Conn. Ct. Common Pleas, 1971-73; judge Conn. Superior Ct., 1973-85, adminstrv. judge, 1978-85, chief adminstrv. judge, civil divsn., 1979-85; assoc. justice Conn. Supreme Ct., Hartford, 1985-87, sr. assoc. justice, 1987-95; chief mediator Sta.-Fed ADR, Inc., 1993-95; mediator Conn. Superior Ct. Annexed Mediation Program, 1996—; asst. prosecuting atty. New London Police Ct., 1951-55. Trustee, New London Pub. Library, Mitchell Coll., Lawrence and Meml. Hosp.; bd. dirs. Holy Cross Alumni, Am. Cancer Soc., New London Fed. Savs. and Loan; chmn. New London Republican Party, 1956-65; nat. committeeman Conn. State Young Reps., 1959-61; legal counsel Conn. State Senate Rep. Minority, 1961-65; campaign mgr. to gubernatorial candidate, 1962; mem. athletic council Holy Cross Coll., 1971-77, chmn., 1972-73; bd. of trustees Mitchell Coll., 1976-89, chmn., 1988-91. Served to lt. (j.g.) USNR, 1942-46. Recipient Columbus award Italian-Am. Civic Assn., 1964; In Hoc Signo award Holy Cross Coll., 1976; 1st Humanitarian award Eastern Conn. chpt. March of Dimes, 1983. Mem. New London Bar Assn., Conn. Bar Assn., Am. Justinian Soc., Holy Cross Alumni Assn. (pres. 1981-82); Conn. Trial Lawyers Assn. (Jud. award). Roman Catholic. Home: 25 Shirley Ln New London CT 06320-2929 Office: 70 Huntington St New London CT 06320-6113

SANTAVICCA, PAMELA FERGUSON, social welfare administrator; b. Plainfield, N.J., Apr. 15, 1949; d. Russell L. and Laura Esther (Telander) Ferguson; children: Daniel, Elizabeth. BA, Douglass Coll., 1971; MEd, Rutgers U., 1972. Cert. elem. tchr., N.J. Tchr. Orchard Road Sch., Montgomery Twp., N.J., 1972-84; county coord. Congrl. Campaign, Centre County, Pa., 1986; dir. Christian edn. St. Andrews Ch., State College, Pa., 1987-88; exec. dir. Food Bank State Coll., 1992—; del. Coun. Human Svcs., Centre County, 1992—, Interfaith Mission, State College, 1992—; rep. County Food Banks, Bellefonte, Pa., 1992—; com. mem. Supercupboard Program, Centre County, 1995—. Committeewoman State Coll. Bd. Dems., 1986—; mem. profl. adv. com. United Way; co-founder Cmty. Safety Net; vestry mem. St. Andrews Episc. Ch., 1988-95, reader, chalice bearer, 1992—; co-founder Cmty. Safety Net, 1996. Named Citizen of Yr., Elks Club of State College, 1996. Mem. NOW, Hunger Project, Leadersip Ctr. County, Rotary Internat. (group study exch. 1996—), Altrusa Internat. Democrat. Episcopalian. Avocations: hiking, reading, gardening, travel, public speaking. Home: 520 W Fairmount Ave State College PA 16801 Office: Food Bank State College 208 W Foster Ave State College PA 16801-4822

SANTE, WILLIAM ARTHUR, II, electronics manufacturing executive; b. N.Y.C., July 16, 1943; s. William Arthur and Grace Elizabeth (Burnat) S.; m. Kathleen Margaret Rourke, July 2, 1966; children: Jennifer, William, Timothy. BS, U. Detroit, 1965; MBA, U. Pitts., 1981. CPA, Mich. Mgr. Deloitte & Touche, Detroit, 1965-78; gen. auditor Rockwell Internat., Pitts., 1978—. Mem. Am. Inst. CPA's, Mich. Assn. CPA's, Inst. Internal Auditors. Republican. Roman Catholic. Clubs: Shannopin (Pitts.), Rivers (Pitts.). Office: Rockwell Internat Corp 625 Liberty Ave Pittsburgh PA 15222-3110

SANTEE, DALE WILLIAM, lawyer, air force officer; b. Washington, Pa., Mar. 28, 1953; s. Robert Erwin and Elsbeth Emma (Bantleon) S.; married; 1 child, Enri De'Von; m. Junko Mori, June 2, 1992. BA, Washington & Jefferson Coll., 1975; MA, U. No. Ariz., 1982; JD, U. Pitts., 1978. Bar: Pa. 1978, U.S. Ct. Mil. Appeals 1979, Calif. 1989. Floor mgr., commn. salesman J.C. Penney Co., Washington, Pa., 1971-76; asst. mgr. Rach Enterprises, Charleroi, Pa., 1977-78; legal intern Washington County Pub. Defender; commd. 2d lt. USAF, 1979, advanced through grades to lt. col., 1996; from asst. staff judge advocate to area def. counsel Luke Air Force Base, Ariz., 1979-81; claims officer 343 Combat Support Group/Judge Advocate, Eielson AFB, Alaska, 1981-83; sr. staff legal adviser Dept. Vet. Affairs, Washington, 1983-89; asst. staff judge advocate Mil. Justice div. Air Force Judge Advocate Gen.'s Office, Washington, 1986-89, 63CSG/Judge Advocate, Norton Air Force Base, Calif., 1989-91; dep. pub. defender Juvenile div. San Diego County, 1990-93, dep. alt. pub. defender, 1993—; dep. staff judge advocate 452 AMW/Judge Advocate, March Air Res. Base, Calif., 1991—; v.p. Neuer Enterprises, Nanjemoy, Md., 1983-89; participant Mgmt. Devel. Seminar, 1988. Mem. San Diego County Rep. Party; pres., co-chmn. legis. com. PTA Zamorano Elem. Sch., San Diego, chmn. SITE com.; mem. San Diego County Child Abuse Coord. Coun., San Diego County Commn. on Children and Youth, San Diego County Juvenile Ct. Mental Health Task Force, San Diego County Unified Sch. Dist. Parent Adv. Coun.; bd. dirs. San Diego County Youth Ct. Program, Pub. Defenders Assn., Train Ct. Apptd. Spl. Advocates for Voices for Children. Decorated Air Force Commendation medal, 1981, 89, Air Force Meritorious Svc. medal, 1991, 96; named Outstanding Young Man of Am., U.S. Jaycees, Montgomery, Ala., 1981; acad. scholar Washington & Jefferson Coll., 1971-75, Beta scholar Washington & Jefferson Coll., 1974, Pa. Senatorial scholar Pa. Senate, 1975, 76, 77, 78. Mem. Pa. Bar Assn., Calif. Bar Assn., San Diego County Bar Assn., San Diego County Psych-Law Soc. Avocations: swimming, softball, stamp and coin collecting, foreign travel. Home: 1156 Corrales Ln Chula Vista CA 91910-7956

SANTER, RICHARD ARTHUR, geography educator; b. Detroit, Sept. 26, 1937; s. Arthur James and Hazel Luella (Houghten) S.; m. Ruth Margaret Boyce, Aug. 29, 1959; children: Carolyn M., Catherine R. BS, Ea. Mich. U., 1959, MS, 1965; PhD, Mich. State U., 1970. Cert. secondary tchr., Mich. Tchr. geography Wyandotte (Mich.) Pub. Schs., 1963-66; prof. geography Ferris State U., Big Rapids, Mich., 1969-96, ret., 1996; cons. Graphic Learning Corp., Tallahassee, 1983, Humanities Coun. West Cen. Mich., Big Rapids, 1987—; coord. govs. conf. Upper Great Lakes Commn., Bid Rapids, 1980. Author: Michigan: Heart of Great Lakes, 1977, Geography of Michigan and the Great Lakes Basin, 1993, (atlas) Green Township Atlas, 1974; contbg. author: Michigan Visions of Our Past, 1989; co-editor, team leader: The Autobiography of Woodbridge N. Ferris, 1995. Mem., mapper Green Twp. Plan Commn., Paris, Mi., 1973-74; co-chmn. Mecosta County Bicentennial Commn., Big Rapids, 1974-75; mem. Mecosta County Zoning Commn., Big Rapids, 1978-81; bd. dirs., elder United Ch., Big Rapids, 1970-81; mem. Mich. conf. United Ch. of Christ, Commn. of Ch. and Pastoral Ministries, 1988-91; chmn. 1993 commn. Ferris State U., 1990-93; mem. bd. of trust Hist. Soc. Mich., 1993-96. 1st Lt. U.S. Army, 1959-62. Recipient Recognition award Population Action Coun., 1983, Certs. of Appreciation, Mich. Sesquicentennial Commn., 1987, The Population Inst., 1987, Nat. Geography Bee, 1989-96. Mem. Assn. Am. Geographers, Nat. Coun. for Geog. Edn. (Mich. coord. 1970-74), Mich. Acad. Sci., Arts and Letters (sect. chmn. 1974-75, 94-95, instn. rep. 1988-89), Phi Delta Kappa (chmn. 1990-91). Presbyterian. Avocation: outdoor nature recreation. Office: Ferris State Univ Dept Social Scis Geography 901 S State St Big Rapids MI 49307-2251

SANTI, ELLYN E. (ELLYN E. WAGNER), mathematics educator. BS, No. Ariz. U., 1971, MA, 1974; postgrad., George Mason U., 1980-82. Cert. tchr., Va. Tchr. math. Flagstaff (Ariz.) Pub. Schs., 1972-76, head math. dept., 1974-76; asst. prof. math. No. Va. C.C., Annandale, Va., 1976—; participant Writing Across the Curriculum Workshops, Annandale, 1992-93. Recipient recognition for outstanding contbns. to edn. No. Va. C.C. Alumni Fedn., 1993. Mem. Am. Math. Assn. Two-Yr. Colls., Va. Math. Assn. Two-Yr. Colls. (regional v.p. 1989-91, coord. spring conf. 1992), Phi Kappa Phi. Avocations: classical piano, ballroom dancing. Office: No Va C C 8333 Little River Tpke Annandale VA 22003-3743

SANTIAGO, BENITO RIVERA, professional baseball player; b. Ponce, P.R., Mar. 9, 1965; m. Bianca Santiago; 1 child, Benny Beth. Baseball player San Diego Padres, 1986-92, Florida Marlins, 1993-94, Cininnati Reds, 1995, Philadelphia Phillies, 1996, Toronto Blue Jays, 1997—. Named Nat. League Rookie of Yr. Baseball Writers' Assn. Am., 1987, Sporting News All-Star Team, 1987, 89, 91, 92; recipient Gold Glove award, 1988-90, Silver Slugger award, 1987-88, 90-91; holder maj. league rookie record for most consecutive games batted safely. Office: Toronto Blue Jays, 1 Blue Jays Way Ste 3200, Toronto, ON Canada M5V 1S1*

SANTIAGO, JULIO VICTOR, medical educator, researcher, administrator; b. San German, Puerto Rico, Jan. 13, 1942. BS, Manhattan Coll., 1963; MD, U. Puerto Rico, 1967. Diplomate Am. Bd. of Internal Medicine, 1975. Fellow in metabolism and endocrinology Washington U., St. Louis, 1972-74; chief resident Barnes Hosp., St. Louis, 1974-75; dir. divsn. of endocrinology and metabolism Dept. of Pediatrics, 1984—; program dir., Diabetes Rsch. and Tng. Ctr. Wash. U. Sch. Medicine, 1987—, prof. of medicine, pediatrics, 1983—. Assoc. editor Diabetes, 1977-79, 91-95, editor, 1995—. Mem. Am. Soc. for Clin. Investigation, Soc. for Pedatric Rsch., Am. Diabetes Assn. Home: 4 Forest Parkway Dr Ballwin MO 63021-5553 Office: Washington U Sch Medicine St Louis Hosp 1 Childrens Place Saint Louis MO 63110

SANTIAGO-HUDSON, RUBEN, actor. Appeared in Broadway play Jelly's Last Jam; appeared in off-Broadway plays including East Texas Hot Links, Measure for Measure, Ceremonies in Dark Old Men; appeared in plays including Seven Guitars (Tony award winner 1996); appeared in films including Blown Away, Solomon and Sheba; appeared on TV shows including NYPD Blue, NY Undercover, Law & Order, The Cosby Mysteries, Another World, The Return of the Hunter, Dear John. Office: Hardin & Curtis 850 7th Ave Ste 405 New York NY 10019-5230

SANTILLAN, ANTONIO, financial company executive; b. Buenos Aires, May 8, 1936; naturalized, 1966; s. Guillermo Spika and Raphaella C. (Abaladejo) S.; children: Andrea, Miguel, Marcos. Grad., Morgan Park Mil. Acad., Chgo., 1954; BS in Psychology, Coll. of William and Mary, 1958. Cert. real estate broker. Asst. in charge of prodn. Wilding Studios, Chgo., 1964; pres. Adams Fin. Services, Los Angeles, 1965—. Writer, producer, dir. (motion pictures) The Glass Cage, co-writer Dirty Mary/Crazy Harry, Viva Knievel; contbg. writer Once Upon a Time in America; TV panelist Window on Wall Street; contbr. articles to profl. fin. and real estate jours. Served with USNR, 1959. Recipient Am. Rep. award San Francisco Film Festival, Cork Ireland Film Fest, 1961. Mem. Writer's Guild Am., L.A. Bd. Realtors, Beverly Hills Bd. Realtors (income/investment divsn. steering com.), Westside Realty Bd. (bd. dirs.), L.A. Ventures Assn. (bd. dirs.), Jonathan Club (L.A.), Rotary, Roundtable, Toastmasters Internat. Avocations: golf, tennis, skiing. Office: Adams Fin Svcs Inc 425 N Alfred St West Hollywood CA 90048-2504

SANTINI, JOHN AMEDEO, educational consultant; b. Detroit, Nov. 4, 1926; s. Amedeo Enrico and Ida Mercurio (LaFata) S.; m. Mary Beverly Bergman, Aug. 11, 1956 (div. 1982); m. Deborah Sewell Stogner, Apr. 28, 1996; children: Maria Bettina, Lucia Bianca, John Amedeo. B.A., U. Chgo., 1948; J.D., Wayne State U., 1953; M.A., U. Mich., 1960; Ed.D., Harvard, 1965. Bar: Mich. 1954. Prodn. engr. Fisher body div. Gen. Motors Corp., 1949-51; pvt. practice Detroit, 1954-56; tchr. elem. and middle grades St. Clair Shores and Grosse Pointe, Mich., 1956-60; elem. sch. prin. Chagrin Falls, Ohio, 1960-62; dir. curriculum study Brockton, Mass., 1963-64; supt. schs. Farmington, Conn., 1964-66, New Haven, 1966-69; prof. edn., chmn. dept. edn. Conn. Coll., New London, 1969-85, edn. cons., 1985—; lectr. edn. Western Res. U., 1962; vis. prof. edn. adminstrn. U. Bridgeport, 1971, U. Conn., 1974; cons. edn., Sarasota (Fla.) County, 1963—, Walpole, Mass., 1964, West Hartford, Conn., 1973. Mem. Old Lyme Park and Recreation Commn.; bd. mgrs. Old Lyme-P.G. Noyes Library, 1980—; mem. arbitration panel Conn. Dept. Edn., basic skills adv. com., 1980—, tchr. prep. program rev. com., 1979—. Served with USAAF, World War II. Mem. ABA (adv. commn. on youth edn. for citizenship), Mich. Bar Assn., Am. Fedn. Musicians, Am., Conn., New Eng. assns. sch. supts., Nat., Conn., Mich. edn. assns., Nat. Orgn. Legal Problems of Edn., AAUP, Conn. Assn. Colls. and Univs. for Tchr. Edn. (pres. 1973-74), Conn. Profs. Ednl. Adminstrn. (pres. 1973-74), Phi Kappa Phi, Phi Delta Kappa. Presbyn. (deacon). Home: 110 Tremain St N Mount Dora FL 32757-5678

SANTLOFER, JONATHAN, artist, educator; b. N.Y.C., Apr. 26, 1946; s. Louis and Edith (Brill) S.; m. Joy Katzman; 1 child, Doria. BFA, Boston U., 1967; MFA, Pratt Inst., 1969. Head art dept. Tower Hill Sch., Wilmington, Del., 1969-73; instr. studio and art history Jersey City (N.J.) State Coll., 1974-80; instr. drawing and painting Columbia U., N.Y., 1988-90; resident painter, instr. Vt. Studio Ctr., 1991; instr. drawing and painting Lacoste Sch. of Arts, 1992; mem. humanities faculty art history New Sch. for Social Rsch., 1976—; resident artist Am. Acad., Rome, 1989-90; Yaddo residency Yaddo Colony, Saratoga Springs, N.Y., 1995, 96, 97. One-man shows include Inst. Contemporary Art, Tokyo, 1978, 85, Franklin & Marshall Coll., Pa., 1981, Betsy Rosenfield Gallery, Chgo., 1982, Pam Adler Gallery, N.Y.C., 1982, 83, 85, Lawrence Oliver Gallery, Phila., 1983, Graham Modern, N.Y.C., 1986, 88, 90, Klein Gallery, Chgo., 1986, 89, The Heckscher Mus., Huntington, N.Y., 1987, Nina Freudenheim Gallery, Buffalo, N.Y., 1987, Ruth Bachofner, L.A., 1991, Galleriea Peccolo, Italy, 1992, James Graham and Sons, N.Y.C., 1994; exhibited in group shows at Graham Modern, N.Y.C., 1988-89, 90-91, 92, Galleria Peccolo, Italy, 1988-89, Andre Zarre, N.Y.C., 1988-89, The Jewish Mus., N.Y.C., 1988-89, Gallery Urban, N.Y.C., 1988-89, PPOW, N.Y.C., 1988-89, Richard Green Gallery, L.A., 1988-89, Barbara Toll Fine Arts, N.Y.C., 1988-89, 92, Nina Freudenheim, Buffalo, 1990-91, Lennon/Weinberg Gallery, N.Y.C., 1993, Santa Monica Mus., 1994, The Drawing Ctr., N.Y.C., 1994, Adam Baumgold Fine Arts, N.Y.C., 1994, others; represented in permanent collections Art Inst. Chgo., Ill., AT&T, Am. Can Co., Amoco Products Co., Boston (Mass.) U. Mus. and Gallery Collection, Buscaglia-Castellani Mus./Gallery, Niagara Falls, N.Y., Chase Manhattan Bank, NA, Chem. Bank, Continental Group, Cooke & Bieler, Pa., Grand Rapids (Mich.) Mus. Art, Grahan Gund, Mass., Indpls. (Ind.) Mus. Art, Inst. Contemporary Art, Japan, others; contbr. articles to profl. jours. Painting grantee Nat. Endowment for the Arts, 1981, 89. Office: care James Graham & Sons 1014 Madison Ave New York NY 10021

SANTMAN, LEON DUANE, lawyer, former federal government executive; b. Phila., July 29, 1930; s. Elmer William and Anna Mary (Moffitt) S.; m. Juliet Gloria Peacock, June 16, 1952; 1 dau., Lorri Leigh Santman Myers. BS, U. S., COAST Guard Acad., 1952; LLB, U. Houston, 1953; LLM, George Washington U., 1968. Bar: Tex. 1963, Md. 1974. Commd. ensign U.S. Coast Guard, 1952, advanced through grades to comdr., 1967, ret., 1972; assoc. gen. counsel Cost of Living Council, Washington, 1972-74; asst. gen. counsel U.S. Dept. Transp., Washington, 1974-77, dir. Materials Transp. Bur., 1977-85; dir. ship ops. Maritime Adminstrn., 1985-88. Episcopalian.

SANTNER, THOMAS, statistics educator, consultant, researcher; b. St. Louis, Aug. 29, 1947; s. Joseph Frank and Margaret Ann (Dolak) S.; m. Gail DeFord, Aug. 29, 1970; children—Emily, Matthew, Abigail, Dominick. BS, U. Dayton, 1969; MS, Purdue U., 1971, PhD, 1973. Asst. prof. Cornell U., Ithaca, N.Y., 1973-80, assoc. prof., 1980-86, prof., 1986-89, dir. stats. ctr., 1982-86; prof. Ohio State U., 1990—, chair dept. statistics, 1992—; cons. Hosp. for Spl. Surgery, N.Y.C., 1983—. Co-author: The Statistical Analysis of Discrete Data, 1989, Design and Analysis if /experiments for Statistical Selection, Screening, and Multiple Comparisons, 1995; co-editor: Design of Experiments: Ranking and Selection, 1984. Contbr. articles to prof. jours. NSF, ASA and IMS fellow; recipient numerous grants. Mem. Inst. Math. Stats., Biometric Soc., Am. Statis. Assn. Home: 1042 Putney Dr Columbus OH 43085-2903 Office: Ohio State U Dept Stats Columbus OH 43210

SANTOMERO, ANTHONY M., business educator; b. N.Y.C., Sept. 29, 1946; s. Camillo and Jean (Oddo) S.; m. Marlena Belviso, Aug. 21, 1971; children: Jill Renee, Marc Anthony. AB, Fordham U., 1968; PhD, Brown U., 1971; EDhe (hon.), Stockholm Sch. Econs., 1992. Successively asst. prof., assoc. prof., prof. fin. Wharton Sch., U. Pa., Phila., 1972-84, R.K. Mellon prof. fin., 1984—, vice dean, dir. grad. div., 1984-87, dep. dean, 1990-94; dir. Wharton Fin. Instns. Ctr., 1995—; asst. prof. econs. Baruch Coll., CUNY, 1971-72; vis. prof. European Inst. Advanced Studies in Mgmt.,

Brussels, 1977-78, Stockholm Sch. Econs., 1989-90, U. Rome, 1994, vis. prof. fin., Tor Vergata, 1994; formerly vis. prof. Ecole Superieure des Sciences Economiques and Commerciales, France, 197-78, Fin. Economists Roundtable, 1997—; bd. dirs. The Zweig Fund, The Zweig Total Return Fund, Temp. Investment Fund Inc., Compass Capital Funds; bd. trustees Mcpl. Fund for Temp. Investment, 1991-95. Author: Current Views on Bank Capital, 1983, Financial Markets, Instruments and Institutions, 1996; assoc. editor Jour. Banking and Fin., 1978—, Jour. Money, Credit and Banking, 1980—, Jour. Econs. and Bus., 1979—, Jour. Bank Rsch., Jour. Fin. Rsch., Jour. Fin. Svc. Rsch., 1992—, Euro Fin. Rev., 1995—; bd. editors Advances in Internat. Banking and Fin., 1993—, European Fin. Mgmt., 1996—; founding co-editor Brookings-Wharton Papers on Financial Policy, 1997—; contbr. numerous articles to profl. jours. Mem. European Fin. Assn. (exec. com. 1984-87), Am. Fin. Assn., Am. Econs. Assn., Am. Assn. Bank Dirs. (adv. bd.). Roman Catholic. Home: 310 Keithwood Rd Wynnewood PA 19096-1224 Office: U Pa Wharton Sch 2336 Steinberg Hal-Dietrich Philadelphia PA 19104

SANTONI, RONALD ERNEST, philosophy educator; b. Arvida, Que., Can., Dec. 19, 1931; s. Fred Albert and Phyllis (Tremaine) S.; m. Marguerite Ada Kiene, June 25, 1955; children: Christina, Marcia, Andrea, Juanita, Jonathan, Sondra. BA, Bishop's U., Lennoxville, Que., 1952; MA, Brown U., 1954; PhD, Boston U., 1961; postgrad., U. Paris-Sorbonne, 1956-57. Asst. prof. philosophy U. Pacific, Stockton, Calif., 1958-61; postdoctoral fellow Yale U., New Haven, 1961-62; asst. prof. philosophy Wabash Coll., Crawfordsville, Ind., 1962-64; mem. faculty Denison U., Granville, Ohio, 1964—; prof. philosophy Denison U., 1968—, chmn. dept., 1971-73, 82-84, 92, Maria Teresa Barney chair in philosophy, 1978—; Peace lectr. Bethel Coll., 1985; vis. scholar Cambridge U., Eng., 1986, 90, 94, 96, also vis. lectr. in philosophy, 1990; vis. fellow Clare Hall, Cambridge U., 1986, 90; vis. fellow in philosophy Yale U., 1975, 81, 93-94; keynote speaker 2d Internat. Conf. on Nuclear Free Zones, Cordoba, Spain, 1985; speaker World Cong. Philosophy, Montreal, Can., 1982, Brighton, U.K., 1988, Internat. Studies Assn., London, 1989, speaker and U.S.A. co-chair Internat. Conf. Internat. Philosophers for Prevention of Nuclear Omnicide, Moscow, 1990; speaker World Congress Universalism, Warsaw, Poland, 1993; del. and raporteur UN meeting of Peace Messenger Orgns., Dagomys, Sochi, USSR, 1991; invited plenary speaker 2d Internat. Cong. Violence and Co-existence, Montreal, Can., 1992; invited participant Colloquium on Technological Risks to Environment, Montreal, Can., 1993; participant, spkr. numerous profl. confs. Contbg. author: Current Philosophical Issues, 1966, Towards an Understanding and Prevention of Genocide, 1984, Nuclear War: Philosophical Perspectives, 1985, Encyclopedic Critical Bibliography of Genocide, 1988, Just War, Nonviolence and Nuclear Deterrence: Philosophers on War and Peace, 1992, The Institution of War, 1991, Violence and Human Co-Existence, 1994; author: Bad Faith, Good Faith and Authenticity in Sartre's Early Philosophy, 1995; editor, contbr. Religious Language and the Problem of Religious Knowledge, 1968; co-editor Social and Political Philosophy, 1963; contbg. editor Internet on the Holocaust and Genocide; contbr. over 125 articles and revs. to profl. jours., also to The Progressive, The Human Quest, Churchman; bd. editors Jour. Peace and Justice Studies. V.p. NAACP, Licking County, 1967; active ACLU; organizer Crawfordsville Human Rels. Coun., 1962-64; mem. nat. exec. com. Episcopal Peace Fellowship, 1968-78; mem. internat. coun. Internat. Inst. on the Holocaust and Genocide, 1985—; mem. nat. coun. Fellowship of Reconciliation, 1988-89; trustee Margaret Hall Sch., Versailles, Ky., 1972-74; nat. bd. dirs. Promoting Enduring Peace, 1982—. Canadian Govt. Overseas fellow Royal Soc. Can., 1956-57; Church Soc. for Coll. Work faculty fellow, 1961-62; Yale postdoctoral rsch. fellow, 1961-62; Soc. for Religion in Higher Edn. postdoctoral fellow, 1972—; Yale rsch. fellow, 1975; guest fellow Berkeley Coll., Yale U., 1975, 81, 93-94, 96, elected assoc. fellow, 1994—; vis. fellow in philosophy Yale U., 1981, 93-94, 96; Robert C. Good faculty fellow Denison U., 1985-86, Robert C. Good Faculty Rsch. fellow, 1993-94; elected life mem. Clare Hall, Cambridge (Eng.) U., 1986; recipient Mellon award for disting. faculty Denison U., 1972, Crossed Keys Faculty of Yr. award Denison U., 1986-87. Mem. Am. Philos. Assn., Ch. Soc. for Coll. Work, Soc. for Phenomenology and Existential Philosophy, Internat. Philosophers for Prevention of Nuclear Omnicide (v.p. 1983-85, v.p. cen. div. 1990-91, internat. pres. 1991-96, exec. com. 1996—), Sartre Soc. of N.Am. (exec. com. 1994—), Sartre Circle, Gandhi-King Soc., War Resisters League, Union of Bi-Nat. Profls. Against Omnicide (v.p. 1978—), Concerned Philosophers for Peace (founding 1980—, pres. 1996-97). Episcopalian. Home: 500 Burg St Granville OH 43023-1005 *Gratitude for what one has been given, commitment to personal growth and integrity, some gracious gall, listening to the world's humiliated, and a recognition that any genuine success is a gift of grace, never fully merited.*

SANTORE, CARRIE-BETH, computer management professional; b. Torrington, Conn., July 28, 1953; d. Michael and Dolores Leonard S. BA History and Am. Studies cum laude, Conn. Coll., 1975; MA History, U. Conn., 1977; MBA Mktg., Va. Polytechnic Inst., 1988. Analyst CIA, Washington, 1980-90; prin. tng. specialist Quality Sys., Inc., Fairfax, Va., 1990-93, dep. dir. ops. programs, 1993-95; mgr. Proposal Ctr. Quality Systems, Inc., Fairfax, Va., 1995-96; tech. publs. mgr. Sci. & Tech. Analysis Corp., Fairfax, Va., 1996-97; prin. Am. Mgmt. Systems, Fairfax, 1997—; Lotus cert. cons., 1994. Bd. dirs., sec. Seminary Walk Condo Assn., Alexandria, Va., 1987-88, editor newsletter, 1986-87; vol. Alexandria Waterfront ARC, 1989-90; mem. com. to devel. internat. studies program Conn. Coll., New London, 1988-89. Mem. SALT, Balt. Washington Info. Systems, AAUW, Women's Nat. Book Assn., Assn. Proposal Mgmt. Profls., Phi Alpha Theta. Avocations: golf, hiking, reading, baseball, travel. Office: Am Mgmt Systems 4114 Legato Rd Fairfax VA 22033-4002

SANTORO, ANTHONY RICHARD, academic administrator; b. Feb. 2, 1939; m. Carol Lynne; 1 child, Melissa. AB, Coll. of the Holy Cross, 1960; MA, U. Calif., 1962; PhD, Rutgers U., 1978. Instr. history Monmouth Coll., West Long Branch, N.J., 1963-67; v.p. for adminstrn., chair depts history and philosophy, registrar Briarcliff Coll., Briarcliff Manor, N.Y., 1967-77; v.p. Devel. and Coll. Rels. Ladycliff Coll., Highland Falls, N.Y., 1977-88; pres. St. Joseph's Coll., Standish, Maine, 1979-87; pres. Christopher Newport U., Newport News, Va., 1987-96, pres. emeritus, disting. prof. history, 1996—. Author: Theophanes Chronographia: A Chronicle of 8th Century Byzantium, 1982; co-author: An Eyewitness to History: The Short History of Nikephoros the Patriarch of Constantinople, 1991. Office: Christopher Newport U Smith Hall 164 Newport News VA 23606-2998

SANTORO, CHARLES WILLIAM, investment banker; b. N.Y.C., Apr. 20, 1959; s. Dino and Dorice (Gillick) S.; m. Vanessa Lee Bishop; 1 child, Olivia Charlotte. BA in Econs., Columbia U., 1982; MBA, Harvard U., 1984. With Morgan Stanley & Co., N.Y.C., 1984-88; sr. v.p., coord. officer European mergers and acquisitions Morgan Stanley Internat., London, 1989-90; mng. dir., head cross border investment banking Smith Barney, Inc., N.Y.C., 1991-93, head investment banking new bus. group, 1993-95; mng. dir., head. indsl. corp. finance Paine Webber Inc., N.Y.C., 1995-96, vice chmn. investment banking, 1996—. Recipient fellowship Harvard Bus. Sch., 1983. Mem. Harvard Club of N.Y., N.Y. Athletic Club, Columbia Coll. Alumni Assn. (co-chmn. class of '82 com. 1982—). Republican. Roman Catholic. Home: 3 Alden Ter Greenwich CT 06831-4422 also: 3 Mallord St, London SW3, England Office: Paine Webber Inc 1285 Avenue Of The Americas New York NY 10019-6028

SANTORUM, RICK, senator; b. Winchester, Va., May 10, 1958; s. Aldo and Catherine (Dughi) S.; m. Karen Garver, June 2, 1990; children: Elizabeth Anne, Richard John, Daniel James. BA with honors, Pa. State U., State College, 1980; MBA, U. Pitts., 1981; JD, Dickinson Sch. Law, 1986. Bar: Pa. 1986. Adminstrv. asst. State Sen. Doyle Corman, Harrisburg, Pa., 1981-86; exec. dir. local govt. com. Pa. State Senate, Harrisburg, 1981-84, exec. dir. transp. com., 1984-86; assoc. atty. Kirkpatrick and Lockhart, Pitts., 1986-90; mem. 102nd-103rd Congresses from 18th Pa. dist., Washington, D.C., 1991-95; U.S. Senator from Pa., 1995—; mem. Agr. Com., Armed Svcs. Com., Rules and Adminstrn. Com., Spl. Com. on Aging. Bd. dirs. Mt. Lebanon Extended Day Program, 1987-91; mem. Child Advocacy Project, 1987-91. Mem. Allegheny County Bar Assn., Tyrolean Soc. Western Pa., Italian Sons and Daus. Assn., Rotary. Republican. Roman Catholic. Avocations: golf, cross country skiing, racquet sports. Home: 127 Seminole Dr Pittsburgh PA 15228-1528 Office: US Senate 120 Russell Senate Office Bldg Washington DC 20510-3803*

SANTOS, ADELE NAUDE, architect, educator; b. Cape Town, South Africa, Oct. 14, 1938; came to U.S., 1973; d. David Francois Hugo and Aletta Adèle Naudé. Student, U. Cape Town, South Africa, 1956-58; Diploma, Archtl. Assn., 1961; MArch in Urban Design, Harvard U., 1963; M in City Planning, U. Pa., 1968, MArch, 1968. Pvt. practice architecture with Antonio de Souza Santos, 1966-73; ptnr. Interstudio, Houston, 1973-79; assoc. prof. architecture Rice U., Houston, 1973-78, prof., 1979; prof. architecture and urban design, dept. architecture U. Pa., Phila., 1981-90; founding dean Sch. Architecture U. Calif., San Diego, 1990-94; pvt. practice architecture and urban design Adele Naude Santos, Architect, Phila., 1979-90, Adele Naude Santos and Assocs., San Diego and Phila., 1991—; prof. architecture Coll. Environ. Design U. Calif., Berkeley, 1994—; founding dean Sch. of Architecture, U. Calif., San Diego, 1990—. Project dir., co-filmmaker for 5 part series, 1979-80. Wheelwright Travelling fellow, Harvard U., 1968; NEA grantee, 1976, Tex. Com. for Humanities grantee, 1979; recipient (with Hugo Naudé) Bronze medal for House Naudé Capt. Inst. South African Architects, 1967, award for public TV program So. Ednl. Communications Assn., 1980, 3d place award Inner city Infill Competition, 1986; winner Internat. Design Competition, Hawaii Loa Coll., hon. mention Cin. Hillside Housing Competition and City Visions, Phila., 1986; winner competition for Franklin/La Brea Affordable Housing Project Mus. Comtemporary Art and Community Redevel. Agy. City L.A., 1988, Pa. Soc. Architects design award for Franklin/La Brea Multi-Family Housing, 1988; winning entry collaborative competition for amphitheater, restaurant and natural history mus., Arts Pk., La., 1989; winner competition for 24-unit residential devel., City of Camden, N.J., 1989, for New Civic Ctr., City of Perris, Calif., 1991. Office: 2527 South St Philadelphia PA 19146-1037 also: 121 2d St 7th Fl San Francisco CA 94105*

SANTOS, EILEEN, management consultant; b. Morristown, N.J., Feb. 27, 1965; d. Angel Jesus and Arsenia (Quiles) S. BS in Engring., Rutgers U., Piscataway, N.J., 1987; MBA, Columbia U., 1992. Assoc. engr. Westinghouse Elec. Corp., Balt., 1987-89; asst. mgr. N.J. Bell, Newark, 1989-90; ops. specialist Philip Morris Mgmt. Corp., N.Y.C., 1992-94; sr. bus. cons. Am. Mgmt. Systems, Inc., Roseland, N.J., 1994-97; mgr. change mgmt. Andersen Cons., Florham Park, N.J., 1997—. chairperson profl. com., Soc. Hispanic Profl. Engrs., Washington, 1988, client svc. team Vols. for Med. Engring, 1988; chairperson pub. rels. com., mem. exec. bd. Coun. of Action for Minority Profls., Newark, 1989; v.p. Hispanic Bus. Assn., 1991. Recipient Cora and Rose Morgan fellowship Columbia U., 1991. Mem. NAFE, Nat. Soc. Hispanic MBAs. Democrat. Roman Catholic. Avocation: folk art collector. Home: 8 Sand Spring Rd Morristown NJ 07960-6706 Office: Andersen Cons 1345 Ave of Americas New York NY 10105

SANTOS, GEORGE WESLEY, physician, educator; b. Oak Park, Ill., Feb. 3, 1928; s. George and Emma (Gast) S.; m. Joanne Agnes Corrigan, June 7, 1952; children: Susan Elizabeth, George Wesley II, Kelly Anne, Amy Coburn. SB, MIT, 1951, MS in Phys. Biology, 1951; MD, Johns Hopkins U., 1955; Doctoris Medicinae Gradum Honoris Cause, U. Munich, 1989. Intern Johns Hopkins Hosp., Balt., 1955-56, asst. resident, 1958-60; scholar Leukemia Soc., N.Y.C., 1961-66; mem. faculty Johns Hopkins Sch. Medicine, Balt., 1962—, assoc. prof. medicine, 1968-73, prof. oncology and medicine, 1973-94; prof. emeritus, 1994—; asst. physician in chief Balt. City Hosp., 1963-77; mem. Cancer Clin. Investigative Rev. Com., 1969-73; mem. extramural sci. adv. bd. Meml. Sloan-Kettering Cancer Ctr., 1977-79; mem. Immunology-Epidemiology Spl. Virus Cancer Program, 1969-73; chmn. bone marrow transplant registry ACS, 1969-73; mem. Internat. Com. Organ Transplant Registry ACS, 1969-73; mem. cell biology-immunology-genetics rsch. evaluation com. VA, 1969-71. Assoc. editor Cancer Rsch., 1978-81; mem. bd. editl. advisors Jour. Immunopharmacology, 1978—; mem. editl. bd. Blood, 1983—. With USNR, 1956-58. Recipient Disting. Achievement in Cancer Rsch. award Bristol Meyers, 1988. Mem. Am. Soc. Hematology, Transplantation Soc. (counselor 1971-73), Am. Assn. Immunologists, Leukemia Soc. Am. (bd. dirs. 1973—), Internat. Soc. Exptl. Hematology (councillor 1973, pres. 1981), Am. Assn. Cancer Rsch., Am. Soc. Clin. Investigation, Nat. Multiple Sclerosis Soc. (chmn. adv. com. on drug devel. 1981-82, mem. adv. com. on drug devel. 1981—). Home: 308B Mariners Point Hilton Head Island SC 29926-1213

SANTOS, GILBERT ANTONIO (GIL), radio and television sportscaster; b. Achusnet, Mass., Apr. 19, 1938; s. Arthur Nunes and Herminia Rego (Torres) S.; m. Roberta Marie Reul, Apr. 19, 1961; children: Mark Joseph, Kathleen Marie. Student, Southeastern Mass. U., New Bedford, 1956-58; grad., New Eng. Broadcast Sch., Boston, 1959. Sportscaster WBSM Radio, New Bedford, 1958-64, WNBH Radio, New Bedford, 1964-70, WBZ Radio/TV, Boston, 1971—. Vol. Easter Seal Soc. Southeastern Mass., 1974-82, Multiple Sclerosis Soc., Mass. chpt., 1995—. Staff sgt. U.S. Army, 1961-63. Named Mass. Sportscaster of Yr., Nat. Sportscasters Assn., 1980, 84, 86, New Eng. Emmy TV Play-By-Play, 1980, 2D AP Best Sportscaster, Play-By-Play Mass., 1976-96, 2 UPI Best in Nation Sportscaster awards, 1988, 90. Roman Catholic. Avocations: reading, gardening, cooking, bicycling, history. Home: 499 King St Raynham MA 02767 Office: WBZ Radio/TV 1170 Soldiers Field Rd Boston MA 02134-1004

SANTOS, LEONARD ERNEST, lawyer; b. Caracas, Venezuela, Aug. 5, 1946; s. Paul Joseph and Frieda (Epstein) S.; m. Jeannie Bernadette Niedermeyer, Oct. 28, 1978; children: Jonathan, Matthew, Andrew. BA cum laude, Tufts U., 1967; JD, NYU, 1971. Bar: Ariz. 1972, D.C. 1972, U.S. Dist. Ct. D.C. 1972, U.S. Ct. Appeals (9th and 5th cirs.) 1972, U.S. Supreme Ct. 1972. Law clk. to cir. judge U.S. Ct. Appeals (9th cir.), San Francisco, 1971-72; assoc. Hogan & Hartson, Washington, 1972-76; sr. atty. internat. affairs U.S. Dept. Treasury, Washington, 1976-83; internat. trade counsel U.S. Senate Fin. Com., Washington, 1983-87; ptnr. Verner, Liipfert, Bernhard, McPherson & Hand, Washington, 1987-89, Perkins Coie, Washington, 1989—. Note and comment editor NYU Law Jour., 1970; contbr. legal publs. Exec. dir. Dole for Pres. campaign, Washington, 1988, 96. Mem. NAFTA (chpt. 19 dispute settlement panels). Republican. Roman Catholic. Avocations: architecture, economics. Office: Perkins Coie 607 14th St NW Washington DC 20005-2000

SANTOS, LISA WELLS, critical care nurse; b. Richardson, Tex., Oct. 25, 1963; d. Malcolm R.N. and Maitland Anne (MacIntyre) Wells; m. Ignacio Santos, Jr., Dec. 17, 1988. Cert. med. asst., x-ray-lab. technician, Tex. Coll. Osteopathy, 1983; ASN, El Centro Coll., 1988; postgrad., U. North Tex.; BS in Bus. Mgmt., Le Tourneau U., 1993; postgrad., U. Phoenix, 1995—. RN, Tex.; cert. in CPR; cert. case mgr., cert. profl. in health care quality; advanced competency certification in continuity of care; assoc. cert. mgr.; cert. disability analyst, fellow. Med. technologist Family Med. Ctr., Dallas, 1984-85, Beltline Med. Clinic, Dallas, 1985-86; nurse, lab. technician Primacare, Dallas, Plano, Richardson, Tex., 1986-88; charge nurse telemetry unit NME Hosp.-RHD Meml. Hosp., Denton, Tex., 1988-89; nurse ICU Denton (Tex.) Regional Med. Ctr.; nurse Angel Touch, Dallas, 1989; nurse cons. Travelers Ins., Richardson, Tex., 1990-91; med. rev. specialist Nat. Group Life, Las Colinas, Tex., 1991-94; mgr. coordinated care Nat. Group Life, 1994-95; pres. San Cal Health Care Options, Lewisville, Tex., 1994-95; clin. dir. PRN Associated Care/ Am. Care Source, Dallas, 1995—. Contbr. articles to profl. jour. Mem. AACN, NAFE, Nat. Assn. Health Care Quality, Nat. Assn. Quality Assurance Profls., Assn. Nurses in AIDS Care, Case Mgmt. Soc. Am., Am. Assn. Law Ethics and Medicine, Am. Assn. Continuity of Care, Alpha Epsilon Delta, Alpha Beta Kappa, Gamma Beta Phi.

SANTSCHI, PETER HANS, marine sciences educator; b. Bern, Switzerland, Jan. 3, 1943; came to U.S., 1976; s. Hans and Gertrud (Joss) S.; m. Chana Hoida, Mar. 28, 1972; children: Rama Aviva, Ariel Tal. BS, Gymnasium, Bern, 1963; MS, U. Bern, 1971, PhD summa cum laude, 1975; Privatdozent, Swiss Fed. Inst. Tech., Zurich, Switzerland, 1984. Lectr. chemistry Humboltianum Gymnasium, Bern, 1968-70; teaching rsch. asst. U. Bern, 1970-75; rsch. scientist Lamont-Doherty Geol. Obs., Columbia U., Palisades, N.Y., 1976-77; rsch. assoc. Lamont-Doherty Geol. Obs. Columbia U., Palisades, N.Y., 1977-81; sr. rsch. scientist Lamont-Doherty Geol. Obs., Columbia U., Palisades, N.Y., 1981-82, Swiss Inst. Pollution Control, Zurich-Duebendorf, Switzerland, 1982-88; prof. oceanography Tex. A&M U., College Station, 1988—; prof. marine scis. Tex. A&M U., Galveston, Tex., 1988—; sect. head chem. oceanography dept. oceanography Tex. A&M U., College Station, 1990—; head isotope geochemistry and radiology sect. Swiss Inst. Water Resources and Water Pollution Control, Zurich, 1983-88; mem. rev. panel on chem. oceanography NSF, 1990-91. Contbr. articles to profl. jours. Cpl. Swiss Army, 1964-65. Mem. AAAS, Am. Chem. Soc., Am. Geophys. Union, Oceanography Soc., Am. Soc. Limnology and Oceanography. Avocation: swimming. Office: Tex A&M U Oceanography Dept Galveston TX 77553-1675

SANTULLI, THOMAS VINCENT, surgeon; b. N.Y.C., Mar. 16, 1915; s. Frank and Amalia (Avagliano) S.; m. Dorothy Muriel Beverly, Apr. 10, 1941 (dec.); children: Thomas Vincent Jr., Robert B.; m. Patricia Rita, May 28, 1982. B.S., Columbia, 1935; M.D., Georgetown U., 1939. Intern N.Y. Polyclinic Hosp., 1939-41, resident, 1941-44; prof. surgery Columbia U., N.Y.C., 1967-81, prof. emeritus, 1981—; chief pediatric surg. service emeritus Babies Hosp., Columbia-Presbyn. Med. Center, N.Y.C., 1955-81; attending surgeon emeritus Presbyn. Hosp., Columbia-Presbyn. Med. Center. Mem. Am. Surg. Assn., Am. Pediatric Surg. Assn. (pres. 1980-81), A.C.S., British Assn. Pediatric Surgeons, N.Y. Pediatric Surg. Soc. (pres. 1967-69). Office: Babies Hosp 3959 Broadway New York NY 10032-1537

SANWICK, JAMES ARTHUR, mining executive; b. Balt., Feb. 15, 1951; s. Alfred George and Catherine Anne (von Sas) S.; m. Brenda Julia Tietz, Sept. 20, 1980; children: Luke Graham, Sierra Catherine. AS, Catonsville (Md.) C.C., 1975; BS, U. No. Colo., 1976; M in Pub. Administn., U. Alaska S.E., 1985. Recreation therapist Md. Sch. for the Blind, Balt., 1974; dir. camp New Horizon United Cerebral Palsy Md., Balt., 1975; sub-dist. mgr. Nat. Park Svc., various, 1976-82; freelance mgmt. cons. Juneau, Alaska, 1982-84; regional mgr. div. labor standards Alaska Dept. Labor, Juneau, 1983-88; adj. faculty sch. bus. and pub. administrn. U. Alaska S.E., Juneau, 1985-93; mgr. Alaska Productivity Improvement Ctr., Juneau, 1989-93; mgr. human resources and pub. affairs Greens Creek Mining Co., Juneau, 1989-93; mgr. human resources, securities and pub. affairs Rawhide Mining Co., Fallon, Nev., 1993—; owner Sierra Bldg. Alternatives, 1995—; bd. dirs. Gov.'s Com. on Employment Disabled Persons, Alaska Acad. Decathalon Inc.; chmn. Job Svc. Employer Com., Alaska, 1989-93; bd. advisors Inst. Mine Tng. U. Alaska S.E., 1989-93. Co-author: (info. phamphlet) Blue Water Paddling in Alaska, 1980; editor: (film) Green's Creek Project, 1990; photographic editor: Inside Passage Mag., 1982, 83; photographer: (book) Death Valley, 1977. Patrolman Nat. Ski Patrol System, Juneau, 1978-83; instr., trainer ARC, Alaska, Utah, Ariz., 1979-82; v.p. bd. dirs. Alaska Acad. Decathlon; mem. Reno Exec. Roundtable, 1995—. Sgt. USMC, 1970-73. Recipient Nat. New Svc. award United Cerebral Palsey, 1975; named Candidate of Yr. Nat. Ski Patrol System, 1979. Mem. Nev. Mining Assn. (human resources com. 1993—), Soc. Human Resources Mgmt., Juneau Ski Club. Avocations: skiing, hiking, scuba diving, guitar, tennis. Office: Rawhide Mining Co PO Box 2070 Fallon NV 89407-2070

SANYOUR, MICHAEL LOUIS, JR., financial services company executive; b. Richmond, Va., Aug. 24, 1930; s. Michael Louis, Sr. and Betty (Toobert) S.; m. Therese Marie McCarthy, June 1, 1951; children: Jeffrey, Mark, Jennifer, Florence, Norman, Ned. A.A., Union Coll., 1952; S.B., Rutgers U., 1954, postgrad., 1978-82; M.B.A., Harvard U., 1956; postgrad., Am. Coll., 1987-92. CLU, ChFC. Vice pres. Harbridge House, Inc., Boston, 1956-63; also dir; corp. v.p. mktg. Volkswagen of Am., Inc., Englewood Cliffs, N.J., 1963-70; pres., chief exec. officer Subaru of Am., Pennsauken, N.J., 1970-75, also dir.; exec. v.p., dir. Sci. Mgmt. Corp., 1975-82; pres., chief exec. officer Wofac Co., Bridgewater, N.J., 1975-82; pres., chief exec. officer, dir. Metrologic Instruments Inc., Bellmawr, N.J., 1982-85; pres., chief operating officer, dir. Avant-Garde Computing, Inc., Mt. Laurel, N.J., 1985-86; principal, dir. CMS Cos., Phila., 1986—; bd. dirs. CSS Industries Inc. Contbr. to: Chief Executive's Handbook, 1975, Am. Mgmt. Assn.'s Publs., 1990. Trustee, pres. West Jersey Chamber Music Soc., 1987-88; councilman Moorestown, N.J., 1988—; bd. dirs. Union League of Phila., Meml. Health Alliance, 1992-97, ARC of Burlington County, 1989-94, Coriell Inst. for Med. Rsch., World Affairs Coun. Phila., 1992—; bd. dirs. Phila. Pres.'s Orgn., vice chmn., 1992-93, chmn., 1993-94; class sec. HBS Class of '56, 1986-96. With USNG, 1948-56. Recipient Alumni award Rutgers U., 1954, awards Am. Cancer Soc., 1978, 79. Mem. World Pres.'s Orgn., Legatus, Am. Mensa Ltd., Automotive Orgn. Team, World Affairs Coun. Phila., South Jersey C. of C. (v.p., dir.), Beta Gamma Sigma, Delta Sigma Pi. Clubs: Harvard (N.Y.C.); Union League (Phila.), Harvard Bus. Sch. (Phila.) (pres. 1980-81, chmn. 1983-84, dir. 1984—); Moorestown Rotary (pres.1987-88, dir.). Home: 201 E Maple Ave Moorestown NJ 08057-2011 Office: 1926 Arch St Philadelphia PA 19103-1444

SANZO, ANTHONY MICHAEL, health care executive; b. Bayonne, N.J., June 13, 1954; married. BA, Allegheny Coll., 1976; MA, Duke U., 1978. Dir. ambulatory care svcs. Meml. Hosp. Burlington County, Mt. Holly, N.J., 1979; adminstrv. resident Presbyn. U. Hosp., Pitts., 1978-79, asst. dir., 1980-82, v.p., 1982-84, sr. v.p., COO, 1985-86; sr. v.p., COO Allegheny Gen. Hosp., Pitts., 1986-87, pres., CEO, 1988—; adj. educator in field. Contbr. articles to profl. jours. Home: Blackburn Rd Sewickley PA 15143-8386 Office: Allegheny Gen Hosp 320 E North Ave Pittsburgh PA 15212-4756

SANZONE, DONNA S., publishing executive; b. Bklyn., Apr. 4, 1949; d. Joseph J. Seitz and Faye (Brooks) Rossman; m. Charles F. Sanzone, Jan. 2, 1972; children: Danielle, Gregory. BA magna cum laude, Boston U., 1970; MA, Northeastern U., 1979. Grad. placement specialist Inst. Internat. Edn., N.Y.C., 1970-72; adminstr. AFS Internat. Scholarships, Brussels, 1972-74; editor Internat. Ency. Higher Edn., Boston, 1974-76; editor G.K. Hall & Co., Pubs., Boston, 1977-81, exec. editor, 1981-91, editor-in-chief, 1991-96; v.p. Oryx Press, Boston, 1996—. Contbg. author: Access to Power, 1981. Mem. ALA, Assn. Am. Pubs., Assn. Coll. and Rsch. Librs., Libr. and Info. Tech. Assn. Office: Oryx Press 18 Pine St Weston MA 02193-1116

SAPAROFF, PETER M., lawyer; b. Boston, Oct. 27, 1942; s. Michael and Delphine (Campbell) S.; m. Lisa Duberg, Feb. 9, 1992; children: Heather, Michael, Allison. AB, Harvard U., 1964, JD, 1967. Bar: Mass. 1967, N.Y. 1981, U.S. Supreme Ct. 1982. Ptnr. Gaston & Snow, Boston, 1973-91, Palmer & Dodge, Boston, 1991-95, Mintz, Levin, Cohn, Fennis, Glovsky & Popeo, Boston, 1995—. Mem. ABA (various coms.). Congregationalist. Avocation: sports. Office: Mintz Levin Cohn Fennis Glovsky & Popeo 1 Financial Ctr Boston MA 02111-2621

SAPER, CLIFFORD BAIRD, neurobiology and neurology educator; b. Chgo., Feb. 20, 1952; s. Julian and Susan Menkin S.; m. Barbara Susan Farby, Aug. 26, 1973; children: Rebecca Michelle, Leah Danielle, Sean Zachary. BS, U. Ill., 1972, MS, 1972; MD, Washington U., 1977, PhD, 1977. Diplomate Am. Bd. Psychiatry and Neurology. Intern Jewish Hosp., St. Louis, 1977-78; resident New York Hosp., N.Y.C., 1978-81; asst. prof. Washington U., St. Louis, 1981-84, assoc. prof., 1984-85; assoc. prof. U. Chgo., 1985-88, prof., 1988-92, chmn. com. on neurobiology, 1987-92; James Jackson Putnam prof. neurology and neurosci. Harvard Med. Sch., 1992—; chmn. dept. neurology Beth Israel Deaconess Med. Ctr., Boston, 1992—. Editor-in-chief Jour. of Comparative Neurology, 1994—; contbr. articles to profl. jours. Mem. Am. Neurol. Assn., Am. Acad. Neurology, Am. Physiol. Soc., Soc. for Neurosci. Office: 330 Brookline Ave Boston MA 02215-5400

SAPERS, CARL MARTIN, lawyer; b. Boston, July 16, 1932; s. Abraham E. and Anne (Herwitz) S.; m. Judith H. Thompson, Nov. 29, 1959; children: Jonathan Simonds, Rachel Elizabeth, Benjamin Lovell. AB, Harvard U., 1953, JD, 1958. Bar: Mass. 1958. Assoc. Hill, Barlow, Goodale & Adams, Boston, 1958-65; ptnr. Hill & Barlow, Boston, 1965-96; of counsel Hill & Barlow, 1997—; counsel Mass. Crime Commn., 1996—; spl. asst. atty. gen. criminal divsn. Commonwealth of Mass., 1963-65; adj. prof. Harvard Grad. Sch. Design, 1983—; spl. cons. Mass. Ethics Commn., 1978-79; mem. Mass. Bd. Registration in Medicine, 1995—, vice chair, 1997—. Moderator Town of Brookline, 1982-91; bd. dirs. Boston Archtl. Ctr., 1993—. With U.S. Army, 1953-55. Mem. AIA (hon., Allied Professions medal 1975), Boston Bar Assn. (coun. 1970-73, 91-94), Am. Arbitration Assn. (bd. dirs. 1987—, Whitney North Seymour medal 1991), Am. Coll. Constrn. Lawyers (bd. govs. 1989—, pres. 1993), Handel & Haydn Soc. (bd. govs. 1988—). Home: 26 Chesham Rd Brookline MA 02146-5811 Office: Hill & Barlow One International Pl Boston MA 02110

SAPERSTEIN, DAVID, novelist, screenwriter, film director; b. N.Y.C.; s. Louis and Celia S.; m. Ellen Mae Bernard; children: Ivan, Ilena. Student,

CCNY Film Inst., CCNY. With CBS-TV Ed Murrow Show-Person To Person; writer, prodr., dir. Skyline Films, Inc., 1963-83; asst. prof. film NYU Grad. Sch., Tisch Sch. Arts, 1992-93; instr. screenwriting Manhattan Marymount Coll., 1996-97. Lyricist 70 pub. songs; theatrical prodns. include musicals Blue Planet Blue, Clowns; author: Cocoon, 1985 (Best seller), Fatal Reunion, 1987, Metamorphosis, 1988, Red Devil, 1989, Funerama, 1994, Dark Again, 1996; movies include Cocoon (Best Original Story for Screen 1985, 2 Acad. awards); writer, dir. My Sister's Keeper, Personal Choice (Beyond the Stars), Hearts & Diamonds; writer Torch, Sara Deri, Queen of America, Italian Ices, Joshua's Golden Band, Roamers, Vets, Do Not Disturb, Snatched, Jack in the Box, SchoolHouse, Point of Honor, Roberto!, The John Gill Story: In Defense of Ivan the Terrible, Joshua's Golden Band, Fighting Back, Babs' Labs, Silyan the Stork; writer, dir. music videos Dr. Bill, Teenage Mutant Ninja Turtles, Fallen Angel, Wowii; segment prodr. for Northstar Ent./PBS Reppies; dir. over 300 TV commls.; writer, dir. over 200 documentaries, corp. and indsl. films, videos including Dance of the Athletes (Emmy nomination), Explorers in Aqua-Space, Rodeo: A Matter of Style. Recipient Cine Golden Eagle award, N.Y. Film Festival award, San Francisco Film Festival award, Venice Film Festival award, Melbourne Film Festival award, N.Y. Art Dirs. award, Chgo. Film Festival award. Mem. Writer Guild of Am., Dir. Guild of Am. Office: Ebbets Field Prodns Ltd Wykagyl Station PO Box 42 New Rochelle NY 10804-0042

SAPERSTEIN, LEE WALDO, mining engineering educator; b. N.Y.C., July 14, 1943; s. Charles Levy and Freda Phyllis (Dornbush) S.; m. Priscilla Frances Hickson, Sept. 16, 1967; children: Adam Geoffrey, Clare Freda. BS in Mining Engring., Mont. Sch. Mines, 1964; DPhil in Engring. Sci., Oxford U., 1967. Registered profl. engr., Ky., Mo., Pa. Laborer, miner, engr. The Anaconda Co., Butte, Mont., and N.Y.C., 1963-64; asst. prof. mining engring. Pa. State U., University Park, 1967-71; assoc. prof. Pa. State U., 1971-78, prof., 1978-87, sect. chmn., 1974-87; prof., chmn. dept. mine engring. U. Ky., Lexington, 1987-93; dean, prof. mining engring. Sch. Mines and Metallurgy U. Mo., Rolla, 1993—; chmn. engring. accreditation commn., 1989-90, bd. dirs. Accreditation Bd. for Engring. and Tech., 1992—, sec. of bd., 1995-97, ABET fellow. Contbr. articles to refereed jours. Rhodes scholar Oxford U., 1964-67. Mem. NSPE, ASEE, AIME, Soc. Mining Engrs. (disting. mem. AIME-Soc. Mining Engrs.), Am. Assn. Rhodes Scholars. Home: 801 Laurel Dr Rolla MO 65401-3841 Office: U Mo 305 V H Mc Nutt Hall Rolla MO 65409-0810

SAPERSTEIN, MARC ELI, religious history educator, rabbi; b. N.Y.C., Sept. 5, 1944; s. Harold Irving and Marcia Belle (Rosenblum) S.; m. Roberta Shapiro, June 17, 1970; children: Sara Michal, Adina Ruth. AB, Harvard U., 1966, PhD, 1977; student, Pembroke Coll., U. Cambridge, Eng., 1966-67; MA, Hebrew U., Jerusalem, 1971, Hebrew Union Coll., N.Y.C., 1972. Ordained rabbi, 1972. Lectr. in Hebrew lit. Harvard U., Cambridge, Mass., 1977-79; lectr. in Jewish studies Harvard U. Divinity Sch., 1979-81, asst. prof. Jewish studies, 1981-83, assoc. prof., 1983-86; Gloria M. Goldstein prof. Jewish history and thought Washington U., St. Louis, 1986-97, chmn. program Jewish and Near Eastern Studies, 1989—; rabbi Temple Beth David, Canton, Mass., 1973-86; Charles E. Smith prof. of Jewish history George Washington U., Washington, 1997—, dir. Judaic studies, 1997—; mem. exec. bd. Cen. Conf. Am. Rabbis, 1985-87. Author: Decoding the Rabbis, 1980, Jewish Preaching, 1200-1800, 1989, Moments of Crisis in Jewish-Christian Relations, 1989, Your Voice Like a Ram's Horn, 1996, also articles; editor: Essential Papers on Messianic Movements and Personalities in Jewish History, 1992. Fellow Charles and Julia Henry Fund, 1966-67, Am. Coun. Learned Socs., 1983-84, Inst. Advanced Studies Hebrew U., Jerusalem, 1989, Am. Acad. for Jewish Rsch., 1994—, Ctr. for Judaic Studies, U. Pa., 1995-96; Danforth Found. Kent fellow, 1973-77. Mem. Assn. Jewish Studies (bd. dirs. 1983—), Phi Beta Kappa. Home: 7445 Oxford Dr Saint Louis MO 63105-2915 Office: George Washington U Dept History Washington DC 20052

SAPHIR, RICHARD LOUIS, pediatrician; b. N.Y.C., May 1, 1933; s. Samuel and Grace (Greenberg) S.; m. Judith Schwartz, Dec. 6, 1958; 1 child, Steven. BA, NYU, 1954; MD, SUNY, N.Y.C., 1958. Diplomate Nat. Bd. Med. Examiners, Am. Bd. Pediatrics. Asst. attending physician Mt. Sinai Hosp., N.Y.C., 1965-71; chief, pediatric svcs. U.S. Naval Hosp., Newport, R.I., 1967-69; asst dir., pediatrics acute care clinic Mt. Sinai Hosp., 1970-78, asst. clin. prof. pediatrics, assoc. attending physician, 1971-82, assoc. clin. prof. pediatrics, 1982-88, attending physician, 1982—, clin. prof. pediatrics, 1988—; mem. bd. dirs. Mt. Sinai Childrens Ctr. Found., N.Y.C., 1987—. Contbr. articles to profl. jours. Chmn. community and adv. com. N.Y.C. Info. and Counseling Program for Sudden Infant Death Syndrome, 1979-81; med. bd. YMHA, N.Y.C., 1982-86. Comdr. USNR, 1967-69. Fellow N.Y. Acad. Medicine (treas. 1987-89), Am. Acad. Pediats. (ednl. program rep. ambulatory care quality improvement program 1992—, com. sci. meetings 1985-97, chmn. prep course 1991-96, editl. bd. Pediat. in Rev. 1997—, ednl. advisor proficiency testing program Am. Acad. Pediats. and Coll. Am. Pathologists), N.Y. Pediat. Soc. (pres. 1978-79), N.Y. County Med. Soc. (vice chmn. com. child welfare 1974-85). Office: BSM Pediatrics PC 55 E 87th St New York NY 10128-1043

SAPICO, FRANCISCO LEJANO, internist, educator; b. Manila, July 18, 1940; came to U.S., 1967; s. Urbano Loyola and Asuncion Limon (Lejano) S.; m. Margaret Mary Armstrong, Nov. 7, 1969; children: Erica Anne, Derek Armstrong. AA, U. Philippines, 1960, MD, 1965. Diplomate Am. Bd. Internal Medicine, Am. Bd. Infectious Diseases. Rotating intern, resident in internal medicine Philippine Gen. Hosp.-U. Philippines, Manila, 1964-67; resident in internal medicine SUNY Upstate Med. Ctr., Syracuse, 1967-69; fellow in infectious diseases UCLA Ctr. for Health Scis., 1969-71; fellow in infectious diseases Wadsworth VA Hosp., L.A., 1971-72, staff physician dept. medicine, 1972-77; physician specialist dept. medicine Rancho Los Amigos Med. Ctr., Downey, Calif., 1977—, chief infectious diseases, 1995—; adj. asst. prof. medicine UCLA Sch. Medicine, 1972-77; asst. prof. medicine U. So. Calif. Sch. Medicine, L.A., 1977-82, assoc. prof., 1982-90, prof., 1990—. Contbr. articles to med. jours., chpts. to books. Judge Fullerton (Calif.) Youth Sci. Fair, 1982-86, Orange County Sci. and Engring. Fair, Fullerton, 1984; coach, asst. coach Fullerton Rangers Youth Soccer Club, 1982-89. Fellow ACP, Infectious Diseases Soc. Am.; mem. Am. Soc. Microbiology, Am. Soc. Tropical Medicine and Hygiene, Infections Disease Assn. Calif. Republican. Avocations: soccer, tennis, camping, fishing, photography. Office: Rancho Los Amigos Med Ctr 7601 Imperial Hwy Downey CA 90242-3456

SAPIENZA, JOHN THOMAS, lawyer; b. South Orange, N.J., Feb. 26, 1913; s. James C. and Rosalie (Gaimo) S.; m. Virginia H. Gignoux, Feb. 12, 1972; children by previous marriage: John Thomas, James K. A.B. summa cum laude, Harvard U., 1934, LL.B. magna cum laude, 1937. Bar: N.Y. 1938, D.C. 1943. Law clk. Judge A.N. Hand, N.Y.C., 1937-38, Justice Stanley Reed, Washington, 1938-39; assoc. firm Wright, Gordon, Zachry & Parlin, N.Y.C., 1939-41; assoc. firm Covington & Burling, Washington, 1941-48, ptnr., 1949-87, ret. ptnr., 1987—; dir. Hiram Walker-Gooderham & Worts Ltd., 1971-86, Hiram Walker & Sons, Inc., 1971-86, Hiram Walker Resources Ltd., 1981-86, Wyman Gordon Co., 1973-83; dir. Am. Security Bank, N.A., 1975-83, dir. emeritus, 1983-88. Pres.: Harvard Law Rev, 1936-37. Trustee George Washington U., 1978-88, hon. trustee, 1988—. Served to lt. comdr. USNR, 1943-46. Mem. Am., D.C., Fed. bar assns., Am. Law Inst., Confrerie des Chevaliers du Tastevin, Phi Beta Kappa. Clubs: Burning Tree (Washington), Metropolitan (Washington) ; Farmington Country (Charlottesville, Va.). Home: 635 Worthington Dr Apt 300 Charlottesville VA 22903-4660 Office: Covington & Burling PO Box 7566 1201 Pennsylvania Ave NW Washington DC 20004-2401

SAPINSKY, JOSEPH CHARLES, magazine executive, photographer; b. N.Y.C., Dec. 13, 1923; s. Simon Moses and Janet (Charles) S.; m. Jane Tomney, Oct. 21, 1970; children—Michael Joseph, Jane Anne, Laura Alexandra. Certificate illustration, Pratt Inst., 1943; certificate advt. design, 1947; postgrad., Colgate U., 1943, Cornell U., N.C. U. Art dir. Today's Living, N.Y. Herald Tribune, N.Y.C., 1960-63; art dir. N.Y. Mag., N.Y.C., 1963-65; asso. art dir., dir. photography Sat. Evening Post, N.Y.C., 1965-67; dir. publs. I.O.S., Geneva, 1967-69; art dir. This Week, N.Y.C., 1969, Jock N.Y. mag., N.Y.C., 1970; dir. publs. I.I.G., London, 1970; art dir. Woman's Day mag., N.Y.C., 1971-83; exec. art dir. Woman's Day Spls., N.Y.C., 1983-92; comml. photographer, 1992—; cons. art dir. Infinity mag., N.Y.C., 1971-73; instr. dept. photography Sch. Visual Arts, N.Y.C., New Sch., N.Y.C. Served with USNR, 1943-46; capt. Res. ret. Recipient numerous art dir. awards. Mem. Am. Soc. Mag. Photographers, Soc. Illustrators, Am. Soc. Mag. Editors, Am. Inst. Graphic Arts, Soc. Publ. Designers, Res. Officers Assn. Home: 76 Bank St New York NY 10014-2124

SAPINSLEY, LILA MANFIELD, state official; b. Chgo., Sept. 9, 1922; d. Jacob and Doris (Silverman) Manfield; BA, Wellesley Coll., 1944; D. Pub. Service, U. R.I., 1971; D. Pedagogy, R.I. Coll., 1973, LHD, Brown U., 1993; m. John M. Sapinsley, Dec. 23, 1942; children—Jill Sapinsley Mooney, Carol Sapinsley Rubenstein, Joan Sapinsley Lewis, Patricia Sapinsley Levy. Mem. R.I. Senate, 1972-84, minority leader, 1974-84; dir. R.I. Dept. Community Affairs, 1985; bd. dirs. Lifespan Corp.; chmn. R.I. Housing and Mortgage Fin. Corp., 1985-87; Commr. R.I. Pub. Utilities Commn., 1987-93. Mem. R.I. Gov.'s Commn. on Women; commr. Edn. Commn. of States; pres. bd. trustees Butler Hosp., 1978-84; trustee R.I. State Colls., 1965-70, chmn., 1967-70; trustee U. R.I., R.I. Coll. Found.; bd. dirs. Hamilton House, Trinity Repertory Co., Lincoln Sch., Wellesley Center for Research on Women, 1980, Providence Pub. Libr. Recipient Alumnae Achievement award Wellesley Coll., 1974; Outstanding Legislator of Yr. award Republican Nat. Legislators Assn., 1984. Republican. Jewish. Home: 25 Cooke St Providence RI 02906-2022

SAPOFF, MEYER, electronics component manufacturer; b. N.Y.C., June 2, 1927; s. Benjamin and Mary (Charney) S. Student, Mohawk Coll., 1946-48, Poly. Inst. Bklyn., 1948-50, 52-53; BS in Elec. Engring. magna cum laude, Poly. Inst. Bklyn., 1950, postgrad., 1952-53; postgrad., MIT, 1951, U. Pa., 1951-52; MS in Elec. Engring., Drexel Inst. Tech., 1952. Rsch. engr. Franklin Inst. Labs., Phila., 1950-52; rsch. fellow sr. grade Poly. Inst. Bklyn., 1952-53; dir. rsch. Victory Engring. Corp., Springfield, N.J., 1953-57; dir. engring. Victory Engring. Corp., Springfield, 1957-63, v.p., 1963-69; cons., sr. staff scientist Keystone Carbon Co., St. Mary's, Pa., 1969-70; pres. Thermometrics, Inc., Edison, N.J., 1970-86, chmn. bd. dirs., 1986-93, sr. staff cons., 1993-96; pres. MS Cons., Princeton, 1993—; cons. in field; program com., chmn. E20.08 Med. Thermometry subcom., chmn. session on thermistors 6th Symposium on Temperature, Measurement and Control in Sci. and Industry. Contbr. articles to profl. jours.; patentee in field. Active Citizens League West Orange, 1962-75, West Orange PTA, 1960-76. With USN, 1945-46. Recipient Indsl. Rsch. IR-100 award, 1974; State of NYU scholar, 1948-50; Poly. Inst. Bklyn. fellow, 1953. Mem. IEEE, ASTM, AAAS, Poly. Inst. Bklyn. Alumni Assn., Am. Ceramic Soc., Internat. Orgn. for Legal Metrology, Am. nat. Standards Inst., Am. Vacuum Soc., Tau Beta Pi, Eta Kappa Nu. Home: 1137 Stuart Rd Princeton NJ 08540-1216 Office: 301 N Harrison St Ste 69 Princeton NJ 08540-3512

SAPOLSKY, HARVEY MORTON, political scientist, educator; b. Haverhill, Mass., Feb. 21, 1939; s. Abraham and Anne Betty (Selig) S.; m. Karen P. Stenbo, Aug. 27, 1966. BA, Boston U., 1961; MPA, Harvard U., 1963, PhD, 1967. Mem. faculty MIT, 1966—, prof. polit. sci., 1977—, dir. comm. forum, 1987-95, dir. def. and arms control program, 1989—; dep. dir. Univ. Health Policy Consortium, 1978-83, assoc. chmn. faculty, 1981-83; vis. prof. U. Mich., 1971-72; cons. Artificial Heart Assessment Panel Nat. Heart and Lung Inst., Washington, 1972-73; mem. Ethics and Health Policy Panel Hastings (N.Y.) Ctr., 1979-80; mem. com. on Fed. Rsch. on Effect of Ionizing Radiation NRC, Washington, 1980-81; mem. com. on Risk Perception and Comm. NRC, 1987-88; mem. Sec. of Energy's Task Force on Alternative Futures for Dept. of Energy Labs., 1994-95. Author: The Polaris System Development, 1972, (with D. Altman and Richard Greene) Health Planning and Regulation, 1981, (with A. Drake, S. Finkelstein) The American Blood Supply, 1982, Science and the Navy, 1990; editor: Consuming Fears: The Politics of Product Risks, 1986; co-editor: Federal Health Programs, 1981, (with S. Altman), 1981, (with R. Crane, W.R. Newman and E. Noam) The Telecommunications Revolution, 1992; also articles. Mem. AAAS (sec. sect. social and econ. scis. 1968-73), Am. Polit. Sci. Assn., Nat. Acad. Social Ins., Coun. on Fgn. Rels. Home: 37 Edgemoor Rd Belmont MA 02178-3916 Office: MIT Def Arms Control Studies Pro E38-600 Cambridge MA 02139

SAPOLU, MANASE JESSE, professional football player; b. Laie, Western Samoa, Mar. 10, 1961. Student, U. Hawaii. Guard San Francisco 49ers, 1983—. Selected to Pro Bowl, 1993, 94; mem. San Francisco 49ers Super Bowl Champions XXIII, 1988, XXIV, 1989, XXIX, 1994. Office: San Francisco 49ers 4949 Centennial Blvd Santa Clara CA 95054-1229*

SAPORTA, JACK, psychologist, educator; b. N.Y.C., Oct. 21, 1927; s. David and Victoria (Fils) S.; m. Judith Hammond, May 28, 1967 (div. 1979); children: David, Victoria. AB cum laude, Adelphi U., 1951; PhD, U. Chgo., 1962. Diplomate Am. Bd. Profl. Psychology; lic. clin. psychologist. Pvt. practice, 1962—; supt. Tinley Park (Ill.) Mental Health Ctr., 1975-78; chief manpower tng. and devel. Ill. Dept. Mental Health, Chgo., 1978-82; dean, prof. Forest Inst. Profl. Psychology, Des Plaines, Ill., 1982-85; coord. studies Fielding Inst., Santa Barbara, Calif., 1984—; prof. Ill. Sch. Profl. Psychology, Chgo., 1985—; mem. adj. faculty psychology Lake Forest Grad. Sch. Mgmt., 1987-97; mem. Ill. State Clin. Psychology Lic. and Disciplinary Com., Springfield, 1984-93; profl. staff Forest Hosp., Des Plaines, 1977-96; mem. staff Luth. Gen. Hosp., Park Ridge, Ill., 1986—. Served with U.S. Army, 1946-47, Germany. Named Educator of Yr., Forest Inst., 1982, Outstanding Faculty Mem. Lake Forest Grad. Sch. Mgmt. Fellow Acad. Clin. Psychology, NTL-Inst. (faculty); mem. APA (accreditation site vis. team), Ill. Psychol. Assn., Chgo. Psychol. Assn. Avocations: tennis, computers, do-it-yourself home projects. Home: 3201 California Ave Rolling Meadows IL 60008-2226

SAPP, DONALD GENE, minister; b. Phoenix, Feb. 27, 1927; s. Guerry Byron and Lydia Elmeda (Snyder) S.; m. Anna Maydean Nevitt, July 10, 1952 (dec.); m. Joann Herrin Mountz, May 1, 1976; children: Gregory, Paula, Jeffrey, Mark, Melody, Cristine. AB in Edn., Ariz. State U., 1949; MDiv, Boston U., 1952, STM, 1960; D Ministry, Calif. Grad. Sch. Theology, 1975. Ordained to ministry Meth. Ch., 1950. Dir. youth activities Hyde Park (Mass.) Meth. Ch., 1950-52; minister 1st Meth. Ch., Peabody, Mass., 1952-54, Balboa Island (Calif.) Community Meth. Ch., 1954-57, Ch. of the Foothills Meth., Duarte, Calif., 1957-63; sr. minister Aldersgate United Meth. Ch., Tustin, Calif., 1963-70, Paradise Valley (Ariz.) United Meth. Ch., 1970-83; dist. supt. Cen. West Dist. of Desert S.W. Conf. United Meth. Ctr., Phoenix, 1983-89. Editor Wide Horizons, 1983-89; contbr. articles to profl. jours. Chaplain City of Hope Med. Ctr., Duarte, 1957-63; trustee Plaza Community Ctr., L.A., 1967-70; corp. mem. Sch. Theology at Claremont, Calif., 1972-80; pres. Met. Phoenix Commn., 1983-85; del. Western Jurisdictional Conf. United Meth. Ch., 1984, 88; bd. dirs. Coun. Chs., L.A., 1963-67, Orange County (Calif.) Human Rels. Coun., 1967-70, Interfaith Counseling Svc. Found., 1982-89, Wesley Community Ctr., Phoenix, 1983-89; mem. gen. conf. United Meth. Ch., 1988. With USN, 1945-46. Mem. Ariz. Ecumenical Coun., Bishops and Exec. Roundtable, Rotary (pres.), Kappa Delta Pi, Tau Kappa Epsilon. Democrat. Avocation: overseas travel. Home: 5225 E Road Runner Rd Paradise Valley AZ 85253

SAPP, WALTER WILLIAM, lawyer, energy company executive; b. Linton, Ind., Apr. 21, 1930; s. Walter J. and Nona (Stalcup) S.; m. Eva Kaschner, July 10, 1957 (dec.); children: Karen Elisabeth, Christoph Walter. AB magna cum laude, Harvard, 1951; JD summa cum laude, Ind. U., 1957. Bar: Ind. 1957, N.Y. 1959, Colo. 1966, U.S. Supreme Ct. 1972, Tex. 1977. Pvt. practice N.Y.C., 1957-60, 63-66; practice in Paris, France, 1960-63, Colorado Springs, 1966-76; assoc. atty. Cahill, Gordon, Reindel & Ohl, Paris, 1960-63, N.Y.C., 1957-60, 63-65; partner Cahill, Gordon, Reindel & Ohl, 1966; gen. counsel Colo. Interstate Corp., 1966-76, v.p., 1968-76, sec., 1971-76, sr. v.p., dir., exec. com., 1973-75, exec. v.p., 1975-76; v.p. Coastal States Gas Corp., 1973-76; sr. v.p., gen. counsel Tenneco, Inc., Houston, 1976-92, sec., 1984-86; pvt. practice Houston, 1992—; Editor-in-chief Ind. U. Law Jour., 1956-57. Trustee Houston Ballet, 1982-85, Awty Internat. Sch., 1989—, vice-chmn., 1994—; bd. dirs. Harris County Met. Transit Authority, 1982-84, Houston Internat. Protocol Alliance, 1992-94, Houston Symphony, 1989—, v.p., 1991-94; adv. bd. Inst. for Internat. Edn. S.W. region, 1987—, chmn., 1992-94, Internat. and Comparative Law Ctr. Southwestern Legal Found., 1976-92. Lt. USNR, 1951-54. Mem. ABA, N.Y. State Bar Assn., Tex. Bar Assn., Assn. Bar City of N.Y., Houston Bar Assn., Order of the Coif, French-Am. C. of C. (bd. dirs. 1987-92), Alliance Francaise Houston (bd. dirs. 1989—, v.p. 1991-94). Mem. United Ch. of Christ. Office: 2108 Quenby St Houston TX 77005-1506

SAPPENFIELD, CHARLES MADISON, architect, educator; b. Columbia, S.C., Mar. 17, 1930; s. Charles Madison and Elizabeth Olive (Moss) S.; m. Mary Frances McGowan Dec. 14, 1963 (div. June 1990); children—Charles Ross, Sarah Kathleen. B.Arch., N.C. State U., 1956; Cert., Denmark's Royal Acad., Copenhagen, 1961. Registered architect, Ind., Tenn., N.C. Asst. prof. N.C. State U., Raleigh, 1956-57, asst. prof., 1961-63; head archtl. firm C.M. Sappenfield, Asheville, N.C. and Muncie, Ind., 1961—; assoc. prof. Clemson U., S.C., 1963-65; prof. architecture Ball State U., Muncie, Ind., 1965-94, prof. emeritus, 1994—, dean, 1965-81, dean emeritus, 1994—, dir. Design Indiana, 1983-88; awards juror Interfaith Forum on Religious Art and Architecture, 1981, Am. Cons. Engrs. Council, 1982; mem. accreditation teams Nat. Archtl. Accrediting Bd., 1967-82. Archtl. works include: Dormitories, U. N.C., Gumpert residence, Dave residence. Pres. Asheville Art Mus., N.C., 1964-65; chmn. Ind. Commn. on Aging, Indpls., 1983-85; pres. Alpha Day Care Ctr. for Elderly, Muncie, 1985; mem. State Planning Adv. Commn., Indpls., 1974-82. Served with U.S. Army. Recipient Gold medal for service Ball State U., 1983; named Sagamore of the Wabash, Gov. of Ind., 1982. Fellow AIA (dir. nat. bd. dirs. 1989-92); mem. Ind. Soc. Architects (pres. 1976), Ind. Archtl. Found. (chmn. 1975), Am. Soc. Landscape Architects (awards juror 1983), Danish Fedn. Architects (hon., Aeresmedallion 1987), Fulbright Alumni Assn., Alpha Rho Chi. Republican. Episcopalian. Lodges: Rotary, Civitan. Avocations: bicycling, racquetball, photography. Home and Office: 2900 W Torquay Rd Muncie IN 47304-3229

SAPPINGTON, SHARON ANNE, school librarian; b. West Palm Beach, Fla., Sept. 15, 1944; d. A. D. and Laura G. (Jackson) Chambless; m. Andrew Arnold Sappington III, June 11, 1966; children: Andrew Arnold IV, Kevin Sean. Student, Fla. So. coll., 1962-64; BA in Edn., U. Fla., 1966; media specialist, U. Ala., 1980. 5th grade tchr. Tates Creek Elem., Lexington, Ky., 1966-68; 4th grade tchr. Sadieville (Ky.) Elem., 1968-69; libr. media specialist A.H. Watwood Elem., Childersburg, Ala., 1980—; guest storyteller Young Author's Conf., Winterboro, Lincoln, Sylacauga, and Fayetteville, Ala., 1982-94; vis. com. mem. Southeastern Accreditation Assn.; program presenter Internat. Reading Assn., Birmingham, Ala., 1983; guest speaker rare children's books "By the Way" TV talk show, 1983. Creator, presenter: (slide presentation) Tellers of Tales and Sketchers of Dreams, 1983, (multimedia programs) Dinosaurs, Teddy Bears, and Wild Things, 1990, Shanghaied in the Beijing Airport, 1994. Circle chmn., Sunday tchr. Grace United Meth. Ch., Birmingham, 1973, 92-95; delivery mem. Meals on Wheels, Birmingham, 1975-76; radio reader for the blind WBHM Pub. Broadcasting, Birmingham, 1980; guest speaker, program presenter Jaycees, Kiwanis, and C. of C., Childersburg, 1993-94. Title I grantee, 1991, Stutz Bearcat grantee, 1992. Mem. AAUW, ALA, Am. Assn. Sch. Librs., Ala. Libr. Assn. (children's and sch. divsn. publicity chmn. 1991-93, chmn. Nat. Libr. Week 1993-94, Outstanding Youth Svcs. award 1989), People to People Internat. (libr. del. to China 1993), Kappa Delta Pi. Democrat. Methodist. Avocations: collector of 19th century illustrated children's literature. Home: 5278 Cornell Dr Birmingham AL 35210-2935 Office: A H Watwood Elem Sch Limbaugh Blvd Childersburg AL 35044

SAPSOWITZ, SIDNEY H., entertainment and media company executive; b. N.Y.C., June 29, 1936; s. Max and Annette (Rothstein) Sapsowitz; m. Phyllis Skopp, Nov. 27, 1957; children: Donna Dawn Chazen, Gloria Lynn Aaron, Marsha Helene Gleit. BBA summa cum laude, Paterson (N.J.) State Coll., 1980. Various fin. and oper. systems positions Metro Goldwyn Mayer, Inc., N.Y.C., 1957-68; exec. v.p., dir. Penta Computer Assoc. Inc., N.Y.C., 1968-70, Cons. Actuaries Inc., Clifton, N.J., 1970-73; exec. v.p., CFO Am. Film. Theatre, N.Y.C., 1973-76, Cinema Shares Internat Distrb. Corp., N.Y.C., 1976-79; sr. cons. Solomon, Finger & Newman, N.Y.C., 1979-80; exec. v.p., chief fin. officer Metro Goldwyn Mayer, Inc., L.A., 1980-85; various positions leading to exec. v.p. fin. and adminstrn., CFO MGM/UA Entertainment Co., Culver City, Calif., 1985-86; also bd. dirs. MGM/UA Entertainment Co., L.A.; fin. v.p.; chief bus. and ops. officer, Office of Pres., dir. United Artists Corp., Beverly Hills, Calif., 1986-87; chmn. bd., CEO MGA/UA Telecommunications Corp., Beverly Hills, 1986-89; sr. exec. v.p., dir., mem. exec. com. MGA/UA Communications Co., 1986-89; chmn., CEO Sid Sapsowitz & Assocs., Inc., 1989—. Pres., Wayne Conservative Congregation, N.J., 1970-77. Mem. Am. Mgmt. Assn., Am. Film Inst., Acad. Motion Picture Arts and Scis., Fin. Exec. Inst., TV Acad. Arts and Scis., KP (chancellor comdr.).

SAPUTRA, DANIEL, agricultural engineering educator; b. Padangsidempuan, Indonesia, Aug. 9, 1958; s. Adam and Hanna Saputra; m. Liniyanti D. Oswari, Sept. 19, 1984; children: Danny Matthew, Joshua Michael, Irene Ruth. Sarjana, Bogor (Indonesia) Agrl. U., 1982; MS in Agrl. Engring., U. Ky., 1988, PhD, 1992. Site mgr. P.T. Layaniraya, Tarakan, Indonesia, 1982-83; supervision head P.T. Trans Intra Asia, West Aceh, Indonesia, 1983-84; lectr. Coll. Agr. U. Sriwijaya, Palembang, Indonesia, 1985—, head food process engring., 1993—. Contbr. articles to profl. jours.; patentee in field. Mem. Am. Soc. Agrl. Engrs., Indonesian Soc. Agrl. Engrs. Seventh Day Adventist. Office: Indralaya Campus, U Sriwijaya Coll Agr, Palembang 30662, Indonesia

SARACHIK, MYRIAM PAULA, physics educator; b. Antwerp, Belgium, Aug. 8, 1933; came to U.S., 1947; d. Solomon and Sarah (Segal) Morgenstein; m. Philip E. Sarachik, Sept. 6, 1954; 1 child, Karen Beth. AB, Barnard Coll., 1954; MS, Columbia U., 1957, PhD, 1960. Rsch. assoc. IBM Watson Labs., Columbia U., N.Y.C., 1960-61; mem. tech. staff Bell Telephone Labs., Murray Hill, N.J., 1962-64; asst. prof. physics CCNY, 1964-67, assoc. prof., 1967-70, prof., 1971—, Disting. prof., 1995—; advisor NSF, NRC. Contbr. articles to profl. jours. Recipient N.Y.C. Mayor's award for excellence in math., phys. and engring. scis., 1995. Fellow Am. Phys. Soc. (various offices and coms.), N.Y. Acad. Scis.; mem. NAS. Office: CCNY Physics Dept Convent Ave and 138 St New York NY 10031

SARAF, KOMAL C., psychologist; b. India, May 9, 1939; came to U.S., 1969; naturalized; s. Ratan Chand and Phula Bai Saraf. BA in Psychology, U. Agra, India, 1960, MA in Psychology, 1963; diploma in med. and social psychology, Ranchi U., India, 1965; PhD in Clin. Psychology, Calif. Sch. Profl. Psychology, 1980. Diplomate Am. Bd. Profl. Disability Cons., Am. Coll. Forensic Examiners; lic. psychologist, Pa., N.J.; cert. therapist in rational emotive therapy. Intern clin. psychology Hosp. for Mental Diseases, Ranchi, 1963-65; asst. rsch. officer India Internat. Ctr., New Delhi, 1965-67; clin. psychologist Rehab. Ctr. for the Visually Handicapped, New Delhi, 1967-68, AABC Sch. for Multiple Handicapped & Brain Injured Children, Jamaica, N.Y., 1969-70; staff clin. psychologist I Trenton (N.J.) Psychiat. Hosp., 1970-74, N.J. State Prison, Trenton, 1974-77; pvt. practice, Morrisville, Pa., 1980—; prin. clin. psychologist youth clinic N.J. Tng. Sch. for Boys, Jamesburg, 1980-96; clin. dir. Ewing Residential Ctr., Trenton, 1996—; instr. Internat. Sch. for Mental Health Practitioners, Morrisville, 1981—, Govt. of India Tchr.'s Tng. Ctr., New Delhi, 1967-68; co-adj. instr. Trenton State Coll., 1975; lectr. in psycho-social adjustment to handicapped persons; chair psychology internship com. Psychol. Svcs. Jersey Dept. Corrections, 1982—. Calif. Sch. Profl. Psychology scholar, 1977-80, Govt. of India scholar, 1963-65. Assoc. fellow Inst. for the Advanced Studies in Rational Emotive Therapy; mem. APA, Internat. Coun. Psychologists (mem. nominating com. 1976-77, co-chair psycho-edn. com. on India 1973-74), Am. Assn. Marriage and Family, N.J. Psychol. Assn. (chair utilization profl. svcs.-pub. 1987-88), Pa. Psychol. Assn., Gen. Psychol. Svcs., Inc., All India Assn. Clin. Psychologists (founder), All India Assn. Mental Retardation (founder). Avocations: traveling, camping, fishing, raquetball, bicycling. Home: 1430 Riverside Dr Trenton NJ 08618-5805

SARAF, SHEVACH, company executive. Chmn., CEO, pres. Solitron Devices, West Palm Beach, Fla. Office: Solitron Devices 3301 Electronics Way West Palm Beach FL 33407-4620

SARASON, IRWIN G., psychology educator; b. Newark, Sept. 15, 1929; s. Max and Anna Sarason; m. Barbara June Ryrholm, Sept. 19, 1953; children: Suzanne, Jane, Donald. BA, Rutgers U., Newark, 1951; MS, U. Iowa, 1953; PhD, Ind. U., 1955. Lic. psychologist, Wash. Intern clin. psychology VA Hosp., West Haven, Conn., 1955-56; asst. prof. psychology U. Wash.,

Seattle, 1956-59, assoc. prof., 1959-65, prof., 1965—. Co-author: Abnormal Psychology, 1972, 8th edit., 1996; editor: Jour. Personality and Social Psychology, 1985-91; author over 250 articles. The Netherlands Inst. for Advanced Study fellow, Wassenaar, 1975, 85. Fellow APA, Japan Soc. for Promotion of Sci., AAAS, Western Psychol. Assn. (pres. 1978-79), Wash. State Psychol. Assn. (pres. 1965). Avocations: travel, music, reading. Home: 13516 42nd Ave NE Seattle WA 98125-3826 Office: U Wash Dept Psychology Seattle WA 98195

SARASTE, JUKKA-PEKKA, conductor; b. Heinola, Finland, 1956. With Finnish Radio Symphony Orch., 1978—, prin. condr., 1987—; prin. condr. Scottish Chamber Orch., 1987-91; music dir. The Toronto Symphony Orch., 1994—. Guest condr. Helsinki Philharm., Beijing Cen. Opera Orch., Symphonic Orch. Chengdu, Rotterdam Philharm. Orch., Chamber Orch. Europe, Bavarian Radio Symphony Orch., Junge Deutsche Philharm., Detroit Orch., Minn. Orch., Vienna Symphony Orch., Rome's Santa Cecilia Orch., Cleve. Orch., Boston Symphony Orch., L.A. Philharm. Orch., others; co-founder Avanti Chamber orch.; condr. more than 39 recs. with Finnish Radio Symphony Orch. and Scottish Chamber Orch. Recipient First prize Scandinavian Conducting Competition, 1981, hon. doctorate fine arts, York U., Toronto, 1995. Office: Radio Symphony Orch, Yleisradio Ja 14, SF-00240 Helsinki 24, Finland also: Toronto Symphony Orch, 212 King St W Ste 550, Toronto, ON Canada M5H 1K5*

SARAVOLATZ, LOUIS DONALD, epidemiologist, physician educator; b. Detroit, Feb. 15, 1950; s. Samuel and Saya Betty (Chonich) S.; m. Yvette Susanne Braymer, Oct. 6, 1990; children: Samuel Francis, Louis Donald II, Stephanie Nicole. BS, U. Mich., 1972, MD, 1974. Fellow Am. Coll. Epidemiology. Internship Henry Ford Hosp., 1974-75, residency, 1975-77, infectious disease fellowship, 1977-79; intern Henry Ford Hosp., Detroit, 1974-75, 1975-77, fellow, 1977-79; dir. hosp. epidemiology Henry Ford Hosp., 1979-82, divsn. head infectious diseases, 1982-96, dir. infectious diseases rsch. lab., 1982-96; prof. medicine Case-Western Res. U., 1993-96, Wayne State U. Sch. Medicine, Detroit, 1996—; clin. prof. medicine U. Mich. Med. Sch., Ann Arbor, 1986-96; mem. AIDS clin. drug devel. com. NIH, 1990-95. Contbr. over 100 articles to profl. publs. Active Blue Ribbon Com. on AIDS State of Mich., Detroit, 1990; chmn. physician com. on AIDS Greater Detroit Health Coun., 1989. Fellow ACP, Infectious Diseases Soc. Am.

SARAZEN, RICHARD ALLEN, media company executive; b. Bklyn., June 27, 1933; s. Nicholas and Anna M. (Isacco) S.; children: Richard, Theresa, Mary, Barbara, David, Russell, Christina, Andrea. B.B.A., Hofstra U., 1955. CPA, N.Y., Pa., Calif. Acct. Arthur Young & Co., N.Y.C., 1955-58; ptnr. Alexander Grant & Co., N.Y.C., 1958-67; v.p. fin. Seeburg Corp., Chgo., 1967-69; mng. ptnr. Alexander Grant & Co., Pitts., Los Angeles, 1969-74; exec. v.p. News Am. Pub., Inc., N.Y.C., 1974-80; chmn. bd. XCor Internat., Inc., N.Y.C., 1980-82; sr. exec. v.p., bd. dir. The News Corp. Ltd., Sydney, Australia, 1982—. Bd. dirs. N.Y.C. Center Found. Mem. AICPA, N.Y. State Soc. CPAs. Republican. Roman Catholic. Club: Chgo. Athletic. Home: 165 Galway Rd Windham NY 12496 Office: News Am Pub Inc 1211 Avenue Of The Americas New York NY 10036-8701

SARAZIN, CRAIG LEIGH, astronomer, educator; b. Milw., Aug. 11, 1950; s. Valley V. and Martha V. (Gustafson) S.; m. Jane Curry, June 12, 1971; children: Stephen N., Andrew T. BS in Physics, Calif. Inst. Tech., 1972; MA in Physics, Princeton U., 1973, PhD in Physics, 1975. Millikan fellow Calif. Inst. Tech., Pasadena, 1975; mem. Inst. Advanced Study, Princeton, N.J., 1975-77; asst. prof. U. Va., Charlottesville, 1977-79, assoc. prof. dept. astronomy, 1979-86, prof., 1986-96, W.H. Vanderbilt prof. astronomy, 1996—, chmn. dept., 1992-95; vis. asst. prof. U. Calif., Berkeley, 1979; vis. scientist Nat. Radio Astronomy Obs., Charlottesville, 1977-82; vis. prof. physics Inst. Advanced Study, 1981-82, Joint Inst. Lab. Astrophysics vis. fellow U. Colo., Boulder, 1985-86; mem. com. on Space Astronomy Astrophysics, Washington, 1984-86, mem. x-ray astronomy working group, 1989-94; mem. Advanced X-ray Astronomy Facility users com., 1993—, Advanced Satellite for Cosmology and Astrophysics users com., 1995—. Author: X-ray Emission from Clusters of Galaxies; contbr. numerous articles to profl. jours. NSF grantee, 1981-86, NASA grantee, 1979-82, 86—; recipient Haren Fischer Physics prize Calif. Inst. Tech., 1971. Mem. Am. Astron. Soc., Internat. Astron. Union. Home: 2574 Kimbrough Cir Charlottesville VA 22901-9516 Office: Leander J McCormick Obs Dept of Astronomy U of Va PO Box 3818 Charlottesville VA 22903-0818

SARBANES, PAUL SPYROS, senator; b. Salisbury, Md., Feb. 3, 1933; s. Spyros P. and Matina (Tsigounis) S.; m. Christine Dunbar, June 11, 1960; children—John Peter, Michael Anthony, Janet Matina. A.B., Princeton, 1954; B.A. (Rhodes scholar), Oxford (Eng.) U., 1957; LL.B., Harvard, 1960. Bar: Md. bar 1960. Law clk. to judge Morris Soper U.S. Ct. Appeals (4th cir.), 1960-61; asso. Piper & Marbury, Balt., 1961-62; adminstrv. asst. Walter W. Heller; chmn. Council Econ. Advisers, 1962-63; exec. dir. Charter Revision Commn., Balt., 1963-64; asso. Venable, Baetjer & Howard, Balt., 1965-70; mem. Md. Ho. of Dels., 1967-71, 92d Congress from 4th Dist. Md., 93d-94th congresses from 3d Dist. Md.; U.S. senator from Md., 1977—, mem. banking, housing and urban affairs com., fgn. rels. com., joint econ. com., senate Dem. policy com. Democrat. Greek Orthodox. Office: US Senate 309 Hart Senate Bldg Washington DC 20510 also: Tower I Ste 100 100 S Charles St Baltimore MD 21201-2725*

SARBIN, HERSHEL BENJAMIN, management consultant, business publisher, lawyer; b. Massillon, Ohio, Dec. 30, 1924; s. Joseph I. and Sarah Charlotte (Reich) S.; m. Susan Challman, July 24, 1973; children by previous marriage: Penelope Sarbin Burke, Richard, Barbara; 1 stepdau., Caroline Cooley. A.B., Western Res. U., 1946; J.D., Harvard U., 1950. Bar: Ill. 1950, N.Y. 1953. Assoc. firm Lewis and MacDonald, N.Y.C., 1953-58; with Ziff-Davis Pub. Co., 1950-81; pub. Popular Photography mag., 1965-66, sr. v.p. co., 1967-74; assoc. pub. Travel Weekly, 1967-68, pub., 1969-74, pres., pub. dir., chief exec. officer photog. div., 1968-69, pres. Pub. Transp. and Travel div., 1970-74; pres. Ziff-Davis Pub. Co., 1974-78; exec. v.p. Ziff Corp., 1978-81, also dir.; chmn., pres. Hershel Sarbin Assocs., Inc., 1981—; vis. assoc. prof. Fla. Internat. U., 1980; mem. exec. com., nat. photography coordinator Pres.'s Council Youth Opportunity, 1968; fed. commr. Nat. Commn. on New Technol. Uses of Copyrighted Works, 1975-78; mem. policy rev. bd. Public Agenda Found.; pres., CEO Cowles Bus. Media, Inc., 1991-95; Sr. Advisor Cowles Media, 1995. Author: (with George Chernoff) Photography and the Law, 1958, rev. edit., 1977. Mem. exec. com. Westchester County (N.Y.) Sch. Bd., 1964-66; mem. ethical practices com. N.Y. Sch. Bd. Assn., 1965-68; pres. Hastings-on-Hudson Bd. Edn., 1966-67. Served with AUS, 1946-47. Mem. Phi Beta Kappa. Clubs: Harvard, Sky (N.Y.C.); Bedford Golf and Tennis (N.Y.). Home: 756 Guard Hill Rd Bedford NY 10506-1042 Office: 6 Riverbend Ctr 911 Hope St Stamford CT 06907-2318

SARBINOFF, JAMES ADAIR, periodontist, consultant; b. Indpls., Dec. 29, 1947; s. James Gill and Eileen Sarbinoff; m. Tamara Lynn Griffith, June 6, 1971. A.B. in Zoology, Ind. U., 1970; D.D.S., Ind. U.-Indpls., 1974, M.S. in Dentistry, 1981. Diplomate Am. Acad. Periodontology; bd. cert. 1994. Gen. practice dentistry, Indpls., 1974-79; gen. practice periodontics, Indpls., 1981—; cons. Marion County Home, Indpls., 1975-79; instr. clin. dentistry Ind. U. Sch. Dentistry, Indpls., 1974-79, assoc. prof., 1981-82. Editor: Perio Probe, 1981. Chmn. dental div. United Way, Indpls., 1983, 84. Recipient Mosby Scholarship Book award Mosby Pub. Co., 1974, Swenson scholar, 1982. Mem. ADA, Am. Acad. Periodontology, Ind. Dental Assn. (alt. del. to conv. 1986-88, del. 1989-97, cons. govt. affairs com.), Indpls. Dist. Dental Soc. (bd. dirs. 1987-92, v.p. 1993-94, chmn. I.D.D.S. mid-winter clin. conf. 1992, pres.-elect 1994, pres. 1995-96). Avocations: skiing; computers, native american art. Office: 6801 Lake Plaza Dr Ste 111A Indianapolis IN 46220-4052

SARCHET, BERNARD REGINALD, retired chemical engineering educator; b. Byesville, Ohio, June 13, 1917; s. Elmer C. and Nellie Myrtle (Huff) S.; m. Lena Virginia Fisher, Dec. 13, 1941; children: Renee Erickson, Dawne, Melanie Koewing. BS in Chem. Engring., Ohio State U., 1939; MS in Chem. Engring., U. Del., 1941. From engr. to dir. comml. devel. Koppers Co., Inc., Pitts., 1941-67; prof. and founding chmn. dept. engring. mgmt. U. Mo., Rolla, 1967-88; mgmt. cons. Sarchet Assocs., Rolla, 1975—. Co-author: Supervisory Management (Essentials), 2nd edit. 1976, Management for Engineers, 1981; contbr. articles to profl. jours. Mem. Planning Commn. Beaver, Pa., 1955-58; dir. Billy Graham Film Crusades, Rolla, 1969-75; area dir. Here's Life America, Rolla, 1977. Recipient Profl. Achievement award U. Del., 1952, Freedom Found. awards, 1974-75, Fellow Mem. awd., Am. Soc. for Engineering Educ., 1992. Fellow Am. Soc. Engring. Mgmt. (founding pres., bd. dirs. 1979—), Am. Soc. Engring. Edn. (chmn. 1976). Achievements include patent on composition for producing detergent polyglycol condensation products; led in developing engineering management for engineers. Home: PO Box 68 Rolla MO 65402-0068

SARDELLA, EDWARD JOSEPH, television news anchor; b. Buffalo, June 2, 1940; s. Joseph Edward and Josephine Jenny (D'Amico) S.; m. Sandra K. Lorenzen, Jan. 17, 1975. BA in Speech Arts, Occidental Coll., L.A., 1962. Radio disc jockey, newsman KWIN/KTIL/KERG, Ashland/Tillamook/Eugene, Oreg., 1966-69; reporter KVAL-TV, Eugene, 1969-70; reporter/anchor KOIN-TV, Portland, Oreg., 1970-72, KMGH-TV, Denver, 1972-74; news anchor/sr. editor KUSA-TV, Denver, 1974—; adj. instr. journalism U. Colo., Boulder, 1984-92. Author: Write Like You Talk, 1984; co-author: The Producing Strategy, 1995. Olympic torchbearer, 1996. Capt. USMC, 1962-66. Recipient Emmy award Nat. Assn. TV Arts and Scis., 1992, 93, 94, 95, 96; named Colo. Broadcaster of Yr., 1997. Office: KUSA-TV 500 E Speer Blvd Denver CO 80203-4187

SARDESON, LYNDA SCHULTZ, nursing, diabetes educator; b. LaPorte, Ind., Nov. 5, 1946; d. Wilbur W. and Helen (Winkfein) Schultz; children: Brian Michael, Eric Matthew. BS, Purdue U., Westville, Ind., 1976. Cert. diabetes educator. Emergency room nurse LaPorte Hosp., inpatient ctr. rep., sr. clin. instr. diabetes edn. program coord.; parish nurse Bethany Luth. Ch., LaPorte; guest presenter 1st Ann. Med. Congress, Izheusk, Russia, 1996. Active N.Am. Cultural Exch. League; past pres. People to People Internat., Vietnam Women's Meml.; mem. bd. elders, chmn. svc. divsn. Bethany Luth. Ch. With AUS, 1967-70. Mem. ANA, ADA, Am. Assn. Diabetes Educators, No. Ind. Assn. Diabetes Educators (sec., bd. dirs.), Am. Legion.

SAREMBOCK, IAN JOSEPH, internist; b. Cape Town, Republic of South Africa, June 9, 1951; m. Ghita Marueen Sarembock; children: Craig Murray, Kerri Lauren. MD, U. Cape Town, 1975, PhD, 1988. Diplomate Am. Bd. Internal Medicine, Am. Bd. Cardiovascular Medicine. Sr. house officer dept. internal medicine U. Cape Town and Groote Schuur Hosp., Cape Town, 1979-80, resident in internal medicine, 1980-83; sr. registrar Cardiac Clinic U. Cape Town and Groote Schuur Hosp., 1985-86; Velva Schrire meml. rsch. fellow Cardiac Clinic Groote Schur Hosp., 1983-85; postdoctoral rsch. assoc. divsn. cardiology Yale U., New Haven, 1986-88; attending cardiologist divsn. cardiology VA Ctr., West Haven, Conn., 1987-88; asst. prof. internal medicine cardiovascular divsn. U. Va. Health Scis. Ctr., Charlottesville, 1988-93, assoc. prof. internal medicine cardiovascular divsn., 1993—, dir. coronary care unit, cardiac catheterization lab., 1988—; cardiology cons. Salem (Va.) VA Med. Ctr., 1988—; lectr., presenter in field; invited prof. Heart-Lung Inst., Utrecht, The Netherlands, 1992; mem. faculty restenosis summits, Cleve. Clinic, 1992, 93, 97. Contbr. articles to profl. pubs. Mem. policy working com., house staff supervision Commonwealth of Va., 1990—. Grantee U. Va. Sch. Medicine, 1989, Beecham Labs., 1989-90, Am. Heart Assn., 1989-91, 91-92, 95—, NIH, 1991-94. Fellow ACP, Coll. Physicians South Africa, Am. Coll. Cardiology (allied health profls. com. 1993—); mem. AAAS, Am. Heart Assn. (bd. dirs. Charlottesville/Albermarle divsn. 1991—, mem. Va. affiliate rsch. peer rev. subcom. 1992—, thrombosis coun. 1987, fellow coun. on clin. cardiology 1989), South African Med. and Dental Coun. Office: U Va Dept Cardiology PO Box 158 Charlottesville VA 22902-0158

SARFATY, SUZANNE, internist and educator; b. Irvington, N.Y., Apr. 11, 1962; d. Sam and Pat (Petrovich) S. BS, Boston U., 1984, MD, 1988, MPH, 1994. Diplomate Am. Bd. Internal Medicine. Intern and resident Boston City Hosp., 1988-91; attending/clin. instr. Boston U., 1991-93, asst. prof. medicine and pub. health, 1995—, asst. dean of student affairs, 1995—. Mem. prof. com. Am. Cancer Soc., Boston, 1991—; mentor Boston Ptnrs. for Edn., 1991—. Recipient Cmty. Svc. award CIBA Geigy, 1986; Dana Farber cancer prevention fellow, 1993-94. Fellow ACP. Avocations: cooking, travel, reading, Spanish language. Home: 11 Verndale St Brookline MA 02146-2423

SARFATY, WAYNE ALLEN, insurance agent, financial planner; b. Rochester, N.Y., Apr. 18, 1951; s. Benjamin and Grace (Rowan) S.; m. Karen Nugent, July 12, 1957, Apr. 18, 1951; children: Melissa A., Gabrielle M. Student, Parsons Coll., 1971-74. Cert. ins. agt. Sales rep. Met. Life, Rochester, N.Y., 1979-81; register rep. Prudential Fin. Svcs., Rochester, 1981-92; owner, broker Wayne A. Sarfaty & Assocs., Rochester, 1992—. Dir. tng. films. Mem. Eagle Club. Recipient Nat. Quality award Nat. Assn. Life Underwriters, 1982-90; named to Million Dollar Round Table, NALU, 1987. Avocations: camping, auto racing, darts. Home: PO Box 182 Cohocton NY 14826-0182

SARGEANT, ERNEST JAMES, lawyer; b. Spokane, Wash., Sept. 26, 1918; s. Ernest Edward and Louise (McWhinnie) S.; m. Helene Sophie Kazanjian, Jan. 29, 1944. B.A. cum laude, Harvard U., 1940, LL.B. magna cum laude, 1947. Bar: Mass. 1947. Assoc. Ropes & Gray, Boston, 1947, 52-56, ptnr., 1956-90, of counsel, 1991—; lectr. law Harvard U. Law Sch., Cambridge, Mass., 1961-62, 65-92; adj. prof. Boston Coll. Law Sch., 1990—. Grad. treas. Harvard Law Rev., Cambridge, 1971—. Capt. U.S. Army, 1942-46, 51-52. Mem. Am. Law Inst. (council), ABA, Boston Bar Assn. Clubs: Union (Boston); Country (Brookline, Mass.). Home: 24 Highgate Wellesley Hills MA 02181-1420 Office: Ropes & Gray 1 International Pl Boston MA 02110-2602

SARGENT, CHARLES LEE, manufacturing company executive; b. Flint, Mich., Mar. 22, 1937; s. Frank T. and Evelyn M. (Martinson) S.; m. Nancy Cook, June 9, 1962; children: Wendy L., Joy A., Candace L. B ME, GM Inst., 1960; MBA, Harvard U., 1962. Reliability engr. AC Spark Plug div. GM, Flint, 1962-63; with Thetford Corp., Ann Arbor, Mich., 1962-95, pres., chmn. bd. dirs., 1974-95; pres., chmn. bd. dirs. Thermassan Corp., 1969-72; chmn. GMI Engring. and Mgmt. Inst., Flint, Mich., 1995—; pres., owner Quality Boat Lifts, Inc., Fort Myers, Fla., 1996—; bd. dirs. First of Am. Bank, Fla.; trustee Lincoln Cons. Schs., 1973-77; GMI Engring. and Mgmt. Inst., Flint, 1989, chmn. 1995—. Patentee in field. Elder Presbyn. Ch. Recipient Entrepreneurial Achievement award GMI, 1989; named Entrepreneur of the Yr., Harvard Bus. Sch. Club of Detroit, 1981. mem. Barton Hills Country Club (bd. dirs. 1985-87, pres. 1987), Harvard Bus. Sch. Club of Detroit (bd. dirs. 1983-93). Avocations: traveling, golf. Home: 3774 Cracker Way Bonita Springs FL 34134-8628

SARGENT, DAVID JASPER, university official; b. Manchester, N.H., Aug. 5, 1931; s. Merton Jasper and Marguerite (Riley) S.; student U. N.H., 1949-51; J.D. magna cum laude, Suffolk U., Boston, 1954, LL.D. (hon.), 1978; m. Shirley Woodbury Swift, Dec. 21, 1951. Bar: N.H., 1954, Mass., 1954; U.S. Supreme Ct. 1978. Assoc. Kowal and Sargent, Boston, 1954-57; mem. faculty Suffolk U. Law Sch., Boston, 1957-73, prof. law, 1961-73, dean, 1973-89, pres., 1989—; chmn. Chief Justice's Commn. Future of the Cts., 1989; cons. Am. Trial Lawyers Assn., 1957-81; mem. Mass. Jud. Selection Com., 1974-77, Nat. Bd. Trial Advocacy, 1978—. Trustee, Anatolia Coll., Thessaloniki, Greece. Recipient Nat. Service award Am. Trial Lawyers Assn., 1968; Outstanding Alumnus award Suffolk U. Law Sch., 1978; hon. mem. Minn. Bar. Mem. ABA, Am. Law Inst., Mass. Bar Assn. (chmn. com. trial practice 1974-77, chmn. subcom. ct. unification 1976), N.H. Bar Assn. Episcopalian. Club: Masons. Contbr. articles to legal publs. Home: 83 Church St Winchester MA 01890-2545 Office: Suffolk U President's Office 25th Fl 1 Beacon St Boston MA 02108-3107*

SARGENT, JAMES CUNNINGHAM, lawyer; b. New Haven, Feb. 26, 1916; s. Murray and Mary Hale (Cunningham) S.; m. Rebecca Porteous Jackson, Jan. 23, 1943; children: Stephen Denny, James Cunningham, Felicity Hale, Sarah Blanchard. Grad., Taft Sch., 1935; B.A., U. Va., 1938, LL.B., 1940. Bar: N.Y. 1940, D.C. 1961. With Clarke & Baldwin, N.Y.C., 1940-41; trial atty. Consol. Edison Co. of N.Y., 1941-51; asst. atty. gen., elections fraud bur. State of N.Y., 1948; law asst. appellate div. N.Y. Supreme Ct., 1951-54; asso. atty. Spence & Hotchkiss, N.Y.C., 1954-55; regional adminstr. SEC, N.Y.C., 1955-56; mem. SEC, 1956-60; asst. gen. counsel CIT Finance Corp., N.Y.C., 1960-64; mem. Whitman & Ransom (and predecessors), 1964-94; guest lectr. corporate securities U. Va. Law Sch., 1958-60, Practicing Law Inst., 1962—. Served from pvt. to capt. USAAF, 1942-46. Mem. St. Andrews Soc., Bar Assn. City N.Y., N.Y. County Lawyers Assn., ABA, Fed. Bar Assn., Fed. Bar Coun., Va. Bar Assn. (hon.), U. Va. Law Sch. Alumni Assn. (pres.), Order of Coif, Sky Club, Univ. Club (N.Y.C.), Church Club (N.Y.C.), Downtown Assn. (N.Y.C.), Capitol Hill Club (Washington), Army-Navy Club (Washington), Farmington Country Club, Phi Delta Phi. Episcopalian. Home: 409 Altamont Cir Charlottesville VA 22903 Office: Gunsel Opton Handler Gottlieb Feiler & Katz 52 Vanderbilt Ave New York NY 10017-3808

SARGENT, JAMES O'CONNOR, freelance writer; b. N.Y.C., June 15, 1918; s. Joseph Hughes and Maryann Josephine (O'Connor) S.; m. Mildred Elizabeth Clark, apr. 19, 1949. Student, British Intelligence Sch., Calcutta, India, summer 1944, Fordham U., 1949-51. Ghostwriter, freelance writer, 1949—; founder Washington Writers Group, Washington, 1960—. Editor, rschr., writer (Bell Aircraft Co. in-house publ.) History of the Helicopter, 1952; author: (novellas) You Don't Bury on Christmas, 1960, Interregnum in a Commune, 1968, The Button Man, 1969, Moon in Pisces, 1970, Death in Saigon, 1971, Last Minuet in Washington, 1973, (MWA Anthology) Killers of the Dream, 1974; (screenplay) Queen Victoria and Lady Flora, 1993; (play) Loss of Innocence, 1994, (with Dakin Williams) Satanic Chapters, 1997; published over 1500 works. Liaison with Peiping Aviators Assn., 1995-97. Maj. USAF, 1942-47. Decorated Bronze Star, Chinese medal of freedom. Mem. 14th USAF Assn., U.S. Liberty of Congress, 528th Fighter Squadron Assn. (officer), Am. Mus. Natural History. Avocations: walking 5 miles per day, genealogy, World War I & II history, friendships. Home: 1019 Stillbrook Rd Pensacola FL 32514-1629

SARGENT, JOSEPH DENNY, insurance executive; b. West Hartford, Conn., Sept. 11, 1929; s. Thomas Denny and Elizabeth (Owen) S.; m. Mary A. Tennant, June 25, 1955; children: Robert Tennant, Thomas Denny II, Mary Diane, Suzanne Davis. Grad., St. Paul's Sch., Concord, N.H., 1948; BA, Yale U., 1952. With Conning & Co., Inc., Hartford, Conn., ptnr., 1957—; mng. ptnr. Conning & Co., Inc., 1986-92; chmn., chief exec. officer Conning & Co., 1986-91, chmn., 1992; chmn. Conning Internat., London, 1986-92; vice chmn. Conning & Co., 1993-95, also bd. dirs., 1993-95; bd. dirs. Beekley Corp., Bristol, Conn., Tenwick Reins., Stamford, Conn., Exec. Risk Ins. Co., Simsbury, Conn., MMI co., Chgo., Blanch, Mpls., Mut. Risk, Bermuda, Policy Mgmt. Sys., Columbia, S.C.; chmn. Conn. Surety Corp., Hartford, Bradley, Foster & Sargent, Hartford, Beazley Furlonge Holdings, Ltd., London; trustee McLean Fund; chmn., treas. SKI Ltd, 1956-96. Past trustee Wadsworth Atheneum; past trustee Children's Svcs. of Conn.; trustee Hartford Hosp. Mem. Yale Club (Hartford), Hartford Club, Hartford Golf Club. Home: 25 Colony Rd West Hartford CT 06117-2215 Office: City Place II 185 Asylum St Hartford CT 06103-3402

SARGENT, JOSEPH DUDLEY, insurance executive; b. Phila., Apr. 16, 1937; s. Gerald Thomas and Nora (Oliver) S.; m. Sheila Reidy, Apr. 27, 1963; children: Moira, Colleen, Joseph, Sean, Liam, Bridget. AB, Fairfield U., 1959. CLU. Agy. sec. The Guardian Life Ins. Co. Am., N.Y.C., 1959-70, v.p., 1970-79, sr. v.p. health ins., 1980-83, sr. v.p. life ins., 1984-88, exec. v.p., 1989-92, pres., 1993—, pres., CEO, 1996, also bd. dirs.; pres.-guardian Ins. and Annuity Co., 1993. Bd. dirs. Life Ins. Mktg. and Rsch. Inst., Life Office Mgmt. Assn., United Way of N.Y.C., The Discovery Mus. Bridgeport. With U.S. Army, 1960-64. Mem. Nat. Assn. Life Underwriters. Republican. Roman Catholic. Avocations: boating, fishing. Home: 90 Lancelot Dr Fairfield CT 06430 Office: Guardian Life Ins Co of Am 201 Park Ave S New York NY 10003-1601

SARGENT, LIZ ELAINE (ELIZABETH SARGENT), safety consulting executive; b. Meadville, Pa., Apr. 17, 1942; d. Melvin Ellsworth and Roberta Jean (Beach) Taylor; m. Lawrence Sargent, Sept. 6, 1969; 1 child, Kathy-Dawn. Student, Allegheny Coll., 1964; AA cum laude, Cuyahoga C.C., Cleve., 1987, Assoc. in Transp. cum laude, 1989. Car distbr. Norfolk and Western R.R., Cleve., 1963-69; account mgr. Ill. Cen. R.R., Cleve., 1970-73; traffic coord. Carlon Pipe, Mantua, Ohio, 1973-75; chief dispatcher X.L. Trucking, Coshocton, Ohio, 1975-77; corp. log auditor Anchor Motor Freight, Beachwood, Ohio, 1977-78; cons. Saf-T, Parma, Ohio, 1978-84; v.p. safety Saf-T, Shaker Heights, Ohio, 1987-91; dir. safety Sherwin Williams, Cleve., 1984-87; pres. Safety Advisors for Transp., Inc., Beachwood, Ohio, 1991—; founder Love Keepers, 1996; speaker Coshocton (Ohio) Traffic Club, 1984, Am. Indsl. Hygiene, Cleve., 1985. Author: Halt Chemical-Safety Procedures, 1983-84, Progressive Insurance, 1987, RL Lipton Co. manual, 1995; contbr. articles to profl. jours. Chairperson intergenerational com. Ch. in Aurora, Ohio, 1984-86, Valley View Village Ch. libr. chairperson, mem. choir; bd. dirs. Shaker Heights Teen Recreational Com., 1984-87. Delta Nu Alpha scholar, 1977. Mem. Ohio Trucking Assn. (nat. safety coun.), Cleve. Bd. Realtors, Motor Fleet Safety Suprs. (nat. com.), Fleet Maintenance Coun., Phi Theta Kappa. Republican. Avocations: interior design, painting, writing poetry and short stories, dried floral arrangements, hiking. Office: Saf-T 14716 Rockside Rd Maple Heights OH 44137-4016

SARGENT, NOEL BOYD, electrical engineer; b. Cleve., Dec. 5, 1943; s. William Boyd and Jennie Parkin (Wheeler) S.; m. Joan Marie Hodan, Aug. 21, 1965; children: Andrew, Jeffrey. BS in Engring., Cleve. State U., 1970. Broadcast engr. Stas. WVIZ-TV, WERE am-fm, WKSU, Cleve., 1960-65; electronics technician NASA-Lewis Rsch. Ctr., Cleve., 1965-70, engr. aero-acoustics, 1970-76, rsch. engr., 1976-83, sr. engr. launch vehicles, 1983-87, tech. asst., 1988—; apptd. Nat. Interagency Coordination Group for Lightning Rsch., 1997. Mem. IEEE, Soc. Automotive Engrs. (vice chmn. Com. AE-4, 1992—, sec. Com. AE-4R, 1988-92, cert. electromagnetic compatibility engr.). Avocations: soccer, amateur radio. Office: NASA-Lewis Rsch Ctr 21000 Brookpark Rd Cleveland OH 44135-3127

SARGENT, PAMELA, writer; b. Ithaca, N.Y., Mar. 20, 1948. BA, SUNY, Binghamton, N.Y., 1968, MA, 1970. Mng. editor, Binghamton, N.Y., 1970-73, asst. editor, 1973-75; Am. editor Bull. Sci. Fiction Writers Am., Johnson City, N.Y., 1983-91. Author: Cloned Lives, 1976, Starshadows, 1977, The Sudden Star, 1979, Watchstar, 1980, The Golden Space, 1982, The Alien Upstairs, 1983, Earthseed, 1983, Eye of the Comet, 1984, Homesmind, 1984, Venus of Dreams, 1986, The Shore of Women, 1986, The Best of Pamela Sargent, 1987, Alien Child, 1988, Venus of Shadows, 1988, Ruler of the Sky, 1993 (Nebula best novelette award 1992, Locus best novelette award 1993, Electric Sci. Fiction award 1993); edit: (anthology) Women of Wonder, 1975, Bio-Futures, 1976, More Women of Wonder, 1976, The New Women of Wonder, 1978, (with Ian Watson) Afterlives, 1986, Women of Wonder, The Classic Years, 1996, Women of Wonder, The Contemporary Years, 1995, Nebula Awards 29, 1995, Nebula Awards 30, 1996, Nebula Awards 31, 1997. Office: care Richard Curtis Assocs Inc 171 E 74th St New York NY 10021-3221

SARGENT, ROBERT GEORGE, engineering educator; b. Port Huron, Mich., June 14, 1937; s. George O. and Marie L. (Roome) S.; m. Dorothy Baum, 1970; 1 dau., Tiffany. BSE, U. Mich., 1959, MS, 1963, PhD, 1966. Elec. engr. Hughes Aircraft Co., Culver City, Calif., 1959-61; faculty mem. Syracuse U., 1966—, asst. prof., 1966-70, assoc. prof., 1970-81, prof. indsl. engring. and ops. research, 1981—, chmn. dept., 1982-85, prof. elec. and computer engring., 1994—; vis. faculty Cornell U., 1981-82, Ctr. Econ. Rsch. Tilburg U., 1996; bd. dirs. Winter Simulation Conf., 1974-84, chmn. bd., 1979-81, gen. chmn., 1977; chmn. TIMS Coll. on Simulation and Gaming, 1978-80. Dept. editor: Communications of Assn. Computing Machinery, 1980-85; editorial adv. bd. ACM Transactions on Modeling and Simulations, 1989—; contbr. articles to profl. jours. Recipient Service award Winter Simulation Conf., 1984. Mem. Assn. Computing Machinery (nat. lectr. 1985-89, Svc. award 1985), Ops. Rsch. Soc. Am., Inst. Mgmt. Scis. (Disting. Svc. award for Simulation 1985), Inst. Indsl. Engrs. (Svc. award 1985), Soc. Computer Simulation (bd. dirs. 1984-87), Computer Soc. of IEEE (mem. exec. com. simulation 1985—). Office: Syracuse U Dept Indsl Engring and Ops Rsch 439 Link Hall Syracuse NY 13244

SARGENT, THOMAS ANDREW, political science educator, university program director; b. Indpls., Apr. 24, 1933; s. Thomas Edward and Inez (Secrest) S.; m. Cecily Constance Fox-Williams, 1965 (dec.); children: Sarah

Beatrice, Andrew Fox; m. 2d Frances Petty, 1987. BA, DePauw U., Greencastle, Ind., 1955; MA, Fletcher Sch. Law and Diplomacy, Tufts U., 1959, MA in Law and Diplomacy, 1968, PhD, 1969. With First Nat. City Bank, N.Y.C., 1959-64, asst. accountant, 1963-64; asst. sec. Irving Trust Co., N.Y.C., 1964-66; mem. faculty Ball State U., Muncie, Ind., 1969-89, dir. London Ctr., 1973-74, chmn. polit. sci. dept., 1977-80, prof. polit. sci., 1979-89, prof. emeritus, 1989—, acting asst. to dean Coll. Scis. and Humanities, 1981-82, assoc. dean Coll. Scis. and Humanities, 1982-85, dir. spl. programs Minnetrista Ctr., 1985-87; dir. E.B. Ball Ctr., Muncie, 1987-89, dir. emeritus, 1989—. Contbg. editor: Ripon Forum, 1973-78. Bd. dirs., exec. v.p. Ea. Ind. Cmty. TV, Muncie, 1974-76, pres., 1976-77; mem. nat. bd. govs. Ripon Soc., Washington, 1976-84; mem. Indpls. Com. Fgn. Rels., 1977—; bd. dirs. Hist. Muncie, Inc., 1979-85, pres., 1980; bd. dirs. Muncie Civic Theatre Assn., 1978-81, 90-96, 1st v.p., 1992-96; exec. dir. Ind. Consortium for Internat. Programs, 1982-88; mem. Ind. Real Estate Commn., 1983-91; trustee DePauw U., 1983—; bd. dirs. Muncie Symphony Orch., 1985-95, pres., 1991-93; mem. bd. govs. Minnetrista Cultural Ctr., Muncie, 1989-94, chmn., 1992-94; trustee Malpas Trust, 1990—, pres., 1997—; bd. dirs. Arts Ind., Inc., 1992—, Muncie Children's Mus., 1994—, v.p., 1996-97, pres. 1997. 1st lt. USAF, 1955-58. Named Sagamore of Wabash, 1988. Mem. Am. Polit. Sci. Assn., Delaware County Hist. Alliance (bd. dirs. 1980-86, 87-95, pres., 1987-91), Soc. Profl. Journalists, Delaware Country Club, Columbia Club (Indpls.), Maxinkuckee Yacht Club (Culver, Ind.), Rotary, Phi Delta Theta. Republican. Methodist. Address: 2207 W Wiltshire Rd Muncie IN 47304-3350

SARGENT, WALLACE LESLIE WILLIAM, astronomer, educator; b. Elsham, Eng., Feb. 15, 1935; s. Leslie William and Eleanor (Dennis) S.; m. Anneila Isabel Cassells, Aug. 5, 1964; children: Lindsay Eleanor, Alison Clare. B.Sc., Manchester U., 1956, M.Sc., 1957, Ph.D., 1959. Research fellow Calif. Inst. Tech., 1959-62; sr. research fellow Royal Greenwich Obs., 1962-64; asst. prof. physics U. Calif., San Diego, 1964-66; mem. faculty dept. astronomy Calif. Inst. Tech., Pasadena, 1966—; prof. Calif. Inst. Tech., 1971-81, Ira S. Bowen prof. astronomy, 1981—; Miller Prof. U. Calif., Berkeley, 1993; Thomas Gold lectr. Cornell U., Ithaca, N.Y., 1994-95; Sackler lectr. Harvard U., Cambridge, Mass., 1995, U. Calif., Berkeley, 1996. Contbr. articles to profl. jours. Alfred P. Sloan fellow, 1968-70. Fellow Am. Acad. Arts and Scis., Royal Soc. (London); mem. Am. Astron. Soc. (Helen B. Warner prize 1969, Dannie Heineman prize 1991), Royal Astron. Soc. (George Darwin lectr. 1987), Astron. Soc. Pacific (Bruce Gold medal 1994), Internat. Astron. Union. Club: Athenaeum (Pasadena). Home: 400 S Berkeley Ave Pasadena CA 91107-5062 Office: Calif Inst Tech Astronomy Dept 105-24 Pasadena CA 91125

SARGENT, WILLIAM WINSTON, anesthesiologist; b. Oshkosh, Wis., Feb. 28, 1933; s. Sprague Spencer and Lila Jane (Gjermundson) S. BS in Medicine, U. Ill., Chicago, 1955, MD, 1957; MS in Anesthesiology, U. Minn., 1967. Diplomate Am. Bd. Anesthesiology. Staff anesthesiologist St. Anthony Hosp., Rockford, Ill., 1960-61, Swedish Am. Hosp., Rockford, 1960-61; instr. anesthesiology U. Minn., Mpls., 1967-74, asst. prof. anesthesiology, 1974-80; staff anesthesiologist St. Luke's Hosp., Duluth, Minn., 1980-95. Contbr. articles to profl. jours. Capt. USAF, 1961-64, France. Fellow Am. Coll. Anesthesiologists; mem. AMA, Am. Soc. Anesthesiologists, Minn. Soc. Anesthesiologists, Minn. State Med. Assn., St. Louis County Med. Soc. Presbyterian.

SARIAN, JIRAIR NERSES, radiologist; b. Aintab, Turkey, Aug. 16, 1915; s. Nerses Sarkis and Nourita Hagop (Philipbossian) S.; BA, Am. U. Beirut, 1937; MD, U. Lausanne (Switzerland), 1940; BD, Nazarene Theol. Sem., 1949; m. Jessie Helen Maghakian, Jan. 28, 1950; children: Norita, June, John. Rotating intern U. Lausanne Hosps., 1940-41, resident, 1941-44, chief asst., 1944-46; rotating intern Herrick Meml. Hosp., Berkeley, Calif., 1950-51; research and teaching fellow dept. oncology and radiology U. Kans. Med. Ctr., Kansas City, 1948-49, dept. radiology Huntington Meml. Hosp., Pasadena, Calif., 1951; practice medicine specializing in radiology, L.A., 1951; asst. clin. prof. radiology U. Calif. Coll. Medicine, Irvine, 1965—; asst. clin. prof. U. Calif., L.A., Sch. of Nursing; med. dir. Union Rescue Mission; treas. bd. trustees Haigazian Coll. Author articles, books and booklets in English, Armenian and French; expert witness radiologist superior and fed. cts. Recipient cert. of appreciation AMA, Am. Roentgen Ray Soc., 1963; Physicians Recognition award AMA, 1969, 72, 76. Diplomate Am. Bd. Radiology. Mem. Armed Forces Inst. Pathology (cert.), AMA, Calif., L.A. County med. assns., Am. Roentgen Ray Soc., Am. Coll. Radiology, Physicians Club. Home: 5305 Shenandoah Ave Los Angeles CA 90056-1036

SARICKS, CHRISTOPHER LEE, transportation analyst; b. Columbus, Ohio, Apr. 19, 1948; s. Ambrose and Reese (Pyott) S.; m. Joyce E. Goering, Aug. 21, 1971; children: Brendan James, Margaret Katherine. BA summa cum laude, U. Kans., 1970; MPhil, London (Eng.) Sch. Econs., 1973. Dir. environ. planning Chgo. Area Transp. Study, 1975-77, regional planning consistency coord., 1977-78; group leader, planning and assessment Pacific Environ. Svcs., Elmhurst, Ill., 1978-79; assoc. transp. systems planner Argonne (Ill.) Nat. Lab., 1979-84, environ. scientist, 1984—; evaluation mgr. NE Ill. ITS Project, 1995-96; Rsch. project rev. and oversight panel Transp. Rsch. Bd., Washington, 1994—, air quality com., 1988—. Contbr. articles to profl. jours. Little league coach Downers Grove, Ill., 1991-92; v.p. Artists Showcase West, Downers Grove, 1988-90, 94—. Recipient Argonne Pacesetter award Argonne Nat. Lab., 1987, Winner Nat. Pub. Radio, 1987. Mem. Air Waste Mgmt. Assn. (land use and transp. com. chair 1988-91, mobile sources com. 1991—), Delta Upsilon (Outstanding Alumni Kans. chpt. 1994). Avocations: hiking, biking, reading, trivia games, piano playing. Home: 1116 61st St Downers Grove IL 60516-1819 Office: Argonne Nat Lab ES-362/2B 9700 Cass Ave # 2B Argonne IL 60439-4803

SARICKS, JOYCE GOERING, librarian; b. Nov. 8, 1948; d. Joe W. and Lovella Goering; m. Christopher L. Saricks, Aug. 21, 1971; children: Brendan James, Margaret Katherine. BA with highest distinction in Eng.& Ger, U. Kans., 1970; MA in Comparative Lit., U. Wis., 1971; MA/MAT in Library Sci., U. Chgo., 1977. Reference librarian Downers Grove (Ill.) Pub. Library, 1977-80, head tech. svcs., 1980-83, coord. lit. and audio svcs., 1983—; presenter workshops in field. Author: (with Nancy Brown) Readers' Advisory Service in the Public Library, 1989, revised edit., 1997. Mem. Read Ill. adv. com., 1990-91. Woodrow Wilson fellow, 1970; recipient Allie Beth Martin award Pub. Library Assn., 1989, No. Ill. Lib. of Yr. award Windy City Romance Writers, 1995. Mem. ALA, Ill. Library Assn., Adult Reading Round Table (founder), Phi Beta Kappa, Delta Phi Alpha, Pi Lambda Theta, Beta Phi Mu. Home: 1116 61st St Downers Grove IL 60516-1819 Office: Downers Grove Pub Library 1050 Curtiss St Downers Grove IL 60515-4606

SARIDIS, GEORGE NICHOLAS, electrical, computers and system engineering educator, robotics and automation researcher; b. Athens, Greece, Nov. 17, 1931; came to U.S., 1961, naturalized, 1971; s. Nicholas and Anna (Tsofa) S.; m. Panayota Dimarogona, Apr. 10, 1985. Diploma in Mech. and Elec. Engring., Nat. Tech. U., Athens, 1955; MS in Elec. Engring., Purdue U., 1962, PhD, 1965. Instr. Nat. Tech. U., 1955-63, Purdue U., West Lafayette, Ind., 1963-65, asst. prof., 1965-70, assoc. prof., 1970-75, prof., 1975-81; prof. elec., computer and system engring. Rensselaer Poly. Inst., Troy, N.Y., 1981-96, dir. Robotics and Automation Lab., 1982-96, prof. emeritus, 1997—; dir. NASA Ctr. for Intelligent Robotic Systems for Space Exploration, 1988-92; engring. program dir. NSF, Washington, 1973; hon. prof. Huazhong U., Wuhan, China. Author: Self-Organizing Control of Stochastic Systems, 1977, Stochastic Processes Estimation and Control, 1995; co-author: Intelligent Robotic Systems: Theory and Applications, 1992, Reliable Plan Selection by Intelligent Machines, 1996, Design of Intelligent Control System based on Hierarchical Stochastic Automata, 1996; also numerous articles, reports. Co-author: Intelligent Robotic Sys.; co-editor, contbg. author: Fuzzy Automata, 1977; editor, contbg. author: Advances in Automation and Robotics, Vol. 1, 1985, Vol. 2, 1990. Fellow IEEE (founding pres. robotics and automation council 1981-84, Centennial medal 1984, Disting. Mem. award 1989); mem. ASME, Soc. Mfg. Engrs./Robotics Internat.-Machine Vision Assn. (sr.), Am. Soc. Engring. Edn., N.Y. Acad. Scis., Acad. Alteus (Greece). Home: 38 Loudonwood E Loudonville NY 12211-1465 Office: Rensselaer Poly Inst Dept Electrical Computer & Sys Engring Sch of Engring Troy NY 12180-3590

SARINO, EDGARDO FORMANTES, physician; b. Laoag City, Ilocos Norte, Philippines, Nov. 6, 1940; s. Epafrodito Cruz and Esperanza Raval Formantes S.; m. Milagros Felix Ona, Dec. 6, 1965; children: Edith Melanie, Edgar Michael, Edenn Michele; came to U.S., 1965, naturalized, 1983. MD, U. of the East, 1964. Rotating intern St. Clare's Hosp., N.Y.C., 1965-66; resident in anatomical pathology Coney Island Hosp., N.Y.C., 1966; resident in gen. surgery Manhattan VA Hosp., N.Y.C., 1966-67, N.Y. U.-Bellevue Med. Ctr., N.Y.C., 1967-68; resident in radiology Manhattan VA Hosp., N.Y.C., 1968-71, fellow in diagnostic radiology, 1971-73; staff radiologist Mercer Med. Ctr., Trenton, N.J., 1973-83; chief nuclear medicine service Louis Johnson VA Med. Ctr., Clarksburg, W.Va., 1983-93, acting chief radiology svc., 1988-92, chief imaging svc., 1993—; clin. assoc. prof. radiology U. W.Va. Sch. Medicine, 1989—; teaching asst. in gen. surgery N.Y. U.-Bellevue Med. Ctr., N.Y.C., 1967-68. Recipient Certificate of Merit, Mallinkrodt Pharm., 1969. Diplomate Am. Bd. Radiology. Mem. Am. Coll. Physician Execs., Soc. Nuclear Med., Am. Coll. Radiology, Radiol. Soc. N.Am., Harrison County Med. Soc., W.Va. Radiol. Soc., Assn. Philippine Practicing Physicans in Am., Philippine Radiol. Soc. Am. Contbr. articles to med. jours. Home: 96 Garden Cir Bridgeport WV 26330-1367 Office: Louis Johnson VA Med Ctr Clarksburg WV 26301

SARIS, PATTI B., federal judge; b. 1951. BA magna cum laude, Radcliffe Coll., 1973; JD cum laude, Harvard U., 1976. Law clerk to Hon. Robert Braucher Mass. Supreme Judicial Ct., 1976-77; atty. Foley Hoag & Eliot, Boston, 1977-79; staff counsel U.S. Senate Judiciary Com., 1979-81; atty. Berman Dittmar & Engel, Boston, 1981-82; chief civil divsn. U.S. Atty.'s Office, 1984-86; U.S. magistrate judge U.S. Dist. Ct. Mass., 1986-89; assoc. justice Mass. Superior Ct., 1989-94; dist. judge U.S. Dist. Ct. Mass., 1994—; mem. com. on civil rules Supreme Judicial Ct. Comments editor civil rights Civil Liberties Law Rev. Bd. trustees Beth Israel Hosp.; active Wexner Heritage Found. Nat. Merit scholar, 1969; recipient award Mothers of Murdered Children, 1993. Mem. Nat. Assn. Women Judges, Am. Jewish Com., Women's Bar Assn. (bd. dirs. 1982-86), Mass. Bar Assn., Mass. Assn. Women Judges, Boston Bar Assn., Boston Inns Ct., Phi Beta Kappa. Office: John W McCormack Courthouse 90 Devonshire St Rm 1805 Boston MA 02109-4501*

SARJEANT, WALTER JAMES, electrical and computer engineering educator; b. Strathroy, Can., Apr. 7, 1944; s. Walter Burns and Margaret (Laurie) S.; m. Ann Richards, June 30, 1972; children: Eric, Cheryl. BSc in Math, Physics, U. Western Ont., Can., 1966, MSc in Physics, 1967, PhD in Physics, 1971. Asst. dir. R&D Gen-Tec Inc., Quebec City, Que., Can., 1971-73; program mgr. Lumonics Rsch. Ltd., Ottawa, Ont., Can., 1973-75; staff scientist Nat. Rsch. Coun., Ottawa, Ont., Can., 1975-78; project leader Los Alamos (N.Mex.) Nat. Lab., 1978-81; James Clerk Maxwell prof. elec. and computer engring. SUNY, Buffalo, 1981—; dir. High Power Electronics Inst. Author: High Power Electronics, 1989. Fellow IEEE; mem. Electromagnetics Acad., Electrostatics Soc., N.Y. Acad. Scis., Rotary, Eta Kappa Nu. Office: SUNY Elec Engring Dept PO Box 601900 312 Bonner Hall Buffalo NY 14260

SARKIS, J. ZIAD, management consultant; b. Beirut, Lebanon, July 8, 1968; arrived in France, 1975; s. Nicolas Ata and Claude (Moussalli) S. BAS in Anthropology, Econs. and Math. with distinction and honors, Stanford U., 1990, MS in Engring. and Mgmt., 1990. Cons. McKinsey & Co., San Francisco, 1990, N.Y.C., 1991-92, Paris, 1992; prin. fin. svcs. practice AT Kearney & Co., N.Y.C., 1992-94; co-founder, sr. ptnr., bd. dirs. Mitchell Madison Group, N.Y.C., 1994—. Gen. sec. Phoenixia-X, Paris, 1993—. Greek Catholic. Office: Mitchell Madison Group 520 Madison Ave New York NY 10022-4213

SARKISIAN, CHERILYN See CHER

SARLE, CHARLES RICHARD, health facility executive; b. Saratoga Springs, N.Y., Sept. 21, 1944; s. John Robert and Marjorie Elizabeth (Swick) S.; m. Marion D. Wallace, June 21, 1968; children: Richard Charles, Robert Edmond. BBA cum laude, Northea. U., 1968; MBA, Babson Coll., 1973. CPA, Mass., Vt.; cert. mental health adminstr. Assn. Mental Health Adminstrs. Staff acct. Price Waterhouse & Co., Boston, 1968-70, George Kanavich, CPA, Wellesley, Mass., 1970-72; controller Human Resource Inst., Boston, 1972-73, adminstr., 1973-77; controller Brattleboro (Vt.) Retreat, 1977-78, dir. adminstrn., 1978-85, v.p., 1985-88, chief exec. officer, 1988-97; pres., CEO Carrier Found., Belle Mead, N.J., 1997—; Speaker in field. Mem. commn. Vt. Health Bldg. Fin. Agy., 1978-90; trustee Austine Sch. for Deaf and Hard of Hearing, 1990—, pres., 1994—; trustee Winston Prouty Ctr. for Child Devel., 1982-97, treas., 1983-90, sec., 1991-97. Recipient recognition award Brattleboro C. of C., 1985. Fellow AICPA, Mass. Soc. CPAs, Am. Coll. Healthcare Execs. (regent Va. br. 1991-95); mem. Am. Hosp. Assn. (del.-at-large 1988-92, del.-at-large to regional policy bd.), Nat. Assn. Pvt. Psychiat. Hosps. (bd. dirs. polit. action com. 1983-93), Nat. Psychiat. Alliance (trustee 1989-96, pres. 1994-96), Vt. Soc. CPAs (Comty. Svc. award 1984), Hosp. Fin. Mgmt. Assn. (mem. hosp. cost com. 1985—), Rescue, Inc. (trustee 1982-83), New Eng. Healthcare Assembly (trustee 1995—). Republican. Avocations: skiing, fishing, tennis, photography. Home: PO Box 840 Belle Mead NJ 08502 Office: Carrier Foundation Rt 601 Belle Mead NJ 08502

SARLEY, JOHN G., broadcast executive, writer; b. Cleve., Mar. 1, 1954; s. Edward James and Ann Sarley. BA, Cleve. State U., 1977. Writer, producer Marschalk Co. Advt., Cleve., 1977-80, DOCSI Corp., Hollywood, Calif., 1980—; pres. Sarley, Bigg & Bedder Inc., Hollywood, 1981—. Recipient Clio awards, 1980, 84, 87, 90, 92, 93, 94, London Internat. Advt. awards Internat. Radio Festival N.Y., Radio Mercury awards, The Globals, N.Y. Festival awards and Promax. Mem. Broadcast Promotion and Mktg. Execs., Hollywood C. of C. Office: Sarley Bigg & Bedder Inc 1644 N Stanley Ave Hollywood CA 90046-2713

SARNA, NAHUM MATTATHIAS, biblical studies educator; b. London, Eng., Mar. 27, 1923; came to U.S., 1951, naturalized, 1959; s. Jacob and Milly (Horonzick) S.; m. Helen Horowitz, Mar. 23, 1947; children: David E. Y., Jonathan D. BA, U. London, 1944, MA, 1946; minister's diploma, Jews Coll., London, 1947; PhD, Dropsie Coll., Phila., 1955; D Hebrew Letters (hon.), Gratz Coll., Phila., 1984; LHD (hon.), Hebrew Union Coll.-Jewish Inst. Religion, 1987; D Hebrew Lit., Hebrew Coll., Boston, 1991. Asst. lectr. Hebrew, Univ. Coll., London, 1946-49; lectr. Gratz Coll., Phila., 1951-57; librarian Jewish Theol. Sem.; also asst. prof. Bible Tchrs. Inst., 1957-63, assoc. prof. of Bible, 1963-65; asso. prof. Bibl. studies Brandeis U., Waltham, Mass., 1965-67; Dora Golding prof. Bibl. studies Brandeis U., 1967-85, prof. emeritus, 1985—, chmn. dept. Near Eastern and Judaic studies, 1969-75, chmn. humanities council, 1980-81; vis. prof. Bible, Dropsie Coll., 1967-68; vis. prof. religion Columbia U., 1964-65, 92, Yale U., 1992-94; vis. disting. prof. Fla. Atlantic U., 1995—. Author: Understanding Genesis, 1966, Exploring Exodus, 1986, Commentary to Genesis, 1989, Commentary to Exodus, 1991, Songs of the Heart: An Introduction to the Book of Psalms, 1993; co-author: A New Translation of the Book of Psalms, 1973, The Book of Job, A New Translation with Introductions, 1980; editor, translator: Jewish Publ. Soc. Bible, 1966-85; editorial bd. Jour. Bibl. Lit, 1973-75, Soc. Bibl. Lit. Monograph Series, 1975—; deptl. editor Ency. Judaica; gen. editor Jewish Publ. Soc. Bible Commentary series, 1974—; editor Proceedings of the American Academy for Jewish Research; mem. editorial adv. bd. Biblical Archaeology Rev., Moment Mag.; contbr. to Ency. Judaica, 1972, Ency. Brit., 1974, Dictionary of the Middle Ages, 1982, Ency. Religion, 1986, Anchor Bible Dictionary, 1992, Oxford Companion to the Bible, 1993; also articles to scholarly jours. Assoc. trustee Am. Sch. Oriental Rsch.; trustee, mem. exec. com. Boston Hebrew Coll.; mem. acad. adv. coun. Nat. Found. Jewish Culture; trustee Annenberg Rsch. Inst., 1990-95. Recipient Jewish Book Ann. award, 1967, Jewish Cultural Achievement award in Bibl. scholarship, 1994, Disting. Humanist award Ohio State U., 1995; Am. Coun. Learned Socs. fellow, 1971-72, Moses A. Dropsie fellow U. Pa., 1993, Inst. Advanced Studies fellow Hebrew U., 1982-83. Fellow Royal Asiatic Soc., Am. Acad. Jewish Research; mem. Soc. Bibl. Lit. and Exegesis, Am. Oriental Soc., Israel Exploration Soc., Archons of Colophon, Palestine Exploration Soc. Bibl. Colloquium, Assn. for Jewish Studies (hon. sec.-treas. 1972-79, pres. 1983-85). Home: 7886 Chula Vista Crescent Boca Raton FL 33433-4101

SARNAT, BERNARD GEORGE, plastic surgeon, educator, researcher; b. Chgo., Sept. 1, 1912; s. Isadore M. and Fanny (Sidran) S.; m. Rhoda Elaine Gerard, Dec. 25, 1941; children: Gerard, Joan. SB, U. Chgo., 1933, MD, 1937; MS, DDS, U. Ill., 1940. Diplomate Am. Bd. Plastic Surgery. Intern Los Angeles County Gen. Hosp., 1936-37; resident oral and plastic surgery Cook County Hosp., Chgo., 1940-41; asst. to Dr. Marshall Davison (gen. surgery), Chgo., 1942-43, Drs. Vilray P. Blair and Louis T. Byars (plastic and reconstructive surgery), St. Louis, 1943-46; practice medicine specializing in plastic surgery Chgo., 1946-56, Beverly Hills, Calif., 1956-91; asst. histology U. Ill. Coll. Dentistry, 1937-40, prof., head dept. oral and maxillofacial surgery, 1946-56; asst. dept. surgery Washington U. Sch. Medicine, St. Louis, 1944-46; prof., dir. dept. oral and plastic surgery St. Louis U. Coll. Dentistry, 1945-46; clin. asst. prof. surgery (plastic surgery) U. Ill. Coll. Medicine, 1949-56; adj. prof. oral biology Sch Dentistry UCLA, 1969—, mem. Dental Rsch. Inst., 1974-95, adj. prof. plastic surgery Sch. Medicine, 1974—; attending staff Cedars-Sinai Med. Ctr., L.A., 1956-91, emeritus, 1991—, mem. staff, sr. rsch. scientist, chief plastic surgery, 1961-81; cons. in gen., plastic and maxillofacial surgery VA Regional Office, Chgo., until 1956; lectr. in field. Sr. author: (with Dr. Isaac Schour) Oral and Facial Cancer, 2d edit., 1957, (with Dr. Daniel Laskin) Surgery of the Temporomandibular Joint, 1964; editor: (with Daniel Laskin) The Temporomandibular Joint A Biological Basis for Clinical Practice, 4th edit., 1991, (with Andrew D. Dixon) Factors and Mechanisms Affecting Growth of Bone, 1982, Normal and Abnormal Bone Growth: Basic and Clinical Research, 1985, Fundamentals of Bone Growth: Methodology and Applications, 1991; contbr. chpts. to textbooks, articles to surg. and sci. jours., other pubs. Co-winner Joseph A. Capps prize for med. rsch., 1940, Frederick B. Noyes prize, 1940; recipient Kerbs award for rsch. plastic and reconstructive surgery, 1950, 1st prize, sr. award Found. Am. Soc. Plastic and Reconstructive surgeons, 1957, Beverly Hills Acad. of Medicine award, 1959, Nat. Achievement award medicine Phi Epsilon Pi, 1964, 1st prize Am. Rhinologic Soc., 1980, medal Hebrew U., Jerusalem, 1985, medal Tel Aviv U., 1985, Disting. Svc. Alumni award U. Chgo. Pritzker Sch. Medicine, 1987, hon. award Am. Soc. Maxillofacial Surgeons, 1990, Dallas B. Phemister Profl. Achievement award Dept. Surgery U. Chgo., 1993, Disting. Alumnus award U. Ill. Coll. Dentistry, 1994, Craniofacial Biology Rsch. award Internat. Assn. for Dental Rsch., 1995, Disting. Scientist award. Fellow ACS, AAAS, Am. Assn. Plastic Surgeons (hon.); mem. Calif. Med. Soc., L.A. Med. Soc., Am. Soc. Plastic and Reconstructive Surgeons, Plastic Surgery Rsch. Coun. (founding mem. 1955, chmn. 1957), Calif. Soc. Plastic Surgeons, Beverly Hills Acad. Medicine (pres. 1962-63), Internat. Assn. Craniofacial Biology, Am. Assn. Phys. Anthropologists, Internat. Assn. Study Dento-Facial Abnormalities (hon.), Sigma Xi, Omicron Kappa Upsilon, Zeta Beta Tau, Phi Delta Epsilon, Alpha Omega (Internat. Achievement medal 1988). Home: 1875 Kelton Ave Apt 301 Los Angeles CA 90025-4575

SARNELLE, JOSEPH R., electronic publishing specialist, magazine and newspaper editor; b. Bklyn., Aug. 24, 1951; s. Alphonse Louis and Julie Lena (Mingarelli) S.; m. Ruth Patricia Cullen, Aug. 5, 1982; children: Cullen Joseph, D'Arcy Emilie. BA, Cornell U., 1973; postgrad., Sch. Visual Arts, N.Y.C., 1976-77, The New Sch., N.Y.C., 1979-80. Graphic artist Lewahl KC Graphics, N.Y.C., 1974-76; editor United Bus. Publs., N.Y.C., 1976-79; mng. editor Lebhar-Friedman Inc., N.Y.C., 1979-88; assoc. mng. editor HomeOwner Mag., N.Y.C., 1988-90; online sys. developer Info. Builders Inc., N.Y.C., 1990—; cons. video Markham-Novelle Pub. Rels., N.Y.C., 1988-89; cons. Best info. Family Media, N.Y.C., 1990-91. Author, dir. (videos) J. Roland Pepe's Guide to New York City, 1980, Underground Roundup, 1981. Recipient McMullen scholar, Cornell U., Regents scholar, State of N.Y., 1969; Best Headline of Year award Lebhar-Friedman Inc., 1982. Office: Info Builders Inc 1250 Broadway New York NY 10001-3701

SARNO, MARIA ERLINDA, lawyer, scientist; b. Manila, Philippines, July 26, 1944. BS in Chemistry magna cum laude, U. Santo Tomas, Philippines, 1967; MS in Chemistry summa cum laude, Calif. State U., Long Beach, 1975; JD cum laude, Western State U., 1993. Bar: Calif. 1994, U.S. Patent Office, 1993. Instr. U. Santo Tomas, Philippines, 1967-68; sr. chemist, analytical rsch. and quality assurance Rachelle Labs., Long Beach, Calif., 1969-74; teaching/rsch. asst. Calif. State U., Long beach, 1971-73; mgr. in charge of radioisotope section Curtis Nuclear Lab., L.A., 1974; assoc. chemist, asst. to dir. quality control Nichols Inst., San Pedro, Calif., 1974-75; mgr. rsch. and devel. Baxter Healthcare, Hyland, Calif., 1975-91; legal coord. sci. affairs Immunotherapy div. Baxter Biotech, Irvine, Calif., 1991-93, mgr. regulatory affairs, 1994-95; pvt. law practice, 1994—. Editorial bd: (tech. editor) Western State U. Law Review; Contbr. articles to profl. jours.; patentee in field. Mem. ABA, Orange County Bar Assn., Los Angeles County Bar Assn., Am. Chem. Soc., Am. Intellectual Property Law Assn., Phi Kappa Phi, Phi Delta Gamma. Home: 12541 Kenobi Ct Cerritos CA 90703-7756

SARNO, PATRICIA ANN, biology educator; b. Ashland, Pa.; d. John Thomas and Anna (Harvest) S. BS, Pa. State U., 1966, MEd, 1971; postgrad. Bucknell U., 1967, Bloomsburg U., 1970. Programmer planetarium, tchr. sci. Pottsville (Pa.) High Sch., 1967; tchr. biology Schuylkill Haven (Pa.) Area High Sch., 1967-91, sci. chmn., coord. dist., 1973-91; lead tchr. sci. Pa. Acad. Suprs. and Curriculum Devel. Dist. Pa. Sch., 1991—; cons. Contbr. to profl. jours. Pa. Edn. Dept., career program Pottsville Hosp. Dow Chem. Co. grantee, 1971. Mem. AAAS, AAUW, NEA, Pa. Edn. Assn. (exec. bd.), Nat. Assn. Biology Tchrs., Nat. Tchrs. Assn., Pa. Assn. Supervision and Curriculum Devel., N.Y. Acad. Scis., Pa. Tchrs. Assn., Am. Inst. Biol. Scis., Pa. Acad. Scis., Pa. State U. Alumni Assn., Schuylkill Haven Edn. Assn., Phi Sigma, Delta Kappa Gamma. Discoverer spider species Atypus snetzingeri, 1973. Home: 49 S Balliet St Frackville PA 17931-1703 Office: Schuylkill Haven HS Schuylkill Haven PA 17972

SARNOFF, LILI-CHARLOTTE DREYFUS (LOLO SARNOFF), artist, business executive; b. Frankfurt, Germany (Swiss citizen), Jan. 9, 1916; came to U.S., 1940, naturalized, 1943; d. Willy and Martha (Koch von Hirsch) Dreyfus; m. Stanley Jay Saroff, Sept. 11, 1948; children: Daniela Martha Bargezi, Robert L. Grad. Reimann Art Sch. (Germany), 1936, U. Berlin, 1936-38; student U. Florence (Italy), 1948-54. Rsch. asst. Harvard Sch. Pub. Health, 1955-69; rsch. assoc. cardiac physiology Nat. Heart Inst., Bethesda, Md., 1954-59; pres. Rodana Rsch. Corp., Bethesda, 1959; v.p. Catrix Corp., Bethesda, 1958-61; inventor FloLite light sculptures under name Lolo Sarnoff, 1968; one-woman shows include Agra Gallery, Washington, 1969, Corning Glass Ctr. Mus., Corning, N.Y., 1970, Gallery Two, Woodstock, Vt., 1970, Gallery Marc, Washington, 1971, 72, Franz Bader Gallery, Washington, 1976, Gallery K, Washington, 1978, 81, Alwin Gallery, London, 1981, Galerie von Bartha, Basel, Switzerland, 1982, Gallery K, Washington, 1982, 83, 84, 85, 87, 88, 89, 90, 91, La Galerie L'Hotel de Ville, Geneva, Switzerland, 1982, Pfalzgalerie, Kaiserlautern, Fed. Republic of Germany, 1985, Gallery K, Washington, 1987-91, Galerie Les Hirondelles, Geneva, 1988, Rockville (Md.) Civic Ctr., 1988, Washington Square Sculpture Group, 1989, Internat. Sculpture Congress, Washington, 1990, Retrospective show Gallery K, Washington, 1995, Sculpture on the Grounds, Rockville, 1996; represented in collections: Fed. Nat. Mortgage Assn., Washington, Brookings Inst., Washington, Corning Glass Ctr. Mus., Nat. Air and Space Museum, Washington, Kennedy Ctr., Washington, Nat. Acad. Sci., Chase Manhattan Bank, N.Y.C., Israel Mus., Jerusalem, Nat. Mus. Women in the Arts, Washington, others. Past trustee Nat. Ballet, Mt. Vernon Coll.; founder, pres. Arts for the Aging, Inc., Bethesda, Md., 1988—; active Washington Opera Soc., Washington Ballet Soc.; bd. overseers Corcoran Gallery Art, 1991. Recipient Gold medal Accademia Italia delle Arti e del Lavoro, 1980, Golda Meir award, 1995. Mem. City Tavern Club (Washington), Cosmos Club. Democrat. Co-inventor electrophrenic respirator; inventor flowmeter. Home: 7507 Hampden Ln Bethesda MD 20814-1331

SARNOFF, MARC DAVID, lawyer; b. Bklyn., Dec. 28, 1959; s. Joel Sarnoff and Alaine (Katz) Stagnitta. BA, U. Tampa, 1981; JD, Loyola U., New Orleans, 1984; postgrad., Tulane U. Bar: La. 1985, Fla. 1986, U.S. Dist. Ct. (so. dist.) Fla. 1986, D.C. 1987. Assoc. Herman, Herman, Katz & Coller, New Orleans, 1984-85; asst. prosecutor Orleans Parish Dist. Atty. Office, New Orleans, 1985-86; assoc. Christenberry & D'Antoni, New Orleans, 1986-87, Law Offices of Howard D. Dillman, Miami, Fla., 1987-91; ptnr. Goldman, Moore and Sarnoff, Miami, 1991-92, Sarnoff & Bayer, Miami, 1992—. Capt. U. Tampa Swimming Team, 1978. Mem. Million Dollar Advs. Forum, Phi Delta Theta (v.p. 1980, 81). Home: 3197 Virginia St Miami FL 33133 Office: Sarnoff & Bayer 3197 Virginia St Miami FL 33133-4545

SARNOFF, THOMAS WARREN, television executive; b. N.Y.C., Feb. 23, 1927; s. David and Lizette (Hermant) S.; m. Janyce Lundon, May 21, 1955; children: Daniel, Timothy, Cynthia. Grad., Phillips Acad., 1939-43; student, Princeton, 1943-45; B.S. in Elec. Engring., Stanford U., 1948, postgrad. Sch. Bus. Adminstrn., 1948-49; D.H.L., Columbia Coll. Engaged in prodn. and sales with ABC, Inc., 1949-51; prodn. Metro-Goldwyn-Mayer, 1951-52; with NBC, 1952-77; v.p. prodn. and bus. affairs NBC (Pacific div.), 1956-60, v.p. adminstrn. West Coast, 1960-62, v.p. charge West Coast, 1962-65, staff exec. v.p. West Coast, 1965-77; pres. NBC Entertainment Corp., 1972-77, Sarnoff Internat. Enterprises, 1977-81, Sarnoff Entertainment Corp., 1981—; exec. v.p. Venturetainment Corp., 1981-87, pres., 1987—. Exec. producer Bonanza: The Next Generation, 1987, Bonanza: The Return, 1993, Back to Bonanza Retrospective, 1993, Bonanza: Under Attack, 1995. Mem. Calif. Commn. for Reform Intermediate and Secondary Edn. Pres., Research Found., St. Joseph Hosp., Burbank, 1965-73, Permanant Charities Com. of Entertainment Industries, 1971-72; nat. trustee Nat. Conf. Christians and Jews. Served with Signal Corps AUS, World War II. Mem. Acad. TV Arts and Scis. (chmn. bd. trustees 1972-74, chmn. past pres.'s coun. 1989-92), Acad. TV Arts and Scis. Found. (pres. 1990—), The Caucus for Prodrs., Writers and Dirs. Office: 2451 Century Hl Los Angeles CA 90067-3510

SAROKIN, H. LEE, retired federal judge; b. Perth Amboy, N.J., Nov. 25, 1928; s. Samuel O. and Reebe (Weinblatt) S.; m. Marjorie Lang, Apr. 23, 1971; children: James Todd, Jeffrey Scott, Abby Jane. A.B., Dartmouth Coll., 1950; J.D., Harvard U., 1953. Bar: N.J. 1954. Assoc. Lasser, Lasser, Sarokin & Hochman, Newark, 1955-58; partner Lasser, Lasser, Sarokin & Hochman, 1958-79; asst. county counsel Union County, N.J., 1959-65; U.S. dist. judge Dist. of N.J., Newark, 1979-94; judge U.S. Ct. Appeals (3d cir.), Newark, 1994-96. Fellow Am. Bar Assn.; mem. Am. Law Inst.; Mem. N.J. Bar Assn., Essex County Bar Assn., Fed. Bar Assn.

SARPY, LEON, lawyer; b. New Orleans, Nov. 25, 1907; s. Henry Leon and Anita Louise (Staigg) S.; m. Courtney Dickinson, July 7, 1938 (dec. Mar. 1945); children: Courtney Anne, H. Leon; m. Eleanor Legier, July 17, 1948 (wid. 1996); 1 son, John Robert. A.B., Loyola U., New Orleans, 1928, LL.B., 1931, LL.D. (hon.), 1961; LL.M., Georgetown U., 1932. Bar: La. 1931. Practice law New Orleans, 1932; mem. firm Chaffe, McCall, Phillips, Toler & Sarpy, 1948—; lectr. Loyola U. Law Sch., 1934-87, prof., 1992—, Sarpy Endowed prof., 1992—; dist. rent atty. OPA, 1942-43; reporter La. Criminal Code, 1942, La. Code Civil Procedure, 1960. Contbr. to legal jours. Chmn. CSC New Orleans, 1952-63; chmn. civic luncheon for Pres. deGaulle of France, 1960; pres. Asso. Catholic Charities New Orleans, 1953-54; mem. Audubon Park Commn., 1963-70; bd. pres. New Orleans United Fund, 1959-60; bd. dirs. Greater New Orleans Homestead Assn., 1940-87; chmn. adv. bd. Convent Good Shepherd, 1957-58; trustee St. Mary's Dominican Coll., 1963-67; chmn. Community Chest of New Orleans, 1970-73; adv. bd. Loyola U., 1964-72, Tulane Admiralty Inst., 1966-87. Mem. La. N.G., 1925-28; Mem. USCG Temp. Res., 1944-45. Decorated Legion of Honor France; named Outstanding Alumnus, Jesuit High Sch., New Orleans, 1964; recipient Brotherhood award NCCJ, 1964, Gold medal St. Mary's Dominican Coll., 1970, Pres.' medal Loyola U., 1989, Alexis deTocqueville award United Way, 1989; named Rex of New Orleans Mardi Gras, 1972; cert. appreciation Outstanding Community Svc. ARC, 1992. Mem. ABA (ho. dels. 1965-70), La. Bar Assn. (pres. 1964-65), New Orleans Bar Assn. (pres. 1950-51), Am. Law Inst., La. Law Inst. (v.p. 1961-68, pres. 1968-73, chmn. 1980-86), Inst. Jud. Adminstrn. (N.Y.), S.W. Legal Found. (chmn. rsch. fellows 1970-72), Order of Coif, Blue Key, Delta Theta Phi, La. Club, Boston Club (New Orleans), Round Table Club (pres. 1964-66), Serra Club (pres. 1960-61), Order of St. Lazarus. Clubs: Boston (New Orleans), Round Table (New Orleans) (pres. 1964-66), Serra (New Orleans) (pres. 1960-61); Order of St. Lazarus. Home: 455 Walnut St New Orleans LA 70118-4933 Office: 2300 Energy Centre 1100 Poydras St New Orleans LA 70163-1101

SARREALS, SONIA, data processing consultant; b. N.Y.C., Sept. 17, 1938; d. Espriela and Sadie Beatrice (Scales) Sarreals; m. Waldro Lynch, Sept. 18, 1981 (div. Oct. 1983). BA in Langs. summa cum laude, CCNY, 1960; cert. in French, Sorbonne, Paris, 1961. Systems engr. IBM, N.Y.C., 1963-69; cons. Babbage Systems, N.Y.C., 1969-70; project leader Touche Ross, N.Y.C., 1970-73; sr. programmer McGraw-Hill, Inc., Hightstown, N.J., 1973-78; staff data processing cons. Cin. Bell Info. Systems, 1978-89; sr. analyst AT&T, 1989-92; lead tech. analyst Automated Concepts Inc., Arlington, Va., 1992-96; tech. cons. Maxim Group, Reston, Va., 1996—. Elder St. Andrew Luth. Ch., Silver Spring, 1992-96. Downer scholar CUNY, 1960, Dickman Inst. fellow Columbia U., 1960-61. Mem. Assn. for Computing Machinery, Phi Beta Kappa. Democrat. Avocations: needlework, sewing. Home: 13705 Beret Pl Silver Spring MD 20906-3030 Office: Maxim Group 11417 Sunset Hills Rd Reston VA 20190-5233

SARRIS, ANDREW GEORGE, film critic; b. Bklyn., Oct. 31, 1928; s. George Andrew and Themis (Katavolos) S.; m. Molly Clark Haskell, May 31, 1969. A.B., Columbia, 1951. Film critic Village Voice, N.Y.C., 1960-89, N.Y. Observer, 1989—; editor-in-chief Cahiers du Cinema in English; instr. Sch. Visual Arts, 1965-67; asst. prof. N.Y. U., 1967-69; assoc. prof. films Columbia Sch. Arts, N.Y.C., 1969-81, prof., 1981—. Author: The Films of Josef Von Sternberg, 1966, Interviews with Film Directors, 1967, The Film, 1968 The American Cinema, 1968, Confessions of a Cultist, 1970, The Primal Screen, 1973, The John Ford Movie Mystery, 1976, Politics and Cinema, 1978. Served with Signal Corps AUS, 1952-54. Guggenheim fellow, 1969. Mem. Am. Film Inst. (dir.), Soc. Cinema Studies, Nat. Soc. Film Critics, N.Y. Film Critics. *I keep on working toward that last deadline.*

SARRY, CHRISTINE, ballerina; b. Long Beach, Calif., May 25, 1946; d. John and Beatrice (Thomas) S.; m. Jim Varriale, Sept. 12, 1984; 1 child, Maximilian Sarry Varriale. With Joffrey Ballet, 1963-64; With Am. Ballet Theatre, 1964-68, prin. dancer, 1971-74; leading dancer Am. Ballet Co., 1969-71; ballerina Eliot Feld Ballet, 1974-81; mem. faculty Ballet Tech., N.Y.C., also freelance guest tchr. Performed ballets for Agnes DeMille, Antony Tudor, Jerome Robbins, Eliot Feld; appeared at White House, 1963, 67; U.S. Dept. State tours include, Russia, 1963, 66, S.Am., 1964, 76, various tours of N.Am., Orient, Europe, various appearances U.S. nat. TV; partnered by Mikhail Baryshnikov.

SARSON, EVELYN PATRICIA See KAYE, EVELYN PATRICIA

SARSON, JOHN CHRISTOPHER, television producer, director, writer; b. London, Jan. 19, 1935; s. Arnold Wilfred and Annie Elizabeth (Wright) S.; m. Evelyn Patricia Kaye, Mar. 25, 1963; children: Katrina May, David Arnold. BA with honors, Trinity Coll., Cambridge, Eng., 1960, MA, 1963. Dir. Granada TV, Manchester, Eng., 1960-63; producer, dir. Sta. WGBH-TV, Boston, 1963-73; pres. Blue Penguin, Inc., Boulder, Colo., 1974—; v.p. TV programming Sta. WYNC-TV, N.Y.C., 1989-90; dir. Pub. Broadcasting Assocs., Newton, Mass.; cons. to numerous pub. TV stations. Creator, producer MAsterpiece Theatre, PBS, 1970-73, Zoom, PBS, 1971-73; producer Live From the Met, PBS, 1977-79, Kid's Writes, Nickelodeon, 1982-83, American Treasure, a Smithsonian Journey, 1986, Spotlight Colorado, 1991, PArenting Works, 1993, Club 303, 1994. Served with Royal Navy, 1956-57. Recipient Emmy award, 1973, 74, Peabody award Ohio State U., 1978, Internat. Emmy award, 1983, Nat. Acad. TV Arts and Scis. Gov.'s award, 1991. Mem. Dirs. Guild Am., Nat. acad. TV Arts and Scis. (gov. Heartland chpt.). Avocations: music; cooking; gardening; travel. Home and Office: 3031 5th St Boulder CO 80304-2501

SARTAIN, JAMES EDWARD, lawyer; b. Ft. Worth, Feb. 9, 1941; s. James F. and May Belle (Boaz) S.; m. Barbara Hardy, Aug. 17, 1962; 1 child, Bethany Sartain Hughes. BA, Tex. A&M U., 1963; LLB, Baylor U., 1966. Bar: Tex. 1966, U.S. Ct. Mil. Appeals, 1971, U.S. Dist. Ct. (no. dist.) Tex. 1974. Staff atty. Dept. Justice, Washington, 1970-72; staff atty. to U.S. Sen. William L. Scott Fairfax, Va., 1972; pvt. practice Ft. Worth, 1973—; sec. Penrose Lumber Co., Abilene, Tex., 1987—, Esprit Comm. Corp., Austin, Tex.; bd. dirs. Emerald Restoration, Inc., Abilene, Tex.; sec. Esprit Comm. Corp., Austin, Tex. Bd. dirs. Ft. Worth Boys Club, 1980-89, Oakwood Cemetery, Ft. Worth, 1979-84. Capt. arty. U.S. Army, Vietnam. Mem. ABA, Abilene Bar Assn., Baylor Law Alumni Assn., Ft. Worth-Tarrant County Bar Assn., Coll. State Bar Tex., Masons, Petroleum Club, Phi Delta Phi. Republican. Presbyterian. Office: 6112 Mccart Ave Ste 201 Fort Worth TX 76133-3380 also: PO Box 450 Abilene TX 79604

SARTOR, ANTHONY JOSEPH, environmental engineer; b. Englewood, N.J., Mar. 28, 1943; s. John and Catherine (Dottino) S. Sr.; m. Maria C. Crisonio, Dec. 26, 1964; children: Lisanne, Colette (twins), John. BS in Engring., Manhattan Coll., 1964; MS in Engring., Mich. U., 1965, PhD, 1968. Devel. engr. Celanese Co., 1968-70; sr. water quality engr. Con Edison, N.Y.C., 1970-72; mgr. environ. affairs N.Y. Power Pool, 1972-74; pres. Sartor Assocs., Warren, N.J., 1974-77; exec. v.p., treas., sec. Paulus, Sokolowski, Sartor, Inc., Warren, 1977—; commr. N.J. Sports and Exposition Authority, 1992. Trustee Richard J. Hughes Found., Inc., 1994-96; mem. Environ. Commn., Fanwood, N.J.; mem. gov.'s transition team N.J. Dept. Environ. Protection. Recipient Disting. Service award Fanwood-Scotch Plains Jaycees. Mem. Am. Chem. Soc., Am. Inst. Chem. Engrs., Na.t Soc. Environ. Engrs., Jaycees (past bd. dirs., pres.), UNICO (Environ. Sci. award), Italian-Am. Club, Sigma Xi, Phi Lambda Upsilon. Club: Italian-Am. (Fairview, N.J.). Office: PO Box 4039 67A Mountain Boulevard Ext Warren NJ 07059-5626

SARTOR, DANIEL RYAN, JR., lawyer; b. Vicksburg, Miss., June 2, 1932; s. Daniel Ryan and Lucy Leigh (Hubbs) S.; m. Olive Guthrie Moss, Oct. 12, 1957; children—Clara M., Daniel Ryan, Walter M. B.A., Tulane U., 1952, LL.B., 1955. Bar: La. 1955. Instr. Tulane U., New Orleans, 1955-56, asst. prof., 1956-57; ptnr. Snellings, Breard, Sartor, Inabnett & Trascher, Monroe, La., 1957—. Contbr. articles to profl. jours. Fellow Am. Coll. Trust and Estate Counsel, Am. Bar Found., La. Bar Found.; mem. La. State Law Inst. (mem. council 1969—, sec. civil law sect. 1969—), La. State Bar Assn. (chmn. sect. on trust estate, probate and immovable property 1973-74, bd. govs. 1974-75). Democrat. Methodist. Clubs: Lotus (Monroe), Tower. Home: 2405 Pargoud Blvd Monroe LA 71201-2326 Office: Snellings Breard Sartor 1503 N 19th St Monroe LA 71201-4941

SARTORE, JOHN THORNTON, lawyer; b. N.Y.C., Nov. 5, 1946; s. Frank Jean and Mary Olive (Wacaser) S.; m. Sally Ann Coppersmith, Feb. 28, 1973; children: Michael, David, Delmy, Jenny. BA, Yale U., 1968; JD, Columbia U., 1971. Bar: Vt. 1972, U.S. Dist. Ct. Vt. 1972, U.S. Ct. Appeals (2d cir.) 1978, N.Y. 1989, U.S. Dist. Ct. (no. dist.) N.Y. 1992. Assoc. Paul, Frank & Collins, Inc., Burlington, Vt., 1971-74, mem., 1974—, pres., CEO, 1994—. Mem. ABA, Am. Coll. Trial Lawyers, Am. Bd. Trial Advocates, Vt. Bar Assn., N.Y. State Bar Assn., Chittenden County Bar Assn., New Eng. Legal Found. (dir.). Office: Paul Frank & Collins Inc One Church St Burlington VT 05402-1307

SARTORELLI, ALAN CLAYTON, pharmacology educator; b. Chelsea, Mass., Dec. 18, 1931; m. Alice C. Anderson, July 7, 1969. B.S., New Eng. Coll. Pharmacy Northeastern U., 1953; M.S., Middlebury (Vt.) Coll., 1955; Ph.D., U. Wis., 1958; M.A. (hon.), Yale U., 1967. Rsch. chemist Samuel Roberts Noble Found., Ardmore, Okla., 1958-60; sr. rsch. chemist Samuel Roberts Noble Found., 1960-61; mem. faculty dept. pharmacology Yale Sch. Medicine, New Haven, Conn., 1961—, prof., 1967—, head devel. therapeutics program Comprehensive Cancer Center, 1974-90, chmn. dept. pharmacology, 1977-84, dep. dir. Comprehensive Cancer Ctr., 1982-84, dir. Comprehensive Cancer Ctr., 1984-93, Alfred Gilman prof. pharmacology, 1987—, prof. epidemiology, 1991—; Charles B. Smith vis. rsch. prof. Meml. Sloan-Kettering Ctr., 1979; William N. Creasy vis. prof. clin. pharmacology Wayne State U., 1983; Mayo Found. vis. prof. oncology Mayo Clinic, 1983; Walter Hubert lectr. Brit. Assn. Cancer Rsch., 1985; Pfizer lectr. in clin. pharmacology U. Conn. Health Ctr., 1985; William N. Creasy vis. prof. clin. pharmacology Bowman Gray Sch. Medicine, 1987; Wellcome vis. prof. basic sci. U. Pitts. Sch. Medicine, 1990; mem. sci. adv. bd. ImmunoGen, Inc., 1981—, U. Ind. Cancer Ctr., 1992, Cancer Inst. N.J., 1993—, Cell Pathways, Inc., 1993—; chmn. cancer sci. adv. bd. ViraChem., Inc., 1986-93, The Liposome Co., 1986—, Vion Pharms., 1993—, bd. dirs., chmn. sci. adv. bd.; chmn. vis. sci. adv. com. Columbia U. Comprehensive Cancer Ctr., 1986—; chmn. pres.'s cancer adv. bd. Fox Chase Cancer Ctr., 1992—; mem. cancer clin. investigation rev. com. Nat. Cancer Inst., 1968-72, mgmt. cons. to dir. divsn. cancer treatment, 1975-77, bd. sci. counselors, divsn. cancer treatment, 1978-81, chmn. com. to establish nat. coop. drug discovery groups, 1982-83, chmn. special review com. Outstanding Investigator grant applications, 1992, chmn. ad hoc contracts tech. rev. group, 1993; mem. instl. rsch. grants com. Am. Cancer Soc., 1971-76, coun. analysis and projection, 1978-79; cons. in biochemistry U. Tex. M.D. Anderson Hosp. and Tumor Clinic, Houston, 1970-76; cons. Sandoz Forschungs-Institut, Vienna, Austria, 1977-80; mem. exptl. therapeutics study sect. NIH, 1973-77, working cadre nat. large bowel cancer project, 1973-76; mem. adv. com. Cancer Rsch. Ctr., Washington U. Sch. Medicine, 1971-75, SLSB Partners, L.P., 1992—; mem. sci. adv. com. U. Iowa Cancer Ctr., 1979-83; mem. external adv. com. Wis. Clin. Cancer Ctr., 1978-79, Duke Comprehensive Cancer Ctr., 1983-94; mem. external adv. bd. U. Ariz. Cancer Ctr., 1982-92, U. So. Calif. Cancer Ctr., 1983-93, Clin. Cancer Rsch. Ctr., Brown U., 1980-86; mem. nat. program com. 13th Internat. Cancer Congress, 1979-81; cons. Bristol-Myers Co., 1982-93, mem. selection com. prize in cancer rsch., 1977-85, chmn., 1979-81, chmn. selection com. award for disting. achievement in cancer rsch., 1989-92; bd. advisors Drug and Vaccine Devel. Corp. (Ctr. for Pub. Resources), 1980-81, Specialized Cancer Ctr., Mt. Sinai Med. Ctr., 1981-90, Grace Cancer Drug Ctr., Roswell Park Meml. Inst., 1986-89; mem. med. and sci. adv. com. grants rev. subcom. Leukemia Soc. Am., 1984-88; bd. dirs. Metastasis Rsch. Soc., 1984-90; mem. program planning com. Mary Lasker-Am. Cancer Soc. Conf., 1986; mem. external sci. rev. com. Massey Cancer Ctr., 1989-94; bd. visitors Moffit Cancer Ctr. U.S. Fla., 1989-94; mem. ad hoc cons. group for cancer ctrs. program Nat. Cancer Adv. Bd., 1989-92; dep. dir. Cancer Prevention Rsch. Unit for Conn., 1989-93, acting dir., 1991-93; mem. nat. bd. Cosmetic Toiletry and Fragnance Assn.'s Look Good...Feel Better Program, 1989-91; mem. organizing com. Conf. on Bioreductive Drug Activation, 1993-94; chmn. bd. special cons. Inst. for Cancer Therapeutics, 1993—. Regional editor Am. Continent Biochem. Pharmacology, 1968—, exec. editor, 1993—; editor-in-chief Cancer Comm., 1969-91, Oncology Rsch., 1993—; editor Handbuch der experimentellen Pharmakologie vols. on antineoplastic and immunosuppressive agts.; editor series on cancer chemotherapy Am. Chem. Soc. Symposium, 1976; exec. editor Pharmacology and Therapeutics, 1975—; mem. editl. bd. Internat. Ency. Pharmacology and Therapeutics, 1972-94, Seminars in Oncology, 1973-83, Chemico-Biol. Interactions, 1975-78, Jour. Meldicinal Chemistry, 1977-82, Cancer Drug Delivery, 1982-85, Jour. Enzyme Inhibition, 1984—, Anti-Cancer Drug Design, 1984—, Jour. Liposome Rsch., 1986-92, In Vivo, 1990—, Cancer Biotherapy, 1992, Cancer Rsch., Therapy, and Control, 1993—, Oncology Reports, 1995—, Molecular and Celleular Differentiation, 1995—; mem. adv. bd. Advances in Chemistry Series, ACS Symposium Series, 1977-80; mem. editl. adv. bd. Cancer Rsch., 1970-71, assoc. editor, 1971-78; assoc. editor Current Awareness in Biol. Scis., Current Advances in Pharmacology and Toxicology, 1983—, Cancer Cells, 1989-91, Jour. Exptl. Therapeutics and Oncology, 1995—; mem. exec. adv. bd. Ency. of Human Biology, 1987-90, Dictionary of Sci. and Tech., 1989-91; editl. cons. Biol. Abstracts, 1984—; contbr. articles to profl. jours. Bd. dirs. Shubert Performing Arts Ctr., 1992—, Shubert Opera Bd., 1991—, chmn., 1993—. Recipient Outstanding Alumni award Northeastern U., 1987, Mike Hogg award M.D. Anderson Cancer Ctr., U. Tex., 1989, Alumni Achievement award Middlebury Coll., 1990. Fellow AAAS, N.Y. Acad. Scis.; mem. Am. Assn. Cancer Rsch. (dir. 1975-78, 84-87, chmn. publs. com. 1981-88, v.p. 1985-86, fin. com. 1985-88, exec. com. 1985-89, chmn. exec. com. 1987, pres. 1986-87, chmn. awards com. 1987, chmn. nominating com. 1993-95, mem. devel. com. 1995—), Am. Chem. Soc., Am. Soc. Microbiology, Am. Soc. Biochemistry and Molecular Biology, Am. Soc. Cell Biology, Am. Soc. Pharmacology and Exptl. Therapeutics (award in exptl. therapeutics 1986, award com. 1988, chmn. 1992), Assn. Am. Cancer Insts. (v.p. 1986, bd. dirs. 1986-89, liaison rep. to Nat. Cancer Inst. 1986, pres. 1987-88, chmn. bd. dirs. 1989), Inst. of Medicine of NAS (com. on govt. industry collaboration in biomed. rsch. and edn. 1989, mem. Forum on Drug Devel. and Regulation 1989—), Conn. Acad. Sci. and Engring., Coun. Biology Editors. Home: 4 Perkins Rd Woodbridge CT 06525-1616 Office: Yale U Dept Pharmacology 333 Cedar St New Haven CT 06510-3206

SARTORI, BRIDGET ANN, home health care nurse; b. Plattsburg, N.Y., July 17, 1957; d. Francis McCarthy and Phyllis (Harvey) McCarthy/Haegler; m. Robert S. Sartori, May 20, 1978; children: Robert F., Ryan R. BSN, Mt. St. Mary's Coll., Newburgh, N.Y., 1990. RN, N.Y. Staff nurse CCU White Plains (N.Y.) Hosp., 1990-91; nurse in home care divsn. Putnam Hosp. Ctr., Carmel, N.Y., 1991—, acting LTHHCP coord. home care divsn., 1995-97; supr. clin. svcs. Homecare, Inc., Brookfield, Conn., 1997—; intravenous therapy nurse Anytime Home Care, Poughkeepsie, N.Y., 1992—; substitute tchr., substitute sch. nurse Dover Union Free Sch. Dist., 1994—; children's adv. Astor Head Start, Dover Plains, N.Y., 1989-92. Mem. rescue squad J.H. Ketcham Hose Co., Dover Plains, 1978—, mem. ladies aus., 1978—, fire prevention officer, 1994-95, corp. sec., 1996; 1st v.p. J.H. Ketcham Hose Co. Fire Police, 1994—; coach Dover Little League, 1994, 95. Recipient Army Nurse Perseverance award U.S. Army, 1990. Republican. Roman Catholic. Avocations: reading, biking. Office: Homecare Inc Home Care Divsn Dept Clinical Svcs Brookfield CT 06814

SARTORI, GIOVANNI, political scientist; b. Florence, Italy, May 13, 1924; s. Dante and Emilia (Quentin) S.; 1 child, Ilaria. PhD, U. Florence, 1956; Doctor honoris causa, U. Genoa, 1992, Georgetown U., 1994, U. Guadalajara, 1996. Assoc. prof. U. Florence, 1956-62, prof., 1962-76, dean faculty of polit. scis., 1968-71; prof. polit. sci. Stanford U., 1976-79; Albert Schweitzer prof. in the humanities Columbia U., N.Y.C., 1979—; fellow Ctr. Advanced Study Behavioral Scis., 1971-72; sr. fellow Hoover Instn., 1976-79. Author: Democratic Theory, 1962, Parties and Party Systems: A Framework for Analysis, 1976, La Politica, 1979, The Theory of Democracy Revisited, 1987, Elementi di Teoria Politica, 1990, Democrazia, 1993, Comparative Constitutional Engineering, 1994. Guggenheim fellow, 1979, Russell Sage Found. fellow, 1988-89. Mem. Am. Acad. Arts and Scis, Accademia dei Lincei. Home: 25 Central Park W Apt 270 New York NY 10023-7253 Office: Sch Internat Affairs 420 W 118th St Rm 1234 New York NY 10027-7213

SARWAR, BARBARA DUCE, school system administrator; b. Mpls., Aug. 9, 1938; d. Harold Taylor and Barbara (Thayer) Duce; m. Mohammad Sarwar, Dec. 28, 1972; 1 child, Barbara Sara Depies. BS, U. Colo., 1972; M Spl. Edn., Ea. N.Mex. U., 1975, Edn. Specialist, 1979. Cert. tchr., adminstr., N.Mex. Tchr. 2d grade, English as 2d lang. Lake Arthur (N.Mex.) Mcpl. Schs., 1972-74; tchr. spl. edn. Artesia (N.Mex.) Pub. Schs., 1974-79, ednl. diagnostician, 1979-88, dir. spl. edn., 1988—. Contbr. to profl. publs. Pres. Altrusa Club Artesia, 1981-82, 86-87, The Arc of Artesia, 1990-92. Named Employee of Yr. Arc of N.Mex., 1994. Mem. Artesia Edn. Assn. (pres. 1978-79), Internat. Reading Assn. (pres. Pecos Valley chpt. 1975-76, sec. N.Mex. unit 1977-78), Nat. Assn. Sch. Psychologists, N.Mex. Sch. Adminstrs. Assn., Assoc. Sch. Curriculm Divsn., Phi Kappa Phi, Phi Delta Kappa. Avocations: reading, sewing, golf. Home: PO Box 1493 Artesia NM 88211-1493 Office: Artesia Pub Schs 1106 W Quay Ave Artesia NM 88210-1826

SARWER-FONER, GERALD JACOB, physician, educator; b. Volkovsk, Grodno, Poland, Dec. 6, 1924; arrived in Can., 1932, naturalized, 1935; s. Michael and Ronia (Caplan) Sarwer-F.; m. Ethel Sheinfeld, May 28, 1950; children: Michael, Gladys, Janice, Henry, Brian. B.A., Loyola Coll. U., Montreal, 1945, M.D. magna cum laude, 1951; D.Psychiatry, McGill U., 1955. Diplomate: Am. Bd. Psychiatry and Neurology. Intern. Univ. Hosps. U. Montreal Sch. Medicine, 1950-51; resident Butler Hosp., Providence, 1951-52, Hosps. Western Res. U., Cleve., 1952-53, Queen Mary Vets. Hosp., Montreal, 1953-55; lectr. psychiatry U. Montreal, 1953-55; lectr., assoc. prof. McGill U., 1955-70; dir. dept psychiatry Queen Elizabeth's Hosp, Montreal, 1964-71; prof. psychiatry U. Ottawa, Ont., 1971—, prof., chmn. psychiatry, 1974-86; dir. dept. psychiatry Ottawa Gen. Hosp., 1971-87; dir. Lafayette Clinic, Detroit, 1989-92; prof. psychiatry and behavioral Neurosciences Wayne State U., Detroit, 1989—; cons. in psychiatry Ottawa Gen. Hosp., Royal Ottawa Hosp., Nat. Def. Med. Ctr., Children's Hosp. of Eastern Ont., Ottawa, Windsor (Ont.) Western Hosp. Ctr., Ottawa Sch. Bd.; Z. Lebensohn lectr. Silbey Meml. Hosp. Cosmos Club, Washington,. 1991. Editor: Dynamics of Psychiatric Drug Therapy, 1960, Research Conference on the Depressive Group of Illnesses, 1966, Psychiatric Crossroads-the Seventies, Research Aspects, 1972, Social Psychiatry in the Late 20th Century, 1993; editor in chief Psychiat. Jour. U. Ottawa, 1976-90, emeritus editor in chief, 1990—; mem. editorial bds. of numerous internat. and nat. profl. jours.; editor numerous audio-video tapes; contbr. to more than 190 articles to profl. jours. Bd. govs. Queen Elizabeth Hosp., Montreal, 1966-71; life gov. Queen Elizabeth Hosp. Found.; cons. Protestant Sch. Bd., Westmount, Que., 1966-71; advisor Com. on Health, City of Westmount, 1969-71. Served to lt. col. Royal Can. A Med. Corps, 1949-62. Recipient Sigmund Freud award Am. assn. Psychoanalytic Physicians, 1982, William V. Silverberg Meml. award Am. Acad. Psychoanalysis, 1990, Poca award Assn. Psychiat. Out Patient Ctrs. Am., 1990; Simon Bolivar lectr. Am. Psychiat. Assn., New Orleans, 1981; Can. Decoration, Knight of Malta. Fellow AAAS, Royal Coll. Physicians and Surgeons (Can., mem. spl. psychiat. com. 1958-64, exec. sec. test psychiat. com. 1987-89), Royal Coll. Psychiatry (Found. fellow), Am. Coll. Neuropsychopharmacology (charter, life), Can. Coll. Neuropsychopharmacology (life, hon. found.), Internat. Coll. Psychosomatic Medicine (sec.-gen. 1979-83), Internat. Psychoanalytical Assn. (mem. program com. 31st congress N.Y. 1979), Am. Psychiat. Assn. (life; mem. com. psychiatry and law 1975-77), Am. Orthopsychiat. Assn. (life), Am. Coll. Psychiatrists (bd. regents 1978-80, emeritus fellow), Am. Psychopathol. Assn., Am. Coll. Psychoanalysts (pres. elect 1983, pres. 1984-85, Henry Laughlin award 1986), Am. Coll. Mental Health Adminstrn. (life), Benjamin Rush Soc. (founding mem., councillor), World Psychiat. Assn. (chair Sci. program VI World Congress 1974, v.p. sect. on edn. 1989—, mem. internat. adv. com. 9th World Congress Rio de Janeiro 1993, mem. nominating com., mem. organizing com. sci. program com. X World Congress in Madrid 1996), Can. Psychiat. Assn. (life), Collegium Internat. Neuropsychopharmacology; mem. Am. Acad. Psychiatry and the Law (sr., pres. 1977, Silver Apple award), Soc. Bio.. Psychiatry (sr. mem., H. Azina Meml. lectr. 1963, pres. 1983-84), Can. Psychoanalytic Soc. (pres. 1977-81), Can. Assn. Profs. of Psychiatry (pres. 1976-77, 82-86), Am. Assn. for Social Psychiatry (v.p. 1987-89, pres. elect 1990, pres. 1992-94), Mich. Psychoanalytic Soc., Cosmos Club, Royal Can. Mil. Inst. Club. Home and Office: 3220 Bloomfield Shr West Bloomfield MI 48323-3300

SASAHARA, ARTHUR ASAO, cardiologist, educator, researcher; b. Del Rey, Calif., May 11, 1927; s. Harold Hango and Blanche (Takayama) S.; m. Alice Ann Guenther, Apr. 2, 1955; children: Ann Mariko, Claire Michiko, Ellen Reiko, Karen Hideko, Mark Tadao. AB, Oberlin Coll., 1951; MD, Case Western Res. U., 1955; AM (hon.), Harvard U., 1974. Diplomate Am. Bd. Internal Medicine. Intern Boston City Hosp., 1955-56; jr. asst. med. resident Mass. Gen. Hosp., Boston, 1956-57; fellow in cardiology West Roxbury VA Med. Ctr., Mass., 1957-58, Children's Hosp. Med. Ctr., Boston, 1958-59; sr. resident in medicine Yale-New Haven Med. Ctr., 1959-60; asst. chief med. svc., dir. cardiopulmonary lab., dep. chmn. rsch. and edn. com. VA Hosp. West Roxbury, 1960-70, chief cardiopulmonary sect., 1971-74, assoc. chief staff for rsch. and edn., 1970-76, chief med. svc., 1974-82; chief med. svc. West Roxbury-Brockton VA Hosp., 1982-87; prof. medicine Harvard Med. Sch., Boston, 1974-93; prof. emeritus Harvard Med. Sch., 1993—; cons. cardiovascular-pulmonary diseases Boston, 1965-87; cons. pediatric cardiology Children's Hosp. Med. Ctr., Boston, 1976-86; physician Brigham and Women's Hosp., Boston, 1979-82, sr. physician, 1982—; dir. Thrombolytics Rsch. Pharm. Products Divsn. Abbott Labs., Abbott Park, Ill., 1987-95, sr. med. dir., 1995-97. Author-editor: Pulmonary Embolic Disease, 1965, Pulmonary Emboli, 1975, Advances in Therapeutic Agents in Thrombosis and Thrombolysis, 1997; contbr. articles to profl. jours.; designer constant infusion med. pump, Harvard Apparatus Co., 1973; editorial bd. Jour. Nuclear Medicine, 1981-83, Am. Jour. Medicine, 1971-72, Circulation, 1973-78, VASA, 1978-85, Jour. Cardiovascular Medicine, 1980-86, Primary Cardiology, 1986-89. With U.S. Army, 1945-47. NIH grantee, 1963-82; VA grantee, 1961-87. Fellow ACP, Am. Coll. Chest Physicians, Am. coll. Cardiology; mem. AAAS, Am. Fedn. Clin. Rsch., Internat. Soc. Thrombosis and Thrombolysis, Alpha Omega Alpha. Democrat. Episcopalian. Home: 221 Mt Vernon St West Newton MA 02165

SASAKI, CLARENCE TAKASHI, surgeon, medical educator; b. Honolulu, Jan. 24, 1941; s. Tsutomu and Carla Harumi (Mirikitani) S.; m. Carolyn Elizabeth Lindahl, June 26, 1967; children: Peter Gordon, John Eric. B.A., Pomona Coll., 1962; M.D., Yale U., 1966. Diplomate: Am. Bd. Otolaryngology. Intern San Francisco Hosp., U. Calif., 1966-67; resident in surgery Dartmouth Med. Sch., 1967-68; resident in otolaryngology Yale U. Med. Sch. Hosps., New Haven, 1970-73, faculty mem., 1973—, assoc. prof., 1977-82, prof. surgery, 1982—, chief sect. otolaryngology, 1981—; Charles Ohse prof. surgery Yale U. Med. Sch. Hosps., 1988—, vice chmn. dept. surgery, 1996. Author: Surgery of the Skull Base, Head and Neck Surgery, Vol. 1 Atlas Otolarynogology, Vocal Fold Physiology, Laryngeal Function in Phonation and Respiration, Neurological Diseases of the Larynx; mem.

editorial bd. profl. jours. Served to maj. M.C. U.S. Army, 1968-70. Recipient award Fowler Triological Soc., 1979. Mem. Am. Acad. Otolaryngology (1st prize clin. rsch.), Am. Soc. Head and Neck Surgery (coun.), Assn. Rsch. Otolaryngology, Am. Laryngol. Rhinol. and Otol. Soc. (coun., sec. ea. sect. 1990), New Eng. Otolaryngology Soc. (pres. 1987, coun.), Assn. Acad. Depts. Otolaryngology (coun.), Am. Laryngol. Assn., Pan Pacific Surg. Assn., Soc. for Neurosci., Soc. Neurovascular Surgery, Soc. for Head and Neck Surgeons, Am. Neurotolog. Soc., Pan Am. Assn. Oto-rhino-laryngology and Bronchoesophagology, Conn. Med. Soc., N.Y. Acad. Scis., Soc. Univ. Otolaryngologists, Collegium ORLAS, Cartesian Soc., Am. Bronchoesophagological Assn., N.Am. Skull Base Soc., Laryngeal. Cancer Assn. (Padua), Am. Otol. Soc., Dysphagia Rsch. Soc. (treas., pres.), Lawn Club, Mory's Assoc., Yale Club, Phi Beta Kappa, Sigma Xi. Office: Yale U Med Sch Dept Surgery PO Box 208041 333 Cedar St New Haven CT 06520-8041

SASAKI, TATSUO, musician; b. Okayama, Japan, Mar. 30, 1944; s. Koichi and Fumiko Sasaki; m. Shigeko Hayashi, Apr. 9, 1972; children: Jun Daniel, Maki Elisabeth. BA in Music, Tokyo U. of Arts, 1965; postgrad., Juilliard Sch. Music, 1965-67. Percussionist Am. Symphony, N.Y.C., 1966-67; solo timpanist Am. Wind Symphony, Pitts., 1966-67; asst. timpanist Israel Philharm. Orch., Tel Aviv, 1967-69; percussionist Japan Philharm. Orch., Tokyo, 1969-72; prin. timpanist Orch. Sinfonica Brazileiro, Rio de Janeiro, 1972-73, San Diego Symphony and San Diego Opera, 1973—; xylophone recitalist in U.S., Europe, Japan; spl. mem. Japan Xylophone Assn., Tokyo, 1971—; dir. Pacific Xylo-Marimba Trio, San Diego, 1974-76; dir., xylophone soloist Internat. Chamber Concert, Dusseldorf, Fed. Republic Germany, 1975—; dir. Sasaki/Rhein Brass Quintet, Dusseldorf, 1988—. Performer (album) Xylophone Artistry, 1983, (compact disk) Xylophone Artistry, Musical Heritage Soc., 1994. Fulbright scholar U.S. govt., 1965-67. Avocations: golfing, skiing, shogi (japanese chess). Home: 5842 Henley Dr San Diego CA 92120-4521 Office: San Diego Symphony 1245 7th Ave San Diego CA 92101-4302

SASENICK, JOSEPH ANTHONY, health care company executive; b. Chgo., May 18, 1940; s. Anthony E. and Caroline E. (Smicklas) S.; m. Barbara Ellen Barr, Aug. 18, 1962; children: Richard Allen, Susan Marie, Michael Joseph. BA, DePaul U., 1962; MA, U. Okla., 1966. With Miles Labs., Inc., Elkhart, Ind., 1963-70; product mgr. Alka-Seltzer, 1966-68, dir. mktg. grocery products div., 1968-70; with Gillette Corp., Boston, 1970-79; dir. new products/new ventures, personal care div. Gillette Corp., 1977; v.p. diversified cos. and pres. Jafra Cosmetics Worldwide, 1977-79; mktg. dir. Braun AG, Kronberg, W. Ger., 1970-73; chmn. mng. dir. Braun U.K. Ltd., 1973-77; with Abbott Labs., North Chicago, 1979-84; corp. v.p., pres. consumer products div. Abbott Labs., 1979-84; pres., chief exec. officer Moxie Industries, 1984-87, Personal Monitoring Technologies, Rochester, N.Y., 1987; pres. Bioline Labs., Ft. Lauderdale, Fla., 1988; mng. dir., ptnr. Vista Resource Group, Newport Beach, Calif., 1988-90; pres., CEO, Alcide Corp., Redmond, Wash., 1991-92, CEO, 1992—. Mem. Columbia Tower Club, El Niguel Club, Wash. Athletic Club. Home: 1301 Spring St Seattle WA 98104-3533 Office: Alcide Corp 8561 154th Ave NE Redmond WA 98052-3557

SASHIN, DONALD, physicist, radiological physicist, educator; b. N.Y.C., Dec. 11, 1937; s. David and Pearl (Taub) S.; m. Kathleen Flaherty, July 24, 1967; children: Deirdre Moira, Courtenay Aileen. BS in Physics, MIT, 1960; MS in Physics, Carnegie Inst. Tech., 1962; PhD in Physics, Carnegie Mellon U., 1968. Instr. Dept. of Radiology U. Pitts., 1967-70, asst. prof. in radiation health, 1970-77; asst. prof. Dept. of Indsl. and Environ. Health Sci. U. Pitts., 1970-77; assoc. prof. Dept. of Radiology U. Pitts., 1989—, 1974—; assoc. prof. Dept. Radiation Health U. Pitts., 1977-89, assoc. prof., 1987-89, assoc. prof. Dept. of Environ. and Occupl. Health, 1989—. Contbr. articles to profl. jours., patentee in field. Recipient Cum Laude award sci. exh., RSNA, 1977, cert. of merit sci. exh., RSNA, 1979. Mem. APS, AAPM, SNM, HPS, IEEE, Sigma Xi. Democrat. Roman Catholic. Avocations: golf, fishing, swimming, sailing. Home: 4360 Centre Ave Pittsburgh PA 15213 Office: PET Facility B 938 PUH 200 Lothrop St Pittsburgh PA 15213-2546

SASLOW, GEORGE, psychiatrist, educator; b. N.Y.C., Dec. 5, 1906; s. Abram and Becky (Zinkoff) S.; m. Julia Amy Ipcar, July 28, 1928; children: Michael G., Rondi, Steven, Marguerite. ScB magna cum laude, Washington Sq. Coll. NYU, 1926; postgrad., U. Rochester, 1926-28; PhD in Physiology, NYU, 1931; MD cum laude, Harvard U., 1940. Instr., asst. prof. biology N.Y. U., 1928-37; vis. research asso. physiology Cornell Med. Coll., 1935-36, U. Rochester Sch. Medicine, 1936-37; research asso. physiology Harvard Sch. Pub. Health, 1937-40; neurology-neurosurgery intern Boston City Hosp., 1940-41; resident Worcester State Hosp., 1941-42; chief resident psychiatry Mass. Gen. Hosp., Boston, 1942-43; staff Mass. Gen. Hosp., 1955-57; instr., successively asst., asso. prof., prof. pychiatry Washington U. Sch. Medicine, 1943-55; staff Barnes Hosp., St. Louis, 1943-55; practice of psychiatry, 1943—; clin. prof. psychiatry Harvard, 1955-57; prof. psychiatry U. Oreg. Med. Sch., Portland, 1957-74; head dept. U. Oreg. Med. Sch., 1957-73, prof. emeritus, 1979—; chief mental health and behavioral sci. edn., chief psychiatry service VA Hosp., Sepulveda, Calif., 1974-79; prof. psychiatry in residence UCLA, 1974-79; mem. Psychiat. Security Rev. Bd., 1983—. Nat. Tng. Labs. fellow. Fellow Am. Psychiat. Assn. (life; mem. task force on nomenclature and stats.), Am. Coll. Psychiatrists (charter); mem. AMA, Assn. for Advancment of Behavioral Therapy, Delta Soc. (bd. dirs. 1986-89). Home: 02403 SW Greenwood Rd Portland OR 97219-8394

SASMOR, JAMES CECIL, publishing representative, educator; b. N.Y.C., July 29, 1920; s. Louis and Cecilia (Mockler) S.; 1 child from previous marriage: Elizabeth Lynn; m. Jeannette L. Fuchs, May 30, 1965. BS, Columbia U., 1942; MBA, Calif. Western U., 1977, PhD, 1979. Cert. Am. Bd. Med. Psychotherapists, sex educator Am. Assn. Sex Educators, Counselors and Therapists, Healthcare Risk Mgr. Am. Inst. Med. Law, diplomate Am. Bd. Sexology, Am. Bd. Disability Analysts (sr. analyst). Advt. sales exec. 1946-59; registered rep. Nat. Assn. Security Dealers, 1956-57; founder, owner J.C. Sasmor Assocs. Publishers' Reps., N.Y.C., 1959-89; co-founder, pres., dir. adminstrn. Continuing Edn. Cons., Inc., 1976—; pub. cons., 1959—; clin assoc., U. So. Fla. Coll. of Medicine, 1987-89; adj. faculty Coll. Nursing, 1980-89, dir. Ednl. Counseling Comprehensive Breast Cancer Ctr., U. So. Fla. Med. Ctr., 1984-89, client librn. mental health inst., 1979-89. Team tchr. childbirth edn. Am. Soc. Childbirth Educators; bd. dirs. Tampa chpt. ARC; pres. Am. Cancer Soc. Sedona, Ariz. Unit, 1995—, co-chmn. adult edn. com.; bd. dirs. Ariz. State Divsn., mem. pub. edn. com.; county nursing ednl. cons. ARC, chmn. instrnl. com. on nursing and health, 1979-85. With USN, 1942-58, PTO; lt. USNR ret. Recipient cert. appreciation ARC, 1979, Dept. Health and Rehab. Svcs. award for Fla. Mental Health Inst. Svc., 1980, Cert. of Appreciation Am. Fgn. Svc. Assn., 1988. Internat. Coun. of Sex Edn. and Parenthood Am. U. fellow, 1981—. Mem. NAACOG (bd. dirs. Tampa chpt.), Nat. Assn. Pubs. Reps. (pres. 1965-66), Am. Soc. Psychoprophylaxis in Obstetrics (dir. 1970-71), Am. Soc. Childbirth Educators (co-founder, dir. 1972—), Internat. Coun. Women's Health Issues (chmn. resources com.), Health Edn. Media Assn., Nursing Educators Assn. Tampa, Lions (bd. dirs. Found. Ariz., pres. Sedona club). Author: Economics of Structured Continuing Education in Selected Professional Journals'; contbr. chpts. to Childbirth Education: A Nursing Perspective; contbr. articles to profl. jours. Home: 235 Arrowhead Dr Sedona AZ 86351-8900 Office: PO Box 2282 Sedona AZ 86339-2282

SASS, ARTHUR HAROLD, educational executive; b. N.Y.C., Nov. 22, 1928; s. Maxwell Sigmund and Alice May (McGillick) S.; m. Eleanore G. Schmidt, Dec. 31, 1949; children: Nancy, Arlene, Susan, Eric. BS, Oswego (N.Y.) State Coll., 1949; EdM, Rutgers U., 1959, postgrad., 1960-68. Cert. chief sch. adminstr. Tchr. Millsboro (Del.) Pub. Sch. System, 1949-51, Eatontown (N.J.) Pub. Sch. System, 1955-66; coord. coop. indsl. edn. Monmouth Regional High Sch., Tinton Falls, N.J., 1966-68; prin. Mt. Holly (N.J.) Pub. Sch. System, 1968-71; supt. schs. Lumberton Twp. (N.J.) Pub. Sch. System, 1971-72, Lacey Twp. (N.J.) Pub. Sch. System, 1972-74; analyst mil. pers. Naval Sea Systems Command, Washington, 1975-79; head employee devel. Naval Rsch. Lab., Washington, 1979-83, 85-90; acad. dir. Naval Res. Engring. Duty Officer Sch., Leesburg, Va., 1983-85; pres. DEVPRO, Inc., Warrenton, Va., 1985—; prin. founder Dept. Def. Sci. and Engring. Apprentice Program; established nation's first fed. svc. high sch. coop. indsl. edn. program, 1967. Author: Guide to the Naval Ammunition Depot, 1967; editor: (brochure) Commodore John Barry-Father of the U.S. Navy, 1976. Chmn. Shade Tree Commn., Little Silver, N.J., 1968-75, Rapidan/Rappahannock (Va.) Cmty. Mental Health Ctrs., 1980-81; deacon Warrenton Ch. of Christ, 1985—, elder, 1995; mem. Va. Gov.'s Adv. Bd. for Emergency Med. Svcs., 1994—. With USN, 1952-55; capt. USNR, 1983-88. Recipient Tng. Officers' Conf. Disting. Svc. award, 1988, Outstanding Contbn. to Engring. Edn. and Rsch award George Washington U., 1991. Mem. Am. Soc. Tng. and Devel., Res. Officers Assn. (v.p. Va. chpt. 1982-83), Naval Res. Assn. (Plimsoll Mark award 1975), Am. Soc. Naval Engrs., Navy League, Wash. Acad. Scis., Tng. Dirs. Forum. Republican. Avocation: outdoor activities. Home and Office: 5268 Ambler Dr Warrenton VA 20187-9201

SASS, NEIL LESLIE, toxicologist; b. Balt., Oct. 24, 1944; s. Samuel and Blanche (Radoon) S.; m. Anita Paige Hoswell, June 29, 1984. BS, Wake Forest Coll., 1966; MS, W.Va. U., 1969, PhD, 1971; MS, Johns Hopkins U., 1984. Commd. officer USPHS, 1966, advanced through grades to capt., 1988, cmdr. Preventive Medicine Unit, 1989; served as rsch. toxicologist med. labs. U.S. Army, Edgewood Arsenal, Md., 1971-74; chief clin. investigations William Beaumont Med. Ctr., El Paso, Tex., 1974-77; toxicologist Bur. of Foods FDA, Washington, 1977-82; spl. asst. to dir. divsn. toxicol. rsch. Ctr. for Food Safety & Applied Nutrition, Washington, 1982—. Jewish. Home: 12900 Fork Rd Baldwin MD 21013-9345 Office: CFSAN/FDA 200 C St SW Washington DC 20204-0001

SASS, RONALD LEWIS, biology and chemistry educator; b. Davenport, Iowa, May 26, 1932; s. Erwin Leese and Flora Alice (Puck) S.; m. Joyce R. Moorhead, 1951 (div. 1968); children: Dennise, Andria; m. Margaret Lee Macy, Apr. 4, 1969; children: Hartley, Dennis. BA, Augustana Coll., Rock Island, Ill., 1954; PhD, U. So. Calif., L.A., 1957. Chemist U.S. Army, Rock Island (Ill.) Arsenal, 1951-54; asst. prof. Rice U., Houston, 1958-62, assoc. prof., 1962-66, prof., 1966—, chmn. biology, 1981-87; co-dir. Rice Ctr. for Edn., Houston, 1988—; chair Rice Earth Sys. Inst., Houston, 1990—, Ecology and Evolutionary Biology, 1995—; cons. EPA, Washington, 1990—, Coll. Bd., N.Y.C., 1988—. Contbr. articles on chemistry, biology and biochemistry to profl. jours. NSF predoctoral fellow U. So. Calif., 1954-57, fellow AEC, 1957-58, Guggenheim fellow, 1965, sr. rsch. fellow NRC, 1988. Mem. Internat. Geospher-Biosphere Program (com. chair 1990—). Avocations: tennis, fishing. Home: 2406 Wordsworth St Houston TX 77030-1834 Office: Rice U Ecology & Evolutionary Biology Houston TX 77251

SASSEEN, ROBERT FRANCIS, university educator; b. Bklyn., June 6, 1932; s. Robert B. and Teresa M. (Regan) S.; divorced; children: Robert V., Christopher J., Patricia M., Timothy P., Katherine A. BA in Polit. Sci, U. Notre Dame, Ill., 1957; MA, U. Chgo., 1959, PhD, 1961. Instr. polit. sci. Marquette U., Milw., 1960-62; asst. prof. honors div. U. Santa Clara, Calif., 1962-65; from lectr. to prof. polit. sci. San Jose (Calif.) State U., 1965-72, chmn. dept., 1971-72, assoc. acad. v.p., dean faculty, 1972-81; pres. U. Dallas, 1981-96. Author articles in field. With AUS, 1951-54. Roman Catholic. Office: U Dallas Dept Politics 1845 E Northgate Dr Irving TX 75062-4736

SASSER, ELLIS A., gifted and talented education educator; b. Norfolk, Va., June 14, 1946; d. Haywood Ellis and Jessie (Johnson) S.; m. R. Wayne Kitsteiner, June 11, 1983. BA, Emory and Henry Coll., 1968; MA, Va. Commonwealth U., 1976; cert. creative problem solving, Ctr. for Creative Learning, Honeoye, N.Y., 1990, cert. advanced creative problem solving, 1990. Primary tchr. Henrico County Pub. Schs., Richmond, Va., 1968-76; tchr. gifted Henrico County Pub. Schs., Richmond, 1976—; tchr. humanities Three Chopt Gifted Ctr. Henrico County Pub. Schs.; gifted adv. bd. Henrico County Programs for the Gifted, Richmond, 1990—. Recipient R.E.B. award for teaching excellence Greater Richmond Community Found., 1989. Mem. AAUW, NEA, Va. Edn. Assn., Henrico Edn. Assn., Coun. for Exceptional Children, Va. Assn. for Gifted Edn., Va. Hist. Soc., Richmond Area Friends of the Gifted, Richmond Symphony Chorus, 1973-94, West of the Blvd. Civic Assn., Delta Kappa Gamma Soc. Internat. (pres. Gamma Chi chpt. 1994-96). Avocations: travel, drawing and painting, reading, photography. Home: 3223 Floyd Ave Richmond VA 23221-2903 Office: Henrico County Pub Schs Three Chopt Elem Sch 1600 Skipwith Rd Richmond VA 23229-5205

SASSER, JAMES RALPH (JIM SASSER), ambassador, former senator; b. Memphis, TN, Sept. 30, 1936; s. Joseph Ralph and Mary Nell (Gray) S.; m. Mary Gorman, Aug. 18, 1962; children: Gray, Elizabeth. Student, U. Tenn., 1954-55; BA, Vanderbilt U., 1958, LLB, 1961. Bar: Tenn. 1961. Ptnr. Goodpasture, Carpenter, Woods & Sasser, Nashville, 1961-76; chmn. Tenn. Dem. Party, 1973-76; mem. U.S. Senate from Tenn., 1977-1994; U.S. Ambassador to China U.S. State Dept., Beijing, China, 1996—. Chmn. Tenn. State Dem. Exec. Com., 1973-76; so. vice chmn. Assn. Dem. State Chmn., 1975-76. Served with USMCR, 1958-65. Mem. ABA, NCCJ (dir. Nashville chpt.), UN Assn., Nashville Com. Fgn. Relations, Am. Judicature Soc. Office: American Embassy Psc 461 Box 50 FPO AP 96521-0050*

SASSER, WILLIAM JACK, retired federal agency administrator, consultant; b. Arcadia, Okla., Aug. 12, 1934; children: Sam, Steve, Susan, Sandra. BS in Sociology and Psychology, Okla. Bapt. U., 1956; postgrad., S.W. Bapt. Sem., 1957-60, George Washington U., 1966. Lic. comml. pilot with instrument rating. Air traffic control specialist S.W. region FAA Air Route Traffic Control Ctr., Ft. Worth, 1963-65, pers. officer, 1970-71; tech. intern FAA, Washington, 1965-66; employee devel. officer S.W. region FAA, Houston and Ft. Worth, 1966-70; chief tng. br. pers. div. Gt. Lakes region FAA, Des Plaines, Ill., 1971-73; with exec. devel. program Gt. Lakes and ctrl. regions FAA, Des Plaines, Kansas City, Mo., 1973-75; asst. chief airports div. ctrl. region FAA, Kansas City, 1975-76, mgr., 1977-87; mgr. airports div. S.W. region FAA, Ft. Worth, 1987-89, dep. regional adminstr. S.W. region, 1989-95; ret. S.W. region, 1995; pvt. cons., 1995—. Home: PO Box 162595 Fort Worth TX 76161

SASSOON, JANET, ballerina, educator; b. Sorabaya, Indonesia, Sept. 2, 1936; came to U.S., 1937; d. Edward and Flora (Bar) S.; m. John Roland Upton Jr., Aug. 7, 1983. Began training with Christensen brothers, Ruby Asquith, and Gisella Caccialanza, San Francisco; Studied with Leo Staats, Lubov Egorova, Olga Preobrajenska, Mathilde Kshessinskaya, Paris, 1951. Dancer Grand Ballet du Marquis de Cuevas, Paris, 1952-55, Chgo., Utah and San Francisco Ballets, 1955; prima ballerina Berlin Ballet, 1956; dir. Acad. of Ballet, San Francisco, 1974-89, assoc. dir., 1989—; condr. master classes in ballet, movement therapy for numerous profl. dancers including Natalia Makarova; vitacullurist, v.p. Three Palms Vineyard, Napa Valley. Avocations: cooking, gardening, writing. Country Home: 1112 Pine St Calislaga CA 94515

SASTRY, KEDARNATH NANJUND, microbiologist, educator; b. Mysore, Karnataka, India, Apr. 28, 1955; came to U.S., 1986; s. N. Nanjund and N. Ratnamma (Rao) S.; m. T.S. Rajeswari, Feb. 16, 1987; 1 child, Omkar Kedarnath. BSc in Biology, U. Mysore, 1973, MSc in Microbiology, 1976; PhD in Microbiology, U. Pune, India, 1984. Rsch. asst. Nat. Inst. Virology, Pune, 1978-81, asst. rsch. officer, 1981-86; asst. prof. pathology and lab. medicine Boston U., 1990—; lectr. in field. Contbr. abstracts and articles to profl. jours. Fellow Indian Coun. Med. Rsch., 1977-78, Children's Hosp., 1986-90. Mem. AAAS. Avocations: reading, chess. Office: Boston U 80 E Concord St Rm S301 Boston MA 02118-2307

SATA, LINDBERGH SABURO, psychiatrist, physician, educator; b. Portland, Oreg., Jan. 6, 1928; s. Charles Kazuo and Ito (Kojima) S.; m. Yuriko Kodama, Aug. 19, 1956; children: Roberta, Camille, Holly, John. BS, U. Utah, 1951, MD, 1958, MS, 1964. Intern U. Utah Coll. Medicine, Salt Lake Gen. Hosp., 1958-59, resident in psychiatry, 1959-62, chief resident in psychiatry, 1961-62; adminstrv. chief resident neurology U. Utah Coll. Medicine, VA Hosp., Salt Lake City, 1960-61; fellow Inst. for Mental Retardation, Letchworth Village, Thiells, N.Y., 1962; intern Behavioral Sci. Intern Program Nat. Tng. Labs., Bethel, Maine, 1966; instr. U. Utah, 1962-64; asst. prof. The Psychiat. Inst. U. Md., Balt., 1964-67, assoc. prof., 1967-68; assoc. prof. U. Wash., Seattle, 1968-77, asst. dean, 1969-70, prof., 1977-78; prof., chmn. St. Louis U. Sch. Medicine, 1978-94, prof. emeritus, chmn. emeritus, 1994—. Fellow Am. Coll. Psychiatrists, Am. Psychiat. Assn., Pacific Rim Coll. Psychiatrists (founding); mem. Am. Assn. for Social Psychiatry. Office: 1606 Riverview Dr NE Auburn WA 98002-3054

SATCHER, DAVID, public health service officer, federal official; b. Anniston, Ala., Mar. 2, 1941; s. Wilmer and Anna S; m. Nola; children: Gretchen, David, Daraka, Daryl. BS, Morehouse Coll., 1963; MD, PhD, Case Western Reserve Univ., 1970. Faculty mem. Sch. Medicine UCLA; faculty mem., chair dept. family medicine King-Drew Med. Ctr., interim dean, 1977-79; dir. King-Drew Sickle Cell Rsch. Ctr.; prof., chmn. dept. cmty. and family medicine Morehouse Sch. Medicine, Atlanta; pres. Meharry Med. Coll., Nashville, 1982-93; dir. Ctrs. for Disease Control and Prevention, Atlanta, 1993—; adminstr. Agy. for Toxic Substances and Disease Registry, 1993—; apptd. mem. Coun. of Grad. Med. Edn., 1986, also chair. Recipient Watts Grassroots award for Cmty. Leadership, 1978, Nat. Conf. Christians and Jews awards, 1985, Nashvillian of Yr. award, 1992, Ebony Mag. Black Achivement award, 1994, Brewslow award in Pub. Health, 1995, Dr. Nathan B. Davis award AMA, 1996. Mem. Inst. Medicine NAS, Phi Beta Kappa, Alpha Omega Alpha. Office: Ctr Disease Control & Prevention 1600 Clifton Rd NE Bldg 16 Atlanta GA 30329-4018

SATCHLER, GEORGE RAYMOND, physicist; b. London, June 14, 1926; came to U.S., 1959; s. George Cecil and Georgina Lillie (Strange) S.; m. Margaret Patricia Gibson, Mar. 27, 1948; children: Patricia Ann, Jacqueline Helen. BA, Oxford U., 1951, MA, 1951, D Phil., 1955, DSc, 1989. Research fellow Clarendon Lab., Oxford U., 1954-59, 71; research assoc. physics dept. U. Mich., 1956-57; physicist Oak Ridge Nat. Lab., 1959-94, assoc. dir. physics div., 1967-74, theoretical physics dir., 1974-76, distinguished research staff mem., 1976-94; rsch. prof. U. Tenn., 1994—. Author: (with D.M. Brink) Angular Momentum, 1962, Introduction to Nuclear Reactions, 1980, Direct Nuclear Reactions, 1983; contbr. research articles to profl. jours. Served with RAF, 1944-48. Corp. rsch. fellow, 1976-94. Fellow Am. Phys. Soc. (mem. exec. com. nuclear physics div. 1974-75, T.W. Bonner prize 1977). Home: 973 W Outer Dr Oak Ridge TN 37830-8608

SATEREN, TERRY, theater technical production; b. Madison, Wis., Dec. 5, 1943; s. Leland Bernhard and Eldora (Johnson) S. BA, Augsburg Coll., 1968. Tech. prodn. dir. Guthrie Theatre, Mpls., 1974-78, dir. prodn., 1985-87; dir. exhibits Sci. Mus. Minn., St. Paul, 1978-85; tech. prodn. dir. Seattle Repertory Theatre, 1987—; cons. acad. and community theaters and museums, 1974—, U. Minn., 1992; Master class lectr. U. Wash., Seattle, 1989-91; adj. prof. U. Wash., 1991-92. Designer: (operas) Three Penny Opera, 1972, Newest Opera in the World, 1972, Don Giovanni, 1973; commd. sculptor numerous inds., chs. and acad. instns., 1966—. Pres.'s scholar Valparaiso (Ind.) U., 1967. Mem. U.S. Inst. Theatre Tech. Avocations: scuba diving, mountain climbing, travel, museums. Home: 7341 23rd Ave NW Seattle WA 98117-5661 Office: Seattle Repertory Theatre 155 Mercer St Seattle WA 98109-4639

SATHE, SHARAD SOMNATH, chemical company executive; b. Bombay, Oct. 10, 1940; came to U.S., 1967; s. Somnath Waman and Kamala S. (Bhave) S. m. Usha Moreshwar Tamhankar, Feb. 6, 1966; children: Vandana, Swapna. BS, U. Bombay, 1960; B in Pharmacy, Banaras Hindu U., 1963; PhD, Ind. U., 1971. Rsch. asst. CIBA Rsch. Ctr., Bombay, 1964-67; postdoctoral fellow Rsch. Triangle Inst., Raleigh, N.C., 1971-73; rsch. chemist Mallinckrodt, Inc., St. Louis, 197-379, tech. supr., 1979-81, group leader, 1981-87, mgr. R & D, 1989-94; assoc. dir. rsch., 1995—. Patentee in field; contbr. articles to profl. jours. Pres. India Student Assn., Bloomington, Ind., 1969-70; mem. bd. of trustees India Assn. of St. Louis, 1980-85; pres. Sangeetha, St. Louis, 1986-87. Fellow Am. Inst. Chemistry, N.Y. Acad. Scis.; mem. Am. Chem. Soc. Avocations: music, tennis, reading. Office: Mallinckrodt Inc 2nd & Mallinckrodt St Saint Louis MO 63147

SATHER, EVERETT NORMAN, accountant; b. Story City, Iowa, July 20, 1935; s. George John and Laura Josephine (Bakka) S.; m. Patricia Ann Johnson, Apr. 24, 1955; children: Kimberly L., Kristine J., Kendall D. Student, Am. Inst. Bus., Des Moines, 1953-55. CPA, Iowa, Nebr., Ill. Office mgr. Story Polk Farm Svc., Nevada, Iowa, 1955-57; office mgr., bookeeper Capital City Electric Co., Des Moines, 1958-59; staff acct. Willard C. Randol, CPA, Des Moines, 1959-60, Ryun, Givens and Co., Des Moines, 1960-63; acct. Everett N. Sather, CPA, Des Moines, 1963-66; acct., ptnr. Denman and Co., Des Moines, 1966—; pres., chmn. Ankeny (Iowa) Nat. Bank, 1972-82; pres. Triple K Ltd., Ankeny, 1983—, Boone (Iowa) Speedways, Inc., 1976-96. Active Polk County Bd. Rev., Des Moines, 1970—; chmn. bd. Greater Des Moines Aviation Expo, 1989-96; treas. Des Moines Grand Prix, 1988-94; bd. dirs. Care Initiatives, 1993—. Mem. AICPA, Ill. Soc. CPAs, Iowa Soc. CPAs, Rotary (bd. dirs. 1990-93, pres. 1994-95), Zagszig Shrine, Scottish Rite, MAsons. Lutheran. Avocation: sports. Office: Denman and Co 1601 22nd St Ste 400 West Des Moines IA 50266-1408

SATHER, GLEN CAMERON, professional hockey team executive, coach; b. High River, Alta., Canada, Sept. 2, 1943. Former professional hockey player; pres., gen. mgr. Edmonton Oilers, Nat. Hockey League, Alta., Can., coach, 1977-89, now alt. gov.; coach winning team in Stanley Cup competition, 1987. Recipient Jack Adams Award for NHL Coach of the Yr., 1986. Office: care Edmonton Oilers, 11230 110th St 2nd Flr, Edmonton, AB Canada T5G 3G8*

SATHRE, LEROY, mathematics educator, consultant; b. Cleve., June 4, 1936; s. Louis and Hazel Irene (Pletcher) S.; m. B. Ann Sathre, May 30, 1968 (div. May 1983); m. Winona Sechrist, Aug. 30, 1984. BA, DePauw U., 1958; MS, U. Fla., 1960; postgrad., U. Calif., Santa Barbara, 1963-65. Reliability engr. N.Am. Aviation, Downey, Calif., 1960-62; statistician Gen. Electric Co., Daytona Beach, Fla., 1965-67; instr. St. Johns River Jr. Coll., Palatka, Fla., 1968-70; prof. Valencia C.C., Orlando, Fla., 1970-94, dept. chmn., 1994—; pres. faculty senate Valencia City Coll., 1974-75; sec., treas. United Community Coll. Faculty of Fla., Tallahassee, 1976-80; textbook reviewer various pubs. Mem. Math. Assn. Am., Fla. Math. Assn. of Two Yr. Colls., Am. Math. Assn. Two Yr. Colls. Democrat. Methodist. Office: Valencia Community Coll 701 N Econlockhatchee Trl Orlando FL 32825-6404

SATHYAMOORTHY, MUTHUKRISHNAN, engineering researcher, educator; b. Sathanur, Tamil Nadu, India, Feb. 21, 1946; s. Kuppusamy and Visalakshi Muthukrishnan; m. Chitra Subbiah, May 26, 1971; children: Mohanakrishnan, Kumaran. B in Civil Engring., U. Madras, India, 1967; M in Engring. Mechanics, Indian Inst. of Tech., Madras, India, 1969, PhD in Aero. Engring., 1973. Lectr. Indian Inst. of Tech., Madras, India, 1969-74; rsch. fellow U. Birmingham, Eng., 1974-76; asst. prof. Clarkson U., Potsdam, N.Y., 1979-82, assoc. prof., 1982-92, assoc. prof., exec. officer, 1992-94, prof., exec. officer, 1994-97, prof., chair, 1997—; vis. rsch. faculty U. Calgary, Can., 1977-79. Contbn. author: Handbook of Civil Engineering Practice, 1988; editor: Material Nonlinearity in Vibrations, 1985; author: Nonlinear Analysis of Structures, 1997. Recipient Appreciation cert. U.S. Army, 1990, Outstanding Advisor award Clarkson U., 1993, Tau Beta Pi Faculty award, 1997. Fellow ASME (mem. nat. student sect. com. 1992-94, mem. gen. awards com. 1994—, Nat. Faculty Advisor award 1993); AIAA (assoc.), Aero. Soc. India. Avocations: overseas travel, camping, photography, fishing. Home: 177 Regan Rd Potsdam NY 13676 Office: Clarkson U Dept Mech & Aeronautical Engr Mech Engring Dept Potsdam NY 13699-5725

SATIN, JOSEPH, language professional, university administrator; b. Phila., Dec. 16, 1920; s. Reuben Philip and Harriet (Price) S.; m. Selma Rosen (dec. 1978); children: Mark, Diane; m. Barbara Jeanne Dodson (dec. 1987); m. Terrye Sagan, 1992. BA, Temple U., 1946; AM, Columbia U., 1948, PhD, 1952. Instr. integrated studies W.Va. U., Morgantown, 1952-54; prof. English and Comparative Lit. Moorhead (Minn.) State U., 1954-63; chmn. dept. English and Journalism Midwestern U., Wichita Falls, Tex., 1963-73; dean Sch. Arts and Humanities Calif. State U., Fresno, 1973-89; mgr. concert series Moorhead State U., 1956-61; mem. nat. bd. cons. NEH, Washington, 1979—; dir. London semester Calif. State U., Fresno, 1982-92, dir. Frank Lloyd Wright Auditorium project. Author: Ideas in Context, 1958, The 1950's: America's "Placid" Decade, 1960, Reading Non-Fiction Prose, 1964, Reading Prose Fiction, 1964, Reading Drama, 1964, Reading Poetry, 1964, Shakespeare and His Sources, 1966, Reading Literature, 1968, The Humanities Handbook (2 Vols.), 1969; editor: Frank Lloyd Wright-Letters to Apprentices, 1982, Letters to Architects, 1984, Letters to Clients, 1986, Treasures of Taliesin, 1985, The Guggenheim Correspondence, 1986, Frank Lloyd Wright: His Living Voice, 1987, Frank Lloyd Wright, The Crowning Decade, 1989; translator: Federico Fellini, Comments on Film, 1987; contbr. to Ency. Internat. Edn., 1978; dir. Univ. Press, Calif. State U., 1982-92. Served with U.S. Army, 1943-46, ETO. Jewish. Avocations: creative writing, music, parcheesi. Home: 65 Maywood Dr San Francisco CA 94127-2007

SATINE, BARRY ROY, lawyer; b. N.Y.C., July 25, 1951; s. Norman S. and Fay (Mekles) S.; m. Janice Bea Halfond, Aug. 4, 1974; children: David, Leah. B.A., CCNY, 1972; J.D., George Washington U., 1975. Bar: N.Y. 1976, D.C. 1977, U.S. Dist. Ct. (so. dist.) N.Y. 1978, U.S. Supreme Ct. 1979, U.S. Dist. Ct. (ea. dist.) N.Y. 1982, U.S. Ct. Appeals (2d cir.) 1989. Trial atty. U.S. Civil Service Commn., Washington, 1975-78; atty. AT&T, N.Y.C., 1978-81, N.Y. Tel. Co., N.Y.C., 1981-82; mem. assoc. Surrey & Morse, N.Y.C., 1982-84, ptnr., 1985; ptnr. Jones, Day, Reavis & Pogue, 1986—. Mem. Assn. of Bar of City of N.Y. (litigation com.). Office: Jones Day Reavis & Pogue 599 Lexington Ave New York NY 10022-6030

SATINOVER, JEFFREY B., psychiatrist, health science facility administrator, lecturer, author; b. Chgo., Sept. 4, 1947; s. Joseph and Sena (Rotman) S.; m. Julie Rachel Leff, June 10, 1982; Sarah Katherine, Anne-Rebecca, Jenny Leigh. BS, MIT, 1971; EdM, Harvard U., 1973; MD, U. Tex., 1982; Diplomate, C.G Jung Institute, Zurich, Switzerland, 1976. Diplomate Am. Bd. Psychiatry and Neurology, added qualifications in geriatric psychiatry. Fellow dept. psychiatry and child psychiatry Yale U., New Haven, 1982-86; founder, exec. dir. Sterling Inst., Stamford, Conn., 1985-92; med. dir. Temenos Inst., Westport, Conn., 1984—; pvt. practice, Westport, 1992—; pres., bd. dirs. C.G. Jung Found. N.Y., 1988-92; bd. dirs., mem. catchment area coun. S.W. Regional Mental Health Bd., 1988-92; William James lectr. psychology and religion Harvard U., 1975; mem. Lower Fairfield County Regional Action Coun. Against Substance Abuse, 1990-92. Author: Homosexuality and the Politics of Truth, 1994, The Empty Self: Gnostic Foundations of Modern Identity, 1994, Feathers of the Skylark, 1996; contbg. author: Jungian Psychotherapy, 1984, Science and the Fragile Self, 1990, Jungian Analysis, 1993, Cracking the Bible Code, 1997; contbr. articles to profl. and pub. policy jours. Founder, mem. exec. bd. com. Save Our Schs., 1994—; bd. dirs. Towrd Tradition; bd. advisors Family Inst. Conn., 1996—; active nat. physician's resource coun. Focus on Family, 1994-97; bd. dirs. Klingberg Family Ctrs., 1994-96. Capt. USAR N.G., 1989-94; maj. USAR, 1995—. Recipient Seymour Lustman Residency Rsch. 2d place award Yale U. psychology dept., 1983, 85. Mem. Am. Psychiat. Assn. (Burroughs-Wellcome fellow 1983-85), Internat. Assn. Analytical Psychology, Aspetuck Valley Country Club, Alpha Omega Alpha. Republican. Jewish. Avocations: tennis, harpsichord, jazz keyboard. Home: 38 Steep Hill Rd Weston CT 06883-1822 Office: 29 E Main St Westport CT 06880-3749

SATINSKAS, HENRY ANTHONY, airline services company executive; b. Kaunas, Lithuania, Dec. 22, 1936; came to U.S., 1949; s. Henry Francis and Donna (Olechnavicius) S.; m. Lucia Aldona Sestakauskas, Dec. 7, 1963; children: Henry Arnold, Paul Steven (dec.), Laura Monica. Student, Drexel U., 1957-60; BS in Bus. Adminstrn., Temple U., 1963. Mgmt. trainee Pub. Service Coordinated Transp., Maplewood, N.J., 1964; asst. garage supr. Jersey City, 1965-66; charter service mgr. Suburban Transit Corp., New Brunswick, N.J., 1966-68; gen. mgr. Ave B and E Byway Transit Co., N.Y.C., 1968-71, St. John's (Newfoundland, Can.) Transp. Commn., 1971-73; asst. dir. transp. planning Montgomery County Govt., Rockville, Md., 1973-76; gen. mgr. Airway Limousine Service subs. Hudson Gen. Corp., Balt., 1976-78; dir. transp. services Airway Services subs. Hudson Gen. Corp., Jamaica, N.Y., 1978-81; v.p. Hudson Gen. Corp., Great Neck, N.Y., 1981—. Mem. adv. coun. on edn. Province of Newfoundland and Labrador, St. John's, 1972; bd. dirs. Greater Jamaica Devel. Corp., 1987-90. Republican. Roman Catholic. Avocations: reading, gardening, travel, biking. Home: 35 Woodvale Dr Syosset NY 11791-1213 Office: Hudson Gen Corp 111 Great Neck Rd Great Neck NY 11021-5402

SATINSKY, BARNETT, lawyer; b. Phila., June 17, 1947; s. Alex and Florence (Talsky) S.; m. Fredda Andrea Wagner, June 17, 1973; children: Meagen, Sara Beth, Jonathan. AB, Brown U., 1969; JD, Villanova U., 1972. Bar: Pa. 1972, U.S. Dist. Ct. (ea. dist) Pa. 1975, U.S. Dist. Ct. (mid. dist.) Pa. 1975, U.S. Ct. Appeals (3d cir.) 1981. Law clk. Phila. Ct. Common Pleas, 1972-73; dep. atty. gen. Pa. Dept. Justice, Harrisburg, 1973-75; 1st asst. counsel Pa. Pub. Utility Commn., Harrisburg, 1975-77, chief counsel, 1977; assoc. Fox, Rothschild, O'Brien & Frankel, LLP, Phila., 1978-81; ptnr. Fox, Rothschild, O'Brien & Frankel, Phila., 1981—. Children Svcs. Rev. com., United Way Southeast Pa., 1984-86; bd. dirs. ACLU, Harrisburg, 1973-74, Voyage House, Inc., 1994-96. Mem. ABA (pub. utility, labor and employment law sects., employee benefits com. 1984—), Pa. Bar Assn. (labor rels., pub. utility law sects. 1980—, pub. utility law com., governing coun. 1991-93), Phila. Bar Assn. (labor law pub. utility law coms. 1980—, chmn. pub. utility law com. 1988-91), Nat. Assn. Coll. and Univ. Attys., Nat. Assn. Regulatory Commrs. (staff subcom. law 1977), Soc. for Human Resource Mgmt., Tau Epsilon Law Soc. Democrat. Jewish. Office: Fox Rothschild O'Brien & Frankel 2000 Market St Philadelphia PA 19103-3231

SATO, EUNICE NODA, former mayor, consultant; b. Livingston, Calif., June 8, 1921; d. Bunsaku and Sawa (Maeda) Noda; m. Thomas Takashi Sato, Dec. 9, 1950; children—Charlotte Patricia, Daniel Ryuichi and Douglas Ryuji (twins). AA, Modesto Jr. Coll., 1941; BA, U. No. Colo., 1944; MA, Columbia U., 1948. Public sch. tchr. Mastodon Twp. Schs., Alpha, Mich., 1944-47; ednl. missionary Reformed Ch. Am., Yokohama, Japan, 1948-51; coun. mem. City of Long Beach, Calif., 1975-86; mayor, 1980-82; sec. corp. bd. Los Angeles County Health Systems Agy., 1978-79. Monthly contbr. articles to 2 neighborhood papers, 1975-86. Bd. dirs. Long Beach chpt. ARC, 1975—, mem. exec. com., 1978-91, 93—, past pres. and v.p., mem. Calif. state svc. coun., A.R.C., 1995—; bd. dirs. Goodwill Industries, 1978-82 ; trustee St. Mary's Bauer Med. Ctr., 1977—; pres. Industry Edn. Coun., Long Beach, 1984-86, mem. exec. bd., 1984—; bd. dirs. Industry Edn. Coun. of Calif.; treas. So. Calif. Consortium of I.E.C., 1984-86, pres., 1988-89; mem. State Adv. Group on Juvenile Justice and Delinquency Prevention, 1983-91, Calif. Coun. Criminal Justice, 1983-95, legis. com. Girl Scout coun. Calif., 1986-92, chair, 1991-92; bd. dirs. Long Beach council Girl Scouts U.S., 1986-92, Region III United Way, 1974-88; mem. Asian Pacific adv. com. Calif. Dept. Rehab., 1985-87, recreation commn. City of Long Beach, 1985-86, pub. safety policy com. League Calif. Cities, 1981-86, community econ. and housing devel. com. So. Calif. Assn. Govts., 1976-86, Calif. Task Force to Promote Self-Esteem and Personal and Social Responsibility, 1987-90; Long Beach chpt. pres. NCCJ, 1987-88; pres. Internat. Community Coun., 1986-87, Japanese Am. Reps., 1987, 88; presdl. appointee Nat. Adv. Coun. Ednl. Rsch. and Improvement, 1991-94; pres. Aux. to Sch. Theology, Claremont, 1990-91, exec. bd. 1989-91; chair selection com. Leadership Long Beach, 1990-91, sec. exec. bd., 1991-92; chair adv. bd. AIESEC, 1990-92, Long Beach Area Rep. Party, 1990-92; asst. sec. cen. com., L.A, 1990-92; sec.-gen. coun. on fin. and administrn. United Meth. Ch., 1992—; appointed by Gov. to commn. on teacher credentialing State Calif., 1994; chair adminstrv. bd. Leisure World Cmty. Ch., 1996; rep. to South Coast Ecumenical Coun., 1993—. Recipient Outstanding Svc. award Long Beach Coord. Coun., 1969, Mother of Yr. award Silverado United Meth. Ch., 1973, Hon. Svc. award Calif. PTA, 1963, Continuing Svc. award, 1974, hon. life membership award Nat. PTA, 1974, Outstanding Laywoman of Yr. award Long Beach Area Coun. Chs., 1976, Woman of Yr. award State Women's Coun.-C. of C., 1979, Long Beach Iternat. Bus. and Profl. Women's Club, Nat. Merit award DAR, 1982, Citizen of Yr. award Los Altos YMCA, 1982, Calif. Cmty. Pool for Handicapped, 1982, Outstanding Citizen award Torch Club of Long Beach, 1983, W. Odie Wright award Industry Edn. Coun., 1990, Humanitarian award NCCJ, 1992, Vol. of Yr. award ARC, 1st Life Membership award Long Beach chpt. UN Assn., Kunsho award of Order of the Sacred Treasure, Gold Rays with rosette from Japanese Govt., 1996. Mem. Alpha Iota (hon.). Republican. Methodist. Home: Bixby Village 551-101 Pittsfield Ct Long Beach CA 90803-2024

SATO, GLENN KENJI, lawyer; b. Honolulu, Jan. 6, 1952; s. Nihei and Katherine (Miwa) S.; m. Donna Mae Shiroma, Apr. 4, 1980 (div. Aug. 1985); m. Nan Sun Oh, Mar. 27, 1987; children: Gavan, Allison, Garrett. BBA, U. Hawaii, 1975; JD, U. Calif., San Francisco, 1977. Bar: Hawaii 1978, U.S. Dist. Ct. Hawaii, 1978, U.S. Ct. Claims 1990. Assoc. Fujiyama, Duffy & Fujiyama, Honolulu, 1978-80, 83-87, ptnr., 1987-95; stockholder Law Offices of Glenn K. Sato, Honolulu, 1980-82; pres. ISL Svcs., Inc., Honolulu, 1983; ptnr. Sato & Thomas, Honolulu, 1995—; vice chmn. Pattern Jury Instrn. Com., State of Hawaii, Honolulu, 1993. Treas. Polit. Action Com., Honolulu, 1993. Mem. Beta Gamma Sigma. Avocations: golf, hunting, target shooting, surfing. Office: Sato & Thomas 1001 Bishop St Ste 770 Honolulu HI 96813-3429

SATO, HIROSHI, materials science educator; b. Matsuzaka, Mie, Japan, Aug. 31, 1918; came to U.S., 1954; s. Masayoshi and Fusae (Ohhara) S.; m. Kyoko Amemiya, Jan. 10, 1947; children: Norie M., Nobuyuki Albert, Erika Michiko. BS, Hokkaido Imperial U., Sapporo, Japan, 1938, MS, 1941; DSc, Tokyo U., 1951. Rsch. assoc. faculty sci. Hokkaido Imperial U., Sapporo, 1941-42, asst. prof. Inst. Low Temperature Sci., 1942-43; rsch. physicist Inst. Phys. and Chem. Rsch., Tokyo, 1943-45; prof. Tohoku Imperial U., Sendai, Japan, 1945-57; rsch. physicist Westinghouse Rsch. Labs., Pitts., 1954-56; prin. scientist Sci. Lab., Ford Motor Co., Dearborn, Mich., 1956-74; prof. materials engring. Purdue U., West Lafayette, Ind., 1974-89, Ross Disting. prof. engring., 1984-89, Ross Disting. prof. emeritus engring., 1989—; affiliate prof. dept. materials sci. U. Washington, Seattle, 1986-89; collaborator Los Alamos (N.Mex.) Nat. Lab., 1989—; vis. prof. U. Grenoble, France, 1967, Tokyo Inst. Tech., 1979, Tech. U. Hannover, Fed. Republic Germany, 1980-81; cons. Oak Ridge (Tenn.) Nat. Lab., 1978, 80. Contbr. over 260 articles to profl. jours., chpts. to books. Recipient U.S. Sr. Scientist award Alexander von Humboldt Found., 1980; fellow John Simon Guggenheim Meml. Found., 1966, Japan Soc. for Promotion Sci., 1979. Fellow Am. Phys. Soc.; mem. Japan Phys. Soc., Am. Ceramic Soc., Metall. Soc.-AIME, Japan Inst. Metals (hon. 1985—, Prize of Merit 1951). Office: Purdue U Sch Materials Engring 1289 Master Dr Lafayette IN 47905-8780

SATO, KAZUYOSHI, pathologist; b. Shibata, Niigata, Japan, Apr. 3, 1930; came to U.S., 1968; s. Katsueita and Kyo (Sakagawa) S.; m. Ann Marie Farrenkopf, July 5, 1964 (dec. Aug. 1983); children: P.T. Sachiko, P. Miyoko, Michael T., Phillip K. Student, Niigata U., Japan, 1954, MD, 1958. Diplomate Am. Bd. Pathology, Anatomic and Clin. Pathology. Intern USAF Hosp., Tachikawa, Japan, 1958-59; intern Ellis Hosp., Schenectady, N.Y., 1959-60, asst. resident in pathology, 1960-61; resident in pathology Free Hosp. for Women, Brookline, Mass., 1961-62; resident in pathology The Children's Hosp. Med. Ctr., Boston, 1962-63, resident in neuropathology, 1963-64; resident fellow in pathology Mayo Grad. Sch. Medicine, Rochester, Minn., 1968-70; dir. labs. Falmouth (Mass.) Hosp., 1972-96; dir. Falmouth Hosp. Service Lab., Sandwich, Mass., 1986-93; pathologist and rsch. assoc. Atomic Bomb Casualty Commn., Nagasaki, Japan, 1964-68; pathologist, chief of pathology USPHS Hosp., Norfolk Va., 1970-72, Falmouth (Mass.) Hosp., 1972—. Recipient Fulbright scholarship, 1959. Fellow Coll. Am. Pathologists, Am. Soc. Clin. Pathologists; mem. Assn. Mil. Surgeons U.S. Home: 88 Two Ponds Rd Falmouth MA 02540-2225 Office: Falmouth Hosp 100 Ter Heun Dr Falmouth MA 02540-2503

SATO, MOTOAKI, geologist, researcher; b. Tokyo, Japan, Oct. 11, 1929; came to U.S., 1955, 63.; s. Iwazo and Kyoko (Ito) S.; m. Ellen B. Levinson, Feb. 11, 1961 (div. Sept. 1978); children: Emily Coates, Alice Isomé, Thomas Bartlett. BS in Geology, U. Tokyo, Japan, 1953, MS in Geology, 1955; PhD in Geology, U. Minn., 1959. Research asst. dept. geophysics Univ. Minn., Mpls., 1956-58; rsch. fellow in geophysics dept. geol. scis. Harvard Univ., Cambridge, Mass., 1958-61; assoc. prof. geology Inst. Thermal Springs Research, Misasa, Tottori, Japan, 1961-63; research geologist U.S. Geological Survey, Washington, 1963-65; geologist, project chief U.S. Geological Survey, Washington/Reston, Va., 1965-95; scientist emeritus U.S. Geological Survey, Washington/Reston, 1995—; prin. investigator Lunar Sample & Sci. Program, NASA, 1971-80. Contbg. author books and articles in profl. jours. Fulbright/Smith-Mundt fellow Inst. Internat. Edn., 1955-57, Gilbert fellow U.S. Geol. Survey, Reston, Va., 1982-83. Mem. Am. Geophysical Union, Geochemical Soc., Geological Soc. Washington (2d v.p. 1982-83), Geochemistry Div. Am. Chem. Soc. Home: 11173 Lake Chapel Ln Reston VA 20191 Office: US Geol Survey 956 National Ctr Reston VA 20192 *Remember that we did not design the way Nature works; Nature designed us, too. So let's listen ever so carefully, with an open mind, to what Nature is trying to tell us.*

SATO, PAUL HISASHI, pharmacologist; b. Mt. Vernon, N.Y., Mar. 22, 1949; s. Yoshio and Lury (Shiogi) S.; m. Jeanne Ellen Courville, June 29, 1996. BS, Jamestown Coll., 1971; MS, NYU, 1972, PhD, 1975. Rsch. assoc. Roche Inst. Molecular Biology, Nutley, N.J., 1975-77; assoc. prof. Mich. State U., East Lansing, 1977—. Office: Mich State U Dept Pharmacology/Toxicol East Lansing MI 48824

SATO, RICHARD MICHIO, consulting engineering company executive; b. Paia, Maui, Hawaii, Dec. 30, 1934; s. Shinichi and Namie (Hanazawa) S.; m. Althea Reiko Ouye; children: Janice Muraoka, Kelvin. BSCE, U. Hawaii, 1956. Registered civil/structural engr., Calif., Hawaii, Guam. Civil and structural engr. Dalton Dalton Assocs., L.A., 1960-62; structural engr. William M. Taggart, SE, L.A., 1962-67; project coord. Office of Univ. Planning U. Hawaii, Honolulu, 1967-69; project engr. T.Y. Lin Hawaii, Honolulu, 1969; pres. Sato & Assocs., Inc. (formerly Richard M. Sato & Assoc. & Sato & Kuniyoshi, Inc.), Honolulu, 1969—. 1st lt. U.S. Army, 1957-59. Mem. Am. Concrete Inst., Prestressed Concrete Inst., Structural Engrs. Assn. Hawaii (pres. 1976), Consulting Engrs. Coun. Hawaii, Hui Kokua Kinipopo (pres. 1993—), U. Hawaii Pres.'s Club, U. Hawaii Alumni Assn., Chi Epsilon. Avocations: golf, sports fan. Office: Sato & Assocs Inc 2046 S King St Honolulu HI 96826-2219*

SATO, TADASHI, artist; b. Maui, Hawaii, Feb. 6, 1923. Student, Honolulu Sch. Art, Bklyn. Mus. Art Sch., New Sch. Soc. Rsch. One man shows include First Hawaiian Ctr., Honolulu, 1997; exhbns. include Guggenheim Mus., N.Y.C., 1954, Honolulu Acad. Arts, 1957, Pacific Heritage Exhibit, L.A., 1963, McRoberts and Tunnard Ltd., London, 1964, White House Festival Arts, Washington, 1965, Berlin Art Festival, 1967, Japanese C. of C., Honolulu, 1993-94, Maui Cmty. and Cultural Assn., 1994; represented in permanent collections Albright-Knox Art Gallery, Buffalo, Guggenheim Mus., Whitney Mus. Am. Art, N.Y.C., Honolulu Acad. Arts, U. Art Gallery, Tucson, (mosaic) Hawaii State Capitol Bldg., State Libr. Aina Haina, Oahu, State Hosp., Kea-lakekua, Hawaii, Wailulu War Meml. Gymnasium, Maui, Krannert Art Mus., Ill., U. Nebr.; executed murals Halekulani Hotel, Honolulu, (mosaic) West Maui Recreation Ctr., (oil) Bay Club, Kapalua, Maui; retrospective Hui No Eau, Makawao, Maui, 1992. Office: PO Box 476 Lahaina HI 96767-0476

SATOLA, JAMES WILLIAM, lawyer; b. Cleve., Aug. 26, 1961; s. William John and Catherine Ann (Recek) S. BS in Zoology, Ohio State U., 1984; JD, Case Western Reserve U., 1989. Bar: Ohio 1989, U.S. Dist. Ct. (no. dist.) Ohio 1990, D.C. 1991, U.S. Ct. Appeals (6th cir.) 1992, U.S. Supreme Ct. 1993. Med. rsch. asst. I U. Hosps. of Cleve., 1985-86; law clk to judge John M. Manos U.S. Dist. Ct. (no. dist.) Ohio, Cleve., 1989-91; assoc. Squire, Sanders & Dempsey, Cleve., 1991—. Articles editor Case Western Reserve Law Rev., Cleve., 1988-89. Mem. Inn of Ct. (assoc.). Republican. Avocations: art, music, golf, landscaping. Home: 2608 Dysart Rd University Ht OH 44118-4409 Office: Squire Sanders & Dempsey 4900 Key Tower 127 Public Sq Cleveland OH 44114-1216

SATO-VIACRUCIS, KIYO, nurse, inventor, entrepreneur, consultant; b. Sacramento, May 8, 1923; d. John Shinji and Mary Tomomi (Watanabe) Sato; m. Gene Viacrucis, Aug. 9, 1958 (div. May 1976); adopted children: Cia, Jon, Paul, Tanya. BS, Hillsdale Coll., 1944; M in Nursing in Grad. Studies/Pub. Health Nursing, Western Res. U., 1951. Cert. health and devel. specialist, Calif., pub. health nurse, Calif., audiologist. Nursery sch. attendant Poston (Ariz.) II Concentration Camp, 1942; staff nurse U. Hosps., Cleve., 1948; pub. health nurse Sacramento County Health Dept., 1948-50, 52-53; sch. nurse U. Oslo, 1953, Sacramento County Schs., 1954-58; presch. nurse Sacramento City Unified Sch. Dist., 1973-85; pvt. practice cons. Blackbird Vision Screening System, Sacramento, 1985—; cons., speaker Blackbird Vision Screening System, 1973—; cons. state task force Vision Screening Guidelines, 1981. Inventor Blackbird presch. vision screening method; cons. vision screening; contbr. articles to profl. jours. Served to capt. USAF, 1951-52. Recipient Excellence in Nursing award RN Mag. Found., 1983. Mem. Nat. Sch. Nurses Assn., Calif. Sch. Nurses Orgn., Japanese Am. Citizens League (pres. 1950), Am. Assn. Ret. Persons, VFW (pub. rels., post surgeon 1985—, cmty. activities 1986—, speaker's bur. Internment of Am. of Japanese Descent and the U.S. Constn.). Democrat. Avocations: writing, pottery, hula dancing, Tai Chi, grandchildren. Home: PO Box 277424 Sacramento CA 95827 Office: Blackbird Vision Screening PO Box 277424 Sacramento CA 95827-7424

SATOVSKY, ABRAHAM, lawyer; b. Detroit, Oct. 15, 1907; s. Samuel and Stella (Benenson) S.; m. Toby Nayer, Sept. 4, 1938 (dec.); children: Sheldon Baer, James Bennett. B.A., U. Mich., 1928, J.D., 1930. Bar: Mich. 1930, U.S. Supreme Ct. 1930. Assoc. William Henry Gallagher, Detroit, 1930-65; Bldg. chmn. lawyers com. United Found. and Torch Dr. Co-chmn. profl. divsn. Allied Jewish Campaign; adv. coun. United Synagogue Am.; del. Jewish Cmty. Coun. Detroit; v.p. Mosies Chetim Orgn. Detroit; bd. dirs. Detroit Svc. Group, past chmn. fgn. mission; active fund raiser Greater Miami United Jewish Appeal; mem. fund dr. com. U. Mich. Law Sch.; trustee Clover Hill Park Cemetery, 1978-81, trustee emeritus, 1982—; bd. dirs. Congregation Sharrey Zedek, Southfield, Mich., past pres., 1959-62. Recipient Sem. award Jewish Theol. Sem. Am., 1952; citation of merit Jewish Welfare Fedn., Detroit; Jerusalem award State of Israel Bond Orgn.; numerous other awards. Mem. ABA, Mich. Bar Assn., Detroit Bar Assn., Oakland County Bar, Nat. Fedn. Jewish Men's Clubs (founder, past pres., hon. life pres., Gt. Lakes regional award 1977, Ma'Asim Tovim (Good Deeds) award 1989), Am. Arbitration Assn., Jewish Hist. Soc. Mich. (mem. adv. bd.), Am. Jewish Hist. Soc., Am. Judicature Soc., Men's Club Congregation Shaarey Zodek (past pres., hon. life pres.), Standard Club, B'nai B'rith (past pres. Detroit), Hadassah (life), Phi Beta Delta (merged with Pi Lambda Phi). Home and Office: 28455 Northwestern Hwy Southfield MI 48034-1823 also: 20379 W Country Club Dr Aventura FL 33180-1629 *With a desire and willingness to improve my profession, my religious beliefs, and help the community, I have devoted a good portion of my time and efforts for those purposes. I, too, have been enriched by the association, have hopefully directed and encouraged others, and hope to continue to do so.*

SATRE, PHILIP GLEN, casino entertainment executive, lawyer; b. Palo Alto, Calif., Apr. 30, 1949; s. Selmer Kenneth and Georgia June (Sterling) S.; m. Jennifer Patricia Arnold, June 30, 1973; children: Malena Anne, Allison Neal, Jessica Lilly, Peter Sterling. BA, Stanford U., 1971; JD, U. Calif.-Davis, 1975; postgrad sr. exec. program MIT, 1982. Bar: Nev. 1975, Calif. 1976. Assoc. Vargas & Bartlett, Reno, 1975-79; v.p., gen. counsel, sec. Harrah's, Reno, 1980-83, sr. v.p., 1983-84, pres. Harrah's East, Atlantic City, 1984; pres., CEO Harrah's Hotels and Casinos, Reno, 1984-91; dir, sr. v.p. Gaming Group The Promus Cos., Inc., Memphis, 1988-91, dir., pres., COO, 1991-94, dir., pres., CEO, 1994-95; pres, CEO Harrahs Entertainment, Inc., 1995—, chmn., pres., CEO, 1997—; dir., treas. Nat. Judicial Coll., Reno. Active The Stanford Athletic Bd., 1996—. Mem. ABA, Nev. Bar Assn., Calif. Bar Assn., Order of Coif, Phi Kappa Phi, Stanford Alumni Assn. (pres. Reno chpt. 1976-77), Young Pres. Orgn., The Bus. Roundtable.

SATTER, LARRY DEAN, biochemist, scientific research administrator; b. Madelia, Minn., July 30, 1937; m. 1966; 1 child. BS, S.D. State U., 1960; MS, U. Wis., 1962, PhD in Biochemistry and Dairy Sci., 1964. Asst. prof. to assoc. prof. dairy sci. U. Wis., Madison, 1964-73, prof., 1973-81; mem. staff U.S. Dairy Forage Rsch. Ctr., U. Wis., USDA, Madison, 1981-87, dir., 1987—. Recipient Am. Feed Mfrs. award, 1977. Mem. Am. Dairy Sci. Assn., Am. Soc. Animal Sci., Am. Inst. Nutrition, Brit. Nutrition Soc. Office: U Wis USDA Dairy Forage Rsch Ctr 1925 Linden Dr W Madison WI 53706-1108*

SATTERFIELD, CHARLES NELSON, chemical engineer, educator; b. Dexter, Mo., Sept. 5, 1921; s. Charles David and Hermine (Weber) S.; m. Anne Pettingell, July 6, 1946; children—Mark Edward, Joye. B.S. cum laude, Harvard U., 1942; M.S., MIT, 1943, Sc.D., 1946. Registered profl. engr., Mass. Asst. prof. chem. engring. Mass. Inst. Tech., Cambridge, 1946-53; asso. prof. Mass. Inst. Tech., 1953-59, prof., 1959—; Lectr. indsl. chemistry Harvard, 1948-57; cons.on rocket propellants Dept. Def., 1952-60; mem. com. chem. kinetics NRC, 1960-66; chmn. ad hoc panel on abatement nitrogen oxide emissions from stationary sources Nat. Acad. Engring., 1970-72; indsl. cons. to major cos. in petroleum and chem. industries. Co-author: Thermodynamic Charts for Combustion Processes, 1949, Hydrogen Peroxide, 1955 (translated into Russian 1957), Role of Diffusion in Catalysis, 1963; author: Mass Transfer in Heterogeneous Catalysis, 1970 (translated into Russian 1976), Heterogeneous Catalysis in Practice, 1980 (translated into Russian 1984), repub. as Heterogeneous Catalysis in Industrial Practice, 1991, also more than 140 tech. papers; mem. editl. adv. bd. Indsl. and Engring. Chemistry, 1966-68, Advances in Chemistry Series, 1971-73, 82-86, Energy and Fuels, 1990—, Applied Catalysis, 1995—. Fellow Am. Acad. Arts and Scis.; mem. Am. Chem. Soc., Am. Inst. Chem. Engrs. (Wilhelm award 1980), Sigma Xi, Tau Beta Pi. Patentee in field. Home: 38 Tabor Hill Rd Lincoln MA 01773-2906 Office: Dept Chem Engring Mass Inst Tech Cambridge MA 02139

SATTERLEE, TERRY JEAN, lawyer; b. Kansas City, Mo., Aug. 28, 1948; d. Charles Woodbury and Francis Jean (Shriver) S.; m. William W. Rice, Jan. 9, 1982; children: Cassandra Jean Rice, Mary Shannon Rice. BA, Kans. U., 1970; JD, U. Mo., 1974. Bar: Mo. 1974. Lawyer Arthur Benson Assocs., Kansas City, Mo., 1974-77, Freilich & Leitner, Kansas City, 1977-78, U.S. Environ. Protection Agy., Kansas City, 1978-83; of counsel Lathrop & Norquist, Kansas City, 1985-87, ptnr., 1987—. Contbr. articles to profl. jours. Chmn. Bd. Zoning Adjustment, Kansas City, 1983-87, Mo. State Pks Adv. Bd., 1997; Kansas City Hazardous Materials com; campaign com. Jackson County Exec; steering com. COMPASS Met. Planning, Kansas City, 1990-93. Mem. Mo. Bar Assn. (chair environ. com. 1990-93), Kansas City Bar Assn. (environ. com. chmn. 1986-90), Natural Resource com., Mo. C. of C. (natural resource coun. 1990-96, bd. dirs. 1997), Kansas City C. of C. (environ. com. chmn. 1992), Women's Pub. Svc. Network. Democrat. Episcopalian. Office: Lathrop & Gage 2345 Grand Blvd Ste 2500 Kansas City MO 64108-2625

SATTERTHWAITE, CAMERON B., physics educator; b. Salem, Ohio, July 26, 1920; s. William David and Mabel (Cameron) S.; m. Helen Elizabeth Foster, Dec. 23, 1950 (div. July 31, 1979); children: Mark Cameron, Tod Foster, Tracy Lynn, Keith Alan, Craig Evan (dec.). B.A., Coll. Wooster, 1942; postgrad., Ohio State U., 1942-44; Ph.D., U. Pitts., 1951. Chemist Manhattan dist. project Monsanto Chem. Co., Dayton, Ohio, 1944-47; research chemist DuPont, Wilmington, Del., 1950-53; researcher, adv. physicist Westinghouse, Pitts., 1953-61; asso. prof. physics U. Ill., Urbana, 1961-63; prof. U. Ill., 1963-79, prof. emeritus, 1979—; prof. physics Va. Commonwealth U., Richmond, 1979-85; prof. emeritus Va. Commonwealth U., 1985—, chmn. dept. physics, 1979-82; program dir. NSF, 1975-76; field sec. Friends Com. on Nat. Legis., 1988-90. Contbr. articles to profl. jours. Sch. dir., Monroeville, Pa., 1959-61; trustee, mem. fin. com. Southeastern Univs. Research Assn., 1980-85; Democratic nominee for U.S. Congress, 1966; del. to Dem. Nat. Conv., 1968, 72. Fellow Am. Phys. Soc.; mem. Fedn. Am. Scientists (chmn. 1968). Patentee in field. Home: Unit # 1 803 S Coler Ave Urbana IL 61801-4009

SATTERTHWAITE, FRANKLIN BACHE, JR., management educator, consultant; b. Mt. Holly, N.J., Apr. 30, 1943; s. Franklin Bache and Emily Vaux (Cresson) S.; m. Antonia Mitchell, Oct. 6, 1987 (div. Oct. 1992); m. Martha Werenfels, May 21, 1994; 1 child, Peter Franklin. AB, Princeton U., 1965; M in Urban Studies, Yale U., 1968, MPhil, 1972, PhD, 1975. Sci. faculty Escola Americiana, Rio Janeiro, Brazil, 1965-66; planner Nat. Inst. Mental Health, Chevy Chase, Md., 1968-70; cons. Battelle Meml. Inst., Columbus, Ohio, 1971-72; touring squash pro W.P.S.A., N.Am., 1976-84; sr. cons. Brown Cronson Assocs., N.Y.C., 1981-87; prin. Frank Satterthwaite, N.Y.C., 1982-95, R.I., 1995—; asst. prof. Johnson & Wales U., Providence, 1993-97, assoc. prof., 1997—; cons. Cost of Living Coun., Washington, 1972-73. Author: The Three-Wall Nick and Other Angles, 1979. Lt. USPHS, 1968-70. Mem. Am. Mktg. Assn., Acad. Mgmt. Avocations: squash (World Profl. Vets. Squash Champion 1984), tennis, golf, piano, travel. Home: 81 Strathmore Rd Cranston RI 02905-3722 Office: Johnson and Wales U 8 Abbott Park Pl Providence RI 02903-3703

SATTERTHWAITE, HELEN FOSTER, retired state legislator; b. Blawnox, Pa., July 8, 1928; d. Samuel J. and Lillian (Schreiber) Foster; B.S. in Chemistry, Duquesne U., 1949; m. Cameron B. Satterthwaite, Dec. 23, 1950 (div. July 1979); children: Mark Cameron, Tod Foster, Tracy Lynn, Keith Alan, Craig Evan (dec.). Biol. technician U.S. Dept. Agr., 1967-68; research asst. Iowa State U. Coll. Agr., 1971; lab. technician U. Ill. Coll. Agr., 1968-70; rsch. chemist E.I. duPont de Nemours & Co., Wilmington, Del., 1951-53; rsch. asst. Gulf R & D, Harmarville, Pa., 1950; natural sci. lab. technician U. Ill. Coll. Vet. Medicine, 1971-74; rep. Gen. Assembly Ill., 1974-92, majority leader, 1991-92, sch. fin. task force, 1990-92, ret., 1993; chairperson House com. on higher edn., 1983-91, vice-chairperson elem. and secondary edn., 1983-91; mem. Commn. on Mental Health and Devel. Disabilities, 1975-85, mem. exec. com., 1977-85, vice chairperson, 1979-85; mem. Commn. to Visit and Examine State Instns., 1977-85, Ill. Coun. Mental Health, 1992-95, task force on global climate change, 1991-96, League Women Voters, treas. 1995—, Bus. & Profl. Women's Club, treas. 1993-94, sec. 1994-95. Bd. dirs. East Central Ill. Health Systems Agy., 1977-79, Champaign County Mental Health Ctr. 1993—, Girls Inc. 1992-96, Champaign County (Ill.) United Way, 1970-74, mem. budget com., 1973-74, mem. joint rev. com. on funding Champaign County Mental Health Programs, 1973; co-chairperson Task Force on Mental Retardation for Champaign County Mental Health Bd., 1973; mem. Ill. Developmental Disability Advocacy Authority, 1977-85, vice chmn., 1979-80; chairperson Ill. House Democratic Study Group, 1979-81; mem. Edn. Commn. of the States, 1985-92; mem. Nat. Conf. State Legis. Commn. on Labor and Edn., 1985-92. Recipient Freshman Legislator of Yr. award Ill. Edn. Assn., 1975; commendation Ill. State's Attys. Assn., 1975; Best Legislator award Ind. Votors Ill., 1976, 78, 80, 82, 84, 86, 88, 90; cert. honor Assn. Students Govts., 1977; Disting. Service cert. Am. Vets. World War II, Korea and Viet Nam, 1977; Environ. Legis. of Yr. award Ill. Environ. Council, 1977, 79, 81, 83; Meritorious Svc. award Champaign County Council on Alcoholism, 1978, Ill. Community Coll. Trustees Assn., 1986; Perfect Voting Record award Ill. Credit Union League, 1979, Ill. Wildlife Fedn., 1979; cert. spl. recognition Ill. Women's Polit. Caucus, 1979, 80, Public Service award Izaak Walton League, 1980, Friend of Edn. award Ill. State Bd. Edn., 1985, Cert. of Appreciation Champaign County Urban League, 1987, Resolution of Honor Ill. Libr. Assn., 1987, 100 percent award Ill. State Coun. Sr. Citizens Orgns., 1989, Dare to be Great award Ill. Women Adminstrs., 1989; named Person of Yr., Champaign County Mental Health Assn., 1981, Pub. Citizen of Yr., Illini Dist. and Ill. chpt. Nat. Assn. Social Workers, 1981, Legislator of Yr., Ill. Assn. Sch. Social Workers, 1989. Mem. Ill. Conf. Women Legislators (co-convenor 1981-83), Nat. Order Women Legislators (dir. Region IV 1982, treas. 1983-84), Delta Kappa Gamma. Quaker.

SATTLER, ROLF, plant morphologist, educator; b. Göppingen, Germany, Mar. 8, 1936; arrived in Can., 1962; s. Otto and Emma (Mayer) S.; m. Liv Hamann, May 1, 1963 (div. 1985). PhD, U. Munich, 1961; DS with honors, Colombo U. Asst. prof. McGill U., Montreal, Que., Can., 1964-69, assoc. prof., 1969-77, prof., 1977—. Author: Organogenesis of Flowers, 1973 (Lawson medal 1974), Biophilosophy, 1986; editor: Theoretical Plant Morphology, 1978, Axioms and Principles of Plant Construction, 1981; contbr. articles to profl. jours. NATO fellow, 1962-64. Fellow Royal Soc. Can., Linnean Soc. London; mem. Can. Bot. Assn., Sci. and Med. Network, Internat. Assn. for New Sci., Sigma Xi. Office: McGill U, 1205 Dr Penfield Ave, Montreal, PQ Canada H3A 1B1

SATTLER, STEPHEN CHARLES, writer, editor, communications consultant; b. Cleve., Feb. 22, 1962; s. Leo Anthony and Gertrude Louise (Hoffman) S.; life ptnr. Cornelius O'Neil O'Farrell, Jr., June 3, 1987. AB in History, Georgetown U., 1995; MS in Mktg., Johns Hopkins U., 1997. Mng. editor Nat. Press, Washington, 1987-88; publs. and membership coord. Amideast, Washington, 1988-91; interim dir. outreach and comm. Am. Coun. on Edn., Washington, 1992—; ptnr. O'Farrell & Sattler, Washington, 1990—. Editor: The Golden Circle, 1987, On My Own: A Single Mother by Choice, 1987, Black Mondays: Worst Decisions of the Supreme Court, 1987, Katharine the Great: Katharine Graham and the Washington Post, 1987; editor: (ref. books) Introduction to the Arab World, 1989, National Guide to Educational Credit for Training Programs, 1992-93, 93-94, Guide to the Evaluation of Educational Experiences in the Armed Services, 1994, GED Candidates in Canada, 1994, The Literacy Proficiencies of GED Examinees, 1995, Guiding Principles for Distance Learning in a Learning Society, 1996, Distance Learning Evaluation Guide, 1996. Sec./newsletter editor Trees for Capitol Hill, Washington, 1993—; vol. Whitman-Walker Food Bank, Washington, 1994—; active mem. Ch. of the Epiphany, Washington, 1993—. Recipient pub. excellence (APEX) awards Comm. Concepts, 1994-97, Bronze Apple award Nat. Ednl. Film and Video Festival, 1989. Mem. Am. Mktg. Assn., Greater Washington Soc. Assn. Execs., The Chemists Club. Democrat. Episcopalian. Avocations: historic preservation, antique automobiles. Home: 1000 Maryland Ave NE Washington DC 20002-5330 Office: Am Coun on Edn Ste 250 1 Dupont Cir NW Washington DC 20036-1193

SATULOFF, BARTH, accounting executive, dispute resolution professional; b. Buffalo, Dec. 13, 1945; s. Bernard and Annette (Lurie) S.; m. Gail Lois Seid Jaffe, Aug. 23, 1992. BBA in Acctg., U. Miami, 1967, MBA, 1969. CPA, Fla., N.Y., Ill., La.; registered securities arbitrator, NYSE, AMEX, NASD; cert. state ct. arbitrator, Fla.; Spl. Master, Fla. pvt. property and land use cases. Staff acct. Price Waterhouse, Miami, Fla., 1969-71; tax specialist Laventhol & Horwath, Miami, 1973-74; mng. dir. Barth Satuloff, CPA, Miami, 1974—; pres., bd. dirs. Satuloff Bros., Inc., Buffalo, 1974-94, Miami, 1994—; sec., treas. Chartered Investment Rsch. Corp., Miami, 1980-89, also bd. dirs. Mem. endowment fund com. U. Miami, 1979; mem. Estate Planning Coun. Greater Miami, 1974; bd. dirs. Fellowship House Found., Miami, 1980; mem. FICPA Polit. Action Com., 1983—, Ctr. for Fine Arts, Hist. Mus. South Fla., The Lowe Art Mus. U. Miami, Met. Mus. Art, N.Y.C. With Fla. N.G., 1970-76. Mem. AICPA (mem. small bus. taxation com. of tax divsn. 1993-96), ABA (sec. dispute resolution, bylaws and directory com. 1994-96, forum on entertainment and sports industries, taxation and bus. law), Fla. Inst. CPAs Ednl. Found., Fla. Inst. CPAs, N.Y. State Soc. CPAs, Ill. Soc. CPAs, Soc. La. CPAs, Miami Country Day Sch. Alumni Assn. (bd. dirs. 1987—, sec. 1987-93, treas. 1994—), Am. Arbitration Assn. (nat. panel arbitrators and mediators), Audubon Soc., Zool. Soc. Fla., Ducks Ultd. (chmn. Miami chpt. 1991-92, 94-95), Trout Unltd., Rocky Mountain Elk Found., Nature Conservancy. Avocations: hunting, fishing, skiing, photography. Home: 9614 SW 134th Ct Miami FL 33186-2253 Office: 9495 Sunset Dr Ste B-275 Miami FL 33173-3253

SATUR, NANCY MARLENE, dermatologist; b. Philipsburg, Pa., Apr. 12, 1953; d. Nicholas and Mary (Kutzer) S.; m. John David Lortscher, Oct. 20, 1979; children: David Nicholas, Glenn William, Stephen John. BS magna cum laude, Pa. State U., 1974; MD, Thomas Jefferson U., 1976. Diplomate Am. Bd. Dermatology. Intern Allentown (Pa.) Gen. Hosp., 1976-77; resident in pathology U. Ill. Hosp., Chgo., 1978-79; resident in dermatology Case Western Res. U. Hosp., Cleve., 1979-82; dermatologist Encinitas, Calif., 1985—; sr. instr. dermatology Case Western Res. U. Hosp., 1982-83, sr. clin. instr. dermatology, 1983-84. Fellow Am. Acad. Dermatology; mem. AMA, Calif. Med. Assn., Am. Soc. Dermatologic Surgery, Am. Soc. Laser Medicine and Surgery, Am. Acad. Cosmetic Surgery, Am. Soc. Lipo-Suction Surgery, San Diego Dermatologic Soc., Pacific Dermatologic Assn. Office: 477 N El Camino Real Ste C308 Encinitas CA 92024-1332

SATURNELLI, ANNETTE MIELE, school system administrator; b. Newburgh, N.Y., Dec. 1, 1937; d. William Vito and Anna (Marso) M.; m. Carlo F. Saturnelli, Oct. 15, 1960; children: Anne, Karen, Carla. BA, Vassar Coll., 1959; MS, SUNY, New Platz, 1978; EdD, NYU, N.Y.C., 1993. Rsch. chemist Lederle Labs/Am. Cyanamid, Pearl River, N.Y., 1959-64; sci. coord. Marlboro (N.Y.) Cen. Sch. Dist., 1974-84; state sci. supr. N.Y. State Dept. Edn., Albany, 1984-86; dir. sci. edn. Newburgh (N.Y.) City Sch. Dist., 1986—; project dir., proposal reviewer NSF, Washington, 1984—; state coord. N.Y. State Sci. Olympiad, 1985-86; mem. Gov. Cuomo's Task Force on Improving Sci. Edn., Albany, N.Y., 1989—; mem. adv. bd. N.Y. State Systemic Initiative, 1993—, N.Y. State Tech. Edn. Network, 1993—. Author: Focus on Physical Science, 1981, 87; editor: Transforming Testing in New York State--A Collection of Past, Present and Future Assessment Practices, 1994. Recipient Presdl. award Excellence in Sci. Tchg., Washington, 1983; NSF 3-yr. summer sci. camp grantee, 1995, 96, 97, N.Y. State Edn. Dept. Workforce Preparation grantee, 1993-94, N.Y. State Edn. Dept. Sch.-to-Work grantee, 1995-96, 96-97, NSF Comprehensive Partnership for Math. and Sci. Achievement grantee, 1996—. Mem. ASCD, Nat. Sci. Tchrs. Assn. (Exemplary Sci. Tchrs. award 1982), N.Y. State Sci. Suprs. (bd. dirs., pres. 1991, Mid Hudson Sch. Study Coun. Excellence in Adminstrn. award 1993), Sci. Tchrs. Assn. N.Y. State (pres. 1993, Outstanding Sci. Tchrs. award 1983, N.Y. State Outstanding Sci. Supr. award 1988, Fellows award 1990), Phi Delta Kappa. Home: 3 Taft Pl Cornwall On Hudson NY 12520-1713 Office: Newburgh Free Acad 201 Fullerton Ave Newburgh NY 12550-3718

SATZ, LOUIS K., publishing executive; b. Chgo., Apr. 28, 1927; s. Harry Addison and Faye (Pollen) S.; m. Adele Wallenstein, Mar. 2, 1976 (dec.); children: Jay, Jonathan. B.S. in Mktg, U. Ill., 1949. Circulation dir. Pubs. Devel. Corp., Chgo., 1953, Guns mag., Jr. Arts and Activities, 1961; wholesaler sales mgr., then v.p., dir. sales Bantam Books, Inc., N.Y.C., 1962-80; sr. v.p., dir. diversified markets Bantam Books, Inc., 1980-84; pub. Passport Books, Lincolnwood, Ill., 1985-88; pres. Louis K. Satz Assocs., Pub. Cons., N.Y.C., 1988-91; ptnr. Scott/Satz Group, Pub. Cons., Walnut Creek, Calif., 1991—; guest lectr. Sarah Lawrence Coll. Pub. Sch., Pace U.; faculty Hofstra U., Denver Pub. Inst.; bd. dirs. N.Y. is Book Country, Brandeis U. Pub. Scholarship Fund, Oscar Dystel Fellowship NYU. Served with AUS, World War II, ETO. Mem. Am. Assn. Pubs. (chmn. small books mktg. div. 1975). Office: Scott/Satz Group 558 Monarch Ridge Dr Walnut Creek CA 94596-2956

SAUCIER, GENE DUANE, state legislator, import/export company executive; b. Dallas, Sept. 25, 1931; s. Albert L. and Myrtle Irene (West) S.; m. Marilyn Emmy Cox, Dec. 27, 1952 (div. Sept. 1980); children: Alan, Steve, Renee; m. Giulia Riga LaCagnina, Nov. 28, 1981. BS in Agronomy Soils, Miss. State U., 1953; MS in Counseling, U. So. Miss., 1970, EdD in Adult Edn., 1978. Builder, developer Saucier Co., Hattiesburg, Miss., 1957-70; dir. admissions U. So. Miss., Hattiesburg, 1970-74, dean spl. acad. svcs., 1974-84, asst. v.p. bus. and fin., 1984-93; rep. Miss. Ho. of Reps., Jackson, 1993—; importer tractors from China. Scoutmaster Boy Scouts Am., 1960-70, chmn. camping and activities Pine Burr Area, 1970. 1st lt. USAF, 1953-56. Named Forrest County Tree Farmer of Yr., 1996, Miss. Tree Farmer Yr., 1996. Mem. Res. Officers Assn., Am. Assn. Collegiate Registrars and Admissions Officers (mem. adv. bd. 1985-86), So. Assn. Collegiate Registrars and Admissions Officers (bd. dirs. 1981, local arrangements chmn. 1981, v.p. admissions and fin. aid 1982-83, pres. 1985-86), Miss. Assn. Collegiate Registrars and Admissions Officdrs, Miss. Forestry Assn. (exec. bd. dirs. 1992-94, bd. dirs. 1992-94), Miss. Nature Conservancy, Forrest/Lamar Forestry Assn. (pres. 1989-92), Sigma Chi, ODK, Phi Delta Kappa, Omicron Delta Kappa. Office: 41 Saucier Rd Hattiesburg MS 39402-9138

SAUCIER, GUYLAINE, broadcast executive; b. Noranda, Québec, Can., June 10, 1946; d. Gérard and Yvette (Thiffault) S. C.A., 1971. Chmn. Can. Broadcasting Corp.-SRC, Ottawa, Ont., Can.; bd. dirs. Petro-Can., Bell Can., Hawker Siddeley, Bank Montreal, Boreal Inc., Tembec; mem. Commn. Inquiry Unemployment Ins. Mem. L'Ordre Comptables Agréé Québec, C. of C. (former pres. Québec), Hillside Tennis, Mt. Royal, St. Denis. Avocation: tennis. Office: Can Broadcasting Corp, 250 Leonark Ave, Ottawa, ON Canada K12 6R5*

SAUCIER LUNDY, KAREN, college dean, educator; b. Hattiesburg, Miss., Oct. 7, 1954; d. William Marshall and Ruth (Landers) S.; m. Joel Christopher Lundy, Dec. 27, 1986; 1 child, Marshall Parker. BS in Nursing, U. So. Miss., 1975; MS in Community Health Nursing, U. Colo. Health Scis. Ctr., 1978; MA in Sociology, U. Colo., Boulder, 1987, PhD in Sociology, 1987. RN. Clin. nurse U. Miss. Med. Ctr., Jackson, 1976-77; clin. specialist HEW, USPHS, Atlanta, 1978-80; clin. instr. U. Miss. Med. Ctr. and Med. Sch., 1980-81; asst. prof. Loretto Heights Coll., Denver, 1983-85; instr. U. Colo., Boulder, 1982-85; prof., dean sch. nursing Delta State U., Cleveland, Miss., 1985-90; assoc. prof. U. So. Miss., Hattiesburg, 1990-92, 1992—; mem. Miss. Bd. Nursing, 1990-94. Author: Community Health, 1987, nursing text, 1991, Family and Community Health Nursing, 1991 (AJN Book of the Year 1991). Vol. Spl. Olympics, Miss., Fla., 1979-80; mem. ARC, 1978-82; cons. Sierra Club, Denver, 1977-78, Headstart, Tampa, Fla., 1978-79; bd. dirs. March of Dimes, Jackson, 1979-81, Am. Cancer Soc., 1985—. Am. Coll. Test Merit scholar 1972-75; USPHS fellow, 1977; named Educator Nurse of Year Miss. Nurses' Assn., 1989. Mem. ANA, Am. Sociol. Assn., So. Sociol. Assn., Nat. League Nursing (accreditation site visitor 1988—), Kappa Delta. Democrat. Avocation: photography. Home: PO Box 927 89 James Switzer Rd Purvis MS 39475-0927 Office: U So Miss Sta Box 5095 Hattiesburg MS 39406-5095

SAUDER, ERIE JOSEPH, manufacturing executive; b. Archbold, Ohio, Aug. 6, 1904; s. Daniel D. and Anna (Schrock) S.; m. Leona Short, June 23, 1927 (dec. Nov. 1974); children: Delmar, Maynard, Myrl; m. Orlyss Alline Short, Feb. 1, 1976. PhD (hon.), Defiance (Ohio) Coll., 1985, North Tech. Coll., Archbold, 1987. Chmn. bd. Sauder Woodworking, Archbold; v.p., bd. dirs. F&M Bank; founder Sauder Farm & Craft Village. Trustee Defiance Coll.; overseer Goshen Coll; treas. Ohio-Eastern Mission Bd., 1978—; pres., bd. trustees Sunshine Children's Home, others. Home: PO Box 261 Archbold OH 43502-0261 Office: Sauder Woodworking Co 502 Middle St Archbold OH 43502-1559

SAUER, DAVID ANDREW, writer, computer consultant; b. Urbana, Ill., Feb. 25, 1948; s. Elmer Louis and Frances (Hill) S. BA, Northwestern U., 1970; MS, Simmons Coll., 1975. Reference libr. Boston U., 1976-78, bibliographer, 1978-84, sci. bibliographer, 1984-88, head Stone Sci. Libr., 1988-94; v.p. info. svcs. CyberHelp, Inc., 1995—. Co-author: Internet for Windows, 1994, WinComm Pro: The Visual Learning Guide, 1995, ProComm Plus V2 for Windows: The Visual Learning Guide, 1995, Access for Windows 95: The Visual Learning Guide, 1995, Cruising America Online 2.5, 1995, Internet for Windows: The America Online 2.5 Edition, 1995, Internet for Windows: The Microsoft Network Edition, 1995, Cruising the Microsoft Network, 1996, Cruising CompuServe, 1996, WinFax Pro 7 for Windows: The Visual Learning Guide, 1996, Windows NT 4.0 Visual Desk Reference, 1997. Mem. S.W. Corridor Project, Boston, 1977-87, Forest Hills Neighborhood Improvement Assn., Boston, 1977-90, Forest Hills/Woodbourne Neighborhood Group, 1991-94. Mem. ALA, Spl. Librs. Assn., San Diego Computer Soc., Highland Casitas Homeowners Assn. (chmn. 1996—). Democrat. Home and Office: 1034 La Tierra Dr San Marcos CA 92069-4617

SAUER, ELISSA SWISHER, nursing educator; b. Williamsport, Pa., Jan. 9, 1935; d. Oliver S. and Emily Louisa (Gehron) Swisher; m. Raymond James Sauer, Nov. 27, 1964. Diploma, Reading Hosp. Sch. Nursing, 1957; BS, Albright Coll., Reading, 1958; MS in Nursing, U. Pa., Phila., 1964. Nurse Community Health and Civic Assn., Ardmore, Pa., 1966-67; pub. health coord. Albert Einstein Med. Ctr., 1967-68; pvt. duty nurse, 1968-73; clin. faculty Schuylkill County AVTS, 1973-74; prof. nursing Reading (Pa.) Area Comunity Coll., 1975-80; oncology nurse adminstr.-educator Comprehensive Community Cancer Ctr., Allentown, Pa., 1981-85; exec. dir. Holy Family Home Health Care, Orwigsburg, Pa., 1985-89; dir. nursing program, chair health svcs. div. Reading Area Community Coll., 1989—. Author: Instructor's Manual and Procedure Manual to accompany Fundamentals of Nursing: Human Health and Function, 2d edit., 1996. Mem. Pa. Nurses Assn. (Dist. 2 dir. 1994—, Adminstr. award 1992), Pa. League for Nursing, Sigma Theta Tau. Home: 1114 Pepper Ridge Dr Reading PA 19606 Office: Reading Area C C PO Box 1706 10 S 2d St Reading PA 19603-1706

SAUER, GEORGIA BOORAS, newspaper writer; b. Kalamata, Greece, May 9, 1946; came to U.S., 1946; d. Peter P. and Angela (Dimopoulos) Booras; m. Mark Sauer, Jan. 4, 1969; children: Peter, Alexander. BS, U. Ill., 1968. Obituary and feature writer Champaign (Ill.)-Urbana Courier, 1966-68; reporter Times-Democrat, Davenport, Iowa, 1968; reporter, travel writer, copy editor Chgo. Tribune, 1969-70, fashion and feature writer, asst. Lifestyle editor, 1971-75; reporter Home Furnishings Daily, Fairchild Publs., N.Y.C., 1970-71; fashion reporter, Sunday women's editor N.Y. Daily News, N.Y.C., 1975-76; fashion editor St. Louis mag., 1981-86; became feature writer St. Louis Post-Dispatch, 1986-91; fashion editor Pitts. Post Gazette, 1993—. Pres. bd. dirs. Ladue Chapel Nursery Sch.; bd. dirs. Martha's Shelter, St. Louis, 1985-91, DG Found. for Visually Impaired Children, St. Louis, 1985-91, St. Louis Pub. Libr., 1987-91, Payback, St. Louis, 1987-91; mem. Jr. League St. Louis and Pitts.; bd. dirs. Three Rivers South, Pitts., Ozanam Cultural Ctr., mem. bd. parents coun. Shadyside acad., mem. devel. com. Greek Orthodox. Office: Pittsburgh Post-Gazette 34 Blvd Of The Allies Pittsburgh PA 15222-1204*

SAUER, GORDON CHENOWETH, physician, educator; b. Rutland, Ill., Aug. 14, 1921; s. Fred William and Gweneth (Chenoweth) S.; m. Mary Louise Steinhilber, Dec. 28, 1944; children: Elisabeth Ruth, Gordon Chenoweth, Margaret Louise, Amy Kieffer.; m. Marion Green, Oct. 23, 1982. Student, Northwestern U., 1939-42; B.S., U. Ill., 1943, M.D., 1945. Diplomate: Am. Bd. Dermatology and Syphilology. Intern Cook County Hosp., Chgo., 1945-46; resident dermatology and syphilology N.Y. U.-Bellevue Med. Center, 1948-51; dermatologist Thompson-Brumm-Knepper Clinic, St. Joseph, Mo., 1951-54; pvt. practice Kansas City, Mo., 1954—; mem. staff St. Luke's, Research, Kansas City Gen. hosps.; asso. instr. U. Kans., 1951-56, vice chmn. sect. dermatology, 1956-58, asso. clin. prof., 1960-64, clin. prof., 1964-93; clin. prof. emeritus, 1993—; head sect. dermatology U. Kans., 1958-70; clin. asso., acting head dermatology sect. U. Mo., 1955-59, cons. dermatology, 1959-67, clin. prof., 1967—; cons. Munson Army Hosp., Ft. Leavenworth, Kans., 1959-68; Mem. dermatology panel, drug efficacy panel Nat. Acad. Sci.-FDA, 1967-69. Author: Manual of Skin Diseases, 1959, 7th edit., 1995, Teen Skin, 1965, John Gould Bird Print Reproductions, 1977, John Gould's Prospectuses and Lists of Subscribers to His Work on Natural History: With an 1866 Facsimile, 1980, John Gould The Bird Man, 1982, John Gould The Bird Man: Associates and Subscribers, 1995, John Gould The Bird Man: Bibliography 2, 1996; editor Kansas City Med. Bull., 1967-69; contbr. articles to profl. jours. Bd. dirs. Kansas City Area coun. Camp Fire Girls Am., 1956-59, Kansas City Lyric Theatre, 1969-74, Kansas City Chamber Choir, 1969-74, Chouteau Soc., 1985—, U. Mo.-Kansas City Friends of Libr., 1988-92; bd. dirs. Mo. br. The Nature Conservancy, 1984-91. Sr. asst. surgeon USPHS, 1946-48. Named Dermatology Found. Practitioner of Yr., 1992. Fellow Am. Acad. Dermatology and Syphilology (dir. 1975-79, v.p. 1980); mem. Mo., Jackson County med. socs., Mo. Dermatol. Soc. (pres. 1974-75), Dermatology Found. (trustee 1978-83), Am. Ornithol. Union, Wilson Ornithol. Soc., Royal Australasian Ornithologists Union, Soc. Bibliography Natural History, Am. Dermatol. Assn., Alpha Delta Phi, Nu Sigma Nu. Presbyterian. Office: 6400 Prospect Ave Kansas City MO 64132-1180 Home: 422 E 55th St Kansas City MO 64110-2454

SAUER, HARRY JOHN, JR., mechanical engineering educator, university administrator; b. St. Joseph, Mo., Jan. 27, 1935; s. Harry John and Marie Margaret (Witt) S.; m. Patricia Ann Zbierski, June 9, 1956; children: Harry John, Elizabeth Ann, Carl Andrew, Robert Mark, Katherine Anne, Deborah Elaine, Victoria Lynn, Valerie Joan, Joseph Gerard. B.S., U. Mo.-Rolla, 1956, M.S., 1958; Ph.D., Kans. State U., 1963. Instr. mech. engring. Kans. State U., Manhattan, 1960-62; sr. engr., cons. Midwest Rsch. Inst., Kansas City, Mo., 1963-70; mem. faculty dept. mech. and aerospace engring. U. Mo., Rolla, 1957—, prof., 1966—, assoc. chmn., 1980-84, dean grad. study, 1984-92; cons. in field; mem. Gov.'s Commn. on Energy Conservation, 1977; mem. Mo. Solar Energy Resource Panel, 1979-83. Co-author: Environmental Control Principles, 1975, 4th edit., 1985, Thermodynamics, 1981, Heat Pump Systems, 1983, Engineering Thermodynamics, 1985, Principles of Heating, Ventilating and Air Conditioning, 1991, 2d edit., 1994; contbr. articles to profl. jours. Pres. St. Patrick's Sch. Bd., 1970-72, St. Patrick's Parish Council, 1975-76. Recipient Ralph R. Teetor award Soc. Automotive Engrs., 1968; Hermann F. Spoehrer Meml. award St. Louis chpt. ASHRAE, 1979; also disting. service award, 1981, E. K. Campbell award of merit, 1983. Mem. ASME, ASHRAE, NSPE, Soc. Automotive Engrs., Am. Soc. Engring. Edn., Mo. Soc. Profl. Engrs., Mo. Acad. Sci., Sigma Xi. Roman Catholic. Home: 10355 College Hills Dr Rolla MO 65401-7726 Office: Dept of Mech Engring U Mo Rolla MO 65401

SAUER, RICHARD JOHN, developer fundraiser; b. Walker, Minn., Nov. 15, 1939; s. Herman and Katherine Elizabeth (Rieder) S.; m. Elizabeth Louise Hornstein, Aug. 18, 1962; children: Michele, Alison, Maria, Peter. BS in Biology, St. John's U., Collegeville, Minn., 1962; MS in Zoology, U. Mich., Ann Arbor, 1964; PhD in Entomology, N.D. State U., 1967. Asst. prof. biology St. Cloud (Minn.) State U., 1967-68; asst. prof., then assoc. prof. entomology Mich. State U., East Lansing, 1968-76, acting assoc. dir. Mich. Agrl. Expt. Sta., 1975-76; prin. entomologist Coop. State Rsch. Svc., USDA, Washington, 1974-75; prof., head dept. entomology Kans. State U., Manhattan, 1976-80; dir. Agrl. Expt. Sta. U. Minn., St. Paul, 1980-89, v.p. agriculture, forestry and home econs., 1983-89; interim pres. U. Minn., Mpls., 1988-89; pres., CEO Nat. 4-H Coun., Chevy Chase, Md., 1989—. Mem. Am. Soc. Assn. Execs. Roman Catholic. Home: 1523 Ivystone Ct Silver Spring MD 20904-5476 Office: Nat 4-H Coun 7100 Connecticut Ave Chevy Chase MD 20815-4934

SAUERACKER, EDWARD, academic administrator; b. Bethpage, N.Y., Apr. 20, 1956; s. William Francis and Carol Veronica (Schuyler) S. BS magna cum laude, Hofstra U., 1978; MPh in Econs., CUNY, 1982, PhD in Econs., 1984. Rsch. asst. CUNY Grad. Ctr., 1978-82; asst. prof. econs. and fin. Baruch Coll., CUNY, 1984-86, asst. dir. Ctr. for Study of Bus. and Govt., 1982-86; asst. dean for assessment SUNY Empire State Coll., Old Westbury, N.Y., 1986—, asst. prof. econs., 1990—; asst. dean for assessment Harry Van Arsdale Jr. Sch. Labor Studies SUNY-ESC, N.Y.C., 1994—; adj. instr. dept. econs. and geography Hofstra U., 1979-84, adj. asst. prof., 1987—; editor Baruch Prospectus, Baruch Coll., CUNY, 1984; cons. in field. Author articles and column. N.Y. state rep. Coun. for Adult and Exptl. Learning, 1993-95; founder, mem. steering com. The Learning Collaborative, 1992—; bd. dirs. Help-Aid-Direction, Inc., 1991; sec. Met. Econ. Assn., 1988-91; trustee Hicksville Pub. Libr., 1994—. Unied Hosp. Fund grantee, 1985-86; CUNY fellow, Hofstra scholar, Danforth nominee; named to Outstanding Young Men of Am.; recipient Excellence in Profl. Svc. award SUNY Emprie State Coll. Mem. Kiwanis (pres. 1994-96, divsn. circle-K chair 1994—), Phi Beta Kappa, Omicron Kappa Epsilon. Home: 43 Jay St Hicksville NY 11801-5855 Office: SUNY Empire State Coll Long Island Ctr PO Box 130 Old Westbury NY 11568-0130

SAUERBREY, ELLEN ELAINE RICHMOND, former radio talk show host; b. Balt., Sept. 9, 1937; d. Edgar Arthur and Ethel Frederika (Landgraf) Richmond; m. Wilmer John Emil Sauerbrey, June 27, 1959. AB summa cum laude in Biology and English, Western Md. Coll., 1959. Biology instr., chmn. sci. dept. Baltimore County Sch. System, 1959-64; dist. mgr. Baltimore County U.S. Census, 1970; Md. Ho. of Dels., Annapolis, 1978-95, minority leader, 1986-95; radio talk show host Sta. WBAL, 1995-96; Rep. candidate for Gov., 1994. Rep. Nat. Committee Woman, Md., 1996— Rules com., 1996; del. Rep. Nat. Convs., 1968, 76, 84, 88, 92, 96, mem. credentials com., 1984, platform com., chmn. subcom. on economy, 1977; vice chmn. Rep. State Ctrl. Com. of Balt. County, 1966-71; trustee Md. Coun. Econ. Edn., Franklin Sq. Hosp.; founder United Citizens for Md.'s Future; mem. govt. activities com. United Cerebral Palsey Ctrl. Md.; nat. chmn. Am. Legis. exec. Coun., 1990-91. Recipient Pvt. Property award Greater Balt. Bd. Realtors, 1984; named Legislator of Yr., Md. Assn. Builders and Contractors, 1982, Am. Legis. Exec. Coun., 1986, Western Md. Coll. Alum of Yr., 1988, Outstanding Legis. Leader, Am. Legis. Exec. Coun., 1992, Rep. Woman of Yr., Md. Rep. Party, 1995. Mem. DAR, Nat. Fedn. rep. Women (Margaret Chase Smith award 1995), Md. Fedn. Rep. Women, Am. Legis. exch. Coun. (chmn. emeritus), Md. Farm Bur., Md. Conservative Union, Beta Beta, Beta, Phi Beta Kappa. Presbyterian. Avocations: gardening, travel.

SAUERHAFT, STAN, public relations executive, consultant; b. N.Y.C., Nov. 25, 1926; s. Al and Rae S.; m. Rosalie Cynthia Tolkin, Oct. 28, 1951; children: Richard Craig, Douglas Clark, Robert James. BA, U. Mich., 1948, MA, 1949. Editor, scriptwriter Paramount News, 1950-51; scriptwriter Hearst Metrotone News, N.Y.C., 1951-52; editor Food Bus. Mag., N.Y.C., 1952-53; acct. supr. Selvage, Lee & Chase, N.Y.C., 1953-55; v.p., mem. creative plans bd. Communications Counselors, Inc. McCann-Erickson, N.Y.C., 1955-59; pres. Chase and Sauerhaft Assocs., N.Y.C., 1959-65; exec. v.p., dir., mem. mgmt. com. Hill & Knowlton, Inc., N.Y.C., 1965-86; vice chmn. bd. , dir. Burson-Marsteller, U.S., 1987-88; vice chmn., dir. Burson-Marsteller Internat., 1988—; instr., lectr. Columbia U. Grad. Sch., 1962-65, NYU Grad. Bus. Sch., 1984-87. Author: The Merger Game, 1971; co-author: Image Wars, 1989; contbr. bus. articles and chpts. to anthologies.

Chmn. West Point Civilian Adv. Com., N.Y., 1980—; mem. exec. com. of bd. Inst. for Pub. Rels. Rsch. and Edn., 1984—, LS&A Coll. of U. Mich., 1990—; mem. adv. bd. U. Mich. Staff sgt. AUS, 1945-46. Coll. of Fellows Pub. Rels. Soc. Am. (nat. accreditation bd. 1981-83), Pub. Rels. Soc. N.Y. (pres. 1983-85); mem. Soc. Profl. Journalists, Authors Guild, Pub. Affairs Coun., Am. Platform Tennis Assn. (v.p.), U. Mich. Alumni Club, Union League Club N.Y. (chmn. pub. affairs com. 1980-84), Burning Tree Country Club (Greenwich, Conn.), Wiindmill Club, Seabrook Island Club (S.C.). Republican. Avocations: golf, platform tennis, bridge. Office: Burson-Marsteller 230 Park Ave S New York NY 10003-1513 *A father's advice to his sons: If you can't outthink them, outwork them. But better yet, try to do both. Also, the best luck seems to befall the hardest workers.*

SAUFER, ISAAC AARON, lawyer; b. Bronx, N.Y., June 16, 1953; s. Solomon and Beatrice (Kanofsky) S.; m. Debra Edith Goldberg, June 26, 1977; children: Suzanne, Nancy, Scott, Daniel, Jonathan. BA, Yeshiva U., N.Y.C., 1975; JD, Bklyn. Law Sch., 1978; LLM in Taxation, NYU, 1982. Bar: N.Y. 1979, N.J. 1986, Fla. 1986, Conn. 1987. Summer intern N.Y. County Dist. Attys. Office, N.Y.C., 1976; legal editor Prentice-Hall, Inc., Englewood Cliffs, N.Y., 1979-80; assoc. Kurzman Karelsen & Frank, LLP, N.Y.C., 1980-85, ptnr., 1986—; adj. asst. prof. NYU Sch. Continuing Edn., N.Y.C., 1988—; lectr. seminars, 1991, 93, 95, 97. Co-author: (N.Y. real property forms) Bergerman & Roth, 1986-87. Office: Kurzman Karelsen & Frank LLP 230 Park Ave Ste 2300 New York NY 10169

SAUFLEY, WILLIAM EDWARD, banker, lawyer; b. Washington, Mar. 7, 1956; s. Franklin Dewit and Ruth Constance (Wright) S.; m. Leigh Ingalls, Jan. 3, 1981. BA, Dartmouth Coll., 1977; JD, U. Maine, 1980. Bar: Maine 1980, U.S. Dist. Ct. Maine 1980. Of counsel Maine Legislature, Augusta, 1981-84; v.p. counsel Maine Savs. Bank, Portland, 1984-88, gen. counsel, sec., 1988-91; corp. sec. The One Bancorp, Portland, 1984-91, gen. counsel, 1989-91; sr. v.p., gen. counsel Fleet Bank of Maine, Portland, 1992-94; of counsel Monaghan, Leahy, Hochadel & Libby, Portland, 1995-96; sr. v.p. Atlantic Bank N.A., Portland, 1996—. Trustee 75 State St Home for Elderly, Portland, 1986-92. Mem. ABA, Maine Bar Assn. (chmn. consumer and fin. instns. law sect.). Democrat. Roman Catholic. Avocations: photography, computers. Home: 51 Bramblewood Dr Portland ME 04103-3796 Office: Atlantic Bank NA PO Box 3849 511 Congress St Portland ME 04104-3489

SAUL, ANN, public relations executive; b. Columbia, Miss.; d. Otto and Ruth (Stamps) Saul. BS in Edn., Miss. Coll., 1961; postgrad., U. Louisville. Staff writer, circulation mgr. Louisville Mag. and Louisville Area C. of C., 1971-77; employee communications staff Brown & Williamson Tobacco Corp., 1977-79; media rels. staff NKC Hosps., 1979-80; pub. rels. and sales promotion staff Am. Temp. Svcs., 1980-82; sr. account supr. Daniel J. Edelman Pub. Rels., Chgo., 1982-87; dr. communication svcs. Nat. Easter Seal Soc., Chgo., 1987-89; v.p. Sam Huff & Assocs., Pub. Rels., Chgo., 1989-91; founder Ann Saul Pub. Rels., 1991—. Mem. Pub. Rels. Soc. Am., Publicity Club of Chgo. (Silver Trumpet 1985, 95, bd. dir.). Avocations: reading, volunteer activities, art, travel.

SAUL, APRIL, photographer; b. Bklyn., May 27, 1955; children: Amy, Nicholas. BA in English, Tufts U.; MA in Mass Comm., U. Minn. Staff photographer Balt. Sun, 1980, Phila. Inquirer, 1981—. Nikon/NPPA Documentary Sabbatical grantee, 1985; recipient Robert F. Kennedy Journalism award, 1983, Budapest award World Press Photo, 1991, Gold medal, Best in Show award Soc. Newspaper Design, 1994; named Photographer of Yr. Pa. Press Photographers Assn., 1993, N.J. Press Photographers Assn., 1993, No. Photographer of Yr. Soc. Newspaper Design, 1994; co-recipient Pulitzer prize for exploratory journalism, 1997. Office: Phila. Inquirer PO Box 8263 Philadelphia PA 19101*

SAUL, B. FRANCIS, II, bank executive; b. Washington, Apr. 15, 1932; s. Andrew Maguire and Ruth Clark (Sheehan) S.; m. Elizabeth Patricia English, Apr. 30, 1960; children: Sharon Elizabeth, B. Francis III, Elizabeth Willoughby, Andrew Maguire II, Patricia English. Grad. Georgetown Prep. Sch., 1950; BS, Villanova U., 1954, DCS (hon.), 1989; LLB, U. Va., 1957. Bar: D.C. 1959. Chmn., pres. B.F. Saul Co., Chevy Chase, Md., 1957—; chmn., trustee B.F. Saul Real Estate Investment Trust Co., Chevy Chase, 1964—; With Chevy Chase Bank, F.S.B., 1969—, chmn., CEO, founder; chmn. Fin. Gen. Bankshares, Inc., 1978-82; chmn., CEO, trustee Saul Ctrs., Inc., 1993—; chmn. bd. dirs. 1st Am. Bankshares, Inc., Washington, 1978-85; dir. Colonial Williamsburg Hotel Properties, Inc., 1983—; mem. Archdiocese fin. coun. for Archbishop of Washington, 1990—; mem. honors com. John F. Kennedy Ctr. Performing Arts, 1995—; mem. trustees coun. Nat Gallery of Arts, 1995—, dir. bd. vis. and govs. Washington Coll., 1995—; mem. bd. advisors CLW Life and Annuity Acquisition Corp., 1994—. Trustee Fed. City Coun., Nat. Geographic Soc., 1985—, Suburban Hosp., 1972-76; dirs. Wadsworth Preservation Trust, 1983—; trustee Brookings Inst., 1987-93, hon. trustee, 1993—; trustee Corcoran Gallery Art, Washington, 1972-90; mem. vis. com. Sch. Architecture U. Va., 1985—; bd. dirs. Garfinckel, Brooks Bros., Miller & Rhoads, 1970-81, Madeira Sch., Greenway, Va., 1978-88, Portsmouth Abbey Sch., R.I., 1979-84, United World Coll. of Am. West, Montezuma, N.Mex., 1982-85, D.C. Fund for Creative Space, 1980-82, D.C. chpt. ARC, 1964-86; mem. Folger Shakespeare Libr. Com., 1985—; pres. D.C. Soc. for Crippled Children, 1973-75. Mem. Mortgage Bankers Assn. Met. Washington (pres. 1968), Nat. Assn. Real Estate Investment Trusts (pres. 1973-74), Alfalfa Club, Alibi Club, Met. Club, Knights of Malta, Chevy Chase Club, Burning Tree Club, Friendly Sons of St. Patrick (pres. 1992), Wianno Club, The Brook Club, Roman Catholic. Home: 1 Quincy St Chevy Chase MD 20815-4226 Office: BF Saul Co 8401 Connecticut Ave Chevy Chase MD 20815-5803

SAUL, GEORGE BRANDON, II, biology educator; b. Hartford, Conn., Aug. 8, 1928; s. George Brandon and Dorothy (Ayers) S.; m. Sue Grau Williams, Mar. 28, 1953. A.B., U. Pa., 1949, A.M., 1950, Ph.D., 1954. From instr. to assoc. prof. Dartmouth, 1954-67; prof. biology Middlebury (Vt.) Coll., 1967—, chmn. dept., 1968-76, 91-93, v.p. acad. affairs, 1976-79; Research asso. Calif. Inst. Tech., 1964-65; NSF postdoctoral fellow U. Zurich, Switzerland, 1959-60; vis. scientist Boyce Thompson Inst. for Plant Research, Yonkers, N.Y., 1972-73. Author papers in field. Fellow AAAS; mem. Pa. Acad. Sci., Genetics Soc. Am., Am. Genetics Assn., N.Y. Acad. Scis., Sigma Xi. Club: Lion. Home: Munger St RR 3 Box 2575 Middlebury VT 05753 Office: Middlebury Coll Dept Biology Middlebury VT 05753

SAUL, JOHN WOODRUFF, III, writer; b. Pasadena, Calif., Feb. 25, 1942; s. John Woodruff and Adeline Elizabeth (Lee) S. Student, Antioch Coll., 1959-60, Cerritos Coll., 1960-61, Mont. State U., Missoula, 1961-62, San Francisco State Coll., 1963-65. In various positions primarily in L.A. and San Francisco, 1965-76. Author: Suffer The Children, 1977, Punish the Sinners, 1978, Cry for the Strangers, 1979, Comes the Blind Fury, 1980, When the Wind Blows, 1981, The God Project, 1982, Nathaniel, 1984, Brainchild, 1985, Hellfire, 1986, The Unwanted, 1987, The Unloved, 1988, Creature, 1989, Second Child, 1990, Sleep Walk, 1990, Darkness, 1991, Shadows, 1992, Guardian, 1993, The Homing, 1994, Black Lightning, 1995, The Blackstone Chronicles, 1997, The Presence, 1997; also other novels under pseudonyms. Bd. dirs. Seattle Theatre Arts, 1978-80; bd. govs. Tellurian Communities, Inc., Madison, Wis.; v.p. Chester Woodruff Found., N.Y.C. Mem. Authors Guild. Democrat. Swedenborgian. Office: care Jane Rotrosen 318 E 51st St New York NY 10022-7803 *For a writer, the education of experience is without doubt the best education.*

SAUL, JULIAN, retail executive; b. 1940. CEO Queen Carpet, Dalton, Ga., 1962—. Office: PO Box 1527 Dalton GA 30722-1527*

SAUL, KENNETH LOUIS, retired utility company executive; b. Columbus, Ohio, Aug. 29, 1923; s. Aloysius Louis and Ruth Geneva (Duke) S.; m. Shirley Ann Todd, Feb. 14, 1953; children: Carl, Deborah, Kenneth, Mark, Lori, Richard. BBA, Ohio State U., 1949. Various mgmt. positions Columbus & So. Ohio Elec. Co., 1955-70, asst. controller, 1970-74; v.p., controller Tucson Elec. Power, 1974-84, sr. v.p., chief fin. officer, 1984-88, also bd. dirs.; bd. dirs. Ohio Steel Products, Columbus, Engrng. Rsch. Assocs., Tucson. Chmn. bd. Bishop Hartley High Sch., Columbus, 1967-73; treas., bd. dirs. United Way, Tucson, 1975-81, Carondelet Health Care, Tucson, 1982-85, St. Joseph's Hosp., Tucson, 1976-82. Staff sgt. USAAF, 1943-45, PTO. Mem. Nat. Assn. Accts., Skyline Country Club (pres. 1979-80), SMOO Investment Club (pres. 1970-73). Republican. Roman Catholic. Avocations: golf, swimming, baseball, football. Home: 560 N Fairhaven Dr Vail AZ 85641-9646

SAUL, NORMAN EUGENE, history educator; b. LaFontaine, Ind., Nov. 26, 1932; s. Ralph Odis and Jessie (Neff) S.; m. Mary Ann Culwell, June 27, 1959; children: Alyssa, Kevin, Julia. B.A., Ind. U.- Bloomington, 1954; M.A., Columbia U., 1959, Ph.D., 1965; postgrad., Leningrad State U. (USSR), 1960-61. Instr. history Purdue U., 1962-65; asst. prof. Brown U., 1965-68; vis. assoc. prof. Northwestern U., 1969-70; assoc. prof. U. Kans., Lawrence, 1970-75, prof. history, 1975—, chmn. dept. history, 1981-89. Author: Russia and the Mediterranean 1797-1807, 1970, Sailors in Revolt, 1978, Distant Friends: The United States and Russia, 1763-1867, 1991, Concord and Conflict: The United States and Russia, 1867-1914, 1996; editor: Russian-American Dialogue on Cultural Relations, 1776-1914, 1997. Fulbright scholar, London, 1954-55, Helsinki, 1968-69; Soviet Am. exch. scholar Internat. Rsch. and Exch. Bd., Moscow, 1973-74, 91-92; fellow Ford Found., 1957-59, Kennan Inst., 1976, 84, 91, 95, 97, Hall Ctr. for Humanities, 1989, 95; recipient Byron Caldwell Smith Book award for Distant Friends Hall Ctr. for Humanities, 1993. Mem. Am. Hist. Assn., Am. Assn. Advancement of Slavic Studies, Kans. State Hist. Soc. Home: 1002 Crestline Dr Lawrence KS 66049-2607 Office: Dept of History U of Kans Lawrence KS 66045

SAUL, RALPH SOUTHEY, financial service executive; b. Bklyn., May 21, 1922; s. Walter Emerson and Helen Douglas (Coutts) S.; m. Bette Jane Bertschinger, June 16, 1956; children: Robert Southey, Jane Adams. B.A., U. Chgo., 1947; LL.B., Yale U., 1951. Bar: D.C. 1951, N.Y. 1952. With Am. Embassy, Prague, Czechoslovakia, 1947-48; assoc. firm Lyeth & Voorhees, N.Y.C., 1951-52; asst. counsel to Gov. N.Y. State, 1952-54; staff atty. RCA, 1954-58; with SEC, 1958-65, dir. div. trading and markets, 1963-65; v.p. corporate devel. Investors Diversified Services, Inc., Mpls., 1965-66; pres. Am. Stock Exchange, N.Y.C., 1966-71; co-CE, chmn. mgmt. com. First Boston Corp., 1971-74; chmn., chief exec. officer INA Corp., Phila., 1975-82, CIGNA Corp., Phila., 1982-84; chmn. Horace Mann Educators Corp.; bd. dirs. PH-II, Inc., Commonwealth Ventures, Am. Bldgs. Co. Trustee Com. for Econ. Devel., Brookings Inst.; chmn. Ednl. Quality Work Force Adv. Bd. With USNR, 1943-46, PTO. Mem. ABA, N.Y. Stock Exch. (regulatory adv. com.), Union League , Merion Golf Club, Links Club. Home: 805 Oxford Crest Villanova PA 19085 Office: Cigna Corp One Logan Square PO Box 7716 18th and Cherry Sts Philadelphia PA 19192

SAUL, STEPHANIE, journalist; b. St. Louis, Jan. 28, 1954; d. Elmer William and Nancy (Cromer) S.; m. Walt Bogdanich, Jan. 2, 1982; children: Nicholas Walter, Peter Eric. BA, U. Miss., 1975. Reporter New Albany (Miss.) Gazette, 1974, Clarion-Ledger, Jackson, Miss., 1975-80, The Plain Dealer, Cleve., 1980-84; nat. corr. Newsday, Melville, N.Y., 1984—. Recipient Silver Gavel award ABA, 1980, George Polk award for regional reporting, 1981, Nat. Press Club award, 1990, IRE award Investigative Reporters and Editors, 1995, Headliner award Atlantic City Press Club, 1995, Roy Howard award Scripps Howard Found., 1995, Pulitzer prize for investigative reporting, 1995. Office: Newsday 235 Pinelawn Rd Melville NY 11747-4226

SAUL, WILLIAM EDWARD, civil engineering educator; b. N.Y.C., May 15, 1934; s. George James and Fanny Ruth (Murokh) S.; m. J. Muriel Held Eagleburger, May 11, 1976. BSCE, Mich. Tech. U., 1955, MSCE, 1961; PhDCE, Northwestern U., 1964. Registerd profl. engr., Wis., Idaho, Mich., profl. structural engr., Idaho. Mech. engr. Shell Oil Co., New Orleans, 1955-59; instr. engrng. mechanics Mich. Tech. U., Houghton, 1960-62; asst. prof. civil engrng. U. Wis., Madison, 1964-67, assoc. prof., 1967-72, prof., 1972-84; dean Coll. Engrng., prof. civil engrng. U. Idaho, Moscow, 1984-90; prof. civil engrng. Mich. State U., East Lansing, 1990—, chair dept. civil and environ. engrng., 1990-95; cons. engr., 1961—; bd. dirs. Idaho Rsch. Found., 1984-90; vis. prof. U. Stuttgart, Germany, 1970-71. Co-editor Conf. of Methods of Structural Analysis, 1976. Fulbright fellow 1970-71; von Humboldt scholar, 1970-71. Fellow ASCE (pres. Wis. sect. 1983-84); mem. NSPE, Mich. Soc. Profl. Engrs., Internat. Assn. Bridge and Structural Engrs., Am. Concrete Inst., Am. Soc. Engrng. Edn., Sigma Xi, Phi Kappa Phi, Tau Beta Pi, Chi Epsilon. Avocations: hiking, reading, travel, gadgets. Home: 1971 Cimarron Dr Okemos MI 48864-3905 Office: Mich State U A349 Engrng Bldg East Lansing MI 48824

SAULMON, SHARON ANN, college librarian; b. Blackwell, Okla., June 13, 1947; d. Ellis Gordon and Willa Mae Overman; 1 child, John Henry. AA, No. Okla. Coll., 1967; BA, Ctrl. State U., 1969, MBA, 1987; MLS, U. Okla., 1974; postgrad., Okla. State U., 1982. Children's libr. Met. Libr. Sys., Oklahoma City, 1969-74, coord. pub. svcs., 1974-77, asst. chief ext. svcs., 1977-80; reference/special projects libr. Rose State Coll., Midwest City, Okla., 1980-91, head libr., 1991—; adj. faculty Rose State Coll., 1983—; program chair Global Okla. Multi-Cultural Festival, 1993; mem. nat. adv. panel for assessment of sch. and pupb. librs. in support of nat. edn. goals, 1995-96; project dir. Internet Tng., 1997; spkr. various civic and profl. orgns. Contbr. articles to profl. jours. Bd. dirs. Areawide Aging Agy., 1974-77; chair Met. Libr. Commn., 1990—, disbursing agt., chair fin. com., 1986-88, long-range planning com., 1985-87; chair bd. dirs. Met. Librs. Network Ctrl. Okla., 1989-90, chair alternative funding com., 1990—, newsletter editor, 1987-89, chair electronic media com., 1987-89. Recipient Outstanding Contbn. award Met. Libr. Sys., Friends of the Libr., 1990, Disting. Svc. award Okla. Libr. Assn., 1995. Mem. AAUW, Am. Libr. Trustee Assn. (pres. 1994-95, 1st v.p., pres. elect 1993-94, newsletter editor 1989-93, chair publs. com. 1987-92, regional v.p. 1985-88, chair speakers bur. com. 1991-92), Assn. Coll. and Rsch. Librs. (Cmty. and Jr. Coll. sect.), Pub. Libr. Assn., Am. Libr. Assn. (mem. legis. com. 1996—, adv. bd. 1996—), Am. Mktg. Assn., Okla. Libr. Assn. (conf. preview editor 1990-91, chair trustees divsn. 1989-90, mem. coms., disting. svc. award 1995, chair divsn. univ. colls. 1996-97). Democrat. Methodist. Avocations: organist, tennis. Office: Rose State Coll Libr 6420 SE 15th St Midwest City OK 73110-2704

SAULS, DON, clergyman; b. Eureka, N.C.; m. Marie Brown; children: Donna, Dale. B in Sacred Lit., Holmes Sch. of the Bible, Greenville, S.C., 1967; MA in Adult Edn., N.C. State U., 1984; postgrad., N.C. Wesleyan Coll. Ordained to ministry Pentecostal Free Will Bapt. Ch., 1966. Pastor Pentecostal Free Will Bapt. Ch., Benson, N.C., 1967-74, gen. dir. Christian Edn. dept., 1971-84, gen. supt., 1984-96; pastor Pikeville Pentecostal Free Well Bapt. Ch., Goldsboro, N.C., 1996—; tchr. Heritage Bible Coll., Dunn, N.C., 1971—, also trustee; chmn. bd. dirs., sec., mem. bd. adminstrn. Pentecostal Fellowship N.Am., 1988-91, Pentecostal and Charismatic Chs. of N.Am.; lectr. U.S. and abroad; host, preacher weekly TV program; frequent radio spkr. Columnist Messienger, 1984—; contbr. articles to jours. in field. Former chmn. bd. dirs. Cape Fear Christian Acad.; pres. Harnett County Helpnet. Mem. Kiwanis (former pres. Dunn club, bd. dirs., dir. children's programs dist. 11). Office: Pentecostal Free Will Bapt Ch 304 S Cottonwood Dr Goldsboro NC 27530-9188

SAUMIER, ANDRE, finance executive; b. Montreal, Que., Can., Aug. 26, 1933; s. Robert and Georgette (Sansoucy) S.; children: Sonia, Genevieve, Verushka. BA, U. Montreal, 1950; LTh, Angelicum U., Rome, 1955; MA, U. Chgo., 1958; MBA, Harvard U., 1962. Rsch. assoc. Battelle Inst., Columbus, Ohio, 1962-63; dir. rsch. Urban Affairs Coun., Ottawa, Ont., Can., 1963-67; asst. dep. minister rural devel., regional devel., urban affairs Govt. of Can., Ottawa, Ont., 1967-75; dep. sec. gen. to cabinet, dep. minister of mines, water & energy Govt. of Que., Quebec City, 1975-79; sr. v.p. Richardson Greenshields Co., Montreal, 1979-85; pres., CEO Montreal Stock Exch., 1985-87; chmn. Saumier Morrisson & Davidson Inc., Investment Bankers, Montreal, 1987-89, Saumier Freres Conseil, Fin. Advisors, Montreal, 1989—; internat. advisor Alpha Capital Inc., Montreal; bd. dirs., chmn. Societe Nat. de L'Amiante, Montreal; chmn. Sebentar Holdings Inc., Unilever Can., Inc., Toronto, Alyvanor Inc., Montreal, Vista Info. Tech. Inc., Montreal, Can. ASEAN Ctr., Singapore; advisor World Resources Inst., Washington, Ministry of Fin. of Indonesia, Jakarta, Ministry of Fin. of Gabon, Libreville, Ministry of Fin. of Kazakhstan, Almaty, Office of Prime Min., Govt. of Vietnam, Hanoi; bur. de consultation de Montreal, City of Montreal, Que. Contbg. author books on environment. Bd. govs. Nouveau-Monde Theater, Montreal, 1983—, Quebec Press Coun. Found. Decorated officer Nat. Order of Niger, 1972, Order of St.-Lazarus of Jerusalem, 1987; recipient Merit award Montreal C. of C., 1985, 88. Home: 65 St Paul W Apt 403, Montreal, PQ Canada H2Y 3S5 Office: Saumier Freres Conseil, 5 Place Ville-Marie Ste 1234, Montreal, PQ Canada H3B 2G2

SAUNDERS, ADAH WILSON, physical education educator; b. Balt.; d. William Llewellyn and Irene Bertha (Dorkins) Wilson; 1 child, Leigh Robert. BS, Hampton U., 1967; MS, Columbia U. Teacher's Coll., 1971. Instr. phys. edn. Hunter Coll., CUNY, N.Y.C., 1967-68, Bronx C.C., N.Y.C., 1968-69; tchr. phys. edn. N.Y.C. Bd. Edn., 1971—, dean students, 1993—; coach N.Y. Jr. Tennis League; dir. summer camps N.Y.C. Dept. of Human Resources, 1969-72. Inventor: (bd. game) The Presidency; patentee: Rollice Shoe, 1991. Mem. Leonardo Da Vinci Sch. Bd. Edn., Corona, N.Y. Grantee N.Y.C. Bd. Edn., The Early Morning Health Club, 1985. Mem. United Fedn. Tchrs., Am. Fedn. Tchrs., Queens C. of C. Home: Apt 7V 41-10 Bowne St Flushing NY 11355-5612 Office: Leonardo Da Vinci Sch 98-50 50th Ave Corona NY 11368-2757

SAUNDERS, ALEXANDER HALL, real estate executive; b. Tallahassee, Oct. 5, 1941; s. Irvin Jasper and Perry Francis (Watson) S.; m. Pamela Wightman, July 24, 1970; 1 child, Anne Marguerite. AA, Norman Coll., 1961; BA, Mercer U., 1966. Planning adminstr. Ga. Dept. Corrections, Atlanta, 1969-70; mgmt. analyst Ga. Dept. Transp., Atlanta, 1970-71, tng. adminstr., 1971-72, asst. to research and devel., 1972-73, adminstr., asst. to dir., 1974-82; pres. ERA Towne Square Realty, Inc., Stone Mountain, Ga., 1982—. Named one of Top Real Estate Execs. in Am., ERA, 1987. Mem. Nat. Assn. Realtors, Ga. Assn. Realtors, DeKalb Bd. Realtors, ERA North Ga. Brokers Coun. (trustee 1983-86, pres. 1988-89, v.p., dir. fin. 1989-), Metro Listing Svc., U.S. C. of C., DeKalb C. of C., Better Bus. Bur., Alpha Tau Omega, Delta Theta Phi. Avocations: tennis, racquet ball, golf.

SAUNDERS, ARLENE, opera singer; b. Cleve., Oct. 5, 1935. MusB, Baldwin-Wallace Coll., 1957. Tchr. voice Rutgers U., New Brunswick, N.J., 1987-88; tchr. classical vocal repertoire Abraham Goodman Sch., N.Y.C., 1987-88; advisor, tchr. vocal dept. NYU, 1990-96, tchr. master classes, head opera dept., 1990-96; tchr. master classes Baldwin Wallace Coll., Santa Fe Opera Co., etc.; founder, dir. Opera Mobilé, Inc., N.Y.C., 1991—; adjudicator Met. Opera Regional Auditions, Liederkranz Voice Auditions, etc. Debut Milan Opera, 1961; Met. Opera debut in Die Meistersinger, 1976; specializes in Strauss and Wagner; performer with Phila. Opera, Lyric Opera, Houston Opera, Covent Garden, London, Teatro Colon, Buenos Aires, San Francisco Opera, Vienna Staatsoper, Paris Opera, Australian Opera, Sydney, Berlin Deutsche Opera, Munich Staatsoper, Hamburg State Opera, 1963-86, Rome Opera, Brussels Opera, Maggio Musicale, Florence, Italy, Geneva (Switzerland) Opera, Berlin Festival, Lisbon Opera, Glyndebourne Festival Opera, Eng., English Opera North, Boston Opera, N.Y.C. Opera; performed world premieres of Beatrix Cenci, 1971, Jakobowsky und der Oberst, 1965, Help, Help, The Globolinks, 1968, Ein Stern Geht Auf Aus Jaakob, 1970 (Gold medal Vercelli (Italy) voice competition); appeared in opera films including Arabella (title role), Meistersaenger (Eva), Marriage of Figaro (Countess), Help, Help the Globolinks (Mme. Euterpova), Der Freischuetz (Agathe), Gasparone (Carlotta); recs. for Philips and Victor. N.Y.C. Mayor's award, 1962; Kammersängerin Hamburg, 1967. Mem. Pi Kappa Lambda (Epsilon Phi chpt.). Address: 535 E 86th St New York NY 10028-7533

SAUNDERS, BRYAN LESLIE, lawyer; b. Newport News, Va., Apr. 18, 1945; s. Raymond Hayes and Lois Mae (Pair) S.; divorced; children: Kelly Brooke, Justin Lee; m. Anne Mason Dunbar, July 15, 1995. BS, East Tenn. State U., 1967; JD, U. Tenn., 1973. Bar: Va. 1973, U.S. Dist. Ct. (ea. dist.) Va. 1973, U.S. Ct. Appeals (4th cir.) 1991. Lawyer Cogdill & Assocs., Newport News, Va., 1973-76; pvt. practice Newport News, 1976—; commr. in chancery Cir. Ct. of Newport News, 1990—. Sgt. U.S. Army, 1968-71. Decorated Bronze star, 1971; recipient Outstanding Svc. to Law Enforcement Newport News and Police Dept., 1986. Mem. Va. Bar Assn., Nat. Assn. Criminal Def. Lawyers, Va. Coll. Criminal Def. Attys., Pi Kappa Phi, Pi Gamma Mu. Avocations: chess, bridge, bowling. Office: 728 Thimble Shoals Blvd Ste C Newport News VA 23606-2574

SAUNDERS, CHARLES ALBERT, lawyer; b. Boulder, Colo., Jan. 18, 1922; s. Charles and Anna (Crouse) S.; m. Betti Friedel, Oct. 18, 1946; children—Melanie, Stephen, Cynthia, Shelley. BA, U. Houston, 1942; LLB, U. Tex., 1945. Bar: Tex. bar 1945. Since practiced in Houston; partner firm Fulbright & Jaworski, L.L.P., 1959—; dir. Brookside Corp. Editor: How To Live-and Die-With Texas Probate, 8 vols., 1968, Texas Estate Administration, 1975. Bd. dirs. Houston Symphony Soc., 1964—; bd. dirs. Am. Lung Assn., San Jacinto, 1965—, pres., 1972-73; past mem. bd. govs. U. Houston. Recipient Leon Jaworski award for cmty. svc. Houston Bar Assn., 1997. Mem. ABA, State Bar Assn., Houston Bar Assn., Am. Coll. Trust and Estate Coun. (regent 1972-80, pres. 1978-79), Internat. Acad. of Estate and Trust Law, Assn. Cmty. TV (bd. dirs. 1970—). Republican. Presbyterian. Home: 19 Willowron Dr Houston TX 77024-7618 Office: Fulbright & Jaworski 1301 Mckinney St Ste 5100 Houston TX 77010-3095

SAUNDERS, CHARLES BASKERVILLE, JR., retired association executive; b. Boston, Dec. 26, 1928; s. Charles Baskerville and Lucy (Carmichael) S.; m. Margaret MacIntire Shafer, Sept. 9, 1950; children—Charles Baskerville III, George Carlton, Margaret Keyser, Lucy C., John R. Grad., St. Mark's Sch., 1946; A.B., Princeton, 1950. News reporter, polit. columnist Ogdensburg (N.Y.) Jour., 1950-51; edn. reporter Hartford (Conn.) Times, 1951-53; asst. dir. pub. relations Trinity Coll., Hartford, 1953-55; asst. dir. pub. info. Princeton, 1955-57; legis. asst. Sen. H. Alexander Smith, 85th Congress, 1957-58; asst. to asst. sec. for legislation HEW, 1958-59; asst. to sec. Arthur S. Flemming, 1959-61, dep. asst. sec. for legislation, 1969-71; asst. to pres. Brookings Instn., 1961-69; dep. commr. of edn. for external affairs U.S. Office Edn., 1971-72; dep. asst. sec. for edn. HEW, 1973-74; dir. govt. relations Am. Council on Edn., 1975-78, v.p. for govt. relations, 1978-87, sr. v.p., 1987-92. Author: Brookings Institution: A Fifty-Year History, 1966, Upgrading the American Police, 1970. Mem. Montgomery County Bd. Edn., 1966-70, Md. Higher Edn. Commn., 1989— (chmn. 1994-95, vice chmn. 1995—); chmn. bd. dirs. Md. Higher Edn. Loan Corp., 1994-95. Republican. Presbyterian. Home: 7622 Winterberry Pl Bethesda MD 20817-4848

SAUNDERS, DAVID ALAN, lawyer; b. Chgo., June 3, 1939; s. Elmer M. and Eleanor (Lindauer) S.; m. Judith Obalil, June 15, 1963; children: Lynn Ellen, Laura Beth. BA, Oberlin Coll., 1961; JD, U. Chgo., 1964. Bar: Ill. 1964, U.S. Dist. Ct. (no. dist.) Ill. 1964, U.S. Ct. Appeals (7th cir.) 1965. Assoc. Hoffman & Davis, Chgo., 1964-69, ptnr., 1969-86; ptnr. Seyfarth, Shaw, Fairweather & Geraldson, Chgo., 1986—; lectr. on pub. fin. for various bar and govt. fin. assns. Active Bd. Ethics, Evanston, Ill., 1986-. Mem. ABA, Chgo. Bar Assn., Nat. Assn. Bond Lawyers, Chgo. Council Lawyers. Home: 1133 Forest Ave Evanston IL 60202-1407 Office: Seyfarth Shaw Fairweather 55 E Monroe St Ste 4200 Chicago IL 60603-5803

SAUNDERS, DEBRA J., columnist; b. Newton, Mass., Dec. 8, 1954. BA in Latin and Greek, U. Mass., Boston, 1980. Asst. dir. Arnold Zenker Assocs., 1982-83; writer/rschr., account exec. Todd Domke Assocs., Sacramento, 1983-84, Russo Watts & Rollins, Sacramento, 1985-86; asst. to Rep. Leader Calif. Legislature, Sacramento, 1987-88; columnist, editl. writer L.A. Daily News, 1988-92; columnist San Francisco Chronicle, 1992—; leader study group on polit. speechmaking Harvard U., Cambridge, Mass., 1984; tchr. editl. and column writing UCLA Ext., 1992. Published in Wall St. Jour., Nat. Review, Weekly Std.; syndicated nationally via Creators Syndicate. Office: San Francisco Chronicle 901 Mission St San Francisco CA 94103-2905

SAUNDERS, DERO AMES, writer, editor; b. Starkville, Miss., Sept. 27, 1913; s. Madison and Erin (Hearon) S.; m. Beatrice Nair, May 23, 1936; children: David, Richard. A.B., Dartmouth Coll., 1935; A.M., Columbia U., 1938. Lectr., lecture mgr., contbr. to various mgs., 1936-42; with Fgn. Econ. Adminstrn., Washington and Cairo, Egypt, 1943-45; chief Fgn. Econ. Adminstrn. (Middle East div.), 1945; asso. editor Fortune mag., 1945-57; v.p. Med. and Pharm. Info. Bur., 1957-59; lectr. Hunter Coll., 1960-61, 67—; assoc. editor Forbes mag., 1960-62, sr. editor, 1962-66, exec. editor, 1966-81, contbg. editor, 1982—. Contbg. author: Why Do People Buy?, 1953, The

Changing American Market, 1954; Editor: The Portable Gibbon, 1952, The Autobiography of Edward Gibbon, 1961; co-editor: The History of Rome, 1958; chmn. editorial bd.: Dartmouth Alumni mag., 1983-85. Pres. Dartmouth Alumni Council, 1970-71; Prin. U.S. civilian rep. Middle East Supply Center, 1945. Clubs: Players (N.Y.C.); Heights Casino (Bklyn.). Home: 446 W 22nd St New York NY 10011-2502 Office: 60 5th Ave New York NY 10011-8802

SAUNDERS, DOROTHY ANN, insurance company executive, sales management; b. Roxbury, N.C., Nov. 29, 1932; d. James William and Anna Bell (Wesley) Rice; m. Bernard L. Lewis, June 10, 1950 (dec. Jan. 1957); m. J.R. Saunders, Nov. 26, 1976 (dec. May 1981). Student, Md. U., 1950-53. Bookeeper, office mgr. IN Cosmetics, Bethesda, Md., 1958; owner, mgr. Donnel's Hall of Gifts, Washington, 1959-63, Gifts, Inc., Washington, 1959-63; with U.S. Govt. Health, Edn., Welfare, Bethesda, 1965-73; owner, mgmt. in sales Dorothy Saunders Ins. Agy., Forest, Va., 1973—; vis. spkr. Bus. & Profl. Woman's Assn., Brookneal, Va., 1986-87; mem. bd. rsch. advisor ABI. Mem. Nat. Trust for Historic Preservation. Fellow Am. Biog. Inst.; mem. Internat. Platform Assn., Am. Lyceum Assn. Democrat. Baptist. Avocation: music. Home and Office: RR 1 Box 166D Huddleston VA 24104-9765

SAUNDERS, GEORGE LAWTON, JR., lawyer; b. Mulga, Ala., Nov. 8, 1931; s. George Lawton and Ethel Estell (York) S.; children: Kenneth, Ralph, Victoria; m. Terry M. Rose. B.A., U. Ala., 1956; J.D., U. Chgo., 1959. Bar: Ill. 1960. Law clk. to chief judge U.S. Ct. Appeals (5th cir.), Montgomery, Ala., 1959-60; law clk to Justice Hugo L. Black U.S. Supreme Ct., Washington, 1960-62; assoc. Sidley & Austin, Chgo., 1962-67, ptnr., 1967-90; founding ptnr. Saunders & Monroe, Chgo., 1990—. With USAF, 1951-54. Fellow Am. Coll. Trial Lawyers; mem. ABA, Ill. State Bar Assn., Chgo. Bar Assn., Order of Coif, Chgo. Club, Tavern Club, Point-O'Woods Club, Quadrangle Club, Law Club, Legal Club, Phi Beta Kappa. Democrat. Baptist. Home: 179 E Lake Shore Dr Chicago IL 60611-1351 Office: Saunders & Monroe 205 N Michigan Ave Chicago IL 60601

SAUNDERS, JAMES C., neuroscientist, educator; b. Elizabeth, N.J., May 8, 1941; s. Charles Oliver and Elizabeth Veronica (Drake) S.; m. Elaine Priscilla Edwards, Oct. 14, 1967; children: Breton Morris, Drew Charles. BA, Ohio Wesleyan U., 1963; MA, Conn. Coll., 1965, U. Pa., 1979; PhD, Princeton U., 1968. Lectr. dept. psychology Monash U., Victoria, Australia, 1969-72; rsch. assoc. Cen. Inst. for Deaf, St. Louis, 1972-73; asst. prof., then prof. dept. otorhinolaryngology U. Pa., Phila., 1973-92, acting dir. Inst. Neurol. Scis., 1980-83, prof., 1984—; guest scientist Karolinska Inst., Stockholm, 1984-85; exec. com. CHABA, Nat. Rsch. Coun., Washington, 1986-89; chmn. disorders rev. com. NIDCD, Bethesda, Md., 1987-89; mem. exec. coun. Assn. Rsch. Otolaryngology, Chgo., 1988-91; mem. com. on hearing and bioacoustics Nat. Inst. on Deafness and Other Communications Disorders. Contbr. chpts., rev. papers to books on biology of hearing; contbr. articles on auditory neurobiology to profl. jours; author abstracts of meeting presentations on hearing. Recipient Basic Sci. Rsch. award Am. Acad. Otolaryngology, 1978, 87, Pa. Acad. Otolaryngology, 1982, Basic Sci. Excellence award (Claude Pepper award) NIDCD, 1988, Lindback award for disting. teaching U. Pa., 1992. Mem. AAAS, Acoustical Soc. Am., Soc. Neurosci., N.Y. Acad. Sci., Sigma Xi (legal cons. effects of noise on hearing). Democrat. Office: U Pa 5 Ravdin ORL 3400 Spruce St Philadelphia PA 19104 Home: 417 Bryn Mawr Ave Bala Cynwyd PA 19004-2619

SAUNDERS, JOHN, broadcast network host; b. Feb. 2, 1955. Student, Western Mich. U., 1974-76, Ryerson Poly., Toronto, 1976. News dir. CKNS Radio, Espanola, Ont., Can., 1978; sports anchor CKNY-TV, Ont., 1978-79, ATV News, New Brunswick, Can., 1979-80, City-TV, Toronto, 1980-82, WMAR-TV, Balt., 1982-86; anchor SportsCenter, NCAA basketball studio host, NHL host ESPN, 1986—; host Baseball Tonight ESPN, 1990-93, NHL telecasts, 1987-88; host NCAA basketball ABC, 1990—, coll. football telecast host, 1992—, NHL host, 1993—; contbr. Wide World of Sports, 1990—; caller play-by-play Toronto Raptors CKVR-TV, 1995—. Office: ESPN ESPN Plaza Bristol CT 06010

SAUNDERS, KENNETH D., insurance company executive, consultant, arbitrator; b. Chgo., Jan. 4, 1927; s. Maurice and Mildred (Cochrane) S.; m. Jean S. Davies, Dec. 17, 1949; children: Karen Saunders Waugh, William Thomas. A.B., Dartmouth Coll., 1949. With Continental Casualty Co., Chgo., 1949-59; asst. v.p. Continental Casualty Co., 1957-59; exec. asst. Standard Accident Ins. Co., Detroit, 1959-62; with Combined Ins. Co. Am., Chgo., 1962-86; v.p. Combined Ins. Co. Am., 1969-74, sr. v.p., 1974-86; with Rollins, Burdick, Hunter, 1986-87. With USMC, 1945-46. Mem. Health Ins. Assn. Am. (com. leader), Chgo. Group Ins. Assn. (past treas., dir.), Internat. Ins. Soc. (charter mem.), Am. Arbitration Assn. (panel). Clubs: Economic (Chgo.), Tavern (Chgo.), Exmoor Country (Ill.), John's Island (Fla.). Office: 1418 Woodhill Dr Northbrook IL 60062-4661

SAUNDERS, MARK A., lawyer; b. N.Y.C., July 9, 1946; s. Phillip George and Florence (Schell) S.; m. Paula Squillante, Sept. 2, 1972; children: David Prescott, Christina Joy. BA cum laude, Fordham U., 1968; JD, U. Va.-Charlottesville, 1972. Bar: N.Y. 1973, U.S. Dist. Ct. (so. dist.) N.Y. 1973, U.S. Ct. Appeals (2d cir.) 1974, U.S. Ct. Appeals (D.C. Cir.) 1987, U.S. Supreme Ct., 1987. Assoc. law firm Donovan Leisure Newton & Irvine, N.Y.C., 1972-75; counsel Morgan Stanley & Co. Inc., N.Y.C., 1975-80; sr. counsel Kennecott Corp., N.Y.C., 1980-82; ptnr. law firm Seki, Jarvis & Lynch, N.Y.C., 1982-84, Blum, Haimoff, Gersen, Lipson & Niedergang, N.Y.C., 1984-87; ptnr.-in-charge securities practice Haight, Gardner, Poor & Havens, N.Y.C., 1987—; mem. faculty Internat. Law Inst., Washington, 1985—; mem. comparative law delegation to govt. of People's Rep. of China, 1986; gen. counsel Softstrip Intrnat. Ltd. subs. Eastman Kodak Co., 1985-87. Author: American Depositary Receipts: An Introduction to U.S. Capital Markets For Foreign Companies, 1993, Fordham Internat Law Jour., 1993, Onr. mng. bd. editors: Va. Jour. Internat. Law, 1971-72; cons. editor China Banking & Finance, 1988-92; mem. adv. bd. The Southwestern Legal Found. Recipient Jervey Fellowship in Fgn. and Comparative Law, Columbia U. Parker Sch. Internat. Law, 1972. Fellow Am. Coll. Investment Counsel; mem. ABA (coms. fed. securities, regulation & internat. securities matters & foreign investment in the U.S.), Assn. of Bar of City of N.Y., Internat. Bar Assn., Legatus, Phi Beta Kappa. Roman Catholic. Home: 3 Nutmeg Dr Greenwich CT 06831-3211 Office: Haight Gardner Poor & Havens 195 Broadway New York NY 10007-3100

SAUNDERS, NORMAN THOMAS, military officer; b. Amityville, N.Y., Oct. 19, 1942; s. Norman George and Marjory (Scott) S.; m. Christine Patricia Miller, Feb. 24, 1968; children: Thomas, Carré. BS, USCG Acad., 1964; MS, Naval Postgrad. Sch., Monterey, Calif., 1972; grad., Nat. War Coll., 1985. Commd. officer USCG, 1964, advanced through grades to Radm., 1991; br. chief edn. and tng. div. USCG, Washington, 1972-76; exec. officer USCGC COURAGEOUS, Port Canaveral, Fla., 1976-78; spl. projects officer personnel div. USCG, Washington, 1978-79, br. chief personnel div., 1979-82; comdg. officer USCGC DEPENDABLE, Panama City, Fla., 1982-84; spl. projects officer research and devel. USCG, Key West, Fla., 1985-86; comdr. USCG Group, Key West, 1986-88; chief intelligence and law enforcement br. 7th CG Dist., Miami, Fla., 1988-90; chief, ops. div. 7th USCG Dist., Miami, 1990-91; comdr. 2nd USCG Dist., St. Louis, 1991-93, mil. personnel command, Washington, 1993-94; asst. commdr. for ops. Office of Law Enforcement and Def. Ops., 1994—. Mem. Mil. Order World Wars, Naval Order U.S., Coast Guard Combat VA, Ret. Officers Assn., Sigma Xi. Republican. Methodist. Avocations: running, tennis, fishing, reading. Home: 13479 Point Pleasant Dr Chantilly VA 20151-2446

SAUNDERS, PAUL CHRISTOPHER, lawyer; b. N.Y.C., May 21, 1941; s. John Richard and Agnes Grace (Kelly) S.; m. Patricia Newman, Sept. 14, 1968; children—Paul Christopher, Michael Eagan. A.B., Fordham Coll., 1963; J.D., Georgetown U., 1966; Certificat d'Études Politiques, Institut d'Études Politiques, Paris, 1962. Bar: N.Y. 1966, D.C. 1967, U.S. Supreme Ct. 1969. Assoc. Cravath, Swaine & Moore, N.Y.C., 1971-77, ptnr., 1977—. Mem. editl. bd. Georgetown Law Jour., 1965-66; editor-in-chief The Advocate, 1969-70. Trustee Fordham U., 1991-96; bd. regents Georgetown U., chmn. bd. visitors Law Ctr., 1992-97; trustee, vice-chmn. Fordham Prep. Sch., 1986-94; v.p., bd. dirs. Legal Aid Soc., 1983-88; bd. dirs., trustee Lawyers Com. for Civil Rights Under Law, 1985—, co-chair 1995-97; bd. trustees Vols. Legal Svc., Inc.; mem. Cardinal's Com. of Laity, 1982-90. Capt. JAGC, U.S. Army, 1967-71. Decorated Knight of Malta, 1982; recipient John Carroll award Georgetown U., 1995. Fellow Am. Bar Found.; mem. ABA, N.Y. State Bar Assn., Assn. of Bar of City of N.Y., London Ct. Internat. Arbitration, Am. Judicature Soc., Phi Beta Kappa, Pi Sigma Alpha. Democrat. Roman Catholic. Clubs: Apawamis, Westchester Country (Rye, N.Y.). Home: 1220 Park Ave New York NY 10128-1733 also: 455 Polly Pk Rd Rye NY 10580-1949 Office: Cravath Swaine & Moore Worldwide Plz 825 8th Ave New York NY 10019-7416

SAUNDERS, PETER PAUL, investor; b. Budapest, Hungary, July 21, 1928; emigrated to Can., 1941, naturalized, 1946; s. Peter Paul and Elizabeth (Halom) Szende; m. Nancy Louise McDonald, Feb. 11, 1956; children: Christine Elizabeth McBride, Paula Marie. Student, Vancouver Coll., 1941-44; B.Com., U. B.C., 1948. Acct. Canadian Pacific Rly. Co., 1948-50; founder, pres. Laurentide Fin. Corp., Ltd., 1950-66, vice chmn., 1966-67; chmn., pres. Coronation Credit Corp. Ltd., Vancouver, B.C., Can., 1968-78, Versatile Corp. (formerly Coronation Credit Corp. and Cornat Industries Ltd.), Vancouver, B.C., Can., 1978-87; prin., pres. Saunders Investment Ltd., Vancouver, 1987—; bd. dirs. Computrol Security Sys. Ltd., Wajax Ltd., Greene Valley Concessions, AXA Pacific Ins. Co., Molnar Capital Corp.; mem. Vancouver adv. bd. Nat. Trust Co. Ltd.; pres., dir. Harlan Fairbanks Co. Ltd. Past pres. Vancouver Symphony Soc., 1968-70, Can. Cancer Soc., B.C. and Yukon Rdgion, 1975-77, Vancouver Art Gallery Assn., 1981-83; chmn. Vancouver Opera Round Table, 1984-92; bd. dirs. B.C. and Yukon Div. Arthritis Soc. Mem. Vancouver Club, Vancouver Lawn Tennis and Badminton Club, Shaughnessy Golf and Country Club, Royal Vancouver Yacht Club, Thunderbird Country Club (Rancho Mirage, Calif.). Avocations: golf, skiing, hunting, boating. Home: 3620 Alexandra St, Vancouver, BC Canada V6J 4B9 Office: Saunders Investment Ltd, PO Box 49352 Bentall Ctr, Vancouver, BC Canada V7X 1L4

SAUNDERS, PHILIP D., professional basketball team executive; b. Cleve., Feb. 23, 1955; m. Debbie Saunders; children: Ryan, Mindy, Rachel and Kimberly (twins). Student, U. Minn. Asst. coach U. Minn Golden Golphers, 1982-86, U. Tulsa, 1986-88; head coach Continental Basketball Assn. Rapid City (S.D.) Thrillers, 1988-89; head coach Continental Basketball Assn. La Crosse (Wis.) Catbirds, 1989-94, gen. mgr., 1991-93, team pres., 1991-94; head coach Continental Basketball Assn. Sioux Falls (S.D.) Skyforce; gen. mgr., head coach Minn. Timberwolves, 1995—. Named CBA Coach of the Yr., 1989, 92. Office: Minn Timberwolves 600 1st Ave N Minneapolis MN 55403-1400*

SAUNDERS, ROGER ALFRED, hotel group executive; b. Brookline, Mass., Feb. 14, 1929; s. Irving Matthew and Shirley (Brown) S.; m. Nina Ann Alexander, Oct. 4, 1953 (dec. 1991); children: Gary L., Jeffrey G., Todd R., Tedd R.; m. Norma Stilson, Aug. 11, 1996. A.B., Miami U., 1951; H.H.D. (hon.), Stonehill Coll., 1981, New Eng. Sch. Law, 1982, Johnson and Wales U., 1990; cert. hotel adminstr., Mich. State U., 1985. Pres., owner Copley Square Hotel, Boston, 1951—; co-owner Lenox Hotel, Boston, 1963—; founder Saunders Hotel Group, Boston, 1962—; trustee Am. Hotel Found., Inc.; bd. dirs. Friends of Copley Sq. Pres. Back Bay Assn., 1974-76, bd. dirs., exec. com.; trustee Women's Edn. and Indsl. Union, 1984-87, bd. dirs., adv. Council Freedom Trail; bd. overseers Children's Hosp., New Eng. Med. Center, Boston, Mus. Fine Arts, 1986-88, 92—; Wang Ctr. for Performing Arts (life trustee); trustee Beth Israel/Deaconess Hosp. Corp.; mem. Boston Kyoto Sister City Found., Corp. Mass. Gen. Hosp., Boston Coordinating Com. (Vault), 1985—; bd. dirs. Boston Mcpl. Research Bur., 1982-87, World Affairs Council Boston; bd. advisors Stonehill Coll.; mem. bd. corp. New Eng. Med. Center Hosp., 1981-94; mem. adv. council Ho. of Reps. Tourism and Travel Caucus, 1980-84; mem. corp. Mus. of Sci., 1982-89 Mass. Gen. Hosp., 1985—; chmn. Mass. Film Commn., 1984; appointed Civilian Aide to Sec. of Army for Mass., 1987—; bd. overseers Boston Symphony Orchestra; mem. exec. com. Creater Boston Conv. and Visitors Bur., 1985—. Served with Air Force N.G., 1951-54. Recipient Hotel and Restaurant Industry Leadership award of New Eng., 1977; Grand Bostonian award Boston's 350th Anniversary Celebration, 1978; resolution of recognition Boston City Council, 1978, 80, 82; Humanitarian award Nat. Jewish Hosp. and Research Ctr., Denver, 1979; cert. of merit U.S. Congl. Travel and Tourism Caucus; Hist. Neighborhood Found. award, 1986; Community Enrichment award Am. Jewish Com., 1990; honoree NCCJ, 1985; named Yankee Travel Exec. of Yr., 1991. Fellow Inst. Cert. Travel Agts.;mem Internat. Assn. of Skal Clubs (exec. com., past pres.), Am. Hotel and Motel Assn. (chmn. 1991), Am. Hotel and Motel Assn. (nat. pres. 1990), New Eng. Innkeepers Assn. (v.p. 1981-85), Mass. Hotel Assn. (pres. 1963-65), Greater Boston Hotel Assn. (bd. dirs., pres. 1966-68), Boston C. of C. (v.p. 1973-78), Confrerie de la Chaine des Rotisseurs (chargé de Mission 1988—), Les Amis de Escoffier (exec. com. 1983—), World Affairs Council Boston (bd. dirs.), Algonquin Club, Badminton and Tennis Club (Boston), Longwood Cricket, Bass Rocks County Club. Founder first non-profit Nat. Ind. Hotel Reservation Center. Office: Saunders Hotel Group 6 Saint James Ave Boston MA 02116-3819

SAUNDERS, RON, lawyer, former state legislator; b. Key West, Fla., Oct. 30, 1954; s. Jack and Edith (Hill) S. BS with high honors, U. Fla., 1976, JD, 1979. Bar: Fla. 1979. Pvt. practice Key West, 1979-94, Tallahassee, 1995—; mem. Fla. Ho. of Reps., 1986-94, chmn. appropriations com., 1990-92, chmn. cmty. affairs com., 1992-94; mem. Fla. Tax and Budget Reform Commn., 1993-94. Pres. Key West Jaycees, 1981-82; chmn. bd. trustees Fla. Keys C.C., 1983-86; pres. Fla. Keys Land and Sea Trust, 1990-91. Named Outstanding Chpt. Pres., Fla. Jaycees, 1982, Outstanding Young Floridian, 1993, Most Effective Mem., Fla. Ho. of Reps., 1991, 92. Mem. Fla. Bar Assn. (bd. govs. young lawyers sect. 1982-86). Democrat. Episcopalian. Address: PO Box 10923 Tallahassee FL 32302-3923

SAUNDERS, RUBIE AGNES, former magazine editor, author; b. N.Y.C., Jan. 31, 1929; d. Walter St. Clair and Rubie Gwendolyn (Ford) S. B.A., Hunter Coll. CUNY, 1950. Editorial sec. Parents Mag. Enterprises, Inc., N.Y.C., 1950-51; editorial asst. Parents Mag. Enterprises, Inc., 1951-53, asst. editor, 1953-54, mng. editor, 1955-60; editor Young Miss mag., 1960-80, editorial dir., 1967-80; instr. Inst. Children's Lit., 1980—. Author: Calling All Girls Party Book, 1966, Marilyn Morgan, R.N., 1969, Marilyn Morgan's Triumph, 1970, Concise Guide to Baby Sitting, 1972, Concise Guide to Smart Shopping and Consumerism, 1973, Quick and Easy Housekeeping, 1977, The Beauty Book, 1983, Good Grooming for Boys, 1989, Good Grooming for Girls, 1989. Bd. dirs. Feminist Press, New Rochelle Coun. on Arts.; mem., pres. New Rochelle Bd. Edn., 1991—. Named Outstanding Grad., 1960, elected to Hunter Coll. Hall of Fame, 1972; recipient 25 Yr. service award Cub Scout Pack 371, Bklyn., 1985. Mem. Westchester-Putnam Sch. Bds. Assn. (exec. com.). Home: 26 Glenwood Ave New Rochelle NY 10801-3602

SAUNDERS, SALLY LOVE, poet, educator; b. Bryn Mawr, Pa., Jan. 15, 1940; d. Lawrence and Dorothy (Love) S. Student, Sophia U., Tokyo, Japan, 1963, U. Pa., Columbia; B.S., George Williams Coll., 1965. Tchr. Shipley Sch., Bryn Mawr, 1962-65, Agnes Irwin Sch., Wynnewood, Pa., 1964-65, Montgomery County Day Sch., Wynnewood, 1962, Miquon (Pa.) Sch., Waldron Acad., Merion, Pa., 1965-66, Phelps Sch., Malvern, Pa., 1965-70, Frankford Friends Sch. Phila., 1965-66, Haverford (Pa.) Sch., 1965-66, Friends Sem. Sch., N.Y.C., 1966-68, Ballard Sch., N.Y.C., 1966-67, Lower Merion Sch., Ardmore, Pa., nights 1967-71, Univ. Settlement House, Phila., 1961-63, Navajo Indian Reservation, Fort Defiance, Ariz., 1963, Young Men's Jewish Youth Center, Chgo., 1964-65, Margaret Fuller Settlement House, Cambridge, Mass., 1958-61; poetry therapist Pa. Hosp. Inst., 1969-74; also drug rehab. house Pa. Hosp. Inst., Phila.; poet in residence Tyrone Guthrie Ctr., Newbliss, Ireland, Aug. 1988; poetry workshop leader Pendle Hill Quaker Ctr., Wallingford, Pa., Apr. 1988; poetry week leader Ferry Beach, Saco, Maine, summer 1988; pioneer in poetry therapy. Poet, 1946—; poems pub. in periodicals including others; author: Past the Near Meadows, 1961, Pauses, 1978, Fresh Bread, 1982, Random Thoughts, 1992, Patchwork Quilt, 1993, Quiet Thoughts and Gentle Feelings, 1996; contbr. poems to newspapers. Mem. Acad. Am. Poets, Nat. Fedn. State Poetry Socs., Am. Poetry League, Nat. League Am. Pen Women, Poetry Therapy Assn. (v.p.), Avalon Orgn., Authors Guild, Nat. Writers Club, Pen and Brush Club, N.H., Pa. poetry socs., Cath. Poetry Soc. (asso.), Fla. State Poetry Soc. (asso.). Episcopalian. Home: 2030 Vallejo St Apt 501 San Francisco CA 94123-4854 Office: 609 Rose Hill Rd Broomall PA 19008-2254 *So often during my life I have found great comfort and strength in writing and reading poetry. With my poetry I want to help others to get in touch with their own powers. Poetry, to me, is a rare and beautiful freedom and this is what I want to share with others.*

SAUNDERS, TERRY ROSE, lawyer; b. Phila., July 13, 1942; d. Morton M. and Esther (Hauptman) Rose; m. George Lawton Saunders Jr., Sept. 21, 1975. BA, Barnard Coll., 1964; JD, NYU, 1973. Bar: D.C. 1973, Ill. 1976, U.S. Dist. Ct. (no. dist.) Ill. 1976, U.S. Ct. Appeals (7th cir.) 1976, U.S. Supreme Ct. 1983. Assoc. Williams & Connolly, Washington, 1973-75; assoc. Jenner & Block, Chgo., 1975-80, ptnr., 1981-86; ptnr. Susman, Saunders & Buehler, Chgo., 1987-94; pvt. practice Law Offices of Terry Rose Saunders, Chgo., 1995—. Author: (with others) Securities Fraud: Litigating Under Rule 10b-5, 1989. Recipient Robert B. McKay award NYU Sch. Law. Mem. ABA (co-chair class actions and derivative suits com. sect. litigation 1992-95, task force on merit selection of judges), Ill. State Bar Assn., Chgo. Bar Assn., NYU Alumni Assn. (bd. dirs. 1985—), Order of Coif, Union League Club. Office: 30 N La Salle St Chicago IL 60602-2502

SAUNDERS, WARD BISHOP, JR., retired aluminum company executive; b. Gilroy, Calif., Nov. 26, 1919; s. Ward Bishop and Lamira (Doan) S.; m. Elaine McDermott, Oct. 11, 1942; children: Douglas L., Myra K., Leslie J. B.S., U. Calif.-Berkeley, 1942; J.D., Stanford U., 1948. Bar: Calif. 1948, U.S. Dist. Ct. (no. dist.) Calif. 1948, U.S. Supreme Ct. 1956. Atty. Kaiser Aluminum & Chem. Corp., Oakland, Calif., 1951-65, div. v.p., 1965-71; v.p. Kaiser Aluminum & Chem. Corp., Oakland, 1971-84; dir. Volta River Authority, Accra, Ghana, Aluminium Bahrain, Manama, Bahrain, Hindustan Aluminium Co., Bombay, India; mng. dir. Volta Aluminium Co. Ltd., Tema, Ghana, 1971-84; pres. Kaiser Aluminum Salaried Retirees Assn., 1991-93. Served to lt. USNR, 1942-46. Mem. State Bar Calif., Alameda County Bar Assn., Kaiser Aluminum Salaried Retirees Assn. (bd. dirs. 1988-94, pres. 1992-93, v.p. 1995—), Commonwealth Club of Calif. Republican. Unitarian. Home: 6123 Estates Dr Oakland CA 94611-3117

SAUNDERS, W(ARREN) PHILLIP, JR., economics educator, consultant, author; b. Morgantown, W.Va., Sept. 3, 1934; s. Warren Phillip and Thelma Marie (Dotson) S.; m. Nancy Lee Trainor, June 16, 1956; children: Kathleen M., Kevin W., Keith A., Kent T., Kristine A. BA, Pa. State U., 1956; MA, U. Ill., 1957; PhD, MIT, 1964. Instr. econs. Bowdoin Coll., Brunswick, Maine, 1961-62; rsch. assoc., from asst. to assoc. prof. econs. Carnegie-Mellon U., Pitts., 1962-70; prof. econs. Ind. U., Bloomington, 1970—; assoc. dean Coll. of Arts and Scis. Ind. U., Bloomington, 1974-78, chmn. dept. econs., 1988-92; cons. Agy. for Instructional Tech., Bloomington, 1976-78, 81-84, 92-93. Author: (books) Political Dimension of Labor-Management Relations, 1986; author, editor: Framework for Teaching Basic Economic Concepts, 1995; (Workbooks) Introduction to Macroeconomics (17th edit.), 1997, Introduction to Microeconomics (17th edit.), 1997; contbr. articles to Am. Econ. Rev., 1964—. Chmn. staff-parish rels. com. First United Meth. Ch., Bloomington, 1982-94. Recipient Vilard award for disting. rsch., Nat. Assn. Econ. Educators, N.Y.C., 1986, Leavey award for edn. Freedoms Found., Valley Forge, Pa., 1986, Disting. Svc. award. Nat. Coun. Econ. Edn., 1995. Mem. Am. Econ. Assn., Midwest Econ. Assn. (1st v.p. 1988-89), Soc. Econs. Educators (pres. 1992-93). Home: 3725 E Brownridge Rd Bloomington IN 47401-4209 Office: Ind Univ Dept Econs Bloomington IN 47405

SAUNDERS, WILLIAM HUNDLEY, JR., retired chemist, educator; b. Pulaski, Va., Jan. 12, 1926; s. William Hundley and Vivian (Watts) S.; m. Nina Velta Plesums, June 25, 1960 (dec. June 1982); children: Anne Michele, Claude William. BS in Chemistry, Coll. William and Mary, 1948; PhD in Organic Chemistry, Northwestern U., 1952. Rsch. assoc. MIT, 1951-53; instr. U. Rochester, 1953-56, from. asst. prof. to assoc. prof., 1956-64, prof. chemistry, 1964-91, faculty sr. assoc., 1991-95, chmn. dept., 1966-70, prof. emeritus, 1996—. Author: Ionic Aliphatic Reactions, 1965; (with A.F. Cockerill) Mechanisms of Elimination Reactions, 1973; (with L. Melander) Reaction Rates of Isotopic Molecules, 1980; contbr. numerous articles to profl. jours. With U.S. Army, 1944-45, ETO. Guggenheim fellow, 1960-61; Sloan Found. fellow, 1961-64; NSF sr. postdoctoral fellow, 1970-71. Mem. Am. Chem. Soc., Royal Soc. Chemistry, Phi Beta Kappa, Sigma Xi, Phi Lambda Upsilon. Democrat. Unitarian. Avocations: bicycling, cross country skiing, travel. Home: 15 Parkwood Ave Rochester NY 14620-3401 Office: U Rochester Dept Chemistry River Sta Rochester NY 14627

SAUNDERS, WILLIAM LOCKWOOD, financial consultant; b. Seattle, Dec. 13, 1911; s. William Guy and Elizabeth (Ruggles) S.; m. Marjorie Allen, Nov. 30, 1945 (dec.); 1 dau., Mary Lee; m. Margaret Cella, Feb. 13, 1959; stepchildren: Joan Aletto, Gail Nelson. B.A., U. Wash., 1948; M.B.A., Northwestern U., 1950. Resident mgr. Drumheller Ehrlichman & White, Aberdeen, Wash., 1933-36; with W.L. Saunders (investments), 1936-42; sales mgr. H. Irving Lee & Co., San Jose, Calif., 1946; fin. cons., 1946-48; with A.G. Becker & Co., Inc., Chgo., 1949—; v.p. A.G. Becker & Co., Inc., 1951—, dir., 1960—; chmn. Oceanatic Steamship Co., 1958-61; pres. Gisholt Machine Co., Madison, Wis., 1963-66; also dir.; chmn. Long Island Tankers, 1958-60; dir. Oregon Am. Lumber Co., 1951-53, Pacific Far East Line, 1957-61, Gilman Engring. & Mfg., 1963, Enterprises Internat., Inc., 1973—, The George E. Taylor Fgn. Affairs INst., 1986—. Bd. dirs. John A. Johnson Found. Served to lt. comdr. USNR, 1943-46. Mem. Bohemian Club (San Francisco), Lighthouse Point Yacht and Racquet Club (Fla.), Beta Gamma Sigma, Alpha Sigma Phi. Congregationalist. Home: The Highlands Seattle WA 98177 also: # 16 1212 Hwy A-1A Hillsboro Bch FL 33062 Office: PO Box 33250 Seattle WA 98133-0250

SAUNDERSON, WILLIAM, Canadian provincial official; m. Meredith Saunderson; children: Janet, Brian, Pamela. BA in History, U. Toronto; Hon.Doctorate, U. Ottawa, 1994. Chartered acct. With firm Clarkson & Gordon (now Ernst & Young), to 1971; co-founder, v.p. Sceptre Investment Counsel Ltd., from 1971; mem. for Eglinton Can. Parliament; min. econ. devel., trade and tourism Province of Ont., 1995—; fin. comptroller Progressive Conservative Nat. Election Campaigns, 1984 88. Active in fundraising for U. Ottawa, Queen Elizabeth Hosp., Toronto, Scouts Can., Rowing Can. Office: Hearst Block, 900 Bay St, Toronto, ON Canada M7A 2E1*

SAUNTRY, SUSAN SCHAEFER, lawyer; b. Bangor, Maine, May 7, 1943; d. William Joseph and Emily Joan (Guenter) Schaefer; m. John Philip Sauntry, Jr., Aug. 18, 1968; 1 child, Mary Katherine. BS in Foreign Service, Georgetown U., 1965, JD, 1975. Bar: D.C. 1975, U.S. Dist. Ct. D.C. 1975, U.S. Ct. Appeals (D.C. cir.) 1975, (4th cir.) 1977, (6th cir.) 1978, (10th cir.) 1983, U.S. Supreme Ct. 1983. Congl. relations asst. OEO, Washington, 1966-68; program analyst EEO Com., Washington, 1968-70, U.S. Dept. Army, Okinawa, 1970-72; assoc. Morgan, Lewis & Bockius, Washington, 1975-83, ptnr., 1983-94; of counsel Howe, Anderson & Steyer, PC, Washington, 1994—. Co-author: Employee Dismissal Law: Forms and Procedures, 1986; contbr. articles to profl. jours. Mem. ABA, D.C. Bar Assn., D.C. Women's Bar Assn., Nat. Assn. Women Bus. Owners, AAUW, Phi Beta Kappa, Pi Sigma Alpha. Democrat. Office: Ste 1050 1747 Pennsylvania Ave NW Washington DC 20006-4604

SAUR, KLAUS G., publisher; b. Pullach, Germany, July 27, 1941; s. Karl-Otto and Veronika (Bossmann) S.; m. Lilo Stangel, Oct. 5, 1940; children: Klaus Peter, Annette. Grad. Comml. Coll. Munich; PhD honorus causa Philipps U., Marburg, Simmons Univ. Coll., Boston. Pub. mgr. Vulkan-Verlag, Essen, 1962-63; pub. K.G. Saur Verlag, Munich, 1963-66, pub., pres., 1966—; hon. prof. U. Glasgow; chmn. export com. German Book Trade, Frankfurt, 1979—, chmn. Deutsche Bibliothek German Nat. Libr., Bowker Co., N.Y., bd. dirs. F.A. Brockhaus/Bibliographisches Inst. A.G./ Mannheim, Reed Reference Pub. Editor, founder World Guide to Libraries. Hon. fellow U. Graz, Austria; hon. senator Ludwig-Maximilian U., Munich. Recipient Munich Honor medal, 1994, Fed. Cross of merit, Hon. medal Fed. Republic of Germany. Mem. German Pubs. Assn. (pres.), Deutsche Bibliothek Frankfurt-Leipzig-Berlin (bd. dirs. 1978, chmn. bd.), Frankfurt Book Fair (chmn. bd.), German Museum Munich (bd. dirs. 1976), Rotary. Office: K G Saur Verlag KG, Ortlerstr 8, D-81373 Munich Germany also: K G Saur 121 Chanlon Rd New Providence NJ 07974-1541

SAURWEIN, VIRGINIA FAY, international affairs specialist; b. Madrid, Feb. 24, 1928; d. George Nelson and Ruth Augusta (Zimmerman) S. BA, Carleton Coll., Northfield, Minn., 1950; MA, U. Denver, 1952. Adminstrv. sec. Collegiate Coun. for UN, Am. Assn. UN, N.Y.C., 1952-55; dir. edn. dept. Am. Assn. UN, N.Y.C., 1955-57; dir. publs. ctr. and program U.S. Com. for UN, UN Assn. U.S., N.Y.C., 1957-63, 63-65; program dir., editor Intercom Ctr. for War/Peace Studies, N.Y.C., 1965-70; non-govtl. orgns. officer UN Devel. Programme, N.Y.C., 1970-75; chief non-govtl. orgns. office Dept. Econ. and Social Affairs, UN, N.Y.C. and Geneva, 1975-88, 89-90; non-govtl. orgn. liaison officer UN Office, Geneva, 1988-89; liaison officer Vienna UN, N.Y.C., 1990; non-govtl. orgn. officer UN Crime Congress, Havana, Cuba, 1990, UN World Conf. on Women, Beijing, China, 1995; sec. com. on non-govtl. orgns. UN, N.Y.C., 1976-87; non-govtl. otgn. officer 19 major confs., 1975-88. Editor: Hommage to a Friend, 1964; updated: A Visual History of the United Nations, 1962; author, editor Intercom, 1968-70, Commitment, 1972-75. Founder, convenor, bd. mem.Women's World Banking, N.Y.C., 1975-85; mem. adv. com. YWCA, N.Y.C., 1960's; mem. bd. Sustainable End of Hunger Found., Accra, Ghana, 1991—. Mem. Soc. Internat. Devel., Fedn. Former Internat. Civil Servants (UN rep., chair non-govtl. affairs com. 1995—), Airedale Terrier Club Am. (bd. dirs. 1990—), Am. Kennel Club (del. rep. Airedale Terrier Club Am., editor Airedale column AKC Gazette), Airedale Terrier Club New Eng. (pres. 1976-77), Airedale Terrier Club Met. N.Y. (pres. 1989-90, 94-96). Democrat. Lutheran. Avocations: womens internat. economic issues, dog breeder, music, chorale singing. Home: 32 Glen Dr South Salem NY 10590

SAUSMAN, KAREN, zoological park administrator; b. Chgo., Nov. 26, 1945; d. William and Annabell (Lofaso) S. BS, Loyola U., 1966; student, Redlands U., 1968. Keeper Lincoln Park Zoo, Chgo., 1964-66; tchr. Palm Springs (Calif.) Unified Sch., 1968-70; ranger Nat. Park Svc., Joshua Tree, Calif., 1968-70; zoo dir. The Living Desert, Palm Desert, Calif., 1970—; natural history study tour leader internat., 1974—; part-time instr. Coll. Desert Natural History Calif. Desert, 1975-78; field reviewer conservation grants Inst. Mus. Svcs., 1987—, MAP cons., 1987—, panelist, 1992—; internat. studbook keeper for Sand Cats, 1988—, for Cuvier's Gazelle, Mhorr Gazelle, 1990—; co-chair Arabian Oryx species survival plan propogation group, 1986-95; spkr. in field. Author Survival Captive Bighorn Sheep, 1982, Small Facilities- Opportunities and Obligations, 1983; wildlife illustrator books, mags, 1970—; editor Fox Paws newsletter Living Desert, 1970—, ann. reports, 1976—; natural sci. editor Desert Mag., 1979-82; compiler Conservation and Management Plan for Antelope, 1992; contbr. articles to profl. jours. Past bd. dirs., sec. Desert Protective Coun.; adv. coun. Desert Bighorn Rsch. Inst., 1981-85; bd. dirs. Palm Springs Desert Resorts Convention and Visitors Bur., 1988-94; bd. dirs., treas. Coachella Valley Mountain Trust, 1989-92. Named Woman Making a Difference Soroptomist Internat., 1989, 93. Fellow Am. Assn. Zool. Parks and Aquariums (bd. dirs., accredation field reviewer, desert antelope taxon adv. group, caprid taxon adv. group, felid taxon adv. group, small population mgmt. adv. group, wildlife conservation and mgmt. com., chmn. ethics com. 1987, mem. com., internat. rels. com., ethics task force, pres'. award 1972-77, outstanding svc. award 1983, 88, editor newsletter, Zool. Parks and Aquarium Fundamentals 1982); mem. Internat. Species Inventory System (mgmt. com., policy adv. group 1980-96), Calif. Assn. Mus. (v.p. 1992-96), Calif. Assn. Zoos and Aquariums, Internat. Union Dirs. Zool. Gardens, Western Interpretive Assn. (so. Calif. chpt.), Am. Assn. Mus., Arboreta and Botanical Gardens So. Calif. (coun. dirs.), Soc. Conservation Biology, Nat. Audubon. Soc., Jersey Wildlife Preservation Trust Internat., Nature Conservancy, East African Wildlife Soc., African Wildlife Found., Kennel Club Palm Springs (past bd. dirs., treas. 1978-80), Scottish Deerhound Club Am. (editor Scottish Deerhounds in N.A., 1983, life mem. U.K. chpt.), Internat. Bengal Cat Soc. (pres. 1994-96). Avocations: pure bred dogs, cats, dressage, painting, photography. Office: The Living Desert 47 900 Portola Ave Palm Desert CA 92260

SAUSSELE, CHARLES WILLIAM, marking systems company executive; b. St. Louis, July 25, 1933; s. Charles W. Sr. and Else (Rein) S.; m. Isobel G. Goodsir, July 22, 1961; children: Jeffrey G., John C. BS in Mech. Engring., U. Mo., Rolla, 1956; M Automotive Engring., Chrysler Inst., Highland Park, Mich., 1958; MBA, Mich. State U., 1978. Rsch. engr. Chrysler Corp., Highland Park, 1956-61; engring. mgr. Holley Carburetor div. Colt Industries, Warren, Mich., 1961-71; sales/mktg. mgr. Borg & Beck div. Borg-Warner, Sterling Heights, Mich., 1971-81; v.p. sales/mktg. Russell Birdsall & Ward Corp., Mentor, Ohio, 1981-86; v.p., gen. mgr. Borries Marking Systems, Ann Arbor, Mich., 1986—; cons. SAB Automotive, Kansas City, Mo., 1981-82. Inventor Diesel Combustion System, Automotive Emission Devel. Capt. U.S. Army, 1956-58. Mem. Soc. Automotive Engrs., Soc. Mfg. Engrs., Pi Tau Sigma. Avocations: travel, sailing, photography, tennis. Home: 37656 N Laurel Park Dr Livonia MI 48152-2662 Office: Borries Marking System 3135 S State St Ste 108 Ann Arbor MI 48108-1653

SAUSVILLE, EDWARD ANTHONY, medical oncologist; b. Albany, N.Y., Apr. 3, 1952; s. Edward Adolphus and Pauline (Zamenick) S.; m. Carol Ann Cassidy, Feb. 1, 1975; children: Justin, Brendan, Elizabeth, Rebecca, Paul. BS, Manhattan Coll., 1973; MD, PhD, Albert Einstein Coll. Medicine, 1979. Med. house staff Brigham & Women's Hosp., Boston, 1979-82; med. staff fellow Nat. Cancer Inst., Bethesda, Md., 1982-85; sr. investigator Nat. Cancer Inst., Bethesda, 1985-88, 90—, assoc. dir. Devel. Therapeutics Program, 1994—; assoc. prof. medicine Georgetown U. Sch. Medicine, Washington, 1988-90. Author: (book chpt.) "Lung Cancer" in Kelley Textbook Internal Medicine, 1989; contbr. articles to New Eng. Jour. Medicine, Jour. Biol. Chemistry, Cancer Rsch. Mem. Am. Assn. Cancer Rsch., Am. Soc. Clin. Oncology, Am. Soc. Biochem. Molecular Biology, Phi Beta Kappa, Alpha Omega Alpha. Achievements include research on mechanisms of bleomycin action; bombesin-related peptide gene expression and response in lung cancer; optimal treatment and staging of cutaneous T-cell lymphoma; preclinical, Phase I and Phase II trials of novel antineoplastic agents. Home: 709 Bonifant Rd Silver Spring MD 20905 Office: Nat Cancer Inst Devel Ther Program EPN 843 Bethesda MD 20892

SAUTE, ROBERT EMILE, drug and cosmetic consultant; b. West Warwick, R.I., Aug. 18, 1929; s. Camille T. and Lea E. (Goffinet) S.; m. Arda T. Darnell, May 18, 1957; children: Richard R., Steven N., Allen K. BS, R.I. Coll. Pharmacy, 1950; MS, Purdue U., 1952, PhD, 1953. Registered pharmacist. Tech. asst. to pres. Lafayette (Ind.) Pharmacal, 1955-56; sr. rsch. and devel. chemist H.K. Wampole Denver Chem. Co., Phila., 1956-57; supt. Murray Hill (N.J.) plant Strong Cobb Arner Inc., 1957-60; adminstrv. dir. rsch. and devel. Avon Products Inc., Suffern, N.Y., 1960-68; dir. rsch. and devel. toiletries div. Gillette Co., Boston, 1968-71; group v.p. Dart Industries, L.A., 1972-75; pres. Saute Cons., Inc., L.A., 1975—; bd. dirs. Joico Labs., Inc., Cosmetics Enterprises, Ltd. Contbr. to books; patentee in field. With U.S. Army, 1953-55. Fellow Soc. Cosmetic Chemists (bd. dirs. 1987-89, 94-96, chmn. Calif. chpt. 1986); mem. AAAS, N.Y. Acad. Scis., Soc. Investigative Dermatology, Am. Assn. Pharm. Scientists, Sigma Xi, Rho Chi. Avocations: travel, art, music, cooking, wine.

SAUTER, MARSHA JEANNE, elementary school educator; b. Ft. Wayne, Ind., Apr. 13, 1951; d. Donald Paul and Juanita Mae (Foltz) Harsch; m. Michael Charles Sauter, Dec. 11, 1971; 1 child, Paul Michael. Student, Ball State U., 1969-71; BS in Edn. summa cum laude, U. Cin., 1974. Cert. tchr., Ohio, Okla. 6th grade tchr. Norwood (Ohio) Schs., 1974-75, 1st grade tchr., 1975-77; kindergarten tchr. Mason (Ohio) Schs., 1979-81; 1st grade tchr. Oak Park Elem. Sch. Bartlesville (Okla.) Schs., 1988—, primary curriculum coord., 1992-96, edn. com., 1991, English/math. textbook selection com., 1992, 93. Jr. H.S. youth advisor Good Shepherd Presbyn. Ch. Bartlesville, 1982-85, Sr. H.S. youth advisor, 1991-92, elder on session, 1985-88, 96—; mem. sunshine squad-crisis line Women Children in Crisis, Bartlesville, 1993—; sec. Bartlesville Cmty. Singers. Grantee Bartlesville Sch. Found. 1992, 94-96. Mem. NEA, Nat. Coun. Tchrs. Math., Tchrs. Assn. of Whole Lang., Nat. Reading Assn., Okla. Reading Assn., Soc. for Prevention of Cruelty to Animals, Okla. Edn. Assn., Toastmasters (Competent Toastmaster award 1993, sec.-treas. 1994-95, v.p. membership 1995-96), Alpha Delta Kappa. Avocations: singing, church, traveling. Home: 365 Turkey Creek Rd Bartlesville OK 74006-8116 Office: Bartlesville Pub Schs Oak Park Elem 200 Forest Park Rd Bartlesville OK 74003-1503

SAUVAGE, LESTER ROSAIRE, health facility administrator, cardiovascular surgeon; b. Wapato, Wash., Nov. 15, 1926; s. Lester Richard Sauvage and Laura Marie Brouillard; m. Mary Ann Marti, June 9, 1956; children: Lester Jr., John, Paul, Helen, Joe, Laura, William, Mary Ann. Student, Gonzaga U., 1942-43, DSc (hon.), 1982; MD, St. Louis U., 1948; Honoris Causa (hon.), Seattle U., 1976. Diplomate Nat. Bd. Med. Examiners, Am. Bd. Surgery, Am. Bd. Thoracic Surgery. Intern King County Hosp., Seattle, 1948-49, surg. resident, 1949-50, sr. resident, 1955-56; sr. resident Children's Med. Ctr., Boston, 1956-58; rsch. assoc. dept. surgery U. Wash., Seattle, 1950-52; sr. resident in thoracic surgery Boston City Hosp., 1958; pvt. practice Pediatric and Cardiovascular Surgeons, Inc., Seattle, 1959-91; founder, med. dir. Hope Heart Inst. (formerly Reconstructive Cardiovascular Rsch. Ctr.), Seattle, 1959—; clin. prof. surgery sch. medicine U. Wash., 1985—; chmn. dept. surgery, dir. surg. edn. Providence Med. Ctr., Seattle; dir. cardiac surgery Children's Orthopedic Hosp. and Med. Ctr.; presenter in field, 1974—. Author: Prosthetic Replacement of the Aortic Valve, 1972; mem. editorial bd. Annals Vascular Surgery; contbr. over 200 rsch. papers to profl. jours. Capt. M.C., U.S. Army, 1952-54. Recipient Vocat. Svc. award Seattle Rotary Club, 1977, Humanitarian award Human Life Found., 1977, Brotherhood award Nat. Conf. Christians and Jews, 1979, Clemson award Soc. Biomaterials, 1982, Jefferson award Am. Inst. Pub. Svc., Seattle Post-Intelligencer, 1983, Gov.'s Disting. Vol. award, 1983, Spotlight award Am. Soc. Women Accts., 1985, Wash. State Medal of Merit, 1987, Seattle 1st Citizen award, 1992. Mem. AMA, Am. Acad. Pediatrics (surg. sect.), Am. Assn. Thoracic Surgery, Am. Coll. Cardiology, Am. Coll. Chest Physicians, Am. Coll. Surgeons, Am. Heart Assn., Am. Pediatric Surg. Assn., Neurovascular Soc. N.Am. (founding mem.), Wash. State Heart Assn., Wash. State Med. Assn., North Pacific Pediatric Soc., North Pacific Surg. Soc., N.W. Soc. Clin. Rsch., Pacific Assn. Pediatric Surgeons, Pacific Coast Surg. Assn., New Eng. Soc. Vascular Surgery (hon.), Seattle Surg. Soc., King County Med. Soc., Internat. Cardiovascular Soc., Soc. Artificial Internal Organs, Soc. Clin. Vascular Surgery (hon.), Soc. Vascular Surgery, Acad. Surg. Rsch., Alpha Omega Alpha, Alpha Sigma Nu. Roman Catholic. Achievements include research in synthetic blood vessel grafts, vascular surgical techniques, prediction and prevention of thrombotic complications of atherosclerosis, endothelial cell function and vascular autografts.

SAUVAGEAU, PHILIPPE, library director; b. Trois-Rivières, Que., Can., June 11, 1940; s. Lorenzo and Laurette (Forest) S. BA, Seminaire St.-Joseph, Trois-Rivieres, 1961; B of Libr. Scis., U. Montréal, 1962. Assoc. libr. Svc. des Bibliothèque de la Mauricie, Trois-Rivières, 1962-64; adminstr. Bibliothèque Régionale du Nord de l'Outaouais, 1964-70, Bibliothèque Centrale de prêt de l'Outaouais et du Saguenay-Lac, St. Jean, 1971-75; dir. Bibliothèque Que., Can., 1975-80; gen. dir. Institut Canadien de Que., 1980-89; pres. gen. dir. Bibliothèque Nationale du Que., 1989—; cons. various orgns. including Agence de Coopèration Culturelle et Technique, Paris, Benin, Senegal, 1986-87, Bibliothèque de L'Assemblee Nationale, Que., 1983. Author: Comment Diffuser La Culture, 1969; contbr. articles to jours. Pres. Secrétariat Permanent des Peuples Francophones, Que., 1979-89; adminstr. Fest. du Film Que., 1986-87; mem. Conf. Canadienne des Arts, 1970—. Decorated Chevalier de l'Ordre des Arts et des Lettres Min. Culture and Communication of the French Govt., 1988; recipient Prix de Développement Culturel "La Laurentienne", Couns. Culture Que., 1986; named adminstr. of cultural devel. Conseil de la Culture de la Region de Que., 1985. Mem. Le Trident (dir. 1976), Com. Internat. des Bibliothèque Publiques, Assn. L'Avancement Scis. et Tech. de la Docum., Can. Libr. Assn., L'Institut Quebecois de Recherche sur la Culture (adminstr. 1991-93). Club: Garnison. Office: Bibliothèque Nat de Quebec, 2275 rue Holt, Montreal, PQ Canada H2G 3H1

SAUVEY, DONALD (ROBERT), retired musical instrument company executive; b. Green Bay, Wis., Mar. 15, 1924; s. Irving and Alice (LaBelle) S.; m. Shirley Ann Capelle, Nov. 24, 1949. Student, Am. TV Lab., 1942-43; cert. electronic tech., Milw. Sch. Engring., 1947. Sales mgr. Conn Organ Co., Elkhart, Ind., 1960-65; dir. mktg. Electro Music, Pasadena, Calif., 1965-70; v.p., gen. mgr. Electro Music, 1970-73, Gulbransen Organ Co. subs. CBS, Chgo., 1973-75; pres., chief exec. officer Hammond Organ Chgo., 1975-85; pres., dir. Hammond Internat. Can., Ltd., Agincourt, Ont.; v.p. Organos Hammond de Mex. S.A. de C.V., Mexico City; dir. Hammond Organ U.K. Ltd., Milton Keynes, Eng., Nihon Hammond, Osaka, Japan, Marmon Co. Mem. businessmen's adv. council Forty-Plus of Chgo., Inc., 1977—. Served with USAAF, 1943-46. Mem. Am. Music Conf. (dir.), Nat. Assn. Music Mchts. Republican. Roman Catholic. Patentee in field.

SAVAGE, BLAIR DEWILLIS, astronomer, educator; b. Mt. Vernon, N.Y., June 7, 1941; s. Rufus Llewellyn and Christine (Burney) S.; m. Linda Jean Wilber, June 25, 1966; children: Reid Hamilton, Keith Wesley. B.Engring. Physics, Cornell U., 1964; M.S., Princeton U., 1966, Ph.D., 1967. Research assoc. Princeton U., 1967-68; asst. prof. U. Wis., Madison, 1968-73, assoc. prof., 1973-78, prof. astronomy, 1978—, chmn. dept., 1982-85; vis. fellow Joint Inst. Lab. Astrophysics, Boulder, Colo., 1974-75; investigator space astronomy projects NASA, 1968—; bd. pres. Wis., Ind., Yale Nat. Optical Astronomy Obs. Telescope Consortium, 1990-96. Contbr. articles to profl. jours. Peyton fellow Princeton U., 1964-66; NASA fellow Princeton U., 1966-67; research grantee NASA, NSF, 1968—. Mem. Am. Astron. Soc. (councilor 1994-97), Internat. Astron. Union, Nat. Rsch. Coun. (space sci. bd. mem. 1985-88, chmn. com. for space astronomy and astrophysics 1985-88, astronomy and astrophysics survey com. 1989-90), Assn. for Univ. Rsch. in Astronomy (bd. dirs. 1989-92), Tau Beta Pi. Home: 4015 Hiawatha Dr Madison WI 53711-3037 Office: Dept Astronomy U Wis 475 N Charter St Madison WI 53706-1507

SAVAGE, CHARLES FRANCIS, lawyer; b. Bklyn., Oct. 2, 1942; s. Charles Lincoln and Frances Regis (Moran) S.; m. Maria Ania Bojcun, July 1, 1967; children: Charles F.I., Michael R. BA, Columbia U., 1963, JD, 1966. Bar: N.Y., 1966, Fla. 1977, Colo. 1981. Assoc. Cadwalader, Wickersham & Taft, N.Y.C., 1966-70; sec., gen. counsel Belco Petroleum Corp., N.Y.C., 1970-75, v.p. planning and devel., 1975-77; also bd. dirs. Belco Petroleum Corp.; v.p., gen. counsel Fla. Gas Co., Winter Park, 1977-78; asst. gen. counsel conservation and solar applications U.S. Dept. of Energy, Washington, 1978-79, dep. gen. counsel legal svcs., 1979-81; v.p.-legal, sec. Ensource, Inc., Denver, 1981-86; ptnr. Holland & Hart, Denver, 1986-93, Heppenstall, Savage, Hilyard & Muller, L.L.C., 1993—. Mem. ABA, N.Y. Bar Assn., Fla. Bar Assn., Colo. Bar Assn., Assn. Bar City N.Y., Denver Bar Assn., N.Y. County Lawyers Assn., Fed. Energy Bar.

SAVAGE, EDWARD WARREN, JR., physician; b. Macon, Ga., July 7, 1933; s. Edward Warren and Mildred Eleanor (Goodwin) S.; m. Carole Porter, June 6, 1959; children: Cheryl, Racheal, Edward Warren. A.B., Talladega Coll., 1955; postgrad., St. Louis U., 1955; M.D., Meharry Med. Coll., 1960. Diplomate: Am. Bd. Obstetrics and Gynecology. Intern St. Joseph's Hosp., Syracuse, N.Y., 1960-61; resident Kings County Hosp.-State U. N.Y., Bklyn., 1963-67; USPHS fellow in gynecol. cancer State U. N.Y. Downstate Med. Center, Bklyn., 1967-69; asst. instr. State U. N.Y. Downstate Med. Center, 1964-66, instr., 1966-69; dir. gynecologic oncology U. Ill., Chgo., 1970-73; asst. prof. U. Ill., 1969-73, asso. prof., 1973; med. dir. King/Drew Med. Ctr., L.A., 1993—; assoc. prof. Sch. Medicine Charles R. Drew Med. Sch., L.A., 1973-80, prof., 1980—, dean clin. affairs, 1993—; mem. staff St. Francis Hosp. of Lynwood, Centinela Hosp. Med. Ctr., UCLA Hosps. and Clinics; adj. assoc. prof. UCLA Sch. Medicine, 1977, prof., 1986—. Contbr. numerous articles to profl. publs. Exec. bd. Los Angeles Community Cancer Control., 1977. Served as capt. M.C. USAF, 1961-63. Fellow ACS, Am. Coll. Obstetricians and Gynecologists; mem. Soc. Gynecologic Oncologists, Am., Western Assn. Gynec. Oncologists (pres. 1980-81), Nat., Golden State med. assns., AAUP, Am. Soc. Colposcopy and Cervical Pathology (dir. 1973-80), Chgo. Gynecol. Soc., Am. Cancer Soc., Ill., Los Angeles Obstet. and Gynecol. Socs. (pres. 1989-90), Charles R. Drew Med. Soc. Office: 12021 Wilmington Ave Los Angeles CA 90059-3019 *I am the product of two wonderful parents whose support and ideals, inclusive of a strong work ethic, allowed me to be prepared for the several fortuitous opportunities that presented themselves. My hope is that somehow my life will be a positive statement to those who know me.*

SAVAGE, JAMES CATHEY, III, lawyer; b. Nashville, June 26, 1947; s. James C. Jr. and Mary (Estes) S.; m. Annette Egan, Aug. 5, 1975 (div.); children: Sean Patrick, Catriona Sarah; m. Clara Parra, Nov. 25, 1986; children: James C. IV, Anthony Joseph. BS, Austin Peay St. U., 1968; JD, Memphis State U., 1973; MS in Criminal Justice, Troy State U., 1977; LLM, John Marshall Law Sch., 1978, Georgetown U., 1981; Diploma of Program Mgmt., Def. Sys. Mgmt. Coll., 1997; LLD (hon.), North Tenn. Bible Inst., 1981. Bar: Tenn. 1973, U.S. Supreme Ct. 1977, D.C. 1981, Md. 1982; cert. tchr. Commd. 1st lt. U.S. Army, 1973, advanced through grades to lt. col, 1988; enlisted ranger and edn. dir. U.S. Army, Vietnam, 1969-70; ins. adjuster Tenn. Co., Molloy & Leary, Bituminious Casualty, 1971-73; judge adv. U.S. Army, Ga., Germany, 1973-77; vets. and contracts atty. V.A. Gen. Counsel, Washington, 1978-82; fgn. mil. sales atty. USAF Electronic Systems Ctr., Hanscom AFB, Mass., 1983-86; chief counsel U.S. Army Materials Tech. Lab, Watertown, Mass., 1986-92, U.S. Army Rsch. Lab, Watertown, Mass., 1992-95; sr. atty. Soldier Sys. Command, Natick, Mass., 1995—; civilian mem. Army Acquisition Corps, 1995—; army reserve asst. counsel Defense Contract Mgmt., Boston, 1992-96; adj. prof. City Colls. Chgo., Troy State U., Phillips Coll., John Marshall Law Sch., Middlesex, C.C., U. of Andes, 1974-92. Weekly show host Assembly (BCAT-TV), Burlington, Mass., 1989-93; contbr. articles to profl. jours. Dep. dir. Internat. Rescue Com./Army Res. Project Resettlement for Refugees, Washington, 1980-82; canvasser Am. Heart Assn., Burlington, 1989-92; lay min. Christian Chs., 1974—; chmn. bd. deacons, mem. pastor/parish, pers., parish counsel and nomination coms. Burlington Congl. Ch., 1986-95, 1st Congl. Ch., Natick, 1995—, missions com., 1997; mem. Christian Legal Soc., 1980—, Inst. Religion and Democracy, 1980—; corp. mem. United Ch. Bd. World Ministries, 1993-94, officer, 1996-97; active Christian Mil. Fellowship, 1984—; comdr., exec. officer New Eng. Selective Svc. Sys., 1986-92; officer Christian Fellowship, 1988—; mem. Cultural Coun. and Cable TV Adv. Bd., Town of Burlington; mem. Cable TV Adv. Bd., Town of Natick; lt. col. civil air patrol CAP Group I Mass., 1988-93. Decorated Bronze Star and 25 other mil. medals; named Mass. Citizen of Yr. Am. Legion, 1985; recipient Exceptional Profl. award, 1985, Excellence in Govt. and Outstanding Community Svc. awards, Boston, 1987, 92, Fed. Exec. Bd., mil., edn. and community svc. recognition resolution Mass. Ho. of Reps., 1992. Mem. Fed. Bar Assn. (nat. chmn. internat. procurement com. 1985-88, vice-chmn. 1979-90, past pres. Mass. chpt. 1985-86, nat. del., Disting. Svc. award), Assn. U.S. Army, New Eng. Chpt. Judge Advocates Assn. (pres./v.p. 1983-86), Res. Officers Assn. (nat. judge adv. 1993-94, state pres. 1993-94, pres.-elect 1992-93, state v.p. for Army 1990-92, state judge adv. 1985-86, pres. William Tudor and N.E. Civil Affairs chpts. 1984-89, Nat. Disting. Svc. awards), Nat. Civil Affairs Assn. (Nat. Disting. Svc. award), DAV (life, Honor Guard Burlington chpt. 113 1985-93), Natick VFW (life, state judge adv. and sr. vice comdr.-All Am. Post 1982-83), Natick AMVETS (life, post comdr.and state judge adv. 1982-83), Natick Am. Legion, 75th Ranger Regiment Assn. (nat. dir. 1987-90), Vietnam Vets. Am. (life, sec. D.C. chpt. 1980), Phi Delta Kappa (treas. Harvard U. chpt. 1990-92), Phi Alpha Delta. Avocations: computers, and guitar and trumpet playing. Home: 15 Lake Shore Rd Natick MA 01760-2007 Office: US Army Soldier Sys Command Kansas St Legal Office Natick MA 01760-5035

SAVAGE, JAMES FRANCIS, editor; b. Boston, July 23, 1939; s. James and Hanora (Enright) S.; m. Sharon Kaye Base, May 29, 1965; 1 son, Sean. A.A., Boston U., 1959, B.S., 1961. Reporter Quincy (Mass.) Patriot Ledger, 1961-63; reporter Miami (Fla.) Herald, 1963-67, investigative reporter, 1967-78, investigations editor, 1978-84, assoc. editor investigations, 1984—; investigative reporter Boston Herald Traveler, 1967. Served with AUS, 1962. Recipient Nat. Headliners award, 1969, Fla. Press Assn. award, 1972, George Polk Meml. award for investigative reporting, 1973, 80, Pub. Service award Nat. A.P. Mng. Editors, 1974, 80, award Fla. Soc. Newspaper Editors, 1974, 75, Nat. Disting. Service award Sigma Delta Chi, 1979, 87, Pulitzer Prize Staff award for Nat. Reporting, 1987, Outstanding Investigative Reporting award Investigative Reporters and Editors, 1988, Disting. Alumni award Boston U. Coll. Communications, 1990, Pulitzer Prize Staff Pub. Svc. award, 1993; Profl. Journalism fellow Stanford, 1974-75. Home: 1004 Orange Is Fort Lauderdale FL 33315-1651 Office: 1 Herald Plz Miami FL 33132-1609

SAVAGE, JOHN EDMUND, computer science educator, researcher; b. Lynn, Mass., Sept. 19, 1939; s. Edmund J. and Eldora A. (Guay) S.; m. Patricia Joan Landers, Jan. 29, 1966; children: Elizabeth, Kevin, Christopher, Timothy. ScB, MIT, 1962, ScM, 1962, PhD, 1965. Mem. tech. staff Bell Telephone Labs., Holmdel, N.J., 1965-67; prof. computer sci. Brown U., Providence, 1967—, chmn. dept. computer sci., 1985-91; vis. prof. U. Paris, 1980-81, Warwick U., Eng., 1991-92; mem. dept. vis. com. elec. engring. and computer sci. MIT, 1991—; cons. in field. Author: The Complexity of Computing, 1976; (with others) The Mystical Machine, 1986; editor: (with Thomas Knight) Advanced Research in VLSI and Parallel Systems, 1992; chmn. editl. bd. Computing Rsch. News, 1990-96; mem. editl. bd. Jour. Computer and Sys. Scis., 1993—; patentee data scrambler, 1970, means and methods for generating permutation of a square, 1976. Mem. MIT Corp. visiting com. dept. elec. engring. and computer sci. Fulbright-Hays grantee, 1973; NSF fellow, 1961, Guggenheim fellow, 1973. Fellow AAAS, IEEE, Assn. Computing Machinery; mem. Computing Rsch. Assn. (bd. dirs. 1990-96), Sigma Xi, Tau Beta Pi. Avocations: reading, skiing, bicycling. Office: Brown U Dept Computer Sci 115 Waterman St Providence RI 02912-9016

SAVAGE, JOHN PATRICK, provincial official; b. Newport, South Wales, N.S., Can., May 28, 1982; married; 7 children. Grad., Queen's Coll. Med. Sch., Belfast, No. Ireland, 1956. Mayor City of Dartmouth, Can., 1985-92; premier, min. intergovtl. affairs, min. aboriginal affairs, pres. exec. coun. Govt. of Nova Scotia, Halifax, 1993—; co-chair Nova Scotia Round Table on Environment and Economy. Active Dartmouth Sch. Bd., 1978, chair bd. dirs., 1984, 85. Office: Office of the Premier, 1700 Granville St 7th Fl PO Box 726, Halifax, NS Canada B3J 2T3

SAVAGE, JOSEPH SCOTT, physician, career officer; b. Malden, Mass., Dec. 30, 1958; s. Joseph Edward and Arlene Barbara (Piniarski) S.; m. Gwendolyn Kieko Uezu, July 4, 1979; 1 child, Colin Eric. BA, Wheaton Coll., 1983; DO, Kirksville Coll. Osteopath. Medicine, 1987. Diplomate Am. Bd. Osteopathic Medical Examiners. Commd. maj. USAF, 1988; coord. EMS svcs. Wright Patterson AFB, Dayton, Ohio, coord. disaster svcs.; attending physician Hosp. USAF Hosp., RAF Lakenheath, Eng., 1988-91, asst. dir. emergency dept., 1990-91; dir. emergency tng. we. Europe divsn. USAF, RAF Lakenheath, Eng., 1990-91; flight surgeon USAF Hosp., Holloman AFB, N. Mex., 1991-92; flight surgeon Space Shuttle contingency opers. USAF, Holloman AFB, N. Mex., 1991-92; resident physician Wright State U./USAF, Dayton, 1992-95; staff physician, instr. tactical medicine USAF Hosp., Wright Patterson AFB, 1995—, EMS dir., 1996—; asst. clin. prof. in emergency medicine Wright State U., 1996—; spl. asst. Dept. Health and Human Svcs., Rockville, Md., 1986; health policy fellow U.S. Senate, Washington, 1988; chief cons. Dayton (Ohio) SWAT Team, 1994-96; keynote spkr. Ohio State EMS, Columbus, 1995. Spl. lectr. Unitarian Universalist Ch., Oakwood, Ohio, 1993. Decorated Commendation medal USAF, 1993; recipient Dir.'s award USPHS U.S. Surgeon Gen., 1987. Mem. Am. Coll. Emergency Physicians. Avocation: fine arts, athlete. Home: 6860 Rose Bud Way Dayton OH 45415 Office: USAF Dept Emergency Svcs Dayton OH 45433

SAVAGE, M. SUSAN, mayor. Student, U. Aix-Marseilles, Aix-en-Provence, France, 1969, City of London Poly., Eng., 1972; BA in Sociology with honors, Beaver Coll., 1974. Pre-trial rep. Phila. Ct. Common Pleas, 1974-75; criminal justice planner Montgomery County Criminal Justice Unit, 1975-77; exec. dir. Met. Tulsa Citizens Crime Com., 1977-87; vol. coord. Vote Yes For Tulsa, 1987; chief of staff to mayor City of Tulsa, 1988-92, mayor, 1992—. Active Lee Elementary Sch. PTA; bd. dirs., treas. Okla. Crime Prevention Assn.; bd. dirs. Youth Svcs. of Tulsa County, 1984-88, pres., 1986-87; co-chair Safe Streets/Enhanced 911 Steering Com., 1987; mem. C. of C. Task Force/Community Edn. Network, 1983. Office: Office of Mayor City Hall Rm 1115 200 Civic Ctr Tulsa OK 74103-3827*

SAVAGE, MICHAEL JOHN KIRKNESS, oil company and arts management executive; b. Birmingham, Eng., Oct. 28, 1934; came to U.S., 1962, naturalized, 1981; s. Leonard W. H. and Hilda C. (Fletcher) S.; m. Elisabeth Karl, June 21, 1965 (div.); m. Virginia Hooper, Aug. 31, 1978; 1 child, Matthew Nicholas. MA in Econs. and Law with honors, Cambridge U., 1958; postgrad., Manchester (Eng.) Bus. Sch., 1965; Diploma in Arabic, Middle E. Ctr. for Arab Studies, Shemlan, Lebanon, 1967. Various positions The British Petroleum Co. Ltd., England, Kuwait, Lebanon, Abu Dhabi, Alaska, Can., U.S., 1958-82; pres. BP Alaska Inc., San Francisco, 1977,

Sohio Petroleum Co., San Francisco, 1978-82; internat. dir. The Brit. Petroleum Co. Ltd., London, 1982; pres. Merlin Petroleum Co., San Francisco, 1983-88, Savage Petroleum Co., Sausalito, Calif., 1992-95; bd. dirs., mng. dir. San Francisco Opera, 1994—; bd. dirs. HS Resources, Inc., San Francisco. Trustee Alaska Pacific U., 1982-86; trustee San Francisco Conservatory of Music, 1983—, chmn., 1990-94. Mem. Brit.-Am. Chamber (San Francisco), Belvedere (Calif.) Tennis Club (bd. dirs. 1994—). Avocations: Music, tennis, skiing, mountain walking. Office: San Francisco Opera War Meml Opera House 301 Van Ness Ave San Francisco CA 94102-4509

SAVAGE, MICHAEL PAUL, medicine educator, interventional cardiologist; b. Wilkes-Barre, Pa., Jan. 25, 1955; s. Peter J. and Olga J. (Sekerchek) S.; m. Kathleen A. Gallagher, June 1989; children: Katherine, Andrew. BA, Wesleyan U., Middletown, Conn., 1976; MD, Jefferson Med. Coll., 1980. Diplomate Am. Bd. Internal Medicine, Am. Bd. Cardiovascular Disease, Nat. Bd. Med. Examiners. Intern, then resident New Eng. Deaconess Hosp.-Harvard U. Med. Sch., Boston, 1980-83; fellow Jefferson Med. Coll., Phila., 1983-86, asst. prof. medicine, 1986-91, assoc. prof., 1991—, dir. cardiac catheterization, 1990—, dir. interventional cardiology sect., 1996—; cons. Johnson & Johnson Interventional Sys. Co., Warren, N.J., 1994—; lectr. coronary angioplasty and cardiac catheterization. Contbr. numerous articles to New Eng. Jour. Medicine, Circulation, Am. Jour. Cardiology, Jour. Am. Coll. Cardiology, chpts. to books. Fellow Am. Coll. Cardiology, Soc. Cardiac Angiography and Interventions, Pa. Med. Soc., Am. Heart Assn., Am. Fedn. for Clin. Rsch. Roman Catholic. Achievements include research in interventional cardiology concerning new techniques in treatment of coronary artery disease, culminating in international, prospective trials demonstrating superiority of implantable coronary stents over conventional balloon angioplasty. Office: Jefferson Med Coll 1025 Walnut St Ste 410 Philadelphia PA 19107-5001

SAVAGE, MICHAEL THOMAS, federal executive; b. Oroville, Calif., Oct. 22, 1934; s. Guy Thomas Savage and Sarah Mery (Bennett) Barber; m. Robin Kendall Ward, Apr. 4, 1966; children: Mark McNeer, Kelly Robin. BA in Polit. Sci., U. Calif., Berkeley, 1956, MA in Polit. Sci., 1959; postgrad., Woodrow Wilson Sch., 1969-70. Field renewal rep. Cmty. Devel. Programs, San Francisco, 1959-64, acting chief, chief of ops. br., 1964-66, dir. field svcs. divsn., 1966-68, dep. regional dir. renewal assistance, 1968-70; various positions Office of Orgn. and Mgmt., Washington, 1970-74, dir. office of mgmt. systems, acting dir., 1974-76, dep. dir. office mgmt., 1976-79; dir. office housing ops. and field monitoring Office of Cmty. Planning and Devel., Washington, 1979-82, program advisor to asst. sec., enterprise zone coord., 1982-86, dep. dir. office block grant assistance and zone coord., 1986-93; dep. dir. Office of Econ. Devel., Washington, 1993—; urban policy advisor Chmn. Ho. Govt. Ops. Com., Washington, 1990-93. Editorial bd.: Econ. Devel. Quar.; contbr. articles to profl. jours. Officer, supporter Great Falls (Va.) Players, 1983—; co-chair No. Va. alumni recruiting com. Pa. State U., No. Va., 1992—. 2d lt. U.S. Infantry, 1959. Recipient Mid Career fellowship Nat. Inst. Pub. Affairs, Washington, 1969; named LEGIS fellow Office Pers. Mgmt., Washington, 1990. Avocations: little theater, softball. Home: 436 River Bend Rd Great Falls VA 22066-4017

SAVAGE, NEVE RICHARD, marketing executive; b. Harrow, Eng., Nov. 18, 1944; came to U.S., 1970, naturalized, 1983; s. Richard Marshall and Joan Muriel (Eperon) S.; m. Ann Elizabeth Freeman, Apr. 29, 1972; children: Sarah-Jane, Megan, Truan. B.A., U. Oxford (Eng.), 1966, M.A., 1968. Account supr. Garland-Compton Advt., London, 1966-70; sr. v.p. Compton Advt., N.Y.C., 1970-77; dir. Compton Advt., 1980-83; exec. v.p. Cadwell Davis Savage Advt., N.Y.C., 1977-82; exec. v.p. internat. Wells, Rich, Greene, Inc., N.Y.C., 1983-86; vice chmn. Kornhauser & Calene Inc., 1986-88; exec. group dir. Ogilvy & Mather, 1988-94; v.p. mktg. AT&T Wireless Svcs., Kirkland, Wash., 1994—.

SAVAGE, PHILLIP HEZEKIAH, federal agency administrator; b. Balt., Aug. 13, 1932; s. Abraham and Ivory F. (Robinson) Shpritz; m. Phyllis Millard; children: Kim Yvette, Jan Miriam, Kirk Phillip; m. Diane Bradford Geers, June 24, 1972; children: Rebekah Ann, Elisabeth Bradford. BA, Morgan State U., 1970; MA, Antioch Sch. Law, 1984. Dir. NAACP, N.Y.C. and Phila., 1960-72, ARA Svcs. Inc., 1972-74; mgr. equal employment opportunity tng. project Gen. Acctg. Office, Washington, 1975-76; dir. equal employment opportunity office SEC, Washington, 1976-84; dir. pub. employment divsn. HUD, Washington, 1984-89, exec. asst. to asst. sec., 1989-92, dep. asst. sec. ops. and mgmt., 1992-94; sr. advisor to supt. D.C. Pub. Schs., 1994-95; sr. advisor, asst. sec. HUD, 1995—. Arbitrator Better Bus. Bur., Office Common Ownership Communities and Office Consumer Affairs, Montgomery County, Md.; past chair Partnership Fund for Compensation of Victims of Hate, Violence, Montgomery County; pres. Interracial Family Circle, v.p. Kenwood Park Citizens Assn.; mem. River Rd. Unitarian Ch. With USAF, 1950-53. Recipient Giraffe award, 1988. Avocations: reading, walking, travelling. Home: 7223 Marbury Ct Bethesda MD 20817-6129 Office: HUD Fair Housing and Equal Opportunity 451 7th St SW Washington DC 20410-0001

SAVAGE, RANDALL ERNEST, journalist; b. Commerce, Ga., Mar. 3, 1939; s. Ernest Kyle and Sara Beatrice (Collins) S.; m. Joyce Carol Martin, Nov. 26, 1964 (div. May 1984); children: Kimberly Dawn, Bradley Kyle; m. Mary Elizabeth Hallmark, Aug. 4, 1984; children: Brock Morgan, Laura Marie, Shaw Hamilton. Student, U. Md.-European Div., RAF Bentwaters, Eng., 1967-69; B.A. in Journalism, U. Ga., 1972. Service sta. worker Collins Service Sta., Commerce, Ga., 1958; billing clk. Benton Rapid Express, Atlanta, 1958-61; truck driver So. Oil Co., High Point, NC, 1964-65; reporter Commerce News, Ga., 1972; sr. spl. projects reporter Macon Telegraph and News, Ga., 1972—. Served with U.S. Army, 1961-64; with USAF, 1966-69. Recipient 3rd place in news AP, Atlanta, 1976, 2nd place in news AP, Atlanta, 1976, 1st place in sports AP, Atlanta, 1984; 2d place in news Green Eyeshades award, 1976; Pulitzer prize, 1985, Outstanding Alumnus award Henry W. Grady Coll. of Journalism and Mass Communication, U. Ga., 1989. Baptist. Avocations: jogging; softball; fishing; freelance writing. Home: 3269 Lennox Dr Macon GA 31204-1054 Office: Macon Telegraph & News Po Box 4167 120 Broadway Macon GA 31201-3444

SAVAGE, ROBERT HEATH, advertising executive; b. Chillicothe, Ohio, Nov. 24, 1929; s. Russell Heath and Frances (Hunt) S.; m. Lorna Dale, May 2, 1970. B.A., Principia Coll., 1951; M.B.A., Harvard U., 1956. Brand mgr. Procter & Gamble, Cin., 1956-60; sr. v.p., mgmt. supr., dir. Ogilvy & Mather, Inc., N.Y.C., 1960-71; mktg. mgr. personal products div. Lever Bros., N.Y.C., 1971; exec. v.p. Botsford Ketchum, Inc., San Francisco, 1972, pres., 1972-78, chmn., 1978-81; pres. KM&G Internat., Inc., 1978-81, Saatchi and Saatchi Compton, Inc., N.Y.C., 1981-83; mng. dir. Henson Assocs., N.Y.C., 1983-86; ptnr. CMA Assocs., Fairfield, Conn., 1987—; mngt. cons., sports and video mktg. cons., 1987—. With USMCR, 1951-54. Mem. Gipsy Trail Club, Naples Bath and Tennis Club, Colliers Reserve Country Club, Brooklawn Country Club. Home and Office: 5 Crooked Mile Rd Westport CT 06880-1124

SAVAGE, RUTH HUDSON, poet, writer, speaker; b. Childress, Tex., Apr. 29, 1932; d. John Floyd and Eula Jemima (Cornelius) Hudson; m. Robert Berkes, Nov. 6, 1950 (div. June 1963); children: Donna, Mike, Kelly, Rex; m. Martin Thomas Savage, Sept. 18, 1965. Pres. Poets of Tarrant County, 1995-96. Author: (book of poetry) Voices in the Wind, 1982, (play) Tumbleweed Christmas, 1989; author of numerous poems; author, performer Audio Poetry Cassette: Simply Savage, 1992; contbg. writer to newspapers; newsletter editor Arlington Women's Shelter, 1988-91; mem. newsletter publicity LWV, Arlington, 1991-92. Dir. Arlington Friends of the Libr., 1987—; judge Tex. Student Poetry, 1987—. Mem. Acad. Am. Poets. Avocations: speaking, writing, costume design, art, costumed dramatic book reviewer. Home: 1700 Ocho Rios Ct Arlington TX 76012

SAVAGE, SCOTT DAVID, broadcast executive; b. Newark, Nov. 10, 1954; s. Philip and Charlotte Jean (Figman) S.; m. Anne Marthine Aldrich, Aug. 24, 1975 (div. Mar. 1992); children: Daniel, Ellen; m. Marilyn Massucci, May 4, 1993. BA, Pa. State U., 1975. Account exec., sales mgr. Stas. WMAJ-AM and WXLR-FM, State College, Pa., 1974-77, Westinghouse Broadcasting Co., Pitts., N.Y.C., Ft. Wayne, Ind., 1977-80; dir. sports mktg. Sta. WTOP-AM, Washington, 1981-84; gen. sales mgr. Sta. WCBM-AM, Balt., 1984-85; sta. mgr., gen. sales mgr. Sta. WNEW-AM, N.Y.C., 1985-88; v.p., gen. mgr. Tex. State Network, Dallas, 1988-90; exec. v.p., COO Pinnacle Broadcasting Co., Dallas, 1990-91; v.p., gen. mgr. Stas. KYNG-FM, Dallas, 1992—. Recipient award of excellence Am. Women in Radio and TV, 1994. Mem. Assn. Radio Mgrs. (pres. 1995).

SAVAGE, STEPHEN MICHAEL, lawyer; b. Norwich, Conn., Apr. 23, 1946; s. Alfred and Iva (Allen) S.; m. Lois Palestine, July 4, 1968; children: Meredith, William, Sam. BA, U. Pa., 1968; JD, Harvard U., 1973. Bar: Ariz. 1973, U.S. Dist. Ct. Ariz. 1973. With Fennemore Craig, Phoenix, 1973—, chmn. mgmt. com., 1988—. Bd. dirs. Ariz. Diabetes Assn., Phoenix, 1983-87, Ariz. Mus. Sci. and Tech., Phoenix, 1992—; chmn. bd. dirs. All Saints' Episcopal Day Sch., Phoenix, 1988; comdr., pres. Mounted Sheriff's Posse Maricopa County, Phoenix, 1992-93. Mem. ABA, State Bar Ariz. (chmn. sect. corp., banking and bus. law 1983-84), Maricopa County Bar Assn., Assn. Corp. Growth, Phoenix Country Club. Avocations: team roping, golf. Office: Fennemore Craig 2 N Central Ave Ste 2200 Phoenix AZ 85004-4406

SAVAGE, SUSAN, 1953, mayor; b. Tulsa, Okla.; married; 2 children. Degree in Criminal Justice and Economics. Past exec. dir. Met. Tulsa Citizens Crime Commn.; mayor City of Tulsa, 1992—; chmn. Indian Nations Coun. Govt. Bd. dirs. Okla. Mcpl. League, others; mem. nationwide panels on 911 svcs., infrastructure devel.; vol. Carver Middle Sch., Booker T. Washington H.S., numerous pub. svc. activies. Mem. U.S. Conf. Mayors (chmn. com. energy and environ.). *

SAVAGE, TERRY RICHARD, information systems executive; b. St. Louis, Oct. 21, 1930; s. Terry Barco and Ada Vanetta (Cochran) S.; m. Gretchen Susan Wood, Sept. 26, 1964; children: Terry Curtis, Christopher William, Richard Theodore. AB, Washington U., St. Louis, 1951, MA, 1952; PhD, U. Pa., 1954. Mgr. system software IBM Rsch., Yorktown Heights, N.Y., 1956-63; dir. data processing Documentation Inc., Bethesda, Md., 1963-64; mgr. info. systems Control Data Corp., Rockville, Md., 1964-67; dir. rsch. Share Rsch. Corp., Santa Barbara, Calif., 1967-68; computer-aided acquisition and logistic support program mgr. TRW, Redondo Beach, Calif., 1968-92; ret., ind. cons. pvt. practice, 1992—; expert witness for various coms. U.S. Congress, 1981, 84, 88, 89. Contbr. articles to profl. jours. Bd. dirs. ABC-Clio Press, Santa Barbara, 1970-75, Help the Homeless Help Themselves, Rancho Palos Verdes, Calif., 1988-94, ChorusLiners, Rancho Palos Verdes, 1983—, Savage Info. Svcs., Inc., Torrance, Calif., 1992—. Mem. Cosmos Club. Home and Office: 30000 Cachan Pl Rancho Palos Verdes CA 90275-5412

SAVAGE, THOMAS JOSEPH, executive, governance and planning consultant, educator, priest; b. Medford, Mass., Oct. 28, 1947; s. Frank James and Viola Augustine (Ballou) S. B.A. summa cum laude, Boston Coll., 1971; M. City Planning, U. Calif.-Berkeley, 1973; M. Pub. Policy, Harvard U., 1982, EdD, 1985. Assoc. Cheswick Ctr., Boston, 1973, dir., 1984—; assoc. Instl. Strategies Assocs., Cambridge, Mass., 1975-87; asst. acad. v.p. Fairfield (Conn.) Univ., 1986-88; pres. Rockhurst Coll., Kansas City, Mo., 1988-96, pres. Nat. Seminars Group., 1991—; adj. faculty Lesley Coll., Cambridge, 1982-85; cons. Lilly Endowment, Indpls., 1983-87; chmn. planning com. Jesuits New Eng. Province, Boston, 1985-88. Author: Seven Steps to a More Effective Board, 1994, The Goverance of Catholic Health Care Institutions, Catholic Health Assn., Spring, 1988; also articles. Del. Bridges for Peace, Soviet Union, 1985; Trustee Regis U., 1989—, U. Detroit Mercy, 1995—, St. Louis U., 1991—, Loyola Marymount, 1994—; bd. dirs. Valentine-Radford Comm., 1992—, Preferred Health Profls., 1992—, Kauffman Found., 1993—, Menninger Clinic, 1993—; co-chair FOCUS (Comprehensive Strategic Plan for Kansas City), 1992—; founding chmn. Brush Creek Ptnrs., 1994-96. Mellon fellow, 1971-73. Mem. Am. Planning Assn., Nat. Policy Assn., AAAS, Assn. Jesuit Colls. and Univs. (bd. dirs. 1989-96), World Future Soc., Bostonian Soc., Phi Beta Kappa. Roman Catholic. Club: Harvard. Address: Nat Seminars Group 6901 W 63d St Shawnee Mission KS 66202

SAVAGE, WALLACE HAMILTON, lawyer; b. Houston, Nov. 21, 1912; s. Homer H. and Mary (Wallace) S.; m. Dorothy Harris, Oct. 12, 1940; children—Virginia Wallace (Mrs. A. Lee McAlester), Dorothy Harris. B.S., U. Va., 1933; J.D., Harvard, 1936. Bar: Tex. 1937, Colo. 1937. Practiced in Dallas; Dallas County chmn., nat. vice chmn. Citizens Com. Hoover Report, 1952-54; mem., dir. Citizen's Com. for Reorgn. Exec. Branch of Govt., 1954-59. Author: A Bait of Perjury, 1970. Mayor pro tem City of Dallas, 1947-49, mayor, 1949-51; chmn. Dallas County Democratic Com., 1952-54, Tex. Dem. Com., 1952-54 . Served as comdr. USNR, 1941-45. Univ. fellow U. Colo., 1936- 37. Mem. Am., Dallas bar assns., State Bar Tex., Phi Delta Phi. Clubs: Dallas Country, Idlewild. Home: 5703 Swiss Ave Dallas TX 75214-4638

SAVAGE, WILLIAM WOODROW, education educator; b. Onley, Va., Jan. 9, 1914; s. Frank Howard and Florence Elmira (Twyford) S.; m. Margaret Jane Clarke; children—Earl R., William W. A.B., Coll. William and Mary, 1937; M.A., U. Chgo., 1946, Ph.D., 1955; student, U. Va., summer 1951. Research editor, div. rural research Fed. Emergency Relief Adminstrn., Richmond, Va., 1935-36; div. mgr. Montgomery Ward & Co., Newport News, Va., 1937-38; statis. worker WPA, Richmond, 1938-39; counselor Va. Consultation Service, Richmond, 1939-42; acting dir. Va. Consultation Service, 1942-45; asst. state supr. guidance and consultation services Va. Dept. Edn., 1946-47; dean Longwood Coll., Farmville, Va., 1947-52; project coordinator, asso. dir. Midwest Adminstrn. Center, U. Chgo., 1952-56; dean Coll. Edn., U. S.C., 1956-65, prof. edn., 1956-79; curator U. S.C. Mus. Edn., 1973-85. Author: Interpersonal and Group Relations, 1968; Co-author: Readings in American Education, 1963; Editor: Work and Training, monthly Va. Bd. Edn, 1941-47, Administrator's Notebook, monthly Midwest Adminstrn. Center, 1954-56, U. S.C. Edn. Report, 1957-65, 67-85; adv. com.: Sch. Rev, 1954-56; Contbr. articles to jours. Mem. visitation and appraisal com. Nat. Coun. for Accreditation Tchr. Edn., 1964-67. Mem. S.C. Assn. Sch. Adminstrs., U. S.C. Soc., Wardlaw Club (pres. 1974-75), Order of White Jacket, Phi Delta Kappa. Methodist. Home: 1100 German School Rd Richmond VA 23225-4275

SAVAGEAU, MICHAEL ANTONIO, microbiology and immunology educator; b. Fargo, N.D., Dec. 3, 1940; s. Antonio Daniel and Jennie Ethelwin (Kaushagen) S.; m. Ann Elisa Birky, July 22, 1967; children—Mark Edward, Patrick Daniel, Elisa Marie. B.S., U. Minn., 1962; M.S., U. Iowa, 1963; Ph.D., Stanford U., 1967, postgrad., 1968-70; postgrad., UCLA, 1967-68. Research fellow UCLA, Los Angeles, 1967-68; lectr. Stanford U., Calif., 1968-69; from asst. to full prof. U. Mich., Ann Arbor, 1970—; sr. research fellow Max Planck Inst., Göttingen, Fed. Republic of Germany, 1976-77; fellow Australian Nat. U., Canberra, 1983-84; prof. microbiology and immunology U. Mich., Ann Arbor, 1978—, chmn. dept., 1982-85, 92—, prof. chem. engring., dir. cellular biotech. labs., 1988-91; dir. NIH trng. program in Cellular Biotechnology, 1991-92; cons. Upjohn Co., Kalamazoo, 1979-81, NIH, Bethesda, Md., 1981-82, 94-95, Synergen, Boulder, Colo., 1985-87, Nat. Rsch. Coun./Howard Hughes Med. Inst., 1997; Found. for Microbiology lectr., 1993-95; vis. prof. dept. biochemistry U. Ariz., Tucson, 1994. Author: Biochemical Systems Analysis, 1976; mem. editl. bd. Math. Scis., 1976-95, editor, 1995—; mem. editl. bd. Jour. Theoretical Biology, 1989-96, mem. adv. bd., 1996—; mem. editl. bd. Nonlinear World, 1992—, Nonlinear Digest, 1992—; co-editor Math. Ecology, 1986—; contbr. articles to profl. jours. Australian Nat. U. fellow, 1983-84; Guggenheim Found., fellow N.Y.C., 1976-77; Fulbright Found., sr. research fellow, Washington, Fed. Republic of Germany, 1976-77; sr. fellow Mich. Soc. Fellows, 1990-94; grantee NIH, NSF, 1964—. Fellow AAAS; mem. Am. Chem. Soc., Am. Soc. Microbiology, IEEE (sr.), Soc. Indsl. and Applied Math., Biophys. Soc., Soc. Gen. Physiologists, Soc. Math. Biology (bd. dirs. 1987-90), Internat. Fedn. Nonlinear Analysts (bd. dirs. 1997—). Office: U Mich Dept Microbiology and Immunology 5641 Med Sci II Ann Arbor MI 48109-0620

SAVARD, DENIS JOSEPH, professional hockey player; b. Pointe Gatineau, Que., Can., Feb. 4, 1961. With Chgo. Black Hawks, 1980-90, 96—, Montreal Canadiens, 1990-93, Tampa Bay Lightning, 1993-96; mem. Stanley Cup championship team 1983; player NHL All-Star games, 1982-84, 86, 88, 91. Recipient Michel Briere trophy, 1979-80. Office: Chgo Blackhawks 1901 W Madison St Chicago IL 60612-2459*

SAVAS, EMANUEL S., public management educator; b. N.Y.C., June 8, 1931; s. John and Olga (Limbos) S.; m. Helen Andrew, Dec. 25, 1955; children: Jonathan, Stephen. BA, U. Chgo., 1951, BS, 1953; MA, Columbia U., 1956, PhD, 1960. Control systems cons. IBM, Yorktown Heights and White Plains, N.Y., 1959-65; urban systems mgr. N.Y.C., 1966-67; 1st dep. city adminstr. Office of Mayor of N.Y.C., 1967-72; chmn. Mayor's Urban Action Task Force, 1969-72; prof. pub. mgmt. Columbia U., N.Y.C., 1972-83; dir. Center for Govt. Studies Columbia U., 1973-83, assoc. dir. Center for Policy Rsch., 1973-81; asst. sec. for policy devel. and rsch. HUD, Washington, 1981-83; prof. mgmt. Baruch Coll., CUNY, 1981-94, prof. public policy, 1994—, dir. public policy program, 1994—, chm. dept. mgmt., 1986-93; dir. Privatization Rsch. Orgn., 1986—; cons. NSF, Nat. Bur. Standards, Am. Paper Inst., Nat. Endowment for Arts, HUD, Dept. Transp., World Bank, AID, U.S. Dept. State, President's Commn. on Privatization, UN, UN Devel. Program, ILO, UNIDO, USIA, also others; mem. voting bd. Blue Cross and Blue Shield Greater N.Y., 1976-79, bd. dirs., 1979-81; mem. Pres.-Elect's Urban Affairs Task Force, 1980, N.Y. State Senate Adv. Commn. on Privatization, 1990-95; mem. Gov. Pataki privatization coun., N.Y., 1995—; dir. U.S.-USSR Joint Project on Mgmt. Cities, 1973-81; advisor on privatization Govt. Poland, 1990-92, Govt. Lesotho, 1992, Govt. Ukraine, 1993, N.Y.C. mayor, 1994—, Govt. South Africa, 1996. Author: Computer Control of Industrial Processes, 1965, Organization and Efficiency of Solid Waste Collection, 1977, Privatizing the Public Sector, 1982, Moscow's City Government, 1985, Privatization, 1987, 12 fgn. edits., others; editor: Alternatives for Delivering Public Services, 1977, Privatization for New York, 1992; mem. editorial bd. Urban Affairs Quar., Privatization Report, Privatization Watch, State and Local Govt. Rev.; contbr. 110 articles to profl. jours. Mem. N.Y.C. Mayor-elect Giuliani transition team, 1993, N.Y. Gov.-elect Pataki transition team, 1994. With U.S. Army, 1953-54, Korea. Recipient Systems Sci. and Cybernetics award IEEE, 1968, Louis Brownlow award Am. Soc. Public Adminstrn., 1970, Honor award Templeton Found., 1989, Leadership award Nat. Coun. Pub.-Private Partnerships, 1993, Outstanding Acad. award Am. Soc. Pub. Adminstrn., 1996. Mem. Sigma Xi, Psi Upsilon. Greek Orthodox. Club: City of N.Y. (trustee 1974-77, Richard Childs award 1979). Office: CUNY Baruch Coll Box F-1228 17 Lexington Ave New York NY 10010-5526

SAVCHENKO, ALLA, ballet mistress; arrived in Can., 1981; Diploma of excellence, Moscow Ballet Sch. Mem. Bolshoi Ballet, 1953-74; ballet mistress, choreographer Sovrenennik Theatre, Moscow, 1974-79; regisseur Royal Winnipeg Ballet, 1981-89, ballet mistress, 1989-90, sr. ballet mistress, 1989—. Leading roles include Humpbacked Horse, The Nutcracker, The Stone Flower, Fire of Paris, Cinderella, Swan Lake, The Sleeping Beauty. Office: Royal Winnipeg Ballet, 380 Graham Ave, Winnipeg, MB Canada R3C 4K2*

SAVEKER, DAVID RICHARD, naval and marine architectural engineering executive; b. San Jose, Calif., Jan. 10, 1920; s. William Thomas and Bernice (Lloyd) S.; m. Jessie Mae Walters, June 19, 1941 (dec. 1995); m. Judy D. Saltzman, July 3, 1995; children: William, Linda, Richard (dec.), Jeffery Whittier. AA, San Jose State Coll., 1939; AB, Stanford U., 1941; cert. in naval architecture, U.S. Naval Acad., 1942; SM, MIT, 1946. Registered profl. engr., Calif. Commd. ensign USN, 1941, advanced through grades to capt., 1960, ret., 1968; assoc. prof. Calif. Poly. State U., San Luis Obispo, 1969-80; pres. D.R. Saveker Naval Architecture, Pismo Beach, Calif., 1980—; assoc. Mac Kinnon Searle Consortium, Alexandria, Va., 1991—. Inventor sinusoidal structure and applications. Research grantee NASA/Stanford Lab., 1973. Mem. Marine Tech. Soc., Soc. Naval Architects and Marine Engrs., Tau Beta Pi. Democrat. Methodist. Club: Cosmos (Washington). Avocations: history, music, water colors. Home: 711 Hanford St Pismo Beach CA 93449-2347

SAVELKOUL, DONALD CHARLES, lawyer; b. Mpls., July 29, 1917; s. Theodore Charles and Edith (Lindgren) S.; m. Mary Joan Holland, May 17, 1941; children: Jeffrey Charles, Jean Marie, Edward Joseph. BA magna cum laude, U. Minn., 1939; JD cum laude, William Mitchell Coll. Law, 1951. Bar: Minn. 1951, U.S. Dist. Ct. Minn. 1952, U.S. Ct. Appeals (8th cir.) 1960, U.S. Supreme Ct. 1971. Adminstrv. work various U.S. govt. depts., including Commerce, War, Labor, Wage Stblzn. Bd., 1940-51; mcpl. judge Fridley, Minn., 1952-53; pvt. practice law Mpls., St. Paul, Fridley, 1951-96; chmn. bd. Fridley State Bank, 1962-95, Blaine State Bank, 1972—; pres. Bahrein, Inc., 1962-95, Blaine Bldg. Corp., 1972—, Babbscha Co., 1962-95; mem. faculty William Mitchell Coll. Law, 1952-59, corp. mem., 1956—; sec. Fridley Recreation and Svc. Co., 1955—; mem. Minn. Legislature, 1967-69. Mem. Gov.'s Com. Workers Compensation, 1965-67, Gov.'s Adv. Coun. on Employment Security, 1957-60; chmn. Fridley Police Civil Svc. Commn., 1962-63; gen. counsel Minn. AFL-CIO Fedn. Labor, 1952-71. 1st lt. AUS, 1943-46. Decorated Bronze Star; recipient Disting. Alumni award Coll. Liberal Arts U. Minn., 1995. Mem. ABA, Minn. Bar Assn. (chmn. 1957-58, bd. dirs. 1958-62, 68-69, labor law sect.), Hennepin County Bar Assn., Justice William Mitchell Soc., Am. Legion, U. Minn. Pres.'s Club, Phi Beta Kappa. Roman Catholic. Office: 916 Moore Lake Dr W Fridley MN 55432-5148

SAVELL, EDWARD LUPO, lawyer; b. Atlanta, Apr. 29, 1921; s. Leon M. and Lillian (Lupo) S.; m. Bettie Patterson Hoyt, Oct. 11, 1944; 1 dau., Mary Lillian Savell Clarke. B.B.A., Emory U., 1947, LL.B., 1949. Bar: Ga. 1948; registered mediator Ga. ADR. Assoc. A.C. Latimer, Atlanta, 1948-53; ptnr. Carter, Latimer & Savell, Atlanta, 1953-56, Woodruff, Latimer & Savell (and successor firms), Atlanta, 1956-87; of counsel Savell & Williams, Atlanta, 1987—; instr. John Marshall Law Sch., 1951-55; dir. Legal Aid Soc., 1955-58; arbitrator Am. Arbitration Assn. and Fulton Superior Ct. Contbr. articles to legal jours. With USAF, 1942-45, CBI. Fellow Internat. Acad. Trial Lawyers (pres. 1978-79, Dean of Acad. 1976); mem. Atlanta Bar Assn. (sec.-treas. 1953-54), ABA, State Bar Ga., Ga. Def. Lawyers Assn. (founder, v.p.), Internat. Assn. Ins. Counsel, Atlanta Claims Assn., Lawyers Club Atlanta, Chi Phi, Phi Delta Phi. Presbyterian. Clubs: Cherokee Town and Country, Commerce, Univ. Yacht (past commodore). Office: Savell and Williams 2600 Marquis I Tower 245 Peachtree Center Ave NE Atlanta GA 30303-1222

SAVENOR, BETTY CARMELL, painter, printmaker; b. Boston, Sept. 2, 1927; d. Harry Hyman and Sally Carmell; m. Jack Savenor, June 1, 1948; children: Alan, Barry, Ronald. Student, Jackson Van Ladau Sch. Fashion, Brandeis U., DeCordova Mus.; BFA, Mass. Coll. Art, 1993. represented by Art 3, Inc., Manchester, N.H., Diane Levine, Boston, Market Barn Gallery, Falmouth, Mass. Exhibited in shows at Guild of Boston Artists, Salmagundi Club, N.Y., Boston Printmakers, U. Mass., Harvard U., Okla. U., Brandeis U., Purdue U., Ind., Attleboro (Mass.) Mus., Western N.Mex. U., Montclair Art Mus., N.J., Duxbury Art Complex, Mass., Morris Mus. Arts & Scis., N.J., George Walker Vincent Smith Mus., Mass., Nat. Gallery, N.Y., Fairleigh Dickinson U., N.J., Fitchburg Art Mus., Mass., Boston C. of C., Fed. Res. Bank of Boston, Adelphi U., N.Y., Stonehill Coll., Cahoon Mus. Am. Art, Midwest Mus. Art, Ind., Allied Artists Am., N.Y., Bentley Coll., Mass., also various traveling exhbns.; represented in permanent collections at Fairfield Med. Assn., Vackerville, Calif., Bank of Boston, Data Products, NEC Info. Sys., Inc., Skowhegan Bank, Maine, Sheraton Corp., Hollywood, Calif. and New Orleans, Meadows Country Club, Fla., First Bank of Concord, N.H., Indian Head Bank, N.H., New Eng. Life Ins. Co., Conn. Mut. Ins. Co., Liberty Mut. Ins. Co., Velcro Mgmt., Jo-Ann Fabrics. Juror for numerous art shows, Mass.; demonstrator for many art socs. Recipient Nicholas Reale Meml. award for graphics Allied Artists Am., Mem. New Eng. Watercolor Soc. (sec. 1983-93, Best Contemporary Watercolor prize 1990), Nat. Assn. Women Artists (prize 1982, 87, 89), Cape Code Art Assn. (Jurors Merit award 1992-94, 1st prize in graphics 1993-95), Am. PEN Women (Best in State award 1983-95), Concord Art Assn. (Gold medal 1985, 1st prize 1991). Democrat. Jewish. Avocations: tennis, swimming, decorating. Home and Studio: 4305 Highland Oaks Cir Sarasota FL 34235-5173

SAVEROT, PIERRE-MICHEL, nuclear waste management company executive. MS, Northwestern U., 1977. Asst. to pres. Jai Corp., Fairfax, Va. Home: 3112 White Daisy Pl Fairfax VA 22031 Office: Jai Corp Ste 200 4103 Chain Bridge Rd Fairfax VA 22031

SAVETH, EDWARD NORMAN, history educator; b. N.Y.C., Feb. 16, 1915; s. Isidor and Eva (Vasa) S.; m. Harriet Obstler, June 22, 1975; 1 child by previous marriage, Henry. B.S.S., CCNY, 1935; M.A., Columbia U., 1937, Ph.D., 1946. Prof. history Grad. Faculty New Sch. for Social Research, N.Y.C., 1960-63; Fulbright prof. Kyoto U., Kyoto, Japan, 1964-65; prof. Dartmouth Coll., 1965-66; Disting. vis. prof. Tex. Lutheran Coll., Seguin, 1966-67; Disting. prof. SUNY-Fredonia, 1967-85; adj. prof. SUNY, Buffalo, 1987—; lectr. USIA, Nepal, 1965, Morocco, 1977; Fulbright prof. Hebrew U., Jerusalem, 1981; vis. prof. U. Rochester, 1972; lectr. Beijing Tchrs. Coll., 1989. Author: American historians and European Immigrants, 1947; author, editor: Understanding the American Past, 1954, Henry Adams, 1963, American History and the Social Sciences, 1964; revisions editor: Ency. Americana, 1962; contbr. numerous articles to mags. Mem. Am. Hist. Assn., Orgn. Am. Historians. Home: 11 High Ct Buffalo NY 14226-3527 Office: SUNY-Buffalo Dept History Buffalo NY 14260

SAVIC, STANLEY DIMITRIUS, physicist; b. Belgrade, Yugoslavia, Dec. 30, 1938; came to the U.S., 1958; s. Dimitrius and Zorka (Vuckovic) S. BS, Roosevelt U., 1962; MS, U. Ill., 1969. Staff scientist Argonne Cancer Rsch. Hosp., Chgo., 1962-63; with radiology staff U. Chgo., 1963-64; v.p. Zenith Electronics Corp., Glenview, Ill., 1964—; chief U.S. del. Internat. Electrotech. Commn., Geneva, 1986-90; lectr. in field, 1984-91; mem. com. FDA, Washington, 1978-81; mem. faculty N.Y. Acad. Fire Scis., Albany, 1991. Author: X-Ray Conference Proceedings, 1968, co-author, 1968; contbr. chpt.: Standards Management, 1990. Apptd. by sec. Dept. Health & Human Svcs. to Tech. Electronic Products Radiation Safety Standards Com., Washington, 1978-81, 93; sec. Holy Resurrection Cathedral, Chgo., 1978-79; divsn. chmn. Crusade of Mercy, United Way, 1988. Mem. IEEE (sr.), N.Y. Acad. Scis., Nat. Fire Protection Assn., ASTM, Electronic Industries Assn. (chmn. safety com. 1983-87, mem. engring. policy coun. 1992—, Disting. Svc. award 1987). Republican. Serbian-Orthodox. Achievements include patent for a safety-related electronic circuit. Office: Zenith Electronics Corp 1000 Milwaukee Ave Glenview IL 60025-2423

SAVICH, RENÉ, broadway theater executive, producer; b. Chgo., Nov. 14, 1947; d. Nicholas and Elizabeth (Szakurski) S. BS, Northwestern U., 1969. Asst. house mgr. Minskoff Theatre, N.Y.C., 1973; mem. mgmt. staff The Shubert Orgn. Inc., N.Y.C., 1975-77, mgr. dept. maintenance, 1977-80; asst. house mgr. The Shubert Theatre, N.Y.C., 1975-77, Plymouth Theatre, N.Y.C., 1978; house mgr. Barrymore Theatre, N.Y.C., 1978-79; mgr. co. The Elephant Man, N.Y.C., 1980; house mgr. Playhouse Theatre, N.Y.C., 1980-81, Cort Theatre, N.Y.C., 1981-85, Golden Theatre, N.Y.C., 1985-86, Booth Theatre, N.Y.C., 1987—. Producer off-Broadway plays including Wine Untouched, 1979, Lou, 1981, Punchy, 1983. Mem. Assn. of Theatrical Press Agts. and Mgrs., Actors Equity Assn., Treas. and Ticket Sellers Union. Office: The Shubert Orgn Inc 234 W 44th St New York NY 10036-3909*

SAVILLE, DUDLEY ALBERT, chemical engineering educator; b. Lincoln, Nebr., Feb. 25, 1933; s. George A. and Alta (Goddard) S.; m. Joy Wagner, Mar. 7, 1959; children: Alexander, Andrea. B.S., U. Nebr., 1954, M.S., 1959; Ph.D, U. Mich., 1966. Engr. Carbide & Carbon Chem. Co. (Institute), W. Va., 1954-55; research engr. Chevron Research Corp. (Richmond), Calif., 1959-61, Shell Devl. Co., Emeryville, Calif., 1966-68; asst. prof. Princeton U. (N.J.), 1968-71, assoc. prof., 1971-77, prof. dept. chem. engring., 1977. Assoc. editor Jour. Physico-Chem. Hydrodynamics, 1980-87; mem. adv. bd. Jour. Colloid Interface Sci., 1992-94; contbr. articles to profl. jours. Served to 1st lt. USAF, 1955-58. Mem. Am. Inst. Chem. Engrs., Am. Chem. Soc., Am. Phys. Soc. Office: Princeton U Dept Chem Engring Princeton NJ 08544

SAVILLE, THORNDIKE, JR., coastal engineer, consultant; b. Balt., Aug. 1, 1925; s. Thorndike and Edith Stedman (Wilson) S.; m. Janet Foster, Aug. 28, 1950; children: Sarah, Jennifer, Gordon. A.B., Harvard U., 1947; M.S., U. Calif.-Berkeley, 1949. Research asst. U. Calif., Berkeley, 1947-49; hydraulic engr. Beach Erosion Bd. and Coastal Engring. Research Center, Ft. Belvoir, Va., 1949-81; chief research div. Beach Erosion Bd. and Coastal Engring. Research Center, 1964-71, tech. dir., 1971-81. Contbr. over 75 articles to engring. and sci. publs. Served with USAAF, 1943-46. Recipient Meritorious Civilian Service award Dept. Army, 1981. Fellow AAAS, Wash. Acad. Scis., ASCE (Huber award 1963, Moffatt-Nichol award 1979, Internat. Coastal Engring. award 1991); mem. Am. Geophys. Union, Internat. Assn. for Hydraulic Rsch., Nat. Acad. Engring., Permanent Internat. Assn. Navigation Congresses (hon., U.S. commr. 1971-78, U.S. commr. emeritus 1987—, U.S. rep. PTC II 1991—), Am. Shore and Beach Preservation Assn. (bd. dirs. 1976—, v.p. 1988-95), Cosmos Club (Washington). Home and Office: 5601 Albia Rd Bethesda MD 20816-3304 *A good leader takes the blame and gives the credit.*

SAVIN, ABBY LURIA, social worker; b. New Haven, Conn., June 29, 1930; d. Jacob J. and Sylvia (Aaronson) Luria; m. Martin Savin, Nov. 7, 1964 (dec. June 1992); 1 child, Ellen Jacqueline Johnson. BS in Human and Cmty. Svc., Empire State Coll., 1981; MSW, So. Conn. State U., 1985. Exec. sec., adminstrv. asst. New Haven YWCA, 1965-83; outreach/intake coord. Cmty. Mediation, New Haven, 1985-86; pre-trial supr. Superior Ct./Cath. Family Svcs., New Haven, 1986-91; case mgr. New Haven Family Alliance, 1991-92, adoption/foster care coord., 1992-96, case mgmt. supr., 1996—; treas. Conn. Coun. on Adoption, 1994; presenter workshops and seminars in field. Recipient Women in Leadership award New Haven YWCA, 1983, 92, cert. of appreciation Tough Love Group, Meriden, Conn., 1989. Mem. AAUW, NASW (bd. dirs. 1992), Conn. Assn. Human Svcs., Conn. Prison Assn., Tutor-Literacy Vols. Greater New Haven. Home: 60 Brooklawn Cir New Haven CT 06515-2303 Office: New Haven Family Alliance 5 Science Park New Haven CT 06511-1966

SAVIN, RONALD RICHARD, chemical company executive, inventor; b. Cleve., Oct. 16, 1926; s. Samuel and Ada (Silver) S.; m. Gloria Ann Hopkins, Apr. 21, 1962; children: Danielle Elizabeth, Andrea Lianne. BA in Chemistry and Lit., U. Cin., 1944-46; BA in Chemistry and Literature, U. Mich., 1948; postgrad., Columbia U., 1948-49, Sorbonne, Paris, 1949-50; grad., Air War Coll., 1975, Indsl. Coll. Armed Forces, 1976. Pres., owner Premium Finishes, Inc., Cin., 1957-91; cons. aerospace and anti-corrosive coatings; inventor Hunting Indsl. Coatings. Contbr. articles on aerospace, marine industry and transp. to profl. jours.; holder 14 patents in field of aerospace and anti-corrosion coatings. With USAF, 1948-55, World War II and Korea, col. Res. 1979, ret. 1986. Mem. Steel Structures Painting Coun., Nat. Assn. Corrosion Engrs., Air Force Assn., Am. Internat. Club (Geneva), Res. Officers Assn., Army Navy Club. Avocations: scientific development, photography, tennis.

SAVINELL, ROBERT FRANCIS, engineering educator; b. Cleve., May 26, 1950; s. Robert D. and Lotte R. Savinell; m. Coletta A. Savinell, Aug. 23, 1974; children: Teresa, Robert, Mark. BSChemE, Cleve. State U., 1973; MS, U. Pitts., 1974, PhD, 1977. Registered profl. engr., Ohio. Rsch. engr. Diamond Shamrock Corp., Painesville, Ohio, 1977-79; assoc. prof. U. Akron, Ohio, 1979-86; prof. Case Western Reserve U., Cleve., 1986—, dir. Ernest B. Yeager Ctr. for Electrochem. Scis., 1991—. Divsn. editor Jour. Electrochem. Soc., 1988-91; N.Am. editor Jour. Applied Electrochemistry, 1991—; contbr. articles to profl. jours. Named Presdl. Young Investigator, NSF, Washington, 1984-89, Outstanding Engring. Alumnus, Cleve. State U., 1984. Mem. AIChE (program chmn. 1986-92), Electrochem. Soc. (divsn. officer 1992—). Avocations: sailing, skiing. Office: Case Western Reserve U Dept Chem Engring AW Smith Bldg Cleveland OH 44106

SAVINETTI, LOUIS GERARD, town councilperson; b. Sea Cliff, N.Y., Sept. 5, 1955; s. Louis Philip and Alice Margaret (Stanco) S.; m. Holly Pinto, Apr. 30, 1983; 1 child, Scott Pinto. BA in Edn., L.I. U., Brookville, N.Y., 1979, MPA, 1987; JD, Touro Sch. Law, Huntington, N.Y., 1996. Asst. dir. Office of County Devel. County of Nassau, Roslyn Harbor, N.Y., 1981-88; asst. to commr. Town of Oyster Bay, N.Y., 1988-92, dep. commr. planning and devel., 1992-96, councilman, 1994—; with Capetola & Doddato, Attys. at Law, Williston Park, N.Y., 1994—. Exec. leader Republican Party, Glen Head, Glenwood Landing and Old Brookville, N.Y., 1992. Founder Geographic Info. Systems Commn., Cmty. Congress Citizens Adv. Bd.; bd. dirs. Syosset Hosp.; founder Fire Adv. Bd., Marine Adv. Bd., Environ. Coordinating Coun. Mem. Grenville Baker Boys and Girls Club Alumni, Glen Head/Glenwood Bus. Assn., L.I. U. Alumni Assn. Episcopalian. Avocations: photography, music. Home: 43 Kissam Ln Glen Head NY 11545-1013

SAVINI, TOM, make-up artist, actor, director; b. Pitts.; m. Nancy Hare, 1984. Film work includes Deathdream, 1972, Deranged, 1974, Martin, 1976, Dawn of the Dead, 1978, Effects, 1980, Eyes of a Stranger, 1980, Friday the 13th, 1980, Friday the 13th IV, The Burning, 1981, Maniac, 1981, The Prowler, 1981, Alone in the Dark, Creepshow, 1982, Midnight, 1983, Friday the 13th-The Final Chapter, 1984, Invasion U.S.A., 1985, Day of the Dead, 1985, The Texas Chainsaw Massacre, Part II, 1987, Monkey-Shines: An Experiment in Fear, 1988, Red Scorpion, 1989, Two Evileyes, 1990, Heartstopper, 1992, Trauma, 1993, H.P. Lovecrafts Necronomicon, 1994, Mr. Stitch, Ghostwriter, Killing Zoe; dir. Night of the Living Dead, 1990; actor appearences include Knightriders, 1981, The Ripper, 1986; dir. Night of the Living Dead, 1990, episodes Tales from The Darkside; writer: Grand Illusions, 1983, Grand Illusions Books II, 1988. *

SAVITS, BARRY SORREL, surgeon; b. Phila., Feb. 14, 1934; s. Frank and Sophia (Cohen) S.; children: George, Frank, Alexander. BA, Princeton U., 1955; MD, U. Pa., 1959; cert. surg. residency, Mt. Sinai Hosp., N.Y.C., 1965. Prof. surgery Project Hope, Ecuador, 1965-66; instr. surgery Albert Einstein Med. Coll., Bronx, N.Y., 1966-67; surgeon LaGuardia Med. Group, Queens, N.Y., 1970-72; dir. surgery St. Mary's Hosp., Bklyn., 1973-91, Kingsbrook Jewish Med. Ctr., Bklyn., 1991—. Vis. surgeon Care-Medico, Afghanistan. Comdr. USN, 1967-69. Fellow ACS (gov. 1991-97); mem. SAGES, Assn. Acad. Surgery, Assn. Surg. Program Dirs., Bklyn. Surg. Soc. (pres. 1992-93). Jewish. Avocations: reading, children. Office: Kingsbrook Jewish Med Ctr 585 Schenectady Ave Brooklyn NY 11203-1822

SAVITSKY, DANIEL, engineer, educator; b. N.Y.C., Sept. 26, 1921; s. Maxim and Anna (Oleksiw) S.; m. Mary Wysocki; children: Jean, James, Anne. BCE, CCNY, 1942; MSc, Stevens Inst. Tech., 1952; PhD, NYU, 1971. Registered profl. engr., N.Y. Structural engr. EDO Corp., College Point, N.Y., 1942-44; aero. rsch. scientist Nat. Adv. Com. for Aero., Langley Field, Va., 1944-47; prof. emeritus Stevens Inst. Tech., Hoboken, N.J., 1947—; chmn. high speed vehicle com. Internat. Towing Tank Conf., 1978-88; cons. Naval Studies Bd., Nat. Rsch. Coun. Author: (with others) Yearbook of Science and Technology, 1987; patentee hydrofoil controls. Fellow Soc. Naval Architects and Marine Engrs. (Adm. Cochrane award 1967, Davidson medal 1996), Am. Soc. Naval Engrs., Niantic Bay Yacht Club (Conn.), Sigma Xi. Roman Catholic. Avocations: sailing, skiing, tennis. Home: 597 Delcina Dr Westwood NJ 07675-6111 Office: Davidson Lab 711 Hudson St Hoboken NJ 07030-5953

SAVITSKY, THOMAS ROBERT, lawyer; b. Pa., Sept. 12, 1952; s. Stanley George and Adele (Kaleda) S.; m. Deborah Ann Sokirka, Jan. 13, 1973; children: Thomas Jason, Raina Alexandra. BS in Biology, Villanova U., 1974; MS in Microbiology, Temple U., 1978; JD, Widener U., 1983. Bar: U.S. Patent and Trademark Office, 1984, Mich. 1985, Tenn. 1988, U.S. Dist. Ct. (ea. dist.) Mich. 1985, U.S. Ct. Appeals (fed. cir.) 1991; cert. quality engr. Am. Soc. for Quality Control, 1981. Microbiologist Warner-Lambert Co., 1978-81; lab. supr. Betz Labs., Trevose, Pa., 1982-84; patent atty. The Dow Chem. Co., Midland, Mich., 1984-87, Eastman Chem. Co., Kingsport, Tenn., 1987-89; sr. patent atty. Eastman Chem. Co., Kingsport, 1989-91, licensing and bus. devel. mgr., 1991-92; asst. counsel Bristol-Myers Squibb Co., Princeton, N.J., 1992—. Mem. ABA, AAAS, Am. Intellectual Property Law Assn., Am. Soc. for Microbiology. Roman Catholic. Home: 26 Meadow Ln Pennington NJ 08534-2113 Office: Bristol-Myers Squibb Co PO Box 4000 Princeton NJ 08543

SAVITT, STEVEN LEE, computer scientist; b. Mpls., May 25, 1949; s. Leonard Robert and Claire (Hurwitz) S.; m. Gloria Lynn Kumagai; children: Mariko, Leilani, Joshua. BSEE, U. Minn., 1971, PhD in Computer Sci., 1992. Founder, CEO Compmark I Corp., Mpls., 1972-83; rsch. sect. head Honeywell, Inc., Mpls., 1983-89; rsch. staff scientist Alliant Techsystems, Inc., Mpls., 1989-96, engring. sect. head, 1996—; co-chair database com. Automatic Target Recognizer Working Group, 1985-87. Mem. IEEE, Japanese-Am. Citizens League. Avocations: piano, classic car collecting, canoeing, tennis, swimming. Home: 332 Westwood Dr N Golden Valley MN 55422-5263

SAVITT, SUSAN SCHENKEL, lawyer; b. Bklyn., Aug. 21, 1943; d. Edward Charles and Sylvia (Dlugatch) S.; m. Harvey Savitt, July 2, 1969 (div. 1978); children: Andrew Todd, Daniel Cory. BA magna cum laude, Pa. State U., 1964; JD, Columbia U., 1968. Bar: N.Y. 1968, U.S. Dist. Ct. (so. and ea. dists.) N.Y. 1973, U.S. Tax Ct. 1973, U.S. Ct. Appeals (2d cir.) 1981, U.S. Supreme Ct. 1980, U.S. Dist. Ct. (no. dist.) N.Y. 1986. Atty. Nassau County Legal Svcs., Freeport, N.Y., 1973-74; asst. corp. counsel City of Yonkers, 1977-78; from assoc. to ptnr. Epstein, Becker & Green, P.C., N.Y.C., 1978-94; ptnr. Winston & Strawn, N.Y.C., 1994—; adj. prof. Elizabeth Seton Coll., Yonkers, 1982-83; mem. NYU exec. coun. Met. Ctr. for Edni. Rsch. Devel. and Tng., 1987-90. Mem. Hastings-on-Hudson (N.Y.) Sch. Bd., 1984-93, v.p., 1986, 87-88, pres., 1989-90, 92-93; bd. dirs. Associated Blind, 1993-95, Search for Change, 1996—. Mem. ABA (internat. law sect., litigation and labor law sect.), N.Y. State Bar Assn. (com. on women and the law, labor law sect.), Women's Bar Assn. (litigation com.), N.Y. State Sch. Bd. Attys. Assn., Pa. State Alumni Club (v.p. Westchester County 1985-87), Phi Beta Kappa, Alpha Kappa Delta, Phi Gamma Mu, Pi Kappa Phi. Office: Winston & Strawn 200 Park Ave New York NY 10166-0005

SAVITZ, MARTIN HAROLD, neurosurgeon; b. Boston, Jan. 20, 1942; s. Nathan and Bernice Beatrice (Segal) S.; m. Susan Rayna Gordon, June 23, 1968 (div. Sept. 1977); 1 child, Sean Isaac; m. Harmony Gwynne Keys, Oct. 28, 1979; 1 child, Ariel Austryn. AB, Harvard U., 1963; MD, Hahnemann, 1969. Diplomate Am. Bd. Neurol. Surgery, Am. Bd. Clin. Neurosurgery, Nat. Bd. Med. Examiners, Am. Bd. Forensic Medicine. Intern Boston City Hosp., 1969-70; resident Mount Sinai Hosp., N.Y.C., 1970-74; clin. instr. dept. neurosurgery Mt. Sinai Sch. Medicine, N.Y.C., 1974-82, asst. clin. prof., 1982-86, assoc. clin. prof., 1986-97; attending neurosurgeon Nyack (N.Y.) Hosp., Good Samaritan Hosp., Rockland County, N.Y., Cmty. Hosp., Dobbs Ferry, N.Y.; mem. pres.'s coun. Harvard Coll., 1991—, marshal of commencement, 1993—; mem. alumni bd. trustees Hahnemann U., 1991-94; 18 vis. lectureships in 8 different countries; head exam com. Am. Bd. Clin. Neurosurgery, 1995—. Contbg. editor Mt. Sinai Jour. Medicine, 1976-90, asst. editor, 1990—; mem. editl. bd. Jour. Orthopaedic Neurol. Medicine and Surgery, 1991—; contbr. 2 chpts. to textbooks, 80 articles to profl. jours. Named Internat. Man of Yr., Internat. Biographical Ctr., 1994. Fellow ACS, Am. Biog. Assn., Internat. Coll. Surgeons (chmn.-elect U.S. sect. neurosurgery, 1992, chmn., 1993, exec. com. 1994, chmn.-elect 1995, chmn. 1996, bd. regents 1997), N.Y. Acad. Medicine, Phila. Coll. Physicians, Am. Acad. Neurol. Orthopaedic Surgery (bd. dirs. 1994—) Am. Forensic Examiners Coll. (ethics com. 1995—), Internat. Biog. Assn.; mem. AMA, AAAS, Am. Assn. Neurol. Surgeons, N.Y. Soc. Neurosurgery, Congress Neurol. Surgeons, N.Y. State Neurosurg. Soc., Internat. Fedn. of Surg. Colls., Internat. Soc. Minimal Intervention in Spinal Surgery, Hastings Ctr., Am. Biographical Inst. (Man of Yr. 1995), N.Y. Acad. Scis., Alpha Omega Alpha, Phi Delta Epsilon. Jewish. Avocations: travel to all 7 continents, photography of rare fauna and flora, archeology. Home: Hobbit Holw New City NY 10956 Office: 55 Old Turnpike Rd Ste 101 Nanuet NY 10954-2449

SAVITZ, MAXINE LAZARUS, aerospace company executive; b. Balt., Feb. 13, 1937; d. Samuel and Harriette (Miller) Lazarus; m. Sumner Alan Savitz, Jan. 1, 1961; children: Adam Jonathan, Alison Carrie. BA in Chemistry magna cum laude, Bryn Mawr Coll., 1958; PhD in Organic Chemistry, MIT, 1961. Instr. chemistry Hunter Coll., N.Y.C., 1962-63; sr. electrochemist Mobility Equipment Rsch. and Devel. Ctr., Ft. Belvoir, Va., 1963-68; prof. chemistry Federal City Coll., Washington, 1968-72; program mgr. NSF, Washington, 1972-74; dir. FEA Office Bldgs. Policy Rshc. U.S. Dept. Energy, Washington, 1974-75, dir. div. indsl. conservation, 1975-76, from dir. div. bldgs. and community systems to dep asst sec., 1975-83; pres. Lighting Rsch. Inst., 1983-85; asst. to v.p. engring. Ceramic Components div. The Garrett Corp., 1985-87; gen. mgr. ceramic components divsn. AlliedSignal Inc., Torrance, Calif., 1987—; bd. dirs. Am. Coun. for Energy Efficient Economy, 1984—, Internat. Inst. Energy Conservation, 1984-94, Energy Found., 1991—; cons. State Mich. Dept. Commerce, 1983, N.C. Alternative Energy Corp., 1983, Garrett Corp., 1983, Energy Engring. Bd., Nat. Rsch. Bd., 1986-93, Office Tech.Assessment, U.S. Congress Energy Demand Panel, 1987-91, nat. materials adv. bd. NRC, 1989-94; bd. dirs. U.S. Advanced Ceramic Assn., 1989—, chmn., 1992; adv. com. div. ceramics/materials ORNL, 1989-92, adv. com. dir., 1992-96; adv. bd. Sec. Energy, 1992—; mem. Def. Sci. Bd., 1993-96; vis. com. adv. tech. Nat. Inst. Standards and Tech., 1993—. Editor Energy and Bldgs.; contbr. articles to profl. jours. Policy com. mem. NAE, 1994—. NSF postdoctoral fellow, 1961, 62, NIH predoctoral fellow, 1960, 61. Mem. Nat. Acad. Engring. Office: AlliedSignal Ceramic Components Divsn 2525 W 190th St Torrance CA 90504-6002

SAVITZ, SAMUEL J., actuarial consulting firm executive; b. Phila., Dec. 23, 1936; s. Paul and Ann (Gechman) S.; BS in Bus. Adminstrn., Temple U., 1958; postgrad. U. Pa., 1960-62, Temple U., 1965; m. Selma Goldberg, June 15, 1958; children: Jacqueline Beverly, Steven Leslie, Michelle Lynn. Pension analyst Provident Mut. Life Ins. Co., Phila., 1958-61; v.p. The Wirkman Co., Phila., 1961-64; pres. Samuel J. Savitz & Assoc., Inc., Phila., 1964-86; chmn. bd., cons. Exec. Compensation Plans, Inc., Phila., 1980-86; sr. prin. Laventhol & Horwath, Phila., 1986-90; chmn., CEO Savitz Orgn., Inc., 1990—; vis. lectr. U. Pa., Phila., 1960, La. State U., 1972-74; faculty Villanova U., 1971-75; cons. in field. Mem. pension com. Fedn. Jewish Agys., Phila., 1960; bd. dirs. Am. com. Weizmann Inst. Sci., 1984-85, Phila. All-Star Forum, 1987-95, Mann Music Ctr., 1992—; bd. trustees Fgn. Policy Rsch. Inst., 1996—. With USAR, 1954-62. Mem. Am. Soc. Pension Actuaries (dir. 1969-75). Jewish. Club: Locust. Contbr. articles in field to profl. jours. Home: 470 Conshohocken State Rd Bala Cynwyd PA 19004-2639 Office: 1845 Walnut St Philadelphia PA 19103-4708

SAVOCA, ANTONIO LITTERIO, technology company executive; b. Cleve., Aug. 10, 1923; s. Peter Louis and Angelina Nancy (Ragonese) S.; m. Charlene Henson, Sept. 27, 1952; 1 child, Gina Savoca Rose. BBA, U. Okla., 1958. Mgr. dept. proposals Wasatch div. Thiokol Corp., Brigham City, Utah, 1963-66, asst. to gen. mgr., 1966-68, dir. fin. and adminstrn., 1968-74, sr. v.p., gen. mgr., 1974-83; pres., chief exec. officer Transpace Carriers, Inc., Greenbelt, Md., 1983-86; mgmt. cons. various cos., 1986-89; pres., chmn., CEO Atlantic Rsch. Corp. subs. Sequa Corp., Alexandria, Va., 1989—; sr. v.p. Sequa Corp., N.Y.C.; bd. dirs. No. Va. Tech. Coun. Chmn. U.S. Savs. Bond Campaign, Alexandria, 1991. Lt. col. USAF, 1942-63; ETO; Korea. Mem. Nat. Assn. Mfrs., Air Force Assn., Assn. U.S. Army, Am. Def. Preparedness Assn., Italy-U.S. Bus. Conf. (bd. dirs.), Navy League, U.S. Space Found., Hon. Utah Cols., The Robert Trent Jones Golf Club, Ogden Golf and Country Club, Tower Club. Republican. Roman Catholic. Office: Atlantic Rsch Corp 1577 Spring Hill Rd Ste 600 Vienna VA 22182-2223

SAVOCCHIO, JOYCE A., mayor; b. Erie, Pa.; d. Daniel and Esther S. BA in History, Mercyhurst Coll., 1965; MEd, U. Pitts., 1969; cert. secondary sch. adminstrn., Edinboro U., 1975; LLD (hon.), Gannon U., 1990. Tchr. social studies Erie Sch. Dist., 1965-85, asst. prin. Strong Vincent High Sch., 1985-89, tchr. coord. high sch. task force, 1971-75; pres. Erie Edn. Assn., 1975-76; mem. coun. City of Erie, 1981-90, pres. coun., 1983, mayor, 1990—; pres. Pa. League League of Cities and Municipalities, Northwestern Pa. Mayors' Roundtable; mem. subcoms. on transp. and comms. U.S. Conf. of Mayors; bd. dirs. State Job Tng. Partnership Bd.; mem., sec. Electoral Coll. for Commonwealth of Pa. Past pres. Erie Hist. Mus.; past mem. editl. bd. Erie Hist. Soc.; mem. Pa. Gov.'s Flagship Commn., Cmty. Task Force on Drug and Alcohol Abuse. Named Woman of Yr., Dem. Women Erie, 1981, Italian Am. Women's Assn., 1987, Outstanding Citizen of Yr., MECA United Cerebral Palsy, 1991; recipient Disting. Alumna award Mercyhurst Coll., 1990, Community Svc. award Roosevelt Mid. Sch., 1990, Disting. Citizen award French Creek coun. Boy Scouts Am., 1991. Roman Catholic. Office: Office of Mayor Mcpl Bldg 626 State St Erie PA 16501-1128

SAVOIA, MICHAEL ANTHONY, engineer; b. S.I., May 28, 1955; s. Michael John and Marie Teresa (Balto) S.; m. Diane Agnes Kotlarczyk, Dec. 29, 1984; children: Sara Marie, Michael Dominic. AAS in Automotive Tech., SUNY, Farmingdale, 1975; BS in Transp. Tech., Western Mich. U., 1977. Cert. quality engr. Product engr. Holley Carburetor, Warren, Mich., 1977-79, Mather Co., Milan, Mich., 1979-84; gen. mgr. U.S. Gasket Products, Saddlebrook, N.J., 1985-86; sr. applications engr. Fed. Mogul Corp., Milan, 1988-93; investments rep. Edward D. Jones & Co., Tecumseh, Mich., 1993—. Patentee in field. Mem. Tecumseh Rotary (pres. 1996-97), Tecumseh Area C. of C. (bd. dirs. 1995—), Tecumseh Area Cmtys. in Schs. (bd. dirs. 1995—). Roman Catholic. Avocations: automotive racing, race engine bldg. Home: 19621 Bethel Church Rd Manchester MI 48158-9504 Office: Edward D Jones & Co 112 N Evans St Ste 4 Tecumseh MI 49286-1555

SAVOIE, LEONARD NORMAN, transportation company executive; b. Manchester, N.H., Aug. 8, 1928; s. Joseph Peter and Angelina (Desmarais) S.; m. Elsie Anne Berscht, June 9, 1951; children: Deborah Anne, Judith Lynn, Andrew Peter. B.S., Queen's U., 1952; M.B.A., U. Detroit, 1955. Indsl. engr. Kelsey-Hayes Can. Ltd., Windsor, Ont., Can., 1952-60; mgmt. cons. P.S. Ross & Partners, Toronto, Ont., 1960-64; pres., gen. mgr. Kelsey-Hayes Can. Ltd., 1964-70; pres., chief exec. officer Algoma Central Ry., Sault Ste. Marie, Ont., 1970-93, vice-chmn., 1993-96; bd. dirs. Can. Gen. Ins. Co., E-L Fin. Corp. Ltd., Empire Life Ins. Co., Newaygo Forest Products Ltd., Gt. Lakes Power Ltd. Bd. dirs. United Appeal. Mem. Profl. Engrs. Ont., Engring. Inst. Can., Canadian, Sault Ste. Marie chambers commerce. Clubs: Rotary, Toronto, Toronto Ry, Sault Ste. Marie Golf. Office: Algoma Cen Ry, 289 Bay St, Sault Sainte Marie, ON Canada P6A 4Z2

SAVOIE, RONALD E., secondary educator; b. Northampton, Mass., Oct. 11, 1948; s. Emery Joseph and Marguerite (Provost) S.; m. Linda Jean Popielarczyk, Oct. 17, 1970; children: Kelly Irene, Ronelle Erin. BA in U.S. History, Assumption Coll., Worcester, Mass., 1970; MEd in History, Westfield (Mass.) State Coll., 1979. Cert. history, social studies, English tchr., Mass., Conn. Tchr. U.S. history, intramural dir., jr. varsity baseball coach St. Michael's High Sch., Northampton, 1970-76; tchr. U.S. history, jr. varsity baseball coach West Springfield (Mass.) High Sch., 1976-77; tchr. U.S. history, intramural dir. Cowing Jr. High Sch., West Springfield, 1977-81; tchr. U.S. history and geography McAlister Mid. Sch., Suffield, Conn., 1981—, coord. social studies dept., 1989-91; mem. Suffield Social Studies Curriculum Bd., coord. 1950's and 1960's interdisciplinary unit; jr. varsity and varsity baseball coach Suffield High Sch., 1984-91. Mem., coach Southampton (Mass.) Youth Athletic Assn., 1979-91; pres. Hampshire Regional Jr.-Sr. High Sch. Booster Club, Westhampton, Mass., 1992—. Mem. NEA, Nat. Coun. for Social Studies, Conn. Coun. for Social Studies, Orgn. Am. Historians, Conn. Edn. Assn., Suffield Edn. Assn. Roman Catholic. Avocations: coaching baseball and softball, reading, golf, listening to 1950-60's music. Home: PO Box 264 Southampton MA 01073-0264 Office: McAlister Mid Sch 260 Mountain Rd Suffield CT 06078-2082

SAVONA, MICHAEL RICHARD, physician; b. N.Y.C., Oct. 21, 1947; s. Salvatore Joseph and Diana Grace (Menditto) S.; m. Dorothy O'Neill, Oct. 18, 1975. BS summa cum laude, Siena Coll., 1969; MD, SUNY, Buffalo, 1973. Diplomate Am. Bd. Internal Medicine. Intern in internal medicine Presbyn. Hosp. Columbia U., N.Y.C., 1973-74, resident in internal medicine, 1974-76; vis. fellow internal medicine Delafield Hosp./Columbia U. Coll. Physicians and Surgeons, N.Y.C., 1974-76; practice medicine specializing in internal medicine Maui Med. Group, Wailuku, Hawaii, 1976-87, gen. practice medicine, 1987—; dir. ICU, Maui Meml. Hosp., also dir. respiratory therapy, CCU., chmn. dept. medicine, 1980—; clin. faculty John A. Burns Sch. Medicine, U. Hawaii, asst. prof. medicine, 1985—, asst. rsch. prof., 1989—. Bd. dirs. Maui Heart Assn.; dir. profl. edn. Maui chpt. Am. Cancer Soc.; mem. Maui County Hosp. Adv. Commn.; mem. coun. Community Cancer Program of Hawaii. Recipient James A. Gibson Wayne J. Atwell award, 1970, physiology award, 1970, Ernest Whitebsky award, 1971, Roche Lab. award, 1972, Pfiser Lab. award, 1973, Phillip Sang award, 1973, Hans Lowenstein M.D. Meml. award, 1973. Mem. AMA, Am. Thoracic Soc., Hawaii Thoracic Soc., Maui County Med. Assn. (past pres.), Hawaii Med. Assn., Hawaii Oncology Group, ACP, SW Oncology Coop. Group, Alpha Omega Alpha, Delta Epsilon Sigma. Office: 1830 Wells St Wailuku HI 96793-2365

SAVORY, MARK, management consultant, insurance company executive; b. Englewood, N.J., Oct. 5, 1943; s. William A. and Marion J. (Garland) S.; m. Rose Marie Proietti, Feb. 5, 1988. BA with honors, Rutgers U., Newark, 1965; MA, Columbia U., 1966; MBA, U. Conn., 1973. Sec.-dir. Hartford (Conn.) Ins. Group, 1971-81; ptnr. Coopers & Lybrand, N.Y.C., 1981-90; nat. dir. ins. cons. Ernst & Young, 1990—; contr. Sullivan & Cromwell, Inc., N.Y.C., 1983—. Contbr. articles to profl. jours. V.p. Tallott Glen Assn., 1985. Capt. USAF, 1966-71. Mem. Internat. Ins. Soc. (bd. govs. 1988—), Heron Soc. (founding). Home: 14 Carla Ct Morristown NJ 07960-5959 Office: Ernst & Young 750 7th Ave New York NY 10019-6834

SAVOY, DOUGLAS EUGENE, bishop, religion educator, explorer, writer; b. Bellingham, Wash., May 11, 1927; s. Lewis Dell and Maymie (Janett) S.; m. Elvira Clarke, Dec. 5, 1957 (div.); 1 son, Jamil Sean (dec.); m. Sylvia Ontaneda, July 7, 1971; children: Douglas Eugene, Christopher Sean, Sylvia Jamila. Student, U. Portland, 1947-8; DST, D Canon and Sacred Law, Jamilian U. of the Ordained, 1980; PhD in Theology, DD (hon.), Tech. Inst. Bibl. Studies, Nev., 1990. Ordained to ministry Internat. Community of Christ Ch., 1962, bishop, 1971. Cardinal head bishop Internat. Community of Christ Ch., 1971—; lectr. in ministerial tng. studies, 1972—; pastor Univ. Chapel, Reno, 1979—; founder Jamilian Parochial Sch., 1976; chancellor, founder Sacred Coll. of Jamilian Theology; pres., founder Jamilian U. of the Ordained, 1980; pres. Advs. for Religious Rights and Freedoms; chmn. World Coun. for Human Spiritual Rights, 1984—; head Jamilian Order of Patriarchs, 1990—; engaged in newspaper pub. West Coast, 1949-56; began explorations in jungles east of Andes in Peru to prove his theory that high civilizations of Peru may have had their origin in jungles, 1967; pres., founder Andean Explorers Club, Found., Reno; pres., Advocates for Religious Rights and Freedoms; chmn., World Coun. for Human Spiritual Rights. Author: Antisuyo, The Search for Lost Cities of the High Amazon, 1970, Vilcabamba, Last City of the Incas, 1970, The Cosolargy Papers, vol. 1, 1970, vol. 2-3, 1972, The Child Christ, 1973, Arabic edit., 1976, Japanese edit., 1981, The Decoded New Testament, 1974, Arabic edit., 1981, The Millenium Edition of the Decoded New Testament, 1983, On The Trail of The Feathered Serpent, 1974, Code Book and Community Manual for Overseers, 1975, Prophecies of Jamil, First Prophecy to the Americas, Vol. 1, 1976, Second Prophecy to the Americas, 1976, The Secret Sayings of Jamil, The Image and the Word, Vol. 1, 1976, Vol. 2, 1977, Project X—The Search For the Secrets of Immortality, 1977, Prophecy to the Races of Man, Vol. 2, 1977, Solar Cultures of The Americas, 1977, Dream Analysis, 1977, Vision Analysis, 1977, Christoanalysis, 1978, The Essaei Document: Secrets of an Eternal Race, 1978, Millennium edit., 1983, The Lost Gospel of Jesus: Hidden Teachings of Christ, 1978, Millennium edit., 1983, Secret Sayings of Jamil, Vol. 3. 1978, Vol. 4, 1979, Prophecy to The Christian Churches, 1978, The Sayings, vol. 4, 1979, Solar Cultures of Oceania, 1979, Prophecy of The End Times, Vol. 4, 1980, The Holy Kabbalah and Secret Symbolism, Vols. 1 and 2, 1980, Solar Cultures of China, 1980, Christotherapy, 1980, Christophysics, 1980, Christodynamics, 1980, Code Book of Prophecy, 1980, The Sayings, vol. 5, 1980, vol. 6, 1981, Solar Cultures of India, 1981, Prophecy on the Golden Age of Light and the Nation of Nations, Vol. 5, 1981, Solar Cultures of Israel, vol. 3, 1981, The Counsels, 1982, Prophecy of the Universal Theocracy, vol. 6, 1982, Prophecy of the New Covenant, vol. 7, 1982, The Book of God's Revelation, 1983, Miracle of the Second Advent, 1984, Clerical Studies in Theology, Book I, Book II, Book III, Book IV, Transformative Theology: The School of Revelation, Transformative Theology: The School of Prophecy, Liturgical Theology: Preparation for Advanced Degrees, 1993; over 300 audio tape rec. lectures, 1974—, numerous others.; documentary film on Gran Vilaya, 1989; wrote, dir. videos Royal Roads to Discovery, Mystery of the Essenes of Old Israel, Secrets From the High Andes of Peru, 1993; contbr. articles on Peruvian cultures to mags., also articles on philosophy and religion; discoverer lost city of Incas at Vilcabamba Cuzco, numerous ancient cities in Amazonia including Gran Pajaten, Gran Vilaya, Monte Peruvia, Twelve Cities of the Condor. Trustee in Trust Episcopal Head Bishop Internat. Community of Christ. Served with AS USNR, 1944-46. Decorated officer Order of the Grand Cross (Republic of Peru), 1989; recipient numerous exploring awards including over 40 Flag awards Andean Explorers Club, 1958-85 and Explorer of the Century trophy Andean Explorers Found., 1988, Silver Hummingbird award Ministry Industry and Tourism of Peru, 1987, medal of Merit Andres Reyes, 1989. Mem. Geog. Soc. Lima, Andean Explorers Found, Ocean Sailing Club, World Coun. for Human Spiritual Rights, Advs. for Religious Rights and Freedoms, Authors Guild. Clubs: Explorers (N.Y.C.); Andean Explorers Found. and Ocean Sailing. Home: 2025 La Fond Dr Reno NV 89509-3025 Office: 643 Ralston St Reno NV 89503-4436 *One who makes dreams come true is that person who gets an idea, figures out how to make it work and then throws all of his energy into the project, stopping at nothing.*

SAVOY, SUZANNE MARIE, critical care nurse; b. N.Y.C., Oct. 18, 1946; d. William Joseph and Mary Patricia (Moclair) S. BS, Columbia U., 1970; M in Nursing, UCLA, 1978. RN, CCRN, cert. CCRN, CS. Staff nurse MICU, transplant Jackson Meml. Hosp., Miami, 1970-72; staff nurse MICU Boston U. Hosp. (Mass.), 1972-74; staff nurse MICU VA Hosp., Long Beach, Calif., 1974-75; staff nurse MIRU Cedars-Sinai Med. Ctr., L.A., 1975-77; critical care clin. nursing specialist Anaheim (Calif.) Meml. Hosp., 1978-81; practitioner, instr. Rush-Presbyn.-St. Luke's Med. Ctr. Coll. Nursing, Chgo., 1982-88; rsch. assoc. dept. neurosurgery, Rush U., 1984-88; clin. rsch. assoc. Medtronic, Inc. Drug Adminstrn. Systems, Mpls., 1988-91; staff nurse critical care Harper Hosp., Detroit, 1992-93; clin. nurse specialist, surg./trauma critical care, Detroit Recieving Hosp., 1993-95; clin. instr. Wayne State U. Coll. of Nursing, Detroit, 1991-96, adj. faculty, 1996—; program coord. Critical Care ACNP-CC MSN, Wayne State U., 1993-96; adult critical care clin. nurse specialist Saginaw Gen. Hosp., 1996—; neurosci. clinician acute stroke unit Harper Hosp., Detroit, 1989; edn. cons. Critical Care Svcs., Inc., Orange, Calif., 1979-81. Co-author articles for profl. jours. Mem. Am. Assn. Neurosci. Nurses (treas. Ill. chpt. 1983-85, pres. 1986-87, SE Mich. chpt. 1992—, bd. dirs., treas., program chair), Am. Assn. Critical Care Nurses (bd. dirs. Long Beach chpt. 1981-82), Am. Assn. Sci. Nursing (mem. rsch. com. 1993-95), Lambda Gamma Phi (bd. dirs. 1994-96), Sigma Theta Tau. Roman Catholic.

SAVRANN, RICHARD ALLEN, lawyer; b. Boston, July 29, 1935; s. Abraham B. and Doris (Curhan) S.; m. Diane Barbara Kleven, Dec. 22, 1957; children: Stephen Keith, Russell Carl. BA, Harvard U., 1956, JD, 1959. Bar: Mass. 1959, U.S. Dist. Ct. Mass. 1963, U.S. Ct. Appeals (1st cir.) 1965. Exec. Klev Bro. Mfg., Derry, N.H., 1959-63; assoc. Law Office of Jerome Rappaport, Boston, 1963-68; asst. atty. gen. Commonwealth of Mass., Boston, 1968-70; ptnr. Newell, Savrann & Miller, Boston, 1970-75; sr. ptnr. Kunian, Savrann & Miller, Boston, 1976-81, Singer, Stoneman, Kunian & Kurland, P.C., Boston, 1981-88, Singer, Kunian * Kurland, P.C., Boston, 1988-90; sr. ptnr, Curhan, Kunian, Goshko, Berwick and Savrann, P.C., Boston, 1990-92; ptnr. Burns and Levinson, Boston, 1993—. Mem. Andover (Mass.) Housing Authority, 1972-90, chmn., 1984-90; pres. Hospice of Greater Lawrence, North Andover, Mass., 1984; bd. dirs. Boston Latin Sch. Found., 1987, clk., 1992—; bd. dirs. Comite Internat. de Sci. pour La Santè et l'Environ., Paris, 1993—. Mem. FBA, Am. Trial Lawyers Assn., Mass. Bar Assn., Indian Ridge Country Club, Eastpointe Country Club (Palm Beach Gardens, Fla.), Harvard Club (Andover) (pres. 1985—). Avocations: golf, opera. Home: 11 Sheridan Rd Andover MA 01810-5109 Office: Burns and Levinson 125 Summer St Boston MA 02110-1616

SAVRIN, LOUIS, lawyer; b. Phila., Jan. 20, 1927; s. William Philip and Anna (Sass) S.; m. Barbara J. Schwimmer, Jan. 16, 1954; children: Jonathan Eric, Philip Wade, Daniel Scott. B.S., N.Y. U., 1948; J.D., U. Pa., 1951. Bar: N.Y. 1952. Atty. tax dept. Arthur Young & Co. (C.P.A.'s), N.Y.C., 1951-55; pvt. practice N.Y.C., 1955—; gen. counsel, sec. Pickwick Internat., Inc., N.Y.C., 1965-77. Assoc. editor: U. Pa. Law Rev, 1949-51. Mem. sch. bd. Dist. 21, Bklyn., 1962-68. With AUS, 1945-46. Mem. N.Y. State Bar Assn., N.Y. County Lawyers Assn., Real Estate Tax Rev. Bar Assn.; mem. B'nai B'rith (pres. lodge 1957-59, named to lodge Hall of Fame 1967, Torch of Freedom award Anti-Defamation League 1982). Club: Mason. Home: 50 Park Ave Apt 17H New York NY 10016 Office: 60 E 42nd St New York NY 10017-5003

SAWABINI, WADI ISSA, retired dentist; b. Jaffa, Palestine, Jan. 14, 1917; s. Issa J. and Julia C. (Malak) S.; m. Harriet Colgate Abbe Lack, Aug. 6, 1949; children—Wadi' Issa, Frederick Lack, Stuart John, Julia Malak. Student, College des Ecoles Chrétiennes, 1924-32; D.D.S., Am. U. Beirut, 1940. Grad. study Forsyth Dental Infirmary, 1940-41; intern Med. Center Hosp. Vt. (formerly DeGoesbriand Meml. Hosp.), Burlington, 1941-42; attending staff; assoc. pvt. practice Dr. Charles I. Taggart, 1942-51; pvt. practice Burlington, 1951-88, ret.; instr. oral pathology U. Vt., 1951-58; dir. U. Vt. (Sch. Dental Hygiene), 1953-72; asst. prof. oral hygiene U. Vt. (Coll. Medicine), 1958-72; chief dental staff Mary Fletcher Hosp., 1958-68, assoc. prof. dept. allied health scis., 1969-72. Mem. adv. bd. Vt. Pub. Health Dept.; mem. Vt. Bd. Health, 1980-86; v.p. bd. dirs. Overlake Day Sch., 1962-63; mem. Ethan Allen Homestead Fundraising Com., 1990—. Paul Harris fellow Burlington Rotary. Fellow Internat. Coll. Dentists (mem. exec. council 1950-54), Am. Coll. Dentists; mem. Vt. Dental Soc. (pres. 1956-57, mem. bd. rev., Disting. Service award 1972), New Eng. Dental Soc., Champlain Valley Dental Soc., C. of C., ADA, Fedn. Dentaire Internat. Republican. Episcopalian (vestryman). Clubs: Mason (Shriner), Rotary (dir. 1955-56, pres. 1961-62), Ethan Allen (Burlington). Home: Bldg O Apt 2 Gardenside Shelburne VT 05482-7316 *I attribute my life's happiness to my alma mater, The American Univeristy of Beirut. It gave me technical expertise and love to seek knowledge, international understandings, and service to fellowman without regard to color nationality or religion.*

SAWALLISCH, WOLFGANG, conductor; b. Munich, Germany, Aug. 26, 1923; s. Wilhelm and Maria (Obermeier) S.; ed. Wittelsbacher Gymnasium of Munich, Musikalische Ausbildung, pvt. music studies; m. S. Mechthild, 1952. Condr., Augsburg, 1947-53; musical dir. Aachen, 1953-58, Wiesbaden, 1958-60, Cologne Opera, 1960-63; condr. Hamburg Philharm. Orch., 1960-73, hon. mem., 1973—; prin. condr. Vienna Symphony Orch., 1960-70, hon. mem.; also prof. Staatliche Hochschule für Musik, Cologne, 1960-63; musical dir. Bayerische Staatsoper Munich, 1971-92, dir. Staatsoper Munich, 1982-92, hon. mem., 1992; permanent condr. Teatro alla Scala, Milan; condr. many festivals; rec. artist U.S. and Britain; hon. condr. NHK Symphony Orch., Tokyo, 1967; artistic dir. Suisse Romande Orch., Geneva, 1973-80; music dir. Phila. Orch., 1993—. Recipient Accademico Onorario Santa Cecilia, 1975, Toscanini Gold Baton, La Scala, 1993; decorated Osterreichisches Ehrenkreuz für Kunst und Wissenschaft, Bundesverdienstkreuz, Bayerischer Verdienstorden, Grosses Bundesverdienstkreuz mit Stern (Fed. Republic Germany), Order of the Rising Sun Japan; recipient Bruckner-Ring, Vienna Symphony Orch., 1980; Bayerisches Maximilians-order für Wissenschaft and Kunst, 1984, Chevalier dans L'ordre National de la Légion d'Honneur de France, 1991. Mem. Richard Strauss Gesellschaft Munich (pres. 1976). Office: Phila Orch 1420 Locust St Philadelphia PA 19102-4223*

SAWCHUK, RONALD JOHN, pharmaceutical sciences educator; came to U.S., 1966; m. Rosslyn Andrea Murison, July 8, 1967; children: David, Heather, Holly. BSc in Pharmacy, U. Toronto, Ont., Can., 1963, MSc in Pharmaceutics, 1966; PhD in Pharm. Chemistry, U. Calif., San Francisco, 1972. Tchg. asst. U. Toronto, 1963-65; pharmacist Toronto, 1966; tchg. asst. U. Calif., 1966-68; instr. pharmaceutics U. Minn., Mpls., 1971-72, asst. prof., 1972-77, assoc. prof., 1982-95, dir. bioanalytical and pharmacokinetic svcs., 1995—, assoc. dir. Clin. Pharmacokinetics Lab., Coll. Pharmacy, 1974-82, dir. Clin. Pharmacokinetics Lab., 1982-95; acting chmn. dep. pharms. U. Minn., 1983-86, dir. grad. studies in pharms., 1983-89, 92-94, dir. bioanalytic and pharmacokinetic svcs., 1995—; mem. organizing com. NATO Advanced Study Inst., Erice, Italy, 1994; cons. antiepileptic drug devel. program NIH/Nat. Inst. of Neurol. Diseases and Stroke, 1991-93; mem. U.S. Pharmacopeia Com. of Revision, 1990-95. Editl. bd. Saudi Pharm. Jour., Jour. Pharm. Scis.; contbr. articles in pharmacokinetics and bioanalysis to sci. jours. Scholar Can. Found. for Advancement of Pharmacy, 1964, NRC Can., 1965-66; Warner-Lambert rsch. fellow, 1965; NIH tng. grantee, 1968-70; recipient Horace T. Morse-Amoco Found. award, 1986, Hallie Bruce Meml. Lectr. award, 1996. Fellow AAAS, Am. Assn. Pharm. Scientists. Achievements include research drug distribution and elimination studies utilizing microdialysis. Home: 1762 20th Ave NW New Brighton MN 55112-5419 Office: U Minn Coll Pharmacy Weaver-Densford Hall 308 Harvard St SE Minneapolis MN 55455-0353

SAWDEI, MILAN A., lawyer; b. Bakersfield, Calif., Aug. 23, 1946. BA, U. Calif., Long Beach, 1969; JD, W.S.U., 1975. Bar: Calif. 1975, U.S. Dist. Ct. (ctrl. dist.) Calif. 1975. House counsel Sanyo Electric, Inc., 1975-77; assoc. counsel Brown Co. (Gulf & Western), 1978-80; divsn. counsel Petrolane, Inc., 1980-83; sr. counsel Bergen Brunswig Corp., Orange, Calif., 1983-90, v.p., chief legal officer, 1990-92, exec. v.p., chief legal officer, sec., 1992—. Mem. ABA, Am. Corp. Counsel Assn., Am. Soc. Corp. Secs., L.A. County Bar Assn. Office: Bergen Brunswig Corp 4000 Metropolitan Dr Orange CA 92868-3502

SAWDEY, RICHARD MARSHALL, lawyer; b. Buffalo, Jan. 8, 1943; s. Marshall Douglas and Eleanor Katherine (Reichman) S.; m. Judith Hollister Helgeson, Aug. 12, 1967; children—David Marshall, Karin Elizabeth. B.S., Mich. State U., 1965; J.D., U. Mich., 1968. Bar: Ill. 1968. Assoc. McBride, Baker, Wienke & Schlosser, Chgo., 1968-73; atty. R.R. Donnelley & Sons, Chgo., 1974-75, asst. sec., 1975-83, sec., 1983-85; v.p., sec., 1985-88; Of counsel Hoogendoorn, Talbot, Davids, Godfrey & Milligan, Chgo., 1988—. Mem. ABA, Chgo. Bar Assn. (chmn. fin. and investment svcs. com. 1994-95). Office: Hoogendoorn Talbot Davids Godfrey & Milligen 122 S Michigan Ave Ste 1220 Chicago IL 60603-6107

SAWHILL, ISABEL VAN DEVANTER, economist; b. Washington, Apr. 2, 1937; d. Winslow B. and Isabel E. Van Devanter; m. John C. Sawhill, Sept. 13, 1958; 1 son, James W. BA, NYU, 1962, PhD, 1968. Policy analyst Office Sec. HEW, 1968-69, Office Mgmt. and Budget, 1969-70; asst. prof. econs. Goucher Coll., Balt., 1969-73; sr. rsch. assoc. Urban Inst., 1973-77, program dir., 1975-77, program dir., sr. fellow, 1980-93; dir. Nat. Commn. Employment Policy, Washington, 1977-79; program assoc. dir. Office Mgmt. and Budget, 1993-95; sr. fellow and Arjay Miller chair in pub. policy Urban Inst., 1995—; vis. prof. Georgetown U. Law Ctr., 1990-91; chairperson rsch. adv. bd. Com. for Econ. Devel., 1995—. Author: The Reagan Record, 1984, Challenge to Leadership, 1988. Past mem. Sec. of Labor's commn. on workforce quality and labor mkt. efficiency, Ctr. Strategic and Internat. Studies commn. on strenghtening of Am., NRC bd. on sci., tech., and econ. policy; bd. dirs. Am. Assembly, Manpower Demonstration Res. Corp.; vice chairperson bd. dirs. Resources of the Future; pres. Nat. Campaign Prevent Teen Pregnancy, 1996—. Mem. Am. Econ. Assn. (mem. exec. com.), Assn. Pub. Polit. Analysis and Mgmt. (pres. 1988), Phi Beta Kappa. Office: 2100 M St NW Washington DC 20037-1207

SAWHILL, JOHN CRITTENDEN, conservationist, economist, university president, government official; b. Cleve., June 12, 1936; s. James Mumford and Mary Munroe (Gipe) S.; AB, Princeton U., 1958; PhD, N.Y. U., 1963; m. Isabel Van Devanter, Sept. 13, 1958; 1 child, James W. With Merrill, Lynch, Pierce, Fenner & Smith, Washington, 1958-60; asst. dean, prof. NYU Sch. Bus. Adminstrn., 1960-63, pres. NYU Washington Sq., 1975-79; dir. credit rsch. and planning Comml. Credit Co., Balt., 1964-66, sr. v.p., 1968-73; sr. assoc. McKinsey & Co., Washington, 1966-68; assoc. dir. natural resources Office Mgmt. and Budget, Washington, 1973-74; adminstr. Fed. Energy Adminstrn., Washington, 1973-75; dep. sec. Dept. Energy, Washington, 1979-80; chmn. U.S. Synthetic Fuels Corp., Washington, 1980; bd. dirs. McKinsey & Co., Inc., Washington, 1980-90, Pacific Gas & Electric Co., NACCO Industries, Vanguard Group. Pres. The Nature Conservancy, Arlington, Va., 1990—; chmn. bd. trustees Whitehead Inst. Biomed. Rsch.; trustee Princeton U.; mem. Coun. on Fgn. Rels.; mem., dir. Trilateral Commn. Mem. AAAS (dir.), Met. Club (Washington), Chevy Chase Club (Md.), River Club (N.Y.C.). Office: The Nature Conservancy 1815 N Lynn St Arlington VA 22209-2003*

SAWICKI, ZBIGNIEW PETER, lawyer; b. Hohenfels, Germany, Apr. 13, 1949; came to U.S., 1951; s. Witold and Marianna (Tukiendorf) S.; m. Katheryn Marie Loman, Aug. 19, 1972; children: James, Jeffrey, Jessica, Jason. BSChemE, Purdue U., 1972; MBA, Coll. St. Thomas, St. Paul, 1977; JD, Hamline U., 1980. Bar: Minn. 1980, U.S. Dist. Ct. Minn. 1981, U.S. Ct. Appeals (8th cir.) 1981, U.S. Patent and Trademark Office 1981, U.S. Ct. Appeals (fed. cir.) 1982, Can. Patent Office 1994, Can. Trademark Office 1995. Process engr. 3-M Co., St. Paul, 1973-75; process engring. supr. Conwed Corp., St. Paul, 1975-77; shareholder, bd. dirs. Kinney & Lange, Mpls., 1980—. Bd. dirs. Orono (Minn.) Hockey Boosters, 1992—. With USAF, 1970-72. Mem. ABA, Am. Intellectual Property Assn., Internat. Trademark Assn., Minn. Intellectual Property Assn. (past treas.), Am. Legion. Home: 4510 N Shore Dr Mound MN 55364-9602 Office: Kinney & Lange 625 4th Ave S Minneapolis MN 55415-1624

SAWIN, NANCY CHURCHMAN, art educator, artist, historian; b. Wilmington, Del., June 21, 1917; d. Sanford W. and Ellen (Quigley) S. BA, Principia Coll., 1938; MA, U. Del., 1940; EdD, U. Pa., 1962; PhD (hon.), Golden Beacom Coll., 1987. With Sanford Sch., Hockessin, Del., 1938-74; dean girls Sanford Sch., 1945-62, head sch., 1962-74; coordinator student services U. Del. Div. Continuing Edn., Newark, 1974-77; ednl. cons. DuPont Co., ICI Ams., 1976-80; chmn. Del. State Sci. Fair com., 1962; mem. com. Jr. Sci. and Humanities Symposium, 1962-76; mem. English, lang. arts adv. com. State Del., 1965-68; sec., dir. Recreation, Promotion and Service, Inc., 1963-74; mem. All-Am. Hockey Team, 1948-59. One-person shows include Ctr. for Creative Arts, 1993—, others; editor: The Eagle, 1961-62; co-pub., illustrator: Between the Bays, 1977, Delaware Sketchbook, 1976, Backroading Throuth Cecil County, 1977, Brick and Ballast, 1985; author, illustrator: Man-O-War My Island Home, 1978, Up the Spine and Down the Creek, 1982, Locks Traps and Corners, 1984, China Sketchbook, 1985, A Hockessin Diary, 1987, Privy to the Council, 1987, The Oulde King's Roade, 1989, North from Wilmington by Oulde Roads and Turnpikes, 1992, Once Upon a Time in the Country, 1994, Sketches of Early Delaware Main Streets, 1997. Trustee Goldey Beacom Coll., pres., 1974-81, 97—, mem. safety coun., 1964-74; pres. Del. Sports Hall of Fame, 1982—; pres. bd. dirs. Del. Soc. for Preservation of Antiquities, 1986-88, chair, 1990—; chair fundraising com. Hockessin County Libr., 1989-94; bd. dirs. Preservation Del., 1996—. 2d lt. CAP, 1942-45. Recipient Medal of Merit, U. Del., 1989, DAR History medal, 1990, Hist. Preservation award New Castle County, 1996, gold medals Del. Sr. Olympic Swimming, 1994, 95, 96, gold medal U.S. Sr. Olympics, 1997, Disting Svc. award Ctr. for Creative Arts, 1997; named to Del. Sports Hall of Fame, 1977; charter mem. U.S. Field Hockey Hall of Fame, 1988; named to Hall of Fame of Del. Women, 1991, Wall of Fame, U. Del., 1991. Mem. AARP, Headmistress Assn. East, Del. Art Mus., Rehoboth Art League, Middle Atlantic States Assn. Colls. and Secondary Schs. (past pres.), Commn. on Secondary Schs., Red Clay Creek Assn., Internat. Fedn. Women's Hockey Assns. (past pres.), U.S. Field Hockey Assn. (past pres., named to Sports Hall of Fame 1987), Del. Field Hockey Assn. (past pres.), Nat. League Am. Pen Women, DAR (History medal), Daus. of Founders and Patriots, Nat. Soc. New Eng. Women, Daus. Colonial Wars, Del. Greenbank Questars (pres. 1993-94), Hockessin Cmty. Club, Delta Kappa Gamma (past pres.), Pi Lambda Theta. Republican. Presbyterian (elder). Club: Quota (pres. Wilmington 1971-73, gov. 10th Dist. 1979-80). Address: North Light Studio 147 Sawin Ln Hockessin DE 19707-9713

SAWINSKI, VINCENT JOHN, chemistry educator; b. Chgo., Mar. 28, 1925; s. Stanley and Pearl (Gapinski) S.; m. Florence Whitman, Aug. 24, 1952; children—Christine Frances, Michael Patrick. B.S., Loyola U., 1948, M.A., 1950, Ph.D., 1962. Instr., asst. prof. chemistry, physiology and pharmacology Loyola U., Chgo., 1949-67; supervisory research chemist VA, Hines, Ill., 1961-66; assoc. prof. chemistry, phys. sci. City Colls. Chgo., 1967-71, prof., 1971-91, prof. emeritus, 1991—, chmn. phys. sci. dept. Wright campus, 1971-91. Contbr. articles to profl. jours. Served with U.S. Army, 1945-46. Fellow AAAS, Am. Inst. Chemists; mem. Am. Chem. Soc., Nat. Sci. Tchrs. Assn., Sigma Xi. Home: 1945 N 77th Ct Elmwood Park IL 60707-3623 Office: 4300 N Narragansett Ave Chicago IL 60634-1591

SAWIRIS, MILAD YOUSSEF, statistician, educator; b. Cairo, Jan. 11, 1922; came to U.S., 1966, naturalized, 1972; s. Youssef Sawiris and Faika Botros Samaan. B.Sc., Cairo U., 1942, diploma in edn., 1944, diploma higher edn., 1959; M.A., U. London, 1963, Ph.D., 1965; M.S., Stanford U., 1975. Tchr. math. Egyptian Govt. schs., 1944-48, 57-61, Sudan Govt. schs., 1948-57; mem. faculty Calif. State U., Sacramento, 1966-86, prof. emeritus, 1986—. Author research papers. Mem. Am. Statis. Assn. Mem. Coptic Orthodox Ch. Home: 8308 Caribbean Way Sacramento CA 95826-1657

SAWOROTNOW, PARFENY PAVLOVICH, mathematician, educator; b. Ust Medveditskaya, Russia, Feb. 20, 1924; came to U.S., 1949, naturalized, 1965; s. Pavel Ivanovich and Anna Davidovna (Soloview) S.; student U. Graz (Austria), 1946-49; MA (Peirce scholar), Harvard U., 1951, PhD (Shattuck fellow), 1955. Teaching fellow Harvard U., 1953-54; instr. math. Cath. U. Am., Washington, 1954-57, asst. prof., 1957-62, assoc. prof., 1962-67, prof., 1967-96, prof. math. emeritus, 1997—. NSF grantee, 1967, 70; with Georgetown U. and George Washington U., 1971-77. Mem. Am. Math. Soc., Math. Assn. Am., Calcutta Math. Soc., N.Y. Acad. Scis., AAUP, Sigma Xi. Mem. Eastern Orthodox Ch. Contbr. articles to and referred papers for math. rsch. jours. Home: 6 Avon Pl Hyattsville MD 20782-3328 Office: Cath U Am Dept Math 4th and Michigan Ave NE Washington DC 20064

SAWTELL, STEPHEN M., private investor, lawyer; b. St. Paul, Jan. 17, 1931; s. William Amos and Helen Mary (Fiegenbaum) S.; m. Helen Elizabeth Wencel, June 27, 1956; children: Stephen, Katherine H. Student, Northwestern U., 1948-50; BSc in Law, U. Nebr., 1956, JD, 1957; postgrad., Stanford U., 1974. Bar: Nebr. 1957. With No. Natural Gas Co. (now Enron, Inc.), Omaha, 1957-85, Dubuque Packing Co. of Omaha, 1987-88, CENI Corp., JinNeb Beef Ltd., Dalien, China, 1987-89; of counsel McMannama and Assocs., Inc., Omaha, 1988—. Pres. Omaha Symphony Assn., 1969-71, Jr. Achievement Omaha, 1975, Omaha Sister City Assn., 1974-83; chmn. Omaha Com. on Fgn. Rels., 1975-81; mem. bd. advisors Salvation Army, 1981—. With AUS, 1952-55. Named Omaha's Outstanding Young Man of Year Omaha Jr. C. of C., 1963. Mem. Masons, Rotary, Omaha Club, Omaha Country Club. Congregationalist. Home: 702 Ridgewood Ave Omaha NE 68114-5360

SAWTELLE, CARL S., psychiatric social worker; b. Boston, July 14, 1927; s. Carl Salvador and Martha (Bellamacina) S.; BA, Suffolk U., Boston, 1951; MSW, Simmons Sch. Social Work, 1953; m. Thelma Florence Ramsay, Aug. 20, 1950; children: Tracy Lynn, Lisa June. Social worker Tewksburry (Mass.) State Hosp., 1952; psychiat. social worker, head psychiat. social worker, dir. clin. social work Taunton (Mass.) State Hosp., 1953-74; 1st dir. clin. social work, Plymouth, Mass., 1974-78; co-founder, v.p. 1st legally established War On Poverty program Triumph, Inc., Taunton; co-founder 1st Greater Taunton Coun. on Alcoholism, 1972. With USCG, 1944-46. 1st lic. social worker in Mass., 1980. Mem. Nat. Assn. Social Workers (co-founder Southeast Mass. chpt. 1957, pres. 1957, Spl. Mass. Chpt. award 1978), Acad. Cert. Social Workers (chmn. 1962-72), Am. Legion, Mass. Mental Health Social Workers Assn. (co-founder, pres. 1972-74, other offices). Created innovated programs, resources, opportunities, svcs. to state mental hosp. patients and their families; mentor to young social workers; contbr. advancement of knowledge, practice quality and standards of psychiat. social work; father of licensing and registration of Social Workers in Mass. Home: 9 Tracywood Rd Canton MA 02021-3501

SAWYER, ANITA DAWN, special education educator; b. Harrison, Ark., July 8, 1963; d. Donnie Frank and Myrtle Darline (Curbow) Coxsey; m. Timothy Clarence Sawyer, Mar. 26, 1988; children: Benjamin Aram, Lukas Ryan, Lauren Nicole. AS, North Ark. Cmty. Tech. Coll., Harrison, 1984; BS in Edn., U. Ctrl. Ark., 1986. Cert. spl. edn.-mildy handicapped grades K-12. Jr. and sr. H.S. spl. educator Omaha (Ark.) Pub. Schs., 1986-91; extended yr. svcs. coord. Boone County Spl. Svcs., Harrison, summer 1987; tchr.-leader summer youth program Job Tng. Partnership Act, Harrison, summer 1991; jr. and sr. H.S. spl. educator Alpena (Ark.) Pub. Schs., 1991; indirect svcs. coord. Omaha (Ark.) H.S., 1986-91, Alpena (Ark.) H.S., 1991-97, dist. spl. olympics coord., Omaha Pub. Schs., 1987-91, Alpena Pub. Schs., 1991—; jr. h.s. spl. educator Trinity Heights Acad., Little Rock, 1997—; adv. bd. mem. Omaha H.S. Future Bus. Leaders Am., 1990-91; coord. transitional svcs. Omaha, 1986-91, Alpena, 1991—; pres. pers. policies com., Alpena, 1995-96. Vol. internat. cert. Omaha (Ark.) and Ark. Spl. Olympics, 1986-91; fundraising and cmty. contact rep. United Way-Omaha (Ark.) H.S., 1989; spl. olympics coach in bowling, basketball, floor hockey and athletics Alpena (Ark.) and Ark. Spl. Olympics, 1991—. Mem. NEA, Ark. Edn. Assn. (bldg. rep., gen. assembly 1986-90), Omaha Edn. Assn. (v.p. 1986-87, pres. 1987-90, rep.), Coun. Exceptional Children, Omaha Booster Club (v.p. 1988-89), Omaha PTO, Alpena PTO. Baptist. Avocations: cooking, reading, crafts, playing piano, singing. Home: 441-A Union Rd Harrison AR 72601 Office: Trinity Heights Acad Learning Disabilites-ADD 1900 N University Ave Little Rock AR 72207

SAWYER, CHARLES HENRY, anatomist, educator; b. Ludlow, Vt., Jan. 24, 1915; s. John Guy and Edith Mabel (Morgan) S.; m. Ruth Eleanor Schaeffer, Aug. 23, 1941; 1 dau., Joan Eleanor. BA, Middlebury Coll., 1937, DSc honoris causa, 1975; student, Cambridge U., Eng., 1937-38; Ph.D., Yale, 1941. Instr. anatomy Stanford, 1941-44; assoc., asst. prof., assoc. prof., prof. anatomy Duke U., 1944-51; prof. anatomy UCLA, Los Angeles, 1951-85; prof. emeritus UCLA, 1985—, chmn. dept., 1955-63, acting chmn., 1968-69, faculty research lectr., 1966-67. Editorial bd.: Endocrinology, 1955-59, Proc. Soc. Exptl. Biology and Medicine, 1959-63, Am. Jour. Physiology, 1972-75; Author papers on neuroendocrinology. Mem. Internat. Brain Research Orgn. (council 1964-68), AAAS, Am. Assn. Anatomists (v.p. 1969-70, Henry Gray award 1984), Am. Physiol. Soc., Am. Zool. Soc., Neurosci. Soc., Endocrine Soc. (council 1968-70, Koch award 1973), Am. Acad. Arts and Scis., Nat. Acad. Scis., Soc. Exptl. Biology and Medicine, Soc. Study Reprodn. (dir. 1969-71, Hartman award 1977), Internat. Neuroendocrine Soc. (council 1972-76), Hungarian Soc. Endocrinology and Metabolism (hon.), Japan Endocrin Soc. (hon.), Phi Beta Kappa, Sigma Xi. Home: 466 Tuallitan Rd Los Angeles CA 90049-1941 Office: U Calif Sch Medicine Dept Neurobiology Los Angeles CA 90024

SAWYER, CHARLES HENRY, art educator, art museum director emeritus; b. Andover, Mass., Oct. 20, 1906; s. James Cowan and Mary Pepperrell (Frost) S.; m. Katharine Clay, June 28, 1934. BA, Yale U., 1929, MA, 1947; student, Harvard Law Sch., 1929-30; student of Fine Arts, Harvard U. Grad. Sch., 1930-32; LHD, Amherst Coll., 1950; DFA, U. New Hampshire, 1951; LHD, Clark U., 1953. Dir. Addison Gallery of Am. Art, art instr. Phillips Acad., Andover, Mass., 1930-40; dir. Worcester (Mass.) Art Mus., 1940-46; dir. divsn. of the arts, prof. history of art Yale U., New Haven, Conn., 1947-56; master Timothy Dwight Coll. Yale U., New Haven, 1947-53; dean Sch. of Architecture and Design, Yale U., New Haven, 1947-56; dir. mus. of art U. Mich., Ann Arbor, 1957-72, prof. history of art, 1957-76, dir. emeritus mus. of art, 1973—; mem. art adv. commn. Harvard U., 1940-58, Cambridge, , Amherst (Mass.) Coll., 1948-60, Smith Coll., Northampton, Mass. 1948-55, U. Notre Dame, Ind., 1973-82, Smithsonian Art Commn., Smithsonian Instn., Washington, 1953-80; trustee Corning (N.Y.) Mus. of Glass, 1950-75; prof. emeritus History of Art, U. Mich., 1977—. Author: (book) Art in English Public Schools, 1936; author various articles, exhibition catalogues etc., 1931—. Mem. Art Commn. State of Mass., Boston, 1940-44, Historic Sites Commn., State of New Hampshire, Concord, 1948-58, Arts Coun., State of Mich., Lansing, 1964-72. Named Hon. Mem. NMAA Commn. Washington, 1985—. Fellow Am. Acad. Arts and Scis.; mem. Assn. Art Mus. Dirs. (hon. mem. 1973—), Century Assn. N.Y., Am. Antiquarian Soc. Episcopalian. Avocations: hist. rsch., gardening. Home: 2 Highland Ln Ann Arbor MI 48104-1727

SAWYER, (L.) DIANE, television journalist; b. Glasgow, Ky., Dec. 22, 1945; d. E.P. and Jean W. (Dunagan) S.; m. Mike Nichols, Apr. 29, 1988. BA, Wellesley Coll., 1967. Reporter Sta. WLKY-TV, Louisville, 1967-70; adminstr. press office White House, 1970-74; rschr. Richard Nixon's memoirs, 1974-78; gen. assignment reporter, then Dept. State corr. CBS News, 1978-81; co-anchor Morning News CBS, from 1981, co-anchor Early Morning News, 1982-84; corr., co-editor 60 Minutes CBS-TV, 1984-89; co-anchor Prime Time Live ABC News, 1989—; co-anchor Day One, 1995, Turning Point. Recipient 2 Peabody awards for Pub. Svc., 1988, Robert F. Kennedy award 10 Emmy awards, Spl. Dupont award, IRTS Lifetime Achievement award. Mem. Coun. Fgn. Rels. Office: PrimeTime Live 147 Columbus Ave Fl 3 New York NY 10023-5900

SAWYER, DOLORES, motel facility executive; b. Shreveport, La., Oct. 16, 1938; d. Orlan B. Greer and Doris Lucile (Sanders) Eckman; m. Raymond Lee Sawyer Jr., June 11, 1960; children: Lisa Kay, Linda Faye. BSN, Northwestern State Coll., 1960; MSN, Tex. Woman's U., 1975. Supr. obstetrics dept. Highland Hosp., Shreveport, La., 1962-64; head nurse (3-11 shift) Scott and White Meml. Hosp., Temple, Tex., 1966-71, dir. of nursing edn., 1975-76; sch. nurse Temple Ind. Sch. Dist., 1971-72; instr. Mary-Hardin Baylor Coll., Belton, Tex., 1972-74; asst. prof., clin. specialist U. Tex. Arlington, 1976-86; v.p. Budget Host Internat., Arlington, Tex., 1986-96, sr. v.p., 1996—. Recipient Amoco Outstanding Tchg. award, 1981. Mem. Sigma Theta Tau. Republican. Methodist. Avocations: reading, tole painting, gardening, crafts, piano. Office: Budget Host Internat 3607 W Pioneer Pkwy Arlington TX 76013-4504

SAWYER, H(AROLD) MURRAY, JR., lawyer; b. Niagara Falls, N.Y., Jan. 10, 1946; s. Harold Murray and Susan (Imbrie) S.; m. Ann Randolph Gawthrop; children: Ann Sawyer Chilton, Amy Greenwood, Harold Murray III. BA, U. N.C., 1968; JD, Vanderbilt U., 1971. Bar: Del. 1971, U.S. Dist. Ct. Del. 1972, U.S. Ct. Appeals (3d cir.) 1972, U.S. Supreme Ct. 1979, Pa. 1981. Assoc. Richards, Layton & Finger, Wilmington, Del., 1971-72; dep. atty. gen. criminal div. State of Del., Wilmington, 1972-73; ptnr. Berg, Komissaroff & Sawyer, Wilmington, 1973-77; founding ptnr. Sawyer Akin & Herron, Wilmington, 1978—; pres. Registered Agents Ltd., Wilmington, 1978—, Am. Incorporators Ltd., Wilmington, 1985—; mem. bd. profl. responsibility Del. Supreme Ct., Wilmington, 1983-96. Contbr. articles to profl. jours. Trustee The Pilot Sch., Wilmington, 1980—; mem. New Castle County Coun., Wilmington, 1980-82, Del. Health Facilities Authority, 1983-92. Mem. ABA, Del. Bar Assn., Rotary (bd. dirs. Wilmington 1992-97, pres. 1995-96), Club Wilmington. Republican. Episcopalian. Avocations: golf, travel, reading. Office: Sawyer Akin & Herron 1220 N Market St PO Box 25047 Wilmington DE 19899-5047

SAWYER, HAROLD S(AMUEL), lawyer; b. San Francisco, Mar. 21, 1920; s. Harold S. and Agnes Veronica (McGugan) S.; m. Marcia Steketee, Aug. 26, 1944; children: Stephen R., David H., Keary W., Mariya Sinclair. AA, Coll. Marin, 1939; BA, U. Calif., Berkeley, 1940; JD, Hastings Coll. U. Calif., San Francisco, 1943. Bar: Calif. 1943, Mich. 1946, U.S. Dist. Ct. (we. dist.) Mich. 1946, U.S. Ct. Appeals (6th cir.) 1947, U.S. Supreme Ct. 1966, D.C. 1978. Lt. USN, 1941-45; assoc. Warner Norcross & Judd, Grand Rapids, Mich., 1945-49, ptnr., 1950-76, 85-93, chmn., CEO, 1967-75; prosecuting atty. Kent County, Grand Rapids, 1975-76; congressman U.S. Ho. Reps., Washington, 1977-85; mem. Mich. Law Revision Com., 1966-69; dir., mem. exec. com. Kysov Indsl. Corp. (NYSE), chmn. bd. dirs. Citation Cos. (AMEX); dir., v.p. Grand Hotel Co., Mackinac Isle, Mich. Bd. dirs. West Mich. Legal Aid Soc., 1985—; dir. Greater Grand Rapids C. of C.; pres. D.A. Blodgett Home for Children, Camp Blodgett Children's Camp. Recipient Nat. Leadership Coun. award, 1977-82, Guardian of Ind. Bus. award, 1977-78, 81-84, Watchdog of the Treasury award, 1977-80, 83-84, Congl. Rep. Party award, Kent County Disting. Svc. award, 1976, March of Dimes Disting. Citizens award, 1984. Fellow Am. Coll. Trial Lawyers, Internat. Acad. Trial Lawyers (bd. dirs. 1965-71), Internat. Soc. Barristers, Am. Bar Found. (life), Mich. Bar Found. (life); mem. Am. Law Inst. (life), U.S. Jud. Conf. (life, 6th cir.). Home: 4100 14 Mile Rd NE Rockford MI 49341-9726

SAWYER, HOWARD JEROME, physician; b. Detroit, Nov. 17, 1929; s. Howard C. and Dorothy M. (Risley) S.; m. Janet Carol Hausen, July 24, 1954; children: Daniel William, Teresa Louise. BA in Philosophy, Wayne State U., 1952, MD, 1962, postdoctoral, 1969-72. Diplomate Am. Bd. Preventive Medicine in Occupational and Environ. Medicine. Intern William Beaumont Hosp., Royal Oak, Mich., 1962-63, resident in surgery, 1963-64; chief physician gen. parts div. Ford Motor Co., Rawsonville, Mich., 1964-66; med. dir. metall. products dept. Gen. Electric Co., Detroit, 1966-73; chem. and metal div. Gen. Electric Co., 1972-73; staff physician Detroit Indsl. Clinic, Inc., 1973-74; pres., med. dir. OccuMed Assocs., Inc., Farmington Hills, Mich., 1974-84; dir. OccuMed div. Med. Service Corp. Am., Southfield, Mich., 1984-86; dir. occupational, environ. and preventive medicine Henry Ford Hosp., 1987-91; pres. Sawyer Med. Cons., P.C., 1991—; adj. asst. prof. occupational and environ. health scis. Wayne State U., 1974—; lectr. Sch. Pub. Health, U. Mich., Ann Arbor, 1977—; cons. med. dir. St. Joe Minerals Corp., 1976-87, Chesbrough Pond's Inc., 1979-83; cons. Anaconda, Bendix, Borg Warner Chems., Fed. Mogul, Gen. Electric, Gt. Lakes Chems., other corps. Contbr. articles to profl. jours., chpts. to textbooks. Fellow Am. Coll. Preventive Medicine, Am. Occupational and Environ. Med. Assn., Mich. Occupational and Environ. Med. Assn. (pres. 1986), Am. Acad. Occupational Medicine; mem. AMA, Detroit Occupational Physicians Assn. (pres. 1984), Mich. State Med. Soc., Oakland County Med. Soc., Am. Indsl. Hygiene Assn., Mich. Indsl. Hygiene Soc. Office: Sawyer Med Cons PC 7072 Edinborough Dr West Bloomfield MI 48322-4025

SAWYER, JOHN, professional football team executive; s. Charles S.; m. Ruth Sawyer; children: Anne, Elizabeth, Catherine, Mary. Pres., part owner Cin. Bengals, Nat. Football League; pres. J. Sawyer Co., Ohio, Miss., Mont., Wyo.; vice pres Cin. Bengals. Office: J Sawyer Co Provident Towers Cincinnati OH 45202-3717 Office: Cin Bengals 200 Riverfront Stadium Cincinnati OH 45202-3500*

SAWYER, MARGO LUCY, artist, educator; b. Washington, May 6, 1958; d. Eugene Douglas and Joan Imogen (Alford) S.; m. Rosario Pizzi, June 20, 1992. BA hons., Chelsea Sch. Art, London, 1980; MFA, Yale U., 1982. Assoc. prof. U. Tex., Austin, 1988—; vis. artist Chelsea Sch. Art, London, 1982—, Sir J.J. Sch. Art, Bombay, India, 1982-83, Baroda Sch. Art, Gujarat, India, 1983, West Surrey Coll. Art & Design, Eng., 1983, Sch. Visual Arts, N.Y.C., 1983, 89, Yale U., New Haven, 1985, Tyler Sch. Art, Rome, 1987, RISD, Rome, 1987, U. Houston, 1994. One-person shows include Brit. Coun., Bombay, India, 1983, Barbara Toll Fine Arts, N.Y.C., 1989, 91, Sagacho Exhibit Space, Tokyo, 1996, Gallery Gallery, Kyoto, Japan, 1996, Internat. House of Japan, Tokyo, 1996others; group shows include Whitechapel Gallery, London, 1979, ICA, London, 1979, 80, Leo Castelli Gallery, N.Y.C., 1986, Portland (Maine) Mus. Art, 1987, U. Md. Art Gallery, Balt., 1988, Meyers/Bloom Gallery, Santa Monica, Calif., 1989, Archer M. Huntington Art Gallery, Austin, Tex., 1990, 91, 92, 93, 94, Harn Mus. Art, Gainesville, Fla., 1992, Laguna Gloria Art Mus., Austin, 1994, Abilene (Tex.) Outdoor Sculpture exhbn., 1995-96; permanent collections include Hyde Park, London, Cityarts Workshop, Paradise Restaurant, L.A., Portland Mus. Art, Samuel O. Harn Mus. Art, U. Fla., Prudential Ins., Chem. Bank, Champion Paper, and various pvt. collections. Am. Acad. Rome fellow, 1986-87, Japan Found. visual arts fellow, 1996; Travel grantee Ford Found., 1981, Fulbright grantee, 1982-83, 95-96, N.Y. State Coun. on Arts grantee, 1987, Travel grantee NEA, 1994. Office: U Tex at Austin Dept Art and Art History Austin TX 78712-1104

SAWYER, MARY CATHERINE, hospital administrator; b. Borger, Tex., Dec. 8, 1931; d. Andrew Rodgers and Mary Elizabeth (Slater) Hill; m. Edmond Eugene Sawyer, Aug. 26, 1963; children: Slater Shane, Anthony Barrett, Maronda Rae. BBA, Tex. Tech U., 1956; cert. in med. records, U. Tex. Med. Br., Galveston, 1957. Registered med. adminstr.; cert. coding specialist. Med. record adminstr. Taylor Hosp., Inc., Lubbock, Tex., 1957-63; pvt. practice cons. Paris, Tex., 1963-79; med. record adminstr., coding specialist St. Joseph's Hosp., Paris, 1979—. Mem. DAR (corr. sec. 1989-91, treas. 1991-93, 1st vice regent 1994-96, def. chmn. 1990-96), Gordon Country Club, Phi Gamma Nu. Methodist. Avocation: genealogy. Home: PO Box 128 Deport TX 75435-0128 Office: St Joseph's Hosp PO Box 9070 Paris TX 75461-9070

SAWYER, NELSON BALDWIN, JR., credit union executive; b. Jacksonville, Fla., Nov. 11, 1948; s. Nelson Baldwin and Nancy (Watson) S.; m. Carla Lee Dowden, Aug. 9, 1986. BA, U. North Fla., 1974. Program cons. State of Fla., Jacksonville, 1974-81; product mgr. Qualified Plan Designs, Inc., Jacksonville, 1981-83, Associated Gen. Contractors, Jacksonville, 1983-86; membership mgr. Calif. Credit Union League, Pomona, 1986-87, comm. mgr., 1987-90; sr. v.p., COO Calif. League Svcs. Corp., Pomona, 1990-93; sr. v.p. Wescorp, San Dimas, Calif., 1994—; chmn. bd. dirs. Calif. Ctr. Credit Union, Product Rsch. Orgn. for Credit Unions. Bd. dirs. Jacksonville C. of C., 1984-85. Mem. U.S. Jaycees (pres. Jacksonville 1983-84, chmn. bd. '84-85, senator, U.S., 1984—, Outstanding Young Man Am. 1983), Am. Soc. Assn. Execs., Fla. Yacht Club. Republican. Episcopalian. Office: WesCorp 924 Overland Ct San Dimas CA 91773-1742

SAWYER, PHILIP NICHOLAS, surgeon, educator, health science facility administrator; b. Bangor, Maine, Oct. 25, 1925; s. Frank S. and Linda (Makanna) S.; m. Grace Makla, June 13, 1953; children: Margaret Ann, Elizabeth Lynn, Susan Jean, Philip Michael. BS, Harvard U., 1947; MD, U. Pa., 1949. Diplomate Am. Bd. Surgery, Am. Bd. Thoracic Surgery. Intern Hosp. of U. Pa., Phila., 1949-50, resident in surgery, fellow, 1953-56; chief resident in surgery, fellow in pathology St. Luke's Hosp., N.Y.C., 1953-57; instr., asst. prof. surgery SUNY Downstate Med. Ctr., Bklyn., 1957-62, assoc. prof., 1962-66, prof., head vascular surgery svc., 1966-84, prof. emeritus, 1985—; pres. Interface Biomed. Labs. Corp.; prof. surgery N.Y. Med. Coll., 1991—; vis. surgeon, head vascular surg. svcs. Kings County Hosp., Bklyn., 1972—; cons. Meth. Hosp., Bklyn.; assoc. attending, head vascular surg. svcs. St. John's Episcopal Hosp., Far Rockaway, N.Y.; attending surgery VA Hosp., Bklyn.; cons. cardiovascular and thoracic surgeon Norwalk (Conn.) Hosp.; cons. vascular surgeon Caledonian Hosp., Bklyn., Pocono Hosp., East Stroudsburg, Pa.; prin. investigator Office Naval Rsch., NIH, Am. Heart Assn., 1953-84, NIH, 1957-86; disting. lectr. worldwide. Founding editor Jour. Investigative Surgery; assoc. editor: Am. Jour. Med. Electronics, Jour. Biomed. Rsch. Engring.; editor: Biophysical Mechanisms in Vascular Homeostasis & Intravascular Thrombosis, 1965, Vascular Grafts, 1976, Modern Vascular Grafts, 1987; co-editor: Surgical Resident's Manual, 1980, Vascular Diseases, Current Controversies, 1981; contbr. over 300 articles to med. jours.; numerous patents on heart valves, vascular grafts, hemostatic agts., vascular wall protective agts. Recipient Clemson award for basic biomaterials rsch. Soc. for Biomaterials, 1985; Markle scholar, 1959-64. Mem. Acad. Surg. Rsch. (Jacob Markowitz award 1986), AAAS, Am. Assn. for Thoracic Surgery, Am. Chem. Soc., Am. Coll. Cardiology, ACS, Am. Coll. Chest Physicians, AMA, Am. Heart Assn., Am. Nuclear Soc., Am. Soc. for Artificial Internal Organs, IEEE, Internat. Cardiovascular Soc., Soc. for Thoracic Surgeons, Soc. Univ. Surgeons, Soc. for Vascular Surgery, European Soc. for Microcirculation, Fedn. Am. Socs. for Exptl. Biology, Cardiovascular Soc. (pres.), Harvard Club (N.Y.C.), Sigma Xi, others. Avocation: collecting historical weapons. Home and Office: 7600 Ridge Blvd Brooklyn NY 11209-3008

SAWYER, RAYMOND LEE, JR., motel chain executive; b. New Orleans, Oct. 7, 1935; s. Raymond Lee Sawyer and Eloise Falvy (Searcy) Easley; m. Dolores Jean Young, June 11, 1960; children: Lisa Kay, Linda Faye. BA, Northwestern State U., 1959. Art dir., advt. mgr. Natural Food and Farming Mag., Atlanta, Tex., 1959-66, editor, 1963-66; asst. editor, editor Tourist Court Jour./Southwest Water Works Jour., Temple, Tex., 1966-73; editor Tourist Court Jour./Southwest Water Works Jour., Temple, 1973-75; founding ptnr., sr. v.p. Budget Host Inns, Ft. Worth, 1975-83, pres., chief exec. officer, 1983—. Named Man of Yr. Motel Brokers Assn. Am., 1974; recipient Bob Gresham Meml. award Nat. Innkeeping Assn., 1975. Mem. Am. Automobile Assn. (mem. lodging adv. panel 1990—). Methodist. Avocations: photography, writing.

SAWYER, RAYMOND TERRY, lawyer; b. Cleve., Oct. 1, 1943; s. R. Terry and Fanny Katherine (Young) S.; m. Katherine Margaret Schneider, Aug. 5, 1972; children: Margaret Young, John Terry. BA, Yale U., 1965; LLB, Harvard U., 1968. Bar: Ohio 1969, U.S. Dist. Ct. (no. dist.) Ohio 1970. Assoc. Thompson Hine & Flory LLP, Cleve., 1968-76, ptnr., 1976-83, 86—; exec. dir. Ohio Housing Fin. Agy., Columbus, 1983-84; counsel to gov. State of Ohio, Columbus, 1984, chief of staff, 1985-86; chmn. Gov.'s commn. on housing, 1989-90; bd. dirs. Premix, Inc., North Kingsville, Ohio. Vol. VISTA, East Palo Alto, Calif., 1968-69; mem. Tech. Leadership Coun., 1987-95, Leadership Cleve., 1986-87, Cleve. Found. Study Commn. on Med. Rsch. Edn., 1991-92; mem. Ohio Bd. Regents, Columbus, 1987-96, chmn., 1992-93; trustee Cleve. Ballet, 1987—, Cleve. Orch., 1993—, Western Res. Hist. Soc.; bd. dirs. Premix, Inc., North Kingsville, Ohio; chmn. George W. Codrington Charitable Found. Named Man of Yr. Womanspace, 1982. Mem. ABA, Ohio State Bar Assn. (chair corp. law com. 1993-95), Clevel. Bar Assn., Yale U. Alumni Assn. (pres. Cleve. chpt. 1980-81), Assn. Yale Alumni (del. 1996-99). Democrat. Presbyterian. Office: Thompson Hine Flory LLP 3900 Key Ctr Cleveland OH 44114-1216

SAWYER, ROBERT MCLARAN, history educator; b. St. Louis, Nov. 12, 1929; s. Lee McLaran and Harrie (Alcock) S.; m. Patricia Ann Covert, Nov. 23, 1955; children—Ann Marie, Lee McLaran, Gail Louise. B.S., S.E. Mo. State Coll., 1952; M.A., U. Ill., 1953; Ph.D., U. Mo., 1966. Tchr. Rolla (Mo.) Public Schs., 1955; asst. prof., then asso. prof. history U. Mo., Rolla., 1956-67; mem. faculty U. Nebr., Lincoln, 1967—; prof. history of edn. U. Nebr., 1969—, chmn. dept. history and philosophy of edn., 1975-81; mem. council U. Nebr. (Coll. Arts and Scis.), 1979—; vis. prof. Ark. State U., Jonesboro, summer 1966; proposal reviewer Nat. Endowment Humanities, 1979. Author: The History of the University of Nebraska, 1929-1969, 1973, The Many Faces of Teaching, 1987, The Art and Politics of College Teaching, 1992, The Black Student's Guide to College Success, 1993, The Handbook of College Teaching, 1994; also articles, revs. Served with AUS, 1953-55. Mem. Orgn. Am. Historians, History Edn. Soc., Am. Ednl. Studies Assn., Soc. Profs. Edn., Phi Alpha Theta, Phi Delta Kappa. Home: 2640 S 35th St Lincoln NE 68506-6623 Office: Univ Nebr 29 Henzlit Hall Lincoln NE 68588

SAWYER, THOMAS C., congressman; b. Akron, Ohio, Aug. 15, 1945; m. Joyce Handler, 1968; 1 child, Amanda. BA, U. Akron, 1968, MA, 1970. Pub. sch. tchr. Ohio; adminstr. state sch. for delinquent boys; legis. agt. Ohio Pub. Utilities Commn.; mem. Ohio House Reps., Columbus, 1977-83; mayor City of Akron, 1984-86; mem. 100th-105th Congresses from 14th Ohio dist., Washington, D.C., 1987—; mem. ec and ed opp com., subcom. employer-employee rels., commerce com., mem. subcom. oversight and investigations com. stds. conduct, mem. transp. and infrastructure com., subcom. surf. transp.; mem. Transp. and Infrastructure com., subcom. surface transp. Democrat. Office: US Ho of Reps 1414 Longworth Bldg Washington DC 20515-3514*

SAWYER, THOMAS EDGAR, management consultant; b. Homer, La., July 7, 1932; s. Sidney Edgar and Ruth (Bickham) S.; BS, UCLA, 1959; MA, Occidental Coll., 1969; PhD, Walden U., 1990; m. Joyce Mezzanatto, Aug. 22, 1954; children—Jeffrey T., Scott A., Robert J., Julie Anne. Project engr. Garrett Corp., L.A., 1954-60; mgr. devel. ops. TRW Systems, Redondo Beach, Calif., 1960-66; spl. asst. to gov. State of Calif., Sacramento, 1967-69; prin., gen. mgr. Planning Rsch. Corp., McLean, Va., 1969-72; dep. dir. OEO, Washington, 1972-74; assoc. prof. bus. mgmt. Brigham Young U., 1974-78; pres. Mesa Corp., Provo, 1978-82, chmn. bd., 1978-82; pres. and dir. Sage Inst. Internat., Inc., Provo, Utah, 1982-88; chmn. bd., CEO Pvt. Telecom Networks, Inc. (name changed to Nat. Applied Computer Techs., Inc.), Orem, Utah, 1988—; chief tech. officer GST Telecommunications (formerly Greenstar Telecomm., Inc.), San Francisco, 1993—; also bd. dirs., Vancouver, Wash., 1995—; dir. Intechna Corp., HighTech Corp., Indian Affiliates, Inc., Greenstar USA, Inc., San Francisco, 1994—. Chmn. Nat. Adv. Council Indian Affairs; chmn. Utah State Bd. Indian Affairs; mem. Utah Dist. Export Coun.; mem. Utah dist. SBA Council; chmn. So. Paiute Restoration Com.; mem. adv. coun. Nat. Bus. Assn.; mem. Utah Job Tng. Coordinating Coun. Served with USMC, 1950-53. Mem. Am. Mgmt. Assn., Am. Soc. Public Adminstrn., Utah Coun. Small Bus. (dir.), Utah State Hist. Soc. (bd. dirs. 1993—). Republican. Mormon. Club: Masons. Author: Assimilation Versus Self-Indentity: A Modern Native American Perspective, 1976, Computer Assisted Instruction: An Inevitable Breakthrough, Current Challenges of Welfare: A Review of Public Assistance As Distributive Justice, 1989, Impact of Failure By Senior Executives to Receive Accurate Critical Feedback on Pervasive Change, 1990, The Promise of Funding a New Educational Initiative Using the Microcomputer, 1988, New Software Models for training and Education delivery, 1989, New Organizations: How They Deviate from Classical Models, 1989, Increasing Productivity in Organizations: The Paradox, 1989, An Introduction and Assessment of Strategic Decision Making Paradigms in Complex Organizations, 1989, The Influence of Critical Feedback and Organizational Climate on Managerial Decision Making, 1990, Future of Technology in Education, 1989. Home: 548 W 630 S Orem UT 84058-6154 Office: 382 E 720 S Orem UT 84058-6342

SAWYER, THOMAS WILLIAM, air force officer; b. Turlock, Calif., Nov. 19, 1933; s. Everett Edward and Marie Georgine (Gunderson) S.; m. Faith Barry Martin, Feb. 16, 1957; children: William Everet, John Martin, Susan Quincy. BS in Mil. Sci., U. Nebr., 1965; MS in Internat. Rels., George Washington U., 1974. Enlisted U.S. Air Force, 1952, commd. and advanced through grades to maj. gen., 1983; comdr. 57th Fighter Squadron, Keflavik, Iceland, 1971-73; chief internat. relations div. Hdqrs. U.S. Air Force, Washington, 1974-77; vice comdr. 20th Air Div., Fort Lee, Va., 1977-78; mil. asst. to Sec. Air Force, 1978-80; comdr. 26th Air Div., Luke AFB, Ariz., 1980-82; dep. ops. NORAD and Space Command, Colorado Springs, Colo., 1982-86; retired USAF, 1986; founder, pres. Aerospace Network Inc., 1986. Bd. dirs. Pikes Peak chpt. ARC, Colo./Wyo. chpt. Am. Def. Preparedness Assn. Decorated Disting. Service medal, Def. Disting. Service medal, Legion of Merit with 2 oak leaf clusters, Silver Star (2). Mem. Phoenix C. of C. (bd. dirs. 1980-82), Colorado Springs C. of C. Avocations: nat. security affairs, woodworking, automobile bldg. Home: 10 W Cheyenne Mountain Blvd Colorado Springs CO 80906-4335 Office: Aerospace Network Inc 10 W Cheyenne Mountain Blvd Colorado Springs CO 80906-4335

SAWYER, WILBUR HENDERSON, pharmacologist, educator; b. Brisbane, Australia, Mar. 23, 1921; s. Wilbur Augustus and Margaret Henderson S.; m. Marian Gholson Kittredge, Nov. 14, 1942 (dec. Mar. 1982); children: Wilbur Kittredge, Robert Kittredge, Thomas Kittredge, Richard Kittredge; m. Pomona Jean Mitchell, Aug. 28, 1982. A.B., Harvard U., 1942, M.D., 1945, PhD, 1950; DSc, Med. Coll. Ohio, Toledo, 1994. Instr. biology Harvard U., Cambridge, Mass., 1950-53; asst. prof. physiology NYU Med. Sch., N.Y.C., 1953-57; asso. prof. pharmacology Columbia U. Coll. Physicians and Surgeons, N.Y.C., 1957-64; prof. Columbia U. Coll. Physicians and Surgeons, 1964-78, Gustavus A. Pfeiffer prof., 1978-90, prof. emeritus, 1991—, spl. lectr., 1993—. Contbr. articles on exptl. endocrinology, physiology and pharmacology to profl. jours. Served to lt. (j.g.) M.C., USN, 1946-48. Recipient Lederle Med. Faculty award NYU, 1955-57; Fulbright-Hays Sr. scholar, 1974; Commonwealth Fund travelling fellow, 1965. Fellow AAAS; mem. Am. Soc. Zoologists, Am. Physiol. Soc., Soc. Gen. Physiologists, Soc. Exptl. Biology and Medicine, Endocrine Soc., Am. Soc. Pharmacology and Exptl. Therapeutics, Harvey Soc., Soc. Endocrinology, Am. Peptide Soc., Alpha Omega Alpha. Home: 1490 Kings Ln Palo Alto CA 94303-2836

SAWYER, WILLIAM DALE, physician, educator, university dean, foundation administrator; b. Roodhouse, Ill., Dec. 28, 1929; s. Cloyd Howard and Eva Collier (Dale) S.; m. Jane Ann Stewart, Aug. 25, 1951; children—Dale Stewart, Carole Ann. Student, U. Ill., 1947-50; MD cum laude, Washington U., St. Louis, 1954; ScD (hon.), Mahidol U., Bangkok, 1988; DPH (hon.), Chiang Mai U., Thailand, 1993. Intern Washington U.-Barnes Hosp., 1954-55, resident, 1957-58, fellow, 1958-60; asst. prof. microbiology Johns Hopkins U., Balt., 1964-67; prof., chmn. dept. microbiology Rockefeller Found.-Mahidol U., Bangkok, 1967-73, Ind. U. Sch. Medicine, Indpls., 1973-80; prof. depts. medicine, microbiology and immunology Wright State U., Dayton, Ohio, 1981-87, dean Sch. Medicine,, 1981-87; pres. China Med. Bd. N.Y., Inc., 1987-97; adj. prof. biology Ball State U., Muncie, Ind., 1978-80; hon. prof. microbiology Sun Yat Sen U. Med. Sci., 1987; hon. prof. Peking Union Med. Coll., 1989; hon. advisor Beijing Med. U.; cons. U.S. Army Med. R & D Command, WHO Immunology Ctr., Singapore, 1969-73; mem. bd. sci. advisers Armed Forces Inst. Pathology, 1975-80, chmn., 1979-80; adj. prof. medicine and microbiology and immunology N.Y. Med. Coll., Valhalla, 1990—; hon. prof. China Med. U., 1995, West China U. Med. Sci., 1995, Zhejiang Med. U., 1995, Jiujang Med. Coll., 1995, Hunan Med. U., 1996, Xian Med. U., 1996, Shanghai Med. U., 1996. Contbr. numerous articles to profl. jours. Mem. Lobund adv. bd. U. Notre Dame. Served to maj. M.C., UAS, 1955-64. Recipient Gold medal of merit Airlangga U., Indonesia, 1992, Pub. Health Recognition award Asia-Pacific Acad. Consortium Pub. Health, 1993, China Health medal, 1996, White Magnolia award, 1996. Fellow ACP; mem. AAAS, Am. Soc. Microbiology (br. pres. 1976), Sci. Rsch. Soc. Am., Am. Fedn. Clin. Rsch., Ctrl. Soc. Clin. Rslch., Infectious Diseases Soc. Am., Soc. Exptl. Biology and Medicine, Am. Acad. Microbiology, Am. Assn. Pathologists, Assn. Am. Med. Colls. (coun. deans 1980-87), Phi Beta Kappa, Sigma Xi, Alpha Omega Alpha. Home: 154 Poppy Hills Cove S Georgetown TX 78628 Office: China Med Bd of NY Inc 750 3rd Ave New York NY 10017-2703

SAWYERS, CLAIRE ELYCE, arboretum administrator; b. Maryville, Mo., May 30, 1957; d. Scott Kirkir and Betty Jane (Alexander) S. BS with distinction, Purdue U., 1978, MAg., 1981; MS, U. Del., 1984. Dir. Scott Arboretum of Swarthmore (Pa.) Coll., Swarthmore, Pa., 1990—. Office: Scott Arboretum 500 College Ave Swarthmore PA 19081-1306

SAWYERS, ELIZABETH JOAN, librarian, administrator; b. San Diego, Dec. 2, 1936; d. William Henry and Elizabeth Georgiana (Price) S. A.A., Glendale Jr. Coll., 1957; B.A. in Bacteriology, UCLA, 1959, M.L.S., 1961. Asst. head acquisition sect. Nat. Library Medicine, Bethesda, Md., 1962-63, head acquisition sect., 1963-66, spl. asst. to chief tech. services div., 1966-69, spl. asst. to assoc. dir. for library ops., 1969-73; asst. dir. libraries for tech. services SUNY-Stony Brook, 1973-75; dir. Health Scis. Library Ohio State U., Columbus, 1975-90, spl. asst. to dir. Univ. librs., 1990—. Mem. Assn. Acad. Health Scis. Library Dirs. (sec./treas. 1981-83, pres. 1983-84), Med. Library Assn., Am. Soc. for Info. Sci., Spl. Libraries Assn., ALA. Office: Ohio State Univ Librs 1858 Neil Ave Columbus OH 43210-1225

SAWYERS, JOHN LAZELLE, surgeon; b. Centerville, Iowa, July 26, 1925; s. Francis Lazelle and Almira (Baker) S.; m. Julia Edwards, May 25, 1957; children: Charles Lazelle, Al Baker, Julia Edwards. A.B., U. Rochester, 1946; M.D., Johns Hopkins U., 1949. Diplomate: Am. Bd. Surgery (dir. 1981-87), Am. Bd. Thoracic Surgery. House officer surgery Johns Hopkins Hosp., Balt., 1949-50; asst. resident, resident in surgery Vanderbilt U. Hosp., Nashville, 1953-58; practice medicine specializing in surgery Nashville, 1958—; surgeon Edwards-Eve Clinic, 1958-60; chief surg. service Nashville Gen. Hosp., 1960-77; surgeon-in-chief St. Thomas Hosp., Nashville, 1977-82; prof. surgery Vanderbilt U., Nashville, chmn. dept. surgery, dir. sect. surg. scis., 1983-94. Bd. dirs. Davidson County unit Am. Cancer Soc. Served from lt. (j.g.) to lt. M.C. USNR, 1950-52. Fellow A.C.S. (gov. 1974-80, pres. Tenn. chpt. 1974); mem. Am. Surg. Assn. 1st v.p. 1994), Southeastern Surg. Congress (pres. 1980), So. Surg. Assn. (pres. 1987), Halsted Soc. (pres. 1981). Home: 403 Ellendale Ave Nashville TN 37205-3401 Office: Vanderbilt U Dept Surgery 1001 Oxford House Nashville TN 37232-4730

SAWYIER, DAVID R., lawyer; b. Chgo., Feb. 2, 1951. BA, Harvard U., 1972, JD, 1977; MA, Oxford U., 1974; diploma law, Cambridge U., 1979. Bar: Ill. 1977, D.C. 1978. Law clerk U.S. Ct. Appeals D.C. cir., 1977-78; ptnr. Sidley & Austin, Chgo. Mem. ABA (bus. law sect.), Chgo. Bar Assn. (futures sect.). Office: Sidley & Austin 1 First Natl Plz Chicago IL 60603-2003

SAX, HELEN SPIGEL, lawyer; b. Phila., June 2, 1915; d. D. Hays and Erna (Sultan) Solis-Cohen; m. Herbert Spigel, Aug. 31, 1939; children—Frank, Robert, James; m. James E. Sax, June 15, 1969. B.A., Swarthmore Coll., 1937; LL.B., U. Pa., 1940. Bar: Ill. 1941, Pa. 1945. With War Labor Bd., Chgo., 1940-41; mem. Wolf Block Schorr & Solis-Cohen, Phila., 1945—. Trustee Rosenbach Mus. and Libr., 1969—, Nat. Mus. Am. Jewish History, 1975—; bd. dirs. Big Bros.-Big Sisters Assn. Phila; mem. women's bd. Thomas Jefferson U. Hosp.; mem. adv. bd. Phila. Found.; mem. Juvenile Justice Alliance-Citizens Crime Commn.; former pres., mem. fin. com. Girl Scouts of Greater Phila. Mem. ABA, Pa. Bar Assn., Phila. Bar Assn., Phila. Lawyers Club, Phi Beta Kappa. Office: Wolf Block Schorr SE Corner 15th Chestnut St Philadelphia PA 19102

SAX, JOSEPH LAWRENCE, lawyer, educator; b. Chgo., Feb. 3, 1936; s. Benjamin Harry and Mary (Silverman) S.; m. Eleanor Charlotte Gettes, June 17, 1958; children—Katherine Elaine Dennett, Valerie Beth, Anne-Marie. Rosen. AB, Harvard U., 1957; JD, U. Chgo., 1959; LLD (hon.), Ill. Inst. Tech., 1992. Bar: D.C. 1960, Mich., 1966, U.S. Supreme Ct. 1969. Atty. Dept. Justice, Washington, 1959-60; pvt. practice law Washington, 1960-62; prof. U. Colo., 1962-65, U. Mich., Ann Arbor, 1966-86; dep. asst. sec. and counselor U.S. Sec. Interior, Washington, 1994-96; vis. prof. U. Calif. Law Sch., Berkeley, 1965-66, 86, U. Paris I, 1981, 82, Stanford Law Sch., 1985; fellow Ctr. Advanced Study in Behavioral Scis., 1977-78; cons. U.S. Senate Com. on Pub. Works, 1970-71; mem. cons. council Conservation Found., 1969-73; mem. legal adv. com. Pres.'s Council on Environ. Quality, 1970-72; mem. environ. studies bd. Nat. Acad. Sci., 1970-73; mem. Mich. Environ. Rev. Bd., 1973-74. Author: Waters and Water Rights, 1967, Water Law, Planning and Policy, 1968, Defending the Environment, 1971, Mountains Without Handrails, 1980, Legal Control of Water Resources, 1991. Bd. dirs. Environ. Law Inst., Washington, 1970-75; trustee Center for Law and Social Policy, 1970-76; regional gov. Internat. Coun. Environmental Law; gov.'s rep. Gt. Lakes Task Force, 1984-85. With USAF, 1960. Fellow AAAS; mem. University Club (San Francisco).

SAX, ROBERT EDWARD, food service equipment company executive; b. Phila., Nov. 2, 1938; s. Sam and Jessie (Sirisky) S.; m. Rochelle E. Sax, Jan. 11, 1959; children: Nathan, Beverly. Student, U. Pa., 1960-66; diploma, Xerox Sys., Chgo., 1987. Pres. Robert E. Sax Assocs., Inc., Blackwood, N.J., 1965-79; sr. sales mgr. Household Internat., Inc., Veron Hills, Ill., 1979-90; v.p. nat. accounts True Food Svc. Equipment, O'Fallon, Mo., 1990—. Author: It's Yours Just Ask, 1975. Pres. ARCH, Berlin, N.J., 1971. Named Man of Yr. Sta. WPEN, Camden, N.J., 1969. Mem. NHRA, RROC, Masons. Home: 305 Old Orchard Rd Cherry Hill NJ 08003-1216

SAX, STANLEY PAUL, manufacturing company executive; b. Cin., Sept. 1, 1925; s. Ben Philip and Goldie (Quitman) S.; children: Steven Jay, David Jay; m. Patricia Moran Leach, June 14, 1970; children: Cathy, Carolyn. A.B., U. Wis., 1948. Researcher Market Research Co. Am., Chgo., 1942; instr. U. Wis., 1948; v.p., dir. Am. Buff Co., Detroit, 1948-57; exec. v.p., dir. Am. Buff Co., Chgo., 1957—; pres. Speedway Buff Co.; pres., chmn. bd., dir. J.J. Siefen Co., 1961—; chmn. bd., pres. Sax Abrasive Corp., 1961—, Sax Cal. Corp., 1962—, Klem Chem. Corp., 1963—, Stan Sax Corp., Seco Chems., Inc., 1965—; chmn. bd. Buckingham Products Co., McAleer Mfg. Co., 1968—, Sax Realty Investment Corp., 1967—, Globe Compound Corp., 1971—, Goodison Mfg. Co., 1972—, Ana, Inc., 1974—; partner S & D Leasing Co. Contbr. articles to profl. jours. Trustee Sax Family Found.; nat. trustee Balt. Mus. Art; bd. dirs. Met. Soc. Crippled Children and Adults. Served to lt. AUS, 1943-46; to lt. col. Res. 1946—. Recipient Wis. scholar award. Mem. Mil. Order World Wars, Metal Finishing Suppliers Assn. (trustee), Detroit C. of C., Detroit Inst. Arts (patron), Friends of Am. Wing (Founders Soc.), Friends of Henry Ford Mus., Pres.'s Soc., Am. Electroplaters Soc., Am. Soc. for Abrasives, Soc. Mil. Engrs., Young President's Orgn., World Presidents Orgn., Chief Execs. Orgn., Amateur Athletic Union, Soc. Die Casting Engrs., Res. Officers Assn., V.F.W., Wis. Alumni Assn., Winterhur Collectors Circle Mt. Vernon 100, Phi Beta Kappa, Alpha Phi Omega, Phi Kappa Phi, Psi Chi, Phi Eta Sigma. Clubs: Elk (Detroit), Rotarian. (Detroit), Economic (Detroit), Renaissance (Detroit); Recess, Army-Navy. Lender furnishings to diplomatic reception rooms, Nat. Portrait Gallery, Smithsonian Inst.; benefactor fine arts com. Dept. State. Home: 1340 Pembroke Dr Bloomfield Hills MI 48304-2653 Office: 101 S Waterman St Detroit MI 48209-3065

SAXBE, WILLIAM BART, lawyer, former government official; b. Mechanicsburg, Ohio, June 24, 1916; s. Bart Rockwell and Faye Henry (Carey) S.; m. Ardath Louise Kleinhans, Sept. 14, 1940; children: William Bart, Juliet Louise Saxbe Blackburn, Charles Rockwell. A.B., Ohio State U., 1940; LL.B., 1948; hon. degrees, Central State U., Findlay Coll., Ohio Wesleyan U., Walsh Coll., Capital U., Wilmington Coll., Ohio State U., Bowling Green State U. Bar: Ohio 1948. Practiced in Mechanicsburg, 1948-55; partner Saxbe, Boyd & Prine, 1955-58; mem. Ohio Gen. Assembly, 1947-48, 49-50; majority leader Ho. Reps., 1951-52, speaker, 1953-54; atty. gen. Ohio, 1957-58, 63-68; partner Dargusch, Saxbe & Dargusch, 1960-63; mem. U.S. Senate from, Ohio, 1969-74; atty. gen. U.S., 1974; ambassador to India, 1975-77; partner firm Chester, Saxbe, Hoffman & Wilcox, Columbus, Ohio, 1977-81; of counsel firm Jones, Day, Reavis & Pogue, Cleve., 1981-84, Pearson, Ball & Dowd (merger Pearson, Ball & Dowd and Reed, Smith & McClay), Washington, 1984-93; ind. spl. counsel Central States Teamsters Pension Fund, 1982—; of counsel Chester Willcox & Saxbe, Columbus, Ohio, 1994—. Served with 107th Cav. AUS, 1940-42; Served with 107th Cav. USAAF, 1942-45; col. Res. Mem. Am., Ohio bar assns., Am. Judicature Soc., Chi Phi, Phi Delta Phi. Republican. Episcopalian. Clubs: Mason (33d degree) (Columbus), University (Columbus), Columbus Athletic (Columbus), Columbus (Columbus), Scioto Country (Columbus); Urbana (Ohio) Country; Burning Tree Country (Bethesda, Md.); Country of Fla. (Boynton Beach). Home: 1171 N Ocean Blvd Gulf Stream FL 33483-7273 Office: 4600 N Ocean Blvd Boynton Beach FL 33435-7312

SAXBERG, BORJE OSVALD, management educator; b. Helsinki, Finland, Jan. 25, 1928; came to U.S., 1950, naturalized, 1966; s. Oskar Valdemar and Martha (Granberg) S.; m. A. Margrete Haug; children: Bo Erland Haug, Bror Valdemar Haug. BA, Swedish Sch. Bus. and Econs., 1950; BS, Oreg. State U., 1952; MS, U. Ill., 1953, PhD, 1958. Teaching asst., instr. U. Ill., 1953-57; prof. dept. mgmt. and orgn. U. Wash., 1957—; asso. dean U. Wash. (Bus. Sch.), 1967-70, chmn. dept. mgmt. and orgn., 1972-76, chmn. faculty senate, 1980-81, chmn. dept. mgmt. and orgn., 1989-93; dir. program in entrepreneurship and innovation, 1989-95; cons. in field. Author: (with R. Joseph Monsen) The Business World, 1967, (with H.P. Knowles) Personality and Leadership Behavior, 1971, (with R.A. Johnson) Management, Systems and Society, 1976, (with B. Mar) Managing High Technology, 1985. Ford Found. fellow, 1960-61. Mem. Am. Sociol. Assn., Rainier Club, Swedish Club (Seattle). Home: 7336 58th Ave NE Seattle WA 98115-6257 Office: Univ Wash Grad Sch Bus 353200 Seattle WA 98195-3200

SAXBY, LEWIS WEYBURN, JR., retired glass fiber manufacturing executive; b. Oak Park, Ill., Dec. 17, 1924; s. Lewis Weyburn Saxby and Dorothy (Porter) Willey; m. Kathryn Hutchinson, 1947 (dec. 1990); m. Kay Taylor, Jan. 23, 1993; children: Steven Lewis, Ann, Jane Porter. BS, U. Calif., Berkeley, 1945; MBA, Stanford U., 1948. Prodn. trainee Owens-Corning Fiberglas Corp., Newark, Ohio, 1948-49; prodn. scheduler Santa Clara, Calif., 1949-51; estimator salesman San Francisco, 1951-52, dept. supr., 1952-56; br. mgr. Sacramento, Calif., 1956-58; br. mgr. Detroit, 1958-60, mgr. supply and contracting East, 1960-61; mgr. supply and contracting Toledo, 1961-66, v.p., mgr. supply and contracting, 1966-70, v.p. mech. products and constrn. services, 1971-74, v.p. mech. ops. div., 1974-78, sr. v.p., 1978-89; bd. dirs. Performance Contracting Group, Am. Borate Co. Bd. dirs., chmn. com. Toledo Conv. and Visitors Bur., 1986-96. Served as ensign USNR, 1943-46. Recipient Gold Leadership award Jr. Achievemnt, Inc., 1981. Mem. Nat. Insulation Contractors (chmn. com. 1984-89, Man of Yr. 1985), Inverness (Toledo) (bd. govs. 1976-80), Toledo Club. Republican. Presbyterian. Avocations: golf, tennis, travel, photography, snorkeling.

SAXE, DEBORAH CRANDALL, lawyer; b. Lima, Ohio, July 23, 1949; d. Robert Gordon and Lois Barker (Taylor) Crandall; m. Robert Saxe, June 3, 1989; children: Elizabeth Sara, Emily Jane. BA, Pa. State U., 1971; MA, UCLA, 1973, JD, 1978. Bar: Calif. 1978, D.C. 1979, U.S. Dist. Ct. D.C. 1979, U.S. Dist. Ct. (ea. dist.) Calif. 1981, , U.S. Dist. Ct. (ctrl. dist.) Calif. 1982, U.S. Dist. Ct. (no. and so. dists.) Calif. 1987, U.S. Ct. Appeals (4th and D.C. cirs.) 1979, U.S. Ct. Appeals (6th cir.) 1985, U.S. Ct. Appeals (8th and 9th cirs.) 1987, U.S. Ct. Appeals (2nd cir.) 1990, U.S. Supreme Ct. 1985. Assoc. Seyfarth, Shaw, Fairweather & Garaldson, Washington, 1978-83; assoc. Jones, Day, Reavis & Pogue, Washington, 1983-85; assoc. Jones, Day, Reavis & Pogue, L.A., 1985-87, ptnr., 1988-97; shareholder Heller Ehrman Shite & McAuliffe, 1997—; judge pro tem, Small Claims Ct., L.A., 1985-88. Co-author: Advising California Employers, 1990, 2d edit., 1995; contbg. editor Employment Discrimination Law, 1989. Bd. dirs. Pediatric and Family Med. Ctr., L.A., 1990—. Mem. ABA (labor law sect. 1978—), Calif. Bar Assn. (labor law sect. 1985—), L.A. County Bar Assn. (labor law sect. 1985—, mem. exec. com. 1988—), Pi Lambda Theta, Phi Beta Kappa. Office: Heller Ehrman White & McAuliffe 601 S Figueroa Fl 40 Los Angeles CA 90017-5704

SAXE, LEONARD, social psychologist, educator; b. N.Y.C., June 12, 1947; s. Theodore and Majorie (Mayers) S.; m. Marion Gardner, Aug. 9, 1970; 1 child, Daniel. BS in Psychology, U. Pitts., 1969, MS in Psychology, 1972, PhD in Social Psychology, 1976. Asst. instr. U. Pitts., 1973-75; asst. then assoc. prof. psychology Boston U., 1976-88, assoc. dir. Ctr. Applied Social Sci., 1982-84, dir., 1984-87; rsch. prof. Heller Sch. Social Welfare Brandeis U., Waltham, Mass., 1988-90, adj. prof. psychology, adj. rsch. prof., 1990—; prof. psychology Grad. Ctr. CUNY, 1991—; head social-personality psychology, 1993-95; Fulbright sr. lectr. U. Haifa, Israel, 1981-82; mem. task force Children's Mental Health Rsch. Inst. Medicine-NAS, 1988-89; rev. coms. HHS-Healthcare Fin. Adminstr. NIMH, Nat. Inst. Drug Abuse, Dept. Edn.; cons., contractor Office Tech. Assessment, U.S. Congress, 1980-88; bd. govs. U. Haifa, 1993—. Author: (with others) Children's Mental Health: Problems and Treatment, 1987, (with M. Fine) Social Experiments: Methods for Design and Evaluation, 1981; editor: (with M.J. Saks) Advances in Applied Social Psychology, Vol. 3, 1986, (with D. Koretz) New Directions for Program Evaluation, 1982, (with D. Bar-Tal) The Social Psychology of Education: Theory and Research, 1978; contbr. chpts. to books, articles to profl. jours.; assoc. and mng. editor Personality and Social Psychology Bull., 1978-81; ad hoc reviewer various jours., book reviewer various pubs. Congl. fellow Office Tech. Assessment, 1979. Fellow APA (bd. dirs. sect. social and ethical responsibility 1985-88, Disting. Contbn. award 1989), AAAS, Soc. Psychol. Study Social Issues (coun. 1982-84, 87-89). Office: CUNY Grad Ctr 33 W 42nd St New York NY 10036-8003

SAXE, THELMA RICHARDS, secondary school educator, consultant; b. Ogdensburg, N.J., Apr. 21, 1941; d. George Francis and Evelyn May (Howell) Richards; m. Kenneth Elwood Meeker, Jr., June 22, 1957 (div. 1965); children: Sylvia Lorraine Meeker Hill, Michelle Louise Meeker Arromando, David Sean (dec.); m. Frederick Ely Saxe, Feb. 18, 1983; stepchildren: Jonathan Kent, Holly Harding Schenker. BA, William Paterson Coll., Wayne, N.J., 1972, MEd, 1975, postgrad., 1983-84; Dyslexia cert., Fairleigh Dickinson U., 1994. Cert. paralegal, dyslexia specialist Fairleigh Dickonson U. Tchr. handicapped Sussex (N.J.)-Wantage Regional Sch. Dist., 1972-75; resource rm. tchr. Sussex County Vo-Tech Sch., Sparta, N.J., 1975-77; learning cons. Sussex County Vo-Tech Sch., 1977-83; learning specialist Bennington-Rutland Supervisory Union, Manchester, Vt., 1986-87; learning cons. Stillwater (N.J.) Twp. Sch., 1987-88, Independence Twp. Cen. Sch., Great Meadows, N.J., 1989; learning cons., tutor in pvt. practice specializing dyslexia Sparta, 1986—; asst. prin. Harmony Twp. Sch., Harmony, N.J., 1989-92; learning cons. Montague (N.J.) Elem. Sch., 1996—; coord. gifted/talented Sussex Vo-Tech, 1980-83; coord. child study team Stillwater Twp. Sch., 1987-88, Montague Twp. Sch., 1996—. Mem. Coun. Exceptional Children, Learning Disabilities Assn., Orton Dyslexia Soc., N.J. Assn. Learning Cos., Kappa Delta Pi. Republican. Presbyterian. Avocations: music, singing, piano, autoharp, skiing, hiking, travel. Home: 17 Park Rd Sparta NJ 07871-2002 Office: Accent on Comm 350A Sparta Ave Sparta NJ 07871-1143

SAXENA, ARJUN NATH, physicist; b. Lucknow, India, Apr. 1, 1932; s. Sheo and Mohan (Piyari) Shanker; came to U.S., 1956, naturalized, 1976; BSc, Lucknow U., 1950, MSc, 1952, profl. cert. in German, 1954; Post MS diploma, Inst. Nuclear Physics, Calcutta, India, 1955; PhD, Stanford U., 1963; m. Veera Saxena, Feb. 9, 1956; children: Rashmi, Amol, Varsha, Ashvin. Rsch. asst. Stanford U., 1956-60; mem. tech. staff Fairchild Semicondr. Co., Palo Alto, Calif., 1960-65; dept. head Sprague Electric Co., North Adams, Mass., 1965-69; mem. tech. staff RCA Labs., Princeton, N.J., 1969-71; pres., chmn. bd. Astro-Optics, Phila., 1972; pres. Internat. Sci. Co., Princeton Junction, N.J., 1973—; disting. vis. scientist Centre de Récherches Nucléaires, Strasbourg, France, 1973, 77; sr. staff scientist, mgr. engring. Data Gen. Corp., Sunnyvale, Calif., 1975-80; mgr. process tech. Signetics Corp., Sunnyvale, 1980-81; Gould AMI scientist, dir. advanced process devel. Gould AMI Semicondrs., Santa Clara, Calif., 1981-87; dir. Ctr. for Integrated Electronics, prof. dept. elec. and computer system engring. Rensselaer Poly. Inst., Troy, N.Y., 1987-96, emeritus prof., 1996—; disting. vis. scientist Inst. Microelectronics, Stuttgart, Germany, 1993-94. Treas. Pack 66, Boy Scouts Am., W. Windsor, N.J., 1970-74. Recipient Disting. Citizen award State of N.J., 1975. Mem. IEEE, Stanford Alumni Assn. (life). Contbr. articles on semicondr. tech., optics, nuclear and high-energy physics to sci. jours., 1953—; patentee in field. Home: 4217 Pomona Ave Palo Alto CA 94306-4312

SAXENA, BRIJ B., biochemist, endocrinologist, educator. PhD, India; DSc, U. Muenster, W.Ger.; PhD, U. Wis., 1961. Asst. prof. biochemistry and endocrinology N.J. Coll. Medicine., 1966-74; assoc. prof. biochemistry Cornell U. Med. Coll., N.Y.C., 1974—; prof. biochemistry Cornell U. Med. Coll., 1974—, prof. endocrinology, 1981—, dir. div. reproductive endocrinology. Contbr. 200 articles to profl. jours. Recipient Career Scientist award N.Y.C. Health Research Council; Upjohn research award; Campoz da Paz award. Fellow Royal Soc. Medicine (London); mem. Am. Soc. Biol. Chemists, AAAS, Endocrine Soc., Harvey Soc., Am. Physiol. Soc., Am. Chem. Soc. Office: Cornell Univ Med Coll 1300 York Ave New York NY 10021-4805

SAXENA, NARENDRA K., marine research educator; b. Agra, India, Oct. 15, 1936; came to U.S., 1969; s. Brijbasi Lal and Sarbati Saxena; m. Cecilia H. Hsi, Mar. 21, 1970; Sarah Vasanti, Lorelle Sarita. Diploma Geodetic Engring., Tech. U., Hanover, Fed. Republic Germany, 1966; D in Tech Scis., Tech. U., Graz, Austria, 1972. Research assoc. geodetic sci. Ohio State U., Columbus, 1969-74; asst. prof. U. Ill., Urbana, 1974-78; asst. prof. U. Hawaii, Honolulu, 1978-81, assoc. prof., 1981-86, prof., 1986—, dept. chmn., 1994—; adj. research prof. Naval Postgrad. Sch., Monterey, Calif., 1984—; co-chmn. Pacific Congresses on Marine Tech., Honolulu, 1984, 86, 88; pres. Pacon Internat. Inc., 1987—. Editor Jour. Marine Geodesy, 1976—. Mem. Neighborhood Bd., Honolulu, 1984. Fellow Marine Tech. Soc. (various offices 1974—); mem. ASCE, Am. Geophys. Union, The Tsunami Soc. (sec. 1985—). Office: U Hawaii Dept Civil Engring Honolulu HI 96822

SAXER, RICHARD KARL, metallurgical engineer, retired air force officer; b. Toledo, Aug. 31, 1928; s. Alexander Albert and Gertrude Minnie (Kuebeler) S.; m. Marilyn Doris Mersereau, July 19, 1952; children—Jane Lynette, Robert Karl, Kris Renee, Ann Luette. Student, Bowling Green State U., 1946-48; BS, U. S. Naval Acad., 1952; MS in Aero. Mechanics Engring., Air Force Inst. Tech., 1957; PhD in Metall. Engring., Ohio State U., 1962; grad., Air Forces Staff Coll., 1966, Indsl. Coll. Armed Forces, 1971. Commd. 2d lt. U.S. Air Force, 1952, advanced through grades to lt. gen., 1976; electronics officer, mech. officer (4th Tactical Support Sqadron, Tactical Air Command), Sandia Base, N.Mex., 1953-54; electronics and mech. officer, spl. weapons assembly sect. supr. (SAC 6th Aviation Depot Squadron), French Morocco, 1954-55; project engr. mech. equipment br. Air Force Spl. Weapon's Center, Kirtland AFB, N.Mex., 1957-59; project officer Nuclear Safety div., 1959-60; assoc. prof. dept. engring. mechanics Air Force Inst. Tech., 1962-66; asso. prof., dep. dept. head USAF Acad., 1966-70; comdr., dir. Air Force Materials Lab., Wright-Patterson AFB, Ohio, 1971-74; dep. for Reentry System Space and Missile Systems Orgn., 1974-77; dep. for aero equipment Aero. Systems Div., 1977-80, dep. for tactical systems, 1980, vice comdr., 1981-83; aero. systems div. dir. Def. Nuclear Agy., 1983-85, ret., 1985; pres. R.K. Saxer & Assocs., 1985-91; CEO Universal Tech. Corp., Dayton, Ohio, 1991—; research and tech. com. materials and structures NASA, 1973-74; chmn. planning group aerospace materials Interagy. Council Materials, 1973-74; mem. Nat. Mil. Adv. Bd., 1971-74, NATO adv. group for research and devel., 1973-74. Contbr. articles to profl. jours. Decorated Def. Disting. Svc. medal, Legion of Merit, Meritorious Service medal USAF, D.S.M., Joint Svc. Commendation medal, Air Force Commendation medal with 3 oak leaf clusters, Army Commendation medal U.S., Def. Superior Service medal, Cross of Gallantry with palm Vietnam, Def. Meritorious Service medal; recipient Disting. award for systems mgmt. Air Force Assn., 1979; Disting. Alumnus award Ohio State U., 1986. Mem. Air Force Assn., Am. Def. Preparedness Assn. (pres. Dayton 1977-78), Sigma Xi, Phi Lambda Epsilon, Alpha Sigma Mu, Masons, Shriners. Home: 215 Dalfaber Ln Springboro OH 45066

SAXL, RICHARD HILDRETH, lawyer; b. Boston, June 3, 1948; s. Erwin Joseph and Lucretia (Hildreth) S. BA, U. Pa., 1970, JD, Rutgers U., Camden, N.J., 1975. Bar: Conn. 1976, U.S. Dist. Ct. Conn. 1976, U.S. Ct. Appeals (2d cir.) 1977. Assoc. Jerry Davidoff, Westport, Conn., 1976-78; ptnr. Davidoff & Saxl, Westport, 1979-94; pvt. practice law offices Richard H. Saxl, Westport, 1994—; lectr. on probate Fairfield (Conn.) U., 1982; condr. probate seminar Sacred Heart U., Fairfield, 1989; condr. real estate seminar Lawyers Forum, Westport, 1992, 93. Mem. Fairfield Town Planning and Zoning Commn., 1981-93, chmn., 1991-93; chair Fairfield Land Acquisition com., 1997—; bd. dirs. Conn. Renaissance, Inc., Norwalk, 1979-82, pres., 1981-82; mem. Fairfield Charter Revision Commn., 1984-85, 92. Recipient Svc. award Conn. Fedn. Planning and Zoning Agys., 1993, cert. of commendation Conn. Jud. Dept., 1985-87. Mem. Conn. Bar Assn., Westport Bar Assn., Pequot Yacht Club. Democrat. Avocations: squash, sailing. Home: 753 Sasco Hill Rd Fairfield CT 06430-6376 Office: 323 Riverside Ave Westport CT 06880-4810

SAXON, JOHN DAVID, lawyer, policy analyst, educator; b. Anniston, Ala., July 21, 1950; s. J.Z. and Sarah Elizabeth (Steadham) S.; m. Elizabeth Lord, Mar. 10, 1973. BA with honors, U. Ala., 1972, JD, 1977; grad. Exec. Program Stanford U., 1986; MA, U. N.C., 1973. Bar: Ala. 1977, U.S. Dist. Ct. (no. dist.) Ala. 1977, U.S. Supreme Ct. 1983, U.S. Dist. Ct. (mid. dist.) Ala. 1989, U.S. Dist. Ct. (so. dist.) Ala. 1990, U.S. Ct. Appeals (11th cir.) 1990, U.S. Ct. Appeals (5th cir.) 1992. Adminstrv. asst. to acting chief exec. officer U. Ala.-University, 1976-77; assoc. Sirote, Permutt, Friend, Friedman, Held & Apolinsky, P.A., Birmingham, Ala., 1977-78; spl. asst. to Vice Pres. U.S., Washington, 1978-79; counsel subcom. on jurisprudence and govt. rels. Com. on Judiciary, U.S. Senate, Washington, 1979-80, counsel Select Com. on Ethics, 1980-83; dir. corp. issues RCA, Washington, 1983-86; Washington rep., Gen. Electric Co., 1986-87; assoc. counsel U.S. Senate Select com. on secret mil. assistance to Iran and the Nicaraguan Opposition, 1987-88; spl. counsel U.S. Senate Armed Svcs. com., 1988; counsel, Johnston, Barton, Proctor, Swedlaw & Naff, Birmingham, 1988-90; atty. Gathings & Davis, Birmingham, 1990-92; ptnr. Cooper, Mitch, Crawford, Kuykendall & Whatley, 1992-95; pres. and prin. John D. Saxon, P.C., 1995—; adj. instr. polit. communication U. Md., 1982-83; instr. speech communication U. Ala.-University, 1973; instr. speech communication and mgmt. Brewer Jr. Coll., Tuscaloosa, 1975-77; adj. instr. civil litigation Samford U., Birmingham, 1977-78; adj. prof. Washington Coll. Law The Am. U., 1988; vis. scholar The Hastings Ctr., 1983; mem. Am. Observer Delegation, Kettering Found., U.S.-China Task Force, 1986; bd. dirs. White House Fellows Found., 1981-84 , pres., 1983-84; mem. bd. advisers Center for Publ. Law and Service, U. Ala. Sch. Law, 1976-83; bd. trustees Farrah Law Soc., 1988-94, vice-chmn., 1990-92, chmn., 1992-94; bd. dirs. exec. com. mem. vice chmn. U. Ala. Law Found., vice chmn., 1996—; mem. Pres.'s Commn. White House Fellowships, 1983-84, 93—; mem. Washington Local Devel. Corp, 1986-88; chmn. Ala. Clinton for Pres. Campaign, 1992, 96; mem. platform com. Dem. Nat. Conv., 1992, del., 1996; treas. Ala. Dem. Party, 1995—; mem. policy adv. com. The Coalition for Excellence in Edn., chmn., 1991-92; dir. The A+ Rsch. Found.; mem. bd. advisors N.E. Ala. Devel. Forum, 1992—, Nat. Governing Bd. Common Cause, 1992-95, Leadership Birmingham Class of 1993-94; mem. pres. adv. coun. Birmingham So. Coll., 1993—; mem. adminstrv. bd. First United Meth. Ch., 1994—; co-pres. Birmingham Boys Choir Found., 1994-96; asst. scoutmaster Troop 57 Boy Scouts of Am.; pres. Southside Baseball, 1995-97; adv. com. The Blackburn Inst., U. Ala.; bd. dir. Miles Coll. Ctr. for Cmty. Econ. Devel., 1995—. Served to 2d lt. U.S. Army, 1974, capt. Res. White House Fellow, 1978-79; named Disting. Mil. Grad., U. Ala., 1972. Mem. ABA (spl. com. litigation sect.), Ala. Bar Assn., Birmingham Bar Assn. (chmn. profl. ethics com. 1991-92, mem. grievance com. 1992—, co-chmn. 1995-96, chmn. 1997—), Ala. Trial Lawyers Assn. (bd. govs. 1990-94, exec. com. 1994—), White House Fellows Assn. (pres. 1983-84), Kiwanis Club (Birmingham), Scabbard and Blade, The Order of Barristers, Bench and Bar (Outstanding Sr. award 1977), Downtown Dem. Club (pres. 1992-93), Omicron Delta Kappa, Omicron Delta Epsilon, Phi Alpha Theta, Pi Sigma Alpha. Methodist. Contbr. articles to newspapers and legal publs., chpts. to books.

SAXTON, H. JAMES, congressman; b. Scranton, Pa., Jan. 22, 1943; s. Hugh R. and Helen M. (Billings) S.; m. Helen Jean Gadomski, June 9, 1965; children—Jennifer, James Martin. B.A., East Stroudsburg State Coll., 1965; postgrad. in elem. edn., Temple U., 1967-68. Tchr. Bordentown Pub. Schs., Bordentown, N.J., 1965-68; realtor Jim Saxton Realty Co., Bordentown, N.J., 1968-85; assemblyman N.J. State Assembly, Trenton, 1975-81; state senator N.J. State Senate, Trenton, 1981-84; mem. 99th-105th Congresses from 13th (now 3rd) N.J. dist., Washington, D.C., 1984—; mem. nat. security com., chmn. resources subcom. on fisheries, wildlife & oceans, mem. joint econ. com.; mem. travel and tourism caucus, maritime caucus, congl. port caucus environ. and energy study conf., Rep. study com., Stripers Ltd. (99th Congress); sec. N.J. Congl. Del., Washington, 1985-89. Active Boy Scouts Am., Burlington Council. Bordentown C. of C. Club: Leadership Found. N.J. Lodge: Elks. Office: US Ho of Reps 339 Cannon Bldg Ofc Bldg Washington DC 20515-3003*

SAXTON, JAMES, congressman; children: Martin, Jennifer. Tchr., small businessman; mem. U.S. Ho. of Reps., Washington, 1984—; vice-chmn. joint econ. com. U.S. Ho. of Reps., 104th Congress, Washington, chmn. Ho. subcom. Fisheries, Wildlife and Oceans; mem. Ho. Nat. Security Com. U.S. Ho. of Reps., Washington. Republican. Office: House Reps 339 Cannon

Bldg Ofc Bldg Washington DC 20515-3003 also: 7 Hadley Ave Toms River NJ 08753-7539 also: 1 Maine Ave Cherry Hill NJ 08002-3010*

SAXTON, LLOYD, psychologist, author; b. Loveland, Colo., Sept. 28, 1929; s. Oliver George and Alice Augusta (Andersen) S.; m. Nancy Alison Roberts, Dec. 17, 1955; children: Perry Brent, Jay Ronald, Barbara Jean. AB in English, U. Calif., Berkeley, 1950, BS in Psychology, 1954; MS in Psychology, San Francisco State U., 1955; PhD in Psychology, U. of the Pacific, Stockton, Calif., 1957. Diplomate Am. Bd. Forensic Examiners (cert. 1996); lic. psychologist, Calif. Intern in clin. psychology Chilldren's Hosp., San Francisco, 1955-56; teaching fellow U. Pacific, San Francisco, 1955-57, instr. psychology, 1957-58, asst. prof. psychology, 1958-60; assoc. prof. psychology Am. Acad. of Asian Studies, San Francisco, 1960-62, prof. psychology, 1962-65; chmn. dept. psychology Coll. of San Mateo, Calif., 1965-75, prof. psychology, 1975-92; pvt. practice San Francisco/Larkspur, 1958—; emeritus, 1995. Author: Individual, Marriage and the Family, 1968, Individual, 9th edit., 1996; author/editor: A Marriage Reader, 1970, The American Scene, 1970. Mem. APA, AAAS, AAUP, Am. Assn. Marriage and Family Therapists, Western Psychol. Assn., Am. Coll. Forensic Examiners, Mensa, Am. Chess Fedn. Democrat. Avocations: chess, sailing, music, ballet, opera. Home and Office: 57 Hatzic Ct Larkspur CA 94939-1971

SAXTON, RUTH OLSEN, educator, dean; b. Spokane, Wash., Apr. 18, 1941; d. O. Martin and Edith M. (Halsey) Olsen; m. Paul Malcom, Mar. 16, 1963; children: Kirsten Teresa, David Malcom, Katherine Blair. BA, Wheaton Coll., 1963; MA, Mills Coll., 1972; PhD, U. Calif., Berkeley, 1986. Calif. C.C. credential. Tchr. English Hyde Park H.S., Chgo., 1963-64; instr. English Coll. of Alameda, Calif., 1972-76, Mills Coll., Oakland, Calif., 1974-85; asst. prof. English Mills Coll., Oakland, 1985-90, assoc. prof. English, 1990—, dean of letters, 1993—; charter mem. Calif. Writing Project Adv. Bd. Editor: Woolf & Lessing: Breaking the Mold, 1994; assoc. editor Woolf Studies Annual. Recipient Outstanding Tchr. award Sears Found., 1990. Mem. MLA, Va. Woolf Soc., Doris Lessing Soc. (newsletter editor 1991—). Democrat. Home: 800 Portal Ave Oakland CA 94610 Office: Mills College 5000 Macarthur Blvd Oakland CA 94613-1301

SAXTON, WILLIAM MARVIN, lawyer; b. Joplin, Mo., Feb. 14, 1927; s. Clyde Marvin and Lea Ann (Farnan) S.; m. Helen Grace Klinefelter, June 1, 1974; children: Sherry Lynn, Patricia Ann Painter, William Daniel, Michael Lawrence. A.B., U. Mich., 1949, J.D., 1952. Bar: Mich. Mem. firm Love, Snyder & Lewis, Detroit, 1952-53; mem. firm Butzel, Long, Detroit, 1953—, dir., chmn., CEO, 1989-96, dir. emeritus, 1997—; lectr. Inst. Continuing Legal Edn.; sec., bd. dirs. Fritz Broadcasting, Inc., 1983—; mem. mediation tribunal hearing panel for 3d Jud. Dist. Mich., 1989—, 6th Jud. Dist., 1994—. Trustee Detroit Music Hall Ctr. Soc. for the Performing Arts, 1984—; trustee Hist. Soc. U.S. Dist. Ct. (ea. dist.) Mich., 1992-95, pres., 1993-95. Recipient Distinguished award Mich. Road Builders Assn., 1987. Master of Bench Emeritus Am. Inn of Court; fellow Am. Coll. Trial Lawyers, Am. Bar Found., Am. Coll. Labor and Employment Lawyers, Mich. Bar Found.; mem. ABA, Detroit Bar Assn. (dir. 1974-79, Goodnow Pres.'s award 1996), Mich. Bar (mem. atty. discipline panel), Detroit Indsl. Rels. Rsch. Assn. (treas. 1980—, v.p. 1982, pres. 1984-85), Mich. Young Lawyers (pres. 1954-55), Am. Law Inst., Fed. Bar Assn., Indsl. Rels. Rsch. Assn. Am. Arbitration Assn., U.S. 6th Cir. Ct. Appeals (life, mem. jud. conf., mem. bicentennial com.), Am. Inn Ct., Cooley Club, Renaissance Club, Detroit Golf Club (dir. 1983-89), Detroit Athletic Club. Office: Butzel Long 150 W Jefferson Ave Ste 900 Detroit MI 48226-4430

SAY, ALLEN, children's writer, illustrator; b. Aug. 28, 1937; s. Masako Moriwaki; m. Deirdre Myles, Apr. 18, 1974; 1 child, Yuriko. Pub. EIZO Pr., Berkeley, 1968. Author, illustrator: Dr. Smith's Safari, 1972, Once Under the Cherry Blossom Tree: An Old Japanese Tale, 1974, The Feast of Lanterns, 1976, The Bicycle Man, 1982, A River Dream, 1988, The Lost Lake, 1989, Tree of Cranes, 1991, Grandfather's Journey, 1993 (Caldecott medal 1994, Boston Globe/Horn Book award 1994), The Stranger in the Mirror, 1995, Emma's Rug, 1996; author: The Innkeeper's Apprentice, 1989, El Chino, 1990; illustrator: A Canticle to the Waterbirds, 1968, Two Ways of Seeing, 1971, Magic and Night River, 1978, The Lucky Yak, 1980, The Secret Cross of Lorraine, 1981, How My Parents Learned to Eat, 1984 (Horn Book honor list 1984, Christopher award 1985), The Boy of the Three Year Nap, 1988 (Boston Globe/Horn Book award 1988, Caldecott honor book 1989). Office: care Houghton Mifflin 222 Berkeley St Boston MA 02116-3748*

SAY, BURHAN, physician; b. Istanbul, Turkey, Feb. 26, 1923; came to U.S. 1951; s. Ethem Serif and Ayse Say; m. Elizabeth E. Jackson, Nov. 5, 1955; children: Ahmet Serif, Daniel Demir. MD, U. Istanbul, 1946. Diplomate Am. Bd. Pediatrics, Am. Bd. Med. Genetics. Asst. prof. pediatrics Hacettepe U., Ankara, Turkey, 1960-64, prof. pediatrics, 1964-73; clin. prof. of pediatrics U. of Okla./Tulsa Med. Coll., 1975—; dir. H.A. Chapman Inst., Tulsa, 1982—; v.p. Children's Med. Ctr., Tulsa, 1988—. Contbr. articles to profl. jours. Pres. Am. Cancer Soc., Tulsa, 1980-90, Great Plains Genetics Soc., Tulsa, 1993. Lt. Turkish Army, 1946-48, Turkey. Fulbright scholar, Boston, 1966-68. Avocation: sports. Home: 6216 E 99th St Tulsa OK 74137-5503 Office: Childrens Med Ctr 5300 E Skelly Dr Tulsa OK 74135-6566

SAYATOVIC, WAYNE PETER, manufacturing company executive; b. Cleve., Feb. 8, 1946; s. Peter and Margaret Ann (Nestor) S.; m. Janice Elaine Zajac, July 27, 1968; children: Jason Scott, Jamie Elizabeth. BA in Econs., Syracuse U., 1967, MBA in Fin., 1969. Fin. mgmt. program Gen. Electric Co., Syracuse, N.Y., 1969-72; fin. and cost acctg. mgr. Lubriquip div. Houdaille Industries Inc., Solon, Ohio, 1972-75; contr. Hydraulics div. Houdaille Industries Inc., Buffalo, 1975-77, Strippit div Houdaille Industries Inc., Akron, N.Y., 1977-79; treas. Houdaille Industries Inc., Ft. Lauderdale, Fla., 1979-86; v.p., treas., sec. Houdaille Industries Inc., Northbrook, Ill., 1986-88; v.p., treas., sec. IDEX Corp., Northbrook, 1988-91, v.p. fin., CFO, sec., 1992-94; sr. v.p. fin., CFO, sec., 1994—. Mem. Mfrs.' Alliance for Productivity & Innovation (fin. coun.). Office: IDEX Corp 630 Dundee Rd Northbrook IL 60062-2762

SAYER, JOHN SAMUEL, retired information systems consultant; b. St. Paul, July 27, 1917; s. Arthur Samuel and Genevieve (Ollis) S.; m. Elizabeth Hughes, June 9, 1940; children: Stephen, Susan, Kathryn, Nancy. BSME, U. Minn., 1940. Registered profl. engr., Del. Sect. mgr. E.I. Du Pont de Nemours & Co, Wilmington, Del., 1940-60; exec. v.p. Documentation, Inc., Washington, 1960-63; v.p. corp. devel. Aurbach Corp., Phila., 1963-65; exec. v.p. Leasco Systems & Rsch., Bethesda, Md., 1966-70, Leasco Info. Products, Silver Spring, Md., 1971-74; pres. Remac Info. Corp., Gaithersburg, Md., 1975-82; cons. John Sayer Assocs., Gaithersburg, 1983-94, ret., 1994; numerous presentations in field. Contbr. numerous articles to profl. jours. Recipient Info. Product of Yr. award Info. Industries Assn., 1973. Mem. ASME, Assn. Info. and Image Mgmt., Am. Inst. Info. Sci. Achievements include direction of work leading to critical path method of planning and scheduling, technical word thesarus, microfiche, data base publishing.

SAYER, MICHAEL, physics educator; b. Newport, Gwent, Wales, Nov. 6, 1935; emigrated to Can., 1960, naturalized, 1965; s. Charles Claude and Elizabeth Mary (Southcott) S.; m. Anne Moira Rogers, Aug. 27, 1960; children: Jane, Suzanne, Andrew, Christopher. BSc, U. Birmingham, Eng., 1957; PhD, U. Hull, Eng., 1961. Registered profl. engr. Postdoctoral fellow U. B.C., Vancouver, 1960-62; asst. prof. physics Queen's U., Kingston, Ont., 1962-67, assoc. prof., 1967-73, prof., 1973—, head dept. physics, 1977-82; assoc. dean for research Faculty Applied Sci. Queen's U., 1984-87; prof. materials and metallurgical engring. Queens U., Kingston, 1990—; sr. indsl. fellow, dir. research Almax Industries Ltd., 1987-88; vis. fellow Sheffield U., Eng., 1972-73; dir. Cansort Devices Ltd., Kingston, 1977—; vis. asst. prof. Trent U., Peterborough, Ont., 1965-66; mem. Can. Engring. Accreditation Bd., 1987-94. Contbr. articles to profl. jours.; patentee in field. Grantee Natural Sci. and Engring. Rsch. Coun. Can., 1962—; recipient Silver medal for Tech. Transfer Can. Award for Excellence, 1986, Bell Can. award Corp. Higher Edn. Forum, 1996. Fellow Royal Soc. Can., Can. Ceramic Soc. (pres. 1987-88, editor Can. Ceramic Quar. 1986—); mem. Am. Ceramic Soc., Materials Rsch. Soc., Assn. Profl. Engrs. Ont. Roman Catholic. Home: 97 Yonge St, Kingston, ON Canada K7M 1E4 Office: Queen's Univ, Dept Physics, Kingston, ON Canada K7L 3N6

SAYERS, KEN W(ILLIAM), writer and public relations executive; b. N.Y.C., July 31, 1942; s. William Verey and Doris Edith (Weale) S.; m. Rose Mary Beirao, Aug. 20, 1965; children: Wendy Elizabeth, Matthew Verey. BA in Journalism, CCNY, 1965; postgrad., Columbia U., 1970. Dep. chief book br. Office Asst. Sec. of Def. for Pub. Affairs, Washington, 1967-69; mgr. rsch. and analysis DMS, Inc., Greenwich, Conn., 1969-72; mgr. rsch. and publs. Lulejian & Assocs., Inc., Falls Church, Va., 1972-74; mgr. internat. pub. affairs Am. Cyanamid Co., Wayne, N.J., 1974-77; various positions IBM Corp., 1977—; pres. Halyard Ptnrs., Ridgefield, Conn., 1994—. Co-author: Anchors and Atoms, It Was a Very Good Year; author: Industrial Lasers; editor: Missiles and Spacecraft, World Aircraft Forecast; contbr. articles to profl. jours. Exec. officer Queens Nautical Cadets, Astoria, N.Y., 1963-65. Lt. USN, 1965-69. Decorated Joint Svc. Commendation medal. Home: 342 Limestone Rd Ridgefield CT 06877-2635 Office: IBM Corp Rt# 100 Somers NY 10589

SAYERS, MARTIN PETER, pediatric neurosurgeon; b. Big Stone Gap, Va., Jan. 2, 1922; s. Delbert Bancroft and Loula (Thompson) S.; m. Marjorie W. Garvin, May 8, 1943; children: Daniel Garvin Sayers, Stephen Putnam Sayers, Julia Hathaway Sayers Bolton, Elaine King Sayers Buck. B.A., Ohio State U., 1943, M.D., 1945; postgrad., U. Pa., 1948-51. Intern Phila. Gen. Hosp., 1945-46; resident in neurosurgery U. Pa. Hosps., Phila., 1948-51; practice medicine specializing in neurosurgery Columbus, Ohio, 1951—; mem. faculty Ohio State U., Columbus, 1951-87, clin. prof. neurosurgery, 1968-87, emeritus; chief dept. pediatric neurosurgery Ohio State U., 1960-87; cons. Bur. Crippled Children Services Ohio.; Neurosurgeon Project Hope, Ecuador, 1964, Ceylon, 1968, Cracow, Poland, 1979. Served as lt. M.C., USN, 1946-48. Mem. Am. Assn. Neurol. Surgeons (chmn. pediatric sect.), Congress Neurol. Surgeons (pres.), Neurosurg. Soc. Am. (pres.), Am. Soc. Pediatric Neurosurgery, Soc. Neurol. Surgeons. Office: 931 Chatham Ln Columbus OH 43221-2417

SAYERS, RICHARD JAMES, newspaper editor; b. Oil City, Pa., Mar. 16, 1947; s. Theodore Roosevelt and Ardella (Hanna) D.; m. Mary Catherine Smith, Nov. 22, 1974; children—Kelly Lyn, Rachel Richelle, Christopher Alan, Shannon Marie. Student, Albany Bus. Coll., Rochester Ins. Tech. Sports writer Rochester Times-Union, N.Y., 1969-74; sports editor Port Huron Times Herald, Mich., 1974-76; exec. sports editor Boston Herald Am., 1976-79; asst. mng. editor Detroit News, 1979-89; sr. editor THE NATIONAL Sports Daily, N.Y.C., 1989-91; editor Conn. Post, Bridgeport, 1991—. Grad. Multicultural Mgmt. Program fellow U. Mo., 1988. Presbyterian. Home: 98 Neponsit St Stamford CT 06902-4445

SAYETTA, THOMAS CHARLES, physics educator; b. Williamsport, Pa., Apr. 12, 1937; s. Morris and Gladys Pauline (Sunderland) S.; m. Patsy Anne Sherrill; 1 child, Susan Leigh. BS in Physics, U. S.C., 1959, PhD in Physics, 1964. Teaching asst. physics dept. U. S.C., Columbia, 1956-59; engr. RCA, Camden, N.J., 1959-60; teaching asst. physics dept. U. S.C., Columbia, 1960-63, rsch. asst. physics dept., 1963-64; prof. physics East Carolina U., Greenville, N.C., 1964—. Asst. editor Internat. Jour.. Math. and Math. Sci., 1979-83. Nat. treas. Chi Beta Phi, 1974-82. With USNR, 1954-62. Mem. Am. Assn. Physics Tchrs., Sigma Xi (pres. East Carolina U. chpt. 1970-71). Avocations: tennis, basketball. Home: 1117 Hillside Dr Greenville NC 27858-4522 Office: Physics Dept East Carolina U Greenville NC 27858

SAYKALLY, RICHARD JAMES, chemistry educator; b. Rhinelander, Wis., Sept. 10, 1947; s. Edwin L. and Helen M. S. BS, U. Wis., Eau Claire, 1970; PhD, U. Wis., Madison, 1977. Postdoctoral Nat. Bur. Standards, Boulder, Colo., 1977-79; asst. prof. U. Calif., Berkeley, 1979-83, assoc. prof., 1983-86, prof., 1986—, vice chmn. dept. chemistry, 1988-91, Miller Rsch. Prof., 1996; Bergman lectr. Yale U., 1987; Merck-Frost lectr. U. B.C., 1988; Bourke lectr. Royal Soc. Chemistry, 1992; Samuel M. McElvain lectr. U. Wis., Madison, 1995; Harry Emmett Gunning lectr. U. Alta., 1995; prin. investigator Lawrence Berkeley Lab., 1983-91; prin. investigator Sci. for Sci. Tchrs., NSF; mem. Laser Sci. Topical Group Fellowship Com., 1993—; mem. internat. steering com. 12th Internat. Conf. on Laser Spectroscopy, 1995; mem. exec. com. Divsn. Chem. Physics, 1995—. Contbr. over 200 articles to profl. jours.; editl. rev. bd. Jour. Chem. Physics, 1993-95, Molecular Physics, 1983—, Chem. Physics Letters, 1987—, Spectroscopy Mag., 1986—, Rev. of Sci. Instruments, 1987-90, Jour. Molecular Spectroscopy, 1995—. Recipient Disting. Alumnus award U. Wis., Eau Claire, 1987, Bomen Michelson prize for spectroscopy, 1989, E.K. Plyler prize for molecular spectroscopy, 1989, E.R. Lippincott medal OSA, SAS, 1992, Disting. Tchg. award U. Calif., 1992, Humboldt sr. scientist award, 1995; fellow Dreyfuss Found., 1979, Churchill fellow Cambridge U., 1995; Presdl. Young Investigator NSF, 1984-88. Fellow Am. Phys. Soc., Royal Soc. Chemistry, Am. Acad. Arts and Scis.; mem. AAAS, AAUP, Optical Soc. Am., Am. Chem. Soc. (Harrison Howe award 1992). Office: Univ California Dept of Chemistry 419 Latimer Hall # 1460 Berkeley CA 94720-1460

SAYLES, EDWARD THOMAS, theatrical producer; b. Auburn, N.Y., Feb. 19, 1952; s. Thomas Edward and Gilda Marie (Campolieto) S.; m. Sue Ann Kocks (div.); children: Austin, Celeste. BA, SUNY, Cortland, 1974; MA, Bowling Green (Ohio) State U., 1980. Producing dir. Uptown Stage, Cortland, 1975-76, Trotwood (Ohio) Circle Theatre, 1976-80, First St., Dayton, 1978-80, Merry-Go-Round Playhouse, Auburn, N.Y., 1980—; instr. SUNY, Cortland, 1975-76, guest prof., 1985-87; N.Y. State Coun. on the Arts, 1986—. Dir., collaborator original plays including Alice in Wonderland, 1985 (Nat. Showcase award 1988), The Long House, 1994; developed middle sch. playwrighting prog. known as Echoes, 1994-97. Trustee Cayuga County United Way, Auburn, 1988-92, Tomato Festival, 1987-89, Cayuga County Arts Coun., 1994-97, Cayuga Mus., 1990-94. Recipient Creative Support award Nat. Endowment for the Arts, 1977-80, Ohio Arts Coun., 1977-80, Dayton (Ohio) Found., 1977-80, N.Y. State Coun. on the Arts, 1980-97. Mem. Owasco Country Club (bd. dirs.), Phi Alpha Theta (v.p. 1973), Alpha Psi Omega (v.p. 1974). Roman Catholic. Office: Merry Go Round Playhouse PO Box 506 Auburn NY 13021-0506

SAYLES, LEONARD ROBERT, management educator, consultant; b. Rochester, N.Y., Apr. 30, 1926; s. Robert and Rose (Sklof) S.; m. Kathy Ripin; children: Robert, Emily. BA with highest distinction, U. Rochester, 1946; PhD in Econs. and Social Sci, MIT, 1950. Asst. prof. Cornell U., 1950-53, U. Mich., 1953-56; prof. emeritus Grad. Sch. Bus. Adminstrn., Columbia U., 1956-91, prof. bus. adminstrn., 1962—, head div. indsl. relations and orgnl. behavior, 1960-72; adviser to adminstr. NASA, 1966-71; sr. rsch. scientist Ctr. for Creative Leadership, Greensboro, N.C., 1988-94; Disting. vis. lectr. McGill U., 1974; bd. govs. Center for Creative Leadership, 1984-88. Author: (with G. Strauss) The Local Union, 1953, Managerial Behavior, 1964, Human Behavior in Organizations, 1966, (with E. Chapple) Measure of Management, 1961, Behavior of Industrial Work Groups, 1958, Individualism and Big Business, 1963, (with W. Dowling) How Managers Motivate, 1971, (with M. Chandler) Managing Large Systems; Organizations for the Future, 1971, 2d edit., 1993, (with G. Strauss) Personnel, 4th edit, 1980, Managing Human Resources, 2d edit, 1981, Leadership, 1979, (with R. Burgelman) Inside Corporate Innovation, 1985, Managing in Real Organizations, 1989, The Working Leader, 1993; mem. editorial bd. Human Orgn., 1957-62. Trustee Seacrest Sch., 1996-97. Fellow Am. Anthropol. Assn.; mem. Phi Beta Kappa.

SAYLES, THOMAS DYKE, JR., banker; b. Newton Center, Mass., Jan. 16, 1932; s. Thomas Dyke and Eleanor (Norton) S.; m. Patricia Blake, Dec. 11, 1954; children: Lynn Diane, Richard Norton, Stephen Dyke. A.B., Dartmouth, 1954; M.A., N.Y. U., 1961. With Mfrs. Hanover Trust Co., N.Y.C., 1958-70; v.p. Mfrs. Hanover Trust Co., 1966-70, sr. v.p., 1970; dir. Summit Trust Co., Summit, N.J., 1968-95; exec. v.p., chief adminstrn. officer Summit Trust Co., 1970, pres., 1971-80, chmn., 1971-94; chmn., pres., chief exec. officer Summit Bancorp., 1974-87, chmn., chief exec. officer, 1987-94, chmn., 1994-95; bd. dirs. Selective Ins. Group., Inc., Summit Bancorp. Trustee Overlook Hosp., 1972-80, Drew U., 1984—, Papermill Playhouse, 1991-95, NCCJ, 1991—, N.J. Israel Commn., 1991; trustee Summit Speech Sch., 1995—, pres., 1996—. With USAF, 1955-58. Mem. Chatham (N.J.) Jr. C. of C. (dir. 1965), N.J. State C. of C. (trustee 1992-95). Clubs: Baltusrol (Springfield); Canoe Brook (Summit), Pine Valley. Home: 58 Lincoln Ave Chatham NJ 07928-2062 Office: Summit Bancorp 382 Springfield Ave Ste 303 Summit NJ 07901-2707

SAYLOR, LARRY JAMES, lawyer; b. Biloxi, Miss., Nov. 7, 1948; s. Rufus Don and Alice Julia (Kidd) S.; m. Mary L. Mullendore, Dec. 27, 1975; children: David James, Stephen Michael. AB in Political Sci., Miami U., Oxford, Ohio, 1970; M in City and Regional Planning, Ohio State U., 1976; JD, U. Mich., 1976. Bar: D.C. 1976, Mich. 1977, U.S. Ct. Appeals (D.C. cir.) 1977, U.S. Ct. Appeals (6th cir.) 1978, U.S. Supreme Ct. 1981, U.S. Ct. Appeals (10th cir.) 1982. Law clk. to presiding judge U.S. Ct. Appeals (D.C. cir.), Washington, 1976-77; ptnr. Miller, Canfield, Paddock and Stone, Detroit, 1977—. Article editor Mich. Law Rev., 1975-76; contbr. articles to profl. jours. 1st lt. USAF, 1970-72. Mem. ABA (antitrust and litigation sects.), Mich. Bar Assn., (chair antitrust sect. 1994-95), D.C. Bar Assn., World Trade Club, Detroit Econ. Club. Avocations: skiing, woodworking. Home: 455 Lakeland St Grosse Pointe MI 48230-1654 Office: Miller Canfield Paddock & Stone 150 W Jefferson Ave Ste 2500 Detroit MI 48226-4432

SAYLOR, MARK JULIAN, editor; b. Wellsville, N.Y., Mar. 19, 1954; s. Richard Samuel and Naomi (Roth) S.; children: Samuel, Benjamin, Katie. BA cum laude, Harvard Coll., 1976. Staff writer Ark. Democrat, Little Rock, 1976-77; staff writer San Jose (Calif.) Mercury News, 1977-81, asst. met. editor, 1981-82, govt. and politics editor, 1982-85; asst. city editor San Diego County edit. LA Times, L.A., 1985-89, city editor San Diego edit., 1989-91, Calif. polit. editor, 1991-95; entertainment editor Business, 1995—. Avocation: chess master. Office: LA Times Times Mirror Sq Los Angeles CA 90053

SAYLOR, PETER M., architect; b. Phila., July 26, 1941; s. Harry T. and Dorothy (Johnson) S.; m. Caroline Metcalf, Apr. 4, 1970; children: Thomas S., Elizabeth B. BArch, U. Pa., 1963, MArch, 1965. Registered arch., Iowa, Pa., N.J., Ind., Wis., Conn., Ohio, Minn. Architect Mitchell-Giurgola, Phila., 1967-70; ptnr. Dagit-Saylor Architects, Phila., 1970—; design critic, juror U. Pa., 1975—; bd. dirs. Found. for Architecture, Phila., 1980-90. V.p. Chestnut Hill Cmty. Assn., Phila., 1979, bd. dirs. 1976-79; bd. dirs. All Saint's Hosp., Wyndmoor, Pa., 1981-86. Recipient various bldg. design award. Fellow AIA (bd. dirs. Phila. chpt. 1973-82, chpt. pres. 1981-82); mem. Pa. Soc. Archs., Chestnut Hill Hist. Soc. (bd. dirs. 1988-95, pres. 1989-92), Phila. Soc. Preservation of Landmarks (bd. dirs. 1989-96, pres. 1993-94), Phila. Mus. Art (friends bd. dirs. 1990-93), Phila. Cricket Club (bd. dirs. 1985-91), Mask and Wig Club (pres. 1980-81, bd. dirs. 1970-84). Republican. Episcopalian. Office: Dagit-Saylor Archs 100 S Broad St Philadelphia PA 19110-1023

SAYLOR, STEVEN WARREN, writer prose, fiction; b. Port Lavaca, Tex., Mar. 23, 1956; s. Lyman Harrison and Lucy Lee (Reeves) S. BA History, U. Tex., 1978. Author: Roman Blood, 1991, Arms of Nemesis, 1992, Catilina's Riddle, 1993 (Lambda Literary award 1994), The Venus Throw, 1995, A Murder on the Appian Way, 1996, The House of the Vestals, 1997; contbr. short stories, essays to numerous mags. Mem. Mystery Writers of Am. (Robert L. Fish Meml. award 1993). Avocations: bicycling, furniture making, travel. Office: St Martins Press 175 5th Ave New York NY 10010-7703

SAYRE, DAVID, physicist; b. N.Y.C., Mar. 2, 1924; s. Ralph E. and Sylvia (Rosenbaum) S.; m. Anne Bowns, Dec. 26, 1947. BS, Yale U., 1944; MS, Auburn U., 1948; PhD, Oxford (Eng.) U., 1951. Staff mem. radiation lab. MIT, Cambridge, 1943-46; rsch. assoc. U. Pa., Phila., 1951-55; mathematician IBM Corp., N.Y.C., 1955-59, corp. dir. programming, 1959-62; mem. rsch. staff IBM T.J. Watson Rsch. Ctr., Yorktown Heights, N.Y., 1962-90, ret., 1990; cons. U.S. Office Naval Rsch., London, 1951; mem. U.S.A. Nat. Com. for Crystallography, 1952-55, 81-84, vice chmn., 1984-86; vis. fellow All Souls Coll., Oxford U., 1972-73; guest scientist dept. physics SUNY, Stony Brook, 1980—; guest rschr. Brookhaven Nat. Lab., Upton, N.Y., 1983—. Co-author: Waveforms, 1947; editor: Computational Crystallography, 1983; co-editor: Structural Studies on Molecules of Biological Interest, 1983, X-Ray Microscopy II, 1988; contbr. numerous articles to profl. jours. Trustee Village of Head-of-the-Harbor, L.I., N.Y., 1975-95. Mem. Am. Crystallographic Assn. (treas. 1952-55, pres. 1983, Fankuchen award 1989). Episcopalian. Achievements include devel. of atomicity-based direct phasing method for x-ray crystallography, (with others) of first FORTRAN compiler and first virtual computer system; contbns. to x-ray microscopy; first observation (with others) of x-ray diffraction pattern from single biol. cell.

SAYRE, EDWARD VALE, chemist; b. Des Moines, Sept. 8, 1919; s. Edward Agnew and Audrey (Vale) S.; m. Virginia Nelle Rogers, Oct. 20, 1943. BS, Iowa State U., 1941; AM, Columbia U., 1943, PhD, 1949. Mgr. rsch. sect. Manhattan Dist. project Columbia U., 1942-45; rsch. chemist Eastman Kodak Rsch. Labs., Rochester, N.Y., 1949-52; sr. chemist Brookhaven Nat. Lab., Upton, N.Y., 1952-84; rsch. phys. scientist Smithsonian Instn., Washington, 1984—; dir. rsch. Museum Fine Arts, Boston, 1975-80, sr. scientist, 1980-84; sr. scientist Alexander von Humboldt Found., 1980; vis. lectr. Stevens Inst. Tech., 1955-61; adj. prof. fine arts Inst. Fine Arts, N.Y. U., 1960-74; disting. vis. prof. Am. U. Cairo, 1970; Regents prof. U. Calif., Irvine, 1972; mem. sci. adv. coun. Winterthur Mus. Contbr. numerous rsch. articles to profl. jours.; assoc. editor Archaeometry, 1969-93, Art and Archaeology Tech. Abstracts, 1970-87, Jour. Archaeol. Sci., 1971-77. Guggenheim fellow, 1969; recipient U.S. sr. scientist award Alexander von Humboldt Found., 1980-81, George von Hevesy medal, 1984, Alumni Disting. Achievement citation Iowa State U., 1996. Fellow Internat. Inst. for Conservation of Hist. and Artistic Works, Am. Inst. for Conservation of Hist. and Artistic Works; mem. Am. Chem. Soc. Club: Cosmos. Home: 2106 Wilkinson Pl Alexandria VA 22306-2540

SAYRE, E(NOCH) PHILLIP, political scientist, state official, retired; b. Humboldt, Iowa, Apr. 19, 1926; s. Enoch Franklin and Grace Irene (Rusk) S.; m. Mary-Ellen Silverstone, May 25, 1957; children: Michael Franklin, Elisabeth Carol Sayre Lozinsky. BA, U. Wash., 1950; postgrad., Georgetown U., 1951-54. Campaign mgr. Congressman Henry M. Jackson and Senator W.G. Magnuson, Skagit County, Wash., 1950; mem. campaign staff Henry M. Jackson for U.S. Senate, Wash., 1953; adminstrv. asst. to Congressman John Lesinski, U.S. Ho. of Reps., Washington, 1954-56; ins. agt. State Mut. Life Assurance Co., Washington, 1956-62; staff assoc. J.D. Marsh & Assocs., Inc., Washington, 1962-64; dir. fin. planning, supr. ins. Capital Plans, Washington, 1964-68; v.p., registered prin. Diversified Planning Corp., Washington, 1968-70; adminstrv. analyst dept. fiscal svcs. Md. Gen. Assembly, Annapolis, 1970-80, sr. adminstrv. analyst, 1980-96; staff dir. Md. Commn. on Intergovtl. Cooperation, 1974-78. Chmn. legis. com. Young Dems. D.C., 1954-56; co-founder Md. Com. for Fair Representation, 1960-62; chmn. issues com. We. Suburban Dem. Club Montgomery County, Md., 1962-64; mem. Md. Constl. Conv. Commn., 1965-67; co-chmn. Dem. Com. for Constn., Md., 1968; mem. steering com. Citizens for Proposed Constn. Md., 1968. Recipient resolution Md. Ho. of Dels., 1963, 65, Young Dem. of Yr. award Young Dems. Md., 1965, Outstanding Civic Achievement award Young Dems. Montgomery County, 1966. Mem. Am. Soc. for Pub. Adminstrn., World Future Soc., Bannockburn Civic Assn., Bannockburn Cmty. Club, Washington Ethical Soc. Avocations: reading, futurist interests, walking, outdoors, nature. Home: 6809 Laverock Ct Bethesda MD 20817-4912

SAYRE, FRANCIS BOWES, JR., clergyman; b. Washington, Jan. 17, 1915; s. Francis Bowes and Jessie Woodrow (Wilson) S.; m. Harriet Taft Hart, June 8, 1946; children: Jessie Wilson, Thomas Hart, Harriet Brownson, Francis Nevin. A.B. cum laude, Williams Coll., 1937, D.D. (hon.), 1963; M.Div., Episcopal Theol. Sch., Cambridge, Mass., 1940; L.H.D. (hon.), Wooster Coll., 1956; D.D. (hon.), Va. Theol. Sch., 1957, Wesleyan U., Conn., 1958, Hobart Coll., 1966; S.T.D. (hon.), Queen's U., Belfast, 1966; Litt.D. (hon.), Lehigh U., Ursinus Coll., 1973. Ordained to ministry Episcopal Ch., 1940; asst. minister Christ Ch., Cambridge, 1940-42; indsl. chaplain Diocese of Ohio, Cleve., 1946-51; rector St. Paul's Ch., East Cleveland, Ohio, 1947-51; dean Washington Cathedral, 1951-78; asso. dir. Woodrow Wilson Internat. Center for Scholars, Washington, 1978-79; Chmn. bd. Detroit Indsl. Mission, 1956-68; chmn. U.S. Com. for Refugees, 1958-61. Bd. dirs. Presbyn. Ministers Fund; pres. Martha's Vineyard Hosp., 1981-83. Served as chaplain USNR, 1942-46. Recipient Clergyman of Yr.

award Religious Heritage Am., 1976; Disting. Pub. Service medal NASA, 1977. Mem. Sigma Phi.

SAYRE, JOHN MARSHALL, lawyer, former government official; b. Boulder, Colo., Nov. 9, 1921; s. Henry Marshall and Lulu M. (Cooper) S.; m. Jean Miller, Aug. 22, 1943; children: Henry M., Charles Franklin, John Marshall Jr., Ann Elizabeth Sayre Taggart (dec.). BA, U. Colo., 1943, JD, 1948. Bar: Colo. 1948, U.S. Dist. Ct. Colo. 1952, U.S. Ct. Appeals (10th cir.) 1964. Law clk. trust dept. Denver Nat. Bank, 1948-49; asst. cashier, trust officer Nat. State Bank of Boulder, 1949-50; ptnr. Ryan, Sayre, Martin, Brotzman, Boulder, 1950-66, Davis, Graham & Stubbs, Denver, 1966-89, of counsel, 1993—; asst. sec. of the Interior for Water and Sci., 1989-93. Bd. dirs. Boulder Sch. Dist. 3, 1951-57; city atty. City of Boulder, 1952-55; gen. counsel Colo. Mcpl. League, 1956-63; prin. counsel No. Colo. Water Conservancy Dist. and mcpl. subdist., 1964-87, spl. counsel, 1987, bd. dirs. dist., 1960-64; former legal counsel Colo. Assn. Commerce and Industry. Lt. (j.g.) USNR, 1943-46, ret. Decorated Purple Heart. Fellow Am. Bar. Found. (life), Colo. Bar Found. (life); mem. ABA, Colo. Bar Assn., Boulder County Bar Assn. (pres. 1959), Denver Bar Assn., Nat. Water Resources Assn. (Colo. dir. 1980-89, 93-95, pres. 1984-86), Denver Country Club, Univ. Club, Mile High Club, Phi Beta Kappa, Phi Gamma Delta, Phi Delta Phi. Republican. Episcopalian. Home: Davis Graham & Stubbs 355 Ivanhoe St Denver CO 80220-5841 Office: Davis Graham & Stubbs PO Box 185 Denver CO 80201-0185

SAYRE, KENNETH MALCOLM, philosophy educator; b. Scottsbluff, Nebr., Aug. 13, 1928; s. Harry Malcolm and Mildred Florence (Potts) S.; m. Lucille Margaret Shea, Aug. 19, 1958 (dec. Apr. 1980); children: Gregory, Christopher, Jeffrey; m. Patricia Ann White, Apr. 4, 1983; 1 child, Michael. A.B., Grinnell Coll., Iowa, 1952; M.A., Harvard U., 1954, Ph.D., 1958. Asst. dean Grad. Sch. Arts and Letters Harvard U., Cambridge, Mass., 1953-56; systems analyst MIT, Cambridge, Mass., 1956-58; from instr. to prof. philosophy U. Notre Dame, Ind., 1958—, dir. Philosophic Inst., 1966—. Author: Recognition, 1965, Consciousness, 1969, Plato's Analytic Method, 1969, Cybernetics and the Philosophy of Mind, 1976, Moonflight, 1977, Starburst, 1977, Plato's Late Ontology, 1983, Plato's Literary Garden, 1995. Served with USN, 1946-48. NSF grantee, 1962-79; NEH fellow, 1995-96. Mem. Am. Philos. Assn., Phi Beta Kappa. Home: 910 Weber Sq South Bend IN 46617-1850 Office: Univ Notre Dame Dept Philosophy Notre Dame IN 46556

SAYRE, LINDA DAMARIS, human resources professional; b. Washington, Nov. 26, 1945; d. Wallace Stanley and Kathryn Louise (McKnight) S. BA in English, Wells Coll., 1967; MA in Sociology, U. Sussex, Brighton, Eng., 1969; postgrad., Rutgers U., 1993—. Human resources specialist N.Y.C. Human Resources Adminstrn., 1967-68; rsch. assoc. Presdl. Campaign Gov. Nelson Rockefeller, N.Y.C., 1968; edml. coord. Isabella Geriat. Ctr., N.Y.C., 1970-72; rsch. assoc. N.Y.C. Mayor's Commn. on City Fins., 1973-75; project mgr. The Urban Acad. for Mgmt., N.Y.C., 1976-80; intern and external tng. cons. Boston and N.Y.C., 1980-83; tng. cons. N.Y.C. Bd. of Edn., N.Y.C., 1983-84; tng. and edn. dir. Gen. Hosp. Ctr., Passaic, N.J., 1984-87; dir. human rels. Bronx (N.Y.) Lebanon Hosp., 1987-90; external cons. Atlanta, N.Y.C., 1990-95; tng. & devel. mgr. BOC Gases, Murray Hill, N.J., 1995—. Mem. steering com. Broadway Dems., N.Y.C., 1974-80, 1993-96, pres., 1975, 77; coord. Carter Presdl. Campaign, N.Y. 20th Congl. Dist., 1976; bd. Westside Cares Food Voucher, N.Y.C., 1993-95. Mem. ASTD (v.p. programs No. N.J. 1985-86, chmn. nat. affairs Atlanta 1991), N.Y. ASTD (v.p. prof. edn. 1993, pres. 1994, past pres. 1995, co-chair adv. coun. 1996, nat. leadership design com. 1995—). Democrat. Avocations: writing, community service. Home: 448 Riverside Dr New York NY 10027

SAYRE, RICHARD LAYTON, lawyer; b. Spokane, Wash., May 21, 1953; s. Charles Layton and Elizabeth Jane (Ward) S.; m. Karen Linda Sayre, Mar. 8, 1979; children: Wendi Sue Jackman, Tracey Lynn Turner. BA, U. Wash., 1976; JD, Gonzaga U., 1979. Bar: Wash. 1979, U.S. Dist. Ct. (ea. and we. dist.) Wash. 1979, U.S. Ct. Appeals (9th cir.) 1986; cert. elder law atty. Nat. Elder Law Found. Deputy prosecuting atty. Spokane County, Spokane, 1979-84; shareholder Underwood, Campbell, Brock & Cerutti, Spokane, 1984-92, Sayre & Sayre P.S., Spokane, 1992—; pres. Nat. Acad. Elder Law Attys., Washington, 1995-96. Potentate, trustee El Katif Shrine Temple, Spokane, 1997—; bd. govs. Shriner's Hosp. for Children, Spokane, 1993-96; exec. officer Order of DeMolay, Washington, 1993—, active mem. internat. supreme coun. Recipient Pro Bono award Spokane County Bar Assn., 1991, Recognition of Achievement & Contribution award Lutheran Social Svcs. of Washington, Idaho, 1992. Mem. Nat. Acad. Elder Law Attys., Spokane Estate Planning Coun. Democrat. Episcopal. Avocations: sailing, skiing. Office: Sayre & Sayre 111 W Cataldo Ave Ste 210 Spokane WA 99201-3203

SAYRE, ROBERT FREEMAN, English language educator; b. Columbus, Ohio, Nov. 6, 1933; s. Harrison M. and Mary (White) S.; (divorced); children—Gordon, Nathan, Laura; m. Hutha Refle, May 7, 1988. B.A., Wesleyan U., Middletown, Conn., 1955; Ph.D., Yale U., 1962. Instr. English U. Ill., Urbana, 1961-63; Fulbright lectr. Lund (Sweden) U., 1963-65; mem. faculty U. Iowa, 1965—, prof. English, 1972—; dir. inter-profl. seminars NEH, 1978, 79; Fulbright lectr. Montpellier, France, 1984; exch. prof. U. Copenhagen, 1988-89; mem. adv. bd. Leopold Ctr. for Sustainable Agr., 1994—. Author: The Examined Self: Benjamin Franklin, Henry Adams and Henry James, 1964, Adventures, Rhymes and Designs of Vachel Lindsay, 1968; Thoreau and the American Indians, 1977; editor: A Week on the Concord and Merrimac Rivers, Walden, The Maine Woods, Cape Cod (H.D. Thoreau), 1985, Take This Exit: Rediscovering the Iowa Landscape, 1989, New Essays on Walden, 1992, American Lives: An Anthology of Autobiographical Writing, 1994; contbr. articles and revs. to profl. jours. Guggenheim fellow, 1973-74. Mem. Am. Studies Assn., MLA. Office: U Iowa English Dept Iowa City IA 52242

SAYRE, ROBERT MARION, ambassador; b. Hillsboro, Oreg., Aug. 18, 1924; s. William Octavius and Mary Sayre; m. Elora Amanda Moyhihan, Dec. 29, 1951; children: Marian Amanda, Robert Marion, Daniel Humphrey. B.A. summa cum laude, Willamette U., 1949; J.D. cum laude (Alexander Welborn Weddell Peace prize 1956), George Washington U., 1956; M.A., Stanford U., 1960; LL.D., Willamette U., 1965. Bar: D.C. 1956, U.S. Ct. Appeals 1956, U.S. Supreme Ct. 1962. Joined U.S. Fgn. Service, 1949; econ. adviser on Latin Am., 1950-52, mil. adviser, 1952-57, officer charge inter-Am. security affairs, 1955-57; polit. counselor embassy Lima, Peru, 1958-59; fin. attache embassy Havana, Cuba, 1960; exec. sec. Task Force Latin Am., State Dept., 1961, officer charge Mexican affairs, 1961-63; dep. dir. Office Caribbean and Mexican Affairs, 1963-64; dir. Office Mexican Affairs, 1964; sr. staff mem. White House, 1964-65; sr. dep. asst. sec. Bur. Inter-Am. Affairs, Dept. State, 1965-68; acting asst. sec. Dept. State, 1967—; Am. ambassador to Uruguay, 1968-69, to Panama, 1969-74; sr. insp. Dept. State, 1974-75, insp. gen., 1975-78; ambassador to Brazil, 1978-81; chmn. U.S. Interdepartmental group on Terrorism, dir. Counter-terrorism and Emergency Planning Dept. State, 1981-84, sr. insp., 1985; ptnr. IRC Group, Inc., 1986-87; adv. to U.S. rep. Orgn. of Am. States, 1985-87, under sec. for mgmt., 1987-94; sr. assoc. Global Bus. Access, Ltd., Washington, 1995—; chair Open Forum Working Group on Internat. Econs. U.S. Dept. State, 1995-96. Sr. councilor Atlantic Coun. Washington Inst. Fgn. Affairs. Capt. AUS, WWII; col. REs., ret. Decorated Soc. Cross (Brazil); Cross of Balboa (Panama); recipient Outstanding Employee award Dept. State, 1952, Superior Honor awards, 1964, 75, Disting. Honor award, 1978, Outstanding Performance award, 1982, 83, 84, 85, Presdl. Meritorious award, 1986, Fgn. Svc. Cup award, 1990, Sec.'s Cert. of Appreciation, U.S. Dept. State, 1996. Mem. Blue Key, Phi Delta Theta, Phi Eta Sigma, Tau Kappa Alpha. Episcopalian. Club: Cosmos, Dacor. Home: 3714 Bent Branch Rd Falls Church VA 22041-1028 Office: Global Business Access Ltd 1825 I St NW Ste 400 Washington DC 20006-5415

SAYSETTE, JANICE ELAINE, vertebrate paleontologist, zoo archaeologist; b. San Francisco, Feb. 27, 1949; d. James Monroe and Isabel Christine (Saysette) Heffern; m. Thomas Arthur Haygood, Aug. 6, 1978 (div. June 1991); children: Grant Thomas, Ian James. AA in Nursing, Ohlone Coll., 1974; BSN, Metro State, 1981; MSN, U. Colo., 1982; MA in Anthropology, Colo. State U., 1990, postgrad., 1991—. Staff nurse Palo Alto (Calif.) VA Hosp., 1974-75, San Jose (Calif.) Hosp., 1975-78, O'Connor Hosp., San Jose, 1978-80; clin. nursing instr. U. No. Colo., Greeley, 1982-87; nursing supr. Poudre Valley Hosp., Ft. Collins, Colo., 1988-89; grad. teaching asst. Colo. State U., Ft. Collins, 1988-90, ind. contractor-zooarchaeology, 1990—; crew mem. U. Wyo. Lookingbill Archaeological Site, 1991; crew chief Denver Mus. Natural History Porqupine Cave Paleontological Site, 1993; lectr., presenter in field. Mem. Am. Soc. Mammalogists, Internat. Coun. Archaeozoology, Soc. Am. Archaeology, Soc. Vertebrate Paleontology. Democrat. Avocation: fly fishing, hiking. Office: Colo State U Dept of Biology Fort Collins CO 80523

SAYWELL, WILLIAM GEORGE GABRIEL, foundation administrator; b. Regina, Sask., Can., Dec. 1, 1936; s. John Ferdinand Tupper and Vera Marguerite S.; m. Helen Jane Larmer; children: Shelley Jayne, William James Tupper, Patricia Lynn. BA, U. Toronto, 1960, MA, 1961, PhD, 1968; LLD (hon.), U. B.C., 1994. Asst. prof. dept. East Asian studies U. Toronto, Ont., Ont., Can., 1963-69; asst. prof. U. Toronto, Ont., Can., 1969-71, assoc. prof., 1971-82, prof., 1982-83, chmn. dept., 1971-76; prof. dept. history, pres. Simon Fraser U., Burnaby, B.C., Can., 1983-93; pres., chief exec. officer Asia Pacific Found. of Can., Vancouver, B.C., 1993—; sinologist and 1st sec. Can. Embassy, Beijing, 1972-73; dir. U. Toronto-York U. Ctr. Modern East Asia, 1974-75; prin. Innis Coll., 1976-79; vice provost U. Toronto, 1979-83; dir. Westcoast Energy, Spar Aerospace, Western Garnet Internat. Author articles and revs. on Chinese affairs to profl. jours. Decorated Order B.C. Office: Asia Pacific Found Can, 666-999 Canada Pl, Vancouver, BC Canada V6C 3E1

SAZEGAR, MORTEZA, artist; b. Tehran, Iran, Nov. 11, 1933; s. Hassan Ali and Zahra (Frootan) S.; m. Patricia Jean Kaurich, July 13, 1959. B.A., U. Tex., El Paso, 1955, B.S., 1956; postgrad., Baylor U. Coll. Medicine, 1956-57, Cornell U., 1958-59. One man exhibitions include, Poindexter Gallery, N.Y.C., 1964, 67, 69, 71, 73, 75, 77, group exhibitions include, Detroit Inst. Arts, 1965, Chgo. Art Inst., 1965, Univ. Art Mus., U. Tex., Austin, 1965, 72, Whitney Mus. Am. Art, 1970, Cleve. Mus. Art, 1972, Corcoran Gallery Art, Washington, 1973, Tyler Sch. Art, Temple U., Phila., 1979; represented in permanent collections, Whitney Mus. Am. Art, N.Y.C., San Francisco Mus. Modern Art, Riverside Mus., N.Y.C., U. Mass., Amherst, Corcoran Gallery Art, Prudential Ins. Corp. Am., Mus. Contemporary Art, Tehran, Iran. Mem. Artists Equity Assn. Democrat. Address: 1223 Homeville Rd Cochranville PA 19330

SAZIMA, HENRY JOHN, oral and maxillofacial surgery educator; b. Cleve., Dec. 25, 1927; s. Henry Charles and Frances (Masin) S.; m. Carol Ann Watson, Sept. 10, 1955; 1 child, Holly Ann Sazima Davani. BS, Case Western Res. U., 1948, DDS, 1953; grad. sch. medicine, U. Pa., 1956-57; grad. sch. edn., Chapman Coll., 1967-69. Diplomate Am. Bd. Oral and Maxillofacial Surgery. Chief maxillfacial div. Naval Support Act, Saigon, Republic of Viet Nam, 1969-70; chmn. dental dept. Naval Med. Ctr., Phila., 1971-73, San Diego, 1979-80; spl. asst. dentistry Sec. Def. Health Affairs, Washington, 1973-77; comdg. officer Naval Dental Ctr., Parris Island, S.C., 1977-79; dep. chief dental div. Bur. Medicine and Surgery, Washington, 1980-82; comdg. officer Nat. Naval Dental Ctr., Bethesda, Md., 1982-83; dir. resources div. Chief Naval Ops., Washington, 1983-84; dep. commdr. for readiness and logistics Naval Med. Command, Washington, 1984-87, ret. rear admiral, 1987; now clin. assoc. prof. oral and maxillofacial surgery Georgetown U. Med. Ctr.; exec. dir. Acad. Dentistry Internat., 1988—; emeritus, 1995; cons., lectr., researcher in field. Co-author: Management of War Injuries, 1977; contbr. articles to profl. jours. Recipient Residents award St. Vincent Charity Hosp., 1957. Fellow Am. Coll. Dentists, Assn. Oran and Maxillofacial Surgeons, Internat. Assn. Oral and Maxillofacial Surgeons, Acad. Dentistry Internat. (Blue Cloud award 1995); mem. Brit. Soc. Oral and Maxillofacial Surgeons, European Assn. Maxillofacial Surgery, Assn. Mil. Surgeons of U.S. (chmn. internat. com. 1984-86, Margetis award 1971), Internat. Coll. Dentists (dep. regent 1971-87), Omicron Kappa Upsilon, Delta Tau Delta, Psi Omega. Republican. Roman Catholic. Club: Mil. Order of CARABAO. Avocations: sports, tennis, music, travel. Home: 4924 Sentinel Dr Apt 105 Bethesda MD 20816-3506 Office: Acad Dentistry Internat Office of Exec Dir Ste 50 5125 Macarthur Blvd NW Washington DC 20016-3300

SBARBARO, ROBERT ARTHUR, banker; b. Bklyn., Jan. 24, 1933; s. John Vincent and Louise Olga (Perigone) S.; m. Kathleen Ann Noonan, Sept. 12, 1959; children—Robert, Paul, Nancy. B.A., Wagner Coll., 1954; grad., Stonier Sch. Banking, Rutgers U., 1977. CFP. Programming mgr. IBM, 1956-59; regional ops. mgr. Univac, 1959-65; asst. v.p., mgr. Computax Corp., N.Y.C., 1965-70; sr. v.p. Irving Trust Co., N.Y.C., 1970-89; pres. SPAR Cons., Montvale, N.J., 1989—. Mem. Montvale (N.J.) Recreation Commn., 1979-80; treas. Pascack Hills High Sch. Parents Assn., 1978-79; trustee Wagner Coll. Served with U.S. Navy, 1954-56. Recipient Alumni Achievement award Wagner Coll., 1987—. Mem. Data Processing Mgmt. Assn., Am. Banking Assn., Data Security Inst., Internat. Assn. for Fin. Planning. Republican. Roman Catholic. Avocation: sports. Home: 14 Sunrise Dr Montvale NJ 07645-1044 Office: SPAR Cons 14 Sunrise Dr Montvale NJ 07645-1044

SBUTTONI, KAREN RYAN, reading specialist; b. Albany, Sept. 9, 1953; d. Patrick Frederick and Virginia Mary (Moore) Ryan; m. Michael James Sbuttoni, Aug. 9, 1975; children: Michael Louis, Ashley Ryan. BS in Bus. Edn., Buffalo State Coll., 1979; MS in Bus. Edn., SUNY, Albany, 1983, MS in Reading, 1991, CAS in reading, 1994. Cert. reading specialist K-12 and bus. edn. 7-12, N.Y. Tchr. Williamsville East H.S., Buffalo, N.Y., spring 1979, East Irondequoit H.S., Rochester, N.Y., 1979-81; reading specialist, mem. admissions com. and outcomes com. Albany Acad., 1992—; tchg. asst. SUNY, Albany, 1992. Religious edn. tchr. St. Pius X Ch., Loudonville, N.Y., 1982-84. Mem. Internat. Reading Assn., Nat. Coun. Tchrs. English. Avocations: skiing, biking, reading, cross-stitching. Office: Albany Acad Academy Rd Albany NY 12208

SCAFE, LINCOLN ROBERT, JR., sales executive; b. Cleve., July 28, 1922; s. Lincoln Robert and Charlotte (Hawkins) S.; student Cornell U., 1940-41; m. Mary Anne Wilkinson, Nov. 14, 1945; children—Amanda Katharine, Lincoln Robert III. Service mgr. Avery Engring. Co., Cleve., 1946-51; nat. service mgr. Trane Co., LaCrosse, Wis., 1951-57; service and installation mgr. Mech. Equipment Supply Co., Honolulu, 1957-58; chief engr. Sam P. Wallace of Pacific, Honolulu, 1958-62; pres. Air Conditioning Service Co., Inc., Honolulu, 1962-84; sales engr. G.J. Campbell & Assocs., Seattle, 1984-89. Served with USNR, 1942-45; PTO. Mem. ASHRAE, Alpha Delta Phi. Clubs: Cornell Hawaii (past pres.); Outrigger Canoe. Republican. Author tech. service lit. and parts manuals; contbr. articles to trade publs. Home: 10721 SW 112th St Vashon WA 98070-3044 Office: GJ Campbell and Assocs 11613 Rainier Ave S Seattle WA 98178-3945

SCAFFIDI, JUDITH ANN, school volunteer program administrator; b. Bklyn., Aug. 2, 1950; d. Anthony William and Rose Virginia (Nocera) S. BA, SUNY, Plattsburg, 1972, MS, 1973; postgrad. Kennedy Learning Ctr., Einstein Coll. Medicine, 1983; PhD (hon.), Internat. U. Bombay, 1993; HHD (hon.), London Inst. Applied Rsch., 1993. Cert. secondary edn. English. VISTA mem. ACTION, N.Y.C., 1976-77; coord. cultural resources N.Y.C. Sch. Vol. Program, N.Y.C., 1977-80; dist. coord. in Bklyn. N.Y.C. Sch. Vol. Program, 1980—; field supr., adj. faculty Coll. for Human Svcs., N.Y.C., 1984-86; adv. coun. chairperson Ret. Sr. Vol. Program in Bklyn., 1983-86; adv. bd. Ret. Sr. Vol. Program in N.Y.C., 1983-86. Mem. Am. Friends Svc. Com., 1994—. Recipient award for svcs. in promotion literacy Internat. Reading Assn. and Bklyn. Reading Coun., 1986, award for outstanding leadership Ret. Sr. Vol. Program, 1986, cert. of appreciation Mayor City of N.Y., 1991,. Mem. NAFE, Cath. Tchrs. Assn. Bklyn. (del. sch. dist. 18, 1982-91), Internat. Platform Assn., World Found. Successful Women, Am. Biog. Inst. (rsch. bd. advisors 1992-93), Am. Biog. Inst. Rsch. Assn. (bd. govs. 1992—), Internat. Parliament for Safety and Peace (dep. mem. and diplomatic passport), Maisson Internat. de Intellectuels (Acad. MIDI), Cath. Alumni Club N.Y., Amnesty Internat. Roman Catholic. Avocations: foreign and domestic travel, reading, walking. Home: 2330 Ocean Ave Apt 3H Brooklyn NY 11229-3036 Office: NYC Sch Vol Program 352 Park Ave S Fl 13 New York NY 10010-1709

SCAFFIDI-WILHELM, GLORIA ANGELAMARIE, elementary education educator; b. Vineland, N.J., June 3, 1960; d. Joseph J. and Gloria (Izzi) Scaffidi; m. Andrew H. Wilhelm, Nov. 7, 1992. BA summa cum laude, Glassboro State Coll., 1982. Cert. tchr. elem. edn., N.J. Tchr. 3rd grade St. Nicholas Sch., Egg Harbor City, N.J., 1982-85; 4th grade tchr. Charles L. Spragg Sch., Egg Harbor City, N.J., 1986—; advisor cheerleading club Egg Harbor City Schs., 1988-91, journalism club, 1989-93, staff mem. yearbook com., 1990-94, 96-97, editor sch. newspaper, 1989-94, 96-97, advisor pub. rels. sch. activities, 1989-94, 96-97. Named Tchr. of Yr., Egg Harbor City Schs., 1989-90. Mem. N.J. Edn. Assn., Kappa Delta Pi. Roman Catholic.

SCAGLIONE, ALDO DOMENICO, literature educator; b. Turin, Italy, Jan. 10, 1925; came to U.S., 1951, naturalized, 1958; s. Teodoro and Angela (Grasso) S.; m. Jeanne M. Daman, June 28, 1952 (dec. June 1986); m. Marie M. Burns, Aug. 28, 1992. D.Modern Letters, U. Torino, 1948. Lectr. U. Toulouse, France, 1949-51; instr. Italian U. Chgo., 1951-52; mem. faculty U. Calif., Berkeley, 1952-68, prof. Italian and comparative lit., 1963-68, chmn. dept. Italian, 1963-65; W.R. Kenan prof. Romance langs., comparative lit. U. N.C., Chapel Hill, 1968-87; prof. Italian NYU, N.Y.C., 1987—, chmn. Italian dept., 1989-93, Erich Maria Remarque prof. lit., 1991—; vis. prof. Romance langs. Yale, 1965-66; vis. prof. comparative lit. Grad. Center, City U. N.Y., 1971-72; vis. prof. Italian, U. Va., fall, 1986; H.F. Johnson research prof. Inst. for Research in Humanities, Madison, Wis., 1981-82; Asso. Columbia U. Renaissance Seminar. Author: Nature and Love in the Late Middle Ages, 1963, Ars Grammatica, 1970, The Classical Theory of Composition, 1972, The Theory of German Word Order, 1981, Komponierte Prosa von der Antike bis zur Gegenwart, 2 vols., 1981, The Liberal Arts and the Jesuit College System, 1986, Knights at Court: Courtliness, Chivalry, and Courtesy from Ottonian Germany to the Italian Renaissance, 1991; also articles; editor: Orlando Innamorato, Amorum Libri, 2 vols., rev. edit., 1963, Francis Petrarch, Six Centuries Later: A Symposium, 1975, Ariosto 1974 in America, 1976, The Emergence of National Languages: A Symposium, 1984, The Divine Comedy and The Encyclopedia of Arts and Sciences, 1987, The Image of the Baroque, 1995, Series L'Interprete and Speculum Artium, Longo Editore, Ravenna, 1976—, (with Peter Lang) Series Studies in Italian Culture: Literature in History, 1989—; editor: Italian Culture, 1978-80; gen. editor: Romance Notes and N.C. Studies in Romance Langs. and Lits., 1971-75; assoc. editor: Romance Philology, 1963—, N.C. Studies in Comparative Literature, 1968-87, Studies in Philology, 1969-87, Amsterdam Studies in the History of Linguistics, 1973—, Annali d'Italianstica, 1983—, The Comparatist, 1983—, Differentia, 1984—, Italica, 1984—; U.S. corr.: Studi Francesi, 1961—. Chmn. Berkeley campus campaign Woodrow Wilson Nat. Found., 1964-65. Served with Italian Liberation Army, 1944-45. Decorated Knight Order of Merit (Italy); Fulbright fellow, 1951; Guggenheim fellow, 1958; Newberry Library sr. resident fellow Chgo., 1965; fellow Southeastern Inst. for Medieval and Renaissance Studies, 1968; fellow Cini Found. Program in Medieval and Renaissance Culture, 1973; fellow German Acad. Exchange, W.Ger., 1977, 80; fellow Rockefeller Found. Conf. and Study Center, Bellagio, Italy, 1978; dir. NEH Seminar for Coll. Tchrs., Chapel Hill, N.C., 1981. Mem. MLA (exec. coun. 1981-85), Internat. Linguistic Assn., N.Am. Assn. for History of Lang. Scis. (pres. 1989-92), Am. Boccaccio Assn. (pres. 1980-81), Am. Assn. Italian Studies (v.p. 1981-83, hon. pres. 1988-89), Renaissance Soc. Am., Dante Soc. Am. (coun. 1975-78, 81-83, 89-92), Am. Assn. Tchrs. Italian, Medieval Acad. Am., Am. Comparative Lit. Assn., Renaissance Soc. No. Calif. (pres. 1962-63). Home: 3 Reading Ave Frenchtown NJ 08825-1013 Office: 24 W 12th St New York NY 10011-8604

SCAIFE, RICHARD MELLON, philanthropist; married; 2 children. Mgr. Scaife Newspapers. Chmn., trustee Sarah Scaife Found., Inc.; donor, chmn., trustee Carthage Found., Allegheny Found. Office: Scaife Family Found 3 Mellon Bank Ctr 525 William Penn Pl Ste 3900 Pittsburgh PA 15219-1708*

SCALA, JAMES, health care industry consultant, author; b. Ramsey, N.J., Sept. 16, 1934; s. Edvigi and Lorene (Hendricksen) S.; m. Nancy Peters, June 15, 1957; children: James, Gregory, Nancy, Kimberly. BA, Columbia U., 1960; PhD, Cornell U., 1964; postgrad., Harvard U., 1968. Staff scientist Miami Valley Labs., Procter and Gamble Co., 1964-66; head life scis., dir. fundamental rsch. Owens Ill. Corp., 1966-71; dir. nutrition T.J. Lipton Inc., 1971-75; dir. health scis. Gen. Foods Corp., 1975-78; v.p. sci. and tech. Shaklee Corp., San Francisco, 1978-85, sr. v.p. sci. affairs, 1986-87; lectr. Georgetown U. Med. Sch., U. Calif.-Berkeley extension. Author: Making the Vitamin Connection, 1985, The Arthritis Relief Diet, 1987, 89, Eating Right for a Bad Gut, 1990, 92, The High Blood Pressure Relief Diet, 1988, 90, Look 10 Years Younger, Feel 10 Years Better, 1991, 93, Prescription for Longevity, 1992, 94, If You Can't/Won't Stop Smoking, 1993; editor: Nutritional Determinants in Athletic Performance, 1981, New Protective Roles for Selected Nutrients, 1989; columnist Dance mag.; contbr. articles on nutrition and health scis. to profl. publs. With USAF, 1953-56. Disting. scholar U. Miami, Fla., 1977, Fla. Atlantic U., 1977. Mem. AAAS, Am. Inst. Nutrition, Am. Coll. Nutrition, Brit. Nutrition Soc., Sports Medicine Coun., Am. Soc. Cell Biology, Inst. Food Technologists, Astron. Soc. Pacific (bd. dirs., chmn. devel. coun.), Am. Dietetic Assn., Olympic Club (San Francisco), Oakland Yacht Club, Sigma Xi. Republican. *I am in awe of the incredible resiliency of living things, but most of all the human spirit.*

SCALA, JOHN CHARLES, secondary education educator, astronomer; b. Summit, N.J., Mar. 20, 1958; s. John Michael and Lola Ann (Bevilacque) S.; m. Virginia Anne Ronen, Oct. 11, 1980; children: Aubrey Lyn, Valerie Anne. BA in Astronomy, Lycoming Coll., 1980. Tchr. Stetson Mid. Sch., West Chester, Pa., 1980-82, Mendham (N.J.) H.S., 1982-83, Hopatcong (N.J.) Mid. Sch., 1983; shipment insp. Ciba-Geigy Pharms., Summit, 1983-87; tchr., dir. planetarium Lenape Valley H.S., Stanhope, N.J., 1987—; adj. prof. astronomy County Coll. Morris, Randolph, N.J., 1983-89, Sussex County C.C., Newton, N.J., 1989—; resource tchr. Am. Astron. Soc., Austin, Tex., 1994—. Merit badge counsellor Morris-Sussex coun. Boy Scouts Am., 1988—. Recipient Gov.'s Recognition award N.J. Dept. Edn., 1991, award A-Plus for Kids Network, 1993; named Tchr. of Yr., Lenape Valley H.S., 1995; Geraldine R. Dodge Found. grantee, summer 1993. Mem. NSTA, Internat. Planetarium Soc., Mid. Atlantic Planetarium Soc., Garden State Planetarium Resource Assn. Avocations: photography, reading, camping. Office: Lenape Valley HS Planetarium Sparta Rd Stanhope NJ 07874

SCALA, MARILYN CAMPBELL, special education educator, writer, consultant; b. Lansing, Mich., June 25, 1942; d. Coral Edward and Eloise (Doolittle) Campbell; children: Nicholas, Anne. BS Edn., U. Mich., 1964; MA Spl. Edn., Columbia U., 1967. Cert. elem. edn., spl. edn. tchr., N.Y. Tchr. physically handicapped Multi-Age, Port Chester, N.Y., 1964-66; tchr. spl. edn. PS 199, N.Y.C., 1966-69, Manhattan Sch. for Seriously Disturbed, N.Y.C., 1969-70; tchr. regular and spl. edn. Munsey Park Sch., Manhasset, N.Y., 1970—. Co-author: Three Voices: An Invitation to Poetry Across the Curriculum; contbr. articles to profl. jours. Recipient Disting. Svc. award Bd. Edn., Manhasset, 1989-90. Mem. Manhasset Edn. Assn. (corr. sec. 1992-95), Tchr. Resource Ctr. Bd., Dist. Shared Decision Making Team, Delta Kappa Gamma. Avocations: reading, writing, travel, museum visits. Office: Munsey Park Sch Hunt Lane Manhasset NY 11030

SCALA, SINCLAIRE MAXIMILIAN, retired aerospace engineer; b. Charleston, S.C., June 27, 1929; s. George and Goldie (Bocker) S.; m. Enid Joan Perlin, Mar. 25, 1951; children: Howard Alexander, Richard Perlin, Susanna Linda. BME cum laude, CCNY, 1950; postgrad., Columbia U., 1950, NYU, 1950-51; MME, U. Del., Newark, 1953; MA, Princeton U., 1955, PhD, 1957; MBA, U. Pa., 1978. Advanced devel. engr. Westinghouse Elec. Corp., Lester, Pa., 1951-53; rsch. fellow Princeton (N.J.) U. James Forrestal Rsch. Ctr., 1953-56; rsch. engr. GE, Phila., 1956-58, cons. high altitude gas dynamics, 1958-59, mgr. high altitude aerodynamics, 1959-64, mgr. theoretical fluid physics, 1964-68, mgr. fluid physics projects, 1968-69, mgr. environ. scis. lab., 1969-73, chief scientist, 1973-74, sr. cons. scientist, 1974-80, tech. dir. ind. R & D program, 1974-80, mgr. adv. weapons concepts, 1980-82, tech. dir. profl. devel. and edn. program, 1974-82, chmn. rsch. & engring. productivity coun., 1979-82; v.p. advanced engring. Fairchild Republic Co., Farmingdale, N.Y., 1982-83, v.p. advanced systems & tech. devel., 1983-84, v.p. strategic def., 1984-85, v.p. research, 1985-86, dir. rsch. and advanced product devel., 1986-87; dir. advanced programs Grumman Aircraft Systems, Bethpage, N.Y., 1987-91; dir. bus. planning Grumman Corp. Ops., Bethpage, 1991-94, ret., 1994; lectr. dept. physics Temple U., Phila, 1960-61; guest lectr. MIT, 1964-66; Colloquium lectr. various univs. to date; gen. chmn. AFOSR/GE Symposium on Dynamics of Manned Lifting Planetary Entry, Phila., 1962; mem. NASA Research &

Tech. Adv. Subcom. on Fluid Mechanics, Washington, 1965-70; mem. indsl. and profl. adv. council dept. aerospace engring. Pa. State U., 1969-73; cons. Engring. & Tech. Socs. Council of Delaware Valley, Inc., Phila., 1980-82; active various symposiums. Contbr. articles to profl. jours.; patentee in field. Pres. Wyncote-West Elkins Park Community Council, Montgomery Co., Pa., 1963-65; v.p. Cheltenham Council Civic Assns., 1964-65; bd. dirs. Parents Assn. Syracuse U., 1969-73; panel mem. Continuing Edn. Com. Commonwealth of Pa., 1976-77. Recipient Alumni award in mech. engring. CCNY, 1950; NYU teaching fellow, 1950-51, Guggenheim fellow, 1953-55, Bakhmeteff fellow, 1955-56. Fellow AIAA (assoc.); mem. Air Force Assn., Am. Def. Preparedness Assn., Am. Soc. Engring. Edn., Assn. for Unmanned Vehicle Systems, Nat. Mgmt. Assn., N.Y. Acad. Sci., Tech. Mktg. Soc. Am., U.S. Space Found., Army Aviation Assn. of Am., World Future Soc., Elfun Soc., Sigma Xi, Tau Beta Pi, Pi Tau Sigma. Home: 2107 Alexis Ct Tarpon Springs FL 34689-2053

SCALES, JAMES RALPH, history educator, former university president; b. Jay, Okla., May 27, 1919; s. John Grover and Katie (Whitley) S.; m. Elizabeth Ann Randel, Aug. 4, 1944 (dec. Aug. 1992); children: Laura (dec.), Ann Catherine. B.A., Okla. Baptist U., 1939; M.A., U. Okla., 1941, Ph.D., 1949; postgrad., U. Chgo., 1941-42, 47-49, U. London, 1958; LL.D., Alderson Broaddus Coll., 1971, Duke U., 1976; Litt.D., No. Mich. U., 1972; L.H.D., Belmont Abbey Coll., 1981, Winston-Salem State U., 1984, William Jewell Coll., 1989. Reporter Miami (Okla.) News Record, 1934-35, Shawnee (Okla.) News-Star, 1935-36; instr. Okla. Baptist U., Shawnee, 1940-42, asst. prof., 1946-47, assoc. prof., 1947-51, prof. history, govt., 1951-61, v.p., 1950-53, exec. v.p., 1953-61, pres., 1961-65; dean arts and scis. Okla. State U., Stillwater, 1965-67; pres. Wake Forest U., Winston-Salem, N.C., 1967-83, Worrell prof. Anglo Am. studies, 1983—; founder Cimarron Rev., 1967—; Mem. Pres.'s Com. Edn. Beyond High Sch., 1957; mem. adv. com. U.S. Army Command and Gen. Staff Coll., Ft. Leavenworth, Kans., 1969-72, chmn., 1971-72; mem. U.S. del. UNESCO, 1978-81. Co-author: Oklahoma Politics: A History, 1983. Okla. del. Dem. Nat. Conv., 1956; bd. dirs. N.C. Civil Liberties Union; trustee Belmont Abbey Coll., 1977-80; mem. Bapt. Joint Com. on Pub. Affairs, 1990—. Signal officer USN, 1942-45. Named to Okla. Hall of Fame, 1983. Mem. Am. Hist. Assn., Am. Polit. Sci. Assn., AAUP, So. Assn. Bapt. Colls. (pres. 1969-70), Am. Guild Organists, N.C. Assn. Ind. Colls. (pres. 1969-71), Winston-Salem C. of C. (dir.), Nat. League for Nursing (hon.), Cherokee West, Phi Beta Kappa, Omicron Delta Kappa, Phi Eta Sigma. Baptist (deacon). Clubs: Rotary (Winston-Salem); University (N.Y.C.); Twin City (Winston-Salem); Bay Hill Golf and Country (Orlando, Fla.); Cape Fear (Wilmington, (N.C.); Miles Grant Country (Port Salerno, Fla.); Reform (London). Home: 5401 Indiana Ave A2 Winston Salem NC 27106-2809

SCALES, RICHARD LEWIS, sales representative; b. Indpls., Nov. 16, 1928; s. Ortho Lorton and Nina L. (Julian) S.; m. E. Jean Rankin, Dec. 21, 1951; children: Richard, Allan, Anne. BSME, Purdue U., 1952. Rsch. and devel. engr. Bell Labs./Western Electric, Chgo., also Whippany, N.J., 1955-58; sales engr. Bodine Electric Co., Chgo., 1958-61; dist. sales mgr. Wabash (Ind.) Magnetics, 1961-66; founder, chmn. bd. (emeritus) Richard Scales Assocs., Wabash, 1966—, RSA Inc., Wabash, 1985—. Contbr. articles to mag. Elder, Presbyn. Ch. Lt. USNR, 1952-55, Korea; past pres. Wabash Rotary Club, Paul Harris award. Republican. Avocations: computers, photography. Home: 550 Sommers Ave Wabash IN 46992-2021 Office: Richard Scales Assocs Inc 84 W Market St Wabash IN 46992-3127

SCALETTA, PHILLIP RALPH, III, lawyer; b. Iowa City, Iowa, Dec. 18, 1949; s. Phillip Jasper and Helen M. (Beedle) S.; m. Karen Lynn Scaletta, May 13, 1973; children: Phillip, Anthony, Alexander. BSIM, Purdue U., 1972, MS, 1972; JD, Ind. U., 1975. Bar: Ind. 1975, U.S. Dist. Ct. Ind. 1975, Ill. 1993. Assoc. Ice Miller Donadio & Ryan, Indpls., 1975-81, ptnr., 1981—. Contbr. articles to profl. jours. Chmn. Ind. Continuing Legal Edn. Found., Indpls., 1989; mem. Environ. Quality Control Water Com., 1988—. Mem. Ind. Bar Assn., Indpls. Bar Assn., Def. Rsch. Inst., Internat. Assn. Def. Counsel, Gyro Club Indpls. (v.p. 1992-93, pres. 1993-94, bd. dirs. 1990—). Avocations: golf, skiing, tennis. Home: 7256 Tuliptree Trl Indianapolis IN 46256-2136 Office: Ice Miller Donadio & Ryan 1 American Sq Indianapolis IN 46282-0001

SCALIA, ANTONIN, United States supreme court justice; b. Trenton, N.J., Mar. 11, 1936; s. S. Eugene and Catherine Louise (Panaro) S.; m. Maureen McCarthy, Sept. 10, 1960; children—Ann Forrest, Eugene, John Francis, Catherine Elisabeth, Mary Clare, Paul David, Matthew, Christopher James, Margaret Jane. A.B., Georgetown U., 1957; student, U. Fribourg, Switzerland, 1955-56; LL.B., Harvard, 1960. Bar: Ohio 1962, Va. 1970. Assoc. Jones Day Cockley & Reavis, Cleve., 1961-67; assoc. prof. U. Va. Law Sch., 1967-70; prof. law U. Va., 1970-74; gen. counsel Office Telecommunications Policy, Exec. Office of Pres., 1971-72; chmn. Adminstrv. Conf. U.S., Washington, 1972-74; asst. atty. gen. U.S. Office Legal Counsel, Justice Dept., 1974-77; vis. prof. Georgetown Law Center, 1977, Stanford Law Sch., 1980-81; vis. scholar Am. Enterprise Inst., 1977; prof. law U. Chgo., 1977-82; judge U.S. Ct. Appeals (D.C. cir.), 1982-86; justice U.S. Supreme Ct., Washington, 1986—. Editor: Regulation mag, 1979-82. Sheldon fellow Harvard U., 1960-61. Office: US Supreme Ct Supreme Ct Bldg 1 1st St NE Washington DC 20543-0002*

SCALISE, CELESTE, lawyer; b. San Antonio, May 15, 1959; d. Robert and Edna (King) Scalise; m. James S. Boyd Jr., Oct. 6, 1984 (div. Dec. 1988); m. Marshall Bruce Lloyd, May 13, 1989 (div. July 1995); m. Khalil Qubrori, Feb. 16, 1997. BA, U. Tex., San Antonio, 1979; JD, Tex. Tech U., 1983. Bar: Tex. 1984, U.S. Ct. Appeals (5th cir.) 1984, U.S. Dist. Ct. (so. dist.) Tex. 1985, U.S. Dist. Ct. (no. dist.) Tex. 1990, U.S. Dist. Ct. (we. dist.) Tex. 1991, U.S. Dist Ct. (ea. dist.) Tex. 1992. Field ops. asst. Bur. of Census U.S. Dept. of Commerce, San Antonio, 1980; title examiner, law clk. Lubbock (Tex.) Abstract & Title Co., 1982-83; assoc. Bonilla & Berlanga, Corpus Christi, Tex., 1983-89; sr. assoc. Heard, Goggan, Blair & Williams, San Antonio, 1989-90; assoc. Denton & McKamie, San Antonio, 1990, Joe Weiss and Assocs., San Antonio, 1990; field litigation office Cigna litigation atty. Law Offices of Sean P. Martinez, San Antonio, 1990—; pres. Fountain Rorm, Inc.; mem. adv. group Camino Real Health Systems Agy., Inc., San Antonio, 1978-80. Mem. substance abuse adv. com. Planned Parenthood Bd., Corpus Christi, 1983-85; vice chair Nueces County Mental Health/Mental Retardation Substance Abuse Com., San Antonio, 1987-89; mem. vestry Trinity Episcopal Ch. Mem. Tex. Bar Assn. (govt. lawyers sect., ins. def.), San Antonio Bar Assn., U. Tex. at San Antonio Alumni Assn., Delta Theta Phi. Episcopalian. Avocations: photography, reading, gem and minerals collector. Home: 2130 W Gramercy Pl San Antonio TX 78201-4822 Office: Law Offices Sean P Martinez 300 Convent St San Antonio TX 78205-3701

SCALISE, FRANCIS ALLEN, adminstrator, consultant; b. Rochester, N.Y., Dec. 16, 1930; s. Sam and Margaret Rose (Seran) Scalise; children: Allen, Stephen. BS in Elem. Edn., SUNY, Brockport, 1952; MEd in Ednl. Adminstrn., U. Rochester, 1956. Tchr. Virgil I. Grissom Sch. 7, Rochester, 1955-60, acting prin., 1960-61; prin. Gen. Elwell S. Otis Sch. 30, Rochester, 1962-67, Susan B. Anthony Sch. 27, Rochester, 1967-71, Dr. Louis A. Cerulli Sch. 34, Rochester, 1971-90; ret., 1990; supr. student tchr. satellite sch., SUNY, Brockport, 1976-90; workshop presenter Wayne County Schs., Goldsboro, N.C., 1988. Team capt. new bldg. drive YMCA, Rochester, 1983; vol. ptnr. Compeer Psychiat. Program, Rochester, 1988; vol. Monroe County Dem. Com., Rochester, 1986, 89, 90. Recipient Community Svc. awards Neighborhood Hope, 1990, Rochester Police Dept., 1990. Mem. Sch. Adminstrs. Assn. N.Y. State, Adminstrs. and Suprs. Assn. Rochester, Phi Delta Kappa. Roman Catholic. Avocations: racquetball, world travel, photography. Home: 1000 East Ave 508 Rochester NY 14607

SCALISH, FRANK ANTHONY, labor union administrator; b. Cleve., Nov. 5, 1940; s. John T. and Tillie M. (Rockman) S.; m. Carla Rita Cinti, 1960; children: John M., Frank A., Tina Marie. Grad. high sch., Cleve. Bus. agt. Local Union #1 Textile Processors Svc. Trades, Health Care Profl. and Tech. Employees Internat., Cleve., 1962—; sec., treas. Local Union #1, Cleve., 1978—; v.p. Internat. Union, Chgo., 1969-84, gen. pres., 1984—. Bd dirs. Cleve. Opera Theater, 1981-84. Recipient Israel Solidarity award Israeli Bonds, 1983. Roman Catholic. Avocations: hunting, fishing, golf, grandchildren. Office: Texile Processors Service Trades Health Care Prof Tech Employees 303 E Wacker Dr Ste 1109 Chicago IL 60601-5212

SCALLEN, THOMAS KAINE, broadcasting executive; b. Mpls., Aug. 14, 1925; s. Raymond A. and Lenore (Kaine) S.; m. Bille Jo Brice; children by previous marriage: Thomas, Sheila, Patrick, Eileen, Timothy and Maureen (twins). BA, St. Thomas Coll., 1949; JD, U. Denver, 1950. Bar: Minn. Asst. atty. gen. State of Minn., Mpls., 1950-55; sole practice Mpls., 1955-57; pres. Med. Investment Corp., Mpls., 1957—, Internat. Broadcasting Corp., Mpls., 1977—; owner Harlem Globetrotters; pres., exec. producer Ice Capades; chmn. bd. dirs. Century Park Pictures Corp., Los Angeles, chmn. bd. dirs. Blaine-Thompson Co., Inc., N.Y.C; chmn. Apache Plastics, Inc., Stockton, Calif. Served with AUS. Mem. World Pres. Orgn., Minn. Club, Calhoun Beach Club, L.A. Athletic Club. Clubs: University (St. Paul, Mpls.), Rochester (Minn.) Golf and Country, Edina (Minn.) Country, Athletic (Mpls.). Home: Heron Cove Windham NH 03087 Office: Internat Broadcasting Corp 80 S 8th St # 4701 Minneapolis MN 55402-2100

SCAMEHORN, JOHN FREDERICK, chemical engineer; b. York, Nebr., Oct. 26, 1953; s. Denver Alonzo and Mary Esther (Weber) S. BSChE, U. Nebr., 1973, MS, 1974; PhD, U. Tex., 1980. Registered profl. engr. Okla., Tex. Rsch. engr. Conoco, Ponca City, Okla., 1974-77; rsch. asst. U. Tex., Austin, 1977-80; rsch. engr. Shell Devel. Co., Houston, 1980-81; prof. U. Okla., Norman, Okla., 1981-92, Asahi glass chair, 1992—; v.p. Surfactant Assoc. Inc., Norman, 1987—; adv. bd. mem. EPA Hazardous Substance Rsch., Manhattan, Kans., 1989-90; organizer 65th Annual Colloid and Surface Sci. Symposium, Norman, 1991; assoc. editr. Jour Am. Oil Chemists Soc., 1986—; host radio show KGOU, Norman, 1984. Editor: Phenomena in Mixed Surfactant Systems, 1986, Surfactant Based Separation Processes, 1989, Solubilization in Surfactant Aggregates, 1995; contbr. articles to profl. jours. Bd. dirs. Opera Guild U. Okla., 1985-86. Recipient Cert. Appreciation ISEC Am. Chem. Soc., 1992. Mem. Am. Oil Chemists Soc. (mem. at large bd. 1990—), Am. Chemical Soc. (chair spearations subdivisn. 1994), Am. Inst. Chemical Engrs. Republican. Achievements include development of new techniques in surfactant-based separation processes, pioneering development of micellar-enhanced ultrafiltration for wastewater/groundwater, clean-up. Office: U Okla 100 E Boyd St Norman OK 73019-1000

SCAMMELL, MICHAEL, writer, translator; b. Lyndhurst, Hampshire, Eng., Jan. 16, 1935; s. Frederick George Talbot and Estelle Constance (Ayling) S.; m. Erika Roettges, Feb. 17, 1962 (div.); m. Rosemary Alise Nossiff, Aug. 11, 1990. BA with 1st Class Honours in Modern Langs., Nottingham (Eng.) U., 1958; PhD in Slavic Langs. and Lits., Columbia U., 1985. Lectr. in English Lang. and Lit. U. Ljubljana, Yugoslavia, 1958-59; instr. Russian Lang. and Lit. CCNY, 1961-63; dir. East European exchange program, N.Y. Inst. Humanities N.Y.U., N.Y.C., 1982-84; prof. dept. Russian Lit. Cornell U., Ithaca, N.Y., 1987-93, chair dept., 1987-92, dir. Soviet and East European Studies program, 1989-92; prof. writing and translation Sch. of the Arts, Columbia U., N.Y.C., 1994-96; bd. dirs. Internat. Ctr. Devel. Policy; freelance translator, N.Y.C. and London, 1962-65, London, 1967-71; lang. supr., programme asst. external svcs. East European divsn. BBC, London, 1965-67; founder, editor Index on Censorship, London, 1972-81; dir. Writers and Scholars Ednl. Trust, London, 1972-81; vis. prof. dept. Russian lit. Cornell U., 1986-87. Author: Blue Guide to Yugoslavia, the Adriatic Coast, 1969, Solzhenitsyn, a Biography, 1984, (L.A. Times Book prize 1984, Silver PEN award 1985); editor: Russia's Other Writers, 1970, La letteratura contemporanea nell'Europa dell'Est, 1977, Unofficial Art from the Soviet Union, 1977, The Solzhenitsyn Files, 1995; translator: Cities and Years (Konstantin Fedin) 1962, Crime and Punishment (Fyodor Dostoyevsky) 1963, The Gift (Vladimir Nabokov) 1963, The Defence (Vladimir Nabokov) 1964, Childhood, Boyhood & Youth (Leo Tolstoy) 1964, My Testimony (Anatoly Marchenko) 1969, To Build a Castle (Vladimir Bukovsky) 1978; author introduction Ressurection (Leo Tolstoy) 1963; contbg. translator various Slavic poetry anthologies; contbr. articles to profl. jours., reviews to newspapers. Internat. adv. com. Robert F. Kennedy Meml. Human Rights award, Washington, 1985-94. Cadet, Brit. Intelligence Corps., 1953-55. Post-grad. fellow Columbia U., 1959-61, sr. vis. fellow 1981-83, fellow, then assoc. fellow NYU, 1982-86, fellow Kennan Inst. Advanced Russian Studies, 1985, Post-doctoral fellow Harvard U., 1986; grantee Rockefeller Found., 1979, Ford Found., 1981-82, Leverhulme Trust, 1981-82, Nat. Endowment for the Humanities, 1993, Guggenheim Found., 1994; recipient Writers' bursary award Arts Coun. Gt. Britain, 1981, Humanities Divsn. award Ford Found., 1982-83. Mem. Internat. PEN (v.p. 1984—), PEN Am. Ctr. (v.p. 1995-96, pres. 1996—), Internat. Acad. Scholarship and the Arts (bd. dirs. 1986—). Avocations: theatre, tennis, sailing. Office: Columbia Univ Writing Divsn Sch Arts 2960 Broadway New York NY 10027

SCAMMON, RICHARD MONTGOMERY, retired political scientist, retired editor; b. Mpls., July 17, 1915; s. Richard Everingham and Julia (Simms) S.; m. Mary Stark Allen., Feb. 20, 1952; 1 dau., Anne Valerie. A.B., U. Minn., 1935; A.M., U. Mich., 1938. Rsch. sec., radio office U. Chgo., 1939-41; with Office Mil. Govt. for Germany, U.S., 1945-48; chief, div. rsch. for Western Europe Dept. of State, 1948-55; dir. Elections Rsch. Center, 1955-61, 65-95; elections cons. NBC News, 1965-89; vis. fellow Am. Enterprise Inst.; mem. Israeli-Am. Electoral Conf., 1989; cons. to State Dept., 1979-80; dir. Bur. Census, Dept. Commerce, 1961-65. Co-author: The Real Majority; Editor: America Votes, America at the Polls. Chmn. U.S. delegation observe elections in, USSR, 1958; chmn. Pres.'s Commn. Registration and Voting Participation, 1963; mem. OAS electoral mission to, Dominican Republic, 1966; mem. Pres.'s Commn. to observe elections in Viet Nam, 1967; chmn. U.S. Select Commn. Western Hemisphere Immigration, 1966-68; pres. Nat. Council on Pub. Polls, 1969-70; mem. Pres.'s Commn. on Fed. Statistics, 1970-71, U.S. delegation Gen. Assembly UN, 1973, U.S. delegation observe elections in El Salvador, 1982; mem. Nat. Bipartisan Commn. on Central Am., 1983-84. Served with U.S. Army, 1941-46. Mem. Am. Polit. Sci. Assn., Am. Acad. Polit. and Social Sci., Acad. Polit. Sci. Club: Cosmos (Washington). Home: 5508 Greystone St Chevy Chase MD 20815-5534

SCANDALIOS, JOHN GEORGE, geneticist, educator; b. Nisyros Isle, Greece, Nov. 1, 1934; s. George John and Calliope (Broujos) S.; m. Penelope Anne Lawrence, Jan. 18, 1961; children: Artemis Christina, Melissa Joan, Nikki Eleni. B.A., U. Va., 1957; M.S., Adelphi U., 1960; Ph.D., U. Hawaii, 1965; D.Sc. (hon.), Aristotelian U. Thessaloniki, Greece, 1986. Assoc. in bacterial genetics Cold Spring Harbor Labs., 1960-62; NIH postdoctoral fellow U. Hawaii Med. Sch., 1965; asst. prof. Mich. State U., East Lansing, 1965-70; assoc. prof. Mich. State U., 1970-72; prof., head dept. biology U. S.C., Columbia, 1973-75; prof., head dept. genetics N.C. State U., Raleigh, 1975-85; disting. univ. research prof. N.C. State U., 1985—; mem. Inst. Molecular Biology and Biotechnology, Research. Ctr. Crete, Greece; vis. prof. genetics U. Calif., Davis, 1969; vis. prof. OAS, Argentina, Chile and Brazil, 1972; mem. recombinant DNA adv. com. NIH. Author: Physiological Genetics, 1979; editor: Developmental Genetics, Advances in Genetics, Current Topics in Medical and Biological Research; co-editor: Isozymes, 4 vols., 1975, Monographs in Developmental Biology, 1968-86; molecular biology editor Physiol. Plant, 1988—. Served with USAF, 1957. Alexander von Humboldt travel fellow, 1976; mem. exchange program NAS, U.S.-USSR. Fellow AAAS; mem. Genetics Soc. Am., Am. Soc. Biochemistry and Molecular Biology, Am. Genetic Assn. (pres.), Soc. Devel. Biology (dir.), Am. Inst. Biol. Scis., Am. Soc. Plant Physiologists, N.Y. Acad. Scis., Sigma Xi. Office: NC State U Dept Genetics PO Box 7614 Raleigh NC 27695

SCANDARY, E. JANE, special education educator, consultant; b. Saginaw, Mich., Sept. 12, 1923; d. Leonard William and Reva Charlotte (Smith) Leipprandt; m. Theodore John Scandary; children: John S., Robert G. BA, Mich. State U., East Lansing, 1945, EdS, 1963, PhD, 1968; MEd, Wayne State U., 1951. Cert. secondary and spl. edn. tchr., Mich. Therapist speech and lang. Ann J. Kellogg Sch., Battle Creek, Mich., 1945-47; supr. speech therapy programs Wayne County Schs., Detroit, 1948-52; supr. programs for phys., hearing and visually impaired Ingham Intermediate Schs., Mason, Mich., 1960-78; spl. edn. cons. Mich. Dept. of Edn., Lansing, 1978-87, Livingston Intermediate Schs., Howell, Mich., 1987—; rsch. assoc. Mich. State U., East Lansing, 1965-66, adj. prof., 1969-75, 81-82; mem. adv. com. China-U.S. Sci. Exchange Program Spl. Edn.; guest lectr. seminars spl. edn. Australia, Eng., Iran, Israel, Aruba, Germany, Scotland. Editor Chronicles newsletter, 1987—; contbr. articles to profl. jours. Vol. Mich. Hist. Mus., 1995—; chair futures com. Mich. Dept. Edn., 1992, editor, chair Task Force Futuresin Spl. Edn. 2000 AD and Beyond, 1992. 1st Chance Early Childhood grantee, 1972-78; recipient Resolution of Tribute Mich. State Senate, 1986; Scandary award for outstanding contbrs. early childhood edn. established in her name, 1990. Mem. Nat. Coun. Exceptional Children (field editor 1976-86, pres. div. physically handicapped 1982-83), Mid-Mich. Art Guild, World Future Soc. Avocations: painting, writing, reading, creative sewing.

SCANDLING, WILLIAM FREDRIC, retired food service company executive; b. Rochester, N.Y., June 17, 1922; s. Fredric D. and Helen T. (Moran) S.; m. Margaret Warner, Apr. 19, 1949 (dec. Oct. 1990); 1 child, Michael; m. Yvette Farquaharson-Oliver, June 1995. A.B., Hobart Coll., 1949, LL.D. (hon.), 1967. Co-founding ptnr. ALS & Co., Geneva, N.Y., 1948, Saga Corp., Geneva, N.Y., 1949; co-founding ptnr. Saga Corp. (ALS and Saga Corp. merged), Menlo Park, Calif., 1962, dir., 1949-86, sec.-treas., 1949-68, pres., 1968-78, founder, dir., 1978-86; dir. Empire Broadcasting Corp., 1975-82; pres. Auburn Broadcasting Corp., Calif., 1975-82, dir., 1982-86. Trustee Hobart and William Smith Coll., Geneva, 1967—, chmn. 1971-82; trustee Deep Springs Coll., Calif., 1984-92, Nat. Council Salk Inst.; chmn., bd. dirs. Community Found. Santa Clara County, Calif., 1988-91. With USAAF, 1943-45. Mem. Kappa Alpha Soc., Menlo Country Club ((Woodside, Calif.), Seneca Yacht Club (Geneva), Genesee Valley Club (Rochester, N.Y.). Home: 134 Tuscaloosa Ave Atherton CA 94027-4017

SCANDURA, JOSEPH MICHAEL, mathematics educator, researcher, software engineer; b. Bay Shore, N.Y., Apr. 29, 1932; s. Joseph and Lucy S.; m. Alice Baker, Aug. 13, 1960; children: Jeanne, Janette, Joseph, Julie. AB, U. Mich., 1953, MA, 1955; PhD, Syracuse U., 1962; postdoctoral, Stanford U., summer 1964, 68-69, U. Calif.-Berkeley, summer 1968, MIT, summer 1972; postgrad., U. Kiel, W.Ger., 1975, Inst. Ednl. Tech., Italy, summer 1978. Tchr. math., sci. White Plains, Bay Shore, 1953-56; instr. math., head wrestling coach Syracuse U., N.Y., 1956-63; asst. prof. edn., math. SUNY-Buffalo, 1963-64; research asst. prof. math. edn. Fla. State U., Tallahassee, 1964-66; dir. instructional systems, structural learning U. Pa., Phila., 1966—; founder, chmn. Intelligent Micro Systems, Narberth, Pa., 1978—; chmn. bd. sci. advisors MERGE Rsch. Inst., 1973; cons. jours., govt. agys., pub. cons., 1967—; cons. U.S. Office Edn., NSF, NAS, Tex. Instruments, Borg-Warner, U.S. Army; organizer, lèctr., participant profl. confs., 1963—; dir. NATO Advanced Study Inst. on Structural Process Theories of Complex Human Behavior, 1977; coach undefeated Ea. Intercollegiate Wrestling Championship Team, 1963. Author: Mathematics - Concrete Behavioral Foundations, 1971, (with others) An Algorithmic Approach to Mathematics - Concrete Behavioral Foundations, 1971, Structural Learning I - Theory and Research, 1973, Problem Solving - A Structural Process Approach with Instructural Implications, 1977, (with A.B. Scandura) Structural Learning and Concrete Operations - An Approach to Piagetian Conservation, 1980, Cognitive Approach to Software Development, 1988, Prodoc (comprehensive suite of software devel. and maintenance tools), 1989, Cognitive Approach to Software Engineering and Re-engineering, 1991, Research on Program Modification under program control, 1992, NATO Advanced Study Inst., 1993, Automated Software Conversions and Re-engineering, 1993; contbr. over 175 articles to profl. jours.; editor: Research in Mathematics Education, 1967, Structural Learning II - Issues and Approaches, 1976, (with C.J. Brainerd) Structural Process Models of Complex Human Behavior, 1978; developer, producer numerous computer-based instructional systems and software devel. systems; patentee in field. Recipient Renssalaer award, 1949, Bausch and Lomb award, 1949, Nat. AAU Wrestling Champion and Outstanding Wrestler award, 1955; Fulbright scholar, 1975-76, 1997—; U.S. Office Edn. fellow, 1978-79. Fellow APA (chmn. E.L. Thorndike award com. 1974-79); mem. AAUP, IEEE, Assn. Computing Machinery, Am. Ednl. Rsch. Assn. (past com. chmn.), Nat. Coun. Tchrs. Math. (past fed. funds com. chmn.), Math. Assn. Am., Psychonomic Soc., Structural Learning Soc. (chmn. 1969-80, 85-88, 95—, editor in chief Jour. Structural Learning 1976-90, Jour. Structural Learning and Intelligent Systems 1990—), Unif. Profs. for Acad. Order, Phi Kappa Phi, Phi Eta Sigma, Phi Delta Kappa. Home: 1249 Greentree Ln Narberth PA 19072-1219 Office: U Pa Instructional Systems Philadelphia PA 19104 *Accomodation to -- as well as leadership of -- groups, institutions and/or societies is an essential ingredient of success in most walks of life. There are circumstances, however, which require inner direction, whether developing a new scientific paradigm or standing firm against political pressures. Although vindication is rarely complete and often delayed, following one's best instincts yields its own rewards—perhaps the satisfaction of ultimately being proven right but more often simply knowing one did what had to be done.*

SCANLAN, JAMES PATRICK, philosophy and Slavic studies educator; b. Chgo., Feb. 22, 1927; s. Gilbert Francis and Helen (Meyers) S.; m. Marilyn A. Morrison, June 12, 1948.;. BA, U. Chgo., 1948, MA, 1950, PhD, 1956. Research fellow Inst. Philos. Research, San Francisco, 1953-55; instr. Case Inst. Tech., Cleve., 1955-56; from instr. to assoc. prof. Goucher Coll., Balt., 1956-68; prof., dir. Slavic Ctr. U. Kans., Lawrence, 1968-70; prof. Ohio State U., Columbus, 1971-91, dir. Slavic Ctr., 1988-91, prof. emeritus, 1992—; vis. rsch. scholar Moscow State U., 1964-65, 69, Acad. Scis. USSR, Moscow, 1978, 93, Russian State U. for the Humanities, 1995; fgn. vis. fellow Slavic Rsch. Ctr., Hokkaido U., Sapporo, Japan, 1987-88. Author: Marxism in the USSR, 1985; editor: Historical Letters by Peter Lavrov, 1967, Soviet Studies in Philosophy, 1987-92, Russian Studies in Philosophy, 1992—, Technology, Culture and Development: The Experience of the Soviet Model, 1992, Russian Thought After Communism, 1994; co-editor: Russian Philosophy, 1965, Marxism and Religion in Eastern Europe, 1976. Served with USMC, 1945-46. Woodrow Wilson Internat. Ctr. fellow, 1982; recipient Translation award Nat. Translation Ctr., 1967, Faculty Research award Fulbright-Hays, 1982-83. Mem. Am. Philos. Assn., Am. Assn. Advancement Slavic Studies, Phi Beta Kappa. Home: 1000 Urlin Ave Apt 206 Columbus OH 43212-3324

SCANLAN, JOHN DOUGLAS, foreign service officer, former ambassador; b. Thief River Falls, Minn., Dec. 20, 1927; s. Paul Douglas and Ruby (Bennes) S.; m. Margaret Anne Calvi; children: Kathleen, Michael, Malia, John. B.A., U. Minn., 1952, M.A. in Russian Studies, 1955. Instr. U. Minn., 1955; Soviet research analyst U.S. Dept. State, Washington, 1956-58; third sec. Am. Embassy, Moscow, 1958-60; cultural attache Am. Embassy, Warsaw, 1961-65; second sec. Am. Embassy, Montevideo, 1966-67; prin. officer Am. Consulate, Poznan, Poland, 1967-69; sr. rep. to U.S. Dept. Defense, Washington, 1969-71; desk officer U.S.-Soviet bilateral relations, 1971-73; polit. counselor Am. Embassy, Warsaw, 1973-75; mem. state exec. seminar Washington, 1975-76; spl. asst. to Dir. Gen. of Fgn. Service, 1976-77; dep. dir. for Europe, USIA, 1977-79; dep. chief Mission in Belgrade, Yugoslavia, 1979-81; dep. asst. sec. of state for European affairs, 1981-82; fgn. affairs fellow Fletcher Sch. Law and Diplomacy, Tufts U., 1983-84; chmn. U.S. del. to Conf. on Security and Coop. in Europe, Cultural Forum Preparatory Conf., Budapest, 1984; amb. to Yugoslavia, Am. Embassy, Belgrade, 1985-89; dep. comdt. U.S. Army War Coll., Carlisle Barracks, Pa., 1989-91; sr. cons. East EUR, ICN Pharmaceutcals Inc.; mem. bd. Am. Drug Co., Project on Ethnic Rels.; mem. Ctr. Strategic and Internat. Studies U.S.-European-Poland Action Commn.; adv. coun. ABA Ctrl. and East European Law Initiative project. Mem. Planning Commn., Falls Church, Va., 1972-73, City Council, 1975-79. Recipient Presdl. Meritorious Service award for Diplomacy, 1984.

SCANLAN, KATHY, sports association administrator. Dir. mgmt. Seattle Parks and Recreation Dept., 1977-80; bus. and ops. mgr. Woodland Park Zoo, 1980-82; dep. dir. Seattle Ctr., 1982-88; exec. v.p. Seattle SuperSonics, 1990-92; prior cons. prin. Scanlan, Sorensen and Potter, Inc.; pres. USA Gymnastics (formerly U.S. Gymnastics Fedn.), 1994—; past exec. dir. World Univ. Games Buffalo '93; exec. v.p. Seattle Organizing Com. for 1990 Goodwill Games, others. Office: USA Gymnastics 201 S Capitol Ave Ste 300 Indianapolis IN 46225-1058

SCANLAN, MICHAEL, priest, academic administrator; b. Far Rockaway, N.Y., Dec. 1, 1931; s. Vincent Michael and Marjorie (O'Keefe) S. BA, Williams Coll., 1953; JD, Harvard U., 1956; MDiv, St. Francis Sem., Loretto, Pa., 1975; LittD (hon.), Coll. Steubenville, 1972; LLD (hon.), Williams Coll., Williamstown, Mass., 1978; PdD (hon.), St. Francis Coll.,

Loretto, Pa., 1987. Ordained priest Roman Catholic Ch., 1964; Cross Pro Ecclesia et Pontifice, 1990. Acting dean Coll. Steubenville, Ohio, 1964-66, dean, 1966-69; rector pres. St. Francis Major Sem., Loretto, Pa., 1969-74; pres. Franciscan U. Steubenville, 1974—; mem. Pa. Fullbright Com., 1974; pres. FIRE Cath. Alliance for Faith, Intercession, Repentence and Evangelism, 1984—. Author: The Power in Penance, 1972, Inner Healing, 1974, A Portion of My Spirit, 1979, The San Damiano Cross, 1983, Turn to the Lord-A Call to Repentance, 1989, The Truth About Trouble, 1989, What Does God Want: A Practical Guide to Making Decisions, 1996; chmn. editl. bd. New Covenant mag., 1985-92. Mem. Diocese of Steubenville Ecumenical Commn., 1964-69; bd. dirs. Rumor Control Ctr., Steubenville, 1968-69, C. of C., Steubenville, 1976-79; bd. trustees St. Francis Prep. Sch., Spring Grove, Pa., 1969-74; vice-chmn., bd. trustees St. Francis Coll., Loretto, Pa., 1969-74; trustee United Way, Steubenville, 1975-80; chmn. nat. svc. com. Cath. Charismatic Renewal, 1975-78. Staff judge adv. USAF, 1956-57. Mem. Assn. Ind. Colls. and Univs. Ohio (sec. 1980-82), Nat. Cath. Edn. Assn. (vice-chmn. 1968-69), Cath. Edn. Assn. Pa. (chmn. sem. divsn. 1973), Ea. Major Sem.Rectors (sec. 1969), Fellowship of Cath. Scholars, Legatus. Roman Catholic. Avocations: tennis, golf. Office: Franciscan U Dept Academic Adminstr University Blvd Steubenville OH 43952 *If you are going to change something, you've got to live on vision, before you live on reality. You have to be so inspired by the vision, that you keep telling everybody until it gets in them, and they start living it with you.*

SCANLAN, RICHARD THOMAS, classics educator; b. St. Paul, May 30, 1928; s. Robert Lawrence and Catherine (Rockstroh) S.; m. Donna Mary Campion, Dec. 29, 1951; children: John, Susan, Catherine, Anne, Margaret. B.S., U. Minn., 1951, M.A., 1952. Tchr. Hastings High Sch., Minn., 1953-55, Edina High Sch., Minn., 1955-67; prof. classics U. Ill., Urbana, 1967—; ednl. cons., 1960-75. Author: Power in Words, 1983; computer courses, 1975, 77; Myths of Greece and Rome, 1986. Pres. bd. trustees Champaign Libr., 1980-92. With U.S. Army, 1946-48, Italy. Named Excellent Tchr. Am. Classical League, 1966; recipient Silver medal Nat. Coun. for Advancement of Edn., 1985. Mem. Am. Philol. Assn., Am. Classical League, Archaeol. Assn., Classical Assn. (Excellent Tchr.award 1974). Roman Catholic. Home: 2103 Noel Dr Champaign IL 61821-6552 Office: Univ of Ill Dept of Classics Urbana IL 61801

SCANLAN, THOMAS CLEARY, publishing executive, editor; b. Birmingham, Mich., May 18, 1957; s. Thomas Matthew and Emily (Cleary) S.; m. Sally Sachs, June 20, 1981; children: Bridget C., Thomas M., Patrick J. BS, St. Louis U., 1979. Salesman Walter Heller Co., Chgo., 1979-82; pub., editor Surplus Record, Inc., Chgo., 1982—. Office: Surplus Record Inc 20 N Wacker Dr Chicago IL 60606-2806

SCANLAN, THOMAS JOSEPH, college president, educator; b. N.Y.C., Mar. 5, 1945; s. Thomas Joseph and Anna Marie (Schmitt) S. BA in Physics, Cath. U. Am., 1967; MA in Math., NYU, 1972; PhD in Bus. Adminstrn., Columbia U., 1978. Prin. Queen of Peace High Sch., North Arlington, N.J., 1972-75; dir. fin., edn. N.Y. Province, Bros. of Christian Schs., Lincroft, N.J., 1978-81; vice chancellor Bethlehem (Israel) U., 1981-87; pres. Manhattan Coll., Bronx, N.Y., 1987—; vice chmn. Commn. Ind. Colls. and Univs., 1996—, First Cova Life Ins. Co., 1993—. Trustee Lewis U., Romeoville, Ill., 1987—; bd. trustees Commn. on Ind. Colls. & Univs., 1994—, Assn. Cath. Colls. and Univs., 1994—. Recipient Pro Ecclesia et Pontifice medal, Pope John Paul II, Vatican City, 1986. Mem. Bros. of Christian Schs., Am. Coun. Edn., Assn. Cath. Colls. and Univs (trustee 1994—), Assn. Am. Colls., Nat. Cath. Edn. Assn., Nat. Assn. Ind. Colls. and Univs., Nat. Collegiate Athletic Assn. (trustee Divsn. I), Metro Atlantic Athletic Assn., Equestrian Order of the Holy Sepulchre of Jerusalem, Phi Beta Kappa, Beta Gamma Sigma. Avocations: tennis, reading, movies. Office: Manhattan Coll Dept of Finance Manhattan Coll Pky Bronx NY 10471-3913

SCANLON, ANDREW, structural engineering educator; b. Bridge of Allan, Scotland, Apr. 16, 1944. BSc with honors, U. Glasgow, Scotland, 1966; PhD, U. Alta., Can., 1972. Civil engr. Pub. Works Can., Saint John, N.B., 1966-67; project engr. N.B. Devel. Corp., Fredericton, 1967-68; teaching asst. U. Alta., Edmonton, 1968-71; structural design engr. Duthie Newby and Assocs., Edmonton, 1971-73; structural divsn. head Reid, Crowther and Ptnrs. Ltd., Edmonton, 1973-78; sr. structural engr. structural evaluation sect. Constrn. Tech. Labs., Inc., 1978-80, mgr. analytical design sect., 1980-82; assoc. prof. civil engring. U. Alta., 1982-83, prof., 1983-87; prof. Pa. State U., University Park, 1987—, dir. transp. structures program. Pa. Transp. Inst., 1993—, acting head dept., 1991. Recipient Le Prix P.L. Pratley award Can. Soc. Civil Engring., 1990. Office: Pa State U 212 Sackett Bldg University Park PA 16802-1408

SCANLON, CHARLES FRANCIS, army officer, retired, defense consultant; b. Nashville, Jan. 31, 1935; s. Francis James Gordon and Dorothy Rose (Compton) S.; m. Barbara Jean Schoen, Oct. 9, 1954; children: Teri, Brett, Ashlyn, Kellie. BA in Polit. Sci., U. Fla., 1960; grad., Command and Gen. Staff Coll., Ft. Leavenworth, Kans., 1970, Naval War Coll., Newport, R.I., 1977; MA in Am. Studies, U. Hawaii, 1974; postgrad., Pa. State U., 1982, Harvard U., 1984, 1992. Commd. 2d lt. U.S. Army, 1960, advanced through grades to maj. gen., 1988; chief collection U.S. Army Europe, Heidelberg, Germany, 1977-78; comdg. officer 66th Mil. Intelligence Brigade, Munich, 1978-80; chief ops. U.S. Army Intelligence and Security Command, Arlington, Va., 1980-82; exec. officer Dept. Army Asst. Chief Staff Intelligence, Washington, 1982-83; dep. commdr. gen. U.S. Army Intelligence and Security Command, Arlington, 1983-85; dir. estimates Def. Intelligence Agy., Washington, 1985-86, dir. attaches, 1986-90; comdg. gen. U.S. Army Intelligence and Security Command, Ft. Belvoir, Va., 1990-93; ret., 1993; pres. Def. and Internat. Consulting Svcs. Internat. Security, Counterintelligence Cons. Svcs., Fairfax Station, Va., 1993—. Decorated Def. D.S.M., Army D.S.M., Nat. Intelligence D.S.M., Legion of Merit with 3 oak leaf clusters, Bronze Star with 2 oak leaf clusters; elected to U.S. Mil. Intelligence Hall of Fame, 1995. Mem. Assn. U.S. Army, Nat. Mil. Intelligence Assn. (pres. 1974-76), Sigma Nu. Baptist. Avocations: boating, scuba diving, racquetball, soaring, reading. Home and Office: 8036 Oak Hollow Ln Fairfax VA 22039-2627 also: 435 Park Ave Satellite Beach FL 32937

SCANLON, DERALEE ROSE, dietitian, educator, author; b. Santa Monica, Calif., Aug. 16, 1950; d. Stanley Ralph and Demba (Runkle) S.; m. Alex Spataru, July 20, 1970 (div. 1974). AA, Santa Monica Coll., 1968; accred. med. record tech., East L.A. Coll., 1980; BS, U. Calif., L.A., 1984. Registered dietitian. V.p. corp. sales, nutrition dir. LIfeTrends Corp., Carlsbad, Calif., 1984-86; dir. media, nutrition Irvine Ranch Farmers Markets, L.A., 1987-88; spokesperson for media Calif. Milk Adv. Bd., San Diego, 1986; nutrition reporter Med-NIWS, L.A., 1990-91; dietitian Sta. ABC-TV The Home Show, L.A., 1991-92, Sta. NBC-TV David Horowitz Fight Back, L.A., 1991-92; dietitian, nutrition reporter Sta. KTTV-TV Good Day L.A., 1994-95; nutritionist Sta. KABC-TV Kids View, 1994—; co-host talk radio show Light and Lively, KABC, 1994—; mgr. Nutrition Svcs. Vitex Foods, Inc., 1995-96; spokesperson Sandoz Nutrition, 1995-96; host nat. cable TV health show To Your Health, 1996-97; mgr. nutrition sci. support Leiner Health Products, 1997—; media spokesperson Lifetime Food Co., Seaside, Calif., 1992—, Interior Design Nutritionals, Provo, Utah, 1993—, Weight Watchers, 1993-94; contbr. writer L.A. Parent Mag., Burbank, Calif., 1991—; syndicated nutrition reporter Live N'Well TV Series, Utah, 1992-93; nutrition educator Emeritus Coll. Sr. Health, Santa Monica, 1990-92; nutrition lectr. Princess Cruises, L.A., 1987; nutrition video host AMA Campaign Against Cholesterol, 1989; lectr. on nutrition and health to various orgns., 1993—; leader seminar series on I.B.S. UCLA Med. Ctr., 1994-95, others; mgr. nutrition sci. support Leiner Health Products, 1997. Author: The Wellness Book of IBS, 1989, Diets That Work, 1991, rev. edit., 1992, 93; newspaper columnist: Ask the Dietitian, 1990-94; columnist Natural Way Mag.; Ask the Dietitian column in The Natural Way Mag., 1995; contbr. articles to profl. jours. Mem. AFTRA, Dietitians in Bus./Comms. (regional rep. 1990-92, So. Calif. chairperson 1991-92, editor nat. newsletter 1994-96), Am. Dietetic Assn. (pub. rels. chair 1985-87), Calif. Dietetic Assn. (Dietitian of Yr. in Pvt. Practice, Bus. and Comm. 1993), Soc. for Nutrition Edn., Nat. Speakers Assn. Avocations: hiking, white water rafting, water skiing, dancing, gardening. Home and Office: 10613 Eastborne Ave Los Angeles CA 90024-5920

SCANLON, DOROTHY THERESE, history educator; b. Bridgeport, Conn., Oct. 7, 1928; d. George F. and Mazie (Reardon) S.; AB, U. Pa., 1948, MA, 1949; MA, Boston Coll., 1953; PhD, Boston U., 1956; postdoctoral scholar Harvard U., 1962-64, 72. Tchr. history and Latin Marycliff Acad., Winchester, Mass., 1950-52; tchr. history Girls Latin Sch., Boston, 1952-57; prof. Boston State Coll., 1957-82, Mass. Coll. Art, 1982-95, prof. emerita, 1995—. Recipient Disting. Svc. award Boston State Coll., 1979, Faculty Award of Excellence, Mass. Coll. Art, 1985, Faculty Disting. Service award, Mass. Coll. Art, 1987. Mem. Pan-Am. Soc., Latin Am. Studies Assn., Am. Hist. Assn., Orgn. Am. Historians, Am. Studies Assn., Am. Assn. History of Medicine, History of Sci. Soc., AAUP, AAUW, Phi Alpha Theta, Delta Kappa Gamma. Author: Instructor's Manual to Accompany Lewis Hanke, Latin America: A Historical Reader, 1974; contbr. Biographical Dictionary of Social Welfare, 1986. Home: 23 Mooring Ln Dennis MA 02638-2321 Office: Mass Coll Art Dept History 621 Huntington Ave Boston MA 02115-5801

SCANLON, EDWARD CHARLES, clinical psychologist; b. Bradford, Pa., Dec. 3, 1931; s. Edward John Scanlan and Martha (Karlous) Charles; m. Constance Morgan, May 19, 1962 (div. Jan. 1976); 1 child, Heather Marie. AB cum laude, SUNY, Buffalo, 1954; EdM, Harvard U., 1958, EdD, 1961; postgrad., Columbia U. Lic. psychologist, Pa. Assoc. prof. Lehigh U., Bethlehem, Pa., 1961-66; acad. dean Montgomery County C.C., Conshohoken, Pa., 1966-69; acting. dir. home sch. Wilkes Coll., Wilkes Barre, Pa., 1968-71; clin. psychologist dept. human svcs. mental health and mental retardation Northampton County Dept. Human Svcs., Easton, Pa., 1972—; vis. prof. clin. psychology Clinic Mental Health and Mental Retardation, Pottsville, Pa., 1971-72. Capt. USAF, 1954-57. Thayer scholar Harvard U. Mem. APA, Pa. Psychol. Assn., Harvard Club of Phila., Lehigh Country Club, Masons, Phi Beta Kappa. Democrat. Anglican. Avocations: classic automobiles, psychoanalytic studies. Office: Bridal Path Woods D-2 Bethlehem PA 18017

SCANLON, EDWARD F., surgeon, educator; b. Waynesburg, Pa., Sept. 15, 1918; s. Hugh and Ellen S.; m. Virginia K. Scanlon, June 26, 1948; children: Cathy, Mary, Sally. B.S., Kenyon Coll., 1940, D.Sc. (hon.), 1983; M.D., Columbia U., 1943. Intern St. Luke's Presbyn. Hosp., Chgo., 1944; resident in surgery St. Luke's Presbyn. Hosp., 1946-50, Meml. Sloan Kettering, N.Y.C., 1950-53; fellow Meml. Sloan Kettering, 1953; mem. staff Evanston Hosp, Ill., 1953-89; chmn. dept. surgery Evanston Hosp, 1974-86; mem. faculty dept. surgery Northwestern U. Med. Sch., Chgo., 1953—, prof. surgery, 1971—, chief surg. oncology, 1974-86, emeritus prof., 1989—. Mem. editorial adv. bd. Cancer Treatment Reports, 1976-80, Jour. Surg. Oncology, 1982-93, Internat. Jour. Breast and Mammary Pathology, 1982-93, Seminars in Surg. Oncology, 1982-93; contbr. articles to med. jours. Bd. dirs. Evanston Hosp., 1977-86. Served with M.C., U.S. Army, 1944-46. Hayes Martin lectr., 1979, James Ewing lectr., 1984; recipient scholarship Shell Intercollegiate Aviation, 1940, Am. Cancer Soc. ann. divisional award, 1978. Fellow ACS (bd. govs. 1971-76); mem. Soc. Surg. Oncology (pres. 1974-75), Am. Cancer Soc. (pres. 1980-81), Internat. Union Against Cancer (com. internat. collaborative activities), Am. Surg. Assn., Soc. Head and Neck Surgeons (treas. 1974), Western Surg. Assn., Central Surg. Assn., Chgo. Surg. Soc., Phi Beta Kappa. Home: 1338 Edgewood Ln Northbrook IL 60062-4716

SCANLON, JANE CRONIN, mathematics educator; b. N.Y.C., July 17, 1922; d. John Timothy and Janet Smiley (Murphy) Cronin; m. Joseph C. Scanlon, Mar. 5, 1953 (div.); children: Justin, Mary, Anne, Edmund. Student, Highland Park Jr. Coll., 1939-41; BS, Wayne State U., 1943; MA, U. Mich., 1945, PhD, 1949. Mathematician Air Force Cambridge Research Center, 1951-54; instr. Wheaton Coll., Norton, Mass., 1954-55; asst. prof. Poly. Inst. Bklyn., 1957-58, asso. prof., 1958-60, prof., 1960-65; prof. math. Rutgers U., New Brunswick, N.J., 1965-91, prof. emerita, 1991—; cons. Singer-Kearfott Div., Naval Research Lab. Office Naval Research Fellow Princeton, 1948-49; Horace H. Rockham Postdoctoral fellow U. Mich., 1950-51, Rutgers Research Council fellow, 1968-69, 72-73; NSF vis. professorship for women Courant Inst., NYU, 1984-85. Author: Fixed Points and Topological Degree in Nonlinear Analysis, 1964, Advanced Calculus, 1967, Differential Equations: Introduction and Qualitative Theory, 1980, 2d edit., 1994, Mathematics of Cell Electrophysiology, 1980, Mathematical Aspects of Hodgkin-Huxley Neural Theory, 1987. Mem. Am. Math. Soc., Soc. for Indsl. and Applied Math., Math. Assn. Am., Internat. Soc. Chronobiology. Home: 110 Valentine St Highland Park NJ 08904-2106 Office: Rutgers U Dept Math New Brunswick NJ 08903

SCANLON, LAWRENCE EUGENE, English language educator; b. Montclair, N.J., Sept. 12, 1927; s. Leo Dudley and Margaret Gertrude (Kennedy) S.; m. Anne Maxwell Sherrerd, Aug. 23, 1952; children: Lawrence Francis, Neal Patrick, Heidi Anne. BA, Wesleyan U., 1951; MA, Rutgers U., 1952; PhD, Syracuse U., 1958. Asst. prof. English Mount Holyoke Coll., South Hadley, Mass., 1958-63; prof. Hartford (Conn.). Coll. for Women, 1963-92. Author: First Came Commodore Perry, 1969, A Memorial of Ebensee, 1994, The Story He Left Behind Him Paddy the Cope, 1994. Justice of the peace Town of East Granby, Conn., 1970-72; v.p. Capital Region Libr. Coun., Hartford, 1970-74. With U.S. Army, 1945-46. Fulbright grantee, Austria, 1952-53, Japan, 1964-65, West Germany, 1980-81, summer grantee NEH, 1974. Avocations: writing, travel, investing. Home: 101 Holcomb St East Granby CT 06026-9531

SCANLON, PETER REDMOND, accountant; b. N.Y.C., Feb. 18, 1931; s. John Thomas and Loretta Dolores (Ryan) S.; m. Mary Jane E. Condon, Mar. 7, 1953; children: Peter, Barbara, Mark (dec.), Brian, Janet. BBA in Acctg., Iona Coll., 1952, LLD (hon.), 1992. CPA, N.Y. Mem. profl. staff Coopers & Lybrand, N.Y.C., 1956-66, ptnr., 1966-91, vice chmn., 1976-82, chmn., chief exec. officer, 1982-91, ret. chmn., 1991—; hon. ptnr. N.Y.C. Partnership, 1991. Lt. USN, 1952-56. Decorated Knight of Malta, Knight Holy Sepulchre; recipient Arthur A. Loftus award Iona Coll., 1974, Trustee award, 1990, Crain's N.Y. All Star award, 1990, Best in Class award Conf. Bd. Youth Edn., 1991. Mem. AICPA, N.Y. State Soc. CPAs, N.Y. Athletic Club. Roman Catholic. Office: Coopers & Lybrand 1251 Ave Of The Americas New York NY 10020-1104

SCANLON, ROSEMARY, economist; b. Inverness, N.S., Can., Dec. 25, 1939; d. Donald Angus and Mary Agnes (MacDonald) MacLellan; A.B., St. Francis Xavier U., N.S., 1959; M.A. (Ford Found. Scholar) U. New Brunswick, 1960; P.M.D., Harvard Bus. Sch., 1981; m. Michael Scanlon, Apr. 24, 1965 (div. 1979); children: Sean Donald, Jennifer; Instrn. econs. Coll. of William and Mary, Williamsburg, Va., 1960-63; asst. prof. Old Dominion U., Norfolk, Va., 1963-65; econ. analyst Port Authority of N.Y. and N.J., 1969-93; sr. economist for regional research, 1977-80, mgr. econ. devel. planning, N.Y.C., 1980-83, chief economist, 1983—; asst. dir. Planning and Devel. Dept., 1985; apptd. dep. state contr., N.Y.C., 1993; bd. dirs. Nova Scotia Power, Inc. bd. dirs. Rsch. Found. SUNY, 1987-93. Recipient Salute to Women in Business award YWCA of N.Y.C., 1980, Outstanding Achievement award, Exec. Dirs. award. Mem. Am. Econ. Assn., Nat. Council for Urban Econ. Devel. (bd. dirs. 1982-88). Author: The Arts as an Industry in N.Y.-N.J., 1983, The Arts as an Industry, 1993, The Regional Economy, 1993; (with others) Cities in a Global Soc., 1989; contbr. articles to profl. jours. Home: 10 Clinton St Apt 9T Brooklyn NY 11201-2710 Office: 270 Broadway New York NY 10007-2306

SCANLON, TERRENCE MAURICE, public policy foundation administrator; b. Milw., May 1, 1939; s. Maurice John and Anne (Hayes) S.; m. Judy Ball, June 14, 1969; children: Michael Mansfield, Justin Ball, Brendan Hayes. BS, Villanova U., 1961. Staff asst. The White House, Washington, 1963-67; with SBA, Washington, 1967-69; with Dept. of Commerce, Washington, 1969-83, mem. office Minority Bus. Enterprise, 1969-80, with Internat. Trade Adminstrn., 1980-81, with Minority Bus. Devel. Agy., 1981-83; mem. Consumer Product Safety Commn., Washington, 1983-89, vice chmn., 1983-84, chmn., 1985, 86-89; v.p., treas. The Heritage Found., Washington, 1989-91, v.p. corp. rels., 1991-94; chmn., pres. Capital Rsch. Ctr., Washington, 1994—. Am. Polit. Sci. Assn. Congl. fellow, 1967-68. Mem. Sovereign Mil. Order of Malta, University Club. Home: 4510 Dexter St NW Washington DC 20007-1115 Office: Capital Rsch Ctr 1513 16th St NW Washington DC 20036-1480

SCANLON, THOMAS MICHAEL, lawyer; b. Indpls., Apr. 20, 1909; s. John H. and Anna C. (Ferriter) S.; m. Grace L. Barnett, July 10, 1937; children: Thomas M., Christopher G. A.B., Butler U., 1932; LL.B., Ind. U., 1935. Bar: Ind. 1935. Asso. Noel, Hickam, Boyd & Armstrong, Indpls., 1935-40; assoc. Barnes, Hickam, Pantzer & Boyd, 1940-43, ptnr., 1943-82; of counsel Barnes & Thornburg, 1982—; mem. Ind. Bd. Law Examiners, 1942-43, 47-52. Co-author: Preparation for Trial. Trustee emeritus Butler U. Served to lt. comdr. USNR, 1943-46. Fellow Am. Bar Found., Ind. Bar Found. (50-yr. award for disting. svc. 1986), Indpls. Bar Found.; mem. ABA (chmn. sect. antitrust law 1973-74), Ind. Bar Assn. (pres. 1955-56), Indpls. Bar Assn., Bar Assn. 7th Fed. Cir. (pres. 1956-57), Am. Law Inst. (life), Am. Coll. Trial Lawyers, Delta Tau Delta, Phi Delta Phi. Clubs: Lawyers of Indianapolis (Indpls.) (pres. 1964-65), Indpls. Literary (Indpls., pres. 1990-91), Woodstock (Indpls.), Players (Indpls., pres. 1962-63). Home: 9570 Copley Dr Indianapolis IN 46260-1430 Office: Merchants Bank Bldg Indianapolis IN 46204-3506

SCANNELL, DALE PAUL, education educator; b. Iowa City, Mar. 3, 1929; s. Paul A. and Florence (Fieseler) S.; children—Steven, Jeffrey, Susan, Janet. B.A., U. Iowa, 1951, M.A., 1955, Ph.D., 1957. Tchr. Iowa City High Sch., 1950-51, 53-57; acting asst. prof. edn. U. Calif. at Berkeley, 1958-59; asst. prof. U. Kans., 1959-62, asso. prof., 1962-64, prof., 1964-67; assoc. dean U. Kans. (Grad. Sch.), 1963-67; prof. edn. U. Iowa, 1967-69; dean Sch. Edn. U. Kans., 1969-85; dean Coll. Edn. U. Md., College Park, 1985-91; prof. edn. Ind. U., Indpls., 1994—; vis. prof., Lester Prof. tchr. edn. U. S.C., 1993-94. Author: (with others) Tests of Academic Progress, 2d edit., 1971, Tests of Achievement and Proficiency, Form T, 1978, Form G, 1985, Form H, 1986, Form J, 1989, (with Oscar Haugh) Form K, 1993, Form L, 1993, Form M, 1995, Writing, Listening.Supplements, 1986, (with A.J. Edwards) Educational Psychology, 1968, (with V.H Noll and Robert Craig) Introduction to Educational Measurement, 4th edit., 1979, (with V.H. Holl and Rachel Noll) Introductory Reading in Educational Measurement, 1972, (with D.B. Tracy) Testing and Measurement in the Classroom, 1975. Served to lt. USAF, 1951-53. Mem. AAUP, AM. Ednl. Research Assn., Nat. Council Measurements in Edn., Phi Delta Kappa. Congregationalist. Club: Kiwanis. Home: 501 Copley Pl Indianapolis IN 46290-1050 Office: IUPUI Dept Edn Indianapolis IN 46202

SCANNELL, THOMAS JOHN, cold metal forming company executive; b. Detroit, Sept. 11, 1954; s. Robert Michael and Mary Frances (Chadwick) S. AS, Henry Ford Community Coll., Dearborn, Mich., 1982; BME, U. Detroit, 1988. Gen. laborer Fed. Screw Works, Romulus, Mich., 1973-82, supr. tool store, 1982-84, tool design engr. III, 1984-86, tool design engr. II, 1986-88, tool design engr. I, 1988-90, mgr. tool engring., 1990—; owner Great Lakes News Distributors, 1986—; exec. v.p. Detroit Hockey Assn. Hockey coach Detroit Police Athletic League. Mem. Soc. Mfg. Engrs. Avocations: golf, skiing, automobile restoration. Office: Fed Screw Works 34846 Goddard Rd Romulus MI 48174-3406

SCANNELL, WILLIAM EDWARD, aerospace company executive, consultant, psychologist; b. Muscatine, Iowa, Nov. 11, 1934; s. Mark Edward and Catharine Pearson (Fowler) S.; m. Barbara Ann Hoemann, Nov. 23, 1957; children: Cynthia Kay, Mark Edward, David Jerome, Terri Lynn, Stephen Patrick. BA in Gen. Edn., U. Nebr., 1961; BS in Engring., Ariz. State U., 1966; MS in Systems Engring., So. Meth. U., 1969; PhD, U.S. Internat. U., 1991. Commd. 2d lt. USAF, 1956, advanced through grades to lt. col., 1972; B-47 navigator-bombardier 98th Bomb Wing, Lincoln Air Force Base, Nebr., 1956-63; with Air Force Inst. of Tech., 1963-65, 68-69; chief mgmt. engring. team RAF Bentwaters, England, 1965-68; forward air contr. 20th Tactical Air Support Squadron USAF, Danang, Vietnam, 1970-71; program mgr. Hdqrs. USAF, Washington, 1971-74, staff asst. Office of Sec. Def., 1974-75, ret., 1975; account exec. Merrill Lynch, San Diego, 1975-77; program engring. chief Gen. Dynamics, San Diego, 1977-79, engring. chief, 1979-80, program mgr., 1980-83; mgr. integrated logistics support Northrop Corp., Hawthorne, Calif., 1984-88; mgr. B-2 program planning and scheduling Northrop Corp., Pico Rivera, Calif., 1988-91; pres. Scannell and Assocs., Borrego Springs, Calif., 1991-97; mem. adj. faculty U.S. Internat. U., San Diego. Decorated DFC with three oak leaf clusters, Air medal with 11 oak leaf clusters. Mem. APA, Calif. Psychol. Assn., Soc. Indsl. and Orgnl. Psychology, Inst. Indsl. Engrs., Coronado Cays Yacht Club, De Anza Country Club, Psi Chi. Republican. Roman Catholic. Home: PO Box 2392 717 Anza Park Trail Borrego Springs CA 92004-2392 Office: Scannell & Assocs PO Box 2392 Borrego Springs CA 92004-2392

SCARBOROUGH, CHARLES BISHOP, III, broadcast journalist, writer; b. Pitts., Nov. 4, 1943; s. Charles Bishop and Esther Francis (Campbell) S.; m. Linda Anne Gross, Dec. 14, 1972; children: Charles Bishop IV, Elizabeth Anne; m. Anne Ford Uzielli, Oct. 2, 1982; m. Ellen Carol Ward, Sept. 25, 1994. B.S., U. So. Miss., 1969. Prodn. mgr. Sta.-WLOX-TV, Biloxi, Miss., 1966-68; reporter, anchorman Sta.-WDAM-TV, Hattiesburg, Miss., 1968-69; reporter, anchorman, mng. editor Sta.-WAGA-TV, Atlanta, 1969-72; reporter, anchorman Sta.-WNAC-TV, Boston, 1972-74, NBC News, N.Y.C., 1974—. Author: (novels) Stryker, 1978, The Myrmidon Project, 1981, Aftershock, 1991. Served with USAF, 1961-65. Recipient awards for journalism AP (9), 1969-72, Emmy awards (22), 1974-94, award Aviation/Space Writers Assn., 1977, 78, 88, UPI award for journalism N.Y. Press Club award, 1988, 89, Sigma Delta Chi award, Deadline Club award, Terry Anderson Journalism award Working Press Assn. N.J., 1992. Mem. Phi Kappa Phi. Office: NBC News 30 Rockefeller Plz New York NY 10112

SCARBOROUGH, JOE, congressman; b. Atlanta, Apr. 9, 1963; m. Melanie Scarborough; Children: Joey, Andrew. BA, U. Ala., 1985; JD, U. Fla., 1990. Atty., 1990—; mem. 104th Congress from 1st Fla. dist., Washington, 1995—, polit. dir. freshman class, 1995—; mem. govt. reform and oversight com., nat. security com., mem. edn. com., co-chmn. New Federalists 105th Congress; bd. dirs. Emerald Coast Pediat. Primary Care, Inc. Mem. Fellowship Christian Athletes, Navy League (bd. dirs.), Rotary,. Republican. Office: US Ho of Reps 127 Cannon Bldg Washington DC 20515-0901

SCARBOROUGH, ROBERT HENRY, JR., coast guard officer; b. Hawkinsville, Ga., Mar. 12, 1923; s. Robert Henry and Janet Augusta (Burton) S.; m. Walterene Brant, July 1, 1946; children—Robert Henry, James Burton. BS, U.S. Mcht. Marine Acad., 1944; BBA, U. Hawaii, 1969, MBA, 1971; M.S., George Washington U., 1971, Armed Forces Staff Coll., 1963, Nat. War Coll., 1971. Commd. lt. (j.g.) USCG, 1949; advanced through grades to vice adm., 1978; chief Office of Ops. USCG, 1974-75, chief of staff, 1975-77, comdr. 9th Coast Guard Dist., 1977-78; vice comdt. USCG, Washington, 1978-82; ret. USCG, 1982; exec. dir. Navy League U.S., 1982-84; pres. Polaris Potomac Corp., 1985—. With USNR, 1942-49. Decorated Legion of Merit, D.S.M. Mem. Beta Gamma Sigma. Office: 5357 37th St N Arlington VA 22207-1312

SCARBROUGH, CLEVE KNOX, JR., museum director; b. Florence, Ala., July 17, 1939; s. Cleve Knox and Emma Lee (Matheny) S. B.S., U. No. Ala., 1962; M.A., U. Iowa, 1967. Asst. prof. art history U. Tenn., 1967-69; dir. Mint Mus. Art, Charlotte, N.C., 1969-76, Hunter Mus. Art, Chattanooga, 1976—; pres. N.C. Mus. Coun., 1976; bd. mem. adv. com. Tenn. Arts Commn., 1976-77, chmn. visual arts com., 1978—; mem. art selection com. TVA, 1983—, Provident Life Ins. Co., 1983—; cons. Mus. Assessment Program, 1984-94; grant evaluator Inst. Mus. Svcs., 1985-86; mem. art adv. com. First Tenn. Corp., 1991; lectr. Tenn. Gov.'s Conf. on the Arts, 1991. Compiler, editor: North Carolinians Collect, 1970, Pre Columbian Art of the Americas, 1971, Graphics by Four Modern Swiss Sculptors, 1972, British Paintings from the North Carolina Museum, 1973, Montain Landscapes by Swiss Artists, 1976. Mem. Chattanooga Landmark Com.; mem. City Planning Bd.; Bd. dirs. Chattanooga Conv. and Visitors Bur., 1977-79; advisor Chattanooga Cen. City Council, 1981-85, Tenn. State Mus., 1981, mem. Am. Federation of Arts Adv. Bd., 1987—. Served with USN, 1962-64. Mem. Am. Assn. Museums (accreditation vis. com. 1985-94), Southeastern Mus. Conf. (coun. 1976-80, 86-88, chmn. publs. com. 1979, rep. to Am. Assn. Mus.; bd. dirs. 1986-88), Rotary. Office: Hunter Mus Art 10 Bluff View St Chattanooga TN 37403-1111

SCARBROUGH, FRANK EDWARD, government official; b. Knoxville, Tenn., Sept. 27, 1942; s. James L. and Anna Dale (Edwards) S.; m. Deborah Griffin, Feb. 4, 1972; 1 child, Elizabeth Anne. BS, U. Tenn., 1964; AM,

Harvard U., 1966, PhD, 1971. Rsch. assoc. U. Bern, Switzerland, 1971-73; instr. U. Pa., Phila., 1973-76; chemist food additive rev. FDA, Washington, 1977-80, chief regulatory affairs staff, 1980-86, dep. dir. Office Nutrition, 1986-89, dir. Office Nutrition, 1989-92, dir. Office Food Labeling, 1992—. Contbe. author: Food Labeling, 1994. Recipient award of merit FDA, 1985, Superior Svc. award USPHS, 1991, Disting. Svc. award HHS, 1993. Mem. Am. Chem. Soc., Am. Soc. Clin. Nutrition, Inst. Food Technologists. Office: FDA Office of Food Labeling 200 C St SW Washington DC 20204-0001

SCARDINA, FRANK JOSEPH, real estate executive; b. Chgo., Feb. 18, 1948; s. Joseph Samuel and Marian Florence (Bogseth) S.; m. Diane Lynne Stern, Sept. 1, 1968; children: Brian Joseph, Kevin Stanley, Adam Charles, Todd Richard. BA in Econs, U. Denver, 1969; JD, U. Calif., Berkeley, 1972. Bar: Calif. 1972. Assoc. Mitchell, Silberberg & Knupp, L.A., 1975-77, Chickering and Gregory, San Francisco, 1972-75; corp. counsel Kaufman and Broad, Inc., L.A., 1978; v.p., gen. counsel Kaufman and Broad, Inc., 1979-80; pres. Kaufman and Broad Communities, Inc., 1981-89, Kaufman and Broad of So. Calif., 1985-90, Birtcher Homes, 1992-93; divsn. pres. Ryland Homes, 1993-94, regional pres. west region, 1994—; pres. M.J. Brock & Sons, Inc., 1994—; vis. lectr. Law Sch. U. So. Calif., 1987-92; mem. L.A. Blue Ribbon Com. for Affordable Housing, 1988. Pres. Bon Vivant Homeowners Assn., 1976-77; founding pres. Lindley Oaks Parents-Tchrs. Assn., 1979-80. Home: 6148 Edinburgh Ct Agoura Hills CA 91301-4141

SCARDINO, ALBERT JAMES, journalist; b. Balt., Sept. 22, 1948; s. Peter Lester and Mary Katherine (Mangelsdorf) S.; m. Marjorie Beth Morris, Apr. 19, 1974; children—Adelaide Katherine Morris, William Brown, Albert Henry Hugh. B.A., Columbia U., 1970; M.J., U. Calif.-Berkeley, 1976. Editor Ga. Gazette, Savannah, 1978-84; corr., editor N.Y. Times, N.Y.C., 1985-89; press sec. Mayor of N.Y.C., 1990-91; ind. journalist, 1991—. Editor, producer documentary film: Guale, 1976 (numerous awards 1976). Recipient Pulitzer Prize, 1984. Mem. Internat. Soc. Weekly Newspaper Editors (bd. dirs. 1983-86, Golden Quill award 1982), Columbia Coll. Alumni Assn. (sec. 1990-93). Home: 19 Empire House, Thurloe Pl, London SW7 2RU, England

SCARDINO, MARJORIE MORRIS, publishing company executive; b. Flagstaff, Ariz., Jan. 25, 1947; d. Robert Weldon and Beth (Lamb) Morris; m. Albert James Scardino, Apr. 19, 1974; children: Adelaide Katherine Morris, William Brown, Albert Henry Hugh. BA, Baylor U.; JD, U. San Francisco. Ptnr. Brannen Wessels & Searcy, Savannah, Ga., 1976-85; pub. Ga. Gazette Pub. Co., Savannah, 1978-85; pres. The Economist Newspaper Group, Inc., N.Y.C., 1985-93; worldwide mng. dir. Economist Intelligence Unit, N.Y.C., 1992-93; chief exec. The Economist Group, London, 1993-97, Pearson P.L.C., London, 1997—; bd. dirs. The Economist Newspaper, Ltd., ConAgra, W.H. Smith; mem. vis. com. New Sch. for Social Rsch., N.Y.C., 1989—. Bd. dirs. Atlantic Coun., 1989, Pub. Radio Internat., 1993—. Office: Pearson PLC, 3 Burlington Gardens, London W1X 1LE, England

SCARF, HERBERT ELI, economics educator; b. Phila., July 25, 1930; s. Louis H. and Lena (Elkman) S.; m. Margaret Klein, June 28, 1953; children: Martha Anne Samuelson, Elizabeth Joan Stone, Susan Margaret Merrell. AB, Temple U., 1951; MA, Princeton U., 1952, PhD, 1954; LHD (hon.), U. Chgo., 1978. With RAND Corp., Santa Monica, Calif., 1954-57; asst. and assoc. prof. stats. Stanford U., Calif., 1957-63, fellow Ctr. for Advanced Study, 1962-63; vis. assoc. prof. Yale U., New Haven, 1959-60, prof. econs., 1963-70, Stanley Resor prof. econs., 1970-78, Sterling prof. econs., 1979—; dir. Cowles Found. Research in Econs., Yale U., 1967-71, 1981-84, div. social sciences, 1971-72, 1973-74. Author: Studies in the Mathematical Theory of Inventory and Production, 1958, Computation of Economic Equilibria, 1973. Editor: Applied General Equilibrium Analysis, 1984. Recipient Lanchester prize Ops. Research Soc. of Am., 1974, Von Neumann medal, 1983; named Disting. fellow Am. Econ. Assn., 1991. Fellow Econometric Soc. (pres. 1983); mem. Am. Acad. Arts and Sciences, Nat. Acad. of Sciences, Am. Philos. Soc. Democrat. Jewish. Clubs: New Haven Lawn (Conn.), Yale (N.Y.C.). Office: Yale U Cowles Found Rsch Econs PO Box 208281 New Haven CT 06520-8281

SCARF, MARGARET (MAGGIE SCARF), author; b. Phila., May 13, 1932; d. Benjamin and Helen (Rotbin) Klein; m. Herbert Eli Scarf, June, 1953; children: Martha Samuelson, Elizabeth Stone, Susan Merrell. BA, South Conn. State U., 1989. Writer in residence Jonathan Edwards Coll., Yale U.; contbg. editor New Republic, Washington, DC, 1978—, Self Mag., N.Y.C., 1991—; writer-in-residence Jonathan Edwards Coll., 1995—; assoc. fellow Jonathan Edwards Coll. Yale U., New Haven, 1979, 81, 83; sr. fellow Bush Ctr. in Child Devel. and Social Policy, Yale U., 1991—; mem. adv. bd. Am. Psychiat. Press, Poynter Fellowship Journalism Yale U., 1995-96. Author: Meet Benjamin Franklin, 1968, Antarctica: Exploring the Frozen Continent, 1970, Body, Mind, Behavior, 1976 (Nat. Media award Am. Psychological Assn. 1977), Unfinished Business: Pressure Points in the Lives of Women, 1981, Intimate Partners: Patterns in Love and Marriage, 1987, Intimate Worlds: Life Inside the Family, 1996; contbr. numerous articles to jours. including N.Y. Times mag. and book rev., Psychology Today; TV appearances include: David Letterman Show, Oprah Wingrey Show, CBS News, Good Morning Am., Today Show, Phil Donahue, numerous others. Recipient Nat. Media award Am. Psychol. Found., 1971, 74, 77, Conn. UN award Outstanding Conn. Women, 1987, cert. commendation Robert T. Morse Writers Competition Am. Psychiat. Assn., 1997; grantee Smith Richardson Found., 1991-94; Ford Found. fellow, 1973-74, Neiman fellow Harvard U., 1975-76, Ctr. Advanced Study in Behavioral Scis. fellow, 1977-78, 85-86, Alicia Patterson Found. fellow, 1978-79. Mem. Conn. Soc. Psychoanalytic Psychologists, Am. Psychiat. Press (mem. adv. bd. 1992), Lawn Club, Elizabethans, PEN Writer's Assn. Avocations: reading, hiking, swimming. Office: Jonathan Edwards Coll Yale U 68 High St East Haven CT 06512-2316

SCARFIOTTI, FERDINANDO, production designer. Prodn. designer: (films) The Conformist, 1971, Death in Venice, 1971, Avanti!, 1972, Last Tango in Paris, 1973, Daisy Miller, 1974, American Gigolo, 1980, Flash Gordon, 1980, Honky Tonk Freeway, 1981, Cat People, 1982, Bring on the Night, 1985, The Last Emperor, 1987 (Academy award best art direction 1987), Mamba, 1988, Toys, 1992 (Academy award nomination best art direction 1992). Office: care Art Directors Guild 11365 Ventura Blvd Ste 315 Studio City CA 91604-3148*

SCARMINACH, CHARLES ANTHONY, lawyer; b. Syracuse, N.Y., Feb. 19, 1944; s. John Louis and Lucy (Egnoto) S.; children: John, Catherine, Karen, Charles, Robert. MA, U. Buffalo, 1965; JD, Syracuse U., 1968. Bar: N.Y. 1968, S.C. 1974. Gen. counsel Sea Pines Co., Hilton Head Island, S.C., 1973-78; sole practice, Hilton Head Island, 1978-83; ptnr. Novit & Scarminach, P.A., Hilton Head Island, 1983-93; bd. dirs. Nations Bank, Hilton Head Island. Chmn. bd. Sea Pines Montessori Sch., Hilton Head Island, 1979-83; bd. dirs. Hilton Head Preparatory Sch., 1984-93, chmn. bd. trustees 1986-93. Maj. U.S. Army, 1968-73. Mem. ABA, S.C. Bar Assn., N.Y. State Bar Assn., Hilton Head Island C. of C. (bd. dirs. 1996—). Democrat. Roman Catholic. Club: Sea Pines. Home: 10 Wood Duck Ct Hilton Head Island SC 29928-4153 Office: Novit Scarminach & Williams PA PO Box 14 Hilton Head Island SC 29938-0014

SCARNE, JOHN, game company executive; b. Steubenville, Ohio, Mar. 4, 1903; s. Fiorangelo and Maria (Tamburro) S.; m. Steffi Kearney, 1956; 1 son, John Teeko. Student pub. schs., Guttenberg, N.J. Pres. John Scarne Games, Inc., North Bergen, N.J., 1950—; gaming cons. Hilton Hotels Internat. Magician stage, screen and television; Author: Scarne on Dice, 1945, Scarne on Cards, 1950, Scarne on Card Tricks, 1950, Scarne on Magic Tricks, 1952, Scarne's New Complete Guide to Gambling, 1962, The Odds Against Me, 1967, Scarne's Encyclopedia of Games, 1973, The Mafia Conspiracy, 1976, Scarne's Guide to Casino Gambling; Scarne's Guide to Modern Poker; Contbr. to: World Book Ency, 1970, Ency. Brit, 1975. Cons. to U.S. Armed Forces, 1941-45. Named Man of Year for Police Chiefs of U.S., 1960. Office: Unit 312 2581 Countryside Blvd Clearwater FL 33761-4515

SCAROLA, JOHN MICHAEL, dentist, educator; b. N.Y.C., Nov. 18, 1934; s. Michael Fidelis and Filomena Mary (Turso) S.; m. Theodora Mary Marty, June 15, 1963; children: Michael A., John P., Stephen A., Robert M., Mary E. BS, Fordham Coll., 1956; DDS, Columbia U., 1960. Instr. Columbia Dental Sch., N.Y.C., 1962-68, asst. clin. prof., 1969-72, course dir. fixed partial dentures, 1969-72, assoc. clin. prof., 1973-86, course dir. prosthodontic elective, 1977-91, clin. prof., 1986—; lectr., clin. prof. postgrad. prostodontics Columbia U., N.Y.C., 1986—, AEGD-Columbia U., N.Y.C., 1990-92, Luth. Med. Ctr., Bklyn., 1993—; cons. in prosthodontics Northport VA Hosp., East Northport, N.Y., 1970-91. Scoutmaster Boy Scouts Am., Port Washington, N.Y., 1976-78; chmn. spl. gifts Bishop's Annual Appeal, St. Peter's-Port Washington, 1977-78; Cath. Youth Orgn. sports coach St. Paul The Apostle, Brookville, N.Y., 1980-83; fundraising com. The Yard, Martha's Vineyard, Mass., 1990; concert com. Musician's Emergency Fund, N.Y.C., 1992. Lt. USNR, 1960-62. Fellow Am. Coll. Dentists (chmn. N.Y. sect. 1994), N.Y. Acad. Dentistry (pres. 1989-90), Greater N.Y. Acad. Prosthodontics (dir. 1993-97); mem. Greater N.Y. Acad. Prosthodontics Found. (dir., pres. 1989-97), N.Y. Acad. Dentistry Endowment Fund (dir., pres. 1992-93). Republican. Roman Catholic. Avocations: golf, opera, classical music, gardening. Home: 83 Fruitledge Rd Brookville NY 11545 Office: 501 Madison Ave New York NY 10022-5602

SCARPA, ANTONIO, medicine educator, biomedical scientist; b. Padua, Italy, July 3, 1942; s. Angelo and Elena (DeRossi) S. MD cum laude, U. Padua, 1966, PhD in Pathology, 1970; MA (hon.), U. Pa., 1978. Asst. prof. biochemistry, biophysics U. Pa., Phila., 1973-76, assoc. prof., 1976-80, prof., 1980-86, dir. biomed. instrumentation group, 1983-86; prof. dept. pathology Jefferson U., Phila., 1986—; prof., chmn. dept. physiology and biophysics Case Western Res. U., Cleve., 1986—, dir. tng. ctr., program project, 1983—, prof. medicine, 1989—; cons. study sect. NIH, Bethesda, 1984—, Am. Heart Assn., Dallas, 1986-91; pres., assoc. chair dept. physiology, 1993-94; vice chair Nat. Caucus Basic Sci. Presidents, Washington. Editor (books): Frontiers of Biological Energetics, Calcium Transport and Cell Function, Transport ATPases, Membrane Pathology, Membrane and Cancer Cells; editor (jours.) Archives Biochemistry and Biophysics, Cell Calcium, Biochemistry Internat.; mem. editorial bd. Circulation Rsch., 1978-81, Biophys. Jour., 1979-82, Jour. Muscle Rsch., 1979—, Magnesium, 1982—, Physiol. Revs., 1982-90, FASEB Jour., 1987-92, Molecular Cellular Biochemistry, 1988—; contbr. numerous articles to profl. jours. Mem. Am. Soc. Physiologists, Am. Soc. Biol. Chemistry, Biophys. Soc. (exec. coun. 1980-83, 85-89, 94-97), U.S. Bioenergetics Group (program chmn. 1974-75, 82, 83, exec. officer 1985-90, assoc. chmn. dept. physiology, pres. 1993-95). Avocations: farming, sailing, painting. Office: Case Western Reserve Univ Dept Of Physiology Cleveland OH 44106

SCARPITTI, FRANK ROLAND, sociology educator; b. Butler, Pa., Nov. 12, 1936; s. Frank and Geneva (Costanza) S.; m. Ellen Louise Canfield, Sept. 5, 1959; children: Susan, Jeffrey. B.A., Cleve. State U., 1958; M.A., Ohio State U., 1959, Ph.D., 1962. Research asso. Ohio State U. Psychiat. Inst., Columbus, 1961-63; asst. prof. Rutgers U., 1963-67; asso. prof. sociology U. Del., 1967-69, prof., 1969—, chmn. dept., 1969-80, 88-94; cons. state and fed. govts.; Bd. dirs. Joint Commn. on Criminology and Criminal Justice Edn. and Standards, 1977-81. Author: Schizophrenics in the Community, 1967, Combatting Social Problems, 1967, Youth and Drugs, 1970, Group Interactions as Therapy, 1974, Social Problems, 1974, 77, 80, Deviance: Action, Reaction, Interaction, 1975, Women, Crime and Justice, 1980, The Young Drug User, 1980, Poisoning for Profit, 1985, Social Problems, 1989, 92, 97, Social Problems: The Search for Solutions, 1994; contbr. articles to profl. jours. Recipient Hofheimer prize for research Am. Psychiat. Assn., 1967; mem. Danforth Found. asso. program. Mem. Am. Sociol. Assn., Am. Soc. Criminology (v.p. 1978-79, pres.-elect 1979-80, pres. 1980-81), AAUP, Alpha Kappa Delta, Phi Kappa Phi, Omicron Delta Kappa. Home: 104 Radcliffe Dr Newark DE 19711-3147

SCARR, SANDRA WOOD, psychology educator, researcher; b. Washington, Aug. 8, 1936; d. John Ruxton and Jane (Powell) Wood; m. Harry Alan Scarr, Dec. 26, 1961 (div. 1970); children: Phillip, Karen, Rebbecca, Stephanie; m. James Callan Walker, Aug. 9, 1982 (div. 1994). AB, Vassar Coll., 1958; AM, Harvard U., 1963, PhD, 1965. Asst. prof. psychology U. Md., College Park, 1964-67; assoc. prof. U. Pa., Phila., 1967-71; prof. U. Minn., Mpls., 1971-77, Yale U., New Haven, 1977-83; Commonwealth prof. U. Va., Charlottesville, 1983-95, chmn. dept. psychology, 1984-90; CEO, chmn. bd. dirs. KinderCare Learning Ctr., Inc., 1995-97; ret., 1997; mem. nat. adv. bd. Robert Wood Johnson Found., Princeton, N.J., 1985-91; coord. coun. psychology SUNY Bd. Regents, N.Y.C., 1984-92; prof. Kerstin Hesselgren, Sweden, 1993-94. Author: Race, Social Class and Individual Differences in IQ, 1981, Mother Care/Other Care, 1984 (Nat. Book award APA 1985), Caring for Children, 1989; editor Jour. Devel. Psychology, 1980-86, Current Directions in Psychol. Sci., 1991-95. Fellow Ctr. for Advanced Studies, Stanford U., Calif., 1976-77; grantee NIH, NSF, others, 1967-95. Fellow AAAS, APA (chmn. com. on human rsch. 1980-83, coun. of reps. 1984-89, bd. dirs. 1988-90, Award for Disting. Contbn. to Rsch. on Pub. Policy 1988), Am. Psychol. Soc. (bd. dirs. 1992—, pres. 1996-97, James McKeen Cattell award 1993); mem. Am. Acad. Arts and Scis. (coun. mem. 1995—), Behavior Genetics Assn. (pres. 1985-86, mem. exec. coun. 1976-79, 84-87), Soc. for Rsch. in Child Devel. (governing coun. 1974-76, 87-93, chmn. fin. com. 1987-89, pres. 1989-91), Internat. Soc. for Study of Behavioral Devel. (exec. bd. 1987-94). Avocations: dogs, gardening. Home: 77-6384 Halawai St Kailua Kona HI 96740

SCARRITT, THOMAS VARNON, newspaper editor; b. Tuscaloosa, Ala., Jan. 28, 1953; s. Charles Wesley and Valerie (Varnon) S.; m. Kathryn Rush Hubbard, Dec. 28, 1973; children: Sara Kathryn, Thomas Varnon Jr. BA in Journalism, U. N.C., 1974; MBA, Samford U., 1995. Reporter The Birmingham (Ala.) News, 1975-79, Washington corr., 1979-83, news editor, 1983-85, editorial page editor, 1986-89, exec. editor, 1989—. Bd. dirs. Literacy Coun. Ctrl. Ala. Mem. Am. Soc. Newspaper Editors, Soc. Profl. Journalists (pres. Ala. profl. chpt. 1988-89), Kiwanis (Birmingham), Phi Beta Kappa. Episcopal. Home: 4240 Clairmont Ave S Birmingham AL 35222-3724 Office: The Birmingham News 2200 4th Ave North Birmingham AL 35202

SCARSE, OLIVIA MARIE, cardiologist, consultant; b. Chgo., Nov. 10, 1950; d. Oliver Marcus and Marjorie Ardis (Olsen) S. BS, North Park Coll., 1970; MD, Loyola U., Maywood, Ill., 1973. Diplomate Am. Bd. Internal Medicine, Am. Bd. Cardiovascular Diseases. Surg. intern Resurrection Hosp., Chgo., 1974; resident in internal medicine Northwestern U., Chgo., 1974-77; cardiovascular disease fellow U. Ill., Chgo., 1977-80; dir. cardiac catherization lab. Cook County Hosp., Chgo., 1981; dir. heart sta. MacNeal Hosp., Berwyn, Ill., 1983; dir. electrophysiology Hines VA Hosp., Maywood, Ill., 1984-85; dir. progressive care Columbus Hosp., Chgo., 1985-88, pvt. practice, 1984—; pvt. practice Ill. Masonic Hosp., Chgo., 1989-96; founder Physician Cons. for Evaluation of Clin. Pathways, Practice Parameters and Patient Care Outcomes, 1991—. Dir. continuous quality improvement Improvement Columbus, 1990-95. Pillsbury fellow Pillsbury Fund, 1980. Fellow Am. Coll. Cardiology; mem. AMA, ACP, Chgo. Med. Assn., Ill. State Med. Assn., Am. Heart Assn., Crescent Countries Found. for Med. Care, Physicians Health Network, Cen. Ill. Med. Review Orgn. Avocations: musician, ballet and tap dancer, actress, model, singer. Home and Office: 2650 N Lakeview Ave Apt 4109 Chicago IL 60614-1833

SCATENA, LORRAINE BORBA, rancher, women's rights advocate; b. San Rafael, Calif., Feb. 18, 1924; d. Joseph and Eugenia (Simas) de Borba; m. Louis G. Scatena, Feb. 14, 1960; children: Louis Vincent, Eugenia Gayle. BA, Dominican Coll., San Rafael, 1945; postgrad., Calif. Sch. Fine Arts, 1948, U. Calif., Berkeley, 1956-57. Cert. elem. tchr., Calif. Tchr. Dominican Coll., 1946; tchr. of mentally handicapped San Anselmo (Calif.) Sch. Dist., 1946; tchr. Fairfax (Calif.) Pub. Elem. Sch., 1946-53; asst. to mayor Fairfax City Recreation, 1948-53; tchr., libr. U.S. Dependent Schs., Mainz am Rhine, Fed. Republic Germany, 1953-56; translator Portugal Travel Tours, Lisbon, 1954; bonding sec. Am. Fore Ins. Group, San Francisco, 1956-60; rancher, farmer Yerington, Nev., 1960—; hostess com. Caldecott and Newbury Authors' Awards, San Francisco, 1959; mem. Nev. State Legis. Commn., 1975; coord. Nevadans for Equal Rights Amendment, 1975-78, rural areas rep., 1976-78; testifier Nev. State Senate and Assembly, 1975, 77; mem. adv. com. Fleischmann Coll. Agr. U. Nev., 1977-80, 81-84; speaker Grants and Rsch. Projects, Bishop, Calif., 1977, Choices for Tomorrow's Women, Fallon, Nev., 1989. Trustee Wassuk Coll., Hawthorne, Nev., 1984-87; mem. Lyon County Friends of Libr., Yerington, 1971—, Lyon County Mus. Soc., 1978; sec., pub. info. chmn. Lyon County Rep. Women, 1968-73, v.p. programs, 1973-75; mem. Lyon County Rep. Ctrl. Com., 1973-74; mem. Marin County Soc. Artists, San Anselmo, Calif., 1948-53; charter mem. Eleanor Roosevelt Fund Women and Girls, 1990, sustaining mem., 1992—; Nev. rep. 1st White House Conf. Rural Am. Women, Washington, 1980; participant internat. reception, Washington, 1980; mem. pub. panel individual presentation Shakespeare's Treatment of Women Characters, Nev. Theatre for the Arts, Ashland, Oreg. Shakespearean Actors local performance, 1977; mem. Nev. Women's History Project, U. Nev., 1996—. Recipient Outstanding Conservation Farmer award Mason Valley Conservation Dist., 1992, Soroptimist Internat. Women Helping women award 1983, invitation to first all-women delegation to U.S.A. from People's Republic China, U.S. House Reps., 1979; Public Forum Travel grantee Edn. Title IX, Oakland, Calif., 1977; fellow World Lit. Acad., 1993. Mem. Lyon County Ret. Tchrs. Assn. (unit pres. 1979-80, 84-86, v.p. 1986-88, Nev. State Outstanding Svc. award 1981, state conv. gen. chmn. 1985), Rural Am. Women Inc., AAUW (br. pres. 1972-74, 74-76, chair edn. found. programs, 1983—, state convention gen. chmn. 1976, 87, state sec. 1970-72, state legis. program chmn. 1976-77, state chmn. internat. rels. 1979-81, state pres. 1981-83, br. travelship, discovering women in U.S. history Radcliffe Coll. State Humanities award 1975, Future Fund Nat. award 1983, Lorraine Scatena endowment gift named in her honor for significant contbns. to the AAUW Ednl. Found., 1997), Mason Valley Country Club, Italian Cath. Fedn. Club (pres. 1986-88), Uniao Portuguesa Estado da Calif. Roman Catholic. Avocations: writing, photography. Home: PO Box 247 Yerington NV 89447-0247

SCATURRO, PHILIP DAVID, investment banker; b. Newark, Dec. 8, 1938; s. Charles and Rose (Montino) S. BA, Williams Coll., 1960; JD, Columbia U., 1963, MBA, 1963. Analyst Ladenburg, Thalmann & Co., Inc., N.Y.C., 1964-67; v.p. Sellin, Forbes & Smith, N.Y.C., 1967; v.p. Allen & Co. Inc., N.Y.C., 1967-71, mng. dir., exec. v.p., 1977—; gen. ptnr. R&S Assocs., N.Y.C., 1972-76; pvt. investor, N.Y.C., 1976-77; bd. dirs., chmn. compensation com., exec. com. United Asset Mgmt. Co.; bd. dirs. Intrenet, Inc., Milford, Ohio, Opal Concepts, Inc., Anaheim, Calif., Hi-Tech Mfg., Inc., Thornton, Colo., Asquith Ct. Ltd., London. Bd. dirs., exec. com., chmn. fin. com., treas. N.Y.C. Opera; trustee, exec. com., chmn. audit com., trustee New Sch. for Social Rsch.; mem. com. on alt. investments Williams Coll. Mem. Univ. Club (N.Y.C.), Century Assn. Avocations: Opera, music, theatre, wine, fly fishing. Office: Allen & Co 711 5th Ave New York NY 10022-3111

SCEIFORD, MARY ELIZABETH, retired public television administrator; b. Erie, Pa., Nov. 30, 1932; d. William Michael and Ellen Elizabeth (Laffer) S. BA, Allegheny Coll., 1954; MS, Univ. Wis., 1960; PhD, Syracuse Univ., 1969. Cert. tchr. Pa., Wis., Ohio. Kindergarten tchr. Lakewood (Ohio) Pub. Schs., 1954-56; grade one/two tchr. Madison (Wis.) Pub. Schs., 1956-59; art tchr. Mt. Lebanon (Pa.) Pub. Schs., 1960-65; tv. tchr. WQED-TV, Pitts., 1965-66; art tchr. Mt. Lebanon Pub. Schs., 1966-67; assoc. dir. Sch. Svcs. WQED-TV, Pitts., 1969-74, dir. sch. svcs., 1974-75; assoc. dir. edn. and children's tv programs Corp. for Pub. Broadcasting, Washington, 1975-96; ret.; adv. bd. Nat. Pub. Broadcasting Archives, College Park, Md., 1993—. Contbr. articles to profl. jours. Bd. trustees Allegheny Coll., 1975—; USA rep. European Broadcasting Union Youth Group, Geneva, Switzerland, 1993-96. Mem. Am. Ednl. Rsch. Assn., ASCD, Assn. Ednl. Communications & Tech., Phi Beta Kappa, Pi Lambda Theta. Avocations: walking, swimming, gardening, piano.

SCELSA, JOSEPH VINCENT, sociologist; b. N.Y.C., Dec. 7, 1945; s. Albert John and Katherine Mary S.; A.A., LIU, 1966, B.A., 1968; M.A., City U. N.Y., 1973, M.S.Ed., 1978; M.A., Columbia U., 1983, Ed.D., 1984; m. Joyce Ann Tisi, Nov. 13, 1981; 1 child, Jonathan. Counselor, tchr. N.Y.C. Bd. Edn., 1970-78, coord. career and occupational edn., 1979; coord. specialized counseling CUNY, 1979-81; pvt. practice counseling, N.Y.C., 1975—; lectr. grad. faculty Herbert H. Lehman Coll., 1980—; dir. Calandra Inst. CUNY, 1984—. Cert. sch. counselor, N.Y. Active Coun. of 1000 Nat. Italian-Am. Found; past vice chair multi cultural adv. bd. N.Y.C. Bd. Edn., 1990-91; N.Y. State Mentoring Program Adv. Bd., 1990—; bd. dirs. Nat. Ethnic Coalition Orgns., 1990—, Coalition Italo-Am. Assn., 1986—; Italian Apostalate, N.Y., 1993. Recipient Disting. Alumni award LIU, 1985, Organizational Leadership award Coalition Italo-Am. Assns., Inc., 1988, Americus award Bronx Community Coll., 1989, Role Model award Club DaVinci, 1990, Inte I-A Student Assn. award, CUNY, 1991, Intergroup Rels. Chancellor's award, 1994, FIERI Leadership award, 1993, Philip Mazzei award, 1993, Ellis Island medal of honor, 1997; named Cavaliere of Order of Merit Republic of Italy, 1992; Italian fellow John Jay Coll., 1993; inductee St. Lucy's Hall of Fame, 1996. Mem. Am. Counseling Assn., Am. Mental Health Counselors Assn. (cert. of recognition 1979, counselor of yr. 1983-84), Nat. Acad. Cert. Clin. Mental Health Counselors, Nat. Bd. for Cert. Counselers, Am.-Italian Hist. Assn., N.Y. State Mental Health Counselors Assn. (past pres., Outstanding Work award 1980), Ill. Club. Home: 41 Carwall Ave Mount Vernon NY 10552-1211 Office: CUNY Grad Ctr 33 W 42nd St New York NY 10036-8003

SCEPANSKI, JORDAN MICHAEL, librarian, administrator; b. Yonkers, N.Y., Nov. 21, 1942; s. Michael James and Margaret (Witko) S.; m. H. Lea Wells, Apr. 18, 1981; children—Kathryn Mary, Jordan Wells, Jennifer Elizabeth. BS, Manhattan Coll., 1964; MLn, Emory U., 1967; postgrad., U. N.C., Charlotte, 1976-77; M.B.A., U. Tenn., Nashville, 1982. Vol. Peace Corps, Turkey, 1964-66; adult services librarian Uniondale Pub. Library, N.Y., 1967-68; various profl. staff positions ALA, Chgo., 1970-73; asst. dir. library, asst. prof. U. N.C., Charlotte, 1974-78; dir. central library Vanderbilt U., Nashville, 1978-84; dir. univ. library and learning resources Calif. State U., Long Beach, 1984-96; exec. dir. Triangle Rsch. Librs. Network, Chapel Hill, N.C., 1996—; mgmt. intern Joint Univ. Librs., Nashville, 1977-78; cons./trainer Assn. Rsch. Librs., 1979; Fulbright lectr. Hacettepe U., Ankara, Turkey, 1981-82; cons. Coll. Charleston, S.C., No. Ky. U., Highlands Heights, Elon Coll., N.C., Calif. State U., L.A., Bloomsburg U.; facilitator, trainer U. Notre Dame, South Bend, Ind., U. Nebr., Lincoln, U. Wyo.; founding mem. IBM Informa; bd. dirs. VTLS Inc.; sr. advisor for libr. affairs Calif. State U. Sys., 1995. Contbr. articles to profl. jours. Served with U.S. Army, 1968-70. Recipient K.G. Saur award Coll. and Research Libraries publ., 1988; sr. fellow UCLA, 1983; faculty/librarian coop. research grantee Council on Library Resources, 1983. Mem. ALA (chair Nat. Libr. Week com. 1980-81, chair internat. rels. round table 1990-91, chair K.S. Sauer Libr. Lit. award com. 1995-96), Western Assn. Schs. and Colls. (accreditation vis. team), Freedom to Read Found., Fulbright Alumni Assn., Jane Austen Soc. N.Am., Beta Phi Mu, Phi Beta Delta. Democrat. Roman Catholic. Office: Wilson Libr CB # 3940 Chapel Hill NC 27599-3940

SCERPELLA, ERNESTO GUILLERMO, physician researcher; b. Lima, Peru, Dec. 11, 1960; came to U.S., 1988; s. Juan Severino and Maria Doris (Porth) S.; m. Patricia Del Carmen Campos, Oct. 29, 1988; 1 child, Ernesto Alessandro. MD, Cayetano Heredia U., 1986. Resident internal medicine U. Miami, 1988-91, fellow spl. immunology, 1994-95, asst. prof. medicine, 1995—; fellow infectious disease U. Tex., Houston, 1991-94; mem. infection control com. Pub. Health Trust-Jackson Meml. Hosp., Miami, 1995—; instr. in histology Cayetano Heredia U., Lima, 1980-81. Author numerous scientific articles on areas related to infectious diseases and AIDS; sci. reviewer for several med. jours. Zeneca travel grant Nat. Found. for Infectious Diseases, 1993. Mem. ACP, AMA, Infectious Diseases Soc. of Am. (HIV/AIDS tng. program 1994), Panamerican Assn. of Infectious Diseases. Office: U Miami Sch Medicine 901 NW 17th St Ste D Miami FL 33136-1135

SCHAAB, ARNOLD J., lawyer; b. Newark, Dec. 26, 1939; s. Robert George and Pauline (Levine) S.; m. Marcia Stecker, 1964 (div. 1978); children: Emily Diana, Genevieve; m. Patricia Caesar, 1981 (div. 1996). BA, New Sch. for Social Rsch., 1962; LLB, Harvard U., 1965. Bar: N.Y. 1967, U.S. Dist. Ct. (so. and ea. dists.) N.Y. 1967. Assoc. Chadbourne & Parke, N.Y.C., 1966-69; ptnr. Anderson, Kill, Olick & Oshinsky, N.Y.C., 1969-78; sr. ptnr. Pryor, Cashman, Sherman & Flynn, N.Y.C., 1978—. Pres. Literacy Ptnrs., Inc.; mem. exec. com. Shaker Mus. and Libr., Old Chatham, N.Y.; mem. vis. com. Milano Grad. Sch. Mgmt. and Pub. Policy, New Sch. for Social Rsch. Fulbright scholar Law Faculty U. Paris, 1966. Fellow N.Y. Bar Found., Am. Bar Found.; mem. ABA (vice chair internat. fin. transactions com., forum com. on constrn. industry), N.Y. State Bar Assn. (chair internat. law and practice sect., chmn. spl. com. free trade in the Ams., ho. of dels., fin. com., long range planning com., by-laws com.), Assn. Bar City N.Y., Univ. Club (chmn. fin. com., chmn. audit com., mem. coun.), Doubles, Old Chatham Hunt Club. Office: Pryor Cashman Sherman & Flynn 410 Park Ave New York NY 10022-4407

SCHAACK, PHILIP ANTHONY, retired beverage company executive; b. Evanston, Ill., June 6, 1921; s. Harry Charles and Lora Mary (Colford) S.; m. Elizabeth Eberhart, Mar. 27, 1943; children: Susan, Laura, Betsy. Student, Northwestern U., 1943; LLD (hon.), Ill. Benedictine Coll., 1977. Vice-pres. Joyce Beverages/Chgo., 1957-60; v.p. Joyce Beverages/Ill., Joliet, 1960-63, exec. v.p., 1963-65, pres., 1965-85; dir. Joyce Beverages/Ill. Retired ir. First Midwest Bank; past chmn., trustee Ill. Benedictine Coll.; vice-chmn. nat. devel. coun. Sisters of Providence. With USN, 1942-45. Mem. Chgo. Golf Club, Innisbrook Golf Club, Minocqua Country Club, Timber Ridge Country Club. Republican. Roman Catholic. Home: 1480 Aberdeen Ct Naperville IL 60564-9797

SCHAAF, MIV, writer, graphic designer, composer; b. Oct. 3, 1920; m. Alfred Musso, 1959; 1 chld, Gia Musso. BA, Mich. State U., 1943; postgrad., Humboldt State U., 1990—. Owner Miv Schaaf Assocs., 1954—; seminar tchr. UCLA, U. Calif. Irvine, Scripps Coll., 1977—; del. White House Conf. Librs., 1979; judge Robert B. Campbell book collection UCLA, 1980; speaker in field. Author: Who Can Not Read About Crocodiles?, 1988; columnist L.A. Times, 1972-87, North Coast Jour., 1993—; writer 156 poems; composer more than 160 songs including Songs of Age and Songs of Rage. Pres. Archtl. Panel, L.A., 1954-72; founder Pasadena Cultural Heritage Commn., 1973. Recipient Premier award Pasadena Heritage, 1977, Met. Coop. Libr. System and Calif. Libr. Assn. award, 1982, Gold Crown award Pasadena Arts Coun., 1983. Avocation: playing cello. Office: PO Box 707 Trinidad CA 95570

SCHAAP, RICHARD JAY, journalist; b. N.Y.C., Sept. 27, 1934; s. Maurice William and Leah (Lerner) S.; m. Barbara M. Barron, June 20, 1956 (div. 1967); children: Renee Beth, Michelle Anne; m. Madeleine Gottlieb, Aug. 29, 1967 (div. 1980); children: Jeremy Albert, Joanna Rose; m. Patricia Ann McLeod, May 17, 1981 ; children—Karen Joan, David Maurice. BS, Cornell U., 1955; MS, Columbia U., 1956. Sr. editor Newsweek, N.Y.C., 1956-63; city editor N.Y. Herald Tribune, 1964-66; correspondent NBC, N.Y.C., 1971-80, ABC, N.Y.C., 1980—; host of The Sports Reporters ESPN, 1990—. Author over 30 books including RFK, 1967, Turned On, 1967, (with Jerry Kramer) Instant Replay, 1968, (with Jimmy Breslin) 44, 1980, Steinbrenner!, 1982, The 1984 Olympic Games, 1984, (with Jerry Kramer) Distant Replay, 1985, (with Billy Crystal) Absolutely Mahvelous, 1986, (with Phil Simms and Phil McConkey) Simms to McConkey, 1987, (with Bo Jackson) Bo Knows Bo, 1990, (with Joe Montana) Montana, 1995, (with Tom Waddell) Gay Olympian, 1996, (with Nick Bollettieri) My Aces My Faults, 1996. Served to lt. U.S. Army, 1957-58. Recipient Emmy awards for Sid Caesar profile 1984, sports features 1986, Tom Waddell profile 1988, commentaries 1992, 94, 96, Columbia Sch. Journalism Alumni award, 1994, Cable Ace award, 1996. Office: ABC News 47 W 66th St New York NY 10023-6201

SCHAAR, SUSAN CLARKE, state legislative staff member; b. Lawrenceville, Va., Dec. 21, 1949; d. Garland Lewis and Frances Virginia (Matthews) Clarke; m. William Berkley Schaar Jr., Nov. 24, 1990. BA, U. Richmond, 1972. Engrossing clk. Senate Va., Richmond, 1974, legis. rsch. analyst, 1974-77; asst. to the clk. Senate of Va., Richmond, 1977-83; asst. clk. Senate Va., Richmond, 1983-90, clk. of the Senate, 1990—. mem. YMCA Model Gen. Assembly Adv. com., Richmond, 1990—; trustee U. Richmond, 1990-94; pres. Richmond Club of Westhampton, 1988-90; mem. Spider Club Athletic Bd., Richmond, 1988-90; bd. assocs. U. Richmond, 1995—. Mem. Am. Soc. Legis. Clks. and Secs. (mem. exec. com. 1995—, sec.-treas. 1996, pres.-elect 1997), Omicron Delta Kappa, Pi Sigma Alpha. Baptist. Office: Senate of Va PO Box 396 Richmond VA 23218-0396

SCHABER, GORDON DUANE, law educator, former judge; b. Ashley, N.D., Nov. 22, 1927; s. Ronald and Esther (Schatz) S. A.B. with distinction, Sacramento State Coll., 1949; J.D. with honors, U. Calif. at San Francisco, 1952; LL.D., McGeorge Sch. Law, 1961, John Marshall Law Sch., 1983, Widener U., Del. Law Sch., 1984; LLD, Southwestern U., 1994. Bar: Calif. 1953. Pvt. practice Sacramento, 1953-65; ptnr. firm Schaber & Cecchettini, Sacramento, 1953-65; prof., asst. dean McGeorge Coll. of Law (now McGeorge Sch. Law of U. Pacific), Sacramento, 1953-56, asst. dean, 1956, acting dean, dean, prof. law, 1957-91, univ. counsellor, disting. prof. law, 1991—; presiding judge Superior Ct. Sacramento County, 1965-70; dir. Air Calif., 1974-81, Westgate Corp., 1979-82, Sacramento Cablevision, 1980-82, Capitol Bank of Commerce, vice chmn., 1987-90; chmn. bd. dirs. River City Cablevision Inc.; mem. Calif. Bd. Control, 1962-64; chmn. Greater Sacramento Plan Com., 1970; cons. on establishment Sch. Law at U. Puget Sound, 1970-71; cons. study on jud. workload Jud. Council Calif., 1971-72; mem. Adv. Com. to Chief Justice Calif. on Superior Ct. Mgmt., 1971; cons. vehicle theft study Calif. Hwy. Patrol, 1972; panelist Sacramento Bee Secret Witness Program, 1971-90; mem. adv. com. to Calif. Office Econ. Opportunity, Calif. Legal Services Expt., 1972; vice chmn. Calif. Ednl. Facilities Authority, 1978—; bd. dirs. Nat. Center Adminstrv. Justice, 1978; mem. President's Adminstrn. Justice Task Force, 1980; mem. Joint Task Force on Student Fin. Aid Com. and Govt. Rels., 1988-90, Com. to Study the Law Sch. Process, 1989-90, Ind. Law Sch. Com., 1989-90; bd. dirs. Witkin Legal Inst., 1996. Author: Contracts in a Nutshell, 1975, 3d rev. edit., 1990, Procedural Guide for the Evaluation and Accreditation of Court Facilities, 1977, (with others) The Twentieth Century and the Courthouse, 1977; contbr. articles to profl. jours., book reviewer. Mem. Telethon gift com. Sacramento-San Joaquin chpt. Muscular Dystrophy Assn., 1980; mem. Sierra Found. for Health (One Hundred Million Dollar Health Trust), 1987—; mem. adv. bd. Performing Arts Fund, Sacramento Bee, 1987—; mem. exec. com. Sacramento Area Commn. on Mather Conversion, 1989-90, Law Sch. Admission Coun., Fin. Aid Svcs. Com., 1989-90; past mem., bd. advisors Mental Health Soc. Sacramento, Better Bus. Bur., LWV; trustee Stanford Homes Found., 1980-87, Hon. Lorenzo Patino Scholarship Trust, 1984, Sierra Found. for Health, 1987—; bd. dirs. Sacramento Regional Found., 1982-87, Sutter Hosps. of Sacramento, 1978; mem. bd. advisors Coll. Pub. Interest Law, Pacific Legal Found., 1974—; vice chmn. Calif. Edn. Facilities Authority, 1978—; chmn. Sacramento County Dem. Ctrl. Com., 1960-64; mem. Dem. State Ctrl. Com., 1960-64, 74-82; founding chair Valley Vision, 1993-95; active numerous other civic coms. Named Sacramento County Young Man of Yr., 1962, Trial Judge of Yr. Calif. Trial Lawyers Assn., 1969, Humanitarian of Yr. Sacramento County Bar Assn., 1990, Sacramentan of Yr. Sacramento C. of C., 1994, Outstanding Alumnus Hastings Coll., 1994; recipient Legal Edn. and Jud. award Am. Trial Lawyers Assn., 1965, Order of Hornet Calif. State U., Sacramento, 1972, award Citizenship and Law Related Edn. Ctr., 1994, Silver Hope award Multiple Sclerosis Soc., 1994. Fellow Am. Bar Found.; mem. ABA (council sect. legal edn. and admissions to bar 1975, chmn. 1981, sec. 1982-92, adv. com. pres.-elect on competence of lawyers continuing edn. 1978, numerous other coms., Robert J. Kutak award 1991), Sacramento Bar Assn. (v.p. 1970), State Bar Calif. (mem. com. legislation 1969-89, spl. com. appellate cts. 1970-72, long range adv. planning com. 1972-89, vice chmn. com. law sch. edn. 1973, chmn. 1974, mem. commn. to study bar examination processes 1976-80, Merit Selection Com., others), Am. Judicature Soc., Order of Coif, Phi Delta Phi. Clubs: Commonwealth, Comstock, Sutter, Sacramento/Capitol, many others. Home: 937 Piedmont Dr Sacramento CA 95822-1701 Office: U Pacific McGeorge Sch Law 3200 5th Ave Sacramento CA 95817-2705

SCHACHMAN, HOWARD KAPNEK, molecular biologist, educator; b. Phila., Dec. 5, 1918; s. Morris H. and Rose (Kapnek) S.; m. Ethel H. Lazarus, Oct. 20, 1945; children—Marc, David. BSChemE, Mass. Inst. Tech., 1939; PhD in Phys. Chemistry, Princeton, 1948; DSc (hon.), Northwestern U., 1974; MD (hon.), U. Naples, 1990. Fellow NIH, 1946-48; instr., asst. prof. U. Calif., Berkeley, 1948-54, assoc. prof. biochemistry, 1954-59, prof. biochemistry and molecular biology, 1959-91, chmn. dept. molecular biology, dir. virus lab., 1969-76, prof. emeritus, dept. molecular and cell biology, 1991-94, prof. grad. sch., 1994—; mem. sci. coun. and sci. adv. bd. Stazione Zoologica, Naples, Italy, 1988—; cons. bd. sci. Meml. Sloan-Kettering Cancer Ctr., 1988—; mem. sci. adv. com. Rsch. ! Am., 1990—; William Lloyd Evans lectr. Ohio State U., 1988, Carl and Gerty Cori lectr., Washington U. Sch. Medicine, 1993; faculty rsch. lectr. U. Calif., Berkeley, 1994; Alta. Heritage Found. for Med. Rsch. vis. prof. U. Alta., 1996. Author: Ultracentrifugation in Biochemistry, 1959; developer of ultracentrifuge as a tool for studying macromolecules of biol. interest; condr. studies on structure and function of regulatory enzyme: aspartate transcarbamylase. Mem. bd. sci. counselors Cancer Biology and Diagnosis divsn. Nat. Cancer Inst., 1989-92; spl. advisor to dir. NIH, 1994—. Lt. USNR, 1945-47. Recipient John Scott award, 1964, Warren Triennial prize Mass. Gen. Hosp., 1965, Alexander von Humboldt award, 1990, Berkeley citation for disting. achievement and notable svc. U. Calif., 1993; Guggenheim Meml. fellow, 1956. Mem. AAAS, NAS (chmn. biochemistry sect. 1990-93, panelist sci. responsibility and conduct of rsch. 1990-92), Am. Chem. Soc. (award in chem. instrumentation 1962, Calif. sect. award 1958), Am. Soc. Biochemistry and Molecular Biology (pres. 1987-88, chmn. pub. affairs com. 1989—, Merck award 1986, Herbert A. Sober award 1994), Fedn. Am. Socs. for Exptl. Biology (pres. 1988-89, pub. affairs exec. com. 1989—, pub. svc. award 1994), Accademia Nazionale Dei Lincei, Sigma Xi. Achievements include development of the ultracentrifuge as a tool for studying macromolecules of biological interest; studies on structure and function of a regulatory enzyme: Aspartate transcarbamylase. Office: U Calif Berkeley Dept Molecular and Cell Bio 229 Stanley Hall # 3206 Berkeley CA 94720-3207

SCHACHT, HENRY BREWER, manufacturing executive; b. Erie, Pa., Oct. 16, 1934; s. Henry Blass and Virginia (Brewer) S.; m. Nancy Godfrey, Aug. 27, 1960; children: James, Laura, Jane, Mary. BS, Yale U., 1956; MBA, Harvard U., 1962; DSc (hon.), DePauw U., 1982; MA (hon.), Yale U., 1988. Sales trainee Am. Brake Shoe Co., N.Y.C., 1956-57; investment mgr. Irwin Mgmt. Co., Columbus, Ind., 1962-64; v.p. fin. Cummins Engine Co., Inc., Columbus, 1964-66; v.p., cen. area mgr. internat. Cummins Engine Co., Inc., London, 1966-67; group v.p. internat. and subsidiaries Cummins Engine Co., Inc., 1967-69; pres. Cummins Engine Co., Inc., Columbus, 1969-77, CEO, 1977-94, chmn., 1977-95; chmn., CEO, Lucent Techs., Murray Hill, N.J., 1995—; bd. dirs. AT&T, Chase Manhattan Corp., Chase Manhattan Bank N.A., Alcoa. Trustee emeritus The Culver Ednl. Found.; active Bus. Coun., Coun. Fgn. Rels.; mem. The Assocs., Harvard Bus. Sch., The Bus. Enterprise Trust; hon. trustee Brookings Instn., Com. Econ. Devel., Yale Corp.; chmn. trustees Ford Found.; sr. mem. Conf. Bd. With USNR, 1957-60. Mem. Tau Beta Pi. Republican. Office: Lucent Techs 600 Mountain Ave New Providence NJ 07974-2008

SCHACHT, HENRY MEVIS, writer, consultant; b. Pasadena, Calif., Feb. 28, 1916; s. Henry and Amelia (Claussen) S.; m. Mary Joan Turnbull, Dec. 30, 1937; children: Henry John, Linda Joan. BA, U. Calif., Berkeley, 1936. Info. specialist U. Calif., Berkeley, 1936-42; dir. agr. NBC, San Francisco, 1942-59, ABC, San Francisco, 1959-60; agrl. columnist San Francisco Chronicle, 1959-93; dir. agrl. info. U. Calif., 1961-65; v.p. corp. relations, corp. sec. Calif. Canners & Growers, San Francisco, 1965-81; freelance writer, 1936—; cons. radio-TV to FAO of UN, Cairo, 1963, Mexico City, 1965, Tokyo, 1966; dir. Calif. Co. for Internat. Trade; dir. Agrl. Issues Ctr., U. Calif. Pres. U.S. Fruit Export Coun., 1972-75; exec. sec. Commn. Calif. Agr. and Higher Edn., 1993-95; adv. bd. Agrl. Issues Ctr. U. Calif., 1990—. Mem. Pub. Relations Soc. Am., Pub. Relations Roundtable San Francisco, Nat. Assn. Farm Broadcasters, Agrl. Relations Council, Nat. Canners Assn. (dir. 1966-81). Home: 60 Hiller Dr Oakland CA 94618-2351

SCHACHT, JOCHEN HEINRICH, biochemistry educator; b. Königsberg, Fed. Republic Germany, July 2, 1939; came to U.S., 1969; s. Heinz and Else (Sprenger) S.; m. Helga Hildegard Seidel, Jan..27, 1967; children: Miriam Helga, Daniel Jochen. BS, U. Bonn, Fed. Republic Germany, 1962; MS in Chemistry, U. Heidelberg, Fed. Republic Germany, 1965, PhD in Biochemistry, 1968. Asst. research chemist, Mental Health Research Inst. U. Mich., Ann Arbor, 1969-72, from asst. prof. to assoc. prof. biochemistry, Dept. Biol. Chemistry & Otolaryngology, 1973-84, prof., 1984—, chmn. grad. program in physiol. acoustics, 1981—; vis. prof. Karolinska Inst., Stockholm, 1979-80; acting dir. Kresge Hearing Rsch. Inst., U. Mich., 1983-84, assoc. dir., 1989—; mem. hearing rsch. study sect. USPHS, NIH, Nat. Inst. Neurol. and Communicative Disorders and Stroke, 1986-89, Task Force Nat. Strategic Rsch. Plan, Nat. Insts. Deafness and Communication Disorders, USPHS, NIH. Mem. editl. bd. Hearing Rsch., 1990—; assoc. editor Audiology & Neuro-Otol., 1995—; contbr. more than 100 articles to profl. jours., book chpts., revs.; co-editor Neurochemistry of Cholinergic Receptors, 1974. Fogarty Sr. Internat. fellow NIH, 1979, Sen. J. Javitz Neurosci. investigator, 1984; recipient Chercheur Etranger rsch. award INSERM, Paris, 1986, 94, Animal Welfare award Erna-Graff Found., Berlin, 1987, Disting. Faculty Achievement award U. Mich., 1989, Employer of Yr. award Nat. Capital Assoc. Coop. Edn. and Gallaudet U., Washington. Mem. Deutsche Gesellschaft für Biologische Chemie, Am. Soc. Neurochemistry, Internat. Soc. Neurochemistry, Soc. for Neurosci., Assn. for Research in Otolaryngology, Am. Soc. Biol. Chemists, Assn. Espanola de Audiologia Exptl. Avocations: photography, travel, birding. Office: U Mich Kresge Hearing Rsch Inst Ann Arbor MI 48109-0506

SCHACHT, LINDA JOAN, broadcast journalist; b. Berkeley, Calif., Sept. 11, 1944; d. Henry Mevis and Mary (Turnbull) S.; m. John Burdette Gage, May 1, 1976; children: Peter Turnbull, Katharine Burdette. BA, U. Calif., Berkeley, 1966, MJ, 1978. Reporter Sta. KQED-TV, San Francisco, 1974-76, Sta. KPIX-TV, San Francisco, 1976—; vis. faculty Grad. Sch. Journalism U. Calif., Berkeley, 1990—. Reporter Dem. conv., 1980 (Emmy award 1981), investigative article on second mortgage brokers, 1977 (Emmy award), on children as witnesses, 1984 (Calif. State Bar award 1985, ABA award 1986). Mem. Nat. Acad. TV Arts and Scis.

SCHACHT, RICHARD LAWRENCE, philosopher, educator; b. Racine, Wis., Dec. 19, 1941; s. Robert Hugo and Alice (Munger) S.; m. Judith Rowan; children: Eric Lawrence, Marshall Robert. B.A., Harvard U., 1963; M.A., Princeton U., 1965, Ph.D., 1967; postgrad, Tübingen U., Fed. Republic Germany, 1966-67. Asst. prof. U. Ill., Urbana-Champaign, 1967-71, assoc. prof., 1971-80, prof. philosophy, 1980—, Jubilee prof. of Liberal Arts and Scis., 1990—, chmn. dept., 1980-91, interim dean Coll. Liberal Arts and Scis., 1994; vis. prof. U. Oreg., 1969, U. Pitts., 1973, U. Mich., 1979; vis. scholar Tübingen U., 1975. Author: Alienation, 1970, Hegel and After, 1975, Nietzsche, 1983, Classical Modern Philosophers, 1984, The Future of Alienation, 1994, Making Sense of Nietzsche, 1995; editor: Nietzsche Selections, 1993, Nietzsche, Genealogy, Morality, 1994, Internat. Nietzsche Studies. Mem. Am. Philos. Assn., N.Am. Nietzsche Soc. (exec. dir.), Internat. Sociol. Assn. (v.p., research com. on alienation theory), AAUP. Office: U Ill Dept Philosophy 105 Gregory 810 S Wright St Urbana IL 61801-3611

SCHACHT, RONALD STUART, lawyer; b. Stamford, Conn., Nov. 7, 1932; s. Saul Albert and Faye Dorothy (Gittleman) S.; m. Natalie Helene Goldman, June 17, 1956; children—Patti Ellen, Bonnie Anne, Cindy Joy. B.S., U. Conn., 1954; LL.B., NYU, 1957, LL.M., 1960. Bar: N.Y. 1957, D.C. 1980. Tax atty. IRS, N.Y.C., 1957-62; assoc. Proskauer Rose Goetz & Mendelsohn, N.Y.C., 1962-69, ptnr., 1969—, mng. ptnr., 1981-84, mem. exec. com., 1985-95; lectr. Practising Law Inst., NYU Inst. Fed. Taxation; adj. assoc. prof. Sch. Continuing Edn. NYU, 1970-72. Bd. dirs. Congregation Agudath Shalom, Stamford, 1968-73; mem. com. Fedn. Jewish philanthropies, N.Y.C., 1972-80. Mem. N.Y. State Bar Assn., Assn. of Bar of City of N.Y., N.Y. County Lawyers Assn. (bd. dirs. 1977-83, chmn. ins. com. 1975-85), Newfield Swim Club (bd. dirs. 1967-70, pres. 1969), Phi Kappa Phi, Gamma Chi Epsilon. Democrat. Jewish. Home: 17280 Antigua Point Way Boca Raton FL 33487 Office: Proskauer Rose 1585 Broadway New York NY 10036-8200

SCHACHTER, BARRY, economist; b. Providence, R.I., Aug. 17, 1954; s. Hyman and Fannie (Dunder) S.; m. Joanne Fitzsimmons, Sept. 13, 1981; 1 child, Devra Fitzsimmons. BS in Econs., Bentley Coll., 1976, AS in Acctg., 1976; MA in Econs., Cornell U., 1979, PhD, 1982. From instr. to asst. prof. dept. Econs. Rutgers U., New Brunswick, N.J., 1980-82; from asst. prof., to assoc. prof. Simon Fraser U., Burnaby, B.C., 1982-88; assoc. prof. Tulane U., New Orleans, 1988-92; fin. economist divsn. econ. analysis Commodity Futures Trading Commn., Washington, 1990-94; fin. economist risk analysis divsn. Comptroller of the Currency, Washington, 1994-97; v.p. market risk dept. Chase Manhattan Bank, 1997—; lectr. U. Pa., 1994, Georgetown U., 1996; vis. asst. prof. U. Utah, Salt Lake City, 1987-88; vis. scholar rsch. dept. Internat. Monetary Fund, Washington, 1992-93; ad hoc referee Can. Coun. Killam Fellowship, 1988, Econ. Inquiry, 1983-84, Fin. Review, 1985, 89-90, Jour. Fin. Rsch. 1987-93, Fin. Mgmt., 1989-90, 93-96, Jour. Bus. and Rsch., 1988, Jour. Fin., 1989, 91, 94, Quar. Jour. Econs., 1989, Jour. Money, Credit and Banking, 1989, Jour. Econ. Theory, 1990, Jour. Banking & Fin., 1990-93, Jour. Fin. Edn., 1990, Review of Quantatative Fin. and Acctg., 1991-92, Internat. Review Econs. and Fin., 1992, Soc. Scis. and Humanities Rsch. Coun. Can. 1993, Rev. Deriv. Res., 1996, Math. Fin., 1994, others; speaker in field; presenter various confs. Book editor and author; contbr. articles to profl. jours., chpts. to books, annuals, proceedings; assoc. editor Internat. Rev. of Fin. Analysis, 1990—, Jour. Derivatives, 1993—, Fin. Mgmt., 1993—, Jour. Banking & Finance, 1995—, Jour. Fin. Engring., 1995—; editor: Derivatives, Regulation and Banking, 1997. Rsch. grantee Simon Fraser Univ., 1982, 84, 86, Inst. Quantitative Rsch. Fin., 1990; recipient Best Paper award Internat. Options Market, 1984. Mem. Am. Econs. Assn., Am. Fin. Assn., Fin. Mgmt. Assn., Internat. Assn. Fin. Engrs. (chair adv. bd. 1996), Western Fin. Assn. Office: Chase Manhattan Bank Market Risk Divsn 270 Park Ave New York NY 10017-2014

SCHACHTER, HARRY, biochemist, educator; b. Vienna, Austria, Feb. 25, 1933; came to Can., 1951; s. Asher and Miriam (Freund) S.; m. Judith Jakubovic, Dec. 23, 1958; children: Aviva, Asher. BA, U. Toronto, 1955, MD, 1959, PhD, 1964. From assist. prof. to assoc. prof. dept. biochemistry U. Toronto, 1964-72, prof., 1972—, chmn., 1984-89; sr. scientist Rsch. Inst. Hosp. for Sick Children, Toronto, 1976—; head biochemistry rsch. divsn. Rsch. Inst. Hosp. for Sick Children, 1976-89.

SCHACHTER, MAX, retired engineering services company executive; b. N.Y.C., Aug. 22, 1913; s. Morris and Rebecca (Sirota) S.; m. Ida Jensky, June 25, 1936; 1 son, Robert. Student, N.Y. U., 1932, CCNY, 1932-36, Cooper Union, 1942. Registered profl. engr., N.Y., N.J. Machine designer Torrington Mfg. Co., Conn., 1941-43, Machine & Tool Design Co., N.Y.C., 1943-48; chief engr. machine design div. Am. Machine & Foundry, Bklyn., 1949-51; chmn. Atlantic Design Co., Inc., Livingston, N.J., 1951-89, ret., 1989. Trustee, now pres. Ruth Gottscho Kidney Found., 1960—. Mem. ASME. Jewish.

SCHACHTER, MICHAEL BEN, psychiatrist, complementary physician; b. Bklyn., Jan. 15, 1941; s. Saul and Ann (Palestine) S.; m. Margaret Josephine Kavanagh, July 22, 1967 (div. Mar. 1979); children: Brian Joseph, Amy, Stefan James; m. Marlene Helen Brodsky, Aug. 22, 1982 (div. Mar. 1993); children: Adam Elliot, Jason Neil; m. Lisa Lackhai, July 19, 1993; 1 child, Seth Andrew. BA, Columbia U., 1961, MD, 1965. Diplomate Am. Bd. Psychiatry and Neurology in Psychiatry, Am. Bd. Chelation Therapy. Med., surg. and pediat. intern Hosp. for Joint Diseases and Med. Ctr., N.Y.C., 1965-66; resident psychiatry Downstate Med. Ctr., Kings County Hosp., Bklyn., 1966-69; staff psychiatrist Bklyn. Cmty. Counseling Ctr., 1968-69; staff psychiatrist Rockland County Cmty. Mental Health Ctr., Pomona, N.Y., 1971, dir. emergency and admissions, 1971-72, dir. outpatient clinic, 1972-74; founder, dir. Schachter Ctr. Complementary Medicine, Suffern, N.Y., 1974—. Author: The Natural Way to a Healthy Prostate, 1995, (with David Sheinkin and Richard Hutton) The Food Connection, 1979, Food, Mind and Mood, 1980, 2d edit., 1987; contbr. articles to profl. jours. Bd. dirs. Am. Bd. Chelation Therapy, 1983-88. Maj. USAF, 1969-71. Recipient Appreciation award NHF, 1979, Carlos Lamar Pioneer Meml. award Am. Acad. Med. Preventics, 1979, Merit award Am. Acad. Craniomandibular Disorders, 1981, Physician's Recognition awards AMA. Fellow Am. Coll. for Advancement in Medicine (v.p. 1985-87, pres.-elect 1987-89, pres. 1989-91); mem. Am. Psychiat. Assn., Am. Acad. Environ. Medicine, Am. Coll. Nutrition, Found. for Advancement Innovative Medicine (v.p. 1986-94, pres. 1994—), Am. Preventive Med. Assn. (bd. dirs. 1993-95). Avocations: running, basketball, swimming, tennis, golf. Office: 2 Executive Blvd Ste 202 Suffern NY 10901-4164

SCHACHTER, OSCAR, lawyer, educator, arbitrator; b. N.Y.C., June 19, 1915; s. Max and Fannie (Javits) S.; m. Mollie Miller, Aug. 9, 1936 (dec. July 1980); children: Judith (Mrs. John Modell), Ellen (Mrs. John P. Leventhal); m. Muriel L. Sackler, June 14, 1982. BSS, Coll. City N.Y., 1936; JD, Columbia, 1939. Bar: N.Y. 1939. Editor-in-chief Columbia Law Rev., 1938-39; pvt. practice N.Y.C., 1939-40; atty. U.S. Dept. of Labor, Washington, 1940; chief nat. defense sect. in law dept. FCC, 1941; sect. of law com. and adviser on internat. communications Bd. of War Communications, 1941-42; prin., divisional asst., adviser on wartime econ. controls and on European liberated areas U.S. Dept. State, 1942-43; asst. gen. counsel UNRRA, 1944-46; drafting officer UNRRA council sessions, 1944-45; legal adv. UNRRA del. to USSR and Poland, 1945; legal counselor UN, 1946-52, dir. gen. legal div., 1952-66; dep. exec. dir., dir. studies UN Inst. for Tng. and Research, 1966-75; lectr. law Yale U. Law Sch., 1955-71; Carnegie lectr. Hague Acad. Internat. Law, 1963-82; Rosenthal lectr. Northwestern U. Law Sch., 1974; prof. Law Sch. and Faculty Internat. Affairs Columbia U., 1975—, Hamilton Fish prof. internat. law and diplomacy Law Sch. and Faculty Internat. Affairs, 1980-85, prof. emeritus Law Sch. and Faculty Internat. Affairs, 1985—; vis. prof Harvard Law Sch., 1982; chmn. legal com. UN Maritime Conf., 1948; legal cons. UNESCO, 1948; past dir. Gen. Legal Div. of UN; served as legal adviser various internat. confs. and UN couns. and coms.; sec. legal adv. com. UN Atomic Energy Commn., 1946-47; vice chmn. Internat. Investment Law Conf., 1958; exec. sec. Internat. Arbitration Conf., 1958; mem. panel arbitrators Internat. Ctr. for Settlement of Investment Disputes, 1980-87; judge Ct. Arbitration in Canada-France Maritime Boundary dispute, 1989-92; expert advisor UN com. on transnational sorps., 1990-93. Author: Relation of Law, Politics and Action in the U.N, 1964, Sharing the World's Resources, 1977, International Law in Theory and Practice, 1985, rev. edit., 1991; co-author: Across the Space Frontier, 1952, Toward Wider Acceptance of UN Treaties, 1971, International Law Cases and Materials, 1980, 3rd edit., 1993, United Nations Legal Order, 2 vols., 1995; contbr. articles and monographs on internat. law, internat. instns., legal philosophy, human rights, internat. peace and security, internat. resources to legal jours.; editor-in-chief Am. Jour. Internat. Law, 1978-84, hon. editor, 1985—; co-editor: Competition in International Business, 1981; editorial bd. Marine Policy. Bd. dirs. Internat. Peace Acad., 1970-82. Recipient Friedman award Columbia Law Sch., 1983, Carl Fulda award U. Tex. Law Sch., 1990, Columbia Law medal for excellence, 1991. Fellow Am. Acad. Arts and Scis., World Acad. Art and Sci.; mem. ABA, Am. Soc. Internat. Law (pres. 1968-70, hon. v.p., exec. coun., hon. pres. 1994-96, Manley Hudson medal 1981, Cert. of Merit for creative scholarship 1992), Coun. on Fgn. Rels., Inst. de Droit Internat. (v.p. 1991—), Internat. Law Assn., Internat. Astronautical Acad., Phi Beta Kappa. Home: 11 E 86th St New York NY 10028-0548 Office: Columbia U Law Sch New York NY 10027

SCHACTER, BRENT ALLAN, oncologist, health facility administrator; b. Winnipeg, Man., Can., June 1, 1942; s. Irvin C. and Claire (Easton) S.; m. Sora Ludwig, Dec. 20, 1981; children: Isanne, Jennifer, Miriam. BSc, U. Man., 1965, MD with honors, 1965. Intern Winnipeg Gen. Hosp., 1965-66, jr. asst. resident, 1967-68; asst. resident in internal medicine Barnes Hosp., St. Louis, 1968-69; clin. fellow hematology Barnes Hosp. and Washington U., St. Louis, 1969-70; rsch. fellow, asst. in medicine U. Tex. Southwestern Med. Sch., Dallas, 1970-72; asst. prof. internal medicine U. Man., Winnipeg, 1972-77, assoc. prof. medicine, 1977-87, prof., 1987—; Nat. Cancer Inst. of Can. Rsch. fellow Man. Cancer Treatment and Rsch. Found., Winnipeg, 1966-67, pres., CEO, 1993—; lectr. in field; sci. officer grant panel C, Nat. Cancer Inst. Can., 1978, mem., 1979-82; mem. Man. Health Rsch. Coun. grant panel, 1982-84, 89-91; adv. bd. Can. Porphyria Found., 1988—. Contbr. numerous articles and abstracts to profl. jours. Recipient Med. Rsch. Coun. Can. Vis. Scientist award, 1986; fellow Muscular Dystrophy Assn., 1964, John S. McEachern Meml. fellow Can. Cancer Soc., 1969-70, Med. Rsch. Coun. Can. fellow, 1970-72; Isbister scholar, 1962, 63, Med. Rsch. Coun. Can. scholar, 1975-80. Fellow Royal Coll. Physicians; mem. AAAS, Royal Coll. Physicians and Surgeons of Can. (specialty com. in med. oncology 1985-94, bd. med. examiners in med. oncology 1987-90, specialty com. in hematology 1989-93, core com. mem. 1990—, chmn. bd. examiners med. oncology 1990-93, mem. regional adv. com. Sask./Man. dist. 1992—), Am. Fedn. for Clin. Rsch., Can. Soc. for Clin. Investigation (awards com. 1980-82, chmn. 1981-82), Am. Assn. for Study of Liver Diseases, Am. Soc. Hematology, Can. Soc. Hematology, Am. Soc. Clin. Oncology, Can. Bone Marrow Transplant Group, Can. Hemophilia Soc. (mem. clinic dirs. group

1990-93, sec-treas. 1991-93), Can. Liver Club. Avocations: cross-country skiing, scuba diving, model railroading. Home: 224 Lamont Blvd, Winnipeg, MB Canada R3P 0E9 Office: Manitoba Cancer Trtmnt Rsch Found, 100 Olivia St, Winnipeg, MB Canada R3E 0V9

SCHAD, THEODORE MACNEEVE, science research administrator, consultant; b. Balt., Aug. 25, 1918; s. William Henry and Emma Margaret (Scheldt) S.; m. Kathleen White, Nov. 5, 1944 (dec. Aug. 1989); children: Mary Jane, Rebecca Christina; m. Margot Cornwell, March 19, 1995. BSCE, Johns Hopkins U., 1939. Registered profl. engr., D.C. Various positions water resources engring. U.S. Army C.E., U.S. Bur. Reclamation, Md., Colo., Oreg. Wash., 1939-54; prin. budget examiner water resources programs U.S. Bur. Budget, Exec. Office of Pres., 1954-58; sr. specialist engring. and pub. works, dep. dir. Congl. Rsch. Svc., Libr. of Congress, 1958-68; staff dir. U.S. Senate Com. Nat. Water Resources, 1959-61; exec. dir. Nat. Water Commn., 1968-73; exec. sec. Environ. Studies Bd., 1973-77; dep. dir. Commn. Natural Resources, NAS, Washington, 1977-83; exec. dir. Nat. Ground Water Policy Forum, 1984-86; sr. fellow Conservation Found., Washington, 1986-; U.S. commr. Permanent Internat. Assn. Nav. Congresses, Brussels, 1963-70, commr. emeritus, 1987—; cons. U.S. Senate Com. Interior and Insular Affairs, 1963, U.S. Ho. of Reps. Com. Sci. and Tech., 1962-65, U.S. Office Saline Water, 1965-67, A.T. Kearney, Inc., Alexandria, Va., 1979-80, Chesapeake Rsch. Consortium, 1984, Ronco Cons. Corp., 1986—, Gambia River Basin Devel. Commn., Dakar, 1986-87, Apogee Rsch. Corp., 1987—, Office Tech. Assessment, U.S. Congress, 1992-95. Contbr. articles to Ency. Brit. and profl. jours. Treas. Nat. Speleol. Found., 1961-65, trustee, 1965—; bd. dirs. Vets. Coop. Housing Assn., Washington, 1958-81, v.p., 1960-72. Recipient Meritorious Svc. award U.S. Dept. Interior, 1950, Icko Iben award Am. Water Resources Assn., 1978, Henry P. Caulfield medal, 1990. Fellow ASCE (treas. Nat. Capital chpt. 1952-55, v.p. 1967, pres. 1968, Julian Hinds prize 1991); mem. AAAS, Nat. Speleol. Soc., Am. Water Works Assn. (hon.), Am. Geophys. Union, Am. Acad. Environ. Engrs., Nat. Acad. Pub. Adminstrn., Permanent Internat. Assn. Nav. Congresses, Internat. Commn. Irrigation and Drainage, Potomac Appalachian Trail Club, Cosmos Club, Colo. Mountain Club (Denver), Seattle Mountaineers Club. Home: 4540-25th Rd N Arlington VA 22207-4102 Office: The Conservation Found 1260-24th St NW Washington DC 20037

SCHADE, CHARLENE JOANNE, adult and early childhood education educator; b. San Bernardino, Calif., June 26, 1935; d. Clarence George Linde and Helen Anita (Sunny) Hardesty; m. William Joseph Jr., Apr. 12, 1958 (div., 1978); children: Sabrina, Eric, Camela, Cynthia; m. Thomas Byron Killens, Sept. 25, 1983. BS, UCLA, 1959. Tchr. dance & pe L.A. Unified Secondary Schs., Calif., 1959-63; dir., instr. (Kindergym) La Jolla YMCA, Calif., 1972-76; instr. older adult San Diego Community Colls., 1977—; artist in residence Wolf Trap/Headstart, 1984-85; workshop leader S.W. Dance, Movement and Acro-Sports Workshop, prime-time adult activities coord., 1988—, Am. Heart Assn., Arthritis Found., Am. Lung Assn., AAHPERD, S.W. Dist. AHPERD, Calif. Assn. Health, Phys. Edn., Recreation and Dance, Head Start, San Diego Assn. Young Children, Calif. Assn. Edn. Young Child, Calif. Kindergarten Assn., So. Calif. Kindergarten Assn., 1997, Assn. Childhood Edn. Internat., IDEA Internat. Assn. Fitness Profls., San Diego C.C., Am. Soc. on Aging, Fourth Internat. Congress Physical Activity, Aging and Sports, 1996, others; cons. to Calif. Gov.'s Coun. on Phys. Fitness, 1993; feature guest Sta. KFMB and KPBS TV shows, San Diego, 1980-88. Author: Move With Me From A to Z, 1982, Move With Me, One, Two, Three, 1988; co-author: Prime Time Aerobics, 1982, Muevete Conmigo, uno, dos, tres, 1990; co-writer: Guide for Physical Fitness Instructors of Older Adults, Grant Project, 1990, The Empowering Teacher, 1990, Handbook for Instructors of Older Adults, 1994. Dir. We Care Found., San Diego, 1977-79, Meet the Author programs San Diego County Schs., 1988—; founder SOLO, San Diego, 1981-83; adminstr., v.p. ODEM chpt. Toastmasters, San Diego, 1982; chmn. People with Arthritis Can Exercise com. San Diego chpt. Arthritis Found., 1994-95; trainer PACE instrs. Nat. Arthritis Found., 1995—. Grantee Video Showcase of Exercises for Older Adults, 1992-93. Mem. AAPHERD (workshop leader), Calif. Assn. Health, Phys. Edn., Recreation and Dance (workshop leader). Avocations: hiking, dancing, traveling. Office: Exer Fun/Prime Time Aerobic 3089C Clairemont Dr Ste 130 San Diego CA 92117-6802

SCHADE, MALCOLM ROBERT, lawyer; b. Holyoke, Mass., Oct. 23, 1950; s. G. Malcolm and Dorothy Jean (Alderman) S.; m. Charlanne Reid Murray, June 26, 1971. BA magna cum laude, Windham Coll., 1971; JD, Columbia U., 1974, postgrad., 1975-76. Bar: N.Y. 1975, Mass. 1975, U.S. Dist. Ct. (so., ea., we. & no. dists.) N.Y. 1975, U.S. Ct. Appeals (2d cir.) 1975, U.S. Ct. Appeals (1st cir.) 1976, U.S. Supreme Ct. 1978, U.S. Dist. Ct. Vt. 1980, U.S. Ct. Appeals (6th cir.) 1985, U.S. Dist. Ct. (ea. dist.) Mich. 1988. Assoc. Kronish, Lieb, Shainswit, Weiner & Hellman, N.Y.C., 1977-79, Skadden Arps Slate Meagher & Flom, N.Y.C., 1980-83; ptnr. Alexander & Green, N.Y.C., 1984-86, Mudge Rose Guthrie Alexander & Ferdon, N.Y.C., 1987-95, Thacher, Proffit & Wood, N.Y.C., 1995—. Rapporteur (book) American Hostages in Iran, 1985. Trustee Windham Coll., Putney, Vt., 1970-71, 76-80, sec., 1977-80, chmn. bd., 1978-80. Mem. Assn. Bar of City of N.Y. (com. on internat. arms control & security affairs 1979-85), Mass. Bar Assn., Comml. Bar Assn. (London, overseas mem.), Down Town Assn., Larchmont Shore Club (bd. dirs. 1995—), Horseshoe Harbor Yacht Club. Congregationalist. Avocations: sailing, hunting, skiing. Home: 24 Beech Rd New Rochelle NY 10804-4304 Office: Thacher Proffitt & Wood Two World Trade Ctr New York NY 10048

SCHADE, STANLEY GREINERT, JR., hematologist, educator; b. Pitts., Dec. 21, 1933; s. Stanley G. and Charlotte (Marks) S.; m. Sylvia Zottu, Mar. 24, 1966; children: David Stanley, Robert Edward. BA in English, Hamilton Coll., 1955; MD, Yale U., 1961. Diplomate Am. Bd. Internal Medicine, Am. Bd. Hematology, Am. Bd. Oncology. Intern, resident, hematology fellow U. Wis., Madison, 1962-66; chief hematology Westside VA Hosp., Chgo., 1971-77; prof. medicine, chief hematology U. Ill., Chgo., 1978—. Contbr. articles to profl. jours. Served to maj. U.S. Army, 1967-69. Fulbright fellow Tubingen, Fed. Republic of Germany, 1956. Fellow Am. Coll. Physicians; mem. Am. Soc. Hematology. Presbyterian. Avocation: medical ethics. Home: 189 N Delaplaine Rd Riverside IL 60546-2060 Office: Westside VA Med Ctr Hematology Sect 820 S Damen Ave Chicago IL 60612-3728

SCHADE, WILBERT CURTIS, educational administrator; b. St. Louis, Jan. 4, 1945; s. Wilbert Curtis and Florence Mary (Allen) S.; m. Jacqueline Siewert, May 14, 1977; children: Benjamin Allen Siewert, Timothy Knorr Siewert. BA, U. Pa., 1967; AM, Washington U., St. Louis, 1970; PhD, Ind. U., 1986. Teaching asst. dept. Romance Lang. Washington U., St. Louis, 1967-68; tchr. French St. Louis Priory Sch., 1970-71; assoc. instr. Dept. French and Italian, Ind. U., Bloomington, 1972-74, 76-80; tchr. French Webster Groves (Mo.) H.S., 1975-76; asst. dir. admissions Beloit (Wis.) Coll., 1980-83, assoc. dir. admissions, 1983-84; dir. coll. placement and dir. admissions Westover Sch., Middlebury, Conn., 1984-90; head upper sch. The Key Sch., Annapolis, Md., 1990-94, interim dir. devel., 1994-95; dir. coll. counseling, tchr. French, head lang. dept. Wasatch Acad., Mt. Pleasant, Utah, 1995-96, asst. headmaster for acad. affairs, 1996—; lectr. in field. Co-editor: African Literature in its Social and Political Dimensions, 1983; contbr. articles to profl. jours. including World Lit. Written in English, Studies in 20th Century Lit. and articles in books. Mem. Anne Arundel County (Md.) Task Force on Year Round Edn., 1994-95; mem. Utah State Office of Edn.'s Fgn. Lang. Instrl. Materials and Textbook Adv. Com., 1996-98. NEH Summer Inst. on African Am. Lit. and Film grantee, 1994. Mem. Nat. Assn. Coll. Admission Counseling (presenter nat. conf. 1985), Rocky Mountain Assn. for Coll. Admission Counseling (exec. bd., chief assembly del. to Nat. Assn.), African Lit. Assn. (exec. com. 1979), Phi Delta Kappa. Soc. of Friends. Avocation: tennis. Home: 47 S 100 W Mount Pleasant UT 84647 Office: Wasatch Acad 120 S 100 W Mount Pleasant UT 84647-1509

SCHADT, JAMES PHILLIP, consumer products executive; b. Saginaw, Mich., Aug. 7, 1938; s. Phillip Jr. and Jean D. (Cardy) S.; m. Barbara L. Soldmann, Aug. 16, 1959; children: Lauren C., Andrew F. BA, Northwestern U., 1960. With Procter & Gamble USA, 1960-73, Pepsi Inc., 1973-78, Consolidated Foods Corp., 1978-81; pres., CEO Cadbury Schweppes Inc., 1981-91; pres., COO Reader's Digest Assoc. Inc., Pleasantville, N.Y., 1991-94, pres., CEO, 1994—, chmn., pres., CEO, 1995—. trustee Am. Enterprise Inst., Norwalk (Conn.) Hosp., Northwestern U. Mem. Am. Assn. Pubs., Bus. Roundtable, Mag. Pubs. Assn., Grocery Mfrs. Assn., Bli Brook Club (Purchase, N.Y.), Chgo. Club, Fairfield Country Hunt Club, Country Club of Fairfield, John's Island Club, Lotos Club. Home: 17 Owenoke Pk Westport CT 06880-6834 Office: Readers Digest Assn Readers Digest Rd Pleasantville NY 10570-7000

SCHAECHTER, MOSELIO, microbiology educator; b. Milan, Italy, Apr. 26, 1928; children: Judy, John. Student Central U., Ecuador, 1947-49; MA, U. Kans., 1952; PhD, U. Pa., 1954. Postdoctoral fellow State Serum Inst., Copenhagen, 1956-58; instr., asst. prof., assoc. prof. U. Fla., Gainesville, 1958-62; from assoc. prof. to disting. prof. dept. microbiology Tufts U., Boston, 1962-95, prof. emeritus 1995—; adj. prof. San Diego State U., 1995—. Editor: Molecular Biology Bacterial Growth, 1985, Escherichia coli and Salmonella Typhimurium, 1987, 95, Mechanisms of Microbiol. Disease, 1989, 92, In the Company of Mushroom, 1997. Mem. Am. Soc. Microbiology (pres. 1985-86, chmn. internat. activities), Am. Soc. Med. Sch. Microbiology Chmn. (pres. 1984-85, chair internat. activities 1986-94), Soc. Gen. Microbiology, Boston Mycol. Club, Sigma Xi. Avocations: field mycology; hiking. Office: San Diego State U Dept Biology San Diego CA 92182

SCHAEFER, ADOLPH OSCAR, JR., advertising agency executive; b. Phila., May 21, 1932; s. Adolph Oscar and Jessie Rae (Brooks) S.; m. Leslie C. Maurer, May 4, 1994; children by previous marriage: Jeffrey S., Andrew C.; adopted children: Scott S., Adrian L. Maurer, Senta G. Maurer. B.S. in Econs., Wharton Sch., U. Pa., 1954. With drug products div. Procter & Gamble, Cin., 1954-56; mfrs. rep. Towle & Son Co., Phila., 1956-61; ptnr. Rockett & Schaefer Advt., Phila., 1961-63; v.p. Eldridge Co., Phila., 1963-64; pres. Schaefer Advt. Inc., Valley Forge, Pa., 1964-87, chmn. bd. dirs., 1987-89; chmn. Direct Strategies, Inc., Devon, Pa., 1989-92; cons. Spotcom, Inc. Mem. editorial adv. bd.: Pa. Gazette, U. Pa., 1970-72. Mem. alumni bd. mgrs. Episcopal Acad., 1969-73; pres. Valley Forge Gallery, Pa., 1992—, Corporate Insights, Valley Forge, Pa. Served with U.S. Army, 1954-56. Mem. Bus. and Profl. Advt. Assn. (Hall of Fame 1993), Pa. Soc. SAR, Union League Club, Phi Gamma Delta. Home: PO Box 752 Valley Forge PA 19482-0752

SCHAEFER, C. BARRY, railroad executive, lawyer, investment banker; b. Elizabeth, N.J., Feb. 23, 1939; s. Carl H. and Evelyn G. (Conk) S.; m. Carol Ann Craft, July 11, 1970; children: Sara Elizabeth, Susan Craft. BS in Engring., Princeton U., 1961; MS in Engring., U. Pa., 1962; LLB, Columbia U., 1965; MBA, NYU, 1970. Bar: N.Y. 1966, Nebr. 1972. With Kelley, Drye, Warren, N.Y.C., 1966-69; asst. gen. counsel Union Pacific Corp., N.Y.C., 1969-72; western gen. counsel Union Pacific R.R. Co., Omaha, 1972-74, v.p., western gen. counsel, 1974-77, v.p. law, 1977-82; sr. v.p. planning and corp. devel. Union Pacific Corp., N.Y.C., 1984-88; exec. v.p. Union Pacific Corp., Bethlehem, Pa., 1988; sr. advisor Dillon Read & Co. Inc., 1989-91; mng. dir. The Bridgeford Group, 1992-97, Beacon Group, 1997—; dir. Ultramar Corp. Nat. bd. dirs. Jr. Achievement, Colorado Springs, Colo., 1986—. Mem. Racquet and Tennis Club (N.Y.C.), Round Hill Club (Greenwich, Conn.), Desert Mountain Club (Scottsdale, Ariz.).

SCHAEFER, CARL GEORGE LEWIS, writer, public relations and advertising executive; b. Cleve.; s. George S. and Margaret (Freyberg) S.; m. Virginia Clark, Sept. 2, 1938; 1 dau., Susan Diane Schaefer Francis. A.B., UCLA, 1931. Freelance mag. writer, 1931; pres. Pacific Intercollegiate Press Assn., 1931-32; reporter Hollywood (Calif.) Citizen-News, 1931-35; with Warner Bros.-Seven Arts, Burbank, Calif., 1935-71; dir. internat. relations Warner Bros.-Seven Arts, 1962-71; owner Carl Schaefer Enterprises, Hollywood, 1971—; bur. chief movie/TV mktg. Movie News, Singapore, Antena, B.A., 1975—; coord. internat. poster competition Hollywood Reporter, 1971-82, dir. spl. projects; exec. com. ShoWest, 1978—. Mem. internat. com. Acad. Motion Picture Arts and Scis., 1940—; chmn. internat. Hollywood Mus., 1964; vice chmn. Hollywood-Wilshire council Girl Scouts U.S., 1957-58; mem. Mayor Los Angeles Council Internat. Visitors, 1964—; mem. interview bd. Los Angeles Police Dept., 1965—; mem. adv. com. West Hollywood Hosp., 1983—; mng. dir. Internat. Festival Adv. Council, 1971—; nat. panel consumer arbitrators Better Bus. Bur. Los Angeles, 1984—; co-founder con. fgn. Oscars Acad. Motion Picture Arts & Scis. Served with OSS, World War II, ETO; ensign Calif. Naval Militia, 1935-36. Decorated Huesped de Honor Mexico; Legion of Honor France; Ordine al Merito Italy; l'Ordre de la Courrenne Belgium; recipient service plaque Acad. Motion Picture Arts and Scis., The Hollywood Reporter Spl. Key Art award, 1990. Mem. Am. Soc. French Legion of Honor, Assn. Motion Picture and TV Producers (chmn. internat. co. 1967-68, 69-70), Publicists Guild Am. (charter), Internat. Press Photo-Journalists (hon.), Fgn. Trade Assn. So. Calif. (past pres., chmn. bd.), Brit.-Am. (dir.), Los Angeles Chambers Commerce, Culver City C. of C., Western Publs. Assn., Am. Bus. Press, Blue Key, Sigma Alpha Epsilon, Alpha Delta Sigma. Republican. Methodist. Clubs: Mason (Los Angeles) (Shriner), Press (Los Angeles), Brit. United Services (Los Angeles). Address: 3320 Bennett Dr Hollywood CA 90068-1704 *When I lose my imagination, I'll be more than happy to cash in the chips whatever—and slink off.*

SCHAEFER, CHARLES JAMES, III, advertising agency executive, consultant; b. Orange, N.J., Dec. 17, 1926; m. Eleanor Anne Montville, Apr. 8, 1961; 1 child, Charles James IV. AB, Dartmouth Coll., 1948, M in Comml. Sci., 1949. V.p. Dickie-Raymond, 1952-67; sr. v.p. Metromedia, 1968-69; exec. v.p., treas. The DR Group, Boston, 1969-76, pres., 1976-87; exec. v.p., dir. Needham Harper Worldwide Inc., N.Y.C., 1984-87; chmn. bd. Marcoa DR Group, Inc., N.Y.C., 1987-88; cons. Rapp Collins Marcoa, N.Y.C., 1989-92; advt. cons., 1992—. Trustee, mem. exec. com. Direct Mktg. Edn]. Found., 1983-89; campaign chairperson United Way Millburn-Short Hills, 1994, 95. With USN, 1945-46. Mem. Direct Mktg. Assn. (chmn. awards com. 1971-76, Hall of Fame com. 1978-81, ethics com. 1981-86), Assn. Direct Mktg. Agys. (pres. 1980-82, gen. chmn. Caples awards 1985, Direct Mktg. Day N.Y. 1988, N.Y. Direct Marketer of Yr. award 1987, Silver Apple award 1989, contbr. to jour.), Dartmouth Club of N.Y. (pres. 1968-70), Lotos Club (bd. dirs. 1985-88, treas. 1987-88), Canoe Brook Country Club (Summit, N.J.). Home and Office: 307 Hobart Ave Short Hills NJ 07078-2207

SCHAEFER, DAN L., congressman; b. Gutenberg, Iowa, Jan. 25, 1936; s. Alvin L. and Evelyn (Everson) S.; m. Mary Margaret Lenney, 1959; children: Danny, Darren, Joel, Jennifer. BA, Niagara U., 1961, LLD (hon.), 1986; postgrad., Potsdam State U., 1961-64. Pub. rels. cons., 1967-83; mem. Colo. Gen. Assembly, 1977-78; mem. Colo. Senate, 1979-83, pres. pro tem, 1981-82, majority whip, 1983; mem. 98th-103rd Congresses from 6th dist. Colo., Washington, 1983—; mem. house small bus. com., 1983, govt. ops. com., 1983, energy and commerce com., 1984-86 (subcom. on fossil and synthetic fuels; commerce, transp. and tourism; oversight/investigations), environ. and energy study com., 1987— (subcoms. on Transp. and Hazardous materials, Telecom. and Fin.), Energy and Commerce ranking Rep Oversight and Investigations, 1993—, Rep. study com.; mem. house sci. and high tech. task force, mil. reforms caucus, congl. grace caucus; mem. adv. com., com. of concern for Soviet Jewry; mem. exec. bd. Environ. and Energy Study Conf., 1995; chmn. Subcom. on Energy and Power House Commerce Com.; mem. Subcom. on Telecom. and Fin., House Vet. Affairs Com., Subcom. on Edn. Training, Employment and Housing, 1995—; co-chmn. The Mainstream Conservative Alliance. Co-chair Nat. Retail Sales Tax Caucus, Congl. Oil and Gas Forum; mem. Spkrs. Task Force on Environ.; founder Nat. Trails Caucus, House Renewable Energy Caucus; pres. Foothills Recreation Bd., 1973-76; sec. Jefferson County Rep. Party, Colo., 1975-76. With USMCR, 1955-57. Recipient Colo. Park and Recreation citation, 1976; named Elected Ofcl. of Yr., Lakewood/South Jeffco C. of C., 1986, 88, 90, Leadership award U.S. Congl. Adv. Bd., Am. Security Coun. Found., Taxpayers Friend award Nat. Taxpayer's Union, 1985-86, 88, 90, 91, 92, 93, 94, 95, Golden Bulldog award Watchdog of Treasury, 1985-86, 87-88, 88-89, 89-90, 91-92, 93-94, 95-96, Spirit of Enterprise award U.S. C. of C., 1995, Nat. Health award Am. Assn. Nurse Anesthetists, 1996, Nat. Security Scorecare Perfect 100 award Ctr. for Security Policy, 1995, Friend of Taxpayer Perfect 100% award Ams. for Tax Reform, 1996; named Guardian of Small Bus., Nat. Fedn. Ind. Bus., 1996. Mem. C. of C., Rotary, Beta Theta Pi. Roman Catholic. Office: House of Representatives 2353 Rayburn Bldg Ofc B Washington DC 20515-3811

SCHAEFER, DAVID ARNOLD, lawyer; b. Cleve., May 3, 1948; s. Leonard and Maxine V. (Bassett) S.; m. Riki C. Freeman, Aug. 8, 1971; children—Kevin, Lindsey, Traci. BS, Miami U., Oxford, Ohio, 1970; MA, Northwestern, U., 1971; JD, Case Western Res. U., 1974. Bar: Ohio 1974, U.S. Dist. Ct. (no. dist.) Ohio 1974, U.S. Ct. Appeals (6th cir.) 1978, U.S. Supreme Ct. 1978. Ptnr. Guren, Merritt et al, 1980-84, Benesch, Friedlander et al, Cleve., 1984-93; McCarthy, Lebit, Crystal & Haiman, Cleve., 1993—; Author: Deposition Strategy, 1981, 2d edit., 1984; contbr. articles to profl. publs. Soccer coach Ohio Amateur Youth Soccer League, Cleve., 1980-81, 84. Mem. ABA, Ohio State Bar Assn., Ohio Acad. Trial Lawyers (Disting. Svc. award 1980, seminar speaker 1982), Fed. Bar Assn. (pres. elect 1991-92, pres. 1992-93), Nat. Inst. Trial Advocacy (faculty), 8th Dist. Jud. Conf. (life). Office: McCarthy Lebit 1800 Midland Bldg 101 W Prospect Ave Cleveland OH 44115-1027

SCHAEFER, FRANK WILLIAM, III, microbiologist, researcher; b. Dayton, Ohio, Sept. 1, 1942; s. Frank William Jr. and Irene Josephine (Krouse) S. BA, Miami U., Oxford, Ohio, 1964; MS, U. Cin., 1970, PhD, 1973. Rsch. assoc. parasitologist U. Notre Dame, South Bend, Ind., 1973-78; U.S. EPA EPA, Cin., 1978—. Mem. AAAS, Am. Soc. Parasitology, Am. Soc. Microbiology, Am. Water Works Assn., Soc. Protozoologists, Sigma Xi. Home: 9948 McCauley Woods Dr Sharonville OH 45241-1489 Office: US EPA 26 Martin Luther King Dr W Cincinnati OH 45220-2242

SCHAEFER, GEORGE A., JR., bank executive. Chmn., pres., CEO Fifth Third Bancorp, Cin. Office: Fifth Third Bancorp 38 Fountain Square Plz Cincinnati OH 45263-0001*

SCHAEFER, GEORGE LOUIS, theatrical producer and director, educator; b. Wallingford, Conn., Dec. 16, 1920; s. Louis and Elsie (Otterbein) S.; m. Mildred Trares, Feb. 5, 1954. BA magna cum laude, Lafayette Coll., 1941, LittD, 1963; postgrad., Yale Drama Sch., 1942; LHD, Coker Coll., 1973. Producer, dir. TV series Hallmark Hall of Fame, 1955-68; freelance producer, dir., 1945—; assoc. dean sch. theater, film and TV UCLA, 1986-91; artistic dir. N.Y.C. Ctr. Theatre Co., 1949-52; dir. Dallas State Fair Musicals, 1952-58; pres. Compass Prodns., Inc., 1959-86. Dir. Broadway prodns. G.I. Hamlet, 1945, Man and Superman, 1947, The Linden Tree, 1948, The Heiress (revival), 1949, Idiot's Delight (revival), 1950, Southwest Corner, 1955, The Apple Cart, 1956, The Body Beautiful, 1958, Write Me a Murder, 1961, The Great Indoors, 1966, The Last of Mrs. Lincoln, 1972, Mixed Couples, 1980; co-prodr. Broadway and London prodns. The Teahouse of the August Moon, 1953; dir., co-prodr. Zenda for L.A. Civic Light Opera Co., 1963; prodr. To Broadway with Love for N.Y. World's Fair, 1964; prodr., dir. TV spls. Do Not Go Gentle Into That Good Night, 1967, A War of Children, Sandburg's Lincoln, 1974-76, In This House of Brede, 1975, Truman at Potsdam, Amelia Earhart, 1976, Our Town, 1977, First You Cry, Orchard Children, 1978, Blind Ambition, Mayflower, 1979, The Bunker, 1981, Jean Harris Trial, 1982, A Piano for Mrs. Cimino, 1982, Deadly Game, 1983, Answers, 1983, Right of Way, 1983, Children in the Crossfire, 1984, Stone Pillow, 1985, Mrs. Delafield Wants to Marry, 1986, Laura Lansing Slept Here, 1988, Let Me Hear You Whisper, 1990, The Man Upstairs, 1992, Harvey, 1996; dir. films An Enemy of the People, Generation, Doctor's Wives, Pendulum, Macbeth; dir. L.A. prodn. Leave It To Jane, 1987; author: From Live to Tape to Film, 1996. Mem. Nat. Council on the Arts, 1983-88. Recipient Emmy awards, 1959, 60, 61, 68, 73, Dirs. Guild Am. TV awards, 1961, 64, 67, 68, Dinneen award Nat. Cath. Theatre Conf., 1964; named Dir. of Yr., Radio-TV Daily, 1957, 60, 63, 65; Am. Theatre fellow, 1995. Mem. Dirs. Guild Am. (v.p. 1961-79, pres. 1979-81), Phi Beta Kappa.

SCHAEFER, GORDON EMORY, food company executive; b. 1932; married. BS, Marquette U., 1956. With Peat, Marwick, Mitchell & Co., 1955-59; treas. Pabst Brewing Co., Milw., 1965-72, v.p. adminstrn., 1972-75, v.p. ops., 1975-76, exec. v.p. ops., 1976-89, cons., 1980—, dir.; pres., dir. Krier Foods Inc., Belgium, Wis., 1981-85, Corrs Beverages, Chgo., 1985-86; dir. bus. devel. Lakeside Packing Co., Manitowoc, Wis., 1989-92; mng. dir. Robertson Assocs., Mfg. Europe Ltd., Cardiff, Wales, U.K., 1993-94; bd. dirs. Fox Fin. Co., Grand Rapids, Mich., Melal Packaging Internat., Denver, Berg Industries, Inc., Marshfield, Wis.; fin. and ops. cons.; owner, operator Schaefer's Orchards. Home: 154 Granville Rd Cedarburg WI 53012-9509

SCHAEFER, HANS-ECKART, pathologist; b. Koblenz, Germany, Sept. 8, 1936; s. Hans and Mathilde (Sellerbeck) S.; m. Birgit Peters, Apr. 19, 1966. Degree in medicine, U. Mainz, Fed. Republic Germany, 1958; postgrad., U. Bonn, Fed. Republic Germany, 1962; MD, U. Bonn, 1963; PhD, U. Köln, Fed. Republic Germany, 1970. Med. diplomate. Resident Kantonales Hosp., Walenstadt, Switzerland, Städtisches Hosp., Pforzheim, Bollmanns Hosp., Nienburg, 1961-63; asst. physician Inst. Pathology U. Bonn, 1963-67; asst. physician Inst. Pathology U. Köln, 1967-73, head dept. ultrastructural pathology, 1973-83; mng. dir. Inst. Pathology U. Freiburg, Fed. Republic Germany, 1983—; also chair gen. and spl. pathology U. Freiburg. Author: Leukopoese and Myeloproliferative Erkrankungen, 1984; co-author: Atlas of Malignant Haematology, 1996; co-editor textbook Allgmeine und Spezielle Pathologie, 1989, 93, 95; exec. editor Pathology Rsch. and Practice. Fellow Heidelberg Acad. Wissenschaften; mem. Gesellschaft Histochemie (pres. 1983-84), Internat. Acad. Pathology, Internat. Soc. Hematology, Deutsche Gesellschaft Pathologie, Soc. Europaea Pneumologica, Deutsche Gesellschaft Säugetierforschung, Deutsche Gesellschaft Arterioskleroseforschung (pres. 1989-92), Deutsche Gesellschaft Hämatologie Onkologie. Avocation: harpsichord playing. Home: Weinbergstrasse 15, D 79249 Merzhausen Federal Republic of Germany Office: Inst Pathology, Alberstrasse 19 PO Box 214, D 79002 Freiburg Germany

SCHAEFER, HENRY FREDERICK, III, chemistry educator; b. Grand Rapids, Mich., June 8, 1944; s. Henry Frederick Jr. and Janice Christine (Trost) S.; m. Karen Regine Rasmussen, Sept. 2, 1966; children: Charlotte, Pierre, Theodore, Rebecca, Caleb. BS in Chem. Physics, MIT, 1966; PhD in Chem. Physics, Stanford U., 1969. From asst. prof. to prof. chemistry U. Calif., Berkeley, 1969-87; Graham Perdue prof., dir. Ctr. for Computational Quantum Chemistry U. Ga., Athens, 1987—; Wilfred T. Doherty prof., dir. Inst. Theoretical Chemistry, U. Tex., Austin, 1979-80; endowed lectr. Nat. U. Mex., 1979, Johns Hopkins U., 1982, Brown U., 1985, U. Canterbury, Christchurch, New Zealand, 1986, U. Kans., 1986, Vanderbilt U., 1988, U. Va., 1988, U. Alta, 1990, U. Guelph, Waterloo, Ont., 1991, Case Western Res. U., 1992, Kans. State U., 1993; Francis A. Schaeffer lectr. Covenant Sem., St. Louis, 1995; Mary E. Kapp lectr. Va. Commonwealth U., 1996; C.S. Lewis lectr. U. Tenn., 1997; George A. Abbott lectr. U. N.D., 1997. Contbr. articles to profl. jours. including The Electronic Structure of Atoms and Molecules: A Survey of Rigorous Quantum Mechanical Results, 1972, Modern Theoretical Chemistry, 1977, Quantum Chemistry, 1983, A New Dimension to Quantum Chemistry, 1994; editor Jour. Molecular Physics, 1991—. Recipient Pure Chemistry award Am. Chem. Soc., 1979, Leo Hendrik Baekeland award, 1983, Centenary medal Royal Soc. Chemistry, London, 1992; Sloan fellow, 1972, Guggenheim fellow, 1976-77; named one of 100 Outstanding Young Scientists in Am., Sci. Digest, 1984, named 3rd Most Highly cited chemist in world Science Watch, 1992. Fellow Am. Phys. Soc., Am. Sci. Affiliation; mem. Internat. Acad. Quantum Molecular Sci., Am. Chem. Soc. (chmn. divsn. phys. chemistry 1992). Presbyterian. Office: U Ga Ctr Computational Quantum Chemistry Athens GA 30602

SCHAEFER, JACOB WERNLI, military systems consultant; b. Paullina, Iowa, June 27, 1919; s. Louis B. and Minnie (Wernli) S.; m. Mary Snow Carter, July 26, 1941; children: Joanna, James, Scott. B.M.E., Ohio State U., 1941, D.Sc. (hon.), 1976. Mem. staff Bell Labs., 1941-84; dir. Kwajalein (Marshall Islands) Field Sta., 1963-65; exec. dir. Holmdel, N.J., 1968-80, Murray Hill, N.J., 1980-81; exec. dir. Mil. Systems Div., Whippany, N.J., 1981-84, ret.; pvt. cons., 1984—. Contbr. articles to profl. jours. Pres. Watchung (N.J.) Sch. Bd., 1954-63; trustee Bancroft Sch., Haddonfield, N.J., 1973—; chmn. Watchung Planning Bd., 1967-95; mem. Watchung Area coun. Boy Scouts Am., 1966-69. Capt. Ordnance Corps AUS, 1942-46. Recipient Disting. Alumnus award Ohio State U., 1966, 95, 2 Outstanding Civilian Svc. medals U.S. Army. Fellow IEEE; mem. Nat. Acad. Engring., ASME, Army Ordnance Assn. Republican. Achievements include patent for command guidance for anti-aircraft missiles, optical tracking systems for anti-aircraft fire control; management of initial cellular telephone system development; responsibility for first electronic PBX development. Home: 115 Century Ln Watchung NJ 07060-6007

SCHAEFER, JAMES LEE, television news producer; b. Lincoln, Nebr., June 21, 1946; s. Francis T. and Margaret O. (O'Keefe) S.; m. Margaret Wheatley, Feb. 1, 1975; children: Blake W., Eliot C., Alexander O. BA, U. Notre Dame, 1968; MA, NYU, 1970. Film editor WKYC-TV, Cleve., 1974-76, prodr., 1976-82; exec. prodr. Storer News Bur., Washington, 1986-88; bur. chief Gillett News Bur., Washington, 1988-91; sr. prodr., writer WJLA-TV, Washington, 1993-94, ops. mgr., 1994-95, exec. prodr., 1995—; cons. for polit conventions Gillett/Wenma, Washington, 1991-92; writer, prodr. WJW-TV, Cleve., 1982-86. Writer, prodr. (TV documentaries) WKYC: Spotlight on Cleveland, 1976 (Emmy award), 35th Anniversary, 1983 (Emmy award), A Holocaust Remembrance, 1994 (Headliner award 1994), Going Back: D-Day , 1995 (RTNDA award 1995); co-prodr. news series Baseball Strike, 1982 (Emmy award). Commr. Arlington (Va.) Little League, 1992-96, ARC (Va.) Babe Ruth Sr. League, 1997—. Recipient Silver Baton N.Y. Festival of Film and TV, 1983. Mem. NATAS (Emmy awards Cleve. chpt. 1976, 79, 80),. Unitarian. Home: 647 N Kenmore St Arlington VA 22201 Office: WJLA-TV 3007 Tilden St NW Washington DC 20008-3075

SCHAEFER, JIMMIE WAYNE, JR., agricultural company executive; b. Anna, Ill., Dec. 26, 1951; s. Jimmie Wayne and Wilma Jean (Kinder) S.; m. Melanie Kugel, Apr. 19, 1981; 1 child Jyoti. BS in Agronomy, So. Ill. U., 1974; MSCI, MERU, Switzerland, 1979. Br. mgr. World Plan Exec. Coun., Nashville, 1975-79; pres. Schaefer & Assoc., Inc., Fairfield, Iowa, 1979-82, J.W. Schaefer Mortgage Co., Fairfield, 1981-1982; chmn., chief exec. officer Soil Techs. Corp., Fairfield, 1982—; chmn., CEO Sunshine Natural Foods, Inc., Fairfield, 1990—, JAT Internat. Inc., Fairfield, 1994—; chmn. bd. Radiance Dairy Coop., Fairfield, 1980-92; bd. dirs. FAE Credit Union, Fairfield, 1982-84; lectr. microalgal applications in agr. to ednl. and rsch. instns. in numerous developing countries; exec. dir. Inst. for Agr. and Environ. Studies, Maharishi U. Mgmt., Fairfield, 1990—. Author: (with others) Turf Integrated Pest Management Systems, 1988; patentee in field. Mem. Am. Soc. Agronomy, Am. Soc. Agrl. Cons. Avocation: gentleman farmer. Home: 2105 185th St Fairfield IA 52556-9204 Office: Soil Techs Corp 2103 185th St Fairfield IA 52556-9232

SCHAEFER, JOHN PAUL, chemist, corporate executive; b. N.Y.C., Sept. 17, 1934; s. Conrad and Meta (Rekelkamm) S.; m. Helen Marie Schwarz, May 18, 1958; children—Ann Marie, Susan Margaret. B.S., Poly. Inst. Bklyn., 1955; Ph.D. in Chemistry, U. Ill., 1958; fellow, Calif. Inst. Tech., 1958-59. Asst. prof. U. Calif. at Berkeley, 1959-60; mem. faculty U. Ariz., 1960—, prof. chemistry, head dept., 1968-70; dean Coll. Liberal Arts U. Ariz., 1970-71, pres., 1971-82; pres. Rsch. Corp., 1982—, also bd. dirs.; chmn. bd. Rsch. Corp. Techs. Inc., 1988—; bd. dirs. Olin Corp., Rsch. Corp. Techs. Bd. dirs. Tucson Airport Authority; bd. govs. U.S.-Israel Binat. Sci. Found., 1972-77. Mem. AAAS, Nat. Audubon Soc., Tucson Audubon Soc. (pres. 1961-65), Am. Chem. Soc., Ariz. Acad., Nature Conservancy, Newcomen Soc., Sigma Xi, Phi Lambda Upsilon, Phi Kappa Phi. Office: Rsch Corp 101 N Wilmot Rd Ste 250 Tucson AZ 85711-3361

SCHAEFER, JON PATRICK, judge, lawyer; b. Fremont, Ohio, Nov. 20, 1948; s. Ellsworth Joseph and Lois Ann (Fought) S.; m. Kathryn Louise Koch, Aug. 21, 1971; children: Heather Marie, Matthew Thomas. BS, Bethel Coll., 1971; JD, Memphis State U., 1974. Bar: Ohio 1974, U.S. Dist. Ct. (no. dist.) Ohio 1977. Ptnr. McKown, Schaefer & McKown Co., L.P.A., Shelby, Ohio, 1974-84; pvt. practice Shelby, 1984-88; acting judge Shelby Mcpl. Ct., 1981-86, judge, 1986—; prosecutor, atty. City of Shelby, 1975-78. Mem. Richland County Dem. Exec. Com., 1975-76; bd. dirs. Shelby chpt. ARC, 1985-94. Recipient Community Svc. award Richland County Sheriff's Dept., 1987. Mem. ABA, Ohio Bar Assn. (mem. unauthorized practice law com.), Richland County Bar Assn. Huron County Bar Assn., Ohio Trial Lawyers Assn., K.C. (grand knight Shelby chpt. 1979-83, Knight of the Yr. award 1984, Cath. Family of Yr. award 1986), Sertoma (pres. Shelby chpt. 1981-82, 90-91, dist. gov. 1985-86, Disting. Gov. award 1986), Shelby C. of C., Ohio Farm Bur., Catawba West Harbor Yacht Club. Avocations: boating, fishing, reading. Home: 65 Independence Dr Shelby OH 44875-1815 Office: Shelby Mcpl Ct 14 Church St Shelby OH 44875-1204

SCHAEFER, LEWIS GEORGE, physicians assistant; b. Flint, Mich., July 23, 1937; s. John George Schaefer (dec.) and Lucile Marie (Burk) Branam; children: Gregory Lewis, Janet Marie. LPN, Letterman Gen. Hosp., San Francisco, 1966; BS, Baylor U., 1974; A in Criminal Justice, Ctrl. Carolina Coll., 1984. Lic. N.C. Physician's asst. U.S. Army, Ft. Bragg, N.C., 1974-78, U.S. Army Civil Svc., Ft. Bragg, N.C., 1978-86, Dept. of Corrections, McCain, N.C., 1994. With U.S. Army, 1954-78. Mem. Corvettes of Am. Roman Catholic. Avocations: collecting class automobiles. Home: 736 Carnegie Dr Fayetteville NC 28311

SCHAEFER, MARILYN LOUISE, artist, writer, educator; b. Cedar Rapids, Iowa, Apr. 22, 1933; d. Henry Richard and Maria Augusta (Dickel) S. AA, Monticello Coll. for Women, 1953; BFA, Cranbrook Acad. Art, 1956, MFA, 1960; MA cum laude, U. Chgo., 1958; MA, St. John's Coll., Santa Fe, 1979. Rsch. asst. editor Encyclopaedia Britannica, Chgo., 1960-63; humanities editor Encyclopedia Americana, N.Y., 1964-68; acquisitions editor Litton Ednl. Pub., N.Y., 1968-70; from instr. to prof. art and advt. design dept. N.Y.C. Tech. Coll. CUNY, 1970—; contbg. editor Encyclopedia Americana, 1979—, Coll. Teaching jour., 1979. Contbr. articles to profl. publs. including Art and Auction mag., Art and Antiques mag., Am. Artist mag., Encyclopedia Americana, 1970—. Luce Found. postgrad. study fellow St. John's Coll., 1976-79; Ingram Merrill Found. grantee, 1983-84. Mem. AAUW, CUNY Acad. Arts and Scis. Home: 306 W 76th St New York NY 10023-8065 Office: NYC Tech Coll CUNY 300 Jay St Brooklyn NY 11201-1909

SCHAEFER, MICHAEL JUDE, industrial control systems engineer; b. Glen Ridge, N.J., Oct. 4, 1954; s. Hubert Emil and Agnes Alice (Boehmer) S.; m. Terry Lynn Vezerian, Jan. 28, 1988; m. Terri Lyn Armitage, July 10, 1993; children: Stephanie, Jessica, Nicole. Student, Grossmont C.C., 1976-78, U. Calif., San Diego, 1978-81; postgrad., U. Calif., San Diego, 1992. Gen. contractor Oakwood Constrn., San Diego, 1981-86; controls specialist Burke Engring., San Diego, 1986-90; control sys. engr. Omega Controls, San Diego, 1990-92, Centaurus Sys., San Diego, 1992-95, Medland Controls, Chula Vista, Calif., 1995—; cons. in field, 1995—. Mem. Instrument Soc. Am., Assn. Profl. Energy Mgrs. Achievements include being control system engineering project leader for seveal landmark highrises, prisons, military bases; performance of proof of concept engineering (hardware) for first bacnet type installation in the world. Home: 9375 E Heaney Cir Santee CA 92071-2926 Office: 2363 Newton Ave # B San Diego CA 92113-3648

SCHAEFER, RHODA PESNER, elementary school educator; b. Bronx, N.Y., Mar. 15, 1947; d. Herman Pesner; m. Alan Jacob Schaefer, Sept. 23, 1967; children: Ira Marc, Melissa Anne. BA, Dominican Coll., Orangeburg, N.Y., 1980; MA in Edn., SUNY, New Paltz, 1987. Cert. tchr., N.Y. Teaching asst. East Ramapo Cen. Schs., Spring Valley, N.Y., 1984-87; tchr. East Ramapo Cen. Sch. Dist., Spring Valley, 1987—; instr. East Ramapo Tchrs.' Ctr., 1988—; adj. prof. L.I. U., 1989—, SUNY, New Paltz, 1994—, Coll. of New Rochelle, N.Y.; mem. Hudson Valley Portfolio Project, 1993-96. Pres., officer PTA, Spring Valley, 1972—. Mem. ASCD, Internat. Reading Assn., N.Y. Reading Assn., Rockland Reading Coun., N.Y. Assn. for Computers and Tech. Edn., Nat. Coun. English Tchrs., Nat. Coun. for Social Studies. Office: Hillcrest Elem Sch Addison Boyce Dr New City NY 10956

SCHAEFER, ROBERT WAYNE, banker; b. Balt., Feb. 28, 1934; s. Roland Elmer and Lillian (Reid) S.; m. Elaine Lennon, May 18, 1963; children: Linda, Karen. Student, Balt. City Coll., 1949-51; BS in Acctg., U. Balt., 1955; MBA in Fin., Loyola Coll., 1971. C.P.A., Md. With First Nat. Bank of Md., Balt., 1951-55, 59—; comptroller First Nat. Bank of Md., 1961—, v.p., 1965-69, sr. v.p., 1969-73, exec. v.p., 1973-96; exec. dir. France-Merrick Founds., Balt., 1996—; instr. accounting N.C. State Coll., 1956-58; instr. accounting, econs., taxes, credit Balt. chpt. Am. Inst. Banking, 1960-66. Mem. Balt. City Sch. Bd., 1973-75, Balt. City Bd. Fin.; bd. dirs., treas. Balt. Area United Fund, 1964-79; past bd. dirs. Balt. coun. Boy Scouts Am., Balt. chpt. ARC, Boys Latin Sch.; trustee, pres. Wesley Home for Aged; bd. dirs. Balt. City Aquarium, Roland Park Country Sch., Md. Gen. Hosp., Western Md. Coll., 1981-92, Lyric Theatre, 1985—, Enoch Pratt Libr., 1986-93, Ind. Coll. Fund Md., 1990—, Coun. on Econ. Edn., YMCA Ctrl. Md., 1992, U. Balt. 1st lt. USMCR, 1956-58. Mem. Bank Adminstrn. Inst. (past pres., bd. dirs. Balt. chpt.), Md. CPA Assn., Fin. Execs. Inst., U. Balt. Alumni Assn. (bd. dirs. 1972—), U. Balt. Found., Valley Country Club. Republican. Methodist (bd. dirs., mem. finance com.). Home: 5903 Meadowood Rd Baltimore MD 21212-2436 Office: France-Merrick Foundations 1st Md Bldg 1122 Kenilworth Dr Baltimore MD 21204-2139

SCHAEFER, THEODORE PETER, chemistry educator; b. Gnadenthal, Man., Can., July 22, 1933; s. Paul Jacob and Margarethe (Wiebe) S.; m. Nicola Caroline Sewell, Dec. 26, 1960; children: Catherine, Dominic, Benjamin. B.S. with Honors, U. Man., 1954, M.S., 1955; D.Phil. (Shell scholar), Oxford (Eng.) U., 1958; D.Sc. (hon. causa), U. Winnipeg, 1982. Prof. chemistry U. Man., Winnipeg, Can., 1958—, Univ. Disting. prof., 1982—; researcher NRC, Ottawa, Can., 1959, 62, Nat. Phys. Lab., Teddington, U.K., 1960, 65, Argonne Nat. Lab., Chgo., 1967, 68; sr. fellow, mem. grants com. NRC, Ottawa.; mem. council Nat. Scis. and Engring. Research Council, Ottawa., 1980-85. Contbr. articles on nuclear magnetic resonance to sci. jours. Recipient Herzberg award Spectroscopy Soc. Can., 1975. Fellow Chem. Inst. Can. (Noranda award 1973), Royal Soc. Can. Home: 210 Oak St, Winnipeg, MB Canada R3M 3R4 Office: Univ of Manitoba, Dept of Chemistry, Winnipeg, MB Canada R3T 2N2 *Persistence can sometimes emulate perspicacity.*

SCHAEFER, WILLIAM DAVID, English language educator; b. Dighton, Mass., May 11, 1928; s. Louis and Elsie K. (Otterbein) S.; m. Josephine R. Lamprecht, Aug. 8, 1958; 1 dau., Kimberly. B.A., NYU, 1957; M.S., U. Wis., 1958, Ph.D., 1962. Mem. faculty UCLA, 1962-90, prof. English, 1970-90, chmn. dept., 1969-71, exec. vice chancellor, 1978-87. Author: James (BV) Thomson: Beyond the City, 1965, Speedy Extinction of Evil and Misery, 1967, Education Without Compromise: From Chaos to Coherence in Higher Education, 1990; contbr. articles to profl. jours., short stories to literary mags. Served with AUS, 1954-56. Fulbright fellow Eng., 1961-62. Mem. MLA (exec. dir. 1971-78). Home: 164 Stagecoach Rd Bell Canyon CA 91307-1044 Office: UCLA 405 Hilgard Ave Los Angeles CA 90095-9000

SCHAEFER, WILLIAM G., lawyer; b. Kansas City, Mo., June 16, 1941; m. Sharon Saylor, Dec. 21, 1963; children: James, Kristen. BA, U. Kans., 1963; JD, Harvard U., 1966. Bar: Ill. 1966, D.C. 1978, Md. 1984. Ptnr. Sidley & Austin, Chgo. and Washington, 1966-74, 78-93; v.p., gen. counsel DeKalb Corp., Ill., 1974-77; spl. counsel Bechel Corp., Gaithersburg, Md., 1993-96; sr. v.p. legal affairs Treasure Chest Advt. Co., Balt., 1996—. Office: Treasure Chest Advt Co 250 W Pratt St Baltimore MD 21201-2423

SCHAEFFER, BRENDA MAE, psychologist, author; b. Duluth, Minn.; d. Ralph J. Bernice M. (Johnson) Furtman; children: Heidi, Gordon III. BA in Sociology, Psychology and English cum laude, U. Minn., 1962; MA in Human Devel., St. Mary's Coll., Winona, Minn., 1976. Lic. psychologist, Minn.; cert. addictions specialist. Mem. faculty Coll. St. Scholastica, Duluth, 1976—; trainer, therapist, communications cons. Transactional Analysis Inst., Mpls., 1984-88; owner, clin. dir. Brenda M. Schaeffer and Assocs., Inc., Healthy Relationships, Inc.; vis. prof. U. Minn., Duluth, 1976—; guest lectr. dep. counseling U. Wis., Superior, 1980-81; nat. and internat. lectr. Author: Is It Love or Is It Addiction, 1987, Loving Me, Loving You, 1991, Signs of Healthy Love, Signs of Addictive Love, Power Plays, Addictive Love, Help Yourself Out; mem. editorial bd. Transactional Analysis Jour.; editor Healthy Relationships newsletter. Planner Lake Superior Task Force, Duluth, 1980-83; bd. dirs., sec. Nat. Coun. Sexual Addictions/Compulsions, 1992—, sec. 1994-95; v.p. H. Milton Erickson Inst. Minn., 1992-93. Mem. Internat. Transactional Analysis Assn. (1975), Transactional Anaylsis Inst. Minn. (founder, pres. 1984-86), U.S. Assn. Transactional Analysis, Northeast Minn. Transactional Analysis Seminar (founder and chairperson 1977-83). Office: 27306 County Road A Spooner WI 54801-9019

SCHAEFFER, EDWIN FRANK, JR., lawyer, finance company executive; b. N.Y.C., Nov. 29, 1930; s. Edwin Frank and Rachel Townsend (Bouchier) S.; m. Joan Cameron Sherwood, Apr. 7, 1956; children: Edwin Frank III, Cameron, Donald. AB, Washington and Lee U., 1952; JD, Harvard U., 1955. Bar: Ky. 1955, U.S. Dist. Ct. (ea. and we. dists.) Ky. 1957, U.S. Ct. Appeals (6th cir.) 1957. Assoc., Bullitt, Dawson & Tarrant, Louisville, 1955-60, ptnr., 1960-63; ptnr. Kincaid, Wilson, Schaeffer, Hembree & Kinser, P.S.C., Lexington, Ky., 1963-79, bd. dirs., chmn. bd. dirs., 1979-93; vice chmn., bd. dirs. Ky. Fin. Co., Inc., 1976-84, chmn., 1984-91; bd. dirs. Ky. Central Life Ins. Co., 1976-93, Central Bank & Trust Co., 1974-93, Bd. dirs. Lexington Philharm., 1970-80, United Way, 1976-80, 84-88, Lexington Ctr. Corp., 1982—, Hospice of Bluegrass, 1985-91. Served with JAGC, AUS, 1955-57. Fellow Am. Bar Found.; mem. Ky. State Bar Assn., Fayette County Bar Assn., Louisville Bar Assn., Greater Lexington C. of C. (bd. dirs. 1986-88). Democrat. Presbyterian. Club: Lexington Country. Address: 200 W Vine St Ste 810 Lexington KY 40507-1620

SCHAEFFER, GLENN WILLIAM, casino corporate financial executive; b. Pomona, Calif., Oct. 11, 1953; s. William Donald and Mary Louise (Miller) S.; m. Deborah Lynn Helfer, Sept. 6, 1974 (div. Apr. 1981); m. Renee Sue Riebel, May 25, 1985. AB summa cum laude, U. Calif., Irvine, 1974, MA, 1975; MFA, U. Iowa, 1977. Fin. cons. Dean Witter, Los Angeles, 1977-78; assoc. Hill and Knowlton, Inc., Los Angeles, 1978-81; v.p. Ramada Inns, Inc., Phoenix, 1981-84; exec. v.p., chief fin. officer Circus Circus Enterprises, Inc., Las Vegas, Nev., 1984-91; pres. Circus Circus Enterprises, Inc., 1991-93; also bd. dirs. Circus Circus Enterprises, Inc., Las Vegas; ptnr. Gold Strike Resorts, Jean, Nev., 1993-95; pres. Circus Circus Enterprises, 1995—. Pres. Hitch fellow U. Calif.-Irvine, 1973-74. Mem. Phi Beta Kappa. Avocations: reading, bicycling. Office: Circus Circus Enterprises 2880 Las Vegas Blvd S Las Vegas NV 89109-1138

SCHAEFFER, LEONARD DAVID, health care executive; b. Chgo., July 28, 1945; s. David and Sarah (Levin) S.; m. Pamela Lee Sidford, Aug. 11, 1968; children: David, Jacqueline. BA, Princeton U., 1969. Mgmt. cons. Arthur Andersen & Co., 1969-73; dep. dir. mgmt. Ill. Mental Health/Devel. Disability, Springfield, 1973-75; dir. Ill. Bur. of Budget, Springfield, 1975-76; v.p. Citibank, N.A., N.Y.C., 1976-78; asst. sec. mgmt. and budget HHS, Washington, 1978, adminstr. HCFA, 1978-80; exec. v.p., COO Student Loan Mktg. Assn., Washington, 1980-82; pres., CEO Group Health, Inc., Mpls., 1983-86; chmn., CEO Blue Cross of Calif., Woodland Hills, 1986—, WellPoint Health Networks Inc., 1992—; bd. dirs. Allergan, Inc., Irvine, Calif., Metra Biosystems; bd. councilors U. So. Calif. Sch. Pub. Adminstrn., 1988—; bd. dirs. exec com. Blue Cross-Blue Shield Assn., Chgo., 1986—; mem. Congl. Prospective Payment Assessment Commn., 1987-93; mem. Pew Health Professions Com., Phila., 1990-93; chmn. bd. trustees Nat. Health Found., L.A., 1992—; chmn. Nat. Inst. Health Care Mgmt., 1993—; mem. Coun. on the Econ. Impact of Health Sys. Change, 1996—. Mem. editorial adv. bd. Managed Healthcare, 1989—. Bd. govs. Town Hall of Calif., L.A., 1989—. Kellogg Found. fellow, 1981-89, Internat. fellow King's Fund Coll., London, 1990—; recipient Citation-Outstanding Svc., Am. Acad. Pediats., 1981, Disting. Pub. Svc. award HEW, Washington, 1980. Mem. Cosmos Club, Princeton Club, Regency Club. Office: Blue Cross of Calif 21555 Oxnard St Woodland Hills CA 91367-4943

SCHAEFFER, REINER HORST, air force officer, retired librarian, foreign language professional; b. Berlin, Lichterfelde, Fed. Republic Germany, Jan. 13, 1938; came to U.S., 1958; s. Immanuel Emil and Wilhelmine (Fahrni) Frei-S.; m. Cathy Anne Cormack, Apr. 6, 1966; 1 child, Brian Reiner. Nat. Cert., Bus. Sch., Thun, Switzerland, 1957; B.G.S. in Bus., U. Nebr., 1970; M.P.A. in Orgnl. Behavior, U. Mo., 1972; Ph.D. in Fgn. Lang. Edn., Ohio State U., 1979. Commd. officer USAF, 1958, advanced through grades to lt. col.; instr. German, French USAF Acad., Colorado Springs, Colo., 1975-77, assoc. prof., 1979-81, chmn. German, 1981, dir. librs., 1982-86, prof., 1986-92, dir. Acad. Librs., 1986—. Mem. People to People, Colorado Springs; bd. dirs. Friends of AF Acad. Librs. Named Disting. Grad. Air Force Inst. Tech, Wright-Patterson AFB, Ohio, 1979; recipient 5 Meritorious Service medals, 5 Air Force Commendation medals. Mem. Am. Assn. Tchrs. of German, Swiss Club (pres. Colorado Springs chpt. 1990-96, chmn.), Pi Alpha Alpha, Alpha Sigma Alpha. Republican. Avocations: skiing; golfing; hiking; soccer. Home: 515 Celtic Ct Colorado Springs CO 80921-1807 Office: Fgn Lang Ctr LLC 315 E Willamette Ave Colorado Springs CO 80903-1115

SCHAEFFER, ROBERT OLLIE, elevator company executive; b. Elgin, Ill., June 21, 1928; s. Ollie Frank and Clara (Bremer) S.; m. Lois Arlene Menke, June 24, 1950; children: Cynthia, Kathryn, Joan, William. BSCE, Purdue U., 1951. Registered profl. engr., Ill., Ind., N.Y., Tex., Mass.; registered real estate broker, Ill. Gen. mgr. passenger conveyor div. Stephens-Adamson Mfg., Aurora, Ill., 1951-63; gen. mgr. escalator div. Montgomery Elevator Co., Moline, Ill., 1963-72; v.p. mfg. Montgomery Elevator Co., Moline, 1972-86, v.p. corp. purchasing, 1986—; bd. dirs. Renew Moline, Ill., Devel. Assn. Rock Island, Rock Island, Ill.; pres. Coxton Devel. Corp. Patentee in field. Mem. planning commn. City of Moline, 1965-70, vice chmn. Moline Planning Commn., 1994—; alderman City of Moline, 1970, 71-72; village trustee Hampton, Ill., 1975-79, mayor, 1984-85; past pres., treas. Tri City Coin Club; past mem. bd. elders Holy Cross Luth. Ch., Moline, past pres. and past sec. congregation; founder new chpt. Western Ill. Nat. Multiple Sclerosis Soc., 1965, past pres., treas. and bd. mem. Named Boss of Yr., Jr. C. of C., 1970. Fellow ASCE; mem. NSPE, Ill. Soc. Profl. Engrs., Am. Standard Safety Code for Elevators, Escalators and Moving Walks (vice chmn. escalator com.), Nat. Assn. Elevator Safety Authorities (dir. 1992—), Nat. Soc. Paper Money Collectors. Republican. Lutheran. Avocations: baseball cards, pocket watches, racing homing pigeons. Home: 2730 30th Street Ct Moline IL 61265-5307

SCHAER, WERNER, computer services executive; b. Olten, Switzerland, Sept. 23, 1940; came to U.S., 1966.; s. Friedrich and Erna Helen (Kreuzberger) S.; m. Marisa Casseres, Dec. 20, 1965; children: Sara Elaine, William Ernest. Diplom in Elec. Engring., Fed. Inst. Tech., Zurich, Switzerland, 1962; MBA, Pepperdine U., 1975. Systems analyst Sperry Rand, Zurich, Geneva, Phila., Washington, 1963-66; dir., v.p. devel. Computer Sci. Corp. Infonet, El Segundo, Calif., 1969-77; pres. Computer Scis. Corp. Europe, S.Am., Brussels, 1978-82; sr. v.p. Computer Scis. Corp. Systems Div., Falls Church, Va., 1983-86; pres. Computer Scis. Corp. Network Integration Div., Herndon, Va., 1987-95; corp. v.p. Telecomms. CSC, 1996—. Mem. IEEE, Armed Forces Communications and Electronics Assn., Zofingia Club (Aarau, Switzerland, pres. 1958). Avocations: violin, tennis, skiing. Home: 12206 Thoroughbred Rd Herndon VA 22071-2007 Office: Computer Scis Corp 3190 Fairview Park Dr Falls Church VA 22042-4510

SCHAFER, ALICE TURNER, retired mathematics educator; b. Richmond, Va., June 18, 1915; d. John H. and Cleon (Dermott) Turner; m. Richard Donald Schafer, Sept. 8, 1942; children: John Dickerson, Richard Stone. AB, U. Richmond, 1936, DSc, 1964; MS, U . Chgo., 1940, PhD (fellow), 1942. Tchr. Glen Allen (Va.) High Sch., 1936-39; instr. math. Conn. Coll., New London, 1942-44; asst. prof. Conn. Coll., 1954-57, asso. prof., 1957-61, prof., 1961-62; prof. math. Wellesley Coll., 1962-80, Helen Day Gould prof. math., 1969-80, Helen Day Gould prof. math. emerita, 1980—, affirmative action officer, 1980-82; prof. math. Marymount U., Arlington, Va., 1989-96; ret., 1996; instr. U. Mich., Ann Arbor, 1945-46; lectr. Douglass Coll., New Brunswick, N.J., 1946-48; asst. prof. Swarthmore (Pa.) Coll., 1948-51, Drexel Inst. Tech., Phila., 1951-53; mathematician Johns Hopkins Applied Physics Lab., Silver Spring, Md., 1945; lectr. Simmons Coll., Boston, 1980-88, Radcliffe Coll. Seminars, Cambridge, Mass., 1980-85. Contbr. articles on women in math. and other articles to math. jours. Recipient Disting. Alumna award Westhampton Coll., U. Richmond, 1977; NSF sci. faculty fellow Inst. for Advanced Study, Princeton, N.J., 1958-59. Fellow AAAS (math. sect. A nominating com. 1979-83, mem.-at-large 1983-86, chair-elect sect. A 1991, chair 1992, retiring chair 1993, Assn. for Women in Math. rep., 1993—), AAUP (chmn. nat. com. W 1980-83, mem. nat. com. 1984-87), Am. Math. Soc. (chmn. postdoctoral fellowship com. 1973-76, affirmative action procedures com. 1980-82, chair com. on Human Rights of Mathematicians 1988-94), Soc. Indsl. and Applied Math., Am. Statis. Assn., Inst. Math. Stats., Nat. Coun. Tchrs. of Math. (chair com. on women 1976-81), Math Assn. Am. (adv. com. for Women and Math. program 1987-89, dir. fund raising 1989-92, lectr. 1982—, chair devel. com. 1988-92), Internat. Congress Mathematicians (mem. fund raising com. 1986), Assn. for Women in Math. (pres. 1973-75, Alice T. Schafer Prize established 1989, chair fund raising com. 1992-94, leader math. del. women mathematicians to China 1990, U.S. chair postsecondary math. edn., U.S./China Joint Conf. on Edn. 1992, co-chair Citizen Amb. program People to People U.S. and China Joint Conf. on Women's Issues 1995, session women in sci. and math., Disting. Svc. award 1996), Emily's List (mem. majority coun.), Cosmos Club, Phi Beta Kappa, Sigma Xi, Sigma Delta Epsilon. Achievements include first study of singularities of space curves in projective differential geometry; research on undulation point of a space curve. Home: 2725 N Pollard St Arlington VA 22207-5038

SCHAFER, CARL WALTER, investment executive; b. Chgo., Jan. 16, 1936; s. MacHenry George and Gertrude (Herrick) S.; 1 child, MacHenry George II. BA with distinction, U. Rochester, 1958. Budget examiner Budget Bur., Exec. Office Pres., Washington, 1961-64, legis. analyst, 1964-66, dep. dir. budget preparation, 1966-68, dir. budget preparation, 1968-69; staff asst. U.S. Ho. of Reps. Appropriations Com., 1969; dir. budget Princeton (N.J.) U., 1969-72, treas., 1972-76, fin. v.p., treas., 1976-87, lectr. indsl. adminstrn., 1975; prin. Rockefeller & Co., Inc., 1987-90; pres. Atlantic Found., Princeton, N.J., 1990—; pres., CEO Palmer Square Inc., 1979-81; trustee, treas. McCarter Theatre Co. Inc., 1974-76; co-chmn. N.J. Gov.'s Task Force on Improving N.J. Econ. and Regulatory Climate, 1982-83; chmn. investment adv. com. Howard Hughes Med. Inst., 1985-92; trustee Am. Bible Soc., 1987-92; trustee, dir. Roadway Express, Inc., Wainoco Oil Corp., Nutraceutix Inc., Electronic Clearing House Inc., The Paine Webber and Guardian Groups of Mut. Funds, Evans Sys., Inc., Harbor Br. Inst. Inc., The Investment Fund for Founds., Hamilton and Co., The Johnson Atelier and Sch. Sculpture, The Banbury Fund; mem. internat. adv. coun. Wm. Sword & Co., Inc.; trustee, chmn. fin. com. Chem. Heritage Found. Mem. Asset Mgmt. Advisors (investment com.), Rockefeller Ctr. Club (N.Y.C.), Phi Beta Kappa. Home and Office: PO Box 1164 Princeton NJ 08542-1164

SCHAFER, EDWARD T., governor; b. Bismarck, N.D., Aug. 8, 1946; s. Harold and Marian Schafer; m. Nancy Jones; children: Edward Thomas Jr., Ellie Sue, Eric Jones, Kari Jones. BSBA, U. N.D., 1969; MBA, Denver U., 1970. Quality control inspector Gold Seal, 1971-73, v.p., 1974, chmn. mgmt. com., 1975-78; owner/dir. H&S Distbn., 1976—; pres. Gold Seal, 1978-85, Dakota Classics, 1986—, TRIESCO Properties, 1986—, Fish 'N Dakota, 1990-94; gov. State of N.D., 1992—. Chmn. N.D. Micro Bus. Mktg. Alliance; pres. N.D. Heritage Group; adv. coun. Distributive Edn. Clubs of Am.; lectr. Hugh O'Brien Leadership Found.; counselor Junior Achievement; dir. Bismarck Recreation Coun.; trustee Missouri Valley Family YMCA; plankowner USS Theodore Roosevelt; ann. support com. Medcenter One Found.; mem. Bismarck State Coll. Found. Mem. NRA, Theodore Roosevelt Assn. (Theodore Roosevelt Medora Found., United Sportsman of N.D., U. N.D. Pres. Club, U. Mary Pres. Club, Bismarck-Mandan Rotary. Republican. Office: Office of Gov 600 E Boulevard Ave Bismarck ND 58505-0660*

SCHAFER, JAMES ARTHUR, physiologist; b. Buffalo, Oct. 10, 1941; s. Joseph James and Gladys Leita (Lighty) S.; m. Margaret Anne Schiefer, Aug. 16, 1964; children: James Arthur Jr., Kirsten Ann. BS, U. Mich., 1963, PhD, 1968. Postdoctoral fellow Gustav-Embden Ctr., Frankfurt, Fed. Republic Germany, 1968-69, Duke U., Durham, N.C., 1969-70; asst. prof. U. Ala., Birmingham, 1970-72, assoc. prof., 1972-76, sr. scientist, prof. dept. physiology, 1976—; prof. dept. medicine Nephrology Res. & Tng. Ctr., Birmingham, 1980—. Editor: Am. Jour. Physiology: Renal, 1983-89; assoc. editor News in Physiol. Scis., 1997—; editl. bd. Jour. Gen. Physiology, 1979—, Kidney Internat., 1990-95; contbr. numerous sci. articles to profl. pub ls. Chmn. rsch. com. Nat. Kidney and Urol. Diseases Adv. Bd.; sec. HHS, 1987-90. Recipient Established Investigator award Am. Heart Assn., 1971-76, Robert F. Pitts. Meml. award Internat. Union Physiol. Scis., Sydney, Australia, 1983, Max Planck-Von Humboldt Rsch. award Govt. of Germany, 1994, Homer W. Smith award Am. S oc. Nephrology and N.Y. Heart Assn., 1993; Jane Coffin Childs Meml. fellow, 1968-69. Mem. Am. Physiol. Soc. (elected councilor 1992-95, pres.-elect 1995-96, pres. 1996-97, past pres. 1997—), Am. Soc. Nephrology (sec.-treas. 1989-92, elected councilor 1992-95, pres.-elect 1995), Am. Soc. Clin. Investigation (hon.), Fedn. Am. Socs. Exptl. Biology (bd. dirs., exec. com. 1996-97, pub. affairs exec. com. 1997—). Avocations: classical music, racquet sports. Office: U Ala Dept Phys & Biophysics 958 BHS Bldg 1918 University Blvd Birmingham AL 35233-2008

SCHAFER, JOHN FRANCIS, retired plant pathologist; b. Pullman, Wash., Feb. 17, 1921; s. Edwin George and Ella Frances (Miles) S.; m. Joyce A. Marcks, Aug. 16, 1947; children—Patricia, Janice, James. B.S., Wash. State U., 1942; Ph.D., U. Wis., 1950. Asst. prof. to prof. plant pathology Purdue U., 1949-68; head dept. plant pathology Kans. State U., 1968-72; chmn. dept. plant pathology Wash. State U., Pullman, 1972-80; integrated pest mgmt. coordinator sci. and edn. USDA, 1980-81, acting nat. research program leader plant pathology Agrl. Research Service, 1981-82; dir. cereal rust lab. USDA, St. Paul, 1982-87, biol. sci. collaborator, 1987-95; retired, 1995; vis. rsch. prof. Duquesne U., 1965-66; adj. prof. plant pathology U. Minn., 1982-92. Contbr. articles to profl. jours., chpts. to books. Served with AUS, 1942-46. Phi Sigma scholar, 1942. Fellow AAAS, Ind. Acad. Sci., Am. Phytopathol. Soc. (past pres.); mem. Am. Soc. Agronomy, Crop Sci. Soc. Am. Achievements include identification of increased resistance to wheat leaf rust by genetic recombination; demonstration of probabilities of virulence to genetic resistance combinations, of tolerance as a mechanism of disease control, of use of cultivaral diversity for disease protection; bred (with others) over 30 disease resistant cultivars of cereal crops, including Arthur wheat. Home: 4949 Snyder Lane Apt 108 Rohnert Park CA 94928-4851

SCHAFER, JOHN STEPHEN, foundation administrator; b. N.Y.C., Sept. 5, 1934; s. Stephen James and Siiri (Halmi) S.; m. Gertrud Rosa Fleischmann, June 14, 1958; children: Sylvia F., John Stephen, Karen D., Kristen H. B.A., Rutgers U., 1956, M.B.A., 1963. Advt. research mgr. Union Carbide Corp., N.Y.C., 1959-65; research mgr. Bus. Week, N.Y.C., 1965-66; v.p. Opinion Research Corp., Princeton, N.J., 1966-80; pres. Am. Econ. Found., Cleve., 1981—, trustee, 1975—; v.p., dir. Ams. for Competitive Enterprise System, Phila., 1970-82. Editor Linde Electric Welding Progress, 1959-62, ORC Pub. Opinion Index, 1968-72, AEF Straight Talk, 1981-82, Bellcore Exch., 1993-94. Polit. pollster Ed Clark for U.S. Pres., 1980; chmn. N.J. Libertarian party, 1983; nat. dir. U.S. Jaycees, 1965-66, v.p. N.J., 1964-65. Served to 1st lt. U.S. Army, 1957-59. Mem. Jr. Chamber Internat. (hon. life), Philosophan Soc., Scabbard and Blade, Delta Phi Alpha. Presbyterian. Home: 114 Walton Palm Rd Panama City Beach FL 32413

SCHAFER, MICHAEL FREDERICK, orthopedic surgeon; b. Peoria, Ill., Aug. 17, 1942; s. Harold Martin and Frances May (Ward) S.; m. Eileen M. Briggs, Jan. 8, 1966; children—Steven, Brian, Kathy, David, Daniel. B.A., U. Iowa, 1964, M.D., 1967. Diplomate: Am. Bd. Orthopedic Surgery. Intern Chgo. Wesley Meml. Hosp., 1967-68; resident in orthopedic surgery Cook County Program, Northwestern U., Chgo., 1968-72; practice medicine specializing in orthopedic surgery Chgo., 1974—; asst. prof. orthopedic surgery Northwestern U., 1977—; Reyerson prof. and chmn. dept. orthopedic surgery; asso. attending orthopedic surgeon Northwestern Meml. Hosp., 1974—; adj. staff Children's Meml. Hosp., Chgo., 1974—; cons. VA Lakeside Hosp., 1974—; adv. bd. Center Sports Medicine, Northwestern U., 1976—; panelist Bur. Health Manpower, HEW, 1976; sec.-treas. Orthopedic Research and Edn. Found. Contbr. articles to med. jours. Served to maj. U.S. Army, 1973-74. Fellow Am. Orthopaedic Assn., Am. Acad. Orthopaedic Surgeons, Assn. Bone and Joint Surgeons; mem. AMA, Am. Orthopedic Soc. Sports Medicine, Ill. Med. Soc., Chgo. Med. Soc., Internat. Soc. Study of Pain, Scoliosis Rsch. Soc. Roman Catholic. Home: 1815 Ridgewood Ln W Glenview IL 60025-2205 Office: 303 E Chicago Ave Chicago IL 60611-3008

SCHAFER, RAYMOND MURRAY, composer, author; b. Sarnia, Ont., Can., July 18, 1933; s. Harold J. and Belle (Rose) S.; m. Jean C. Reed, Sept. 18, 1975. Studies with John Weinzweig, Royal Conservatory of Music, 1950-55; L.R.S.M., Royal Coll. and Royal Acad. Music, London, 1954. Artist in residence Meml. U. Nfld., 1963-65; prof. communications studies Simon Fraser U., Burnaby, B.C., Can., 1965-75; author, composer multimedia composition Ra, multimedia composition Princess of the Stars,, 1985. Author: British Composers in Interview, 1963, The Composer in the Classroom, 1965, Ear Cleaning, 1967, The New Soundscape, 1969, The Book of Noise, 1970, When Words Sing, 1970, The Rhinoceros in the Classroom, 1974, E.T.A. Hoffmann and Music, 1975, Creative Music Education, 1976, The Tuning of the World, 1977, The Chaldean Inscription, 1978, The 16 Scribes, 1982, On Canadian Music, 1984, Dicamus et Labyrinthos, 1985, The Thinking Ear, 1986; novel Smoke, 1976; Composer: various works including Music for the Morning of the World, 1972, From the Tibetan Book of the Dead, 1968, String Quartet, 1970, Miniwanka, 1973, Son of Heldenleben, 1968. Recipient Arts award Can. Council, 1968-69, Fromm Music Found. award, 1969, Serge Koussevitzky Music Found. award, 1969, Can. Music Coun. medal, 1972, Leger prize, 1978, Priz Arthur Honegger, 1980, 1st Glenn Gould Prize, 1987, Banff Ctr. Sch. Fine Arts Nat. award, 1985; Guggenheim fellow, 1976. Mem. Can. League Composers. Can. Music Council, Sinfonia, Phi Mu Alpha.

SCHAFER, ROBERT LOUIS, agricultural engineer, researcher; b. Burlington, Iowa, Aug. 1, 1937; s. Marion Louis and Pansy (Head) S.; m. Carolyn Louise Henn, Aug. 1, 1959; 1 child, Elizabeth Diane. BS, Iowa State U., 1959, MS, 1961, PhD, 1965. Agrl. engr. Agrl. Rsch. Svc., USDA, Ames, Iowa, 1959-64, Auburn, Ala., 1964-95. Co-author: Advances in Soil Dynamics, 1994; contbr. articles to profl. jours. Fellow Am. Soc. Agrl. Engrs. (McCormick Case Gold medal 1997). Home: PO Box 188 Loachapoka AL 36865-0188

SCHAFER, RONALD WILLIAM, electrical engineering educator; b. Tecumseh, Nebr., Feb. 17, 1938; s. William Henry and Esther Sophia (Rinne) S.; m. Dorothy Margaret Hall, June 2, 1960; children: William R., John C. (dec.), Katherine L., Barbara Anne. Student, Doane Coll., Crete, Nebr., 1956-59; BEE, U. Nebr., 1961, MEE, 1962; PhD in Elec. Engring., MIT, 1968. Mem. tech. staff Bell Labs., Murray Hill, N.J., 1968-74; John O. McCarty prof. elec. engring. Ga. Inst. Tech., Atlanta, 1974—, Inst. prof., 1991—; chmn. bd. Atlanta Signal Processors Inc., 1983—. Co-author: Digital Signal Processing, 1974, Digital Processing of Speech Signals, 1979, Speech Analysis, 1979, Discrete-Time Signal Processing, 1989, Computer-Based Exercises for Signal Processing Using Matlab, 1995. Recipient Class of 34 Disting. Prof. award Ga. Inst. Tech., 1985. Fellow IEEE (Emanuel R. Piore award 1980, Edn. medal 1992), Acoustical Soc. Am.; mem. IEEE Acoustics Speech and Signal Processing Soc. (soc. award 1982), AAAS, Nat. Acad. Engring. Democrat. Methodist. Lodge: Kiwanis. Office: Ga Inst of Tech Dept of Elec Engring Atlanta GA 30332-0250

SCHAFER, SHARON MARIE, anesthesiologist; b. Detroit, Mar. 23, 1948; d. Charles Anthony and Dorothy Emma (Schweitzer) Pokriefka; m. Timothy John Schafer, Nov. 12, 1977; children: Patrick Christopher, Steven Michael. BS in Biology, Wayne State U., 1971, MD, 1975. Diplomate Am. Bd. Anesthesiology. Intern, resident Sinai Hosp. Detroit, 1975-78; pvt. practice anesthesiology Troy, Mich., 1988—. Mem. AMA, Am. Soc. Anesthesiologists. Roman Catholic. Home and Office: 5741 Folkstone Dr Troy MI 48098-3154

SCHAFER, THOMAS WILSON, advertising agency executive; b. Youngstown, Ohio, Sept. 12, 1939; s. Kenneth Charles and Clara Louise (Wilson) S.; m. Anne Kernwein, Jan. 22, 1972; children: Charles Kenneth, Bret Thomas. B.A., Colgate U., 1962. Salesman Gen. Foods Corp., 1962-65; sr. ptnr. Tatham EURO RSCG Advt., Chgo., 1965-93; chmn. Schafer Rsch., Inc., Savannah, Ga., 1993—. Past dir. Off the Street Club. Mem. Chgo. Advt. Fedn. (past exec. v.p.). Clubs: Bob O'Link Golf, Saddle and Cycle, Off The Street. Home: 5 Modena Rd Savannah GA 31411-2136 Office: Schafer Rsch Inc 5 Modena Rd Savannah GA 31411-2136

SCHAFER, WILLIAM HARRY, electric power industry administrator; b. South Portsmouth, Ky., Aug. 22, 1936; s. William Harry and Mary Minnie (Papillon) S. AS, Franklin U., 1980; BA, Capitol U., 1987; MS, Greenwich U., 1992. Cert. fraud examiner; cert. protection profl.; cert. profl. mgr. With Columbus (Ohio) region Am. Electric Power (formerly Columbus So. Power), 1969—, risk mgmt. coord., 1989—; cons. in loss prevention field. First aid instr. Franklin County ARC, Columbus, 1965-93; mem. Simon Kenton coun. Boy Scouts Am., Columbus. Named Ky. Col., Gov. Ky., 1974, Ky. Adm., 1994, Hon. (Ohio) Lt. Gov., 1974; recipient Columbus Mayor's award for Voluntary Svc., 1982, Outstanding Comty. Svc. award Ohio Senate, 1982, Humanitarian Achievement award Columbus Dispatch newspaper, 1983, Silver Beaver award Boy Scouts Am., 1979, 50 Yr. Vets. award, 1997; James E. West fellow Boy Scouts Am., 1995. Mem. Nat. Assn. Cert. Fraud Examiners, Acad. Security Educators and Trainers, Am. Soc. Indsl. Security, Valley Forge Hist. Soc. (life), Ky. Hist. Soc. (life), U.S. Capitol Hist. Soc. (supporting founding mem.), Nat. Safety Coun. (camping com. 1974-86), Nat. Fire Protection Assn. (edn. com. 1989-93), Children's Club-Children's Hosp. (charter), Masons, Shriners. Methodist. Avocations: back-packing, travel, humanities. Home: 60 Broadmeadows Blvd Apt 327 Columbus OH 43214-1152 Office: Am Electric Power Columbus Region 215 N Front St Columbus OH 43215-2255

SCHAFF, BARBARA WALLEY, artist; b. Plainfield, N.J., May 6, 1941; d. Miron M. and Silvia S. (Solott) Walley; m. John A. Schaff, Apr. 10, 1963 (div. 1992); children: Elizabeth A., Joshua L. BA, Syracuse U., 1963; cert., Pa. Acad. Fine Arts, 1994; grad., China Nat. Acad. Fine Art, Hangzhou, 1994. Clay artist Stockton, N.J., 1968-88; advisor to faculty BFA program Kean Coll., Union, N.J., 1987—; painter Phila., 1989—; mem. adv. bd. Hunterdon Art Ctr., Clinton, N.J., 1988, 89; workshop leader, U.S. and Can. One woman shows include N.J. State Mus., Trenton, 1985, Lee Sclar Gallery, Morristown, N.J., 1986, Howe Gallery, Kean Coll., Union, 1989, ITT Boston Sheraton, 1995, Thos. Moser Cabinetmakers, Phila., 1995, Ciboulette, Phila., 1997, So. Vt. Art Ctr., Manchester, 1997; exhibited in group shows Newark Mus., 1973, 77, Morris Mus., Morristown, N.J., 1973, 77, Carnegie Ctr., Princeton, N.J., 1984, Newman Galleries, Phila., 1986, Ednl. Testing Svc., Princeton, 1987, Monarch Title Nat., San Angelo (Tex.) Mus. Art, 1989, U.S. Artists, Phila., 1992, 93, China Nat. Acad. Fine Art, 1994, Morris Gallery, Mus. Am. Art, Phila., 1994, Am. Drawing Biennial V, Muscarelle Mus. Art, Williamsburg, Va., 1996, Phila. Mus. Art Members' Dining Room, 1996, Fellowship of Pa. Acad. Fine Arts, Woodmere Mus., 1996, others; represented in permanent collections N.J. State Mus., Trenton, Fuller Mus. Art, Brockton, Mass., also corp. collections; commns. include N.J. Natural Gas, Wall, 1983, Bell Comms. Rsch., Red Bank, N.J., 1985, Kenneth Endick, Boca Raton, Fla., 1987; works featured in N.J. Mag., Star Ledger, N.Y. Times, Am. Artists, An Illustrated Survey of Leading Contemporaries. Recipient Medal of Excellence for promotion and design Art Dirs. Club N.J., 1986; fellow N.J. State Coun. on Arts, 1984-85, resident fellow Va. Ctr. Creative Arts, 1996. Mem. Fellowship of Pa. Acad. of Fine Arts (com. mem., exhibitor 1986, 87, 94, Mable Wilson Woodrow Meml. award 1994), Artist Equity. Avocations: gardening, cooking, music, sailing. Home: 1520 Spruce St Philadelphia PA 19102 Office: Barbara Schaff Studio 314 Brown St Philadelphia PA 19123-2202

SCHAFFER, DAVID IRVING, lawyer; b. N.Y.C., Oct. 17, 1935; s. Frank and Edith (Montlack) S.; m. Lois Ann Warshauer, June 16, 1957; children: Susan Edith Wenig, Eric Michael. B.A., U. Pa., 1956; LL.B., Harvard U., 1959. Bar: N.Y. 1960. Assoc. Shearman & Sterling, N.Y.C., 1960-65; sec., counsel Yale Express System, Inc., N.Y.C., 1965-66; sr. v.p., gen. counsel, sec. Avis, Inc., Garden City, N.Y., 1966-83; v.p., gen. counsel U.S. Surgical Corp., Norwalk, Conn., 1983-86; of counsel Meltzer, Lippe, Goldstein, Wolf & Schlissel, P.C., Mineola, N.Y., 1986-89, ptnr., 1989—; past pres. Nassau County Legal Aid Soc., 1984-86. Bd. dirs. United Community Fund, Great Neck, N.Y., 1980, L.I. Venture Group, 1988—. With USAR, 1960. Mem. ABA, N.Y. State Bar Assn., Nassau County Bar Assn., Harvard Club. Democrat. Home: 31 Amherst Rd Great Neck NY 11021-2910 Office: Meltzer Lippe Goldstein Wolf & Schlissel PC 190 Willis Ave Mineola NY 11501-2639

SCHAFFER, EDMUND JOHN, management consultant, retired engineering executive; b. N.Y.C., July 28, 1925; m. Muriel Spiro, Aug. 22, 1948; children: Diane Schaffer Garretson, Elaine Schaffer Luks. BS in Indsl. Engring., Syracuse U., 1950. Sr. staff indsl. engr. Carborundum Co., Niagara Falls, N.Y., 1952-60; mgr. mfg. Ford Motor Co., Detroit, 1952-60; sr. indsl. engr. ITT, N.Y.C., 1960-69, v.p., dir. worldwide indsl. engring. and mfg., 1969-82, ret., 1982; mgmt. cons. Short Hills, N.J., 1983—. With USN, 1943-47. Mem. Canoe Brook Country Club, Johns Island Country Club, Interlachen Country Club. Home: 63 Slope Dr Short Hills NJ 07078-1953

SCHAFFER, EUGENE CARL, education educator; b. Phila., May 10, 1944. BA, Temple U., 1968, EdD, 1976. Dir. field experience Valparaiso U., Valparaiso, Ind., 1974-76; prof. curriculum and instrn. U. N.C., Charlotte, 1976-91, chair dept. mid., secondary and K-12 edn., 1994—. Co-author: Recent Advances in School Effects Research, 1994; contbr. articles to profl. jours. Recipient Fulbright scholarship, Japan rsch. fellowship. Mem. Am. Edn. Rsch. Assn., Phi Delta Kappa. Home: 5838 Newcombe Ct Charlotte NC 28277-2590

SCHAFFER, JAMES MASON, foundation administrator; b. Detroit, Aug. 27, 1954; s. James Albert Schaffer and Patricia Jean (Mason) Tillman; m. Jennifer Lee Yoder, Aug. 27, 1988; children: Abigail, William. BA, Mich. State U., 1981; MPA, NYU, 1994. Ambudsman Covenant House, N.Y.C., 1981-83; dir. logistics, asst. to chmn. AmeriCares Found., New Canaan, Conn., 1983-86, 90-92; dir. devel. Emmaus House, N.Y.C., 1986-87, Legal Action Ctr. for Homeless, N.Y.C., 1987-88; mgr. resource devel. TechnoServe, Norwalk, Conn., 1988-90; dir. devel. Hole in the Wall Gang Fund, New Haven, 1992-96, St. Luke's Cmty. Svcs., Stamford, Conn., 1996—; bd. dirs. Internat. Svc. Agys., Washington, 1988-92, Part of the Solution, Bronx; chmn. bd. dirs. Nat. Gardening Assn., Burlington, Vt.; mem. bd. advisors Outer Island, Stony Creek, Conn. With USAF, 1974-78. Mem. Nat. Soc. Fund Raising Execs., Phi Kappa Phi, Phi Alpha. Roman Catholic. Home: 32 Woodside Rd Guilford CT 06437-1801

SCHAFFER, JEFFREY L., lawyer; b. L.A., Aug. 21, 1952. AB, U. Calif., Berkeley, 1974; JD, U. Calif., 1979. Bar: Calif. 1979, U.S. Dist. Ct. (no. dist.) Calif., U.S. Ct. Appeals (9th cir.) 1985. Mem. Howard, Rice, Nemerovski, Canady, Falk & Rabkin, San Francisco; panelist Continuing Edn. Bar, 1983-92, computer law inst. U. So. Calif., 1986. Assoc. editor Calif. Law REv., 1977-79. Mem. ABA (bus. law sect.), Am. Bankruptcy Inst., State Bar Calif. (bus. law sect., mem. debtor/creditor and bankruptcy com. 1987-90, 96—), Bar Assn. San Francisco (comml. law and bankruptcy sect., co-chair barristers club's bankruptcy and comml. law com. 1984-85), Berkeley Law Found., Order of Coif, Phi Beta Kappa. Office: Howard Rice Nemerovski Canady Falk & Rabkin 3 Embarcadero Ctr Ste 7 San Francisco CA 94111-4003

SCHAFFER, KENNETH B., communications executive, satellite engineer, inventor, consultant; b. N.Y.C., Oct. 19, 1947; s. Louis and Rose (Paul) S.; m. Alla Fyodorovna Kliouka, Aug. 26, 1993; 1 child, Kibo Louis. BA, CCNY, 1969. Pres., founder Sound Images, Inc., N.Y.C., 1969-72; exec. v.p. Douglas Internat., N.Y.C., 1972-75; pres., founder Ken Schaffer Group, Inc., N.Y.C., 1975-82, Orbita Techs. Corp., N.Y.C., 1981-86; v.p., founder Belka Internat. Inc., N.Y.C. and Moscow, 1986-91; pres., founder Belcom, Inc., N.Y.C., Moscow, and Almaty, 1991-96, also bd. dirs.; cons. wireless, satellite, internetworking, Russia. Profiled in The New Yorker, 1991. Recipient Golden Ace award Cable TV Assn., 1989. Mem. Am. Radio Relay League, Aircraft Owners and Pilots Assn., Internet Soc., Moscow Comml. Club. Achievements include invention of wireless guitar, satellite system to intercept internal Soviet television. Avocations: flying, amateur radio, internetworking. Home: 21 W 58th St New York NY 10019

SCHAFFER, ROBERT (BOB SCHAFFER), congressman; b. Cin., July 24, 1962; s. Robert James and Florence Ann (Bednar) S.; m. Maureen Elizabeth Menke, Feb. 8, 1986; children: Jenniffer and Emily (twins), Justin, Sarah. BA in Polit. Sci., U. Dayton, 1984. Speechwriter republican caucus Ohio Gen. Assembly, 1984-85; legis. asst. State of Ohio, Columbus, 1985; majority adminstrv. asst. Colo. Senate, Denver, 1985-87, mem., 1987-96; mem. 105th Congress, U.S. Ho. of Reps. from 4th Colo. dist., Washington, 1997—; commr. Colo. Advanced Tech. Inst., 1988—; proprietor No. Front Range Mktg. and Distbn., Inc. Mem. Mental Health Bd. Larimer County, 1986-87; mem. com. on human svcs. Nat. Conf. State Legislatures; campaing co-chair Arnold for Lt. Gov.; Republican candidate for Lt. Gov. of Colo., 1994. Named Nat. Legislator of Yr., Rep. Nat. Legislators Assn., 1995, Taxpayer Champion, Colo. Union of Taxpayers, 1995, Bus. Legislator of the Yr. Colo. Assn. Commerce and Industry, Named Guardina Small Bus. Nat. Fedn. Ind. Bus. Mem. Jaycees (Mover and Shaker award 1989), KC. Roman Catholic. Avocations: backpacking, skiing, baseball, painting, reading. Home: 3284 Silverthorne Dr Fort Collins CO 80526-2766 Office: US Ho Reps 2121 Cannon House Office Bldg Washington DC 20515

SCHAFFER, SETH ANDREW, lawyer; b. Bklyn., Jan. 7, 1942; m. Karen (Kiki) Cohn, Dec. 1, 1968; children: Amanda, Julia, James. BA in Econs. magna cum laude, Harvard U., 1963, LLB cum laude, 1967; postgrad., Cambridge (Eng.) U., 1964. Bar: N.Y. 1970, U.S. Dist. Ct. (so. dist.) N.Y. 1973, U.S. Ct. Appeals (2d cir.) 1973, U.S. Supreme Ct. 1980. Tchr. math. and econs. York (Pa.) Country Day Sch., 1967-68; assoc. dir. Vera Inst. Justice, 1969-72; asst. U.S. atty. U.S. Dist. Ct. (so. dist.) N.Y., 1972-75; chief counsel Moreland Act Commn. on Nursing Homes, N.Y.C., 1975-76; of counsel Stanley S. Arkin, P.C., Attys. at Law, 1976-77; v.p., gen. counsel, sec. of univ. NYU, N.Y.C., 1977-93, sr. v.p., gen. counsel, sec., 1993—; pres. Nat. Assn. Coll. and Univ., trustee Hosp. for Joint Diseases. Dir. Not for Profit Coordinating Com. N.Y. Henry fellow Cambridge U., Eng., 1964. Mem. Assn. Bar City N.Y., Phi Beta Kappa. Home: 14 Washington Mews New York NY 10003-6608 Office: NYU 70 Washington Sq S New York NY 10012-1019

SCHAFFER, TERESITA CURRIE, federal official; b. Washington, Sept. 28, 1945; d. Francis and Teresita (Sparre) Currie; m. Howard B. Schaffer, Oct. 25, 1971; children: Michael C., Christopher S. AB, Bryn Mawr Coll., 1966; Cert., Institut d'Etudes Politiques, Paris, 1965; postgrad., Georgetown U., 1973-74. Embassy officer U.S. Embassy, Tel Aviv, 1967-69; econ. officer U.S. Embassy, Islamabad, Pakistan, 1975-77; sci. attache U.S. Embassy, New Delhi, 1977-79; polit. analyst U.S. Dept. State, Washington, 1969-71, economist, 1972-73; div. chief, dir. Office Trade U.S. Dept. State, Washington, 1980-84; dir. Office Egyptian Affairs U.S. Dept. State, Washington, 1987-89, dep. asst. sec. for Near East and South Asia, 1989-92; amb. to Sri Lanka and Maldives U.S. Embassy, Colombo, Sri Lanka, 1992-95; dir. fgn. svc. inst. Dept. State, Arlington, Va. Author: Profile of Women in Bangladesh, 1986, Survey of Development Projects and Activities for Women in Bangladesh, 1986; chmn. editorial bd. Fgn. Svc. Jour., 1972-74. Mem. Am. Fgn. Svc. Assn. Office: Foreign Svc Inst 4000 Arlington Blvd Arlington VA 22204*

SCHAFFLER, MITCHELL BARRY, research scientist, anatomist, educator; b. Bronx, N.Y., Apr. 10, 1957; s. Walter and Shirley (Balter) S. BS, SUNY, Stony Brook, 1978; PhD, W.Va. U., 1985. Rsch. fellow in radiobiology U. Utah, Salt Lake City, 1985-87; asst. prof. U. Calif., San Diego, 1987-90; assoc. prof. and sect. head anatomy Bone and Joint Ctr. Henry Ford Health Scis. Ctr., Detroit, 1990—, Case Western Res. U., 1990—; adj. prof. Anatomy U. Mich., Ann Arbor, 1990—. Mem. editl. bd. Bone, Jour. Orthop. Rsch.; contbr. articles to profl. jours. Grantee Whitaker Found., 1988, NIH, 1991—, NASA, 1996—. Mem. Am. Assn. Anatomists, Am. Assn. Phys. Anthropology, Am. Soc. Bone Mineral Rsch., Orthop. Rsch. Soc., Sigma Xi, Phi Kappa Phi. Achievements include rsch. in skeletal biology, osteoporosis, osteoarthritis, and biomechanics. Office: Henry Ford Hlth Scis Ctr Bone and Joint Ctr 2799 W Grand Blvd Detroit MI 48202-2608

SCHAFFNER, BERTRAM HENRY, psychiatrist; b. Erie, Pa., Nov. 12, 1912; s. Milton and Gerta (Herzog) S. Student, Harvard U., 1928-29, 32-33; AB, Swarthmore Coll., 1932; MD, Johns Hopkins U., 1937; diploma, William Alanson White Inst., 1953. Diplomate Am. Bd. Psychiatry, Am. Bd. Neurology. Intern Johns Hopkins Hosp., Balt., 1937-38; resident in neurology Mt. Sinai Hosp., N.Y.C., 1938-39; resident in psychiatry Bellevue Hosp., N.Y.C., 1939-40, N.Y. State Psychiat. Inst., N.Y.C., 1946-47; pvt. practice psychiatry and psychoanalysis N.Y.C., 1947—; lectr. Sch. Nursing Cornell U., N.Y.C., 1950-60; mem. faculty, clin. supr. in psychotherapy William Alanson White Inst. Psychoanalysis, 1960—, med. dir. HIV svc., clin. supr. psychoanalysis, 1993—; cons., editor confs. Josiah Macy Jr. Found., 1949, 50, 51; cons. U.S. Children's Bur., 1946-47, Bur. Mental Health, V.I., 1954-60, World Fedn. Mental Health, 1958-68, others; mem. N.Y. County dist. bd. Com. on Gay and Lesbian Issues; cons. WHO, 1960-67; founder, exec. dir. U.S.-Caribbean Aid to Mental Health, Inc., 1960-68; organizer Biennial Caribbean Confs. for Mental Health, 1959-65; organizer, cons. Caribbean Fedn. for Mental Health, 1959-65; mem. rsch. study Pre-Soviet Russian Family in the Research in Contemporary Cultures, Columbia U., 1949-51. Mem. editl. bd. Jour. of Gay and Lesbian Psychotherapy, 1987—; author: Father Land: A Study of Authoritarianism in the German Family, 1948; contbr. numerous articles to profl. publs. Mem. acquisitions com. The Bklyn. Mus., 1995—; trustee Bklyn. Mus. of Art. Recipient Adolf Meyer award for Disting. Svc. on Behalf of Improved Care and Treatment of the Mentally Ill in the Caribbean, 1961. Fellow AMA (life), Am. Psychiat. Assn. (chmn. 1983-86, mem. com. on AIDS N.Y. County dist. br. 1989-92, life), Am. Acad. Psychoanalysis (life), Caribbean Psychiat. Assn.; mem. Group for Advancement of Psychiatry (chair internat. rels. com. 1960-65, chair com. on human sexuality 1987—). Avocations: collecting Asian and Indian art. Home and Office: 220 Central Park S New York NY 10019

SCHAFFNER, CHARLES ETZEL, consulting engineering executive; b. N.Y.C., July 21, 1919; s. Louis C. and Christina (Etzel) S.; m. Olga T. Stroedecke, Feb. 13, 1943; children—Charles Etzel II, Linda Jean. B.C.E., Cooper Union, 1941, C.E., 1952; M.C.E., Bklyn. Poly. Inst., 1944; B.S.S.E., U. Ill., 1945, N.Y. U.; D.Sci (hon.), Iona Coll., 1983. Jr. engr. Moran Proctor, Freeman & Mueser, N.Y.C., 1941; instr. Cooper Union, 1941-44; mem. faculty Bklyn. Poly. Inst., 1946-70, prof. engring., 1957-70, adj. prof., 1970-72, asst. dean, 1954-57, assoc. dean, 1957-58, dean, dir. planning, 1958-62, v.p. adminstrn., 1962-70; v.p. Syska & Hennessy, Inc., 1970-73, sr. v.p., 1973-76, exec. v.p., 1976-85, vice chmn., 1985-86, cons., 1987—, also dir.; chmn. nat. adv. bd. Summer Inst. Young Engring. Tchrs., 1959-63; mem. adv. panel NSF, 1960-70; chmn. exec. bd. N.Y.C. Bldg. Code Project, 1962-66; mem. panel 421.00 adv. to bldg. research div. Inst. Applied Tech., Nat. Bur. Standards, 1966-69; mem. bldg., constrn. adv. council Dept. Bldgs. City N.Y., 1966—; mem. bldg. research adv. bd. NRC, 1972-79, vice chmn., 1973-77; chmn., 1977-78, Mayor's Bldg. and Constrn. Adv. Council, 1971-73; exec. dir. Mayor's Fire Safety Com., 1971-73; mem. N.Y.C. Constrn. Industry Advisory Council, 1973—; v.p., bd. dirs. N.Y. Bldg. Congress, 1967-71, sec., 1971-75, chmn. govtl. affairs com., 1977-78, pres., 1979-83, chmn. council pres., 1983-87, chmn. council bus. and labor, 1987-88. Contbr. articles profl. jours. Commr. edn. dist., Locust Valley, N.Y., 1956-59, pres., 1958-59; commr. edn., pres. Central Dist. 3, Oyster Bay, N.Y., 1959-63; Trustee Cooper Union, 1975-78; trustee Cooper Union Research Found. Served with AUS, 1944-46. Named Outstanding Alumnus Cooper Union, 1966; Good Scout of Yr. Boy Scouts Am., 1979; recipient Disting. Alumnus award Poly. Alumni Assn., Alumnus of Year, 1972. Mem. Operation Democracy, ASCE (Civil Engr. of Year 1969), ASTM, Am. Arbitration Assn. (bd. arbitrators), Am. Soc. Engring. Edn. (v.p., gen. council 1965-67, v.p. fin. 1974-77, dir. 1965-67, 74-77, 78-81, pres. 1979-80), Nat. Inst. Bldg. Scis. (exec. com. consultative council 1978-82, dir. 1982-88), Engrs. Joint Council (dir. 1976-79), Am. Assn. Engring. Socs. (bd. govs. 1979-81, chmn. ednl. affairs council 1979-80), Am. Concrete Inst., N.Y. State Sch. Bds. Assn., N.Y. State Soc. Profl. Engrs. (dir. Nassau County chpt., Engr. of Year, Kings County chpt. 1968), Cooper Union Alumni Assn. (pres. 1973), Tau Beta Pi, Chi Epsilon, Omega Delta Phi. Clubs: Municipal, Nassau. Home and Office: Linden Farms Rd Locust Valley NY 11560

SCHAFFNER, CYNTHIA VAN ALLEN, writer, researcher; b. Washington, Jan. 28, 1947; d. James Alfred and Abigail Fifthian (Halsey) Van Allen; m. Robert Todd Schaffner, June 11, 1972; 1 child, Hilary Van Allen. BA, Western Coll., 1969; MAT, Simmons Coll., 1971; postgrad., Cooper-Hewitt, N.Y.C., 1994—. Editor Mademoiselle mag., N.Y.C., 1972-79; dir. devel. Am. Acad. in Rome, N.Y.C., 1987-89. Author: Discovering American Folk Art, 1991; co-author: Folk Hearts, 1984, American Painted Furniture, 1997; also mag. articles. Co-chairperson Fall Antiques Show, N.Y.C., 1979-93; trustee Mus. Am. Folk Art, N.Y.C., 1980-95. Lisa Taylor fellow, 1995, 96. Mem. Coll. Art Assn., Decorative Arts Soc., Cosmopolitan Club, Southampton Colonial Soc. (trustee 1996—). Avocations: canoeing, gardening, antiquing. Home: 850 Park Ave New York NY 10021-1845

SCHAFFNER, ROBERT JAY, JR., nurse practitioner; b. Mechanicsburg, Pa., Feb. 25, 1949; s. Robert J. Sr. and Bertha May (Books) S.; m. Ellen Gail Hirsch, Sept. 7, 1974 (div.). BA in English, Edn., U. Mass., 1972; BSN, SUNY, Albany, 1986, DD (hon.), 1986; MS, U. Rochester, 1989; MBA, Simon Grad. Sch. Bus. Adminstr, 1992. RN, N.Y., Mass.; cert. dietitian-nutritionist, N.Y. Head of math. Lear Sch. Inc., Miami, Fla., 1974-81; critical care nurse Strong Meml. Hosp. U. Rochester, N.Y., 1983-86, asst. clinician burn ICU, 1986-89, clin. specialist, nurse practitioner, 1990—; clin. assoc. faculty U. Rochester, 1992—; nurse practitioner J.L. Norris Clinic, Rochester, 1993—; exec. com. profl. Nursing Orgn., Rochester, 1988-90, chair-elect, 1989; co-founder Men in Nursing Orgn., Rochester, chair, 1991-92, v.p. Am. assembly, 1993—; mem. nursing faculty com. Regents Coll., 1992—; presenter in field; ceo RSA Assocs., 1986—. Author: poetry (A Best New Poet of 1988, Golden Poet award 1989, Poet of Merit, Am. Poetry Assn. 1989); contbr. articles to profl. jours. CPR instr., disaster action team vol., ARC, 1987—; blood pressure monitor ARC, Boston, 1982-83. Recipient Eleanor Hall award, 1989, Outstanding Svc. award SUNY; Mary Riddle scholar Newton Wellesley Sch. Nursing, 1983; Commonwealth Exec. Nurse fellow, 1989; named Internat. Citizen of Yr. Hutt River Province, 1996, Lee Cohen award, 1996. Mem. AACN, Am. Burn Assn., Am. Soc. Parenteral and Enteral Nutrition, N.Y. State Nurses Assn. (Ross utrition group), Genesee Valley Nurses Assn. (bd. dirs. 1995-97), SUNY-Albany Alumni Assn. (v.p., trustee 1989-95), U. Mass. Alumni Assn. (nominations com.), Sigma Theta Tau (chair fin. com.). Avocations: painting, bicycling, windsurfing, weight lifting, motorcycling. Home: 71 S Estate Dr Webster NY 14580-2809 Office: U Rochester Med Ctr 601 Elmwood Ave PO Box 667 Rochester NY 14642

SCHAFFNER, ROBERTA IRENE, medical, surgical nurse; b. Vero Beach, Fla., Oct. 5, 1926; d. Robert Wesley and Harriett Louise (Davis) Routh; m. David Leonard Schaffner, Apr. 25, 1947 (div. July 1975); children: Penny Routh S., David Leonard II. Mem. cadet nurse corps, Charity Hosp., New Orleans, La., 1944-45; ADA, Montgomery County C.C., Blue Bell, Pa., 1978; BSN, Gwynedd (Pa.) Mercy Coll., 1982, MSN, 1984. RN Pa. Med.-surg. nurse Chestnut Hill Hosp., Phila., 1978—; mem. delegation to study health care delivery sys., Moscow, Tbillisi, Azerbeijan, Kiev, 1981, Shanghai, Beijing, Nanjing, Hong Kong, 1984, Milan, Pisa, Bologna, Florence, Rome, Sorento, Naples, 1985. Cadet U.S. Nurse Corps, 1945. Mem. Oncology Nursing Soc., Sigma Theta Tau. Republican. Home: 1600 Church Rd # A 214 Wyncote PA 19095-1926 Office: Chestnut Hill Hosp 8835 Germantown Ave Philadelphia PA 19118-2718

SCHAICH, WILLIAM L., physics educator; b. Springfield, Oct. 15, 1944; s. Wilbur Allison and Lillian Luella (Halfaker) S.; m. Georgia Jeann Loebrich, Dec. 23, 1966; children: Amy C., Lucy B. BS, Denison U., 1966; MS, Cornell U., 1968, PhD, 1970. Post doctoral fellow Bristol, U.K., 1970-71; research asst. U. Calif., LaJolla, Calif., 1971-73; asst. prof. Ind. U., 1973-76, assoc. prof., 1976-80, prof., 1980—. Contbr. articles to profl. jours. Fellow Am. Physical Soc. Office: Ind U Swain Hall W Bloomington IN 47405

SCHAIE, K(LAUS) WARNER, human development and psychology educator, researcher; b. Stettin, Germany (now Poland), Feb. 1, 1928; came to U.S., 1947, naturalized, 1953; s. Sally and Lottie Louise (Gabriel) S.; m. Coloma J. Harrison, Aug. 9, 1953 (div. 1973); 1 child, Stephan; m. Sherry L. Willis, Nov. 20, 1981. A.A., City Coll. San Francisco, 1951; B.A., U. Calif.-Berkeley, 1952; M.S. U. Wash., 1953, Ph.D., 1956. Lic. psychologist, Calif., Pa. Postdoctoral fellow Washington U., St. Louis, 1956-57; asst. prof. psychology U. Nebr., Lincoln, 1957-1964, assoc. prof., 1964-68; prof., chmn. dept. psychology W.Va. U., Morgantown, 1964-73; prof. psychology, dir. Gerontology Research Inst., U. So. Calif., 1973-81; Evan Pugh prof. human devel. and psychology, dir. Gerontology Ctr., Pa. State U., University Park, 1981—; mem. devel. behavior study sect. NIH, Bethesda, Md., 1970-72, chmn., 1972-74, chmn. human devel. and aging study sect., 1979-84, mem. expert panel in comml. airline pilot retirement, 1981, data and safety bd. shep project, 1984-91. Author: Developmental Psychology; A Life Span Approach, 1981; Adult Development and Aging, 1982, 4th rev. edit., 1996, Intellectual Development in Adulthood: The Seattle Longitudinal Study, 1996; editor: Handbook of Psychology of Aging, 1977, 4th rev. edit., 1996, Longitudinal Studies of Adult Development, 1983, Cognitive Functioning and Social Structure over the Life Course, 1987, Methodological Issues in Research on Aging, 1988, Social Structure and Aging: Psychological Processes, 1989, Age Structuring in Comparative Perspective, 1989, The Course of Later Life, 1989, Self-Directedness: Cause and Effects Throughout the Life Course, 1990, Aging, Health Behaviors and Health Outcomes, 1992, Caregiving Systems: Formal and Informal Helpers, 1993, Societal Impact on Aging: Historical Perspectives, 1993, Adult Intergenerational Relations: Effects of Societal Change, 1995, Older Adults Decision Making and the Law, 1996; editor Ann. Rev. Gerontology and Geriatrics vol. 7, 1987, vol. 11, 1991; contbr. articles to profl. jours. Fellow APA (coun. reps. 1976-79, 83-86, Disting. Contbn. award 1982, Disting. Scientific Conbns. award, 1992), Gerontol. Soc. (Kleemeier award 1987, disting. mentorship award 1996), Am. Psychol. Soc.; mem. Psychometric Soc., Internat. Soc. Study Behavioral Devel. Unitarian. Avocations: hiking; stamps. Home: 425 Windmere Dr # 3A State College PA 16801 Office: Pa State U Dept Human Devel & Family Studies University Park PA 16802

SCHAIRER, GEORGE SWIFT, aeronautical engineer; b. Pitts., May 19, 1913; s. Otto Sorg and Elizabeth Blanche (Swift) S.; m. Mary Pauline Tarbox, June 20, 1935; children: Mary Elizabeth, George Edward, Sally Helen, John Otto. With Bendix Aviation Corp., South Bend, Ind., 1935-37, Consol. Vultee Aircraft Corp., San Diego, 1937-39; joined Boeing Airplane Co., Seattle, 1939, successively chief aerodynamicist, chief engr. aerodynamics and powerplant, 1948-51, chief tech. staff, 1951-56, asst. chief engr., 1956-57, dir. research, 1957-59, v.p. research and devel., 1959-73, v.p. research, 1973-78, cons., 1978-88; mem. sci. adv. group USAAF, 1945-46; mem. com. on aerodynamics NACA; mem. tech. adv. panel on aeros. Dept. Def., 1954-61; sci. adv. bd. USAF, 1955-60; cons. ops. evaluation group USN, 1961; panel sci. and tech. manpower Pres.'s Sci. Adv. Com., 1962-64; sci. adv. com. Def. Intelligence Agy., 1966-70; mem. aeros. and space engring. bd. NRC, 1977-79. Contbr. articles to profl. jours. Trustee A Contemporary Theatre. Recipient Spirit of St. Louis award ASME, 1959, Guggenheim medal, 1967. Fellow AIAA (hon. fellow, Sylvanus Albert Reed award 1950, Wright Bros. lectr. 1964); mem. NAE, NAS, Internat. Acad. Astronautics, Am. Helicopter Soc., Soc. Naval Architects and Marine Engrs., Sigma Xi, Sigma Tau. Address: 4242 Hunts Point Rd Bellevue WA 98004-1106

SCHAKE, LOWELL MARTIN, animal science educator; b. Marthasville, Mo., June 6, 1938; s. Martin Charles and Flora Olinda (Rocklage) S.; m. Wendy Anne Walkinshaw, Sept. 11, 1959; children: Sheryl Anne, Lowell Scott. BS, U. Mo., 1960, MS, 1962; PhD, Tex. A&M U., 1967. Asst. prof. Tex. A&M U., College Station, 1965-67, assoc. prof., 1969-72, prof., 1972-84; asst. prof., area livestock specialist Tex. A&M U., Lubbock, 1967-69; prof., head animal sci. dept. U. Conn., Storrs, 1984-92; prof., chmn. animal sci. dept. Tex. Tech. U., Lubbock, 1992-95; developer applied animal ethology program Tex. A&M U., 1970, New Eng. Biotech Conf. series, 1990, S.W. Beef Forum, 1993; chmn. Am. Registry of Profl. Animal Scientist Com. on Profl. Stds., 1988; chmn. Nat. Com. Exec. Officers of Animal Vet., Dairy and Poultry Sci. Depts., 1992; cons. Alpart, Kingston, Jamaica, 1975, U.S. Feeds Grain Coun., 1970-73, A.O. Smith Products Inc., 1968-92, Humphrey Land & Cattle Co., Dallas, 1980-86; lectr. in field. Author: Growth and Finishing of Beef Cattle, A Class Handbook, 1982; contbr. articles to profl. jours. Recipient Innovative Teaching award Tex. A&M U., 1978. Mem. Am. Soc. Animal Sci., Plains Nutrition Coun. (adv. bd. 1967-80, sec.-treas. 1994-95, founder), Nat. Assn. Colls. and Tchrs. Agr., Am. Registry Profl. Animal Scientists (dir. for Northeast 1987-89), Coun. for Agr. Sci. and Tech. World Conf. on Animal Prodn., Am. Soc. Dairy Sci., Gamma Sigma Delta. Republican. Club: Tiger (College Station) (pres.). Avocations: fishing, gardening, outdoor work. Home: 13542 Carlos Fifth Ct Corpus Christi TX 78418-6913

SCHALEBEN, ARVILLE, newspaper editor, writer, educator; b. Brown County, Minn., Jan. 25, 1907; s. Wilhelm and Lina (Helling) S.; m. Ida Androvandi, Sept. 14, 1935; children: Joy Schaleben Lewis, Susan Schaleben Wilson, Mary Schaleben Totero, Will. B.A., U. Minn., 1929. With Milw. Jour., 1929-72, reporter, asst. city editor, then city editor, 1936-46, asst. mng. editor, 1946-59, mng. editor, 1959-62, exec. editor, 1962-66, asso. editor, 1966-72; v.p. The Jour. Co., 1962-68, dir., 1960-72; editor-in-residence U. Wis., Madison, 1972—; also vis. prof. U. Wis.; vis. prof. Medill Sch. Journalism, Northwestern U., 1972—; Riley prof. journalism Ind. U., Bloomington, 1972; lectr. U. Wis., Milw., 1976-77. Author: Your Future in Journalism; editorial bd. This Week mag.; contbr. anthologies: Folks Say of Will Rogers, The American Dream, Headlining America, News Stories of 1933, News Stories of 1934, Fifty and Feisty. Pres. Androvandi, Ltd., Milw. Dir. Fox Point (Wis.) Sch. Bd., 1942-48; mem. President's Com. for Handicapped, 1950-58; chmn. Nicolet High Sch. bldg. com., 1953. Named Wis. Journalist of Year, Soc. Profl. Journalists, 1975, 80; recipient Honor al Merito award N.Am. Assn. of Venezuela. Mem. Wis. AP Assn. (pres.), AP Mng. Editors Assn. (dir.; chmn. news research com. 1965, mem. media competition com., new methods com., com. future newspapers, co-editor 50-yr. associated press history, regent 1965—), Am. Newspaper Pubs. Assn. (mem. news research center steering com. 1964-72), Am. Soc. Newspaper Editors (co-chmn. edn. com., mem. research com., com. edn. for journalism, com. minorities), Internat. Press Inst., Soc. South Pole, Antarctican Soc., Sigma Delta Chi (chmn. Wis. 1958, mem. prof. goals com.). Congregationalist (past chmn. bldg. com.). Clubs: Milw. Press (pres. 1936-39, mem. Found.), Milw. Press (pres. Found. 1975-85, knight of Golden Quill, 1979), Ozaukee Country (Mequon, Wis.), Makai Golf and Tennis (Princeville, Hanalei, Hawaii). Home: 8254 N Gray Log Ln Milwaukee WI 53217-2862 Office: 333 W State St Milwaukee WI 53203-1305 also: U Wis-Madison Vilas Communications H Madison WI 53706 *In our good earth's eternity, not one among us is more enduring than the least among us unless he so lives to lengthen mankind's future.*

SCHALL, ALVIN ANTHONY, federal judge; b. N.Y.C., Apr. 4, 1944; s. Gordon William and Helen (Davis) S.; m. Sharon Frances LeBlanc, Apr. 25, 1970; children: Amanda Lanford, Anthony Davis. BA, Princeton U., 1966; JD, Tulane U., 1969. Bar: N.Y. 1970, U.S. Dist. Ct. (so. and ea. dists.) N.Y. 1973, U.S. Ct. Appeals (2d crct.) 1974, D.C. 1980, U.S. Dist. Ct. D.C. 1991, U.S. Ct. Appeals (D.C. crct.) 1991, U.S. Ct. Fed. Claims 1982, U.S. Ct. Appeals (fed. crct.) 1987, U.S. Supreme Ct. 1989. Assoc. Shearman & Sterling, N.Y.C., 1969-73; asst. U.S. atty. ea. dist. N.Y. Borough of Bklyn., 1973-78, chief appeals div., 1977-78; trial atty. civil div. U.S. Dept. Justice, Washington, 1978-87, sr. trial counsel, 1986-87, asst. to atty. gen., 1988-92; ptnr. Perlman & Ptnrs., Washington, 1987-88; judge U.S. Ct. Appeals (fed. crct.), Washington, 1992—. Office: 717 Madison Pl NW Washington DC 20439-0002

SCHALL, LAWRENCE DELANO, economics educator, consultant; b. Los Angeles, Nov. 5, 1940; s. Lee and Lillian (Seltzow) S.; m. Betty Jane Kay, Aug. 6, 1982; children: Michael Kay, Adam Kent. BA, UCLA, 1962; MA in Econs., U. Chgo., 1967, PhD in Econs., 1969. CPA, Wash. Sec.-treas. Permco Inc., Los Angeles, 1959-61; acting asst. prof. econs. U. Wash., Seattle, 1968-69, asst. prof., 1969-72, assoc. prof., 1972-76, prof., 1976—. Author: (with C. W. Haley) The Theory of Financial Decisions, 1972, 2d edit., 1979, Introduction to Financial Management, 1977, 6th edit., 1991, (with K. Henderson and R. May) Evaluating Business Ventures, 1982; contbr. articles to profl. jours. Recipient Bank of Am. Excellence award, 1983, Burlington No. Found. award, 1986, First Interstate Bank award, 1990, Andrew V. Smith award, U. Wash., 1992. Mem. Am. Econ. Assn., Am. Fin. Assn., Fin. Mgmt. Assn., Fin. Execs. Inst. Office: U Wash Sch Bus Adminstrn 261 Mackenzie Hall Dj # 10 Seattle WA 98195

SCHALLENKAMP, KAY, academic administrator; b. Salem, S.D., Dec. 9, 1949; d. Arnold B. and Jennie M. (Koch) Krier; m. Ken Schallenkamp, Sept. 7, 1970; children: Heather, Jenni. BS, No. State Coll., 1972; MA, U. S.D., 1973; PhD, U. Colo., 1982. Prof. No. State Coll., Aberdeen, S.D., 1973-88, dept. chair, 1982-84, dean, 1984-88; provost Chadron (Nebr.) State Coll., 1988-92, U. Wis., Whitewater, 1992-97; pres. Emporia (Kans.) State U., 1997—; cons. North Ctrl. Assn., nursing homes, hosps. and ednl. instns. Contbr. articles to profl. jours. Commr. North Ctrl. Assn., 1995—. Bush fellow, 1980; named Outstanding Young Career Woman, Bus. and Profl. Women's Club, 1976. Mem. Am. Speech and Hearing Assn. (cert.), Rotary. Avocation: martial arts. Office: Emporia State U 1200 Commercial St Emporia KS 66801-5057

SCHALLER, GEORGE BEALS, zoologist; b. Berlin, May 26, 1933; s. Georg Ludwig S. and Bettina (Byrd) Iwersen; m. Kay Suzanne Morgan, Aug. 26, 1957; children: Eric, Mark. BS. in Zoology, BA in Anthropology, U. Alaska, 1955; Ph.D. in Zoology, U. Wis., 1962. Research assoc. Johns Hopkins U., Balt., 1963-66; research zoologist Wildlife Conservation Soc., Bronx, 1966—; adj. assoc. prof. Rockefeller U., N.Y.C., 1966—; research assoc. Am. Mus. Natural History. Author: The Mountain Gorilla, 1963 (Wildlife Soc. 1965), The Year of the Gorilla, 1964, The Deer and the Tiger, 1967, The Serengeti Lion, 1972 (Nat. Book award 1973), Golden Shadows, Flying Hooves, 1973, Mountain Monarchs, 1977, Stones of Silence, 1980, The Giant Pandas of Wolong, 1985, The Last Panda, 1993. Ctr. Advanced Study in Behavioral Scis. fellow, Stanford U., 1962; fellow Guggenheim Found., 1971; decorated Order of Golden Ark (The Netherlands), 1978, Explorers medal, Explorers Club, 1990; recipient gold medal World Wildlife Fund, 1980; Cosmos prize Japan, 1996. Recipient Tyler Environ. prize, 1997.

SCHALLER, JAMES PATRICK, lawyer; b. Hazleton, Pa., July 12, 1940; s. James Albert and Florence P. (McDermott) S.; M. Madeleine Bial, Apr. 12, 1969; 1 child, James Joseph. B.A., King's Coll., Pa., 1965; J.D., George Washington U., 1969. Bar: Va. 1969, D.C. 1969, Md. 1990, U.S. Dist. Ct. D.C. 1969, U.S. Ct. Appeals (D.C. cir.) 1969, U.S. Supreme Ct. 1972. Assoc., Jackson Gray & Laskey, Washington, 1968-72; ptnr., dir. Jackson & Campbell, P.C., and predecessor, Washington, 1972—; bd. govs. D.C. (Unified) Bar, 1979-82; sec. Nat. Inst. Trial Advocacy, 1974-86; chair com. unauthorized practice D.C. Ct. Appeals, 1982-90. Bd. editors Dist. Lawyer, 1977-88. Served with USN, 1958-61. Fellow Am. Coll. Trial Lawyers, Am. Bar Found., Charles Fahy Am. Inn of Ct. (pres. 1994-96, D.C. state chair 1996—), D.C. Circuit Jud. Conf., Jud. Conf. D.C., The Barristers, Bar Assn. D.C. (chair young lawyers sect. 1974-75, dir. 1975-76), ABA (bd. editors 1986—), Va. Bar Assn., D.C. Def. Lawyers Assn. (sec. 1974-75, v.p. 1975-76), Order of Malta, John Carroll Soc., Phi Delta Phi, Delta Sigma Rho, Tau Kappa Alpha. Roman Catholic. Office: Jackson & Campbell PC 1120 20th St NW Washington DC 20036-3406

SCHALLER, JANE GREEN, pediatrician; b. Cleve., June 26, 1934; d. George and May Alice (Wing) Green; children: Robert Thomas, George Charles, Margaret May. A.B., Hiram (Ohio) Coll., 1956; M.D. cum laude, Harvard U., 1960. Diplomate Am. Bd. Pediatrics, Am. Bd. Med. Examiners. Resident in pediatrics Children's Hosp.-U. Wash., Seattle, 1960-63; fellow immunology Children's Hosp. U. Wash., 1963-65; mem. faculty U. Wash. Med. Sch., 1965-83, prof. pediatrics, 1975-83; head div. rheumatic diseases Children's Hosp., Seattle, 1968-83; prof., chmn. dept. pediatrics Tufts U. Sch. Medicine/New Eng. Med. Ctr., 1983—; pediatrician-in-chief Floating Hosp. for Children, Boston, 1983—; vis. physician Med. Rsch. Coun., Taplow, Eng., 1971-72. Author articles in field.; Editorial bds. profl. jours. Bd. dirs. Seattle Chamber Music Festival, 1982-85; trustee Boston Chamber Music Soc., 1985—; mem. Boston adv. coun. UNICEF, tech. advisor UN Study on the Impact of Armed Conflict on Children, 1995-97. Mem. Inst. Medicine of NAS, AAAS (sci. and human rights program), Soc. Pediatric Rsch., Am. Pediatric Soc., Am. Acad. Pediatrics (mem. exec. com. section on internat. child health, head children's rights prog., rep. to UNICEF), Internat. Pediatric Assn. (spl. cons.), Am. Coll. Rheumatology, New Eng. Pediatric Soc. (pres. 1991-93), Assn. Med. Sch. Pediatric Chmn. (exec. com. 1986-89, rep. to coun. on govt. affairs and coun. of acad. socs.), Com. Health in So. Africa (exec. com. 1986—), Physicians for Human Rights (exec. com. 1986—, founding pres. 1986-89), Aesculapian Club (pres. 1988-89), Harvard U. Med. Sch. Alumni Coun. (v.p. 1977-80, pres. 1982-83), Internat. Rescue Com. (med. adv. com., women's commn. for refugee women and children), Mass. Women's Forum, Internat. Women's Forum, Tavern Club, Saturday Club. Office: Floating Hosp for Children 750 Washington St # 286 Boston MA 02111-1526

SCHALLER, JOANNE F., nursing consultant; b. Columbus, Ga., July 15, 1943; d. John Frank and Ethel Beatrice (Spring) Lanzendorfer; m. Robert Thomas Schaller, Jan. 22, 1977; 1 child, Amy. BS, Pacific Luth. U., 1969; M in Nursing, U. Wash., 1971. House supr. UCLA Hosp., 1971-72; outpatient supr. Harborview Hosp., Seattle, 1973-75; outpatient clinic and emergency room supr. U. Wash. Hosp., Seattle, 1975-77; co-author, researcher with Robert Schaller MD Seattle, 1977-87; prin. Nursing Expert-Standards of Care, Seattle, 1987—; cons. Wash. State Trial Lawyers, Wash. Assn. Criminal Def. Lawyers, 1989—; founder, CEO Present Perfect, Seattle, 1991—; appt. Breast Cancer cons. UWMC, 1995—. Contbr., editor articles to profl. jours. Bd. dirs. Pacific Arts Ctr., 1992—; vol. guardian ad litem King County Juvenile Ct., 1978—; vol. Make a Wish Found. U.S. Bank, 1984—, Multiple Sclerosis Assn., 1986—, Am. Heart Assn., 1986—, Internat. Children's Festival, 1987—, Seattle Children's Festival, 1987—, Seattle Dept. Parks and Recreation Open Space Com., 1990—, Pacific N.W. Athletic Congress, 1991—, Wash. Fed. Garden Clubs Jr. Advisor, 1992—, Fred Hutchison Cancer Rsch. Ctr., 1993—; mem. parent coun. Seattle Country Day Sch., 1986-96—, volunteer, U.S. Rowing events; mem. Photo Coun. Seattle Art Mus., 1986—, Native Am. Coun., 1989—; mem. N.W. Coun. Seattle Art Mus., 1992—, mem. NAOO Coun. Seattle Art Mus., 1989—, Plestcheeff Inst. Decorative Arts, 1992—; mem. fundraiser Children's Hosp. Med. Ctr., 1977—, Breast Cancer Fund, 1994—, Susan G. Komen Breast Cancer Found., 1994—. Named 1st Migrant Health Care Nurse, State of Wash., 1969, 1st Am. nurse visiting China, 1974. Mem. AAUW, ANA, Wash. State Nurses Assn., U. Wash. Alumni Assn. Avocations: photography, writing, gardening, hiking, music. Home and Office: 914 Randolph Ave Seattle WA 98122-5267

SCHALLERT, EDWIN GLENN, lawyer; b. L.A., Aug. 7, 1952; s. William Joseph and Rosemarie Diane (Waggner) S. AB, Stanford U., 1974; JD, Harvard U., 1981, MPP, 1981. Bar: N.Y. 1974, U.S. Ct. Appeals (7th cir.) 1986, U.S. Ct. Appeals (2d cir.) 1989, U.S. Dist. Ct. (so. dist.) N.Y. 1975. Legis. aid to U.S. rep. Les Aspin Washington, 1975-78, law clk. to Hon. J. Skelly Wright, 1981-82, law clk. to Hon. Thurgood Marshall, 1982-83; assoc. Debevoise & Plimpton, N.Y.C., 1983-89, ptnr., 1989—. Mem. Internat. Inst. for Strategic Studies, Coun. Fgn. Rels. (term mem. 1983-88), Phi Beta Kappa. Democrat. Avocation: tennis. Office: Debevoise & Plimpton 875 3d Ave New York NY 10022-6225

SCHALLY, ANDREW VICTOR, endocrinologist, researcher; b. Poland, Nov. 30, 1926; came to U.S., 1957; s. Casimir Peter and Maria (Lacka) S.; m. Ana Maria Comaru, Aug., 1976. B.Sc., McGill U., Can., 1955, Ph.D. in Biochemistry, 1957; 18 hon. doctorates. Research asst. biochemistry Nat. Inst. Med. Research, London, 1949-52; dept. psychiatry McGill U., Montreal, Que., 1952-57; research assoc., asst. prof. physiology and biochemistry Coll. Medicine, Baylor U., Houston, 1957-62; assoc. prof. Tulane U. Sch. Medicine, New Orleans, 1962-67, prof., 1967—; chief Endocrine Polypeptide and Cancer Inst. VA Med. Ctr., New Orleans; sr. med. investigator VA, 1973—. Author several books; contbr. articles to profl. jours. Recipient Van Meter prize Am. Thyroid Assn., 1969; Ayerst-Squibb award Endocrine Soc., 1970; William S. Middletown award VA, 1970; Ch. Mickle award U. Toronto, 1974; Gairdner Internat. award, 1974; Borden award Assn. Am. Med. Colls. and Borden Co. Found., 1975; Lasker Basic Research award, 1975; co-recipient Nobel prize for medicine, 1977; USPHS sr. research fellow, 1961-62. Mem. NAS, AAAS, Endocrine Soc., Am. Physiol. Soc., Soc. Biol. Chemists, Soc. Exptl. Biol. Medicine, Internat. Soc. Rsch. Biology Reprodn., Soc. Internat. Brain Rsch. Orgn., Mex. Acad. Medicine, Nat. Acad. Medicine Brazil, Acad. Medicine Venezuela, Acad. Medicine Poland, Acad. Sci. Hungary, Acad. Sci. Russia. Home: 5025 Kawanee Ave Metairie LA 70006-2547 Office: VA Hosp 1601 Perdido St New Orleans LA 70112-1207

SCHAMA, SIMON, historian, educator, author; b. London, England, Feb. 13, 1945; married; 2 children. BA, Cambridge (Eng.) U., 1966, MA in History, 1969. Univ. prof. Columbia U.; sr. assoc. Ctr. European Studies Harvard U., Cambridge, Mass., 1980-93. Author: Patriots and Liberators: Revolution in the Netherlands, 1780-1813, 1977 (Wolfson prize for history 1977, Leo Gershoy Meml. prize Am. Hist. Assn. 1978), Two Rothschilds and the Land of Israel, 1979, The Embarrassment of Riches: An Interpretation of Dutch Culture in the Golden Age, 1987, Citizens: A Chronicle of the French Revolution, 1989 (NCR prize for non-fiction), Dead Certainties, 1991, Landscape and Memory, 1995. Office: Columbia U Dept History New York NY 10027

SCHAMBRA, PHILIP ELLIS, federal agency administrator, radiobiologist; b. Saginaw, Mich., Nov. 8, 1934; s. William Philip and Gwendolyn Maude (Leister) S.; m. Uta Gertrude Bossel, Mar. 30, 1967 (div. Aug. 1981); children: Eric William Philip, Kirsten Uta, Heidi Maren; m. Donita Bartels Feldman, Aug. 15, 1990. BA, Rice U., 1956; PhD, Yale U., 1961. Examiner Office of Mgmt. and Budget Exec. Office of Pres., Washington, 1968-71, staff mem. Coun. on Environ. Quality, 1971-74; assoc. dir. Nat. Inst. Environ. Health Scis., Research Triangle Park, N.C., 1974-81; chief internat. coordination Fogarty Internat. Ctr. NIH, Bethesda, Md., 1981-84; sci. attache U.S. Embassy, New Delhi, 1984-88; dir. Fogarty Internat. Ctr. NIH, Bethesda, Md., 1988—. Contbr. articles on radiobiology to profl. jours. Recipient Superior Svc. award USPHS, 1989; Nat. Cancer Inst. fellow, 1958, Rsch. fellow NASA, 1964. Mem. AAAS. Avocations: sailing, racquetball. Home: 9104 Drumaldry Dr Bethesda MD 20817-3341 Office: NIH Fogarty Internat Ctr 9000 Rockville Pike Bethesda MD 20814-1436

SCHANBERG, SAUL MURRAY, pharmacology educator; b. Clinton, Mass., Mar. 22, 1933; m. Rachel Weinbaum, Dec. 18, 1956; children: Laura E., Linda S. B.A., Clark U., 1954, M.A., 1956; Ph.D., Yale U., 1961, M.D., 1964. Cons. Calif. Dept. Mental Health, 1962-65; intern in pediatrics Albert Einstein Med. Ctr., N.Y.C., 1964-65; rsch. assoc. NIMH, 1965-67; asst. prof. Duke U. Med. Ctr., Durham, N.C., 1967-69, assoc. prof., 1969-73, prof. of pharmacology, 1973—; prof. psychiatry Duke U. Med. Ctr., 1983—; assoc. dean Duke U. Med. Ctr. Sch., 1987-93, chair phamacology, 1987-92. Cons. USPHS, Rockville, Md., 1983-84. NIMH grantee, 1968; NIH grantee, 1967. Fellow Am. Coll. Neuropsychopharmacology. Home: 1604 Pinecrest Rd Durham NC 27705-5832 Office: Duke U PO Box 3813 Durham NC 27710-3813

SCHANDER, MARY LEA, police official; b. Bakersfield, Calif., June 11, 1947; d. Gerald John Lea and Marian Lea Coffman; BA (Augustana fellow) Calif. Luth. Coll., 1969; MA, UCLA, 1970; m. Edwin Schander, July 3, 1971. Staff aide City of Anaheim (Calif.) Police Dept., 1970-72, staff asst., 1972-78, sr. staff asst., 1978-80; with Resource Mgmt. Dept., City of Anaheim, 1980-82; asst. to dir. Pub. Safety Agy., City of Pasadena Police Dept., 1982-85, spl. asst. to police chief, 1985-88, adminstrv. comdr., 1988-92, police comdr., 1992—; freelance musician; publisher Australian Traditional Songs, 1985, Songs in the Air of Early California, 1994; lectr. Calif. Luth. Coll.; instr. Calif. State U., Northridge; cons. City of Lodz, Poland, Internat. Assn. Chiefs of Police; speaker, panelist League of Calif. Cities, Pasadena Commn. on Status of Women; mcpl. mgmt. asst. CLEARS; instr. Calif. State U., Northridge. Producer (cable TV program) Traditional Music Showcase. Contbr. articles in field to profl. jours. Bd. dirs. Women At Work, Step Up Adv. Program; mem. Inst. Bd. Corrections. Recipient Police Chief's Spl. award City of Pasadena, 1987, Women at Work Medal of Excellence, 1988. Mem. Nat. Womens Political Caucus, Nat. Ctr. for Women in Policing, Pasadena Arts Coun., L.A. County Peace Officers, Internat. Assn. Chiefs of Police, Rotary. Home: PO Box 50151 Pasadena CA 91115-0151 Office: Pasadena Police Dept 207 N Garfield Ave Pasadena CA 91101-1748

SCHANFARBER, RICHARD CARL, real estate broker; b. Cleve., June 11, 1937; s. Edwin David and Helen (Newman) S.; m. Barbara A. Berger, Dec. 21, 1958 (div. Sept. 1981); children: Edwin Jeffrey, Lori Jo, Tammy Joy. Grad., NYU, 1959. Cert. profl. standards instr.; cert. energy instr.; cert. tchr. Ohio; lic. FCC broadcasters. Pres. Erieview Realty Inc., Gates Mills, 1961—, Miller Warehouse, Gates Mills, 1968—, ERI Travel Co., Gates Mills, 1974—, ERI Sales Co., Gates Mills, 1979—, Eastgate Travel Svcs., Gates Mills, Ohio, 1987—. Pres. Shaker Hts. (Ohio) Alumni Assn., 1986—, Cleve. Area Bd. Realtors, 1981, Cleve. Warehouseman Assn., 1977-79; chmn. City of Cleve. Landmarks Commn., 1984—. Mem. NRA (life), Nat. Assn. Realtors, Ohio Assn. Realtors, Cleve. Growth Assn., Cleve. Area Bd. Realtors, Mayfield Twp. Hist. Soc., Great Lakes Sci. Ctr., Rock and Roll Hall of Fame Mus. Republican. Jewish. Avocations: woodworking, coin collecting, antiques, travel. Home: 6719 Sandalwood Dr Gates Mills OH 44040-9619

SCHANFIELD, FANNIE SCHWARTZ, community volunteer; b. Mpls., Dec. 25, 1916; d. Simon Zouberman and Mary (Schmilovitz) Schwartz; m. Melvin M. Stock, Oct. 27, 1943 (dec. Apr. 1944); 1 child, Moses Samuel Schanfield; m. Abraham Schanfield, Aug. 28, 1947; children: David Colman, Miriam Schanfield Kieffer. Student, U. Minn., 1962-75. Author: My Thoughts, 1996, Son, I Have Something to Tell You, 1997, Ma, I Wrote It Down, 1997. Bd. dirs. Jewish Cmty. Ctr., Mpls., 1975-96, chairperson older adult needs, 1982-88; past pres. Bnai Emet Women's League, Mpls., 1988-90; rschr., advocate Hunger Hennepin County, Mpls., 1969-75; sec. Joint Religious Legis. Coalition; v.p., bd. dirs. Cmty. Housing Svc., Mpls., 1971-85. Recipient Citation of Honor, Hennepin County Commn., 1989, Lifetime Achievement award Jewish Comty. Ctr. Greater Mpls., 1995. Mem. NOW, Lupus Found. Minn., Internat. Soc. Poets, Hadassah (prs. 1967-69, Citation 1969). Jewish. Avocations: needlepoint, rug hooking, writing. Home: 3630 Phillips Pky Minneapolis MN 55426-3792

SCHANFIELD, MOSES SAMUEL, geneticist, educator; b. Mpls., Sept. 7, 1944; s. Abraham and Fanny (Schwartz) S. BA in Anthropology, U. Minn., 1966; AM in Anthropology, Harvard U., 1969; PhD in Human Genetics, U. Mich., 1971. Postdoctoral fellow in immunology U. Calif. Med. Ctr., San Francisco, 1971-74, rsch. geneticist, 1974-75; head of blood bank Milw. Blood Ctr., 1975-78; asst. dir. ARC, Washington, 1978-83; exec. dir. Genetic Testing Inst., Atlanta, 1983-85; lab. dir. Analytical Genetic Testing Ctr., Atlanta and Denver, 1985—; adj. asst. prof. Med. Coll. Wis., Milw., 1976-78; adj. assoc. prof. George Washington U., Washington, 1979-83, Emory U., Atlanta, 1984-89; adj. assoc. prof. Univ. Kans., 1992—; affiliated faculty Colo. State Univ., Fort Collins, 1992—; mem. Nat. Forensic DNA Rev. Panel for the Blind DNA Proficiency Testing, 1996, Nat. Forensic DNA Review Panel, Nat. Inst. of Justice. Author, editor: Immunobiology of the Erythrocyte, 1980, International Methods of Forensic DNA Analysis, 1996; contbg. author: Immunogenetic Factors and Thalassaemia of Hepatitis, 1975; contbr. articles to profl. publs. Recipient Gold medal Latin Am. Congress Hemotherapy and Immunohematology, 1979, R&D 100 award, 1993. Fellow Am. Acad. Forensic Sci.; mem. Am. Soc. Crime Lab. Dirs., Am. Soc. Human Genetics, Human Biology Coun., Phi Kappa Phi. Achievements include discovery of the biological function of GC protein as vitamin D transport protein, of 2 sources of errors in DNA sizings. Office: Analytical Genetic Testing Ctr Ste 201 7808 Cherry Creek South Dr Denver CO 80231-3231

SCHANK, ROGER CARL, computer science and psychology educator; b. N.Y.C., Mar. 12, 1946; s. Maxwell and Margaret (Rosenberg) S.; children: Hana, Joshua. B.S., Carnegie Inst. Tech., 1966; M.A., U. Tex., 1967, Ph.D., 1969; M.A. (hon.), Yale U., 1976. Asst. prof. linguistics and computer sci. Stanford (Calif.) U., 1968-74; rsch. fellow Inst. Semantics and Cognition, Castagnola, Switzerland, 1973-74; assoc. prof. computer sci. Yale U., New Haven, Conn., 1974-76, prof. computer sci. and psychology, 1976-89, chmn. dept. computer sci., 1980-85; John Evans prof. computer sci., psychology and edn., dir. Inst. for Learning Scis. Northwestern U., Evanston, Ill., 1989—; pres., chmn. bd. Cognitive Sys., Inc., New Haven, 1981-88; pres., chmn. Computeach, Inc., 1982-88; pres. Learning Scis. Corp., 1995—. Author: Conceptual Information Processing, 1975, Dynamic Memory, 1982, (with others) Scripts, Plans, Goals and Understanding, 1977, Cognitive Computer, 1984, Explanation Patterns, 1986, The Creative Attitude, 1988, Tell Me A Story, 1990, reprinted with new forward, 1995, The Connoisseur's Guide to the Mind, 1991, Engines for Education, 1995, Virtual Learning: A Revolutionary Way to Build a Highly Skilled Workforce, 1996; editor Cognitive Sci. Jour.; inventor computer programs. Mem. Cognitive Sci. Soc. (founder). Office: Northwestern U Inst Learning Scis 1890 Maple Ave Evanston IL 60201-3155

SCHANNEP, JOHN DWIGHT, brokerage firm executive; b. Newport News, Va., May 23, 1934; s. Dwight Bahney and Harriet Louise (Quinn) S.; m. Helen Ann Harris, June 21, 1958; children: John Barton, Dwight David, Timothy Michael, Marie Louise. BS, U.S. Mil. Acad., 1956. Commd. 1st lt. U.S. Air Force, 1956; resigned, 1960; account exec. Dean Witter Reynolds, Phoenix, 1960-68, v.p., resident mgr., Tucson, 1968-83, sr. v.p., 1983-89, ret.; pres. Tucson Stock/Bond Club, 1971-72; bd. dirs. SNEDCO. Author, pub. Schannep Timing Indicator Quar. Letter, 1980—. Pres. Big Bros. Tucson, 1972-74. Mem. Nat. Assn. Security Dealers (Ariz. committeeman and chmn. 1971-73), Tucson C. of C. (v.p. 1971), Pinetop Lakes Golf and Country Club (treas. 1990-91, pres. 1991-93), West Point Soc. (pres. 1967), Lions (pres. Phoenix chpt. 1966). Republican. Episcopalian. Home: 5191 E Hill Place Dr Tucson AZ 85712-1346 Office: Dean Witter Reynolds 7070 N Oracle Rd Ste 100 Tucson AZ 85704-4338

SCHAPERY, RICHARD ALLAN, engineering educator; b. Duluth, Minn., Mar. 3, 1935; s. Aaron and Nellie (Slovut) S.; m. Mable Etta Burns, June 14, 1957; 1 child, Phillip Randal. BS in Mech. Engring. with high distinction, Wayne State U., 1957; MS, Calif. Inst. Tech., 1958, PhD in Aeros, 1962. Mem. faculty Purdue U., Lafayette, Ind., 1962-69; prof. civil and aerospace engring. Tex. A.&M. U., College Station, 1969-80, Disting. prof., 1980-90, Alumni prof., 1980-85, TEES chair, 1985-89, R.P. Gregory chair, 1989-90; dir. Mechanics and Materials Center, 1972-90; The Cockrell Family Regents chair in engring., prof. U. Tex., Austin, 1990—; Cons. industry, govt.; editor-in-chief Internat. Jour. of Fracture, 1996—. Contbr. to profl. jours. and books. Gen. Motors Corp. fellow, 1958, Woodrow Wilson fellow, 1960, Douglas Aircraft fellow, 1961; Purdue XL grantee, 1963; recipient machinery's award for design, 1957; Disting. Achievement award for rsch. Tex. A&M U., 1978, Disting. Engring. Alumni award Wayne State U., 1992. Fellow Soc. Engring. Science; mem. AIAA, Am. Ceramic Soc., Sigma Xi, Omicron Delta Kappa, Tau Beta Pi. Home: 7133 Valburn Dr Austin TX 78731-1812 Office: U Tex Dept Aerospace/Mechanics Engring Austin TX 78712

SCHAPIRO, DONALD, lawyer; b. N.Y.C., Aug. 8, 1925; s. John Max and Lydia (Chaitkin) S.; m. Ruth Ellen Goldman, June 29, 1952 (dec. Aug. 1991); m. Linda N. Solomon, Oct. 10, 1993; children: Jane G., Robert A. A.B., Yale U., 1944, LL.B., 1949. Bar: N.Y. 1949. Assoc. Paul, Weiss, Rifkind, Wharton & Garrison, N.Y.C., 1949-51; asst. chief counsel subcom. ways and means com. on adminstrn. revenue laws U.S. Ho. of Reps., Washington, 1951-52; assoc. Barrett, Smith, Schapiro, Simon & Armstrong, N.Y.C., 1952-55; partner Barrett, Smith, Schapiro, Simon & Armstrong, 1955-88; ptnr. Chadbourne & Parke, 1988—; vis. lectr. law Yale U. Law Sch., 1949-78, 94-95, instr. law and econs., 1945-49. Mem. Order of Coif, Phi Beta Kappa, Phi Delta Phi. Home: 1035 5th Ave New York NY 10028-0135 Office: Chadbourne & Parke 30 Rockefeller Plz New York NY 10112

SCHAPIRO, JEROME BENTLEY, chemical company executive; b. N.Y.C., Feb. 7, 1930; s. Sol and Claire (Rose) S.; B.Chem. Engring., Syracuse U., 1951; postgrad. Columbia U., 1951-52; m. Edith Irene Kravet, Dec. 27, 1953; children: Lois, Robert, Kenneth. Project engr. propellents br. U.S. Naval Air Rocket Test Sta., Lake Denmark, N.J., 1951-52; with Dixo Co., Inc., Rochelle Park, N.J., 1954—, pres., 1966—; lectr. detergent standards, drycleaning, care labeling, consumers standards, orgns., U.S., 1968—; U.S. del. spokesman on drycleaning Internat. Standards Orgn., Newton, Mass., 1971, Brussels, 1972, U.S. del. spokesman on dimensional stability of textiles, Paris, 1974, Ottawa, 1977, Copenhagen, 1981; chmn. U.S. del. com. on consumer affairs, Geneva, 1974, 75, 76, spokesman U.S. del. on textiles, Paris, 1974, mem. U.S. del. on care labeling of textiles, The Hague, Holland, 1974, U.S. del., chmn. del. council com. on consumer policy, Geneva, 1978, 79, 82, Israel, 1980, Paris, 1981; leader U.S. del. com. on dimensional stability of textiles, Manchester, Eng., 1984; fed. govtl. appointee to Industry Functional Adv. Com. on Standards, 1980-81; legal expert drycleaning techniques and procedures. Mem. Montclair (N.J.) Sch. Study Com., 1968-69; co-founder Jewish Focus, Inc., 1991, pub. Catskill/Hudson Jewish Star. 1st lt. USAF, 1952-53. Fellow ASTM (chmn. com. D-12 Soaps and Detergents 1974-79, mem. standing com. on internat. standards 1980-84, hon. mem. award com. D-13, textiles); mem. AIChE, Am. Nat. Standards Inst. (vice chmn. bd. dirs., 1983-85, exec. com. 1979-81, 83-85, bd. dir. 1979-85, fin. com. 1982-85, chmn. consumer council 1976, 79, 80, 81, mem. steering com. to advise Dept. Commerce on implementation GATT agreements 1976-77, mem. exec. standards coun., 1977-79), internat. standards coun., chmn. internat. consumer policy adv. com. 1978-86), Am. Assn. Textile Chemists and Colorists (mem. exec. com. on rsch. 1974-77, chmn. com. on dry cleaning 1976-88, vice chmn. internat. test methods com., 1982-86) Am. Chem. Soc., Standards Engring. Soc. (cert.), Internat. Standards Orgn. (mem. internat. standards steering com. for consumer affairs 1978-81), Nat. Small Bus. Assn. (assoc. trustee 1983-85). Jewish (v.p., treas. temple). Lodge: Masons. Home: PO Box 771 Wurtsboro NY 12790-0771 Office: 158 Central Ave PO Box 7038 Rochelle Park NJ 07662-4003

SCHAPIRO, MARY, federal agency administrator, lawyer; b. N.Y.C., June 19, 1955; d. Robert D. and Susan (Hall) S.; m. Charles A. Cadwell, Dec. 13, 1980. BA, Franklin and Marshall Coll., 1977; JD, George Washington U., 1980. Bar: D.C. 1980. Trial atty., 1980-81; counsel to chmn. Commodity Futures Trading Commn., 1981-84; gen. counsel Futures Industry Assn., 1984-88; commr. SEC, Washington, 1988-94; chmn. Commodity Futures Trading Commn. (CFTC), Washington, 1994-96; pres. NASDR, Washington, 1996—. Office: NASDR 1735 K St NW Washington DC 20006-1516*

SCHAPIRO, MIRIAM, artist; b. Toronto, Ont., Can., Nov. 15, 1923; d. Theodore and Fannie (Cohen) S. BA, State U. Iowa, 1945, MA, 1946, MFA, 1949; hon. doctorate, Wooster Coll., 1983, Calif. Coll. Arts and Crafts, 1989, Mpls. Coll. Art and Design, 1994, Miami U., 1995, Moore Coll. Art, Phila., 1995. co-orginator Womanhouse, Los Angeles, 1972, Heresies mag., N.Y.C., 1975; co-originator feminist art program Calif. Inst. Arts, Valencia, 1971; founding mem. Feminist Art Inst., N.Y.C.; mem. adv. bd. Women's Caucus for Art; assoc. mem. Heresies Collective; lectr. dept. art history U. Mich., 1987. Works in numerous books and catalogues; numerous one-woman shows including, Galerie Liatowitsch, Basel, Switzerland, 1979, Lerner Heller Gallery, N.Y.C., 1979, Barbara Gladstone Gallery, N.Y.C., 1980, Spencer Mus. Art, Lawrence, Kans., 1981, Everson Mus., Syracuse, N.Y., 1981, Galerie Rudolf Zwirner, Cologne, Fed. Republic Germany, 1981, Staatagalerie, Stuttgart, Fed. Republic Germany, 1983, Dart Gallery, Chgo, 1984, Bernice Steinbaum Gallery/Steinbaum Krauss Gallery, N.Y.C., 1986, 88, 90, 91, 94, 97, Brevard Art Ctr. and Mus., Melbourne, Fla., 1991, Guild Hall Mus., East Hampton, N.Y., 1992, ARC Gallery, Chgo., 1993, James Madison U., Harrisburg, Va., 1996, Nat. Mus. Am. Art Smithsonian Inst., Washington, 1997. others; retrospective exhbn., Wooster (Ohio) Coll. Art Mus., 1980; exhibited in numerous group shows, including, Palais de Beaux Arts, Brussels, 1979, Inst. Contemporary Art, Phila., 1979, Delahunty Gallery, Dallas, 1980, Indpls. Mus., 1980, Va. Mus., Richmond, 1980, Laguna Gloria Mus., Austin, Tex., 1980, R.O.S.C., Dublin, Ireland, 1980, Biennale of Sydney, Australia, 1982, Zurich, Switzerland, 1983, Sidney Janis Gallery, N.Y.C., 1984, Am. Acad. Arts and Letters, N.Y.C., 1985, Mus. Modern Art, N.Y.C., 1988, Whyte Mus. Can. Rockies, Banff, Alta., 1991, Nat. Mus. Women in Arts., Wash., 1993, Jane Voorhees Zimmerli art mus. Rutger's U., New Brunswick, N.J., 1994, Mus. of F.A. Boston, 1994, Santa Barbara Mus. of Art, 1994, Hudson River Mus. of Westchester, Yonkers, N.Y., 1995, Mus. of Contemporary Arts, Los Angeles, Calif. Bronx Mus. of the Arts, N.Y., 1995, Columbus (Ga.) Mus., 1996, Parrish Mus., Southampton, N.Y., 1997, Austin (Tex.) Mus., 1997; represented in permanent collections, Hirshhorn Mus., Washington, Bklyn. Mus., Met. Mus. Art, N.Y.C., Mus. Contemporary Art, San Diego, Mpls. Inst. Art, Mulvane Art Center, Topeka, Nat. Gallery Art, Washington, N.Y.U., Peter Ludwig Collection, Aachen, Germany, Stanford U., Palo Alto, Calif., Univ. Art Mus., Berkeley, Calif., Whitney Mus., N.Y.C., Worcester (Mass.) Art Mus., Santa Barbara (Calif.) Mus. Art, Nat. Mus. Am. Art Smithsonian Inst., Washington, also others; author: (books) Women and the Creative Process, 1974, Rondo: An Artists Book, 1988; sculpture Anna and David, Rosslyn, Va., 1987. Guggenheim fellow, 1987, Nat. Endowment for Arts fellow; grantee Ford Found.; recipient numerous other grants and fellowships. Mem. Coll. Art Assn. (past dir.). Office: Steinbaum Krauss Gallery 132 Greene St New York NY 10012-3242 *Process and ideology in an opulent, multilayered, eccentric and hopeful abstract art: 1. The need for order and stability. 2. The need to destroy order and stability in order to find something else. 3. Finding something else. Pattern, itself an architectural species, reflects order and stability. Then a need to create chaos as though life itself were taking place. Finally the bonding layer by layer, the interpenetration of paint, fabric, photograph, tea towel, ribbon, lace, and glue. A collage: a simultaneity; a visual dazzlement, a multi-layering, a final message for the senses. And the ideology which inspires the work itself? That is feminism, the wish to have the art speak as a woman speaks. To be sensitive to the material used as though there were a responsibility to history to repair the sense of omission and to have each substance in the collage be a reminder of a woman's dreams. All of my works are auto-biographical. They are about the yearnings of a woman who decided a long tim*

SCHAPP, REBECCA MARIA, museum director; b. Stuttgart, Fed. Republic Germany, Dec. 12, 1956; came to U.S., 1957; d. Randall Todd and Elfriede Carolina (Scheppan) Spradlin; m. Thomas James Schapp, May 29, 1979. AA, DeAnza Coll., 1977; BA in Art, San Jose State U., 1979, MA in Art Adminstrn., 1985. Adminstrv. dir. Union Gallery, San Jose, Calif., 1979-82; from mus. coordinator to dep. dir. de Saisset Mus. Santa Clara (Calif.) U., 1982-92, dir., 1993—. Mem. San Francisco Mus. Modern Art; bd. dirs. Works of San Jose, v.p. 1983-85. Mem. Non-Profit Gallery Assn. (bd. dirs.). Democrat. Avocations: racquetball, walking, bicycling, camping. Office: De Saisset Museum Santa Clara Univ 500 El Camino Real Santa Clara CA 95050-4345

SCHAPPELL, ABIGAIL SUSAN, speech, language and hearing therapist; b. York, Pa., May 25, 1952; d. Felix and Ann (Getty) DeMoise; m. Gery Mylan Schappell, Oct. 20, 1979; 1 child, Jonathan Michael. BS with Master's equivalency, U. Va., 1974; postgrad., Bloomsburg U., 1975-77. Lic. speech-lang. pathologist, Pa. Speech-lang.-hearing specialist dept. pub. welfare Hamburg (Pa.) Ctr., 1975; judge deaf posters and essays Virginville (Pa.) Grange, 1990—, tchr. emergency pers. on communicating with deaf and hard of hearing, 1991, 92; leader demonstrations and workshops on sign lang. and dysphagia, non-verbal comms., active listening to various orgns., 1978—. Pub: (Boy Scouts Coun. manual), Scouting for the Handicapped, Hawk Mountain, 1981-82. Sign/del. to conf. Bible Sch. dir., mem. Zion's United Ch. of Christ, Windsor Castle, Pa., 1985—; rep. nat. triann. conv. Penn Laurel coun. Girl Scouts U.S.A., 1975; instr. ARC. Named Virginville Grange Comty. Citizen of Yr., 1994-95, Outstanding Young Woman of Am., 1984. Mem. AAUW, Am. Assn. Mental Retardation (presenter at state conf. 1994, regional conf. 1995, mem. Region 9 core com. for speech 1976), Pa. Speech and Hearing Assn., Berks Deaf and Hard of Hearing Svcs., Schuykill Haven Bus. and Profl. Women (pres 1983-84, involvement on dist. and state level, Young Careerist local, dist. and state honors 1980-81), Yorktown chpt. DAR, Smithsonian Assocs., Order Ea. Star (mem., chaplain Blue Mountain chpt. 1981, 82), Hamburg Area Soccer Assn. (sec. 1989-94), Young Careerist Alumni Assn. (life). Republican. Avocations: massage, signing, music. Home: 531 S 4th St Hamburg PA 19526 Office: Hamburg Ctr Old RR 22 Hamburg PA 19526

SCHAR, STEPHEN L., lawyer; b. Chgo., Oct. 19, 1945; s. Sidney and Lillian (Lieberman) S.; m. Jessica S. Feit, Aug. 17, 1980; children: Scott Andrew, Elizabeth Loren. B.A., U. Chgo., 1967; J.D., DePaul U., 1970. Bar: Ill. 1970, U.S. Dist. Ct. (no. dist.) Ill. 1970. Assoc. Aaron, Aaron, Schimberg & Hess, Chgo., 1970-77, ptnr., 1977-80; ptnr. Aaron, Schimberg, Hess, Rusnak, Deutsch & Gilbert, 1980-84, Aaron, Schimberg, Hess & Gilbert, 1984, Aaron, Schimberg & Hess, 1984, D'Ancona & Pflaum, 1985—; instr. estate planning Loyola U., Chgo., 1978-79. Bd. dirs. Jewish Children's Bur. Chgo., 1982—, pres., 1996—; pres. Faulkner Condominium Assn., Chgo., 1980-82, Carl Sandburg Village Homeowners Assn., Chgo., 1981-82. Mem. Ill. Bar Assn., Chgo. Bar Assn. (pres. probate practice div. III 1979), Chgo. Estate Planning Council. Home: 2155 Tanglewood Ct Highland Park IL 60035-4231 Office: D'Ancona & Pflaum 30 N La Salle St Ste 2900 Chicago IL 60602-2502

SCHARF, PETER MARK, Sanskrit and Indian studies educator; b. New Haven, Conn., June 14, 1958; s. Roy Herbert and Candida Maria (Boccuzzi) S. BA in Philosophy, Wesleyan U., 1981; postgrad., Brown U., 1982-83; PhD in Sanskrit, U. Pa., 1990. Computer analyst, programmer, 1981-83; teaching asst. U. Pa., 1985-86, postdoctoral fellow in linguistics, 1990-91, 93, 94; lectr. in classics Brown U., Providence, 1992—; vis. lectr. religious studies U. Va., 1992; presenter in field. Author: The Denotation of Generic Terms in Ancient Indian Philosophy: Grammar, Nyaya, and Mimamsa, 1996; contbr. articles to profl. jours. Outstanding High Sch. Sr.'s Semester scholar, 1976; Fgn. Lang. and Area Studies fellow, 1983-85, Jr. rsch. fellow Am. Inst. Indian Studies, 1986-88, Mellon grad. fellow, 1988-89, U. Pa. Dean's fellow, 1989-90. Mem. Am. Oriental Soc., Assn. for Asian Studies, Bhandarkar Oriental Rsch. Inst. (life). Avocations: chess, photography, transcendental meditation, mountain climbing. Office: Brown U Dept Classics PO Box 1856 Providence RI 02912-1856

SCHARF, WILLIAM, artist; b. Media, Pa., Feb. 22, 1927; s. Lester William and Ebba (Anderson) S.; m. Diana Denny, Mar. 11, 1947 (div. 1951); 1 child, William Denny; m. Sally Kravitch, Mar. 25, 1956; 1 child, Aaron Anderson. Student, Barnes Found., 1946-47; cert. in painting, Pa. Acad. of Fine Arts, 1947. Instr. Mus. Modern Art, N.Y.C., 1964, Sch. Visual Arts, N.Y.C., 1965-73, San Francisco Inst. Fine Arts, 1963, 66, 69, 74, 89. One-man shows include David Herbert Gallery, N.Y.C., 1960, 62, San Francisco Inst. Fine Arts, 1969, Neuberger Mus., Purchase, N.Y., 1976, High Mus., Atlanta, 1978, Armstrong Gallery, N.Y.C., 1987, U. Mich. Mus. Art, Ann Arbor, 1993; exhibited in group shows at Guggenheim Mus., N.Y.C., 1982, Hirschl-Adler Gallery, N.Y.C., 1980, Smith-Anderson Gallery, Palo Alto, Calif., Nat. Mus. Am. Art, Washington, 1987, 91, 92, Am. Acad. and Inst. Arts and Letters, N.Y.C., 1989, 91; represented in permanent collections Boston Inst. Contemporary Art, Bklyn Mus., Solomon r. Guggenheim Mus., N.Y.C., Newark Mus., Nat. Mus. Am. Art, Smith Coll. Mus., Northampton, Mass., Zimmerli Mus., Rutgers U., New Brunswick, N.J., U. Mich. Mus. art., Phillips Collection, Washington, The Neuroscis. Inst., San Diego. Trustee Rothko Found., N.Y.C., 1979-87; instr. Art Student's League, N.Y., 1987-97. With USAF, 1945-46. Emmlen Cresson fellow Pa. Acad. Fine Arts, 1948. Mem. Artist Equity Assn., Soc. of Illustrators.

SCHARFF, JOSEPH LAURENT, lawyer; b. New Orleans, Oct. 2, 1935; s. Joseph Roy and Celia Ray (Rosenhein) S.; m. Mary Susan Greulach, June 29, 1963; children: Catherine Elizabeth, Robert Laurent, Anne Victoria. BS in Journalism, Northwestern U., 1957; JD, Harvard U., 1964. Bar: D.C. 1965, U.S. Supreme Ct. 1970, U.S. Ct. Appeals (D.C. cir.) 1965, U.S. Ct. Appeals (2nd cir.) 1980, U.S. Ct. Appeals (5th cir.) 1973, U.S. Ct. Appeals (10th cir.); U.S. Ct. Claims 1965. From assoc. to ptnr. Pierson, Ball & Dowd, Washington, 1964-89; ptnr. Reed Smith Shaw & McClay, Washington, 1989-95, counsel, 1996. Mem. ABA (fair trial-free press com. 1973-76, com. reps. media 1985-95, co-chmn. 1989-92), Fed. Comm. Bar Assn., Soc. Profl. Journalists, Radio-TV News Dirs. Assn. (counsel 1965-95, Disting. Svc. award 1987, Media Inst. First Amendment Adv. Coun., J. Laurent Scharff Legal Internship established 1996). Home and Office: 12000 Turf Ln Reston VA 20191-2123 Office: Reed Smith Shaw and McClay 1301 K St NW Washington DC 20005-3317

SCHARFF, MATTHEW DANIEL, immunologist, cell biologist, educator; b. N.Y.C., Aug. 28, 1932; s. Harry and Constance S.; m. Carol Held, Dec. 19, 1954; children—Karen, Thomas, David. AB, Brown U., 1954, DrMedSci (hon.), 1994; MD, NYU, 1959. House officer II and IV med. service Boston City Hosp., 1959-61; research asso. NIH, 1961-63; asst. prof. Albert Einstein Coll. Medicine, Yeshiva U., Bronx, N.Y., 1963-67; asso. prof. Albert Einstein Coll. Medicine, Yeshiva U., 1967-71, prof. dept. cell biology, 1971—, chmn. dept., 1972-83, dir. div. biol. scis., 1975-81; asso. dir. Cancer Center, 1975-86, dir., 1986-95. Served with USPHS, 1961-63. Recipient Alumni Achievement award NYU Sch. Medicine, 1980, N.Y. Acad. Medicine medal, 1990, Commemorative award Albert Einstein Coll. Medicine, 1993, hon. Dr. Med. Sci., Brown U., 1994. Mem. Am. Assn. Immunologists, Am. Soc. Clin. Investigation, Nat. Acad. Scis., Am. Acad. Arts and Sci., Phi Beta Kappa, Sigma Xi, Alpha Omega Alpha. Office: Albert Einstein Coll Med Cancer Ctr 1300 Morris Pk Ave Bronx NY 10461-1926

SCHARFMAN, SCOTT PHILLIP, investment banker; b. N.Y.C., May 14, 1962; s. Melvin Allen and Helen (Brachfeld) S.; m. Heidi M. Grasberger, June 30, 1996; 1 child, Olivia Helen. AB cum laude, Princeton (N.J.) U., 1986. Co-founder, pres. Students for the Exploration and Devel. of Space, 1980-86; analyst The First Boston Corp., N.Y.C., 1986-88, assoc., 1988-91; assoc. The Blackstone Group, N.Y.C., 1991-92, v.p., 1992-94; mng. dir. equity capital markets Bear, Stearns & Co., Inc., N.Y.C., 1994—. Mem. Princeton Club of N.Y., Princeton Campus Club (trustee), Sigma Xi. Office: 245 Park Ave New York NY 10167-0002

SCHARLAU, CHARLES EDWARD, III, natural gas company executive; b. Chgo., Apr. 24, 1927; s. Charles Edward II and Esther (Powell) S.; m. Clydene Yvonne Sloop, Aug. 13, 1960; children: Caryn, Robin, Greg, Charles, Marti. LLB, U. Ark., 1951. Bar: Ark. 1951, U.S. Dist. Ct. (western dist.) Ark. 1951, U.S. Supreme Ct. 1958. Atty. Ark. Western Gas Co., Fayetteville, 1951-61, v.p., 1961-68, pres., 1968-78; pres., chmn. S.W. Energy Co., Fayetteville, 1978—; bd. dirs. C.H. Heist Co., Clearwater, Fla., McIlroy Bank and Trust Co., Fayetteville. Chmn. U. Ark. Devel. Coun., 1989-97; trustee U. Ark., 1997—. With USMC, 1945-46. Mem. ABA, Ark. Bar Assn., So. Gas Assn., Nat. Assn. Mfrs. (bd. dirs. 1986-89), Am. Gas Assn. (bd. dirs. 1987-90), U. Ark. Alumni Assn. (pres. 1972-73), Ark. C. of C. (pres. 1977-79), Beta Gamma Sigma. Methodist. Avocations: reading, tennis, canoeing, sports. Home: 1506 Sunset Pl Fayetteville AR 72701-1627 Office: Southwestern Energy Co 1083 Sain St Fayetteville AR 72703-6206

SCHARLEMANN, ROBERT PAUL, religious studies educator, clergyman; b. Lake City, Minn., Apr. 4, 1929; s. Ernst Karl and Johanna Meta (Harre) S. Student, Northwestern Coll., Watertown, Wis., 1946-49; B.A., Concordia Coll. and Sem., St. Louis, 1952; B.D., Concordia Coll. and Sem., 1955; Dr. theol., U. Heidelberg (Germany), 1957. Ordained to ministry, Lutheran Ch., 1960. Instr. philosophy Valparaiso U., 1957-59; postdoctoral fellow Yale U., 1959-60; pastor Bethlehem Luth. Ch., Carlyle, Ill., 1960-62, Grace Luth. Ch., Durham, N.C., 1962-63; asst. prof. religion U. So. Calif., 1963-64, assoc. prof., 1964-66; assoc. prof. religion U. Iowa, Iowa City, 1966-68, prof., 1968-81; Commonwealth prof. religious studies U. Va., Charlottesville, 1981—; Fulbright-Hayes prof. U. Heidelberg, 1975-76. Author: Thomas Aquinas and John Gerhard, 1964, Reflection and Doubt in the Thought of Paul Tillich, 1969, The Being of God, 1981, Inscriptions and Reflections, 1989, The Reason of Following, 1991; editor Jour. of Am. Acad. Religion, 1980-85; contbr. articles to profl. jours. Mem. Am. Acad. Religion, Am. Theol. Soc., European Soc. Culture, Soc. for Philosophy of Religion. Office: U Va Dept Religious Studies Charlottesville VA 22903

SCHAROLD, MARY LOUISE, psychoanalyst, educator; b. Wichita Falls, Tex., Mar. 3, 1943; d. Walter John and Louise Helen (Hartmann) Baumgartner; m. William Ballew McCollum, Aug. 23, 1964 (div. 1981); m. Harry Karl Scharold, June 19, 1982; children: Margaret Louise, Walter Ballew. BA with highest distinction, U. Kans., 1964; MD, Baylor Coll. Med., 1968; postgrad. Topeka Inst. for Psychoanalysis, 1981. Diplomate Am. Bd. Psychiatry and Neurology. Intern Meml. Baptist. Hosp., Houston, 1968-69; resident in psychiatry Baylor Coll. Med., Houston, 1969-72, chief resident, 1971-72; practice of medicine specializing in psychoanalysis, Houston, 1972—; asst. prof. Baylor Coll. Med., Houston, 1973-76, asst. clin. prof., 1981-84, assoc. clin. prof., 1984—; dir. Baylor Psychiat. Clinic, Houston, 1973-76; co-dir. Rice U. Psychiat. Service, Houston, 1981-82; asst. clin. prof. U. Kans. Sch. Medicine, Kansas City, 1977-81; teaching assoc. Topeka Inst. Psychoanalysis, 1980-81; instr. Houston-Galveston Psychoanalytic Inst., 1984-86, teaching analyst, 1986-90, tng. and supervising analyst, 1990—, v.p., 1994-96, pres. 1996—; Adv. bd. Leavenworth Mental Health Assn., Kans., 1977-81. Watkins scholar U. Kans., 1961-64. Fellow Am. Psychiatric Assn. (chmn. Tex. peer review 1984-88); mem. Am. Psychiat. Assn., Am. Psychoanalytic Assn. (cert. 1982, peer rev. com. 1985-90, prof. ins. commn. 1986-93, bd. profl. stds., 1994—, CME com., 1994—, mem. exec. coun. 1994-96, cert. com. 1994—), Am. Group Psychotherapy Assn., Houston Psychiatric Soc. (v.p. 1984-85, pres. elect 1985-86, pres. 1986-87), Houston-Galveston Psychoanalytic Soc. (sec.-treas. 1984-86, pres.-elect 1986-88, pres. 1988-90, alter councillor 1994-96), Psychiat. Assn. (quality assurance com. 1986-87), Houston Group Psychotherapy Soc. (adv. bd. 1984-85), Mortar Bd., Phi Beta Kappa, Delta Phi Alpha, Alpha Omega Alpha, Hilltopper, Pi Beta Phi Alumni Assn. Republican. Lutheran. Office: 3400 Bissonnet St Ste 170 Houston TX 77005-2153

SCHARP-RADOVIC, CAROL ANN, choreographer, classical ballet educator, artistic director; b. Ypsilanti, Mich., Aug. 9, 1940; d. John Lewis and Mary Vivien (Alther) Keeney; m. Jack Laurel Scharp, July 28, 1958 (div. July 1970); children: Kathryn E., Mark A.; m. Srecko Radovic, Nov. 15,

1989. Studied with Pereslavic, Danilova; student, Harkness Ballet, N.Y.C., Joffrey Ballet, N.Y.C., Eglevsky Ballet, N.Y.C., Briansky Ballet, Darvesh Ballet, N.Y.C.; studied with Jurgen Schneider, Am. Ballet Theatre, 1983-93; studied with Janina Cunova, Luba Gulyeava, Australian Ballet Co., 1983-93; studied with Ninel Kurgapkina, Ludmila Synelnikova, Genhrich Mayorov, Kirov Ballet, 1987-89; studied with Ludmila Sakharova, Perm Ballet, 1993; studied with Ludmila Synelnikova, Bolshoi Ballet Sch., Moscow, 1989; studied with Inna Zubkhovskaya, Alex. Stiopin, Lydia Goncharova, Valentina Chistova, Mararita Zagurskaya, Valentina Rumyantsema, Vaganova Ballet Acad., St. Petersburg, Russia, 1993. Ballet mistress Adrian (Mich.) Coll., 1982-84; founder, artistic dir. Ann Arbor (Mich.) Ballet Theatre, 1980—; studied with Janina Cunova; studied with Luba Gulyeava Kirov Ballet, 1984; former regional field judge Nat. Ballet Achievement Fund; dir. seminars Marygrove Coll., Detroit. Choreographer Cinderella, 1980, Nightingale, 1980, Nutcracker, 1984, Carnival of the Animals, 1981, Carmen, 1983, Midsummer Nights Dream, 1982, Vivaldi's Spring, 1990, Opulence, 1984, La Boutique Fantasque, 1995, Handel's Alcina, 1985, Gymnopedie, 1985, Gershwin's Preludes, 1996, Ravel's Bolero, 1997, Dracula, 1997, others. Ruth Mott grantee for choreography, 1982. Mem. Mich. Dance Assn. Avocations: gardening, reading, writing. Home: 6476 Huron River Dr Dexter MI 48130-9796 Office: CAS Ballet Theatre Sch Ann Arbor Ballet Theatre 548 Church St Ann Arbor MI 48104-2514

SCHATT, PAUL, newspaper editor; b. N.Y.C., Aug. 31, 1945; divorced; children: Suzannah, Andrew. BA with distinction Polit. Sci., English, Ariz. State U., 1967. Editor Ariz. Republic, 1964-66, reporter, 1965-74, urban affairs editor, 1974-75, asst. city editor, 1975-79, chief asst. city editor, 1979-82, asst. met. editor, 1985-86, met. editor, 1986-88, editor edit. pages, 1993—; asst. editor Ariz. Mag., 1981-82, editor, 1982-85; editor edit. pages Phoenix Gazette, 1988-93, The Ariz. Republic, 1993—; vis. lectr. Pub. Affairs Journalism, Ariz. State U., 1976—, instr. Mass. Comm. Dept., 1974-76; dir. Eugene C. Pulliam Fellowship. Phoenix program, 1990—; writing coach, 1989; del. Pre White House Conf. Librs., 1991. v.p. Crisis Nursery, 1984-87, bd. dirs. 1980-87; exec. bd. Hospice of the Valley, 1980-87; pres. Friends of Phoenix Pub. Libr., 1985-86, bd. dirs. 1986—; bd. trustees 1st Amendment Congress, 1989—; bd. dirs. Camelback Hosps. 1982-89, chmn. bd. dirs. 1986-87, Cactus Pine Coun. Girl Scouts Am., 1988-89, Sun Sounds Inc., 1982-89, Valley Leadership Inc., 1991—, alum. assn., 1985-89, Ariz. Zool. Soc., 1991—, Barrow Neurol. Found., 1991—, Kids Voting, 1991-93, Barry Goldwater Inst., 1991-93, Ariz. Club, 1991—. With Ariz. Nat. Guard, 1966-79. Recipient Montgomery award Outstanding Svc. to Community Friends of Phoenix Pub. Libr., 1989; profl. Journalism fellow Stanford U., 1970-71. Mem. Am. Soc. Newspaper Editors, Soc. Profl. Journalists (pres. Valley of Sun chpt. 1974-75, 83-84, exec. bd. 1988-92), Sigma Delta Chi (co-chair nat. convention 1974). Office: The Ariz Republic Editorial Dept 200 E Van Buren St Phoenix AZ 85004-2238

SCHATTEN, GERALD PHILLIP, cell biologist, reproductive biologist, educator; b. N.Y.C., Nov. 1, 1949; s. Frank and Sylvia Schatten; m. Heather Aronson, July 4, 1994; children, Daniel, Madeline. BS, U. Calif., Berkeley, 1971, PhD, 1975. Instr. U. Calif., Berkeley, 1975; postdoctoral fellow Rockefeller Found., 1976-77; from asst. prof. to prof. Fla. State U., Tallahassee, 1979-86; prof. molecular biology, zoology and obstetrics gynecology U. Wis., Madison, 1986—, dir. integrated microscopy resource for biomed. rsch., 1986-92, dir. gamete and embryo biol. tng. program, 1989—; program dir. Mellon Ctr. of Excellence in Reproductive Biology, 1996—; dir. gamete and embryo biol. tng. program U. Wis., Madison, 1989—; exec. bd. UNESCO Internat. Cell Rsch. Orgn., 1995—; co-dir. frontiers in reprodn. course Maine Biol. Lab., Woods Hole, Mass., 1998—. Recipient Rsch. Career Devel. award NIH, 1981-86. Office: Univ Wis 1117 W Johnson St Madison WI 53706-1705

SCHATZ, IRWIN JACOB, cardiologist; b. St. Boniface, Man., Can., Oct. 16, 1931; came to U.S., 1956, naturalized, 1966; s. Jacob and Reva S.; m. Barbara Jane Binder, Nov. 12, 1967; children: Jacob, Edward, Stephen and Brian (twins). Student, U. Man., Can.), Winnipeg, 1951, M.D. with honors, 1956. Diplomate: Am. Bd. Internal Medicine. Intern Vancouver (B.C.) Gen. Hosp., 1955-56; resident Hammersmith Hosp., U. London, 1957, Mayo Clinic, Rochester, Minn., 1958-61; head sec. peripheral vascular disease Henry Ford Hosp., Detroit, 1961-68; assoc. prof. medicine Wayne State U., 1968-71, chief sect. cardiovascular disease, 1969-71; assoc. prof., assoc. dir. sect. cardiology U. Mich., 1972-73, prof. internal medicine, 1973-75; prof. medicine John A. Burns Sch. Medicine, U. Hawaii, 1975—, chmn. dept. medicine, 1975-90. Author: Orthostatic Hypotension, 1986; contbr. numerous articles to med. jours. Rockefeller Found. scholar, 1991. Master ACP (bd. govs. 1984-89, Laureate award Hawaii chpt. 1992); fellow Am. Coll. Cardiology (bd. govs. 1980-84); mem. Am. Heart Assn. (fellow couns. cardiology and circulation), Am. Fedn. Clin. Rsch., Asian-Pacific Soc. Cardiology (v.p. 1987-91), Accreditation Coun. for Grad. Med. Edn. (chmn. residence rev. com. internal medicine 1993-95), Hawaii Heart Assn. (pres.), Western Assn. Physicians, Am. Autonomic Soc. (chmn. bd. govs., pres. 1996-98), Pacific Interurban Club. Jewish. Home: 4983 Kolohala St Honolulu HI 96816-5126 Office: 1356 Lusitana St Honolulu HI 96813-2421

SCHATZ, LILLIAN LEE, playwright, molecular biologist, educator; b. N.Y.C., Apr. 8, 1944; d. Joseph Louis and Rose (Zakalik) S. BA in Biology, SUNY, Buffalo, 1965, MA in Biology, 1970. Cert. h.s. tchr. biology, chemistry, gen. sci., N.Y., 1968. Rsch. asst. dept. biology SUNY at Buffalo, 1965-68, rsch. asst. dept. pharmacology Sch. Medicine, 1969; rsch. assoc. dept. biology SUNY, Buffalo, 1971-74; cancer rsch. scientist dept. viral oncology Roswell Park Meml. Inst., Buffalo, 1969-70; tchr. biology Kenmore East Sr. H.S., Buffalo, 1970-71; playwright Buffalo, 1976—; presenter workshop Rosa Coplon Jewish Home and Infirmary, Buffalo, N.Y., 1982, N.Y. State Community Theater Assn., 1982. Plays include Solomon's Court, 1979, Neshomah, 1983, Bernie, 1985, The Jonah Men, 1991; contbr. rsch. articles to sci. jours. Charter mem. B'not Israel Group Buffalo chpt. Hadassah, life mem. Recipient N.Y. State Regents Coll. Scholarship, 1961-65; semi-finalist Sergel Drama prize Ct. Theatre, U. Chgo., 1985, Nat. Play Award Competition Nat. Repertory Theatre Found., 1981; Playwriting fellow, N.Y. State Creative Artists Pub. Svc. fellow, 1980-81, Roswell Park Meml. Inst. fellow, 1962, Summer Sci. fellow. Democrat. Jewish. Avocations: art, genealogy. Home and Office: 31 Twyla Pl Buffalo NY 14223-1526

SCHATZ, MONA CLAIRE STRUHSAKER, social worker, educator, consultant, researcher; b. Phila., Jan. 4, 1950; d. Milton and Josephine (Kivo) S.; m. James Fredrick Struhsaker, Dec. 31, 1979 (div.); 1 child, Thain Mackenzie. BA, Metro State Coll., 1976; postgrad., U. Minn., 1976; MSW, U. Denver, 1979; D in Social Work/Social Welfare, U. Pa., 1986. Teaching fellow U. Pa., Phila., 1981-82; asst. prof. S.W. Mo. State U., Springfield, 1982-85; assoc. prof. Colo. State U., Ft. Collins, 1985—, field coord., 1986-88, dir. non-profit agy. adminstrn. program, 1995—, project dir. Edn. and Rsch. Inst. for Fostering Families, 1987—, dir. youth agy. adminstrn. program Am. Humanics, 1988-90; cons. Mgmt. and Behavioral Sci. Ctr., The Wharton Sch. U. Pa., 1981-82; resource specialist So. N.J. Health Sys. Agy., 1982; adj. faculty mem. U. Mo., Springfield, 1994; med. social worker Rehab. and Vis. Nurse Assn., 1985-90; mem. Colo. Child Welfare Adv. Com., Family Conservation Initiative; internat. cons. and trainer Inst. for Internat. Connections, Russia, Latvia, Albania, U.S., Hungary, Ukraine, Romania, 1992—. Contbr. articles to profl. jours. Cons., field rep. Big Bros./Big Sisters of Am., Phila., 1979-83; acting dir., asst. dir. Big Sisters of Colo., 1971-78; owner Polit. Cons. in Colo., Denver, 1978-79; active Food Co-op, Ft. Collins, Foster Parent, Denver, Capital Hill United Neighbors, Adams County (Denver) Social Planning Coun., Co., Colo. Justice Coun., Denver, Regional Girls Shelter, Springfield; bd. dirs. Crisis Helpline and Info. Svc. Scholar Lilly Endowment, Inc., 1976, Piton Found., 1978; recipient Spl. Recognition award Big Bros./Big Sisters of Am., 1983, Recognition award Am. Humanics Mgmt. Inst., 1990. Mem. Inst. Internat. Connections (bd. dirs.), Coun. Social Work Edn., Group for Study of Generalist Social Work, Social Welfare History Group, Nat. Assn. Social Workers (nominating com. Springfield chpt., state bd. dirs., No. Colo. rep.), Student Social Work Assn. Colo. State U. (adv. 1986-89), Permanency Planning Coun. for Children and Youth, NOW (treas. Springfield chpt. 1984-85), Student Nuclear Awareness Group (advisor), Student Social Work Assn. (advisor), Har Shalom, Alpha Delta Mu. Democrat. Avocations: cooking, traveling, reading, biking, sewing. Office: Colo State U Social Work Dept Fort Collins CO 80523

SCHATZBERG, ALAN FREDERIC, psychiatrist, researcher; b. N.Y.C., Oct. 17, 1944; s. Emanuel and Cila (Diamand) S.; m. Nancy R. Silverman, Aug. 27, 1972; children: Melissa Ann, Lindsey Diamand. BS, NYU, 1965, MD, 1968; MA (hon.), Harvard U., 1989. Diplomate Nat. Bd. Med. Examiners, Am. Bd. Psychiatry and Neurology. Intern Lenox Hill Hosp., N.Y.C., 1968-69; resident in psychiatry Mass. Mental Health Ctr., Boston, 1969-72; clin. fellow in psychiatry Harvard Med. Sch., Boston, 1969-72, asst. prof. psychiatry, 1977-82, assoc. prof., 1982-88, prof., 1988-91; interim psychiatrist-in-chief McLean Hosp., Belmont, Mass., 1984-86, dir. depression rsch. facility, 1985—, svc. chief, 1982-84, 86-88; psychiatrist adv. panel Eli Lilly & Co., Indpls., 1986-93; clin. dir. Mass. Mental Health Ctr., Boston, 1988-91; Kenneth T. Norris, Jr. prof. psychiatry and behavioral scis. Stanford U., 1991—, chmn. dept. psychiatry and behavioral scis. Sch. Medicine, 1991—; cons. AMA Videoclinics, Chgo., 1979-83; mem. AMA/FAA panel on health regulations, Chgo., 1984-86; mem. NIH Biol. Psychopathology and Clin. Neurosci. Intitial Rev. Group, 1991-95, chmn., 1993-94. Co-author: Manual of Clinical Psychopharmacology, 1986, 3d edit., 1997; contbr. more than 200 articles, book chpts. to profl. publs.; co-editor: Depression: Biology, Psychodynamics and Treatment, 1978, Hypothalamic-Pituitary-Adrenal Axis, 1988, Textbook of Psychopharmacology, 1995; mem. editl. bd. McLean Hosp. Jour., 1975-88, Jour. Psychiat. Rsch., 1986—, Integrative Psychiatry, 1990—, Harvard Rev. Psychiatry, 1992—, Archives of Gen. Psychiatry, 1995—, Psychoneuroendocrinology, 1995—, Annals Psychiatry, 1992—, Anxiety, 1993, Jour. Clin. Psychopharmacology, 1993—; assoc. editor-in-chief Depression, 1992—. Maj. USAF, 1972-74. Rsch. grantee NIMH, 1984-87, 94—, Poitras Charitable Found., 1985-93. Fellow Am. Psychiat. Assn., Am. Coll. Neuropsychopharmacology (coun. 1995—), Am. Psychopath. Assn.; mem. Am. Coll. Psychiatrists, Mass. Psychiat. Soc. (coun. 1987-90), No. Calif. Psychiat. Soc. Avocations: travel, theater, tennis, swimming, fine arts. Office: Stanford U Sch Medicine 401 Quarry Rd Rm 300 Stanford CA 94305-5548

SCHATZKI, GEORGE, law educator; b. 1933. A.B., Harvard U., 1955, LLB, 1958, LLM, 1965. Teaching fellow Harvard U., Cambridge, Mass., 1963-65; prof. law U. Tex.-Austin, 1965-79; dean U. Wash. Sch. Law, Seattle, 1979-82, prof., 1979-84; dean U. Conn. Sch. Law, Hartford, 1984-90, prof., 1984—; vis. prof. law U. Pa., Phila., 1973-74, Harvard U., Cambridge, Mass., 1977-78; vis. lectr. law Yale U., New Haven, 1993, 96. Co-author: Labor Relations and Social Problems: Collective Bargaining in Private Employment, 1978, Labor and Employment Law, 1988, 2d edit., 1995. Office: U Conn Law Sch 55 Elizabeth St Hartford CT 06105-2213

SCHAUB, HARRY CARL, lawyer; b. Hazleton, Pa., Feb. 3, 1929; s. Harry J. and Lida M. (Fisher) S.; m. Kathryn Klindt Deans, Aug. 14, 1982; children: Lisa A., Irene Cannon, Christian K. BA, U. Pa., 1950; JD, Yale U., 1955; postgrad., Columbia U., 1962. Bar: Pa. 1955. Assoc. Montgomery, McCracken, Walker & Rhoads, Phila., 1955-62; ptnr. Montgomery, McCracken, Walker & Rhoads, 1963—; consul Republic of Austria to State of Pa., 1978-84, consul gen., 1984—. Contbr. articles to profl. jours. V.p., bd. dirs. Luth. Ch. of Holy Communion, Phila., 1975-88; bd. dirs. YMCA Cen., Phila., 1986-91, dean 1997—; chmn. bd. dirs. Consular Corps Coll., 1987-96; mem. The Athenaeum of Phila., 1976—. Capt. U.S. Army, 1951-53. Decorated Golden Medal of Honor 1st class (Austria), 1992; recipient Johann Strauss award City of Vienna, 1979. Mem. ABA, Pa. Bar Assn., Phila. Bar Assn., Internat. Bar Assn., Am. Soc. Internat. Law, Am. Coun. on Germany, Austrian Soc. Pa. (v.p., bd. dirs. 1981-97), John Peter Zenger Law Soc. (founder, bd. dirs., pres. 1994-96), Union League of Phila., Rittenhouse Club, Mil. Order Fgn. Wars, The Franklin Inn, The Penn Club, Phi Beta Kappa, Pi Gamma Mu. Democrat. Lutheran. Home: 1420 Locust St Unit 7K Philadelphia PA 19102 Office: Montgomery McCracken 123 S Broad St Philadelphia PA 19109-1029

SCHAUB, JAMES HAMILTON, engineering educator; b. Moundsville, W.Va., Jan. 27, 1925; s. Carroll Franklin and Lilian Hoyle (Hutchison) S.; m. Malinda Katherine Bailey, June 15, 1948. Student, George Washington U., 1942-43; B.S. in Civil Engring., Va. Poly. Inst., 1948; S.M. in Civil Engring., Harvard U., 1949; Ph.D., Purdue U., 1960. Registered profl. engr., Va. Soils engr. Ore. Hwy. Dept., 1949-50, 51-52; lab. dir. Palmer and Baker, Inc., Mobile, 1952-55; asst. prof. civil engring. Va. Poly. Inst., 1955-58; instr., research engr. Purdue U., 1958-60; prof. civil engring., chmn. dept. W.Va. U., 1960-67, assoc. dean engring., 1967-69; prof. civil engring., chmn. dept. U. Fla. at Gainesville, 1969-87, Disting. Service prof., 1984-92, NSF faculty fellow, 1975-76, affiliate prof. dept. history, 1977-92, Disting Svc. prof. emeritus, 1992—; acad. visitor dept. history of sci. and tech. Imperial Coll., U. London, 1975-76; Edwin P. Conquest chair humanities Va. Mil. Inst., 1986; vis. prof. Swarthmore Coll., spring 1988; cons. engr. to state, fed. and pvt. agys. and cos., 1960—. Co-author 2 books; author tech. papers. Served with inf. AUS, 1943-46; with C.E. 1950-51, ETO, Korea. Recipient Eminent Career award Coll. Engring, U. Fla., 1987. Mem. ASCE (named Engr. of Year, Fla. sect. 1974, William H. Wisely award 1986), Am. Pub. Works Assn. (pres. chpt. 1983-84, nat. dir.-at-large 1983-89), Order of Engr., Golden Key, Chi Epsilon, Phi Kappa Phi, Kappa Sigma, Sigma Xi, Tau Beta Pi. Episcopalian. Home: 4401 NW 15th Pl Gainesville FL 32605-4509

SCHAUB, MARILYN MCNAMARA, religion educator; b. Chgo., Mar. 24, 1928; d. Bernard Francis and Helen Katherine (Skehan) McNamara; m. R. Thomas Schaub, Oct. 25, 1969; 1 dau., Helen Ann. B.A., Rosary Coll., 1953; Ph.D., U. Fribourg, Switzerland, 1957; diploma, Ecole Biblique, Jerusalem, 1967. Asst. prof. classics and Bibl. studies Rosary Coll., River Forest, Ill., 1957-69; prof. Bibl. studies Duquesne U., Pitts., 1969-70, 73—; participant 8 archeol. excavations, Middle East; adminstrv. dir. expedition to the Southeast Dead Sea Plains, Jordan, 1989—; hon. assoc. Am. Schs. Oriental Rsch., 1966-67, trustee, 1986-89; Danforth assoc., 1972-80. Author: Friends and Friendship for St. Augustine, 1964; translator: (with H. Richter) Agape in the New Testament, 3 vols, 1963-65. Mem. Soc. Bibl. Lit., Catholic Bibl. Assn., Am. Acad. Religion. Democrat. Home: 25 Mckelvey Ave Pittsburgh PA 15218-1452 Office: Duquesne U Theology Dept Pittsburgh PA 15282

SCHAUB, SHERWOOD ANHDER, JR., management consultant; b. Rahway, N.J., Jan. 8, 1942; s. Sherwood Anhder Sr. and Doris (Beecher) S.; m. Diane Katherine Wells, July 29, 1967; children: Whitney, Kristen. BBA with honors, Nichols Coll., 1964; postgrad. in bus. adminstrn., Fairleigh Dickinson U., 1965-69. Cert. mgmt. cons. Dir. Gilbert Lane, N.Y.C., 1965-67; exec. v.p. Ward Clancy, N.Y.C., 1967-71; founder, chmn., CEO, sr. mng. ptnr. Goodrich & Sherwood Co., N.Y.C. 1971-94, chmn., Goodrich & Sherwood Assocs., Inc., 1994—; CEO Reed, Cuff & Assocs., 1980-86; CEO Exec. Change, Inc., 1978; mem. adv. bd. Paine Webber; mem. Schwarzkopf Cup select com., 1992-95; pres. House of Hamilton, 1995, Trans Link Am., 1995, chmn.; mem. bd. Restaurant Assocs., NPD Corp. Author: Breakpoints, 1986; contbr. articles on mgmt. to mags. and profl. jours. Congl. advisor Pres. Ronald Reagan, 1986; head Bus. Task Force N.Y. for Reagan Adminstrn., 1987-89; bd. dirs. Conn. Pub. Broadcasting; trustee Nichols Coll., 1992-96, mem. exec. com., 1995, head presidl. search com. 1995. Decorated Knight Comanderie de Bordeaux 1993 (France); named Outstanding Alumnus, Nichols Coll., 1994; elected to U.S. 100 Top Recruiters, 1990-96. Mem. Nat. Assn. Corp. and Profl. Recruiters, Young Pres. Orgn. (bd. dirs. 1986-88, vice chmn. met. chpt. sounding bd., hospitality, edn. chmn., chpt. chmn. elect 1989), Pvt. Pilots Assn., World Pres. Orgn., Safari Club Internat. (bd. dirs., 1987-89, chpt. chmn. 1996), U.S. Equestrian Team. Congregationalist. Clubs: Chemists, University, Westfield Tennis, New Canaan Racquet, New Cannan Field, Am. Friends of Game Conservancy, Rolling Rock, Weston Gun Club, Mashomak Field and Game, Econ. of N.Y., Explorers (fellow), Madison Ave. Sports Car Driving & Chowder Society, Greenwich Polo, Ducks Unlimited (sponsor, co-chmn. So. Conn. 1994-96), Advt. Sportsmen of N.Y. (bd. dirs., treas.), Sandanona Club (Millbrook, N.Y.). Avocations: scuba diving, equestrian riding, big and small game hunting, antiques, sporting clays shooting. Office: Goodrich & Sherwood Assocs Inc 521 5th Ave New York NY 10175

SCHAUB, THERESA MARIE, early childhood educator; b. Milw., Oct. 12, 1951; d. Joseph and Mary (Huberty) S. BS in Early Childhood, U. Wis., 1975. Cert. exceptional-edn.-early childhood, Wis. Kindergarten tchr. Sacred Heart, Milw., 1981-82, Ebenezer Child Care, Milw., 1982-83; presch.-head tchr. Ragamuffin Child Care, Milw., 1984-85, 86-87; asst. dir., head tchr. Country Kare, Albuquerque, 1985-86; kindergarten tchr. Holy Angels Sch., Milw., 1987-90, St. Rose Sch., Milw., 1990-94; head start tchr. Children's Outing Assn., Milw., 1994-96, Parkman Sch., Milw., 1996, Andrew S. Douglas Sch., Milw., 1996—; supportive cons. St. Rose Sch., Milw., 1990-94, peer mediation supr., 1991-94, AV coord., 1990-94; parent vol. com. Children's Outing Assn., 1995-96. Author: ABC's of Peace, 1990. Pres. Young Dems.; vol. Homeless Shelter Casa Maria Hospitality, Milw., 1975-80; vol. tchr. Peacemakers Camp, Milw., 1992; bd. dirs. Clear Horizons Food Coop., Milw., 1978. Mem. Milw. Peace Ctr., NAEYC, Sierra Club, NOW, Nat. Audubon Soc., Wis. Edn. for Social Responsibility, Habitat for Humanity. Avocations: hiking, snowshoeing, traveling, listening to music, aerobics. Office: Parkman Sch 3620 N 18th St Milwaukee WI 53206-2362

SCHAUBLE, JOHN EUGENE, physical education educator; b. Paterson, N.J., Aug. 14, 1949; s. Charles Eugene and Rosemary (White) S.; children: Sarah, Angela. BA, Bemidji State U., 1973, BS, 1974; MA, U. Ala., 1984. Cert. tchr. health, phys. edn., K-12; cert. swimming coach/level 4; cert. aquatic mgr.; cert. pool operator, ARC water safety instr., lifeguard instr., waterfront lifeguard instr., first aid instr., CPR instr. Northeast area dir. Phys. Fitness Inst. of Am., Albany, N.Y., 1974-75; head swim coach Lake Forest (Ill.) Swim Club, 1975-78; asst. swim coach/grad. asst. U. Ala., Tuscaloosa, 1978-79; head swim coach Palm Springs (Calif.) Swim Team, 1979-80; asst. swim coach Ft. Lauderdale (Fla.) Swim Team, 1980-82; aquatic dir., head swim coach Briarwood of Richmond Aquatic Club, Richmond, Va., 1982-83; head swimming coach, intramural coord. William Rainey Harper Coll., Palatine, Ill., 1983-85; boys/girls asst. swim coach Sch. Dist. 211, Palatine, 1985-90; nat. coach Palatine Swim Team, 1983-92; head boys and girls swim coach Adlai E. Stevenson High Sch., Lincolnshire, Ill., 1990-96, aquatic coord., 1990—; asst. girls track and field coach Adlai E. Stevenson High Sch., 1992—; head coach Patriot Aquatic Club, 1992-94; fund raising com. U.S. Swimming, Inc., Colorado Springs, Colo., 1990—; coaches rep. Ill. Swimming, Inc., Aurora, 1990-94, bd. dirs., tech. planning com., others. Nominated Coach of Yr., Nat. Jr. Coll. Athletic Assn., Ft. Pierce, Fla., 1984; named Sectional Coach of Yr. Ill. High Sch. Assn. Mem. Ill. Swimming Assn. (nominated Coach of Yr. coll. div., 1984), Nat. Interscholastic Swimming Coaches Assn., Am. Swimming Coaches Assn., Am. Coll. Sports Medicine, Nat. Strength and Conditioning Assn., AAPHERD, NEA. Republican. Roman Catholic. Avocations: computer, running, swimming, tennis, weight tng. Home: 504 Spruce Dr Apt 1A Palatine IL 60074-2315 Office: 1 Stevenson Dr Lincolnshire IL 60069-2824

SCHAUBMAN, AVERI LYN, social worker; b. N.Y.C., Nov. 2, 1955; d. Gerald Eli and Toby (Cohen) S.; m. Bruce Alan Stoebner, June 18, 1989. BA, Clark U., Worcester, Mass., 1976; MSW, U. Denver, 1979. Lic. clin. social worker; cert. practitioner neuro-linguistic programming. Child care worker ARCHway, Inc., Worcester, 1976-77; social worker Cen. Denver Youth Div., 1979-80; asst. dir. Roundup Fellowship, Denver, 1980-85; clinical social worker Cherry Creek Sch. Dist., Aurora, Colo., 1985—; pvt. practice Denver, 1988—; cons. Colo. Dept. of Edn., Denver, 1982-93; pro bono mental health care Mental Health Assn. of Colo., 1988-89. Project Dir. Research-needs assessment, 1981. Bd. dirs. Chestor House, Inc., Boulder, Colo., 1985-90. Recipient Chan Carmen Meml. Mental Health award, 1997; grantee Colo. Autism Project Devel. Disabilities Coun., 1981. Mem. NASW, Assn. Persons with Severe Handicaps (Colo. chpt. sec. 1984-86), Denver Assn. Retarded Citizens, Nat. Autism Soc. (Colo. chpt. bd. mem. 1979-83). Democrat. Avocations: backpacking, cross-country skiing, gourmet cooking. Home: 2554 Hudson St Denver CO 80207-3232

SCHAUER, CATHARINE GUBERMAN, public affairs specialist; b. Woodbury, N.J., Sept. 24, 1945; d. Jack and Anna Ruth (Felipe) Guberman; m. Irwin Jay Schauer, July 4, 1968; children: Cheryl Anne, Marc Cawin. AB, Miami-Dade Jr. Coll., 1965; BEd, U. Miami, 1967; postgrad. Mercer U., 1968, MPA, Troy State U., 1995. Writer, Miami (Fla.) News, 1962-63; tchr. Dade County Schs., Miami, Fla., 1967-68; coord. pub. info. Macon Jr. Coll. (Ga.), 1968-69; writer Atlanta Jour., 1969-72; editor Ridgerunner newspaper, Woodbridge, Va., 1973-75; pub. info. specialist Dept. Interior, Washington, 1980-82; writer Dept. Army, Ft. Belvoir, Va., 1982-84, chief prodn., design and editl., publs. div., 1984-85; head writer-editor SE region U.S. Naval Audit Svc., Virginia Beach, Va., 1986; pub. affairs specialist, tech. rep. for vis. ctr. ops., NASA Langley, 1986-90, project mgr., chmn. 75th anniversary yr., 1991-92; NASA Langley Rsch. Ctr., Hampton, Va., 1987-89, acting head Office Pub. Svcs., 1989, pub. affairs officer for space NASA Langley, 1993—; columnist, writer Potomac News, Woodbridge, 1972-85; guest lectr. George Washington U. Grad. Sch. Contbr. articles to profl. jours. Historian, publicity chmn. PTO, Woodbridge, 1974; publicity chmn. Boy Scouts Am., Woodbridge, 1974-83, Girl Scouts U.S., Woodbridge, 1974-79; bd. dirs. Congregation Ner Tamid, Woodbridge, 1984-85. Recipient Outstanding Tng. Devel. Support award U.S. Army, 1983; 1st place news writing award and 1st place for advt. design Fla. Jr. Coll. Press Assn., 1964, 1st place feature writing award, 1964, 1st place news writing award Sigma Delta Chi, 1965, 70th anniversary team NASA, 1988, Long Duration Exposure Facility Team award NASA, Combined Fed. Campaign Spl. award for Outstanding Svc. to Va. Peninsula, 1996. Mem. Va. Press Women (1st Pl. Govt. Mags. 1991, 3d Pl. Govt. Brochures 1991, 1st Pl. Govt. Brochures 1993, 1st Pl. Govt. Media Campaign 1993, 2nd Pl. Pub. Svc. Campaign, 1996, 1st Pl. Govt. Pub. Svc. Campaign 1996, 1st Pl. Pub. Svc. Campaign 1997), Women in Comms., Nat. Fedn. Press Women (life, 1st Pl. Govt. Mag. 1991, 1st Pl. Govt. Media Campaign 1993, 96, 1st Pl. Govt. Internal Comm. Campaign 1996), Internat. Assn. Bus. Communicators (1st Place Mktg. Campaign award 1996, 1st Pl. award of excellence Pub. Svc. Campaign, 1996). Democrat. Office: NASA Langley Rsch Ctr Mail Code 160 Hampton VA 23681-0001

SCHAUER, FREDERICK FRANKLIN, legal educator; b. Newark, Jan. 15, 1946; s. John Adolph and Clara (Balayti) S.; m. Margery Clare Stone, Aug. 25, 1968 (div. June, 1982); m. Virginia Jo Wise, May 25, 1985. AB, Dartmouth Coll., 1967, MBA, 1968; JD, Harvard U., 1972. Bar: Mass. 1972, U.S. Supreme Ct. 1976. Assoc. Fine & Ambrogne, Boston, 1972-74; asst. prof. law W.Va. U., Morgantown, 1974-76, assoc. prof., 1976-78; assoc. prof. Coll. William and Mary, Williamsburg, Va., 1978-80, Cutler prof., 1980-83; prof. of law U. Mich., Ann Arbor, 1983-90; Frank Stanton prof. of 1st Amendment Kennedy Sch. of Govt., Harvard U., Cambridge, Mass., 1990—, acad. dean, 1997—; vis. scholar, mem. faculty law Wolfson Coll. Cambridge (Eng.) U., 1977-78; vis. prof. Law Sch., U. Chgo., 1990; vis. fellow Australian Nat. U., 1993; William Morton Disting. Sr. fellow in humanities Dartmouth Coll., 1991; vis. prof. law Harvard Law Sch., 1996; Ewald Disting. vis. prof. law U. Va., 1996, vis. prof. govt. Dartmouth Coll., 1997. Author: The Law of Obscenity, 1976, Free Speech: A Philosophical Enquiry, 1982 (ABA cert. merit 1983), Supplements to Gunther Constitutional Law, 1983-96, Playing by the Rules: A Philosophical Examination of Rule Based Decision-Making in Law and Life, 1991, The First Amendment: A Reader, 1992, 2d edit., The Philosophy of Law, 1995; contbr. articles to profl. jours. Mem. Atty. Gen.'s Commn. on Pornography, 1985-86. Served with Mass. Army N.G., 1970-71. NEH fellow, summer 1980. Fellow Am. Acad. Arts and Scis.; mem. Am. Philos. Assn., Am. Soc. for Polit. and Legal Philosophy (v.p. 1996—), Assn. Am. Law Schs. (chmn. sect. constl. law 1984-86). Office: Kennedy Sch of Govt Harvard U Cambridge MA 02138

SCHAUER, WILBERT EDWARD, JR., lawyer, manufacturing company executive; b. Milw., Oct. 28, 1926; s. Wilbert Edward and Gertrude (Nickel) S.; m. Genevieve Stone, June 23, 1951; children—Jeffrey Edward, Constance Emily, Gregory Wilbert, Martha Ann, Jennifer Caroline. B.B.A., U. Wis., 1949, M.B.A., 1950, J.D., 1950. Bar: Wis. 1950. Accountant Pub. Service Commn. Wis., 1950-52; with Rexnord, Inc., Milw., 1952-87; v.p. finance, treas. Rexnord, Inc., 1968-76, v.p. fin. and law, 1977-78, exec. v.p. fin. and adminstrn., 1978-86, vice chmn., 1986-87. Alderman, Brookfield, Wis., 1958-68; pres. Common Council, 1966-68. Mem. Milw. Club, Westmoor Country Club (Brookfield, Wis.), Bluemond Golf and Country Club, Moorings Country Club. Home: 3215 Gulf Shore Blvd N # Ph4 Naples FL 34103

SCHAUF, VICTORIA, pediatrician, educator, infectious diseases consultant; b. N.Y.C., Feb. 17, 1943; d. Maurice J. and Ruth H. (Baker) Bisson; m. Michael Delaney; 2 children. BS with honors in Microbiology, U. Chgo., 1965, MD with honors, 1969. Intern pediatrics U. Chgo. Hosp., 1969-70; resident pediatrics Sinai Hosp. of Balt., 1970-71; chief resident pediatrics Children's Hosp. Nat. Med. Ctr., Washington, 1971-72; rsch. trainee NIH, Bethesda, Md., 1972; asst. prof. microbiology Rush Med. Coll., Chgo., 1972-

74; prof. pediatrics, head pediatric infectious diseases U. Ill., Chgo., 1974-84; med. officer FDA, Rockville, Md., 1984-86; chmn. dept. pediatrics Nassau County Med. Ctr., East Meadow, N.Y., 1986-90; prof. pediatrics SUNY, Stony Brook, 1987-94; vis. prof. Rockefeller U., 1990-92; mem. vis. faculty Chiang Mai (Thailand) U., 1978; mem. ad hoc com. study sects. NIH, Bethesda, 1981-82; bd. dirs. Pearl Stetler Rsch. Fond., Chgo., 1982-84; cons. FDA, 1987-88, 93-95, Can. Bur. Human Prescription Drugs, Ottawa, 1990—, biotech. investors, 1993—; course dir. pediatric infectious diseases rev. course Cornell U. Med. Coll., N.Y.C., 1994, faculty, 1995. Co-author: Pediatric Infectious Diseases: A Comprehensive Guide to the Subspecialty, 1997; prodr. TV programs in field; contbr. articles to profl. jours., chpts. to books. Vol. physician Cook County Hosp., Chgo., 1974-84; mem. adv. com. Nat. Hansen's Disease Ctr., La., 1986, Nassau County Day Care Coun., N.Y., 1988-90; mem. adv. bd. Surg. Aid to Children of World, N.Y., 1986-90. Am. Lung Assn. grantee U. Ill., 1977; recipient contract NIH, U. Ill., 1978-81, grantee, 1979-84. Fellow Infectious Diseases Soc. Am.; mem. Pediatric Infectious Diseases Soc. (exec. bd.), Soc. Pediatric Rsch., Am. Pediatric Soc., AAAS, Am. Soc. Microbiology, Am. Acad. Pediatrics, Phi Beta Kappa, Alpha Omega Alpha. Avocation: walking.

SCHAUFUSS, PETER, dancer, producer, choreographer, ballet director; b. Copenhagen, Denmark, Apr. 26, 1950; s. Frank Schaufuss and Mona Vangsaae S. Student, Royal Danish Ballet Sch. Apprentice with Royal Danish Ballet, 1965; soloist Nat. Ballet Can., 1967-68, Royal Danish Ballet, 1969-70; prin. with LFB, 1970-74, N.Y.C. Ballet, 1974-77, Nat. Ballet Can., 1977-83; artistic dir. London Festival Ballet (now English Nat. Ballet), 1984-90; ballet dir. Deutsche Oper Berlin, 1990-93, Royal Danish Ballet, 1994-95; guest appearances in Can., Denmark, France, Germany, Italy, Japan, U.K., U.S.A., USSR, Austria, S.Am.; presented BBC TV series Dancer, 1984; numerous other TV appearances; created roles include Rhapsodie Espagnole, The Steadfast Tin Soldier (Balanchine), Phantom of the Opera (Petit), Verdi Variations, Orpheus (MacMillan); ballets produced include La Sylphide (London Festival Ballet, Stuttgart Ballet, Roland Petit's Ballet de Marseille, Deutsche Oper Berlin, Teatro Comunale Firenze, Vienna State Opera, Opernhaus Zurich, Teatro dell'Opera di Roma, Hessisches Staatstheater Wiesbaden, Ballet du Rhin, Royal Danish Ballet), Napoli (Nat. Ballet Can., Teatro San Carlo, Naples, English Nat. Ballet, formerly London Festival Ballet), Folktale (Deutsche Oper Berlin), Dances from Napoli (London Festival Ballet), Bournonville (Aterballetto), The Nutcracker (London Festival Ballet, Graz Opera Ballet, Deutsche Oper Berlin), Giselle (Deutsche Oper Berlin, Royal Danish Ballet), Tchiakovsky Trilogy (Deutsche Oper Berlin), Sleeping Beauty (Deutsche Oper Berlin), Swan Lake (Deutsche Oper Berlin); staging of Romeo and Juliet (Royal Danish Ballet); producer, choreographer (Royal Danish Ballet) Hamlet, 1996, Jury. Decorated officer Order of the Crown (Belgium); recipient Solo award 2d Internat. Ballet Competition, Moscow, 1973, Star of the Yr. award Abendzeitung, Munich, 1978, Evening Std. award, 1979, Soc. of West End Theatres Ballet award (now Oliver), 1979, Manchester Evening News Theatre awards-dance, 1986, Laker Olprisen, Copenhagen, 1988, Berlin Co. award for best ballet prodn. Berlinerzeitung, 1991, Edinburgh Festival Critics prize, 1991, Critics prize Edinburgh Festival, 1991; named Knight of the Dannebrog, 1988. Office: care Papoutsis Rep Ltd, 18 Sundial Ave, London SE25 4BX, England

SCHAUMBURG, HERBERT HOWARD, neurology educator; b. Houston, Tex., Nov. 6, 1932; m. Joanna Jane Austin; children: Barnabas Paul, Kristin Elizabeth. AB cum laude, Harvard Coll., 1956; MD, Washington U., 1960. Instr. in neurology Albert Einstein Coll. of Medicine, N.Y.C., 1964-67, asst. prof. neurology, 1967-69, assoc. prof. neurology, 1972-76, prof., 1976—, vice chmn., 1977-84, acting chmn., 1984-86, chmn., 1986—; instr. pathology Harvard Med. Sch., Boston, 1969-71. Mem. Am. Acad. Neurology, Am. Assn. Neuropathologists, Am. Neurol. Assn., Soc. Toxicology, Soc. Neurosci. Home: 616 King Ave City Island Bronx NY 10464 Office: Albert Einstein Coll Medicine 1300 Morris Park Ave Bronx NY 10461-1926

SCHAUPP, JOAN POMPROWITZ, trucking company executive, writer; b. Green Bay, Wis., Sept. 29, 1932; d. Joseph and Helen Elizabeth (Vander-Linden) Pomprowitz; m. Robert James Schaupp, Sept. 4, 1956; children: Margaret Schaupp Siebert, Frederick, John Robert, Elizabeth Schaupp Sidles. BS cum laude, U. Wis., 1954; cert. in theology, St. Norbert Coll., 1979; MA, U. Wis., Green Bay, 1982; DMin, Grad. Theol. Found., 1996. Woman's editor Green Bay Press-Gazette, 1955-56; freelance writer Green Bay, 1957-75; sec.-treas., dir. L.C.L. Transit Co., Green Bay, 1962-70; dir. P & S Investment Co., Green Bay, 1982—, mgmt. cons., 1984-89, dir. strategic planning, 1992, vice chmn., 1994—; pres. The Manna Co., Green Bay, 1992—. Author: Jesus Was a Teenager, 1972, Woman Image of Holy Spirit, 1975 (Thomas Moore Book award), Elohim: A Search for a Symbol for Human Fulfillment, 1995. Master gardener De Pere (Wis.) Beautification Com., 1991-92; lector St. Francis Xavier Cathedral, Green Bay, 1991-92. Mem. Am. Acad. Religion, Nat. Fedn. Press Women, Nat. Press Club, Soc. Bibl. Lit., Equestrian Order of the Holy Sepulchre Jerusalem (lady comdr. with star), Secular Franciscan Order (vice min. Assumption Province 1991-92), Franciscans Internat. Avocations: gardening, walking, swimming. Home: PO Box 358 De Pere WI 54115-0358

SCHAUT, JOSEPH WILLIAM, banker; b. Cleve., May 30, 1928; s. Francis Xavier and Emma Gertrude (Urmann) S.; m. Susan Stiver, Apr. 23, 1955; children: Deborah Anne Schaut Payne, Gregory F., Mary Theresa Schaut Bentley, Michael J. B in Social Sci. in Econs., Georgetown U., 1950, JD, 1953. Bar: D.C. 1953, U.S. Mil. Ct. Appeals 1953, U.S. Dist. Ct. D.C. 1953, U.S. Ct. Appeals (D.C. cir.) 1953, Ohio 1954. Tax analyst Republic Steel Corp., Cleve., 1953-60, asst. to sec., 1960-67, asst. sec., 1967-81; dir. corp. properties Republic Steel Corp., 1976-84; corp. sec. Republic Steel Corp., Cleve., 1981-84; bus. cons., 1984-85; sr. trust officer AmeriTrust Co. Nat. Assn., 1986-92; sr. trust officer Soc. Nat. Bank, Cleve., 1992-93, v.p., 1993-96; v.p. Mellon Bank F.S.B., 1996—. Served to col. USAR, 1950-78. Recipient award Silver Beaver Greater Cleve. council Boy Scouts Am., 1975. Mem. Am. Soc. Corp. Secs. (dir. 1976-79), Ohio State Bar Assn., Greater Cleve. Growth Assn., Delta Theta Phi, Pi Gamma Mu. Roman Catholic. Office: Skylight Office Tower 1660 W 2nd St Ste 920 Cleveland OH 44113-1454

SCHAWLOW, ARTHUR LEONARD, physicist, educator; b. Mt. Vernon, N.Y., May 5, 1921; s. Arthur and Helen (Mason) S.; m. Aurelia Keith Townes, May 19, 1951; children: Arthur Keith, Helen Aurelia, Edith Ellen. BA, U. Toronto, Ont., Can., 1941, MA, 1942, PhD, 1949, LLD (hon.), 1970; DSc (hon.), U. Ghent, Belgium, 1968, U. Bradford, Eng., 1970, U. Ala., 1984, Trinity Coll., Dublin, Ireland, 1986; DTech (hon.), U. Lund, Sweden, 1987; DSL (hon.), Victoria U., Toronto, 1993. Postdoctoral fellow, rsch. assoc. Columbia U., 1949-51, vis. assoc. prof., 1960; rsch. physicist Bell Tel. Labs., 1951-61, cons., 1961-62; prof. physics Stanford (Calif.) U., 1961-91, also J.G. Jackson-C.J. Wood prof. physics, 1978, prof. emeritus, 1991—, exec. head dept. physics, 1966-70, acting chmn. dept., 1973-74. Author: (with C.H. Townes) Microwave Spectroscopy, 1955; Co-inventor (with C.H. Townes), optical maser or laser, 1958. Recipient Ballantine medal Franklin Inst., 1962, Thomas Young medal and prize Inst. Physics and Phys. Soc., London, 1963, Schawlow medal Laser Inst. Am., 1982, Nobel prize in physics, 1981, Nat. Medal of Sci., NSF, 1991, Arata award High Temperature Soc. Japan, 1994, Ronald H. Brown Am. Innovator award U.S. Dept. Commerce, 1996; named Calif. Scientist of Yr., 1973, Marconi Internat. fellow, 1977; named to Am. Inventors Hall of Fame, 1996. Fellow Am. Acad. Arts and Scis., Am. Phys. Soc. (coun. 1966-70, chmn. div. electron and atomic physics 1974, pres. 1981), Optical Soc. Am. (hon. mem. 1983, dir.-at-large 1966-68, pres. 1975, Frederick Ives medal 1976); mem. NAS, IEEE (Liebmann prize 1964), AAAS (chmn. physics sect. 1979), Am. Philos. Soc., Royal Irish Acad. (hon.). Office: Stanford U Dept Physics Stanford CA 94305

SCHAYES, ADOLF, retired basketball player; b. N.Y.C., May 19, 1928. With Syracuse Nationals, 1948-63; with Phila. 76ers, 1963-64, coach, 1963-66; coach Buffalo, 1970-72. Named Rookie of Yr., NBL, 1949, Hall of Fame, 1972, NBA 25th Anniversary All-Time Team, 1970, Coach of Yr., NBA, 1966. Achievements include leading NBA in free throw shooting, 1958, 60, 62; All-Am., 1948; mem. Championship Team, 1955; All-NBA First Team, 1952-55, 57, 58; All-NBA Second Team, 1950, 51, 56, 59-61; twelve-time NBA All-Star game; all-time leading rebounder Phila. 76ers, 1948-64. Office: c/o Basketball Hall of Fame PO Box 179 Springfield MA 01101-0179

SCHECHNER, RICHARD, theater director, author, educator; b. Newark, Aug. 23, 1934; s. Sheridan and Selma Sophia (Schwarz) S.; m. Carol Martin; children: Samuel MacIntosh, Sophia Martin. BA, Cornell U., 1956; postgrad., Johns Hopkins U., 1957; MA, State U. Iowa, 1958; PhD, Tulane U., 1962. Asst. prof. theatre Tulane U., 1962-66, assoc. prof., 1966-67; prof. performance studies NYU, 1967-91, Univ. prof., 1991—; co-founder, co-dir. New Orleans Group, 1965-67; founder, dir. Performance Group, N.Y.C., 1967-80; founder, artistic dir. East Coast Artists, 1991—; bd. dirs. Theatre Comms. Group, 1977-78; advisor Internat. Theatre Inst., 1975-77, Ctr. Performance Rsch., Aberwrystwich, Wales, 1993—; pres. Bunch of Exptl. Theatres, 1975, 77, Fulbright Theatre Discipline Com., 1988-91. Author: Public Domain, 1968, Environmental Theater, 1973 (with others) Theatres, Spaces, Environments, 1975, Essays on Performance Theory, 1977, 2d edit. 1988, (with others) Makbeth, 1977, The End of Humanism, 1982, Performative Circumstances, 1983, Betweeen Theater and Anthropology, 1985, (with Samuel MacIntosh-Schechner) The Engleburt Stories: North to the Tropics, 1987, The Future of Ritual, 1993; editor: Dionysus in 69, 1970; co-editor: Free Southern Theater, 1968, Ritual, Play, and Performance, 1976, By Means of Performance, 1990; gen. editor: (serieis) Worlds of Performance, 1993—, Grotowski Sourcebook, 1997; editor: The Drama Rev., 1962-69, 85—, contbg. editor, 1971-85; adv. editor Jour. Ritual Studies, 1987—; adv. editor Text and Performance Quar., 1988—; dir. Dionysus in 69, 1968, Macbeth, 1969, Commune, 1970, The Tooth of Crime, 1972, Mother Courage, 1975, The Marilyn Project, 1975, Oedipus, 1977, Cops, 1978, The Balcony, 1979, The Red Snake, 1981, Richard's Lear, 1981, The Cherry Orchard, 1983, Prometheus Project, 1985, Don Juan, 1987, Tomorrow He'll Be Out of the Mountains, 1989, Ma Rainey's Black Bottom, 1992, Faust/Gastronome, 1993, Three Sisters, 1997, The Oresteia, 1995. Served with AUS, 1958-60. Recipient Modello prize, 1985, Contbns. to Theatre Spl. award New England Theatre Conf., 1991, Work in Theatre award Towson State U., 1991; grantee John D. Rockefeller 3d Fund, 1971-72, 76, Asian Cultural Coun., 1988, 95; Guggenheim fellow, 1976, Fulbright fellow, 1976, 83, N.Y. Inst. Humanities fellow, 1987-94, NEH sr. rsch. fellow, 1988, Am. Inst. Indian Studies, 1997. Office: NYU 721 Broadway 6th Fl Washington Sq New York NY 10003

SCHECHTER, ARTHUR LOUIS, lawyer; b. Rosenberg, Tex., Dec. 6, 1939; s. Morris and Helen (Brilling) S.; m. Joyce Proler, Aug. 26, 1965; children: Leslie Schechter Karpas, Jennifer Schechter Rosen. BA, U. Tex., 1962, JD, 1964; postgrad. U. Houston, 1964-65. Bar: Tex. 1964, U.S. Dist. Ct. (ea. and so. dists.) Tex. 1966, U.S. Ct. Appeals (5th cir.), U.S. Supreme Ct. 1976, cert. Tex. Bd. Legal Specialization to Personal Injury Trial Law, 1964-94. Pres. Arthur L. Schechter & Assocs., 1992-94, Schechter & Marshall, L.L.P., 1994—; spkr. Marine Law Seminar, 1983; spkr. in field. Contbr. to Law Rev., 1984. Bd. dirs. Theatre Under the Stars, Houston, 1972-78, Congregation Beth Israel, Houston, 1972-84, pres., 1982-84; pres. Am. Jewish Com., Houston, 1982-84, chmn. fgn. rels. com., chmn. United Jewish Campaign exec. com., chmn. 1993-94; pres. Jewish Fedn. Ctr. Houston, 1994-96; mem. fin. coun. Nat. Dem. Orgn., 1979; mng. trustee, mem. fin. com. Dem. Nat. Com., 1992—, fin. chmn. Tex. Clinton/Gore '96; vice chair Clinton/Gore Jewish Leadership Coun., 1996; v.p., exec. com. Nat. Jewish Dem. Coun., 1992—; mem. Leadership Cir., Dem. Senatorial Campaign Com.; mem. Deans Council, U. Tex. Law Sch. Found., Austin, 1981-84, U.S. Holocaust Coun., 1994—; pres. Beth Israel Congregation, 1988-90; bd. trustees Schlenker Sch. Coun. Recipient Svc. award Congregation Beth Israel, 1976, Samuel Kartt Leadership award, 1997, Pres. award NAACP, 1992, Love award Child Advocate Houston, Benefactor award Jewish Chautaqua Soc., 1995, Nat. Am. Jewish Com. Human Rels. award, 1996. Mem. ATLA, Tex. Trial Lawyers Assn. (chmn. admiralty sect., presenter 1985-87), Jewish Fedn. Houston (bd. mem., v.p., pres. 1994—), Houston Trial Lawyers Assn., Houston Bar Assn. Democrat. Jewish. Home: 19A Westlane Houston TX 77019

SCHECHTER, AUDREY, medical, surgical nurse; b. N.Y.C., July 6, 1934; d. Abraham and Ruth (Greenwald) Levine; m. Edwin Schechter, Sept. 1, 1957; children: Laurie, Michael. Diploma, Bellevue Sch. of Nursing, 1957; BSN, SUNY, Albany, 1987; MSN, Coll. Of New Rochelle, 1991. CCRN, TNCC. Crit. care nurse The Stamford (Conn.) Hosp., 1970-90, clin. nurse specialist, 1991-94; pacemaker testing nurse Cardiol. Assocs., Darien, Conn., 1974-87; preceptor/mentor for master's students Pace U., Purchase, N.Y., 1991-93; nurse Lyme Vaccine Investigation Study, Stamford, 1995—; asst. dir. of nursing Mediplex of Stamford, 1995—; leader for arthritis self-help classes, Arthritis Found., 1994-95; chart rev. Malpractice Legal Cons., Conn., 1994; mem. speaker's bur., Arthritis Found., 1994-95. Devel.: (in-house manual) Orthopedic Learning Manual, Bony Fragments - Orthopedic Bits and Pieces, 1990-94. Mem. AACN (treas. Fairfield County chpt. 1982-90). Avocations: reading, walking, theater, exercise workshops. Home: 158 Four Brooks Rd Stamford CT 06903-4624

SCHECHTER, GERALDINE POPPA, hematologist; b. N.Y.C., Jan. 16, 1938; d. Josif and Victoria (Nosi) P.; m. Alan Neil Schechter, Feb. 6, 1965; children: Daniele Malka, Andrew M.R. AB, Vassar Coll., Poughkeepsie, N.Y., 1959; MD, Columbia U., 1963. Diplomate Am. Bd. Internal Medicine, Am. Bd. Hematology. Intern, resident Presbyn. Hosp., N.Y.C., 1963-65; resident, fellow, rsch. assoc. VA Med. Ctr., Washington, 1965-70, staff physician, 1970-74, chief hematology, 1974—; asst., assoc. prof. medicine George Washington U., Washington, 1971-81, prof. medicine, 1981—; mem. hematology com. Am. Bd. Internal Medicine, Phila., 1985-91, bd. dirs., 1990-95, residency review com. internal medicine, 1996—. Mem. editl. bd. Blood, 1985-89; contbr. articles to hematologic jours. Office: VA Med Ctr Hematology Sect 50 Irving St NW Washington DC 20422-0001

SCHECHTER, ROBERT SAMUEL, chemical engineer, educator; b. Houston, Feb. 26, 1929; s. Morris S. and Helen Ruth Schechter; m. Mary Ethel Rosenberg, Feb. 15, 1953; children: Richard Martin, Alan Lawrence (dec.), Geoffrey Louis. B.S. in Chem. Engring, Tex. A&M U., 1950; Ph.D. in Chem. Engring, U. Minn., 1956. Registered profl. engr., Tex. Asst. prof. chem. engring. U. Tex. at Austin, 1956-60, assoc. prof., 1960-63, prof., 1963—; adminstrv. dir. Ctr. Statis. Mechs. and Thermodynamics, 1968-72, chmn. dept. chem. engring., 1970-73, chmn. petroleum engring., 1975-78, E.J. Cockrell, Jr. prof. chem. and petroleum engring., 1975-81, Dula and Ernie Cockrell prof. engring., 1981-83, Getty prof. engring., 1984-85, Getty Oil Centennial chair in Petroleum Engring., 1985-89, W.A. (Monty) Moncrief Centennial Endowed chair in Petroleum Engring., 1989—; vis. prof. U. Edinburgh, Scotland, 1965-66; Disting. vis. prof. U. Kans., spring 1968; vis. prof. U. Brussels, 1969; Disting. Lindsay lectr. Tex. A&M U., 1993; cons. in field. Author: Variational Method in Engineering, 1967, (with G.S.G. Beveridge) Optimization—Theory and Practice, 1970, Adventures in Fortran Programming, 1975, (with B.B. Williams and J.L. Gidley) Acidizing Monograph, 1979, (with D.D. Shah) Enhanced Oil Recovery by Surfactants and Polymers, 1979; (with Maurice Bourrel) Microemulsions and Related Systems, 1988, Oil Well Stimulation, 1991; contbr. (with D.D. Shah) numerous articles to profl. jours. Served to 1st lt., Chem. Corps AUS, 1951-53. Decorated Chevalier Order Palmes Academique; recipient Outstanding Teaching award U. Tex., 1969, Outstanding Paper award, 1973, Gen. Dynamics award for Excellence in Engring. Teaching, Gen. Dynamics Corp., 1987, Sr. Rsch. award Engring. Rsch. Coun. of Am. Soc. Engring. Educators, 1991. Mem. AIME, Am. Inst. Chem. Engrs., Am. Chem. Soc., Soc. Petroleum Engrs. (John Franklin Carll award 1994), Nat. Acad. Engrs., Sigma Xi, Tau Beta Pi. Developer methods of measuring surface viscosity and ultra low inter-facial tensions; discoverer instability of thermal diffusion. Home: 4700 Ridge Oak Dr Austin TX 78731-4724

SCHECHTER, STEPHEN L., political scientist; b. Washington, Nov. 28, 1945; s. William J. and Blossom (Rapaport) S.; m. Stephanie A. Thompson, Feb. 16, 1993; 1 child, Sarah J.; 1 stepdaughter: Kelly Anne Thompson. BA, Syracuse U., 1967; PhD, U. Pitts., 1972. Acting dir. Ctr. for Study of Federalism/Temple U., 1973-76; asst. to full prof. polit. sci. Russell Sage Coll., Troy, N.Y., 1977—; exec. dir. N.Y. State Commn. on Bicentennial of U.S. Constitution, 1986-90; dir. Coun. for Citizenship Edn. Russell Sage Coll., N.Y., 1990—; coord. We The People, 1992—; pres. N.Y. State Coun. on Social Edn., 1992-93; presenter workshops in field; sr. rsch. advisor N.Y. State Commn. on the Capital Region, 1995-97. Co-editor: World of the Founders: New York Communities in the Federal Period, 1990, Contexts of the Bill of Rights, 1990, New York and the Union, New York and the Bicentennial, 1990; editor: Roots of the Republic: American Founding Documents Interpreted, 1990, others; contbr. articles to profl. jours., chpts. to books in field; editor: Social Sci. Record, 1993-96. Chmn. Rensselaer County Bicentennial Commn., 1991; commr. Albany City Charter Revision Commn., 1997-98. Mem. Nat. Coun. Social Studies (state del. 1991), Internat. Assn. Ctrs. for Fed. Studies (co-founder 1976), Am. Polit. Sci. Assn., N.Y. State Acad. Pub. Adminstrn., others. Office: Russell Sage Coll 45 Ferry St Troy NY 12180-4115

SCHECKNER, SY, former greeting card company executive; b. N.Y.C., Aug. 8, 1924; s. Morris and Bella S.; m. Georgene W. Carrigan, Aug. 17, 1974; children: Barry David, Michael Matthew, Jeri Bella,. Student, CCNY, U. Pitts., U. Ill. Sr. v.p., dir. Papercraft Corp., Pitts, 1956-75, Am. Greetings Corp., Cleve., 1975-85; pres. Knomark, Inc., Plus Mark, Inc.; gen. ptnr. Doubletree Investments. Vice chmn. bd. trustees Tusculum Coll., Greeneville, Tenn. Served with U.S. Army, 1942-45. Decorated Purple Heart. Office: 1480 S Military Trl West Palm Beach FL 33415-9176

SCHECTER, ARNOLD JOEL, preventive medicine educator; b. Chgo., Dec. 1, 1934; s. Benjamin and Leonore Natalie (Lyon) S.; m. Martha-Jean Berenson, Feb. 14, 1964; children: Benjamin, David, Anna. BA in Liberal Arts, U. Chgo., Chgo., 1954, BS in Physiology-Neurophysiology, 1957; MD, Howard U., 1962; MPH, Columbia U., 1975. Diplomate Am. Coll. Preventive Medicine; med. lic., Ky., N.Y., N.J. Postdoct. Harvard Med. Sch., Boston, 1962-65, instr. dept. medicine, 1964-65; intern Beth Israel Hosp., Boston, 1966; gen. practitioner, sr. aviation med. examiner West Point, Ky., 1969-70; dir. inpatient rehab. ctr., drug and alcohol rehab. program Region Eight Mental Health and Mental Retardation Bd., Inc., Louisville, 1971-72; asst. prof. dept. psychiatry drug and alcohol programs SUNY, Bklyn., 1973-75; clin. assoc. prof. dept. preventive medicine N.J. Med. Sch., Newark, 1975-79; prof. dept. preventive medicine SUNY, Binghamton, 1979—; cons. U.S. EPA, Washington, 1985-86, WHO, 1986-90; dir. clin. rsch. in drug abuse, coord., faculty mem. Career Tchr. Tng. Ctr., 1972-75; assoc. dir. office primary health care edn., office of the dean N.J. Med. Sch., 1976-79; advisor Environ. Defense Fund, 1991-92, Nat. Vets. Legal Svcs. Project, 1991-92; co-founder assoc. editor The Am. Jour. Drug and Alcohol Abuse, N.Y.C., 1973-78, editorial bd. 1978—; editorial adv. bd. Substance and Alcohol Actions/Misuse, Elmsford, N.Y., 1979—; presenter in field. Author: Rehabilitation Aspects of Drug Dependence, 1977, Treatment Aspects of Drug Dependence, 1978, Biomedical Issues in Drug Abuse, 1981, Sociological Issues in Drug Abuse, 1981; author (with H. Alksne, E. Kaufman) Drug Abuse: Modern Trends, Issues and Perspectives, 1978, Critical Concerns in the Field of Drug Abuse, 1978; editor: Dioxins and Health, 1994; contbr. over 120 articles to profl. jours. including Organo-Halogen Compounds, Chemosphere, Women & Health, Toxicology and Applied Pharmacology, Am. Jour. Physiology, Am. Jour. Pub. Health, Jour. Occupl. and Environ. Health, Occupl. and Environ. Health, Environ. Health Perspectives; editor: Dioxins and Health, 1994. Major M.C., U.S. Army, 1967-69. Recipient Pacesetter award Commonwealth Mass., 1990. Fellow ACP, Am. Coll. Preventive Medicine, Am. Coll. Occupational Medicine; mem. APHA, AAAS, Assn. Tchrs. Preventive Medicine, Am. Coll. Epidemiology, Microscopy Soc. Am., Am. Soc. for Cell Biology, Am. Occupational Medicine Assn., Soc. for Epidemiologic Rsch., N.Y. Acad. Scis., N.Y. State Occupational Medicine Assn., N.Y. State Med. Soc., Broome County Med. Soc. Achievements include discovery of dioxin contamination of body tissues of general population of the U.S., that PCB transformer fires can lead to contamination of buildings by dioxins, elevated dioxin body burden from Agent Orange in Vietnamese and in American Vietnam Veterans; development of congener specific tissue analysis as biomarker for dioxin exposure. Home: 88 Aldrich Ave Binghamton NY 13903-1451 Office: SUNY Health Sci Clin Campus PO Box 1000 Binghamton NY 13902-1000

SCHECTER, WILLIAM PALMER, surgeon; b. N.Y.C., Dec. 14, 1947; s. Benjamin Robert and Ann Georgina (Saunders) S.; m. Gisela Franziska Fohlmeister, Sept. 1, 1974; children: Samuel Chaim, Anna Ruth. AB in Polit. Sci., Harpur Coll., Binghamton, N.Y., 1968; MD, Albany Med. Coll., 1972. Diplomate Am. Bd. Surgery, Am. Bd. Anesthesiology. Rotating intern San Francisco Gen. Hosp., 1972-73; resident in anesthesiology Mass. Gen. Hosp., Boston, 1973-75; resident in surgery U. Calif., San Francisco, 1976-79; pvt. practice San Francisco, hand surgery fellow, 1979-80; chief of surgery San Francisco Gen. Hosp., 1994—; prof. clin. surgery U. Calif., San Francisco, 1994—.

SCHEEDER, LOUIS, theater producer, director, educator; b. N.Y.C., Dec. 26, 1946; s. Louis W. and Julia H. (Callery) S. BA in English Lit., Georgetown U., 1968; postgrad., Sch. of Arts, Columbia U., 1968-69; MA in Performance Studies, NYU, 1995. Founder, dir. The Classical Studio NYU, 1991—; dir. NYU Tisch Sch. of the Arts, Shakespeare Ensemble, 1989-90; mem. adv. council Nat. Com. on Arts and Edn., 1977-82; mem. D.C. Commn. on Arts and Humanities, 1976-80; bd. advs. New Playwrights' Theatre of Washington, 1975-82; asst. stage mgr. Arena Stage, Washington, 1969-70; dir., producer Folger Theatre Group, Washington, 1973-81; cons. Ctr. for Renaissance and Baroque Studies U. Md., 1984-91; asst. dir. Royal Shakespeare Co. Stratford-Upon-Avon, Eng., 1988. Dir., prodr. plays including Creeps (Am. premiere), 1973, The Farm (Am. premiere), 1974, The Collected Works of Billy the Kid (Am. premiere), 1975, Henry V, 1976, The Fool (Am. premiere), 1976, Mummer's End (world premiere), 1977, Teeth 'n' Smiles (Am. premiere), 1977, Two Gentlemen of Verona, 1977, Mackerel (world premiere), 1978, Black Elk Speaks (tour), 1978, Richard III, 1978, Whose Life Is It Anyway? (Am. premiere), 1978, Richard II, 1978, As You Like It, 1979, Custer (Kennedy Ctr.), 1979, Charlie and Algernon (Kennedy Ctr.), 1980, Crossing Niagara (Am. premiere), 1981, Love's Labour's Lost, 1981; also dir. Broadway, Off Broadway, regional prodns. including (Broadway) Charlie and Algernon, 1980, (Off Broadway) Creeps, 1973, Passover, 1986, (Off-Off-Broadway) The Gettysburg Sound Bite, 1989, Brunch at Trudy and Paul's, 1990, The Christmas Rules, 1991, The Monkey Business, 1992; dir. All's Well That Ends Well, 1990; dance: dir. Near Ruins, Ruby, 1996, Let's Go Thundering, 1997; prodr. How I Got That Story (Off Broadway), 1982, Diamonds (Off Broadway), 1984, Today, I Am a Fountain Pen (Off Broadway), 1986; dir. Man. Theatre Ctr., 1982, 83, 84, Nat. Arts Ctr., Ottawa, Ont., Can., 1984, Hedda Gabler, Ctr. Stage, Toronto, 1985, Reg: Life in the Trees, GeVa Theatre, 1991; asst. dir. Broadway prodn. Carrie, 1988. Recipient Dixon award Georgetown U., 1968, Alumni Achievement award Georgetown U. Alumni Club Met. Washiington, 1981, Mayors Arts award, D.C., 1982, Acad. Excellence award NYU, 1995. Mem. Soc. Stage Dirs. and Choreographers, Episc. Actors Guild (coun. 1990-96). Home: 7 Stuyvesant Oval New York NY 10009-1901

SCHEEL, NELS EARL, financial executive, accountant; b. Spencer, Wis., Sept. 25, 1925; s. Roland Edward and Louise Ernestine (Hake) S.; m. Elaine Marie Carlisle, Aug. 28, 1949; children: Thomas W., John E., Martha L., Mark A., Mary E. BS, Youngstown Coll., 1949; MBA, U. Pa., 1950. CPA, Ohio. Staff acct. Lybrand Ross Bros., Cleve., 1950-54; asst. controller Century Foods, Youngstown, Ohio, 1954-62; treas., controller The Bailey Co., Cleve., 1962-63, Golden Dawn Foods, Sharon, Pa., 1963-82; v.p., chief fin. officer Peter J. Schmitt Co., Sharon, 1982-89; cons. to industry Columbiana, 1989—; part-time faculty Youngstown (Ohio) State U., 1954-94; bd. mem. Sovereign Cirs., Inc., North Jackson, Ohio, 1992—, bd. chmn., 1995—. Pres. Crestview Bd. Edn., Columbiana, Ohio, 1970-81. Staff sgt. AUS, 1943-46, PTO, hon. discharge. Mem. Am. Inst. CPA's, Ohio Soc. CPA's.

SCHEELE, PAUL DRAKE, former hospital supply corporate executive; b. Elgin, Ill., Aug. 6, 1922; s. Arthur R. and Helen M. (Christiansen) S. B.A., Coe Coll., 1944; M.B.A., Harvard, 1947. With Am. Hosp. Supply Corp., 1947—; pres. Harleco div., Phila., 1966-68; group v.p. Am. Hosp. Supply Corp., 1968-70; exec. v.p., also pres. internat. group Am. Hosp. Supply Corp., Evanston, Ill., 1970-74, v.p., asst. to chmn. bd., 1974-81. Chmn. bd. trustees Coe Coll. Served to 1st lt., inf. AUS, 1943-46. Mem. Harvard Bus. Sch. Club, Harvard Club Fla., Econ. Club (Chgo.), Tau Kappa Epsilon, Pi Delta Epsilon.

SCHEELER, CHARLES, construction company executive; b. Balt., June 20, 1925; s. George F. and Catherine Louise (Seward) S.; m. Mary Katherine Scarborough, Aug. 22, 1953; children—Charles P., George D., Donald C. B.S., U. Md., 1948, LL.B., 1952. Bar: Md. 1952; CPA, Md. With C. J.

Langenfelder & Son., Inc., Balt., 1949—; exec. v.p., treas. C. J. Langenfelder & Son., Inc., 1974-77, pres., chief exec. officer, 1977-95; chmn. bd. Rosedale Fed. Savs. & Loan Assn. Served with USN, 1943-46, PTO. Mem. AICPA, Md. Assn. CPAs. Office: 8427 Pulaski Hwy Baltimore MD 21237-3022

SCHEELER, JAMES ARTHUR, architect; b. Pontiac, Ill., Dec. 20, 1927; s. Aman B. and Jane (Steele) S.; m. Barbara Jean Lloyd, Sept. 2, 1950; children: James Erich, Carl Aman, Orissa Jane Elizabeth. B.S. with highest honors, U. Ill., 1951, M.S., 1952; postgrad., U. Liverpool, 1952-53. Grad. asst. U. Ill., Urbana, 1950-52; draftsman-designer Lundeen & Hilfinger, Bloomington, Ill., 1952-53; designer Skidmore, Owings & Merrill, Chgo., 1955-59; partner Richardson, Severns, Scheeler & Assos., Inc., Champaign, Ill., 1959-65; v.p., treas. Richardson, Severns, Scheeler & Assos., Inc., 1965-71; vice chmn. bd., dir. Prodn. Systems for Architects and Engrs., Inc., 1973-81; vis. critic U. Ill., 1959-60. Mem. Plan Commn., Champaign, 1966—, chmn., 1969-71; mem. Champaign County Regional Planning Commn., 1967-71; bd. dirs. Nat. Center for a Barrier-Free Environment, 1978—, pres., 1981. Served with USN, 1946-47. Recipient various archtl. awards.; Francis J. Plym fellow, 1953-54; Fulbright fellow, 1953. Fellow AIA (treas. Ctrl. Ill. chpt. 1967-68, sec. 1968-69, pres. 1970-71, nat. dep. exec. v.p. 1971-76, pres. corp. 1974-78, exec. v.p. 1971-76, pres. corp. 1974-78, exec. v.p. 1977-78, program devel. group exec. 1976-85, sr. exec. 1985-88, v.p. design practice group 1989, resident fellow 1990—), Internat. Union of Archs. Profl. Practice Commn. (sec. 1994—), Fedn. Colls. Archs. Republic Mex. (hon.); mem. Ill. Arts Coun. (archtl. adv. bd. 1966-71), Montessori Soc. Champaign-Urbana (dir. 1964-66), Gargoyle, Scarab, Phi Kappa Phi, Lambda Chi Alpha, Lambda Alpha. Episcopalian. Address: 11179 Saffold Way Reston VA 22090-3824

SCHEER, JULIAN WEISEL, business executive, author; b. Richmond, Va., Feb. 20, 1926; s. George Fabian and Hilda (Knopf) S.; m. Suzanne Fugler Huggan, Oct. 9, 1965; 1 child, Hilary Susannah; children by previous marriage: Susan, David Scott, George Grey. AB, U. N.C., 1950. Reporter Mid-Va. Publs., Richmond, 1939-43; asst. dir. Sports Info, UNC, 1947-53; pres. Scheer Syndicate, Chapel Hill, N.C., 1947-53; columnist, reporter Charlotte (N.C.) News, 1953-62; asst. adminstr. pub. affairs NASA, 1962-71; ptnr. Sullivan, Murray & Scheer, Washington, 1971-76; sr. v.p. corp. affairs LTV Corp., Dallas, 1976-93; ptnr. Murray, Scheer, Tapia and Montgomery, Washington, 1993—; bd. dirs. several corps. Free-lance writer, author. Trustee Highland Sch., adv. coun. Washington Coll.; bd. dirs. Sch. Journalism, U. N.C. With U.S. Mcht. Marine, 1943-46; with USNR, 1946-53. Mem. Algonquin Soc., City Tavern Club, Sigma Delta Chi, Pi Lambda Phi. Home: 8303 Old Dumfries Rd Catlett VA 20119-1940

SCHEER, MILTON DAVID, chemical physicist; b. N.Y.C., Dec. 22, 1922; s. Abraham and Lena (Brauner) S.; m. Emily Hirsch, June 23, 1945; children—Jessica, Richard Mark, Julia Rachel. B.S., CCNY, 1943; M.S., N.Y. U., 1947, Ph.D., 1951. Chemist Bd. Econ. Warfare, Guatemala, C. Am., 1943-44; research asst. N.Y. U., 1947-50; combustion scientist U.S. Naval Air Rocket Test Sta., Dover, N.J., 1950-52; phys. chemist U.S. Bur. Mines, Pitts., 1952-55; research scientist Gen. Electric Co., Cin., 1955-58; phys. chemist Nat. Bur. Standards, Washington, 1958-68; chief photochemistry sect. Nat. Bur. Standards, 1968-70, chief phys. chemistry div., 1970-77; dir. Center for Thermodynamics and Molecular Sci., Nat. Measurement Lab., 1977-80; research scientist chem. kinetics div. Ctr. for Chem. Physics, Nat. Measurement Lab., 1981-85; ptnr. McNesby & Scheer Research Assocs., 1985-89; rsch. cons. U.S. Dept. Energy, Germantown, Md., 1990-94; vis. prof. U. Md., 1980-81; Fulbright scholar U. Rome, 1982-83. Contbr. numerous articles to profl. jours. Served with USN, 1944-46. Fellow Am. Inst. Chemists, AAAS; mem. Am. Chem. Soc., Am. Phys. Soc. Home: 15100 Interlachen Dr Apt 512 Silver Spring MD 20906-5605

SCHEER, R. SCOTT, physician; b. N.Y.C., Oct. 24, 1938; s. Leonard and Josephine (Holtschl) S.; m. Beverly Joan Henry Scheer, Dec. 27, 1940; children: Kirsten Leigh, Laura Lynn. AB, Cornell U., 1960; MD, SUNY, Buffalo, 1965. Diplomate Am. Bd. Radiology, Am. Bd. Nuc. Medicine, Nat. Bd. Med. Examiners. Intern Santa Barbara (Calif.) Cottage Hosp., 1965-66; resident Cornell Univ.-N.Y. Hosp., 1966, Phila. Gen. Hosp., 1968-71; staff radiologist Meth. Hosp., Phila., 1971-72; assoc. dir. radiology Coatesville (Pa.) Hosp., 1972-77; dir. dept. radiology Norristown (Pa.) State Hosp., 1973-93; dir., chief exec. officer Med. Imaging Svcs., Chester Springs, Pa., 1977—; dir. radiology Scranton (Pa.) Imaging Ctr., 1993-94; cons. radiologist Oxford Valley Imaging Ctr., 1992-95, mng. ptnr., 1995-97; cons. radiol. expert, 1981—; attending radiologist Pottstown Meml. Med. Ctr., 1977-93; cons. in MRI, Fonar Corp., 1990-92; cons. radiologist U.S. Radiology Assocs., 1996—. Capt. U.S. Army Med. Corps, 1966-68. Recipient N.Y. State Regents Med. scholarship, 1961. Mem. AMA, Am. Coll. Radiology, Nat. Bd. Med. Examiners (cert.), Radiol. Soc. N.Am., Pa. Med. Soc., Pa. Radiol. Soc., soc. of Magnetic Resonance in Medicine, Chester County Med. Soc., Am. Inst. of Ultrasound in Medicine, Pa. Coll. Nuclear Medicine, Union League of Phila., Valley Forge Mountain Racquet Assn. Republican. Presbyterian. Avocations: photography, gardening, tennis. Office: Med Imaging Svcs 1420 Conestoga Rd Chester Springs PA 19425-1901

SCHEERER, ERNEST WILLIAM, dentist; b. Wabash, Ind., May 18, 1932; s. Ernest William and Anna Lucille (Bahler) S.; m. Ingrid Elvy Yvonne, Sept. 28, 1973. BS, Purdue U., 1954; DDS, Ind. U., 1961. Intern The Queen's Hosp., Honolulu, 1961-62; assoc. Pvt. Dental Practice, Honolulu, 1963-65; owner Pvt. Solo Dental Practice, Honolulu, 1965-75; ptnr. Dental Adminstrn., Honolulu, 1975-78; v.p. Scheerer & West Dental Corp., Honolulu, 1978—; chief Dept. Dentistry Queen's Hosp., Honolulu. Contbr. various clin. articles to profl. jours. Mem. Big Bros., Hawaii, 1968-74. Mem. Master Acad. Gen. Dentistry, Hawaii Acad. Gen. Dentistry (past pres.), Am. Coll. Dentists, ADA, Hawaii Dental Assn. (treas.), Internat. Acad. Gnathology, Pierre Fauchard Soc., Fedn. Dental Internat., Am. Equilibration Soc., Acad. of Osseointegration, Am. Acad. Esthetic Dentistry, Am. Coll. Dentists O.K.U., Hawaii Med. Libr. (sec.), Elks. Mem. United Ch. of Christ. Club: Pacific. Avocations: tennis, travel, Hawaiian music. Office: Scheerer & West Inc 735 Bishop St Ste 211 Honolulu HI 96813-4816

SCHEETZ, SISTER MARY JOELLEN, English language educator; b. Lafayette, Ind., May 20, 1926; d. Joseph Albert and Ellen Isabelle (Fitzgerald) S. A.B., St. Francis Coll., 1956; M.A., U. Notre Dame, 1964; Ph.D., U. Mich., 1970. Tchr. English, Bishop Luers High Sch., Fort Wayne, Ind., 1965-67; acad. dean St. Francis Coll., Fort Wayne, 1967-68; pres. St. Francis Coll., Ft. Wayne, Ind., 1970-93; pres. emeritus; English lang. prof. St. Francis Coll., Ft. Wayne, Ind., 1993—. Mem. Nat. Coun. Tchrs. English, Delta Epsilon Sigma. Office: St Francis Coll 2701 Spring St Fort Wayne IN 46808-3939

SCHEFFER, LUDO CAREL PETER, educational researcher, consultant; b. Bussum, The Netherlands, Sept. 3, 1960; s. Lukas Albert and Alida Johanna Theodora (Kassenaar) S.; m. Gwynne Rochelle Smith, oct. 1, 1994; 1 child, William Alexander. PhD, Free U., Amsterdam, The Netherlands, 1987, U. Pa., 1995. Cons., trainer Shell Netherlands, Rotterdam, 1987-88; cons. trainee Hollandse Beton Groep, The Hague, The Netherlands, 1988; rsch. asst. lit. rsch. ctr. U. Pa., Phila., 1988-90; rsch. asst. Nat. Ctr. on Adult Lit., Phila., 1990-91, lit. fellow, 1991-93, project dir., 1993—. Co-author: Students At Risk: Pitfalls and Promising Plans, 1993; (newsletter) NCAL Connections, 1994. Bd. dirs. CHAMP, Phila., 1991, Shelter Lit. Network, Pila., 1992; exec. dir., chair Shelnet, Phila., 1993. Recipient Cmty. Leadership award Internat. Ho. of Phila., 1991; named Phi Beta Delta scholar, 1992. Mem. APA (assoc.), Am. Ednl. Rsch. Assn., New Eng. Ednl. Rsch. Assn., Jean Piaget Soc., Amnesty Internat., Habitat for Humanity, So. Poverty Law Ctr., Phila. Concerned About Housing. Avocations: reading, arts, sports. Home: 507 S 45th St Philadelphia PA 19104

SCHEFFLER, ISRAEL, philosopher, educator; b. N.Y.C., Nov. 25, 1923; s. Leon and Ethel (Grünberg) S.; m. Rosalind Zuckerbrod, June 26, 1949; children: Samuel, Laurie. B.A., Bklyn. Coll., 1945, M.A., 1948; M.H.L., Jewish Theol. Sem., 1949; Ph.D. (Ford fellow 1951), U. Pa., 1952; A.M. (hon.), Harvard U., 1959; D.H.L. (hon.), Jewish Theol. Sem., 1993. Mem. faculty Harvard U., 1952-92, prof. edn., 1961-62, prof. edn. and philosophy, 1962-64, Victor S. Thomas prof. edn. and philosophy, 1964-92, professor emeritus, 1992—, hon. research fellow in cognitive studies, 1965-66, co-dir. Research Ctr. for Philosophy of Edn., 1983—; Fellow Center for Advanced Study in Behavioral Scis., 1972-73. Author: The Language of Education, 1960, The Anatomy of Inquiry, 1963, Conditions of Knowledge, 1965, Science and Subjectivity, 1967, Reason and Teaching, 1973, Four Pragmatists, 1974, Beyond the Letter, 1979, Of Human Potential, 1985, Inquiries, 1986, In Praise of the Cognitive Emotions, 1991, Teachers of My Youth, 1995, Symbolic Worlds, 1997; co-author: Work, Education and Leadership, 1995; editor: Philosophy and Education, 1958, 66; co-editor: Logic and Art, 1972; contbr. articles to profl. jours. Recipient Alumni award of merit Bklyn. Coll., 1967, Disting. Svc. medal Tchrs. Coll., Columbia, 1980, Benjamin Shevach award Boston Hebrew Coll., 1995; Guggenheim fellow, 1958-59, 72-73; NSF grantee, 1962, 65. Mem. Am. Acad. Arts and Scis., Am. Philos. Assn., Philosophy Edn. Soc., Nat. Acad. Edn. (charter), Philosophy of Sci. Assn. (prs. 1973-75). Office: Harvard U Larsen Hall Cambridge MA 02138

SCHEFFLER, LEWIS FRANCIS, pastor, educator, research scientist; b. Springfield, Ohio, Oct. 13, 1928; s. Lewis Francis and Emily Louise (Kloker) S.; m. Willa Pauline Cole, Aug. 9, 1949 (div. 1978); children: Lewis F. Fischer, Richard Thomas, Gary Arlen, Tonni Kay; m. Mary Lee Smith, Apr. 18, 1978; stepchildren: Kimberly McCollum, Jeffrey McIlroy, Kerry Buell. BA in Liberal Arts, Cin. Bible Seminary, 1950; AA in Bus., Jefferson Coll., 1989; MAT, Webster U., 1989. Quality assurance Tectum Corp., Newark, 1954-57; rsch. group leader Owens-Corning Fiberglas, Granville, Ohio, 1957-64; tech. asst. to v.p. R&D and Engring., 1960-63; rsch. administr. Modiglas Fibers Corp., Bremen, Ohio, 1965-68; dir. R & D Flex-O-Lite Corp., St. Louis, 1968-71; pastor Christian Ch., St. Louis, 1972-75; police commns. Brentwood (Mo.) Police Dept., 1975-87; pastor Christian Ch., Potosi, Mo., 1988-89, Slater (Mo.) Christian Ch., 1989-93, Clark (Mo.) Christian Ch., 1994—; asst. prof. English lang. and lit. Mo. Valley Coll., Marshall, 1989-93; adj. prof. theology Mo. Sch. Religion, 1993—; adj. prof. English Moberly Area C.C., 1996—; organizing co-chmn. aerospace composite materials com. ASTM, 1961; mem. exec. bd. Northwest Area Christian Ch., 1989-93; mem. Coun. of Areas of Mid-Am. Region Christian Ch., 1990-93; cons. in field. Contbr. articles to profl. jours. Patentee in field. Money raiser United Appeal, chaplaincy Blessing Hosp., Quincy, Ill., 1974; vol. Ill. Divsn. Children and Family Svcs., 1972-75; sec. exec. com. N.W. Area Christian Ch. (Disciples of Christ), 1992-94. Mem. Medieval Acad. Am., Mo. Philol. Assn. Avocations: philosophy and pomology. Home: 701 Walnut Laddonia MO 63352-9710 *Now and then, God has so touched people in such a way that, recognizing it, we think "So that's what God must be like!" and our ethical and moral sensitivities are heightened.*

SCHEFFMAN, DAVID THEODORE, economist, management educator, consultant; b. Milaca, Minn., Dec. 1, 1943; s. David Theodore and Fern Virginia (Maas) S.; m. Cathy Schutz, May 11, 1989. BA, U. Minn., 1967; PhD, MIT, 1971. Lectr. Boston Coll., 1970-71; from asst. prof. to assoc. prof. Univ. Western Ont., London, Can., 1971-81; sr. economist FTC, Washington, 1979-82, dep. dir., 1983-86, dir., bur. econs., 1985-88; Justin Potter prof., prof. bus. strategy and mktg. Vanderbilt U., Nashville, 1989—; prof., dir. Inst. Applied Econs. Concordia U., Montreal, Que., Can., 1982-83; adj. prof. Georgetown U. Law Ctr., Washington, 1986; cons. Ont. Econ. Coun., Toronto, 1973-81, GM, 1977, Ctrl. Oil Inquiry, Ottawa, Ont., 1982-84, Ctrl. Govt., Ottawa, 1979—, Can. Competition Tribunal, 1987-89, Can. Bur. Competition Policy, 1988-91, U.S. Sentencing Commn., 1988-89, PepsiCo, 1989-93, Kraft Gen. Food, 1989-92, PacifiCorp, 1989-93, NERA, 1991-93, Boeing, 1992—, LECG, 1993—, Berwind Industries, Inc., 1993-95, Comm. Ctrl., Inc., Applied Innovation, Inc., TEC, 1995—, Nortel, 1995, Coca Cola, 1996—. Author: Speculation and Monopoly in Urban Development: Analytical Foundations, 1977, An Economic Analysis of Provincial Land Use Policies in Ontario, 1980, Social Regulation in Markets for Consumer Goods and Services, 1982, An Economic Analysis of the Impact of Rising Oil Prices on Urban Structure, 1983, Strategy, Structure, and Antitrust in the Carbonated Soft Drink Industry, 1992. Recipient Dissertation Fellowship award NSF, 1967-68; vis. scholar U. Minn., 1978. Mem. Am. Econ. Assn., Strategic Mgmt. Soc., Am. Mgmt. Assn., Am. Mktg. Assn. Office: Owen Grad Sch Mgmt Vanderbilt U Nashville TN 37203

SCHEFTNER, GEROLD, marketing executive; b. Milw., June 1, 1937; s. Arthur Joseph and Alice Agnes (Gregory) S.; m. Chantal Scheftner; children: Mark A., Mary L., Michael D. Student, Milw. Bus. Inst., 1953, Great Lakes Naval Acad. Sch. Dental-Med. Surgery, USAF, 1955-56, USAF Inst., 1959, Marquette U., 1959-60. Territorial rep. Mossey-Otto Co., Milw., 1960-63; with Den-Tal-Ez Mfg. Co., Des Moines, 1963—; dir. fgn. affairs Den-Tal-Ez Mfg. Co., 1969-71; dir. Far Ea. affairs, 1971-72, exec. dir. internat. sales/mktg., 1973, v.p., gen. mgr. internat. ops., 1974—, also corp. dir., 1969—; chmn. bd. Den-Tal-Ez Ltd., Gt. Britain, 1974—; prs., mktg. specialist Heraeus/Jelenko; pres. S&S Scheftner, Ltd., Biel/Bienne, Mainz, Germany; adviser Kuwait M.O.H., Saudi Arabia; pres., mktg. specialist Productivity Tng. Corp., Calif., Tek-Scan Inc., subs. GE, Boston, Swift Instruments, Cosmetique SA Worben, Switzerland, specialist Infection Control Dental Surgery & Labs.;therapy equipment and apparatus Relaxodont (dental patient anxiety relaxer), Temple U., 21st Century Group, Jacksonville, Fla., OralSafe, Inc., Temecula, Calif.; mfr. disposable dental surgery instruments for WHO, Geneva. Pub. Zahn Dental Co. Catalog. Bd. dirs. Dist. Export Coun. Iowa, 1976-77; mem. Lake Panorama (Iowa) Devel. Assn., 1972-73; chmn. World Trade Coun. Iowa, 1976-77; adv. bd. bldg. program St. Charles Boys Home, Milw., 1963. With USAF, 1955-59. Recipient Presdl. Mgr. of Yr. award Den-Tal-Ez Co., 1967, Lectr. award Faculdade de Odontologia, U. Ribeirao Preto, Brazil, 1974. Mem. Am. Dental Trade Assn., Am. Dental Mfrs. Assn., Hong Kong Dental Trade Assn. (hon.), Saudi Dental Soc. (advisor sci. dental products, concepts), Internat. Platform Assn., Greater Des Moines C. of C. (dir. 1976-77), Lions. Republican. Office: S&S Scheftner Internat, Silbergasse 6, Hardernstrasse 12, CH-3250 Lyss Switzerland *Live enthusiastically, expand your natural attributes, be truthful and sincere, assume responsibility, avoid prejudice of the innocent, respect authority, live for today, but improve tomorrow-pray consistently and confidently, love and be loved, be proud of your noble heritage of being an American.*

SCHEIB, GERALD PAUL, fine art educator, jeweler, metalsmith; b. L.A., Dec. 26, 1937; s. Harry William and Olive Bauer (Cartwright) S.; m. Elizabeth Ann Galligan, Dec. 27, 1965 (div. 1978); children: Gregory Paul, Geoffrey Paul; m. Dedra Lynn True, Oct. 1, 1983; 1 child, Adam True. AA, East L.A. Jr. Coll., 1959, BA, Calif. State U., L.A., 1962, MFA, 1968. Cert. life teaching credential in fine arts, secondary and coll. tchr., Calif. Secondary tchr. art L.A. Unified Sch. Dist., 1963-77; prof. fine art L.A. Community Coll. Dist., 1977—; pres. faculty senate L.A. Mission Coll., San Fernando, Calif., 1983-84; bargaining unit rep., AFT Coll. Guild Local 1521; elected Arts and Letters chair L.A. Mission Coll., 1993; owner, mgr. Artificers Bench, Sylmar, Calif., 1976—. Policy bd. mem. The Calif. Arts Project, 1995-97. With USNR, 1955—. Recipient of tribute City of L.A., 1983, Citizen of Month award, Los Angeles County, 1983. Mem. Calif. Art Edn. Assn. (membership chmn. 1985-87, pres.-elect 1989-91, pres. 1991-93, Calif.'s Outstanding Art Educator in Higher Edn. 1994-95), San Fernando Active 20-30 Club (pres. 1981-82), Nat. Assn. Scholars, Sons of Union Vets of Civil War, U.S. Naval Cryptologic Vets. Assn. Republican. Avocations: collecting antiques, creating custom jewelry. Office: 13356 Eldridge Ave Sylmar CA 91342-3200

SCHEIBE, KARL EDWARD, psychology educator; b. Belleville, Ill., Mar. 5, 1937; s. John Henry and Esther Julia (Friesen) S.; m. Elizabeth Wentworth Mixter, Sept. 10, 1961; children: David Sawyer, Robert Daniel. B.S., Trinity Coll., 1959; Ph.D., U. Calif.-Berkeley, 1963; M.A. (hon.), Wesleyan U., 1973. Faculty mem. Wesleyan U., Middletown, Conn., 1963—, prof. psychology, 1973—, chmn. dept., 1973-76, 79-81, 86-88; v.p. Stonington Inst., 1984-91; dir. Saybrook Counseling Ctr., 1990—; vis. prof. U. So. Calif., 1974; dir. rev. panels NSF Sci. Profl. Devel. Program, 1975-81; cons. Am. Council Edn., 1975-81. Author: Beliefs and Values, 1970, Mirror, Masks, Lies and Secrets, 1979, Studies in Social Identity, 1983, Self Studies: The Psychology of Self and Identity, 1995. Trustee Trinity Coll., Hartford, Conn., 1977-83; moderator congregation First Ch. of Christ, Middletown, 1981-82. Woodrow Wilson fellow, 1959; NSF fellow, 1961; NIMH research grantee, 1964-68; Fulbright fellow Cath. U. Sao Paulo, Brazil, 1972-73, 84. Mem. Am. Psychol. Assn., New Eng. Psychol. Assn., Eastern Psychol. Assn., Conn. Acad. Arts and Scis., Phi Beta Kappa. Congregationalist. Home: 11 Long Ln Middletown CT 06457-4046 Office: Wesleyan U Dept Psychology Middletown CT 06459

SCHEIBEL, ARNOLD BERNARD, psychiatrist, educator, research director; b. N.Y.C., Jan. 18, 1923; s. William and Ethel (Greenberg) S.; m. Madge Mila Ragland, Mar. 3, 1950 (dec. Jan. 1977); m. Marian Diamond, Sept. 1982. B.A., Columbia U., 1944, M.D., 1946; M.S., U. Ill., 1952. Intern Mt. Sinai Hosp., N.Y.C., 1946-47; resident psychiatry Barnes and McMillan Hosp., St. Louis, 1947-48, Ill. Neuropsychiat. Inst., Chgo., 1950-52; asst. prof. psychiatry and anatomy U. Tenn. Med. Sch., 1952-53, assoc. prof., 1953-55; assoc. prof. UCLA Med. Center, 1955-67, prof. psychiatry and anatomy, 1967—, mem. Brain Rsch. Inst., 1960—, acting dir. Brain Rsch. Inst., 1987-90, dir., 1990-95; cons. VA hosps., Los Angeles, 1956—. Contbr. numerous articles to tech. jours, chpts. to books.; editorial bd.: Brain Research, 1967-77, Developmental Psychobiology, 1968—, Internat. Jour. Neurosci., 1969—, Jour. Biol. Psychiatry, 1968—, Jour. Theoretical Biology, 1980—. Mem. Pres.'s Commn. on Aging, Nat. Inst. Aging, 1980—. Served with AUS, 1943-46; from lt. to capt. M.C. AUS, 1948-50. Guggenheim fellow (with wife), 1953-54, 59. Fellow Am. Acad. Arts and Scis., Norwegian Acad. Scis., Am. Psychiat. Assn. (life); mem. AAAS, Am. Neurol. Assn., Soc. Neuorosci., Pyschiat. Rsch. Assn. Am. Assn. Anatomists, Soc. Biol. Psychiatry (Luckman Tchg. award 1997), So. Calif. Psychiat. Assn. Home: 16231 Morrison St Encino CA 91436-1331 Office: Dept of Med Research UCLA Los Angeles CA 90024 *Intense personal tragedy can embitter life and choke off further personal creativity. It may also offer the opportunity to open new doors in the discovery of self. I am more aware than ever of my good fortune in having the opportunity to teach, to continue investigative work in the structure and function of the brain, and to give love and care to those who need it. I am more than ever convinced that loving and being loved is the greatest good that we can know, the state in which we most nearly fulfill our roles as human beings.*

SCHEIBEL, JAMES ALLEN, volunteer service executive; b. St. Paul, Aug. 30, 1947; s. Donald Louis and Beverly Wanda (Call) Urista; m. Mary Pat Lee, July 10, 1987.. AA, Nazareth Hall, 1967; BA, St. John's U., 1969; Hon. Doctorate, Coll. St. Catherine, 1993. City coun. aide to Joanne Showalter St. Paul, 1978-79; vol. 15th anniversary VISTA, 1979-80; v.p. Mondale's Youth Employment Task Force, Washington, 1980-81; assoc. dir. Citizen Heritage Ctr., St. Paul, 1981-82; city coun. mem. City of St. Paul, 1982-89, mayor, 1990-94; v.p., dir. domestic vol. svc. programs Corp. Nat. Svc., Washington, 1994—; mem. nat. adv. coun. Ctr. for Global Org., 1990—; chmn. U.S. Conf. of Mayors Task Force on Hunger, 1990-94; mem. Lifelong Literacy Project, St. Paul, 1990-94; mem., bd. dirs. Nat. Law Ctr. on Homelessness and Poverty. Mem. Partnership for Democracy, Washington, 1988-91. Recipient Spurgeon award, 1985, Am. Jewish Com. Humanitarian award, 1990, Chip Fricke award Nagasaki Sister City Com., 1993, Bravo award St. Paul C. of C., 1993. Office: Corp for Nat Svc Office of CEO Domestic Volunteer Svc Program 1201 New York Ave NW Washington DC 20525-0001

SCHEIBEL, KENNETH MAYNARD, journalist; b. Campbell, Nebr., May 17, 1920; s. G. Alfred and Rachel Christine (Koch) S.; m. Helen Schmitt, May 14, 1955 (div. Sept. 1977); children: Victor Warren Schmitt, William Becker Schmitt, Kenneth Jr., Sally. Student, George Washington U., 1938-41; BA, U. Va., 1947, MA, 1949. Mag. salesman Periodical Pubs. Service Bur., Inc., 1935-38; reporter Internat. News Service, Washington, 1940-41, Wall St. Jour., Washington, 1949-51; Washington corr. Gannett Newspapers, 1951-63; syndicated columnist N.Am. Newspaper Alliance, 1963-64; chief Washington bur. Donrey Media Group, 1964-67; founder, bur. chief Washington Bur. News, 1967—; founder nat. syndicated column Washington Farm Beat, 1970-85; Washington corr. Wis. State Jour., 1963-66, LaCrosse (Wis.) Tribune, 1963-66, Billings (Mont.) Gazette, 1964-71, V.I. Network, 1966-67, Moline (Ill.) Daily Dispatch, 1967-68, Drovers' Jour., 1967-68, Newport News (Va.) Daily Press & Times Herald, 1969-71, Packer Pub. Co., 1964-74, Gasoline Retailer, 1966-67, Okla., Farmer Stockman; congl. corr. F-D-C Reports, 1975-77; Washington columnist Farm Jour., 1960-75; covered nat. polit. convs., campaigns; v.p. Fraser Assos. (public relations), Washington, 1976-79; Congl. broadcast interviewer. Contbr. nat. mags., newspaper syndicates. Incorporator War Meml. of Korea, Washington, 1981; editor Nat. Ctr. Fin. and Econ. Info., U.S.-Saudi Arabian Joint Econ. Commn., Riyadh, 1985-86. Capt. AUS, 1941-46, 755th Tank Bn., 1942-45, Europe, North Africa, Italy. Decorated Bronze star, U.S. Army Occupation medal, Combat Infantryman badge; co-recipient Croix De Guerre (France), Thoth award for excellence in pub. rels., 1980. Mem. Izaak Walton League Am., White House Corrs. Assn., Overseas Press Club of Am., Am. Radio Relay League, Sigma Chi. Presbyn. Clubs: Nat. Press (Washington) (financial sec., gov. 1969-73, vice chmn. bd. 1971), dir. Nat. Press Bldg. Corp. (Washington) (1973, v.p., pres. club and bldg. corp. 1974). Home: 1325 18th St NW Apt 302 Washington DC 20036-6505 *The greatest sins are timidity and self indulgence, the greatest virtue is to love. Live each day, don't fret about yesterday or tomorrow. Enjoy the senses, learn from others, and never forget that both love and hate are returned.*

SCHEIBER, HARRY N., law educator; b. N.Y.C., 1935. BA, Columbia U., 1955; MA, Cornell U., 1957, PhD, 1961; MA (hon.), Dartmouth Coll., 1965. instr. to assoc. prof. history Dartmouth Coll., 1960-68, prof., 1968-71; prof. Am. history U. Calif., San Diego, 1971-80; prof. law Boalt Hall, U. Calif., Berkeley, 1980—, chmn. jurisprudence and social policy program, 1982-84, 90-93, assoc. dean, 1990-93, 96—; The Stefan Riesenfeld Prof., 1991—; vice chair Univ. Academic Senate, 1993-94. chair, 1994-95; Fulbright disting. sr. lectr., Australia, 1983, marine affairs coord. Calif. Sea Grant Coll. Program, 1989—; vis. rsch. prof. Law Inst. U. Uppsala, Sweden, 1995. Chmn. Littleton Griswold Prize Legal History, 1985-88; pres. N.H. Civil Liberties Union, 1969-70; chmn. Project '87 Task Force on Pub. Programs, Washington, 1982-85; dir. Berkeley Seminar on Federalism, 1986—; cons. judiciary study U.S. Adv. Commn. Intergovernmental Rels., 1985-88; dir. NEH Inst. on Constitutionalism, U. Calif., Berkeley, 1986-87, 88-91. Recipient Sea Grant Colls. award, 1981-83, 84-85, 86-96; fellow Ctr. Advanced Study in Behavioral Scis., Stanford Calif., 1967, 71; Guggenheim fellow, 1971, 88; Rockefeller Found. humanities fellow, 1979, NEH fellow, 1985-86; NSF grantee, 1979, 80, 88-89; Fellow U. Calif. Humanities Rsch. Inst., 1989. Mem. Am. Hist. Assn., Orgn. Am. Historians, Am. Soc. Intl. Law, Agrl. History Soc. (pres. 1978), Econ. History Assn. (trustee 1978-80), Law and Soc. Assn. (trustee 1979-81, 1996—), Am. Soc. Legal History (dir. 1982-86, 90-93, 96—), Nat. Assessment History and Citizenship Edn. (chmn. nat. acad. bd. 1986-87), Marine Affairs and Policy Assn. (bd. dirs. 1991-96), Ocean Governance Study Group (steering com. 1991—), Internat. Coun. Environ. Law. Author numerous books including: (with L. Friedman) American Law and the Constitutional Order, 1978, 2d edit. 1988; contbr. articles to law revs.and social sci. jours., 1963—. Office: U Calif Berkeley Law Sch Boalt Hall Berkeley CA 94720-2150

SCHEIBER, STEPHEN CARL, psychiatrist; b. N.Y.C., May 2, 1938; s. Irving Martin and Frieda Olga (Schor) S.; m. Mary Ann McDonnell, Sept. 14, 1965; children: Lisa Susan, Martin Irving, Laura Ann. BA, Columbia Coll., 1960; MD, SUNY, Buffalo, 1964. Diplomate Am. Bd. Psychiatry and Neurology. Intern Mary Fletcher Hosp., Burlington, Vt., 1964-65; resident in psychiatry Strong Meml. Hosp., Rochester, N.Y., 1967-70; asst. prof. U. Ariz., Tucson, 1970-76, assoc. prof., 1976-81, prof., 1981-86; exec. sec. Am. Bd. Psychiatry and Neurology, Inc., Deerfield, Ill., 1986-89; exec. v.p. Am. Bd. Psychiatry and Neurology, Inc., 1989—; adj. prof. psychiatry Northwestern U., Chgo. and Evanston, 1986—, Med. Coll. Wis., Milw., 1986—. Co-editor: The Impaired Physician, 1983, Certification, Recertification and Lifetime Learning in Psychiatry, 1994; contbr. articles to profl. jours. Mem. med. adv. com. Casas de los Ninos, Tucson, 1974-86; mem. mental health adv. com. Tucson Health Planning Coun., 1974-75; med. student interviewer Office of Med. Edn., 1975; mem. Glenbrook (Ill.) Norht H.S. Boosters Club, 1988-91; treas. Robert E. Jones Found., 1988-96. Surgeon USPHS, 1965-67. Grantee Group Therapy Outcome Studies on Inpatient Service, 1980, Dialysis and Schizophrenia Pilot Project NIH, 1978; recipient Outstanding Tchr. award U. Ariz., 1986. Fellow Am. Psychiat. Assn. (chmn. imparied physician com. 1985-88, cons. 1988-92), Am. Coll. Psychiatrists (bd. regents 1992—, treas. 1995—), Am. Assn. Dirs. Psychiat. Residency Tng. (pres. 1981-82), Assn. Acad. Psychiatry (Parliamentary sec. 1979*84, treas. 1984-88, pres.-elect 1988-89, pres. 1989-90), Group for Advancement of Psychiatry (invited mem., chmn. mem. edn. com. 1987-91, bd. dirs., sec. 1993-97, pres.-elect 1997), Oracle Heights Club (pres. 1983-84).

Democrat. Jewish. Office: Am Bd Psychiatry & Neurology 500 Lake Cook Rd Ste 335 Deerfield IL 60015-4939

SCHEICH, JOHN F., lawyer; b. Bklyn., Aug. 6, 1942; s. Frank A. and Dorothy (O'Hara) S. BA, St. John's U., N.Y.C., 1963, JD, 1966; postgrad., John Marshall Law Sch., Chgo., 1968. Bar: N.Y. 1967, U.S. Ct. Internat. Trade Admission 1969, U.S. Dist. Ct. (ea. and so. dists.) N.Y. 1971, U.S. Ct. Appeals (2d cir.) 1971, U.S. Supreme Ct. 1975, Pa. 1980. Spl. agt. FBI U.S. Dept. Justice, Washington, 1966-69; asst. dist. atty. Queens County, Kew Gardens, N.Y., 1969-72; pvt. practice John F. Scheich, P.C., Richmond Hill, N.Y., 1970-76, 79-91; ptnr. Raia & Scheich, P.C., Richmond Hill, N.Y., 1976-79; sr. ptnr. Scheich & Goldsmith, P.C., Richmond Hill, Hicksville, N.Y., 1991-95, Scheich, Goldsmith & Dreishpoon, P.C., Richmond Hill, Hicksville, 1996—; lectr. estate planning Nat. Bus. Inst., 1994; mem. assigned counsel panel for indigent defendants in major felony and murder cases 9th and 11th jud. dists. N.Y. State Supreme Ct., Queens County, 1972-94; lectr. Lawyers in the Classroom, 1979-91; chmn. arbitration panel Civil Ct. City of N.Y., 1981-90; bd. dirs. Ra-Li Brokerage Corp., v.p., 1975—; adv. bd. 1st Am. Title Ins. Co. Am., 1995—. Editor: Conashaugh Courier, 1989-92; mem. editorial bd., 1988-92; contbg. columnist, 1981-89. Mem. Com. for Beautification of East Norwich, N.Y., 1983—, bd. dirs., 1993-96, pres. 1996—; mem. Holy Name Soc. of Our Lady of Perpetual Help Ch., 1963—, sec., 1965-67, v.p., 1969-71, pres., 1971-73; bd. dirs. Conashaugh Lakes Cmty. Assn., Milford, Pa., 1981-90, organizing mem. Conashaugh Lakes Owners interim com., 1977-81, sec. 1981-82, v.p. 1982-84, pres. 1984-86, past pres. 1986-88; mem. St. Edward's Syosset, N.Y. Sch. Bd., 1986-90; parish coun. Our Lady of Perpetual Help, 1976-82, pres. 1978-80, fin. com., adv. to pastor, 1970-82, chmn. fin. com., 1979-82; bd. dirs. Northslope II Homeowners Assn., Shawnee-on-Delaware, Pa., 1988-90, 92-94; mem. East Norwich Rep. Club, 1982—, bd. dirs. 1984-87, 93—, v.p. 1987-89, pres. 1989-93; nat. trust and estate assoc. Meml. Sloane Kettering Cancer Ctr., 1994—; active Internat. Wine Ctr., 1985—, St. Edward the Confessor Ch., Syosset, N.Y., 1982—, St. Vincent Ch., Dingman Hills, Pa., 1977—, St. Dominic's Ch., Oyster Bay, N.Y., 1982—, Lincoln Ctr. Performing Arts, Inc., 1985—, Nat. Rep. Senatorial Com., 1988—, Bravo Soc., 1994—, Concern for Dying, 1984—, Sea Cliff Chamber Players, 1992—; mem. Nassau County Rep. Com., 1993—, St. John Vianney Roman Catholic Ch., St. Pete Beach, Fla., 1994—, Performing Arts Ctr. Pinellas County, St. Petersburg, Fla., 1994—. Recipient J. Edgar Hoover award, 1967, award of appreciation, Civil Trial Inst., St. John's U. Sch. of Law, 1991, 95, Disting. Svc. award, 1992, cert. of appreciaiton Conashaugh Lakes Cmty. Assn., 1990, Dist. Svc. award Kiwanis Club, 1992, Cert. of Merit for Disting. Svc. award Nassau County Exec. Hon. Thomas Gulotta, 1989, Presdl. Order of Merit award Pres. George Bush, 1991, Order of Merit award Nat. Rep. Senatorial Com., 1994; named one of Best Trial Lawyers in the U.S., Town and Country mag., 1985. Mem. ABA (cert. of appreciation Am. Bar Endowment 1992), ATLA, Pa. State Bar Assn., N.Y. State Bar Assn., Queens County Bar Assn., Nassau County Bar Assn., N.Y. State Trial Lawyers Assn., Ciminal Cts. Bar Assn., Internat. Platform Assn., John Marshall Lawyers Assn. (bd. dirs., pres. 1992—), Soc. Former Spl. Agts. of FBI, N.Y. State Assn. Criminal Def. Lawyers, St. John's Coll. Alumni Assn., Asst. Dist. Attys. Assn. Queens County, St. John's U. Sch. of Law Alumni Assn., St. John's Prep. Sch. Alumni Assn., Friends of the Arts of Nassau County, Inc., Cath. Lawyers Guild of Queens County, N.Y., KC, Brookhaven Wine Lovers Soc., East Norwich Civic Assn., Phi Alpha Delta. Avocation: collecting fine wines. Home: 170 Sugar Toms Ln East Norwich NY 11732-1153 Office: Scheich Goldsmith & Dreishpoon PC 10342 Lefferts Blvd Jamaica NY 11419-2012 also: 109 Newbridge Rd Hicksville NY 11801-3908 also: 3901 Conashaugh Trl Box 4042, Conashaugh Lakes Milford PA 18337

SCHEIDLER, JAMES EDWARD, business executive; b. Chippewa Falls, Wis., Mar. 11, 1946; s. Clifford James and Mary Margaret (Roch) S.; m. Ellen Marie Swiontek, Aug. 23, 1970; children: Matthew, Nathan, Mary. BA in Econs. and History, U. Wis., Eau Claire, 1968, MA in Tchg. in History, 1975. Tchr., coach Campbellsport (Wis.) Sch. Dist., 1968-69, Reedsburg (Wis.) Sch. Dist., 1969-72; salesman IBM, Madison, Wis., 1973-78; salesman, mktg. mgr. WAF Inst. Raltech, Madison, 1978-85; nat. accounts and nat. sales mgr. Spacesaver Corp., Ft. Atkinson, Wis., 1985-92; mgr. plan devel. and govt. rels. Wis. Physican Svcs., Madison, 1992-96; v.p. Tiziani Enterprises, Madison, 1996—. Chmn. Madison Night at County Stadium, 1980-84; mem. steering com. Wis. Basketball Coaches All Star Game, Madison, 1983—; founder, chmn. Badger Classic, high sch. basketball tournament, Madison, 1986—; mem. Queen of Peace Sch. Bd., Madison, 1987-89; pres. Edgewood H.S. Athletic Assn., Madison, 1991—; bd. trustees Edgewood H.S., Madison, 1995—; pres. U. Wis. Basketball Boosters, 1977, 88. Named to Hall of Fame, Wis. Basketball Coaches, 1993. Mem. U. Wis.-Eau Claire Alumni Assn. (bd. dirs. 1989—, pres. 1996-97), Mendota Gridiron Club. Roman Catholic. Avocations: golf, reading, youth sports, music. Home: 21 Frederick Cir Madison WI 53711-1646

SCHEIDT, W. ROBERT, chemistry educator, researcher; b. Richmond Heights, Mo., Nov. 13, 1942; s. Walter Martin and Martha (Videtich) S.; m. Kathryn Sue Barnes, Aug. 9, 1964; children: Karl Andrew, David Martin. BS, U. Mo., 1964; MS, U. Mich., 1965, PhD, 1968; postdoctoral studies, Cornell U., 1970. Asst. prof. U. Notre Dame, Ind., 1970-76, assoc. prof., 1976-80, prof., 1980—; vis. prof. U. Wash., Seattle, 1980, U. Paris (Orsay), France, 1991; mem. review sect. Metallobiochemistry NIH, Bethesda, 1991—. Contbr. articles to profl. jours. Fellow AAAS; mem. Am. Chem. Soc. (assoc. editor Chem. Revs. jour. 1980-85), Am. Crystallographic Assn., Sigma X. Democrat. Office: U Notre Dame Dept Chemisty Notre Dame IN 46556

SCHEIE, PAUL OLAF, physics educator; b. Marietta, Minn., June 24, 1933; s. Olaf Johan and Selma Pricilla (Varhus) S.; m. Mary Anna Harrison, May 18, 1963; children—Eric, Maren. BA, St. Olaf Coll., Northfield, Minn., 1955; MS, U. N.Mex., 1957; PhD, Pa. State U., 1965. Asst. prof. physics Oklahoma City U., 1958-63; asst. prof. biophysics Pa. State U., State Coll., 1965-73; prof. physics Tex. Luth. Univ., Seguin, 1973—, interim acad. dean, 1976. Contbr. articles to profl. publs. Recipient Faculty Alumni award, Tex. Luth. Coll., 1985. Mem. Biophys. Soc., AAAS, Am. Assn. Physics Tchrs., Am. Phys. Soc., Royal Micros. Soc., Sigma Xi. Lutheran. Lodge: Lions. Avocations: woodworking, gardening. Home: 207 Leonard Seguin TX 78155-5110 Office: Tex Luth Univ Dept Physics 1000 W Court St Seguin TX 78155-5978

SCHEIFLY, JOHN EDWARD, retired lawyer; b. Mexico, Mo., Aug. 25, 1925; s. Luke Clauser and Isabella (Sprankle) S.; m. Patricia Ann Lenhart, Dec. 27, 1947; children: John Edward, Jan Ellen. Sc.B., Brown U., 1945; J.D., Washington and Lee U., 1948. Bar: W.Va. 1948, Calif. 1954. Practice law L.A., 1953—; mem. firm Baker, Scheifly & Porter, Huntington, W.Va., 1949-53, McClean, Salisbury, Petty & McClean, L.A., 1953-57, Willis, Butler, Scheifly, Leydorf & Grant (and predecessors), L.A., 1958-81, Bryan, Cave, McPheeters & McRoberts, L.A., 1981-84; mem. firm Morgan, Lewis & Bockius, L.A., 1984-90, counsel, 1990—; lectr. tax law U. So. Calif., 1960-74. Author lectr. fed. tax matters profl. publs., insts. Dir. Presbyn. Intercommunity Hosp., Whittier, Calif., 1994—. Lt. USNR, 1943-46, 51-53. Mem. ABA (mem. coun. sect. taxation 1974-77), State Bar Calif., Los Angeles County Bar Assn. (chmn. tax sect. 1965-66), Jonathan Club (L.A.), Hacienda Golf Club (LaHabra, Calif.), Monterey Country Club (Palm Desert, Calif.). Home: 9441 Friendly Woods Ln Whittier CA 90605-1658 Office: Morgan Lewis & Bockius 801 S Grand Ave Los Angeles CA 90017-4613

SCHEIMAN, EUGENE R., lawyer; b. Bklyn., July 15, 1943. BA, L.I. U., 1966; JD cum laude, Bklyn. Law Sch., 1969. Bar: N.Y. 1970, U.S. Dist. Ct. (so. and ea. dists.) N.Y. 1971, U.S. Ct. Appeals (1st cir.) 1972, U.S. Ct. Appeals (5th cir.) 1973, U.S. Ct. Appeals (4th cir.) 1974, U.S. Supreme Ct. 1976, U.S. Ct. Appeals (2nd cir.) 1977, U.S. Ct. Appeals (fed. cir.), U.S. Ct. Appeals (11th cir.) 1989, U.S. Ct. Appeals (3rd cir.) 1990. Mem. Baer Marks & Upham, N.Y.C. Rsch. editor Bklyn. Law Rev., 1968, editor-in-chief, 1969. Mem. ABA (sect. on individual rights and responsibilities), N.Y. State Bar Assn., Assn. Bar. City of N.Y. (mem. com. comm. and media law), Philonomic Honor Soc. Office: Baer Marks & Upham 805 3rd Ave New York NY 10022-7513

SCHEIMER, LOUIS, film and television producer; b. Pitts., Oct. 19, 1928; s. Sam and Lena (Kessler) S.; m. Jay Wucher, Dec. 29, 1953; children—Lane, Erika. BFA, Carnegie Inst. Tech., 1952. With various animation studios, 1955-62; founder, pres. Filmation Studios, Woodland Hills, Calif., 1962-89; pres. Lou Scheimer Prodns., Woodland Hills, Calif., 1989—. Producer: (animated TV programs) Archie, 1968, Fat Albert, 1972 (Wilbur award, Scott Newman Drug Abuse Prevention award 1985), Star Trek, 1973 (Emmy award 1974), Isis, 1975, Tarzan, 1976, Space Academy, 1977, He-Man and Masters of the Universe, 1983, She-Ra Princess of Power, 1985, Ghostbusters, 1986, BraveStarr, 1987, Arch Angels, 1995 (feature film) Pinocchio and the Emperor of the Night, 1987, Happily Ever After, 1989. Recipient Christopher award, 1972, Emmy award, 1979. Mem. Nat. Acad. TV Arts and Scis., Motion Picture Acad. Jewish. Office: Lou Scheimer Prodns 20300 Ventura Blvd Ste 145 Woodland Hills CA 91364-2448

SCHEIN, EDGAR HENRY, management educator; b. Zurich, Switzerland, Mar. 5, 1928; came to U.S., 1939, naturalized, 1944; s. Marcel and Hilde (Schoenbeck) S.; m. Mary Louise Lodmell, July 28, 1956; children—Louisa, Elizabeth, Peter. Ph.B., U. Chgo., 1946, B.A., 1947; B.A., Stanford U., 1948, M.A., 1949; Ph.D., Harvard U., 1953. Teaching asst. statistics Stanford U., 1947-49; teaching asst. social psychology Harvard U., 1949-52; research psychologist, neuropsychiatry div. Walter Reed Army Inst. Research, also chief social psychology sect., 1952-56; mem. faculty MIT, 1956—, prof. orgnl. psychology and mgmt., 1964—, chmn. orgn. studies group Sloan Sch. Mgmt., 1972-81, Sloan Fellows prof. mgmt., 1978—; mem. bd., exec. com. Nat. Tng. Labs., 1962-64; cons. to govt. and industry, 1956—. Author books and articles in field. Served to capt. AUS, 1950-56. Recipient Aux. Research award Social Sci. Research Council, 1958. Mem. Am. Psychol. Assn., Am. Sociol. Assn., Phi Beta Kappa, Sigma Xi. Office: MIT Sloan Sch Mgmt Cambridge MA 02139

SCHEIN, GERALD D., publishing executive. Pres., pub. Real Estate Forum, N.Y.C. Office: Real Estate Forum 111 8th Ave New York NY 10011-5201

SCHEIN, HARVEY L., communications executive; b. N.Y.C., Sept. 15, 1927; s. Morris and Matilda (Feld) S.; m. Joy Carol Gitlin, Dec. 11, 1963; children: Mark David, Justin Harris. A.B., NYU, 1949; LL.B., Harvard U., 1952. Bar: N.Y. 1953. Asso. Rosenman, Colin, Kaye, Petschek & Freund, N.Y.C., 1952-58; gen. atty. Columbia Records div. CBS, also asst. sec. CBS, 1958-60, div. v.p. internat., 1961-67; pres. CBS Internat. div., 1968-71, CBS Columbia Group, 1971-72; pres., chief exec. officer Sony Corp. Am., 1972-77, chmn., 1977-78; exec. v.p. Warner Communications Inc., 1978-80; pres. Warner Plays, Inc., 1978-80; pres., chief exec. officer Polygram Corp., 1980-83; exec. v.p., dir. News America Pub. Inc., 1983-88; pres., chief exec. officer Skyband Inc., 1983-88; v.p., bd. dirs. Internat. Fedn. Phonographic Industries, 1969-73; mem. Marconi Internat. Fellowship Council; mem. adv. council Partners of the Americas; asst. sec. Franklin D. Roosevelt Found., 1952-58. Editor: Harvard Law Rev., 1951-52. Served with USNR, 1945. Mem. Phi Beta Kappa.

SCHEIN, PHILIP SAMUEL, physician, educator, pharmaceutical executive; b. Asbury Park, N.J., May 10, 1939; s. Irving and Henrietta (Setzer) S.; m. Dorothy Rosenfeld, May 28, 1967; children: Deborah, Andrew. A.B., Rutgers U., 1961; M.D., SUNY, Syracuse, 1965. Diplomate Am. Bd. Internal Medicine (chmn. med. oncology com. 1980-83). Intern Beth Israel Hosp., Boston, 1966-68, resident, 1968-69, 70-71; sr. house officer Radcliffe Infirmary, Oxford, Eng., 1969-70; instr. medicine Harvard U., 1970-71; sr. investigator Nat. Cancer Inst., Bethesda, Md., 1971-74, head clin. pharm. sect., 1973-74; dir. div. med. oncology Georgetown U. Hosp., 1974-83; sci. dir. Georgetown U. Cancer Ctr., 1974-83; v.p. clin. R & D worldwide Smith Kline and French Labs., Phila., 1983-86; chmn., CEO U.S. Biosci., 1987—; cons. oncology Walter Reed Gen. Hosp., Washington, 1971-84, Clin. Ctr., NIH, 1971-84; assoc. prof. medicine and pharmacology Georgetown U., 1974-77, prof., 1977—; adj. prof. medicine Brown U., 1983—, medicine and pharmacology U. Penn., 1983-, pharmacology Temple U., 1984—; mem. Nat. Pancreatic Cancer Project, 1974-79, Nat. Cancer Adv. Bd., 1994—; chmn. Gastrointestinal Tumor Study Group, 1974-83; FDA adv. com. on oncology drugs, 1979-81, Mid-Atlantic Oncology Program. Fellow Royal Soc. Medicine, ACP, Royal Coll. Physicians London, Royal Coll. Physicians Glasgow; mem. Am. Soc. Clin. Oncology (bd. dirs. 1979-83, pres. 1983), Am. Assn. Cancer Research, Am. Soc. Clin. Investigation, Am. Soc. Hematology, Assn. Am. Physicians, Merion Cricket Club, Am. Soc. Clin. Pharmacology Therapeutics, Sigma Xi, Alpha Omega Alpha. Club: Union League. Research on mechanisms of action of cancer chemotherapy drugs, prediction and prevention drug toxicity, treatment malignant and hematologic diseases. Office: US Bioscience 100 Front St Conshohocken PA 19428-2800

SCHEIN, VIRGINIA ELLEN, psychologist; b. Rahway, N.J., June 23, 1943; d. Jacob Charles and Anne S.; m. Rupert F. Chisholm. BA cum laude, Cornell U., 1965; PhD, N.Y.U., 1969. Lic. psychologist, Pa. 1 child, Alexander Nikos. Sr. research assoc. Am. Mgmt. Assn., N.Y.C., 1969-70; mgr. personnel research Life Office Mgmt. Assn., N.Y.C., 1970-72; dir. personnel research Met. Life Ins. Co. N.Y.C., 1972-75; asso. prof. Sch. Mgmt. Case Western Res. U., Cleve., 1975-76; vis. asso. prof. Sch. Orgn. and Mgmt., Yale U., New Haven, 1976-77; assoc. prof. mgmt. Wharton Sch. U. Pa., Phila., 1977-80; mgmt. cons. Virginia E. Schein, PhD, P.C., 1975—; assoc. prof. psychology Bernard M. Baruch Coll., City U. N.Y., 1982-85; prof. mgmt. Gettysburg Coll., Pa., 1986—, chair mgmt. dept., 1993-95. Co-author: Power and Organization Development, 1988; Author: Working from the Margins, 1995; mem. editorial rev. bds. Women Mgmt. Rev., Acad. Mgmt. Execs.; contbr. articles to profl. jours. Bd. dirs. Keystone Rsch. Ctr., Family Planning Ctr., Survivors, Inc., past pres. bd.; bd. dirs. Pvt. Industry Coun. Mem. Am. Psychol. Assn. (council reps. 1978-80, com. on women 1980-83), Met. Assn. Applied Psychology (pres. 1973-74), Acad. Mgmt., (rep. orgn. devel. div. 1979-81, mem. exec. com. women mgmt. divsn.), Internat. Assn. Applied Psychology, Am. Psychol. Assn., Psi Chi. Office: Gettysburg Coll Dept Mgmt Gettysburg PA 17325

SCHEINBAUM, DAVID, photography educator; b. Bklyn., Apr. 14, 1951; s. Louis and Rhoda (Feerman) S.; m. Vicki Golden, May 30, 1973 (div. 1975); m. Janet Ann Goldberg-Russek, Mar. 21, 1982; stepchildren: Jonathan Russek, Andra Russek; 1 child, Zachary. BA, CUNY, 1973. Instr. photography Pace U., N.Y.C., 1974-75, LaGuardia (N.Y.) Community Coll., 1975-78; assoc. prof. art Coll. Santa Fe, 1979-81, 82—, assoc. prof. of art photography, 1981—, full prof., 1996—; printer, asst. to Beaumont Newhall, Santa Fe, 1980-93; printer to Eliot Porter, Santa Fe, 1980-90; co-dir. Scheinbaum & Russek, Ltd., Santa Fe, 1979—. Author: (photographs) Bisti, 1987, Miami Beach: Photographs of an American Dream, 1990, Ghost Ranch: Land of Light, 1997; photography exhbns. include Pace U., 1974, Midtown Y Gallery, N.Y., 1977, Santa Fe Gallery for Photography, 1979, 81, The Armory for the Arts, Santa Fe, 1980, 1981, Sea Breeze Gallery, Block Island, R.I., 1982, Highlands U., Las Vegas, N.Mex., 1982, Gov's Gallery, Santa Fe, 1982, Santa Fe Festival for the Arts, 1982, Coll. Santa Fe, 1983, Dem. Conv., San Francisco, 1984, Mus. Natural History, Albuquerque, Bisti/Miami Beach Photogroup Coral Gables, Fla., 1990, Ctr, Met. Studies U. Mo., St. Louis, 1988, Earthscope Expo '90 Photo Mus., Osaka, Japan, 1990, Jamestown C.C., N.Y., 1990, Neikrug Photo Gallery Internat., Tokyo, 1987, Albuquerque Mus., 1998, Mus. Fine Arts, Santa Fe, 1998, Gallery of Contemporary Photography, 1998; in permanent collections Norton Gallery Mus., West Palm Beach, Fla, Amon Carter Mus., Ft. Worth, N.Mex. State U., Las Cruces, Ctr. Creative Photography, Tucson, Ariz., Mus. Fine Arts, Santa Fe, Bklyn. Mus., U. Okla., Norman, Bibliothèque Nationale France, Paris, Gernsheim Collection. U. Tex., Austin, Albuquerque Mus., Rockwell Mus., Corning, N.Y., Chase Manhattan Bank, N.Y. Pub. Libr., Fogg Art Mus., Harvard U., Met. Mus. Art, N.Y.C., Frito-Lay Collection, Kans. City, Expo 90 Photo Mus., Osaka, Coll. Art Gallery, SUNY, New Paltz, N.Y., Univ. Art Mus., U. N.Mex., Corcoran Gallery Art, Washington, Colorado Springs Fine Art Ctr. Inducted Wall of Fame Kingsborough C.C., N.Y., 1994. Mem. N.Mex. Coun. on Photography (founder, v.p., bd. dirs.), Santa Fe Ctr. Photography (bd. dirs. 1978-85). Jewish. Home: 369 Montezuma Ave # 345 Santa Fe NM 87501-2626 Office: Coll Santa Fe Saint Michaels Dr Santa Fe NM 87501

SCHEINBERG, LABE CHARLES, physician, educator; b. Memphis, Dec. 11, 1925; m. Louise Goldman, Jan. 6, 1952: children: Susan, David, Ellen, Amy. AB, U. N.C., 1945; MD, U. Tenn., 1948. Intern Wesley Meml. Hosp., Chgo., 1949; resident psychiatry Elgin (Ill.) State Hosp., 1950; resident, asst. neurology Neurol. Inst., N.Y., 1952-56; mem. faculty Albert Einstein Coll. Medicine, 1956-93, prof. neurology, asst. dean, 1968-69, assoc. dean, 1969-70, prof. rehab. medicine and psychiatry, dean, 1970-72; dir. neurology Hosp., 1966-73; dir. dept. neurology and psychiatry St. Barnabas Hosp., Bronx, N.Y., 1974-79; prof. neurology emeritus Albert Einstein Coll. Medicine, N.Y.C., 1995—. Cons. editor: N.Y. Acad. Scis., 1964, 84; founding editor-in-chief Jour. Neurologic Rehab., Rehab. Reports, Multiple Sclerosis Rsch. Reports. Served as capt. M.C. USAF, 1951-52. Fellow Am. Acad. Neurology; mem. Am. Neurol. Assn., Am. Assn. Neuro-pathology, Am. Soc. Exptl. Pathology, Phi Beta Kappa, Alpha Omega Alpha. Home: 9 Oak Ln Scarsdale NY 10583-1621

SCHEINBERG, PERITZ, neurologist; b. Miami, Fla., Dec. 21, 1920; s. Mendel and Esther Dobrisch (Asch) S.; m. Chantal D'Adesky, Mar. 12, 1971; children: Philip Asch, Richard David, Marissa. A.B. in Chemistry, Emory U., 1941, M.D., 1944. Diplomate: Am. Bd. Internal Medicine, Am. Bd. Psychiatry and Neurology. Intern Grady Hosp., Atlanta, 1944-45; resident in internal medicine and neurology Grady Hosp. and Duke U. Hosp., 1946-50; research asst. prof. physiology U. Miami Med. Research Unit, Miami, Fla., 1950-53; asso. prof. neurology U. Miami Med. Research Unit, 1955-57, prof. neurology, 1957—; chmn. dept. neurology U. Miami Sch. Medicine, 1961—. Author, editor books in field.; contbr. articles to profl. jours. Served with M.C. USNR, 1945-46, 53-55. Fellow ACP, Am. Acad. Neurology; mem. Am. Neurol. Assn. (pres. 1981), Assn. Univ. Profs. Neurology (pres. 1977-78), Am. Heart Assn., Nat. Multiple Sclerosis Soc. (mem. med. adv. bd.). Democrat. Jewish. Office: U Miami Jackson Meml Med Ctr 1611 NW 12th Ave Miami FL 33136-1005

SCHEINBLUM, ANITA FRANUSISZIN, pediatrics nurse; b. Durham, N.C., Aug. 22, 1965; d. Alfred John and Nancy A. (Atkins) F. BSN, Emory U., 1988. RN Fla.; cert. pediatric advanced life support. Staff nurse Children's Hosp. Med. U. of S.C., 1988-89; clin. nurse II, charge nurse pediatric ICU N.C. Children's Hosp., Chapel Hill, 1989-92; pediatric home care nurse Interim Healthcare, N.Y.C., 1993-95; pediat. and neonatal ICU nurse Fla. Hosp., Orlando, Fla., 1995—; chmn. primary nursing com. pediatric ICU; instr. in field. Altrusa Women's Club scholar, 1984-88. Mem. Alpha Chi Omega, Sigma Theta Tau, Rho Lambda.

SCHEINDLIN, RAYMOND PAUL, Hebrew literature educator, translator; b. Phila., May 13, 1940; s. Irving and Betty (Bernstein) S.; m. Shira Ann Joffe, Mar. 1969 (div. 1981); children—Dov Baer, Dahlia Rachel; m. Janice Clair Meyerson, 1986. B.A., U. Pa., 1961; M.H.L., Jewish Theol. Sem., N.Y.C., 1963; Ph.D., Columbia U., N.Y.C., 1971. Ordained rabbi, 1965. Asst. prof. McGill U., Montreal, Que., Can., 1969-72; asst. prof. Cornell U., Ithaca, N.Y., 1972-74; assoc. prof. Jewish Theol. Sem. of Am., N.Y.C., 1974-85, prof. Hebrew lit., 1985—, provost, 1984-90; dir. Shalom Spiegel Inst. of Medieval Hebrew Lit., 1996—; rabbi Congregation Baith Israel Anshei Emes, Bklyn., 1979-82; mem. publ. com. Jewish Publ. Soc., Phila., 1985-90; mem. internat. adv. com. Ctr. for Judaic Studies U. Pa., 1995—; mem. bd. acad. advisors Catalan Mus. Jewish Culture, Gerona, Spain, 1993—; mem. editl. com. Jewish Quar. Rev., 1995—. Translator: (novella) Of Bygone Days by Mendele Mokher Seforim, 1973, Jewish Liturgy: A Comprehensive History by Ismar Elbogen, 1993; author: Form & Structure in the Poetry of Al-Mu'tamid Ibn 'Abbad, 1974, 201 Arabic Verbs, 1978, Wine, Women, and Death: Medieval Hebrew Poems on the Good Life, 1986, The Gazelle: Medieval Hebrew Poems on God, Israel and the Soul, 1991, Chronicles of the Jewish People, 1996, (libretto) Miriam and the Angel of Death, 1984; mem. editorial com. Prooftexts, 1988—, Edebiyat, 1992—, Studies in Muslim-Jewish Relations, 1992—. Guggenheim fellow, 1988, Annenberg Inst. fellow, 1993; sr. assoc. fellow Oxford Centre for Postgrad. Hebrew Studies. Mem. Soc. for Judeo-Arabic Studies (exec. com.), World Union for Jewish Studies , Assn. Jewish Studies, Jewish Publ. Soc. (bd. dirs. 1987-93). Home: 420 Riverside Dr New York NY 10025-7773 Office: Jewish Theol Sem Am 3080 Broadway New York NY 10027-4650

SCHEINDLIN, SHIRA A., federal judge; b. Washington, Aug. 16, 1946; d. Boris and Miriam Joffe; m. Stanley Friedman, May 22, 1982; 2 children. BA cum laude, U. Mich., 1967; MA in Far Ea. Studies, Columbia U., 1969; JD cum laude, Cornell U., 1975. Bar: N.Y. 1976. With Stroock, Stroock & Lavan, 1975-76; law clerk to Hon. Charles L. Brieant, Jr. U.S. Dist. Ct. (so. dist.) N.Y., 1976-77; asst. U.S. atty. Ea. Dist. N.Y., 1977-81; gen. counsel N.Y.C. Dept. of Investigation, 1981-82; U.S. magistrate U.S. Dist. Ct. (ea. dist.) N.Y., 1982-86; with Budd, Larner, Gross, Rosenbaum, Greenberg & Sade, Short Hills, N.J., 1986-90, ptnr., 1990; ptnr. Herzfeld & Rubin, N.Y.C., 1990-94; endispute mem. Judicial Panel, 1992-94; judge U.S. Dist. Ct. (so. dist.) N.Y., 1994—; adj. prof. law Bklyn. Law Sch., 1983—; mem. 2d Cir. Conf. Planning Com., So. Dist. Adv. Com., 1991-94. Recipient Spl. Achievement award Dept. of Justice, 1980. Mem. Fedn. Bar Coun. (trustee 1986-88, 90—, v.p. 1988-90), N.Y. State Bar Assn. (chair comml. and fed. litigation sect. 1991-92), N.Y. County Lawyers Assn. (bd. dirs. 1992-95, chair tort sect. 1992-94), Assn. of Bar of City of N.Y. Office: US Courthouse 500 Pearl St Rm 1050 New York NY 10007-1316

SCHEINER, JAMES IRA, engineering company executive; b. Mpls., May 7, 1944; s. Samuel L. and Sally Scheiner; m. Kristin Scofield; children: Alec, Zachary, Meredith. BS in Civil Engring., U.S. Mil. Acad., 1965; MPA, MCE, Princeton U., 1967. Registered profl. engr., Pa. Cons., prin. transp. consulting divsn. Booz-Allen and Hamilton, 1971-79; dep. sec. adminstrn. Pa. Dept. Transp., 1979-83; sec. revenue Commonwealth of Pa., 1983-87; v.p. Huth Engrs., Inc., 1987-88; pres. Stoner Assocs., Inc., 1988-91; pres., COO Benatec Assocs., Inc., 1991—. Contbr. articles to profl. jours. Vice chair area bd. Leadership Harrisburg; group chair 1993 campaign cabinet capital region United Way; mem. Pa. Chamber Bus. and Industry Bd.; mem. Harsco Bd.; trustee Harrisburg Area C.C. Capt. CE, U.S. Army, Vietnam, 1967-71. Decorated Bronze Star, Purple Heart; recipient Disting. Svc. award Nat. Gov.'s Assn., 1986. Office: Benatec Assocs 101 Erford Rd Camp Hill PA 17011-1808*

SCHEINFELD, JAMES DAVID, travel agency executive; b. Milw., Nov. 11, 1926; s. Aaron and Sylvia (Rosenberg) S.; children from previous marriage: John Stephen, Shaina, Robert Alan; m. Elna Magnusson, 1994. BA in Econs. magna cum laude, U. Wis., 1949. With Manpower, Inc., 1948-78, salesman, Chgo., 1949-51, br. mgr., 1951-53, nat. sales mgr., Milw., 1953-56, dir. sales, corp. sec., 1956-59, v.p. sales, 1959-62, exec. v.p. mktg., 1962-65, exec. v.p. (sr.), chief ops. officer, 1965-76, v.p. spl. projects, 1976-78, mem. exec. com., bd. dirs., 1959-76, cons., 1978-84; exec. v.p., chief exec. officer, bd. dirs. Transpersonal, Inc., Any Task Inc., Manpower Argentina, Manpower Europe, Manpower Ltd. (U.K.), Manpower Australia, Manpower Japan, Manpower Germany GmbH, Manpower Norway, Manpower Denmark, Manpower Venezuela, 1966-76; pres. Travway Internat. Inc. - Funway Holidays, Funjet, 1976-81, Aide Svcs., Inc., Tampa, Fla., 1976-81; pres., chief exec. officer Travelpower Inc., 1976-84; sr. v.p. Carlson Travel Network, 1984—; mem. Hickory Travel Systems Inc., 1977-85, bd. dirs. 1978-85, pres., 1980-82, pres. emeritus, 1982—. Contbr. articles to profl. jours. Chmn. Cancer Crusade Milw. County, 1970; bd. dirs. Sinai-Samaritan Med. Ctr., Better Bus. Bur. Milw., 1979-90, Found. for Santa Barbara City Coll., 1989—, pres., 1996—; trustee Santa Barbara Med. Found. Clinic, 1990—; trustee U. Wis.-Milw. Found., 1981-91; mem. bus. adv. bd. U. Wis.-Milw., 1987—; mem. adv. bd. Sch. Fine Arts, U. Wis.-Milw., 1986-93; chmn. bus. adv. bd. Santa Barbara City Coll., 1988-92; dir. Santa Barbara Trust for Hist. Preservation, 1995—; mem. Greater Milw. Com., 1984—. With USNR, 1944-46. Mem. Nat. Assn. Temporary Svcs. (pres. 1975-76, bd. dirs. 1969-77), Univ. Club Milw., La Cumbre Country Club (Santa Barbara), Rotary Club of Montecito Calif. Home: 129 Rametto Rd Santa Barbara CA 93108-2317 Office: 9076 N Deerbrook Trail Milwaukee WI 53223-2474 *I do not often walk or look back where my footprints are. I prefer to walk that part of the beach I have never walked before. I am a person who thinks more about tomorrow than yesterday . . . more about what can be done than what has been done . . . more about challenges than accomplishments. Looking back is helpful only if I can find a sign to help me in my future.*

SCHEINHOLTZ, LEONARD LOUIS, lawyer; b. Pitts., June 2, 1927; s. Bernard A. and Marie (Getzel) S.; m. Joan R. Libenson, Aug. 16, 1953; children: Stuart, Nancy, Barry. B.A., U. Pa., 1948, M.A., 1949; LL.B., Columbia U., 1953. Bar: Pa. 1954, U.S. Ct. Appeals (3d cir.) 1959, U.S. Ct.

Appeals (6th cir.) 1968, U.S. Supreme Ct. 1972, U.S. Ct. Appeals (4th cir.) 1973, U.S. Ct. Appeals (5th cir.) 1981, U.S. Ct. Appeals (11th cir.) 1991, U.S. Ct. Appeals (2d cir.) 1993. Assoc. Reed, Smith, Shaw & McClay, Pitts., 1953-62, spl. ptnr., 1962-64, gen. ptnr., 1964—, head labor dept., 1980-86; dir. Am. Arbitration Assn., N.Y.C., 1980-96. Author: Exemption Under the Anti-Trust Laws for Joint Employer Activity, 1982, The Arbitrator as Judge and Jury: Another Look at Statutory Law in Arbitration, 1985. Vice chmn. Pa. AAA Fedn., Harrisburg, 1982-85 ; chmn. W. Pa. AAA Motor Club, 1979-82; trustee Montefiore Hosp., Pitts., 1976-79. Served with USN, 1945-46. Mem. ABA, Pa. Bar Assn., Allegheny County Bar Assn. Republican. Jewish. Home: 746 Pinoak Rd Pittsburgh PA 15243-1153 Office: Reed Smith Shaw & McClay Mellon Sq 435 6th Ave Pittsburgh PA 15219-1809

SCHEINKMAN, JOSÉ ALEXANDRE, economics educator; b. Rio de Janeiro, Brazil, Jan. 11, 1948; s. Samuel and Sara (Lerner) S.; m. Michele Zitrin, Dec. 14, 1969; 1 child, Andrei Zitrin. B.A., U. Fed. Rio de Janeiro, 1969; M.S., Instituto de Matematica Pura e Aplicado, Brazil, 1970; M.A., U. Rochester, 1972, Ph.D., 1973. Asst. prof. econs. U. Chgo., 1973-76, assoc. prof., 1976-81, prof., 1981-86, Alvin H. Baum prof. economics, 1987—, chmn. econs. dept.; v.p. Goldman, Sachs & Co., 1987-89; vis. prof. Instituto de Matematica Pura e Aplicado Brazil, 1979-80, Fundação Getulio Vargas, Brazil, 1979-80, U. Paris, 1985-94; external Prof. Sante Fe Inst., 1989—; Harry Johnson lectr. Royal Econ. Soc./Assn. Univ. Tchrs. in Econs., 1989; cons. Ministry of Planning, Brazil, 1981. Editor: General Equilibrium Growth and Trade, 1975, Jour. Polit. Economy, Chgo., 1983-94; contbr. articles to profl. jours. NSF grantee. Fellow AAAS, Econometric Soc. Home: 5719 S Kenwood Ave Chicago IL 60637-1743 Office: Univ Chicago 1126 E 59th St Chicago IL 60637-1539

SCHEINMAN, STANLEY BRUCE, venture capital executive, lawyer; b. N.Y.C., Nov. 13, 1933; s. Samuel and Sadie (Seiffer) S.; m. Susan L. Elstein (dec.); m. Janet L. Donnely, Dec. 30, 1975 (dec.); children: Catherine Amy, Anthony Paul, Sarah Jean, Norah Jane. AB, Cornell U., 1954; MBA, CCNY, 1957; JD (Harlan Fisk Stone scholar), Columbia U., 1960. Bar: N.Y. 1960. Assoc. firm Cravath, Swaine & Moore, N.Y.C., 1960-62; capital projects officer, legis. programs staff coord. AID, Washington, 1962-64; sr. exec. officer Bur. Pvt. Enterprise AID, 1982-83; v.p. fin. and adminstrn. svcs. industries div., also v.p., counsel internat. div. PepsiCo. Inc., 1965-70; v.p. fin. and adminstrn. pharm. divsn. Revlon, Inc., 1970-72; sr. v.p. MCI Comm., 1972-76; pres., COO FSC Corp., Pitts., 1976-81; pres. New Venture Capital Corp., Washington, 1984-85; prin. Re Venture Assocs., Salisbury, Conn., 1985-86; chmn., CEO Internat. 800 Telcom Corp., Geneva, 1987-88; pres., CEO Zurich Depository Corp., Manhasset, N.Y., 1988-89; exec. v.p. AMIF&S Ltd., N.Y.C., 1989-91; pres. IT Svc. Corp., Westport, Conn., 1991-92; v..p. ops. and bus. devel. EQ Corp., Westport, 1992-95; exec. v.p., CFO Computer Products and Svcs. Inc., Wilton, Conn., 1995—; pres., CEO T & C Internat. Ltd., London, 1996—. Mem. Assn. of Bar of City of N.Y., Fin. Execs. Inst., Internat. Execs. Assn., Paris-Am. Club, Fgn. Svc. Club, Cornell Club. Home: PO Box 3355 Westport CT 06880-8355 Office: 206 Danbury Rd Wilton CT 06897-4004

SCHEINMAN, STEVEN JAY, medical educator; b. Monticello, N.Y., Oct. 22, 1951; married; 2 children. AB summa cum laude, Amherst Coll., 1973; MD cum laude, Yale U., 1977. Diplomate Am. Bd. Internal Medicine in nephrology; lic. physician, N.Y., Conn. Resident internal medicine Yale-New Haven Hosp., 1977-80; chief resident internal medicine Upstate Med. Ctr., Syracuse, N.Y., 1980-81, fellow nephrology, 1981-83; fellow nephrology Yale-New Haven Hosp., 1983-84; asst. prof. medicine SUNY Health Sci. Ctr., Syracuse, 1984-90, asst. prof. pharmacology, 1988-90, assoc. prof. medicine and pharmacology, 1990-94, prof. medicine and pharmacology, 1994—, chief nephrology sect. dept. medicine, 1994—; vis. scientist MRC Molecular Medicine Group, Royal Postgrad. Med. Sch., Hammersmith Hosp., London, 1992, 95; vis. scholar dept. biochemistry U. Oxford, 1985; attending physician U. Hosp., Syracuse, Crouse-Irving Meml. Hosp., Syracuse, VA Med. Ctr., Syracuse; dir. Nephrology Fellowship Program, 1993—; spkr. seminars, confs., orgns. Mem. editl. bd. Yale Jour. Biology and Medicine, 1975-77; contbr. articles to profl. jours. Recipient Lange award Yale U. Sch. Medicine, 1976, Resident Merit award Conn. chpt. ACP, 1980, NIH Nat. Rsch. Svc. award, 1981-83, NIH clin. investigator award, 1985-90, Charles R. Ross Rsch. award SUNY-Health Sci. Ctr., 1992; grantee Nat. Inst. Arthritis Diabetes Digestive and Kidney Diseases, 1981-83, 85-90, 95—, Am. Heart Assn., 1985, 88-90, 90-91, 92-95, 95—, NATO, 1995—. Mem. Am. Soc. Clin. Investigation, Am. Fedn. Med. Rsch., Am. Soc. Nephrology, Internat. Soc. Nephrology, Am. Physiol. Soc., Am. Soc. Bone and Mineral Rsch., Am. Heart Assn. Coun. on Kidney, Assn. Subspecialty Profs., Phi Beta Kappa. Home: 24 University Ave Hamilton NY 13346 Office: SUNY Health Sci Ctr 750 E Adams St Syracuse NY 13210-2306

SCHELBERT, HEINRICH RUEDIGER, nuclear medicine physician; b. Wuerzberg, Germany, Nov. 5, 1939. MD, J. Maximillian U., Wuerzburg, Germany, 1964. Diplomate Am. Bd. Nuclear Medicine. Intern Mercy Med. Ctr., Phila., 1966-67; resident Mercy Med. Ctr., 1967-68, 70-71; resident cardiology U. Dusseldorf, Germany, 1971-72; fellow cardiology, resident nuclear medicine U. Calif., San Diego, 1968-69, 72-73; hosp. assoc. UCLA Med. Ctr., 1977—; prof. radiol. scis. UCLA Sch. Medicine, L.A., 1980-93, prof. pharmacol. and radiol. scis., 1993—. Recipient Georg von Hevesy prize 2d Internat. Congress World Fedn. Nuclear Medicine and Radiation Biology, 1978, 3d Internat. Congress World Fedn. Nuclear Medicine and Radiation Biology, 1982. Fellow Am. Coll. Cardiology; mem. Am. Heart Assn. (disting. scientific achievement award 1989), Soc. Nuclear Medicine (Herrman L. Blumgart pioneer lectr. award 1989). Office: UCLA Sch Medicine Dept Molecular & Med Pharm 23-120 CHS Los Angeles CA 90095-1735

SCHELER, BRAD ERIC, lawyer; b. Bklyn., Oct. 11, 1953; s. Bernard and Rita Regina (Miller) S.; m. Amy Ruth Frolick, Mar. 30, 1980; children: Ali M., Maddie H., Zoey B. BA magna cum laude, Lehigh U., 1974; JD, Hofstra U., 1977. Bar: N.Y. 1978, U.S. Dist. Ct. (so. and ea. dists.) N.Y. 1978. Assoc. Weil, Gotshal & Manges, N.Y.C., 1977-81; sr. ptnr., chmn. bankruptcy and restructuring practice Fried, Frank, Harris, Shriver & Jacobson, N.Y.C., 1981—. Rsch. editor Hofstra U. Law Rev., 1975-77. Treas., bus. mgr. Trustees of Gramercy Park, N.Y.C., 1979-87. Mem. ABA (bus. bankruptcy com. corp. banking and bus. law sect., creditors' rights com. litig. sect.), N.Y. State Bar Assn., Assn. Bar City of N.Y. (com. on bankruptcy and corp. reorgn. 1991-94), Sigma Alpha Mu (v.p. 1973). Jewish. Home: 32 Maple Hill Dr Larchmont NY 10538-1614 Office: Fried Frank Harris 1 New York Plz New York NY 10004

SCHELL, ALLAN CARTER, retired electrical engineer; b. New Bedford, Mass., Apr. 14, 1934; s. Charles Carter and Elizabeth (Moore) S.; m. Shirley T. Sardiner; children: Alice Rosalind, Cynthia Anne. B.S., MIT, 1956, M.S.E.E., 1956, Sc.D., 1961; student, Tech. U. Delft, Netherlands, 1956-57. Research physicist Air Force Cambridge Research Labs., Bedford, Mass., 1956-76; Guenter Loeser Meml. lectr. Air Force Cambridge Research Labs., 1965; dir. electromagnetics directorate Rome Air Devel. Ctr., Bedford, 1976-87; chief scientist Hdqrs. USAF Systems Command, 1987-92; chief scientist, dep. dir. sci. and tech. Hdqrs. USAF Materiel Command, 1992-94; dir. Electro; vis. assoc. prof. MIT, 1974; chair dept. of elec. engring. adv. coun. U. Pa., 1992-94. Contbr. articles to profl. jours.; patentee in field (9). Served as lt. USAF, 1958-60. Recipient Fulbright award, 1956-57, Meritorious Exec. award U.S. Govt., 1989; NSF fellow, 1955-56, 60-61. Fellow IEEE (bd. dirs. 1981-82, editor IEEE Press 1976-79, Procs. of IEEE 1990-92), Antennas and Propagation Soc. of IEEE (pres. 1978, editor tran. 1969-71, John T. Bolljahn award 1966), Internat. Sic. Radio Union, Air Force Assn., Sigma Xi, Tau Beta Pi.

SCHELL, BRAXTON, lawyer; b. Raleigh, N.C., Feb. 24, 1924; s. Marshall H. and Margaret (Newsom) S.; m. Ann Cooper Knight, Mar. 30, 1951 (div. 1982); children: Braxton, Richard Knight, James Gray.; m. Mary Rehill, Apr. 16, 1983. Student, N.C. State Coll., 1942-43; B.S., U. N.C., 1948, J.D. with honors, 1951. Bar: N.C. 1951. Since practiced in Greensboro; assoc. Smith, Moore, Smith, Schell & Hunter, Greensboro, 1951-56; ptnr. Smith, Moore, Smith, Schell & Hunter, 1956-85, Smith, Helms, Mullis, and Moore, 1986-87, Schell, Bray, Aycock, Abel & Livingston, 1987—; gen. counsel Flagler Sys. and The Breakers Palm Beach, Inc.; bd. dirs. Kenan Transport Co. Assoc. editor: N.C. Law Rev. 1950-51. Chmn. Special Liason Tax Com. Southeastern Region, 1960-61; bd. dirs. N.C. Outward Bound Sch., 1975-88, chmn., 1977-80; trustee Outward Bound, Inc., 1978-81; bd. dirs. William R. Kenan Fund for Pvt. Enterprise, Arts and Enging., Tech. and Sci. Served with USAAF, 1942-45. Fellow Am. Bar Found.; mem. Am., N.C. bar assns., Order of Coif, Phi Beta Kappa. Presbyn. Clubs: Greensboro Country (pres. 1971-72), Greensboro City (dir. 1980—). Home: 422B Fisher Park Cir Greensboro NC 27401-1615 Office: Schell Bray Aycock Abel & Livingston 1500 Renaissance Pla Greensboro NC 27420

SCHELL, CATHERINE LOUISE, family practice physician; b. Niskayuna, N.Y., Jan. 27, 1948; m. Richard J. Rathe, Jan. 7, 1986. BA, Ind. U., 1970, MA, 1974; MLS, Simmons Coll., 1975; MD, Am. U. Caribbean, Montserrat, 1983. Diplomate Am. Bd. Family Practice. Libr. Calder Med. Libr., U. Miami, Fla., 1975-78; libr., dir. Mercy Hosp., Miami, 1978-79; libr. Miami-Dade C.C., 1978-80; intern Med. Coll. Ga., Rome, 1983; resident U. Wyo., Cheyenne, 1985-87; staff physician Vets. Hosp., Cheyenne, 1986-88, Dept. of Army, U.S. Dept. Def., Ft. Devens, Mass., 1988-90, Vets. Hosp., Lake City, Fla., 1990-93; staff physician, fellow Vets. Hosp., Gainesville, Fla., 1993-95; geriatrics fellow U. Fla., 1993-95; physician Dept. of Navy, 1995-96; locums, 1996—. Tchr. ESL YMCA Internat., Taipei, Taiwan, 1970-71. Title IIB fellow Simmons Coll., 1974-75; Ford Found. grantee, Ind. U., 1969-70. Fellow Am. Acad. Family PRactice; mem. Acad. Health Sci., Med. Libr. Assn.

SCHELL, JAMES MUNSON, financial executive; b. Kalamazoo, Mich., Mar. 25, 1944; s. Frank John and Shirley I. S.; m. Susan O'Laughlin, Aug. 6, 1966; children: Karen, Michael, Ryan. B.A., Vanderbilt U., 1966; M.B.A., Washington U., 1968. Dir. term and internat. financing Chrysler Fin. Corp., Troy, Mich., 1976-79, v.p., treas., 1980-81; v.p. domestic treasury Am. Express Co., N.Y.C., 1981-82; v.p. fin. resources Hertz Corp., N.Y.C., 1982-83; v.p., chief fin. officer Clabir Corp., Greenwich, Conn., 1983-84; v.p., treas. Fairchild Industries, 1985-87; ind. fin. cons., 1987—; bd. dirs. Jackson-Jordan Corp., CTI Industries. Republican. Roman Catholic. Home: 40 Stony Brook Rd Darien CT 06820-4326

SCHELL, JOAN BRUNING, information specialist, business science librarian; b. N.Y.C., June 9, 1932; d. Walter Henry and Gertrude Emily (Goossen) Bruning; m. Harold Benton Schell, Aug. 27, 1955 (div. 1978); children: Jeffrey Mark, Sue Lynne. AB, Wittenberg U., 1954; postgrad., Syracuse U., 1963, U. Md., 1965-66; MLS, U. Pitts., 1968. Actuarial, claims asst. Nationwide Ins., Columbus, Ohio, 1954-57; tech. report typist Cornell U., Ithaca, N.Y., 1957; bus. libr. asst. U. Pitts., 1969; bus. reference libr. Dallas Pub. Libr., 1971-73, Pub. Libr. Cin. and Hamilton County, Cin., 1973-79; book selection coord. Pub. Libr. Cin. & Hamilton County, Cin., 1979-83, asst. to main libr., 1983-85; literacy tutor Cin. LEARN, 1985-89; recorder feminist lit. Womyn's Braille Press, Mpls., 1985-89; wellness program asst. Times Pub. Co., St. Petersburg, Fla., 1989-96, Taoist Tai Chi Soc., 1995—; dir. Wittenberg U., Springfield, Ohio, 1988—; bd. dirs. Crazy Ladies Ctr. Inc., Cin., 1989-93; coord. Fla. west coast Old Lesbians Organizing for Change, 1993-95; sec., trustee Clio Found., Inc., 1995—; docent Fla. Internat. Mus., 1994—. Compiler: (reference source) Greater Cincinnati Business Index, 1975-79; editor: New Reference Materials, 1983, 84. Mem. Tampa Bay YWCA Women's Guild, St. Petersburg, 1991-95; vol. NOW Elect Women Campaign, St. Petersburg, 1990-92, Senator Helen G. Davis Reelection, St. Petersburg, 1992. Mem. ALA, Spl. Librs. Assn. (treas., archivist 1974-83), Am. Assn. Individual Investors, Laubach Literary Action, Taoist Tai Chi Soc., Beta Phi Mu Libr. Sci. Hon., Phi Delta Gamma Grad. Women Hon. Avocations: travel, reading, figure skating fan, yoga, swimming. Address: PO Box 7472 Saint Petersburg FL 33734-7472

SCHELL, NORMAN BARNETT, physician, consultant; b. N.Y.C., May 25, 1925; s. Jack and Ada Sylvia (Rosen) S.; m. Lila Barbara Mendelsohn, Aug. 27, 1950; children: Martin, Judith, Steven. AB cum laude, NYU, 1946, MD, 1950; MPH, Harvard U., 1971. Diplomate Am. Bd. Pediats., Am. Bd. Preventive Medicine, Nat. Bd. Med. Examiners; lic. physician, N.Y. Rotating intern Beth Israel Hosp., N.Y.C., 1950-51; asst. resident in pediats. Mt. Sinai Hosp., N.Y.C., 1951-52; clin. fellow in pediats. N.Y.-Cornell Med. Ctr., N.Y.C., 1952-53; pvt. practice Jericho and Hicksville, N.Y., 1956-69; pub. health physician Nassau County Health Dept., Mineola, N.Y., 1969-76, dep. commr., 1976-90; asst. prof. preventive medicine SUNY, Stony Brook, 1974-90; pediat. cons. N.Y. State Health Dept., 1956-69, HEW Project Head Start, N.Y.C., 1968-75; emeritus pediat. staff Nassau County Med. Ctr. Author: Keys to Childhood Illnesses, 1992; contbr. articles to profl. jours. Lt. M.C., USN, 1953-55, capt. M.C., USNR, 1981-85. Recipient Physician Recognition award AMA, 1970, Grade 1A Health Officer N.Y. State Health Dept., 1973. Fellow Am. Acad. Pediats. (com. on sch. health 1971-77, citation com. on med. edn. 1977), Am. Coll. Preventive Medicine, N.Y. Acad. Medicine; mem. Am. Coll. Legal Medicine (assoc.), Nassau County Med. Soc. (chmn. sch. health com.), Harvard Club N.Y.C., West Point Club, Phi Beta Kappa. Avocations: photography, classical music, computer technology. Home and Office: 63 Birchwood Park Dr Jericho NY 11753-2238

SCHELLEN, NANDO, opera director; b. The Hague, The Netherlands, Oct. 11, 1934; came to U.S., 1993; m. Deborah Raymond, June 19, 1991; 4 children. Mng. dir. Netherlands Opera, 1969-79, assoc. gen. dir., 1979-87; gen. artistic dir. Sweelinck Conservatory of Music, Amsterdam, 1990-93; gen. dir. Indpls. Opera, 1993-96; freelance stage dir., 1982—. Home: 209 E 45th St Indianapolis IN 46205-1711

SCHELLENBERG, KARL ABRAHAM, biochemist; b. Hillsboro, Kans., July 13, 1931; s. Theodore R. and Alma Alice (Groening) S.; m. Elizabeth Joan Booker, Aug. 20, 1955; children: Robert, Elizabeth, Richard, Margaret. BS, Coll. William and Mary, 1953; MD, Johns Hopkins U., 1957; PhD, Harvard U., 1964. Asst. prof. Johns Hopkins U., Balt., 1963-68; asso. prof. physiol. chemistry Johns Hopkins U., 1968-73; prof., chmn. dept. biochemistry Eastern Va. Med. Sch., Norfolk, 1973—; mem. adv. bd. NSF Middle Atlantic Mass Spectrometry Lab.; mem. adv. com. dept. chem. scis. Old Dominion U.; mem. adv. com. dept. chemistry Coll. William and Mary. Contbr. articles to profl. jours. John and Mary R. Markle Found. scholar, 1965-70; NIH grantee. Mem. Nat. Bd. Med. Examiners (biochemistry test com. 1989-92), Assn. Am. Med. Schs. (panel on the gen. profl. edn. of the physician 1982-84), Assn. Med. Sch. Depts. Biochemistry (sec. 1987-91), Am. Soc. Biol. Chemists, Am. Chem. Soc., N.Y. Acad. Scis., Va. Acad. Scis., Oxygen Soc., Phi Beta Kappa, Sigma Xi (Tidewater, Va. chpt. sec. 1990-91, pres. 1992-93, pres. 1995-96). Club: Pithotomy. Patentee in field. Home: 1332 Lakeview Dr Virginia Beach VA 23455-4130 Office: Eastern Va Med Sch PO Box 1980 Norfolk VA 23501-1980

SCHELLENBERGER, ROBERT EARL, management educator and department chairman; b. Janesville, Wis., July 25, 1932; s. Ervin William and Adelaide Louise (Keller) S.; m. Linda Eula Todd, Dec. 30, 1961; children: Brian T., Keith W., Heidi L. BSBA, U. Wis., 1958, MBA, 1959; PhD, U. N.C., 1963. Personnel supr. Libby McNeill and Libby, Janesville, Wis., 1957-58; from asst. prof. to assoc. prof. chmn. div. stats. dept. bus U. Md., College Park, 1963-68; chair dept. mgmt. So. Ill. U., Carbondale, Ill., 1968-70; dir. planning Sch. Human Resources Devel. So. Ill. U., Carbondale, 1970-71, prof. mgmt., 1968-71; vis. prof., dir. program evaluation Babcock Grad. Sch. Mgmt., Wake Forest U., Winston-Salem, N.C., 1971-73; prof. dept. mgmt. Temple U., Phila., 1973-81, from chmn. dept. mgmt. to asst. to acad. vice chancellor, 1975-77; prof. decision scis. dept. East Carolina U., Greenville, N.C., 1981—, chmn. decision scis. dept., 1989-95; pres. Md. Rsch. and Cons., Hyattsville, 1964-67; v.p. Ea. Acad. Mgmt., 1967; cons. Comml. Credit Corp., Balt., 1966. Author: Managerial Analysis, 1967, Policy Formulation, 1978, 2d edit., 1982; co-editor Jour. of Econs. and Bus., 1976; developer (software package) MANYSYM, 1965, 68, 78, 82, 86. Chmn. Utilities Com., Carbondale, 1970-72. Title IV NDEA fellow U. N.C., 1960-62, Earhart Jr. fellow U. Wis. Mem. Assn. for Bus. Simulation, SE Decision Scis. Inst., Decision Scis. Inst. (bd. dirs. 1974-77), Beta Gamma Sigma. Office: East Carolina U Decision Scis Dept Greenville NC 27858

SCHELLER, SANFORD GREGORY, printing company executive; b. Newark, July 7, 1931; s. John Arthur Scheller and Harriet (Gregory) Tate; m. Marjory Meyer, Dec. 31, 1950; children: Sanford Gregory Jr., Douglas Meyer, Bradford John, Frances Scheller Lavin, Eric Bruce. BBA, Westminster Coll., New Wilmington, Pa., 1953. V.p., gen. mgr. St. Regis Corp., N.Y.C., 1978-84, Champion Internat., Stamford, Conn., 1984-85; pres., chief exec. officer Treasure Chest Advt., Glendora, Calif., 1986-95; vice chmn. Big Flower Press Holdings, Inc., N.Y.C., 1995—. Republican. Office: Big Flower Press Holdings Ste 28 13000 Sawgrass Village Cir Ponte Vedra Beach FL 32082-5021

SCHELLHAAS, LINDA JEAN, toxicologist, consultant; b. South Haven, Mich., Apr. 27, 1956; d. Richard Louis and Virgene Frieda (Lietzke) Plankenhorn; m. Robert Wesley Schellhaas, May 27, 1990. BA in Biology, Albion Coll., 1978. Pathology rsch. asst. Internat. R&D Corp., Mattawan, Mich., 1978-80; toxicology rsch. coord. Borriston Labs., Inc., Temple Hills, Md., 1980-84; quality assurance coord. Tegeris Labs., Inc., Temple Hills, Md., 1984-85; good lab. practice compliance specialist, staff scientist Dynamac Corp., Rockville, Md., 1985-90; dir. quality assurance Pathology Assocs., Inc., Frederick, Md., 1992-94; pres., regulatory compliance specialist Quality Reviews, Inc., Falling Waters, W.Va., 1990—; instr. regulatory compliance tng. seminars, 1990—. Contbr. articles to profl. jours. Mem. Soc. Quality Assurance, Albion Coll. Fellows, Pi Beta Phi, Phi Beta Kappa. Avocations: sheep, goat and poultry husbandry, raising sheep-herding dogs, needlework, animal welfare. Office: Quality Reviews Inc 1204 Berkeley Dr Falling Waters WV 25419-9657

SCHELLHAAS, ROBERT WESLEY, counselor, songwriter, musician; b. Pitts., Feb. 27, 1952; s. Albert Wesley and Florence Elizabeth (Smiley) S.; children: Matthew L., Abigail K., David A.; m. Linda Jean Plankenhorn, May 27, 1990. BA, Thiel Coll., 1974; MDiv, Gordon-Conwell Theol. Sem., 1977; PhD, Calif. Grad. Sch. Theology, Glendale, 1986. Ordained minister Congl. Ch., 1978. Pastor Congl. chs., Everett, Peabody, Mass., 1976-80; chaplain U.S. Army, 1980-88; owner/founder Schellware, Everett, Mass., 1977-89; v.p., founder Quality Revs., Inc., Falling Waters, 1989—; also bd. dirs. Quality Reviews, Inc., Falling Waters; staff scientist Dynamac Corp., 1989-90; dir. Creative Alternatives Recording, Pub., 1992—; career cons. Author: Toyosaurus Wrex, 1986, Intimacy: Theological and Behavioral Implications, 1986, Personality Preference Inventory (P.P.I.), 1988, Led Zeppelin: My Night as the Right Fifth Member, 1996; ad editor/author: AIDS Ministry in Perspective, 1988, Army monthly newsletters, 1980-85, various pub. articles. V.p. Ft. Stewart (Ga.) Sch. Bd., 1980-82; profl. counselor AIDS Ministry; Cub Scout leader Boy Scouts Am., 1981-85; missions dir. Children's Sand and Surf Missions, 1976-79; founder Smiley/Schellhaas Musicians' Endowed Scholar Fund, Laroche Coll., Pitts., 1995. Maj. USAR, 1988—. Recipient Mayor's award in Photography, Everett, 1976. Mem. DAV, SAR, Internat. Found. Gender Edn., Assn. Clin. Pastoral Counseling, Am. Philatelic Soc. Avocations: photography, philately, bodysurfing, fishing. Office: Quality Reviews Inc 1204 Berkeley Dr Falling Waters WV 25419-9657

SCHELLING, JOHN PAUL, lawyer, consultant; b. Chgo., Aug. 24, 1924; s. Lawrence C. and Hattie (La Bonte) S.; m. V. Jacqueline Davis, Aug. 27, 1945; children: Lawrence, Donna Schelling Scheer, Gloria Schelling Boughers. Student, St. Mary's Coll., Winona, Minn., 1942-43, U. Ill., 1946-47; J.D., Loyola U., Chgo., 1950; postgrad., U. Chgo., 1954-55. Bar: Ill. 1950, Va. 1986. Assoc. McMahon & Plunkett, Chgo., 1950-51; mem. indsl. relations staff Union Asbestos & Rubber Co., Chgo., 1951-56; fin. mgr. Land-Air, Inc. subs. Dynalectron Corp., Chgo., 1956-60; sec. Dynalectron Corp., McLean, Va., 1960-65; v.p. Dynalectron Corp., McLean, 1962-71, v.p., gen. counsel, 1972-76, sr. v.p. fin. and adminstrn. group, 1977-78, sr. v.p. adminstrn. group, 1979-84, sr. v.p. adminstrn. group, gen. counsel, 1984-86, ret., 1986; chmn. Esop com. DynCorp, 1987-97. Bd. dirs., v.p. Potomac Hills Citizens Assn., McLean, 1963-64; organizer, bd. dirs., v.p. Highland Swim Club, McLean, 1964-67; bd. dirs. McLean Orch., 1984-86; trustee Fairfax Couty Pub. Schs. Edn. Fund., 1984-86; bd. dirs. Shorewood Property Owners Assn., 1990—, sec.-treas., 1990-92, pres., 1992-95, v.p., 1995—; treas. Lake Anna Civic Assn., 1994—. With USNR, 1943-46. Mem. D.C. Bar Assn., Va. Bar Assn., Tanyarb Country Club (bd. dirs. 1996), Delta Theta Phi. Home and Office: 167 Laurelwood Dr Mineral VA 23117

SCHELLING, THOMAS CROMBIE, economist, educator; b. Oakland, Calif., Apr. 14, 1921; s. John M. and Zelda M. (Ayres) S.; m. Corinne T. Saposs, Sept. 13, 1947 (div. 1991); children: Andrew, Thomas, Daniel, Robert; m. Alice M. Coleman, Nov. 8, 1991. AB, U. Calif., Berkeley, 1943; PhD, Harvard U., 1951. U.S. govt. economist Copenhagen, Paris, Washington, 1948-53; prof. econs. Yale U., 1953-58, Harvard U., Cambridge, Mass., 1958—; prof. econs. and pub. affairs U. Md., College Park, 1990—; sr. staff mem. RAND Corp., 1958-59; chmn. rsch. adv. bd. Com. Econ. Devel., 1978-81, 84-85; mem. sci. adv. bd. USAF, 1960-64, def. sci. bd., 1966-70; mem. mil. econ. adv. panel CIA, 1980-85; trustee Aerospace Corp., 1984-93. Author: National Income Behavior, 1951, International Economics, 1958, The Strategy of Conflict, 1960, Arms and Influence, 1966, Micromotives and Macrobehavior, 1978, Choice and Consequence, 1984; co-author: Strategy and Arms Control, 1961. Recipient Frank E. Seidman Disting. award in polit. economy, 1977. Fellow Am. Acad. Arts and Scis., AAAS, Assn. for Pub. Policy Analysis and Mgmt., Am. Econ. Assn. (pres. 1991, Disting. mem. award); mem. NAS (rsch. award, 1993), Inst. Medicine, Ea. Econ. Assn. (pres. 1996). Office: Univ Md Sch Pub Affairs College Park MD 20742

SCHELLMAN, JOHN A., chemistry educator; b. Phila., Oct. 24, 1924; s. John and Mary (Mason) S.; m. Charlotte Green, Feb. 10, 1954; children: Heidi M., Lise C. AB, Temple U., 1948; MS, Princeton U., 1949, PhD, 1951; PhD (hon.), Chalmers U., Sweden, 1983, U. Padua, Italy, 1990. USPHS postdoctoral fellow U. Utah, 1951-52, Carlsberg Lab., Copenhagen, 1953-55; DuPont fellow U. Minn., Mpls., 1955-56; asst. prof. chemistry U. Minn., 1956-58; assoc. prof. chemistry Inst. Molecular Biology, U. Oreg., Eugene, 1958-63; prof. chemistry, rsch. assoc. Inst. Molecular Biology, U. Oreg., 1963—; vis. Lab. Chem. Physics, Nat. Inst. Arthritis and Metabolic Diseases, NIH, Bethesda, Md., 1980; vis. prof. Chalmers U., Sweden, 1986, U. Padua, Italy, 1987. Contbr. articles to profl. jours. Served with U.S. Army, 1943-46. Fellow Rask-Oersted Found., 1954, Sloan Found., 1959-63, Guggenheim Found., 1969-70. Fellow Am. Phys. Soc.; mem. NAS, Am. Chem. Soc., Am. Soc. Biochemistry and Molecular Biology, Am. Acad. Arts and Scis., Biophys. Soc., Phi Beta Kappa, Sigma Xi. Democrat. Home: 780 Lorane Hwy Eugene OR 97405-2340 Office: Univ Oreg Inst Molecular Biology Eugene OR 97403

SCHELM, ROGER LEONARD, information systems specialist; b. Kingston, N.Y., July 29, 1936; s. Frederick G. and Elizabeth M. (Wojciechowski) S.; m. Gloria Mae Dutterer, June 13, 1958; children: Sandra Lee Kern, Theresa Jean Sollitto, Ginger Lisa Teesdale. B.A. in Polit. Sci., Western Md. Coll., 1958; M.A. in Pub. Adminstrn., Am. U., 1970; postgrad., U. Md., 1960-62. Analytic equipment programmer Nat. Security Agy., Ft. Meade, Md., 1958-60; computer cons. various cons. firms Balt. and Washington, 1960-68; mgr. army plans and programs Informatics Inc., Bethesda, Md., 1968; mgr. def. programs Automation Tech. Inc., Wheaton, Md., 1968-69; dir. advanced planning Genasys Corp., Washington, 1969-71; mgr. info. systems Ins. Co. North Am., Phila., 1971-72, sect. mgr. computing ops., 1972-74; mgr. tech. services INA Corp., Phila., 1974-75; mem. spl. tech. projects INA Corp. merger with Conn. Gen. Ins. Co. to form CIGNA Corp. 1982, Phila., 1975-76, asst. dir. tech. services, 1977, asst. dir. spl. tech. projects, 1977-78, asst. dir. adminstrn., 1978-79, asst. dir. resource mgmt., data ctr. design, contingency planning, 1979-80; dir. corp. info. tech. now CIGNA Corp., Phila., 1981-82, dir. planning and control ops. div., 1982-83, v.p. strategic planning, systems div., 1983-84, v.p. applied research/expert systems, systems div., 1984-92; co-founder, pres. Schelm Internat., Inc., Cherry Hill, N.J., 1992—; mem. adj. faculty Camden Coll., N.J., 1978-82; mem. Camden County EDP Adv. Com., 1980-82; mem. faculty Drexel U., Phila., 1983-95. Author: Ednl. Computer mag., 1982; mem. editl. adv. bd., author Small Sys. World mag., 1982-84; mem. editl. adv. bd. Spang-Robinson Report, 1986-87, Machine Intelligence News, 1987-93, AI Expert mag., 1985-88; cons. editor Expert Sys. Jour., 1987-91. Tech. advisor various sch. bds., colls., univs. and non-profit orgns. Served to capt. U.S. Army, 1959. Mem. Am. Assn. Artificial Intelligence, Assn. Computing Machinery (founder Delaware Valley chpt. vice. chmn., program chmn. 1983-84, chmn. 1984-85, founder Del. Valley Spl. Interest Group in Artificial Intelligence, 1985, vice chmn. 1985-87), World Future Soc. Home: 506 Balsam Rd

Cherry Hill NJ 08003-3202 Office: Schelm Internat Inc PO Box 172 Cherry Hill NJ 08003-0172

SCHELSKE, CLAIRE L., limnologist, educator; b. Fayetteville, Ark., Apr. 1, 1932; s. Theodore J. and Ida S. S.; m. Betty Breukelman, June 2, 1957; children—Cynthia, John, Steven. A.B., Kans. State Tchrs. Coll., Emporia, 1955, M.S., 1956; Ph.D., U. Mich., 1961. Tchg. and rsch. asst. dept. biology Kans. State Tchrs. Coll., 1952-55, vis. instr., summer 1960; teaching fellow dept. zoology U. Mich., 1955-57; asst. prof. radiol. health dept. environ. health U. Mich. (Sch. Public Health); asst. research limnologist Gt. Lakes Research Div., Inst. Sci. and Tech., 1967-68, assoc. rsch. limnologist, 1969-71, rsch. limnologist, 1971-87; asst. dir. Gt. Lakes Research Div., Inst. Sci. and Tech. (Gt. Lakes Research Div.), 1970-72, acting dir., 1973-76, assoc. prof. limnology, dept. atmospheric and oceanic sci., 1976-87; assoc. prof. natural resources Sch. Natural Resources, 1976-86, prof., 1986-87; Carl S. Swisher prof. water resources U. Fla., Gainesville, 1987—; research fellow Inst. Fisheries Research, Mich. Dept. Conservation, 1957-60; research assoc. U. Ga. Marine Inst., 1960-62; fishery biologist, supervisory fishery biologist, chief Estuarine Ecology Program, Bur. Comml. Fisheries, Radiobiol. Lab., Beaufort, N.C., 1962-66; adj. asst. prof. dept. zoology N.C. State U., Raleigh, 1964-66; tech. asst. Office Sci. and Tech., Exec. Office of Pres., Washington, 1966-67; cons. Ill. Atty. Gen., 1977-79. Author: (with J.C. Roth) Limnological Survey of Lakes Michigan, Superior, Huron and Erie, 1973. Recipient Disting. Alumnus award Emporia State U. (formerly Kans. State Tchrs. Coll.), 1989. Fellow AAAS, Am. Inst. Fishery Rsch. Biologists (regional and dist. dir. South-Cen. Gt. Lakes chpt. 1977-80); mem. Am. Soc. Limnology and Oceanography (sec. 1976-85, v.p. 1987-88, pres. 1988-90), Ecol. Soc. Am. (assoc. editor 1972-75), Internat. Assn. Gt. Lakes Rsch. (editl. bd. 1970-73, chmn. 20th Conf. 1977, assoc. editor 1984-93), Soc. Internat. Limnology. Home: 2738 SW 9th Dr Gainesville FL 32601-9003 Office: U Fla Dept Fisheries and Aquatic Scis 7922 NW 71st St Gainesville FL 32653-3071

SCHEMNITZ, SANFORD DAVID, wildlife biology educator; b. Cleve., Mar. 10, 1930; s. David Arthur Schemnitz; m. Mary Margaret Newby, July 8, 1958; children: Ellen Kay, Steven, Stuart. Student, U. Wis., 1948-50; BS in Wildlife, U. Mich., 1952; MS in Wildlife, U. Fla., 1953; PhD in Wildlife, Olka. State U., 1958. Cert. wildlife biologist. Conservation aide State of Mich. Dept. Conservation, Ann Arbor, 1951-52; game research biologist State of Minn. Dept. Conservation, St. Paul, 1958-59; asst. prof. wildlife Pa. State U., University Park, 1960-61; prof. wildlife resources U. Maine, Orono, 1962-75; dept. head fish and wildlife sci. N.Mex. State U., Las Cruces, 1975-81, prof. wildlife scis., 1981—. Editor: Wildlife Management Techniques Manual, 1980; contbr. articles to profl. jours. Fulbright Prof. Council for Internat. Exchange Scholars, Kathmandu, Nepal, 1983, Kenya, 1990. Mem. Am. Soc. Mammalogists, The Wildlife Soc. (life, S.W. regional rep. 1979-80), Ecol. Soc. Am., Wilson Ornithol. Soc., N.Mex. Wildlife Fedn. (bd. dirs. 1983—), Sigma Xi. Home: 8105 Dona Ana Rd Las Cruces NM 88005-6307

SCHENCK, BENJAMIN ROBINSON, insurance consultant; b. N.Y.C., July 21, 1938; s. John T. and Harriet Buffum (Hall) S.; m. Sally V. Sullivan, Aug. 27, 1960; children: Steven T., Elizabeth F., Timothy S. B.A., William Coll., Williamstown, Mass, 1960; LL.B., Harvard U., 1963. Bar: N.Y. 1964, Mass. 1978. Asst. counsel to gov. State of N.Y., Albany, 1963-66; assoc. Bond, Schoeneck & King, Syracuse, N.Y., 1966-68; dep. supt., 1st dep. sup. and supt. State of N.Y. Dept. Ins., N.Y.C., 1968-75; sr. v.p. Shearson Hayden Stone Inc., N.Y.C., 1975-77; sr. v.p. State Mut. Life Assurance Co. Am., 1977-86, exec. v.p., 1986-89; pres. Worcester Mut. Ins. Co., 1979-83, Cen. Mass. Health Care, Inc., Worcester, 1989-93. Home: 85 Stockbridge Rd Lee MA 01238-9308 Office: 63 State Rd Great Barrington MA 01230-1223

SCHENCK, FREDERICK A., business executive; b. Trenton, May 12, 1928; s. Frederick A. and Alwilda M. (McLain) S.; m. Quinta Chapman, Jan. 25, 1974. Student, Howard U., 1948-50; B.S., Rider Coll., 1958, M.A., 1976. With N.J. Dept. Community Affairs, 1967-72; dir. youth and family services div. N.J. Dept. Human Svs., 1972-74; dep. dir. adminstrn. purchase and property div. N.J. Treasury Dept., 1974-77; secretarial rep. Fed. Region II, Dept. Commerce, 1977-78; dep. under sec. Dept. Commerce, 1978-79; sr. v.p. adminstrn. Resorts Internat. Hotel Casino, Atlantic City, 1979-88; v.p. personnel Cunard Lines Ltd., N.Y.C., 1988-93; self employed mgmt. cons. Secaucus, N.J., 1995—; bd. dirs. Bur. Nat. Affairs Inc.; mem. adv. com. on judicial conduct N.J. Supreme Ct. With USNR, 1946-48. Mem. N.J. Gov.'s Commn. on Disabled; bd. dirs. Bur. Nat. Affairs Inc. With USNR, 1946-48. Mem. Am. Soc. Public Adminstrn., N.J. C. of C. Presbyterian. Club: Sundowners, Nat. Guardsmen, Inc. Home: 569 Sanderling Ct Secaucus NJ 07094-2220

SCHENCK, JACK LEE, retired electric utility executive; b. Morgantown, W.Va., Aug. 2, 1938; s. Ernest Jacob and Virginia Belle (Kelley) S.; m. Rita Elizabeth Pietschmann, June 7, 1979; 1 son, Erik. B.S.E.E., B.A. in Social Sci., Mich. State U., 1961; M.B.A., NYU, 1975. Engr. AID, Tunis, Tunisia, 1961, Detroit Edison Co., 1962-63; engr., economist OECD, Paris, 1963-70; v.p. econ. policy analysis Edison Electric Inst., N.Y.C. and Washington, 1970-81; v.p., treas. Gulf States Utilities Co., Beaumont, Tex., 1981-92, sr. v.p., CFO, 1992-94; cons. on electric utility restructuring and privatization in the former Soviet Union, 1994—. Mem. Internat. Assn. Energy Econs., Triangle Club, Eta Kappa Nu. Republican.

SCHENCK, JOHN FREDERIC, physician; b. Decatur, Ind., June 7, 1939; s. John C. Schenck and Mildred Blosser; m. Jane Stark, Oct. 12, 1962 (div. 1982); children: Brooke, Kimberly, David; m. Susan J. Kalia, Oct. 8, 1994; 1 stepchild, Tania. BS in Physics, Rensselaer Poly. Inst., 1961, PhD in Physics, 1965; MD, Albany Med. Coll., 1977. Intern Albany (N.Y.) Med. Ctr. Hosp., 1977-78; staff scientist electronics lab GE, Syracuse, N.Y., 1965-73; staff mem., sr. scientist corp. R & D ctr. GE, Schenectady, N.Y., 1973—; assoc. prof. electrical engring. Syracuse U., 1970-73; mem. med. staff Ellis Hosp., Schenectady, 1981—; adj. asst. prof. dept. radiology U. Pa., 1983—; chmn. Workshop on Advances in Magnetic Resonance Imaging Safety and Compatibility, McLean, Va., 1996. Contbr. articles to profl. jours; 12 patents in field of magnetic resonance imaging. Recipient S.S. Greenfield award Am. Assn. Physicists in Medicine, 1993; Nat. Merit Scholar, 1957-61; NSF fellow, 1962-63;. Mem. IEEE, AAAS, Internat. Soc. Magnetic Resonance in Medicine, Am. Phys. Soc., N.Y. Acad. Sci., Sigma Xi. Home: 4914 Ravine Ct Ann Arbor MI 48105-9442 Office: GE Corp Rsch Devel Bldg K1 NMR Schenectady NY 12309

SCHENDEL, DAN ELDON, management consultant, business educator; b. Norwalk, Wis., Mar. 29, 1934; s. Leonard A. and Marian T. (Koch) S.; B.S. in Metall.Engring., U. Wis., 1956; M.B.A., Ohio State U., 1959; Ph.D. (Ford Found. fellow), Stanford U., 1963; m. Mary Lou Sigler, Sept. 1, 1956; children: Suzanne, Pamela, Sharon. With ALCOA, 1956, U.S. Civil Service, 1959-60, SRI, 1963-65; prof. mgmt., dir. exec. edn. programs Purdue U., 1965-85; vis. prof. U. Mich., 1988-89, U. Chgo., 1990-91; pres. Strat egic Mgmt. Assocs., Inc. Served with USAF, 1956-59. Fellow Acad. Mgmt.; mem. Strategic Mgmt. Soc. (founding pres., exec. dir.), Strategic Leadership Forum. Club: Lafayette Country. Author: (with others) Strategy Formulation: Analytical Concepts, 1978, Divided Loyalties, 1980, Fundamental Issues in Strategy, 1994; editor: (with others) Strategic Management: A New View of Business Policy and Planning, 1979; founding editor Strategic Mgmt. Jour., 1980—. Home: 1327 N Grant St West Lafayette IN 47906-2463 Office: Krannert Grad Sch Mgmt Purdue U West Lafayette IN 47907

SCHENDEL, STEPHEN ALFRED, plastic surgery educator, craniofacial surgeon; b. Mpls., Oct. 10, 1947; s. Alfred Reck and Jeanne Shirley (Hagquist) S.; m. Susan Elizabeth Brown, Aug. 15, 1969; children: Elliott, Mélisande. BA, St. Olaf Coll., Northfield, Minn., 1969; BS with high distinction, U. Minn., 1971, DDS, 1973; diplome asst. etranger with high honors, U. Nantes, France, 1980; MD, U. Hawaii, 1983. Diplomate Am. Bd. Plastic Surgery, Nat. Bd. Med. Examiners, Nat. Bd. Dental Examienrs, Am. Bd. Oral and Maxillofacial Surgery (adv. com., bd. examiner 1991-95). Fellow in oral pathology U. Minn. Sch. Dentistry, Mpls., 1972; pvt. practice gen. dentistry, then oral-maxillofac. surgery, Honolulu, 1974-75, 80-83; resident in gen. dentistry Queen's Med. Ctr., Honolulu, 1973-74; intern, then resident in oral and maxillofacial surgery Parkland Meml. Hosp., Dallas, 1975-79; resident in gen. surgery Baylor U. Med. Ctr., Dallas, 1983-84; resident in gen. surgery Stanford (Calif.) U. Med. Ctr., 1984-86, resident in plastic surgery, 1986-89, acting assoc. prof. surgery, 1989-91, assoc. prof., 1991-95, head div. plastic and reconstructive surgery, 1992—, dir. residency tng., 1992-97, chmn. dept. functional restoration, 1994—, prof., 1995—; head plastic surgery, dir. Craniofacial Ctr. Lucile Salter Packard Children's Hosp., Stanford; asst. to Dr. Paul Tessier, Paris, 1987-88; asst. dept. stomatology and maxillofacial surgery Centre Hospitalier Regional Nantes, 1979-80; referee Am. Jour. Orthodontics and Dentofacial Orthopedics, 1990—; asst. clin. prof. surgery U. Hawaii John A Burns Sch. Medicine, Honolulu, 1980-84; mem. med. bd. Lucile Salter Packard Children's Hosp. at Stanford, 1991—. Assoc. editor Selected Readings in Oral and Maxillofacial Surgery, 1989—; mem. edtl. bd. Jour. Cranio-Maxillofacial Surgery; contbr. articles and abstracts to med. and dental jours., chpts. to books. Recipient Disting. Alumnus award St. Olaf Coll., 1993; Fulbright fellow, Nantes, 1979-80, Chateaubriand fellow Govt. of France, 1987-88. Fellow ACS, Am. Acad. Pediat.; mem. European Assn. Cranio-Maxillofacial Surgeons, Am. Soc. Pediat. Plastic Surgeons, Soc. Baylor Surgeons (founding), French Assn. Maxillofacial Surgeons (fgn.), Am. Cleft Palate-Craniofacial Assn., Am. Soc. Plastic and Reconstructive Surgeons (sec. 1996—), Am. Soc. Maxillofacial Surgeons, Assn. Acad. Chairmen Plastic Surgery, Zedplast (bd. dirs. 1993—), Calif. Med. Assn. (mem. sci. adv. panel on plastic surgery 1992-96), Omicron Kappa Upsilon. Avocations: fly fishing, painting and sculpture. Office: Stanford U Med Ctr NC-104 Div Plastic-Reconstr Surg Stanford CA 94305

SCHENK, JOHN ERWIN, environmental engineer; b. Ann Arbor, Mich., Nov. 16, 1940; s. Erwin Karl and Erma Ida (Burkhardt) S.; m. Nancy Ann Klabunde, Feb. 27, 1965; children: Timothy John, Laura Ann. BS, U. Mich., 1963, MS, 1964, PhD, 1969. Cert. profl. engr., Mich. Exec. v.p. Environ. Control Tech., Ann Arbor, Mich., 1969-86; from v.p. to pres. ENCOTEC, Inc., Ann Arbor, 1986—. Mem. Water Environment Fedn., Mich. Water Pollution Control Assn. (com. 1978-85). Avocations: gardening, fishing. Office: ENCOTEC Inc 3985 Research Park Dr Ann Arbor MI 48108-2219

SCHENK, JOSEPH BERNARD, museum director; b. Glendale, Ariz., Mar. 28, 1953; m. Jacqueline Van Lienop; children: Brian, Stuart. BA in Mus. Staff Preparation, Huntingdon Coll., 1974; MA in Art Edn., Ball State U., 1979; postgrad., U. Calif., Berkeley, 1986. Exhibits asst. Hunter Mus. of Art, Chattanooga, 1974-75; asst. dir. Alford House/Anderson Fine Arts Ctr., Anderson, Ind., 1976, exec. dir., 1976-79; exec. dir. Okefenokee Heritage Ctr., Waycross, Ga., 1979-83; dir. So. Forest World, Waycross, 1979-83, Chattahoochee Valley Art Mus., LaGrange, Ga., 1983-88, Mobile (Ala.) Mus. of Art, 1988—; bd. dirs. U.S. Sports Acad. Art Mus.; v.p. Ala. Mus. Assn., 1994-96, pres., 1996—; adv. panelist Visual Arts Fellowships, Ala. State Coun. on the Arts, 1994-95, Profl. Touring Panel Ga. Coun. for Arts, 1983-84, PRACSO Panel Ga. Coun. for Arts, 1984-86, Arch. & Environ. Arts Ind. Arts Commn., 1978-79, Mus. Ind. Arts Commn., 1977-79; Ind. rep. Small Mus. Com. Midwest Mus. Conf., 1978-79. Pub. numerous art catalogs; editor newsletter Ga. Assembly of Community Arts Agys., 1987-88. Art juror at numerous pub. and pvt. art shows; bd. dirs. Ga. Alliance for Arts Edn., 1982-84, Assn. Ind. Mus., 1979, Mobile Arts Coun., 1989-90, Ga. Assembly Community Arts Agys., 1986-88; commr. Madison County Hist. Home, Anderson, 1977-79; mem. dedication com., cons. Krannert Fine Arts Ctr., Anderson Coll., 1979; mem. com. forest festival tourism and conventions Waycross/Ware County C. of C., 1979-83; bd. dirs. Southeastern Ga. Travel and Tourism Assn., 1981-83, sec., 1981-82, pres., 1982-83. Grantee Nat. Endowment for Arts, Ala. State Coun. on Arts, Mobile Arts Coun., Ga. Endowment for Humanities, Ga. Coun. Arts, Ala. Arts Found., Inst. Mus. Svcs., Ga. Gov.'s Intern Program, others; recipient Spark Plug of Yr. award Waycross Jaycees, 1981; Mus. Mgmt. Inst. scholar, 1986. Mem. Am. Assn. Mus., Southeastern Mus. Conf., Ala. Mus. Assn. (v.p. 1994—), Rotary, Mobile United. Home: 6401 Sugar Creek Dr S Mobile AL 36695-2926 Office: Mobile Museum of Art PO Box 8426 4850 Museum Dr Mobile AL 36689

SCHENK, QUENTIN FREDERICK, retired social work educator, mayor; b. Fort Madison, Iowa, Aug. 25, 1922; s. Fred Edward John and Ida (Sabrowsky) S.; m. Patricia J. Kelley, Aug. 6, 1946 (div. Apr. 1970); children: Fred W. (dec. 1972), Patricia, Karl, Martha; m. Emmy Lou Willson, May 23, 1970. B.A., Willamette U., 1948; M.S., U. Wis., 1950, M.S. in Social Work, 1953, Ph.D., 1953. Asst. prof. social work U. Wis.-Madison, 1953-55, prof., chmn. extension social work, 1961-63; prof., former dean Sch. Social Welfare, Milw., 1962-68, prof. emeritus, 1990—; assoc. prof. U. Mo., 1955-61; project specialist Ford Found., 1968-71; Spl. cons. on urban mission in Africa United Presbyn. Ch., 1971—, World Council Chs., 1971—; adviser to Haile Sellassie I U., Addis Ababa, Ethiopia, 1968-71; Alderman City of Cedarburg (Wis.), 1974-82, mayor, 1982-86. Author: (with Emmy Lou Schenk) Pulling Up Roots, 1978, Welfare Society and the Helping Professions, 1981; author sect. on Ethiopia, Welfare in Africa, 1987; contbr. articles, bulls., reports to profl. lit. Mem. Nat. Trust for Hist. Preservation, Wis. Hist. Preservation Negotiating Bd.; chmn. bd. Guest House, Milw., 1987-89; mem. Sierra Club, Planned Parenthood, Unitarian Fellowship Eau Claire, ACLU, Dem. Party of Wis. Pilot USNR, 1942-46. Decorated Air medal with 3 gold stars, DFC; recipient Presdl. citation Pres. Harry Truman, 1948. Mem. AAUP, Am. Sociol. Assn., Am. Assn. Ret. Persons, Coun. on Social Work Edn., Aircraft Owners and Pilots Assn. Home: # 409 550 Graham Ave Apt 409 Eau Claire WI 54701-5200

SCHENK, SUSAN KIRKPATRICK, geriatric psychiatry nurse, educator, consultant; b. New Richmond, Ind., Nov. 29, 1938; d. William Marcius and Frances (Kirkpatrick) Gaither; m. Richard Dee Brown, Aug. 13, 1960 (div. Feb. 1972); children: Christopher Lee, David Michael, Lisa Catherine; m. John Francis Schenk, July 24, 1975 (widowed Apr. 1995). BSN, Ind. U., 1962; postgrad., U. Del., 1973-75. RN, PHN, BCLS; cert. community coll. tchr., Calif. Staff nurse, then asst. dir. nursing Bloomington (Ind.) Hosp., 1962-66; charge nurse Newark (Del.) Manor, 1967-69; charge nurse GU Union Hosp., Terre Haute, Ind., 1971-72; clin. instr. nursing Ind. State U., Terre Haute, 1972-73; clin. instr. psychiatric nursing U. Del., Newark, 1974-75; psychiatric nursing care coord. VA Med. Ctr., Perry Point, Md., 1975-78; nurse educator Grossmont Hosp., La Mesa, Calif., 1978-90, cmty. rels. coord., 1990-91; dir. psychiat. svcs. Scripps Hosp. East County, El Cajon, Calif., 1991—; tech. advisor San Diego County Bd. Supervisors, 1987; tech. cons. Remedy Home and Health Care, San Diego, 1988; expert panelist Srs. Speak Out, KPBS-TV, San Diego, 1988; guest lectr. San Diego State U., 1987. Editor: Teaching Basic Caregiver Skills, 1988; author, performer tng. videotape Basic Caregiver Skills, 1988. Mem. patient svcs. com. Nat. Multiple Sclerosis Soc., San Diego, 1986-89; bd. dirs. Assn. for Quality and Participation, 1989. Adminstrn. on Aging/DHHS grantee, 1988. Mem. Am. Psychiat. Nurses Assn., Ind. U. Alumni Assn. (life), Mensa, Sigma Theta Tau. Avocations: bluegrass banjo, piano, gardening, reading. Home: 9435D Carlton Oaks Dr Santee CA 92071-2582 Office: Scripps Hosp East County 1688 E Main St El Cajon CA 92021-5204

SCHENK, WORTHINGTON GEORGE, JR., surgeon, educator; b. Buffalo, Feb. 10, 1922; s. Worthington George and Edna (Klein) S.; m. Jean L.K. Lyon, Mar. 9, 1946; children: Martha, Lura, Worthington George III, Elsa, Gregory, Molly, Andrew. B.A., Williams Coll., 1942; M.D., Harvard U., 1945. Diplomate: Am. Bd. Surgery. With U. Buffalo, 1948-66, assoc. prof. surgery, 1959-66; prof. surgery SUNY, Buffalo, 1966-85; acting chmn. dept. surgery SUNY, 1969-72, chmn., 1972-85; dir. surgery Erie County Med. Ctr., Buffalo, 1966-85; ret., 1985. Editorial bd. Current Surgery; contbr. articles to profl. jours. Mem. AMA, Am. So. surg. assns., Am. Assn. Surgery Trauma, Soc. Univ. Surgeons, Soc. Vascular Surgery (past treas., pres. 1976), Soc. Clin. Surgery (sec. 1966-72), Internat. Cardiovascular Soc., ACS, Soc. for Surgery of Alimentary Tract, Surg. Biology Club, Phi Beta Kappa. Home: 38 Front Ave Hanford Bay Silver Creek NY 14136 *It has been a great pleasure to have been involved in the development of vascular surgery from its inception. Retrospectively, my basic laboratory type research contributions now give me the greatest satisfaction, far more than any number of surgical operations. Next in importance is the satisfaction of having turned out more than 25 research fellows.*

SCHENKEL, PETER, food company executive. CEO So. Foods Group, Dallas. Office: Southern Foods Group PO Box 279000 Dallas TX 75227*

SCHENKEL, SUZANNE CHANCE, natural resource specialist; b. Phila., Mar. 12, 1940; d. Henry Martyn Chance II and Suzanne (Sharpless) Jameson; m. John Lackland Hardinge Schenkel, June 15, 1963; children: John Jr., Andrew Chance. BS in Edn., Tufts U., 1962. Tchr. Roland Pk. Country Sch., Balt., 1962-65; exec. dir. Mass. Citizens' Com. for Dental Health, Springfield, 1981-83; pub., editor Women's Investment Newsletter, Longmeadow, Mass., 1985-89; pub. affairs officer USDA's Soil Conservation Svc., Amherst, Mass., 1990-93; resource conservationist divsn. conservation & ecosys. assistance USDA's Natural Resources Conservation Svc., Washington, 1993-97; ops. partnership liaison East Regional Office, Beltsville, Md., 1997—; staff Merchant Marine and Fisheries com. U.S. Ho. of Reps., Washington, 1993. Author Wetlands Protection and Management Act. Chmn. Longmeadow (Mass.) Conservation Commn., 1984-90; supr. Hampden County (Mass.) Conservation Dist., 1985-90; bd. dirs., v.p. League of Women Voters of Mass., Boston, 1974-85; exec. com. Water Supply Citizens' Adv. Com.; adv. bd. Water Resources Authority, Mass., 1979-90. Mem. Soil and Water Conservation Soc., Nat. Assn. Conservation Dists. Episcopalian. Avocations: golf, tennis, sailing. Home: 1052 Carriage Hill Pky Annapolis MD 21401-6505 Office: USDA Natural Resources STe 100 11710 Beltsville Dr Ste 100 Beltsville MD 20705-3102

SCHENKELBACH, LEON, safety consultant, author, educator; b. N.Y.C., Sept. 1, 1917; s. Max and Gussie (Weiner) S.; m. Lucille Ross, Oct. 6, 1946. Student CCNY, 1934-35, Cooper Union Inst., 1938-39; A.S., Connecticut Bd. for State Acad. Awards, 1975. Enlisted as pvt. U.S. Army, 1941, advanced through grades to lt. col., 1961; safety mgr. U.S. P.O. Dept., N.Y.C., 1946-62; safety dir. U.S. Army, Bklyn., 1962-66, Bayonne, N.J., 1964-66; safety mgr. Dept. Def., Hartford, Conn., 1966-69; systems safety mgr. U.S. Army, Rock Island, Ill., 1969-73; retired, 1973; cons. safety to bus., industry, legal profession and academia, Cromwell, Conn., 1974—; mem. adj. faculty Hartford Grad. Ctr., Conn., 1977—, U. New Haven, West Haven, Conn., 1978—; mem. Safety Specialists & Indsl. Hygiene Delegation to Peoples' Republic of China, 1983, lectr., 1985; lectr. to personnel at Ministry Metall. Industry, Beijing, Safety Tech. Research Inst., Wuhan, other personnel in Xian, Huangshi, Shanghai; systems safety cons., USN, 1985; lectr. in field. Author: Safety Management Primer, 1975; Safe Driving Primer, 1979; Mem. budget com. United Way of Iowa/Ill. Quad-Cities, 1970-74; bd. dirs. World Affairs Conf. of Iowa/Ill. Quad-Cities, 1970-74. Mem. Am. Def. Preparedness Assn. (v.p. Hartford/Springfield chpt. 1979-84), Am. Soc. Safety Engrs. (pres. Nutmeg chpt. 1979-80), Conn. Safety Soc. (pres. 1978-79), Ret. Officers Assn. Democrat. Jewish. Home and Office: 44 Silo Way Bloomfield CT 06002-1652

SCHENKENBERG, MARY MARTIN, principal; b. Oakland, Calif., Nov. 29, 1944; d. Leo Patrick and Florence Kathryn (Brinkoetter) Martin; m. Philip Rawson Schenkenberg III, Aug. 20, 1966; children: Philip Rawson IV, Amy Lynn, Stephen Patrick. BA in English, Fontbonne Coll., 1966; MA Teaching in English, St. Louis U., 1975, PhD in English, 1991. Cert. tchr., Mo. Asst. prof. Fontbonne Coll., St. Louis, 1978-85; English dept. chair Nerinx Hall High Sch., St. Louis, 1979-89; asst. prof. Webster U., St. Louis, 1986-89; co-prin. Nerinx Hall High Sch., St. Louis, 1989-92, prin., 1992—; adj. prof. St. Louis U., 1985-89; advanced placement reader Ednl. Testing Svc., Princeton, N.J., 1986-89. Author: (with others) The English Classroom in the Computer Age, 1991. Bd. pres. Mary, Queen of Peace Sch., St. Louis, 1977. Mem. ASCD, Nat. Coun. Tchrs. English, Greater St. Louis Tchrs. English (bd. dirs. 1989—). Roman Catholic. Avocations: tennis, theater, travel. Office: Nerinx Hall High Sch 530 E Lockwood Ave Webster Grvs MO 63119-3217*

SCHENKER, ALEXANDER MARIAN, Slavic linguistics educator; b. Cracow, Poland, Dec. 20, 1924; came to U.S., 1946, naturalized, 1952; s. Oskar and Gizela (Szaminski) S.; m. Krystyna Czajka, Oct. 15, 1970; children: Alfred R., Michael J., Catherine I. Student, Stalinabad Pedagogical Inst., 1943-46, U. Paris, 1947-48; M.A., Yale U., 1950, Ph.D., 1953. Asst. in instrn. Yale U., New Haven, 1950-52; instr. Yale U., 1952-56, asst. prof., 1956-63, asso. prof., 1963-67, prof. Slavic linguistics, 1967—; vis. prof. Slavic linguistics U. Calif., Berkeley, 1969-70. Author: Polish Declension, 1964, Beginning Polish, 2 vols., rev. edit., 1973, The Dawn of Slavic: Introduction to Slavic Philology, 1996; editor: Fifteen Modern Polish Short Stories, 1970, American Contributions to the 10th Internat., Congress of Slavists Linguistics, 1988; co-editor: For Wiktor Weintraub, 1975, The Slavic Literary Languages, 1980, Studies in Slavic Linguistics and Poetics, 1982. Mem. Conn. Acad. Arts and Scis., Polish Inst. Arts/Scis., Am. Assn. Tchrs. Slavic and E. European Langs., Am. Assn. Advancement Slavic Studies. Home: 145 Deepwood Dr Hamden CT 06517-3451 Office: Yale U Dept Slavic Langs and Lits PO Box 208236 New Haven CT 06520-8236

SCHENKER, CARL RICHARD, JR., lawyer; b. Portland, Oreg., Feb. 28, 1949; s. Carl Richard and Frances Emily (Cole) S.; m. Susan Sherman Richardson, Mar. 29, 1986. BA, Stanford U., 1971, JD, 1974. Bar: Calif. 1974, D.C. 1977, U.S. Dist. Ct. (so. dist.) Calif. 1977, U.S. Supreme Ct. 1978, U.S. Dist. Ct. D.C. 1980, U.S. Ct. Appeals (5th and 11th cirs.) 1981, U.S. Ct. Appeals (D.C. cir.) 1983, U.S. Ct. Appeals (2d cir.) 1992. Law clk. to Hon. Shirley M. Hufstedler U.S. Ct. Appeals (9th cir.), L.A., 1974-75; law clk. to Hon. Lewis F. Powell, Jr. U.S. Supreme Ct., Washington, 1975-76; assoc. O'Melveny & Myers, Washington, 1976-82, ptnr., 1982—. Pres. Stanford Law Review, 1973-74; contbr. articles to profl. jours. Mem. ABA, Fed. Bar Assn., D.C. Bar Assn., Phi Beta Kappa. Office: O'Melveny & Myers 555 13th St NW Washington DC 20004-1109

SCHENKER, ERIC, university dean, economist; b. Vienna, Austria, Feb. 24, 1931; came to U.S., 1939, naturalized, 1945; s. Adolph and Olga (Strauss) S.; m. Virginia Martha Wick, Apr. 14, 1963; children: David, Richard, Robert. B.B.A., CCNY, 1952; M.S., U. Tenn., 1955; Ph.D., U. Fla., 1957. Asst. prof. Mich. State U., 1957-59; mem. faculty U. Wis.-Milw., 1959—, prof. econs., 1965—; dean U. Wis.-Milw. (Sch. Bus. Adminstrn.), 1976—; dir. Urban Research Center, 1974-76; asso. dir. Center Great Lakes Studies, 1967-74, sr. scientist, 1974—; asso. dean Coll. Letters and Scis., 1963-69; bd. dirs. Am. Med. Bldgs., Ampco Metal; cons. in field. Author: The Port of Milwaukee: An Economic Review, 1967; co-author: Port Planning and Development as Related to Problems of U.S. Ports and the U.S. Coastal Environment, 1974, The Great Lakes Transportation System, 1976, Port Development in the United States, 1976, Maritime Labor Organizations on the Great Lakes-St. Lawrence Seaway System, 1978, Great Lakes Transportation System in the 80s, 1986; also monographs and articles. Sr. mem. Milw. Bd. Harbor Commrs., 1960-72, chmn., 1965-68; chmn. panel on future port requirements of U.S., Maritime Transp. Research Bd., Nat. Acad. Scis., 1973-76, chmn. panel on reducing tankbarge pollution, 1980-81; mem. pilotage adv. bd. to U.S. sec. transp., 1972-75; trustee Mt. Sinai Med. Ctr, 1984-88; mem. Econ. Progress Authority of Milw. Met. Sewerage Dist., 1983-88, Marine Bd., NAS, 1982-83, Gov.'s Coun. on Econ. Issues, 1983—. Served with AUS, 1952-54. Mem. Am. Econs. Assn., So. Econs. Assn., Phi Kappa Phi, Alpha Kappa Psi, Beta Gamma Sigma, Beta Alpha Psi. Home: 2254 W Dunwood Rd Milwaukee WI 53209-1818

SCHENKER, LEO, retired utility company executive; b. Vienna, Austria, Jan. 3, 1922; came to U.S., 1952, naturalized, 1959; s. Max and Selda Lea (Podhorcer) S.; m. Alda R. Tinson, Jan. 20, 1949; children: Michael Gregory, Deborah Anne. B.S. with first class honors, U. London, 1942; M.A. in Sci. (Can. Inst. Steel Constrn. fellow), U. Toronto, 1950; Ph.D., U. Mich., 1954. Mng. dir. METAG Ltd., London, 1945-48; asst. rsch. engr. Hydro-Electric Power Commn. of Ont. (Can.), Toronto, 1948-52; rsch. assoc. U. Mich., Ann Arbor, 1952-54; with Bell Telephone Labs., 1954-87, various positions, dir. mil. electronic tech., 1968-71; dir. Loop Maintenance Systems Lab., 1971-80, exec. dir. Central Office Ops. div., 1980-83, exec. dir. network system planning div., 1983-84, exec. dir. tech. info. div., 1984-87; adj. prof. electrical engring. Cooper Union, N.Y.C. Served with RAF, 1942-45. Recipient Duggan medal Can. Inst. Steel Constrn., 1950. Fellow IEEE, Sigma Xi, Phi Kappa Phi. Patentee communications tech. field.

SCHENKER, MARC BENET, preventive medicine educator; b. L.A., Aug. 25, 1947; s. Steve and Dosella Schenker; m. Heath Massey, Oct. 8; children: Yael, Phoebe, Hilary. BA, U. Calif., Berkeley, 1969; MD, U. Calif., San Francisco, 1973; MPH, Harvard U., Boston, 1980. Instr. medicine Harvard U., Boston, 1980-82; asst. prof. medicine U. Calif., Davis, 1982-86, assoc. prof., 1986-92, prof., 1992—, chmn. dept. epidemiology and preventive medicine, 1995—. Fellow ACP; mem. Am. Thoracic Soc., Am. Pub. Health Assn., Soc. Epidemiologic Rsch., Am. Coll. Epidemiology, Soc. Occupl. Environ. Health, Internat. Commn. Occupl. Health, Phi Beta Kappa, Alpha Omega Alpha. Office: Dept Epidemiology and Preventive Medicine TB 168 Davis CA 95616-8638

SCHENKER, STEVEN, physician, educator; b. Poland, Oct. 5, 1929; came to U.S., 1943, naturalized, 1946; s. Alfred and Ernestyna S.; m. Sally Ann Wood, May 11, 1956; children: Julie C. Schenker Burn, Steven A., David S., Andrew G., Jennifer E.; m. Jo Ann Neumann, Nov. 24, 1985. B.A., Cornell U., 1951, M.D., 1955. Intern Harvard Service-Boston City Hosp., 1955-56, resident in medicine, 1956-58; asst. prof. medicine U. Cin. Sch. Medicine, 1961-63; asst. prof. U. Tex., Southwestern Sch. Medicine, 1963-67, assoc. prof. medicine, 1967-70; prof. medicine, biochemistry, dir. div. gastroenterology Vanderbilt U. Sch. Medicine, Nashville VA Hosp., 1970-82; prof. medicine and pharmacology, dir. div. gastroenterology U. Tex. Sch. Medicine, San Antonio, 1982—; chmn. study sect. Nat. Inst. on Alcohol Abuse and Addiction, 1980-83; chmn. study sects. VA, 1985-88. Editor: Hepatology, 1985-90. Contbr. numerous articles in field to profl. jours. Recipient Markle award, 1963; Career Devel. award NIH, 1968; Jurzykowski Found. for Research in Medicine award, 1979, Alcoholism Research Soc. award 1987. Mem. Am. Assn. for Study Study of Liver Diseases (pres. 1980), Am. Soc. Clin. Investigation, Assn. Am. Physicians, Am. Gastroent. Soc., Am. Soc. Pharm. and Exptl. Therapeutics, Am. Soc. Clin. Nutrition, Internat. Soc. for Study of Liver Diseases, Alpha Omega Alpha. Home: 26025 Mesa Oak Dr San Antonio TX 78255-3533 Office: U Tex Med Sch San Antonio TX 78284

SCHENKKAN, ROBERT FREDERIC, writer, actor; b. Chapel Hill, N.C., Mar. 19, 1953; s. Robert Frederic Sr. and Jean (McKenzie) S.; m. Mary Anne Dorward, Dec. 1, 1984; children: Sarah Victoria, Joshua McHenry. BA in Theatre Arts, U. Tex., 1975; MFA in Acting, Cornell U., 1977. Author: (plays) Final Passages, 1981, The Survivalist, 1982 (best of the fringe award Edinburgh Festival 1984), Tachinoki, 1987, Tall Tales, 1988 (Playwrights Forum award 1988, Best One Act Plays 1993), Heaven on Earth, 1989 (Julie Harris Playwright award Beverly Hills Theatre Guild 1989), The Kentucky Cycle, 1991 (Pulitzer prize for drama 1992, L.A. Drama Critics Circle Best Play award 1992, Penn Ctr. West award 1993, Best Play Tony award nominee 1993, Best Play Drama Desk award nominee 1993), Conversations with the Spanish Lady and Other One-Act Plays, 1993, (films) The Quiet American, 1997, Crazy Horse, 1996, The Long Ride Home, 1995. Grantee Vogelstein Found., 1982, Arthur Found., 1988, Fund for New Am. Plays grantee 1990, Calif. Arts Coun. grantee, 1991. Mem. Writers Guild, Dramatists Guild, Actors Equity, SAG, Ensemble Studio Theatre.

SCHENKMAN, JOHN BORIS, pharmacologist, educator; b. N.Y.C., Feb. 10, 1936; s. Abraham and Theresa (Moses) S.; m. Deanna Owen, June 5, 1960; children: Jeffrey Alan, Laura Ruth. BA in Chemistry, Bklyn. Coll., 1960; PhD in Biochemistry, SUNY Upstate Med. Ctr., Syracuse, 1964. Postdoctoral fellow U. Pa. Johnson Found., Phila., 1964-67, Inst. Protein Research Osaka U., Japan, 1967-68, Inst. Toxicology Tübingen U., Fed. Republic Germany, 1968; asst. prof. Yale U. Sch. Medicine, New Haven, 1968-71, assoc. prof., 1971-78; prof., dept. head. U. Conn. Health Ctr., Farmington, 1978-87; prof. U. Conn., Farmington, 1987—, dir. grad. program cellular and molecular pharmacology, 1995—. Contbr. articles to profl. jours. Served as sgt. U.S. Army, 1953-55. Research grantee NIH, NSF; recipient Research Career Devel award NIH, 1971-76. Mem. Am. Soc. Biochemists and Molecular Biologists, AM. Soc. Pharmacology Exptl. Therapeutics, Brit. Biochemistry Soc., Soc. Toxicology, Am. Med. Sch. Pharmacologists (councilor 1987-88). Jewish. Avocations: fishing, botany, wine making. Office: U Conn Sch Medicine Dept Phamacology Farmington CT 06030-1505

SCHEPISI, FRED, producer, director, screenwriter; b. Melbourne, Australia, Dec. 26, 1939. Student, Assumption Coll., Marcellin Coll. assessor student films Swinburne Inst. Tech., Melbourne; with govt. sponsored exptl. Film Fund; founder prodn. co. The Film Ho. Dir. films including Libido, 1973, Barbarosa, 1982, Iceman, 1984, Plenty, 1985, Roxanne, 1987; prodr., dir. The Russia House, 1990, Mr. Baseball, 1992, Six Degrees of Separation, 1993, I.Q., 1994; screenwriter, dir., prodr. The Devil's Playground, 1976 (Best Film award Australian Film Inst.), The Chant of Jimmie Blacksmith, 1978, A Cry in the Dark, 1988 (Best Screenplay award Australian Film Inst.). Address: ICM 8942 Wilshire Blvd Beverly Hills CA 90211*

SCHEPPACH, RAYMOND CARL, JR., association executive, economist; b. Hamden, Conn., Mar. 28, 1940; s. Raymond Carl and Margret (Barrie) S.; m. Anna Roberts, July 14, 1962 (div. Nov. 1978); children: Kristine, Raymond Scott; m. Trevia Dean, Apr. 28, 1985. B.A., U. Maine, 1962; M.A., U. Conn., 1965, Ph.D., 1970. Vice pres., sr. cons. Jack Faucett Assocs., Chevy Chase, Md., 1969-75; asst. dir. natural resources and commerce Congl. Budget Office, Washington, 1976-80, dep. dir. office, 1980-82; exec. dir. Nat. Govs. Assn., Washington, 1982—. Author: State Projections of the Gross national Product, 1970 and 1980, Transportation Productivity: Measurement and Policy Applications, 1975, Energy Policy Analysis and Congressional Action, 1982, New Directions in Economic Policy: An Agenda for the 1980's, 1984. Served to capt. U.S. Army, 1962-64. Mem. Am. Econ. Assn. Home: 4078 Rosamora Ct Mc Lean VA 22101-5807 Office: Nat Govs Assn 444 N Capitol St NW Ste 267 Washington DC 20001-1512

SCHEPPS, VICTORIA HAYWARD, lawyer; b. Brockton, Mass., June 11, 1956; d. William George and Lucy Victoria (Mitcheroney) Hayward; m. Frank Schepps, Sept. 18, 1982; children: Frank IV, Lucia. BA, Suffolk U., 1977; JD, U. San Diego, 1981. Instr., Northeastern U., Boston, 1981-83; assoc. Hoffman & Hoffman, Boston, 1983-85, Mark J. Gladstone, P.C., 1985-87; Doktor, Hirschberg & Schepps, 1987-88, Schepps & Reilly, 1988-90; pvt. practice Law Office of Victoria Hayward Schepps, Stoughton, Mass., 1990— . Mem. Mass. Bar Assn., Mass. Conveyancing Assn., Mass. Assn. Bank Counsel, Inc. Democrat. Roman Catholic. Office: 6 Cabot Pl Ste 9 Stoughton MA 02072-4625

SCHER, ALLAN JOSEPH, oncologist, consultant; b. Bklyn., June 2, 1935; s. David E. and Helen (Elbogen) S.; m. Linda Ronni Tash, Apr. 2, 1966; children: Michael B., Lauren J. BA, Yeshiva U., 1957; MD, Albert Einsten Coll. of Medicine, 1962. Diplomate Nat. Bd. Med. Examiners, 1963, Am. Bd. Radiology, 1967; lic. N.Y. 1963, Calif. 1966, N.J. 1968. Intern Bronx-Lebanon Hosp. Ctr., N.Y., 1962-63; resident in radiology Kings County Hosp., Bklyn., 1963-66; asst. chief radiation therapy USNR, San Diego, 1966-68; chief radiation oncology Morristown (N.J.) Meml. Hosp., 1968-86; cons. in radiation therapy Hackettstown (N.J.) Community Hosp., 1973-91; asst. adj. radiologist Beth Israel Hosp. Ctr., N.Y.C., 1966; clin. asst. instr. Kings County Hosp., 1969-71; clin. asst. prof. radiology Rutgers Med. Sch., 1974—; adj. asst. prof. allied health Fairleigh Dickinson U., Teaneck, N.J., 1975-85; cons. in radiation therapy Community Med. Ctr., Morristown, 1970-80. Presented numerous papers at various medical symposia. Mem. Coun. on Cancer, N.J., 1972-73, med. com. Riverside Hospice, 1976-79. State of N.Y. Med. Edn. and Rsch. Found. fellow, 1966-67. Fellow N.J. Acad. Medicine (sec. radiation therapy sect. 1975-76, chmn. 1976-77), Am. Coll. Radiology (alternate councillor 1981-84, councillor 1984-87); mem. AMA, Am. Soc. Therapeutic Radiology and Oncology, N.J. Oncology Soc. (co-founder, treas. 1975-77, trustee 1984-86, treas. 1987-88, sec. 1988-89, v.p. 1989-90, pres. 1990-91), N.J. Med. Soc. (sec. radiology sect. 1971-72, chmn. 1972-73, mem. ad hoc com. on atomic energy plants 1976), Radiology Soc. N.J. (sec. 1977-78, v.p. 1978-79, pres.-elect 1979-80, pres. 1980-81, mem. exec. com. 1972-94, chmn. radiotherapy sect. 1972-94, 96), Morris County Med. Soc., Albert Einstein Coll. Medicine Alumni Assn. (mem. bd. govs. 1975-78), N.J. Assn. Med. Specialty Socs. (v.p. 1980, pres. 1981), Acad. Medicine of N.J. (mem. exec. com. 1991). Jewish. Avocations: skiing, archaeology. Office: Radiation Oncologists of NW NJ 100 Madison Ave Morristown NJ 07960-6013

SCHER, HOWARD DENNIS, lawyer; b. Ft. Monmouth, N.J., Apr. 23, 1945; s. George Scher and Rita (Eitches) Zar; children: Seth Micah, Eli David. BA, Brandeis U., 1967; JD, Rutgers U., 1971. Bar: Pa. 1971, U.S. Dist. Ct. (ea. dist.) Pa. 1971, U.S. Ct. Appeals (3rd cir.) 1971, U.S. Supreme Ct. 1975. Asst. city solicitor City of Phila., 1971-73; assoc. Goodis, Greenfield, Henry & Edelstein, Phila., 1973-77; assoc. Montgomery, McCracken, Walker & Rhoads, Phila., 1977-80, ptnr., 1980—. V.p. Jewish Employment Vocat. Svcs., Phila., 1988—; trustee Fedn. of Jewish Agys. of Greater Phila.; dir. Akiba Hebrew Acad., Merion, Pa.; mem. pres.'s coun. Brandeis U. Fellow Am. Coll. Trial Lawyers; mem. ABA, Pa. Bar Assn., Phila. Bar Assn., Brandeis U. Alumni Assn. (v.p. 1983-87). Home: 2222 Locust St Philadelphia PA 19103-5511 Office: Montgomery McCracken Walker & Rhoads 123 S Broad St Philadelphia PA 19109-1029

SCHER, IRVING, lawyer; b. N.Y.C., July 22, 1933; s. Charles and Tillie (Ballenberg) S.; m. Amy Lynn Katz, June 8, 1985; 1 child, Sara Katz-Scher. BA, City Coll. N.Y., 1955; JD, Columbia U., 1962. Bar: N.Y. 1963. Assoc. Weil, Gotshal & Manges, N.Y.C., 1962-69, ptnr., 1969—; adj. prof. NYU Sch. Law, 1972—; co-chmn. ann. anti-trust law inst. Practicing Law Inst., N.Y.C., 1976—; adv. bd. Antitrust and Trade Regulation Reports, 1980—. Editor Columbia Law Rev., 1960-61, revs. editor, 1961-62; editor, co-author: Antitrust Advisor, 4th edit., 1995; contbr. articles to profl. jours. Served as lt. USNR, 1955-59. Recipient Harlan Fiske Stone scholarship Columbia Law Sch., 1960-62, Nat. Scholarship award Columbia Law Sch., 1961-62, Gluck scholarship Columbia Law Sch., 1960-61. Mem. ABA (chmn. antitrust law section 1988-89), N.Y. State Bar Assn. (chmn. antitrust law section 1980-81). Jewish. Avocations: skiing, theater. Office: Weil Gotshal & Manges 767 5th Ave New York NY 10153-0001

SCHER, ROBERT SANDER, instrument design company executive; b. Cin., May 24, 1934; s. Stanford Samuel and Eva (Ordan) S.; m. Audrey Erna Gordon, Oct. 21, 1961; children: Sarahh, Alexander, Aaron. SB, MIT, 1956, SM, 1958, Diploma in Mech. Engring., 1960, ScD, 1963. Rsch. and teaching asst. MIT, Cambridge, Mass., 1957-62; control system engr. RCA, Hightstown, N.J., 1963-65; engring. mgr. Sequential Info. System, Elmsford, N.Y., 1965-71; tech. dir. Teledyne Gurley, Troy, N.Y., 1971-78, v.p. engring., 1978-86, pres., 1986-92; pres. Encoder Design Assocs., Clifton Park, N.Y., 1993—. Co-author patent Linear Digital Readout, 1975. Mem. ASME, Optical Soc. Am. Jewish. Avocation: chamber music. Home: 2 Laurel Oak Ln Clifton Park NY 12065-4712

SCHER, STEVEN PAUL, literature educator; b. Budapest, Hungary, Mar. 2, 1936; came to U.S., 1957, naturalized, 1963; Diploma in piano, Bela Bartok Conservatory of Music, Budapest, 1955; B.A. cum laude, Yale U., 1960, M.A., 1963, Ph.D., 1966. Instr. German, Columbia U., N.Y.C., 1965-67; asst. prof. German, Yale U., New Haven, 1967-70; assoc. prof. Yale U., 1970-74; prof. German and comparative lit. Dartmouth Coll., Hanover, N.H., 1974—; chmn. dept. Dartmouth Coll., 1974-80, acting chmn. dept., 1982-83, Ted and Helen Geisel 3d Century prof. humanities, 1984-89; vis. prof. U. Paderborn, Fed. Republic Germany, summer 1980, Karl-Franzens-U. Graz, Austria, summer 1984; grant reviewer Guggenheim Found., NEH, Am. Council Learned Socs., others; cons. univ. presses and scholarly jours.; lectr. throughout world. Author: Verbal Music in German Literature, 1968; editor: (with Charles McClelland) Postwar German Culture: An Anthology, 1974, 2d edit., 1980, Interpretationen: Zu E.T.A. Hoffmann, 1981, (with Ulrich Weisstein) Literature and the Other Arts. Proc. of IXth Congress of Internat. Comparative Lit. Assn., Innsbruck, vol. 3, 1981, Literatur und Musik. Ein Handbuch zur Theorie und Praxis eines komparatistischen Grenzgebietes, 1984, Music and Text: Critical Inquiries, 1992; contbr. articles and essays to scholarly jours. Morse fellow, 1969-70; Humboldt fellow, 1972-73; Yale Coll. scholar, 1957-60, grad. fellow, 1960-62; DAAD grantee U. Munich, 1964-65. Mem. MLA (chmn. bibliography com. of div. lit. 1972-86), Am. Comparative Lit. Assn., Internat. Comparative Lit. Assn., Internat. P.E.N. Club. Home: 102 S Main St Hanover NH 03755-2040 Office: Dartmouth College Dept German Dartmouth Hall Hanover NH 03755

SCHER, VALERIE JEAN, music critic; b. Chgo., Jan. 31, 1952; d. Jacob and Klema (Seider) S.; m. David Clark Elliott, Sept. 6, 1980; children: Sabrina, Travis. B in Performance Piano, Northwestern U., Evanston, Ill., 1974, M in Music History, 1976, postgrad., 1978. Asst. music critic Chgo. Daily News, 1975-78; asst. music and dance critic Chgo. Sun-Times, 1978-82; dance critic, asst. music critic Phila. Inquirer, 1982-83; music and dance critic San Diego Tribune, 1984-91, music, dance and theater critic, 1991-92; music critic San Diego Union-Tribune, 1992—. Mem. Music Critics Assn. Avocations: horseback riding, gardening, cooking. Office: San Diego Union-Tribune 350 Camino De La Reina San Diego CA 92108-3003

SCHERAGA, HAROLD ABRAHAM, physical chemistry educator; b. Bklyn., Oct. 18, 1921; s. Samuel and Etta (Goldberg) S.; m. Miriam Kurnow, June 20, 1943; children: Judith Anne, Deborah Ruth, Daniel Michael. B.S., CCNY, 1941; A.M., Duke U., 1942, Ph.D., 1946, Sc.D. (hon.), 1961; Sc.D. (hon.), U. Rochester, 1988, U. San Luis, 1992, Technion, 1993. Teaching, research asst. Duke U., 1941-46; fellow Harvard Med. Sch., 1946-47; instr. chemistry Cornell U., 1947-50, asst. prof., 1950-53, assoc. prof., 1953-58, prof., 1958-65, Todd prof. chemistry, 1965-92, Todd prof. chemistry emeritus, 1992—, chmn. dept., 1960-67; vis. assoc. biochemist Brookhaven Nat. Lab., summers 1950, 51, cons. biology dept., 1950-56; vis. lectr. div. protein chemistry Wool Rsch. Labs., Melbourne, Australia, 1959; vis. prof. Soc. for Promotion Sci., Japan, Aug. 1977; mem. tech. adv. panel Xerox Corp., 1969-71, 74-79; mem. biochemistry tng. com. NIH, 1963-65, reviewers rsch., 1995—; mem. rsch. career award com. NIGMS, 1967-71; commn. molecular biophysics Internat. Union for Pure and Applied Biophysics, 1965-69, mem. commn. macromolecular biophysics, 1969-75, pres., 1972-75, mem. commn. subcellular and macromolecular biophysics, 1975-81; adv. panel molecular biology NSF, 1960-62; Welch Found. lectr., 1962, Harvey lectr., 1968, Gallagher lectr., 1968, Lemieux lectr., 1973, Hill lectr., 1976, Venable lectr., 1981; co-chmn. Gordon Conf. on Proteins, 1963; mem. coun. Gordon Rsch. Confs., 1969-71. Author: Protein Structure, 1961, Theory of Helix-Coil Transitions in Biopolymers, 1970; co-editor Molecular Biology, 1961-86; mem. editl. bd. Physiol. Chemistry and Physics, 1969-75, Mechanochemistry and Motility, 1970-71, Thrombosis Rsch., 1972-76, Biophys. Jour., 1973-75, Macromolecules, 1973-84, Computers and Chemistry, 1974-84, Internat. Jour. Peptide and Protein Chemistry, 1982—; corr. PAABS Revista, 1971-73; mem. editl. adv. bd. Biopolymers, 1963—, Biochemistry, 1969-74, 85—, Structural Chemistry, 1989-93, Jour. Computational Polymer Sci., 1991—, Jour. Biomolecular NMR, 1991—, Jour. Biomed. Sci., 1994—, Jour. Am. Chem. Soc., 1995—. Mem. Ithaca Bd. Edn., 1958-59; Bd. govs. Weizmann Inst., Israel, 1970—; mem. staff Naval Research Lab. Project, Air Force OSRD Project, World War II. Fulbright, Guggenheim fellow Carlsberg Lab., Copenhagen, 1956-57, Weizmann Inst., Israel, 1963; NIH Spl. fellow Weizmann Inst., 1970; Fogarty scholar NIH, 1984, 86, 88-91; recipient Townsend Harris medal CCNY, 1970, Chemistry Alumni Sci. Achievements award, 1977, Kowalski medal Internat. Soc. Thrombosis and Haemostatis, 1983, Linderstrøm-Lang medal Carlsberg Lab., 1983, Internat. Soc. of Quantum Chemistry and Quantum Pharmacology award in Theoretical Biology, 1993, Stein & Moore award Protein Soc., 1995; named Hon. mem. Soc. Polymer Sci. Japan, 1995. Fellow AAAS; mem. NAS, Am. Peptide Soc. (hon.), Am. Chem. Soc. (chmn. Cornell sect. 1955-56, mem. exec. com. div. biol. chemistry 1966-69, vice chmn. divsn. biol. chemistry 1970, chmn. divsn. biol. chemistry 1971, Eli Lilly award 1957, Nichols medal 1974, Kendall award 1978, Pauling award 1985, Mobil award 1990, Repligen award 1990, IBM award for computers in chem. and pharm. rsch. 1997), Am. Soc. Biol. Chemists, Biophys. Soc. (coun. 1967-70), Am. Acad. Arts and Scis., N.Y. Acad. Scis. (hon. life), Hungarian Biophys. Soc. (hon.), Phi Beta Kappa, Sigma Xi, Phi Lambda Upsilon. Home: 212 Homestead Ter Ithaca NY 14850-6220

SCHERAGA, JOEL DOV, economist; b. Bklyn., Mar. 29, 1955; s. Morton G. and Susanna (Rothberg) S. AB, Brown U., 1976, MA, 1979, PhD, 1981. Rsch. asst. Jet Propulsion Lab., summer 1974, 75; geophys. rsch. asst. Brown U., Providence, 1976-77, teaching asst., 1977-80; instr. U. R.I., Providence, 1979-80; asst. prof. Rutgers U., New Brunswick, N.J., 1981-87; vis. asst. prof. Princeton (N.J.) U., 1985-86; sr. economist U.S. EPA, Washington, 1987-91, br. chief, 1991-95, divsn. dir., 1995—; sr. economist Nat. Acid Precipitation Assessment Program, Washington, 1989-90. Author: Problems and Issues in Microeconomics, 1985; contbr. articles to profl. publs. Tchr. Hebrew, Congregation Har Shalom, Potomac, Md., 1987. Mem. Am. Econs. Assn., Soc. Govt. Economists (book rev. editor 1988-90), Ea. Econs. Assn. (program com. 1985-88). Avocations: flying, sky diving, running, softball, bowling. Home: 545 N Piedmont St Arlington VA 22203 Office: EPA Mail Code 2174 401 M St SW Washington DC 20460-0001

SCHERECK, WILLIAM JOHN, retired historian, consultant; b. Chgo., Dec. 22, 1913; s. Frank and Adele (Schubert) S.; m. Flora Blanche George, May 19, 1943; children: Linda, William Jr.,Ralph, Florian. Student Wofford Coll., 1950-51; BS in Sociology, U. Wis.,952, po stgrad., 1952-53. With Crawford County (Wis.) Welfare Dept., 1938-42; with State Hist. Soc. Wis., Madison, 1953-79, rsch. asst., 1954-55, field services supr., 1956-59, head Office Local History, 1960-79, Wis. Coun. Local History, from 1961, ret.; now researcher ancient histories and religions; Wm J. Ess Desktop Publs. include Safe Karate, How to Get Out of Bed, Ghosts of the Battlefield. Active Girls Scouts U.S.A., Spartanburg, S.C., 1947-48, Boy Scouts Am., Madison, 1956-58. 2d lt. U.S. Army, 1942-45. Decorated Bronze Star; recipient 1st place award S.C. State Coll. Press Assn., 1951, Crusade for Freedom awards, 1951, 1st place award for Sounds of Heritage, Am. Exhbn. Ednl. Radio and TV, 1955. Author, distbr. Simplified System of Cataloging local Hist. Soc. and Mus. Mem. Am. Legion, Ret. Officers Assn., Am. Fedn. State, County and Mcpl. Employees, Am. Fedn. of Police, Wis. Alumni Assn., Am. Assn. Ret. Persons. Methodist. Author How to Get Out of Bed, Ghosts of the Battlefield, Safe Karate; award winning poet; contbr. articles to mags. and newspapers. Home: 11013 W Harmony Dr Lodi WI 53555

SCHERER, A. EDWARD, nuclear engineering executive; b. Bklyn., May 23, 1942; s. Samuel M. and Margie Scherer. BS in Mech. Engring., Worcester Poly. Inst., 1963; MS in Nuclear Engring., Pa. State U., 1965; MBA, Rensselaer Poly. Inst., Hartford, Conn., 1978. Registered profl. engr., Mass. Asst. to project mgr. Combustion Engring., Inc., Windsor, Conn., 1968-70, reactor project engr., test evaluation engr., 1970-73, asst. project mgr., 1973-75, mgr. nuclear licensing, 1975-80, dir. nuclear licensing, 1980-90, v.p. nuclear quality ABB Combustion Engring. Nuclear Power, 1990-92, v.p. regulatory affairs ABB Combustion Engring. Nuclear Fuel, 1992-93; v.p. bus. devel. ABB Combustion Engring. Nuclear Ops., 1993-96; mem. tech. adv. com., mem. issues mgmt. com., mem. standardization oversight com. NUMARC, Washington; mem. Indsl. Profl. Adv. Coun., 1991-96, Pa. State U., chmn. nuc. engring., 1995-96. Contbr. articles to profl. jours. Mem. Penn State Indsl. Profl. Adv. Coun., 1991-96 (chmn. nuclear engring. 1996). Capt. U.S. Army, 1965-67, South Vietnam. Named Outstanding Engring. Alumnus, Pa. State U., 1995. Fellow ASME; mem. Am. Nuclear Soc., Sigma Xi, Alpha Epsilon Pi (internat. pres. 1982-84, fiscal control bd. 1986—, v.p. Found. 1985—).

SCHERER, FREDERIC MICHAEL, economics educator; b. Ottawa, Ill., Aug. 1, 1932; s. Walter King and Margaret (Lucey) S.; m. Barbara A. Silbermann, Aug. 17, 1957; children: Thomas, Karen S. Main, Christina. AB with honors, U. Mich., 1954; MBA with high distinction, Harvard U., 1958, PhD, 1963; D (hon.), Univ. Hohenheim, 1996. Asst. prof. Princeton (N.J.) U., 1963-66; prof. econs. U. Mich., Ann Arbor, 1966-72; chief economist FTC, Washington, 1974-76; prof. econs. Northwestern U., Evanston, Ill., 1976-82; Joseph Wharton prof. polit. economy Swarthmore (Pa.) Coll., 1982-89; Larsen prof. pub. policy and mgmt. Harvard U., Cambridge, Mass., 1989—; vis. prof. Ctrl. European U., Prague, 1993-94; Arthur Andersen disting. visitor U. Cambridge, U.K., 1997. Author: The Weapons Acquisition Process, 1964 (Lancaster prize 1964), Industrial Market Structure and Economic Performance, 1970, 3d rev. edit., 1990, The Economics of Multi-Plant Operation, 1975, Innovation and Growth, 1984, International High-Technology Competition, 1992, Competition Policies for an Integrated World Economy, 1994, Industry Structure, Strategy and Punblic Policy, 1996; co-author: Mergers, Sell-Offs and Economic Efficiency, 1987; mem. editl. bd. Jour. Indsl. Econs., 1982-89, Jour. Econ. Lit., 1989—; assoc. editor Ency. Econs., 1983—. Mem. adv. panel NSF, Washington, 1980-83, U.S. Office Tech. Assessment, 1989-93, U.S. Bur. of the Census, 1997—. Sr. research fellow Internat. Inst. Mgmt., 1972-74, Am. Stats. Assn. Census fellow, 1989-90; Baker scholar Harvard U., 1957; grantee NSF, 1970, 79, 82; O'Melveny & Myers Centennial Rsch. grantee, 1989, Sloan Fedn. grantee, 1996. Mem. European Assn. for Rsch. in Indsl. Econs. (co-founder 1974), Internat. J.A. Schumpeter Assn. (pres. 1988-90), Brit-N.Am. Com., Am. Econ. Assn. (v.p. 1988), Indsl. Orgn. Soc. (pres. 1992), So. Econ. Assn. (v.p. 1990). Democrat. Roman Catholic. Avocations: listening to music, musicology. Home: 48 Pier 7 Charlestown MA 02129 Office: Harvard U John F Kennedy Sch Govt Cambridge MA 02138

SCHERER, HAROLD NICHOLAS, JR., electric utility company executive, engineer; b. Plainfield, N.J., Apr. 5, 1929; s. Harold Nicholas and Nora (McDonough) S.; m. Jane Neely, Sept. 6, 1952 (div.); children—Anne Scherer McConnell, Peter; m. Patricia Condon, May 4, 1974; stepchildren: James, John, Joseph, Jeffery Ludwig, Jean Ludwig Ransdell. B.E., Yale U., 1951; M.B.A., Rutgers U., 1955. Registered profl. engr., N.J., Mass. Various engring. positions Pub. Service Electric and Gas Co., Newark, 1951-63; various engring. positions Am. Electric Power Service Corp., N.Y.C., 1963-68, asst. chief elec. engr., 1968-69, chief elec. engr., 1969-73, v.p. elec. engr., 1973-82; sr. v.p. elec. engring. Am. Electric Power Service Corp., Columbus, Ohio, 1982-90; also dir. Am. Electric Power Service Corp., until 1990; pres. Commonwealth Electric Co., Wareham, Mass., 1990-93, Cambridge Electric Light Co., Canal Electric Co., Com/Steam Co., 1990-93; bd. dirs. Commonwealth Electric Co., Cambridge Electric Light Co., Com/Steam Co., Commonwealth Svcs. Co., Canal Electric Co.; cons. utility mgmt. and engring., 1993—; mem. joint U.S.-USSR working group on power transmission, 1975-81, joint U.S.-Italy working group on power transmission, 1979-88; vice-chmn. Am. Nat. Stds., N.Y.C., 1985-87; v.p. U.S. Nat. Com., 1985-93, pres., 1993—, chmn. U.S. tech. com. Internat. Conf. on Large High Voltage Electric Sys., 1985-91, internat. adminstrv. coun., 1988—, internat. exec. com., 1993—; mem. engring. rev. bd. Bonneville Power Adminstrn., 1984-94; chmn. elec. sys. and equipment com. Edison Electric Inst., 1989-90, pres. power engring. edn. found., 1992-96; chmn. blue-ribbon panel Pacific Coast Blackouts, Bonneville-Power Adminstrn., 1996-97. Contbr. articles to profl. jours. Pres. N.J. Jr. C. of C., 1960-61; councilman City of Plainfield, 1963-65; mem. Watchung (N.J.) Hills Regional H.S. Bd. Edn., 1970-72; pres. Woods at Josephinum Civic Assn., Worthington, Ohio, 1983-84. Recipient Clayton Frost award U.S. Jaycees, 1961, Young Man of Yr. award Plainfield Jaycees, 1963, Lifetime Achievement award T&D Mag., 1990. Fellow IEEE (v.p. power engring. soc. 1988-89, pres. 1990-91), William Habirshaw award for transmission and distbn. engring. 1986, Disting. Mem. award Internat. Conf. on Large High Voltage Electric Systems 1996); mem. NAE, Tau Beta Pi, Beta Gamma Sigma. Republican. Home and Office: 467 Bay Ln Centerville MA 02632-3352

SCHERER, KARLA, foundation executive, venture capitalist; b. Detroit, Jan. 13, 1937; d. Robert Pauli and Margaret (Lindsey) S.; m. Peter R. Fink, Sept. 14, 1957 (div. July 1989); children: Christina Lammert, Hadley McKenzie Tolliver, Allison Augusta Scherer; m. Theodore Souris, Sept. 5, 1992. Student, Wellesley Coll., 1954-55; BA, U. Mich., 1957. Chmn. Karla Scherer Found., Detroit, 1989—; advisor on shareholders' rights; speaker on corp. governance to various univs. and profl. assns.; condr. workshops in field; leader only successful proxy contest of maj. U.S. publicly held corp., 1988. Trustee Eton Acad., Birmingham, Mich., 1989—; mem. vis. com. Fordham U. Grad. Sch. Bus. Adminstrn.; former mem. bd. dirs. Cottage Hosp., Univ. Liggett Sch., Music Hall, Detroit League for Handicapped; former mem. adv. bd. Wellesley Coll; former mem. Rep. Dennis M. Hertel's Candidate Selection Com. for Armed Svcs. Acads.; mem. U. Mich. Ctr. for the Edn. of Women Leadership Coun. Named Outstanding Woman Leader of Yr. Oakland U., 1990, one of Metro Detroit's Dynamic Women Women's Econ. Club, 1992, Entrepreneur of Yr. Finalist, 1993. Mem. Am. Mgmt. Assn. (gen. mgmt. coun. for growing orgns.), Women's Forum Mich., Econ. Club Detroit (bd. dirs. 1991—), Women's Econ. Club Detroit, Detroit Club, Detroit Athletic Club, Country Club Detroit, Grosse Pointe Club, Renaissance Club (bd. dirs. 1995—). Office: 100 Renaissance Ctr Ste 1680 Detroit MI 48243-1009

SCHERER, NORBERT FRANZ, chemistry educator; b. Milw., July 9, 1960; s. Franz and Ilse Scherer; m. Seung-Eun Choi, June 2, 1990; children: Matthew S., Amanda, Andrew. BS, U. Chgo., 1982; PhD, Caltech., 1989. NSF postdoctoral fellow U. Chgo., 1989-91, postdoctoral assoc., 1991-92; asst. prof. chemistry U. Pa., Phila., 1992-97; prof. chemistry U. Chgo., 1997—. Contbr. articles to sci. publs. Recipient Nat. Young Investigator award NSF, 1993-98; David and Lucile Packard fellow, 1993-98, Arnold and

Mabel Beckman fellow, 1994-96, Alfred P. Sloan fellow, 1997; Camille Dreyfus tchr.-scholar, 1996. Mem. Am. Chem. Soc., Am. Phys. Soc., Optical Soc. Am. Office: U Chgo Dept Chemistry 4735 S Ellis Ave Chicago IL 60637

SCHERER, ROBERT DAVISSON, retired business and association executive; b. Ironton, Ohio, Jan. 27, 1929; s. Albert C. and Lois (Davisson) S.; m. Margaret Jane Harsh, June 18, 1951; children: Gary, Mark, Thomas. BS in Agr., Ohio State U., 1950. With sales and mktg. depts. Landmark and affiliates, 1955-75; v.p. food div. Landmark, Inc., Columbus, Ohio, 1975-81, sr. v.p. adminstrn., 1982-83, exec. v.p., chief exec. officer, 1983-85; exec. v.p., chief oper. officer Countrymark, Inc., Delaware, Ohio, 1985-86; pres., chief exec. officer Nat. Coop. Bus. Assn., Washington, 1986-93; pres. AGLANDS, Inc., 1993—. Bd. dirs. CARE, N.Y.C. then Atlanta, 1988—, Overseas Co-op. Devel. Commn., Washington, 1986-93, vols. in Overseas Devel. Assistance, Washington, 1986-93; bd. dirs. exec. com. Internat. Co-op. Alliance, Geneva, 1987-93; agr. rep. alumni adv. coun. Ohio State U., 1983-89; mem. Bennett Round Table of Farm Found., AID Adminstr.'s Adv. Com. on Voluntary Fgn. AID, 1988-93; bd. dirs. Citizens Network, Nat. Agrl. Adv. Com., 1987-93. Recipient Disting. Alumni award Ohio State U. Coll. Agr., 1983, Exec. of Yr. award Profl. Secs. Internat., Cen. Ohio, 1984. Mem. Gamma Sigma Delta. Republican. Home: 610 Garden Pky Circleville OH 43113-1422

SCHERER, RONALD CALLAWAY, voice scientist, educator; b. Akron, Ohio, Sept. 11, 1945; s. Belden Davis and Lois Ramona (Callaway) S.; children: Christopher, Maria. BS, Kent State U., 1968; MA, Ind. U., 1972; PhD, U. Iowa, 1981. Research asst. U. Iowa, Iowa City, 1979-81, asst. research scientist, 1981-83, adj. asst. prof., 1983-88, adj. assoc. prof., 1988—; adj. asst. prof. U. Denver, 1984-86; asst. adj. prof. U. Colo., Boulder, 1984-93, adj. assoc. prof., 1993—; research scientist The Denver Ctr. for the Performing Arts, 1983-88, sr. scientist, 1988-96; lectr. voice and speech sci. Nat. Theatre Conservatory, Denver, 1990-94; asst. clin. prof. Sch. Medicine U. Colo., Denver, 1988—; assoc. prof. Bowling Green State U, OH, 1996—; adj. assoc. prof. U. Okla., 1992—; affiliate clin. prof. U. No. Colo., 1993—; Oberlin Coll. affiliate scholar, 1996—; mem. exec. and legis. bd. Nat. Ctr. for Voice and Speech, 1990-96. Author: (with Dr. I. Titze) Vocal Fold Physiology: Biomechanics, Acoustics and Phonatory Control, 1983; contbr. articles to profl. jours. Nat. Inst. Dental Research fellow, 1972-76. Fellow Internat. Soc. Phonetic Scis. (auditor 1988-91); mem. Internat. Arts Medicine Assn., Am. Speech-Lang.-Hearing Assn., Acoustical Soc. Am., Internat. Assn. Logopedics and Phoniatrics, Am. Assn. Phonetic Scis. (nominating com. 1985-87), Collegium Medicorum Theatri, Sigma Xi, Pi Mu Epsilon. Office: Bowling Green State U Dept Comm Disorders Bowling Green OH 43403

SCHERER, SUZANNE MARIE, artist, educator; b. Buffalo, Sept. 12, 1964; d. Robert Henry Scherer and Judith Louise Le Bar; m. Pavel Victorovich Ouporov, Oct. 25, 1991. AA, Broward C.C., 1984; BFA magna cum laude, Fla. State U., 1986; MFA summa cum laude, Bklyn. Coll., 1989; postgrad., Surikov State Art Acad., Moscow, 1989-91. Educator Bklyn. Mus., 1987-89; profl. artist N.Y.C., 1989—; guest lectr. Bklyn. Coll., 1992, Pa. Sch. Art and Design, Lancaster, 1996; artist-in-residence Lancaster Mus. and Pa. Sch. Art and Design, 1996; lectr. Lancaster Mus. Artist: The Trouble with Testosterone and Other Essays on the Biology of the Human Predicament, by Robert M Sapolsky, 1997, Bataille's Eye, 1997, The Basics of Buying Art, 1996, Monumental Propaganda, 1994, Genesis: A Living Conversation, 1996; artist (jour.) the Scis. 1995-96, (TV) Genesis: A Living Conversation, 1996, (radio) Radio Free Europe: Interview with Raya Vail, 1995, WBAI-FM: Interview with Charles Finch, 1994; solo exhbns. include Lancaster (Pa.) Mus. Art, 1996, H. Ferzt Gallery, N.Y.C., 1994, Ctrl. House of Artist-New Tretyakov Gallery, Moscow, 1991, Spaso House Gallery, Residence of Am. Amb., Moscow, 1991; group exhbns. include Bass Mus. Art, Miami Beach, Fla., 1996, Schmidt Bingham Gallery, N.Y.C., 1996, Kemper Mus. Contemporary Art, Kansas City, Mo., 1995, Smithsonian Instn., 1995, Dalaenas Mus., Fawn, Sweden, 1995, Brit. Consulate, 1995, Desaisset Mus., Santa Clara, Calif., 1994, N.Y. Acad. Scis., N.Y.C., 1996; pub. collections include N.Y. Pub. Libr., N.Y.C., Bob Blackburn's Printmaking Workshop Collection, N.Y.C., Lancaster Mus. Art, Min. Culture, Moscow, Russian Acad. Art, Moscow. Mem. Internat. Women's Orgn., Moscow, 1989-91. Grantee Internat. Rsch. and Exchs. Bd., 1989; Visual Arts Residency grantee Mid-Atlantic Arts Found., 1996. Democrat. Avocations: reading, visiting museums, collecting art and artifacts, photography. Home and Office: Scherer and Ouporov 2d Fl 97 President St Brooklyn NY 11231

SCHERF, CHRISTOPHER N., foundation administrator; b. N.Y.C., Aug. 8, 1950; s. Richard Edward and Doris Margaret (Farley) S.; m. Diane Frances Koenig, Nov. 13, 1981; children: Casey Lyn, Donna Streit, Donald Makofske. BA, U. Md., 1972. Sports writer Hagerstown (Md.) Morning Herald, 1973, UPI, N.Y.C., 1973-77, The Courier-Jour., Louisville, 1977-78; mgr. media rels. N.Y. Racing Assn., Jamaica, 1978-82; dir. svc. bur. Thoroughbred Racing Assns. of N.Am., 1982-88, exec. v.p., 1988—; also bd. dirs. Thoroughbred Racing Assns. of N.Am., Elkton, Md.; bd. dirs. TRA Ins. Co., TRA Enterprises, Inc.; govt. affairs comm. Am. Horse Coun., 1988—. Co-author: Pro Basketball'76-'77, 1976, Pro Basketball '77-'78, 1977. Mem. Turf Publicists Am., Nat. Turf Writers Assn., Am. Soc. Assn. Execs. Office: Thoroughbred Racing Assn(TRA) 420 Fair Hill Dr Elkton MD 21921-2573

SCHERF, JOHN GEORGE, IV, lawyer; b. Tuscaloosa, Ala., Oct. 12, 1962; s. John G. III and Roberta Cannon (Timmons) S.; m. Lorie Lankford, Feb. 12, 1994; 1 child, Austin Tyler. AA, Okaloosa Walton Jr. Coll., Niceville, Fla., 1983; BA in Psychology, U. West Fla., 1987; JD, Samford U., 1991. Bar: Ala. 1992, U.S. Dist. Ct. (no. dist.) Ala. 1994. Clk., assoc. Taylor & Taylor, Birmingham, Ala., 1992-93; assoc. Frank S. Buck, P.C., Birmingham, 1993-95; pvt. practice Birmingham, 1995—. Mem. ATLA, Ala. Bar Assn., Ala. Trial Lawyers Assn., Birmingham Bar Assn. Democrat. Methodist. Home: 611 Springs Ave Birmingham AL 35242-4851 Office: Scherf Griffin & Davis LLC 2122 1st Ave N Birmingham AL 35203-4202

SCHERGER, JOSEPH E., family physician, educator; b. Delphos, Ohio, Aug. 29, 1950; m. Carol M. Wintermute, Aug. 7, 1973; children: Adrian, Gabriel. BS summa cum laude, U. Dayton, 1971; MD, UCLA, 1975. Family practice residency U. Wash., Seattle, 1975-78; clin. instr. U. Calif. Sch. Medicine, Davis, 1978-80, asst. clin. prof., 1980-84, assoc. clin. prof., 1984-90, clin. prof., 1990—, dir. predoctoral program, 1991-92; med. dir. family practice and community medicine Sharp Healthcare, San Diego, 1992—. Recipeient Hippocratic Oath award UCLA, Calif. Physician of Yr. award Am. Acad. Family Physicians. Mem. Inst. Medicine of NAS, Am. Acad. Family Physicians, Soc. Tchrs. Family Medicine. Home: 13188 Windbreak Rd San Diego CA 92130-1821 Office: Sharp Healthcare 3571 Corporate Ct San Diego CA 92123-2415

SCHERICH, EDWARD BAPTISTE, retired diversified company executive; b. Inland, Nebr., Dec. 3, 1923; s. Clarence H. and Clara E. (Baptiste) S.; m. Hyacinth Rau, Aug. 11, 1945 (div. 1980); children: Carol, Eileen, John.; m. Antoinette Currera, 1981; 1 stepdau., Sylvia McNamara. B.B.A., Tulane U., 1948. Acct. Colo. Milling & Elevator Co., Denver, 1948-50; accountant, office mgr. Southdown, Inc., New Orleans, 1950-55; controller Southdown, Inc., 1955-69; v.p. finance, sec., treas. Southdown Sugars Inc., New Orleans, 1970-73; v.p., sec., treas. Southdown Land Co., New Orleans, 1971-75; sec.-treas. Southdown, Inc., Houston, 1975-78; v.p., sec. Southdown, Inc., 1979-84, treas., 1980-83; ind. fin. cons., 1984—; pres. Valmax Inc., 1989—. Served in USNR, 1943-45. Mem. Beta Gamma Sigma. Home: 633 Brouilly Dr Kenner LA 70065-1101 Office: PO Box 641307 Kenner LA 70064-1307

SCHERICH, ERWIN THOMAS, civil engineer, consultant; b. Inland, Nebr., Dec. 6, 1918; s. Harry Erwin and Ella (Peterson) S.; student Hastings Coll., 1937-39, N.C. State Coll., 1943-44; B.S., U. Nebr., 1946-48; M.S., U. Colo., 1948-51; m. Jessie Mae Funk, Jan. 1, 1947; children—Janna Rae Scherich Thornton, Jerilyn Mae Scherich Dobson, Mark Thomas. Civil and design engr. U.S. Bur. Reclamation, Denver, 1948-84, chief spillways and outlets sect., 1974-75, chief dams br., div. design, 1975-78, chief tech. rev. staff, 1978-79, chief div. tech. rev. Office of Asst. Commr. Engring. and Rsch. Ctr., 1980-84; cons. civil engr., 1984—. Mem. U.S. Com. Internat. Commn. on Large Dams. Served with AUS, 1941-45. Registered profl. engr., Colo. Fellow ASCE; mem. NSPE (nat. dir. 1981-87, v.p. southwestern region 1991-93), Profl. Engrs. Colo. (pres. 1977-78), Jefferson County West C. of C. Republican. Methodist. Home and Office: 3915 Balsam St Wheat Ridge CO 80033

SCHERMER, JUDITH KAHN, lawyer; b. N.Y.C., Feb. 28, 1949; d. Robert and Barbara Kahn; m. Daniel Woodrough Schermer; 1 child, Sarah Nicole. BA, U. Chgo., 1971; JD, William Mitchell Coll. Law, 1987. Bar: Minn. 1987, U.S. Dist. Ct. Minn. 1987. Advt. and promotion specialist U. Chgo. Press, 1971-75; systems analyst Allstate Ins. Co., Northbrook, Ill., 1975-78, Lutheran Brotherhood, Mpls., 1980-83; polit. aide Mpls. City Coun., 1986-87; ptnr. Schermer & Schermer, Mpls., 1987—. Pres., Feminist Caucus, assoc. chair 5th dist., state exec. com. Dem. Farm Labor Party; bd. dirs. Women Candidates Devel. Coalition. Mem. ATLA, Minn. Trial Lawyers Assn. (bd. govs., chair employment law sect.), Minn. State Bar Assn., Minn. Women Lawyers, Nat. Employment Law Assn. Home: 4624 Washburn Ave S Minneapolis MN 55410-1846 Office: Schermer and Schermer Lumber Exch Bldg 10 S 5th St Ste 700 Minneapolis MN 55402-1033

SCHERR, ALLAN LEE, computer scientist, executive; b. Balt., Nov. 18, 1940; s. Morris and Sarah (Kratzmar) S.; m. Marsha Kahn, Sept. 2, 1962 (div. 1974); children: Elise A., Stephanie L.; m. Linda Martin, June 8, 1980; 1 child, Katherine M. B.E.E., MIT, 1962, M.E.E., 1962, Ph.D.E.E., 1965. Mgr. time sharing option design System Devel. div. IBM, Poughkeepsie, N.Y., 1967-70; mgr. multiple virtual storage (MVS) project IBM, 1971-74; mgr. distributed systems programming System Communications div. IBM, Kingston, N.Y., 1977-80; dir. communications programming IBM, 1980-81; dir. communications and applications systems corp. staff IBM, Armonk, N.Y., 1981-83; dir. engring. and programming systems products div. IBM, White Plains, N.Y., 1983-86; dir. integrated applications info. systems div. IBM, Milford, Conn., 1986-88, v.p. devel. and integration application systems div., 1988-89, application solutions dir. architecture and devel., Application Solutions Line Bus., 1990-91; v.p. tech. World Wide Cons. Practices IBM Cons. Group, Milford, Conn., 1991-93; ind. cons. bus. process engring., info. tech., tech. mgmt. Weston, Conn., 1993-94; sr. v.p. software engring. EMC Corp., Hopkinton, Mass., 1994—; seminar leader Werner Erhard & Assocs., N.Y.C., 1982-90. Author: An Analysis of Time-Shared Computer Systems, 1966 (Grace Murray Hopper award Assn. Computing Machinery 1975); patentee in field. Mem. The Hunger Project, San Francisco, 1977—. IBM fellow, 1984. Fellow IEEE; mem. Sigma Xi, Tau Beta Pi, Eta Kappa Nu. Democrat. Home: 12 Doeskin Dr Framingham MA 01701-5016

SCHERR, BARRY PAUL, foreign language educator; b. Hartford, Conn., May 20, 1945; s. Joseph and Helen Lillian (Shapiro) S.; m. Sylvia Egelman, Sept. 8, 1974; children: Sonia, David. AB magna cum laude, Harvard U., 1966; AM, U. Chgo., 1967, PhD, 1973. From acting asst. prof. to asst. prof. U. Washington, Seattle, 1970-74; from asst. prof. to prof. Russian Dartmouth Coll., Hanover, N.H., 1974—, chair dept. Russian, 1981-90, 96—, chair program Linguistics, Cognitive Sci., 1989-96; ad hoc svc. Bd. Examiners State N.H. Teacher Certification; co-dir. seminar Soviet Union for Secondary Sch. Tchrs., 1984; co-organizer Internat. Conf. Russian Verse Theory, 1987, Internat. Conf. Anna Akhmatova and the Poets of Tsarskoe Selo, 1989. Author: Russian Poetry: Meter, Rhythm and Rhyme, 1986, Maxim Gorky, 1988; co-trans. The Seeker of Adventure, Alexander Grin, 1989; mem. editorial bd. Slavic and East European Jour., 1978-88; co-editor: Russian Verse Theory: Procs. of the 1987 Conference at UCLA, 1987, ORUS! Studia litteraria Slavica in honorem Hugh McLean, 1995, A Sense of Place: Tsarskoe Selo and Its Poets, 1993; co-translator, co-editor Maksim Gorky: Selected Letters, 1997; contbr. articles to profl. jours. Scholar Harvard Coll., 1963-66; fellow NDEA, 1966-69; grantee Internat. Rsch. and Exchange Bd., 1969-70, NEH, 1987, 89, U.S. Dept. Edn., 1987-89, Dartmouth Coll. Sr. Faculty, 1988; summer rsch. grantee Grad. Sch., Inst. Comparative and Fgn. Area Studies U. Wash., 1973. Mem. MLA (mem. exec. com. assoc. dept. fgn. langs. 1983-85, del. assembly 1986-88), Am. Assn. Advancement Slavic Studies, Am. Assn. Tchrs. Slavic and East European Langs. (pres. 1987-88, founder, past pres. No. New England chpt., numerous coms.). Office: Dartmouth Coll Russian Dept 44 N College St Hanover NH 03755-1801

SCHERR, JAMES E., sports association executive; m. April Scherr; 1 child, Evan. BS, U. Nebr.; MBA, Northwestern U. Exec. dir., treas. USA Wrestling, Colorado Springs, Colo., 1990—; bd. dirs. USA Wrestling, Athlete Adv. Com., U.S. Olympic Com.; trustee U.S. Olympic Found.; mem. TV and mktg. commn. FILA. Placed 5th in freestyle wrestling, Seoul Olympics, 1988; recipient silver medal World Championship, 1987, 89, bronze medal 1986 World meet, three U.S. Nationals titles, 2 World Cup gold medals, NCAA Championship, Outstanding Freestyle Werstler, U.S. Nationals, 1989. Office: USA Wrestlintg 6155 Lehman Dr Colorado Springs CO 80918-3439

SCHERR, LAWRENCE, physician, educator; b. N.Y.C., Nov. 6, 1928; s. Harry and Sophia (Schwartz) S.; m. Peggy L. Binenkorb, June 13, 1954; children: Cynthia E., Robert W. AB, Cornell U., 1950, MD, 1957. Diplomate Am. Bd. Internal Medicine (bd. dirs., sec.-treas. 1979-86). Intern Cornell Med. divsn. Bellevue Hosp. and Meml. Ctr., 1957-58, asst. resident, 1958-59, rsch. fellow cardiorenal lab., 1959-60, chief resident, 1960-61, co-dir. cardiorenal lab., 1961-62, asst. vis. physician, 1961-63, assoc. vis. physician, 1963-65, dir. cardiology and renal unit, 1963-67, assoc. dir., 1964-67, vis. physician, 1966-68; physician to out-patients N.Y. Hosp., 1961-63, asst. attending physician, 1963-66, assoc. attending physician, 1966-71, attending physician, 1971—; asst. attending physician Sloan-Kettering Cancer Ctr., 1962-71, cons., 1971—; chmn. dept. medicine North Shore Univ. Hosp., 1967—, dir. acad. affairs, 1969-93, sr. v.p. med. affairs, 1993—; asst. in medicine Med. Coll. Cornell U., 1958-59; rsch. fellow N.Y. Heart Assn., 1959-60, instr. medicine, 1960-63, asst. prof., 1963-66, assoc. prof., 1966-71, David J. Greene disting. prof., 1971-96, assoc. dean, 1969-96; David J. Greene prof. medicine, assoc. dean NYU Sch. Medicine, 1996—; career scientist Health Rsch. Coun., N.Y.C., 1962-66; tchg. scholar Am. Heart Assn., 1966-67; pres. N.Y. State Bd. Medicine, 1974-75; bd. dirs. Nat. Bd. Med. Examiners, 1976-80; chmn. Accreditation Coun. for Grad. Med. Edn., 1988, N.Y. State Coun. on Grad. Edn., 1987-92. Contbr. articles to profl. jours. Lt. USNR, 1950-53. Fellow N.Y. Acad. Medicine, Am. Heart Assn. (coun. on clin. cardiology); mem. ACP (master, chmn. and gov. Downstate N.Y. region II 1975-80, regent 1980-86, chmn. bd. regents 1985-86; nat. pres.-elect 1986-87, pres. 1987-88, pres. emeritus), AMA, Am. Fedn. Clin. Rsch., Harvey Soc., N.Y. Med. Soc., Nassau County Med. Soc., Assn. Am. Med. Colls., Am. Clin. and Climatologic Assn. Home: 19 Doral Dr Manhasset NY 11030-3907 Office: N Shore Univ Hosp Manhasset NY 11030

SCHERSTEN, H. DONALD, management consultant, realtor, mortgage broker; b. Titusville, Pa., Nov. 6, 1919; s. H.J. and Clara (Brown) S.; m. Katherine Conley; 1 dau. by previous marriage, Sandra S. Hotard. B.S., Temple U., 1941; postgrad., Tulsa U., 1946-48, Columbia U., 1955. With Creole Petroleum Corp. (affiliate Exxon Corp.), 1948-69, successively dist. field chief accountant Cabimas, Venezuela, coordinator procedures, fin. statements and audits, asst. controller, 1951-62; controller Creole Petroleum Corp. (affiliate Exxon Corp.), Caracas, 1962-69; gen. auditor Exxon Corp., N.Y.C., 1969-74; coordinator math., computers, systems Exxon Corp., 1975-76; pres. H. Donald Schersten & Assocs. (Mgmt. Cons.), 1977—, R.J. Reynolds Nabisco, 1977-78; lic. real estate agt., 1985—; lic. mortgage broker, 1986—. Pres. council Am. Ch. Caracas, 1960. Served to 1st lt. AUS, 1942-45. Named to Accelt. Alumni Hall of Fame, Temple U., 1985. Mem. Am. Petroleum Inst. (chmn. audit com. 1974-76), Inst. Internal Auditors (cert.), U.S. Power Squadrons, USCG Aux. (comdr. 1984). Clubs: Internat. Safari Big Game Hunting, Toastmasters (past pres. Caracas chpt.), Los Rancheros Deep Sea Fishing. Avocations: champion/Classic Billfish Tourn. 1973, Cabo San Lucas, Mexico. Home: 4693 Glebe Farm Rd Sarasota FL 34235-1806

SCHERZER, JOSEPH MARTIN, dermatologist; b. Newark, July 2, 1946; s. Louis and Gertrude (Brodnick) S.; m. Anna Stella Meed, June 24, 1971; children: Jeanine Rebecca and Michael Ira. BA cum laude, Rutgers U., 1968; MD, Albert Einstein Med. Coll., 1972. Diplomate Am. Bd. Dermatology; spl. cert. in Dermopathology. Intern Manhattan Vet. Adminstrn. Hosp., N.Y.C., 1972-73, med. resident, 1973-74; resident in dermatology NYU Med. Ctr., 1974-76; owner, president Scottsdale (Ariz.) Skin and Cancer Ctr., Ltd., 1976—; asst. instr. Bellevue (N.Y.) Med. Ctr., 1976 (fall). Founding mem. Nat. Orgn. Physicians Who Care, 1985; mem. Scottsdale C.C. Jazz Ensemble, 1989. Recipient Outstanding Svc. award Scottsdale C.C. Jazz Ensemble, 1989, 1990; named Jazz Performer of Yr., 1992, Jazz Instrumentalist of Yr., 1993. Mem. AMA, Am. Acad. Dermatology; Phoenix Dermatology Soc. (v.p. 1978-79, sec.-treas. 1983-84, pres. 1984-85), Ariz. Med. Assn., Assn. Am. Physician/Surgeons, (founding pres. Ariz. chpt. 1995-96), Maricopa County Med. Soc., Internat. Soc. Dermatopathology, Am. Soc. Dermatopathology. Avocations: photography, music, poetry, reading, writing. Office: Scottsdale Skin Cancer Ctr 10900 N Scottsdale Rd Ste 502 Scottsdale AZ 85254-5236

SCHETKY, LAURENCE MCDONALD, metallurgist, researcher; b. Baguio, The Philippines, July 15, 1922; s. Gerald Laurence and Ethyl Jane (McDonald) S.; m. Diane Heiskell, Dec. 12, 1977 (div. Feb. 1986); m. Karen Searles, July 12, 1986 (div. Oct. 1994); 1 child, Mark Christian; m. Margarita A. Smith, Oct. 27, 1995. BSChemE, Rensselaer Poly Inst., Troy, N.Y., 1943, MMetE, 1948, PhD, 1953. Registered profl. engr., Mass. Rsch. fellow MIT, Cambridge, 1953-59; v.p. rsch. Alloyd Electronics, Inc., Cambridge, 1959-63; dir. R & D Internat. Copper Rsch. Assn., Inc., N.Y.C., 1963-83; pres. Memory Metals, Inc., Stamford, Conn., 1983-86; v.p., chief scientist Memry Corp., Brookfield, Conn., 1987—; dir. Photoetching Engring., Inc., Milford, Mass., 1985—. Editor: Beryllium Technology, 2 vol., 1966, The Metallurgy of Copper, 13 vols., 1966-83; author: (with others) Copper in Iron and Steel, 1982; contbr. over 100 articles to physics and metallurgy jours. With USN, 1944-46, PTO. Rsch. fellow Alcoa Corp., 1948-53. Fellow Am. Soc. Metals Internat. (life), Brit. Inst. Metals; mem. AIME (life). Republican. Episcopalian. Achievements include 5 patents in Electron Beam Technology, Vapor Phase Deposition, Shape Memory Actuators. Home: 77 Rock House Rd Easton CT 06612-1003 Office: Memry Corp 57 Commerce Dr Brookfield CT 06804-3405

SCHEU, DAVID ROBERT, SR., historic site director; b. Milw., Feb. 8, 1944; s. Oscar Charles Jr. and Dorothy Marie (Schmitz) S.; m. Deborah Singleton Hill, Feb. 3, 1968; children: David R. Jr., Stephanie Ann Scheu Aman. BS in Engring., U.S. Naval Acad., 1967; MBA, U. So. Ill., Edwardsville, 1980. Commd. ensign USN, 1967, advanced through grades to capt., 1988; served on USS Sterett, 1967-69, USS Buchanan, 1970-71; stationed at US Naval Acad., 1971-74; served on USS Berkeley, 1975-77; stationed at Fleet Combat Tng. Ctr. Pacific, 1977-80; served on USS Hepburn, 1980-81, USS New Jersey, 1981-83, USS Edson, 1984-86; stationed at Comcargru Seven, 1986-89, Mil. Sealift Command, 1989-91; dir. Battleship N.C. Meml., Wilmington, N.C., 1991—. Bd. dirs. Travel Coun. N.C., Raleigh, 1991—, N.C. Maritime History Coun., Beaufort, 1991—, Cape Fear Coast Conv. and Visitors Bur., Wilmington, 1992—, Hist. Naval Ships Assn., 1994—, N.C. Heritage, Inc., Raleigh, 1996—, S.E. Tourism Soc., Atlanta, 1996—. Mem. U.S. Naval Inst., Navy League U.S., S.E. Tourism Soc., Ret. Officers Assn. Roman Catholic. Avocations: sailing, jogging. Office: USS NC Battleship Meml PO Box 480 Wilmington NC 28402-0480

SCHEU, LYNN MCLAUGHLIN, scientific publication editor; b. Lancaster, Ohio, July 9, 1942; d. Franklin Neil and Carol Lois (Bigham) McLaughlin; m. Richard V. Scheu, Apr. 16, 1966; children: David Edward, Michael Patrick. BS, Auburn U., 1964; postgrad., Ohio State U., 1964-66. English, French tchr. Reynoldsburg (Ohio) H.S., 1966-70; adj. curator mollusks Mus. History & Sci., Louisville, 1978-85; editor Am. Conchologist, Louisville, 1987—; chairperson Lambis Group, 1996; mem. editl. adv. bd. Bailey Matthews Shell Mus. and Ednl. Found., Sanibel, Fla., 1988—. Editor (website) The Conchologist's Information Network (ConchNet). Mem. exec. bd. Friends of Libr., Louisville, 1989-95; mem. Mayor's Task Force on Librs., Louisville, 1988-89. Mem. Conchologists Am. (bd. dirs. 1987—). Avocations: shell collecting, fossils, landscape gardening, genealogy. Home and Office: 1222 Holsworth Ln Louisville KY 40222-6616

SCHEUER, JAMES, physician, educator, researcher; b. N.Y.C., Feb. 21, 1931; s. Sidney Henry and Linda (Ullman) S.; m. Ruth Lucas, Dec. 15, 1961; children:Kim, Jeff, Greg. BA, U. Rochester, 1952; MD, Yale U., 1956. Diplomate in internal medicine and cardiovascular disease Am. Bd. Internal Medicine. Med. intern Bellevue Hosp., N.Y.C., 1956-57; NIH fellow in cardiology Mt. Sinai Hosp., N.Y.C., 1957, 59, resident in internal medicine, 1958-60; rsch. fellow in internal medicine N.Y. Hosp.-Cornell Med. Ctr., N.Y.C., 1962-63; rsch. assoc. Inst. for Muscle Disease, N.Y.C., 1962-63; trainee in metabolism and nutrition Grad. Sch. Pub. Health/U. Pitts., 1963-64; from instr. to assoc. prof. medicine U. Pitts. Sch. medicine, 1964-72; prof. medicine, assoc. prof. to prof. physiology Albert Einstein Coll. Medicine, Bronx, N.Y., 1972—; dir. divsn. cardiology Albert Einstein Coll. Medicine/Montefiore Med. Ctr, Bronx, 1972-87, vice chmn. dept. medicine, 1980-87, Baumritter prof., chmn. dept. medicine, 1990—; lectr. and vis. prof. in field. Mem. editl. bd. Cardiology, 1970-75, Circulation Rsch., 1975-81, others; contbr. numerous articles to profl. jours. Recipient awards and grants in field. Fellow ACP, Am. Coll. Cardiology; mem. AAAS, Assn. Am. Physicians, Assn. Profs. Medicine (exec. com. 1994—), Am. Fedn. for Clin. Rsch., Am. Heart Assn. (fellow coun. on circulation, coun. on clin. cardiology), Am. Physiol. Soc., Am. Soc. for Clin. Investigation, Assn. Univ. Cardiologists, Cardiac Muscle Soc., Ctrl. Soc. for Clin. Rsch., Internat. Soc. for Heart Rsch., N.Y. Acad. Sci., N.Y. Heart Assn., Soc. for Exptl. Biology and Medicine, N.Y. Cardiology Soc., Eastern Inter Urban Clin Club. Office: Albert Einstein Coll Med 1300 Morris Park Ave Bronx NY 10461-1926

SCHEUER, PAUL JOSEF, chemistry educator; b. Heilbronn, Germany, May 25, 1915; came to U.S., 1938; s. Albert and Emma (Neu) S.; m. Alice Elizabeth Dash, Sept. 5, 1950; children: Elizabeth E., Deborah A., David A., Jonathan L.L. BS with high honors, Northeastern U., Boston, 1943; MA, Harvard U., 1947, PhD, 1950. Asst. prof. chemistry U. Hawaii, Honolulu, 1950-55, assoc. prof. chemistry, 1956-61, prof. chemistry, 1961-85, prof. chemistry emeritus, 1985—; vis. prof. Orsted Inst., U. Copenhagen, 1977, 89; Toyo Suisan vis. prof. U. Tokyo, 1992. Author: Chemistry of Marine Natural Products, 1973, editor 12 series, 1978-93; contbr. more than 265 articles to profl. jours. Spl. agt. U.S. Army, 1944-46, ETO. Recipient Rsch. Achievement award Am. Soc. Pharmacognosy, 1994, Regents award for rsch. excellence U. Hawaii, 1972; named P.J. Scheuer award Marine Chemists, 1992; NATO fellow, 1975. Fellow AAAS, Royal Soc. Chemistry; mem. Am. Chem. Soc. (sect. chair 1956, 87, Hawaii sect. award 1996, Ernest Guenther award 1994), Northeastern U. Alumni Assn. (Disting. Alumni award 1984). Office: U Hawaii Chemistry Dept 2545 The Mall Honolulu HI 96822-2233

SCHEUERLE, ANGELA ELIZABETH, geneticist; b. Syracuse, N.Y., Aug. 13, 1962; d. William Howard and Jane Frances (Walker) S.; m. Alan Joseph Eynan. BS in Biology magna cum laude, U. of the South, 1984; MD, U. South Fla., 1988. Resident in pediatrics Children's Hosp. Med. Ctr., Cin., 1988-91; fellow Inst. for Molecular and Human Genetics Baylor Coll. Medicine, Houston, 1991-95; asst. prof. pediatrics, divsn. med. genetics U. Tex. Med. Sch., Houston, 1995—; mem. instnl. ethics com. Hermann Hosp.; mem. bioethics subcom. Lyndon Banes Johnson Gen. Hosp.; mem. instnl. ethics com. Humana Hosp. Vol. Tampa (Fla.) Big Bros./Big Sisters, 1978-82; trustee St. Mark's Episcopal Sch.; mem. bioethics com. Episcopal Diocese of Tex. Fellow Am. Acad. Pediatrics, Am. Coll. Med. Genetics; mem. Am. Soc. Human Genetics, Phi Beta Kappa, Sigma Xi, Alpha Epsilon Delta. Democrat. Avocations: horseback riding, photography, crossword puzzles. Office: UTHSC-Houston Dept Pediats Divsn Med Genetics 6431 Fannin MSB 3.144 Houston TX 77030

SCHEUPELEIN, ROBERT JOHN, government official; b. Brookhaven, N.Y., May 9, 1932; s. Ernest and Mary (Leonowitz) S.; m. Kathleen Ehrensberger (div. 1980). BA in Chemistry, U. Miami, 1955, MS in Phys. Chemistry, 1956; PhD in Phys. Chemistry, U. Utah, 1961; postgrad., Harvard U., 1982. Rsch. assoc. dermatology Harvard Med. Sch., Cambridge, Mass., 1962-68, assoc. in biophysics and dermatology, 1968-70, prin. assoc. in biophysics, 1970-77; chief dermal and ocular toxicology br. Bur. Foods, FDA, Washington, 1977-79, dir. div. food animal additives, 1979-82; dep. dir. Office Toxicological Scis., Ctr. for Food Safety and Applied Nutrition, Washington, 1983-88, dir. Office Toxicological Scis., 1988-92, dir. Office Rsch. Skills, 1992-94; prin. The Weinberg Group Inc, Washington, 1994—; course dir. skin biology and physiology Harvard-MIT Program in Health Sci., 1971-76; mem. White House USTP Task Force on Chem. Carcinogens,

Washington, 1983-85; mem. task force on risk assessment and risk mgmt. HHS, Washington, 1984-85; mem. risk assessment subcom. Nat. Sci. and Tech. Coun., 1994—. Editor: Biological Basis for Risk Assessment of Dioxins, 1991; contbr. articles to sci. jours., chpts. to books. Capt. USAR, 1961-62. Recipient sci. lit. award Soc. Cosmetic Chemists, 1968, citation Bur. Roods, FDA, 1980, award of merit FDA, 1987; sr. exec. fellow Harvard U. John F. Kennedy Sch. Govt., 1982. Mem. AAAS; mem. Soc. for Risk Analysis. Avocations: tennis, woodworking, ballroom dancing, writing. Home: 5140 Maris Ave Alexandria VA 22304-1963*

SCHEVILL, JAMES ERWIN, poet, playwright; b. Berkeley, Calif., June 10, 1920; s. Rudolph and Margaret (Erwin) S.; m. Margot Helmuth, Aug. 2, 1966; children (by previous marriage): Deborah, Susanna. BS, Harvard U., 1942; MA (ad eundem), Brown U.; LHD (hon.), R.I. Coll., 1986. Mem. faculty San Francisco State Coll., 1959-68, prof. English, 1968, dir. Poetry Center, 1961-68; prof. Brown U., 1969-85, prof. emeritus, 1985—; reader various univs., insts., and orgns. Author: (poems) Tensions, 1947, The American Fantasies, 1951, The Right to Greet, 1955, Selected Poems 1945-59, 1959, Private Dooms & Public Destinations: Poems 1945-62, 1962, The Stalingrad Elegies, 1964, Release, 1968, Violence & Glory: Poems 1962-68, 1969, The Buddhist Car & Other Characters, 1973, Pursuing Elegy: A Poem About Haiti, 1974, The Mayan Poems, 1978, Fire of Eyes: A Guatemalan Sequence, 1979, The American Fantasies: Collected Poems 1945-81, 1983, The Invisible Volcano, 1985, Ghost Names/Ghost Numbers, 1986, Ambiguous Dancers of Fame: Collected Poems 1945-86 Vol. II, 1987, Winter Channels, 1994, The Complete American Fantasies, 1996; (biographies) Sherwood Anderson: His Life and Work, 1951, The Roaring Market and the Silent Tomb, 1956, Bern Porter: A Personal Biography, 1993; (plays) High Sinners, Low Angels, 1953, The Bloody Tenet, 1957, Voices of Mass. and Capital A, 1958, The Black President and Other Plays, 1965, Lovecraft's Follies, 1971, Breakout: In Search of New Theatrical Environments, 1973, Cathedral of Ice, 1975, reprinted in internat. anthology Plays of the Holocaust, 1988, Oppenheimer's Chair, 1985, Collected Short Plays, 1986, Monologue on S.J. Perelman, 1986, Time of the Hand and Eye, 1986, Mother O Or The Last American Mother, 1990, (with Mary Gail) The Garden on F Street, 1992, The Phantom of Life: A Melville Play, 1993, Five Plays, 1993; (novel) The Arena of Ants, 1977; (rec.) Performance Poems, 1984; (translation) The Cid, 1961; editor: Six Historians (by F. Schevill), 1956, (with others) Wastepaper Theatre Anthology, 1978; plays produced in various theaters in U.S. including Guthrie Theatre, Mpls., Magic Theatre, San Francisco, La Mama, N.Y.C., Trinity Repertory Co., Providence, Goodman Theatre, Chgo., Berkeley Repertory Theatre, R.I. Playwrights Theatre, Volkstheater, Rostock, German Dem. Republic, others. Served to capt. AUS, 1942-46. Ford Found. grantee, 1954, 60-61, R.I. Com. on Humanities grantee, 1975; Fund Advancement Edn., 1953-54, Office for Advanced Drama Research fellow, 1957, Rockefeller fellow, 1964, Guggenheim fellow, 1981, McKnight fellow, 1984; recipient Performance prize Nat. Theatre Competition, 1945, 2d prize Phelan Biography Competition, 1954, 2d prize Phelan Drama Competition, 1958, William Carlos Williams award, 1965, Roadsted Found. award, 1966, Gov.'s award R.I., 1975, Best Story of Yr. award Ariz. Quart., 1977; story selected for O. Henry Awards Prize Stories, 1978; award in lit. Am. Acad. and Inst. Arts and Letters, 1991; work commd. by Nat. Council Chs., 1956-61, Fromm Found., 1959, Trinity Repertory Co., R.I. Hosp., 1986, Providence Coll., 1986, Magdalena Group, 1992. Home: 1309 Oxford St Berkeley CA 94709-1424 Office: Brown U Dept English Providence RI 02912

SCHEWE, DONALD BRUCE, archivist, library director; b. Cleve., Oct. 28, 1943; s. Norman Edward and Theodora (Robinson) S.; m. Charlene R. Wenz, June 10, 1965; children: Amanda Marie, Ann Elizabeth. BA, U. Nebr., 1964, MA, 1968; PhD, Ohio State U., 1971. Archivist Franklin D. Roosevelt Library, Hyde Park, N.Y., 1972-77, supervisory archivist, 1977-79, asst. dir., 1979-81; dir. Carter Presdl. Materials Project, Atlanta, 1981-86, Jimmy Carter Library, Atlanta, 1986—. Editor: Franklin D. Roosevelt and Foreign Affairs, 1981. With U.S. Army, 1964-66, Vietnam, ret. lt. col. Mem. Assn. Records Mgrs. and Adminstrs., Soc. Ga. Archivists, Orgn. Am. Historians, Inst. of Cert. Records Mgrs. (pres. 1996—). Episcopalian. Lodge: Rotary. Office: Jimmy Carter Libr 441 Freedom Pky Atlanta GA 30307-1498

SCHEXNAYDER, BRIAN EDWARD, opera singer; b. Port Arthur, Tex., Sept. 18, 1953; s. Leonard and Dorothy (Carrier) S.; m. Sherri Scallan, Oct. 2, 1976. BA in Music, U. Southwestern La., 1976; postgrad., Juilliard Sch. Music, 1976-80. Performances with Met. Opera, N.Y.C., Paris Opera Co., Edmonton (Alta., Can.) Opera Co., New Orleans Opera Co., Santiago (Chile) Opera, Winnipeg (Man., Can.), St. Petersburg (Fla.) Opera, Jackson (Miss.) Opera Co., San Francisco Opera, Frankfurt Opera, Hamburg Staatsoper Opera, Oper der Studt Bonn, Spoleto (Italy) Festival of Two Worlds, Cin. Opera, Fla. Grand Opera. Mem. Am. Guild Musicians. Avocations: computers, billiards, remote control airplanes.

SCHEXNAYDER, CHARLOTTE TILLAR, state legislator; b. Tillar, Ark., Dec. 25, 1923; d. Jewell Stephen and Bertha (Terry) Tillar; m. Melvin John Schexnayder Sr., Aug. 18, 1946; children: M. John Jr., Sarah Holden, Stephen. BA, La. State U., 1944, postgrad., 1947-48. Asst. editor La. Agrl. Extension, Baton Rouge, 1944; editor The McGehee (Ark.) Times, 1945-46, 48-53; editor, co-publisher The Dumas (Ark.) Clarion, 1954-85, publisher, 1985—; mem. Ark. Ho. of Reps., Litte Rock, 1985—, asst. speaker pro tem, 1995—; pres. Ark. Assn. Women, 1955, Nat. Newspaper Assn., Washington, 1991-92, Ark. Press. Assn., Little Rock, 1982, Nat. Fedn. Press Women, Blue Springs, Mo., 1977-78, Litte Rock chpt. Soc. Profl. Journalists, 1973; mem. pres.'s coun. Winrock Internat., 1990—. Editor: Images of the Past, 1991. 1st woman mem. Ark. Bd. Pardons and Parole, 1975-80; mem. Ark. Legis. Coun., 1985-92; v.p. Desha County Mus., 1989—; dir. Dumas Indsl. Found., 1986—; mem. exec. com. Ark. Ctrl. Radiation Therapy Inst., 1991-92; mem. adv. bd. Ark. Profl. Women Achievement, 1992—; vice chair Ark. Rural Devel. Commn., 1991-96; mem. Winrock Internat. Adv. Coun., 1991—; chmn. Ark. Rural Devel. Commn., 1996-97; founding incorporator, bd. dirs. Ark. Waterways Commn., 1996—. Named Disting. Alumnus Ark. A&M Coll., 1971, Woman of Achievement Nat. Fedn. Press Women, 1970, Outstanding Arkansan C. of C., 1986; recipient Ark. Profl. Women of Distinction award No. Bank, Little Rock, 1990, Emma McKinney award Nation's Top Cmty. Newspaper Woman, 1980, Journalist award Nat. Conf. of Christians and Jews, 1989, Lifetime Achievement award Nat. Fedn. Press Women, 1992, Outstanding Svc. award Ark. Assn. Elem. Prins., Disting. Svc. award Ark. Press Assn., 1993; named to La. State U. Alumni Hall of Distinction, 1994, Disting. Svc. award Internat. Soc. Weekly Newspaper Editors, 1996, Golden Svc. award Ark. Press Assn., 1996, State Leadership award Ark. Waterways Commn., 1996; named one Top 100 Ark. Women, Ark. Bus., 1995, 96, 97. Mem. Pi Beta Phi (Crest award 1992), Ark. Delta Coun. (chmn. of bd. dirs. 1989—). Democrat. Roman Catholic. Home: 322 Court St Dumas AR 71639-2718 Office: Clarion Publishing Co Inc 136 E Waterman St Dumas AR 71639-2227

SCHEY, JOHN ANTHONY, metallurgical engineering educator; b. Sopron, Hungary, Dec. 19, 1922; came to U.S., 1962; s. Mihaly and Hedvig Terez (Topfl) S.; m. Margit Maria Sule, Sept. 13, 1926; 1 child, John Francis. Diplome metall. engring., Tech. U., Sopron, 1946; candidate tech. scis., Acad. Scis., Budapest, Hungary, 1953; D of Engring. (hon.), U. Stuttgart, 1987, U. Heavy Industry, Miskolc, Hungary, 1989. Cert. mfg. engr.; registered profl. engr. Chief technologist Iron and Metal Works, Csepel, Hungary, 1947-51; reader Tech. U., Miskolc, Hungary, 1951-56; dept. head Brit. Aluminium Co. Research Labs., 1957-62; metall. advisor Ill. Inst. Tech. Research Inst., Chgo., 1962-68; prof. U. Ill., Chgo., 1968-74; prof. U. Waterloo, Ont., Can., 1974-88, disting. prof. emeritus, 1988; resource person Niagara Inst., Ontario, 1980; course dir. Forging Industry Assn., Cleve., 1978; cons. to various corps. in U.S. and Can. Author: Tribology in Metalworking, 1983, Introduction to Manufacturing Processes, 2d edit., 1987; patentee in field. Recipient W.H.A. Robertson award Inst. Metals, 1966. Fellow Am. Soc. Metals, Soc. Mfg. Engrs. (Gold Medal award 1974); mem. Nat. Acad. Engring., Can. Inst. Mining and Metallurgy (Dofasco award 1984); fgn. mem. Hungarian Acad. Scis. Avocations: music, history, impact of technology on soc.

SCHIAFFINO, S(ILVIO) STEPHEN, retired medical society executive, consultant; b. Bklyn., Nov. 1, 1927; s. Stephen Anthony and Jane (DiDonato) S.; m. Josephine Rose Bovello, Apr. 25, 1954; children—Susan, Stephen. BS, Georgetown U., 1946, MS, 1948, Ph.D. in Biochemistry, 1956. Research biochemist div. nutrition FDA, Washington, 1948-50; asst. br. chief div. FDA, 1954-60; mgr. chemistry dept. Hazelton Labs., Vienna, Va., 1960-61; with NIH, 1961—; scientist adminstr. NIH (Nat. Cancer Inst.), 1961-64, asst. chief research grants rev. br., 1964-69, chief., 1969-72, asso. dir. for sci. rev., 1972-78, dep. dir. div. research grants, 1978-86; sr. sci. advisor office of extramural research and tng., office of dir. NIH, 1986-87; exec. officer, sci. officer Am. Soc. for Clin. Nutrition, Bethesda, Md., 1987-93; cons., 1993—; cons. in field. Served with AUS, 1950-53. Recipient Superior Service award FDA, 1960, Superior Service award NIH, 1969. Mem. AAAS, Am. Soc. for Clin. Nutrition., Am. Inst. Nutrition.

SCHIAVELLI, MELVYN DAVID, academic administrator, chemistry educator, researcher; b. Chgo., Aug. 8, 1942; s. Gene James and Frances Elizabeth (Giacomo) S.; m. Virginia Farrell, Sept. 10, 1966; children—Timothy, Karen. BS in Chemistry, DePaul U., 1964; PhD in Chemistry, U. Calif., Berkeley, 1967. Rsch. assoc. Mich. State U., East Lansing, 1967-68; from asst. prof. to assoc. prof. chemistry Coll. William and Mary, Williamsburg, Va., 1968-80; prof. chemistry Coll. William and Mary, Williamsburg, 1980-94, chmn. dept. chemistry, 1978-84, dean Faculty Arts and Scis., 1984-86; provost Coll. William and Mary, 1986-93, acting pres., 1992; prof. chem. and biochem., provost U. Del., Newark, 1994—. Contbr. articles to profl. jours., 1969—. Grantee NSF Petroleum Rsch. Fund, 1969-90. Mem. Am. Chem. Soc., Royal Inst. Chemists, Sigma Xi. Roman Catholic. Office: U Del Office Univ Provost 129 Hullihen Ct Newark DE 19711-3649

SCHIAVELLO, BRUNO, mechanical engineer; b. Gerocarne, Italy, July 12, 1945; came to the U.S., 1982; s. Francesco and Marianna (Sirgiovanni) S. BS in Mech. Engring., U. Rome, 1974; MS in Fluid Dynamics, Von Karman Inst., 1975. Registered profl. engr., Italy. Hydraulic rschr. Worthington SpA, Desio, Italy, 1975-79, product engr., 1979-82; assoc. dir. hydraulics McGraw Edison-Worthington, Mountainside, N.J., 1982-83, dir. hydraulics, 1983-85; mgr. fluid dynamics Dresser Pump Divsn., Harrison, N.J., 1985-93; dir. fluid dynamics Ingersoll Dresser Pumps, Phillipsburg, N.J., 1993—; mem. adv. com. pump symposium Tex. A&M U., College Station, 1984—; lectr. Von Karman Inst., 1978, Conf. Norwegian Chartered Engrs., 1986, 88; contbr. articles to profl. jours. Mem. Am. Assn. Mech. Engrs., Soc. Hydrotechnique de France, Internat. Assn. Hydraulic Rsch., AIAA. Achievements include development of computer prediction methods for pump performance, advanced designs of pump leading to performance improvement and/or cost reduction of centrifugal and mixed flow pumps, single and multistage; designed two-phase flow pumps. Home: 246 Millburn Ave Apt C Millburn NJ 07041-1724

SCHIAVI, RAUL CONSTANTE, psychiatrist, educator, researcher; b. Buenos Aires, Argentina, Jan. 7, 1930; came to U.S. 1956; s. Constantino and Maria (Acquier) S.; m. Michelle deMiniac, Aug. 26, 1960; children; Isabelle, Nadine, Viviane. MD, U. Buenos Aires, 1953. Diplomate Am. Bd. Psychiatry and Neurology. Fgn. asst. psychiatry U. Paris, 1955-56; resident in psychiatry U. Pa., Phila., 1956-59; instr. psychiatry U. Pa., 1959-61; assoc. College de France, Paris, 1961-63; asst. prof. psychiatry Cornell U., N.Y.C., 1963-66; assoc. prof. psychiatry SUNY, Downstate Med. Ctr., Bklyn., 1966-71, Mt. Sinai Sch. Medicine, N.Y.C., 1971-78; prof. psychiatry Mt. Sinai Sch. Medicine, 1978-96, emeritus prof. psychiatry, 1996—; fellow Found. Fund for Rsch. in Psychiatry, 1958-63; cons. NIMH, 1966-70, 77-81 (Rsch. Sci. Devel. award 1966, grantee 1976-95); dir. human sexuality program Mt. Sinai Sch. Medicine, 1973-96; advisor WHO, 1989. Contbr. articles to profl. jours., chpts. to books; co-editor Jour. Sex and Marital Therapy; mem. editl. bd. Archives of Sexual Behavior, Hormones and Behavior, Psychosomatic Medicine, Revista Latinoamericana de Sexologia, Quaderni de Sessuologia Clinica, Revista Argentina de Sexualidad Humana, Annual Rev. Sex Rsch. Recipient Masters and Johnson award Soc. for Sex Therapy and Rsch., 1991; grantee NIH, 1977-80, 87-95, others. Fellow Am. Psychopathol. Assn., Psychiat. Rsch. Soc., Am. Psychiat. Assn. (life fellow, cons. 1989, Excellence in Edn. award 1992)); mem. AAAS, Am. Psychosomatic Soc. (coun. 1985-88), Internat. Acad. Sex Rsch. (pres. 1995-96), Soc. Sex Therapy and Rsch. (pres. 1984-86), Sex Info and Edn. Coun. of U.S. (bd. dirs. 1979-83), Internat. Soc. Psychoneuroendocrinology, Sigma Xi.

SCHIAVINA, LAURA MARGARET, artist; b. Springfield, Mass., Nov. 27, 1917; d. Joseph A. and Egidia (Bernini) Schiavina; student Traphagen Sch. of Fashion, 1944-46, U. R.I., 1967, Cornell U., 1968, Art Students League, 1973-74. With Eastern States Farmers Exchange, Springfield, 1935-44; with Marsh & McLennan, 1944-75, adminstrv. asst., 1971-75, librarian Wm. M. Mercer, Inc. subs., 1975-80; represented by Z Gallery, N.Y.C. One-woman shows at Little Gallery, Barbizon Hotel, N.Y.C., 1968, Galerie Internat., N.Y.C., 1969, Z Gallery, N.Y.C., 1993, 94; exhibited in group shows at Westfield (Mass.) Coll., 1968, Nat. Acad., N.Y.C., 1969, Bergen Mus. of Art and Sci., Paramus, N.J., 1991, Stuhr Mus. of the Prairie Pioneer, Grand Isle, Nebr., 1990, Nat. Soc. of Painters in Casein and Acrylic, 1992, 94, Washington & Lee U., Lexington, Va., 1993, Darke County Ctr. for Arts, Greenville, Ohio, 1993, NLAPW 1992 Biennial Sumner Mus., Washington, 1992, 1994 Biennial Cork Gallery, N.Y.C.; Lever House, N.Y.C., 1973, 74, 83, 84, 85, 86, 87, 95, Queensboro C.C. Gallery, 1984, 94, 96, Cork Gallery, N.Y.C., 1984, 93, 94, Westbeth Gallery, N.Y.C., 1985, 88, Nat. Arts Club, 1986, 88—, Isis Gallery, 1986, Morin-Miller Galleries, 1988; also various exhbns. with Wall St. Art Assn., Nat. Art. League and Jackson Heights Art Club, Audubon Artists, 1969, 86, 88—, Salmagundi Club, 1996—, Nat. Assn. Women Artists travel show centennial exhibits at 5 art ctrs. and mus., 1989, and ann. exhbns., 1989—, QCC Art Gallery Collection; represented in pvt. collections. Active Flushing Coun. on Culture and the Arts. Recipient numerous prizes, awards. Mem. Wall St. Art Assn. (v.p. 1972-76), Audubon Artists, Inc., Nat. Art League, Burr Artists Inc., Nat. Assn. Women Artists, N.Y. Artists Equity, Nat. League Am. Pen Women, Jackson Heights Art Club (pres. 1970-71), The Catholic Fine Arts Soc., Salmagundi Club. Home: 35-25 78th St Jackson Heights NY 11372 Studio: 41 Union Sq W # 406 New York NY 10003-3208

SCHIAVO, MARY FACKLER, news consultant, lawyer, educator; b. Pioneer, Ohio, Sept. 4, 1955. AB cum laude, Harvard U., 1976; MA, Ohio State U., 1977; JD, NYU, 1980. Bar: Mo. 1980, U.S. Dist. Ct. (we. dist.) Mo. 1980, U.S. Ct. Appeals (8th cir.) 1983, U.S. Ct. Appeals (10th cir.) 1985, U.S. Supreme Ct. 1990, D.C. 1993, Md. 1994. Assoc. law firm, Kansas City, Mo., 1980-82; asst. U.S. atty. we. dist. Mo. U.S. Dept. Justice, Kansas City, 1982-85, fed. prosecutor organized crime and racketeering strike force, 1985-86; White House fellow, spl. asst. to U.S. Atty. Gen. U.S. Dept. Justice, Washington, 1987-88; exec. dir. Bush/Quayle '88 Campaign, State of Mo., 1988; atty. law firm, Kansas City, 1989; asst. sec. labor-mgmt. standards U.S. Dept. Labor, Washington, 1989-90; insp. gen. U.S. Dept. Transp., Washington, 1990-96; aviation consultant ABC News, 1996—; prof. The Ohio State U., Columbus, 1997—; instr. U.S. Atty. Gen.'s Adv. Inst., Washington, 1986, 88, FBI Acad., Quantico, Va., 1988; guest lectr. NYU Sch. Law, 1986, 88, 91; bd. dirs. Dept. Labor Acad., 1989-90; bd. dirs. White House Fellows Assn. and Found., 1992-96, 2d v.p., 1992-93, chair ann. meeting, 1993, 1st v.p., 1993-94, pres. 1994-95; mem. Pres.'s Coun. on Integrity and Efficiency, 1990-96, Pres.'s Commn. on White House Fellowships, 1994-95. Bd. dirs. Root-Tilden Scholarship program NYU, 1982-89. Recipient Thompson award Ohio State U. Alumni, 1988, Aviation Laurel citation Aviation Week and Space Tech. mag., 1992, Aviation Laurel award Aviation Week and Space Tech. mag., 1995; named one of Top Ten Coll. Women in U.S., 1975, one of ten Outstanding Young Working Women in Am., 1987, Kansas City Career Woman of Yr., 1988; Ohio State U. fellow, 1976-77; U.S.-Japan Leadership fellow, 1995; Root-Tilden legal scholar NYU, 1977-79. Mem. ABA (ho. of dels. 1986-89, assembly del. 1986-89, litigation sect. complex crimes com.), Mo. Bar Assn. (bd. govs. 1986-89, chmn. pro bono task force 1984-86, young lawyers coun. 1983-86, Outstanding Svc. award 1986), Women Fgn. Policy Group. Avocations: pilot, ventriloquist. Office: The Ohio State U Columbus OH 43210

SCHIAZZA, GUIDO DOMENIC (GUY SCHIAZZA), educational association administrator; b. Phila., May 17, 1930; s. Guido and Claudina (DiPrinzio) S.; m. Irmgard Heidi Reissmueller, May 15, 1954. BA, Pa. State U., 1952; postgrad., St. Joseph's U., 1954-55, Villanova U., 1954-55, Temple U., 1955-58. Cert. tchr., Pa.; cert. clinician, ednl. specialist, instructional specialist, sch. psychologist, guidance counselor, reading specialist. Speech therapist, lang. arts instr. Commonwealth of Pa., Dept. Edn., 1956-59; founder, clinician, instr., dir., bd. pres. Communicative Arts Ctr., Inc., Drexel Hill, Pa., 1958, Communication Skills Community Resources Ctr., Inc., Drexel Hill, Pa., 1958, 1964—; charter mem. exec. bd., bd. pres. United Pvt. Acad. Schs., Assn. of Pa., Drexel Hill, 1966—; exec. bd. govs., bd. chmn. The Accrediting Commn., Drexel Hill, 1971—; charter mem. Pa. State Univ. Radio and TV Guild, University Park, Pa., 1951—; mem. legis. action com., Pa. State U., Univ. Park, 1988—; cons. communications skills, The Accrediting Commn., 1971—, United Pvt. Acad. Schs. Assn., Pa., 1966—. Founder, chmn., CEO Am. Ednl. Group, 1991—; chmn. CEO Internat. Ednl. Group, 1991—; CEO Cmty. Resources Ctr., Drexel Hill, 1991—, project coord. Energy Quest, 1992—; active Nat. Com. to Preserve Social Security and Medicare, Washington, 1986—, Am. Imigration Control Found., Monterey, Va., 1987—, English First, Springfield, Va., 1988—; mem. pres.'s coun. Rep. Nat. Com., 1989—, Nat. Rep. Senatorial Com., 1989—, Rep. Presdl. Task Force, 1989—. 1st Lt. Signal Corps, U.S. Army, 1952-54. Recipient Svc. award United Pvt. Acad. Sch. Assn. Pa., Monroeville, Pa., 1978, Disting. Achievement and Svc. award Bd. Govs. of the Accrediting Commn., Downington, Pa., 1980, Dr. Charles Boehm Edn. of Yr. award University Park, Pa., 1990, Loyal and Dedicated Svc. award The Accrediting Commn., 1974. Mem. NEA, Libr. Congress (chartered), Internat. Platform Assn., Pa. Edn. Assn., Jefferson Ednl. Found., World Affairs Coun. Phila., Heritage Found., Nat. Trust for Hist. Preservation, Nat. Congl. Club, Pa. State U. Nittany Lions Club, Pa. State U. Alumni Assn., Pa. State U. Football Lettermen's Club, Pa. State U. Varsity "S" Club. Republican. Roman Catholic. Avocations: music, home and garden design, automotive design, reading, golf. Office: The Accrediting Commn 436 Burmont Rd Drexel Hill PA 19026-3630

SCHICHLER, ROBERT LAWRENCE, English language educator; b. Rochester, N.Y., May 16, 1951; s. Alfred James and Elizabeth Johanna (Flugel) S. BA in English, SUNY, Geneseo, 1974, MA in English, 1978; PhD of English, Binghamton U., 1987. Writer, asst. adminstr. Artists-in-Residence Program, Rochester, N.Y., 1978-79; substitute tchr. City Sch. Dist., Rochester, 1980-82; instr. English Talmudical Inst. Upstate N.Y., Rochester, 1981-82, Binghamton (N.Y.) U., 1983-84; rsch. asst. Medieval and Renaissance Texts and Studies, Binghamton, 1985-86; adj. asst. prof. Rochester Inst. Tech., 1987-89; assoc. prof. English Ark. State U., State University, 1989—; adj. asst. prof. Monroe C.C., Rochester, 1987-89. Author: King of the Once Wild Frontier: Reflections of a Canal Walker, 1993; editor: Lady in Waiting: Poems in English and Spanish, 1994, Abstracts of Papers in Anglo-Saxon Studies, 1988—, Ctr. for Medieval and Early Renaissance Studies, Binghamton, 1986-94, Spillway Pubs., Rochester, 1992—; asst. editor: Old English Newsletter, 1986-87, Mediaevalia, Binghamton, 1988-89; contbr. articles to profl. jours. Active Pres's. Nat. Steering Com., 1995—. Mem. Internat. Soc. Anglo-Saxonists, Internat. Ctr. Medieval Art, Medieval Acad. Am., Modern Lang. Assn. Am., South Cen. Modern Lang. Assn., Ark. Philol. Assn. Home: 726 Southwest Dr Apt K-2 Jonesboro AR 72401-7074 Office: Dept English and Philosophy Ark State U State University AR 72467-1890

SCHICK, EDGAR BREHOB, German literature educator; b. Phila., June 28, 1934; s. Claude Ernest and Martha Henrietta (Brehob) S.; m. Margaret Barbara Buehl, Feb. 12, 1938; children: Susanne, Christina. AB magna cum laude, Muhlenberg Coll., 1955; MA, Rutgers U., 1962, PhD, 1965. Asst. prof. German SUNY, Binghamton, 1963-68; asst. to pres. SUNY, Albany, 1968-72, asst. prof., 1968-72; v.p. acad. affairs St. John Fisher Coll., Rochester, N.Y., 1972-78, exec. v.p., 1978-80, assoc. prof., 1972-80; pres. Nasson Coll., Springvale, Maine, 1980-83; provost, v.p. acad. affairs, prof. Eastern Ill. U., Charleston, 1984-87; exec. dir. Bd. Trustees, Md. State Univs. & Colls., Annapolis, 1987-88; vice chancellor for policy and planning U. Md. System, Adelphi, 1988-91; sr. fellow Am. Assn. State Colls. and Univs., 1991-94; cons. Assn. Governing Bds., 1993-95; chmn. visitation team Mid. States Assn. Colls. and Schs., Phila., 1975-79; cons. IBM, Yorkville, N.Y., 1968, Nat. Luth. Campus Ministry, 1968-85, USAID, 1992-95. Author: Metaphorical Organicism in the Early Herder, 1971, Shared Visions of Public Higher Education Governance: Structures and Leadership Styles That Work, 1992, The "Local Board" in Multi-Campus Public Universities, 1994; contbr. articles on German lit. and higher edn. to profl. jours. Bd. dirs. United Way, 1981-82, Maine Ind. Colls. Assn., 1981-93, Deaton Hosp., Balt.; v.p. Christ Luth. Ch. Found., Balt.; mem. Accreditation Bd. for Engring. Tech.; pres. Oakleigh Forest Civic Assn. Univ. fellow, Rutgers U., New Brunswick, N.J., 1962-63; grantee Carnegie Found., Dept. HEW. Mem. Am. Assn. Higher Edn., Am. Assn. Univ. Adminstrs., Am. Assn. Tchrs. German, Assn. for Instl. Rsch., Soc. for Coll. and Univ. Planning, Thomas Mann Soc., Nat. Soc. Fund-Raising Execs. Lutheran. Home: 106 Quinn Rd Severna Park MD 21146-3015

SCHICK, HARRY LEON, investment company executive; b. N.Y.C., Oct. 24, 1927; s. Martin and Sadie (Spitz) S.; m. Eleanor Alter, Oct. 17, 1982; m. Inge Nussbaum, Oct. 12, 1964 (div. Nov. 1971); 1 child, Susan. A.B. magna cum laude, Bklyn. Coll., 1947; M.S., Columbia U., 1948; postgrad., NYU, 1948-52. Securities analyst Sutro Bros., N.Y.C., 1948-52; asst. to pres. Clairdale Enterprises, Inc., N.Y.C., 1953-66; mgr. arbitrage dept. First Manhattan Co., N.Y.C., 1966-69, gen. ptnr., 1969-91, ltd. ptnr., 1992—; lectr. Donaldson Sch. Orgn. and Mgmt., Yale U., New Haven, 1978-88, NYU Grad. Sch. Bus. Adminstrn., N.Y.C., 1977; lectr. in field. Bd. overseers Libr. of Jewish Theol. Sem.; trustee Washington Inst. for Near East Policy. Mem. Inst. Chartered Fin. Analysts, Am. Fin. Assn., Am. Econ. Assn., N.Y. Soc. Security Analysts (bd. dirs. 1975-76), Beta Gamma Sigma. Jewish. Home: 215 E 68th St Apt 15Y New York NY 10021-5726 Office: First Manhattan Co 437 Madison Ave New York NY 10022-7001

SCHICK, IRVIN HENRY, academic administrator, educator; b. Wilkes-Barre, Pa., Aug. 10, 1924; s. Irvin and Elizabeth (Valentine) S.; diploma Bliss Elec. Sch., 1947; B.E.E. with distinction, George WashingtonU., 1958; M.S. in Elec. Engring. (NSF fellow), U. Md., 1961; m. Marilyn Freeman, July 17, 1954 (dec. Aug. 1961); m. Marjorie Bletch Beach, Dec. 23, 1967; 1dau., Carolyn Patricia. Engring. asst. Jeddo-Highland Coal Co. (Pa.), 1942-43; instr. Bliss Elec. Sch., Washington, 1947-50; prof. math. and elec. engring., dept. head Montgomery Coll., Rockville, Md., 1950-65, dir. extension, 1965-67, dean adminstrn., 1967-75, adminstrv. v.p., 1975-78, prof. emeritus, adminstrv. v.p. emeritus, 1978—. Tchr., tutor, cons. indsl. cos. 1949—. Served with USAAF, 1943-46. Mem. AAUP, Montgomery County Edn. Assn., Md. State Tchrs. Assn., IEEE, Am. Assn. Sch. Adminstrs., Internat. Platform Assn., Bliss Elec. Soc. (bd. govs.,past pres., Tent Troupe Theatrical Organ. (bd. govs.), Theta Tau, Sigma Tau (past pres.), Sigma Pi Sigma, Tau Beta Pi. Home: 105 Fleetwood Ter Silver Spring MD 20910-5512

SCHICK, MICHAEL WILLIAM, public relations consultant; b. San Antonio, July 17, 1956; s. Lawrence Martin and Jeanne Frances (McCuen) S.; m. Diana Lynn McGinty, Mar. 14, 1988; children: Tiffany Michele, Jessica Diane. B in Media Arts with honors, U. S.C., 1979. Dir. prodns., asst. v.p. S.C. Savs. & Loan League, Columbia, 1978-81; dep. press sec. to U.S. Sen. Strom Thurmond Washington, 1981-85; sr. assoc. Civic Svc. Inc., Washington, 1985—. Co-founder, chmn. First Monday Night, McLean, Va., 1981-94; Fourth Presbyn. Ch., Bethesda, Md., 1988—; chmn. Creative Living Internat., Reston, 1988—. Mem. Am. Assn. Polit. Conss., Washington Internat. Trade Assn., U.S./China Bus. Coun. Republican. Avocations: golf, tennis, soccer, sailing, guitar. Home: 11560 Brass Lantern Ct Reston VA 20194-1221 Office: Civic Svc Inc 1050 Connecticut Ave NW Ste 870 Washington DC 20036

SCHICKEL, RICHARD, writer, film critic, producer; b. Milw., Feb. 10, 1933; s. Edward J. and Helen (Hendricks) S.; children: Erika Tracy, Jessica Avery. BS, U. Wis., 1955. Sr. editor Look mag., 1957-60, Show mag., 1960-63; freelance writer, 1963—; film critic Life mag., 1965-72, Time mag., 1973—; cons. Rockefeller Bros. Fund, 1964, Rockefeller Found., 1965; lectr. in history art Yale, 1972, 76; adj. prof. film, U. S. Calif., 1989; pres. Lorac Prodns., 1986—. Author: The World of Carnegie Hall, 1960, The Stars, 1962, Movies: The History of an Art and an Institution, 1964, The Gentle Knight, 1964, The Disney Version, 1968, The World of Goya, 1968, Second Sight: Notes on Some Movies, 1972, His Picture in the Papers, 1974, Harold Lloyd: The Shape of Laughter, 1974, The Men Who Made the Movies, 1975, The World of Tennis, 1975, The Fairbanks Album, 1975, Singled Out, 1981,

Cary Grant, A Celebration, 1984, D.W. Griffith; An American Life, 1984, James Cagney, A Celebration, 1985, Intimate Strangers: The Culture of Celebrity, 1985, Striking Poses, 1987, Schickel on Film, 1989, Brando: A Life In Our Times, 1991, Double Indemnity, 1992, Clint Eastwood: A Biography, 1996; co-author: Lena, 1965, The Platinum Years, 1974, Hollywood at Home, 1990 (novel) Another I, Another You, 1978; co-editor: Film 67-68, 1968; producer, dir., writer (TV series) The Men Who Made the Movies, 1973; producer, writer: (TV spls.) Life Goes to the Movies, 1976, SPFX, 1980, Cary Grant, A Celebration, 1989; producer, writer, dir.: (TV spls.) Funny Business, 1978, Into the Morning: Willa Cather's America, 1978, The Horror Show, 1979, James Cagney: That Yankee Doodle Dandy, 1981, From Star Wars to Jedi: The Making of a Saga, 1983, Minnelli on Minnelli; Liza Remebers Vincent, 1987, Gary Cooper: American Life, American Legend, 1989, Myrna Loy: So Nice to Come Home To, 1990, Barbara Stanwyck: Fire and Desire, 1991, Eastwood & Co.: Making Unforgiven, 1992, Hollywood on Hollywood, 1993, Elia Kazan: A Director's Journey, 1995, The Moviemakers, 1996, The Harry Hausen Chronicles, 1997. Recipient Book prize Brit. Film Inst., 1985; Guggenheim fellow, 1964. Mem. Nat. Soc. Film Critics, N.Y. Film Critics, Dirs. Guild Am., Writers Guild Am.

SCHICKELE, PETER, composer; b. Ames, Iowa, July 17, 1935; s. Rainer Wolfgang and Elizabeth (Wilcox) S.; m. Susan Sindall, Oct. 27, 1962; children: Karla, Matthew. B.A., Swarthmore Coll., 1957; M.S., Julliard Sch. Music, 1960; PhD (hon.), Swarthmore, 1980. Composer-in-residence Los Angeles High Sch., 1960-61; faculty Swarthmore Coll., 1961-62, Juilliard Sch. Music, 1961-65, Aspen Festival Music, Colo., 1963. Composer: scores for films The Crazy Quilt, 1965, Funny Man, 1967, Silent Running, 1972, several non-theatrical and TV films; arranger for: Joan Baez albums Noel, 1966, Joan, 1967, Baptism, 1968; composer mus. score for film at Tex. pavilion of Hemisfair, San Antonio, 1968; TV appearances include: Profile on the Arts, Camera Three, Bach 'N' Roll, 13 Stars for 13, Dick Cavett Show, Mike Douglas Show, David Frost Show, ABC Comedy News, Tonight Show with Johnny Carson; comedian, recorded: An Evening with P.D.Q. Bach, 1968, P.D.Q. Bach: 1712 Overture and Other Musical Assaults, 1989, Oedipus Tex and Other Choral Calamities, 1990, WTWP-Classical Talkity-Talk Radio, 1991, Music for an Awful Lot of Winds and Percussion, 1992, other comedy albums; mem., The Open Window, chamber-rock trio, 1967-71; composer and lyricist: Oh Calcutta; composer String Quartet No. 1, American Dreams and numerous works for orch., chorus, piano, chamber music, band, organ, voice and instruments, 1953—; creator, host Schickele Mix, Pub. Radio Internat., family concerts with Am. Symphony Orch., 1994—; author: The Definitive Biography of P.D.Q. Bach. Recipient Gershwin Meml. award, 1959, Elizabeth Tow Newman Contemporary Music award, 1964, Grammy awards, 1990-93, Deems Taylor award; Ford Found. grantee. Mem. ASCAP, Am. Music Ctr., Assn. Classical Music, Am. Fedn. Musicians. Avocation: crossword puzzles. Office: ICM Artists care Stewart Warkow 40 W 57th St New York NY 10019-4001*

SCHIDLOW, DANIEL, pediatrician, medical association administrator; b. Santiago, Chile, Oct. 23, 1947; m. Sally Rosen; children: David, Michael, Jessica. Grad., U. Chile, 1972. Diplomate Am. Bd. Pediatrics, Am. Bd. Pediatric Pulmonology; lic. in D.C., Pa., N.J. Rotating intern U. Chile Hosp., U. Chile Sch. Medicine, 1971-72, resident in internal medicine, instr. phys. diagnosis, 1972-73; resident, emergency rm. physician in pediatrics E.G. Cortes Hosp. Children, U. Chile, 1973-74; resident in pediatrics Albert Einstein Coll. Medicine Bronx (N.Y.)-Lebanon Hosp. Ctr., 1974-76; fellow pediatric pulmonary medicine St. Christopher's Hosp. Children, Phila., 1976-78; chief sect. pediatric pulmonology dept. pediatrics St. Christopher's Hosp. Children, 1983-94, sr. v.p. clin. affairs, 1994—; from asst. to assoc. prof. pediatrics sch. medicine Temple U., Phila., 1978-90, prof., 1990-94, dep. chmn. dept. pediatrics, 1991-94; prof., sr. vice chmn. dept. pediatrics Allegheny U. of Health Scis., Phila., 1994—, Med. Coll. Pa., Phila., 1994—, Hahnemann Sch. Medicine, Phila., 1994—; sr. v.p. clin. affairs St. Christopher's Hosp. Children, 1978—, dir. fellowship tng. and edn. program sect. pediatric pulmonology, 1979-91, assoc. dir. pediatric pulmonary and cystic fibrosis ctr., 1981-83, med. dir. dept. respiratory therapy, 1982-88, project dir. Phila. pediatric pulmonary ctr., 1983-86, dir. cystic fibrosis ctr., 1983—, chair capital campaign com. dept. pediatrics, 1987, mem. exec. com. med. staff, 1988—, mem. various coms.; courtesy staff Lancaster (Pa.) Gen. Hosp., 1980-82; cons. divsn. rehab. Pa. Dept. Health, 1983—; mem. promotions com. dept. pediatrics sch. medicine Temple U., 1986—, chmn. com. appointments clin.-educator track 1991—; attending staff no. divsn. Albert Einstein Med. Ctr., 1987—; cons. Nat. Ctr. Youth Disabilities, 1987—; mem. med. adv. coun. Cystic Fibrosis Found., Bethesda, Md., 1987—, trustee, 1990—, med. dir. home care svcs., 1991—, various other positons; consulting staff Temple U. Hosp., 1988—; mem. organizing com. N.Am. Cystic Fibrosis Conf., 1990-93, co-chmn., 1992—; co-chmn. Nat. Concensus Conf. Pulmonary Complications Cystic Fibrosis, McLean, Va., 1992; mem. adv. bd. Phila. Parenting Assocs., 1992—. Reviewer Jour. Pediatrics, Am. Jour. Diseases Children, others. Named Illustrious Guest, City of LaPlata, Argentina, 1992. Fellow Am. Acad. Pediatrics (Pa. chpt., sect. diseases chest), Am. Coll. Chest Physicians (sect. cardiopulmonary diseases children); mem. AAAS, Am. Thoracic Soc. (mem. nominating com. 1993—), Am. Fedn. Clin. Rsch., Chilean Pediatric Soc. (hon.), Pa. Thoracic Soc., Ea. Soc. Pediatric Rsch., Phila. Pediatric Soc. Home: 315 N Bowman Ave Merion Station PA 19066-1523 Office: St Christopher's Hosp Chldn Office Med and Acad Affairs Erie Ave at Front St Philadelphia PA 19134

SCHIEBLER, GEROLD LUDWIG, physician, educator; b. Hamburg, Pa., June 20, 1928; s. Alwin Robert and Charlotte Elizabeth (Schmoele) S.; m. Audrey Jean Lincourt, Jan. 8, 1954; children: Mark, Marcella, Kristen, Bettina, Wanda, Michele. BS, Franklin and Marshall Coll., 1950; MD, Harvard U., 1954. Intern pediatrics and internal medicine Mass. Gen. Hosp., Boston, 1954-55, resident, 1955-56; resident pediatrics U. Minn. Hosp., Mpls., 1956-57, fellow pediatric cardiology, 1957-58, rsch. fellow, 1958-59; rsch. fellow sect. physiology Mayo Clinic and Mayo Found., 1959-60; asst. prof. pediatric cardiology U. Fla., 1960-63, assoc. prof., 1963-66, prof., 1966-92, Disting. Svc. prof., 1992—, chmn. dept. pediatrics, 1968-85, assoc. v.p. for health affairs for external rels., 1985—; dir. div. Children's Med. Svcs., State of Fla., 1973-74. Author: (with L.P. Elliott) The X-ray Diagnosis of Congenital Cardiac Disease in Infants, Children and Adults, 1968, 2d edit., 1979, (with L.J. Krovetz and I.H. Gessner) Pediatric Cardiology, 2d edit., 1979. Mem. AAAS, Inst. Medicine NAS, Am. Acad. Pediatrics (Abraham Jacobi award 1993), AMA (Benjamin Rush award 1993), Am. Coll. Cardiology, Soc. Pediatric Rsch. (emeritus), Fla. Pediatric Soc. (exec. com.), Fla. Heart Assn. (past pres.), Fla. Med. Assn. (past v.p., bd. govs., pres. 1991-92), Phi Beta Kappa, Alpha Omega Alpha. Home: 2115 NW 15th Ave Gainesville FL 32605-5216

SCHIEFELBUSCH, RICHARD L., research administrator; b. Osawatomie, Kans., July 23, 1918; s. Edward Francis and Emma (Martie) S.; m. Ruth Lenore Magee, Sept. 20, 1942; children—Lary, Carol, Jean. B.S., Kans. State Tchrs. Coll., 1940; M.A. in Speech Pathology and Psychology, U. Kans., 1947; Ph.D. in Speech Pathology, Northwestern U., 1951. Mem. faculty U. Kans., Lawrence, 1946-89, prof. speech pathology and audiology, 1959-69; dir. Speech and Hearing Clinic Schiefelbusch Speech and Hearing Clinic, Lawrence, 1949-56; dir. Bur. Child Research U. Kans., Lawrence, 1955-90, Univ. Disting. prof., 1969-89; Univ. Disting. prof. emeritus, 1989—; chmn. child lang. grad. degree program U. Kans., Lawrence, 1983-89, interim dir. Gerontology Ctr., 1989-91; interim dir. Inst. for Life Span Studies Schiefelbusch Inst. for Life Span Studies, Lawrence, 1989-90; dir. Kans. Center Mental Retardation and Human Devel., Lawrence, 1969-89; co-dir. Kans. Research Inst. Learning Disabilities, Lawrence, 1977-81; sr. scientist VA Hosp., Topeka, 1991-93; cons. in field, dir. research grants. Author book series Language Intervention; also numerous articles in field; mem. editorial bds. profl. jours. Served with USAAF, 1941-46. Recipient Disting. Service award Nat. Assn. for Retarded Citizens, 1983; Disting. Achievement award Pittsburg State U., 1985, Disting. Accomplishment award Am. Assn. Univ. Affiliated Programs, 1987; Fulbright scholar, Australia, 1986. Fellow Am. Assn. Mental Deficiency (Spl. award 1975, Edn. award 1986), Am. Speech and Hearing Assn. (assn. honoree 1976, v.p. edn. and sci. affairs 1980-82); mem. Council Exceptional Children. Home: 3113 Campfire Dr Lawrence KS 66049-2012 Office: U Kans Bur Child Rsch Lawrence KS 66045

SCHIEFFELIN, GEORGE RICHARD, educational consultant; b. N.Y.C., July 3, 1930; s. George McKay and Louise (Winterbotham) S. B.A., Hobart Coll., 1953. Ednl. cons. Denver, 1956-62, New Haven, 1962-89, Tampa, Fla., 1989—; dir. Charles Scribner's Sons, N.Y.C., Scribner Book Stores, N.Y.C., Pubs. Realty Co., N.Y.C., 1962-83, Macro Communications, N.Y.C., 1975-83; asst. to lt. gov. of Colo., 1958-59. Trustee Hobart and William Smith Colls., 1969-78, Rocky Mountain Coll., 1989-93, adv. com. Rocky Mountain Coll., 1993—. With AUS, 1953-55. Mem. Morristown Field Club, Univ. Club (Denver), Princeton Club (N.Y.C.), Williams Club.

SCHIEFFER, BOB, broadcast journalist; b. Austin, Tex.; m. Patricia Penrose; children: Susan, Sharon. B.A. in Journalism, Tex. Christian U. Reporter Ft. Worth Star-Telegram; news anchorman Sta. WBAP-TV, Dallas-Ft. Worth; with CBS News, 1969—, Pentagon corr., 1970-74, White House corr., 1974-79, chief Washington corr., 1982—; anchorman CBS Sunday Night News, 1973-74, Sunday edit. CBS Evening News, 1976—, Monday-through-Friday edits. Morning, 1979-80; co-anchorman CBS Morning News, from 1985; also participant CBS news spls. and spl. reports, including Peace and the Pentagon, 1974, Watergate-The White House Transcripts, 1974, The Mysterious Alert, 1974, 1976, Ground Zero, 1981; Democratic Nat. Conv., 1976, Republican Nat. Conv., Campaign '72; and mem. Emmy award-winning team CBS Evening News with Walter Cronkite, 1971; currently moderator Face the Nation CBS News, chief Washington corr.; co-anchor CBS Weekend News/Sunday News, N.Y.C. Author: (with Gary Paul Gates) The Acting President, 1989. Recipient various awards Sigma Delta Chi, various awards Tex. Associated Broadcasters, various awards AP Mng. Editors; co-recipient Emmy awards. Office: care CBS News Weekend/Sunday News 524 W 57th St New York NY 10019-2902*

SCHIEFFER, J. THOMAS, professional baseball team executive. Pres. Texas Rangers. Office: Texas Rangers 1000 Ballpark Way Arlington TX 76011-5168*

SCHIEKOFER, SUSAN, advertising executive; m. Richard Schiekofer; 2 children. With Ted Bates' Coll. Tng. Program, Wunderman, Ricotta and Kline; sr. ptnr., assoc. media dir. Ogilvy & Mather Direct, 1984—. Office: Ogilvy & Mather Direct 309 W 49th St New York NY 10019-7316

SCHIELE, PAUL ELLSWORTH, JR., educational business owner, writer; b. Phila., Nov. 20, 1924; s. Paul Ellsworth Sr. and Maud (Barclay) S.; m. Sarah Irene Knauss, Aug. 20, 1946; children: Patricia Schiele Tiemann, Sandra Schiele Kicklighter, Deborah Schiele Hartigan. AT, Temple U., 1949; BA, LaVerne U., 1955; MA, Claremont Associated Colls., 1961; PhD, U.S. Internat. U., San Diego, 1970. Cert. sec. tchr., Calif. 1961. Tchr. sci. and math. Lincoln High Sch., Phila., 1956-57, Ontario (Calif.) Sch. Dist., 1957-65; math. and sci. cons. Hacienda La Puente U. Sch. Dist., Calif., 1965-75; asst. prof. Calif. State U., Fullerton, 1975-83; pres., owner Creative Learning Environments and Resources, Glendora, Calif., 1983—, cons. sci. curriculum, 1985—; dir. title III project ESEA, 1974-75, cons. for project, 1975-77; cons. in field. Author: Primary Science, 1972, 2d edit., 1976, (novel) Under Cover of Night, 1995, Chasing the Wild Geese, 1996, Deception Appearances, 1997; editor: A Living World, 1974, 2d edit., 1986; writer 9 sound filmstrips, model units for sci. and math. activity books, 10 sci. activities for L.A. Outdoor Edn. Program, 1980; editor 21 sci. and math. activity books, 1975-76; writer, co-dir. (TV) Marine Biology Series, 1970-71; contbr. numerous articles to profl. mags., 1960-85; writer and designer of 2 sci. ednl. games; designer in field. Apptd. adv. com. Sci. and Humanities Symposium Calif. Mus. Sci. and Industry, 1974; mem. State Sci. Permit Com., Tide Pools of Calif. Coast, 1974-75; active Playhouse 90, Pasadena (Calif.) Playhouse; mem. Friends of Libr., Friends Libr. Found. Mem. Internat. Platform Assn., ABI Rsch. Assn. (bd. govs.), Calif. Elem. Edn. Assn. (hon.), Nat. PTA (hon.), Calif. Inter-Sci. Coun. (pres., chmn. 1971, 72), Elem Sch. Scis. Assn. (past pres., bd. dirs.), Phi Delta Kappa (chartered). Republican. Lutheran. Avocations: travel, etchings, art collecting, fencing. Home: 231 Catherine Park Dr Glendora CA 91741-3018

SCHIER, DONALD STEPHEN, language educator; b. Ft. Madison, Iowa, Sept. 10, 1914; s. Francis and Marcella (Kenny) S. B.A., State U. Iowa, 1936; M.A., Columbia U., 1937, Ph.D., 1941. Mem. faculty State Tchrs. Coll., Bemidji, Minn., 1939-41, 41-42, Ill. Inst. Tech., 1946; mem. faculty Carleton Coll., Northfield, Minn., 1946-80; prof. French Carleton Coll., 1953-80; vis. prof. U. Wis., 1964-65; Brown tutor in French U. of South, Sewanee, Tenn., 1980-81. Author: Louis-Bertrand Castel, 1942; editor: (with Scott Elledge) The Continental Model, 1960, 2d edit., 1970; (Bertrand de Fontenelle), Nouveaux Dialogues des morts, 1965, rev. edit., 1974; translator: Letter on Italian Music (Charles de Brosses), 1978. Mem. selection com. Young Scholar Program, Nat. Found. Arts and Humanities, 1966-67. Served to capt. AUS, 1942-46. Mem. MLA, Am. Assn. Tchrs. French, Am. Soc. Eighteenth-Century Studies. Home: 750 Weaver Dairy Rd Apt 1106 Chapel Hill NC 27514-1441

SCHIER, MARY JANE, science writer; b. Houston, Mar. 10, 1939; d. James F. and Jerry Mae (Crisp) McDonald; B.S. in Journalism, Tex. Woman's U., 1961; m. John Christian Schier, Aug. 26, 1961; children—John Christian, II, Mark Edward. Reporter, San Antonio Express and News, 1962-64; med. writer Daily Oklahoman, also Oklahoma City Times, 1965-66; reporter, med. writer Houston Post, 1966-84; sci. writer, univ. editor U. Tex. M.D. Anderson Cancer Ctr., 1984—. Recipient award Tex. Headliners Club, 1969, Tex. Med. Assn., 1972-74, 76, 78, 79, 80, 82 Tex. Hosp. Assn., 1974, 82, Tex. Public Health Assn., 1976, 77, 78, others. Mem. Houston Press Club Ednl. Found. (pres 1992—). Lutheran. Home: 9742 Tappenbeck Dr Houston TX 77055-4102 Office: 1515 Holcombe Blvd Houston TX 77030-4009

SCHIERHOLZ, WILLIAM FRANCIS, JR., real estate developer; b. St. Louis, Oct. 14, 1921; s. William Francis and Florence Cecelia (Wuensch) S.; m. Joan Flavin, Sept. 7, 1947; children—Margaret Ann, John W., William Francis, III. B.S. in Engring. Adminstrn, Washington U., St. Louis, 1943. Vice pres., gen. mgr. Fuel Oil of St. Louis, 1949-55; pres. Chemtech Industries, Inc., St. Louis, 1956-87, chmn. bd., 1991—; with real estate devel. Habitech Devel. Corp., Chesterfield, Mo., 1989-91; bd. dirs. Commerce Bank St. Louis; pres. Affiliated Chem. Group, Ltd., Bermuda; commr. Mo. Hwy. and Transp. Commn., 1982-87. Chmn. Mo. State Com. Reponsible Consumerism, 1977-78; mem. exec. bd. St. Louis area coun. Boy Scouts Am., adv. bd. INROADS, also chmn.; bd. dirs. Jr. Achievement of Miss. Valley; commr. Mo. Highway and Transp. Commn., 1982-87. Served to capt. USAAF, 1943-46. Mem. U.S. C. of C., Mo. C. of C. (dir., exec. com., Man of Yr. 1981), St. Louis Regional Commerce and Growth Assn. (dir., exec. com., chmn.), Am. Assn. Indsl. Mgmt. (pres. 1976, dir), Chem. Mfg. Assn., NAM, Presidents Assn, Chem. Industry Council Greater St. Louis (pres. 1970), Backstoppers, Affiliated Chem. Group (pres. 1966), Rotary Club St. Louis (pres. 1981-82), Beta Theta Pi (pres. alumni assn. 1967). Clubs: Univ., Mo. Athletic, Rotary (pres. 1981-82). Office: Chemtech Industries Inc 732 Crown Industrial Ct # L Chesterfield MO 63005-1107

SCHIESER, HANS ALOIS, education educator; b. Ulm, Germany, July 15, 1931; came to U.S., 1965; s. Alois and Anna (Stegmann) S.; m. Margret H. Schröer, June 6, 1962; children: Peter, Elisabeth. BA, Kepler Gymnasium, Ulm, 1952; MA in Philosophy, Passau, Fed. Republic Germany, 1959; EdM, Pedagogic Acad., Weingarten, Fed. Republic Germany, 1962; PhD, Loyola U., 1970. Head tchr. Pestalozzischule, Ulm, 1964-65; learning disabilities tchr. Jeanine Schultz Meml. Sch., Skokie, Ill., 1966-67; co-dir. Oak Therapeutic Sch., Evanston, Ill., 1967-70; assoc. prof. to prof. edn. DePaul U., Chgo., 1969-91, prof. emeritus, 1991—; cons. various indsl. and bus. tng. programs, 1978-91; program cons. Delphian Soc., L.A., 1977-90; rschr., tchr. in Germany, 1991—; active in tchrs. edn. Midwest Montessori Tchr. Tng. Ctr., Evanston, Ill.; mem. adv. bd. Verein Psychol.; founding dean Acad. Culture, History and Religion, Chelyabinsk, Russia, 1995. Author chpts. in books; contbr. numerous articles U.S. and German publs.; adv. bd. Am. Edits. Sociology, Dushkin Pub. Group, 1985-91. Pres. N.Am. Family Svc. Found., Oak Lawn, Ill., 1974-91; bd. dirs. S.O.S. Children's Villages USA, Washington, 1986-94; pres. emeritus S.O.S. Children's Village Ill., Inc., Chgo.; pub. policy expert Domestic Issues Heritage Found., 1991—; bd. govs. Invest-in-Am. Nat. Found., Phila., 1988-90. Rsch. grantee DePaul U., 1985-86, Rsch. sabbatical, 1989. Mem. Am. Ednl. Studies Assn., Nat. Soc. for Study of Edn., Philosophy of Edn. Soc. U.S.A., Soc. Educators and Scholars (bd. dirs. 1984-90), Am. Montessori Soc., Thomas More Gesellschaft/Amici Mori Europe, Phi Delta Kappa (pres. Zeta chpt., Chgo. 1973-75). Home: Veilchenweg 9, D-89134 Bermaringen Germany also: 136 Dodge Ave Evanston IL 60202-3661 Office: DePaul U 2320 N Kenmore Ave Chicago IL 60614-3210

SCHIESS, BETTY BONE, priest; b. Cin., Apr. 2, 1923; d. Evan Paul and Leah (Mitchell) Bone; m. William A. Schiess, Aug. 28, 1947; children: William A. (dec.), Richard Corwine, Sarah. BA, U. Cin., 1945, MA, Syracuse U., 1947; MDiv, Rochester Ctr. for Theol. Studies, 1972. Ordained priest Episcopal Ch., 1974; priest assoc. Grace Episc. Ch., Syracuse, N.Y., 1975; mem. N.Y. Task Force on Life and Law (apptd. by gov.) 1985—; chaplain Syracuse U., 1976-78, Cornell U., Ithaca, N.Y., 1978-79; rector Grace Episc. Ch., Mexico, N.Y., 1984-89; cons. Women's Issues Network Episc. Ch. in U.S., 1987—; writer, lectr., cons. religion and feminism, 1979—. Author: Take Back the Church, Indeed The Witness, 1982, Creativity and Procreativity: Some Thoughts on Eve and the Opposition and How Episcopalians Make Ethical Decisions, Plumline, 1988, Send in the Clowns, Chrysalis, Journal of the Swedenborg Foundation, 1994; contbr. forward to book. Bd. dirs. People for Pub. TV in N.Y., 1978, Religious Coalition for Abortion Rights; trustee Elizabeth Cady Stanton Found., 1979; mem. policy com. Coun. Adolescent Pregnancy; mem. N.Y. State Task Force Life and the Law, 1983—. Recipient Gov.'s award Women of Merit in Religion, 1984, Ralph E. Kharas award ACLU Cen. N.Y., 1986 Goodall disting. alumna award & Hills Sch., 1988, Human Rightes award Human Rights Commn. of Syracuse and Onondaga County, N.Y., 1989; inducted into Nat. Women's Hall of Fame, 1994. Mem. NOW (Syracuse), Internat. Assn. Women Ministers (dir. 1978, pres. 1984-87), Na'amat U.S. (hon. life), Mortar Bd., Theta Chi Beta. Democrat. Home and Office: 107 Bradford Ln Syracuse NY 13224-1901 Office: Episcopal Cmty Anabel Taylor Hall Cornell U Ithaca NY 14850

SCHIESSLER, ROBERT WALTER, retired chemical and oil company executive; b. Honesdale, Pa., Oct. 2, 1918; s. Walter A. and Josephine (Herzog) S.; m. Betty Hartman, June 5, 1939; children—Lynn Alice, Dale Ann; m. Florence Cutler, Aug. 16, 1968. B.S., Pa. State U., 1939, Ph.D., 1944; M.S., McGill U., 1941. Research chemist Gen. Electric Co., Schenectady, 1941; from instr. to asso. Prof. chemistry and dir. Am. Petroleum Inst. Research Pa. State U., 1942-55; chemistry and physics cons., 1946-55; tech. dir. Central Research div. Mobil Oil Co., Paulsboro and Princeton, N.J., 1950-60; mgr. central research div., asst. gen. mgr. research dept. Central Research div. Mobil Oil Co., 1960-62, gen. mgr. research dept., 1962-67; v.p. research Mobil Research & Devel. Corp., 1967-68; chmn., pres. Indsl. Reactor Labs., Inc., 1966-67; mgr. long-range planning Mobil Oil Corp., 1968-72, gen. mgr. real estate and land devel., 1972-83; chmn. Mobil Land Devel. Corp., 1972-83; pres. Sandvik, Inc., 1983-84; chmn. bd. trustees Gordon Rsch. Conf., Inc., 1957; mem. bd. Am. Chem. Soc. Peroleum Rsch. Fund, 1955-59, 60-63; Rsch. chemist Can. govt., 1940-41. Co-Author: Chemistry of Petroleum Hydrocarbons, 1954, Discoverer method for prodn. super-explosive used by U.S. and Can., World War II. Recipient award in petroleum chemistry Am. Chem. Soc., 1953; named outstanding young man State Coll. of Pa., outstanding young man Jr. C. of C., 1952; recipient Wisdom award, 1970. Fellow Am. Inst. Chemists, AAAS (v.p. for chemistry, chmn. chemistry sect. 1960); mem. Am. Chem. Soc., AAUP, Sigma Xi, Phi Lambda Upsilon, Phi Eta Sigma. Home: 1500 Palisade Ave Fort Lee NJ 07024

SCHIFF, ANDREW NEWMAN, physician, venture capitalist; b. N.Y.C., Aug. 31, 1965; s. David T. and Martha Elisabeth (Lawler) S. BS in honors, Brown U., 1987; MD, Cornell U., 1990. Diplomate Am. Bd. Internal Medicine, Nat. Bd. Med. Examiners. Resident, intern internal medicine N.Y. Hosp.; clin. assoc. in medicine N.Y. Hosp.-Cornell U., N.Y.C., 1993-94, assoc. dir. primary care residency program, 1994—; assoc. dir. med. rsch. Ctr. on Addiction/Substance Abuse Columbia U., N.Y.C., 1993-95; ptnr. Kuhn, Loeb & Co., N.Y.C., 1994—. Dep. dir. campaign scheduling Campaign to Re-Elect Mario Cuomo, N.Y.C., 1994; tech. advisor Gov.'s Health Care Adv. Bd., Albany, 1994; mem. presdl. transitional team for HHS, Clinton/Gore Presdl. Transition Team, Washington, 1992; bd. dirs. Henry St. Settlement, N.Y.C., 1993—, Youth Counseling League, N.Y.C., 1988—, Reaching Up, Inc., 1994—; mem. fin. com. Cornell U. Med. Coll., N.Y.C., 1995. Office: Cornell Internal Med Assocs 505 E 70th St # 4 New York NY 10021-4872

SCHIFF, DAVID TEVELE, investment banker; b. N.Y.C., Sept. 3, 1936; s. John Mortimer and Edith Brevoort (Baker) S.; m. Martha Elisabeth Lawler, May 11, 1963; children: Andrew Newman, David Baker, Ashley Reynolds. B.Engring., Yale U., 1958. Trainee Chem. Bank N.Y. Trust, N.Y.C., 1959-62; analyst Madison Fund, N.Y.C., 1962; assoc., then partner Kuhn, Loeb & Co., N.Y.C., 1963-77; vice chmn. Kuhn Loeb & Co. Inc., 1977; mng. dir. Lehman Bros. Kuhn Loeb Inc., N.Y.C., 1977-83; also dir. Lehman Bros. Kuhn Loeb Inc.; mng. ptnr. Kuhn, Loeb & Co. (formerly KLS Enterprises), 1984—; chmn. Touchwood Records, LLC, 1995—; dir., vice chmn. Am. Crown Life Ins. Co., N.Y.C., 1981-95; bd. dirs. Crown Life Ins. Co., Toronto, 1971-92; mem. lower Manhattan adv. bd. Chem. Bank, 1977-85. Trustee Met. Mus. Art, Citizens Budget Commn., N.Y.C., Greater N.Y. coun. Boy Scouts Am., 1965-91; trustee, chmn. bd. Wildlife Conservation Soc.; trustee Beekman Downtown Hosp., 1966-82, chmn., 1975-79; trustee Brooks Sch., North Andover, Mass., 1972-90, treas., 1987-90; bd. govs. Yale U. Art Galleries, 1973-97, Fed. Hall Meml. Assn.; adv. bd. dirs. Outward Bound, Inc.; mem. Provident Loan Soc. N.Y.; bd. dirs. Am. Hosp. of Paris Found., N.Y.C., 1987. With AUS, 1959. Mem. Econ. Club N.Y.C., Pilgrims U.S., Brook Club, Century Assn., River Club, Maroon Creek Club (Aspen, Colo.), Mill Reef Club (Antigua), Yale Club N.Y.C., Am. Bugatti Club, Vintage Sports Car Club Am. Republican. Episcopalian. Home: 770 Park Ave New York NY 10021-4153 Office: 485 Madison Ave Fl 20 New York NY 10022-5803

SCHIFF, DONALD WILFRED, pediatrician, educator; b. Detroit, Sept. 11, 1925; s. Henry and Kate (Boesky) S.; m. Rosalie Pergament; children: Stephen, Jeffrey, Susan, Douglas. Student, Wayne State U., 1943-44, Oberlin Coll., 1944-45; MD, Wayne State U., 1949. Diplomate Am. Bd. Pediatrics. Intern Detroit Receiving Hosp., 1949-50; resident in pediatrics U. Colo., 1954-55, chief resident in pediatrics, 1955-56; instr. U. Colo. Health Scis. Ctr., Denver, 1956-59, asst. clin. prof., 1959-69, assoc. clin. prof., 1969-78, clin. prof., 1978-87, prof., 1987—; pvt. practice Littleton (Colo.) Clinic, 1956-86, chmn. bd., 1973-79; med. dir. HMO Colo., Denver, 1980-86; med. dir. Child Health Clinic The Children's Hosp., Denver. Contbr. articles to profl. jours. Bd. dirs. Sch. Dist. VI, Colo., 1962; pres. Arapahoe Mental Health Clinic, Denver, 1968-70, bd. dirs., 1964-70; adv. coun. State of Colo. Medicaid, Denver, 1981—. With USN, 1944-46, USPHS, 1952-54, Turtle Mountain Indian Reservation, N.D. Recipient 25 Yrs. Teaching award U. Colo. Sch. Medicine, 1981. Mem. Am. Acad. Pediatrics (chmn. Colo. chpt. 1973-79, alternate dist. chmn. 1977-81, chmn. dist. 8 1981-86, nat. pres. 1988-89), Rocky Mountain Pediatric Soc., Colo. Med. Soc. Home: 600 Front Range Rd Littleton CO 80120-4052 Office: The Children's Hosp Child Health Clinic Box BO32 1056 E 19th Ave Denver CO 80218-1007

SCHIFF, EUGENE ROGER, medical educator, hepatologist; b. Cin., Jan. 3, 1937; s. Leon and Augusta (Miller) S.; m. Dana Kendall, Dec. 27, 1965; children: David, Lisa. BA, U. Mich., 1958; MD, Columbia U., 1962. Diplomate Am. Bd. Internal Medicine, Am. Bd. Gastroenterology, Nat. Bd. Med. Examiners. Intern and med. resident Cin. Gen. Hosp., 1962-64; med. resident Parkland Meml. Hosp., Dallas, 1966-67; USPHS postdoctoral fellow in gastroenterology Southwestern Med. Sch., U. Tex., Dallas, 1967-69; asst. prof. medicine U. Miami (Fla.) Sch. Medicine, 1969-74, assoc. prof., 1974-78, prof., 1978—, chief div. hepatology, 1971—, dir. Ctr. for Liver Diseases, 1982—; chief hepatology sect. VA Med. Ctr., Miami, 1971—; chmn. adv. com. on gastrointestinal drugs FDA, Rockville, Md., 1983-85, 88-92, mem. adv. com. on blood safety, 1997—. Co-editor: Diseases of the Liver, 5th edit., 1982, 6th edit., 1987, 7th edit. 1993. Bd. dirs. Am. Digestive Health Found., 1996—, chmn. digestive health initiative on viral hepatitis, 1996—. Lt. comdr. USPHS, 1964-66. Master Am. Coll. Gastroenterology; fellow ACP (gov. Fla. chpt. 1984-88); mem. AMA, Am. Assn. for Study of Liver Diseases (sec.-treas. 1991-96, councilor 1997—), Am. Bd. Internal Medicine (subspecialty bd. gastroenterology), Internat. Assn. for Study of Liver Diseases, Am. Gastroenterology Assn. (chmn. Biliary Disorders sect. 1993-95), Argentine Soc. Gastroenterology (hon.). Jewish. Home: 10445 SW 109th St Miami FL 33176-3455 Office: U Miami 1500 NW 12th Ave Ste 1101 Miami FL 33136-1038

SCHIFF, GARY STUART, academic administrator, educator; b. Bklyn., Mar. 27, 1947; s. Jacob and Lillian (Grumet) S.; divorced; children: Jeremy Jay, Rina Joy. BA, Bin Hebrew Lit., Yeshiva U., 1968; MA, Columbia U., 1970, Cert. in Middle East Studies, 1973, PhD, 1973; DHL (hon.), Gratz Coll., 1997. Asst. prof. Jewish studies and polit. sci. CUNY, 1973-76; dir. Mid. East affairs Nat. Jewish Community Rels. Coun., N.Y.C., 1976-78; exec. asst. to pres. Acad. for Ednl. Devel., N.Y.C., 1978-83; pres. Gratz Coll., Melrose Park, Pa., 1983-97. Author: Tradition and Politics: The Religious Parties of Israel, 1977, The Energy Education Catalog, 1981; contbr. articles to profl. jours. Grantee NEH, Ford Found., Danforth Found., Woodrow Wilson Found., William Penn Found., Pew Charitable Trusts. Mem. Assn. of Colls. of Jewish Studies (bd. dirs.), Assn. for Israel Studies (v.p.), Coun. for Jewish Edn. (bd. dirs.), Assn. for Jewish Studies, World Jewish Congress (governing bd.), Am. Jewish Com. (N.Y. chpt. bd. dirs., Phila. chpt. communal affairs commn.). Avocations: liturgical music, boating, cats. Home: 14180 Kentmore Park Rd Kennedyville MD 21645

SCHIFF, GUNTHER HANS, lawyer; b. Cologne, Germany, Aug. 19, 1927; came to U.S., 1936; s. Hans and Alice (Goldstein) S.; m. Katharine MacMillan, Jan. 27, 1950 (div. 1957); children: Eric Alan, Mary Alice; m. JoAnn R. Schiff; children: Jage, Hans Judson. B.S.F.S., Georgetown U., 1949, J.D., 1952. Bar: D.C. 1952, Calif. 1953. Assoc., ptnr., of counsel various firms, Beverly Hills, Calif., 1954-94; pvt. practice Beverly Hills, Calif., 1994—; sec. Los Angeles Copyright Soc., Beverly Hills, 1975-76. Contbr. articles to profl. jours. Pres. Beverly Hills Civil Svc. Commn., 1984-85, 88-89; pres. Free Arts for Abused Children, 1993-94, dir.; chmn. Rent Control Rev. Bd., Beverly Hills, 1980-84; trustee Young Musicians Found. With USNR, 1945-46. Mem. Beverly Hills Bar Assn. (chmn. Resolutions Com. 1977-78), Los Angeles County Bar Assn., ABA, U.S. Copyright Soc., Los Angeles Copyright Soc., Calif. Yacht Club. Avocations: sailing; skiing; golfing. Home: 612 N Foothill Rd Beverly Hills CA 90210-3404 Office: Law Office Gunther H Schiff 9430 W Olympic Blvd Beverly Hills CA 90212-4552

SCHIFF, JOHN JEFFERSON, insurance company executive; b. Cin., Apr. 19, 1916; s. John Jefferson and Marguerite (Cleveland) S.; m. Mary Reid, July 26, 1941; children: John Jefferson, Suzanne, Thomas R. BSc in Commerce, Ohio State U., 1938. Vice chmn. Cin. Ins. Co., 1979—; pres. Cin. Fin. Corp., 1979-91, chief exec. officer, 1987-91; chmn., exec. com. Cin Fin Corp., 1991—; v.p. Deaconess Hosp. of Cin., Griffith Found. for Ins. Chmn. Cin. Art Mus.; trustee Am. Inst. for Property and Liability Underwriters, USS Constitution Museum; chmn. investment com. Navy League of the U.S.; Great Living Cincinnatian, Feb. 7, 1997. Served to lt. comdr. Supply Corps, USN, 1942-46. Named Ins. Man of Yr. in Cin., Cin. Ins. Bd., 1977. Mem. Cin. C. of C. (v.p. 1972). Republican. Methodist. Clubs: Queen City, Western Hills Country, Cin. Country, Royal Poinciana Golf, Naples Yacht Club. Home: 1926 Beech Grove Dr Cincinnati OH 45233-4912 Office: Cin Fin Corp PO Box 145496 Cincinnati OH 45250-5496

SCHIFF, MARGARET SCOTT, newspaper publishing executive. V.p., controller, personnel adminstr. Washington Post. Office: Washington Post Co 1150 15th St NW Washington DC 20071-0001

SCHIFF, MARTIN, physician, surgeon; b. Phila., July 16, 1922; s. Isidore and Cecelia (Miller) S.; m. Mildred Tepley, Jan. 5, 1946; children: Denise Schiff Simon, Michael, David. BS, Pa. State U., 1943; MD, U. Calif.-Irvine, 1951. Intern L.A. County Gen. Hosp., 1950-51; gen. practice medicine specializing in bariatrics L.A., 1951—; mem. staff Brotman Meml. Hosp.; lectr. L.A. area community colls. Author: Eat & Stay Slim, 1972, Miracle Weight-Loss Guide, 1976, One-Day-At-A-Time Weight Loss Plan, 1980, (5 tapes) Weight Loss Plan for Health, Happiness & A Longer Life Span, 1982, The Thin Connection, 1986. Lt. USN, 1943-45, PTO. Mem. AMA, Calif. Med. Assn., L.A. Med. Assn., Am. Soc. Weight Control Specialists. Home: 1220 Corsica Dr Pacific Palisades CA 90272-4016 Office: 12900 Venice Blvd Los Angeles CA 90066-3543

SCHIFF, ROBERT, health care consultancy company executive; b. N.Y.C., Jan. 7, 1942; s. Henry and Jeanette (Levine) S.; m. Adrianne Bendich, Aug. 16, 1964 (div. July 1979); children: Jorden, Debra; m. Joann McTaggart, Aug. 24, 1986. BS, CCNY, 1964; MS, Iowa State U., 1966; PhD, U. Calif., Davis, 1968. Asst. prof. anatomy Tufts U. Sch. Medicine, Boston, 1969-72; mgr. serology rsch. Hyland divsn. Baxter Labs., Costa Mesa, Calif., 1972-74; dir. R & D J.T. Baker Diagnostics, Bethlehem, Pa., 1974-77; dir. diagnostic R & D Hoffmann-LaRoche, Nutley, N.J., 1977-80; group v.p. Warner Lambert Co., Morris Plains, N.J., 1980-82; pres., CEO Schiff & Co., Inc., West Caldwell, N.J., 1982—; Del. Nat. Commn. for Clin. Lab. Stds., 1979-80; vice chmn. R & D Coun. N.J., 1980-82; bd. dirs. E.P.I. subs. E-Z-EM, Westbury, N.Y., 1991—. Contbr. numerous articles to profl. jours.; patentee in field. Aid to Cancer Rsch. grantee, Mass., 1970. Mem. N.Y. Acad. Sci., Regulatory Affairs Profl. Soc. (cert.), Am. Soc. Quality Control (cert. quality auditor), Am. Assn. Clin. Chemistry, Sigma Xi. Avocation: licensed pilot. Office: Schiff & Co 1129 Bloomfield Ave West Caldwell NJ 07006-7123

SCHIFF, STEFAN OTTO, zoologist, educator; b. Braunschweig, Germany, July 22, 1930; came to U.S., 1941, naturalized, 1943; s. Walter and Johanne Ilse (Muller) S.; m. Laura Frances Ward, June 6, 1957; children—Sena, Stefanie. B.S., Roanoke Coll., 1952; Ph.D., U. Tenn., 1964. USPHS trainee, 1961-63; mem. faculty George Washington U., Washington, 1964—, prof. zoology, 1976-95, prof. emeritus, 1995, chmn. dept. biol. scis., 1977-87, dir. grad. genetics program, 1971-95. Author: Twenty-One Afternoons of Biology, 3d edit., 1986, Buttons: Art in Miniature, 1980. Lutheran. Home: 10710 Howerton Ave Fairfax VA 22030-2917 Office: George Washington U Lisner Hall 321 Washington DC 20052

SCHIFF, STEVEN HARVEY, congressman, lawyer; b. Chicago, Ill., Mar. 18, 1947; s. Alan Jerome and Helen M. (Ripper) S.; m. Marcia Lewis, Nov. 8, 1968; children: Jaimi, Daniel. BA, U. Ill., Chgo., 1968; JD, U. N.Mex., 1972. Bar: N.Mex. 1972, U.S. Dist. Ct. N.Mex. 1972, U.S. Ct. Appeals (10th cir.) 1980. Asst. dist. atty. Dist. Atty.'s Office, Albuquerque, 1972-77, sole practice, 1977-79; asst. city atty. City of Albuquerque, 1979-81; dist. atty. State of N.Mex., Albuquerque, 1981-89; mem. 101st-104th Congresses from 1st N.Mex. dist., Washington, D.C., 1989—; mem. govt. reform & oversight com. U.S. House of Reps., mem. judiciary com. and standards of ofcl. conduct com., chmn. sci. subcom. on basic rsch.; lectr. U. N.Mex., Albuquerque, 1981—. Chmn. Bernalillo County Rep. Party Conv., Albuquerque, 1984, 87, staff judge adv. N.Mex. Air N.G. Col. JAGC, USAFR. Recipient Law Enforcement Commendation medal SR, 1984. Mem. ABA, Albuquerque Bar Assn., N.Mex. Bar Assn. Republican. Jewish. Club: Civitan. Lodge: B'nai Brith (pres. 1976-78). Home: 804 Summit Ave NE Albuquerque NM 87106-2045 Office: House of Reps 2404 Rayburn Bldg Washington DC 20515-3101 also: 625 Silver Ave SW Ste 140 Albuquerque NM 87102

SCHIFFER, CLAUDIA, model. Model Guess? jeans, 1989—, Revlon cosmetics, Chanel. Runway debut in Chanel fashion show, 1990; appeared on covers of Mademoiselle, Cosmopolitan, Vogue, and over 100 others. Office: Elite Model Agy 111 E 22nd St New York NY 10010-5403*

SCHIFFER, DANIEL L., gas company executive; m. Sheila Schiffer; children: Michael, Eric. AB, Bklyn. Coll., 1964; JD, Cornell U., 1967. Law clk. U.S. Ct. Appeals (2d cir.); pvt. practice N.Y.C.; spl. asst. N.Y. Pub. Svc. Commn., N.Y.C.; now sr. v.p., gen. counsel, sec. MCN Energy Group, Inc., 1989—. Trustee Botsford Gen. Hosp. Mem. ABA, Mich. State Bar Assn., Detroit Bar Assn., Fed. Energy Bar Assn. Avocations: sports, reading, bridge. Office: MCN Corp 500 Griswold St Detroit MI 48226-3700

SCHIFFER, JOHN PAUL, physicist; b. Budapest, Hungary, Nov. 22, 1930; came to U.S., 1947, naturalized, 1953; s. Ernest and Elisabeth (Tornai) S.; m. Marianne Tsuk, June 28, 1960; children: Celia Anne, Peter Ernest. AB, Oberlin Coll., 1951; MS, Yale U., 1952, PhD, 1954. Research asso. Rice Inst., Houston, 1954-56; asst. physicist Argonne (Ill.) Nat. Lab., 1956-59, asso. physicist, 1960-63, sr. physicist, 1964—, assoc. dir. physics div., 1964-79, 83—, dir. physics div., 1979-82; prof. physics U. Chgo., 1968—; vis. asso. prof. Princeton, 1964; vis. prof. U. Rochester, N.Y., 1967-68; mem. adv. coms. nuclear physics Nat. Acad. Scis.; mem. program adv. or rev. coms. Los Alamos Meson Physics Facility, 1971-73, Ind. U. Cylotron Facility, 1974-77, Lab. for Nuclear Sci., M.I.T., 1975-79, Lawrence Berkeley Lab, Bevalac, 1978-80, Swiss Inst. Nuclear Research, 1981-85, Max Planck Inst. Nuclear Physics, 1982-85; mem. physics adv. panel NSF, 1971-73; mem. Nuclear Sci. Adv. Com. Dept. Energy/NSF, 1981-85, chmn., 1983-85; chmn. program adv. com. CEBAF, 1986-91; chmn. subcom. Implementation of 1989 Long Range Plan for Nuclear Sci.; chair Com. on Nuclear Physics, NRC, 1996—. Editor: Comments on Nuclear and Particle Physics, 1971-75; assoc. editor Revs. Modern Physics, 1972-77; mem. editorial bd. Phys. Rev. C, 1983-85; editor: Physics Letters, 1978—; mem. editorial com. ann. revs. of nuclear and particle sci., 1987-91; contbr. articles on nuclear structure physics and nuclear reactions to phys. jours. and books. Mem. cold fusion panel Dept. Energy, 1989. Recipient Alexander V. Humboldt Found. sr. U.S. scientist award, 1973-74; Wilbur Cross medal Yale U., 1985; Guggenheim fellow, 1959-60. Fellow AAAS (mem. coun., chair physics sect. 1992-93), Am. Phys. Soc. (chmn. div. nuclear physics 1975-76, Tom W. Bonner prize 1976); mem. NAS, Royal Danish Acad. Scis. and Letters. Research on nuclear structure, Mössbauer effect, heavy-ion reactions, pion interactions in nuclei, quark searches, condensation in confined cold plasmas. Office: Physics Division Argonne Nat Lab Argonne IL 60439

SCHIFFER, LOIS JANE, lawyer; b. Washington, Feb. 22, 1945; d. Benjamin and Clara (Goldberg) S. BA, Radcliffe Coll., 1966; JD, Harvard U., 1969. Bar: Mass. 1969, D.C. 1971, U.S. Supreme Ct. 1973. Legal svcs. lawyer Boston Legal Assistance Project, 1969-70; ct. law clk. D.C. Circuit Ct., Washington, 1970-71; assoc. Leva, Hawes, Symington, Martin, Oppenheimer, Washington, 1971-74; lawyer Ctr. for Law and Social Policy, Washington, 1974-78; chief gen. litigation sect. Land and Natural Resources div. U.S. Dept. Justice, Washington, 1978-81, spl. litigation counsel, 1981-84; gen. counsel Nat. Pub. Radio, Washington, 1984-89; ptnr. Nussbaum & Wald, Washington, 1989-93; acting asst. atty. gen. environ. and natural resources divsn. U.S. Dept. Justice, Washington, 1993-94, asst. atty. gen. environ. and natural resources divsn., 1994—; adj. prof. environ. law Georgetown U. Law Ctr., Washington, 1986—. Bd. dirs. Women's Legal Def. Fund, 1975-86, Am. Rivers, 1989-93; bd. dirs. ACLU/NCA, 1982-93, pres., 1988-90. Fellow Am. Bar Found.; mem. Phi Beta Kappa. Democrat. Jewish. Avocations: reading, movies, hiking. Home: 4640 Brandywine St NW Washington DC 20016-4449

SCHIFFMAN, GERALD, microbiologist, educator; b. N.Y.C., May 22, 1926; s. Samuel and Mollie (Brookner) S.; m. Lillian Ebert, July 12, 1951; children: Stewart, Howard. B.A. cum laude, NYU, 1948, Ph.D., 1954. Asst. prof. and disting. prof. microbiology Coll. Physicians and Surgeons, Columbia U., N.Y.C., 1960-63; asso. prof. dept. research medicine and microbiology U. Pa., Phila., 1963-70; prof. SUNY Health Sci. Ctr., Bklyn., 1970-97, disting. svc. prof., 1995-97, prof. emeritus, 1997; cons. Contbr. articles to profl. jours. Served in U.S. Army, 1943-45, ETO. Decorated Bronze Star; recipient Nichols award, 1947; Atomic Energy fellow, 1948-52; NIH grantee, 1974-94. Mem. Am. Assn. Immunologists, Am. Chem. Soc., Am. Soc. Microbiology, AAAS, Harvey Soc., Soc. Complex Carbohydrates, Sigma Xi, Phi Beta Kappa, Mu Chi Sigma, Pi Mu Epsilon. Jewish. Office: 450 Clarkson Ave Brooklyn NY 11203-2012

SCHIFFMAN, HAROLD FOSDICK, Asian language educator; b. Buffalo, Feb. 19, 1938; s. Merl and Mathilda (Keller) S.; m. Marilyn Gail Hornberg, June 10, 1978; 1 son, Timothy Marc Rajendran. B.A., Antioch Coll., 1960; M.A., U. Chgo., 1966, Ph.D., 1969. Lectr. anthropology U. Calif.-Davis, 1966-67; asst. prof. U. Wash., Seattle, 1967-73, assoc. prof., 1973-78, prof., 1978-95, chmn. dept. Asian langs., 1982-87; prof. South Asian studies U. Pa., Phila., 1995—, acad. dir. Penn Lang. Ctr., Luce prof. lang. learning, 1995—; Trustee Am. Inst. Indian Studies, Chgo., 1979-82; lang. dir. Southeast Asian Summer Studies Inst., 1992-93, mem. lang. adv. com., 1993-94. Author: A Grammar of Spoken Tamil, 1979, A Reference Grammar of Spoken Kannada, 1983, Linguistic Culture and Language Policy, 1996; co-editor: Dravidian Phonological Systems, 1975; co-author: Language and Society in South Asia, 1981. Pres. bd. dirs. Seattle Pro Musica (choral group), 1976-78; mem. Pacific Northwest Chamber Chorus, Seattle, 1983-87. Sr. fellow Am. Inst. Indian Studies, 1976, 78; grantee U.S. Office Edn., 1971, 74, 78, NEH, 1984-87, Smithsonian Inst., 1984-87, Fulbright Rsch., 1993-94. Mem. Assn. Asian Studies (S. Asia council 1982-85), Am. Inst. Indian Studies (trustee 1979-82), Soc. S. Indian Studies (sec.-treas. 1973-75), Internat. Assn. Tamil Research (v.p. 1987-89). Quaker. Office: U Pa Dept South Asian Studies 820 Williams Hall Philadelphia PA 19104-6305

SCHIFFMAN, JOSEPH HARRIS, literary historian, educator; b. N.Y.C., June 13, 1914; s. Samuel and Norma Minnie (Berger) S.; m. Elizabeth Selsbee, Nov. 29, 1941; children: Jessica, Joshua. BA, L.I. U., 1937; MA, Columbia U., 1947; PhD, NYU, 1951. Instr. dept. English, L.I. U., 1945-49, asst. prof., 1949-51, assoc. prof., 1951-58, coord. grad. program Am. studies, 1956-58; prof. English Dickinson Coll., Carlisle, Pa., 1958-79, James Hope Caldwell prof. Am. studies, 1968-79, emeritus prof., 1979—, prof. continuing edn., 1979-86, 90-96, chmn. dept. English, 1959-69; sr. Fulbright vis. prof., India, 1964, U. Bordeaux (France), 1965-66, U. Indonesia, 1981-82; vis. prof. Grad. Sch. U. Pa., 1960, 67, New Coll., U. South Fla., spring 1981; lectr. U. P.R., 1984, Lifetime Learning, Sarasota, 1984-88, Elderhostel U., Del., 1995; fgn. expert vis. prof. East China Normal U., Shanghai, 1985; founding dir. Am. Studies Rsch. Centre, India, 1964, Am. adv. com., 1990—; lectr. French Ednl. Radio System, 1966, acad. specialist program, Malaysia, Internat. Communication Agy., 1982; PhD theses examiner various univs., India, 1970-82; friend Internat. Am. Studies & Lang. Seminar, Salzburg, Austria; lectr. numerous orgns. including Mark Twain Assn. N.Y., Walt Whitman Birthplace Assn., MLA, Am. Studies Assn., Rotary, Pa. Writers Group, Jewish Community Ctr., Bosler Free Libr., AAUW, YWCA, Bethany Retirement Community, U.S.-China Peoples Friendship Assn., Sr. Action Ctr., Pa. Poets Soc., Harrisburg Manuscript Club, Golden Age Club, Encore Books and Music, Cumberland County Med. Soc. Alliance. With U.S. Army, 1942-45, ETO. Recipient Lindback Found. Disting. Teaching award, 1962, Fulbright-Hays award U.S. State Dept., 1964, 65, 81, Alumni award L.I. U., 1976. Mem. Am. Studies Assn. (pres. Met. N.Y. chpt. 1958-59), MLA (head Am. lit. internat. bibliography com. 1961-64), Nat. Council Tchrs. English. Author: (with Lewis Leary) American Literature: A Critical History from Its Beginning to the Present, Ency. World Lit., 1973, William Faulkner, A Dramatic Evocation, 1981; contbr. articles on Am. writers to lit. jours.; contbr. introductions to Looking Backward (Edward Bellamy), 1959, Brook Farm (Lindsay Swift), 1961, Three Shorter Novels of Herman Melville, 1962; editor: Edward Bellamy, Selected Writings on Religion and Society, 1955, Edward Bellamy, The Duke of Stockbridge, 1962; recs. including Idealist, Activist, The Haunted Chamber, The World a Ship, In Search of America, The Roaring Twenties, A Utopian Dream, also revs. to scholarly jours. Home: 551 S Hanover St Carlisle PA 17013-3919 Office: Dickinson Coll Carlisle PA 17013

SCHIFFMAN, LOUIS F., management consultant; b. Poland, July 15, 1927; s. Harry and Bertha (Fleder) S.;m. Mina R. Hankin, Dec. 28, 1963; children: Howard Laurence, Laura Lea. BChemE, NYU, 1948, MS, 1952, PhD, 1955. Rsch. engr. Pa. Grade Crude Oil Assn., Bradford, 1948-50; teaching fellow in chemistry NYU, 1950-54; rsch. chemist E.I. duPont de Nemours & Co., Wilmington, Del., 1954-56, Atlantic Refining Co., Phila., 1956-59; project leader, group leader, head corrosion sect. Amchem Products Inc., Ambler, Pa., 1959-70; pres. Techni Rsch. Assocs. Inc., Willow Grove, Pa., 1970—, real estate developer: ptnr. Bay Properties Co., Bay Club Marina, Margate, N.J., Willow Grove (Pa.) Assocs.; pub., editor Patent Licensing Gazette, 1968—, World Tech., 1975—; panelist on forum patents and inventions Delaware Valley Industry, 1973; mem. adv. oversight com. NSF, 1975, moderator energy conf. ERDA, Washington, 1976, Las Vegas, 1977; mem. adv. group in small bus. R&D programs Dept. Def., 1980. Editor: (with others) Guide to Available Technologies, 1985; contbr. to Encyclopedia of Chemical Technology, 1967; contbr. articles to profl. jours. Patentee in field. Recipient Founders Day award NYU, 1956. Fellow Am. Inst. Chemists; mem. Am. Chem. Soc., N.Y. Acad. Scis., Lic. Execs. Soc., Tech. Transfer Soc., Assn. Univ. Tech. Mgrs., Assn. Small Rsch. Cos. (editorial contbr. newsletter), Sigma Xi, Phi Lambda Upsilon. Home: 1837 Merritt Rd Abington PA 19001-4606 Office: Techni Rsch Assocs Inc PO Box T Willow Grove PA 19090-0922

SCHIFFMAN, ROBERT STANLEY, environmental test equipment manufacturing executive; b. Passaic, N.J., Jan. 25, 1944; s. Saul and Lillian (Gold) S.; m. Anita Joyce Sikeman, Aug. 15, 1965; children: Caren L., Glenn H., Robyn L. BSBA in Mgmt., Clark U., 1965; MBA in Mktg., Seton Hall U., 1970. Chmn., pres., CEO, bd. dirs. Tenney Engring. Inc., Union, N.J., 1977—. Mem. Inst. Environ. Sci. (sr.), Aircraft Owners and Pilots Assn. Office: Tenney Engring Inc 1090 Springfield Rd Union NJ 07083-8119

SCHIFFMAN, SUSAN STOLTE, medical psychologist, educator; b. Chgo., Aug. 24, 1940; d. Paul R. and Mildred (Glicksman) Stolte; m. Harold Schiffman (div.); 1 child, Amy Lise; m. H. Troy Nagle, July 22, 1989. BA, Syracuse U., 1965; PhD, Duke U., 1970. Lic. psychologist, N.C. Postdoctoral fellow Duke U., Durham, N.C., 1970-72, asst. prof., 1972-77, assoc. prof., 1978-83, full prof., 1983—; cons., mem. adv. bd. Nestle, Vevey, Switzerland, 1990, Fragrance Rsch. Fund, N.Y.C., 1986—, and others. Author: Introduction to Multidimensional Scaling: Theory, Methods and Applications, 1981, Flavor Set-Point Weight Loss Cookbook, 1990. Nat. Inst. Aging grantee, 1972—. Mem. Assn. Chemoreception Scis., European Chemoreception Rsch. Orgn., Soc. for Neurosci. Office: Duke U Med Sch Dept Psychiatry Box 3259 Durham NC 27708-0086

SCHIFFNER, CHARLES ROBERT, architect; b. Reno, Sept. 2, 1948; Robert Charles and Evelyn (Keck) S.; m. Iovanna Lloyd Wright, Nov. 1971 (div. Sept. 1981); m. Adrienne Anita McAndrews, Jan. 22, 1983. Student, Sacramento Jr. Coll., 1967-68, Frank Lloyd Wright Sch. Architecture, 1968-77. Registered architect, Ariz., Nev., Wis. Architect Taliesin Associated Architects, Scottsdale, Ariz., 1977-83; pvt. practice architecture Phoenix, 1983—; lectr. The Frank Lloyd Wright Sch. of Architecture, 1994, 95. Named one of 25 Most Promising Young Americans Under 35, U.S. mag., 1979; recipient AIA Honor award Western Mountain Region, 1993, Western Home awards Sunset Mag., 1989, 91, AIA Ariz. Merit award, 1993 and numerous others. Home: 5202 E Osborn Rd Phoenix AZ 85018-6137 Office: Camelhead Office Ctr 2600 N 44th St Ste 208 Phoenix AZ 85008-1565

SCHIFFRIN, ANDRE, publisher; b. Paris, June 12, 1935; came to U.S., 1941; s. Jacques and Simone (Heymann) S.; m. Maria Elena de la Iglesia, June 14, 1961; children—Anya, Natalia. B.A. summa cum laude, Yale U., 1957; M.A. with 1st class honors, Cambridge U., Eng., 1959. With New Am. Library, 1959-63; with Pantheon Books, Inc., N.Y.C., 1962-90, editor, then editor in chief, mng. dir., 1969-90; pub. Schocken Books subs. Pantheon Books Inc., 1987-90; pres. Fund for Ind. Pub., N.Y.C., 1990—; dir., editor in chief The New Press, N.Y.C., 1990—; vis. fellow Davenport Coll., 1977-79; vis. lectr. Yale U., 1977, 79; bd. dirs. The New Press, N.Y.C. Contbr. articles to profl. jours., N.Y. Times Book Rev., Nation, New Republic. Mem. coun. Smithsonian Instn., 1969—; bd. dirs. N.Y. Coun. for Humanities, 1978—, mem. exec. com., 1979-80; bd. dirs. N.Y. Civil Liberties Union; mem. freedom to pub. com. Assn. Am. Pubs., 1976-78; mem. vis. com. history dept. Princeton U., 1978—; mem. freedom to read com. AAUP, 1985—; mem. U.S. cultural del. to Peoples Republic China, 1983, 87; mem. vis. com. grad. faculty The New Sch., 1995—. Mellon fellow Clare Coll., 1957, hon. scholar, 1959; hon. fellow Trumbull Coll., Yale U., 1979—; Fulbright travel grantee, 1958-59. Fellow N.Y. Inst. for the Humanities. Home: 250 W 94th St New York NY 10025-6954 Office: The New Press 450 W 41st St New York NY 10036-6807

SCHIFLETT, MARY FLETCHER CAVENDER, health facility executive, researcher, educator; b. El Paso, Tex., Sept. 23, 1925; d. John F. and Mary M. (Humphries) Cavender; 1 son, Joseph Raymond. BA in Econs. with honors, So. Meth. U., 1946, BS in Journalism with honors, 1947; MA in English, U. Houston, 1971. Writer, historian Office Price Adminstrn., Dallas, 1946-47; asst. editor C. of C. Publs., Dallas, 1947-48; bus. writer Houston Oil, 1948-49; market analyst Cravens-Dargan, Ins., Houston, 1949-52; bus. writer Bus. Week and McGraw-Hill Pub. Co., Houston, 1952-56; freelance writer in bus. econs., banking and ins., 1956-68; spl. projects coord. Ctr. for Human Resources, Houston, 1969-73; dir. publs. Energy Inst., U. Houston, 1974-78; sr. rsch. assoc. Inst. Labor and Indsl. Rels., 1973-80, mem. adj. faculty Coll. Architecture, 1976-85, dir. Ctr. for Health Mgmt., Coll. Bus. Adminstrn., 1980-83; assoc. dir. rsch. and planning Tex. Med. Ctr., Inc., Houston, 1984; dir. spl. projects and pub. affairs Tex. Med. Ctr., 1985-92, asst. v.p., 1993-95, assoc. v.p., 1995—. Bd. dirs. Third Ward Redevelopment Coun., 1993—, Houston Acad. Motion Pictures, 1986-90, Houston World Trade Assn., 1988-91, Friends Hermann Pk., 1995—, mem. exec. com., 1996—. Pres., Houston Ct. Humanities, 1978-80; project dir. Houston Meets Its Authors I-IV, 1980-84; pub. program dir. Houston: Internat. City, 1980-83. Named One of Houston's Women of Yr. YMCA, 1988. Mem. Internat. Coun. Indsl. Editors, World Future Soc., Tex. Folklore Soc., Friends of Libr., Houston C. of C. (future studies com. 1975-84, small bus. coun. 1981-83), Nat. Assn. Bus. Economists, AIA (profl. affiliate), Mortar Bd., Theta Sigma Phi, Alpha Theta Phi, Delta Delta Delta. Methodist. Club: Downtown (pres. 1987-89), River Oaks Rotary (bd. dirs. 1996—, Paul Harris fellow 1996. Author: (with others) Dynamics of Growth, 1977, Applied Systems and Cybernetics, 1981, The Ethnic Groups of Houston, 1984, Names and Nicknames of Places and Things, 1986. Office: Tex Med Ctr 406 Jesse H Jones Libr Bldg Houston TX 77030

SCHIFRIN, LALO, composer; b. Buenos Aires, June 21, 1932. Student, Juan Carlos Paz and Olivier Messiaen.; PhD (hon.), RISD, 1989. Tchr. composition UCLA, 1970-71; guest condr. Israel Philharm, L.A. Philharm, L.A. Chamber Orch., Indpls. Symphony, Atlanta Symphony. Argentinian rep., Internat. Jazz Festival, Paris, 1955, formed own jazz group; composer for stage, modern dance, TV; with Dizzy Gillespie's band, 1962; film and TV composer, Hollywood, Calif., 1964—; compositions: (for ballet) Jazz Faust, 1963, (for orch.) Piano Concerto # 1, 1986, Cantos Aztecas, 1989, Concerto for guitar and orch., 1986, Concerto for double bass and orch., 1987, Three tangos for flute, harp and strings, 1987, Dance concertantes for clarinet and orch., 1990, Impressions for trumpet and orch., 1990, La Nouvelle Orleans Woodwind Quitet, 1991, Concerto # 2, 1992, Cantares Argentinos, 1992, Symphony # 1 for orch., 1993 (opera) The Trial of Louis XVI, 1988; theme for TV series Mission: Impossible (2 Grammy awards); film scores include The Cincinnati Kid, 1965, Cool Hand Luke, 1967, The Fox, 1968; film scores include Kelly's Heroes, 1970, W.U.S.A., 1970, Pussycat, Pussycat, I Love You, 1970, Bullit, 1970, Dirty Harry, 1971, THX-1138, 1971, The Beguiled, 1971, Magnum Force, 1973, The Four Musketeers, 1975, The Eagle Has Landed, 1977, Voyage of the Damned, 1976, Rollercoaster, 1977, Telefon, 1977, Boulevard Nights, 1979, The Concorde-Airport '79, 1979, Competition, 1981, Sudden Impact, 1984, The Sting II, 1985, The Fourth Protocol, 1987, The Fourth Protocol, 1987; TV series The Young-Lawyers, Mannix, 'Mission Impossible', Starsky and Hutch; writer orchestration for Grand Finale medley for Carreras, Domingo and Pavarotti, Rome, 1991; commd. Steinway Found piano concerto The Americas, selected by Nat. Symphony Orch., 1992. Recipient 4 Grammy awards, 1967, 1969, 1986, 6 Acad. award nominations Acad. Motion Picture Arts and Scis., 1966, 67, 75, 77, 80, 82, Walk of Fame award Hollywood C. of C.; chevalier de l'Ordre des Arts et des Lettres French gov. *

SCHIFSKY, CHARLES MARK, magazine editor; b. St. Paul, May 19, 1962; s. William Charles and Kathleen Jeanne (Lau) S.; m. Gina Marie Gelsomino, Oct. 8, 1994; 1 child, Amanda Jeanne. BA in Journalism and Pub. Rels., U. St. Thomas, St. Paul, 1987. With Bill Schifsky Enterprises, St. Paul, 1977-87; pub. rels. rep. Ramsey County Info. Office, St. Paul, 1987; clutch specialist Gary Ormsby Racing, Auburn, Calif., 1988-90; co-crew chief Jack Clark Racing, Indpls., 1990-91; assoc. editor Car Craft mag. Peterson Pub. Co., L.A., 1992-93, editor, 1993—. Mem. Motor Press Guild, Nat. Hot Rod Assn. (mem. top fuel world championship team 1989). Avocations: travel, photography, golf, motorsports. Office: Petersen Pub/Car Craft Mag 6420 Wilshire Blvd Los Angeles CA 90048-5502

SCHIFTER, RICHARD, lawyer, government official; b. Vienna, Austria, July 31, 1923; came to U.S., 1938; s. Paul and Balbina (Blass) S.; m. Lilo Krueger, July 3, 1948; children: Judith, Deborah, Richard P., Barbara, Karen. BS in Social Sci. summa cum laude, CCNY, 1943; LLB, Yale U., 1951; DHL (hon.), Hebrew Union Coll., 1992. Bar: Conn. 1951, D.C. 1952, U.S. Supreme Ct. 1954, Md., 1958. Assoc. Fried, Frank, Harris, Shriver & Jacobson, Washington, 1951-57, ptnr., 1957-84; dep. U.S. rep. with rank of ambassador UN Security Council, N.Y.C., 1984-85; asst. sec. of state for human rights and humanitarian affairs Dept. State, Washington, 1985-92; U.S. rep. UN Human Rights Commn., Geneva, 1983-86, 93; spl. asst. to pres., counselor Nat. Security Coun., Washington, 1993-97, spl. advisor to

Sec. of State, 1997—; head U.S. del. Conf. on Security and Cooperation in Europe Experts Meeting on Human Rights, Ottawa, Ont., Can., 1985, Dem. Insts., Oslo, 1991; bd. dirs. U.S. Inst. Peace, 1986-92; mem. Congl. Commn. on Security and Cooperation in Europe, 1986-92. V.p., pres. Md. Bd. Edn., Balt., 1959-79; chmn. Md. Gov.'s Commn. on Funding Edn. of Handicapped Children, 1975-77, Md. Values Edn. Commn., 1979-83, Montgomery County Dem. Cen. Com., Md., 1966-70; del. Dem. Nat. Conv., 1968; bd. govs., chmn. Nat. Adv. Com., Am. Jewish Com., 1992-93. With U.S. Army, 1943-46, ETO. Recipient Disting. Svc. award Sec. of State, 1992. Mem. Phi Beta Kappa. Democrat. Jewish. Home: 6907 Crail Dr Bethesda MD 20817-4723 Office: Nat Security Coun Washington DC 20506

SCHILD, RAYMOND DOUGLAS, lawyer; b. Chgo., Dec. 20, 1952; s. Stanley Martin and Cassoundra Lee (McArdle) S.; m. Ellen Arthea Carstensen, Oct. 24, 1987; children: Brian Christopher, Melissa Nicole. Student, U.S. Mil. Acad., 1970; BA summa cum laude, De Paul U., 1974, JD magna cum laude, 1982; M in Life Scis., Order of Essenes, 1996. Bar: Ill. 1982, U.S. Dist. Ct. (no. dist.) Ill. 1982, U.S. Ct. Appeals (7th cir.) 1982, Idaho 1989, U.S. Dist. Ct. Idaho 1989, U.S. Ct. Appeals (9th cir.) 1989, U.S. Supreme Ct. 1990. Assoc. Clausen, Miller, Gorman, Caffrey & Witous, Chgo., 1982-84; law clk. to chief judge law divsn. Cir. Ct. Cook County, Chgo., 1984-85; assoc. John G. Phillips & Assocs., Chgo., 1985-87, Martin, Chapman, Park & Burkett, Boise, Idaho, 1988-89; pvt. practice Boise, 1989-90; pres. Martin, Chapman, Schild & Lassaw, Chartered, Boise, 1990-96; bd. dirs. Image Concepts Internat., Inc., Boise; lectr. on legal edn. ICLE and NBI, 1993—. Co-host legal radio talk show KFXD, 1994; legal columnist Idaho Bus. Rev., 1988-96. Mem. adv. bd. Alliance for the Mentally Ill, Boise, 1991—, Parents and Youth Against Drug Abuse, Boise, 1991-92; fair housing adminstr. Sauk Village (Ill.) Govt., 1987-88; instr. Ada County Youth Ct., Boise, 1992—. Schmitt fellow DePaul U., 1974; recipient award of merit Chgo. Law Coalition, 1987. Mem. ATLA, Idaho Trial Lawyers' Assn., Ill. State Bar Assn., Idaho State Bar Assn., Boise Estate Planning Counsel, Shriners (temple atty. 1994—), Masons (jr. steward 1992). Avocations: tennis, trombone, writing, music.

SCHILDHAUSE, SOL, lawyer; b. N.Y.C., Sept. 5, 1917; s. Jacob and Fannie (Gerber) S.; m. Phyllis Sydell, May 23, 1943 (divorced); children: Susan Schildhause Tash, Peter, Richard. BS, CUNY, 1937; JD, Harvard U., 1940. Bar: N.Y. 1941, D.C. 1972, U.S. Ct. Claims 1975, U.S. Supreme Ct. 1978. Mng. ptnr. Sta. KOMA-AM, Oklahoma City, 1956-57; adminstrv. law judge FCC, Washington, 1963-66, chief cable TV bur., 1966-73; ptnr. D.C. office Farrow, Schildhause & Wilson, 1973-93; chmn. bd., gen. counsel The Media Inst., Washington; lectr. Practicing Law Inst., 1985. Mem. ABA (asst. chmn. cable TV com. 1986), FCC Bar Assn. Democrat. Jewish. Club: Harvard (Washington).

SCHILDKNECHT, CALVIN E(VERETT), chemist, consultant, writer; b. Frederick, Md., Aug. 15, 1910; s. Calvin Ezra and Edith Julia (Fisher) S.; m. Althea Jean Schneider, Nov. 21, 1942; children—David, Eric. B.S., Gettysburg Coll., 1931; Ph.D., Johns Hopkins U., 1936. Research chemist DuPont Co., Arlington, N.J., 1936-43; with dept. research and devel. Gen. Aniline & Film, Easton, Pa. and N.Y.C., 1943-51, Celanese Corp. Am., Summit, N.J., 1951-53; assoc. prof. chemistry Stevens Inst. Tech., Hoboken, N.J., 1953-59; prof. Gettysburg Coll., 1959-79, prof. emeritus, cons., 1953—; lectr. in field. Author: Vinyl and Related Polymers, 1952; Polymer Processes, 1956; Allyl Compounds and Their Polymers, 1973; (with Irving Skeist) Polymerization Processes, 1977, Monocacy and Catoctin, Vols. I-III, 1985-94. Contbr. to encys. and profl. jours. Patentee in field. Mem. Am. Chem. Soc., Audubon Soc., Adams and Frederick County Hist. Soc., Sigma XI. Club: Appalachian Mt. Avocations: butterfly gardening, early local history, luminescence of postage stamps. Home: 1075 Old Harrisburg Rd Gettysburg PA 17325

SCHILLER, ARTHUR A., architect, educator; b. N.Y.C., July 23, 1910; s. Valentine and Rose (Bayer) S.; m. Anne O'Donnell, June 12, 1937; children: Valerie Schiller Schaefer, Virginia Schiller Waicul, Eileen Schiller Toomey. BArch, NYU, 1933; diploma, Beaux Arts Inst. Design, N.Y.C., 1935; MArch, MIT, 1939. Registered profl. architect, N.Y. Architect U.S. Govt., Washington, 1936-38, N.Y.C. Dept. Parks, 1938-47; chief architect Bd. Higher Edn., N.Y.C., 1947-51, dir. architecture and engring., 1951-67; coord. campus planning Queens Coll., N.Y.C., 1967-73; adj. prof. N.Y. Inst. Technology, Old Westbury, 1973-91; cons. Triboro Bridge Authority, N.Y.C., 1946; lectr. CCNY, 1957-67. Mayor Village of Plandome Manor, N.Y., 1965-87, trustee, 1960-65; trustee Sci. Mus. L.I. 1986—. Named Man of Yr. AARP, 1990, Sr. Citizen of Yr. Nassau County, State of N.Y., 1992 . Fellow AIA (pres. Queens chpt. 1957-58); mem. N.Y. State Assn. Architects (dir. 1959-60), Assn. Univ. Architects (emeritus), U.S. Power Squadron (comdr. 1961-62, budget dir. 1988-91), Elks (life). Avocations: boating, gardening, conducting defensive driving courses for older citizens. Home: 15 Luquer Rd Manhasset NY 11030-1015

SCHILLER, DONALD CHARLES, lawyer; b. Chgo., Dec. 8, 1942; s. Sidney S. and Edith (Lastick) S.; m. Eileen Fagin, June 14, 1964; children—Eric, Jonathan. Student, Lake Forest Coll., 1960-63; J.D., DePaul U., 1966. Bar: Ill. 1966, U.S. Dist. Ct. (no. dist.) Ill. 1966, U.S. Supreme Ct. 1972. Ptnr. Schiller, DuCanto & Fleck (formerly Schiller & Schiller and Schiller & DuCanto), Chgo., 1966—; chair domestic rels. adv. com. Cir. Ct. Cook County, 1993—, exec. com., 1986-93; speaker profl. confs. Contbr. chpts. and articles to profl. publs. Mem. steering com. on juvenile ct. watching, LWV, 1980-81. Recipient Maurice Weigle award Chgo. Bar Found., 1978, Disting. Alumni award, DePaul U., 1988, various certs. of appreciation profl. groups: named One of Am.'s Best Divorce Lawyers, Town and Country, 1985, The Nat. Law Jour., 1987, The Best Lawyers in Am., 1987, 89, 91, 93, One of Chgo's. Best Div. Lawyers, Crain's Chgo. Bus., 1981, Today Chgo. Woman, 1985, Inside Chgo. mag., 1988. Fellow Am. Bar Found., Am. Acad. Matrimonial Lawyers (chair continuing legal edn. 1993-94); mem. ABA (bd. govs. 1994—, chmn. family law sect. 1985-86, Ill. State del. 1980-84, mem. Ho. of Dels. 1984, editor-in-chief Family Law Newsletter 1977-79; mem. editorial bd., assoc. editor Family Adv. Mag. 1979-84, speaker at confs. and meetings), Ill. Bar Assn. (chmn. family law sect. 1976-77, editor Family Law Bull. 1976-77, bd. govs. 1977-83, treas. 1981-84, v.p. 1984-86, pres. 1987-88, chmn. various coms., lectr., incorporator Ill. State Bar Assn. Risk Retention Group, Inc. 1988, pres. 1988-89), Chgo. Bar Assn., Am. Coll. Family Law Trial Lawyers (diplomate). Office: Schiller DuCanto & Fleck 200 N La Salle St Ste 2700 Chicago IL 60601-1020

SCHILLER, ERIC M., lawyer; b. Detroit, Mar. 19, 1946; s. Stanley Schiller and Sara (Barliant) Benson; m. Jill E. Friedman, Aug. 16, 1970; children: Colin, Daniel, Jonathan. BA, Ind. U., 1968; JD, Northwestern U., 1971. Bar: Ill. 1971. Assoc. Sonnenschein Nath & Rosenthal, Chgo., 1971-78, ptnr., 1978—; mem. exec. com., policy and planning com. Sonnenschein, Nath & Rosenthal, 1971—; lectr. ALI-ABA. Exec. bd. dirs. Anti-Defamation League of Chgo., 1989-92. Mem. ABA, Chgo. Bar Assn., Am. Coll. Real Estate Attys., The Law Club of Chgo., John Henry Wigmore Club of Northwestern U. Law Sch. (exec. com. 1990-93), The Standard Club, The Met. Club, Lake Shore Country Club. Home: 7 Rockgate Ln Glencoe IL 60022-1250 Office: Sonnenschein Nath & Rosenthal 8000 Sears Tower Chicago IL 60606-6328

SCHILLER, FRANCIS, neurologist, medical historian; b. Prague, Czechoslovakia, Jan. 23, 1909; came to U.S., 1950; s. Friedrich and Luise (Manheimer) S. MD, German U., Prague, 1933. Diplomate Am. Bd. Psychiatry and Neurology. With U. Calif. Med. Sch., San Francisco, 1951-79, clin. prof. neurology, 1972, emeritus prof. neurology, 1979; neurologist Kaiser Permanente Med. Group, San Francisco, 1953-78; cons. neurology Pub. Health Svc., San Francisco, 1978-81, VA Compensation & Pension, San Francisco, 1984—; sr. lectr. history and health sci. U. Calif., San Francisco, 1962—. Author: Paul Broca, 1824-80, 1979, A Möbius Strip, 1981; contbr. articles to profl. jours. Fellow Am. Acad. Neurology, San Francisco Neurology Soc.; mem. Internat. Acad. History of Medicine, Bay Area History of Medicine Club (pres. San Francisco cht. 1975-76). Avocations: gardening, piano. Home: 2730 Wawona St San Francisco CA 94116-2866 Office: U Calif Dept History of Health Scis Box 0726 Parnassus Ave 458 San Francisco CA 94122-2721

SCHILLER, HERBERT IRVING, social scientist, author; b. N.Y.C., Nov. 5, 1919; s. Benjamin Franklin and Gertrude (Perner) S.; m. Anita Rosenbaum, Nov. 5, 1946; children: Daniel T., P. Zachary. B in Social Sci., CCNY, 1940; MA, Columbia U., 1941; PhD, NYU, 1960. Teaching fellow CCNY, 1940-41, lectr. econs., 1949-59; economist U.S. Govt., 1941-42, 46-48; mem. faculty Pratt Inst., Bklyn., 1950-63; prof. econs., chmn. dept. social studies Pratt Inst., 1962-63; research asso. prof. Bur. Econ. and Bus. Research, U. Ill. at Urbana, 1963-65, research prof., 1965-70; prof. communication U. Calif., San Diego, 1970-90, prof. emeritus, 1990—; lectr. Bklyn. Acad. Music, 1961-66; vis. fellow Inst. Policy Studies, Wash., 1968; vis. prof. U. Amsterdam, 1972-74; Thord-Gray vis. lectr. U. Stockholm, 1978; vis. prof. comms. Hunter Coll., CUNY, 1978-79, Am. U., 1991-93, NYU, 1993—. Author: Mass Communications and American Empire, 1969, rev. edit., 1992, Superstate: Readings in the Military-Industrial Complex, 1970, The Mind Managers, 1973, Communication and Cultural Domination, 1976, Who Knows: Information in the Age of the Fortune 500, 1981, Information and the Crisis Economy, 1984, Culture Inc.: The Corporate Takeover of Public Expression, 1989, Information Inequality, 1996, (with others) Hope and Folly: The U.S. and UNESCO, 1945-85, 1989; editor Quar. Rev. Econs. and Bus., 1963-70; co-editor: Triumph of the Image: The Media's War in the Persian Gulf, 1992, Beyond National Sovereignty: International Communication in the 1990s, 1993, Invisible Crises, 1996. Served with AUS, 1942-45, MTO. Mem. AAAS, Internat. Assn. Mass Communication Research (v.p.), Internat. Inst. Communications (trustee 1978-84), AAUP (sec. Ill. U.), Phi Beta Kappa. Home: 7109 Monte Vista Ave La Jolla CA 92037-5326 Office: U Calif San Diego La Jolla CA 92093

SCHILLER, JAMES JOSEPH, lawyer; b. Cleve., July 1, 1933; s. Jacob Peter and Helen Elizabeth (Tosh) S.; m. Sara Brooke Wilson, Oct. 24, 1964; children: Charles A., Brooke V.G., Kristan W. BS, Case Inst. Tech., 1955; JD, U. Mich., 1961. Bar: Ohio 1962. Assoc. Marshman, Hornbeck & Hollington, Cleve., 1961-68; ptnr. Marshman, Snyder & Seeley, Cleve., 1968-73, Zellmer & Gruber, Cleve., 1973-80, Weston, Hurd, Fallon, Paisley & Howley, Cleve., 1980-88, Porter, Wright, Morris & Arthur, Cleve., 1989-95, Schiller & Ryan, Cleve., 1995—. Campaign mgr. John J. Gilligan for Gov. of Ohio, Cuyahoga County, 1970; campaign dir. U.S. Senator Howard M. Metzenbaum, Cleve., 1973; mem. Ohio Dem. Com., 1970-73; dep. registrar motor vehicles Dept. Hwy. Safety, Cuyahoga County, 1971-74; trustee Greater Cleve. Regional Transit Authority, 1985-87; vestryman Christ Episcopal Ch., Shaker Heights, Ohio, 1974-76, 90-93, clk., 1974-76, sr. warden, 1992-93; chmn. bd. suprs. ChristCh. Found., 1995—; trustee Recovery Resources, 1988—, chmn. bd. dirs., exec. com., 1994-96; trustee Ohio Ch. Orch., exec. com., 1996—; trustee Cleve. Ballet, 1997—. Lt. j.g. USNR, 1955-58. Recipient Cert. Commendation Bd. County Commrs., 1987. Mem. ABA, Ohio State Bar Assn. (ethics com. 1986-88), Cleve. Bar Assn., Rowfant Club (fin. com. 1988, coun. Fellowes 1990-91, 95—, advocate 1992-95), Union Club, Cleve. Skating Club. Avocations: sailing, skiing, restoring furniture. Home: 13415 Shaker Blvd Cleveland OH 44120 Office: James J Schiller & Assocs The Arcade 401 Euclid Ave Ste 332 Cleveland OH 44114-2402

SCHILLER, LAWRENCE JULIAN, motion picture producer, director; b. N.Y.C., Dec. 28, 1936; s. Isidore and Jean (Liebowitz) S.; children: Suzanne, Marc, Howard, Anthony, Cameron. B.A., Pepperdine Coll., 1958. Photojournalist Life mag., 1959-69, Paris Match, 1960-69, London Sun. Times, 1960-69. Producer, dir.; (films) Hey, I'm Alive, The Winds of Kitty Hawk, Marilyn, Raid on Short Creek, An Act of Love, The Executioner's Song (Emmy award), Peter the Great (Emmy award), By Reason of Insanity, Margret Brourke-White Story, Plot to Kill Hitler, Double Jeopardy; author: American Tragedy, Sunshine, Marilyn; collaborator: (with Albert Goldman) Lenny Bruce (with Eugene Smith) Minamata, (with Norman Mailer) The Executioner's Song (Pulitzer prize 1980), Oswald's Tale; (with O.J. Simpson) I Want To Tell You. Chmn. bd. dirs. Am.-Soviet Film Initiative, 1988; Am. del. Moscow Internat. Forum on Peace, 1987; mem. USSR-USA Bi-Lateral Talks, 1988. Recipient numerous awards in photojournalism Nat. Press Photographers Assn., Acad. award for The Man Who Skied Down Everest, 1975. Mem. Nat. Press Photographers Assn., Calif. Press Photographers Assn., Dirs. Guild of Am., Acad. of Motion Picture Arts and Scis. Democrat. Jewish.

SCHILLER, PIETER JON, venture capital executive; b. Orange, N.J., Jan. 14, 1938; s. John Fasel and Helen Roff (Roberts) S.; m. Elizabeth Ann Williams, Nov. 20, 1965; children—Cathryn Ann, Suzanne Elizabeth. B.A. in Econs. with honors, Middlebury (Vt.) Coll., 1960; M.B.A., N.Y. U., 1966. Fin. analyst Merck & Co., Inc., N.Y.C., 1960-61; fin. analyst, asst. div. controller, dir. auditing, then asst. controller Allied Chem. Corp., N.Y.C. and Morristown, N.J., 1961-75; treas. Allied Chem. Corp., 1975-79, v.p. planning and devel., 1979-83; Allied Corp. exec. v.p. diagnostic ops. Allied Health & Sci. Products Co., 1983-86; pres. subs. Instrumentation Lab., Lexington, Mass., 1983-86; gen. ptnr. Advanced Tech. Ventures, Boston, 1986—; bd. dirs. Anthra Pharms., Inc., Princeton, N.J., Afferon Corp., Phoenix, HealthShare Tech., Acton, Mass., Endius, Inc., Plainville, Mass., Mass., CollaGenex Pharms., Inc., Newtown, Pa., Novoste Corp., Norcross, Ga. Chmn. bd. trustees Newark Boys Chorus Sch., 1976-78, pres. bd., 1974-76; trustee Colonial Symphony Soc., 1978-85, v.p., 1980-82, pres. 1982-83, Morris Mus., Morristown, Concord (Mass.) Mus., 1994-96, v.p. 1996—; bd. dirs. New Eng. Coun., Boston, 1983-86, Middlebury Coll. Alumni Assn., 1989—, v.p. 1992-94, pres. 1994-96; chmn. allocations com. United Way of Morris County, 1974-79, v.p. bd. dirs., mem. exec. com., 1979-80; trustee Morris Mus. Arts and Scis., 1980-83. Mem. Fin. Execs. Inst. Republican. Episcopalian. Avocations: skiing, photography. Home: 18 S Meadow Ridge Concord MA 01742-5328

SCHILLER, SOPHIE, artist, graphic designer; b. Moscow, Feb. 10, 1940; came to U.S., 1974; d. Samuel and Rebecca (Lagovier) Elinson; m. Mikhail Schiller, Apr. 29, 1960; 1 child, Maria. Student, Moscow State Art Sch., 1954-58; MA, Moscow Inst., 1964; cert. in graphic and book design, Mass. Coll. Art, 1977. Graphic artist Progress Pub. House, Moscow, 1964-70, Popular Sci. mag., Moscow, 1970-74; artist, graphic designer Boston, 1974—; freelance graphic designer Harvard Press, Boston, M.E. Sharpe Pub., N.Y., Ginn Press, Simon & Schuster, Boston, Tech. Rev., MIT, Cambridge, Mass. One person shows include Galleria del Corso, Rome, 1974, Wennigar Gallery, Boston, 1977; exhibited in group shows Taganka Exhibit, Moscow, 1962, Moscow Artists Union, 1962, Am. Painters in Paris Exhbn., 1975, Unofficial Art from Soviet Union, Washington, 1977, Mariland Gallery, St. Mary's City, 1977, Bard Coll., N.Y., 1991, Rose Art Mus., Brandeis U., Boston, 1992, Tofias Gallery, Boston, 1994, Zimmerly Art Mus., Rutgers U., N.J., 1995; group shows include The Dorland-Haight Gallery, Milton, Can., 1993. Mem. Nat. Mus. Women in the Arts. Avocations: travel, hiking, collecting children's art. Home and Studio: 63 University Rd Brookline MA 02146-4532

SCHILLER, WILLIAM RICHARD, surgeon; b. Bennett, Colo., Jan. 14, 1937; s. Francis T. and Frances M. (Finks) S.; m. Beverlee Schiller; children from previous marriage: Julie, Lisa. B.S., Drury Coll., Springfield, Mo., 1958; M.D., Northwestern U., 1962. Diplomate Am. Bd. Surgery; cert. of added qualifications in surg. critical care, 1987, recertified in surg. critical care, 1994. Intern Passavant Meml. Hosp., Chgo., 1962-63; resident Northwestern U. Clin. Tng. Program, Chgo., 1963-68; assoc. prof. surgery Med. Coll Ohio, Toledo, 1970-78; prof. surgery U. N.Mex, Albuquerque, 1978-83; dir. Trauma Ctr. St. Joseph's Hosp., Phoenix, 1983-89; dir. burn and trauma ctr. Maricopa Med. Ctr., Phoenix, 1989—; clin. prof. surgery U. Ariz. Health Sci. Ctr.; prof. surgery Mayo Grad. Sch. Medicine, Rochester, Minn. Contbr. chpts. to books, articles to profl. jours. Served as maj. M.C. U.S. Army, 1968-70, Vietnam. Fellow ACS; mem. Am. Assn. Surgery of Trauma, Cen. Surg. Assn., Western Surg. Assn., Soc. Surgery of Alimentary Tract, Am. Burn Assn., Internat. Soc. of Surgery. Republican. Home: 8226 E Via De La Escuela Scottsdale AZ 85258-3054 Office: Burn and Trauma Ctr Maricopa Med Ctr 2601 E Roosevelt St Phoenix AZ 85008-4973

SCHILLING, ARLO LEONARD, bank executive; b. Huntington, Ind., Oct. 13, 1924; s. Jacob Howard and Nova Elnora (Rusher) S.; m. Gloria Ann Wygant, Oct. 20, 1946; children: Nancy, Emily, Janey. BS in Edn., Huntington Coll., 1948; MS in Edn., Ind. U., 1950; PhD in Econ., Edn., Psychology, Purdue U., 1958. Tchr. Avilla Pub. Schs., Ind., 1948-52; prin. Coesse Pub. Schs., Ind., 1952-55, Montpelier Pub. Schs., Ind., 1955-56; instr. Purdue U., West Lafayette, Ind., 1956-58; asst. supt. Elkhart Pub. Schs., Ind., 1958-60; pres. North Cen. Coll., Naperville, Ill., 1960-75; chmn., dir., vice chair chmn. Harris Bank Naperville, 1975-94; ret.; vice chmn. Paramount Arts Centre Endowment, Aurora, Ill., 1983—; interim pres. Bank Fox Valley, Westmont, 1975-80. Life trustee North Ctrl. Coll., Naperville, 1960—; mem. pres.'s adv. coun. Sch. Edn., Purdue U., West Lafayette, Ind. With U.S. Army, 1943-45, ETO. Mem. NEA, Rotary (pres. 1968), Phi Delta Kappa, Kappa Delta Pi. Republican. Methodist. Avocations: gardening, reading, public speaking, fund raising. Home: 38 W 55 Deerpath Rd Batavia IL 60510-9464

SCHILLING, DAVID AUGUST, management educator; b. Camden, N.J., Feb. 2, 1951; s. Spencer August and Ruth Elaine (Halvorsen) S.; m. Catherine Petersen. BS in Physics with honors, Miami U., 1972; PhD, Johns Hopkins U., 1976. Asst. prof. mgmt. scis. Am. U., Washington, 1976-78; asst. prof. mgmt. scis. Ohio State U., Columbus, 1978-83, assoc. prof. mgmt. scis., 1983-87, assoc. prof., dir. MBA program prof. mgmt. scis., 1987-88, assoc. prof., chmn. mgmt. scis., 1988-89, prof., chmn. mgmt. scis., 1989—. Contbr. articles to profl. jours. Mem. Phi Beta Kappa. Home: 2226 Picket Post Ln Columbus OH 43220-2918 Office: Ohio State U Columbus OH 43210-1399

SCHILLING, EMILY BORN, editor, association executive; b. Lawton, Okla., Oct. 2, 1959; d. George Arthur and Sumiko (Nagamine) Born; m. Mark David Schilling, June 26, 1995. BS, Ball State U., 1981. Cert. rural electric communicator Nat. Rural Electric Coop. Assn. Feature writer The News-Sentinel, Fort Wayne, Ind., 1981-83; wire editor The Noblesville (Ind.) Daily Ledger, 1983; staff writer Ind. Statewide Assn. Rural Electric Coops., Indpls., 1983-84, mng. editor, 1984-85, editor, 1985—. Author: Power to the People, 1985. Mem. Coop. Communicators Assn. (Michael Graznak award 1990), Internat. Assn. Bus. Communicators (award of excellence dist. 7 1985), Elec. Women's Round Table Inc. (Power award 1994), Electric Inst. Ind., Nat. Electric Cooperatives Statewide Editors Assn. Office: Ind Statewide Assn RECs 720 N High School Rd Indianapolis IN 46214-3756

SCHILLING, EYDIE ANNE, science educator, consultant; b. Columbus, Ohio, June 17, 1965; d. Phyllis Anne (Helsel) Radugge. BS in Bilog. Scis., Ohio State U., 1989, MA in Sci. Edn., 1994. Cert. tchr., Ohio; comprehensive sci., biology sci. gen. sci. Tchr. integrated 7th and 8th grade sci. Wynford Middle Sch., Bucyrus, Ohio, 1989-93; tchr. tech. biology and integrated 8th grade sci. Ridgedale Jr./Sr. H.S., Marion, Oho, 1993-94; tech. chemistry and integrated 8th grade sci. Ridgedale Jr./Sr. H.S., Marion, 1994-95; tchr. biology, chemistry, tech. biology Teays Valley H.S., Asheville, Ohio, 1995-96; cons. Tech.-Prep. Consortium, Marion, 1993-95, Marion County Schs., 1993-95, Buckeye Assessment Teams in Sci., Columbus, 1995—; mem. math-sci. adv. subcom. Ctrl. Ohio Regional Profl. Devel. Ctr., Columbus, 1995—; instr. Project Discovery, Columbus, 1995—; tchr. biology, chemistry Tech. Prep II Teays Valley H.S., Ashville, Ohio, 1995—; coach high sch. girls track, high sch. cross country Teays Valley Schs., Ashville, 1995—. Grantee Project Discovery, Columbus, 1991; intern Young Exptl. Scientist C.O.S.I., Columbus, 1991, 92. Mem. Nat. Sci. Tchrs. Assn., Sci. Elem. Coun. Ohio (presenter conf. 1995-96), Ohio State Univ. Alumni, Phi Delta Kappa. Republican. Lutheran. Home: 1039 Vernon Rd Bexley OH 43209-2467 Office: Teays Valley Schs SR 752 Ashville OH 43103

SCHILLING, FREDERICK AUGUSTUS, JR., geologist, consultant; b. Phila., Apr. 12, 1931; s. Frederick Augustus and Emma Hope (Christoffer) S.; m. Ardis Ione Dovre, June 12, 1957 (div. 1987); children: Frederick Christopher, Jennifer Dovre. BS in Geology, Wash. State U., 1953; PhD in Geology, Stanford U., 1962. Computer geophysicist United Geophys. Corp., Pasadena, Calif., 1955-56; geologist various orgns., 1956-61, U.S. Geol. Survey, 1961-64; underground engr. Climax (Colo.) Molybdenum Co., 1966-68; geologist Keradamex Inc., Anaconda Co., M.P. Grace, Ranchers Exploration & Devel. Corp., Albuquerque and Grants, N.Mex., 1968-84, Hecla Mining Co., Coeur d'Alene, Idaho, 1984-86, various engring. and environ. firms, Calif., 1986-91; prin. F. Schilling Cons., Canyon Lake, Calif., 1991—. Author: Bibliography of Uranium, 1976. Del. citizen amb. program People to People Internat., USSR, 1990-91. With U.S. Army, 1953-55. Fellow Explorers Club; mem. Geol. Soc. Am., Am. Assn. Petroleum Geologists, Soc. Mining Engrs., Internat. Platform Assn., Adventurers' Club Inc. L.A., Masons, Kiwanis, Sigma Xi, Sigma Gamma Epsilon. Republican. Presbyterian. Avocation: track and field. Office: F Schilling Cons 30037 Steel Head Dr Canyon Lake CA 92587-7460

SCHILLING, JANET NAOMI, nutritionist, consultant; b. North Platte, Neb., Mar. 1, 1939; d. Jens Harold and Naomi Frances (Meyer) Hansen; children: Allan Edward III, Karl Jens. BS, U. Neb., 1961; MS, Ohio State U., 1965; MPH, U. Calif., Berkeley, 1991. Registered dietitian. Tchr. home econs. Peace Corps., Dimbokro, Ivory Coast, 1962-64; cons. nutrition Wis. Divsn. Health, La Crosse, 1966-67, 69; dietary cons. Cozad (Neb.) Community Hosp., 1968; instr. Viterbo Coll., La Crosse, 1974-81; lectr. U. Wis., La Crosse, 1982-84; teaching asst. ESL Sch. Dist. La Crosse, 1984-87; nutrition educator Women, Infant, and Children Program, 1988-89; nutrition cons. Vis. Nurses, LaCrosse, 1987-89; dietitian Merrithew Meml. Hosp., Martinez, Calif., 1992; pub. health nutrition cons. Women Infant & Childrens Program Policy and Compliance Unit, Sacramento, 1995; nutrition cons. Wis. Winnebago Nation, 1991; pediatric dietitian in Romanian Orphanges thru World Vision, 1993; nutritionist Contra Costa Head Start & Child Devel., 1994. Author: Life in the Nutrition Community, 1980, Life in the Nutrition Cycle II, 1980; co-author: Nutrition Activities, 1984, Recipe Book of Nutritious Snacks, 1985. Mem. LaCrosse Sch. Dist. Nutrition Task Force, 1976-88; Sunday sch. tchr., supr. Our Savior's Luth. Ch., 1975-86, chmn. Mobile Meals, 1982-86; v.p. membership booster club Ctrl. H.S. LaCrosse, 1985-87, pres., 1987-88; bd. dirs. YMCA, LaCrosse, 1982-88; mem. No. Calif. Returned Peace Corps vols., 1990—; mem. Glide Ch. Housing Task Force, 1995—; trustee East Bay Habitat for Humanity, 1995—. Mem. AAUW (pres. 1978-80, Named Grant scholar 1981), APHA, LaCrosse Area Dietetic Assn. (1st pres. 1968-69, Outstanding Dietitian Yr. 1985), Wis. Dietetic Assn. (chmn. educators 1983-85), No. Wis. Dietetic Assn. (pres. 1982), Am. Dietetic Assn. (educators practice group 1978-90), LaCrosse Jaycees (Carol award 1973), Calif. Dietetic Assn. (pediat. practice group chmn. 1997-98). Democrat. Avocations: running, swimming, biking. Home: 1604 Roger Ct El Cerrito CA 94530-2028

SCHILLING, JOHN ALBERT, surgeon; b. Kansas City, Mo., Nov. 5, 1917; s. Carl Fielding and Lottie Lee (Henderson) S.; m. Lucy West, June 8, 1957 (dec.); children: Christine Henderson, Katharine Ann, Jolyon David, John Jay; m. Helen R. Spelbrink, May 28, 1979. A.B. with honors, Dartmouth Coll., 1937; M.D., Harvard U., 1941. Diplomate Am. Bd. Surgery (chmn. 1969). Intern, then resident in surgery Roosevelt Hosp., N.Y.C., 1941-44; mem. faculty U. Rochester (N.Y.) Med. Sch., 1945-53, asst. prof. surgery, 1955-56; prof. surgery, head dept. U. Okla. Med. Sch., 1956-74; prof. surgery U. Wash. Med. Sch., Seattle, 1974—; chmn. dept. U. Wash. Med. Sch., 1975-83, prof. emeritus, 1988—; mem. bd. sci. counselors Nat. Cancer Inst., chmn., 1969; also mem. diagnosis subcom. breast cancer task force; chmn. adv. com. to surgeon gen. on metabolism of trauma Army Med. Research and Devel. Command; mem. surgery study sect., div. research grants NIH; chief surgery USAF Sch. Aviation Medicine, 1953-55; cons. Surgeon Gen. USAF, 1959-75. Author articles, chpts. in books, abstracts, reports.; editorial bd. Am. Jour. Surgery, Annals of Surgery. Served to maj. M.C. USAF, 1953-55. Grantee Army Office Surgeon Gen., 1956-80. Mem. ACS (bd. govs., chmn. com. surg. edn. in med. schs., 1st v.p. 1977-78), Am. S., Western, Pan-Pacific, N. Pacific, Pacific Coast surg. assns., Soc. Univ. Surgeons, Southwestern Surg. Soc., Central Surg. Soc., Southern Surgical Congress (hon. mem. 1978), Okla. Surg. Assn. (pres. 1970-71, hon. mem. 1974) Am. Assn. Surgery Trauma, Surg. Biology Club, Am. Physiol. Soc., Soc. Surg. Chmn., Am. Trauma Soc., Seattle Surg. Soc., Soc. Exptl. Pathology, Soc. Surgery Alimentary Tract, Explorers Club, Alpha Omega Alpha. Clubs: Yacht (Seattle), University (Seattle). Home: 9807 Lake Washington Blvd NE Bellevue WA 98004-5431 Office: Dept Surgery (RF-25) Univ Wash Medical Sch Seattle WA 98195

SCHILLING, JOHN MICHAEL, golf course executive; b. Hiawatha, Kans., Nov. 23, 1951; s. George H. and Darlene J. (Wachter) S.; m. Pamela S. Hischke, Sept. 5, 1969; children: John II, James. Student Highland Coll., 1971-72; BS in Journalism, U. Kans., 1974. Assoc. editor Kans. Electric

Coops., Topeka, 1975-76, editor, 1976-79; editor Golf Course Supts. Assn. Am., Lawrence, Kans., 1978-79, mktg. dir., 1979-83, exec. dir., 1983-93; pres. St. Andrews Corp., Lawrence, 1994—. Contbr. articles to profl. jours. Mem. Am. Soc. Assn. Execs., Nat. Assn. Expn. Mgrs., Am. Advt. Fedn., U.S. Golf Assn., Nat. Golf Found. (bd. dirs.), Internat. Assn. Golf Adminstrs. Republican. Lutheran. Club: Alvamar Country (Lawrence). Avocations: golf, boating, coaching, breeding dogs, reading, computers. Home: 854 E 1259 Rd Lawrence KS 66042-9460 Office: St Andrews Corp PO Box 3407 Lawrence KS 66046

SCHILLING, RICHARD M., lawyer, corporate executive; b. Green Bay, Wis., June 15, 1937; s. Merlin Schilling; m. Eileen M. Schilling, Sept. 6, 1959; children: Sherry Schilling Harlan, Rick. BS, U. Green Bay, 1959; LLB, Harvard, 1962. Atty. with Schiff, Hardin & Waite, Chgo., 1962-69; corp. atty. Sundstrand Corp., Rockford, Ill., 1969—. Mem. Chgo. Bar Assn., Winnebago County Bar Assn., ABA, Machinery and Allied Products Inst. Office: Sundstrand Corp PO Box 7003 4949 Harrison Ave Rockford IL 61125

SCHILLING, WARNER ROLLER, political scientist, educator; b. Glendale, Calif., May 23, 1925; s. Jule Frederick and Pauline Frances de Berri (Warner) S.; m. Jane Pierce Metzger, Jan. 27, 1951 (dec. Nov. 1983); children: Jonathan, Frederick. A.B., Yale U., 1949, M.A., 1951, Ph.D., 1954. Research fellow Center Internat. Studies, Princeton U., 1953-54; asst. prof. internat. relations Mass. Inst. Tech., 1957-58; mem. faculty Columbia, 1954—, prof. govt., 1967-73, James T. Shotwell prof. internat. relations, 1973—; dir. Inst. War and Peace Studies, 1976-86; cons., occasional lectr. in field. Co-author: Strategy, Politics and Defense Budgets, 1962, European Security and the Atlantic System, 1973, American Arms and a Changing Europe, 1973; Contbr. numerous articles to jours. Served with USAAF, 1944-46. Guggenheim fellow, 1964-65; resident fellow Bellagio Study and Conf. Center, 1975. Mem. Internat. Inst. Strategic Studies, Council Fgn. Relations. Club: Leonia Democratic. Home: 496 Park Ave Leonia NJ 07605-1243 Office: 420 W 118th St New York NY 10027-7213

SCHILLING, WILLIAM RICHARD, aerospace engineer, research and development company executive; b. Manheim, Pa., Jan. 12, 1933; s. William Thomas and Ora Lee (Worley) S.; m. Patricia Elise Brigman, June 8, 1957; 1 child, Duane Thomas. BCE, Va. Poly. Inst., 1956; MS in Structural Engring., Pa. State U., 1959; MS in Aero. Engring., U. So. Calif., 1961, Engrs. Degree in Aerospace Engring., 1966. Aerodynamist Douglas Aircraft Co., Santa Monica, Calif., 1956-64; study chmn. Research Analysis Corp., McLean, Va., 1964-72; div. mgr. Sci. Applications, Inc., McLean, 1972-78; pres., chief exec. officer McLean Rsch. Ctr., Inc., 1978-89; exec. v.p. Wackenhut Applied Techs. Ctr., Fairfax, Va., 1989-91; dir. bus. devel., dir. sys. rsch. divsn., bd. dirs. Internat. Devel. and Resources, Inc., Falls Church, Va., 1991—; pres. Systems Rsch. Corp., Falls Church, 1991—; pres., bd. dirs. LaMancha Co., Santa Fe, 1985-89. Contbr. numerous articles to profl. jours. Chmn. com. Boy Scouts Am., McLean, 1968-78; vol. Am. Heart Assn., McLean, 1984-89; bd. dirs., chief exec. officer Internat. Housing Devel., McLean, 1986—. Mem. Assn. U.S. Army, Am. Def. Preparedness, Va. C. of C. Baptist. Avocations: classical lit., art, music, travel. Home: 6523 Old Dominion Dr Mc Lean VA 22101-4613 Office: Internat Devel & Resources 10560 Main St Fairfax VA 22030-7182

SCHILLINGER, EDWIN JOSEPH, physics educator; b. Chgo., July 14, 1923; s. Edwin Joseph and Marie (Wolf) S.; m. Carmelita Larocco, Aug. 27, 1949; children—Rosemarie, Mary, Ann, Edwin, Jerome, Elizabeth. B.S., DePaul U., 1944; M.S., U. Notre Dame, 1948, Ph.D., 1950. Mem. faculty DePaul U., Chgo., 1950—, prof. physics, 1963-88, prof. emeritus, 1988—, chmn. dept., 1952-68, 76-79, dean Coll. Liberal Arts and Scis., 1966-70, acting dean, 1980-81; ednl. cons. Served with AUS, 1944-46. Decorated Purple Heart; recipient merit award Chgo. Tech. Socs., 1976; AEC fellow, 1948-50. Fellow Am. Phys. Soc.; mem. Am. Assn. Physics Tchrs., AAAS, Ill. Acad. Sci., Chgo. Acad. Tech. (charter mem.), Sigma Xi. Roman Catholic. Home: 7724 W Peterson Ave Chicago IL 60631-2246

SCHILLING-NORDAL, GERALDINE ANN, secondary school educator; b. Springfield, Mass., Feb. 4, 1935; d. Robert Milton and Helen Veronica (Ewald) Schilling; m. Reidar Johannes Nordal. BS, Boston U., 1956, MEd, 1957; postgrad., Springfield Coll., Anna Maria Coll. Tchr. art Agawam (Mass.) Jr. H.S., 1957-58; tchr. art Agawam H.S., 1958—, K-12 art acad. coord., 1995-96, head art dept., 1970-95; instr. oil painting univ. ext. course Agawam Night Sch., 1957-58; instr. creative arts Agawam Evening Sch., 1973-80. Active Agawam Town Report Com., 1967-77, Agawam Hist. Commn., 1979-87, Agawam Arts and Humanities Com., 1979-85, Agawam Minerva Davis Libr. Study Com., 1987-95, Agawam Cultural Coun., 1994-97; sec. Agawam Town Beautification Com., 1974-87; mem. town tchrs. rep. Agawam Bicentennial Com., 1975-77; chmn. 40th anniversary St. John the Evangelist Ch., Agawam, 1986, co-chmn. 50th anniversary com., 1996, mem. renovation com., 1983; decoration chmn. town-wide Halloween parties, Agawam, 1971-93; recruiter Miss Agawam Pageant; appeal vol. Cath. Charity, 1995—; mem. Agawam Cath. Womens Club, 1995—, banquet com., 1997. Mem. NEA, ASCD, Agawam Edn. Assn. (sec. 1970-74, 76-77), Hampden County Tchrs. Assn., Mass. Tchrs. Assn., Mass. Art Edn. Assn., Nat. Art Edn. Assn., New Eng. Art Edn. Assn., Mass. Alliance for Art Edn., Am. Assn. Ret. Persons, Mass. Cath. Order Foresters, West Springfield Neighborhood House Alumni Assn. (pres. 1966, advisor 1968), West Springfield H.S. Alumni Assn. (3d v.p. 1968-70, 1st v.p. 1970-71, pres. 1972-74), Boston U. Alumni Club Springfield Area (organizer area giving campaigns 1957-62, class agt. 1985—, mem. area scholarship com. 1995—), Am. Legion (life), Zeta Chi Delta (pres. 1955-56), Delta Kappa Gamma (Alpha chpt., art chairperson, reservation chmn. art work and hist. archives, hospitality). Office: Agawam Sr High Sch 760 Cooper St Agawam MA 01001-2177

SCHILLINGS, DENNY LYNN, history educator; b. Mt. Carmel, Ill., June 28, 1947; s. Grady Lynn and Mary Lucille (Walters) S.; m. Karen Krek; children: Denise, Corinne. AA, Wabash Valley Coll., 1967; BEd, Ea. Ill. U., 1969, MA in History, 1972; postgrad., Chgo. State U.; MA in Adminstrn., Govs. State U., 1996; postgrad., Ill. State U., No. Ill. U. Grad. asst. dept. history Ea. Ill. U., Charleston, 1969; tchr. Edwards County High Sch., Albion, Ill., 1969-70, Sheldon (Ill.) High Sch., 1971-73, Homewood-Flossmoor (Ill.) High Sch., 1973—; participant, con. Atlantic Coun. U.S. and NATO, Washington, 1986, Internat. Soviet-U.S. Textbook Project Conf., Racine, Wis., 1987; moderator Soviet-U.S. Textbook Study: Final Report, Dallas, 1987; chair history content adv. com. Ill. Tchr. Certification Requirements Com. 1986; mem. Ill. State Bd. Edn., Com. to Establish Learner Outcomes, 1984, Joint Task Force on Admission Requirements Ill. State Bd. on Higher Edn., 1986—; mem. adv. com. for Jefferson Found. Sch. Programs, 1987-90, Ill. State Bd. Edn.'s Goals Assessment Adv. Com., 1987-90. Author: (with others) Economics, 1986, The Examination in Social Studies, 1989, Links Across Time and Place: A World History, 1990, Illinois Government Text, 1990, Challenge of Freedom, 1990; author: The Living Constitution, 1991, 2d edit., 1997; co-editor: Teaching the Constition, 1987; reviewer, cons. for ednl. instns. and organizations; chair editorial bd. Social Edn., 1983; contbg. editor Social Studies Tchr., 1987-88. Mem. steering com. Homewood-Floosmoor High Sch. Found., 1983-84. Mem. NEA, Am. Hist. Assn. (James Harvey Robinson prize com. 1990-91), Ill. Assn. Advancement History, Ill. Coun. Social Studies (v.p. 1981, editor newsletter 1979-84, pres. 1983), Ill. Edn. Assn. (Gt. Lakes coord. com. 1982-83), Nat. Coun. Social Studies (publs. bd. 1983-86, bd. dirs. 1987-90, 94-96, exec. com. 1989-90, chair conf. com. 1989-90, pres. 1993-94, program planning com. 1989, 91), World History Assn., Phi Alpha Theta. Avocations: computers, reading. Home: 18447 Aberdeen St Homewood IL 60430-3525 Office: Homewood-Flossmoor High Sch 999 Kedzie Ave Flossmoor IL 60422-2248

SCHILPLIN, YVONNE WINTER, educational administrator; b. Mahnomen, Minn., May 26, 1946; d. Milo Joseph and Lucille Margaret (Schoenborn) Winter; m. Frederick Colegrove Schilplin III, Dec. 30, 1975; children: Frederick IV, Chad. Student, St. Cloud State U., 1964. Retail fashion buyer Fandel's Dept. Store, St. Cloud, Minn., 1968-75; mem. graduation standards exec. com. Minn. Dept. Edn., Mpls., 1988—; mem. Annandale (Minn.) Sch. Bd. Dist. 876, 1988-94, chmn., 1991-94; co-owner, cons. Am. Rsch. Grant Writing & Tng., Inc., 1993—. Edn. chmn. Minn. PTA, Mpls., 1989-91; mem. legis. com. St. Cloud Reading Rm., 1991-92, v.p., 1996—; liaison for sch. bd. Annandale PTA, 1989-94; co-chmn. Living Wax Mus., Minn. Pioneer Park, 1991-92; mem. facilities planning com. Sch. Dist. 876, mid. sch. steering com. Recipient Minn. Sch. Bd. Mem. of Yr., 1994. Mem. Stearns County Hist. Soc., Minn. Sci. Mus., St. Cloud Country Club. Avocations: reading, tennis, herb and flower garden, fishing, fashion modeling. Home: RR 3 Annandale MN 55302-9803

SCHILSKY, RICHARD LEWIS, oncologist, researcher; b. N.Y.C., June 6, 1950; s. Murray and Shirley (Cohen) S.; m. Cynthia Schum, Sept. 24, 1977; children: Allison, Meredith. BA cum laude, U. Pa., Phila., 1971; MD with honors, U. Chgo., 1975. Diplomate Nat. Bd. Med. Examiners, Am. Bd. Internal Medicine (subspecialty med. oncology); lic. physician, Mo., Ill. Intern, resident medicine Parkland Meml. Hosp., Southwestern Med. Sch., Dallas, 1975-77; clin. assoc. medicine br. and clin. pharmacology br. Divsn. Cancer Treatment, Nat. Cancer Inst., Bethesda, Md., 1977-80, cancer expert clin. pharmacology br., 1980-81; asst. prof. dept. internal medicine U. Mo. Sch. Medicine, Columbia, 1981-84; asst. prof. dept. medicine U. Chgo. Pritzker Sch. Medicine and Michael Reese Med. Ctrs., 1984-86, assoc. prof. dept. medicine, 1986-89; assoc. dir. joint sect. hematology and med. oncology U. Chgo. and Michael Reese Med. Ctrs., 1986-89; assoc. prof. dept. medicine, assoc. dir. sect. U. Chgo. Pritzker Sch. Medicine, 1989-91, prof. dept. medicine sect. hematology-oncology, 1991—; dir. U. Chgo. Cancer Rsch. Ctr., 1991—; chmn. Cancer and Leukemia Group B, Chgo., 1995—; Vivian Saykaly vis. prof. oncology McGill U., 1962; mem. sci. com. 7th Internat. Congress on Anti-Cancer Chemotherapy, 1997; mem. adv. panel on hematologic and neoplastic disease U.S. Pharmacopeial Conv., 1991-95; bd. dirs. Assn. Am. Cancer Insts., 1995—; mem. cancer ctr. support grant rev. com. Nat. Cancer Inst., NIH, 1992-95; mem. expert panel on advances in cancer treatment, 1992-93; mem. Cancer Ctrs. Working Group, 1996-97; mem. Oncologic Drugs Adv. Com. FDA, 1996—. Mem. editl. bd. Investigational New Drugs, 1988-95, Jour. Clin. Oncology, 1990-93, Contemporary Oncology, 1991-95, Jour. Cancer Rsch. and Clin. Oncology, 1991—, Seminars in Oncology, 1997—; assoc. editor Clin. Cancer Rsch., 1994—; contbr. articles to profl. jours., chpts. to books. With USPHS, 1977-80. Recipient Spl. Advancement for Performance award VA, 1983, Fletcher Scholar award Cancer Rsch. Found., 1989; grantee VA, 1981-87, Am. Cancer Soc., 1983-86, 92-95, Ill. Cancer Coun., 1985-86, Michael Reese Inst. Coun., 1985-86, Nat. Cancer Inst., 1987, 88-90, Burroughs-Wellcome Co., 1987-88, NIH/Nat. Cancer Inst., 1988—. Fellow ACP; mem. AAAS, Am. Soc. Clin. Oncology (chmn. pub. rels. com. 1994—), Am. Assn. Cancer Rsch. (chmn. Ill. state legis. com. 1992—), Am. Fedn. Clin. Rsch. (senator Midwest sect. 1983-84, councilor 1983-86, chmn.-elect 1987-88, chmn. 1988-89), Am. Assn. Cancer Edn., Am. Soc. Clin. Pharmacology and Therapeutics, Ctrl. Soc. Clin. Rsch., N.Y. Acad. Scis., Assn. Am. Cancer Insts. (bd. dirs. 1995—), Chgo. Soc. Internal Medicine, Sigma Xi, Alpha Epsilon Delta, Alpha Omega Alpha. Office: U Chgo Cancer Rsch Ctr 5841 S Maryland Ave Chicago IL 60637-1463

SCHIMBERG, A(RMAND) BRUCE, retired lawyer; b. Chgo., Aug. 26, 1927; s. Archie and Helen (Isay) S.; m. Barbara Zisook; children: Geoffrey, Kate. PhB, U. Chgo., 1949, JD, 1952. Bar: Ohio 1952, Ill. 1955, U.S. Supreme Ct. 1987. Assoc. Paxton & Seasongood, Cin., 1952-55; ptnr. Schimberg, Greenberger, Kraus & Jacobs, Chgo., 1955-65, Leibman, Williams, Bennett, Baird & Minow, Chgo., 1965-72; ptnr. Sidley & Austin, Chgo., 1972-92, counsel, 1993-94; ret., 1994; lectr. U. Chgo., 1953-54; gen. counsel Comml. Fin. Assn., 1978-94; past mem. editl. bd. Lender Liability News. Mng. and assoc. editor U. Chgo. Law Rev., 1951-52; contbr. articles to legal jours. Bd. dirs. U. Chgo. Law Sch. Alumni Assn., 1969-72; dir. vis. com. U. Chgo. Law Sch., 1980-83. Mem. ABA (chmn. subcom. and charter mem. comml. fin. svcs. com.), Am. Coll. Comml. Fin. Lawyers (pres. 1994-95, bd. regents), Ill. Bar Assn. (chair comml. banking, bankruptcy sect. 1972-73), Chgo. Bar Assn. (chair ucc com., 1966, bd. mgrs. 1968-70, chair judiciary com. 1971-72), Law Club Chgo., Mid-Day Club, Lake Shore Country Club. Home: 132 E Delaware Pl Apt 5002 Chicago IL 60611-1442

SCHIMBERG, BARBARA HODES, organizational development consultant; b. Chgo., Nov. 30, 1941; d. David and Tybe Zisook; children from previous marriage: Brian, Valery; m. A. Bruce Schimberg, Dec. 29, 1984. BS, Northwestern U., 1962. Ptnr. Just Causes, cons. not-for-profit orgns., Chgo., 1978-86; cons. in philanthropy, community involvement, and organizational devel., 1987—; Chgo. cons. Population Resource Ctr., 1978-82. Woman's bd. dirs. Mus. Contemporary Art; bd. dirs., vice chmn. Med. Rsch. Inst. Coun., Michael Reese Med. Ctr.; bd. dirs., chmn. Midwest Women's Ctr.; trustee Francis W. Parker Sch.; bd. dirs. Women's Issues Network Found., 1991—, pres., 1993-94; mem. adv. bd. Med. Rsch. Inst. Coun., Children's Meml. Hosp. Mem. ACLU (adv. com.). Office: 132 E Delaware Pl Apt 5002 Chicago IL 60611-4944

SCHIMBERG, HENRY AARON, soft drink company executive; b. Chgo., Mar. 3, 1933; s. Arnold and Judith (Aaron) S.; m. Linda Waxberg, June 21, 1975; children: Aaron David, Alexis Leigh. BA, Beloit Coll., 1954. Exec. v.p. Nehi Royal Crown Corp., Chgo., 1970-76; pres. Royal Crown Bottling Co., Los Angeles, 1976-79; pres. bottling ops. Royal Crown Cola Co., Rolling Meadows, Ill., 1979-82; pres., CEO, bd. dirs. Coca-Cola Bottling Midwest, Mpls., 1982-91, Cen. States Coca-Cola Bottling Co., Springfield, Ill., 1985-91, Coca-Cola Bottling Co. of St. Louis, 1986-91, Cin. Coca-Cola Bottling Co., 1986-91, Mid-States Coca-Cola Bottling Co., Paducah, Ky., 1986-91; pres., COO, bd. dirs. Johnston Coca-Cola Bottling Group, Chattanooga, Tenn., 1986-91, Coca-Cola Enterprises Inc., Atlanta, 1991—, Pacific Coca-Cola Bottling Co., Bellevue, Wash., 1992—, Austin Coca-Cola Bottling Co., Dallas; bd. dirs. Johnston So. Co., Chattanooga. Cpl. U.S. Army, 1954-56. Mem. Minn. Soft Drink Assn. (bd. dirs. 1983—), Wis. Soft Drink Assn., Ill. Soft Drink Assn. (pres. 1974-76), Nat. Soft Drink Assn. (exec. bd. 1986—, chmn. 1994-96), Coca-Cola Bottlers Assn. (bd. govs. 1986—). Jewish. Avocations: tennis, skiing. Office: Coca-Cola Enterprises Inc 2500 Windy Ridge Pkwy SE Atlanta GA 30339-5677

SCHIMEK, DIANNA RUTH REBMAN, state legislator; b. Holdrege, Nebr., Mar. 21, 1940; d. Ralph William and Elizabeth Julia (Wilmot) Rebman; m. Herbert Henry Schimek, 1963; children: Samuel Wolfgang, Saul William. AA, Colo. Women's Coll., 1960; student, U. Nebr., Lincoln, 1960-61; BA magna cum laude, U. Nebr., Kearney, 1963. Former tchr. and realtor; mem. Nebr. Legislature, Lincoln, 1989—, chmn. govt., mil. and vets. affairs com., 1993-94, vice chair urban affairs com., 1995—; bd. dirs. First Security Nat. Bank. Dem. Nat. committeewoman, 1984-88; chmn. Nebr. Dem. Com., 1980-84, mem. exec. com., 1987-88; past pres., sec. bd. dirs. Downtown Sr. Ctr. Found., 1990-96; mem. exec. bd. Midwest Coun. of State Govts., 1995—, co-chair health and human svcs. com., 1995—; exec. dir. Nebr. Civil Liberties Union, 1985; bd. dirs. Nebr. Repertory Theater, Exon Found., 1997—; mem. adv. bd. Martin Luther Home, 1997—. Mem. Nat. Conf. State Legislators Women's Network (bd. dirs. 1993-96), P.E.O., Soroptimists, NAACP. Democrat. Unitarian. Home: 2321 Camelot Ct Lincoln NE 68512-1457 Office: Dist # 27 State Capital Lincoln NE 68509

SCHIMELPFENIG, C(LARENCE) W(ILLIAM), JR., retired chemistry educator; b. Dallas, Apr. 8, 1930; s. Clarence William and Hulda Anna Louise (Borchardt) S.; m. Dorothy Marie Massey, Apr. 28, 1956; children: Laurel Ann, Gretchen Marie, Michael William. BS, North Tex. State U., 1953, MS, 1954; PhD, U. Ill., 1957. Asst. prof. George Washington U., Washington, 1957-59, U. North Tex., Denton, 1959-62; rsch. chemist E.I. du Pont de Nemours and Co., Wilmington, Del., 1962-72; asst. prof. SUNY, Buffalo, 1973-75, Erskine Coll., Due West, S.C., 1975-76; assoc. prof. Tex. Wesleyan Coll., Ft. Worth, 1976-81, U. North Tex., Denton, 1981-82; prof. chemistry Dallas Bapt. U., 1982-91; adj. prof. chemistry U. Tex., Arlington, 1991-96; curator (part-time vol.) Libr. Spl. Collections, U. Tex., Dallas, 1995—. Patentee chlorination method, moistenable hot melt adhesive; contbr. articles to profl. jours. Dist. commr. Boy Scouts of Am., Wilmington, Del., 1972; mem. Crime Watch Bd., Pantego, Tex., 1987-91; mem. Planning and Zoning Commn., Pantego, 1991—; elder Hanover Presbyn. Ch., Wilmington. Recipient grants Robert A. Welch Found., Houston, 1960-62, '78-81, Silver Beaver award, Boy Scouts of Am., 1973. Mem. Am. Chem. Soc. (program dir. meeting-in-miniature, Dallas-Ft. Worth 1981), Sigma Xi, Alpha Chi Sigma, Phi Lambda Upsilon. Republican. Presbyterian. Avocations: gardening, nature study. Home: 2008 Silver Leaf Dr Pantego TX 76013-3126

SCHIMKE, DENNIS J., state legislator; m. Olive Schimke; 3 children. BS, U. N.D., MS. Bison rancher, tchr. physics; rep. Dist. 28 N.D. Ho. of reps., 1990-92, rep. dist. 26, 1995—, mem. edn. and agr. com. Home: PO Box 525 Edgeley ND 58433-0525

SCHIMMEL, PAUL REINHARD, biochemist, biophysicist, educator; b. Hartford, Conn., Aug. 4, 1940; s. Alfred E. and Doris (Hudson) S.; m. Judith F. Ritz, Dec. 30, 1961; children: Kirsten, Katherine. A.B., Ohio Wesleyan U., 1962; postgrad., Tufts U. Sch. Medicine, 1962-63, Mass. Inst. Tech., 1963-65, Cornell U., 1965-66, Stanford U., 1966-67, U. Calif., Santa Barbara, 1975-76; Ph.D., Mass. Inst. Tech., 1966; DSc (hon.), Ohio Wesleyan U., 1996. Asst. prof. biology and chemistry MIT, 1967-71, assoc. prof., 1971-76, prof. biochemistry and biophysics, 1976-92, John D. and Catherine T. MacArthur prof. biochemistry and biophysics, 1992—; mem. NIH Study Sect. Physiol. Chemistry, 1975-79; indsl. cons. on enzymes and recombinant DNA. Author: (with C. Cantor) Biophysical Chemistry, 3 vols., 1980; mem. editl. bd. Archives Biochemistry, Biophysics, 1976-80, Nucleic Acids Rsch., 1976-80, Jour. Biol. Chemistry, 1977-82, Biopolymers, 1979-88, Internat. Jour. Biol. Macromolecules, 1983-89, Trends in Biochem. Scis., 1984—, Biochemistry, 1989—, Accounts of Chem. Rsch., 1989-94, European Jour. Biochemistry, 1991—, Protein Sci., 1991-94, Proc. Nat. Acad. Scis., 1993—. Alfred P. Sloan fellow, 1970-72. Fellow AAAS (chmn. Amory prize com. 1995-96), Am. Acad. Arts and Scis.; mem. NAS (class II biochemistry sect. rep. 1995-96), Am. Chem. Soc. (Pfizer award 1978, chmn. divsn. biol. chemistry 1984-85) Am. Soc. for Biochemistry and Molecular Biology (chmn. nominating com. 1990, awards com. 1995), Ribonucleic Acid Soc. Office: MIT Dept Biology Cambridge MA 02139

SCHIMMER, BARRY MICHAEL, rheumatologist; b. Newark, Jan. 7, 1945; s. Emanuel and Florence Pearl (Haflich) S.; m. Naomi Ann Raicer, May 24, 1970; children: Alexandra Tamar, Rebecca Tal. BA, Rutgers U., 1966; MD, Albert Einstein Coll. Medicine, Bronx, N.Y., 1970. Diplomate Am. Bd. Internal Medicine, subspecialty rheumatology. Intern Hosp. U. Pa., Phila., 1970-71, med. resident, 1971-73; clin. rsch. assoc. Harvard Med. Sch., Boston, 1973-75; clin. assoc. prof. medicine U. Pa. Sch. Medicine, Phila., 1978-95, Thomas Jefferson U., Phila., 1995—; chief rheumatology sect. Pa. Hosp., Phila., 1978—; chmn. grants and scholarship com. Arthritis Found., Ea. Ga. chpt., Phila., 1988-96; med. sec. rheumatology subspecialty bd. Am. Bd. Internal Medicine, Phila., 1990—; chmn. grants and scholarship com. Harry R. Kellman Acad., Cherry Hill, N.J., 1984-91. Fellow ACP, Am. Coll. Rheumatology; mem. Phila. Rheumatism Soc., Alpha Omega Alpha, Phi Beta Kappa. Avocations: classical music, opera. Office: Pa Rheumatology Assoc 822 Pine St # 1C Philadelphia PA 19107-6124

SCHIMPF, JOHN JOSEPH, real estate developer; b. Paterson, N.J., May 19, 1949; s. Joseph Stephen and Veronica Barbara (Blad) S.; m. Barbara Ann Reid, June 3, 1972; children: Laryn Michelle, Brian Scott, Alysson Marie. BA magna cum laude in Spanish Lit., Seton Hall U., 1971; MA in Comparative Lit., U. Wis., 1974, MA in Spanish Lit., 1975; MBA in Fin. and Mktg., Columbia U., 1977. Corp. loan officer petroleum div. Chase Manhattan Bank, N.Y.C., 1977-79; mgr. treasury ops. Marsh & McLennan Cos., Inc., N.Y.C., 1980-81; exec. v.p., dir. Hovnanian Enterprises, Inc., Red Bank, N.J., 1981—; bd. dirs. Hovnanian Enterprises, Inc., Red Bank, N.J., New Fortis Corp., King, N.C. Trustee Brookdale C.C. Found., Lincroft, N.J., Emmanuel Cancer Found., Iselin, N.J.; mem. adv. bd. to chancellor Seton Hall U. Served to 1st lt. U.S. Army, 1971-73. Mem. Nat. Assn. Indsl. and Office Parks, Nat. Assn. Sr. Living Industries. Roman Catholic. Avocations: reading, art, racquetball. Office: Hovnanian Enterprises Inc 10 Hwy 35 PO Box 500 Red Bank NJ 07701*

SCHIMPFF, STEPHEN CALLENDER, internist, oncologist; b. Cleve., Nov. 23, 1941; s. Leo Donald and Lorraine (McClintock) S.; m. Carol Rawstrom, Sept. 2, 1963; 1 child, Elizabeth Callender. BA, Rutgers U., 1963; MD, Yale U., 1967. Diplomate Am. Bd. Internal Medicine, Am. Bd. Med. Examiners. Intern Yale-New Haven Hosp., 1967-68, resident, 1968-69; acting head med. svc. Balt. Cancer Rsch. Program, 1970-71, sr. investigator, 1973-76, head. infection rsch. sect., 1976-81; head infectious diseases and microbiology sect. U. Md., Balt., 1981-83, prof. medicine, 1979, prof. oncology, head divsn. infectious disease, 1979-85, Am. Cancer Soc. prof. oncology, 1985-89, dir. Cancer Ctr., 1982-85; exec. v.p. U. Md. Med. System, 1985—; Co-founder Multinat. Assn. for Supportive Care in Cancer, 1988—. Editor: Comprehensive Textbook Oncology, 1986, 91, Recent Results in Cancer Research—Infectious Complications in Bone Marrow Transplantation, 1993; contbr. articles to profl. jours. Bd. dirs. Md. Hosp. Edn. Inst., 1987—, vice chmn. 1992—, sec. 1991-92; bd. dirs. Md. Cancer Consortium, 1990—; bd. dirs. Md. Easter Seal Soc., 1989-92, vice chmn., 1990-92; leader Girl Scouts U.S., 1982. Fellow ACP, Infectious Diseases Soc. Am.; mem. Am. Soc. Clin. Oncology (sec., treas. 1985-88), Am. Assn. Cancer Rsch., Md. Assn. Nonprofit Orgns. (bd. dirs. 1991—, vice chmn. 1991-94, chmn. 1994—), Alpha Omega Alpha. Home: 10129 Pasture Gate Ln Columbia MD 21044-1735 Office: U Md Med System 22 S Greene St Baltimore MD 21201-1544

SCHINDEL, DONALD MARVIN, lawyer; b. Chgo., Jan. 5, 1932; s. Harry L. and Ann (Schiff) S.; m. Alice Martha Andrews, Apr. 24, 1960; children—Susan, Judith, Andrea. B.S. in Acctg., U. Ill., 1953; J.D., U. Chgo., 1956. Bar: Ill. 1956. Ptnr. Sonnenschein, Nath & Rosenthal, Chgo., 1956—. Author: Estate Administration and Tax Planning for Survivors, 1987, supplements, 1988—. Pres. Congregation Beth Or, Deerfield, Ill., 1983-85. Fellow Am. Coll. Trust and Estate Counsel; mem. Chgo. Estate Planning Council, ABA, Ill. Bar Assn., Chgo. Bar Assn. (chmn. probate practice com. 1981-82). Clubs: Metropolitan, East Bank (Chgo.). Avocations: tennis, photography, carpentry, running, juggling. Home: 636 Rice St Highland Park IL 60035-5012 Office: Sonnenschein Nath & Rosenthal 8000 Sears Tower 233 S Wacker Dr Chicago IL 60606-6306

SCHINDERLE, ROBERT FRANK, retired hospital administrator; b. Mayville, Wis., Aug. 3, 1923; m. Elizabeth, June 23, 1949; children—David, Gary, Mary, Brian. B.S., Marquette U., 1949; M.S., Northwestern U., 1959. Asst. office mgr. Western Leather Co., Milw., 1949-51; mgr. bus. office St. Francis Hosp., Peoria, Ill., 1951-55; credit mgr. Mercy Hosp., Chgo., 1955-59, asst. to adminstr., 1957-58, controller, 1958-59, asst. adminstr., 1959-65; asst. adminstr. St. Joseph Hosp., Joliet, Ill., 1965-70, assoc. adminstr., 1970-71, adminstr., 1971-76, exec. dir., 1976-86; dir. corp. legis. affairs and devel. Franciscan Sisters Health Care Corp., Mokena, Ill., 1986-89, ret.; chmn. Areawide Hosp. Emergency Services Council. Bd. dirs. Region IX Health Systems Agy., Our Lady of Angels Retirement Home, Joliet, Joliet YMCA, St. Joseph Coll. Nursing, Joliet. Fellow Am. Coll. Hosp. Adminstrs.; mem. Am. Hosp. Assn., Ill. Hosp. Assn. (chmn. 1975-76), Catholic Hosp. Assn. (dir.), Ill. Cath. Hosp. Assn. (chmn. 1972-73). Roman Catholic. Lodges: Rotary, Elks, KC. Home: 408 W Newkirk Dr Plainfield IL 60544-1838

SCHINDLER, ALBERT ISADORE, physicist, educator; b. Pitts., June 24, 1927; s. Jonas and Esther (Nass) S.; m. Phyllis Irene Liberman, June 17, 1951; children—Janet Mae, Jerald Scott, Ellen Susan. B.S., Carnegie Inst. Tech., 1947, M.S., 1948, D.Sc., 1950. Research asst. Carnegie Inst. Tech., Pitts., 1947-50, research physicist, 1950-51; supervisory rsch. physicist Naval Rsch. Lab., Washington, 1951-75; assoc. dir. research for material sci. and component tech. Naval Research Lab., 1975-85; prof. materials engring. and physics Purdue U., West Lafayette, Ind., 1985-92, cons., 1992—, dir. Ind. Ctr. for Innovative Superconductor Tech., 1988-91, dir. Midwest Superconductivity Consortium, 1990-91; dir. div. materials rsch. NSF, Washington, 1988-90; cons. Recipient E.O. Hulburt award Naval Research Lab., 1956, Nat. Capitol award for applied sci., 1962, Pure Sci. award Naval Research Lab.-Sci. Research Soc. Am., 1965, award Washington Acad. Scis., 1965, USN Disting. Achievement in Sci. award, 1975, Alumni Merit award Carngie Mellon U., 1976, Sr. Exec. Service award Dept. Navy, 1983. Fellow Am. Phys. Soc.; mem. Sigma Xi. (dir.). Home: 6615 Sulky Ln Rockville MD 20852-4344

SCHINDLER, ALEXANDER MOSHE, rabbi, organization executive; b. Munich, Germany, Oct. 4, 1925; s. Eliezer and Sali (Hoyda) S.; m. Rhea Rosenblum, Sept. 29, 1956; children—Elisa Ruth, Debra Lee, Joshua Michael, Judith Rachel, Jonathan David. B in Social Sci., CCNY, 1950; B in Hebrew Letters, Hebrew Union Coll., 1951, M in Hebrew Letters, 1953, DD (hon.), 1977; DHL (hon.), U. S.C., 1987, Lafayette U., 1988; DD (hon.),

Hamilton Coll., 1990; LLD (hon.), Coll. of Holy Cross, 1994, Wittenberg U., 1995; DHL (hon.), Hebrew Union Coll., 1996. Ordained rabbi, 1953. Asst. rabbi Temple Emanuel, Worcester, Mass., 1953-56; assoc., rabbi Temple Emanuel, 1956-59; dir. New Eng. council Union Am. Hebrew Congregations, 1959-63, nat. dir. edn., 1963-67, v.p., 1967-72, pres.-elect, 1972, pres., 1973-96, pres. emeritus, 1996—; mem. exec. bd. Conf. Pres. Major Am. Jewish Orgns., 1967—, chmn., 1976-78; mem. exec. bd. Hebrew Union Coll./Jewish Inst. Religion, 1967-96; v.p. Meml. Found. for Jewish Culture, 1967—, chmn. exec. com., 1994-96, pres. 1996—; v.p. World Jewish Congress; mem. exec. com. World Zionist Orgn., 1973-96; mem. exec. com. Joint Distbn. Com., 1987—, sec., 1992-94; bd. govs. Hebrew Union Coll., 1973-96; v.p. World Union for Progressive Judaism. Author: From Discrimination to Extermination, 1950; lit. editor: CCAR Jour., 1959-63; founding editor: Dimensions, Reform Judaism's quar. religious thought, 1966—; editor: Reform Judaism's graded text book series, 1963-67. Served with AUS, 1943-46. Decorated Bronze Star, Purple Heart; recipient Solomon Bublick prize Hebrew U. Jerusalem, 1978; Townsend Harris medal CCNY, 1979. Mem. Am. Assn. Jewish Edn. (exec. bd. 1963-67), Ctrl. Conf. Am. Rabbis (exec. bd. 1967-96). Home: 6 River Ln Westport CT 06880-1925 Office: Union Am Hebrew Congregations 838 5th Ave New York NY 10021-7012 *To live life fully, clinging to its many gifts with all my might—and then, paradoxically, to let go when life compels us to surrender what it gave.*

SCHINDLER, BARBARA FRANCOIS, school administrator; b. Chgo., Oct. 28, 1935; d. Harry and Nellie Irene (Lewis) Francois; m. Charles A. Schindler, Jan. 29, 1955; children: Marian, Susan, Neal. BA, U. Tex., 1960; MA, U. Okla., 1975, PhD, 1984. Cert. tchr., Okla. Tchr. Norman (Okla.) Pub. Schs., 1972-86; exec. dir. Dem. Party Okla., Oklahoma City, 1986-87; tchr. Moore (Okla.) Pub. Schs., 1987-88; curriculum supr. Oklahoma City Pub. Schs., 1988—; mem. sch. bd. Moore-Norman Vocat.-Tech. Sch., Norman, 1979-83; bd. dirs. Law-Related Edn., Oklahoma City; chair Okla. Close-Up, Oklahoma City, 1990-92; community planner U.S.-Japan Ednl. Initiative, 1993. Contbr. chpt. to book For the Man, the Myth and the Era, 1987; author: (supplementary materials) The Oklahoma Story, 1980. Nat. Del. Dem. Party Conv., N.Y.C., 1980, Atlanta, 1988; county party chair Dem. Party, Cleveland County, 1985-87. Recipient Excellence in Teaching award Profl. Educators, 1975; Fulbright fellow, 1992, NEH fellow, 1988; grantee Japan Study Tour Found., 1990. Mem. ASCD, Nat. Coun. for Social Studies (com. mem. 1988—), Nat. Coun. for Econ. Edn. (bd. dirs. 1990—), Okla. Edn. Assn. (bd. dirs. 1978-85), Phi Delta Kappa. Avocations: bridge, hiking. Home: 2000 Morgan Dr Norman OK 73069-6525

SCHINDLER, CHARLES ALVIN, microbiologist, educator; b. Boston, Dec. 27, 1924; s. Edward Esau and Esther Marian (Weisman) S.; m. Barbara Jean Francois, Jan. 14, 1955; children: Marian Giffin, Susan, Neal. BS in Biology, Rensselaer Poly. Inst., 1950; MS, U. Tex., 1956, PhD, 1961. Commd. officer USAF, 1951, advanced through grades to maj., 1965; asst. dir. for biology and medicine at atomic weapons tests Armed Forces Spl. Weapons Project, Camp Mercury, Nev., 1953; rsch. scientist USAF, 1954-68; tchr. Norman (Okla.) Pub. Schs., 1968-86; asst. prof. U. Okla., Flagler Coll., 1968-86; cons., sci. supr. Oklahoma City (Okla.) Sch. Dist., 1989-93; cons. Mead Johnson Rsch. Ctr., Evansville, Ind., 1962-72. Contbr. articles to profl. jours. Coun. mem. Norman (Okla.) City Coun., 1967-81, 83-85. Fellow Charles E. Lewis Fellowship Com., Austin, Tex., 1958; rsch. grantee NSF, Norman, 1972. Mem. Soc. Gen. Microbiology, Sigma Xi. Achievements include U.S. and foreign patents on the bacteriolytic agent Lysost aphin. Avocations: electronics, photography, bridge. Home: 2000 Morgan Dr Norman OK 73069

SCHINDLER, DONALD WARREN, biopharmaceutical engineer, consultant; b. Westfield, N.J., Apr. 2, 1925; s. Wilbur Vincent and Francis Lillian (Hollberg) S.; m. Scot N. Stahl, Sept. 7, 1947 (div. Aug. 1971); children: Leslie, Mark, Wendy (dec. 1971); m. Gail Robertson Hoff, July 26, 1972 (div. Dec. 1975); m. Dorothy Jean Martin, July 1, 1980; children: William, Bruce, Judy, Patricia, Donna, Holly, Larry. AB in Biol. Scis., Marietta (Ohio) Coll.; postgrad., Rutgers U. Dir. biol. mfg. Ortho Pharm. Corp., Raritan, N.J., 1951-59; mgr. biol. mfg. Warner-Lambert Pharm. Co., Morris Plains, N.J., 1959-74; gen. mgr. Fisher Sci. Diagnostics Div., Orangeburg, N.Y., 1978-82; pres. SRC Assocs., Park Ridge, N.J., 1974-94, Schindler Assocs., Montvale, N.J., 1994—; mem. adv. bd. Okla. Immunological Labs., Oklahoma City, 1972-78; cons. Serono Labs., Inc., Boston, 1982-91, U. Minn., Mpls., 1984-91, Ares Applied Rsch. N.V. Gen., 1982-90. Pres. Passaic Twp. Sch. Bd., Stirling, N.J., 1964-70; trustee 1st Congl. Ch., Park Ridge, N.J., 1987-90; deacon 1st Presbyn. Ch., Myersville, N.J., 1968-71; regional dir. tng. Boy Scouts Am. Watchung Area coun., Plainfield, N.J., 1968-71. With USNR, 1942-46, PTO. Mem. VFW, Am. Chem. Soc., Am. Inst. Chemists, Am. Legion, N.Y. Acad. Scis., Newcomen Soc., Parenteral Drug Assn., Internat. Soc. Pharm. Engrs., U.S. Equestrian Team, Am. Horse Shows Assn., U.S. Combined Tng. Assn., Pharms. Mfg. Assn., Beta Beta Beta, Alpha Sigma Phi. Republican. Office: Schindler Assocs Ste 101 150 Upper Saddle River Rd Montvale NJ 07645-1027

SCHINDLER, JUDI(TH KAY), public relations executive, marketing consultant; b. Chgo., Nov. 23, 1941; d. Gilbert G. and Rosalie (Karlin) Cone; m. Jack Joel Schindler, Nov. 1, 1964; 1 child, Adam Jason. BS in Journalism, U. Ill., 1964. Assoc. editor Irving Cloud Publs., Lincolnwood, Ill., 1963-64; asst. dir. publicity Israel Bond Campaign, Chgo., 1965-69; v.p. pub. relations Realty Co. of Am., Chgo., 1969-70; dir. pub. relations Pvt. Telecommunications, Chgo., 1970-78; pres. Schindler Communications, Chgo., 1978—; del. White House Conf. on Small Bus., Washington, 1980, 86; mem. adv. bd. Entrepreneurship Inst., Chgo., 1988-92. Bd. dirs. Family Matters Comty. Ctr.; mem. Chgo. bd. Roosevelt U.; leader luncheon coun. YWCA, Chgo., 1987, 89-90, 92; appointee small bus. com. Ill. Devel. Bd., 1988-89. Named Nat. Women in Bus. Adv. SBA, 1986, Chgo. Woman Bus. Owner of Yr., Continental Bank and Nat. Assn. Women Bus. Owners, 1989, Ill. Finalist Entrepreneur of Yr. award, 1991, 92. Mem. Nat. Assn. Women Bus. Owners (pres. Chgo. chpt. 1980-81, nat. v.p. membership 1988-89), Small Bus. United of Ill., Publicity Club Chgo., Alpha Epsilon Phi. Office: Schindler Comm 500 N Clark St Chicago IL 60610-4202

SCHINDLER, KEITH WILLIAM, software engineer; b. Selma, Calif., May 27, 1959; s. George Junior and Doris Angelynn (Young) S. BSEE in Computer Sci. with honors, U. Calif., Berkeley, 1982. Programmer Summit Group, Berkeley, 1979-81; jr. programmer Control Data, Inc., Sunnyvale, Calif., 1983; assoc. mem. tech. staff Symbolics, Inc., Chatsworth, Calif., 1987-88; sr. mem. tech. support Graphics div. Symbolics, L.A., 1988-90; software engr. Sidley, Wright & Assoc., Hollywood, Calif., 1990-92; cons. Out-Takes, Inc., L.A., 1992—; pres. Schindler Imaging Inc., San Jose, Calif., 1997—; tech. dir. Sidley-Wright & Assoc., Hollywood, 1990-92, Movie Time Cable Channel, Hollywood, 1990, Video Image, Marina Del Rey, Calif., 1990; cert. developer Apple Computer, Inc., 1991—, Truevision, Inc., 1990—; developer software Out-Takes' Digital Photography System; dir. software applications devel. Pixera Corp., Los Gatos, Calif., 1997—, project leader, Cupertino, Calif., 1995-96. Patentee in field. Mem. Soc. Motion Picture and TV Engrs., Tau Beta Pi. Democrat. Avocations: mountain biking, hiking, chess, racquetball. Office: Schindler Imaging 14580 Story Rd San Jose CA 95127-3446

SCHINDLER, MARVIN SAMUEL, foreign language educator; b. Boston, Jan. 2, 1932; s. Edward Esau and Esther Marian (Wiseman) S.; m. Roslyn Frances Abt, Aug. 11, 1974; children: Daniel Mark, Lore Elaine, Inge-Marie, Neal Elliott. B.A., U. Mass., 1953; M.A., Ohio State U., 1955, Ph.D., 1965. Instr. German Pa. State U., Pottsville, 1955-59; asst. prof. Ohio State U., 1965-67; asso. prof. German, asso. dean Grad. Sch. Arts and Scis., U. Va., Charlottesville, 1967-71; prof. German, chmn. dept. fgn. langs. No. Ill. U., DeKalb, 1971-74; prof. German, chmn. dept. Romance and Germanic langs. and lits. Wayne State U., Detroit, 1974-83; dir. Jr. Yr. in Germany Programs Wayne State U., 1975—. Author: The Sonnets of Andreas Gryphius, 1971; asso. editor: German Quar, 1971-78. Fulbright fellow, 1961-62; ehrensenator Albert-Ludwigs Universität, Freiburg;Bundesverdienstkreuz, 1. Klasse, Fed. Republic of Germany. Mem. Am. Assn. Tchrs. German (exec. council), MLA, Assn. Depts. Fgn. Langs. (exec. com., pres. 1981), Midwest Modern Lang. Assn. Home: 10075 Lincoln Dr Huntington Wd MI 48070-1507 Office: 487 Manoogian Hall Wayne State Univ Detroit MI 48202

SCHINDLER, PESACH, rabbi, educator, author; b. Munich, Germany, Apr. 11, 1931; came to U.S., 1940; s. Alexander Moshe and Esther (Zwickler) S.; m. Shulamith Feldman, June 30, 1954; children: Chaya, Gita, Meyer, Nechama, Avi. BA, CCNY Bklyn. Coll., 1953; MS, Yeshiva U., 1964; PhD, NYU, 1972; D Pedagogy (hon.), Jewish Theol. Sem., N.Y.C., 1987. Ordained rabbi, 1956. Dir. edn. Congregation Adath Israel, Toronto, Ont., Can., 1959-65; asst. dir. edn. United Synagogue of Am., N.Y.C., 1965-72; dir. Ctr. for Conservative Judaism United Synagogue of Am., Jerusalem, 1972—; asst. prof. Hebrew U., Jerusalem, 1975—; faculty U. Toronto Sch. Theology Jewish Studies Program in Jerusalem, 1986—, Sem. Jewish Studies, Jerusalem, 1988—; mem. internat. bd. Yad Vashem, Jerusalem, 1980—. Author: Hasidic Responses to the Holocaust in the Light of Hasidic Thought, 1990; contbr. numerous articles to profl. jours. Founding mem. Hebrew U. Orch., Jerusalem, 1988. Mem. Rabbinical Assembly (rabbinic ct. on conversion 1988-92, com. on Jewish law 1990-93), Educators Assembly, Jerusalem Long Distance Running Club (chmn. 1984-87). Office: United Synagogue Conservative Judaism, PO Box 7456, Jerusalem 94205, Israel *Therfore faith is confrontation with the incredulous and with doubt. The struggle for redemption is therefore confrontation with the non-redemptive. Both represent a form of creation ex-nihilo—a marvelous gift from the Almighty to even the humblest human being, His partner in the constant drama in the response to life.*

SCHINDLER, WILLIAM STANLEY, retired public relations executive; b. Detroit, Jan. 4, 1933; s. William Henry and Katherine (Schilling) S. Student, Wayne State U., 1950-53. Sr. v.p. Campbell-Ewald Co., Warren, Mich., 1968-85; v.p. pub. rels. Detroit Med. Ctr., 1985-92; interim v.p. Wayne State U., Detroit, 1993; cons. to bus., univs., and founds.; v.p. Sandusky Pub. Co., Mich. Editor: Progress Report-New Detroit, Inc, 1969. Past mem. Detroit Hist. Commn., Detroit Fire Commn.; chmn. Detroit CSC; past pres. Detroit Hist. Soc., Hist. Soc. Mich.; mem. Gov's. Sesquicentennial Commn.; bd. dirs. Adult Well-Being Svcs., Sacred Heart Rehab. Ctr., Brush Park Devel. Authority, Harper Hosp. Aux. With U.S. Army. 1954-56. Decorated Commendation Medal with pendant. Mem. Pub. Rels. Soc. Am., Adcraft Club Detroit, Detroit Press Club, Soms Whiskey Rebellion, Recess Club, Univ. Club, Detroit Athletic Club, Prismatic Club, Box 12 Club. Home: 8741 W Wescott Dr Peoria AZ 85382-3694

SCHINK, FRANK EDWARD, electrical engineer; b. N.Y.C., May 14, 1922; s. Frank and Elizabeth (Kreps) S.; m. Barbara Jean McCally, Oct. 26, 1946; children: Stephen Frank, Thomas Ross. BEE, Bklyn. Poly. (now Poly. U. N.Y.), 1952, MEE, 1955. Registered profl. engr., N.Y., N.J. Elec. engr. George G. Sharp, Naval Architect, N.Y.C., 1940-43, 45, Anaconda Co., N.Y.C., 1946-59, Anaconda-Jurden Assocs., N.Y.C., 1959-61; sr. engr. M.W. Kellogg Co., N.Y.C., 1961-62; sr. engr. Port Authority of N.Y. & N.J., N.Y.C., 1962-77, cons. engr., 1977-84, chief elec. engr., 1984-89; pvt. practice elec. cons. Cranford, N.J., 1989—; mem. various coms. ELECTRO Confs., 1976-96, past bd. dirs.; mem. adv. coun. N.J. Union County Transp., Westfield, 1977-79; mem. Port Authority Maintenance Improvement coun., N.Y.C., 1979-80; mem. com. IEEE Vehicular Tech. Conf., 1993; lectr. seminars Internat. Elec. Exposition and Congress, 1986, 87, Power Engrng. Soc. Chpts. Cong., 1996. Author/editor: Environmental Impact Assessment, 1977; contbr. articles to profl. jours. Pres. Brookside Civic Assn., Cranford, 1960-62; chmn. Cub Scout and Boy Scouts Troops, Cranford, 1960-65; capt. United Fund, Cranford, 1962; tchr. Am. Coun. for Emigres, N.Y.C., 1975. With U.S. Army, 1943-45, ETO. Fellow IEEE (vice chmn. region I 1986-87; chmn. N.Y. sect. 1984-85, vice chmn. 1982-84, treas. 1981-82, editor N.Y. sect. Monitor 1989-90, life mem. com. 1994-97; also various coms.); mem. IEEE Power Engring Soc. (ad com. 1978-87, exec. com. 1983-87, chpts. rep. 1976-80, chmn. Winter Power Confs., N.Y. 1990—), IEEE Industry Applications Soc. (coun. mem. 1977-90), Tau Beta Pi, Eta Kappa Nu. Republican. Methodist. Home and Office: 14 Middlebury Ln Cranford NJ 07016-1622

SCHINK, JAMES HARVEY, lawyer; b. Oak Park, Ill., Oct. 2, 1943; s. Norbert F. and Gwendolyn H. (Hummel) S.; m. Lisa Wilder Haskell, Jan. 1, 1972 (div. 1980); children—David, Caroline, Elizabeth; m. April Townley, Aug. 14, 1982. BA, Yale U., 1965, JD, 1968. Bar: Ill. 1968, Colo. 1982. Assoc. Sidley & Austin, Chgo., 1968; law clk. to judge U.S. Ct. Appeals, Chgo., 1968-69; assoc. Kirkland & Ellis, Chgo., 1969-72, ptnr., 1972—. Sustaining fellow Art Inst. Chgo. Mem. ABA, Ill. Bar Assn., Chgo. Bar Assn., Chgo. Club, Univ. Club, Saddle and Cycle Club, Mid-Am. Club, Econ. Club of Chgo., Chgo. Yacht Club, Denver Athletic Club, Vail Racquet Club, Yale Club of N.Y.C., Point O' Woods Golf and Tennis Club (Benton Harbor, Mich.). Republican. Presbyterian. Home: Apt 408 480 N McClurg Ct Chicago IL 60611 Office: Kirkland & Ellis 200 E Randolph St Ste 6100 Chicago IL 60601-6436

SCHINKEL, CLAUS, chemical company executive; b. Mexico City, July 27, 1925; s. Claus and Erna (Gautier) S.; m. Helga Elisabeth Dobler, Dec. 10, 1949 (div. July 1965); children: Susana, Hildegard, Ingrid, Claus-Werner; m. Dulce Maria Garcia-de-Presno, Oct. 28, 1977. Degree in chem. engring., U. Nacional Autonoma Mex., 1948. Mgr. Schinkel, S.A., Mexico City, 1949-57; CEO, dir. Consultores Industriales, S.A., Mexico City, 1957-77, Depositos Unidos, S.A. de C.V., Mexico City, 1957-92, Tecnica Quimica, S.a. de C.V., Mexico City, 1957-96, Grupo T.Q. Asesores, S.A. de C.V., Mexico City, 1988-96. Mem. Soc. Exalumnos de Facultad de Quimica, Colegio Aleman Alexander von Humboldt, A.C., Rotary Club (pres. Ajusco Pedregal Club 1989-90). Lutheran. Avocations: tennis, archeology. Home: Fuego 31, 01900 Mexico City Mexico Office: High Purity De Mexico, Calle Diez # 123, 09070 Mexico City Mexico

SCHINNERER, ALAN JOHN, entrepreneur; b. Long Beach, Calif., June 8, 1925; s. Walter John and Esther Schinnerer; m. Barbara Elaine Daniger, Aug. 17, 1951 (div. Aug. 1971); children: Gregory, Scott, Brett, Vicky. AA, Long Beach City Coll., 1948; B of Elec. Engring., U. So. Calif., 1952, postgrad. law, 1956-57, postgrad. bus., 1958-59. Purchasing agt. McCulloch Corp., Los Angeles, 1952-56; systems engr. Hughes Aircraft Co., Culver City, Calif., 1956-59; sales engr. Gilfillan Corp., Los Angeles, 1959-61; mktg. specialist N.Am. Rockwell Corp., Downey, Calif., 1961-68; sr. project engr. Hughes Aircraft Co., El Segundo, Calif., 1968-74, dir. satellite tests, 1974-76, assoc. program mgr., 1976-84; pres., owner, founder Calif. Classic Boats, Long Beach, Calif., 1979—; founding ptnr. Looking Glass Cellars, Murrieta, Calif., 1995—. Author: (catalog) Parts for Antique and Classic Chirs-Craft, Dodge, Gar Wood and Hacker runabouts, 1979-96. Bd. dirs. Antique Powercraft Hist. Soc., 1984-85. Served with USN, 1943-46, PTO. Mem. Antique and Classic Boat Soc. (founding pres. So. Calif. chpt. 1983-86), Garwood Soc., Delta Tau Delta. Republican. Clubs: Chris-Craft Antique Boat, Porsche of Am., Tahoe Yacht, Sierra. Home: 5581 Ridgebury Dr Huntington Beach CA 92649-4825 Office: Calif Classic Boats 3267 E Grant St Long Beach CA 90804-1212

SCHIPPER, MERLE, art historian and critic, exhibition curator; b. Toronto, Ont., Can.; came to U.S., 1943; d. Leon J. and Libby (Genesove) Solway; m. Bernard Schipper, May 22, 1943 (div. Jan. 1980); children: Lee, Amy Schipper Howe. BA, U. Toronto, 1943; MA, UCLA, 1970, PhD, 1974. Instr. extension UCLA, 1974-78, 83-84, lectr. summer session, 1977-79, 84; vis. artist grad. sch. Claremont (Calif.) U., 1979; lectr. U. So. Calif., L.A., 1985; corr. L.A. ARTNews, N.Y.C., 1985-87; columnist ARTScene, L.A., 1987—; project dir. Santa Monica (Calif.) Arts Found., 1987-89; art book reviewer L.A. Daily News, 1990-91; organizer Congress Internat. Assn. Art Critics, 1991; mem. pub. art panel Santa Monica Arts Commn., 1966—; mem. artist selection panel Met. Transp. Assn., Chinatown Sta., 1993. Panelist, mem. grants com. Art Orgn. Dept. Cultural Affairs, L.A., 1984-85; mem. selection com. of sculpture installation Calif. Med. Ctr., L.A., 1986; mem. Rev. Com. Hist. Resources Survey Project, L.A., 1978-85, So. Calif. Com. for Contemporary Art Documentation, L.A., 1985-89. Rsch. fellow Indo-U.S. Subcommn., 1988; travel grantee Ptnrs. of Ams., 1989. Mem. Coll. Art Assn., Internat. Assn. Art Critics. Home and Office: # 6 10650 Eastborn Ave Los Angeles CA 90024

SCHIPPER, MICHAEL, academic administrator; b. N.Y.C., Nov. 26, 1942; s. Eddie and Gertrude S.; m. Janet Lynne Altmann, Nov. 1, 1947; children: Adam, Julie. AA, U. Houston, 1964, BS, 1964; MA, Bradley U., 1968; postgrad., Harvard U., 1986-90. Dir. human resources Choate Symms Health Svcs., Arlington, Mass., 1981-85, Marlbrough (Mass.) Hosp., 1985-87, Sts. Meml. Med. Ctr., Lowell, Md., 1991-94; v.p. human resources Lakeshore Hosp., Manchester, N.H., 1987-91; v.p. Roger Williams U., Bristol, R.I., 1994—. With USMC. Mem. Squantum Assn., Bristol Yacht Club. Avocation: boating. Home: 86 Kickemuit Ave Bristol RI 02809-4404 Office: Roger Williams U 1 Old Ferry Rd Bristol RI 02809-2923

SCHIPPERS, DAVID PHILIP, lawyer; b. Chgo., Nov. 4, 1929; s. David Philip and Angela Marie (Lyons) S.; m. Jacquelin Joyce Liautaud, Apr. 19, 1952; children: David P. III, Kathleen M., Antoinette M., Ann L., Colleen M., Thomas M., Kevin D., Mary A., Patrick F., Peter A. BA, Loyola U., Chgo., 1955, JD, 1959. Bar: Ill. 1959, U.S. Dist. Ct. (no. dist.) Ill. 1959, U.S. Ct. Appeals (7th cir.) 1962, U.S. Supreme Ct., 1966, U.S. Dist. Ct. (so. dist.) Ill. 1973, U.S. Ct. Appeals (9th cir.) 1976, U.S. Ct. Claims 1979, U.S. Ct. Appeals (3d, 4th, 6th, 8th cirs.) 1981, U.S. Ct. Appeals (fed. cir.) 1983, Wis. 1985, U.S. Ct. Mil. Appeals 1987. Service rep. Ill. Bell Telephone Co., Chgo., 1950-59; assoc. Pope, Ballard, Uriell, Kennedy, Shepard & Fowle, Chgo., 1959-62; asst. atty. U.S. Dept. Justice, Chgo., 1962-63, spl. asst. atty. gen., 1963-64, chief organized crime and racketeering sec., 1964-67; ptnr. Schippers & Bailey, Chgo., 1967—; adj. prof. Willamette U., Salem, Oreg., 1972—, Loyola U. Sch. Law, Chgo., 1972—; lectr. J.A.G. Sch., Maxwell AFB, Ala., 1988, 89. Active Cath. League Religious Freedom, Chgo., 1986—; Ill. Dept. Law Enforcement Merit Bd., Springfield, 1987-93; Ill. Crime Investigating Com., Chgo., 1969. Decorated knight Equestrian Order of the Holy Sepulchre, 1995—; recipient Alumni medal of Excellence, Loyola U., 1967, citation Loyola U. Alumni Assn., 1970. Mem. ABA, Fed. Bar Assn., Ill. Bar Assn., Chgo. Bar Assn., Am. Arbitration Assn., Am. Trial Lawyers Assn., Ill. Trial Lawyers Assn., Appellate Lawyers Assn., Nat. Assn. Criminal Def. Lawyers, Chgo. Crime Commn., Fed. Criminal Investigators Assn., Markey Inn of Ct. Club. Office: Schippers & Bailey 36th Fl 20 N Clark St Fl 36 Chicago IL 60602-4109

SCHIRBER, ANNAMARIE RIDDERING, speech and language pathologist, educator; b. Somerset County, N.J., Dec. 18, 1941; d. Pieter C. and Marie Louise (Kerk) Riddering; m. Eric R. Schirber, Aug. 25, 1960; children: Stefan Rene, Ashley Brooke. BA in Speech and Hearing Therapy, Rutgers U., 1964; MA in Edn. of Deaf and Hard of Hearing, Smith Coll., 1968; postgrad., Rutgers U., 1987-93. Cert. tchr. of deaf, hard of hearing, spl. edn., speech correctionist, speech-lang pathologist, N.J. Speech therapist Manatee County Bd. Edn., Bradenton, Fla., 1968-69; speech-lang. specialist Lawrence Twp. Pub. Schs., Lawrenceville, N.J., 1969—; adj. instr. comm. dept. Trenton (N.J.) State Coll., 1983-87; vis. lectr. Rutgers U., New Brunswick, 1993. Author: Teaching Auditory Processing Skills to Children, 1994; co-author: (with Erica Winebrenner) Speech Activities for Children, 1994, Language Activities to Teach Children at Home, 1994. Mem. exec. com. Women's Coll. Symposium, Princeton, N.J., 1982-84; mem. nat. alumnae admissions com. Smith Coll., Northampton, Mass., 1984-86. Grantee Lawrence Twpw. Bd. Edn., 1973, 89, 90. Mem. N.J. Speech-Lang. and Hearing Assn. (legis. com. 1996), Ctrl. Jersey Speech-Lang. and Hearing Assn. (exec. com. 1984, v.p. 1985, pres. 1986-87). Office: Lawrence Twp Pub Schs Princeton Pike Trenton NJ 08648

SCHIRMEISTER, CHARLES F., lawyer; b. Jersey City, June 18, 1929; s. Charles F. and Louise P. (Schneider) S.; m. Barbara Jean Fredericks, Feb. 9, 1952; children—Pamela, Charles Bradford. B.A., U. Mich., 1951; LL.B., Fordham U., 1956. Bar: N.Y. 1956, U.S. Dist. Ct. (so. dist) N.Y., U.S. Ct. Appeals (2d cir.), U.S. Supreme Ct. 1961. Asst. dist. atty. N.Y. County (N.Y.), 1956-61; assoc. Reid & Priest, N.Y.C., 1961-71, ptnr., 1971-94; chmn. bd. trustees, deacon, Community Congregational Ch., Short Hills, N.J.; trustee Ocean Grove (N.J.) Camp Meeting Assn. Served to capt. USMC, 1951-53. Mem. ABA, N.Y. County Lawyers Assn., Fed. Bar Coun., Sigma Alpha Epsilon. Republican. Clubs: University (N.Y.C.), Canoe Brook Country Club (Summit, N.J.). Avocations: tennis, oenology, golf. Home: 15 Beechcroft Rd Short Hills NJ 07078-1648 Office: Reid & Priest 40 W 57th St New York NY 10019-4001

SCHIRN, JANET SUGERMAN, interior designer; b. Jersey City, N.Y.; d. Oscar H. and Mary (Lustig) S.; 1 child, Martha. BFA, Pratt Inst.; MFA, Columbia U.; postgrad. in Architecture, U. Ill. Tchr. N.Y.C. Bd. Edn.; dir. N.Y.C. Bd. Adult Edn.; pres. Janet Schirn Design Group, Chgo., N.Y.C., 1950—; prin. The J S Collection, N.Y.C., 1978—; adj. prof. So. Ill. U., 1991-92; mem. adv. bd. Du Pont Co., Monsanto, 1981-89, So. Ill. U., 1990-95. Contbr. articles to interior design mag. Bd. dirs. Washington Archtl. Forum, 1992-96, Chgo. Archtl. Assistance Ctr., 1975, pres., 1982; adv. bd. mem. Mundelein Coll. dept. interior architecture, 1978; mem. Met. Planning Coun., Chgo., 1980—, Art Resources Tchg., 1984-95—; mem. aux. bd. Sch. of Art Ins., Ill. Arts Alliance, 1992—. Recipient award Chgo. Lighting Inst., 1989, 92, 93, 95, Villeroy and Boch gold award, 1990, Designer mag. residential award, 1990, Edward Fields 1st prize Rug Design, 1981, 91, 1st prize project awards ASID, 1993, 95, 96. Mem. UNESCO (steering com. tall bldgs. and urban habitat coun.), Am. Soc. Interior Designers (nat. pres. 1986, nat. treas. 1984, regional v.p. 1981, pres. Ill. chpt. 1977-78, nat. dir. 1979-83, chmn. pub. affairs 1989), Illuminating Engring. Soc., Am. Inst. Architects (nat. urban planning and design com. 1981-85), Chgo. Network, Internat. Fedn. Interior Designers (exec. bd. dirs. 1992-96). Home: 220 E Walton St Chicago IL 60611-1534 Office: Janet Schirn Design Group 401 N Franklin St Chicago IL 60610-4400 also: 521 5th Ave New York NY 10175 also: 821 Delaware Ave SW Washington DC 20024-4207

SCHIRO, JAMES J., brokerage house executive; m. Tomasina Schiro; 2 children. Grad., St. John's U., D of Comml. Sci. (hon.), 1995; grad., Amos Tuck Sch. Exec. Program. With Price Waterhouse, 1967—, ptnr., 1979, chmn. mining spl. svcs. group, 1979-88, nat. dir. merger and acquisitions svcs., vice chmn., mng. ptnr. N.Y. met. region; mng. ptnr. Price Waterhouse, N.Y.C.; chmn., sr. ptnr. Price Waterhouse LLP, N.Y.C.; mem. U.S. Firm's Mgmt. com., World Firm's Gen. Coun.; bd. govs. World Econ. Forum; treas., exec. com. U.S. Coun. for Internat. Bus.; chairperson Bus. Improvement Dist. task force N.Y.C. Partnership/C. of C. econ. devel. com.; mem. leadership com. Lincoln Ctr. Consolidated Corp. Fund. Mem. leadership com. Lincoln Ctr. Consolidated Corp. Fund; mem. N.Y. steering com. Accts. Coalition on Liability Refor; chairperson fin. com., bd. trustees McCarter Theatre, Princeton, N.J. Recipient Ellis Island Medal of Honor, 1994, St. John's U. Alumni Pietas medal, 1992, Avenue of the Americas Assn.'s Gold Key award, 1992. Mem. AICPA, N.Y. State Soc. of Pub. Accts., Regional Plan Assn. (bd. dirs.). Office: Price Waterhouse LLP 1177 Avenue Of The Americas New York NY 10036-2714

SCHIRRA, WALTER MARTY, JR., business consultant, former astronaut; b. Hackensack, N.J., Mar. 12, 1923; s. Walter Marty and Florence (Leach) S.; m. Josephine Cook Fraser, Feb. 23, 1946; children: Walter Marty III, Suzanne Karen. Student, Newark Coll. Engring., 1940-42; B.S., U.S. Naval Acad., 1945; D. Astronautics (hon.), Lafayette Coll., U. So. Calif., N.J. Inst. Tech. Commd. ensign U.S. Navy, 1945, advanced through grades to capt., 1965; designated naval aviator, 1948; service aboard battle cruiser Alaska, 1945-46; service with 7th Fleet, 1946; assigned Fighter Squadron 71, 1948-51; exchange pilot 154th USAF Fighter Bomber Squadron, 1951; engaged in devel. Sidewinder missile China Lake, Calif., 1952-54; project pilot F7U-3 Cutlass; also instr. pilot F7U-3 Cutlass and FJ3 Fury, 1954-56; ops. officer Fighter Squadron 124, U.S.S. Lexington, 1956-57; assigned Naval Air Safety Officer Sch., 1957, Naval Air Test Ctr., 1958-59; engaged in suitability devel. work F4H, 1958-59; joined Project Mercury, man-in-space, NASA, 1959; pilot spacecraft Sigma 7 in 6 orbital flight, Oct. 1962; in charge operations and tng. Astronaut Office, 1964-69; command pilot Gemini 6 which made rendezvous with target, Gemini 7, Dec. 1965; comdr. 11 day flight Apollo 7, 1968; ret., 1969; pres. Regency Investors, Inc., Denver, 1969-70; chmn., chief exec. officer ECCO Corp., Englewood, Colo., 1970-73; chmn. Sernco, Inc., 1973-74; with Johns-Manville Corp., Denver, 1974-77; v.p. devel. Goodwin Cos., Inc., Littleton, Colo., 1978-79; ind. cons., 1979-80; dir. Kimberly Clark, 1983-91. Decorated D.F.C.(3), Air medal (2), Navy D.S.M.; recipient Distinguished Service medal (2) NASA, Exceptional Service medal. Fellow Am. Astronautical Soc., Soc. Exptl. Test Pilots. Home and Office: PO Box 73 Rancho Santa Fe CA 92067-0073

SCHISGAL, MURRAY JOSEPH, playwright; b. N.Y.C., Nov. 25, 1926; s. Abraham and Irene (Sperling) S.; m. Reene Schapiro, June 29, 1958; children: Jane, Zachary. Student, Bklyn. Conservatory of Music, 1948, L.I. U., 1950; LLB, Bklyn. Law Sch., 1953; BA, New Sch. Social Research, 1959.

Author: The Typists and The Tiger, London, 1960, N.Y.C., 1963, Ducks and Lovers, London, 1961, Knit One, Purl Two, Boston, 1963, Luv (One of the Best Plays of 1964-65), London, 1963, N.Y.C., 1964, Fragments, Windows and other plays, 1965, Best Short Plays, 1981, 83, 85; contbr. to Best Short American Plays 1994-1995; original TV plays The Love Song of Barney Kempinski, 1966, Natasha Kovolina Pipishinski, 1976; off-Broadway Fragments, 1967, The Basement, 1967; Jimmy Shine, 1968, 69, Shooting Towards the Millinneum, 1997, Playtime, 1997; Broadway The Chinese, N.Y.C., 1970 (pub. in Best Short Plays of the World Theatre 1973), Dr. Fish, 1970, An American Millionaire, 1974, All Over Town, 1974 (pub. Best Plays 1974-75); screenplay The Tiger Makes Out, 1967, The Pushcart Peddlers, prod. off-off-Broadway, 1979; novel Days and Nights of a French Horn Player, 1980, Walter and the Flatulist; prod. off-Broadway The Downstairs Boys, 1980, The Songs of War, 1989; prod. regional theatre A Need for Brussels Sprouts, 1981, Play Time, Denver Ctr. Theatre, 1991, The Japanese Foreign Trade Minister, Cleve. Playhouse, 1992, 74 Georgia Ave., 1992, Circus Life, 1992; prod. Broadway Twice Around the Park, 1982; Other Plays, 1983, Closet Madness and Other Plays, 1984, Popkins, Paris, 1990, Play Time, 1991, The Songs of War, 1989; prod. Off Broadway The New Yorkers, 1984, Circus Life, 1995; prodr. Extensions, 1994; co-author: screenplay Tootsie (Winner Los Angeles Film Critics, N.Y. Film Critics, Nat. Soc. Film Critics, Writers Guild Am. award for best comedy); author Luv and Other Plays, 1983, The Rabbi and the Toyota Dealer, 1985, Jealousy, There are No Sacher Tortes in Our Society, 1985, Old Wine in a New Bottle, 1987, Road Show, 1987, Man Dangling, 1988, Oatmeal and Kisses, 1990, (with others) Best Short American Plays of 1991, 92-93, Sexaholics and Other Plays, 1995, Extensions, 1994, Circus Life, 1995, The Artist and The Modul (Best Am. Short Play), 1994-95, Play Time (Published by Dramatists Play Svc., 1997). Recipient Vernon Rice award otustanding achievement off-Broadway Theatre, 1963; Outer Circle award Outstanding Theatre, 1963; named Outstanding Playwright, 1963. Office: care Arthur B Greene Internat Creative Mgmt 101 Park Ave Fl 43 New York NY 10178

SCHIZER, ZEVIE BARUCH, lawyer; b. Bklyn., Dec. 19, 1928; s. David and Bertha (Rudavsky) S.; m. Hazel Gerber, Aug. 23, 1962; children: Deborah Gail, Miriam Anne, David Michael. BA magna cum laude, NYU, 1950; JD, Yale U., 1953. Bar: N.Y. 1954, U.S. Dist. Ct. (so. and ea. dist.) N.Y. 1959, U.S. Ct. Appeals (2d cir.) 1959, U.S. Supreme Ct. 1959. Assoc. Guzik & Boukstein, N.Y.C., 1953-54; teaching fellow NYU Sch. Law, 1954-55; assoc. Philips, Nizer, Benjamin & Krim, N.Y.C., 1955-56, Aranow, Brodsky, Einhorn & Dann, N.Y.C., 1956-57; asst. counsel jud. inquiry Appellate Divsn. 2nd Dept., Bklyn., 1957-62; assoc. Hays, Porter, Spanier & Curtis, N.Y.C., 1963-68, ptnr., 1968-85; sec. United Aircraft Products, Inc., Dayton, Ohio, 1970-83; ptnr. Schizer & Schizer, N.Y.C., 1985—. Trustee Bklyn. Pub. Libr., 1966—, pres. 1985-88, N.Y. Young Dem. Club, N.Y.C., 1960-61; trustee East Midwood Jewish Ctr., Bklyn., 1991—. Mem. N.Y. County Lawyers Assn. (mem. profl. ethics com., mem. com. on profl. discipline), Phi Beta Kappa. Democrat. Jewish. Home: 1134 E 23rd St Brooklyn NY 11210-4519 Office: Schizer & Schizer 3 New York Plz New York NY 10004-2442

SCHLAFER, DONALD HUGHES, veterinary pathologist; b. Sidney, N.Y., July 15, 1948; s. Donald Hughes and Mildred (Gamewell) S., Jr.; m. Judith Ann Appleton, Aug. 2, 1980; children: Nathan James, Russell Matthew. BS, Cornell U., 1971, MS, 1975; DVM, N.Y. State Coll. Vet. Medicine, Ithaca, 1974; PhD, Coll. Vet. Medicine, Athens, Ga., 1982. Diplomate Am. Coll. Vet. Pathologists, Am. Coll. Theriogenologists (exec. com. 1993-96), Am. Coll. Vet. Microbiologists. Gen. practice vet. medicine Guilderland Animal Hosp., Altamont, N.Y., 1975-77; resident dept. vet. pathology U. Ga., Athens, 1977-79; research pathologist USDA Plum Island Animal Disease Ctr., Greenport, N.Y., 1975-82; asst. prof. dept. vet. pathology Cornell U., Ithaca, 1982-88, assoc. prof., 1988-97, prof. comparative reproductive pathology, 1997—, dir. Bovine Research Ctr., 1982-91; cons. in field, 1983—. Contbr. articles to profl. publs. Mem. AVMA, Soc. for Study of Reprodn., Soc. for Theriogenology (exec. com. 1993-96). Office: T6016 Coll Vet Medicine Cornell U Ithaca NY 14853

SCHLAFLY, HUBERT JOSEPH, JR., communications executive; b. St. Louis, Aug. 14, 1919; s. Hubert J. and Mary Ross (Parker) S.; m. Leona Martin, June 12, 1944. B.S. in Elec. Engring, U. Notre Dame, 1941; post-grad., Syracuse U. extension, 1946-47. Electronics engr. Gen. Electric Co., Schenectady, 1941-44, Syracuse, 1946-47; project engr. Radiation Lab., Mass., Inst. Tech., 1944-45; dir. TV research 20th Century-Fox Film Corp., N.Y.C., 1947-51; a founder Teleprompter Corp., N.Y.C., 1951, v.p., 1951-74, pres., 1971-72, exec. v.p. tech. devel., 1972-74; pres. Transponder Corp., Greenwich, 1977-86; chmn., chief exec. officer Portel Services Corp., 1984-86; chmn., pres. Portel Services Network, Inc., 1987-91, chmn. bd., 1991—; cons. in field; industry coord., chmn. exec. com., cable tech. adv. com. FCC, 1972-75; adviser com. telecom. Nat. Acad. Engring.; advisor Sloan Commn. Cable Comms.; mem. engring. adv. coun. U. Notre Dame, 1977—, vice chmn., 1983, chmn., 1984; lectr. in field; dir., sec. Milbrook Corp., 1994—. Author: Computer in the Living Room. Bd. govs. Milbrook Club, 1993—. Recipient Engring. Honor award U. Notre Dame, 1976, Nat. Acad. T.V. Arts and Scis. Emmy award, 1992. Fellow Soc. Motion Picture and TV Engrs.; mem. IEEE (Delmer Ports award 1979, life), Nat. Cable TV Assn. (chmn. standards com. 1965-69, chmn. domestic satellite com. 1971-73, chmn. future svcs. com. 1972, assns. com. 1981, Outstanding Tech. Achievements award 1974), Cable TV Pioneers, Electronic Industries Assn. (chmn. broadband cable sect. 1971-73, founding chmn. broadband communications com.), Soc. Cable TV Engrs. (sr.), Fairfield Found. (hon.); named Notre Dame alumni Man of Yr., 1992. Roman Catholic. Clubs: Milbrook Country, Rotary (pres. Greenwich club 1991-92), Knights of Malta, Knight St. Gregory the Great. Patentee in field. Home and Office: 27 Orchard Dr Greenwich CT 06830-6711

SCHLAFLY, PHYLLIS STEWART, author; b. St. Louis, Aug. 15, 1924; d. John Bruce and Odile (Dodge) Stewart; m. Fred Schlafly, Oct. 20, 1949; children: John F., Bruce S., Roger S., Phyllis Liza Forshaw, Andrew L., Anne V. BA, Washington U., St. Louis, 1944, JD, 1978; MA, Harvard U., 1945; LLD, Niagara U., 1976. Bar: Ill. 1979, D.C. 1984, Mo. 1985, U.S. Supreme Ct. 1987. Syndicated columnist Copley News Svc., 1976—; pres. Eagle Forum, 1975—; broadcaster Spectrum, CBS Radio Network, 1973-78; commentator Cable TV News Network, 1980-83, Matters of Opinion sta. WBBM-AM, Chgo., 1973-75. Author, pub.: Phyllis Schlafly Report, 1967—; author: A Choice Not an Echo, 1964, The Gravediggers, 1964, Strike From Space, 1965, Safe Not Sorry, 1967, The Betrayers, 1968, Mindszenty The Man, 1972, Kissinger on the Couch, 1975, Ambush at Vladivostok, 1976, The Power of the Positive Woman, 1977, First Reader, 1994; editor: Child Abuse in the Classroom, 1984, Pornography's Victims, 1987, Equal Pay for Unequal Work, 1984, Who Will Rock the Cradle, 1989, Stronger Families or Bigger Government, 1990, Meddlesome Mandate: Rethinking Family Leave, 1991. Del. Rep. Nat. Conv., 1956, 64, 68, 84, 88, 92, 96, alt., 1960, 80; pres. Ill. Fedn. Rep. Women, 1960-64; 1st v.p. Nat. Fedn. Rep. Women, 1964-67; mem. Ill. Commn. on Status of Women, 1975-85; nat. chmn. Stop ERA, 1972—; mem. Ronald Reagan's Def. Policy Adv. Group, 1980; mem. Commn. on Bicentennial of U.S. Constn., 1985-91; mem. Adminstrv. Conf. U.S., 1983-86. Recipient 10 Honor awards Freedoms Found., Brotherhood award NCCJ, 1975; named Woman of Achievement in Pub. Affairs St. Louis Globe-Democrat, 1963, one of 10 most admired women in world Good Housekeeping poll, 1977-90. Mem. ABA, DAR (nat. chmn. Am. history 1965-68, nat. chmn. bicentennial com. 1967-70, nat. chmn. nat. def. 1977-80, 83-95), Ill. Bar Assn., Phi Beta Kappa, Pi Sigma Alpha. Office: Eagle Forum 7800 Bonhomme Ave Saint Louis MO 63105-1906

SCHLAGEL, RICHARD H., philosophy educator; b. Springfield, Mass., Nov. 22, 1925. BS in Pre-Med cum laude, Springfield Coll., 1949; MA in Philosophy, Boston U., 1952, PhD, 1955. Instr. philosophy Coll. of Wooster, 1954-55; instr. Clark U., 1955-56; asst. prof. George Washington U., 1956-62, assoc. prof., 1962-68, prof., 1968—, chmn. dept., 1965-69, 70-71, 77-83, named Elton prof. philosophy, 1986; sabbatical, Paris, with travel throughout Europe, 1962-63, 69-70, 76-77, 83-84, 90-91. Author: From Myth to Modern Mind: A Study of the Origins and Growth of Scientific Thought, vol. 1, Theogony through Ptolemy, vol. 2, 1995, Copernicus through Quantum Mechanics, 1996, Contextual Realism: A Metaphysical Framework for Modern Science, 1986; contbr. articles and reviews to profl. jours. Borden Parker Browne fellow, 1953-54. Mem. AAUP, Am. Philos. Assn., Washington Philosophy Club (v.p. 1964-65, pres. 1965-66). Office: George Washington U Dept Philosophy Washington DC 20052

SCHLAGER, SEYMOUR IRVING, physician; b. Hannover, Germany, Apr. 20, 1949; came to U.S., 1956; s. Conrad and Helen (Topol) S. BS, U. Ill., Chgo., 1969, MS, 1973, PhD, 1975; MD, U. Miami, Fla., 1985; JD, William H. Taft U., Santa Ana, Calif., 1997. Diplomate Nat. Bd. Med. Examiners, Am. Bd. Forensic Medicine. Rsch. scientist Nat. Cancer Inst., Bethesda, Md., 1975-80; assoc. prof. U. Notre Dame, Ind., 1980-83; resident in internal medicine U. Chgo., 1985-88; practicing physician Med. Care Group, Ltd., Skokie, Ill., 1988-89; head AIDS/antiviral venture Abbott Labs., Abbott Park, Ill., 1989-91; v.p. R&D Acad. Pharms., Inc., Lake Bluff, Ill., 1996—; dir. clin. studies divsn. pharmacology dept. medicine Chgo. Med. Sch., North Chicago, Ill., 1996—; mem. expert adv. bd. WHO, Geneva, 1981-83; physician cons. Ill. Dept. Rehab. Svcs., Springfield, Ill., 1988-89; bd. govs. Midwest Immunology Assn., Chgo., 1983-85. Author: Environmental Science and Technology, 1977, Clinical Management of Infectious Diseases, A Guide to Diagnosis and Therapy, 1997, Products Liability Law, A Review and Analysis, 1997; contbr. 187 articles to sci. and med. jours. Bd. dirs. Am. Cancer Soc., Indpls., 1980-83; mem. AMA-Physicians Against Domestic Violence, Chgo., 1992—. Recipient Honored Scientist award Chgo. Assn. Immunology, 1983. Mem. Am. Coll. Legal Medicine (physician assoc.), Am. Coll. Forensic Examiners (adv. bd. profl. stads. 1995—), Am. Soc. Law, Medicine and Ethics, Crescent Counties Found. for Med. Care. Republican. Jewish. Avocations: music, fitness, biking, tennis, reading. Office: Chgo Med Sch Dept Medicine Divsn Clin Pharmacology 3333 Green Bay Rd North Chicago IL 60064-3037 also: Acad Pharms 21 Skokie Valley Rd Lake Bluff IL 60044-1816

SCHLAGETER, ROBERT WILLIAM, museum administrator; b. Streator, Ill., May 10, 1925; s. Herman Pete and Ida (Ladtkow) S.; divorced; children—David Michael, Robert William. Diploma, Karl Ruprecht Univ., Heidelberg, Fed. Republic Germany, 1950; BA, U. Ill., 1950, MFA, 1957. Asst. prof. U. Tenn., Knoxville, 1952-58; dir. Mint Mus. Art, Charlotte, N.C., 1958-66; assoc. dir. Downtown Gallery, N.Y.C., 1966, Ackland Art Ctr., U. N.C., Chapel Hill, 1967-76; dir. Cummer Gallery Art, Jacksonville, Fla., 1976-92, dir. emeritus, 1992—; fine arts cons. corp. and pvt. collecting, 1993—. Author: (exhbn. catalogue) Winslow Homer's Florida, George Inness' Florida, Martin Johnson Heade Florida, Robert Henri-George Bellows. Served with U.S. Army, 1943-45, ETO. Home: 5201 Atlantic Blvd Apt 2 Jacksonville FL 32207-2473

SCHLAIFER, CHARLES, advertising executive; b. Omaha, July 1, 1909; s. Abraham Schlaifer; m. Evelyn Chaikin, June 10, 1934 (dec. Oct. 1978); children: Arlene Lois Silk, Roberta Semer; m. Ann Mesavage, July 31, 1980. Privately ed.; LittD (hon.), John F. Kennedy Coll., 1969. Newspaper reporter Omaha, 1926-29; advt. dir. Publix Tri-States Theatres, Nebr., Iowa, 1929-37; mng. dir. United Artists Theatres, San Francisco, 1937-42; nat. advt. cons. United Artists Prodrs., 1937-42; nat. advt. mgr. 20th Century-Fox Film Corp., N.Y.C., 1942-45; v.p. charge advt. and pub. rels. 20th Century-Fox Film Corp., 1945-49; pres. Charles Schlaifer & Co., Inc., N.Y.C., 1949—; vis. prof. New Sch. Social Rsch.; expert witness U.S. Congl. and Senatorial coms. on mental health, 1949—. Author: Advertising Code, Motion Picture Assn., 1948; co-author: Action for Mental Health, 1961, Heart's Work, 1991; contbr. articles to psychiat. jours. Mem. Pres.'s Com. Employment Handicapped, 1960—; founder, co-chmn. Nat. Mental Health Com., 1949-57; mem. nat. mental health adv. council Surgeon Gen. U.S., 1950-54; sec.-treas. Joint Commn. Mental Illness and Health, 1955-61; vice chmn. Found. Child Mental Welfare, 1963; mem. Gov.'s Youth Coun. State N.Y.; chmn. N.Y. State Mental Hygiene Facilities Improvement Corp., 1963—, White House Conf. Children, 1970; sec.-treas., bd. dirs. Joint Commn. Mental Health Children; chmn. N.Y. State Facilities Devel. Corp., 1963-78; mem. adv. council NIMH, 1976—; bd. dirs. Hillside Hosp., League Sch. For Seriously Disturbed Children, Menninger Found., Nat. Mental Hygiene Com. Recipient Social Conscience award Karen Horney Clinic, 1972; Hon. fellow Postgrad. Ctr. Mental Health. Fellow Am. Psychiat. Assn. (hon.), Brit. Royal Soc. Health (hon.), Am. Orthopsychiat. Assn. (hon.); Mem. Nat. Assn. Mental Health (founder), Acad. for Motion Picture Arts and Scis., Harmonie Club. Home and Office: 150 E 69th St New York NY 10021-5704

SCHLAIN, BARBARA ELLEN, lawyer; b. N.Y.C., May 28, 1948; d. William and Evelyn (Youdelman) S.; B.A., Wellesley Coll., 1969; M.A., Columbia U., 1970; J.D., Yale U., 1973. Bar: N.Y. 1974, U.S. Dist. Ct. (so. dist.) N.Y. 1974, U.S. Ct. Appeals (2d cir.) 1975, U.S. Dist. Ct. (ea. dist.) N.Y. 1977. Assoc. firm Donovan Leisure Newton & Irvine, N.Y.C., 1973-76, Graubard Moskovitz McGoldrick Dannett & Horowitz, N.Y.C., 1976-79; atty. McGraw-Hill, Inc., N.Y.C., 1979-80, asst. gen. counsel, 1980-86, v.p., assoc. gen. counsel, asst. sec., 1986—. sec. proprietary rights com. Info. Industry Assn., 1982-83. Author outlines Practicing Law Inst., 1983, 84, 85, 86, 88; contbr. numerous articles to profl. jours. Bd. dirs., v.p., sec. Dance Research Found., N.Y.C., 1983-86, chmn. 1986—. Phi Beta Kappa scholar, Durant scholar Wellesley Coll., 1967-69. Mem. ABA, Assn. Am. Pubs. (lawyers com. 1979—), Assn. Bar City N.Y. (communications law com. 1985-88). Office: The McGraw-Hill Companies 1221 Avenue Of The Americas New York NY 10020-1001

SCHLARMAN, STANLEY GERARD, bishop; b. Belleville, Ill., July 27, 1933. Student, St. Henry Prep. Sem., Belleville, Gregorian U., Rome, St. Louis U. Ordained priest Roman Catholic Ch., 1958, consecrated bishop, 1979. Titular bishop of Capri and aux. bishop of Belleville, 1979-83; bishop of Dodge City Kans., 1983—. Office: Diocese of Dodge City PO Box 137 910 Central Ave Dodge City KS 67801-4513*

SCHLATTER, GEORGE H., producer, director, writer; b. Birmingham; m. Jolene Brand; two children. Student, Pepperdine U. Producer numerous shows including (TV series) Dinah Shore Shows, 1957-62, 60-62, Judy Garland Show, 1963, Steve Lawrence Show, 1965, Colgate Comedy Hour, 1967, Laugh-In, 1967-73, 76-77, Bill Cosby Series, 1972-73, Cher, 1975, Real People, 1979; (TV spls.) Grammy Awards 1965, 68, 69, 70, Jonathan Winters, 1964, Meredith Willson, 1964, Danny Thomas, 1964, 65, Ernie Ford, 1967, Laugh-In, 1967, Dinah Shore, 1969, Doris Day, 1974, Cher, 1975, Diana Ross, 1975, Goldie Hawn, 1975, Goldie & Liza Together, 1980, Joe Piscopo, 1986, George Schlatter's Comedy Club Spl., 1988, Beverly Hills 75th Anniversary, 1989, Sammy Davis Jr. 60th Anniversary Celebration, 1989, 25th Anniversary of the Jerry Lewis Labor Day Telethon, 1990, Sinatra 75th: The Best is Yet to Come, 1990, Soc. of Singers Salute to Frank Sinatra, 1990, Real People Reunion Spl., 1991, A Party for Richard Pryor, 1991, (charitable events) Thalians Tribute to Marianne and Kenny Rogers, 1981, Sun Valley Ski Tournament, 1985, 86, Am. Cinematheque Tribute to Eddie Murphy, 1986, to Bette Midler, 1987, to Robin Williams, 1988, Tel Aviv Found. Cinematheque Tribute to Goldie Hawn and Stan Kamen, 1987, AIDS Project Los Angeles Benefit, 1987, Big Sisters Benefit, 1988, Beverly Hills 75th Anniversary Honoring Frank Sinatra, 1989, Paul Newman/Joanne Woodward Event for the Scott Newman Found., 1990, Carousel of Hope Ball (Barbara/Marvin Davis Diabetes Found., 1990. Recipient 5 Emmys, 22 Emmy nominations, Golden Globe awards, Image awards, Monitor awards, Dirs. Guild award, Producers Guild award, Writer's Guild award ; named Internat. Radio and TV Man of Yr.; awarded a star on Hollywood Blvd.'s Walk of Fame. Avocations: skiing, horseback riding, sailing, scuba diving. Office: William Morris Agy 151 S El Camino Dr Beverly Hills CA 90212-2704*

SCHLECKSER, JAMES HENRY, sales and engineering executive; b. Rahway, N.J., Sept. 16, 1962; s. Henry and Mary Ellen (Counihan) S.; m. Denise Priscille Bergeron, July 2, 1988. B of Chem. Engring., U. Del., 1984; MBA, U. Conn., 1988. Cert. engr.-in-tng., Del. Product engr. Rogers Corp., Manchester, Conn., 1984-86; asst. corp. sec. R/MAT Inc., Manchester, 1986-88; product supr. Rogers Corp., Manchester, 1986-88; product mgr. J.M. Ney Electronics, Bloomfield, Conn., 1988-90; sales mgr. Ney Ultrasonics, Bloomfield, 1990-92; dir. sales and engring. NEY Ultrasonics, Bloomfield, 1992-95; pres. General Eastern, Woburn, Mass., 1995—; chmn. Ultrasonic Industry Standards, Dayton, Ohio, 1994. Author: (book chpt.) Modern Plastics Ency., 1988; contbr. articles to profl. jours. including Soc. Vacuum Coaters, Circuits Assembly, Plastics Engring. Chmn. Internat. Spl. Olympics, Bolton, Conn., 1995; exec. com. Canon Greater Hartford Open, Cromwell, Conn., 1988-94; dir. Hartford Jaycees, 1990-92. Recipient Brownfield award Jaycees, 1989, State Champion Pub. Speaking, 1990. Mem. Soc. Automotive Engrs. (bd. dirs. local chpt. 1989). Home: 23 Woodhaven Dr Andover MA 01810-2822

SCHLEEDE, GLENN ROY, energy market and policy consultant; b. Lyons, N.Y., June 12, 1933; m. Sandra Christine Klafehn, Dec. 27, 1958; children: Kristen M., Kimberly J., Kendall E. BA, Gustavus Adolphus Coll., 1960; MA, U. Minn., 1968; advanced mgmt. program, Harvard U., 1987. Research asst. Indsl. Relations Ctr., U. Minn., Mpls., 1960-61; mgmt. intern, then contractor personnel specialist AEC, Argonne, Ill. and Germantown, Md., 1961-65; asst. chief div. natural resources U.S. Office Mgmt. and Budget, Exec. Office of Pres., Washington, 1965-72, exec. assoc. dir., 1981; dep. assoc. dir. Office of Policy Analysis, AEC, Germantown, 1972-73; assoc. dir. energy and sci. Domestic Council, The White House, Washington, 1973-77; sr. v.p. Nat. Coal Assn., Washington, 1977-81; pres. New Eng. Energy Inc., Westborough, Mass., 1982-92, also bd. dirs.; v.p. New Eng. Power Service Co., Westborough, 1982-92, also bd. dirs.; v.p. New Eng. Electric System, Westborough, 1986-92; pres., CEO, dir. Energy Market and Policy Analysis, Inc., Reston, Va., 1992—. Author numerous speeches, papers and congl. testimony on various nat. energy policy issues. Recipient Disting. Alumni in Bus. award Gustavus Adolphus Coll. Alumni Assn., St. Peter, Minn., 1987. Republican. Lutheran. Avocations: reading, travel, carpentry. Home: 1414 Hemingway Ct Reston VA 20194-1241 Office: Energy Market and Policy Analysis Inc PO Box 3875 Reston VA 20195-1875

SCHLEEDE, LORI GERAINE, primary education educator; b. East Patchogue, N.Y., Mar. 20, 1964; d. Robert Hupfer and Sandra Jean Geraine; m. John F. Schleede, June 25, 1989. BS in Edn., Seton Hall U., 1986; MS in Edn., L.I. U., 1990. Notary public. Substitute tchr. So. Country Sch. Dist., East Patchogue, 1986-88; adminstrv. asst. Hermon E. Swezey Co., Inc., Bellport, N.Y., 1986-88; real estate salesperson Cully Reality, Patchogue, N.Y., 1987-89; permanent substitute William Floyd Sch. Dist., Mastic, N.Y., 1988; kindergarten tchr. So. County Sch. Dist., East Patchogue, 1988-93; sch. rep. union-ednl. problems com. So. Country Sch. Dist., East Patchogue, mem. bldg. planning team, mem. assessment com., trainer perceptual screening; adminstr. for Head Start, Brevard County, Fla., 1994—. Dir. programs Space Coast Early Intervention Ctr., 1997—. Mem. Internat. Reading Assn., Nat. Assn. for Edn. Young Children, Assn. for Edn. Young Children Internat., North Shore Reading Coun. (treas. 1992-93). Republican. Roman Catholic. Avocations: gardening, boating, biking, reading, photography.

SCHLEGEL, FRED EUGENE, lawyer; b. Indpls., July 24, 1941; s. Fred George and Dorothy (Bruce) S.; m. Jane Wessels, Aug. 14, 1965; children: Julia, Charles, Alexandra. BA, Northwestern U., 1963; JD with distinction, U. Mich., 1966. Bar: Ind. 1966. Assoc. lawyer Baker & Daniels, Indpls., 1966-72, ptnr., 1972—; vice chmn. Meridian St. Preservation Commn., Indpls., 1975-90; bd. dirs. Indpls. Water Co., IWC Resources Corp. Contbr. articles to profl. jours. Chmn. Indpls. Pub. Schs. Edn. Found., 1988-90; pres. Festival Music Soc., 1974-75, 79, 86-87; bd. dirs. Indpls. Symphony Orch., 1991—, Arts Coun. Indpls. Mem. ABA, Ind. Bar Assn., Fed. Energy Bar Assn., Northwestern U. Alumni Club Indpls. (pres. 1992-94). Republican. Presbyterian. Office: Baker and Daniels 300 N Meridian St Ste 2700 Indianapolis IN 46204-1750

SCHLEGEL, JOHN FREDERICK, management consultant, speaker, trainer; b. Ogden, Utah, Dec. 18, 1944; s. Max Joseph and Mary Georgia (Whittaker) S.; m. Priscilla Mary Hecht, Sept. 8, 1967. BS in Pharmacy, U. Pacific, 1967; D of Pharmacy, U. So. Calif., 1972, postdoctoral fellow, 1972-73, MS in Edn., 1980; ScD in Pharmacy (hon.), Mass. Coll. Pharmacy, 1984, L.I. U., 1985. Lic. pharmacist, Calif., Nev.; cert. assoc. exec. Chief pharmacist U. So. Calif. Sch. Pharmacy, Los Angeles, 1967-73, dir. pharmacy admissions, 1973-75; dir. office student affairs Am. Assn. Colls. Pharmacy, Alexandria, Va., 1975-77, asst. exec. dir., 1977-81, exec. dir., 1981-84; chief exec. officer Am. Pharm. Assn., Washington, 1984-89; exec. v.p., chief exec. officer Am. Acad. Facial Plastic and Reconstructive Surgery, Washington, 1989-92; pres. Schlegel & Assocs., Chevy Chase, Md., 1992—; cons. U.S. Govt., VA, HHS, various pharm. cos., assns. and schs. pharmacy. Contbr. over 60 articles on pharmacy, health care and assn. mgmt.; presenter in field. Nat. del. White House Conf. on Aging, Washington, 1981. Disting. alumnus U. So. Calif. Sch. Pharmacy, 1985, U. the Pacific Sch. Pharmacy, 1987. Fellow Am. Soc. Assn. Execs.; mem. Am. Soc. Assn. Execs., Am. Pharm. Assn., Am. Assn. Med. Soc. Execs., Group Health Assn. (trustee, officer), Greater Washington Soc. Assn. Execs., Phi Delta Chi (charter, bd. counsellors). Avocations: tennis, classical music, gardening. Office: 7423 Lynnhurst St Chevy Chase MD 20815-3101

SCHLEGEL, JOHN PETER, academic administrator; b. Dubuque, Iowa, July 31, 1943; s. Aaron Joseph and Irma Joan (Hingtgen) S. BA, St. Louis U., 1969, MA, 1970; BDiv, U. London, 1973; DPhil, Oxford U., 1977. Joined Soc. of Jesus, 1963, ordained priest Roman Cath. Ch., 1973. From asst. prof. to assoc. prof. Creighton U., Omaha, 1976-79, asst. acad. v.p., 1978-82; dean Coll. Arts and Scis. Rockhurst Coll., Kansas City, Mo., 1982-84, Marquette U., Milw., 1984-88; exec. and acad. v.p. John Carroll U., Cleve., 1988-91; pres. U. San Francisco, 1991—; cons. Orgn. for Econ. Devel. and Cooperation, Paris, 1975-76. Author: Bilingualism and Canadian Policy in Africa, 1979; editor: Towards a Redefinition of Development, 1976; contbr. articles to profl. jours. Mem. Milwaukee County Arts Coun., 1986-88, Mo. Coun. on Humanities, Kansas City, 1984; trustee St. Louis U., 1985-91, Loyala U. Chgo., 1988-95, Loyola U. New Orleans, 1995—, St. Ignatius H.S., Cleve., 1990-91, Loyola Coll. in Md., 1992—; bd. dirs. Coro Found., Commonwealth Club Calif., Calif. Coun. on World Affairs, 1997—. Oxford U. grantee, 1974-76; Govt. of Can. grantee, 1977-78. Mem. Am. Coun. on Edn., Can. Studies in U.S., Olympic Club, Univ. Club, Bohemian Club. Avocations: racquet sports, classical music, cooking, hiking. Office: U San Francisco Office of Pres 2130 Fulton St San Francisco CA 94117-1080

SCHLEICHER, NORA ELIZABETH, banker, treasurer, accountant; b. Balt., Aug. 10, 1952; d. Irvin William and Eleanor Edna S.; m. Ray Leonard Settle Jr., July 27, 1985. AA cum laude, Anne Arundel Community Coll., 1972; BS summa cum laude, U. Balt., 1975. CPA, Md. Staff auditor Md. Nat. Bank, Balt., 1975-76, sr. staff auditor, 1976-77, supr. auditing dept., 1977-78; full charge acct. Wooden & Benson, CPA's, Balt., 1978-81; asst. to treas. First Fed. Savs. & Loan Assn., Annapolis, Md., 1981, asst. treas., 1982-83, v.p., 1984; v.p., treas. First Fed. Savs. & Loan Assn. (now First Annapolis Bank), 1984—. Bd. dirs., treas. Coll. Manor Community Assn. Mem. AICPA, Md. Assn. CPA's, Fin. Mgrs. Soc., Coll. Manor Community Assn. (bd. dirs., treas.). Methodist. Office: First Annapolis Savs Bank 1832 George Ave Annapolis MD 21401-4103

SCHLEIFER, THOMAS C., management consultant, author, lecturer. BS in Constrn. Mgmt., E. Carolina U., 1989, MS in Constrn. Mgmt., 1990; PhD, Herriot-Watt U., 1994. Owner Schleifer Bros., Inc., Hanover, N.J., 1964-75; owner, founder, pres., internat. cons. firm CMA Cons. Group, Morristown, N.J., 1976-86; dir. appropriate tech., vol. Habitat for Humanity, Americus, Ga., 1987-88; assoc. prof. Ariz. State U., Tempe, 1990-92; eminent scholar Del E. Webb Sch. Constrn., Ariz. State U., 1993-94; vis. prof. East Carolina U., 1989-90; former chmn. continuing edn. com. Associated Gen. Contractors Am.; lectr. and presenter in field. Author: Construction Contractors' Survival Guide, 1990, Glossary of Suretyship and Related Terms, 1981; contbr. articles to profl. jours. Bd. advisors Habitat for Humanity Internat., 1989—. Mem. Am. Inst. Constructors (bd. dirs. 1990-93), Am. Arbitration Assn. (N.J. adv. coun. 1968-75), Am. Concrete Inst. (edn. com. 1972-76), Associated Gen. Contractors Am. (chmn. continuing edn. com. 1970-76), Assn. Advancement 3d World (internat. adv. coun. 1988-91). Home and Office: 5625 N 75th Pl Scottsdale AZ 85250-6471

SCHLEIN, MIRIAM, author; children: Elizabeth Weiss, John Weiss. B.A. in Psychology, Bklyn. Coll., 1947. Author over 85 books for children, natural sci. books, concept books, story books, picture books, including: A Day at the Playground, 1951, The Four Little Foxes, 1952 (Jr. Lit. Guild selection), Shapes, 1952, Go with the Sun, 1952, Tony's Pony, 1952, Fast is Not a Ladybug, 1953 (Boys' Club Am. Jr. Book award 1953), When Will the World Be Mine?, 1953 (Caldecott Honor Book, Am. Libr. Assn. 1954), The Sun Looks Down, 1954, How Do You Travel?, 1954, Heavy is a Hippopotamus, 1954, Elephant Herd, 1954 (Jr. Lit. Guild selection, Herald Tribune Honor Book award 1954), Oomi, the New Hunter, 1955, Little Red Nose, 1955, It's About Time, 1955, City Boy, Country Boy, 1955 (Jr. Lit. Guild selection), Puppy's House. 1955, Big Talk, 1955, Lazy Day, 1955, Henry's Ride, 1956, Something for Now, Something for Later, 1956, Deer in the Snow, 1956, The Big Cheese, 1957 (Jr. Lit. Guild selection), Little Rabbit, The High Jumper, 1957, Amazing Mr. Pelgew, 1957, A Bunny, A Bird, A Funny Cat, 1957, Here Comes Night, 1957, The Bumblebee's Secret, 1958, Home: The Tale of a Mouse, 1958, Herman McGregor's World, 1958, The Raggle Taggle Fellow, 1959, Little Dog Little, 1959, The Fisherman's Day, 1959, Kittens, Cubs and Babies, 1959, My Family, 1960, The Sun, the Wind, the Sea and the Rain, 1960, Laurie's New Brother, 1961, Amuny, Boy of Old Egypt, 1961, The Pile of Junk, 1962 (Jr. Lit. Guild selection), Snow Time, 1962, The Snake in the Carpool, 1963, Who?, 1963, The Big Green Thing, 1963, The Way Mothers Are, 1963, Big Lion, Little Lion, 1964, Billy, the Littlest One, 1966, The Best Place, 1968, My House, 1971, Moon-months and Sun-days, 1972, The Rabbit's World, 1973, Juju Sheep and the Python's Moonstone, 1973, What's Wrong with Being a Skunk?, 1974, Metric: The Modern Way to Measure, 1975, The Girl Who Would Rather Climb Trees, 1975, Giraffe: The Silent Giant, 1976 (Childrens' Book of Yr. Child Study Assn. 1976), Bobo, the Troublemaker, 1976, Antarctica: The Great White Continent, 1978, I Hate It, 1978, On the Track of the Mystery Animal, 1978, I, Tut: The Boy Who Became Pharaoh, 1979, Snake Fights, Rabbit Fights and More: A Book About Animal Fighting, 1979 (Outstanding Sci. Trade Book for Children Nat. Sci. Tchrs. Assn./Children's Book Council Joint Com. 1979), Lucky Porcupine!, 1980 (Outstanding Sci. Trade Book for Children Nat. Sci. Tchrs. Assn./Children's Book Council Joint Com. 1980), Billions of Bats, 1982 (Outstanding Sci. Trade Book for Children Nat. Sci. Tchrs. Assn./Children's Book Council Joint Com. 1982), Our Holidays, 1983, Project Panda Watch, 1984 (Children's Sci. Book award N.Y. Acad. Sci. 1985), What the Elephant Was, 1986, The Dangerous Life of the Sea Horse, 1986 (Outstanding Sci. Trade Book for Children Nat. Sci. Tchrs. Assn./Children's Book Council Joint Com. 1986), Pigeons, 1989, Big Talk, 1990, The Year of the Panda, 1990 (Outstanding Sci. Trade Book for Children Nat. Sci. Tchrs. Assn./Children's Book Council Joint Com. 1990), That's Not Goldie, 1990, Jane Goodall's Animal World: Elephants, Hippos, Gorillas, Pandas, 1990, I Sailed With Columbus, 1991, Discovering Dinosaur Babies, 1991 (Outstanding Sci. Trade Book for Children Nat. Sci. Tchrs. Assn./Children's Book Council Joint Com. 1991), Let's Go Dinosaur Tracking, 1991, Squirrel Watching, 1992, Secret Land of the Past, 1993, Just Like Me, 1993, Before the Dinosaurs, 1996, The Puzzle of the Dinosaur-Bird: The Story of Archaeopteyx, 1996, More than One, 1996 (Jr. Lit. Guild selection), Sleep Safe, Little Whale, 1997 (Book of the Month Club alternate); contributor: (as Miriam Weiss) Redbook, McCall's, Ladies Home Jour., Good Housekeeping, Univ. Rev., Creative Living, Colorado Quar.; included in anthologies; transl. into Danish, Swedish, Italian, French, Dutch, Norwegian, German, Braille. Mem. Authors Guild, PEN Am. Center (children's book com.), Nat. Writers Union. Home and Office: 19 E 95th St New York NY 10128

SCHLENDER, WILLIAM ELMER, management sciences educator; b. Sawyer, Mich., Oct. 28, 1920; s. Gustav A. and Marie (Zindler) S.; m. Lela R. Pullen, June 9, 1956 (dec. June 1983); m. Margaret C. Krahn, Mar. 3, 1987. A.B., Valparaiso U., 1941; M.B.A., U. Denver, 1947; Ph.D., Ohio State U., 1955. With U.S. Rubber Co., 1941-43, 46; asst. prof., assoc. prof. bus. adminstrn. Bowling Green State U., 1947-53; asst. prof. bus. orgn., prof. Ohio State U., 1954-65, asst. dean, 1959-62; assoc. dean Ohio State U. (Coll. Commerce and Adminstrn.), 1962-63; prof. mgmt. U. Tex., 1965-68, chmn. dept., 1966-68; dean Cleve. State U. Coll. Bus. Adminstrn., 1968-75, prof. mgmt., 1975-76; Internat. Luth. Laymen's League prof. bus. ethics Valparaiso (Ind.) U., 1976-79, Richard E. Meier prof. mgmt., 1983-86, Richard E. Meier prof. emeritus, 1986—; vis. assoc. prof. mgmt. Columbia U., 1957-58; vis. prof. mgmt. U. Tex., Arlington, 1981-82; cons. in field; bd. govs. Internat. Ins. Soc., 1972-90; bd. dirs. Carrier Enterprises. Author: (with M.J. Jucius) Elements of Managerial Action, 3d edit, 1973, (with others) Management in Perspective: Selected Readings, 1965; Editor: (with others) Management in a Dynamic Society, 1965; Contbr. (with others) articles to profl. jours. Served with AUS, 1943-45. Decorated Bronze Star. Recipient Exec. Order Ohio Comodr. for outstanding contbn. to growth and devel. of state. Fellow Acad. Mgmt.; mem. Indsl. Rels. Rsch. Assn. (pres. N.E. Ohio chpt. 1971-72), Internat. Coun. Small Bus., Am. Legion, Tau Kappa Epsilon, Soc. for Case Rsch., Beta Gamma Sigma, Sigma Iota Epsilon, Pi Sigma Epsilon, Alpha Kappa Psi, Phi Kappa Phi, Rotary. Home: PO Box 446 Sawyer MI 49125-0446 Office: Coll Bus Adminstrn Valparaiso U Valparaiso IN 46383 *I resolved long ago that where I worked and what I did would be guided not by prestige considerations, but by the answers to three questions: (1) Will my work allow me to grow by discovering and developing my capabilities? (2) Will it make a significant contribution to my profession and to the community? (3) Will I enjoy doing it? My career, and my personal philosophy, have these underlying guidelines.*

SCHLENSKER, GARY CHRIS, landscaping company executive; b. Indpls., Nov. 12, 1950; s. Christian Frederick and Doris Jean (Shannon) S.; m. Ann Marie Tobin, Oct. 27, 1979; children: Laura Patricia, Christian Frederick II. Student, Purdue U., 1969-71, 73; A Bus. Adminstrn., Clark Coll., 1979; cert. emergency med. technician, Ind. Vocat. Tech. Inst., Lafayette, 1974. Salesman Modern Reference, Indpls., 1971; orthopaedic technician St. Elizabeth Hosp., Lafayette, 1973-75, asst. mgr. ambulance service, 1975; sales asst. Merck, Sharpe & Dohme, Oakbrook, Ill., 1975-77; v.p. Turfco, Inc., Zionsville, Ind., 1977-84; pres. Turfscape, Inc., Zionsville, 1984—; speaker Midwest Turf Conf., 1991. With U.S. Army, 1971-73. Mem. ASTM (erosion control subcom.), BBB, Nat. Fedn. Ind. Bus., Midwest Turf Found., Ohio Turf Found., Internat. Erosion Control Assn., U.S. C. of C., Ind. C. of C., Zionsville C. of C., Phi Kappa Psi. Presbyterian. Avocations: woodworking, golf.

SCHLENTZ, ROBERT JOSEPH, reliability engineer; b. Chgo., Dec. 9, 1940; s. Harold Joseph and Katherine (Dufalo) S.; m. Eileen Ellen Pride, May 10, 1969; children: Julie Joann, Karen Katherine. BS in Physics, DePaul U., 1963, MS in Physics, 1965. Registered profl. engr., Minn. Assoc. rsch. scientist U. Notre Dame, Ind., 1966-68; dept. mgr. electro magnetic compatibility, staff engr. Medtronic, Fridley, Minn., 1968-77; project engr. Maico Hearing Instruments, Edina, Minn., 1977-83; sr. specialist reliability enging. 3M (Minn. Mining & Mfg.), St. Paul, 1983—. Treas. Mpls. Dem. Farmer-Labor Com., Mpls., 1985-88. Mem. IEEE (sr., twin cities sect. chair), Minn. Soc. Profl. Engrs. (bd. dirs.). Roman Catholic. Avocations: music, science fiction, politics. Home: 3040 Buchanan St NE Minneapolis MN 55418-2251 Office: 3M 3M Center Saint Paul MN 55144-0001

SCHLESINGER, ARTHUR (MEIER), JR., writer, educator; b. Columbus, Ohio, Oct. 15, 1917; s. Arthur M. and Elizabeth (Bancroft) S.; m. Marian Cannon, 1940 (div. 1970); children: Stephen Cannon, Katharine Kinderman, Christina, Andrew Bancroft; m. Alexandra Emmet, July 9, 1971; 1 son, Robert Emmet Kennedy. AB summa cum laude, Harvard U., 1938, mem. Soc. of Fellows, 1939-42; postgrad. (Henry fellow), Cambridge (Eng.) U., 1938-39; hon. degrees, Muhlenberg Coll., 1950, Bethany Coll., 1956, U. N.B., 1966, New Sch. Social Rsch., 1966, Tusculum Coll., 1966, R.I. Coll., 1969, Aquinas Coll., 1971, Western New Eng. Coll., 1974, Ripon Coll., 1976, Iona Coll., 1977, Utah State U., 1978, U. Louisville, 1978, Northeastern U., 1981, Rutgers U., 1982, SUNY-Albany, 1984, U. N.H., 1985, U. Oxford, 1987, Akron U., 1987, Brandeis U., 1988, U. Mass., Boston, 1990, Hofstra U., 1991, Adelphi U., 1992, Dominican Coll., 1992, Mt. Ida Coll., 1993, Middlebury Coll., 1994, Roosevelt U., 1995, Lynn U., 1996, No. Ill. U., 1996. With OWI, 1942-43, OSS, 1943-45; assoc. prof. history Harvard U., 1946-54, prof., 1954-62; vis. fellow Inst. Advanced Study, Princeton, N.J., 1966; Schweitzer prof. humanities CUNY, 1966-95; cons. Econ. Cooperation Adminstrn., 1948, Mutual Security Adminstrn., 1951-52; spl. asst. to Pres. of U.S., 1961-64; mem. jury Cannes Film Festival, 1964; mem. Adlai E. Stevenson campaign staff, 1952, 56; chmn. Franklin Delano Roosevelt Four Freedoms Found., 1983—; trustee Robert F. Kennedy Meml., Twentieth Century Fund.; adv. Arthur and Elizabeth Schlesinger Library. Author: Orestes A. Brownson, 1939, The Age of Jackson, 1945 (Pulitzer prize for history 1946), The Vital Center, 1949, (with R.H. Rovere) The General and the President, 1951, The Age of Roosevelt Vol. I: The Crisis of the Old Order 1919-1933, 1957 (Francis Parkman prize Soc. Am. Historians 1957, Frederic Bancroft prize Columbia U. 1958), The Age of Roosevelt Vol. II: The Coming of the New Deal, 1958, The Age of Roosevelt Vol. III: The Politics of Upheaval, 1960, Kennedy or Nixon: Does It Make Any Difference?, 1960, The Politics of Hope, 1963, (with John Blum) The National Experience, 1963, A Thousand Days, 1965 (Pulitzer prize for biography 1966, Nat. Book award 1966), The Bitter Heritage, 1967, The Crisis of Confidence, 1969, The Imperial Presidency, 1973 (Sidney Hillman Found. award 1973), Robert Kennedy and His Times, 1978 (Nat. Book award 1979), The Cycles of American History, 1986, The Disuniting of America, 1991; contbr. articles to mags. and newspapers; film reviewer: Show mag, 1962-64, Vogue, 1967-72, Saturday Rev., 1977-80, Am. Heritage, 1981-82; editor: Harvard Guide to American History, 1954, Guide to Politics, 1954, Paths to American Thought, 1963, The Promise of American Life, 1967, The Best and the Last of Edwin O'Connor, 1970, History of American Presidential Elections 1789-1972, 1971, 1972-1984, 1986, The Coming to Power, 1972, The Dynamics of World Power: A Documentary History of United States Foreign Policy 1945-1973, 1973, History of U.S. Political Parties, 1973, Congress Investigates, 1975, The American Statesman, 1982, The Almanac of American History, 1983, Running for President, 1994; screenwriter: (teleplay) The Journey of Robert F. Kennedy. Served with AUS, 1945. Decorated comdr. Order of Orange-Nassau (The Netherlands), Ordem del Libertador (Venezuela); recipient Nat. Inst. and Am. Acad. Arts and Letters gold medal in history and biography, 1967, Ohio Gov.'s award for history, 1973, Eugene V. Debs award in edn., 1974, Fregene prize for lit. (Italy), 1983; Guggenheim fellow, 1946; Am. Acad. Arts and Letters grantee, 1946. Mem. Am. Hist. Assn., Orgn. Am. Historians, Soc. Am. Historians (pres. 1989-92), Am. Acad. and Inst. Arts and Letters (pres. 1981-84, chancellor 1984-87), Am. Philos. Soc., Mass. Hist. Soc., Colonial Soc. Mass., Russian Acad. Scis., Franklin and Eleanor Roosevelt Inst. (co-chmn. 1983—), ACLU, Coun. Fgn. Rels., Ams. for Dem. Action (nat. chmn. 1952-54), Century Assn., Knickerbocker Club, Phi Beta Kappa. Democrat. Unitarian. Home: 455 E 51st St New York NY 10022-6474 Office: CUNY 33 W 42nd St New York NY 10036-8003

SCHLESINGER, B. FRANK, architect, educator; b. N.Y.C., Sept. 17, 1925; s. Augustus and Ethel (Brower) S.; m. Draga A. Christy; children: Jeff, Nike, Katherine, Daniel, Christy Anna; 1 stepson, Frances L. Haley Jr. Student, Middlebury Coll., 1946-48; BS, U. Ill., 1950; MArch, Harvard U., 1954. Draftsman Hugh Stubbins Assocs., 1953-55, Marcel Breuer, 1955-56; pvt. practice architecture Princeton, N.J., 1956-59, Doylestown, Pa., 1959-69, Phila., 1969-71, Washington, 1971—; instr. archtl. design U. Pa., 1957-60; vis. critic Columbia Sch. Architecture, 1962-63, U. Pa., 1965; KEA disting. prof. Sch. Architecture, U. Md., 1971, prof. architecture, 1971—. With USNR, 1943-46. Wheelwright fellow Harvard U., 1963; recipient design awards Pa. Soc. Archs., 1960-65, 69, 84, Bronze medal, 1965, Silver medal, 1973, Design awards Progressive Arch., 1966-67, 69, 72, 74, Design awards Interfaith Forum on Religion, Art and Arch., 1987, 92. Fellow AIA (Design awards Phila. chpt. 1960-61, 63-65, 68-69, No. Va. chpt. 1975, Washington chpt. 1990, 92, 95); mem. Harvard Grad. Sch. Design Alumni Assn. (pres. 1971-73), Associated Harvard Alumni (dir. 1972). Address: 1015 33rd St NW # 806 Washington DC 20007

SCHLESINGER, EDWARD BRUCE, neurological surgeon; b. Pitts., Sept. 6, 1913; s. Samuel B. and Sara Marie (Schlesinger) S.; m. Mary Eddy, Nov. 1941; children—Jane, Mary, Ralph, Prudence. B.A., U. Pa., 1934, M.D., 1938. Diplomate Am. Bd. Neurosurgery. Mem. faculty Columbia Coll. Phys. and Surg., N.Y.C., 1946—; prof. clin. neurol. surgery Columbia Coll. Phys. and Surg., 1964—, Byron Stookey prof., chmn. dept. neurol. surgery, 1973-80, Byron Stookey prof. emeritus, 1980—; dir. neurol. surgery Columbia Presbyn. Hosp., 1973-80, pres. med. bd., 1976-79; cons. in neurosurgery Presbyn. Hosp., 1980-87, cons. emeritus, 1987—. Author rsch. publs. on uses, effects of curare in disease, lesions of central nervous system, localization of brain tumors using radioactive tagged isotopes, genetic problems in neurosurgery and spinal disorders. Trustee Matheson Found., Sharon (Conn.) Hosp. Recipient emeritus rsch. award Presbyn. Hosp. Fellow N.Y. Acad. Scis., N.Y. Acad. Medicine; mem. AAAS, AMA, Am. Assn. Neurol. Surgeons, Harvey Soc., Neurosurg Soc. Am. (pres. 1970-71), Soc. Neurol. Surgeons, Am. Assn. Surgery of Trauma, Am. Rheumatism Soc., Am. Coll. Clin. Pharmacology and Chemotherapy, Ea. Assn. Electroencephalographers, Sigma Xi. Achievements include investigation of clinical pathological markers of genetic disorders and the syndromes created. Home: PO Box 3239 Fort Lee NJ 07024-9239 Office: 710 W 168th St New York NY 10032-2603

SCHLESINGER, HARVEY ERWIN, judge; b. N.Y.C., June 4, 1940. BA, The Citadel, 1962; JD, U. Richmond, 1965. Bar: Va. 1965, Fla. 1965, U.S. Supreme Ct. 1968. Corp. counsel Seaboard Coast Line R.R. Co., Jacksonville, Fla., 1968-70; chief asst. U.S. atty. Middle Dist. Fla., Jacksonville, 1970-75, U.S. magistrate judge, 1975-91, U.S. Dist. judge, 1991—; adj. prof. U. N. Fla., 1984-91; mem. adv. com. on Fed. Rules of Criminal Procedure to U.S. Supreme Ct., 1986-93; mem. Judicial Conf. Adv. Com. on the Admin. of the Magistrate Judges system, 1996—, chmn. U.S. Dist. Ct. Forms Task Force, Washington, 1983—. Served to capt. JAGC U.S. Army, 1965-68. Bd. dirs. Pine Castle Ctr. for Mentally Retarded, Jacksonville, 1970-87 , pres., 1972-74. chmn. bd. dirs., 1973-74, 76, trustee Pine Castle Found., 1972-76; trustee Congregation Ahavath Chesed, Jacksonville, 1970—, v.p., 1975-80, pres., 1980-82; v.p. S.E. council Union Am. Hebrew Congregations, 1984-88; asst. commissioner for exploring N. Fla. council Boy Scouts Am., 1983-86, exec. com., 1986—; mem. Boy Scouts Am. Nat. Jewish com. on Scouting, Irving, Tex., 1986-93, recipient Silver Beaver award Boy Scouts Am., 1986, Fla. Sesquicentennial Commn., 1995-96; trustee River Garden Home for Aged, 1982—, sec., 1985; co-chmn. bd. govs. Jacksonville chpt. NCCJ, 1983—, presiding co-chmn. 1984-89, nat. bd. trustees, N.Y.C., 1986-93. Recipient George Washington Medal Honor, Freedoms Found, Valley Forge, Pa, 1987, Silver Medallion Humanitarian award Nat. COnf. Christians and Jews, 1992. Mem. ABA (fed. rules of evidence and criminal procedure com. 1979—, Nat. Conf. Special Court Judges, 1975, 90, conf. newsletter editor, 1988-90, Nat. Conf. Fed. Trial Judges, 1990—, chmn. Legislation com., 1996—; Flascher award 1989), Va. Bar Assn., Fla. Bar Assn., Fed. Judges Assn., Nat. Council U.S. Magistrates (pres. 1987, v.p. 1985, pres. elect 1986, sec. 1983, treas. 1984), Jacksonville Bar Assn., Fed. Bar Assn. (pres. Jacksonville chpt. 1974, 75, 81-82), Am. Judicature Soc., Chester Bedell Am. Inns of Ct. (pres. 1992-96. Lodge: Rotary (Paul Harris fellow, pres. S. Jacksonville club), Mason (past master, past venerable master, knights commander of Ct. Honour, Scottish rite bodies), Shriner. Office: 311 W Monroe St PO Box 1740 Jacksonville FL 32201

SCHLESINGER, JAMES RODNEY, economist; b. N.Y.C., Feb. 15, 1929; s. Julius and Rhea (Rogen) S.; m. Rachel Mellinger, June 19, 1954; children: Cora K., Charles L., Ann R., William F., Emily, Thomas S., Clara, James Rodney. A.B. summa cum laude, Harvard U., 1950, A.M., 1952, Ph.D., 1956. Asst. prof., then assoc. prof. U. Va., 1955-63; sr. staff mem. RAND Corp., 1963-67; dir. strategic studies, 1967-69; asst. dir. Bur. Budget, 1969, acting dep. dir., 1969-70; asst. dir. Office Mgmt. and Budget, 1970-71; chmn. AEC, 1971-73; dir. CIA, Feb.-July 1973; U.S. sec. def., 1973-75; vis. scholar Johns Hopkins Sch. Advanced Internat. Studies, 1976-77; asst. to Pres., 1977; sec. Dept. Energy, 1977-79; counselor Ctr. for Strategic and Internat. Studies, Georgetown U., 1979—; sr. adv. Lehman Bros., 1979—; cons. in field. Author: The Political Economy of National Security, 1960, America at Century's End, 1989; co-author: Issues in Defense Economics, 1967. Frederick Sheldon prize fellow Harvard U., 1950-51. Mem. Phi Beta Kappa. Republican. Presbyterian. Office: Lehman Bros 800 Connecticut Ave NW Washington DC 20006-2709

SCHLESINGER, JOHN RICHARD, film, opera and theater director; b. London, Feb. 16, 1926; s. Bernard Edward and Winifred Henrietta (Regensburg) S. B.A., Balliol Coll., Oxford U., 1950. Dir. BBC TV, 1958-60. Dir. feature films including Terminus, 1961 (Golden Lion award Venice Film Festival, Brit. Acad. award), A Kind of Loving, 1962 (Golden Bear award Berlin Film Festival), Billy Liar, 1963, Darling, 1965 (N.Y. Critics award, Acad. nomination), Far From the Madding Crowd, 1966, Midnight Cowboy, 1968 (Acad. award best dir., best film, Brit. Acad. award best dir., best film), Sunday Bloody Sunday, 1970 (David di Donatello award, Brit. Acad. award best dir., best film), Day of the Locust, 1974, Marathon Man, 1976, Yanks, 1979 (Nat. Bd. Rev. award, New Std. award), Honky Tonk Freeway, 1980, Separate Tables, 1982, An Englishman Abroad, 1983 (Brit. Acad. award best single drama, Broadcasting Press Guild award best single drama, Barcelona Film Festival award best fiction film), The Falcon and the Snowman, 1983, The Believers, 1986, Madame Sousatzka, 1988, Pacific Heights, 1991, The Innocent, 1993, Cold Comfort Farm (BBC/ Thames), 1994, Eye for an Eye, 1995, Bafta Fellowship, 1996, Sweeney Todd, 1997, TV films including An Englishman Abroad (BBC), 1983 (David Wark Griffith award for best TV film), A Question of Attribution (PBS), 1992 (Brit. Acad. award best single drama); plays including Days in the Trees, 1966, I and Albert, 1972, Heartbreak House, 1974, Julius Caesar, 1977, True West, 1981, operas including Les Contes d'Hoffmann, 1980-81 (Soc. West End Theatre award), Der Rosenkavalier, 1984-85, Un Ballo in Maschera, 1989; assoc. dir. Nat. Theatre, London, 1973-80. Served with Royal Engrs., 1944-48. Recipient David di Donatello Spl. Dir. award, 1980, Shakespeare prize, 1981, The Hamptons Internat. Film Festival Disting. Achievement award, 1995; BAFTA fellow, 1996. Office: United Talent Agy Attn Jeremy Zimmer 9560 Wilshire Blvd Beverly Hills CA 90212

SCHLESINGER, JOSEPH ABRAHAM, political scientist; b. Boston, Jan. 4, 1922; s. Monroe Jacob and Millie (Romansky) S.; m. Mildred Saks, Sept. 9, 1951; children: Elizabeth Hannah, Jacob Monroe. Student, Hobart Coll., 1938-40; A.B., U. Chgo., 1942; A.M., Harvard U., 1947; Ph.D., Yale U., 1955. Instr. Boston U., 1947-49; teaching fellow Wesleyan U., Middletown, Conn., 1952-53; mem. faculty Mich. State U., East Lansing, 1953—; prof. polit. sci. Mich. State U., 1963—; vis. prof. U. Calif., Berkeley, 1964-65. Author: How They Became Governor, 1957, Ambition and Politics: Political Careers in the United States, 1966, Political Parties and the Winning of Office, 1991, also articles. Del. Ingham County (Mich.) Democratic Conv., 1966-68. Served with AUS, 1943-45. Cowles fellow, 1950-51; Block fellow, 1951-52; grantee Social Sci. Research Council, 1955-57, 68-69; recipient Distinguished Faculty award Mich. State U., 1976, Sr. Fulbright award for Rsch. Western Europe, 1990—. Mem. Am. Polit. Sci. Assn. (coun. 1981-83, 1st ann. award for outstanding pub. paper 1986, Samuel Eldersveld award for lifetime achievement 1993), Midwest Polit. Sci. Assn. (v.p. 1969-70), So. Polit. Sci. Assn., Mich. Conf. Polit. Scientists, Acad. Polit. Sci. Democrat. Jewish. Home: 930 Roxburgh Ave East Lansing MI 48823-3131 Office: Dept Polit Sci Mich State Univ East Lansing MI 48824

SCHLESINGER, MILTON J., virology educator, researcher; b. Wheeling, W.Va., Nov. 26, 1927; s. Milton J. and Caroline (Oppenheimer) S.; m. Sondra Orenstein, Jan. 30, 1955. BS, Yale U., 1951; MS, U. Rochester, 1953; PhD, U. Mich., 1959. Rsch. assoc. U. Mich., Ann Arbor, 1953-56, 59-60; guest rsch. investigator Inst. Superiore di Sanita, Rome, 1960-61; rsch. assoc. MIT, Cambridge, 1961-64; asst. prof. virology Washington U. Sch. Medicine, St. Louis, 1964-67, assoc. prof., 1967-72, prof., 1972—; chmn. exec. coun. divsn. biol. and biomed. scis., 1992-94; vis. scientist Imperial Cancer Rsch. Fund, London, 1974-75; vis. scholar Harvard U., Cambridge, 1989-90, 95-96; mem. adv. panels Am. Heart Assn., Dallas, 1975-78, NSF, Washington, 1978-82; mem. sci. adv. bd. Friedrich Miescher Inst., Basel, Switzerland, 1988—, chmn., 1992—; nat. lectr. Sigma Xi, 1991-93. Editor: Heat Shock, 1982, Togaviridae of Flaviviridae, 1986, Lipid Modification of Proteins, 1992, (monographs) The Ubiquitin System, 1988, Stress Proteins, 1990; mem. editl. bd. virology, 1975-92, Jour. Biol. Chemistry, 1982-87, Molecular and Cellular Biology, 1983-92. Bd. dirs. ACLU, St. Louis, 1966-72, Coalition for Environ., St. Louis, 1989-92. Mem. AAAS, Am. Biol. Chemistry and Molecular Biology, Am. Soc. Microbiology, Am. Soc. Virologists, Am. Chem. Soc., Protein Soc. Office: Dept Molecular Micro 8230 Washington U Med Sch 660 S Euclid Ave Saint Louis MO 63110-1010

SCHLESINGER, ROBERT WALTER, microbiologist, microbiology educator emeritus; b. Hamburg, Germany, Mar. 27, 1913; came to U.S., 1938, naturalized, 1943; s. Emil and Flora (Strelitz) S.; m. Adeline P. Sacks, Jan. 7, 1942; children: Robert, Ann. Student, U. Hamburg Med. Sch., 1931-34; M.D., U. Basel, Switzerland, 1937. Guest investigator Inst. Bacteriology and Hygiene, U. Basel, 1937-38; intern Beekman Hosp., N.Y.C., Stamford (Conn.) Hosp., 1938-40; fellow, asst. pathology and bacteriology Rockefeller Inst., N.Y.C., 1940-46; assoc. research prof. pathology, head virus research lab. U. Pitts. Sch. Medicine, 1946-47; assoc. mem., div. infectious diseases Pub. Health Research Inst., City of N.Y., Inc., 1947-55; prof., chmn. dept. microbiology St. Louis U. Sch. Medicine, 1955-63; prof. dept. microbiology U. Medicine and Dentistry N.J.-Robt. Wood Johnson Med. Sch., Piscataway, 1963-83, emeritus disting. prof., 1984—, chmn., 1963-80, also acting dean.; cons. Sec. War, 1946; mem., chmn. virology study sect. NIH; mem., chmn. microbiology and infectious disease adv. com. Nat. Inst. Allergy and Infectious Disease, NIH; mem. adv. com. Nat. Cancer Inst.; mem. cell biology and virology adv. com. Am. Cancer Soc. Editor: Virology; contbr. articles to sci. jours., chpts. to books. Served as capt. M.C. AUS, 1944-46. Recipient Humboldt award Fed. Republic Germany, 1981; Guggenheim fellow, 1972-73. Mem. Am. Acad. Microbiology, Am. Assn. Immunologists, Am. Soc. Microbiology, Am. Soc. Cancer Rsch., AAAS, Am. Soc. Virology, N.Y. Acad. Scis., Sigma Xi, Alpha Omega Alpha. Home and Office: 7 Langley Rd Falmouth MA 02540-1809

SCHLESINGER, SANFORD JOEL, lawyer; b. N.Y.C., Feb. 8, 1943; s. Irving and Ruth (Rubin) S.; children: Merideth, Jarrod, Alexandra; m. Suzanne Beth Mangold, 1994; 1 stepchild, Mariel Mangold. BS in Govt. with hons., Columbia U., 1963; JD, Fordham U., 1966. Bar: N.Y. 1966, U.S. Dist. Ct. (so. and ea. dists.) N.Y. 1967, U.S. Ct. Appeals (2d cir.) 1968, U.S. Ct. Internat. Trade 1969, U.S. Tax Ct. 1993, U.S. Supreme Ct. 1978. Assoc. Frankenthaler & Kohn, N.Y.C., 1966-67; asst. atty. gen. trusts and estates bur. charitable found. div. State of N.Y., N.Y.C., 1967-69; ptnr. Rose & Schlesinger, N.Y.C., 1969-81, Goldshmidt, Oshatz, Powsner & Saft, N.Y.C., 1981-85; ptnr., head trusts and estates dept. Shea & Gould, N.Y.C., 1985-93; ptnr., head wills and estates dept. Kaye, Scholer, Fierman, Hays & Handler, N.Y.C., 1993—; adj. faculty Columbia U. Sch. Law, 1989-94; adj. prof. N.Y. Law Sch., 1978—; adj. prof. grad. program in estate planning U. Miami Sch. Law, 1995—; mem. estate planning adv. com. Practising Law Inst., 1990—; bd. advisors and contbrs. Jour. of S Corp. Taxation, 1989-96; lectr. in field; condr. workshops in field. Author: Estate Planning for the Elderly Client, 1984, Planning for the Elderly or Incapacitated Client, 1993; columnist, mem. editl. bd. Estate Planning mag., 1995—; contbr. articles to profl. jours. Mem. adv. bd. Inst. Fed. Taxation NYU, 1988-96, chmn., 1993-94; mem. legis adv. com. Scarsdale (N.Y.) Sch. Bd., 1981-83, mem. nominating com., 1979-82; pres. dist. 17 N.Y.C. Cmty. Sch. Bd., 1970-71; mem. fin. and estate planning adv. bd. Commerce Clearing House, 1988—. Fellow Am. Coll. Trust and Estate Counsel; mem. ABA (chmn. social security and other govt. entitlements com. 1990-91, chmn. probate and trust com.-estate planning, drafting charitable giving coms., 1992-94), Internat. Acad. Estate & Trust Law (Academician 1992—), Nat. Acad. Elder Law Attys., Bklyn. Bar Assn., Assn. of Bar of City of N.Y., N.Y. State Bar Assn. (treas. trusts and estates sect. 1991-92, sec. trusts and estates sect. 1992-93, chmn. trusts and estates sect. 1994-95, chmn. exec. com. 1st jud. dist. 1987-91, jour. bd. editors 1995—). Avocations: baseball, writing. Office: Kaye Scholer Fierman Hays & Handler 425 Park Ave New York NY 10022-3506

SCHLESINGER, STEPHEN LYONS, horticulturist; b. N.Y.C., July 24, 1940; s. Nathan and Gertrude (Lyons) S.; m. Barbara Bernthal, Feb. 17, 1963; children—Adam Lyons, Lauren Elizabeth. B.A., Williams Coll., 1962; student, U. Paris, 1960-61; M.A. in French, Columbia U., 1964; postgrad., Rutgers U., 1995. Lectr. in French Hunter Coll., 1963-64; lectr. in French Columbia U., summers 1963-64; adminstrv. asst. John Simon Guggenheim Meml. Found., N.Y.C., 1965-67, asst. sec., 1967-70, assoc. sec., 1970-73, sec., 1973-88, spl. cons., 1988-89; ind. cons., 1989-90; assoc. dir., dir. maj. gifts The Corella and Bertram F. Bonner Found., Princeton, N.J., 1990-91; nurseryman Dubrow's Nurseries, Livingston, N.J., 1990-95; garden ctr. horticulturist, 1995—. Woodrow Wilson fellow, 1962-63. Home: 17 Prospect Ter Montclair NJ 07042-3204 Office: DuBrow's Nurseries 251 W Northfield Rd Livingston NJ 07039-2610

SCHLESS, PHYLLIS ROSS, investment banker; d. Lewis H. and Doris G. Ross; m. Aaron Backer Schless, July 7, 1970; 1 son, Daniel Lewis Ross. Cert., N.Y. Playhouse Sch. of Theatre, 1962, N.Y. Sch. Interior Design, 1964; B.A. in Econs., Wellesley Coll., 1964; M.B.A., Stanford U., 1966. Assoc. internat. fin. Kuhn Loeb & Co., N.Y.C., 1966-70; fin. cons., 1971-73; sr. fin. analyst Trans World Airlines, N.Y.C., 1974-75; corp. fin., mergers and acquisitions Lazard Freres & Co., 1976-79; dir. mergers and acquisitions Am. Can Co., Greenwich, Conn., 1979-82; v.p. mergers and acquisitions Bear, Stearns & Co., N.Y.C., 1982-84; sr. v.p. corp. acquisitions Integrated Resources, 1984-85; chmn., chief exec. officer Ross Fin. Svcs.

Group Inc., 1985—; supervisory dir. Merrill Lynch HYTS Funds, 1991-96; bd. dirs. Calvery Hosp. Fund Bd., 1992—, chair investment com., 1995—; trustee A.E. Tinker Fund, 1993—; trustee Nat. Child Labor Com., 1981-95, chmn., 1992-94; trustee New World Found., 1986-92, chair fin. com., treas. 1988-92; bd. dirs. Stanford Bus. Sch. Club, N.Y., 1994—; adj. faculty NYU, 1996—. Pres. Greater Bridgeport nat. Coun. Jewish Women, 1971-73, bd. dirs., 1974-75; bd. dirs. Girls Clubs Am., 1975-89, mem. exec. com., 1982-89, pres., 1984-86; bd. dirs. Pauline Koner Dance Co., 1979-81, So. Conn. Child Guidance Clinic, 1981-83, New Canaan United Way, 1981-83; treas. Wellesley Class '64, 1984-89. Mem. Univ. Club. Home: 12 E 86th St New York NY 10028 Office: Ross Fin Svcs Group Inc 122 E 42nd St Ste 4005 New York NY 10168-4099

SCHLESSINGER, BERNARD S., retired university dean; b. Toronto, Ont., Can., Mar. 19, 1930; came to U.S., 1938, naturalized, 1948; s. Morris and Eleanor Schlessinger; m. June Hirsch, Dec. 21, 1952; chldren: Rashelle, Jill, Joel. B.S., Roosevelt U., 1950; M.S., Miami U., Oxford, Ohio, 1952; Ph.D., U. Wis., 1955; M.L.S., U. R.I., 1975. Research chemist Am. Can Co., Barrington, Ill, 1955-56; dept. head Chem. Abstracts, Columbus, Ohio, 1958-66; info. researcher Olin Corp., New Haven, 1966-68; asst. dir. Library Sch., So. Conn. State Coll., New Haven, 1968-74; prof. library sci. U. S.C., 1975-77; dean Library Sch. U. R.I., Kingston, 1977-82; prof. Sch. Libr. Sci. Tex. Woman's U., Denton, 1982-92; ret., 1992. Contbr. articles to profl. jours. Served with USAF, 1956-58. Named Outstanding Alumnus U. R.I. Grad. Library Sch., 1978. Mem. ALA, Tex. Library Assn., Sigma Xi, Phi Lambda Upsilon, Beta Phi Mu. Home: 15707 Hamilton St Omaha NE 68118-2339

SCHLEUSENER, RICHARD AUGUST, college president; b. Oxford, Nebr., May 6, 1926; s. August William and Katherine Charlotte (Albrecht) S.; m. Elaine Emma Wilhelm, June 12, 1949; children: Kathryn Jeanne Schleusener Miller, Richard Dennis, Rand Lee, Debra Sue, Jeffrey Thomas. BS, U. Nebr., 1949, DSc (hon.), 1984; MS, Kans. State U., 1956; PhD, Colo. State U., 1958; postgrad., MIT, 1951-52. Rsch. engr. Colo. State U., 1958-64, dir. Inst. Atmospheric Sci.; prof., head dept. meteorology S.D. Sch. Mines and Tech., Rapid City, 1965-74, v.p., dean engrng., 1974-75, acting pres., 1975-76, pres., 1976-86; pres. Black Hills Regional Eye Inst. Found., 1987-96, ret., 1996; cons. weather modification U.S. Dept. Interior, 1964—, U.S. Forest Svc., 1966—, UNESCO, 1971—, also pvt. firms. Contbr. articles to tech. jours. With USAF, 1950-55. Mem. Am. Meteorol. Soc., Am. Geophys. Union, Rotary, Sigma Xi, Beta Sigma Psi. Lutheran. Home: 315 S Berry Pine Rd Rapid City SD 57702-1923

SCHLEY, REEVE, III, artist; b. N.Y.C., Mar. 11, 1936; s. Reeve and Elizabeth (Boies) S.; m. Georgia Terry, Oct. 5, 1968; children: Marie B., Reeve T. B.A., Yale U., 1959; M.F.A., U. Pa., 1962; studied with, Josef Buchty, Munich, 1954-55. Instr. watercolor NAD, N.Y.C., 1981—. Exhibited in group shows including Spook Farm Gallery, Farm Hills, N.J., 1958, Hunterdon County Art Ctr. Ann., 1959, Pa. Acad., 1966, N.J. State Mus., Trenton, 1967, Tenn. Fine Arts Ctr., Nashville, 1973, Okla. Art Ctr., Oklahoma City, 1974, Butler Inst. Am. Art, Youngstown, Ohio, 1974, Drew U., 1975, Silvermine Guild Artists, 1975, NAD, 1977-78, Bklyn. Mus., 1984; one-man shows Vendo Nubes Gallery, Chestnut Hill, Pa., 1967, 71, Phila. Art Alliance, 1969, Spook Farm Gallery, 1970, Saratoga (N.Y.) Gallery, 1972-75, Graham Gallery, N.Y., 1973-97, N.J. State Mus., 1978, Hull Gallery, Washington, 1978, 80, Byck Gallery, Louisville, 1979, Peale House Gallery, Pa. Acad. Fine Arts, 1980, Gallerie Arnoldi-Livie, Munich, 1985, New Orleans Acad. Fine Arts, 1985, 96; represented in permanent collections N.J. State Mus., Trenton, NAD, Newark Mus., Bklyn. Mus., Yale U. Art Gallery, Heublein Collection, Somerset County Coll., Tenneco Chems. Recipient Ranger Fund purchase prize NAD, 1981, 85, cert. of merit, 1978, 95; Best in Show award Hunterdon County Art Ctr., 1974, Laura M. Gross Meml. award Silvermine Guild Artists, 1975, purchase prize Somerset County Coll. Tri-State Exhbn., 1975, 2d prize for watercolor Sumerset Art Assn., 1975; Cresson travel scholar Pa. Acad. Fine Arts, 1962; fellow N.J. Coun. Arts, 1979.

SCHLEY, WAYNE ARTHUR, political consultant; b. Hamilton, Mont., May 22. AA, Shasta Coll., 1960; BS, Sacramento State U., 1963; MS, Am. U., 1974; postgrad., U. Alaska, 1970, Harvard U. Cert. high sch. tchr. (lifetime), Calif. Dept. Edn. Tchr., admin. Placer H.S., Auburn, Calif., 1963-70; spl. asst. to Sen. Ted Stevens, Washington, 1971-77; staff dir. minority and majority subcom. civil svc. Post Office and Gen. Svcs., Washington, 1977-86; minority staff dir. Senate Com. on Rules and Adminstrn., Washington, 1987-92; commr. U.S. Postal Rate Commn., Washington, 1992-95; cons. on legis. and postal issues Washington, 1995—. Chmn. Calif. Teenage Reps., 1963-64; regional v.p. Calif. Young Reps., 1964-66, state sgt. at arms, 1966-67; mem. Placer County Rep. Ctrl. Com., 1965-70. Recipient Cert. of Achievement, JFK Sch. Govt. Harvard U., 1982. Home and Office: 614 Massachusetts Ave NE Washington DC 20002-6006

SCHLEY, WILLIAM SHAIN, otorhinolaryngologist; b. Columbus, Ga., Sept. 21, 1940; s. Frances Brooking Schley and Susie (Smith) Mathews. BA, Emory U., 1962, MD, 1966. Intern mixed surg. The Roosevelt Hosp., N.Y.C., 1966-67, resident in surgery, 1967-68; resident in otorhinolaryngology N.Y. Hosp.-Cornell Med. Ctr., N.Y.C., 1970-73; clin. instr. otorhinolaryngology Cornell U. Med. Coll., 1972-75, clin. asst. prof., 1975-81, assoc. prof., 1982—, acting chmn. dept. otorhinolaryngology, 1988-94, chmn. dept. otorhinolarygology, 1994—; Otorhinolaryngologist to putpatients with pvt. patient privileges N.Y. Hosp., 1973-75, asst. attending otorhinolaryngologist with pvt. patient privileges, 1975-81, assoc. attending, 1992—, acting otorhinolaryngologist-in-chief, 1988-94, otorhinolaryngologist-in-chief, 1994—; assoc. asst. surgeon otolaryngology Manhattan Eye, Ear, Nose and Throat Hosp., 1988—; v.p. and sec. med. bd. N.Y. Hosp., 1994—; mem. co-chmn. vis. day com. The N.Y. Hosp.-Cornell Med. Ctr., 1995—; pres. N.Y. Hosp.-Cornell Med. Coll. Alumni Coun., 1996—. Author: (with others) Pulmonary Diseases of the Fetus Newborn and Child, 1978; contbr. numerous articles to profl. publs. Vestry St. James Ch., N.Y.C., 1994-97; mem. ad hoc bd. visitors Emory U., 1994-95. Lt. comdr. USNR. Recipient Eagle Scout Boy Scouts Am., 1954. Fellow ACS (Manhattan dist. #2 com. on applicants 1991—); mem. Am. Acad. Otolaryngology-Head and Neck Surgery, Med. Soc. State of N.Y., N.Y. State Soc. Otolaryngology-Head and Neck Surgery (exec. coun. 1974-80, dist. dir. 1980), County Med. Soc. N.Y., N.Y. Laryngol. Soc. (sec.-treas. 1981-84, v.p. 1984-85, pres. 1985-86), N.Y. Bronchoscopic Soc. (v.p. 1986-94, pres. 1994—), Assn. Emory Alumni (bd. govs. 1990-97, pres.-elect 1993-94, pres. 1994-95), Omicron Delta Kappa. Episcopalian. Avocations: astronomy, ornithology. Home: 320 E 72nd St New York NY 10021-4769 Office: NY Hosp Starr 541 525 E 68th St New York NY 10021-4873

SCHLICHTEMEIER-NUTZMAN, SUE EVELYN, training consultant; b. Omaha, May 30, 1950; d. StuarTaylor and LaVera YVaughn (Conn) S.; m. Ronald E. Sorensen, Dec. 2, 1972 (div. Aug., 1984); m. Wade Edwin Nutzman, Aug. 27, 1988. BA in Journalism, U. Nebr., 1972, MA in Tng. and Devel., 1988, postgrad., 1989—. Advt. mgr. Burton Harpsichord Co., Lincoln, 1970-71; editorial asst. Nebr. Natural Resources Commn., Lincoln, 1971-72; editor Nebr. Personnel Dept., Lincoln, 1972-73; public info. specialist Governor's Budget Office, Lincoln, 1973-74; mental health cons. Mentl Health Ctr., Lincoln, 1974-81; tng. cons., keynote speaker Lincoln, 1977—; adj. advt. instr., U. Nebr., Lincoln, 1977-81, diversity instr., 1992—, orgn. cons., 1990—, dir. math camp, 1993—, team bldg. tnr. 1993—, motivational spkr. Author: Seeds of Change, 1985, Assertiveness Training, 1990, Help in the Aftermath, 1995; contbr. feature articles and reviews to newspapers and other pubs. Organist, youth music dir., trustee, historian, Nehawka (Nebr.) United Meth. Ch., 1985-93; dir. Community Youth Music Program, Nehawka, 1988-93; sec. Conestoga Found Bd., Murray, Nebr. 1988-92; treas. Conestoga Bd. Edn., Murray, 1988-92; project leader 4-H, 1993—; dir. Math Camp, 1993—, mem. steering com. Conestoga, 1994—; mem. Eastern Nebr. Regional Math Sci. Coalition, 1995—; many other civic and charitable roles as vol. Recipient fellowship U. Nebr., Lincoln, 1991-92. Mem. ASTD, Bus. and Profl. Women (keynote spkr. 1991-92), Missouri Valley Adult Edn. Assn., Adult and Continuing Edn. Assn. Nebr., Internat. Platform Speakers Assn., Am. Bus. Women's Assn. (keynote speaker 1993, tng. strategic planning cons., 1996, natl. keynotes, 1995-96), U. Nebr. Alumni Assn. (life). Democrat. Avocations: flower gardening, piano, art, reading, writing. Home and Office: Tng Plng Cons 3412 Mount Pleasant Dr Nehawka NE 68413-2424

SCHLICHTING, CATHERINE FLETCHER NICHOLSON, librarian, educator; b. Huntsville, Ala., Nov. 18, 1923; d. William Parsons and Ethel Louise (Breitling) Nicholson; BS, U. Ala., 1944; MLS, U. Chgo., 1950; m. Harry Fredrick Schlichting, July 1, 1950 (dec. Aug. 1964); children: James Dean, Richard Dale, Barbara Lynn. Asst. librarian U. Ala. Edn. Library, Tuscaloosa, summers 1944-45; librarian Sylacauga (Ala.) High Sch., 1944-45, Hinsdale (Ill.) High Sch., 1945-49; asst. librarian Centre for Children's Books, U. Chgo., 1950-52; instr. reference dept. library Ohio Wesleyan U., Delaware, 1965-69, asst. prof., 1969-79, asso. prof., 1979-85, prof., 1985—, curator Ohio Wesleyan Hist. Collection, 1986—, student personnel librarian, 1966-72, adviser Mortar Bd., 1969-72, mem. exec. com., 1973-79, 85-86, sec. com., 1973-74, 76-77. Mem. adminstrv. bd. Methodist Ch., 1963-81, chmn. adminstrv. bd., 1985—, mem. Council on Ministries, 1975-81, chmn., 1975-77. Recipient Algernon Sidney Sullivan award U. Ala., 1944. Ohio Wesleyan U.-Mellon Found. grantee, 1972-73, 84-85; GLCA Teaching fellow, 1976-77. Mem. ALA, Ohio Library Assn., Midwest Acad. Librarian Conf., Acad. Librarians Assn. Ohio (dir. 1984-86), AAUP (chpt. sec. 1967-68, chpt. exec. com. 1973-78), United Meth. Women (v.p. Mt. Vernon dist. 1989-92, pres. 1994—), Kappa Delta Pi, Alpha Lambda Delta. Democrat. Clubs: Ohio Wesleyan U. Womans (exec. bd. 1969-72, 77-79, 81-84, pres. 1969-70, sec. 1977-78), History (pres. 1971-72, v.p. 1978-79), Fortnightly (pres. 1975-76, 87-88), Am. Field Service (pres. Delaware chpt. 1975-76) (Delaware). Author: Introduction to Bibliographic Research: Basic Sources, 4th edit., 1983; Checklist of Biographical Reference Sources, 1977; Audio-Visual Aids in Bibliographic Instruction, 1976; Introduction to Bibliographic Research: Slide Catalog and Script, 1980; info. cons. (documentary) Noble Achievements: The History of Ohio Wesleyan 1942-92, 1992, 150 Years of Excellence: A Pictoral View of Ohio Wesleyan University, 1992. Home: 414 N Liberty St Delaware OH 43015-1232 Office: Ohio Wesleyan U La Beeghly Library Delaware OH 43015

SCHLICHTING, NANCY MARGARET, hospital administrator; b. N.Y.C., Nov. 21, 1954. BA, Duke U., 1976; MBA, Cornell U., 1979. Adminstrv. resident Meml. Hosp. Cancer, N.Y.C., 1978; fellow Blue Cross-Blue Shield Assn., Chgo., 1979-80; asst. dirs. ops. Akron (Ohio) City Hosp., 1980-81, assoc. dir. planning, 1981-83, exec. v.p., 1983-88; exec. v.p. Riverside Meth. Hosps., Columbus, Ohio, 1988-92, pres., COO, 1992-93, pres., CEO, 1993-96; pres. Ea. region Cath. Health Initiatives, Aston, Pa., 1996-97; exec. v.p. Summa Health Sys., Akron, Ohio, 1997—. Home: 320D Village Pointe Dr Akron OH 44313 Office: Summa Health Sys 525 E Market St Akron OH 44304-1619 also: Cath Health Initiatives One McIntyre Dr Aston PA 19014-1196

SCHLICKAU, GEORGE HANS, cattle breeder, professional association executive; b. Haven, Kans., Nov. 2, 1922; s. Albert Rudulph and Florence Elsabe (Wittorff) S.; m. Lois Marie Ritthaler, Apr. 26, 1955; children: Bruce Alan, Susan Marie, James Darwin, Nancy Ann. Grad. high sch. Breeder registered Schlickau Hereford cattle, Haven, 1943—; pres. Reno County (Kans.) Hereford Assn., 1947-56, treas., 1956-58; dir. Reno County Cattleman's Assn., 1970-74, sec., 1970-71, treas., 1974; dir. Kans. Hereford Assn., 1955-71, 84-90, v.p., 1959, pres., 1960, 61; mem. organizing bd. Kans. Bull Test Sta., county committeeman Kans. Livestock Assn., 1960-75, bd. dirs., 1976-80, v.p. purebred coun., 1990-91, pres. purebred coun., 1992-93; bd. dirs. Am. Hereford Assn., 1969-75, v.p., 1973-74, pres., 1974-75; bd. dirs. Am. Nat. Cattleman's Assn., 1974-76; mem. fgn. trade com. Nat. Cattlemsn's Assn., 1990-93. Contbr. articles in field to profl. jours.; exhibitor, also winner numerous awards at major cattle shows across country; guest speaker, judge at numerous Hereford cattle events across country. Host ann. judging sch. and contest for Future Farmers Am. and 4-H youth, 1940-84; dir. Kans. Nat. Jr. Livestock Show, 1973—, sec., 1982-83, chmn., 1984-85, bd. govs., 1988—; bd. dirs. Haven State Bank, 1962—, Equus Beds Groundwater Mgmt. Dist. 2, 1975-79, Beef leader Haven 4-H Club, 1947-67; mem. Haven H.S. Bd., 1962-65, clk., 1964-65; mem. agrl. adv. com. Hutchinson (Kans.) Cmty. Jr. Coll., Kans., 1974-82; adv. Am. Jr. Hereford Assn., 1977-82; pres. Parent-Tchr. League Luth. Sch., 1979-80, 83-84; mem. zoning bd. City of Haven, 1985-88; bd. dirs. Ark Valley Electric Coop Assn., 1984-96, v.p., 1986-90, pres. 1990-93, Dist. IV Kans. Electric Coop., 1986-96, chmmn., 1992; bd. dirs. Kans. Coop. Coun., 1994-96; vice chmn. KACRE, 1992, chmn. 1993; adv. coun. mem. Arthur Capper Coop. Ctr., 1994-96. Recipient Am. Farmer Degree award Future Farmers Am., 1942, Reno County Outstanding Young Farmer award Hutchinson Jaycees, 1959, Kans. Hereford Herdsman of the Year award High Plains Jour., 1960, Soil Conservation award Kans. Bankers Assn., 1968, Hon. State Farmer Degree award Future Farmers Am., 1972, Kans. Hereford Breeder of Yr., 1976, Portrait Gallery Outstanding Livestock Breeder award Kans. State U. Block and Bridle Club, 1978, Reno County 4-H Family of Yr. award, 1987, Reno County Farm Focus Family award Hutchinson C. of C., 1989, Stockman of Yr. award Kansas Livestock and Meat Industry Coun., 1994; named Kans. Seedstock Producer of Yr. BIF, 1988; Kans Jr. Livestock Show dedicatory, 1991, Master Farmer, Master Farm Homemaker, 1991. Mem. Kans. Wheat Growers Assn., Kans. Farm Bur., Haven Industries, Inc., Kansas City (Kans.) Hereford Club, Kans. State U. Block and Bridle Club (hon. mem.), Haven Booster Club (sec. 1952-53, pres. 1954-56), Future Farmers Am. (mem. adv. com. Haven chpt. 1971—). Lutheran (mem. sch. bd. 1967-70, chmn. 1969-70; chmn. ch. bd. 8 yrs., chmn. congregation 1984-88, elder 1977-79). Home: 14506 S Victory Rd Haven KS 67543

SCHLICKE, CARL PAUL, retired surgeon; b. Bklyn., Mar. 16, 1910; s. Carl Paul and Eunice Gertrude (Hope) S.; m. Hilda Meek Hinckley, Aug. 30, 1937; children: Paul Van Waters, Suzanne Parker. AB, UCLA, 1931; MD, Johns Hopkins Med. Sch., 1935; MS in Surgery, U. Minn., 1940. Diplomate Am. Bd. Surgery. Intern John Hopkins Hosp., Balt., 1935; asst. resident in surgery L.I. (N.Y.) Coll. Hosp., 1936-37; fellow in surgery Mayo Clinic, Rochester, Minn., 1937-42; surgeon Rockwood Clinic, 1946-79, sr. surgeon, 1951-75; clin. assoc. prof. surgery U. Wash., Seattle, 1969-75, clin. prof., 1975-82; retired Rockwood Clinic, 1979; clin. prof. emeritus U. Wash., Seattle, 1982—; staff St. Lukes Hosp., 1946-51, Sacred Heart Hosp., 1950-79, chmn. surg. dept., 1958-75; cons Spokane (Wash.) Vets. Hosp., Fairchild AFB Hosp. Author: Working Together: A History of a Medical Group Practice, 1980, General George Wright, Guardian of the Pacific Coast, 1988, Spokane and Inland Empire Blood Bank, 1990; contbr. over 70 articles to profl. jours., 16 articles to hist. jours. Fellow ACS (gov., regent, 1st v.p.), mem. AMA, Spokane County Med. Soc., Washington State Med. Assn. (pres. 1965-66), Am. Surg. Assn. (2d v.p. 1976), Spokane Surg. Soc. (pres. 1960), North Pacific Surg. Assn. (pres. 1964), Western Surg. Assn. (pres. 1972), Pacific Coast Surg. Assn. (pres. 1976-77), Internat. Soc. Surgery, Soc. Surgery Alimentary Tract, Surgeon's Travel Club, Mayo Clinic Alumni Assn. (pres. 1968), Barber Surgeons Pacific NW, Alpha Omega Alpha, Sigma Xi. Republican. Avocations: swimming, canoeing, listening to jazz music. Home: 826 E Overbluff Rd Spokane WA 99203-3445

SCHLICKEISEN, RODGER OSCAR, non-profit environmental organization executive; b. Houston, Jan. 24, 1941; s. Oscar and Elvene Alice (Rennemo) S.; m. Susan Jane Culver, May 23, 1970; 1 child, Derek. BA, U. Wash., 1963; MBA, Harvard U., 1965; DBA, George Washington U., 1978. Loan officer Export-Import Bank of U.S., Washington, 1968-70; pres. Gryphon, Inc., Washington, 1970-74; group dir. com. on budget U.S. Senate, Washington, 1974-79; assoc. dir. econs. and govt. U.S. Office of Mgmt. and Budget, Washington, 1979-80; v.p. Craver, Mathews, Smith & Co., Falls Church, Va., 1980-81, CEO, 1981-87; chief of staff Office of U.S. Senator Max Baucus, Washington, 1987-91; pres., CEO Defenders of Wildlife, Washington, 1991—; bd. dirs. Island Resources Found., St. Thomas, V.I., Ctr. for Policy Alternatives, Washington, Natural Resources Coun. of Am., Washington; bd. advisors Environ. Comms. Orgn., L.A., 1992—, Environ. Media Assn., L.A., 1992—. Contbr. articles to profl. publs. Va. state chmn. Common Cause, 1971-74; mem. League of Conservation Voters, Washington. Mem. Soc. for Conservation Biology. Office: Defenders of Wildlife 1101 14th St NW Washington DC 20005-5601

SCHLICKMAN, J. ANDREW, lawyer; b. Washington, Mar. 28, 1952. AB, Georgetown U., 1974; JD, U. Chgo., 1978. Bar: Ill. 1978, U.S. Supreme Ct. 1987. Ptnr. Sidley & Austin, Chgo. Coord. author: International Environmental Law and Regulation, 1991, 2d edit., 1994. Mem. ABA, Ill State Bar Assn., Chgo. Bar Assn. Office: Sidley & Austin 1 First Natl Plz Chicago IL 60603-2003

SCHLIEBS, CHARLES ALLAN, lawyer; b. Kansas City, Mo., Dec. 3, 1950; s. Edgar Emil and Elsie Elizabeth (Rosher) S.; m. Melanie Emily Schuldis, Nov. 15, 1981. BA, BS in Econ., U. Pa., 1972; JD, Vanderbilt U., 1975. Bar: Mo. 1975, U.S. Supreme Ct. 1979, Pa. 1984. Assoc. Blackwell Sanders Matheny Weary & Lombardi, Kansas City, 1975-79, ptnr., 1980-82, various corp. positons, 1982-88; ptnr. Jones, Day, Reavis & Pogue, Pitts., 1988-89, adminstv. ptnr., 1989—; mem. adv. bd. U. Pitts. Sch. Law Ctr. Internat. Legal Edn., 1995—, mem. internat. adv. bd. U. Pitts. Grad. Sch. Pub. and Internat. Affairs, 1990—, Duquesne U., Palumbo Sch. Bus. Adminstrn., Pitts., 1990—. Mem. ABA, Internat. Bar Assn., Pa. Bar Assn., Duquesne Club. Home: 10 Myrtle Hill Rd Sewickley PA 15143-8700 Office: Jones Day Reavis & Pogue 1 Mellon Bank Ctr Pittsburgh PA 15258-0001

SCHLIEVE, HY C. J., principal; b. Mandan, N.D., Apr. 4, 1952; s. Calvin L. and Loretta L. (Johnson) S.; m. Terri Ann Hansen, Dec. 30, 1977; children: Derek, Aaron, Jessica. BA, N.D. State U., 1974, MS, 1984; EdD, Calif. Coast U., 1994. Tchr., coach Halliday (N.D.) Pub. Sch., 1974-75, Drake (N.D.) Pub. Sch., 1975-76, Montpelier (N.D.) Pub. Sch., 1976-81; prin. Unity Pub. Sch., Petersburg, N.D., 1981-83, Page (N.D.) Pub. Sch., 1983-85; supt. Wolford (N.D.) Pub. Sch., 1985-87, Garrison (N.D.) Pub. Schs., 1987-93; prin. Buhl Joint Sch. Dist. 412, Idaho, 1993-95, Oconto Falls Area Sch. Dist., Wis., 1995—; com. mem. NDASA Rsch. and Evaluation, Garrison, 1988-93; fiscal agt. Mo. Hills Consortium, McLean County, N.D., 1989-93; cons. asbestos Garrison Pub. Sch. Dist., 1987-93. Sec. Govtl. Affairs Com., Garrison, 1987-93; mem. Tourism Com., Garrison, 1988-92, Econ. Devel. Com., 1988-89. Recipient Nat. Superintendent of the Yr. awd., North Dakota, Am. Assn. of School Administrators, 1992. Mem. Nat. Assn. Secondary Sch. Prins. (prin. assessor tng. 1990), NSBA Fed. Policy Coords. Network. Avocations: golf, hunting, fishing, bowling, outdoor activities. Home: 175 N Farm Rd Oconto Falls WI 54154-1220 Office: Oconto Falls High Sch 408 Cedar Ave Oconto Falls WI 54154-1253*

SCHLINGER, WARREN GLEASON, retired chemical engineer; b. Los Angeles, May 29, 1923; s. William McKinley and Esther (Gleason) S.; m. Katharine S. Stewart, June 29, 1947: children: Michael S., Norman W., Sarah Lynne. BS, Calif. Inst. Tech., 1944, MS, 1946, PhD, 1949. Registered profl. engr., Calif. Instr. Calif. Inst. Tech., Pasadena, 1949-53; chem. engr. Texaco Inc., Montebello, Calif., 1953-61, supr. research, 1961-69, mgr., 1969-81, assoc. dir., 1981-87, ret. 1987; cons. 1987—. Contbr. numerous articles to profl. publs. Patentee in field. Fellow Am. Inst. Chem. Engrs. (Chem. Engrng. Practice award 1981, So. Calif. sect. Tech. Achievement award 1976; Electric Power Research Inst. Achievement award 1985); mem. NAE, Am. Chem. Soc., Sigma Xi, Tau Beta Pi. Clubs: Jonathan (Los Angeles); Calif. Country (Whittier). Home: 3835 Shadow Grove Rd Pasadena CA 91107-2241

SCHLITT, WILLIAM JOSEPH, III, metallurgical engineer; b. Columbus, Ohio, June 12, 1942; s. William Joseph Jr. and Florence (McCall) S.; m. Anne Marie Ritchie, Apr. 1, 1994. BS in Metall. Engring., Carnegie Inst. Tech., 1964; PhD in Metallurgy, Pa. State U., 1968. Registered profl. engr., Tex. Scientist Kennecott Minerals Co., Salt Lake City, 1968-75, sr. scientist, 1975-76, mgr. hydrometallurgy dept., 1977-81, prin. program mgr., 1981-82; process staff mgr. Brown & Root, Inc., Houston, 1982-83, mgr. tech., 1983-93, product line mgr. chems., 1993-94; mgr. process tech. Davy Nonferrous Divsn. of Kvaerner Metals, San Ramon, Calif., 1994—; mem. oversight com. soln. mining NSF, Socoro, N.Mex., 1977-79; mem. oversight com. smelter flue dust Environ. Prot. Agy., Butte, Mont., 1978-79; mem. internat. adv. bd. In Situ jour., N.Y.C., 1988—. Editor: In Situ Uranium Leaching and Ground Water Restoration, 1979, Leaching and Recovering Copper from As-Mined Materials, 1980 (Publ. Bd. Commendation 1981), Gold and Silver-Leaching, Recovery and Economics, 1981, Interfacing Technologies in Solution Mining, 1982 (Publ. Bd. Commendation 1983), Salts and Brines '85, 1985; assoc. editor: (handbook) SME Mining Engineering Handbook, 1992; contbr. more than 35 tech. articles to profl. jours., trade publs., and proc. volumes including Metall. Transactions B, AIME Transactions, In Situ, Minerals and Metall. Processing. Pres. Ft. Bend County Kennel Club, Richmond, Tex., 1988-90. Trainee NSF, 1984-88. Mem. Soc. Mining Engrs. (bd. dirs. 1984-95, chmn. mining and exploration divsn. 1986-87), The Metall. Soc. (bd. dirs. 1982-83), Can. Inst. Mining and Metallurgy, Sigma Xi, Tau Beta Pi, Phi Kappa Phi. Achievements include patents in field. Avocation: licensed dog show judge. Office: Davy Internat Davy Nonferrous Divsn 2440 Camino Ramon Ste 100 San Ramon CA 94583-4293

SCHLITTER, STANLEY ALLEN, lawyer; b. Decorah, Iowa, Jan. 27, 1950; s. Joseph Everett and Lillian Helena (Helgerson) S.; m. Sheila Lynn Edwards, Sept. 24, 1977; children: Stephanie Anne, Joseph Allen, John Edward. BS, Iowa State U., 1972; JD, U. Iowa, 1977. Bar: Ill. 1977, U.S. Dist. Ct. (no. dist.) Ill. 1977, U.S. Ct. Appeals (7th cir.) 1981, U.S. Ct. Appeals (Fed. cir.) 1982, D.C. 1989. Assoc. Kirkland & Ellis, Chgo., 1977-84, ptnr., 1984-88; ptnr. Kirkland & Ellis, Washington, 1988-91, Jenner & Block, Chgo., 1991—. Mem. ABA, IEEE, Am. Intellectual Property Law Assn. Office: Jenner & Block One IBM Plaza Chicago IL 60611-3608

SCHLITTLER, GILBERTO BUENO, former United Nations official, lecturer; b. Piracicaba, Sao Paulo, Brazil, Oct. 6, 1934; came to U.S., 1963; s. Zacharias and Sebastiana (Bueno) S.; m. Ana Maria Amaral, Oct. 5, 1963 (div. Nov. 1973); children: Joao-Paulo, Leonardo. B in Social and Polit. Scis., U. Sao Paulo, 1956; MPA, NYU, 1970. Adminstrn. officer Sao Paulo State Civil Svc., 1957-62; polit. affairs officer UN, N.Y.C., 1964-78, sr. polit. affairs officer, 1979-82, dir. Gen. Assembly affairs, 1983-88, dir. Security Coun., 1988-92, dir. spl. assignments, 1992, dir. Americas divsn., 1992-94, dir. Guatemala unit, 1994-95, spl. envoy of sec.-gen. for the Guatemala Peace Process, 1995-96; mgmt. cons. Brazilian Investment Cos., Sao Paulo, 1958-63; lectr. on UN questions, 1965—; mem. faculty NYU Sch Continuing Edn. Editor: Historia Social de Sao Paulo, 1964; editor newspaper Folha da Manha, 1956-58. Mem. UN Panel of Counsel in Disciplinary and Appeals Cases, 1966-78; mem., chmn. UN Joint Appeals Bd., 1978-92; mem. UN Discrimination Panel, 1975. U. Sao Paulo scholar, 1953-56, Music Composition scholar, 1954. Mem. Met. Mus. Art. Christian. Avocations: music (piano), literature, theatre, fine arts, travel. Home: 420 E 23rd St Apt 13-g New York NY 10010-5037

SCHLODER, JOHN E., museum director. BS, Duquesne U., 1969; diplôme d'Ancien Elève, L'Ecole du Louvre, Paris, 1973; licence L'Institut d'Art et d'Archéologie, U. Paris-Sorbonne, 1973, doctorat L'Institut d'Art et d'Archéologie, 1988; MPhil, Columbia U., 1980. Chargé de Mission Musée du Louvre, Paris, 1979-82; asst. curator Cleve. Mus. Art Edn Dept., 1982-85, assoc. curator, 1985-86, adminstr. pub. programs, 1986-88, asst. dir. edn and pub. programs, 1988-92; dir. Birmingham (Ala.) Mus. Art, 1992—; vis. prof. Colégio Andrews, Rio de Janeiro, Brazil, 1980-81, Vaculdade Candido Mendes, Rio de Janeiro, 1981-82; adj. prof. dept. art history Case Western Res. U., Cleve., 1984-92; lectr. in field. Mus. rep. Northeastern Ohio Inter-Mus. Coun., 1984-92; trustee Cleve. Sch. Arts, 1991-92; active Southeast Mus. Conf., 1992—; mem. Leadership Birmingham, 1994-95; bd. dirs. Op. New Birmingham, 1993—; mem. Birmingham Olympic programming com., mem. outreach com., 1994—. Lurcy Trust fellowship, 1975, Columbia U. Traveling fellowship, 1975, 76, U. Cambridge, Eng. Leverhulme fellowship, 1977, Kellogg Project fellowship Smithsonian Instn., 1987; scholarship J. Paul Getty Trust, 1989; vis. Scholar grantee The Japan Found., 1995; recipient French Govt. award, 1975, award of achievement for best cmty. event Northern Ohio Live Mag., 1991. Mem. Am. Assn. Mus., Assn. Art Mus. Dirs., Internat. Lab. for Visitor Studies, Visitor Studies Assn., Ala. Mus. Assn., Birmingham Area Mus. Assn., Soc. de l'Historie de l'Art Français, Rotary Club Birmingham. Home: 3110 Carlisle Rd Birmingham AL 35213 Office: Birmingham Mus Art 2000 8th Ave N Birmingham AL 35203-2205

SCHLOEMANN, ERNST FRITZ (RUDOLF AUGUST), physicist, engineer; b. Borgholzhausen, Germany, Dec. 13, 1926; came to U.S., 1954, naturalized, 1965; s. Hermann Wilhelm and Auguste Wilhelmine (Koch) S.; m. Gisela Mattiat, June 19, 1955 (dec. 1990); children: Susan C., Sonia G., Barbara I.; m. Sally (Duren) Heatter, Nov. 5, 1994. BS, U. Göttingen, Fed. Republic of Germany, 1951, MS, 1953, PhD, 1954. With rsch. div. Raytheon Co., Lexington, Mass., 1955-94, electronics sys. divsn., 1994-95; ind. cons. Weston, Mass., 1995—; cons. scientist, 1964-95; vis. assoc. prof. Stanford U., 1961-62; vis. prof. U. Hamburg, Germany, 1966. Assoc. editor:

Jour. Applied Physics, 1974-76; contbr. numerous articles to profl. jours. Recipient T.L. Phillips award for Excellence in Tech., 1990. Fellow IEEE, Am. Phys. Soc., Sigma Xi. Democrat. Unitarian. Achievements include patents in field of magnetic materials and their application to microwave technology. Home & Office: 38 Brook Rd Weston MA 02193-1713

SCHLOERB, PAUL RICHARD, surgeon, educator; b. Buffalo, Oct. 22, 1919; s. Herman George and Vera (Gross) S.; m. Louise M. Grimmer, Feb. 25, 1950; children: Ronald G., Patricia Johnson, Marilyn A. Hock, Dorothy E. Schloerb Hoban, Paul Richard. A.B., Harvard U., 1941; M.D., U. Rochester, 1944. Intern U. Rochester Med. Sch., 1944-45, asst. resident, 1947-48, instr. surgery, 1952; research fellow, resident Peter Bent Brigham Hosp., Boston, 1948-52; mem. faculty U. Kans. Med. Ctr., Kansas City, 1952-79, prof. surgery, 1964-79, 88—, dean for research, 1972-79, dir. nutritional support svc., 1993—; prof. surgery U. Rochester (N.Y.) Med Ctr., 1979-88, adj. prof. surgery, 1988-90; surgeon Strong Meml. Hosp., 1979-88, dir. Surg. ICU, 1979-85, dir. surg. nutritional support service. Contbr. over 100 articles to profl. jours. Served to lt. (j.g.), M.C. USNR, 1944-45; to lt. 1953-55. Mem. AMA, ACS, AAAS, Am. Surg. Assn., Soc. U. Surgeons, Am. Physiol. Soc., Internat. Soc. Surgery, Ctrl. Surg. Assn., Am. Assn. for Surgery of Trauma, Am. Assn. Cancer Rsch., Biomed. Engring. Soc., Am. Inst. Nutrition, Am. Soc. Clin. Nutrition, Sigma Xi. Office: Dept Surgery U Kansas Med Ctr Kansas City KS 66160

SCHLOM, JEFFREY BERT, research scientist; b. N.Y.C., June 22, 1942; s. David and Anna (Klein) S.; children: Amy Melissa, Steven Michael. BS (Pres.'s scholar), Ohio State U., 1964; MS, Adelphi U., 1966; PhD, Rutgers U., 1969. Instr. Columbia Coll. Phys. and Surg., 1969-71, asst. prof., 1971-73; chmn. breast cancer virus segment Nat Cancer Inst., NIH, Bethesda, Md., 1973-76; chief lab. tumor immunology and biology Nat Cancer Inst., NIH, 1983—, head exptl. oncology sect., 1976-83; prof. George Washington U., Washington, 1975—; disting. lectr. Can. Cancer Soc., 1985. Mem. numerous editorial bds.; contbr. numerous articles to profl. jours. Recipient Dir.'s award NIH, 1977, 89, Tech. Transfer award NIH, 1994, 95, 96, Disting. Scientist award Turin U., 1996, others. Mem. Am. Assn. Cancer Rsch. (Rosenthal award 1985), Am. Soc. Cytology (Basic Rsch. award 1987). Office: Insts of Health Bldg 10 Rm 8B07 Bethesda MD 20892

SCHLOSBERG, RICHARD T., III, newspaper publishing executive. Pub., CEO L.A. Times. Office: LA Times Times Mirror Sq Los Angeles CA 90053*

SCHLOSE, WILLIAM TIMOTHY, health care executive; b. West Lafayette, Ind., May 16, 1948; s. William Fredrick and Dora Irene (Chitwood) S.; m. Linda Lee Fletcher, June 29, 1968 (div. 1978); children: Vanessa Janine Schlose Hubert, Stephanie Lynn; m. Kelly Marie Martin, June 6, 1987; 1 child, Taylor Jean Martin-Schlose. Student, Bowling Green State U., 1966-68, Long Beach City Coll., 1972-75; teaching credential, UCLA, 1975. Staff respiratory therapist St. Vincent's Med. Ctr., L.A., 1972-75; cardio-pulmonary chief Temple Community Hosp., L.A., 1975-76; adminstrv. dir. spl. svcs. Santa Fe Meml. Hosp., L.A., 1976-79; mem. mktg. and pub. rels. staff Nat. Med. Homecare Corp., Orange, Calif., 1979-81, Medtech of Calif., Inc., Burbank, Calif., 1981-84; regional mgr. Mediq Health Care Group Svcs., Inc., Chatsworth, Calif., 1984-88; pres. Baby Watch Homecare, Whittier, Calif., 1988-90, Tim Schlose and Assocs., Orange, Calif., 1990—; staff instr., Montebello (Calif.) Adult Schs. Author: Fundamental Respiratory Therapy Equipment, 1977; mem. editl. adv. bd. RT, The Jour. Respiratory Car Practitioners, 1997. With USN, 1968-72. Mem. Am. Assn. Respiratory Care, Calif. Soc. Respiratory Care (past officer), Nat. Bd. Respiratory Care, Nat. Assn. Apnea Profls., Am. Assn. Physicians Assts., L.A. Pediatric Soc., Calif. Perinatal Assn., Saleen Owners Enthusiasts Club, SVT Cobra Owner's Club So. Calif., Mustang Club Am. Republican. Methodist. Avocations: boating, automobile racing, automobile restoration, wrist watch collecting, fly fishing. Office: Tim Schlose and Assocs 910 E Chapman Ave Orange CA 92866-2109

SCHLOSS, HOWARD MONROE, federal agency administrator; b. New Orleans, Jan. 30, 1960; m. Deborah Tawney; children: Michael Austin, Lindsay Taylor. BFA in Journalism, So. Meth. U., 1982. Copy editor Fort Worth Star-Telegram, asst. to the op-ed page editor, 1983-87; writer, editor UPI, Dallas, 1982; dep. comm. dir., comm. dir. Dem. Congl. Campaign Com., 1987-91; acct. supr. Powell Tate, 1991-93; dep. asst. sec. for pub. affairs Treasury Dept., 1994-95, asst. sec. for pub. affairs, 1995—. Office: Dept of Treasury Pub Affairs 1500 Pennsylvania Ave NW Washington DC 20220

SCHLOSS, IRVING STEVEN, lawyer; b. N.Y.C., Feb. 3, 1945; s. Arthur and Bianca (Steinberger) S.; m. Christine Skeeles, June 28, 1970; children: Tracy, David. AB magna cum laude, Harvard Coll., 1966; LLB, Yale U., 1970. Bar: Conn. 1972, U.S. Dist. Ct. Conn. 1972, U.S. Ct. Appeals (2d cir.) 1973, U.S. Tax Ct. 1985. Law clerk for Judge Spottswood Robinson, III (D.C. cir.) U.S. Ct. Appeals, Washington, 1970-71; ptnr. Tyler, Cooper & Alcorn, New Haven, 1976—. Contbr. articles to profl. publs. Bd. dirs. Guilford (Conn.) Free Libr., 1986-92, Shoreline Found., Guilford, 1984-93, New Haven Symphony Orch., 1995—; vol. CPTV Auction, West Hartford, 1987-88; mem. Rep. Town Coun., Guilford, 1987-91. Recipient Man of Yr. award Guilford YMCA, 1990. Mem. ABA, Conn. Bar Assn. (chmn. sect. corps. and other bus. orgns. 1988-90), New Haven Conn. Bar Assn., Quinnipiack Club.

SCHLOSS, NATHAN, economist; b. Balt., Jan. 14, 1927; s. Howard L. and Louise (Levi) S.; BS in Bus., Johns Hopkins U., 1950; m. Rosa Montalvo, Mar. 1, 1958; children: Nina L., Carolyn D. Buyer, Pacific Coast gen. merchandise office Sears Roebuck & Co., Los Angeles, 1955-60, staff asst. econ. research dept., Chgo., 1960-63; sr. market analyst corp. rsch. dept. Montgomery Ward & Co., Chgo., 1963-65; rsch. mgr. real estate dept. Walgreen Co., Chgo., 1970-72; v.p. rsch. and planning Maron Properties Ltd., Montreal, Que., Can., 1972-74; corp. economist, fin. analyst Real Estate Rsch. Corp., Chgo., 1974-88, sr. v.p., 1986-88, treas., chief fin. analyst, 1982-88; economist Office of Ill. Atty. Gen., Chgo., 1988—; cons. economist, since 1965—; mem. com. on price indexes and productivity fgn. labor Bus. Research Adv. Council of Bur. Labor Stats., Dept. Labor, 1979-88, also chairperson (1985-86), com. on employment and unemployment. Recipient Commendable Svc. award Dept. Labor, 1987. Mem. Plan Commn., Village of Wilmette, Ill., 1975-77, mem. tech. adv. com. on employment and tng. data Ill. Employment and Tng. Coun., 1979-82; mem. tech. adv. com. Ill. Job Tng. Coordinating Council, 1983-87. Mem. Am. Mktg. Assn., Nat. Assn. Bus. Economists, Ill. Econ. Assn., Lambda Alpha. Contbr. articles on fin. and market analysis of real estate to profl. jours. Home: 115 Hollywood Ct Wilmette IL 60091-3122 Office: 100 W Randolph St Chicago IL 60601

SCHLOSS, SAMUEL LEOPOLD, JR., retired food service executive, consultant; b. Montgomery, Ala., Mar. 30, 1926; s. Samuel Leopold and Amelia (Strauss) S.; m. Burke Hart Klein; children: Stephen, Alyce, Adam. BS in Indsl. Engring., Ga. Inst. Tech., 1947; MS in Indsl. Engring., Columbia U., 1948. Sec. Schloss and Kahn Inc., Montgomery, 1948-56, pres., 1956-86, chmn., 1986-94. Pres. Montgomery Acad., 1979-80, bd. dirs. emeritus, 1982; control bd. Montgomery Com. of One Hundred, 1984-86; bd. dirs. YMCA Metro Bd., Ctrl. Ala. Red Cross, 1996. Capt. USAFR, 1960. Mem. Montgomery C. of C. (pres. 1983), Standard Club (pres. 1964), Capital City Club (bd. govs. 1977-80), Rotary (pres. 1972-73), Montgomery Country Club. Republican. Office: Union Bank Tower 60 Commerce St Ste 1210 Montgomery AL 36104-3562

SCHLOSSBERG, FRED PAUL, elementary education educator; b. N.Y.C., May 30, 1944; s. Alexander and Mae S.; divorced; 1 child, Elan. BSBA, Boston U., 1966; M of Phys. Edn., NYU, 1983. Tchr. elem. sch. N.Y.C. Bd. Edn., 1966—; coach local basketball team, North Bellmore, N.Y., 1988—, local baseball team, North Bellmore, 1988-92. Vol. Alcoholics Anonymous, West Hempstead, N.Y., 1987-93; tutor Literacy Vols. Am. Democrat. Avocations: physical fitness, dealer of sports and non-sports cards, comic books and memorabilia, music, travel. Home: 3678 Ocean Ave Seaford NY 11783

SCHLOSSBERG, STEPHEN I., management consultant; b. Roanoke, Va., May 18, 1921; s. Morris Joseph and Jennie (Weinstein) S.; m. Mary Coleman Bazelon, 1953 (div. 1958); m. Nancy Kamin, June 6, 1963; children: Mark Jay, Karen Jean. BS in Commerce, U. Va., 1956, LLB, 1957. Asst. mgr. Kanns, Inc., Roanoke, Va., 1945-49; mem. labor organ. staff Internat. Ladies Garment Workers Union, N.Y.C., 1949-54; assoc., ptnr. Van Arkel & Kaiser, Washington, 1957-61; spl. asst. to dir. Fed. Mediation and Conciliation Service, Washington, 1961-63; gen. counsel, dir. govt. relations Internat. Union UAW, Detroit, 1963-81; ptnr. Zwerdling, Schlossberg, Leibig & Kahn, Washington, 1981-85; dept. under sec. for labor-mgmt. relations and coop. programs U.S. Dept. Labor, Washington, 1985-87; spl. advisor to dir. gen. and dir. Washington br. ILO, 1987-94; sr. cons. The Kamber Group, Washington, 1995—; cons., advisor in field; former mem. Presdl. Adv. Bd. on Ambassadorial Appointments, Presdl. Commn. on Indsl. Competiveness; adj. prof. law Georgetown U. Law Ctr., 1962-63, 84-85. Author: Organizing and the Law, 1967, 2d edit. (with Frederick Sherman), 1971, 3d edit. (with Judith Scott), 1983, 4th edit., 1991. Served to staff sgt. U.S. Army, 1941-45, ETO. Mem. ABA (commn. on nat. inst. justice, former co-chmn. internat. labor law com., sect. on labor law, former mem. consortium on legal services, former mem. spl. com. on election law), Order of Coif, Raven Soc., Omicron Delta Kappa. Home: 2801 New Mexico NW # PH17 Washington DC 20007 Office: The Kamber Group 1920 L St NW Washington DC 20036-5004

SCHLOSSER, ANNE GRIFFIN, librarian; b. N.Y.C., Dec. 28, 1939; d. C. Russell and Gertrude (Taylor) Griffin; m. Gary J. Schlosser, Dec. 28, 1965. BA in History, Wheaton Coll., Norton, Mass., 1962; MLS, Simmons Coll., 1964; cert. archives adminstrn. Nat. Archives and Records Service, Am. U., 1970. Head UCLA Theater Arts Library, 1964-69; dir. Louis B. Mayer Libr., Am. Film Inst., L.A., 1969-88, dir. film/TV documentation workshop, 1977-87; head Cinema-TV Libr. and Archives of the Performing Arts, U. So. Calif., L.A., 1988-91; dir. Entertainment Resources Seminar, 1990; dir. rsch. libr. Warner Bros., 1991—. Project dir.: Motion Pictures, Television, Radio: A Union Catalogue of Manuscript and Special Collections in the Western U.S., 1977. Active Hollywood Dog Obedience Club, Calif. Numerous grants for script indexing, manuscript cataloging, library automation. Mem. Soc. Calif. Archivists (pres. 1982-83), Theater Library Assn. (exec. bd. 1983-86), Women in Film, Spl. Librs. Assn.. Democrat. Episcopalian. Avocations: running, swimming, reading, dog obedience training. Office: Warner Bros Rsch Libr 5200 Lankershim Blvd Ste 100 North Hollywood CA 91601-3100

SCHLOSSER, HERBERT S., broadcasting company executive; b. Atlantic City, Apr. 21, 1926; s. Abraham and Anna (Olesker) S.; m. Judith P. Gassner, July 8, 1951; children: Lynn C., Eric M. A.B. summa cum laude, Princeton, 1948; LL.B., Yale, 1951. Bar: N.Y. 1952. Assoc. firm Wickes, Riddell, Bloomer, Jacobi & McGuire, N.Y.C., 1951-54, Phillips, Nizer, Benjamin, Krim & Ballon, N.Y.C., 1954-57; with NBC, 1957-78; v.p., gen. mgr. Calif. Nat. Prodns., Inc. sub. NBC, 1960-61, dir. talent and program adminstrn., 1961-62, v.p. talent and program adminstrn., 1962-66; v.p. programs West Coast NBC, 1966-72; exec. v.p. NBC-TV Network, 1972-73, pres., 1973-74, mem. bd. dirs., 1973-78; pres. NBC, Inc., 1974-78, CEO, 1977-78; exec. v.p. RCA, 1978-85; sr. advisor broadcasting and entertainment Schroder & Co., Inc., N.Y.C., 1986—; pres. RCA cable sub. RCA, RCA Internat. Audio Visuals, Inc.; ptnr. Arts and Entertainment Cable Network, RCA/Columbia Home Video; bd. dirs. Ctrl. European Media Enterprises, Ltd., Data Broadcasting Corp., U.S. Satellite Broadcasting Co., Inc. Trustee Internat. Radio and TV Found., 1972-74; former mem. govs. Ford's Theatre Soc.; former trustee Nat. Urban League; chmn. bd. Am. Mus. of the Moving Image. With USNR, 1944-46. Recipient Humanitarian award NCCJ, 1974, Gold Brotherhood award, 1978. Mem. Assn. of Bar of City of N.Y., Am., N.Y. State bar assns., Council on Fgn. Relations, Acad. TV Arts and Scis., Advt. Council (past dir.), Yale Law Sch. Assn., Internat. Radio and TV Soc. (trustee 1973-74), Hollywood Radio and TV Soc. (trustee 1970-72), Phi Beta Kappa (pres. alumni assn. So. Calif. 1970-72, mem. Phi Beta Kappa assocs.). Club: Princeton (N.Y.). Office: Schroder & Co Incing Image Equitable Ctr 787 7th Ave New York NY 10019-6018

SCHLOSSMAN, JOHN ISAAC, architect; b. Chgo., Aug. 21, 1931; s. Norman Joseph and Carol (Rosenfeld) S.; m. Shirley Goulding Rhodes, Feb. 8, 1959; children: Marc N., Gail S. Mewhort, Peter C. Student, Grinnell Coll., 1949-50; BA, U. Minn., 1953, BArch, 1955; MArch, MIT, 1956. Registered architect, Ill., Fla. Archtl. designer The Architects Collaborative, Cambridge, Mass., 1956-57; architect Loebl Schlossman & Hackl and predecessors, Chgo., 1959-65, assoc., 1965-70, prin., 1970—; bd. overseers Coll. Arch. Illinois Inst. Tech., Chgo.; founding bd. dirs. Chgo. Archtl. Assistance Ctr., 1974-79. Chmn. Glencoe Plan Commn., Ill., 1977-82; trustee Com. for Green Bay Trail, Glencoe, 1970-77, Chgo. Arch. Found., 1971-75, Graham Found. for Advanced Studies in Fine Arts, 1995—; bd. dirs. Merit Music Program, Chgo., 1983-93, pres., 1988-90, hon. trustee 1996. Named dir. for life Young Men's Jewish Council, Chgo., 1971; Rotch travelling scholar, 1957. Fellow AIA (trustee ins. trust 1971-76, chmn. ins. com. 1974-75, v.p. Chgo. chpt. 1975, chmn. architects liability com. 1976, 80-82, hon. found. trustee 1995—), Archtl. Soc. of Art Inst. Chgo., Tavern Club (gov. 1986-88, v.p. 1990), The Arts Club, Alpha Rho Chi,. Office: Loebl Schlossman & Hackl 130 E Randolph St Ste 3400 Chicago IL 60601-6313

SCHLOSSMAN, STUART FRANKLIN, physician, educator, researcher; b. N.Y.C., Apr. 18, 1935; s. Abe and Pearl (Susser) S.; m. Judith Seryl Rubin, May 25, 1958; children: Robert, Peter. BA magna cum laude, NYU, 1955, MD, 1958; MA, Harvard U., 1975. Intern in medicine med. divsn. III Bellevue Hosp., N.Y.C., 1958-59, asst. resident in medicine med. divsn. III, 1959-60; Nat. Found. fellow dept. microbiology Coll. Physicians Columbia U., N.Y.C., 1960-62; asst. physician med. svc. Vanderbilt Clinic, Coll. Physician USPHS, Washington, 1960-62; Ward hematology fellow dept. internal medicine Sch. Washington U., St. Louis, 1962-63; rsch. assoc. lab. biochemistry Nat. Cancer Inst. USPHS, Washington, 1963-65; clin. instr. in medicine Sch. of Medicine George Washington U., 1964-65; assoc. in medicine, dir. blood bank Beth Israel Hosp., Boston, 1965-66; instr. Med. Sch. Harvard U., Boston, 1966-68, asst. physician, 1967-68, chief clin. immunology, 1971-73; physician Beth Israel Hosp., Boston, 1968—; from asst. to assoc. prof. medicine Harvard Med. Sch., Boston, 1968-77, prof., 1977—, Baruj Benacerraf prof. medicine, 1990—, chief divsn. tumor immunology and immunotherapy, 1973—; sr. physician Brigham and Women's Hosp., Boston, 1976—. Mem. editorial bd. Jour. of Immunology, 1969-74, Cellular Immunology, 1970—, Human Immunology, 1979-84, Clin. Immunology and Immunopathology, 1979—, Hybridoma, 1980—, Cancer Investigation, 1981, Stem Cells, 1981, Cancer Revs., 1984—, Internat. Jour. of Cell Cloning, 1983-86; mem. adv. bd. Cancer Treatment Reports, 1976-80; assoc. editor Human Lymphocyte Differentation, 1980-82; contbr. numerous articles to profl. jours. Recipient Solomon Berson Achievement award, 1984, Robert Koch prize and medal, 1984. Fellow AAAS; mem. NAS, Am. Soc. Hematology, Am. Soc. Immunologists, Am. Soc. Clin. Investigation, Assn. Am. Physicians, Inst. of Medicine, Alpha Omega Alpha. Office: Dana-Farber Cancer Inst 44 Binney St Boston MA 02115-6013

SCHLOTFELDT, ROZELLA MAY, nursing educator; b. DeWitt, Iowa, June 29, 1914; d. John W. and Clara C. (Doering) S. BS, State U. Iowa, 1935; MS, U. Chgo., 1947, PhD, 1956; DSc (hon.), Georgetown U., 1972, Adelphi U., 1979, Wayne State U., 1983, U. Ill., Chgo., 1985, Kent State U., 1987, U. Cin., 1989, Case Western Res. U., 1996; LHD (hon.), Med. U. S.C., 1976. Staff nurse State U. Iowa, VA Hosp., 1935-39; instr., supr. maternity nursing (State U. Iowa), 1939-44; asst. prof. U. Colo. Sch. Nursing, 1947-48; asst., then assoc. prof. Wayne State U. Coll. Nursing, 1948-55; prof., assoc. dean Wayne State U. Coll. Nursing (Coll. Nursing), 1957-60; dean Frances Payne Bolton Sch. Nursing, Case Western Res. U., 1960-72, prof., 1960-82, prof., dean emeritus, 1982-95; vis. prof. Rutgers U., 1984-89, 90—, U. Pa., 1985-86; spl. cons. Surgeon Gen.'s Adv. Group on Nursing, 1961-63; mem. nursing research study sect. USPHS, 1962-66; mem. Nat. League for Nursing-USPHS Com. on Nursing Edn. Facilities, 1962-64; mem. com. on health goals Cleve. Health Council, 1961-66; mem. Cleve. Health Planning and Devel. Commn., 1969-72; adv. com. div. nursing W.K. Kellog Found., 1959-67; v.p. Ohio Bd. Nursing Edn. and Nurse Registration, 1970-71, pres., 1971-72; mem. Nat. Health Services Research Tng. Com., 1970-71; mem. supply and edn. panel Health Manpower Com., 1966-67; rev. com. Nurse Tng. Act, 1967-68; bd. visitors Duke U. Med. Center, 1968-70; mem. council, exec. com. Inst. Medicine of Nat. Acad. Scis., 1971-75; mem. nat. adv. health services council Health Services and Mental Health Adminstrn., 1971-75; mem. def. adv. com. on women in services Dept. Def., 1972-75; bd. mem., treas. Nursing Home Adv. and Research Council, 1975-96; mem. adv. panel Health Services Research Commn. on Human Resources, Nat. Acad. Sci., 1977-85; cons. Walter Reed Army Inst.; adv. council on nursing, U.S. VA, 1965-69, chmn., 1966-69; mem. Yale U.; Council Com. on Med. Affairs, 1981-86; mem. adv. bd. Scholarly Inquiry for Nursing Practice, 1987—. Mem. editorial bd.: Advances in Nursing Sci, Inquiry, 1982-85, Jour. Nursing Edn., 1982-91; contbr. numerous articles to profl. jours. Bd. vis. Syracuse U., 1990—. Served to 1st lt. Army Nurse Corps, 1944-46. Recipient Disting. Svc. award U. Iowa, 1973, Case Western Res. U., 1991, N. Watts Lifetime Achievement award, 1995; named Living Legend, Am. Acad. Nursing, 1995. Fellow Am. Acad. Nursing (v.p. 1975-77, Living Legend award 1995), Nat. League Nursing; mem. ANA (chmn. commn. on nurse edn. 1967-70, mem. com. for studying credentialling 1976-79, adv. com. W.K. Kellogg Nat. Fellowship program 1981-85), Pi Lambda Theta, Sigma Theta Tau (nat. v.p. 1948-50, selection com., disting. lectr. program 1986-87, Founders award for creativity 1985). Home: 1111 Carver Rd Cleveland Heights OH 44112-3635 Office: 2121 Abington Rd Cleveland OH 44106-2333

SCHLOTTERBECK, WALTER ALBERT, manufacturing company executive, lawyer; b. N.Y.C., Dec. 22, 1926; s. Albert Gottlob and Maria Louise (Fritz) S.; m. Pauline Elizabeth Hoerz, Sept. 2, 1951; children—Susan, Thomas, Paul. A.B., Columbia U., 1949, LL.B., 1952. Bar: N.Y. 1953. Counsel Gen. Electric Co. (various locations), 1952-87; v.p., corp. counsel Gen. Electric Co., N.Y.C., 1970-77; sec. Gen. Electric Co., 1975-76; gen. counsel Gen. Electric Co. (various locations), 1976-87, sr. v.p., 1977-87. Served with USNR, 1944-46. Home: 201 Overlake Dr E Medina WA 98039-5331

SCHLOTZHAUER, VIRGINIA HUGHES, parliamentarian; b. Washington, July 24, 1913; d. William and Secy Alice (Royston) Hughes; m. Elbert O. Schlotzhauer, May 16, 1936; children: Carol Schlotzhauer Hinds, Jean Schlotzhauer Sumner, Jude Schlotzhauer Wilson. AB in LS, George Washington U., 1934. Mem. libr. staff George Washington U., Washington, 1934; various clerical positions U.S. Govt., ARC, Washington, Phoenix, mid-1930s; cons. parliamentarian Washington, 1967—; cons. Nat. Parliamentarian Edn. Project for Colls. and Univs. sponsored by Am. Inst. Parliamentarians funded by William Randolph Hearst Found., 1993-95; presenter seminars. Author: A Parliamentarian's Book of Limericks, 1984; (with others) Parliamentary Opinions, 1982, Parliamentary Opinions II, 1992; primary contbr./cons. column Parliamentary Jour.; contbr. articles to profl. publs. Mem. steering and bylaws coms., sec. Nominating Conv. for Endorsement of Candidates for Bd. Edn., Montgomery County, Md., 1966; election reporter ABC-LWV, Prince George's County, Md., 1970s; v.p., bylaws com. Planned Parenthood Am., Prince George's County, late 1960s and 70s; group leader, bd. dirs., sec., trustee Potomac Area coun. Camp Fire Girls, Md. and D.C. area, 1940s and 50s; participant nonpartisan and Dem. polit. campaigns; judge various contests Future Bus. Leaders Am., Washington, 1970s. Co-recipient (parliamentary book in Spanish) Las Asociaciones y Normas Procesales para sics Asambleas Deliberationas by Lcda Domingo Rivera-Rivera dedicated in her honor, 1996. Mem. AAUW (life, named gift Bethesda-Chevy Chase br. 1962, named gift Md. divsn. 1972), Am. Inst. Parliamentarians (cert. profl. parliamentarian, mem. adv. coun. or bd. dirs. 1966—, pres. D.C. chpt. 1966-68, opinions com. 1974—, chmn. 1974-78, cons., named changed to Virginia Schlotzhauer D.C. chpt. 1984), Nat. Assn. Parliamentarians (profl. registered parliamentarian, mem. coms.), D.C. Assn. Parliamentarians (founding pres., 1st hon. pres., Achievement award 1976), Westerners. Avocations: travel, writing, poetry, gardening, Spanish language and culture. Home and Office: 9819 Indian Queen Point Rd Fort Washington MD 20744-6904

SCHLUETER, DAVID ARNOLD, law educator; b. Sioux City, Iowa, Apr. 29, 1946; s. Arnold E. and Helen A. (Dettmann) S.; m. Linda L. Boston, Apr. 22, 1972; children: Jennifer, Jonathan. BA, Tex. A&M U., 1969; JD, Baylor U., 1971, LLM, U. Va., 1981. Bar: Tex. 1971, D.C. 1973, U.S. Ct. Mil. Appeals 1972, U.S. Supreme Ct. 1976. Legal counsel U.S. Supreme Ct., Washington, 1981-83; assoc. dean St. Mary's U., San Antonio, 1984-89, prof. law, 1986—; reporter Fed. Adv. Com. on Criminal Rules, 1988—; chmn. JAG adv. coun., 1974-75. Author: Military Criminal Justice: Practice and Procedure, 1982, 4th edit., 1996; (with others) Military Rules of Evidence Manual, 1981, 3d edit., 1991, Texas Rules of Evidence Manual, 1983, 4th edit., 1995, Texas Evidentiary Foundations, 1992, Military Evidentiary Foundations, 1994, Military Criminal Procedure Forms, 1997; contbr. articles to legal publs. Maj. JAGC, U.S. Army, 1972-81. Fellow Am. Law Inst., Tex. Bar Found. (life), Am. Bar Found. (life); mem. ABA (vice chmn. criminal justice sect. coun. 1991-94, vice chmn. com. on criminal justice and mil. 1983-84, chmn. standing com. on mil. law 1991-92, chmn. editl. adv. bd., Criminal Justice Mag., 1989-91), Tex. Bar Assn. Republican. Lutheran. Office: St Marys U Sch Law 1 Camino Santa Maria St San Antonio TX 78228-5433

SCHLUETER, ERIKA MANRIQUEZ, civil engineer research scientist; b. Santiago, Chile; came to U.S., 1980; d. Javier Bustos Manriquez and Constantina Vilos Anso; m. Ross Donald Schlueter, May, 1981; children: Dietrich, Kurt. B of Civil Constrn., Cath. U., Santiago, 1980; postgrad., MIT, 1980-81, San Jose State U., 1983; MS in Civil Engring., U. Wash., 1986; PhD in Engring. Sci., U. Calif., Berkeley, 1995. Instr. continuing edn. Cath. U., Santiago, 1975-77, tchg. asst., 1976-77; hydrogeologist Celzac Co., Santiago, 1978; med. asst. Stanford (Calif.) U. Med. Ctr., 1981, fin. aids analyst, 1981-82; homemaker Pleasanton, 1986-88; rsch. asst. Lawrence Berkeley Nat. Lab. U. Calif., Berkeley, 1988-95; rsch. scientist Lawrence Berkeley Nat. Lab. U. Calif., Berkeley, 1995—. Contbr. numerous articles to profl. jours. Fulbright fellow, 1980-81, Jane Lewis fellow, 1990-91. Mem. ASCE, Soc. Petroleum Engrs., Am. Geophys. Union, Soc. Exploration Geophysicists (Award of Merit 1994-95). Republican. Roman Catholic. Home: 780 Cragmont Ave Berkeley CA 94708-1345 Office: Lawrence Berkeley Nat Lab MS 44B 1 Cyclotron Rd Berkeley CA 94720

SCHLUETER, LINDA LEE, law educator; b. L.A., May 12, 1947; d. Dick G. Dulgarian and Lucille J. Boston; m. David A. Schlueter, Apr. 22, 1972; children: Jennifer, Jonathan, BA, U. So. Calif., 1969; JD, Baylor U., 1971. Bar: D.C. 1973, U.S. Supreme Ct. 1976, Ct. Mil. Appeals, 1990. Govt. rels. specialist hdqrs. U.S. Postal Svc., Washington, 1973-75; staff atty. Rsch. Group, Inc., Charlottesville, Va., 1979-81; pvt. practice Washington, 1981-83; asst. prof. law Sch. Law St. Mary's U., San Antonio, 1983-87, assoc. prof., 1987-90, prof., 1990-94; presenter law Tex. Women Scholars Program, Austin, 1986, 87; bd. dirs Inst. for Comparative and Internat. Legal Rsch. Author: Punitive Damages, 1981-89, 3rd edit., 1995, ann. suppls., Legal Research Guide: Patterns and Practice, 1986, 3rd edit., 1996; editor Cmty. Property Jour. , 1986-88, Cmty. Property Alert, 1989-90; assoc. editor Modern Legal Sys. Cyclopedia, 20 vols., 1990, ann. suppls. Mem. ABA, Bexar County Women's Bar Assn., San Antonio Conservation Soc., Order of Barristers, Phi Alpha Delta. Republican. Lutheran.

SCHLUTER, GERALD EMIL, economist; b. Carroll, Iowa, June 9, 1942; s. Emil and Violetta Marie (Witt) S.; m. Carolyn Jean Finnell, Apr. 27, 1968; 1 child, Deborah Jean. BS, Iowa State U., 1964, MS, 1966, PhD, 1971. Rsch. asst. econs. Iowa State U., Ames, 1964-66, rsch. assoc. econs., 1966-70; agrl. economist Econ. Rsch. Svc. USDA, Washington, 1970-84, supervisory economist Econ. Rsch. Svc., 1984—; econs. instr., Washington, 1983—, USDA Grad. Sch., Washington, 1979-83. Editor: (jour.) Agrl. Econs., 1984-87; author: (econs. series) Food & Fiber System, 1972; cotbr. over 90 articles to profl. jours. Mem. property com. Bethany Luth. Ch., Alexandria, Va., 1983-88; coach Lee-Mt. Vernon Soccer Assn., Alexandria, 1982-83. Mem. Am. Agrl. Econs. Assn., So Regional Sci. Assn. (coun. 1992-95), Am. Econ. Assn., Western Agrl. Econs. Assn., Northeastern Agrl. and Resource Econs. Assn., So. Agrl. Econs. Assn. Avocations: fishing, youth soccer, personal computers. Home: 3877 Manzanita Pl Alexandria VA 22309-1479 Office: USDA Econ Rsch Svc 1301 New York Ave NW Rm 924 Washington DC 20005-4708

SCHLUTER, PETER MUELLER, electronics company executive; b. Greenwich, Conn., May 24, 1933; s. Fredric Edward and Charlotte (Mueller) S.; m. Jaquelin Ambler Lamond, Apr. 18, 1970 (div. June 1990); children:

Jane Randolph, Charlotte Mueller, Anne Ambler. BME, Cornell U., 1956; postgrad. Harvard U. Grad. Sch. Bus. Adminstrn., 1982. Sr. engr. Thiokol Chem. Corp., Brigham City, Utah, 1958-59; asso. Porter Internat. Co., Washington, 1960-65, v.p., 1965-66, pres., treas., dir., 1966-70; pres., treas. dir. Zito Co., Derry, N.H., 1970-72; internat. bus. cons., Washington, 1972-74; v.p., dir. Buck Engring. Co. Inc. (now named Lab-Volt Sys., Inc.), Farmingdale, N.J., 1975, pres., CEO, dir., 1975—; hon. mem. City and Guilds of London Inst. Mem. Republican Inaugural Book and Program Com., 1969; mem. cmty. adv. bd. Monmouth coun. Girl Scouts U.S.; mem. adv. council Monmouth (N.J.) U. Sch. Bus. Admin.; bd. dirs. United Way of Monmouth County.; trustee Monmouth Med. Ctr.; N.Am. rep., mem. presidium WORLDDIDAC, Bern, Switzerland, v.p., 1996—. Recipient Golden Osprey award So. Monmouth County C. of C., 1995. Fellow City and Guilds of London Inst. (hon.); mem. World Assn. Mfrs. and Distributors of Ednl. Materials (N.Am. rep.), Metropolitan Club Washington, Rumson Country Club, Pi Tau Sigma. Home: 4 Quaker Ln Little Silver NJ 07739-1806 Office: PO Box 686 Farmingdale NJ 07727-0686

SCHLUTH, MICHAEL VERNON, advertising agency executive; b. Phila., Aug. 8, 1944; s. Frank Charles and Charlotte Laurel (Hanwell) S.; A.S. in Mktg., La Salle Coll., 1968; m. Nancy Jane Weller, Jan. 14, 1967; children—Lori Ann, Donna Jean, Michael Philip; m. Susan Katherine Nice, Sept. 10, 1988; 1 child, Brendan Hunter. Advt. sales rep. Phila. Newspapers, Inc., 1968-75; pres. Alstin Advt., Inc., Phila., 1975—; owner, pres. Lordon-Michaelson Assocs., 1984—. Bd. dirs. Phila affiliate Nat. Human Resources Assn., 1995. Served with U.S. Army, 1963-65. Office: 1435 Walnut St Philadelphia PA 19102-3219

SCHMALBECK, RICHARD LOUIS, university dean, lawyer; b. Chgo., Dec. 31, 1947; s. George Louis and Betty Jeanne (Strecker) S.; m. Linda Michaels; children: Suzanne, Sabine. AB in Econs. with honors, U. Chgo., 1970, JD, 1975. Bar: Ohio 1975, D.C. 1977. Asst. to dir. and economist Ill. Housing Devel. Authority, Chgo., 1971-73; assoc. Vorys, Sater, Seymour & Pease, Columbus, Ohio, 1975-76; spl. asst. to assoc. dir. for econs. and govt. Office of Mgmt. and Budget, Washington, 1976-77; assoc. Caplin & Drysdale, Washington, 1977-80; assoc. prof. law Duke U., Durham, N.C., 1980-84, prof. law, 1984-90, 93—, vice chmn. acad. coun., 1984-85; dean U. Ill. Coll. Law, Champaign, 1990-93. Assoc. editor U. Chgo. Law Rev., 1974-75; contbr. articles to profl. jours. Mem. ABA (articles editor jour. 1977-80), Am. Law Inst., Phi Beta Kappa. Office: Duke University Sch of Law PO Box 90360 Durham NC 27708-0360

SCHMALE, ALLEN LEE, financial services company executive; b. Addieville, Ill., Feb. 12, 1933; s. Arnold August and Leona Karoline (Becker) S.; m. Lorraine Marie Loyet, July 19, 1952; children: Judith Ann, Arnold August II, Michelle Lee, René Cerise, Allen Kent. CLU, ChFC. Salesman Western & So. Life Ins. Co., St. Louis, 1955-56, Monarch Life Ins. Co., St. Louis, 1956-58, Mass. Indemnity & Life Ins., St. Louis, 1958-65; pres. Schmale Fin. Svcs., Inc., Okawville, Ill., 1965-88, chmn., 1988—, also bd. dirs. Trustee Village of Okawville, 1976-80, mem. bus. devel. com.; vice chmn. Washington County (Ill.) Rep. Com.; coord. Edgar for Gov., Ill., 1990, 94; pres. St. Peters Ch., 1975-77; br. officer Walnut St. Securities Inc. Recipient Contbns. to Growth award Belleville (Ill.) Area Coll., 1977. Mem. Am. Soc. CLU and ChFC, East Side Life Underwriters (pres. 1971-72), Million Dollar Roundtable, Ill. Life Underwriters (bd. dirs. 1975-78), Nat. Assn. Life Underwriters (del. 1971), Estate Planning Coun. St. Louis, Okawville Comty. Club (pres. 1974-76). Republican. Avocation: golf. Home: 5304 County Highway 6 Okawville IL 62271-2530 Office: Schmale Fin Svcs Inc 611 S Front St Okawville IL 62271-2121

SCHMALENBERGER, JERRY LEW, pastor, seminary educator; b. Greenville, Ohio, Jan. 23, 1934; s. Harry Henry and Lima Marie (Hormel) S.; m. Carol Ann Walthall, June 8, 1956; children: Stephen, Bethany Allison, Sarah Layton. BA, Wittenberg U., 1956, DDiv (hon.), 1984; MDiv, Hamma Sch. Theology, Springfield, Ohio, 1959, D of Ministry, 1976. Ordained to ministry Luth. Ch., 1959. Dir. Camp Mowana, Mansfield, Ohio, 1958-59; pastor 3d Luth. Ch., Springfield, 1959-61, 1st Luth. Ch., Bellefontaine, Ohio, 1961-66; sr. pastor 1st Luth. Ch., Tiffin, Ohio, 1966-70, Mansfield, 1970-79; sr. pastor St. John's Luth. Ch., Des Moines, 1979-88; pres. Pacific Luth. Theol. Sem., Berkeley, Calif., 1988-96, prof. parish ministry, 1988—; co-dir. Iowa Luth. Hosp. Min. of Health Program, Des Moines, 1986-88; Roland Payne lectr. Gbarnga (Liberia) Sch. Theology, 1987; lectr. Luth. Theol. Sem., Hong Kong, 1994, The United Theol. Coll., Kingston, Jamaica, 1994; guest prof. The Augustana Hochschule, Germany, 1996. Author: Lutheran Christians' Beliefs Book One, 1984, Book Two, 1987, Iowa Parables and Iowa Psalms, 1984, Saints Who Shaped the Church, 1986, Stewards of Creation, 1987, Nights Worth Remembering, 1989, The Vine and the Branches, 1992, Call to Witness, 1993, Plane Thoughts on Parish Ministry, 1994, Invitation to Discipleship, 1995, The Preacher's Edge, 1996, Preparation for Discipleship, 1997; columnist Rite Ideas, 1987-88. Bd. dirs. Grand View Coll., Des Moines, 1980-88, Wittenberg U., Springfield, Ohio, 1974-87, Luth. Social Services of Iowa, 1980-87, chmn. pre fund drive, 1988; bd. dirs. Planned Parenthood of Mid-Iowa, Des Moines, 1987-88; dir. Evang. Outreach/Luth. Ch. Am., 1983-85; mem. Iowa Luth. Hosp. Charitable Trust, 1986-88; chair Com. for Homeless Fund, Des Moines, 1986. Named Outstanding Alumni Wittenberg U., 1965, Young Man of Yr. Tiffin Jaycees, 1965, Man of Yr. Bellefontaine Jaycees, Disting. Alumni award Trinty Sem., Columbus, 1989. Mem. NAACP, Acad. Preachers, Acad. Evangelists (organizer 1986—), Kiwanis, Rotary. Avocations: historical research and writing, travel, boating. Home and Office: 162 Pelican Loop Pittsburg CA 94565-2004 *Personal philosophy: Not perfect, but forgiven, we find real life in living ours for others.*

SCHMALENSEE, RICHARD LEE, economist, government official, educator; b. Belleville, Ill., Feb. 16, 1944; s. Fred and Marjorie June (Veigel) S.; SB, MIT, 1965, PhD, 1970; m. Edeth Diane Hawk, Aug. 19, 1967; children: Alexander Clayton, Nicholas Hawk. Asst. prof., assoc. prof. econs. U. Calif., San Diego, 1970-77; assoc. prof. applied econs. Sloan Sch. Mgmt. MIT, Cambridge, Mass., 1977-79, prof., 1979-86, prof. econs. and mgmt., 1986-89, Gordon Y Billard prof., 1988—, dir. MIT Ctr. for Energy and Environ. Policy Rsch., 1991—; dep. dean Sloan Sch., 1996—; dir. L.I. Lighting, Co.; mem. Pres.'s Coun. Econ. Advisors, 1989-91; NSF grantee, 1975-77, 81-83; research fellow U. Louvain (Belgium), 1973-74, 85. Fellow AAAS, Econometric Soc.; mem. Am. Econ. Assn. (nominating com. 1987, exec. com. 1993-95). Author: The Economics of Advertising, 1972; The Control of Natural Monopoly, 1979; co-author: Markets for Power, 1983, Economics, 1988; co-editor: Handbook of Industrial Organization, 1989; mem. editorial bd. Jour. Indsl. Econs., 1981-89, Am. Econ. Rev., 1982-86, Internat. Jour. Indsl. Orgns., 1982-89, Jour. Econs. & Mgmt. Strategy, 1993—, Jour. Econ. Perspectives, 1993—. Home: 20 Malia Ter Chestnut Hill MA 02167-1326 Office: MIT 50 Memorial Dr Rm E52-456 Cambridge MA 02142-1347

SCHMALSTIEG, WILLIAM RIEGEL, Slavic languages educator; b. Sayre, Pa., Oct. 3, 1929; s. John William and Dorothy Augusta (Riegel) S.; m. Emily Lou Botdorf, Mar. 28, 1952; children: Linda, Roxanne. BA, U. Minn., 1950; postgrad., Columbia U., 1952; MA, U. Pa., 1951, PhD, 1956; PhD (hon.), Vilnius U., 1994. Instr. U. Ky., Lexington, 1956-59; asst. prof. Lafayette Coll., Easton, Pa., 1959-63; assoc. prof. U. Minn., Mpls., 1963-64; prof. Pa. State U., University Park, 1964—, head dept. Slavic langs., 1969-91; mem. Internat. Commn. Balto-Slavic Linguistics, 1973—; appointed Edwin Erle Sparks prof. Slavic Lang., 1990. Author: (with L. Dambriunas and A. Klimas) An Introduction to Modern Lithuanian, 1966, 4th edit., 1990, 5th edit., 1993, An Old Prussian Grammar, 1974, Studies in Old Prussian, 1976, Indo-European Linguistics, 1980, An Introduction to Old Church Slavic, 1976, 2d edit., 1983, A Lithuanian Historical Syntax, 1988; (with Warren Held and Janet Gertz) Beginning Hittite, 1988, A Student Guide to the Genitive of Agent in the Indo-European Languages, 1995, An Introduction to Old Russian, 1995; editor Gen. Linguistics, 1971-82. Served to 1st lt. U.S. Army, 1952-54. NEH grantee, 1978-79, Fulbright grantee and exch. scholar Acad. Scis., Vilnius, USSR, 1986; recipient Humanities medal Pa. State U., 1983, Friend of Lithuania award Knights of Lithuania, 1990; named Disting. Alumnus Breck Sch., 1990. Mem. Assn. Advancement Baltic Studies (pres. 1982-84), Am. Assn. Tchrs. of Slavic and East European Langs. Episcopalian. Home: 814 Cornwall Rd State College PA 16803-1430 Office: Dept Slavic Langs Pa State U University Park PA 16802

SCHMALTZ, ROY EDGAR, JR., artist, art educator; b. Belfield, N.D., Feb. 23, 1937; s. Roy and Mercedes (Martin) S.; m. Julia Mabel Swan, Feb. 1, 1958; children: Liese Marlene, Jennifer Lynn, Gregory Jason. Student Otis Art Inst., Los Angeles, 1959-60, U. Wash., 1960-61, Akademie der Bildenden Kunste, Munich, W. Ger., 1965-66; B.F.A., San Francisco Art Inst., 1963, M.F.A., 1965. Lectr. art Coll. of Notre Dame, Belmont, Calif., 1968-70, M. H. De Young Meml. Art Mus., San Francisco, 1968-70; prof. art St. Mary's Coll. of Calif., Moraga, 1969—, chmn. dept. art; mem. artists' bd. San Francisco Art Inst., 1989-92; exhbns. include: Seattle Art Mus., 1959, M. H. De Young Meml. Art Mus., 1969, Frye Art Mus., Seattle, 1957, San Francisco Mus. Modern Art, 1971, U. Calif.-Santa Cruz, 1977, Fine Arts Mus. of San Francisco, 1978, Oakland Art Mus., 1979, Rutgers U., Camden, N.J., 1979, Springfield (Mo.) Art Mus., 1980, Butler Inst. Am. Art, Youngstown, Ohio, 1981, Huntsville (Ala.) Mus. Art, 1982, Haggin Mus., Stockton, Calif., 1982, U. Hawaii-Hilo, 1983, Alaska State Mus., Juneau, 1981, Tex. State U., San Marcos, 1980, Crocker Art Mus., Sacramento, 1982, Hearst Art Gallery, 1986; group exhbns. include San Francisco Internat. Airport Gallery, 1987, Solano Coll., Fairfield, Calif., 1988, U. Del., Newark, 1988, San Francisco Art Inst., 1989, Natsoulas Gallery, Davis, Calif., 1989, Bedford Regional Ctr. Arts, Walnut Creek, Calif., 1989, Contemporary Realist Gallery, San Francisco, 1994, Hearst Art Gallery, Moraba, Calif., 1995; represented in permanent collections: Richmond Art Ctr. (Calif.), U. Hawaii-Hilo, Las Vegas Art Mus. (Nev.), Hoyt Mus. and Inst. Fine Arts, New Castle, Pa., Frye Art Mus., San Francisco Art Inst., M. H. De Young Meml. Art Mus., Mills Coll., Oakland, Amerika-Haus, Munich, Contra Costa County Art Collection, Walnut Creek, Calif., Western Wash. U., Bellingham, Clemson U., S.C.; dir. Hearst Art Gallery, St. Mary's Coll.; vis. artist lectr. Academie Art Coll., San Francisco, 1971, grad. program Lone Mountain Coll., San Francisco, 1973-74. Coach Little League Baseball Team, Concord, Calif., 1982; mem. artist's bd. San Francisco Art Inst., 1989-93. Fulbright fellow, 1965-66; Frye Art Mus. traveling fellow, 1957; recipient Painting award All Calif. Ann., 1965; Nat. Watercolor award Chautauqua Inst., 1980; Seattle Art Assn. Painting award, 1957; San Francisco Art Inst. award, 1961; Otis Art Inst. award, 1959; Walnut Creek Civic Art Ctr. award, 1982, San Francisco Art Commn. award, 1985, Calif. State Fair Art award, 1985, Sears award for excellence in leadership, 1989-90. Mem. Coll. Art Assn., Fine Arts Mus. of San Francisco, AAUP, San Francisco Art Inst. Alumni Assn. Home: 1020 Whistler Dr Suisun City CA 94585-2929 Office: Saint Marys Coll Dept Art Moraga CA 94575

SCHMALZ, CARL NELSON, JR., artist, educator, printmaker; b. Ann Arbor, Mich., Dec. 26, 1926; s. Carl Nelson and Esther Dorothy (Fowler) S.; m. Dolores Irene Tourangeau, Dec. 2, 1950; children: Stephen Theodore (dec.), Mathew Nelson, Julia Irene. A.B., Harvard U., 1948, M.A., 1949, Ph.D., 1958; M.A. (hon.), Amherst Coll., 1969. Teaching fellow in fine arts Harvard U., Cambridge, Mass., 1950-52; asst. prof. Bowdoin Coll., Brunswick, Maine, 1953-62; curator, asst dir. Walker Art Mus., 1953-62; asst. prof. Harvard U., 1960; prof. Amherst Coll., 1962-95, prof. emeritus, 1995—; lectr. in field. Author: Watercolor Lessons from Eliot O'Hara, 1974, Watercolor Your Way, 1978, Finding and Improving Your Painting Style, 1986, paperback, 1992; exhibited in one-man shows including Cambridge (Mass.) Art Assn., 1948, Laing Gallery, Portland, Maine, 1955, Amherst (Mass.) Coll., 1963, U. Mass., 1965, W.C. Rawls Mus., Va., 1972, Concord (Mass.) Art Assn., 1974, Govt. House, Hamilton, Bermuda, 1979, Jones Library, Amherst, Mass., 1979, The Arlington, Kennebunkport, Maine, 1980, Harmon-Meek Gallery, Naples, Fla., 1987, 91, 92, Gallery at 6 Deering St., Portland, Maine, 1987, 91, Fretz Gallery, Portland, 1987-88; exhibited in group shows including Jordan Marsh Co., 1947, 48, 50, 71-73, Colby Coll., 1958, Carnegie Inst., Pitts., 1963, FAR Gallery, N.Y.C., 1964-68, Am. Watercolor Soc., 1966, 68, 70, Bowdoin Coll. Mus., 1973, Balt. Watercolor Soc., 1976, Boston Atheneum, 1979, Watercolor U.S.A. Honor Soc., 1989, 91, Maine Art Gallery, 1991, Rolly-Michaux Gallery, Boston, 1995; represented in permanent collections: Walker Art Mus., Brunswick, Maine, Jones & Laughlin Steel Corp., Diners Club Am., Kalamazoo Art Center, Hampshire Coll., Zanesville Art Inst., Blue Cross/Blue Shield, Philharmonic Ctr. for the Arts, Naples, Fla.; work published in various pubs. including The Artist's Guide for Using Color, 1992, The Artist's Mag., 1994, Splash 3: Ideas and Inspirations, 1994. Mem. exec. bd. Interfaith Housing Corp., Amherst, 1966-76; pres. bd. trustees Amherst Day Sch., 1966-69; mem. Pelham Arts Lottery Coun., 1984-90; v.p. bd. dirs. Portland Mus. Art, 1957-62. Bacon fellow, 1951; recipient 1st prize watercolor Cambridge Art Assn. Ann., 1947; 1st prize for traditional watercolor Virginia Beach Boardwalk Show, 1965; South Mo. Trust purchase award Watercolor U.S.A., 1970; 1st prize watercolor 30th Ann. Kennebunk River Club Show, 1985. Mem. Coll. Art Assn., Watercolor U.S.A. Honor Soc. Democrat.

SCHMALZRIED, MARVIN EUGENE, financial consultant; b. Dighton, Kans., Nov. 11, 1924; s. Carl D. and Marie M. (Bahm) S.; m. Jean Landino, Nov. 27, 1946; children—Darlene, Candace, Cynthia, Derek, Valerie, Rebecca. B.B.A., Northwestern U., 1949; LL.B., U. Conn., 1955. Bar: Conn. bar 1955; C.P.A., Conn. Acct. Webster, Blanchard & Willard, CPA's (named changed to Price Waterhouse & Co.), Hartford, Conn., 1950-55; contr., asst. treas. J.B. Williams Co., Glastonbury, Conn., 1955-57; treas., sec. Curtis 1000, Inc. (name changed to Am Bus. Products, Inc.), Atlanta, 1957-61; asst. to pres. Am. Home Products Corp., N.Y.C., 1961-63, comptroller, 1964-67, v.p., 1967-72, sr. v.p., 1972-84; pres. Venda Vid, Inc., N.Y.C., 1986-90; sr. v.p. View-Master Ideal Group, Inc., N.Y.C., 1987-90; exec. v.p. Strategics Inc., 1993-95; bd. dirs. Am. Bus. Products, Inc., Atlanta. Recipient Gold medal Conn. Soc. C.P.A.'s, 1953. Mem. AICPA, ABA, Old Greenwich Friday Evening Reading Soc. (pres.). Club: Darien Country. Home and Office: 26 Cove Ave Norwalk CT 06855-2400

SCHMANDT-BESSERAT, DENISE, archaeologist, educator; b. Ay, France, Aug. 10, 1933; came to U.S., 1965, naturalized, 1970; d. Victor and Jeanne (Crabit) Besserat; m. Jurgen Schmandt, Dec. 27, 1956; children: Alexander, Christopher, Phillip. Ed., Ecole du Louvre, 1965. Research fellow in Near Eastern Archaeology Peabody Mus. Harvard U., Cambridge, Mass., 1969-71; fellow Radcliffe Inst., Cambridge, 1969-71; asst. prof. Middle Eastern studies U. Tex., Austin, 1972-81, assoc. prof., 1981-88, prof., 1988—; acting chief curator U. Tex. Art Mus., 1978-79; vis. assoc. prof. U. Calif., Berkeley, 1987-88. Author: Before Writing, 1992, How Writing Came About, 1996; adv. editor Tech. and Culture, 1978-92; mem. editl. bd. Written Communication, 1993-95, Visible Lang., 1985—; contbr. articles to profl. jours. Recipient Kayden Nat. U. Press Book award, 1992; Wenner-Gren Foun. grantee, 1970-71, NEA grantee, 1974-75, 77-78, ACLS grantee, 1984, Deutscher Akademischer Austauschdienst grantee, 1986, NEH grantee, 1992; NEH fellow, 1979-80, U. Wis. Inst. for Rsch. in Humanities fellow,, 1984-85, USIA, Am. Ctr. Oriental Rsch. fellow, 1994-95, 97. Mem. Am. Oriental Soc., Archeol. Inst. Am. (governing bd. 1983-89), Am. Anthropol. Assn., Am. Schs. of Oriental Rsch., Centro Internationale Ricerche Archeologiche Anthropologiche e Storiche (Rome). Office: U of Tex Austin TX 78712

SCHMEIDLER, NEAL FRANCIS, engineering executive; b. Hays, Kans., Feb. 29, 1948; s. Cyril John and Mildred Mary (Karlin) S.; m. Lorrinda Mary Brungardt, Jan. 31, 1950; children: Lori Ann, LaNette Renee, Lance Edward, LeAnna Karleen. BS in Math., Fort Hays State U., 1970; MS in Indsl. Engring., Kans. State U., 1973. Master engr. Trans World Airlines, Inc., Kansas City, Mo., 1973-78; chief indsl. engr. U.S. Dept. of the Army, Fort Carson, Colo., 1978-80; staff indsl. engr. U.S. Dept. of Agriculture, Washington, 1980-83; tech. dir. Tech. Applications, Inc., Alexandria, Va., 1983-86; v.p. engring. and tech. svcs. div. Standard Tech., Inc., Bethesda, Md., 1986-88; dir. indsl. engring. and ops rsch. svcs. Operational Technologies Svcs., Inc., Vienna, Va., 1989-91; founder, pres. OMNI Engring. and Tech., Inc., McLean, Va., 1989—; dir. No. Va. Tech. Coun., 1993-95. Guest (radio talk show) Basically Business, 1991; contbr. articles to profl. jours. Mem. info. tech./telecommunications infrastructure com. Commonwealth of Va. Gov.'s Regional Econ. Devel. Adv. Couns., 1994. Named Sr. Engr. of Yr., D.C. Coun. of Engring. and Archtl. Socs., 1991; recipient Spl. Act or Svc. award U.S. Dept. of Army, 1980. Mem. ABA (small bus. com. 1991-92), Inst. Indsl. Engrs. (sr., nat. capital chpt. bd. dirs. 1986-93, Award of Excellence 1982), Air Traffic Control Assn., Am. Soc. for Quality Control, No. Va. Tech. Coun., Human Factors and Ergonomics Soc., Washington Acad. Scis. (bd. mgrs. 1993-96), Kappa Mu Epsilon, Sigma Pi Sigma. Office: OMNI Engring & Tech Inc 7921 Jones Branch Dr # 530 Mc Lean VA 22102-3306

SCHMELER, MARK RAYMOND, occupational therapist; b. Cowansville, Que., Can., Aug. 20, 1966; s. Frank Raymond and Wilma Marie (Murphy) S.; m. Christina I. Rabij, Dec. 11, 1993. BS, Syracuse U., Utica, N.Y., 1989; MS, U. Buffalo, 1993. Cert. Assistive Tech. Practitioner. Occupational therapist New Eng. Rehab. Hosp., Portland, Maine, 1989-91; rsch. fellow U. Buffalo, 1991-93; dir. rehab. tech. svc. Westchester County Med. Ctr., Valhalla, N.Y., 1993-96; instr. rehab. tech. N.Y. Med. Coll., Valhalla, N.Y., 1993-96; asst. prof. rehab. sci. & tech. U. Pitts., 1996—, sr. evaluation specialist Ctr. Assistive Tech. Med. Ctr., 1996—. Inventor Rehab. Engring. Soc. N.Am., 1992, 93. Mem. Am. Occupational Therapy Assn., Rehab. Engring. Soc., World Fedn. Occupational Therapy. Republican. Roman Catholic. Avocations: skiing, bicycling, travel. Office: U Pitts Med Ctr 200 Lothrop St Pittsburgh PA 15213-2546

SCHMELING, GARETH, classics educator; b. Algoma, Wis., May 28, 1940; married. B.A., Northwestern Coll., 1963; M.A. (Knapp fellow), U. Wis., 1964, Ph.D. (Knapp travelling grantee 1965-66, Univ. fellow 1967-68), 1968. Asst. prof. classics U. Va., 1968-70; assoc. prof. U. Fla., 1970-74, prof., 1974—, chmn. classics, 1974—, chmn. humanities, 1974-76, dir. Center for Studies in Humanities, 1978-87, prin. investigator Humanities Perspectives on Professions, 1975-87, acting chmn. dept. philosophy, 1986-88; vis. prof. U. Colo., Boulder, 1992; panelist, research div. Nat. Endowment for Humanities, also mem. nat. bd. consultants. Translator and author Introduction: Cornelius Nepos: Lives of Famous Men, 1971; author: Petronius' Satyricon, 1971, Ovid's the Art of Love, 1972, Chariton and the Rise of Ancient Fiction, 1974, Homer's the Odyssey, 1974, A Bibliography of Petronius, 1977, Xenophon of Ephesus, 1980, Historia Apollonii Regis Tyri, 1988, The Novel in the Ancient World, 1996; contbr. numerous articles, revs. to profl. jours.; editor: Newsletter Petronian Soc. 1970—; editorial com.: U. Fla. Press Humanities Monographs, 1978—. Named 1 of 5 Tchrs. of Yr. for Arts and Scis. U. Fla., 1973; recipient Rome prize Am. Acad., 1977-78; U. Va. faculty fellow, summer 1969, summer 1970; U. Fla. fellow, summer 1971, summer 1974; Nat. Endowment for Humanities fellow, 1973-74; Am. Council Learned Socs. summer fellow, 1974; Am. Philos. Soc. grantee, 1970, 71, 72, 77-78, 84-85; U. Fla. grantee, 1977-78. Fellow Am. Acad. in Rome; mem. Am. Philol. Assn., Am. Classical League, Vergilian Soc., Classical Assn. of Middle West and South (sec.-treas. 1975-82, pres. 1985-86). Home: 320 NW 30th St Gainesville FL 32607-2524 Office: Dept Classics U Fla Gainesville FL 32611

SCHMELTZER, DAVID, lawyer; b. N.Y.C., Mar. 8, 1930; s. Harry Schmeltzer and Julia Hoffman Liebman; m. Louise Rose Levy, June 10, 1962; 1 child, Daniel Havram. BA, L.I. U., 1957; LLB, Bklyn. Law Sch., 1960. Bar: N.Y. 1961. Assoc. Charles Struckler Law Office, N.Y.C., 1960-61; mng. atty. Otterbourg, Steindler, Houston & Rosen, N.Y.C., 1961-62; pub. counsel U.S. Maritime Adminstrn., Washington, 1962-66; atty. Dept. Commerce, Washington, 1966; asst. chief counsel Nat. Hwy. Traffic and Safety Ad, Washington, 1967-73; asst. gen. counsel Consumer Product Safety Commn., Washington, 1973-75, dep. gen. counsel, 1975-77, acting gen. counsel, 1976-77, dir. compliance, 1977—; instr. U. Md. Univ Coll., College Park, 1979-90; mng. dir. Inst. Safety Analysis, Rockville, Md., 1981; vice-chmn. Internat. Consumer Product Health and Safety Orgn., 1995, 96, mem. exec. com., 1995—; contbr. papers and lectures for consumer safety orgns. for European Cmty. and Chinese nat. govt. and provincial govts. Avocation: tennis. Home: 9424 Garden Ct Potomac MD 20854-3964 Office: US Cons Prod Safety Commn Compliance Office 4330 E West Hwy Bethesda MD 20814-4408

SCHMELTZER, EDWARD, lawyer; b. N.Y.C., Aug. 22, 1923; s. Harry A. and Julia (Hoffman) S.; m. Elizabeth Ann Cooper, June 19, 1949; children: Henry Cooper, Elizabeth Sabine. B.A., Hunter Coll., 1950; M.A., Columbia U., 1951; J.D., George Washington U., 1954. Bar: D.C. 1954, U.S. Supreme Ct 1958. Economist PHA, 1951-53; econ. cons., 1953-54; trial atty. Fed. Maritime Bd. Maritime Adminstrn., 1955-60; dir. bur. domestic regulation Fed. Maritime Commn., 1961-66, mng. dir., 1966-69; ptnr. Morgan, Lewis & Bockius, 1969-76, Schmeltzer, Aptaker & Shepard, 1976—; U.S. rep. 12th Diplomatic Conf. on Internat. Maritime Law, Brussels, 1967, 13th Diplomatic Conf., Brussels, 1968. Mem. bd. editors: Jour. Maritime Law and Commerce; Contbr. articles to profl. jours. Served with USAAF, 1943-46. Recipient Fed. Maritime Commn.; Distinguished Service award, 1969. Mem. Maritime Adminstrv. Bar Assn. (pres. 1971-73). Club: Cosmos (Washington). Home: 10412 Buckboard Pl Rockville MD 20854-3805 Office: The Watergate 2600 Virginia Ave NW Washington DC 20037-1905

SCHMELZER, HENRY LOUIS PHILLIP, lawyer, financial company executive; b. Concord, Mass., Aug. 10, 1943; s. Frank Elden and Carroll (Blanning) S.; m. Cynthia E. Livingston, Sept. 28, 1978. B.A., U. Maine, 1965; J.D., George Washington U., 1968. Bar: Mass. 1971. Atty. State Mut. Life Assurance Co., Worcester, Mass., 1970-72; various positions New Eng. Securities Corp., Boston, 1972-90, pres., dir., 1991-92; v.p. New Eng. Mut. Life Ins. Co., 1983-87; pres., trustee New Eng. Funds, 1992—. bd. dirs. Back Bay Advisors, Maine Bank & Trust Co. Bd. overseers U.S.S. Constitution Mus. Capt. M.I., U.S. Army, 1968-70, Vietnam; mem. divsn. capital campaign steering com. Am. Cancer Soc. Decorated Bronze Star with oak leaf cluster; recipient Vietnamese Cross for Gallantry. Mem. Investment Co. Inst. (legis. com.), Boston Com. on Fgn. Rels., Portland (Maine) Yacht Club. Unitarian. Office: New Eng Funds LP 399 Boylston St Ste 10 Boston MA 02116-3305

SCHMEMANN, SERGE, journalist; b. Paris, Apr. 12, 1945; arrived in U.S., 1951; s. Rev Alexander and Juliana (Ossorguine) S.; m. Mary Schidlovsky, Sept. 13, 1970; children: Anne, Alexander, Nathalie. BA cum laude, Harvard U., 1967; MA, Columbia U., 1971; LittD (hon.), Middlebury Coll., 1995. Desk editor AP, N.Y.C., 1972-75, UN corr., 1975-77, South Africa corr., 1977-79, Moscow corr., 1979-80; Moscow bur. chief N.Y. Times, 1980-87, 91-95, Bonn bur. chief, 1987-90, Jerusalem bur. chief, 1995—. Contbr. articles to profl. publs. With U.S. Army, 1968-70, Vietnam. Recipient Hal Boyle award, Overseas Press Club, 1986, Pulitzer Prize for Coverage of German Reunification, 1991. Mem. Phi Beta Kappa. Avocations: piano, carpentry. Office: NY Times 229 W 43rd St New York NY 10036-3913

SCHMERLING, ERWIN ROBERT, counselor, retired physicist; b. Vienna, Austria, July 28, 1929; came to U.S., 1955, naturalized, 1962; s. Heinrich H. and Lily (Goldsmith) S.; m. Esther M. Schmerling, Apr. 5, 1957; children: Susan D., Elaine M. BA, Cambridge U., 1950, MA, 1954, PhD in Radio Physics, 1958; grad., Advanced Mgmt. Program, Harvard, 1969, Fed. Exec. Inst., 1975. Asst. prof. elec. engring. Pa. State U., University Park, 1955-60, assoc. prof., 1960-62, 63-64; staff scientist NASA-Hdqrs., Washington, 1962-63, program chief ionospheric physics, magnetospheric physics, space plasma physics, 1964-82; asst. dir. space and earth scis. Goddard Space Flight Ctr., NASA, Greenbelt, Md., 1984-86; chief data system scientist Office Space Science and Applications NASA Hdqrs., Washington, 1986-88; SAIS program scientist NASA, Washington, 1988-89; data system scientist solar system exploration div. NASA Hdqrs., Washington, 1989-90, program mgr. astrophysics data systems, 1991-94; counselor Svc. Corps of Retired Execs. (SCORE); mem. U.S. coms. III and IV Internat. Sci. Radio Union, 1985—, sec. U.S. Com. III, 1966-69, chmn., 1969-72; chmn. subcom. C1 Com. Space Rsch. (COSPAR), 1984-88; mem. Adv. Group Aerospace Research and Devel., 1978-85; vis. scholar Stanford U., 1983; cons. RCA, Gen. Electric, 1959-62. Contbr. papers to profl. jours. Recipient medal for contbns. to internat. geophys. programs Soviet Geophys. Soc., 1985. Fellow IEEE (mem. wave propagation standards com.); mem. Am. Geophys. Union, AAAS, Sigma Xi. Home: 9917 La Duke Dr Kensington MD 20895-3140

SCHMEROLD, WILFRIED LOTHAR, dermatologist; b. Munich, Germany, Dec. 30, 1919; came to U.S., 1956; s. Wilhelm and Frieda (Hinterwinkler) S.; m. Perlette J. Joers, 1962 (div. Apr. 1974); children: Klaus, John, Will, James, Susan, Paul, Carl, Mike, Tom, Marianne. Abiturient, Altes Realgymnasium, 1938; MD, U. Munich, 1945. Bd. cert. dermatologist, dermatopathologist. Intern U Munich Med. Faculty, 1945-46; asst. UN Hosp., Munich, 1946-50, Max Plank Inst., Munich, 1951-52, U. Erlangen, Germany, 1952-53, U. Munich, 1953-56; intern Fairview Park Hosp., Cleve., 1956-57; asst. U. Ill., Chgo., 1957-60, instr., 1960-75, clin. asst. prof., 1975—; dermatologist pvt. practice, Carol Stream, Ill., 1959—, dermatopathologist, 1978—. Contbr. articles to profl. jours. Charter mem.

founders club Ctrl. DuPage Hosp., Winfield, Ill., 1963. Fellow AMA, Am. Acad. Dermatology (life), German Dermatological Soc. (life), Am. Soc. Dermatopathology, Ill. Dermatological Soc., Ill. State Med. Soc., Chgo. Dermatological Soc. Roman Catholic. Avocations: opera, travel, anthropology, archaeology, history. Office: Mona Kea Med Park 507 Thornhill Dr # B Carol Stream IL 60188-2703

SCHMERSE, TRACI JO, financial services company executive; b. Rockford, Ill., Jan. 24, 1959; d. Paul Eugene and Barbara Jean (Nelson) Hutmacher; m. Mike Schmerse, May 10, 1986 (div. Jan. 1988). AS, Rock Valley Coll., Rockford, Ill., 1982; BS in Biology, Rockford Coll., 1985. Mktg. asst. Pioneer Fin. Svcs., Rockford, 1989-90, mktg. analyst, 1990-91, exec. adminstrv. asst., 1991—, asst. corp. sec., 1994-96, sr. mktg. liaison, 1996—. Office: Pioneer Fin Svcs Inc 304 N Main St Rockford IL 61101-1019

SCHMERTMANN, JOHN HENRY, civil engineer, educator, consultant; b. N.Y.C., Dec. 2, 1928; s. Johannes Conrad Schmertmann and Margarete Anna-Marie (Carstens) Schmertmann Ottesen; m. Pauline Anne Grange, Aug. 11, 1956; children: Carl, Gary, Neil, Joy. B.S.C.E., MIT, 1950; M.S.C.E., Northwestern U., 1954, Ph.D. in Civil Engring., 1962. Registered profl. engr., Fla. Soils engr. Mueser Rutledge Cons. Engrs., N.Y.C., 1951-54; soils engr. C.E., U.S. Army, Wilmette, Ill., 1954-56; asst. prof. civil engring. U. Fla., Gainesville, 1956-62; assoc. prof. U. Fla., 1962-65, prof., 1965-79, adj. prof., prof. emeritus; prin. Schmertmann & Crapps, Inc., Gainesville, 1979—; postdoctoral fellow Norwegian Geotech. Inst., Oslo, 1962-63; vis. scientist div. bldg. research NRC Can., Ottawa Ont., 1971-72. Author numerous profl. papers. Fellow ASCE (br. pres. 1972, Collingwood prize 1956, Norman medal 1971, State of the Art award 1977, Middlebrooks award 1981, Terzaghi lectr. 1989), Fla. Engring. Soc.; mem. Nat. Acad. Engring., ASTM (subcom. chmn. 1974—). Republican. Lutheran. Avocation: sport fishing. Office: Schmertmann & Crapps Inc 4509 NW 23rd Ave Ste 19 Gainesville FL 32606-6570

SCHMERTZ, ERIC JOSEPH, lawyer, educator; b. N.Y.C., Dec. 24, 1925; married; 4 children. A.B., Union Coll., 1948, LL.D. (hon.), 1978; cert., Alliance Francaise, Paris, 1948; J.D., NYU, 1954. Bar: N.Y. 1955. Internat. rep. Am. Fedn. State, County and Mcpl. Employees, AFL-CIO, N.Y.C., 1950-52; asst. v.p., dir. labor tribunals Am. Arbitration Assn., N.Y.C., 1952-57, 59-60; indsl. relations dir. Metal Textile Corp. subs. Gen. Cable Corp., Roselle, N.J., 1957-59; exec. dir. N.Y. State Bd. Mediation, 1960-62, corp. dir., 1962-68; labor-mgmt. arbitrator N.Y.C., 1962—; mem. faculty Hofstra U. Sch. Bus., 1962-70; prof. Hofstra U. Sch. Law, 1970—, Edward F. Carlough disting. prof. labor law, 1981—, dean Sch. Law, 1982-89; of counsel Rivkin, Radler, Kremer, 1989—; commr. labor rels. City of N.Y., 1990-91; 1st Beckley lectr. in bus. U. Vt., 1981; bd. dirs. Wilshire Oil Co.; mem. N.Y. State Pub. Employment Rels. Bd., 1991—; cons. and lectr. in field. Co-author: (with R.L. Greenman) Personnel Administration and the Law, 1978; contbr. chpts. to books, articles to profl. jours., to profl. law confs., seminars and workshops. Mem. numerous civic orgns. Served to lt. USN, 1943-46. Recipient Testimonial award Southeast Republican Club, 1969; Alexander Hamilton award Rep. Law Students Assn.; Eric J. Schmertz Disting. Professorship Pub. Law and Pub. Svc. established Hofstra Law Sch., 1993. Mem. Nat. Acad. Arbitrators, Am. Arbitration Assn. (law com., Whitney North Seymour Sr. medal 1984), Fed. Mediation and Conciliation Svc., N.Y. Mediation Bd., N.J. Mediation Bd., N.J. Pub. Employment Rels. Bd., Hofstra U. Club, Princeton Club. Office: 275 Madison Ave New York NY 10016-1101

SCHMERTZ, HERBERT, public relations and advertising executive; b. Yonkers, N.Y., Mar. 22, 1930; s. Max and Hetty (Frank) S.; children: Anthony, Lexy, Nicole, Thomas, Conor. AB, Union Coll., 1952, LLD (hon.), 1977; LLB, Columbia U., 1955. Bar: N.Y. State 1958. With Am. Arbitration Assn., N.Y.C., 1955-61; gen. counsel, asst. to dir. Fedn. Mediation and Conciliation Svc., N.Y.C., 1961-66; with Mobil Oil Corp., N.Y.C., 1966—; pres. Mobil Shipping and Transp. Co., 1973-74; v.p. pub. affairs Mobil Oil Corp., 1974-88; pres. The Schmertz Co., Inc., N.Y.C., 1988—, Washington, 1990—. Author: Good-bye to the Low Profile, 1986; co-author Takeover, 1980. Appointee Pres.'s Commn. on Broadcasting to Cuba, U.S. Adv. Commn. on Pub. Diplomacy; mem. adv. coun. NYU Sch. Arts; bd. dirs. USO Met. N.Y.C.; trustee Media Inst.; bd. govs. Media and Society Seminars Columbia U. Grad. Sch. Journalism. Served with CIC U.S. Army, 1955-57. Mem. Coun. Fgn. Rels., N.Y. Athletic Club. Democrat. Jewish. Office: Schmertz Co Inc 10 Rockefeller Plz Fl 3 New York NY 10020-1903 also: Schmertz Co Washington 1300 N 17th St Ste 1330 Arlington VA 22209

SCHMERTZ, MILDRED FLOYD, editor, writer; b. Pitts., Mar. 29, 1925; d. Robert Watson and Mildred Patricia (Floyd) S. B.Arch., Carnegie Mellon U., 1947; M.F.A., Yale U., 1957. Archtl. designer John Schurko, Architect, Pitts., 1947-55; assoc. editor Archtl. Record, N.Y.C., 1957-65; sr. editor Archtl. Record, 1965-80, exec. editor, 1980-85, editor-in-chief, 1985-90; vis. lectr. Yale Sch. Architecture, 1979—. Editor, contbr.: New Life for Old Buildings; other books on architecture and planning. Bd. mgrs. Jr. League, City of N.Y., 1964-65; commr. N.Y. Landmarks Preservation Commn., 1988-91. Fellow AIA; mem. Archtl. League N.Y., Mcpl. Art Soc. N.Y., Century Assn. (N.Y.C.). Home and Office: 310 E 46th St New York NY 10017-3002

SCHMETTERER, JACK BAER, federal judge; b. Chgo., Apr. 12, 1931; s. Samuel and Gertrude (Schiff) S.; m. Joan L. Ruther, Mar. 18, 1956; children: Laura, Mark, Kenneth. BA, Yale U., 1952, JD, 1955. Bar: Ill. 1956. Instr. polit. sci. Yale U., New Haven, 1954-55, U. Ga., 1957-58; ptnr. Schmetterer & Schmetterer, Chgo., 1958-63; asst. U.S. atty. U.S. Dist. Ct. (no. dist.) Ill., Chgo., 1963-68, 1st asst. U.S. atty., 1968-70; ptnr. Freeman, Schmetterer, Freeman & Salzman, Chgo., 1970-71; 1st asst. states atty. State's Atty. of Cook County, Chgo., 1971-73; ptnr., head of litigation Gottlieb & Schwartz, Chgo., 1974-85; U.S. bankruptcy judge U.S. Bankruptcy Ct. (no. dist.) Ill., Chgo., 1985—; vis. prof. U. Ill., Chgo., 1974-76. Bd. dirs. Cook County Ct. Watchers, Inc., until 1985, Better Govt. Assn., until 1985; former mem. Northbrook Village Bd., North Shore Mass Transit Dist. Bd. With U.S. Army, 1956-58. Mem. ABA, Fed. Bar Assn. (pres. Chgo. chpt. 1993-94), John Howard Assn. (v.p., bd. dirs.), Legal Club Chgo., Law Club, Mackey-Wigmore Inn of Ct., Decalogue Soc. Office: US Bankruptcy Ct # 600 219 S Dearborn St Apt 600 Chicago IL 60604

SCHMETZER, ALAN DAVID, psychiatrist; b. Louisville, Sept. 3, 1946; s. Clarence Fredrick and Catherine Louise (Wootan) S.; m. Janet Lynn Royce, Aug. 25, 1968; children: Angela Beth, Jennifer Lorraine. BA, Ind. U., 1968, MD, 1972. Diplomate Am. Bd. Psychiatry and Neurology with added qualifications in addiction psychiatry. Intern, Ind. U. Hosps., Indpls., 1972-73, resident, 1972-75; dir. clinics PCI, Inc., Anderson, Beech Grove and Kokomo, Ind., 1975-79; psychiat. cons. Community Addiction Svcs. Agy., Indpls., 1975-80; instr. psychiatry in primary care Family Practice Residency Programs, St. Francis Hosp., St. Vincent's Hosp. and Ind. U. Hosps., Indpls., 1975-91; med. dir. Child Guidance Clinic of Marion County, Indpls., 1980-81; chmn. psychiatry dept. St. Francis Hosp., Beech Grove, 1980-82; med. dir. Crisis Intervention Unit, Midtown Mental Health Ctr., 1980-90; dir. Midtown Mental Health Ctr., 1990-96, med. dir. 1996—; coord. emergency psychiat. svcs. Ind. U. Med. Ctr., Indpls., 1980-90; asst. prof. psychiatry, 1975-94, assoc. prof. psychiatry, 1994—, coord. psychiat. edn. of med. students, 1989-95, asst. chmn. dept. psychiatry, 1993-96, dir. psychiatric edn., 1995—; chief pyschiatry Wishard Meml. Hosp., 1990—; primary psychiat. cons. Ind. Dept. of Mental Health, 1988-89. Maj. Ind. N.G., 1972-79. Decorated Army Commendation medal; recipient Residents award for outstanding teaching 1985, 90, Roeske Excellence in Teaching award 1992. Fellow Am. Psychiat. Assn., Am. Ortho-psychiat. Assn.; mem. AMA (Physicians Recognition award 1978—), Ind. Med. Assn., Indpls. Med. Soc., Am. Psychiat. Assn., Ind. Psychiat. Soc. (pres. 1989-90, 97—), Am. Orthopsychiat. Assn., Am. Acad. Clin. Psychiatry, Alpha Phi Omega, Phi Beta Pi, Psi Chi, Alpha Epsilon Delta. Presbyterian. Clubs: Athenaeum Turnverein, Columbia. Contbr. articles to profl. jours. Office: Midtown CMHC 1001 W 10th St Indianapolis IN 46202-2859

SCHMID, HARALD HEINRICH OTTO, biochemistry educator, academic director; b. Graz, Styria, Austria, Dec. 10, 1935; Came to U.S., 1962; s. Engelbert and Annemarie (Kletetschka) S.; m. Patricia Caroline Igou, May 21, 1977. MS, U. Graz, 1957, LLD, 1962, PhD, 1964. Rsch. fellow Hormel inst. U. Minn., Austin, 1962-65, rsch. assoc., 1965-66, asst. prof., 1966-70, assoc. prof., 1970-74, prof., 1974—; cons. NIH, Bethesda, Md., 1977—; acting dir. Hormel inst. U. Minn., 1985-87, exec. dir., 1987—; lectr. Mayo Med. Sch., Rochester, Minn., 1990—. Mng. editor Chemistry and Physics of Lipids, Elsevier Sci. Publs., Amsterdam, The Netherlands, 1984—; contbr. numerous articles to profl. jours. Rsch. grantee NIH, 1967—. Mem. AAAS, Am. Soc. Biochemistry and Molecular Biology, Am. Chem. Soc., The Oxygen Soc. Avocations: yacht racing, downhill skiing, tennis, classical music. Home: 2701 2nd Ave NW Austin MN 55912-1195 Office: U Minn Hormel Inst 801 16th Ave NE Austin MN 55912-3679

SCHMID, LYNETTE SUE, child and adolescent psychiatrist; b. Tecumseh, Nebr., May 28, 1958; d. Mel Vern John and Janice Wilda (Bohling) S.; m. Vijendra Sundar, June 13, 1987; children: Jesse Christopher Mikaéle, Eric Lynn Kalani, Christina Elizabeth Ululani. BS, U. Nebr., 1979; MD, U. Nebr., Omaha, 1984; postgrad., U. Mo., 1984-89. Diplomate Am. Bd. Med. Examiners, Am. Bd. Psychiatry and Neurology. Child and adolescent psychiatrist Fulton (Mo.) State Hosp., 1990-91, Mid-Mo. Mental Health Ctr., Columbia, Mo., 1991-96; clin. asst. prof. psychiatry U. Mo., Columbia, 1990-96. Contbr. articles to profl. jours. Mem. Am. Psychiat. Assn., Am. Acad. Child and Adolescent Psychiatry, Ctrl. Mo. Psychiat. Assn. (sec.-treas. 1992-93, pres.- elect 1993-94, pres. 1994-95), U. Nebr. Alumni Assn., Phi Beta Kappa, Alpha Omega Alpha. Republican. Baptist. Avocations: walking, reading, studying scripture.

SCHMID, PATRICIA JEAN, personnel professional; b. Terre Haute, Ind., Mar. 12, 1948; d. LeRoy Benjamin and Sue Jean (Nickerson) Patterson; 1 child, Peggy Marie. BA, U. Iowa, 1971, MA in English, 1973, EdS, 1973. Related edn. chair Ivy Tech Coll., Richmond, Ind., 1974-84; sec. Am. Water Sys., Richmond, 1984-86, cmty./employee rels. mgr., 1986-88, asst. dir. pers. devel., 1988-96, dir. pers. svcs., 1996—; lectr. EEOC, N.Y.C., Phil. Health Maintenance, 1991-95. Editor mag. Am. Water, 1994—. Mem. econ. edn. adv. coun. Ind. U. East, Richmond, 1988. Mem. ASTD (dir. utilities industry group 1992-95), Am. Water Works Assn., Phi Beta Kappa. Presbyterian. Office: Am Water Sys 1025 Laurel Oak Rd Voorhees NJ 08043-3506

SCHMID, RUDI (RUDOLF SCHMID), internist, educator, academic administrator, scientist; b. Switzerland, May 2, 1922; came to U.S., 1948, naturalized, 1954; s. Rudolf and Bertha (Schiesser) S.; m. Sonja D. Wild, Sept. 17, 1949; children: Isabelle S., Peter R. BS, Gymnasium Zurich, 1941; MD, U. Zurich, 1947; PhD, U. Minn., 1954. Intern U. Calif. Med. Center, San Francisco, 1948-49; resident medicine U. Minn., 1949-52, instr., 1952-54; research fellow biochemistry Columbia U., 1954-55; investigator NIH, Bethesda, Md., 1955-57; assoc. medicine Harvard U., 1957-59, asst. prof., 1959-62; prof. medicine U. Chgo., 1962-66; prof. medicine U. Calif., San Francisco, 1966-91, prof. emeritus, 1991—, dean Sch. Medicine, 1983-89, assoc. dean internat. rels., 1989-95; Cons. U.S. Army Surgeon Gen., USPHS, VA. Mem. editorial bd. Jour. Clin. Investigation, 1965-70, Blood, 1962-75, Gastroenterology, 1965-70, Jour. Investigative Dermatology, 1968-72, Annals Internal Medicine, 1975-79, Proceedings Soc. Exptl. Biology and Medicine, 1974-84, Chinese Jour. Clin. Scis., Jour. Lab. Clin. Medicine, 1991—, Hepatology Comm. Internat. (Japan), 1993—; cons. editor Gastroenterology, 1981-86. Served with Swiss Army, 1943-48. Master ACP; fellow AAAS, N.Y. Acad. Scis., Royal Coll. Physicians; mem. NAS, Am. Acad. Arts and Scis., Assn. Am. Physicians (pres. 1986), Am. Soc. Clin. Investigation, Am. Soc. Biol. Chemistry and Molecular Biology, Am. Soc. Hematology, Am. Gastroenterol. Assn., Am. Assn. Study Liver Disease (pres. 1965), Internat. Assn. Study Liver (pres. 1980), Swiss Acad. Med. Scis. (mem. senate), Leopoldina, German-Am. Acad. Coun. (exec. com.). Research in biochemistry, metabolism of hemoglobin, heme, prophyrins, bile pigments, liver and muscle. Home: 211 Woodland Rd Kentfield CA 94904-2631 Office: U Calif Med Sch Office of Dean PO Box 0410 San Francisco CA 94143-0410

SCHMID, WILFRIED, mathematician; b. Hamburg, Germany, May 28, 1943; came to U.S., 1960; s. Wolfgang and Kathe (Erfling) S. BA, Princeton U., 1964; MA, U. Calif., Berkeley, 1966, PhD, 1967. Asst. prof. math. U. Calif., Berkeley, 1967-70; prof. math. Columbia U., 1970-78, Harvard U., 1978—; vis. mem. Inst. for Advanced Study, Princeton, 1969-70, 75-76; vis. prof. U. Bonn, 1973-74. Editor Springer Ergebnisse der Mathematik; contbr. articles to profl. jours. Sloan fellow, 1968-70, Guggenheim fellow, 1975-76, 88-89. Home: Silver Hill Rd Lincoln MA 01773 Office: Harvard U Dept Mathematics Cambridge MA 02138

SCHMIDHAMMER, ROBERT HOWARD, environmental executive, engineering consultant; b. Altoona, Pa., May 13, 1931; s. Leo Anselm and Audrey Norma (Dibert) S.; m. Elaine Carol Jones, Dec. 18, 1954 (dec. Nov., 1986); children: Linda K., Raymond J.; m. Patricia M. Burgess, Feb. 29, 1996. BSME/ BSCE, Finlay Engring. Coll., Kansas City, Mo., 1958; grad. studies Engring. & Constrn. Mgmt., Various Schs., 1960-72. Constrn. mgr., consulting engr. Developers and individuals, different locations, 1960-87; sr. project mgr. Marcor Environ. Corp., Rochester, N.Y., 1987-90; engring. cons., environ. svcs. AAC Contracting, Inc., Rochester, N.Y., 1990—; cons. pvt. practice, Rochester, 1990—; bd. dirs. 3 non-pub. corps. Contbr. articles to environ. jours. Bd. dirs. various civic orgns. With USAF, 1950-53, Korea. Mem. Rochester Engring. Soc. (fin. cons.), Rochester Lions Club (officer/dir.), Rochester C. of C., Assn. Facilities Engrs., Cert. Hazardous Materials Mgrs. (Finger Lakes chpt.), Construction Specifications Inst., VFW, Am. Legion, Bldg. Owners and Mgmt. Assn. Republican. Roman Catholic. Avocations: collector stamps and coins, sailing. Home: 36 Rogers Ave Rochester NY 14606-1827 Office: AAC Contracting Inc Engring and Environ Svcs Rochester NY 14611

SCHMIDHAUSER, JOHN RICHARD, political science educator; b. N.Y.C., Jan. 3, 1922; s. Richard J. and Gertrude (Grabinger) S.; m. Thelma Lorraine Ficker, June 9, 1952; children: Steven, Paul, Thomas, John C., Martha, Sarah, Susan. B.A. with honors, U. Del., 1949; M.A., U. Va., 1952, Ph.D., 1954. Instr. U. Va., 1952-54; prof. constl. law U. Iowa, 1954-64, prof. polit. sci., 1967-73; prof. polit. sci. U. So. Calif., 1973-92, prof. emeritus, 1993—; mem. 89th Congress 1st dist. Iowa.; research fellow Research Inst. on Jud. Process, Social Sci. Research Council, 1958; sr. fellow law and behavorial scis. U. Chgo., 1959-60; Talbot vis. prof. govt. U. Va., 1982-83. Author: The Role of Supreme Court as Final Arbiter in Federal-State Relations, 1789-1957, 1958, The Supreme Court; Its Politics, Personalities and Procedures, 1960, Constitutional Law in the Political Process, 1963, (with Berg) The Supreme Court and Congress, 1972, (with Berg and Hahn) American Political Institutions and Corruption, 1976, (with Totten) Whaling in Japan-U.S. Relations, 1978, Judges and Justices, 1979, Constitutional Law in American Politics, 1984, Comparative Judicial Politics, 1987; also numerous articles in jours. Chmn. Citizens Action Com. for Fair Representation in Iowa Legislature, 1961; dist. chmn. Operation Support Pres. Kennedy and Johnson, 1961—; chmn. Johnson County Dem. Ctrl. Com., 1961-64; del. Iowa Dem. Convs., 1956, 58, 60, 62; mem. Dem. Nat. Com. Alumni Coun., 1986—; chmn. Santa Barbara, Calif. Dem. Ctrl. Com., 1991-92; mem. exec. com. Los Padres chpt. of the Sierra Club, 1992-96; sec. Santa Barbara Dem. League, 1993-96. With USNR, 1941-45, PTO. Recipient Raubenheimer award U. So. Calif., 1991, Golden Key award for Comparative Rsch, 1991. Mem. Iowa City Mgr. Assn. (bd. reps. 1956-59, chmn. handbook revision 1958), Internat. Polit. Sci. Assn. (chmn. research com. for comparative jud. studies 1980-88), Am. Polit. Sci. Assn., Midwestern Polit. Sci. Assn., Western Polit. Sci. Assn. (v.p., program chmn. 1980-81, pres.-elect 1981-82), AAUP (sec.-treas. State U. Iowa 1958-59, mem. com. on relationship fed. and state govt. to higher edn., mem. exec. com. U. So. Calif. chpt. 1983-92), Humanities Soc., Raven Soc., Phi Beta Kappa, Phi Kappa Phi. Unitarian (chmn. Iowa City Soc. Men's Club 1960-61). Home: 726 Arbol Verde St Carpinteria CA 93013-2508 *For the young today the opportunity for a good education puts them at the threshold of great opportunities. I encourage them to enjoy that with the same spirit that my generation experienced.*

SCHMIDLY, DAVID J., university official and dean, biology educator; b. Levelland, Tex., Dec. 20, 1943; m. Janet Elaine Knox, June 2, 1966; children: Katherine Elaine, Brian James. BS in Biology, Tex. Tech U., 1966, MS in Zoology, 1968; PhD in Zoology, U. Ill., 1971. From asst. prof. to prof. dept. wildlife fisheries scis. Tex. A&M U., College Station, 1971-82, prof., 1982-96, head dept. wildlife, 1986-92; CEO, campus dean Tex. A&M U., Galveston, 1992-96; chief curator Tex. Coop. Wildlife Coll., College Station, 1983-86; v.p. Tex. Inst. Oceanography, 1992-96; v.p. rsch. and grad studies, dean grad. sch. Tex. Tech U., Lubbock, 1996—, prof. biol. scis., 1996—, charter mem. faculty senate, 1983-85; cons. Nat. Park Svc., Wildlife Assocs., Walton and Assocs., Continental Shelf Assn., LGL; lectr. various workshops and seminars; press adv. com. Tex. A&M U., 1983-96; charter mem. Tex. A&M U. Faculty Senate, 1983-85, chmn. Scholarship Com., 1978-82. Author: The Mammals of Trans-Pecos Texas including Big Bend National Park and Guadalupe Mountains National Park, 1977, Texas Mammals East of the Balcones Fault Zone, 1983, The Bats of Texas, 1991, The Mammals of Texas, 1994; contbr. articles to profl. jours. Trustee Tex. Nature Conservancy, 1991—. Recipient Dist. Prof. award Assn. Grad. Wildlife and Fisheries Scis., 1985, Donald W. Tinkle Rsch. Excellence award Southwestern Assn. Naturalists, 1988, Diploma Recognition La Universidad Autonoma de Guadalajara, 1989, La Universidad Autonoma de Tamaulipas, 1990. Fellow Tex. Soc. Sci. (bd. dirs. 1979-81); mem. AAAS, Am. Soc. Mammalogists (life, editor Jour. Mammalogy 1975-78), Am. Inst. Biol. Scis. (bd. dirs. 1993—, coun. affiliate socs. 1989—), Am. Naturalist, Soc. Marine Mammalogy (charter mem.), Soc. Systematic Zoology, The Wildlife Soc. Soc. Conservation Biology, Nat. Geog. Sci. Soc., S.W. Assn. Naturalists (life mem., bd. govs. 1980-86, 91—, pres. 1981, trustee 1986—), Tex. Mammal Soc. (pres. 1985-86), Assn. Systematic Collections (bd. dirs.), Chihuahuan Desert Rsch. Inst. (v.p. bd. scientists 1982—, bd. dirs. 1991), Mexican Soc. Mammalogists, Sigma Xi (v.p. 1986-87, pres. 1987-88), Disting. Scientist award 1991), Beta Beta Beta. Phi Sigma, Phi Kapa Phi. Home: 4404 15th St Lubbock TX 79416 Office: Tex Tech U Holden Hall Box 41033 Lubbock TX 79409-1033

SCHMIDMAN, JO ANN, artistic director. BFA, Boston U., 1970. Performer Joseph Chaikin's Open Theatre, N.Y.C.; artistic dir., writer, actor, prodr., light and concept designer Omaha Magic Theatre, 1968—; project dir., fiscal agt. for more than 90 found., corp., govt. grants; lectr. internationally; condr. workshops in ensemble acting, directing, collaborative theatre, performance art and storytelling; tchr. playwriting and poetry at various univs., 1993-96; writing Team mem. of Framework, visual performing arts, reporter Theatre Program, NEA, 1980—, mem. artistic advancement com., 1987-89, 92, chmn., 1988-89, mem. theatre overview panel, 1988; mem. Japanese-Am. Fellowship Com., 1987. Contbg. writer: 100,001 Horror Stores of the Plains, 1976, This Sleep Among Women, 1978, Running Gag, 1980 (commd. perfs. 1980 Winter Olympics); dir., performer: (with Sora Kimberlain) Yellow Strapping, 1980, (with Kimberlain) Blue Tube, 1980, (with Kimberlain) White Out, 1980, (with Kimberlain) Reflected Light, 1980, Change Yer Image, 1981, Aliens Under Glass, 1982, Velveeta Meltdown, 1982, Watch Where We Walk, 1983, (with Megan Terry) X-Rayed-Iate: E-Motion in Action, 1984, Astro*Bride, 1984, (with Terry) Sea of Forms, 1986, (with Terry) Walking Through Walls, 1987, (with Terry) Babes Unchained, (with Terry) Body Leaks, 1990, Belches on Couches, 1993; dir.: (with Terry, Kimberlain, and Calif. State students) Cancel That Last Thought or See the 270 Foot Woman in Spandex, 1989, (with Terry and Kimberlain) Sound Fields, 1991, (with Terry) Remote Control, 1994, (with Terry) Star Path Moon Stop, 1995-96; editor (with Terry) Right Brain Vacation Photos, 1972-92; performer: Terminal, Open Theatre, 1971-73; contbg. writer, performer: Mutation Show and Nightwalk, Open Theatre, 1970-73 (Obie award); prodr., dir., performer numerous plays. Artist-in-the-Schs. in Performing Arts grantee Nebr. Arts Coun., tours with Omahta Magic Theatre: U.S., Asia, (Korea), 1995, 96. Home: 2309 Hanscom Blvd Omaha NE 68105-3143 Office: Omaha Magic Theatre 325 S 16th St Omaha NE 68102-2208

SCHMID-SCHOENBEIN, GEERT WILFRIED, biomedical engineer, educator; b. Albstadt, Baden-Wurttemberg, Germany, Jan. 1, 1948; came to U.S., 1971; s. Ernst and Ursula Schmid; m. Renate Schmid-Schoenbein, July 3, 1976; children: Philip, Mark, Peter. Vordiplom, Liebig U., Giessen, Germany, 1971; PhD in Bioengring., U. Calif., San Diego, 1976. Staff assoc. dept. physiology Columbia U., N.Y.C., 1976-77, sr. assoc., 1977-79; asst. prof. dept. applied mechs. & engring. scis. U. Calif., San Diego, 1979-84, assoc. prof., 1984-89, prof., 1989-94, prof. dept. bioengring., 1994—. Editor: Frontiers in Biomechanics, 1986, Physiology and Pathophysiology of Leukocyte Adhesion, 1994. Recipient Melville medal ASME, 1990. Fellow Am. Inst. for Med. & Biol. Engring., Am. Heart Assn.; mem. Biomed. Engring. Soc. (pres. 1991-92), Am. Microcirculatory Soc., European Microciculatory Soc., Am. Physiol. Soc. Achievements include bioengineering research of cardiovascular disease and lymphology. Office: U Calif San Diego Dept Bioengineering La Jolla CA 92093-0412

SCHMIDT, ADOLPH WILLIAM, retired ambassador; b. McKeesport, Pa., Sept. 13, 1904; s. Adolph and Louise (Schmidt) S.; m. Helen Sedgley Mellon, June 27, 1936; children—Helen Schmidt Claire, Thomas M. A.B., Princeton U., 1926, LL.D. (hon.), 1977; M.B.A., Harvard U., 1929; certificates, U. Dijon, U. Berlin and U. Paris, Sorbonne, 1926-27; LL.D. (hon.), U. Pitts, 1954, U. N.B., 1973; L.H.D., Chatham Coll., 1965, Carnegie-Mellon U., 1981. Officer Mellon Nat. Bank and affiliated orgns., Pitts., 1929-42; chmn. bd., dir. Columbia Radiator Co., McKeesport, 1939-42; mem. exec. com., dir. Pitts. Coal Co., 1940-42; v.p., gov. T. Mellon & Sons, Pitts., 1946-69; trustee A.W. Mellon Ednl. and Charitable Trust, pres., 1954-65; trustee Old Dominion Found., 1941-69, Carnegie Inst., 1965-92; ambassador to Can. Ottawa, Ont., 1969-74; U.S. del. Conf. on North Atlantic Community, Bruges, Belgium, 1957, Atlantic Congress, London, Eng., 1959, Atlantic Conv. NATO Nations, Paris, France, 1962; adviser to U.S. delegation Econ. Commn. for, Europe, Geneva, Switzerland, 1967; bd. govs. Atlantic Inst., Paris; bd. dirs. Atlantic Council U.S., Washington. Co-founder Pitts. Playhouse, 1934, Pitts. Symphony, 1937; pres. Presbyn.-Univ. Hosp., 1946-47; 1st chmn. Three Rivers Arts Festival, 1960; pres., chmn. Allegheny Conf. on Community Devel., Pitts., 1956-61; vice chmn. Urban Redevel. Authority, 1954-59; 1st chmn. Southwestern Pa. Regional Planning Commn., 1960; mem. bus. and internat. coms. Nat. Planning Assn., 1955-69; mem. Can.-Am. Com., 1974-80; chmn. Pa. State Planning Bd., 1955-68; dir. Population Crisis Com., Washington, 1965-69, Population-Environment Balance, Inc., 1973-89; mem. bd. visitors and govs. St. Johns Coll., Annapolis, Md. and Santa Fe, N.Mex., also chmn., 1956, 62; mem. grad. council Princeton U. Served from capt. to lt. col. U.S. Army, 1942-46; with OSS in Africa and Europe; Allied Control Commn. Berlin. Awarded Bronze Star, Two Battle Stars; Benjamin Rush award Allegheny Co. Med. Soc., 1950; David Glick award World Affairs Council, 1965. Mem. Coun. Fgn. Rels., Mil. Order World Wars, Coun. Am. Ambs. Republican. Presbyterian. Clubs: Links, Anglers (N.Y.C.); Duquesne (Pitts.), Pitts. Golf; Laurel Valley Golf, Rolling Rock (Ligonier, Pa.); Metropolitan (Washington). Home: RR 4 Ligonier PA 15658-9804

SCHMIDT, ALLEN EDWARD, religious denomination administrator; b. Barriere, B.C., Can., Oct. 30, 1932; s. Ernst Waldemar and Agda Elvira (Rosen) S.; m. Catherine Edith Lee, June 19, 1954; children: Rebecca Lee Wade, Leanne Ruth Birdwell, Joseph Allen. BA with honors, Hardin-Simmons U., 1957; MDiv, Golden Gate Bapt. Sem., 1962. Owner, operator trucking co. Barriere, 1949-52; founding pastor Temple Bapt. Ch., Fairfield, Calif., 1960-61, Pike Rd. Bapt. Ch., Surrey, B.C., 1961-66, Royal Heights Bapt. Ch., Delta, B.C., 1966-81; Can. ch. coord. N.W. Bapt. Conv., Portland, Oreg., 1981; exec. dir., treas. Can. Conv. of So. Baptists, Cochrane, Alta., Can., 1985—. Pres. PTA, Surrey, 1977-79, Surrey Ministerial, 1975-77, N.W. Bapt. Conv., Portland, 1976-78, exec. bd. dirs., chmn., 1971-75. Home: 128 Riverview Cir, Cochrane, AB Canada T0L 0W4 Office: Can Conv So Baptists, Bag 300, Cochrane, AB Canada T0L 0W0

SCHMIDT, ARTHUR, film editor. Editor: (films) (with Jim Clark) The Last Remake of Beau Geste, 1977, Coal Miner's Daughter, 1980 (Academy award nomination best film editing 1980), The Escape Artist, 1982, Firstborn, 1984, The Buddy System, 1984, (with Harry Keramidas) Back to the Future, 1985, Fandango, 1985, (with Gib Jaffe) Ruthless People, 1986, Who Framed Roger Rabbit?, 1988 (Academy award best film editing 1988), (with Keramidas) Back to the Future II, 1989, (with Keramidas) Back to the Future III, 1990, (with Dov Hoenig) The Last of the Mohicans, 1992, Death Becomes Her, 1992, (with Jim Miller) Addams Family Values, 1993, Forrest Gump, 1994 (Academy award best film editing 1994), The Birdcage, 1996. Office: care Motion Picture Editors 7715 W Sunset Blvd Ste 220 Los Angeles CA 90046-3912

SCHMIDT, BARNET MICHAEL, communications and electronic engineer; b. New Milford, N.J., June 30, 1958; s. Frank Lowell and Lee (Fishkin) S. BSEE, Stevens Inst. Tech., 1980, BS Computer Sci., 1980, MSEE, 1985. Comml. pilot/instrument. Electronic engr. Cessna Aircraft Co., Boonton, N.J., 1980-81; sr. systems engr. Timeplex Corp., Unisys Co., Woodcliff Lake, N.J., 1981-85; mem. tech. staff, cons. AT&T Bell Labs., Holmdel, N.J., 1985-90; mem. tech. staff Bell Comms. Rsch., Piscataway, N.J., 1990-95; mem. tech. staff Network Transmission Sys. Lab. AT&T Bell Labs., Holmdel, N.J., 1995—; cons. engr. Computer Scis. Corp., El Segundo, Calif., 1986-90. 3 Patents in field. Mem. IEEE. Achievements include inventing neural-network based intelligent systems for isolating hidden troubles in telecommunications networks; inventing of novel adaptive filter synthesis techniques; developer of optimal SONET network architectures and routing methods; developer of robust fault tolerant optical transmission sys. and network surveillance sys. Office: AT&T Bell Labs Bell Comms Rsch Inc Crawfords Corner Rd RMIL633 Holmdel NJ 07733-1988

SCHMIDT, BERLIE LOUIS, agricultural research administrator; b. Treynor, Iowa, Oct. 2, 1932; s. Hans Frederick and Louisa Amalie (Guttau) S.; m. Joanne Doris Bruning, Sept. 4, 1954 (dec. Apr. 1982); children: Brian, Luanne Schmidt Code, Kevin, Kimberly Schmidt Nelson, Christy Schmidt Mash; m. Bonnijane G. Mehlhop, June 14, 1986. B.S., Iowa State U., 1954, M.S., 1959, Ph.D., 1962. Soil scientist Soil Conservation Svc. USDA, Council Bluffs, Iowa, 1954-57; grad. rsch. assoc. Iowa State U., Ames, 1957-62; asst. prof. agronomy Ohio State U., Wooster, 1962-65, assoc. prof., 1965-69; prof., assoc. chmn. dept. agronomy Ohio State U., Columbus, 1969-75, prof., chmn. dept. agronomy, 1975-86, prof., coord. Conservation Tillage Systems Program, 1986-87; prof. emeritus Ohio State U., Washington, 1987—; nat. program leader, soil and water rsch. Coop. State Rsch., Edn. and Extension Svc., USDA, Washington, 1987—; program dir. Nat. Rsch. Initiative Competitive Rsch. Grants Program, 1994—. Editor: Determinants of Soil Loss Tolerance, 1982; contbr. articles to sci. jours. Elder Worthington United Presbyterian Ch., Worthington, Ohio, 1983. With U.S. Army, 1954-56, PTO. Fellow Am. Soc. Agronomy, Ohio Acad. Sci., Soil Sci. Soc. Am.; mem. Soil and Water Conservation Soc. Am. (Outstanding Mem. award All-Ohio chpt. 1977), Internat. Soc. Soil Sci., Coun. Agrl. Sci. and Tech. Republican. Home: 2103 Kedge Dr Vienna VA 22181-3211 Office: USDA CSREES 808 Aerospace Bldg Washington DC 20250-2210

SCHMIDT, BRUCE RANDOLPH, science administrator, researcher; b. N.Y.C., June 19, 1948; s. Charles Henry and Beverly (Quinby) S.; m. Jackie Gillmor, Aug. 14, 1971; children: Valerie, Michael. BS in Fisheries Mgmt., Utah State U., 1970; MS in Wildlife and Fisheries Sci., S.D. State U., 1975. Fisheries technician Alaska Dept. Fish & Game, King Salmon, summer 1969, fisheries technician, crew leader, summer 1970; biol. aide, temporary Utah Divsn. Wildlife Resources, Dutch John, summer 1971; fisheries rsch. biologist Utah Divsn. Wildlife Resources, Lake Powell, 1971-72; rsch. project leader Utah Divsn. Wildlife Resources, Flaming Gorge, 1977-83; fisheries sect. planner Utah Divsn. Wildlife Resources, Salt Lake City, 1983-84, chief of fisheries, 1984-94; rsch. asst. S.D. State U., Brookings, 1973-74; fisheries rsch. biologist S.D. Dept. Game & Fish, Webster, 1975-77; rsch. sect. supr. Oreg. Dept. Fish & Wildlife, Corvallis, 1994—; chair N.Am. Fisheries Leadership Workshop, Snowbird, Utah, 1990; Oreg. coord. Gov.'s Coastal Salmon Restoration Initiative, a multi-agy. and local cmty. coop. effort to restore salmon populations. Lead author: (statewide mgmt. plan) A Conceptual Management Plan for Cutthroat Trout in Utah, 1995. Valedictorian Utah State U., 1970. Mem. Am. Fisheries Soc. (pres. adminstr.'s sect. 1990). Home: 3146 NW Greenbriar Pl Corvallis OR 97330-3431 Office: Oregon Dept Fish & Wildlife 28655 Highway 34 Corvallis OR 97333-2227

SCHMIDT, CHARLES T., JR., labor and industrial relations educator. Prof., dir. labor and indsl. rels. rsch., labor arbitrator. Office: University of Rhode Island Labor Research Ctr Adams House Kingston RI 02881

SCHMIDT, CHAUNCEY EVERETT, banker; b. Oxford, Ia., June 7, 1931; s. Walter Frederick and Vilda (Saxton) S.; m. Anne Garrett McWilliams, Mar. 3, 1954; children: Carla, Julia, Chauncey Everett. B.S., U.S. Naval Acad., 1953; M.B.A., Harvard U., 1959. With First Nat. Bank, Chgo., 1959-76; v.p., gen. mgr. br. First Nat. Bank, London, Eng., 1965-68; v.p. for First Nat. Bank, Europe, Middle East, Africa, 1968-69; sr. v.p. First Nat. Bank, Chgo., 1969-72; exec. v.p. First Nat. Bank, 1972, vice chmn. bd., 1973, pres., 1974-76; chmn. bd., chief exec. officer, dir. Bank of Calif. N.A., San Francisco, 1976—; chmn. bd., pres., chief exec. officer, dir. BanCal Tri-State Corp., 1976—; dir. Amfac, Inc., Honolulu; mem. Adv. Council Japan-U.S. Econ. Relations; adv. bd. Pacific Rim Bankers Program. Exec. bd. and pres. San Francisco Bay Area council Boy Scouts Am.; council SRI Internat.; bd. dirs. Bay Area Council; bd. govs. San Francisco Symphony; trustee U.S. Naval War Coll. Fedn., Newport, R.I. Served with USAF, 1953-56. Mem. Assn. Res. City Bankers, Am. Bankers Assn., Internat. Monetary Conf., Calif. Bankers Clearing House Assn. (dir.), Calif. Roundtable (dir.), Japan-Calif. Assn. Clubs: Comml. (Chgo.); Bankers (San Francisco), Bohemian (San Francisco). Home: 40 Why Worry Ln Woodside CA 94062-3654 Office: 3000 Sand Hill Rd Ste 158 Menlo Park CA 94025-7116

SCHMIDT, CHUCK, professional football team executive; b. Detroit, Jan. 22, 1947; m. Sharon Schmidt; children: Scott, Krista, Matthew. Degree in bus., U. Mich.; grad. degree in fin., Wayne State U. Formerly with Ernst and Whinney; CPA Detroit Lions, from 1976, also contr., then v.p. fin., until 1987, exec. v.p., chief oper. officer, 1989—. Bd. dirs., sec., treas. Detroit Lions Charities; bd. dirs. CATCH, Pontiac (Mich.) Devel. Found. Office: Detroit Lions 1200 Featherstone Rd Pontiac MI 48342-1938*

SCHMIDT, CLARENCE ANTON, financial consultant; b. Chgo., Nov. 28, 1935; s. Clarence Lawrence and Anna Elizabeth (Leske) S.; m. Anne Louise Wolfer, Feb. 28, 1959; children: J. Paul, Carolyn Anne Schmidt Noll. BS in Indsl. Mgmt., Carnegie-Mellon U., 1957, MS in Indsl. Adminstrn., 1958. ChFC; CLU. Cost engr. Eastman Kodak Co., Rochester, N.Y., 1958-65; supr. cost engring. Eastman Kodak Co., Rochester, 1965-67; corp. mgr. fin. plans Litton Industries, Beverly Hills, Calif., 1967-69; v.p. fin. machine tool group Litton Industries, Hartford, Conn., 1969-72; v.p. fin., CFO, Hillenbrand Industries, Batesville, Ind., 1972-76, Consol. Aluminum Corp., St. Louis, 1976-79; spl. agt. Northwestern Mut. Life, St. Louis, 1979-85; fin. counselor Cigna Fin. Advisors, St. Louis, 1985-93; fin. cons. Clarence A. Schmidt, ChFC, St. Louis, 1994—. Bd. dirs. Luth. Ministries Assn., St. Louis, 1983-91, pres., 1988-90. Mem. Am. Soc. CLU's and ChFC's (instr. wealth accumulation 1994), Internat. Assn. for Fin. Planning, Nat. Assn. Life Underwriters, Estate Planning Coun. St. Louis. Republican. Avocations: tennis, bridge. Office: 139 Ladue Oaks Dr Saint Louis MO 63141-8129

SCHMIDT, CLAUDE HENRI, retired research administrator; b. Geneva, Switzerland, May 6, 1924; came to U.S., 1935; s. Roger Auguste Schmidt and Lucette (Henriette) Wuhrman; m. Melicent Esther Hane, June 25, 1953; children—Valerie Lynn, Jeffrey Allan. A.B., Stanford U., 1948, M.A., 1950; Ph.D., Iowa State U., 1956. With Agrl. Rsch. Svc., USDA, 1956-88; rsch. entomologist Orlando, Fla., 1956-62; project leader Fargo, N.D., 1964-67; br. chief Beltsville, Md., 1967-72; area dir. N. Cen. region Fargo, 1972-82, lab. dir., 1982-88, acting dir. Red River Valley Agrl. Rsch. Ctr., 1988; collaborator, 1988-94; chair Cass County Control Bd., 1994—; entomologist IAEA, Vienna, Austria, 1962-64; sec. Nat. Mosquito Fish and Wildlife Commn., Washington, 1968-72. Editor Leafy Spurge News, 1994—; contbr. articles to profl. jours. Served with AUS, Signal Corps 1942-46, to 1st lt. Med. Service Corps, 1950-53. Fellow Washington Acad. Sci., AAAS; mem. Am. Mosquito Control Assn. (pres. 1981-82), Am. Chem. Soc., Entomol. Soc. Am. Republican. Lodge: Elks. Home: 1827 3rd St N Fargo ND 58102-2335

SCHMIDT, CYRIL JAMES, librarian; b. Flint, Mich., June 27, 1939; s. Cyril August and Elizabeth Josephine S.; m. Martha Joe Meadows, May 22, 1965; children: Susan, Emily. BA, Cath. U. Am., 1962; MSLS, Columbia U., 1963; Ph.D., Fla. State U., 1974. Asst. bus. and industry dept. Flint Pub. Library, 1963-65; reference librarian Gen. Motors Inst., Flint, 1965; asso. librarian S.W. Tex. State U., San Marcos, 1965-67; head undergrad. libraries, asst. prof. Ohio State U., 1967-70; dir. libraries SUNY, Albany, 1972-79; also mem. faculty SUNY (Sch. Library and Info. Sci.); univ. librarian Brown U., Providence, 1979-81; exec. v.p. Rsch. Libraries Group, Stanford, Calif., 1981-89; prin. cons. Schmidt & Assocs., Palo Alto, Calif., 1989—; univ. prof., libr. San Jose (Calif.) State U., 1992—. Author papers in field. Libr. Svcs. Act fellow, 1962-63, Higher Edn. Act fellow, 1970-72. Mem. ALA, ACLU, Pi Sigma Alpha, Beta Phi Mu. Home: 244 Forest Ave Palo Alto CA 94301-2510 Office: San Jose State U 1 Washington Sq San Jose CA 95112-3613

SCHMIDT, DANIEL EDWARD, IV, lawyer; b. N.Y.C., Dec. 17, 1946; s. Daniel Edward III and Mary (Mannion) S.; m. Gail Kennedy, Sept. 5, 1980; children: Kathryn Kennedy, Michael Kennedy. BA, St. Lawrence U., 1971; postgrad., New Sch., 1972; JD, St. John's U., 1975. Bar: N.Y. 1976; cert. arbitrator. From asst. counsel to assoc. gen. counsel Prudential Property & Casualty, Holmdel, N.J., 1975-81, assoc. gen. counsel, divsn. head, 1981-83; v.p., assoc. gen. counsel, asst. sec. Prudential Reins Co., Newark, 1983-84; dir., v.p., gen. counsel, corp. sec. Scor U.S. Group, N.Y.C., 1984-86, dir., sr. v.p., gen. counsel, corp. sec., 1986-89; dir., exec. com., sr. v.p., gen. counsel, corp. sec. Sorema N.A. Group, N.Y.C., 1989-94, dir., exec. com., exec. v.p., group gen. counsel, 1995—; dep. gen. mgr., gen. counsel, corp. sec. Sorema Internat. Holding, N.V., The Netherlands, 1993-96, U.S Counsel, Groupama, 1996—; pvt. practice reins. arbitrator, umpire, Little Silver, N.J., 1987—; reins. lectr. Wingdale, N.Y., 1986—; bd. dirs. ARIAS (U.S.), N.Y.C. Chmn. editl. bd. Arias- U.S. Quar. Bd. dirs., exec. com. ARC, Monmouth County, Shrewsbury, N.J., 1981-84; judge Ecclesiastical Trial Ct., Episcopal Diocese of N.J. With U.S. Army, 1967-70. Mem. ABA, Am. Arbitration Assn. (panel comml. arbitrators), N.Y. Bar Assn., Assn. Internat. Droit des Assureurs (U.S. chpt.), Bamm Hollow Country Club. Episcopalian. Avocations: golf, tennis, skiing. Home: 628 Little Silver Point Rd Little Silver NJ 07739-1737 Office: Sorema NA Group 199 Water St Fl 20 New York NY 10038-3526

SCHMIDT, EDWARD CRAIG, lawyer; b. Pitts., Nov. 26, 1947; s. Harold Robert and Bernice (Williams) S.; m. Elizabeth Lowry Rial, Aug. 18, 1973; children: Harold Robert II, Robert Rial. BA, U. Mich., 1969; JD, U. Pitts., 1972. Bar: Pa. 1972, U.S. Dist. Ct. (we. dist.) Pa. 1972, U.S. Ct. Appeals (3d. cir.) 1972, U.S. Ct. Appeals (D.C. cir.) 1975, U.S. Supreme Ct. 1981, U.S. Ct. Appeals (9th cir.) 1982, U.S. Ct. Appeals (4th cir.) 1982, U.S. Ct. Appeals (6th cir.) 1987, U.S. Ct. Appeals (11th cir.) 1990, U.S. Ct. Appeals (2d cir.) 1992, U.S. Ct. Appeals (4th cir.) 1994. Assoc. Rose, Schmidt, Hasley & Di Salle, Pitts., 1972-77, ptnr., 1977-90, Jones, Day Reavis & Pogue, Pitts.; mem. adv. com. Superior Ct. Pa., 1978-80. Co-editor; Antitrust Discovery Handbook-Supplement, 1982; asst. editor: Antitrust Discovery Handbook, 1980; contbr. articles to profl. jours. Bd. dirs. Urban League, Pitts., 1974-77. Mem. Supreme Ct. Hist. Soc., Pa. Bar Assn., D.C. Bar Assn., Allegheny County Bar Assn. (pub. rels. com. coun. civil litigation sect. 1977-80), Internat. Acad. Trial Laywers, Acad. Trial Lawyers Allegheny County (bd. govs. 1985-87), U. Pitts. Law Alumni Assn. (bd. govs. 1980). Clubs: Rolling Rock (Ligonier, Pa.), Duquesne (Pitts.), Longue Vue (Pitts.). Republican. Home: 159 Washington St Pittsburgh PA 15218-1351 Office: Jones Day Reavis & Pogue One Mellon Bank Ctr 31st Fl 500 Grant St Pittsburgh PA 15219-2502

SCHMIDT, FRED (ORVAL FREDERICK SCHMIDT), editor; b. Lone Wolf, Okla., Sept. 17, 1922; s. Otto Frederick and Mabel Marie (Johnson) S.; m. Eleanor Minerva Austin, Jan. 15, 1949; 1 son, Frederick Curtis. Student, U. Okla., 1941-42, Chgo. Sch. Photography, 1947-48. Photographer, color technician James Israel Studio, Mt. Vernon, Ohio, 1949-55; from adminstrv. asst. to mng. editor Profl. Photographers Am., Inc., 1955-74; editorial dir. Photomethods, N.Y.C., 1974-85, Internat. TV, 1983-85, Photo/Design, 1984-85; exec. editor Video Mgr., 1985-88; cons. editor Tape/Disc Bus., 1987-89; tchr. photojournalism Milw. Area Tech. Coll., 1965-66, mem. adv. bd., 1972-74; lectr. No. Ill. U., 1968-73; sec. Profl. Photographers, Ohio, 1954-55. Co-author: Opportunities in Photography, 1978. Bd. advisers Chgo. Internat. Film Festival, 1967-75. Served with USCGR, 1942-46. Recipient Nat. award Profl. Photographers Am., 1964, award of Nikola Tesla medal World Coun. Profl. Photographers, 1995. Mem. Am. Soc. Photographers (hon. assco.), Yugoslavia Fedn. Profl. Photographers (hon.), Profl. Photographers of Israel, Internat. TV Assn. (Svc. award). Home and Office: 138 Joralemon St Brooklyn NY 11201-4714

SCHMIDT, GENE EARL, hospital administrator; b. Goessel, Kans., Aug. 5, 1942; s. Arthur K. and Hedwig (Neufeld) S.; m. Marcia K. Hiebert, June 24, 1966; 1 child, William. BA in Social Scis., Bethel Coll., 1964; MHA, U. Minn., 1970. Adminstr. Brook Lane Psychiat. Ctr., Hagerstown, Md., 1966-68; exec. dir. Community Mental Health Ctr., Indpls., 1970; asst. adminstr. Children's Hosp., Columbus, Ohio, 1970-73; exec. v.p. St. Francis Hosp., Miami Beach, Fla., 1973-86; pres. Hutchinson (Kans.) Hosp. Corp., 1986—. Pres. Am. Cancer Soc., Hutchinson, 1990-92; bd. dirs. Tng. and Evaluation Ctr. for Handicapped, ARC, Hutchinson, 1988—, chmn., 1993; mem. advance gifts chmn. United Way, Hutchinson, 1992. Fellow Am. Coll. Healthcare Execs.; mem. Kans. Hosp. Assn. (bd. dirs. 1989-94), Greater Hutchinson C. of C. (chmn. 1992), Rotary. Republican. Presbyterian. Home: 2503 Briarwood Ln Hutchinson KS 67502-1803 Office: Hutchinson Hosp 1701 E 23rd Ave Hutchinson KS 67502-1105

SCHMIDT, GEORGE, physicist; b. Budapest, Hungary, Aug. 1, 1926; s. Laszlo Schmidt and Katalin Wellisch; m. Katalin Varkonyi, June 26, 1955; children: Franklin R., Ronald W. Diploma in Elec. Engring., Tech. U., Budapest, 1950; PhD in Physics, Hungarian Acad. Scis., Budapest, 1956; M in Engring., Stevens Inst. Tech., 1961. Sr. lectr. Israel Inst. Tech., Haifa, Israel, 1957-58; asst. prof. Stevens Inst. Tech., Hoboken, N.J., 1959-61, assoc. prof., 1961-63, prof. physics, 1963-83, George Meade Bond prof. physics and engring. physics, 1983-92; prof. emeritus Stevens Inst. Tech., Hoboken, 1992—; vis. prof. U. Wis., 1965, UCLA, 1972-73; vis. scientist Culham Labs., Culham, Eng., 1965, Ecole Polytechnique, Paris, 1979-80; cons. Sci. Applications Inc., Washington, 1981—, Poly. U. of N.Y., 1984—, Berkeley Assocs., Washington, 1985. Author: Physics of High Temperature Plasmas, 1966, 2nd rev. edit., 1979; contbr. sci. articles to profl. jours. Recipient Research award Stevens Inst. Tech., 1961. Fellow Am. Phys. Soc.; mem. N.Y. Acad. Scis. Office: Stevens Inst of Tech Dept Of Physics Hoboken NJ 07030

SCHMIDT, HAROLD EUGENE, real estate company executive; b. Cedar Rapids, Iowa, Oct. 12, 1925; s. Alfons W. and Lillie (Schlegel) S.; m. Lucy Hermann, Apr. 13, 1957; children: Harold, Sandra. B.S. in Civil Engring, U. Iowa, 1949; M.S. in San. Engring, MIT, 1953. Research and devel. engr. Chgo. Pump Co., 1949-51; engr. A.B. Kononoff, Miami, Fla., 1956-58; with Gen. Devel. Corp., Miami, 1958-82; v.p. utilities, asst. v.p. ops. Gen. Devel. Corp., 1967-72, v.p., 1972-81, v.p. community div., 1973-81, sr. v.p., 1981-82; pres. Gen. Devel. Utilities Inc., 1972-82, Kingsway Properties, Inc., 1982—; dir. Port Charllote Bank, Fla. Served to capt. USAF, 1951-56. Mem. Am. Water Works Assn., Water Pollution Control Fedn., Sigma Xi, Chi Epsilon. Home and Office: 12313 SW Kingsway Cir Arcadia FL 34266-8734

SCHMIDT, HERMAN J., former oil company executive; b. Davenport, Iowa, Feb. 26, 1917; s. Herman and Lillian (Beard) S.; m. Eileen Carpenter, Dec. 20, 1967; children: Paul David, Sarah Louise. AB, U. Iowa, 1938; JD, Harvard U., 1941. Bar: N.Y. 1943. With Cravath, Swaine & Moore, 1941-44, 47-51; tax counsel Socony Mobil Oil Co. Inc. (now Mobil Corp.), N.Y.C., 1951-55, adminstrv. asst. to gen. counsel, 1955, assoc. gen. counsel, 1955-56, gen. counsel, 1956-59, exec. v.p., 1959-74, vice chmn., 1974-78, dir., 1957-78; pres. Mobil Internat. Oil Co., 1959-63; bd. dirs. H.J. Heinz Co., MAPCO, Inc., Hon Industries, Inc. Former chmn. bd. trustees Am. Enterprise Inst.; hon. life trustee U. Iowa Found. Served to 1st lt. M.I. Corps, AUS, 1944-47. Mem. Harvard Law Rev. Assn., Blind Brook Club (Ryebrook, N.Y.), Phi Beta Kappa, Phi Gamma Delta. Home: 15 Oakley Ln Greenwich CT 06830-3025

SCHMIDT, JAKOB EDWARD, medical and medicolegal lexicographer, physician, author, inventor; b. Riga, Livonia, Latvia, June 16, 1906; came to U.S., 1924, naturalized, 1929; s. Michael E. and Rachel I. (Goldman) S. Grad., Balt. City Coll., 1929; Ph.G., U. Md., 1932, BS in Pharmacy, 1935, MD, 1937, postgrad., 1939. Intern Sinai Hosp., Balt.; gen. practice medicine Balt., 1940-53; resident Charlestown, Ind., 1953—; indsl. physician Ind. Ordnance Works, 1953-54; med. and medicolegal lexicographer, 1950—; pres. Sculptural Med. Jewelers, 1973-76; mem. revision com. U.S. Pharmacopeia XI. Columnist What's the Good Word, Balt. Sun; Sharpen Your Tongue, Am. Mercury; The Medical Lexicographer, Modern Medicine; Medical Semantics, Medical Science; Underworld English, Police; Medical Vocabulary Builder, Trauma; English Word Power and Culture, Charlestown Courier, Understanding Med. Talk; assoc. med. editor, Trauma, 1959-88; editor: Medical Dictionary, 1959—; compiler: 50,000-word vocabulary test, 1956; contbr. numerous articles to med. jours., lay press, including Esquire, Playboy, also to press svcs., including UPI, NANA, others; cons. JAMA on med. terminology, also cons. med. terminology to legal profession and cts., to mfrs. on med. tradenames and trademarks; author: Terminology of Sensual Emotions, 1954, Medical Terms Defined for the Layman, 1957, REVERSICON, A Physician's Medical Word Finder, 1958, Medical Discoveries, Who and When, 1959, Dictionary of Medical Slang and Related Expressions, 1959, Narcotics, Lingo and Lore, 1959, The Libido, Its Scientific, Lay, and Slang Terminology, 1960, Baby Name Finder—The Source and Romance of Names, 1961, Schmidt's Illustrated Attorneys' Dictionary of Medicine and Word Finder, 1962, One Thousand Elegant Phrases, 1965, Medical Lexicographer, A Study of Medical Terminology, 1966, The Cyclopedic Lexicon of Sex Terminology, 1967, Police Medical Dictionary, 1968, Practical Nurses' Medical Dictionary, 1968, A Paramedical Dictionary, 1969, 2d edit., 1973, Structural Units of Medical and Biological Terms, 1969, English Word Power for Physicians and other Professionals, 1971, English Idioms and Americanisms, 1972, English Speech for Foreign Students, 1973, Textbook of Medical Terminology, 1973, Visual Aids for Paramedical Vocabulary, 1973, Analyzer of Medical-Paramedical Vocabulary, 1973, Index of Medical-Paramedical Vocabulary, 1974, Schmidt Diccionario para Auxiliares de la Medicina, 1976, Literary Foreplay, 1983, Romantic's Lexicon, 1987, Schmidt's Illustrated Attorneys' Dictionary of Medicine and Word Finder, 18th edit., 4 vols., 1981, 28th edit., 5 vols., 1995. Recipient Owl gold medal Balt. City Coll., 1929; Rho Chi gold medal U. Md. Sch. Pharmacy, 1932; gold medal for excellence in all subjects, 1932; cert. of honor U. Md. Sch. Medicine, 1937; award and citation N.Y. met. chpt. Am. Med. Writers' Assn., 1959. Mem. Am. Dialect Soc., Natural History Soc., Am. Name Soc., Am. Med. Writers' Assn., Internat. Soc. Gen. Semantics, AMA, Med. and Chirurgical Faculty of Md., Balt. City Med. Soc., Nat. Assn. Standard Med. Vocabulary, Nat. Soc. Lit. and Arts, Authors' Guild, Authors' League, Am. Mus. Natural History, Cousteau Soc., Smithsonian Instn., Planetary Soc., Nat. Writers' Club, Rho Chi, others. Achievemants include invention of iodine-pentoxide-shunt method and apparatus for detection of carbon monoxide in oxygen, atmosphere, and medicinal gases; shock-proof electric fuse; magnetic needle finger ring; prosthetic mammary papilla; discovered effect of cesium and related metals on oxidation of organic matter in lakes, ponds and drinking water, the TV eye phenomenon, others. Home: 934 Monroe St Charlestown IN 47111-1557

SCHMIDT, JAMES CRAIG, retired bank executive, bankruptcy examiner; b. Peoria, Ill., Sept. 27, 1927; s. Walter Henry and Clara (Wolfenbarger) S.; m. Jerrie Louise Bond, Dec. 6, 1958; children: Julie, Sandra, Suzanne. Student, Ill. Wesleyan U., 1945, 48-50, Ph.B. in Bus. Adminstrn, 1952; postgrad., U. Ill. Coll. Law, 1950-52; J.D., DePaul U., 1953. Spl. agt. Fidelity & Deposit Co., Chgo., 1956-58; with Home Fed. Savs. & Loan Assn., San Diego, 1958-67; asst. sec. bus. and transp. State of Calif., 1967-69; vice-chmn., pres. Gt. Am. Bank, San Diego, 1969-88; pres. Conf. Fed. Savs. and Loans of Calif., 1974-75; mem. Calif. Toll Bridge Authority, 1969-74; mem. Calif. State Transp. Bd., 1972-78; past chmn. San Diego Bal. Commn. Task Force. Pres. San Diego Holiday Bowl Football Game, 1986; dir. Friends of Legal Aid; bd. dirs. Greater San Diego Sports Assn., dir., San Diego Hwy. Devel. Assn., San Diego County Taxpayers Assn. Mem. Calif. Bar Assn., Ill. Bar Assn., Calif. League Savs. Instns. (chmn. 1986-87), Calif. C. of C. (bd. dirs. 1987-90), U.S. Savs. Instn. League (exec. com. 1983-86), Univ Club, mem. Catfish Club, Sigma Chi, Phi Delta Phi. Office: Ste 0-2 8380 Hercules St La Mesa CA 91942-2922

SCHMIDT, JANIS ILENE, elementary education educator; b. Wyandot County, Ohio., Feb. 4, 1930; d. Floyd Dale and Edith June (Clark) Herbert; m. William Frederick Schmidt, Aug. 27, 1950; children: Lon William, Randy Floyd. BS, Findlay Coll., 1968; MEd, Ashland Coll., 1986. Cert. elem. tchr., Ohio. Elem. tchr. Wharton (Ohio) Elem., 1950-52, Upper Sandusky (Ohio) Schs., 1967—. Author: Improvement of Retention, 1986. Officer Beta Usando Literary Club, Upper Sandusky, 1993; mem. Wyandot Meml. Hosp. Guild, 1980-95, North Salem Luth. Ch. Tchr., officer, 1950—, Tri-G Mothers League, 1953-80. Jennings scholar The Martha Holden Jennings Found., Ohio, 1969-73. Mem. Internat. Reading Assn. (com. chmn. 1990). Republican. Lutheran. Avocations: golf, boating, bicycling, gardening, sewing. Home: 569 N Warpole St Upper Sandusky OH 43351-9332 Office: East Sch 401 3rd St Upper Sandusky OH 43351-1105

SCHMIDT, JEAN MARIE, microbiology educator; b. Waterloo, Iowa, June 5, 1938; d. John Frederick and Opal Marie (Lowe) S. BA, U. Iowa, 1959, MS, 1961; PhD, U. Calif., Berkeley, 1965. NIH postdoctoral fellow U. Edinburgh, Scotland, 1965-66; asst. prof. Ariz. State U., Tempe, 1966-71, assoc. prof., 1971-79, prof. microbiology, 1979—, assoc. dir. for biology Cancer Rsch. Inst., 1982—, acting chair dept. microbiology, 1988-89. Author: (with others) Bergey's Manual of Systematic Bacteriology, 1989; contbr. articles to jours. NSF grantee, 1981. Fellow AAAS; mem. Am. Soc. Microbiology (divsn. chmn. 1979-80), Phi Beta Kappa, Sigma Xi. Democrat. Methodist. Avocations: backpacking, photography, piano.

SCHMIDT, JOHN RICHARD, agricultural economics educator; b. Madison, Wis., July 3, 1929; s. Oscar John and Alma Theodora (Ula) S.; m. Rosemary Pigorsch, Oct. 7, 1951; children: Janet, Deborah, Allen. B.S., U. Wis., 1951, M.S., 1953; Ph.D., U. Minn., 1960. Asst. prof. agr. econs. U. Wis., Madison, 1956-61, assoc. prof., 1961-65, prof., 1965-95, prof. emeritus, 1995—, chmn. dept., 1966-70; owner, mgr. JRS Computing Svcs., Madison, 1995—; farm mgmt. cons. Am. Farm Bur. Fedn., Chgo., 1962; cons. Banco de Mexico, 1972-84, IBRD (World Bank), 1973—; Agrl. Devel. Bank Iran, 1974-76; mem. adv. bd. Internat. Devel. Inst., 1983. Contbr. articles to tech. jours., also monographs, bulls. Bd. dirs. U. Wis. Credit Union, 1968-77, pres., 1969-75; mem. com. Wis.-Upper Mich. Synod Sem., 1972-75, mem. ch. coun. 1967-69, 72-75, pres. 1974-75. Mem. Am. Agrl. Econs. Assn., Western Farm Econs. Assn., Rotary, Delta Theta Sigma (nat. sec. 1962-64), Gamma Sigma Delta (pres. Wis. chpt. 1975). Lutheran. Home: 106 Frigate Dr Madison WI 53705-4426 Office: JRS Computing Svcs 6601 Grand Teton Plz Ste 4 Madison WI 53719-1049

SCHMIDT, JOHN THOMAS, neurobiologist; b. Louisville, Sept. 25, 1949; s. Adolph William and Olivia Ann (Hohl) S.; m. Marilyn Joan Gough, Jan. 6, 1979; children: Sarah, Benjamin. BS in Physics, U. Detroit, 1971; PhD in Biophysics, U. Mich., 1976. Postdoctoral assoc. Nat. Inst. for Med. Rsch., London, 1976-77, Vanderbilt U. Med. Sch., Nashville, 1977-80; asst. prof. biol. scis. SUNY, Albany, 1980-85, assoc. prof. biol. scis., 1985-94, prof. biog. scis., 1994, dir. Neurobiology Rsch. Ctr., 1988—. Editor: Activity-Driven CNS Changes, 1991. Mem. Soc. for Neuroscis. (treas. Hudson Berkshire chpt. 1981-83, pres. 1987-89), N.Y. Acad. Scis. Office: SUNY Neurobiology Rsch Ctr 1400 Washington Ave Albany NY 12222-0100

SCHMIDT, JOSEPH DAVID, urologist; b. Chgo., July 29, 1937; s. Louis and Marian (Fleigel) S.; m. Andrea Maxine Herman, Oct. 28, 1962. BS in Medicine, U. Ill., 1959, MD, 1961. Diplomate Am. Bd. Urology. Rotating intern Presbyn. St. Luke's Hosp., Chgo., 1961-62, resident in surgery, 1962-63; resident in urology The Johns Hopkins Hosp., Balt., 1963-67; faculty U. Iowa Coll. Medicine, Iowa City, 1969-76; faculty U. Calif., San Diego, 1976—, prof., head div. urology, 1976—, vice-chmn. dept. surgery, 1985—; cons. U.S. Dept. Navy, San Diego, 1976—; attending urologist Vets. Affairs Dept., San Diego, 1976—. Author, editor: Gynecological and Obstetric Urology, 1978, 82, 93. Capt. USAF, 1967-69. Recipient Francis Senear award. U. Ill., 1961. Fellow Am. Coll. of Surgeons; mem. AMA, Am. Urol. Assn. Inc., Alpha Omega Alpha. Avocations: collecting antique medical books, manuscripts. Office: U Calif Med Ctr Divsn Urology 200 W Arbor Dr San Diego CA 92103-1911

SCHMIDT, JOSEPH W., lawyer; b. Jeffersontown, Ky., July 6, 1946; s. A.W. and Olivia Ann (Hohl) S.; m. Angela Petchara Apiradee, Dec. 20, 1969; children: Narissa Ann, Suriya Christine. BA in Psychology, Bellarmine Coll., 1969; AB in Commerce, U. Md., Bangkok, 1972; JD,

Columbia U., 1975. Bar: N.Y. 1976. Law clk. to presiding judge U.S. Dist. Ct. (so. dist.), N.Y., 1975-76; assoc. Breed, Abbott & Morgan, N.Y.C., 1976-83, ptnr., 1983-93; ptnr. Whitman Breed Abbott & Morgan, 1993-96, Coudert Bros., N.Y.C., 1996—. Adminstrv. editor Columbia Jour. of Law and Social Problems, 1974-75. Woodrow Wilson fellow, 1968; Harlan Fiske Stone scholar, 1975. Mem. ABA, Assn. of Bar of the City of N.Y., N.Y. Bar Assn., Am. Coll. Investment Counsel. Avocations: skiing, reading. Office: Coudert Bros 1114 Avenue Of The Americas New York NY 10036-7703

SCHMIDT, JULIUS, sculptor; b. Stamford, Conn., June 2, 1923; s. Louis Frank and Susie (Koment) S.; m. Carolyn Marsha Wolf (div.); children: Ania J., Ianos; m. Mary Katherine Powers, 1981 (div.); 1 child, Araan J. Student, Okla. A&M U., 1950-51; B.F.A., Cranbrook Acad. Art, 1952, M.F.A., 1955; student, Ossip Zadkine, Paris, 1953, Accademia di Belle Arti, Florence, Italy, 1954. Chmn. sculpture dept. Kansas City Art Inst., 1954-59, R.I. Sch. Design, 1959-60, U. Calif.-Berkeley, 1961-62, Cranbrook Acad. Art, 1962-70, U. Iowa, Iowa City, 1970-93; ret., 1993. 34 one-man shows 1953—; exhibited in group shows Allen Meml. Art Mus., Oberlin, Ohio, 1958, Arts Club of Chgo., Mus. Modern Art, N.Y.C., 1960, Whitney Mus., 1960-63, Gallerie Claude Bernard, paris, 1960, Guggenheum Mus., 1962, San Francisco Mus. Art, 1962, Phila. Art Alliance, 1963, Battersea Park, London, 1963, Sai Paolo Bienal, Brazil, 1963, White House Festival of Arts, Washington, 1965, Bienale Middleheim, Belgium, 1971; represented in permanent collections Nelson Gallrey-Atkins Mus., Kansas City, Mo., Art Inst., Chgo., Mus. Modern Art, N.Y.C., Mus. U. Nebr., Whitney Mus. Art, N.Y.C., Krannert Art Mus., Urbana, Ill., Washington, U., Walker Art Center, Mpls., Albright-Knox Mus., Buffalo, Detroit Inst. Art, U. Calif. Art Mus., Cranbrook Acad. Art, Mich., Princeton Mus. Art, Hirschhorn Mus., Washington, Numerous others. Served with USNR, World War II. Guggesheim fellow, 1963-64; recipient two air medals, USNR. Address: 5 Highview Knls NE Iowa City IA 52240-9149

SCHMIDT, KAREN ANNE, travel company executive, state legislator; b. L.A., Nov. 27, 1945; d. Ernest Potter and Anne Ruth (Cieslar) Jacobi; m. Gary Manning Schmidt, Jan. 30, 1970 (div. Jan. 1984); children: Geoffrey, Gavin; m. Simeon Robert Wilson III, Mar. 20, 1993. Student, Ariz. State U., 1963-66. Stewardess TWA, Kansas City, Mo., 1966-67, Western Airlines, L.A., 1967-68; sales rep. Delta Airlines, Atlanta, 1968-70; owner Go Travel Svc., Bainbridge Island, Wash., 1971—; mem. Wash. Legislature, 1980—, chmn. transp. policy & budget com. and organized crime com. Named Legislator of Yr. Hwy. Users Fedn., 1992, 95, Legislator of Yr. Wash. State Patrol, 1995, Maritime Legis. of Yr., 1997. Mem. Bainbridge Island C. of C. (dir. 1971-81, pres. 1976), Rotary (named Woman of the Yr. 1979). Office: Go Travel Svc 155 Madrone Ln N Bainbridge Is WA 98110-1862 also: Wash Ho of Reps 328 Jlob Olympia WA 98504

SCHMIDT, KAREN LEE, marketing consultant, management consultant; b. Milw., Oct. 14, 1953; d. Walter K. and Marilyn V. Schmidt. BSBA, Colo. State U., 1975; postgrad., U. Louisville, 1978-79. Sales rep. STSC, Inc., Bethesda, Md., 1979-81; regional software sales mgr. Xerox Corp., L.A., 1981-85; cen. region mgr. Datext, Inc., Boston, 1985-87; regional mgr. Systems Software Assocs., Chgo., 1987-88; dir. bus. devel. Andersen Cons., Chgo., 1988-94; nat. dir. mktg. fin. svcs. KPMG, N.Y.C., 1994-95; chief mktg. officer Quantra Corp., Chgo., 1995—.

SCHMIDT, KARL A., lawyer; b. Stockton, Calif., Sept. 18, 1947. BS, U. Calif., Berkeley, 1969, JD, 1974. Bar: Calif. 1974. Mem. Pillsbury Madison & Sutro, L.A. Mem. ABA. Office: Pillsbury Madison & Sutro Citicorp Plz 725 S Figueroa St Ste 1200 Los Angeles CA 90017-5443

SCHMIDT, KATHLEEN MARIE, lawyer; b. Des Moines, June 17, 1953; d. Raymond Driscoll and Hazel Isabelle (Rogers) Poage; m. Dean Everett Johnson, Dec. 21, 1974 (div. Nov. 1983); children: Aaron Dean, Gina Marie; m. Ronald Robert Schmidt, Feb. 7, 1987. BS in Home Econs., U. Nebr., 1974; JD, Creighton U., 1987. Bar: Nebr. 1987, U.S. Dist. Ct. Nebr. 1987, U.S. Ct. Appeals (8th cir.) 1989, U.S. Supreme Ct. 1991. Apprentice printer, journeyman Rochester (Minn.) Post Bull., 1978-82; dir. customer info. Cornhusker Pub. Power Dist., Columbus, Nebr., 1982-83; artist Pamida, Omaha, 1983; offset artist Cornhusker Motor Club, Omaha, 1983-84; assoc. Lindahl O. Johnson Law Office, Omaha, 1987-88; pvt. practice Omaha, 1988-90; ptnr. Emery, Penke, Blazek & Schmidt, Omaha, 1990-91; pvt. practice, Omaha, 1992—; atty. in condemnation procs. Douglas County Bd. Appraisers, Omaha, 1988—. Mem. Millard Sch. Bd., Omaha, 1989-96, treas. 1991, 92; mem. strategic planning com. Millard Sch. Dist., 1990; mem. Omaha Mayor's Master Plan Com., 1991-94. Named hon. mem. Anderson Mid. Sch., Omaha, 1991. Mem. Nebr. Bar Assn., Omaha Bar Assn. (spkrs. bur. 1992—), Nat. Sch. Bd. Assn. (del. federal rels. network 1991-96, cert. recognition 1991), Nebr. Sch. Bd. Assn. (presenter 1991, 92, award of achievement 1991, 94). Republican. Lutheran. Home: 15936 Cuming St Omaha NE 68118-2241 Office: 399 N 117th St Ste 305 Omaha NE 68154-2562

SCHMIDT, KLAUS DIETER, management consultant, university administrator, marketing and management educator; b. Eisenach, Germany, May 8, 1930; came to U.S., 1949, naturalized, 1952; s. Kurt Heinrich and Luise (Kruger) S.; B.A. in Econs., U. Calif., Berkeley, 1951; M.B.A., Stanford U., 1953; Ph.D. in Bus. Adminstrn., Golden Gate U., 1978; m. Lynda Hollister Wheelwright, June 29, 1950; children: Karen, Claudia. Buyer, jr. mdse. mgr. Broadway Hale, 1952-54; sales mgr. Ames Harris Neville Co., 1954-56, ops. mgr., 1956-57; gen. mgr. Boise Cascade Corp., 1957-60; pres., chmn. bd. Kimball-Schmidt Inc., San Rafael, Calif., 1960-73, chmn. subs. Kalwall Pacific, 1962-67, chmn. subs. AFGOA Corp., 1966-69; asst. prof. mgmt. and mktg. San Francisco State U., 1970-75, assoc. prof. mgmt., 1975-80, prof. mgmt. and mktg., 1980-85, chmn. dept. mgmt. and mktg., 1979-85, prof. emeritus, 1989—, assoc. dean sch. bus. emeritus, 1985-88; chmn. Schmidt Cons. Group, 1988—; dir. Ctr. for World Bus., 1976-88, dir. U.S.-Japan Inst., 1981-88, editor-in-chief Sch. Bus. Jours., 1980-88; U.S. negotiator for Pres. Carter White House on Afghanistan issue, 1980-88; mem. Dept. Commerce Dist. Export Council, 1982-88; research cons. SRI Internat. Republican. Mem. Alpha Deta Phi, Beta Gamma Sigma. Club: University (San Francisco). Author 20-booklet series Doing Business In ..., Stanford Rsch. Inst., 1978-80. Office: PO Box 269 Brooklin ME 04616-0269

SCHMIDT, KLAUS FRANZ, advertising executive; b. Dessau, Germany, May 25, 1928; came to U.S., 1951; naturalized, 1957; s. Franz and Elfriede (Klamroth) S.; m. Gisela Garbrecht, June 19, 1954; children: Dagmar Schmidt Etkin, Ena Schmidt. Student, Coll. of Journalism, Aachen, Germany, 1947-48, Sch. of Design and Printing, Bochum, Germany, 1948-50; BA, Wayne State U., 1956. Printer, compositor, 1948-56; type dir. Mogul Williams & Saylor, N.Y.C., 1956-59, Doyle, Dane, Bernbach, N.Y.C., 1959-61; type dir. Young & Rubicam, N.Y.C., 1961-68, v.p., dir. print ops., 1968-75, v.p., dir. creative support, 1975-85, sr. v.p., mgr. prodn. svcs., 1985-91; advt./graphic arts cons., 1991—; co-organizer Vision Congress Internat. Ctr. for Communications Arts & Scis., N.Y.C., 1965, 67, 69, 77; chmn., bd. trustees Internat. Ctr. Typographic Arts, N.Y.C. 1969-70. Am. editor Der Druckspiegel, 1957-64; contbg. editor Print Mag., 1968—, The Dunn Report, 1991-95. Recipient Typomundus award, 1964, Internat. Book Exhbn. award, Leipzig, Germany, 1965. Mem. Print Advt. Assn. (chmn. N.Y. chpt. 1969-71, nat. sr. v.p. 1971-75), Am. Assn. Advt. Agys. (chmn. subcom. on phototypography 1969-75), Digital Distbn. of Advt. to Publ. Assn. (vice chmn. 1991-95), N.Y. Type Dirs. Club (pres. 1984-86, awards 1962, 64-66, 68, 69), N.Y. Art Dirs. Club (v.p. 1984-86), Advt. Prodn. Club (pres. 1982-84), Gravure Advt. Coun. (chmn. 1970-72). Home and Office: 549 Munroe Ave Sleepy Hollow NY 10591-1333

SCHMIDT, L. LEE, JR., university official; b. Mullinville, Kans., Oct. 2, 1937; s. Lester Lee and Mary (Gilliam) S.; m. Sarah Sue Lookingbill, Aug. 12, 1961; children: Suzanne, Jon. B.S. in Bus. Adminstrn., U. Ark., 1962, Ph.D., 1971; M.B.A., Tex. Tech U., 1963. CPA, Colo. Audit sr. Ernst & Young, Fort Worth, 1963-66; mgr. acctg. The Western Co., Fort Worth, 1966-67; asst. prof. U. Tex.-Arlington, 1967-68; instr. U. Ark., Fayetteville, 1968-71; prof. acctg., chmn. dept. Colo. State U., Ft. Collins, 1971-87, assoc. dean Coll. Bus., 1988-92; assoc. dean Coll. Bus. Adminstrn., U. Tex., El Paso, 1992-96; dean Coll. Bus. and Tech. Tex. A&M U., Commerce, 1996—; speaker in field. Contbr. articles to profl. jours. Served with USN, 1955-58. Earhart Found. fellow, 1968-69. Mem. AICPA, Am. Acctg. Assn., Fin. Execs. Inst., Beta Gamma Sigma, Beta Alpha Psi. Office: Tex A&M U-Commerce Coll Bus & Techtrn Commerce TX 75429-3011

SCHMIDT, L(AIL) WILLIAM, JR., lawyer; b. Thomas, Okla., Nov. 22, 1936; s. Lail William and Violet Kathleen (Kuper) S.; m. Diana Gail (div. May 1986); children: Kimberly Ann, Andrea Michelle; m. Marilyn Sue, Aug. 11, 1990; stepchildren: Leland Darrell Mosby, Jr., Crystal Rachelle Mosby. BA in Psychology, U. Colo., 1959; JD, U. Mich., 1962. Bar: Colo. 1962, U.S. Dist. Ct. Colo. 1964, U.S. Tax Ct. 1971, U.S. Ct. Appeals (10th cir.) 1964. Ptnr. Holland & Hart, Denver, 1962-77, Schmidt, Elrod & Wills, Denver, 1977-85, Moye, Giles, O'Keefe, Vermeire & Gorrell, Denver, 1985-90; of counsel Hill, Held, Metzger, Lofgren & Peele, Dallas, 1989—; pvt. practice law Denver, 1990—; lectr. profl. orgns. Author: How To Live-and Die-with Colorado Probate, 1985, A Practical Guide to the Revocable Living Trust, 1990; contbr. articles to legal jours. Pres. Luth. Med. Ctr. Found., Wheat Ridge, Colo., 1985-89; pres. Rocky Mountain Prison and Drug Found., Denver, 1986—; bd. dirs. Luth. Hosp., Wheat Ridge, 1988-92; bd. dirs. Denver Planned Giving Roundtable, Bonfils Blood Ctr. Found., Planned Giving Adv. Group of Nat. Jewish Hosp. Fellow Am. Coll. Trust and Estate Counsel (Colo. chmn. 1981-86); mem. ABA, Am. Judicature Soc., Rocky Mtn. Estate Planning Coun. (founder, pres. 1970-71), Greater Denver Tax Counsel Assn., Am. Soc. Magicians, Denver Athletic Club, Phi Delta Phi. Republican. Baptist. Avocation: magic. Office: 1050 17th St Ste 1700 Denver CO 80265-1050 also: Law Offices of Gregory J Morris 300 S 4th St Las Vegas NV 89101-6014

SCHMIDT, LAURA LEE, elementary and middle school gifted and talented educator, special education educator; b. South Bend, Ind., Sept. 6, 1960; d. Max A. and Sandra Lee (Engmark) Tudor; m. William Michael Schmidt, Aug. 7, 1982; children: Sandra Lorena, Charlotte Lee. BA, U. Ky., 1982; postgrad., Augustana Coll., Sioux Falls, S.D., U. S.D.; MEd, S.D. State U., 1991. Cert. elem. K-8, spl. edn. K-12, mid./jr. h.s., gifted edn. K-12, S.D. Spl. edn. tchr. Owen County Sch. Dist., Owenton, Ky.; elem. sch. tchr. White River (S.D.) Sch. Dist.; elem. and music tchr. St. Liborius Sch., Orient, S.D.; spl. edn. and chpt. I tchr. Cresbard (S.D.) Sch.; gifted edn. tchr., spl. edn. tchr. Douglas Mid. Sch., Douglas Sch. Dist., Box Elder, S.D. Easter seals camp counselor; vol. Spl. Olympics; accompianist high sch. choir. Mem. Dir. Spl. Edn., Mortar Board, Lambda Sigma. Home: 614 Bluebird Dr Box Elder SD 57719-9509

SCHMIDT, MAARTEN, astronomy educator; b. Groningen, Netherlands, Dec. 28, 1929; came to U.S., 1959; s. Wilhelm and Antje (Haringhuizen) S.; m. Cornelia Johanna Tom, Sept. 16, 1955; children: Elizabeth Tjimkje, Maryke Antje, Anne Wilhelmina. BSc, U. Groningen, 1949; PhD, Leiden U., Netherlands, 1956; ScD, Yale U., 1966. Sci. officer Leiden Obs., The Netherlands, 1953-59; postdoctoral fellow Mt. Wilson Obs., Pasadena, Calif., 1956-58; mem. faculty Calif. Inst. Tech., 1959-95, prof. astronomy, 1964-95, exec. officer for astronomy, 1972-75, chmn. div. physics, math. and astronomy, 1975-78; mem. staff Hale Obs., 1959-80, dir., 1978-80; emeritus. Co-winner Calif. Scientist of Yr. award, 1964. Fellow Am. Acad. Arts and Scis. (Rumford award 1968); mem. Am. Astron. Soc. (Helen B. Warner prize 1964, Russell lecture award 1978), NAS (fgn. assoc., recip. James Craig Watson Medal, 1991), Internat. Astron. Union, Royal Astron. Soc. (assoc., Gold medal 1980). Office: Calif Inst Tech 105 24 Robinson Lab 1201 E California Blvd Pasadena CA 91125-0001

SCHMIDT, MARK JAMES, state public health official; b. Milw., July 16, 1955; s. Warren J. and Carolyn Juel (Gissing) S.; m. Janet M. Schmidt, Oct. 5, 1991; 1 child, Andrew T.; stepchildren: Nathan A. and Aaron M. Stotts. BA, U. Wis., Eau Claire, 1977; MSc., Ill. State U., 1978. Dir. debate U. No. Iowa, Cedar Falls, 1978-79; dir. comm. Ill. Rep. Party, Springfield, 1979-83; asst. to adminstr. driver svc. dept. Office of the Sec. State, Springfield, Ill., 1983-91; dir. pub. affairs Ill. Dept. Cen. Mgmt. Svcs., 1991-95; asst. dir. Ill. Dept. Pub. Health, Springfield, 1995—; guest lectr. polit. comm. Ill. State U., Normal, 1980; cons. 6th Congl. Dist. Rep. Com., Lombard, Ill., 1985-90; rep. Ill. Drivers Lic. Compact Com., Falls Church, Va., 1987-91; mem. Ill. Rural Health Assn.; bd. dirs. Ill. Rural Ptnrs., Inc., 1995-97, co-chmn. pub. sector, 1997—. Editor: Driver's Handbook (annual) Rules of the Road, 1984-91; editor Driver Svcs. Dept. newsletter, 1988-91; contbr. articles to profl. jours. Debate strategist Fahner for Atty. Gen. Ill., 1982, Bertini for Congress, Chgo., 1982; advisor Richard Austin for Congress, Springfield, Ill., 1984; coord. Citizens for Jim Edgar, Springfield, 1985-91; chmn. pub. info. subcom. Ill. Comml. Drivers License Program, 1989-91. Recipient Gov. Adminstrs. Recognition award Ill. Primary Health Care Assn., 1997. Fellow Ill. Pub. Health Leadership Inst.; mem. Masons, Order Eastern Star. Republic. Methodist. Home: 37 Meander Pike Chatham IL 62629-1569 Office: Ill Dept Pub Health 535 W Jefferson St Springfield IL 62702-5058

SCHMIDT, MICHAEL JACK, former professional baseball player; b. Dayton, Ohio, Sept. 27, 1949; m. Donna Wightman; children: Jessica Roe, Jonathan Michael. BBA, Ohio U., Athens. With Phila. Phillies, 1972-89; co-owner Mike Schmidt's Phila. Hoagies; spokesperson Participate in the Lives Am. Youth NIKE. Nat. League Player in All-Star Game, 1974, 76, 77, 79-84, 86, 87; named Most Valuable player, National League, 1980,1981, 1986., Most Valuable Player 1980 World Series; recipient 10 Golden Glove awards; inducted into Baseball Hall of Fame, 1995. Address: Baseball Hall of Fame PO Box 590 Cooperstown NY 13326*

SCHMIDT, PATRICIA FAIN, nurse educator; b. Chgo., June 17, 1941; d. Lawrence D. and Catherine B. (Schira) Fain; m. Donald W. Schmidt, July 16, 1966; children: Kathryn, Kristine, Michael. BSN, Coll. of St. Teresa, 1963; MSN, Marquette U., 1965; EdD, U.S. Internat. U., 1981. Instr. Coll. of St. Teresa, Winona, Minn.; asst. prof. San Diego State U.; assoc. prof. nursing Palomar Coll., San Marcos, Calif. Mem. Sigma Theta Tau. Home: 12573 Utopia Way San Diego CA 92128-2229

SCHMIDT, PATRICIA RUGGIANO, education educator; b. Ft. Bragg, N.C., Jan. 13, 1944; d. Samuel and Elva (Beckmann) Ruggiano; m. Thomas Jay Schmidt, Nov. 11, 1967; children: Thomas Jay Jr., Anthony Charles. BA cum laude, Potsdam (N.Y.) Coll., 1965; MEd, U. Mass., 1966; EdD, Syracuse U., 1993. Cert. tchr. elem. tchr. (nursery sch. to grade 6), N.Y. State, K-12 reading tchr., N.Y. State. Elem. tchr. Liverpool (N.Y.) Pub. Schs., 1966-68; reading specialist Fayetteville-Manlius (N.Y.) Schs., 1973-91; grad. asst. Syracuse U., 1991-92, adj. instr., 1992-93; adj. instr. Oswego (N.Y.) Coll., 1992-93, Le Moyne Coll., Syracuse, 1992-93; asst. prof. edn. LeMoyne Coll., Syracuse, 1993—; treas./negotiator for N.Y. State United Tchrs., Fayetteville-Manlius Tchrs. Assn., 1984-91; N.Am. del. to Eastern Europe for rsch. exchange and study People to People, Budapest, St. Petersburg, Moscow, 1993; presenter in field. Author: One Teacher's Reflections: Implementing Multicultural Literacy Learning, 1996; contbr. article to profl. jour. William Sheldon fellow, 1992-93. Mem. Internat. Reading Assn., Am. Ednl. Rsch. Assn., Nat. Reading Conf., N.Y. State Reading Assn., Kappa Delta Pi, Phi Delta Kappa. Avocations: skiing, golf, gardening, hiking, travel. Home: RD 3 Ray Rd Canastota NY 13032 Office: Le Moyne Coll 212 Reilly Hall Syracuse NY 13214

SCHMIDT, PAUL JOSEPH, physician, educator; b. N.Y.C., Oct. 22, 1925; s. Joseph and Anna (Schwanzl) S.; BS Fordham U., 1948; MS, St. Louis U., 1952; MD, NYU, 1953; m. Louise Kern Fredericks, June 18, 1953; children: Damien, Matthew, Thomas, Maria. Intern, St. Elizabeth's Hosp., Boston, 1953-54; staff assoc. Nat. Microbiol. Inst., Bethesda, Md., 1954-55; chief blood bank dept. NIH, Bethesda, Md., 1955-74, asst. chief clin. pathology dept., 1963-65; sr. asst. surgeon, USPHS, 1954, advanced through grades to med. dir., 1964-74; assoc. clin. prof. pathology, then clin. prof. Georgetown U., Washington, 1965-75; dir. S.W. Fla. Blood Bank, Inc., Tampa, 1975-90, pres. 1987-90; head transfusion medicine, Transfusion Medicine Acad. Ctr., 1991—; prof. pathology U. So. Fla., Tampa, 1975—; cons. com. on Blood, AMA, 1964-69; tech. adv. Blood Transfusion Rsch. div. US Army, 1966-74; res. adv. com. Blood Program, ARC, 1967-73; com. Human Rsch., ARC, 1968-74; council on Immunohematology, Am. Soc. Clin. Pathologists, 1968-74; com. Anticoagulant Solutions, NRC-Nat. Acad. Sci., 1968-70; com. Plasmapheresis, NRC-Nat. Acad. Sci., 1969-70; com. Blood Bank Programs, N.Y.C., 1969-70; com. Component Therapy, NRC-Nat. Acad. Sci., 1969; com. standards, Am. Assn. Blood Banks, 1970-85 (chmn. 1981-85); Task Force on Blood Banking, dept. HEW, 1972-73; adv. com. Blood Diseases and Resources, Nat. Heart Lung Blood Inst., 1975-79; cons. to surgeon gen. U.S. Navy, 1976; dir. clin. svcs. ARC Blood Svcs., San Juan, P.R., 1993-95; clin. prof. pathology U. P.R., 1993—, Koppisch lectr., 1994; Molthan Meml. lectr. Pa. Assn. Blood Banks, 1995. Mem. svc. and rehab. com. Fla. div. Am. Cancer Soc., 1976-84; bd. dirs. ARC, Tampa 1978-83 (v.p. 1980); com. Transfusion Transmitted Viruses, Coll. Am. Pathologists 1981-91; com. Transfusion Medicine, Coll. Am. Pathologists, 1981-92; bd. dirs. Am. Blood Commn., 1985-87. Served with U.S. Army, 1944-46. Recipient Jour. Club Rsch. award, NYU, 1952, Silver medal Spanish Red Cross, 1960; Emily Cooley award Am. Assn. Blood Banks, 1974, John Elliott award, 1993. Diplomate Am. Bd. Pathology, Nat. Bd. Med. Examiners. Fellow Coll. Am. Pathologists (emeritus); mem. Am. Assn. Blood Banks (pres. 1987-88), Internat. Assn. History Medicine, Internat. Soc. Blood Transfusion, Fla. Assn. Blood Banks (pres. 1980-81), Cosmos, Rotary. Roman Catholic. Contbr. articles to profl. jours., editorial bd. Transfusion, 1968—, Annals Clinical Lab. Sci., 1971-74, Blood, 1976-77; editor: Progress in Transfusion and Transplantation, 1972; described etiology of renal failure after hemolytic blood transfusion reactions, 1967, Rh null disease, 1967. Office: PO Box 2125 Tampa FL 33601-2125

SCHMIDT, PAUL WICKHAM, lawyer; b. Milw., June 25, 1948; s. Edmund Julian and Barbara (Wickham) S.; m. Cathryn Ann Piehl, June 27, 1970; children: Thomas Wickham, William Piehl, Anna Patchin. BA cum laude, Lawrence U., 1970; JD cum laude, U. Wis., 1973. Bar: Wis. 1973, U.S. Dist. Ct. (we. dist.) Wis. 1973, U.S. Supreme Ct. 1982, D.C. 1988. Atty. advisor Bd. Immigration Appeals, Washington, 1973-76; gen. atty. office of gen. counsel Immigration and Naturalization Service, Washington, 1976-78, acting gen. counsel, 1979-81, 86-87, dep. gen. counsel, 1978-87; assoc. Jones, Day, Reavis & Pogue, Washington, 1987-89, ptnr., 1990-92; mng. ptnr. Fragomen, Del Ray & Bernsen, P.C., Washington, 1993-95; chmn. Bd. of Immigration Appeals, Falls Church, Va., 1995—. Mem. ABA, D.C. Bar Assn., Wis. Bar Assn., Fed. Bar Assn. (immigration sect.). Avocations: crew volunteer, gardening, camping, history. Home: 711 S View Ter Alexandria VA 22314-4923 Office: Bd Immigration Appeals Skyline Tower 5107 Leesburg Pike Ste 2400 Falls Church VA 22041-3234

SCHMIDT, PETER GUSTAV, shipbuilding industry executive; b. Tumwater, Wash., Dec. 3, 1921; s. Peter G. and Clara Louise (Muench) S.; m. Elva Mary Ingalls, Dec. 3, 1945; children: Mimi Schmidt Fielding, Jill Schmidt Crowson, Janet Schmidt Mano, Hans. BSME, U. Wash., 1948; MS in Naval Architecture and Marine Engring., U. Mich., 1950. Naval architect Nat. Steel Shipbldg. Corp., San Diego, 1950-52, Carl J. Nordstrom/P. Spaulding, Seattle, 1952-53; pres. Marine Constrn. & Design Co., Seattle, 1953—, Astilleros Marco Chilena Ltd., Santiago, Chile, 1960—, Marco Peruana S.A., Lima, Peru, 1965—, Campbell Industries, San Diego, 1979—. Author papers on fishing gear and vessels. Served to lt (j.g.) USN, 1942-45, PTO. Recipient Puget Sound's Maritime Man of Yr. award Puget Sound Press Assn., 1975, Naval Arch. and Marine Engring. Merit award U. Mich., 1996. Mem. Soc. Naval Architects and Marine Engrs., Wash. State Boatbuilders Assn. (pres. 1956-58), Alpha Delta Phi. Avocations: competitive sailing, classical music. Office: Marine Constrn & Design 2300 W Commodore Way Seattle WA 98199-1226

SCHMIDT, PHILIP S., mechanical engineering educator. Prof. dept. mech. engring. U. Tex., Austin, Douglass prof. Recipient Ralph Coats Roe award ASEE, 1992; named Carnegie Found. Tex. Prof. of Yr., 1994. Office: Univ Tex Dept Mech Engring Austin TX 78712

SCHMIDT, RAYMOND PAUL, naval career officer, historian, government official; b. Western, Nebr., Sept. 14, 1937; s. Reuben Edward and Angeline Agnes (Kudlik) S.; m. Roberta Ruth Schrom, June 11, 1961; 1 child, Douglas Craig. B in Edn., History and Social Sci., U. Nebr., 1958; postgrad., U. Md., 1960-62, The Am. U., 1975-81; M in History, U. Wis., 1966. Instr. math. and social sci. Sr. High Sch., Bellevue, Nebr., 1958-59; ensign USN, 1959, advanced through grades to capt., 1981; historian, archivist Naval Security Group Command USN, Washington, 1968-81, sr. congl. security policy rev. officer Office Naval Intelligence, 1981-82, sr. res. forces advisor Dept. Def., 1982-88, head Navy info. security policy, 1988—; history instr. James Madison Meml. High Sch., Madison, Wis., 1966-68; mem. U.S. Nat. Disclosure Policy Com. Team, Japan, Thailand, 1989, Germany, 1991, leader, Albania, 1995. Author: (with others) Naval Officers Guide, 1983, And I Was There, 1985; contbr. articles to profl. jours. Pres. North Ashburton Citizens Assn., Bethesda, Md., 1982—; Merit badge counselor Boy Scouts Am., 1974-93; info. officer U.S. Naval Acad., Annapolis, Md., 1978-93; spkr. Pearl Harbor Symposium Adm. Nimitz Found., Tex., 1991, symposium moderator, 1992; active Montgomery County Planning Bd. Citizens Adv. Com., Md., 1989-94. Named Hon. Admiral Great Navy of State of Nebr., 1983. Mem. DAV (life), Nat. Classification Mgmt. Soc. (editor Viewpoints 1991-96), Nat. Trust Hist. Preservation, Am. Hist. Assn., U.S. Naval Inst. (life, contbr.), Res. Officers Assn. (life), Ret. Officers Assn. (life), Naval Res. Assn. (life, sec./treas. 1966-68), U. Nebr. Alumni Assn. (life), Naval Intelligence Profls., U.S. Naval Cryptologic Vets. Assn., Colonial Williamsburg Found., Phoenix Soc. Unitarian. Home: 6205 Lone Oak Dr Bethesda MD 20817-1743

SCHMIDT, RICHARD ALAN, management company executive; b. Chgo., Aug. 5, 1943; s. Herman and Lillian (Hirsch) S.; married; children: Mollee A., Michael A. Student, Bradley U., 1966. Purchasing agt. U.S. Ry. Equipment Co., Chgo., 1969-71; product mgr. Lift Parts Mfg. Co., Chgo., 1971-73; gen. mgr. Systems Products Co., Chgo., 1973-74, Highlift Equipment Co., Columbus, Ohio, 1974-81; dir. to pres. Schmidt Mgmt. Inc., Columbus, 1979-88; owner Aero Devel., Inc., Columbus, 1988-90; chmn., CEO Stellar Asset Mgmt., Inc., Naples, Fla., 1990-97; CEO Paradiam, LLC, Miami, Fla., 1997—; pres. Sandcastle Boats, Inc.; pvt. pilot, rated instr. Multi Engine Land & Sea; scuba diver, dive master rating. Columnist material mgmt., 1979; editor, pub. The Risk Report, 1991-97; bus. editor WNPL-TV News; editor-in-chief The Stellar Stock Report, 1997—. Dep. sheriff Perry County, Ohio. Mem. Internat. Materials Mgmt. Soc. (cert. in materials mgmt. and handling, pres. Columbus chpt. 1977, internat. pres. 1977-78), Naples C. of C. (pres. club 1991—), Mensa.

SCHMIDT, RICHARD MARTEN, JR., lawyer; b. Winfield, Kans., Aug. 2, 1924; s. Richard M. and Ida (Marten) S.; m. Ann Downing, Jan. 2, 1948; children—Eric, Gregory, Rolf (dec.), Heidi. A.B., U. Denver, 1945, J.D., 1948. Bar: Colo. bar 1948, D.C. bar 1968. Dep. dist. atty. City and County of Denver, 1949-50; mem. firm McComb, Zarlengo, Mott & Schmidt, Denver, 1950-54; ptnr. Schmidt & Van Cise (and predecessor), Denver, 1954-65; 65; gen. counsel USIA, 1965-68; ptnr. Cohn and Marks, Washington, 1969—; counsel spl. agrl. investigating subcom. Counsel Am. Soc. Newspaper Editors, 1968—; mem. Gov.'s Coun. Local Govt., Colo., 1963-64; chmn. Mayor's Jud. Adv. Com., Denver, 1963-64, Gov.'s Supreme Ct. Nominating Com., 1964-65; mem. Gov.'s Oil Shale Adv. Com., 1963-65, Colo. Commn. on Higher Edn., 1965; mem. bd. Nat. Press Found., 1993—. Trustee U. Denver. Mem. ABA (chmn. standing com. on assn. comms. 1969-73, chmn. forum com. on comms. 1979-81, co-chmn. nat. conf. lawyers and reps. of media 1984—, mem. commn. on lawyer advt. 1964—), Colo. Bar Assn. (gov.), Denver Bar Assn. (pres. 1963-64), D.C. Bar Assn., Cosmos Club (Washington). Episcopalian. Home: 115 5th St SE Washington DC 20003-1123 Office: Cohn and Marks 1333 New Hampshire Ave NW Washington DC 20036-1511

SCHMIDT, ROBERT CHARLES, JR., finance executive; b. Oklahoma City, Apr. 2, 1942; s. Robert Charles and Francis Laura (Schiele) S.; m. Susan G. Dietz-Felbinger, Nov. 8, 1974; children: Laura Stewart, Elizabeth Berry. B.A., Westminster Coll., Fulton, Mo., 1964; postgrad., U. Okla., 1972, London Grad. Sch. Bus. Studies, 1974-76. Exec. trainee First Nat. Bank in St. Louis, 1967-68, comml. banker, 1968-74, v.p., mgr. client services div., 1974-76; v.p. treasury ops. Am. Express Co., N.Y.C., 1976-81, dep. treas., 1981-86; chmn. bd. Am. Express Export Credit Corp., 1982-86; group v.p., gen. mgr. Nat. Data Corp., Atlanta, 1986-88, exec. v.p., 1988-89; exec. v.p. Capital Guaranty Corp., San Francisco, 1989-91; pres. Tampsco Enterprises, Inc., St. Louis, 1993; ptnr. The Whitelaw Group, St. Louis, 1994-96; pres. SCM Group, Inc., St. Louis, 1996—; cons. City of N.Y., 1977. Loaned exec. United Fund, St. Louis, 1973; trustee Congl. Summer Assembly Edn. Fund, 1993—, Anglican Inst., 1996. Served with U.S. Army, 1965-67. Decorated Army Commendation medal; recipient cert. of merit USO, 1966,

Alumni Achievement award Westminster Coll., 1977. Mem. Treas. Group (chmn. 1982-83), Noonday Club (St. Louis), Crystal Downs Country Club (Frankfort, Mich.), Beta Theta Pi. Republican. Episcopalian. Office: 230 S Bemiston Ave Ste 300 Saint Louis MO 63105-1907

SCHMIDT, ROBERT MILTON, physician, scientist, educator; b. Milw., May 7, 1944; s. Milton W. and Edith J. (Martinek) S.; children Eric Whitney, Edward Huntington. AB, Northwestern U., 1966; MD, Columbia U., 1970; MPH, Harvard U., 1975; PhD in Law, Medicine and Pub. Policy, Emory U., 1982. Diplomate Am. Bd. Preventive Medicine. Resident in internal medicine Univ. Hosp. U. Calif.-San Diego, 1970-71; resident in preventive medicine Ctrs. Disease Control, Atlanta, 1971-74; commd. med. officer USPHS, 1971; advanced through grades to comdr., 1973; dir. hematology div. Nat. Ctr. for Disease Control, Atlanta, 1971-78, spl. asst. to dir., 1978-79, inactive res., 1979—; clin. asst. prof. pediatrics Tufts U. Med. Sch., 1974-86; clin. asst. prof. medicine Emory U. Med. Sch., 1971-81, clin. asst. prof. community health, 1976-86; clin. assoc. prof. humanities in medicine Morehouse Med. Sch., 1977-79; attending physician dept. medicine Wilcox Meml. Hosp., Lihue, Hawaii, 1979-82, Calif. Pacific Med. Ctr., San Francisco, 1983—; dir. Ctr. Preventive Medicine and Health Research, 1983—, dir. Health Watch, 1983—; sr. scientist Inst. Epidemiology and Behavioral Medicine, Inst. Cancer Research, Calif. Pacific Med. Ctr., San Francisco, 1983-88; prof. hematology and gerontology, dir. Ctr. Preventive Medicine and Health Rsch., chair health professions program San Francisco State U., 1983—; cons. WHO, FDA, Washington, NIH, Bethesda, Md., Govt. of China, Mayo Clinic, Rochester, Minn., Northwestern U., Evanston, Ill., U. R.I., Kingston, Pan Am. Health Orgn., Inst. Pub. Health, Italy, Nat. Inst. Aging Rsch. Ctr., Balt., U. Calif., San Diego, U. Ill., Chgo., Columbia U., N.Y.C., Brown U., Providence, U. Calif., L.A., Harvard U., Boston, U. Chgo., Emory U., Atlanta, Duke U., N.C., U. Tex., Houston, Ariz. State U., U. Hawaii, Honolulu, U. Paris, U. Geneva, U. Munich, Heidelberg U., U. Frankfurt, U. Berlin, Cambridge (Eng.) U., U. Singapore, others; vis. rsch. prof. gerontology Ariz. State U., 1989-90; mem. numerous sci. and profl. adv. bds., panels, coms. Mem. editorial bd. Am. Jour. Clin. Pathology, 1976-82, The Advisor, 1988—, Generations, 1989—, Alternative Therapies in Health and Medicine, 1995—, Aging Today, 1997; book and film reviewer Sci. Books and Films, 1988—; author: 17 books and manuals including Hematology Laboratory Series, 4 vols., 1979-86, CRC Handbook Series in Clinical Laboratory Science, 1976—; assoc. editor: Contemporary Gerontology, 1993—; contbr. over 270 articles to sci. jours. Alumni regent Columbia U. Coll. Physicians and Surgeons, 1980—. Northwestern U. scholar, 1964-66; NSF fellow, 1964-66; Health Professions scholar, 1966-70; USPHS fellow, 1967-70; Microbiology, Urology, Upjohn Achievement, Borden Rsch. and Virginia Kneeland Frantz scholar awards Columbia U., 1970; recipient Am. Soc. Pharmacol. and Exptl. Therapy award in pharmacology, 1970, Commendation medal USPHS, 1973, Leadership Recognition awards San Francisco State U., 1984-89, 91-94, Meritorious Performance and Profl. Promise award, 1989, Meritorious Svc. award, San Francisco State U., 1992, Student Disting. Teaching and Svc. award Pre-Health Professions Student Alliance, 1992. Fellow ACP (commentator ACP Jour. Club/Annals of Internal Medicine 1993—), AAAS (med. scis. sect.), Royal Soc. Medicine (London), Gerontol. Soc. Am., Am. Geriatrics Soc., Am. Coll. Preventive Medicine (sci. com.), Am. Soc. Clin. Pathology, Internat. Soc. Hematology; mem. AMA, APHA, Am. Med. Informatics, Internat. Commn. for Standardization in Hematology, Am. Soc. Hematology, Internat. Soc. Thrombosis and Hemostasis, Acad. Clin. Lab. Physicians and Scientists, Am. Assn. Blood Banks, Nat. Assn. Advisors for Health Professions (bd. dirs.), Am. Assn. Med. Informatics (chair prevention and health evaluation informatics WG), Calif. Coun. Gerontology and Geriatrics, Am. Coll. Occupl. and Environ. Medicine, Assn. Tchrs. Preventive Medicine (edn. com., rsch. com.), Am. Soc. Microbiology, Am. Soc. Aging (editl. bd. 1990—, Dychtwald Pub. Speaking award 1991), N.Y. Acad. Scis., Internat. Health Evaluation Assn. (v.p. for Ams. 1992—, bd. dirs., pres. 1994—), Cosmos Club, Golden Key (hon. faculty mem.), Army and Navy Club (Washington), Harvard Club (N.Y.), Havard Club (San Francisco), Sigma Xi, others. Home: 25 Hinckley Walk San Francisco CA 94111-2303 Office: Health Watch Ctr 2100 Webster St Ste 508 San Francisco CA 94115-2381

SCHMIDT, RONALD HANS, architect; b. Hoboken, N.J., Sept. 9, 1938. BArch., Syracuse U., 1961. Sr. designer Skidmore, Owings & Merrill, N.Y.C., 1963-68; ptnr., dir. archtl. design Grad. Partnership, Newark, 1968-81; pres., chief exec. officer Ronald Schmidt & Assocs., P.A., Hackensack, N.J., 1981—. Vice chmn. Bergen County (N.J.) Econ. Devel. Corp.; mem. bd. regents Felician Coll.; mem. exec. com. Network of Opportunity. Recipient numerous awards. Office: 222 Grand Ave Englewood NJ 07631-4352

SCHMIDT, RONALD R., academic administrator. BA, Point Loma Nazarene Coll.; MA, U. So. Calif.; EdD, Brigham Young U. Rsch. asst. office of lt. gov. State of Calif., Sacramento, 1966; faculty dept. sociology and polit. sci. Am. River Coll., Sacramento, 1966-69, chmn. divsn. behavioral scis., 1970-77; assoc. dir. master planning Los Rios C.C. Dist., Sacramento, 1977, devel. officer, 1977-80; exec. dir., sec. Los Rios Found., Sacramento, 1978-80; dir. devel. Friends U., Wichita, Kans., 1980-82; v.p. instnl. advancement So. Nazarene U., Bethany, Okla., 1982-86; exec. v.p., chief ops. officer Young Life Found., Colorado Springs, Colo., 1986-91; exec. v.p., chief ops. officer Colo. Christian U., Lakewood, Colo., 1992-93, pres., 1993—; cons. Statewide Vocat. Ednl. Needs Assessment Project, Calif. C.C., The Gallup Orgn., Johns Hopkins U., So. Regional Edn. Bd.; v.p. Assn. Nazarene Bldg. Profls., chmn. State Liaison Com., Pub. Svc./Social Work Edn.; co-dir. Human Svcs. Career Devel. Project, Intergovtl. Personnel Act Grant Project; pres. Los Rios C.C. Dist. Divsn. Chmn.'s Assn. State rep. Calif. C.C. Assn. Home: 8063 S Zephyr St Littleton CO 80123-5536

SCHMIDT, RUTH ANN, college president emerita; b. Mountain Lake, Minn., Sept. 16, 1930; d. Jacob A. and Anna A. (Ewert) S. B.A., Augsburg Coll., Mpls., 1952; M.A., U. Mo., 1955; Ph.D., U. Ill., 1962; LLD, Gordon Coll., 1987. Asst. prof. Spanish Mary Baldwin Coll., Staunton, Va., 1955-58; asst. prof. Spanish SUNY-Albany, 1962-67, assoc. prof., 1967-78, dean of humanities, 1971-76; prof. and provost Wheaton Coll., Norton, Mass., 1978-82; pres. Agnes Scott Coll., Decatur, Ga., 1982-94, pres. emerita, 1994—; chmn. Women's Coll. Coalition, 1986-88. Author: Ortega Munilla y sus novelas, 1973, Cartas entre dos amigos del teatro, 1969. Trustee Gordon Coll., Wenham, Mass., 1980-86, Lyon Coll., 1993—; bd. dirs. DeKalb C. of C., 1982-85, Atlanta Coll. Art, 1984-94; mem. exec. com. Women's Coll. Coalition, 1983-88; v.p. So. Univ. Conf., 1993. Named Disting. Alumna Augsburg Coll., 1973. Mem. Assn. Am. Colls. (dir. 1979-82, treas. 1982-83), Soc. Values in Higher Edn., Am. Coun. Edn. (commn. on women in higher edn. 1985-88), AAUW, Assn. Pvt. Colls. and Univs. Ga. (pres. 1987-89), Internat. Women's Forum, Young Women's Christian Assn. Acad. Women Achievers. Democrat. Presbyterian.

SCHMIDT, RUTH A(NNA) M(ARIE), geologist; b. Bklyn., Apr. 22, 1916; d. Edward and Anna M. (Range) S. AB, NYU, 1936; MA, Columbia U., 1939, PhD, 1948. Cert. profl. geologist. Geologist U.S. Geol. Survey, Washington, 1943-56; dist. geologist U.S. Geol. Survey, Anchorage, 1956-63; prof., chmn. geology dept. U. Alaska, Anchorage, 1959-84; cons. geologist Anchorage, 1964—; lectr. Elder Hostels, Alaska Pacific U., Anchorage, 1988-89, U. Alaska, Anchorage, 1994; coord. Engring. Geol. Evaluating Group, Alaskan 1964 Earthquake, Anchorage, 1964; environ. cons. Trans Alaska Pipeline, Office of Gov., Anchorage, 1975-76. Editor: Alaska geology field trip guide books, 1984, 89; contbr. articles to profl. jours. Trustee, pres. Brooks Range Libr., Anchorage, 1979-91; bd. dirs., com. chmn. Anchorage Audubon Soc., 1989—; mem. exec. bd., chmn. various coms. Alaska Ctr. Environment, Anchorage. Fellow AAAS, Arctic Inst. N.Am. (bd. govs. 1983-94), Geol. Soc. Am.; mem. Am. Inst. Profl. Geologists (charter), Am. Assn. Petroleum Geologists, Internat. Geol. Congress (del.), Alaska Geol. Soc. (hon. life mem., bd. dirs. 1993-95), Sigma Xi. Avocations: photography, gardening, hiking.

SCHMIDT, SANDRA JEAN, financial analyst; b. Limestone, Maine, Mar. 21, 1955; d. Dale Laban and Marie Audrey (Bailey) Winters; m. Lee Lloyd Schmidt, Oct. 20, 1973; children: Colby Lee, Katrina Leesa. AA summa cum laude, Anne Arundel Community Coll., 1987; BS summa cum laude, U. Balt., 1990. CPA, Md. Enlisted U.S. Army, 1973, traffic analyst, 1973-85, resigned, 1985; auditor Md. State Office of Legislative Audits, Balt., 1990-93; fin. analyst Md. Ins. Adminstrn., Balt., 1993—. Tutor Anne Arundel County Literacy Coun., Pasadena, Md., 1990—; mentor U. Balt., 1991; host family Am. Intercultural Student Exchange, 1992—. Mem. AICPA, Am. Soc. Women Accts., Md. Assn. CPAs, Soc. Fin. Examiners, U. Balt. Alumni Assn., Alpha Chi, Beta Gamma Sigma, Phi Theta Kappa. Republican. Baptist. Home: 7716 Pinyon Rd Hanover MD 21076-1585

SCHMIDT, STANLEY ALBERT, editor, writer; b. Cin., Mar. 7, 1944; s. Otto Elliott William and Georgia (Metcalf) S.; m. Joyce Mary Tokarz, June 9, 1979. BS, U. Cin., 1966; MA, Case Western Res. U., 1968, PhD, 1969. Asst. prof. physics Heidelberg Coll., Tiffin, Ohio, 1969-78; free-lance writer Lake Peekskill, N.Y., 1968—; editor Analog Sci. Fiction and Fact Dell Mags., N.Y.C., 1978—; mem. bd. advisors Nat. Space Soc., Washington, 1982—. Author: Newton and the Quasi-Apple, 1975, The Sins of the Fathers, 1976, Lifeboat Earth, 1978, Analog Yearbook II, 1981, Analog's Golden Anniversary Anthology, 1980, Analog: Readers' Choice, 1981, Analog's Children of the Future, 1982, Analog's Lighter Side, 1982, Analog: Writers' Choice, 1983, War and Peace: Possible Futures from Analog, 1983, Aliens from Analog, 1983, Writer's Choice, Vol. II, 1984, From Mind to Mind, 1984, Analog's Expanding Universe, 1986, Tweedlioop, 1986, Unknown, 1988, Unknown Worlds, 1989, Analog Essays in Science, 1990, Writing Science Fiction and Fantasy, 1991, Aliens and Alien Societies, 1995; contbr. stories to science fiction mags., articles to mags., chpts. to books. Mem. Sci. Fiction and Fantasy Writers Am., Am. Assn. Physics Tchrs., Am. Fedn. Musicians. Avocations: photography, hiking, linguistics, cooking, flying. Office: Analog Sci Fiction 1270 Avenue Of The Americas New York NY 10020

SCHMIDT, STANLEY EUGENE, retired speech educator; b. Harrington, Wash., Dec. 14, 1927; s. Otto Jacob and Ella Genevieve (Wilson) S.; m. Randall Lee, Stephen Douglas. BS in Edn., U. Idaho, 1956; MEd in Adminstrn., U. Oreg., 1958; MA in Speech, Wash. State U., 1975. Supt., tchr., coach Rose Lake (Idaho) Sch. Dist. # 35, 1949-55; forensics coach, speech tchr. Jefferson H.S., Portland, Oreg., 1955-65; dir. forensics Portland C.C., 1965-93, lead speech instr., 1979-82, subject area chmn., 1986-90; adj. prof. speech U. Portland, 1987-93; parliamentarian faculty senate, 1975-80. Co-author anthology: The Literature of the Oral Tradition, 1963. Chmn., precinct committeeman Rep. Party, Kootenai County, Idaho, 1951-53; mem. Easter Seal Soc., Portland, 1980—; pres. Kootenai County Tchrs. Assn., 1953-54, North Idaho Edn. Assn., 1954-55, Oreg. Speech Assn., 1960-61, Oreg. C.C. Speech Assn., 1971-72. Recipient Excellence award U.S. Bank, Portland, 1993, Merit award N.W. Forensic Assn., 1992. Mem. Portland Rose Soc., Royal Rosarian, Masons (jr. grand deacon 1990-91, jr. grand steward 1991-92, grand orator, 1992-93, dist. dep. 1986-90, 32d deg. Scottish Rite, comdr. 1989-90), Cryptic Masons of Oreg. (grand orator 1994-95), Tualitin Valley Shrine Club, Shriners (pres. 1991, bd. dirs. 1989—), Red Cross of Constantine (St. Laurence Conclave, recorder 1993—, dir. of the work 1989—). Baptist. Avocations: rose gardening, stamps, coins, fishing, sports. Home: 5460 SW Palatine St Portland OR 97219-7259

SCHMIDT, STEPHEN CHRISTOPHER, agricultural economist, educator; b. Isztimer, Hungary, Dec. 20, 1920; came to U.S., 1949, naturalized, 1965; s. Francis Michael and Anne Marie (Angeli) S.; m. Susan M. Varszegi, Dec. 20, 1945; children—Stephen Peter, David William. Dr.Sc., U. Budapest, Hungary, 1945; Ph.D., McGill U., Montreal, Que., Can., 1958. Asst. head dept. Hungary Ministry Commerce, Budapest, 1947-48; asst. prof. U. Ky., Lexington, 1955-57, Mont. State U., Bozeman, 1957-59; asst. prof. U. Ill., Urbana-Champaign, 1959-63, assoc. prof., 1963-70, prof. agrl. mktg. and policy, 1970-91, prof. emeritus, 1991—. Fulbright grantee Bulgaria, 1992-93; Ford Found. fellow, 1959; Agrl. Devel. Coun. grantee, 1966, U. Man. Rsch. fellow, 1968-69, Ford Found. rsch. grantee, 1973, 74, Whitehall found. grantee, 1979, Internat. Inst. Applied Systems Analyses (Laxenburg, Austria) rsch. scholar, 1976-77, USDA Intergovtl. Personnel Act grantee, 1983-84. Mem. Am. Agrl. Econs. Assn. (award 1979), Internat. Assn. Agrl. Economists, Am. Assn. Advancement Slavic Studies, Ea. Econ. Assn., Sigma Xi, Gamma Sigma Delta. Office: 1301 W Gregory Dr Urbana IL 61801-3608

SCHMIDT, TERRY LANE, health care executive; b. Chgo., Nov. 28, 1943; s. LeRoy C. and Eunice P. Schmidt; children: Christie Anne, Terry Lane II. B.S., Bowling Green State U., 1965; M.B.A. in Health Care Adminstrn, George Washington U., 1971. Resident in hosp. adminstrn. U. Pitts. Med. Center, VA Hosp., Pitts., 1968-69; adminstrv. asst. Mt. Sinai Med. Center, N.Y.C., 1969-70; asst. dir. Health Facilities Planning Council of Met. Washington, 1970-71; asst. dir. dept. govtl. relations A.M.A., Washington, 1971-74; pres. Terry L. Schmidt Inc. Physician Svcs. Group, San Diego, 1974—; exec. dir., chief operating officer Emergency Health Assocs. P.C., Phoenix, 1989-91, Charleston Emergency Physicians, S.C., S.C., 1990-95, Joplin Emergency Physican Assocs., 1991-92, Big Valley Med. Group, 1991-92, Blue Ridge Emergency Physicians, P.C., 1992-93, Berkeley Emergency Physicians, P.C., 1992-95; pres. Med. Cons. Inc., 1983-84; v.p. Crisis Communications Corp. Ltd., 1982-90; pres. Washington Actions on Health, 1975-78; partner Washington counsel Medicine and Health, 1979-81; pres. Ambulance Corp. Am., La Jolla, Calif., 1984-87; chmn., pres. Univ. Inst., 1992—; lectr., part-time faculty dept. health care adminstrn. George Washington U., 1969-84, preceptor, 1971-84; adj. prof. grad. sch. Pub. Health San Diego State U., 1995—, preceptor, 1989—; asst. prof. Nat. Naval Sch. Health Care Adminstrn., 1971-73; faculty CSC Legis. Insts., 1972-76, Am. Assn. State Colls. and U. Health Tng. Insts.; mem. adv. com. ambulatory care standards Joint Commn. Accreditation of Hosps., 1971-72; guest lectr. health care adminstrn. Nat. U., San Diego, 1992-93; adj. prof. Bus. Adminstrn. U.S. Internat. U., San Diego, 1994-95. Author: Congress and Health: An Introduction to the Legislative Process and the Key Participants, 1976, A Directory of Federal Health Resources and Services for the Disadvantaged, 1976, Health Care Reimbursement: A Glossary, 1983; mem. editl. adv. bd. Nation's Health, 1971-73; contbr. articles to profl. jours. Bd. dirs. Nat. Eye Found., 1976-78. Mem. Med. Group Mgmt. Assn., Hosp. Fin. Mgmt. Assn., Assn. Venture Capital Groups (bd. dirs. 1984-89), San Diego Venture Group (chair 1984-87), U. Calif. San Diego Venture Group (chair 1984-87), U. Calif. San Diego Faculty Club, Univ. Club (life), Nat. Dem. Club (life), Nat. Rep. Club (life), Capitol Hill Club (life), Alpha Phi Omega (pres. Bowling Green alumni chpt. 1967-70, sec.-treas. alumni assn. 1968-71). Office: 7770 Regents Rd Ste 113-611 San Diego CA 92122-1937

SCHMIDT, THOMAS CARSON, international development banker; b. York, Pa., Oct. 15, 1930; s. George Small and Josephine Foot (Reifsnider) S.; m. Lucy Carter Searby, Aug. 21, 1954 (div. May 1980); children: Peter, Lucy, Thomas.; m. Robin G. Berry, Nov. 26, 1983; 1 stepdau., Julia Barclay. A.B., Princeton U., 1952; M.Div., Va. Sem., 1955; Ph.D. in Policy Scis., SUNY, 1971. Ordained priest Episcopal Ch., 1955; rector St. Alban's Ch., Bogota, Colombia, 1955-58; asst. St. James, New London, Conn., 1958-61; rector St. Andrew's, Longmeadow, Mass., 1961-68; on leave serving Diocese Zululand-Swaziland, South Africa, 1965-66; mgmt. cons., 1968-71, asst. commr. edn. State of R.I., 1971-73; mem. R.I. Gov.'s Policy and Program Rev. Staff Providence, 1973-75; commr. edn. State of R.I., 1975-80; v.p. Partners of the Americas, 1980-81; mgmt. cons. nat. and fgn. firms, 1981-83, 94—; pub. adminstrn. specialist Internat. Bank Reconstrn. and Devel. (World Bank), 1983-89, sr. gen. educator, 1989-94. Chmn. manpower task force R.I. Health Sci. Edn. Coun., 1973-75, mem. exec. bd., 1973-75; mem. edn. com. Maine Coun. Chs.; bd. dirs. Comty. Bldg. Trust. Mem. Internat. Soc. Ednl. Planners (treas. 1973), Internat. Assn. Applied Social Scientists, Council Chief State Sch. Officers (bd. dirs. 1976-80), State Higher Edn. Exec. Officers Assn. (legis. com.), Am. Assn. State Colls. and Univs. (legis. com.), SUNY Buffalo Alumni Assn. (dir.). Home: 142 Rock Schoolhouse Bristol ME 04539-8803

SCHMIDT, THOMAS JOSEPH, JR., lawyer; b. New Haven, Jan. 16, 1945; s. Thomas Joseph and Rosemary (O'Shaughnessy) S.; m. Linda Diane Crider, Nov. 16, 1974; children: Elizabeth Anne, Thomas Joseph III, Karen Diana. AB, Xavier U., 1967; JD, U. Cin., 1970. Bar: Ohio 1970, U.S. Ct. Mil. Appeals 1970. Commd. 2d lt. U.S. Army, 1967, advanced through grades to capt., 1969-75; legal officer U.S. Army Corps Engrs., Ft. Hayes, Ohio, 1967-68, Ft. Knox, Ky., 1969-70; atty. U.S. Army JAGC, Ft. Benning, Ga., 1971-75; asst. counsel Midland Enterprises Inc., Cin., 1975-77, assoc. gen. counsel, 1977-83, gen. counsel, 1983-87, gen. counsel, sec., 1987-95, v.p., gen. counsel and sec., 1995—. Republican. Roman Catholic. Office: Midland Enterprises Inc 300 Pike St Cincinnati OH 45202-4222

SCHMIDT, THOMAS WALTER, airport executive; b. St. Paul, Nov. 16, 1938; s. Elmer John and Margaret Elizabeth (Cunnien) S.; m. Roxanne B. Therrien, Mar. 1, 1980; children: Susan, Johnette, Holly. BA, U. Minn., 1961. Accredited airport exec. Dir. aviation Burlington (Vt.) Internat. Airport, 1970-83; asst. dir. aviation McCarran Internat. Airport, Las Vegas, Nev., 1983-89; exec. dir. Capital Region Airport Authority, Lansing, Mich., 1989—. Dir., mem. exec. com. Greater Lansing Conv. and Visitors Bur., Lansing, 1993—; dir. Capital Choice program C. of C., Lansing, 1995—. Mem. Mich. Athletic Club. Office: Capital Region Airport Authority Capital City Airport Lansing MI 48906

SCHMIDT, WALDEMAR ADRIAN, pathologist, educator; b. L.A., Aug. 22, 1941; s. Waldemar Adrian and Mary Charlotte (Parker) S.; m. Karmen LaVer Bingham, Feb. 1, 1963; children: Rebecca, Sarah, Waldemar, Diedrich. BS, Oreg. State U., 1965; PhD, U. Oreg., 1969, MD, 1969. Intern U. Oreg. Hosps. and Clinics, Portland, 1969-70, resident, 1970-73; pathologist LDS Hosp., Salt Lake City, 1973-77; prof. pathology U. Tex. Med. Sch., Houston, 1977-91, Oreg. Health Sci. U. and VA Med. Ctr., Portland, 1991—. Author: Principles and Techniques of Surgical Pathology, 1982; editor Cytopathology Annual, 1991—. Asst. scoutmaster Boy Scouts Am., Houston, 1982-91. Maj. U.S. Army, 1970-76. Mem. Coll. Am. Pathologists (program com.), Sigma Xi, Alpha Omega Alpha. Avocations: photography, silviculture. Office: VA Med Ctr 3710 SW Us Veterans Hospital Rd Portland OR 97201-2964

SCHMIDT, WAYNE WILLIAM, museum director, curator; b. Chicago, Ill., Mar. 31, 1945; s. Walter William and Gloria Louise (Schoenfeldt) S.; m. Kathleen Keating Anderson, Mar. 31, 1979 (div. May 1991); 1 child, Robert Joseph; m. Margaret Ann Brooks; children: Jessica, Samantha. BA cum laude, Northeastern Ill. U., Chgo., 1971, attended, 1972-75. Sta. mgr. Inflight Svcs., N.Y.C., 1968-79; pres., CEO Great Lakes Naval and Maritime Mus., Chgo., 1979-86; exec. dir., COO Intrepid Sea-Air-Space Mus., N.Y.C., 1986-90; cons. Chgo., 1990-92; dir. Nat. Mus. Transp., St. Louis, 1992—; adv. Nat. Park Svc., Washington, 1993; v.p. Historic Naval Ships N.Am., Phila., 1976-80; adv. Assn. Railroad Mus., Phila., 1996—. cons. Webster's Illus. Dictionary, 1994-95, Arm. Accreditation Standards, 1996-97. V.p. Nationalities Coun. Ill., Chgo., 1970-80; mem. Internat. Naval Review, N.Y.C., 1986, Commissioning Com. U.S.S. Chgo., CHgo., 1986; sec/-treas. Zachary and Elizabeth Fisher Armed Svcs. Found., N.Y.C., 1988-90. Served with USNR, 1963-65. Mem. Am. Assn. Mus., Navy League, St. Louis Mus. Collaborative, 1993—. Republican. Roman Catholic. Avocations: sailing, golf, scale modeling, photography. Home: 1016 Parkfield Terr Ballwin MO 63021 Office: Nat Mus Transp 3015 Barrett Station Rd St. Louis MO 63122

SCHMIDT, WILLIAM ARTHUR, JR., lawyer; b. Cleve., Oct. 2, 1939; s. William Arthur and Caroline (Jäger) S.; m. Gerilyn Pearl Smith, Sept. 30, 1967; children: Deborah, Dawn, Jennifer. BSBA, Kent State U., 1962; JD, Cleve. State U., 1968. Bar: Ohio 1968, Ill. 1990. Contract specialist NASA-Lewis, Cleve., 1962-66, procurement analyst, 1967-68; atty. Def. Logistics Agy., Alexandria, Va., 1968-73; assoc. counsel Naval Sea Sys. Command, Arlington, Va., 1973-75; procurement policy analyst Energy R & D Adminstrn., Germantown, Md., 1975-76; sr. atty. U.S. Dept. Energy, Germantown, 1976-78; counsel spl. projects U.S. Dept. Energy, Oak Ridge, Tenn., 1978-83; judge Agr. Bd. Contract Appeals, Washington, 1983-87; adminstrv. judge HUD, Washington, 1987; chief legal counsel Fermilab, Batavia, Ill., 1987-92; gen. counsel Univ. Rsch. Assn., Inc., Washington, 1992—. Co-author: (NASA handbook) R & D Business Practices, 1968. Mem. Fed. Bar Assn. (past pres. East Tenn. 1978-83, 25 Yr. Svc. award 1994), Ill. Bar Assn., Bd. Contract Appeals Judges Assn. (dir.-sec. 1986-88), Sr. Execs. Assn., Delta Theta Phi (dist. chancellor 1978-83), Sigma Chi. Republican. Lutheran. Avocations: boating, choir, civil war history. Home: 7209 Bloomsbury Ln Spotsylvania VA 22553-1944 Office: Univ Rsch Assn Inc 1111 19th St NW Ste 400 Washington DC 20036-3627

SCHMIDT, WILLIAM C., chemical company executive; b. Niles, Mich., Sept. 27, 1938; s. Felix A. and Anna (Reifschneider) S.; m. Bethany Ann Boyd, Dec. 17, 1966; 1 child, Craig W. B.B.A., U. Mich., 1960, M.B.A., 1961. Cert. Mgmt. Acct. Various acctg. positions Dow Chem. Co., Midland, Mich., 1961-73; controller Dow Chem. Pacific Ltd., Hong Kong, 1973-78; area controller Dow Chem. Co., Midland, Mich., 1978-82, asst. corp. controller, 1982—; v.p., chief fin. officer DowElanco, Indpls., 1989—; bd. dirs. Mycogen Corp. Chmn. bd. dirs. Midland Hosp. Ctr., 1986-89; bd. dirs. Mid-Mich. Health Care Corp., 1983-89, chmn. bd., 1986-88; treas., bd. dirs. Indpls. Symphony Orch., 1992—. Cpl. U.S. Army, 1962-64. Mem. Inst. Mgmt. Accts., Inst. Cert. Mgmt. Accts. (regent 1985-89), Am. Indsl. Health Coun. (treas. 1986-87), Fin. Execs. Inst., Ind. C. of C. (bd. dirs. 1992—). Methodist. Home: 4958 St Charles Pl Carmel IN 46033-5936 Office: DowElanco 9330 Zionsville Rd Indianapolis IN 46268-1053

SCHMIDT-BOVA, CAROLYN MARIE, vocational school administrator, consultant; b. Jacksonville, Fla., Sept. 1, 1948; d. Leonard Stephen and Marianne Vesta (Ruscher) S.; m. Edward W. Bova. EdB, SUNY, Buffalo, 1980, MEd, 1981; cert. advanced study, SUNY, Brockport, 1988. Cert. tchr., N.Y., SDA Work Study Coord. Instr. Erie Bd. Coop. Edn. Svcs., Lancaster, N.Y., 1977-82, Orleans-Niagara Bd. Coop. Ednl. Svcs., Medina, N.Y., 1982—; adj. instr. SUNY, Buffalo, 1988—; cons. N.Y. Dept. Edn., Albany, 1982—, facilitator, 1982-85, regional resource person, 1985—; bd. dirs. Inst. for Curriculum Advancement; mem. adv. com. Sch. Dist. Reorganization Ctrl. Western Regional Study. Leader Girl Scouts U.S.A., Buffalo. Tchr. Intern award Tchrs. Ctr., Lockport, N.Y., 1989; N.Y. Disting. Occupational edn. award, 1991. Mem. ASCD, Am. Vocat. Assn., Vocat. Indsl. Clubs Am. (advisor, Advisor of Yr. N.Y. State 1994-95, Buffalo State Coll. Vocat. Tech. Edn. Excellence award 1995-96), N.Y. State Tchrs. Vocat. Assn. (regional rep.), Buffalo State Coll. Alumni (adv. bd. dirs. vocat. tech. programs), Phi Delta Kappa, Epsilon Pi Tau, Iota Lambda Sigma. Home: 5894 Fisk Rd Lockport NY 14094-9224 Office: Orleans-Niagara Bd Ednl Svc 3181 Saunders Settlement Rd Sanborn NY 14132-9487

SCHMIDT-NELSON, MARTHA ALICE, communications and training executive, ergonomist; b. Boston. BA, Clark U., 1981; MA, Columbia U., 1984. Cert. profl. ergonomist. Human factors engr. AT&T, Piscataway, N.J., 1984-87; mgr. instructional tech. devel. Dynamics Rsch. Corp., Andover, Mass., 1987—. Office: Dynamics Rsch Corp 60 Frontage Rd Andover MA 01810-5423

SCHMIDT-NIELSEN, BODIL MIMI (MRS. ROGER G. CHAGNON), physiologist; b. Copenhagen, Denmark, Nov. 3, 1918; came to U.S., 1946, naturalized, 1952; d. August and Marie (Jorgensen) Krogh; m. Knut Schmidt-Nielsen, Sept. 20, 1939 (div. Feb. 1966); children: Astrid, Bent, Bodil; m. Roger G. Chagnon, Oct. 1968. D.D.S., U. Copenhagen, 1941, D.Odont., 1946, DPhil., 1955; D.Sc. (hon.), Bates Coll., 1983. Faculty Duke, Durham, N.C., 1952-64; prof. biology Case Western Res. U., Cleve., 1964-71, chmn. dept., 1970-71, adj. prof., 1971-74; trustee Mt. Desert Island Biol. Lab., Maine, research scientist, 1971-86, exec. com., 1978-85, v.p., 1979-81, pres., 1981-85; adj. prof. Brown U., Providence, 1972-78, dept. physiol. U. Fla., Gainesville, 1987—; Mem. tng. grant com. NIGMS, 1967-71. Author: August and Marie Krogh, Lives in Science, 1995; editor: Urea and the Kidney, 1970; assoc. editor Am. Jour. Physiology: Regulatory, Integrative and Comparative Physiology, 1978-81. Trustee Coll. of Atlantic, Bar Harbor, Maine, 1972-92. Recipient Career award NIH, 1962-64, John Simon Guggenheim Meml. fellow, 1952-53; Bowditch lectr., 1958, Jacobaeus lectr., 1974. Fellow AAAS (de. coun. 1977-79), N.Y. Acad. Scis., Am. Acad. Arts and Scis.; mem. Am. Physiol. Soc. (coun. 1971-77, pres. 1975-76, Ray G. Daggs award 1989, Orr Reynolds award 1994, August Krogh lectr. 1994), Soc. Exptl. Biology and Medicine (coun. 1969-71). Research, publs. on biochemistry of saliva, water metabolism of desert animals, urea excretion, peristalsis of renal pelvis and concentrating mechanism, comparative kidney physiology, comparative physiology of excretory organs. Home: 4426 SW 103rd Ct Gainesville FL 32608-7146 Office: U Fla Dept Physiology Gainesville FL 32605

SCHMIDT-NIELSEN, KNUT, physiologist, educator; b. Norway, Sept. 24, 1915; came to U.S., 1946, naturalized, 1952; s. Sigval and Signe Torborg

(Sturzen-Becker) Schmidt-N. Mag. Scient., U. Copenhagen, 1941, Dr. Phil., 1946; Dr. Med. (hon.), U. Lund, Sweden, 1985; D in Philosophy (hon.), U. Tondheim, Norway, 1993. Research fellow Carlsberg Labs., Copenhagen, 1941-44, Carlsberg Labs. (U. Copenhagen), 1944-46; research assoc. zoology Swarthmore (Pa.) Coll., 1946-48; docent U. Oslo, Norway, 1947-49; research assoc. physiology Stanford U., 1948-49; asst. prof. Coll. Medicine, U. Cin., 1949-52; prof. physiology Duke U., Durham, N.C., 1952—; James B. Duke prof. physiology Duke U., 1963—; Harvey Soc. lectr., 1962; Regents' lectr. U. Calif. at Davis, 1963; Brody Meml. lectr. U. Mo., 1962; Hans Gadow lectr. Cambridge (Eng.) U., 1971; vis. Agassiz prof. Harvard, 1972; Wellcome vis. prof. U. S.D., 1988; mem. panel environmental biology NSF, 1957-61; mem. sci. adv. com. New Eng. Regional Primate Center, 1962-66; mem. nat. adv. bd. physiol. research lab. Scripps Instn. Oceanography, U. Calif. at San Diego, 1963-69, chmn., 1968-69; organizing com. 1st Internat. Conf. on Comparative Physiology, 1972-80; pres. Internat. Union Physiol. Scis., 1980-86, mem. U.S. nat. com. 1966-78, vice chmn. U.S. nat. com., 1969-78; mem. subcom. on environmental physiology U.S. nat. com. Internat. Biol. Programme, 1965-67; mem. com. on research utilization uncommon animals, div. biology and agr. Nat. Acad. Scis., 1966-68; mem. animal resources adv. com. NIH, 1968; mem. adv. bd. Bio-Med. Scis., Inc., 1973-74; chief scientist Scripps Instn. Amazon expdn., 1967. Author: Animal Physiology, 3d. edit, 1970, The Physiology of Desert Animals; Physiological Problems of Heat and Water, 1964, How Animals Work, 1972, Animal Physiology; Adaptation and Environment, 1975, 2d edit., 1979, 3d edit., 1983, Scaling: Why is Animal Size So Important?, 1984; sect. editor Am. Jour. Physiology, 1961-64, 70-76; editor Jour. Applied Physiology, 1961-64, 70-76; mem. editorial bd. Jour. Cellular and Comparative Physiology, 1961-66, Physiol. Zoology, 1959-70, Am. Jour. Physiology, 1971-76, Jour. Applied Physiology, 1971-76, Jour. Exptl. Biology, 1975-79, 83-86; cons. editor: Annals of Arid Zone, 1962—; hon. editorial adv. bd. Comparative Biochemistry and Physiology, 1962-63; chief editor News in Physiol Scis., 1985-88, cons. editor, 1988—; contbr. articles to sci. publs. Guggenheim fellow, 1953-54; grantee Office Naval Rsch., 1952-54, 58-61, UNESCO, 1953-54, Office Q.M. Gen., 1953-54, Office Surgeon Gen., 1953-54, NIH, 1955-86, NSF, 1957-61, 59-60, 60-61, 61-63; recipient Rsch. Career award USPHS, 1964-85, Internat. prize for biology Japan Soc. for the Promotion of Sci., 1992. Fellow AAAS, N.Y. Acad. Sci., Am. Acad. Arts and Scis.; mem. NAS, N.C. Acad. Sci. (Poteat award 1957), Am. Physiol. Soc., Am. Soc. Zoologists (chmn. div. comparative physiology 1964), Soc. Exptl. Biology, Royal Danish Acad., Acad. Scis. (France) (fgn. assoc.), Royal Norwegian Soc. Arts and Sci., Norwegian Acad. Scis. and Letters, Physiol. Soc. London (assoc.), Royal Soc. London (fgn.); hon. mem. Am. Soc. Zoologists, Harvey Soc., Zool. Soc. London, Deutsche Ornitologengesellshaft. Office: Duke Univ Dept Zoology Box 90325 Durham NC 27708-0325

SCHMIEDER, CARL, jeweler; b. Phoenix, Apr. 27, 1938; s. Otto and Ruby Mable (Harkey) S.; m. Carole Ann Roberts, June 13, 1959; children: Gail, Susan, Nancy, Amy. Student Bradley Horological Sch., Peoria, Ill., 1959-61; BA, Pomona Coll., 1961; Owner timepiece repair svc., Peoria, 1959-61; clock repairman Otto Schmieder & Son, Phoenix, 1961-65, v.p., 1965-70, pres., 1970—, chief exec. officer, 1970—. Mem. subcom. Leap Commn., 1966; area rep. Pomona Coll., 1972-76. Cert. jeweler; cert. gemologist, gemologist appraiser; recipient Design award Diamonds Internat., 1965, Cultured Pearl Design award, 1967, 68, Diamonds for Christmas award, 1970; winner Am. Diamond Jewelry Competition, 1973; bd. dirs. Lincoln Hosp., 1983—, Ariz. Mus., 1984-88; delegate White House Conf. on Small Bus., 1986, 95; chmn. Gov.'s Conf. on Small Bus., 1988-91; col. Confederate Air Force. Mem. Am. Gem. Soc. (dir. 1973-86, nat. chmn. nomenclature com. 1975-77, chmn. membership com. 1977-81, officer 1981-86), Ariz. Jewelers Assn. (Man of Yr. 1974), Jewelers Security Alliance (dir. 1974-78), Jewelers Vigilance Com. (dir. 1981-87), Jewelry Industry Council (dir. 1982-88), 24 Karat Club So. Calif., Exptl. Aircraft Assn., Warbirds of Am. (dir. 1990—), Deer Valley (Ariz.) Airport Tenants Assn. (dir. 1980-90, pres. 1983-90), Ariz. C. of C. (bd. dirs. 1985-89), Small Bus. Council (bd. dirs. 1985-89, chmn. 1988, del. to White House Conf., 1986, 95, chmn. Govs. Conf. on small bus. 1988-89), Nat. Small Bus. United (bd. dirs. 1990-94), Kiwanis (pres. Valley of Sun chpt. 1975-76), Friends of Iberia, Rotary. Republican. Methodist. Home: 1016 W Rovey Phoenix AZ 85013 Office: Park Ctrl Phoenix AZ 85013

SCHMIEL, DAVID GERHARD, clergyman, religious education administrator; b. Cedarburg, Wis., Dec. 10, 1931; s. Gerhard August and Frieda Helena (Labrenz) S.; m. Shirley Ann Friede, July 6, 1957; children: Mark, Peter, Steven, Daniel, Julia. BA, Northwestern Coll., 1953; ThD, Concordia Sem., 1967. Pastor St. Paul's Luth. Ch., Gresham, Nebr., 1958-60, Onalaska, Wis., 1960-62; prof. St. Paul's Coll., Concordia, Mo., 1962-70; prof., dean Concordia Coll., St. Paul, 1970-81; dir. instrn. Concordia Sem., St. Louis, 1981-82; pres. Concordia Coll., Ann Arbor, Mich., 1983-91; dir. theol. edn. svc. Luth. Ch.-Mo. Synod, St. Louis, 1991-93; pres. Concordia Theol. Sem., Ft. Wayne, Ind., 1993-95, ret., 1995. Author: Via Propria and Via Mystica...Gerson, 1969. Found. for Reformation Rsch. Jr. fellow, Southeastern Inst. for Medieval and Renaissance Studies, Jr. fellow, 1965, 66, 68.

SCHMIT, DAVID E., lawyer; b. Charleston, W.Va., Feb. 18, 1947. BSEE, U. Cin., 1969, MSEE, 1976; JD, No. Ky. U., 1975. Bar: Ohio 1975, U.S. Patent and Trademark Office. Mem. Frost & Jacobs, Cin. Office: Frost & Jacobs 2500 PNC Ctr 201 E 5th St Cincinnati OH 45202-4117

SCHMIT, LUCIEN ANDRÉ, JR., structural engineer; b. N.Y.C., May 5, 1928; s. Lucien Alexander and Eleanor Jessie (Donley) S.; m. Eleanor Constance Trabish, June 24, 1951; 1 son, Lucien Alexander, III. B.S., MIT, 1949, M.S., 1950. Structures engr. Grumman Aircraft Co., Bethpage, N.Y., 1951-53; research engr., aeroelastic and structures lab. MIT, 1954-58; asst. prof. engring. (Case Inst. Tech.), 1958-60, assoc. prof., 1961-63, prof., 1964-70; prof. engring. and applied sci. UCLA, 1970-91, Rockwell prof. aerospace engring. emeritus, 1991—; mem. sci. adv. bd. USAF, 1977-84. Contbr. numerous articles on analysis and synthesis of structural systems, finite elements methods, design of fiber composite components and multidisciplinary design optimization to profl. jours. Fellow AIAA (Design Lecture award 1977, Structures, Structural Dynamics and Materials award 1979, Multidisciplinary Design Optimization award 1994), ASCE, Am. Acad. Mechanics; mem. NAE. Home: 545 3rd Ave S Edmonds WA 98020-4103

SCHMITT, BERNARD W., bishop. Ordained priest Roman Cath. Ch., 1955, ordained to episcopacy, 1988. Titular bishop Walla Walla, Wash., 1988-89; bishop Diocese of Wheeling-Charleston, W.Va., 1989—. Office: Chancery Office Box 230 1300 Byron St Wheeling WV 26003-3315*

SCHMITT, FREDERICK ADRIAN, gerontologist, neuropsychologist; b. Cin., July 22, 1953; s. Werner and L. Gerlinde (Adrian) S.; m. Melinda Greenlese, Oct. 16, 1984. B.S., Rensselaer Poly., 1975; Ph.D., U. Akron, 1982. Lic. psychologist, N.C., Ky. Postdoctoral fellow Duke Aging Ctr., Durham, N.C., 1981-83, fellow in geriatrics, 1983-84; vis. asst. prof. psychology, U. N.C., Chapel Hill, 1984-85; rsch. assoc. Duke Med. Ctr., Durham, 1984-85; dir. neuropsychology svc. U. Ky., Lexington, 1985—, assoc. prof. neurology, 1990—, adj. prof. psychiatry, adj. prof. dept. psychology; assoc. Sanders-Brown Ctr. on Aging; cons. NIMH Office AIDS Programs, Am. Found. for AIDS Rsch.; co-dir. Memory Disorders Clinic. Contbr. chpts. to books, articles to profl. jours. Mem. AAAS, APA, Am. Acad. Neurology, Nat. Acad. Neuropsychology, N.Y. Acad. Sci, Gerontol. Soc. Am., Internat. Neuropsychol. Soc., Soc. for Research Child Devel., Soc. for Neurosci. Mem. of Baha'i Faith. Office: U Ky Dept Neurology Chambers Bldg Annex 4 Rm 228E Lexington KY 40536

SCHMITT, GEORGE FREDERICK, JR., materials engineer; b. Louisville, Nov. 3, 1939; s. George Frederick and Jane Limbird (Hurst) S.; m. Ann Cheatham, July 31, 1965; 2 children. BS, U. Louisville, 1962, MS, 1963; MBA, Ohio State U., 1966. Chief integration and ops. divsn. USAF Materials Directorate, Wright Lab., Wright Patterson AFB, Ohio, 1966—; advanced engring devel. mgr. USAF Materials Lab., Wright Patterson AFB, Ohio, 1986-90; chief plans and programs br. USAF Materials Lab., Wright AFB, Ohio, 1989-90, asst. chief nonmetallic materials divsn., 1990-96; guest lectr. U. Dayton, 1970, 95, Cath. U., 1973, U. Mich., 1975. Contbr. articles profl. jours. Mem. Kettering (Ohio) Civic Band, 1965—, Affiliate Socs. Council of Dayton, 1972-81. Served to 1st lt. USAF, 1963-66. Named Fed. Profl. Employee of Yr. Dayton, 1972, One of Ten Outstanding Engrs., Engrs. Week, 1975, Air Force Meritorious Civilian Svc. award, 1994. Fellow Soc. for Advancement Materials and Process Engrs. (Best Paper award 1973, nat. sec. 1975-76, nat. membership chmn. 1977-79, nat. v.p. 1979-81, nat pres. 1981-82, chmn. long-range planning com. 1983-87, trustee 1991—, chmn. Internat. SAMPE Symposium 1996), AIAA (assoc., materials tech. com.); mem. ASTM (rec. sec. 72-75, chmn. com. on erosion and wear 1976-79, chmn. liaison subcom. 1979-83, award of merit 1981), Am. Chem. Soc., Affiliate Socs. Coun. Dayton (chmn. 1978-79). Republican. Lutheran. Home: 1500 Wardmier Dr Dayton OH 45459-3354 Office: WL Materials Directorate MLB Wright-Patterson AFB 2941 P St Bldg 654 Dayton OH 45433-7749

SCHMITT, GEORGE JOSEPH, chemist; b. Farmingdale, N.Y., June 21, 1928; s. Joseph Frank and Carolyn (Henych) S.; m. E. Christine Schneider, Feb. 10, 1952; children: Paul, Carol, Mark, David. BS in Chemistry, Bklyn. Poly. Inst., 1950; PhD in Chemistry, SUNY, Syracuse, 1960. Chemist Am. Cyanamid, Bound Brook, N.J., 1953-57; chemist Allied Chem., Morristown, N.J., 1960-61, group leader, 1961-63, assoc. dir. rsch., 1963-69, mgr. rsch., 1969-80, dir. Polymer Lab., 1980-89, dir. Structural Polymers Lab., 1989-94; ret.; adv. bd. N.J. R & D Coun., 1982-85. 1st lt. U.S. Army, 1950-53. Named NSF fellow, 1957-60. Mem. Am. Chem. Soc., Soc. for Advancement Materials and Processing Engring., Sigma Xi. Achievments include research on polymer synthesis, structure/property relationships, bipolar membranes, advanced composites, bioresorbable polymers, electrically conducting polymers, composite armor.

SCHMITT, HOWARD STANLEY, minister; b. Waterloo, Ont., Can., Oct. 19, 1933; came to U.S., 1971; s. Delton Howard and Beulah (Weber) S.; m. Dorothy Jean West, May 20, 1960; children: Valerie Jean Schmitt Jones, Jeffrey Howard. B Theology, Toronto Bible Coll., Ont., Can., 1963. Ordained to ministry Mennonite Ch., 1963. Pastor Wanner Mennonite Ch., Cambridge, Ont., 1960-71, Calvary Mennonite Ch., Ayr, Ont., 1964-69, S. Union Mennonite Ch., West Liberty, Ohio, 1971-83; hosp. chaplain Mary Rutan Hosp., Bellefontaine, Ohio, 1983-85; dir. devel. Adriel Sch., West Liberty, Ohio, 1985-86; pastor Bay Shore Mennonite Ch., Sarasota, Fla., 1986-95, Sharon Mennonite Ch., Plain City, Ohio, 1995—; sec. Mennonite Conf. Ont., Cambridge, 1970-71; overseer Ohio Conf. Mennonites, West Liberty, 1972-78, 84-86; moderator Southeast Mennonite Conf., Sarasota, 1989-92; mem. Mennonite Ch. Gen. Bd., 1991-95. Vice chair Mary Rutan Hosp. Bd., 1978-83. Recipient 13 Yrs. Svc. award Vol. Chaplains Group, Mary Rutan Hosp., 1985. Mem. Sarasota Mennonite Mins. Fellowship (past, sec., chmn.), Plain City Pastors' Fellowship, Ctrl. Ohio Mennonite Pastor Peer Group.

SCHMITT, JOHANNA MARIE, plant population biologist, educator; b. Phila., Mar. 12, 1953; d. William Francis and Laura Belle (Wear) S.; m. Darrell Marion West, Aug. 6, 1983. BA, Swarthmore (Pa.) Coll., 1974; PhD, Stanford U., 1981. Postdoctoral rsch. assoc. Duke U., Durham, N.C., 1981-82; asst. prof. Brown U., Providence, 1982-87, assoc. prof. biology, 1987-94, prof., 1994—; mem. adv. panel NSF on population biology, 1989; mem. R.I. Task Force, New Eng. Plant Conservation program, 1991—. Assoc. editor Evolution, 1990-92; contbr. articles to profl. jours. including Evolution, Ecology, Am. Naturalist, Jour. Ecology, Nature. Bd. dirs. Sojourner House, Providence, 1989-92. NSF grad. fellow, 1974, mid. career fellow, 1992-93; rsch. grantee, 1984—; recipient faculty award for women, 1991—. Mem. Soc. for Study of Evolution (coun. mem. 1990-92, exec. v.p. 1994-95), Bot. Soc. Am., Ecol. Soc. Am., Am. Soc. Naturalists (v.p. 1997). Achievements include research on ecological genetics of natural plant populations: density-dependent phenomena, gene flow and population structure, inbreeding depression, the evolution of sex, maternal effects, seed ecology, natural selection, evolution of plasticity, adaptive significance of phytochrome, ecological risks of transgenic plants. Office: Brown Univ Dept Ecology & Evolution Providence RI 02912

SCHMITT, KARL MICHAEL, retired political scientist; b. Louisville, Ky., July 22, 1922; s. Edward Peter and Mary Ann (Iula) S.; m. Grace Bernadette Leary, June 18, 1949; children: Karl, Edward, Barbara, William, Michael. B.A., Cath. U. Am., 1947, M.A., 1949; Ph.D., U. Pa., 1954. Teaching asst. U. Pa., 1948-50; instr. history Niagara U., 1950-54, asst. prof., 1954-55; research analyst U.S. Dept. State, 1955-58; asst. prof. dept. govt. U. Tex., 1958-63, assoc. prof., 1963-66, prof., 1966-91, prof. emeritus, 1991—, chmn., 1975-80; vis. prof. U. Calif., Los Angeles, summer 1959, Nat. War Coll., 1970-71; vis. sr. fellow U. Manchester, Eng., 1988-89; cons. Dept. of State, 1962-70. Author: Communism in Mexico; A Study in Political Frustration, 1965, Mexico and the United States, 1821-1973: Conflict and Coexistence, 1974, others. Contbr. articles to profl. jours. Served with U.S. Army, 1943-45. Decorated Purple Heart. Mem. Tex. Cath. Hist. Assn. (pres. 1976-77). Roman Catholic. Home: 2603 Pinewood Ter Austin TX 78757-2136 Office: Dept Govt U Tex Austin TX 78712

SCHMITT, MARY ELIZABETH, postal supervisor; b. Detroit, Sept. 16, 1948; d. Jerome Ferdinand and Margaret Ellen (Beauregard) S. BS, Ea. Mich. U., 1979. Waitress, hostess Mr. Steak, Westland, Mich., 1969-70; mgr. housewares K-Mart, Ypsilanti, Mich., 1971, asst. mgr., jewelry, 1972; postal clk. U.S. Postal Svc., Ann Arbor, Mich., 1972-88, postal supr., 1988—. Crisis intervention counselor Ozone House, Ann Arbor, 1978; convenor Gray Panthers of Huron Valley, Ann Arbor, 1979-80; active Greenpeace. Mem. LWV, Nat. Assn. Postal Suprs., Ann Arbor Postal Fed. Credit Union (v.p. 1987—), Sierra Club, Ancestry Club. Roman Catholic. Avocations: travel, reading, hiking, canoeing, geneaology. Home: PO Box 1833 Ann Arbor MI 48106-1833 Office: US Postal Svc 2075 W Stadium Blvd Ann Arbor MI 48103-7011

SCHMITT, NANCY CAIN, public and corporate relations executive, writer; b. Fayetteville, N.C., June 12, 1942; d. Carlton White and Cleo Margaret (Parnell) Cain; m. Louis Dennis Schmitt, July 13, 1974 (div.). BA, Wake Forest U., 1960-64. Intern Winston-Salem (N.C.) Jour.-Sentinel, 1963-64; reporter Gastonia (N.C.) Gazette, 1964-66; copy editor, reporter Twin City Sentinel, Winston-Salem, 1966-67; entertainment editor Fayetteville Observer, 1967-78; lifestyle editor Anchorage Times, 1978-83; pub. rels. specialist Multivisions Cable TV Co., Anchorage, 1983-84; editor Alaska Jour. of Commerce, Anchorage, 1984-85; sr. comms. specialist U.S. Postal Svc., 1985—. Author: How to Care for Your Car: A Women's Guide to Car Care in Alaska, 1978 (nat. award 1979); mem. editl. bd. Episc. Diocean of Alaska, Fairbanks, 1983-86; contbr. articles to profl. jours. and nat. publs. Recipient Asst. Postmaster Gen.'s award for excellence, USPS Legis. Affairs Corp. Rel. Sr. VP Opportunity award, Sr. Op-Ed Writing award. Mem. Nat. Fedn. Press Women (nat. bd. dirs. 1990-91, pres. 1997—), Pub. Rels. Soc. Am., Alaska Press Women (pres. treas., sec., communicator of achievement, recipient numerous awards), Alaska Press Club (recipient 3 awards), Rotary Internat. (bd. dirs. 1991-92). Home: 6716 E 16th Ave Apt A Anchorage AK 99504-2513 Office: U S Postal Svc Corp Rels 3720 Barrow St Anchorage AK 99599-9998

SCHMITT, PAUL JOHN, history and geography educator; b. Pitts., Jan. 25, 1951; s. Phillip John and Adeline Marie (Barnhart) S.; m. Ruth Margaret Glass, June 20, 1987. BS, Ariz. State U., 1976, BA in Edn., 1978; MA, U. Nev., Las Vegas, 1994. Registration clk. Hermosa Inn Resort, Scottsdale, Ariz., 1978-79, asst. mgr., 1979-82; convention svc. mgr. Carefree (Ariz.) Inn Resort, 1982-84; tchr. Tonopah (Nev.) High Sch., 1984-85; reservation clk. Desert Inn Country Club and Spa, Las Vegas, Nev., 1985-92; prof. history C.C. of So. Nev., Las Vegas, 1992—. Mem. Assn. Am. Geographers, Orgn. Am. Historians, Am. Western History Assn., Orgn. Am. Historians, Phi Alpha Theta, Gamma Theta Upsilon. Avocations: reading, photography, horseback riding. Office: CC So Nev Cheyenne Campus Dept Regional Studies 3200 E Cheyenne Ave # C North Las Vegas NV 89030-4228

SCHMITT, ROLAND WALTER, retired academic administrator; b. Seguin, Tex., July 24, 1923; s. Walter L. and Myrtle F. (Caldwell) S.; m. Claire Freeman Kunz, Sept. 19, 1957; children: Lorenz Allen, Brian Walter, Alice Elizabeth, Henry Caldwell. BA in Math, U. Tex., 1947, BS in Physics, 1947, MA in Physics, 1948; PhD, Rice U., 1951; DSc (hon.), Worcester Poly. Inst., 1985, U. Pa., 1985; DCL (hon.), Union Coll., 1985; DL (hon.), Lehigh U., 1986; DSc (hon.), U. S.C., 1988, Universite De Technologie De Compiegne, 1991; DL (hon.), Coll. St. Rose, 1992, Russell Sage, 1993, Hartford Grad. Ctr., 1995, Ill. Inst. Tech., 1996, Rensselaer Polytechnic Inst., 1997. With GE, 1951-88; R & D mgr. phys. sci. and engring. GE, Schenectady, 1967-74; mgr. energy sci. and engring. R & D GE, 1974-78, v.p. corp. R & D, 1978-82, sr. v.p. corp. R & D, 1982-86, sr. v.p. sci. and tech., 1986-88, ret., 1988; pres. Rensselaer Poly. Inst., Troy, N.Y., 1988-93; bd. dirs. Gen. Signal Corp., Reveo Corp.; bd. advisors ILINC, 1996—; mem. tech. adv. bd. Chrysler Corp.; 1990-93; past pres. Indsl. Rsch. Inst.; mem. energy rsch. adv. bd. U.S. Dept. Energy, 1977-83; chmn. CORETECH, 1988-93; mem. Com. on Japan, NRC, 1988-90, Comml. Devel. Ind. Adv. Group, NASA, 1988-90; exec. com. Coun. on Competitiveness, 1988-93; chmn. NRC Panel on Export Controls, 1989-91; mem. Dept. Commerce Adv. Commn. on Patent Law Reform, 1990-92; mem. adv. bd. Oak Ridge Nat. Lab., 1993—; chmn. Motorola's Sci. Adv. Bd., 1995—; chmn. rsch. priority panel for NRC Future of Space Sci., 1994-95. Trustee N.E. Savs. Bank, 1978-84; bd. advisors Union Coll., Schenectady, 1981-84, Argonne Univs. Assn., 1979-82, RPI, 1982-88; bd. govs. Albany Med. Ctr. Hosp., 1979-82, 88-90; bd. dirs. Sunnyview Hosp. and Rehab. Ctr., 1978-86, Coun. on Superconductivity for Am. Competitiveness, 1987-89; mem. exec. com. N.Y. State Ctr. for Hazardous Waste Mgmt., 1988-89; chmn. Office of Tech. Assessment adv. panel on industry and environment; mem. Nat. Commn. Ill. Inst. Tech., 1993-94. With USAAF, 1943-46. Recipient RPI Community Svc. award, 1982, award for disting. contbns. Stony Brook Found., 1985, Rice U. Disting. Alumni award, 1985, IRI Medalist award, 1989, Royal Swedish Acad. of Engring. Sci., 1990, Arthur M. Bueche award Nat. Acad. of Engring., 1995; named Fgn. Assn. of Engring. Acad. of Japan, U. Albany Found. Acad. Laureate, 1997; named to Jr. Achievement Capital Region Bus. Hall of Fame, 1996. Fellow AAAS, IEEE (Centennial medal 1984, Engring. Leadership award 1989, Founders medal 1992, Hoover medal 1993), Am. Phys. Soc. (Pake award 1993), Am. Acad. Arts and Scis.; mem. NAE (coun., Beuche award 1995), Am. Inst. Physics (chmn. 1993—), Coun. Sci. Soc. Pres. (chair 1993—), N.Y. Acad. Scis. (pres. coun. 1993—), Nat. Sci. Bd. (chmn. 1982), Dirs. Indsl. rsch., Rensselaer Alumni Assn. (Disting. alumni award 1993). Office: PO Box 240 Rexford NY 12148-0240

SCHMITT, WILLIAM HOWARD, cosmetics company executive; b. Sterling, Ill., Oct. 27, 1936; s. Alfred William and Katherine Henrietta (Skow) S.; m. Antionette Marie Payne, Mar. 22, 1960; children: Hilary Ann, Andrea Kay, Joseph Michael. BS in Pharmacy, Drake U., 1958. Rsch. assoc. G.D. Searle, Skokie, Ill., 1963-66; assoc. dir. rsch. Alberto Culver, Melrose Park, Ill., 1966-71; dir. product devel. Chesebrough-Pond's USA, Trumbull, Conn., 1971-74; dir. internat. Chesebrough-Pond's Inc., Trumbull, Conn., 1974-83, group dir. R&D, 1983-85, v.p. R&D, 1985-89, sr. v.p. R&D, 1989—; chmn. sci. adv. commn. Cosmetics, Toiletry and Fragrance Assn., Washington, 1994—. Author: (with others) An Overview of World-Wide Regulatory Programs, 1984; editor: Cosmetics and Toiletries Industry, 1992, 2nd edit., 1996 (CIBS award 1996); patentee in toiletry and cosmetics field. Lt. USAF, 1959-62. Mem. Soc. Cosmetic Chemists, Am. Assn. for Dental Rsch. Avocations: boating, hunting, fishing. Office: Chesebrough-Ponds Inc 40 Merritt Blvd Trumbull CT 06611-5413

SCHMITT, WOLFGANG RUDOLF, consumer products executive; b. Koblenz, Germany, Mar. 12, 1944; s. Josef H. and M.H. (Baldus) S.; m. Toni A. Yoder, June 30, 1974; children: Christopher, Corey, Clayton. BA, Otterbein Coll., 1966; AMP, Harvard U. Bus. Sch., 1986. With Rubbermaid Inc., Wooster, Ohio, 1966—, pres., gen. mgr. housewares products div., 1984-91, exec. v.p., bd. dirs., 1987-91, pres., chief operating officer, 1991—; chmn., CEO, 1993—; bd. dirs. Parker Hannifin Corp., Kimberly-Clark Corp. Bd. dirs. Otterbein Coll., 1992—. Avocations: horticulture, tennis, sailing. Office: Rubbermaid Inc 1147 Akron Rd Wooster OH 44691-2501

SCHMITTEN, ROLLAND ARTHUR, government official; b. Wenatchee, Wash., Aug. 26, 1944; s. Raymond Earl and Waunita (Hughes) S.; m. Barbara Rae Regan, Aug. 14, 1965; children: Jennifer Suzanne, Heidi Elizabeth, Rolland Arthur. B.S., Wash. State U., 1966. Logging supt. Schmitten Lumber Co., Cashmere, Wash., 1970-73, owner, mgr., 1977-82; regional land mgr. The Pack River Co., Spokane, Wash., 1973-77; dir. Wash. State Dept. Fisheries, Olympia, 1981-83; dep. chief of staff Office of Gov., Olympia, 1983-84, exec. asst., 1984—; N.W. regional dir. Nat. Marine Fisheries Service, 1985-93, asst. adminstr., 1993—; v.p. Keep Washington Green, 1978-81; mem. Western Legis. Forestry Task Force, Wash., 1978-81, Nat. Conf. of State Legislatures, 1977-81. Councilman Cashmere City, 1973-77; mem. Chelan County Port Commn., 1977; mem. Wash. Ho. of Reps., 1976-81; mem. Bd. Natural Resources, 1983—, Columbia River Fisheries Commn., 1981-83. Served to capt. USMC, 1966-70, Viet Nam. Named Conservationist of Yr., N.W. Salmon and Steelhead Council, 1981, Alumni of Yr., Wash. State U. Sch. Forestry, 1983; recipient Outstanding Community Achievement of Vietnam Vets. award Pres. Carter, 1979, U.S. Forest Service 75th Anniversary award, 1980. Mem. Internat. Pacific Salmon Fisheries Commn. (chmn. 1981-84), North Pacific Fisheries Mgmt. Council. Republican. Presbyterian. Home: 800 Nitley Rd Silver Spring MD 20904 Office: Nat Marine Fisheries Svc 1315 E West Hwy Silver Spring MD 20910-3285

SCHMITTER, CHARLES HARRY, electronics manufacturing company executive, lawyer; b. Paterson, N.J., Feb. 4, 1928; s. Charles and Jennie (Schoe) S.; m. Margaret Ann Roose, Oct. 24, 1964 (dec. Dec. 1989). A.B. magna cum laude, Rutgers U., 1948; J.D., Columbia, 1953. Bar: N.Y. bar 1956, Mich. bar 1960. Asso. atty. firm Cravath, Swaine & Moore, N.Y.C., 1955-59; asst. sec. Ford Motor Co., 1959-64; corp. sec. Sperry Rand Corp. (now Unisys Corp.), N.Y.C., 1964-87, ret., 1987. Served with AUS, 1953-55. Mem. Am. Bar Assn., Am. Soc. Corp. Secretaries, Phi Alpha Delta, Theta Chi. Club: Rockefeller Center Luncheon (N.Y.C.). Home: 420 E 51st St New York NY 10022-8014

SCHMITZ, CHARLES EDISON, evangelist; b. Mendota, Ill., July 18, 1919; s. Charles Francis Schmitz and Lucetta Margaret (Foulk) Schmitz Kaufmann; m. Eunice Magdalene Ewy, June 1, 1942; children: Charles Elwood, Jon Lee. Student, Wheaton Coll., 1936-37, 38, 39; BA, Wartburg Coll., Waverly, Iowa, 1940; BD, Wartburg Theol. Sem., Dubuque, Iowa, 1942, MDiv, 1977. Ordained to ministry Luth. Ch., 1942. Founding pastor Ascension Luth. Ch., L.A., 1942-48, Am. Evang. Luth. Ch., Phoenix, 1948-65; dir. intermountain missions, founding pastor 14 Evang. Luth. Parishes, Calif., Ariz., N.Mex., Fla., 1948-65; evangelist Am. Luth. Ch., Mpls., 1965-73; sr. pastor Peace Luth. Ch., Palm Bay, Fla., 1973-89; pastor-at-large Am. Evang. Luth. Ch., Phoenix, 1989—; charter mem. Navajo Luth. Mission, Rock Point, Ariz., 1960—; pastoral advisor Ariz. Luth. Outdoor Ministry Assn., Prescott, 1958-65, 89—; Kogudus Internat. Retreat master and chaplain, Fla., Berlin and Marbach, Germany, 1990; mem. transition team Fla. Synod, Evang. Luth. Ch. Am., 1985-89. Author: Evangelism for the Seventies, 1970; co-author: ABC's of Life, 1968; assoc. editor Good News mag., 1965-71. Founder, chmn. Ariz. Ch. Conf. on Adult and Youth Problems, 1956-65; vice chmn. synod worship & ch. music com. Am. Luth. Ch., Mpls., 1960-66; chmn. Space Coast Luth. Retirement Ctr., Palm Bay, Fla., 1985-89; chaplain Ariz. chpt. Luth. Brotherhood, 1991—. Named Citizen of Yr., Palm Bay C. of C., 1979. Mem. Nat. Assn. Evangelicals, German Am. Nat. Congress (nat. chaplain), Lions (officer Phoenix and Palm Bay clubs 1952—, Ariz. Dist. 21A chaplain 1994-95), Kiwanis (bd. dirs. L.A. chpt. 1942-48). Republican. Home: 12444 W Toreador Dr Sun City West AZ 85375-1926 *The truly modern person today who, like the scribes of old, would aspire to fulfillment in leadership would do well to remember Jesus' words: "Therefore every scribe who has been trained for the Kingdom of Heaven is like the master of a household who brings out of his treasure what is new and what is old." (Matt. 13:52).*

SCHMITZ, DANIEL DEAN, mechanical engineer; b. Moorhead, Minn., Apr. 8, 1964; s. Thomas Oswin and Diane Marie (Bruski) S. Student, Bismarck State Coll., 1983-85; BS, N.D. State U., 1987. Registered profl. engr. N.D., Minn., N.Y., Pa., Ga., Va., Mont. Mech. engr. Crisafulli Pump Co., Glendive, Mont., 1988-90, Beazely Engring., PC, Bismarck, N.D., 1990-93; mech. engr., dir. design and product prodn., project mgr. Henning, Metz, Hartford & Assocs., Inc., Fargo, N.D., 1993-95; chief mech. engr. SSR Engr., Inc., East Grand Forks, Minn., 1995—. Mem. ASHRAE, NSPE, Am. Soc. Plumbing Engrs. Avocations: boating, waterskiing, restoring vehicles, bicycling. Office: SSR Engrs Inc PO Box 471 East Grand Forks MN 56721

SCHMITZ, DENNIS MATHEW, English language educator; b. Dubuque, Iowa, Aug. 11, 1937; s. Anthony Peter and Roselyn S.; m. Loretta D'Agostino, Aug. 20, 1960; children—Anne, Sara, Martha, Paul, Matthew. B.A., Loras Coll., 1959; M.A., U. Chgo., 1961. Instr. English Ill. Inst. Tech., Chgo., 1961-62, U. Wis., Milw., 1962-66; asst. prof. Calif. State U., Sacramento, 1966-69, assoc. prof., 1969-74, prof., 1974—; poet-in-residence, 1966—. Author: We Weep for Our Strangeness, 1969, Double Exposures, 1971, Goodwill, Inc., 1976, String, 1980, Singing, 1985, Eden, 1989, About Night: Selected and New Poems, 1993. Recipient Discovery award Poetry Center, N.Y.C., 1968; winner First Book Competition Follett Pub. Co., 1969; di Castagnola award Poetry Soc. Am., 1986; Shelley Meml. award Poetry Soc. Am., 1987; NEA fellow, 1976-77, 85-86, 92-93, Guggenheim fellow, 1978-79. Mem. PEN, Assoc. Writing Programs. Roman Catholic. Office: Calif State U Dept English 6000 J St Sacramento CA 95819-2605

SCHMITZ, DOLORES JEAN, primary education educator; b. River Falls, Wis., Dec. 27, 1931; d. Otto and Helen Olive (Webster) Kreuziger; m. Karl Matthias Schmitz Jr., Aug. 18, 1956; children: Victoria Jane, Karl III. BS, U. Wis., River Falls, 1953; MS, Nat. Coll. Edn., 1982; postgrad., U. Minn., Mankato, 1969, U. Melbourne, Australia, 1989, U. Wis., Milw., 1989, Carroll Coll., 1990, Cardinal Stritch, 1990. Cert. tchr., Wis. Tchr. Manitowoc (Wis.) Pub. Schs., 1953-56, West Allis (Wis.) Pub. Schs., 1956-59, Lowell Sch., Milw., 1960-63, Victory Sch., Milw., 1964; tchr. Palmer Sch., Milw., 1966-84, 86-94, unit leader, 1984-86; ret., 1994; co-organizer Headstart Tchg. Staff Assn., Milw., 1968; insvc. organizer Headstart and Early Childhood, Milw., 1969-92; pilot tchr. for Whole Lang., Hi-Scope and Math. Their Way, 1988-93; bd. dirs. Cuurriculum Devel. Ctr. of Milw. Edn. Ctr., 1993-94. Author: (curriculum) Writing to Read, 1987, Cooperation and Young Children (ERIC award 1982), Kindergarten Curriculum, 1953. Former supporter Milw. Art Mus., Milw. Pub. Mus., Milw. County Zoo, Whitefish Bay Pub. Libr., Earthwatch Riveredge Nature Ctr.; vol. fgn. visitor program Milw. Internat. Inst., 1966-94, holiday folk fair, 1976-94, Earthwatch, 1989; lobbyist Milw. Pub. Sch. Bd. and State of Wis., 1986-93; coord. comty. vols., 1990-94. Grantee Greater Milw. Ednl. Trust, 1989. Mem. NEA (life), ASCD, Milw. Kindergarten Assn. (rec. sec. 1986-93), Nat. Assn. for Edn. of Young Children, Tchrs. Applying Whole Lang., Wis. Early Childhood Assn., Milw. Tchrs. Ednl. Assn. (co-chmn. com. early childhood 1984-86), Assn. for Childhood Edn. Internat. (charter pres. Manitowoc chpt. 1955-56), Milw. Educating Computer Assn., Alpha Psi Omega. Roman Catholic. Avocations: bicycling, nature. Home: 312 8th Ave N Apt 1 Tierra Verde FL 33715-1800 *Like a very old song said-Accentuate the POSITIVE, eliminate the negative,and don't mess with Mr. In-Between. Life is better for you and everyone around you if these "rules" are followed. Success=If it is to be, it is up to me. I can.*

SCHMITZ, FRANCIS DAVID, lawyer; b. Milw., July 13, 1950; s. Joseph Francis and Helen Julia (Rudzik) S.; m. Elizabeth Ann Brinker, Dec. 12, 1975; children: Sarah, Catherine. BA, St. Norbert Coll., 1972; MBA, So. Ill. U., 1975; JD, Marquette U., 1983. Bar: Wis. 1983, U.S. Dist. Ct. (ea. and we. dists.) Wis. 1983, U.S. Ct. Appeals (7th cir.) 1985. Law clk. to judge U.S. Ct. Appeals (7th cir.), Chgo., 1983-84; asst. U.S. atty. for ea. dist. Wis. U.S. Dept. Justice, Milw., 1984—, chief criminal divsn., 1992-96, chief econ. crimes, 1996—. Capt. U.S. Army, 1973-80, col. USAR, 1980—. Mem. State Bar Wis., Assn. U.S. Army. Roman Catholic. Avocations: flyfishing, jogging. Office: Office US Atty 517 E Wisconsin Ave Milwaukee WI 53202-4504

SCHMITZ, ROBERT ALLEN, publishing executive, investor; b. Chgo., Jan. 19, 1941; s. John and Lee (Zeal) S.; m. Jenny Ann Quest, Aug. 23, 1969 (div.); children: Alexander, Nicholas, Lara, Maximilian. BA with distinction, U. Mich., 1963; MBA, MIT, 1965. Asst. to pres. Lima (Peru) Light and Power Co., 1965-67; acquisition analyst W.R. Grace Co., N.Y.C., 1967-69; asst. to chmn. N.W. Industries, N.Y.C., 1969-70; prin. McKinsey & Co., Inc., N.Y.C., 1970-82; v.p. books Dow Jones & Co., N.Y.C., 1982-88; chmn., pres., chief exec. officer Richard D. Irwin, Inc., Homewood, Ill., 1983-89; pres., founder Quest Capital Ltd., 1989—; investment cons. Soros Fund Mgmt., 1990-92; mgn. dir., sr. ptnr. Trust Co. of the West, 1993—; mem. adv. bd. Coll. Commerce De Paul U., Chgo., 1985—; bd. dirs. Adams Rite Sabre, Inc., Glendale, Calif., Superior Fireplace Co., Fullerton, Calif., Houston Foods Co., Chgo., Archibald Candy Co., Chgo., US Media Group, Inc., Crystal City, Mo., Ctrl. Valley Publ., Merced, Hobby Products Co., Inc., Penrose, Colo., Automated Bar Controls, Vacaville, Calif. Pres. Cultural Arts Ctr. Found., Homewood, Ill. Mem. Assn. Am. Pubs. (chmn. higher edn. divsn. 1989), Nature Conservancy (trustee N.Y. state chpt.). Office: Trust Co of the West 200 Park Ave Ste 2200 New York NY 10166-0005

SCHMITZ, ROGER ANTHONY, chemical engineering educator, academic administrator; b. Carlyle, Ill., Oct. 22, 1934; s. Alfred Bernard and Wilma Afra (Aarns) S.; m. Ruth Mary Kuhl, Aug. 31, 1957; children—Jan, Joy, Joni. B.S. in Chem. Engring., U. Ill., 1959; Ph.D. in Chem. Engring., U. Minn., 1962. Prof. chem. engring. U. Ill., Urbana, 1962-79; Keating-Crawford prof. chem. engring. U. Notre Dame, Ind., 1979—, chmn. dept. chem. engring., 1979-81, dean engring., 1981-87; v.p., assoc. provost U. Notre Dame, 1987-95; cons. Amoco Chems., Naperville, Ill., 1966-77; vis. prof. Calif. Inst. Tech., Los Angeles, 1968-69, U. So. Calif., Los Angeles, 1968-69. Contbr. articles to profl. jours. Served with U.S. Army, 1953-55. Guggenheim Found. fellow, 1968. Mem. Nat. Acad. Engring., Am. Inst. Chem. Engrs. (A.P. Colburn award 1970, R.H. Wilhelm award 1981), Am. Chem. Soc., Am. Soc. for Engring. Edn. (George Westinghouse award 1977). Roman Catholic. Home: 16865 Londonberry Ln South Bend IN 46635-1444 Office: U Notre Dame 301 Cushing Hall Notre Dame IN 46556

SCHMITZ, SHIRLEY GERTRUDE, marketing and sales executive; b. Brackenridge, Pa., Dec. 19, 1927; d. Wienand Gerard and Florence Marie (Grimm) S. BA, Ariz. State U., 1949. Tchr., guidance counselor Mesa High Sch., Ariz., 1949-51; area mgr. Field Enterprises Ednl. Corp., Phoenix, 1951-52, dist. mgr., 1952, regional mgr., 1953-55, br. mgr., Montreal, Que., Can., 1955-61, nat. supr., Chgo., 1961-63, asst. sales mgr., 1963-65, nat. sales mgr., 1965-70; v.p., gen. sales mgr. F.E. Compton Co. div. Ency. Brit., Chgo., 1970-71, exec. v.p., dir. sales, 1971-73; pres. CHB Port-A-Book Store, Inc., 1973-76; gen. mgr. Bobbs-Merrill Co., Inc., Indpls., 1976-82; v.p. sales U.S. Telephone Communications of Midwest, Inc., Chgo., 1982-83; exec. v.p. sales and market devel. Entertainment Publs., Corp., Birmingham, Mich., 1983-89, sr. v.p. mktg. and sales, Troy, Mich., 1989-92; prin. S.G. Schmitz and Assocs., Chgo., 1992—; bd. advisors Ctr. Advancement of Small Bus., Ariz. State U. Sch. Bus; bd. dirs. Spectral, Inc.; mem. pres.'s cabinet capital fund raising campaign Ariz. State U. Home: 93 Miller Rd Lake Zurich IL 60047-1395

SCHMOKE, KURT L., mayor; b. Balt., Dec. 1, 1949; m. Patricia Schmoke; children: Katherine, Gregory. BA, Yale U., 1971; JD, Harvard U., 1976. Former assoc. Piper & Marbury; former pvt. practice; asst. U.S. atty Balt.; state's atty. Maryland, 1982-87; mayor Baltimore, 1987—; apptd. mem. White House Domestice Policy Staff, 1977-78; former mem. Gov.'s Commn. on Prison Overcrowding; former mem. Md. Criminal justice Coord. Coun. & Task Force to Reform Insanity Def.; founder Balt. Community Devel. Financing Corp., 1988—. Rhodes Scholar Yale U. Office: Office of the Mayor 250 City Hall Baltimore MD 21202-3417*

SCHMOLKA, LEO LOUIS, law educator; b. Paris, Apr. 25, 1939; came to U.S., 1944; s. Francis and Irene S.; m. Lucille J. Schoenbaum, July 29, 1965; children—Andrew, Gregory. A.B., Dartmouth Coll., 1960; LL.B., Harvard U., 1963; LL.M., NYU, 1971. Bar: N.Y. 1964. Assoc. Weil, Gotshal and Manges, N.Y.C., 1964-71; ptnr. Weil, Gotshal and Manges, 1971-81, of counsel, 1981—; adj. asst. prof. law NYU Sch. of Law, 1971-75; adj. assoc. prof. law NYU Law Sch., 1975-76, adj. prof., 1977-80, assoc. prof., 1981-84, prof., 1985—, mem. faculty, dir. IRS/NYU continuing profl. edn. program, 1987—; cons. U.S. Treasury Dept. Office Tax Policy, Washington, 1994-95, Am. Law Inst., 1979-86, U. Miami (Fla.) Estate Planning Inst., 1976-80; vis. adj. prof. law U. Miami Sch. Law, 1977, 80; vis. lectr. continuing legal edn. various univs. and tax insts., 1973—. Contbr. articles to legal jours. Fellow Am. Coll. Trust and Estate Counsel; mem. ABA, N.Y. State Bar Assn. (chmn. com. on income taxation estates and trusts 1973-75, estate and gift tax 1976-77, mem. exec. com. tax sect. 1978), Internat. Acad. Estate and Trust Law (academician). Office: NYU Sch Law 40 Washington Sq S Rm 430 New York NY 10012-1005

SCHMOLL, HANS JOACHIM, internal medicine, hematology, oncology educator; b. Hannover, Germany, June 21, 1946; s. Johannes and Edeltraut (Schneider) S. MD, Med. U. Hannover, 1970, PhD, 1982. Rsch. assoc. Med. U., Hannover, 1971-84, prof. medicine and hematology-oncology, 1984-95; prof. medicine and hematology dept. hematology and oncology Martin Luther U., Halle-Wittenberg, Germany, 1996—. Author: Kompendium Intern Onkologie, 1986, 2nd edit., 1996. Home: Ludwig Barnay Strasse 9, D-30175 Hannover Germany Office: Martin Luther Univ, Dept Hematology/Oncology, D-06120 Halle-Saale Germany

SCHMOLL, HARRY F., JR., lawyer, educator; b. Somers Point, N.J., Jan. 20, 1939; s. Harry F. Sr and Margaret E. Schmoll; m. Rita L. Miescier, Aug. 29, 1977. BS, Rider Coll., 1960; JD, Temple U., 1967. Bar: Pa., D.C. 1969, N.J. 1975. With claims dept. Social Security Adminstrn., Phila., 1960-67; staff atty. Pa. State U., State College, 1968-69; regional dir. Pa. Crime Commn., State College, 1969-70; campaign aide U.S. Senator Hugh Scott, Harrisburg, Pa., 1970; pvt. practice law, State College, 1970-74, Manahawkin, N.J., 1975-96; instr. criminal justice Pa. State U., University Park, 1969-74, assoc. prof. criminal justice, bus. law Burlington County Coll., Pemberton, N.J., 1974-92, prof., 1992—, pres. elect edn. assn., 1992-93, 96-97, pres. edn. assn., 1993-94, 97—; judge mcpl. ct., Stafford Twp., 1982-85. Gen. counsel German Heritage Coun. of N.J., Inc.; mem. Barnegat Twp. Rent Control Bd., 1991, Barnegat Twp. Zoning Bd., 1994. Author: New Jersey Criminal Law Workbook, 1976, 2nd edit. 1979. Mem. Stafford Twp. Com., 1979-81, dep. mayor, 1979. Trustee Pheasant Run Homeowners Assn., Barnegat, N.J., 1992-95. Mem. Pa. Bar Assn., N.J. Bar Assn., German-Am. Club of So. Ocean County (past pres.). Office: 72 Peppergrass Dr S Mount Laurel NJ 08054

SCHMULTS, EDWARD CHARLES, lawyer, corporate and philanthropic administrator; b. Paterson, N.J., Feb. 6, 1931; s. Edward M. and Mildred (Moore) S.; m. Diane E. Beers, Apr. 23, 1960; children: Alison C., Edward M., Robert C. BS, Yale U., 1953; JD, Harvard U., 1958. Bar: N.Y. 1959, D.C. 1974. Assoc. White & Case, N.Y.C., 1958-65, ptnr., 1965-73, 77-81; gen. counsel Treasury Dept., Washington, 1973-74; undersec. Treasury Dept., 1974-75; dep. counsel to Pres. U.S., 1975-76; dep. atty. gen. of U.S. Dept. Justice, Washington, 1981-84; sr. v.p. external rels., gen. counsel GTE Corp., Stamford, Conn., 1984-94; lectr. securities laws. Bd. dirs. Greenpoint Fin. Corp., Germany Fund, Ctrl. European Equity Fund; chmn. bd. trustees Edna McConnell Clark Found., Refugee Policy Group. With USMC, 1953-55. Mem. Am. Bar Assn., Assn. Bar City N.Y., Adminstrv. Conf. U.S. (council 1977-84), Sakonnet Golf Club, Met. Club. Clubs: Sakonnet Golf (Little Compton, R.I.); Metropolitan (Washington).

SCHMUTZ, CHARLES REID, university foundation executive; b. Youngstown, Ohio, Jan. 26, 1942; s. Charles Edward and Alice Mae (Bliss) S.; m. Judith Rhodes Seiple, June 19, 1965; children: Charles Reid Jr., Andrew Edward, Jill Caroline. AB in Econs., Brown U., 1964. Lab. technician The Standard Slag Co., Youngstown, 1964-65; direct salesman The Standard Slag Co., Cleve., 1965-69; mktg. and prodn. scheduler The Standard Slag Co., Youngstown, 1969-73, mktg. and indsl. engr., 1973-85, gen. mgr., v.p. ops., 1985-89; pres. Youngstown State U. Found., 1989—; bd. dirs. StanCorp., Youngstown. Bd. dirs. Youngstown Playhouse, Jr. Achievement Mahoning Valley. Named to Hall of Fame, Ohio Aggregates Assn., 1990. Mem. Rotary. Methodist. Avocations: golf, tennis.

SCHMUTZHART, BERTHOLD JOSEF, sculptor, educator, art and education consultant; b. Salzburg, Austria, Aug. 17, 1928; came to U.S., 1958, naturalized, 1963; s. Berthold Josef and Anna (Valaschek) S. Student, Acad. for Applied Art, Vienna, Austria, 1956. Cert. fed. tchr., Austria. Prof. Wekschulheim Felbertal, Salzburg, 1951-58; sculptor Washington, 1959-60; tchr. Longfellow Sch., Bethesda, Md., 1960-63; prof., chmn. dept. sculpture Corcoran Sch. Art, Washington, 1963-94, prof. emeritus, 1994—; lectr. Smithsonian Instn., Washington, 1968-84. One-man shows include Fredericksburg Gallery Fine Art, Va., 1967-73, Franz Bader Gallery, Washington, 1978, 81, 83, 86, 88; group shows include Nat. Collection Fine Arts, Washington, 1961-70, High Mus. Art, Atlanta, 1965, Ark. Art Ctr., Little Rock, 1966, Birmingham Mus. Art, Ala., 1967, Hirschhorn Mus. and Sculpture Garden, Washington, 1981, Nat. Gallery Modern Art, New Delhi, 1990; represented in permanent collections Hirschhorn Collection; designer fountain, Gallery of Modern Art, Fredericksburg, 1967; author: The Handmade Furniture Book, 1981; contbr. articles to profl. jours. Fine arts panelist D.C. Commn. for Arts, 1973-79; chmn. bd. Market Five Gallery, Washington, 1978-82; bd. dirs. Franz Bader Gallery, Washington, 1981-86; trustee Arts for the Aging, Inc., Washington, 1990—. Recipient 1st prize Washington Religious Arts Council, 1960, for sculpture, Little Rock, 1966, Louisville, 1968, Silver medal Audubon Soc., Washington, 1971. Mem. Guild for Religious Architects, Artists Equity Assn. (pres. D.C. chpt. 1973-75), AAUP, Am. Austrian Soc. (pres. 1968-70, exec. com.), Soaring Soc. Am. Home: 32 Layline Ln Fredericksburg VA 22406-4061

SCHNABEL, JOHN HENRY, retired music educator; b. Evansville, Ind., Mar. 15, 1915; s. Arthur John and Myrtle L. (Walters) S.; m. Emily H. Wepfer, June 28, 1938; children: Jack D. (dec.), Julia Belle Schnabel Klinke, Diane Schnabel Williams Clayton (dec.), Kathlee Mae Schnabel Wong. B.S., Evansville Coll., 1939; Mus.M., Northwestern U., 1947; Ed.D., Ind. U., 1954; B. A. in Fine Arts, So. Ill. U.-Edwardsville, 1975. Dir. bands Evansville Coll., 1937-39; supr. music Carlisle-Haddon Twp. schs., Carlisle, Ind., 1939-42; supr. music, dir. bands Jasper (Ind.) High Sch., 1942-49; asso. prof. music, dir. bands Panhandle A. and M. Coll., Goodwell, Okla., 1949-52; prin. Stratford (Tex.) Ind. Sch., 1952-53; grad. asst. Ind. U., 1953-54; vis. prof. Miami U., Oxford, Ohio, 1954-55; dir. admissions Park Coll., Parkville, Mo., 1955-57; registrar, dir. admissions So. Ill. U., Edwardsville, 1957-67, mem. faculty, 1957-80, prof. edn., 1973-80, prof. emeritus, 1980—, head fine arts div., 1961-62, dir. teaching learning centers, 1972-75, coordinator computer based instrn. lab., 1977-80; cons. computer assisted instrn., 1980-90, mgmt. cons., 1980—, ret., 1996; chmn. bd., chief exec. officer George G. Fetter Co., Louisville, 1970—. Author: An Evaluation of Extra-Class Activities, 1966, Ten Years of University Progres, 1967; others; condr. workshops in oboe and watercolor. Oboist, mem. bd. dirs. Alton (Ill.) Civic Symphony, 1957-61; oboist other orchs., 1929—; adv. council Ednl. Resources Info. Center Ednl. Facilities, U. Wis., Madison, 1965-67; Bd. dirs. Alton Meml. Hosp., 1967—. Served with AUS, 1945. Mem. Assn. Collegiate Registrars (chmn. facilities com. 1965-67), Am. Assn. Collegiate Registrars and Admissions Officers, Am. Assn. Sch. Adminstrs., Council Ednl. Facilities Planning, Am. Assn. Higher Edn., Assn. Ednl. Data Systems, Assn. Devel. Computer Based Instrnl. Systems, Internat. Double Reed Soc. (patron), Phi Delta Kappa, Phi Mu Alpha, Kappa Kappa Psi. Methodist. Club: Rotary. Home and Office: 2305 Fairview Dr Alton IL 62002-5627

SCHNABEL, ROBERT VICTOR, retired academic administrator; b. Scarsdale, N.Y., Sept. 28, 1922; s. Frederick Victor and Louise Elizabeth (Frick) S.; m. Ellen Edyth Foelber, June 7, 1946; children: Mark F., Philip P. Student, Concordia Sem., St. Louis, 1943-45; AB, Bowdoin Coll., 1944; MS, Fordham U., 1951, PhD, 1955; LLD (hon.), Concordia Coll., 1988. Tchr. St. Paul's Sch., Ft. Wayne, Ind., 1945-49; prin. St. Matthew's Sch., N.Y.C., 1949-52; asso. supt. edn. Central Dist., Luth. Ch.-Mo. Synod, 1952-56; asst. prof. philosophy Concordia Sr. Coll., Ft. Wayne, 1956-60, assoc. prof., 1960-65, prof., acad. dean, 1966-71; pres. Concordia Coll., Bronxville, N.Y., 1971-76; acad. v.p., dean Wartburg Coll., Waverly, Iowa, 1976-78; pres. Valparaiso (Ind.) U., 1978-88; cons. Luth. Edn. Conf. N.Am., 1977-88. Contbr. articles to profl. jours. Mem. AAUP, Luth. Acad. Scholarship, Assoc. Colls. Ind., Nat. Assn. Ind. Colls. and Univs., Rotary, Phi Delta Kappa. Office: Valparaiso Univ 23 Huegli Hall Valparaiso IN 46383

SCHNABEL, ROCKWELL ANTHONY, ambassador; b. Amsterdam, Holland, Dec. 30, 1936; came to U.S., 1957; s. Hans and Wilhelmina S.; m. Marna Belle Del Mar, 1964; children: Mary Darrin, Christy Ann, Everton Anthony. Student, Trinity Coll., Haarlem, Netherlands, 1951-56. Pres. Unilife Assurance Group S.H. Luxembourg, 1974-78; dir. Bateman Eichler Hill Richards, Los Angeles, 1967-82, sr. v.p., 1969-82, vice chmn. bd., chmn. exec. com., 1978-82; pres. Bateman Eichler Hill Richard Group, Los Angeles, 1981-83; amb. to Finland U.S. Dept. State; under sec. for travel and tourism U.S. Dept. Commerce, Washington, 1989-91, dep. sec., 1991-92, acting sec. of commerce, 1992-93; ptnr. Trident Capital LLP Inc., L.A., 1992—; bd. dirs. Internat. Game Tech., Amax Gold Inc., Cyprus Amax Minerals Inc., CSG Systems Inc., Pegasus Sys. Anasazi Inc. Past pres. L.A. Pension Bd., Calif., 1982; mem. L.A. Olympic Organizing Com., 1983-84. With Air N.G., 1958-64. Decorated comdr. Order of Good Hope, South Africa, Grand Cross of Lion of Finland; recipient Gold medal Dutch Govt., U.S. Dept. Commerce, medal of honor the Netherlands Olympic Com. Mem. L.A. Beach Club, Calif. Club, L.A. Country Club. Office: Trident Capital Inc 11100 Santa Monica Blvd Los Angeles CA 90025-3384

SCHNABLE, GEORGE LUTHER, chemist; b. Reading, Pa., Nov. 26, 1927; s. L. Irvin and Laura C. (Albright) S.; m. Peggy Jane Butera, May 4, 1957; children: Lee Ann, Joseph G. BS, Albright Coll., 1950; MS, U. Pa., 1951, PhD, 1953. Project engr. Lansdale (Pa.) Tube Co., 1953-58; engring. specialist Philco Corp., Lansdale, 1958-61; mgr. materials and processes Philco-Ford Corp., Blue Bell, Pa., 1961-71; head process rsch. RCA Labs., Princeton, N.J., 1971-80, head device physics and reliability, 1980-87; head device physics and reliability David Sarnoff Rsch. Ctr., Princeton, 1987-91; ind. tech. cons. Schnable Assocs., Lansdale, 1991—. Author: (with others) Advances in Electronics and Electron Physics, 1971, The Chemistry of the Semiconductor Industry, 1987, Microelectronics Reliability, 1989, Microelectronics Manufacturing Diagnostics Handbook, 1993; editor spl. issue RCA Rev., 1984; divsn. editor Jour. of Electrochem. Soc., 1978-90; contbr. 80 articles to profl. publs. With U.S. Army, 1946-47. Fellow AAAS, Am. Inst. Chemists, Electrochem. Soc. (chm. Phila. sect. 1969-71); mem. IEEE (sr.) (assoc. guest editor Proceedings 1974), Alpha Chi Sigma, Phi Lambda Upsilon, Sigma Xi. Achievements include 39 patents (several with others); contributions to semiconductor device fabrication technology and reliability. Home and Office: Schnable Assocs 619 Knoll Dr Lansdale PA 19446-2925

SCHNACK, GAYLE HEMINGWAY JEPSON (MRS. HAROLD CLIFFORD SCHNACK), corporate executive; b. Mpls., Aug. 14, 1926; d. Jasper Jay and Ursula (Hemingway) Jepson; student U. Hawaii, 1946; m. Harold Clifford Schnack, Mar. 22, 1947; children: Jerrald Jay, Georgina, Roberta, Michael Clifford. Skater, Shipstad & Johnson Ice Follies, 1944-46; v.p. Harcliff Corp., Honolulu, 1964—, Schnack Indsl. Corp., Honolulu, 1969—, Nutmeg Corp., Cedar Corp.; ltd. ptnr. Koa Corp. Mem. Internat. Platform Assn., Beta Sigma Phi (chpt. pres. 1955-56, pres. city council 1956-57). Established Ursula Hemingway Jepson art award, Carlton Coll., Ernest Hemingway creative writing award, U. Hawaii. Office: PO Box 3077 Honolulu HI 96802-3077 also: 1200 Riverside Dr Reno NV 89503-5459

SCHNACK, LARRY GENE, university chancellor; b. Harlan, Iowa, Mar. 19, 1937; s. Alvin and Twyla (Kulbom) S.; m. Carol Jean Hansen, Sept. 1, 1955; children—Lorrie, Kevin, Mark, Rachelle. B.S. in Gen. Sci., Iowa State U., 1958, Ph.D. in Organic Chemistry, 1965. Tchr. Emmons High Sch., Minn., 1958-61; mem. faculty, adminstr. U. Wis.-Eau Claire, 1965—, prof. chemistry, 1981—, chancellor, 1985—; bd. dirs. No. States Power Co. Mem. Eau Claire Area Indsl. Devel. Corp., Momentum Chippewa Valley. Recipient DuPont Teaching award Iowa State U., 1965, Disting. Service award Nat. Residence Hall Hon., Eau Claire, Wis., 1984. Mem. Eau Claire Country Club, Rotary (past pres. local club), Eau Claire C. of C. Office: U Wis Office of Chancellor Eau Claire WI 54702-4004

SCHNACKENBERG, ROY LEE, artist; b. Chgo., Jan. 14, 1934; s. Elmer J. and Hazel (Bard) S.; children: Marke, Douglas; m. Shirley Goldman, 1986. B.F.A., Miami U., Oxford, Ohio, 1956. One-man shows include, Joachim Gallery, Chgo., 1962, Main St. Galleries, Chgo., 1963, 64, 66, 68-69, Michael Wyman Gallery, Chgo., 1972, Esther Robles Gallery, Los Angeles, 1973; group exhbns. include print and drawing biennial, Art Inst. Chgo., 1961, Chgo. and Vicinity Show Art Inst. Chgo., 1961, 62, 64, 66-69, 73, 78, Soc. Contemporary Art, Art Inst. Chgo., 1962, 70, New Horizons in Sculpture, Chgo., 1962, 2d ann. art dealers show, N.Y.C., 1963, Ill. Biennial Show, Champaign, 1965, 67, Twelve Chgo. Artists, Walker Mus., Mpls., 1965, also, , Mulvane Art Center, Topeka, 1965, 50 States of Art Exhibit, Burpee Mus., Rockford, Ill.; Recent Aquisitions Exhbn., Whitney Mus., 1967, also, ann. exhbn. painting and sculpture, 1967, 68-69, 69-70, No. Ill. U. group exhbn., Normal, 1968-69, Western Ill. U. show, Macomb, 1968-69, Ill. Arts Council traveling Sculpture exhbn., 1968-69, Des Moines Art Center exhbn., New Am. Realists, Konsthallen, Gotenborg, Sweden, 1970, The Art of Playboy World Tour, Milan, 1971,, Dept. Interior Bicentennial Exhbn., Corcoran Gallery, Washington, 1976,; nat. tour 200 Years of Illustration, N.Y. Hist. Soc.; Zriny-Hayes Gallery, Chgo., 1978, Mitchell Mus., Champaign, Ill., 1980, Continuity and Change, Chgo. Artists, 1983, Snead Gallery, Rockford, Ill., 1985, 89, 91, 93, 94, Chgo. Arts Club; executed mural Crucible, South Chgo. Savs. Bank, 1977; 2d ann. art dealers executed mural, S.E. Savs. & Loan, 1979; represented in permanent collections, Whitney Mus. Am. Art, N.Y.C., Art Inst. Chgo., Mus. Contemporary Art, Chgo., Burpee Art Mus., Rockford, Ill., others. Served with AUS, 1956-58. Recipient Joseph R. Shapiro award New Horizons in Sculpture, Chgo., 1962; Slobe award, 1964; Viehler award, 1965; Logan medal, 1973; Municipal award, 1974; all Art Inst. Chgo.; recipient purchase prize Burpee Mus., 1965, Copley Found. award N.Y.C., 1967. Mem. Arts Club of Chgo., Chgo. Yacht Club.

SCHNAIBERG, ALLAN, sociology educator; b. Montreal, Que., Can., Aug. 20, 1939; came to U.S., 1964; s. Harry and Belle (Katzoff) S.; m. Edith L. Harshbarger, Sept. 1, 1981; children by previous marriage: Lynn Renee, Jill Ann. B.S., McGill U., 1960; M.A., U. Mich., 1964, Ph.D., 1968. Analytical chemist Can. Nat. Rys., Montreal, 1960-61; materials and process engr. Canadair, Ltd., Montreal, 1961-63; asso. dir. West Malaysian Family Survey, Kuala Lumpur, 1966-67; prof. sociology Northwestern U., Evanston, Ill., 1969—; chmn. dept. sociology Northwestern U., 1976-79; cons. Wissenschaftszentrun, Berlin. Author: The Environment: From Surplus to Scarcity, 1992; co-author: Environment and Society: The Enduring Conflict, 1994, Local Environmental Struggles: Citizen Activism in the Treadmill of Production, 1996; co-editor: Distributional Conflicts in Environmental Resource Policy, 1986. Population Council fellow, 1967-68; Nat. Inst. Child Health and Human Devel. research grantee, 1970-72. Mem. Am. Sociol. Assn. (Disting. Contbn. award environ. sociology sect. 1984, chmn. environ. and tech. div. 1991-93), Soc. for Study Social Problems (chmn. environ. problems divsn. 1978-80, mem. C. Wright Mills com. 1979). Home: 6615 N Fairfield Ave Chicago IL 60645-4405 Office: 1810 Chicago Ave Evanston IL 60208-0812 *Learn conventional wisdom, but be prepared to challenge it at all times. What most people agree upon is often wrong, though they won't welcome you bringing this to their attention.*

SCHNAITMAN, WILLIAM KENNETH, finance company executive; b. Talbot County, Md., May 12, 1926; s. William and Catherine Almeda (Cheezum) S.; m. Beverly June Marshall, July 13, 1963. Student, Strayer Bus. Sch., Balt., 1943. Clk. Comml. Credit Co., Balt., 1946-70; asst. sec. Comml. Credit Co., 1970-72, treas., 1972-75, dir. cash mgmt., 1976-87, ret., 1987. With AUS, 1944-46, ETO. Home: 12520 Wye Ln Wye Mills MD 21679-2050

SCHNALL, DAVID JAY, management and administration educator; b. Bklyn., Mar. 20, 1948; married; 3 children. BA in polit. sci., Yeshiva U., 1969, MS in Jewish studies, 1972; MA in polit. sci., Fordham U., 1971, PhD, 1974. Ordained min. Yeshiva U., 1972. Adj. prof. dept. polit. sci. Fordham U., 1971-73; adj. prof. dept. social sci. Rockland Cmty. Coll. SUNY, 1972-73; adj. prof. Judaic studies Bklyn. Coll. CUNY, 1974-76; assoc. prof. dept. polit. sci. Coll. S.I. CUNY, 1972-79; prof. dept. pub. adminstrn. L.I. U., 1979-91; Herbert Schiff prof. mgmt. and adminstrn. Yeshiva U., 1991—; cons. Hadassah Women's Zionist Orgn., 1979-80, Jewish Cmty. Rels. Coun. N.Y., 1985-86, Ctr. Mgmt. Analysis, 1981—, Health Exec. Assistance League, 1985—, United Jewish Appeal, Fedn. of Jewish Philanthropies, Jewish Bd. Family Svcs., N.Y. Gov.'s Office of Employee Rels. Author: The Jewish Agenda: Essays in Contemporary Jewish Life, 1987, Beyond the Green Line: Israeli Settlements West of the Jordan, 1984, Radical Dissent in Contemporary Israeli Politics: Cracks in the Wall, 1979, Ethnicity and Suburban Local Politics, 1975; co-editor: Crisis and Challenge: The Jewish Family in the 21st Century, 1995, Contemporary Issues in Health Care, 1984; contbr. articles to profl. jours. Mem. Orthodox Caucus, N.Y., 1991—, Nat. Orthodox Leadership Conf., N.Y., 1993-95; mem. Coun. on Social Work Edn.; mem. Rabbinical Coun. of Am. Grantee Lucius Littauer

Found., CUNY Rsch. Found., Sigma Xi, Meml. Foun. Jewish Culture, L.I. U. Rsch. Coun.; fellow Nat. Def. Edn. Program, N.Y. State Pub. Adminstrn. Program, Fordham U. Grad. Coun. Mem. Phi Beta Kappa, Pi Sigma Alpha, Pi Alpha Alpha. Democrat. Jewish. Avocations: writing, traveling. Office: Yeshiva Univ B1205 500 W 185th St New York NY 10033-3201

SCHNALL, EDITH LEA (MRS. HERBERT SCHNALL), microbiologist, educator; b. N.Y.C., Apr. 11, 1922; d. Irving and Sadie (Raab) Spitzer; AB, Hunter Coll., 1942; AM, Columbia U., 1947, PhD, 1967; m. Herbert Schnall, Aug. 21, 1949; children: Neil David, Carolyn Beth. Clin. pathologist Roosevelt Hosp., N.Y.C., 1942-44; instr. Adelphi Coll., Garden City, N.Y., 1944-46; asst. med. mycologist Columbia Coll. Physicians and Surgeons, N.Y.C., 1946-47, 49-50; instr. Bklyn. Coll., 1947; mem. faculty Sarah Lawrence Coll., Bronxville, N.Y., 1947-48; lectr. Hunter Coll., N.Y.C., 1947-67; adj. assoc. prof. Lehman Coll., City U. N.Y., 1968; asst. prof. Queensborough Community Coll., City U. N.Y., 1967, assoc. prof. microbiology, 1968-75, prof., 1975—, adminstr. Med. Lab. Tech. Program, 1985—; vis. prof. Coll. Physicians and Surgeons, Columbia U., N.Y.C., 1974; advanced biology examiner U. London, 1970—. Mem. Alley Restoration Com., N.Y.C., 1971—; mem. legis. adv. com. Assembly of the State of N.Y., 1972. Mem. Community Bd. 11, Queens, N.Y., 1974—, 3d vice-chmn., 1987-92, 2nd vice chmn., 1992—; public dir. of bd. dirs. Inst. Continuing Dental Edn. Queens County, Dental Soc. N.Y. State and ADA, 1973—. Rsch. fellow NIH, 1948-49; faculty rsch. fellow, grantee-in-aid Rsch. Found. of SUNY, 1968-70; faculty rsch. grant Rsch. Found. City U. N.Y., 1971-74. Mem. Internat. Soc. Human and Animal Mycology, AAAS, Am. Soc. Microbiology (coun., N.Y.C. br. 1981—, co-chairperson ann. meeting com. 1981-82, chair program com. 1982-83, v.p. 1984-86, pres. 1986-88), Med. Mycology Soc. N.Y. (sec.-treas. 1967-68, v.p. 1968-69, 78-79, archivist 1974—, fin. advisor 1983—, pres. 1969-70, 79-80, 81-82), Bot. Soc. Am., Med. Mycology Soc. Americas, Mycology Soc. Am., N.Y. Acad. Scis., Sigma Xi, Phi Sigma. Clubs: Torrey Botanical (N.Y. State); Queensborough Community Coll. Women's (pres. 1971-73) (N.Y.C.). Editor: Newsletter of Med. Mycology Soc. N.Y., 1969-85; founder, editor Female Perspective newsletter of Queensborough Community Coll. Women's Club, 1971-73. Home: 21406 29th Ave Flushing NY 11360-2622

SCHNAPF, ABRAHAM, aerospace engineer, consultant; b. N.Y.C., Aug. 1, 1921; s. Meyer and Gussie (Schaeffler) S.; m. Edna Wilensky, Oct. 24, 1943; children: Donald J., Bruce M. BSME, CCNY, 1948; MSME, Drexel Inst. Tech., 1953. Registered profl. engr., N.J. Devel. engr. on lighter-than-air aircraft Goodyear Aircraft Corp., Akron, Ohio, 1948-50; mgr. fire control system def. electronics RCA, Camden, N.Y., 1950-55, mgr. airbourne navigation system, aerospace weapon system, 1955-58; program mgr. TIROS/TOS weather satellite systems RCA Astro-Electronics, Princeton, N.J., 1958-70, mgr. satellite programs, 1970-79, prin. scientist, 1979-82; cons. Aerospace Systems Engring., Willingboro, N.J., 1982—; lectr., presenter on meteor. satellites, space tech., communication satellites. Sgt. USAF, 1943-46. Recipient award Nat. Press Club Washington, 1975, award Am. Soc. Quality Control-NASA, 1968, Pub. Svc. award NASA, 1969, cert. of appreciation U.S. Dept. Commerce, 1984, RCA David Sarnoff award; inducted into Space Tech. Hall of Fame, 1992; named to 5000 Personalities of the World, named Internat. Man. of Yr. 1992-93. Fellow AIAA; mem. Am. Astro. Soc., Am. Meterol. Soc., Space Pioneers, N.Y. Acad. Scis. (mem. think tank week sessions 1980's), N.J. Arbitration Soc. Home and Office: 41 Pond Ln # 160 Willingboro NJ 08046-2756

SCHNAPP, ROGER HERBERT, lawyer; b. N.Y.C., Mar. 17, 1946; s. Michael Jay and Beatrice Joan (Becker) S.; m. Candice Jacqueline Larson, Sept. 15, 1979; 1 child, Monica Alexis. *Father Michael Jay Schnapp was a respected entrepreneur and businessman on the East Coast until his retirement. He introduced innovative approaches in each of the industries in which he held leadership positions. Daughter Monica Alexis Schnapp attends the Pegasus School, a school which specializes in the education of intellectually gifted children* BS, Cornell U., 1966; JD, Harvard U., 1969; postgrad. Pub. Utility Mgmt. Program, U. Mich., 1978. Bar: N.Y. 1970, U.S. Ct. Appeals (2d cir.) 1970, U.S. Supreme, 1974, U.S. Dist. Ct. (so. dist.) N.Y. 1975, U.S. Ct. Appeals (4th and 6th cirs.) 1976, U.S. Ct. Appeals (7th cir.) 1977, U.S. Dist. Ct. (so. dist.) N.Y. 1975, U.S. Dist. Ct. (no. dist.) Calif. 1980, U.S. Ct. Appeals (8th cir.) 1980, Calif., 1982, U.S. Dist. Ct. (cen. dist.) Calif. 1982, U.S. Ct. Dist. (ea. dist.) Calif., 1984. Atty. CAB, Washington, 1969-70; labor atty. Western Electric Co., N.Y.C., 1970-71; mgr. employee rels. Am. Airlines, N.Y.C., 1971-74; labor counsel Am. Electric Power Svc. Corp., N.Y.C., 1974-78, sr. labor counsel, 1978-80; indsl. rels. counsel Trans World Airlines, N.Y.C., 1980-81; sr. assoc. Parker, Milliken, Clark & O'Hara, L.A., 1981-82; ptnr. Rutan & Tucker, Costa Mesa, Calif., 1983-84, Memel, Jacobs, Pierno, Gersh & Ellsworth, Newport Beach, Calif., 1985-86, Memel, Jacobs & Ellsworth, Newport Beach, 1986-87; pvt. practice, Newport Beach, 1987—; AV rated by Martindale Hubbell; bd. dirs. Dynamic Constrn., Inc., Laguna Hills, Calif., 1986—; commentator labor rels. Fin. News Network; commentator Sta. KOCN Radio, 1990-91; lectr. Calif. Western Law Sch., Calif. State U.-Fullerton, Calif. State Conf. Small Bus.; lectr. collective bargaining Pace U., N.Y.C.; lectr. on labor law Coun. on Edn. in Mgmt.; Nat. Vice Chmn., Finance Committee, National Republican Senatorial Committee, N.E. regional coord. Pressler for Pres., 1979-80. Mem. Bus. Rsch. Adv. Coun. U.S. Dept. Labor, Labor Law Consulting Group; bd. dirs. Legal Specialization; trustee Chapman U., 1991-95. Mem. Calif. Bar Assn., Labor Law Consulting Group, Calif. Bd. of Legal Specialization, Balboa Bay Club, The Ctr. Club. Republican. Jewish. Author: Arbitration Issues for the 1980s, 1981, A Look at Three Companies, 1982; editor-in-chief Indsl. and Labor Rels. Forum, 1964-66; columnist Orange County Bus. Jour., 1989-91; contbr. articles to profl. publs. Office: PO Box 9049 Newport Beach CA 92658-1049 *During a 28-year career in employment law, Roger Schnapp has been highly successful in assisting international, nationwide and California employers (including nonprofit organizations) with union avoidance and decertification of existing union representatives, with collective bargaining negotiations providing significant relief from limitations on management's ability to manage, with the development of individualized personnel policies and procedures which permitted these employers to manage in the most cost effective manner and in litigation before courts (including the Supreme Court of the United States), administrative agencies and arbitrators.*

SCHNARE, ROBERT EDEY, JR., library director; b. Morristown, N.J., Dec. 31, 1944; s. Robert Edey and Olive Margaret (Flatt) S.; m. MaryKay Wise, Aug. 29, 1970; 1 child, Katharine Grace. BA, William Paterson Coll., 1967; MLS, U. Pitts., 1968; MA, U. Conn., 1971. Reference libr. history dept. Conn. State Libr., Hartford, 1968-73; head spl. collections U.S. Mil. Acad. Libr., West Point, N.Y., 1973-86; libr. dir. U.S. Naval War Coll., Newport, R.I., 1986—; chmn. Consortium of R.I. Acad. and Rsch. Librs., Providence, 1991-93; bd. dirs. Coalition of Libr. Aovocates, Providence, 1991—; chmn. edn. and tng. com. R.I. Preservation Planning Grant, 1991-92; del. White House Conf. on Libr. and Info. Svcs., 1990—; chmn. preservation working group New England Libr. Network, Newton, Mass., 1992—; mem. com. on mgmt. Anne S.K. Brown Mil. Collection, 1987—; mem. Mid-Atlantic Archivist Conf., 1973—; mem. preservation working group Fed. Libr. Info. Ctr. Com., 1991—. Publ. editor Conservation Adminstrn. News, 1979-87, mem. editl. bd., 1987-94; contbr. articles to profl. jours., chpt. to book; compiler Union List of Mil. Edn. Coordinating Com. Library Resources, 1994. Chmn. gifted adv. coun. Providence Bd. Edn., 1990-92; chmn. stewardship St. Martin's Episcopal Ch., Providence, 1990; vol. Providence schs., 1992—. Named Disting. Grad., William Paterson Coll., 1985; recipient Disting. Svc. award Conservation Adminstrn. News, 1987, 94, Dept. of the Army's Comdr.'s award for civilian svc. U.S. Mil. Acad., 1987, Navy Dept.'s Meritorious Civilian Svc. award Naval War Coll., 1995. Mem. ALA (chmn. William Young Boyd Mil. Novel award jury 1997), Spl. Librs. Assn., Assn. for Study Conn. History, New Eng. Archivists. Office: US Naval War Coll Libr 686 Cushing Rd Newport RI 02841-1201

SCHNECK, GARY ALAN, securities broker; b. Larned, Kans., Apr. 17, 1953; s. Lawrence and Janice H. (Younkin) S.; m. Beverly Jane Taylor, Mar. 29, 1980; 1 child, Eric Lawrence. BSME, Kans. State U., 1975, MSME, 1976. CFP. Design engr. Fisher Controls, Marshalltown, Iowa, 1976-78; process control engr. Celanese Chem., Pampa, Tex., 1978-81; process control group leader Celanese Chem., Pampa, 1981-83; securities broker Edward D. Jones & Co., Borger, Tex., 1983—; ltd. ptnr. Jones Fin. Cos., Maryland Heights, Mo., 1986—. Chmn. Hutchinson County Red Cross, Borger, 1987-88; v.p. Frank Phillips Coll. Devel. Corp., Borger, 1991-92. Mem. Borger C. of C. (pres. 1991-92, bd. dirs. 1997), Borger Independ. Sch. Dist. (trustee 1996), Rotary (pres. 1988-89, named Paul Harris fellow 1989). Republican. Methodist. Avocations: flying, boating, golfing, tennis, travel. Office: Edward D Jones & Co 605 W 3rd St Borger TX 79007-4007

SCHNECK, JEROME M., psychiatrist, medical historian, educator; b. N.Y.C., Jan. 2, 1920; s. Maurice and Rose (Weiss) S.; m. Shirley R. Kaufman, July 24, 1943. AB, Cornell U., 1939; MD, SUNY-Bklyn., 1943. Diplomate Am. Bd. Psychiatry and Neurology. Intern Interfaith Med. Ctr., 1943; mem. psychiat. staff Menninger Clinic, Topeka, 1944-45; chief psychiatry and sociology dept. Fort Missoula, Mont., 1946, Camp Cooke, Calif., 1947; mem. psychiat. staff L.I. Coll. Hosp., 1947-48, Kings County Hosp., 1948-70, SUNY Hosp., Bklyn., 1955-70; assoc. vis. psychiatrist Kings County Hosp., 1949-70; mem. psychiat. staff State U. Hosp., Bklyn., 1955-70; pvt. practice N.Y.C., 1947—; attending psychiatrist St. Vincent's Hosp. and Med. Ctr. N.Y., 1970—, hon. sr. psychiatrist, 1990—; psychiat. cons. VA Regional Office, 1947-48, N.Y. State Dept. Social Svcs., 1977-83, N.Y. State Dept. Civil Svc., 1978-84, N.Y. State Office Ct. Adminstrn., 1978-85, N.Y. State Dept. Edn., 1981-83; dir. Mt. Vernon Mental Hygiene Clinic, 1947-52; assoc. chief psychiatrist Westchester County Dept. Health, 1949-50, cons., 1951-52; clin. instr. L.I. Coll. Medicine, 1947-50; clin. assoc. SUNY Coll. Medicine, Bklyn., 1950-53, asst. prof., 1955-58, assoc. prof., 1958-70; supervising psychiatrist Community Guidance Svcs., 1955-70; cons. coun. on mental health AMA, 1956-58; cons. NBC, 1962, Ctr. Rsch. in Hypnotherapy, 1964-70; vis. lectr. N.Y. Med. Coll.-Met. Hosp., 1965; faculty Am. Inst. Psychotherapy and Psychoanalysis, 1970-85. Author: Hypnosis in Modern Medicine, 1953, 2d edit., 1959, Spanish lang. edit., 1962, 3rd edit., 1963, Studies in Scientific Hypnosis, 1954, A History of Psychiatry, 1960, The Principles and Practice of Hypnoanalysis, 1965 (Best Book award Soc. For Clin. and Exptl. Hypnosis 1965); editor: Hypnotherapy, Hypnosis and Personality, 1951; author over 400 med. and sci. publs., book chpts., articles; mem. bd. editors: Personality: Symposia on Topical Issues, 1960-61, Jour. Integrative and Eclectic Psychotherapy, 1986-89; contbg. editor Psychosomatics, 1961-75; mem. editorial bd. Voices—The Art and Science of Psychotherapy, 1965; features editor The Interne, 1942, co-editor, 1943. Capt. AUS, 1945-47. Recipient Clarence B. Farrar award Clarke Inst. of Psychiatry, U. Toronto, 1976. Fellow AAAS, APA, Am. Med. Authors, Acad. Psychosomatic Medicine, Am. Psychiat. Assn. (life), Soc. for Clin. and Exptl. Hypnosis (life, founder, founding pres. 1949-56, exec. coun. 1949—, assoc. editor jour. 1953—, Award of Merit 1955, Gold medal 1958, Bernard B. Raginsky award 1966, Shirley Schneck award 1970, Roy M. Dorcus award 1980, Spl. Presdl. award 1986), Am. Acad. Psychotherapists (co-founder, v.p. 1956-58), Am. Med. Writers Assn., Am. Soc. Psychoanalytic Physicians (founding fellow, bd. dirs. 1958-62), Am. Soc. Clin. Hypnosis (life mem.), Internat. Soc. Clin. and Exptl. Hypnosis (co-founder, bd. dirs. 1958-68, founding fellow), Internat. Acad. Eclectic Psychotherapists (charter fellow); mem. AMA, Soc. Acad. Achievement (charter), Soc. Apothecaries London, Inst. Practicing Psychotherapists, Pan Am. Med. Assn. (v.p. sect. clin. hypnosis 1960-65, N.Am. v.p. 1966), N.Y. Soc. Med. History (exec. com. 1956-62), Am. Bd. Med. Hypnosis (founder, pres. 1958-60, life bd. dirs.), Inst. Rsch. in Hypnosis Inc. (bd. dirs., bd. editors 1957-70), Am. Assn. History Medicine, History of Sci. Soc., Assn. Advancement Psychotherapy (charter) Can. Med. History Assn., N.Y. Soc. for Clin. Psychiatry (chmn. com. on history of psychiatry), Charles F. Menninger Soc., Sigma Xi. Address: 26 W 9th St New York NY 10011-8971

SCHNECK, PAUL BENNETT, computer scientist; b. N.Y.C., Aug. 15, 1945; s. Irving and Doris (Grossman) S.; m. Marjorie Ann Axelrod, Feb. 5, 1967; children: Phyllis Adele, Melanie Jane. BS, Columbia U., 1965, MS, 1966; PhD, NYU Courant Inst. Math. Scis., 1979. Computer scientist Inst. for Space Studies, N.Y.C., 1970-76; program mgr. Goddard Space Flight Ctr., Greenbelt, Md., 1976-79; asst. to dir. Goddard Space Flight Ctr., Greenbelt, 1979-80, chief info. extraction div., 1980-81, asst. dir., 1981-83; head info. sci. div. Office of Naval Rsch., Arlington, Va., 1983-85; dir. Supercomputing Rsch. Ctr., Bowie, Md., 1985-93; chief scientist Inst. Defense Analyses, 1993; fellow Mitre Corp., McLean, Va., 1993-96, dir. info. sys. and fellow, 1994-96; dir. info. sys. and fellow Mitretek Systems, Inc., McLean, Va., 1996-97; chief technologist MRJ Tech. Solutions, Fairfax, Va., 1997—; vice chmn. bd. Nat. Info. Tech. Ctr., 1993, chmn. bd., CEO, 1994, exec. com., 1994-97; mem. adv. bd. Inst. Computational Sci. and Informatics, George Mason U., 1995—; mem. adv. bd. computer scis. U. Md., College Park, 1989-95; tchr. Columbia U., Johns Hopkins U., U. Md. Author: Supercomputer Architecture, 1987; contbr. articles to Ency. of Computer Sci. and Tech., Ann. Rev. of Computer Sci., Ency. Phys. Sci. and Tech. Yearbook. Fellow IEEE, Assn. for Computing Machinery; mem. Brit. Computer Soc., Engring. Coun. (chartered engr., Eng.). Achievements include management of Massively Parallel Processor project, 1980-81; design and implementation of the science supervisory system in use at NASA from 1968-83, on the IBM 360/95 and 370/165, and the Amdahl 470/V6, V7; and of the vector/parallel compiler. Office: MRJ Tech Solutions 10560 Arrowhead Dr Fairfax VA 22030-7305

SCHNECK, STUART AUSTIN, retired neurologist, educator; b. N.Y.C., Apr. 1, 1929; s. Maurice and Sara Ruth (Knapp) S.; m. Ida I. Nakashima, Mar. 2, 1956; children—Lisa, Christopher. B.S. magna cum laude, Franklin and Marshall Coll., 1949; M.D., U. Pa., 1953. Diplomate Am. Bd. Psychiatry and Neurology (bd. dirs., sec. 1990-91, v.p. 1991-92, pres. 1992-93). Intern Hosp. U. Pa., Phila., 1953-54; resident in medicine U. Colo. Med. Center, Denver, 1954-55, 57-58, resident in neurology, 1958-61; instr. neurology U. Colo. Sch. Medicine, 1959-61; instr. neuropathology Columbia U., N.Y.C., 1961-63; vis. fellow in neurology Vanderbilt Clinic, Columbia-Presbyn. Med. Center, N.Y.C., 1961-63; asst. prof. neurology and pathology U. Colo., 1963-67, assoc. prof., 1967-70, prof., 1970-95, assoc. dean clin. affairs Sch. Medicine, 1984-89, emeritus prof., 1996—; cons. Fitzsimons Army Hosp., VA, Nat. Jewish Hosp.; pres. med. bd. Univ. Hosp., Denver, 1983-89, bd. dirs., 1989-90. Contbr. articles to profl. jours. Served with USAF, 1955-57. USPHS fellow, 1961-63. Mem. AAAS, Am. Acad. Neurology, Am. Assn. Neuropathologists, Am. Neurol. Assn., Alpha Omega Alpha (bd. dirs. 1979-89, treas., pres. 1990-93).

SCHNEE, ALIX SANDRA, historic site administrator; b. Bern, Switzerland, May 9, 1949; d. Alexander and Helen Louise (Jurkops) S.; m. Enrico Anthony Giordano, Jan. 16, 1982; 1 child, Alexander Cole Giordano. BA, Am. U., 1971; EdD, Colgate U., N.Y.C., 1987. Edn. specialist Horace Mann Lincoln Inst., N.Y.C., 1982-83; program coord. Tchrs. Coll. Colgate U., 1985-87; cons. The Harlem Sch. for Arts, N.Y.C., 1989-90; evaluator N.Y. Coun. for Humanities Colgate U., 1991; cons. The Dalton Sch., N.Y.C., 1990-92; hist. site mgr. Philipse Manor Hall State Hist. Site N.Y. State, Yonkers, 1992—; adj. prof. N.Y. Inst. Tech., N.Y.C., 1992; mem. Landmarks Planning Commn., Yonkers, 1997, Property Coun. Lyndhurst, N.Y., 1996-97; mem. exec. com. Lower Hudson Conf., Elmsford, N.Y., 1993—; bd. dirs. Hudson River Comty. Assn. Mem. adv. com. Yonkers Foxfire Sch. Mem. Downtown Yonkers Mgmt. Assn., East Yonkers Rotary. Avocations: art, swimming, tennis. Home: 94 Grove St Yonkers NY 10701 Office: Philipse Manor Hall State Hist Site PO Box 496 Yonkers NY 10702

SCHNEEMAN, BARBARA OLDS, agricultural studies educator; b. Seattle, Oct. 3, 1948; d. William Arthur and Rose (Antush) Olds; m. Paul Schneeman, Mar. 23, 1974; 1 child, Eric. BS in Food Sci. and Tech., U. Calif., Davis, 1970; PhD in Nutrition, U. Calif., Berkeley, 1974. NIH postdoctoral fellow gastrointestinal physiology Children's Hosp., Oakland, Calif., 1974-76; asst. prof. nutrition dept. nutrition and food sci. & tech. U. Calif., Davis, 1976-82, assoc. prof. nutrition, 1982-86, prof. nutrition, nutritionist, 1986—, prof. dept. internal medicine divsn. clin. nutrition, 1986—, assoc. dean Coll. Agrl. and Environ. Scis., 1985-88, chair dept. nutrition, 1988-93, dean Coll. Agrl. and Environ. Scis., 1993—, dir. programs. divsn. agr. and natural resources, 1993—; vis. scientist Cardiovascular Rsch. Inst., U. Calif., San Francisco, 1991-92; lectr. women in sci. series Coll. St. Catherine, St. Paul, 1987; adv. dir. Blue Cross Calif., 1992-95; mem. dietary guidelines for Ams. adv. com. to Secs. of Agr., Health and Human Svcs., 1989-90, 94-95; mem. expert panel on food safety and nutrition Inst. Food Technologists, 1985-91; mem. external adv. bd. Post Ctr. for Nutrition and Health, 1989-90; councilor Soc. for Exptl. Biology and Medicine, 1988-91. Assoc. editor Jour. Nutrition, 1991-94; contbg. editor Nutrition Revs., 1982-90; editl. bd. Jour. Nutrition, 1982-87, Procs. for Soc. Exptl. Biology and Medicine, 1985-91, Acad. Press: Food Sci. and Nutrition, 1988—. Fellow NDEA, U. Calif., Berkeley; food sci. scholar; recipient Outstanding Cmty. Svc. award Tierra del Oro coun. Girl Scouts U.S., 1995, Future Leaders award for rsch. Nutrition Found., 1978-80, Samuel Cate Prescott award for rsch. Inst. Food Tech., 1985, Farma Food Internat. Fibre prize, Copenhagen, 1989. Mem. AAAS, Inst. Food Technologists (sec.-treas. nutrition divsn. 1988-89), Am. Physiol. Soc., Am. Inst. Nutrition (treas. 1989-92), Am. Heart Assn. (fellow arteriosclerosis coun.). Office: U Calif Davis Coll Agrl and Environ Scis Davis CA 95616

SCHNEEMANN, CAROLEE, painter, performing artist, filmmaker, writer; b. Pa., Oct. 12, 1939. B.A., Bard Coll., 1960; M.F.A., U. Ill., 1961. Originated Kinetic Theater, 1962; with Judson Dance Theater, 1962-66; performance works, film showings throughout U.S. and Europe; (erotic film) Fuses, 1964-68, Kitch's Last Meal, 1973-78; (video tapes) Up To and Including Her Limits, 1974-77, Interior Scroll—The Cave, 1995; performance installations include Art Inst. Chgo., 1980; performance tour Fresh Blood—A Dream Morphology, France, Belgium, Holland, 1981, Enter...Vulva, 1996, 97; (books) Parts of a Body House Book, 1972, Cezanne, She Was A Great Painter, 1974, ABC—We Print Anything—In the Cards, 1979, More than Meat Joy, Complete Performance Works and Selected Writings, 1979 and 1997; exhbns. Whitney Mus., 1984, 85, 93, 95, Mus. Modern Art, N.Y.C., 1992, 95, 96, Ctr. Georges Pompidou, Paris, 1995, 96, New Mus., N.Y.C., 1992, 95, 96, 97, Retrospective at New Mus. Contemporary Art, 1996/97. Guggenheim fellow 1993; grantee NEA, 1974, 77-78, 83, Gottlieb Found., 1987, Pollock-Krasner Found., 1996. Office: 437 Springtown Rd New Paltz NY 12561-3027

SCHNEEWIND, JEROME BORGES, philosophy educator; b. Mt. Vernon, N.Y., May 17, 1930; s. Jerome John and Charlotte (Borges) S.; m. Elizabeth G.R. Hughes, Feb. 23, 1963; children: Sarah, Rachel, Hannah. B.A., Cornell U., 1951; M.A., Princeton U., 1953, Ph.D., 1957. Instr. philosophy U. Chgo., 1957-60, Princeton U., 1960-61; asst. prof. Yale U., 1961-63; asso. prof. philosophy U. Pitts., 1964-68, prof., 1968-75, dean Coll. Arts and Scis., 1969-73; v.p., provost Hunter Coll., CUNY, 1975-81; prof. philosophy Johns Hopkins U., Balt., 1981—, chmn. dept., 1981-91; philosophy adviser Ency. Americana, 1967—; mem. adv. bd. sci. tech. and values program NEH, 1975-78; mem. Coun. for Phil. Studies, 1975-80. Author: Backgrounds of English Victorian Literature, 1970, Sidgwick's Ethics and Victorian Moral Philosophy, 1977; editor: Moral Philosophy From Montaigne to Kant, 1990; editorial bd. Victorian Studies, 1968-75, The Monist, 1969-76, Am. Philosophy Quar., 1975-77, Philos. Studies, 1975-78, Jour. of History Ideas, 1985—, pres. bd. dirs., 1988—; contbr. articles on ethics and history of ethics to publs. Served with Signal Corps, AUS, 1954-56. Mellon postdoctoral fellow, 1963-64; Guggenheim fellow, 1967-68; Am. Council Learned Socs. grantee, 1973; NEH sr. fellow, 1974, Ctr. for Advanced Study in the Behavioral Scis., 1992-93. Fellow AAAS; mem. Am. Philos. Assn. (exec. com. Ea. divsn. 1964-67, chmn. com. on teaching philosophy 1973-78, nominating com. 1986-88, v.p. Ea. divsn. 1994-95, pres. 1995-96). Office: Philosophy Dept Johns Hopkins U Baltimore MD 21218

SCHNEIBEL, VICKI DARLENE, public relations administrator; b. Astoria, Oreg., Mar. 11, 1946; d. Howard Stanley and Sally (Thompson) Brandt; m. Lawrence Walter Schneibel, Mar. 18, 1967. AAS, Anchorage Community Coll., 1986; BA, Alaska Pacific U., 1991, MAT, 1994. Cert. profl. sec. Clk. typist The Oregonian, Portland, Oreg., 1964-67; statis. typist Rader Pneumatics, Inc., Portland, Oreg., 1967-71; sec., bookkeeper Larry's Custom Remodeling, Portland, Oreg., 1971-73; bookkeeper Tualatin Hills Pk. & Recreation Dist., Portland, Oreg., 1973-74; pvt. sec. Aloha (Oreg.) Community Bapt. Ch., 1974-79; exec. sec. Hyster Sales Co., Tigard, Oreg., 1979-83, 1st Nat. Bank of Anchorage, 1983-84; office mgr. Control Data Alaska, Anchorage, 1984-86; human resource adminstr. Westmark Hotels, Inc., Anchorage, 1986—; cmty. adv. bd. mgr. Holland Am. Line (parent co. Westmark Hotels, Inc.), 1996—; Cmty. Advisory Bd. Mgr. for Holland America Line (parent co. of Westmark Hotels, Inc.). Author: Let Sleeping Moose Lie, Good Dog!, 1994. Active Anchorage Women's Commn., 1995—, Alaska Worksite Wellness Alliance. Mem. ASTD, Am. Mgmt. Assn., Soc. For Human Resource Mgmt. Lutheran. Avocations: reading, tennis, walking, writing, camping. Home: 6646 Cimarron Cir Anchorage AK 99504-3945 Office: Holland Am Lines 510 L St Ste 400 Anchorage AK 99501-1956

SCHNEIDER, ADELE SANDRA, clinical geneticist; b. Johannesburg, South Africa, Mar. 21, 1949; came to U.S., 1976, naturalized, 1981; d. Michael and Annette (Sive) S.; m. Gordon Mark Cohen, July 2, 1978; children: Jeffrey, Brian, Adrienne. MB, BChir, Witwatersrand U., Johannesburg, South Africa, 1973. Intern in internal medicine Baragwanath Hosp., Johannesburg, 1974, intern in gen. surgery, 1974; sr. house officer in pediatrics Coronation Hosp., Johannesburg, 1975; sr. house officer in radiation therapy Johannesburg Gen. Hosp., 1975-76; resident in pediatrics Wilmington (Del.) Med. Ctr., 1976-78; fellow in clin. genetics and metabolic diseases Children's Hosp. of Phila., 1978-81, staff physician Cystic Fibrosis Clinic, 1987-88; staff pediatrician Children's Rehab. Hosp., Phila., 1981-82, dir. pediatrics, 1982-87, acting med. dir., 1984-85; clin. instr. dept. pediatrics Jefferson Med. Coll., Phila., 1982-84, clin. asst. prof. dept. pediatrics, 1984—; clin. geneticist Hahnemann Univ. Hosp., Phila., 1987-90, asst. clin. prof. dept. pediatrics and neoplastic diseases, 1987-90; clin. geneticist Albert Einstein Med. Ctr., Phila., 1990-92, acting dir. med. genetics, 1992-93, dir. clin. genetics program, 1993—; mem. courtesy faculty Sch. Medicine Temple U., Phila., 1987; clin. geneticist St. Christopher's Hosp. for Children, Phila., 1987; genetics cons. dept. pediatrics Bryn Mawr (Pa.) Hosp.; presenter, lectr. in field. Contbr. articles to profl. jours. Bd. dirs. Phila. Parenting Associates, 1986-93. Fellow Am. Coll. Med. Genetics; mem. Am. Soc. Human Genetics, Am. Chem. Soc. Office: Albert Einstein Med Ctr Dept Pediatrics 5501 Old York Rd Philadelphia PA 19141-3001

SCHNEIDER, ALLAN STANFORD, biochemistry neurosience and pharmacology educator, biomedical research scientist; b. N.Y.C., Sept. 26, 1940; s. Harry and Edith (Gonsky) S.; m. Mary-Jane Beekman Tunis, Dec. 14, 1968; children: Henry Seth, Joseph Benjamin. B.Chem. Enging., Rensselaer Poly. Inst., 1961; M.S., Pa. State U., 1963; Ph.D., U. Calif.-Berkeley, 1968. Chem. engr. E.I. du Pont de Nemours & Co. Exptl. Sta., Wilmington, Del., 1963-64; postdoctoral fellow Weizmann Inst. Sci., Rehovot, Israel, 1969-71; staff fellow NIH, Bethesda, Md., 1971-73; assoc. Sloan-Kettering Inst. Cancer Research, N.Y.C., 1974-80, assoc. mem., 1980-85; asst. prof. Cornell U. Grad. Sch. Med. Scis., N.Y.C., 1974-80, assoc. prof. biochemistry, 1981-83, assoc. prof. cell biology and genetic, 1983-85, chmn. biochemistry unit Sloan-Kettering div., 1982-83; assoc. prof. pharmacology and toxicology Albany (N.Y.) Med. Coll., N.Y., 1985-86, prof. pharmacology and toxicology, 1986-94; prof. pharmacology and neurosci. Albany (N.Y.) Med. Coll., 1995—; dir. grad. studies Albany (N.Y.) Med. Coll., N.Y., 1987-91; vis. prof. Weizmann Inst. Sci., Rehovot, Israel, 1987; vis. rsch. scholar U. Bergen, Norway, 1989, 95. Contbr. chpts to books, sci. articles to profl. jours. Rsch. grantee Am. Cancer Soc., 1980-83, Am. Heart Assn., 1977-82, 90-93, NIH, 1982-93, NSF, 1977-79, Cystic Fibrosis Found., 1980-82; established investigator Am. Heart Assn., 1977-82. Mem. Am. Soc. Biochemistry and Molecular Biology, Biophys. Soc., Soc. Neurosci., Am. Heart Assn. (coun. on basic sci. 1977-95), Phi Lambda Upsilon, Tau Beta Pi (internat. sci. adv. com. for chromaffin cell biology 1987-93). Achievements include first isolation and characterization of chromaffin cells of the adrenal gland now widely used as a model neuronal cell culture system; determination of the relation between cytosolic calcium signals and neurohormone (adrenaline) secretion, relevant to cellular mechanism of hormone and neurotransmitter release; spectroscopic characterization of protein structure in situ in biomembranes and cells; theoretical and experimental analysis of optical activity spectra of turbid biological suspensions; research on neurochemistry of adrenal chromaffin cells, regulation of hormone and neurotransmitter release and mechanisms of nicotine dependence. Office: Dept Pharmacology & Neurosci Albany Med Coll A 136 Albany NY 12208

SCHNEIDER, ARTHUR PAUL, retired videotape and film editor, author; b. Rochester, N.Y., Jan. 26, 1930; s. Mendell Phillip and Frieda (Bl) S.; m. Helen Deloise Thompson, June 5, 1954; children: Robert Paul, Lori Ann. Student, U. So. Calif., 1953. With NBC, 1951-68, film and videotape editor, 1953-60, developer double system method of editing video tape, 1958; pres. Burbank (Calif.) Film Editing, Inc., 1968-72, Electronic Video Industries Inc., 1977-79; supr. video tape editing Consol. Film Industries Inc.,

Hollywood, Calif., 1972-76, editorial supr., 1980-83; pvt. practice editing, 1983-88; cons., lectr., author. Film and tape editor all: Bob Hope shows, 1960-67; supr. NBC kinescope and video tape editors (1966-67); video tape editor: Laugh-In Series, 1967-68; video tape editor: Comedy Shop Series, 1977-80; post-prodn. cons. to Video Systems and Broadcast Engrng. mag.; video tape editor: TV series Sonny & Cher, 1973, Sonny Comedy Revue, 1974, Tony Orlando and Dawn, 1974, Hudson Bros., summer, 1974, Dean Martin Series, 1975-76, Mickey Mouse Club Series, Walt Disney Prodns., 1976, Redd Foxx Series, 1977; (author: Electronic Post Production and Videotape Editing, 1989 (pub. in Chinese 1995), Electronic Post Production Terms and Concepts, 1990; contbg. author: Association of Cinema and Video Laboratores (ACVL) Handbook, 5th edit., 1995, Focal Guide to Electronic Media CDRom Version, 1997, Jump Cut: Memoirs of a Pioneer Television Editor, 1997; contbr. articles to publs. in field. Recipient Broadcast Preceptor award San Francisco State U., 1975; named hon. Ky. Col. Mem. Acad. Television Arts and Scis. (Emmy nominations and Emmy award for video tape editing 1966, 68, 73, 84, gov. 1977-80, sec. 1980-81), Am. Cinema Editors (life), Soc. Motion Picture and TV Engrs., Delta Kappa Alpha (life). Home: PO Box 156 Fish Camp CA 93623-0156

SCHNEIDER, ARTHUR SANFORD, physician, educator; b. Los Angeles, Mar. 24, 1929; s. Max and Fannie (Ragin) S.; m. Edith Kadison, Aug. 20, 1950; children: Jo Ann Schneider Farris, William Scott, Lynnellen. B.S., UCLA, 1951; M.D., Chgo. Med. Sch., 1955. Diplomate Am. Bd. Internal Medicine, Am. Bd. Pathology. Intern, Wadsworth VA Hosp., Los Angeles, 1955-56; resident Wadsworth VA Hosp., 1956-59, chief clin. pathology sect., 1962-68; mem. faculty UCLA, 1961-75, clin. assoc. prof., 1971-75; chmn. dept. clin. pathology City of Hope Med. Ctr., Duarte, Calif., 1968-75; prof., chmn. dept. clin. pathology Whittier Coll., 1974-75; prof., chmn. dept. pathology Chgo. Med. Sch., 1975—; chief lab. service VA Med. Ctr., North Chicago, Ill., 1975-86, chief lab. hematology, 1986-94. Contbr. numerous chpts. to books and articles to med. jours. Served to capt. M.C., USAF, 1959-61. Fellow ACP, Coll. Am. Pathologists, Am. Soc. Clin. Pathologists; mem. AAUP, AMA, Internat. Acad. Pathology, Am. Assn. for Investigative Pathology, Assn. Pathology Chairmen, Acad. Clin. Lab. Physicians and Scientists, Am. Soc. Hematology, Am. Assn. Blood Banks, Am. Soc. Clin. Rsch., Ill. Med. Soc., Lake County Med. Soc., Sigma Xi, Alpha Omega Alpha, Phi Delta Epsilon. Office: Chgo Med Sch 3333 Green Bay Rd North Chicago IL 60064-3037

SCHNEIDER, BENJAMIN, psychology educator; b. N.Y.C., Aug. 11, 1938; s. Leo and Rose (Cohen) S.; m. H. Brenda Jacobson, Jan. 29, 1961; children: Lee Andrew, Rhody Yve. BA, Alfred U., 1960; MBA, CUNY, 1962; PhD, U. Md., 1967. Lic. psychologist, Md. Asst. prof. adminstrv. scis. and psychology Yale U., New Haven, 1967-71; prof. psychology-mgmt. U. Md., College Park, 1971-79, prof. psychology and mgmt., 1982—; John A. Hannah prof. orgnl. behavior Mich. State U., East Lansing, 1979-82; v.p. Orgnl. and Pers. Rsch., Inc. Author: (with D.T. Hall) Organizational Climates and Careers, 1973, Staffing Organizations, 1976, 2d edit. (with N. Schmitt), 1986; (with F.D. Schoorman) Facilitating Work Effectiveness, 1988, Organizational Climate and Culture, 1990, (with D.E. Bowen) Winning the Service Game, 1995; mem. editl. rev. bd. Acad. Mgmt. Jour., 1971-86, Adminstrv. Sci. Quar., 1976-82, Jour. Applied Psychology, 1988—, Brit. Mgmt. Jour., 1989—, Internat. Jour. Svc. Industry Mgmt., 1989—, Pers. Psychology, 1994—. Fulbright grantee, 1973-74. Fellow APA, Am. Psychol. Soc., Soc. for Indsl. and Orgnl. Psychology (pres. 1984-85), Acad. Mgmt. (pres. orgnl. behavior div. 1982-83), Orgnl. and Personnel Rsch., Inc. (v.p., cons. to mgmt.). Home: 8122 Thoreau Dr Bethesda MD 20817-3105 Office: U Maryland Dept Psychology College Park MD 20742

SCHNEIDER, CALVIN, physician; b. N.Y.C., Oct. 23, 1924; s. Harry and Bertha (Green) S.; A.B., U. So. Calif., 1951, M.D., 1955; J.D., LaVerne (Calif.) Coll., 1973; m. Elizabeth Gayle Thomas, Dec. 27, 1967. Intern Los Angeles County Gen. Hosp., 1955-56, staff physician, 1956-57; practice medicine West Covina, Calif., 1957—; staff Inter-Community Med. Ctr., Covina, Calif. Cons. physician Charter Oak Hosp., Covina, 1960—. With USNR, 1943-47. Mem. AMA, Calif., L.A. County med. assns. Republican. Lutheran. Office: 224 W College St Covina CA 91723-1902

SCHNEIDER, CARL EDWARD, law educator; b. Exeter, N.H., Feb. 23, 1948; s. Carl Jacob and Mabel Dot (Jones) S.; m. Joan L. Wagner, Jan. 6, 1976. BA, Harvard Coll., 1972; JD, U. Mich., 1979. Curriculum specialist Mass. Tchrs. Assn., Boston, 1972-75; law clk. to judge U.S. Ct. Appeals (D.C. cir.), Washington, 1979-80; law clk. Potter Stewart U.S. Supreme Ct., Washington, 1980-81; asst. prof. law U. Mich., Ann Arbor, 1981-84, assoc. prof. law, 1984-86, prof. law, 1986—. Author: (with Margaret F. Brinig) An Invitation to Family Law, 1996; editor: (book) The Law and Politics of Abortion, 1980; contbr. articles to profl. jours. Fellow Am. Council of Learned Socs., Ford Found., 1985; life fellow Clare Coll., Cambridge. Mem. Order of Coif. Office: U Mich Law Sch 625 S State St Ann Arbor MI 48109-1215

SCHNEIDER, CARL WILLIAM, lawyer; b. Phila., Apr. 27, 1932; s. Nathan J. and Eleanor M. (Milgram) S.; m. Mary Ellen Baylinson; children—Eric, Mark, Adam, Cara. B.A., Cornell U., 1953; LL.B. magna cum laude, U. Pa., 1956. Bar: Pa. 1957. Law clk. U.S. Ct. Appeals (3d cir.), Phila., 1956-57; sr. law clk. U.S. Supreme Ct., Phila., 1957-58; assoc. Wolf, Block, Schorr and Solis-Cohen, Phila., 1958-65; ptnr. Wolf, Block, Schorr and Solis-Cohen, 1965—; spl. advisor divsn. corp. fin. SEC, Washington, 1964; lectr. securities law U. Pa., 1968-70, vis. assoc. prof., 1978-81, acting dir. Ctr. for Study Fin. Instns.; bd. editors and advisors Rev. Securities and Commodities Regulations. Author: SEC Consequences of Corporate Acquisitions, 1971; also numerous articles; mem. editl. adv. bd. Securities Regulation Law Jour., Securities Regulation and Law Report. Pres. Found. of Jewish Families and Children's Svc., Phila.; bd. dirs. Phila. Geriatric Ctr. Mem. ABA, Fed. Bar Assn., Pa. Bar Assn., Phila. Bar Assn. (chmn. sect. corp. banking and bus. law 1972). Home: 235 Linden Dr Elkins Park PA 19027-1341 Office: Wolf Block Schorr Packard Bldg 12th Fl SE Corner 15 Chestnut St Philadelphia PA 19102

SCHNEIDER, CAROLYN ALICE BRAUCH, elementary education educator; b. N.Y.C., Dec. 15, 1946; d. Elliott David and Marie Alice (Giroux) B.; m. Thom J. Schneider, Aug. 3, 1978; children: Logan, Whitney, Brock. BS, U. Bridgeport, 1968. Tchr. phys. edn. Westview (Colo.) Elem. Sch., 1968-72, McElwain (Colo.) Elem. Sch., 1972-75; tchr. phys. edn., health Northglenn (Colo.) Mid. Sch., 1975—, coach gymnastics, 1975-84, coach track, volleyball, 1975—; coach North Area Soccer Assn., Thornton, Colo., 1995-96, 96-97 Rec (competitive), 97— U-11B/Explosion White coach traveling competitive team; instr., bldg. supr. Northglenn Recreation Dept., 1969-84, mem. sch. improvement team, rep. Dist. Sch. Improvement Team. Mem. NEA, AAHPERD, Colo. Edn. Assn., Am. Health Assn. Roman Catholic. Avocation: sports.

SCHNEIDER, CHARLES I., newspaper executive; b. Chgo., Apr. 6, 1923; s. Samuel Hiram and Eva (Smith) S.; m. Barbara Anne Krause, Oct. 27, 1963; children: Susan, Charles I. Jr., Kim, Karen, Traci. BS, Northwestern U., 1944. Indsl. engr., sales mgr., v.p. mktg. and sales Curtis-Electro Lighting Corp., Chgo., 1945-54, pres., 1954-62; pres. Jefferson Electronics, Inc, Santa Barbara, Calif., 1962-64; pres. 3 sub., v.p., asst. to pres. Am. Bldg. Maintenance Industries, Los Angeles, 1964-66; group v.p. Times Mirror Co., Los Angeles, 1966-88, ret.; pvt. investor and cons., 1988—; bd. dirs. Jeppesen Sanderson, Inc., Denver, Graphic Controls Corp., Buffalo, Regional Airports Improvement Corp. Bd. regents Northwestern U., Evanston, Ill.; trustee, past pres. Reiss-Davis Child Study Center, L.A.; bd. govs., past pres. The Music Ctr.; trustee the Menninger Found.; pres. St. John's Hosp. and Health Ctr. Found., Santa Monica, Calif. Served with AUS, 1942-44. Mem. Chief Execs. Orgn. (past pres., bd. dirs.). Clubs: Standard (Chgo.); Beverly Hills Tennis (Calif.); Big. Ten of So. Calif. Avocations: tennis, squash, music, reading. Home: 522 N Beverly Dr Beverly Hills CA 90210-3318 *An individual's growth and success as a manager are in direct proportion to his or her ability to develop, motivate and lead able, capable people.*

SCHNEIDER, DAN W., lawyer, consultant; b. Salem, Oreg., Apr. 28, 1947; s. Harold Otto and Frances Louise (Warner) S.; m. Nancy Merle Schmalzbauer, Mar. 29, 1945; children: Mark Warner, Edward Michael. BA cum laude, St. Olaf Coll., 1969; JD, Willamette U., 1974; LLM, Columbia U., 1975. Bar: Oreg. 1974, D.C. 1978, Ill. 1987. Trial atty. U.S. Dept. Justice Antitrust, Washington, 1975-79; dep. assoc. dir. U.S. SEC, Washington, 1979-86; gen. ptnr. Schiff Hardin & Waite, Chgo., 1986-95; name ptnr. Smith Lodge & Schneider, Chgo., 1995—; bd. dirs. NygaarArt, Northfield, Minn. Contbr. articles to profl. jours. Trustee, sec. Ill. Acad. Fine Arts, Chgo., 1990—; mem. adv. bd. Steensland Art Mus., Northfield, 1990—. Recipient 1st prize Nathan Burkan Law Essay Competition ASCAP, N.Y., 1974, Christie award Securities Transfer Assn., 1987. Mem. Met. Club. Chgo., Monroe Club. Avocations: art collecting, art writing, music composition. Office: Smith Lodge & Schneider 55 W Monroe St Chicago IL 60603-5001

SCHNEIDER, DANIEL SCOTT, pediatric cardiologist; b. Mitchell, S.D., July 17, 1953; s. Robert George and Lois Irene (Theis) S.; m. Lisa Anne Magri, Oct. 22, 1988; children: Elizabeth, Emily, Luisa. BS, Creighton U., 1975, MD, 1979. Diplomate Am. Bd. Pediat., Am. Bd. Pediat. Cardiology. Commd. ensign USN, 1979, advanced through grades to comdr., 1992; pediat. cardiologist Childrens Hosp. of the Kings Dau., Norfolk, Va., 1992—. Named Tchr. of Yr. Portsmouth Naval Hosp. Pediat. Residents, 1992. Mem. tidewater Down Syndrome Assn. (profl. adv. 1993—), Alpha Sigma Nu, Alpha Omega Alpha. Roman Catholic. Office: Childrens Hosp the Kings Daus 601 Childrens Ln Norfolk VA 23507-1910

SCHNEIDER, DAVID J., psychology educator, academic administrator; b. Indpls., July 24, 1940; s. Joseph C. and Ruby Marie (Disque) S.; m. Doris Elizabeth Lieben, Dec. 21, 1962; children: Kristen Lynn, Caitlin Ann. BA, Wabash Coll., 1962; PhD, Stanford U., 1966. Asst. prof. Amherst (Mass.) Coll., 1966-71; assoc. prof. Brandeis U., Waltham, Mass., 1971-75; assoc. prof. U. Tex. San Antonio, 1975-78, prof., 1978-88; prof. Rice U., Houston, 1989—; vis. asst. prof. Stanford (Calif.) U., 1970-71; vis. prof. Ind. U., Bloomington, 1987-88; chmn. psychology Rice U., 1990-96. Author: Person Perception, 1979, Introduction to Social Psychology, 1988; editor (periodical) Social Cognition, 1980-92. Home: 2107 Southgate Blvd Houston TX 77030-2111 Office: Rice Univ PO Box 1892 Psychology Dept 6100 S Main Houston TX 77251

SCHNEIDER, DAVID MILLER, lawyer; b. Cleve., July 27, 1937; s. Earl Philip and Margaret (Miller) S.; children: Philip M., Elizabeth Dale. B.A., Yale U., 1959; LL.B., Harvard U., 1962. Assoc. Baker & Hostetler, Cleve., 1962-72, ptnr., 1972-89; chief legal officer Progressive Casualty Ins. Co., Cleve., 1989—; sec. The Progressive Corp., Cleve., 1989—. Trustee Alcoholism Svcs. of Cleve., 1977—, pres., 1980-82, chmn., 1982-84; v.p. Ctr. for Human Svcs., Cleve., 1980-83; trustee Cleve. chpt. NCCJ, 1986—. Mem. ABA, Ohio Bar Assn., Bar Assn. Cleve., Union Club, Tavern Club, Hunt Club, Town Club (Jamestown, N.Y.), Ojibway Club (Pointe au Baril, Ont., Can.). Republican. Episcopalian. Home: 2767 Belgrave Rd Cleveland OH 44124-4601 Office: The Progressive Corp 6300 Wilson Mills Rd Cleveland OH 44143-2109

SCHNEIDER, DENNIS RAY, microbiology educator; b. Sinton, Tex., June 10, 1952; m. Cynthia Diane Schatte, Aug. 21, 1976; 2 children. BA with honors, U. Tex., 1974, PhD, 1978. Post-doctoral fellow Behringwerke AG, Marburg/Lahn, West Germany, 1978-79, U. Mo. Med. Sch., Columbia, 1980-81; rsch. microbiologist New Eng. Nuclear, N. Billerica, Mass., 1981-82; R&D dir. Austin (Tex.) Biol. Lab., 1982-88; adj. assoc. prof. U. Tex., Austin, 1986—; R&D devel. dir. Micro-Bac Internat., Austin, 1988-94; v.p. Micro-Bac Internat., Round Rock, Tex., 1994—. Author: Bioremediation: A Desktop Manual for the Environmental Professional; author chpt. Microorganism Adaptation to Host Defense. Grantee NASA, 1988, 92, 93. Mem. AAAS, Am. Soc. for Microbiology, Mensa, Profl. Assn. Dive Instrs. Avocations: scuba diving, fictional writing. Office: Micro-Bac Internat 3200 N I H 35 Round Rock TX 78681-2410

SCHNEIDER, DONALD FREDERIC, banker; b. N.Y.C., Nov. 12, 1939; s. Charles and Lillian (Anton) S.; m. Mary Patricia McCafferty, Sept. 7, 1963; children—Laurie, John. B.S., Lehigh U., 1961; M.B.A., N.Y. U., 1968. Mgmt. trainee Marine Midland Bank, N.Y.C., 1961-65, asst. sec., 1965-68, asst. v.p., 1968-69, v.p., 1969-79; v.p. 1st Nat. Bank Chgo., 1979-87; fin. cons. Cigna Individual Fin. Svcs. Co., Chgo., 1987; v.p. Irving Trust Co./Bank of N.Y., 1987-90, Citibank N.A., N.Y.C., 1990-96; MMS Assocs., Inc., 1997—; mem. corp. trust activities com. Am. Bankers Assn., fiduciary and securities ops. exec. com. Mem. Am. Soc. Corporate Secs. (pres. Chgo. region 1987), Securities Transfer Assn. Home and Office: 88 Penwood Rd Basking Ridge NJ 07920-2240

SCHNEIDER, DONALD J., trucking company executive; b. 1935. BA, St. Norbert Coll., 1957; MBA, U. Pa. CEO Schneider Transport Inc., Green Bay, Wis., 1957—, Schneider National. Office: Schneider National PO Box 2545 Green Bay WI 54306*

SCHNEIDER, DUANE BERNARD, English literature educator, publisher; b. South Bend, Ind., Nov. 15, 1937; s. William H. and Lillian L. (Pitchford) S.; children: Jeffrey, Eric, Lisa, Emily. B.A., Miami U., Oxford, Ohio, 1958; M.A., Kent State U., 1960; Ph.D., U. Colo., 1965. Instr. engring. English U. Colo., 1960-65; asst. prof. English Ohio U., Athens, 1965-70, assoc. prof., 1970-75, prof., 1975—, chmn. Faculty Senate, 1981-83, chmn. dept. English, 1983-86; dir. Ohio U. Press, 1986-95; editor, pub. Croissant & Co., 1968—. Author: (with others) Anais Nin: An Introduction, 1979. Mem. Thomas Wolfe Soc. (trustee, pres. 1979-81). Home: 9909 Farralone Ave Chatsworth CA 91311

SCHNEIDER, EDWARD LEE, botanic garden administrator; b. Portland, Oreg., Sept. 14, 1947; s. Edward John and Elizabeth (Mathews) S.; m. Sandra Lee Alfarone, Aug. 2, 1968; children: Kenneth L., Cassandra L. BA, Ctrl. Wash. U., 1969, MS, 1971; PhD, U. Calif., Santa Barbara, 1974. From asst. to assoc. prof. botany S.W. Tex. State U., San Marcos, 1974-84, prof., 1984-94, chmn. biology dept., 1984-89, dean sci., 1989-92; exec. dir. Santa Barbara (Calif.) Botanic Garden, 1992—. Author: The Botanical World; contbr. articles to profl. jours. Recipient Presdl. Rsch. award S.W. Tex. State U., 1986, Disting. Alumnus award Ctrl. Wash. U., 1996; grantee NSF, 1980, 90. Fellow Tex. Acad. Sci. (pres. 1992-93); mem. Internat. Water Lily Soc. (bd. dirs., sec. 1989-96, inducted into Hall of Fame), Internat. Pollination Congress, Nat. Coun. Deans. Home: 1140 Tunnel Rd Santa Barbara CA 93105-2134 Office: Santa Barbara Botanic Garden 1212 Mission Canyon Rd Santa Barbara CA 93105-2126

SCHNEIDER, EDWARD LEWIS, medicine educator, research administrator; b. N.Y.C., June 22, 1940; s. Samuel and Ann (Soskin) S. BS, Rensselaer Poly. Inst., 1961; MD, Boston U., 1966. Intern and resident N.Y. Hosp.-Cornell U., N.Y.C., 1966-68; staff fellow Nat. Inst. Allergy and Infectious Diseases, Bethesda, Md., 1968-70; research fellow U. Calif., San Francisco, 1970-73; chief, sect. on cell aging Nat. Inst. Aging, Balt., 1973-79, assoc. dir., 1980-84, dep. dir., 1984-87; prof. medicine, dir. Davis Inst. on Aging U. Colo., Denver, 1979-80; dean Leonard Davis Sch. Gerontology U. So. Calif., L.A., 1986—, exec. dir. Ethel Percy Andrus Gerontology Ctr., 1986—, prof. medicine, 1987—, William and Sylvia Kugel prof. gerontology, 1989—; sci. dir. Buck Ctr. for Rsch. in Aging, 1989—; cons. MacArthur Found., Chgo., 1985-93, R.W. Johnson Found., Princeton, N.J., 1982-87, Brookdale Found., N.Y.C., 1985-89. Editor: The Genetics of Aging, 1978, The Aging Reproductive System, 1978, Biological Markers of Aging, 1982, Handbook of the Biology of Aging, 1985, 95, Interrelationship Among Aging Cancer and Differentiation, 1985, Teaching Nursing Home, 1985, Modern Biological Theories of Aging, 1987, The Black American Elderly, 1988, Elder Care and the Work Force, 1990. Med. dir. USPHS, 1968—. Recipient Roche award, 1964. Fellow Gerontology Soc., Am. Soc. Clin. Investigation; mem. Am. Assn. Retired Persons, U.S. Naval Acad. Sailing Squadron (coach 1980-86). Office: U So Calif Andrus Gerontology Ctr Los Angeles CA 90089-0191

SCHNEIDER, EDWARD MARTIN, retired physician; b. Cleve., May 12, 1922; s. Sol S. and Beatrice Hilda (Sicherman) S.; m. Jane H. Einstein, June 18, 1950; children: Douglas A., Robert S. Student, Northwestern U., 1940-43; MD, U. Cin., 1946. Diplomate Am. Bd. Internal Medicine. Intern Mt. Sinai Hosp., Cleve., 1946-47, asst. resident medicine, 1947-48, sr. asst. resident medicine, 1950-51; fellow in medicine Cin. Gen. Hosp., 1951-52; asst. prof. of medicine U. Okla. Sch. Medicine, Oklahoma City, 1952-57; sr. physician gastroenterology Miner's Meml. Hosp. Assn., McDowell, Ky., Beckley, W.Va., 1957-61; chief of medicine Cameron Meml. Hosp., Bryan, Ohio, 1961-62; chief medical rsch. sect. Upjohn Co., Kalamazoo, Mich., 1962-67; pvt. practice Woodland Hills, Calif., 1968-81. Author 17 rsch. papers. Capt. M.C., AUS, 1948-50. Fellow Am. Coll. Physicians, Am. Coll. Gastroenterologists; mem. Assn. Mil. Surgeons (life), Am. Assn. Study Liver Disease (emeritus), Soc. of Sigma Xi. Avocations: ham radio operating, music appreciation. Home: 20676 Fairmount Blvd Apt 205 Cleveland OH 44118-4850

SCHNEIDER, GEORGE, internist, endocrinoligist; b. Boston, Oct. 29, 1939; s. Morris and Doris (Saslovsky) S.; m. Patricia Marian Seymour, aug. 2, 1964; children: Andrew Gordon, Pamela Robin. AB, Harvard U., 1961; MD, Tufts U., Boston, 1965. Diplomate Am. Bd. Internal Medicine, Am. Bd. Internal Medicine in Endocrinology and Metabolism. Intern Bellevue Hosp., N.Y.C., 1965-66, asst. resident, 1966-67; assoc. resident Strong Meml. Hosp., Rochester, N.Y., 1969-70; fellow Yale U. Sch. of Medicine, New Haven, Conn., 1970-72; chief of endocrinology VA Hosp., East Orange, N.J., 1972-80, Beth Israel Med. Ctr., Newark, 1980—; pvt. practice endocrinology Roseland, N.J., 1980—; chief endocrinology Beth Israel Hosp., Newark, 1986—; med. dir. diabetes treatement ctr. Beth Israel Hosp., Newark, 1980—. Contbr. over 36 articles to profl. jours., 1970-90. Lt. cmmdr. USPHS, 1967-69. Fellow ACP, Am. Coll. Endocrinology; mem. AMA, Acad. Medicine of N.J., Am. Diabetes Assn., Endocrine Soc., Alpha Omega Alpha. Avocations: tennis, travel, water sports, fishing, fine dining. Office: 204 Eagle Rock Ave Roseland NJ 07068-1718

SCHNEIDER, GEORGE T., obstetrician-gynecologist; b. New Orleans; s. George Edmond Schneider and Erna Marie Kraft; 1 child, Lynne Schneider Cantrell. Diploma, U. Heidelberg, Fed. Republic Germany, 1938; BS, Tulane U., 1941, MD, 1944. Intern Touro Infirmary, New Orleans, 1944-45, resident ob-gyn, 1945-47; resident ob-gyn U.S. Naval Hosp., Creat Lakes, Ill., 1947-48; vice chmn. Ochsner Med. Instns., New Orleans, 1960-86, cons., 1986—; prof. ob-gyn Sch. Medicine, La. State U., New Orleans, 1965—. Contbr. numerous articles to profl. jours. Bd. dirs. Assn. Internat. Edn., Houston, 1984—, YMCA New Orleans, 1985—, Am. Cancer Soc. La. Lt. USNR, 1945. Recipient Cert. of Merit Cancer Soc. El Salvador, 1980; named hon. counsul Honduras, 1988. Fellow ACS, Am. Coll. Ob-Gyn; mem. Ob-Gyn Soc. New Orleans (past pres.), Internat. Soc. Reproductive Medicine (past pres.), Hospitaliers Order St. Lazarus. Presbyterian. Office: Ochsner Med Instns 1514 Jefferson Hwy New Orleans LA 70121-2429

SCHNEIDER, GEORGE WILLIAM, horticulturist, educator, researcher; b. East Canton, Ohio, Apr. 4, 1916; s. John W. and Cleta (Harter) S.; m. Bernice M. Youtz; children: William Wayne, George Russell. BS, Ohio State U., 1938, MS, 1939; PhD, Rutgers U., 1950. Grad. instr. Ohio State U., Columbus, 1939; instr. N.Mex. State Coll., Las Cruces, 1939-46; asst. prof. Rutgers U., New Brunswick, N.J., 1946-50; from assoc. prof. to prof. horticulture N.C. State U., Raleigh, 1950-58; head dept. horticulture U. Ky., Lexington, 1958-60, assoc. dir. extension, 1960-69, prof. hort., 1969—; chmn. extension bd. U. Wis., Madison, 1966, ECOP Com. on Devel., Washington, 1968-69. Author: Fruit Growing, 1963; contbr. articles to profl. jours. Chmn. First Meth. Ch., Lexington, 1965. Lt. (j.g.) USN, 1943-46, ATO. Fellow AAAS, Am. Soc. Hort. Sci. (pomology chmn.). Home: 249 Greenbriar Rd Lexington KY 40503-2633

SCHNEIDER, GRETA SARA, economist, financial consultant; b. Bklyn., May 26, 1954; d. Irving Victor and Anne Joyce (Goldberg) S. BA, MA, CUNY, 1975, MA, 1976, PhD, 1977. Writer, cons. Pitts., 1972-73; cons. Flushing, N.Y., 1973-85; sr. writer, cons. Buck Cons. Inc., N.Y.C., 1985-86; chmn., CEO Schneider Cons. Inc., N.Y.C., 1986-90; pvt. cons. Greta Schneider Cons., N.Y.C., 1991—; prin. Schneider Consulting Group, 1996—; lectr. The Learning Annex, 1995-96, others; advisor Am. Women's Econ. Devel. Corp., 1988—. Author: Exploding the Bankruptcy Mystique, 1993. Mem. Little Theatre Group, Marathon Cmty. Ctr., Little Neck, N.Y., 1980-83; founder, pres. Bankruptcy Anonymous, 1996; hon. mem. bd. dirs. Am. Biographical Inst. Nat. Adv. Bd., 1996. Cambridge Biographical Inst. fellow, 1993. Mem. AFTRA, Nat. Assn. Women Bus. Owners, Nat. Assn. Bus. Communicators, Internat. Platform Assn., Employee Assistance Profls. Assn., Soc. Human Resource Mgmt., U.S. C. of C., Writers Guild Am., Rotary. Avocations: chef, pilot, tennis, chess, speech coach. Home: 252-37 60th Ave Little Neck NY 11362-2423 Office: 130 W 30th St Fl 5 New York NY 10001-4004

SCHNEIDER, HAROLD JOEL, radiologist; b. Cin., Aug. 9, 1923; s. Henry W. and Sarah Miriam (Hauser) S.; m. Mary Zipperstein, Dec. 23, 1945; children—Jill, Elizabeth, Ann, Jane. M.D., U. Cin., 1947. Diplomate: Am. Bd. Radiology. Intern Cin. Gen. Hosp., 1947-48, resident in radiology, 1953-56; resident in surgery Holzer Hosp. and Clinic, Gallipolis, Ohio, 1948-49; gen. practice medicine Dayton, Ohio, 1949-50; asst. prof. radiology U. Ala. Med. Sch., Birmingham, 1956-59; assoc. prof. radiology U. Cin. Med. Center, 1959-69, prof. radiology, 1969-91, prof. emeritus, 1991—; dir. diagnostic radiology Christian R. Holmes Hosp., 1959-91; former cons. Cin. VA Hosp. Contbr. articles to profl. jours. Served to 1t. USNR, 1950-52. Named to U. Cin. Athletic Hall of Fame, 1995. Fellow Am. Coll. Radiology; mem. Radiol. Soc. N.Am., Am. Roentgen Ray Soc., Ohio Radiol. Soc., Ohio Med. Soc., Greater Cin. Radiol. Soc., Cin. Acad. Medicine. Home: 7290 Elbrook Ave Cincinnati OH 45237-2946

SCHNEIDER, HOWARD, lawyer; b. N.Y.C., Mar. 21, 1935; s. Abraham and Lena (Pincus) S.; m. Anne Evelyn Gorfinkle; children—Andrea Rose, Jeffrey Winston. AB, Cornell U., 1956, JD with distinction, 1959. Bar: N.Y. 1959, D.C. 1976. Assoc., then ptnr. Stroock & Stroock, N.Y.C., 1959-75; gen. counsel Commodity Futures Trading Commn., Washington, 1975-77, Rosenman & Colin, N.Y.C., 1977—. Contbr. articles to profl. jours. Served to capt. USAR, 1956-66. Mem. Assn. Bar of City of N.Y. (chmn. com. 1982—), Harmonie Club (N.Y.C.). Republican. Jewish. Home: 830 Park Ave New York NY 10021 Office: Rosenman & Colin 575 Madison Ave New York NY 10022-2511

SCHNEIDER, JAMES FREDERICK, judge; b. Balt., Nov. 18, 1947; s. Joseph F. and Mary L. S. B.A., U. Balt., 1969, J.D., 1972. Bar: U.S. Dist. Ct. Md. 1973, U.S. Ct. Appeals 1972. Law clk. to judge Supreme Bench Balt., 1972-73; asst. state's atty. for Balt., 1973-78; gen. equity master to Supreme Bench Balt., 1978-82; judge U.S. Bankruptcy Ct. for Dist. Md., 1982—; historian, archivist Supreme Bench Balt. Recipient Silver Key award Law Student div. Am. Bar Assn., U. Balt., 1972. Mem. ABA, Bar Assn. Balt. City, Md. State Bar Assn., Heuisler Honor Soc. Author: The Story of the Library Company of the Baltimore Bar, 1979; The Centennial of the Bar Association of Baltimore City, 1980, (with H.H. Walker Lewis) A Bicentennial History of the United States District Court for the District of Maryland 1790-1990, 1990, A Century of Striving for Justice (Centennial History of the Maryland State Bar Association), 1996. Office: US Bankruptcy Ct 101 W Lombard St Baltimore MD 21201-2626

SCHNEIDER, JAMES JOSEPH, military theory educator, consultant; b. Oshkosh, Wis., June 18, 1947; s. Joseph Edward and Virginia Gertrude Schneider; m. Peggy L. Spees, July 28, 1973 (dec. May 1976); m. Claretta Virginia Burton, Nov. 11, 1984; children: Kevin, Jason, Jenifer, Julie. BA, U. Wis., Oshkosh, 1973, MA, 1974; PhD, U. Kans., 1992. Planning evaluator Winnegago County, Oshkosh, 1978-80; ops. rsch. analyst Tng. and Doctrine Command Analysis Ctr., Ft. Leavenworth, Kans., 1980-84; prof. mil. theory Sch. Advanced Mil. Studies U.S. Army Command and Gen. Staff Coll., Ft. Leavenworth, 1984—; adj. assoc. prof. history Russian and East European Studies Ctr., U. Kans., 1994—. Author: (monograph) Exponential Decay of Armies in Battle, 1985, The Structure of Strategic Revolution, 1994; also numerous articles. With U.S. Army, 1965-68, Vietnam. Recipient medal for civilian achievement Dept. Army, 1989, Bronze Order of St. George, U.S. Cav. Assn., 1990. Mem. Am. Hist. Assn., Mil. Ops. Rsch. Soc. Office: U S Army Command/Gen Staff Coll Sch Advanced Mil Studies Fort Leavenworth KS 66027

SCHNEIDER, JAN, obstetrics and gynecology educator; b. Prague, Czechoslovakia, Dec. 10, 1933; came to U.S., 1963, naturalized, 1967; s.

Evzen and Erika S.; m. Sandra Wilson, May 20, 1961; children—Hana, Donald, Kathryn, Jonathan. M.B., U. London, 1957; M.P.H., U. Mich., 1967. Prof. ob-gyn, chief obstetric service dept. ob-gyn U. Mich. Med. Sch., Ann Arbor, 1963-77; prof., chmn. ob-gyn Med. Coll. Pa. and Hahnemann Med. Sch. Allegheny U., Phila., 1978—. Editor: (with R. J. Bolognese and R. H. Schwarz) Perinatal Medicine, 2d edit, 1981. Fellow Am. Coll. Obstetricians and Gynecologists, Soc. Perinatal Obstetricians, Am. Gynecol. and Obstet. Soc., Phila. Obstet. Soc. Presbyterian. Office: Med Coll Pa 3300 Henry Ave Philadelphia PA 19129-1121

SCHNEIDER, JANE HARRIS, sculptor; b. Trenton, N.J., Jan. 2, 1932; d. Leon Harris and Dorothy (Perlman) Rosenthal; m. Alfred R. Schneider, July 25, 1953; children: Lee, Jeffry, Elizabeth. BA, Wellesley Coll.; postgrad., Columbia U., Coll. New Rochelle. Exhibited work in numerous group and one-person shows including June Kelly Gallery, 1988, 90, 93, 95, 97, Nassau County Mus. Fine Art, Roslyn, N.Y., 1988, Alternative Mus., N.Y.C., 1985, Phila. Art Alliance, 1984, Atrium Gallery, St. Louis, 1993, 96, Bill Bace Gallery, 1992, Triplex Gallery, N.Y.C., 1991, Rockland Ctr. for Arts, West Nyack, N.Y., 1990, Hudson River Mus., Yonkers, N.Y., 1989, Sculpture Ctr., N.Y.C., 1988, Quietude Gardens Gallery, East Brunswick, N.J., 1997, Isis Conceptual Lab., West Branch, Iowa, 1997, many others; sculpture represented in numerous pub. and pvt. collections, including Fine Arts Mus. L.I., 1985, Davis Mus. and Cultural Ctr., Wellesley, Mass., Patterson (N.J.) Mus., N.J. State Mus., Trenton, Ark. Art Ctr., Little Rock. Avocations: swimming, gardening. Studio: 75 Grand St New York NY 10013-2235

SCHNEIDER, JANET M., arts administrator, curator, painter; b. N.Y.C., June 6, 1950. d. August Arthur and Joan (Battaglia) S.; m. Michael Francis Sperendi, Sept. 21, 1985. BA summa cum laude, Queens Coll., CUNY, 1972; spl. study fine arts Boston U. Tanglewood Inst., 1971. With Queens Mus., Flushing, N.Y.C., 1973-89, curator, 1973-75, program dir., 1975-77, exec. dir., 1977-89. Collections arranged include: Sons and others, Women Artists See Men (author catalog), 1975, Urban Aesthetics (author catalog), 1976, Masters of the Brush, Chinese Painting and Calligraphy from the Sixteenth to the Nineteenth Century (co-author catalog), 1977, Symcho Moszkowicz: Portrait of the Artist in Postwar Europe (author catalog), 1978, Shipwrecked 1622, The Lost Treasure of Philip IV (author catalog), 1981, Michaelangelo: A Sculptor's World (author catalog), 1983, Joseph Cornell: Revisited (author catalog), 1992, Blueprint for Change: The Life and Times of Lewis H. Latimer (co-author catalog), 1995. Chmn. Cultural Instns. Group, N.Y.C., 1986-87; mem. N.Y.C. Commn. for Cultural Affairs, 1991-93; bd. dirs. N.Y.C. Partnership, 1987-88, Gallery Assn. N.Y. State 1979-81; exec. dir. Cultural Inst. Group, 1995—. Mem. Artists Choice Mus. (trustee 1979-82), Am. Assn. Mus., Phi Beta Kappa.

SCHNEIDER, JAYNE B., school librarian; b. Cin., Nov. 9, 1950; d. Neil Kendrick and Edith (Dilworth) Bangs; m. James R. Bronn, June 9, 1973 (div. 1979); m. Arthur Schneider, July 11, 1986; 1 stepdaughter, Heather. BS in Elem. Edn., Ea. Ky. U., 1973; MA in Libr. Sci., Spaulding U., 1978. Tchr., 1st & 2d grades Fort Thomas (Ky.) Pub. Schs./Ruth Moyer Elem., 1973-78; libr. Lassiter Middle Sch., Ky., 1973—; presenter Nat. Middle Sch. Assn., St. Louis, 1988, Denver, 1989, Assn. of Ind. Media Educators, 1992. Mem. Ky. Hist. Soc., Friends of the Libr.; co-capt. Block Watch. Named Superstar Ky. Ednl. TV; Owen Badgett grantee Louisville Community Grant, 1988. Mem. NEA, ALA, AASL, PTSA (life), Nat. Mid. Sch. Assn., Jefferson County Sch. Media Assn. (treas. 1982-83, sec. 1991-92, newsletter editor 1992-93, pres.-elect 1993-94, pres. 1994-95, nomination chairperson 1996—), Ky. Sch. Media Assn. (bd. dirs. 1994-95). Presbyterian. Avocations: genealogy, collecting antique glass, knitting. Home: 2553 Kings Hwy Louisville KY 40205-2646 Office: Lassiter Mid Sch 8200 Candleworth Dr Louisville KY 40214-5552

SCHNEIDER, JOANNE, artist; b. Lima, Ohio, Dec. 4, 1919; d. Joseph and Laura (Office) Federman; m. Norman Schneider, May 15, 1941; children—Melanie Schneider Tucker, Lois Schneider Oppenheim. B.F.A., Syracuse U., 1941. One-man shows John Heller Gallery, N.Y.C., 1954, 55, 57, 58, Tirca Karlis Gallery, Provincetown, Mass., 1963, Frank Rehn Gallery, N.Y.C., 1965, 66, 69, 72, 75, Elaine Benson Gallery, Bridgehamton, N.Y., 1972, 74, 79, 85, St. Mary's Coll., St. Mary's City, Md., 1978, Alonzo Gallery, N.Y.C., 1978, Discovery Art Gallery, Clifton, N.J., 1978; group shows include Whitney Mus., N.Y.C., Pa. Acad. Arts, Corcoran Galleries, Washington, Toledo Mus., U. Nebr., Everson Mus., Syracuse, N.Y.; represented in permanent collections Met. Mus. Art, N.Y.C., Colby Coll., Syracuse U., Butler Inst., St. Mary's Coll., U. Notre Dame, Guild Hall, East Hampton, N.Y. Recipient Audubon Artists Stanley Grumbacher Meml. award, 1972. Address: 35 E 75th St New York NY 10021-2761 *A life spent in pursuit of creative expression is a fuller, more satisfying life.*

SCHNEIDER, JOHN ARNOLD, business investor; b. Chgo., Dec. 4, 1926; s. Arnold George and Anna (Wagner) S.; m. Elizabeth C. Simpson, Oct. 20, 1951; children: Richard Ward, William Arnold, Elizabeth Anne. B.S., U. Notre Dame, 1948. Exec. assignments with CBS-TV in, Chgo. and N.Y.C., 1950-58; v.p., gen. mgr. sta. WCAU-TV, Phila., 1958-64; sta. WCBS-TV, N.Y.C., 1964-65; pres. CBS TV Network, 1965-66, CBS/Broadcast Group, 1966-69, 71-77; exec. v.p. CBS, Inc., 1969-71, sr. v.p., from, 1977; pres., chief exec. officer Warner Amex Satellite Entertainment Corp., 1979-84. Trustee, mem. exec. com. U. Notre Dame; trustee Com. for Econ. Devel. Served with USNR, 1943-46. Roman Catholic. Club: Indian Harbor Yacht. Home: 155 Clapboard Ridge Rd Greenwich CT 06831-3304

SCHNEIDER, JOHN HOKE, health science administrator; b. Eau Claire, Wis., Sept. 29, 1931; div.; 2 children. B.S. in Chemistry, U. Wis., Madison, 1953, M.S. in Exptl. Oncology, 1955, Ph.D., 1958. Rsch. asst. McArdle Meml. Lab., U. Wis., 1953-58; asst. prof. biochemistry Am. U. Beirut, 1958-61, Vanderbilt U. Med. Sch., 1961-62; editor in chief Biol. Abstracts, Phila., 1962-63; grants assoc. tng. program NIH, Bethesda, Md., 1963-64; sci. and tech. info. specialist, office program planning and analysis Nat. Cancer Inst., 1964-74, dir. internat. cancer rsch. data bank program, 1974-84, sci. rev. adminstr., grants rev. br., 1984-89, program dir. cancer tng. br., 1989-96 retired, ret., 1996. Author numerous papers on nucleic acid rsch., info. sci., and classification rsch. Recipient numerous achievement awards. Mem. AAAS, Phi Beta Kappa, Sigma Xi. Home: 8414 Donnybrook Dr Chevy Chase MD 20815

SCHNEIDER, KAREN LEE, psychotherapist; b. Houston, July 16, 1965; d. Robert Louis and Gloria Jean (Craft) S. B Religious Edn., Bayridge Christian Coll., 1991; MA, Houston Grad. Sch. Theology, 1991. Asst. dir., tchr. Tchrs. Listening to Children, Houston, 1987-91; asst. dir., psychotherapist TLC Counseling & Tng. Ctr., Houston, 1991—, co-developer esteem enhancing discipline, 1987, co-developer self-esteem measure for young children-TLC esteem scale, rschr., co-developer anti-violence/anti-gang program, 1991—; rschr., co-analyst anti-soc. behavior in children and adolescents TLC program Houston and Spring Br. Pub. Schs., 1995-97, psychotherapist TLC anti-gang program, 1996; v.p., co-founder Luminé, Inc., Houston, 1989—; lectr. on esteem enhancing dipscipline, 1987—. Author: TLC Theory and Technique, 1991, (booklets) TLC Philosophy, 1993; contbr. articles to profl. jours.; appeared in TV news programs, 1991—. Vol. psychotherapist Houston Pub. Schs., 1994-95, Mayor's TLC Anti-Gang Program, 1996, TLC Anti-Violence Program, 1995-97, mem. summit meetings, 1994—, Houston Police Dept. Cmty. Outreach Dept., 1995-96. Recipient benefit concert Musicians Band Together to UnPlug Violence, Houston, 1995; grantee Amoco, 1995, Houston Endowment, 1995, Mayor's Anti-Gang Office, Houston, 1996. Mem. Am. Counseling Assn., Am. Mental Health Counselors Assn. Methodist. Avocations: dancing, acting, painting, bicycling, music. Office: TLC Counseling & Tng Ctr 50 Briar Hollow Ln Ste 303E Houston TX 77027-9305

SCHNEIDER, MARK, political science educator; b. N.Y.C., Oct. 28, 1946; s. Irving and Ida (Schwartz) S.; m. Susan Roth, June 27, 1986; children: Johanna, Elizabeth. BA, Bklyn. Coll., 1967; PhD, U. N.C., 1974. Asst. prof. polit. sci. U. Mich., Ann Arbor, 1973-74; asst. prof. polit. sci. SUNY, Stony Brook, 1974-78, assoc. prof., 1978-85, prof., 1985—, chmn. dept., 1986—; Fulbright sr. lectr., India, 1980-81. Author: The Competitive City, 1989, Public Entrepreneurs, 1995; contbr. articles to profl. jours. Mem. Am. Polit. Sci. Assn., Midwest Polit. Sci. Assn. Office: SUNY Dept Polit Sci Stony Brook NY 11794

SCHNEIDER, MARK LEWIS, government official; b. Newark, Dec. 31, 1941; s. Benjamin and Ruth (Kobran) S.; m. Susan Gilbert, June 20, 1965; children: Aaron Mitchell, Miriam Beth. A.B. in Journalism with honors, U. Calif., Berkeley, 1963; M.A. in Polit. Sci., San Jose State Coll., 1965. Reporter UPI, San Francisco, 1963-64, San Francisco Call Bull., 1965; vol. Peace Corps, El Salvador, 1966-68; reporter Washington News Call Bull., 1969-70; mem. staff U.S. Senate Judiciary Subcom., 1970-71; legis. asst. to Sen. Edward M. Kennedy, 1971-77, 80-81; dep. asst. sec. for human rights Dept. State, Washington, 1977-79; mem. del. UN Gen. Assembly, 1978, UN Human Rights Commn., 1979; coordinator policy planning, sr. advisor Pan Am. Health Orgn., 1981-93; adminstr. for Latin Am. and Caribbean USAID, 1993—; lectr. Kennedy Inst. Politics, Harvard U., 1976; adj. prof. Georgetown U., 1996. Bd. dirs. Internat. Human Rights Law Group, 1981-92. Fulbright fellow, 1976; Recipient F.W. Richardson award Calif. Press Assn., 1963. Mem. Am. Polit. Sci. Assn., Latin Am. Studies Assn. Democrat. Jewish. Home: 3517 Tilden St NW Washington DC 20008-3122

SCHNEIDER, MARTIN AARON, photojournalist, ecologist, engineer, writer, artist, television director, public intervenor, educator, university instructor, lecturer; b. N.Y.C., Sept. 23, 1926; s. Morris and Florence (Frohlich) S. Stuyvesant Science, 1941-44, CUNY, 1947-52. Editor in chief Nocturne; freelance artist, 1941—, freelance photographer, 1954—; photojournalist Life, Time, Newsweek, Sports Illustrated, N.Y. Times, NBC-TV, Ency. Britannica, Mpls. Tribune, Handball Illustrated, Time Annual Year in Review, Grolier Ency., Crowell-Collier Ency., NBC Startime, Variety, Time-Life: Ecology, Saturday Review of Literature, 1960—; ecologist, USPHS, U.S. Senate, U.S. EPA, N.Y.C.EPA, N.Y. State Dept. Environ. Conservation, N.Y.C. Dept. Air Pollution, 1964—; product safety engineer, designer, builder, crash-safety, pollution and radiation monitoring, multi-alternate fuel, laboratory vehicle, 1967—, instr., lectr. NYU, Cornell U., Ithaca, NY, New Sch. Social Rsch., N.Y.C., SUNY, Albany, Cooper Union, N.Y.C., CUNY, Iowa U., lectr. in field, 1969—; pub. intervenor, N.Y.C. Health Dept., N.Y. State Health Dept., N.Y. State Dept. Environ. Conservation, Gov. Rockefeller's State Study Commission for N.Y.C. (Scott Commission), U.S. District Ct., N.Y. Supreme Ct.; People of N.Y.C., N.Y.C. Council, N.Y. Attorney General, 1970—. TV news guest NBC Today, CBS, ABC, 1970—; radio news guest NBC, CBS, NPR, 1970, TV and radio commentator, NBC, CBS, ABC, PBS, Fox, 1970—; author: Breath of Death, 1972, Consumer Genocide, 1992; The Schneider Tapes, 1996, War Against War, ed. 1996, Crash Genocide: Millions Killed by Suppressed Safety, 1996; co-author: America-Photographic Statements, 1972, Eye of Conscience, 1974; dir., prodr., writer, cinematographer (TV documentaries) Environment Crusade, CBS, 1970, The Poisoned Air, CBS, 1970, Killers of the Environment, NBC, 1971, Censorship of Pollution Solutions by Media and Government, PBS, 1974, No Justice for Victims-Criminals Only, 1992; contbr. N.Y. Times, Ency. Britannica, Macmillan Ency. of Photographic Artists, N.Y. Village Voice "White Earth Ranger: Ecology's Batman", New World Or No World (Frank Herbert) 1970—; photography exhibited at Mus. Modern Art, N.Y.C., 1958—, George Eastman House Mus., Rochester, N.Y., 1963, 64—, Libr. Congress, 1970, Smithsonian Instn., 1972—, Art Inst. Chgo., 1973—, Whitney Mus., N.Y.C., 1978—; painting exhibited at Guggenheim Mus., N.Y.C., 1974; film exhibited at Am. Mus. Natural History, N.Y.C., 1969-72. Served with U.S. Army Paratroopers, 1944-46, PTO. Fellowship grantee Creative Artists Pub. Svc., 1977, 78; recipient TV Franny Consumer Advocacy award, 1974, for work that was a basis for the first Clean Air Act of 1970. Jewish. Office: 1501 Broadway Ste 2907 New York NY 10036-5601 *Where millions are endangered where my work makes a difference--despite gunfire, vehicle sabotage, seizure of home and all possessions, censorship--there is no dream for me in moving mere mountains, but only in moving man to move himself.*

SCHNEIDER, MATHIEU, hockey player; b. N.Y., June 12, 1969. Hockey player Montreal Canadiens Nat. Hockey League, 1990-95, hockey player N.Y. Islanders, 1995-96, hockey player Toronto Maple Leafs, 1996—; mem. Stanley Cup championship team, 1993; played All-Star Game, 1996. Office: Toronto Maple Leafs, 60 Carlton St, Toronto, ON Canada M5B 1L1

SCHNEIDER, MATTHEW ROGER, lawyer; b. N.Y.C., Nov. 7, 1948; s. Theodore David Schneider and Rosalind (Schwartz) Werner; m. Marjorie Ann Friedlander, Mar. 6, 1976; children: Adam Benjamin, Emily Beth. BA, Cornell U., 1970; student, Georgetown U., 1971; JD, Cath. U., Washington, 1974. Bar: D.C. 1976, U.S. Dist. Ct. D.C., 1994. Staff asst. U.S. Senate Jud. Com., Washington, 1973-74; counsel U.S. Senate Govt. Ops. Com., Washington, 1974-77; spl. asst. Office of Sec. Def., Washington, 1977-79; dir. legis. affairs SEC, Washington, 1979-81, sr. counsel, divsn. corp. fin., 1981-82; chief of staff U.S. Senator Jeff Bingaman, Washington, 1983-85; prin. Law Office Matthew Schneider, Washington, 1985-87; ptnr. Willkie, Farr & Gallagher, Washington, 1987-95, Garvey, Schubert & Barer, 1996—. Bd. dirs. Capitol Hill Hosp., Washington, 1981-87, Epilepsy Found. for Nat. Capital Area; chmn. conflict resolution subcom. Epilepsy Found. Am. Avocations: biking, singing, guitar. Office: Garvey Schubert & Barer 5th Fl 1000 Potomac St NW Ste 5 Washington DC 20007-3501

SCHNEIDER, MELVIN FREDERICK, retired secondary music educator; b. Lark, Wis., Mar. 7, 1904; s. Charles Phillip and Amelia (Thiele) S.; m. Naomi Jessie Manshardt, Sept. 14, 1940. BMus, U. Wis., 1930, MA, 1948, postgrad., to 1955. Tchr. orch., chorus and math. high sch., South Beloit, Ill., 1930-32; tchr. orch., band and social studies high sch., Oregan, Wis., 1932-35, Wisconsin Dells, Wis., 1935-37, Prairie du Sac, Wis., 1937-40; rschr. in music edn. U. Wis., Madison, 1940-45, U. No. Iowa, Cedar Falls, 1945-60; ind. rschr. in music edn. Cedar Falls, 1960—; voice and string instr., instrument repair instr. Mem. String Tchrs. Assn. (a founder), Music Educators Nat. Conf. (award for 50 yrs. of svc.), Cedar Falls C. of C., Phi Delta Kappa. Republican. Congregationalist. Home: 1615 Merner Ave Cedar Falls IA 50613-3522

SCHNEIDER, MICHAEL JOSEPH, biologist; b. Saginaw, Mich., Apr. 21, 1938; s. Michael Elias and Jane (Moffitt) S.; m. Janet Marie Potter, Nov. 24, 1967. B.S., U. Mich., 1960; M.S., U. Tenn., 1962; Ph.D. (Hutchinson Meml. fellow 1963-64, John M. Coulter research fellow 1964-65), U. Chgo., 1965. Resident research asso. Nat. Acad. Scis., Beltsville, Md., 1965-67; USPHS fellow U. Wis., Madison, 1967-68; asst. prof. biology Columbia U., 1968-73; mem. faculty U. Mich., Dearborn, 1973—, prof. biology, 1975—, chmn. dept. natural scis., 1975-80, 83-89, assoc. provost for acad. affairs, 1990, interim provost, vice chancellor for acad. affairs, 1991; vis. prof. Plant Research Lab., Mich. State U., East Lansing, 1980-81. Contbr. articles profl. jours. Mem. AAAS, Am. Soc. Plant Physiologists, Am. Soc. Photobiology, Sigma Xi. Home: 4654 Mulberry Woods Cir Ann Arbor MI 48105-9767 Office: U Mich-Dearborn Dept Nat Scis Dearborn MI 48128-1491

SCHNEIDER, NICHOLAS MCCORD, planetary scientist, educator; b. Appleton, Wis., Dec. 17, 1956; s. Ben Ross Jr. and Mackay (McCord) S. BA in Physics and Astronomy, Dartmouth Coll., 1979; PhD in Planetary Sci., U. Ariz., 1988. Asst. prof. lab. for atmospheric & space physics and astrophysical planetary & atmospheric scis. U. Colo., Boulder, 1990—. Recipient Presdl. Young Investigator award NSF, 1991. Mem. Am. Astron. Soc. (divsn. for planetary scis.), Am. Geophys. Union. Office: Univ Colo Lab Atmospheric & Space Physics CB392 Boulder CO 80309-0392

SCHNEIDER, NORMAN M., business executive; b. N.Y.C., Feb. 5, 1911; s. David and Edith S.; m. JoAnne Federman, May 15, 1940; children: Melanie Schneider Tucker, Lois Schneider Oppenheim. B.A., U. Scranton, 1932. Partner Norsid Co., N.Y.C., 1932-46; founder, pres. Allison Mfg. Co., N.Y.C., 1946-70; pres. and chmn. leisure products div. Beatrice Co. Inc., Chgo., 1970-81; mgmt. cons. Beatrice Co. Inc., 1981-86; pres. Schneider Assocs., N.Y.C., 1987—; former mem. N.Y. Bd. Trade; bd. dirs. Park Electrochem. Corp., Toys R Us, Datascope Corp. Recipient Man of Yr. award Boy Scouts Am. Mem. Explorers Club, Harmonie Club. Office: 46 E 70th St New York NY 10021-4928

SCHNEIDER, PAM HORVITZ, lawyer; b. Cleve., Nov. 29, 1951; m. Milton S. Schneider, June 30, 1973; 1 child, Sarah Anne. BA, U. Pa., 1973; JD, Columbia U., 1976. Bar: N.Y. 1977, Pa. 1979. Assoc. White & Case, N.Y.C., 1976-78; assoc. Drinker Biddle & Reath, Phila., 1978-84, ptnr., 1984—. Contbr. articles to profl. jours. Fellow Am. Coll. Trust and Estate Counsel (regent); mem. ABA (vice chair real property probate and trust law sect.), Internat. Acad. Estate and Trust Law (academician). Office: Drinker Biddle & Reath 1345 Chestnut St Philadelphia PA 19107-3426

SCHNEIDER, PETER, film company executive; m. Hope Schneider; 2 children. BA in Theater, Purdue U. Mng. dir. St. Nicholas Theater, Chgo., 1976-80; gen. mgr. Apollo Theater Prodns., London, 1980-83; dir. Olympic Arts Festival, L.A., 1984; with Walt Disney Studios, 1985—; pres. Walt Disney Theatrical Prodns. Walt Disney Pictures, Burbank, Calif., 1996—; dir. plays The WPA, Playwrights Horizon, Circle Repertory Theater, N.Y.C. Office: Walt Disney Pictures 500 S Buena Vista St Burbank CA 91521

SCHNEIDER, PETER RAYMOND, political scientist; b. Muskogee, Okla., Aug. 8, 1939; s. Leo Frederick and Tillie Oleta (Cannon) S.; m. Anne Larason, Jan. 22, 1964 (div. 1983); children: Christopher, Geoffrey; m. Adrienne Armstrong, Dec. 19, 1986; 1 child, Robbie. BS, Okla. State U., 1966, MS, 1968; PhD, Ind. U., 1974. News editor No. Va. Sun, Arlington, 1961-62; news writer AP, Balt., 1962, Balt. News-Am., 1962-65; asst. prof. U. Oreg., Eugene, 1974-76; pres. Inst. of Policy Analysis, Eugene, 1976-83; v.p. Am. Justice Inst., Sacramento, 1983; dir. Ctr. for Assessment of The Juvenile Justice Ctr., Sacramento, 1983; v.p. Nat. Partnership, Washington, 1985; sr. rsch. scientist Pacific Inst. for Rsch. and Evaluation, Bethesda, Md., 1984-92, dir. justice div., 1986-89; pres. Inst. of Policy Analysis, Vienna, Va., 1992-95; CEO IPA Internat., Inc., Vienna, 1995—. Contbr. numerous articles to profl. jours., chpts. to books. Recipient Julia Lathrop award Am. Criminal Justice Assn., 1985. Mem. Am. Polit. Sci. Assn., Am. Restitution Assn., Pi Sigma Alpha, Sigma Delta Chi, Phi Kappa Phi, Omicron Delta Kappa, Phi Kappa Theta. Avocations: flying, tennis, selling wine. Home: 9025 Streamview Ln Vienna VA 22182-1726 Office: IPA Internat Inc 8133 Leesburg Pike Ste 360 Vienna VA 22182-2706 *In a career devoted to the pursuit of knowledge, I have learned that nothing - absolutely nothing - is worth more than lessons learned from painful personal experience. To my regret, I usually learned such lessons after the opportunities toprofit from them had already passed. If I could do it over again I would be more daring and venturesome and make my mistakes early, while there was still plenty of time to invest the information.*

SCHNEIDER, PHYLLIS LEAH, writer, editor; b. Seattle, Apr. 19, 1947; d. Edward Lee Booth and Harriet Phyllis (Ebbinghaus) Russell; m. Clifford Donald Schneider, June 14, 1969; 1 child, Pearl Brooke. B.A., Pacific Luth. U., 1969; M.A., U. Wash., 1972. Fiction, features editor Seventeen Mag., N.Y.C., 1975-80; mng. editor Weight Watchers Mag., N.Y.C., 1980-81; editor YM mag., N.Y.C., 1981-86. Author: Parents Book of Infant Colic, 1990, Kids Who Make a Difference, 1993, Straight Talk on Women's Health: How to Get the Health Care You Deserve, 1993, Hot Health Care Careers, 1993, What Kids Like To Do, 1993. Recipient Centennial Recognition award Pacific Luth. U., 1990. Democrat. Episcopalian.

SCHNEIDER, RAYMOND CLINTON, architect, educator; b. Smyrna, N.Y., Dec. 10, 1920; s. George William and Helen (Carey) S.; m. Margaret Maude Pearce, Sept. 16, 1943 (dec. Aug. 1982); children: Stephen Eric, Martha Anne (dec.), Pearce Clinton; m. Ruth Brown Martsolf, Jan. 2, 1983 (div. Jan. 1986); m. Gertraude R. McMullen, May 28, 1986 (div. Sept. 1988); life ptnr. M. Maxine La Shell (dec. Jan. 1996). B.S. in Architecture, Kans. State U., 1949, M.S. in Edn, 1952; Ed.D., Stanford U., 1955. Registered architect, Kans. Architect firms in Salina and Manhattan, Kans., 1947-51; assoc. dir. sch. planning lab., asso. dir. W. Regional Center Ednl. Facilities Lab., also research asso., lectr. edn. Stanford U., Palo Alto, 1955-62; head personnel subsystems sect., systems tech. lab. Sylvania Corp., Mountain View, Calif., 1962-63; dir. research and planning Porter, Gogerty, Meston, San Jose, Calif., 1963-64; assoc. prof. edn. and architecture U. Wash., Seattle, 1964-78; prof. architecture and edn. U. Wash., 1978-82, prof. emeritus, 1983—; asst. to dean, 1964-73, dir. grad. program architecture, 1976-83, exhibiting artist and sculptor, 1946—, cons. in field. Author articles in field, chpts. in books. Served with AUS, 1942-46. Kellogg fellow, 1953-54; Masonite Co. fellow, 1954-55; Borg-Warner Co. fellow, 1954-55. Mem. VFW (life), Am. Legion. Address: 4406 SW 29th Ter Topeka KS 66614-3102

SCHNEIDER, RICHARD GRAHAM, lawyer; b. Bryn Mawr, Pa., Aug. 2, 1930; s. Vincent Bernard and Marion Scott (Graham) S.; m. Margaret Peter Fritz, Feb. 15, 1958; children: Margaret W., Richard Graham, John F. BA, Yale U., 1952; JD, U. Pa., 1957. Bar: Pa. 1958. Assoc. Dechert Price & Rhoads, Phila., 1957-66; ptnr. Dechert Price & Rhoads, 1966-95; of counsel, 1995—. Case editor U. Pa. Law Rev., 1956-57. Trustee Baldwin Sch., Bryn Mawr, 1971-79; trustee Episcopal Acad., Merion, Pa., 1976-83. 1st lt. USAF, 1952-54, PTO. Mem. ABA, Pa. Bar Assn., Phila. Bar Assn., Order of Coif, Merion Cricket Club, Merion Golf Club, Yale Club (pres. 1966-68). Republican. Presbyterian. Office: Dechert Price & Rhoads 4000 Bell Atlantic Tower 1717 Arch St Philadelphia PA 19103-2713

SCHNEIDER, RICHARD T(HEODORE), optics research executive, engineer; b. Munich, July 29, 1927; came to U.S., 1961; s. Wilhelm and Martha E. (Hofmann) S.; m. Lore M. Reinhard, May 16, 1950; children: Ursula M. Schneider Long, Richard W. Diploma in physics, U. Stuttgart, Fed. Republic of Germany, 1958, PhD, 1961. Registered profl. engr. Calif. Teaching asst. U. Stuttgart, 1958-61; sect. chief Allison div. Gen. Motors Corp., Indpls., 1961-65; assoc. prof. U. Fla., Gainesville, 1965-68, prof., 1968-88, prof. emeritus, 1988-90; pres. Eye Rsch. Lab., Inc., Alachua, Fla., 1984-90; chief scientist RTS Labs., Inc., Alachua, 1984-92; cons. Allison div. Gen. Motors Corp., Indpls., 1965-67; IPA assignment Eglin AFB, Ft. Walton Beach, Fla., 1983; liaison scientist USN Office Naval Rsch., London, 1975. Editor: Uranium Plasmas, 1971; patentee in field; contbr. articles to profl. jours. Recipient Medal for Exceptional Sci. Achievement, NASA, 1975, Outstanding Tech. Achievement award, Fla. Engring. Soc., 1978. Mem. Optical Soc. Am., Am. Phys. Soc., Internat. Soc. for Optical Engring., Sigma Xi, Tau Beta Pi (Eminent Engr. 1970). Avocation: flying airplanes. Home: 12903 NW 112th Ave Alachua FL 32615 Office: Eye Rsch Lab 1663 Technology Ave Alachua FL 32615-9499

SCHNEIDER, ROB, actor. Appeared in films Home Alone 2, 1992, Surf Ninjas, 1993, Demolition Man, 1993, The Beverly Hillbillies, 1993, Judge Dredd, 1995, The Adventures of Pinocchio, 1996, (tv series) Men Having Babies, 1995—. Office: United Talent Agy 9560 Wilshire Blvd 5th Fl Beverly Hills CA 90212*

SCHNEIDER, ROBERT E., II, lawyer; b. 1939. BS, Purdue U., 1962; JD, Ind. U., 1966. Bar: Ind. 1966. Trust officer Ind. Nat. Bank, 1969-74, legal counsel, 1974-79; sr. v.p., gen. counsel, sec. INB Fin. Corp., Indpls., 1979-93; 1st v.p., sec. and cashier NBD Bank N.A., Indpls., 1993—. Office: NBD Bank NA 1 Indiana Sq Indianapolis IN 46204-2004

SCHNEIDER, ROBERT EDWARD, insurance company executive, actuary; b. Hartford, Conn., June 3, 1950; s. F. Russell and Barbara (Carey) S.; m. Catherine Genetti, Sept. 9, 1978; children: Christopher Michael, Andrew Robert. AB, Middlebury Coll., 1972. Asst. actuary Nat. Life Ins. Co., Montpelier, Vt., 1972-75, New Eng. Life Ins. Co., Boston, 1975-77; assoc. actuary New Eng. Mut. Life Ins. Co., Boston, 1977-81, 2d v.p. then v.p., actuary, 1981-84, sr. v.p., actuary, 1984-91, exec. v.p., CFO, 1991—; bd. dirs. New Eng. Securities Corp., Boston. Mem. editorial bd. Actuarial Digest, Atlanta, 1986-88. Bd. dirs. Exec. Service Corps of New Eng., Boston, 1987-93. Fellow Soc. of Actuaries, Can. Inst. Actuaries; mem. Am. Acad. Actuaries. Roman Catholic. Home: 52 Westminster Rd Newton MA 02159-2355 Office: New England Life Ins Co 501 Boylston St Boston MA 02116-3706

SCHNEIDER, ROBERT JAY, oncologist; b. Miami, Fla., May 31, 1949; s. Irving and Ethel (Pack) S.; m. Barbara Cunningham, June 1, 1974; children: Matthew, Kirsten. Student, Washington U., 1967-69; BA cum laude, Boston U., 1971; MD, Albert Einstein Coll. Medicine, N.Y.C., 1975. Diplomate Am. Bd. Internal Medicine, Am. Bd. Oncology; lic. physician, N.Y. Intern, jr. and sr. resident internal medicine Bronx Mcpl. Hosp., N.Y.C., 1975-78; fellow med. oncology Meml. Sloan-Kettering Cancer Ctr., N.Y.C., 1978-80, adj. attending physician/cons. dept. medicine, 1981—; asst. prof. medicine N.Y. Med. Coll., Valhalla, 1980-81; clin. instr. medicine Cornell U. Med.

Coll., 1978-80; jr. clin. faculty fellow Am. Cancer Soc., 1980-81; mem. N.Y. Met. Breast Cancer Group, 1990—; cons. cancer program No. Westchester Hosp. Ctr., Mt. Kisco, N.Y., 1981-82; mem. staff Westchester County Med. Ctr., Valhalla, N.Y., No. Westchester Hosp. Ctr., Mt. Kisco, Meml. Sloan-Kettering Cancer Ctr., N.Y.C. Contbr. articles to profl. jours. Mem. adv. bd. Cancer Care, Inc. Conn., 1997—. Recipient Clin. Fellowship award Am. Cancer Soc., 1978-79. Mem. Am. Soc. Clin. Oncology, Westchester County Med. Soc., N.Y. State Med. Soc., Woodway Country Club. Republican. Presbyterian. Achievements include research in detection and treatment of early breast cancer, the human spirit in the fight against cancer, salvage chemotherapy with etoposide, ifosfamide and cisplatin in refractory germ cell tumors. Office: 439 E Main St Mount Kisco NY 10549-3404

SCHNEIDER, ROBERT JEROME, lawyer; b. Cin., June 22, 1947; s. Jerome William and Agnes (Moehringer) S.; m. Janice Loraine Eckhoff, Dec. 13, 1968; children: Aaron Haisley, Jared Alan, Margot Laraine. BS in Mech. Engring., U. Cin., 1970, JD, 1973. Bar: Ill. 1973, U.S. Dist. Ct. (no. dist.) Ill. 1973, U.S. Ct. Appeals (7th cir.) 1973, U.S. Ct. Appeals (fed. cir.) 1973-82. Ptnr. Mason, Kolehmainen, Rathburn & Wyss, Chgo., 1973-82; ptnr., asst. chmn. patents, chmn. intellectual property dept. McDermott, Will & Emery, Chgo., 1982-94; ptnr. chmn., intellectual dept. Keck Mahin & Cate, Chgo., 1994—. Mem. ABA, ASME, Ill. Bar Assn., Chgo. Bar Assn., Licensing Execs. Soc., Intellectual Property Law Assn. Chgo. (sec. 1981-83), Fedn. Internat. des Conseils en Proriete Industrielle, Assn. Internationale Pour la Protection de la Propriété Industrielle, Internat. Trademark Assn., Am. Intellectual Property Law Assn., Inter-Pacific Bar Assn., Tower Club (bd. govs. 1988—, v.p. 1994-95, pres. 1995—). Republican. Roman Catholic. Home: 1609 Asbury Ave Winnetka IL 60093-1303 Office: Keck Mahin & Cate 77 W Wacker Dr Chicago IL 60601

SCHNEIDER, ROY, United States Virgin Islands government official. Gov. Govt. of U.S. V.I., St. Thomas. Office: Office of Gov Kogens Glade Saint Thomas VI 00802*

SCHNEIDER, SOL, electronic engineer, consultant, researcher; b. N.Y.C., Feb. 24, 1924; s. David and Naomi F. Schneider; m. Rhoda B. Schneider, Apr. 16, 1950; children: Sandra E., Barry. BA, CUNY Bklyn. Coll., 1946; MS, NYU, 1949. Supervisory physicist U.S. Army Electronics Tech. and Devices Lab., Ft. Monmouth, N.J., 1948-80, chief pulse power and plasma devices, 1956-80; cons. Rockwell Internat., Canoga Park, Calif., 1980-81, U.S. Army Pulse Power Ctr., Ft. Monmouth, 1982—, SRI, Internat., Menlo Park, Calif., 1983-91, Vitronics, Inc., Eatontown, N.J., 1987-96, Berkeley Rsch. Assocs., Springfield, Va., 1996—; adj. prof. Southwestern Ctr. for Elec. Engring. Edn., St. Cloud, Fla., 1980-86; cons. Los Alamos (N.Mex.) Nat. Lab., 1980-81; mem. USN Pulsed Power Tech. Adv. Group, Washington, 1978-80, SDIO Pulsed Power Tech. Adv. Group, 1983-93; assoc. mem. Adv. Group on Electronic Devices, Dept. Def., Washington, 1970-80. Contbr. articles to profl. jours.; holder 14 patents. With U.S. Army, 1943-46, ETO. Recipient Spl. Act award Sec. Army, 1963, U.S. Army R&D Achievement award Dept. Army, 1963, 78, Army Sci. award, 1978. Fellow IEEE (life; chmn./editor symposium proc. 1957-80, chmn. emeritus power modulator symposium 1981—, co-chmn. high voltage workshop 1989-90, exec. com. 1991—, High Voltage award 1991, Germeshausen award 1992); mem. Am. Phys. Soc. (exec. com. gaseous electronics conf. 1961-66, sec. 1964, exec. com. electron and atomic physics divsn. 1965-66). Home: 100 Arrowwood Ct Red Bank NJ 07701-6717

SCHNEIDER, STEPHEN HENRY, climatologist, environmental policy analyst, researcher; b. N.Y.C., Feb. 11, 1945; s. Samuel and Doris C. (Swarte) S.; married, 1995; 2 children from previous marriage. BS, Columbia U., 1966, MS, 1967, PhD in Mechanical Engring., 1971; DSc (hon.), N.J. Inst. Tech., 1990, Monmouth Coll., 1991. NAS, NRC postdoctoral research assoc. Goddard Inst. Space Studies NASA, N.Y.C., 1971-72; fellow advanced study program Nat. Ctr. Atmospheric Research, Boulder, Colo., 1972-73, scientist, dep. head climate project, 1973-78, acting leader climate sensitivity group, 1978-80, head visitors program and dep. dir. advanced study program, 1980-87; sr. scientist Nat. Ctr. Atmospheric Research, Boulder, 1980-96; head interdisciplinary climate systems sect. Nat. Ctr. Atmospheric Research, Boulder, Colo., 1987-92; prof. biol. scis. dept., sr. fellow Inst. Internat. Studies Stanford (Calif.) U., 1992—; affiliate prof. U. Corp. Atmospheric Rsch. Lamont-Doherty Geol. Obs., Columbia, U., 1976-83; mem. Carter-Mondale Sci. Policy Task Force, 1976; Clinton-Gore sci. advisor, 1992, 96; sci. advisor, interviewee Nova Sta. WGBH-TV, Planet Earth, Sta. WQED-TV; mem. internat. sci. coms. climatic change, ecology, energy, environ. edn., food and pub. policy; expert witness congl. coms.; mem. Def. Sci. Bd. Task Force on Atmospheric Obscuration; lead author intergovernmental panel on climate change Working Group I, 1995-96. Author: (with Lynne E. Mesirow) The Genesis Strategy: Climate and Global Survival, 1976, (with Lynne Morton) The Primordial Bond: Exploring Connections Between Man and Nature Through Humanities and Science, 1981, (with Randi S. Londer) The Coevolution of Climate and Life, 1984, Global Warming: Are We Entering the Greenhouse Century?, 1989, (with W. Bach) Interactions of Food and Climate, 1981, (with R.S. Chen and E. Boulding) Social Science Research and Climate Change: An Interdisciplinary Appraisal, 1983, (with K.C. Land) Forecasting in the Social and Natural Sciences, 1987, (with P. Boston) Scientists on Gaia, 1990; editor-in-chief: The Encyclopedia of Climate and Weather, 1996, Laboratory Earth: The Planetary Experiment We Can't Afford to Lose, 1997; editor: Climatic Change, 1976—; contbr. sci. and popular articles on theory of climate, influence of climate on soc., relation of climatic change to world food, population, energy, development and environ. policy issues, environ. aftereffects of nuclear war, carbon dioxide greenhouse effect, pub. understanding sci., environ. edn. Recipient Louis J. Battan Author's award Am. Meteorol. Soc., 1990; named one of 100 Outstanding Young Scientists in Am. by Sci. Digest, 1984; MacArthur Found. Prize fellow John D. and Catherine T. MacArthur Found., 1992. Fellow AAAS (Westinghouse award 1991), Scientists Inst. for Pub. Info.; mem. U.S. Assn. Club Rome, Am. Meteorological Soc., Am. Geophysical Union, Fedn. Am. Scientists, Soc. Conservation Biology, Soc. Ecol. Economics. Office: Stanford U Dept Biol Scis Stanford CA 94305-5020

SCHNEIDER, STEVEN L., company executive. Pres., CEO Trion, Inc., Sanford, N.C. Office: 101 Mcneill Rd Sanford NC 27330-9451

SCHNEIDER, THOMAS AQUINAS, surgeon, educator; b. St. Charles, Mo., Dec. 22, 1934; s. Vincent Augustine and Anna Maria (Marheineke) S.; m. Joyce Elaine Diehr, June 7, 1958; children: Lisa, Thomas, Dawn, Tracy. BS, Loras Coll., 1954; MD, St. Louis U., 1958. Diplomate Am. Bd. Surgery. Resident surgery St. Louis City Hosp., 1958-63; pvt. practice St. Charles, 1963—; clin. instr., St. Louis U., 1966-91, asst. clin. prof. 1991—; med. dir. vascular lab. St. Joseph Health Ctr., St. Charles, 1991—, dir. trauma svc. 1981-91. Fellow ACS; mem. Mo. Com. on Trauma, St. Louis Surg. Soc. (councilor 1988-91, v.p. 1996-97), St. Louis Vascular Soc. (pres. 1993-95), Hodgen Club (pres. 1988), Alpha Omega Alpha. Roman Catholic. Avocations: golf, music, history. Office: 300 1st Capitol Dr Saint Charles MO 63301-2844

SCHNEIDER, THOMAS PAUL, prosecutor; b. June 5, 1947; s. Milton and Gloria (Bocaner) S.; m. Susan G. Stein, May 31, 1987; children: Rachel Jenny, Daniel Joshua. BA with honors, U. Wis., 1972, JD, 1972. U.S. atty. U.S. Dept. Justice, Milw., 1993—. Mem. Wis. Bar Assn., Milw. Bar Assn. Democrat. Jewish. Office: US Attys Office 517 E Wisconsin Ave Milwaukee WI 53202-4504

SCHNEIDER, THOMAS RICHARD, hospital administrator; b. Cin., July 16, 1944; s. Richard Arthur and Janet (Tingley) S.; m. Judith Ann Johnson, June 10, 1967; children: Gregory Thomas, Marcia Kay, Jill Elise. BS in Bus. Adminstrn., Miami U., Oxford, Ohio, 1966; MHA, U. Minn., 1968. Asst. adminstr. Meml. Hosp. of South Bend, Ind., 1971-77, Ft. Hamilton-Hughes Meml. Hosp., Hamilton, Ohio, 1977-82; assoc. adminstr. Ft. Hamilton-Hughes Meml. Hosp., 5, Ohio, 1982-84, assoc. adminstr., chief oper. officer, 1984-85, v.p. ops. and profl. svcs., 1985-91; adminstr. Shriners Hosp. for Children, Shreveport, La., 1992—; chmn. health careers Greater Cin. Hosp. Coun., 1983-90; mem. adv. bd. Xavier U. Ctr. for Health Mgmt. Edn., Cin., 1985-91; trustee Cmty. Blood Ctr., Dayton, Ohio, 1985-91. Trustee, 1st v.p. YMCA of Hamilton-Fairfield, 1990; chmn. city charter comms. com. City of Hamilton, 1990; chmn. pub. svc. div. United Way of Hamilton-Fairfield, 1988-90. Mem. Med. Svc. Corps. USN, 1968-71. Recipient disting. svc. award YMCA, 1982, great American family award of honor, 1990, proclamation Mayor and City Coun. of Hamilton, 1992. Fellow Am. Coll. Healthcare Execs.; mem. Rotary Internat., Masons, Shriner. Republican. Methodist. Avocations: fishing, golf, boating, reading, clowning. Home: 535 Northpark Dr Bossier City LA 71111 Office: Shriners Hosp 3100 Samford Ave Shreveport LA 71103-4239

SCHNEIDER, VALERIE LOIS, speech educator; b. Chgo., Feb. 12, 1941; d. Ralph Joseph and Gertrude Blanche (Gaffron) S. BA, Carroll Coll., 1963; MA, U. Wis., 1966; PhD, U. Fla., 1969; cert. advanced study Appalachian State U., 1981. Tchr. English and history Montello High Sch. (Wis.), 1963-64; dir. forensics and drama Montello High Sch., 1963-64; instr. speech U. Fla., Gainesville, 1966-68, asst. prof. speech, 1969-70; asst. prof. speech Edinboro (Pa.) State Coll., 1970-71; assoc. prof. speech East Tenn. State U., Johnson City, 1971-76, prof. speech, 1976—; instr. newspaper course Johnson City Press Chronicle, 1979, Elizabethton Star, Erwin Record, Mountain City Tomahawk, Jonesboro Herald and Tribune, 1980; mem. investor panel USA Today, 1991-92. Editor East Tenn. State U. evening and off-campus newsletter, 1984-91; assoc. editor: Homiletic, 1974-76; columnist Video Visions, Kingsport Times-News (Tenn.), 1984-86; book reviewer Pulpit Digest, 1986-90; contbr. articles on speech to profl. jours. Chmn. AAUW Mass Media Study Group Com., Johnson City, 1973-74. Recipient Creative Writing award Va. Highlands Arts Festival, 1973; award Kingsport (Tenn.) Times News, 1984, 85, Tri-Cities Met. Advt. Fedn., 1983, 84; Danforth assoc., 1977; finalist Money mag. contest 'Best Personal Fin. Mgrs.', 1994. Mem. Speech Communication Assn. (Tenn. rep. to states adv. council 1974-75), So., Tenn. (exec. bd. 1974-77, publs. bd. 1974-78, pres. 1977-78), Religious Speech Communication Assn. (Best article award 1976), Tenn. Basic Skills Council (exec. bd. 1979-80, v.p. 1980-81, pres. 1981-82), AAUW (v.p. chpt. 1974-75, pres. 1975-76, corp. rep. for East Tenn. State U. 1974-76), Am. Assn. Continuing Higher Edn., Bus. and Profl. Women's Club (chpt. exec. bd. 1972-73, v.p. 1976-77), Mensa, Delta Sigma Rho-Tau Kappa Alpha, Phi Delta Kappa, Delta Kappa Gamma, Pi Gamma Mu. Presbyterian. Home: 3201 Buckingham Rd Johnson City TN 37604-2715 Office: East Tenn State U PO Box 23098 Johnson City TN 37614-0124

SCHNEIDER, WILLIAM CHARLES, aerospace consultant; b. N.Y.C., Dec. 24, 1923; s. Charles J. and Margaret (Stoeffler) S.; m. Roseann Vasco, Oct. 6, 1964; children: Catherine M., Jeanne M., Robert J., Robert Sherer. BS, MIT, 1949; MS, U. Va., 1952; D in Engring., Cath. U. Am., 1976. Rsch. scientist NACA Langley Rsch. Ctr., Hampton, Va., 1949-55; asst. br. head Air-to-Air Missiles Bur. Aeros., Washington, 1955-60; dir. space vehicles USN Bur. Weapons, Washington, 1960-61; dir. space systems Internat. Tel. & Tel., Nutley, N.J., 1961-63; dep. dir. Gemini program Office Manned Space Flight NASA Hdqrs., Washington, 1963-65; dir., dep. dir. operations, mission dir. Office Manned Space Flight NASA Hdqrs. (Gemini program), 1965-66; dir. Apollo Applications Missions, 1966-67, Apollo Mission dir., 1967-68, dir. Skylab program, 1968-74, dep. assoc. adminstr. for space transp. systems, 1974-78, assoc. adminstr. for space tracking and data systems, 1979-80; v.p. mgmt. and product assurance Systems Group Computer Scis. Corp., Falls Church, Va., 1980-83; v.p. control systems Computer Scis. Corp., Falls Church, 1983-85, v.p. devel., 1985-90; cons., 1990—; mem. life scis. strategic planning bd. NASA, life scis. div. working group, aerospace medicine adv. com. NASA, mem. space sta. adv. com.; mem. adv. space tech. com. NRC; bd. dirs. Spacetech Inc. Mem. bd. visitors Cath. U. Served with USNR, 1942-46. Recipient Exceptional Service medal NASA, 1965, Distinguished Service medal, 1968-73, Outstanding Leadership medal, 1980; Apollo Group Achievement award, 1969; Astronautics Engr. award, 1974; Robert J. Collier trophy, 1974; Am. Astronautical Soc. Space Flight award, 1974. Fellow AIAA, Internat. Acad. Astronautics, Planetary Soc., Am. Astron. Soc. (v.p.); mem. VFW, Armed Forces Comm. and Electronics Assn., Energy Mgmt. and Control Soc., NASA Alumni League (treas.), Brit. Interplanetary Soc. Home and Office: 11801 Clintwood Pl Silver Spring MD 20902-1707

SCHNEIDER, WILLIAM GEORGE, former life insurance company executive; b. Shenandoah, Iowa, Jan. 18, 1919; s. Fred M. and Abba F. (Ferguson) S.; m. Phyllis Welch, Mar. 28, 1943; children—Stephen F., Richard W. B.A., State U. Iowa, 1940; postgrad., N.Y. U. With Met. Life Ins. Co., 1940-41, 45-46; with Bankers Life Co. (now named Prin. Fin. Group), Des Moines, 1946-84; sr. v.p. Bankers Life Co., 1970-82, exec. v.p., 1982-84, ret., 1984. Served with AUS, 1941-45. Fellow Soc. Actuaries; mem. Am. Acad. Actuaries, Phi Beta Kappa. Republican. Clubs: Des Moines, Des Moines Golf and Country. Home: 3662 Ingersoll Ave Apt 414 Des Moines IA 50312-3422

SCHNEIDER, WILLIAM GEORGE, chemist, research consultant; b. Wolseley, Sask., Can., June 1, 1915; s. Michael and Phillipina (Krauschaar) S.; m. Jean Purves, Sept. 2, 1940; children: Judith Schneider Saunders, Joanne Schneider Spurrier. B.Sc., U. Sask., 1937, M.Sc., 1939, D.Sc., 1969; Ph.D., McGill U., 1941, D.Sc., 1970; D.Sc. (hon.), York U., 1966, Meml. U., 1968, McMaster U., 1969, Laval U., 1969, Moncton U., 1969, U. N.B., 1970, U. Montreal, 1970, Acadia U., 1976, U. Regina, 1976, Ottawa U., 1978; LL.D., U. Alta., 1968, Laurentian U., 1968. Head phys. chemistry sect., div. chemistry NRC Can., Ottawa, Ont., 1946-63; dir. div. pure chemistry NRC Can., 1963-65, v.p., 1965-67, pres., 1967-80; research cons., 1980—. Author: (with J.A. Pople, H.J. Bernstein) High Resolution Nuclear Magnetic Resonance, 1959; contbr. articles to profl. jours. Decorated Order of Can., 1977. Fellow Royal Soc. Can. (Henry Marshall Tory medal), Royal Soc. London, Chem. Inst. Can. (medal 1969, Montreal medal 1973); mem. Internat. Union Pure and Applied Chemistry (pres. 1983-85). Office: Unit # 2, 65 Whitemarl Dr, Ottawa, ON Canada K1L 8J9

SCHNEIDER, WILLYS HOPE, lawyer; b. N.Y.C., Sept. 27, 1952; d. Leon and Lillian (Friedman) S.; m. Stephen Andrew Kals, Jan. 21, 1979; children: Peter, Josefine. AB, Princeton U., 1974; JD, Columbia U., 1977. Bar: N.Y. 1978, U.S. Dist. Ct. (ea. and so. dists.) N.Y. 1978, U.S. Tax Ct. 1979. Law clk. to hon. Jack B. Weinstein U.S. Dist. Ct. (ea. dist.) N.Y., Bklyn., 1977-78; assoc. Paul, Weiss, Rifkind, Wharton & Garrison, N.Y.C., 1978-83; ptnr. Kaye, Scholer, Fierman, Hays & Handler, N.Y.C., 1983—. Contbr. articles to profl. jours. Mem. ABA, N.Y. State Bar Assn., Assn. of Bar of City of N.Y. Home: 320 W End Ave New York NY 10023-8110 Office: Kaye Scholer Fierman Hays & Handler 425 Park Ave New York NY 10022-3506

SCHNEIDER-CRIEZIS, SUSAN MARIE, architect; b. St. Louis, Aug. 1, 1953; d. William Alfred and Rosemary Elizabeth (Fischer) Schneider; m. Demetrios Anthony Criezis, Nov. 24, 1978; children: Anthony, John and Andrew. BArch, U. Notre Dame, 1976; MArch, MIT, 1978. Registered architect, Wis. Project designer Eichstaedt Architects, Roselle, Ill., 1978-80, Solomon, Cordwell, Buenz & Assocs., Chgo., 1980-82; project architect Gelick, Foran Assocs., Chgo., 1982-83; asst. prof. Sch. Architecture U. Ill., Chgo., 1980-86; exec. v.p. Criezis Architects, Inc., Evanston, Ill., 1986—. Graham Found. grantee MIT, 1977, MIT scholar, 1976-78; Prestressed Concrete Inst. rsch. grantee, 1981. Mem. AIA, Chgo. Archtl. Club, Chgo. Women in Architecture, Am. Solar Energy Soc., NAFE, Jr. League Evanston, Evanston C. of C. Roman Catholic. Avocations: tennis, swimming. Office: 1007 Church St Ste 101 Evanston IL 60201-5910

SCHNEIDERMAN, DAVID ABBOTT, publisher, journalist; b. N.Y.C., Apr. 14, 1947; s. Robert D. and Mary (Torres) S.; m. Peggy Rosenthal, Sept. 19, 1981. BA, Johns Hopkins U., 1969, MA, 1970. Asst. to the editor op-ed page N.Y. Times, 1970-74, dep. editor, 1974-78; editor in chief Village Voice, N.Y.C., 1979-87, pub., 1985-88, 91—, pres., 1985—; publ. 7 Days, N.Y.C., 1988-90; pres. Stern Pub., 1995—; chmn. L.A. (Calif.) Weekly Inc., 1995—; mem. libr. coun. Johns Hopkins U. Office: Village Voice 36 Cooper Sq New York NY 10003-7118 also: LA Weekly 6715 Sunset Blvd Los Angeles CA 90028-7107

SCHNEIDERMAN, IRWIN, lawyer; b. N.Y.C., May 28, 1923; s. Meyer and Bessie (Klein) S.; m. Roberta Haig, Nov. 28, 1966; 1 child, Eric T. BA, Bklyn. Coll., 1943; LLB cum laude, Harvard U., 1948; DHL (hon.), Bklyn. Coll., 1993. Bar: N.Y. 1949, D.C. 1952. Assoc. Cahill Gordon & Reindel, N.Y.C., 1948-59, ptnr., 1959-89, sr. counsel, 1990—; spl. cons. to chmn. SEC, 1981-82, mem. adv. com. on tender offers, 1983. Trustee Bklyn. Coll. Found., 1983—; co-chmn. N.Y.C. Opera, 1993—; bd. dirs. WNYC Found., 1989—, City Ctr. Music and Drama, Inc., 1990—, N.Y.C. NARAL, 1990—, Lincoln Ctr. for Performing Arts, Inc., 1994—. Lt. (j.g.) USNR, 1943-46. Mem. Harvard Club. Home: 203 E 72nd St New York NY 10021-4568 Office: Cahill Gordon & Reindel 80 Pine St New York NY 10005-1702

SCHNEITER, GEORGE MALAN, golfer, development company executive; b. Ogden, Utah, Aug. 12, 1931; s. George Henery and Bernice Slade (Malan) S.; B. Banking and Fin., U. Utah, 1955; m. JoAnn Deakin, Jan. 19, 1954; children: George, Gary, Dan, Steve, Elizabeth Ann, Michael. With 5th Army Championship Golf Team U.S. Army, 1955-56; assoc. golf pro Hidden Valley Golf Club, Salt Lake City, 1957; golf pro Lake Hills Golf Club, Billings, Mont., 1957-61, sec., 1957-61, pres., 1964—; pres. Schneiter Enterprises, Sandy, Utah, 1974—; developer Schneiter's golf course, 1973—, and subdiv., 1961—; player PGA tour 1958-78; sr. player PGA tour, 1981—. With U.S. Army, 1955-56. Winner Utah sect. Sr. Championship, Wyo. Open Super Sr. Championship, Salt Lake City Parks Tournament, Vernal Brigham Payson Open, Yuma Open, Ariz.; named U.S. Army Ft. Carson Post Golf Champ, 5th Army Championship Golf Team, 1955-56. Mem. PGA, Am. Mormon, Salt Lake City C. of C., Internat. Golf Course Superintants Assn. Office: 2009 Brassy Dr Las Vegas NV 89122-2033 *Personal philosophy: I think everyone should try to make the world a better place to live than it was when we entered it and we should try to help each other and live in peace.*

SCHNEITER, GEORGE ROBERT, government executive; b. Louisville, Oct. 30, 1937. BSME, Purdue U., 1959, MSME, 1962, PhD in Mech. Engring., 1966. Rsch. asst., instr. rocket propulsion Purdue U., 1960-65; dir. Advanced Ballistic Reentry Sys. program Aerospace Corp., 1965-73; dep. dir. Dept. of Def. SALT Task Force Office of Sec. of Def., 1978-81, sr. advisor to Sec. of Def.'s Rep. to SALT del., 1973-78; team leader for study on Advanced Tactical Aircraft Ctr. for Naval Analyses, 1982-86; dir. strategic aeronautical and theater nuclear sys. Office of Dir. Def. Rsch. & Engring., Office of Sec. of Def., 1986-88; dir. strategic and space sys. Office of Under Sec. of Def., Office of Sec. of Def., 1988-94, dir. strategic and tactical sys., 1994—. Recipient Meritorious Exec. Presdl. award, 1980, 89. Fellow AIAA (assoc.). Office: Dept of Defense Dir Strategic Tactical Sys 3090 Defense Pentagon Washington DC 20301-3090

SCHNELL, CARLTON BRYCE, lawyer; b. Youngstown, Ohio, Jan. 1, 1932; s. Carlton Wilhelm and Helen Jean (Alexander) S.; m. Dorothy Stewart Apple, Aug. 15, 1953; children—Laura, Margaret, Heidi. B.A., Yale U., 1953, LL.B., 1956. Bar: Ohio 1956. Assoc. Arter & Hadden, Cleve., 1956-65, ptnr., 1966-96, mng. ptnr., 1977-82; mng. ptnr. Arter & Hadden, Washington, 1982-84. Exec. comm. mem. Greater Cleve. Growth Assn., Cleve., 1983—; chmn. Build Up Cleve., 1981-89; profl. chmn. United Way, Cleve., 1983; co-chmn. Charter Rev. Commn., Cleve., 1983-84; pres. Citizen's League Rsch. Inst., 1992-95. Named Vol. of Yr., Leadership Cleve., 1985. Mem. Tex. Club Cleve. (pres. 1972-73), Cleve. Tax Inst. (chmn. 1978), Ohio C. of C. (trustee 1977-80). Republican. Presbyterian. Clubs: Union, Pepper Pike. Avocations: golf; tennis. Home: 31450 Shaker Blvd Cleveland OH 44124-5153 Office: Arter & Hadden 1100 Huntington Blvd Cleveland OH 44115

SCHNELL, GEORGE ADAM, geographer, educator; b. Phila., July 13, 1931; s. Earl Blackwood and Emily (Bernheimer) S.; m. Mary Lou Williams, June 21, 1958; children: David Adam, Douglas Powell, Thomas Earl. BS, West Chester U., 1958; MS, Pa. State U., 1960, PhD, 1965; postdoctoral study, Ohio State U., 1965. Asst. prof. Coll. SUNY, New Paltz, 1962-65, assoc. prof., 1965-68, prof. geography, 1968—, founding chmn. dept., 1968-94; vis. assoc. prof. U. Hawaii, summer, 1966; cons. cmty. action programming, 1965 ; manuscript reader, cons. to several pubs., 1967—; founder, founding bd. dirs. Inst. for Devel., Planning and Land Use Studies, 1986—; cons. Mid-Hudson Pattern for Progress, 1986, Open Space Inst., 1987, Mid-Hudson Regional Econ. Devel. Coun., 1989, Urban Devel. Corp., 1989-90, 93, Tech. Devel. Ctr., 1991, Catskill Ctr., 1991, Ednl. Testing Svc., 1993-94, 96, 97; consulting editor Exams Unltd., Albany, N.Y., 1995—; mem. exec. bd. dirs. Hudson Valley Study Ctr.; cons. depts. of geography, 1988—. Author: (with others) The Local Community: A Handbook for Teachers, 1971, The World's Population, Problems of Growth, 1972, Pennsylvania Coal: Resources, Technology, Utilization, 1983, West Virginia and Appalachia: Selected Readings, 1977, Hazardous and Toxic Wastes: Technology, Management and Health Effects, 1984, Environmental Radon: Occurrence, Control and Health Hazards, 1990, Natural and Technological Disasters: Causes, Effects and Preventive Measures, 1992, Conservation and Resource Management, 1993; co-author: (with M.S. Monmonier) The Study of Population: Elements, Patterns, Processes, 1983, Map Appreciation, 1988, Medicine and Health Care into the 21st Century, 1995; editor: (with G.J. Demko and H.M. Rose) Population Geography: A Reader, 1970; contbr. articles to profl. jours.; presneter papers to more than 70 ann. meetings of scholarly and profl. socs. Appt. mem. local bds. and coms. Town and Village of New Paltz, and New Paltz Ctrl. Sch. Dist., 1965—; elder Reformed Ch. of New Paltz. With AUS, 1952-54. Recipient Excellence award N.Y. State/United Univ. Professions, 1990; Disting. Alumnus award West Chester U., 1994. Mem. Assn. Am. Geographers, Pa. Geog. Soc. (mem. editl. bd. Pa. Geographer, Disting. Geographer award 1994), Pa. Acad. Sci. (assoc. editor jour. 1988—). Home: 29 River Park Dr New Paltz NY 12561-2636 Office: SUNY at New Paltz Dept Geography 75 S Manheim Blvd New Paltz NY 12561-2400

SCHNELL, JOSEPH, dancer; b. Marin County, Calif.. Student, Sch. Am. Ballet, 1983; scholarship student, The Joffrey Ballet Sch., 1984-85. Dancer Joffrey II Dancers, N.Y.C., 1984, The Joffrey Ballet, N.Y.C., 1987—. Address: Joffrey Ballet 70 E Lake St Ste 1300 Chicago IL 60601-5907*

SCHNELL, ROBERT LEE, JR., lawyer; b. Mpls., Sept. 20, 1948; s. Robert Lee and Dorothy Mae (Buran) S.; m. Jacqueline Irene Husak, Dec. 19, 1969 (div. Aug. 1988); children: Robert Lee III, Elizabeth Anne, Jennifer Irene; m. Julie Ann Bemlott, Sept. 29, 1989; children: Helen Bridget, Michael Henry. BA cum laude, Princeton U., 1970; JD magna cum laude, Harvard U., 1974. Bar: Minn. 1974, U.S. Dist. Ct. Minn. 1974, U.S. Ct. Appeals (8th cir.) 1975, U.S. Supreme Ct. 1990. Assoc. Faegre & Benson, Mpls., 1974-81, ptnr., 1982—. Bd. dirs. United Way of Mpls., 1992-93. Office: Faegre & Benson 2200 Norwest Ctr 90 S 7th St Minneapolis MN 55402-3903

SCHNELL, ROGER THOMAS, retired military officer, state official; b. Wabasha, Minn., Dec. 11, 1936; s. Donald William and Eva Louise (Barton) S.; m. Barbara Ann McDonald, Dec. 18, 1959 (div. Mar. 1968); children: Thomas Allen, Scott Douglas. A in Mil. Sci., Command and Gen. Staff Coll., 1975; A in Bus. Adminstn., Wayland Bapt. U., 1987. Commd. 2d lt. Alaska N.G., 1959, advanced through grades to col., 1975; shop supt. Alaska N.G., Anchorage, 1965-71, personnel mgr., 1972-74, chief of staff, 1974-87, dir. logistics, 1987; electrician Alaska R.R., Anchorage, 1955-61, elec. foreman, 1962-64; dir. support personnel mgmt. Joint Staff Alaska N.G., 1988-92, ret.; personnel mgr. State of Alaska, 1992; asst. commr. dept. mil. and vets. affairs State of Alaska, Ft. Richardson, 1992-95, dep. commr. dept. mil. and vets. affairs, 1995—. Bd. dirs. Meth. Trust Fund. Mem. Fed. Profl. Labor Relations Execs. (sec. 1974-75), Alaska N.G. Officers Assn. (pres. 1976-78, bd. dirs. 1988—), Am. Legion, Amvets. Republican. Methodist. Lodge: Elks. Avocations: traveling, photography. Home: 6911 Hunt Ave Anchorage AK 99504-1891 Office: Dept Mil and Vets Affairs State of Alaska PO Box 5800 Camp Denali Bldg # 4900 Anchorage AK 99505-5800 *Personal philosophy: Success is built on honesty, hard work, determination, committment and the ability to make personal sacrifices to strive for high professional goals. Always keep a positive attitude and treat each person as you would like to be treated.*

SCHNELL, RUSSELL CLIFFORD, atmospheric scientist, researcher; b. Castor, Alta., Can., Dec. 12, 1944; s. Henry Emmanuel and Anna (Traudt) S.; m. Suan Neo Tan, May 25, 1974; children: Alicia, Ryan. BSc with distinction, U. Alta. (Can.), Edmonton, 1967; BSc, Meml. U., St. John's, Nfld., Can., 1968; MSc, U. Wyo., 1971, PhD, 1974. Research scientist U. Wyo., Laramie, 1971-74, Nat. Ctr. Atmospheric Research and NOAA, Boulder, Colo., 1974-76; dir. Mt. Kenya study World Meteorol. Orgn. div. UN, Nairobi, Kenya, 1976-78; research scientist U. Colo., Boulder, 1979-82, dir. Arctic Gas and Aerosol Sampling Program, 1982-92, fellow Coop. Inst. Research in Environ. Scis., 1985-92; dir. Mauna Loa Observatory, Hilo, Hawaii, 1992—; mem. aerobiology com. Nat. Acad. Sci., 1976-79; cons. UN,

Geneva, 1977-80, Shell Devel., Modesto, Calif., 1978-79, Holme, Roberts & Owen, 1990-92; mem. adv. bd. Frost Tech., Norwalk, Conn., 1983-85; bd. dirs. TRI-S Inc., Louisville, Colo., Magee Sci.,. Editor Geophys. Research Letters, Arctic Haze Edit., 1983-84; discovered bacteria ice nuclei, 1969; patentee in field; contbr. articles to profl. jours. Bd. dirs. Boulder Valley Christian Ch., 1978-91; chmn. Boulder Council Internat. Visitors, 1983-85. Rotary Internat. fellow, 1968-69. Mem. Am. Geophys. Union, AAAS, Am. Meteorol. Soc. (cert. cons. meteorologist), Internat. Assn. Aerobiology, Soc. Cryobiology, Sigma Xi, Sigma Tau. Avocations: travel, real estate investing, public speaking, flying. Office: Mauna Loa Observatory PO Box 275 Hilo HI 96721-0275

SCHNELLE, KARL BENJAMIN, JR., chemical engineering educator, consultant, researcher; b. Canton, Ohio, Dec. 8, 1930; s. Karl Benjamin and Kathryn Emily (Hollingsworth) S.; m. Mary Margaret Dabney, Sept. 8, 1954; children: Karl Dabney, Kathryn Chappell. BS, Carnegie Mellon U., 1952, MS, 1957, PhD, 1959. Registered profl. engr., Tenn. Chem. engr., shift foreman Organics area Pitts. Plate Glass Co., New Martinsville, W.Va., 1952-54; asst. prof. chem. engring. Vanderbilt U., 1958-61, assoc. prof., 1961-64, assoc. prof. environ. and air resources engring., 1967-70, prof., 1970-80, chmn. div. socio-technol. systems, 1972-75, chmn. environ. and water resources engring., 1975-76, chmn. environ. engring. and policy mgmt. dept., 1976-80, chmn. chem. engring. dept., 1980-88, prof. chem. and environ. engring., 1980—; Alexander Heard disting. svc. prof., 1995-96; v.p. ECCE, Nashville, 1983-88, pres., 1989—; mem. Air Pollution Control Bd., State Tenn., 1978-82, 82-87; Fulbright prof. U. Liege, Belgium, 1977; invited prof. Universite Catholique de Louvain, Belgium, 1982; vis. prof. chem. engring. Danish Tech. Inst., Lyngby, Denmark, 1988-89. Fellow AICE; mem. Air and Waste Mgmt. Assn., Instrument Soc. Am., Am. Soc. Engring. Edn., Am. Soc. Environ. Engrs., Sigma Xi, Phi Kappa Phi, Tau Beta Pi. Office: Vanderbilt U PO Box 1604 Station B Nashville TN 37235

SCHNELLER, EUGENE S., sociology educator; b. Cornwall, N.Y., Apr. 9, 1943; s. Michael Nicholas and Anne Ruth (Gruner) S.; m. Ellen Stauber, Mar. 24, 1968; children: Andrew Jon, Lee Stauber. BA, L.I. U., 1967; AA, SUNY, Buffalo, 1965; PhD, NYU, 1973. Rsch. asst. dept. sociology NYU, N.Y.C., 1968-70; project dir. Montefiore Hosp. and Med. Ctr., Bronx, N.Y., 1970-72; asst. prof. Med. Ctr. and sociology Duke U., Durham, N.C., 1973-75; assoc. prof., chmn. dept. Union Coll., Schenectady, 1975-79, assoc. prof., dir. Health Studies Ctr., 1979-85; prof., dir. Sch. Health Adminstrn. and Policy, Ariz. State U., Tempe, 1985-91, assoc. dean rsch. and adminstrn. Coll. Bus., 1992-94; dir. L. William Seidman Rsch. Ctr., Tempe, 1992-94, counselor to pres. for health profl. edn., 1994-96; clin. prof. cmty. and family medicine U. Ariz., 1995—; prof., dir. Sch. Health Adminstrn. and Policy Ariz. State U., 1996—; vis. rsch. scholar Columbia U., N.Y.C., 1983-84; chmn. Western Network for Edn. in Health Adminstrn., Berkeley, Calif., 1987-92; commr. Calif. Commn. on the Future Med. Edn., 1996—; mem. Ariz. Medicaid Adv. Bd., 1990-92, Ariz. Data Adv. Bd., 1989-91, Ariz. Health Care Group Adv. Bd., 1989; mem. health rsch. coun. N.Y. State Dept. Health, 1977-85; fellow Accrediting Commn. on Edn. for Health Svcs. Adminstrn., 1983-84. Author: The Physician's Assistant, 1980; mem. editorial bd. Work and Occupations, 1975-93, Hosps. and Health Svcs. Adminstrn., 1989-92, Health Adminstrn. Press, 1991-94; Health Mgmt. Review, 1996; contbr. articles to profl. jours., chpt. to book. Trustee Barrow Neurol. Inst., Phoenix, 1989-95; chair nat. adv. com. Nat. Adv. Com. of the Investigator Awards in Health Svcs. Rsch. Robert Wood Johnson Found., 1993-96. Mem. APHA, Am. Sociol. Assn., Assn. Univ. Health Programs Health Adminstrn. (bd. dirs. 1990-96, chmn. bd. dirs. 1994-95). Home: 11843 N 114th Way Scottsdale AZ 85259 Office: Ariz State U Sch Health Admin & Policy Tempe AZ 85287

SCHNEPS, JACK, physics educator; b. N.Y.C., Aug. 18, 1929; s. Elias and Rose (Rephen) S.; m. Lucia DeMarchi, Mar. 11, 1960; children: Loredana, Melissa, Leila. B.A., N.Y. U., 1951; M.S., U. Wis., 1953, Ph.D., 1956. Asst. prof. physics Tufts U., 1956-60, asso. prof., 1960-63, prof., 1963—, chmn. dept. physics, 1980-89, Vannevar Bush chair, 1995—; vis. scientist European Orgn. Nuclear Research, Geneva, Switzerland, 1965-66; lectr. Internat. Sch. Elementary Particle Physics, Yugoslavia, 1968; vis. research fellow Univ. Coll., London, Eng., 1973-74; vis. prof. Ecole Polytechnique, Palaiseau, France, 1982-83, The Technion, Haifa, Israel, 1989-90, Coll. de France, Paris, 1997. Contbg. author: Methods in Subnuclear Physics, Vol. IV, 1970; editor Proc. of Neutrino 88, 1989; contbr. articles to profl. jours. NSF postdoctoral fellow U. Padua, Italy, 1958-59. Fellow Am. Phys. Soc.; mem. European Phys. Soc., AAUP, Phi Beta Kappa, Sigma Xi. Home: 3 Foxcroft Rd Winchester MA 01890-2407 Office: Dept Physics Tufts U Medford MA 02155

SCHNERING, PHILIP BLESSED, investment banker; b. Detroit, Dec. 26, 1917; s. Otto Young and Dorothy (Russell) S.; m. Ruth Scott, June 10, 1940; children: Sally, Sandra, Philip S., Judith, Wendy. BA, U. Chgo., 1939. Salesman, retail crew worker, factory trainee Curtiss Candy Co., Chgo., 1938-40, salesman supr., 1940, dist. field mgr., 1941-43, asst. to pres., 1943-48, v.p., div. sales mgr., 1948-53, exec. v.p., 1953-58; dir. comml. devel. McCormick & Co., Inc., Balt., 1958-64; exec. v.p. Farboil Co., Balt., 1965-66; pres. Bowen Co., Balt., 1966-72; investment banker, 1973—; chmn. bd. Curtiss Breeding Svc., Cary, Ill. Vice pres. Balt. Boy Scouts Am.; past pres., dir. Balt. coun. Camp Fire Girls; chmn. nat. bd., dir. fin. com. Nat. Camp Fire Girls; trustee Nat. Coun. Crime and Delinquency; chmn. Md. Commn. Crime and Delinquency; assoc. trustee Northwestern U. Mem. Am. Mgmt. Assn., Soc. Am. Archaeology, Antique Auto Club, Balt. Yacht Club, Green Spring Valley Hunt Club. Home: 13801 York Rd N-10 Cockeysville MD 21030

SCHNIER, DAVID CHRISTIAN, marketing executive, author; b. Marion, Ohio, Aug. 26, 1942; s. Frederick George William and Dorothy LaVerne (Keller) S. AA, Sinclair Community Coll., Dayton, Ohio, 1976; BS in Edn., U. Dayton, 1979. Adminstr. various depts. VA Ctr., Dayton, 1964-66; tutorial dir. Sinclair Community Coll., 1975-81; pres. Go Blue Enterprises, Dayton, 1987—, Bobby Driscoll Fan Club, Dayton, 1988—; minister of music Ch. of the Holy Angels, Dayton, 1980—. Author: The Sea Eagle, 1951; soloist Hope Luth. Ch., Dayton, 1995—, St. Mark's Luth. Ch., Dayton, 1996—, St. Paul's Evang. Luth. Ch. Active Am. Gay/Lesbian Atheists, Inc., Freedom From Religion Found., Inc., Fundamentalists Anonymous; soloist Hope Luth. Ch., Dayton, 1995—, St. Paul Evang. Ch., 1996—, St. Luke's United Ch. of Christ, Dayton, 1996—, St. Mark's Luth. Ch., Dayton, 1996—. Mem. ASPCA, People for Ethical Treatment of Animals, N.Am. Man/Boy Love Assn., Circus Hist. Soc., The Cousteau Soc., Greenpeace, Scrabble Players Club No. 215 (dir. Dayton chpt. 1983-85), Nat. Geographic Soc., Nat. Audubon Soc., Columbus Assn. Performing Arts, Fellowship Christian Magicians, Dayton Mus. Natural History (life). Roman Catholic. Avocations: classical music, spectator sports, choir, motion pictures. Home and Office: 601 Bowen St Dayton OH 45410-2422

SCHNITZER, ARLENE DIRECTOR, art dealer; b. Salem, Oreg., Jan. 10, 1929; d. Simon M. and Helen (Holtzman) Director; m. Harold J. Schnitzer, Sept. 11, 1949; 1 child, Jordan. Student, U. Wash., 1947-48; BFA (hon.) Pacific NW Coll. Art., 1988. Founder, pres. Fountain Gallery of Art, Portland, Oreg., 1951-86; exec. v.p. Harsch Investment Corp., 1951—. Apptd. to Oreg. State Bd. Higher Edn., 1987-88; former bd. dirs. Oreg. Symphony Assn., v.p. Oreg. Symphony; former bd. dirs. U.S. Dist. Ct. Hist. Soc.; former bd. dirs. Boys and Girls Club, 1988—; mem. Gov.'s Expo '86 Commn., Oreg.; mem. exec. com., former bd. dirs. Artquake; former mem. adv. bd. Our New Beginnings; past bd. dirs. Artists Initiative for a Contemporary Art Collection; former trustee Reed Coll., 1982-88; mem. exec. com. bd. dirs. N.W. Bus. Com. for Arts.; trustee, mem. exec. com. Oreg. Health Scis. Univ. Found.; mem. arts acquisition and collections com. Portland Art Mus.; mem. Nat. Com. for the Performing Arts, Kennedy Ctr., 1995—; adv. bd. Svcs. to Children and Families, Orgn.; bd. trustees Oreg. Jewish Cmty. Found., 1996—; mem. Nat. Coun. Fine Arts Mus. San Francisco, 1995—. Recipient Aubrey Watzek award Lewis and Clark Coll., 1981, Pioneer award U. Oreg., 1985, Met. Arts Commn. award, 1985, White Rose award March of Dimes, 1987, Disting. Svc. award Western Oreg. State Coll. 1988, Oreg. Urban League Equal Opportunity award 1988, Gov's. award for Arts, 1987, Woman of Achievement award YWCA, 1987, Disting. Svc. award U. Oreg., 1991, SAFECO Art Leadership award ArtFair/Seattle, 1994, Portland First Citizen award Portland Met. Assn. Realtors, 1995, Tom McCall Leadership award, 1995; honored by Portland Art Assn., 1979, Northwest Bus. Com. for the Arts, 1997, Arts Champions, 1997. Mem. Univ. Club, Multnomah Athletic Club, Portland Golf Club. Office: Harsch Investment Corp 1121 SW Salmon St Portland OR 97205-2000

SCHNITZER, BERTRAM, hematopathologist; b. Frankfurt, Germany, June 21, 1929; arrived in Can., 1940; s. Robert Julius and Eva (Rosen) S.; m. Anna-Ercoli, June 2, 1959; children: Bret, Robert, Stefan. BS, NYU, 1952; MD, U. Basle, Switzerland, 1958. Lic. physician, Conn., Va., Mich.; diplomate in anatomic pathology and clin. pathology Am. Bd. Pathology. Intern Balt. City Hosps., 1958-59; resident pathology Georgetown U. Hosp., Washington, 1959-63; pathologist, hematopathologist Armed Forces Inst. Pathology, Washington, 1963-66; instr. pathology U. Mich., Ann Arbor, 1966-67, asst. prof., 1967-69, assoc. prof., 1969-73, prof. pathology, dir. hematopathology, 1973—; cons. VA Hosp., Ann Arbor, 1966—; mem. hematology test com. Am. bd. Pathology, 1980-85. Co-author: Monocytes, Monocytosis and Monocytic Leukemia, 1973, Refractory Anemia, 1975; contbr. articles to profl. jours., chpts. to books; cover photograph Sci., 1972. Recipient First DiGuglielmo Prize in Hematology Italian Nat. Soc., Rome, 1976, S.W. Oncology Group grantee U.S. Govt., Washington. Mem. Soc. Hematopathology (pres. 1988-90), Am. Soc. Clin. Pathologists (expert panel hematology com. 1986—, com. on continuing edn. spl. topics 1989—), Am. Soc. Hematology, Internat. Inflammation Club. Achievements include research on tumors of the head and neck, surgical pathology of lymph nodes and neoplastic hematology. Office: U Mich Dept Pathology Ann Arbor MI 48109-0602

SCHNITZER, IRIS TAYMORE, financial management executive, lawyer; b. Cambridge, Mass., Aug. 3, 1943; d. Joseph David and Edith (Cooper) Taymore; m. Stephen Mark Schnitzer, Sept. 10, 1966. BA in Econs., Boston U., 1967; JD, Mass. Sch. Law, 1996. Bar: Mass. 1996; lic. real estate broker, life ins. advisor, life ins. and health ins. broker; registered rep. NASD; CFP; CLU; cert. in fin. counseling, advanced pension planning. Real estate broker Woods Real Estate, Braintree, Mass., 1968; real estate broker, property mgr. Village Gate Realty, Brockton, Mass., 1969; agt. Prudential Ins., Boston, 1970-73; supr. edn. and advanced underwriting, agt. Northwestern Mutual Life, Boston, 1973-78; fin. planning cons. Iris Taymore Schnitzer Assocs., Boston, Mass., 1973-79; trainer fin. planners Gerstenblatt Co., Newton, Mass., 1978-79; founder, pres. The Fin. Forum, Inc., Boston, 1979-91, TFF, Inc. at the Chase Exchange, N.Y.C., 1980-83; pres. I&S Assocs., Boston, 1991-93; v.p. Fleet Investment Svcs., Boston, 1993—; bd. dirs., clk. Mister Tire, Inc., Abington, Mass.; arbitrator Nat. Assn. Securities Dealers, 1992—. Contbr. articles to profl. jours. Chmn. credit com., bd. dirs. Mass. Feminist Fed. Credit Union, Boston, 1975-77; bd. dirs. Ledgewood, Brookline, Mass., 1967-70, LWV, Brockton, Mass., 1968-70, NOW, Boston, 1972-73; bd. govs. Women's City Club, Boston, 1976-80; pres. Mass. divsn. Women's Equity Action League, 1977-79; life mem. Navy League U.S, Boston, 1985—; treas., bd. dirs. Festival of Light and Song, 1989-92; bd. dirs. Achievement Rewards for Coll. Scientists, Boston, 1991-93, 94-95; mem. steering com. Fleet Bank of Mass. United Way, 1994, 95; co-chair task group to establish Girls' Bank of Patriots' Trail Girl Scout Coun., 1996—. Named One of the Best Fin. Planners in the U.S., Money Mag., 1987, to Mutual Funds Panel, Sylvia Porter's Personal Fin. Mag., 1988, 89. Fellow Mass. Bar Found.; mem. Am. Assn. Individual Investors (pres. Boston chpt. 1987-89, bd. dirs. 1985-95), Mass. Bar Assn., Boston Bar Assn., Women's Bar Assn. of Mass., Boston Estate Planning Coun., Boston Club. Republican. Jewish. Avocations: sailing, gardening, interior and fashion design, animals, classical music. Office: Fleet Investment Svcs MABOFO5A 75 State St Boston MA 02109

SCHNITZER, JAN EUGENIUSZ, medical educator, scientist; b. Pitts., June 24, 1957. BSChemE, Princeton U., 1980; MD, U. Pitts., 1985. Assoc. rsch. scientist Sch. Medicine Yale U., New Haven, Conn., 1985-90; asst. prof. San Diego Sch. Medicine U. Calif., La Jolla, 1990-93; asst. prof. Harvard Med. Sch., Boston, 1994-95, assoc. prof., 1995—. Mem. editl. bd. Am. Jour. Physiology-Heart, 1993—, Microvascular Rsch., 1997—. Recipient Established Investigator award Am. Heart Assn. and Genentech, 1993—; grantee NIH, 1889—, CaP Cure award Assn. for the Cure of Cancer of the Prostate, 1995. Office: Harvard Med Sch Beth Israel Hosp Path 330 Brookline Ave Boston MA 02215-5400

SCHNITZER, ROBERT C., theater administrator; b. N.Y.C., Sept. 8, 1906; s. Louis and Clara (diBilliani) S.; m. Marcella Abels Cisney, June 7, 1953. Grad., Horace Mann Sch. for Boys, 1923; A.B., Columbia U., 1927. State dir. Del., asst. dep. nat. dir. Fed. Theatre Project, 1936-39; exec. dir. Civic Theatre, Kalamazoo, Mich., 1939-40; faculty Vassar Coll., 1941-42, Smith Coll., 1942-43, Columbia U. Sch. Dramatic Arts, 1948-54; cons. Martha Graham Sch. Dance, Rollins Sch. Theatre, Randall Sch. Theatre, Dramatic Workshop of New Sch., Denver Red Rocks Theatre, Utah Centennial, 1945-49; vets. counselor Nat. Theater Conf., 1945-46; gen. mgr. ANTA Exptl. Theatre, 1946-47, Cheryl Crawford Prodns., 1952-53, Gilbert Miller Prodns., 1953-54, Am. Nat. Theatre and Acad. Internat. Cultural Exch., 1954-60; gen. mgr. overseas tour Theatre Guild Am. Repertory Co., 1960-61; exec. dir. Profl. Theatre Program U. Mich., Ann Arbor, prof. theatre arts, 1961-73, prof. emeritus and exec. dir. emeritus, 1974—; co-founder, exec. dir. Univ. Resident Theatre Assn., 1969-74; cons., 1974—; del. U.S. Nat. Conf. on UNESCO, 1953-57, 1st Inter-Am. Conf. Exch. Persons, 1958; vis. theatre expert German Fgn. Office Cultural Exch. Program, 1965; cons. to pres. U. Bridgeport for Coll. Fine Arts, 1975-87; disting. vis. prof. U. Miami, Fla., 1980, U. Bridgeport, Conn., 1981; co-founder Westport Arts Ctr., 1984, interim pres.,1 985, v.p., 1986, chmn. bd., 1987-89, chmn. emeritus, 1989—; mem. Fulbright selection com. theatre arts, 1955-59, Mich. Coun. Arts, 1961-73; hon. bd. dirs. Westport/Weston Arts Coun., 1969-84. Stage mgr., actor, Theatre Guild, Walter Hampden, Katherine Cornell, other Broadway cos., 1927-36; owner, dir., Robin Hood Summer Theatre, Arden, Del., 1933-40; gen. mgr. U.S. participation, Denmark Hamlet Festival, Elsinore, 1949, 1st Am. Ballet Theatre tour, Europe, 1950, U.S. ofcl. participation, Berlin Festivals, 1951-53, U.S. participation, Congress Cultural Freedom Festival, Paris, 1952, U.S. Salute to France, Paris, 1955; arranged visits to U.S., Greek Nat. Theatre, 1952, Yugoslav Nat. Folk Ballet, 1956, Shanta Rao East Indian Dance Co., 1957; Contbr. articles in field to various publs. Mem. Weston (Conn.) Commn. Arts, 1995—. Served with ARC, 1943-45, CBI. Recipient Pres.'s Citation U. Mich., 1971, Arts Mgmt. Career award for svcs. to Am. theater, 1971, Sidney Howard award, 1951; Rockefeller Found. grantee, 1948; grad. fellow in theater adminstrn. named in his honor U. Mich., 1974; Robert C. Schnitzer theater memorabilia collection established at George Mason U. Mem. Coll. Fellows of Am. Theatre (life), Actors Equity Assn., Am. Nat. Theatre and Acad., Assn. Theatrical Press Agts. and Mgrs., Nat. Coun. Arts and Govt., Nat. Theatre Conf., Theatre Libr. Assn., U.S Inst. Theatre Technicians, The Players Club, The Century Club. Home: 9 Riverbank Rd Weston CT 06883-2316

SCHNITZLEIN, HAROLD NORMAN, anatomy educator; b. Hannibal, Mo., Aug. 29, 1927; s. Harold Daniel and Martha Anna (Wilhelm) S.; m. Harriett Elizabeth Scheidker, June 2, 1949; children: Jan Elizabeth, Paul Norman, Daniel Richard, Thomas Harry. AB, Westminster Coll., Fulton, Mo., 1950; MS, St. Louis U., 1952, PhD, 1954. USPHS fellow Dept. Anatomy St. Louis U., 1951-54; instr. anatomy U. Ala., Birmingham, 1954-57, asst. prof., 1957-62, assoc. prof., 1962-70, prof., 1970-73; chmn., prof. anatomy U. S. Fla. Coll. Medicine, Tampa, 1973-78, prof., 1978-85, prof. anatomy and radiology, 1985-93, prof. anatomy, radiology, neurology, 1985-93; clin. prof. radiology U. Diagnostic Inst., Tampa, 1993-94, prof. emeritus anatomy, 1995—. Coeditor: Correlative Comparative Anatomy Vertebrate Tel., 1982, Imaging Anatomy: Head and Spine, 2d edit., 1990. Sgt. USAAF, 1946-47. Office: U Diagnostic Inst Dept Anatomy Tampa FL 33612

SCHNOBRICH, ROGER WILLIAM, lawyer; b. New Ulm, Minn., Dec. 21, 1929; s. Arthur George and Amanda (Reinhart) S.; m. Angeline Ann Schmitz, Jan. 21, 1961; children: Julie A. Johnson, Jennifer L. Holmers, Kathryn M. Kubinski, Karen L. Holetz. BBA, U. Minn., 1952, JD, 1954. Bar: Minn. 1954. Assoc. Fredrikson and Byron, Mpls., 1956-58; pvt. practice Mpls., 1958-60; ptnr. Popham Haik, Schnobrich & Kaufman, Mpls., 1960—; bd. dirs. numerous corps., Mpls. With U.S. Army, 1954-56. Mem. ABA, Minn. Bar Assn., Hennepin County Bar Assn., Order of Coif, Law Rev. Roman Catholic. Avocations: family, jogging, reading, golf. Home: 530 Waycliff Dr N Wayzata MN 55391-1385 Office: Popham Haik Schnobrich & Kaufman 3300 Piper Jaffray Tower 222 S 9th St Minneapolis MN 55402-3389

SCHNOLL, HOWARD MANUEL, investment banking and managed asset consultant; b. Milw., June 6, 1935; s. Nathan P. and Della (Fisher) S.; m. Barbara Ostach, Dec. 3, 1988; children: Jordan, Terry, Jeffrey, Robert, Tammy, Daniel. BBA, U. Wis., 1958. CPA, Wis.; cert. mgmt. cons. Mng. ptnr. Nankin, Schnoll & Co., S.C., Milw., 1966-86; mng. ptnr., bd. dirs. BDO Seidman, 1986-90; pres., chief oper. officer Universal Med. Bldgs., L.P., Milw., 1990, also bd. dirs.; pres. Howard Schnoll & Assocs., Milw., 1991; mng. dir. Grande, Schnoll & Assocs., Milw., 1992-93; exec. mng. dir., COO Glaisner, Schilffarth, Grande & Schnoll, Ltd., Milw., 1993—. Bd. dirs. Milw. World Festival, Inc., 1968—, City of Festivals Parade, Milw., 1983—, Aurora Health Care Ventures, Milw. Heart Rsch. Found., Milw. Heart Inst., Arthritis Found.; pres. Milw. Coun. on Alcoholism and Drug Dependance, 1993—, bd. dirs.; treas. Am. Heart Assn., Milw., 1978-82; capt. United Way, Milw., 1985; mem. Greater Milw. Com. Nat. Found. Ileitis and Colitis, Milw. chpt. Served to sgt. U.S. Army, 1956-63. Mem. AICPA, Wis. Inst. CPAs, Acct. Computer Users Tech. Exchange, Brynwood Country Club (bd. dirs., treas.), B'nai Brith (pres. 1960-62). Jewish. Avocations: golf, tennis. Office: Glaisner Schilffarth Grande & Schnoll 250 E Wisconsin Ave Ste 800 Milwaukee WI 53202-4205

SCHNOOR, JEFFREY ARNOLD, lawyer; b. Winnipeg, Man., Can., June 22, 1953; s. Toby and Ray (Kass) S. BA, U. Man., 1974, LLB, 1977. Bar: Man. 1978. Assoc. McJannet Weinberg Rich, Winnipeg, 1977-84, ptnr., 1984-86; exec. dir. Man. Law Reform Commn., Winnipeg, 1986—; pres. Fedn. Law Reform Agys. Can., 1995—; del. Uniform Law Conf. Can., mem. steering com. 1995—, chair civil sect., 1996—. Trustee, mem. exec. com. United Way of Winnipeg, 1990—, treas., 1991-92, pres., 1994-95, mem. R&D 2000 steering com., 1995—; chair cmty. rels. com. United Way of Can., 1996—. Named Queen's Counsel Govt. of Man., 1992; recipient Chair's award of distinction United Way of Winnipeg, 1997. Mem. Law Soc. Man. (lectr. bar admission course 1981—), Man. Bar Assn. (governing coun. 1988—, life mem.), Can. Bar Assn. (legis. and law reform com. 1994—). Avocations: travel, languages, performing arts, fitness. Home: 104 Harvard Ave, Winnipeg, MB Canada R3M 0K4 Office: Man Law Reform Commn, 405 Broadway 12th Fl, Winnipeg, MB Canada R3C 3L6

SCHNUCK, CRAIG D., grocery stores company executive; b. 1948. MBA, Cornell U., 1971. With Schnuck Markets, Inc., Hazelwood, Mo., 1971—, v.p., 1975-76, exec. v.p., sec., 1976-83, pres., chief exec. officer, 1983—, also bd. dirs. Office: Schnuck Markets Inc 11420 Lackland Rd Saint Louis MO 63146-3559*

SCHNUCKER, ROBERT VICTOR, history and religion educator; b. Waterloo, Iowa, Sept. 30, 1932; s. Felix Victor and Josephine (Maasdam) S.; m. Anna Mae Engelkes, Sept. 18, 1955; children: Sarai Ann, Sar Victor, Christjahn Dietrich. AB, NE Mo. State U., 1953; BD, U. Dubuque, 1956; MA, U. Iowa, 1960, PhD, 1969. Ordained to ministry Presbyn. Ch., 1956/. Pastor United Presbyn. Ch. USA, Springville, Iowa, 1956-63, Meth.-Presbyn. Ch., Labelle, Mo., 1976-97; asst. prof. N.E. Mo. State U., Kirksville, 1963-65, assoc. prof., 1963-65, prof., 1969—; dir. Thomas Jefferson U. Press; supr. Bible exam. Presbyn. Ch. USA, Louisville, 1977-89; bd. dirs. Ctr. for Reformation Rsch., St. Louis, 1984—; pres. Conf. of Hist. Jours., 1993. Author: A Glossary of Terms for Western Civilization, 1975, Helping Humanities Journal Survive, 1985, History Assessment Test, 1990; editor: Calviniana, 1989, Historians of Early Modern Europe, 1976-93, 97, Network News Exch.., 1978-88; pres. 1st and 2d Editing History, Conf. for Hist. Jour., 1985-97; book rev. editor, mng. editor 16th Century Jour., 1972—; pub. 16th Century Essays and Studies, 1980—; contbr. articles to profl. jours. Fellow Soc. Sci. Study of Religion, 1988; NEH grantee for jour. pubs., 1980. Mem. AAUP, Am. Acad. Religion, Renaissance Soc. Am., Am. History Assn. (chmn. Robinson prize com. 1987), Am. Soc. Ch. History, Soc. History of Edn., Soc. Bibl. Lit., Soc. for Reformation Rsch., Soc. Scholarly Pubs., Soc. for Values in Higher Edn., Conf. for Hist. Jour., Am. Coun. Learned Soc. (exec. bd. conf. adminstr. officers 1993-96, sec. 1994, chmn. 1995-96), Conf. Faith and History, 16th Century Studies Cons. (exec. sec. 1972—). Office: Truman State U Thomas Jefferson Univ Press MC1111L Kirksville MO 63501

SCHNUR, ROBERT ARNOLD, lawyer; b. White Plains, N.Y., Oct. 25, 1938; s. Conrad Edward and Ruth (Mehr) S.; children: Daniel, Jonathan. BA, Cornell U., 1960; JD, Harvard U., 1963. Bar: Wis. 1965, Ill. 1966. Assoc. Michael, Best & Friedrich, Milw., 1966-73, ptnr., 1973—; chmn. Wis. Tax News, 1983-90; adj. prof. tax law U. Wis. Law Sch., 1988—. Capt. U.S. Army, 1963-65. Fellow Am. Coll. Tax Counsel; mem. ABA, Wis. Bar Assn. (chmn. tax sect. 1986-88), Milw. Bar Assn. Home: 929 N Astor St Milwaukee WI 53202-3454 Office: Michael Best Friedrich 100 E Wisconsin Ave Milwaukee WI 53202-4107

SCHOBER, ROBERT CHARLES, electrical engineer; b. Phila., Sept. 20, 1940; s. Rudolph Ernst and Kathryn Elizabeth (Ehrisman) S.; m. Mary Eve Kanuika, Jan. 14, 1961; children: Robert Charles, Stephen Scott, Susan Marya. BS in Engring. (Scott Award scholar), Widner U., 1965; postgrad., Bklyn. Poly. Extension at Gen. Electric Co., Valley Forge, Pa., 1965-67, U. Colo., 1968-69, Calif. State U.-Long Beach, 1969-75, U. So. Calif., 1983-84. Engr. Gen. Electric Co., Valley Forge, 1965-68, Martin Marietta Corp., Denver, 1968-69; sr. engr. Jet Propulsion Lab., Pasadena, Calif., 1969-73, sr. staff, 1986—; mem. tech. staff Hughes Semiconductor Co., Newport Beach, Calif., 1973-75; prin. engr. Am. Hosp. Supply Corp., Irvine, Calif., 1975-83; sr. staff engr. TRW Systems, Redondo Beach, Calif., 1983-84; cons. Biomed. LSI, Huntington Beach, Calif. Mem. IEEE (student br. pres. 1963-65), Soc. for Indsl. and Applied Math., Assn. for computing Machinery, Tau Bea Pi. Republican. Patentee cardiac pacemakers. Current Work: Develop large scale integrated circuits for computer, spacecraft, and military, as well as commercial applications; design high speed signal processing integrated circuits; instrumental in starting the quest for low power integrated circuits; actively persuing the advancment of ultra low power technology; provides dissemination through public domain distribution of a low power MOSIS cell library, workshops and publications. Subspecialties: application specific microprocessor architecture design; ultra low power analog and digital systems and integrated circuits; integrated circuit design; focal plane electronic signal processing arrays, neural networks; synchro converter electronics; sigma-delta analog to digital converters and signal processing electronics; implantable medical devices including cardiac pacemakers, defibulators and hearing aids. Office: Jet Propulsion Lab 4800 Oak Grove Dr Pasadena CA 91109-8001

SCHOBINGER, RANDY ARTHUR, state legislator. Student, Minot State U., 1991-96. Warehouseman Minot; senator State of N.D., Bismarck; Movers, Inc.; vice chmn. transp. com. State Senate of N.D., mem. edn. com.; endorsed candidate of the N.D. Repub. Party for State Treasurer, 1996. Office: ND State Capitol 600 Easy St Bismarck ND 58504-6239

SCHOBORG, THOMAS WILLIAM, urologist; b. Covington, Ky., Oct. 14, 1949; s. William Henry and Adelma Barbara (Timmerman) S.; m. Josephine Ann Valenti, oct. 6, 1973; children: Thomas William, Christopher J. BA in Zoology, U. Cin., 1969; MD, Emory U., 1973. Diplomate Am. Bd. Urology. Resident Univ. Hosp., Jacksonville, Fla., 1973-78, chief resident in urology, 1978-79; chief urology Ga. Bapt. Med. Ctr., Atlanta, 1981; assoc. prof. urology Med. Coll. Ga., Augusta, 1985—; bd. dirs. Nat. Kidney Found. Ga., Atlanta, 1986—. Contbr. articles to profl. jours. Coach youth baseball East Side Baseball, Marietta, Ga., 1993—. Recipient Upjohn Achievement award, 1979. Mem. AMA, Am. Urol. Assn., Atlanta Urol. Assn., Soc. Laparoscopic Surgeons, Endourol. Soc. Roman Catholic. Avocation: collecting nautical antiques and shipwreck artifacts. Office: Atlanta Urol Group PC 285 Boulevard NE Ste 215 Atlanta GA 30312-4208

SCHOCHOR, JONATHAN, lawyer; b. Suffern, N.Y., Sept. 9, 1946; s. Abraham and Betty (Hechtor) S.; m. Joan Elaine Brown, May 31, 1970; children: Lauren Aimee, Daniel Ross. BA, Pa. State U., 1968; JD, Am. U., 1971. Bar: D.C. 1971, U.S. Dist. Ct. D.C. 1971, U.S. Ct. Appeals (D.C. cir.) 1971, Md. 1974, U.S. Dist. Ct. Md. 1974, U.S. Ct. Appeals (4th cir.) 1974, U.S. Supreme Ct. 1986. Assoc., McKenna, Wilkinson & Kittner, Washington, 1970-74; assoc. Ellin & Baker, Balt., 1974-84; ptnr. Schochor,

Federico & Staton, Balt., 1984—; lectr. in law; expert witness to state legis. Assoc. editor-in-chief American U. Law Rev., 1970-71. Mem. ABA, Assn. Trial Lawyers Am. (state del. 1991, state gov. 1992-95), Am. Bd. Trial Advocates (membership com. 1994—), Am. Bd. Trial Advocates, Am. Judicature Soc., Md. State Bar Assn. (spl. com. on health claims arbitration 1983), Md. Trial Lawyers Assn. (bd. govs. 1986-87, mem. legis. com., 1985-88, chmn. legis. com. 1986-87, sec. 1987-88, exec. com. 1987-92, v.p. 1987-88, pres.-elect 1989, pres. 1990-91), Balt. City Bar Assn. (legis. com. 1986-87, spl. com. on tort reform 1986, medicolegal com. 1989-90, circuit ct. for Balt. City task force-civil document mgmt. system 1994—), Bar Assn. D.C., Internat. Platform Assn., Phi Alpha Delta. Office: Schochor Federico & Staton PA 1211 Saint Paul St Baltimore MD 21202-2705

SCHOCK, ROBERT NORMAN, geophysicist; b. Monticello, N.Y., May 25, 1939; s. Carl Louis and Norma Elizabeth (Greenfield) S.; m. Susan Esther Benton, Nov. 28, 1959; children: Pamela Ann, Patricia Elizabeth, Christina Benton. B.S., Colo. Coll., 1961; M.S., Rensselaer Poly. Inst., 1963, Ph.D., 1966; postgrad., Northwestern U., 1963-64. Cert. Calif. state wine judge. Jr. geophys. trainee Continental Oil Co., Sheridan, Wyo., 1960; jr. geologist Texaco In., Billings, Mont., 1961; teaching asst. Rensselaer Poly. Inst., Troy, N.Y., 1961-63, research asst., 1964-66; research assoc. U. Chgo., 1966-68; sr. research scientist Lawrence Livermore Nat. Lab., U. Calif., 1968—, group leader high pressure physics, 1972-74, sect. leader geoscis. and engring., 1974-76, div. leader earth scis., 1976-81, head dept. earth scis., 1981-87, energy program leader, 1987-92, dep. assoc. dir. for energy, 1992—; pres. Pressure Sys. Rsch. Inc.; mem. faculty Chabot Coll., 1969-71; dir. Alameda County Flood Control and Water Conservation Dist., 1984-86; mem. adv. panel on geoscis. U.S. Dept. Energy, 1985-87; chair adv. com. U. Calif. Energy Inst., 1992—; mem. rsch. adv. com. Gas Rsch. Inst., Chgo., 1995—. Mem. editl. bd. Rev. Sci. Instruments, 1975-77; assoc. editor Jour. Geophys. Rsch., 1978-80; bd. assoc. editors 11th Lunar and Planetary Sci. Conf., 1980; mem. adv. bd. Physics ans Chemistry of Minerals, 1983-97; rsch. and publs. on high pressure physics, solid state physics, physics of earth interior, rock deformation, energy R&D and energy policy. Fulbright sr. fellow U. Bonn (Germany), 1973; vis. research fellow Australian Nat. U. Canberra, 1980-81. Mem. AAAS, Am. Geophys. Union, Sigma Xi, Commonwealth of Calif. Club, Cosmos Club (Washington). Office: Lawrence Livermore Nat Lab PO Box 808 Livermore CA 94551-0808

SCHOCK, WILLIAM WALLACE, pediatrician; b. Huntingdon, Pa., Aug. 15, 1923; s. Clarence and Mabel (Decker) S.; m. Doris Ann Wilson, July 1, 1944; 1 child, William Wallace. Student, Juniata Coll., 1941-43; MD, Temple U., 1947. Intern Conemaugh Valley Meml. Hosp., Johnstown, Pa., 1946-48; resident Women AFB, Cheyene, Wyo., 1951-52; pvt. practice medicine Huntingdon, 1948-50; pediatrician Warren AFB Hosp., 1951-52; chief outpatient svc. USAF, Cheyene, Wyo., 951-52; pvt. practice medicine specializing in pediatrics Huntingdon, 1952—; pediatrician J. C. Blair Meml. Hosp.; local pub. health pediatrician. Pres. Huntingdon chpt. Am. Cancer Soc., 1955-57; bd. dirs. local chpt. Am. Heart Assn., 1955-62; mem. Am. Security Coun., Rep. Nat. Com., 2d Amendment Found. With AUS, 1942-45, USAF, 1950-52. Recipient Wisdom award Leon Gutterman, Wisdom Hall of Fame, 1970. Fellow Royal Soc. Health; mem. AMA, Pa. Med. Soc., Huntingdon County Med. Soc. (past pres.), Med. Alumni Assn. Temple U., Am. Assn. Mil. Surgeons U.S., Am. Acad. Pediatrics (assoc.), Internat. Platform Assn., Phi Rho Sigma, Huntingdon Country Club, Heidelburg Country Club (Altoona, Pa.), U.S. Senatorial Club, Rotary. Republican. Presbyterian. Home and Office: RR 2 Box 69 Huntingdon PA 16652-9115

SCHOCKAERT, BARBARA ANN, operations executive; b. Queens, N.Y., Dec. 13, 1938; d. Lawrence Henry and Eleanor Veronica (Tollner) Grob; children: Donna Ann, Don. Student, Ocean County Coll., Toms River, N.J., 1987, 94—. Cert. notary pub. V.p. ops. Am. Vitamin Products, Inc., Freehold, N.J., 1977-89, v.p. ops. Foods Plus div., 1990-94, sales coord., 1994—; assoc. Ocean County Realty, Toms River, N.J., 1987-90, Crossroads Realty, Toms River, 1990—. Contbg. author: Greatest Poems of the Western World, 1989 (Golden Poet award). Past pres. mayor's adv. com., past pres. of help line Town of Jackson, N.J.; past bd. dirs. Big Bros. of Ocean County; speaker community svc. orgns. Named Woman of Yr., Jaycees, 1974; recipient Capitol award Nat. Leadership Coun., 1991, Silver Bowl award for 1st pl. poetry contest, 1996. Mem. N.J. Realtors Assn., Internat. Platform Assn., Alpha Beta Gamma. Home: 977 Fairview Dr Toms River NJ 08753-3064 Office: 500 Halls Mill Rd Freehold NJ 07728-8811

SCHOECK, RICHARD J(OSEPH), English and humanities scholar; b. N.Y.C., Oct. 10, 1920; s. Gustav J. and Frances M. (Kuntz) S.; m. Reta R. Haberer, 1945 (div. 1976); children: Eric R., Christine C., Jennifer A.; m. Megan S. Lloyd, Feb. 19, 1977. MA, Princeton U., 1949, PhD, 1949. Instr. English Cornell U., 1949-55; from asst. prof. to assoc. prof. U. Notre Dame, 1955-61; prof. English U. Toronto, 1961-71; head dept. English St. Michael's Coll., 1965-70; prof. vernacular lit. Pontifical Inst. Mediaeval Studies, Toronto, 1964-71; dir. rsch. activities Folger Shakespeare Libr., also dir. Folger Inst. Renaissance and 18th Century Studies, 1970-74; adj. prof. English Cath. U. Am., 1972; prof. English, medieval and renaissance studies U. Md., 1974-75; prof. English and humanities U. Colo., Boulder, 1975-89, prof. emeritus, 1987—; chmn. dept. integrated studies U. Colo., 1976-79; chmn. comparative lit., 1983-84; prof. Anglistik Univ. Trier, 1987-90, head dept., Geschäftsführer, 1988-89; adj. prof. English U. Kans., Lawrence, 1990—; Vincent J. Flynn prof. Letters Coll. St. Thomas, 1969; vis. prof. Princeton U., 1964, U. Dallas, 1985; vis. fellow Inst. Advanced Studies in Humanities, Edinburgh, 1984-85; vis. scholar Corpus Christi Coll., Oxford, 1994; fellow Assn. Advancement Edn., 1952-53, Yale U., 1959-60, Can. Coun. 1967-68, Ctr. for the Book, Brit. Libr., 1995-96; cons. NEH: bd. dirs. Natural Law Inst. U. Notre Dame; advisor Italian Acad. for Advanced Studies in Am., 1993. Author: The Achievement of Thomas More, 1976, Intertexuality and Renaissance Texts, 1984, Erasmus Grandescens, 1988 (poems) The Eye of a Traveller, 1992, The Knights Book (poems), 1993, Erasmus of Europe, Vol. I, The Making of a Humanist, 1467-1500, 1990, Vol. II The Prince to Humanists, 1501-1536, 1993; contbr. numerous articles, papers, revs. to jours. and mags.; editor: Delehaye's Legends of the Saints, 1961, Editing 16th Century Texts, 1966 (Roger Ascham), The Scholemaster, 1966, Shakespeare Quar., 1972-74, Acta Conventus Neo-Latini Bononiensis, 1985; gen. editor: The Confutation of Tyndale, 3 vols., 1973; co-editor: Voices of Literature, 2 vols., 1964, 66, Chaucer Criticism, 2 vols, 1960, 61, Style, Rhetoric and Rhythm: Essays by M.W. Croll, 1966, Acta Conventus Neo-Latini Torontonensis, 1991; former gen. editor: Patterns of Literary Criticism; spl. editor Canada vol. Rev. Nat. Literatures, 1977, Sir Thomas Browne and the Republic of Letters, 1982, A Special Number of English Language Notes, 1982; gen. editor (series) Renaissance Masters, 1992—; mem. editl. bds. profl. jours. Served with U.S. Army, 1940-46. Guggenheim Found. fellow, 1968-69, Fulbright fellow, 1983; recipient Centennial medal U. Colo., 1976, Falconer Madan award Bibliographi Soc., London, 1997, 1st prize Mellen Poetry Competition, 1997; grantee Can. Coun., UNESCO, Am. Coun. Learned Socs., U. Toronto, U. Colo. Fellow Royal Soc. Can., Royal Hist. Soc.; mem. Internat. Assn. Neo-Latin Studies (pres. 1976-79), MLA, Renaissance Soc. Am., PEN (N.Y.), Can. Humanities Assn., Internat. Assn. U. Profs. English, Assn. Can. Studies in U.S. Home: 232 Dakota St Lawrence KS 66046-4710 *More than a thousand years ago Bede summed up what are for me the principles of my professional career: I have always thought it fitting to learn and to teach and to write.*

SCHOEFFMANN, RUDOLF, consulting engineer; b. Linz, Austria, May 25, 1926; s. Rudolf and Anna (Hartl) S.; m. Herta Buttinger, Apr. 20, 1954; children: Monka M.B., Margit M.A., Rudolf M.G. Ing., Engring. Sch. Linz, 1944; Dipl.Ing., Tech. U. Vienna, Austria, 1951. Constructor Vöest, Linz, 1951-55, constrn. group leader, 1955-65, mgr., 1959-65, divsn. mgr., 1965-72; cons. Allis Chalmers Corp., Milw., 1972-81; dir. and cons. Rokop-Davy, Stockton, Eng., 1980-82; pvt. cons. engr. Linz, 1973—. Contbr. articles to profl. jours. Recipient Silver Cross of Merit, Pres. of Austria, 1969. Mem. Club of Engrs. and Architects, Chamber of Cons. Engrs., Golf Club of Linz. Roman Catholic. Achievements include 18 patents. Avocations: golf, skiing, swimming, chess.

SCHOELLER, DALE ALAN, nutrition research educator; b. Milw., June 8, 1948; s. Arthur B. and Anne Clare (Maas) S.; m. Madeline Mary Juresh, Aug. 22, 1970; children: Nicholas Paul, Gregory Scott, Erica Lee. BS with honors, U. Wis., Milw., 1970; PhD, Ind. U., 1974. Postdoctoral fellow Argonne (Ill.) Nat. Lab., 1974-76; from asst. prof. to prof., also rsch. assoc. U. Chgo., 1976-91, assoc. prof., 1991—, prof., 1996; assoc. prof. U. Wis., Madison, 1997—; chmn. com. on human nutrition and nutritional biology U. Chgo., 1991-97. Author: (book chpt.) Obesity, 1992; co-author: (book chpt.) Annual Review of Nutrition, 1991. Achievements include development of stable isotope methods for the study of human energy metabolism including first human use of doubly labeled water for measurement of free-living total energy expenditure. Avocations: coaching youth sports including basketball, baseball and hockey. Mem. Am. Soc. Nutritional Scis. (Mead Johnson award 1987), Am. Soc. for Clin. Nutrition, Am. Soc. for Mass Spectrometry, N.Am. Soc. for Study of Obesity. Office: U Wis Dept Nutrition 1415 Linden Dr Madison WI 53706-1527

SCHOEMANN, RUDOLPH ROBERT, lawyer; b. Chgo., Nov. 2, 1930; s. Rudolph and Anna Elise (Claus) S.; m. Florence Margaret Olivier, May 17, 1952 (div.); children—Peggy Ann Schoemann Salathe, Rudolph Robert III, Richard Randolph (dec.), Rodney Ryan; m. Marie Louise Gandolfo Webb, Dec. 2, 1983. Student, Wabash Coll., Crawfordsville, Ind., 1946-47; B.C.S., Loyola U. of South, New Orleans, 1959, J.D., 1952; B.A., Tulane U., 1966, LL.M. in Admiralty Law, 1981, LL.M. in Internat. Law, 1989; postgrad. U. New Orleans, 1981-82. Bar: La. 1952, U.S. Supreme Ct. 1959, U.S. Ct. Appeals (5th cir.) 1952, U.S. Ct. Appeals (11th cir.) 1981, U.S. Ct. Appeals (D.C. cir.) 1982, U.S. Dist. Ct. Md. 1957, U.S. Dist. Ct. (ea. dist.) La. 1952, U.S. Dist. Ct. (we. dist.) La. 1960, U.S. Dist. Ct. (mid. dist.) La. 1952, U.S. Ct. Mil. Appeals, 1953, U.S. Ct. Customs and Patent Appeals 1953, U.S. Ct. Claims 1953. Assoc. James J. Morrison, New Orleans, 1952-54; ptnr. Smith & Schoemann, New Orleans, 1955-60, Schoemann & Gomes, 1961-63, Schoemann, Gomes, Ducote & Collins, 1963-67, Schoemann, Gomes & Ducote, 1968-74, Rudolph R. Schoemann, 1974-77, Schoemann & Golden, 1978-79, Schoemann, Swaim, Morrison & Cockfield, 1979-80, Schoemann & Assocs., 1980—(all New Orleans). Served with La. N.G., 1949-52, to 1st lt. JAGC, U.S. Army, 1952-53; capt. Res. ret. Mem. ABA, La. Bar Assn., New Orleans Bar Assn., La. Def. Assn., New Orleans Def. Assn., Def. Research Inst., Soc. Naval Architects and Marine Engrs., Fed. Bar Assn. Democrat. Lutheran. Address: 3670 Gentilly Blvd New Orleans LA 70122-4910

SCHOEN, ALVIN E., JR., environmental engineer, consultant; b. Milford, Conn., Jan. 3, 1945; s. Alvin E. and Thelma (Trerrace) S.; m. Mary Ann Kosik; 1 child, Matthew S. BA in Math., U. Conn., 1968, BS in Engring., 1971; MSCE, Polytechnic Inst. of N.Y., 1977; PhD in Environ. Engring., U. Okla., 1994. Registered profl. engr., Ohio, Maine, N.Y., Conn., Mass., N.H., Va., Okla., N.J.; Diplomate Am. Acad. Environ. Engrs. Field engr. Mobil Oil Corp., Scarsdale, N.Y., 1973-76, engring. supr., 1976-80; project engr. Mobil Oil Corp., Fairfax, Va., 1980-82; group leader, process engr. Mobil Oil Corp., Oklahoma City, 1985-89; environ. engr. rsch. and devel. Mobil Oil Corp., Princeton, N.J., 1989-96; project engr. Arabian Am. Oil, Dhahran, Saudi Arabia, 1982-85; pres. A.E. Schoen & Assocs. Inc., Skillman, N.J., 1996—; commr. Inland Wetlands Commn., Brookfield, Conn., 1978-80, Environ. Commn., Montgomery Twsp, N.J., 1992-93. 1st lt. C.E., U.S. Army, 1968-70, Vietnam. Fellow ASCE; mem. Nat. Soc. Profl. Engrs., Water Environ. Fedn., Lions Clubs Internat., Rotary Internat. Office: AE Schoen & Assocs Inc PO Box 131 Skillman NJ 08558

SCHOEN, STEVAN JAY, lawyer; b. N.Y.C., May 19, 1944; s. Al and Ann (Spevack) S.; m. Cynthia Lukens; children: Andrew Adams, Anna Kim. BS, U. Pa., 1966; JD, Cornell U., 1969; MPhil in Internat. Law, Cambridge U. (Eng.), 1980. Bar: N.Mex. 1970, N.Y. 1970, U.S. Supreme Ct. 1976, U.S. Tax Ct. 1973, U.S. Ct. Internat. Trade 1982. Nat. dir. Vista law recruitment U.S. OEO, Washington, 1970-71; atty. Legal Aid Soc. of Albuquerque, 1971-73; chief atty., spl. asst. atty. gen. N.Mex. Dept. Health and Social Svcs., Albuquerque, 1973-77; ptnr. Brennan, Schoen & Eisenstadt, 1979-89, Stevan J. Schoen P.A., 1989-89; probate judge, Sandoval County, 1990—; arbitrator, NYSE. mem. N.Mex. Supreme Ct. Appellate Rules Com., 1982-92; chmn. rules com. Com. on Fgn. Legal Cons., 1993, Jud. Edn. Planning Com.; mem. Children's Code Rules Com., 1976-78; bd. edn. Bernalillo Pub. Sch. Dist., 1996-97. Mem. Mayor's Albuquerque Adv. Com. on Fgn. Trade Zone, 1992-94; v.p. Placitas Vol. Fire Dept., 1974-86. Recipient Cert. for Outstanding Svc. to Judiciary N.Mex. Supreme Ct., 1982, cert. of Appreciation, N.Mex. Supreme Ct., 1992, Cert. of Appreciation, N.Mex. Sec. of State, 1980, Cert. of Appreciation, U.S. OEO, 1971, Pro Bono Pub. Svc. award 1989, cert. Recognition Legal Aid, 1994, award Las Placitas Assn., 1996. Mem. Am. Judges Assn., Nat. Coll. Probate Judges, State Bar N.Mex. (past chmn. real property, probate and trust sect. 1989, Outstanding Contbn. award 1989, task force on regulation of advt. 1990-91, past chmn. appellate practice sect. 1991, past chmn. internat. law sect. 1991-92, commn. on professionalism 1992-95, organizing com. U.S.-Mex. law inst. 1992), N.Mex. Probate Judges Assn. (chmn. 1993—), Oxford-Cambridge Soc. N.Mex. (sec.), N.Mex. Assn. Counties (adv. bd.). Home: 14 Rainbow Valley Rd Placitas NM 87043-8801 Office: 5700 Harper Dr NE Ste 430 Albuquerque NM 87109-3573

SCHOEN, WILLIAM JACK, financier; b. Los Angeles, Aug. 2, 1935; s. Jack Conrad and Kathryn Mabel (Stegmayer) S.; m. Sharon Ann Barto, Oct. 1, 1966; children: Kathryn Lynn, Karen Anne, Kristine Lea, William Jack. BS in Fin. magna cum laude, U. So. Calif., 1960, MBA, 1963. Mktg. mgr. Anchor Hocking Glass Co., 1964-68; v.p. sales and mktg. Obear-Nester Glass Co., 1968-71; pres. Pierce Glass Co., Port Allegheny, Pa., 1971-73; pres., chief exec. officer, dir. F.&M. Schaefer Brewing Co., N.Y.C., 1973-81; now chmn., pres. Wilshar Mgmt. Co. Inc., Naples, Fla., 1981—; chmn., pres. Health Mgmt. Assocs. Inc., Naples, 1983—; also bd. dirs. Health Mgmt. Assocs. Inc.; bd. dirs. 1st Union Nat. Bank Fla., Horace Mann Ins. Co. Contbr. to indsl. publns. Served with USMC, 1953-56, Korea. Mem. Naples Yacht Club, Port Royal Club, Quail Creek Country Club, Phi Kappa Phi. Republican. Episcopalian.

SCHOENBAUM, DAVID LEON, historian; b. Milw., Mar. 26, 1935; s. Milton Lionel and Leah (Hertz) S.; m. Tamara Holtermann, June 6, 1963; children—Michael, Miriam. B.A., U. Wis.-Madison, 1955, M.A., 1958; D.Phil., St. Antony's Coll., Oxford U., 1965. Reporter Waterloo Courier, Iowa, 1957-58; copy editor Mpls. Tribune, 1958-59; asst. prof. Kent State U., Ohio, 1966-67; from asst. prof. to prof. history U. Iowa, Iowa City, 1967—; guest prof. U. Freiburg, Fed. Republic Germany, 1974-75, U. Bonn, Fed. Republic Germany, 1989; prof. U.S. Naval War Coll., Newport, R.I., 1976-77, Johns Hopkins Univ. Sch. of Advanced Internat. Studies, Bologna Ctr., Bologna, Italy, 1991-93; occasional free-lance journalist. Author: Hitler's Social Revolution, 1966, The Spiegel Affair, 1968, Zabern 1913, 1983, The United States and The State of Israel, 1993; co-author: (with Elizabeth Pond) The German Question and Other German Questions, 1996. Fulbright grantee, Bonn. Fed. Republic Germany, 1959, sr. scholar, 1973-74, 88-89, 96-97; Guggenheim grantee, 1975, German Marshall Fund U.S. grantee, 1986—; sr. scholar Truman Presdl. Library, Independence, Mo., 1982-83; fellow Woodrow Wilson Ctr. , 1984-85, German Soc. Fgn. Affairs, Bonn, 1988-89. Jewish. Avocation: chamber music (violin and viola). Home: 617 Holt Ave Iowa City IA 52246-2917 Office: U Iowa Dept History Iowa City IA 52242

SCHOENBERG, APRIL MINDY, nursing administrator; b. Nassau, N.Y., June 2, 1955; d. Robert and Eleanor (Marks) Christian; m. Gerald Duggan, 1979 (div.); children: Lance, Craig, Danielle; m. Bruce Schoenberg; 1 child, Michael. BSN, Long Island U., 1978. Intravenous cert., 1994, cen. line intravenous cert., 1995; cert. Nassau Fire Commn. Head nurse Sunrise Manor Nursing Home, Bayshore, N.Y., 1982-87; unit coord. East Neck Nursing Ctr., Babylon, N.Y., 1987-89; dir. nursing svcs., asst. dir. nursing svcs. Oceanside (N.Y.) Care Ctr., 1988-91; PRI nurse, medicare nurse, rehab. coord., MDST coord. Ctrl. Island Health Care, Plainview, N.Y., 1993-95; reviewer, monitor restraints and psychoactive medications Quality of Care Mgmt., N.Y.C., 1995—; RN discharge planner Northshore Hosp. Plainview (N.Y.), 1995—; Asst. info. Tumor Registry Northshore Hosp., Manhasset, N.Y., 1975. Assoc. mem. Am. Mus. Natural History; sponsor Child Reach, 1984—. Mem. N.Y. State Nurses Assn., Multiple Sclerosis Soc., Nat. Trust Hist. Preservation (elected), The Nature Conservancy Soc. (elected). Avocations: puzzles, bowling, racquetball, reading, speed walking.

SCHOENBERG, LAWRENCE JOSEPH, computer services company executive; b. N.Y.C., July 4, 1932; s. Samuel and Selma (Shapiro) S.; m. Barbara Brizdle, Sept. 15, 1990; children: Douglas, Eric, Julie. A.B., U. Pa., 1953, M.B.A., 1956. Sr. systems analyst IBM, N.Y.C., 1956-59; asst. mgr. systems Litton, Orange, N.J., 1959-61; sr. cons. Computer Scis., N.Y.C., 1961-63; exec. v.p. Automation Scis., N.Y.C., 1963-65; chmn., chief exec. officer AGS Computers, Mountainside, N.J., 1966-91; chmn. ITAA (formerly ADAPSO), Arlington, Va., 1983; bd. dirs. Penn-Am. Group, Inc., Merisel Inc., Sungard Inc., Cellular Tech. Svcs. Co., Inc.; chmn. Gov. Tech. Svcs., Inc. Contbr. articles to profl. jours. Trustee Charles Babbage Inst., Dickinson Coll.; assoc. trustee U. Pa. Cpl. U.S. army, 1953-55. Mem. Software Industry Assn. (dir. 1976-91), Orange Lawn Tennis Club, Germantown Cricket Club, Longboat Key Club, Racquet Club of East Hampton. Office: GTSI Inc PO Box 8460 Longboat Key FL 34228-8460

SCHOENBERG, MARK GEORGE, government agency administrator; b. Bklyn., Nov. 22, 1947; s. Abraham Arthur and Ruth Millie (Dunn) S. BA, Columbia U., 1971, postgrad., 1972-73; postgrad., N.C. State U., 1971-72. Research asst. NIMH-sponsored project at N.C. State U., Raleigh, 1971-72; asst. to pres. Key Electric Ltd., Glen Oaks, N.Y., 1973-76; gen. mgr. Key Electric Ltd., Los Angeles, 1976; asst. to pres. Kalsan Electric, Hempstead, N.Y., 1977; asst. mgr. Lincoln Inn, Rockville Ctr., N.Y., 1978; expert, cons. EPA, Washington, 1978; assoc. dir. U.S. Regulatory Council, Washington, 1979-82; exec. dir. Regulatory Info. Service Ctr., Washington, 1982—. Mem. Sr. Exec. Assn., Train Collectors Assn., Lionel Collectors Club Am. Avocations: healthy gourmet cooking, early music, wine collecting. Office: Regulatory Info Svc Ctr Gen Svcs Adminstrn 18th & F Sts NW Washington DC 20405

SCHOENBERGER, JAMES EDWIN, federal agency administrator; b. Dayton, Ohio, Sept. 7, 1947; s. Harry Robert and Elizabeth Jane (Hollenkamp) S.; m. Aura Victoria Montana, June 24, 1977; children: David, Eric. BS in Civil Engring., Purdue U., 1969; MBA, Harvard U., 1971. V.p. ops. for midwestern housing developer Herman Devel. Group, Indpls., 1971-74; various positions New Communities Adminstrn. and with sec. HUD, Washington, 1974-77, assoc. dep. asst. sec., 1981-83; dir. land utilization Peabody Coal Co., St. Louis, 1977-81; sr. v.p. ops. The Investment Group, Washington, 1983-86; gen. dep. asst. fed. housing commr. U.S. HUD, Washington, 1987-89, assoc. gen., dep. asst. sec., 1990—. Roman Catholic. Avocation: computers. Office: HUD 451 7th St SW Rm 9106 Washington DC 20410-0001

SCHOENBERGER, STEVEN HARRIS, physician, research consultant; b. Cleve., Nov. 26, 1950; s. Stanford L. and Irene (Gold) S. BA, Tulane U., 1972; MD, U. Autonoma Guadalajara, Mex., 1976. Diplomate Am. Bd. of Urology. Asst. prof. Tulane U. Sch. Medicine, New Orleans, 1983—; rsch. assoc. Delta Regional Primate Rsch. Ctr., Covington, La., 1983-85; chmn. laser com., Lawrence and Meml. Hosp., New London, Conn., 1989—, rsch. cons. Pfizer Med. Group, Groton, Conn., 1989—. Fellow ACS, Am. Soc. Laser Medicine and Surgery; mem. Soc. Univ. Urologists, N.Y. Acad. Scis., New Eng. Escadrille. Office: 3 Shaws Cv Ste 206 New London CT 06320-4968

SCHOENBUCHER, BRUCE, health physicist; b. Dec. 15, 1943; s. Albert King and Alice Elizabeth (Thomson) S.; m. Patty Jo Parry, Feb. 3, 1965 (div. Feb. 1980); children: Teresa Marie, Bonnie Lynn Schoenbucher Mendoza; m. Nancy Lippincott, Jan. 3, 1987; 1 child, Carly Cramer Cutler. BS in Radiation Protection Engring., Tex. A&M U., 1977, MS in Nuclear Engring., 1982. Lic. med. physicist, Tex.; cert. healthcare safety profl. Health physicist nuclear sci. ctr. Tex. A&M U., College Station, 1971-75, health physicist Coll. Vet. Medicine, 1977-79; mgr. radiation safety programs U. Tex. Med. Br., Galveston, 1980-88, asst. dir. environ. health and safety, 1984-88, radiation safety officer, dir. environ. health and safety, 1988—; radiation safety officer Burn Inst Shriners Hosp. for Crippled Children, Galveston, 1991—; presenter in field. Contbr. articles to profl. publs. With USN, 1962-71. Mem. APHA, Health Physics Soc. (med. sect. exec. bd. 1993-96, mem. pub. info. com. 1981-84, chmn. 1982-84), South Tex. Chpt. Health Physics Soc. (chmn. ad hoc com. on licensure of med. physicists, chmn. fin. com. 1986-88, treas. 1980-85, pres-elect 1985-86, pres. 1986-87), Am. Assn. Physicists in Medicine, Am. Biol. Safety Assn., Am. Soc. Safety Engrs., Laser Inst. Am., Nat. Fire Protection Assn., Tex. Safety Assn., Galveston C. of C., U.S. Coast Guard Auxilliary, Phi Kappa Phi, Sigma Nu Epsilon, Tau Beta Pi. Office: U Tex Med Br 301 University Blvd Galveston TX 77555-5302

SCHOENDIENST, ALBERT FRED (RED SCHOENDIENST), professional baseball coach, former baseball player; b. Germantown, Ill., Feb. 2, 1923; m. Mary Eileen O'Reilly; children: Colleen, Cathleen, Eileen, Kevin. Infielder St. Louis Cardinals, 1945-56, 61-63, N.Y. Giants, 1956-57, Milw. Braves, 1957-61; coach St. Louis Cardinals, 1961-64, 1979-95, now special assistant to gen. mgr., mgr., 1964-77; coach Oakland Athletics, Calif., 1977-78. Mem. Nat. League All-Star team, 10 times, player in 9 games; mem. World Series Championship team, 1946, 57; managed team to World Series Championship, 1967; inducted into Major League Baseball Hall of Fame, 1989. Office: Saint Louis Cardinals 250 Stadium Plz Saint Louis MO 63102-1722*

SCHOENE, KATHLEEN SNYDER, lawyer; b. Glen Ridge, N.J., July 24, 1953; d. John Kent and Margaret Ann (Bronder) Snyder. BA, Grinnell Coll., 1974; MS, So. Conn. State Coll., 1976; JD, Washington U., St. Louis, 1982. Bar: Mo. 1982, U.S. Dist. Ct. (we. and ea. dists.) Mo. 1982, Ill. 1983. Head libr. Mo. Hist. Soc., St. Louis, 1976-79; assoc. Peper, Martin, Jensen, Maichel & Hetlage, St. Louis, 1982-88, ptnr., 1989—; bd. dirs. Legal Svcs. of Eastern Mo. Author: (with others) Missouri Corporation Law and Practice, 1985; contbr. articles to profl. jours. Trustee Grinnell (Iowa) Coll., ex officio voting mem., 1991-93; bd. dirs. Jr. League St. Louis, 1995-96, Leadership Ctr. Greater St. Louis, 1995-96, FOCUS St. Louis, 1996—. Mem. ABA, Nat. Health Lawyers Assn., Nat. Assn. Bond Lawyers, The Mo. Bar, Ill. State Bar Assn., Bar Assn. Met. St. Louis (treas. 1991-92, sec. 1992-93, v.p. 1993-94, pres.-elect 1994-95, pres. 1995-96, chairperson small bus. com. 1987-88, mem. exec. com. 1988-96, chairperson bus. law sect. 1988-89, mem. exec. com. young lawyers sect. 1988-90), St. Louis Bar Found. (bd. dirs. 1994—, v.p. 1995-96, pres. 1996—). Home: 7824 Cornell Ave Saint Louis MO 63130-3701 Office: Peper Martin Jensen Maichel & Hetlage 720 Olive St Fl 24 Saint Louis MO 63101

SCHOENER, THOMAS WILLIAM, zoology educator, researcher; b. Lancaster, Pa., Aug. 9, 1943; s. Harold Cloyd and Alta Marjorie (Hewitt) S.; m. Susan L. Keen, 1985. BA, Harvard Coll., 1965, PhD, 1969. Asst. prof. Harvard Coll., Cambridge, Mass., 1972-73, assoc. prof., 1973-75; assoc. prof. U. Wash., Seattle, 1975-76, prof., 1976-80; prof. U. Calif., Davis, 1980—, chairperson sect. evolution and ecology divsn. biol. scis., 1993—. Mem. editl. bd. dirs. Oecologia, 1984-93; past mem. editl. bd. Evolution, Am. Naturalist, Sci., Acta Oecologia; contbr. chpts. to books, articles to profl. jours. Recipient MacArthur prize Ecol. Soc. Am., 1987; grantee NSF, 1975—, Nat. Geog. Soc.; jr. fellow Harvard U., 1969-72; Guggenheim fellow, 1992-93. Mem. NAS, AAAS, Am. Acad. Arts and Scis., Am. Ornithologists Union (elective), Am. Soc. Naturalists, Ecol. Soc. Am., Am. Soc. Ichthyologists and Nerpetologists, Cooper Ornithol. Soc., Wilson Ornithol. Soc., Am. Arachnological Soc., Bahamas Nat. Trust. Avocations: weight lifting; reading. Office: U Calif Sect Evolution and Ecology Davis CA 95616

SCHOENFELD, HANNS-MARTIN WALTER, accounting educator; b. Leipzig, Germany, July 12, 1928; came to U.S., 1962, naturalized, 1968; s. Alwin and Lisbeth (Kirbach) S.; m. Margit Frese, Aug. 10, 1956; 1 child, Gabriele. MBA, U. Hamburg, Fed. Republic Germany, 1952, DBA, 1954; PhD, U. Braunschweig, Fed. Republic Germany, 1966. Pvt. practice acctg. Hamburg, 1948-54; bus. cons. Europe, 1958-62; faculty accountancy U. Ill., Champaign/Urbana, 1962—; prof. acctg., bus. adminstrn. U. Ill., Urbana, 1967—, Weldon Powell prof. acctg., 1976, 80-81, H. T. Scovill prof. acctg., 1985-94; prof. emeritus, 1994—, Office of West European Studies, 1994—; lectr., cons. in bus. and acctg., Eng., Belgium, Austria, Denmark, Brazil, Mex., Germany, Poland, Indonesia, Japan, Switzerland, Hungary, Czechoslovakia, 1962—; vis. prof. econs. U. Vienna, Austria, 1984—, Handelshochschule, Leipzig, Germany, 1996—. Author: numerous books including Management Dictionary 2 vols., 4th edit, 1971, Cost Accounting, 8th edit, 1974-95, Management Development, 1967, Cost Terminology and Cost Theory, 1974, (with J. Sheth) Export Marketing: Lessons from Europe, 1981, (with H.P. Holzer) Managerial Accounting and Analysis in Multinational

Enterprises, 1986, (with L. Noerreklit) Resources of the Firm, 1996. With German Army, 1944-45. Recipient Dr. Kausch prize for internat. integration of acctg. U. St. Gall, Switzerland, 1996. Mem. Am. Acctg. Assn. (chmn. internat. sect. 1976-77), Acad. Acctg. Historians (v.p. 1976-77, pres. 1978-79, Hour Glass award for best book publs. 1975), Acad. Internat. Bus., German Profs. Bus. Adminstrn., German Assn. Indsl. Engring., European Acctg. Assn., Council of European Studies, Internat. Assn. for Acctg. Edn. and Rsch., Beta Gamma Sigma, Beta Alpha Psi. Home: 1014 Devonshire Dr Champaign IL 61821-6620 Office: U Ill Dept Acctg 360 Commerce Bldg W 1206 S 6th St Champaign IL 61820-6915

SCHOENFELD, HENRY F., insurance executive; b. Germany, May 1, 1928; came to U.S., 1938; s. Solomon and Alice (Cohen) S.; children: Judith A. Morrison, Betsey L. Collins. BS in Indsl. Engring., Pa. State U., 1951. CLU; CPCU. Inds. engr. The Martin Co., Balt., 1951, Markel Svc., Richmond, Va., 1954-55; ins. agy. The Apple & Bond Co., Balt., 1955-60; ptnr. Hecht Schoenfeld Ins. Agy., Balt., 1960-62; v.p. Wolman Hecht & Schoenfeld, Balt., 1962-64; pre. Schoenfeld Ins. Assocs. Inc., Balt., 1964—; instr. Johns Hopkins U., Balt., 1966-68; mem. nat. agts. adv. bd. Hartford, 1972, Atlantic Ins. Co., 1982-85, Zurich Am. Ins. Co., 1987-90, Northbrook Ins. Co., 1991-95. Mem. Har Sinai Congregation Balt., treas. 1982-83, 90-92, 1st v.p. 1992-96. 1st lt. U.S. Army, 1951-54. Mem. Am. Soc. CLU's (past pres. Balt. chpt.), Soc. CPCU's (past pres. Md. chpt.), Balt. Assn. Ind. Ins. Agts. (past pres.), Balt. Assn. Life Underwriters, Profl. Ins. Agts., Million Dollar Roundtable, Penn State-Mt. Nittany Soc., Jewish Vocat Svc. (bd. mem.), Assoc Jewish Fedn. of Balt. (past bd. mem.), Suburban Club Baltimore County (past bd. mem.). Home: 2001 Wiltonwood Rd Stevenson MD 21153 Office: Schoenfeld Ins Assocs Inc 110 E Lombard St Baltimore MD 21202-5541

SCHOENFELD, JIM, professional hockey coach. Head coach Washington Capitols, 1994-97, Phoenix Coyotes, 1997—. Office: Phoenix Coyotes One Renaissance Sq 1 N Ctrl Ste 1930 Phoenix AZ 85004*

SCHOENFELD, MICHAEL P., lawyer; b. Bronx, N.Y., Oct. 17, 1935; s. Jack and Anne S.; B.S. in Acctg., N.Y.U., 1955; LL.B., LL.D., Fordham U., 1958; m. Helen Schorr, Apr. 3, 1960; children—Daniel, Steven, Tracy, Admitted to N.Y. bar, 1959, U.S. Supreme Ct., 1963; atty. Am. Home Assurance Co., N.Y.C., 1958-62; ptnr. firm Schoenfeld & Schoenfeld, Melville, 1959—; v.p. Interstate Brokerage Corp., 1965-84, pres., 1984—; ptnr. Melville Realty Co., 1977—; legal adv. various bus. orgns. Vice pres., trustee Temple Beth David, Commack, N.Y., 1972-75; chmn. Community Action Com. of Dix Hills and Commack, 1970-72, Dix Hills Planning Bd., 1972-74; treas. Dix Hills Republican Club, 1976-80; mem. Huntington (N.Y.) Zoning Bd. Appeals, 1980-91, chmn., 1986-89. Recipient United Jerusalem award Israel Bond Drive, 1977; City of Hope Service award; George Bacon award Fordham Law Sch. Mem. N.Y. State Bar Assn., Suffolk County Bar Assn. Home: 14 Clayton Dr Dix Hills NY 11746-5517 Office: 999 Walt Whitman Rd Huntington Station NY 11747-3007

SCHOENFELD, ROBERT LOUIS, biomedical engineer; b. N.Y.C., Apr. 1, 1920; s. Bernard and Mae (Kizelstein) S.; m. Helene Martens, Jan. 22, 1944 (div. 1965); children: David, Joseph, Paul; m. Florence Moskowitz, Dec. 11, 1965 (dec. 1989); children: Nedda, Bethany; m. Shulamith Stechel, July 8, 1990. BA, Washington Square Coll., 1942; BSEE, Columbia U., 1944; MEE, Poly. Inst. Bklyn., 1949, DEE, 1956. Rsch. assoc. Columbia U. Med. Sch., N.Y.C., 1947-51; rsch. fellow Sloan Kettering Cancer Rsch. Inst., N.Y.C., 1951-56; assoc. prof. Poly. Inst. Bklyn., 1947-54; assoc. prof. Rockefeller U., N.Y.C., 1957-90, prof. emeritus, 1990—. Contbr. articles to profl. jours. Lt. Signal Corps, U.S. Army, 1944-46, ETO. Fellow IEEE (mem. editl. bd. 1965-75, Centennial medal 1985), Am. Inst. for Med. and Biol. Engring. Democrat. Jewish. Achievements include pioneering application of computer automation to biological laboratory experiments. Office: Rockefeller U 1230 York Ave New York NY 10021-6307

SCHOENFELD, THEODORE MARK, industrial engineer; b. N.Y.C., July 10, 1907; s. Emil and Serena (Kertesz) S.; widowed; 1 child, Edward Lawrence. BS, CCNY, 1930; Grad. Cert. Pub. Adminstrn., NYU, 1938; Grad. Cert. Indsl. Engring., Stevens Inst. Tech., 1945. Profl. engr., Calif. Newspaperman Daily News Record, Christian Sci. Monitor, N.Y.C., 1930-33; asst. dir. methods and systems City of New York, 1934-41; adminstrv. officer U.S. Dept. of State, N.Y.C., 1944-45; chief indsl. engr. MGM Internat. Films Corp., N.Y.C., 1945-48; indsl. engr. and mgmt. cons. George S. May Co., N.Y.C., Park Ridge, Ill., 1949-73; exec. v.p. Ramco Mfg. Co., Roselle Park, N.J., 1974-91; vol. medicare counselor, chmn. outreach com., cert. lectr. CHIME, Princeton, N.J., 1992—. Author: The Safety Shield Story, 1984; contbg. author: Worldwide Multi-National Symposium, 1976. Dir. U.S. Peace Corps Aux., N.Y.C. and L.I., 1968-69; v.p. Bklyn. Soc. for Ethical Culture, N.Y.C., 1964-79, pres., 1980-85. With field artillery U.S. Army, 1943-44. Recipient Legis. commendation N.J. Senate, 1982, Nat. Chem. award with honors Chem. Processing Mag., 1980, with highest honors, 1982; named Disting. Engr. of U.S., Engring. Joint Coun., 1983; named to Cambridge/Oxford list of persons who in the course of history have contributed to the advancement of sci., 1985. Fellow Am. Inst. Chemists, N.J. Inst. Chemists (mem. gov. coun. 1988—); mem. Am. Inst. Indsl. Engrs. (nat. divs. dir. 1974-75), Princeton Ethical Humanist Fellowship (pres., 1986-87, treas. 1989—, founder). Democrat. Achievements include inventing the Spra-Gard - most widely used safety device against hazardous chemical fluids used by chemical and atomic plants throughout the world; inventing the first safety shield to protect against hydrofluoric acid, first effective safety shield for expansion joints, "Gain Sharing Plan" used by automobile dealer service departments throughout the U.S.; creating secondary distribution pattern for flowers resulting in sales of flowers by supermarkets and green grocers throughout the U.S. Home: 86 C Empress Plaza Cranbury NJ 08512

SCHOENFELD, WALTER EDWIN, manufacturing company executive; b. Seattle, Nov. 6, 1930; s. Max and Edna Lucille (Reinhardt) S.; m. Esther Behar, Nov. 27, 1955; children—Lea Anne, Jeffrey, Gary. B.B.A., U. Wash., 1952. Vice pres., dir. Sunshine Mining Co., Kellogg, Idaho, 1964-69, First N.W. Industries, Inc. (Seattle Super Sonics), 1968-79; chmn. bd., pres. Schoenfeld Industries, Inc. (diversified holding co.), 1968-93; vice chmn., acting pres., CEO, Vans, Inc., 1993—; ptnr. Seattle Mariners Baseball Club, 1977-81, Seattle Sounds Soccer Club, 1974-79; v.p., dir. Chief Execs. Orgn., 1987—; bd. dirs. Hazel Bishop Cosmetics; bd. dirs., vice chmn. Vans Shoes, 1993—; chmn., CEO Van's Inc., 1993—; chmn. Schoenfeld Neckwear Corp., Seattle, 1983-87, Taylor & Burke Ltd., U.K., 1987-88, Schoenfeld Group, Seattle, 1987-88; trustee Seattle Found., 1987-85, N.W. Artificial Kidney Ctr., Seattle, 1967-88. Bd. dirs. Wash. China Rels. Coun., 1980—, Sterling Recreation Orgn., 1985-90; chmn. Access Long Distance of Washington; bd. govs. Weizmann Inst. Sci., Rehovot, Israel, 1980—; trustee Barbara Sinatra Children's Ctr., Eisenhower Hosp., Rancho Mirage, Calif., 1990—. With AUS, 1952-55, Korea. Recipient various service awards. Mem. Chief Execs. Orgn., Seattle C. of C., Ranier Club, Seattle Yacht Club, Tamarisk Country Club (Rancho Mirage, Calif.), Mission Hills Country Club, Glendale Country Club (Bellevue, Wash.), Alpha Kappa Psi. Office: 2001 6th Ave Ste 2550 Seattle WA 98121-2522

SCHOENHARD, WILLIAM CHARLES, JR., health care executive; b. Kansas City, Mo., Sept. 26, 1949; s. William Charles S. and Joyce Evans (Thornsberry) Bell; m. Kathleen Ann Klosterman, June 3, 1972; children: Sarah Elizabeth, Thomas William. BS in Pub. Adminstrn., U. Mo., 1971; M of Health Adminstrn. with honors, Washington U., St. Louis, 1975. V.p., dir. gen. svcs. Deaconess Hosp., St. Louis, 1975-78; assoc. exec. dir. St. Mary's Health Ctr., St. Louis, 1978-81; exec. dir. Arcadia Valley Hosp., Pilot Knob, Mo., 1981-82, St. Joseph Health Ctr., St. Charles, Mo., 1982-86; exec. v.p., COO SSM Health Care Sys., St. Louis, 1986—; bd. dirs. Mark Twain Bank, 1986—; regent Mo.-Gateway area Am. Coll. Healthcare Execs., 1997—. Contbr. articles to profl. jours. Pres. Shaw Neighborhood Improvement Assn., St. Louis, 1979-80; mem. adv. bd. St. Louis chpt. Lifeseekers, 1985-94; mem. bd. mgrs. Kirkwood-Webster (Mo.) YMCA, 1990-96, sec., 1996; mem. nat. adv. coun. Healthcare Forum, 1992—; mem. healthcare adv. bd. Sanford Brown Colls., 1992-94; mem. leadership excellence com. Cath. Health Assn. U.S., 1993—; mem. steering com. Greater St. Louis Healthcare Alliance, 1994-95; bd. dirs. St. Andrews Mgmt. Svcs., Inc., 1994—; bd. dirs. Lindenwood Coll., 1997—. With USN, 1971-72, Vietnam. Fellow Am. Coll. Health Care Execs.; mem. Mid-Am. Transplant Assn. (bd. dirs. 1995—), Am. Legion, Navy League U.S., Univ. Club St. Louis, Phi Eta Sigma, Pi Omicron Sigma, Delta Upsilon, Delta Sigma Pi. Roman Catholic. Avocations: reading, walking. Home: 420 Fairwood Ln Saint Louis MO 63122-4429 Office: SSM Health Care System 477 N Lindbergh Blvd Saint Louis MO 63141-7813

SCHOENHERR, JOHN (CARL), artist, illustrator; b. N.Y.C., July 5, 1935; s. John Ferdinand and Frances (Braun) S.; m. Judith Gray; children: Jennifer L., Ian G. BFA, Pratt Inst., 1956. Painter/illustrator book: Owl Moon, 1987 (Caldecott medal 1988); exhbn. Hiram Blauvelt Art Mus., 1997. Recipient World Sci. Fiction award World Sci. Fiction Conv., London, 1965, silver medal Phila. Acad. Natural Sci., 1984, purchase award Hiram Blauvelt Art Mus., 1994. Mem. Am. Soc. Mammalogists, Soc. Illustrators, Soc. Animal Artists (medal 1979, 85). Home and Office: 135 Upper Creek Rd Stockton NJ 08559-1209

SCHOENRICH, EDYTH HULL, academic administrator, physician; b. Cleve., Sept. 9, 1919; d. Edwin John and Maud Mabel (Kelly) Hull; m. Carlos Schoenrich, Aug. 9, 1942; children: Lola, Olaf. AB, Duke U., 1941; MD, U. Chgo., 1947; MPH, John Hopkins U., 1971. Diplomate Am. Bd. Internal Medicine, Am. Bd. Preventive Medicine. Intern John Hopkins Hosp., Balt., 1948-49, asst. resident medicine, 1949-50, postdoctoral fellow medicine, 1950-51, chief resident, pvt. wards, 1951-52; asst. chief, acting chief dept. chronic and cmty. medicine Balt. City Hosp., Balt., 1963-66; dir. svc. to chronically ill and aging Md. State Dept. Health, Balt., 1966-74; dir. divsn. pub. health adminstrn. Sch. Pub. Health, John Hopkins U., Balt., 1974-77, assoc. dean academic affairs, 1977-86, dir. part time profl. programs and dep. dir. MPH program, 1986—, prof. dept. health policy and mgmt., 1974—, joint appointment medicine, 1978—. Contbd. articles to profl. jours. Bd. trustees Friends Life Care Cmty., 1984—; Kennedy-Krieger Inst., Balt., 1985—, Vis. Nurses Assn., 1990—. Recipient Stebbins medal John Hopkins U., 1989. Fellow Am. Col. Physicians, Am. Coll. Preventive Medicine; mem. Assn. Tchrs. Preventive Medicine, Am. Pub. Health Assn., Med. Chirurg. Soc. Md., Balt. City Med. Soc., Phi Beta Kappa, Alpha Omega Alpha, Delta Omega. Avocations: gardening, music, theater, swimming. Home: 1402 Boyce Ave Baltimore MD 21204-6512 Office: Johns Hopkins Univ Sch Pub Health 615 N Wolfe St Baltimore MD 21205-2103

SCHOEPPEL, JOHN FREDERICK, mechanical and electrical engineer, consultant; b. South Bend, Ind., Oct. 25, 1917; s. Frederick Otto and Helen S.; m. Jacqueline Mae Gall, Apr. 17, 1949; children: Pamela Jo, Sonja Lou. BSc, Northwestern U., Evanston, Ill., 1939. Devel. engr. Honeywell, Inc., Mpls., 1939-47; mgr. flight references Lear, Inc., Grand Rapids, Mich., 1947-60; gen. mgr. instrn. and control divsn. Pneumo, Grand Rapids, Mich., 1960-66; dir. new products NWL Corp., Kalamazoo, 1966-71; v.p., gen. mgr. Sundstrand Data Control, Redmond, Wash., 1971-73; exec.. v.p. Veriflo Corp., Richmond, Calif., 1974-90, cons. R & D, 1990—. Contbr. articles to profl. jours. Mem. ASTM, Semiconductor Equipment Mfrs. Inst. (com. 1990-92), SEMATECH Standards (com. 1991-93). Republican. Achievements include patents for Autopilots, Gyros, Flight Reference Display, Equipment for Semiconductor Production, Automatic Autopilot; development of two gyro stable platforms for aircraft outpilot, modern all-attitude flight displays for Airforce and Navy. Avocations: advanced woodworking, photography, sound systems.

SCHOESLER, MARK GERALD, state legislator, farmer; b. Ritzville, Wash., Feb. 16, 1957; s. Gerald E. and Dorothy (Heinemann) S.; m. Ginger J. Van Aelst, Apr. 8, 1978; children: Veronica, Cody. AA, Spokane (Wash.) C.C., 1977. Mem. Wash. Ho. of Reps., Olympia, 1992—; vice chair agr. ecology, mem. rules, agr. and ecology, fin. chair joint adminstrv. rules rev. coms., 1995-96. Pres. Wash. Friends Farms and Forests, 1991-92; mem. Cmty. Econ. Revitalization Bd. Mem. Wash. Assn. Wheat Growers (dir. 1990-92). Republican. Mem. United. Ch. Christ. Home: Rte 1 Box 151 Ritzville WA 99169

SCHOETTGER, THEODORE LEO, city official; b. Burton, Nebr., Sept. 2, 1920; s. Frederick and Louise Cecelia (Gierau) S.; m. Kathlyn Marguerite Hughey, June 3, 1943; children—Gregory Paul, Julie Anne. B.S. in Bus. Adminstrn. with Distinction, U. Nebr., 1948. C.P.A., Calif. Sr. acct. Haskins & Sells, Los Angeles, 1948-55; controller Beckman Instruments, Inc., Fullerton, Calif., 1955-58; corp. chief acct. Beckman Instruments, Inc., 1958-60; treas. Docummun Inc., Los Angeles, 1960-77; fin. dir. City of Orange, Calif., 1977-93. Mem. fin. com., treas., bd. dirs. Childrens Hosp. Served to lt. USNR, 1942-45. Mem. Calif. Soc. CPA's (nat. dir., v.p., past pres. Los Angeles chpt.), Fin. Execs. Inst., Mcpl. Fin. Officers Assn., Beta Gamma Sigma, Alpha Kappa Psi. Methodist. Clubs: Jonathan, Town Hall. Home: 9626 Shellyfield Rd Downey CA 90240-3418

SCHOETTLE, FERDINAND P., legal educator; b. Phila., Aug. 17, 1933; s. Ferdinand P. and Helen Louise (White) S.; m. E. Bok, Feb. 13, 1965 (div. 1976); m. D. Jean Thomson, Nov. 24, 1979 (div. 1982); children—Michael, Derek. B.A. in History, Princeton U., 1955; LL.D., Harvard U., 1960, M.A. in Econs., 1978, Ph.D., 1983. Bar: Pa. 1961, Minn. 1968. Asst., U.S. Senator J.S. Clark, Washington, 1961-62; assoc. Morgan, Lewis & Bockius, Phila., 1963-67; prof. law U. Minn. Law Sch., Mpls., 1967—; vis. prof. Harvard U., 1972-74, Uppsala U., Sweden, 1984; guest scholar Brookings Inst., Washington, 1992-93. Co-author: State and Local Taxes, 1974; editor: Tax Policy Notes, 1993—; contbr. articles to profl. jours. Served to lt. USN, 1955-57. Mem. sailing U.S. Olympic Team, 1956, 60. Mem. ABA (chmn. taxes and revenue com. 1979-82), Am. Law Inst. Home: 3104 Dumbarton Ave NW Washington DC 20007 Office: U Minn Sch Law Minneapolis MN 55455

SCHOETTLER, GAIL SINTON, state official; b. Los Angeles, Oct. 21, 1943; d. James and Norma (McLellan) Sinton; children: Lee, Thomas, James; m. Donald L. Stevens, June 23, 1990. BA in Econs., Stanford U., 1965; MA in History, U. Calif., Santa Barbara, 1969, PhD in History, 1975. Businesswoman Denver, 1975-83; exec. dir. Colo. Dept. of Personnel, Denver, 1983-86; treas. State of Colo., Denver, 1987-94, lt. govern., 1995—; bd. dirs. Nat. Jewish Hosp.; chair Colo. Commn. Indian Affairs, Aerospace States Assn.; mem. bd. trustees U. No. Colo., 1981-87. Mem. Douglas County Bd. Edn., Colo., 1979-87, pres., 1983-87; trustee U. No. Colo., Greeley, 1981-87; pres. Denver Children's Mus., 1975-85. Recipient Disting. Alumna award U. Calif. at Santa Barbara, 1987, Trailblazer award AAUW, 1997. Mem. Nat. Women's Forum (bd. dirs. 1981-89, pres. 1983-85), Internat. Women's Forum (mem. bd. dirs. 1981-89, pres. 83-85), Women Execs. in State Govt. (bd. dirs. 1981-87, chmn. 1988), Leadership Denver Assn. (bd. dirs. 1987, named Outstanding Alumna 1985), Nat. Congress Lt. Govs., Stanford Alumni Assn., Denver Rotary. Democrat.

SCHOETZ, DAVID JOHN, JR., colon and rectal surgeon; b. Milw., Oct. 29, 1948; s. David John and Beverly (Rogers) S.; m. Ruthanne Brennan, Mar. 25, 1972; children: Elizabeth Anne, David John III. BA, Coll. of Holy Cross, 1970; MD, Med. Coll. Wis., Milw., 1974. Resident in surgery Boston U. Med. Ctr., 1974-81; resident in colon/rectal surgery Lahey Clinic Med. Ctr., Burlington, Mass., 1981-82, staff colon-rectal surgeon, 1982—, chmn. dept. colon-rectal surgery, 1987—. Fellow ACS, Am. Soc. Colon and Rectal Surgeons. Office: Lahey Clinic Med Ctr 41 Mall Rd Burlington MA 01803-4136

SCHOFIELD, ANTHONY WAYNE, judge; b. Farmington, N.Mex., Mar. 5, 1949; s. Aldred Edward and Margueriete (Knudsen) S.; m. Rebecca Ann Rosecrans, May 11, 1971; children: Josie, Matthew Paul, Peter Christian, Addie, Joshua James, M. Thomas, Jacob L., Daniel Z. BA, Brigham Young U., 1973, JD, 1976. Bar: Utah 1976, U.S. Dist. Ct. Utah 1976, U.S. Ct. Appeals (7th and 10th cirs.) 1977. Law clk. to hon. judge A. Sherman Christansen U.S. Dist. Ct. Utah, Salt Lake City, 1976-77; assoc. Ferenz, Bramhall, Williams & Gruskin, Agana, Guam, 1977-79; pvt. practice American Fork, Utah, 1979-80; assoc. Jardine, Linebaugh, Brown & Dunn, Salt Lake City, 1980-81; mem., dir. Ray, Quinney & Nebeker, Provo, Utah; judge 4th Jud. Dist. Ct., Provo, Utah, 1993—. Bishop Mormon Ch., American Fork, 1985-88; commr. American Fork City Planning Commn., 1980-85; trustee American Fork Hosp., 1984-93. Mem. Cen. Utah Bar Assn. (pres. 1987, 91). Avocations: photography, music. Office: 125 N 100 W Provo UT 84601-2849

SCHOFIELD, CALVIN ONDERDONK, JR., bishop; b. Delhi, N.Y., Jan. 6, 1933; s. Calvin O. and Mabel (Lenton) S.; m. Elaine Marie Fullerton, Aug. 3, 1963; children: Susan Elaine, Robert Lenton. B.A., Hobart Coll., 1959, S.T.D. (Hon.), 1980; M.Div., Berkeley Div. Sch., 1959, D.D. (hon.), 1979; D.D. (hon.), U. of the South, 1981. Ordained priest Episcopal Ch., 1962; curate St. Peter's Episcopal Ch., St. Petersburg, Fla., 1962-64; vicar St. Andrew's Episcopal Ch., Miami, Fla., 1964-70; rector St. Andrew's Episcopal Ch., 1970-78; bishop coadjutor Diocese S.E. Fla., Miami, 1978-79, bishop, 1980—; exec. bd. Presiding Bishops Fund for World Relief; exec. coun. Episcopal Ch., 1991—. Regent U. of the South, Sewanee, Tenn., 1988—. Capt. chaplain corps USNR, 1960-85; ret., 1985. Mem. Naval Res. Assn., Naval Inst. Republican. Office: 525 NE 15th St Miami FL 33132-1411*

SCHOFIELD, HERBERT SPENCER, III, insurance executive; b. Mineola, N.Y., May 21, 1942; s. Herbert Spencer Jr. and Katherine Joan (Alcott) S.; divorced; children: Scott, Kate; m. Ruth Marie Mayers, July 14, 1985. BA, Lafayette Coll., Easton, Pa., 1965. CLU, ChFC, cert. ins. cons. Spl. agt. Northwestern Mut., Norwalk, Conn., 1974-93; personal ins. agt. various cos. by contract, Norwalk, 1974-93; pres. Schofield & Co., Glenbrook, Conn., 1993—. Mem. Nat. Assn. Life Underwriters, Estate Planning Coun. Southwestern Fairfield County (exec. bd. 1988-93, 1st v.p. membership 1990-91, pres. 1991-92), S.W. Conn. Assn. Life Underwriters (treas. 1977-80), Nat. Trust for Hist. Preservation. Roman Catholic. Avocations: photography, walking, 18th and 19th century American antiques. Office: Schofield & Co PO Box 2916 Stamford CT 06906-0916

SCHOFIELD, JAMES ROY, computer programmer; b. Reedsburg, Wis., Aug. 16, 1953; s. G. C. Schofield and Margaret (Collies) Tverberg. BA, Carleton Coll., 1976. Programmer Brandon Applied Systems, San Francisco, 1977-78, Rand Info. Systems, San Francisco, 1979-83; systems programmer IBM, San Jose, Calif., 1983-91; programmer Office of Instnl. Rsch./U. Calif., Berkeley, 1991-94, Datis Corp., San Mateo, Calif., 1994-95, Compuware Corp., Los Gatos, Calif., 1995-96, Pacific Bell, San Ramon, Calif., 1996—. Mem. Assn. for Computing Machinery, Assn. for Computing Machinery Spl. Interest Group in Computers and Soc., Phi Beta Kappa. Avocations: guitar, reading, swimming. Home: PO Box 25143 San Mateo CA 94402-5143 Office: Pacific Bell 2600 Camino Ramon San Ramon CA 94583-5009

SCHOFIELD, JOHN TREVOR, environmental management company executive; b. Manchester, Eng., Mar. 1, 1938; s. John and Hilda May (Mumford) S.; m. Jennifer Ann Wood, June 4, 1960 (div. Aug. 1980); children: Karen Jane, Alistair John; m. Susan B. West, July 24, 1982; 1 child, Kimberly. BS, U. Manchester, 1959. Dir. European ops. Borg-Warner Chem. Corp., Amsterdam, The Netherlands, 1964-70; mng. dir. Tunnel Holdings PLC, London, 1970-78; chief exec. officer, pres. Stablex Corp., Radnor, Pa., 1978-81; sr. v.p. Internat. Tech. Corp., Torrance, Calif., 1981-91; pres., CEO, chmn. Thermatrix Inc., San Jose, Calif., 1992—; mem. adv. bd. Cupertino Nat. Bank; bd. dirs. Phys. Scis., Inc.; sec.-treas. Environ. Export Coun. U.S.A. Mem. Bd. Calif. Environ. Bus. Coun. (co-chmn.), Environ. Tech. Adv. Coun. for Calif. Avocation: public speaking, gourmet cooking. Office: Thermatrix Inc 101 Metro Dr Ste 248 San Jose CA 95110-1343

SCHOFIELD, JOHN-DAVID MERCER, bishop; b. Somerville, Mass., Oct. 6, 1938; s. William David and Edith Putnam (Stockman) S. BA, Dartmouth Coll., 1960; MDiv, Gen. Theol. Sem., N.Y.C., 1963, DD (hon.), 1989. Joined Monks of Mt. Tabor, Byzantine Cath. Ch., 1978; ordained priest Episcopal Ch. Asst. priest Ch. of St. Mary the Virgin, San Francisco, 1963-65, Our Most Holy Redeemer Ch., London, 1965-69; rector, retreat master St. Columba's Ch. and Retreat House, Inverness, Calif., 1969-88; bishop Episcopal Diocese of San Joaquin, Fresno, Calif., 1988—; aggregate Holy Transfiguration Monastery, 1984—; bishop protector Order Agape and Reconciliation, Chemainus, B.C., Can., 1990—. Episcopal visitor to Community of Christian Family Ministry, Vista, Calif., 1991—; trustee Nashotah House Sem., Wis., 1991—; bd. dirs. Fresno Leadership Found., 1996—. Mem. Episcopal Synod of Am. (founder 1989), Episcopalians United (bd. dirs. 1987—). Republican. Office: Diocese of San Joaquin 4159 E Dakota Ave Fresno CA 93726-5227

SCHOFIELD, PAUL MICHAEL, finance company executive; b. Wilmington, Del., Mar. 30, 1937; s. John Edward and Sabina A. (Clarke) S.; m. Carol Ann Hane, July 11, 1964; children—Paul Michael, Andrew Clarke, Dennis Charles. B.A., LaSalle U., Phila., 1960; postgrad., U. Del., 1963. Asst. treas. Sears Roebuck Acceptance Corp., Wilmington, Del., 1971-73, asst. v.p., 1973-74, treas., 1974-83, v.p., treas., 1983-87; pres., treas. Discover Credit Corp., Wilmington, 1987—. Campaign capt. United Way of Del., 1978; campaign capt. Boys Club Del., 1979. Mem. Del. Fin. Assn. (treas.), Phila. Treas. Club. Democrat. Roman Catholic. Club: Irish Culture of Del. (treas. 1980). Avocations: reading; golf; woodworking. Home: 2014 Delaware Ave Wilmington DE 19806-2208 Office: Discover Credit Corp 3711 Kennett Pike Wilmington DE 19807-2102

SCHOFIELD, ROBERT E(DWIN), history educator, academic administrator; b. Milford, Neb., June 1, 1923; s. Charles Edwin and Nora May (Fullerton) S.; m. Mary-Peale Smith, June 20, 1959; 1 son, Charles Stockton Peale. A.B., Princeton, 1944; M.S., U. Minn., 1948; Ph.D., Harvard, 1955. Research asst. Fercleve Corp. and Clinton Labs., Oak Ridge, 1944-46; research assoc. Knolls Atomic Power Lab., Gen. Electric Co., 1948-51; asst. prof., then assoc. prof. history U. Kans., Lawrence, 1955-60; mem. faculty Case Western Res. U., Cleve., 1960-79, prof. history of sci., 1963-72, Lynn Thorndike prof. history of sci., 1972-79; prof. history Iowa State U., Ames, 1979-93, prof. emeritus, 1993—, dir. grad. program history tech. and sci., 1979-92; mem. Inst. Advanced Study, 1967-68, 74-75; Sigma Xi nat. lectr., 1978-80. Author: The Lunar Society of Birmingham, 1963, Scientific Autobiography of Joseph Priestley: Selected Scientific Correspondence, 1966, Mechanism and Materialism: British Natural Philosophy in an Age of Reason, 1970, (with D.G.C. Allan) Stephen Hales: Scientist and Philanthropist, 1980. Served with AUS, 1945-46. Fulbright fellow, 1953-54; Guggenheim fellow, 1959-60, 67-68. Fellow Am. Phys. Soc., Royal Soc. Arts; mem. History of Sci. Soc., Soc. History Tech., Midwest Junto History of Sci., Am. Soc. 18th Century Studies, Acad. Internat. d'Histoire des Scis. (corr.). Home: 44 Sycamore Rd Princeton NJ 08540-5323

SCHOGGEN, PHIL H(OWARD), psychologist, educator; b. Tulsa, Aug. 28, 1923; s. Walter B. and Emma F. (Alexander) S.; m. Maxine F. Spoor, June 28, 1944; children: Leida, Christopher, Ann, Susan. AB in Psychology, Park Coll., 1946; MS, U. Kans., Lawrence, 1951, Ph.D. in Psychology, 1954. Asst. prof. psychology U. Oreg., 1957-62, asso. prof., 1962-66; prof., chmn. dept. psychology George Peabody Coll., 1966-75; prof. York U., Toronto, Ont., Can., 1975-77; prof. human devel. and family studies N.Y. State Coll. Human Ecology, Cornell U., 1977-90, prof. emeritus, 1990—, chmn. dept., 1977-82. Author: (with R. G. Barker) Qualities of Community Life, 1973; Behavior Settings: A Revision and Extension of Roger G. Barker's Ecological Psychology, 1989. Served with USNR, 1944-46, 50-51. Mem. APA. Home: 121 Vossland Dr Nashville TN 37205-3617

SCHOGT, HENRY GILIUS, foreign language educator; b. Amsterdam, May 24, 1927; s. Johannes Herman and Ida Jacoba (Van Rijn) S.; m. Corrie Frenkel, Apr. 2, 1955; children—Barbara, Philibert Johannes, Elida. B.A. in French, U. Amsterdam, 1947, B.A. in Russian, 1948, M.A. in Russian, 1951, M.A. cum laude in French, 1952; Ph.D. in French, U. Utrecht, 1960. Docent Russian U. Groningen, The Netherlands, 1953-63; sr. lectr. French U. Utrecht, The Netherlands, 1954-63; master asst. gen. linguistics U. Paris, 1963-64; vis. lectr. Russian and French Princeton (N.J.) U., 1964-66; prof. French and linguistics U. Toronto, Ont., Can., 1966-92. Author: books including Les causes de la double issue de e fermé tonique libre en français, 1960, Le système verbal du français contemporain, 1968, Sémantique synchronique, synonymie, homonymie, polysémie, 1976, (with Pierre Léon and Edward Burstynsky) La phonologie, 1977, Linguistics, Literary Analysis and Literary Translation, 1988. Fellow Royal Soc. Can.; mem. Société de linguistique de Paris, Can. Linguistic Assn. Home: 47 Turner Rd, Toronto, ON Canada M6G 3H7 Office: Dept French, Univ Toronto, Toronto, ON Canada M5S 1J4 *My ideas and goals in life are closely connected with the ideals of a socialist system of distribution of wealth and of individual responsibility towards one's fellow human beings and towards society.*

SCHOLDER, FRITZ, artist; b. Breckenridge, Minn., Oct. 6, 1937. Student, Wis. State Coll., 1956-57; AA, Sacramento City Coll., 1958; BA, Sacramento State Coll., 1960; MFA, U. Ariz., 1963, DFA (hon.), 1985; DFA (hon.), Ripon Coll., Wis., 1984, Concordia Coll., Minn., 1986; HHD (hon.), Coll. Sante Fe; DFA (hon.), U. Wis., Superior, 1993. Teaching asst. art Univ. Ariz., 1962-64; instr. art history, advanced painting Inst. Am. Indian Arts, 1964-69; artist in residence Dartmouth Coll., 1973; guest artist Santa Fe Art Inst., 1987, Okla. Art Inst., 1980-81, 88, Am. U., Washington, 1990. One-man shows: Crocker Art Gallery, Sacramento, 1959, Coll. Santa Fe, 1967, Roswell (N.Mex.) Art Center, 1969, Tally Richards Gallery Contemporary Art, Taos, N.Mex., 1971, 73, 75, 78, 79, St. John's Coll., Santa Fe, 1972, Cordier & Ekstrom, N.Y.C., 1972, 74, 76, 78, 90, Gimpel & Weitzenhoffer, N.Y.C., 1977, Graphics 1 and 2, Boston, 1977, Smith Andersen Gallery, Palo Alto, Calif., 1979, Plains Mus., Moorhead, Minn., 1980, 1981-89, Scottsdale Center for Arts, 1981, Tucson Mus. Art, 1981, Weintraub Gallery, N.Y.C., 1981, ACA Galleries, N.Y.C., 1984, 86, Sena Galleries West, Santa Fe, N.Mex., 1986, 87, Louis Newman Galleries, L.A., 1985, 87, 90-94, Schneider Mus. Art, Ashland, Oreg., 1990, Alexander Gallery, N.Y., 1991, Riva Yares Gallery, Scottsdale, Ariz., 1992, 94, Neiman Fine Art Gallery, Santa Fe, 1996, Thorne-Sagendorph Art Mus. Keene, 1996; exhibited group shows: Carnegie Art Inst., Butler Inst. Am. Art, Calif. Palace of Legion of Honor, Houston Mus. Fine Arts, Dallas Mus. Fine Arts, San Francisco Mus. Art, Denver Art Mus., Ft. Worth Art Center, Basel Art 5, Linden Mus., Stuttgart, Philbrook Art Center, Oakland Art Mus., Tucson Art Center, N.Mex. Art Mus., Edinburgh Art Festival, Museo de Bellas Artes, Buenos Aires, Biblioteca Nacional, Santiago, Chile, Mus. voor Land-en-Volkenkunder, Rotterdam, Amerika Haus, Berlin Festival, Center for Arts of Indian Am., Washington, Yellowstone Art Center, Nat. Mus. Modern Art, Tokyo, Kyoto, Japan, also other fgn. and Am. shows, Smithsonian tour, Bucharest, Berlin, London, Ankara, Madrid, Belgrade, Athens, 1972-73; represented in permanent collections: Mus. Modern Art, N.Y.C., Art Inst. Chgo., Center Culturel Americain, Paris, Art Gallery Toronto, NEA, Houston Mus. Fine Arts, Boston Fine Arts Mus., Milw. Art Mus., Portland (Oreg.) Art Mus., Dallas Mus. Fine Arts, Bur. Indian Affairs, Mus. N.Mex., Smithsonian Instn., Bklyn. Mus., Phoenix Art Mus., San Diego Fine Arts Gallery, Okla. Art Center, Brigham Young U., Heard Mus., Phoenix, Bibliotheque Nat., Paris, San Francisco Mus. Art, Hermitage Mus., Leningrad, others; Included in: American Prints and Printmakers; Subject of: PBS film Fritz Scholder, 1976, PBS film Fritz Scholder, An American Portrait, 1983; author: Fritz Scholder Lithograph, 1975, 1983, Scholder/Indians, Fritz Scholder, Rizzoli, Fritz Scholder, Paintings and Monotypes, Afternoon Nap, 1991, Live Dog/Evil God, 1992, Fritz Scholder, A Survey of Paintings, 1993, Remnants of Memory, 1993, Fritz Scholder's Book of Symbols for Children, 1994, Fritz Scholder, Thirty Years of Sculpture, 1994, Rot/Red, 1995; guest artist Santa Fe Art Inst., 1987, Taos Inst. Art, 1990, Am. U., Washington, 1990. Recipient Ford Found. purchase award, 1962, 1st prize W.Va. Centennial Exhbn., 1973, purchase prize 13th S.W. Print Drawing Show, 1963, Hallmark purchase award, 1965, 1st prize Scottsdale Indian Nat., 1966, Grand prize Washington Biennial Indian Show, 1967, Grand prize Scottsdale Indian Nat., 1969, jurors award S.W. Fine Arts Biennial, 1970, 71, 72, prize in painting Am. Acad. and Inst. Arts and Letters, 1977, award in painting AAAL, 1977, internat. prize in lithography Intergrafiks, Berlin, 1980, 90, N.D. Gov.'s award in arts, 1981, N.Mex. Gov.'s award, 1983, Societaire Salon d'Automne, Paris, 1983, Golden Plate award Am. Acad. Achievement, 1985, Third prize Intergrafiks, 1990, Laird Leadership award in the arts U. Wis., Stevens point, 1995, Visionary award Inst. Am. Indian Arts; John Hay Whitney fellow, 1962-63. Address: 118 Cattletrack Rd Scottsdale AZ 85251 *I Believe in Art, Love, and Magic.*

SCHOLEFIELD, ADELINE PEGGY, therapist; b. Bklyn., Nov. 23, 1932; d. C. Joseph and Connie (Campbell) Taylor; m. Paul Robert Scholefield, June 26, 1954; children: Debra, Robert, Scott, Colin, Colleen, Heidi, Alan, Gene, Timothy, Christina, Holly, Shawn. Cert. radiol. technician, NYU, 1953; BS, N.H. Coll., 1989; MS in Human Svc., Springfield Coll., 1991. Registered radiol. technician, N.Y.; lic. mental health therapist. X-ray technician St. Elizabeth's Hosp., N.Y.C., 1951-53, St. Joseph' Hosp., Lowell, Mass., 1954-67; owner, operator Maplewood Farm Family Care, Peperell, Mass., 1968—, Lauranne Village, Laconia, N.H., 1979-81; issues aide Offices of Senator Edward M. Kennedy, Boston, 1984-85, health and human svc. rep., 1985-87; liaison Dept. Social Svcs., Boston, Fitchbourg, Mass., 1988—, mem. steering com. of adv. coun.; sec. Statewide Adv. Coun., 1992. Foster parent Maplewood Farm, Pepperell, 1956—; staff Dem. State Com., Boston, 1987; sec. pers. bd. Town of Pepperell, 1989-90; vol. support/group loss and bereavement therapist, Naukeag Hosp., Ashbourham, Mass., 1993—, vol. therapist, 1991—; mem. adv. com. Coun. of Aging Commn.; mem. St. Josph's Parish Coun., Pepperell; ad hoc com. VA Hosp.; bd. dirs. Adult Foster Care Com. of Am. Named Foster Parent of Yr. State of Mass., Boston, 1985; recipient commendation for family care VA, Bedford, Mass., 1971-73, 76, 81; Goldie Rogers award Dept. Social Svcs., 1994, Commr. award, 1996. Mem. Mass. Assn. Profl. Foster Care, Lioness Club (charter). Roman Catholic. Avocations: music, reading. Home and Office: 1 Chestnut St # 183 Pepperell MA 01463-1013

SCHOLEFIELD, PETER GORDON, health agency executive; b. Newport, Wales, June 26, 1925; emigrated to Can., 1947, naturalized, 1952; s. Tom and Margaret (Bithell) S.; m. Erna Mary Cooper, Sept. 29, 1951; children—David, John, Paul. B.Sc., U. Wales, 1944, M.Sc., 1946, D.Sc., 1960; Ph.D., McGill U., Montreal, Que., Can., 1949. From research fellow to prof. biochemistry McGill U., 1949-65, dir. cancer research unit, 1965-69; asst. exec. dir. Nat. Cancer Inst. Can., Toronto, 1969-80; exec. dir. Nat. Cancer Inst. Can., 1980-91, spl. adviser to chief exec. officer, 1991-92; dir. grants and awards Alta. Heritage Found. for Med. Rsch., Edmonton, 1992-94; coord. acad. affairs Samuel Lunenfeld Rsch. Inst. Mt. Sinai Hosp., Toronto, 1994—; chair rsch. policy com., bd. dirs. Alzheimer Soc. of Can., 1994—. Home: 161 Allanhurst Dr, Islington, ON Canada M9A 4K5 Office: Mt Sinai Hosp, Samuel Lunenfeld Rsch Inst, 600 University Ave Rm 970, Toronto, ON Canada M5G 1X5

SCHOLER, SUE WYANT, state legislator; b. Topeka, Oct. 20, 1936; d. Zint Elwin and Virginia Louise (Achenbach) Wyant; m. Charles Frey Scholer, Jan. 27, 1957; children: Elizabeth Scholer Truelove, Charles W., Virginia M. Scholer McCal. Student, Kans. State U., 1954-56. Draftsman The Farm Clinic, West Lafayette, Ind., 1978-79; assessor Wabash Twp., West Lafayette, 1979-84; commr. Tippecanoe County, Lafayette, Ind., 1984-90; state rep. Dist. 26 Ind. Statehouse, Indpls., 1990—; asst. minority whip, 1992-94, Rep. whip, 1994—; mem. Tippecanoe County Area Plan Commn., 1984-90. Bd. dirs. Crisis Ctr., Lafayette, 1984-89, Tippecanoe Arts Fedn., 1990—, United Way, Lafayette, 1990-93; mem. Lafayette Conv. and Visitors Bur., 1988-90. Recipient Salute to Women Govt. and Politics award, 1986, United Sr. Action award, Outstanding Legislator award, 1993, Small Bus. Champion award, 1995, Ind. Libr. Fedn. Legislator award, 1995. Mem. Ind. Assn. County Commrs. (treas. 1990), Assn. Ind. Counties (legis. com. 1988-90), Greater Lafayette C. of C. (ex-officio bd. 1984-90), Tippecanoe Profl. Women, LWV, P.E.O., Purdue Women's Club (past treas.), Kappa Kappa Kappa (past pres. Epsilon chpt.)., Delta Delta Delta (past pres. alumnae, house corp. treas.). Republican. Presbyterian. Avocations: golf, needlework, reading. Home: 807 Essex St West Lafayette IN 47906-1534 Office: Indiana Statehouse Rm 3A-7 Indianapolis IN 46204

SCHOLES, EDISON EARL, army officer; b. McCaysville, Ga., Aug. 16, 1939; s. Alvin L. and Marie (Plemmons) S.; m. Elva E. Bussey, June 4, 1961; children: Juana Kimberly Scholes, Tracy Michele Scholes Heller, Michael Lee. BS in Physics cum laude, No. Ga. Coll., 1961; MS in Ops. Rsch., Naval Postgrad. Sch., 1970; postgrad., Army War Coll., 1980, Harvard Def. Policy Seminar, 1991. Commd. 2d lt. U.S. Army, 1961, advanced through grades to maj. gen., 1991; comdr. A Detachment, 10th Spl. Forces Group, 1st Spl. Forces U.S. ArmyEurope, 1963-66; comdr. Co. D, 2d Bn.(Abn.), 8th Cav., 1st Cav. Div. U.S. Army, Republic of Vietnam, 1967-68; comdr. 1st Bn., 23d Inf., 2d Inf. Div. U.S. Army, Republic of Korea, 1976-77; comdr. 2d Tng. Bn., Sch. Brigade, U.S. Army Inf. Sch. U.S. Army, Ft. Benning, Ga., 1978-79, comdr. 1st Inf. Tng. Brigade, U.S. Army Infantry Tng. Ctr., 1983-85; dep. commanding gen. chief of staff 3d U.S. Army/U.S. Army Cen. Command U.S. Army, Ft. McPherson, Ga., 1986-88; asst. div. comdr. 82d Airborne Div. U.S. Army, Ft. Bragg, N.C., 1988-89, chief of staff XVIII Airborne Corps, 1989-90; chief of staff joint task force-south, Op. Just Cause U.S. Army, 1989-90; dep. commanding gen. XVIII Airborne Corps, Operation Desert Shield/Desert Storm U.S. Army, Saudi Arabia, Iraq, 1990-91; dep. commanding gen. XVIII Airborne Corps U.S. Army, Ft. Bragg, 1991-93; dep. comdr. Allied Land Forces, S.E. Europe NATO, 1993-95; postgrad. Harvard Def. Policy Seminar, 1991; program gen. mgr. Saudi Arabia N.G. Modernization Program, Vinnell Arabia, 1995—. Decorated Disting. Svc. medal with oak leaf cluster, Silver Star, Legion of Merit with oak leaf cluster, Bronze Star with V device and 4 oak leaf clusters, Purple Heart with oak leaf cluster, 6 Air medals, Army Commendation medal with V device and oak leaf cluster, Armed Forces Expeditionary medal, Vietnam Svc. medal with 6 campaign stars, Southwest Asia Svc. medal with 3 campaign stars, Combat Infantry badge, Expert Infantry badge, Army Gen. Staff badge, Meritorious Svc. medal, Nat. Def. Svc. medal with oak leaf cluster, Kuwait Liberation medal; Cross of Gallantry with Silver and Bronze Stars and Palm (Republic of Vietnam), S.W. Asia Svc. medal with 3 stars; numerous other domestic and foreign awards and skill badges. Mem. 82d Airborne Divsn. Assn., Spl. Forces Assn. (chpt. XXXIV), U.S. Army Ranger Assn., Assn. of U.S. Army, Spl. Ops. Assn., VFW, Officers' Club. Baptist. Avocations: running, reading, camping, fishing. Office: Vinnell Corp Unit 61322 Box A2-r APO AE 09803-1322

SCHOLL, ALLAN HENRY, retired school system administrator, education consultant; b. Bklyn., May 6, 1935; s. Joseph Arnold and Edith (Epstein) S.; m. Marina Alexandra Mihailovich, July 3, 1960. BA, UCLA, 1957; MA, U. So. Calif., 1959, PhD in History, 1973. Lic. gen. secondary tchr. (life), administrv. svcs. (life), jr. coll. tchr. (life) Calif. Tchr. social studies L.A. Unified Sch. Dist., 1960-82, adviser social studies sr. high schs. div., 1982-84, dir. secondary history, social scis. Office Instrn., 1984-91; instr. history L.A. City Coll., 1966-69, U. So. Calif., L.A., 1968-69, Community Coll., Rio Hondo, Calif., 1972-74, Cerritos (Calif.) Coll., 1973-74; dir. ALMAR Ednl. Cons., Pasadena, Calif., 1991—; curriculum developer, writer history tchg. and resource guides; cons. Pasadena Unified Sch. Dist., 1987-88, Coll. Bd., 1980-88, Autry Mus. Western Heritage, 1992—, L.A. Unified Sch. Dist. Office Gifted Programs, 1995—; edn. cons. Am. Odyssey, 1991; cons. H.S. govt. and U.S. history textbooks, 1987; lectr. in history and art history. Author: United States History and Art, 1992; co-author: 20th Century World History: The Modern Era, 1993, History of the World: The Modern Era, 1994, History of the World, 1995; co-developer, contbr.: The Treatment of People of African Descent in Nazi Occupied Europe, 1995, The Holocaust Timeline, 1995, Those Who Dared: Rescuers and Rescued, 1995; cons. Anne Frank in Historical Perspective, 1995; contbr. articles to profl. jours. Bd. dirs. Pasadena Chamber Orch., 1977-78, Pasadena Symphony Orch., 1984-85, Pasadena Centennial Com., 1985; mem. exec. bd., chmn. edn. com. Martyrs Meml. and Mus. of Holocaust of L.A., 1992—; mem. Ednl. adv. bd. Autry Mus. of Western Heritage, 1992—. With U.S. Army, 1958-59. NDEA fellow Russian lang. studies, 1962; Chouinard Art Inst. scholar, 1952. Mem. Am. Hist. Assn., Nat. Coun. Social Studies, Calif. Coun. Social Studies, Soc. Calif. Social Studies Assn. (bd. dirs. 1982-84), Assoc. Adminstrs. L.A. (legis. coun. 1983-85), Crohn's and Colitis Found. Am., Phi Alpha Theta. Avocations: reading, hiking, travel, art history, opera. *Personal philosophy: I have always believed that to achieve in life one should work hard and never give up. That is the only way we can ever hope to make a lasting contribution to society.*

SCHOLL, DAVID ALLEN, federal judge; b. Bethlehem, Pa., Aug. 20, 1944; s. George Raymond and Beatrice Roberta (Weaver) S.; m. Cynthia Ann Schuler Vetere, June, 1966 (div. 1972); m. Portia Elizabeth White, May 26, 1973; children: Tracy, Xavier; 1 stepchild, Sierra Milan. AB, Franklin & Marshall Coll., 1966; JD, Villanova U., 1969. Bar: Pa. 1969, U.S. Dist. Ct. (ea. dist.) 1970, U.S. Ct. Appeals (3d cir.) 1971, U.S. Tax Ct. 1975, U.S. Supreme Ct. 1975. Staff atty. Community Legal Services, Inc., Phila., 1969-73, 77-80; exec. dir. Delaware County Legal Assistance Assn., Chester, Pa., 1973-76; mng. atty. Lehigh Valley Legal Services, Bethelehem, Allentown, Pa., 1980-86; judge U.S. Bankruptcy Ct., Phila., 1986-94, chief judge, 1994—. Bd. dirs. Phila. Vols. for Indigent Program, 1988-94, Consumer Bankruptcy Assistance Project, 1992—. Recipient Joseph Harris award Ba'Hais of Lehigh Valley, Bethelehem, 1984. Mem. Pa. Bar Assn. (chairperson consumer law commn., 1983-86), Northampton County Bar Assn. Avocations: baseball, rock music. Home: 118 N Highland Ave Bala Cynwyd PA 19004-3027 Office: US Bankruptcy Ct 3118 US Courthouse 900 Market St Philadelphia PA 19107-4228

SCHOLLANDER, WENDELL LESLIE, JR., lawyer; b. Ocala, Fla., May 17, 1943; s. Wendell Leslie and Martha Dent (Perry) S.; m. Jayn Mary Cochran, Aug. 22, 1970; 1 son, Wendell Leslie III. BS, U. Pa., 1966, MBA, 1968; student law, Stetson U., 1969-70; JD, Duke U., 1972. Bar: N.C. 1977, Tenn. 1972, Fla. 1987. With Container Corp. Am., Fernandina, Fla., 1968-69; assoc. firm Miller, Martin, Chattanooga, 1972-75; asst. counsel R.J. Reynolds Industries, Inc., 1975-78, assoc. counsel, 1978-79, sr. assoc. counsel, 1979-82, sr. counsel, 1982-85; gen. counsel RJR Archer, Inc., Winston-Salem, N.C., 1979-85; of counsel Finger, Parker & Avram, Winston-Salem, 1985-87; ptnr. Schollander, Winston-Salem, 1987—; gen. counsel Splty. Tobacco Council, 1985-87. Mem. ABA, N.C. Bar Assn., Forsyth County Bar Assn., Mensa, SAR, Phi Delta Phi, Kappa Sigma. Presbyterian. Home: 2011 Georgia Ave Winston Salem NC 27104 Office: 2000 W 1st St Ste 509 Winston Salem NC 27104-4225

SCHOLNICK, ROBERT J., college dean, English language educator; b. Boston, June 22, 1941; s. I. Allen and Ruth (Kleiman) S.; m. Sylvia Bette Huberman, June 21, 1964; children: Joshua David, Jonathan Ben. BA, U. Pa., 1962; MA, Brandeis U., 1964, PhD, 1969. Asst. prof. English Coll. William and Mary, Williamsburg, Va., 1967-74, assoc. prof., 1974-80, prof., 1980—, dean grad. studies, 1986-96, founding dir. Am. studies program, 1981; chair applied sci. Coll. William and Mary, Williamsburg, 1986-88; bd. dirs. Univ. Press of Va., Charlottesville, 1988-92; mem. adv. bd. Am. Periodicals. Author: Edmund Clarence Stedman, 1977; editor Am. Lit. and Sci., 1992; contbr. articles to profl. jours. NEH fellow Coll. Tchrs., 1986-87. Mem. MLA, Rsch. Soc. for Am. Periodicals (founding pres.), Am. Studies Assn., Soc. for Sci., Va. Consortium Sci. and Engring. Univs. (bd. dirs. 1992-96), B'nai B'rith Va. (Hillel svc. award 1986), Phi Beta Kappa. Avocations: distance running, arts. Home: 149 Indian Springs Rd Williamsburg VA 23185-3938 Office: Coll William and Mary Williamsburg VA 23185

SCHOLSKY, MARTIN JOSEPH, priest; b. Stafford Spring, Conn., Jan. 16, 1930; s. Sigmund Felix and Mary Magdalen (Wysocki) S. BA, St. John's Sem., 1952, MA in History, 1956; MA in Classical Greek, Cath. U. of Am., 1966. Ordained priest Roman Cath. Ch., 1956. Asst. pastor St. Peter's Ch., Hartford, Conn., 1956-61; prin. St. Peter's Sch., Hartford, 1956-58; instr. St. Thomas Sem., Bloomfield, Conn., 1961-67; admissions dir. St. Thomas Sem., Bloomfield, 1965-67; vocations dir. Archdiocese of Hartford, 1967-78; chaplain Newington (Conn.) Children's Hosp., 1961-78; weekend asst. St. Mary's Ch., Newington, 1961-78; pastor St. Bartholomew Ch., Manchester, Conn., 1978-90; dean Manchester Deanery, 1989-91; spiritual dir. St. Thomas Aquinas High Sch., New Britain, Conn., 1991-92; weekend asst. St. Francis of Assis Ch., South Windsor, Conn., 1991-92; instr. Holy Apostle's Sem. & Coll., Cromwell, Conn., 1988-94; pastor St. Mary's Ch., East Hartford, Conn., 1992—. Contbr. articles to profl. jours. Home: 36 Griswold St Manchester CT 06040-3928 Office: St Marys Ch East East Hartford CT 06108 *Conscience is not our own personal feelings about things; rather, it is our innate awareness of the rightness and wrongness of our deeds as God sees them, an awareness, often denied, that still remains the measure by which God will ultimately judge us all.*

SCHOLTEN, MENNO NICO, mortgage banker; b. Assen, Drenthe, Netherlands, June 18, 1943; came to U.S., 1949; s. Nico Menno and Hennie (Nienhuis) S.; m. Susan Sumnar, Aug. 11, 1973; 1 child, Paul Menno. BArch., U. Calif., Berkeley, 1967; MBA, DePaul U., 1980. Registered architect. Architect various, including Skidmore, Owings & Merrill, others, Chgo., 1968-78, Knight Architects, Engrs. and Planners, Chgo., 1978-81, 1989-92; asst. v.p. constrn. lending adminstr. First Nat. Bank of Chgo., 1981-85; v.p. real estate group First Tex. Savs., Dallas, 1985-87; mgr. constrn. lending Household Internat. (Household Bank), Prospect Heights, Ill., 1992-94; pres. The Mesu Group, Ltd., Evanston, Ill., 1995—. Patentee chair design, 1979. Recipient award of merit Chgo. Assn. of Commerce and Industry and Internat. Trade Club of Chgo., 1979. Mem. AIA (Chgo. chpt.), Homebuilders Assn. of Greater Chgo., Am. Guild Organists (bd. dirs., treas. 1991-94), Calif. Scholarship Fedn. (life mem.), Delta Mu Delta., Intl. Platform Assn., Mortgage Bankers of Am. Avocations: tennis, skiing. Home: 3521 Central St Evanston IL 60201-4915

SCHOLTEN, PAUL, obstetrician, gynecologist, educator; b. San Francisco, Oct. 14, 1921; s. Henry Francis and Gladys (Lamborn) S.; m. Marion Lucy O'Neil, Feb. 7, 1948; children: Catherine Mary (dec.), Anne Marie, Pauline Marie, Joseph, Stephen, John. AB, San Francisco State U., 1943; postgrad., Stanford U., 1946-47; MD, U. Calif., San Francisco, 1951. Diplomate Am. Bd. Ob-Gyn. Intern San Francisco Gen. Hosp., 1951-52; resident in ob-gyn U. Calif., San Francisco, 1952-55; pvt. practice specializing in ob-gyn San Francisco, 1955-80; coll. physician Student Health Svc. San Francisco State U., 1956-80, dir. women's svcs. Student Health Svc., 1980-91; pvt. practice San Francisco, 1991—; part-time ship's surgeon Delta Lines, 1980-84; assoc. clin. prof. Med. Sch., U. Calif., San Francisco, 1955—, assoc. clin. prof. Nursing Sch., 1987—; preceptor Med. Sch., Stanford U., 1989-91; lectr. on health and wine at numerous univs., profl. groups. Contbr. articles to profl. publs., chpts. to books. Cons. U.S. Wine Inst.; sci. advisor Calif. State Adv. Bd. on Alcohol-Related Problems, 1980-86; bd. dirs. A.W.A.R.E., Century Coun. Sgt. U.S. Army, 1944-46. Mem. AMA, Calif. Med. Assn., Pan Am. Med. Assn., San Francisco Med. Soc. (editor 1971—, historian, past pres.), San Francisco Gynecol. Soc., Am. Coll. Ob-Gyn., Soc. Med. Friends of Wine (bd. dirs. 1955—, past pres.), San Francisco Wine and Food Soc. (bd. dirs. 1960—, past pres.), Internat. Wine and Food Soc. (gov. 1989—, Bronze medal 1989), San Francisco State U. Alumni Assn. (bd. dirs. 1962—), German Wine Soc., Sierra Club. Republican. Roman Catholic. Home and Office: 121 Granville Way San Francisco CA 94127-1133

SCHOLTZ, ROBERT ARNO, electrical engineering educator; b. Lebanon, Ohio, Jan. 26, 1936; s. William Paul and Erna Johanna (Weigel) S.; m. Laura Elizabeth McKeon, June 16, 1962; children: Michael William, Paul Andrew. BSEE, U. Cin., 1958; MSEE, U. So. Calif., 1960; PhD, Stanford U., 1964. Co-op student Sheffield Corp., Dayton, Ohio, 1953-58; MS and PhD fellow Hughes Aircraft Co., Culver City, Calif., 1958-63, sr. staff engr., 1963-78; prof. U. So. Calif., L.A., 1963—; vis. prof. U. Hawaii, 1969, 78; cons. LinCom Corp., L.A., 1975-81, Axiomatix Inc., L.A., 1980-86, JPL, Pasadena, 1985, Tech. Group, 1987-89, TRW, 1989, Pulson Comm., 1992-93, Colley-Godward, Palo Alto, 1994. Co-author: Spread Spectrum Comm., 3 vols., 1984, Spread Spectrum Communications Handbook, 1994, Basic Concepts in Information Theory and Coding, 1994; contbr. numerous articles to profl. jours. (recipient Leonard G. Abraham Prize Paper award 1983, Donald G. Fink Prize award 1984, Signal Processing Soc. Sr. Paper award 1992). Pres., South Bay Community Concert Orgn., Redondo Beach, Calif., 1975-79. Fellow IEEE (bd. govs. info. theory group 1981-86, bd. govs. communication soc. 1981-83, chmn. fin. com. NTC 1977, program chmn. ISIT 1981). Office: U So Calif Comm Scis Inst Dept Elec Engring Los Angeles CA 90089-2565

SCHOLZ, CHRISTOPHER HENRY, geophysicist, writer; b. Pasadena, Calif., Feb. 25, 1943; s. Joseph George and Elizabeth (Ochsner) S.; m. Paula Hanna, May 19, 1962 (div. 1978); children: Erich Frederich, Adrienne Louise; m. Yoshiko Yanagisawa, Feb. 8, 1986; 1 child, Morika Tsujimura. BS, U. Nev., 1964; PhD, MIT, 1967. Rsch. fellow Calif. Inst. Tech., Pasadena, 1967-68; rsch. assoc. Lamont-Doherty Geol. Obs., Columbia U., N.Y.C., 1968-70; sr. rsch. assoc. Lamont-Doherty Geol. Obs., Columbia U., 1970—, assoc. prof. geology, 1971-75, prof., 1975—. Author: The Mechanics of Earthquakes and Faulting, 1990, Fieldwork: A Geologist's Memoir of the Kalahari, 1997; contbr. articles on earthquakes, deformation of the earth, mech. properties of rock to profl. jours. A.P. Sloan fellow, 1975-77; C.I. Green fellow, 1980-81. Fellow Am. Geophys. Union; mem. Seismol. Soc. Am., Médaille du Collége de France. Office: Lamont-Doherty Earth Obs Palisades NY 10964

SCHOMER, HOWARD, retired clergyman, educator, social policy consultant; b. Chgo., June 9, 1915; s. Frank Michael and Daisy (Aline) S.; m. Elsie Pauline Swenson, Mar. 23, 1942 (dec. Nov. 1996); children: Karine, Mark, Paul, Ellen. B.S. summa cum laude, Harvard U., 1937, postgrad., 1939-40; student, Chgo. Theol. Sem., 1938-39, 40-41, D.D., 1954; LL.D., Olivet Coll., 1966. Ordained to ministry Congl. Ch., 1941. Student pastor Fitzwilliam, N.H., Oak Park, Ill.; asst. dean U. Chgo. Chapel., 1940-41; counsellor Am. history Harvard U., 1939-40; civilian pub. service Am. Friends Service Com., 1941-45; Am. Bd. Mission fellow to chs. of Europe Chambon-sur-Lignon, France, 1946-55; history tchr., work camp dir. Coll. Cevenol; founder internat. conf. center Accueil Fraternel, Permanent Conf. Protestant Chs. in Latin Countries of Europe; asst. to rapporteur UN Commn. on Human Rights, UN Econ. and Social Council, 1947-48; inter-church aid sec. for Europe World Council Chs., Geneva, 1955-58; pres., prof. ch. history Chgo. Theol. Sem., 1959-66; exec. dir. dept. specialized ministries Div. Overseas Ministries, Nat. Council Chs., N.Y.C., 1967-70; participant integration demonstrations in Ala., Ga., Washington, Chgo., SCLC, 1960-66; world issues sec. United Ch. Bd. World Ministries, 1971-80; Indochina liaison officer World Council of Chs., 1970-71; United Ch. of Christ officer for social responsibility in investments, 1972-81; founder, dir. Corp. Adv. Services, 1980-90; founder, mem. United Ch. Christ Working Group with United Ch. in German Democratic Rep. and Fed. Rep. of Germany, 1977-86; vis. prof. religion and society Andover Newton Theol. Sch., 1981; vis. lectr. Manchester Coll., St. John's U.; Woodrow Wilson vis. fellow Drew U., 1981; pres. Internat. Fellowship of Reconciliation, 1959-63, v.p., 1963-65; participant 1st-3d assemblies World Council Chs., Amsterdam, 1948, Evanston, 1954, New Delhi, 1961; rep. UN non-govt. orgn. UNIAPAC, 1979-85; pastoral assoc. First Congl. Ch. (United Ch. Christ), Montclair, N.J., 1983-89; delegated observer Vatican Council II, 1963; v.p. Am. Friends Coll. Cevenol., 1981-89; bd. dirs. Interfaith Center for Corp. Responsibility, 1973-81; chmn. exec. com. Freedom of Faith - A Christian Com. for Religious Rights, 1978-81; mem. nat. adv. bd. N.Y. State Martin Luther King Jr. Inst. for Nonviolence, 1989-92. Translator: The Prayer of the Church Universal (Marc Boegner), 1954; editor: The Oppression of Protestants in Spain, 1955, the Role of Transnational Business in Mass Economic Development, 1975; editor-at-large Christian Century, 1959-70; contbr.; Business, Religion and Ethics-Inquiry and Encounter, 1982, Aspects of Hope, 1993; articles to religious and interdisciplinary publs.; corr. in U.S. for Évangile et Liberté, 1988—. Past co-chmn. Chgo. Com. for Sane Nuclear Policy; bd. dirs. World Conf. on Religion and Peace, 1974-84, sec. for Kampuchea issues, 1979-81; former trustee Am. Waldensian Aid Soc.; mem. internat. council Internat. Ctr. Integrative Studies, 1984-91, bd. dirs., 1987-91; trustee Internat. Inst. for Effective Communication, 1987-93; bd. dirs. Alternative Lifelong Learning, 1992—, Cambodian Found. for Justice, Peace and Devel., 1993—. Mem. ACLU, Wider Quaker Fellowship, Fellowship Reconciliation, Ctr. for Theology and the Natural Scis., Outlook Club (Berkeley), Harvard Club San Francisco, Phi Beta Kappa. Home: 110 41st St Apt 512 Oakland CA 94611-5240 *The human capacity to hope and the power of hope to achieve either good or evil are astonishing. Reasonable hope for the better calls simply for dedicated effort. Mystical hope for the perfect demands consecrated surrender.*

SCHOMMER, CAROL MARIE, principal. Prin. Madonna High Sch. Recipient Blue Ribbon, 1990-91. Office: Madonna High Sch 4055 W Belmont Ave Chicago IL 60641-4700*

SCHOMMER, TRUDY MARIE, pastoral minister, religion education; b. Wayzata, Minn., May 18, 1937; d. Edward and Gertrude (Mergen) S. BA, Coll. St. Catherine, St. Paul, 1966; MA, Manhattanville Coll., 1971, Pacifica Grad. Inst., 1996. Joined Order of Franciscan Sisters of Little Falls, Minn., 1955. Dir. religious edn. St. Pius X, White Bear Lake, Minn., 1971-77; campus min., theology tchr. St. Cloud (Minn.) State Univ., 1977-81; pastoral min. St. Galls, St. Elizabeth, Milw., 1981-85; dir. religious edn. St. Alexander's, Morrisonville, N.Y., 1985-90; pastoral min. of religious edn. St. Mary's, Bryantown, Md., 1990-91; diocesan dir. religious edn. Diocese of New Ulm, Minn., 1991—; exec. bd. mem. Nat. Assembly Religious Women, Chgo., 1974-78. Author: Easiest Gospel Stories Ever, 1993; book reviewer Sister's Today, 1988-91. Mem. Network, Washington, 1978—. Mem. Nat. Cath. Edn. Assn., Nat. Parish Coords. and Dirs. Democrat. Roman Catholic. Home and Office: 408 Preston St NW Preston MN 55965-1002 *Life is an adventure: a time each of us is given to explore and discover the many ways Christ's life and love permeates the whole world. Life is a challenge: together as Christians we face the many challenges and difficulties of life.*

SCHON, ALAN WALLACE, lawyer, actor; b. Mpls., Nov. 27, 1946; s. Hubert Adelbert and Jennie (Jamieson) S.; m. Linda Kay Long, June 14, 1969; 1 child, Cynthia Anne. BA, U. Minn., 1969; JD, William and Mary Coll., 1973; grad. Command & Gen. Staff Coll., U.S. Army, 1984. Bar: Minn. 1973, U.S. Dist. Ct. Minn., Alaska 1986, U.S. Dist. Ct. Alaska, U.S. Ct. Appeals (9th cir.) 1988, Va. 1995. Prin. Schon Law Office, Fairbanks, Alaska, 1986-94; owner, pub. Nordland Pub. Co., Hampton, Va., 1991-94; dep. city atty. mcpl. bonds, environ. law, pub.-pvt. econ. devel. funding environ. law City of Hampton, Va., 1994—; nationwide environ. group mgr. Delphi Info. Network, Gen. Videotex Corp., Cambridge, Mass., 1991-94. Author, pub. EnvironLaw, 1991-94; editor William and Mary Law Rev., 1970-73; performer Va. Opera, Norfolk, 1995-96; film actor Day of the Jackal, 1996, Quest: Flight 427, 1996. Dir. Alaska State Fair, Fairbanks, 1987-91, Fairbanks Light Opera Theater, Fairbanks, 1991-94; dir., sec. Riding for Am., Inc., 1993—; dir. Interior Alaska Econ. Devel. Ctr., 1993-94. Maj. U.S. Army, 1974-86. Mem. Fairbanks C. of C. (chmn. environ. concerns com. 1992-94). Avocations: outdoor sports, arts. Home: 13 Keeton Ct Hampton VA 23666-2271 Office: Office of City Atty 22 Lincoln St Hampton VA 23669-3522

SCHONBERG, ALAN ROBERT, management recruiting executive; b. N.Y.C., Oct. 23, 1928; s. Julius and Evelyn (Guzik) S.; m. Carole May Kreisman, Dec. 27, 1975; children: William, Evelyn, David, Jeffrey. Nat. sales mgr. Majestic Specialties, Inc., Cleve., 1953-63; pres. Internat. Personnel, Inc., Cleve., 1963-65, Mgmt. Recruiters Internat., Inc., Cleve., 1965—. Pres., bd. dirs. Jewish Vocat. Service, Cleve., 1983—; trustees Mt. Sinai Hosp. , Cleve., bd. dirs. Cleve. Jewish News; gen. chmn. Welfare Fund Campaign; v.p. Jewish Family Svcs. Assn.; trustee Am. Jewish Commn., Mt. Sinai Med. Ctr., Hebrew Immigrant Aid Soc. Named one of Cleve.'s 86 Most Interesting People, Cleve. Mag., 1986, Man of Yr. local chpt. Orgn. through Rehab. and Tng., 1996, Entrepreneur of Yr. Inc. Mag., Merrill Lynch Ernst & Young, 1995. Mem. Internat. Franchise Assn., Internat. Confederation Pvt. Employment Agys. Assns., Am. Mgmt. Assn., Assn. Human Resource Cons. (chmn. 1980—), Org. for Rehab. and Training (ORT). Avocation: world travel. Office: Mgmt Recruiters Internat Inc 200 Public Sq Fl 31 Cleveland OH 44114-2301

SCHÖNBERG, BESSIE, dance educator; b. Hanover, Germany, Dec. 27, 1906; m. Dimitry Varley Jan. 6, 1934. Student, U. Oreg., 2 yrs.; studied with Martha Hill, Martha Graham; BA, Bennington Coll., 1936. Dancer Martha Graham Dance Co., N.Y.C., 1931; asst. to Martha Hill Bennington Coll. and/or Bennington Sch. of the Dance, 1933-35, 34-41; dance instr. Sarah Lawrence Coll., Bronxville, N.Y., 1936-41, head dance dept., 1941-75, 1941, prof. emerita, 1975—; tchr. dance dept. Juilliard, N.Y.C., 1993—; guest tchr. Ohio State U., Wesleyan U., U. N.H., George Mason U., The Art of Movement Ctr., London, Contemporary Dance Ctr., London, Dance Theater Workshop, N.Y.C., Dance Theatre Harlem, N.Y.C., NYU Tisch Grad. Sch. of Arts; dance cons. Hunter Coll., N.Y.C., Oberlin (Ohio) Coll., Dennison U., Wesleyan U.; mem. appeals bd. N.Y. State Coun. on Arts; mem. adv. panel NEA Dance Program; chmn., bd. dirs. Dance Theater Workshop. Appeared in Martha Graham's dances including Primitive Mysteries, Ceremonials, Heretic, Project in Movement for a Divine Comedy. Mentor fellow NEA, 1994; recipient citation Assn. Am. Dance Cos., 1975, Lifetime Achievement in Dance Bessie award, 1987-88, Gov. Arts award N.Y. State, 1989, Ernie award Dance/USA, 1994; The N.Y. Dance and Performance Awards are named in her honor as The BESSIES.

SCHONBERG, HAROLD CHARLES, music critic, columnist; b. N.Y.C., Nov. 29, 1915; s. David and Minnie (Kirsch) S.; m. Rosalyn Krokover, Nov. 28, 1942; m. Helene Cornell, May 10, 1975. BA cum laude, Bklyn. Coll., 1937; MA, NYU, 1938; LittD, Temple U., 1964; LHD, Grinnell Coll., 1967. Assoc. editor Am. Music Lover, 1939-41; contbr. editor Mus. Digest, 1946-48; music critic N.Y. Sun, 1946-50; contbg. editor, record columnist Mus. Courier, 1948-52; music and record critic N.Y. Times, 1950-60, sr. music critic, 1960-80, cultural corr., 1980-85; columnist on The Gramophone of London, 1948-60; judge many internat. piano competitions. Author: The Guide to Long-Playing Records, Chamber and Solo Instrumental Music, 1955, The Collector's Chopin and Schumann, 1959, The Great Pianists, 1963, The Great Conductors, 1967, Lives of the Great Composers, 1970, Grandmasters of Chess, 1973, Facing the Music, 1981, The Glorious Ones--Classical Music's Legendary Performers, 1985, Horowitz: His Life and Music, 1992; illustrated own articles with caricatures; contbg. editor Internat. Ency. Music and Musicians, New Grove Dictionary of Music and Musicians. Served as 1st lt. Airborne Signal Corps AUS, 1942-46. Recipient Pulitzer prize for criticism, 1971. Clubs: Manhattan Chess, Century Assn., Army and Navy. Home: 160 Riverside Dr New York NY 10024-2106

SCHONBERG, WILLIAM PETER, aerospace, mechanical, civil engineering educator; b. N.Y.C., Mar. 25, 1960; s. Christian and Tamara (Kalnev) S.; m. Jane Heminover, Sept. 7, 1986; children: Christina Carol, Richard William. BSCE cum laude, Princeton U., 1981; MS in Engring., Northwestern U., 1983, PhD, 1986. Asst. prof. civil engring. U. Ala., Huntsville, 1986-91, assoc. prof., 1991-94, prof., 1994—, chair civil and environ. engring. dept., 1995—; mem. working group NASA Boeing Space Sta., 1987-90. Contbr. articles to profl. publs. Recipient rsch. and creative works award U. Ala.-Huntsville Found., 1992; Walter P. Murphy fellow, 1981-82, summer faculty fellow NASA, 1987, 88, 94, 95, Air Force Office Sci. Rsch., 1992, 93; grantee U. Ala.-Huntsville Rsch. Inst., 1987-92. Mem. AIAA (sr., Young Engr. of Yr. award 1990, Lawrence Sperry award 1995), ASME, ASCE, Am. Acad. Mechanics, Tau Beta Pi. Avocations: astronomy, stamps, mystery novels, rock & roll music, travel. Office: U Ala Huntsville 4701 University Dr NW Huntsville AL 35899-0100

SCHÖNEMANN, PETER HANS, psychology educator; b. Pethau, Fed. Republic Germany, July 15, 1929; came to U.S., 1960, naturalized, 1965; s. Max Paul Franz and Hertha Anna (Kahle) S.; m. Roberta Dianne Federbush, Jan. 29, 1962; children: Raoul Dieter, Nicole Deborah. Vordiplom in Psychologie, U. Munich, 1956; Hauptdiplom in Psychologie, U. Goettingen, 1959; Ph.D., U. Ill., 1964. Thurstone postdoctoral fellow U. N.C., 1965-66; asst. prof., then assoc. prof. Ohio State U., 1966-69; postdoctoral fellow Ednl. Testing Service, Princeton, N.J., 1967-68; vis. prof. Technische Hochschule, Aachen, Fed. Republic Germany, 1981; mem. faculty Purdue U., 1969—, prof. psychology, 1971—; vis. prof. Univs. Munich, Bielefeld and Braunschweig, 1984-85, Nat. Taiwan U., 1992. Author papers in field. Recipient Found. for the Advancement of Outstanding Scholarship award, Taiwan, 1996. Mem. Soc. Multivariate Exptl. Psychology. Office: Dept Psychol Scis Purdue U Lafayette IN 47907

SCHONFELD, GUSTAV, medical educator, researcher; b. Mukacevo, Ukraine, May 8, 1934; came to U.S., 1946; s. Alexander Schonfeld and Helena Gottesmann; m. Miriam Steinberg, May 28, 1961; children: Joshua Lawrence, Julia Elizabeth, Jeremy David. BA, Washington U., St. Louis, 1956, MD, 1960. Diplomate Am. Bd. Internal Medicine. Intern. Bellevue Med. Ctr. NYU, 1960-61, resident in internal medicine, 1961-63; chief resident in internal medicine Jewish Hosp., St. Louis, 1963-64; NIH trainee in endocrinology and metabolism Washington U., St. Louis, 1964-66, instr. medicine, 1965-66, asst. prof. medicine, 1968-70, assoc. prof. preventive medicine and medicine, 1972-77, prof. preventive medicine and prof. internal medicine, 1977-86, William B. Kountz prof. medicine, 1987-96, August A. Busch prof. medicine, head dept. internal medicine, 1996—, dir. atherosclerosis and lipid rsch. ctr., 1972-96, acting head dept. preventive medicine, 1983-86, mem. exec. faculty Sch. Medicine, 1983-86, chmn. whole univ. faculty senate coun., 1995—; rsch. assoc. Cochran VA Hosp., St. Louis, 1965-66, clin. investigator, 1968-70, cons. in internal medicine, 1972—; rsch. flight med. officer USAF Sch. Aerospace Medicine, Brooks AFB, Tex., 1966-68; asst. physician Barnes Hosp., St. Louis, 1972-86; assoc. physician Barnes Hosp., 1986—; clin. instr. medicine Harvard U. Med. Sch., Boston, 1970-72; assoc. prof. metabolism and human nutrition, asst. dir. Clin. Rsch. Ctr. MIT, Boston, 1970-72; mem. rsch. com. Mo. Heart Assn., 1978-80; expert witness working group on atherosclerosis Nat. Heart, Lung and Blood Inst., 1979, Nat. Diabetes Adv. Bd., 1979; mem. endocrinologic and metabolic drugs adv. com. USPHS, FDA, 1982-86; mem. nutritional study sect. NIH, 19844-88, spl. reviewer metabolism study sect.; mem. adult treatment guidelines panel Nat. Cholesterol Edn. Program, 1986—; mem. Consenseus Devel. Conf. on Triglyceride, High Density Lipoprotein and Coronary Heart Disease, 1992—; cons. Am. Egg Bd., Am. Dairy Bd., Inst. Shortening and Edible Oils, Ciba-Geigy, Sandoz, Fournier, Parke-Davis, Bristol-Meyers Squibb, Monsanto/Searle. Editor: Atherosclerosis; past mem. editorial bd. Jour. Clin. Endocrinology and Metabolism, Jour. Clin. Investigation; mem. editorial bd. Jour. Lipid Rsch. Recipient Berg Prize in Microbiology, 1957, 58, Faculty/Alumni award Washington U., 1995; named Physician honoree Am. Heart Assn. Mo. Affiliate, 1995; grantee merit status NIH. Fellow ACP; mem. Assn. Am. Physicians, Am. Soc. for Clin. Investigation, Am. Physiol. Soc., Am. Soc. Biol. Chemists, Am. Inst. Nutrition, Am. Diabetes Assn., Am. Heart Assn. (program com. coun. on atherosclerosis 1977-80, 86-88, nat. com. 1980-84, pathology rsch. com. 1980-83, budget com. 1991, awards com. 1992), Endocrine Soc., Alpha Omega Alpha. Office: Washington U Sch Medicine Box 8046 660 S Euclid Saint Louis MO 63110

SCHONFELD, WILLIAM ROST, political science educator, researcher; b. N.Y.C., Aug. 28, 1942; s. William A. and Louise R. (Rost) S.; m. Elena Beortegui, Jan. 23, 1964; children: Natalie Beortegui, Elizabeth Lynn Beortegui. Student, Cornell U., 1960-61; B.A. cum laude with honors, NYU, 1964; M.A., Princeton U., 1968, Ph.D., 1970. Research asst. Princeton U., 1966-69, research assoc., 1969-70, vis. lectr., 1970; asst. prof. polit. sci. U. Calif.-Irvine, 1970-75, assoc. prof., 1975-81, prof., 1981—, dean Sch. Social Scis., 1982—; sr. lectr. Fond. Nat. de Sci. Politique, Paris, 1973-74; researcher Centre de Sociologie des Organisations, Paris, 1976-78. Author: Youth and Authority in France, 1971, Obedience and Revolt, 1976, Ethnographie du PS et du RPR, 1985. Recipient Disting. Teaching award U. Calif.-Irvine, 1984; Fulbright fellow Bordeaux, France, 1964-65; Danforth grad. fellow, 1964-69; Fulbright sr. lectr. Paris, 1973-74; NSF-CNRS Exchange of Scientists fellow Paris, 1976-78; Ford Found. grantee France, Spain, 1978-79; finalist Prof. Yr. Council for Advancement and Support of Edn., 1984. Mem. Am. Polit. Sci. Assn., Assoc. Francaise de Sci. Pol., Phi Beta Kappa. Office: U Calif Sch Social Scis Irvine CA 92697

SCHONHOLTZ, JOAN SONDRA HIRSCH, banker, civic worker; b. N.Y.C., Sept. 8, 1933; d. Joseph G. and Mildred (Klebanoff) Hirsch; m. George J. Schonholtz, Aug. 21, 1951; children: Margot Beth, Steven Robert, Barbara Ellen. Student, Vassar Coll., 1950-52; B.A., Barnard Coll., 1954; postgrad., Am. U., 1963. Chmn. bd. dirs., founding mem. Grand Bank (formerly) 1st Women's Bank of Md., Rockville, 1976—; chmn. FWB Bancorp., Rockville, 1982—, Grand Banc Inc. Pres. Ft. Benning Med. Wives, Ga., 1962-63; sec. Montgomery County Women's Med. Aux., Md., 1968; bd. dirs. Svc. Guild of Washington, 1968-77, sec., 1969-70, pres., 1975-77; bd. dirs. Pilot Sch. for Blind Multiple Handicapped Children, Washington, 1968-77; bd. dirs. Strathmore Hall Arts Ctr., N. Bethesda, Md., 1992—; spl. gifts chmn. Cancer Soc. Montgomery County, 1968, 69; mem. Washington Adv. Coun. on Deaf-Blind Children, 1972-74; chmn. Friends of Wash. Adventist Hosp., Takoma Park, Md., 1993-94. Recipient Outstanding Service award Service Guild of Washington, 1969. Republican. Jewish. Clubs: Vassar, Barnard. Home: 10839 Lockland Rd Potomac MD 20854-1855

SCHONHORN, HAROLD, chemist, researcher; b. N.Y.C., Apr. 2, 1928; s. Benjamin and Dorothy (Gitlin) S.; m. Esther Matesky, Jan. 17, 1954; children: Deborah, Jeremy. BS, Bklyn. Coll., 1950; PhD, N.Y. Polytech. U., 1959. Mem. tech. staff Bell Labs., Murray Hill, N.J., 1961-84; v.p. R & D Polyken Tech. div. Kendall Co., Lexington, Mass., 1984-93; pres. Schonhorn Consultants, 1993—. Contbr. over 100 articles to profl. jours. Pres. B'nai B'rith Lodge, Summit, N.J., 1970. With U.S. Army, 1953-55, Korea. Mem. Am. Chem. Soc. Achievements include 15 patents.

SCHONWETTER, RONALD SCOTT, physician, educator; b. Miami Beach, Fla., Apr. 24, 1958; s. Morris Jack and Joyce (Trager) S.; m. Rita A. Nemitoff, Mar. 2, 1986; children: Sara Wendi, Rachel Elana, Jonathan Harris. BA in Chemistry and Psychology with high honors, Emory U., 1979; MD, U. South Fla., 1984. Diplomate Am. Bd. Internal Medicine, Nat. Bd. Med. Examiners. Intern Baylor Coll. Medicine, Houston, 1984-85, resident in primary care internal medicine, 1985-87; fellow geriat. medicine Baylor Coll. Medicine and VA Med. Ctr., Houston, 1987-89; asst. prof. medicine divsn. geriatric medicine, dept. internal medicine, coll. medicine U. South Fla., Tampa, 1989-94, assoc. prof. medicine divsn. geriat. medicine, 1994—; assoc. med. dir. Hospice Hillsborough, Inc., Tampa, 1989-92, med. dir., 1992—, med. dir. palliative care clinic, 1993—; med. dir. Univ. Village Nursing Ctr., Tampa, 1989-94; staff physician Tampa Gen. Hosp. Skilled Nursing Facility, 1989—; cons. internist suncoast gerontology memory disorder clinic Coll. Medicine, U. South Fla., 1989-93; mem. hospice steering com., 1993—; vice chmn. Am. Bd. Hospice and Palliative Medicine, 1996—; presenter in field. Contbr. articles to profl. jours. Recipient New Investigator award Am. Geriatric Soc. and Merck U.S. Human Health, 1994. Fellow ACP, Am. Geriatrics Soc. (mem. ethics com. 1992—); mem. Am. Med. Dirs. Assn. (cert. med. dir.), Nat. Hospice Orgn. (coun. hospice profls. 1994—), Gerontol. Soc. Am., Acad. Hospice Physicians. Jewish. Office: U South Fla Coll Medicine Dept Internal Medicine Divsn Geriatric Medicine 12901 Bruce B Downs Blvd Tampa FL 33612-4742

SCHOOLAR, JOSEPH CLAYTON, psychiatrist, pharmacologist, educator; b. Marks, Miss., Feb. 28, 1928; s. Adrian Taylor and Leah (Covington) S.; m. Betty Jane Peck, Nov. 2, 1960; children—Jonathan Covington, Cynthia Jane, Geoffrey Michael, Catherine Elizabeth, Adrian Carson. A.B., U. Tenn., Memphis, 1950, M.S., 1952; Ph.D., U. Chgo., 1957, M.D., 1960. Diplomate Am. Bd. Psychiatry and Neurology. Chief drug abuse research TRIMS, Houston, 1966-72; assoc. prof. U. Tex. Grad. Sch. Biomed. Scis., Houston, 1968—; prof. psychiatry Baylor Coll. Medicine, Houston, 1975—, prof. pharmacology, 1974—, chief div. psychopharmacology, 1973—; dir. Tex. Research Inst. Mental Scis., Houston, 1972-85; mem. Nat. Bd. Med. Examiners' Task Force on Drug Abuse and Alcoholism, 1982—; mem. Drug Abuse Adv. Com., FDA, Washington, 1983-85, chmn., 1984; chmn. profl. needs planning task force Nat. Inst. Drug Abuse, Washington, 1977—. Editor: Current Issues in Adolescent Psychiatry, 1973, Research and the Psychiatric Patient, 1975, The Kinetics of Psychiatric Drugs, 1979, Serotonin in Biological Psychiatry - Advanced in Biochemical Psychopharmacology, 1982. Cons. Parents' League Houston, 1972-74; mem. coordinating com. Citizens Mental Health Service, Houston, 1976; mem. acad. com. for study of violence Houston Police Dept., 1979; bd. dirs. Can-Do-It, Houston, 1982—. Served to 1st lt. U.S. Army, 1945-47. Recipient Eugen Kahn award Baylor Coll. Medicine, Houston, 1964. Fellow Am. Psychiat. Assn., Am. Coll. Psychiatrists; mem. Am. Coll. Neuropsychopharmacology, Collegium Internationale NeuroPsychopharmacologicum, Am. Soc. Pharmacology and Exptl. Therapeutics. Episcopalian. Home: 2222 Sunset Blvd Houston TX 77005-1530 Office: Baylor Coll Medicine One Baylor Pla PO Box 25302 Houston TX 77265-5302*

SCHOOLEY, CHARLES EARL, electrical engineer, consultant; b. Archie, Mo., Sept. 18, 1905; s. Charles Elias and Virginia Maria (Bone) S.; m. Dorothy S. Alexander, Apr. 29, 1934 (dec. 1965); 1 dau., Dorothy Virginia; m. Dolores Harter, Apr. 1966 (dec. 1993). B.S. in Elec. Engring, U. Mo., 1928. Registered profl. engr., Ga. With Ozark Utilities Co., Bolivar Telephone Co., Mo. Pacific R.R.; transmission engr. Long Lines dept. Am. Tel. & Tel. Co., St. Louis, Kansas City, N.Y.C., 1927-44; co-axial carrier engr., elec. coordination engr. Am. Tel. & Tel. Co., N.Y.C., 1944-48; div. engr. Am. Tel. & Tel. Co., Washington, 1948-49; facility engr., engr. transmission, comml. devel. engr. Am. Tel. & Tel. Co., 1949-51, toll dialing engr., plant extension engr., system planning engr., operating and engring. dep., 1951-53, asst. chief engr., dir. customer products planning, 1956-57; chief engr. So. Bell Tel. & Tel. Co., Atlanta, 1953-55; v.p. operations, dir. Ind. Bell Telephone Co., Indpls., 1957-59; dir. operations, mem. bd. long lines dept. Am. Tel. & Tel. Co., N.Y., 1959-66; dir., v.p. Transpacific Communications Co., Transocean Cable Ship Co., Eastern Tel. & Tel. Co., 1960-66, 9 other Am. Tel. & Tel. subs; v.p., treas., dir. Eds, Inc., Sharon, Conn., 1970-85. Vice pres. Berkshire Hills (Conn.) Music and Dance Assn., 1970-78; v.p., treas. Wingspread Found., 1977—; trustee Brevard (N.C.) Music Ctr., 1994—. Recipient Disting. Service to Engring. medal U. Mo., 1960. Fellow IEEE; mem. Ga. Engring. Soc., Met. Club (N.Y.C.), Hendersonville (N.C.) Country Club, QEBH U. Mo., Delta Upsilon (bd. dirs. 1962-70), Eta Kappa Nu. Address: PO Box 746 Hendersonville NC 28793-0746 also: PO Box 633 Winter Haven FL 33882-0633 also: 210 Crooked Creek Rd Hendersonville NC 28739-6822

SCHOOLEY, OTIS BRYSON, III, commercial airport executive. BA in Bus. Adminstrn./Acctg., Calif. State U.; cert. in exec. mgmt., U. Calif., Irvine. Asst. dir. John Wayne Airport, Orange County, Calif., 1991—; chmn. Calif. Transp. Commn.'s Tech. Adv. Com. on Aviation. Mem. So. Calif. Assn. of Govt. (aviation tech. adv. com.), Calif. Assn. of Airport Execs., Am. Assn. of Airport Execs. Office: John Wayne Airport Orange County 3151 Airway Ave Bldg K-101 Costa Mesa CA 92626-4607

SCHOOLMAN, ARNOLD, neurological surgeon; b. Worcester, Mass., Oct. 31, 1927; s. Samuel and Sarah (Koffman) Schulman; m. Gloria June Feder, Nov. 10, 1963; children: Hugh Sinclair, (Jill) Annette. Student, U. Mass., 1945-46; BA, Emory U., 1950; PhD, Yale U., 1954, MD, 1957. Diplomate Am. Bd Neurol. Surgery, Nat. Bd. Med. Examiners. Intern U. Calif. Hosp., San Francisco, 1957-58; resident in neurol. surgery Columbia-Presbyn. Med. Ctr., Neurol. Inst. N.Y., N.Y.C., 1958-62; instr. neurol. surgery U. Kans. Sch. Medicine, Kansas City, 1962, asst. prof. surgery, 1964; assoc. prof. U. Mo. Sch. Medicine, Kansas City, 1976; chief sect. neurosurgery Research Med. Ctr., Kansas City, 1982; dir. Midwest Neurol. Inst., 1982-83. Patentee in field. Served with USN, 1946-48. Fellow ACS (mem. Mo. chpt.); mem. AMA, Mo. State Med. Assn., Kansas City Med. Soc., Kansas City Neurosurg. Soc. (pres. 1984-85), Kansas City Neurol. Soc., Rocky Mountain Neurosurg. Soc., Am. Assn. Neurol. Surgeons, AAAS, Mo. Neurol. Soc., Internat. Coll. Surgeons, Congress Neurol. Surgeons, Brit. Royal Soc. Medicine, Phi Beta Kappa, Sigma Xi. Avocation: pilot. Home: 8705 Catalina St Shawnee Mission KS 66207-2351 Office: 1000 E 50th St Ste 310 Kansas City MO 64110-2215

SCHOOLS, CHARLES HUGHLETTE, banker, lawyer; b. Lansing, Mich., May 24, 1929; s. Robert Thomas and Lillian Pearl (Lawson) S.; B.S., Am. U., 1952, M.A., 1958; J.D., Washington Coll. of Law, 1963; LL.D., Bethune-Cookman U., 1973; m. Rosemarie Sanchez, Nov. 22, 1952; children—Charles, Michael. Dir. phys. plant Am. U., 1952-66; owner, 1957—, Gen. Security Co., Washington, 1969—; chmn., pres. Consol. Ventures Ltd.; pres., chmn. bd. McLean Bank (Va.), 1974—, Instl. Environ. Mgmt. Services; chmn. bd. Harper & Co.; chmn., pres. Community Assos. of Va., Associated Real Estate Mgmt. Services; dir. Computer Data Systems Inc., DAC Devel. Ltd., Am. Indsl. Devel. Corp., Intercoastal of Iran; mem. Met. Bd. Trades. Pres., McLean Boys' Club; bd. dirs. D.C. Spl. Olympics, Nat. Kidney Found.; trustee Bethune Cookman Coll., Western Md. Coll., Randolph Macon Acad. Served with USAAF, 1946-47, USAF, 1947-48. Mem. Va. C. of C., Profl. Businessman's Orgn., Alpha Tau Omega. Democrat. Clubs: Georgetown of Washington, Touchdown of Washington, Univ. of Washington, Washington Golf and Country, Pisces (Washington); Halifax (Daytona Beach, Fla.); Masons. Home: 1320 Darnall Dr Mc Lean VA 22101-3006 Office: 1313 Dolley Madison Blvd Mc Lean VA 22101-3926

SCHOONHOVEN, RAY JAMES, retired lawyer; b. Elgin, Ill., May 24, 1921; s. Ray Covey and Rosina Madeline (Schram) (White) S.; m. Marie Theresa Dunn, Dec. 11, 1943; children: Marie Kathleen, Ray James, Jr., Pamela Suzanne, John Philip, Rose Lynne. B.S.C., U. Notre Dame, 1943; J.D., Northwestern U., 1948. Bar: Ill. 1949, U.S. Supreme Ct. 1954, D.C. 1973, U.S. Ct. Mil. Appeals 1954. Assoc. Seyfarth, Shaw Fairweather & Geraldson, Chgo., 1949-57, ptnr., 1957-92; ret.; chief rulings and ops. br. Wage Stabilization Bd. Region VII, Chgo., 1951-52. Book rev. editor: Ill. Law Rev., 1948. Served to lt.comdr. USNR, 1942-62. Mem. ABA, Ill. State Bar Assn., Chgo. Bar Assn., D.C. Bar Assn., Chgo. Athletic Assn., Univ. Club. Chgo., Order of Coif. Republican. Roman Catholic. Home: 6636 N Ponchartrain Blvd Chicago IL 60646-1428 Office: Seyfarth Shaw Fairweather & Geraldson 55 E Monroe St Ste 4200 Chicago IL 60603-5803 *I work hard to preserve our free enterprise system and, hopefully, to make such contribution to our society that it is better for my having been a part of it.*

SCHOONMAKER, SAMUEL VAIL, III, lawyer; b. Newburgh, N.Y., Sept. 1, 1935; s. Samuel V. Jr. and Catherine (Wilson) S.; m. Carolyn Peters, Sept. 18, 1965; children: Samuel V. IV, Frederick P. BA magna cum laude, Yale U., 1958, JD, 1961. Bar: Conn. 1961, U.S. Dist. Ct. Conn. 1961, U.S. Dist. Ct. (so. and ea. dist.) N.Y. 1964, U.S. Ct. Appeals (2d cir.) 1964, U.S. Supreme Ct. 1965. Pres. Schoonmaker & George, P.C., Greenwich, Conn., 1996—; assoc. Cummings & Lockwood, Stamford, Conn., 1970-96, ptnr., 1961-70, co-mng. ptnr., 1987-90, mng. ptnr., 1990-94, chmn. exec. com., 1987-94; founder, pres. Schoonmaker & George, PC, Greenwich, Conn., 1996—; state trial referee Conn. Superior Ct., 1989; pres. Schoonmaker Family Assn., New Paltz, N.Y., 1975-77. Sr. topical editor Conn. Bar Jour., 1977-81; mem. bd. editors Fairshare and America Jour., 1992; contbr. articles to profl. jours. Chmn. Conn. Child Support Commn., 1984-86; mem. Conn. Family Support Com., 1986-90; mem. Darien (Conn.) Rep. Town Com., 1974-76, rep. town meeting, 1990—; pres. Youth Tennis Found. New Eng., Needham, Mass., 1975-77; pres. New Eng. Lawn Tennis Assn., 1977-79 (Man of Yr. award 1979). Fellow Am. Acad. Matrimonial Lawyers Conn. (bd. mgrs., Disting. Svc. award 1988), Internat. Acad. Matrimonial Lawyers, Am. Bar Found.; mem. ABA (chmn. family law sect. 1982-83), Conn. Bar Assn. (chmn. family law sect. 1971-74), Conn. Bus. and Industry Assn. (bd. dirs. 1993—), S.W. Conn. Bus. and Industry Assn. (bd. dirs. 1990—), Pub. Defenders Assn. (chmn.), Wee Burn Country Club (Darien, Conn., asst. sec.), Yale Club (N.Y.C.), Phi Beta Kappa. Avocation: tennis, platform tennis. Home: 231 Old Kings Hwy Darien CT 06820 Office: Schoonmaker & George PC PO Box 5059 5 Edgewood Ave Greenwich CT 06831-5059

SCHOONMAKER POWELL, THELMA, film editor; b. 1940; m. Michael Powell, 1984 (dec. 1990). Editor: (films) Who's That Knocking at My Door, 1968, Woodstock, 1970 (Academy award nomination best film editing 1970), Raging Bull, 1980 (Academy award best film editing 1980), The King of Comedy, 1983, After Hours, 1985, The Color of Money, 1986, The Last Temptation of Christ, 1988, New York Stories ("Life Lessons"), 1989, GoodFellas, 1990 (Academy award nomination best film editing 1990), Cape Fear, 1992, The Age of Innocence, 1993, A Personal Journey with Martin Scorsese Through American Movies, 1995, Casino, 1995 (Academy award nomination best film editing 1995), Kundun, 1997. Office: Cappa Prodns 445 Park Ave Fl 7 New York NY 10022-2606

SCHOONOVER, JACK RONALD, judge; b. Winona, Minn., July 23, 1934; s. Richard M. and Elizabeth A. (Hargeisheimer) S.; student Winona State Coll., 1956-58; LLB, U. Fla., 1962; m. Ann Marie Kroez, June 18, 1965; children: Jack Ronald, Wayne J. Bar: Fla. 1962. Atty. Wotitzky, Wotitzky & Schoonover, 1962-69, Schoonover, Olmsted & Schwarz, 1969-75; spl. asst. state's atty., State of Fla., 1969-72; city atty. City of Punta Gorda, Fla., city judge, 1973-74; judge 20th Jud. Cir. Ct., Ft. Myers, Fla., 1975-81, 2d Dist. Ct. Appeal, 1981—, chief judge, 1990-92; atty. Charlotte County Sch. Bd., 1969-75, Charlotte County Zoning Bd., Charlotte County Devel. Authority; mem. unauthorized practice law com. 12th Jud. Cir., mem. grievance com. 20th Jud. Cir.; adj. prof. Edison C.C. Tchr. Charlotte County Adult Edn. Assn. Served with USAF, 1952-56. Mem. Am. Legion. Home: 1224 Stratton Ct W Lakeland FL 33813-2348 Office: PO Box 327 Lakeland FL 33802-0327

SCHOONOVER, JEAN WAY, public relations consultant; b. Richfield Springs, N.Y.. AB, Cornell U., 1941. With D-A-Y Pub. Rels., Ogilvy & Mather Co., N.Y.C., 1949-91, D-A-Y Pub. Rels. Inc. and predecessor, N.Y.C., 1949—; owner, pres. Dudley-Anderson-Yutzy Pub. Rels. Inc. and predecessor, N.Y.C., 1970—; chmn. Dudley-Anderson-Yutzy Pub. Relations Inc. and predecessor, 1984-88; merger with Ogilvy & Mather, 1983; sr. v.p. Ogilvy & Mather U.S., 1984-91; vice chmn. Ogilvy Pub. Relations Group, 1986-91; ind. cons., 1992—; pres. YWCA of the City of N.Y., 1994—; mem., historian, Pub. Relations Seminar; mem. U.S. Dept. Agriculture Agribusiness Promotion Council, 1985—. Trustee Cornell U., 1975-80; mem. Def. Adv. Com. on Women in Svcs., 1987-89. Named Advt. Woman of Yr. Am. Advt. Fedn., 1972, one of Outstanding Women in Bus. & Labor, Women's Equity Action League, 1985; recipient Matrix award, 1976, Nat. Headliner award, 1984, N.Y. Women in Comm., 1976, Leadership award Internat. Orgn. Women Bus. Owners, 1980, Entrepreneurial Woman award Women Bus. Owners N.Y., 1981, Women of Distinction award Soroptimists Internat. N.Y., 1995. Mem. Women Execs. in Pub. Rels. N.Y.C. (pres. 1979-80), Pub. Rels. Soc. Am., Pub. Rels. Soc. N.Y. (pres. 1979), Womens Forum, Women's City Club. Home: 25 Stuyvesant St New York NY 10003-7505

SCHOONOVER, MARGARET See LEFRANC, MARGARET

SCHOPLER, JOHN HENRY, psychologist, educator; b. Fuerth, Fed. Republic Germany, Nov. 5, 1930; came to U.S., 1938, naturalized, 1943; s. Ernest H. and Erna (Oppenheimer) S.; m. Janice E. Hough, Dec. 12, 1969; children: Kari, Lisa, Andrew, David. B.A., U. Rochester, 1952; M.A., U. N.Mex., 1953; Ph.D., U. Colo., 1958. Mem. faculty U. N.C., Chapel Hill, 1957—; asso. prof. psychology U. N.C., 1964-69, prof., 1969—, chmn. dept., 1976-83; NSF sr. postdoctoral fellow London Sch. Econs. and Polit. Sci., 1966-67, Kenan prof., 1983-84. Author: (with Chester Insko) Experimental Social Psychology, 1972; co-founder, asso. editor: (with John Thibaut) Jour. Exptl. Social Psychology, 1964-69; contbr. (with Chester Insko) articles to profl. jours. Fulbright scholar, 1974-75. Fellow Am. Psychol. Assn., Soc. Psychol. Study Social Issues, N.C. Psychol. Assn.; mem. Soc. Explt. Social Psychology. Office: U NC Dept Psychology Chapel Hill NC 27514

SCHOPPMANN, MICHAEL JOSEPH, lawyer; b. N.Y.C., May 17, 1960; s. Fred Richard and Dorothy Ann (Wood) S.; m. Marlene Elizabeth Macbeth, Nov. 21, 1987; children: Michael, Steven. BS, St. John's U., 1982; JD, Seton Hall U., 1985. Bar: N.J. 1985, U.S. Dist. Ct. N.J. 1986, U.S. Supreme Ct. 1992, D.C. 1993, N.Y. 1994. Assoc. Baker Garber Duffy & Baker, Hoboken, N.J., 1985-87; counsel Johnstone Skok Loughlin & Lane, Westfield, N.J., 1987-90; prin. Kern Augustine Conroy & Schoppmann, Bridgewater, N.J., 1990—. Author, editor: (text) Basic Health Law, 1993.. Mem. ABA, Assn. Trial Lawyers Am., N.J. Bar Assn. (chair adminstrv. law sect. 1994—), Bar Assn. Washington, N.Y. Bar Assn., Somerset County Bar Assn. Office: Kern Augustine Conroy & Schoppmann 1120 Us Highway 22 Bridgewater NJ 08807-2944

SCHOPPMEYER, MARTIN WILLIAM, education educator; b. Weehawken, N.J., Sept. 15, 1929; s. William G. and Madeleine M. (Haas) S.; m. Marilyn M. Myers, Aug. 9, 1958; children: Susan Ann, Martin William. B.S., Fordham U., 1950; Ed.M., U. Fla., 1955, Ed.D., 1962. Tchr. Fla. pub. schs., 1955-59; instr., then asst. prof. U. Fla., 1960-63; assoc. prof., then prof. edn. Fla. Atlantic U., Boca Raton, 1963-68; dir. continuing edn. Fla. Atlantic U., 1965-67; mem. faculty U. Ark., Fayetteville, 1968—; prof. edn. U. Ark., 1971-93; univ. prof. U. Ark., Fayetteville, 1993—; program coord. for ednl. adminstrn. U. Ark., 1983-90; mem. Nat. Adv. Coun. Edn. Professions Devel., 1973-76; exec. sec. Ark. Sch. Study Coun., 1976—; evaluator instructional tng. program Nat. Tng. Fund, 1978; bd. dirs. Women's Ednl. and Devel. Inst., 1977-80, Nat. Sch. Devel. Coun., sec., 1989-90, v.p. 1990, pres., 1990-92; mem. oversight com. South Conway (Ark.) County Sch. Dist.; mem. state commn. to study effect of Amendment 59 to Ark. Constn. Author books, monographs, articles in field. Mem. president's coun. Subiaco Acad., 1984-90; chmn. Subiaco Sch. Bd., 1990-93, mem., 1993—. With U.S. Army, 1951-53, Korea. Recipient numerous fed. grants. Mem. NEA, Ark. Edn. Assn. (past chpt. pres.), Ark. Assn. Ednl. Adminstrs., KC, Rotary, Kappa Delta Pi, Phi Delta Kappa, Delta Tau Kappa. Roman Catholic. Home: 2950 Sheryl Ave Fayetteville AR 72703-3542 Office: U Ark 231 Grad Edn Bldg Fayetteville AR 72701 *The only really sound investment for a family, a community, or a society is that money spent for the education of its youth.*

SCHOR, JOSEPH MARTIN, pharmaceutical executive, biochemist; b. Bklyn., Jan. 10, 1929; s. Aaron Jacob and Rhea Iress (Kay) S.; children: Esther Helen, Joshua David, Gideon Alexander, Eric, Neil; m. Laura Sharon Strumingher, June 14, 1992. BS magna cum laude, CCNY, 1951; PhD, Fla. State U., 1957. Sr. rsch. chemist Armour Pharm. Co., Kankakee, Ill., 1957-59, Lederle Labs., Pearl River, N.Y., 1959-64; dir. biochemistry Endo Labs., Garden City, N.Y., 1964-70; head dept. biochemistry DuPont and Endo Labs., 1970-77; v.p. sci. affairs Forest Labs., N.Y.C., 1977-94; sr. v.p. sci. affairs emeritus, Forest Labs, 1995—. Editor, contbr.: Chemical Control of Fibrinolysis-Thrombolysis, 1970. Contbr. articles to profl. jours. Patentee in field. USPHS fellow, 1955-57. Fellow Am. Inst. Chemists (cert. profl. chemist); mem. Am. Chem. Soc. (chmn. Nassau County subsect. 1971-72), Internat. Soc. on Thrombosis and Hemostasis, N.Y. Acad. Scis., AAAS, Phi Beta Kappa, Sigma Xi. Home: 28 Meleny Rd Locust Valley NY 11560-1221

SCHOR, LAURA STRUMINGHER, academic administrator, historian; b. N.Y.C., June 24, 1945; d. David Charles and Esther Rachel (Pearl) Gross; children: Eric Alain, Neil Remy; m. Joseph Martin Schor, June, 1992. BA, Queens Coll., CUNY, 1967; MA, U. Rochester, 1970, PhD, 1974. Asst. prof. SUNY, Fredonia, 1973-79; assoc. prof., dir. women's studies U. Cin., 1979-85, prof., vice provost, 1985-89; prof., provost, v.p. acad. affairs Hunter Coll., CUNY, N.Y.C., 1989—. Author: Women and the Making of the Working Class, 1979, What Were Little Boys and Girls Made Of?, 1984, The Odyssey of Flora Tristan, 1988, Les Jolies Femmes d'Edouard de Beaumont, 1994. Mem. Internat. Soc. for Study European Ideas, Am. Hist. Assn., French Hist. Assn., Phi Beta Kappa. Office: CUNY-Hunter Coll Office of Provost 695 Park Ave New York NY 10021-5024

SCHOR, STANLEY SIDNEY, mathematical sciences educator; b. Phila., Mar. 3, 1922; s. Joseph and Dorothy (Abrams) S.; m. Irene Sternberg, June 19, 1949; children—Mark, Robin, Randi. A.B., U. Pa., 1943, A.M., 1950, Ph.D., 1952; certificate, U. Cin., 1944. Instr. U. Pa., Phila., 1950-53, asst. prof. stats., 1953-58, assoc. prof., 1958-64, dir. Nat. Periodic Health Exam. Research Group, 1958-64; dir. dept. biostats. AMA, Chgo., 1964-66; prof. biostats. Chgo. Med. Sch., 1964-66; prof., chmn. dept. biometrics Temple U. Med. Sch., 1966-75, adj. prof., 1975-85; vis. prof. Tel Aviv U., 1973-74, Med. Coll. Pa., 1979; exec. dir. Cbards, Merck Sharp & Dohme, West Point, Pa., 1975-91; clin. prof. Hahnemann Med. Sch., 1975-85; cons. in field. Author: Fundamentals of Biostatistics, 1968; mem. editorial staff Jour. Trauma, 1955-91, Jour. AMA, 1964-91, Chest, 1966-91; contbr. articles to profl. jours. Served with AUS, 1943-46. Recipient Career Achievement award Pharm. Rsch. and Mfrs. Am., 1996, Stanley S. Schor fellowship in biostatistics U. N.C. and Merck. Fellow Am. Public Health Assn., Am. Statis. Assn. (Career Achievement award), Phila. Coll. Physicians; mem. AAUP, Biometric Soc., Royal Soc. Health, Pi Gamma Mu. Home: 3912 S Ocean Blvd Apt 1105 Highland Beach FL 33487

SCHOR, SUZI, lawyer, psychologist; b. Chgo., Feb. 1, 1947; d. Samuel S. and Dorothy Helen (Hineline); 1 child, Kate. BABA, Ind. U., 1964; MBA Mktg., Northwestern U., 1967, JD, 1970; PhD in Fine Arts (hon.), U. Nev., PhD in Clin. Psychology, 1989. Bar: Ill., 1971. Pvt. practice L.A., 1971-80; v.p. legal affairs Little Gypzy Mgmt., Inc., Beverly Hills, Calif., 1980—; mem. Pres.'s Coun. on Alcoholism. Author: 13th Step to Death, 1995; contbg. author Wine and Dine Mag.; contbr. articles to profl. jours. Bd. dirs. Nat. Ctr. for Hyperactive Children, L.A., 1989-91, sec. Rainbow Guild Cancer Charity, L.A., 1985-89, ind. cons. Jewish Legal Aid, L.A., 1988—; campaign coord. advisor Dem. Nat. Campaign, L.A., 1990, 94; donor mem. L.A. Coun. on World Affairs. Recipient Poet of Yr. award Nat. Libr. and Assn. of Poetry, 1995. Mem. ABA (criminal justice com. 1994), AAUW, NAADAC, CAADAC, L.A. Breakfast Club (chmn. entertainment 1988-90), Rotary, Mensa. Jewish. Avocations: singing, skiing, writing.

SCHORE, NILES, lawyer; b. N.Y.C., Mar. 27, 1950; s. Harold G. and Hilda (Werner) S.; m. Anne Dunlap Vaughan, May 18, 1979. BS, U. Pa., 1971; JD, George Washington U., 1975. Bar: Pa. 1975, Ga. 1980. Co.-dir., mng. atty. Keystone Legal Svcs., Clearfield, Pa., 1981-82; dir. Elderly Law Project, Phila., 1983-88; staff atty. Pa. Health Law Project, Chester, 1988-89; counsel, exec. dir. Pa. Sen. Urban Affairs and Housing Commn., Harrisburg, 1989-94, Pa. Sen. Pub. Health & Welfare Commn., Harrisburg, 1995—; chair consumer com. Pa. Intragovtl. Coun. on Long Term Care, Harrisburg, 1988-89; mem. Atty. Gen.'s Task Force on Violence Against the Elderly, Harrisburg, 1987-88; mem. children, families and health com. Assembly on State Issues, Nat. conf. State Legislatures, 1993—. Author: An Advocate's Guide to Medical Assistance Eligibility in Pennsylvania, 2d edit., 1988. Mem. Pa. Bar Assn. Democrat. Jewish. Home: 168 W Marshall Rd Lansdowne PA 19050 Office: Sen Pa Rm 543 Main Capitol Bldg Harrisburg PA 17120

SCHORE, ROBERT, social worker, educator; b. N.Y.C., July 29, 1934; s. David and Helen S.; married, three children. Student, Mesivta Tifereth Jerusalem, N.Y.C., 1947-48; BA, CCNY, 1955; MS, Columbia U., 1959; cert. advanced study, SUNY, New Paltz, 1985; postgrad., Postgrad. Ctr. for Mental, Health, 1967, Inst. for Rational-Emotive, Therapy, Bank St. Coll., 1984, Rockland Conservatory Music, 1992—. Diplomate Clin. Social Work, NASW; cert. social worker, impartial hearing officer, sch. dist. adminstr., supr. sch. social workers, N.Y. Social worker Dept. Social Svcs./Child Placement Svcs., N.Y.C., 1956-58, Edwin Gould Found., N.Y.C., 1959-63; supr. with NIMH dem. project Shield Inst., Bronx, N.Y., 1963-65; sch. social worker N.Y.C. Bd. Edn. Bur. Child Guidance, Bronx, 1965-80; sch. social worker Com. on Spl. Edn., Bronx, 1980-85, High Sch. Clin. Svcs., Bronx, 1986-91; pvt. practice West Nyack, N.Y., 1992-95; psychotherapist Ind. Consultation Ctr., Bronx, 1967, Rockland County Mental Health Ctr., Monsey, N.Y., 1968-69; rsch. assoc., editor/NIMH demo project Nathan Kline Inst., Orangeburg, N.Y., 1968-85; instr. CCNY, 1966; field instr. NYU, 1970-73; adj. prof. Rockland C.C., Suffern, N.Y., 1993—; fair hearing officer N.Y. State Edn. Dept., 1992—; adminstrv. intern Clarkstown Sch. Dist., West Nyack, 1984-85; workshop leader in field. Editor: Orb Mag., 1950-51; contb. chpts. to books, articles to profl. jours. Supr., cons. Vol. Counseling Svc., New City, N.Y., 1992-94; bd. dirs. Rockland Hebrew Day Sch., 1986; violinist Riverdale Orchestra, Suburban Symphony of Rockland, Ramapo Orchestral Soc., N.Y. With USAR, 1957-63. Mem. Am. Fedn. Tchrs., N.Y. State United Tchrs., United Fedn. Tchrs., Acad. Cert. Social Workers, Am. Radio Relay League, Crystal Radio Club. Jewish. Avocations: photography, music, violin, piano, amateur radio. Office: PO Box 276 Monsey NY 10952-0276

SCHORER, SUKI, ballet teacher; b. Boston; d. Mark and Ruth (Page) S.; 1 child, Nicole. Studied with, George Balanchine. Dancer San Francisco Ballet, 1956-59, N.Y.C. Ballet, 1959-72; prin. dancer N.Y.C. Ballet Co., 1968-72, artistic assoc. lecture demonstration program, 1972-95; mem. faculty Sch. Am. Ballet, 1972—; internat. guest tchr. and lectr. specializing in Balanchine tng. and technique; artist dir., tchr. on Balanchine Essays (videos). Author (monograph) Balanchine Pointework, 1995; created roles in Balanchine's Harlequinade, Don Quixote, Midsummer Night's Dream, Jewels, La Source, Raymonda Variations; repertory included prin. roles in Apollo, Serenade, Concerto Barocco Symphony in C, La Somnambula, Stars and Stripes, Tarantella, Valse Fantaisie, The Nutcracker, Brahams Schoenberg, La Valse, Western Symphony, Ivesiana, Divertimento # 15, Ballet Imperial, others. Recipient Disting. Tchr. in Arts award Nat. Found. Advancement in Arts, 1997. Office: Sch of Am Ballet 70 Lincoln Center Plz New York NY 10023-6548

SCHORGL, THOMAS BARRY, arts administrator; b. St. Louis, Mar. 1, 1950; s. Francis William and Janet Sarah (Peterson) S.; m. Elizabeth Ann Eades, Aug. 6, 1977; children: Matthew, Ann, Joseph. BFA, U. Iowa, 1973, MA in Drawing, 1974; MFA in Printmaking, Miami U., Oxford, Ohio, 1976; apprenticeship, Atelier, Garrigue, France, 1976; postgrad., U. Notre Dame, 1979. Comml. artist R.H. Donnelly, Chgo., 1977; curator Art Ctr. Inc., South Bend, Ind., 1977-78, dir. acting, 1978, exec. dir., 1978-81; account exec. James P. Carroll & Assocs., South Bend, 1981-83; exec. dir Ind. Arts. Commn., Indpls., 1983-94; pres., CEO Culture Works, Dayton, Ohio, 1994-97; CEO Cmty. Partnership for Arts and Culture, Cleve., 1997—; cons. in field. Chmn. Arts Midwest, 1989-91, treas., 1987, 88; panelist Nat. Endowment for Arts, 1985-90, chmn. grants panel Art is Basic to Edn., 1986-89; bd. dirs. Ohio Citizens for Arts, 1994—. Mem. Great Lakes Arts Alliance (sec., treas. 1983-85, merger com.), Affiliated State Arts Agys. Upper Midwest (chmn. program com. 1985—), Arts Midwest (chmn. 1989-91), Nat. Assembly of State Arts Agys. (bd. dirs. 1991—). Avocations: visual arts, antiques, endurance sports. Office: Cleve Found 1422 Euclid Ave Ste 1400 Cleveland OH 44115-2001

SCHORLING, WILLIAM HARRISON, lawyer; b. Ann Arbor, Mich., Jan. 7, 1949; s. Otis William Schorling and Ruthann (Bales) Schorling Moorehead; m. Lynne Ann Newcomb, June 1, 1974; children: Katherine Pearce, Ann Oury, John Roberts. BA cum laude, Denison U., 1971; JD cum laude, U. Mich., 1975. Bar: Pa. 1975, U.S. Ct. Appeals (3d cir.) 1977. Ptnr. Eckert, Seamans, Cherin & Mellott, Pitts., 1984-89, Klett Lieber Rooney & Schorling, P.C., Pitts., 1989—; lectr. Pa. Bar Inst., Harrisburg, 1983—, Comml. Law League, N.Y.C., 1984—, Profl. Edn. Systems, Inc., Eau Claire, Wis., 1986—, Southwest Legal Found., Dallas, 1994—; founders' coun. Comml. Fin. Assn. Edn. Found., 1991—; bd. dirs. Consumer Bankruptcy Assistance Project, 1995—. Contbr. articles to profl. jours. Fellow Am. Bar Found.; mem. ABA (chmn. bus. bankruptcy com., lectr. 1988—), Am. Banker Inst. (lectr. 1994—), Phila. Bar Assn. (lectr. 1996—), E. Dist. Bankruptcy Assn., Pa. Bar Assn. (lectr. 1983—), Allegheny County Bar Assn. (chmn. bankruptcy and comml. law sect. 1991), The Com. of Seventy (chair subcom. issues 1997—), Longue Vue Club, Duquesne Club, Rivers Club, Pa. Soc. Presbyterian. Home: 5600 Northumberland St Pittsburgh PA 15217-1238 Office: Klett Lieber Rooney & Schorling 2 Logan Sq 12th Fl Philadelphia PA 19103-6901

SCHORNACK, JOHN JAMES, accountant; b. Chgo., Nov. 22, 1930; s. John Joseph and Helen Patricia (Patrickus) S.; m. Barbara Anne Lelli, June 5, 1965; children: Mark Boyd, Anne Marguerite Trueman, Erin Keeley Schornack Dickes, Tracy Bevan. BS, Loyola U., 1951; MBA, Northwestern U., 1956; grad., Advanced Mgmt. Program, Harvard Bus. Sch., 1969. With Ernst & Young (formerly Arthur Young & Co.), 1955-91, partner, 1964-91; firm dir. personnel Ernst & Young LLP (formerly Arthur Young & Co.), N.Y.C., 1966-71; asst. mng. ptnr. N.Y.C. office Ernst & Young LLP (formerly Arthur Young & Co.), 1971-72, mng. ptnr., 1972-74, mng. ptnr. Chgo. office, 1976-85, mng. ptnr. Midwest region, vice chmn., 1985-91; mem. mgmt. com. Arthur Young & Co.; mgmt. com. Arthur Young & Co.; vice chmn., mng. ptnr. Midwest region Ernst & Young, 1989-91; bd. dirs., chmn. Ernst & Young Found., 1981-91; chmn., bd. dirs., CEO Kraft Seal Corp.; chmn., bd. dirs. Binks James & Corp., Franklin Park, Ill., North Shore Bancorp, Inc., Wintrust Fin. Corp. Pres. Chgo. Youth Ctrs., 1979-95; bd. govs. Chgo. Symphony, 1979-85, trustee, 1985—; vol. United Way, 1975-92, dir., 1989-92; vis. adv. com. sch. accountancy DePaul U., 1980-83; mem. Loyola U. Citizens Bd., 1977-94, chmn., 1993-94; mem. adv. com. Northwestern U. Grad. Sch. Mgmt., 1967-91; coun. U. Chgo. Grad. Sch. Bus., 1982-91; bd. dirs. Met. Planning Coun., 1992-95; trustee Kohl Children's Mus., 1994—, Lyric Opera, 1984-92, Cath. Theol. Union, 1992—, Graham Found., 1992—; trustee Barat Coll., 1983—, vice chmn., 1985-90, chmn., 1990—; trustee St. Francis Hosp., 1986—, vice chmn., 1991-94. Mem. AICPA, Am. Acctg. Assn., Ill. Soc. CPA's, Midwest-Japan Assn. (chmn. 1983—), Japan Am. Soc., 410 Club, Economic Club, Tavern Club, Chgo. Club, Glen View Club, Ocean Club. Home: 314 Regent Wood Northfield IL 60093-2762 Office: Ernst & Young LLP Midwest Regional Office 233 S Wacker Dr Chicago IL 60606-6306 also: Kraft Seal Corp 13777 W Laurel Dr Lake Forest IL 60045-4530

SCHORR, ALAN EDWARD, librarian, publisher; b. N.Y.C., Jan. 7, 1945; s. Herbert and Regina (Fingerman) S.; m. Debra Genner, June 11, 1967; 1 son, Zebediah. BA, CUNY, 1966; MA, Syracuse U., 1967; postgrad., U. Iowa, 1967-71; MLS, U. Tex., 1973. Tchr., rsch. asst. dept. history U. Iowa, 1967-70; govt. publs. and map libr., asst. prof. Elmer E. Rasmuson Libr., U. Alaska, 1973-78; assoc. prof., dir. libr. U. Alaska, Juneau, 1978-84; prof., dean univ. libr. Calif. State U., Fullerton, 1984-86; pres. The Denali Press, Juneau, 1986—; freelance indexer and bibliographer; vis. lectr. Birmingham (Eng.) Poly., 1981; mem. Alaska Ednl. Del. to China, 1975. Author: Alaska Place Names, 1974, 4th edit., 1991, Directory of Special Libraries in Alaska, 1975, Government Reference Books, 1974-75, 1976, 1976-77, 1978, Government Documents in the Library Literature 1909-1974, 1976, ALA RSBRC Manual, 1979, Federal Documents Librarianship 1879-1987, 1988, Hispanic Resource Directory, 1988, 3d edit., 1996, Refugee and Immigrant Resource Directory, 1990, 92, 94; editor: The Sourdough, 1974-75, Directory of Services for Refugees and Immigrants, 1987, 3d edit., 1993, Guide to Smithsonian serial publs., 1987 ; book reviewer, columnist: S.E. Alaska Empire, 1979—, L.A. Times; contbr. articles to profl. jours. Mem. Auke Bay (Alaska) Vol. Fire Dept.; mem. Juneau Borough Cemetery Adv. Com., 1980-81, Juneau Borough Libr. Adv. Com., 1981-82, Am. Book Awards Com., 1980; mem. strategic com. Juneau Sch. Bd., Juneau Bd. Edn., 1991—, chmn. facilities com., 1994-96, chmn. policy com., 1996—. Mem. ALA (reference and subscription books rev. com. 1975-86, reference and adult services div. publs. com. 1975-77, Nat. Assn. Hispanic Publications, Mudge citation commn. 1977-79, 84-86, Dartmouth Coll. Medal Commn., Governing Council 1977-84, Dewey medal com. 1984-85, Denali Press award), Alaska Library Assn. (exec. bd. 1974-75, nominating com. 1977-79), Pacific N.W. Library Assn. (rep. publs. com. 1973-75), Assn. Coll. and Research Libraries (publ. com. 1976-80), Spl. Libraries Assn. (assoc. editor geography and map div. bull. 1975-76), Soc. for Scholarly Pub., Internat. Assn. Ind. Pubs (bd. dirs. 1990-92, 95—), Pub. Mktg. Assn., PEN Ctr. USA West, Amnesty Internat., Explorers Club N.Y., No. Pub. Consortium (regional rep. 1993-96), Wash. Athletic Club. Office: PO Box 1535 Juneau AK 99802

SCHORR, ALVIN LOUIS, social worker, educator; b. N.Y.C., Apr. 13, 1921; s. Louis and Tillie (Godiner) S.; m. Ann Girson, Aug. 21, 1948; children—Jessica Lee, Kenneth L., Wendy Lauren. B.S.S., CCNY, 1941; M.S.W., Washington U., St. Louis, 1943; D.H.L., Adelphi U., 1975. With Family Service No. Va., 1956-58; family life specialist Office Commr. Social Security, 1958-62; vis. prof. London (Eng.) Sch. Econs., 1962-63; acting chief long range research Social Security Adminstrn., 1963-64; dir. research and planning Office Econ. Opportunity, 1965-66; dep. asst. sec. Dept. Health, Edn. and Welfare, 1967-69; prof. social policy, dir. income maintenance project Brandeis U., 1969-70; dean Grad. Sch. Social Work, N.Y.U., 1970-73; gen. dir. Community Service Soc. N.Y., 1973-77; vis. prof. Cath. U. Am., 1977-79; Leonard W. Mayo prof. Case Western Res. U., 1979-92, Leonard W. Mayo prof. emeritus, 1992—; Fulbright sr. rsch. scholar, 1962-63; vist. prof. Hebrew U., Jerusalem, 1986, Fla. Internat. U., 1995, N.Mex. State U., 1996; vis. scholar London Sch. Econs., 1991-92. Author: Filial Responsibility in the Modern American Family, 1961, Slums and Social Insecurity, 1963, Social Services and Social Security in France, 1964, Poor Kids, 1966, Explorations in Social Policy, 1968, Children and Decent People, 1974, Jubilee for Our Times, 1977, Thy Father and Thy Mother, 1980, Common Decency: Domestic Policies After Reagan, 1986, Economic Development in Cleveland: A Dissenting View, 1991; The British Personal Social Services: An Outside View, 1992. Recipient Disting. Service in Social Welfare award Washington U. Alumni Assn., 1969; recipient Michael Schwerner award, 1972. Fellow Nat. Acad. Social Ins.; mem. Phi Beta Kappa. Home: 1701 E 12th St Apt 14tw Cleveland OH 44114-3237 Office: Case Western Res U Mandel Sch Appl Social Sci Cleveland OH 44106

SCHORR, BRIAN LEWIS, lawyer, business executive; b. N.Y.C., Oct. 5, 1958; s. Philip I. and Hannah Schorr; m. Amy B. Horowitz, Aug. 19, 1984; 2 children. BA magna cum laude, MA, Wesleyan U., Middletown, Conn., 1979; JD, NYU, 1982. Bar: N.Y. 1983, D.C. 1985, U.S. Supreme Ct. 1988. Assoc. Paul, Weiss, Rifkind, Wharton & Garrison, N.Y.C., 1982-90, ptnr., 1991-94; exec. v.p., gen. counsel Triarc Cos., Inc., N.Y.C., 1994—; mem. bd. advisors Jour. Ltd. Liability Cos.; lectr. CLE programs. Author: Schorr on New York Limited Liability Companies and Partnerships, 1994; contbr. articles to legal jours. Vice pres. Bronx (N.Y.) H.S. Sci. Endowment Fund, Inc. Mem. ABA, N.Y. State Bar Assn., Assn. Bar City N.Y. (chmn. com. on corp. law 1993-96, co-chmn. joint drafting com. N.Y. ltd. liability co. law), Tri Bar Opinion Com., Bronx H.S. Sci. Alumni Assn. (trustee). Office: Triarc Cos Inc 280 Park Ave New York NY 10017-1216

SCHORR, DANIEL LOUIS, broadcast journalist, author, lecturer; b. N.Y.C., Aug. 31, 1916; s. Louis and Tillie (Godiner) S.; m. Lisbeth Bamberger, 1967; children: Jonathan, Lisa. B.S.S., CCNY, 1939; hon. doctorate, Kalamazoo Coll., Columbia Coll., Chgo., Wilkes U., Nebr. Wesleyan U., L.I. U., Brandeis U., Spartus Coll. Asst. editor Jewish Telegraphic Agy., 1934-41; news editor ANETA (Netherlands) News Agy. in N.Y., 1941-48; free-lance corr. N.Y. Times, Christian Sci. Monitor, London Daily Mail, 1948-53; Washington corr. CBS News; also spl. assignments CBS News, Latin Am. and Europe, 1953-55; reopened CBS Moscow Bur., 1955; roving assignments U.S. and Europe, 1958-60; chief CBS News Bur., Germany, Central Europe, 1960-66; Washington corr. CBS, 1966-76; Regents prof. U. Calif., Berkeley, 1977; columnist Des Moines Register-Tribune Syndicate, 1977-80; sr. Washington corr. Cable News Network, 1980-85; sr. analyst Nat. Public Radio, 1985—. Author: Don't Get Sick in America!, 1971, Clearing the Air, 1977. Decorated officer Orange Nassau (The Netherlands), Grand Cross of Merit (Germany); recipient citations of excellence for radio-TV reporting Soviet Union Overseas Press Club, 1956, Best TV Interpretation of Fgn. News award 1963, ACLU and others awards for pub. suppressed Congsl. intelligence report, Emmy awards for coverage of Watergate, 1972, 73, 74, Peabody award for lifetime of uncompromising reporting of highest integrity, 1992, George Polk award for radio commentary L.I. U., 1994, Disting. Svc. award Am. Soc. Journalism and Mass Comm., 1994, Golden Baton award for lifetime achievement A.I. DuPont Columbia U., 1996; inducted in Hall of Fame Soc. Profl. Journalists, 1991. Mem. Am. Fedn. Radio-TV Artists, Council on Fgn. Relations N.Y.C. *Journalism, for more than a half century, has been both profession and outlook on life. I have always felt myself the observer and nonparticipant, the quintessential outsider. I have pursued the sense of things behind the appearance of things, the meaning behind the manipulation. I have fought, with dubious success, against the blurring of the media line between reality and fantasy.*

SCHORR, LISBETH BAMBERGER, child and family policy analyst, author, educator; b. Munich, Jan. 20, 1931; d. Fred S. and Lotte (Krafft) Bamberger; m. Daniel L. Schorr, Jan. 8, 1967; children—Jonathan, Lisa. BA with highest honors, U. Calif., Berkeley, 1952; LHD (hon.), Wilkes U., 1991, U. Md., 1994. Med. care cons. U.A.W. and Community Health Assn., Detroit, 1956-58; asst. dir. Dept. Social Security AFL-CIO, Washington, 1958-65; acting chief CAP Health Svcs., OEO, 1965-66; chief program planning Office for Health Affairs, OEO, Washington, 1967; dir. project effective intervention Harvard U., Cambridge, Mass.; cons. Children's Def. Fund, Washington, 1973-79; scholar-in-residence Inst. of Medicine, 1979-80; chmn. Select Panel on Promotion Child Health, 1979-80; adj. prof. maternal and child health U. N.C., Chapel Hill, 1981-85; lectr. social medicine Harvard U. Med. Sch., 1984—; dir. project on effective interventions Harvard U., 1988—; nat. coun. Alan Gutmacher Inst., 1974-79, 82-85; pub. mem. Am. Bd. Pediatrics, 1978-84; vice chmn. Found. for Child Devel., 1978-84, bd. dirs., 1976-84, 86-94; mem. coun. Nat. Ctr. for Children in Poverty, 1987-96; mem. children's program adv. com. Edna McConnell Clark Found., 1987-97; bd. dirs. Pub. Edn. Fund Network, 1991-93; co-chair Roundtable on Comprehensive Cmty. Inititatives Aspen Inst., 1992—, chair roundtable steering com. on evaluation, 1994—; mem. bd. on children and families NAS, 1993-95; mem. nat. Commn. State and Local Pub. Svcs., 1992-94; mem. task force on young children Carnegie Corp., 1994; mem. sec.'s adv. com. Head Start quality and expansion, 1993-94; trustee City Yr., 1994—; mem. exec. com. Harvard Project on Schooling and Children. Author: Within Our Reach: Breaking the Cycle of Disadvantage, 1988, Common Purpose: Strengthening Families and Neighborhoods to Rebuild America, 1997. Recipient Dale Richmond Meml. award Am. Acad. Pediatrics, 1977, 9th Ann. Robert F. Kennedy Book award, 1989, Nelson Cruikshank award nat. Coun. Sr. Citizens, 1990, Porter prize, 1993. Mem. Inst. Medicine, NAS, Nat. Acad. on Social Ins., Phi Beta Kappa. Home: 3113 Woodley Rd NW Washington DC 20008-3449

SCHORR, MARTIN MARK, forensic psychologist, educator, writer; b. Sept. 16, 1923; m. Dolores Gene Tyson, June 14, 1952; 1 child, Jeanne Ann. Student Balliol Coll., Oxford (Eng.) U., 1945-46; AB cum laude, Adelphi U., 1949; postgrad., U. Tex., 1949-50; MS, Purdue U., 1953; PhD, U. Denver, 1960; postgrad., U. Tex. Diplomate in psychology; diplomate Am. Bd. Profl. Disability Cons., Am. Bd. Forensic Examiners, Am. Bd. Forensic Medicine; lic. clin. psychologist. Chief clin. psychol. svcs. San Diego County Mental Hosp., 1963-67; clin. dir. human services San Diego County, 1963-76; pvt. practice, forensic specialist San Diego, 1962—; forensic examiner superior, fed. and mil. cts., San Diego, 1962—; prof. abnormal psychology San Diego State U., 1965-68; chief dept. psychology Center City (Calif.) Hosp., 1976-79; cons. Dept. Corrections State of Calif., Minnewawa, 1970-73, Disability Evaluation Dept. Health, 1972-75, Calif. State Indsl. Accident Commn., 1972-78, Calif. Criminal Justice Adminstrn., 1975-77, Vista Hill Found., Mercy Hosp. Mental Health, Foodmaker Corp., Convent Sacred Heart, El Cajon, FAA Examiner. Author: Death by Prescription, 1988; dir. Alpha Centauri Prodns. Recipient award for aid in developing Whistle Blower Law Calif. Assembly, 1986. Fellow Internat. Assn. Social Psychiatry, Internat. Biog. Assn. (life: Great Britain), Am. Coll. Forensic Examiners (life), Am. Bd. Forensic Med.; mem. AAAS, PEN, APA, Am. Acad. Forensic Scis. (qualified med. evaluator), Internat. Platform Assn., World Mental Health Assn., Mystery Writers Am., Nat. Writers Club, Mensa. Home: University City 2970 Arnoldson Ave San Diego CA 92122-2114 Office: 275 F St Chula Vista CA 91910-2820 *Personal philosophy: Some wag once said that the hardest thing one learns in life is which bridge to cross and which to burn!.*

SCHORR, MARVIN G., technology company executive; b. N.Y.C., Mar. 10, 1925; s. Samuel and Fannie (Smolen) S.; m. Rosalie Yorshis, Dec. 22, 1957; children: Eric Douglas, Susan Ellen. BS, Yale U., 1944, MS, 1947, PhD, 1949. Research asst., instr. Yale U., New Haven, 1946-47; project dir. physics and electronics div. Tracerlab, Inc., 1940-51; exec. v.p., treas. Tech/Ops., Inc., Boston, 1951-62, pres., chief exec. officer, 1962-88, chmn. 1988—; spl. cons. USAF, 1951-52; dir. Mass. Tech. Devel. Corp., 1973-76, chmn. bd., 1976-83; dir. Ealing Corp., 1965-76, Hysil Mfg. Co., 1965-78, Dynamics Research Corp., 1978-85, Helix Tech. Corp., Costar Corp. Mem. nuclear engrng. adv. com. Lowell Inst. Tech., 1958-68; trustee Park Sch., 1974-80; trustee Am. Coll. Greece, 1970-82, chmn. exec. com., 1980-82, hon. trustee, 1982—; trustee New Eng. Deaconess Hosp., 1972—, vice chmn. bd., 1978-81, chmn., 1981-86. Served with U.S. Army, 1944-46. Fellow AAAS; mem. IEEE, Ops. Research Soc. Am., Am. Phys. Soc., Young Pres. Orgn. (chmn. New Eng. chpt. 1967-68), Boston Com. Fgn. Relations, The Forty-Niners, World Bus. Council, Chief Execs. Orgn., Internat. Bus. Ctr.-Chief Exec. Officers Round Table, Explorers Club. Clubs: Cosmos (Washington); Harvard, St. Botolph, Union (Boston); Yale (Boston and N.Y.C.); Longwood Cricket (Brookline, Mass.). Home: 330 Beacon St Boston MA 02116-1153 Office: Tech/Ops Corp 1 Beacon St Boston MA 02108-3107

SCHORR, S. L., lawyer; b. N.Y.C., Feb. 19, 1930; s. Charles and Clara (Lerech) S.; m. Eleanor Daru, Mar. 23, 1956; children: Lewis, Andrew, Emily, Roberta. Student, L.I. U., 1948-50; LLB, Bklyn. Law Sch., 1953. Bar: N.Y. 1955, Ariz. 1962, U.S. Dist. Ct. Ariz. 1962, U.S. Supreme Ct. 1979. Planning commr. Pima County, Tucson, 1959-62; asst. city mgr. Tucson, 1962-63; ptnr. Lewis and Roca, Tucson, 1988—; co-chair Continuing Legal Edn. Seminar on Ballot Box Zoning, U. Ariz., 1991, Ariz. State Bar Continuing Legal Edn. Seminar on Land Use Regulation and Litigation, 1977, 86, 89, 95. Bd. dirs. Pima Coll., 1966-67; mem. Commn. on Improved Govtl. Mgmt., Tucson, 1974-77, Gov.'s Econ. Planning and Devel. Adv. Bd., Phoenix, 1983-85; chmn. Gov.'s Task Force on Seriously Mentally Ill, Phoenix, 1989-91. Mem. Ariz. Bar Assn., Pima County Bar Assn. Democrat. Office: Lewis and Roca 1 S Church Ave Ste 700 Tucson AZ 85701-1621

SCHORR-RIBERA, HILDA KEREN, psychologist; b. N.Y.C., May 2, 1942; d. Leon and Rosa Schorr-Ribera; m. Ira Eli Wessler, Aug. 6, 1971; children: Mike, Daniel. BA, Hunter Coll., 1963; MEd, U. No. Fla., 1982; PhD, U. Pitts., 1988. Lic. psychologist, Pa.; diplomate Am. Bd. Forensic Examiners;diplomate, fellow Am. Bd. Med. Psychotherapists and Psychodiagnosticians, Am. Bd. Forensic Medicine. Psychotherapist South Hills Interfaith Ministries, Bethel Park, Pa., 1989-92, Profl. Psychol. Assn. of Greater Pitts., 1992; pvt. practice psychologist Pitts., 1993; group facilitator Burger King Cancer Caring Ctr., Pitts., 1989—, Allegheny Hospice, Pitts., 1994-96; child therapist Forbes Hospice, Pitts., 1993—; psychol. evaluator Washington (Pa.) County Ct., 1993—, Allegheny County Ct., Pitts., 1995—. Author: (with others) Educating the Child With Cancer, 1993. Keynote speaker on illness and bereavement to hosps., schs., and agys., Pitts., 1989—. Mem. APA, Am. Soc. Clin. Hypnosis, Am. Acad. Experts in Traumatic Stress, Am. Counseling Assn., Am. Coll. Forensic Examiners, Pa. Psychol. Assn., Greater Pitts. Psychol. Assn. Avocations: music, bilingual activities, reading, walking, traveling. Office: 117 Ridgeway Ct Pittsburgh PA 15228-1729

SCHORSCH, ISMAR, clergyman, Jewish history educator; b. Hannover, Germany, Nov. 3, 1935; m. Sally Korn; children: Jonathan, Rebecca, Naomi. BA, Ursinus Coll., 1957; MA, Columbia U., 1961, PhD, 1969; MHL, Jewish Theol. Sem. Am., 1962; LittD (hon.), Wittenberg U., 1989, Ursinus Coll., 1990, Gratz Coll., 1995, Russian State U., 1996. Ordained rabbi, 1962. Instr. Jewish Theol. Sem., N.Y.C., 1964-68; asst. prof. Jewish Theol. Sem. Am., N.Y.C., 1970-72, assoc. prof., 1972-76, prof., 1976—, dean Grad. Sch., 1975-79, provost, 1980-84; asst. prof. Jewish history Columbia U., N.Y.C., 1968-70; bd. dirs. Leo Baeck Inst., 1976, mem. exec. com., 1980, pres., 1985-86, 90—, mem. editorial bd. of yearbook, 1987. Author: From Text to Context: The Turn to History in Modern Judaism, 1994; contbr. articles to Judaism, also other profl. publs. Chancellor Jewish Theol. Sem., 1986—. Chaplain U.S. Army, 1962-64. Recipient Clark F. Ansley award Columbia U. Press, 1969; NEH fellow, 1979-80. Fellow Am. Acad. Jewish Rsch. Office: Jewish Theol Sem 3080 Broadway New York NY 10027-4650

SCHORSKE, CARL EMIL, historian, educator; b. N.Y.C., Mar. 15, 1915; s. Theodore A. and Gertrude (Goldschmidt) S.; m. Elizabeth Gilbert Rorke, June 14, 1941; children: Carl Theodore, Anne (Mrs. J. L. Edwards), Stephen James, John Simon, Richard Robert. AB, Columbia U., 1936; MA, Harvard U., 1937, PhD, 1950; DLitt (hon.), Wesleyan U., 1967, Bard Coll., 1982, Clark U., 1983, New Sch. Social Rsch., 1986, Miami U., 1987, SUNY, Stony Brook, 1988, Monmouth Coll., 1994; DPhil (hon.), U. Salzburg, 1986. Prof. history Wesleyan U., Middletown, Conn., 1946-60; prof. history U. Calif.-Berkeley, 1960-69; prof. history Princeton U., 1969-80, emeritus, 1980—. Author: (with Hoyt Price) The Problem of Germany, 1947, German Social Democracy 1905-17, 1955, Fin-de-Siècle Vienna, 1980. Served to lt. (j.g.) USNR, 1943-46; with OSS, 1941-46. Recipient Austrian Cross of Honor for arts and scis., 1979, Pulitzer prize for gen. nonfiction, 1981, Grand prize for cultural edn. City of Vienna, 1985; named Officer, French Order Arts and Letters, 1987, Great Silver medal of Honor, Austria, 1996; MacArthur fellow, 1981-86. Fellow Royal Acad. Fine Arts Netherlands (hon.); mem. Am. Acad. Arts and Scis., Austrian Acad. Scis. (corr.), Am. Hist. Assn. (council 1964-68, Disting. Scholar award 1992), Ctr. Advanced Study Behavioral Sci., Inst. Advanced Study., Getty Ctr. Home: 106 Winant Rd Princeton NJ 08540-6738

SCHOTLAND, DONALD LEWIS, neurologist, educator; b. Orange, N.J., Sept. 21, 1930; s. Joseph Henry and Elsie (Block) S.; m. Estherina Shems, Jan. 11, 1976; children: John, Thomas, Peter. AB, Harvard U., 1952, MD, 1957; spl. student, MIT, 1955-56; MA (hon.), U. Pa., 1973. Diplomate: Am. Bd. Psychiatry and Neurology. Intern U. Ill. Research and Edn. Hosp., 1957-58; asst. resident in neurology Columbia Presbyn. Med. Center, N.Y.C., 1958-61; asst. neurologist Columbia Presbyn. Med. Center, 1961-65, asst. attending neurologist, 1965-66; asst. in neurology Coll. Physicians and Surgeons, Columbia U., N.Y.C., 1960-61; vis. fellow in neurology Coll. Physicians and Surgeons, Columbia U., 1961-64, assoc. in neurology, 1964-66, asst. prof. neurology, 1966-67; assoc. prof. Sch. Medicine U. Pa., Phila., 1967-72, prof. Sch. Medicine, 1972—; speaker profl. confs., U.S., Can., Italy, Japan, China, France, Israel, Finland; dir. Henry M. Watts, Jr. Neuromuscular Disease Rsch. Ctr., 1974-90. Editor: Diseases of the Motor Unit, 1982; contbr. articles, papers to profl. publs. Served to 1st lt. USAR, 1958-65. NIH postdoctoral fellow, 1961-64; recipient Research Career Devel. award, 1966-67, various grants NIH and Muscular Dystrophy Assn. Fellow Coll. of Physicians of Phila.; mem. Am. Acad. Neurology, Am. Neurol. Assn., Phila. Neurol. Soc., Muscular Dystrophy Assn. (sci. adv. com. 1974-86, chmn. fellowship com. 1974-86, chmn. 6th Internat. Conf. 1980). Home: 1310 Wyngate Rd Wynnewood PA 19096-2455 Office: Hosp of Univ Pa 3400 Spruce St Philadelphia PA 19104

SCHOTT, JEFFREY BRIAN, software engineer; b. Phila., Nov. 6, 1960; s. Roger and Alice (Heist) S.; m. Christina Marion Gummel, Apr. 23, 1983; children: Ryan Jeffrey, Kristin Alexis. AS, Pierce Jr. Coll., 1980. Dir. data factory and warehouse IMS Am., Plymouth Meeting, Pa.; sr. cons. Aston Brooke, Plymouth Meeting, 1995—; Internet and Data Warehouse arch.; lectr. in field. Architect: (distributed extract system) Xponent Backend, 1992; co-inventor xponent geo-spatial product estimation; Internet and data warehouse architect. Avocations: boating, swimming, walking. Home: 119 Jasen Dr Chalfont PA 18914 Office: Aston Brooke 610 W Germantown Pike Ste 450 Plymouth Meeting PA 19462-1050

SCHOTT, JOHN (ROBERT), international consultant, educator; b. Rochester, N.Y., Jan. 30, 1936; s. John and Ellen (Waite) S.; m. Diane Elizabeth Dempsey, June 19, 1963; children: Elizabeth Anne (dec.), Jennifer, Jared Reed, George Kermit Alexander. BA magna cum laude, Haverford Coll., 1957; postgrad., Oxford U., 1957-59; PhD, Harvard U., 1964. Resident tutor in govt. Eliot House, Harvard Coll., Cambridge, Mass., 1960-64; inst. polit. sci. Wellesley (Mass.) Coll., 1964-66; policy planning specialist AID, Washington, 1966-67; chief Title IX div. AID, Washington, 1967-68; vis. prof. polit. devel. Fletcher Sch. Law & Diplomacy, Tufts U., Medford, Mass., 1968-70; sr. v.p. Thunderbird Grad. Sch. Internat. Mgmt., Phoenix, 1970-71; cons. internat. affairs Francestown, N.H., 1971-74; pres. Schott & Assocs., Inc., Jaffrey Center, N.H., 1974-93; mem. U.S. Del. World Assembly Internat. Secretariat for Voluntary Service, New Delhi, 1967; advisor Office Prime Minister Royal Thai Govt., Bangkok, 1978-80, Minister Cooperatives Govt. of Indonesia, Jakarta, 1983-84; research asst. spl. appointment The Brookings Inst., Washington, 1960-61;. Author: Kenya Tragedy: European Colonization in East Africa, 1964, Frances' Town: History of Francestown, N.H., 1972, A Five-Year Comprehensive Plan for Development of Agricultural Cooperatives in Thailand, 1979, Recana-Komprehensip Pengembangan Kud, Jakarta, Indonesia, 1985, also various govt. reports and articles in profl. jours. and regional publs.; editor: An Experiment in Integrated Rural Development, 1978. Bd. of Selectmen, Francestown, N.H., 1975-78; trustee Spaulding Youth Ctr., Tilton, N.H., 1971-82, 85-89, pres. bd. trustees, 1972-75; trustee Internat. Inst. Rural Reconstrn., N.Y.C., 1979-89, mem. exec. con., 1985-89, bd. trustees N.H. Pub. Radio, 1990-96, chmn., 1993-95; mem. spl. study commn. Coop. Extension Svc. State of N.H., 1980-81, also mem. scenic and cultural by-ways com., 1993-96; forestry rep. County Extension Coun., Hillsboro County, N.H., 1979-82; pres. N.H. Timberland Owner's Assn., 1989-90, bd. dirs., 1988-91; chmn. N.H. chpt. The Nature Conservancy, 1990-93, hon. trustee, 1993—, chmn. N.H. Timber-Tourism Coalition, 1990-94; vice-chmn, Foresters Lic. Bd. State of N.H., 1990-95; bd. trustees Cheshire Med. Ctr., 1992-94, RiverMead Retirement Cmty., Peterborough, N.H., 1993—, chmn., 1996—. Rotary Found. fellow, 1957-58, Coslett Found. fellow, 1958-59, Harvard Arts & Scis. fellow, 1959-60, Fulbright scholar, 1962-63. Mem. Am. Forestry Inst. (cert. tree farmer). Home and Office: Schott & Assocs Inc PO Box 660 Jaffrey NH 03452-0660

SCHOTT, MARGE, professional baseball team executive; b. 1928; d. Edward and Charlotte Unnewehr; m. Charles J. Schott, 1952 (dec. 1968). Owner Schottco, Cin.; ltd. ptnr. Cin. Reds, 1981-84, gen. ptnr., 1984—, owner, pres., 1985—, chief exec. officer. Office: Cin Reds 100 Cinergy Field Cincinnati OH 45202*

SCHOTTENFELD, DAVID, epidemiologist, educator; b. N.Y.C., Mar. 25, 1931; m. Rosalie C. Schaeffer; children: Jacqueline, Stephen. AB, Hamilton Coll., 1952; MD, Cornell U., 1956; MS in Pub. Health, Harvard U., 1963. Diplomate Am. Bd. Internal Medicine, Am. Bd. Preventive Medicine. Intern in internal medicine Duke U., Durham, N.C., 1956-57; resident in internal medicine Meml. Sloan-Kettering Cancer Ctr., Cornell U. Med. Coll., N.Y.C., 1957-59; Craver fellow med. oncology Meml. Sloan-Kettering Cancer Ctr., 1961-62; clin. instr. dept. pub. health Cornell U., N.Y.C., 1963-67, asst. prof. dept. pub. health, 1965-70, assoc. prof. dept. pub. health, 1970-73, prof. dept. pub. health, 1973-86; John G. Searle prof., chmn. epidemiology sch. pub. health U. Mich., Ann Arbor, 1986—, prof. internal medicine, 1986—; vis. prof. epidemiology U. Minn., Mpls., 1968, 71, 74, 82, 86; W.G. Cosbie lectr. Can. Oncology Soc., 1987. Editor: Cancer Epidemiology and Prevention, 1982, 2d edit., 1996; author 9 books; contbr. more than 170 articles to profl. jours. Served with USPHS, 1959-61. Recipient Acad. Career award in Preventive Oncology, Nat. Cancer Inst., 1980-85. Fellow AAAS, ACP, Am. Coll. Preventive Medicine, Am. Coll. Epidemiology, Armed Forces Epidemiology Bd.; mem. Phi Beta Kappa. Office: U of Mich Sch Pub Health Dept Epidemiology 109 Observatory St Ann Arbor MI 48109-2029

SCHOTTENHEIMER, MARTIN EDWARD, professional football coach; b. Canonsburg, Pa., Sept. 23, 1943; m. Patricia Schottenheimer; children—Kristen, Brian. B.A., U. Pitts., 1964. Football player Buffalo Bills, NFL, 1965-68, Boston Patriots, 1969-70; real estate developer Miami and Denver, 1971-74; asst. coach World Football League, Portland, 1974, N.Y. Giants, 1975-77, Detroit Lions, 1978-79; asst. coach Cleve. Browns, 1980-84, head coach, 1985-88; head coach Kansas City Chiefs, 1989—. Office: Kansas City Chiefs 1 Arrowhead Dr Kansas City MO 64129-1651*

SCHOTTENSTEIN, JAY L., retail executive; b. 1954. Grad., Ind. U. With Schottenstein Stores, Columbus, Ohio, vice chmn., exec. v.p., CEO, 1992—. Office: Schottenstein Stores 1800 Moler Rd Columbus OH 43207-1680*

SCHOTTER, ANDREW ROYE, economics educator, consultant; b. N.Y.C., June 6, 1947; s. I. Harvey and Sara (Rothstein) S.; m. Anne Howland, June 7, 1970; children: Geoffrey, Elizabeth. BS, Cornell U., 1969; MA, PhD, NYU, 1974. Asst. prof. Syracuse (N.Y.) U., 1974-75; asst. prof. NYU, 1975-81, assoc. prof., 1981-86; prof., chmn. econs. dept. NYU, N.Y.C., 1989—, chmn. C.V. Starr Ctr. for Applied Econs., 1986-89; vis. asst. prof. Cornell U., Ithaca, 1974-75; vis. prof. U. Venice, 1993; cons. Gulf & Western Corp., N.Y. 1987, Pegalis & Wachsman, Great Neck, N.Y., 1987-88, Nat. Econ. Rsch. Assocs., White Plains, N.Y., 1989—. Author: Economic Theory of Social Institutions, 1981, Free Market Economics: A Critical Appraisal, 1985, 2d edit., 1990, Microeconomics: A Modern Approach, 1993; mem. editl. bd.: Am. Econ. Rev., 1995—. Grantee Office of Naval Rsch., 1980-85, NSF, 1988-90; recipient Kenan Enterprise award, 1993. Mem. Am. Econ. Assn., Econometric Soc. Office: NYU Dept Econs 269 Mercer St New York NY 10003-6633

SCHOTTLAND, EDWARD MORROW, hospital administrator; b. N.Y.C., Aug. 5, 1946; s. Leo Edward and Harriet (Morrow) S.; m. Nancy Resnick, June 25, 1977; 1 child, David. BA, Queens Coll., CUNY, 1968; MPS, Cornell U., 1973. Asst. adminstr. Mercy Hosp., Rockville Centre, N.Y., 1973-75, asst. adminstr. and dir. planning, 1975-79; pres. Kosair Crippled Children's Hosp., Louisville, 1979-81, sr. v.p., chief adminstrv. officer Kosair Children's Hosp., Louisville, 1983-89; v.p. NKC, Inc., Louisville, 1981-83, sr. v.p., 1983-89; exec. v.p., COO The Miriam Hosp., Providence, R.I., 1989-96; sr. v.p. Lifespan, Providence, R.I., 1995-96; sr. v.p. System Integration, Lifespan, 1996—; mem. Gov.'s Adv. Council on Med. Assistance, 1985-89. Chmn. Jefferson County Child Abuse Authority, Louisville, 1981-83, dir., 1979-86; bd. dirs. Suicide Prevention and Edn. Ctr., Louisville, 1982-86, HARI, 1990—, Interfaith Healthcare Ministries, v.p., 1994—, RIMRIN, Inc., 1994—; bd. trustee Barrington (R.I.) Pub. Libr.; chmn. bd. Beavertail Prodns., 1995—. Recipient Baldrige award Examiner, 1997. Fellow Am. Coll. Health Execs. (regent 1994—); mem. Nat. Assn. Children's Hosps. and Related Institutions (bd. dirs., 1986-89). Home: 3 Stratford Rd Barrington RI 02806-3617 Office: The Miriam Hosp 164 Summit Ave Providence RI 02906-2853

SCHOULTZ, LARS, political scientist, educator; b. San Gabriel, Calif., Aug. 23, 1942; s. Ture Wilhelm and Bernice (Bowie) S.; m. Jane Volland, Jan. 18, 1969; children: Nils Gibson, Karina Anne. BA, Stanford U., 1964, MA, 1966; PhD, U. N.C., 1973. Prof. Miami U., Oxford, Ohio, 1973-77, U. Fla., Gainesville, 1977-79; William Rand Kenan Jr. prof. polit. sci. U. N.C., Chapel Hill, 1979—. Author: Human Rights and U.S. Policy Toward Latin America, 1981, National Security and U.S. Policy Toward Latin America, 1987, The Populist Challenge, 1983. Sgt. U.S. Army, 1966-67. MacArthur fellow in internat. peace and security MacArthur Found., 1990-91, Fulbright fellow, Rockefeller Found. fellow, Ford Found. fellow, Social Sci. Rsch. Coun., Woodrow Wilson fellow, 1994-95. Mem. Latin Am. Studies Assn. (pres. 1991-92, v.p. 1990-91). Democrat. Home: 250 Glandon Dr Chapel Hill NC 27514-3816 Office: U NC Inst Latin Am Studies Chapel Hill NC 27599

SCHOUMACHER, BRUCE HERBERT, lawyer; b. Chgo., May 23, 1940; s. Herbert Edward and Mildred Helen (Wagner) S.; m. Alicia Wesley Sanchez, Nov. 4, 1967; children: Liana Cristina, Janina Maria. BS, Northwestern U., 1961; MBA, U. Chgo., 1963, JD, 1966. Bar: Nebr. 1966, U.S. Dist. Ct. Nebr. 1966, Ill. 1971, U.S. Dist. Ct. (no. dist.) Ill. 1971, U.S. Ct. Appeals (7th cir.) 1979, U.S. Supreme Ct. 1982, U.S. Ct. Fed. Claims 1986. Assoc. Luebs, Tracy & Huebner, Grand Island, Nebr., 1966-67; assoc. McDermott, Will & Emery, Chgo., 1971-76, ptnr., 1976-89; ptnr. Querrey & Harrow, Ltd., Chgo., 1989—; instr. bus. adminstrn. Bellevue Coll., Nebr., 1967-70; lectr. U. Md., Overseas Program, 1970. Author: Engineers and the Law: An Overview, 1986; contbg. author: Construction Law, 1986; co-author: Successful Business Plans for Architects, 1992; contbr. articles to profl. jours. Served to capt. USAF, 1967-71, Vietnam. Decorated Bronze Star, 1971. Fellow Am. Coll. Constrn. Lawyers; mem. ABA, AIA (profl. affiliate), Nebr. Bar Assn., Ill. State Bar Assn. (ad hoc com. large law firms 1992—, chmn. membership and bar activities com. 1988-89, coun. ins. law sect. 1986-91, mem. spl. com. on computerized legal rsch. 1986-87), Chgo. Bar Assn. (chmn. fed. civil procedure com. 1982-83), Def. Rsch. Inst., Ill. Assn. Def. Trial Counsel, Chgo. Bldg. Congress (bd. dirs. 1985—, sec. 1987-89, 95—, v.p. 1989-91), Western Soc. Engrs. (assoc.), The Legal Club, The Law Club, Tower Club (Chgo.), Univ. Club Chgo., Pi Kappa Alpha, Phi Delta Phi. Republican. Methodist. Office: Querrey & Harrow Ltd 180 N Stetson Ave Chicago IL 60601-6710

SCHOW, TERRY D., state official; b. Ogden, Utah, Dec. 14, 1948; s. Hugh Stuart Sloan and Minnie Aurelia (Ellis) Mohler; m. June Hansen, Feb. 14, 1973; children: Amy, Jason. AD, Honolulu C.C., 1975; BA, Chaminade U., 1975. Cert. in mgmt., Utah. Spl. and criminal investigator State of Utah, Ogden, 1976-83, lead investigator, 1984-92; investigator Fed. Govt., Salt Lake City, Denver, 1983-84; mgr. State of Utah, Ogden, 1992—. Mem. Gov.'s Coun. on Vets. Issues, 1989—, chmn., 1990—; mem. State of Utah Privatization Policy Bd., 1989-92; chmn. 1st Congressional Dist. Utah Rep. Party, 1982-83, mem. state exec. com., 1982-83; chmn. legis. dist Weber County Rep. Party, Ogden, 1987-91, 93—; trustee Utah's Vietnam Meml., Salt Lake City, 1988—; leader Boy Scouts Am., Ogden, 1985—; mem. citizens' adv. com. Ogden City Neighborhood Redevel., 1996—. Sgt. U.S. Army, 1967-70, 72-76; Vietnam. Decorated Bronze Star, 1970, Combat Inf. Badge, 1970; recipient Championship Team Trophy Pistol U.S. Army, 1975. Mem. DAV (life Weber chpt. 4, comdr. 1994, state comdr. 1995—), NRA (life), VFW, AL (comdr. Ogden post 9 1996-97, dist. vice comdr. 1996-97), Utah Peace Officers Assn., Utah Pub. Employees Assn. (bd. dirs. 1988-89, v.p. 1989-92, pres. 1992-93, chmn. Ogden Valley dist.), Kiwanis (Ogden chpt. pres. 1992-93, pres. Layton chpt. 1985-86, named Kiwanian of Yr. 1982-83, lt. gov. divsn. 3 ut/ld dist. Kiwanis internat. bd. dirs., 1995—, homeless vets. fellow Ogden 1992—, Weber County vets. meml. com. 1994—). Republican. Mormon. Avocations: woodworking, photography, scouting. Home: 4045 Bona Villa Dr Ogden UT 84403-3203 Office: State of Utah Office Recoveries 2540 Washington Blvd Fl 4 Ogden UT 84401-3112

SCHOWALTER, JOHN ERWIN, child and adolescent psychiatry educator; b. Milw., Mar. 15, 1936; s. Raymond Phillip and Martha (Kowalke) S.; m. Ellen Virginia Lefferts, June 11, 1960; children: Jay, Bethany. BS, U. Wis.-Madison, 1957, MD, 1960. Diplomate Am. Bd. Psychiatry and Neurology (com. on cert. in child psychiatry 1983-85, chmn. 1986-87, bd. dirs. 1993—, chmn. com. added qualifications forensic psychiatry 1993-97); cert. in adult and child psychiatry also psychoanalysis. Intern in pediatrics Yale-New Haven Hosp., 1960-61; asst. resident in psychiatry Cin. Gen. Hosp., 1961-63; fellow in child psychiatry Yale Child Study Ctr., 1963-65; psychiatrist Mental Hygiene Clinic U.S. Army, Ft. Ord, Calif., 1965-67; asst. prof. Yale U. Child Study Ctr., New Haven, 1967-70, assoc. prof. Sch. Medicine, 1970-75, dir. tng., 1971-96, prof. pediatrics and psychiatry, 1975—, chief child psychiatry, 1982-90, dir. child psychiatry clin. svcs., 1990—, Albert J. Solnit prof. child psychiatry and pediatrics, 1989—; mem. publ. com. Yale U. Press, 1992—; mem. sci. adv. bd. Sophia Found. Med. Rsch., Rotterdam, The Netherlands, 1984-89; dir. mental health and substance abuse Yale Preferred Health Plan, 1995—. Co-author: The Family Handbook of Adolescence, 1979; contbr. numerous articles, book revs.; mem. editorial bd. Pediatrics, 1976-81, Children's Health Care, 1977—, Jour. Am. Psychoanalytic Assn., 1978, Pediatrics in Rev., 1978-85; asst. editor Jour. Am. Acad. Child and Adolescent Psychiatry, 1988—; co-editor Yearbook Psychiatry and Applied Mental Health, 1988—. Capt. U.S. Army, 1965-67. Fellow Am. Acad. Child and Adolescent Psychiatry (sec. 1985-87, pres. 1989-91, Simon Wile award 1996), Am. Coll. Psychiatrists, Am. Acad. Pediatrics; mem. Am. Pediatric Soc., Am. Psychoanalytic Assn. (cert. adult and child), Group for Advancement Psychiatry (com. on child psychiatry 1981, bd. dirs. 1989-91, pres. 1993-95), Assn. for Care of Children's Health (pres. 1984-86), AMA (residency rev. com. for psychiatry 1983-87, 89-94), Soc. Profs. Child Psychiatry (pres. 1984-86), We. New Eng. Inst. Psychoanalysis (mem. faculty in child psychoanalysis 1980—, supervisor child psychoanalysis 1984—, pres. 1986-88), Conn. and New Haven med. socs., Conn. Coun. Child Psychiatrists (pres. 1979-81), Benjamin Rush Soc., DARE Am. (mem. sci. adv. panel), others, Sigma Xi. Lutheran. Home: 606 Ellsworth Ave New Haven CT 06511-1636 Office: Yale U Child Study Ctr PO Box 207900 230 S Frontage Rd New Haven CT 06520-7900

SCHOWALTER, WILLIAM RAYMOND, college dean, educator; b. Milw., Dec. 15, 1929; s. Raymond Philip and Martha (Kowalke) S.; m. Jane Ruth Gregg, Aug. 22, 1953; children: Katherine Ruth, Mary Patricia, David Gregg. BS, U. Wis., 1951; postgrad., Inst. Paper Chemistry, 1951-52; MS, U. Ill., 1953, PhD, 1957; PhD (hon.), Inst. Nat. Poly. Lorraine, France, 1996. Asst. prof. dept. chem. engring. Princeton U., 1957-63, assoc. prof., 1963-66, prof., 1966-86, Class of 1950 prof. engring. and applied sci., 1986-89, acting chmn. dept. chem. engring., 1971, chmn. dept. chem. engring., 1978-87, assoc. dean Sch. Engring. and Applied Sci., 1971-77; dean Coll. Engring. U. Ill., Urbana, 1989—; Sherman Fairchild disting. scholar Calif. Inst. Tech., 1977-78; vis. fellow U. Salford, Eng., 1974; vis. sr. fellow Sci. Rsch. Coun., U. Cambridge, Eng., 1970; cons. to chem. and petroleum cos.; editl. adv. bd. McGraw-Hill Pub. Co., 1964-92; co-chmn. Internat. Seminar for Heat and Mass Transfer, 1970; vis. com. for chem. engring. MIT, 1979-87, Lehigh U., 1980-87; mem. vis. com. Sch. Engring., Stanford U., 1990—; evaluation panelist Ctr. Chem. Engring. Nat. Bur. Standards, 1982-88, chmn., 1986-88; mem. commn. engring. and tech. sys. NRC, 1983-88; engring. rsch. bd., 1984-86, com. on chem. engring. frontiers; adv. coun. chem. engring. Cornell U., 1983-91; adv. coun. Sch. Engring., Rice U., 1986-92; adv. com. Ill. Inst. Tech., 1992—; acad. adv. bd. Sematech Corp., 1992—; internat. adv. panel Nat. U. Singapore, 1996—; Reilly lectr. in chem. engring. U. Notre Dame, 1985, Van Winkle lectr. in chem. engring. U. Tex., Austin, 1986, David M. Mason lectr. chem. engring. Stanford U., 1987; bd. dirs. BankIll. Trust Co. Author: Mechanics of Non-Newtonian Fluids, 1978; co-author: Colloidal Dispersions, 1989; mem. editl. com. Ann. Rev. Fluid Mechanics, 1974-80, Internat. Jour. Chem. Engring., 1974-94, Indsl. and Engring. Chemistry Fundamentals, 1975-78, Jour. Non-Newtonian Fluid Mechanics, 1976—, AIChE Jour., 1979-83; contbr. articles to profl. jours. Mem. Ill. Gov.'s Sci. Adv. Com., 1989-96. Served with U.S. Army, 1953-55. Decorated officier des Palmes Académiques (France), 1995; recipient Disting. Svc. citation Coll. Engring., U. Wis., Madison, 1983; Guggenheim fellow, 1987-88. Fellow AIChE (William H. Walker award 1982, bd. dirs. 1992-94), Am. Acad. Arts and Scis.; mem. Am. Soc. Engring. Edn. (exec. com. engr. deans coun. 1992-95), NAE (awards com. 1986-88, chmn. 1987, acad. adv. bd. 1991-94, chmn. 1992-94, coun. 1994—, Lectr. award chem. engring. divsn. 1971), Am. Chem. Soc., Soc. Rheology (exec. com. 1977-79, v.p. 1981-83, pres. 1983-85, Bingham medal 1988), Sigma Xi, Tau Beta Pi, Phi Lambda Upsilon, Phi Eta Sigma. Home: 1846 Maynard Dr Champaign IL 61821-5268

SCHRADE, ROLANDE MAXWELL YOUNG, composer, pianist, educator; b. Washington, Sept. 13; d. Harry Robert and Isabelle Martha (Maxwell) Young; m. Robert Warren Schrade, Dec. 21, 1949; children: Robelyn, Rhonda Lee, Rolisa, Randolph, Rorianne. Pupil Harold Bauer, N.Y.C., Vittorio Giannini; student, Manhattan Sch. Music, Juilliard Sch. Music.. Debut as concert pianist Town Hall, N.Y.C., 1953, Nat. Gallery, Washington, 1954; founder, dir. ann. performances Sevenars Concerts, Inc., Worthington, Mass., 1968—, music dir., 1975—, also broadcasts, 1984, 85; recitalist radio Sta. WGMS-FM, Washington; mem. music faculty Allen-Stevenson Sch., N.Y.C., 1968-89; v.p., treas. Sevenars Music House, Inc., N.Y.C., 1968—. Concerts include Lincoln Ctr., Alice Tully Hall, 1980, 93, Sevenars Concerts, Inc., ann. music festival, Worthington, Mass., 1968—, tour, N.Z., 1982, 84; featured N.B.C. Today Show with Schrade family pianists, 1993; named Steinway Piano Co. Global Artist List; appearances PM Mag., TV, 1980, 81; composer, pub. and recorded over 100 songs; albums include America 76, Original and Traditional Songs for Special Days, 1988; editor: songs of Carrie Jacobs Bond, Boston Music Co. Mem. ASCAP, DAR (Bicentennial award 1972), Mut. Artists Mgmt. Alliance (founder, bd. dirs.). Episcopalian. Home and Office: 30 E End Ave Ste 3A New York NY 10028-7053 also: Sevenars Worthington MA 01098

SCHRADER, HARRY CHRISTIAN, JR., retired naval officer; b. Sheboygan, Wis., Aug. 4, 1932; s. Harry Christian and Edna Flora (Stubbe) S.; m. Carol Joan Gossman, June 23, 1956; 1 child, Mary Clare. BS, U.S. Naval Acad., 1955; MS, U.S. Naval Postgrad. Sch., 1963. Commd. ensign USN, 1955, advanced through grades to vice adm., 1982; comdr. U.S.S. Tawasa, 1963-64, U.S.S. A. Hamilton, 1970-72, U.S.S. Jackson, 1972-73, U.S.S. Gilmore, 1973-75, U.S.S. Long Beach, 1975-78; dir. MLSF Amphibious, Mine Warfare and Advanced Vehicles div. Office Naval Ops.,

Washington, 1978-80; comdr. Cruiser Destroyer Group One, San Diego, 1980-82, Naval Surface Forces, U.S. Pacific Fleet, San Diego, 1982-85; ret. USN, 1985; mgr. Middle East/NATO programs, autonetics div. Rockwell Internat., Anaheim, Calif., 1985-87; pres. Coronado (Calif.) Tech. Internat., 1987; bd. dirs. Continental Maritime Industries, Inc.; adv. bd. Levine-Fricks, Recco, Inc. Mem. Am. Def. Preparedness Assn., San Diego Oceans Found. (mem. adv. bd.), Sigma Xi.

SCHRADER, HELEN MAYE, retired municipal worker; b. Akron, Ohio, June 8, 1920; d. Simon P. and Helen Cecelia (Fennessy) Eberz; widowed; children: Alfred E., Kathleen Therese Schrader Wein. Notary pub., Ohio. Insp., clk. Fed. Govt. agys., 1940; stenographer Chem. Warfare divsn. USAF, Akron, 1954; clk., stenographer VA; elected clk./treas. of twp. Springfield (Ohio) Twp., 1956-92. Sec. Springfield Dem. Club, Akron, 1957—; sec., treas. Springfield Twp. Civic Club, 1980—. Mem. Summit County Assn. of Trustees and Clks. (sec. 1959-78, 83-92, Svc. plaque 1979, 92). Roman Catholic. Avocations: needlework, flower arranging, crossword puzzles. Home: 693 Neal Rd Akron OH 44312-3709

SCHRADER, HENRY CARL, civil engineer, consultant; b. Chgo., Jan. 5, 1918; s. Henry Fred and Helene (Arkenberg) S.; m. Marium Warner, Aug. 22, 1942; children: Henry Carl, Gary Warner. BSCE, U. Ill., 1940, MSCE, 1959; diploma Indsl. Coll. Armed Forces, Ft. McNair, D.C., 1962. Registered profl. engr., Ill., Va., Md., D.C., Pa., Mass., N.C. Commd. 2nd lt., U.S. Army, 1940; advanced through grades to maj. gen., 1971; dist. engr. Corps of Engrs., Okinawa, Ryukus Island, 1962-64; chief systems analysis Office Chief Staff Dept Army, Washington, 1966-67, dir. mgmt. info. systems, 1967-70; comdr. 18th Engr. Brigade, Vietnam, 1970-71, comdr. Computer Systems Command, Ft. Belvior, Va., 1971-73; ret., 1973; prin. mktg. Dalton Dalton Newport, Washington, 1973-84; v.p. URS Dalton, 1984-86; v.p. URS Greiner, Inc. (formerly URS Cons., Inc.), Virginia Beach, Va., 1986—; specialist high speed ground transp. systems, 1978—. Decorated Air Medal with 2 clusters, Disting. Svc. medal with cluster, Legion of Merit with 3 clusters; Engr. Yr. award Dept. Civil Engring. U. Ill., 1971. Fellow ASCE, Soc. Am. Mil. Engrs. (dir. 1979-86); mem. NSPE, Am. Rd. and Transportation Bldrs. Assn. (bd. dirs. 1982-95, pres. planning and design div. 1988-90, pres. pub./pvt. ventures div. 1990-92, railroads adv. coun. 1977—), Am. Ry. Engring. Assn., High Speed Rail Assn. (bd. dirs. 1982—, vice chmn. 1990-92, chmn. membership com. 1985—), Army and Navy Club, Bethesda Country Club (dir. 1983-86), Farmington Country Club. Republican. Episcopalian.

SCHRADER, KEITH WILLIAM, mathematician; b. Neligh, Nebr., Apr. 22, 1938; s. William Charles and Gail (Hughes) S.; m. Carol Jean Taylor, Dec. 26, 1960; children: Jeffrey, Melinda. B.S., U. Nebr., 1959, M.S., 1961, Ph.D., 1966; postgrad., Stanford U., 1961-63. Engr. Sylvania Co., Mountain View, Calif., 1962-63; asst. prof. dept. math U. Mo.-Columbia, 1966-69, assoc. prof., 1969-78, prof., 1978-79, chmn. dept. math. prof., 1979-82, 85-88, prof. dept. math., 1988—. Bd. dirs. Schrader Inst. Early Learning, Columbia, 1970-83; mem. Planning And Zoning Commn., 1980-90. NASA grantee, 1967-68; NSF grantee, 1969-70. Mem. Am. Math. Soc., Sigma Xi, Sigma Phi Epsilon. Office: Dept Math U Mo Columbia MO 65211-0001

SCHRADER, KEN, professional race car driver; b. Fenton, Mo., May 29, 1955; m. Ann Schrader; children: Dorothy, Sheldon Bradley. Professional race car driver 1971—, winner Lakehill Speedway Track championship, raced in NASCAR Winston Cup races 1984—, winner Hendrick Motorsports, 1988, 2-time winner Busch Clash, winner 3 consecutive Daytona 500 Poles, winner 1991 Budweiser 500. Named 1985 NASCAR Rookie of Yr. Office: c/o NASCAR PO Box 2875 Daytona Beach FL 32120-2875

SCHRADER, LAWRENCE EDWIN, plant physiologist, educator; b. Atchison, Kans., Oct. 22, 1941; s. Edwin Carl and Jenna Kathryn (Tobiason) S.; m. Elfriede J. Massier, Mar. 14, 1981. BS, Kans. State U., 1963; PhD, U. Ill., 1967; grad., Inst. Ednl. Mgmt., Harvard U., 1991. Asst. prof. dept. agronomy U. Wis., Madison, 1969-72; assoc. prof. U. Wis., 1972-76, prof., 1976-84; prof., head dept. agronomy U. Ill., Urbana, 1985-89; dean Coll. Agr. and Home Econs. Wash. State U., Pullman, 1989-94, prof. dept. horticulture, 1994—; chief competitive rsch. grants office Dept. Agr., Washington, 1980-81; trustee, treas. Agrl. Satellite Corp., 1991-94. Contbr. chpts. to books, articles to profl. jours. Active Consortium for Internat. Devel., 1989-94, chair fin. com., vice chair exec. com., 1990-92, trustee 1989-94; mem. exec. com. Coun. Agrl. Heads of Agr., 1992-94. Capt. U.S. Army, 1967-69. Recipient Soybean Researchers Recognition award 1983, Disting. Service award in Agriculture Kansas State U., 1987; Romnes Faculty fellow U. Wis., 1979. Fellow AAAS (steering group sect. agr. 1991-95, chair-elect sect. on agr., food and renewable resources 1995-96, chmn. 1996-97, past chmn. 1997-98), Am. Soc. Agronomy, Crop Sci. Soc. Am.; mem. Am. Soc. Plant Physiologists (sec. 1983-85, pres.-elect 1986, pres. 1987), Am. Chem. Soc., Blue Key, Sigma Xi, Gamma Sigma Delta, Phi Kappa Phi, Phi Eta Sigma, Alpha Zeta. Methodist. Home: 3504 Crestview Rd Wenatchee WA 98801-9668 Office: Wash State U Tree Fruit Rsch & Extension Ctr 1100 N Western Ave Wenatchee WA 98801-1230

SCHRADER, LEE FREDERICK, agricultural economist; b. Okawville, Ill., Mar. 11, 1933; s. Fred and Alma (Koenemann) S.; m. Martha Ellen Kohl, Dec. 27, 1958; children—Mark, Katherine, Amanda. B.S., U. Ill., 1955; M.S., Mich. State U., 1958; Ph.D., U. Calif., Berkeley, 1961. Buyer Lever Bros. Co., N.Y.C., 1961-64; economist Armour & Co., Chgo., 1965-66; mem. faculty Sch. Agr. Purdue U., West Lafayette, Ind., 1966—; prof. agrl. econs. Sch. Agr. Purdue U., 1971—. Author: (with R.A. Goldberg) Farmers' Cooperatives and Federal Income Taxes, 1975; contbr. articles to profl. jours. Served with U.S. Army, 1955-57. Mem. Am. Agrl. Econs. Assn. Home: 128 Seneca Ln West Lafayette IN 47906-2041 Office: Purdue U Dept Agrl Econs West Lafayette IN 47907

SCHRADER, MARTIN HARRY, retired publisher; b. Queens, N.Y., Nov. 26, 1924; s. Harry F. and Ida (Spiess) S.; m. Cecelia Sofer, July 7, 1957; children: Howard, Daniel, Esther. B.A., Queens Coll., 1946. Vice pres. Alfred Auerbach & Co., 1950-60; dir. mktg. House Beautiful mag., N.Y.C., 1960-65; pub. spl. publs. div. House Beautiful mag., 1965-69; pub. Town and Country mag., N.Y.C., 1969-77, Harpers Bazaar, 1977-91; retired, 1991—; v.p. Hearst Mags., 1983-91; lectr. merchandising Fairleigh Dickinson U., 1958-61, Parson Sch. Design, 1976—, Merchandising New Sch. Grad. Ctr., 1984; advt. Cosmetics Plus, N.Y.C.; cons. Columbia Journalism Rev., Sports Traveler Mag., Reed Reference Pub. Pro-bono pub. Westchester Arts News/Westchester Arts Coun.; author bi-weekly column Gannett Suburban Newspapers, quarterly column Westchester 60 Plus Mag.; editor spl. sect. Westchester/Fairfield County Bus. Jour., 1996—. Former nat. adv. bd. Salk Inst., La Jolla, Calif.; bd. govs. Coty Fashion Critics Awards.; bd. dirs. Mother's Day Found., Ednl. Found. Fashion Industries. Recipient Human Relations award Am. Jewish Com., 1979. Mem. U.S. Lawn Tennis Assn. (umpire's com. 1961-94). Jewish (trustee temple 1965-94).

SCHRADER, MICHAEL EUGENE, columnist, editor; b. Jersey City, Apr. 3, 1938; s. Eugene Charles and Anne Veronica (Kane) S. BA in Latin, NYU, 1961, MA in English, 1963; postgrad., UCLA, 1965-67, 68-69, Trinity Coll., Dublin, 1967-68, U. Copenhagen, Denmark, 1970. Asst. editor Macmillan Co., N.Y.C., 1962-64; teaching asst. U. Ill., Urbana, 1964-65; teaching asst., rsch. asst. UCLA, 1965-67, 68-69; sr. copy editor Dell Pub. Co., N.Y.C., 1971-72; copy chief Sat. Rev. mag., N.Y.C., 1972-76, Penthouse mag., N.Y.C., 1976-82; assoc. editor Med. Econs. mag., Oradell, N.J., 1982; sr. copy editor Woman's World mag., Englewood, N.J., 1983-84; book reviewer, sr. copy editor Nation's Restaurant News, N.Y.C., 1985—. Columnist: From the Bookshelf, in Nation's Restaurant News, 1988—. Friend of Bobst Libr., NYU, 1994—, established Anne Kane Schrader Cookbook and Nutrition Collection. Recipient Danish Marshall award U. Copenhagen, 1970; Fulbright scholar, 1967-68. Mem. Internat. Assn. Culinary Profls., James Beard Found. (assoc., judge food and beverage book awards 1991-94). Democrat. Roman Catholic. Avocations: reading fiction and poetry, growing house plants, travel, movies, theater. Home: 10 Waterside Plz Apt 4 H New York NY 10010-2610 Office: Lebhar-Friedman Inc Nation's Restaurant News 425 Park Ave New York NY 10022-3506

SCHRADER, PAUL JOSEPH, film writer, director; b. Grand Rapids, Mich., July 22, 1946; s. Charles A. and Joan (Fisher) S.; m. Jeannine Oppewall (div.); m. Mary Beth Hurt, Aug. 6, 1983. B.A., Calvin Coll., 1968; M.A., UCLA., 1970. Film critic Los Angeles Free Press, Coast mag., 1970-71; editor Cinema mag., 1970. Author: Transcendental Style in Film: Ozu, Bresson, Dreyer, 1972, Schrader on Schrader, 1989; screenwriter: The Yakuza, 1975, Taxi Driver, 1976, Obsession, 1976, Rolling Thunder, 1978, Raging Bull, 1980, The Mosquito Coast, 1986, The Last Temptation of Christ, 1988, Heat, 1996; screenwriter, prodr.: Old Boyfriends, 1978; screenwriter, dir.: Blue Collar, 1977, Hardcore, 1978, American Gigolo, 1979, Mishima: A Life in Four Chapters, 1985, Light of Day, 1987, Light Sleeper, 1992Witch-hunt, 1994, Touch, 1997; dir.: Cat People, 1982, Patty Hearst, 1988, The Comfort of Strangers, 1990. Address: 9696 Culver Blvd Ste 203 Culver City CA 90232-2753 Office: William Morris Agy 1325 Ave of the Americas New York NY 10019*

SCHRADER, ROBERT GEORGE, lawyer; b. White Plains, N.Y., Apr. 28, 1961; s. George Louis and Florence Rose (Smith) S.; m. Virginia Alexander Kurtz, Apr. 20, 1991; children: Robert George, Jr., de Grasse Alexandra. BA in Microbiology, Fla. Atlantic U., 1983; diploma, U. San Diego Paris Inst. for Comparative Law, 1986; JD cum laude, Nova U., 1987. Bar: Fla. 1987, U.S. Dist. Ct. (so. dist.) Fla. 1987, U.S. Ct. Intrenat. Trade 1988. Jud. intern to honorable Norman C. Roettger Jr. U.S. Dist. Ct. (so. dist.) Fla., Ft. lauderdale, 1986; assoc. Sandler, Travis & Rosenberg, P.A., Miami, Fla., 1987-92; ptnr. Schrader & Zhang, P.A., North Miami, Fla., 1992-94, Sandler, Travis & Rosenberg P.A., 1994—; of counsel Ruden, McClosky, Smith, Schuster & Russel, P.A., 1995—; adjunct prof. Fla. Internat. U., 1994—; adj. prof. law internat. trade and fin. Nova Southeastern U. Law Sch., 1997—. Editor jour. Customs and Trade Update, 1988-95; editor newsletter N.B.W.C.A., 1988-95; contbr. articles to profl. jours.; panel mem. TV program Immigration and Beyond, 1992. Mem. Bus. Vols. for the Arts, Miami, 1990-93; vol. of yr., mem. adv. bd. Camillus House, Miami, 1991-95; bd. dirs., legal counsel Inner City Childrens Dance Co., Miami, 1991-92; com. person Broward Rep. Exec. Com. Recipinet UP and Comer award Price Waterhouse/South Fla. Mag., 1994; Fla. Atlantic U. faculty scholar, 1983, Goodwin scholar, 1984-86. Episcopalian. Avocations: gourmet chef, Shaolin kung fu, cycling, scuba diving, gardening. Office: Ruden McClosky 200 E Broward Blvd Fort Lauderdale FL 33301-1963

SCHRADER, THOMAS F., utilities executive; b. Indpls., 1950. Grad., Princeton U., 1972, 78. Pres., chief exec. officer Wis. Gas Co., Milw. Office: Wis Gas Co 626 E Wisconsin Ave Milwaukee WI 53202-4603

SCHRADER, WILLIAM JOSEPH, accountant, educator; b. Leroy, Tex., Sept. 21, 1929; s. Rudolph L. and Lela V. (Gaylor) S.; m. Nancy L. Etnier, Mar. 22, 1953 (dec. 1974); children: Diana, Dale (dec. 1974), Frank; m. Mary Kuhns Maserick, Mar. 6, 1976. BBA, Baylor U., 1950; MBA, Ind. U., 1951; PhD, U. Wash., 1959. CPA, Tex. Acct. Texaco, New Orleans, 1949, A.C. Upleger & Co. (C.P.A.'s), Waco, Tex., 1949-50; instr. U. Wash., Seattle, 1952-54; asst. prof. to prof. accounting Pa. State U., University Park, 1954-91; head dept. accounting and mgmt. info. systems Pa. State U., 1976-86; prof. emeritus, 1992—; bd. dirs. various firms including Ceramic Finishing Co., Ultran Labs., Inc., Applied Sci. Labs., Inc., Cenco Assocs. Inc., 1968—; gen. ptnr. investment partnerships; Fulbright prof. U. Dar es Salaam, 1973-75; vis. prof. U. Zimbabwe, 1987; dir. linkage project with U. Zimbabwe, 1982-87; resident advisor mgmt. tng. project U. West Indies, 1989-90; mem. bd. advs. Inst. of Chartered Accts. of The Caribbean, 1988—; trustee Alpha Real Estate and Mortgage Trust. Author: Income Measurement by Products and Periods, 1959, (with Malcom & Willingham) Financial Accounting: An Events Approach, 1981; contbr. articles to profl. publs. including Jour. of Risk and Ins., Acctg. Rev., Abacus, Fin. Exec., Acctg. Horizons, Acctg. Historians Jour. Active Centre County (Pa.) Task Force on Housing, 1969-70; trustee Fair Housing Inc. Liquidating Trust. Mem. AICPA, AAUP, Am. Acctg. Assn., Acad. Acctg. Historians. Baptist. Clubs: Am. Philatelic Soc, Am. Philatelic Research Library. Home: 305 Adams Ave State College PA 16803-3606 Office: 240 Beam Bus Adminstrn Bldg University Park PA 16802

SCHRADY, DAVID ALAN, operations research educator; b. Akron, Ohio, Nov. 11, 1939; s. Marvin G. and Sheila A. (O'Neill) S.; m. Mary E. Hilt, Sept. 1, 1962; children: Peter, Patrick, Matthew. BS, Case Inst. Tech., 1961, MS, 1963, PhD, 1965. Prof., chmn. Naval Postgrad. Sch., Monterey, Calif., 1974-76, dean acad. planning, 1976-80, provost and acad. dean, 1980-87, prof. ops. rsch., 1988—; Disting. prof. Naval Postgrad. Sch., Monterey, 1995—; vis. prof. Cranfield Inst. Tech./Royal Mil. Coll. of Sci., Shrivenham, Eng., fall 1987-spring 88. Contbr. articles to profl. jours. Recipient Goodeve medal Ops. Rsch. Soc., U.K., 1992. Fellow Mil. Ops. Rsch. Soc. (pres. 1978-79, Wanner Meml. award 1994); mem. Ops. Rsch. Soc. Am. (pres. 1983-84, Kimball medal 1994), Internat. Fedn. Ops. Rsch. Socs. (hon. treas. 1988—), Inst. Mgmt. Scis. Avocation: guitar, motor sports. Office: Naval Postgrad Sch Dept Ops Rsch Monterey CA 93943-5000

SCHRAG, ADELE FRISBIE, business education educator; b. Cynthiana, Ky., May 7, 1921; d. Shirley Ledyard and Edna Kate (Ford) S.; m. William Albert Schrag, Apr. 6, 1963; 1 stepchild, Marie Carol. B.S., Temple U., 1942; M.A., N.Y. U., 1944, Ph.D., 1961. Tchr. Manor Twp. High Sch., Millersville, Pa., 1942-43, Downingtown (Pa.) Sr. High Sch., 1943-50; instr., asst. prof. Temple U. Sch. Bus. and Pub. Administrn., Phila., 1950-60; prof. bus. edn. and vocat. edn. Coll. Edn., 1960-85, sr. prof. edn., 1985-88, prof. emeritus, 1988—; vis. lectr. N.Y. U.; cons. Phila. Community Coll., 1967-82. Editor: Business Education for the Automated Office, 1964; author: (with Estelle L. Popham and Wanda Blockhus) A Teaching-Learning System for Business Education, 1975, How to Dictate, 1981, Office Procedures Update, 1982, (with Robert Poland) A Teaching System for Business Subjects, 1988; contbr. articles to profl. jours., chpts. to books. Trustee Meth. Hosp., 1981-85, Sun Cities Symphony Assn., 1988-93, Maricopa Habitat for Humanity, 1994—. Recipient Profl. Panhellenic award, 1963; Kensington High Sch. Alumnae award, 1972. Mem. Soc. Automation in Bus. Edn. (pres. 1969-73, dir. 1974), Nat. Assn. Bus. Tchr. Edn. (pres. 1983-84), Bus. Edn. Certification Council, Phi Gamma Nu (nat. treas. 1952-54, nat. sec. 1954-56), Delta Pi Epsilon (policy commn. for bus. and econ. edn. 1975-78, dir. research found. 1978-83, pres. research found. 1983). Home: 14515 W Granite Valley #644 Sun City West AZ 85375

SCHRAG, EDWARD A., JR., lawyer; b. Milw., Mar. 27, 1932; s. Edward A. and Mabel Lena (Baumbach) S.; m. Leslie Jean Israel, June 19, 1954; children: Amelia Marie Schrag Prack, Katherine Allison Schrag Roberts, Edward A. III (dec.). B.S. in Econs, U. Pa., 1954; J.D., Harvard, 1960. Bar: Ohio 1961. Assoc., then firm partner, now of counsel Vorys, Sater, Seymour and Pease, Columbus, 1960—; sec. Ranco Inc., 1972-87; trustee Lake of Woods Water Co., 1972-91; mem. Ohio div. Securities Adv. Com. Mem. Downtown Area Com., 1970-74. Served to lt. (j.g.) USNR, 1954-57. Mem. ABA, Ohio Bar Assn. (chmn. corp. law com. 1986-88, chmn. securities regulation subcom., spl. com. bus. cts., bd. govs., corp. counsel sect., chmn. 1991-93), Columbus Bar Assn., Columbus Area C. of C., Navy League, Alpha Tau Omega, Beta Gamma Sigma, Phi Sigma Alpha, Pi Gamma Mu. Episcopalian. Clubs: Capital, Crichton, Ohio State U. Pres.'s. Home: 9400 White Oak Ln Westerville OH 43082-9606 Office: Vorys Sater Seymour & Pease PO Box 1008 52 E Gay St Columbus OH 43216-1008

SCHRAG, PETER, editor, writer; b. Karlsruhe, Germany, July 24, 1931; came to U.S., 1941, naturalized, 1953; s. Otto and Judith (Haas) S.; m. Melissa Jane Mowrer, June 9, 1953 (div. 1969); children: Mitzi, Erin Andrew; m. Diane Divoky, May 24, 1969 (div. 1981); children: David Divoky, Benaiah Divoky; m. Patricia Ternahan, Jan. 1, 1988. A.B. cum laude, Amherst Coll., 1953. Reporter El Paso (Tex.) Herald Post, 1953-55; asst. sec., asst. dir. publs. Amherst Coll., 1955-66, instr. Am. Studies, 1960-64; asso. edn. editor Sat. Rev., 1966-68, exec. editor, 1968-69; editor Change mag., 1969-70; editor at large Saturday Rev., 1969-72; contbg. editor Saturday Review/Education, 1972-73; editorial adv. bd. The Columbia Forum, 1972-75; editorial bd. Social Policy, 1971—; contbg. editor More, 1974-78, Inquiry, 1977-80, The Am. Prospect, 1995—; editorial page editor Sacramento Bee and McClatchy Newspapers, 1978-96, contbg. editor, 1996—; vis. lectr. U. Mass. Sch. Edn., 1970-72; fellow in profl. journalism Stanford U., Palo Alto, Calif., 1973-74; lectr. U. Calif. at Berkeley, 1974-78, 90—; Pulitzer Prize juror, 1988-89. Author: Voices in the Classroom, 1965, Village School Downtown, 1967, Out of Place in America, 1971, The Decline of the Wasp, 1972, The End of the American Future, 1973, Test of Loyalty, 1974, (with Diane Divoky) The Myth of the Hyperactive Child, 1975, Mind Control, 1978; contbr. articles. Mem. adv. com. Student Rights Project, N.Y. Civil Liberties Union, 1970-72; mem. Com. Study History, 1958-72; trustee Emma Willard Sch., 1967-69; bd. dirs. Park Sch., Oakland, Calif., 1976-77, Ctr. for Investigative Reporting, 1979-81; bd. visitors Claremont Grad. Sch.; mem. bd. advisors Pub. Policy Inst. Calif. Guggenheim fellow, 1971-72; Nat. Endowment for Arts fellow, 1976-77. Office: Sacramento Bee 21st & Q St Sacramento CA 95852

SCHRAG, PHILIP GORDON, law educator; b. Chgo., Apr. 12, 1943; s. Louis Phillip and Lala D. (Fineman) S.; m. Emily Shiling, June 7, 1964 (div. Aug. 1985); children: David, Zachary; m. Lisa Gabrielle Lerman, Dec. 29, 1985; children: Samuel Lerman, Sarah. AB, Harvard U., 1964; LLB, Yale U., 1967. Bar: N.Y. 1967, D.C. 1981. Asst. counsel NAACP Legal Def. & Edn. Fund Inc., N.Y.C., 1967-70; consumer adv. City of N.Y., 1970-71; assoc. prof. law Columbia U., N.Y.C., 1971-73, prof. law, 1973-77; dep. gen. counsel ACDA, Washington, 1977-81; prof. law Georgetown U., Washington, 1981—; cons. Consumer Protection Bd., N.Y., 1975, Carter-Mondale Transition Planning, 1976, Gov.'s Adv. Coun., P.R., 1970. Author: Counsel for the Deceived, 1972, Consumer Protection Law, 1973, Behind the Scenes: The Politics of a Constitutional Convention, 1985, Listening for the Bomb, 1989. Del. Statehood Constnl. Conv., D.C., 1982; chair Consumer's Adv. Coun., N.Y.C., 1968-70.

SCHRAGE, ROSE, educational administrator; b. Montelimar, France, Apr. 15, 1942; came to U.S., 1947; d. Abraham and Celia (Silbiger) Levine; m. Samuel Schrage, Dec. 12, 1935 (dec. 1976); children: Abraham, Leon. BRE, Beth Rivkah Tchrs. Sem., Bklyn., 1968; Paralegal, Manpower Career Devel. Agy., Bklyn., 1973; MS, L.I. U., 1975; Advanced Cert. Ednl. Adminstrn., Bklyn. Coll., 1983. Cert. sch. dist. adminstr., guidance counselor, tchr., asst. prin. Sec. N.Y.C., 1964-68; police adminstrv. aide N.Y.C. Police Dept., 1974-75; coordinator state reading aid program Sch. Dist. 14, Bklyn., 1977-78, project dir. Title VII, 1978-81, asst. dir. reimbursable fed. and state programs, 1981-85, dist. bus. mgr., 1985-94, asst. prin., 1994—; chmn. N.Y.C. Bd. Edn. IMPACT Com., Bklyn., 1986—. Author (poem): Never Again, 1983; contbg. editor Chai Today; contbr. articles on current affairs and concerns to profl. jours. Del. Republican. Jud. Conf., 1968; founder, pres Concerned Parents, Bklyn., 1977; radio co-host Israeli War Heroes Fund-Radiothon, Bklyn.; family counselor local social agys., Bklyn.; co-founder cmty. vol. ambulance Hatzalah, 1977. Recipient Cert. of Appreciation as vol. regional coord. N.Y. State Mentoring Program N.Y. Gov. Cuomo, 1991. Mem. Am. Assn. Sch. Adminstrs., Assn. Orthodox Jewish Tchrs. (v.p. exec. bd.), N.Y. State Assn. Sch. Bus. Ofcls., N.Y.C. Assn. Sch. Bus. Ofcls., Coun. Suprs. and Adminstrs. Avocations: tennis, needlepoint, piano, reading, communal activities.

SCHRAGER, MINDY RAE, business professional; b. Paterson, N.J., Jan. 18, 1958; d. Julius Maxwell and Miriam (Max) S.; m. Jim Flannery, 1993. BA, Dickinson Coll., 1979; MBA, Babson Coll., 1981. ASQC cert. quality mgr. Cons., Nolan Norton & Co., Lexington, Mass., 1981-86; mgr. Logos Corp., Dedham, Mass., 1986-87; supr. resource ctr., customer satisfaction mgr., distribution quality mgr., dir. of quality for worldwide distribution, Motorola ISG, Mansfield, Mass., 1987-95; dir. quality, dir. bill payment ops. Fidelity Investments, Boston, 1995—. Co-author: Non Product Quality: The Cornerstone for Sucess, Continuous Improvement of the Selling Process. Mem. NAFE, Am. Soc. Quality Control (founder, chmn. 1992-94, bus. process improvement com.), Assn. for Rsch. and Enlightenment, Assn. Quality and Participation (co-founder Boston chpt. 1990, v.p. 1991-92, pres. 1992-93) Avocation: ballroom dance. Home: 43 Bradford Rd Framingham MA 01701-3381 Office: Fidelity Investments 82 Devonshire St # 1F Boston MA 02109-3605

SCHRAM, MARTIN JAY, journalist; b. Chgo., Sept. 15, 1942; s. Marlo Joseph and Charleene Janice (Fidler) S.; m. Patricia Stewart Morgan, May 23, 1964; children—Kenneth Marlo, David Morgan. B.A., U. Fla., 1964. Reporter The Miami (Fla.) News, 1964-65; reporter Newsday, Garden City, N.Y., 1965-67; mem. Washington bur. Newsday, 1967-69, White House corr., 1969-73, chief Washington bur., sr. editor paper, 1973-79; writer on the presidency Washington Post, 1979-81, nat. affairs writer, 1981-86; assoc. editor, editor Sunday edits. Chgo. Sun-Times, 1986-87; asst. mng. editor, editor Sunday edits. Rocky Mountain News, Denver, 1987-88; polit. columnist United Feature Syndicate, Newspaper Enterprise Assn., 1989-94, Scripps Howard News Svc., Washington, 1994—; commentator Cable News Network, 1988—; nat. editor Washingtonian Mag., 1988-90; fellow Gannett Ctr. for Media Studies, Columbia U., 1985-86; guest scholar Woodrow Wilson Internat. Ctr., 1990-91. Author: Running for President, A Journal of the Carter Campaign, 1976, Running for President: 1976, The Carter Campaign, 1977; (with others) The Pursuit of the Presidency, 1980, The Great American Video Game: Presidential Politics in the Television Age, 1987, Speaking Freely, 1995; co-editor: Mandate for Change, 1993. Recipient James Wright Brown Meml. award Sigma Delta Chi, 1965, Lowell Mellet award Pa. State U., 1988. Office: 1090 Vermont Ave NW Ste 1000 Washington DC 20005-4905

SCHRAM, RONALD BYARD, lawyer; b. Detroit, Sept. 7, 1942; s. Byron Canby and Mary Louise (Byard) S.; m. Carol Lorraine Anderson, July 19, 1969; children: Laura Mary, Alison Leigh. BA, Dartmouth Coll., 1964; MA in Econs., Cambridge U., England, 1966; JD, U. Mich., 1969, LLM, 1970, SJD, 1971. Bar: Mass. 1970. Assoc. Ropes & Gray, Boston, 1970-78, ptnr., 1978—. Trustee Dartmouth Coll., Hanover, N.H., 1981-92, Dartmouth-Hitchcock Med. Ctr., Lebanon, N.H., 1983-93, New Eng. Sports Mus., Cambridge, Mass., 1984—, Derby Acad., Hingham, Mass., 1982-89. Keasbey Found. fellow, Phila., 1964-66; George M. Humphrey fellow in law econ. policy, U. Mich. Law Sch., Ann Arbor, 1969-70. Mem. Boston Bar Assn., Am. Acad. Hosp. Attys., Phi Beta Kappa. Office: Ropes & Gray 1 International Pl Boston MA 02110-2602

SCHRAM, STEPHEN C., professional basketball team executive; m. Patricia Wilcox; children: Parker, Caitlin. Diploma, U. Wyo.; MBA, MAAP, Duke U., 1984. Legis. asst. U.S. Sen. Malcolm Wallop, Washington; assoc. Morgan Stanley, 1984, v.p. fixed income securities divsn.; exec. Brookwood Investments, 1991—; vice chmn. bd. dirs. Boston Celtics; pres. Boston Celtics Ltd. Partnership; pres., vice-chmn. Boston Celtics Comm. Ltd. Partnership; bd. dirs. Aexco Petroleum, MPO Videotronics. Office: Celtics Ltd Partnership 151 Merrimac St Boston MA 02114-4714*

SCHRAMEK, TOMAS, ballet dancer; b. Bratislava, Czechoslovakia, Sept. 11, 1944; emigrated to Can., 1968, naturalized, 1973; s. Hans and Valeria (Neudorfer) S. BFA, Acad. Mus. and Theatre Arts, Bratislava, 1968. Mem. Sluk, Slovakia folk dance ensemble, 1959-68, prin. dancer, 1964-68; dancer Nat. Ballet Can., 1969-71, soloist, 1971-73, prin. dancer, 1973-91, prin. character artist, ballet master, 1991—. Mem. Actors Equity Assn., Assn. Can. TV and Radio Artists. Home: 205 Belsize Dr. Toronto, ON Canada M4S 1M3 Office: Nat Ballet Canada, 470 Queens Quay West, Toronto, ON Canada M5V 3K4

SCHRAMM, BERNARD CHARLES, JR., advertising agency executive; b. Balt., Jan. 23, 1928; s. Bernard C. and Juliet Marie (Barranger) S.; m. Florence Mae Fangman, 1950; children: Stephanie Schramm McDaniel, Carol Schramm Molander, Bernard Charles III, Claudia Schramm Chitwood. Student, Balt. Poly. Inst., 1942-46. Prodn. mgr. Van Sant, Dugdale & Co., Balt., 1946-52; media dir. AWL Advt., Balt., 1952-55; dir. prodn. Henry J. Kaufman Assocs., Washington, 1955-58; exec. v.p. Avalon Hill Co., Balt., 1958-64; v.p. Cargill, Wilson & Acree Advt., Richmond, Va., 1964-68; pres. William Cook Advt. Inc. (now The William Cook Agy. Inc.), Jacksonville, Fla., 1968-89; chmn. bd. William Cook Advt. Inc. (now The William Cook Agy. Inc.), Jacksonville, 1989—; bd. dirs. Otis F. Smith Found., chmn., 1991-93. Mem. exec. com., v.p. United Way N.E. Fla., 1982-87, bd. dirs., 1982-93; bd. dirs. N.E. Fla. chpt. ARC, 1976-89, chmn., 1980-81; bd. dirs. Fla. C.C. Found., 1976-89. Mem. Am. Assn. Advt. Agys. (chmn. Fla. coun., 1984-85, elected vice-chmn. So. Region Bd. of Govs., 1988—, chmn., 1989, nat. bd. dirs., mem. agy. mgmt. com., elected chmn. So. Region Bd. Govs. 1989), Jacksonville area C. of C., San Jose Club, River Club (Jacksonville), Ponte Vedra Club. Republican. Roman Catholic. Avocations: golf, reading, spectator sports. Home: 1220 Journeys End Ln

Jacksonville FL 32223-1753 Office: William Cook Agy Inc 225 Water St Ste 1600 Jacksonville FL 32202-5149

SCHRAMM, DAVID NORMAN, astrophysicist, educator; b. St. Louis, Oct. 25, 1945; s. Marvin M. and Betty Virginia (Math) S.; m. Judith J. Gibson, 1986; children from previous marriage: Cary, Brett. SB in Physics, MIT, 1967; PhD in Physics, Calif. Inst. Tech., 1971. Rsch. fellow in physics Calif. Inst. Tech., Pasadena, 1971-72; asst. prof. astronomy and physics U. Tex., Austin, 1972-74; assoc. prof. astronomy, astrophysics, physics Enrico Fermi Inst. and Coll. U. Chgo., 1974-77, prof., 1977—, Louis Block prof. phys. scis., 1982—, prof. conceptual founds. of sci., 1983—, acting chmn. dept. astronomy and astrophysics, 1977, chmn., 1978-84, v.p. for rsch., 1995—, Louis Block disting. svc. prof. in phys. scis., 1996—; resident cosmologist Fermilab, 1982-84; cons., lectr. Adler Planetarium, Lawrence Livermore Lab., Los Alamos Nat. Lab.; organizer sci. confs.; frequent lectr. in field; chmn. bd. trustees Aspen Ctr. for Physics; bd. on physics and astronomy, exec. com. NRC, 1990—, chair, 1993—, mem. com. aviation weather systems aeronautics and space engring. bd., 1994—; bd. dirs. Astron. Rsch. Consortium, 1990—; pres. Big Bang Aviation, Inc.; bd. overseers Fermi Nat. Accelerator Lab., 1990—. Co-author: The Advanced Stages of Stellar Evolution, 1977, From Quarks to the Cosmos: Tools of Discovery, 1989, The Shadows of Creation: Dark Matter and the Structure of the Universe, 1991; author: The Big Bang and Other Explosions in Nuclear & Particle Astrophysics, 1996; co-editor: Supernovae, 1977, Fundamental Problems of Stellar Evolution, 1980, Essays in Nucleosynthesis, 1981, Gauge Theory and the Early Universe, 1988, Dark Matter in the Universe, 1990, The Big Bang and Other Explosions in Nuclear and Particle Astrophysics, 1996; editor profl. jours.; columnist Outside mag.; contbr. over 350 articles to profl. jours. Recipient Gravity Rsch. Found. prize, 1980, Humboldt award Fed. Republic Germany, 1987-88, Einstein medal Evotos U., Budapest, Hungary, 1989, Grad. Teaching award U. Chgo., 1994. Fellow Am. Acad. Arts and Scis., Am. Phys. Soc. (Lilienfeld prize 1993), Meteor. Soc.; mem. Nat. Acad. Sci., Am. Astron. Soc. (Helen B. Warner prize 1978, exec. com. planetary sci. divsn. 1977-79, sec.-treas. high energy astrophysics divsn. 1979-81), Am. Assn. Physics Tchrs. (Richtmeyer prize 1984), Astron. Soc. Pacific (Robert J. Trumpler award 1974), Internat. Astron. Union (commns. on cosmology, stellar evolution, high energy astrophysics), Aircraft Owners and Pilots Assn., British-N Am. Com., Hungarian Acad. Scis. (hon.), Alpine Club, Sigma Xi. Achievements include development of the cosmological interface with particle physics and the use of cosmological arguments to constrain fundamental physics; use of big bang to form the principle argument regarding the cosmological density of normal matter. Home: 155 N Harbor Dr Apt 5203 Chicago IL 60601-7381 Office: U Chgo AAC 140 5640 S Ellis Ave Chicago IL 60637-1433 also: 150 Pitkin Mesa Dr Aspen CO 81611-1075

SCHRAND, RICHARD HENRY, broadcaster; b. Cin., Nov. 1, 1957; s. Edward August and Jane Marie (Scheib) S.; m. Deborah Fortner, 1979 (div. 1985); 1 chld, Cynthia Lanette; m. Sharon Lynn Lassandro, Dec. 24, 1986; 1 child, Courtney Lynne. Student, Ohio State U., 1975-76, No. Ky. U., 1976-77. Intern WCPO-TV, Cin., 1971-75; producer WKRC-TV, Cin., 1975-79; pub. affairs dir., reporter, anchor WCSC-TV, Charleston, S.C., 1979-83; actor Phila. Experiment, L.A., 1984; asst. promotion dir. WLWT-TV, Cin., 1983-86; spl. projects coord. KXAS-TV, Dallas/Ft. Worth, 1986-87; mgr. media svcs. NBC TV Network, Burbank, Calif., 1987-89; pres. Cyn-Court Enterprises, Burbank, 1989-91; mktg. dir. WPTA-TV, Ft. Wayne, Ind., 1991-92; v.p., gen. mgr. Branson (Mo.) Broadcasting Corp., 1992-95; dir. spl. projects/nat. media, graphics and advt. creator Jim Owens & Assocs., 1995—; gen. mgr. Jim Owens Radio, Inc., Nashville, 1992-94. Bd. dirs. Project Graduation, Dallas/Ft. Worth, 1986-87; mem. Muscular Dystrophy Assn., Charleston, 1980-83; publicist Housing Now, L.A., 1988. Recipient Local Emmy award Nat. Assn. TV Arts and Scis., 1975, award Broadcast Promotion and Mktg. Exec., Seattle, 1992. Avocations: guitar, writing, singing, golf.

SCHRAUT, KENNETH CHARLES, mathematician, educator; b. Hillsboro, Ill., May 19, 1913; s. Charles Frederick and Theresa (Panska) S.; m. Virginia Haury, Feb. 5, 1952; 1 dau., Marilyn Szorc. A.B. with honors, U. Ill., 1936; M.A., U. Cin., 1938, Ph.D., 1940. Vis. instr. U. Notre Dame, summer 1940; instr. dept. math. U. Dayton, (Ohio), 1940-41; asst. prof. U. Dayton, 1941-44, assoc. prof., 1944-48, prof., 1948-72, chmn. dept. math., 1954-72, Disting. Service prof., 1972—, project dir. Research Ctr., 1951-54; vis. lectr. Ohio State U. Grad. Sch., 1946-49; acting prof. U. Cin. Grad. Sch., 1958-60; dir. NSF Math. Inst., Cath. U., Ponce, P.R., summer 1959, U. Dayton, 1961-69, 72; chmn., bd. dirs. Honor Seminars of Met. Dayton, 1987-93. Recipient Lackner award, 1987. Mem. Am. Math. Soc., Math. Assn. Am., Am. Soc. Engring. Edn. (chmn. math. sect. 1967-68, 78-79, mem. exec. com. 1969-73, 76, program chmn. 1977-78), Sigma Xi, Pi Mu Epsilon. Home: 448 Mirage Dr Kokomo IN 46901-7037

SCHRAUTH, WILLIAM LAWRENCE, banker, lawyer; b. Bklyn., Apr. 25, 1935; s. William L. and Louise (Rowland) S.; m. Nancy T. Tollner, Dec. 26, 1959; children—Christopher W., Anne, Michael J., Catherine A. B.A., St. Bonaventure U., Olean, N.Y., 1956; J.D., Fordham U., 1960. Bar: N.Y. 1960. Ptnr., Evans, Severn, Bankert & Peet and predecessor firms, Utica, N.Y., 1962-73; v.p. The Savs. Bank of Utica, 1973-74, exec. v.p., 1974-77, pres., 1977—; trustee RSI Retirement Trust. Pres. bd. dirs. Oneida County Ind. Dem. Corp., Cmty. Found. of Herkaire and Oneida Counties Inc.. Republican. Office: The Savs Bank of Utica 233 Genesee St Utica NY 13501-2811

SCHREADLEY, RICHARD LEE, writer, retired newspaper editor; b. Harrisburg, Pa., Jan. 3, 1931; s. Harry Leroy and Flora Rebecca (McQuilken) S.; m. Doris Arlene Sheaffer, Dec. 18, 1952; 1 child, Rhys Leroy. B.A., Dickinson Coll., 1952; M.A., Tufts U., 1968, M.A.L.D., 1969, Ph.D., 1972. Reporter The News and Courier, Charleston, S.C., 1975; asso. editor The Evening Post, Charleston, 1975-76; editorial page editor The Evening Post, 1976-77, editor, 1977-81; exec. editor The Evening Post and The News and Courier, 1981-88; assoc. editor and sr. writer mil. and polit. affairs The News and Courier, 1989. Author: From the Rivers to the Sea, The United States Navy in Vietnam, 1992, Virtue and Valor, The Washington Light Infantry in Peace and in War, 1996. Chmn. Fgn. Affairs Forum of Charleston, 1987-88, mem. steering com., 1989. Served to comdr. USN, 1949-52, 56-73. Mem. Navy League, Ret. Officer Assn., Washington Light Infantry, Army-Navy Club of Washington, Country Club of Charleston. Home: 812 Clearview Dr Charleston SC 29412-4511

SCHRECK, ROBERT A., JR., lawyer; b. Buffalo, July 22, 1952. BS in Bus. Adminstrn., Georgetown U., 1974; MBA, Northwestern U., 1975, JD, 1978. Bar: Ill. 1978. Ptnr. McDermott, Will & Emery, Chgo., 1978—. Mem. ABA, Chgo. Bar Asns., Chgo. Soc. Clubs. Office: McDermott Will & Emery 227 W Monroe St Chicago IL 60606-5016

SCHRECKINGER, SY EDWARD, advertising executive, consultant; b. Bklyn., Jan. 10, 1937; s. Robert and Bessie (Gable) S.; m. Linda Fiarman, Mar. 4, 1962; children: Jamie Fran, Jon Gary. B.F.A., Pratt Inst., 1958. Art dir. Sudler and Hennesey, N.Y.C., 1958-61; sr. art dir. Marschalk Co., N.Y.C., 1961-63; group supr. Grey Advt., N.Y.C., 1963-66; v.p., assoc. creative dir. Hicks & Greist, N.Y.C., 1966-69; sr. v.p., assoc. creative dir. Young & Rubicam Inc., N.Y.C., 1969-88; advert. and mktg. cons. Oceanside, N.Y., 1988—. Recipient Lion Venice Internat. Film Festival, 1972, Andy Ad Club, N.Y., 1965, 86, award Internat. Bus. Assn., Best award Hollywood Radio & TV Soc., 1971, Clio Am. TV Comml. Festival, 1967, 72, 82, 85, Effy, 1985. Jewish.

SCHREIBER, ALAN HICKMAN, lawyer; b. Muncie, Ind., Apr. 4, 1944; s. Ephriam and Clarrisa (Hickman) S.; m. Phyllis Jean Chamberlain, Dec. 22, 1972; children—Jennifer Aline, Brett Justin. Student DePauw U., 1962-64; B.S. in Bus., Ind. U., 1966, J.D., 1969. Bar: Fla. 1971, U.S. Dist. Ct. (so. dist.) Fla. Asst., State Atty.'s Office, Ft. Lauderdale, Fla., 1971-76; pub. defender 17th Jud. Circuit, Ft. Lauderdale, 1976—; cons. Fla. Bar News on Criminal Law, 1982; lobbyist for indigent funding, Fla., 1980—; apptd. to Supreme Ct. Com. on Racial and Ethic Bias; co-chair Chiles-MacKay task force on criminal justice. Contbr. articles to profl. jours. Mem. Dem. Exec. Com., Ft. Lauderdale, 1980; mem. Plantation Dem. Club, 1983; campaign chmn. Goldstein for Atty. Gen. Fla., 1982. Named Young Dem. of Yr., Broward County Young Dems., 1980; Man of Yr., Jewish War Vets., 1982; recipient B'nai B'rith Pub. Servant award, 1990. Mem. Fla. Bar Assn., Broward County Bar Assn., ABA, Nat. Legal Aid Defenders Assn., Phi Alpha Delta. Home: 885 Orchid Dr Fort Lauderdale FL 33317-1221 Office: 201 SE 6th St Fort Lauderdale FL 33301-3303

SCHREIBER, BERTRAM MANUEL, mathematics educator; b. Seattle, Nov. 4, 1940; s. Isador and Amy (Hurwitz) S.; m. Rita Ruth Stusser, June 30, 1963; children: Susannah M. Schreiber Bechhofer, Deborah H. Schreiber Shapiro, Abraham D., Elisabeth T. BA, Yeshiva U., 1962; MS, U. Wash., 1966, PhD, 1968. Asst. prof. Wayne State U., Detroit, 1968-71, assoc. prof., 1971-78, prof., 1978—, chair dept. math., 1987-90; vis. prof. Hebrew U., Jerusalem, 1975, Mich. State U., East Lansing, 1982-83, Nat. U. Singapore, 1992, U. New South Wales, Australia, 1992, Indian Statis. Inst., 1993, Tata Inst. Fund Res., Bombay, 1993, Bar Ilan U., 1993, Tel Aviv U., 1993, U. Utrecht, The Netherlands, 1993, U. Wroclaw, Poland, 1993. Contbr. articles to profl. jours. NSF grantee, 1968-87; Sci. and Engring. Rsch. Coun. Gt. Britain fellow U. Edinburgh, Scotland, 1976. Mem. Am. Math. Soc., Math. Assn. Am., Israel Math. Union, Edinburgh Math. Soc. Achievements include research in the fields of harmonic analysis, topological groups, and probability theory. Office: Wayne State U Dept Math Detroit MI 48202

SCHREIBER, EILEEN SHER, artist; b. Denver; d. Michael Herschel and Sarah Deborah (Tannenbaum) Sher; student U. Utah, 1942-45, N.Y.U. extension, 1966-68, Montclair (N.J.) State Coll., 1975-79; also pvt. art study; m. Jonas Schreiber, Mar. 27, 1945; children—Jeffrey, Barbara, Michael. Exhibited Morris Mus. Arts and Scis., Morristown, N.J., 1965-73, N.J. State Mus., 1969, Lever House, N.Y.C., 1971, Paramus (N.J.) Mus., 1973, Newark Mus., 1978, Am. Water Color Soc., Audubon Artists, N.A.D. Gallery, N.Y.C., Pallazzo Vecchio Florence (Italy), Art Expo 1987, 1988, Newark Mus., 1991-92; represented in permanent collections Tex. A&M U., Sunbelt Computers, Phoenix, Ariz., State of N.J., Morris Mus., Seton Hall U., Bloomfield (N.J.) Coll., Barclay Bank of Eng., N.J., Somerset Coll., NYU, Morris County State Coll., Broad Nat. Bank, Newark, IBM, Am. Telephone Co., RCA, Johnson & Johnson, Champion Internat. Paper Co., SONY, Mitsubishi, Celanese Co., Squibb Corp., Nabisco, Nat. Bank Phila., NYU, Data Control, Sperry Univac, Ga. Pacific Co., Pub. Svc. Co. N.J., Diane Levine Gallery, Boston, Southwest Gallery, Long Beach Isl., N.J., others; also pvt. collections. Recipient awards N.J. Watercolor Soc., 1969, 72, Marian E. Halpern Memorial award Nat. Assn. Women Artists, 1970; 1st award in watercolor Hunterdon Art Center, 1972, Best in Show award Short Hills State Show, 1976, Tri-State Purchase award Somerset Coll., 1977, Art Expo, N.Y.C. 1987, 88, ; numerous others. Mem. Nat. Assn. Women Artists (chmn. watercolor jury; Collage award 1983, Marian Halpren meml. award 1995), Nat., N.J. Artists Equity, Printmaker Coun. Visual Artists (1st award in printmaking 1996). Home: 22 Powell Dr West Orange NJ 07052-1337

SCHREIBER, EVERETT CHARLES, JR., chemist, educator; b. Amityville, N.Y., Nov. 13, 1953; s. Everett Charles Sr. and Mary Elizabeth (Johnston) S.; m. Jane Karen Sklenar, July 19, 1980. BS, Pace U., 1975; PhD, U. Nebr., 1980. Rsch. assoc. SUNY, Stony Brook, 1980-82; asst. dir. rsch. Muscular Dystrophy Assn., N.Y.C., 1983-84; rsch. assoc. SUNY, 1984-86; spectroscopist G.E. NMR Instruments, Fremont, Calif., 1986-87; quality assurance engr. Varian NMR Instruments, Palo Alto, Calif., 1987-89, tech. tng. specialist, 1989-95, sr. tech. support chemist, 1995-96, sr. chemist, 1996—. Author of tng. texts in engring. and computers; editor Megabytes. V.p. Old Bailey Pl. Home Owners Assn., Fremont, 1989, 95-97, pres., 1990-93, bd. mem., 1994-95, v.p., 1995-96, pres., 1996-97; treas. Young Life, Mission Valley, Fremont, 1993-96. Mem. Am. Chem. Soc., Biophys. Soc., N.Y. Acad. Scis., Soc. Magnetic Resonance in Medicine. Republican. Roman Catholic. Avocations: photography, computers, model trains, music. Office: Varian NMR Instruments 3120 Hansen Way Palo Alto CA 94304-1030

SCHREIBER, GEORGE RICHARD, association executive, writer; b. Ironton, Ohio, July 4, 1922; s. George Joseph and Marie Frances (Heitzman) S.; m. Veva Jeanette Hopkins, May 14, 1945; children—Susan (Mrs. Arlan Shorey), George, Ellen (Mrs. Norman Hodge). A.B., St. Joseph's Coll., Rensselaer, Ind., 1943, L.H.D., 1974; M.A., U. Chgo., 1944. Exec. editor Billboard mag., 1945-60; editor, pub. Vend mag., 1946-66; editorial dir. Billboard Publs., 1966-70; pres., chief exec. officer Nat. Automatic Mdsg. Assn., Chgo., 1970-88, pres. emeritus, 1988—; pres., chief exec. Sunrise Books, 1994—; mem. staff and faculty U. Chgo., 1944-46. Author: Verses from the River Country, 1941, What Makes News, 1943, Automatic Selling, 1954, A Concise History of Vending in the U.S.A, 1965, revised 2d edit., 1990, The Bobby Baker Affair—How to Make Millions in Washington, 1964; contbg. author: Handbook of Modern Marketing, 1986, Vending For Investors-How to Spot Phony Deals, 1994, 2d edit., 1996. Chmn. Glenview (Ill.) Plan Commn., 1962-64, mayor, 1964-67; chmn. Region 1, Chgo. Area Transp. Study Group, 1962-63; bd. dirs. Rockefeller Meml. Chapel, U. Chgo., 1944-45; trustee St. Joseph's Coll., 1964—, chmn., 1970-76, life trustee, 1978—. Recipient Jesse H. Neal award for editorial achievement, 1964; dedication of St. Joseph's Coll. (Ind.) G. Richard Schreiber Dept. Humanities, 1987. Mem. The Authors Guild Inc., Am. Bus. Press (editorial bd.), Assn. Econs. Council, Am. Soc. Assn. Execs., Tavern Club, Internat. Club, Tower Club. Home: 735 Ravine Ave Lake Bluff IL 60044-2625

SCHREIBER, HARRY, JR., management consultant; b. Columbus, Ohio, Apr. 1, 1934; s. C. Harry and Audrey (Sard) S.; BS, Mass. Inst. Tech., 1955; MBA, Boston U., 1958; m. Margaret Ruth Heinzman, June 12, 1955; children: Margaret Elizabeth Schreiber Yeager, Thomas Edward, Amy Katherine Schreiber Garcia. CPA, N.Y. Accountant truck and coach div. Gen. Motors Corp., Pontiac, Mich., 1955; instr. Mass. Inst. Tech., 1958-62; pres. Data-Service, Inc., Boston, 1961-65; pres. Harry Schreiber Assos., Wellesley, Mass., 1965; mgr., nat. dir. merchandising consulting Peat, Marwick, Mitchell & Co., N.Y.C., 1966-70, partner, Chgo., 1970-75; chmn. bd. Close, Martin, Schreiber & Co., 1975-82; partner Deloitte Haskins & Sells, 1983-85; chmn. bd. Harry Schreiber & Assocs., Ltd., 1985—. Pub. Retail Working Papers, 1991—. Staff, Work Simplification Conf. Lake Placid, N.Y., 1960-61; Tobe retailing lectr. Harvard Bus. Sch., 1964. Served to 1st lt. AUS, 1956-58. Mem. Am. Inst. Indsl. Engrs. (chmn. data-processing div. 1964-66, chpt. v.p. 1961, 65, chmn. retail industries div. 1976-78), Com. Internat. Congress Transp. Confs., Assn. for Computing Machinery, Assn. for Systems Mgmt., Inst. Mgmt. Scis., Retail Rsch. Soc., Retail Fin. Execs., Nat. Retail Fedn. (retail systems specifications com., acctg. stds. com.), Food Distbn. Research Soc. (dir. 1972-78, pres. 1974), Japan-Am. Soc. Chgo. Republican. Methodist. Clubs: MIT Faculty; Hidden Creek Country (Reston, Va.), Chester River Yacht and Country Club (Chestertown, Md.); Army and Navy (Washington); Plaza (Chgo.). Home: 107 High St Chestertown MD 21620-1515 Office: 105 High St Chestertown MD 21620-1515

SCHREIBER, JAMES RALPH, obstetrics, gynecology researcher; b. Rosebud, Tex., May 29, 1946; m. Lester B. and Jane Elinore (Hodges) S.; m. Mary Celia Schmitt, Aug. 16, 1968; children: Lisa, Joseph, Laura, Cynthia. BA, Rice U., 1968; MD, Johns Hopkins U., 1972. Cert. Am. Coll. Ob-Gyn, Am. Bd. Reproductive Endocrinology. Intern. ob-gyn. U. So. Calif. Los Angeles County Hosp., 1972-73, resident ob-gyn., 1973-74, 76-78; fellow reproductive endocrinology NIH, Bethesda, Md., 1974-76; asst. prof. ob-gyn U. Calif., San Diego, 1978-82; assoc. prof. U. Chgo., 1982-87, prof., 1988-91; prof., chmn. dept. Washington U., St. Louis, 1991—. Contbr. articles to profl. jours. Grantee NIH, 1978—. Mem. Endocrine Soc., Soc. Gynecologic Investigation. Home: 22 Frontenac Estates Saint Louis MO 63131-2600 Office: Washington U Sch Medicine Dept Ob-Gyn 4911 Barnes Hospital Plz Saint Louis MO 63110-1003

SCHREIBER, KURT GILBERT, lawyer; b. Milw., Aug. 22, 1946; s. Raymond R. and Mildred L. (Kleist) S.; m. Nelda Beth Van Buren, May 3, 1974; children—Katharine Anne, Matthew Edward. A.B. in Econs., Cornell U., 1968; J.D., U. Mich., 1971. Bar: Wis. 1971, Tex. 1979. Internat. atty. Tenneco Internat. Holdings Co., London, 1974-78; atty. Tenneco Inc., Houston, 1978-80; 2d v.p., asst. gen. counsel Am. Gen. Corp., Houston, 1980-83, v.p., gen. counsel, 1983-84, sr. v.p., gen. counsel, 1984-93, sr. v.p., corp. sec., 1993-94; pvt. practice Houston, 1994-96; exec. v.p., gen. counsel Direct Gen. Corp., Nashville, 1996—. Fellow Tex. Bar Found.; mem. ABA, Wis. Bar Assn., Tex. Bar Assn., Cumberland Club. Home: 524 Turtle Creek Dr Brentwood TN 37027

SCHREIBER, MARVIN MANDEL, agronomist, educator; b. Springfield, Mass., Oct. 17, 1925; s. William and Florence Schreiber; m. Phyllis E. Altman, Dec. 18, 1949; 1 child, Michelle. BS, U. Mass., 1950; MS, U. Ariz., 1951; PhD, Cornell U., 1954. Asst. prof. dept. agronomy Cornell U., Ithaca, N.Y., 1954-59; assoc. prof. dept. botany and plant pathology Purdue U., West Lafayette, Ind., 1959-73—, prof., 1973—; rsch. agronomist Agrl. Rsch. Svc. USDA, West Lafayette, 1959—. Fellow AAAS, Am. Soc. Agronomy, Weed Sci. Soc. Am.; mem. Internat. Weed Sci. Soc. (pres. 1979-81), Controlled Release Soc., Coun. Agrl. Sci. and Tech., Sigma Xi. Avocations: golf, gardening. Office: Dept Botany & Plant Pathology Purdue U Lilly Hall Life Scis West Lafayette IN 47907

SCHREIBER, MELVYN HIRSH, radiologist; b. Galveston, Tex., May 28, 1931; s. Edward and Sue Schreiber; m. Laurentina; children—William, Diane, Karen, Lori. M.D., U. Tex. Med. Br., Galveston, 1955. Diplomate: Am. Bd. Radiology (trustee 1987—). Intern U. Tex. Med. Br., Galveston, 1955-56; resident U. Tex. Med. Br., 1956-59, asst. prof. radiology, 1961-64, asso. prof., 1964-67, prof., 1967—, chmn. dept. radiology, 1976-91. Author: Old Dog, New Tricks, A Collection of Essays, 1995. Served as capt. M.C. U.S. Army, 1959-61. Markle Found. scholar, 1963-68. Fellow Am. Coll. Radiology; mem. Assn. Univ. Radiologists (pres. 1974-75). Office: U Tex Med Br Dept Radiology Galveston TX 77555

SCHREIBER, PAUL SOLOMON, lawyer; b. Krakow, Poland, Mar. 29, 1941; came to U.S., 1949; s. John and Betty (Silber) S.; m. Joan A. Perlmutter, Mar. 20, 1971; children: Douglas Arun, Stacey Lauren. BS, CCNY, 1963; LLB, NYU, 1966, LLM, 1967; postgrad., U. Paris, 1967-68. Bar: N.Y. 1966. Assoc. Marshal, Bratter, Greene, Allison & Tucker, N.Y.C., 1969-76, ptnr., 1976-82; ptnr. Kramer, Levin, Naftalis, Nessen, Kamin & Frankel, N.Y.C., 1982-94, Shearman & Sterling, N.Y.C., 1994—; bd. dirs. Harbor Trust Co., Hoboken, N.J., 1985-92. Editor: Annual Survey Am. Law; co-author articles, papers and revs. Trustee, v.p. Park Ave. Synagogue, N.Y.C., 1985—; bd. dirs. Am. Friends of the Rambam Med. Ctr., N.Y.C., 1989—, N.Y.C. chpt. of Nat. Multiple Sclerosis Soc., 1991—, Sch. for Strings, 1994-96; bd. overseers Rabbinical Sch. Jewish Theol. Sem., 1995-96. Arthur Garfield Hayes fellow; Ford Found. fellow. Democrat. Jewish. Office: Shearman & Sterling 599 Lexington Ave New York NY 10022-6030

SCHREIBER, SALLY ANN, lawyer; b. El Paso, Tex., July 23, 1951; d. Warren Thomas and Joyce (Honey) S.; children: Amanda Honey, Ryan Thorp Luther. BBA, U. N.Mex., 1973; JD, Stanford U., 1976. Bar: Calif. 1976, Tex. 1977. Assoc. Johnson & Swanson, Dallas, 1976-81, ptnr., 1981-89; mem. firm Johnson & Gibbs, P.C., Dallas, 1989-93; of counsel Cox & Smith, Inc., Dallas, 1993-94; shareholder Munsch Hardt Kopf Harr & Dinan, P.C., Dallas, 1994—; spkr. Advanced Mgmt. Rsch. Internat., Dallas, 1984, U. Tex., Austin, 1984, 89, 91, 93, Houston, 1994, Dallas, 1995, State Bar of Tex., Dallas, 1989, Lubbock, Arlington, San Antonio, 1990, Houston, 1994, South Tex. Coll. Law, Houston, 1990, 94, U. Houston, 1996, 97, Dallas, 1996, 97, Dallas Bus. Jour., 1997. Editor Stanford U. Law Rev., 1975-76; co-author paper Internat. Bar Assn., 1986. Bd. dirs. The Lyric Opera of Dallas, 1982-86, bd. trustees, 1986-90; mem. law sch. bd. vis. Stanford (Calif.) U., 1981-84; dir. Tex. Bus. Law Found., 1989—, treas. 1994-96, sec. 1996—. Mem. ABA, Tex. Bar Assn. (revision corp. law com. 1981—, vice chair 1993—, ptnrship. law com. 1985—, ltd. liability company com. 1992—, opinion com. 1989—, bus. law sect. coun. 1996—), Calif. Bar Assn., Dallas Bar Assn. Home: 2737 Purdue Ave Dallas TX 75225-7910 Office: Munsch Hardt Kopf Harr & Dinan PC 4000 Fountain Pl 1445 Ross Ave Dallas TX 75202-2812

SCHREIBER, WILLIAM FRANCIS, electrical engineer; b. N.Y.C., Sept. 18, 1925. BS, Columbia U., 1945, MS, 1947; PhD, Harvard U., 1953. Jr. engr. Sylvania Elec. Products, Inc., 1947-49; rsch. assoc. Harvard U., Cambridge, Mass., 1953; rsch. physicist Technicolor Corp., 1953-59; prof. elec. engring. Mass. Inst. Tech., Cambridge, 1959-90, dir. advanced tv rsch. program, 1983-89. Fellow IEEE; mem. Nat. Acad. Engring., Sigma Xi. Office: MIT M/S 36-545 Cambridge MA 02139

SCHREIER, PETER, tenor; b. Meissen, Germany, July 29, 1935. Ed., Dresden Hochschule für Musik, Germany. With Dresden State Opera, Germany, 1959-63, Berlin Staatsoper, Germany, 1963. Appearances include Vienna State Opera, Salzburg Festival, La Scala, Milan, Sadler's Wells, London, Met. Opera, N.Y.C., Teatro Colon, Buenos Aires; recital debut London, 1978; debut as conductor, 1969; has conducted recordings of several choral works by J.S. Bach and Mozart. Office: Kammersänger, Calberlastr 13, D-01326 Dresden Germany

SCHREINER, ALBERT WILLIAM, physician, educator; b. Cin., Feb. 15, 1926; s. Albert William and Ruth Mary (Neuer) S.; m. Jean Tellstrom, Dec. 12, 1953; 1 child, David William. BS, U. Cin., 1947, MD, 1949. Diplomate: Am. Bd. Internal Medicine. Clin. investigator VA Hosp., Cin., 1957-59, chief med. service, 1959-68, dir. dept. internal medicine, 1968-93; dir. resident program internal medicine Christ Hosp., Cin., 1978-87; mem. faculty U. Cin. Coll. Medicine, 1955—, assoc. prof. medicine, 1962-67, prof. internal medicine, 1967—; attending physician Cin. Gen. Hosp., 1957—; cons. to med. dir. Gen. Electric, 1987—; med. dirs. United Home Care Hospice, 1993—, United Home Care Agy. Contbr. articles to tech. jours. Bd. dirs., chmn. health com. Community Action Commn., 1968-701 trustee Drake Meml. Hosp., 1975-78, Leukemia Found. Southwest Ohio, Cancer Control, Am. Cancer Soc., bd. dirs. Hamilton County unit, 1990; bd. dirs. Gamble Inst. Med. Rsch., Cin., 1991—. Fellow ACP; mem. N.Y. Acad. Scis., Am. Fedn. Clin. Rsch., Ohio Med. Assn., Ohio Soc. Internal Medicine (trustee 1978, sec.-treas. 1981-85, v.p. 1982-83, pres. 1984-85), Clin. Soc. Internal Medicine (pres. 1979-80), Assn. Program Dirs. Internal Medicine, Am. Soc. Clin. Rsch. Program Dirs. Internal Medicine, Am. Leukemia Soc. (med. adv. exec. bd.), Am. Cancer Soc. (bd. dirs. Hamilton County unit 1990), Phi Beta Kappa, Sigma Xi. Episcopalian. Home: 8040 S Clippinger Dr Cincinnati OH 45243-3248 Office: 2139 Auburn Ave Cincinnati OH 45219-2906

SCHREINER, GEORGE E., nephrologist, educator, writer; b. Buffalo, Apr. 26, 1922; s. George Frederick and Eleanor (Kreig) S.; m. Joanne Baker, Apr. 3, 1948; children: George F., Mary E., Meredith Schreiner Maclay, William P., Sara B. Schreiner Kendall, Lise Schreiner Salmon, Peter K., Robert P. (dec.). AB magna cum laude, Canisius Coll., 1943, HLD (hon.), 1973; MD cum laude, Georgetown U., 1946, HLD, 1973, ScD (hon.), 1987. Intern Boston City Hosp., 1946-47; fellow in nephrology N.Y. U., 1947-50; resident in medicine Washington VA Hosp., 1950-51; dir. renal clinic Georgetown U. Hosp., 1951-52, 55-61, instr. medicine, 1955-58, asst. prof. medicine, 1958-61, asso. prof. medicine, dir. renal and electrolyte div., 1961-70, prof. medicine, dir. nephrology div., 1970-87, Disting. prof. medicine, 1987—; mem. staff Arlington Hosp., D.C. Gen. Hosp.; cons. VA Hosp., Walter Reed Army Hosp., Speakers Bur., Merck, Hoechst-Roussel, Baxter, George E. Schreiner Premed. Ctr., Canisius Coll. Editor in chief Am. Soc. Artificial Internal Organs, 1957-86, editor emeritus, 1986—; editor in chief: Procs. of Clin. Dialysis, Transplant Forum and Controveries in Nephrology, 1979-84; co-editor: 20 Years Nephrology at Grosshadern; contbr. chpts. to books, articles to profl. jours. Bd. dirs. Washington Heart Assn.; bd. trustees Internat. Soc. for Art Orgns., 1986—; bd. sponsors Nat. Kidney Found.; governing bd. Ctr. for Crisis Counseling, Washington; mem. com. academics, com. devel., bd. trustees Canisius Coll., Buffalo, 1988-94. Recipient Davidson award Med. Soc. D.C., Pres.'s award, 1979, David Hume award Nat. Kidney Found., 1980, Pub. Svc. award NASA, Nettuno d'Argento award U. Bologna, 1988, Achievement award Am. Assn. Kidney Patients, Laureate award Am. Coll. Physicians, Washington; guest of honor Greece Soc. Nephrology-Internat. Congress on Acute Renal Failure. Fellow ACP, Royal Soc. Physicians and Surgeons (Glasgow, Walton lectr.); mem. Soc. Exptl. Biology, Nat. Drug Rsch. Bd., Am. Soc. Physiology, Am. Soc. Pharmacology and Clin. Therapeutics, So. Salt, Water and Kidney Club, Am. Soc. Artificial Internal Organs (past pres.), Internat. Soc. Artificial Organs (life trustee), Nat. Kidney Found. (past pres.), Internat. Soc. Nephrology (pres. 1978-81, past pres., mem. exec. com. 1981-84), Am. Soc. Nephrology (past pres., co-editor in chief Nephron, John Peters award 1989), Assn. Am. Physicians, Am. Soc. Clin. Investigation, Am. Fedn. for Clin. Rsch. (past pres., past treas.), D.C. Med. Soc., Washington Heart Assn. (past pres.), Renal Transplant Physicians, Coun. Transplantation, Am. Soc. Hypertension, Am. Clin. and Climatologic Assn., Wash. Acad. Medicine (admission com. 1987-90, chmn. 1990), Cosmos Club (Washington), Duckwoods Country Club (Kitty Hawk, N.C.), Tralee Golf Club (Kerry, Ireland). Roman Catholic. Home and Office: PO Box 199 Great Falls VA 22066-0199 Office: Georgetown U Hosp 3800 Reservoir Rd NW Washington DC 20007-2113

SCHREINER, JOHN CHRISTIAN, economics consultant, software publisher; b. Los Angeles, Nov. 2, 1933; s. Alexander and Margaret S.; m. Marie Nielsen, June 19, 1967; children: Christian Alexander, Carl Arthur, Elizabeth, Nathan Alexander. B.S.M.E., U. Utah, 1958; M.B.A., Harvard U., 1960; Ph.D., UCLA, 1970. Chartered fin. analyst. Design engr. Eimco Corp., Salt Lake City and N.Y.C., 1957-59; credit exec. James Talcott, Inc., N.Y.C. and Boston, 1960-65; lectr. mgmt. U. Utah, 1965-66; mem. faculty Grad. Sch. Mgmt., U. Minn., Mpls., 1969-84; chmn. dept. fin. and ins. Grad. Sch. Mgmt., U. Minn., 1973-74, 76-81; pres. The Sebastian Group, Inc., 1984—; dir. Deluxe Corp.; cons. to corps. and govt. agys. Co-author: Executive Recruiting: How Companies Obtain Management Talent, 1960; contbr. articles to profl. jours. Mem. Fin. Execs. Inst., Fin. Analysts Fedn., Tau Beta Pi, Phi Kappa Phi. Republican. Mem. Ch. Jesus Christ of Latter-day Saints (missionary, Ger. 1953-56). Club: Harvard Bus. Sch. Minn. Office: The Sebastian Group Inc 5730 Duluth St Minneapolis MN 55422-4000

SCHREMPF, DETLEF, professional basketball player; b. Leverkusen, Germany, Jan. 21, 1963. Student, U. Washington. Forward Dallas Mavericks, 1985-89, Indiana Pacers, 1989-93, Seattle Supersonics, 1993—; player West German Olympic Team, 1984, 92. Recipient Sixth Man award NBA, 1991, 92; mem. NBA All-Star team, 1993. *

SCHRENK, W(ILLI) JUERGEN, health care company executive; b. Dachau, Germany, June 19, 1945; came to U.S., 1972; s. Willi Schrenk and Irmgard (Urbanek) Meinhardt; m. Ruth Halfenberg, Nov. 10, 1971; 1 child, Ralph Michael. PhD, U. Cologne, Germany, 1972. Rsch. fellow Harvard Med. Sch., Boston, 1972-73; guest scientist Nat. Cancer Inst., Bethesda, Md., 1972-73; asst. rsch. prof. U. Calif., Santa Barbara, 1974-77; sr. scientist Abbott Labs., North Chicago, Ill., 1977-79; sci. dir. Boehringer Mannheim GmbH, Tutzing, Germany, 1979-85; sr. dir. R & D Boehringer Mannheim Corp., Indpls., 1986-89; sr. v.p. R & D Gen-Probe, San Diego, 1989-90; v.p. R & D Wampole Labs., Cranbury, N.J., 1990-94; v.p. tech. mgmt. Corange Internat. Ltd., Bermuda, 1994-95; sr. v.p. tech. mgmt., v.p. bus. devel. therapeutics Boehringer Mannheim Group, Gaithersburg, Md., 1996—, sr. v.p. bus. devel. therapeutics divsn., 1997—. Contbr. articles to profl. jours; patentee in field. Established nature preserves in U.S. and Fed. Republic of Germany, 1975-85. Fellow Fed. Republic of Germany, 1964-70, Deutsche Forschungs-Gemeinschaft, 1972-74. Mem. Nature Conservancy, World Wildlife Fund. Avocations: nature photography, skiing, hiking, traveling. Home: 1 Stream Valley Ct Laytonsville MD 20882-1273 Office: Boehringer Mannheim Tech Off 101 Orchard Ridge Dr Gaithersburg MD 20878-1952

SCHREYER, WILLIAM ALLEN, retired investment firm executive; b. Williamsport, Pa., Jan. 13, 1928; s. William L. and Elizabeth (Engel) S.; m. Joan Legg, Oct. 17, 1953; 1 child, DrueAnne Frazier. BA, Pa. State U., 1948. With Merrill Lynch, Inc. and predecessors, N.Y.C., 1948-93; CEO Merrill Lynch & Co., N.Y.C., 1984-92, chmn., 1985-93; chmn. emeritus, 1993—; bd. dirs. Schering-Plough Corp., Callaway Golf Co., Deere & Co., Iridium LLC, Willis Corroon Group. Trustee Ctr. for Strategic and Internat. Studies, Pa. State U., 1986—, chmn. bd. trustees, 1993-96. With USAF, 1955-56. Mem. Econ. Club N.Y., River Club, Links Club, Saturn Club, Springdale Golf Club, Bedens Brook Club, Eldorado Country Club, Georgetown Club, Met. Club, Old Baldy Club, Tournament Players Club, Nassau Club, The Carnegie Club at Skibo Castle, Knights of Malta. Roman Catholic. Office: Merrill Lynch & Co Inc 800 Scudders Mill Rd Plainsboro NJ 08536-1606

SCHRIBER, THOMAS JUDE, computer and information systems educator, researcher; b. Flint, Mich., Oct. 28, 1935; s. Francis Charles and Alma Marie (Jeannot) S.; m. Cornelia Ann Sneed, June 24, 1967; children: Sarah Elizabeth, John Cornelius, Maria Adams. B.S., U. Notre Dame, 1957; M.S.E., U. Mich., 1958, M.A. in Math., 1959, Ph.D., 1964. Asst. prof. Eastern Mich. U., Ypsilanti, 1963-66; asst. prof. U. Mich., Ann Arbor, 1966-69, assoc. prof., 1969-72, prof. Grad. Sch. Bus. Adminstrn., 1972—; chmn. simulation using GPSS U. Mich., 1969-92, U. Louvain, Belgium, 1987-89; vis. scholar Stanford U., Palo Alto, Calif., 1972-73, Swiss Fed. Tech. U., Zurich, 1987, Nat. U. Singapore, 1995; cons. Ford Motor Co., Dearborn, Mich., 1970-72, Stanford Research Inst., Palo Alto, 1973, Monsanto Chem. Co., St. Louis, 1978, Wolverine Software Corp., Annandale, Va., 1981-94, Occidental Petroleum, 1982, Exxon Prodn. Research, Houston, 1984-85, Gen. Motors Corp., Troy, Mich., 1984-85, Electronic Data Systems, Troy, 1985-86; chmn. bd. Winter Simulation Conf. Series, 1981-83; mem. U.S.-USSR Joint Sci. and Tech. Exchange Agreements, Moscow, 1977. Author: Fundamentals of Flowcharting, 1969, FORTRAN Case Studies for Business Applications, 1970, Simulation Using GPSS, 1974, An Introduction to Simulation Using GPSS/H, 1991; editor: FORTRAN Applications in Business Administration, 3 vol. series, 1970, 71, 74; co-author: Managing and Controlling Growing Harbour Terminals, 1997; co-editor: Proceedings of the 1976 Bicentennial Winter Simulation Conference, 1976; assoc. editor: Internat. Jour. of Flexible Mfg. Systems, 1987—. NSF fellow, 1957-60; Fulbright fellow, 1961; Office Naval Research grantee, 1981-83. Fellow Decision Scis. Inst.; mem. Assn. Computing Machinery (nat. lectr. 1969-70), INFORMS (recipient Disting. Svc. award Coll. of Simulation 1996), Soc. for Computer Simulation. Roman Catholic. Home: 2116 Dorset Rd Ann Arbor MI 48104-2604 Office: U Mich Grad Sch Bus Adminstrn Ann Arbor MI 48109

SCHRIEFFER, JOHN ROBERT, physics educator, science administrator; b. Oak Park, Ill., May 31, 1931; s. John Henry and Louise (Anderson) S.; m. Anne Grete Thomsen, Dec. 30, 1960; children: Anne Bolette, Paul Karsten, Anne Regina. BS, MIT, 1953; MS, U. Ill., 1954, PhD, 1957, ScD, 1974; ScD (hon.), Tech. U., Munich, Germany, 1968, U. Geneva, 1968, U. Pa., 1973, U. Cin., 1977, U. Tel Aviv, 1987, U. Ala., 1990. NSF postdoctoral fellow U. Birmingham, Eng., also; Niels Bohr Inst., Copenhagen, 1957-58; asst. prof. U. Chgo., 1958-59; asst. prof., then assoc. prof. U. Ill., 1959-62; prof. U. Pa., Phila., 1962-79; Mary Amanda Wood prof. physics U. Pa., 1964-79; Andrew D. White prof. at large Cornell U., 1969-75; prof. U. Calif., Santa Barbara, 1980-91, Chancellor's prof., 1984-91, dir. Inst. for Theoretical Physics, 1984-89; Univ. prof. Fla. State U., Tallahassee, 1992—, Univ. Eminent Scholar prof., 1995—, chief scientist Nat. High Magnetic Field Lab., 1992—. Author: Theory of Superconductivity, 1964. Mem. Pres.' Com. on Nat. Medal of Sci., 1996. Guggenheim fellow Copenhagen, 1967; Los Alamos Nat. Lab. fellow; Recipient Comstock prize Nat. Acad. Sci.; Nobel Prize for Physics, 1972; John Ericsson medal Am. Soc. Swedish Engrs., 1976; Alumni Achievement award U. Ill., 1979; recipient Nat. Medal of Sci., 1984; Exxon faculty fellow, 1979-89. Fellow Am. Phys. Soc. (v.p. 1994, pres.-elect 1995, pres. 1996, past pres. 1997, Oliver E. Buckley solid state physics prize 1986); mem. NAS (coun. 1990—), Am. Acad. Arts and Scis., Coun. Nat. Acad. Sci., Royal Danish Acad. Scis. and Letters, Acad. Sci. USSR, Nat. Medal Sci. com. Office: Fla State UNHMFL 1800 E Paul Dirac Dr Tallahassee FL 32310

SCHRIER, ARNOLD, historian, educator; b. N.Y.C., May 30, 1925; s. Samuel and Yetta (Levine) S.; m. Sondra Weinshelbaum, June 12, 1949; children—Susan Lynn, Jay Alan, Linda Lee, Paula Kay. Student, Bethany Coll., W.Va., 1943-44, Ohio Wesleyan U., 1944-45; B.S., Northwestern U., 1949, M.A., 1950, Ph.D. (Social Sci. Research Council fellow, Univ. fellow), 1956. Asst. prof. history U. Cin., 1956-61, assoc. prof., 1961-66, prof., 1966-95, dir. grad. studies history, 1969-78, Walter C. Langsam prof. modern European history, 1972-95; Walter C. Langsam prof. history emeritus, 1995—; vis. asst. prof. history Northwestern U., Evanston, Ill., 1960; vis. assoc. prof. history Ind. U., Bloomington, 1965-66; vis. lectr. Russian history Duke U., 1966; disting. vis. prof. U.S. Air Force Acad., 1983-84; dir. NDEA Inst. World History for Secondary Sch. Tchrs., U. Cin., 1965; Am. del. Joint U.S.-USSR Textbook Study Commn., 1989. Author: Ireland and the American Emigration, 1958, reissued, 1970, paperback edit., 1997, The Development of Civilization, 1961-62, Modern European Civilization, 1963, Living World History, 1964, rev., 1993, Twentieth Century World, 1974, History and Life: the World and Its People, 1977, rev., 1993, A Russian Looks at America, 1979. Pres. Ohio Acad. History, 1973-74, Midwest Slavic Conf., 1980. Served with USNR, 1943-46, 52-54. Recipient Disting. Svc. award Ohio Acad. History, 1992; Am. Council Learned Socs. fgn. area fellow, 1963-64. Mem. World History Assn. (v.p. 1986-88, pres. 1988-90). Home: 10 Diplomat Dr Cincinnati OH 45215-2073 Office: Univ Cincinnati Dept History Mail Location 373 Cincinnati OH 45221

SCHRIER, ROBERT WILLIAM, physician, educator; b. Indpls., Feb. 19, 1936; s. Arthur E. and Helen M. Schrier; m. Barbara Lindley, June 14, 1959; children: David, Debbie, Douglas, Derek, Denise. BA, Depauw U., 1957; MD, Ind. U., 1962. Intern Marion County (Ind.) Hosp., 1962; resident U. Wash., Seattle, 1963-65; asst. prof. U. Calif. Med. Ctr., San Francisco, 1969-72, assoc. mem., 1970-72, assoc. dir. renal div., 1971-72, assoc. prof., 1972; prof., head renal disease U. Colo. Sch. Med., Denver, 1972-92, prof., chmn. Dept.of Medicine, 1976—. Pres. Nat. Kidney Found., 1984-86. With U.S. Army, 1966-69. Mem. ACP (master), Am. Soc. Nephrology (treas. 1979-81, pres. 1983), Internat. Soc. Nephrology (treas. 1981-90, v.p. 1990-95, pres. 1995-97), Am. Clin. and Climatol. Assn. (v.p. 1986), Assn. Am. Physicians (pres. 1994-95), Western Assn. Physicians (pres. 1982), Inst. of Medicine, Nat. Acad. of Scis., Alpha Omega Alpha. Office: U Colo Health Scis Ctr Dept Medicine 4200 E 9th Ave Denver CO 80220-3706

SCHRIER, STANLEY LEONARD, physician, educator; b. N.Y.C., Jan. 2, 1929; s. Harry and Nettie (Schwartz) S.; m. Peggy Helen Pepper, June 6, 1953; children: Rachel, Leslie, David. A.B., U. Colo., 1949; M.D., Johns Hopkins U., 1954. Diplomate Am. Bd. Internal Medicine (chmn. subsplty. bd. hematology). Intern Oster Med. Service, Johns Hopkins Hosp., 1954-55; resident U. Mich., Ann Arbor, 1955-56, U. Chgo. Hosp., 1958-59; sr. asst. surgeon USPHS, 1956-58; instr. medicine Stanford Sch. Medicine, Calif., 1959-60; asst. prof. medicine Stanford Sch. Medicine, 1960-63, assoc. prof., 1963-72, prof. medicine, 1972-95, chief divsn. hematology, 1968-94; vis. scientist Weizmann Inst., Rehovot, Israel, 1967-68; vis. prof. Oxford U., Eng., 1975-76, Hebrew U., Jerusalem, 1982-83. John and Mary Markle scholar, 1961; recipient Kaiser award Stanford U., 1972, Kaiser award Stanford U., 1974, 75, David Rytand award, 1982, Eleanor Roosevelt Union Internationale Contre le Cancer award, 1975-76. Fellow ACP; mem. Am. Soc. Hematology, Am. Physiol. Soc., Soc. Exptl. Biology and Medicine, Am. Soc. Clin. Investigation, Western Assn. Physicians, Assn. Am. Physicians. Democrat. Jewish. Office: Stanford U Sch Medicine 300 Pasteur Dr Palo Alto CA 94304-2203

SCHRIESHEIM, ALAN, research administrator; b. N.Y.C., Mar. 8, 1930; s. Morton and Frances (Greenberg) S.; m. Beatrice D. Brand, June 28, 1953; children: Laura Lynn, Robert Alan. BS in Chemistry, Poly. Inst. Bklyn., 1951; PhD in Phys. Organic Chemistry, Pa. State U., 1954; DSc (hon.), No. Ill. U., 1991; PhD (hon.), Ill. Inst. Tech., Chgo., 1992; Laureate, Lincoln Acad., 1996. Chemist Nat. Bur. Standards, 1954-56; with Exxon Research & Engring. Co., 1956-83, dir. corp. research, 1975-79; gen. mgr. Exxon Engring., 1979-83; sr. dep. lab. dir., chief operating officer Argonne Nat. Lab., 1983-84, lab. dir., CEO, 1984-96, dir. emeritus, 1996—; prof. chemistry dept. U. Chgo., 1984-96, lectr. bus. sch., 1997—, lectr. Bus. Sch., 1996—; prin. Washington Adv. Group, 1996—; Karcher lectr. U. Okla., 1977; Hurd lectr. Northwestern U., 1980; Rosensteil lectr. Brandeis U., 1982; Welch Found. lectr., 1987; com. svc. NRC, 1980—; vis. com. chemistry dept. MIT, 1977-82; mem. vis. com. mech. engring. and aerospace dept. Princeton (N.J.) U., 1983-87, mem. vis. com. chemistry dept., 1983-87; mem. Pure and Applied Chemistry Com.; del. to People's Republic of China, 1978; mem. Presdl. Nat. Commn. on Superconductivity, 1989-91, U.S.-USSR Joint Commn. on Basic Sci. Rsch, 1990-93; mem. U.S. nat com. Internat. Union Pure and Applied Chemistry, 1982-85; mem. magnetic fusion adv. com. Div. Phys. Scis. U. Chgo. Magnetic Fusion adv. com. to U.S. DOE, 1983-86; mem. Dept. Energy Rsch. Adv. Bd., 1983-85, Congl. Adv. Com. on Sci. and Tech., 1985-96; mem. vis. coms. Stanford (Calif.) U., U. Utah, Tex. A&M U., Lehigh U.; bd. govs. Argonne Nat. Lab.; mem. adv. com. on space systems and tech. NASA, 1987-93; mem. nuclear engring. and engring. physics vis. com. U. Wis., Madison; mem. Coun. Gt. Lakes Govs. Regional Econ. Devel. Commn. 1987—, rev. bd. Compact Ignition Tomamak Princeton U., 1988-91; advisor Sears Investment Mgmt. Co., 1988-89; bd. dirs. Petroleum Rsch. Fund, ARCH Devel. Corp., HEICO, Rohm and Haas Co., Valley Indsl. Assn., Coun. on Superconductivity for Am. Competitiveness; mem. State of Ill. Commn. on the Future of Pub. Svc., 1990-92; co-chair Indsl. Rsch. Inst. Nat. Labs./Industry Panel, 1984-87; mem. Nat Acad. Engring. Adv. Commn. on Tech. and Soc., 1991-92, Sun Electric Corp. Bd., 1991-92, U.S. House of Reps. subcom. on Sci.-Adv. Group on Renewing U.S. Sci. Policy, 1992-96; mem. Chgo. Acad. of Scis. acad. coun., 1994—; mem. adv. bd. Chemtech; mem. sr. action group on R&D investment strategies Ctr. for Strategic & Internat. Studies 1995; bd. vis. Astronomy and Astrophysics Pa. State U., 1995—. Adv. bd. Chemtech, 1970-85; editl. bd. Rsch. & Devel., 1988-92, Superconductor Industry, 1988-95; patentee in field. Mem. spl. vis. com. Field Mus. of Natural History, Chgo., 1987-88; bd. dirs. LaRabida Children's Hosp. and Rsch. Ctr., 1987-95, Children's Meml. Hosp., Children's Meml. Inst. for Edn. and Rsch.; trustee The Latin Sch. of Chgo., 1990-92; adv. bd. WBEZ Chicagland Pub. Radio Cmty., 1990-96; mem. Conservation Found. DuPage County, 1983-96, Econ. Devel. Adv. Commn. of DuPage County, 1984-88, State of Ill. Gov.'s Commn. on Sci. and Tech., 1986—, Inst. for Ill. Council Advisors, 1988—, Ill. Coalition Bd. Dirs., 1989—, Inst. for Ill. Adv. Rev. Panel, 1986-88, NASA Sci. Tech. Adv. Com. Manpower Requirements Ad Hoc Rev. Team, 1988-91, State of Ill. Gov. Sci. and Exec. com., 1989—, U. Ill. Engring. Vis. com., Urbana-Champaign, 1986-95; trustee Tchrs. Acad. for Math. and Sci. Tchrs. in Chgo., 1990—; bd. visitors astronomy & astrophysics Pa. State U., 1995—. Recipient Outstanding Alumni Fellow award Pa. State U., 1985; laureate Lincoln Acad. Ill., 1996; Disting. fellow Poly. U., 1989. Fellow AAAS (coun. del. chem. sect. 1986-92, bd. dirs. 1992-96, sci. engring. and pub. policy com. 1992, standing com. audit 1992, selection com. to bring FSU scientists to ann. mtg. 1995—), N.Y. Acad. Scis.; mem. NAE (adv. com. tech. and soc. 1991-92, chair study fgn. participation in U.S. R&D 1993-96, mem. program adv. com. 1992-94, NRC com. on dual use tech. 1996-97), AIChE (AIChE award com. 1992—), Am. Chem. Soc. (petroleum chemistry award 1969, chmn. petroleum divsn., councilor, com. on chemistry and pub. affairs 1983-91, joint bd. coun. com. on sci. 1983-87, award in petroleum chemistry com. 1995-96), Am. Mgmt. Assn. (R&D coun. 1988—), Nat. Conf. Advancement Rsch. (conf. com. 1985—, site selection com. 1994, conf. com. 50th ann. 1996), Am. Petroleum Inst. (rsch. coord. coun.), Am. Nuclear Soc., Rohm and Haas (bd. dirs.), Indsl. Rsch. Inst. (fed. adv. com. to Fed. Sci. and Tech. Com. 1992-96, co-chmn. Nat. Labs. Indsl. Panel 1984-87, sr. action group on R&D Investment Strategies), Ctr. Strategic and Internat. Studies (sr. action group 1995-96), Carlton Club (bd. govs. 1992—), Cosmos Club, Comml. Club, Econ. Club, Comml. Club, Sigma Xi, Phi Lambda Upsilon. Home: 1440 N Lake Shore Dr Apt 31ac Chicago IL 60610-1686 Office: Argonne Nat Lab 9700 Cass Ave Argonne IL 60439-4803

SCHRIEVER, BERNARD ADOLPH, management consultant; b. Bremen, Germany, Sept. 14, 1910; came to U.S., 1917, naturalized, 1923; s. Adolph Niholaus and Elizabeth (Milch) S.; m. Dora Brett, Jan. 3, 1938; children: Brett Arnold, Dodie Elizabeth Schriever Moeller, Barbara Alice Schriever Allan. B.S., Tex. A&M U., 1931; M.S.M.E., Stanford U., 1942; D.Sc. (hon.), Creighton U., 1958, Rider Coll., 1958, Adelphia Coll., 1959, Rollins Coll., 1959; D.Aero. Sci. (hon.), U. Mich., 1961; D.Eng. (hon.), Bklyn. Poly. Inst., 1961; LL.D. (hon.), Loyola U., Los Angeles, 1960. Commd. 2d lt. U.S. Army Air Force, 1938; advanced through grades to gen. U.S. Air Force, 1961; comdr. ICBM Program, 1954-59, AFSC, 1959-66; ret., 1966; chmn. bd. Schriever & McKee, Washington, 1971-87; cons. B.A. Schriever, 1987—. Decorated D.S.M., D.S.M. with oak leaf cluster, Legion of Merit, Air medal, Purple Heart; named to Aviation Hall of Fame, 1980; recipient Forrestal award, 1987. Hon. fellow AIAA; mem. NAE, Am. Astron. Soc., Air Force Assn. Club: Burning Tree. Home: 4501 Dexter St NW Washington DC 20007-1116 Office: 2300 M St NW Ste 900 Washington DC 20037-1434

SCHRIEVER, FRED MARTIN, energy, environmental and information technology, satellite systems executive; b. N.Y.C.; s. Samuel and Sara S.; m. Cheri G. Spatt; children: Melissa Ann, Elizabeth Ellen. BME, Poly. U. N.Y., 1956, MME, 1958. Registered profl. engr., N.Y., Wash. cert. mgmt. cons. Chief engr. divsn. Sperry Corp., N.Y.C., 1956-64; ptnr. Booz, Allen and Hamilton, N.Y.C. and Washington, 1964-71; sr. v.p. Reliance Group Holdings, Inc., N.Y.C., 1971-96; chmn., pres. RCG Internat. Inc., N.Y.C., 1971-96; chmn. Eurosat Holdings, Inc., 1995-97; Bd. dirs. Hagler Bailly Inc. Fellow Inst. of Dirs., Inst. Mgmt. Consultants U.K.; mem. ASME, Inst. Mgmt. Cons., Chemists Club. Club: Metropolitan. Home: PO Box 32 Westport CT 06881-0032

SCHRIMSHER, JERRY JAMES, diversified financial services company executive; b. Homegrove, Tex., July 23, 1935; s. Archie A. and Lennie S.; m. Sherry L. Moore, July 29, 1966; children: Tasia C., Jerry J. II, Stan A. B of Career Arts in Mgmt./Aviation, Dallas Bapt. U., 1986; M of Liberal Arts, So. Meth. U., 1992. CLU, ChFC; registered investment advisor, SEC. Gen. foreman Tex. Instruments, Inc., Dallas, 1960-70; v.p. I.R.A., Dallas, 1970-74; pres. Am. Retirement, Dallas, 1974—; mem. Dallas Estate Planning, 1982; accident counselor FAA, Dallas, 1973—. Contbr. articles to profl. jours. With USAF, 1956-60. Mem. U.S. Parachute Assn. (life, bd. dirs. 1970-84), Tex. Parachute Assn. (pres. 1968-69), Dallas Parachute Assn. (pres. 1968-83, chief pilot 1979-83, chief instr. 1965-76). Avocations: flying, skydiving, photography. Home and Office: 1315 Cheyenne Dr Richardson TX 75080-3706

SCHRIVER, JOHN ALLEN, emergency medicine physician; b. Buffalo, Aug. 11, 1937; s. James George and Mary Louise (Anderson) S.; divorced; children: Leslie, Lynn, Randall, Angela. BS, Bethany Coll., 1959; MD, SUNY, Buffalo, 1963. Cert. in internal medicine and emergency medicine. Rotating intern U.S. Naval Hosp., St. Albans, N.Y., 1963-64; resident in internal medicine Oreg. Health Scis. U., Portland, 1968-71; pvt. practice in internal medicine Salem, Oreg., 1971-73; fellow in critical care U. So. Calif., L.A., 1973-74; staff physician Hollywood Presbyn. Hosp., L.A., 1974-76; chief emergency medicine Oreg. Health Scis. U., Portland, 1976-90, Yale U. Sch. Medicine, New Haven, 1991—. With USN, 1964-68. Mem. Alpha Omega Alpha. Avocation: 20th-century history. Home: 215 Bartlett Dr Madison CT 06443 Office: Yale U Sch Medicine Sect Emergency Medicine 464 Congress Ave New Haven CT 06519-1313

SCHRIVER, JOHN T., III, lawyer; b. Evanston, Ill., May 18, 1945. AB, Coll. of Holy Cross, 1967; JD, Georgetown U., 1971. Bar: Ill. 1971, Fla. 1972. Ptnr. McDermott, Will & Emery, Chgo. Mem. ABA, Chgo. Bar Assn., Fla. Bar. Office: McDermott Will & Emery 227 W Monroe St Chicago IL 60606-5016

SCHROCK, HAROLD ARTHUR, manufacturing company executive; b. Goshen, Ind., Apr. 10, 1915; s. Arthur E. and Anna (Shaner) S.; m. Thelma A. Hostetler, Sept. 3, 1938; children—Sara (Mrs. William Barrett), Susan (Mrs. John Graff), Cinda (Mrs. Stephen McKinney), Douglas. B.A, Goshen Coll., 1937. Chmn. bd. dirs. Starcraft Co., Goshen, 1967-71; pres. Goshen Sash & Door Co., Smoker-Craft, Inc., New Paris, Earthway Products, Bristol, Inc., Goshen Iron & Metal Co.; chmn. 1st Nat. Bank of Goshen; v.p. Ind. Capital Co., Ft. Wayne; pres. Ivy Terrace, Inc., Goshen, Marque, Inc., Goshen. Past pres. Greater Goshen Assn., Jr. Achievement, Goshen Gen. Hosp., Goshen Pub. Library; pres. Goshen Hosp. Found. Mem. Goshen C. of C. (pres. 1952). Republican. Lutheran (v.p. vestry). Clubs: Elcona Country (Goshen), Maplecrest Country (Goshen); John's Island (Vero Beach, Fla.); Rotary (past pres.). Home: 510 Carter Rd Goshen IN 46526-5210 Office: US 33 E Goshen IN 46526 Also: Goshen Sash & Door Co Inc 603 E Purl St Goshen IN 46526-4044

SCHROCK, SIMON, retail executive; b. Oakland, Md., Dec. 28, 1936; s. Noah and Cora (Burkholder) S.; m. Eva Lena Yoder, June 7, 1959 (dec. Apr. 1962); m. Pauline Yoder, Sept. 29, 1963; children: Janice Yvonne, Eldon Laverne, Ivan Dale. With Eastern States Farm Supply Co., Oakland, Md., 1957-59, Children's Hosp., Washington, 1959-61, Copp Properties, 1961-75; pres. Choice Books of No. Va., Fairfax, 1975—; chmn. Lighthouse Lit., 1976—. Author: Get on With Living, 1976, Price of Missing Life, 1981, One-Anothering, 1986, Vow-Keepers Vow-Breakers, A Smoother Journey, 1994. Contbr. articles to ch. jours. Bishop Faith Christian Fellowship, Catlett, Va., 1981—. Avocations: traveling; camping; biking. Office: 11923 Lee Hwy Fairfax VA 22030-6708

SCHROCK, THEODORE R., surgeon; b. Berne, Ind., Oct. 21, 1939; s. N.J. and M.A. Schrock; married. BA, U. Calif., 1961; MD, U. Calif., San Francisco, 1964. Diplomate Am. Bd. Surgery. Intern U. Calif. Hosps., San Francisco, 1964-65, resident, 1965-67, 69-71; fellow Mass. Gen. Hosp., Boston, 1967-69; interim chmn. dept. surgery U. Calif. San Francisco Med. Ctr., 1993—. Fellow ACS; mem. Am. Gastroenterological Assn., Am. Soc. Colon and Rectal Surgery, Am. Soc. Gastroenterological Endoscopy, Soc. Surgery Alimentary Tract. Office: U Calif San Francisco Dept Surgery 513 Parnassus Ave # 320 San Francisco CA 94122-2722

SCHRODER, DIETER KARL, electrical engineering educator; b. Lübeck, Germany, June 18, 1935; came to U.S., 1964; s. Wilhelm and Martha (Werner) S.; m. Beverley Claire Parchment, Aug. 4, 1961; children: Mark, Derek. BSc, McGill U., Montreal, Que., Can., 1962, MSc, 1964; PhD, U. Ill., 1968. Sr. engr. research and devel. sect. Westinghouse Electric Corp., Pitts., 1968-73, fellow engr., 1973-77, adv. engr., 1977-79, mgr., 1979-81; prof. elec. engring. Ariz. State U., Tempe, 1981—; researcher Inst. Solid-State Physics, Freiburg, Fed. Republic Germany, 1978-79. Author: Advanced MOS Devices, 1987, Semiconductor Material and Device Characterization, 1990; patentee in field; contbr. articles to profl. jours. Fellow IEEE (disting. nat. lectr. 1993-94); mem. Electrochem. Soc., Sigma Xi, Eta Kappa Nu. Mem. Baha'i Faith. Home: 1927 E Bendix Dr Tempe AZ 85283-4203 Office: Ariz State U Dept Elec Engring Tempe AZ 85287-5706

SCHRÖDER, HARALD BERTEL, aerospace industry executive; b. Stockholm, Dec. 31, 1924; s. Bertel and Selma Katarina (Kraepelien) S.; m. Kjerstin Sjögren, Mar. 17, 1949; children: Göran, Hans, Henrik. M in Aeronautics Engring., Swedish Royal Inst. Tech., Stockholm, 1948. Developmental engr. SAAB-Scania AB, Linköping, Sweden, 1957-62, program mgr. SAAB Viggen Fighter Program, 1962-68, v.p. aircraft sector, 1971-83; sr. v.p. SAAB aircraft div., gen. mgr. SAAB-Aircraft div., 1983-87; exec. v.p. SAAB-Scania AB, Linköping, Sweden, 1987-91; pres. Industry Group JAS AB, 1980-91; adviser to pres. Saab Mil. Aircraft, 1991-95; bd. dirs. Aero. sch. Inst. Sweden, 1987-91. Mem. Royal Swedish Acad. War Scis., Swedish Assn. Def. Industries (pres. 1987-89, bd. dirs. 1986-91), Swedish Aerospace Industries Assn. (pres. 1991-94), European Aerospace Industries Assn. (v.p. 1992-94). Home: Banergatan 53, 11522S Stockholm Sweden

SCHRODER, JACK SPALDING, JR., lawyer; b. Atlanta, July 10, 1948; s. Jack Spalding Sr. and Van (Spalding) S.; m. Karen Keyworth, Sept. 1, 1973; children: Jack Spalding III, James Edward. BA, Emory U., 1970; JD, U. Ga., 1973. Bar: Ga. 1973, U.S. Dist. Ct. (no. dist.) Ga. 1973, U.S. Ct. Appeals (5th cir.) 1973, U.S. Ct. Appeals (11th cir.) 1982. Assoc. Alston & Bird, Atlanta, 1973-78, ptnr., 1978—. Author: Credentialing: Strategies for a Changing Environment/BNA's Health Law and Business Series, 1996, co-editor, contbg. author: Georgia Hospital Law manual, 1979, 84,92. Bd. dirs. Rsch. Atlanta, 1996—; participant Leadership Ga., Atlanta, 1986. United Way (chmn. legal div.), Atlanta, 1980. Mem. ABA (vice chmn. medicine and law com. 1989-90), Am. Acad. Healthcare Attys. (bd. dirs. 1994—, chmn. med. staff and physician rels. com. 1991-94), Ga. Acad. Hosp. Attys. (pres. 1981-82), State Bar Ga. (bd. govs. 1987-89), Atlanta Coun. Younger Lawyers (pres. 1977-78), Atlanta Bar Assn. (pres. 1982-83), Atlanta Bar Found. (pres. 1991-95). Office: Alston & Bird 1 Atlantic Ctr 1201 W Peachtree St NW Atlanta GA 30309-3400

SCHRODER, JOHN L., JR., retired mining engineer; b. Martinsburg, W.Va.. BS in Mining Engring., W.Va. Sch. Mines, MS, 1941. Registered profl. engr., W.Va., Ky. Jr. engr. H.C. Frick Coke Co. U.S. Steel, Uniontown, Pa., 1941-44; prodn., safety engr. Gay Coal and Coke Gay Mining Cos., 1946-49.; asst. engr. mine planning U.S. Steel, Gary, W.Va., 1949-51, asst. chief engr., 1951-1953; chief engr. U.S. Steel, Lynch, Gary, Ky., 1953-1958; gen. supt. U.S. Steel, Lynch, 1958-70; gen. mgr. coal ops. U.S. Steel, Pitts., 1970-79, v.p. coal ops. resource devel., 1979-81, pres. subsidiary U.S. Steel Mining Co., Inc., 1981-83, ret., 1983; spl. asst. to the pres. Am. Mining Congress, 1983-84; dean Coll. Mineral and Engry Resources W.Va. U., 1984-91, ret., 1991; chmn. Mine Insps. Exam. Bd.; mem Govs. Moore's Energy Task Force. Lt. j.g. USN, 1944-46. Recipient Howard N. Evanson award Soc. Mining, Metallurgy and Exploration, 1991.

Mem. AIME (Erskine Ramsay medal 1992), Nat. Mine Rescue Assn., W.Va. Coal Mining Inst., Old Timers Club, King Coal Club. Office: 228 Maple Ave Morgantown WV 26505-6666

SCHRODI, TOM, instructional services director; b. Belleville, Ill., Sept. 24, 1942; s. Walter Joseph and Emma Elizabeth (Bleiker) S.; m. Elizabeth Agnes Clark Schrodi, Aug. 19, 1967; children: Lisa, Tammy, Dawn. BS, Ea. Mich. U., Ypsilanti, 1964; MS, Ea. Mich. U., 1965. Calif. Adminstrv. Credential K-12 and Adult, Calif. Standard Svcs. Credential, Supr. 7-12, Calif. C.C. Credential in History, Calif. Standard Teaching Credential in History. Federal and state project writer Orange Unified Sch. Dist., 1975-80, coord. spl. programs, 1976-79, adminstrv. asst. spl. programs, 1979-80, adminstr. of curriculum, 1980-85, dir. instrnl. svcs., 1985—; coord. career edn. Orange County Consortium K-14, 1972-75; instr. Ctrl. County Regional Occupation Program, 1973-75, Whittier Coll., 1974-82; guest lectr. Calif. State U., Long Beach, 1972-80; cons. Calif. State Dept. Edn., Imperial County Dept. Edn. Author: Visual Communications Cluster Curriculum Guide, 1977, Social Studies Review, 1974, Le Mot Educational Services, 1972; co-author: California's Career Education State Plan, 1978, Comprehensive Career Education System, 1977, Monograph, 1973, Needs Assessment, 1972. Named ASCA Adminstr. of Yr. Curriculum and Instrn., 1993. Mem. Business Industry Coun., Orange Unified Curruculum Coun., Articulation Coun., Partnership Network, Dist. Negotiation Team, ASCD, Calif. Indsl. Edn. Assn., Intercultural Edn. Commn., Orange Suburbia Kiwanis Club, Orange High Sch. Faculty Club, Profl. Assn. Orange Educators. Office: Orange Unified Sch Dist 370 N Glassell St Orange CA 92866-1032

SCHROEDER, AARON HAROLD, songwriter; b. Bklyn., Sept. 7, 1926; s. Max and Pearl (Miller) S. m. Abby Steinberg, Oct. 31, 1967; 1 child, Rachel Amy. Student, music and art high schs., N.Y.C. Contact man Warner Bros. Music, Mills Music; profl. mgr. Charley Barnett; owner A. Schroeder Internat., Ltd. and subs. cos., N.Y.C., 1960-77; founder, pres. Musicor Records, N.Y.C., 1960-65. Mus. dir. film The Four Musketeers; producer TV spl. country music, 1979; composer songs for Fund Drives Berkshire United Way, 1986-87, N.Y. State Dept. Agr., Fairview Hosp., 1988, Operation Earth, 1990; composer songs Not as a Stranger, I Got Stung, Mandolins in the Moonlight, Stuck on You, Twixt Twelve and Twenty, Fools Hall of Fame, Because They're Young, French Foreign Legion, Time and the River, I'm Gonna Knock on Your Door, Rubber Ball, It's Now or Never, Big Hunk of Love, Today's Teardrops, Good Luck Charm, Once She Was Mine; film theme Four Musketeers, She Can Put Her Shoes Under My Bed Anytime, If I Could Only Touch Your Life, We're All In the Same Boat; score for motion picture and TV series Lucky Luke including original songs The Lonesomest Cowboy In the West, Lopin' Along, Lotta Legs' Hotel, Put Your Pistol Back in Your Holster, Cowboy's Lament, numerous others; composer for PBS Pilot "Grover's Corner", 1990, PBS spl. Chanukah at Grover's Corner, 1992; sponsored and pub. numerous award-winning songwriters. Mem. ASCAP (elections bd.), NARAS (gov. 1962). Home: RR 2 Box 118 Great Barrington MA 01230-9808 Office: 200 W 51st St Ste 706 New York NY 10019-6208

SCHROEDER, ALFRED CHRISTIAN, electronics research engineer; b. West New Brighton, N.Y., Feb. 28, 1915; s. Alfred and Chryssa (Weishaar) S.; m. Janet Ellis, Sept. 26, 1936 (dec.); 1 dau., Carol Ann Schroeder Castle.; m. Dorothy Holloway, Nov. 21, 1981. BS, MIT, 1937, MS, 1937. Mem. tech. staff David Sarnoff Rsch. Ctr. RCA, Princeton, N.J., 1937—. Contbr. articles to profl. jours. Recipient RCA Lab. awards, 1947, 50, 51, 52, 57, 70. Fellow IEEE (Vladimir Zworykin award 1971); mem. AAAS, Optical Soc. Am., Soc. Motion Picture and TV Engrs. (David Sarnoff Gold medal 1965), Soc. Info. Display (Karl Ferdinand Braun prize 1989), Sigma Xi. Quaker. Achievements include 75 patents for color TV products including shadow mask tube. Home: Pennswood Village Apt I-114 Newtown PA 18940 Office: SRI Internat David Sarnoff Rsch Ctr Princeton NJ 08540

SCHROEDER, ARNOLD LEON, mathematics educator; b. Honolulu, May 27, 1935; s. Arnold Leon and Wynelle (Russell) S.; BS in Math., Oreg. State U., 1960, MS in Stats., 1962; NSF Insts. at UCLA, 1964, U. So. Calif., 1965; m. Maybelle Ruth Walker, Nov. 9, 1956; children: Steven, Michael, Wendy. Assoc. prof. math. Long Beach (Calif.) C.C., 1962—; computer cons. McDonnell-Douglas Corp., 1966-74, statis. researcher in med. and social sci., 1976-80; cons. statis. software including SPSS, BMDP, and Fortran, 1980—; dir. Schroeder's Statis. Svcs. Author: Statistics/Math Note's for Colleges, 1986—. Chmn. bd. elders Grace Bible Ch., South Gate, Calif., 1985-92. Served with USAF, 1953-57. Mem. Faculty Assn. Calif. C.C., C.C. Assn., Am. Bowlers Tour (life). Home: 5481 E Hill St Long Beach CA 90815-1923 Office: 4901 E Carson St Long Beach CA 90808-1706

SCHROEDER, CHARLES EDGAR, banker, investment management executive; b. Chgo., Nov. 17, 1935; s. William Edward and Lelia Lorraine (Anderson) S.; m. Martha Elizabeth Runnette, Dec. 30, 1958; children: Charles Edgar, Timothy Creighton, Elizabeth Linton. BA in Econs., Dartmouth Coll., 1957; MBA, Amos Tuck Sch., 1958. Treas. Miami Corp., Chgo., 1969-78, pres., 1978—; chmn., bd. dirs Blvd. Bank of Chgo., 1981-91; chmn. Blvd. Bancorp., Inc., 1991-94; bd. dirs. Nat.-Standard Co., Niles, Mich. Trustee Northwestern Meml. Hosp., 1985-93, Northwestern U., 1989—. Lt. (j.g.) USN, 1958-60. Mem. Fin. Analysts Soc. of Chgo., Chgo. Club, Glen View Club, Michigan Shores Club, Comml. Club. Office: Miami Corp 410 N Michigan Ave Chicago IL 60611-4213

SCHROEDER, DAVID HAROLD, health care facility executive; b. Chgo., Oct. 22, 1940; s. Harry T. and Clara D. (Dexter) S.; m. Clara Doorn, Dec. 27, 1964; children: Gregory D., Elizabeth M. BBA, Kans. State Coll., 1965; MBA, Wichita State U., 1968; postgrad., U. Ill., 1968-69. CPA, Ill.; cert. healthcare fin. profl. Supt. cost acctg. Boeing Co., Wichita, Kans., 1965-68; sr. v.p., treas. Riverside Med. Ctr., Kankakee, Ill., 1971—; treas. Riverside Health System, 1982—, Kankakee Valley Health Inc., 1985—, Health Info. Systems Coop., 1991—; v.p., treas. Oakside Corp., Kankakee, 1982—; bd. dirs. Harmony Home Health Svc., Inc., Naperville, Ill.; mem. faculty various profl. orgns.; adj. prof. econs. divsn. health adminstrn. Gov.'s State U., University Park, Ill., 1990-95; trustee Riverside Found. Trust, 1989—, RMC Found., 1989—, Sr. Living Ctr., 1989—. Contbg. author: Cost Containment in Hospitals, 1980; contbr. articles to profl. jours. Trustee Riverside Found. Trust, 1989—, RMC Found., 1989—, Sr. Living Ctr., 1989—, Alzheimer Found., 1996—, Alzheimer's Assn., 1997; pres. Riverside Employees Credit Union, 1976-79; founder Kankakee Trinity Acad., 1980, Riverview Hist. Dist., Kankakee, 1982; pres. Kankakee County Mental Health Ctr., 1982-84, United Way Kankakee County, 1984-85; chmn. Ill. Provider Trust, Naperville, 1983-85; mem. adv. bd. Students in Free Enterprise, Olivet Nazarene U., Kankakee, 1989—; pres. adv. coun. divsn. health adminstrn., preceptor Gov.'s State U., 1987—; trustee, treas. Am. Luth. Ch.; wish granter Make a Wish Found., 1994—; dir. Kankakee County Hist. Soc., 1995. Capt. U.S. Army, 1969-71. Fellow Am. Coll. Healthcare Execs., Healthcare Fin. Mgmt. Assn. (pres. 1975-76), Fin. Analysts Fedn.; mem. AICPA, Ill. Hosp. Assn. (chmn. coun. health fin. 1982-85), Inst. Chartered Fin. Analysts, Nat. Assn. Accts., Fin. Exec. Inst., Ill. CPA Soc., Healthcare Fin. Mgmt. Assn. (William G. Follimer award 1977, Robert H. Reeves award 1981, Muncie Gold award 1987, Founders medal of honor 1990), Investment Analysts Soc. Chgo., Inc., Kankakee County Hist. Soc. (dir. 1995—), Classic Car Club Am., Packard Club, Kiwanis (pres.), Masons, Alpha Kappa Psi, Sigma Chi. Avocations: classical automobile restoration, architectural preservation, computers. Home: 901 S Chicago Ave Kankakee IL 60901-5236 Office: Riverside Med Ctr 350 N Wall St Kankakee IL 60901-2901 *Life's four important questions: Why? Why not? Why not you? Why not now?.*

SCHROEDER, DONALD J., orthopedic surgeon; b. Omaha, Nebr., Nov. 5, 1938; s. Frances A. and Maire L. (Schlueter) S.; m. Patricia A. Speer, Feb. 11, 1962 (div. June 1980); children: Cynthia, Douglas; m. Carol E. Schaan, Aug. 20, 1983. BS, Creighton U., 1960, MD, 1964. Diplomate Am. Bd. Orthopedic Surgery. Intern Detroit Receiving Hosp., 1964-65; resident in orthopedic surgery Wayne State U., Detroit, 1964-71; resident with affiliate hosp. Shriners Hosp., St. Louis, 1969-70; attending surgeon Sacred Heart Gen. Hosp., Eugene, Oreg., 1971—; resident orth. surgery Wayne State U.; attending surgeon Sacred Heart Gen. Hosp., Eugene, Oreg., 1971—. Pres. Marist Found., Eugene, 1993. Smith Kline fellow, 1964. Fellow Am. Acad. Orthopedic Surgeons; mem. AMA (alt. del. 1993—), Oreg. Med. Assn. (pres. 1993-94), Lane County Med. Soc. (pres. 1987-88), Western Orthopedic Assn., Alpha Omega Alpha. Republican. Roman Catholic. Avocation: buffalo ranching. Office: 1180 Patterson St Eugene OR 97401-3619

SCHROEDER, DONALD PERRY, retired food products company executive; b. Danville, Ill., Nov. 2, 1930; s. Donald Joseph and Pauline Hannah (Critchfield) S.; m. Barbara Ann Engle, Jan. 6, 1951; children: Patricia Ann Schroeder Capizzi, Helen Schroeder Marrano, Jeffrey Joseph. Student, Purdue U., 1949, Stanford U., 1982. Mgr. Schroeders I.G.A. Supermarket, Danville, 1950-57; specialist retail meat J.M. Jones Co., Champaign, Ill., 1957-59, mgr. retail zone, 1959-62, dir. meat ops., 1962-67; dir. customer services Olean (N.Y.) Wholesale Grocery Co., 1967-70; nat. dir. meat Ind. Grocers Alliance, Chgo., 1970-74; dir. meat ops. Fleming Cos., Inc., Topeka, 1974-83; v.p. meat., produce ops. Fleming Cos., Inc., Oklahoma City, 1983-88, v.p. meat ops., 1988-89, ret., 1989; chmn. meat council Ind. Grocers Alliance, Chgo., 1962-87. Bd. dirs. Big Bros./Sisters Greater Oklahoma City, 1984-87, North Side YMCA, Oklahoma City, 1988-90. Mem. Nat. Livestock and Meat Bd. (universal meat cut identity com. 1970-73), United Fresh Fruit and Vegetable (bd. dirs. 1984-87). Republican. Roman Catholic. Avocations: yard and garden work, golf, fishing. Home: 5 Charnela Ln Hot Springs Village AR 71909-3030

SCHROEDER, EDMUND R., lawyer; b. N.Y.C., Feb. 6, 1933; s. Robert C. and Rose A. (Garramone) S.; m. Elaine P. Diserio, Jan. 21, 1961; children: Edmund Jr., Christopher, Elizabeth. AB cum laude, Harvard U., 1953, LLB, 1958. Assoc. Archibald R. Graustein, N.Y.C., 1958-61, Root, Barrett, Cohen, Knapp & Smith, N.Y.C., 1961-67; ptnr. Barrett Knapp Smith & Schapiro, N.Y.C., 1967-88, Lord Day & Lord/Barrett Smith, N.Y.C., 1988-94, Cadwalader, Wickersham & Taft, N.Y.C., 1994—; mem. adv. com. Commodity Futures Trading Commn. on Definition and Regulation of Market Instruments, 1975-76. Contbr. articles to profl. jours. Bd. dirs. Orch. St. Luke's N.Y.C., 1987—, chmn. exec. com., 1993—; bd. trustees The United Way of Scarsdale-Edgemont, 1990-92; mem. Scarsdale Bd. Edn., 1976-79; co-founder, 1st chmn. Edn. Through Music, Inc., N.Y.C., 1991—; bd. trustees Hoff-Barthelson Music Sch., Scarsdale, 1974—, chmn. bd., 1986-90, hon. chmn., 1990—; bd. trustees The Nat. Guild Comty. Schs. Arts, Englewood, N.J., 1992-96; bd. advisors Sacred Heart/Mt. Carmel Sch. for Arts, Mt. Vernon, 1995—; arbitrator Am. Arbitration Assn., Nat. Futures Assn. Mem. ABA (chmn. com. futures regulation 1981-85), Bar Assn. City of N.Y. (founder, 1st chmn. com. futures regulation 1976-81), N.Y. State Bar Assn. (com. comty. and future law and regulation 1996—), Scarsdale Golf Club. Office: Cadwalader Wickersham & Taft 100 Maiden Ln New York NY 10038-4818

SCHROEDER, EDWIN MAHER, law educator, law library administrator, university dean; b. New Orleans, June 25, 1937; s. Edwin Charles and Lucille Mary (Maher) S.; m. Marietta Louise DeFazio, Aug. 1, 1936; children—Edwin Charles II, Jonathan David, Margaret Louise. A.A., St. Joseph Sem., St. Benedict, La., 1957; Ph.B., Gregorian U., Rome, 1959; J.D., Tulane U., 1964; M.S., Fla. State U., 1970. Bar: Mass. 1964. Teaching fellow Boston Coll. Law Sch., 1964-65; asst. prof. law U. Conn., 1965-68; asst. prof., asst. law librarian U. Tex., 1968-69; asst. prof. Fla. State U., 1969-71, assoc. prof., 1971-75, prof., 1975—, dir. Law Library, 1969—, asst. dean Coll. Law, 1979-83, assoc. dean Coll. Law, 1983-93. Mem. ABA, Am. Assn. Law Libraries (v.p. Southeastern chpt. 1983-84, pres. 1984-85), Order of Coif, Beta Phi Mu. Roman Catholic. Home: 806 Middlebrooks Cir Tallahassee FL 32312-2439 Office: Law Libr Fla State U Coll Law Tallahassee FL 32306-1043

SCHROEDER, FRED ERICH HARALD, humanities educator; b. Manitowoc, Wis., June 3, 1932; s. Alfred William and Sissel Marie (Lovell) S.; m. Janet June Knope, Aug. 21, 1954; 1 child, Erich Karl. BS, U. Wis., 1960; MA, U. Minn., 1963, PhD, 1968. Elementary sch. tchr. various locations, Wis., 1952-60; asst. prof. English U. Minn., Duluth, 1968-71, assoc. prof. English, 1971-74, prof. behavioral sci., 1977-82, prof. humanities, 1974-96, dir. Ctr. for Am. Studies, 1986-87, dir. Inst. Interdisciplinary Studies, 1987-90, dir. dept. humanities and classics, 1989-90, dir. grad. liberal studies, 1992-95, prof. emeritus, 1996—. Author: Joining the Human Race: How To Teach Humanities, 1972, Outlaw Aesthetics: Arts and the Public Mind, 1977; editor Interdisciplinary Humanities (formerly Humanities Edn. jour.), 1983-95, 5000 Years of Popular Culture, 1980, 20th Century Popular Culture in Museums and Libraries, 1981, Front Yard America: The Evolution and Meanings of a Domestic Vernacular Landscape, 1993; lectr., writer Nat. Humanities Series, 1969-71. Mem. Minn. Humanities Commn., 1985-90. Woodrow Wilson Nat. Found. fellow, 1960-61, dissertation fellow 1963; NEH scholar, 1969-70; Inst. for Human Values in Medicine fellow, 1976. Mem. Am. Culture Assn. (pres. 1984-87), Nat. Assn. Humanities Edn. (pres. 1987-89, exec. sec.-treas. 1989-96), Am. Assn. for State and Local History (seminar instr. 1978-82), Popular Culture Assn. Avocations: collecting art, woodworking, gardening. Home: 5756 N Shore Dr Duluth MN 55804-9660

SCHROEDER, FREDRIC KAUFFMANN, federal commissioner; b. Lima, Peru, May 6, 1957; s. Florence Schroeder; m. Cathlene Ann Nusser, Jan. 3, 1981; children: Carrie Ann, Matthew Stephen. BA in Psychology, San Fransisco State U., 1977, MA in Spl. Edn., 1978, postgrad., 1980; PhD in Ednl. Adminstrn., U. N. Mex. Cert. elem. and secondary adminstrn.; spl. edn., N. Mex. Tchr., coord. Albuquerque Pub. Schs., 1980-86; exec. dir. N. Mex. Commn. for the Blind, 1986-94; commr. Rehab. Svcs. Adminstrn. U.S. Dept. Edn., 1994—; cons. City of Albuquerque, 1985, Minn. Acads. for Deaf and Blind, 1985, Gulf South Rsch. Inst., New Orleans, 1986, Metro. Ctr. for Ind. Living, 1988. Contbr. articles to profl. jours. Office: US Dept Edn 330 C St SW Washington DC 20201-0001

SCHROEDER, GERALD F., judge; b. Boise, Idaho, Sept. 13, 1939; s. Frank Frederick and Josephine Ivy (Lucas) S.; m. Carole Ann McKenna, 1967; children: Karl Casteel, Erich Frank. BA magna cum laude, Coll. of Idaho (now Albertson Coll. of Idaho), 1961; JD, Harvard U., 1964. Bar: Idaho 1965. Assoc. Moffett, Thomas, Barrett & Blanton, Boise, 1965-66; pvt. practice Boise, 1966-67; asst. U.S. atty. Dept. Justice, Boise, 1967-69; judge Ada County Probate Ct., Boise, 1969-71; magistrate State of Idaho, Boise, 1971-75; dist. judge U.S. Dist. Ct. (4th dist.) Idaho, 1975-95; justice Idaho Supreme Ct., 1995—; instr. Boise Bar Rev., 1973—; adj. faculty law Boise State U., 1986-95; former mem. Gov. Coun. on Crime and Delinquency. Author: Idaho Probate Procedure, 1971; (novel) Trianle of the Sons-Phenomena, 1983; contbr. chpt. to history text. Bd. dirs. Boise Philharm. Assn., 1978-81; adminstrv. and dist. judge 4th dist. State of Idaho, 1985-95. Toll fellow Nat. Coun. State Govt., 1990. Mem. Idaho Bar Assn., Boise Racquet and Swim Club (pres. bd. dirs. 1991-93).

SCHROEDER, HAROLD KENNETH, JR., lawyer; b. Buffalo, Aug. 6, 1936; s. Harold Kenneth and Margaret Mary (Mescall) S.; m. Jean Louise Benbenek, Aug. 20, 1958; children: Mary Margaret, Mark, Keith, Kurt, Jennifer. BS, Canisius Coll., 1958; JD, U. Buffalo, 1961; ML, Georgetown U., 1962. Bar: N.Y. 1961, D.C. 1961, U.S. Dist. Ct. (we. dist.) N.Y. 1961, Fla. 1979, U.S. Ct. Appeals (2nd cir.) 1981. Trial atty. U.S. Dept. Justice, Washington, 1962-63; spl. asst. U.S. Atty. D.C. Washington, 1962-63; U.S. Atty. Western Dist. N.Y. U.S. Dept. Justice, Buffalo, 1969-72; ptnr. Hodgson, Russ, Andrews, Woods & Goodyear, Buffalo, 1963-69, sr. ptnr., 1972—; chmn. fed. merit selection panel U.S. Magistrate Judge We. Dist. N.Y., 1989, 92, 94; merit selection panel Fed. Pub. Defender We. Dist. N.Y., 1991, 95; mem. U.S. Civil Justice Reform Act, N.Y. Author: (with others) Law and Tactics in Federal Criminal Cases, 1964. V.p. Orchard Park, N.Y. Ctrl. Sch. Dist., 1972-76, Buffalo Sem., 1972-88. E. Barrett Prettyman fellow Georgetown U., 1961; recipient Disting. Alumnus award U. Buffalo Law Sch., 1996. Mem. Western N.Y. Def. Trial Lawyers Assn. (Def. Trial Lawyer of Yr. 1996), Erie County Bar Assn. Avocation: tennis. Home: 3872 Baker Rd Orchard Park NY 14127 Office: Hodgson Russ Andrews Woods & Goodyear 1800 One M&T Plaza Buffalo NY 14203

SCHROEDER, HARRY WILLIAM, JR., physician, scientist; b. Mpls., Minn., Oct. 1, 1952; s. Harry Williams Sr. and Maria de los Angeles (Melendez) S.; m. Dixie Lee Douglas, Nov. 24, 1979; children: Harry William III, Elena, Jeannette. BS, Tex. A&M U., 1974; PhD, Baylor Coll. Medicine, 1979, MD, 1981. Vis. fellow Yale U., New Haven, 1980; intern, then resident in internal medicine U. Ky., Lexington, 1981-84; sr. fellow med. genetics U. Wash., Seattle, 1984-88; rsch. assoc. Howard Hughes Med. Inst., Seattle, 1986-88; asst. prof. medicine and microbiology U. Ala., Birmingham, 1988-93, assoc. prof. medicine & microbiology, 1993—. RJR Nabisco scholar in immunology, 1989. Fellow Am. Coll. Med. Genetics (founder 1993), Molecular Medicine Soc.; mem. AAAS, Am. Soc. Human Genetics, Am. Fedn. Med. Rsch., Am. Assn. Immunologists, Clin. Immunology Soc., Soc. for Molecular Recognition, So. Soc. for Clin. Investigation, Am. Coll. Rheumatologists. Office: U Ala TI 378 UAB Station Birmingham AL 35294

SCHROEDER, HENRY WILLIAM, publisher; b. Cleve., Wis., Sept. 7, 1928; s. Henry and Esther Julia (Kammann) S. ; m. Dorothy Hildebrand, Aug. 18, 1956 (div.); children: Susan Schroeder Smith, Katherine Jean Duhamel; m. Elizabeth Churbuck, Aug. 15, 1977 (dec.); children: Joy, Bill, Stephen; m. Mary Vae Legler, Feb. 15, 1992; 1 child, Derek Legler. BS, U. Wis., 1957, MS, 1959. Info. dir. Wis. Farm Bur., Madison, 1960-63; asst. dir. pub. rels. Credit Union Internat., Madison, 1963-65; editor, co-pub. Verona Press (Wis.), Oreg. Observer (Wis.), 1966—, also v.p. Southwest Suburban Publs., Inc., 1966-80; co-pub. Fitchburg Star, 1974—, also pres. Southwest Suburban Publs. and Schroeder Publs., Inc., 1980—; pub. Blade-Atlas, Blanchardville, Wis., 1977-83; pres., pub. Leader Publ. Corp., Evansville, Wis., 1981-88; pub. Cmty. Herald Newspapers Corp., 1988—, Monona Herald and McFarland Life newspapers, Clinton (Wis.) Topper, 1994—; pub. Country Courier, Hinckley, Ill. Mem. Gov.'s UN Commn., 1974. Served with USNR, 1949-53. Mem. Wis. Newspaper Assn. (pres. 1983-84), Wis. Newspaper Assn. (bd. dir. 1973-86, 94—), WNA Found. (pres. 1990-91), Madison Press Club, Madison Advt. Fedn., Nat. Newspaper Assn. (govt. affairs conf., chmn. services com., state chmn., Better Newspaper Contest), Suburban Newspapers Am., Verona C. of C. (pres. 1970, 91), Madison Club, East Madison Optimists (bd. dirs. 1993—, pres. 1995-96), Masons (master 1970, bd. dirs. jour. 1990-93, pres. jour., bd. dirs. 1993—), Shriners, Royal Order Jesters. Republican. Office: Verona Press 120 W Verona Ave Verona WI 53593-1315

SCHROEDER, HERMAN ELBERT, scientific consultant; b. Bklyn., July 6, 1915; s. Henry W. and Caroline (Schmidt) S.; m. Elizabeth Barnes, June 13, 1938; children: Nancy Schroeder Tarczy, Edward L., Peter H., Martha L. Schroeder Lewis. A.B. summa cum laude, Harvard, 1936, A.M., 1937, Ph.D., 1939. With E.I. du Pont de Nemours & Co., Wilmington, Del., 1938-80; asst. dir. R&D E.I. du Pont de Nemours & Co., 1957-63, dir. R&D, 1963-80; pres. Schroeder Sci. Svcs., Inc., 1980—; sci. cons. Met. Mus. Art, N.Y.C., Smithsonian Instn., Winterthur Mus. Mem. Chester County Sch. Bd., Unionville, Pa., 1950-56; pres. Assn. Harvard Chemists, 1955-56; mem. vis. com. Harvard Chemistry Dept., 1960-72; mem. sci. adv. com. Winterthur Mus.; trustee, chmn. research com. U. Del. Research Found., 1976-84, former v.p. Recipient award Internat. Inst. Synthetic Rubber Producers, 1979, Lavoisier medal DuPont, 1992. Mem. AAAS, Am. Chem. Soc. (Charles Goodyear medal 1984), N.Y. Acad. Scis., Phi Beta Kappa, Alpha Chi Sigma. Home and Office: 74 Stonegates 4031 Kennett Pike Greenville DE 19807-2037 *A life in industrial research has been for me both challenging and rewarding. Forces which impel me are largely the compulsion to look for the new, to change for the better, be it by finding better ways to do things or by inventing products to make the world function better. Gratifyingly, these often make the world aesthetically more pleasant and sometimes cleaner. I am concerned by the growing hostility of society to science and to developments that ensure a more comfortable life and safer food and energy than would otherwise be possible.*

SCHROEDER, JOHN H., university chancellor; b. Twin Falls, Idaho, Sept. 13, 1943; s. Herman John and Azalia (Kimes) S.; m. Sandra Barrow; children: John K., Andrew Barrow. BA, Lewis and Clark Coll., Portland, Oreg., 1965; MA, U. Va., 1967, PhD, 1971. Instr. history U. Wis., Milw., 1970-71, asst. prof., 1971-76, assoc. prof., 1976-86, prof., 1986—, Am. Coun. on Edn. fellow, 1982-83, assoc. dean, 1976-82, asst. to vice chancellor, 1982-85, acting vice chancellor, 1985-87, vice chancellor, 1987-90, chancellor, 1990—; Louis M. Sears Meml. lectr. Purdue U., 1978; bd. dirs. Columbia Health Sys., Inc. Author: Mr. Polk's War: American Opposition and Dissent, 1973, The Commercial and Diplomatic Role of the American Navy 1829-1861, 1985. Bd. dirs. Greater Milw. Com., Milw. Boys and Girls Club, Milw. Pub. Policy Forum, Greater Milw. Edn. Trust, Wis. Jr. Achievement, Commn. on Urban Agenda; mem. Milw. Conf. on Employment, Edn. and Race, Milw. Quality Edn. Commn. Recipient Edward and Rosa Uhrig award U. Wis.-Milw., 1974, Disting. Teaching award AMOCO/U. Wis.-Milw., 1975. Mem. Orgn. Am. Historians, Soc. for History of Early Republic, Soc. for History Am. Fgn. Rels., Nat. Assn. State Univs. and Land Grant Colls. (bd. dirs.), Rotary. Office: U Wis Chapel Hall PO Box 413 2310 E Hartford Ave Milwaukee WI 53201-3165

SCHROEDER, JOYCE KATHERINE, state agency administrator, research analyst; b. Moline, Ill., Apr. 1, 1951; d. Reinhold J. and Miriam-May Schroeder. BS in Math., U. Ill., 1973, MA in Ops. Rsch., 1978. Underwriter, programmer Springfield, Ill., 1973-76; ops. rsch. analyst Ill. Dept. Transp., Springfield, 1976-78, data analyst, 1978-80, team leader, fatal accident reporting sys., 1980-83, mgr. safety project evaluation, 1983-92, mgr. accident studies and investigation, 1992—; sys. engring. del. to China China Assn. for Sci. and Tech., 1986; mem. staff Driving While Intoxicated Adv. Coun. and Task Force, State of Ill., 1983-86, 89-92, Gov. Task Force on Occupant Protection, 1988-90, Ill. Traffic Safety Info. Sys. Coun., 1993-95. Vol. Animal Protective League, Springfield; leaderbd. co-chairperson LPGA Rail Classic, Springfield, 1983-87; amb. of goodwill Lions of Ill. Found., 1993, trustee, 1995—. Lions Clubs Internat. Melvin Jones fellow, 1993, Lions of Ill. Found. fellow, 1995. Mem. Lions of Ill. Found. (amb. of goodwill 1993, trustee 1995—, treas. found. bd. 1996—), Springfield Lincoln Land Lions Club (charter pres. 1988-90, treas. 1993-95, news editor 1995—), Lions Club (dist. gov. Ill. 1992-93, state membership coord. 1994-96, Melvin Jones fellow 1993), Past. Dist. Gov. Assn. (sec.-treas. 1993—), Phi Kappa Phi, Kappa Delta Pi. Avocations: dogs, travel, music, sports, humanitarian svc. Office: Ill Dept Transp 3215 Executive Park Dr Springfield IL 62703-4514

SCHROEDER, MARY MURPHY, federal judge; b. Boulder, Colo., Dec. 4, 1940; d. Richard and Theresa (Kahn) Murphy; m. Milton R. Schroeder, Oct. 15, 1965; children: Caroline Theresa, Katherine Emily. B.A., Swarthmore Coll., 1962; J.D., U. Chgo., 1965. Bar: Ill. 1966, D.C. 1966, Ariz. 1970. Trial atty. Dept. Justice, Washington, 1965-69; law clk. Hon. Jesse Udall, Ariz. Supreme Ct., 1970; mem. firm Lewis and Roca, Phoenix, 1971-75; judge Ariz. Ct. Appeals, Phoenix, 1975-79, U.S. Ct. Appeals (9th cir.), Phoenix, 1979—; vis. instr. Ariz. State U. Coll. Law, 1976, 77, 78. Contbr. articles to profl. jours. Mem. ABA, Ariz. Bar Assn., Fed. Bar Assn., Am. Law Inst. (coun. mem.), Am. Judicature Soc., Soroptimists. Office: US Ct Appeals 9th Cir 6421 Courthouse-Fed Bldg 230 N 1st Ave Phoenix AZ 85025-0230

SCHROEDER, PATRICIA SCOTT (MRS. JAMES WHITE SCHROEDER), former congresswoman; b. Portland, Oreg., July 30, 1940; d. Lee Combs and Bernice (Lemoin) Scott; m. James White Schroeder, Aug. 18, 1962; children: Scott William, Jamie Christine. B.A. magna cum laude, U. Minn., 1961; J.D., Harvard U., 1964. Bar: Colo. 1964. Field atty. NLRB, Denver, 1964-66; practiced in Denver, 1966-72; hearing officer Colo. Dept. Personnel, 1971-72; mem. faculty U. Colo., 1969-72, Community Coll., Denver, 1969-70, Regis Coll., Denver, 1970-72; mem. 93d-104th Congresses from 1st Colo. dist., 1973-96; co-chmn. Congl. Caucus for Women's Issues, 1976-96; dir. New Solutions for a New Century, Inst. for a Civil Soc.; prof. Princeton U.; pres., CEO Assn. Am. Pubs., Washington, 1997—; mem. Ho. of Reps., ranking minority mem. judiciary subcom. on the Constitution, mem. Nat. Security Com. Inducted, National Women's Hall of Fame, 1995. Congregationalist. Office: Assn Am Pubs # 700 1718 Connecticut Ave NW Ste 700 Washington DC 20009-1148

SCHROEDER, PAUL HERMAN, entomologist; b. Elmer, N.J., Sept. 26, 1930; s. Harry and Emily (Blumke) S.; m. Janet Elma Wiedrich, Feb. 8, 1964; children: Paula, Jana, David, Krista. BS, Rutgers U., 1952, MS, 1960, PhD, 1963. County agrl. agt. Passaic County N.J., Paterson, 1952-57; rsch. asst. Rutgers U., New Brunswick, N.J., 1957-63; biologist entomology and nematology Niagara Chem. Divsn. FMC, Middleport, N.Y., 1963-64; nematologist Niagara Chem. Divsn. FMC, Middleport, 1964-66, mgr. field rsch., 1966-70; mgr. Gasport (N.Y.) Rsch. Field Sta. Niagara Chem. Divsn. FMC, 1970-71; nematologist Castle & Cook Corp., Dole Divsn., Honolulu and Lanai City, Hawaii, 1971-76; product devel. mgr. Union Carbide Corp., Agrl. Products Divsn., Salinas and Jacksonville, 1976-80; registration specialist US EPA, Washington, 1980-92, efficacy reviewer and registration mgr., 1992—. Mem. Entomol. Soc. Am., Soc. Nematologists, Sigma Xi. Home: 14626 Batavia Dr Centreville VA 20120-1325 Office: US EPA 401 M St Washington DC

SCHROEDER, STEVEN ALFRED, medical educator, researcher, foundation executive; b. N.Y.C., July 26, 1939; s. Arthur Edward and Norma (Scheinberg) S.; m. Sally B. Ross, Oct. 21, 1967; children: David Arthur, Alan Ross. BA, Stanford U., 1960; MD, Harvard U., 1964; LHD (hon.), Rush U., 1994; DSc (hon.), Boston U., 1996, U. Mass. Med. Ctr. Am. Bd. Internal Medicine. Intern and resident in internal medicine Harvard Med. Service, Boston City Hosp., 1964-66, 68-70; asst. prof., then assoc. prof. George Washington Med. Ctr., Washington, 1971-76; vis. prof. St. Thomas' Hosp. Med. Sch., London, 1982-83; prof. medicine, chief div. gen. internal medicine, mem. Inst. Health Policy Studies U. Calif., San Francisco, 1976-90; pres. Robert Wood Johnson Found., Princeton, N.J., 1990—; cons. various govtl. and philanthropic health orgns.; chair internat. adv. com. faculty medicine Ben Gurion U., Israel. Sr. editor Current Medical Diagnosis and Treatment, 1987-93; mem. editorial bd. New Eng. Mag.; contbr. numerous articles to profl. jours. Mem. U.S. Prospective Payment Assessment Commn., 1983-88. With USPHS, 1966-68. Master ACP; mem. Physicians for Social Responsibility, Am. Pub. Health Assn., Assn. Am. Physicians, Inst. Medicine, Soc. Gen. Internal Medicine (past pres.), Phi Beta Kappa, Alpha Omega Alpha. Home: 49 W Shore Dr Pennington NJ 08534-2006 Office: Robert Wood Johnson Found PO Box 2316 Princeton NJ 08543-2316

SCHROEDER, WILLIAM JOHN, electronics executive; b. Havre de Grace, Md., June 9, 1944; s. William Martin and Dorothy Jeanne (McLaughlin) S.; m. Marilee Jane Alne, May 28, 1966; children: Kristen, Kari Britt, Kimberley. BSEE, Marquette U., 1967, MSEE, 1968; MBA, Harvard U., 1972. Devel. engr. Honeywell Inc., Mpls., 1968-70; mgmt. cons. McKinsey & Co., Los Angeles, 1972-76; mgr. product planning Memorex Corp., Santa Clara, Calif., 1976-78; pres. Priam Corp., San Jose, Calif., 1978-85, chmn., 1985-86; pres. Conner Peripherals, Inc., San Jose, 1986-89, vice chmn., 1989-94; CEO Arcada Software Inc., a Conner Co., 1993-94; pres., CEO Diamond Multimedia Systems, Inc., San Jose, Calif., 1994—; bd. dirs. Xircom Corp., Thousand Oaks, Calif., MetaTools Inc., Carpenteria, Calif., CNF Transp., Inc., Palo Alto, Calif. Office: Diamond Multimedia Systems Inc 2880 Junction Ave San Jose CA 95134-1922

SCHROEDER, W(ILLIAM) WIDICK, religion educator; b. Newton, Kans., Nov. 12, 1928; s. William Fredric and Irene (Widick) S.; m. Gayle Eadie, Sept. 1, 1956; children: Scott David, Carla Gayle. BA, Bethel Coll., 1949; MA, Mich. State U., East Lansing, 1952; BDiv, Chgo. Theol. Sem., 1955; PhD, U. Chgo., 1960; DD (hon.), Chgo. Theol. Seminary, 1995. Ordained to ministry Congl. Christian Ch., 1955. Instr. Mich. State U., East Lansing, 1953-54, U. Chgo., 1958-60; from asst. prof. to prof. religion and society Chgo. Theol. Sem., 1960-94, prof. emeritus, 1994—; vis. fellow Mansfield Coll., Oxford, Eng., 1966; vis. lectr. Yale U., 1970; vis. scholar Ctr. for Process Studies, Claremont, Calif., 1976; vis. lectr. in ethics and soc. Divinity Sch. U. Chgo., 1967-71, 76; editor Rev. of Religious Rsch., 1964-69. Author: (with Victor Obenhaus) Religion in American Culture: Unity and Diversity in a Midwestern County, 1964; Cognitive Structures and Religious Research, 1970; (with Victor Obenhaus, Larry A. Jones and Thomas P. Sweetser) Suburban Religion: Churches and Synagogues in the American Experience, 1974; (with Keith A. Davis) Where Do I Stand? Living Theological Options for Contemporary Christians, 1973, rev. edit., 1975, 3d edit., 1978; Flawed Process and Sectarian Substance: Analytic and Critical Perspectives on the United Church of Christ General Synod Pronouncement, Christian Faith: Economic Life and Justice, 1990, Toward Belief: Essays in the Human Sciences, Social Ethics, and Philosophical Theology, 1996; co-editor: (with Philip Hefner) Belonging and Alienation: Religious Foundations for the Human Future, 1976; (with Gibson Winter) Belief and Ethics: Essays in Ethics, the Human Sciences and Ministry in Honor of W. Alvin Pitcher, 1978; (with John B. Cobb, Jr.) Process Philosophy and Social Thought, 1981; (with Perry LeFevre) Spiritual Nurture and Congregational Development, 1984, Pastoral Care and Liberation Praxis: Essays in Personal and Social Transformation, 1986, Creative Ministries in Contemporary Christianity, 1991; (with Franklin I. Gamwell) Economic Life: Process Interpretations and Critical Responses, 1988. Mem. Am. Acad. Religion, Am. Sociol. Assn., Soc. for the Sci. Study of Religion, Religious Rsch. Assn., Ctr. for Process Studies, Soc. Christian Ethics. Home: 6315 Longwood Rd Libertyville IL 60048-9447 Office: Chgo Theol Sem 5757 S University Ave Chicago IL 60637-1507 *The aims of existence are aesthetic satisfaction and intensity of feeling. In facilitating these aims, the Divine Reality is the locus of potentiality, the mediator of experience, the evoker of feeling and the ultimate recipient of all that has become.*

SCHROEPFER, GEORGE JOHN, JR., biochemistry educator; b. St. Paul, June 15, 1932; s. George John and Catherine Rita (Callaghan) S.; children: Lisa Marie Schoepfer Schwartz, Cynthia Marie Schoepfer Winzenried, Stephanie Marie, Jeanine Marie Schroepfer Smith, Dana Marie Schroepfer Rethwisch. BS, U. Minn., 1955, MD, 1957, Phd, 1961. Intern U. Minn. Hosps., 1957-58; rsch. fellow depts. biochemistry and internal medicine U. Minn., 1958-61, asst. prof. biochemistry, 1963-64; rsch. fellow chemistry dept. Harvard U., Cambridge, Mass., 1962-63; asst. prof. biochemistry U. Ill., 1964-67, assoc. prof., 1967-70; dir. Sch. Basic Med. Scis. U. Ill., Urbana, 1968-1970; prof. U. Ill., 1970-72; prof. biochemistry and chemistry Rice U., Houston, 1972-83, Ralph and Dorothy Looney prof. biochemistry, prof. chemistry, 1983—, dir. lab. basic med. sci., 1987—, chmn. biochemistry dept., 1972-84, sci. dir. Inst. Biosci. and Bioengring., 1987—; vis. scientist Med. Rsch. Coun. Unit Hammersmith Hosp., London, 1961-62; mem. subcom. on biochem. nomenclature NAS, 1965-68; mem. biochemistry, tng. com. Nat. Inst. Gen. Med. Scis. NIH, 1970-73, ad-hoc com. tng. in biochemistry, 1974; cons. Am. Cyanamid Co., 1984-90, undergrad. biol. scis. edn. panel Howard Hughes Med. Inst., 1988; vis. prof. Sci. and Tech. Agy. Japan, 1993. Assoc. editor Lipids, 1969-76; mem. editl. bd. Jour. Biol. Chemistry, 1974-79, Jour. Lipid Rsch., 1983-88, Current Pharm. Design, 1995—. Fellow AAAS, Arteriosclerosis Coun. of Am. Heart Assn.; mem. Am. Chem. Soc., Am. Soc. Biochemistry and Molecular Biology, Am. Soc. Mass Spectrom, Sigma Xi, Alpha Omega Alpha. Office: Rice U Dept Biochem PO Box 1892 Houston TX 77251-1892

SCHROER, BERNARD JON, industrial engineering educator; b. Seymour, Ind., Oct. 11, 1941; s. Alvin J. and Selma A. (Mellencamp) S.; m. Kathleen Dittman, July 5, 1963; children: Shannon, Bradley. BSE, Western Mich. U., 1964; MSE, U. Ala., 1967; PhD, Okla. State U., 1972. Registered profl. engr., Ala. Mech. designer Sandia Labs., Albuquerque, 1962-63; engr. Teledyne Co., Huntsville, Ala., 1964-67, Boeing Co., Huntsville, 1967-70, Computer Sci. Corp., Huntsville, 1970-72; dir. Johnson Ctr. U. Ala., 1972-91, prof., 1991—, chmn. dept. indsl. and sys. engring., 1991-94, assoc. v.p. rsch., 1994—; mem. adv. coun. Energy Dept., Montgomery, Ala., 1980-86; bd. dirs So. Solar Energy Ctr., Atlanta, 1980-83; mem. gov.'s cabinet State of Ala., Montgomery, 1982. Author: Modern Apparel Manufacturing Systems and Simulation, 1991; contbr. articles to profl. jours. Named Outstanding Engr., Robotics Internat., 1986, Outstanding Engr., Ala. Soc. Profl. Engrs., 1987; recipient summer traineeship NSF, 1971. Fellow Inst. Indsl. Engr. (pres. 1972, 86, Outstanding Engr. 1973, 77); mem. NSPE, Soc. Computer Simulation, Tech. Transfer Soc., Huntsville Rotary. Lutheran. Home: 716 Owens Dr SE Huntsville AL 35801-2034 Office: U Ala Coll Engring Huntsville AL 35899

SCHROER, EDMUND ARMIN, utility company executive; b. Hammond, Ind., Feb. 14, 1928; s. Edmund Henry and Florence Evelyn (Schmidt) S.; m. Lisa V. Strope; children: James, Fredrik, Amy, Lisa, Timothy, Suzanne. BA, Valparaiso U., 1949; JD, Northwestern U., 1952. Bar: Ind. 1952. Pvt. practice law Hammond, 1952—; assoc. Crumpacker & Friedrich, 1952; ptnr. Crumpacker & Schroer, 1954-56; assoc., then ptnr. Lawyer, Friedrich, Petrie & Tweedle, 1957-62; ptnr. Lawyer, Schroer & Eichhorn, 1963-66; sr. ptnr. Schroer, Eichhorn & Morrow, Hammond, 1967-77; pres., chief exec. officer No. Ind. Pub. Svc. Co., Inc., Hammond, 1977-93; chmn. No. Ind. Pub. Svc. Co., Hammond, 1978-93, chmn., chief exec. officer, 1989-93, also bd. dirs.; chmn., pres., chief exec. officer NIPSCO Industries, Inc., 1987-93; cons. NIPSCO Industries Inc., Hammond, 1993-96; also bd. dirs.; asst. dist. atty., No. Ind., 1954-56; trustee Ill. Ins. Exch., 1993-95. Trustee Sch. Bd., Munster, Ind., 1969-71, pres., 1971; fin. chmn. Rep. Party, Hammond, 1958-62; del. Ind. Rep. Conv., 1958, 60, 64, 66, 68. Mem. Fed. Bar Assn., Am. Gas Assn. (chmn. 1986), Rotary (pres. Hammond club 1968). Lutheran. Home and Office: No Ind Pub Svc Co 5265 Hohman Ave Hammond IN 46320-1722

SCHROETER, DIRK JOACHIM, mechanical engineer; b. Solingen, Germany, Mar. 2, 1949; came to U.S., 1957; s. Joachim Willi and Doris Irmgard (Kroeber) S.; m. Melissa Dickerson, Apr. 20, 1974; 1 child, Keira Melissa. BSME, SUNY, Buffalo, 1971, MSME, 1973. Commd. 2d lt. USAF, 1971, advanced through grades to lt. col., 1992; acquistion project officer Guided Bomb Unit-System Program Office, Eglin AFB, Fla., 1972-77; requirements officer Launch Vehicles Deputate, L.A. Air Force Sta., Calif., 1977-79; mem. tech. staff radar systems Hughes Aircraft Co., El Segundo, Calif., 1979-81; mem. profl. staff Lockheed Martin Electronics and Missiles, Orlando, Fla., 1981—; acquisition officer space div. Air Force Res., L.A. Air Force Sta., 1979-81; electronic engr. aero. systems ctr. Air Force Material Command, Wright-Patterson AFB, 1981-93. Editor: Computer Aided Engring. Bulletin, 1982-86; author: (guide) Industrial Modernization Improvement Program-Quick Reference to Modernization, 1986. Judge Orange County Sci. and Engring. Fair, Orlando, Fla., 1985-88. Recipient Commendation medal USAF, 1979, Meritorious Svc. medal USAF, 1993. Mem. AIAA (interactive computer graphics tech. com. 1983-86), Soc. Automotive Engrs. Republican. Methodist. Achievements include development of neutral (IGES and text-based) database: Martin Integrated Neutral Graphics and Engring. Libr. used for computer graphics and file exchange for computer aided acquisition and logistic support with suppliers and customers. Home: 4309 Winderlakes Dr Orlando FL 32835-2607 Office: Lockheed Martin Electronics Electronics and Missiles 5600 Sand Lake Rd # 135 Orlando FL 32819-8907

SCHROLL, EDWIN JOHN, theater educator, stage director; b. Watertown, N.Y., Feb. 14, 1941; s. Clarence Edwin and Frances Lucille (Snyder) S. BS, Lyndon State Coll., 1966; MS, Oswego State U., 1971. Cert. tchr. N.Y. English tchr. jr. high sch. Watertown (N.Y.) Sch. System, 1966-67; English tchr. high sch. Belleville (N.Y.) Cen. Sch., 1967-71; English tchr. high sch. Massena (N.Y.) Cen. Sch., 1971-96, drama and speech tchr., 1988—, drama coach, 1975—, forensics coach; engr., announcer, programmer Pathways to Peace program Sta. WNCQ, Watertown, 1967-92. Cinematographer, writer, narrator, prodr. (documentaries) The United States: A Bicentennial Tour, 1976, Europe on $100 a Day, 1986; cinematographer (TV film) Partying, 1989; dir. various high sch. prodns.; actor various community prodns. Bd. dirs. Youth in Action, 1993-94; active Nat. Family Opinion, 1991—; state advocate Ednl. Theatre Assn., 1996; del. Citizens Ambassador Program of People to People Internat. Theatre Edn. Delegation to China, 1996. Mem. Nat. Geog. Soc., Ednl. Theatre Assn., Archaeology Inst. Am., Am. Film Inst., Nat. Trust Hist. Preservation. Republican. Mem. LDS Ch. Avocations: stamp and coin collecting, gardening, historical research, genealogy, travel. Home: PO Box 216 143 S Murray St Cape Vincent NY 13618 Office: Massena Sch System 290 Main St Massena NY 13662-1901

SCHROPP, JAMES HOWARD, lawyer; b. Lebanon, Pa., June 20, 1943; s. Howard J. and Maud E. (Parker) S.; m. Jo Ann Simpson, Sept. 4, 1965; children: James A., John C., Jeffrey M., Jeremy M. BA, U. Richmond, 1965; JD, Georgetown U., 1973. Bar: D.C. 1973, U.S. Supreme Ct. 1980. Asst. gen. counsel SEC, Washington, 1973-79; ptnr. Fried, Frank, Harris, Shriver & Jacobson, Washington, 1979—; adj. prof. Georgetown U., Washington, 1982-86; mem. faculty Na.t Inst. for Trial Advocacy. Mem. ABA (discovery com. litigation sect. 1984-86, tender offer litigation subcom. corp. banking and bus. law sect. 1985-86, task force on broker-dealer compliance supervisory procedures 1987-89). Office: Fried Frank Harris Shriver & Jacobson 1001 Pennsylvania Ave NW Washington DC 20004-2505

SCHROTE, JOHN ELLIS, retired government executive; b. Findlay, Ohio, May 6, 1936; s. Millard L. and Alberta (Ellis) S.; m. Rachel Daly, Mar. 2, 1957; children: James D., Gretchen Schrote Kent. BS in Agriculture, Ohio State U., 1958; MBA, Xavier U., 1964. Buyer-expediter McGraw Constrn. Co., Middletown, Ohio, 1958-59; buyer Armco Corp., Middletown, 1959-66; adminstrv. asst. Congressman D.E. Lukens, Washington, 1967-71; prin. asst. dir. OEO, Washington, 1971-72; spl. asst. sec. USDA, Washington, 1972-76, nat. rep. congl. com., 1976-79, acting asst. sec., 1981-82; adminstrv. asst. Congressman F.J. Sensenbrenner, Jr., Washington, 1979-81, 1984-89; dep. dir. presdl. pers. office The White House, 1982-83; exec. v.p. Bishop Bryant & Assocs., Washington, 1983-84; asst. to sec. and dir. congl. affairs Dept. Interior, Washington, 1989, dep. asst. sec. policy mgmt. and budget, 1989-91, asst. sec. policy mgmt. and budget, 1991-93; retired, 1993. Mem. Nat. Policy Forum, The Environ. Policy Coun., 1994, N.C. Seafood Indsl. Park Authority; chmn. Currituck County Econ. Devel. Bd., Currituck County Rep. Exec. Com., 3d Dist. Rep. Exec. Com., N.C. State Rep. Exec. Com.; chmn. Currituck County Ext. Svc. Adv. Leadership Coun.; chmn., bd. dirs. Currituck County 4-H Found.; v.p. Ocean Hills Property Owners Assn.; sec.-treas. bd. dirs. 60 Found. Mem. Carolla Bus. Assn. Episcopalian. Home: PO Box 209 Corolla NC 27927

SCHROTH, PETER W(ILLIAM), lawyer, management and law educator; b. Camden, N.J., July 24, 1946; s. Walter and Patricia Anne (Page) S.; children: Laura Salome Erickson-Schroth, Julia James. AB, Shimer Coll., 1966; JD, U. Chgo., 1969; M in Comparative Law, U.Chgo., 1971; SJD, U. Mich., 1979; postgrad., U. Freiburg, Fed. Republic Germany, Faculté Internationale pour l'Enseignement de Droit Comparé; MBA, Rensselaer Poly. Inst., 1988. Bar: Ill. 1969, N.Y. 1979, Conn. 1985, Mass. 1990; solicitor Supreme Ct. England and Wales 1995. Asst. prof. So. Meth. U., 1973-77; fellow in law and humanities Harvard U., 1976-77, vis. scholar, 1980-81; assoc. prof. N.Y. Law Sch., 1977-81; prof. law Hamline U., St. Paul, 1981-83; dep. gen. counsel Equator Bank Ltd., 1984-87; v.p., dep. gen. counsel Equator Holdings Ltd., 1987-94, v.p., gen. counsel, 1994—; adj. prof. law U. Conn., 1985-86, Western New Eng. Coll., 1988—, adj. prof. of mgmt. Rannselaer Poly. Inst., 1988—. Author: Foreign Investment in the United States, 2d edit., 1977; (with Stiefel) Products Liability: European Proposals and American Experience, 1981, Doing Business in Sub-Saharan Africa, 1991; bd. editors Am. Jour. Comparative Law, 1981-84, 91—, Conn. Bar Jour., N.Y. Internat. Law Rev., Jour. Bus. in Developing Nations; contbr. articles to profl. jours. Mem. ABA (editor in chief ABA Environ. Law Symposium 1980-82), Am. Soc. Comparative Law (bd. dirs. 1978-84, 91—), Am. Fgn. Law Assn., Internat. Bar Assn., Internat. Law Assn. (com. multinat. banking), Acad. Internat. Bus., Conn. Civil Liberties Union (bd. dirs. 1985-92), Environ. Law Inst. (assoc.), Columbia U. Peace Seminar (assoc.), Hartford Club (bd. govs. 1995—), Am. Corp. Counsel Assn. (pres. Conn. chpt.), Conn. Bar Assn. (chair sect. of internat. law). Office: Equator House 45 Glastonbury Blvd Glastonbury CT 06033-4411

SCHROTH, THOMAS NOLAN, editor; b. Trenton, N.J., Dec. 21, 1920; s. Frank David and Loretta (Nolan) S.; m. Colette Streit, May 1, 1948 (div. 1958); 1 child, Valerie; m. Patricia Wiggins, Sept. 27, 1958; children: Jennifer, Amy, Anne. Student, Tuck Sch. Bus. Adminstrn., 1942; AB, Dartmouth Coll., 1943. Reporter Time, Washington, 1946-47, UPI, Boston, 1947-48; reporter, news editor Bklyn. Eagle, 1948-51, mng. editor, 1951-55; editorial adviser Magnum Photos, Inc., N.Y.C., 1955; exec. editor, pub. Congl. Quar. Inc. and Editorial Research Reports, Washington, 1955-68; founder, editor Nat. Jour. Ctr. Polit. Rsch., Washington, 1969-70; communications adviser Pub. Broadcasting Environment Ctr., Washington, 1970-71; asst. dir. pub. affairs for communications EPA, Washington, 1970-71, cons., 1972; exec. editor The Ellsworth (Maine) American, 1972-77; co-pub.-editor (with Patricia Schroth) Maine Life Mag., Sedgwick, 1977-81; editorial cons. U. Maine, Bangor, 1976-90; mng. editor South-North News Svc., Hanover, N.H., 1987-91; co-pub. New Leaf Pubs., Sedgwick, Maine, 1990—; mem. Am. Press Inst. Seminar for Mng. Editors, 1953. Editor: Congress and the Nation, 1946-64--A Review of Government and Politics in the Postwar Years; editor Improving the U. of Maine trustee's pamphlet. Elected selectman Town of Sedgwick, 1989-94; bd. dirs. Blue Hill (Maine) Meml. Hosp., 1978-93, Bangor Symphony Orch., 1981-87; bd. dirs., v.p. Island Nursing Home, Deer Isle, Maine, 1985—; mem. Maine State Dem. Com., Augusta, 1985-92; bd. dirs. Downeast Transp., Inc., 1993—. 1st lt. Army Airways Comm. Sys., USAAF, WWII. Mem. Sigma Delta Chi. Avocations: gardening, walking, music. Home and Office: 50 Benjamin River Rd Sedgwick ME 04676-9729

SCHRUM, JAKE BENNETT, university administrator; b. Greenville, Tex., Feb. 9, 1946; s. Jake M. and Julia (Bennett) S.; m. Alice Woodman, Dec. 28, 1968; children: Julia Elizabeth, Emily Katharine. B.A., Southwestern U., 1968; M.Div., Yale U., 1973; postgrad. Harvard U., 1983. Ordained to ministry Methodist Ch., 1969. Devel. officer Yale U., New Haven, 1973-77; dir. devel. Muhlenberg Coll., Allentown, Pa., 1977-78; v.p. Tex. Wesleyan Coll., Fort Worth, 1978-82; v.p. univ. rels. Southwestern U., Georgetown, Tex., 1982-85; v.p. Emory U., Atlanta, 1985-91; pres. Tex. Wesleyan U., 1991-97; chmn. CASE, 1995-96; bd. dirs. Bd. Ind. Colls. & Univs. Tex., 1994-95, Bd. Tex. Ind. Coll. Found., Found. Ind. Higher Educators, 1995—; trustee United Way; adv. bd. Fort Worth Habitat for Humanity. Named Man of Yr., Bnai Brith North Tex., 1995. Mem. Coun. Advancement and Support Edn. (bd. dirs. Europe), Nat. Assn. Ind. Colls. and Univs. (bd. dirs., exec. com. 1995—), Rotary. Avocations: golf, public speaking. Office: Texas Wesleyan University 1201 Wesleyan St Fort Worth TX 76105-1536

SCHTEINGART, DAVID EDUARDO, internist; b. Buenos Aires, Oct. 17, 1930; came to U.S., 1957; s. Mario and Flora (Garfunkel) S.; m. Monica Naomi Starkman, July 3, 1960; children: Miriam, Judith, M. Daniel. MD, U. Buenos Aires, 1955. Diplomate Am. Bd. Internal Medicine. Fellow Mt. Sinai Hosp., N.Y.C., 1957-58, Maimonides Hosp., Bklyn., 1958-59; fellow U. Mich., Ann Arbor, 1959-62, instr., 1962-63, asst. prof., 1963-68, assoc. prof., 1968-72, prof., 1972—. Contbr. articles to profl. jours., books. Pres. Beth Israel Congregation, Ann Arbor, 1974-79, Hebrew Day Sch., Ann Arbor, 1984-86, Jewish Fedn. Washtenaw County, Ann Arbor. Recipient rsch. grants NIH, Bethesda, Md., 1985—. Fellow Am. Coll. Physicians; mem. Endocrine Soc., N.Y. Acad. Scis., Am. Soc. Clin. Nutrition, Cen. Soc. Clin. Rsch., Am. Fedn. Clin. Rsch. Jewish. Avocations: tennis, running, community activities. Office: U Mich Med Sch 1150 W Medical Center Dr Ann Arbor MI 48109-0726

SCHUBART, MARK ALLEN, arts and education executive; b. N.Y.C., May 24, 1918; s. Henry Allen and Pauline (Werner) S. Student pvt. schs., U.S. and France; studied, piano with Celia Wolberg, theory with Marion Nugent, flute with Ruth Freeman, composition with Roger Sessions. Assoc. editor Eton Pub. Corp., 1937-40; asst. music editor newspaper PM, 1940-44; music editor N.Y. Times, 1944-46; dir. pub. activities Juilliard Sch. Music, 1946-49, dean, v.p., 1949-62; exec. dir. The Lincoln Center Fund, Lincoln Center Performing Arts, Inc., N.Y.C., 1963-66; dir. edn. Lincoln Center Performing Arts, Inc., 1966-75; dir. Lincoln Center Inst., 1975-90, pres., 1990-95, chmn., 1995—. Composer two song cycles, opera, concert overture, songs.; Author: Performing Arts Institutions and Young People; Contbr. articles profl. jour. Home: 30 Park Ave New York NY 10016-3801 Office: 70 Lincoln Center Plz New York NY 10023-6548

SCHUBEL, JERRY ROBERT, marine science educator, scientist, university dean; b. Bad Axe, Mich., Jan. 26, 1936; s. Theodore Howard and Laura Alberta (Gobel) S.; m. Margaret Ann Hostetler, June 14, 1958; children: Susan Elizabeth, Kathryn Ann. BS, Alma Coll., 1957; MA in Teaching, Harvard U., 1959; PhD, Johns Hopkins U., 1968. Rsch. assoc. Chesapeake Bay Inst., Johns Hopkins U., Balt., 1968-69, rsch. scientist, 1969-74, adj. rsch. prof., assoc. dir., 1973-74; dir. Marine Sci. Rsch. Ctr., SUNY, Stony Brook, 1974-83; dean, leading prof. SUNY, Stony Brook, 1983-94; acting dir. Waste Mgmt. Inst., SUNY, Stony Brook, 1985-87; provost SUNY, Stony Brook, 1986-89; dir. COAST Inst., SUNY, Stony Brook, 1989; Disting. Svc. prof. SUNY, Stony Brook, 1994-95, prof. emeritus, 1995—; pres., CEO The New Eng. Aquarium, Boston, 1994—; hon. prof. East China Normal U., Shanghai, 1985—; sec. exec. com. Commn. on Food, Environment and Renewable Resources, 1993, chair steering com., 1994; mem. governing bd. Regional Marine Rsch. Program, Greater N.Y. Bight, 1993-94. Author: The Living Chesapeake, 1981, The Life and Death of the Chesapeake Bay, 1986; (with H.A. Neal) Solid Waste Management and the Environment, 1987, Garbage and Trash: Can We Convert Mountains Into Molehills?, 1992; editor: (with B. C. Marcy Jr.) Power Plant Entrainment, 1978; (with others) The Great South Bay, 1991; sr. editor Coastal Ocean Pollution Assement News, 1981-86; co-editor in chief Estuaries, 1986-88; editorial bd. CRC Revs. in Aquatic Scis.; contbr. articles to profl. jours. Mem. adv. bd. Environ. Sci. Com. Outer Continental Shelf, Minerals Mgmt. Scs., 1984-86, chmn., 1986; bd. dirs. N.E. Area Remote Sensing Sys., 1983-85, L.I. Incubator Corp.; v.p. L.I. Forum for Tech., 1989-92; chair Mass. Outfall Monitoring Task Force, 1995—; mem. sci. adv. bd. EPA, 1996—; commr. Nat. Rsch. Coun.'s Commn. on Engring. Tech. Systems, 1996—; mem. vis. com. for MITs Dept. of Ocean Engring., 1995—; trustee Natural Heritage Insts., 1995—. Recipient L.I. Sound Am. Environment Edn. award, 1987, Stony Brook U. medal, 1989, Matthew Fontaine Maury award, 1990, Ben Gurion U. medal, 1993; Alfred P. Sloan fellow, 1959. Mem. Nat. Acad. Sci. (marine bd. 1989-94, exec. com. 1990, vice chair 1991-94, chair 1992-94, com. on Coastal Ocean 1989-93), Nat. Assn. State Univ. and Land Grant Colls. (bd. dirs. marine divsn., chmn. 1986-88), L.I. Environ. Coun., L.I. Marine Resources Adv. Coun. (chair 1990-94), L.I. Rsch. Inst. (bd. dirs. 1992-94), L.I. Environ.-Econ. Roundtable (co-chair 1991-92), Suffolk County Recycling Commn., (chmn. 1987-88), Estuarine Rsch. Fedn. (v.p. 1982-83, pres. 1985-87), N.Y. Sea Grant Inst. (chmn. governing bd. 1988-90, gov.'s task force on coastal resources 1990-91), The Nature Conservancy (trustee L.I. chpt. 1991-94), Franklin Electronic Pubs. (bd. dirs. 1991—), Taproot (bd. dirs. 1988-93, vice chair 1990-93), Sigma Xi, Phi Sigma Pi. Avocation: photography. Home: 10 Thacher St Apt 115 Boston MA 02113-1753 Office: New England Aquarium Central Wharf Boston MA 02110-3399

SCHUBERT, BARBARA SCHUELE, performing company executive; b. Cleve., Feb. 21, 1939; d. William Edward and Mildred Marianne (Matousek) Schuele; m. John Dwan Schubert, June 15, 1963; children: William Edward, Christopher John, David Matthew. BS in Social Scis., John Carroll U, 1962, MA in English, 1967; MEd, 1980. Cert. secondary tchr., elem. remedial reading tchr., Ohio. Tchr. Sch. on Magnolia, Cleve., 1980-82, Ruffing Montessori, Cleve., 1982-83; tchr. English U. Sch., Chagrin Falls, Ohio, 1983-86; gen. mgr. Ohio Ballet, Akron, 1987-90, assoc. dir., 1990—; bd. trustees Ohio Ballet, 1974-87. Bd. dirs. John Carroll U., 1990—; active Beaumont Sch., Ballet Guilds Internat. Roman Catholic. Club: Cleve. Skating. Office: Ohio Ballet 354 W Market St Akron OH 44303-2027

SCHUBERT, FRED ERIC, electrical engineer, educator; b. Stuttgart, Germany, Feb. 8, 1956; came to U.S., 1985; s. Konrad and Martha Ruth (Reichert) S.; m. Jutta Maria Lukai, Feb. 22, 1980; children: Anne F., Martin F., Ursula V. Diploma in Engring. with honors, U. Stuttgart, 1981, D in Engring. with honors, 1986. Rsch. assoc. Max Planck Inst., Stuttgart, 1981-85; mem. tech. staff, prin. investigator AT&T Bell Labs., Murray Hill, N.J., 1985-95; prof. dept. elec. and computer engring. Ctr. for Photonics Rsch., Boston U., 1995—. Author: Doping in III-V Semiconductors, 1993; editor: Delta Doping of Semiconductors, 1996; patentee in field. Postdoctoral fellow AT&T, 1985-87; recipient Lit. prize Verein Deutscher Elektrotechnikes, 1994. Mem. IEEE (sr.), Am. Phys. Soc., Optical Soc. Am., Verein Deutscher Elektrotechniker (lit. prize 1994), Material Rsch. Soc. Roman Catholic. Achievements include several patents involving doping of III-V semiconductors and several patents on high efficiency light emitting diodes. Home: 49 Angela St Canton MA 02021-2251 Office: Boston U Dept Elec and Computer Engring 8 St Mary's St Boston MA 02215

SCHUBERT, GLENDON, political scientist, educator; b. Oneida, N.Y., June 7, 1918; s. Glendon Austin and Agnes (Rogers) S.; m. Elizabeth Josephine Neal (dec. 1949); children: Frank, James; m. Elizabeth Harris; children: Susan, Kathleen, Robin. A.B., Syracuse U., 1940, Ph.D., 1948. Mem. faculties Syracuse U., 1946-48, UCLA, 1948-49, Howard U., 1949-50, Rutgers U., 1950-51, Franklin and Marshall Coll., 1951-52, Mich. State U., 1952-67, U. Minn., 1955; William Rand Kenan Jr. prof. polit. sci. U. N.C. at Chapel Hill, 1967-68; u. prof. York U., 1968-70; u. prof. polit. sci. U. Hawaii, 1970—; rsch. prof. polit. sci. So. Ill. U. at Carbondale, 1986-91; Fulbright lectr. U. Oslo, Norway, 1959-60; fellow Center for Advanced Study in Behavioral Scis., 1960-61; sr. scholar in residence Center for Cultural and Tech. Interchange Between East and West, U. Hawaii, 1963-64, 65; Fulbright-Hays research scholar, Netherlands, 1977; NSF faculty fellow U. Groningen, Netherlands, 1977-78; NATO sr. fellow, U.K.; fellow Netherlands Inst. Advanced Study Humanities and Social Sci., Wassenaar, Netherlands, 1978-79. Author over 25 books; assoc. editor for biosocial behavior The Behavioral and Brain Sci.; adv. editor Jour. Social and Evolutionary Systems, 1980—; assoc. editor Politics and the Life Scis., 1980-90; contbr. articles to profl. jours. in biobehavioral and polit. sci., and pub. policy. Served with Signal Intelligence U.S. Army, 1942-46. Decorated Bronze Star; recipient Regents' medal and award for excellence in research U. Hawaii, 1975. Mem. Internat. Soc. Polit. Psychology, Am. Polit. Sci. Assn. (past mem. exec. coun.), Assn. Polit. Life Scis. (past pres.), Internat. Soc. Human Ethology, Phi Beta Kappa. Address: 92 King George Dr Boxford MA 01921

SCHUBERT, GUENTHER ERICH, pathologist; b. Mosul, Iraq, Aug. 17, 1930; s. Erich Waldemar and Martha Camilla (Zschitzschmann) S.; m. Gisela Schultz, June 13, 1959; children: Frank, Marion, Dirk. MD, University, Heidelberg, Germany, 1957; pvt. docent in pathology, University, Tuebingen, Germany, 1966. Asst. med. dir. University Tuebingen, Fed. Republic of Germany, 1966-76; head Inst. Pathology, Wuppertal, Fed. Republic of Germany, 1976-96; chair of pathology U. Witten-Herdecke, Fed. Republic of Germany, 1985-96. Co-author: Coloratlas of Cytodiagnosis of the Prostate, 1975, Endoscopy of the Urinary Bladder, 1989; author: Textbook of Pathology, 1981, 87. Mem. Wissenschaftlicher Beirat, Bundesarztekammer, Bonn, Germany, 1976-85; pres. Medizinisch Naturwissenschaftliche Gesellschaft, Wuppertal, 1984-85, Onkologischer Schwerpunkt, Wuppertal, 1985-93, OSP Bergisch-Land, 1992-95, Bergische Arbeitsgemeinschaft fur Gastroenterologie, Wuppertal, 1987-88, 90-91, 94-95. Mem. Deutsche Gesellschaft fur Pathologie, Deutsche Gesellschaft fur Nephrologie, Deutsche Gesellschaft fur Urologie, Internat. Acad. of Pathology, Lions. Avocations: music, diving, photography. Home: Am Anschlag 71, D-42ii3 Wuppertal 1, Germany Office: Inst of Pathology, Heusner Strasse 40, 42 283 Wuppertal 2, Germany

SCHUBERT, HELEN CELIA, public relations executive; b. Washington City, Wis.; d. Paul H. and Edna (Schmidt) S. BS, U. Wis., Madison. Dir. pub. rels. United Cerebral Palsy, Chgo., 1961; adminstrv. dir. Nat. Design Ctr., Chgo., 1962-67; owner Schubert Pub. Rels., Chgo., 1967—; bd. dirs. Fashion Group, Chgo., 1988-95. Mem. women's bd. Am. Cancer Soc., Chgo., 1988-96, Art Resources in Tchg., Chgo., 1988-92. Recipient Comm. award Am. Soc. Interior Designers, Chgo., 1979, 83, 88, 94; named to Chgo. Women's Hall of Fame City of Chgo., 1990. Fellow Nat. Home Fashion League; mem. Women's Ad Club Chgo. (pres. 1981-83, Woman of Yr. award 1987), Women in Comm. (pres. 1969-70, Matrix award Lifetime Achievement 1996), Am. Advt. Fedn. (lt. gov. 1983-85). Lutheran. Home: 1400 N Lake Shore Dr Chicago IL 60610-1674

SCHUBERT, JOHN EDWARD, former banker; b. Rochester, N.Y., Jan. 22, 1912; s. Charles A. and Matilda M. (von Rohr) S.; m. Margaret Cecelia la Plante, Nov. 11, 1939 (dec. Jan. 1977); children: Susan R. (Mrs. Dennis E. Coyne), Patricia S. (Mrs. Daniel L. Starks); m. Florence Margaret Moran, Nov. 14, 1977 (dec. Dec. 1978); m. Rita H. Strowe, Mar. 27, 1993. Student, Syracuse U., 1929-30; grad., Rochester Bus. Inst., 1932; hon. degree accounting, 1955; grad., Rutgers U. Grad. Sch. Banking, 1950. With Security Trust Co., Rochester, 1930-44; with Community Savs. Bank, Rochester, 1944-77; pres., chief exec. officer Community Savs. Bank, 1965-73, chmn., chief exec. officer, 1973-75, chmn., 1976-77; dir. Seneca Towers, Inc., Rochester Mgmt. Inc.; realtor Real Estate Bd. Rochester; assoc. Red Barn Properties, Inc. Bd. dirs. Met. Rochester Found., Inc., Sr. Citizens Homes, Inc.; bd. dirs. Automobile Club Rochester, pres., 1977; trustee emeritus Rochester Inst. Tech. Mem. Oak Hill Country Club (v.p. 1964-67, bd. govs. 1962-68, 78-81), Beta Gamma Sigma (hon. U. Rochester chpt.). Home: 18 Winding Brook Dr Fairport NY 14450-2541 Office: 6 Schoen Pl Pittsford NY 14534-2026

SCHUBERT, RICHARD FRANCIS, consultant; b. Trenton, N.J., Nov. 2, 1936; s. Yaro and Frances Mary (Hustak) S.; m. Sarah Jane Lockington, Aug. 24, 1957; children: Robyn, David. BA cum laude, Eastern Nazarene Coll., 1958; LLB, Yale U., 1961. Bar: Pa. 1962, U.S. Supreme Ct 1972. Arbitration atty. Bethlehem Steel Corp., Pa., 1961-66; asst. mgr. labor relations Bethlehem Steel Corp., 1966-70; exec. asst. to undersec. labor Washington, 1970; gen. counsel labor, 1971-73, dep. sec. labor, 1973-75; asst. to v.p. indsl. relations Bethlehem Steel Corp., 1973, asst. v.p. public affairs, 1975-77, v.p. public affairs, 1977-79, pres., 1979-80, vice chmn., 1980-82; pres. ARC, 1982-89; pres., CEO Points of Light Found., 1990-95; bd. dirs. Weirton Steel, Mgmt. Tng. Corp. Bd. dirs. Nat. Alliance Bus., Inst. Ethics, Cmty. Hope, Inc.; chmn. Internat. Youth Found., Biorelease Inc., Nazarene Compassionate Ministries; chmn. Peter F. Drucker Found. Mem. Pa. Bar Assn., Northampton County Bar Assn., Coun. on Fgn. Rels., Am. Iron and Steel Inst. (past chmn. com. on internat. trade), Ctr. Excellence Govt., Ea. Nazarene Alumni Assn. (pres. 1969-73), Phi Alpha Delta. Mem. Ch. of Nazarene. Home: 7811 Old Dominion Dr Mc Lean VA 22102-2425 Office: 1155 Connecticut Ave NW Ste 416 Washington DC 20036-4306

SCHUBERT, RONALD HAYWARD, retired aerospace engineer; b. Bklyn., Aug. 25, 1932; s. John and Joan Sarah (Hayward) S.; m. Dorothy May Smith, Mar. 5, 1953 (div. 1961); children: Marcus H., Malcolm F., Ronald J. (dec.), Ann E.; m. Linda Jane van der Ploeg, Mar. 6, 1961 (div. 1988). BA cum laude, Ohio State U., 1956. Assoc. engr. Hughes Aircraft Co., Fullerton, Calif., 1957-61; physicist Nat. Cash Register Co., Dayton, Ohio, 1962-63; sr. research engr. Lockheed Missiles and Space Co., Sunnyvale, Calif., 1963-90. Served as staff sgt. USMC, 1951-54. Recipient Hon. mention Woodrow Wilson Fellowship Com. Mem. Phi Beta Kappa. Democrat. Roman Catholic. Achievements include pioneering work in reconnaissance satellite orbit concealment; devel. of digital computer simulations for all aspects of the aerospace vehicle, its mission and environment; guidance system and autopilot specialist. Home: 201 W California Ave Apt 1023 Sunnyvale CA 94086-5035

SCHUBERT, WILLIAM HENRY, curriculum studies educator; b. Garrett, Ind., July 6, 1944; s. Walter William and Mary Madeline (Grube) S.; children by previous marriage: Ellen Elaine, Karen Margaret; m. Ann Lynn Lopez, Dec. 3, 1977; children: Heidi Ann, Henry William. BS, Manchester Coll., 1966; MS, Ind. U., 1967; PhD, U. Ill., 1975. Tchr., Fairmount, El Sierra and Herrick Schs., Downers Grove, Ill., 1967-75; clin. instr. U. Wis., Madison, 1969-73; tchg. asst., univ. fellow U. Ill., Urbana, 1973-75; asst. prof. U. Ill., Chgo., 1975-80, assoc. prof., 1981-85, prof., 1985—, coord. secondary edn., 1979-82; coord. instrl. leadership, 1979-85, dir. grad. studies Coll. Edn., 1983-85, coord. grad. curriculum studies, 1985—, coord. edn. studies, 1990-94, chair area curriculum and instruction, 1990-94; vis. assoc. prof. U. Victoria (B.C., Can.), 1981; disting. vis. prof. U. S.C., 1986. Elected Internat. Acad. Edn., Stockholm, 1997. Mem. Internat. Acad. Edn., Profs. of Curriculum (factotum 1984-85), Soc. for Study of Curriculum History (founding mem., sec.-treas. 1981-82, pres. 1982-83), Am. Ednl. Rsch. Assn. (chmn. creation and utilization of curriculum knowledge 1980-82, program chmn. curriculum studies div. 1982-83, sec. Div. B 1989-91), Am. Assn. Colls. for Tchr. Edn., John Dewey Soc. (bd. dirs. 1986-95, chair awards com., 1988-90, co-chair lectures commn., 1989-91, pres. elect, 1990-91, pres. 1992-93), ASCD (steering com. of curriculum com. 1980-83, pubs. com. 1987-90, internat. polling panel 1990—), Am. Ednl. Studies Assn., World Coun. for Curriculum and Instrn., Soc. for Profs. of Edn. (exec. bd. 1997—), Nat. Soc. for Study of Edn., Inst. Dem. in Edn., Masons, Scottish Rite, Phi Delta Kappa, Phi Kappa Phi (pres. U. Ill.-Chgo. chpt. 1981-82). Author: (with Ann Lopez) Curriculum Books: The First Eighty Years, 1980; author: Curriculum: Perspective, Paradigm, and Possibility, 1986; (with Edmund C. Short and George Willis) Toward Excellence in Curriculum Inquiry, 1985; editor: (with Ann Lopez) Conceptions of Curriculum Knowledge: Focus on Students and Teachers, 1982, (with George Willis) Reflections from The Heart of Ednl. Inquiry: Understanding Curriculum and Teaching Through the Arts, 1991, (with William Ayers) Teacher Lore: Learning From Our Own Experience, 1992, (with George Willis, R. Bullough, C. Kridel, J. Holton) The American Curriculum: A Documentary History, 1993; assoc. editor: Ednl. Theory; former mem. editl. bd. Ednl. Studies; former cons. editor Phenomenology and Pedagogy; adv. bd. Teaching Edn., Pi Lamda Theta Pubs., 1995—; mem. editl. bd. Ednl. Theory; cons. editor Jour. Curriculum and Supervision; editorial bd. Curriculum and Teaching; reviewing editor Jour. Gang Behaviour; editor: book series Student Lore, SUNY Press, 1990—; cons. editor Jour. Curriculum Discourse and Dialogue; contbr. over 200 articles and chpts. to profl. publs. Home: 727 S Ashland Ave Chicago IL 60607-3165 Office: U Ill Coll Edn M/C 147 1040 W Harrison St Chicago IL 60607-7129

SCHUCHART, JOHN ALBERT, JR., utility company executive; b. Omaha, Nov. 13, 1929; s. John A. and Mildred Vera (Kessler) S.; m. Ruth Joyce Schock, Dec. 2, 1950; children: Deborah J. Kelley, Susan K. Felton. BS in Bus, U. Nebr., 1950; grad., Stanford U. Exec. Program, 1968. With No. Natural Gas Co., Omaha, 1950-71, asst. sec., 1958-60, mgr. acctg., 1960-66, adminstrv. mgr., 1966-71; v.p., treas. Intermountain Gas Co., Boise, Idaho, 1972-75, chief fin. officer, 1973-75; fin. v.p. and treas., chief fin. officer Mont.-Dakota Utilities Co. (now MDU Resources Group, Inc.), Bismarck, N.D., 1976-77, pres., chief oper. officer, 1978-80, pres., 1980-92, CEO, 1980-94, chmn. bd., 1983—, also dir. Contbr. articles to profl. jours. Trustee Bismarck YMCA, N.D. chpt. Nature Conservancy; mem. bd. regents U. Mary, Bismarck; bus. adv. bd. Coll. Bus., Mont. State U., Billings. With AUS, 1951-53. Recipient Am. Gas Assn. Order of Acctg. Merit award, 1968, 78, Scroll and Merit award Adminstrv. Mgmt. Soc., 1972, U. Nebr. at Omaha citation of Alumnus Achievement, 1987, Coll. of Bus. Disting. Achievement award, 1989, CEO of Yr. award Fin. World Mag., 1993, Commn. and Leadership award Dist. 20 Toastmasters Internat., 1994. Mem. Apple Creek Country Club, Mpls. Athletic Club, Elks, Delta Sigma Pi. Republican. Methodist. Home: 1014 Cottage Dr Bismarck ND 58501-2458 Office: MDU Resources Group Inc 400 N 4th St Bismarck ND 58501-4022

SCHUCK, CARL JOSEPH, lawyer; b. Phila., Nov. 21, 1915; s. Joseph and Christina (Schadl) S.; m. Mary Elizabeth Box, June 7, 1941; children: Mary Ann (dec.), John, James, Catherine, Christopher. BS, St. Mary's Coll., 1937; postgrad., U. So. Calif., 1937-38; JD, Georgetown U., 1941. Bar: D.C. 1940, Calif. 1943, U.S. Supreme Ct. 1952. Atty. Dept. Justice, Washington, 1940-42, Alien Property Custodian, San Francisco, 1942-44; mem. firm Overton, Lyman & Prince, L.A., 1947-79, profl. corp. mem. firm, 1979-85; lectr. Practising Law Inst., 1973; Del. 9th Cir. Jud. Conf., 1963-80, chmn. lawyer-dels. com., 1972, mem. exec. com., 1976-80, chmn. exec. com., 1977-78, mem. sr. adv. bd., 1989-95; mem. disciplinary bd. State Bar Calif., 1970-71. Fellow Am. Coll. Trial Lawyers (chmn. com. on complex litigation 1979-81, regent 1981-85), L.A. County Bar Assn. (trustee 1974-76), Phi Alpha Delta. Club: Chancery (pres. 1984-85). Home and Office: 16916 Hierba Dr Apt 254 San Diego CA 92128-2677

SCHUCK, JOYCE HABER, author; b. N.Y.C., Dec. 9, 1937; d. Frank F. and Florence (Smith) H.; m. Stephen Martin Schuck, June 15, 1958; children: William David, Thomas Allen, Ann Elizabeth. BA in Human Svcs. and Counseling, Loretto Hts. Coll., Denver, 1982. Counselor, tchr. Vision Quest, Colorado Springs, 1979-82; cons., program designer for govt. agys. Colorado Springs, 1982-85; author, 1987—; asst. to cons. Volusia County Dept. Corrections, Daytona Beach, Fla., 1982; cons. student svcs. program Pikes Peak C.C., Colorado Springs, 1982; cons., designer Juvenile Probation of El Paso County, Colorado Springs, 1982, 4th Jud. Dist./Dist. Atty.'s Office, Colorado Springs, 1984. Author: Political Wives, Veiled Lives, 1991. Co-founder Community Transitions, Colorado Springs, 1984; coord. El. Paso County Shape Up Program, 1982; v.p. Community Coun. of Pikes Peak Region, Colorado Springs, 1983, Women's Found. of Colo., Denver, 1987. Recipient Mayor's award for civic leadership City of Colorado Springs, 1983. Mem. Jr. League of Colorado Springs (sustaining), Salon de Femme (founding). Avocations: tennis, skiing, hiking.

SCHUCK, PETER HORNER, lawyer, educator; b. N.Y.C., Apr. 26, 1940; s. Samuel H. and Lucille (Horner) S.; m. Marcy Cantor, June 26, 1966; children: Christopher, Julie. BA with honors, Cornell U., 1962; JD cum laude, Harvard U., 1965, MA, 1969; LLM, NYU, 1966; MA (hon.), Yale U., 1982. Bar: N.Y. State 1966, D.C. 1972. Practiced law N.Y.C., 1965-68; teaching fellow in govt. Harvard U., 1969-71; cons. (Center for Study of Responsive Law), Washington, 1971-72; dir. Washington office Consumers Union, 1972-77; dep. asst. sec. for planning and evaluation HEW, Washington, 1977-79; vis. scholar Am. Enterprise Inst. for Public Policy Research, Washington, 1979; assoc. prof. law Yale U., 1979-81, prof., 1981-86, Simeon E. Baldwin prof. law, 1986—, dep. dean, 1993-94; vis. prof. Georgetown U. Law Ctr., 1986-87, NYU Law Sch., fall 1994; lectr. profl., acad., bus., univ., govt. and citizen groups. Author: The Judiciary Committees, 1975, Suing Government, 1983, Citizenship without Consent, 1985, Agent Orange on Trial, 1986, enlarged edit., 1987; editor: Tort Law and the Public Interest, 1991, Foundations of Administrative Law, 1994, Paths to Inclusion, 1997; contbr. articles and revs. to profl. and popular publs. Guggenheim fellow, 1984-85; recipient Silver Gavel award ABA, 1987. Jewish.

SCHUCK, THOMAS ROBERT, lawyer, farmer; b. Findlay, Ohio, Feb. 7, 1950; s. Robert Damon and Katherine Margaretta (Beynon) S.; m. Pamela Lee Bakan, Sept. 2, 1979. BA, DePauw U., 1972; MA, U. Kent, U.K., 1974; JD, Harvard U., 1976. Bar: Ohio 1976, U.S. Dist. Ct. (no. dist.) Ohio 1977, U.S. Dist. Ct. (so. dist.) Ohio 1979, Ariz. 1990, U.S. Ct. Appeals (6th cir.) 1978, U.S. Ct. Appeals (9th cir.) 1991. Law clk. U.S. Dist. Ct., Cleve., 1976-79; assoc. Taft, Stettinius & Hollister, Cin., 1979-87, ptnr., 1987—; owner, operator Rural Hill Farm; participant Ohio Bench Bar Conf., Columbus, 1990, 91; barrister Am. Inn of Ct., 1986-87, LEAD Clermont, 1997—; mem. bar exam com. U.S. Dist. Ct. (so. dist.) Ohio. Contbg. author: Aids and the Law, 2d edit. 1992; contbr. articles to profl. jours. Trustee Mental Health Svcs. East, Inc., Cin., 1985-91; mem. Clermont County Mental Health Bd., Batavia, Ohio, 1992—; mem. Clermont County Mental Retardation Developmental Disabilities Levy Steering Com., 1996; mem. May Festival Assocs., Cin., 1984-86; spl. gifts com. Cin. Art Acad., 1987; mem. WGUC Radio Cmty. Bd., 1984-86. Rotary Internat. Found. grad. fellow, 1972. Mem. FBA (pres. Cin. chpt. 1994-95, v.p. 6th cir. 1996—), Cin. Bar Assn., Potter Stewart Am. Inn of Ct. (barrister 1986-87), U.S. Rowing Assn. (asst. referee), Harvard Club Cin. (pres. 1995-96), Camargo Hunt Club, Masons, Phi Beta Kappa, Delta Chi, Phi Eta Sigma, Sigma Delta Chi. Republican. Methodist. Avocations: reading, photography. Home: PO Box 615 189 State Route 133 Felicity OH 45120-0615 Office: 1800 Star Bank Ctr 425 Walnut St Cincinnati OH 45202

SCHUDEL, HANSJOERG, international business consultant; b. Wald, Switzerland, Sept. 27, 1937; s. Rene and Alice S. Ed., Coll. Bus. Adminstrn., Zurich, Switzerland. With Byk-Gulden, Konstanz, Germany and Sao Paulo, Brazil, 1962-69, Hicksville, N.Y., 1964-69; pres., chief exec. officer, dir. Stinnes Corp., N.Y.C., 1971-83; exec. officer Stinnes A.G., Muelheim, Fed. Republic of Germany, 1978-83; rep. for the Americas First Arab Pacific Corp. Ltd., Chappaqua, N.Y., 1984—. Mem. German-Am. C. of C. (bd. dirs. 1976-83), Internat. World Travelers Club, Swiss Soc., Confrerie de la Chaine des Rotisseurs, Order des Coteaux de Champagne, Foothills Assn. (bd. dirs.). Office: First Arab Pacific Corp Ltd 1275 4th St Ste 307 Santa Rosa CA 95404-4049

SCHUDER, RAYMOND FRANCIS, lawyer; b. Wickford, R.I., Dec. 27, 1926; s. Rollie Milton and Selma (Ball) S.; AB, Emory U., 1949, JD, 1951; m. Betty Jo Williams, Mar. 14, 1948; children: Gregg Williams, Glen Arva. Bar: Ga. 1951. With Trust Co., Ga., Atlanta, 1951-54; assoc. firm Wheeler, Robinson & Thurmond, Gainesville, Ga., 1954-59; pvt. practice law, Gainesville, 1959-70, 76-96; ptnr. Schuder & Brown, Gainesville, 1971-76; Mcpl. ct. judge, Gainesville, 1956-60, 73-75, Magistrate ct. judge, 1985—; bd. dirs. Lanier Securities, Inc. Supr. Upper Chattahoochee Soil and Water Conservation Dist., 1971-74; chief exec. officer, bd. dirs. Charles Thompson Estes Found., Inc., Gainesville. Cpl. USMCR, 1944-50; 1st lt. USAR, ret. Mem. State Bar Ga. (gov. 1966-70), Gainesville-Northeastern (pres. 1969-70) Bar Assn., Am. Legion, V.F.W., Elks. Methodist. Home: 2224 Riverside Dr Gainesville GA 30501-1232

SCHUELE, DONALD EDWARD, physics educator; b. Cleve., June 16, 1934; s. Edward and Mildred (Matousek) S.; m. Clare Ann Kirchner, Sept. 5, 1956; children: Donna, Karen, Melanie, Judy, Rachel, Ruth. BS, John Carroll U., Cleve., 1956, MS, 1957; PhD, Case Inst. Tech., 1962. Instr. physics and math. John Carroll U., 1956-59; part-time instr. physics Case Inst. Tech., 1959-62, instr., asst. prof., assoc. prof., 1962-70; mem. tech. staff Bell Telephone Labs., 1970-72; assoc. prof. physics Case Western Res. U., 1972-74, prof., 1974—, dean undergrad. coll., 1973-76, chmn. dept. physics, 1976-78; vice dean Case Inst. Tech., 1978-83, v.p. for undergrad. and grad. studies, 1983-84, dean, 1984-86, prof. physics, 1986-88, dean math. and natural sci., 1988-89, Albert A. Michaelson prof. physics, 1989—, acting chmn. elec. engring. and applied physics, 1992-93; cons. in field. Co-editor: Critical Revs. in Solid State Scis, 1969-84; contbr. articles to profl. jours.; patentee in field. Mem. adv. bd. St. Charles Borromeo Sch., 1970-72; pres. Seed Found., 1986-89; trustee St. Mary's Sem., 1980-93; mem. Olympic Sports Equipment and Tech. Com., 1982-93; trustee Newman Found., 1983—, Northeastern Ohio Sci. Fair, 1983—; mem. Diocesan Pastoral Coun., 1992-94; active Rep. Presdl. task force. NSF Faculty fellow, 1961-63; recipient Disting. Physics Alumnus award John Carroll U., 1983. Mem. Am. Phys. Soc. (vice chair Ohio sect. 1995-96, chair 1996-97), Am. Assn. Physics Tchrs., North Coast Thermal Analysis Soc., Newman Apostolate, Case Alumni Coun. (life, treas. 1992—), Sigma Xi, Alpha Sigma Nu, Tau Beta Pi. Republican. Roman Catholic. Achievements include patents fluid pressure device, impact wrench torque calibrator. Home: 4892 Countryside Rd Cleveland OH 44124-2513 Office: Case Western Res U 10900 Euclid Ave Cleveland OH 44106-1712

SCHUELER, BETTY JANE, writer, counselor; b. Washington, Feb. 21, 1944; d. Grover Cleveland and Mary (Bruce) Sherlin; m. Gerald Joseph Schueler, Aug. 17, 1963; children: Diane Sue, Joseph Carroll, Andrew Tyson, Crystal Ann. AA, Harford C.C., Bel Air, Md., 1975; BS, SUNY, Albany, 1992; MS in Adminstrn., Ctrl. Mich. U., 1993; PhD in Interdisciplinary studies, The Grad. Sch. Am., 1996. Lic. profl. marriage and family counselor. Owner Copy Cats, Aberdeen, Md., 1975-88; instr. Harford C.C., Bel Air, Md., 1978-84; owner Compucats Computer Store, Aberdeen, 1982—, Harford Writers Group, Aberdeen, 1988—, Creative Sales and Svc., Aberdeen, 1988—; computer cons., Aberdeen, 1982—, tutor, Aberdeen, 1989—. Co-author: (with Gerald J. Schueler) Coming Into the Light, 1989, Enochian Yoga, 1990, Enochian Workbook, 1993, Angels Message to Humanity, 1996; contbr. articles to profl. jours. Bd. dirs. Friends of the Harford County Librs., Riverside, Md., 1991—; treatment foster parent FACETS, Belcamp, Md., 1992—. Adult scholar Harford County C. of C., Bel Air, 1992. Mem. Am. Counseling Assn., Internat. Assn. Marriage and Family Counselors, Assn. Multicultural Counseling and Devel. Democrat. Methodist. Avocations: reading, crafts, music, art, sports. Office: Harford Writers Group 680 W Bel Air Ave Aberdeen MD 21001-2217

SCHUELER, JOHN R., newspaper executive. Pres., COO The Orange County Register, Santa Ana, Calif. Office: The Orange County Register 625 N Grand Ave Santa Ana CA 92701-4347

SCHUELKE, JOHN PAUL, religious organization administrator; b. Benton Harbor, Mich., Nov. 5, 1934; s. Alwin E. and Martha M. (Schoeneberg) S.; m. Noreta H. Petersen, Sept. 9, 1956; children: Alvin, Mary, Sheryl, Brian. BS in Acctg., U. Wyo., 1957; LLD (hon.), Concordia U., Irvine, Calif., 1983. CPA. From acct. to sr. acct. Colo. Interstate Gas Co., Colorado Springs, 1957-63; staff acct. Arthur Anderson & Co., Denver, 1963-64; mgr. fin. control Colo. Interstate Corp., Colorado Springs., 1964-67, dir. fin. control, 1967-71; adminstrv. v.p. mfg. divsn. Marsh Instrument Co. subs. Colo. Mfg. Corp., Skokie, Ill., 1971-72; exec. dir. bd. dirs., COO Luth. Ch.-Mo. Synod, St. Louis, 1972—; Lectr. in field. Asst. scoutmaster Boy Scouts Am., Colorado Springs; governing bd. Com. Luth. Coop., Luth. Svcs. in Am.; former mem. governing bd. Luth. Coun.-USA; mem. St. Matthew Luth Ch., St. Louis. Recipient God and Country award Eagle Scout. Mem. Alpha Kappa Psi, Gamma Delta (former pres.). Avocations: traveling, fishing, reading.

SCHUELLER, THOMAS GEORGE, lawyer; b. Budapest, Hungary, Oct. 4, 1936; came to U.S., 1938; s. Herbert H. and Edith (Geiringer) S.; m. Sandra Burke, Sept. 3, 1960 (div. Apr. 1982); children: Katherine, Matthew, John. AB cum laude, Amherst Coll., 1958; LLB, Harvard U., 1962. Bar: N.Y. 1963. Salesman Gen. Mills. Inc., Utica, N.Y., 1958-59; assoc. Hughes Hubbard & Reed, N.Y.C., 1962-69, ptnr., 1969—. Bd. dirs., sec. Ballet Hispanico, N.Y.C., 1987—. Mem. ABA, Assn. of Bar of City of N.Y., Phi Beta Kappa. Home: 169 E 78th St New York NY 10021-0405 Office: Hughes Hubbard & Reed 1 Battery Park Plz New York NY 10004-1405 also: 108 Fairchild Rd Sharon CT 06069

SCHUELLER, WILLIAM ALAN, dermatologist; b. Xenia, Ohio, Apr. 14, 1939; s. John Waldo and Jeanne Evelyn (Tipton) S.; m. Joyce Anne Smith, June 22, 1963; children: Robert Alan, Thomas Alan. BA, Ohio State U., 1961; MD, Case Western Reserve U., 1966. Diplomate Am. Bd. Dermatology. Intern Charleston (S.C.) Naval Hosp., 1966-67; resident in dermatology San Diego Regional Med. Ctr., 1969-72; commd. ensign U.S. Navy, 1965; avanced through grades to comdr. U.S. Navy, various, U.S., 1975; resigned U.S. Navy, 1975; pvt. practice in dermatology Johnson City, Tenn., 1976—; active staff Johnson City Med. Ctr., 1976—; cons. staff North Side Hosp., Johnson, City, Tenn. Fellow Am. Acad. Dermatology; mem. AMA, So. Med. Assn., Tenn. Med. Assn., Soc. Investigative Dermatology. Mem. Unitarian Ch. Avocation: amateur radio. Office: 1611 W Market St Johnson City TN 37604-6018

SCHUELLER, WOLFGANG AUGUSTUS, architectural educator, writer; b. Aachen, Germany, Sept. 10, 1934; came to U.S., 1964; s. Sepp and Mathilde (Kalff) S.; m. Ria Herpers, Apr. 22, 1960; 1 child, Uschi. Diploma in Engring. in Civil Engring., FH Aachen, Germany, 1960; BS in Archtl. Engring. with honors, N.D. State U., 1966; MSCE in Structural Engring., Lehigh U., 1968; BArch, Syracuse U., 1971. Registered profl. engr., N.Y., Pa. Supr. constrn., structural engr. Hochtief A.G., Munich and Essen, Fed. Republic of Germany, 1960-63; structural designer Green Blanksteen Russel Assocs., Winnipeg, Man., Can., 1963-64; structural engr. Pioneer Svc. and Engring. Co., Chgo., 1966-67, Richardson, Gordon Assocs., Pitts., 1968-69; prof. architecture Syracuse U (N.Y.), 1971-82, Va. Poly. Inst., Blacksburg, 1982-94, U. Fla., Gainesville, 1994—; vis. prof. Ministry Univ. Affairs Thailand, 1996. Author: Highrise Building Structures, 1977, Horizontal-Span Building Structures, 1983, The Vertical Building Structure, 1990, The Design of Building Structures, 1996. Mem. ASCE, Nat. Soc. Archtl.Engrs., Soc. for History of Tech., Coun. on Tall Bldgs. and Urban Habitat, Sigma Xi, Phi Kappa Phi, Tau Beta Pi. Achievements include rsch., presentation of papers, workshops, book critiques, seminars, and pub. lects. on relationship between bldg. sci., structures in particular, and architecture. Avocations: classical music (opera), jazz, history of art, jogging. Office: U Fla Coll Arch Gainesville FL 32611-5702

SCHUEPPERT, GEORGE LOUIS, financial executive; b. Merrill, Wis., July 1, 1938; s. George Henry and Eleanor Natalie (Pautz) S.; m. Kathleen Kay Carpenter, May 6, 1967; children—Steven Andrew, Stephanie Roanne, Stenning Karl. B.B.A., U. Wis., Madison, 1961; M.B.A., U. Chgo., 1969. Treas., controller Steiger-Rathke Devel. Co., Phoenix, 1964-65; various positions Continental Ill. Nat., Chgo., 1965-76, 1981-86; mng. dir. Continental Ill. Ltd., London, 1977-81; sr. v.p. Continental Ill. Nat. Bank, Chgo., 1982-86; ptnr. Coopers & Lybrand, Chgo., 1986-87; exec. v.p. fin. CBI Industries Inc, Oak Brook, Ill., 1987-95; also bd. dirs. CBI Industries Inc, Oak Brook, 1987-95; exec. v.p., CFO Outboard Marine Corp., Waukegan, Ill., 1996—; bd. dirs. Wells Mfg. Co., Barrington Bank & Trust Co. Bd. dirs., chmn. fin. com. Gt. Books Found.; bd. advisors CPA's for Pub. Interest; chmn., bd. dirs. De Paul U. Gov. Asst. Program. Lt. (j.g.) USN, 1961-64. Recipient Herfurth award U. Wis., 1960. Mem. Econ. Club Chgo. (bd. dirs., chmn. membership com.). Republican. Avocations: history; civic affairs; architecture; travel; golf. Home: 97 Otis Rd Barrington IL 60010-5129 Office: Outboard Marine Corp 100 E Sea Horse Dr Waukegan IL 60085-2141

SCHUERHOLZ, JOHN BOLAND, JR., professional baseball executive; b. Baltimore, MD, Oct. 1, 1940; s. John Boland and Maryne (Wyatt) S.; m. Ellen Louise Lawson, June 21, 1963; 1 dau., Regina Marie Reagan; m. Karen Louise Wiltse, Sept. 18, 1978; 1 son, Jonathan Lawrence. B.E., Towson State U., 1962; postgrad., Loyola Coll. (Md.), 1964-66. Tchr. various schs., 1962-66; adminstrv. asst. Balt. Orioles, 1966-68; adminstrv. asst. Kansas City Royals, 1968-70, asst. farm dir., 1970-75, farm dir., 1975, dir. scouting and player devel., 1976-79, v.p. player personnel, 1979-81, exec. v.p., gen. mgr., 1981-90; exec. v.p., gen. mgr. Atlanta Braves, 1990—. Served with AUS, 1966-72. Lutheran. Office: Atlanta Braves PO Box 4064 Atlanta GA 30302-4064*

SCHUERMAN, JOHN RICHARD, social work educator; b. Scotts Bluff, Nebr., Feb. 27, 1938; s. Lawrence and Mildred Jeanette (France) S.; m. Charlotte Kavaloski, Sept. 12, 1964; children: Gabrielle Ann, Matthew

Lawrence. B.S., U. Chgo., 1960, M.A., 1963, Ph.D., 1970. Social worker Ill. Dept. Mental Health, Chgo., 1963-65; mem. faculty Sch. Social Service Adminstrn., U. Chgo., 1968—, prof. social work, 1978—, asso. dean, 1970-79; mem. Ill. Mental Health Planning Bd., 1971-73; cons. in field. Author: Research and Evaluation in the Human Services, 1983, Multivariate Analysis in the Human Services, 1983, Putting Families First: An Experiment in Family Preservation, 1994. Editor jour. Social Service Rev.; research on child welfare, use of artificial intelligence in social welfare. Home: 1229 E 50th St Chicago IL 60615-2908 Office: 969 E 60th St Chicago IL 60637-2640

SCHUERMAN, NORBERT JOEL, school superintendent; b. DeWitt, Nebr., Dec. 26, 1934; s. Edwin J. and Martha (Finkbeiner) S.; m. Charlette Ann Detling, Aug. 6, 1960; children: Robert, Brenda, Todd. B of Music Edn., U. Nebr., 1957, MEd, 1959, EdS in Ednl. Mgmt. and Supervision, 1964, EdD, 1967. Cert. profl. tchr. (life), Nebr. Tchr. Clatonia-Bennet (Nebr.) Pub. Sch., 1954-58; tchr., prin. Mullen (Nebr.) Pub. Sch., 1958-61; prin. Ainsworth (Nebr.) Pub. Sch., 1961-63; sr. high sch. vice prin. Lincoln (Nebr.) Pub. Sch., 1963-66, 67-69; sr. high sch. prin. Arapahoe County Sch. Dist. 6, Littleton, Colo., 1969-74; from asst. supt. to assoc. supt. to supt. Omaha Pub. Schs., 1974-97; trustee, mem. exec. com. Nebr. Coun. Econ. Edn., 1985—; bd. dirs. Nat. Study Sch. Evaluation, 1986-90, Charles Drew Health Ctr., 1985-95, Fontenelle Forest, 1987-92, 95—; bd. trustees Western Heritage Mus., 1994—; mem. exec. com. Coun. Gt. City Schs., 1988—; mem. Nat. Urban Edn. Task Force, 1990—; mem. Nat. Adv. Bd. for Active Citizenship Today, 1992—; mem. bd. advisors Close Up Found., 1992—; mem. adminstrs. adv. com. U. Nebr.-Lincoln Tchrs. Coll. Mem. adv. com. Mid-Am. coun. Boy Scouts Am., 1984—; coun. regents Big Bros./Big Sisters of Midlands, Omaha, 1986—; bd. dirs. United Way of Midlands, 1985—; adv. bd. Omaha Children's Mus., 1988—. Named Nebr. Supt. of Yr., 1991; recipient Disting. Svc. award Nebr. Coun. Sch. Adminstrs., 1988, awards of honor Nat. Sch. Pub. Rels. Assn., 1991, Nebr. PTA Outstanding PTA Advocate award; named to Exec. Educator mag.'s Top 100 Sch. Execs., 1993. Mem. Am. Assn. Sch. Adminstrs. (urban schs. com. 1992—), Nebr. Coun. Sch. Adminstrs., Omaha Sch. Adminstrs. Assn., North Ctrl. Assn. (bd. dirs. 1983-89, chmn. 1987-88), Large City Schs. Supts. (pres. 1992-93), NCCJ (bd. dirs. 1990—), Nebr. Schoolmasters Club, Urban League of Nebr., Nat. Congress Parents and Tchrs. (hon. life), Nebr. Congress Parents and Tchrs. (hon. life), Phi Delta Kappa, Omicron Delta Kappa. Home: 4007 N 94th St Omaha NE 68134-3927 Office: Omaha Sch Dist 3215 Cuming St Omaha NE 68131-2000

SCHUESSLER, KARL FREDERICK, sociologist, educator; b. Quincy, Ill., Feb. 15, 1915; s. Hugo and Elsa (Westerbeck) S.; m. Lucille Smith, June 27, 1946; children—Thomas Brian. B.A., Evansville (Ind.) Coll., 1936; M.A., U. Chgo., 1939; Ph.D., Ind. U., 1947. Sociologist Ill. State Prison, 1938; tchr. Highland Park (Ill). High Sch., 1939-40; instr. Vanderbilt U., 1946-47; mem. faculty Ind. U., 1947—, prof. sociology, 1960-76, Distinguished prof. sociology, 1976—, chmn. dept., 1961-69; rsch. cons. Thammasat U., Bangkok, Thailand, 1963; vis. prof. UCLA, 1957, U. Calif.-Berkeley, 1965-66, U. Wash., 1967; guest scholar Ctr. for Survey Rsch., Mannheim (Germany) U., 1979-80, vis. prof., 1980-81; fellow Inst. Sociology, U. Hamburg, Germany, summer 1983; mem. adv. panel sociology NSF, 1962-63; mem. behavioral sect. NIH, 1964-68; mem. social sci. rsch. study sect. NIMH, 1968-69, social sci. tng. study sect., 1969-73; mem. NRC, 1970-75. Author: (with J.H. Mueller) Statistical Reasoning in Sociology, 1961; Social Research Methods; Analyzing Social Data, 1971; (with H. Costner) Statistical Reasoning in Sociology, 3d edit, 1977; (with Dagmar Krebs) Soziale Empfindungen: Ein Interkultureller Skalenvergelich bei Deutschen und Amerikanern, 1987; also numerous articles.; editor: (with Cohen and Lindesmith) The Sutherland Papers, 1956, (with E.H. Sutherland) On Analyzing Crime, 1972, (with Demerath and Larsen) Public Policy and Sociology, 1975, Am. Sociol. Rev., 1969-71, Sociol. Methodology, 1977-79, Musical Taste and Social Background, 1980, Measuring Social Life Feelings, 1982. Served to lt. USNR, 1942-46. Fellow AAAS; mem. Am. Sociol. Assn., Am. Statis. Assn. Home: 1820 E Hunter Ave Bloomington IN 47401-5284

SCHUESSLER FIORENZA, ELISABETH, theology educator; b. Tschanad, Romania, Apr. 17, 1938; parents German citizens; d. Peter and Magdalena Schuessler; m. Francis Fiorenza, Dec. 17, 1967; 1 child, Chris. MDiv, U. Wuerzburg, Federal Republic of Germany, 1962; Dr of Theology, U. Muenster, Federal Republic of Germany, 1970; Lic. Theol, U. Wuerzburg, 1963. Asst. prof. theology U. Notre Dame, South Bend, Ind., 1970-75, assoc. prof., 1975-80, prof., 1980-84; instr. U. Muenster, 1966-67; Talbot prof. New Testament Episcopal Div. Sch., Cambridge, Mass., 1984-88; Krister Stendahl prof. div. in scripture and interpretation Harvard U., Cambridge, Mass., 1988—; Harry Emerson Fosdick vis. prof. Union Theol. Sem., N.Y.C., 1974-75; guest prof. U. Tuebingen, Federal Republic of Germany, 1987, Cath. Theol. faculty Luzern, Switzerland, 1990. Author: Der Vergessene Partner, 1964, Priester für Gott, 1972, The Apocalypse, 1976, Invitation to the Book of Revelation, 1981, In Memory of Her, 1983, Bread not Stone, 1984, Judgement or Justice, 1985, Revelation: Vision of a Just World, 1991, But She Said - Feminist Practices of Biblical Interpretation, 1992, Discipleship of Equals: A Critical Feminist Ekklesialogy of Liberation, 1993, Jesus: Miriam's Child and Sophia's Prophet, Critical Issues in Feminist Christology, 1994; editor: Searching the Scriptures, 2 vols, 1993, 94, The Power of Naming, 1996; founding co-editor Jour. Feminist Studies in Religion; also editor other works. Mem. Am. Acad. Religion, Soc. Bibl. Lit. (past pres.). Office: Harvard Div Sch 45 Francis Ave Cambridge MA 02138-1911

SCHUETTE, BILL, state senator; b. Midland, Mich., Oct. 13, 1953. Student, U. Aberdeen, 1974-75; B.S. in Fgn. Svc., Georgetown U., 1976; J.D., U. San Francisco, 1979. Bar: U.S. Supreme Ct. 1985. Atty. Midland, Mich., 1981—; Mich. field coordinator George Bush for Pres., 1979; Mich. polit. dir. Reagan/Bush for Pres., 1980; mem. 99th-101st Congresses from 10th Mich. dist., Washington, 1985-91, Mich. Senate, 1994—; dir. Mich. Dept. Agr., 1991-93. Office: PO Box 30036 Lansing MI 48909-7536

SCHUETTE, CHARLES A., lawyer; b. Columbus, Ind., Feb. 24, 1942. BBA, U. Okla., 1964, JD, 1967. Bar: Okla. 1967, Fla. 1970, U.S. Supreme Ct. 1979, U.S. Dist. Ct. (so. dist.) Fla. 1982, U.S. Dist. Ct. (mid. dist.) Fla. 1982. With Akerman, Senterfitt & Eidson P.A., Miami. Mem. Dade County Homeless Trust. Fellow Am. Bar Found.; mem. ABA, Fla. Bar, Okla. Bar Assn., Dade County Bar Assn. Office: Akerman Senterfitt & Eidson PA 1 SE 3rd Ave # 28flr Miami FL 33131-1700

SCHUETTE, MICHAEL, lawyer; b. Manitowoc, Wis., Apr. 19, 1937; s. Elmer A. and Mary Irene (Hart) S.; m. Mary Dare Whiteside, Oct. 28, 1961; 1 child, Sharon Mary. B.S., Northwestern U., 1959, J.D., 1962. Bar: Ill. 1962, U.S. Dist. Ct. (no. dist.) Ill. 1962. With Lord, Bissell & Brook, Chgo., 1961—, ptnr, 1971—; dir. Corralitos Astron. Research Assn., Horizons for Blind. Mem. ABA (past chmn. coal com. natural resources sect.), Chgo. Bar Assn. Club: Law (Chgo.). Home: 711 Carriage Hill Dr Glenview IL 60025-5405 Office: Lord Bissell & Brook 115 S La Salle St Chicago IL 60603-3801

SCHUETTE, OSWALD FRANCIS, physics educator; b. Washington, Aug. 20, 1921; s. Oswald Frances and Mary (Moran) S.; m. Kathryn E. Cronin, June 7, 1947; children: Patrick Thomas, Mary Kathryn, Elizabeth Anne. B.S., Georgetown U., 1943; Ph.D., Yale U., 1949. Assoc. prof. physics Coll. William and Mary, 1948-53; Fulbright research prof. physics Max Planck Inst. for Chemistry, 1953-54; sci. liaison officer U.S. Naval Forces, Germany, 1954-58; mem. staff Nat. Acad. Scis., Washington, 1958-60; dep. spl. asst. for space Office Sec. Def., Washington, 1961-63; prof. physics dept. U. S.C., 1963-92, dit. prof. emeritus, 1992—; vis. prof. Inst. Exptl. Physics, U. Vienna, 1980. Lt. USNR, 1944-46. Fellow AAAS; mem. Am. Phys. Soc., Am. Assn. Physics Tchrs., S.C. Acad. Sci., Sigma Xi. Home: 4979 Quail Ln Columbia SC 29206-4624

SCHUETZENDUEBEL, WOLFRAM GERHARD, engineering executive; b. Germany, Feb. 17, 1932; came to U.S., 1958; s. Gerhard Egon and Kaethe (Warmbier) S.; m. Ingeborg Jutta Lesch, Dec.15, 1960. BME, Tech. U. Berlin, 1956, MME, MS in Power Engring., 1958; DSc in Nuclear Engring., U. Beverly Hills, L.A., 1979. Registered profl. engr., Calif. asst. mgr. boiler engring. dept. Riley Stoker Corp., Worcester, Mass., 1958-61; sect. mgr. systems devel. Combustion Engring., Inc., Windsor, Conn., 1961-68; various tech. mgmt. positions Gen. Atomic Co. (subs. Gulf Oil Corp.), San Diego, 1968-79; dir. utilities Solvent Refined Coal Internat., Inc. (subs. Gulf Oil Corp.), Denver, 1979-81, Gulf Oil Corp., Houston, 1981-82; pres. Endyne Internat., Inc., Houston, 1982-84; v.p. engring. and technology, sr. v.p. ops. Blount Energy Resource Corp., Montgomery, Ala., 1984-91; v.p. Birwelco-Montenay Inc., Miami, Fla., 1991—; fgn. corr. Resch Verlag, Munich, 1975—; bd.dirs. W&E Umwelttechnik A.G., A Previous Blount Co., Zurich, Switzerland, 1986-89. Patentee in field; author, co-author, translator tech. and sci. works. Fellow ASME (past chmn. nuclear heat exchanger com.); mem. Nat. Assn. Corrosion Engrs. (cert. corrosion specialist), Assn. German Profl. Engrs., Assn. Energy Engrs. (sr. mem.), Cogeneration Inst., Integrated Waste Svcs. Assn., Solid Waste Assn. N.Am. Home: 801 Timberlane Rd Pike Road AL 36064-2208 Office: Birwelco-Montenay Inc 3225 Aviation Ave Miami FL 33133-4741

SCHUG, KENNETH ROBERT, chemistry educator; b. Easton, Pa., Aug. 27, 1924; s. Howard Lester and Marion Henry (Hulbert) S.; m. Miyoko Ishiyama, June 13, 1948; children: Carey Tyler, Carson Blake, Reed Porter. Student, Johns Hopkins U., 1942-43; B.A., Stanford U., 1945; Ph.D., U. So. Calif., 1955. Instr. Seton Hall Coll., South Orange, N.J., 1948-50; research assoc. U. Wis.-Madison, 1954-56; instr. Ill. Inst. Tech., Chgo., 1956-59, asst. prof., 1959-65, assoc. prof., 1965-75, prof. chemistry, 1975—, chmn. dept. chemistry, 1976-82, 85-87, 89-90; project dir. Chgo. Area Health and Med. Careers Program, 1979—; project co-dir. Sci. and Math. Initiative for Learning Enhancement, 1985—; project dir. Howard Hughes Med. Inst. Undergrad. Biol. Scis. Program, 1992—; cons. Argonne (Ill.) Nat. Lab., 1960-62. Co-author: Eigo Kagoku Ronbun no Kakikata, 1979; contbr. articles to profl. jours. Trustee Michael Reese Health Plan, Chgo., 1976-91, Michael Reese Found., 1991—; bd. dirs. Hyde Park Consumers Coop. Soc., 1982-94. Fulbright scholar, 1964-65; grantee in field. Mem. Am. Chem. Soc. (dir., officer Chgo. sect. 1978-84). Home: 1466 E Park Pl Chicago IL 60637-1836 Office: Ill Inst Tech Div Chemistry IIT Ctr Chicago IL 60616

SCHUH, FRANK JOSEPH, drilling engineering company executive, consultant; b. Columbus, Ohio, Feb. 3, 1935; s. Sebastian and Elizabeth (Zorn) S.; m. Alice Virgene Kasler, June 16, 1956; children: Dwain Joseph, Michael James, Barbara Ann. BS in Petroleum Engring., Ohio State U., 1956, MS in Petroleum Engring., 1956. Registered profl. engr., Ohio. Drilling and rsch. engr. Atlantic Refining Co., Tex., La., 1956-62; mem. drilling engring. staff, dir. engring. Atlantic Richfield Co., Dallas, 1962-82; mgr. drilling rsch., sr. advisor Atlantic Richfield Co., Plano, Tex., 1982-86; v.p. Enertech Engring. & Tech., Dallas, 1986-87; pres. Drilling Tech., Inc., Plano, 1987—; v.p. Supreme Resources Corp., Dallas, 1988-92; founder, 1st pres. Drilling Engring. Assn., Dallas, 1983-85. Author: Drilling Equations, 1975; patentee horizontal drilling, high frequency measurement system; 26 other patents. Precinct, region chmn. Rep. Party, Dallas, 1964-74; vol. bldg. com. Mary Immaculate Ch., Dallas, 1965-66; mem. tech. engring. and devel. com. Ocean Drilling Program, Bryan, Tex., 1980—. Recipient outstanding achievement in field of engring. award Nat. Engrs. Coun., 1980, Robert Earl McConnell award Am. Inst. Mining Engrs., 1994, Ohio State Univ. Coll. of Engring. Benjamin G. Lamme Meritorious Achievement medel, 1995. Mem. NAE, Soc. Petroleum Engrs. (nat. bd. dirs. 1983-86, Drilling Engring. award 1986, Disting. Mem. award 1989), Am. Petroleum Inst. (chmn. com. 6, 1985-88, svc. citation 1986), Am. Assn. Drilling Engrs., Soc. Ind. Profl. Earth Scientists, Petroleum Engrs. Club (pres. 1974-75), Ohio State U. Alumni Club (pres. 1968-69), Dallas-Ft. Worth Oilman's Club (handicapper 1973-86). Avocations: golf, sailing. Office: Drilling Tech Inc 5808 Wavertree Ln Ste 1000 Plano TX 75093-4513

SCHUH, G(EORGE) EDWARD, university dean, agricultural economist; b. Indpls., Sept. 13, 1930; s. George Edward and Viola (Lentz) S.; m. Maria Ignez, May 23, 1965; children: Audrey, Susan, Tanya. BS in Agrl. Edn, Purdue U., 1952, DAgr (hon.), 1992; MS in Agrl. Econs., Mich. State U., 1954; MA in Econs, U. Chgo., 1958, PhD, 1961; prof. (hon.), Fed. U. Vicosa, Brazil, 1965; hon. doctorate, Purdue U., 1992. From instr. to prof. agrl. econs. Purdue U., 1959-79; dir. Center for Public Policy and Public Affairs, 1977-78; dep. undersec. for internat. affairs and commodity programs Dept. Agr., Washington, 1978-79, chair bd. for internat. food and agrl. devel., 1995—; prof. agrl. and applied econs., head dept. U. Minn., 1979-84; dir. agr. and rural devel. World Bank, Washington, 1984-87; dean Humphrey Inst. for Pub. Affairs, U. Minn., 1987—, Orville and Jane Freeman Endowed chair, 1996—; program advisor Ford Found., 1966-72; sr. staff economist Pres.'s Coun. Econ. Advisors, 1974-75. Author, editor profl. books; contbr. numerous articles to profl. publs. Served with U.S. Army, 1954-56. Fellow AAAS, Am. Acad. Arts and Scis., Am. Agrl. Econs. Assn. (Thesis award 1962, Pub. Rsch. award 1971, Article award 1975, Policy award 1979, Publ. of Lasting Value award 1988, bd. dirs. 1977-80, pres.-elect 1980-81, pres. 1981-82); mem. Internat. Assn. Agrl. Econs., Am. Econ. Assn., Brazilian Soc. Agrl. Economists. Office: Humphrey Ctr U Minn 301 19th Ave S Minneapolis MN 55455-0429

SCHUHMANN, REINHARDT, JR., metallurgical engineering educator, consultant; b. Corpus Christi, Tex., Dec. 16, 1914; s. Reinhardt and Alice (Shuford) S.; m. Betsy Jane Hancock, Aug. 29, 1937; children—Martha Schuh, Alice Bishop. Student, Calif. Inst. Tech., 1929-31; B.S. in Metall. Engring., Mo. Sch. Mines, 1933; M.S. in Metall. Engring., Mont. Sch. Mines, 1935; Sc.D. in Metallurgy, MIT, 1938; DEng (hon.), Purdue U., 1993. Instr. to assoc. prof. MIT, Cambridge, 1938-54; prof. metall. engring. Purdue U., West Lafayette, Ind., 1954-64, head Sch. Metall. Engring., 1959-64, Ross prof. engring., 1964-81, Ross prof. engring. emeritus, 1981—; Battelle vis. prof. Ohio State U., Columbus, 1966-67; Kroll vis. prof. Colo. Sch. Mines, Golden, 1977; metall. engring. cons., 1946—. Author: Metallurgical Engineering, 1952; contbr. articles to profl. jours.; co-inventor Q-S oxygen process, oxygen sprinkle smelting. Fellow Metall. Soc. of AIME (charter; James Douglas Gold medal 1970, Mineral Industry Edn. award 1975, Extractive metallurgy lectr. 1965, Extractive metallurgy Sci. awards 1959, 77), Am. Soc. for Metals, AAAS; mem. Nat. Acad. Engring., Am. Chem. Soc. Democrat. Episcopalian. Club: Parlor (pres. 1963-64)(Lafayette). Lodge: Rotary. Avocations: classical music; hiking. Home: 2741 N Salisbury St # 2412 West Lafayette IN 47906-1499 Office: Purdue U Sch Materials Engring West Lafayette IN 47907

SCHULBERG, BUDD, author; b. N.Y.C., Mar. 27, 1914; s. Benjamin P. and Adeline (Jaffe) S.; m. Virginia Ray, July 23, 1936 (div. 1942); 1 dau., Victoria; m. Victoria Anderson, Feb. 17, 1943 (div. 1964); children: Stephen, David; m. Geraldine Brooks, July 12, 1964 (dec. 1977); m. Betsy Anne Langman, June 9, 1979; children: Benn Stuart, Jessica A. Student, Deerfield Acad., 1931-32; AB cum laude, Dartmouth Coll., 1936, LLD, 1960; LittD, Long Island U., 1983; DHL, Hofstra U., 1987. Boxing editor Sports Illustrated; pres., prodr. Schulberg Prodns.; founder, dir. Watts Writers Workshop, L.A., 1965—; founder, chmn. Frederick Douglass Creative Arts Ctr., N.Y.C., 1971—. Screenwriter, Hollywood, 1936-39; writer "The Schulberg Report", Newsday Syndicate; author: What Makes Sammy Run?, 1941, The Harder They Fall, 1947, The Disenchanted, 1950, Some Faces in the Crowd, 1953, Waterfront, 1955 (Christopher award 1955), Sanctuary V, 1969, The Four Seasons of Success, 1972, Loser and Still Champion: Muhammad Ali, 1972, Swan Watch, 1975, Everything that Moves, 1980, Moving Pictures: Memories of a Hollywood Prince, 1981, Love, Action, Laughter and Other Sad Tales, 1990, Sparring with Hemingway: And Other Legends of the Fight Game, 1995; editor: From the Ashes: Voices of Watts, 1967; screenwriter: (films) (with Samuel Ornitz) Little Orphan Annie, 1938, (with F. Scott Fitzgerald) Winter Carnival, 1939, (with Dorothy Parker) Weekend for Three, 1941, (with Martin Berkeley) City without Men, 1943, Government Girl, 1943, On the Waterfront, 1954 (Academy award best original story and screenplay 1954, N.Y. Critics award 1954, Fgn. Corrs. award 1954, Screen Writers Guild award 1954, Venice Festival award 1954), A Face in the Crowd, 1957 (German Film Critics award 1957), Wind across the Everglades, 1958, (teleplays) The Pharmacist's Mate, 1951, Paso Doble. A Question of Honor, A Table At Ciro's; playwright: The Disenchanted: A Play in Three Acts, 1958, What Make's Sammy Run?, 1959, (musical) Senor Discretion Himself, 1985; contbr. to Sports Illustrated, Life, N.Y. Times Book Rev., Esquire, Newsday Syndicate, Los Angeles Times Book Rev., N.Y. Times Sunday Mag., Playboy. Bd. dirs. Westminster Neighborhood Assn., L.A., 1965-68, Inner City Cultural Ctr., L.A., 1965-68; mem. nat. adv. commn. on black participation John F. Kennedy Ctr. for Performing Arts; trustee Humanitas Prize. Lt. (j.g.) USNR, 1943-46, assigned to OSS. Awarded Army Commendation Ribbon for gathering photog. evidence of war crimes for Nuremberg Trial, 1945-46; recipient Susie Humanitarian award B'nai B'rith, Image award NAACP, Journalism award Dartmouth Coll., Merit award Lotos Club., L.A. Community Svc. award, 1966, B'hai Human Rights award, 1968, spl. award for Watts Writers Workshop, New Eng. Theater Conf., 1969, Amistad award, award for work with black writers Howard U., Prix Literaire, Deauville Festival 1989, World Boxing Assn. Living Legend award, 1990, Westhampton Writers Lifetime Achievement award, 1989, Southampton Cultural Ctr. 1st Annual Literature award, 1992, Heritage award Deerfield Acad., 1986. Mem. Dramatists Guild, ASCAP, Authors Guild N.Y.C. (mem. council), ACLU, Writers Guild East (mem. coun.), Boxing Writers Am., P.E.N., Sphinx (Dartmouth), The Players Club, Phi Beta Kappa. Office: Miriam Altshuler Lit Agy RR # 1 Box 5 Old Post Rd Red Hook NY 12571 Also: The Artists Agy care Mickey Freiberg 10000 Santa Monica Blvd Ste 300 Los Angeles CA 90067-7007

SCHULBERG, JAY WILLIAM, advertising agency executive; b. N.Y.C., July 17, 1939; s. Perry and Esther (Eagle) S.; m. Kathryn Carmel Nicholson, Sept. 18, 1968. BS (Founder's Day award 1961), NYU, 1961. With Seagram's Inc., 1962, Grumman Aircraft Co., 1963-66; With Foote, Cone & Belding Inc., 1967-68; with Ogilvy & Mather, Inc., N.Y.C., 1968-87; exec. v.p., head creative dept. Ogilvy & Mather, Inc., 1985-87, also mem. U.S. coun. dirs., 1988—; vice chmn., chief creative officer, bd. dirs. Bozell Worldwide, N.Y.C., 1987—; also bd. dirs. Bozell, N.Y.C., operating bd.; bd. dirs. Ogilvy & Mather Worldwide, chmn., exec. com. Creator advt. campaigns for Am. Express, Bahamas, TWA, Maxwell House Coffee, Country Time, Gen. Foods, Duracell, Hardees, Brit. Tourism, Hershey's, Huggies, Merrill Lynch, N.Y. Times, Excedrin, Milk "Mustache", Tyco, USAF, Mass. Mut., Vanity Fair, Vassrette, others. Developed Big Apple campaign, N.Y.C. With AUS, 1962. Recipient Art Dirs. Club awards, One Show awards, Andy awards, Addy awards, Cannes, Hollywood Festival awards, 6 David Ogilvy awards; named Creative Dir. of Yr. Adweek Mag., 1986. Mem. The One Club, Internat. Rescue Com. (bd. dirs.).

SCHULER, JAMES JOSEPH, vascular surgeon; b. Aurora, Ill., Feb. 12, 1946; s. Ella Schuler; m. Catherine Weller, 1969; children: James Jr., Matthew. BS, St. John's U., 1968; MD with hons., U. Ill., 1972, MS in Biochemistry, 1975. Diplomate Am. Bd. Surgery, Am. Bd. Vascular Surgery. Intern U. Ill., Chgo., 1972-73, resident, 1973-78, chief resident, 1978-79, instr., 1975-79, asst. prof., 1980-85, assoc. prof., 1985-92, prof. surgery, 1992—, chief divsn. vascular surgery, 1988—; lectr. Cook County Grad. Sch., Chgo., 1991—; attending surgeon Cook County Hosp., Chgo., 1992—, West Side Vets. Hosp., Chgo., 1979—. Assoc. editor: Civilian Vascular Trauma, 1992; co-author numerous book chpts.; contbr. articles to profl. jours. Vascular Surgery fellow U. Ill., 1979-80; rsch. grantee numerous granting bodies, 1980—. Fellow ACS; mem. Am. Venous Forum, Soc. for Vascular Surgery, Western Surg. Assn., Internat. Soc. for Cardiovascular Surgery, Midwestern Vascular Surg. Soc., Alpha Omega Alpha. Republican. Roman Catholic. Avocations: hunting, fishing. Office: U Ill Hosp 1740 W Taylor St Ste 2200 Chicago IL 60612-7232

SCHULER, ROBERT HUGO, chemist, educator; b. Buffalo, Jan. 4, 1926; s. Robert H. and Mary J. (Mayer) S.; m. Florence J. Forrest, June 18, 1952; children: Mary A., Margaret A., Carol A., Robert E., Thomas C. BS, Canisius Coll., Buffalo, 1946; PhD, U. Notre Dame, 1949. Asst. prof. chemistry Canisius Coll., 1949-53; asso. chemist, then chemist Brookhaven Nat. Lab., 1953-56; staff fellow, dir. radiation research lab. Mellon Inst., 1956-76, mem. adv. bd., 1962-76; prof. chemistry, dir. radiation research lab. Carnegie-Mellon U., 1967-76; prof. chemistry U. Notre Dame, Ind., 1976—; dir. radiation lab. U. Notre Dame, Ind., 1976-95, dir. emeritus, 1995—; John A. Zahm prof. radiation chemistry U. Notre Dame, 1986—; Raman prof. U. Madras, India, 1985-86; vis. prof. Hebrew U., Israel, 1980. Author articles in field. Recipient Curie medal Poland, 1992. Fellow AAAS; mem. Am. Chem. Soc., Am. Phys. Soc., Chem. Soc., Radiation Research Soc. (pres. 1975-76), Sigma Xi. Club: Cosmos. Office: U Notre Dame Radiation Lab Notre Dame IN 46556

SCHULER, ROBERT LEO, appraiser, consultant; b. Cin., June 15, 1943; s. Del D. and Virginia D. (Heyl) S.; m. Shelagh J. Moritz, Aug. 11, 1962; children: Robert C., Sherry L. V.p. Comprehensive Appraisal Service, Inc., Cin., 1977—; bd. dirs. Hamilton County Regional Planning Commn., Cin., 1987-88; mem. exec. com., past pres. OKI Regional Coun. Govts., Cin., 1981-92. Councilman City of Deer Park, Ohio, 1979-86; trustee Sycamore Twp., 1988-92; Ohio state rep. 36th dist., 1993—. Mem. Am. Assn. Cert. Appraiser (sr.), Cin. Bd. Realtors, Ohio Assn. Realtors, Jaycees (v.p.). Republican. Roman Catholic. Home: 3648 Jeffrey Ct Cincinnati OH 45236-1544 Office: PO Box 36442 Cincinnati OH 45236-0442

SCHULER, THEODORE ANTHONY, retired civil engineer, retired city official; b. Louisville, July 1, 1934; s. Henry R. and Virginia (Meisner) S.; m. Jane A. Bandy, July 29, 1979; children: Marc, Elizabeth, Eric, Ellen. BCE, U. Louisville, 1957, M.Engring., 1973. Registered profl. engr., Tenn., Ky. Design, constrn. engr. Brighton Engring. Co., Frankfort, Ky., 1960-65; design engr. Hensley-Schmidt Inc., Chattanooga, 1965-68, assoc. mem., 1969-73, sr. assoc. mem., 1973-75, prin., asst. v.p., head Knoxville office, 1975-81; chief planning engr. engring. dept. City of Knoxville, 1981-96, ret., 1996. Served to lt. (j.g.) USNR, 1957-60. Fellow ASCE. Home: 5907 Adelia Dr Knoxville TN 37920-5801

SCHULHOF, MICHAEL PETER, entertainment, electronics company executive; b. N.Y.C., Nov. 30, 1942; s. Rudolph B. and Hannelore (Buck) S.; m. Paola Nissim, Apr. 17, 1969; children: David Kenneth, Jonathan Nissim. BA, Grinnell Coll., 1964, DSc (hon.), 1990; MS, Cornell U., 1967; PhD (NSF fellow), Brandeis U., 1970. Lic. comml. pilot. Am. research fellow Brookhaven Nat. Lab., Uptown, N.Y., 1969-71; asst. to v.p. mfg. CBS Records, Inc., N.Y.C., 1971-73, mem. exec. com., bd. dirs., 1987—; gen. mgr. bus. products div. Sony Corp., N.Y.C., 1973-77, v.p., 1977-78, sr. v.p., 1978-86; pres. Sony Industries, N.Y.C., 1978-86; chmn. Digital Audio Disc Corp., Terre Haute, Ind., 1986-96; pres. Sony Software Corp., 1991-96; pres., CEO Sony Corp. Am., 1993-95; chmn. bd. dirs. Quadriga Art Inc., 1980—; bd. dirs. Sony Corp., Japan, Sony Corp. Am., Sony Pictures Entertainment, Materials Rsch. Corp.; chmn. Sony Music Entertainment. Contbr. articles to profl. jours. Patentee audio disc apparatus, 1986. Trustee Brandeis U., 1990—, Mus. TV and Radio, N.Y.C., Lincoln Ctr. for Performing Arts, Inc., N.Y.C., The Brookings Instn., Washington; bd. dirs. Ctr. on Addiction and Substance Abuse at Columbia U., N.Y.C.; mem. investment and svcs. policy adv. com. to U.S. Trade Rep.; active Coun. Fgn. Rels. NSF fellw Brandeis U. Mem. Am. Phys. Soc. (dir. 1978), Computer and Bus. Equipment Mfrs. Assn. (dir.), Am. Radio Relay League, Aircraft Owners and Pilots Assn., Guggenheim Mus., Whitney Mus., Harmony Club, Gipsy Trail Club, East Hampton Tennis Club, Profile Club, Fenway Golf Club, Atlantic Golf Club. Office: 375 Park Ave New York NY 10152-0002

SCHULHOFER, STEPHEN JOSEPH, law educator, consultant; b. N.Y.C., Aug. 20, 1942; s. Joseph and Myrelle S.; m. Laurie Wohl, May 28, 1975; children: Samuel, Jonah. AB, Princeton U., 1964; LLB, Harvard U., 1967. Bar: D.C. 1968, U.S. Dist. Ct. (ea. dist.) Pa. 1973, U.S. Supreme Ct. 1973. Law clk. U.S. Supreme Ct., Washington, 1967-69; assoc. Coudert Freres, Paris, 1969-72; prof. law U. Pa., Phila., 1972-86; prof. U. Chgo., 1986—. speedy trial reporter U.S. Dist. Ct., Wilmington, Del., 1975-80; cons. U.S. EPA, Washington, 1977-78, U.S. Sentencing Commn., Washington, 1987-94. Author: Prosecutorial Discretion and Federal Sentencing Reform, 1979. Editor: Criminal Law and its Processes, 1983, 89, 95; contbr. articles to profl. jours. Trustee, Community Legal Services, Inc., Phila., 1981-86. Walter Meyer grantee Am. Bar Found., 1984. Mem. ACLU (Ill. bd. dirs. 1993—), Law and Soc. Assn. Office: U Chgo Law Sch 1111 E 60th St Chicago IL 60637-2702

SCHULIAN, JOHN (NIELSEN SCHULIAN), screenwriter, author; b. L.A., Jan. 31, 1945; s. John and Estella Katherine (Nielsen) S.; m. Paula Lynn Ellis, Aug. 20, 1977 (div. Oct. 1984). BA, U. Utah, 1967; MS, Northwestern U., 1968. Copy editor Salt Lake City Tribune, 1968; reporter Balt. Evening Sun, 1970-75; sportswriter Washington Post, 1975-77; sports columnist Chgo. Daily News, 1977-78, Chgo. Sun-Times, 1978-84, Phila. Daily News, 1984-86; staff writer Miami Vice, Universal City, Calif., 1986-87, story editor, 1987; story editor The Slap Maxwell Story, North Hollywood, Calif., 1987-88; exec. story editor TV series Wiseguy, Hollywood, 1988-89; co-producer TV series Midnight Caller, Burbank, Calif., 1989-90; supervising producer Midnight Caller, 1990-91; co-exec. producer TV series Reasonable Doubts, Burbank, Calif., 1991-92; creative cons. TV series The Untouchables, L.A., 1992-93; co-exec. producer TV series Hercules, Universal City, Calif., 1994-96; co-creator Xena: Warrior Princess, Universal City, Calif., 1995; assoc. prodr. (documentary) Ben Johnson: Third Cowboy on the Right, 1996; co-exec. prodr. (TV series) Lawless, 1996-97. Author: Writers' Fighters and Other Sweet Scientists, 1983; contbg. editor Panorama mag., 1980-81; syndicated columnist UP Syndicate; commentator Nat. Pub. Radio, 1985-86; cons. The Reader's Catalog, 1989; contbr. articles to Playboy, Gentlemen's Quar., Sports Illustrated, The National, L.A. Times; included in The Best Am. Sports Writing, 1994. Mem. Pacific Coast League Hist. Soc. With U.S. Army, 1968-70. Recipient Nat. Headliners Club award, 1980, Column Writing award AP Sports Editors, 1979, 82, Best Sports Stories award, 1983, 84, Nat Fleischer Excellence in Boxing Journalism award Boxing Writers Assn. Am., 1985. Mem. Writers Guild Am., Phi Beta Kappa. Office: Creative Artists Agy United Talent Agy 9830 Wilshire Blvd Beverly Hills CA 90212-1804

SCHULLER, DAVID EDWARD, cancer center administrator, otolaryngology; b. Cleve., Oct. 20, 1944; m. Carole Ann Hauss, June 24, 1967; children: Rebecca, Michael. BA, Rutgers U., 1966; MD cum laude, Ohio State U., 1970. Diplomate Am. Bd. Otolaryngology 1975. Intern dept. surgery U. Hosps. Cleve., 1970-71; resident dept. otolaryngology Ohio State U., Columbus, 1971-72; resident dept. surgery U. Hosps. Cleve., 1972-73; fellow head and neck surgery Pack Med. Found. with John Conley, N.Y.C., 1973; resident dept. otolaryngology Ohio State U. Hosps., Columbus, 1973-75; fellow head and neck oncology and facial plastic and reconstructive surgery U. Iowa, Iowa City, 1975-76; from clin. instr. to prof. and chmn. dept. otolaryngology The Ohio State U., Columbus, 1971—; dir. Compehensive Cancer Ctr. & Arthur G. James Cancer Hosp. and Rsch. Inst., Columbus, 1988—; prof. sect. oral biology, Coll. Dentistry The Ohio State U., 1990—; mem., chmn. various coms. Ohio State U. Hosps. and Coll. Medicine, 1976—; dir. CCC head and neck oncology program Ohio State U., 1977—, hosps. physician flr. coord. 10th flr., 1977-82, dir. laser-microsurgery teaching and rsch. lab., 1987-88; mem. various coms. Grant Hosp., 1980-84; mem. Accreditation Coun. for the Grad. Med. Edn. Residency Review Com. for Otolaryngology, 1985—, chmn., 1988—; vis. prof., lectr., ACS prof. clin. Oncology, 1989-94. numerous instns. Author: (books) (with others) Otolaryngology-Head and Neck Surgery-4 Vols., 1986, Textbook of Otolaryngology-7th Edit., 1988, Otolaryngology-Head and Neck Surgery-Update I, 1988, Musculocutaneous Flaps in Head and Neck Reconstructive Surgery, 1989, Otolaryngology-Head and Neck Surgery Update II, 1990, Otorinolaringologia-Cirugia de Cabeza y Culleo, 1991, Otolaryngology-Head and Neck Surgery-4 Vols., 1992; contbr. chpts. to books and articles to profl. jours.; mem. editorial bd. New Horizons in Otolaryngology/Head and Neck Surgery, 1982-87, The Laryngoscope, 1986—, Am. Jour. Otolaryngology, 1988—, Facial Plastic Surgery Internat. Quar. Monographs, 1992—; mem. rev. bd. Jour. Head and Neck Surgery, 1985—; mem. editorial rev. bd. Otolaryngology-Head and Neck Surgery, 1990—; reviewer New Eng. Jour Medicine, 1992—. Trustee Ohio Cancer Found., 1988—; dir. Am. Bd. Otolaryngology, 1988—. Recipient Cert. of Appreciation, Scioto Meml. Hosp., 1982, Edmund Prince Fowler award Triological Soc., 1984; Henry Rutgers scholar Rutgers U., 1965-66; grantee Nat. Cancer Inst., 1980-88, 90—, Bremer Found., 1982-83, 87-88, Photomedica Inc., 1986-89, Upjohn Co., 1986-90, others. Mem. AMA (mem. rev. panel Archives of Otolaryngology-Head and Neck Surgery 1984—), Am. Cancer Soc. (mem. instl. grant rev. com. 1980—, chmn. rehab. com. Franklin County unit 1981-82, mem. profl. edn. com. 1981—, chmn. 1982-85, v.p. 1982-83, pres. 1986, 87, trustee Ohio divsn. 1988—), Am. Assn. Cosmetic Surgeons, Am. Acad. Facial Plastic and Reconstructive Surgery (mem. rsch. com. 1977-82, chmn. residency rels. com. 1982-85, mem. program com. 1982-85, v.p. mid. sect. 1983-87, chmn. by-laws com. 1988—, treas. 1988—, Honor award 1989), Am. Coll. Surgeons, Am. Cleft Palate Assn., Assn. Am. Cancer Insts., Am. Soc. Head and Neck Injury, Am. Acad. Otolaryngology Head and Neck Surgery (mem. editorial bd. self-instructional package program 1982—, del. bd. govs. 1982-87, Honor award 1983), Am. Soc. Laser Medicine and Surgery, Am. Laryngological, Rhinological, Otological Soc., Inc., Am. Laryngological Assn., Am. Soc. Clin. Oncology (mem. program com. 1989—), Am. Assn. Cancer Researchers, Am. Soc. Head and Neck Surgery (mem. coun. 1983-86, chmn. scholastic and fellowship award com. 1984-86, mem. profl. rels. and pub. edn. com. 1989—), Southwest Oncology Group (chmn. head and neck com. 1983—), Collegium ORLAS, Ohio State Med. Assn. (pres. sect. otolaryngology 1987—), Ohio Soc. Otolaryngology (pres. 1985, 86, 87), Acad. Medicine of Columbus and Franklin County, Columbus E.E.N.T. Soc., Franklin County Acad. Medicine (mem. profl. rels. c 1982—), Head and Neck Intergroup (vice-chmn. 1984-86, chmn. 1986-89), Assn. Rsch. Otolaryngology, Ohio State U. Med. Alumni Soc. (class rep. 1980—, v.p. 1987-88, pres. 1989-90), Med. Forum, Med. Review Club, Order of Hippocrates (charter), Alpha Omega Alpha. Office: 456 W 10th Ave Columbus OH 43210-1240 also: Ohio State Univ Comp Cancer Ctr 300 W 10th Ave Columbus OH 43210-1240

SCHULLER, DIANE ETHEL, allergist, immunologist, educator; b. Bklyn., Nov. 27, 1943; d. Charles William and Dorothy Schuller. AB cum laude with honors in Biology, Bryn Mawr Coll., 1965. Diplomate Am. Bd. Allergy and Immunology, Am. Bd. Pediatrics, Nat. Bd. Med. Examiners. M.D., SUNY Downstate Med. Sch., Bklyn., 1970. Intern, then resident in pediatrics Roosevelt Hosp., N.Y.C., 1970-72, resident in allergy Cooke Inst. Allergy, 1972-74; assoc. in pediatrics Geisinger Med. Center, Danville, Pa., 1974-78, dir. dept. pediatric allergy, immunology and pulmonary diseases 1978-95; asst. clin. prof. pediatrics Hershey Med. Coll., Pa. State U., 1974-79, assoc. clin. prof., 1979-88; clin. prof. Jefferson Med. Coll., Phila., 1989-95; dir. pediatric allergy, immunology, pulmonology Pa. State U., Milton S. Hershey Med. Coll., 1995—, prof. pediatrics, 1995—. Bd. dirs. Central Pa. Lung and Health Assn.; bd. dirs., exec. com. Am. Lung Assn. of Pa., sec., 1992— ; chmn. Susquehanna Valley Lung Assn., 1983—; mem. scholarship com. Bryn Mawr Club, N.Y., 1970-75; mem. Columbia-Montour Home Health Svcs. Adv. Group of Profl. Personnel, 1975-95. Editl. bd. Annals of Allergy, Asthma and Immunology. Recipient Physicians Recognition award AMA, 1973-76, 74-76, 75-78, 79-82, 83-86, 1987-90, 91-94, 95—. Fellow Am. Acad. Pediatrics, Am. Coll. Allergy Asthma and Immunology (2d v.p. 1988, bd. regents 1989-92, exec. com. 1990-93, v.p. 1992-93, pres.-elect 1993-94, pres. 1994-95), Am. Assn. Clin. Immunology and Allergy (regional dir., exec. com.), Joint Coun. Allergy and Immunology (bd. dirs. 1986-95; treas. of joint coun. 1991-93), Am. Acad. Allergy and Immunology; mem. Am. Assn. Cert. Allergists, Pa., N.Y. State allergy socs., N.Y. State, N.Y. County med. socs. Office: Milton S Hershey Med Coll Pa State U Hershey PA 17033 also: 11 Brandywine Hershey PA 17033

SCHULLER, EDDIE, engineering executive; b. Cluj, Romania, Feb. 11, 1956; came to U.S., 1974; s. Francisco B. and Yolanda B. (Kohn) S.; m. Anne P. foster, Sept. 17, 1989; stepchildren: Beth, Sarah. BS in Elec. Engring., U. Ill., Chgo., 1981; MBA, So. Ill. U., 1985; MS in Elec. Engring., Calif. State U., 1993. Engr. Gen. Dynamics, San Diego, 1981-84; v.p. mktg. Hytech Micronics Corp., Encinitas, Calif., 1983-86; mem. tech. staff Interstate Electronics Corp., Anaheim, Calif., 1984-86; sr. engr. Norden Systems, Santa Ana, Calif., 1986-88; pres. Schuller Investment Corp./HP Riders, Anaheim, 1986—; sr. specialist Rockwell Internat./Boeing N.Am., 1988—. Recipient Service award Evanston (Ill.) Police Dept., 1980. Mem. IEEE, Am. Soc. Mil. Engrs., Soc. Old Crows. Jewish. Office: Schuller Investment/HP Riders 18885 Deodar St Fountain Vly CA 92708-7222

SCHULLER, EDWIN ARTHUR, osteopathic physician; b. Darby, Pa., Nov. 12, 1950; s. Edwin Arthur and Rita Mary (McCully) S.; m. Elizabeth Anne Hellmig, Apr. 3, 1971 (div. Jan. 1985); children: Elizabeth Adrienne, Alexandra Lynn, Jamie Christine; m. Peggy L. Smythe; stepchildren: Barry V. Krewson, Daniel L. Krewson. BS in Biology, Villanova U., 1972; DO, Phila. Coll. Osteo. Medicine, 1976. Diplomate Nat. Bd. Examiners in Osteo. Medicine and Surgery, Am. Bd. Emergency Medicine, Am. Bd. Family Practice, Am. Bd. Addiction Medicine; cert. sr. examiner in disability and in vocat. rehab., Pa. Rotating intern Zieger-Botsford Osteo. Hosps., Farmington Hills, Mich., 1976-77, staff physician, emergency medicine physician, 1977-80; resident in ob-gyn. BiCounty Gen. Hosp., Warren, Mich., 1976-77, St. Joseph Mercy Hosp., Pontiac, Mich., 1976-77; staff physician, adminstr. Women's and Crisis Clinic, Common Ground, Inc., Birmingham, Mich., 1978-79; dir. emergency svcs. Zieger Osteo. Hosp., Detroit, 1979; pvt. practice family practice, emergency, addiction medicine Phila., 1980—; cons. in emergency medicine, family practice and mgmt., Detroit, 1977-81; mem. med. bd. for family practice, spinal injuries and substance abuse Radnor Twp. Sch. Dist., 1995—; prin. investigator rsch. study Pfizer, Inc., 1993-94, Glaxo, Inc., 1993; asst. clin. prof. emergency medicine Mich. State U., 1979-80; instr. Widener U. Sch. Law, 1993—; chief med. cons. for addiction medicine Pa. Dental Assn., 1989-90. Author: (poetry) Beyond the Wind...Ahead of the Storm, 1979. Bd. dirs. Common Ground, Inc., Mich., 1979. With M.C., USAF, 1973-80. Recipient T. J. Liljestrand Tchg. award Met. Hosp., 1981, Clin. Rsch. award Boehringer-Ingelheim Co., 1984. Mem. AMA, Pa. Med. Soc., Pa. Osteo. Med. Assn., Phila. County Med. Soc., Am. Osteo. Coll. of Family Practitioners, Am. Soc. Addiction Medicine, Am. Coll. Profl. Execs., Phi Sigma Gamma. Avocations: miniature Schnauzers, sailing, snorkeling, writing. Office: Brookhaven Med Ctr 206 W State St Media PA 19063-3113

SCHULLER, GUNTHER ALEXANDER, composer; b. N.Y.C., Nov. 22, 1925; s. Arthur E. and Elsie (Bernartz) S.; m. Marjorie Black, June 8, 1948; children: Edwin Gunther, George Alexander. Student, St. Thomas Choir Sch., N.Y.C.; MusD (hon.), Manhattan Sch. Music, 1987, Northeastern U., 1967, U. Ill., 1968, Colby Coll., 1969, Williams Coll., 1975, Cleve. Inst. Music, 1977, New Eng. Conservatory Music, 1978, Rutgers U., 1980, Manhattan Sch. Music, 1987, Oberlin Coll., 1989. tchr. Manhattan Sch. Music, 1950-63; head composition dept. Tanglewood, 1963-84; pres. New Eng. Conservatory of Music, 1967-77; artistic dir. Berkshire Music Center, Tanglewood, 1969-84, Festival at Sandpoint, 1985—; founder, pres. Margun Music Inc., 1975, GM Recs., 1980. French horn player, Ballet Theatre, then prin. horn player, Cin. Symphony Orch., 1943-45, prin. French horn, Met. Opera Orch., 1945-59, Concerto #1 for Horn, 1945; composer: Quartet for Four Double Basses, 1947, Fantasy for Unaccompanied Cello, 1951, Recitative and Rondo for Violin and Piano, 1953, Music for Violin, Piano and Percussion, 1957, Contours, 1958, Woodwind Quintet, 1958, Seven Studies on Themes of Paul Klee, 1959, Spectra, 1960, Six Renaissance Lyrics, 1962, String Quartet No. 2, 1965, Symphony, 1965, opera The Visitation 1966, opera Fisherman and His Wife, 1970, Capriccio Stravagante, 1972, The Power Within Us, 1972, Tre Invenzioni, 1972, Three Nocturnes, 1973, Four Soundscapes, 1974, Concerto No. 2 for Orch., 1975, Triplum II, 1975, Horn Concerto No. 2, 1976, Violin Concerto, 1976, Diptych for organ, 1976, Sonata Serenata, 1978, Contrabassoon Concerto, 1978, Deaï for 3 orchs., 1978, Trumpet Concerto, 1979, Octet, 1979, Eine Kleine Posaunenmusik, 1980, In Praise of Winds (Symphony for Large Wind Orch.), 1981, Symphony for Organ, 1982, Concerto Quaternio, 1983, Concerto for Bassoon and Orch., 1984, Farbenspiel (Concerto No. 3 for Orch.), 1985, On Light Wings (piano quartet), 1984; author: Horn Technique, 1962, Early Jazz: Its Roots and Development, 1968, Musings: The Musical Worlds of Gunther Schuller, 1985, The Swing Era, 1989; premiere of Symphony for Brass and Percussion, Cin., 1950, Salzburg Festival, 1957, Dramatic Overture, N.Y. Philharm., 1956, String Quartet, Number 1 Contemporary Arts Festival, U. Ill., 1957, String Quartet Number 3, 1986, Concertino for Jazz Quartet and Orch, Balt. Symphony Orch., 1959, Seven Studies on Themes of Paul Klee, Ford Found., commn., Minn. Symphony, 1959, Spectra, N.Y. Philharm. 1960, Music for Brass Quintet, Coolidge Found., Library of Congress, 1961, Concerto No. 1 for Orch, Chgo. Symphony Orch., 1966, Triplum, N.Y. Philharm. commd. Lincoln Center, 1967, Aphorisms for Flute and String Trio commd, Carlton Coll. Centennial, 1967, Eine Kleine Posaunenmusik, 1980, In Praise of Winds, 1983, Concerto Quaternio, N.Y. Philharm., 1983, Duologue for Violin and Piano, Library of Congress, 1984, Farbenspiel, Berlin Philharm., 1985, Concerto for Viola and Orch., 1985, String Quartet No. 3, 1986, Chimeric Images, 1988, Concerto for String Quartet and Orchestra, 1988, Concerto for Flute and Orchestra, 1988, On Winged Flight: A Divertimento for Band, 1989, Chamber Concerto, 1989, Concerto for Piano Three Hands, 1989, Phantasmata for Violin and Marinba, 1989, 5 Impromptus Eng. Horn and String Quartet, 1989, Impromptus and Cadenzas, 1990, Hommage à Rayechla for 8 cellos/or multiples thereof, 1990, A Trio Setting for clarinet, violin, piano, 1990, Violin Concert No. 2, 1991, Sonata Fantasia for piano, 1992, Ritmica Melodia Armonia for orchestra, 1992, Of Reminiscences and Reflections for orchestra, 1993 (Pulitzer Prize for music 1994), Brass Quintet No. 2, 1993, The Past is in the Present for orchestra, 1994, Sextet for left hand piano and woodwind quintet, 1994, Concerto for organ and orchestra, 1994, Mondrian's Vision, 1994, Magnificat and Nuncdimittis (choir), 1994, Lain out for it (jazz ensemble), 1994, Brass Quintet No. 2, 1994, Rush Hour an 23d, 1994, Blue Dawn into White Heat (concert band), 1995, An Are Ascending, 1996,. Guggenheim fellow, 1962, 63, MacArthur fellow, 1991; recipient Creative Arts award Brandeis U., 1960, Deems Taylor award ASCAP, 1970, Alice M. Ditson Conducting award, 1970, Rodgers and Hammerstein award, 1971, Friedheim award, 1988, William Schuman award Columbia U., 1989, Down Beat Lifetime Achievement award, 1993, Pulitzer prize in music, 1994, BMI Lifetime Achievement award, 1994, Gold medal Am. Acad. Arts and Letters, 1997, Order of Merit Cross Fed. Republic Germany, 1997; named Composer of Yr., Mus. Am., 1995. Mem. Nat. Inst. Arts and Letters, Am. Acad. Arts and Scis. Address: care Margun Music Inc 167 Dudley Rd Newton Center MA 02159-2830 also: care Festival at Sandpoint PO Box 695 Sandpoint ID 83864-0695

SCHULMAN, CLIFFORD A., lawyer; b. Dec. 6, 1947; s. George and Henrietta Schulman; m. Michele Weissman, June 28, 1969; 1 child, David Michael. B.S. in Journalism and Communications cum laude, U. Fla., 1969, J.D., 1972. Bar: Fla. 1972, U.S. Supreme Ct. 1981, U.S. Ct. Appeals (5th cir.) 1975. Law clk. to Eugene P. Spellman, Miami, Fla., 1970-71; research aide to Judge Norman Hendry, Miami, 1972-73; asst. county atty. Met. Dade County, Miami, 1973-79; ptnr. Greenberg, Traurig, Askew, Hoffman, Lipoff, Rosen & Quentel, Miami, 1979—. Editor-in-chief continuing legal edn. manual Environ. Regulation and Litigation in Fla., 1981 edit. Mem. Gov.'s Task Force on Biscayne Bay Rules, 1978; del. 57th biennial conv. Am. Hebrew Congregations, 1983. Served to capt. USAR, 1969-73. Mem. Fla. Bar (co-editor environ. law sect. newsletter 1977-80; exec. council environ. and land use law sect. 1979-83, sec.-treas. 1981-83, chmn. 1984-85). Home: 21311 NE 23rd Ave Miami FL 33180-1007 Office: Greenberg Traurig Hoffman Lipoff Rosen & Quentel PA 1221 Brickell Ave Miami FL 33131-3224

SCHULMAN, GRACE, poet, English language educator; b. N.Y.C.; d. Bernard and Marcella (Freiberger) Waldman, m. Jerome L. Schulman, Sept. 6, 1959. Student, Bard Coll., Johns Hopkins U.; BS, Am. U., 1955; MA, NYU, 1960, PhD, 1971. Prof. Baruch Coll., N.Y.C., 1971—; poetry editor The Nation, N.Y.C., 1971—. Author: (poetry) Burn Down the Icons, 1976, Hemispheres, 1984, For That Day Only, 1994, (critical study) Marianne Moore: The Poetry of Engagement; translator (postry) At the Stone of Losses, Carmi/Present Tense Award. Fellow Yaddo, 1973, 75, 77, 79, 81, 93, MacDowell Colony, 1973, 75, 77, Rockefeller Inst., 1986, fellow in poetry N.Y. Found. for Arts, 1995; recipient Delmore Schwartz Meml. award for poetry, 1996. Mem. PEN (past v.p.), Poetry Soc. Am., Nat. Book Critics Cir., Authors Guild. Home: 1 University Pl Apt 14F New York NY 10003-4519

SCHULMAN, HAROLD, obstetrician, gynecologist, perinatologist; b. Newark, Oct. 26, 1930; m. Rosemarie Vincenti; childrne: Stanley H., Sandra C., Gina M. B.S., U. Fla., 1951; M.D., Emory U., 1955. Diplomate Am. Bd. Ob-Gyn., Am. Bd. Maternal and Fetal Medicine; registered diagnostic med. sonographer. Intern Jackson Meml. Hosp., Miami, Fla., 1955-56; resident Jackson Meml. Hosp., 1958-61; instr. dept. ob-gyn. U. Miami (Fla.) Sch. Medicine, 1961; instr., asst. prof. dept. ob-gyn. Temple U. Sch. Medicine, Phila., 1961-65; asst. prof. dept. ob-gyn. Albert Einstein Coll. Medicine, Bronx, 1965-67; assoc. prof. Albert Einstein Coll. Medicine, 1968-71, prof., 1971—, acting dept. chmn., 1972-73, chmn., 1973-80; assoc. dir. dept. ob-gyn Bronx Mcpl. Hosp. Ctr., 1967-70, dep. dir., 1970-72; chmn. dept. ob-gyn. Winthrop U. Hosp., Mineola, N.Y., 1984-93; prof. ob-gyn SUNY, Stony Brook;, 1984-93; chmn. dept. ob-gyn. Lawnwood Regional Med. Ctr., Ft. Pierce, FL, 1995—. Contbr. articles to profl. pubs. Served to capt. U.S. Army, 1956-58. Am. Cancer Soc. fellow, 1959-60; USPHS trainee, 1965-66. Fellow Am. Coll. Obstetricians and Gynecologists (vice chmn. Dist. II 1972-75); mem. Bronx County Obstet. Soc. (pres. 1974), Soc. for Gynecologic Investigation, AAAS, Assn. Profs. of Ob-Gyn., Obstet. Soc. (sec. 1978-80, pres. 1982-83), N.Y. Obstetrical Soc., Soc. Perinatal Physicians, Am. Gynecologic and Obstetric Soc., Am. Gynecol. Obstetrics, N.Y. Obstetics Soc. (pres. 1982), Phi Beta Kappa, Alpha Omega Alpha; hon. mem. Miami Ob-Gyn. Soc., South Atlantic Obstetricians and Gynecologists Soc., Buffalo Gynecologic and Obstetric Soc. (E.G. Winkler meml. lectr.), Croatian Ultrasound Soc. (hon.). Democrat. Jewish. Office: 4605 N A1A Vero Beach FL 32963-1345

SCHULMAN, MARK ALLEN, market research company executive; b. Phila., Nov. 15, 1945; s. Morris and Ida (Dunn) S. AB, Washington Coll., Chestertown, Md., 1967; MA, U. Wis., 1968; PhD, Rutgers U., 1979. Dir., div. experimental studies U. Md. Ea. Shore, Princess Anne, Md., 1972-75; sr. project dir. Eagleton Inst. Poll Rutgers U., New Brunswick, N.J., 1975-77; sr. v.p. Louis Harris and Assocs., Inc., N.Y.C., 1977-81; pres. Schulman, Ronca & Bucuvalas, Inc., N.Y.C., 1981—. Bd. visitors and govs. Washington Coll., 1990—; mem. adv. bd. New Sch./Mannes Coll. Jazz Program, 1997—. Mem. Am. Assn. Pub. Opinion Rsch. (pres. N.Y. chpt. 1994-95, sec./treas. 1997-98). Office: Schulman Ronca & Bucuvalas Inc 145 E 32nd St New York NY 10016-6055

SCHULMAN, SIDNEY, neurologist, educator; b. Chgo., Mar. 1, 1923; s. Samuel E. and Ethel (Miller) S.; m. Mary Jean Diamond, June 17, 1945; children—Samuel E., Patricia, Daniel. B.S., U. Chgo., 1944, M.D., 1946. Asst. prof. neurology U. Chgo., 1952-57, asso. prof., 1957-65, prof., 1965-75, Ellen C. Manning prof., div. biol. scis., 1975-93, Ellen C. Manning prof. emeritus, 1993—. Served with M.C. AUS, 1947-49. Mem. Am. Neurol. Assn., U. Chgo. Med. Alumni Assn. (pres. 1968-69), Chgo. Neurol. Soc. (pres. 1964-65). Home: 5000 S East End Ave Chicago IL 60615-3140 Office: U Chgo Culver Hall 1025 E 57th St Chicago IL 60637-1508

SCHULMAN, TOM, screenwriter. BA, Vanderbilt Univ. Writer: (films) Dead Poets Society, 1989 (Academy award best original screenplay 1989), What About Bob?, 1991; co-writer: (films) Honey, I Shrunk the Kids, 1989, Second Sight, 1989, Medicine Man, 1992; exec. prodr.: (films) Indecent Proposal, 1993; writer, dir.: (film) Eight Heads in a Duffel Bag, 1997. Office: care CAA 645 Tuallitan Rd Los Angeles CA 90049

SCHULT, THOMAS PETER, lawyer; b. Great Falls, Mont., Sept. 12, 1954; s. Peter Henry and Louise (de Russy) S.; m. Margo C. Soulé, Sept. 18, 1982. BS in Russian History, U. Va., 1976, JD, 1979. Bar: U.S. Dist. Ct. (we. dist.) Mo. 1979, U.S. Ct. Appeals (10th cir.) 1983, U.S. Ct. Appeals (7th, 8th and 11th cirs.) 1984, U.S. Ct. Appeals (5th cir.) 1985, U.S. Supreme Ct. 1987, U.S. Ct. Appeals (9th cir.) 1988. Ptnr. Lathrop Koontz & Norquist, Kansas City, Mo., 1979-89, Bryan Cave, Kansas City, 1989-94; Stinson, Mag & Fizzell, Kansas City, 1994—. Committeeman Jackson County Reps., Kansas City, 1984—. Mem. ABA (products liability com.), Products Liability Adv. Coun., Mo. Bar Assn. (lectr. continuing legal edn.), Fedn. of Ins. and Corporate Counsel, Def. Rsch. Inst. Episcopalian. Office: Stinson Mag & Fizzell 1201 Walnut St Ste 2800 Kansas City MO 64106-2136

SCHULTE, BRUCE JOHN, lawyer; b. Burlington, Iowa, June 27, 1953; s. James Andrew and Julia Germaine (Van Dale) S.; m. Mary E. Guest, July 1984 (div. Feb. 1995); children: James, John. BA in Am. Studies, U. Notre Dame, 1975; JD, U. Iowa, 1978. Bar: Iowa 1978, U.S. Dist. Ct. (so. dist.) Iowa 1979, U.S. Ct. Appeals (8th cir.) 1982, Minn. 1988, U.S. Dist. Ct. Minn. 1988, Ill. 1989. Law clk. Justice K. David Harris Supreme Ct. Iowa, Des Moines, 1978-79; ptnr. Dailey, Ruther, Bauer, Schulte & Hahn, Burlington, Iowa, 1979-87; atty. Bennett, Ingvaldson & McInerny, Mpls., 1988; gen. counsel Blackwood Corp., St. Paul, 1988-89; publs. editor Nat. Inst. for Trial Advocacy-U. Notre Dame, Ind., 1989-91; asst. dean pub. affairs Chgo. (Ill.) Kent Coll. Law, 1991-94; dep. dir. assoc. rels. West Pub., Eagan, Minn., 1995-97; dir. mktg., v.p. acad. consulting Performance Comm. Group, Chgo., 1997—; key person com. ATLA, 1984-88; mem. commn. on jud. dists. Supreme Ct. Iowa, 1987-88; publs. com. Nat. Law Firm Mktg. Assn., 1993-94. Author: Persuasive Expert Testimony, 1990, Laser Disc Technology in the Courtroom, 1990; editor: Cases and Materials on Evidence, 1991, Modern State and Federal Evidence, 1991, Problems and Cases for Legal Writing, 1991. Mem. state ctrl. com. Iowa Dem. party, 1984-88; devel. com. Frances Xavier Ward Sch., Chgo., 1993—; mem. cmty. task force Chgo. (Ill.) Downtown Circulator Project, 1994-96; v.p. pub. affairs U. Notre Dame Alumni Class of 1975. Notre Dame scholar U. Notre Dame, Ind., 1971-72; recipient Spectra award Internat. Assn. Bus. Communicators, 1993, Silver Trumpet, Publicity Club Chgo., 1994. Mem. ABA (mem. tech. com. lawyers conf. jud. adminstrn. divsn. 1995—), Ill. Bar Assn. (mem. standing com. legal edn. and admission to bar 1993—), Chgo. Bar Assn. (mem. law office tech. com. 1995—), Assn. Am. Law Schs., Chgo. Pub. Rels. Forum (treas. 1997), Notre Dame Club Chgo. (co-chair Hesburgh Forum com. 1993—, trustee 1995—, sec. 1997—). Avocations: sailing, choir, gardening. Home and Office: 10312 S Prospect Ave Chicago IL 60643-2825

SCHULTE, DAVID MICHAEL, investment banker; b. N.Y.C., Nov. 12, 1946; s. Irving and Ruth (Stein) S.; m. Nancy Fisher, June 30, 1968; children: Michael B., Katherine F. BA, Williams Coll., 1968; postgrad., Exeter Coll., Oxford (Eng.) U., 1968-69; JD, Yale U., 1972. Bar: D.C. 1973. Law clk. to Mr. Justice Stewart, U.S. Supreme Ct., 1972-73; spl. asst. to pres. N.W. Industries, Inc., Chgo., 1973-75; v.p. corp. devel. N.W. Industries, Inc., 1975-79, exec. v.p., 1979-80; sr. v.p. Salomon Bros., Chgo., 1980-84; mng. ptnr. Chilmark Ptnrs., Chgo., 1984—. Editor-in-chief: Yale Law Jour, 1971-72. John E. Moody scholar Exeter Coll., Oxford U., 1968-69. Mem. Washington Bar Assn., Chgo. Club, Racquet Club, Bryn Mawr Country Club. Office: Chilmark Ptnrs 875 N Michigan Ave Ste 2100 Chicago IL 60611-1803

SCHULTE, FRANCIS B., archbishop; b. Philadelphia, PA, Dec. 23, 1926. Grad., St. Charles Borromeo Sem. Ordained priest Roman Catholic Ch., 1952. Apptd. titular bishop of Afufenia and aux. bishop of Phila., 1981-85; bishop Wheeling-Charleston, W.Va., 1985-89; archbishop New Orleans, 1989—. Office: 7887 Walmsley Ave New Orleans LA 70125-3431*

SCHULTE, FREDERICK JAMES, newpaper editor; b. Mpls., June 6, 1952; s. Philip William and Katherine Louise (Regan) S. BA, U. Va., 1974. Contbg. editor, feature writer Washington Times, 1974-75; news reporter Internat. Med. News Group, Washington, 1976-78; med. writer, gen. assignment reporter Sun-Sentinel, Ft. Lauderdale, Fla., 1978-83, investigative team leader, 1983-88, asst. regional editor, 1988-90, investigations editor, 1990—. Author: Fleeced! Telemarketing Rip-Offs and How to Avoid Them., 1995. Recipient Excellence in Med. Journalism award Fla. Med. Assn., 1983, 1st Pl. Investigative Reporting award Fla. Press Club, 1983, 1st Pl. Sustained Coverage award Inland Daily Press Assn., 1983, Non-deadlin Reporting prize Sigma Delta Chi, 1983, Green Eyeshade award Sigma Delta Chi, 1983, 1st Pl. Pub. Svc. award Fla. Press Club, 1986, 87, 89, 90, Media Merit award Assn. Trial Lawyers Am., 1986, 1st Pl. award Big Bros./Big Sisters Am., 1987, 1st Pl. Pub. Svc. award Fla. Soc. Newspaper Editors, 1987, Children's Express Jounalism award, 1987, 1st Pl. Investigative Reporting award Unity Awards in Media, 1987, Pulitzer Prize finalist, 1987, Worth Bingham Meml. Fund prize, 1989, 96, Freedom of Info. award AP Mng. Editors Assn., 1990, Lowell Thomas award, 1992, John Hancock award, 1992, Silver Gavel award ABA, 1992, Depth Reporting award Fla. Soc. Newpaper Editors, 1993, Pub. Affairs/Social Issues Reporting award Unity Awards in Media, 1993, George Polk award L.I. U., 1993, Gerald Loeb award U. Calif., 1994; Pulitzer prize finalist for best reporting, 1996; Alicia Patterson Found. fellow, 1997. Mem. Investigative Reporters and Editors (S.E. regional coord., Disting. Investigative Reporting award 1985). Office: Sun-Sentinel 200 E Las Olas Blvd Fort Lauderdale FL 33301-2248

SCHULTE, HENRY FRANK, journalism educator; b. Lincoln, Nebr., Sept. 24, 1924; s. Henry F. and Neva Irene (Arnold) S.; m. Irene Nef, May 12, 1951; children: Nancy, Susanne; m. Ann M. Raleigh, Dec. 4, 1993. AB, McGill U., 1951; MS, Columbia, 1952; PhD, U. Ill., 1966. Editor-corr. U.P.I., London, 1954-56; mgr. U.P.I., Spain, 1956-62; assoc. prof. journalism Pa. State U., 1965-69; chmn. newspaper dept. Syracuse (N.Y.) U., 1969-72, prof. journalism, 1980-94; dean Newhouse Sch. Pub. Communications, 1972-80; cons. Nat. Endowment for Arts; dir. WCNY-TV/FM; external examiner U. W.I., 1975-78; cons. external degree program U. State of N.Y. Author: The Spanish Press, 1470-1966: Print, Power and Politics, 1968; Editor, pub.: Mingote's World, 1957. Chmn. Jesse H. Neal awards judging Assn. Bus. Pubs. Served with AUS, 1945-46. Mem. Internat. Press Inst., Inter-Am.

Press Assn., Soc. Profl. Journalists, Women in Communications, Assn. for Edn. in Journalism, N.Y. State Soc. Newspaper Editors (exec. sec. 1969-73), Assn. Edn. in Journalism/Am. Newspaper Publishers Assn. (regional liaison officer 1976-81), Overseas Press Club. Club: Hillsboro (Hillsboro Beach, Fla.). Home: 89 Mccoy Rd Jaffrey NH 03452-5121

SCHULTE, HENRY GUSTAVE, college administrator; b. Seattle, Oct. 14, 1920; s. John Henry and Alma (Winter) S.; m. Joan Noel Burton, Aug. 20, 1949; children—Steven Craig, Scott John, Jane Martha. B.A. in Econs. and Bus., U. Wash., 1948. With D.K. MacDonald & Co., Seattle, 1952-67, asst. treas., 1957-60, treas., 1960-67; bus. mgr. legal firm Bogle, Gates, Dobrin, Wakefield & Long, Seattle, 1967; adminstr. Child Devel. and Mental Retardation Ctr. U. Wash., Seattle, 1968-86; mem. steering com. mental retardation research ctrs. group Nat. Inst. Child Health and Human Devel., 1971-85. Mem. exec. bd., treas. Assn. Univ. Affiliated Facilities, 1974-77. Served with AUS, 1940-45. Mem. Soc. Research Adminstrs. (mem. exec. com. 1971-72), Am. Assn. Mental Deficiency. Office: U Wash Box 357920 Seattle WA 98195-7920

SCHULTE, JEFFREY LEWIS, lawyer; b. N.Y.C., July 24, 1949; s. Irving and Ruth (Stein) S.; m. Elizabeth Ewan Kaiser, Aug. 13, 1977; children: Andrew Riggs, Ian Garretson, Elizabeth Alexandra. BA, Williams Coll., 1971; postgrad., Harvard U., 1971-72; JD, Yale U., 1976. Bar: Pa. 1978, Ga. 1993. Law clk. to hon. John J. Gibbons U.S. Ct. Appeals (3d cir.), Newark, 1976-77; assoc. Schnader, Harrison, Segal & Lewis, Phila., 1977-84, ptnr., 1985-92; founding ptnr. Schnader, Harrison, Segal & Lewis, Atlanta, 1992—, exec. com., 1994—. Contbr. articles to profl. jours. Bd. dirs. North Ardmore (Pa.) Civic Assn., pres., 1990; bd. dirs. Main Line YMCA, chmn., 1989-91; active Ardmore (Pa.) Alliance Project. Mem. ABA, Pa. Bar Assn., State Bar Ga., Phila. Bar Assn., Atlanta Bar Assn. (chmn. comm. and media rels. com.), World Trade Ctr. Atlanta, Atlanta Venture Forum, Bus. and Tech. Alliance, Yale Club of Ga. (bd. dirs. 1996-97), Williams Club Atlanta, Merion Cricket Club, Weekapaug Yacht Club (R.I.), Weekapaug Tennis Club, Phi Beta Kappa. Office: Schnader Harrison Segal & Lewis 303 Peachtree St NE Ste 2800 Atlanta GA 30308-3252

SCHULTE, JOSEPHINE HELEN, historian, educator; b. Foley, Ala., May 9, 1929; d. Mathias and Theresia (Honner) S. AA, Sacred Heart Jr. Coll., Cullman, Ala., 1949; BS in History, Spring Hill Coll., 1957; MA in History, U. So. Miss., 1961; MA in German, Trinity U., San Antonio, 1976; PhD in History, Loyola U., Chgo., 1969. Steamship agt. Gulf Steamship Agy., Mobile, Ala., 1949-58; translator banks in Mobile, 1949-62; German tchr. Brookley Field AFB, Mobile, 1951-62; adminstrv. asst., rsch. assoc. So. Inst. Mgmt., Louisville, 1959-60; spl. lectr. Spring Hill Coll., Mobile, 1960-63; teaching fellow Loyola U., Chgo., 1962-66; asst. prof. Latin Am. history U. of Americas, Mexico City, 1967-70; from assoc. prof. to prof. St. Mary's U., San Antonio, 1970—, coord. Latin Am. studies program, 1972-90, grad. advisor in history, 1973-94; invited to read a paper Internat. Coloquy, U. Lima, Peru, 1991, U. Yucatan, Mex., 1992, U. Maritima, Valparaiso, Chile, 1993; book reviewer. Author: (with Raymond Schmandt) Civil War Chaplains--A Document From A Jesuit Community, 1962, The Spring Hill College Diary, 1861-65, Gabino Barreda y su mision diplomatica en Alemania, 1878-79 Historia Mexicana, 1974; translator: El Positivismo en Mexico, 1974. Grantee OAS, 1966-67, Newberry Library, 1978, Spanish Govt. and OAS, 1981-82; Fulbright grantee, 1983. Mem. Southwestern Conf. L.Am. Studies, German Geneal. Soc., Cath. Hist. Assn., Gottscheer Rsch. Assn. (bd. dirs.). Roman Catholic. Avocations: photography, genealogy, crocheting, collecting postcards and slides, travel. Home: Eagles Nest 5211 Fredericksburg Rd #933 San Antonio TX 78229

SCHULTE, STEPHEN CHARLES, lawyer; b. Evanston, Ill., June 26, 1952; s. George John and Mary Ruth (Lamping) S.; m. Kathleen Ann O'Donnell, Sept. 4, 1982; children: Kate, Maureen, John. BA magna cum laude, St. Louis U., 1973, JD, 1976. Bar: Ill. 1976, U.S. Dist. Ct. (no. dist.) Ill. 1976, U.S. Ct. Appeals (7th cir.) 1991. Atty. Perz & McGuire, Chgo., 1976-83; ptnr. Winston & Strawn, Chgo., 1983—. Founder, bd. dirs. Greater Orgn. for Less Fortunate (GOLF), Chgo., 1982—; fundraiser for Maryville Acad.; mem. Glenview Park Dist. Commn., 1989—, v.p., 1991-92, pres., 1992-93. Mem. ABA, Ill. State Bar Assn., Chgo. Bar Assn., Ill. Trial Lawyers Assn., Ill. Assn. Def. Trial Counsel, Chgo. Vol. Legal Svcs., Nat. Legal Aid Defender Assn., Phi Beta Kappa. Avocations: basketball, baseball, golf, music, travel. Home: 941 Club Cir Glenview IL 60025-2918 Office: Winston & Strawn 35 W Wacker Dr Chicago IL 60601-1614

SCHULTE, STEPHEN JOHN, lawyer, educator; b. N.Y.C., July 7, 1938; s. John and Marjorie (Fried) S.; m. Patricia Walker, June 6, 1962 (div.); children: Susan Jean, Jeffrey David, Elizabeth Ann; m. Margaret Van Doren Cook, Mar. 12, 1975. BA, Brown U., 1960; JD, Columbia U., 1963. Bar: N.Y. 1964. Assoc. Lowenstein, Pitcher, Hochkiss & Parr, N.Y.C., 1963-66, Fried, Frank, Harris, Shriver & Jacobson, N.Y.C., 1966-69; founding ptnr. Schulte Roth & Zabel, N.Y.C., 1969—; adj. prof. law Benjamin N. Cardozo Law Sch., Yeshiva U., 1992—, bd. dirs., 1995—; adj. prof. law Fordham U., 1992—, vice chmn., bd. dirs. Cardozo Law Sch.; lectr. securities law field; panelist various forums. Trustee Choate Rosemary Hall Sch., Wallingford, Conn., 1982—, chmn. investment and fin. com., 1984-85, chmn. devel. com., 1985-86, chmn. nominating com., 1986-89, chmn. bd. trustees, 1990-95. Mem. ABA, N.Y. State Bar Assn. (com. on securities regulation), Assn. Bar City N.Y. (com. on securities regulation, chmn. subcom. on disclosure policy and tender offers), Norfolk Country Club. Office: Schulte Roth & Zabel 900 3rd Ave New York NY 10022-4728

SCHULTE, STEPHEN THOMAS, employee benefits director; b. St. Louis, Apr. 4, 1952; s. Francis and Janet M. (Besand) S.; m. Virginia Lynn King, Aug. 23, 1986. BS, U. Mo., St. Louis, 1973, MBA, 1978. CPA. Mo. Staff auditor Elmer Fox and Co., St. Louis, 1973-79; fin. auditor Brown Group, Inc., St. Louis, 1979-80, sr. fin. systems analyst, 1980-82, mgr. pension benefits, 1982-88, mgr. savings and retirement, 1988-91, dir. employee benefits, 1991—. Instr. Jr. Achievement, St. Louis, 1980-91. Mem. AICPA, U. Mo. Sch. Bus. Alumni Assn. (bd. dirs. 1992-94), Employee Benefits Assn. (bd. dirs. 1992—), EDP Auditors Assn. (bd. dirs. 1975-80), Beta Alpha Psi. Avocations: fishing, travel, gardening. Office: Brown Group Inc 8300 Maryland Ave Saint Louis MO 63105-3645

SCHULTES, RICHARD EVANS, retired botanist, biology educator; b. Boston, Jan. 12, 1915; s. Otto Richard and Maude Beatrice (Bagley) S.; m. Dorothy Crawford McNeil, Mar. 26, 1959; children: Richard Evans II, Neil Parker and Alexandra Ames (twins). AB cum laude, Harvard U., 1937, AM, 1938, PhD, 1941; MH (hon.), Universidad Nacional de Colombia, Bogotá, 1953; DSci (hon.), Mass. Coll. Pharmacy, 1987. Plant explorer, NRC rsch. fellow Harvard Bot. Mus., Cambridge, Mass., 1941-42; research asso. Harvard Bot. Mus., 1942-53; curator Orchid Herbarium of Oakes Ames, 1953-58, curator econ. botany, 1958-85, exec. dir., 1967-70, dir., 1970-85; Guggenheim Found. fellow, collaborator U.S. Dept. Agr., Amazon of Colombia, 1942-43; plant explorer in S.Am., Bur. Plant Industry, 1944-54; prof. biology Harvard U., 1970-72, Paul C. Mangelsdorf prof. natural scis., 1973-81, Edward C. Jeffrey prof. biology, 1981-85, emeritus prof., 1985—; adj. prof. pharmacognosy U. Ill., Chgo., 1975—; Hubert Humphrey vis. prof. Macalaster Coll., 1979; field agt. Rubber Devel. Corp. of U.S. Govt., in S.Am., 1943-44; collaborator Instituto Argronômico Norte, Belém, Brazil, 1948-50; hon. prof. Universidad Nacional de Colombia, 1953—, prof. econ. botany, 1963; bot. cons. Smith, Kline & French Co., Phila., 1957-67; mem. NIH Adv. Panel, 1964; mem. selection com. for Latin Am. Guggenheim Found., 1964-85; mem. sci. adv. bd. Palm Oil Rsch. Inst., Malaysia, 1980-89; mem. sci. adv. bd. Shaman Pharmaceuticals, 1988—; chmn. Ethnobotany Specialist Group, Internat. Union Nature, Switzerland; chmn. on-site visit U. Hawaii Natural Products Grant NIH, 1966, Deutche Gesellschaft für Arzneiphanzenforchung, Berlin, 1967, III Internat. Pharm. Congress, São Paulo, I Amazonian Biol. Symposium, Belém, Brazil, Symposium Ethnpharmacologic Search for Psychoactive drugs, San Francisco; Laura L. Barnes Annual lectr. Morris Arboretum, Phila., 1969; Koch lectr. Rho Chi Soc., Pitts., 33d Internat. Congress Pharm. Sci., Stockholm, 1971; vis. prof. econ. botany, plants in relation to man's progress Jardín Botánico, Medellín, Colombia, 1973; Cecil and Ida H. Green vis. lectr. U. B.C., Vancouver, Can., 1974; co-organizer Internat. Symposium Erythdroxylon, Equador, 1979, co-dir. phase VII Alpha Helix Rsch. plant medicines Witoto, Bora Indianas, Peru, 1977, 2d Philip Morris Symposium, Richmond, Va., 1975, I Solanacese Conf., U. Birmingham, Eng., 1977, Soc. of Americanists, Manchester, Eng., 1982, Salah Workshop for Conservation of Wildlands, Sultanate of Oman, 1983, Symposium of Environ. Protection, 1992, Etnobotanica-92, Córdoba, Spain, 1992, Spruce Meml. Symposium, Castle Howard, Yorkshire, Eng., 1993, INDERENA Bogotá, 1988, others; organizer Internat. Symposium Erythroxylon, Equador, 1979; vis. scholar Rockefeller Study Conf. Centre, Bellagio, Italy, 1980, 88; cons. Rubber Rsch. Inst., Malaysia, 1988—. Author: (with P. A. Vestal) Economic Botany of the Kiowa Indians, 1941, Native Orchids of Trinidad and Tobago, 1960, (with A. F. Hill) Plants and Human Affairs, 1960, rev. edit., 1968, (with A. S. Pease) Generic Names of Orchids—their Origin and Meaning, 1963, (with A. Hofmann) The Botany and Chemistry of Hallucinogens, 1973, rev. edit., 1980, Hallucinogenic Plants, 1976, Plants of the Gods, 1979, Plant Hallucinogens, 1976, (with W.A. Davis) The Glass Flowers at Harvard, 1982, Where the Gods Reign, 1987, El Reino de los Dioses, 1988, (with R.F. Raffauf) The Healing Forest, 1990, Vine of the Soul: Medicine Men of the Colombian Amazon—Their Plants and Rituals, 1992; contbg. author: Ency. Biol. Scis, 1961, Ency. Brit, 1966, 83, Ency. Biochemistry, 1967, McGraw-Hill Yearbook Sci., Tech, 1937-85, New Royal Horticulture Dictionary (ethnobotany chpt., 1992); author numerous Harvard Bot. Mus. Leaflets.; Asst. editor: Chronica Botanica, 1947-52; editor: Bot. Mus. Leaflets, 1957-85, Econ. Botany, 1962-79; mem. editorial bd. Lloydia, 1965-76, Altered States of Consciousness, 1973—, Jour. Psychedelic Drugs, 1974—; co-editor: series Psychoactive Plants of the World, Yale U. Press, 1987—; mem. adv. bd.: Horticulture, 1976-78, Jour. Ethnopharmacology, 1978—, Soc. Pharmacology, 1976—, Elaeis, 1988—, Flora of Ecuador, 1976—, Jour. Latin Am. Folklore, Ethnobotany (India) (also founding mem.), 1989—, Environ. Awareness (India) 1988—, Bol. Mus. Goeldi (Brazil), 1987—, Environ. Conservation (Geneva), 1987—; contbr. numerous articles to profl. jours. Mem. governing bd. Amazonas 2000, Bogotá; assoc. in ethnobotany Museo del Oro, Bogotá, 1974—; chmn. NRC panels, 1974, 75; mem. NRC Workshops on Natural Products, Sri Lanka, 1975, participant numerous sems., congresses, meetings; mem. adv. bd. Fitzhugh Ludlow Libr., Native Land Found., 1980, Morgan Meml. Archives Chadron State Coll., 1987—, Albert Hofmann Found.; v.p. Margeret Mee Amazon Trust, Royal Bot. Gardens. Deocrated Orden de Victoria Regia, Cruz de Boyacá (Colombia); recipient award, 1981, gold medal for conservation presented by Duke of Edinburgh, 1984, Tyler prize for environ. achievement, 1984, Mass. Gov.'s recognition award Nat. Sci. Week, 1985, cert. of merit Bot. Soc. Am., 1991, Jannaki-Ammal medal, 1992, Linnean medal, 1992, medal Harvard U., 1992, Martín de la Cruz medal, 1992, George Sobert Unite Medal of Honor, Mass. Hortucultural Soc., 1995; grantee Rockefeller Found., 1982. Fellow Am. Acad. Arts and Scis., Am. Coll. Neuropsychopharmacology (sci. spkr. San Juan, P.R. 1984), Third World Acad. Scis., Acad. Scis. India, Internat. Soc. Naturalists; mem. NAS, Linnean Soc. (London), Academia Colombiana Ciéncias Exactas, Fisico-Quimicas y Naturales, Inst. Ecuatoriano Ciéncias Naturales, Soc. Sci. Antonio Alzate (Mexico), Argentine Acad. Scis., Am. Orchid Soc. (life hon.), Pan Am. Soc. New Eng., Soc. Mexicana Micologie (hon.), Assn. Amigos Jardines Botánicos (life), Soc. Econ. Botany (organizer ann. meeting 1961, Disting. Botanist of Yr. 1979), New Eng. Bot. Club (pres. 1954-60), Internat. Assn. Plant Taxonomy, Am. Acad. Achievement, Am. Soc. Pharmacognosy, Phytochem. Soc. N.Am., Soc. Colombiana Orquideologia, Soc. Ethnobot. India, Assn. Tropical Biology, Internat. Soc. Ethnobiology, Soc. Cubana Botánica, Sigam Xi (pres. Harvard chpt. 1971-72, medal 1985), Phi Beta Kappa, Beta Nu chpt. Phi Sigma (first hon.). Unitarian (vestryman Kings Chapel, Boston 1974-76, 82-85). Home: 501 Lexington St N 105 Waltham MA 02154 Office: Harvard Univ Mus Oxford St Cambridge MA 02138

SCHULTHEIS, EDWIN MILFORD, dean, business educator; b. N.Y.C., Apr. 15, 1928; s. Milford Theodore and Lillian May (Hill) S.; BS, Hofstra Coll., 1950; MBA, N.Y. U. Grad. Sch. Bus. Adminstrn., 1958, EdD, Sch. Edn., 1972; m. Joan Edna Bruckner, June 23, 1956. Officer mgr., sales rep. Topton Rug Mfg. Co., N.Y.C., 1950-54; area mgr., trainer Mobil Oil Co., N.Y.C., 1954-62; coord. distributive edn. North Babylon (N.Y.) Pub. Schs., 1962-88; prof. bus. adminstrn. SUNY, Farmingdale, 1970-91; asst. prof. edn. NYU, 1973—; dir. edn. Syracuse (N.Y.) U., 1973-78; chmn. bus. mktg. and indsl. edn. depts. North Babylon (N.Y.) Pub. Schs., 1988-91, chmn. dept. bus. adminstrn. Five Towns Coll., Seaford, N.Y., 1991-92; divsn. chmn. bus. and tech. Five Towns Coll., Dix Hills, N.Y., 1992—, dean instrn., 1993—, dep. dean of faculty, 1993—, assoc. dean, 1996-97; test writer, cons. N.Y. State Dept. Edn., Albany, 1965—; textbook reviewer McGraw-Hill Book Co., N.Y.C., 1967-69; cons. Cornell U., 1975; dist. adviser Distributive Edn. Clubs N.Y., 1970, bd. govs. , trustee, 1975-78; mem. curriculum adv. council Suffolk County (N.Y.) Distributive Edn. Assn., 1967—. Author: Content and Structure of Belief-Disbelief Systems, 1972. Elder Presbyn. Ch., U.S.A. Named N.Y. State Tchr. of Yr., 1976; Outstanding Tchr. in N.Y. State, 1978; recipient Outstanding Svc. award Distributive Edn. Clubs. N.Y., Suffolk County Distributive Edn. Assn., Tchr. Excellence award N.Y. State, 1980, Citation for Excellence in Edn. Gov. Mario Cuomo N.Y., 1991, Citation Excellence in Teaching Babylon Twp., 1991. Mem. Acad. Mgmt., Am. Petroleum Inst., Am. Security Coun., Suffolk County Assn. Distributive Edn. Tchrs. (mem. exec. bd. 1962-74), N.Y. State (pres. 1975-78), L.I. Distributive Edn. Assns. (hon. life, exec. bd. 1972-75), N.Y. State Occupational Edn. Assn. (v.p. 1975-78), L.I. Bus. Edn. Chmns. Assn. (hon. life), Distributive Edn. Clubs Am. (regional leader 1972-75, hon. life 1991), Phi Delta Kappa, Kappa Delta Pi, Sigma Alpha Lambda, Phi Sigma Eta. Presbyterian (ordained ruling elder). Club: Bellport (N.Y.) Golf. Author: Modern Petroleum Marketing, 1971. Home: 14 Thorn Hedge Rd Bellport NY 11713-2616 Office: Five Towns Coll Dix Hills NY 11746-6055

SCHULTZ, ALBERT BARRY, engineering educator; b. Phila., Oct. 10, 1933; s. George D. and Belle (Seidman) S.; m. Susan Resnikov, Aug. 25, 1955; children—Carl, Adam, Robin. B.S., U. Rochester, 1955; M.Engring., Yale U., 1959, Ph.D., 1962. Asst. prof. U. Del., Newark, 1962-65; asst. prof. U. Ill., Chgo., 1965-66, assoc. prof., 1966-71, prof., 1971-83; Vennema prof. U. Mich., Ann Arbor, 1983—. Contbr. numerous articles to profl. jours. Served to lt. USN, 1955-58. Rsch. Career award NIH, 1975-80; Javits Neurosci. Investigator award NIH, 1985-92. Mem. NAE, Internat. Soc. for Study Lumbar Spine (pres. 1981-82), ASME (chmn. bioengring. div. 1981-82, H.R. Lissner award 1990), Am. Soc. Biomechanics (pres. 1982-83, Borelli award 1996), U.S. Nat. Com. on Biomechanics (chmn. 1982-85), Phi Beta Kappa. Office: U Mich 3112 GG Brown Lab Ann Arbor MI 48109-2125

SCHULTZ, ALVIN LEROY, retired internist, endocrinologist, university health science facility administrator; b. Mpls., July 27, 1921; s. Maurice Arthur and Elizabeth Leah (Gershin) S.; m. Martha Jean Graham, Aug. 14, 1947; children: Susan Kristine, David Matthew, Peter Jonathan, Michael Graham. BA, U. Minn.-Mpls., 1943, MD, 1947, MS, 1952. Diplomate Am. Bd. Internal Medicine. Intern Ohio State U., Columbus, 1946-47; resident internal medicine U. Minn. Hosps., Mpls., 1949-52; instr. medicine U. Minn.-Mpls., 1952-54, asst. prof., 1954-59, assoc. prof., 1959-65, prof., 1965-88, prof. emeritus, 1988—; asst. chief medicine Mpls. VA Hosp., 1952-54; dir. endocrine clinic U. Minn., 1954-59; dir. medicine and rsch. Mt. Sinai Hosp., Mpls., 1959-65; chief of medicine Hennepin County Med. Ctr., Mpls., 1965-88; chmn. bd. acad. practice plan Hennepin Faculty Assocs., 1983-87; sr. v.p. med. affairs HealthOne Corp., 1988-92; med. affairs officer HealthSpan, 1993-94; dir. strategic planning, chmn. med. advisory coun. Phoenix Alliance, Inc., St. Paul. Assoc. editor: Jour. Lab. and Clin. Medicine, 1966-69, Modern Medicine, 1960—; editorial bd.: Minn. Medicine, 1965-94; Data Centrum, 1984-87; contbr. articles profl. jours. Bd. dirs. Planned Parenthood of Minn., 1970-75, Hennepin County Med. Philanthropic Found., 1976-86. Capt. U.S. Army, 1947-49. Fellow ACP (Minn. gov. 1983-86; chmn. bd. govs. 1987-88, regent 1988-94); mem. Cen. Soc. Clin. Rsch., Am. Fedn. Clin. Rsch., Endocrine Soc., Am. Thyroid Assn., Minn. Med. Assn. (ho. of dels. 1980-85), Coun. of Med. Splty. Socs. (bd. dirs. 1987-92, v.p. 1988-89, pres. 1990-91), Minn. Assn. Pub. Teaching Hosps. (pres. 1983-84), Hennepin County Med. Soc. (dir. 1977-81, pres. 1988-89, chmn. bd. dirs. 1989-90), Golden Valley Country (Mpls.), NW Racquet (Mpls.). Jewish. Avocations: golf, photography, music, reading, computer science. Home: 5127 Irving Ave S Minneapolis MN 55419-1125

SCHULTZ, ARTHUR JOSEPH, JR., retired trade association executive; b. Detroit, June 20, 1918; s. Arthur Joseph and Olive U. (Beauchesne) S.; m. Barbara Farnan, Aug. 20, 1942; children: Arthur, Robert, William, Barbara, John, Karen. Student, Naval War Coll., 1956-57, Brookings Inst., 1962, Naval Line Sch., 1947-48, U. Detroit, 1937-39. Joined U.S. Navy, 1940, commd. ensign, 1940, advanced through grades to capt., 1950; comdg. officer Com. Strike/S. NATO, Verona, Italy, 1959-61, Naval Air Sta., Grosse Ile, Mich., 1961-63, ret., 1963; pres. Chrysler Corp. subs., Highland Park, Mich., 1971-75; dep. adminstr. VA, Washington, 1975-77; pres. Steel Shipping Container Inst., Union, N.J., 1977-89; ret., 1989. Vice pres. Detroit Aviation Commn., 1968-77; bd. dirs. United Way Union County, Elizabeth, N.J., 1981-85, sec./treas., 1983-85; chmn. Hazardous Materials Adv. Com., Washington, 1984-85. Decorated Navy Cross; recipient Meritorious Service award VA, 1977. Mem. Am. Soc. Assn. Execs., Soc. Automotive Engrs., Mil. Order World Wars, Boca Royale Golf and Country Club (Fla.). Republican. Roman Catholic. Home: 55 Cayman Isles Blvd Englewood FL 34223-1832

SCHULTZ, ARTHUR LEROY, clergyman, educator; b. Johnstown, Pa., June 14, 1928; s. Elmer Albert Robert and Alice Lizetta (Flegal) S.; m. Mildred Louise Stouffer, Nov. 29, 1948; children: Thomas Arthur, Rebecca Louise. BA, Otterbein Coll., 1949; MDiv, United Theol. Sem., 1952; MEd, U. Pitts., 1955, PhD, 1963. Sr. min. Albright United Meth. Ch., Pitts., 1952-56; dir. pub. rels. Otterbein Coll., Westerville, Ohio, 1956-65, adj. prof. religion and philosophy, 1990--; pres. Albright Coll., Reading, Pa., 1965-77, Ashland (Ohio) Coll., 1977-80; exec. dir. Cen. Ohio Radio Reading Svc., Columbus, 1980-84; parish min. Ch. Master United Meth., Westerville, 1984-89; min. of visitation Ch. Messiah United Meth., Westerville, 1991—; pres. Pa. Assn. Colls. & Univs., Harrisburg, 1974-75. Trustee Reading Hosp., 1967-77, Wyoming Sem., Kingston, Pa., 1971-80; v.p. Found. for Ind. Colls. Pa., Harrisburg, 1972-73; pres. Pa. Coun. on Alcohol Problems, Harrisburg, 1968-76; pres. Westerville (Ohio) Hist. Soc., 1986-89, Westerville Area Ministerial Assn., 1992-93. Named Outstanding Young Man of the Year Jr. C. of C., Westerville, Ohio, 1960. Mem. Brookstone Cmty. Assn. (sec. bd. trustees 1994—), Rotary (charter pres. 1959, dist. gov. 1965-66, dist. sec.-treas. 1982-93), Masons, Shriners, Torch Club. Republican. Methodist. Avocations: collecting post cards, golf, tennis, travel. Home: 151 Sandstone Loop Westerville OH 43081-4599

SCHULTZ, ARTHUR WARREN, communications company executive; b. N.Y.C., Jan. 13, 1922; s. Milton Warren and Genevieve (Dann) S.; grad. U. Chgo.; D.Letters (hon.), Rosary Coll.; m. Elizabeth Carroll Mahan, 1949 (div. 1987); children—Arthur Warren, John Carroll (dec.), Julia Hollingsworth; m. Susan Keefe, 1988. With Foote, Cone & Belding Communications, Chgo., 1948-82, v.p., 1957-63, sr. v.p., dir., 1963-69, exec. v.p., 1969, chmn. bd., CEO, 1970-81, chmn. exec. com., CEO, 1981-82; dir. Chgo. Sun-Times Co.; vice chmn. Chgo. Sun-Times Newspaper Co., 1989-94. Pres. Cook County Sch. Nursing, 1963-64, Welfare Council Met. Chgo., 1965-67; mem. bus. adv. council Urban League Chgo., 1971-82; chmn. Nat. Com. to Save Am.'s Cultural Collections, 1990-94; mem. Pres.'s Com. on Arts and Humanities, 1984-93; bd. dirs. Chgo. Crime Commn., 1965-71, Community Fund Chgo., 1966-67, Better Bus. Bur., 1970-78, Lyric Opera Chgo., 1967-77, Chgo. Council Fgn. Relations, 1977-86, Chgo. Public TV, 1978-82, Chgo. Central Area Com., 1978-82; trustee YWCA, 1962-74, Calif. Coll. Arts and Crafts, 1985-87; trustee Art Inst. Chgo., 1975—, chmn. bd., 1981-84; trustee U. Chgo., 1977—, Santa Barbara Mus. Art, 1988—, pres., 1989-92. Editor Caring for Your Collections. Served to 1st lt. USAAF, 1943-45. Recipient Alumni Service award U. Chgo., 1986. Mem. Montecito Retirement Assn. (pres. 1996, bd. dirs.), Am. Assn. Advt. Agys. (dir. 1968-71, 74-76, chmn. Chgo. council 1964-65, chmn. Central region 1970-71), Delta Kappa Epsilon. Episcopalian. Clubs: Commercial, Valley (Montecito, Calif.), Birnam Wood. Home and Office: 2072 China Flat Rd Santa Barbara CA 93108-2211

SCHULTZ, BARBARA MARIE, insurance company executive; b. Chgo., Sept. 9, 1943; d. Edwin and Bernice (Barstis) Legner; m. Ronald J. Schultz Sr., May 1, 1965; 1 child, Ronald J. Grad. high sch., Chgo. Account rep. Met. Ins. Co., Aurora, Ill., 1981—; qualifier Met. Life Leaders Conf., 1990. Fellow Nat. Assn. Life Underwriters (edn. chmn. 1988-91, nat. quality award Robert L. Rose award 1990), Life Underwriters Tng. Coun. (chmn. 1986-88, citation 1987), South Cook County Assn. Life Underwriters (edn. chmn. 1988-91). Roman Catholic. Avocations: boating, aerobics, fishing. Office: Met Ins Co 15255 94th Ave Orland Park IL 60462-3800

SCHULTZ, CARL HERBERT, real estate management and development company executive; b. Chgo., Jan. 9, 1925; s. Herbert V. and Olga (Swanson) S.; m. Helen Ann Stevesson, June 6, 1948; children: Mark Carl, Julia Ann. B.S. in Gen. Engring., Iowa State U., 1948. With Schultz Bros. Co., 1948—; mdse. mgr. and store planner Schultz Bros. Co., Chgo., 1962-70; v.p. Schultz Bros. Co., Lake Zurich, Ill., 1968-72; pres. Schultz Bros. Co., 1972—, Ill. Schultz Bros. Co., Ind. Schultz Bros. Co., Iowa Schultz Bros. Co., Wis. Schultz Bros. Co. Mem. Lake Bluff (Ill.) Zoning Bd. Appeals, 1976-85, chmn., 1978-85. Served with U.S. Army, 1944-46. Mem. Lake Zurich Indsl. Coun. (sec. 1976), Assn. Gen. Mdse. Chains (dir. 1975-86, exec. com. 1983-86, chmn. nat. conv. 1982), Ill. Retail Mchts. Assn. (dir. 1984-89), Wis. Retail Fedn. (dir. 1981-89). Presbyterian. Club: Bath and Tennis (Lake Bluff). Home: 701 E Center Ave Lake Bluff IL 60044-2607 Office: 785 Oakwood Rd Ste 102S Lake Zurich IL 60047-1549

SCHULTZ, CAROLE LAMB, community volunteer; b. Corning, N.Y., May 14, 1946; d. Arthur Martin and Jane Ursula (Oehler) Lamb; m. John Charles Schultz, July 13, 1968; children: David Michael, Geoffrey Brian. BS in Math. magna cum laude, St. Lawrence U., Canton, N.Y., 1968. Systems engr. IBM, Williamsport, Pa., 1968-71; invited attendee Gov.'s Cong. of Bus./Edn. Partnerships, Harrisburg, Pa., 1991. Helped establish Children's Hands-on Mus., Children's Discovery Workshop, 1979-88. Treas. Jr. League Williamsport, Inc., 1980-82, cmty. v.p., 1985-86, pres.-elect, 1986-87, pres., 1987-88; area II coun. mem. Assn. Jr. Leagues Internat., Inc., 1988-90, chair nominating com., 1989-90; NE regional coun. United Way Am., 1993—; pers. chair Faxon-Kenmar United Meth. Ch., Williamsport, 1991-92; trustee St. Lawrence U., 1988—, chair honors com., 1994—; ednl. tech. adv. com. Williamsport Area Sch. Dist., 1994—; 2d v.p., sec., divsn. chair, planning mem. Lycoming United Way, Williamsport, 1991—, vice-chair campaign 1992, chair campaign 1993; candidate Williamsport Area Sch. Bd., 1989; panelist Leadership Lycoming, 1987, mentor, 1990—; chair steering com. Lycoming County Sch.-to-Work Partnership, 1995—; cmty. adv. bd. Williamsport-Lycoming Found., 1995—; bd. govs. Cmty. Arts Ctr. Recipient Lycoming County Brotherhood award, 1996, Lycoming United Way award 1997. Mem. AAUW (program v.p. 1973-75, pres. 1975-77, treas. Pa. conv. 1973, 85, Woman of Yr. 1981), Williamsport-Lycoming C. of C. (chair edn. subcom. on partnerships 1991-92), Lycoming Bus.-Edn. Coalition (exec. com., steering com., co-chair task force on skills/curriculum), Phi Beta Kappa. Methodist. Avocations: swimming, travel, music, art, French. Home: 300 Upland Rd Williamsport PA 17701-1852

SCHULTZ, CLARENCE CARVEN, JR., sociology educator; b. Temple, Tex., Oct. 31, 1924; s. Clarence Carven Sr. and Bea Alice (Newton) S.; m. Margie Frances Beran, Oct. 29, 1943; children: Timothy Wayne, Theresa Bea. BS, SW Tex. State U., 1948, MA, 1949; PhD, U. Tex., 1970; AA (hon.), Lee Coll., 1989. Adminstrv. asst. Interstate Theatres, Temple, 1941-42; advt. sales rep. Temple Daily Telegram, 1942-43; asst. mgr. McClellan Stores, Tex., 1946-47; history and sociology instr. S.W. Tex. State U., San Marcos, 1949-52, from asst. prof. to prof., 1965-90, prof. emeritus, 1991; chmn. dept. sociology and anthropology SW Tex. State U., San Marcos, 1971-76, dean Sch. Liberal Arts, 1977-78; teaching fellow U. Tex., Austin, 1952-53; mem. faculty Lee Coll., Baytown, Tex., 1953-65, chmn. div. social scis., 1961-65; curriculum cons. to various pub. schs.; presenter workshops in field. Author: Practical Probation: Handbook, 1972; editor: Family Perspectives, 1975; contbr. articles to profl. jours., chpt. to book. Ens. USNR, 1943-46. Recipient S.W. Tex. Pedogog Teaching Excellence award, 1973, 74, Disting. Tchr. award S.W. Tex. State U. Alumni Assn., 1976, S.W. Tex. Presdl. award for excellence in teaching, 1985, Award of Honor, S.W. Tex. State U. Alumni Assn., 1991; named Piper Prof., Minnie Stevens Piper Found., 1976, Outstanding Former Instr., Lee Coll. Former Students' Assn., 1988; appointed Adm. in Tex. Navy by State Gov., 1969. Mem. NEA-Ret., Tex. Ret. Tchrs. Assn., Tex. State Tchrs. Assn., San Marcos Area Ret. Tchrs., Alpha Chi, Alpha Kappa Delta. Methodist. Home: 604 Franklin Dr San Marcos TX 78666-2426 Office: SW Tex State U Dept Sociology Anthrop San Marcos TX 78666

SCHULTZ, CLARENCE JOHN, minister; b. Morris Twp., Wis., Aug. 4, 1937; s. Clarence John Sr. and Ella Mae (Feavel) S.; m. Doroland Kay King, Aug. 24, 1957 (dec. Jan. 1974); children: Sharon Kay, Susan May Schultz Rogers; m. Martha Ann Aylor, Apr. 5, 1975. BS, Bryan Coll., 1960.

Ordained to ministry Conservative Congl. Ch., 1961. Min. 1st Congl. Ch., Herreid, S.D., 1961-66, Immanuel Evang. Congl. Ch., Sheboygan, Wis., 1966-77, Hope Congl. Ch., Superior, Wis., 1977-83, Zion Evang. Ch., Scottsbluff, Nebr., 1983-89; min. 1st Congl. Ch., Buffalo Center, Iowa, 1989-92, Kenosha, Wis., 1992—. Mem. Conservative Congl. Christian Conf. (rec. sec. 1973-82, v.p. 1994-96, pres. 1996—, Rocky Mountain area rep. 1987-89, endorser of chaplains 1988—, mem. credentials com. 1988—), Rotary (mem. ch. chaplain com. 1993-95). Avocations: amateur radio, golf. Home: 7023 Pershing Blvd Kenosha WI 53142-1723 Office: First Congl Ch 5934 8th Ave Kenosha WI 53140-4006

SCHULTZ, DALE WALTER, state senator; b. Madison, Wis., June 12, 1953; s. Walter Albert and Lillian (Fortman) S.; m. Rachel Weiss, June 20, 1981; children: Katherine Ann, Amanda. BBA, U. Wis., 1975. Farm mgr. Hillpoint, Wis., 1975—; adminstrv. and legis. asst. Wis. State Senate, Madison, 1976-79; planning analyst State of Wis., Madison, 1979-82, rep., 1982-91; senator Wis. State Senate, Madison, 1991—; chair ins. com. Wis. State Seante, Madison, 1995—; mem. audit com. joint com. rev. adminstrv. rules Wis. State Senate. Mem. citizens adv. bd. Sauk County (Wis.) Health Care Ctr.; mem. Sauk County Farm Bur. Recipient Disting. Svc. award FFA, 1994; named Legislator of Yr., Wis. Tech. Coll. Assn., 1994-95, Guardian of Small Bus., Nat. Fedn. Ind. Bus., 1994, Legislator of Yr., Vietnam Vets. Assn., 1994. Republican. Club: Rod & Gun (Hillpoint, Wis.). Lodges: Lions, Masons. Home: 515 N Central Ave Richland Center WI 53581-1702 Office: PO Box 7882 Madison WI 53707-7882

SCHULTZ, DANIEL JOSEPH, manufacturing executive, writer; b. St. Louis, Dec. 10, 1945; s. Abraham Y. and Isabelle (Balk) S.; m. Karen Lynn Hanson, Aug. 3, 1980; children: Brian, David, Rebecca, Jacob. BA, Pershing Coll., 1968; MA, Webster U., 1974, MBA, 1975; PhD, Greenwich U., Hilo, Hawaii, 1992. Exec. Std. Register Co., St. Louis, 1972-75, Schultz Co., St. Louis, 1975—; cons. in field, 1975—. Author: The Crisis Within, 1993. Leader Boy Scouts Am., St. Louis, 1980—. Capt., pilot USAF, 1968-72, Vietnam. Decorated DFC. Fellow Internat. Soc. for Philos. Inquiry (dir. pub. rels. 1994—); mem. Am. Fighting Arts Assn. (Shodan 1st degree Black Belt, 1986, Nidan 2nd Degree Black Belt, 1990). Republican. Avocations: martial arts, reading, writing, outdoors. Home: 60 Muirfield Ct Saint Louis MO 63141-7372 Office: Schultz Co 14090 Riverport Dr Maryland Hts MO 63043-4805

SCHULTZ, DENNIS BERNARD, lawyer; b. Detroit, Oct. 15, 1946; s. Bernard George and Madeline Laverne (Riffenberg) S.; m. Andi Lynn Leslie, Apr. 18, 1967; 1 child, Karanne Anne. BS, Wayne State U., 1970; JD, Detroit Coll. Law, 1977. Bar: Mich. 1977, U.S. Dist. Ct. (ea. dist.) Mich., U.S. Ct. Appeals (6th cir.), U.S. Dist. Ct. (we. dist.) Pa. V.p. Barkay Bldg. Co., Ferndale, Mich., to 1976; law clk. Hon. George N. Bashara, Mich. Ct. Appeals, Detroit, 1977; shareholder Butzel Long, Detroit, 1978—. Editor Detroit Coll. Law Rev., 1977. Detroit Coll. Law Alumni Assn. scholar, 1976, Mich. Consolidated Gas Co. scholar, 1977. Mem. Detroit Bar Assn., Mich. Bar Assn. Republican. Roman Catholic. Avocations: boating, biking, golf. Office: Butzel Long 150 W Jefferson Ave Ste 900 Detroit MI 48226-4430

SCHULTZ, DOUGLAS GEORGE, art museum director; b. Oakland, Calif., Oct. 3, 1947; s. Leon H. and Teresa (deMonte) S. A.B., U. Calif., Berkeley, 1969, M.A. in History of Art, 1972; grad., Inst. Arts Adminstrn., Harvard U., 1971. Summer intern Nat. Gallery of Art, Washington, 1970; curatorial intern Albright-Knox Art Gallery, Buffalo, 1972; asst. curator Albright-Knox Art Gallery, 1973-75, asso. curator, 1975-76, curator, 1977-79, chief curator, 1980-83, dir., 1983—; adj. prof. art history SUNY, Buffalo, 1975-79; mem. adv. bd. Arts Council of Buffalo and Erie County 1975—. Office: Albright-Knox Art Gallery 1285 Elmwood Ave Buffalo NY 14222-1003

SCHULTZ, EILEEN HEDY, graphic designer; b. Yonkers, N.Y.; d. Harry Arthur and Hedy Evelyn (Morchel) S. B.F.A., Sch. Visual Arts, 1955. Staff artist C.A. Parshall Studios, N.Y.C., 1955-57; editorial art dir. Paradise of the Pacific, Honolulu, 1957-58; graphic designer Adler Advt. Agy., N.Y.C., 1958-59; art dir. Good Housekeeping Mag., N.Y.C., 1959-82; creative dir. advt. and sales promotion Good Housekeeping Mag., 1982-86; creative dir. Hearst Promo, 1986-87; pres. Design Internat., N.Y.C., 1987—; creative dir. The Depository Trust Co., 1987—. Art dir., editor, designer, 50th Art Directors Club Annual, 1973; columnist: Art Direction, 1969—. Dir. Sch. Visual Arts, N.Y.C., 1978—; trustee Sch. Art League, 1978—; advisor Fashion Inst. Tech., 1979—; mem. adv. commn. N.Y.C. Community Colls., 1979—. Named Yonkers Ambassador of Good Will to Netherlands, 1955; recipient Outstanding Achievement Sch. Visual Arts Alumni Soc., 1976, Sch. Art League Youth award, 1976. Mem. Art Dirs. Club (pres. 1975-77), Soc. Illustrators (pres. 1991-93), Joint Ethics Com. (chmn. 1978-80), Am. Inst. Graphic Arts, Soc. Publ. Designers, Type Dirs. Club.

SCHULTZ, FRANKLIN M., retired lawyer; b. Cin., June 16, 1917; s. Max and Goldie (Wise) S.; m. Jean Carol Barnett, Apr. 5, 1946 (dec. 1981); children: William B., John M., Katherine, Caroline; m. Virginia B. Henderson, Sept. 4, 1983. BA, Yale U., 1939, LLB, 1942. Bar: Ohio 1947, D.C. 1954, Mass. 1985, U.S. Supreme Ct. 1954. Atty. Fed. Power Commn., 1946-47; assoc. prof. Sch. Law, Ind. U., Bloomington, 1947-53; with firm Purcell & Nelson, Washington, 1953-80; ptnr. Purcell & Nelson, 1957-80, Reavis & McGrath, Washington, 1980-85; lawyer-in-residence Sch. Law, Washington and Lee U., 1985, vis. prof., 1991-94, ret., 1994; vis. prof. Sch. Law, U. Iowa, 1986-90; lectr. Sch. Law, George Washington U., 1958-59; vis. prof. Sch. Law, U. Va., 1975; mem. ednl. appeal bd. U.S. Dept. Edn., 1974-82. Contbr. articles to profl. jours. Trustee Nantucket Land Coun., 1992—. Served to capt. AUS, 1942-46. Decorated Bronze stars. Mem. ABA (mem. council adminstrv. law sect. 1966-69, chmn. 1970-71, del. ho. of dels. 1972-74), D.C. Bar (gen. counsel 1977-79, mem. legal ethics com. 1976-81), Am. Law Inst., Am. Bar Found., Adminstrv. Conf. U.S. (council 1980-82). Home: 1953 Marthas Rd Alexandria VA 22307-1966

SCHULTZ, FREDERICK HENRY, investor, former government official; b. Jacksonville, Fla., Jan. 16, 1929; s. Clifford G. and Mae (Wangler) S.; m. Nancy Reilly, Aug., 1951; children: Catherine G., Frederick H., Clifford G., John R. B.A., Princeton U., 1951; postgrad., U. Fla. Sch. Law, 1954-56. With Barnett Nat. Bank, Jacksonville, 1956-57; owner, operator investment firm, from 1957; mem. Fla. Ho. of Reps., 1963-70, speaker of the house, 1968-70; chmn. bd. Barnett Investment Svcs., Inc.; dir. Barnett Banks Inc., to 1979; vice chmn. bd. govs. Fed. Res. System, Washington, 1979-82; bd. dirs. Barnett Banks, Inc., Am. Heritage Life Ins. Co., S.E. Atlantic Inc., Riverside Group, Inc., Wickes Lumber Co. Served to lt. U.S. Army, 1952-54, Korea. Decorated Bronze Star. Roman Catholic. Office: PO Box 1200 Jacksonville FL 32201-1200

SCHULTZ, GREGORY PAUL, health center official; b. Two Rivers, Wis., Nov. 16, 1961; s. Paul Gerald and Carol Jean (Steffel) S. BS in Health Info. Adminstrn., U. Wis., Milw., 1991; M Health Care Adminstrn., Cardinal Stritch Coll., Milw., 1996. Dir. med. records St. Camillus Health Ctr., Wauwatosa, Wis., 1990-96; with W. Tropicana Med. Ctr., Las Vegas, 1996—. Mem. Am. Health Info. Mgmt. Assn. (registered record administr.), Wis. Health Info. Mgmt. Assn. (long term care publs. team 1993—). Democrat. Roman Catholic. Avocations: travel, walking, working out. Office: W Tropicana Med Ctr 4845 S Rainbow Blvd Ste 401 Las Vegas NV 89103-4750

SCHULTZ, HOWARD MICHAEL, registered nurse; b. Bronx, N.Y., Aug. 18, 1944; s. Sidney and Jeanette (Fineman) S.; m. Ellen Einhorn (div. 1970); children: Marni Rae, Robert Alan. AS, Miami Dade C.C., 1983. RN, Fla.; cert. phys. asst. N.Y. Respiratory tech. Biscayne Med. Ctr., North Miami Beach, 1978; cert. respiratory tech. Cedars of Lebanon Hosp., Miami, 1978-83; nurse Mt. Sinai Med. Ctr. Greater Miami, Miami Beach, 1983-87; customer support specialist Non Invasive Monitoring Sys., Miami Beach, 1987-88; nurse Mt. Sinai Med. Ctr. Greater Miami, 1988—; CEO, pres. Nurseware, Lauderhill, Fla., 1995—. Mem. Am. Assn. Critical Care Nurses, Assn. Nurses in AIDS Care (pres. Broward chpt. 1994-95), Broward PC Assn. Home: 1718 NW 56th Ave Lauderhill FL 33313

SCHULTZ, JEROME SAMSON, biochemical engineer, educator; b. Bklyn., June 25, 1933; s. Henry Herman and Sally (Warburg) S.; m. Jane Paula Schwartz, Sept. 1, 1955; children: Daniel Stuart, Judith Nyquist, Kathryn Hubbard. BS in Chem. Engring., Columbia U., 1954, MS, 1956; PhD in Biochemistry, U. Wis., 1958. Group leader biochem. rsch. Lederle Labs., N.Y., 1958-64; asst. prof. dept. chem. engring. U. Mich., Ann Arbor, 1964-67, assoc. prof., 1967-70, prof., 1970-77, chmn., 1977-85; sect. head, emerging engring. techs. NSF, Washington, 1985-86, dep. dir. cross-disciplinary rsch., 1986-87; dir. Ctr. for Biotech. and Bioengring. U. Pitts., 1987—, prof. chem. engring., 1987—, prof. medicine, 1990—, dir. bioengring. program, 1991—. Editor Biotechnology Progress, 1988—; contbr. articles to profl. jours.; patentee in field. NIH rsch. career devel. awardee, 1970-75. Fellow Am. Inst. for Med. and Biol. Engring. (pres. 1995); mem. AAAS, Nat. Acad. Engring., Am. Chem. Soc. (past chmn. biochem. tech. divsn.), AIChE (past chmn. food and bioengring. divsn., Bioengring. award 1984), Am. Soc. Artificial Internal Organs, Nat. Acad. Engring., Sigma Xi, Phi Lambda Upsilon, Tau Beta Pi. Home: 111 Bentley Dr Pittsburgh PA 15238-2501 Office: U Pitts Ctr Biotechnol & Bioengring 300 Technology Dr Pittsburgh PA 15219-3122

SCHULTZ, KAREN ROSE, clinical social worker, author, publisher, speaker; b. Huntington, N.Y., June 16, 1958; d. Eugene Alfred and Laura Rose (Palazzolo) Squeri; m. Richard S. Schultz, Apr. 8, 1989. BA with honors, SUNY, Binghamton, 1980; MA, U. Chgo., 1982. Lic. clin. social worker, Ill. Unit dir., adminstr. Camp Algonquin, Ill., 1981; clin. social worker United Charities Chgo., 1982-86; social worker Hartgrove Hosp., Chgo., 1986-87; pvt. practice, Oak Brook, Ill., 1987—; owner, founder Inner Space pub. Co., 1993; trainer, speaker various groups, schs. and orgns., DuPage County, Ill., 1988-89; group leader Optifast Program, Oak Park and Aurora, Ill., 1989-90; instr. social work Morraine Valley C.C., Palos Hills, Ill., 1989-90; instr. eating disorders Coll. of Dupage, Glen Ellyn, Ill., 1990-92, mem. eating disorder com., 1989—, tchr. intuition and counseling, 1995—. Author: The River Within, 1993, Shelter in the Forest, 1998; editor, contbg. author The River Within newsletter, 1989—. Com. mem. DuPage Consortium, 1987-89. Mem. NASW (registerd, diplomate), acad. Cert. Social Workers, Nat. Speakers Assn., Profl. Speakers Ill., Toastmasters Interant., Women Entrepreneurs DuPage. Avocations: creative writing, aerobics, yoga, personal growth. Office: 900 Jorie Blvd Ste 234 Oak Brook IL 60523-2230

SCHULTZ, LOUIS EDWIN, management consultant; b. Foster, Nebr., Aug. 8, 1931; s. Louis Albert and Lula Pusey (Cox) S.; m. Mary Kathleen Peck, Mar. 3, 1962; children: Kurt Michael, Kristen Leigh. BSEE, U. Nebr., 1959; MBA, Pepperdine U., 1974. Mktg. mgr. Bell & Howell, Pasadena, Calif., 1962-70; dir. mktg. Cogar Corp., Utica, N.Y., 1970-71; product mgr. Pertec Corp., L.A., 1971-73; gen. mgr. Control Data Corp., Mpls., 1973-84; founder, pres. Process Mgmt. Internat., Inc., Mpls., Minn., 1984—; adv. bd. Inst. for Productivity Through Quality, U. Tenn., Knoxville, 1982-84; bd. dirs. Corcom Cos., Inc. Author: Managing in the Worldwide Competitive Society, 1984, Quality Management Philosophies, 1985, Profiles in Quality, 1994; co-author: Quality Handbook for Small Business, 1994, Deming, The Way We Knew Him, 1995. Mem. Gov.'s Commn. on Productivity, St. Paul, 1986; chmn. Wirth Park Tree Restoration Com., Mpls., 1983; mem. Productivity Planning Com., St. Paul, 1985—. Staff sgt. USMC, 1952-54; advisor to Deming Forum, 1985—; judge Minn. Quality award, 1992. Recipient Profl. Partnership award U. Minn., 1987. Mem. Am. Soc. Performance Improvement (bd. dirs. 1984-89, outstanding svc. award), Minn. Coun. for Quality (bd. dirs. 1987—), Human Sys. Mgmt. (edtl. bd.), Asia-Pacific Orgn. Quality Control, Toastmasters Internat. Republican. Methodist. Office: Process Mgmt Inst 150 S 5th St Ste 1300 Minneapolis MN 55402-4213

SCHULTZ, LOUIS MICHAEL, advertising agency executive; b. Detroit, Aug. 24, 1944; s. Henry Richard and Genevieve (Jankowski) S.; children: Christian David, Kimberly Ann. B.A., Mich. State U., 1967; M.B.A., Wayne State U., 1970. Staff Campbell-Ewald, Warren, Mich., 1967-74; v.p. group dir. Campbell-Ewald, 1975-77, sr. v.p., assoc. dir., 1977-82, group sr. v.p., 1982-83, exec. v.p., 1984-87; exec. v.p. Lintas: USA, 1987—; chmn. Lintas: WW Media Coun., 1991; mem. devel. council IPG, N.Y.C., 1984—; pres., CEO CE Comm., 1994—; bd. dirs. Campbell-Ewald. Advisor, Detroit Renaissance Com., 1981-84. With USAR, 1967-73. Mem. NATAS, Am. Women in Radio and TV, Am. Mktg. Assn., Detroit Advt. Assn., Ad. Club N.Y. (bd. dirs.), Adcraft Club, Marco Polo Club, Old Club, Hidden Valley Club, Longboat Key Club, Detroit Athletic Club. Republican. Roman Catholic. Avocations: golf; tennis; travel. Home: 2899 Pheasant Ring Dr Rochester Hls MI 48309 Office: CE Comms 30400 Van Dyke Ave Warren MI 48093-2368

SCHULTZ, LOUIS WILLIAM, judge; b. Deep River, Iowa, Mar. 24, 1927; s. M. Louis and Esther Louise (Behrens) S.; m. D. Jean Stephen, Nov. 6, 1949; children: Marcia, Mark, Paul. Student, Central Coll., Pella, Iowa, 1944-45, 46-47; LL.B., Drake U., Des Moines, 1949. Bar: Iowa. Claims supr. Iowa Farm Mut. Ins. Co., Des Moines, 1949-55; partner firm Harned, Schultz & McMeen, Marengo, Iowa, 1955-71; judge Iowa Dist. Ct. (6th dist.), 1971-80; justice Iowa Supreme Ct., 1980-93; county atty. Iowa Couty, 1960-68; ret., 1993. Served with USNR, 1945-46. Mem. Am. Bar Assn., Iowa Bar Assn. (bd. govs.), Iowa Judges Assn. (pres.). Office: U Iowa Coll Law # 1488 Iowa City IA 52242

SCHULTZ, MICHAEL, stage and film director, film producer; b. Milw., Nov. 10; s. Leo Schultz and Katherine (Frances) Leslie; m. Gloria Jean Jones. Ed., U. Wis., Marquette U. Dir. stage plays Song of the Lusitanian Bogey, Negro Ensemble Co., N.Y.C., 1968, and London, 1968, Kongi's Harvest, God Is a (Guess What), Does A Tiger Wear a Necktie, 1969; Broadway debut The Reckoning, 1969, Operation Sidewinder, Dream on Monkey Mountain, 1970, Mulebone, Lincoln Ctr., 1991; dir. films including To Be Young, Gifted and Black, 1971, Cooley High, 1975, Car Wash, 1976, Greased Lightning, 1977, Which Way Is Up?, 1977, Sgt. Pepper's Lonely Hearts Club Band, 1978, Scavenger Hunt, 1979, Carbon Copy, 1981, Bustin Loose, 1983, The Last Dragon, 1985, Krush Groove, 1985, Disorderlies, 1987, Livin' Large, 1991, Ceremonies in Dark Old Men; dir. TV films Benny's Place, 1982, For Us The Living, 1983, The Jerk, Too, 1984, Timestalkers, 1986, Rock n' Roll Mom, 1988, Jury Duty, 1989, Hammer and Slammer, 1990, Dayo, 1992, Picket Fences, 1993-94, Young Indiana Jones, 1994, 95, 96, (episodic TV) Picket Fences, Chicago Hope, Jag, Touched by a Angel, The Promised Land, Sisters. Office: PO Box 1940 Santa Monica CA 90406-1940

SCHULTZ, PAUL NEAL, electronic publishing executive; b. Evanston, Ill., Nov. 3, 1957; s. Edward Delfus and Loretta Mae (Fraine) S.; m. Robin Lyn Davis, May 27, 1989; children: Kyle Neal, Caitlyn McKenzie, Sophie Davis. BS in Bus. & Mktg., No. Ill. U., 1979. Territory mgr. Burroughs Corp., Chgo., 1979-81; sr. mktg. rep. Mead Data Cen., Chgo., 1981-84, br. mgr., 1984-90, nat. sales dir. LEXIS Document Svcs. divsn., 1990—; cons. ABA Law Office of Future Com., Chgo., 1985, 86; speaker Chgo. Bar Assn. Tech. Com., Chgo., 1986, 87, 88. Mem. Credit Mgrs. Assn., Comml. Fin. Assn. (adv. bd. dirs.), Equipment Lessors Assn., Western Assn. Equipment Lessors. Roman Catholic. Avocations: golf, fishing, hunting, skiing. Home: 285 S Valley Rd Barrington IL 60010-4748 Office: Lexis Document Svcs 135 S La Salle St Ste 2200 Chicago IL 60603-4303

SCHULTZ, PETER G., chemistry educator. PhD, Calif. Inst. Tech., 1984. Mem. faculty chemistry dept. U. Calif., Berkeley, 1985—, now prof.; founding scientist Affymax Rsch. Inst., 1988; investigator Howard Hughes Med. Inst., 1994—; founder Symyx Techs., 1995—. NIH Postdoctoral fellow, MIT; recipient Nobel Laureate Signature award for Grad. Edn. in Chemistry, Pure Chemistry award, Arthur C. Cope award, Am. Chem. Soc., 1990, Alan T. Waterman award NSF, 1988, Ernest Orlando Lawrence Meml. award U.S. Dept. Energy, 1991, Wolf Prize in Chemistry, 1994, Eli Lilly award Am. Chem. Soc., 1991, DuPont Merck Young Investigator award, 1992, Humboldt Rsch. award for Sr. U.S. Scientist, 1992, Calif. Scientist of Yr. award, 1995. Mem. NAS, Am. Acad. Arts and Scis. Office: U Calif Dept Chemistry Berkeley CA 94720

SCHULTZ, RICHARD CARLTON, plastic surgeon; b. Grosse Pointe, Mich., Nov. 19, 1927; s. Herbert H. and Carmen (Huebner) S.; m. Pauline Zimmermann, Oct. 8, 1955; children: Richard, Lisa, Alexandra, Jennifer. McGregor scholar, U. Mich., 1946-49; M.D., Wayne State U., 1953. Diplomate Am. Bd. Plastic Surgery. Intern Harper Hosp., Detroit, 1953-54; resident in gen. surgery Harper Hosp., 1954-55, U.S. Army Hosp., Fort Carson, Colo., 1955-57; resident in plastic surgery St. Luke's Hosp., Chgo., 1957-58, U. Ill. Hosp., Chgo., 1958-59, VA Hosp., Hines, Ill., 1959-60; practice medicine specializing in plastic surgery Park Ridge, Ill., 1961-96; retired, 1996; clin. asst. prof. surgery U. Ill. Coll. Medicine, 1966-70, assoc. prof. surgery, 1970-76, prof., 1976—, head div. plastic surgery, 1970-87; pres. med. staff Lutheran Gen. Hosp., Park Ridge, 1977-79; vis. prof. U. Pitts., 1972, U. Miss., 1973, U. Pisa, Italy, 1974, Jikei U. Coll. Medicine, Tokyo, 1976, Ind. U., 1977, U. Helsinki, 1977, U. N.Mex., 1978, U. Milan, 1981, So. Ill. Sch. Medicine, 1982, Tulane U. Med. Sch., 1983, Shanghai 2d Med. Coll., 1984, U. Guadalajara (Mex.), 1986, Gazi U., Turkey, 1988, U. Coll. Medicine Tsuksba, Japan, 1996, Taegu (Korea) U., 1996; participant, guest surgeon Physicians for Peace, Turkey and Greece, 1988, Israel and Occupied Ters., 1990, Egypt, 1991, Luthuania, Estonia, 1993 (team leader); leader citizen amb. People to People Internat. Del. Plastic Surgeons to Albania & Russia, 1994. Author: Facial Injuries, 1970, 3d edit., 1988, Maxillo-Facial Injuries from Vehicle Accidents, 1975, Outpatient Surgery, 1979. Mem. sch. bd., Lake Zurich, Ill., 1966-72, pres., 1968-72; pres. Chgo. Found. for Plastic Surgery, 1966—. Served to capt. M.C., AUS, 1955-57. Recipient research award Ednl. Found. Am. Soc. Plastic and Reconstructive Surgery, 1964-65, Med. Tribune Auto Safety award, 1967, Robert H. Ivy award, 1969, Disting. Sci. Achievement award Wayne U. Coll. Medicine Alumni, 1975; Sanvenero-Rosselli award, 1981; Fulbright scholar U. Uppsala, Sweden, 1960-61. Fellow ACS (pres. local commn. on trauma 1985-87); mem. Am. Assn. Plastic Surgeons (trustee 1990-91), Am. Soc. Plastic and Reconstructive Surgeons, Midwestern Assn. Plastic Surgeons (pres. 1978-79), Chgo. Soc. Plastic Surgeons (pres. 1970-72), Midwestern Assn. Plastic Surgeons (pres. 1978-79), Am. Soc. Maxillofacial Surgeons (pres. 1988-89, award of honor 1986), Am. Assn. Automotive Medicine (pres. 1970-71, A. Merkin award 1982), Am. Cleft Palate Assn., Am. Soc. Aesthetic Plastic Surgery, Tord Skoog Soc. Plastic Surgeons (pres. 1971-75), Can. Soc. Plastic Surgery, Chilean Soc. Plastic Surgery (corr.), Japanese Soc. Plastic Surgery (corr.), Cuban Soc. Maxillofacial Surgery (corr.), Korean Soc. Plastic Surgery. Home: 1440 Irvine Ln Montecito CA 93108 Office: 12825 N Northport Point Rd Northport MI 49670-0764

SCHULTZ, RICHARD DALE, national athletic organizations executive; b. Grinnell, Iowa, Sept. 5, 1929; s. August Henry and Marjorie Ruth (Turner) S.; m. Jacquilyn Lu Duistermars, June 26, 1949; children: Robert Dale, William Joel, Kim Marie. BS, Cen. Coll., Pella, Iowa, 1950; EdD Honoris Causa, Cen. Coll., 1987; LLD (hon.), Wartburg Coll., 1988, Alma Coll., 1989, Luther Coll., 1991; Phd, U.S. Sports Acad., 1993; LLD, Daniel Webster Coll., 1997. Head basketball coach, athletic dir. Humboldt (Iowa) High Sch., 1950-60; freshman basketball coach U. Iowa, Iowa City, 1960-62; head baseball coach, assoc. basketball coach U. Iowa, 1962-70, head basketball coach, 1970-74, asst. v.p., 1974-76; dir. athletics and phys. edn. Cornell U., Ithaca, N.Y., 1976-81; dir. athletics U. Va., Charlottesville, 1981-87; exec. dir. NCAA, Mission, Kans., 1987-94; pres. Global Sports Enterprises, 1994-95; exec. dir. U.S. Olympic Com., Colorado Springs, Colo., 1995—; mem. honors ct. Nat. Football Found. and Hall of Fame, Nat. Basketball Hall of Fame, 1992; chmn. bd. NCAA Found., 1989; organizer Iowa Steel Mill, Inc.; bd. trustees Gettysburg Coll., 1996—. Author: A Course of Study for the Coaching of Baseball, 1964, The Theory and Techniques of Coaching Basketball, 1970; Contbr. articles to mags. Bd. dirs. Fellowship of Christian Athletes, 1986, chmn., 1990, chmn. Multiple Sclerosis, 1974-75; mem. Knight Found. Commn. on Intercollegiate Athletics, 1990—; mem. adv. com. on svc. acad. athletic programs Def. Dept. Recipient Disting. Alumni award Ctrl. Coll., Pella, 1970, Lifetime Svc. award U. Iowa, 1994, Corbett award Nat. Assn. Collegiate Dirs. Athletics, 1994, medal of honor Ellis Island, 1997; mem. Basketball Hall of Fame Honor Ct., 1992, Sportsman of Yr. award Marine Corp., 1997; inducted into Iowa Baseball Hall of Fame, 1993. Mem. Nat. Assn. Coll. Basketball Coaches, Ea. Coll. Athletic Assn. (mem. exec. com. 1980-81), Am. Basketball Coaches Assn. (Award of Honor 1994), Am. Football Coaches Assn. (lifetime membership award 1995). Home: 3670 Twisted Oak Cir Colorado Springs CO 80904-2138 Office: US Olympic Com One Olympic Plz Colorado Springs CO 80909

SCHULTZ, RICHARD MARTIN, electronics application engineering executive; b. Chgo., June 6, 1954; s. Richard J. and Rose Mary (Bianchi) S.; m. Gina Marie Ehlers, June 19, 1976; children: Erin Michelle, Nicole Kathryn. BSEE, Rose-Hulman, 1976. Engring. technician Honeywell Comml. Div., Arlington Heights, Ill., 1972-76, design engr., 1976-77; sr. design engr. Honeywell Comml. Div., Arlington Heights, 1978-79, Honeywell Bldg. Svcs. Div., Arlington Heights, 1979-80, Tex. Instruments Inc., Arlington Heights, 1980-81; dir. engring. URL Inc. OEM Group, Elk Grove, Ill., 1981, 82; pres. R.M. Schultz & Assocs. Inc., Crystal Lake, Ill., 1981—, McHenry, Ill., 1988—; pres. Enclave Corp., McHenry, 1988—. Inventor, patentee in field. Mem. McHenry County Solid Waste Com., McHenry, 1990, McHenry County Indsl. Coun., McHenry, 1988—, Corp. Presidents Roundtable, Schaumburg, Ill., 1986-88. Named to Virgil Order of the Arrow, 1970. Mem. McHenry C. of C. Republican. Avocations: hunting, fishing, reading, racquetball. Home: 3370 Executive Dr Marengo IL 60152-9180 Office: R M Schultz & Assocs Inc 1809 S State Route 31 Mc Henry IL 60050-8292*

SCHULTZ, RICHARD OTTO, ophthalmologist, educator; b. Racine, Wis., Mar. 19, 1930; s. Henry Arthur and Josephine (Wagoner) S.; m. Diane Haldane, Sept. 29, 1990; children: Henry Reid, Richard Paul, Karen Jo. B.A., U. Wis., 1950, M.S., 1954; M.D., Albany Med. Coll., 1956; M.Sc., U. Iowa, 1960. Diplomate: Am. Bd. Ophthalmology. Intern, Univ. Hosps., Iowa City, 1956-57; resident in opthalmology Univ. Hosps., 1957-60; chief ophthalmology sect. div. Indian health USPHS, Phoenix, 1960-63; practice medicine specializing in ophthalmology Phoenix, 1963; NIH spl. fellow in ophthalmic microbiology U. Calif., San Francisco, 1963-64; clin. assoc. U. Calif., 1963-64, research assoc., 1963-64; assoc. prof., chmn. dept. ophthalmology Marquette U. Sch. Medicine (now Med. Coll. Wis.), Milw., 1964-68; prof., chmn. Marquette U. Sch. Medicine (now Med. Coll. Wis.), 1968—; dir. Eye Inst.; dir. ophthalmology Milw. Regional Med. Ctr.; mem. nat. adv. eye coun. NIH, 1984-88; cons. VA regional ctr. Milw. Children's, Columbia, Froedert and St. Mary's hosps., Milw. Contbr. articles to profl. jours. Served with USPHS, 1960-63. Fellow Am. Acad. Ophthalmology, ACS, Am. Ophthal. Soc.; mem. Assn. Univ. Profs. Ophthalmology (trustee, pres. 1978), AMA, Am., Milw. ophthalmol. socs., Assn. Research Vision and Ophthalmology, N.Y. Acad. Scis., Research to Prevent Blindness, Oxford Ophthalmol. Congress (Eng.), State Med. Soc. Wis., Wis. Soc. Prevention Blindness, Med. Soc. Milw. County, Milw. Acad. Medicine. Home: 12500 W Grove Ter Elm Grove WI 53122-1973 Office: 8700 W Wisconsin Ave Milwaukee WI 53226-3512

SCHULTZ, ROBERT J., retired automobile company executive; b. 1930. BSME, Mich. State U., 1953, MBA, 1969. With GM Corp., 1955-92, chief engr., 1977-81, gen. mgr. Delco Elecs. div., 1981-84; group dir. engr. Chevrolet, Pontiac, Can. Group, 1984-85; group v.p. GM of Canada Group GM Corp., 1985-90; vice chmn. GM Corp., Detroit, 1990-92; ret., 1993; also chmn., pres., chief exec. officer GM Hughes Electronics Corp.; bd. dirs. OEA, Inc., Nat. Digitronics Corp., TexCo Comm. Bd. trustees Calif. Inst. Tech. With USAAF, 1953-55. Mem. NAE.

SCHULTZ, ROBERT VERNON, entrepreneur; b. Sterling, Ill., July 2, 1936; s. Wilbur Henry and Eleanor Grace (Love) S.; m. Shelly I. Shaw, Feb. 12, 1970; children: Robert G., Trina R., Cherie A. BBA, Lincoln Mgmt. Sch. of Chgo., 1971; BA in Acctg., Rockford Sch. of Bus., 1975; BS in Christian Edn., Moody Bible Inst., 1980. Asst. to v.p. DeKalb Ogle Tel. Co., Rochelle, Ill., 1969-74; mktg. mgr. Chambers Owen Inc., Rockford, Ill., 1960-69; owner, pres. Schultz Mgmt. and Mktg., St. Charles, Ill., 1970—; pres., owner Investment Internat. Inc., North Aurora, 1988—, Diamond Publs. Inc., North Aurora, 1987—; owner Schultz Internat. Inc., Princeton, Ill.; bus. cons. Network Bus. Opportunity Entrepreneurs Chgo. 1970—; owner Schultz Internat. Inc., Princeton. Editor-in-chief, owner, pres., chmn. bd. Ill. Car Mart, 1988. With U.S. Army, 1957-59. Recipient Quick Silver award Ambs. Internat., 1990. Mem. Internat. Platform Assn., Internat. Speakers Platform Assn., Jaycees (pres. 1968). Republican. Avocation: pilot. Home: PO Box 185 Princeton IL 61356-0185 Office: Schultz Internat Inc PO Box 185 Princeton IL 61356-0185

SCHULTZ, SAMUEL JACOB, clergyman, educator; b. Mountain Lake, Minn., June 9, 1914; s. David D. and Anna (Eitzen) S.; m. Eyla June Tolliver, June 17, 1943; children: Linda Sue, David Carl. Grad., St. Paul Bible Inst., 1936; AA, Bethel Coll., 1938; BA, John Fletcher Coll., 1940; BD, Faith Theol. Sem., 1944; MST, Harvard U., 1945, ThD, 1949. Ordained to ministry Christian and Missionary Alliance Ch., 1944; pastor First Meth. Ch., Pine River, Minn., 1940-41, Waldo Congl. Ch., Brockton, Mass., 1944-45, Evang. Bapt. Ch., Belmont, Mass., 1945-47; prof. Gordon Coll., Boston, 1946-47, Bethel Coll. and Sem., St. Paul, 1947-49, St. Paul Bible Inst., 1948-49; prof. Wheaton (Ill.) Coll., 1949-80, prof. emeritus, 1980—, Samuel Robinson prof. Bible and theology, 1955-80, chmn. Bible and philosophy dept., 1957-63, chmn. div. Bibl. edn. and philosophy, 1963-67, chmn. div. Bibl. studies, 1972-79; prof. Old Testament and Bible Exposition Trinity Coll. Grad. Sch. (name now Tampa Bay Theol. Sem.), Dunedin (now Holiday), Fla., 1987-93; prof. Old Testament St. Petersburg (Fla.) Theol. Sem., adj. prof. St. Petersburg Jr. Coll., 1995—; interim supply pastor Bible Ch. Winnetka, Ill., 1951, 60; resident supply pastor South Shore Bapt. Ch., Hingham, Mass., 1958-59. Author: The Old Testament Speaks, 1960, 3d edit., 1980, 4th edit., 1990, Law and History, 1964, The Prophets Speak, 1968, Deuteronomy-Gospel of Love, 1971, The Gospel of Moses, 1974, 79, Interpreting the Word of God, 1976, Leviticus-God Dwelling Among His People, 1983, The Message of the Old Testament, 1986; contbr. Deuteronomy commentary to The Complete Biblical Libr., 1996. Mem. bd. edn. Bethel Coll. and Sem., 1960-65; historian Conservative Congregation Christian Conf., 1980-86; bd. dirs. Inst. in Basic Youth Conflicts, 1965-80, Congl. Christian Hist. Soc., 1984-96, Brookwoods Christian Camps and Confs., Inc., Alton, N.H., 1978—; trustee Gordon-Conwell Sem., South Hamilton, Mass., 1980—, Lexington (Mass.) Christian Acad., 1987—. NYU study grantee Israel, 1966, Wheaton Coll. Alumni research grantee, 1958; recipient Alumnus of the Yr. award Crown Coll., 1996. Mem. Soc. Bibl. Lit., Evang. Theol. Soc. (editor Jour. 1962-75), Near East Archaeol. Soc. (sec., bd. dir.), Wheaton Coll. Scholastic Honors Soc., Phi Sigma Tau. Book the Living and Active Word of God dedicated in his honor, 1983. Home: 143 East St Lexington MA 02173-1913 *Love the Lord your God with all your heart and with all your soul and with all your strength and your neighbor as yourself.*

SCHULTZ, STANLEY GEORGE, physiologist, educator; b. Bayonne, N.J., Oct. 26, 1931; s. Aaron and Sylvia (Kaplan) S.; m. Harriet Taran, Dec. 25, 1960; children: Jeffrey, Kenneth. A.B. summa cum laude, Columbia U., 1952; M.D., N.Y. U., 1956. Intern Bellevue Hosp., N.Y.C., 1956-57; resident Bellevue Hosp., 1957-59; research assoc. in biophysics Harvard U., 1959-62, instr. biophysics, 1964-67; assoc. prof. physiology U. Pitts., 1967-70, prof. physiology, 1970-79; prof., chmn. dept. physiology U. Tex. Med. Sch., Houston, 1979—, prof. dept. internal medicine, 1979—; cons. USPHS, NIH, 1970—; mem. physiology test com. Nat. Bd. Med. Examiners, 1974-79, chmn., 1976-79. Editor Am. Jour. Physiology, Jour. Applied Physiology, 1971-75, Physiol. Revs., 1979-85, Handbook of Physiology: The Gastrointestinal Tract, 1989-91—; mem. editl. bd. Jour. Gen. Physiology, 1969-88, Ann. Revs. Physiology, 1974-81, Current Topics in Membranes and Transport, 1975-81, Jour. Membrane Biology, 1977—, Biochim. Biophys. Acta, 1987-89; assoc. editor Ann. Revs. Physiology, 1977-81; assoc. editor News in Physiol. Scis., 1989-94, editor, 1994—; contbr. articles to profl. jours. Served to capt. M.C. USAF, 1962-64. Recipient Research Career award NIH, 1969-74; overseas fellow Churchill Coll., Cambridge U., 1975-76. Mem. AAAS, Am. Heart Assn. (estab. investigator 1964-68), Am. Physiol. Soc. (councillor 1989-91, pres.-elect 1991-92, pres. 1992-93, past pres. 1993-94), Fed. Am. Soc. Exptl. Biology (exec. bd. 1992-95), Biophys. Soc., Soc. Gen. Physiologists, Internat. Cell Rsch. Orgn., Internat. Union Physiol. Scis. (chmn. internat. com. gastrointestinal physiology 1977-80, chmn. U.S. nat. com. 1992—), Assn. Am. Physicians, Am. Assn. Ob-Gyn. (hon. fellow), Assn. Chmn. Depts. Physiology (pres. 1985-86), Sigma Xi, Phi Beta Kappa. Home: 4955 Heatherglen Dr Houston TX 77096-4213

SCHULTZ, STEVEN T., hotel executive. Sr. v.p. devel. La Quinta Inns, Inc., San Antonio. Office: La Quinta Inns Inc 112 E Pecan St PO Box 2636 San Antonio TX 78299-2636

SCHULTZ, T. PAUL, economics educator; b. Ames, Iowa, May 24, 1940; s. Theodore W. and Esther (Werth) S.; m. Judith Hoenack, Sept. 16, 1967; children: Lara, Joel, Rebecca. BA, Swarthmore Coll., 1961; PhD, MIT, 1966; MA (hon.), Yale U., 1974. Cons. Joint Econ. Com., Washington, 1964; researcher econs. dept. Rand Corp., Santa Monica, Calif., 1965-72, dir. population research, 1968-72; prof. econs. U. Minn., Mpls., 1972-75; prof. econs. Yale U., New Haven, 1974—, dir. Econ. Growth Ctr., 1983-96; cons. World Bank, Rockefeller Found.; mem. com. on population NAS, Washington, 1987-89, 90-93. Author: Structural Change in a Developing Country, 1971, Economics of Population, 1981; editor: (books) The State of Development Economics, 1988, Investment In Women's Human Capital, 1995, (periodical) Research in Population Economics, 1985, 88, 91, 96; assoc. editor Jour. Population Econs., 1991—, Econ. of Edn. Rev., 1993—, China Econ. Rev., 1994—. Fellow AAAS (population resources environ. com. 1985-89, nomination com. 1987-90); mem. Am. Econ. Assn., Econometrics Soc., Population Assn. Am. (bd. dirs. 1979-81), Internat. Union for Sci. Study Population, Soc. for Study Social Biology (bd. dirs. 1986-89), European Soc. for Population Econs. (bd. dirs., pres. 1997), Econ. Rsch. Forum for Arab Countries (trustee 1993—). Office: Yale U Econ Growth Ctr PO Box 208269 27 Hillhouse Ave New Haven CT 06520-8269

SCHULTZ, THEODORE WILLIAM, retired economist, educator; b. Arlington, S.D., Apr. 30, 1902; s. Henry Edward and Anna Elizabeth (Weiss) S.; m. Esther Florence Werth; children: Elaine, Margaret, T. Paul. Grad., So. Dak. Agr., Brookings, S.D., 1924; B.S., S.D. State Coll., 1927, D.Sc. (hon.), 1959; M.S., U. Wis., 1928, Ph.D., 1930; LL.D. (hon.), Grinnell Coll., 1949, Mich. State U. in 1962, U. Ill., 1968, U. Wis., 1968, Cath. U. Chile, 1979, U. Dijon, France, 1981; LL.D., N.C. State U., 1984. Mem. faculty Iowa State Coll., ames, 1930-43; prof., head dept. econs. and sociology Iowa State Coll., 1934-43; prof. econs. U. Chgo., 1943-72, chmn. dept. econs., 1946-61, Charles L. Hutchinson Disting. Service prof., 1952-72, prof. emeritus, 1972—; econ. adviser, occasional cons. Com. Econ. Devel., U.S. Dept. Agr., Dept. State, Fed. Res. Bd., various congl. coms., U.S. Dept. Commerce, FAO, U.S. Dept. Def., Germany, 1948, Fgn. Econ. Adminstrn., U.K. and Germany, 1945, IBRD, Resources for the Future, Twentieth Century Fund, Nat. Farm Inst., others.; dir. Nat. Bur. Econ. Research, 1949-67; research dir. Studies of Tech. Assistance in Latin Am.; bd. mem. Nat. Planning Assn.; chmn. Am. Famine Mission to India, 1946; studies of agrl. developments, central Europe and Russia, 1929, Scandinavian countries and Scotland, 1936, Brazil, Uruguay and Argentina, 1941, Western Europe, 1955. Author: Redirecting Farm Policy, 1943, Food for the World, 1945, Agriculture in an Unstable Economy, 1945, Production and Welfare in Agriculture, 1950, The Economic Organization of Agriculture, 1953, Economic Test in Latin America, 1956, Transforming Traditional Agriculture, 1964, The Economic Value of Education, 1963, Economic Crises in World Agriculture, 1965, Economic Growth and Agriculture, 1968, Investment in Human Capital: The Role of Education And of Research, 1971, Human Resources, 1972, Economics of the Family: Marriage, Children, and Human Capital, 1974, Distortions of Agricultural Incentives, 1978, Investing in People: The Economics of Population Quality, 1981, Restoring Economic Equilibrium: Human Capital in the Modernizing Economy, 1990, The Economics of Being Poor, 1993, Origins of Increasing Returns, 1993; co-author: Measures for Economic Development of Under-Developed Countries, 1951; editor: Jour. Farm Econs., 1939-42; contbr. articles to profl. jours. Research fellow Center Advanced Study in Behavioral Sci., 1956-57; recipient Nobel prize in Econs., 1979. Fellow Am. Acad. Arts and Scis., Am. Farm Econs. Assn., Nat. Acad. Scis.; mem. Am. Agrl. Econ. Assn., Am. Econ. Assn. (pres. 1960, Walker medal 1972), Am. Philos. Soc., Royal Econ. Soc., Nat. Acad. Edn.; others. Home: 5620 S Kimbark Ave Chicago IL 60637-1606 Office: U Chgo Dept Econs 1126 E 59th St Chicago IL 60637-1539*

SCHULTZ, VICTOR M., physician; b. Pitts., Aug. 14, 1932; s. Irvin and Rose (Reiss) S. BS, Kent (Ohio) State U., 1955; MD, Ohio State U., Columbus, 1958. Diplomate Am. Bd. Dermatology. Pvt. practice Santa Monica, Calif., 1965—. Fellow Am. Acad. Dermatology, Pacific Dermatologic Assn.; mem. AMA, Am. Coll. Physicians, Calif. Med. Assn., L.A. County Med. Assn. Avocations: skiing, tennis, golf, music, swimming. Office: 2336 Santa Monica Blvd Ste 201 Santa Monica CA 90404-2067

SCHULTZ, WARREN ROBERT, manufacturing administrator; b. Chgo., June 29, 1949; s. Warren Gimbel and Helen Catherine (Mattes) S.; m. Mary Elise Nunnally, Mar. 31, 1973; children: Warren Thomas, Gregory James. BS in Aerospace Engring., U.S. Naval Acad., 1971. Commd. ensign USN, 1971, advanced through grades to lt., 1975, resigned, 1976; process engr. Corning Glass Works, Harrodsburg, Ky., 1976-78, quality control supr., 1978; project engr., elec. supr. Manville Corp., Etowah, Tenn., 1978-82; plant engr. Manville Corp., Waterville, Ohio, 1982-86, prodn. supt., 1986-89, furnace expansion project spl. assignment coord., 1989-92, prodn. supt. fiberglass dept., 1992-93, prodn. supt. material and sliver depts., 1993; plant mgr. Johns Manville Corp., Waterville, 1993-97, sr. mfg. mgr., 1997—; Waterville Planning Commn., 1995—. Religious tng. instr., St. Joseph's Ch., Maumee, Ohio, 1984-85, mem. parish coun., 1989-91; coach Anthony Wayne Area Little League Baseball Assn., Waterville, 1983-86. Republican. Roman Catholic. Avocations: racquetball, golf. Home: 201 Harvest Ln Waterville OH 43566-1156 Office: Schuller Corp PO Box 517 Toledo OH 43697-0517

SCHULTZE, CHARLES LOUIS, economist, educator; b. Alexandria, Va., Dec. 12, 1924; s. Richard Lee and Nora Woolls (Baggett) S.; m. Rita Irene Hertzog, Sept. 6, 1947; children: Karen M., Kevin C., Helen K., Kathleen, Carol, Mary. A.B., Georgetown U., 1948, M.A., 1950; Ph.D., U. Md., 1960. Mem. staff Pres.'s Council Econ. Advisers, 1952, 54-58; chmn. Pres.'s Council Econ. Advisors, 1977-81; assoc. prof. econs. Ind. U., 1959-61; prof. econs. U. Md., 1961-87; asst. dir. U.S. Bur. of Budget, 1962-64, dir., 1965-67; sr. fellow Brookings Instn., Washington, 1968-76, 81-96, emeritus, 1997—. Author: (with others) Setting National Priorities, 6 vols., 1970, 71, 72, 73, 83, 90, The Public Use of Private Interest, 1977, Other Times, Other Places, 1986, (with others) Barriers to European Growth, 1987, (with others) An American Trade Strategy, 1990, Memos to the President, 1992. Served with AUS, 1943-46. Decorated Purple Heart, Bronze Star. Mem. Am. Econ. Assn. (pres. 1984). Office: Brookings Instn 1775 Massachusetts Ave NW Washington DC 20036-2188

SCHULZ, CHARLES MONROE, cartoonist; b. Mpls., Nov. 26, 1922; s. Carl and Dena (Halverson) S.; m. Joyce Halverson, Apr. 18, 1949 (div. 1972); children: Meredith, Charles Monroe, Craig, Amy, Jill; m. Jean Clyde, 1973. LHD (hon.), Anderson Coll., 1963; DHL (hon.), St. Mary's Coll. of CA, 1969. Cartoonist St. Paul Pioneer Press, Sat. Eve. Post, 1948-49. Created syndicated comic strip Peanuts, 1950—; author of many collections of Peanuts strips and cartoons; screenwriter of several teleplays and feature films based on the Peanuts strip; exhbns. include Around the World and Home Again: A Tribute to the Art of Charles M. Schulz, 1994—, Around the Moon and Home Again: A Tribute to the Art of Charles M. Schulz, 1995—. With U.S. Army, 1943-45. Recipient Outstanding Cartoonist award Nat. Cartoonist Soc., 1955, 1964; Yale Humor award, 1956; School Bell award, Nat. Edn. Assn., 1960; Peabody award and Emmy award for CBS cartoon special "A Charlie Brown Christmas", 1966; Charles M. Schulz award for contribution to the field of cartooning, United Feature Syndicate, 1980; inducted into Cartoonists Hall of Fame. Mem. Nat. Cartoonists Soc. Office: Number One Snoopy Place Santa Rosa CA 95401 also: United Media 200 Madison Ave 4th Fl New York NY 10016

SCHULZ, HELMUT WILHELM, chemical engineer, environmental executive; b. Berlin, July 10, 1912; came to U.S., 1924; s. Herman Ludwig Wilhelm and Emilie (Specka) S.; m. Colette Marie Francoise Prieur, Mar. 6, 1954; children: Raymond A., Caroline P., Roland W., Robert B., Thomas F. BS, Columbia U., 1933, ChemE, 1934, PhD, 1942. Rsch. engr. to mng. dir. Union Carbide Corp., Charleston, W.Va., 1934-69; spl. asst. to dir. def. rsch. and engring. U.S. Dept. of Def., Washington, 1964-67; spl. asst. to U.S. commr. of edn. U.S. Dept. of Edn., Washington, 1971; sr. rsch. scientist, adj. prof. Columbia U., N.Y.C., 1972-85; pres., chief exec. officer Dynecology, Inc., Harrison, N.Y., 1974—; chmn. Brandenburg Energy Corp., Harrison, 1979—. Contbr. articles to profl. jours. Mem. N.Y.C. Mayor's Sci. and Tech. Adv. Coun., 1973-74; bd. dirs. Charleston Symphony Orch., 1956-62, Am. Cancer Soc., W.Va., 1954-58; chmn. W.Va. AEC, Charleston, 1962-64. Grantee in field. Fellow AIChE; mem. N.Y. Acad. Scis., Am. Chem. Soc. (emeritus), N.Y. Yacht Club, Cosmos Club. Achievements include patents; centrifugation cascade for enrichment of fissionable uranium isotope; high acceleration rocket motor; tar-free, slagging coal/waste gasifier; enhanced oil recovery process; synthesis of ethanol from ethylene and steam; waste-to-energy conversion processes, and 60 others. Home: 611 Harrison Ave Harrison NY 10528-1406

SCHULZ, JOHN JOSEPH, communications educator. BA in Journalism, U. Minn., 1962; MPhil, Oxford U., 1979, DPhil, 1981. Newswriter, reporter Voice of Am. News, Washington, 1971-72; corr. Voice of Am. News, Hong Kong, 1972-74; bur. chief Voice of Am. News, Tokyo, 1974-77; commentator BBC, London, 1977-79; coverage editor Voice of Am., 1979-82; deputy dir. Voice of Am. News Divsn., 1982-84; South Asia corr. Voice of Am. News, Islamabad, Pakistan, 1987-89; thinktank analyst Oxford Analytica, 1977-79, 84-88; prof. Nat. War Coll., Washington, 1989-91; sr. corr. Voice of Am. News, 1984-87, 91-92; assoc. dir. publs. The Arms Control Assn., 1992-95; prof. internat. comms. Coll. Comms. Boston U., 1995-97, acting chair dept. mass. comms., advt., and pub. rels., 1997—; editor Arms Control Today, 1992-95; presenter in field. Contbr. articles to profl. jours. With USAF, 1963-71. Decorated 3 DFC, silver star, air medals, gallantry crosses, USAF; recipient disting. alumni award U. Mont., 1995. Office: Coll Communications 640 Commonwealth Ave Boston MA 02215-2422

SCHULZ, JUERGEN, art history educator; b. Kiel, Germany, Aug. 18, 1927; came to U.S., 1938; s. Johannes Martin Askan Schulz and Ilse (Lebenbaum) Hiller; m. Justine Hume, Sept. 1951 (div. 1968); children: Christoph (dec.), Ursula, Catherine; m. anne Markham, May 19, 1969; 1 child, Jeremy. BA, U. Calif., Berkeley, 1950; PhD in History of Art, U. London, 1958. Reporter San Francisco Chronicle, 1950-51; copy editor UPI, London, 1952-53; from instr. to prof. history of art U. Calif., 1958-68; prof. Brown, Providence, 1968-90, Andrea V. Rosenthal prof. history art and architecture, 1990-95; mem. Inst. for Advanced Study, Princeton, N.J., 1971-72. Author: Venetian Painted Ceilings of the Renaissance, 1968, Printed Plans and...Views of Venice, 1971, La cartografia tra scienza e arte, 1990; also articles. Staff sgt. U.S. Army, 1945-48. Decorated grande ufficiale Ordine della Stella della Solidarieta della Repubblica Italiana; Guggenheim fellow, 1966-67. Mem. Ateneo Veneto, Centro Internaz. di Studi di Architettura A. Palladio. Office: Brown U Dept History Art and Architecture PO Box 1855 Providence RI 02912-1855

SCHULZ, KAREN ALICE, medical and vocational case manager; b. Detroit, Aug. 18, 1952; d. Donald E. and Ethel B. (Johnston) Wallinger; m. Kirk C. Hamlin (dec. Sept. 1987); m. Paul R. Schulz, Feb. 19, 1993; children: Jennifer, Carolyn. BA, Concordia U., 1974; MA, Wayne State U., 1991. Case mgr. IntraCorp., Southfield, Mich., 1990-92, S. Yangouyian Assocs., Southfield, 1992-93, Comprehensive Case Mgmt. Svcs., Dearborn, Mich., 1993—; mem. faculty Detroit Coll. Bus., Dearborn, 1993—; sch. dir. Ross Career Schs., Oak Park, Mich., 1980-90; Cert. rehab. counselor, addictions counselor, Am. Bd. Disability Analysts, Am. Bd. Med. Psychotherapists; lic. profl. counselor. Mem. NAFE, Am. Counseling Assn., Mich. Self Insurers Orgn. Office: Comprehensive Case Mgmt Svcs PO Box 7455 Dearborn MI 48121-7455

SCHULZ, KEITH DONALD, corporate lawyer; b. Burlington, Iowa, Dec. 20, 1938; s. Henry Carl and Laura Iral (Bowlin) S.; m. Emily Brook Roane, Apr. 19, 1985; children: Keith Jr., Sarah, Christine, Stefan. BA, U. Iowa, 1960, JD, 1963. Bar: Iowa 1963, Ill. 1966, Wis., 1990. Dep. Sec. of State, State of Iowa, Des Moines, 1965-66; atty. AT&T, Chgo., 1966-67; sec., gen. counsel Borg-Warner Acceptance Corp., Chgo., 1967-74; asst. gen. counsel Borg-Warner Corp., Chgo., 1974-84, v.p., gen. counsel, 1984-88; of counsel Bell, Boyd & Lloyd, Chgo., 1988—; chmn., CEO Downtown Ptnrs., Inc., 1995-96. Contbr. articles to Harvard Bus. Rev., Jour. for Corp. Growth. Chmn. bd. dirs. Vol. Legal Svcs. Found., Chgo., 1984-91; bd. dirs. Southeast Iowa Symphony Orch., Heritage Trust Fund. Mem. Iowa Bar Assn., Chgo. Bar Assn. (chmn. corp. law depts. com. 1983-84), Wis. Bar Assn., Assn. Gen. Counsel, Am. Soc. Corp. Secs., Law Club of Chgo. Clubs: University, Economic (Chgo.). Avocations: tennis, bicycling, skiing. Office: Bell Boyd & Lloyd 70 W Madison St Chicago IL 60602

SCHULZ, LAWRENCE A., lawyer; b. Buffalo, Jan. 5, 1941. BA, SUNY, Buffalo, 1966, JD, 1969. Bar: N.Y. 1970, U.S. Dist. Ct. (we. dist.) N.Y. 1970, U.S. Ct. Appeals (2d cir.) 1972, U.S. Supreme Ct. 1974, U.S. Ct. Appeals (4th cir.) 1982, U.S. Dist. Ct. (no. dist.) N.Y. 1990. Mem. Saperston & Day P.C., Buffalo; pvt. practice, Orchard Park, N.Y.; confidential asst. to appellate divsn. 4th Dept., 1975-81; mem. N.Y. State Jury Selection Uniform Rules Task Force, 1977, Chief Judge's Drafting Com. C. Administrn. Stds. and Policies, 1977-78. Revision editor New York Appellate Practice, 1994, 95. With USN, 1958-62. Mem. N.Y. State Bar Assn. (com. cts. appellate jurisdiction, legis. policy com.), Erie County Bar Assn. (appellate practice com., practice and procedure in city, county and state cts. com., comml. and bankruptcy com.), Monroe County Bar Assn. Office: PO Box 1050 17 Pine Ter Orchard Park NY 14127

SCHULZ, MARIANNE, accountant; b. East Orange, N.J.; d. Clifford W. Schulz; m. James A. Willits, Dec. 29, 1991; children: Lukas James, Laura Christine. BA in Bus., U. Wash., 1979. Cert. mgmt. acct. Contr. Farwest Spl. Products, Bellevue, Wash., 1974-88; acct. Lakeside Industries, Bellevue, Wash., 1988—. Mem. Inst. Mgmt. Accts. (bd. dirs. 1990-92, v.p. 1992-93).

SCHULZ, MARY ELIZABETH, lawyer; b. New Ulm, Minn., Oct. 6, 1950; d. Paul F. and Elizabeth B. (Wichtel) S. BA cum laude, Mankato State U., 1972; JD, So. Meth. U., 1976. Bar: Tex., 1976, Ky., 1992, Ohio, 1993. Atty. Kagay, Turner, Eyres & Robertson, Dallas, 1976-78; asst. regional counsel U.S. EPA, Dallas, 1978-86; atty. Gardere & Wynne, Dallas, 1986-89, Valvoline, Inc., Lexington, Ky., 1989-90; counsel Olin Corp., E. Alton, Ill., 1990-92; sr. environ. counsel B.F. Goodrich Co., Akron, Ohio, 1992—. Mem. ABA. Office: B F Goodrich Co 4020 Kinross Lakes Pkwy Richfield OH 44286-9368

SCHULZ, MICHAEL JOHN, fire and explosion analyst, consultant; b. Milw., Oct. 7, 1958; s. John F. and JoAnn E. (Carlson) S.; m. Donna M. Guzman; children: Kari L., Brian M. BS in Fire and Safety Engring. Tech., U. Cin., 1996; grad., U.S. Fire Adminstrn. Acad. Cert. fire and explosion investigator; cert. fire protection specialist; cert. fire investigation instr.; cert. fire svc. instr. II. Fire investigator Cedarburg (Wis.) Police Dept., 1979-90; capt., fire investigator Cedarburg (Wis.) Fire Dept., 1981-90; sr. staff expert John A. Kennedy & Assoc., Hoffman Estates, Ill., 1990—; cons. U.S. Fire Adminstrn.; instr. fire tech. and police sci. depts. Milw. (Wis.) Area Tech. Coll.; instr. fire sci. tech. dept. William Rainey Harper C.C.; lectr. in field. Author: Manual for the Determination of Electrical Fire Causes, 1988, Guide for Fire and Explosion Investigations, 1992, 95. Recipient Common Coun. Commendation, City of Cedarburg, Wis., 1986; named Firefighter of Yr., Ozaukee County Assn. Fire Depts., 1985. Mem. ASTM, Nat. Assn. Fire Investigators (bd. dirs. 1987—, nat. cert. bd. 1987—, chmn. edn. com., editor The Nat. Fire Investigator, Man of Yr. 1991), Nat. Fire Protection Assn. (tech. com. on fire investigations 1985—, fire svc. sect., sect. rep. tech. com. on fire investigations 1985-92, sec. rep. nat. conf. on fire investigation instrn., mem. bd. dirs. fire sci. and tech. educators sect.), Fire Marshal's Assn. N.Am. (assoc.), Nat. Inst. Bldg. Scis. (reviewing mem. fire rsch. sub-com.), Bldg. Ofcls. and Code Adminstrs. Internat., So. Bldg. Code Congress Internat., Internat. Bldg. Code Ofcls., Internat. Assn. Arson Investigators (John Charles Wilson scholarship award 1982), Ill. Chpt. Internat. Assn. Arson Investigators, Internat. Soc. Fire Svc. Instrs., Nat. Conf. Fire Investigation Instrn. (bd. dirs.), Wis. Soc. Fire Svc. Instrs., Ky. Cols. Republican. Lutheran. Avocation: amateur radio. Office: John A Kennedy & Assocs 2155 Stonington Ave Ste 118 Hoffman Estates IL 60195

SCHULZ, RALPH RICHARD, publishing consultant; b. N.Y.C., June 5, 1928; s. Harry and Margaret (Faecher) S.; m. Joyce S. Woolf, Sept. 9, 1951; children: Laura Stern, Barbara Tejerina, Susan. BS in Chemistry, CCNY, 1950. Asst. editor McLean-Hunter Pub. Co., Toronto, Can., 1950; assoc. editor McGraw-Hill Pub. Co., N.Y.C., 1951-60, mng. editor, 1960-68, editor-in-chief, 1968-73; dir. McGraw-Hill World News, N.Y.C., 1973-76; v.p. editorial dept. McGraw-Hill Pubs. Co., N.Y.C., 1976-84; sr. v.p. editorial dept. McGraw-Hill, Inc., N.Y.C., 1985-92; pub. cons., 1992—; v.p. DeSilva & Phillips Inc., N.Y.C.; adj. prof. Grad. Sch. Bus. Adminstrn., Fordham U., 1990—. Author to numerous mag. on bus. and sci. Trustee Correspondents Fund, N.Y.C., 1979—; bd. dirs. Bus. Press Ednl. Found., N.Y.C., 1986—, McGraw-Hill Found., N.Y.C. 1987-92, Copyright Clearence Ctr., N.Y.C., 1983-92. Petty officer USN, 1946-48. Recipient Honor award for disting. svc. in journalism Ohio U., 1972, Jesse H. Neal Editorial Achievement award Am. Bus. Press, 1972. Mem. Am. Soc. Mag. editors (exec. com. 1984-88), Overseas Press Club Am. (bd. dirs. 1969-73), Nat. Press Club, Players Club (bd. dirs. 1974-78), Silurians, Sigma Delta Chi. Office: DeSilva & Phillips Inc 444 Park Ave S New York NY 10016-7321

SCHULZ, RAYMOND ALEXANDER, medical marketing professional, consultant; b. Paris, June 2, 1946; s. Helmut W. and Colette (Prieur) S.; m. Dixie Lee Suzanne Specht, Apr. 9, 1977 (div. Dec. 1990); children: Christopher, William. BA in Physics, W.Va. U., 1970; MS in Computer Sci., Columbia U., N.Y.C., 1975. Sr. programmer Meml. Sloan Kettering Cancer Ctr., N.Y.C., 1972-74; program coord. Neurol. Inst. Columbia Presbyn. Hosp., N.Y.C., 1974-76; engring. mgr. EMI Med. Systems, Northbrook, Ill., 1976-78; product mgr. Johnson & Johnson (Technicare), Solon, Ohio, 1978-80; group product mgr. Siemens Corp., Iselin, N.J., 1982-82; mktg. mgr. Toshiba Am. Med. Systems (formerly Diasonics MRI), South San Francisco, 1983-92; dir. mktg. Voxel, Laguna Hills, Calif., 1992—. Contbr. over 70 papers on the application of holography to a variety of med. specialties to profl. publs. Recipient first prize Roentgen Centenary Congress, 1995. Mem. Am. Assn. Physicists in Medicine, N.Y. Acad. Scis., Internat. Soc. Magnetic Rsch. in Medicine, Larchmont Yacht Club, Commonwealth Club Calif., Eta Kappa Nu. Avocations: skiing, running, hiking, swimming, mountainbiking. Office: Voxel 26081 Merit Cir Ste 117 Laguna Hills CA 92653-7017

SCHULZ, RICHARD BURKART, electrical engineer, consultant; b. Phila., May 21, 1920; s. Herman G. Schulz and Laura (Burkart) Luckenbill; m. Jeannette Charlotte Vollmer, Nov. 22, 1958; 1 child, Steven Edward. BSEE, U. Pa., 1942, MSEE, 1951. Rsch. assoc. U. Pa., Phila., 1942-46; owner Electro-Search, Phila., 1947-55; program devel. coord. Armour Rsch. Found., Chgo., 1955-61; chief electro-interference United Control Corp., Redmond, Wash., 1961-62; chief electro-compatibility Boeing Co., Seattle, 1962-70; staff mgr. S.W. Rsch. Inst., San Antonio, 1970-74; sci. advisor IIT Rsch. Inst., Annapolis, Md., 1974-83; mgr. EMC and TEMPEST Xerox Corp., Lewisville, Tex., 1983-87; EMC cons. Carrollton, Tex., 1987—. Contbr. 4 chpts. to Handbook on EMC, 1995; contbr. articles to profl. jours. Named Life Master Am. Contract Bridge League. Fellow IEEE (life; Centennial medal 1984, Standards plaque 1991); mem. IEEE Soc. on Electromagnetic Compatibility (life; treas. 1966-67, pres. 1968, bd. dirs. 1961-89, chmn. internat. conf. 1968, tech. program chmn. internat. conf. 1993, L.G. Cumming plaque 1980, Richard R. Stoddart award 1988), Nat. Assn. Radio and TV Engrs., Toastmasters Club. Republican. Lutheran. Home and Office: 2030 Cologne Dr Carrollton TX 75007-2334

SCHULZ, RUDOLPH WALTER, university dean emeritus; b. Chgo., Aug. 10, 1930; s. Walter Adolph and Minna Louise (Burmeister) S.; m. Charlotte Helen Adams, Sept. 8, 1956; children: Stephanie Sue, Kyle Scott. B.S. Northwestern U., 1954, Ph.D., 1958; M.A., Stanford, 1955. Lectr., research asso. Northwestern U., 1956-58, instr. 1958-59; asst. prof. psychology Carnegie-Mellon U., 1959-60; asst. prof. U. Iowa, 1960-64, asso. prof., 1964-66, prof., 1966-95, prof., 1970-73, dean for advanced studies, 1976-91; cons. in field; mem. NSF fellowship selection panel, 1962-68; NSF vis. scientist, 1962-76; bd. dirs. Midwest Univs. Consortium for Internat. Activities, Inc., 1977-91. Cons. editor: Jour. Exptl. Psychology, 1962-74, Jour. Verbal Learning and Verbal Behavior, 1964-74, Contemporary Psychology, 1970-81; editor: Psychonomic Science, 1971-72, Memory and Cognition, 1972-76; Contbr. articles to profl. jours. Served with USNR, 1950-52. Decorated Air medal; Gold research fellow U. Iowa, 1963; NSF research grantee, 1964-76. Fellow Am. Psychol. Assn., AAAS (mem. council 1974-75), Am. Psychol. Soc. (charter); mem. Psychonomic Soc., Midwestern Psychol. Assn. (sec.-treas. 1973-76, pres. 1978), Sigma Xi. Home: 8 Fairview Knls NE Iowa City IA 52240-9147

SCHULZ, RUSSELL EUGENE, musician, educator, composer; b. Harvard, Ill., July 29, 1944; s. Friederich Wilhelm and Helen (DeVries) Schulz; m.

Suzanne Widmar, Aug. 26, 1967 (div. Sept. 1995); children: John Frederick, Karl Andrew. MusB, Valparaiso U., 1966; SMM, Union Theol. Sem., N.Y.C., 1968; DMA, U. Tex., 1974; postgrad., Royal Sch. Ch. Music, London, summer 1976. Dir. music Univ. United Meth. Ch., Austin, 1971-93, Good Shepherd Episcopal Ch., Austin, 1993—; lectr. Austin (Tex.) Presbyn. Theol. Sem., 1975-91; prof. Episcopal Theol. Sem. S.W., Austin, 1974—; dean Evergreen Music Conf., 1981-87; mem. Standing Commn. on Ch. Music, Episcopal Ch., 1978-85. Editor: (hymnal) Songs of Thanks and Praise, 1980; co-editor: New Hymnal for Colleges and Schools, 1992; chmn. The Hymnal 1982, 1985. Recipient Disting. Alumnus award Valparaiso U., 1988. Mem. Hymn Soc. U.S. and Can. (pres. 1988-90), Order of St. John of Jerusalem. Office: PO Box 2247 Austin TX 78768-2247

SCHULZ, WILLIAM FREDERICK, human rights association executive; b. Pitts., Nov. 14, 1949; s. William F. and Jean Smith; m. Beth Graham, 1993. AB, Oberlin Coll., 1971; MA, Meadville/Lombard Theol. Sch., 1973, DMin, 1975, DDiv, 1987; MA, U. Chgo., 1974; DHL, Nova Southea. U., 1995. Minister First Parish Unitarian Universalist, Bedford, Mass., 1975-78; dir. social responsibility Unitarian Universalist Assn., Boston, 1978-79, exec. v.p., 1979-85, pres., 1985-93; exec. dir. Amnesty Internat. USA, 1994—; bd. trustees Meadville/Lombard Theol. Sch., 1996—. Author: Finding Time and Other Delicacies, 1992; editor, contbr. Transforming Words: Six Essays on Preaching, 1984, 2d edit., 1996. Recipient Albert Francis Christie prize, 1973, 75. Mem. ACLU, Unitarian Universalist Mins. Assn., Coun. Fgn. Rels. Democrat. Home: 10 Castle Harbor Rd Huntington NY 11743-1209

SCHULZE, ARTHUR EDWARD, biomedical engineer, researcher; b. Richmond, Tex., Nov. 22, 1938; s. Arthur Dorwin and Ida (Bockhorn) S.; m. Sharon Kay Havemann, Sept. 2, 1962; children: Keith E., Mark A. BSEE, U. Tex., 1962, MSEE, 1963; MS Biomed. Sci., U. Tex., Houston, 1968. Registered profl. engr., Tex. Sr. aerosystems engr. Gen. Dynamics, Ft. Worth, 1963-67; rsch. assoc. U. Tex. Grad. Sch. Biomed. Scis., Houston, 1967-68; mgr., biomed. engr. SCI Systems, Inc., Houston, 1968-74; v.p. Telecare, Inc., Houston, 1974-79; gen. mgr. Tex. Sci. Corp., Houston, 1979-81; dir. R & D Narco Bio-Systems, Houston, 1981-84; pres. Narco Bio-Systems, 1984-86; v.p. Lovelace Sci. Resources, Inc., Houston, 1986-92; pres. Healthcare Tech. Group, 1993—. Contbr. articles to sci. publs. Mem. IEEE, Aerospace Med. Assn., Assn. Advancement Med. Instrumentation, AAAS, Biomed. Technology Club. Avocations: photography, beekeeping. Home: 8807 Mobud Dr Houston TX 77036-5321 Office: Healthcare Tech Group 6901 Corporate Dr Ste 111 Houston TX 77036-5119

SCHULZE, ERIC WILLIAM, lawyer, legal publications editor, publisher; b. Libertyville, Ill., July 8, 1952; s. Robert Carl and Barbara (Mayo) S. BA, U. Tex., 1973, JD, 1977. Bar: Tex. 1977, U.S. Dist. Ct. (we. dist.) Tex. 1987, U.S. Ct. Appeals (5th cir.) 1987, U.S. Dist. Ct. (ea. and so. dists.) Tex. 1988, U.S. Dist. Ct. (no. dist.) Tex. 1989, U.S. Supreme Ct. 1989; bd. cert. civil appellate law Tex. Bd. Legal Specialization, 1990—. Rsch. asst. U. Tex., Austin, 1978; legis. aide Tex. Ho. of Reps., Austin, 1979-81; editor Tex. Sch. Law News, Austin, 1982-85; assoc. Hairston, Walsh & Anderson, Austin, 1986-87; ptnr. Walsh, Anderson, Underwood, Schulze & Aldridge, Austin, 1988—, mng. ptnr., 1993—; editor Tex. Sch. Adminstrs. Legal Digest, Austin, 1986-92, co-pub., 1991—, mng. editor, 1992—. Editor: (legal reference books) Texas Education Code Annotated, 1982-85; editl. adv. com. West's Edn. Law Reporter, 1996—. Del. Tex. State Democratic Conv., 1982, Travis County Dem. Conv., 1982, 84, 86. Recipient Merit award for pubs. Internat. Assn. Bus. Communicators-Austin br., 1983, Merit award for authorship Coll. of State Bar Tex., 1992. Mem. Fed. Bar Assn., Am. Bar Assn., Tex. Bar Assn., Travis County Bar Assn., Bar Assn. of 5th Cir., Defense Rsch. Inst., Nat. Council Sch. Attys., Tex. Council Sch. Attys., Nat. Orgn. Legal Problems in Edn., Toastmasters (pres. Capital City chpt. 1995). Home: 3416 Mt Bonnell Cir Austin TX 78731 Office: Walsh Anderson Underwood Schulze & Aldridge PO Box 2156 Austin TX 78768-2156

SCHULZE, FRANZ, JR., art critic, educator; b. Uniontown, Pa., Jan. 30, 1927; s. Franz and Anna E. (Krimmel) S.; m. Marianne Gaw, June 24, 1961 (div. 1975); children: F. C. Matthew, Lukas; m. Stephanie Mora, 1992. Student, Northwestern U., 1943; Ph.B., U. Chgo., 1945; B.F.A., Sch. Art Inst. Chgo., 1949, M.F.A., 1950; postgrad., Acad. Fine Arts, Munich, Germany, 1956-57. Instr. art Purdue U., 1950-52; chmn. dept. art Lake Forest (Ill.) Coll., 1952-58, artist-in-residence, 1958-61, prof. art, 1961—, Hollender prof. art, 1974-91; art critic Chgo. Daily News, 1962-78, Chgo. Sun-Times, 1978-85; adj. prof. U. Ill., Chgo., 1996; Chgo. corr. in art Christian Sci. Monitor, 1958-62; art and arch. critic The Chicagoan, 1973-74; mem. vis. com. dept. art U. Chgo., 1974—. Author: Art, Architecture and Civilization, 1969, Fantastic Images: Chicago Art Since 1945, 1972, 100 Years of Chicago Architecture, 1976, Stealing Is My Game, 1976, Mies van der Rohe: A Critical Biography, 1985, The University Club of Chicago: A Heritage, 1987, Mariotti, 1988; editor: Mies van der Rohe: Critical Essays, 1989, Mies van der Rohe Archive, 1993; co-editor Chicago's Famous Buildings, 1993, Philip Johnson: Life and Work, 1994; contbg. editor Art News, 1973—, Inland Architect, 1975-94; corr. editor Art in Am., 1975—. Trustee Ragdale Found., Lake Forest, 1981—. Recipient Harbison award for tchg. Danforth Found. of St. Louis, 1971; Adenauer fellow, 1956-57; Ford Found. fellow, 1964-65; Graham Found. for Advanced Studies in the Fine Arts fellow, 1971, 81, 93; NEH fellow, 1982, 88; Skidmore Owings & Merrill Found. fellow, 1983; recipient Disting. Svc. award Chgo. Phi Beta Kappa Soc., 1972; Hon. Mention Hitchcock Book award Soc. Archtl. Historians, 1987. Mem. AAUP, Coll. Art Assn. (bd. dirs. 1983-86), Archives Am. Art (adv. com.), Soc. Archtl. Historians. Office: Lake Forest Coll Dept Art Lake Forest IL 60045

SCHULZE, RICHARD HANS, engineering executive, environmental engineer; b. Buffalo, May 28, 1933; s. Hans Joachim and Lucy (Kawczynska) S.; m. Jacqueline Van Luppen, Nov. 2, 1967 (div. Aug. 1979); children: Richard Hans Jr., Linda, John; m. Enika Grooters, Aug. 29, 1987. BSME, Princeton U., 1954; MBA, Northwestern U., 1958. Registered profl. engr., Tex. Rsch. analyst U.S. Steel Corp., Pitts., 1958-60; chief engr. G&H Rsch. and Devel., McKeesport, Pa., 1960-62; cons. Mgmt. and Mktg. Inst., N.Y.C., 1962-63, IITRI mgmt. consulting divsn., N.Y.C., 1963-64; market analyst plastics divsn. Mobil Chem. Co., N.Y.C., 1964-66; market devel. mgr. Mobil Chem. Co., Jacksonville, Ill., 1966-68; dist. sales mgr. Mobil Chem. Co., Dallas, 1967-71; pres. Ecology Audits, Inc. (Core Labs.), Dallas, 1971-74; pres. Trinity Cons., Inc., Dallas, 1974-97, chmn. bd. dirs., 1997—; instr. over 200 short courses on dispersion moedling of air pollutants throughout world. Contbr. articles to Jour. of Air and Waste Mgmt. Assn., Atmospheric Environ., others; presented papers at sci. symposiums, seminars, confs. Mem. Dallas Symphony Assn., Mus. of Art; bd. dirs. Dallas Opera, 1993—; elder Preston Hollow Presbyn. Ch., 1996—; commr. to Grace Presbytery, 1996—. Lt. (j.g.) USNR, 1954-56. Mem. ASME, TAPPI (air quality com.), Am. Acad. Environ. Engrs. (diplomate), Am. Chem. Soc., Am. Meteorol. Soc., Air and Waste Mgmt. Assn. (bd. dirs. 1986-89, 90-93, v.p. 1988-89, 1st v.p. 1990-91, pres. 1991-92, past pres. 1992-93, chmn. honors and awards com. 1996-97), Nat. Soc. for Clear Air (U.K.), Soc. Petroleum Engrs. (chmn. environ. health and safety award com. 1994-95), Soc. for Risk Analysis, Semi-Condr. Safety Assn., Verein Deutscher Ingenieure, Assn. Francaise des Ingénieurs et Techniciens Environ., Dallas Bar Assn., Inst. Profl. Environ. Practice (qualified environ. profl., trustee 1993-95). Home: 7619 Marquette St Dallas TX 75225-4412 Office: Trinity Cons Inc 12801 N Central Expy Ste 1200 Dallas TX 75243-1733

SCHULZE, RICHARD M., consumer products executive; b. 1941. With No. States Sales Co., 1962—; now chmn., CEO, dir. Besy Buy Co., Inc., Eden Prairie, Minn. Office: Best Buy Co 7075 Flying Cloud Dr Eden Prairie MN 55344-3532*

SCHUMACHER, ELIZABETH SWISHER, garden ornaments shop owner; b. Webster City, Iowa, Apr. 1, 1940; d. Andrew Dale and Harriet Elizabeth (Hodson) Swisher; m. H. Ralph Schumacher Jr., July 13, 1963; children: Heidi Ruth, Kaethe Beth. BS, U. Colo., 1961; student, Barnes Found. Sch Horticulture, 1978. Owner Garden Accents, West Conshohocken, Pa., 1979—; lectr. on garden ornaments, hillside gradening, water in the garden, 1979—; exhibitor designer show house Vassar Coll., Phila. area sites, 1984—, Phila. Flower Show, 1996—. Contbr. articles to Fine Gardening, Green Scene, Gardens and Landscapes. Recipient Outstanding Landscaping award Pa. Nurserymen's Assn., 1972, Residential Beautification award Upper Merion Twp., 1974, 76, 86, Exhibit of Distinction award Phila. Flower Show, 1989, 1st prize Comml. Exhibit, 1996, Best of Philly, Phila. Mag., 1996. Mem. Pa. Hort. Soc. (hotline vol. 1987-94). Office: Garden Accents 4 Union Hill Rd W Conshohocken PA 19428-2719

SCHUMACHER, GEBHARD FRIEDERICH BERNHARD, obstetrician-gynecologist; b. Osnabrueck, Fed. Republic Germany, June 13, 1924; came to U.S., 1962; s. Kaspar and Magarete (Pommer) S.; m. Anne Rose Zanker, Oct. 24, 1958; children: Michael A., Marc M. M.D., U. Goettingen and Tuebingen, 1951; Sc.D. equivalent in obstetrics and gynecology, U. Tuebingen, 1962. Intern U. Tuebingen Med. Sch., 1951-52; tng. biochemistry Max Planck Inst. Biochemistry, Tuebingen, 1952-53; tng. biochemistry and immunology Max Planck Inst. Virus Research, 1953-54; resident in ob-gyn U. Tuebingen, 1954-59, tng. internal medicine, 1959, asst. scientist in ob-gyn and biochem. research, 1959-62, dozent in ob-gyn, 1964-65; Research assoc. in immunology Inst. Tb Research, U. Ill. Coll. Medicine, 1962-63; research assoc., asst. prof. ob-gyn U. Chgo., 1963-64; assoc. prof. ob-gyn asst. prof. biochemistry Albany Med. Coll. of Union U., 1965-67; research physician, div. labs. and research N.Y. State Dept. Health, Albany, 1965-67; assoc. prof. ob-gyn U. Chgo.-Chgo. Lying-In Hosp., 1967-73, chief sect. reproductive biology, 1971-91, prof. Immunology, 1974-91; prof. Biol. Sci. Collegiate Divsn. U. Chgo., 1982-96; prof. emeritus U. Chgo., 1996—; cons. WHO, NIH, other nat. and internat. orgns.; mem. tech. and sci. adv. bds. Family Health Internat., Cistron Tech. Inc. Author: (with Beller) The Biology of the Fluids of the Female Genital Tract, 1979; (with Dhindsa) Immunological Aspects of Infertility and Fertility Regulation, 1980; (with Kaiser) Human Reproduction, Fertility, Sterility, Contraception, German edit., 1981, Spanish edit., 1986; contbr. articles to profl. jours. Fellow Am. Coll. Obstetricians and Gynecologists; mem. Soc. Gynecologic Investigation, Am. Soc. Reproductive Medicine, Soc. Study of Reprodn., Am. Acad. Reproductive Medicine, Am. Soc. Cytology, Am. Soc. Investigative Pathology, Am. Soc. Andrology, Chgo. Assn. Reproductive Endocrinologists (pres. 1985-86), N.Y. Acad. Scis., Deutsche Gesellschaft für Gynakologie und Geburtshilfe, Gesellschaft für Biologische Chemie, Deutsche Gesellschaft für Immunologie, Gesellschaft Deutscher Naturforscher und Aerzte. Home and Office: 557 Hamilton Wood Homewood IL 60430-4403

SCHUMACHER, HANS H., steel company executive; b. Bad Polzin, Prussia, Germany, Nov. 20, 1933; came to U.S., 1960; s. Karl Heinrich and Helene Erna Martha (Droese) S.; m. Anke Margarethe Johannssen, July 10, 1963 (div. Apr. 1964). BSME, Engring. Acad., Wismar, Germany, 1954; MSc in Mech. Engring, Germany, 1993. Engr. shop and prodn. Mathias Thesen Werft, Wismar, Fed. Republic Germany, 1954-55; project engr. Hauni Maschinenfabrik, Hamburg, Fed. Republic Germany, 1955-56; marine engr. Schlieker Werft, Hamburg, 1956-60; liaison engr. Schlieker Werft, N.Y.C., 1960-62; asst. supr. Hudson Engring. Co., Hoboken, N.J., 1960; marine engr. J.J. Henry Co., Inc., N.Y.C., 1962-63; resident engr. Voest-Alpine Internat. Corp., N.Y.C., 1963-65, pres., dir., 1965—; chmn. Voest-Alpine Can. Corp., Vancouver, B.C., 1987; bd. dirs. Va. Crews Coal Co., Welch, W.Va., Third Colony Corp., N.Y.C.; chmn. Vaico, Inc., N.Y.C.; vice chmn. Voest Alpine Internat. Corp., through 1993. Avocations: swimming, antiques. Address: 180 E 79th St Ph A New York NY 10021-0437

SCHUMACHER, H(ARRY) RALPH, internist, researcher, medical educator; b. Montreal, Feb. 14, 1933; s. H. Ralph and Dorothy (Shreiner) S.; m. Elizabeth Jean Swisher, July 13, 1963; children: Heidi Ruth, Kaethe Beth. B.S., Ursinus Coll., 1955; M.D., U. Pa., 1959. Intern Denver Gen. Hosp., 1959-60; resident in medicine Wadsworth VA Hosp., L.A., 1960-62, fellow in rheumatology, 1962-63; fellow in rheumatology Robert B. Brigham Hosp. and Harvard U. Med. Sch., Boston, 1965-67; chief arthritis-immunology ctr. VA Med. Ctr., Phila., 1967—; faculty mem. U. Pa. Sch. Medicine, Phila., 1967—, prof. medicine, 1979—, acting arthritis div. chief, 1978-80, 91-95; vis. scholar NIH, 1994—. Author: Gout and Pseudogout, 1978, Essentials of a Differential Diagnosis of Rhematoid Arthritis, 1981, Rheumatoid Arthritis, 1988, Case Studies in Rheumatology for the House Officer, 1989, Atlas of Synovial Fluid and Crystal Identification, 1991, A Practical Guide to Synovial Fluid Analysis, 1991; editor: Primer on Rheumatic Diseases, 1981—, Jour. Clin. Rheumatology, 1994—; mem. editorial bd. Jour. Rheumatology, 1973—, Arthritis and Rheumatism, 1981-88, Revue du Rhumatisme, 1992—, Brit. Jour. Clin. Practice, 1992—, New European Rheumatology, 1993—, Japanese Jour. Rheumatology, 1993—; contbr. articles to profl. jours.; lectr., author gardening. Pres. Eastern Pa. chpt. Arthritis Found., 1980-82; chmn., founder Phila. Garden Tours, 1987—; bd. dirs. Hemochromatosis Research Found., 1984—, Am. Bd. Med. Advancement China, 1983—. Served with M.C. USAF, 1963-65. Recipient Van-Breeman award The Netherland Rheumatism Soc., 1988, Philip Hench award Assn. Mil. Surgeons, 1986, Hollander award Arthritis Found., 1996; Deposition VA grantee, 1967-95, NIH grantee, 1981, 94—. Fellow ACP; mem. Am. Coll. Rheumatology (pres. Southeastern region 1981-82), Phila. Rheumatism Soc. (pres. 1980), Phila. Electron Microscopy Soc. (chmn. 1975-76), Rheumatism Soc. Mex., Rheumatism Soc. Australia, Rheumatism Soc. Colombia, Rheumatism Soc. Chile, Rheumatism Soc. Republic of China, Rheumatism Soc. Argentina, Med. Soc. Argentina, Fedn. Clin. Rsch., AAAS. Office: Hosp U Pa 3400 Spruce St Philadelphia PA 19104 *I try to teach meticulous observation and questioning of dogma both in daily care of patients and in laboratory investigation of the poorly understood rheumatic diseases.*

SCHUMACHER, HENRY JEROLD, former career officer, business executive; b. Torrance, Calif., June 17, 1934; s. Henry John and Rene (Wilcox) S.; m. Barbara Howell, Aug. 24, 1958; children: Sheri Lynn, Henry Jerold II. Student, Stanford U., 1953; B.S., U.S. Mil. Acad., 1957; M.S., Northeastern U., Boston, 1965; M.B.A., Auburn U., 1977. Commd. lt. U.S. Army, 1958, advanced through grades to maj. gen., 1982; army attaché Moscow, 1969-71; chief communications ops. Vietnam, 1971-72; exec. officer Office Chief of Staff, 1972-75; comdr. U.S. Army Communications Command, Panama, 1977-79; dir. network integration, Office Asst. Chief of Staff Automation and Communications, Dept. Army, 1979-81; comdr. The White House Communications Agy., Washington, 1981-82; chief U.S. Army Signal Corps, 1981-83; ret., 1983; sr. v.p. Visa Internat., 1983-86; chief oper. officer Fuel Tech., Inc., Stamford, Conn., 1986-87; pres. IMM Systems, Phila., 1987-89; exec. v.p. Cylink Corp., Sunnyvale, Calif., 1990-95; exec. dir. Hiller Mus. of No. Calif. Aviation History, Redwood City, 1995—. Decorated Def. D.S.M., D.S.M., Legion of Merit. Home: 156 Normandy Ct San Carlos CA 94070-1519 Office: Hiller No Calif Aviation Mus 601 Skyway San Carlos CA 94070-2702

SCHUMACHER, JOEL, film writer, director; b. N.Y.C., Aug. 29, 1939; s. Francis and Marian (Kantor) S. BA, Parsons U., 1965. Costume designer: (stage) The Time of the Cuckoo, 1974, (films) Play It As It Lays, 1972, The Last of Sheila, 1972, Blume In Love, 1973, Sleeper, 1973, The Prisoner of Second Avenue, 1975, Interiors, 1978; screenwriter: Car Wash, 1976, Sparkle, 1976, The Wiz, 1978; screenwriter, dir.: (films) D.C. Cab, 1983, St. Elmo's Fire, 1985, (TV movies) The Virginia Hill Story, 1974, Amateur Night at the Dixie Bar and Grill, 1979; dir.: The Incredible Shrinking Woman, 1981, The Lost Boys, 1987, Cousins, 1989, Flatliners, 1990, Dying Young, 1991, Falling Down, 1993, The Client, 1994, Batman Forever, 1995, A Time to Kill, 1996, Batman & Robin, 1997; exec. prodr.: Foxfire, 1985, Slow Burn, 1986; writer, exec. prodr.: (TV pilot) Now We're Cookin', 1983; prodn. designer: Killer Bees, 1974. also: Joel Schumacher Productions 400 Warner Blvd Burbank CA 91522*

SCHUMACHER, JON LEE, lawyer; b. Rochester, N.Y., Feb. 28, 1937; s. Howard Alexander and Ruth (Simmons) S.; m. Katherine Truesdell, Apr. 22, 1967; children: Sara Truesdell, Howard Alexander II. AB, Princeton U., 1959; JD, U. Va., 1964. Bar: N.Y. 1964. With Nixon Hargrave Devans & Doyle L.L.P., Rochester, 1964—; mem. mgmt. com. Nixon, Hargrave, Devans & Doyle, Rochester, 1986-90, mng. ptnr., 1988-90. Co-author Charitable Giving and Solicitation. Bd. dirs., officer Rochester Area Found., Inc., 1987-94, United Way, 1986—; pres. estate planning Coun. Rochester, 1986-87. Fellow Am. Coll. Trusts and Estate Counsel; mem. ABA, N.Y. State Bar Assn. (exec. com. trusts and estates law sect. 1985, 88, 94—, chmn. 1997, chmn. estate planning com. 1992-94), Monroe County Bar Assn. (found. pres. 1995-97), Country Club of Rochester, Genesee Valley Club. Republican. Presbyterian. Avocations: walking, opera. Home: 550 Allens Creek Rd Rochester NY 14618-3406 Office: Nixon Hargrave Devans & Doyle Clinton Sq PO Box 1051 Rochester NY 14603-1051

SCHUMACHER, JOSEPH CHARLES, chemical engineer; b. Peru, Ill., Sept. 15, 1911; s. Joseph F. and Josephine (Mattes) S.; m. Theresa Flynn, Jan. 28, 1933; children—John Christian, Kathleen Schumacher Hoffman, Stephen Joseph, Paul; m. Mary Margaret Maher, Jan. 5, 1985. Student, U. Ill., 1928-30; A.B., U. So. Calif., 1946. Research chemist, prodn. supr. Carus Chem. Co., LaSalle, Ill., 1931-40; research and devel. chem. engr. Fine Chems., Inc., Los Angeles, 1940-41; co-founder Western Electro-chem. Co., Los Angeles, 1941, v.p., dir. research, 1941-54, dir.; dir. research Am. Potash & Chem. Corp., 1954-56, v.p. research, 1956-67; v.p. AFN Inc., 1956-67, Kerr-McGee Chem. Corp., 1967-69; founder J.C. Schumacher Co., Oceanside, Calif., 1971, pres., 1971-74, chmn. bd., 1974-86. Regional editor Electrochem. Soc. Jour., 1953-59; co-author, editor Perchlorates; mem. editorial adv. bd. Research Mgmt., 1963-69; contbr. articles to profl. jours.; patentee in chem. products, processes and apparatus. Trustee Whittier Coll., 1968-77. Recipient Honors award U. So. Calif. Chemistry Alumni Soc., 1962. Mem. Electrochem. Soc. (Vittorio de Nora Diamond Shamrock Engring. and Tech. gold medal 1982), Am. Chem. Soc., Planetary Soc., Sigma Xi, Phi Kappa Theta. Roman Catholic. Clubs: Los Angeles Country, Jonathan. Home and Office: 2220 Ave of Stars West Tower # 704 Los Angeles CA 90067

SCHUMACHER, LARRY P., health facility administrator; b. Waseca, Minn., Apr. 26, 1959; s. James H. and Judith A. (Voight) S.; m. Casey A. Hager, June 26, 1982; children: Matthew, Nicholas, Nathan, Mark. Diploma, Burge Sch. Nursing, 1980; BSN, S.W. Mo. State U., 1983; MS in Nursing, Ind. U., 1985. RN, Iowa; cert. nursing adminstr. advanced, 1989. Dir. critical care and med. nursing Rsch. Med. Ctr., Kansas City, Mo.; v.p. nursing and anesthesia St. Joseph Mercy Hosp., Mason City, Iowa; v.p. patient care svcs. Mercy Hosp., Mason City, Iowa; v.p. patient svcs., chief nursing officer North Iowa Mercy Health Ctr., Mason City; sr. vp. clin. integration, chief nursing officer North Iowa Mercy Health Network. Mem. ACHE, ANA, Nat. League Nursing, Am. Orgn. Nurse Execs. Home: 115 10th St NW Mason City IA 50401-2016

SCHUMACHER, ROBERT DENISON, banker; b. Evanston, Ill., Dec. 16, 1933; s. Frank Ade and Dorothy Ormonde (Hilton) S.; m. Mary Ann Montgomery, Aug. 25, 1956; children—Stephen Michael, Jeffrey Hilton. B.A., Williams Coll., 1956; postgrad., Grad. Bus. Sch. N.Y. U., 1957-59; P.M.D., Harvard Bus. Sch., 1966. With Irving Trust Co., N.Y.C., 1956-89, sr. v.p., 1977-89, mgr. adminstrv. services, 1987-89, ret., 1989. Treas. Calvary, Holy Communion and St. George's Episcopal Ch., 1976-79, warden, 1980-86, 89-93; trustee The Church Club, 1993—, treas., 1994—. Mem. The Church Club. Republican. Home: 431 E 20th St New York NY 10010-7502

SCHUMACHER, ROBERT JOSEPH, petroleum company executive; b. Independence, Kans., Mar. 7, 1929; s. Arthur V. and Margaret F. (Templeman) S.; m. Edith Katherine Kelly, Sept. 30, 1950; children: Mary Beth Schumacher Millett, Kathy, Kyle, William. BS in Commerce, Tex. Christian U., 1950; M Profl. Acctg., U. Tex., 1951. CPA, Tex. Staff acct. Sproles & Woodard, CPA's, Ft. Worth, 1950-52; sec., treas. Sojourner Drilling Corp., Abilene, Tex., 1952-68; ind. oil and gas operator, Ft. Worth, 1967-73; pres., chief exec. officer Texland Petroleum, Inc., Ft. Worth, 1973—; chmn., chief exec. officer Pride Refining, Inc., Abilene, 1989-93; pres., CEO Texland Petroleum Inc., Ft. Worth, Tex., 1973—; bd. dirs. Aztec Mfg. Co., Ft. Worth. Staff sgt. U.S. Army, 1946-48. Republican. Roman Catholic.

SCHUMACHER, THERESA ROSE, singer, musician; b. Muskegon, Mich.; d. Boles and Marguerite (Lassard) Pietkiewicz; m. Glenn O. Schumacher, 1968 (div. 1988); children: Pamela Harrington Boller, Daniel Mark Harrington. BS in Sociology, Fairmont State Coll., 1975. Active W.Va. U. Symphony Choir, 1988—, 93 Fairmont State Coll. Choir; musician with spl. knowledge of music from 1735-1850, Nat. Park Svcs., 1989—; appeared on W.Va. Pub. Radio. Mem. AAUW, Bus. And Profl. Women Assn., W.Va. Poetry Soc., Morgantown, W.Va. Poetry Soc., W.Va. Writers. Avocations: special knowledge of cacti and succlents, storytelling, writing poetry, country and folk music. Home: PO Box 162 Mannington WV 26582-0162

SCHUMACHER, THOMAS, film company executive. Grad., UCLA. Past mem. staff L.A. Music Ctr. Mark Taper Forum; past sr. v.p. feature animation Walt Disney Pictures, Burbank, Calif., exec. v.p. feature animation and theatrical prodns., 1996—; line prodr. Olympic Arts Festival, 1984; asst. gen. mgr. L.A. Ballet; co-founder, assoc. dir. L.A. Festival of the Arts, 1987; mem. edn. coun. L.A. Music Ctr.; bd. dirs. Rachel Rosenthal Co. Prodr. film The Rescuers Down Under, 1990; exec. prodr. film The Lion King, 1994. Office: Walt Disney Pictures 500 S Buena Vista St Burbank CA 91521

SCHUMACHER, WILLIAM JACOB, retired army officer; b. Scranton, Pa., Apr. 15, 1938; s. Jacob and Kathryn Isabel (Williams) S.; m. Sandra Dee Caryl, July 23, 1960; children: Caryl Lee, Leslie Karen. BSEE, Lafayette Coll., 1960; MS in Aerospace Engring., Pa. State U., 1970. Commd. 2d lt. U.S. Army, 1960, advanced through grades to brig. gen., 1989; asst. prof. dept. engring. U.S. Mil. Acad., West Point, N.Y., 1970-73; student Def. Systems Mgmt. Coll., Ft. Belvoir, Va., 1975; asst. project mgr. Office of Project Mgr., Rock Island (Ill.) Arsenal, 1976-78; asst. mgr. conventional ammunition and guided missiles div. Cannon Arty. Weapons System, Picatinny (N.J.) Arsenal, 1978-81; comdg. officer Iowa Army Ammunition Plant, Burlington, 1981-83; student U.S. Army War Coll., Carlisle, Pa., 1983-84; project mgr. for Hellfire Missile U.S. Army Missile Command, Huntsville, Ala., 1984-87; program exec. officer Close Combat Missiles, Huntsville, 1987-88, Fire Support, Huntsville, 1988-90; dep. ammunition, asst. sec. army rsch., devel., acquisition Hdqrs. Army Materiel Command, Washington, 1990-92; dep. comdg. officer Strategic Def. Command, Huntsville, 1992; retired, tech. cons. Garber Internat. Assoc., Inc., Arlington, Va., 1992; gen. mgr. strategic systems Martin Marietta, Arlington, Va., 1992-96; exec. v.p. Bunyard Enterprises, Inc., Alexandria, Va., 1996—. Mem. Assn. U.S. Army, Am. Def. Preparedness Assn., Phi Kappa Phi. Avocations: swimming, gardening, book collecting.

SCHUMACKER, RANDALL ERNEST, educational psychology educator; b. Oakes, N.D., May 26, 1951; s. Ernest and Helen (Jackson) S.; m. Joanne Cummins, July 24, 1952; children: Rachel Ann, Jamie Maureen. AA, William Rainey Harper Jr. Coll, 1970; BS, Western Ill. U., 1972; MS, So. Ill. U., 1978, PhD, 1984. Rsch. asst. So. Ill. U., Carbondale, 1980-84, assoc. dir. computing, 1984-87; asst. prof. U. North Tex., Denton, 1988-90, assoc. prof., 1991—, rsch. assoc. prof. Unit Health Svcs. Dept. Family Medicine, 1995—; vis. prof. So. Ill. U., 1980-84; vis. scholar U. Chgo., 1996; cons. Tex. Acad. Math. & Sci., Denton, 1993, Carrollton-Farmers Br. (Tex.), 1991-94, Profl. Devel., 1989-92; presenter in field. Contbr. articles to profl. jours. Mem. Am. Psychol. Assn., Am. Ednl. Rsch. Assn., Southwest Ednl. Rsch. Assn., Am. Statis. Assn., Midwestern Ednl. Rsch. Assn., Nat. Coun. Measurement Edn., Phi Delta Kappa. Republican. Lutheran. Avocations: sailing, golf, gardening. Office: U North Tex Coll Edn Denton TX 76203

SCHUMAKER, JAMES FREDERICK, foreign service officer; b. Macon, Ga., Oct. 12, 1947; s. Frederick L. Schumaker and Laura (Flowers) Bappert. BA, Trinity Coll., 1969. Interpreter U.S. Army, Washington, 1969-73; fgn. svc. officer U.S. Dept. of State, Washington, 1973—; amb. aide U.S. Embassy, Belgrade, Yugoslavia, 1974-76; ops. ctr. U.S. Dept. of State, 1976-77; amb. aide U.S. Embassy, Moscow, 1977-79; political military officer Washington, 1979-81; with Office Soviet Union Affairs, Washington, 1981-85; deputy prin. officer U.S. Consulate Gen., Leningrad, USSR, 1985-87; deputy chief of mission U.S. Embassy, Kabul, Afghanistan, 1988-89; deputy political counselor U.S. Embassy, Moscow, 1989-91; deputy dir. Office of Ind. States and Commonwealth Affairs, 1991-94; deputy chief of mission U.S. Embassy, Kiev, Ukraine, 1995—. With U.S. Army, 1969-73. Mem. Am. Fgn. Svc. Assn. Office: Am Embassy Kiev U S Dept State Washington DC 20521-5850

SCHUMAKER, LARRY LEE, mathematics educator; b. Aberdeen, S.D., Nov. 5, 1939; s. Lee B. and Irene Elizabeth (Kelly) S.; m. Gerda Ingeborg Boguszewski, June 10, 1963; 1 child, Annabel Louise. BS in Math., S.D.

Sch. of Mines, 1961; MS in Math., Stanford U., 1962, PhD in Math., 1966. Staff mathematician Hughes Aircraft Co., Culver City, Calif., 1961-63; research asst. Stanford U., 1964-65, instr. computer sci. dept., 1966; research mem. Math. Research Ctr., U. Wis., Madison, 1966-68; asst. prof. to assoc. prof. U. Tex., 1968-74, prof. of math., 1974-79; prof. math. Tex. A&M U., 1981-88; dir. Ctr. for Approximation Theory Texas A&M U., 1981-88; prof. of math. Vanderbilt U., Nashville, 1988—; visiting prof. and researcher in field. Author: Approximation Functions, 1967, Approximation Theory I, 1973, Approximation Theory II, 1976, Spline Functions: Basic Theory, 1980, Approximation Theory IV, 1983, Approximation Theory V, 1986, Topics in Multivariate Approximation, 1987, Mathematical Methods in Computer-aided Geometric Design, 1989, Approximation Theory VI, 1989, Approximation Theory VI, Part II, 1989, Approximation Theory VII, 1992, Curves and Surfaces, 1991, Mathematical Methods in Computer-aided Geometric Design II, 1992, Numerical Methods of Approximation Theory, Vol. 9, 1992, Recent Advances in Wavelets, 1993, Curves and Surfaces in Geometric Design, 1994, Wavelets, Images, and Surface Fitting, 1994, Mathematical Methods for Curves and Surfaces, 1995, Approximation Theory VIII, Vol. 1, 1995, Vol. 2, 1995. Recipient Humboldt Prize Humboldt Found., 1989, Centennial Outstanding Grad. award S.D. Sch. Mines and Tech., 1985, Student Coun. Tchg. Excellence award Tex. A&M U., 1981; named Humboldt fellow, 1978-79. Mem. Soc. for Indsl. & Applied Math., Am. Math. Soc., The Math. Assn. Am.. Office: Vanderbilt U Dept Of Math Nashville TN 37240

SCHUMAN, GERALD EUGENE, soil scientist; b. Sheridan, Wyo., July 5, 1944; s. George and Mollie (Michael) S.; m. Mabel F. Kaisler, Mar. 27, 1965; children: William G., Kara L. BS in Soil Sci., U. Wyo., 1966; MS in Soil Sci., U. Nev., 1969; PhD in Agronomy, U. Nebr., 1974. Cert. profl. soil scientist. Soil scientist USDA Agrl. Rsch. Svc., Reno, 1966-69, Lincoln, Nebr., 1969-75; soil scientist USDA Agrl. Rsch. Svc., Cheyenne, Wyo., 1975-77, soil scientist, rsch. leader, 1977—; reclamation cons. HKM Assocs., Billings, Mont., 1986-88. Co-editor: Reclaiming Mine Soils, 1987, symposium proc. Soil and Overburgen in Reclamation, 1983; contbr. articles to profl. jours., book chpts. Mem., pres., elder, trustee Our Savior Luth. Ch., Cheyenne, 1975—. Recipient Profl. of Yr. award Orgn. Profl. Employees of USDA, 1988. Fellow Soil Sci. Soc. Am., Am. Soc. Agronomy (cert.), Soil and Water Conservation Soc. (bd. dirs. 1986-89, commendation 1980), Soil Sci. Soc. Am.; mem. Am. Soc. Surface Mining and Reclamation (nat. exec. com. 1991-93, pres. 1992-93, Reclamation Rsch. award 1991), Soc. for Range Mgmt. (Man of the Range award Wyo. sect. 1993, Outstanding Achievement award 1995), Internat. Soil Sci. Soc. Avocations: fishing, hunting, traveling. Office: High Plains Grasslands Rsch Sta 8408 Hildreth Rd Cheyenne WY 82009-8809

SCHUMAN, HOWARD, sociologist, educator; b. Cin., Mar. 16, 1928; s. Robert A. and Esther (Bohn) S.; m. Josephine Miles, Sept. 1, 1951; children—Marc, Elisabeth, David. Student, U. Chgo., 1947-48; A.B., Antioch Coll., 1953; M.S. in Psychology, Trinity U., 1956; Ph.D. in Sociology, Harvard, 1961. Research asso. Harvard, 1961-64; asst. prof. U. Mich., Ann Arbor, 1964-67; asso. prof. U. Mich., 1967-71, prof. sociology, 1971—, chmn. dept., 1970-73, dir. Detroit Area Study, 1965-71, program dir. Survey Research Ctr., 1974—, dir. Survey Research Ctr., 1982-90, prof. emeritus, rsch. scientific emeritus, 1996—. Author: (with others) Economic Development and Individual Change, Racial Attitudes in Fifteen American Cities, Conversations at Random, Black Racial Attitudes, Questions and Answers in Attitude Surveys, Racial Attitudes in America. Served with AUS, 1954-56. Guggenheim fellow, 1980-81, Ctr. Advanced Study Behavioral Scis. fellow, 1985-86. Fellow Am. Acad. Arts and Scis., Soc. for Personality and Social Psychology; mem. Am. Sociol. Soc., Am. Assn. for Pub. Opinion Rsch. (pres. 1985-86). Home: HC 31 Box 477 Phippsburg ME 04562-9708

SCHUMAN, PATRICIA GLASS, publishing company executive, educator; b. N.Y.C., Mar. 15, 1943; d. Milton and Shirley Rhoda (Goodman) Glass; m. Alan Bruce Schuman, Aug. 30, 1964 (div. 1973); m. Stan Epstein, June 14, 1997. AB, U. Cin., 1963; MS, Columbia U., 1966. Libr. trainee Bklyn. Pub. Libr., 1963-65; tchr. libr. Brandeis High Sch., N.Y.C., 1966; asst. prof. libr. N.Y. Tech. Coll., Bklyn., 1966-71; assoc. editor Sch. Libr. Jour., N.Y.C., 1970-73; sr. editor R.R. Bowker Co., N.Y.C., 1973-76; pres. Neal-Schuman Pubs., N.Y.C., 1976—; vis. prof. St. John's U., Queens, N.Y., 1977-79, Columbia U., N.Y.C., 1981-90, Pratt Inst., 1993—; cons. N.Y. State Coun. on Arts, 1987, Office Tech. Assessment, U.S. Congress, 1982, 84, Coord. Coun. Lit. Mags., N.Y.C., 1987, NEH, 1980, Temple U., 1978-80; bd. visitors Sch. Libr. and Computer Studies Pratt Inst., 1987—; juror Best of Libr. Lit., 1980-88; mem. adv. bd. Sch. Libr. and Info. Studies, Queens Coll., 1989-91. Author: Materials for Occupational Education, 1973, 2d edit., 1983 (Best Edn. Book award 1973), Library Users and Personnel Needs, 1980, Your Right to Know: The Call for Action, 1993; editor: Social Responsibilities and Libraries, 1976; mem. editorial bd. Urban Acad. Libr., 1987-89, Multicultural Review, 1991—; contbr. articles to profl. jours. Bd. dirs. Women's Studies Abstracts, Albany, N.Y., 1970-74, Pratt Inst. Sch. of Libr. and Info. Studies, 1993—, Ctr. for Publ., NYU, 1996—; mem. Com. To Elect Major Owens to U.S. Congress, 1983, N.Y.C. Mayor's Com. for N.Y. Pub. Ctr., 1984-85. Recipient Fannie Simon award Spl. Librs. Assn., 1984, Disting. Alumni award Columbia U., 1992; U.S. Office Edn. fellow, 1969. Mem. ALA (councillor 1971-79, 84-88, exec. bd. 1984-88, 90—, treas. 1984-88, chmn. legis. com. 1989-90, 94—, v.p., pres.-elect 1990-91, pres. 1991-92, Disting. Coun. Svc. award 1979, 88, Equality award 1993), ALA, N.Y. Libr. Assn., Assn. for Libr. and Info. Sci. Edn., Spl. Librs. Assn. Office: Neal-Schuman Pubs Inc 100 Varick St New York NY 10013-1506

SCHUMAN, STANLEY H., epidemiologist, educator; b. St. Louis, Dec. 29, 1925; married, 1952; 8 children. MD, Washington U., St. Louis, 1948; MPH, U. Mich., 1960, DPH, 1962; LLD (hon.), Clemson U., 1996. Diplomate Am. Bd. Pediatrics. Intern Jewish Hosp., St. Louis, 1948-49; resident Children's Hosp., St. Louis, 1950-51, Grady Hosp., 1953; clin. instr. pediatrics, sch. medicine Wash. U., 1954-59; from asst. prof. to prof. epidemiology, sch. pub. health U. Mich., Ann Arbor, 1962-73; prof. epidemiology in family practice, coll. medicine Med. U. S.C., Charleston, 1974—, prof. pediatrics, 1976—; med. dir. Agromedicine Program, Clemson Med. U., S.C., 1984—; project dir. S.C. Pesticide Study Ctr., EPA, 1981-84. Author: Epidemiology, 1986, Environmental Epidemiology for the Busy Clinician, 1997, AG-MED, Rural Practitioner's Guide, 1997; editor Jour. Agromedicine, 1994—. Mem. Am. Epidemiol. Soc., Soc. Epidemiol. Rsch., Coun. Agrl. Sci. Tech., Sigma Xi. Achievements include research on pesticide health effects; field trials with young drivers; epidemiology in family practice; cancer of the esophagus, agricultural and occupational medicine. Home: 1019 Scotland Dr Mount Pleasant SC 29464-3612 Office: Med U SC Agromedicine Program 171 Ashley Ave Charleston SC 29425-0001

SCHUMANN, ALICE MELCHER, medical technologist, educator, sheep farmer; b. Cleve., Sept. 1, 1931; d. John Henry and Marian Louise (Clark) M.; m. Stuart McKee Struever, Aug. 21, 1956 (div. June 1983); children: Nathan Chester, Hanna Russell; m. John Otto Schumann, July 3, 1985. BS, Colby Coll., New London, N.H., 1953. Cert. tchr.; cert. med. technologist. Rschr. Lakeside Hosp., Cleve., 1953-54, Bambridge (Ohio) Schs., 1954-55, Shalersville (Ohio) Schs., 1955-56, Richtnior Sch., Overland, Mo., 1956-57; sci. tchr. Tonica (Ill.) High Sch., 1956-58, Morton Grove (Ill.) High Sch., 1958-60, Univ. Chgo. Lab Sch., 1960-65; co-founder Ctr. for Am. Archeology, dir. flotation rsch. U. Chgo. Campus, Kampsville, Ill., 1957-71, head of supplies distbn., dir. food svcs. dept.; head mailing dept. Found. for Ill. Archeology, Evanston and Kampsville, Ill., 1971-83; sheep farmer, wool processor Gravel Hill Farm, Kampsville, 1983—. Vol. Mt. Sinai Hosp., Cleve., 1948-49; tchr. Title I Dist. 40, Kampsville, 1970-71. Recipient Beverly Booth award Colby Coll., 1953, 1st prize for hand spun yarn DeKalb County Fair, Sandwich, Ill., 1987, 88. Mem. Precious Fibers Found., Natural Colored Wool Growers Assn., Farm Bur. of Calhoun County. Avocations: wool growing, spinning wool and cotton, knitting, raising Great Pyrenees guard dogs for sheep, gardening. Home and Office: Gravel Hill Farm RR 1 Box 121A Kampsville IL 62053-9720

SCHUMER, CHARLES ELLIS, congressman; b. Brooklyn, N.Y., Nov. 23, 1950; s. Abraham and Selma (Rosen) S.; m. Iris Weinshall, 1980; 1 child, Jessica Emily. BA magna cum laude, Harvard U., 1971, J.D. with honors, 1974. Bar: N.Y. 1975. Mem. staff U.S. Senator Claiborne Pell, 1973; assoc. Paul, Weiss, Rifking, Wharton and Garrison, 1974; mem. N.Y. State Assembly, 1975-80, chmn. subcom. on city mgmt. and governance, 1977, chmn. com. on oversight and investigation, 1979; mem. 97th-98th Congresses from 16th N.Y. Dist., 99th-105th Congresses from 10th (now 9th) N.Y. dist., Washington, D.C., 1985—; mem. Banking & Fin. Svcs. Com., ranking minority mem. jud. subcom. on crime. Mem. B'nai Brith, Phi Beta Kappa. Democrat. Jewish. Office: US House of Reps Rayburn House Office Bldg Rm 2211 Washington DC 20515*

SCHUMER, WILLIAM, surgeon, educator; b. Chgo., June 29, 1926; s. Solomon and Gussie (Gross) S.; children—Scott, Fern. M.B., Chgo. Med. Sch., 1949, M.D., 1950; M.S., U. Ill., 1966. Diplomate: Am. Bd. Surgery. Intern Mt. Sinai Hosp. Med. Center, Chgo., 1949-50; resident Mt. Sinai Hosp. Med. Center, 1950-54; asst. prof. surgery Chgo. Med. Sch., 1959-65, asst. prof. cardiovascular research, 1964-65; attending surgeon, then asst. chief surgery Mt. Sinai Hosp., Chgo., 1962-65; attending surgeon Hines (Ill.) VA Hosp., 1960-63, VA West Side Hosp., Chgo., 1963-64; dir. surg. service U. Calif. at Davis, Sacramento County Med. Center, 1965-67; chief surg. service VA West Side Hosp., 1967-75; assoc. prof. surgery faculty Abraham Lincoln Sch. Medicine, U. Ill., Chgo., 1967-69; prof. surgery Abraham Lincoln Sch. Medicine, U. Ill., 1969-75; prof. biol. chemistry Grad. Coll., U. Ill. Med. Center, Chgo., 1974-75; mem. staff U. Ill. Hosp., 1967-75; surgery, chmn. dept. U. HEalth Scis./Chgo. Med. Sch., North Chicago, Ill., 1975-90, disting. prof., 1990—; chief surg. service North Chicago VA Med. Center, 1975-79, attending surgeon, 1979-80, chief gen. surg. sect., 1980-82, attending surg. sect., 1983—; chmn. dept. surgery Mt. Sinai Med. Center, Chgo., 1990—; prof. biochemistry U. Health Scis. Chgo. Med. Sch., 1977—, also prof. critical care medicine, disting. prof., 1990—; Mem. numerous coms. VA. Co-editor: Corticosteroids in the Treatment of Shock: Principles and Practice, 1974, Advances in Shock Research, Vol. 2, 1979, Vol. 4, 1980, Vol. 6, 1981, Molecular and Cellular Aspects of Shock and Trauma, Vol. 3, 1983-88; assoc. editor: Circulatory Shock, 1976-79, editor, 1979-88, cons. editor, 1988—; contbr. numerous articles to profl. jours, chpts. to books. Recipient Disting. Alumnus award, 1974, Honors Achievement award Angiology Research Found., 1965, Morris L. Parker award for meritorious research Chgo. Med. Sch., 1976; also numerous awards for sci. exhibits and films. Mem. AAAS, AAUP, ACS, AMA, Am. Assn. Surgery of Trauma, Am. Physiol. Soc., Am. Surg. Assn., Assn. Am. Med. Colls., Assn. VA Surgeons (pres. 1976), Ctrl. Soc. Clin. Rsch., Ctrl. Surg. Soc., Midwest Surg. Soc., Ill. Surg. Soc., Chgo. Shock Soc. (pres. 1978-79), Collegium Internat. Chirurgiae Digestivae, Digestive Disease Found., Inst. Medicine Chgo., N.Y. Acad. Scis., Reticuloendothelial Soc., Soc. Internat. de Chirurgie, Soc. Surgery Alimentary Tract, Soc. Critical Care Medicine, Internat. Fedn. Surg. Colls., Soc. Univ. Surgeons, Surg. Infection Soc., Warren H. Cole Soc., Alumni Assn. U. Ill., Alumni Assn. Chgo. Med. Sch. (prees. Chgo. chpt.), Minn. Surg. Soc. (hon.), Sigma Xi, Alpha Omega Alpha. Office: Mt Sinai Hosp Med Ctr U Health Scis Chgo Med Sch California Ave at 15th St Chicago IL 60608

SCHUMM, STANLEY ALFRED, geologist, educator; b. Kearny, N.J., Feb. 22, 1927; s. Alfred Henry and Mary Elizabeth (Murdock) S.; m. Ethel Patricia Radli, Sept. 3, 1950; children: Brian Murdock, Mary Theresa, Christine Ann. BA, Upsala Coll., 1950; PhD, Columbia U., 1955. Research geologist U.S. Geol. Survey, Denver, 1955-67; prof. geology Colo. State U., Ft. Collins, 1967-86, Univ. disting. prof., 1986—, acting asso. dean, 1973-74; vis. prof. U. Calif., Berkeley, 1959-60, U. Witwatersrand, South Africa, 1975; fellow U. Sydney, Australia, 1964-65, U. New South Wales, 1988; vice chmn. U.S. Nat. Com. Quaternary Rsch., 1967-70, 75-82; dist. vis. scientist U. tex., 1970; vis. lectr. numerous univs. in U.S., vis. scientist N.Z., Europe, Can., Venezuela, Brazil; vis. scientist Polish Acad. Sci., 1969; cons. to govt. agys., engring. firms; prin. geomorphologist, dir. Water Engring. Tech., Davis, Calif., and Ft. Collins, Colo., 1980-81; sr. assoc. Ayres Assocs., Ft. Collins; prin. investigator rsch. projects NSF, 1969-92, Colo. Agrl. Expt. Sta., 1970-75, Army Rsch. Office, 1970-80, 82-93, Office Water Rsch. and Tech., 1974-83, Nat. Park Svc., 1975-77, Fed. Hwy. Adminstrn., 1978-80, Soil Conservation Svc., 1980-85, NASA, 1984-88, Smithsonian Inst., 1986-87, Can. Internat. Devel. Agy., 1991-92. Author: The Fluvial System, 1977, To Interpret the Earth, 1991; co-author: Incised Channels, 1984, Geomorphology, 1985, Experimental Fluvial Geomorphology, 1987; editor: United States Contribution to Quaternary Research, 1969, River Morphology, 1972, Slope Morphology, 1973, Drainage Basin Morphology, 1977, Physical Geography of W.M. Davis, 1980, The Variability of Large Alluvial Rivers, 1994; contbr. chpts. to sci. books, articles to profl. jours. Served with USNR, 1944-45. Recipient Disting. Alumnus award Upsala Coll., 1980, L.W. Durrell award Colo. State U., 1980, Linton award Brit. Geomorphology Rsch. Group, 1981, Warren prize Nat. Acad. Sci., 1986, Best Paper award Soc. Sedimentary Geology, 1996; Harkness fellow U. Canterbury, N.Z., 1983; fellow Japanese Soc. for Advancement of Sci., 1983, Dept. Agr., Republic of South Africa, 1984, Australian Nat. U., 1988; named honor scientist Colo. State U. chpt. Sigma Xi, 1986. Fellow AAAS, Geol. Soc. Am. (asso. editor 1973-75, vice chmn. geomorphology div. 1978-79, chmn. 1979-80, Kirk Bryan award 1979); mem. Am. Geophys. Union (Horton award 1958, assoc. editor 1973-75), ASCE, Internat. Geog. Union, Assn. Am. Geographers, Internat. Assn. Quaternary Research, Am. Quaternary Assn. (councillor), Sigma Xi (pres. Colo. State U. chpt. 1987-88, honor scientist 1987). Home: 1308 Rollingwood Ln Fort Collins CO 80525-1946 Office: Colo State U Dept Earth Resources Fort Collins CO 80525 also: Ayres Assocs 3665 John F Kennedy Pky Fort Collins CO 80525-3152 also: Mussetter Engring 419 Canyon Ave Fort Collins CO 80521

SCHUNK, ROBERT WALTER, space physics research administrator; b. N.Y.C.. BS, NYU, 1965; PhD in Phys. Fluids, Yale U., 1970. Fellow space physics Inst. Sci. and Tech., U. Mich., 1970-71; rsch. assoc. geophysicist Yale U., 1971-73; rsch. assoc. space physics U. Calif., San Diego, 1973-76; assoc. prof. Utah State U., Logan, 1976-79, prof. physics, 1979—; mem. Com. Solar Terrestrial Rsch., Geophys. Rsch. Bd., Nat. Acad. Sci., 1979-82, Nat. Ctr. Atmospheric Rsch. Computer Divsns. Adv. Panel, 1980-83; prin. invester Solar Terrestrial Theory Program, 1980—. Assoc. editor Jour. Geophys. Rsch., 1977-80. Recipient Gov.'s Medal Sci. & Tech., Utah, 1988. Fellow Am. Geophys. Union; mem. AAAS. Home: Utah State U Ctr Atmospheric Space Logan UT 84322-4405

SCHUNKE, HILDEGARD HEIDEL, accountant; b. Indpls., Nov. 24, 1948; d. Edwin Carl and Hildegard Adelheid (Baumbach) S. BA, Ball State U., Muncie, Ind., 1971, MA in German/English, 1973, MA in Acctg., 1975. CPA, Ind., Calif. Exch. teaching grad. asst. Padagogische Hochschule, Germany, 1971-72; teaching grad. asst. German/acctg. Ball State U., Muncie, 1972, 74-75, asst. prof. acctg., 1975-78; investing rschr. Family Partnership, Muncie, 1977-83; staff acct. Am. Lawn Mower Co., Muncie, 1984-88, G&J Seiberlich, CPAs, St. Helena, Calif., 1988-89, R.A. Gullotta, MBA, CPA, Sonoma, Calif., 1989-90; plant acct. Napa Pipe Corp., Napa, Calif., 1990—; continuing edn. instr. Calif. Soc. CPAs, Redwood City, 1990. ESOL instr. Napa County Project Upgrade, 1988-92; ticketing and refreshments com. North Ba Philharmonic Orch., Napa, 1988—, North Bay Wind Ensemble, Napa, 1988—. Mem. AICPAs, Calif. Soc. CPAs, Ind. Soc. CPAs, Inst. Internal Auditors, Environ. Auditing Roundtable, Am. Soc. Quality Control. Avocations: gardening, transcribing, translating and reading German. Home: 1117 Devonshire Ct Suisun City CA 94585-3343 Office: Napa Pipe Corp 1025 Kaiser Rd Napa CA 94558-6257

SCHUPAK, LESLIE ALLEN, public relations company executive; b. Spokane, Wash., Apr. 5, 1945; s. Leo and Henrietta (Neumann) S.; m. Dianne Barbara Goldin, June 23, 1968; 1 child, Adam J. BS, Boston U., 1967, MS, 1971. Asst. to pres., account exec. Sperber Assocs., Inc., Boston, 1968-69; account supr. Wilcox & Williams, N.Y.C., 1969-70; v.p., mgr. Daniel J. Edelman, Inc., N.Y.C., 1970-72; mng. ptnr. Kanan, Corbin, Schupak & Aronow, Inc., N.Y.C., 1972—. Pres. Whippoorwill Lake Property Owners Assn., Chappaqua, N.Y., 1984-88; mem. exec. com. Coll. Comm., Boston U. With U.S. Army, 1968-73. Mem. Nat. Investor Rels. Inst., Donald Ross Soc., Metropolis Country Club (White Plains, N.Y.), Desert Mountain Club (Scottsdale, Ariz.), Met. Golf Assn. Avocations: golf; tennis; fly fishing. Home: 2 Whippoorwill Close Chappaqua NY 10514-2330 Office: KCS&A Pub Rels 820 2nd Ave New York NY 10017-4504

SCHUPP, RONALD IRVING, clergyman, civil rights leader; b. Syracuse, N.Y., Dec. 10, 1951; s. George August and Shirley Louise (Mitchell) S. Ordained ministry, Old Country Ch., 1972; ordained Bapt. ministry, 1976; cert., Moody Bible Inst., 1986, 1988; advanced cert., Evang. Tng. Assn., 1992; cert., Emmaus Bible Coll., 1996, 97. Missionary, asst. pastor The Old Country Ch. Inc., Chgo., 1972-76; missionary Solid Rock Bapt. Ch., Chgo., 1976-89, Marble Rock Missionary Bapt. Ch., Chgo., 1990—; asst. dir. Uptown Community Orgn., Chgo., 1974-76; dir. Chgo. Action Ctr., 1978-80; bd. dirs. West Englewood United Orgn./Clara's House Shelter, 1991-95 (Recipient Appreciation award, 1992), assoc. chaplain, 1991-95; bd. dirs. America's Soup Kitchen on Wheels, Inc., 1996—, organizer, 1996—, nat. chaplain 1996—; mem. steering com. 1st Congl. Dist. Ministerial Assn., Chgo., 1993-95, chair housing com., 1993-95. Contbr. articles and poems to periodicals. Mem. Nat. Coalition for the Homeless, 1991—, Nat. Union of the Homeless, 1992—, Chgo. Coalition for the Homeless, 1988—, vol. organizer, 1988-94, mem. empowerment adv. com., 1991-94; mem. Homeless on the Move for Equality, 1990-92, bd. dirs. 1991-92; mem. Chgo. Peace Coun., 1984-87, Voice of Homeless, San Jose, Calif., 1993—, Kansas City Union of Homeless, 1993—; active Pledge of Resistance, Chgo., 1985—; rep. Chgo. Welfare Rights Orgn., 1986-88; activist Chgo. Clergy and Laity Concerned, 1981-87; founding mem. People's Campaign for Jobs, Housing and Food, Chgo., 1992—, chaplain, 1992—; founding mem., missionary People's Ministry Without Walls, Chgo., 1993—; rep. Lakota Nat. Organizing Com., 1993—, League of Indigenous Sovereign Nations of Western Hemisphere, 1993—; supporting mem. Autonomous Chgo. chpt. Am. Indian Movement of Ill., 1994—, Chgo. Native Am. Urban Indian Retreat, 1994—; rep. Kasigluk Elders Conf., Alaska, 1994—; pres., co-founder Citizens Taking Action, Chgo., 1995-97, chair, steering com., 1995-97, mem. action com., bd. dirs., 1995—; mem., nat. organizer and outreach coord. Nat. People's Campaign, 1995—; organizer Chgo. Pure Food Campaign, 1995—, Chgo. People's Conv. Coalition, 1996. Recipient letter of commendation Chgo. Fire Dept., 1983, proclamations Mayor Richard M. Daley, Chgo., 1991, 92, 93, 94, 97, Mayor Joan Barr, Evanston, Ill., 1993, Mayor Lorraine H. Morton, Evanston, 1994; commendation resolution Chgo. City Coun., 1993, South African elections vigil support resolution Chgo. City Coun., 1994; tribute in congl. record Congressman Bobby L. Rush, 1993, Sen. Carol Moseley Braun, 1994; initiated Wa-kin-ya-wicha-ho Thunder Voice by trad. Lakota Elders, 1993; initiated Kiyuyakki Aurora by Inuit Elder Etok, 1994; initiated by Ninth Khalkha Jetsun Dhampa, 1996; named Lobsang Dhondup (Good Heart Wish Fulfilled) by Abbot Konchok Tsering, 1997; portfolio on file at Smithsonian Instn., Nat. Civil Rights Mus., UN Libr., Vatican Libr. Mem. Operation Push, Inc. (citation 1990), NAACP, ACLU, Chgo. Free South Africa (steering com. 1984-94), UN Assn. of USA, World Jewish Congress (diplomat), Transafrica, Am. Indian Movement (nat.), Internat. Campaign for Tibet, Tibetan Alliance Chgo. Democrat. Avocations: bicycle riding, poetry. Home and Office: 6412 N Hoyne Ave Apt 3A Chicago IL 60645-5638 *Look inward and see your soul, look outward and serve humanity.*

SCHUR, JEFFREY, advertising executive; b. Capetown, Cape of Good Hope, Union of South Africa, May 3, 1946; Canadian citizen; came to U.S., 1992; s. Lionel Harry and Dorothy (Siman) S.; m. Lucille Stella Breakey, Nov. 30, 1965; children: David Leon, Cynthia-Jean. Diploma in Mktg., Cape Coll. for Advanced Tech. Edn., Capetown, 1970. Account exec. J. Walter Thompson, Capetown and Johannesburg, Republic of South Africa, 1969-71; account dir. Ogilvy & Mather, Johannesburg, 1971-76; internat. vp. Latin Am. base Ogilvy & Mather, N.Y.C., 1976-78; account dir. Ogilvy & Mather, Toronto, Ont., Can., 1977-80; gen. mgr., pres. Saatchi & Saatchi, Toronto, 1980-84; pres., chief exec. officer Needham Harper Can., Toronto, 1985-86, Schur Peppler & Assocs., Toronto, 1986-89, Doner Schur Peppler, Toronto, 1989-92; exec. v.p. Earle Palmer Brown, N.Y.C., 1992-94; ptnr. Doig, Elliott, Schur Inc., N.Y.C., 1994—. Dir. Outward Bound, Toronto, 1980-83, Can. Liver Found., Toronto, 1984-86, Toronto Family Svc. Assn., 1985, York Mills Valley Assn., Toronto, 1990-92, Children's Aid, Toronto, 1991-92, S.A. Defence Forces 1st Parachute Bn., 1964-73. Mem. Chartered Inst. Mktg. (lectr. 1971-73, examiner 1973-74, edn. chmn. 1974-75, rsch. award 1970), Vintage Sports Car Club Am., Royal Marsh Harbour Yacht Club. Avocations: skiing, scuba, vintage racing cars, gardening. Home: 55 Shore Rd Old Greenwich CT 06870-1814 Office: Doig Elliott Schur Inc 58A W 15th St New York NY 10011-6835

SCHUR, LEON MILTON, economist, educator; b. Milw., Jan. 11, 1923; s. Ben and Bertha (Stein) S.; m. Edith Laiken, Sept. 4, 1949; children—Julie Miriam, Claudia Laiken, Amy Ruth. Student, U. Wis., 1941-43, Dartmouth, 1943-44; B.A., U. Wis., 1946, Ph.D., 1955. From instr. to prof. econs. La. State U., 1954-64; prof. econs., dir. Ctr. Econ. Edn. U. Wis., Milw., 1964-95, acting chancellor, 1979-80, chmn. dept. econs., 1987-92; vis. prof. Tulane U., 1961, U. Wis., 1962; dir. Univ. Nat. Bank., Wis. Coun. Econ. Edn., 1964—. Contbr. articles to profl. jours. Bernard F. Sliger chair econ. edn. Fla. State U., 1989-96; dir. Discovery World Mus. Sci., Econs. and Tech., 1978-90. From seaman to lt. (j.g.) USNR, 1943-46. Mem. Am. Econ. Assn., Am. Finance Assn., Am. Assn. U. Profs., Wis. Econ. Assn. (pres. 1975-77), Phi Eta Sigma, Beta Gamma Sigma. Jewish. Home: 173 W Suburban Dr Milwaukee WI 53217-2336

SCHUR, SUSAN DORFMAN, public affairs consultant; b. Newark, Feb. 27, 1940; d. Norman and Jeanette (Handelman) Dorfman; children: Diana Elisabeth, Erica Marlene. BA, Goucher Coll., 1961. Adminstr. fed. housing, fgn. aid, anti-poverty programs, 1961-67; mem. Mass. Housing Appeals Com., 1977-86; mem., v.p. Bd. of Alderman, Newton, Mass., 1974-81; mem. Mass. Ho. of Reps., 1981-94; pvt. pub. affairs cons., Newton, Mass., 1995—. Mem. Newton Dem. City Com., 1970—.

SCHURE, ALEXANDER, university chancellor; b. Can., Aug. 4, 1920; s. Harry Joshua and Bessie (Ginsberg) S.; m. Dorothy Rubin, Dec. 8, 1943 (dec. June 1981); children: Barbara, Matthew, Louis, Jonathan; m. Gail Doris Strollo, Sept. 12, 1984. AST in Elec. Engring, Pratt Inst., 1943; BS, CCNY, 1947; MA, NYU, 1948, PhD, 1950, EdD, 1953; D in Engring. Sci., Nova U., 1975; DSc, N.Y. Inst. Tech., 1976; LLD, Boca Raton Coll., 1976, L.I. U., 1983; LHD, Columbia Coll., Calif., 1983; D of Pedagogy, N.Y. Chiropractic Coll., 1985. Asst. dir. Melville Radio Insts., N.Y.C., 1945-48; pres. Crescent Sch. Radio and TV, Bklyn., 1948-55, Crescent Electronics Corp., N.Y.C., 1951-55, N.Y. Tech. Inst., Bklyn., 1953-55; pres., chancellor N.Y. Inst. Tech., 1955-91, chancellor emeritus, 1991—; pres., CEO, chancellor The Univ. Fedn., Inc., 1995—; founder Computer Graphics Lab NY Inst. Tech., 1985-91; chancellor, CEO Nova U., 1970-85; mem. Fla. State Bd. Ind. Colls. and Univs., 1991—; pres. Vidbits, Inc.; dir. Seversky Electronatom Corp., Executone Inc; cons. N.Y. State Dept. Edn., U.S. Office Edn., UNESCO; mem. Regents Regional Coordinating Council for Post-Secondary Edn. in N.Y.C., 1973—, Nassau County Consortia on Higher Edn., L.I., 1971—, Alfred P. Sloan Found. adv. com. for expanding minority opportunities in engring., 1974; rep. to Nat. Assn. State Adv. Council, 1975—; chmn. N.Y. Title IV Adv. Council, 1975-77; mem. steering com. L.I. Regional Adv. Council, 1974—; chair Regents Adv. Council on Learning Techs., 1986-88; mem., trustee exec. com. Commn. Ind. Colls. and Univs.; mem. adv. council learning technologies N.Y. State Dept. Edn., 1982—; mem. Accreditation Task Force for Council on Postsecondary Accreditation/SHEEBO Project on Assessing Long Distance Learning Via Telecommunications (Project ALLTEL), 1982—; mem. N.Y. State Motion Picture and TV adv. bd., chairperson tech. com.; dir. numerous research projects; expert witness Ho. Reps. com. of Commn. on Sci. and Astronautics; mem. adv. coun. Fla. State Bd. Ind. Colls. and Univs. Author and-or editor textbooks, film producer; designer automatic teaching machine; built one of first computer-controlled anthropomorphic speech devices, 1959; patentee in field. Pres. bd. dirs., trustee L.I. Ednl. TV Coun., Garden City; bd. dirs. Coun. Higher Ednl. Instns., N.Y.C., 1973-83. Served with Signal Corps AUS, 1942-45. 1st inductee Fine Arts Mus. of Long Island's Computer Hall of Fame, 1986. Mem. IEEE (L.I. sect. Gruenwald award 1988), N.Y. Acad. Sci., Am. Inst. Engring. Edn., N.E.A., Electronic Industries Assn. (chmn. task force curriculum devel.), Phi Delta Kappa, Delta Mu Delta, Eta Kappa Nu. *The world is an ever changing, ever challenging reality, filled with opportunities for individual fulfillment and success. A positive philosophy toward life does much to make the realization of individual potential an actuality.*

SCHURE, MATTHEW, college president; b. N.Y.C., May 26, 1948; s. Alexander and Dorothy (Rubin) S.; m. Judith Z. Birchman, Aug. 12, 1973; children: Jared, Deborah. BA magna cum laude with high honors in Psychology, Queens Coll., 1969; MA, Columbia U., 1970, MPH, 1976, PhD, 1976. Lic. psychologist, N.Y. Mem. faculty N.Y. Inst. Tech., Old

Westbury, 1969—, research assoc., instr., asst. prof., assoc. prof. behavioral scis., 1969-70, counselor, 1970-72, assoc. dir. Human Resources Devel. Ctr., 1973-77, assoc. dean acad. assessment, 1977-78, dir. Human Resources Devel. Ctr., 1978-81, pres., 1982—; dep. provost, chmn. dept. community medicine N.Y. Coll. Osteo. Medicine, 1981-91. Author: Hannah's Trial: Our Triumph Over Infertility, 1981; contbr. articles and papers in field to profl. pubs. Trustee Commn. on Ind. Colls. and Univs., 1983-86, St. Barnabas Hosp., L.I. Regional Adv. Coun. on Higher Edn.; chmn. bd. trustees N.Y. State Higher Edn. Svcs. Corp., 1993-96; mem. N.Y. State Coun. on Problem Gambling, 1995; chmn. program com. Pvt. Industry Coun., Town of Oyster Bay. Mem. APA, Nassau County Psychol. Assn., Am. Assn. Colls. of Osteo. Medicine (trustee), Phi Beta Kappa. Office: NY Inst Tech PO Box 8000 Old Westbury NY 11568-8000

SCHURMAN, DAVID JAY, orthopedic surgeon, educator; b. Chgo., Apr. 25, 1940; s. Shepherd P. and Dorothy (Laskey) S.; m. Martha Ellen Rocker, Mar. 8, 1967; children: Hilary Sue, Theodore Shepherd. BA, Yale U., 1961; MD, Columbia U., 1965. Intern Baylor U., Houston, 1965-67; resident in gen. surgery Mt. Sinai Hosp., N.Y.C., 1966-67; resident in orthop. surgery UCLA, 1969-72; asst. rsch. surgeon UCLA Med. Sch., 1972-73; asst. prof. orthopedic surgery Stanford Med. Sch., 1973-79, assoc. prof., 1979-87, prof., 1987—. Capt. USAF, 1967-69. Fellow NIH, 1972-73; grantee NIH, 1976—. Mem. Am. Orthopaedic Assn. (bd. dirs. 1994-95), Clin. Orthopaedics and Related Rsch. (bd. dirs. 1994—), Assn. Bone and Joint Surgeons (v.p. 1996-97, pres.-elect1997-98). Office: Stanford U Sch of Medicine R144 Divsn Orthop Surgery 300 Pasteur Dr Palo Alto CA 94304-2203

SCHURZ, FRANKLIN DUNN, JR., media executive; b. South Bend, Ind., May 22, 1931; s. Franklin Dunn and Martha (Montgomery) S.; m. Robin Rowan Tullis, Nov. 22, 1975 (div. 1985). A.B., Harvard U., 1952, M.B.A., 1956, A.M.P., 1984. Exec. asst. South Bend Tribune, 1956-60, dir., 1961-76, sec., 1970-75, assoc. pub., 1971-72, editor, pub., 1972-82, exec. v.p., 1975-76, pres., 1976-82; asst. pub. Morning Herald and Daily Mail, Hagerstown, Md., 1960-62; pub. Morning Herald and Daily Mail, 1962-70, editor, 1966-70; pres. Schurz Communications, Inc., 1982—, treas., 1983-89. Chmn. Ind. Arts Commn., 1979-81; bd. regents St. Marys Coll., Notre Dame, Ind., 1977-83; chmn. adv. coun. Coll. Arts and Letters Notre Dame U., 1980-82; bd. dirs. Ind. Endowment Ednl. Excellence Inc., Indpls., 1987-90; mem. pres.'s coun. Ind. U., Bloomington, 1988—. 2d lt. U.S. Army, 1952-54. Recipient Presdl. Award of Merit Nat. Newspaper Assn., 1965, Frank Rogers award Rotary, South Bend, 1980. Mem. Am. Press Inst. (bd. dirs. 1985-94), AP (chmn. audit com. 1979-84), Chesapeake AP Assn. (past pres.), Md.-Del.-D.C. Press Assn. (past pres.), The Press-Enterprise (bd. dirs. 1992—), Hoosier State Press Assn. (past pres.), Newspaper Advt. Bur. (past bd. dirs.), South Bend Mishawaka Area C. of C. (pres. 1980-82), Am. Soc. Newspaper Editors, Inst. Newspaper Fin. Execs. (past pres.), South Bend Country Club, Nat. Press Club, Soc. Profl. Journalists. Presbyterian. Home: 1329 E Erskine Manor Hl South Bend IN 46614-2186 Office: Schurz Communications Inc 225 W Colfax Ave South Bend IN 46626-1000

SCHURZ, SCOTT CLARK, journalist, publisher; b. South Bend, Ind., Feb. 23, 1936; s. Franklin Dunn and Martha (Montgomery) S.; m. Kathryn Joan Foley, Aug. 5, 1967; children: Scott Clark, Alexandra Carol, John Danforth. B.A., Denison U., 1957. Asst. instr. U. Md., 1957-58; adminstrv. asst. South Bend Tribune, 1960-66; circulation cons. Imperial Valley Press, El Centro, Calif., 1966; asst. to pub. Bloomington (Ind.) Herald-Times/Bedford Times-Mail, 1966-70, pub., 1970—; personnel mgr. Bloomington Herald-Times, 1969-72, promotion mgr., 1969-81, dir. promotions, 1981-86, editor-in-chief, 1977—; editorial chmn. Bedford Times-Mail, 1972-81, editor-in-chief, 1981—; pub., editor-in-chief Sunday Herald Times; pres. Herald-Times, Inc., dir., v.p.; dir. Schurz Communications, Inc. Pres., Bloomington Boys' Club, 19701, Jr. Achievement Monroe County, 1971-73; bd. dirs. United Way Monroe County, 1979-81. Served with U.S. Army, 1958-60. Mem. Internat. Newspaper Mktg. Assn. (pres. 1986), Inland Daily Press Assn. (pres. 1989), Newspaper Assn. Am. (bd. dirs. 1992-95), Inter-Am. Press Assn. (bd. dirs. 1995—), Hoosier State Press Assn. (pres. 1989-97), Newspaper Advt. Bur. (bd. dirs. 1987-92). Republican. Presbyterian. Office: Herald Times Inc 1900 S Walnut St Bloomington IN 47401-7720

SCHUSSLER, THEODORE, lawyer, physician, educator, consultant; b. N.Y.C., July 27, 1934; s. Jack and Fannie (Blank) S.; m. Barbara Ann Gordon, June 18, 1961; children: Deborah, Jonathan, Rebecca. B.A. in Polit. Sci., Bklyn. Coll., 1955; LL.B., Bklyn. Law Sch., 1958; J.D., Bklyn. Law Sch., 1967; M.D., U. Lausanne (Switzerland), 1974. Bar: N.Y. 1959, U.S. Dist. Ct. (so. and ea. dists.) N.Y. 1975, U.S. Tax Ct. 1961, U.S. Ct. Appeals (2d cir.) 1962, U.S. Supreme Ct. 1975. Clerkship and practice, N.Y.C., 1956, 58-59; legal editor tax div. Prentice-Hall, Inc., Englewood Cliffs, N.J., 1956; vol. criminal law div. Legal Aid Soc., N.Y.C., 1959; atty. legal dept. N.Y.C. Dept. Welfare, 1959-60; sole practice, N.Y.C., 1960—; sr. staff asst. IBM-Indsl. Medicine Program, 1969-70, 74-76; intern in medicine St. Vincent's Med. Center of Richmond, S.I., N.Y., 1976-77, resident emergency medicine, 1977-79; resident in gerontology, chief house physician Carmel Richmond Nursing Home, S.I., 1978-80; surg. rotation emergency dept. Met. Hosp. Ctr., 1979; house physician dept. medicine Richmond Meml. Hosp. and Health Ctr., 1979-80; gen. practice medicine, 1980—; attending physician, former chief dept. family practice, former chmn. med. care evaluation, med. records and by-laws coms., former physician, advisor emergency dept., former mem. blood transfusion, credential's, emergency dept. coms., former mem. exec. com., mem. med. staff Community Hosp. of Bklyn., 1980-94; attending physician Meth. Hosp., Bklyn., 1984-92; supervising emergency dept. physician, dept. ambulatory care Meth. Hosp., Bklyn., 1980-83; attending physician Kings Hwy. Hosp., 1981-88, coord. emergency dept., 1981; clin. instr. dept. preventive medicine and community health, Downstate Med. Ctr. SUNY, Bklyn., 1981-88, clin. asst. prof., 1988—, SUNY Health Science Ctr., med. dir. divsn. devel. disabilities Mishkon-Jewish Bd. Family & Children's Svc., Bklyn., 1982—; primary care physician Jewish Home and Hosp. for Aged, N.Y.C., 1993-94; cons. in gerontology Palm Beach Home for Adults, Bklyn., 1980-92; cons. indsl. medicine IBM, 1990-92; tchr., instr., lectr., prof., 1954—; med.-legal cons. to professions of medicine and law. Dem. County Committeeman, 44th Assembly Dist., Bklyn., del. to judicial conv.; mem. exec. bd. United Ind. Dems. Bklyn. Capt. (med. corp.) USAR. Recipient Pub. and Community Svc. award United Ind. Dems. 44th assembly dist., Bklyn. Fellow Am. Coll. Legal Medicine; mem. Am. Coll. Emergency Physicians (past bd. dir. N.Y. chpt., past chmn. medico-legal com. N.Y. chpt.), Assn. Arbitrators of Civil Ct. of N.Y. (small claims divsn., arbitrator), United Univ. Professions, Bklyn. Law Sch. Alumni Assn. (bd. dirs.), Delta Sigma Rho. Author: Torts; Jurisdiction and Practice in Federal Courts; Constitutional Law; Conflict of Laws; contbr. articles to profl. jours. Home and Office: 760 E 10th St Apt 6H Brooklyn NY 11230-2352

SCHUSTER, CARLOTTA LIEF, psychiatrist; b. N.Y.C., Sept. 16, 1936; d. Victor Filler and Nina Lincoln (Rayevsky) Lief; m. David Israel Schuster, Sept. 2, 1962; 1 child, Amanda. BA, Barnard Coll., 1957; MD, NYU, 1964. Cert. Am. Bd. Psychiatry and Neurology; cert. addiction psychiatry. Intern Lenox Hill Hosp., N.Y.C., 1964-65; resident St. Luke's Hosp., N.Y.C., 1965-68; fellow Inst. Sex Edn., U. Pa., Phila., 1968-69; instr. N.Y. Med. Coll., N.Y.C., 1969-72; asst. attending Met. Hosp., N.Y.C., 1969-72; assoc. attending St. Luke's-Roosevelt Hosp. Ctr., N.Y.C., 1972—; staff psychiatrist Silver Hill Found., New Canaan, Conn., 1972-95; clin. assoc. instr. Columbia U., N.Y.C., 1990—; chief substance abuse svc. Silver Hill Found., New Canaan, 1976-95; clin. faculty dept. psychiatry Sch. Medicine NYU, 1995—; dir. recovery clinic Bellevue Hosp., N.Y.C., 1995—. Author: Alcohol and Sexuality, 1988; co-author: Chapter in Advances in Alcohol and Substance Abuse, 1987; contbr. chpt. Mental Health in the Workplace, 1993. Mem. Am. Psychiat. Assn., Am. Med. Soc. on Addictions, Am. Acad. Addication Psychiatry. Democrat. Jewish. Avocations: cooking, attending concerts, opera, films. Office: 207 E 30th St New York NY 10016-8230

SCHUSTER, CHARLES ROBERTS, federal government scientist; b. Woodbury, N.J., Jan. 24, 1930; s. Charles Roberts and Ruth E. S.; m. Chris-Ellyn Johanson, Nov. 1972. AB, Gettysburg Coll., 1951; MS, U. N.Mex., 1953; PhD, U. Md., 1962. Prof. psychiatry and behavioral scis. U. Chgo., 1972—, dir. rsch ctr. drug abuse, 1973-86, acting chmn. dept. psychiatry, 1985-86; dir. Nat. Inst. on Drug Abuse, Rockville, Md., 1986-92; sr. rsch. scientist Balt., 1992-95; prof. psychiatry Wayne State U., Detroit, 1995—; mem. Dept. Health Human Svcs. Commn. on Orphan Diseases, 1987-89, Com. on Problems Drug Dependence, Inc., 1978—; chmn. expert com. WHO, 1975, expert adv. panel on drug dependence. Author: Behavioral Pharmacology, 1968, Drug Dependence, 1970; contbr. over 150 articles to profl. jours. Fellow AAAS, Am. Psychol. Assn. (pres. div. 28 1977-78), Am. Coll. Neuropsychopharmacology; mem. Behavioral Pharmacology Soc. (pres. 1976-78), Inst. Medicine. *

SCHUSTER, ELAINE, civil rights professional, state official; b. Detroit, Sept. 26, 1947; d. William Alfred and Aimee Isabelle (Cote) LeBlanc; m. James William Schuster, Sept. 6, 1969; 1 child, Cambrian James. BA, Wayne State U., 1972, postgrad., 1974-75, paralegal cert., 1991. Asst. payments Mich. Dept. Social Svcs., Detroit, 1972-73; rights rep. Mich. Dept. Civil Rights, Detroit, 1973-80, 82-87, 90, asst. dir. div., 1987-90, supr., 1993-97, dir. Svc. Ctr., 1997—; court adminstr. Chippewa-Ottawa Conservation Ct., Bay Mills, Mich., 1980-82; quality assurance coord. State Mental Health Facility, Southgate, Mich., 1991-93; acting interim dir. Mich. Indian Commn., Detroit, 1995. Author: Critique, An Indian Tours Michilimackinac, 1981; contbr. articles and poems to mags. and profl. jours. Bd. dirs. Tri-County Native Ams., Warren, Mich., 1982-89, sec. Native Am. Sesquicentennial subcom., Mich., 1987; mem. Linking Lifetimes, mentor program for Native Am. youth, 1992-93; sec., newsletter editor various civic orgns.; also other polit. and civic activities. Native Am. fellow Mich. State U., 1989. Mem. ACLU (bd. dirs. Union-Oakland county 1987-88). Democrat. Avocations: exploring local historical and natural places of interest, research, fitness. Office: Mich Dept Civil Rights 1200 6th St Detroit MI 48226

SCHUSTER, GARY FRANCIS, public relations executive; b. Detroit, Jan. 26, 1942; s. Dwayne Alger and Mary Elizabeth (Cullen) S.; m. Barbara Anne Leopold, Aug. 30, 1968; children—Rory Anne, Reid Patrick. B.S. in Journalism/Psychology, Wayne State U., 1966. Gen. assignment reporter Royal Oak (Mich.) Tribune, 1966-68; gen. assignment reporter Detroit News, 1968-70, state capital corr., 1970-74; bur. chief Detroit News, Lansing, 1974-75; chief asst. city editor Detroit News, Detroit, 1975-76; city editor Detroit News, 1976-77, news editor, 1977-78, Washington Bur. chief, 1978-85, White House corr., 1978-85; White House corr. CBS News, 1985-86; pvt. practice media cons., 1986-87; v.p. corp. relations Union Pacific Corp., 1987—. Mem. White House Corrs. Assn. (pres. 1985-86), Saucon Valley Country Club (Bethlehem, Pa.). Roman Catholic.

SCHUSTER, INGEBORG IDA, chemistry educator; b. Frankfurt, W. Ger., Oct. 30, 1937; came to U.S. 1947; d. Ludwig Karl and Mariluise (Kautetzky) S. BA, U. Pa., 1960; MS, Carnegie Inst. Tech., Pitts., 1963; PhD, Carnegie Inst. Tech., 1965. Postdoctoral fellow Bryn Mawr (Pa.) Coll., 1965-67; asst. prof. chemistry Pa. State U., Abington, 1967-73; assoc. prof. chemistry Pa. State U., 1973-83, prof. chemistry, 1983—. Contbr. articles to profl. jours. Huff fellow, 1966; E. Gerry fellow, 1982. Mem. Am. Chem. Soc. Republican. Roman Catholic. Avocations: skiing, violin, cartooning. Office: Pa State Univ 1600 Woodland Rd Abington PA 19001-3918

SCHUSTER, KAREN SUTTON, administrator; b. New Brunswick, N.J., Aug. 26, 1952; d. Alfred Michael and Carmen (Collado) Sutton; m. Derek Vance Schuster, May 31, 1976; children: Sloane, Brooke, Devon, Megan, Christopher. BA, Hofstra U., 1974; postgrad., NYU, 1987-89. Asst. to dir. Mus. Am. Folk Art, N.Y.C., 1975-76, acting dir., 1976-77, bd. dirs., exec. com. officer, 1980-88, gallery dir., 1989-92, dir. ops., 1992-94, dep. dir. planning and adminstrn., 1994-95; v.p. Sotheby's, N.Y.C., 1995—, sr. v.p. ops., 1996—. Bd. dirs. Family Dynamics, N.Y.C., 1976-80. Mem. Cosmopolitan Club (younger members chmn.), Maidstone Club, Coral Beach Club. Democrat. Episcopalian. Home: 79 E 79th St Apt 9 New York NY 10021-0202 Office: Sotheby's 1334 York Ave New York NY 10021-4806

SCHUSTER, MARVIN MEIER, physician, educator; b. Danville, Va., Aug. 30, 1929; s. Isaac and Rosel (Katzenstein) S.; m. Lois R. Bernstein, Feb. 19, 1961; children: Roberta, Nancy, Cathy. BA, BS, U. Chgo., 1951; MD, 1955. Diplomate Am. Bd. Internal Medicine. Intern Kings County Hosp., Bklyn., 1955-56; resident Balt. City Hosp., 1956-58; Johns Hopkins Hosp., Balt., 1958-61; prof. medicine and psychiatry Johns Hopkins U. Sch. Medicine, Balt., 1976—, chief digestive disease divsn. Author: Gastrointestinal Disorders: Behavioral and Physiological Basis for Treatment; Keeping Control: Understanding and Managing Fecal Incontinence; editor: Gastrointestinal Motility Disorders, 1981, Atlas of Gastrointestinal Motility, 1994; contbr. chpts. to textbooks, articles to profl. jours.; mem. editl. bd. Gastroenterology, 1978-81, Gastrointestinal Endoscopy, 1979-81, Psychosomatics, 1979—, Am. Jour. Gastroenterology, 1993—. Bd. dirs. Am. Cancer Soc., 1975—, pres., 1984-86; chmn. med. adv. bd. Balt. Ostomy Assn., 1966—. Recipient St. George Disting. Service award Am. Cancer Soc., 1979. Fellow ACP, Am. Psychiat. Assn., Am. Gastroent. Assn. (chmn. audiovisual com. 1975-78); mem. Am. Soc. Gastrointestinal Endoscopy (governing bd. 1975-78), Am. Coll. Gastroenterology (pres. 1996) Am. Physiol. Soc., AAUP. Democrat. Jewish. Research on gastroenterology and application of biofeedback to gastrointestinal control. Home: 10 Red Cedar Ct Baltimore MD 21208-6305 Office: Marvin M Schuster Digestive and Motility Disorders Ctr 4940 Eastern Ave Baltimore MD 21224-2735

SCHUSTER, PHILIP FREDERICK, II, lawyer, writer; b. Denver, Aug. 26, 1945; s. Philip Frederick and Ruth Elizabeth (Robar) S.; m. Barbara Lynn Nordquist, June 7, 1975; children: Philip Christian, Matthew Dale. BA, U. Wash., 1967; JD, Willamette U., 1972. Bar: Oreg. 1972, U.S. Dist. Ct. Oreg. 1974, U.S. Ct. Appeals (9th cir.) 1986, U.S. Supreme Ct. 1986. Dep. dist. atty. Multnomah County, Portland, Oreg., 1972; title examiner Pioneer Nat. Title Co., Portland, 1973-74; assoc. Buss, Leichner et al, Portland, 1975-76; from assoc. to ptnr. Kitson & Bond, Portland, 1976-77; pvt. practice Portland, 1977-95; ptnr. Dierking and Schuster, Portland, 1996—; arbitrator Multnomah County Arbitration Program, 1985—; student mentor Portland Pub. Schs., 1988—. Contbg. author OSB CLE Publ., Family Law; contbr. articles to profl. jours. Organizer Legal Aid Svcs. for Community Clinics, Salem, Oreg. and Seattle, 1969-73; Dem. committeeman, Seattle, 1965-70. Mem. ABA, ATLA, NAACP (exec. bd. Portland, Oreg. chpt. 1979—), ACLU, Multnomah Bar Assn. (Vol. Lawyers Project), Internat. Platform Assn., Alpha Phi Alpha. Avocations: river drifting, camping, swimming, jogging/walking, karate. Office: 1500 NE Irving St Ste 540 Portland OR 97232-4209 *Hard work and perseverance are the keys to accomplishing any goal. Protecting and nurturing our children and our environment are life's most noble goals. Success is the pursuit of these goals.*

SCHUSTER, ROBERT PARKS, lawyer; b. St. Louis, Oct. 25, 1945; s. William Thomas Schuster and Carolyn Cornforth (Daugherty) Hathaway; 1 child, Susan Michele. AB, Yale U., 1967; JD with honors, U. of Wyo., 1970; LLM, Harvard U., 1971. Bar: Wyo. 1971, U.S. Ct. Appeals (10th cir.) 1979, U.S. Supreme Ct. 1984, Utah 1990. Dep. county atty. County of Natrona, Casper, Wyo., 1971-73; pvt. practice law, Casper, 1973-76; assoc. Spence & Moriarity, Casper, 1976-78; ptnr. Spence, Moriarity & Schuster, Jackson, Wyo., 1978—. Trustee U. Wyo., 1985-89; Wyo. Dem. nominee for U.S. House of Reps., 1994; polit. columnist Casper Star Tribune, 1987-94. Ford Found. Urban Law fellow, 1970-71; pres. United Way of Natrona County, 1974; bd. dirs. Dancers Workshop, 1981-83; chair Wyo. selection com. Rhodes Scholarship, 1989—; mem. bd. visitors Coll. Arts and Scis., U. Wyo., 1991—; mem. Dem. Nat. Com., 1992—; mem. Wyo. Public Policy Forum, 1992—. Mem. ABA, ATLA, Wyo. Trial Lawyers Assn. Home: PO Box 548 Jackson WY 83001-0548 Office: Spence Moriarity & Schuster 15 S Jackson St Jackson WY 83001

SCHUSTER, SEYMOUR, mathematician, educator; b. Bronx, N.Y., July 31, 1926; s. Oscar and Goldie (Smilowitz) S.; m. Marilyn Weinberg, May 2, 1954; children: Paul Samuel, Eve Elizabeth. B.A., Pa. State U., 1947; A.M., Columbia U., 1948; Ph.D., Pa. State U., 1953; postgrad. (fellow), U. Toronto, 1952-53. Instr. Pa. State U., 1950-52; instr. Poly. Inst. N.Y., 1953-54, asst. prof., 1954-56, assoc. prof., 1956-58; vis. assoc. prof. Carleton Coll., Northfield, Minn., 1958-59, assoc. prof., 1959-63, prof. math., 1968—, chmn. dept., 1973-76, William H. Laird prof. math. and liberal arts, 1992-94, William H. Laird prof. emeritus, 1994—; vis. assoc. prof. U. N.C., Chapel Hill, 1961; research assoc. math. dept. U. Minn., Mpls., 1962-63, assoc. prof., 1963-65; assoc. prof. Minn. Math Center, 1965-68, dir. coll. geometry project, 1964-74; dir. Acad. Year Inst. for Coll. Tchrs., 1966-67, NSF Faculty fellow, 1970-71; vis. scholar U. Calif., Santa Barbara, 1970-71, U. Ariz., 1990; guest scholar Western Mich. U., 1976, 81; vis. prof. Western Wash. U., 1983, U. Oreg., 1986. Author: (with K. O. May) Undergraduate Research in Mathematics, 1961, Elementary Vector Geometry, 1962, (with P.C. Rosenbloom) Prelude to Analysis, 1966; also research articles on geometry, graph theory, and analysis.; cons. editor Xerox Pub. Co., 1962-71; assoc. editor, editorial bd.: Am. Math. Monthly, 1969-86; assoc. editor: Indian Jour. Math. Edn, 1976-86; co-producer 12 films on geometry. Served with USNR, 1944-46. Recipient Honor award Am. Film Festival, 1967, Golden Eagle award Cine Film Festival, 1967, 68; named found. fellow Inst. for Combinatorics and Applications. Mem. Math. Assn. Am., Am. Math. Soc., Sigma Xi, Pi Mu Epsilon. Home: 316 Sumner St E Northfield MN 55057-2843

SCHUSTER, STEPHEN FOWLER, lawyer; b. Louisville, Nov. 11, 1943; s. Samuel Y. and Gladys (Fowler) S.; m. Joan Hardy, May 9, 1970; children: David, Elizabeth, AB, Cath. U. Am., 1966; JD, U. Louisville, 1969. Bar: KY. 1969, U.S. Dist. Ct. (ea. and wes. dists.) Ky. 1970, U.S. Ct. Appeals (6th cir.). Ptnr. Ogden, Sturgill & Welch (now Ogden Newell & Welch), Louisville, 1969—. Mem. ABA, Ky. Bar Assn. Office: Ogden Newell & Welch 1 Riverfront Plz Ste 1200 Louisville KY 40202-4222

SCHUSTER, TODD MERVYN, biophysics educator, biotechnology company executive; b. Mpls., June 27, 1933; s. David Theodore and Ann (Kaluser) S.; m. Nancy Joanne Barnes, Jan. 25, 1958; 1 child, Lela Alexa. B.A., Wayne State U., 1958, M.S., 1960; Ph.D., Washington U., 1963. Research assoc. Max Planck Inst. Phys. Chemistry, Goettingen, W.Ger., 1963-66; asst. prof. SUNY-Buffalo, 1966-70; assoc. prof. U. Conn., Storrs, 1970-75, prof. biochemistry, biophysics, 1975—, dept. head, 1977-81, dir. Biotech. Ctr., 1986-90; pres., founder Xenogen Inc., 1986-90; vis. prof. Ind. U., Bloomington, 1975, U. Peking, People's Republic of China, 1987; McCollum-Pratt vis. prof. Johns Hopkins U., Balt., 1979-80; mem. NIH grant rev. panels, biophysics and biophys. chemistry panel, 1971-75, biomed. scis. postdoctoral fellowship panel, 1976, Sickle Cell Disease Adv. Panel, 1977; mem. biol. instrumentation rev panel NSF, 1984-90, biol. facilities, 1987-90, sci. and tech. ctrs., 1988-90; mem. BBS adv. coun. NSF, 1989-92; chmn. adv. com. Nat. Cell Culture Ctr., 1990—; program dir. Nat. Analytical Untracentri Fugation Facility, 1987-94. Contbr. research articles on rapid reaction kinetics, biopolymers, hemeprotein structure and function, virus structure and assembly to profl. jours. USPHS fellow, 1959-63, 63-66. Mem. AAAS, Am. Chem. Soc., Conn. Acad. Sci. and Engring., Biophys. Soc., Protein Soc., Am. Soc. Biol. Chemists, Am. Soc. Virology. Home: 6 Garland Rd West Hartford CT 06107 Office: U Conn Dept Molecular and Cell Biology PO Box 125 Storrs Mansfield CT 06268-0125 also: Xenogen Inc 321 Fisher Bldg Detroit CT 06269-3125

SCHUT, DONNA SUE, elementary education educator; b. Sioux Center, Iowa, Mar. 23, 1961; d. James Martin and Gertrude (Buyert) Intveld; m. Eric Peter Schut, July 21, 1958; 1 child, Alyssa Nichole. BA, Northwestern Coll., Orange City, Iowa, 1983, MA, 1990. Lic. tchr., Iowa. Tchr. Sioux Center Community Schs., 1983—, dept. head social studies dept., 1989-91, 4th grade team leader, 1994-96; supr. student tchrs. Northwestern Coll., Orange City, 1986-87, 88-89, 90-91, 92-93, 94-95, 96-97. Mem. N.W. Iowa Reading Assn. (bldg. rep. 1983—), Sioux Center Edn. Assn., Nat. Coun. for Tchrs. Math., Iowa Coun. for Social Studies, Geographic Alliance Iowa, Assn. Supervision and Curriculum Devel., Internat. Reading Assn. Avocations: reading, baking, collecting cats, spending time with family. Office: Kinsey Elem Sioux Center Community Schs 397 10th St SE Sioux Center IA 51250

SCHUTT, WALTER EUGENE, lawyer; b. Cleve., July 27, 1917; s. Erle Minchin and Elizabeth (Eastman) S.; A.B., Miami U., Oxford, Ohio, 1939; J.D., U. Cin., 1948; m. Dorothy Louise Gilbert, Apr. 18, 1942; children: Gretchen Sue, Stephen David, Elizabeth Ann, Robert Barclay. Admitted to Ohio bar, 1948, U.S. Dist. Ct. (so. dist.) Ohio 1953, U.S. Supreme Ct. bar, 1962, U.S. Tax Ct. 1983, U.S. Ct. Appeals (6th cir.) 1986. Practiced in Wilmington, Ohio, 1948—; city solicitor, Wilmington, 1950-53. Mem. Wilmington Bd. Edn., 1958-65; chmn. Clinton County chpt. ARC, 1951-53; Wilmington chmn. Cin. Symphony Orch. Area Artists Series, 1969-71; trustee Wilmington Coll., 1962-74, sec., 1966-74; trustee Quaker Hill Found., Richmond, Ind., 1970-75, Friends Fellowship Community, Inc., 1986-93; rep. U.S. preparations com. 6th Internat. Assembly World Council of Chs., 1982. Served to 1st lt. USAAF, 1943-46. Decorated D.F.C.; recipient Disting. Service award Wilmington Jr. C. of C., 1953. Mem. Am. Bar Assn. (arms control and disarmament com. 1977-80), Ohio State Bar Assn., Clinton County Bar Assn. (past pres.), World Peace Through Law Ctr. Mem. Soc. of Friends (presiding clk. Friends United Meeting 1978-81, rep. to bd. Nat. Council Chs. of Christ 1985-96; presiding clk. Friends com. on. nat. legis. 1984-87). Club: Rotary. Home: 81 Columbus St Wilmington OH 45177-1801 Office: Thorne Bldg 36 1/2 N South St Wilmington OH 45177-2254

SCHUTTA, HENRY SZCZESNY, neurologist, educator; b. Gdansk, Poland, Sept. 15, 1928; came to U.S., 1962, naturalized, 1967; s. Jakub and Janina (Zerbst) S.; m. Henryka Kosmal, Apr. 29, 1950; children—Katharine, Mark, Caroline. M.B., B.S., U. Sydney, Australia, 1955, M.D., 1968. Jr. resident, then sr. resident St. Vincent's Hosp., Sydney, 1956-58; acad. registrar, house physician Nat. Hosp. Nervous Diseases, London, 1958-62; neurologist Pa. Hosp., Phila., 1962-73; asso. prof. neurology U. Pa. Med. Sch., 1963-73; prof. neurology, chmn. dept. SUNY Downstate Med. Center, Bklyn., 1973-80; prof. U. Wis. Med. Sch., 1980-95, chmn. dept. neurology, 1980-95. Research on bilirubin encephalopathy, cerebral edema, degeneration and regeneration of muscle. Home: 3510 Blackhawk Dr Madison WI 53705-1406 Office: U Hosp 600 Highland Ave Madison WI 53792-0001

SCHUTTER, DAVID JOHN, banker; b. Erie, Pa., Apr. 21, 1945; s. Donald John and Ruth Margaret (Hilbert) S. m. Ellen Carol Hoffman, June 18, 1967; children: David, Erica. BS with honors and distinction, Pa. State U., 1967; postgrad., Mich. State U., 1967-68, Ohio State U., 1973-75; cert., Stonier Grad. Sch. Banking, 1981. Asst. v.p. Huntington Nat. Bank, Columbus, Ohio, 1973-80; v.p. Ameritrust Co., Cleve., 1980-81, v.p., mgr. asset based lending dept., 1981-86, sr. v.p. secured lending div., 1986-89, dep. sr. loan adminstr., 1989-90, sr. cred. pol. off., 1990-92; sr. v.p., regional credit exec. Soc. Nat. Bank, Cleve., 1992-94; exec. v.p., chief credit officer, 1994-97; exec. v.p., sr. lending officer Eastern U.S. Key Bank NA, Cleve., 1997—; pres. AT Comml. Corp., 1986-96; panelist Robert Morris Assocs., Cleve., 1981, 93, mem., 1986—, Cleve. Bar Assn., 1986. Served to capt. U.S. Army, 1968-72. Mem. Nat. Comml. Fin. Assn. (bd. dirs. 1986—), Beta Gamma Sigma, Omicron Delta Epsilon. Office: Key Bank NA 127 Public Sq Cleveland OH 44114-1216

SCHUTZ, DONALD FRANK, geochemist, healthcare corporate executive; b. Orange, Tex., Sept. 22, 1934; s. Theodore J. and Mildred Irene (Chandler) S.; m. Beatriz Valera, May 18, 1958; children: Delfino, Celita. BS in Geology cum laude, Yale U., 1956, PhD in Geology, 1964; MA in Geology, Rice U., 1958. Research staff geologist Yale U., New Haven, 1963-64; mgr. nuclear geochemistry dept. Teledyne Isotopes, Westwood, N.J., 1968-70, v.p., 1970-75, pres., 1975-93; engring. group exec. Teledyne, Inc., Westwood, 1989-92; chief scientist Teledyne Environ. Systems, 1992-93; gen. mgr. Teledyne Brown Engring. Environ. Svcs., 1993—; v.p. Teledyne Environ., Inc., 1996—; mem. low level waste adv. com. N.J. Dept. Environ. Protection, Trenton, 1988-90; chmn. com. on radioactive materials N.J. BIA, Trenton, 1980-88. Pres. Children's Aid and Adoption Soc. N.J. Inc., Bogota, 1976-95, Am. Amateur Judo Found., River Vale, N.J., 1979-89; bd. dirs. Yale U. Alumni Fund, 1989-94; co-chmn. Children's Aid and Family Svcs. Inc., 1995-96. Recipient Antarctic Service medal U.S. Congress, 1964. Mem. Geochem. Soc., Am. Nuclear Soc. (chmn. no. N.J. sect. 1988-89, environ. scis. divsn., bd. dirs., chair 1995-96, pub. policy com. 1991—), Am. Assn. Engring. Soc. Internat. Affairs (standing com. sustainable devel. 1995—), Geol. Soc. Am., Soc. Petroleum Engrs., Am. Assn. Radon Sci. and Tech. (pres. 1986-89, treas. 1990-95), Am. Assn. Petroleum Geologists, Yale Alumni Assn. (bd. dirs. Bergen County and vicinity chpt. 1989—), Sigma Xi. Office: Teledyne Brown Engring Environ Svcs 50 Van Buren Ave Westwood NJ 07675-3242

SCHUTZ, HERBERT DIETRICH, publishing executive; b. Munich, July 16, 1922; came to U.S., 1924; naturalized, 1930; s. Anton Friedrich and Maria Hedwig (Gross) S.; m. Suzanne Cameron, Mar. 22, 1971; children: Leslie, Suzanne; children by previous marriage: Prescott (dec.), Peter, Jeffrey, Elizabeth. BS, Harvard Coll., 1944. Ptnr. N.Y. Graphic Soc . Ltd., Greenwich, Conn., 1946-66, pres., editor in chief, 1966-81, chmn. bd., 1982-84; v.p. Time Inc., N.Y.C., 1966-81; chmn., pres. Schutz and Co., Fine Arts, Greenwich, 1982—. Served to 1st lt. USMC, 1943-46. Mem. Harvard Club (N.Y.C.), Belle Haven Club, Field Club. Home and Office: The Barn Dewart Rd Greenwich CT 06830-3417 also: East End Rd Fishers Island NY 06390

SCHUTZ, JOHN ADOLPH, historian, educator, former university dean; b. L.A., Apr. 10, 1919; s. Adolph J. and Augusta K. (Gluecker) S. AA, Bakersfield Coll., 1940; BA, UCLA, 1942, MA, 1943, PhD, 1945. Asst. prof. history Calif. Inst. Tech., Pasadena, 1945-53; assoc. prof. history Whittier (Calif.) Coll., 1953-56, prof., 1956-65; prof. Am. history U. So. Calif., L.A., 1965-91; chmn. dept. history U. So. Calif., 1974-76, dean social scis. and communication, 1976-82. Author: William Shirley: King's Governor of Massachusetts, 1961, Peter Oliver's Origin and Progress of the American Rebellion, 1967, The Promise of America, 1970, The American Republic, 1978, Dawning of America, 1981, Spur of Fame: Dialogues of John Adams and Benjamin Rush, 1980, A Noble Pursuit: A Sesquicentennial History of the New England Historic Genealogical Society, 1995, Legislators of the Massachusetts General Court, 1691-1780, 1997; joint editor: Golden State Series; contbg. author: Spain's Colonial Outpost, 1985, Generations and Change: Genealogical Perspectives in Social History, 1986, Making of America: Society and Culture of the United States, 1990, rev. edit., 1992. Trustee Citizens Rsch. Found., 1985—. NEH grantee, 1971; Sr. Faculty grantee, 1971-74. Mem. Am. Hist. Assn. (pres. Pacific Coast br. 1972-73, sec.-treas. 1995-96), Am. Studies Assn. (pres. 1974-75), Mass. Hist. Soc. (corr.), New Eng. Hist. Geneal. Soc. (trustee 1988—, editor, author intro. book Boston Merchant Census of 1789, 1989, rec. sec. 1995—), Colonial Soc. Mass. (corr.). Home and Office: 1100 White Knoll Dr Los Angeles CA 90012-1353 *The excitement of collegiate activities makes each year an adventure in learning and a renewal of one's youth.*

SCHUTZE, CHARLES R., lawyer; b. Osaka, Japan, Oct. 19, 1950; s. Alexander J. and Chieko (Teranishi) S.; m. Marsha Lynn Gutweiler, Sept. 25, 1992. BS, Fordham U., 1972; MBA, Iona Coll., 1980; JD, Pace U., 1987. Bar: Wis. 1990, Conn. 1988, U.S. Dist. Ct. (we. and ea. dists.) Wis. 1990, U.S. Ct. Appeals (7th cir.) 1991, U.S. Tax Ct. 1991, U.S. Dist. Ct. Conn. 1988, U.S. Supreme Ct. 1995. Staff acct. Peat, Marwick, Mitchell, White Plains, N.Y., 1972-73; acct. supervisor Dorr-Oliver Inc., Stamford, Conn., 1973-77; acctg. mgr. Arnold Bakers, Greenwich, Conn., 1977-79; dir. acctg. & taxes Howmet Turbin & Components, Greenwich, 1979-87; pvt. practice law Greenwich, Madison, 1987-90, 92—; atty. Stolper Koritzinsky Brewster, Madison, Wis., 1990-92. Mem. AICPA, ATLA, Nat. Assn. Accts. Avocation: computer programming. Office: 237 North St Madison WI 53704-4980

SCHUUR, DIANE JOAN, vocalist; b. Tacoma, Dec. 10, 1953; d. David Schuur. Ed. high sch., Vancouver, Wash. Albums include Pilot of My Destiny, 1983, Deedles, Schuur Thing, 1986, Timeless (Grammy award for female jazz vocal 1986), Diane Schuur and the Count Basie Orchestra (Grammy award for female jazz vocal 1987), Talkin' 'Bout You, 1988, Pure Schuur, 1991 (reached #1 on Billboard contemporary jazz chart, nominated for Grammy award 1991), In Tribute, 1992, Love Songs, 1993 (Grammy nomination, Best Traditional Vocal), 1993 (Grammy nomination, The Christmas Song), (with B.B. King) Heart to Heart, 1994 (entered at #1 on Billboard contemporary jazz chart), Love Walked In, 1996, Blues For Schuur, 1997; performed at the White House, Monterey Jazz Festival, Hollywood Bowl; toured Japan, Far East, South Am., Europe. *"There is no plateau that can't be reached, no obstacle that can't be overcome if you believe in yourself and your higher power".*

SCHUUR, ROBERT GEORGE, lawyer; b. Kalamazoo, Dec. 5, 1931; s. George Garrett and Louise Margaret (DeVries) S.; m. Susan Elizabeth White, Sept. 28, 1968; children—Arah Louise Adele, Jeremiah Donald Garrett. A.B., U. Mich., 1953, LL.B., 1955. Bar: Mich. 1955, N.Y. 1956. Assoc. Reid & Priest, N.Y.C., 1955-65, ptnr., 1966—. Served with USN, 1956-58. Mem. ABA, N.Y. State Bar Assn., Assn. of Bar of City of N.Y., Phi Beta Kappa. Club: University (N.Y.C.). Home: 163 E 82nd St New York NY 10028-1856 Office: Reid & Priest 40 W 57th St New York NY 10019-4001

SCHUYLER, DANIEL MERRICK, lawyer, educator; b. Oconomowoc, Wis., July 26, 1912; s. Daniel J. and Fannie Sybil (Moorhouse) S.; m. Claribel Seaman, June 15, 1935; children: Daniel M., Sheila Gordon. AB summa cum laude, Dartmouth Coll., 1934; JD, Northwestern U., 1937. Bar: Ill. 1937, U.S. Supreme Ct. 1942, Wis. 1943. Tchr. constl. history Chgo. Latin Sch., 1935-37; assoc. Schuyler & Hennessy (attys.), 1937-42, ptnr., 1946-48; ptnr. Schuyler, Richert & Stough, 1948-58, Schuyler, Stough & Morris, Chgo., 1958-76, Schuyler, Ballard & Cowen, 1976-83; ptnr. Schuyler, Roche & Zwirner, P.C., 1983-96, of counsel, 1996—; treas., sec. and controller B-W Superchargers, Inc. div. Borg-Warner Corp., Milw., 1942-46; lectr. trusts, real property, future interests Northwestern U. Sch. Law, 1946-50, asso. prof. law, 1950-52, prof., 1952-80, prof. emeritus, 1980—. Author: (with Homer F. Carey) Illinois Law of Future Interests, 1941; supplements, 1947, 54; (with William M. McGovern, Jr.) Illinois Trust and Will Manual, 1970; supplements, 1972, 74, 76, 77, 79, 80, 81, 82, 83, 84; contbr. to profl. jours. Rep. nominee for judge Cook County Cir. Ct., 1958; bd. dirs., life mem. United Cerebral Palsy Greater Chgo., Lawrence Hall Youth Svcs. Fellow Am. Bar Found.; mem. ABA (past mem. ho. of dels., past chmn. sect. real property, probate and trust law), Chgo. Estate Planning Coun. (past pres., Dist. Svc. award 1977), Am. Coll. Trust and Estate Counsel (past pres.), Chgo. Bar Assn. (past chmn. coms. on trust law and post-admission edn., past bd. mgrs.), Ill. Bar Assn. (past chmn. real estate and legal edn. sects., past bd. govs.), Wis. Bar Assn., Legal Club, Law Club, Univ. Club, Order of Coif, Phi Beta Kappa, Phi Kappa Psi. Home: 909 W Foster Ave Apt 403 Chicago IL 60640-2510 Office: Schuyler Roche & Zwirner PC 130 E Randolph St Ste 3800 Chicago IL 60601-6317

SCHUYLER, JANE, fine arts educator; b. Flushing, N.Y., Nov. 2, 1943; d. Frank James and Helen (Oberhofer) S. BA, Queens Coll., 1965; MA, Hunter Coll., 1967; PhD, Columbia U., 1972. Asst. prof. art history Montclair State Coll., Upper Montclair, N.J., 1970; assoc. prof. C.W. Post Coll., L.I. Univ., Greenvale, N.Y., 1971-73, adj. assoc. profl, 1977-78; coord. fine arts, asst. prof. York Coll., CUNY, Jamaica, 1973-77, 78-87, assoc. prof., 1988-92, prof. 1993-96, prof. emerita 1996—. Author: Florentine Busts: Sculpted Portraiture in the Fifteenth Century, 1976; contbr. articles to profl. jours. Mem. fine arts com. Internat. Women's Arts Festival, 1974-76; pres. United Cmty. Dems. of Jackson Heights, 1987-89. N.Y. Columbia U. summer travel and rsch. grantee, 1969; recipient PSC-CUNY Rsch. award, 1990-91. Mem. Coll. Art Assn., Nat. Trust for Hist. Preservation, Renaissance Soc. Am. Roman Catholic. Home: 35-37 78th St Jackson Heights NY 11372

SCHUYLER, ROBERT LEN, investment company executive; b. Burwell, Nebr., Mar. 4, 1936; s. Norman S. and Ilva M. (Hoppes) S.; m. Mary Carol Huston, June 13, 1958; children: Kylie Anne, Nina Leigh, Melynn Kae, Gwyer Lenn. BS, U. Nebr., 1958; MBA, Harvard U., 1960. Asst. to treas. Potlatch Forests, Inc., Lewiston, Idaho, 1962-64; dir. corp. planning Potlatch Forests, Inc., San Francisco, 1964-66; mgr. fin. analysis Weyerhaeuser Co., Tacoma, 1966-68; mgr. investment evaluation dept. Weyerhaeuser Co., 1968-70, v.p. fin. and planning, 1970-72, sr. v.p. fin. and planning, 1972-85, exec. v.p., chief fin. officer, 1985-91; mng. ptnr. Nisqually Ptnrs., Tacoma, 1991-95; chief exec. officer, bd. dirs. Grande Alberta Paper, Ltd., 1992—; past mem. nat. adv. bd. Chem. Bank, U. Wash. MBA program, coun. fin. exec. Conf. Bd., Pvt. Sector Coun., exec. com. Am. Paper Inst.; bd. dirs. Multicare Health Sys., Paragon Trade Brands Inc., One Sport, Inc. Vice chmn. Santa Fe County Bd. Econ. Advirs.; vice chmn. Santa Fe Bus. Incubators. Mem. Anglers Club, Sangre de Cristo Flyfishers, Las Campanas Golf & Country Club,. Home and Office: 46 Hollyhock Cir Santa Fe NM 87501-8595

SCHWAAB, RICHARD LEWIS, lawyer, educator; b. Oconomowoc, Wis., Nov. 15, 1945. s. Thomas L. and Phyllis N. (Lord) S.; m. Lynn Louise Howie; children: Amy, William, Andrew, Matthew. BSChemE, U. Wis., 1967; JD with honors, George Washington U., 1971, LLM in Internat. Law with highest honors, 1979. Bar: Va. 1971, U.S. Dist. Ct. (ea. dist.) Va. 1979, U.S. Supreme Ct. 1980, U.S. Ct. Appeals (fed. cir.) 1982. Ptnr., Stepno, Schwaab & Linn, Arlington, 1972-74, Bacon & Thomas, Arlington, 1974-78, Schwartz, Jeffery, Schwaab, Mack, Blumenthal & Evans, P.C., Alexandria, 1978-88; ptnr. in charge, chair dept. intellectual property Foley & Lardner, Washington, 1988—; lectr. law George Washington U., 1978-88, George Mason U., 1989—. Max Planck Inst. Fgn. and Internat. Patent, Copyright and Competition Law fellow, 1971-72. Mem. ABA, Am. Intellectual Property Law Assn., Va. State Bar (gov. 1974-78), Am. Soc. Internat. Law, Internat. Patent and Trademark Assn., Internat. Fedn. Indsl. Property Attys., Christian Legal Soc., Phi Kappa Phi, Tau Beta Pi. Co-author Patent Practice, 6 vols., 1976-95; International Patent Law: EPC & PCT, 3 vols., 1978; Intellectual Property Protection for Biotechnology Worldwide, 1987; contbr. articles to profl. jours. Home: 6326 Karmich St Fairfax VA 22039-1621 Office: Foley & Lardner 3000 K St NW Ste 500 Washington DC 20007-5109

SCHWAB, ARTHUR JAMES, lawyer; b. Pitts., Dec. 7, 1946; s. Earl Walter and Helen Alice (Gascoine) S.; m. Karen Jenny, Sept. 2, 1967; children: John Arthur, Ellen Katherine, David Earl. Student, Muskingum Coll., 1964-65; AB, Grove City Coll., 1968; JD, U. Va., 1972. Bar: Pa. 1972, N.J. 1985, U.S. Dist. Ct. (we. dist.) Pa. 1972, U.S. Dist. Ct. (ea dist.) Pa. 1978, U.S. Dist. Ct. (no. dist.) Ohio 1979, U.S. Dist. Ct. S.C. 1980, U.S. Dist. Ct. N.Mex. 1981, U.S. Dist. Ct. Mass. 1984, U.S. Dist. Ct. N.J. 1984, U.S. Ct. Appeals (3d cir.) 1972, U.S. Ct. Appeals (11th cir.) 1982, U.S. Ct. Appeals (4th cir.) 1982, U.S. Ct. Appeals (8th cir.) 1991, U.S. Ct. Appeals (9th cir.) 1995, U.S. Supreme Ct. 1975. Ptnr. Reed, Smith, Shaw and McClay, Pitts., 1973-90; ptnr., chair of litigation Buchanan Ingersoll, Pitts., 1990—. Mem. editorial bd. Va. Law Rev., Sch. Law U. Va., Charlottesville, 1972. Bd. dirs. Grove City (Pa.) Coll. Mem. Pa. Bar Assn. (sec. civil litigation sect.), Acad. Trial Lawyers Allegheny County (bd. dirs.), Allegheny County Bar Assn., (past pres. civil litigation sect.), Am. Inns of Ct. (pres.-elect Pitts. chpt.), Duquesne Club, Rivers Club. Republican. Presbyterian. Home: 3000 Old Orchard Ct Gibsonia PA 15044 Office: Buchanan Ingersoll One Oxford Ctr 301 Grant St Ste 20 Pittsburgh PA 15219-1408

SCHWAB, CHARLES R., brokerage house executive; b. Sacramento, 1937; m. Helen O'Neill; 5 children. Stanford U., 1959, Postgrad., 1961. Formerly mut. fund mgr. Marin County, Calif.; founder brokerage San Francisco, 1971; now chmn., CEO Charles Schwab & Co., Inc. Author: How to be Your Own Stockbroker, 1984. Republican. Office: Charles Schwab & Co Inc 101 Montgomery St San Francisco CA 94104-4122*

SCHWAB, EILEEN CAULFIELD, lawyer, educator; b. N.Y.C., Feb. 11, 1944; d. James Francis and Mary Alice (Fay) Caulfield; m. Terrance W. Schwab, Jan. 4, 1969; children: Matthew Caulfield, Catherine Grimley, Claire Gillespie. BA, Hunter Coll., 1965; JD, Columbia U., 1971; BA magna cum laude. Bar: N.Y. 1972, U.S. Dist. Ct. (so. and ea. dists.) N.Y. 1975, U.S. Ct. Appeals (2d cir.) 1975, U.S. Tax Ct. 1980, U.S. Ct. Appeals (10th cir.) 1993. Assoc. Poletti Friedin, N.Y.C., 1971-72, Hughes Hubbard & Reed, N.Y.C., 1972-75, Davis Polk & Wardwell, N.Y.C., 1975-81; dep. bur. chief Charities Bu., Atty. Gen. of N.Y., 1981-82; counsel Brown & Wood, N.Y.C., 1983—, ptnr., 1984; adj. prof. N.Y. Law Sch.; mediator atty. disciplinary com. first dept., N.Y. Co-chmn. gift planning adv. com. Archdiocese of N.Y.C.; dir. Cath. Found. for the Future, Cath. Communal Fund, Friends of Hunter Coll. Libr.; mem. profl. advisors coun. to Lincoln Ctr. Fellow Am. Coll. Trust and Estate Counsel; mem. N.Y. State Bar Assn., Assn. Bar City N.Y., Phi Beta Kappa. Democrat. Roman Catholic.

SCHWAB, FRANK, JR., management consultant; b. Brookline, Mass., Dec. 19, 1932; s. Frank Sr. and Phyllis (Robinson) F. BA, Rutgers U., 1952; MBA, Harvard Bus. Sch., 1956. Cert. mgmt. cons. Internal auditor Champion Paper, Inc., Hamilton, Ohio, 1956-57; mgmt. engr. Champion Paper, Inc., Pasadena, Tex., 1957-58; cons., assoc. Booz Allen & Hamilton, N.Y.C., 1958-65; dir. trans. planning Planning Rsch. Corp., L.A., 1965; pres., CEO F.R. Schwab & Assocs., N.Y.C., 1965-82; pres., co-CEO Fenvessy & Schwab, N.Y.C., 1982-87; pres., CEO Anderson & Schwab, N.Y.C., 1987—; bd. dirs. Sugarland Oil Corp., N.Y.C., mfrs. and svcs. divsn. Nat. Mining Assn., Washington; mem. adv. bd. GeoBiotics, Inc., Hayward, Calif. With Nat. Mining Hall of Fame & Mus., Leadville, Colo., 1992—. 1st lt., U.S. Army, 1952-54, Korea. Decorated Nat. Def. Svc. medal, Korean Svc. medal with bronze star, Commendation ribbon with medal pendant, UN Svc. medal. Mem. Inst. Mgmt. Cons. (pres. N.Y. chpt. 1975-77), Am. Arbitration Assn. (panel arbitrator), Mil. Order Fgn. Wars (vet. companion), Maidstone Club, Union Club, River Club, King Coal Clubs. Republican. Avocation: tennis. Office: Anderson & Schwab Inc 444 Madison Ave New York NY 10022-6903

SCHWAB, GEORGE DAVID, social science educator, author; b. Nov. 25, 1931; s. Arkady and Klara (Jacobson) S.; BA, City Coll. N.Y., 1954; MA, Columbia, 1955, PhD, 1968; m. Eleonora Storch, Feb. 27, 1965; children: Clarence Boris, Claude Arkady, Solan Bernhard. Lectr., Columbia Coll., N.Y.C., 1959; lectr. CUNY, 1960-68, asst. prof. history, 1968-72, assoc. prof. history, 1973-79, prof., 1980—. Mem. Columbia U. Seminar on the History of Legal and Polit. Thought and Institutions; dir. Conf. History and Politics, CUNY. Trustee, pres., mem. exec. com. Nat. Com. Am. Fgn. Policy. Mem. Am. Hist. Assn., Am. Polit. Sci. Assn. Author: Dayez: Beyond Abstract Art, 1967; Enemy oder Foe, 1968; Switzerland's Tactical Nuclear Weapons Policy, 1969; The Challenge of the Exception: An Introduction to the Political Ideas of Carl Schmitt, 1970, 2d edit., 89; Appeasement and Detente, 1975, 81; Carl Schmitt: Political Opportunist?, 1975; translator: The Concept of the Political with Comments by Leo Strauss (Carl Schmitt), 1976, 96; Legality and Illegality as Instruments of Revolutionaries in their Quest for Power: Remarks Occasioned by the Outlook of Herbert Marcuse, 1978; The German State in Historical Perspective, 1978; Ideology: Reality or Rhetoric?, 1978; Ideology and Foreign Policy, 1978, 81; The Decision: Is the American Sovereign at Bay?, 1978; State and Nation: Toward a Further Clarification, 1980; American Foreign Politics at the Crossroads, 1980; Carl Schmitt: Through a Glass Darkly, 1980; From Quantity and Heterogeneity to Quality and Homogeneity: Toward a New Foreign Policy, 1980; Toward an Open-Society Bloc, 1980; Eurocommunism: The Ideological and Political Theoretical Foundations, 1981; American Foreign Policy at the Crossroads, 1982; A Decade of the National Committee on American Foreign Policy, 1984; trans. Political Theology: Four Chapters on the Concept of Sovereignty (Carl Schmitt), 1985, 88; The Destruction of a Family, 1987; Elie Wiesel: Between Jerusalem and New York, 1990; The Broken Vow, the Good Obtained, 1991; Thoughts of a Collector, 1991; Carl Schmitt Hysteria in the United States, 1992; Contextualizing Carl Schmitt's Concept of Grossraum, 1994; (translation) The Leviathan in the State Theory of Thomas Hobbes (Carl Schmitt), 1996; editor Am. Fgn. Policy Interests; series Global Perspectives in History and Politics. Office: CUNY New York NY 10036

SCHWAB, GLENN ORVILLE, retired agricultural engineering educator, consultant; b. Gridley, Kans., Dec. 30, 1919; s. Edward and Lizzie (Sauder) S.; married; children: Richard, Lawrence,Mary Kay. BS, Kans. State. U., 1942; MS, Iowa State U., 1947, PhD, 1951; postdoctoral, Utah State U., 1966. Registered profl. engr., Ohio. Instr. to prof. agrl. engring. Iowa State U., Ames, 1947-56; prof. agrl. engring. Ohio State U., Columbus, 1956-85, ret., 1985; prof. emeritus Ohio State U., Columbus, Ohio, 1985—; cons. Powell, Ohio, 1985—; bd. dirs. Internat. Water Mgmt. Program, Columbus. Co-author: Soil and Water Conservation Engineering, 4th edit., 1993, Agricultural and Forest Hydrology, 1986, Soil and Water Management Systems, 4th edit., 1996; contbr. articles to profl. jours. Served to capt. U.S. Army, 1942-46. Fellow Am. Soc. Agrl. Engrs. (bd. dirs. soil and water div. 1976-78, Hancock Brick and Tile Drainage Engr. 1968, John Deere medal 1987), Am. Soc. Engrs. Edn., Am. Soc. Testing Materials, Soil and Water Conservation Soc. Am., Am. Geophysical Union, Internat. Commn. Irrigation and Drainage. Avocations: rock polishing, wood working, photography, traveling. Home: 2637 Summit View Rd Powell OH 43065-8879

SCHWAB, HAROLD LEE, lawyer; b. N.Y.C., Feb. 5, 1932; s. Harold Walter and Beatrice (Braverman) S.; m. Rowena Vivian Strauss, June 12, 1953; children: Andrew, Lisa, James. B.A., Harvard Coll., 1953; LL.B., Boston Coll., 1956. Bar: N.Y. 1957, U.S. Ct. Mil. Appeals 1958, U.S. Dist. Cts. (so. and ea. dist.) N.Y. 1967, U.S. Ct. Appeals (2d cir.) 1971, U.S. Supreme Ct. 1971, U.S. Dist. Ct. (no. dist.) N.Y. 1974, U.S. Ct. Appeals (D.C. cir.) 1986, U.S. Dist. Ct. (we. dist.) N.Y. 1988, U.S. Ct. Appeals (11th cir.) 1988, U.S. Ct. Appeals (5th cir.) 1991. Vice pres. H.W. Schwab Textile Corp., N.Y.C., 1959-60; assoc. Emile Z. Berman & A. Harold Frost, N.Y.C., 1960-67, ptnr., 1967-74; sr. ptnr. Lester Schwab Katz & Dwyer, N.Y.C., 1974—; lectr. N.Y. State Bar Assn., N.Y. County Lawyers Assn. Served to lt. col. USAFR. Fellow Internat. Acad. Trial Lawyers; mem. ABA, ASTM, Soc. Automotive Engrs., Assn. for Advancement of Automotive Medicine, Product Liability Adv. Council, N.Y. State Bar Assn. (chmn. trial Lawyers sect. 1980-81), Am. Bd. Trial Advs. (pres. N.Y. chpt. 1982-83), Fedn. Ins. and Corp. Counsel (v.p. 1979-80), Assn. of Bar of City of N.Y. N.Y. County Lawyers Assn., N.Y. State Trial Lawyers Assn., Def. Assn. N.Y., Harvard Club of N.Y., Drug and Chem. Club. Contbr. articles to legal jours.; editor Trial Lawyers Sect. Newsletter-N.Y. State Bar Assn., 1981-84; mem. editorial bd. Jour. Products and Toxics Liability, 1976-96. Home: 205 Beach # 142D St Neponsit NY 11694 Office: Lester Schwab Katz & Dwyer 120 Broadway New York NY 10271-0002

SCHWAB, HERMANN CASPAR, banker; b. N.Y.C., Jan. 8, 1920; s. Hermann Caspar and Ruth (Bliss) S.; m. C. Meteer Shanks, July 5, 1955; children: Henry R., Lesley Schwab Forman, Margery Schwab Weekes, Stuart Taylor, George Bliss, Katharine Lambard Schwab Kimmick. Grad., St. Marks Sch., 1937, Yale U., 1941. With Hanover Bank, 1941-44, 46-55, asst. sec., 1949-53, asst. v.p., 1953-55; ptnr. Dick & Merle Smith, 1956; v.p. Empire Trust Co., 1957-66, sr. v.p., 1965-66; with Bank N.Y., 1966-67; sr. v.p. Schroder Trust Co., N.Y.C., 1967-73, dir., 1970-73; pres., dir. Cheapside Dollar Fund Ltd., N.Y.C., 1970-88; sr. v.p. Schroder Capital Mgmt. Inc., N.Y.C., 1973-84, cons., 1984-88; chmn., dir. Schroder Capitol Funds Inc., 1988—. Mayor Oyster Bay Cove, N.Y., 1973-85, trustee, 1965—; trustee St. Lukes-Roosevelt Hosp. Ctr. 2d lt. inf., AUS, 1943-46. Mem. Piping Rock Club (Locust Valley, N.Y.). Home: 34 Northern Blvd Oyster Bay NY 11771-4105

SCHWAB, HOWARD JOEL, judge; b. Charleston, W.Va., Feb. 13, 1943; s. Joseph Simon and Gertrude (Hadas) S.; m. Michelle Roberts, July 4, 1970; children: Joshua Raphael, Bethany Alexis. BA in History with honors, UCLA, 1964, JD, 1967. Bar: Calif. 1968, U.S. Dist. Ct. (cen. dist.) Calif. 1968, U.S. Ct. Appeals (9th cir.) 1970, U.S. Supreme Ct. 1972. Clk. legal adminstrn. Litton Industries, L.A., 1967-68; dep. city atty. L.A., 1968-69; dep. atty. gen. State of Calif., L.A., 1969-84; judge Mcpl. Ct. L.A. Jud. Dist., 1984-85; judge Superior Ct. Superior Ct. L.A. County, L.A., 1985—; mem. faculty Berkeley (Calif.) Judicial Coll., 1987—. Contbr. articles to profl. jours. Recipient CDAA William E. James award Calif. Dist. Atty.'s Assn., 1981. Mem. San Fernando Valley Bar Assn., Inn. of Ct., Phi Alpha Delta. Democrat. Jewish. Avocations: history, book collecting. Office: LA Superior Ct 6230 Sylmar Ave Van Nuys CA 91401-2712

SCHWAB, JAMES CHARLES, urban planner; b. Oceanside, N.Y., Dec. 20, 1949; s. Charles Francis and Hazel Dorothy (Waters) S.; m. Jean Catlett, June 8, 1985; 1 child, Jessica. BA in Polit. Sci., Cleve. State U., 1973; MA in Urban & Regional Planning, U. Iowa, 1985, MA in Journalism, 1985. Purchasing agt. Kaufman Container Co., Cleve., 1973-75; rsch. assoc. No. Ohio Project on Nat. Priorities, Cleve., 1975-76; sales rep. Met. Life Ins. Co., Willoughby Hills, Ohio, 1976-78; exec. dir. Iowa Pub. Interest Rsch. Group, Iowa City, 1979-81; rsch. asst. Legis. Extended Assistance Group, Iowa City, 1982-85; asst. editor Am. Planning Assn., Chgo., 1985-90, sr. rsch. assoc., 1990—. Author: Raising Less Corn and More Hell, 1988, Industrial Performance Standards for a New Century, 1993, Deeper Shades of Green, 1994; author, prin. investigator: Planning for Post-Disaster Recovery and Reconstruction, 1997; editor Zoning News, 1990—, Environment and Devel., 1992-96; contbr. articles to profl. publs. Chmn. Environ. Concerns Working Group, Met. Chgo. synod Evang. Luth. Ch. Am., 1989—; chmn. Task Force on Care of Creation, Region 5, Dubuque, Iowa, 1992-93; mem. ch. coun. Augustana Luth. Ch., Chgo., 1990-93. Mem. Soc. Midland Authors (bd. dirs., newsletter editor 1990-95, membership sec. 1995—, chmn. biography awards 1995-96, pres. 1997—), Soc. Environ. Journalists, Soc. Profl. Journalists, Investigative Reporters and Editors, Am. Planning Assn., Am. Inst. Cert. Planners. Lutheran. Avocations: travel, reading history, health club workouts, ethnic restaurants. Home: 1755 N Campbell Ave Chicago IL 60647-5205 Office: Am Planning Assn 122 S Michigan Ave Ste 1600 Chicago IL 60603-6107

SCHWAB, JOHN HARRIS, microbiology and immunology educator; b. St. Cloud, Minn., Nov. 20, 1927; s. John David and Katherine (Harris) S.; m. Ruth Ann Graves, Sept. 1, 1951; children: Stewart, Thomas, Anna, Kellogg. BS, U. Minn., 1949, MS, 1950, PhD, 1953. Asst. prof. U. N.C., Chapel Hill, 1953-67, prof., 1967—; Cary C. Boshamer prof., 1982—; scientist Lister Inst. Preventive Medicine, London, 1960, MRC Rheumatism Rsch, Unit, Taplow, England, 1968, Radiobiol. Inst., Rijswijk, The Netherlands, 1975, Pasteur Inst., Paris, 1985. Contbr. articles to profl. jours. and chpts. to books. Recipient Faculty Scholar award Josiah Macy Jr. Found., 1975; NIH Spl. fellow, 1960, 68; Fogarty Internat. fellow NIH, Paris, 1985. Mem. Am. Soc. Mibrobiology (editor Infection and Immunity jour. 1980-85), Am. Assn. Immunologists, AAAS.

SCHWAB, JOHN JOSEPH, psychiatrist, educator; b. Cumberland, Md., Feb. 10, 1923; s. Joseph L. and Eleanor (Cadden) S.; m. Ruby Baxter, Aug. 4, 1945; 1 dau., Mary Eleanor. BS, U. Ky., 1946; MD, U. Louisville, 1946; MS in Physiology (Med. fellow), U. Ill., 1949; postgrad., Duke U., 1951-52, U. Fla., 1959-61. Diplomate: Nat. Bd. Med. Examiners. Intern Phila. Gen. Hosp., 1947-48; resident medicine Louisville Gen. Hosp., 1949-50; edn. officer med. coll. U. Yokohama, 1952-54; internist, psychosomaticist Holzer Clinic, Gallipolis, Ohio, 1954-59; resident psychiatry U. Fla. Hosp., 1959-61; NIMH Career tchr. U. Fla., Gainesville, 1962-64, mem. faculty, 1961-73, prof. psychiatry and medicine, 1967-73, dir. cons. liaison program, 1964-67, resident tng. dir., 1965-71; prin. investigator Fla. Health Study, 1969-74; prof., chmn. dept. psychiatry and behavioral scis. Sch. Medicine U. Louisville, 1973-91, prof. psychiatry, 1991-93, prof. emeritus, 1993—, assoc. dir. clin. psychopharm. rsch., 1991—; chmn. epidemiologic studies rev. com. Ctr. for Epidemiologic Studies, NIMH, 1973-75, cons. psychiatry br., 1975-92; cons. Old Order Amish Study of Depression, 1978—; vol. vis. lectr. Howard U., 1992; ann. vis. lectr. U. Wurzburg, Germany, hon. faculty, 1992—; vis. prof. El-Azar U., Cairo, 1991; prin. investigator LSVL Family Health Study, 1982—. Author: Handbook of Psychiatric Consultation, 1968; also articles; co-author: Sociocultural Roots of Mental Illness: An Epidemiologic Survey, 1978, Social Order and Mental Health, 1979; first author: Family Mental Health, 1993; assoc. editor Psychosomatics, 1965-86; co-editor: Man for Humanity: On Concordance V. Discord in Human Behavior, 1972, Social Psychiatry, vol. l, 1974, The Psychiatric Examination, 1974, 1st Annual Family Mental Health History, Epidem, Clinical Perspectives, 1993; co-edited 9 books, 11 Monograph, and over 250 articles. Capt. USAMC, 1949-54. Fellow Am. Coll. Psychiatrists (regent 1977-79), Collegium Internat. Neuro-Psychopharmacologicum, World Assn. Social Psychiatry, AAAS, Am. Psychiat. Assn. (chmn. council research and devel. 1974-75); mem. AMA, Acad. Psychosomatic Medicine (exec. 1965-72, pres. 1970-71), Group for Advancement Psychiatry (bd. dirs. 1985-87), So. Assn., Jefferson County Med. Soc., Ky. Psychiat. Assn., Am. Assn. Social Psychiatry (pres. 1971-73), Alpha Omega Alpha (Outstanding Performance award for Affirmative Action U. Louisville 1986), World Assn. Soc. Psychiatry (internat. adv. com., Rome, 1991), Psychiatrists for Better Psychiat. (pres. 1990—), U. of the World (co-chair health, edn. com. 1992—). Research on applicability of psychiatric concepts to general medicine, sociocultural aspects of mental illness; establishing guidelines for identification and management of medical patients whose illnesses are complicated by emotional stress; epidemiology of mental illness; depression and the family; clinical psychopharmacology, historical and epidemiologic perspectives on the family. Home: 6217 Innes Trace Rd Louisville KY 40222-6008

SCHWAB, KENNETH LYNN, college president; b. Wolcott, Ind., Feb. 5, 1947; m. Patrician N. Schwab; children: Kempten, Carlton, Christopher. BS, Purdue U., 1969; MEd, U. N.C., 1972; EdD, Ind. U., 1978. Spl. edn. tchr. Defiance (Ohio) City Schs., 1969-70; asst. dean students Guilford Coll., Greensboro, N.C., 1970-74, dean of students, 1974-86, asst. to pres. for instnl. planning, 1980-86; sr. v.p. for instnl. planning, 1986-88; exec. v.p. for adminstrn. U. S.C., Columbia, 1988-91; pres., CEO Centenary

Coll. La., Shreveport, 1991—. Fellow Am. Coun. on Edn. Office: Centenary College of La PO Box 41188 Shreveport LA 71134-1188

SCHWAB, PAUL JOSIAH, psychiatrist, educator; b. Waxahachie, Tex., Jan. 14, 1932; s. Paul Josiah and Anna Marie (Baeuerle) S.; m. Martha Anne Beed, June 8, 1953; children: Paul Josiah III, John Conrad, Mark Whitney. BA, N. Cen. Coll., 1953; MD, Baylor U., 1957. Diplomate Am. Bd. Psychiatry and Neurology. Intern Phila. Gen. Hosp., 1957-58; clin. assoc. Nat. Cancer Inst., Bethesda, Md., 1958-60; resident in internal medicine U. Chgo., 1960-62, resident psychiatry, 1962-65, chief resident and instr. psychiatry, 1965; pvt. practice Naperville, Ill., 1965—; lectr. psychiatry U. Chgo., 1968-74, assoc. prof., 1974-79; clin. assoc., 1979-86, clin. assoc. prof., 1986—; dir. residency tng. U. Chgo., 1976-79, dir. in-patient unit and day treatment program, 1975-79. Contbr. articles to profl. jours. Bd. trustees North Ctrl. Coll., chair liaison com., 1983—, vice-chmn. acad. and student affairs com., 1983-92, vice chair admissions, fin. aid and student devel., 1992-95; pres. North Ctrl. Coll. Alumni Assn., 1979-80. Recipient Outstanding Alumnus, North Ctrl. Coll., 1983. Fellow Am. Psychiat. Assn. (life, Nancy C.A. Roeske award 1991); mem. AMA, Am. Soc. Clin. Psychopharmacology, Acad. Clin. Psychiatrists, Alpha Omega Alpha. Democrat. Methodist. Office: 1200 Tall Oaks Ct Naperville IL 60540-9494

SCHWAB, SUSAN CARROLL, university dean. BA in Polit. Economy, Williams Coll., 1976; MA in Applied Econs., Stanford U., 1977; PhD in Pub. Adminstrn., George Washington U., 1993. U.S. trade negotiator Office of Pres.'s Spl. Trade Rep., Washington, 1977-79; trade policy officer U.S. Embassy, Tokyo, 1980-81; chief economist, legis. asst. for internat. trade for Senator John C. Danforth, 1981-86, legis. dir., until 1989; asst. sec. commerce, dir. gen. U.S. and Fgn. Comml. Svc. Dept. Commerce, 1989-93; with corp. strategy office Motorola, Inc., Schaumburg, Ill., 1993-95; dean U. Md. Sch. Pub. Affairs, College Park, 1995—. Office: U Md Sch Pub Affairs College Park MD 20742

SCHWAB, TERRANCE WALTER, lawyer; b. Pitts., May 19, 1940; m. Eileen Caulfield, Jan. 4, 1969; children: Matthew Caulfield, Catherine Grimley, Claire Gillespie. BA magna cum laude, Harvard U., 1962; LLB cum laude, Columbia U., 1966. Assoc. Milbank, Tweed, Hadley & McCloy, N.Y.C., 1966-70; assoc. Kelley, Drye & Warren, N.Y.C., 1970-74, ptnr., 1975-96; sr. v.p., gen. counsel internat. dept. The Sanwa Bank Ltd., N.Y.C., 1996—; lectr. various profl. orgns. Assoc. editor: Law Practice of Alexander Hamilton, 1964-1980; contbr. articles to profl. jours. Trustee, chmn. St. Luke's Chamber Ensemble, N.Y.C., 1980-82; trustee, sec. Caramoor Ctr. for Music and Arts, Katonah, N.Y., 1971—; trustee Sch. of Convent of Sacred Heart, N.Y.C., 1987—, chmn., 1990-93. Mem. ABA, N.Y. State Bar Assn., Assn. of Bar of City of N.Y., Harvard Club, Deutscher Verein, Swiss Soc. N.Y. Office: The Sanwa Bank Ltd 55 E 52nd St New York NY 10055-0002

SCHWABE, ARTHUR DAVID, physician, educator; b. Varel, Germany, Feb. 1, 1924; came to U.S., 1938, naturalized, 1943; s. Curt and Frieda (Roseno) S. M.D., U. Chgo., 1956. Intern UCLA Med. Center, 1956-57, asst. resident, then assoc. resident medicine, 1957-59, chief resident medicine, 1960-61, USPHS fellow gastroenterology, 1959-60; now mem. staff; chief gastroenterology Harbor Gen. Hosp., Torrance, Calif., 1962-67; cons. Wadsworth VA Center, Los Angeles; mem. faculty UCLA Med. Sch., 1961—, asst. prof. medicine, 1962-67, assoc. prof., 1967-71, prof., 1971-89, chief div. gastroenterology, 1967-88, vice chmn. dept. medicine, 1971-74, emeritus prof., 1989—. Contbr. articles to profl. jours. Served with AUS, 1943-46. Recipient UCLA Golden Apple award sr. class UCLA, 1967, 70, Outstanding Tchr. award UCLA Med. House Staff, 1968, 78, Disting. Teaching award UCLA, 1971, S.M. Mellinkoff Faculty award, 1983; Edward F. Kraft scholar, 1951; Ambrose and Gladys Bowyer fellow medicine, 1958-59. Fellow ACP; mem. Am. Gastroenterol. Assn., N.Y. Acad. Sci., So. Calif. Soc. Gastroenterology (pres. 1969), Western Assn. Physicians, Western Soc. Clin. Investigation, Western Gut Club (chmn. 1969-70), Alpha Omega Alpha. Office: 10833 Le Conte Ave Los Angeles CA 90095-3075

SCHWABE, CALVIN WALTER, veterinarian, medical historian, medical educator; b. Newark, Mar. 15, 1927; s. Calvin Walter and Marie Catherine (Hassfeld) S.; m. Gwendolyn Joyce Thompson, June 7, 1951; children: Catherine Marie, Christopher Lawrence. BS, Va. Poly. Inst., 1948; MS, U. Hawaii, 1950; DVM, Auburn U., 1954; MPH, Harvard U., 1955, ScD, 1956. Diplomate Am. Coll. Vet. Preventive Medicine. From assoc. prof. to prof. parasitology and epidemiology, chmn. dept. tropical health, and asst. dir. Sch. Pub. Health, Am. U. Beirut, 1956-66; mem. Secretariat of WHO, Geneva, 1964-66; prof. epidemiology Sch. Vet. Medicine, also Sch. Medicine, U. Calif., Davis, 1966-91, chmn. dept. epidemiology and preventive medicine, 1966-70; assoc. dean Sch. Vet. Medicine, U. Calif., Davis, 1970-71, adj. prof. Agrl. History Ctr., 1984-91, prof. emeritus, 1991—; cons. Futurevet Assocs., Davis and Pedreguer,, Spain, 1991—; cons. WHO, UN Environ. Program, FAO, NIH, Pan Am. Health Orgn., UNICEF, Nat. Rsch. Coun.; univ. lectr. U. Sask.; Fulbright vis. prof. Univ. Coll. East Africa, Cambridge (Eng.) U., U. Khartoum; Srinivasan Meml. lectr. U. Madras; Spink lectr. comparative medicine U. Minn.; Franklin lectr. scis. and humanities Auburn U.; Entwhistle lectr. Cambridge U.; Schofield lectr. U. Guelph; mem. Am. Rsch. Ctr. Egypt. Author: Veterinary Medicine and Human Health, 1969, 84, What Should a Veterinarian Do?, 1972, Epidemiology in Veterinary Practice, 1977, Cattle, Priests and Progress in Medicine, 1978, Unmentionable Cuisine, 1980, Development Among Africa's Migratory Pastoralists, 1996; also articles. Recipient Karl F. Meyer Gold Headed Cane award Am. Vet. Epidemiology Assn., 1985, Disting. Alumnus award Auburn U., 1992. Fellow Am. Pub. Health Assn. (governing coun. 1974-76); mem. AVMA, Am. Soc. Tropical Medicine and Hygiene, History of Sci. Soc., Sudan Studies Assn. Democrat. Mem. Soc. of Friends. Avocations: collecting musical instruments, cooking, raising bamboos. Home (winter): 849 A St Davis CA 95616-1916 Home (summer): Apartado 90, Pedreguer Alicante 03750, Spain

SCHWABE, JOHN BENNETT, II, lawyer; b. Columbia, Mo., June 14, 1946; s. Leonard Wesley and Hazel Fern (Crouch) S. A.B., U. Mo.-Columbia, 1967, J.D., 1970. Bar: Mo. 1970, U.S. Dist. Ct. (we. dist.) Mo. 1970, U.S. Ct. Mil. Appeals 1971, U.S. Supreme Ct. 1973. Owner, prin. John B. Schwabe, II Law Firm, Columbia, 1974—, St. Louis, 1984—. Trustee, lay leader, mem. adminstrv. bd. Wilkes Blvd. United Meth. Ch., 1974-79, chmn. pastor-parish relations com., 1984-85 ; mem. Friends of Music, Columbia, 1979—, bd. dirs., 1979-81; bd. dirs. Mo. Symphony Soc., 1984-85 . Served to capt. JAGC, USAF, 1970-74. Mem. ABA, Boone County Bar Assn. (sec. 1977-79), Bar Assn. Met. St. Louis, Assn. Trial Lawyers Am., Mo. Assn. Trial Attys., Personal Injury Lawyers Assn., Lawyers Assn. St. Louis, Columbia C. of C., Am. Legion, Phi Delta Phi. Methodist. Club: Wilkes Men's (pres. 1977-79) (Columbia). Office: John B Schwabe II Law Firm Locust Bldg 1015 Locust St Ste 900 Saint Louis MO 63101-1323

SCHWALBE, MARY ANNE, nonprofit committee executive; b. N.Y.C., Mar. 31, 1934; d. James Alfred Goldsmith and Emily (Goetz) Buck; m. Douglas Schwalbe, Dec. 5, 1959; children: Douglas, William, Nina. BA, Radcliffe Coll., 1955; cert., London Acad. Music & Dramatic Art, 1956. Asst. dir. Theatre Comm. Group, N.Y.C., 1962-65; dir. admissions Radcliffe Coll., Cambridge, Mass., 1971-75; asst. dean admissions Harvard/Radcliffe, Cambridge, 1975-79; dir. coll. counseling Dalton Sch., N.Y.C., 1979-85; head upper sch. Nightingale-Bamford Sch., N.Y.C., 1985-90; staff dir. Women's Commn., N.Y.C., 1990-94; staff liaison Internat. Rescue Com., N.Y.C., 1994—; chair adv. bd. Refugee Women Coun., N.Y.C., 1995—. Elder Madison Ave. Presbyn. Ch., N.Y.C., 1985—; bd. dirs. Marymount Manhattan Coll., N.Y.C., 1991—, Searac, Washington, 1992—, Brearley Sch., N.Y.C., 1994—. Recipient Gayle Wilson award Nat. Assn. Coll. Admissions Counselors, 1985, Harvard U. Alumni award, 1993, Leadership award Marymount Manhattan Coll., 1995. Office: Internat Rescue Com 122 E 42nd St New York NY 10168-0002

SCHWALM, FRITZ EKKEHARDT, biology educator; b. Arolsen, Hesse, Germany, Feb. 17, 1936; came to U.S., 1968; s. Fritz Heinrich and Elisabeth Agnes (Wirth) S.; m. Renate Gertrud Streichhahn, Feb. 10, 1962; children—Anneliese, Fritz-Uwe, Karen. PhD, Philipps U., Germany, 1964; Staatsexamen, Philipps U., 1965. Educator boarding sch., Kiel, Fed. Republic Germany, 1956-57; lectr. Folk Universitetet, Stockholm, Sweden, 1959-60; research assoc. U. Witwatersrand, Johannesburg, South Africa, 1966-67, U. Notre Dame, South Bend, Ind., 1968-70; asst. prof., then assoc. prof. Ill. State U., Normal, Ill., 1970-82; assoc. prof. biology, then prof., chair dept. Tex. Woman's U., Denton, 1982—, dir. Animal Care Facility, 1990—, chmn. pro tem grad. coun., 1991-92; coord., chmn. S.W. Conf. for Devel. Biology, Denton, 1985, 90, 96. Author: (monograph) Insect Morphogenesis, 1988; mem. editl. bd. Palmer Jour. Rsch.; contbr. articles to profl. jours. Vice pres. PTA, Normal, 1975. Fellow Anglo-Am. Corp. South Africa, 1966, 67; NATO advanced research fellow, Freiburg, Fed. Republic Germany 1977. Mem. Soc. for Integrative and Comparative Biology, Deutsche Zoologische Gesellschaft, Soc. for Devel. Biology, Phi Kappa Phi (chpt. pres. 1993-96). Home: 1116 Linden Dr Denton TX 76201-2721 Office: Tex Woman's U Biology Sci Rsch Lab Denton TX 76204

SCHWAM, MARVIN ALBERT, graphic design company executive; b. Newark, Apr. 18, 1942; s. Meyer and Fannie (Lerman) S.; m. Jeanette Fein, June 13, 1964; children: Frederic, Matthew. BFA, Cooper Union, 1964. Staff artist Doremus & Co., 1964-66; mgr. Flowerental Corp., N.Y.C., 1966-68; pres. M. Schwam Floralart, N.Y.C., 1968-75; exec. v.p., bd. chmn. Florenco Foliage Systems Corp., N.Y.C., 1975-88; pres. Am. Christmas Decorating Service Inc., N.Y.C.; chmn. bd. Am. Christmas Decorations, Ltd., 1989—; pres. Marc Shaw Graphics, Inc., N.Y.C., Florenco Graphics Systems, Inc.; exec. v.p. Display Arts Worldwide, 1975-88; pres. Creative Animations, Inc., 1988-90; creative dir., v.p. Rennoc Animations, Inc., 1988-90; pres. Almar Communications, Ltd., 1990—, Sayso Communications, Ltd., 1990—, Gay Entertainment TV, Inc., 1992—. Industry chmn. March of Dimes, 1975-78, pres. bd. dirs. Happi Found. for Autistic People, N.Y.C.; trustee Nat. Found. Jewish Genetic Diseases; patron Young Adult Inst. and Workshop, Inc.; co-chmn. restaurant, hotel and entertainment industry luncheon Boy Scouts Am., 1988—; chmn. benefit com. Plan Internat. USA, 1991-92. Recipient award of merit for service to Gen. Motors Corp., 1978, award for Highlight of Christmas, Citibank/Citicorp Center, 1978, Disting. Service award Coler Hosp., 1982-86, Sr. Citizens of Roosevelt Island. Mem. Mcpl. Art Soc. N.Y., Am. Mus. Natural History, Alumni Assn. Cooper Union (2d Century Soc. fellow), Internat. Platform Assn. Designer largest artificial Christmas tree in U.S., Radio City Music Hall, N.Y.C., 1979; decorator Pulitzer Fountain, N.Y.C., 1979-80 Christmas season; chief designer Town Sq., New Orleans, Christmas, 1981, Albany (N.Y.) Tricentennial, 1986; interior landscape designer La. State Pavillion World's Fair, New Orleans, 1984; co-chmn. Nat. Restaurant, Hotel and Entertainment Industry Luncheon, N.Y.C., 1988—. Home: 7 E 17th St New York NY 10003-1913 Office: Am Christmas Decorations Inc 280 E 134th St Bronx NY 10454-4407

SCHWAN, ALFRED, food products executive. Pres., CEO Schwan Sales Enterprises, Inc., Marshall, Minn., 1965—. Office: Schwan Sales Enterprises 115 W College Dr Marshall MN 56258-1747*

SCHWAN, HERMAN PAUL, electrical engineering and physical science educator, research scientist; b. Aachen, Germany, Aug. 7, 1915; came to U.S., 1947, naturalized, 1952; s. Wilhelm and Meta (Pattberg) S.; m. Anne Marie DelBorello, June 15, 1949; children: Barbara, Margaret, Steven, Carol, Cathryn. Student, U. Goettingen, 1934-37; PhD, U. Frankfurt, 1940; Habilitation in physics and biophysics, 1946; DSc (hon.), U. Pa., 1986. Rsch. scientist, prof. Kaiser Wilhelm Inst. Biophysics, 1937-47, asst. dir., 1945-47; rsch. scientist USN, 1947-50; prof. elec. engring., prof. elec. engring. in phys. medicine, assoc. prof. phys. medicine U. Pa., Phila., 1950-83, Alfed F. Moore prof. emeritus, 1983—; dir. electromed. divsn. U. Pa., 1952-73, chmn. biomed. engring., 1961-73, program dir. biomed. engr. tng. program, 1960-77; vis. prof. U. Calif., Berkeley, 1956, U. Frankfurt, Germany, 1962, U. Würzburg, Germany, 1986-87; lectr. Johns Hopkins U., 1962-67, Drexel U., Phila., 1983-90; W.W. Clyde vis. prof. U. Utah, Salt Lake City, 1980; 10th Lauristan Taylor lectr. Nat. Council Radiation Protection and Measurements, 1986; Fgn. sci. mem. Max Planck Inst. Biophysics, Germany, 1962—; cons. NIH, 1962-90; chmn. nat. and internat. meetings biomed. engring. and biophysics, 1959, 61, 65; mem. nat. adv. council environ. health HEW, 1969-71; mem. coms. NAS-NRC, 1968-87. Co-author: Advances in Medical and Biological Physics, 1957, Therapeutic Heat, 1958, Physical Techniques in Medicine and Biology, 1963; editor: Biol. Engring, 1969; co-editor: Interactions Between Electromagnetic Fields and Cells, 1985; mem. editorial bd. Environ. Biophysics, IEEE Transactions Med. Biol. Engring., Jour. Phys. Med. Biol., Nonionizing Radiation, Bioelectromagnetics; contbr. articles to profl. jours. Recipient Citizenship award Phila., 1952, 1st prize AIEE, 1953, Achievement award Phila. Inst. Radio Engring., 1963, Rajewsky prize for biophysics, 1974, U.S. sr. scientist award Alexander von Humboldt Found., 1980-81, Biomed. Engring. Edn. award Am. Soc. Engring. Edn., 1983, d'Arsonval award Bioelectromagnetics Soc., 1985. Fellow IEEE (Morlock award 1967, Edison medal 1983, Centennial award 1984, Phila. Sect. award 1991, chmn. and vice chmn. nat. profl. group biomed. engring. 1955, 62-68), AAAS, Am. Inst. Med. and Biol. Engring.; mem. NAE, Am. Standards Assn. (chmn. 1961-65), Biophys. Soc. (publicity com., council, constn. com.), German Biophys. Soc. (hon.), Soc. for Cryobiology, Nordic (Scandinavian) Bioimpedance Club (hon.), Internat. Fedn. Med., and Biol. Engring., Bioelectromagnetics Soc., Biomed. Engring. Soc. (founder, dir. 1968-71), Sigma Xi, Eta Kappa Nu. Achievements include discovery of counterion relaxation; dielectric spectroscopy of cells and tissues; nonlinearity law of electrode polarization; research on nonionizing radiation biophysics; fundamentals electromagnetic bioengineering; first standard for safe exposure to electrical fields; development of biomedical engineering and education. Home: 99 Kynlyn Rd Wayne PA 19087-2849 also: 162 59th St Avalon NJ 08202-1207 Office: U Pa Dept Bioengring D2 Hayden Hall Philadelphia PA 19104

SCHWAN, LEROY BERNARD, artist, retired educator; b. Somerset, Wis., Dec. 8, 1932; s. Joseph L. and Dorothy (Papenfuss) S.; student Wis. State U., River Falls, 1951-53, Southeastern Signal Sch., Ga., 1954; children from previous marriage: David A., Mark J., William R., Catherine L., Maria E. BS, U. Minn., 1958, MEd, 1960, postgrad., 1961-64; postgrad. No. Mich. U., 1965, Tex. Tech. U., 1970, So. Ill. U., 1978, U. Iowa, 1980, EdD (hon.), 1988. Head art dept. Unity Pub. Schs., Milltown, Wis., 1958-61; instr. art Fridley Pub. Schs., Mpls., 1961-64; asst. prof. art No. Mich. U., Marquette, 1964-66; asst. prof. art Mankato (Minn.) State Coll., 1966-71, assoc. prof., 1971-74, tchr. off-campus grad. classes Northeast Mo. State U., John Wood Community Coll.; dir. Art Workshop Educultural Center, 1968; dir. art edn. Quincy (Ill.) Pub. Schs., 1974-78, art tchr., 1978-88, ret. 1988; tchr. art to mentally retarded children, Faribault, Minn., Owatonna, Minn., Mankato, Lake Owasso Children's Home, St. Paul; dir. art workshops, Mankato, 1970, St. Paul, 1972, 73, 74, 75; dir. workshops tchrs. mentally retarded Mankato, 1971, Faribault, 1972, Omaha, 1972-73, Quincy, 1974, 79, 82, 84-86, asst. adj. Ill. VA Home, 1980—; one-man shows: Estherville Jr. Coll., 1968, Mankato State Coll., 1968, 71, 73,97, Farmington, Wis., 1970, 71, 91, Good Thunder, Minn., 1972, Quincy, 1975, 77, 84, Mankato, Minn., 1975, Western Ill. U., 1979, St. Croix River Valley Arts Coun. Gallery, Osceola, Wis., 1993, 94, 95, 96, The Northern Ctr. for the Arts, Amery, Wis., 1994; exhibited in group shows: Pentagon, Washington, 1955, U. Minn., 1958, No. Mich. U., 1965, St. Cloud State Coll., 1967, Moorhead State Coll., 1967, Bemidji (Minn.) State Coll., 1967, MacNider Mus., Mason City, Iowa, 1969, 72, 73, 74, Gallery 500, Mankato, Minn., 1970, Rochester, Minn., 1972, Minn. Mus., St. Paul, 1973, Hannibal, Mo., 1976, 77-78, Quincy, Ill., 1976, 77, 85, Ill. Art Educators Show, 1984-85, Tchrs. Retirement Art Show, Springfield, Ill., 1987, Phipps Ctr. Arts, Hudson, Wis., 1997; producer ednl. TV series, 1964-65, also 2 shows Kids Komments, Sta. WGEM, Quincy; mural commd. Gem City Coll., 1977. Webelos leader Twin Valley council Boy Scouts Am., 1968-69. Bd. dirs. Polk County Hist. Soc., 1993—. Served with Signal Corps, AUS, 1954-56. Recipient cert. of accomplishment Sec. Army, 1955, Golden Poet award, 1985, 86, 88, 90, 91, Silver Poet award 1989. Mem. Nat. Art Edn. Assn., Ill. Art Edn. Assn., Cath. Order Foresters, Am. Legion, Phi Delta Kappa. Author: Art Curriculum Guide Unity Public Schs., 1961; Portrait of Jean, 1974; Schwan's Art Activities, 1984, Poems of Life, 1995; co-author: Bryant-Schwan Design Test, 1971, Bryant-Schwan Art Guide, 1973; contbr. articles to profl. jours., poems to Am. Poetry Assn. publs., 1984-94, Nat. Libr. Poetry publs., 1991-96. Home: 849 County Road H New Richmond WI 54017-6209

SCHWANAUER, FRANCIS, philosopher, educator; b. Zsámbék, Hungary, Jan. 20, 1933; came to U.S., 1959; s. Georg and Maria (Keller) S.; m. Johanna Maria Koelln, Sept. 29, 1957; children: Stephan Michael, Miriam Frances. Maturum, Ulrich von Hutten Gymnasium, Korntal, Germany, 1954; PhD, U. Stuttgart, Germany, 1959. Asst. prof. Lebanon Valley Coll., Annville, Pa., 1960-62, U. Maine, Orono, 1962-65; asst. prof. U. So. Maine, Portland Gorham, 1965-67, assoc. prof., 1967-72, prof., 1972—. Author: Truth is a Neighborhood with Nothing in Between, 1977, Those Fallacies by Slight of Reason, 1978, No Many is not a One (For the Case is Comparison), 1981, The Flesh of Thought is Pleasure or Pain, 1982, To Make Sure is to Cohere, 1982, Philosophical Fact and Paradox, 1987, Fables from the Fox, 1991. Grantee John Anson Kittredge Ednl. Fund, 1991, 93. Mem. New England Philos. Assn., Internat. Platform Assn. Democrat. Roman Catholic. Avocation: fishing. Home: 4 Woodmont St Portland ME 04102-2709

SCHWANDA, TOM, religious studies educator; b. E. Stroudsburg, Pa., Oct. 23, 1950; s. Theodore Frank and Madlyn Betty (Backensto) S.; m. Grace Elaine Dunning, July 30, 1977; children: Rebecca Joy, Stephen Andrew. Student, Worcester Polytechnic Inst., 1968-69; BA in Econ., Moravian Coll., 1969-72; student, Gordon-Conwell Sem., 1972-74; MDiv, New Brunswick Sem., 1975; DMin, Fuller Theol. Sem., 1992. Ordained to ministry Reformed Ch. in Am., 1975. Pastor Wanaque (N.J.) Reformed Ch., 1975-87; pastor congl. care Immanuel Reformed Ch., Grand Rapids, Mich., 1987-92; interim sr. pastor Remembrance Reformed Ch., Grand Rapids, 1992-93; rsch. fellow H. Henry Meeter Ctr. for Calvin Studies Calvin Coll., Grand Rapids, 1993-95; instr. spirituality and worship Bethlehem Ctr. for Spirituality, Grand Rapids, 1993—; dir. Reformed Spirituality Network, Grand Rapids, 1992—; assoc. for family ministry and spiritual formation Reformed Ch. in Am., 1995—; organizer, convener Gathering Reformed Spirituality, 1993, 94, 95, 97; chair spirituality com. Synod of Great Lakes, 1989—, mem. Christian discipleship com., 1988-94; mem. ch. life, evangelism, missions com. South Grand Rapids Classics, chair, 1992; mem. commn. on worship Reformed Ch. in Am., 1978-94; mem. care of students com. Passaic Classis, 1975, 87, chair, 1978, 83-86, pres., 1979. Contbr. articles to religious jours.; author poetry; manuscript reader, evaluator religious pub. co. Established, managed Wanaque Cmty. Food Pantry, 1977-87; vol. Domestic Crisis Ctr., Grand Rapids, 1988—; bd. dirs. Nat. Inst. Rehabilitation Engring., Hewitt, N.J., 1984—, pres. bd. dirs., 1986—. Recipient Barnabas award Iglesia Cristiana Ebenezer, 1987. Mem. Czechoslovak Soc. Arts and Sci., Czechoslovak Hist. Conf., Soc. for Study of Christian Spirituality. Avocations: running, landscaping, genealogy/family history. Home and Office: 6125 Capitan Dr SE Grand Rapids MI 49546-6721

SCHWANK, JOHANNES WALTER, chemical engineering educator; b. Zams, Tyrol, Austria, July 6, 1950; came to U.S., 1978; s. Friedrich Karl and Johanna (Ruepp) S.; m. Lynne Violet Duguay; children: Alexander Johann, Leonard Friedrich, Hanna Violet. Diploma in chemistry, U. Innsbruck, Austria, 1975, PhD, 1978. Mem. faculty U. Mich., Ann Arbor, 1978—, assoc. prof. chem. engring., 1984-90, acting dir. Ctr. for Catalysis and Surface Sci., 1985-90, prof., interim chmn. dept. chem. engring., 1990-91, assoc. dir. Electron Microbeam Analysis Lab., 1990—; chmn. dept. chem. engring., 1991-95; prof. chem. engring. U. Mich., Ann Arbor, 1995—; vis. prof. U. Innsbruck, 1987-88, Tech. U. Vienna, 1988; cons. in field. Patentee bimetallic cluster catalysts, hydrodesulfurization catalysts and microelectronic gas sensors; contbr. over 70 articles to sci. jours. Fulbright-Hays scholar, 1978. Mem. AAAS, Am. Chem. Soc., Am. Inst. Chem. Engrs., Mich. Catalysis Soc. (sec.-treas. 1982-83, v.p. 1983-84, pres. 1984-85), Am. Soc. Engring. Edn. Home: 2335 Placid Way Ann Arbor MI 48105-1295 Office: U Mich Dept Chem Enging 2300 Hayward St Ann Arbor MI 48109-2136

SCHWANN, WILLIAM JOSEPH, publisher, musician, discographer; b. Salem, Ill., May 13, 1913; s. Henry W. and Effie A. (Garthwait) Schwann; m. Aire-Maija Kutvonen, June 1, 1959. Student, Louisville Conservatory Music, 1930-31; A.B., U. Louisville, 1935, D.Mus. (hon.), 1969; D.Mus. (hon.), New Eng. Conservatory Music, 1982; postgrad., Boston U. Sch. Music, 1935-36, Harvard U., 1937-38. Organist, music dir. various chs. Louisville, 1930-35; organ concerts, broadcasts, 1930-40; tchr. organ, piano, organist, music dir. Boston area, 1935-50; music revs. Boston Herald, Boston Transcript, others, 1937-39; owner Record Shop, Cambridge, Mass., 1939-53; mem. staff Radiation Lab., MIT, 1942-45; compiler, pub. 1st Long Playing Record Catalog now known as monthly Schwann-1 Record and Tape Guide, 1949, Artist Listing LP Catalog, semi-ann. Schwann-2 Record and Tape Guide, Schwann Children's Rec. Catalog, Basic Rec. Library, Basic Jazz Record Library, 1953-83, Schwann Record Catalog (now known as quarterly Schwann Opus and Schwann Spectrum Catalogs, ann. Schwann Artist Listing Catalog), 1984—; pres., treas. W. Schwann, Inc., 1957-77; pres., pub., chief exec. officer ABC Schwann Publications, Inc., 1976-83. Editor: White House Record Library Catalog (listing 2,000 RIAA LP record collection presented to White House), Vol. I, 1973, Vol. II, 1981. Trustee Marlboro Sch. Music, Boston Ballet Co.; bd. dirs. Greater Boston Youth Symphony Orch., Longy Sch. Music, Cambridge Soc. Early Music. Recipient Disting. alumnus award U. Louisville, 1980, 1st Alumni Fellows award, 1990, Citation for Disting. Svcs., Music Libr. Assn. Am., 1983, George Peabody medal for outstanding contbns. to music in Am. Peabody Inst., Johns Hopkins U., 1984; Hon. Gold Record award for 35 yrs. of svc. to music industry and pub. Recording Industry Assn. Am., 1984; Disting. Pub. Svc. to Profession Silver medal Boston U., 1985, Disting. Alumni award, 1994; Arion award Cambridge Soc. Early Music, 1991. Mem. Nat. Audubon Soc. (life), Nat. Parks and Conservation Assn. (life), New Eng. Wild Flower Preservation Soc.(life), Save-the-Redwoods League (life), Soc. for Protection N.H. Forests (life), Am. Forestry Assn. (life), Trustees of Reservations (life), Wilderness Soc. (life), Izaak Walton League (life), Nature Conservancy (life), Appalachian Mountain Club (life), Sierra Club (life), Sigma Alpha Iota (hon.). Clubs: St. Botolph, Harvard of Boston, Harvard Mus. Assn. Home and Office: 26 Old Winter St Lincoln MA 01773-3406

SCHWANTNER, JOSEPH, composer, educator; b. Chgo., Mar. 22, 1943; m. Janet Elaine Rossate; 2 children. B.Mus., Chgo. Conservatory Coll.; M.Mus., Northwestern U., 1966, D.Mus., 1968. Teaching fellow Northwestern U., 1966-68; mem. faculty Chgo. Conservatory Coll., 1967-68; asst. prof. Pacific Lutheran U., 1968-69, Ball State U., 1969-70; successively asst. prof., assoc. prof., prof. Eastman Sch. Music, U. Rochester, 1970—; composer-in-residence St. Louis Symphony Orch., 1982-84. Compositions include Aftertones of Infinity (Pulitzer prize for music 1979), Diaphonia Intervallum, Chronicon, Autumn Canticle, Consortium, In Aeternum, Modis Caelestis, Canticle for the Evening Bells, Elixir, Wild Angels of the Open Hills, And the Mountains Rising Nowhere, Sparrows. Recipient Faricy award, 1965, BMI Student award, 1965, 66, 67, Bearns prize Columbia U., 1967; Nat. Inst. Arts and Letters Charles Ives scholar, 1970; N.Y. State Council on Arts Creative Arts Public Service grantee, 1973; NEA grantee; Guggenheim fellow, 1978-79. Office: Eastman Sch Music 26 Gibbs St Rochester NY 14604-2505*

SCHWARCZ, HENRY PHILIP, geologist, educator; b. Chgo., July 22, 1933; s. Arthur and Zita Elizabeth (Strauss) S.; m. Molly Ann Robinson, Dec. 20, 1964; 1 child, Joshua Arthur. A.B., U. Chgo., 1952; M.Sc. in Geochemistry, Calif. Inst. Tech., 1955, Ph.D. in Geology, 1960. Rsch. assoc. E. Fermi Inst., U. Chgo., 1960-62; prof. geology McMaster U., Hamilton, Ont., Can., 1962—, chmn., assoc.mem. dept. anthropology, 1988-91, univ. prof., 1996—; mem. assoc. com. on meteorites NRC of Can., 1978-86; vis. fellow Clare Hall Coll. Cambridge U., 1991-92, Australian Nat. U., 1995; vis. prof. Hebrew U., Jerusalem, 1992; assoc. mem. dept. anthropology U. Toronto, 1993—; mem. panel refs. Rivista di Antropologia (Roma). Assoc. editor Geochimica et Cosmochimica Acta, 1984-96, Jour. Human Evolution, 1994—, Geoarchaeology, 1994—; mem. editorial bd. Jour. Archaeol. Sci., 1986—; contbr. articles to profl. jours., chpts. to books. Fulbright fellow, Pisa, Italy, 1968-69, Killam fellow Can. Coun., 1993—. Fellow Royal Soc. Can., Geol. Soc. Am. (Archeol. Geol. Div. award 1991); mem. Geochem. Soc., Lithoprobe NSERC 1991—), Am. Quaternary Assn., Acad. III Sci. (mem. coun.), Geol. Soc. Am. (chmn. archeol. geol. divsn.). Avocations: playing violin, drawing. Office: McMaster Univ, Dept Geology, Hamilton, ON Canada L8S 4M1

SCHWARCZ, STEVEN LANCE, law educator, lawyer; b. N.Y.C., Nov. 10, 1949; s. Charles and Elinor Schwarcz; m. Susan Beth Kolodny, Aug. 24, 1975; children: Daniel Benjamin, Rebekah Mara. BS summa cum laude, in Aero. Engring., New York U., 1971; JD, Columbia U., 1974. Bar: N.Y. 1975, U.S. Dist. Ct. (so. dist.) N.Y. 1975. Assoc. Shearman & Sterling, N.Y.C., 1974-82, ptnr., 1983-89; ptnr, chmn. structured fin. practice group Kaye, Scholer, Fierman, Hays & Handler, 1989-96; adj. prof. law Yeshiva

U., Benjamin N. Cardozo Sch. Law, N.Y.C., 1983-92; vis. lectr. Yale Law Sch., 1992-96; lectr. in law Columbia Law Sch., 1992-96; prof. law Duke U. Sch. Law, 1996—. Contbr. articles to profl. jours. Chmn. Friends of the Eldridge St. Synagogue, N.Y.C., 1979—, Legis. Drafting Rsch. Fund. Recipient First Prize award Pub. Speaking Contest, NYU, 1971; George Granger Brown scholar, 1971; NSF grantee in Math., 1969. Fellow Am. Coll. Commercial Fin. Lawyers; mem. Am. Law Inst., Assn. of Bar of City of N.Y. (environ. law com. 1975-78, nuclear tech. com. 1979-81, sci. and law com. 1985—, chmn. 1987—). Tau Beta Pi. Jewish. Office: Duke U Sch Law Box 90360 Science Dr & Towerview Rd Durham NC 27708

SCHWARCZ, THOMAS H., surgeon; b. Portsmouth, Ohio, Nov. 26, 1954; s. Andrew and Edith Schwarcz; m. Kathleen Schwarcz, Sept. 5, 1992; 1 child, John. BA, Ohio State U., 1976, MD, 1979. Diplomate Am. Bd. Surgery, gen. surgery and gen. vascular surgery. Asst. prof. surgery U. Ill. Coll. Medicine, Chgo., 1986-89; asst. prof. surgery U. Ky. Coll. Medicine, Lexington, 1989-92, assoc. prof., 1992—; chief surg. svc. VA Med. Ctr., Lexington, 1995—. Mem. Internat. Soc. Cardiovascular Surgery, Soc. Vascular Surgery, Assn. VA Surgeons, So. Assn. Vascular Surgery, Midwestern Vascular Surg. Soc. Office: VA Med Ctr 2250 Leestown Rd Lexington KY 40511-1052

SCHWARK, HOWARD EDWARD, civil engineer; b. Bonfield, Ill., Aug. 31, 1917; s. Edward F. and Florence M. (Schultz) S.; m. Arlene M. Highbarger, Sept. 28, 1940 (dec. May 1990); m. Carol D. Kehoe, June 1, 1991; children: Timothy Kehoe, Maureen Kehoe, Colleen Corbin. Student St. Viators Coll., Bourbonnias, Ill., 1935-37; BS, U. Ill., 1942. Asst. to county supt. hwys. Ford County (Ill.), 1941-43; engr. E. I. DuPont de Nemours Co., 1942; asst. county supt. hwys. Kankakee County (Ill.), 1946-52, county supt. hwys., 1952-82; bd. dirs. First Am. Bank, Kankakee Devel. Corp.; adviser county rds. FHWA, 1973-82; spl. cons. ESCA Consultants, Urbana, Ill., 1982—, v.p., 1988—. Co-chmn., Rep. Finance Com., 1962-66; pres. Kankakee Pk. Dist., 1959-70; mem. tech. adv. com. to Ill. Transp. Study Commn., 1975-82; trustee, pres. Azariah Buck Old People's Home, ret.; mem. exec. bd. Rainbow coun. Boy Scouts Am.; bd. dirs. Soil and Water Conservation Svc., 1967-74. Served with AUS, 1943-46. Recipient Disting. Alumnus award Civil Engring. Alumni Assn. U. Ill., 1975; Disting. Svc. award U.S. Dept. Transp., 1982; Spl. Achievement award as road adv. for Region 5, FHWA, 1982. Mem. Nat. Soc. Profl. Engrs. (life), Nat. Assn. County Engrs. (life mem., v.p. North Central region 1979-81, Urban County Engr. of Yr. award 1982), Ill. Soc. Profl. Engrs. (life), Ill. Assn. County Supts. Hwys. (life mem., pres. 1970), Ill. Engring. Coun. (pres. 1971-72), Am. Road and Transp. Builders Assn. (life mem., dir. county div. 1969-75, dir. 1975-81, pres. county div. 1975; Outstanding Service award transp. ofcls. div. 1981, Ralph R. Bartelsmeyer award 1983), Kankakee Area C. of C. (dir. 1960-74), Am. Soc. Profl. Engrs., Western Soc. Engrs., Twp. Ofcls. Ill., Freelance Photographers Assn., Ill. Wildlife Fedn. Lutheran. Lodges: Rotary, South Wilmington Sportsman. Home: 319 Berkshire Ct Bourbonnais IL 60914-1552

SCHWARTZ, AARON ROBERT, lawyer, former state legislator; b. Galveston, Tex., July 17, 1926; s. Joseph and Clara (Bulbe) S.; m. Marilyn Cohn, July 14, 1951; children: Richard Austin, Robert Allen, John Reed, Thomas Lee. Pre-law student, Tex. A&M U., 1948; J.D., U. Tex., 1951. Bar: Tex. 1951. Mem. Tex. Ho. of Reps., 1955-59; Mem. Tex. Senate, 1960-81, past chmn. rules, jurisprudence and natural resources coms.; chmn. Tex. Coastal & Marine Coun., U.S. Coastal States Orgn.; adj. legis. prof. Bates Law Sch., U. Houston. Contbr. articles to profl. jours. Mem. exec. com. Galveston Bay Fond.; apptd. to Tex. Oil Spill Oversight Commn., 1993. Served with USN, 1944-46, 2d lt. USAFR, 1948-53. Recipient conservation and legis. awards, Outstanding Citizen award Galveston Jr. C. of C., 1981, Man of Yr., People of Vision award Galveston chpt. Soc. for Prevention of Blindness, 1986, Disting. Service award Nat. Hurricane Conf., Tex. Coastal Mgmt. Adv. Com., 1987, Lifetime Coastal Achievement award, 1997. Mem. Tex. State Bar Assn., Galveston County Bar Assn. Democrat. Jewish. Home: PO Box 3398 Galveston TX 77552-0398

SCHWARTZ, ALAN E., lawyer; b. Detroit, Dec. 21, 1925; s. Maurice H. and Sophia (Welkowitz) S.; m. Marianne Shapero, Aug. 24, 1950; children: Marc Alan, Kurt Nathan, Ruth Anne. Student, Western Mich. Coll., 1944-45; BA with distinction, U. Mich., 1947; LLB magna cum laude, Harvard U., 1950; LLD (hon.), Wayne State U., 1983, U. Detroit, 1985. Bar: N.Y. 1951, Mich. 1952. Assoc. Kelley, Drye & Warren, N.Y.C., 1950-52; mem. Honigman, Miller, Schwartz & Cohn, Detroit, 1952—; spl. asst. counsel N.Y. State Crime Commn., 1951; dir. Unisys Corp., Detroit Edison Co., Core Industries Inc., Handleman Co., Howell Industries, Inc., Pulte Corp. Editor: Harvard Law Rev., 1950. Dir. Detroit Symphony Orch.; v.p., bd. dirs. United Found.; bd. dirs. Detroit Renaissance, Detroit Econ. Growth Corp., New Detroit, Jewish Welfare Fedn. Detroit; trustee Community Found. for Southeastern Mich., Detriot Med. Ctr., Interlochen Arts Acad., Skillman Found.; adv. mem. Arts Commn., City of Detroit. Served as ensign Supply Corps, USNR, 1945-46. Recipient Mich. Heritage Hall of Fame award, 1984, George W. Romney award for lifetime achievement in volunteerism, 1994. Mem. Mich. Bar Assns. Clubs: Franklin Hills Country; Detroit, Economic (dir.). Home: 4120 Echo Rd Bloomfield Hills MI 48302-1941 Office: Honigman Miller Schwartz & Cohn 2290 1st National Bldg Detroit MI 48226

SCHWARTZ, ALAN GIFFORD, sport company executive; b. N.Y.C., Nov. 7, 1931; s. Kevie Waldemar and Vera (Isaacs) S.; m. Roslyn Smulian, Sept. 6, 1958; children: Steven, Andrew, Sally, Elizabeth. BS, Yale U., 1952; MBA, Harvard U., 1954. Ptnr. Gifford Investment Co., Chgo., 1954—; CEO Tennis Corp. of Am., Chgo., 1969—, chmn. bd., 1974—; chmn. exec. com. First Colonia Bankshares, Chgo., 1984—; dir. Mich. Ave. Nat. Bank, Chgo., Comtrex Systems, Inc., Mt. Laurel, N.J.; trustee Roosevelt U., 1994—; mem. bd. dirs. Inst. European & Asian Studies, 1993—, U.S. Tennis Assn., 1994—. Contbr. articles to profl. jours.; editorial cons. Club Industry mag., 1985—. Bd. dirs. Grad. Sch. of Bus., Duke U., Durham, N.C., 1977—, McCormick Boys and Girls Club, 1989—. Elected to Club Industry Hall of Fame, 1987. Mem. Standard Club of Chgo. Jewish. Avocations: travel, tennis. Office: Tennis Corp of Am 2020 W Fullerton Ave Chicago IL 60647-3351*

SCHWARTZ, ALAN LEIGH, pediatrician, educator; b. N.Y.C., Apr. 25, 1948; s. Robert and Joyce (Goldner) S.; m. Judith Child, June 22, 1974; 1 child, Timothy Child. BA, Case Western Res. U., 1974, PHD in Pharmacology, 1974, MD, 1976. Diplomate Am. Bd. Pediatrics. Intern Children's Hosp., Boston, 1976-77, resident, 1976-78, fellow Dana Farber Cancer Inst., 1978-80; instr. Harvard Med. Sch., Boston, 1980-81, asst. prof., 1981-83, assoc. prof., 1983-86; prof. pediatrics, molecular biology and pharmacology Washington U. Sch. Medicine, St. Louis, 1986—, chmn. dept. pediatrics, 1995—; vis. scientist MIT, Boston, 1979-82; mem. sci. adv. bd. Nat. Inst. Child Health and Human Devel., NIH, Bethesda, Md., 1988-94; investigator Am. Heart Assn. Alumni Endowed Prof. Pediatrics, Wash. U. Sch. Medicine, 1987—. Office: Washington U Sch Medicine Dept Pediatrics Box 8116 One Children's Pl Saint Louis MO 63110-1093

SCHWARTZ, ALAN VICTOR, advertising agency executive; b. Detroit, July 12, 1948; s. Seymour and Adeline (Goldstein) S.; m. Linda Toba Dershowitz, Aug. 20, 1981; children: Stacy Ilana, Andrew Robert. B.S. with honors, Lehigh U., 1970; M.B.A. with highest honors, Cornell U., 1972. C.P.A., N.Y. Mgr. Price Waterhouse, Huntington, N.Y., 1972-79; v.p. dir. fin. control Doyle Dane Bernbach, N.Y.C., 1979-81; v.p. chief fin. officer Bernard Hodes Advt., N.Y.C., 1981-84, sr. v.p., chief operating and fin. officer, 1984-87, exec. v.p., chief operating and fin. officer, 1987—. bd. mgrs. Evans Tower, treas. 1991-92, pres. 1991-92; Vice campaign chmn. United Way, L.I., 1978. Mem. Nat. Assn. Accts. (various directorships and treas.), N.Y. State Soc. C.P.A.s, Lehigh Alumni Assn. (pres. L.I. chpt. 1977-79, treas. 1975-77). Office: Bernard Hodes Advt 555 Madison Ave New York NY 10022-3301

SCHWARTZ, ALFRED, university dean; b. Chgo., Jan. 8, 1922; s. Isadore and Lena (Ziff) S.; m. Delle Weiss, Aug. 26, 1945; children: Reid Mitchell, Karen Ruth. B.Ed., Chgo. Tchrs. Coll., 1944; M.A. in Polit. Sci., U. Chgo., 1946, Ph.D. in Ednl. Adminstrn., 1949. Tchr. Chgo. pub. schs., 1944-45; contact officer VA, 1946; instr. U. Chgo. Lab. Sch., 1946-50; assoc. prof. edn. Drake U., 1950-56, U. Del.; also exec. sec. Del. Sch. Study Council, 1956-58; dean (Univ. Coll.); prof. Coll. Edn., Drake U., 1958-85, dean, 1964-79, 80-84, dean emeritus, 1985; acting v.p. acad. adminstrn. Coll. Edn., Coll. Edn., 1979-80; cons., 1985—; adviser Iowa Dept. Pub. Instrn.; mem. coordinating bd. Nat. Council Accreditation for Tchr. Edn.; chmn. tchr. edn. and adv. com. Iowa Dept. Pub. Instrn. Author: (with Harlan L. Hagman) Administration in Profile for School Executives, 1954, (with Stuart Tiedeman) Evaluating Student Progress, 1957, (with Willard Fox) Managerial Guide for School Principals, 1965. Mem. Gov.'s Commn. State-Local Relations. Mem. World Council on Curriculum and Instrn., Iowa Assn. Colls. for Tchr. Edn. (pres., exec. sec.), Am. Profs. for Peace in Middle East, Am. Ednl. Research Assn., Iowa Edn. Assn., NEA, Phi Delta Kappa, Kappa Delta Pi. Home: 3450 3rd Ave Apt 511 San Diego CA 92103-4939

SCHWARTZ, ALLEN G., federal judge; b. Bklyn., Aug. 23, 1934; s. Herbert and Florence (Safier) S.; m. Joan Ruth Teitel, Jan. 17, 1965; children: David Aaron, Rachel Ann, Deborah Eve. BBA, CCNY, 1955; LLB, U. Pa., 1958. Bar: N.Y. 1958. Asst. dist. atty. Office of Dist. Atty., N.Y. County, 1959-62; assoc. firm Paskus Gordon & Hyman, N.Y.C., 1962-65; ptnr. firm Koch Lankenau Schwartz & Kovner, N.Y.C., 1965-69, Dornbush Mensch Mandelstam & Schwartz, N.Y.C., 1969-75; mem. Schwartz & Schreiber, P.C., N.Y.C., 1975-77; corp. counsel City of N.Y., 1978-81; mem. Schwartz Klink & Schreiber, P.C., 1982-87; ptnr. Proskauer Rose Goetz & Mendelsohn, N.Y.C., 1987-94; judge U.S. Dist. Ct. (so. dist.) N.Y., N.Y.C., 1994—; mem. ex officio N.Y.C. Bd. Ethics, 1978-81; pro bono sports commr. City of N.Y., 1982-83. Research editor: U. Pa. Law Rev, 1957-58. Recipient Award of Achievement, Sch. Bus. Alumni, Soc. of the City Coll., 1981, Hogan-Morgantau Assocs. award, 1980, Corp. Coun. ann. award, 1995, Frank S. Hogan Assocs. award, 1995. Office: US Courthouse 500 Pearl St Rm 1350 New York NY 10007-1316

SCHWARTZ, AMY ELIZABETH, editorial writer, columnist; b. N.Y.C., July 26, 1962; d. Stuart Grad and Doris (Greenburg) S.; m. Eric S. Koenig, Jan. 11, 1997. BA, Harvard U., 1984. Rschr. Harper's mag., N.Y.C., 1984; reporter, rschr. The New Republic, Washington, 1985; rschr., writer The Washington Post, 1985-89, editorial writer, 1989—, columnist, 1993—. Vol. tchr. Jewish Study Ctr., Washington, 1993-94. Recipient Bernie Harrison Meml. award for commentary Washington-Balt. Newspaper Guild, 1992, 94, 95; Humboldt Found. Chancellor scholar, Bonn, Germany, 1990-91. Mem. Newspaper Guild. Jewish. Office: Washington Post Editorial Page 1150 15th St NW Washington DC 20071-0001

SCHWARTZ, ANNA JACOBSON, economic historian; b. N.Y.C., Nov. 11, 1915; married; four children. BA, Barnard Coll., 1934; MA, Columbia U., 1935, PhD, 1964; LittD (hon.), U. Fla., 1987; ArtsD (hon.), Stonehill Coll., 1989; LLD (hon.), Iona Coll., 1992. Researcher USDA, 1936, Columbia U. Social Sci. Research Council, 1936-41; mem. sr. research staff Nat. Bur. Econ. Research Inc., N.Y.C., 1941—; instr. Bklyn. Coll., 1952, Baruch Coll., 1959-60; adj. prof. econs. grad. CCNY, 1967-69, grad. sch. CUNY, 1986—, NYU Grad. Sch. Arts and Sci., 1969-70; hon. vis. prof. City U. Bus. Sch., London, 1984—. Mem. editorial bd. Am. Econ. Rev., 1972-78, Jour. Money, Credit and Banking, 1974-75, 84—, Jour. Monetary Econs., 1975—, Jour. Fin. Svcs. Rsch., 1993—; contbr. numerous articles to profl. jours. Disting. fellow Am. Econ. Assn., 1993. Mem. Western Econ. Assn. (pres. 1987-88). Office: Nat Bur Econ Research 50 East 42nd St 17th Fl New York NY 10017-5405

SCHWARTZ, ANTHONY, veterinary surgeon, educator; b. Bklyn., July 30, 1940; s. Murray and Miriam Sarah (Wittes) S.; m. Claudia Rosenberg, July 21, 1963; children: Thomas Frederick, Eric Leigh. Student, Mich. State U., 1957-58; DVM, Cornell U., 1963; PhD, Ohio State U., 1972. Diplomate Am. Coll. Vet. Surgeons (bd. of regents 1989-92). Gen. practice vet. medicine Huntington, N.Y., 1963-66; resident in surgery Animal Med. Ctr., N.Y.C., 1968-69; resident in surgery Ohio State U., Columbus, 1969-70, asst. prof., head sect. small animal surgery, 1973; asst. prof. then assoc. prof. comparative medicine Yale U. Sch. Medicine, New Haven, 1973-79; assoc. prof. then prof., chmn. dept. surgery, assoc. dean clin. edn. Tufts U. Sch. Vet. Medicine, Boston, 1979-89; assoc. dean clin. edn. Tufts U. Sch. Vet. Medicine, 1989-93, prof., chmn. dept. surgery, assoc. dean academic affairs, 1993-97, assoc. dean for acad. and outreach programs, 1997—; cons. U.S. Surg. Corp., Norwalk, Conn., 1975—. Author: (with others) Small Animal Surgery, 1989, Complications in Small Animal Surgery, 1996; editl. bd. Vet. Surgery, 1987-90, Jour. Investigative Surgery, 1987—; assoc. editor: Textbook of Small Animal Surgery, 1985; contbr. articles to profl. jours. Capt. U.S. Army Vet Corps, 1966-68. Recipient 1st prize N.Y. State Vet. Med. Soc., 1963; Robert Wood Johnson Health Policy fellow, Washington, 1988-89; NIH grantee, 1975-84. Mem. AVMA (legis. planning com. 1989-92, coun. on govt. affairs 1992-97), AAAS, Am. Assn. Immunologists, Am. Assn. Vet. Clinicians, Assn. Am. Vet. Med. Colls. (Washington, exec. dir., treas. 1992-93), Nat. Acads. of Practice, Mass. Vet. Med. Assn. (animal welfare com. 1990—, chmn. 1990-91), Sigma Xi, Phi Kappa Phi. Democrat. Jewish. Office: Tufts U Sch Vet Medicine 200 Westboro Rd North Grafton MA 01536-1828

SCHWARTZ, ARTHUR ALAN, surgeon; b. N.Y.C., Sept. 16, 1945; s. Philip and Selma (Galen) S.; m. Ann Mass, June 14, 1969 (div. Mar. 1986); 1 child, Chelsea Lara; m. Lorie Jane Lybeck, Mar. 26, 1988; 1 child, Spencer Loren. BA, Columbia Coll., 1965; MD, NYU, 1969. Diplomate Am. Bd. Surgery. Surg. intern N.Y. Hosp.-Cornell Med. Ctr., N.Y.C., 1969-70; surg. resident Peter Bent Brigham Hosp., Children's Hosp., Harvard Med. Sch., Boston, 1970-73; surg. chief resident UCLA Harbor Gen. Hosp., Torrance, Calif., 1973-75, asst. prof. surgery, 1975-78; pvt. practice surgery Aspen (Colo.) Valley Hosp., 1978-92; surgeon No. Calif. Trauma Group, San Jose, Calif., 1992-93; pvt. practice surgery Santa Cruz, Calif., 1993—. Fellow ACS; mem. Santa Cruz Med. Soc. Avocations: running, hiking, rock & roll. Home: 2520 N Rodeo Gulch Rd Soquel CA 95073-9713 Office: 1505 Soquel Dr Santa Cruz CA 95065-1716

SCHWARTZ, ARTHUR JAY, lawyer; b. Atlanta, May 28, 1947; s. William B. Jr. and Sonia (Weinberg) S.; m. Joyce Straus, Aug. 12, 1972; children: Tracy Jill, Allison Jaye. BA, U. N.C., 1969; JD, Emory U., 1972. Bar: Ga. 1972, U.S. Dist. Ct. (no. dist.) Ga. 1972, U.S. Ct. Appeals (11th cir.) 1972. Ptnr. Smith, Gambrell & Russell, Atlanta, 1972-88, chmn. exec. com., mng. ptnr., 1988-89, 92-93, 96-97; sec., bd. dirs. Lamin Art, Inc., Chgo., 1984—; bd. dirs. Am. Jewish Com., Atlanta, 1982-84, The Temple, Atlanta, 1983-85, 94-97. Served with USAR, 1970-72. Mem. Am. Technion Soc. Atlanta (v.p., bd. dirs. 1980-87), Buckhead Club (bd. dirs. 1987—). Avocations: tennis, running, boating. Office: Smith Gambrell & Russell 3343 Peachtree Rd NE Atlanta GA 30326-1022

SCHWARTZ, ARTHUR ROBERT, food writer, critic, consultant; b. N.Y.C., Mar. 24, 1947; s. Lawrence and Sydell Bedona (Sonkin) S.; m. Elaine Billie Rothseid, Aug. 16, 1969 (div. 1982). BS in Bus. and Journalism, U. Md., 1968; MA, CUNY, Bklyn., 1970. Editor Bklyn. Graphic, 1968-69; food and wine writer Newsday, L.I., N.Y., 1969-79; exec. food editor N.Y. Daily News, 1979-89, restaurant critic, 1979-96; talk show host WOR Radio, N.Y.C., 1992—; lectr. New Sch. for Social Rsch., N.Y.C., 1987—; TV reporter Sta. WNYW-TV Fox-5, N.Y.C., 1989; syndicated food critic. Author: Cooking in a Small Kitchen, 1979, What To Cook When You Think There's Nothing in the House to Eat, 1992, Soup Suppers, 1994; contbr. author: Better Times; also numerous mag. articles. Home and Office: 320 E 42nd St New York NY 10017-5900

SCHWARTZ, AUBREY EARL, artist; b. N.Y.C., Jan. 13, 1928; s. Louis and Clara S. Student, Art Students League, Bklyn. Mus. Art Sch., 1969-94; Prof. emeritus Harpur Coll., SUNY, Binghamton, 1994—; prof. art Harpur Coll., SUNY, Binghamton, 1969—. One-man shows Grippi Gallery, N.Y.C., 1958, Art U.S.A., N.Y. Coliseum, N.Y.C., 1959, Contemporary Graphic Art, U.S. State Dept., 1959, group shows include Whitney Mus. Am. Art, N.Y.C., 1957; represented in permanent collections Nat. Gallery Art, Washington, Bklyn. Mus. Art, Phila. Mus. Art, Library Congress, Washington, Art Inst. Chgo. Recipient 1st prize for graphic art Boston Arts Festival 1960; Guggenheim fellow, 1958-60; Tamarind fellow, 1960; N.Y. State CAPS fellow, 1973-74. Home: 104 Main St Afton NY 13730

SCHWARTZ, BARRY FREDRIC, lawyer, diversified holding company executive; b. Phila., Apr. 16, 1949; s. Albert and Evelyn (Strauss) S.; m. Sherry L. Handsman, Mar. 21, 1985; children: Fanny Rose, Abraham David. AB cum laude, Kenyon Coll., 1970; JD, Georgetown U., 1974. Bar: Pa. 1974, Ill. 1974, U.S. Ct. Appeals (7th cir.) 1975, U.S. Ct. Appeals (3d cir.) 1978, U.S. Ct. Appeals (4th cir.) 1979, U.S. Ct. Appeals (6th cir.) 1981, U.S. Supreme Ct. 1981, N.Y. 1992. Assoc. Sachnoff, Schrager, Jones & Weaver, Chgo., 1974-76; ptnr. Wolf, Block, Schorr & Solis-Cohen, Phila., 1976-89; exec. v.p. gen. counsel MacAndrews & Forbes Holdings, Inc., N.Y.C., 1989—; dir. Franklin Mut. Series Fund Inc., 1994. Mem. alumni coun. Kenyon Coll., Gambier, Ohio, 1985; chmn., bd. dirs. Pub. Interest Law Ctr. Phila., 1989; dir. Greenwich (Conn.) Jewish Fedn., 1991-96; trustee Temple Sholom, Greenwich; dir. Westchester Holocaust Commn.; dir. Greenwich Basketball Assn. Home: 143 Park Ave Greenwich CT 06830-4849 Office: MacAndrews & Forbes Holdings Inc 35 E 62nd St New York NY 10021-8016

SCHWARTZ, BARRY STEVEN, lawyer; b. Bklyn., Mar. 12, 1950; s. Joseph and Helen (Lipkin) S.; m. Sherry Licht Cooper, Feb. 18, 1984; 1 child, Jennifer. BA, NYU, 1972; JD, Cath. U. Am., 1975. Bar: N.Y. 1976, U.S. Dist. Ct. (so. dist.) 1976, N.J. 1979, U.S. Ct. Appeals (2d cir.) 1988. Assoc. Seavey, Fingerit & Vogel, N.Y.C., 1976-81; pvt. practice law N.Y.C., 1980—; of counsel Seavey, Fingerit, Vogel, Oziel & Skoller, N.Y.C.; atty. West New York (N.J.) Rent Control Board, 1984-86. Assoc. editor Cath. U. Law Rev., 1974-75. Mem. ABA, N.Y. State Bar Assn., Masons (master Audubon-Gotham club 1986). Avocations: music, reading, travel. Home: 6 Corn Mill Ct Saddle River NJ 07458-1232 Office: Seavey Fingerit Vogel Oziel 60 E 86th St New York NY 10028-1009

SCHWARTZ, BERNARD, law educator; b. N.Y.C., Aug. 25, 1923; s. Isidore and Ethel (Levenson) S.; m. Aileen Haas, Apr. 18, 1950; 1 child, Brian Michael. BSS, CCNY, 1944; LLB, NYU, 1944; LLM, Harvard U., 1945; PhD, Cambridge (Eng.) U., 1947, LLD, 1956; Doctorat d'Universite, U. Paris, 1963. Bar: N.Y. 1945. Mem. law faculty NYU, 1947-92, Edwin D. Webb prof. law, 1963-92; Chapman Disting. prof. law U. of Tulsa, 1992—; cons. Hoover Commn., 1955; chief counsel, staff dir. spl. subcom. legislative oversight U.S. Ho. Reps., 1957-58; Tagore Law lectr., Calcutta, India, 1984; corr. mem. Nat. Acad. Law and Social Scis., Argentina, 1986—. Author: French Administrative Law and the Common Law World, 1954, The Supreme Court, 1957, The Professor and the Commissions, 1959, Introduction to American Administrative Law, 1962, The Reins of Power, 1963, Commentary on the Constitution of the U.S., 5 vols., 1963-68, The Roots of Freedom, 1967, Legal Control of Government, 1972, Constitutional Law: A Textbook, 1972, 2d edit., 1979, The Law in America, 1974, Administrative Law, 1976, 3d edit., 1991, The Great Rights of Mankind, 1977, expanded edit., 1992, Administrative Law: A Casebook, 1977, 4th edit., 1994, Super Chief: Earl Warren and His Supreme Court, 1983, Inside the Warren Court, 1983, The Unpublished Opinions of the Warren Court, 1985, Some Makers of American Law, 1985, Swann's Way: The School Busing Case and the Supreme Court, 1986, Behind Bakke: The Supreme Court and Affirmative Action, 1988, The Unpublished Opinions of the Burger Court, 1988, The Ascent of Pragmatism: The Burger Court in Action, 1990, The New Right and the Constitution, 1990, Constitutional Issues: Freedom of the Press, 1992, Main Currents in American Legal Thought, 1993, A History of the Supreme Court, 1993, The Unpublished Opinions of the Rehnquist Court, 1996, Decision: How The Supreme Court Decides Cases, 1996, A Book of Legal Lists, 1997, Thomas Jefferson and Bolling v. Bolling, 1997. Ann. Survey Am. Law dedicated in his name, 1988. Mem. ABA. Office: U Tulsa Coll Of Law Tulsa OK 74104

SCHWARTZ, BERNARD, physician; b. Toronto, Can., Nov. 12, 1927; s. Samuel and Gertrude (Levinsky) S.; children: Lawrence Frederick, Karen Lynne, Jennifer Carla, Ariane Samara. M.D., U. Toronto, 1951; M.S., State U. Iowa, 1953, Ph.D., 1959. Intern U. Hosps., State U. Iowa, 1951-52, resident ophthalmology, 1951-54; research fellow U. Iowa, 1954-58; asst. prof. to assoc. prof. Downstate Med. Center fo State U. N.Y., 1958-68; prof. ophthalmology Tufts U., 1968-93, chmn. dept., 1968-90, prof. emeritus ophthalmology, 1993—. Author: Syphilis and the Eye; Editor in chief of: Survey of Ophthalmology, 1968—; Contbr. articles to profl. jours. Dir. Mass. Soc. Prevention of Blindness. Fellow Am. Acad. Ophthalmology, ACS; mem. Assn. Rsch. in Ophthalmology, New Eng. Ophthalmol. Soc., N.Y. Acad. Medicine, N.Y. Acad. Scis., Soc. Française D'Ophthalmologie, Sigma Xi. Home: 180 Beacon St Boston MA 02116-1401 Office: 20 Park Plz Ste 535 Boston MA 02116-4303

SCHWARTZ, BERNARD L., electronics company executive; b. 1925. BBA, CCNY, 1948. Ptnr. Schnee, Hover & Schwartz, 1948-62; sr. v.p. APL Corp., Fla., 1962-68; with Leasco Corp., 1969-72; chmn. bd., chief exec. officer Leasco Corp., Miami Beach, 1969-72; with Loral Corp., N.Y.C., 1972—, former pres., 1973-81, chmn., chief exec. officer, 1972—, also dir.; chmn., chief executive officer, K&F Industries, Inc. With USAAF, 1943-45. Office: Loral Corp 600 3rd Ave Fl 36 New York NY 10016-2001*

SCHWARTZ, BRUCE F., writer; b. Bklyn., Nov. 1, 1952; s. Paul I. and Mildred H. (Herman) S.; m. Cheryl A. Ferrier, July 24, 1983; children: Jason Scott, Lindsay Robyn. BA, So. Conn. State U., 1975; MS, U. Bridgeport, 1977. Broadway producer various musicals, N.Y.C., 1978-82; prof. U. Bridgeport, Conn., 1990-92. Author: A Tangled Web, 1986, The RH Factor, 1992, The Mystery of Oogilly Boogilly, 1995, The Third Millennium, 1996; composer/lyricist: Alice in Wonderland, 1972, The Exception and the Rule, 1973, Alcestis, 1974, Goin' Crazy, 1976, Bojangles, 1978; actor, dir. various prodns., 1970-78. Recipient Lincoln Ctr. award for performing arts, N.Y.C., 1969-70. Democrat. Avocations: cooking, baseball, travel, theatre.

SCHWARTZ, CARL EDWARD, artist, printmaker; b. Detroit, Sept. 20, 1935; s. Carl and Verna (Steiner) S.; m. Kay Joyce Hofmann, June 18, 1955 (div.); children: Dawn Ellen, Cari Leigh; m. Frieda Nelson, Oct. 17, 1982 (div.); m. Dinah Lee Wilson, Jan. 20, 1996. BFA, Art Inst. Chgo. Sch.-U. Chgo., 1957. tchr. art , Chgo., N. Shore Art League, Suburban Fine Arts Center, Deerpath Art League. One-man shows include, South Bend (Ind.) Art Center, Feingarten Gallery, Chgo., 1960, Bernard Horwich Center, Chgo., Covenant Club, Chgo., Barat Coll., Chgo. Pub. Library, Alverno Coll., 1020 Art Center, Rosenberg Gallery, Peoria (Ill.) Art Guild, 1977, Ill. State Mus., 1977 Ill. Inst. Tech., 1978, Miller Gallery, Chgo., 1979, Union League Club, Chgo., 1982, Art Inst. Rental and Sale Gallery, Chgo., 1982, Horwich Gallery, Chgo., 1983, Lake Forest (Ill.) Coll., 1983, Campanile-Capponi Contemporary Gallery, Chgo., 1987, Nagata Gallery, Ft. Myers, Fla., 1988, Jan Cicero Gallery, Chgo., 1990; numerous group shows include 9th Ann. Michigana Exhbt, Detroit (Cloetingh and Deman award 1959), Hyde Park Art Center, Chgo., 1960 (5th Ann. Jury Exhbn. prize), Spectrum Exhbn. '63, Chgo. (1st prize), New Horizons Exhbt, Chgo., 1960 (Joseph Shapiro award), Nat. Design Center, Chgo., 1965 (New Horizons in Painting 1st prize), 3d Ann. Chgo. Arts Competition, 1962 (1st prize), Union League Club, Chgo., 1967 (2d prize), N. Shore Art League Ann. Drawing and Print Show, Chgo., 1965 (1st prize), Artists Guild Chgo., 1965 (prize), McCormack Pl., Chgo., 1965 (1st prize), Detroit Art Inst., 1965 (Commonwealth prize), Park Forest (Ill.) Art Exhbn, 1969 (Best of Show), 14th Ann. Virginia Beach (Va.) Show, 1969 (Best of Show), Suburban Fine Arts Center, Highland Park, Ill., 1970 (prize), 15th Ann. Virginia Beach Show, 1970 (prize), 32d Ann. Artists Guild, Chgo., 1970 (2d prize), N. Shore Art League Print and Drawing Show, 1970 (prize), 16th Ann. Virginia Beach Show, 1971 (2d prize), Ill. State Fair, 1972 (prize), Artists Guild Chgo., 1972 (1st prize), 17th Ann. Virginia Beach Exhbt, 1972 (1st prize), Artists Guild 50th Fine Art Exhbn., Chgo., 1973 (prize), Dickinson State U., 1973 (prize), N. Shore Art League Print Exhbn, 1973 (prize), Lakehurst Exhbt, 1974 (prize), Union League Art Exhbt, 1974 (1st prize), Artists Guild Fine Arts Exhbn., 1974 (best of Show), Bluegrass Painting Exhbn, Louisville, 1975 (award), Union League Art Exhbn, 1976 (prize); represented in permanent collections, Brit. Mus., London, Smithsonian Inst., Washington, Art Inst. Chgo., Jan Cicero Gallery, Chgo., Foster Harmon Gallery, Sarasota, Fla. Home: 6150 Briarwood Ter Fort Myers FL 33912 *I am a painter of light. I'm intrigued and fascinated with form. To me, there are two worlds-the one we all live in, and the one that I create. Painting is the discipline by which I constantly rediscover both of these worlds.*

SCHWARTZ, CARL ROBERT EMDEN, psychiatrist and educator; b. N.Y.C., Feb. 23, 1955. AB magna cum laude, Harvard U., 1976, MD, 1981. Intern in pediatrics Children's Hosp. Med. Ctr., Boston, 1981-82; resident in psychiatry Mass. Gen. Hosp., Boston, 1982-84, chief resident acute psychiatry svc., 1984-85, postgrad. fellow in psychoanalytic psychotherapy, 1985-86, staff psychiatrist psychiat. neurosci. program, 1995—; postdoctoral rsch. fellow clin. rsch. tng. program Mass. Mental Health Ctr., Boston, 1986-88, staff psychiatrist, 1988—; Ethel DuPont-Warren rsch. fellow Harvard Med. Sch., Boston, 1985-86, Warren-Whitman-Richardson fellow, 1988-90, instr. psychiatry, 1988—. Recipient scientist devel. award NIH, 1990-95; Fiske fellow Harvard U..-Trinity Coll., Eng., 1976-77. Mem. APA, Soc. Rsch. in Child Devel., Soc. Rsch. Child and Adolescent Psychopathology, Phi Beta Kappa. Office: Harvard Med Sch 74 Fenwood Rd Boston MA 02115-6113

SCHWARTZ, CAROL LEVITT, government official; b. Greenville, Miss., Jan. 20, 1944; d. Stanley and Hilda (Simmons) Levitt; m. David H. Schwartz (dec.); children: Stephanie, Hilary, Douglas. BS in Spl. and Elem. Edn., U. Tex., 1965. Mem. transiton team Office of Pres. Elect, 1980-81; con. office presdl. personnel The White House, Washington, 1981; cons. U.S. Dept. Edn., Washington, 1982; pres. sec. U.S. Ho. Reps., Washington, 1982-83; mem.-at-large Coun. of D.C., Washington, 1985-89, 97—; candidate for mayor, Washington, 1986, 94; vice chmn. Nat. Edn. Commn. on Time and Learning, 1992-94, Nat. Adv. Coun. on Disadvantaged Children, 1974-79; lectr. in field; radio commentator, 1990-91. Regional columnist Washington Jewish Week, 1995-97. Mem. D.C. Bd. Edn., 1974-82, v.p., 1977-80; bd. dirs. Met. Police Boys and Girls Club, 1st v.p., 1989-93, pres., 1994-96, chmn. membership com., 1984-93; mem. adv. com. Am. Coun. Young Polit. Leaders, 1982-90; mem. Nat. Coun. Friends Kennedy Ctr., 1984-91; bd. dirs. Whitman-Walker Clinic, 1988—, v.p., 1995-96; bd. dirs. St. John's Child Devel. Ctr., 1989-91, Hattie M. Strong Found., 1995—; trustee Kennedy Ctr. Cmty. and Friends Bd., 1991—, chmn. ednl. task force, 1993—; trustee Jewish Coun. on Aging, 1991-93; v.p. adv. bd. Am. Automobile Assn., 1988—; bd. dirs. Washington Hebrew Congregation, 1995—. Mem. Cosmos Club. Republican. Jewish.

SCHWARTZ, CHARLES, JR., federal judge; b. New Orleans, Aug. 20, 1922; s. Charles and Sophie (Hess) S.; m. Patricia May, Aug. 31, 1950; children—Priscilla May, John Putney. BA, Tulane U., 1943, JD, 1947. Bar: La. 1947. Ptnr. Guste, Barnett & Little, 1947-70; practiced in New Orleans, until 1976; ptnr. firm Little, Schwartz & Dussom, 1970-76; dist. counsel Gulf Coast dist. U.S. Maritime Adminstrn., 1953-62; judge U.S. Dist. Ct. (ea. dist.) La., New Orleans, 1976—; mem. Fgn. Itelligence Surveillance Ct., 1992—; prof. Tulane U. Law Sch.; lectr. continuing law insts.; mem. Jud. Conf. Com. U.S. on implementation of jury system, 1981-85; mem. permanent adv. bd. Tulane Admiralty Law Inst., 1984—. Bd. editors Tulane Law Rev. Pres. New Orleans unit Am. Cancer Soc., 1956-57; v.p., chmn. budget com. United Fund Greater New Orleans Area, 1959-61, trustee, 1953-65; bd. dirs. Cancer Assn. Greater New Orleans, 1958—, pres., 1958-59, 72-73; bd. dirs. United Cancer Council, 1963-85, pres., 1971-73; mem. com. on grants to agencies Community Chest, 1965-87; men's adv. com. League Women Voters, 1966-68; chmn. com. admissions of program devel. and coordination com. United Way Greater New Orleans, 1974-77; mem. comml. panel Am. Arbitration Assn., 1974-76; bd. dirs. Willow Wood Home, 1979-85, 1989-92; bd. mgrs. Touro Infirmary, 1992—; trustee Metairie Park Country Day Sch., 1977-83; mem. La. Republican Central Com., 1961-76; mem. Orleans Parish Rep. Exec. Com., 1960-75, chmn., 1964-75; mem. Jefferson Parish Rep. Exec. Com., 1975-76; del. Rep. Nat. Conv., 1960, 64, 68; mem. nat. budget and consultation com. United Community Funds and Coun. of Am., 1961; bd. dirs. Community Svcs. Coun., 1971-73. Served to 2d lt. AUS, 1943-46; maj. U.S. Army Res.; ret. Mem. La. Bar Assn. New Orleans Bar Assn. (legis. com. 1970-75), Fed. Bar Assn., Fgn. Rels. Assn. New Orleans (bd. dirs. 1957-61), 5th Cir. Dist. Judges Assn. (pres. 1984-85), Lakewood Country Club (bd. dirs. 1967-68, pres. 1975-77). Office: US Dist Ct C-317 US Courthouse 500 Camp St New Orleans LA 70130-3313

SCHWARTZ, CHARLES D., broadcast executive; b. Phila., Sept. 6, 1948; s. Howard I. and Jane (Cohen) S.; m. Susan Greenspan, June 28, 1970; children: Daniel, Michael, Amy. BFA, U. Cin., 1970. Media planner, buyer Grey Advt., Inc., N.Y.C., 1970-71; account exec. CBS Radio Spot Sales, CBS, Inc., N.Y.C., 1971-74; retail sales mgr. Sta. WCBS-AM, CBS, Inc., N.Y.C., 1974-75; sales mgr. CBS Radio Spot Sales, CBS, Inc., N.Y.C., 1975-76; gen. sales mgr. Sta. WBBM-AM, CBS, Inc., Chgo., 1976-79; v.p., gen. mgr. Sta. WCAU-AM, CBS, Inc., Phila., 1979-80; pres., chief operating officer Newsystems Group, Inc., Phila., 1980-87; pres., chief executive officer, chmn. Panache Broadcasting, Phila., 1987—. Bd. govs. Cardiovascular Inst., Allegheny U., Phila., 1988—, mem. exec. com., 1988—. Avocations: writing, travel. Office: Ste 250 166 E Levering Mill Rd Bala Cynwyd PA 19004-2664*

SCHWARTZ, CHARLES FREDERICK, retired economist, consultant; b. Balt., May 2, 1916; s. Charles Herzog and Cora (Miller) S.; m. Marika Rupis, June 7, 1941; children: Mary Louise Schwartz Solomon, Charles Anthony. BA, U. Va., 1936, MA, 1937, PhD, 1939; postgrad., Va. Poly. Inst., 1937-38, Georgetown U., 1941-42. Instr. rural econs. U. Va., 1939-41; economist nat. income div. Office Bus. Econs., U.S. Dept. Commerce, 1941-51, asst. chief, 1951-56, asst. dir. Office Bus. Econs., 1956-59; chief N.Am. div. Western Hemisphere Dept., IMF, 1959-62, asst. dir. Western Hemisphere Dept., 1962-66, dep. dir. rsch. dept., 1966-79, dir. adjustment studies, 1979-83; chmn. investment com. Staff Retirement Plan, IMF, 1979-85, spl. cons., office mng. dir., 1983-86; cons., 1987—; cons. Exec. Office of Pres., mem. adv. coms. on balance of payments stats., 1963-65, 75-76. Author publs. on nat. income, the world economy. Recipient gold medal for exceptional svc. Dept. Commerce, 1951. Mem. Internat. Assn. Rsch. in Income and Wealth, Conf. on Rsch. in Income and Wealth (chmn., exec. com. 1961-62), Am. Econ. Assn., Am. Statis. Assn., Phi Beta Kappa, Theta Delta Chi. Home: 7504 Honeywell Ln Bethesda MD 20814-1028

SCHWARTZ, CHARLES PHINEAS, JR., replacement auto parts company executive, lawyer; b. Chgo., Apr. 23, 1927; s. Charles Phineas and Lavinia Duffy (Schulman) S.; m. Joan Straus, Aug. 12, 1954 (div. 1971); children: Alex, Ned, Debra, Emily; m. Susan Lamm Hirsch, Dec. 18, 1976. A.B., U. Chgo., 1945; LL.B., Harvard U., 1950. Bar: Ill. 1950, N.Y. 1951, U.S. Supreme Ct. 1955. Assoc. Szold & Brandwen, N.Y.C., 1950-52; rsch. assoc., teaching fellow Harvard U. Law Sch., Cambridge, Mass., 1952-56; pvt. practice Chgo., 1956-61; ptnr. Straus, Blosser & McDowell, Chgo., 1961-67; fin. and bus. cons. Chgo., 1967-75, 93—; pres., chief exec. officer Champion Parts Inc., Oak Brook, Ill., 1975-86, chmn. bd., chief exec. officer, 1986-92; chmn. emeritus Champion Parts Inc., Oak Brook, 1992—; dir. Supercrete Ltd., Winnipeg, Man., Can., 1964-80, Athey Products Corp., Raleigh, N.C., 1967-86. Trustee, officer Hull House Assn., Chgo., 1958-70; dir., officer Chgo. Fedn. Settlements, 1972-79; dir., officer, pres. Friends of the Parks, Chgo., 1982—; dir., officer, pres. Hyde Park Coop. Soc., 1962-68; pres. U. Cho. Lab. Schs. Parents Assn., 1970-72, 75-77; trustee KAM Isaiah Isrel Congregation, 1975-85; bd. dirs. Chgo. Hearing Soc., 1996—. Served with USNR, 1945-46. Recipient Boulton Meml. award for disting. bus. statesmanship and dedicated service rendered to the entire auto parts rebuilding industry Automotive Parts Rebuilders Assn., 1987. Mem. ABA, Motor Equipment and Mfrs. Assn. (dir. 1977-81), Automotive Pres. Coun., Heavy Duty Bus. Forum, Automotive Sales Coun., Soc. Automotive Engrs., Automotive Parts Rebuilders Assn. (dir., officer, chmn. 1988—), Chgo. Coun. Lawyers, Heavy Vehicle Maintenance Group (officer 1994—), Quadrangle Club (Chgo.), Harvard Club (N.Y.C.). Jewish. Clubs: Quadrangle (Chgo.); Harvard (N.Y.C.). Office: 230 E Ohio St Ste 120 Chicago IL 60611-3266

SCHWARTZ, CHARLES WALTER, lawyer; b. Brenham, Tex., Dec. 27, 1953; s. Walter C. and Annie (Kuehn) S.; m. Kay Anne Kern, Sept. 24, 1996. BS, U. Tex., Austin, 1975, MA, 1980, JD, 1977; LLM, Harvard U., 1980. Bar: Tex. 1977; bd. cert. civil appellate law Tex. Bd. Legal Specialization. Law clk. to judge U.S. Ct. Appeals (5th cir.), Austin, Tex., 1977-79; assoc. Vinson & Elkins L.L.P., Houston, 1980-86, ptnr., 1986—. Contbr. articles to law revs. Fellow Coll. of State Bar of Tex.; mem. ABA, Tex. Bar Assn., Tex. Bar Found., Houston Bar Found., Houston Bar Assn., Am. Law Inst., Tex. Law Rev. Assn., Bar Assn. of 5th Cir. Home: 2825 Albans Rd Houston TX 77005-2309 Office: Vinson & Elkins LLP 2300 First City Tower 1001 Fannin St Houston TX 77002-6706

SCHWARTZ, DALE MARVIN, lawyer; b. Columbus, Ga., Aug. 20, 1942; s. Sanford and Florence (Casper) S.; m. Susan Ellis, Sept. 12, 1965; children: Lori, Leslye, Laine. Student, Vanderbilt U., 1959-60, George Wash. U., 1964; AB, U. Ga., 1965, JD, 1968. Bar: Ga. 1968, U.S. Ct. Appeals 1975, U.S. Supreme Ct. 1977. Ptnr. Troutman Sanders, Atlanta, 1968-97; prin. Dale M. Schwartz & Assoc., Atlanta, 1997—; S.E. counsel to State of Israel, 1976—; mem. Ga. adv. bd. U.S. Civil Rights Commn., 1986-97, chmn., 1991-97; lead counsel Marial Cuban Class Action Litigation, 1981-88; guest Nightline, 60 Minutes, 20/20, CNN, others; adj. prof. Emory U. Sch. Law, 1988—. Editor: Ga. Law Rev., 1966-68, Ga. State Bar Jour., 1966-68; editl. bd. Immigration Policy and Law, 1988—. Gen. counsel Dem. Party Ga., Atlanta, 1978-80; S.E. chmn. Statue of Liberty Ellis Island Found., N.Y.C., 1985-86; mem. nat. bd. dirs., S.E. vice chmn. Anti-Defamation League, N.Y.C. and Atlanta, 1984—, chmn., 1993-95; pres. Jewish Family Svcs., Atlanta, 1984-88; v.p., bd. dirs. Hebrew Immigrant Aid Soc., N.Y.C., 1984—, v.p., 1990—; bd. dirs. Ctr. for Human Rights and Constl. Law, L.A., 1987—, Atlanta Jewish Fedn., 1979-94, Am. Jewish Congress, N.Y.C., 1986-88; pres. Coll. Young Dems. Recipient Young Leadership award Atlanta Jewish Fedn., 1981, Civic Leader award Ga. State U. chpt. Mortar Bd., 1982, Law and Social Action award Am. Jewish Congress, 1984, Civil Liberties award ACLU, Atlanta, 1987. Fellow Am. Immigration Law Found. (gen. counsel 1993—); mem. ABA (coordinating com. on immigration law 1987-94, co-chmn. immigration law com. sect. litigation 1990-92), State Bar Ga., Am. Immigration Lawyers Assn. (bd. dirs. 1980—, nat. pres. 1986-87, Jack Wasserman award for litigation excellence 1988). Avocations: amateur radio, photography, stamp collecting. Home: 650 River Chase Pt NW Atlanta GA 30328-3554 Office: Ste 450 River Edge One 5500 Interstate North Pky Atlanta GA 30328-4662

SCHWARTZ, DANIEL BENNETT, artist; b. N.Y.C., Feb. 16, 1929; s. Bennett Henry and Lillian (Blumenthal) S.; m. Judith Nancy Kass, June 12, 1955 (div. 1980); 1 child, Claudia Bennet. Grad., High Sch. of Music and Art, N.Y.C., 1946; student, Art Students League, 1946, Y. Kuniyoshi; BFA, R.I. Sch. Design, 1949. Instr. pvt. painting class, 1965-81, 90-95, Parsons Sch. Design, 1983. One man shows include Davis Galleries, N.Y.C., 1955, 56, 58, 60, Hirschl & Adler Galleries, N.Y.C., 1963, Maxwell Galleries, San Francisco, 1964, Babcock Galleries, N.Y.C., 1967, F.A.R. Galleries, N.Y.C., 1970, Armstrong Galleries, N.Y.C., 1985, 87, Hammer Galleries, N.Y.C., 1994; exhibited in group shows at Albany Inst. History and Art, Am. Fedn. Arts, Butler Inst. Am. Art, Libr. of Congress, Nat. Acad. Design, Pa. Acad. Fine Art, Whitney Mus. Art, Collection Nat. Portrait Gallery, others; subject of various articles. Louis C. Tiffany Found. grantee, 1956, 60; recipient Purchase prize Am. Acad. Arts and letters, 1964, 84, 11 Gold medals Soc. Illustrators, N.Y.C., 1960-85, Obrig prize for painting Nat. Acad. Design, 1990, winner 1st Benjamin Altman Figure prize, 1992. Mem. Century Assn., elected mem. Nat. Acad of Design, 1997. Avocation: jazz piano. Home and Office: 48 E 13th St New York NY 10003-4631

SCHWARTZ, DANIEL C., lawyer; b. Pa., 1943. AB, Stanford U., 1965; JD, George Washington U., 1969. Bar: D.C. 1969. Asst. to dir. Bur. Competition, FTC, Washington, 1973-75, asst. dir. evaluation, 1975-77, dep. dir., 1977-79; gen. counsel Nat. Security Agy., Washington, 1979-81; ptnr. Bryan Cave LLP, Washington. Mem. ABA. Office: Bryan Cave LLP 700 13th St NW Washington DC 20005-3960

SCHWARTZ, DAVID ALAN, infectious diseases and placental pathologist, educator; b. Phila., May 20, 1953; s. Harold Martin and Thelma (Bell) S; m. Stephanie Baker, May 16, 1993. BA, U. Pitts., 1974, MS in Hygiene, 1977; D in Medicine, Far Eastern U., Manila, The Philippines, 1984. Intern, resident in anatomic pathology sch. medicine Hahnemann U., Phila., 1984-87, chief resident sch. medicine, 1987-88; instr. Harvard U. Sch. Medicine, Boston, 1988-89; asst. prof. pathology Emory U. Sch. Medicine, Atlanta, 1989-94, assoc. prof., 1994—; rsch. scientist Ctrs. for Disease Control, Atlanta, 1992—; asst. prof. medicine (infectious disease) Emory U. Sch. Medicine, Atlanta, 1995—; vis. prof. U. Mayor San Simon, Bolivia, 1993—; cons. in AIDS, CDC, Atlanta, 1992—; cons. in Chagas' disease U.S. AID, Washington, Bolivian Min. Health, La Paz, 1992—; chmn. pathology subcom. Women and Infants Transmission study NIH; pathology cons. Bangkok-CDC HIV Study, 1993—. Co-editor: Pathology of Infectious Diseases; mem. editl. bd. Ann. clin. Lab. Sci., Arch. Pathol. Lab. Medicine; mem. editl. rev. com. Human Pathology; contbr. numerous articles to profl. jours. and chpts. to texts. Recipient Pathology Resident Rsch. award Am. Soc. Clin. Pathologists, 1985; Pediat. AIDS Found. scholar, 1993—; Syphilis Rsch. grantee Ctrs. for Disease Control, 1991, Placental Infections Rsch. grantee Emory Med. Care Found., 1991—, Placental HIV Rsch. grantee NIH, 1991—. Fellow Coll. Am. Pathologists, Coll. Physicians Phila., Internat. Acad. Pathology, Assn. Clin. Scientist, Sigma Xi. Jewish. Achievements include characterization of pathologic features of emerging infections including human microsporidiosis and other parasitic infections; development of new diagnostic methods for pathologic identification of infectious agents; description of molecular pathologic techniques for identification of viruses and parasites. Office: Grady Meml Hosp 80 Butler St SE Atlanta GA 30335-3800

SCHWARTZ, DONALD, chemistry educator; b. Scarsdale, N.Y., Dec. 27, 1927; s. Harry A. and Ethel S.; m. Lois Schwartz, Sept. 8, 1948; children: Leanne, Mark W., Scott B., Bradley F. B.S., U. Mo., 1949; M.S., Mont. State U., 1951; Ph.D., Pa. State U., 1955. Program dir. NSF, 1966-68; asso. dean Grad. Sch., Memphis State U., 1968-70; dean advanced studies Fla. Atlantic U., Boca Raton, 1970-71; v.p., acting pres. State U. N.Y., Buffalo, 1971-74; chancellor Ind. U.-Purdue U., Ft. Wayne, Ind., 1974-78; chancellor, prof. U. Colo., Colorado Springs, 1978-83, prof., 1983-93, prof. emeritus, 1993—; cons. in field. Author papers structure of coal and organo-titanium compounds, also on higher edn. Bd. dirs. Colorado Springs Osteo. Found., 1985—. Served with USCG, 1945. Research fellow AEC, 1953-55; N.Y. State fellow, 1947-48. Mem. Am. Chem. Soc., AAAS, Sigma Xi, Phi Lambda Upsilon, Phi Delta Kappa. Clubs: Rotary, Country of Colo, Shriners. Home: 21 Sanford Rd Colorado Springs CO 80906-4219 Office: U of Colo Cragmor Rd Colorado Springs CO 80907 *Each can become all that he or she is capable of being through education, hard work and compassion for other human beings. This I believe.*

SCHWARTZ, DONALD FRANKLIN, communication educator; b. Jamestown, N.D., Feb. 20, 1935; s. Frank William and Mabel Esther (Williams) S.; m. Lois Carolyn Bonnema, June 26, 1965; children: Daria, Karin, Marc. B.S., N.D. State U., 1957, M.S., 1961; Ph.D., Mich. State U., 1968. Asst. dir. pub. rels. N.D. State U., Fargo, 1959-66, chmn. social scis., 1969-71, chmn. communication, 1967-79; instr. communication Mich. State U., East Lansing, 1966-67; vis. scientist U.S. Dept. Agr., Washington, 1979-80; prof. communication Cornell U., Ithaca, N.Y., 1980—, chmn. dept., 1980-85, dir. undergrad. studies, 1995—; vis. scholar U. N.Mex., 1994. Contbr. articles to profl. jours. Recipient Outstanding Svc. award Future Farmers Am., 1976, Svc. award USDA, 1980, A.D. White Prof. of Yr. award, 1993. Mem. AAUP, Internat. Comm. Assn. (sec., pub. rels. interest group 1992-93), Am. Acad. Mgmt., Am. Soc. Pers. Adminstrn. (chpt. pres. 1976-77), Pub. Rels. Soc. Am. (nat. faculty advisor student assn. 1989-90, vice-chair educators sect. 1992, Pres.'s Citation for Leadership 1990, nat. ednl. affairs com. 1993-96). Roman Catholic. Office: Cornell U Dept Communication 311 Kennedy Hall Ithaca NY 14853-4203

SCHWARTZ, DONALD LEE, lawyer; b. Milw., Dec. 8, 1948; s. Bernard L. and Ruth M. (Marshall) S.; m. Susan J. Dunst, June 5, 1971; children: Stephanie Jane, Cheryl Ruth. BA, Macalester Coll., 1971; JD, U. Chgo., 1974. Bar: Ill. 1974. Assoc. Sidley & Austin, Chgo., 1974-80, ptnr., 1980-88; ptnr. Latham & Watkins, Chgo., 1988—. Chmn. Ill. Conservative Union, 1979-81, bd. dirs. 1977-85. Served with U.S. Army, 1971-77. Mem. ABA (uniform comml. code com., comml. fin. svcs. commn.), Ill. Bar Assn. (sec. coun. banking and bankuprtcy sect. 1982-83), Chgo. Bar Assn. (chmn. comml. law com. 1980-81, fin. insts. com. 1982-83), Ivanhoe Country Club, Monroe Club, Met. Club. Republican. Episcopalian. Avocation: golf. Home: 191 Park Ave Glencoe IL 60022-1351 Office: Latham & Watkins Ste 5800 Sears Tower Chicago IL 60606

SCHWARTZ, DORIS RUHBEL, nursing educator, consultant; b. Bklyn., May 30, 1915; d. Henry and Florence Marie (Shuttleworth) S. BS, NYU, 1953, MS, 1958. RN, N.Y. Staff nurse Meth. Hosp., Bklyn., 1942-43; pub. health nurse Vis. Nurse Assn., Bklyn., 1947-51; pub. health nurse Cornell U. Med. Coll., Cornell-N.Y. Hosp. Sch. Nursing, N.Y.C., 1951-61, tchr. pub. health nursing, geriatric nursing, 1961-80; ret., 1990; sr. fellow U. Pa. Sch. Nursing, Phila., 1981-90; mem. bd. dirs. Elders With Adult Dependants. Author: Give Us to Go Blithely, 1990 (Book of Yr. award Am. Jour. Nursing 1991); sr. author: The Elderly Chronically Ill Patient: Nursing and Psychosocial Needs, 1963; co-author: Geriatrics and Geriatric Nursing, 1983 (Book of Yr. award Am. Jour. Nursing 1984); contbr. articles to profl. jours. Mem. adv. com. nursing WHO, Geneva, 1971-79; adv. com. Robert Wood Johnson Found., Teaching Nursing Home Project, Princeton, N.J., U. Pa. Wharton Sch. Study of Continuing Care Retirement Communities, 1981-83; vol. Foulkeways Continuing Care Retirement Cmty., Gwynedd, Pa. Served to capt. N.C., U.S. Army, 1943-47, PTO. Rockefeller fellow U. Toronto, 1950-51, Mary Roberts fellow Am. Jour. Nursing, 1955, Fogarty fellow NIH, 1975-76; recipient Diamond Jubilee Nursing award N.Y. County RNs Assn., 1979. Fellow Inst. Medicine of NAS, APHA (Disting. Career award nursing sect. 1979), Am. Acad. Nursing (charter, coun. 1973-74); mem. ANA (Pearl McIver award 1979), Soroptimist (v.p. N.Y.C. club 1974-75), Sigma Theta Tau (Founders award 1979, Mentor award Alpha Upsilon chpt. 1992). Democrat. Mem. Soc. of Friends. Avocations: travel; writing; people.

SCHWARTZ, EDWARD ARTHUR, lawyer, foundation executive; b. Boston, Sept. 27, 1937; s. Abe and Sophie (Gottheim) S.; children: Eric Allen, Jeffrey Michael. AB, Oberlin Coll., 1959; LLB, Boston Coll., 1962; postgrad., Am. U., 1958-59, Northeastern U., 1970; postgrad. exec. program, Stanford U., 1979. Bar: Conn. 1962, Mass. 1965. Legal intern Office Atty. Gen. Commonwealth of Mass., 1961; assoc. Schatz & Schatz, Hartford, Conn., 1962-65, Cohn, Reimer & Pollack, Boston, 1965-67; v.p., gen. coun. sec. Digital Equipment Corp., Maynard, Mass., 1967-88; pres. New Eng. Legal Found., Boston, 1990—, also bd. dirs.; vis. prof. law Boston Coll., 1986, adj. prof., 1987-89; also bd. dirs.; bd. dirs. The Computer Mus. Editor Boston Coll. Indsl. and Comml. Law Rev, 1960-62, Ann. Survey Mass. Law, 1960-62. Mem. ABA, Mass. Bar Assn.,Boston Bar Assn. Home: 62 Todd Pond Rd Lincoln MA 01773-3808

SCHWARTZ, EDWARD J., federal judge; b. 1912. Judge Mcpl. Ct. and Superior Ct., San Diego; judge U.S. Dist. Ct. for So. Dist. Calif., former chief judge, now sr. judge. Office: US Dist Ct Courtroom 1 940 Front St San Diego CA 92101-8994*

SCHWARTZ, ELEANOR BRANTLEY, academic administrator; b. Kite, Ga., Jan. 1, 1937; d. Jesse Melvin and Hazel (Hill) Brantley; children: John, Cynthia. Student Mercer U., Ga., 1954-55; student U. Va., 1955, Ga. Southern Coll., 1956-57, BBA, Ga. State U., 1962, MBA, 1963, DBA, 1969. Adminstrv. asst. Fin. Agy., 1954, Fed. Govt., Va., Pa., Ga., 1956-59; asst. dean admissions Ga. State U., Atlanta, 1961-66, asst. prof., 1966-70; assoc. prof. Cleve. State U., 1970-75, prof. and assoc. dean, 1975-80; dean, Harzfeld prof. U. Mo., Kansas City, 1980-87, vice chancellor acad. affairs, 1987-91, interim chancellor, 1991-92, chancellor, 1992—; disting. vis. prof. Berry Coll., Rome, Ga., N.Y. State U. Coll., Fredonia, Mons U., Belgium; cons. pvt. industry, U.S., Europe, Can.; bd. dirs. ANUHCO, Rsch. Med. Ctr., United Group of Mutual Funds, Waddell & Reed Funds, Inc., Torchmark/United Funds, Toy and Miniature Mus., Menorah Med. Ctr. Found., NCCJ, Econ. Devel. Corp. of Kansas City, Midwest Grain Products, Silicon Prairie Tech. Assn., Mo. Planning Coun. for Devel. Disabilities, 1995—, Am. Coun. Edn. Commn. on Minorities in Higher Edn., 1995—, Assn. Gov. Bds. Univs. and Colls., 1995—. Author: Sex Barriers in Business, 1971, Contemporary Readings in Marketing, 1974; (with Muczyk and Smith) Principles of Supervision, 1984. Chmn., Mayor's Task Force in Govt. Efficiency, Kansas City, Mo., 1984; mem. community planning and research council United Way Kansas City, 1983-85; bd. dirs. Jr. Achievement, 1982-86. Recipient Disting. Faculty award Cleve. State U., 1974, Cleve., 60 Women of Achievement Girls Scouts Council Mid Continent, 1983; named Career Woman of Yr. Kansas City, Mo., 1989; recipient disting. svc. award Kansas State U., 1992. Mem. Am. Mktg. Assn., Acad. Internat. Bus., Am. Mgmt. Assn., Am. Case Research Assn., Internat. Soc. Study Behavioral Devel., Phi Kappa Phi, Golden Key, Alpha Iota Delta.

SCHWARTZ, ELI, economics educator, writer; b. N.Y.C., Apr. 2, 1921; s. Israel and Tillie (Shapiro) S.; m. Renee S. Kartiganer, Aug. 29, 1948; children: Pamela F., Alan G. B.S., Denver U., 1943; M.A., U. Conn., 1948; Ph.D., Brown U., 1952. Instr. U. R.I., Kingston, 1947-48; asst. instr. Brown U., Providence, 1948-51; chief regional economist Office Price Stblzn., Boston, 1951-53; lectr. Mich. State U., East Lansing, 1953-54; asst. prof. econs. Lehigh U., Bethlehem, Pa., 1954-58, assoc. prof., 1958-62, prof., 1962-91, Charles Macfarlane prof. econs., 1978-91, chmn. dept. econs., 1978-84, ret., 1991; cons. econs. and fin., expert witness Schwartz-Aronson Assocs., Bethlehem, 1965—. Author: Corporate Finance, 1962, Trouble in Eden, 1980; editor: Managing Municipal Finance, 1980, 83, 87, 96, Restructuring the Thrift Industry, 1989, Theory and Application of the Interest Rate, 1993. With U.S. Army, 1943-46, ETO. Recipient sr. teaching Lehigh U., 1972; Earhart Found. grantee, 1978. Mem. Am. Econs. Assn., Am. Fin. Assn., Nat. Assn. Forensic Econs. (founding mem.). Jewish. Home: 3185 W Cedar St Allentown PA 18104 Office: Lehigh U Dept Econs Rauch Ctr 621 Taylor St Bethlehem PA 18015-3117 *If I have achieved any success it is because I am interested in the subject matter of my field. I am fortunate to enjoy reading, teaching, consulting and writing.*

SCHWARTZ, ELLIOTT SHELLING, composer, author, music educator; b. Bklyn, Jan. 19, 1936; s. Nathan and Rose (Shelling) S.; m. Dorothy Rose Feldman, June 26, 1960; children: Nina, Jonathan. AB, Columbia U., 1957, MA, 1958, EdD, 1962. Instr. music U. Mass., Amherst, 1960-64; from asst. prof. music to assoc. prof. Bowdoin Coll., Brunswick, Maine, 1964-75, prof. music, 1975—; vis. prof. music Ohio State U., Columbus, 1988-92; vis. composer Trinity Coll. Music, London, 1967, U. Calif. Coll. Creative Studies, Santa Barbara, 1970, 73, 74; composer, pianist, commentator British Broadcast Corp, London, 1972, 74, 78, 83; vis. research musician Center Music Expt., La Jolla, Calif., 1978-79; disting. vis. prof. Ohio State U., 1985-86; music cons. Holt, Rinehart & Winston, Random House, Schirmer Books, N.Y.C., 1977—; vis. fellow Robinson Coll., Cambridge U., U.K., 1993-94. Composer: Island, 1970 (Internat. Gaudeamus prize 1970), Chamber Concertos I-IV, 1977-81, Extended Piano, 1980, Dream Music With Variations, 1983, Four Ohio Portraits, 1986, Memorial in Two Parts, 1989, Elan, 1990, Rows Garden, 1993, Equinox, 1994, Timepiece, 1994, Chiaroscuro, 1995, Reflections, 1995, Rainbow, 1996; author: Electronic Music: A Listener's Guide, 1973, Music: Ways of Listening, 1982, (with Daniel Godfrey) Music Since 1945: Issues, Materials and Literature, 1993; editor: (with Barney Childs) Contemporary Composers on Contemporary Music, 1967; contbr. articles to profl. jours. Nat. Endowment for Arts composition grantee, 1974, 76, 82; Rockefeller Found. residence fellow Bellagio, Italy, 1980, 89; MacDowell Colony resident fellow, 1965, 66; Yaddo residence fellow, 1977; recipient Maine State award Maine Commn. Arts and Humanities, 1970, McKim Commn., 1986. Mem. Am. Music Ctr. (v.p. 1981-87), Coll. Music Soc. (nat. coun. 1982-88, pres. 1988-90), Am. Soc. Univ. Composers (nat. coun. 1968-72, nat. chmn. 1983-88), Am. Composers Alliance (governing bd. 1994—). Home: PO Box 451 South Freeport ME 04078-0451 Office: Bowdoin Coll Dept Music Brunswick ME 04011

SCHWARTZ, ESTAR ALMA, lawyer; b. Bklyn., June 29, 1950; d. Henry Israel and Elaine Florence (Scheiner) Sutel; m. Lawrence Gerald Schwartz, June 28, 1976 (div. Dec. 1977); 1 child, Joshua (dec.). JD, N.Y.U., 1980. owner Estaris Paralegal Svc., Flushing, N.Y., 1992—. Mgr., ptnr. Scheiner, Scheiner, DeVito & Wytte, N.Y.C., 1966-81; fed. govt., social security fraud specialist DHHS, OI, OIG, SSFIS, N.Y.C., 1982-83; pensions Todtman, Epstein, et al, N.Y.C., 1983-85; office mgr., sec. Sills, Beck, Cummis, N.Y.C., 1985-86; office mgr., bookkeeper Philip, Birnbaum & Assocs., N.Y.C., 1986-87; office mgr., sec. Stanley Posses, Esq., Queens, N.Y., 1989-90. Democrat. Jewish. Avocations: needlepoint, horseback riding, tennis, bowling, writing children's stories. Home and Office: 67-20 Parsons Blvd Apt 2A Flushing NY 11365-2960

SCHWARTZ, GARRY ALBERT, advertising executive; b. Toledo, Ohio, Jan. 4, 1949; s. Albert Theodore Otto and Ethel Anna (Weiler) S. BA in Speech, Adrian Coll., 1971; MA in Communication, Bowling Green State U., 1972; postgrad., Ind. U., 1974. Creative dir. S & L Advt. & P.R., Toledo,

1976-78; instr. U.S. Savings League Inst., Toledo, 1977; conf. leader Aeroquip Corp., Jackson, Mich., 1978-79; sales promotion supr. Aeroquip Corp., Jackson, 1979-87, advt. display mgr., 1987-88, sr. writer, producer, video, pub. rels., 1988-89, advt. prodn. supr., 1989-91; sr. copywriter Donald L. Arends, Inc., Oak Brook, Ill., 1992-96, Alexander Mktg. Svcs., Inc., Grand Rapids, Mich., 1996—. Mem. Lambda Iota Tau, Iota Beta Sigma, Pi Kappa Delta. Avocations: painting, stamp collecting. Home: 2745 Birchcrest Dr SE Grand Rapids MI 49506 Office: Alexander Mktg Svcs Inc PO Box 601 Grand Rapids MI 49516-0601

SCHWARTZ, GERALD, public relations and fundraising agency executive; b. N.Y.C., June 22, 1927; s. George and Martha F. S.; m. Felice P. Schwartz, June 25, 1950; children: Gary R., Gregg R., Wendy L. Student N.C. State U., 1944-45; AB, U. Miami, Fla., 1949, BS, 1950, postgrad., 1966-67. Staff writer Miami Herald, 1941-44; publicity dir. U.S. Army in Europe, 1946-48; editor Miami Beach Sun, 1950-51; fund raising and pub. rels. counselor, Miami, 1952-58; press sec. to Gov. Nebr., 1959-60; exec. v.p. Bar-Ilan U., Ramat Gan, Israel, Israel, 1960-61; prin. Gerald Schwartz Agy., Miami, Fla., 1962—. Dep. chmn. Dem. Midwest Conf., 1958-60; pres. Am. Zionist Fedn. So. Fla., 1970-73, 86-92; nat. v.p. Am. Zionist Fedn., 85-89, 91-93; pres. Pres.'s council Zionist Orgn. Am., 1983-85; bd. dirs. Temple Emanu-El of Greater Miami, Papanicolaou Cancer Research Inst., Miami, 1962-80; vice chmn. Urban League of Greater Miami, 1983-87; vice chmn. City of Miami Beach Planning Bd., 1953-55; bd. dirs. Greater Miami Symphony, 1982-87, Miami Beach Taxpayers Assn.; pres. Civic League Miami Beach, 1985-87; nat. chmn. Friends of Pioneer Women/Na'amat, 1984-97; pres. Greater Miami chpt. Assn. Welfare of Soldiers in Israel, 1983-86; chmn. City of Miami Beach Hurricane Def. Com., 1978-86, 90-97; trustee South Shore Hosp. and Med. Ctr., Miami, 1987—; exec. vice chmn. South Shore Med. Ctr. Found., 1989—; bd. govs. Barry U., 1985-86; chmn. Econ. Devel. Coun. City of Miami Beach, 1985-91; bd. dirs. Crimestoppers of Dade County, 1991-94; bd. dirs., adminstrv. com. Jewish Nat. Fund of Am., 1995—, v.p. Greater Miami Region, 1996—; mem. exec. bd. State of Israel Bonds Orgn., 1996—. Served with U.S. Army, 1944-46. Recipient Jerusalem Peace award State of Israel Bonds, 1978., Jerusalem 3000 award State Of Israel, 1996. Mem. Pub. Rels. Soc. Am. (accredited; treas. So. Fla. chpt. 1962-64), Am. Pub. Rels. Assn. (pres. chpt. 1960-61), Am. Assn. Polit. Cons, Nat. Assn. Fund Raising Execs. (pres. chpt. 1977-78), Miami Beach Taxpayers Assn. (bd. dirs. 1994—), Miami Internat. Press Club (bd. dirs. 1991—), Miami Beach C. of C. (v.p. 1978-80, 81-84, 86-87, pres.-elect 1988-90, trustee 1990—), Lead and Ink, Tiger Bay Club (pres. 1986-88), Prime Minister's Club of State of Israel (Greater Miami chmn. 1997—), B'nai B'rith (pres. lodge 1964-66), Theta Omicron Pi, Omicron Delta Kappa, Alpha Delta Sigma (pres. chpt. 1965-67), Zeta Beta Tau. Office: Gerald Schwartz Agy 600 Alton Rd Miami FL 33139-5502

SCHWARTZ, GORDON FRANCIS, surgeon, educator; b. Plainfield, N.J., Apr. 29, 1935; s. Samuel H. and Mary (Adelman) S.; m. Rochelle DeG. Krantz, Sept. 5, 1959; children—Amory Blair, Susan Leslie. A.B., Princeton U., 1956; M.D., Harvard U., 1960; MBA, U. Pa., 1990. Intern N.Y. Hosp.-Cornell Med. Ctr., N.Y.C., 1960-61; resident in surgery Columbia-Presbyterian Med. Ctr., N.Y.C., 1963-68; instr. surgery Columbia U., N.Y.C., 1966-68; assoc. in surgery U. Pa., Phila., 1968-70; dir. clin. services Breast Diagnostic Ctr. Jefferson Med. Coll., 1973-78, asst. prof. surgery, 1970-71, assoc. prof., 1971-78, prof., 1978—; practice medicine specializing in surgery and diseases of breast, Phila., 1968—; founder, chmn. acad. com. Breast Health Inst., 1990—; edtl. bd. The Breast Jour., 1994—. Author: (with R.H. Guthrie, Jr.) Reconstructive and Aesthetic Mammoplasty, 1980, (with Douglas Marchant) Breast Disease: Diagnosis and Treatment, 1981, Atlas of Breast Surgery, 1997; mem. editl. bd. The Breast-Ofcl. Jour. of the European Soc. of Mastology, 1996—; contbr. more than 150 articles to profl. jours. Mem. Pa. Gov.'s Task Force on Cancer, 1976-82; mem. breast cancer task force Phila. chpt. Am. Cancer Soc.; mem. clin. investigation rev. com. Nat. Cancer Inst., 1992-95. Served to capt. AUS, 1961-63. NIH Cancer Control fellow, 1968-69. Mem. ACS, AMA, AAUP, Assn. for Acad. Surgery, Allen O. Whipple Surg. Assn., Soc. Surg. Oncology, Internat. Cardiovasc. Soc., Soc. for Surgery Alimentary Tract, Am. Soc. Clin. Oncology, Soc. for Study Breast Diseases (pres. 1981-83), Soc. Internat. Senologie (treas. 1982-90, v.p. 1990-92, sci. com. 1992—), Pa. Med. Soc., Am. Soc. Transplant Surgeons, N.Y. Acad. Scis., Am. Soc. Artificial Internal Organs, Am. Radium Soc., Philadelphia County Med. Soc., Italian Soc. Senology (hon.), Greek Surg. Soc. (hon.), Union League, Locust Club, Princeton Club (pres. Phila. 1989-91), Princeton Club (N.Y.C.), Princeton Terrace Club, Nassau Club, Phi Beta Kappa, Sigma Xi, Alpha Omega Alpha, Nu Sigma Nu. Republican. Jewish. Home: 1805 Delancey Pl Philadelphia PA 19103-6606 Office: 1015 Chestnut St Fl 510 Philadelphia PA 19107-4305

SCHWARTZ, HARRY, journalist; b. N.Y.C., Sept. 10, 1919; s. Sam and Rose (Schnell) S.; m. Ruth E. Blumner, June 8, 1941; children: William Daniel (dec.), John Leonard, Robert Steven. BA, Columbia U., 1940, MA, 1941, PhD, 1943. Economist War Prodn. Bd., 1942-43; economist OSS, 1944-46; asst. prof. econs. Syracuse U., 1946-48, assoc. prof., 1948-51, prof., 1951-53; mem. editorial bd. N.Y. Times, N.Y.C., 1951-79; disting. prof. SUNY, New Paltz, 1967-79; vis. prof. med. econs. Coll. Physicians and Surgeons, Columbia U., 1974, 78-79, writer in residence dept. surgery, 1979-87; columnist Pharm. Exec. mag., 1981—, Scrip mag., 1984—, Am. Med. News, 1989-91; Backman lectr. med. ethics Hebrew Union Coll., 1981; mem. Nat. Bd. Med. Examiners, 1979-83; Mem. exec. com. N.Y. Blood Center, 1973-87. Author: Russia's Soviet Economy, 1949, China, 1966, Prague's 200 Days, 1968, The Case for American Medicine, 1972, Breakthrough: The Discovery of Modern Medicines at Janssen, 1990; columnist Pvt. Practice mag., 1979-91, editor, 1980-84; mem. editl. bd. Psychiat. Times, 1985-94; contbr. numerous articles to profl. jours., newspapers, including Wall St. Jour., N.Y. Times, USA Today. With U.S. Army, 1943-45. Jewish. Home: PO Box 1169 Scarsdale NY 10583-9169

SCHWARTZ, HARRY KANE, lawyer; b. Phila., Apr. 20, 1934; s. M. Murray and Minne G. (Schoenfeld) S.; m. Marinda Kelley, June 20, 1961; children: Anthony Clark, Amanda Lyle. B.A. summa cum laude, Harvard Coll., 1955; Fulbright fellow, Worcester Coll., Oxford U., 1955-56; LL.B. magna cum laude, U. Pa., 1959. Bar: Pa. 1960, D.C. 1961, U.S. Supreme Ct. 1965. Law clk. U.S. Ct. of Appeals, Washington, 1960-61; asst. U.S. atty., 1961-62; atty. SEC, 1962-63; legis. asst. U.S. Sen. Joseph S. Clark, 1963-66; counsel U.S. Senate Subcom. on Employment, Manpower and Poverty, 1966-68; ptnr. Dechert Price & Rhoads, 1969-76; asst. sec. for legislation and intergovtl. relations HUD, Washington, 1977-78; staff adv. domestic policy staff White House, 1978-79; ptnr. Lane & Edson (P.C.), 1979-88, Dewey, Ballantine, Bushby, Palmer & Wood, Washington, 1988-92; dir. Ctr. Preservation Policy Studies, Nat. Trust for Hist. Preservation, 1992-93; spl. projects advisor Office of Cultural Resources, Nat. Park Svc., 1994-95; of counsel Shulman, Rogers, Gandal, Pordy & Ecker, P.A., 1995-96; dir. Phila. Urban Coalition, 1974-76; nat. task force dir. Carter-Mondale Campaign, 1976. Dir. Preservation Action, 1994—, Preservation Md., 1996—. Served with Army N.G., 1961-65. Fellow Salzburg Seminar in Am. Studies, 1964. Mem. Am., Pa., Phila. bar assns., Order of Coif, Phi Beta Kappa. Democrat. Jewish. Club: Cosmos.

SCHWARTZ, HENRY GERARD, surgeon, educator; b. N.Y.C., Mar. 11, 1909; s. Nathan Theodore and Marie (Zagat) S.; m. Edith Courtenay Robinson, Sept. 13, 1934; children: Henry G., Michael R., Richard H. A.B., Princeton, 1928; M.D., Johns Hopkins, 1932. Diplomate: Am. Bd. Neurol. Surgery (chmn. 1968-70). Denison fellow with Prof. O. Foerster, Breslau, Germany, 1931; surg. house officer Johns Hopkins Hosp., 1932-33; NRC fellow Harvard Med. Sch., 1933-35, instr. anatomy, 1935-36; fellow neurol. surgery Washington U. Med. Sch., St. Louis, 1936-37; instr., asst. prof., assoc. prof. neurol. surgery Washington U. Med. Sch., 1937-46, prof., 1946-88, August Busch prof. emeritus, 1988—; acting surgeon-in-chief Barnes and Allied hosps., 1965-67; chief neurosurgeon Barnes, St. Louis Children's hosps., 1946-74; cons. neurosurgeon St. Louis City, Jewish, Los Alamos (N.M.) hosps.; cons. to surgeon gen. USPHS. to surgeon gen. U.S. Army.; Mem. subcom. neurosurgery NRC; del. World Fedn. Neurosurgery. Mem. editorial bd. Jour. Neurosurgery, chmn. 1967-69, editor, 1975-84. Served with AUS, 1942-45. Decorated Legion of Merit; recipient ofcl. citation and commendation Brit. Army, Harvey Cushing medal, 1979. Fellow ACS (adv. council on neurosurgery 1950, 60, v.p. 1972-73); mem. Soc. Neurol. Surgeons (pres. 1968-69), Am. Acad. Neurol. Surgery (pres. 1951-52), Harvey Cushing Soc. (pres. 1967-68), Am. Neurol. Assn. (hon.), Assn. Research Nervous and Mental Disease, Central Neuropsychiat. Assn. Am., Assn. Anatomists, So. Neurosurg. Soc. (pres. 1953-54), Soc. Med. Cons. to Armed Forces, Am. Surg. Assn. (v.p. 1975-76), Soc. de Neuro-Chirurgie de Langue Francaise, Excelsior Surg. Soc., Johns Hopkins Soc. Scholars, Soc. Internat. de Chirugie (Alpha Omega Alpha leader Am. medicine 1978), World Fedn. Neurosurg. Socs. (hon. pres.), Sigma Xi, Alpha Omega Alpha. Home: 2 Briar Oak Saint Louis MO 63132-4204 Office: Washington U Sch Med Dept Neurosurgery 660 S Euclid Ave Saint Louis MO 63110-1010

SCHWARTZ, HERBERT FREDERICK, lawyer; b. Bklyn., Aug. 23, 1935; s. Henry and Blanche Theodora (goldberg) S.; m. Gail Lubets, Jan. 23, 1960; children: Wendy Helene, Karen Anne, Peter Andrew; m. Nan Budde Chequer, Mar. 13, 1987; stepchildren: Elizabeth Guthrie, Anne Hamilton, Laura Dunham. BSEE, MIT, 1957; MA in Applied Econs., U. Pa., 1964, LLB, 1964. Assoc. Fish & Neave, N.Y.C., 1964-70; jr. ptnr. Fish & Neave, 1970-71, ptnr., 1972—, mng. ptnr., 1985-91; lectr. law U. Pa., Phila., 1980-89, adj. prof., 1990—. Mem. adv. bd. PTC Jour., Washington, 1983; author: "Patent Law and Practice," Federal Judicial Center, 1988, 2d. edition, 1995; contbr. articles to profl. jours. Vice-chmn. Jr. Yacht Racing Assn. of L.I. Sound, 1985-88. 1st lt. U.S. Army, Signal Corps, 1957-59. Mem. U.S. Trademark Assn., Assn. of Bar of City of N.Y., Am. Intellectual Property Lawyers Assn., N.Y. Intellectual Property Lawyers Assn., Am. Coll. Trial Lawyers, Am. Law Inst., Order of Coif, N.Y. Yacht Club, Riverside Yacht Club (bd. govs.). Avocation: racing sailboats. Home: 24 Cherry Tree Ln Riverside CT 06878-2629 Office: Fish & Neave 1251 Avenue Of The Americas New York NY 10020-1104

SCHWARTZ, HILDA G., retired judge; b. N.Y.C.; d. Solomon and Anna Leah (Rubin) Ginsburg; m. Herman N. Schwartz, Feb. 21, 1930; 1 child, John Michael. BS, Washington Sq. Coll. of NYU; LLB, NYU, 1929. Bar: N.Y. 1930. Pvt. practice, 1930-46; sec., bur. head, trial commr. Bd. Estimate, N.Y.C., 1946-51; city magistrate City of N.Y., 1951-58, city treas., head dept. finance, 1958-62, dir. finance, 1962-64, judge civil ct., 1965-71; justice state supreme ct. State of N.Y., 1972-83; ret., 1983; counsel to law firm, 1984; chmn. law com. Bd. Magistrates, 1953-58; chmn. home term panel judges, 1954-56; judge adolescent ct., 1953-58. Mem. welfare adv. bd. N.Y. Jr. League, 1953-56; bd. mgrs. Greenwich House, 1946-48; v.p. Young Dem. club 1935-37; trustee Village Temple, 1956-61, chair dedication com., 1957; chair exec. bd. Coun. Org. Am. Jewish Congress, 1958; hon. chair, bd. dirs. Women's League for Histadrut, 1959; vice-chair Greenwich Village Fresh Air Fund, 1962; co-chair community breakfast State of Israel Bonds, 1956; bd. dirs. Washington Sq. Outdoor Art Exhibit, 1950-58, Washington Sq. Coll. Alumni Assn., 1967. Recipient Citation by Women for Achievement, 1951, Award of Merit Women Lawyers Assn. State of N.Y., 1957, Scroll of Key award Key Women, 1959, Honor award Am. Jewish Congress Coun. of Orgns., 1959, Honor award Greenwich Village Community for State of Israel Bonds, 1960, Mother of Yr. award Justice Lodge Masons, 1960, First Egalitarian award Aegis Soc., Fed. Negro Civil Svc. Orgns., 1961, Honor award B'nai B'rith, 1963, Interfaith award, 1963, Alumni Achievement award NYU Washington Sq. Coll. Alumni Assn., 1968; named Woman of Achievement Fedn. Jewish Women Orgns., 1959, Patron ann. bridge, Cath. Ctr. NYU, 1960. Mem. ABA, Assn. of Bar of City of N.Y. (mem. lectr., legal aid, matrimonial law, profl. and jud. ethics coms.), N.Y. State Assn. Women Judges (hon. mem., bd. dirs., Outstanding Jud. Achievement award 1983), Supreme Ct. Justices Assn. of City of N.Y. (bd. dirs. 1976-89), Ins. Arbitrator Forums (arbitrator), N.Y. County Lawyers Assn. (profl. ethics com.), N.Y. State Bar Assn. (jud. sabbaticals com.), N.Y. Women's Bar Assn. (past pres., founder, mem. adv. bd., scroll of honor 1958, Disting. Svc. award 1977, Lifetime Contbn. to Justice award 1984), Nat. Assn. Women Judges, Assn. Supreme Ct. Justices State of N.Y. (community rels., retirement and pensions, jud. sabbaticals coms.), Hadassah (hon. mem. N.Y. chpt. 1961), United HIAS Women's Div. (life), Emerald Soc. (hon. mem. 1961), Histadrut (hon. mem. 1960), Iota Tau Tau (hon.). Office: 43 5th Ave New York NY 10003-4368

SCHWARTZ, HOWARD ALAN, periodontist; b. Paterson, N.J., Dec. 27, 1944; s. Samuel and Ruth (Dimond) S.; m. Rita Blumenthal, Dec. 29, 1968; children: Andrew David Schwartz, Steven Austin Schwartz. BS, Fairleigh Dickinson U., 1967, DDS, 1970; cert. in periodontology, Georgetown U., 1972. State Dental Lic. N.J., N.Y., Mass., Pa., Md., Washington. Clin. instr. in periodontics Georgetown U., 1970-72; chief resident Periodontal Section Dept. Dentistry Veteran's Adminstrn. Hosp., Washington, 1972; asst. prof. Periodontics and Oral Medicine Fairleigh Dickinson U. Sch. Dentistry, Hackensack, N.J., 1972-73, part time clin. asst. prof. Periodontics and Oral Medicine, 1973-79, part time clin. assoc. prof. Periodontics and Oral Medicine, 1979-87, part time clin. prof. Periodontics and Oral Medicine, 1987-89; pvt. practice Periodontics and Oral Medicine, 1972—. Author: (with W.A. Gibson) Immunofluorescent Demonstration of IgG, IgM, and IgA in Human Dental Plaque, (with others) Histochemical Localization of Selected Dehydrogenases in Frozen Sections of Human Dental Plaque, (with others) Salvary Composition as related to Dental Calculus Formation in Humans. Mem. Dentist's Div. Com., Hon. Cabinet, United Jewish Community of Bergen County, 1984-85. Fellow Am. Coll. Dentists, Internat. Coll. Dentists. Mem. Am. Dental Assn., Am. Acad. Periodontology, N.J. Dental Assn. (trustee, treas. 1994-96, v.p. 1996-97, pres.-elect 1997—), Internat. Assn. Dental Rsch., Northeastern Soc. Periodontists, Am. Acad. Oral Medicine, N.J. Soc. Periodontology, Bergen County Dental Soc. (pres. 1989-90), Am. Coll. Dentists, Internat. Coll. Dentists. Jewish. Avocations: running, photography, computers. Home: 10 Wood Hollow Trl Saddle River NJ 07458-1346 Office: 97 N Dean St Englewood NJ 07631-2806

SCHWARTZ, HOWARD JULIUS, allergy educator; b. N.Y.C., Nov. 24, 1936; s. Henry and Edna Betty (Herman) S.; m. Gertrude H. Blody, July 1, 1962; children: Adam David, Kaila Jessica, Michael Jonathan. BA, Bklyn. Coll., 1956; MD, Albert Einstein Coll. Medicine, 1960. Diplomate Am. Bd. Allergy and Immunology, Am. Bd. Internal Medicine; lic. allergist Mass., N.Y., Ohio, Nat. Bd. Med. Examiners. Intern, then asst. resident NYU Med. Services, Bellevue Hosp., N.Y.C., 1960-63, chief resident medicine, psycho-med. div., 1963-64; teaching asst. dept. medicine NYU, N.Y.C., 1961-66; clin. and research fellow in allergy and immunology Mass. Gen. Hosp., Boston, 1966-68; USPHS trainee in medicine Case Western Res. U., Cleve., 1967-71, asst. prof. medicine, 1971-74, mem. Phase II respiratory com., 1971—, mem. hosp. utilization and rev. com., 1975-77, assoc. clin. prof. medicine, 1977-87, clin. prof. medicine, 1987—; asst. physician Univ. Hosps. Cleve., 1968-71, assoc. physician, 1971—, chief allergy clinic, 1972—; staff physician pulmonary sect. Cleve. VA Med. Ctr., 1974-80, cons. in allergy, 1980—; attending physician and cons. in allergy Hillcrest Hosp., Cleve.; cons. staff medicine Mt. Sinai Hosp., Cleve. Author: Hospital Management of the Adult with Status Asthmaticus in Current Therapy of Allergy, 1974, Acute Asthma, Hospital Management-Adult in Current Therapy of Allergy, 1978, Allergic Reactions to Insect Stings in Current Therapy, 1983, also book chpts. and abstracts; contbr. several articles to profl. jours. Served to capt. U.S. M.C., 1964-69. Fellow Am. Acad. Allergy (cutaneous allergy com. 1972-73, penicillin allergy study group 1972—, insect allergy com. 1974—, com. on alternate forms of therapy 1977—, audiovisual com. 1979-81, edn. council 1979-81, chmn. sci. and workshop com. 1982-83, chmn. com. on Am. insects 1980—), Am. Coll. Chest Physicians (com. on allergy 1976—), Am. Coll. Allergy; mem. AMA, Am. Assn. Immunology, Am. Thoracic Soc. (ad hoc com. on definition asthma, allergy, clin. immunology assembly 1979—, program com. 1979-80), Am. Acad. Allergy and Immunology (research council 1980—, sci. and workshop com. 1982—, com. on allergen standardization 1983—, com. on awards, meml. and commemorative lectureships 1984, chmn. com. on anephybis 1992—), Am. Coll. Allergists (com. on insect reactions 1984), Am. Soc. Internal Medicine (com. on internal medicine subspltys. socs. 1984), Asthma and Allergy Found. Am. (med. sci. council 1985), Cen. Soc. Clin. Research, Cleve. Acad. Medicine (health ins. rev. com. splty. panel 1979—), Cleve. Allergy Soc. (sec. treas. 1971, v.p. 1971-72, pres. 1972-74), Cleve. Chest Soc., Cleve. Course in Pulmonary Disease (planning com. 1971-77), Med. Advances Inst. Ohio (allergy com. 1972-73), Midwest Allergy Forum (chmn. 1974, exec. com. 1973-77), Ohio Soc. Allergy and Immunology (program com. 1973-75, sec., treas. 1990, 91, pres.-elect 1991, 92, pres. 1992, 93). Office: Univ Suburban Health Ctr 1611 S Green Rd Cleveland OH 44121-4128

SCHWARTZ, HOWARD WYN, health facility administrator; b. Mpls., June 12, 1951; s. Jerry Schwartz and Geraldine (Berg) Brooks; m. Jeannie Marie Holtzmann, Aug. 2, 1975; children: Abigail Jorene, Rachel Elizabeth. BA cum laude, U. Minn., 1973, MBA, 1982. Acct. Med. Sch., U. Minn., 1973-77, bus. mgr. dept. neurology, 1977-79, adminstr. found. edn. dept., 1979-82, sr. adminstrv. dir., instr. dept. radiology, 1982—; pres. Bus. Mgmt. Svcs., Golden Valley, Minn., 1979—; lectr., author Topics in Radiology Adminstrn., 1984—. Editor-in-chief: RADWORKS Workload Measurement Manual, 1985-87; editor: Radiology Management, 1985-87, Purchasing the Radiology Information System, 1991, Current Concepts in Radiology Management, 1991; contbr. articles to profl. jours. Mem. Cystic Fibrosis Found., Minn., 1980—; chmn. Human Rights Commn., Robbinsdale, 1982-84; sec. Coord. Coun. Minority Concerns, 1984-85; chmn. imaging tech. adv. com. Univ. Hosp. Consortium, 1989-92; dir. Univ. Hosp. Consortium Svcs. Corp., 1990-92, Nat. Summit on Manpower, 1989-92; treas. Tech. Learning Campus Site Coun., Dist. 281, 1990-91, chmn. Bond Referendum campaign, 1995; pres. Armstrong H.S. Parent Assn., Dist. 281, 1991-92. Fellow Am. Healthcare Radiology Adminstrn. (regional pres. 1986-87, nat. pres. 1988-89, sec. edn. found. 1990-91, bd. dirs. edn. found. 1993-95, Outstanding Author award 1990, 93, 96, Midwest Region Disting. Mem. award 1991, Gold award 1991); mem. Radiologists Bus. Mgrs. Assn., Delta Kappa Epsilon. Home: 7400 Winnetka Heights Dr Golden Valley MN 55427-3549 Office: U Minn Hosp 420 Delaware St SE Minneapolis MN 55455-0374

SCHWARTZ, ILENE, psychotherapist, educator; b. Phila., June 19, 1942; d. Israel Gerson and Susan (Soloway) Schiffman. BS, Temple U., 1970; MEd, Antioch U., 1990. Counselor pvt. practice, Phila., 1978—; cons., crisis counselor in the field; instr. psychology and education, 1974-79. Mem. AAUW, Am. Counseling Assn., Freud Friends.

SCHWARTZ, IRVING DONN, architect; b. Chgo., June 11, 1927; s. Simon S. and Rose P. (Pilot) S.; children: Charles, Linda. B.S., U. Ill., 1949, B.S. in Architecture, 1965, M.S. in Architecture, 1972. Registered architect, Ill., Ind., Fla., D.C., Ohio, Ga., Ala., Calif., N.H., Va., Md., Pa, Tenn., La., N.J., Tex., Mo., N.C., S.C. Chief standard cost and indsl. engring. Lanzit Corrugated Box Co., Chgo., 1950-53; pres. Kaufman, Inc., Champaign, Ill., 1953-60; v.p. Hart Mirror Plate Co., Grand Rapids, Mich., 1953-60; asso. Richardson, Severns, Scheeler & Assos., Inc., Champaign, 1960-71; pres. IDS, Inc., Champaign, 1971-83, ADI, Dallas, 1983-86, IDS/B, Inc., Dallas, 1986—; prof. architecture Grad. Sch. Architecture, U. Ill., 1976-83; assoc. prof. design U. North Tex.; cons. in field. Mem. Champaign County Devel. Council; mem. Model Community Coordinating Council, Champaign; co-chmn. bldg. com. Mercy Hosp.; bd. frat. affairs U. Ill.; bd. dirs. United Fund. Served to 2d lt. U.S. Army, 1945-47. Recipient archtl. design research award, graphic design citation Progressive Architecture mag., 1974, Gold Key Design award Hospitality Mag., 1994. Fellow Am. Soc. Interior Designers (treas. 1976, nat. pres. 1978, Louis Tregre award 1992, Nat. design award 1983); mem. AIA (Design award 1983), Nat. Council Archtl. Registration Bds., Nat. Council Interior Design Qualifications (bd. dirs., pres. 1980), Tex. Assn. Interior Design (pres. 1993). Club: Standard (Chgo.). Home: 4443 Westway Ave Dallas TX 75205-3630 Office: IDS/B Inc 2777 N Stemmons Fwy Ste 1650 Dallas TX 75207-2229

SCHWARTZ, IRVING LEON, physician, scientist, educator; b. Cedarhurst, N.Y., Dec. 25, 1918; s. Abraham and Rose (Doniger) S.; m. Felice T. Nlerenberg, Jan. 12, 1946; children: Cornelia Ann, Albert Anthony, James Oliver. AB, Columbia U., 1939; MD, NYU, 1943. Diplomate: Am. Bd. Internal Medicine. Intern, then asst. resident Bellevue Hosp., N.Y.C., 1943-44, 46-47; NIH fellow physiology NYU Coll. Medicine, N.Y.C., 1947-50; Am. Physiol. Soc. Porter fellow, also Gibbs meml. fellow in clin. sci. Rockefeller Inst., N.Y.C., 1950-51, Am. Heart Assn. fellow, 1951-52, asst., then assoc., 1952-58; asst. physician, then assoc. physician Rockefeller Inst. Hosp., 1950-58; sr. scientist Brookhaven Nat. Lab., Upton, N.Y., 1958-61, research collaborator, 1961—; attending physician Brookhaven Nat. Lab. Hosp., 1958—; Joseph Eichberg prof. physiology, dir. dept. U. Cin. Coll. Medicine, 1961-65; dean grad. faculties Mt. Sinai Med. and Grad. Schs., CUNY, 1965-80, prof. physiology and biophysics, chmn. dept., 1968-79, exec. officer biomed. scis. doctoral program, 1969-72, Dr. Harold and Golden Lamport disting. prof., 1979—; dir. Ctr. Peptide and Membrane Research Mt. Sinai Med. Ctr., 1979-87; dean emeritus Mt. Sinai Grad. Sch. Biol. Scis., 1980—. Contbr. articles to sci. publs. Pres. Life Scis. Found., 1962—. Served from 1st lt. to capt., M.C. AUS, 1944-46. Recipient Solomon A. Berson Med. Alumni Achievement award NYU Sch. Medicine, 1973. Fellow A.C.P.; mem. Am. Physiol. Soc., Soc. Exptl. Biology and Medicine, Am. Soc. Clin. Investigation, Am. Fedn. Clin. Research, Biophys. Soc., Endocrine Soc., Harvey Soc., Soc. for Neurosci., Am. Heart Assn., John Jay Assos. Columbia Coll., AAAS, N.Y. Acad. Sci., Sigma Xi, Alpha Omega Alpha. Home: 1120 5th Ave New York NY 10128-0144 also: 9 Thorn Hedge Rd Bellport NY 11713-2615 Office: Mt Sinai Med Ctr 100th St and Fifth Ave New York NY 10029 also: Med Rsch Ctr Brookhaven Nat Lab Upton NY 11973 *The excitement and stimulation that comes from a productive collaboration with other people has been a major source of satisfaction in my life. I feel privileged to have had the opportunity to interact with a wide range of imaginative and inspiring colleagues, students and friends, including my wife of 50 years, whose extraordinary career emphasized the importance of idealism, commitment, persistence and a felicitous blending of focus and flexibility.*

SCHWARTZ, JEROME MERRILL, lawyer; b. Pittsfield, Mass., Oct. 3, 1952; s. Harry and Pauline (Bricker) S.; m. Gail Eileen Schulman, May 29, 1977; children: Karen Beth, Steven Robert. BSEE magna cum laude, U. Mich., 1974, JD magna cum laude, 1977. Bar: Mich. 1977, U.S. Ct. Appeals (6th cir.) 1979, U.S. Supreme Ct. 1990. Assoc. Dickinson, Wright, Moon, Van Dusen & Freeman, Detroit, 1977-83, ptnr., 1984—. Bd. dirs., past chmn. Am. Heart Assn. Mich.; mem. regional adv. bd. Anti-Defamation League. Mem. Detroit Bar Assn., Assn. for Corp. Growth Inc., Comml. Fin. Assn. Edn. Found. (adv. bd.), Nat. Assn. Securities Dealers (panel of arbitrators). Office: 500 Woodward Ave Ste 4000 Detroit MI 48226-3423

SCHWARTZ, JOHN J., association executive, consultant; b. New Rochelle, N.Y., Aug. 28, 1919; s. Edwin Benner and Marjorie Helen (James) S.; m. Katharine S. Sprackling, Jan. 6, 1942; children: Christopher Louis. Grad. high sch., New Rochelle; student, Mercersburg Acad., 1938. Campaign dir. John Price Jones Inc., N.Y.C., 1946-50; dir. pub. relations and fund raising Travelers Aid Soc. N.Y., N.Y.C., 1950-55; dir. devel. Community Service Soc., N.Y.C., 1955-57, Near East Found., N.Y.C., 1957-60; v.p. G.A. Brakeley & Co. Inc., N.Y.C., 1960-61; dir. devel. Fgn. Policy Assn., N.Y.C., 1962-64; founding pres. Greater N.Y. Nat. Soc. of Fund Raising Execs., 1964; asst. v.p. for crusade Am. Cancer Soc., N.Y.C., 1964-66; exec. dir. Am. Assn. Fund Raising Counsel, N.Y.C., 1966-68, exec. v.p., 1968-72, pres., 1972-87; founding bd. mem. Ind. Sector, Washington, 1980-85, mem. com. to measurably increase giving; mem., former pres. Com. on Nat. Ctr. for Charitable Stats.; spl. cons. to Com. on Pvt. Philanthropy and Pub. Needs., 1973; chair pvt. adv. group Nat. Assn. Attys. Gen. Model Law Project. Author: Modern American Philanthropy; A Personal Account, 1994. Mem. adv. bd. mgmt. fund-raising cert. program NYU; mem. adv. coun. Grad. Sch. Mgmt. and Urban Professions, New Sch. Social Rsch.; active formation of 5 borough coalitions Daring Coals for Caring Soc., N.Y.C., 1987; cons. Ind. U. Ctr. on Philanthropy, 1988-91, Cmty. Counselling Svc. Co., Inc., 1988-91; pres. Nat. Philanthropy Day, 1988-90, mem. hon. com., 1981; bd. dirs.-at-large USA World Fund Raising Coun., 1993; pres. Friends of Westport Libr., 1995-97. Capt. USAAF, 1941-46; PTO. Recipient Disting. Profl. Service to Philanthropy award Am. Assn. Fund-Raising Counsel, N.Y., 1976, Outstanding Agy. Profl. award United Way Am., Alexandria, 1982. Mem. Nat. Charities Info. Bur. (bd. dirs. 1978-94), Nat. Soc. Fund-Raising Execs. (bd. dirs. 1964-90, past pres.), Fairfield County Nat. Soc. Fund-Raising Dirs. (bd. dirs. 1992—), Am. Assn. Ret. Persons (bd. dirs. Andrus Found. 1983-90), 501C-3 Soc., Princeton Club (N.Y.C.). Democrat. Unitarian. Avocations: writing history, ship models.

SCHWARTZ, JOHN NORMAN, health care executive; b. Watertown, Minn., Dec. 13, 1945; s. Norman O. and Marion G. (Tesch) S. BA, Augsburg Coll., Mpls., 1967; MHA, U. Minn., 1969. Adminstrv. resident Luth. Hosp. and Med. Ctr., Wheat Ridge, Colo., 1968-69; asst. adminstr. St. Luke's Hosp., Milw., 1969-73, med. adminstr., 1973-75, v.p., 1975-84; sr.

v.p. and chief oper. officer Good Samaritan Med. Ctr., Milw., 1984-85, pres. and chief exec. officer, 1985-88; exec. v.p. Aurora Health Care Inc., Milw., 1988-89; gen. mgr. SmithKline Beecham Clin. Labs., Schaumburg, Ill., 1989-90; chief exec. Trinity Hosp. of Advocate Health Care, Chgo., 1991—; bd. dirs. Samaritan Health Plan, Milw., 1984-89. Bd. dirs. Gt. Lakes Hemophilia Found., Milw., 1975-89, Gov.'s appointee to Coun. on Hemophilia and Related Blood Disorders, Madison, 1978, Sullivan Chamber Ensemble, Milw., 1975-84, South Chgo. YMCA, 1993—; bd. dirs. S.E. Chgo. Devel. Commn., 1996—. Recipient Bd. Mem. of Yr. award Great Lake's Hemophilia Found., 1986, Outstanding Cmty. Leadership award Stony Island C. of C., 1996. Fellow Am. Coll. Healthcare Execs. (regent 1993—). Lutheran. Avocations: jogging, photography, music, choral singing. Office: Trinity Hosp 2320 E 93rd St Chicago IL 60617-3909

SCHWARTZ, JOSEPH, retired container company executive; b. N.Y.C., Apr. 22, 1911; s. Nathan and Ida (Estrich) S.; m. Hazel Shapiro, Dec. 25, 1932; children—Arlene Schwartz Bornstein, Linda Schwartz Rosenbaum. Grad., high sch. Ptnr. Mut. Paper Co., Lynn, Mass., 1928-38; treas. Allied Container Corp., Hyde Park, Mass., 1938-56; pres., treas. Allied Container Corp., Dedham, Hyde Park, 1956-84; chmn. bd. Cargal, Ltd., Lod Israel; ret. v.p. Union Camp Corp., Wayne, N.J. Fellow Brandeis U. Home: #307 3960 Oaks Clubhouse Dr Apt 307 Pompano Beach FL 33069-3645

SCHWARTZ, JOSEPH, English language educator; b. Milw., Apr. 9, 1925; s. Alfred George and Mary (Brandt) S.; m. Joan Jackson, Aug. 28, 1954; 1 son, Adam. B.A., Marquette U., 1946, M.A., 1947; Ph.D., U. Wis., 1952. Teaching asst. Marquette U., Milw., 1946-47; instr. Marquette U., 1947-48, 50-54, asst. prof., 1954-59, assoc. prof., 1959-64, prof., 1964-90, chmn. dept. English, 1963-75, prof. emeritus, 1990—; teaching fellow U. Wis., 1948-50; Chmn. region X Woodrow Wilson Nat. Fellowship Found., 1967-73; pres. bd. edn. Archdiocese of Milw., 1977-79. Author: A Reader for Writers, 3d edit., 1971, Perspectives on Language, 1963, Province of Rhetoric, 1965, Poetry: Meaning and Form, 1969, Hart Crane: A Critical Bibliography, 1970, Hart Crane: A Descriptive Bibliography, 1972, Exposition, 2d edit., 1971, Hart Crane: A Reference Guide, 1983; sr. editor: Renascence Mag., 1978—. Recipient Distinguished Alumni award Marquette U. Sch. Speech, 1967, Outstanding Tchr. award Marquette U., 1974; Ford Found. grantee, 1956; Am. Council Learned Socs. grantee, 1972, 89; HEW grantee, 1966, 67. Mem. Nat. Coun. Tchrs. English (nat. dir. 1965-68), Modern Lang. Assn., Midwest Modern Lang Assn. (exec. com. 1973-76), Fellowship of Cath. Scholars (bd. dirs. 1987-90), Conf. on Christianity and Lit. (bd. dirs. 1987-90), Phi Beta Kappa, Alpha Sigma Nu (hon.). Republican. Roman Catholic. Home: 8516 W Mequon Rd # 112 Thiensville WI 53097-3100 Office: Marquette U PO Box 1888 Renascence Brooks Hall Milwaukee WI 53201-1888

SCHWARTZ, JUDY ELLEN, cardiothoracic surgeon; b. Mason City, Iowa, Oct. 5, 1946; d. Walter Carl and Alice Nevada (Moore) Schwartz. B.S., U. Iowa, 1968, M.D., 1971 Johns Hopkins U.,M.P.H., 1996,Diplomate Am. Bd. Surgery, Am. Bd. Thoracic Surgery, Am. Bd. Med. Mgmt. Intern Nat. Naval Med. Center, Bethesda, Md., 1971-72, gen. surgery resident, 1972-76, thoracic surgery resident, 1976-78, staff cardiothoracic surgeon, 1979-82, chief cardiothoracic surgeon, 1982-83; chmn. cardiothoracic surg. dept. Naval Hosp., San Diego, 1983-85, quality assurance program dir., 1985-88, exec. officer Rapidly Deployable Med. Facility Four, 1986-88; asst. prof. surgery Uniformed Services Univ. Health Scis., Bethesda, 1983—; sr. policy analyst quality assurance Profl. Affairs and Quality Assurance, 1988-90, dep. dir. quality assurance, 1990; dir. clin. policy Health Svcs. Ops., Washington, 1990-94; head performance evaluation and improvement Nat. Naval Med. Ctr., 1994—; cardiothoracic speciality cons. to naval med. command U.S. Navy, Washington, 1983-84; Dept. Defense rep. to Joint Commn. Accreditation Health Care Orgn. task force on info. mgmt., 1990-93, chmn. 1991-93, task force on .IMS Tech., 1993-94; chmn. info. mgmt. workshop Fed. Health Care Study Commn.'s Corrd. Fed. Health Care, 1993. Contbr. articles to various publs. Fellow Am. Coll. Cardiology, Am. Coll. Surgeons (com. allied health pers. 1985-91, exec com. 1987-91, accreditation review com. edn. physician asst. 1988-94, treas. accreditation review com. 1991-93, sr. mem. com. allied health pers. 1991-94); mem. AMA, Am. Thoracic Soc., Am. Med. Women's Assn., Am. Mgmt. Assn., Am. Coll. Physician Execs. Lutheran. Office: Nat Naval Med Ctr 8901 Wisconsin Ave Bethesda MD 20814-3708

SCHWARTZ, KESSEL, modern language educator; b. Kansas City, Mo., Mar. 19, 1920; s. Henry and Dora (Tennenbaum) S.; m. Barbara Lewin, Apr. 3, 1947; children: Joseph David, Deborah, Edward, Michael. B.A., U. Mo., 1940, M.A., 1941; Ph.D., Columbia U., 1953. Asst. instr. U. Mo., 1940-42; dir. cultural ctrs. in Nicaragua, Ecuador, cultural observer in Costa Rica State Dept., 1946-48; instr. Hofstra, Hamilton, Colby colls., 1948-53; asst. prof. U. Vt., 1953-57; assoc. prof., then prof. modern langs., chmn. dept. U. Ark., 1957-62; prof. modern langs. U. Miami, Fla., 1962-90; chmn. dept. U. Miami, 1962-64, 74-83, dir. grad. studies, 1964-65, 83-90, now emeritus prof.; vis. prof. U. N.C., Chapel Hill, 1966-67. Author: The Ecuadorian Novel, 1953, An Introduction to Modern Spanish Literature, 1967, The Meaning of Existence in Contemporary Hispanic Literature, 1969, Vicente Aleixandre, 1970, Juan Goytisolo, 1970, A New History of Spanish American Fiction, 1972 (named Outstanding Acad. Book of Year, Am. Assn. Coll. and Research Librarians), Studies on Twentieth Century Spanish and Spanish American Literature, 1983; co-author: A New History of Spanish Literature, 1961, rev. edit., 1991, A New Anthology of Spanish Literature, 1968; assoc. editor Hispania, 1965-84; editorial adv. bd.: Anales de Literatura Española Contemporánea Folio; Fiestas (Goytisolo), notes and introduction, 1964; contbr. numerous articles to profl. jours., chpts. to books, ency. Nat. patronato Letras de Oro Spanish Literary Prizes. Served with AUS, 1942-46. July 14, 1989 declared Kessel Schwartz Day in Coral Gables, Miami and Dade County by mayors' proclamation. Mem. MLA (group sec. 1964, group chmn. 1965, chmn. nominating com. for modern Spanish lit. 1966-68), Am. Assn. Tchrs. Spanish and Portuguese (chmn. Peninsular lit. sect. 1972), Internat. Assn. Hispanists, Phi Beta Kappa (pres. So. Fla. chpt. 1977), Phi Sigma Iota, Sigma Delta Pi (nat. Order of Don Quijote award 1984, Order of Discoverers award 1989), Pi Delta Phi, Delta Phi Alpha, Omicron Delta Kappa. Home: 6400 Maynada St Miami FL 33146-3318 *If men loved one another sufficiently, we might not need our legal systems. Given our imperfect nature as human beings, we must believe in some higher goals to give meaning to our lives but be ever vigilant that in the pursuit of success we do not infringe upon the happiness of others or confuse the means with the end.*

SCHWARTZ, LEON, foreign language educator; b. Boston, Aug. 22, 1922; s. Charles and Celia (Emer) S.; m. Jeanne Gurtat, Mar. 31, 1949; children—Eric Alan, Claire Marie. Student, Providence Coll., 1939-41; B.A., U. Calif. at Los Angeles, 1948; certificat de phonetique, U. Paris, 1949; M.A, U. So. Cal., 1950, Ph.D., 1962. Tchr. English, Spanish and Latin Redlands (Calif.) Jr. High Sch., 1951-54; high sch. tchr. Spanish and French, 1954-59; prof. French Calif. State U., Los Angeles, 1959-87, emeritus, 1987—, chmn. dept. fgn. langs. and lit., 1970-73. Author: Diderot and the Jews, 1981. Served as 2d lt. USAAF, 1942-45. Decorated Air medal with 5 oak leaf clusters; recipient Outstanding Prof. award Calif. State U. at Los Angeles, 1976. Mem. Am. Assn. Tchrs. French, Modern and Classical Lang. Assn. So. Calif., Western Soc. 18th Century Studies, Am. Soc. 18th Century Studies, Société Diderot, Phi Beta Kappa, Phi Kappa Phi, Pi Delta Phi, Sigma Delta Pi, Alpha Mu Gamma. Office: Calif State U Dept Modern Langs and Lit Los Angeles CA 90032

SCHWARTZ, LILLIAN FELDMAN, artist, filmaker, art analyst, author, nurse; b. Cin., July 13, 1927; d. Jacob and Katie (Green) Feldman; m. Jack James Schwartz, Dec. 22, 1946; children: Jeffrey Hugh, Laurens Robert. RN, U. Cin., 1947; Dr. honoris causa, Kean Coll., 1988. Nurse Cin. Gen. Hosp., 1947; head supr. premature nursery St. Louis Maternity Hosp., 1947-48; cons. AT&T Bell Labs., Murray Hill, N.J., 1968-97; pres. Computer Creations Corp., Watchung, N.J., 1989—; cons. Bell Communications Research, Morristown, N.J., 1984-92, Lucent Technologies/Bell Labs. Innovations, 1996—; artist-in-residence Sta. WNET, N.Y.C., 1972-74; cons. T.J. Watson Rsch. Lab. IBM Corp., Yorktown, N.Y., 1975, 82-84; vis. mem. computer sci. dept. U. Md., College Park, 1974-80; adj. prof. fine arts Kean Coll., Union, N.J., 1980-82, Rutgers U., New Brunswick, N.J., 1982-83; adj. prof. dept. psychology NYU, N.Y.C., 1985-86, assoc. prof. computer sci.; guest lectr. Princeton U., Columbia U., Yale U., Rockefeller U.; mem. grad. faculty Sch. Visual Arts, N.Y.C., 1990—. Co-author: The Computer Artist's Handbook; contbd. articles to profl. jours including Scientific Am., 1995; contbr. chpts. to books, also Trans. Am. Philos. Soc., vol. 75, Part 6, 1985; one-woman shows of sculpture and paintings include Columbia U., 1967, 68, Rabin and Krueger Gallery, Newark, 1968; films shown at Met. Mus., N.Y.C., Franklin Inst., Phila., 1972, U. Toronto, 1972, am. Embassy, London, 1972, L.A. County Mus., Corcoran Gallery, Washington, 1972, Whitney Mus., N.Y.C., 1973, Grand Palais, Paris, Musee Nat. d'Art Moderne, Paris, IBM, and others. Recipient numerous art and film awards, Emmy award Mus. Modern Art, 1984, Computer Graphics World Smithsonian awards for virtual reality, art analysis, inventing computer medium for art and animation, 1993; named Outstanding Alumnus, U. Cin., 1987; grantee Nat. Endowment for Arts, 1977, 81, Corp. Pub. Broadcasting, 1979, Nat. Endowment Composers and Librettists, 1981. Fellow World Acad. of Art and Sci.; mem. NATAS, Am. Film Inst., Info. Film Prodrs. Am., Soc. Motion Picture and TV Engrs., Internat. Sculptors Assn., Centro Studi Pierfrancescani (Sansepolcro, Italy, founding mem.). Pioneer in use of computers as art media; commd. to create computer poster and TV comml. for opening New Mus. Modern Art, 1984; discovered identities of the Mona Lisa, hidden and surface, 1987, and identified steps DaVinci made in transforming Isabella, Duchess of Aragon, into the Mona Lisa using his own features as the model, 1993; discovered perspective used by DaVinci in The Last Supper, 1988; identified time of day and tree of thorns in Piero della Francesca's Resurrection; discovered Elizabeth I is model for Martin Droeshout engraving of Shakespeare, 1991; performed first transmission of computer drawing between U.S. and Germany, 1990; used morphing algorithms to determine Leonardo's creative decision-making steps in transforming the Duchess of Aragon into the Mona Lisa using his own features to segue; discovered method Leonardo used to create his Grotesques, 1994; discovered new Renaissance illusion of another figure in a painting of Christ, 1996, rediscovered Renaissance illusion published in visual computer, 1997. *I have always been provoked by and concerned with the mechanical and technological world around me. I enjoy experimenting with traditional media and combining them with technology today. For example, I used computers as an art medium when computers were solely programmed for scientific purposes. By using the computer to understand the creative process I have made clear the intent of the great masters and applied their decision-making steps to my own work. The excitement in creating is to discover and to make a new world. My present success was achieved in part by being able to make new rules and not be hindered by old or obvious solutions.*

SCHWARTZ, LITA LINZER, psychologist, educator; b. N.Y.C., Jan. 14, 1930; d. Aaron Jerome and Dorothy Claire (Linzer) Linzer; m. Melvin Jay Schwartz, June 18, 1950 (div. 1983); children: Arthur Lee, Joshua David, Frederic Seth. AB, Vassar Coll., 1950; EdM, Temple U., 1956; PhD, Bryn Mawr Coll., 1964. Diplomate Am. Bd. Forensic Psychology, Am. Bd. Profl. Psychology; lic. psychologist, Pa. Part-time instr., counselor Pa. State U., Ogontz, Campus, Abington, 1961-66, asst. prof. ednl. psychology, 1966-71, assoc. prof., 1971-76, prof., 1976-93, disting. prof., 1993-95, prof. women's studies, 1993-95, disting. prof. emerita, 1995—; pvt. practice, 1964—; cons. in field. Recipient Humanitarian Award N.Y. Philanthropic League, 1973, Christian R. and Mary F. Lindback award, 1982, Outstanding Tchr. award Pa. State U. Coll. Edn. Alumni, 1982. Fellow APA, Am. Orthopsychiatric Assn.; mem. Am. Bd. Forensic Psychology, Soc. Reproductive Medicine, Internat. Council of Psychologists (bd. dirs. 1995-96), Assn. Tchr. Educators (Tchr. Laureate 1993-94), Assn. Family and Conciliation Cts., Nat. Assn. for Gifted Children, Pa. Assn. Gifted Children, Soc. for Advancement of Field Theory (exec. bd. 1991-93), Acad. Family Mediators (Pa. and Del. Valley chpts., evaluation com. child custody mediation project Del. Valley), Ethnic Studies Assn. Del. Valley (co-chair program com. 1986-88), Psi Chi. Author: American Education, 1969, 74, 78; Educational Psychology, 1972, 77; The Exceptional Child: A Primer, 1975, 79; Exceptional Students in the Mainstream, 1984; (with Natalie Isser) The American School and The Melting Pot, 1985, 89, (with Florence W. Kaslow) The Dynamics of Divorce, 1987; (with Natalie Isser) The History of Conversion and Contemporary Cults, 1988; Alternatives to Infertility: Is Surrogacy the Answer?, 1991, Why Give Gifts to the Gifted?: Investing in a National Resource, 1994; editor: Mid-Life Divorce Counseling, 1994, (with Florence W. Kaslow) Painful Partings: Divorce and its Aftermath, 1997; contbr. over 60 articles to profl. jours., numerous chapters to books. Office: Pa State U Ogontz Campus Abington PA 19001

SCHWARTZ, LLOYD, music critic, poet; b. N.Y.C., Nov. 29, 1941; s. Sam and Ida (Singer) S. BA, Queens Coll., N.Y.C., 1962; MA, Harvard U., 1963, PhD, 1976. Classical music editor Boston Phoenix, 1977—; co-dir. creative writing U. Mass., Boston, 1982—, dir. creative writing, 1990—; classical music critic Fresh Air Nat. Pub. Radio, Phila., 1987—; prof. English U. Mass., Boston, 1986—. Author: (poems) These People, 1981, Goodnight, Gracie, 1992, (play) These People: Voices for the Stage, 1990; editor: Ploughshares, 1979, Elizabeth Bishop and Her Art, 1983; actor The Spider's Web, 1975-82; dir. These People: Voices for the Stage, 1990, (operas) L'Heure Espagnol (Ravel), 1972, Mavra (Stravinsky), 1973. Recipient Pulitzer prize for criticism, 1994; NEA creative writing fellow in poetry, 1990. Mem. PEN (exec. com. New Eng. chpt. 1983—) PEN Am., Poetry Soc. Am., MLA, New Eng. Poetry Club. Avocations: collecting old recordings, books. Home: 27 Pennsylvania Ave Somerville MA 02145-2217 Office: Boston Phoenix 126 Brookline Ave Boston MA 02215-3920

SCHWARTZ, LLOYD MARVIN, newspaper and magazine correspondent, broadcaster; b. Bklyn., Mar. 6, 1923; s. Philip and Celia W. Schwartz; m. Doris Grossman, May 19, 1946; children: Ellen, Philip, Laura. BA, NYU, 1944. NYU corr. N.Y. Times, 1942-44; news editor, writer Trade Union Courier, 1943-44; reporter Lima (Ohio) News, 1945; reporter, The White House corr. Fairchild Publs., Washington, 1945-65; Washington bur. chief Fairchild Publs., 1965-88; Congl. corr. Fairchild News Service, 1977-88; panelist, news broadcaster Voice of Am., AFL-CIO, Fairchild Broadcast News and WJR-Detroit; Congl. corr. Van Dahl Publs., Albany, Oreg., 1980-90, mem. Senate and Ho. of Reps. Press Galleries, 1946-93; Congl. corr. Linn's Stamp News, Sidney, Ohio, 1990-92; cons. Rsch. Inst. of Am. Democrat. Jewish.

SCHWARTZ, LOUIS BROWN, legal educator; b. Phila., Feb. 22, 1913; s. Samuel and Rose (Brown) S.; m. Berta Wilson, Mar. 29, 1937 (div. 1954); children: Johanna, Victoria; m. Miriam Robbins Humboldt, Sept. 16, 1964. B.S. in Econs, U. Pa., 1932, J.D., 1935. Bar: Pa. 1935, U.S. Supreme Ct. 1942. Atty. SEC, Washington, 1935-39; chief gen. crimes and spl. projects sect. Dept. Justice, 1939-43, chief judgment and enforcement sect. antitrust div., 1945-46; also mem. inter-departmental coms. on war crimes and status-of-forces treaties; prof. law U. Pa. Law Sch., 1946-83, Benjamin Franklin prof., 1964-83; prof. law Hastings Coll. Law, U. Calif., 1983—; vis. prof. Harvard U., Columbia U., U. Calif. at Berkeley, Cambridge (Eng.) U.; Ford vis. Am. prof. Inst. Advanced Legal Studies, U. London (Eng.), 1974; vis. disting. prof. Ariz. State U., 1980; mem. Atty. Gen.'s Nat. Com. Study Antitrust Laws, 1954-55, Pa. Gov.'s Commn. on Penal and Correctional Affairs, 1956-60; adv. commn. Revision Pa. Penal Code, 1963-68; nat. adv. council Nat. Defender Project, 1964-69; dir. Nat. Commn. on Reform of Fed. Criminal Laws, 1968-71; co-reporter Model Penal Code Am. Law Inst., 1962; cons. FTC, Dept. Justice, other agencies. Author: Free Enterprise and Economic Organization, 1959, 6th edit. (with John J. Flynn, Harry First) titled Antitrust and Government Regulation, 1983-85 (2 vols.), Le Système Pénal des Etats-Unis, 1964, Law Enforcement Handbook for Police, 1970, 2d edit., 1979, Proposed Federal Criminal Code, (with Comments and Working Papers), 1971; contbr. numerous articles to profl. jours. Served as lt. (j.g.) USNR, 1944-45. Mem. Ams. Democratic Action (nat. bd.), Am. Law Inst. (adv. com. pre-arraignment code), Order of Coif. Home: 2955 Pierce St San Francisco CA 94123-3824 Office: U Calif Hastings Coll Law 200 Mcallister St San Francisco CA 94102-4707

SCHWARTZ, LOUIS WINN, ophthalmologist; b. Pa., Apr. 19, 1942; s. Edward and Sylvia Beatrice (Winn) S.; m. Linda Weinberg, June 14, 1964; children: Joanne Karen, Geoffrey Paul. AB, Bowdoin Coll., 1963; MD, Jefferson Med. Coll., 1967. Diplomate Am. Bd. Ophthalmology. Intern Phila. Gen. Hosp.-U. Pa., 1967-68; resident in ophthalmology Wills Eye Hosp., Phila., 1970-73; ophthalmologist Ophthalmic Assocs., Lansdale, Pa., 1973—; attending surgeon Wills Eye Hosp. Glaucoma Svc., Phila., 1984—; clin. assoc. prof. ophthalmology Jefferson Med. Coll., Phila., 1984—; chief ophthalmology North Penn Hosp., 1995—. Co-author: Laser Therapy of Anterior Segment, 1988, 7 other books; assoc. editor Contact Lens Assn. Ophthalmology Jour., 1988; contbr. numerous articles to profl. jours. Recipient Honor award Am. Acad. Ophthalmology, 1988. Mem. AMA, Am. Glaucoma Soc., Pa. Acad. Ophthalmology, InterCounty Ophthalmol. Soc. (pres. 1985-86), Ophthalmic Club Phila. (pres. 1985-86). Office: Ophthalmic Assocs 1000 N Broad St Lansdale PA 19446-1138

SCHWARTZ, LYLE H., materials scientist, science administrator; b. Chgo., Aug. 2, 1936; s. Joseph K. Schwartz and Helen (Shefsky) Bernards; divorced; children—Ara, Justin; m. Celesta Sue Jurkovich, Sept. 1, 1973. B.S. in Sci. Engring., Northwestern U., 1959, Ph.D. in Materials Sci., 1964. Prof. materials sci. Northwestern U., Evanston, Ill., 1964-84, dir. Materials Research Ctr., 1979-84; dir. materials sci. and engr. lab. Nat. Inst. Standards and Tech., Dept. Commerce, Gaithersburg, Md., 1984-97; pres. Associated Univs., Inc., 1997—; cons. Argonne Nat. Labs., Ill., 1965-79; vis. scientist Bell Telephone Labs., Murray Hill, N.J., 1971-73. Author: (with J.B. Cohen) Diffraction From Materials, 1977, 2d edit., 1987; also numerous articles and papers. NSF fellow, 1962-63; recipient Presdl. Rank Award of Meritorious Exec. for outstanding govt. svc., 1990. Fellow Am. Soc. for Metals; mem. AAAS, AIME, Nat. Acad. Engring., Am. Phys. Soc., Am. Crystallography Assn., Materials Rsch. Soc., Sigma Xi.

SCHWARTZ, LYLE VICTOR, advertising executive; b. N.Y.C., Feb. 14, 1959; s. Seymour and Sylvia (Geen) S.; m. Marjorie Yellen, Apr. 5, 1987; children: Brittany, Aaron, Scott. BS, Hunter Coll., 1982. Jr. analyst Met. Sunday Newspaper, N.Y.C., 1978-82; media analyst BBDO, N.Y.C., 1982-83; sr. analyst Young & Rubicam, N.Y.C., 1983-85, project dir., 1985-86, supr., 1986-88, group supr., 1988-90, v.p., 1990-94, sr. v.p., 1994—. Recipient Media All Star award Cable Advt. bur./Nat. Cable Corp., 1995. Mem. ARF (cert. of appreciation 1992). Democrat. Jewish. Avocations: managing T Ball team, bowling league, golf, stamp collecting, basketball. Home: 40 Overbrook Dr Airmont NY 10952 Office: Young & Rubicam 285 Madison Ave New York NY 10017-6401

SCHWARTZ, MARILYN, columnist. Columnist Dallas Morning News. Office: The Dallas Morning News Communications News PO Box 655237 Dallas TX 75265*

SCHWARTZ, MARSHALL ZANE, pediatric surgeon; b. Mpls., Sept. 1, 1945; s. Sidney Shay and Peggy Belle (Lieberman) S.; m. Michele Carroll Walker, Oct. 16, 1971; children: Lisa, Jeffrey. BS, U. Minn., 1968, MD, 1970. Diplomate Am. Bd. Surgery, Am. Bd. Pediatric Surgery,. Intern N.Y. Hosp., N.Y.C., 1970-71; resident in gen. surgery U. Minn., Mpls., 1971-73, 75-76, rsch. fellow, 1974-75; jr. resident in pediatric surgery Children's Hosp. Med. Ctr., Harvard Med. Sch., 1973-74, sr. resident in pediatric surgery, 1976-77, chief resident in pediatric surgery, 1977-78; instr. Med. Sch. Harvard U., Boston, 1978-79; asst. in surgery Childrens Hosp. Med. Ctr., Boston, 1978-79; asst. prof. Med. Br. U. Tex., Galveston, 1979-81, assoc. prof. Med. Br., 1981-83, chief. pediatric surgery Med. Br., 1980-83; assoc. prof. U. Calif., Davis, 1983-86, prof., 1986-92, chief pediatric surgery, 1983-92, programmatic subcom., 1984-86, vice chmn. faculty Sch. Medicine, 1990-91, chmn. faculty Sch. Medicine, 1991-92; prof. surgery and pediatrics George Washington Sch. Medicine, 1992-96, Thomas Jefferson Sch. Medicine, 1996—; surgeon-in-chief, chmn. dept. pediatric surgery Children's Nat. Med. Ctr., Washington, 1992-96; assoc. med. dir., assoc. chmn. dept. surgery Dupont Hosp. for Children, Wilmington, Del., 1996—. Editorial bd. Journal of Pediatric Surgery, 1988—. Pres. bd. dirs. Sacramento Children's Hosp. Found., 1990-92; vice chmn. Bd. of Childrens Faculty Assocs., Childrens Nat. Med. Ctr. Recipient Basil O'Connor Rsch. award March of Dimes Found., 1981, Young Investigator award NIH, 1982, Found. for Children Rsch. award, 1982, James W. McLaughlin award U. Tex., 1983. Fellow ACS; mem. Am. Surg. Assn., Soc. Univ. Surgeons, Am. Pediatric Surg. Assn., Soc. Surgery of the Alimentary Tract, Pacific Assn. of Pediatric Surgeons (pres.). Jewish. Avocations: skiing, fishing, wood working. Office: Dupont Hosp for Children 1600 Rockland Rd Wilmington DE 19803-3607

SCHWARTZ, MARVIN, lawyer; b. Phila., Nov. 3, 1922; s. Abe and Freda (Newman) S.; m. Joyce Ellen Sidner, Sept. 7, 1947; children: John Burkhart, Daniel Bruce, Pamela Louise Pier. LL.B., U. Pa., 1949. Bar: Pa. 1950, N.Y. 1951, D.C. 1955. Law sec. to judge U.S. Ct. Appeals, 3d Circuit, Phila., 1949-50; law sec. to Justice Burton U.S. Supreme Ct., Washington, 1950-51; assoc. Sullivan & Cromwell, N.Y.C., 1951-60, ptnr., 1960-92, sr. counsel, 1993—; mediator U.S. Dist. (so. dist.) N.Y., N.Y. Supreme Ct. Comml. Divsn.; arbitrator Am. Arbitration Assn., N.Y. Stock Exch., Nat. Assn. Securities Dealers. Spl. master appellate divsn. 1st dept. Supreme Ct. N.Y.; chmn. Zoning Bd. of Adjustment, Alpine, N.J., 1966-74; mem. Planning Bd., Alpine, 1966-67; bd. overseers emeritus U. Pa. Law Sch. With Signal Corps U.S. Army, 1943-46. Mem. ABA, N.Y. Bar Assn., D.C. Bar Assn., Am. Coll. Trial Lawyers (sec. 1986-88, bd. regents 1981-86, chmn. Downstate N.Y. com. 1976-78), Am. Law Inst. (adviser complex litigation project), Univ. Club (N.Y.C.), Litchfield (Conn.) Country Club. Democrat. Jewish. Office: Sullivan & Cromwell 125 Broad St New York NY 10004-2400

SCHWARTZ, MELVIN, physics educator, laboratory administrator; b. N.Y.C., Nov. 2, 1932; s. Harry and Hannah (Shulman) S.; m. Marilyn Fenster, Nov. 25, 1953; children: David N., Diane R., Betty Lynn. A.B., Columbia U., 1953, Ph.D., 1958, DSc honoris causa, 1991. Assoc. physicist Brookhaven Nat. Lab., 1956-58; mem. faculty Columbia U., N.Y.C., 1958-66; prof. physics Columbia U., 1963-66, Stanford U., Calif., 1966-83; cons. prof. Stanford U., 1983-91; chmn. Digital Pathways, Inc., Mountain View, Calif., 1970-91; assoc. dir. high energy and nuclear physics Brookhaven Nat. Lab., Upton, N.Y., 1991-94; prof. physics Columbia U., N.Y.C., 1991-94, I.I. Rabi prof. physics, 1994—. Co-discoverer muon neutrino, 1962. Bd. govs. Weizmann Inst. Sci. Recipient Nobel prize in physics, 1988, John Jay award Columbia Coll., 1989, Alexander Hamilton medal Columbia U., 1995; Guggenheim fellow, 1968. Fellow Am. Phys. Soc. (Hughes award 1964); mem. NAS. Home: 456 Riverside Dr Apt 11A New York NY 10027 Office: Columbia U Dept Physics New York NY 10027

SCHWARTZ, MICHAEL, university president, sociology educator; b. Chgo., July 29, 1937; s. Norman and Lillian (Ruthenberg) S.; m. Ettabelle Slutsky, Aug. 23, 1959; children: Monica, Kenneth, Rachel. BS in Psychology, U. Ill., 1958, MA in Indsl. Relations, 1959, PhD in Sociology, 1962; LLD (hon.), Youngstown State U., 1990. Asst. prof. sociology and psychology Wayne State U., Detroit, 1962-64; asst. prof. sociology Ind. U., Bloomington, 1964, assoc. prof. sociology, 1966-70; prof., chmn. dept. sociology Fla. Atlantic U., Boca Raton, 1970-72, dean Coll. Social Sci., 1972-76; v.p. grad. studies and research Kent (Ohio) State U., 1976-78, interim pres., 1977, acting v.p. acad. affairs, 1977-78, v.p. acad. and student affairs, 1978-80, provost, v.p. acad. and student affairs, 1980-82, pres., 1982-91; pres. emeritus and trustee's prof. Kent State U., 1991—; trustee Ctrl. State U., 1996—; acting dir. Inst. for Social Rsch., Ind. U., 1966-67; tng. cons. Operation Head Start in Ind., 1964-70; cons. Office of Manpower, Automation and Tng., U.S. Dept. Labor, 1964-65. Cons. editor, Sociometry, 1966-70, assoc. editor, 1970; reader Am. Sociol. Rev. papers; author: (with Elton F. Jackson) Study Guide to the Study of Sociology, 1968; contbr. articles to profl. jours., chpts. to books. Chmn. Mid-Am. Conf. Coun. Pres.; rep. Nat. Coll. Athletic Assn. Pres.'s Commn.; corps evaluators North Ctrl. Assn. Colls. and Schs.; mem. bd. visitors Air U., USAF; mem. Akron (Ohio) Regional Devel. Bd., N.E. Ednl. TV of Ohio, Inc., N.E. Ohio Univs. Coll. Medicine; trustee Akron Symphony Orch. Assn.; mem. State of Ohio Post-Secondary Rev. Entity, 1995; mem. Assn. of Governing Bds. Commn. on Strengthening the Presidency. Recipient Disting. Tchr. award Fla. Atlantic U., 1970-71, Meritorious Svc. award Am. Assn. State Colls. and Univs., 1990; Michael Schwartz Ctr., Kent State U., named in his honor, 1991. Mem. Ohio Tchr. Edn. and Cert. Adv. Commn., Akron Press Club, Cleve. Press Club, Pine Lake Trout Club. Office: Kent State U 405 White Hall Kent OH 44242

SCHWARTZ, MICHAEL ALAN, physician; b. N.Y.C., Dec. 13, 1944; s. David Henry and Ray Schwartz; m. Joan Kay Clayton, Jan. 12, 1979; children: Dana, David, Elizabeth. AB, Princeton, 1965; MD, Cornell U., 1969. Intern, medicine N.Y. Hosp., Cornell, 1969-70; resident, psychiatry N.Y. Hosp., Cornell, Westchester, 1970-74; clin. assoc. NIMH, Washington, 1972-74; asst. prof. psychiatry Cornell Med. Coll., N.Y.C., 1974-76; assoc. to prof. of psychiatry N.Y. Med. Coll., 1976-92; prof. and vice chmn. dept. psychiatry Case Western Res. U., Cleve., 1992—; plenary spkr. symposium on advances in neurosci. Decade of the Brain, WHO, Chinese Psychiat. Assn. Editor: (with Manfred Spitzer, Christoph Mundt, Friedrick Uehlein) Phenomenology, Language, and Schizophrenia, 1992, (with John Sadler and Osborn Wiggins) Psychiatric Diagnostic Classification, 1994; asst. editor Integrative Psychiatry, 1990—; mem. editl. bd. Comprehensive Psychiatry, 1991—, Jour. of Personality Disorders, 1992—; assoc. editor Philosophy, Psychiatry, Psychology, 1993—; co-editor: history and philosopy Current Opinion in Psychiatry, 1994—; contbr. articles to numerous sci. jours. Recipient Medaille des Hopitaux de Marseille, 1997. Fellow Am. Psychiat Assn., Assn. for Advancement of Philosophy and Psychiatry (pres. 1991-94, founding pres. 1994—), Am. Psychopathol. Assn., Ind. Psychiat. Assn. of Russia (hon.), Soc. Italiana per la Psicopatologia (hon.), Ind. Psychiat. Assn. Russia (hon.). Home: 34650 Cedar Rd Gates Mills OH 44040 Office: Univ Hosps of Cleve Dept Psychiatry 11100 Euclid Ave Cleveland OH 44106-1736

SCHWARTZ, MICHAEL ALAN, engineering executive; b. Cleve., Aug. 14, 1949; s. Marc Albert and Helene (Dimond) S.; m. Chrysanthi Karmaniolas, Dec. 7, 1985; children: Andrew Michael, Alison Hyatt, Peter Nicholas. BSME, U. Cinn., 1972. Registered profl. mech. engr., Ill. Project engr. A. B. Dick Co., Niles, Ill., 1972-73; v.p. Mars Lithograph, Inc., Highland Heights, Ohio, 1973-77; dir. engring. Smith RPM, Inc., Lenexa, Kans., 1977-80; exec. v.p. DEV Industries, Inc., Bensenville, Ill., 1980—; pres. Tradestar Expo Ltd., Bensenville, 1992—. Patentee method of press conversion, offset spray dampener. Staff photographer Cinn. News Record, 1970-72; comml. photographer Com. to Elect Gerald Springer, Cinn., 1972. Named Ill. Exporter of Yr., U.S. C. of C., 1990. Mem. European Newspaper Assn. Avocations: cabinet making, golf, radio control equipment.

SCHWARTZ, MICHAEL ROBINSON, health administrator; b. St. Louis, Mar. 18, 1940; s. Henry G. and Edith C. (Robinson) S.; children: Christine, Richard; m. Kathleen Nowicki, Dec., 9, 1989. AB, Dartmouth Coll., 1962; MHA, U. Minn., 1964. Asst. in adminstrn. Shands Teaching Hosp., Gainesville, Fla., 1966-67; asst. dir. Shands Teaching Hosp., Gainesville, 1967-68, assoc. dir., 1968-73; assoc. adminstr. St. Joseph Mercy Hosp., Pontiac, Mich., 1973-76; pres. St. Joseph Mercy Hosp., 1976-85; exec. v.p. Mercy Health Svcs., Farmington Hills, Mich., 1985-96; chief oper. officer Mercy Health Svcs., Farmington Hills, 1988-96; exec. v.p. Ea. Mich. region Sisters of Mercy Health Corp., 1991-92; pvt. practice Birmingham, Mich., 1996—; non-resident lectr. U. Mich., 1982-93; cons. prof. Oakland U., 1980-88; asst. prof. hosp. adminstrn. U. Fla., 1967-73; pres. Eastern Mich. Regional Bd. Sisters of Mercy Health Corp., 1976-79; bd. dirs. Lourdes Nursing Home, 1973-83, v.p., 1974, pres., 1975; bd. dirs. Oakland Livingston Human Svc. Agy., 1977-81; bd. dirs. Mercy Sch. Nursing, 1976-84, v.p., 1981-84; bd. dirs. United Way-Pontiac/North Oakland, 1976-85, v.p., 1982-84; bd. dirs. Oakland Health Edn. Program, 1977-85, treas., 1978-79; bd. dirs. Blue Cross/Blue Shield of Mich. 1982-86, coms. 1978-86, chair hosp. contingent to participating hosp. agreement adv. com., 1989-96; bd. dirs. Greater Detroit Area Health Coun., 1983-88, 93-96; chmn. bd. dirs., pres. Accord Ins. Co. Ltd., 1983-88; chmn. bd. dirs. Mercy Health Plans, 1986-96; chmn. bd. dirs. Venzke Svc. Co., 1983-88, pres., 1983-84; chmn., bd. dirs., pres. Venzke Ins. Co. Ltd., 1988-96; bd. dirs. Mercy Info. Systems, 1986-92, Pontiac Devel. Found., 1984-86; mem. audit and fin. com. Am. Healthcare Systems, 1988-92; mem. S.E. Mich. Hosp. Coun., chmn. pub. rels. com., 1983-85, bd. dirs. Hosp. Fund 1986-96; trustee Sisters of Mercy Health Corp., 1991-93, sec. bd. trustees, 1993. With U.S. Army, 1964-66. Fellow Am. Coll. Healthcare Execs. (mem. exec. com. on higher edn. 1990-93, Mich Regent's award 1992); mem. Mich. Hosp. Assn. (at-large rep. corp. bd. 1990-96, exec. com. 1992-96), Am. Healthcare Systems Risk Retention Group (bd. dirs. 1990-91), Pontiac Urban League (pers. com. 1979), Comprehensive Health Planning Coun. (com. mem. 1976-81).

SCHWARTZ, MILES JOSEPH, cardiologist; b. Richmond, Va., Aug. 7, 1925; s. Hugo and Ella (Kramer) S.; m. Margery Baer Irish, June 7, 1956 (div. 1972); children: Elizabeth, James, Margaret; m. Katherine Rush, May 26, 1980. BS, Queens Coll., 1947; MD, N.Y.U., 1951. Diplomate Am. Bd. Internal Medicine, Am. Bd. Cardiovascular Disease. Intern Mt. Sinai Hosp., N.Y.C., 1951-52, resident, 1953-54; resident Bronx (N.Y.) VA Hosp., 1952-53, fellow, 1954-55, asst. med. sect. chief, 1956-58; resident, then chief resident St. Luke's Hosp., 1955-56; asst. attending physician St. Luke's Hosp. Ctr., N.Y.C., 1959-64, assoc. attending physician, asst. cardiologist, 1959-69, assoc. cardiologist, 1969, chief hypertension clinic, 1959-81, attending physician, dir. cardiography, 1970—, clin. dir. pvt. med. svc., 1974-78; assoc. dir. medicine St. Luke's/Roosevelt Hosp. Ctr., N.Y.C., 1978-84, dir. clin. cardiology tng. program, 1966—, assoc. dir. divsn. cardiology, 1989—, acting dir. divsn. cardiology, 1995-96; cons. Sharon (Conn.) Hosp., 1976-91; prof. clin. med., Columbia U. Coll. of P & S. With USNR, 1944-46. Fellow ACP, Am. Coll. Cardiology, Alpha Omega Alpha. Jewish. Avocations: walking, reading, travel. Home: 217 W Queens Dr Williamsburg VA 23185 Office: St Luke's/Roosevelt Hosp 1111 Amsterdam Ave New York NY 10025-1716 also: 102 E 81st St New York NY 10028

SCHWARTZ, MILTON LEWIS, federal judge; b. Oakland, Calif., Jan. 20, 1920; s. Colman and Selma (Lavenson) S.; m. Barbara Ann Moore, May 15, 1942; children: Dirk L., Tracy Ann, Damon M., Brooke. A.B., U. Calif. at Berkeley, 1941, J.D., 1948. Bar: Calif. bar 1949. Research asst. 3d Dist. Ct. Appeal, Sacramento, 1948; dep. dist. atty., 1949-51; practice in Sacramento, 1951-79; partner McDonough, Holland, Schwartz & Allen, 1953-79; U.S. dist. judge Eastern Dist. Calif., U.S. Dist. Ct., Calif., 1979—; prof. law McGeorge Coll. Law, Sacramento, 1952-55; mem. Com. Bar Examiners Calif., 1971-75. Pres. Bd. Edn. Sacramento City Sch. Dist., 1961; v.p. Calif. Bd. Edn., 1967-68; trustee Sutterville Heights Sch. Dist. Served to maj. 40th Inf. Divsn. AUS, 1942-46, PTO. Named Sacramento County Judge of Yr., 1990; Milton L. Schwartz Am. Inn of Court named in his honor, Davis, Calif. Fellow Am. Coll. Trial Lawyers; mem. State Bar Calif., Am. Bar Assn., Am. Bd. Trial Advocates, Anthony M. Kennedy Am. Inn of Ct. (pres. 1988-90, pres. emeritus 1990—). Office: US Dist Ct 1060 US Courthouse 650 Capitol Mall Sacramento CA 95814

SCHWARTZ, MIRIAM CATHERINE, biology educator; b. Tarlac, Luzon, Philippines, Mar. 9, 1964; came to U.S., 1980; d. Conrado Palarca and Elena Obcena (Domingo) Estanislao; m. Jason Jay Schwartz, July 20, 1987. BS in Biology, Calif. State U., L.A., 1985; PhD, Purdue U., 1992. Rsch. asst., rsch. assoc. dept. biol. sci. Purdue U., West Lafayette, Ind., 1988-93, teaching asst., instr., 1988-93; postdoctoral fellow sch. med. Emory U., Atlanta, 1993-94; biology lectr. Spelman Coll., Atlanta, 1994-95. Contbr. articles to profl. jours. Aux. vol. Emory Univ. Hosp., Atlanta, 1993-95. Mem. Phi Kappa Phi, Golden Key Nat. Honor Soc. Avocations: playing piano, reading business history and political science, hiking, cooking. Office: Spelman Coll Atlanta GA 30314

SCHWARTZ, MISCHA, electrical engineering educator; b. N.Y.C., Sept. 21, 1926; s. Isaiah and Bessie (Weinstein) S.; m. Lillian Mitchnick, June 23, 1957 (div.); 1 son, David; m. Charlotte F. Berney, July 12, 1970. B.E.E., Cooper Union, 1947; M.E.E., Poly. Inst. Bklyn., 1949; Ph.D. in Applied Physics (Sperry Gyroscope grad. scholar), Harvard U., 1951. Project engr. Sperry Gyroscope Co., 1947-52; mem. faculty Poly. Inst. Bklyn., 1952-74, prof. elec. engring., 1959-74, head dept., 1961-65; prof. elec. engring. and computer sci. Columbia U., N.Y.C., 1974-88, Charles Batchelor prof. elec. engring., 1988-96, Charles Batchelor prof. emeritus, 1996—, dir. Ctr. for Telecommunications Research, 1985-88; part-time tchr. Adelphi Coll., 1951-52, CCNY, 1952; cons. radiation physicist Montefiore Hosp., N.Y.C., 1954-56; vis. prof. sys. sci. dept. UCLA, 1964; vis. prof. dept. elec. engring. and computer sci. Columbia U., 1973-74; vis. prof. dept. electronic and elec. engring. U. Coll., London, 1995; vis. prof. dept. elec. and computer engring. U. Calif., San Diego, 1997; chmn. Commn. C, U.S. Nat. Com. Internat. Union Radio Sci., 1977-80; vis. scientist IBM Rsch., 1980, 94, NYNEX Sci. and Tech., 1986; vis. mem. tech. staff AT&T Bell Labs., 1995; cons. in field. Author: Information Transmission, Modulation and Noise, 4th edit., 1990, (with L. Shaw) Signal Processing, 1975, Computer Communication Network Design and Analysis, 1977, Telecommunications Networks, 1987, Broadband Integrated Networks, 1996; editor, contbr.: Communication Systems and Techniques, 1966, reissued, 1995. Served with AUS, 1944-46. NSF sci. faculty fellow, 1965-66; recipient Disting. Vis. award Australian-Am. Ednl. Found., 1975, Vis. Scientist award Nippon Tel. & Tel., 1981, Tchg. award Columbia U., 1984, Gano Dunn award Cooper Union, 1986, Mayor's award for excellence in tech., City of N.Y., 1995; finalist Mayor's Awards for Excellence in Sci. & Tech., City of N.Y., 1992. Fellow AAAS, IEEE (chmn. adminstrv. com. profl. group info. theory 1964-65, bd. dirs. 1978-79, bd. govs. Comm. Soc. 1973-79, v.p. 1982-83, pres. 1984-85, Edn. medal 1983, IEEE Centennial Hall of Fame 1984, Region 1 award for leadership in mgmt. Ctr. for Telecom. Rsch. 1990, Edwin Armstrong award for contbns. to telecomm. 1994); mem. NAE, AAUP (chpt. pres. 1970-72), Assn. for Computing Machinery, Sigma Xi, Tau Beta Pi, Eta Kappa Nu. Home: 66 Maple Dr Great Neck NY 11021-1928 Office: Columbia U Schapiro CEPSR Rm 806 New York NY 10027

SCHWARTZ, MURRAY LOUIS, lawyer, educator, academic administrator; b. Phila., Oct. 27, 1920; s. Harry and Isabelle (Friedman) S.; m. Audrey James, Feb. 12, 1950; children: Deborah, Jonathan, Daniel. BS, Pa. State U., 1942; LLB, U. Pa., 1949; LLD (hon.), Lewis and Clark Coll., 1977. Bar: Pa. 1950, U.S. Ct. Appeals (D.C. cir.) 1950, U.S. Supreme Ct. 1954. Chemist Standard Oil Ind., Whiting, 1942-44; law clk. Fred M. Vinson, Chief Justice U.S., 1949-51; assoc. firm Shea, Greenman, Gardner & McConnaughey, Washington, 1951-53; spl. asst. to U.S. atty. gen. Office Solicitor Gen., 1953-54; 1st dept. city solicitor City Phila., 1954-56; assoc. firm Dilworth, Paxson, Kalish & Green, Phila., 1956-58; prof. law Law Sch., UCLA, 1958-91, dean, 1969-75; David G. Price and Dallas P. Price prof. of law UCLA, 1988-89, exec. vice chancellor, 1988-91; vice chancellor academic affairs U. Calif., Santa Barbara, 1991-92, interim sr. v.p. acad. affairs, 1992-93; chmn. exec. com., bd. dirs. Social Sci. Rsch. Coun., 1981-85; bd. dirs. Mattel, Inc. Author: (with K.L. Karst and A.J. Schwartz) The Evolution of Law in the Barrios of Caracas, 1973, Law and the American Future, 1976, Lawyers and the Legal Profession, 2d edit. 1985; contbr. articles to profl. jours. Served to lt. (j.g.) USNR, 1944-46. Home: 1339 Marinette Rd Pacific Palisades CA 90272-2626

SCHWARTZ, MURRAY MERLE, federal judge; b. 1931. BS, Wharton Sch. U. Pa., 1952; LLB, U. Pa., 1955; LLM, U. Va., 1982. Part-time referee in bankruptcy Dist. of Del., 1969-74; judge U.S. Dist. Ct. Del., 1974—, chief judge, 1985-89. Author: The Exercise of Supervisory Power by the Third Circuit Court of Appeals, 1982. Mem. ABA, Del. State Bar Assn., Am. Judicature Soc. Office: US Dist Ct Lockbox 44 844 N King St Wilmington DE 19801-3519

SCHWARTZ, NEENA BETTY, endocrinologist, educator; b. Balt., Dec. 10, 1926; d. Paul Howard and Pauline (Shulman) S. A.B., Goucher Coll., 1948, D.Sc. (hon.), 1982; M.S., Northwestern U., 1950, Ph.D., 1953. From instr. to prof. U. Ill. Coll. Medicine, Chgo., 1953-72; asst. dean for faculty U. Ill. Coll. Medicine, 1968-70; prof. physiology Northwestern U. Med. Sch., Chgo., 1973-74; Deering prof. Northwestern U., Evanston, Ill., 1974—, chmn. dept. biol. scis., 1974-78, acting dean, Coll. Arts and Scis., 1996—. Contbr. chpts. to books, articles to profl. jours. NIH research grantee, 1955—. Fellow AAAS; mem. Am. Acad. Arts Scis., Endocrine Soc. (v.p. 1970-71, mem. coun. 1979-83, pres. 1982-83, Williams award 1985), Soc. for Study of Reprodn. (dir. 1975-77, exec. v.p. 1976-77, pres. 1977-78, Carl Hartman award 1992), Am. Physio. Soc., Soc. for Neurosci., Phi Beta Kappa. Home: 1511 Lincoln St Evanston IL 60201-2338

SCHWARTZ, NORMAN L., lawyer; b. N.Y.C., Nov. 2, 1935; s. Louis and Rose (Tendlar) S.; m. Sandra Jean Coffae, Nov. 20, 1960; children: Debra, Cathy. BBA cum laude, Ohio State U., 1957, JD summa cum laude, 1960; LLM in Taxation, Georgetown U., 1968. Bar: Ohio 1960, D.C. 1968, Fla. 1991, U.S. Ct. Claims 1986, U.S. Tax Ct. 1961, U.S. Supreme Ct. 1967. Pvt. practice Columbus, Ohio, 1960-61, Dayton, Ohio, 1962-64; atty. IRS, Washington, 1964-68; ptnr. Cohen and Uretz, Washington, 1969-85, Morgan, Lewis & Bockius, Washington, 1985-88; atty. Arthur Andersen LLP, Sarasota, Fla., 1988—. Served with USAF, 1961-62; capt. Ohio Air NG 1960-64. Mem. ABA (chmn. com. on S corps. 1973-74 tax sect.). Democrat. Jewish. Avocations: reading, jogging. Home: 4761 Pine Harrier Dr Sarasota FL 34231-3360 Office: Arthur Andersen LLP 2805 Fruitville Rd Sarasota FL 34237-5318

SCHWARTZ, PERRY LESTER, information systems engineer, consultant; b. Bklyn., July 29, 1939; s. Max David and Sylvia (Weinberger) S.; m. Arlene Metz, Jan. 24, 1960; 3 children. BEE, CUNY, 1957-62; MS in Indsl. Engring. and Computer Sci., NYU, 1967. Registered profl. engr., N.J.; registered profl. planner, N.J.; cert. mediator and arbitrator, expert witness comm. Microwave engr. Airbourne Inst. Lab., Deer Park, N.Y., 1962-63, ITT Fed. Labs., Nutley, N.J., 1963-64; program mgr. Western Electric Co., N.Y.C., 1964-69; dept. head RCA, Princeton, N.J., 1970-71; dir. engring. Warner Communications Inc., N.Y.C., 1972-74; cons. engr. Intertech Associates, Marlboro, N.J., 1974—; adj. faculty CCNY, 1962-71, Ocean County Coll., Toms River, N.J., 1981-83, Rutgers U., New Brunswick, N.J., 1984-87; lectr. N.J. Dept. Edn., 1994, 95. Mem. Am. Cons. Engrs. Coun., Nat. Assn. Radio and Telecom. Engrs. (sr. mem., charter mem., cert. master engr. in wire and RF, Cert. of Distinction 1994-95), IEEE (sr.), Intelligent Bldgs. Inst. Found. (steering com., trustee 1982-89), Nat. Soc. Profl. Engrs., Cons. Engrs. Coun. N.J., N.Y. Acad. Sci., Zeta Beta Tau (chpt. founder 1958), K.P. Office: Intertech Assoc 77-55 Schanck Rd Ste B-9 Freehold NJ 07728

SCHWARTZ, PETER EDWARD, physician, gynecologic oncology educator; b. N.Y.C., Mar. 28, 1941; s. Bernard and Marcia (Firkser) S.; m. Arlene Harriet Eigen, Aug. 18, 1966; children: Bruce, Andrew, Kenneth. BS, Union Coll., Schenectady, N.Y., 1962; MD, Yeshiva U., N.Y.C., 1966; MA (hon.), Yale U., 1985. Diplomate Am. Bd. Ob-Gyn., Am. Bd. Gynecol. Oncology. Surg. intern U. Ky. Med. Ctr., Lexington, 1966-67; resident in ob-gyn. Yale-New Haven Hosp., 1967-71; fellow in gynecol. oncology U. Tex. M.D. Anderson Hosp., Houston, 1973-75; asst. prof. Yale U. Sch. Medicine, New Haven, 1975-80, assoc. prof., 1980-85, prof., 1985—, now vice chmn. dept. ob-gyn., 1992—. Maj. USAF, 1971-73. John Slade Ely Prof. of obstetrics and gynecology at Yale U. (hon. chair). Office: Yale U Sch Medicine Dept Ob-Gyn 333 Cedar St New Haven CT 06510-3206

SCHWARTZ, RENEE GERSTLER, lawyer; b. Bklyn., June 18, 1933; d. Samuel and Lillian (Neulander) Gerstler; m. Alfred L. Schwartz, July 30, 1955; children—Carolyn Susan, Deborah Jane. A.B., Bklyn. Coll., 1953; LL.B., Columbia U., 1955. Bar: N.Y. 1956, U.S. Dist. Ct. (so. and ea. dists.) N.Y. 1956, U.S. Ct. Appeals (2d cir.) 1956, U.S. Dist. Ct. D.C. 1983, U.S. Supreme Ct. 1986. Asspc. Botein, Hays & Sklar, N.Y.C., 1955-65, ptnr., 1965-89, Kronish, Lieb, Weiner & Hellman, N.Y.C., 1990—. Bd. dirs. New Land Found., N.Y.C., 1965—. Mem. Bar Assn. City N.Y. Home: 115 Central Park W New York NY 10023-4153 Office: Kronish Lieb Weiner & Hellman 1114 Avenue Of The Americas New York NY 10036-7703

SCHWARTZ, RICHARD BRENTON, English language educator, university dean, writer; b. Cin., Oct. 5, 1941; s. Jack Jay and Marie Mildred (Schnelle) S.; m. Judith Mary Alexis Lang, Sept. 7, 1963; 1 son, Jonathan Francis. AB cum laude, U. Notre Dame, 1963; AM, U. Ill., 1964, PhD, 1967. Instr. English U.S. Mil. Acad., 1967-69; asst. prof. U. Wis.-Madison, 1969-72, assoc. prof., 1972-78, prof., 1978-81; assoc. dean U. Wis.-Madison (Grad. Sch.), 1977, 79-81; prof. English, dean Grad. Sch., Georgetown U., Washington, 1981—, interim exec. v.p. for main campus academic affairs, 1991-92; interim exec. v.p. for the main campus Georgetown U., Washington, 1995-96; mem. exec. bd. Ctr. Strategic and Internat. Studies, 1981-87. Author: Samuel Johnson and the New Science, 1971 (runner-up Gustave O. Arlt prize), Samuel Johnson and the Problem of Evil, 1975, Boswell's Johnson: A Preface to the Life, 1978, Daily Life in Johnson's London, 1983, Japanese edit., 1990, After the Death of Literature, 1997, (novel) Frozen Stare, 1989; editor: The Plays of Arthur Murphy, 4 vols., 1979, Theory and Tradition in Eighteenth-Century Studies, 1990; contbr. articles to profl. jours. Served to capt. U.S. Army, 1967-69. Nat. Endowment Humanities grantee, 1970, 87; Inst. for Research in Humanities fellow, 1976; Am. Council Learned Socs. fellow, 1978-79; H.I. Romnes fellow, 1978-81. Mem. Mystery Writers Am., Johnson Soc. So. Calif., Am. Soc. Eighteenth-Century Studies, Coun. Grad. Schs., N.E. Assn. Grad. Schs. (exec. com. 1986-88), Assn. Grad. Schs. in Cath. Univs. (exec. com. 1984-87), Assn. Literary Scholars and Critics, N. Am. Conf. Brit. Studies, George Town Club, Alpha Sigma Nu, Alpha Sigma Lambda. Roman Catholic. Home: 4132 41st St N Arlington VA 22207-4802 Office: Georgetown Univ Grad Sch Washington DC 20057

SCHWARTZ, RICHARD DERECKTOR, sociologist, educator; b. Newark, Apr. 26, 1925; s. Selig and Tillie (Derecktor) S.; m. Emilie Zane Rosenbaum, June 30, 1946; children: David, Margaret Jane, Deborah. B.A., Yale U., 1947, Ph.D. in Sociology, 1952; LL.D. (hon.), Am. Internat. Coll., 1977. Research fellow Inst. Human Relations, Yale, 1951-54, instr., asst. prof. sociology and law, 1953-61; faculty Northwestern U., Evanston, 1961-71; prof. sociology Northwestern U., 1964-71, prof. sociology and law, 1966-71; dir. Council Intersocietal Studies, 1965-70, co-dir. law and social sci. program, 1967-70; dean, provost Faculty of Law and Jurisprudence, State U. N.Y. at Buffalo, 1971-76; Ernest I. White rsch. prof. law Syracuse U., 1977—; rsch. cons. Nat. Coun. Juvenile Ct. Judges, 1961-68; lecture tour for U.S. Embassy, India, 1968; adviser U.S. Dept. Justice, 1977-80; cons. U.S. Dept. Transp., 1968-69, Nat. Conf. Commrs. on Uniform State Laws, 1968-70, ABA, 1979-83; mem. com. law enforcement and adminstrn. of justice NAS, 1975-85; fellowship referee Russell Sage Found., 1970-77, NEH, 1972-77, NSF, 1978-81; mem. bd. edn., Orange, Conn., 1954-61; mem. exec. com. Am. Friends Svc. Com., Middle Atlantic Region, 1987-92; chmn. Am. Coalition for Middle East Dialogue, 1990-93. Author: (with others) Society and the Legal Order, 1970, Criminal Law, 1974, Nonreactive Measures in the Social Sciences, 1980, Handbook of Regulation and Administrative Law, 1994; founding editor: Law and Soc. Rev., 1966-69. Served with USNR, 1943-45. Ctr. for Advanced Study in Behavioral Scis. fellow, 1989-90. Fellow AAAS; mem. ABA (nonprofl. legal edn. com. 1986-89), Am. Sociol. Assn., Law and Soc. Assn. (pres. 1972-75). Jewish. Home: 15 Clarmar Rd Fayetteville NY 13066-1603 Office: Syracuse U Coll Law Syracuse NY 13244-1030 *I believe that we could create a better way of life if we structured society to encourage-rather than to penalize-altruism. Although I have not yet contributed much toward achieving such a society, the effort to do so has been satisfying.*

SCHWARTZ, RICHARD FREDERICK, electrical engineering educator; b. Albany, N.Y., May 31, 1922; s. Frederick William and Mary Hoyle (Holland) S.; m. Ruth Louise Feldman, Oct. 25, 1945 (div. Oct. 1977); children: Kathryn Gail, Frederick Earl, Karl Edward, Eric Christian, Frieda Diane; m. Margaret Camp Boes, May 29, 1982. BEE, Rensselaer Poly. Inst., Troy, N.Y., 1943, MEE, 1948; PhD, U. Pa., 1959. Registered profl. engr., Pa., Mich. Instr. Rensselaer Poly. Inst., Troy, 1947-48; engr. Radio Corp. Am., Camden, N.J., 1948-51; instr. U. Pa., Phila., 1951-53, rsch. assoc., 1953-59, asst. prof. electrical engring., 1959-62, assoc. prof. electrical engring., 1962-73; prof. elec. engring. Mich. Tech. U., Houghton, 1973-85, dept. head, 1973-79; prof. elec. engring. SUNY, Binghamton, 1985-95, prof. emeritus, 1995—; vis. asst. prof. U. Mich., Ann Arbor, 1960; cons. Pa. Bar Assn. Endowment, Armstrong Cork Co., Am. Electronics Labs., Inc., IBM, RCA, City of Phila., GE. Co-author: The Eavesdroppers, 1959; contbr. 40 papers to various pubs. Active Delaware County Symphony, Pa., 1967-72, Keeweehaw Symphony Orch., Houghton, 1973-85, Ctr. for Tech. and Innovation, Endicott, N.Y., 1995—. With U.S. Army, 1942-46. Mem. IEEE (sr., life), AAAS, NSPE, Am. Soc. Engring. Edn., N.Y. Soc. Profl. Engrs. (Broome chpt., Engr. of Yr. 1995, Contbns. to Edn. award 1996), Acoustical Soc. Am., Audio Engring. Soc., Catgut Acoustical Soc., Order of the Engr., Sigma Xi, Eta Kappa Nu, Tau Beta Tau. Democrat. Unitarian. Achievements include patents for tuning sys., 1954, oscillator frequency control, 1954, transistor amplifier with high undistorted output, 1954. Home: 2624 Bornt Hill Rd Endicott NY 13760 Office: SUNY Dept Electrical Engring PO Box 6000 Binghamton NY 13902-6000

SCHWARTZ, RICHARD HARVEY, pediatrician; b. Bklyn., July 6, 1938; s. Hy and Ruth (Marshak) S.; m. Rose Lynne Hass, May 29, 1960; children: Lisa, Keith, Keira. BA, George Washington U., 1960; MD, Georgetown U., 1965. Diplomate Am. Acad. Pediatrics, Am. Soc. Addiction Medicine. Intern U.S. Army, 1965-66, resident, 1969-71; pediatrician Vienna (Va.) Pediatric Assn., 1972—. Contbr. articles to profl. jours. Maj. U.S. Army, 1965-69. Mem. AMA (Outstanding Contbn. in Adolescent Medicine award 1990), Am. Acad. Pediatrics (rsch. award 1989). Jewish. Avocations: walking, travel. Office: Vienna Pediatric Assn 410 Maple Ave W Vienna VA 22180-4224

SCHWARTZ, RICHARD JOHN, electrical engineering educator, researcher; b. Waukesha, Wis., Aug. 12, 1935; s. Sylvester John and LaVerne Mary (Lepien) S.; m. Mary Jo Collins, June 29, 1957; children: Richard, Stephan, Susan, Elizabeth, Barbara, Peter, Christopher, Margarett. BSEE, U. Wis., 1957; SM, MIT, 1959, ScD, 1962. Mem. tech. staff Sarnoff Rsch. Labs. RCA, Princeton, N.J., 1957-58; instr. MIT, Cambridge, 1961-62; v.p. Energy Conversions, Inc., Cambridge, 1962-64; assoc. prof. Purdue U., West Lafayette, Ind., 1964-71, prof., 1972—, head dept., 1985-95, dean engring., 1995—, dir. Optoelectronic Ctr., 1986-89; bd. dir. Nat. Elec. Engring. Dept. Heads Assn.; solar cells cons., 1965—. Contbr. chpts. to books, articles to profl. jours. Served to 2nd lt. U.S. Army, 1957-58. Recipient Disting. Svc. medal U. Wis., 1989, Centennial medal, 1991. Fellow IEEE. Achievements include development of high intensity solar cells, of surface charge transfer device, and of numerical models for solar cells. Office: Purdue U 1280 Engring Adminstrn West Lafayette IN 47907

SCHWARTZ, ROBERT, automotive manufacturing company executive, marketing executive; b. Atlantic City, N.J., Mar. 9, 1939; s. Robert A. and Irene (Davis) S.; m. Judith H. Amole, Apr. 30, 1961. B.S., Drexel U., 1961; M.B.A., Wash. State U., 1962. With Ford Motor Co., 1964-70; dist. mgr. Simplicity Mfg., Port Washington, Wis., 1970-71; zone mgr. Am. Motors Corp., Boston, 1971-72, N.Y.C., 1972-74; dir. sales ops. Am. Motors Corp., Detroit, 1975; regional mgr. Am. Motors Corp., 1975-76; gen. mgr. Am. Motors Corp. (U.S. sales), 1976-80; mng. dir. Am. Motors Corp. (N.Am. sales and distbn.), 1981-83; pres. Am. Motors Sales Corp., Detroit, 1978-81, v.p. N.Am. sales, 1981-83; v.p. sales and mktg. Rolls-Royce Motors Inc., Lyndhurst, N.J., 1983-85, pres., CEO, 1986-89; pres. Motors Mgmt., Neptune, N.J., 1989-93; pres., CEO Automotive Ventures, Inc., Wayne, N.J., 1993—. Mem. Metropolitan Club (N.Y.C.).

SCHWARTZ, ROBERT GEORGE, retired insurance company executive; b. Czechoslovakia, Mar. 27, 1928; came to U.S., 1929, naturalized, 1935; s. George and Frances (Antoni) S.; m. Caroline Bachurski, Oct. 12, 1952; children: Joanne, Tracy, Robert G. BA, Pa. State U., 1949; MBA, NYU, 1956. With Met. Life Ins. Co., N.Y.C., 1949-93, v.p. securities, 1962-70, v.p., 1970-75, sr. v.p., 1975-78, exec. v.p., 1979-80, vice chmn. bd., 1980-83, chmn. investment com., 1980-93, chmn. bd., 1983-93, chmn. bd., pres., chief exec. officer, 1989-93; bd. dirs. Met. Life Ins. Co., Potlatch Corp., San Francisco, Lowe's Cos., Inc., North Wilkesboro, N.C., COMSAT Corp., Bethesda, Md., Mobil Corp., Fairfax, Va., Reader's Digest Assn., Inc., Consol. Edison Co. of N.Y., Lone Star Industries, Inc., Stamford, Conn., Ascent Entertainment Group, Inc., Denver, Horatio Alger Assn. Trustee Com. for Econ. Devel.; bd. visitors Smeal Coll., Pa. State U., mem. nat. devel. coun. With AUS, 1950-52. Mem. Bus. Coun., Sky Club, Blind Brook Country Club, Alpha Chi Rho. Office: MetLife Bldg 200 Park Ave Ste 5700 New York NY 10166-0005

SCHWARTZ, ROBERT M., lawyer; b. Phila., Aug. 6, 1940; s. Nathan and Miriam (Albus) S.; m. Karen Leaf, Feb. 11, 1966; children: Eric, Lauren. BS, Pa. State U., 1962; JD, Villanova U., 1965. Bar: Pa. 1965, U.S. Ct. Appeals (3rd cir.) 1965. Law clk. to presiding justice Common Pleas Ct. Montgomery County, Norristown, Pa., 1965; v.p., assoc. counsel Commonwealth Land Title Ins. Co., Phila., 1969-73; ptnr. in charge bus. dept., mem. exec. com. White and Williams, Phila., 1973—. Speaker numerous lectures and seminars in field. Mem. regional exec. com. civil rights com. and regional bd. trustees Anti-Defamation League; bd. dirs., mem. facilities and legal coms. Police Athletic League. Mem. Phila. Bar Assn. (chmn. real property com. 1981, exec. bd. real property sect. 1983-89, 91, chmn. real property sect. 1986), Am. Coll. Real Estate Lawyers (best lawyers in Am. award 1989—), Am. Land Title Assn. (leader's counsel group 1993—), Order of Coif. Republican. Jewish. Avocations: bridge, tennis. Office: White and Williams 1650 Market St Philadelphia PA 19103-7301

SCHWARTZ, ROBERT TERRY, professional association executive; b. Irvington, N.J., Sept. 29, 1950; s. Edward Herman and Harriet Selma (Rosenstein) S.; m. Carol Fawn Mullenix, July 27, 1975; children: Zachary Jacob,

Allison Lizabeth. BFA, Kansas City Art Inst., 1973; M of Indsl. Design, R.I. Sch. Design, 1975. Red Cross project dir. R.I. Sch. Design, Providence, 1975-76; head indsl. design/architecture ARC Nat. Hdqrs., Washington, 1976-88; dir. sci. and tech. Health Industry Mfrs. Assn., Washington, 1988-90; exec. dir., COO Worldesign Found., Great Falls, Va., 1990—, Indsl. Designers Soc. Am., Great Falls, 1990—; provider expert testimony before Congress, 1994, commencement address, Kansas City Art Inst., 1995. Contbr. chpts. to books, articles to profl. jours.; presenter in field; holder 5 patents, 1 trademark. Recipient Project of Merit award Indsl. Design Mag., 1985, Cert. of Achievement, ARC, 1988, Louis B. Tiffany award ARC, 1987, numerous others; Nat. Endowment for the Arts grantee, 1984, 92, 94; EPA grantee, 1992. Mem. Am. Soc. Assn. Execs., Greater Washington Soc. Assn. Execs., Am. Design Coun. (ofcl. rep.). Avocations: Edison antiquities collecting, sailing. Office: Indsl Designers Soc Am 1142 Walker Rd Great Falls VA 22066-1836

SCHWARTZ, ROBERT WILLIAM, management consultant; b. N.Y.C., Oct. 23, 1944; s. Edward and Bertha R. S.; m. Gail Beth Greenbaum, Mar. 18, 1967; children: Jill, Evan. BS, Cornell U., 1967; postgrad., SUNY, Albany, 1970. Assoc. IBM, 1967-68; cons. Peat, Marwick, Mitchell & Co., Albany, 1970-71; v.p. Security Gen. Svcs., Inc., Rochester, N.Y., 1971-73; v.p. fin. and adminstrn. Gardenway Mfg. Co., Troy, N.Y., 1973-77; exec. v.p. United Telecommunications Corp., Latham, N.Y., 1977-79; pres. United Telecommunications Corp., Latham, 1980-82; also bd. dir. United Telecommunications Corp.; pres., chmn. Winsource, Inc., Albany, 1982-85, Schwartz Heslin Group, Inc., 1985—; bd. dirs. Caddim Corp., Union Nat. Bank, Albany, ESARCO Internat., Inc., Springfield, Mo., LBO Capital Corp., Detroit; adj. prof. Rochester Inst. Tech., 1971-73. Bd. dirs. United Cerebral Palsy of Capital Dist., 1973—; trustee Newman Found., Rensselaer Poly. Inst., 1974-78, Gov. Clinton coun. Boy Scouts Am., SUNY Found. Mem. Am. Mgmt. Assn., Esarco Internat., N.Am. Tel. Assn., Assn. for Systems Mgmt., Ft. Orange Club, Econ. Club, Corenell Club (N.Y.C.). Republican. Home: 2 Myton Ln Albany NY 12204-1310 Office: 120 Defreest Dr Troy NY 12180-8360

SCHWARTZ, ROSELIND SHIRLEY GRANT, podiatrist; b. N.Y.C., Apr. 23, 1922; d. Joseph and Amy (Jacobs) Grant; m. Herman Schwartz, Dec. 19, 1943 (dec. Sept., 1980); children: Arthur Zachary, Raymond Dana. BA, NYU, 1943; D Podiatry cum laude, L.I. U., 1947, DPM, 1970; postgrad., L.A. Trade Tech. Coll., 1973-75. Notary pub., Calif. Pvt. practice Podiatry N.Y.C., 1947-73; cons. L.A., 1973-76, travel cons., 1974—; owner, mgr. Ros Travel, N.Y.C., 1995—. Bd. dirs. Welfare League for Retarded Children, 1955-73, chmn. Annual Souvenir Jour., 1955-65, Annual Luncheon, 25th anniversary, 1968, pres., 1969-70; pres. Sisterhood of Community Ctr. of Israel, N.Y., 1966-67; Cub den mother Boy Scouts Am., N.Y., 1960-63; class mother Pub. Schs., N.Y., 1960-66, pres. Parents' Assn. Jr. High Sch., N.Y., 1966-69; bd. dirs., pres. Barrington-Terryhill Condominium Assn., 1981—; vol. UCLA, 1981—; mem. Adv. Coms., Nurse Anesthesists, Infant & Child Care, 1981—. Recipient testimonial Community Ctr. Israel, Bronx, N.Y., 1971, award for devoted leadership Welfare League, 1963, 65. Mem. ARC, IATA, Assn. Wives of Physicians, Podiatry Soc. N.Y. State, Bus. and Profl. Women. Avocations: collecting stamps and coins, travel. Home and Office: Ros Travel 269 W 11th St Apt 3C New York NY 10014-2414

SCHWARTZ, ROY RICHARD, holding company executive; b. N.Y.C., Mar. 27, 1943; s. Julius and Mildred (Friedman) S.; m. Sharon Massler, June 3, 1965; children: Lisa Beth, Meridith Sara, Greg Mathew. AB, Washington Coll., Chestertown, Md., 1964; JD, Columbia U., 1967. Asst. counsel N.Y.C., 1967-68; assoc. Blumberg, Singer, N.Y.C., 1968-72, Kelly, Drye, N.Y.C., 1969-72; U.S. counsel U.S. Imasco Ltd., N.J., 1972-74; sr. U.S. counsel Imasco Ltd., N.J., 1974-78; pres. Imasco Holdings, N.J., 1978-82; v.p. Imasco Resources, Montreal, 1983; v.p. corp. devel. Imasco Ltd., Montreal, 1984-89, sr. v.p., 1989—; bd. dirs. Ulster Petroleums Ltd. Mem. Univ. Club. Office: Imasco Ltd, 600 de Maisonneuve Blvd W, Montreal, PQ Canada H3A 3K7

SCHWARTZ, RUTH WAINER, physician; b. New London, Wis.; d. Louis M. and Kathryn Ann (Schwall) W.; m. Seymour I. Schwartz, June 18, 1949; children: Richard, Kenneth, David. BS, U. Wis., 1947, MD, 1950. Diplomate Am. Bd. Ob-Gyn. Intern Genesee Hosp., Rochester, N.Y., 1950; resident Strong Meml. Hosp., Rochester, N.Y., 1951-54; pvt. practice gyn. Rochester, 1954-95; prof. U. Rochester, 1995—; examiner Am. Bd. Ob-Gyn., 1976-95, bd. dirs., 1981-89; dir. colposcopy, dysplasia and DES Clinic, colposcopy and laser tutor Genesee Hosp.; prof. ob-gyn. U. Rochester Sch. Medicine and Dentistry, dir. Menopause Ctr.; pres. med. staff Genesee Hosp., 1972-74; bd. dirs. Genesee Health Svc., 1972-75, ARC, med. adv. com.; trustee Rochester Acad. Medicine, 1975-78; vis. prof. U. Kuwait Med. Sch., 1984, U. Toledo Sch. Medicine, 1985, U. N.Mex. Sch. Medicine, 1989. Contbr. numerous articles to med. jours. and chpts. to med. textbooks; cons. editor and contbr. to The Merck Manual, 15th edit., 1983, 16th edit., 1987, 17th edit., 1991. Mem. med. adv. bd. N.Y. State Task Force on Child Abuse. Named one of Best Women Doctors in Am., Harper's Bazaar mag., Nov., 1985. Mem. ACS, ACOG, (health care commn., Women in Ob-Gyn task force, patient edn. com. 1979-83, asst. sec. 1994-95, task force on hysterectomy 1987-89, vice chmn. fin. coun. 1996=99, adv. bd. dist. II 1993-96, sec. 1993-96), Am. Soc. Colposcopy and Colpomicroscopy, Gynecologic Laser Soc. (bd. dirs.), Am. Fertility Soc., N.Y. State Med. Assn., Monroe County Med. Soc. (maternal mortality com., pub. health Com.). Home: 18 Lake Lacoma Dr Pittsford NY 14534-3956

SCHWARTZ, SAMUEL, business consultant, retired chemical company executive; b. Moose Jaw, Sask., Can., Nov. 12, 1927; came to U.S., 1951, naturalized, 1965; s. Benjamin and Rose (Becker) S.; m. Margaret Patterson, Feb. 20, 1956; children: Michael R., Thomas R., David C., Janet C. BA, U. Sask., 1948, B in Commerce, 1950; MBA, Harvard U., 1953. Research assoc. Harvard Bus. Sch., Boston, 1953-57; with Conoco Inc., 1957-83; sr. v.p. coordinating and planning Conoco Inc., Stamford, Conn., 1974-75; sr. v.p. corp. planning Conoco Inc., 1975-78, sr. v.p. adminstrv., 1978-80, group sr. v.p. adminstrv., 1980-83; sr. v.p. adminstrv. E.I. duPont de Nemours & Co., Wilmington, Del., 1983-87, sr. v.p., corp. plans dept., 1987-88; dir. Conoco Inc. Consol. Coal Co., 1981-88. Trustee Inst. for the Future, Menlo Park, Calif., 1975-92, Henry du Pont Winterthur Mus., Winterthur, Del., trustee, 1984—, chmn., 1994—.

SCHWARTZ, SEYMOUR IRA, surgeon, educator; b. N.Y.C., Jan. 22, 1928; s. Samuel and Martha (Paul) S.; m. Ruth Elaine Wainer, June 18, 1949; children: Richard, Kenneth, David. BA, U. Wis., 1947; MD, NYU, 1950; PhD (hon.), U. Lund, Sweden, 1989; FRCS (hon.), y. Intern Strong Meml. Hosp., Rochester, N.Y., 1950-51, resident, 1951-52, 54-57; asst. prof. surgery U. Rochester, N.Y., 1959-63, assoc. prof, 1963-67, prof., 1967—, chmn. dept., 1987—, dir. surg. rsch., 1962-82; nat. cons. USAF, 1968-77; mem. surgery study sect. A, NIH, 1974-78. Co-author: Mapping of America, 1980, Surgical Reflections, 1991, Mapping of the French and Indian War, 1994; co-editor: Maingot's Abdominal Operations, 2 edits.; editor-in-chief: Year Book of Surgery, 6 edits., 1969—. Bd. mgrs. Strong Meml. Hosp., Rochester. Lt. (j.g.) USN, 1952-54. Recipient Sesquicentennial medal U. S.C., 1974, Acrel medal Swedish Surg. Assn., 1974, Yandell medal U. Louisville (Ky.), 1978, Roswell Park medal, 1989, Albert Kaiser medal, 1992; John and Mary R. Markle scholar in acad. medicine, 1960. Fellow ACS (regent 1988, chmn. bd. regents 1994—, programs and ethics com. 1989—, Disting. Svc. award 1986), Royal Coll. Surgeons Edinburgh (hon.), Ctrl. Surg. Soc. (pres. 1981-82), So. Surg. Soc., Soc. Univ. Surgeons, Soc. Clin. Surgery (pres. 1985), Am. Surg. Assn. (pres. 1993-94), Am. Antiquarian Soc., Grolier Club (N.Y.C.), Cosmos Club (Washington), Genesee Valley Club, Phi Beta Kappa, Alpha Omega Alpha. Avocation: collecting antique maps. Office: U Rochester Med Ctr 601 Elmwood Ave Rochester NY 14642-0001

SCHWARTZ, SHIRLEY E., chemist; b. Detroit, Aug. 26, 1935; d. Emil Victor and Jessie Grace (Galbraith) Eckwall; m. Ronald Elmer Schwartz, Aug. 25, 1957; children: Steven Dennis, Bradley Allen, George Byron. BS, U. Mich., 1957, Detroit Inst. Tech., 1978; MS, Wayne State U., 1962, PhD, 1970. Asst. prof. Detroit Inst. Tech., 1973-78, head divsn. math. sci., 1976-78; mem. rsch. staff BASF Wyandotte (Mich.) Corp., 1978-81, head sect. functional fluids, 1981; sr. staff rsch. scientist GM, Warren, Mich., 1981—. Contbr. articles to profl. jours.; patentee in field. Recipient Gold award Engrng. Soc. Detroit, 1989, lifetime achievement award Mich. Women's Hall of Fame, 1996. Fellow Soc. Tribologists and Lubrication Engrs. (treas. Detroit sect. 1981, vice chmn. 1982, chmn. 1982-83, chmn. wear tech. com. 1987-88, bd. dirs. 1985-91, assoc. editor 1989-90, contbg. editor 1989—, Wilbur Deutsch award 1987, P.M. Ku award 1994); mem. Am. Chem. Soc., Soc. In Vitro Biology, Soc. Automotive Engrs. (Excellence in Oral Presentation award 1986, 91, 94, Arch T. Colwell Merit award 1991, Lloyd L. Withrow Disting. Spkr. award 1995), Mich. Women's Hall of Fame (lifetime achievement award 1996), Mensa, Classic Guitar Soc. Mich., U.S. Power Squadrons, Detroit Navigators, Sigma Xi. Lutheran. Office: GM Rsch & Devel Ctr Mail Code 480-106-160 30500 Mound Rd Warren MI 48092-2031 *I've spent a number of very pleasant hours trying to make water behave like oil and alcohol behave like gasoline—a quest not much different from that of the ancient alchemists, who also spent their time trying to convert one substance to another.*

SCHWARTZ, STEPHEN BLAIR, retired information industry executive; b. Chgo., Oct. 19, 1934; s. Herbert S. and Gertrude (Weinstein) S.; m. Nancy Jean Astrof, Dec. 18, 1955; children: Debra Lee Schwartz Zaret, Susan Beth Schwartz Derene. B.S. in Indsl. Engrng., Northwestern U., 1957. With IBM Corp., 1957-92; various mgmt. positions, dir. product programs Harrison, N.Y., to 1977, v.p. Systems Communications div., 1977-81; v.p. Armonk, N.Y., 1982-90; v.p. Am. Far East Corp. subs. IBM Corp. Tokyo, 1982-84; pres., CEO Satellite Bus. Systems, McLean, Va., 1984; v.p., asst. group exec. Telecommunications, 1985-86, v.p., pres. Systems Products Div., 1986-88, v.p., gen. mgr. Application Bus. Systems, 1988-90; sr. v.p. market driven quality Stamford, Conn., 1990-92; bd. dirs. Niagara Mohawk Power Corp., MFRI, Inc. Mem. PGA Nat. Golf Club (Palm Beach Gardens, Fla.). Republican. Jewish.

SCHWARTZ, STEPHEN JAY, lawyer; b. Portland, Maine, Sept. 6, 1960; s. Jack Leonard and Sara Belle (Modes) S.; m. Susan Greenspun, Oct. 25, 1987; children: Leonard Samuel, Andrew Joseph, Jack Edward. BA with distinction, U. Maine, 1982; JD, Santa Clara U., 1985. Bar: Maine 1985, U.S. Dist. Ct. Maine 1985. Asst. dist. atty. Prosecutorial Dist. No. 1 York County, Alfred, Maine, 1986-87; ptnr. Schwartz & Schwartz, P.A., Portland, Maine, 1987—; mem. criminal rules adv. com. Maine Supreme Jud. Ct., 1991—. Comments editor Santa Clara Law Rev., 1985; editor Maine Defender, 1992-95; mem. editl. adv. com. Maine Bar Jour., 1990—. Pres. Jewish Fedn. and Cmty. Coun. of So. Maine, Portland, 1994-96. Recipient Richard D. Aronson Young Leadership award Jewish Fedn. and Cmty. of So. Maine, 1994. Mem. ABA, ATLA, Maine State Bar Assn. (chmn. criminal law sect. 1991-92, mem. jud. evaluation com.), Cumberland Bar Assn., Maine Trial Lawyers Assn., Nat. Assn. Criminal Def. Lawyers, Maine Assn. Criminal Def. Lawyers (founder, 1st pres. 1992-93), Pi Sigma Alpha, Sigma Phi Epsilon. Office: Schwartz & Schwartz PA 482 Congress St PO Box 15337 Portland ME 04112-5337

SCHWARTZ, STEPHEN LAWRENCE, composer, lyricist; b. N.Y.C., Mar. 6, 1948; s. Stanley Leonard and Sheila Lorna (Siegel) S.; m. Carole Ann Piasecki, June 6, 1969; children—Scott Lawrence, Jessica Lauren. Student, Juilliard Sch. Music, 1960-64; B.F.A., Carnegie-Mellon U., 1968. Works include: title song for play and film Butterflies Are Free, 1969; (theatre) music and new lyrics Godspell, 1971, four songs, adaptation and direction Working, 1978, music for 3 songs Personals, 1985, (with Leonard Bernstein) English texts for Leonard Bernstein's Mass, 1971, music and lyrics Pippin, 1972, The Magic Show, 1974, The Baker's Wife, 1976, Children of Eden, 1991, lyrics Rags, 1986, (films) Life with Mikey, 1993, Pocahontas, 1995 (Acad. award for best original score 1996, Acad. award for best original song 1996), The Hunchback of Notre Dame, 1996; (juvenile) The Perfect Peach, 1977, The Trip, 1983. Recipient Drama Desk awards, 1971, 78, Grammy awards, 1971, 96, Golden Globe award, 1996. Mem. ASCAP, Nat. Acad. Rec. Arts and Scis., Am. Motion Picture Arts Soc. Address: c/o Paramuse Artists Assocs 1414 Ave of the Americas New York NY 10019

SCHWARTZ, SUSAN LYNN HILL, principal; b. Portland, Ind., Aug. 15, 1951; d. Leland Alfred and Marjorie (Halberstadt) Hill; m. William Samuel Schwartz, July 6, 1974; children: Angelica Martinique, Allysia Dominica. BA, DePauw U., 1973; MA, Ball State U., 1976; postgrad., Tri-Coll. U., Fargo, N.D., 1986, Ind. U., 1993—. Cert. tchr. and aminstr., Ind., N.D. 2d and 3d grade tchr. Jay Sch. Corp., Portland, 1973-76; 1st to 3d grade tchr. Minot (N.D.) Pub. Schs., 1976-80; prin. elem. sch. Ward County Schs., Minot, 1980-82, LaPorte (Ind.) Schs., 1988-96; prin. kindergarten to 5th grade Western Wayne Schs., Cambridge City, Ind., 1996-97; mem. State Sch. Evaluation Team, Bismarck, N.D., 1980-81. Bd. dirs. Am. Cancer Soc., Muncie, Ind., 1985-88, Richmond, Ind., 1992—, Suzuki Music Assn., Muncie, 1986-87; mem./leader Work Area on Edn.-Meth., Muncie, 1985-87; philanthropic chair Delaware County Welcome Wagon, Muncie, 1982-88; treas./fin. sec. Christian Women's Club, Muncie, 1983-86; pres. N.D. State U. Sch. Adminstrs. Assn., Fargo, 1980-81; mem. Wayne County Step Ahead Edn. Com., 1991—; bd. mem. United Way. Named Outstanding Young Educator, Jaycees, 1980, Outstanding Young Career Woman, Bus. and Profl. Women, 1981. Mem. Phi Delta Kappa, Pi Lambda Theta, Delta Kappa Gamma, Psi Iota Xi. Methodist. Avocations: golf, racquetball, bridge. Home: 12522 W Us Highway 40 Cambridge City IN 47327-9485 Office: Western Wayne Elem Sch 801 E Delaware Cambridge City IN 47327

SCHWARTZ, THEODORE B., physician, educator; b. Phila., Feb. 14, 1918; s. William F. and Fanny (Farkas) S.; m. Genevieve Etta Bangs, Jan. 9, 1948; children: Richard, Steven, Michael, David, Jonathan, Thomas. B.S., Franklin and Marshall Coll., 1939; M.D., Johns Hopkins U., 1943. Diplomate Am. Bd. Internal Medicine (bd. govs., 1970-78, sec.-treas., 1976-78). Intern Osler Clinic, Johns Hopkins Hosp., 1943-44; asst. resident medicine Salt Lake City Gen. Hosp., 1946-47, resident medicine, 1947-48; fellow medicine Duke U. Med. Sch., 1948-50, asso. medicine, asst. prof. medicine, 1950-55; dir. sect. endocrinology and metabolism Rush-Presbyn.-St. Luke's Med. Center, Chgo., 1955-82; attending physician Rush-Presbyn.-St. Luke's Med. Center, 1960—; chmn. dept. medicine Rush-Presbyn.-St. Lukes's Med. Center, 1970-82; cons. endocrinology Hines (Ill.) VA Hosp., 1956-71, Great Lakes Naval Hosp., 1960-74; prof. medicine U. Ill. Coll. Medicine, 1960-71; prof., chmn. dept. medicine Rush Med. Coll., 1971-82; prof. medicine U. Wash., Seattle, 1982-96; chief med. services VA Med. Ctr., Boise, 1982-86; mem. Am. Bd. Med. Spltys., 1972-79; cons. endocrinology 1997—. Editor: Yearbook of Endocrinology, 1964-86, endocrinology article Ency. Brit., 1985—; contbr. articles to profl. jours. Bd. dirs. Boise Art Mus., 1984-92. Served with M.C. AUS, 1944-46. Decorated Bronze Star. Fellow ACP (publs. com. 1973-78, chmn. subcom. on aging 1982-85, mem. health and pub. policy com.), Am. Assn. Clin. Endocrinology (hon.), Am. Coll. Endocrinology (hon.); mem. Assn. Program Dirs. Internal Medicine (councilor 1978-80), Am. Fedn. Clin. Rsch., Am. Diabetes Assn., Diabetes Assn. Greater Chgo. (bd. dirs.), Am. Soc. Clin. Investigation, Am. Clin. and Climatol. Assn., Am. Thyroid Assn., Endocrine Soc., Ctrl. Clin. Rsch. Club, Ctrl. Soc. Clin. Rsch., Chgo. Soc. Internal Medicine (pres. 1966-67), Phi Beta Kappa, Alpha Omega Alpha. Address: 200 Lee St Evanston IL 60202-1450

SCHWARTZ, VICTOR ELLIOT, lawyer; b. N.Y.C., July 3, 1940. AB summa cum laude, Boston U., 1962; JD magna cum laude, Columbia U., 1965. Bar: N.Y. 1965, Ohio 1974. Law clk. to judge So. Dist. N.Y., 1965-67; from asst. to assoc. prof. law U. Cin., 1967-72, prof., 1972-79, acting dean, 1973-74; vis. prof. U. Va. Law Sch., 1970-71; adj. prof. law U. Cin., 1985—; ptnr. firm Crowell & Moring, Washington; sr. ptnr. firm Fed. Interagy. task Force on Products Liability, 1976; bd. dirs. Am. Tort Reform Assn.; chmn. Civil Justice Task Force, Am. Legis. Exch. Coun.; adj. prof. law Georgetown U., 1987—; chmn. Dept. of Commerce Task Force on Product Liability and Accident Compensation, 1977-80. Author: Comparative Negligence, 1974, 3d edit., 1994; (with Prosser and Wade) Cases and Materials on Torts, 1976, 9th edit., 1994, How to Prepare for the Multi-State Bar Examination, 1977, Products Liability: Cases and Trends, 1987, Products Liability: Asset Trends, 1988, (with Lee and Kelly) Multistate Legislation, 1985; editor: Columbia Law Rev., 1965; prin. draftsman: Model Uniform Product Liability Act. Recipient Sec. of Commerce award for disting. svc.; named One of 100 Most Influential Attys. in U.S., Nat. Law J, 1994, 97. Mem. ABA (chmn. products liability com. 1979, uniform laws com. 1981, torts and ins. practice sect.), Am. Law Inst. (life, adv. com. Restatement Third of Torts), Phi Beta Kappa. Office: Crowell & Moring 1001 Pennsylvania Ave NW Washington DC 20004-2505 *The greatest joys in life are found in one's relationships, be it business, romance or friendship, with other people.*

SCHWARTZ, WILLIAM, lawyer, educator; b. Providence, May 6, 1933; s. Morris Victor and Martha (Glassman) S.; m. Bernice Konigsberg, Jan. 13, 1957; children: Alan Gershon, Robin Libby. A.A., Boston U., 1952, J.D. magna cum laude, 1955, M.A., 1960; postgrad., Harvard Law Sch., 1955-56; LHD (hon.), Hebrew Coll., 1996. Bar: D.C. 1956, Mass. 1962, N.Y. 1989. Prof. law Boston U., 1955-91, Fletcher prof. law, 1968-70, Roscoe Pound prof. law, 1970-73, dean Sch. of Law, 1980-88, dir. Ctr. for Estate Planning, 1988-91; univ. prof. Yeshiva U., N.Y.C., 1991—; of counsel Swartz & Swartz, 1973-80; v.p. for acad. affairs, chief acad. officer Yeshiva U., N.Y.C., 1993—; counsel Cadwalader, Wickersham and Taft, N.Y.C., Washington, L.A., Charlotte, 1988—; mem. faculty Frances Glessner Lee Inst., Harvard Med. Sch., Nat. Coll. Probate Judges, 1970, 77, 78, 79, 88; gen. dir. Assn. Trial Lawyers Am., 1968-73; reporter New Eng. Trial Judges Conf., 1965-67; participant Nat. Met. Cts. Conf., 1968; dir. Mass. Probate Study, 1976—; chmn. spl. com. on police procedures City of Boston, 1989, 91; bd. dirs. UST Corp., chmn. of co., 1993-94, chmn. bd. dirs., 1996—; bd. dirs. Viacom Inc., Viacom Internat. Inc.; mem. adv. com. WCI Steel, Inc.; mem. legal adv. com. N.Y. Stock Exch. Author: Future Interests and Estate Planning, 1965, 77, 81, 86, Comparative Negligence, 1970, A Products Liability Primer, 1970, Civil Trial Practice Manual, 1972, New Vistas in Litigation, 1973, Massachusetts Pleading and Practice, 7 vols., 1974-80, Estate Planning and Living Trusts, 1990, The Convention Method: The Unused Amending Superhighway, 1995, Jewish Law and Contemporary Dilemmas and Problems, 1997, others; note editor: Boston U. Law Rev., 1954-55; property editor: Annual Survey of Mass. Law, 1960—; contbr. articles to legal jours. Bd. dirs. Kerry Found.; trustee Hebrew Coll., 1975—, Salve Regina Univ.; rep. Office Public Info., UN, 1968-73; chmn. legal adv. panel Nat. Commn. Med. Malpractice, 1972-73; examiner of titles Commonwealth of Mass., 1964—; spl. counsel Mass. Bay Transp. Authority, 1979; trustee Yeshiva U. Recipient Homer Albers award Boston U., 1955, John Ordronaux prize, 1955; Disting. Service award Religious Zionists Am., 1977; William W. Treat award; William O. Douglas award. Fellow Am. Coll. Probate Counsel; mem. ABA, Am. Law Inst., Mass. Bar Assn. (chmn. task force tort liability), N.Y. State Bar Assn., Assn. Bar City N.Y., Nat. Coll. Probate Judges (hon. mem.), Phi Beta Kappa. Office: 500 W 185th St New York NY 10033-3201 *I have been guided by the maxim: "Ideals are like stars. You cannot touch them with your hands, but like the seafaring man, if you choose them as your guide and follow them, you will reach your destiny."*

SCHWARTZ, WILLIAM A(LLEN), broadcasting and cable executive; b. Detroit, Nov. 29, 1938; m. Marlene J. Cohen; children: Jonathan, Cynthia, Michael. BA in Mktg. and Broadcasting, Wayne State U., 1961; postgrad. Bernard Baruch Grad. Sch. Bus.Mgr. research projects NBC, 1963-66; asst. dir. research Columbia Pictures, 1966; v.p., gen. mgr. Sta. WUAB-TV, Cleve., 1968-73; v.p. ops. Telerep, Inc., N.Y.C., 1973-74; v.p. gen. mgr. Sta. KTVU-TV, Oakland, Calif., 1974-79; pres. Cox Broadcasting div., Atlanta, 1979-81; pres. Cox Communications, Inc., Atlanta, 1981-87, chief exec. officer, 1983-87; pres., chief operating officer Cox Enterprises, Inc., Atlanta, 1985-87; chmn., chief exec. officer Capital Cable, 1988—; pres., chief exec. officer Cannell Communications, L.P., 1989-95, First Media Television, L.P., 1995—. Office: 400 Perimeter Center Ter NE Atlanta GA 30346-1227

SCHWARTZ, WILLIAM B., JR., ambassador; b. Atlanta, Nov. 14, 1921; s. William B. and Ruth (Kuhn) S.; m. Sonia Weinberg, Dec. 3, 1942; children—William B., Arthur Jay, Robert C. B.S., U. N.C., 1942. Various positions, then v.p. Nat. Service Industries, Atlanta, 1945-68; pres. Weine Investment Corp., Atlanta, 1969-77; amb. to Bahamas, 1977-81; bd. dirs. Weine Investment Corp., Balco Energy, Phenix Supply, Artex Internat. Mem. pres.'s council Brandeis U., 1966—, chancellor's club U. N.C., Bd. Councillors Carter Ctr., Emory U.; trustee, past chmn. Atlanta chapt. Am. Jewish Com.; chmn. Chatham Valley Found.; bd. dirs. Met. Atlanta Rapid Transit Authority, 1969-76, vice chmn., 1971-73; bd. dirs. Big Bros. Atlanta, Atlanta Jewish Welfare Fedn.; former mem. Pres.'s Council Oglethorp U.; former mem. bd. dirs. Jewish Home for the Aged; chmn. bd. visitors Emory U., 1966-74. Served with USN, 1942-45. Recipient Man of Yr. award Am. Jewish Com., 1972. Mem. Coun. Am. Ambs. Clubs: Standard (Atlanta), Commerce (Atlanta); East Hill (Nassau), Lyford Cay (Nassau); Longboat Key (Fla.); City (Sarasota). Lodges: B'nai Brith, Masons, Shriners. Home: 2724 Peachtree Rd Atlanta GA 30305 also: 1211 Gulf Of Mexico Dr Longboat Key FL 34228

SCHWARTZBERG, MARTIN M., chemical company executive; b. N.Y.C., Dec. 10, 1935; s. Morris H. and Anne C. (Steskanin) S.; m. Florence M. Bloom, Sept. 22, 1957; children: Steven E., Michael C., Scott A. B ChemE, NYU, 1956; MBA, Wayne State U., 1965. Asst. to div. mgr. Pennwalt Corp., Phila., 1969-72, mgr. mktg. service, 1972-74, asst. to chief exec. officer, 1974-76, mng. dir. chems. Europe, 1976-78, mng. dir. splt. chems., 1978-80, pres. agrichems. div., 1980-85, pres. inorganic chems. div., 1985, v.p. chems., 1985-87, sr. v.p. chems., 1987-89; group pres. Elf Atochem N.Am., Inc. (formerly Pennwalt Corp.), Phila., 1990-94, ret., 1995. Bd. dirs. Camden County chpt. ARC. Served with U.S. Army, 1959. Mem. Sigma Iota Epsilon. Avocations: volleyball, golf.

SCHWARTZBERG, PAUL DAVID, lawyer; b. N.Y.C., July 25, 1959; s. Melvin and Zelda Zara (Jacobs) S.; m. Ellen Beth Fassler; children: Joanne Lynn, Marc. BA, Hampshire Coll., 1982; JD cum laude, Vt. Law Sch., 1987. Bar: Vt. 1988, N.Y. 1988. Pres. Environ. Law Found., Inv., N.Y., 1987—; environ. atty. Town of Patterson, N.Y., 1990-93; real estate specialist N.Y.C. Dept. Environ. Protection, 1993—; spl. environ. atty. Town of New Paltz, 1996; facilty assoc. Lincoln Inst. Land Policy, Cambridge, Mass., 1990-93; admissions assoc. Hampshire Coll., Amherst, Mass., 1989—; student advisor SUNY, Empire State Coll., White Plains, N.Y., 1990-94; presenter in field. Producer radio program Let's Talk Trash, 1989-90 (2 AP Broadcasters award 1990); mem. Vt. Law Rev., 1985. Sec.-treas. Putnam Arts Coun., Mahopac, N.Y., 1988-89; campaign advance Walter F. Mondale Presdl. Campaign, 1984, Hart Presdl. Campaign, 1984, Peter Shapiro Govtl. Campaign, N.J., 1985, Sen. Patrick Leahy Campaign, Vt., 1986. Mem. Am. Planning Assn. (Meritorious Svc. award for pub. participation 1991). Avocations: skiing, photography, bicycling. Office: NYC Dep Rte 28A Shokan NY 12481

SCHWARTZEL, CHARLES BOONE, lawyer; b. Louisville, Jan. 4, 1950; s. Charles Joseph and Rosemary Jane (Redens) S.; m. Rose Marie Carlisi, June 20, 1980; children: Sally Ann, Charles Gerard. BA, Vanderbilt U., 1972; JD, U. Tex., 1975. Bar: Tex. 1975. Atty. Vinson & Elkins L.L.P., Houston, 1975—, ptnr., 1983—. Contbr. articles to profl. jours. Councilman City of West University Place, Tex., 1985-89; vol. Trees For Houston, 1985—. Fellow Am. Coll. Trust and Estate Counsel; mem. ABA (chmn. real property, probate and trust law sect. com. on creditors' rights in estates and trusts 1989-93), Tex. Bar Assn., Houston Bar Assn. Roman Catholic. Office: Vinson & Elkins LLP 1001 Fannin St Ste 1935 Houston TX 77002-6706

SCHWARTZHOFF, JAMES PAUL, foundation executive; b. Waukon, Iowa, June 24, 1937; s. Harold J. and Mary (Regan) Schwartzhoff; m. Mary Lou Hess, Apr. 23, 1960; children: Tammara, Eric, Stephanie, Mark, Laurie, Michelle, Steven. B, U. Iowa, 1962. Asst. chief auditor Wis. Dept. Tax, Madison, 1962-67; mgr. treas. dept. Mead Johnson and Co., Evansville, Ind., 1967-69; v.p., treas. Kettering Found., Dayton, Ohio, 1969—; chmn., treas. bd. Pastoral Counseling Ctr., Dayton, 1975-81; treas. Ohio River Rd. Runners, Dayton, 1986-87. Treas. Nat. Issues Forums Inst., Coun. Pub. Policy Edn., Ctr. for Community and Ednl. Devel.; mem. Donor's Forum Ohio Fin. Com., 1990-92; mem. investment com. U. Dayton; adv. com. JMB Endowment and Found. Realty Funds, 1991-94. Cpl. U.S. Army, 1957-59. Mem. AICPA, Found. Fin. Officers Group, Southern Ohio Pension Fund Group. Avocations: bicycling, backpacking, photography, woodworking. Office: Kettering Found 200 Commons Rd Dayton OH 45459-2788

SCHWARTZMAN, ANDREW JAY, lawyer; b. N.Y.C., Oct. 4, 1946; s. Joel Jay and Theresa (Greenhauff) S.; m. Linda Lazarus, June 8, 1986. AB, U. Pa., 1968, JD, 1971. Bar: N.Y. 1972, D.C. 1974, Temporary Emergency Ct. of Appeals 1977, U.S. Dist. Ct. D.C. 1978, U.S. Ct. Appeals (D.C. cir.) 1981, U.S. Ct. Appeals (2nd cir.) 1987, U.S. Supreme Ct. 1980, U.S. Ct. Appeals (7th, 8th, 9th cirs.) 1991. Staff counsel United Ch. of Christ Office of Communication, N.Y.C., 1971-74; atty. adv. Fed. Energy Office, FEA, Washington, 1974-77; sr. atty. adviser U.S. Dept. Energy, Washington, 1977-78; bd. dirs. Safe Energy Communication Council, pres. bd. dirs., 1989—; adv. panel Study on Communications Systems for an Information Age, U.S. Office of Tech. Ctr. for Democracy and Tech., 1996— Assessment; exec. dir. Media Access Project, Washington, 1978—; lectr. Fairleigh Dickinson U., 1972-73; bd. dirs. Telecommunications Research Action Ctr.; mem. comms. coun. forum Aspen Inst. on Comms. and Soc., 1992—; mem. bd. dirs. Min. Media & Telecomms. Conf., 1994—. Contbr. Les Brown's Dictionary of Television, 3d edit., 1992, articles to legal jours. Recipient Everett Parker award United Ch. of Christ, 1991. Mem. ABA, Fed. Communications Bar Assn., U. Pa. Alumni Assn. Home: 3624 Military Rd NW Washington DC 20015-1724 Office: Media Access Project 1707 L St NW Ste 400 Washington DC 20036-4213

SCHWARTZMAN, DAVID, economist, educator; b. Montreal, Que., Can., Apr. 22, 1924; came to U.S., 1954, naturalized, 1964; s. Joseph and Jeannette (Zurick) S.; m. Gertrude Schneiderman, June 17, 1951; children—Michael, Jason, Paul. B.A., McGill U., 1945; postgrad., U. Minn., 1945-46; Ph.D., U. Calif. at Berkeley, 1953. Lectr. McGill U., 1948-51; economist Dominion Bur. Statistics, 1951-53, United 5to $1.00 Stores, Can., 1953-54; instr. Columbia, 1954-58; assoc. prof. N.Y. U., 1958-60; assoc. prof. New Sch. for Social Research, N.Y.C., 1960-64; prof. New Sch. for Social Rsch., 1964—, chmn. dept. econs., 1966-69, 76, 83-84; mem. staff Nat. Bur. Econ. Research, 1963-69; prof. environ. medicine and community health state U. N.Y. Downstate Med. Center, part-time, 1969-70; Cons. Royal Commn. on Farm Machinery, Ottawa, Can., 1968-70, U.S. Bur. Census, 1973, anti-trust div. U.S. Dept. Justice, 1973, U.S. Council on Wage and Price Stability, Exec. Office of Pres., 1975-76; adj. mem. Com. on Trade Regulation, N.Y. County Lawyers' Assn., 1976-85; Bd. advisors Inst. Health Economics and Social Studies, 1976-80. Author: Oligopoly in the Farm Machine Industry, 1970, Decline of Service in Retail Trade, 1971, The Expected Return from Pharmaceutical Research, 1975, Innovation in the Pharmaceutical Industry, 1976, Games of Chicken: Four Decades of Nuclear Policy, 1988, Economic Policy: An Agenda for the Nineties, 1989, The Japanese Television Cartel: A Study Based on Matsushita v. Zenith, 1993, Black Unemployment: Part of Unskilled Unemployment, 1997; contbr. articles to profl. jours. Mem. Am. Econ. Assn. Home: 285 Central Park W New York NY 10024-3006 Office: New Sch for Social Rsch Dept Econs 65 5th Ave New York NY 10003-3003

SCHWARY, RONALD LOUIS, motion picture producer; b. The Dalles, Oreg., May 23, 1944; s. Mitchell Louis and Lorraine (Ablan) S.; children: Brian L., Neil L. BS, U. So. Calif., 1967. Pres. Schwary Enterprises, L.A., 1985—. Prodr. (motion pictures) Ordinary People, 1980 (Golden Globe award 1981, Acad. award 1981), Absence of Malice, 1981, Tootsie, 1982, A Soldier's Story, 1984, Batteries Not Included, 1987, Havana, 1990, Scent of a Woman, 1992, Cops and Robbersons, 1994, Sabrina, 1995, Mirror Has Two Faces, 1996; (TV series) Tour of Duty, 1987. Mem. Dirs. Guild Am. Republican. Roman Catholic.

SCHWARZ, BERTHOLD ERIC, psychiatrist; b. Jersey City, N.Y., Oct. 20, 1924; s. Berthold Theodore D. and Thyra I.W. (Ericson) S.; m. Ardis Marilyn Peterson, Jan. 22, 1955; children: Lisa Thyra, Eric Rolf. AB, Dartmouth Coll., 1945; MD, NYU, 1950; MS, Mayo Grad. Sch. Medicine, 1957. Intern Mary Hitchcock Meml. Hosp., Hanover, N.H., 1950-51; psychiatrist, researcher pvt. practice, Montclair, N.J., 1955-82; Mayo Found., Rouchester, M.N., 1951-55; psychiatrist, researcher pvt. practice, Vero Beach, Fla., 1982—; cons. Essex County Hosp. Ctr., Cedar Grove, N.J., 1965-82, Med. Correctional Assn., Ossining, Casining, N.Y., 1960-72; exec. dir. Internat. Psychosomatics Inst., Mountain Lakes, N.J., 1995—. Contbr. articles to profl. jours. With USNR, 1943-45. Fellow AAAS, Am. Psychiat. Assn., Am. Soc. Physical Rsch., Am. Geriatric Soc. Republican. Avocations: UFOs, paranormal aspects, swimming, walking. Home: 1070 Reef Rd #305 Vero Beach FL 32963 Office: 642 Azalea Ln Vero Beach FL 32963-1832

SCHWARZ, EGON, humanities and German language educator, author, literary critic; b. Vienna, Austria, Aug. 8, 1922; came to U.S., 1949, naturalized, 1956; s. Oscar and Erna S.; m. Dorothea K. Klockenbusch, June 8, 1950; children—Rudolf Joachim, Caroline Elisabeth, Gabriela Barbara. Ph.D., U. Wash., 1954. Mem. faculty Harvard U., 1954-61; mem. faculty dept. Germanic langs. and lit. Washington U., St. Louis, 1961—, prof. German, 1963—, Rosa May Disting. Univ. prof. in the Humanities, 1975-93, prof. emeritus, 1993—; vis. prof. U. Hamburg, Fed. Republic Germany, 1962-63, U. Calif., Berkeley, 1963-65, Middlebury Coll., 1969, U. Calif.-Irvine, 1977, U. Tübingen, 1986; William Evans prof. U. Otago, Dunedin, N.Z., 1984; Disting. scholar Ohio State U., Columbus, 1987, U. Graz, Austria, 1989, 93, U. Siegen, 1993-94. Author: Hofmannsthal und Calderon, 1962, Joseph von Eichendorff, 1972, Das verschluckte Schluchzen-Poesie und Politik bei Rainer Maria Rilke, 1972, Keine Zeit für Eichendorff: Chronik unfreiwilliger Wanderjahre; an autobiography, 1979, revised and expanded, 1992, Dichtung, Kritik, Geschichte: Essays zur Literatur 1900-1930, 1983, Literatur aus vier Kulturen: Essays und Besprechungen, 1987, also numerous other books. Recipient Joseph von Eichendorff medal, 1986, Austrian Medal of Honor for Arts and Scis., 1991, Alexander von Humboldt prize for fgn. scholars, 1995; Guggenheim fellow, 1957-58, Fulbright fellow, 1962-63, sr. fellow NEH, 1970-71, fellow Ctr. for Interdisciplinary Studies, Bielefeld, Germany, 1980-81; grantee Am. Coun. Learned Socs., 1962-63. Mem. MLA (hon.), Am. Assn. Tchrs. German, German Acad. Lang. and Lit. Home: 1036 Oakland Ave Saint Louis MO 63122-6565 Office: Washington U German Dept Saint Louis MO 63130 *When I was young, heroic phantasies were closer to my heart than ethical ones, desires of self-fulfillment stronger than the hopes for an equitable world. Today my horizon is broader in that I wish for a society where personal satisfactions are not achieved at the expense of others, where the earth which one generation inherits is not left more depleted to the next, a society which does not coerce other societies.*

SCHWARZ, GERARD, conductor, musician; b. Weehawken, N.J., Aug. 19, 1947; s. John and Gerta (Weiss) S.; m. Jody Greitzer, June 23, 1984; children: Alysandra, Daniel, Gabriella, Julian. BS, Juilliard Sch., 1972, MA, 1972; DFA (hon.), Fairleigh Dickinson U., Seattle U.; DMus (hon.), U. Puget Sound. Trumpet player Am. Symphony Orch., 1965-72, Am. Brass Quintet, 1965-73, N.Y. Philharm., 1973-77; trumpet player, guest condr. Aspen Music Festival, 1969-75, bd. dirs., 1973-75; music dir. Erick Hawkins Dance Co., 1967-72, SoHo Ensemble, 1969-75, Eliot Feld Ballet Co., N.Y.C., 1972-78; Music Sch. Princeton (N.J.) U.; music dir. N.Y. Chamber Symphony, 1977—, L.A. Chamber Orch., 1978-86, White Mountains (N.H.) Music Festival, 1978-80, Music Today at Merkin Concert Hall, N.Y.C., 1988-89; music advisor Mostly Mozart Festival, Lincoln Ctr., N.Y.C., 1982-84, music dir., 1984—; music advisor Seattle Symphony, 1983-84, prin. condr., 1984-85, music dir., 1985—; artistic advisor Tokyu Bunkamura's Orchard Hall, Japan, 1994—; mem. faculty Juilliard Sch., N.Y.C., 1975-83, Mannes Coll. Music, 1973-79, Montclair (N.J.) State Coll., 1975-80; guest condr. various orchs. including Phila. Orch., L.A. Philharmonic, St. Louis, Buffalo, Detroit, San Francisco, Atlanta, Houston, Pitts., Minn., Jerusalem Symphony, Israel Chamber Orch., Moscow Philharmonic, Moscow Radio Orch., Orch. Nat. de France, Paris, London Symphony Orch., Frankfurt Radio, Stockholm Radio, Helsinki Philharm., Ensemble InterContemporain, Monte Carlo Philharm., Nat. Orch. Spain, English Chamber Orch., London Symphony, Scottish Chamber Orch., City of Birmingham (Eng.) Symphony, Nouvel Orchestre Philharmonique, Sydney (Australia) Symphony, Melbourne (Australia) Symphony, Orchestre National de Lyon, France, Orchestre Philharm. de Montpellier, France, Washington Opera, Da Capo Chamber Players, 20th Century Chamber Orch., Chamber Music Soc. Lincoln Ctr., San Francisco Opera, Seattle Opera, Tokyu Bunkamura, Japan, Residentie Orch. of The Hague, The Netherlands, St. Louis Symphony, London Mozart Players, Kirov Orch., St. Petersburg, Russia, Tokyo Philharm., Royal Liverpool (Eng.) Philharm., Vancouver (Can.) Symphony Orch., City of London Symphonia, Evian Festival in France, 1994; also numerous appearances on TV; rec. artist Columbia, Nonesuch, Vox, MMO, Desto, Angel, Delos records; record: Seattle Symphony 1994-95 Season, 1995. Bd. dirs. Naumburg Found., 1975—. Recipient award for concert artists Ford Found., 1973, Grammy award nominee, Mumms Ovation award, Record of Yr. awards, Ditson Condrs. award Columbia U., 1989; named Condr. of Yr., Musical Am. Internat. Directory of Performing Arts, 1994.

SCHWARZ, GLENN VERNON, editor; b. Chgo., Nov. 24, 1947; s. Vernon Edward and LaVerne Louise (Schuster) S.; m. Cynthia Frances Meisenhoelder, June 17, 1984; 1 child, Chloe. BA, San Francisco State U., 1970. Sports writer San Francisco Examiner, 1970-87, sports editor, 1988—. Fundraiser San Francisco Zoological Soc., 1987—. Mem. AP Sports Editors, Baseball Writers Assn. Am. (bd. dirs. 1986-87). Avocation: nature travel. Office: San Francisco Examiner 110 5th St San Francisco CA 94103-2918

SCHWARZ, J(AMES) CONRAD, psychology educator; b. Hartford, Conn., Sept. 19, 1936; s. William Merlin and Violet May (List) S.; m. Lois J. Stonebraker, 1956 (div. 1981); m. Carolina A.B. Herfkens, Oct. 12, 1984. BS, Pa. State U., 1958; MA, Ohio State U., 1961, PhD, 1963. Lic. clin. psychologist, Conn.; cert. psychologist, N.Y. Rsch. asst. Pa. State U., 1957-58; psychol. trainee Chillicothe (Ohio) VA N.P. Hosp., 1958-60; psychol. intern Columbus (Ohio) VA Out-Patient Clinic, 1960-61; instr. psychology Bowling Green (Ohio) State U., 1962-64, asst. prof., 1964-65; asst. prof., mem. teaching faculty grad. tng. Syracuse U, 1965-70, assoc. prof., 1970-72; assoc. prof., mem. teaching faculty grad. tng. program U. Conn., Storrs, 1972-75, prof., mem. teaching faculty grad. tng. program, 1975—; pvt. practice clin. psychology Mansfield Ctr., Conn., 1973-94, North Windham, Conn., 1995-96; asst. field assessment officer Peace Corps Tng. Programs, 1967-68; clin. psychology cons. VA Out-Patient Clinic, Syracuse, 1968-72, Onodaga Co. Mental Health Clinic, Syracuse, 1969-72; with Windham Pub. Schs.-Project Self-Search, 1974-76; cons. Ea. Conn. Mental Health Group, 1974-83, Bermuda Govt., Child Devel. Project, 1979-82, Optimum Resource, Inc., Software for Learning Disabled Children. Author: Deck-a-Dot Manual: An Educational Card Game Program to Develop Arithmetic Readiness, 1970; If This Is Love, Why Do I Feel So Insecure?, 1989, 90, Teacher's Manual for Optimum Resource Reading Program, 1991; cons. editor Devel. Psychology, 1981-84; co-developer The Optimum Resource Reading Program, 1991; contbr. articles to profl. jours. USPHS fellow, 1958-59, 61-62; grantee Nat. Lab. Early Childhood Edn. Ctr. Syracuse U., 1968-71, NIMH, 1978-83, 84-85, Nat. Inst. Alcohol Abuse and Addiction, 1986-89, U. Conn. Rsch. Found., 1985-87. Mem. APA (div. clin., family psychology), Soc. Rsch. in Child Devel., Sigma Xi, Phi Beta Kappa, Psi Chi, Phi Eta Sigma, Phi Kappa Phi. Avocations: tennis, landscape gardening. Office: U Conn Dept Psychology 406 Babbidge Rd Storrs Mansfield CT 06269-1020

SCHWARZ, JOHN J.H., state senator, surgeon; b. Chgo., Nov. 15, 1937; s. Frank William and Helen Veronica (Brennan) S.; m. Anne Louise Ennis, Jan. 16, 1971 (dec. Feb. 1990); 1 child, Brennan Louise. BA, U. Mich., 1959; MD, Wayne State U., 1964. Physician, surgeon Battle Creek, Mich., 1974—; mayor City of Battle Creek, 1985-87; senator State of Mich., 1987—, pres. pro tempore, 1994—. Trustee Olivet Coll., 1991—, Wayland Acad., 1992-96. Lt. comdr. USN, 1965-67. Mem. AMA, Am. Coll. Surgeons, Am. Soc. for Head & Neck Surgery. Republican. Roman Catholic. Office: State Senate State Capital Lansing MI 48909

SCHWARZ, JOSEPH EDMUND, artist; b. Hartford, Conn., May 13, 1929; s. Jules and Dora (Sklarinsky) S.; m. Jean Bunker Chalmers, Jan. 29, 1951; children: David Bunker, Dina Ruth, Jonathan Chalmers, Adam Jules; m. Sarah Rollings, Oct. 21, 1971. B.F.A., Ohio Wesleyan U., 1950; M.F.A., U. Ill., 1952; Ph.D., Ohio State U., 1957. instr. Ohio State U., 1952-57; assoc. prof. U. Ga., 1957-68; prof., dir. grad. studies Va. Commonwealth U., 1968-73; prof. U. Maine- Machias, 1973-74, Auburn U., Montgomery, Ala., 1977—, head dept. fine arts, 1977—. Exhibited group shows, Butler Art Inst. Ann., 1949-55, Southeastern Ann., Atlanta, 1957, 59-61, 66-67, Chrysler Show, Provincetown, Mass., 1958, Hunter Gallery Ann., Chattanooga, 1960-62, 67, Whitney Ann., N.Y.C., 1958, Montgomery Mus.; represented pub. art collections, Butler Art Inst., Atlanta High Mus., Ball State U., Temple Beth Israel, Hartford, LaGrange Coll. U. Ga. Sch. Law. Home: 165 Vivian Ln Wetumpka AL 36093-2409 Office: Dept Fine Arts Auburn U Montgomery AL 36177 *As a humanist and as a painter, my life's goal is to be actually what I hope I am, that is to realize myself, to develop fully whatever it is that makes my life unique. I want my paintings to be records of my ideas and values, and if it should be that my being and my work have specialty, then I would hope that others would find there compassion and passion, a witnessing of human joy and pain and, finally, affirmation of the beauty of man and of human life.*

SCHWARZ, JOSEPHINE LINDEMAN, retired ballet company director, choreographer; b. Dayton, Ohio, Apr. 8, 1908; d. Joseph and Hannah (Lindeman) S. D.F.A. (hon.), U. Dayton, 1974; H.H.D. (hon.), Wright State U., 1983. Founder, dir. Schwarz Sch. Dance, Dayton, 1927-84, Exptl. Group for Young Dancers (now Dayton Ballet), 1937-79; mem. Weidman Theatre Dance Co., 1934-37; guest tchr., lectr., choreographer Hunter Coll., N.Y.C., YM-YWHA, N.Y.C., also regional dance companies in, Cleve., Phila., Indpls., Houston; pres. N.E. Regional Ballet Assn., 1961; chmn. dance adv. panel Ohio Arts Council, 1967-70; founder, program dir. Nat. Craft Choreography Confs., 1968-70; dance advisory panels Nat. Endowment for Arts, 1975-78; also Ohio Arts Council, 1975-78. Profl. dancer Adolph Bolm's Ballet Intime, Ravinia Opera Ballet, Chgo., 1925-27; European study and performances, 1929-30; author articles. Recipient award Ohio Arts Council, 1977, Spl. Achievement award YWCA, 1982, Brotherhood award Dayton chpt. NCCJ, 1984, Pegasus award Ohioana Library Assn., 1987, Northeast award Regional Dance Am., 1990; inducted into Ohio Women's Hall of Fame, 1991. Mem. Nat. Assn. Regional Ballet (bd. dirs. 1970-75), Am. Dance Guild (award 1985), Friends Dayton Ballet, Dayton Art Inst. Jewish. Home: 350 Ponca Pl # 122 Boulder CO 80303-3802 *There are no short cuts.*

SCHWARZ, MARK, sports correspondent; b. Apr. 19, 1959. BA in Psychology, Cornell U., 1981. Disc jockey WVBR-FM, Ithaca, N.Y., 1978-86; sports reporter KUTV-TV, Salt Lake City, 1986-88; sports anchor, reporter WJXT-TV, Jacksonville, Fla., 1988-90; west coast corr. SportsCenter ESPN, 1990—. Office: ESPN ESPN Plaza Bristol CT 06010

SCHWARZ, MICHAEL, lawyer; b. Brookline, Mass., Oct. 19, 1952; s. Jules Lewis and Estelle (Kosberg) S. BA magna cum laude, U. No. Colo., 1975; postgrad. U. N.Mex., 1977, JD, 1980; Rsch. reader in Negligence Law, Oxford U., 1978; diploma in Legal Studies, Cambridge U., 1981. Bar: N.Mex. 1980, U.S. Dist. Ct. N.Mex. 1980, U.S. Ct. Appeals (10th, D.C., and Fed. cirs.) 1982, U.S. Ct. Internat. Trade, 1982, U.S. Tax Ct. 1982, U.S. Supreme Ct. 1983, N.Y. 1987. VISTA vol., Albuquerque, 1975-77; rsch. fellow N.Mex. Legal Support Project, Albuquerque, 1978-79; supr. law Cambridge (Eng.) U., 1980-81; law clk. to chief justice Supreme Ct. N.Mex., Santa Fe, 1981-82; pvt. practice law, Santa Fe, 1982—; spl. prosecutor City of Santa Fe, 1985; spl. asst. atty. gen., 1986-88; mem. editorial adv. com. Social Security Reporting Svc., 1983-95. Author: New Mexico Appellate Manual, 1990, 2nd. edit., 1996; contbr. articles to profl. jours. Vice dir. Colo. Pub. Interest Rsch. Group, 1974; scoutmaster Great S.W. Area coun. Boy Scouts Am., 1977-79; mem. N.Mex. Acupuncture Licensing Bd., 1983. Recipient Cert. of Appreciation Cambridge U., 1981, Nathan Burkan Meml. award, 1980, N.Mex. Supreme Ct. Cert. Recognition, 1992, 93, 95. Mem. ABA (litigation com. on profl. responsibility, litigation com. on pretrial practice and discovery), ATLA, Am. Arbit. Assn., Bar Assn. U.S. Dist. Ct. Dist. N.Mex., State Bar N.Y., N.Mex. State Bar (bd. dirs. employment law sect. 1990-96, chair employment law sect. 1991-92), N.Y. Bar Assn., First Jud. Dist. Bar Assn. (treas. 1987-88, sec. 1988-89, v.p. 1989-1990, pres. 1990-91, local rules com. mem. 1989-92), N.Mex. Supreme Ct. (standing com. on profl. conduct 1990—, hearing officer, reviewing officer disciplinary com. 1993—), Am. Inns. of Ct. N.Mex. (barrister), Nat. Employment Lawyers Assn. (Nat. chpt., N.Mex. chpt.), Sierra Club, Amnesty Internat., Internat Wolf Ctr. Home and Office: PO Box 1656 Santa Fe NM 87504-1656

SCHWARZ, PAUL WINSTON, judge, lawyer, business company executive; b. Sacramento, Sept. 24, 1948; s. Egon Ferdinand and Louise (Fulcher) S.; m. Virginia Adams, July 12, 1987; children: Austin Winston, Julie Adams. BA in Philosophy, Calif. State U., San Jose, 1971; JD, Santa Clara U., 1974. Bar: Pa. 1975, U.S. Supreme Ct. 1978, D.C. Ct. Appeals 1987, Va. 1992. Commd. 2d. lt. U.S. Army, 1971, advanced through grades to lt. col., 1992; corp. counsel Oracle Corp., Bethesda, Md., 1992-93; sec., v.p. and corp. counsel Oracle Complex Systems Corp., Arlington, Va., 1992-93; counsel McAleese & Associates, P.C., Washington, DC, 1993-94; apptd. U.S. adminstrv. law judge, 1994. Author: A Roadmap into the World of Federal Contracts, 1989. Decorated Legion of Merit, U.S. Army Gen. Staff Badge award. Mem. ABA (chmn. com. on pub. contract law gen. practice sect. 1991, vice-chmn. judiciary com. 1995), Army and Navy Country Club, Army and Navy Club Washington D.C., Nat. Soc. SAR. Episcopalian. Avocations: swimming, pistol. Home: 5336 Sugar Hill Dr Houston TX 77056-2028

SCHWARZ, RALPH JACQUES, engineering educator; b. Hamburg, Germany, June 13, 1922; naturalized, 1944; s. Simon J. and Anna (Schoendorff) S.; m. Irene Lassally, Sept. 9, 1951; children: Ronald Paul, Sylvia Anne. B.S., Columbia U., 1943, M.S., 1944, Ph.D., 1949; postgrad., Poly. Inst. Bklyn., 1944-45, N.Y. U., 1946-47. Registered profl. engr., N.Y. Mem. faculty Columbia U., 1943-92, prof. elec. engring., 1958-92, chmn. dept., 1958-65, 71-72, assoc. dean acad. affairs Faculty Engring. and Applied Sci., 1972-75, acting dean, 1975-76, 80-81, vice dean, Thayer Lindsley prof., 1976-92, Thayer Lindsley prof. emeritus, 1992—; cons. systems analysis, communications and noise theory, 1945—; vis. assoc. prof. UCLA, 1956; adviser Inst. Internat. Edn., 1952-65; vis. scientist IBM Research Center, 1969-70. Author: (with M.G. Salvadori) Differential Equations in Engineering Problems, 1954, (with B. Friedland) Linear Systems, 1965. Bd. dirs. Armstrong Meml. Research Found.; trustee Associated Univs., Inc., 1980-92. Fellow IEEE (chmn. circuit theory group 1963-65, Centennial medal 1984); mem. Communications Soc. (bd. govs.), Am. Soc. Engring. Edn., AAAS, Sigma Xi, Tau Beta Pi, Pi Mu Epsilon, Eta Kappa Nu. Home: 33 Wood Ln New Rochelle NY 10804-3709 Office: Columbia U Engring Sch 116th St And Broadway New York NY 10027

SCHWARZ, RICHARD HOWARD, obstetrician, gynecologist, educator; b. Easton, Pa., Jan. 10, 1931; s. Howard Eugene and Blanche Elizabeth (Smith) S.; m. Patricia Marie Lewis, Mar. 11, 1978; children by previous marriage: Martha L., Nancy Schwarz Tedesco, Paul H., Mary Katherine Schwarz Murray. MD, Jefferson Med. Coll., 1955; MA (hon.), U. Pa., 1971. Diplomate Am. Bd. Ob-Gyn. (examiner 1977-95). Intern, then resident Phila. Gen. Hosp., 1955-59; prof. U. Pa., Phila., 1963-78; prof., chmn. Downstate Med. Ctr., Bklyn., 1978-90, dean, v.p. acad. affairs, 1983-89, provost, v.p. clin. affairs, 1988-93, interim pres., 1993-94, prof. ob.-gyn., 1990-96, disting. Svc. prof. ob.-gyn. emeritus, 1996; chmn. ob.-gyn. N.Y. Meth. Hosp., Bklyn., 1996—; prof. ob.-gyn. Cornell U. Med. Coll., N.Y.C., 1996—; obstetrical cons. March of Dimes Birth Defects Found., 1995—. Author: Septic Abortion, 1968. Editor: Handbook of Obstetric Emergencies, 1984, mem. editorial bd. jour. Ob-Gyn., Milw., 1983-87; contbr. articles to profl. jours. Bd. dirs. March of Dimes, N.Y.C., 1985-95. Capt. USAF, 1959-63. Mem. Am. Coll. Obstetricians and Gynecologists (chmn. dist. 2 1984-87, v.p. 1989-90, pres. elect 1990-91, pres. 1991-92). Republican. Presbyterian. Office: NY Meth Hosp 506 6th St Brooklyn NY 11215-3609

SCHWARZ, RICHARD WILLIAM, historian, educator; b. Wataga, Ill., Sept. 11, 1925; s. George William and Mildred (Imschweiler) S.; m. Joyce Frances Anderson, June 11, 1950; children: Constance Kay, Richard Paul, Dwight Luther. BA, Andrews U., 1949; MS, U. Ill., 1953; MA, U. Mich., 1959, PhD, 1964. Tchr.-librarian Broadview Acad., La Grange, Ill., 1949-53, Adelphian Acad., Holly, Mich., 1953-55; instr. history Andrews U., 1955-58, asst. librarian, 1955-56, acting librarian, 1956-58, asst. prof., 1958-63, assoc. prof., 1963-68, prof., 1968-89, acting chmn. dept. history and polit. sci., 1964-66, prof. emeritus, 1989—, chmn., 1966-77, v.p. acad. adminstrn., 1977-87; reference libr. Berrien Springs Community Libr., 1990-93; vis. instr. Mich. State U., 1967; book reviewer Library Jour., 1957-77. Author: John Harvey Kellogg, M.D, 1970, Lightbearers to the Remnant, 1979; bd. editors: Studies in Adventist History, 1971-83. Del. Berrien County Republican Conv., 1966, 68, 74. Served with USNR, 1944-46. Mem. Assn. 7th-Day Adventists Historians (pres. 1987), Phi Beta Kappa, Phi Alpha Theta, Phi Kappa Phi. Home: 113 Oakwood Pl Hendersonville NC 28792-9521

SCHWARZ, ROBERT DEVLIN, art dealer; b. Atlantic City, N.J., July 11, 1942; s. Frank Samuel and Marie (Devlin) S.; m. Pamela Pillion; children: Robert, Jr., Elizabeth, Jonathan. BS, Dickinson Coll., 1964. Curator Stephen Girard Collection, Phila., 1970-80; pres., curator The Schwarz Gallery, Phila., 1981—; pres., owner. Author: Catalogue of the Stephen Girard Collection, 1980, A Gallery Collects Peale, 1987, One hundred Fifty Years of Philadelphia Still-Life Painting, 1997. Mem. bd. dirs. Conservation Ctr., 1995. Mem. Art Dealers Assn. Am., Art and Antiques Dealers League Am. Republican. Presbyterian. Office: The Schwarz Gallery 1806 Chestnut St Philadelphia PA 19103-4902

SCHWARZ, STEVEN E., electrical engineering educator, administrator; b. L.A., Jan. 29, 1939; s. Carl and Lillian Schwarz; m. Janet Lee Paschal, July 27, 1963. BS, Cal Tech, 1959, MS, 1961, PhD, 1964; AM, Harvard U., 1962. From asst. prof. to prof. elec. engring. U. Calif., Berkeley, 1964—, assoc. dean Coll. Engring., 1991—. Author: Electromagnetics for Engineers, 1990; co-author: Electrical Engineering, An Introduction, 1984, 93; contbr. articles to profl. jours. Guggenheim fellow, 1971-72. Fellow IEEE. Office: U Calif Berkeley Electrical Engring Dept 231 Cory Hall Berkeley CA 94720-1771*

SCHWARZ, WOLFGANG, psychologist; b. Stuttgart, Ger., Oct. 30, 1926; s. Mole and Edith (Gutstein) S.; brought to U.S., 1934, naturalized, 1940; A.B., N.Y. U., 1948, A.M., 1949, Ph.D., 1956; m. Cynthia Mae Johnson, Sept. 12, 1949 (div.); children—Amy Maria, Casey Andrew, Darcy Lynn, Priscilla Anne, Lydia Beth, Emily Jane; m. Susan Decker, 1976; children—Jaime Bartholomew, Noah. Intern, Bellevue Med. Center, N.Y., 1949-51; chief psychology Rip Van Winkle Med. Found., Hudson, N.Y., 1951-53; dir. psychology Hillcrest Med. Center, Tulsa, 1953-56, Hollywood Presbyn. Hosp., Los Angeles, 1956-58; cons. psychology Cedars Lebanon Hosp., Los Angeles, 1956-58; spl. cons. to D.C. Govt., 1959-61, NIH, Bethesda, Md., 1962-64; dir. psychol. research Mass. Dept. Mental Health, Boston and Malden, 1965-68; individual practice clin. psychology, Tulsa, 1953-56, Beverly Hills, Calif., 1956-59, Washington, 1959-63, Concord and Malden, Mass., 1963-73, Mt. Kisco, N.Y., 1973—; lectr. U. Tulsa, 1953-54, Hillcrest Med. Center, Tulsa, 1953-56, Los Angeles State Coll., 1956-57; asst. prof. Howard U., 1961; asso. prof. George Washington U., 1961-62; vis. research asst. Harvard Psychiatry, Lab., 1966-68; prof. Malden Hosp., 1968-71; cons. No. Westchester Hosp., 1974—, United Hosp., 1975—, Four Winds Hosp., 1975-80; cons. psychology Peace Corps, Mass., 1969—. Mem. exec. com. Mayor's Model City Program, Malden, 1967-68. Served with USNR, 1945-46. Recipient Founder's Day award N.Y. U., 1956, Individual award USPHS/NIH, 1960-64. Diplomate Am. Bd. Profl. Psychology. Mem. Am., N.Y., Mass. psychol. assns., Washington Soc. History of Medicine (exec. com. 1963-64), N.Y. Acad. Scis., Psi Chi, Beta Lambda Sigma. Author: A Survey of the Mental Health Facilities in the District of Columbia, 1961; co-author: Hermann Rorschach, M.D.: His Life and Work in Yearbook of Inernational, 1996, also articles. Home: 81 Paulding Dr Chappaqua NY 10514-2818 Office: 121 Smith Ave Mount Kisco NY 10549-2815

SCHWARZENEGGER, ARNOLD ALOIS, actor, author; b. Graz, Austria, July 30, 1947; came to U.S., 1968, naturalized, 1983; s. Karl and Aurelia (Jedrny) S.; m. Maria Owings Shriver, Apr. 26, 1986; children: Katherine Eunice, Christina Aurelia, Patrick. BA in Bus. and Internat. Econs., U. Wis., Superior. Owner prodn. co. and real estate. Actor: (films) Stay Hungry, 1976 (Golden Globe award 1976), Pumping Iron, 1977, The Villain, 1979, Conan, The Barbarian, 1982, Conan, The Destroyer, 1983, The Terminator, 1984, Commando, 1985, Red Sonja, 1985, Raw Deal, 1986, Predator, 1987, Running Man, 1987, Red Heat, 1988, Twins, 1988, Total Recall, 1990, Kindergarten Cop, 1990, Terminator 2: Judgement Day, 1991, The Last Action Hero, 1993, True Lies, 1994, Junior, 1994, Terminator 2: 3-D, 1996, Jingle All the Way, 1996, Eraser, 1996, Crusade, 1996, Batman & Robin, 1997, With Wings of Eagles, 1997; (TV spl.) Sinatra: 80 Years My Way, 1995; (TV movies) The Jayne Mansfield Story, 1980; dir. TV movie Christmas in Connecticut, 1992; host A Very Special Christmas Story; dir. The Switch, Tales from the Crypt, HBO, 1990; author: Arnold: The Education of a Bodybuilder, 1977, Arnold's Bodyshaping for Women, 1979, Arnold's Bodybuilding for Men, 1981, Arnold's Encyclopedia of Modern Bodybuilding, 1985; prodr. bodybuilding video tape. Nat. weight tng. coach Spl. Olympics; vol. prison rehab. programs; chmn. Pres.'s Coun. on Phys.

Fitness and Sports, 1990. Bodybldg. champion, 1965-80; named Jr. Mr. Europe, 1965, Best Built Man of Europe, 1966, Mr. Europe, 1966; Internat. Powerlifting Championship, 1966, German Powerlifting Championship, 1968; IFFB (Internat. Fedn. Body Builders) Mr. Internat., 1968, IFFB Mr. Universe (amateur), 1969; NABBA (Nat. Assn. Body Builders) Mr. Universe (amateur), 1967, NABBA Mr. Universe (profl.), 1968, 69, 70; Mr. World, 1970; IFFB Mr. Olympia, 1970, 71, 72, 73, 74, 75, 80; recipient Golden Globe award for Best Newcomer in Films, 1976, Timmie Award The Touchdown Club, 1990; named Video Star Yr. VSDA, 1990; voted Internat. Star of 1984, ShoWest. Office: care ICM 8942 Wilshire Blvd Beverly Hills CA 90211-1934*

SCHWARZER, WILLIAM W, federal judge; b. Berlin, Apr. 30, 1925; came to U.S., 1938, naturalized, 1944; s. John F. and Edith M. (Daniel) S.; m. Anne Halbersleben, Feb. 2, 1951; children: Jane Elizabeth, Andrew William. AB cum laude, U. So. Calif., 1948; LLB cum laude, Harvard U., 1951. Bar: Calif. 1953, U.S. Supreme Ct. 1967. Teaching fellow Harvard U. Law Sch., 1951-52; asso. firm McCutchen, Doyle, Brown & Enersen, San Francisco, 1952-60; ptnr. McCutchen, Doyle, Brown & Enersen, 1960-76; judge U.S. Dist. Ct (no. dist.) Calif., San Francisco, 1976—; dir. Fed. Jud. Ctr., Washington, 1990-95; sr. counsel Pres.'s Commn. on CIA Activities Within the U.S., 1975; chmn. U.S. Jud. Conf. Com. Fed.-State Jurisdiction, 1987-90; mem. faculty Nat. Inst. Trial Advocacy, Fed. Jud. Ctr., All-ABA, U.S.-Can. Legal Exch., 1987, Anglo-U.S. Jud. Exch., 1994-95, Salzburg Seminar on Am. Studies; disting. prof. Hastings Coll. Law U. Calif. Author: Managing Antitrust and Other Complex Litigation, 1982, Civil Discovery and Manadatory Disclosure, 1994, Federal Civil Procedure Before Trial, 1994; contbr. articles to legal publs., aviation jours. Trustee World Affairs Coun. No. Calif., 1961-88; chmn. bd. trustees Marin Country Day Sch., 1963-66; mem. Marin County Aviation Commn., 1969-76; mem. vis. com. Harvard Law Sch., 1981-86. Served with Intelligence, U.S. Army, 1943-46. Fellow Am. Coll. Trial Lawyers (S. Gates award 1992), Am. Bar Found.; mem. ABA (Meador Rosenberg award 1995), Am. Law Inst., San Francisco Bar Assn., State Bar Calif., Coun. Fgn. Rels. Office: 450 Golden Gate Ave San Francisco CA 94102

SCHWARZKOPF, GLORIA A., education educator, psychotherapist; b. Chgo., Apr. 20, 1926; m. Alfred E. Grossenbacher. BE, Chgo. State U., 1949, MEd in Libr. Sci., 1956. Cert. nat. recovery specialist, reality therapist; libr. sci. endorsement; cert. hypnotherapist; nat. forensic counselor. Tchr. Chgo. Bd. Edn., 1949-91, inservice trainer in substance abuse, 1990, 91; co-therapist ATC outpatient unit Ingalls Meml. Hosp., Chgo., 1981-86; recovery specialist Interaction Inst., Evergreen Park, Ill., 1993-95; instr. Govs. State U., University Park, Ill., 1987, 91, South Suburban Coll., South Holland, Ill., 1991, Prairie State Coll., Chicago Heights, Ill., 1993, 96. columnist Peoples Choice Weekly, 1991-93. Citizens Amb. Program del. to Russia and Czechoslovakia, 1996. Recipient Sci. Tchr. of Yr. award, 1976, Svc. Recognition award, 1985, IMSA Recognition award, 1988; grantee Chgo. Pub. Sch., 1981. Mem. NEA, Nat. Assn. Forensic Counselors, Sci. Tchrs. Assn., Ill. Alcoholism Counselors Alliance, Nat. Alcoholism Coun., Am. Assn. Hypnotherapists, Am. Assn. Behavioral Therapists, Soc. of Am. for Recovery (nat. cert. recovery specialist). Home: 2216 W 91st St Chicago IL 60620-6238

SCHWARZLOSE, RICHARD ALLEN, journalism educator; b. Chgo., Mar. 18, 1937; s. Paul Fowler and Muriel Beth (Kingsley) S.; m. Sally Jean Frye, July 27, 1963; children: Daniel Frye, Rebecca Frye. BS in Journalism, U. Ill., 1959, MA in Polit. Sci., 1960, PhD in Communications, 1965. Reporter, telegraph editor News-Gazette, Champaign, Ill., 1955-62; asst. prof. journalism Purdue U., West Lafayette, Ind., 1965-68; from asst. prof. to prof. journalism Northwestern U., Evanston, Ill., 1968—, assoc. dean Sch. Journalism, 1989-93. Author: Newspapers: A Reference Guide, 1987, Nation's Newsbrokers, 2 vols., 1989-90; author monograph; contbr. numerous articles to profl. jours. Peterson rsch. grantee Am. Antiquarian Soc., Worcester, Mass., 1984. Mem. Assn. for Edn. in Journalism and Mass Communications, Soc. Profl. Journalists, Assn. for Practical and Profl. Ethics. Unitarian. Avocations: biking, conducting seminars with adult groups. Home: 2712 Payne St Evanston IL 60201-2028 Office: Northwestern U Medill Sch Journalism Evanston IL 60208

SCHWARZROCK, SHIRLEY PRATT, author, lecturer, educator; b. Mpls., Feb. 27, 1914; d. Theodore Ray and Myrtle Pearl (Westphal) Pratt; m. Loren H. Schwarzrock, Oct. 19, 1945 (dec. 1966); children: Kay Linda, Ted Kenneth, Lorraine V. BS, U. Minn., 1935, MA, 1942, PhD, 1974. Sec. to chmn. speech dept., U. Minn., Mpls., 1935, instr. in speech, 1946, team tchr. in creative arts workshops for tchrs., 1955-56, guest lectr. Dental Sch., 1967-72, asst. prof. (part-time) of practice adminstrn. Sch. Dentistry, 1972-80; tchr. speech, drama and English, Preston (Minn.) H.S., 1935-37; tchr. speech, drama and English, Owatonna (Minn.) H.S., 1937-39, also dir. dramatics, 1937-39; tchr. creative dramatics and English, tchr.-counselor Webster Groves (Mo.) Jr. H.S., 1939-40; dir. dramatics and tchr.-counselor Webster Groves Sr. H.S., 1940-43; exec. sec. bus. and profl. dept. YWCA, Mpls., 1943-45; tchr. speech and drama Covent of the Visitation, St. Paul, 1958; editor pro-tem Am. Acad. Dental Practice Adminstrn., 1966-68; guest tchr. Coll. St. Catherine, St. Paul, 1969; vol. mgr. Gift Shop, Eitel Hosp., Mpls., 1981-83, Edina Cmty. Resource Pool, 1992-95; cmty. citizen mem. planning, evaluating, reporting com. Edina Pub. Sch. System, 1993-96; tutor for reading, writing, and speaking, 1993-96; cons. for dental med. programs Normandale C.C., Bloomington, Minn., 1968; cons. on pub. rels. to dentists, 1954-96; guest lectr. to various dental groups, 1966-95; lectr. Internat. Congress on Arts and Communication, 1980, Am. Inst. Banking, 1981; condr. tutorials in speaking and profl. office mgmt., 1985-96; owner Shirley Schwarzrock's Exec. Support Svc., 1989—; cons. to mktg. communications mgr. Ergodyne Corp., St. Paul, 1991-92; freelance editor med. support bus., 1992. Author books (series): Coping with Personal Identity, Coping with Human Relationships, Coping with Facts and Fantasies, Coping with Teenage Problems, 1984; individual book titles include: Do I Know the "Me" Others See?, My Life-What Shall I Do With It?, Living with Loneliness, Learning to Make Better Decisions, Grades, What's So Important About Them, Anyway?, Facts and Fantasies About Alcohol, Facts and Fantasies About Drugs, Facts and Fantasies About Smoking, Food as a Crutch, Facts and Fantasies About the Roles of Men and Women, You Always Communicate Something, Appreciating People-Their Likenesses and Differences, Fitting In, To Like and Be Liked, Can You Talk With Someone Else? Coping with Emotional Pain, Some Common Crutches, Parents Can Be a Problem, Coping with Cliques, Crises Youth Face Today, Effective Dental Assisting, (with L.H. Schwarzrock) 1954, 59, 67, (with J.R. Jensen) 1973, 78, 82, (with J.R. Jensen, Kay Schwarzrock, Lorraine Schwarzrock) 1990, Workbook for Effective Dental Assisting, 1960, 68, 73, (with Lorraine Schwarzrock), 1978, 82, 90, Manual for Effective Dental Assisting, 1968, 73, 78, 82, 90; (with Donovan F. Ward), Effective Medical Assisting, 1969, 76; Workbook for Effective Medical Assisting, 1969, 76, Manual for Effective Medical Assisting, 1969, 76; (with C.G. Wrenn) The Coping with Series of Books for High School Students, 1970, 73; The Coping With Manual, 1973, Contemporary Concerns, of Youth, 1980. Pres. University Elem. Sch. PTA, 1955-56; vol. judge Minn. State Hist. Day Program, 1944—. Fellow Internat. Biog. Assn.; mem. Minn. Acad. Dental Practice Adminstrn. (hon.), Minn. Historical Soc., 1992—, Minn. Geneaolgical Soc., 1992—, Zeta Phi Eta (pres. 1948-49), Eta Sigma Upsilon. Home: 7448 W Shore Dr Edina MN 55435-4022 *Growing up as a latch key child, challenged to accomplish adult tasks accompanied by "You can do it Kid," provided me with the ability to face challenges from scrubbing floors to delving deeply into research. Assured that there is a solution to every problem, I absorbed the knowledge and skills my professors taught, developed my creativity and spiritual awareness, and learned to listen sensitively and compassionately. This training enabled me to draw forth creative expression from adolescents, respond to their many needs, and to develop adults' communication skills in numerous settings.*

SCHWARZSCHILD, MARTIN, astronomer, educator; b. Potsdam, Germany, May 31, 1912; came to U.S., 1937, naturalized, 1942; s. Karl and Else (Rosenbach) S.; m. Barbara Cherry, Aug. 24, 1945. Ph.D., U. Goettingen, 1935; D.Sc. (hon.), Swarthmore Coll., 1960, Columbia U., 1973; DSc, Princeton U., 1992. Research fellow Inst. Astrophysics, Oslo (Norway) U., 1936-37, Harvard U. Obs., 1937-40; lectr., later asst. prof. Rutherfurd Obs., Columbia U., 1940-47; prof. Princeton U., 1947-50, Higgins prof. astronomy, 1950-79. Author: Structure and Evolution of the Stars. Served to 1st lt. AUS, 1942-45. Recipient Dannie Heineman prize Akademie der Wissenschaften zu Goettingen, Germany, 1967, Albert A. Michelson award Case Western Res. U., 1967, Newcomb Cleveland Prize AAAS, 1987, Rittenhouse Silver medal, 1966, Prix Janssen Société astronomique de France, 1970, Medal from l'Assn. Pour le Developpement Internat. de l'Observatoire de Nice, 1986, Gerlach-Adolph von Muenchausen Medaille Goettingen U., 1987, Dirk Brouwer award Am. Astron. Soc., 1991, Balzan prize, 1994. Fellow Am. Acad. Arts and Scis.; mem. Internat. Astron. Union (v.p. 1964-70), Akademie der Naturforscher Leopoldina, Royal Astron. Soc. (asso., Gold medal 1969, Eddington medal 1963), Royal Astron. Soc. Can. (hon.), Am. Astron. Soc. (pres. 1970-72), Nat. Acad. Scis. (Henry Draper medal 1961), Soc. Royale des Sciences de Liege (corr.), Royal Netherlands Acad. Sci. and Letters (fgn.), Royal Danish Acad. Sci. and Letters (fgn.), Norwegian Acad. Sci. and Letters, Astron. Soc. Pacific (Bruce medal 1965), Am. Philos. Soc., Royal Soc. (fgn.), Sigma Xi.

SCHWARZTRAUBER, SAYRE ARCHIE, former naval officer, maritime consultant; b. Zion, Ill., June 23, 1929; s. Archie Douglas and Eleanor Miriam (Sayrs) S.; BS cum laude, Maryville (Tenn.) Coll., 1951; MA, Am. U., 1964, PhD, 1970; m. Beryl Constance Stewart, June 27, 1953; children: Sayre Archie, Beryl Ann, Heidi, Holly. Commd. ensign U.S. Navy, 1952, advanced through grades to rear adm., 1976; comdr. River Squadron 5, Vietnam, 1968-69, U.S.S. Decatur, guided missile destroyer, 1970-71, Navy Recruiting Area 4, 1974-76; dep. chief staff Supreme Command Atlantic (NATO), 1976-79; co-dir. U.S.-Spanish Combined Staff, Madrid, 1979-81; dir. Inter-Am. Def. Coll., Washington, 1981-83; ret., 1983; apptd. rear adm. U.S. Maritime Service, 1984; supt. Maine Maritime Acad., 1984-86; mem. Sec. of Navy Adv. Com., 1986-90; nat. and internat. lectr. strategic naval and maritime matters, 1973—. Ruling elder Presbyn. Ch. U.S.A., 1965-86. Decorated Def. Disting. Service medal, Legion of Merit; Cross of Gallantry (Vietnam); Gran Cruz de Mérito (Spain); recipient Alfred Thayer Mahan award Navy League, 1974. Mem. SAR (pres. Cape Cod chpt. 1993-95, state reg. and genealogist 1992—), Gamewardens of Vietnam, Nat. Geneal. Soc., U.S. Naval Inst., Am. Legion, VFW, Mil. Order World Wars, Mensa, Phi Kappa Phi, Pi Gamma Mu, Pi Sigma Alpha, Theta Alpha Phi. Author: The Three-Mile Limit of Territorial Seas, 1972, Schwarztrauber, Stewart and Related Families, 1995; editor Mass. Maritime Mag., 1987-90; contbr. articles, essays and revs. to profl. jours. Home and Office: PO Box 589 Osterville MA 02655-0589

SCHWEBACH, GERHARD HERMANN, microbiologist; b. Asch, Czechoslovakia, Feb. 27, 1944; came to U.S., 1957; s. Leonard Valentine and Gertrude Margareta (Rogler) S.; m. Janet Elaine Peterson, July 1, 1966; children: Derek, Heidi, Daniel, Adam, Nathan, Elisabeth. MS, Brigham Young U., Provo, Utah, 1967; Cert. in Med. Tech., Malcolm grow Med. Ctr., Andrews AFB, Md., 1976. Cert. med. technologist. Honorarium prof. U. Colo., Colorado Springs, 1976-82; sci. instr. Pikes Peak C.C., Colorado Springs, 1988-92, Nat. Coll., Colorado Springs, 1992—; sr. microbiologist Water Resources divsn. City of Colorado Springs, 1982—; cons./rschs. Schwebach Environ. and Pub. Health Svcs., Colorado Springs, 1994—. Author: Practical Guide to Microbial and Parasitic Diseases, 1980; contbr. articles to profl. jours. Cub master Boy Scouts Am., Colo., 1977-79, explorer advisor, Utah, 1972-74; cmty. soccer coach Parks and Recreation, Colorado Springs, 1986-88. Capt. USAF, 1969-79. Decorated Air Force commendation medal with oak leaf cluster, meritorious svc. medal. Mem. AAAS, Coll. Allied Health Profls. of Am. (pres. 1979-97), Am. Soc. Microbiology, Am. Soc. Clin. Pathologists, Soc. Risk Analysis. Republican. LDS. Achievements include development of appropriate fecal coliform, total coliform and fecal streptococcus indicator levels for certain water reuse applications. Avocations: camping, soccer. Home: 3160 Meander Cir Colorado Springs CO 80917 Office: City of Colorado Springs PO Box 1103 Colorado Springs CO 80947

SCHWEBEL, MILTON, psychologist, educator; b. Troy, N.Y., May 11, 1914; s. Frank and Sarah (Oxenhandler) S.; m. Bernice Lois Davison, Sept. 3, 1939; children: Andrew I., Robert S. AB, Union Coll., 1934; MA, SUNY, Albany, 1936; PhD, Columbia U., 1949; Cert. in Psychotherapy, Postgrad. Ctr. Mental Health, N.Y.C., 1958. Lic. psychologist, N.Y., N.J.; diplomate Am. Bd. Examiners Profl. Psychology. Asst. prof. psychology Mohawk Champlain Coll., 1946-49; asst. to prof. edn., dept. chmn., assoc. dean NYU, 1949-67; dean, prof. Grad. Sch. Edn., Rutgers U., New Brunswick, N.J., 1967-77; prof. Grad. Sch. Applied and Profl. Psychology, 1977-85, prof. emeritus, 1985—; vis. prof. U. So. Calif., U. Hawaii; postdoctoral fellow Postgrad. Ctr. Mental Health, N.Y.C., 1954-58, lectr. psychology, 1958-60; cons. NIMH, U.S., state and city depts. edn., ednl. ministries in Europe, Asia, univs. and pub. schs.; pvt. cons. psychologist and psychotherapist, 1953—. Author: A Guide to a Happier Family, 1989, Personal Adjustment and Growth, 1990, Student Teachers Handbook, 3d edit., 1996, Interests of Pharmacists, 1951, Health Counseling, 1953, Who Can Be Educated?, 1968; editor: Mental Health Implications of Life in the Nuclear Age, 1986, Facilitating Cognitive Development, 1986, Promoting Cognitive Growth Over the Life Span, 1990, Behavioral Science and Human Survival, 1965, The Impact of Ideology on the I.Q. Controversy, 1975; editor Peace & Conflict: Jour. Peace Psychology, 1993—; co-editor Bull. Peace Psychology, 1991-94; mem. editl. bd. Am. Jour. Orthopsychiatry, Readings in Mental Health, Jour. Contemporary Psychotherapy, Jour. Counseling Psychology, Jour. Social Issues, others. Mem. sci. adv. bd. Internat. Ctr. for Enhancement of Learning Potential, 1988—; trustee Edn. Law Ctr., 1973-81, Nat. Com. Employment Youth, Nat. Child Labor Com., 1967-75, Union Exptl. Colls. and Univs., 1976-78; pres. Nat. Orgn. for Migrant Children, 1980-85; pres. Inst. of Arts and Humanities, 1984-95. Served with AUS, 1943-46, ETO. Met. Applied Rsch. Coun. fellow, 1970-71. Fellow APA, Am. Psychol. Soc., Am. Orthopsychiatry Assn., Soc. Psychol. Study Social Issues, Jean Piaget Soc. (trustee), Am. Ednl. Rsch. Assn., N.Y. Acad. Scis., Psychologists for Social Responsibility (pres.), Inst. Arts and Humanities Edn. (pres.), Sigma Xi. Home: 1050 George St Apt 17L New Brunswick NJ 08901-1025 Office: Rutgers U Grad Sch Applied and Profl Psychology Piscataway NJ 08854

SCHWEBEL, RENATA MANASSE, sculptor; b. Zwickau, Germany, Mar. 6, 1930; d. George and Anne Marie (Simon) Manasse; came to U.S., 1940, naturalized, 1946; m. Jack P. Schwebel, May 10, 1955; children: Judith, Barbara, Diane. BA, Antioch Coll., 1953; MFA, Columbia U., 1961; student Art Students League, 1967-69. Cartographer, Ecostate, Inc., Ridgewood, N.J., 1949; display artist Silvestri, Inc., Chgo., 1950-51; asst. Mazzolini Art Found., Yellow Springs, Ohio, 1952; one-person show Columbia U., 1961, Greenwich Art Barn, Conn., 1975, Sculpture Ctr., N.Y.C., 1979, Pelham Art Ctr., N.Y., 1981, New Rochelle Libr. Gallery, N.Y., 1980, outdoor installation Alfresco, Katonah Gallery, 1989, Berman/Daferner Gallery, N.Y.C., 1992-93; exhibited in group shows Stamford Mus., Conn., 1967, 96, Hudson River Mus., Yonkers, N.Y., 1972, 74, Wadsworth Atheneum, Hartford, 1975, Silvermine New Eng. Anns., 1972, 76, 80, 95, Silvermine Gallery, 1991, New Britain Mus. Am. Art, Conn., 1974, Sculptors Guild Anns., 1974—, Imprimatur Gallery, St. Paul, 1985, Bergen County Mus., N.J., 1983, Sculpture Ctr., N.Y.C., 1978-88, Katonah Gallery, N.Y., 1986-90, Cast Iron Gallery, N.Y.C., 1991, 93, Kyoto (Japan) Gallery, 1993; traveling show exhibited in Am. cultural ctrs. in Egypt and Israel, 1981, FFS Gallery, N.Y.C., 1994, 95; represented in permanent collection S.W. Bell, Columbia U., Colt Industries, Am. Airlines, ComCraft Industries, Nairobi, Grüber Haus, Berlin, Mus. Fgn. Art, Sofia, Bulgaria. Bd. dirs. Fine Arts Fedn., N.Y., 1985-87; trustee Sculpture Ctr., 1980-88, chmn. exhbn. com., 1986-88; mem. adv. bd. Pehlham Art Ctr., 1982. Mem. Sculptors Guild (bd. dirs., pres. 1980-83), Antioch Coll. Assn. (bd. dirs. 1971-77), Ams. for Peace Now (bd. dirs. 1991—), Nat. Assn. Women Artists (Willis Meml. prize 1974, Medal of Honor 1981, Paley Meml. award 1979), Audubon Artists (Chaim Gross award 1980, medal of honor 1982, Rennick award 1986, 90, 92, 95), Conn. Acad. Fine Arts, N.Y. Soc. Women Artists, Artists Equity N.Y., Katonah Gallery (artist mem. 1986-90). Home: 10 Dogwood Hills Pound Ridge NY 10576-1508

SCHWEBEL, STEPHEN MYRON, judge, arbitrator; b. N.Y.C., Mar. 10, 1929; s. Victor and Pauline (Pfeffer) S.; m. Louise Ingrid Nancy Killander, Aug. 2, 1972; children: Jennifer, Anna. BA in Govt. magna cum laude with highest honors in govt., Harvard U., 1950; postgrad., Cambridge (Eng.) U., 1950-51; LLB, Yale U., 1954; LLD, Bhopal (India) U., 1983; LLD (hon.), Hofstra U., 1997. Bar: N.Y. 1955, U.S. Supreme Ct. 1965, D.C. 1976. Dir. UN hdqrs. office World Fedn. UN Assns., 1950-53; lectr. Am. fgn. policy various univs. U.S. State Dept., India, 1952; research, drafting asst. to Trygve Lie for writing of In the Cause of Peace, 1953; assoc. White & Case, N.Y.C., 1954-59; asst. prof. law Harvard U., Cambridge, Mass., 1959-61; asst. legal advisor U.S. Dept. State, Washington, 1961-66, dep. legal advisor, 1973-81; exec. dir. Am. Soc. Internat. Law, Washington, 1967-72; Burling prof. internat. law Sch. of Advanced Internat. Studies, Johns Hopkins U., Washington, 1967-81; judge Internat. Ct. Justice, The Hague, The Netherlands, 1981—; v.p. Internat. Ct. Justice, The Hague, 1994-97, pres., 1997—; spl. rep. Micronesian claims U.S. Dept. State, 1966-71; legal adviser U.S. del. 16th-20th and 4th Spl. Gen. Assemblies UN; U.S. assoc. rep. Internat. Ct. Justice, 1962, U.S. dep. agt., 1979-80, U.S. counsel, 1980; U.S. rep., chmn. U.S. del. to 1st session UN Spl. Com on Principles Internat. Law concerning friendly relations and cooperation among states, Mexico City, 1964; U.S. rep. on adv. com. UN Program Assistance in Teaching, Study, Dissemination and Wider Appreciation Internat. Law, 1966-74; U.S. counsel Franco-Am. Air Arbitration, 1978; legal adv. U.S. del. to 32d and 33d WHO Assemblies, Geneva, 1979-80; vis. prof. internat. law Australian Nat. U., Canberra, 1969; U.S. rep., chmn. del. 3d session UN Spl. Com. on Question Defining Aggression, Geneva, 1970; counselor internat. law U.S. Dept. State, 1973; U.S. rep., chmn. del. 2d and 4th sessions UNCTAD Working Group on Charter Econ. Rights and Duties of States, Geneva, 1973, Mexico City, 1974; U.S. alt. rep. UN Econ. and Social Council, Geneva, 1974; legal adviser U.S. del. Conf. Internat. Econ. Coop., Paris, 1975; mem. U.S. Tripartite Adv. Com. on Internat. Labor Standards, 1980, Internat. Law Commn., UN, Geneva, 1977-81; spl. rapporteur internat. watercourses Internat. Law Commn., UN, 1977-81, chmn. drafting com., 1978; mem. bd. arbitration Brit. Petroleum v. Iran and Nat. Iranian Oil Co., pres. arbitration tribunal Marine Dr. Ltd. v. Ghana Investments Ctr. and Govt. of Ghana, 1988-90; chmn. or party-apptd. arbitrator internat. comml. arbitration tribunals, 1988—, arbitral tribunal Eritrea-Yemen Arbitration, 1996—; mem. exec. com. Commn. Study Orgn. Peace, 1948-61; adv. joint com. law internat. transactions Am. Law Inst. and Am. Bar Assn., 1959-61; nat. chmn. Collegiate Council for UN, 1948-50; pres. Internat. Student Movement for UN, 1950-51; undergrad. orator Harvard U. Commencement, 1950; mem. adv. bd. Ctr. Oceans Law and Policy U. Va., 1975-81; vice chmn. Sec. State's Adv. Com. Pvt. Internat. Law, 1978-79, chmn., 1979-81; mem. internat. adv. bd. Cambridge U. Ctr. for Rsch. in Internat. Law, 1983—, mem. bd. electors Whewell Professorship in Internat. Law U. Cambridge, 1983—; mem. overseers' com. to visit Harvard U. Law Sch., 1991-97; cons. Ford. Found., 1990; chmn. supervisory bd. Telders Internat. Law Moot Court Competition, The Hague, Netherlands, 1993—, vis. lect. Cambridge U., 1957, Inst. Universitaire de Hautes Etudes Internationales, Geneva, 1980; Carnegie lectr. Hague Acad. Internat. Law, 1972; Brown lectr. Cath. U., 1983; Lauterpacht. lectr., Cambridge U., 1983; jurisprudential lectr. U. Wash., 1985; Otto Walter Internat. Fellow, N.Y. Law Sch., 1987; Sherrill lectr. Yale U., 1988; Centennial Morris vis. prof. Chgo.-Kent Coll. of Law, 1988; Page Disting. vis. jurist U. Kans., 1988; Allison lectr. Suffolk Law Sch., 1989; Regents' lectr. U. Calif. Berkeley, 1990; Wing-Tat Lee lectr. Loyola U., 1990; Ford Found. lectr. U. N.Mex., U. Wash., U. Ind., Vanderbilt U., U. Minn., 1991, U. Calif., L.A., U. Houston, U. Miami, Emory U., Notre Dame U., 1992, U. Iowa, U. Pitts., 1993; Ben C. Green lectr. Case Western Res. U., 1992; Blaine Sloan lectr. Pace U., 1993; Hauser lectr. NYU Law Sch., 1994; Goff lectr., Hong Kong Polytechnic Law Faculty, 1994; Freshfields lectr. U. London, 1996; pres. Adminstrv. Tribunal Internat. Monetary Fund, 1994—. Author: The Secretary-General of the United Nations, 1952, International Arbitration: Three Salient Problems, 1987, Justice in International Law, 1994; editor: The Effectiveness of International Decisions, 1971; mem. editorial bd. Am. Jour. Internat. Law, 1967-81, hon. mem., 1996—; chmn. editorial adv. com. Internat. Legal Materials, 1967-73. Frank Knox fellow Harvard U., 1950-51; recipient Gherini prize Yale Law Sch., 1954, medal of Merit, 1997, Pres. medal Johns Hopkins U., 1992, Harold Weill medal NYU, 1992. Mem. ABA, Am. Soc. Internat. Law (exec. v.p. 1967-73, hon. v.p. 1982-95, hon. pres. 1996—), Internat. Law Assn., Inst. Droit Internat., Coun. Fgn. Rels., Acad. of Experts (v.p. 1995—), Harvard Club (N.Y.C.), Athenaeum (London), Haagsche Club (The Hague), Cosmos Club (Washington), Phi Beta Kappa. Avocations: music, cycling.

SCHWEBER, SILVAN SAMUEL, physics and history educator; b. Strasbourg, France, Apr. 10, 1928; came to U.S., 1942, naturalized, 1951; s. David and Dora (Edelman) S.; m. Myrna Tapper, June 21, 1951 (div. Feb. 1965); m. Miriam Fields, June 14, 1965; children: Libby Ann, Abigail, Simone Aviva, Howard. B.S., CCNY, 1947; M.S., U. Pa., 1949; Ph.D., Princeton U., 1952. Instr. Princeton U., 1951-52; mem. Inst. Advanced Study, Princeton, N.J., 1955; faculty Brandeis U., Waltham, Mass., 1955—; prof. physics Brandeis U., 1961—, Koret prof. history of ideas, 1982—, dir. Dibner Inst. in History of Sci. and Tech., 1987-89, chmn. physics dept., 1958-61, 64-65, 74-76, chmn. Sch. Sci., 1963-64, 79-80, chmn. history of ideas, 1982-88; vis. prof. MIT, 1961-62, 69-70, Hebrew U., Jerusalem, 1971-72, 80-82, Harvard U., spring semester 1986, 87, 91, fall 1991; vis. fellow Harvard U., 1976-78, 83-84, assoc. history of sci., 1986—. Author: Quantum Field Theory, 2d edit., 1961, QED and the Men Who Made It, 1994. Proctor fellow Princeton U., 1952, NSF postdoctoral fellow Cornell U., 1952-54, sr. postdoctoral fellow Carnegie Inst. Tech., 1955. Fellow AAAS, Am. Acad. Arts and Scis.; mem. Am. Phys. Soc., History of Sci. Soc., Phi Beta Kappa, Sigma Xi. Home: 22 Turning Mill Rd Lexington MA 02173-1318 Office: Brandeis U Dept Physics Waltham MA 02254

SCHWED, PETER, author, retired editor and publisher; b. N.Y.C., Jan. 18, 1911; s. Frederick and Bertie (Stiefel) S.; m. Antonia Sanxay Holding, Mar. 6, 1947; children: Katharine Holding (Mrs. Eric F. Wood), Peter Gregory, Laura Sanxay (Mrs. Michael Sirico), Roger Eaton. Grad., Lawrenceville (N.J.) Sch., 1928; student, Princeton U., 1929-32. Asst. v.p. Provident Loan Soc. N.Y., 1932-42; with Simon & Schuster, Inc., N.Y.C., 1946-84; v.p., exec. editor Simon & Schuster, Inc., 1957-62, exec. v.p., 1962-66, pub. trade books, 1966-72, chmn. editorial bd., 1972-82, editorial chmn. emeritus, 1982-84, dir., 1966-72. Author: Sinister Tennis, 1975, God Bless Pawnbrokers, 1975, The Serve and the Overhead Smash, 1976, Hanging in There, 1977; (with Nancy Lopez) The Education of a Woman Golfer, 1979, Test Your Tennis IQ, 1981, Turning the Pages, 1984, Overtime: A 20th Century Sports Odyssey, 1987, How to Talk Tennis, 1988, Quality Tennis after 50...Or 60...Or 70...Or..., 1990, The Common Cold Crusade: A Novel Not to be Sneezed At, 1994, Plum to Peter: Letters of P.G. Wodehouse to his Editor, 1996; compiler: The Cook Charts, 1949; editor: (with H.W. Wind) Great Stories From the World of Sports, 1958; (with Allison Danzig) The Fireside Book of Tennis, 1972; contbr. articles to jours. Trustee Lawrenceville Sch., 1968-72. Capt. F.A. AUS, World War II. Decorated Bronze Star, Purple Heart. Mem. Authors Guild, Century Assn. Democrat. Home: 151 W 86th St New York NY 10024-3401 *I suppose my guiding principle has been to face up to problems and difficult situations as immediately as I can, even if taking more time to think about them might have resulted in better ideas and actions. But an honest, un-Machiavellian handling of matters, without putting them off while brooding about them, has always struck me as effective when I do it, and appealing when others do. I try to carry this principle through with everyone, from my wife and children, through my associates, to community affairs. It gives me a reputation ranging from bluntness to rudeness with those whose favorite I may not be, but I would hope one of respect and admiration with those about whom I care.*

SCHWEGMAN, MONICA JOAN, artist; b. Hamilton, Ohio, Apr. 19, 1958; d. David Michael and LaVerne Henrietta (Mergy) Kiley; m. Craig Alfred Schwegman, Oct. 6, 1978; children: Craig, Sarah. Student, U. Cin., 1976-78; AAS, Brookdale C.C., 1978; postgrad., Kansas City Art Inst., 1990. Mgmt. trainee coll. coop. Marshall Fields, Chgo., 1977-78; decorator, cons. Sears, Toms River, N.J., 1985-88; artist, owner studio and gallery Lampasas, Tex., 1990-94; chmn. Keystone Art Alliance, Lampasas, 1991-94; art dir. Theatre for Lampasas, 1993-94. Exhibited in group shows at Gallery One, Marble Falls, Tex., Found Art, Lampasas, KBVO TV Set Design, Austin, Tex., Breckenrdige Fine Arts Ctr., Pasillo De Artes Gallery, Austin, Contemporary Art Exhibit, Lampasas, Gannon U., Erie, Pa., Glass Growers Gallery, Erie, Barnes & Noble, Erie, Springhill, Erie, Erie Art Mus., 1997. Instr. art City of Lampasas/Sports, 1993. Mem. Lampasas C. of C. (mem. tourism com. 1993). Republican. Roman Catholic. Avocations: reading, aerobics, volleyball.

SCHWEI, MICHAEL ALLEN, doctoral student; b. Milw., July 10, 1956; s. Allen Jacob and Darlene Ann Schwei. BS in Edn., U. Wis., Milw., 1978; MEd, Stephen F. Austin State U., 1995. Cert. tchr., Tex.; cert. in mid-mgmt. With Marino Constrn. Co., Milw., 1978-80; tchr. English Houston Ind. Sch. Dist., 1980-81; tchr. math, computer literacy, journalism Humble

(Tex.) Ind. Sch. Dist., 1981-96; mid. sch. asst. prin. Pflugerville (Tex.) Ind. Sch. Dist., 1996-97; doctoral student in educational leadership Stephen F. Austin State U., Nacogdoches, Tex., 1997—. Named T.P. and Jenny Lou White Outstanding Adminstrn. Edn. Student, Stephen F. Austin State U. Alumni Assn., 1995-96. Mem. ASCD, Assn. of Tex. Profl. Educators, Tex. Assn. Secondary Sch. Adminstrs., Phi Delta Kappa. Avocations: backpacking, outdoor sports. Home: 3101 Wells Branch Pkwy #222 Austin TX 78728 Office: Stephen F Austin State U 2911 Chimney Rock #6 Nacogdoches TX 75961

SCHWEICKART, JIM, advertising executive, broadcast consultant; b. Toledo, June 25, 1950; s. Norman Marvin and Anne Belle (Cress) S.; m. Deborah J., Aug. 14, 1971; children: Jennifer, Kimberly, Stephen. BA in Polit. Sci, Taylor U., Upland, Ind., 1972. News anchor, announcer Sta. WCMR, Elkhart, Ind., 1967-71; news anchor, disc jockey Sta. WWHC, Hartford City, Ind., 1971-72; gen. mgr. Sta. WTUC, Taylor U., 1971; news dir. Sta. WCMR, Elkhart, 1972-74; news anchor Sta. WOWO, Fort Wayne, Ind., 1974-78, Sta. KDKA, Pitts., 1978-79; gen. mgr. Sta. WBCL-FM, Fort Wayne, 1979-85; owner advt. agy., broadcast cons. Fort Wayne, 1984—. Bd. dirs. Christians for Polit. Alternatives; elder bd. Blackhawk Bapt. Ch.; chmn. sch. bd. Blackhawk Christian Sch. Republican. Baptist.

SCHWEICKART, RUSSELL LOUIS, communications executive, astronaut; b. Neptune, N.J., Oct. 25, 1935; s. George L. Schweickart; children: Vicki Louise, Russell and Randolph (twins), Elin Ashley, Diana Croom; m. Nancy Kudriavetz Ramsey; step-children: Matthew Forbes Ramsey, David Scot Ramsey. B.S. in Aero. Engring, Mass. Inst. Tech., 1956, M.S. in Aeros. and Astronautics, 1963. Former research scientist Mass. Inst. Tech. Exptl. Astronomy Lab.; astronaut Johnson Manned Spacecraft Center, Houston, lunar module pilot (Apollo 9, 1969); dir. user affairs Office of Applications, NASA; sci. adv. to Gov. Edmund G. Brown, Jr. State of Calif., 1977-79; chmn. Calif. Energy Commn., 1979-83, commr., 1979-85; pres., founder Assn. Space Explorers, 1985—; pres. NRS Communications, San Francisco, 1991-94; exec. v.p. CTA Comml. Systems, Rockville, Md., 1994—; cons. and lectr. in field. Trustee Calif. Acad. Sci. Served as pilot USAF, 1956-60, 61; Capt. Mass. Air N.G. Recipient Distinguished Service medal NASA, 1970, Exceptional Service medal NASA, 1974, De La Vaulx medal FAI, 1970, Spl. Trustees award Nat. Acad. TV Arts and Scis., 1969. Fellow Am. Astronautical Soc.; mem. Soc. Exptl. Test Pilots, AIAA, Sigma Xi. Club: Explorers. Office: CTA Comml Systems 6116 Executive Blvd Ste 800 Rockville MD 20852-4920*

SCHWEIG, MARGARET BERRIS, retired meeting and special events consultant; b. Detroit, Mar. 23, 1928; d. Jacob Meyer and Anne Lucille (Schiller) Berris; m. Eugene Schweig Jr., Nov. 24, 1951 (dec.); children: Eugene III, John A., Suzanne. Student, U. Mich., 1945-47. Founder, pres. St. Louis Scene, Inc., 1975-94; ret. Mem. St. Louis Conv. and Visitors Commn., St. Louis Forum. Mem. Meeting Planners Internat., Am. Soc. Assn. Execs., Profl. Conv. Mgmt. Assn., Nat. Assn. Exposition Mgrs., Internat. Spl. Events Soc., Hotel Sales Mgmt. Assn. (bd. dirs. 1977-80), Regional Commerce and Growth Assn., The Network (pres. 1980-81).

SCHWEIKER, MARK S., lieutenant governor; b. Bucks County, Pa., 1953; s. John and Mary S.; m. Katherine Schweiker; children: Brett, Eric, Kara. BS, Bloomsburg U., 1975; MA in Adminstrn., Rider U., 1983. Merrill Lynch, McGraw Hill; Supr. Middletown Twp., 1979; commr. Bucks County, Pa., 1987-94; lt. gov., pres. of the senate, chmn. of the bd. of pardons State of Pa., 1995—, chmn. prime coun., chmn. local govt. adv. coun., chmn. gov.'s exec. coun. recycling devel. and waste reduction, dir. Pa. weed and seed program; former chmn. Dela. Valley Regional Fin. Authority. Former bd. dirs. Bucks County United Way. Recipient Alumnus of Yr. Bloomsburg U., 1990, Outstanding Svc. to Conservation award Nature Conservancy Pa. Branch, 1993, Tech. Advocate of Yr. Tech. Coun. Ctrl. Pa., 1996. Office: 200 Main Capitol Building Harrisburg PA 17120-0022

SCHWEIKER, RICHARD SCHULTZ, trade association executive, former senator, former cabinet secretary; b. Norristown, Pa., June 1, 1926; s. Malcolm Alderfer and Blanche (Schultz) S.; m. Claire Joan Coleman, Sept. 10, 1955; children: Malcolm C., Lani, Kyle, Richard S. Jr., Lara Kristi. BA, Pa. State U., 1950; D of Pub. Svcs. (hon.), Temple U., 1970; D.Sc. (hon.), Georgetown U., 1981. Bus. exec., 1950-60; mem. 87th-90th congresses from 13th Dist. Pa., mem. house armed services and govt. ops. coms.; U.S. senator from Pa., 1969-80; mem. appropriations com., ranking mem. Labor-HEW subcom., ranking mem. health and human resources com., ranking mem. health subcom.; sec. HHS, 1981-83; pres. Am. Council Life Ins., Washington, 1983-94; bd. dirs. Tenet Healthcare Corp., LabOne Inc.; chmn. Partnership for Prevention, 1991—. Alt. del. Nat. Rep. Conv., 1952, 56, del., 1972, 80; designated v.p. candidate with Reagan for Pres. of U.S., 1976. Served with USNR, World War II. Recipient Disting. Alumnus award Pa. State U., 1970, Dr. Charles H. Best award Am. Diabetes Assn., 1974, Outstanding Alumnus of Yr. award Phi Kappa Sigma, 1982, Gold medal Pa. Assn. Broadcasters, 1982, Nat. Outstanding Svc. award Headstart, 1983, Pub. Svc. Gold medal Surgeon Gen. U.S., 1988, Govt. Achievement award Juvenile Diabetes Found., 1990, Disting. Achievement award Nat. Coun. on Aging, 1991, John Newton Russell award Nat. Assn. Life Underwriters, 1992; named Outstanding Young Man of Yr., Jr. C. of C., 1960. Mem. Phi Beta Kappa. Address: 904 Lynton Pl Mc Lean VA 22102-2113

SCHWEIKERT, NORMAN CARL, musician; b. Los Angeles, Oct. 8, 1937; s. Carl Albert and Hilda (Meade) S.; m. Sally Hardin Haizlip, July 22, 1961; 1 son, Eric Carl. Mus.B. performer's certificate in horn, Eastman Sch. Music, 1961. teaching assoc. Northwestern U., 1973-75, assoc. prof. (part-time), 1975—; horn instr. Nat. Music Camp, Interlochen, 1967; curator Leland B. Greenleaf Collection Mus. Instruments, Interlochen, 1970-71. Successively 4th, 2d and 3d horn with, Rochester Philharmonic, Civic and Eastman-Rochester symphonies, 1955-62, 64-66, instr. horn, mem., Interlochen (Mich.) Arts Quintet, Interlochen Arts Acad., 1966-71, 1st horn, Rochester Chamber Orch., 1965-66, Midland (Mich.) Symphony Orch., 1969-71, 1st horn, soloist, Northwestern Mich. Symphony Orch., 1966-71, Chgo. Little Symphony, tours, 1967, 68, asst. 1st horn, soloist, Chgo. Symphony Orch., 1971-75, 2d horn, Chgo. Symphony Orch., 1975—; appearances with, Eastman Chamber Orch., Rochester Bach Festival, Aspen Festival Orch., Moravian Music Festival, Alaska Festival, Peninsula Music Festival, Rochester Brass Quintet, Canterbury Wind Quintet, Westchester Brass Quintet, Eastman Wind Ensemble, Chgo. Symphony Winds, Quadrangle Chamber Players, Washington Island Music Festival; soloist, New Japan Philharmonic, rec. artist for, Mercury, Columbia, Everest, C.R.I., Capitol. Mark Ednl., London-Decca, DGG, RCA Victor records, Sheffield Lab, Koch; recitals, also lecture demonstrations.; Contbr. articles to profl. jours. Served with AUS, 1962-64. Recipient certificate of merit City Chgo., 1971. Mem. Internat. Horn Soc. (hon., chmn. organizing com., sec.-treas. 1970-72, adv. coun. 1972-76), Am. Mus. Instrument Soc., Phi Mu Alpha Sinfonia (life alumni mem.), Pi Kappa Lambda. Home: 1491 Edgewood Rd Lake Forest IL 60045-1314 Office: care Chgo Symphony Orch 220 S Michigan Ave Chicago IL 60604-2501

SCHWEITZER, GEORGE, communications executive; b. N.Y.C., 1951. BS in Broadcasting and Film, Boston U., 1972. Prodn. supr. CBS-TV, N.Y.C., 1972-76; dir. comms. Sta. CBS-TV, N.Y.C., 1979; v.p. comms. and ops. CBS Sports, N.Y.C., 1980-82; v.p. comms. and info. CBS, N.Y.C., 1982-87, sr. v.p. comms., 1988-91, sr. v.p. mktg. and comms., 1991-94, exec. v.p. mktg. and comms., 1994—; v.p., dir. copr. rels. Young & Rubicam, 1987-88. Office: Sta CBS-TV 51 W 52nd St New York NY 10019-6119

SCHWEITZER, GEORGE KEENE, chemistry educator; b. Poplar Bluff, Mo., Dec. 5, 1924; s. Francis John and Ruth Elizabeth (Keene) S.; m. Verna Lee Pratt, June 4, 1948; children: Ruth Anne, Deborah Keene, Eric George. BA, Central Coll., 1945, ScD in Philosophy, 1964; MS, U. Ill., 1946, PhD in Chemistry, 1948; MA, Columbia U., 1959; PhD in History, NYU, 1964. Asst. Central Coll., 1943-45; fellow U. Ill., 1946-48; asst. prof. chemistry U. Tenn., 1948-52, assoc. prof., 1952-58, prof., 1960-69, Alumni Distinguished prof., 1970—; cons. to Monsanto Co., Proctor & Gamble, Internat. Tech., Am. Cyanamid Co., AEC, U.S. Army, Massengill; lectr. colls. and univs. Adv. bd. Va. Intermont Coll. Author: Radioactive Tracer Techniques, 1950, The Doctorate, 1966, Genealogical Source Handbook, 1979, Civil War Genealogy, 1980, Tennessee Genealogical Research, 1981, Kentucky Genealogical Research, 1981, Revolutionary War Genealogy, 1982, Virginia Genealogical Research, 1982, War of 1812 Genealogy, 1983, North Carolina Genealogical Research, 1983, South Carolina Genealogical Research, 1984, Pennsylvania Genealogical Research, 1985, Georgia Genealogical Research, 1987, New York Genealogical Research, 1988, Massachusetts Genealogical Research, 1989, Maryland Genealogical Research, 1991, German Genealogical Research, 1992, Ohio Genealogical Research, 1994, Indiana Genealogical Research, 1996, Illinois Geological Research, 1997; also 155 articles. Faculty fellow Columbia U., 1958-60. Mem. Am. Chem. Soc., Am. Philos. Assn., History Sci. Soc., Soc. Genealogists, Phi Beta Kappa, Sigma Xi. Home: 407 Ascot Ct Knoxville TN 37923-5807

SCHWEITZER, MELVIN L., commissioner, lawyer; b. N.Y.C., Oct. 27, 1944. BA, NYU, 1966; JD, Fordham U., 1969. Bar: N.Y. 1969. Atty. Rogers & Wells, N.Y.C.; commr. The Port Authority of N.Y. and N.J., 1993—; assoc. Rogers & Wells, N.Y.C., 1969-74, ptnr., 1975—; mem. Gov. Commn. on N.Y. Fin. Svcs.Industry, 1989—. Counsel, law chmn. N.Y. State Dem. Com., 1974-85. Mem. Assn. Bar City N.Y., Phi Sigma Alpha. Office: Rogers & Wells 200 Park Ave New York NY 10166-0005

SCHWEITZER, THEODORE GOTTLIEB, III, United Nations administrator; b. Hannibal, Mo., Aug. 28, 1942; s. Theodore Gottlieb Jr. and Dorothy Lois (Burnett) S. Cert. in French Lang., U. Paris, 1968; BA, U. Iowa, 1970, MA, 1974. Cert. Thai Lang. Am. Univ. Alumnae Assn., Bangkok, 1976, profl. tchr., Iowa. Tchr., librarian Lewis County Schs., Ewing, Mo., 1971-73; head librarian Internat. Sch., Bangkok, 1974-76; info. officer U.S. Army, Udorn, Thailand, 1974-76; dir. media services Am. Sch., Teheran, 1976-77; dir. media svcs. Am. Sch., Isfahan, Iran, 1977-78; refugee officer UN HCR, Geneva and Bangkok, 1979—; founder S.E. Asia Rescue Found., Ft. Walton Beach, Fla., 1981—, Hanoi Fgn. Langs. U., 1992-94. Author: (with Malcolm McConnell) Inside Hanoi's Secret Archives-Solving the MIA Mystery, 1995. Spl. rep. to Vietnam, Office of the Sec. of Def., Washington, 1992-94. With USAF, 1959-62. Recipient Award of merit SOS Boat people Com., San Diego, 1982, replica of Nobel Peace Prize, UN High Commr. for Refugees, 1981. Mem. Mensa. Republican. Baptist. Avocations: writing, reading, scuba diving, photography, private pilot. Home: 762 Sailfish Dr Fort Walton Beach FL 32548-6041 Office: UN High Commr for Refuges, Palais Des Nations, Geneva Switzerland

SCHWEIZER, KARL WOLFGANG, historian, writer; b. Mannheim, Fed. Republic Germany, June 30, 1946; came to U.S., 1988; s. Ernest Schweizer; m. Elizabeth Wild, 1969; 1 child, Paul. BA in History, Wilfrid Laurier U., Can., 1969; MA, U. Waterloo, Can., 1970; PhD, Cambridge U., 1976. Prof. history Bishop's U., Lenoxville, Que., Can., 1976-88; chmn. dept. Bishop's U., Can., 1978-79, 82-84, 86; prof., chmn. humanities dept. N.J. Inst. Tech., Newark, 1988-93, prof. history dept. social sci. and policy studies, 1993—; grad. faculty Rutgers U., 1993—; vis. lectr. U. Guelph, Can., 1978-80; rsch. assoc. Russian Rsch. Ctr., Ill., 1979-80; acad. visitor London Sch. Econs., 1986, 94, vis. scholar, 1986-87, Queens U., Ont., Can., 1986-87; vis. fellow Darwin Coll., Cambridge, 1987, 94, Princeton U., 1994, Yale U., 1994. Author: Francois de Callieres: The Art of Diplomacy, 1983, Lord Bute: Essays in Reinterpretation, 1988, England, Prussia and the Seven Years War, 1989, Frederick the Great, William Pitt and Lord Bute, 1991, (with J. Osborne) Cobbett in His Times, 1990, Lord Chatham, 1993, Francois de Callieres: Diplomat of the Sun King, 1995; co-author: The Origins of War in Early Modern Europe, 1987, British Prime Ministers, 1997; editor: The Devonshire Political Diary, 1757-1762, 1982, Diplomatic Thought 1648-1815, 1982, Warfare and Tactics in the 18th Century, 1984; co-editor: (with J. Black) Essays in European History 1648-1815 in Honour of Ragnhild Hatton, 1985, Politics and the Press in Hanoverian Britain, 1989, Herbert Butterfield: Essays on the History of Science, 1997; contbr. numerous articles to profl. jours. and mags. Mem. N.J. Gov.'s Adv. Panel on Higher Edn. Restructuring, 1994. Recipient thesis defence award Can. Coun., 1976, travel awards Peterhouse Coll., 1971-73, Adelle Mellen prize for outstanding contbn. to scholarship Edwin Mellen Press, 1989, Citation award N.J. Writer's Conf., 1993; fellow U. Waterloo, 1969-70, Province of Ont., 1969-70, Can. Coun., 1970-75; named Wilfred Laurier Proficiency scholar, 1966-69; rsch. grantee Bishop's U., 1977, 78, 80, 82, 83, postdoctoral rsch. grantee Can. Coun., 1977-78, 82-83, grantee Inter-Univ. Ctr. for European Studies, 1978, 81, conf. grantee S.S.H.R.C., 1985; travel grantee NEH, 1991, N.J. Com. for Humanities. Fellow Royal Hist. Soc.; mem. Internat. Commn. on History of Internat. Rels., Cambridge Hist. Soc., North American Conf. on Brit. Studies, Can. Assn. Scottish Studies, Can. Assn. 18th Century Studies, Inst. Hist. Rsch. Avocations: music, writing, reading. Home: 37 Lenape Trl Chatham NJ 07928-1812 Office: Dept Social Scis and Policy Studies NJ Inst Tech Newark NJ 07102

SCHWEIZER, KENNETH STEVEN, physics educator; b. Phila., Jan. 20, 1953; s. Kenneth Paul and Grace Norma (Fischer) S.; m. Janis Eve Pelletier, Oct. 18, 1986; children: Gregory Michael, Daniel Patrick. BS, Drexel U., 1975; MS, U. Ill., 1976, PhD, 1981. Postdoctoral rsch. assoc. AT&T Bell Labs., Murray Hill, N.J., 1981-83; sr. mem. tech. staff Sandia Nat. Labs., Albuquerque, 1983-91; prof. materials sci. engring. and chemistry U. Ill., Urbana, 1991—; chmn. polymers divsn., 1994—. Contbr. articles to profl. jours. Recipient Sandia award for Excellence, 1990, R&D 100 award, 1992, Award for Scientific Achievement in Materials Chemistry DOE, 1996. Fellow Am. Phys. Soc. (John H. Dillon medal 1991, DOE Materials Chemistry award 1996); mem. Am. Chem. Soc., Soc. Rheology, Sigma Xi, Pi Mu Epsilon. Office: U Ill Dept Materials Sci Engring 1304 W Green St Urbana IL 61801-2920

SCHWEIZER, PAUL DOUGLAS, museum director; b. Bklyn., Nov. 26, 1946; s. Alvin Charles and Marie Gertrude (Scholtz) S.; m. Jane Kulczycki, June 10, 1978. BA, Marietta Coll., Ohio, 1968; MA, U. Del., 1975, PhD, 1979; postgrad. Mus. Mgmt. Inst., U. Calif., Berkeley, 1990. Instr. art history St Lawrence U., Canton, N.Y., 1977-78; asst. prof. St. Lawrence U., Canton, N.Y., 1978-80; curator St. Lawrence U. (Brush Gallery), Canton, N.Y., 1977-78; dir. St. Lawrence U., Canton, N.Y., 1979-80, Munson-Williams-Proctor Inst. Mus. Art, Utica, N.Y., 1980—. Author exhbn. catalog; contbr. articles to profl. jours. Bd. dirs. Remington Art Mus., Ogdensburg, N.Y., 1979-80; bd. dirs. Williamstown (Mass.) Regional Art Conservation Lab., 1981-92, pres., 1988-92. Rsch. grantee Nat. Endowment for Arts, 1978. Mem. Coll. Art Assn., Assn. Art Mus. Dirs., N.Y. State Assn. Art Mus. (trustee 1993-95), Mus. Assn. N.Y. (councilor 1995—), Gallery Allocation of N.Y. (bd. dirs. 1996—), Otsego Sailing Club, Alpha Sigma Phi, Omicron Delta Kappa. Office: Munson-Williams-Proctor Inst Mus Art 310 Genesee St Utica NY 13502-4764

SCHWELB, FRANK ERNEST, federal judge; b. Prague, Czechoslovakia, June 24, 1932; came to U.S., 1947; s. Egon and Caroline (Redisch) S.; m. Taffy Wurzburg, Apr. 9, 1988. BA, Yale U., 1949-53; LLB, Harvard U., 1958. Bar: N.Y. Ct. Appeals 1958, U.S. Dist. Ct. (so. and ea. dists.) N.Y. 1960, U.S. Ct. Appeals (2d cir.) 1961, U.S. Supreme Ct. 1965, U.S. Ct. Appeals (4th cir.) 1968, D.C., D.C. Ct. Appeals, U.S. Dist. Ct. D.C. 1972. Assoc. Mudge, Stern, Baldwin & Todd, N.Y.C., 1958-62; trial atty. Civil Rights Div. U.S. Dept. Justice, Washington, 1962-69, chief eastern sect., 1969, chief housing sect., 1969-79, spl. counsel for litigation, 1979; spl. counsel rev. panel on new drug regulation HEW, Washington, 1976-77; assoc. judge Superior Ct. D.C., Washington, 1979-88, D.C. Ct. Appeals, Washington, 1988—; instr. various legal edn. activities. Contbr. articles to profl. jours. With U.S. Army, 1955-57. Named Younger Fed. Lawyer of Yr., Fed. Bar Assn., 1967. Mem. Bar Assn. of D.C., Assn. of Bar of City of N.Y., World Peace Through Law Ctr., World Assn. Judges, Nat. Lawyers Club. Avocations: tennis, table tennis, sports, Gilbert and Sullivan musicals, Shakespeare. Home: 4879 Potomac Ave NW Washington DC 20007-1539 Office: DC Ct Appeals 500 Indiana Ave NW Washington DC 20001-2131

SCHWEMM, JOHN BUTLER, printing company executive, lawyer; b. Barrington, Ill., May 18, 1934; s. Earl M. and Eunice (Butler) S.; m. Nancy Lea Prickett, Sept. 7, 1956; children: Catherine Ann, Karen Elizabeth. AB, Amherst Coll., 1956; JD, U. Mich., 1959. Bar: Ill. 1959. With Sidley & Austin, Chgo., 1959-65; with legal dept. R.R. Donnelley & Sons Co., Chgo., 1965-69; gen. counsel R.R. Donnelley & Sons Co., 1969-75, v.p., 1971-75, pres., 1981-87, chmn., 1983-89, dir., 1980-92; bd. dirs. William Blair Mut. Funds, Inc., Walgreen Co., USG Corp. Life trustee Northwestern U., Chgo. Mem. Law Club Chgo., Order of Coif, Phi Beta Kappa. Clubs: Chgo., Univ., Mid-Am., Comml., Hinsdale (Ill.) Golf, Old Elm. Home and Office: 2 Turvey Ct Downers Grove IL 60515-4530

SCHWENDEMAN, PAUL WILLIAM, lawyer; b. Chgo., Apr. 7, 1945; s. Oscar and Edna Dorothy (Ellis) S.; m. Shirley Anne Starke; children: Paul A., John E., Thomas D. BA in Econs., Carleton Coll.; MSJ, Northwestern U.; JD, Duquesne U. Bar: Pa. 1978. Mgr. divsn. ops. Greater Waterbury (Conn.) C. of C., 1971-75; v.p. Greater Pitts. C. of C., 1975-78; assoc. Kirkpatrick & Lockhart, Pitts., 1978-84, ptnr., 1984—. Lt. USNR, 1971. Office: Kirkpatrick & Lockhart 1500 Oliver Building Bldg Pittsburgh PA 15222-2312

SCHWENGER, FRANCES, library director; b. Hamilton, Ont., Can., Oct. 20, 1936. BA in Psychology and English, U. Western Ont., 1970; MLS, U. Toronto, 1972. Head cataloguing health scis. libr. McMaster U., 1972-74; with Hamilton Pub. Libr., 1974-82, head ctrl. libr., 1980-82; asst. dir. Met. Toronto Ref. Libr., 1982-86, CEO, 1986—. Mem. ALA, Can. Libr. Assn., Ont. Libr. Assn., Internat. Assn. Met. City Librs., Internat. Fedn. Libr. Assns. and Instns. (mem. standing com. pub. librs. 1993—). Office: Met Toronto Libr Bd, Reference Libr 789 Yonge St, Toronto, ON Canada M4W 2G8

SCHWENKE, ROGER DEAN, lawyer; b. Washington, Oct. 18, 1944; s. Clarence Raymond and Virginia Ruth (Gould) S.; m. Carol Lynne Flenniken, Nov. 29, 1980; 1 son, Matthew Robert; stepchildren: Tracy L. Wolf Dickey, Mary M. Wolf. BA, Ohio State U., 1966; JD with honors, U. Fla., 1969. Bar: Fla. 1970. Instr. Coll. Law, U. Fla., Gainesville, 1969-70; assoc. Carlton, Fields, Ward, Emmanuel, Smith & Cutler, P.A., Tampa, Fla., 1970-74, ptnr., 1975—, adminstr., dept. head Real Estate, Environ. and Land Use Dept., 1978—; adj. prof. Coll. Law, Stetson U., St. Petersburg, Fla., 1979-80. Author chpt. in Environmental Regulation and Litigation in Florida, 1987; contbr. articles to profl. jours. Mem. diocesan coun. Episc. Diocese SW Fla., 1978-86, mem. standing com., 1989-92. Recipient Gertrude Brick Law Rev. prize U. Fla., 1969. Fellow Am. Coll. Real Estate Lawyers (bd. govs. 1985-88), Am. Law Inst.; mem. ABA (standing com. on environ. law 1980—, coun. real property sect. 1988-95), Fla. Bar Assn., Air & Waste Mgmt. Assn., Order of Coif, Greater Tampa C. of C. (chmn. environ. coun. 1980-81), Tampa Club. Democrat. Office: Carlton Fields PO Box 3239 Tampa FL 33601-3239

SCHWENN, LEE WILLIAM, retired medical center executive; b. Morrisonville, Wis., Dec. 23, 1925; s. LeRoy William and Vivian Mae (Kramer) S.; m. Glenna Edith Mehne, Jan. 16, 1947; 1 son, William Lee. B.S., U. Wis., 1948; M.P.H., U. N.C., 1956. Tchr. pub. schs. Appleton, Wis., 1948-52; teaching cons. Wis. Health Dept., 1952-53; adminstrv. asst. Madison (Wis.) Health Dept., 1953-57; adminstrv. cons. U.S. Children's Bur., Atlanta Regional Office, 1957-58; adminstr. USPHS, Washington, 1958-66; assoc. dir. D.C. Dept. Health, 1966-70, D.C. Dept. Human Resources, 1970-71; exec. v.p. Maimonides Med. Center, Bklyn., 1971-88, pres., 1988-89, spl. cons. Bd. Trustees, 1989-96. Recipient Distinguished Pub. Service award D.C. Govt., 1970. Mem. Delta Omega. Home: 1007 Westminster Dr Greensboro NC 27410-4551

SCHWERDT, LISA MARY, English language educator; b. Coral Gables, Fla., Feb. 7, 1953; d. Henry G. and Dilys Doris (Bandurske) S. BS, Fla. Internat. U., 1973, BA, 1977; MA, Purdue U., 1979, PhD, 1984. Cert. secondary educator English, spl. edn., Fla. English instr. Green Sch. of English, Tokyo, Japan, 1973-75; spl. edn. tchr. Carol City (Fla.) Elem. Sch., 1975-77; grad. instr. Purdue U., West Lafayette, Ind., 1977-85; asst. prof. U. North Ala., Florence, 1985-89; adj. lectr. U. Cen. Fla., Orlando, 1989-90, Rollins Coll., Winter Pk., Fla., 1989-90; assoc. prof. English Calif. U. of Pa., 1990—, interim assoc. dean, 1995—. Author: Isherwood's Fiction, 1989; contbr. articles and book revs. to profl. jours. Mem. Sierra Club, Pitts., 1990—, Planned Parenthood, Pitts., 1986—. Grantee Purdue Found., 1982; recipient Excellence in Teaching award Purdue U., 1979, 81. Mem. MLA, Coll. English Assn., Nat. Coun. Tchrs. English, N.E. MLA, Pa. Coll. English Assn., Soc. for the Study of Narrative Lit., Soc. for Health and Human Values. Unitarian. Home: 5337 California Ave Bethel Park PA 15102-3821 Office: Calif U of Pa Dept English California PA 15419

SCHWERIN, HORACE S., marketing research executive; b. N.Y.C., Jan. 18, 1914; s. Paul and Rose (Lewis) S.; m. Lorraine Roth, June 14, 1941 (div. Dec. 1969); children—Barbara, Bruce; m. Enid May Highton, Apr. 28, 1973. B.S., Lafayette Coll., 1935; M.A., Kings Coll., London (Eng.) U., 1936; M.S., U. Paris, France, 1937. Gen. mgr., research dir., cons. N.Y. advt. agys., 1936-41; pres. Research Analysts, Inc., 1946; chmn. bd. Schwerin Research Corp., N.Y.C., Toronto, London, Hamburg, to 1968; chmn., pres. Horace Schwerin & Assos., Englewood Cliffs, N.J., 1968-72; dir. marketing devel. Campbell Soup Co., Camden, N.J., 1972—, v.p. market planning Canned Food div., 1977-82, mktg. strategy cons., 1982—; CEO, chmn. Schwerin Murphy, Inc., 1991—. Author: (with Henry H. Newell) Persuasion in Marketing, 1981; also articles on market research, nutrition, use of govt. data bases. Served as capt. U.S. Army, 1946. Decorated Legion of Merit with oak leaf cluster; inducted into Market Rsch. Coun. Hall of Fame, 1992. Mem. Am. Mktg. Assn., Market Rsch. Coun., Can. Club (N.Y.C.), Princeton Club (N.Y.C.). Methodist. Home: 5D Toll Gate Of Moorestown Moorestown NJ 08057 Office: 633 E Main St Moorestown NJ 08057-3059

SCHWERIN, KARL HENRY, anthropology educator, researcher; b. Bertha, Minn., Feb. 21, 1936; s. Henry William and Audrey Merle (Jahn) S.; m. Judith Drewanne Altermatt, Sept. 1, 1958 (div. May 1975); children: Karl Frederic, Marguerite DelValle; m. Partha Louise Hake Buell, Jan. 25, 1979; stepchildren: Tamara, Brent, Taryn. BA, U. Calif., Berkeley, 1958; PhD, UCLA, 1965. Instr. Los Angeles State Coll., 1963; asst. prof. anthropology U. N.Mex., Albuquerque, 1963-68, assoc. prof., 1968-72, prof., 1972—, asst. chmn. dept. anthropology, 1983-85, chmn. dept. anthropology, 1987-93; prof. invitado Inst. Venezolano de Investigaciones Cientificas, Caracas, 1979. Author: Oil and Steel Processes of Karinya Culture Change, 1966, Antropologia Social, 1969, Winds Across the Atlantic, 1970; editor: Food Energy in Tropical Ecosystems, 1985; contbr. articles to profl. jours. V.p. Parents without Ptnr., Albuquerque, 1976-77. Grantee Cordell Hull Found., Venezuela, 1961-62, N.Y. Zool. Soc., Honduras, 1981; Fulbright scholar Cañar, Ecuador, 1969-70, Paris, 1986. Fellow Am. Anthrop. Assn.; mem. Am. Ethnol. Soc., Am. Soc. Ethnohistory (pres. 1975), Southwestern Anthropol. Assn. (co-editor Southwestern Jour. Anthropology 1972-75), N.Mex. Cactus and Succulent Soc. (v.p. 1970-71), Maxwell Mus. Assn. (bd. dirs. 1984-85), Internat. Congress of Americanists (35th-40th, 43d, 46th, 48th, 49th), Sigma Xi (chpt. pres. 1980-81). Avocations: photography, gardening, hiking, camping, cycling. Office: U NMex Dept Anthropology Albuquerque NM 87131

SCHWERIN, WARREN LYONS, real estate developer; b. N.Y.C., Sept. 1, 1938; s. Clarence M. III and Helena (Lyons) S.; children: Kathryn Amy, James Warren. BA, Trinity Coll., 1960. Founding ptnr. Omega Properties, N.Y., 1961-70; pres. Arlen Shopping Ctrs., N.Y., 1970-73; pres., co-founder Related Properties, Inc., N.Y.C., 1973—. Past pres. Long Island Hearing and Speech Soc., past treas., trustee Buckley Country Day Sch.; trustee L.I. U.; mem. bd. overseers Southampton Coll.; bd. dirs. League for the Hard of Hearing, Indian River Land Trust, Marine Bank, Vero Beach, Fla. Mem. Internat. Council of Shopping Ctrs., Urban Land Inst. Office: Care Warren Lyons Schwerin 2 Manhatteville Road Purchase NY 10577

SCHWERING, FELIX KARL, electronics engineer, researcher; b. Cologne, Nordrhein-Westfalen, Federal Republic of Germany, June 4, 1930; came to U.S., 1964; s. Felix Bernhard and Maria (Heinrichs) S. BS, U. Aachen, Federal Republic of Germany, 1951, Diplom-Ingenieur, 1954, PhD, 1957. Asst. prof. U. Aachen, Federal Republic of Germany, 1956-58; electronic scientist U.S. Army R & D Labs., Fort Monmouth, N.J., 1958-61; project leader AEG-Telefunken, Ulm, Federal Republic of Germany, 1961-64; rsch. scientist U.S. Army Communication Electronics Command (CECOM), Fort Monmouth, N.J., 1964-96, ret., 1996; guest rschr. U.S. Army Communication Electronics Command (CECOM), Fort Monmouth, 1996—; vis. lab. assoc. U.S. Army Rsch. Office, Rsch. Triangle, N.C., 1984-85; vis. prof. N.J. Inst. Tech., Newark, 1986—, Rutgers U., New Brunswick, N.J., 1973-87, Monmouth U., 1996—. Author: (with others) Millimeter Wave Antennas,

1988; author and editor (with others) Microwave Antennas, 1989; mem. editorial bd. Microwave and Optical Tech. Letters, 1988—; contbr. over 30 articles to profl. jours.; patentee in field. Fellow IEEE (Best Paper award Antennas and Propagation Soc. 1961, 82), Internat. Sci. Radio Union, Am. Geophys. Union, Armed Forces Comm. Electronics Assn., Sigma Xi. Roman Catholic. Office: US Army Comm Elec Command Amsel Rd St # WL Fort Monmouth NJ 07703

SCHWETZ, BERNARD ANTHONY, toxicologist; b. Cadott, Wis., Nov. 27, 1940; married; 4 children. BS in Biology, U. Wis., Stevens Point, 1962; DVM, U. Minn., 1967; MS in Pharmacology, U. Iowa, 1968, PhD in Pharmacology, 1970. Diplomate Am. Bd. Toxicology. USPHS trainee dept. vet. physiology and pharmacology U. Minn., 1964-66; USPHS trainee dept. pharmacology U. Iowa, 1966-70; toxicologist Dow Chem. U.S.A., Midland, Mich., 1970-78, dir. toxicology rsch. lab., 1978-82; chief sys. toxicity br. divsn. toxicology rsch. and testing NIEHS, Research Triangle Park, N.C., 1982-92, acting dir. environ. toxicology program, 1993; dir. Nat. Ctr. for Toxicol. Rsch., Jefferson, Ark., 1993—; assoc. commr. for sci. FDA, Rockville, Md., 1994—; adj. prof. U. Ark. for Med. Scis., 1993—, Mich. State U., East Lansing, 1973-82, N.C. State U., Raleigh, 1985-93. Assoc. editor Fundamental and Applied Toxicology, 1983-86, editor, 1986-92; editl. adv. bd. Environ. Health Perspectives, 1984-93, Critical Revs. in Toxicology, 1984—; contbr. numerous articles to profl. publs. Recipient Arnold J. Lehman award Soc. of Toxicology, 1991, Dir.'s award NIH, 1991, Founders award Chem. Industry Inst. of Toxicology, 1994, FDA Commr.'s Spl. citation, 1995. Mem. AVMA, Soc. Toxicology (charter mem. Mich. chpt., councilor 1984-86, pres. N.C. chpt. 1987, pres. reproductive toxicology speciality sect. 1986, pres.-elect south ctrl. chpt. 1997), Teratology Soc. (treas. 1978-82), Behavioral Teratology Soc., Phi Zeta. Avocations: fishing, photography. Office: Nat Ctr Toxicol Rsch HFT-1 3900 Nctr Rd Jefferson AR 72079-9501

SCHWIER, PRISCILLA LAMB GUYTON, television broadcasting company executive; b. Toledo, Ohio, May 8, 1939; d. Edward Oliver and Prudence (Hutchinson) L.; m. Robert T. Guyton, June 21, 1963 (dec. Sept. 1976); children—Melissa, Margaret, Robert; m. Frederick W. Schwier, May 11, 1984. B.A., Smith Coll., 1961; M.A., U. Toledo, 1972. Pres. Gt. Lakes Communications, Inc., 1982—; vice chmn. Seilon, Inc., Toledo, 1981-83, also dir. Contbr. articles to profl. jours. Trustee Wilberforce U., Ohio, 1983—, Planned Parenthood, Toledo, 1979-83, Maumee Valley Country Day Sch., Toledo; bd. dirs. N.W. Ohio Hospice, 1991—. Episcopal Ch., Maumee, Ohio, 1983—; bd. trustees Toledo Hosp., Maumee Country Day Sch., 1986-92; pres. Edward Lamb Found., 1987—. Democrat. Episcopalian. Home and Office: 345 E Front St Perrysburg OH 43551-2131

SCHWIETZ, ROGER L., bishop. Ordained priest Roman Cath. Ch., 1967, consecrated bishop, 1990. Bishop Diocese of Duluth, Minn., 1989—. Home: 2830 E 4th St Duluth MN 55812-1502 Office: Diocese of Duluth Duluth MN 55812-1502*

SCHWIMMER, DAVID, actor; b. Queens, N.Y., Nov. 12, 1966. BS in Speech/Theater, Northwestern U., 1988. Co-founder The Lookingglass Theater Co., Chgo., 1988; actor Friends, 1994—. Stage appearances include West, The Odyssey, Of One Blood, In the Eye of the Beholder, The Master and Margarita; dir. The Jungle, The Serpent, Alice in Wonderland; TV appearances include Monty NYPD Blue, L.A. Law, The Wonder Years; film appearances include Flight of the Invader, 1991, Crossing the Bridge, 1993, Twenty Bucks, 1993, The Pallbearer, 1995, The Pallbearer, 1996, Apt Pupil, 1997, (TV movie) A Celebration of Life, 1997; appeared in, dir. (film) Since You've Been Gone, 1997. Office: The Gersh Agy 232 N Canon Dr Beverly Hills CA 90210-5302*

SCHWIMMER, SIGMUND, food enzymologist; b. Cleve., Sept. 20, 1917; s. Solomon and Sarah (Brown) S.; m. Sylvia Klein, Dec. 18, 1941; children—Susan, Elaine. Student Ohio State U., 1935-36; B.S., George Washington U., 1940; M.S., Georgetown U., 1941, Ph.D., 1943. From lab. asst. to research chemist USDA, Washington and Berkeley, Calif., 1936-62; adj. prof. biology Calif. Inst. Tech., Pasadena, 1963-65; chief research biochemist USDA, Berkeley, 1966-72, collaborator emeritus, 1975—; adj. prof. dept. nutritional scis. U. Calif.-Berkeley, 1985—; sr. expert biochemistry UN Indsl. Devel. Orgn., Haifa, Israel, 1973-74; cons. food enzymology, Berkeley, 1980—; lectr. dept. biotech. food engring. Israel Inst. Tech., Haifa, 1973; vis. scientist Food Industry Rsch. and Devel. Inst., Hsinchu, Taiwan, 1992. Contbr. articles to profl. jours.; editor, Biochem. Sci. Biotech., Cambridge, Eng., 1983—, Trends in Biochemistry, Trends in Biotechnology, 1983—, Jour. Food Biochemistry, 1977—; author: Source Book of Food Enzymology, 1982 (Jour. Assn. Coll. and Research Librarians award 1983). Fellow John S. Guggenheim, NSF; recipient Superior Service award USDA, 1949, 59, Agrl. and Food Chemistry Divsn. award Am. Chem. Soc., 1996. Fellow Inst. Food Technologists; mem. Am. Soc. Biol. Chemists, Sigma Xi. Office: Western Regional Ctr USDA 800 Buchanan St Berkeley CA 94710-1105 Office: U Calif Dept Nutritional Sci Berkeley CA 94720

SCHWIND, MICHAEL ANGELO, law educator; b. Vienna, Austria, July 2, 1924; came to U.S., 1951; s. Siegfried and Sali (Salner) S. J.D., U. Central, Ecuador, 1949; LL.M. in Internat. Law, NYU, 1953, LL.B., 1957. Bar: Ecuador 1949, N.Y. 1957, U.S. Supreme Ct. 1967. Pvt. practice N.Y.C., 1957-69; Lectr. law NYU Sch. Law, 1959-63, adj. asst. prof., 1963-64, assoc. prof., 1964-67, prof., 1967-94, prof. emeritus, 1994—; dir. Inter-Am. Law Inst., Inst. Comparative Law, NYU Sch. Law, 1967-71. Bd. editors Am. Jour. Comparative Law, 1971-97. Mem. Am. Assn. Comparative Study Law (bd. dirs.), Am. Fgn. Law Assn. (bd. dirs. 1980-83, 84-87, 88-91, 93-96, v.p. 1983-84, 91-93, 96—), Am. Soc. Internat. Law. Office: NYU Sch Law 40 Washington Sq S Rm 321 New York NY 10012-1005

SCHWINKENDORF, KEVIN NEIL, nuclear engineer; b. Newberg, Oreg., Mar. 11, 1959; s. Waldemar Adolf and Hattie Bertha (Baumgarten) S. BS, Oreg. State U., 1981, MS, 1983; PhD, U. Wash., 1996. Reg. profl. engr., Wash. Advanced engr. UNC Nuclear Industries, Richland, Wash., 1983-84, engr., 1986-87; sr. engr. Westinghouse Hanford Co., Richland, 1987-96, Fluor Daniel Northwest, Richland, 1996—; v.p. numerical methods, Analyst Devel. Corp., Scappoose, Oreg., 1990—. Designer: (ballistics software) PC-Bullet-ADCs, 1990 (Best Paper award 1992); author tech. publ. in field. Participant March of Dimes Walk-a-Thon, Richland, 1989, 90. Mem. Am. Nuclear Soc., NSPE, NRA, Soc. Computer Simulation, Safari Club Internat., Tau Beta Pi. Republican. Avocations: hunting, target shooting, personal computing, model building, bicycling. Home: 1121 Pine St Richland WA 99352-2135 Office: FDNW Criticality & Shielding MSIN HO-35 Engring Dept PO Box 1050 Richland WA 99352

SCHWOLSKY, PETER M., gas industry executive, lawyer, partner; b. Apr. 29, 1946. BA cum laude, U. Pa., 1968; JD, U. Mich., 1971. Pvt. practice, 1971-73; asst. to gen. counsel N.Y. Stock Exch., 1973-75; atty. Conn. Gen. Life Ins. Co., 1975-77; legis. asst. Sen. Lowell P. Weicker, Conn., 1977-79; counsel Electric Power Rsch. Inst., Washington, 1979-86; ptnr. Steptoe & Johnson, Washington, 1986-91; exec. v.p. N.J. Resources Corp., Princeton, 1991-95; sr. v.p., chief legal officer Columbia Gas Sys. Inc., Reston, Va., 1995—. Contbr. articles to profl. jours. Mem. ABA, D.C. Bar Assn., Conn. Bar Assn. Office: 12355 Sunrise Valley Dr Reston VA 20191-3458

SCHWYN, CHARLES EDWARD, accountant; b. Muncie, Ind., Oct. 12, 1932; s. John and Lela Mae (Oliver) S.; m. Mary Helen Nickey, May 25, 1952 (dec.); children: Douglas, Craig, Beth; m. Madelyn Steinmetz. BS, Ball State U., 1957. CPA, Calif., D.C. With Haskins, Sells & Orlando, Chgo., Orlando, Fla., 1958-67; mgr. Deloitte, Haskins & Sells, Milan, Italy, 1967-70, San Francisco, 1970-80; with Deloitte, Haskins & Sells (now Deloitte & Touche), Oakland, Calif., ptnr. in charge, 1980-92, ret., 1992. Bd. dirs. Jr. Ctr. Art and Sci., 1982-89, pres., 1987-88; bd. dirs., trustee Oakland Symphony, 1982-86, 89-91; bd. dirs. Oakland Met. YMCA, 1984-89, Oakland Police Activities League, 1981-91, Joe Morgan Youth Found., 1982-91, Summit Med. Ctr., 1989-94, 96—, Marcus A. Foster Ednl. Inst., 1986-95, pres., 1991-93; bd. dirs. Greater Oakland Internat. Trade Ctr., 1996; mem. adv. bd. Festival of Lake, 1984-89, U. Oakland Met. Forum, 1992—; co-chmn. Commn. for Positive Change in Oakland Pub. Schs.; mem. campaign cabinet United Way Bay Area, 1989; bd. regents Samuel Merritt Coll., 1994—; chmn., bd. regents, 1996—; chief of protocol, City of Oakland, 1996—; bd. dirs. Greater Oakland Internat. Trade Ctr., 1996—. With USN, 1952-56. Recipient Cert. Recognition Calif. Legis. Assembly, 1988, Ctr. for Ind. Living award, Oakland Bus. Arts award for outstanding bus. leader Oakland C. of C., 1992; date of job retirement honored in his name by Oakland mayor. Mem. AICPA (coun. 1987-90), Oakland C. of C. (chmn. bd. dirs. 1987-88, exec. com. 1982-89), Oakland Met. C. of C., pres., 1996, Calif. Soc. CPAs (bd. dirs. 1979-81, 83-84, 85-87, pres. San Francisco chpt. 1983-84), Nat. Assn. Accts. (pres. Fla. chpt. 1967), Claremont Country Club (treas., bd. dirs. 1989—), Lakeview Club (bd. govs. 1987-92), Oakland 100 Club (pres. 1994), Rotary (bd. dirs. Oakland club 1986-88, 91-92, treas. 1984-86, pres. 1991-92). Office: Office of Protocol City of Oakland 530 Water St Oakland CA 94607-3746

SCIAME, JOSEPH, university administrator; b. Bklyn., Sept. 9, 1941; s. Joseph and Sophie (Pintacuda) S. EdB, St. John's U., 1971. Fin. aid officer, asst. to dean of admissions St. John's U., Jamaica, N.Y., 1967-71, dir. fin. aid, 1971-82, dean fin. aid, 1982, v.p. fin. aid and student svcs., 1982-94, v.p. for govt. and community rels., 1994—; mem. Gov. Commn. on Sch. Achievement, 1971—, chairperson, 1993—; pres. N.Y. Assn. Student Fin. Aid Adminstrn., 1980-82, Ea. Assn. Student Fin. Aid Adminstrn., 1986-87. Chmn. bd. ethics Town of North Hempstead, N.Y., 1984—; nat. chmn., bd. dirs. Garibaldi-Meucci Mus., N.Y., 1987-93. Decorated cavaliere del Merito della Repubblica Italiana; recipient Lifetime Membership award Ea. Assn., 1995, Achievement award N.Y. State Fin. Aid Adminstrs., 1982, Congl. Record award, 1979, 91, 93, 94, 95. Mem. Nat. Assn. Student Fin. Aid Adminstrs. (chmn. 1987-88, Disting. Svc. award 1988, Leadership award 1994), Assn. Equestrian Order Holy Sepulchre (knight grand cross 1991, knight invested 1980), Order Sons of Italy in Am. (lodge pres. 1974-78, state pres. 1993-97), Futures in Edn. Found. (vice chair 1991-93, chair 1994-97). Roman Catholic. Avocations: walking, cooking, gardening, reading, lecturing. Home: 6 Jones St New Hyde Park NY 11040-1616 also: Trout Ln Southampton NY 11968 Office: St John's Univ Off VP Govt & Community Rels Jamaica NY 11439

SCIANCE, CARROLL THOMAS, chemical engineer; b. Okemah, Okla., Feb. 16, 1939; s. Carroll Elmer and Winifred (Black) S.; BS in Chem. Engring., U. Okla., 1960, M in Chem. Engring., 1964, PhD, 1966; m. Anita Ruth Fischer, Jan. 30, 1960; children: Steven, Frederick, Thomas, Erica. With E.I. duPont de Nemours & Co., Inc., 1966-95, planning mgr. nylon intermediates div., petrochem. dept., Wilmington, Del., 1978-80, tech. mgr., 1980-83, dir. engring. rsch., engring. dept., 1983-87, prin. cons. corp. research and devel. planning div., 1987-89; mgr. petroleum products R & D divsn., Conoco, Inc., 1989-93; dir. Environ. Tech. Partnerships, ctrl. R & D dept. DuPont, 1993-95; pres. Sci. Cons. Svcs., Inc., 1995—; sr. lectr. U. Tex., Austin, 1996—. Mem. math. scis. and edn. bd. NRC, 1987-89, adv. bd. NIST for Chem. Sci. & Tech., 1988-94. Served as officer USAR, 1961-63. Fellow Am. Inst. Chem. Engrs. (bd. dirs. materials engring. and scis. div. 1986-92, chmn. new tech. com. 1990-92, govt. rels. com. 1993-96); mem. Fedn. Materials Socs. (v.p. 1988-92, pres. 1993-94), Am. Chem. Soc. (mem. environ. R & D com. 1995—), N.Y. Acad. Scis., Sigma Xi. Home: 16658 Forest Way Austin TX 78734

SCIARRA, JOHN J., physician, educator; b. West Haven, Conn., Mar. 4, 1932; s. John and Mary Grace (Sanzone) S.; m. Barbara Crafts Patton, Jan. 9, 1960; children: Vanessa Patton, John Crafts, Leonard Chapman. BS, Yale U., 1953; MD, Columbia U., N.Y.C., 1957, PhD, 1963. Asst. prof. Columbia U., N.Y.C., 1964-68; prof., dept. head U. Minn. Med. Sch., Mpls., 1968-74; prof. Northwestern U. Med. Sch., Chgo., 1974—; chmn. ob-gyn Northwestern Meml. Hosp., Chgo., 1974—. Editor Gyn-Ob Reference Series, 1973—, Internat. Jour. Gyn-Ob, 1985—. V.p. med. affairs Chgo. Maternity Ctr., Chgo., 1974—. Fellow Am. Coll. Ob-Gyn. (chmn. internal affairs com. 1985-89); mem. Internat. Fedn. Ob-Gyn. (pres. elect 1988-91), Assn. Profs. Ob-Gyn. (sec. 1976-79, pres. 1980), Am. Assn. Maternal and Neonatal Health (pres. 1980-89, coun. resident edn. in ob-gyn. 1988—), Gyn-Ob Found., Am. Fertility Soc. (Hartman award 1965, bd. dirs. 1971-73), Assn. Profs. Ob-Gyn. (sec.-treas. 1987—), Cen. Assn. Ob-Gyn. (trustees 1986—), Yale Club N.Y.C., Carleton Club Chgo. Club: Yale (N.Y.C.); Carleton (Chgo.). Avocation: photography, food, wine. Office: Northwestern U Med Sch 333 E Superior St Chicago IL 60611-3056*

SCIFRES, CHARLES JOEL, agricultural educator; b. Foster, Okla., June 1, 1941; married, 1961; 2 children. BS, Okla. State U., 1963, MS, 1965; PhD in Agronomy, Botany, U. Nebr., 1969. Asst. rsch. agronomist range ecology Agrl. Rsch. Svc. USDA, 1965-68; asst. prof. range mgmt. Tex. A&M U., 1968-69, assoc. prof. range ecology and improvements, 1969-76, prof. range ecology and improvements, 1976-87; prof., head dept. agronomy Okla. State U., 1987-90; assoc. dir. Okla. Agrl. Exptl. Sta., 1990-94; dean, assoc. v.p. divsn. agr. Dale Bumpers Coll. Agr., Food & Life Sci., U. Ark., 1994—. Mem. Weed Sci. Soc. Am., Soc. Range Mgmt., Sigma Xi. Achievements include research in development of vegetation manipulation systems for rangeland resources; management for maximum productivity of usable products from the resource while maintaining its ecological integrity; persistence and modes of dissipation of herbicides from the range ecosystem; life history of key range species and community dynamics following manipulation. Office: U Ark Rm 205 Coll Agr Food and Life Sci Fayetteville AR 72701

SCIFRES, DONALD R., semiconductor laser, fiber optics and electronics company executive; b. Lafayette, Ind.; m. Carol Scifres. B.S., Purdue U., 1968; M.S., U. Ill., 1970, Ph.D., 1972. Research and teaching asst. U. Ill., Urbana, 1968-72; research fellow, area mgr. Xerox Corp., Palo Alto, Calif., 1972-83; founder, pres., CEO SDL, Inc., San Jose, Calif., 1983—, dir., 1983—, chmn., 1992—; nat. lectr. IEEE Quantum Electronics Soc., 1979. Bd. editors Jour. Fiber and Integrated Optics, 1978; mem. editorial adv. bd. Photonics Spectra, 1992—; contbr. articles to tech. jours.; patentee in field. Recipient Disting. Engring. Alumni award Purdue U., 1990, Outstanding Elec. Engr. award, 1992; recipient Engring. Alumni award U. Ill., 1991, Alumni Honor award, 1993; U. Ill. fellow, 1968; Gen. Telephone and Electronics fellow, 1970-72. Fellow IEEE (Jack Morton award 1985), IEEE Lasers and Electro-Optics Soc. (pres. 1992, Engring. Achievement award 1994), Optical Soc. Am. (Edward H. Land medal 1996); mem. Am. Phys. Soc. (George E. Pake prize 1997), Lasers and Electro-Optics Mfg. Assn. (bd. dirs. 1992—, sec. 1994, pres. 1996), Nat. Acad. Engring., Tau Beta Pi, Eta Kappa Nu, Phi Eta Sigma. Office: SDL Inc 80 Rose Orchard Way San Jose CA 95134-1356

SCIOLARO, CHARLES MICHAEL, cardiac surgeon; b. Kansas City, Kans., July 5, 1958; s. Gerald Michael and Charleen Gwen Sciolaro; m. Vicki Lynn Mizell, Sept. 29,. BA in Biology and Chemistry magna cum laude, Mid Am. Nazarene Coll., 1980; MD magna cum laude, U. Kans., Kansas City, 1984. Diplomate Am. Bds. Gen. Surgery, Thoracic and Cardiac; lic. Ariz., Calif., La., Fla., Kans.; cert. advanced cardiac life support, advanced cardiac life support instr., advanced trauma life support, Calif. x-ray supr. and operator, transesophageal echocardiography. Intern gen. surgery Tucson hosps. surg. program U. Ariz., 1984-85, resident gen. surgery, 1985-86, 87-89, chief resident gen. surgery, 1989-90; biochemistry rsch. fellow U. Kans., Kansas City, 1978-79; instr. surgery Loma Linda U. Med. Ctr., Tucson, 1991-92; staff physician St. Francis Cabrini Hosp., Alexandria, La., 1993-96, Rapides Regional Med. Ctr., Alexandria, 1993-96; instr. surgery Loma Linda (Calif.) U. Med. Ctr., 1991-93; physician divsn. cardiac, thoracic and vascular surgery MacArthur Surg. Clinic, Alexandria, 1993-96, Kanza Multispecialty Clinic, Kansas City, 1996—; staff physician Providence Med. Ctr., Kansas City, 1996—, Bethany Med. Ctr., 1996—; emergency rm. physician, cons. Nat. Emergency Corp., Tucson, 1986-87; part-time emergency care attendent Veteran's Med. Ctr., Tucson, 1985-89, Cigna Urgent Care, 1985-89; with divsn. cardiac, thoracic and vascular surgery MacArthur Surg. Clin., Alexandria, 1993-96. Author: (manuscripts) Aortic Coarctation in Infants, 1991; researcher, lectr. and presenter in field. Mem. ACS, Am. Coll. Cardiologists, Am. Coll. Chest Physicians, La. Med. Soc., Kans. Med. Soc., Wyandotte Med. Soc., Rapides Med. Soc., Southea. Surg. Congress, Soc. Thoracic Surgery, Internat. Soc. Intraoperative Cardiovasc. Ultrasound, Internat. Coll. Surgons, Kans. Med. Soc., Wyandotte County Med. Soc., Internat. Platform Assn., Phi Delta Lambda. Republican. Avocations: photography, golf, softball. Home: 12839 Century St Shawnee Mission KS 66213 Office: Kanza 21 N 12th St Ste 300 Kansas City KS 66102-5174

SCIPIONE, RICHARD STEPHEN, insurance company executive, lawyer; b. Newton, Mass., Aug. 27, 1937; s. Charles John and Alice (Scotto) S.; m. Lois Mugford, Aug. 29, 1964; children: Jeffrey Charles, Douglas Loring. BA, Harvard U., 1959; LLB, Boston U., 1962. Bar: Mass. 1962. Atty. John Hancock Mut. Life Ins. Co., Boston, 1965-69, asst. counsel, 1969-74, assoc. counsel, 1975-79, sr. assoc. counsel, 1980-82, 2d v.p., counsel, 1982-84, v.p., gen. solicitor, 1984-85, sr. v.p. and gen. solicitor, 1986-87, gen. counsel, 1987—. Bd. dirs. New England Legal Found., John Hancock Advisers/Distbrs.; trustee John Hancock Mutual Funds. Served to capt. U.S. Army, 1962-65. Mem. ABA (dir. New Eng. Coun.), Assn. Life Ins. Counsel (gov. 1994—), Chatham Yacht Club, South Shore Country Club. Office: John Hancock Mut Life Ins Co Box 111 John Hancock Pl Boston MA 02117

SCIRE, FRANK JACKSON, retired radar scientist; b. Bklyn., July 15, 1928; s. Marco and Marianna (Bianco) S.; m. Jacqueline Deleranko, June 21, 1958; children: Marianne, Mark, Paul. BS in EE, Pratt Inst., 1952; MS in EE, NYU, 1958; PhD in EE, Polytech. Inst. Bklyn., 1967. Mem. tech. staff Bell Telephone Labs., N.Y.C., 1952-54; mgr. missile electronics Maxson Electronics, N.Y.C., Great River, N.Y., 1954-63; dept. head advanced radar systems Sperry, Unisys, Paramax, Great Neck, N.Y., 1963-93; radar scientist rep. U.S. on NATO Adv. Bd. for NIAG-16, Washington and N.Y.C. at NATO Countries, 1985-86; advanced radar tech. coord. Unisys Tech. Transfer Team, Great Neck, N.Y., 1990-92; radar cons. for defense and air traffic, Unisys and Alcott, N.Y., 1993-94. Contbr. articles to profl. jours., papers to sci. confs. Tutor calculus and stats., for referred coll. students, Melville, N.Y., 1970-80; asst. soccer coach St Elizabeth Parish, Melville, N.Y., 1979; asst. baseball coach Little League, Huntington, N.Y., 1981. Mem. IEEE, Mus. Natural History, Sigma Xi, Tau Beta Pi. Republican. Roman Catholic. Achievements include patents on missile guidance, hi-radar visibility in the presence of clutter and jamming, electronic scanning; provided radar solution to USAF for the DEW line detection, tracking, identification of low-flying hostile aircraft by incorporating simultaneously hi data rates with long dwell times; designed and developed a mobile solid state radar capable of extracting aircraft space, time data over land or sea in a sustained severe clutter-jamming environment. Home and Office: Advanced Radar Consulting 19 Saxon St Melville NY 11747

SCIRICA, ANTHONY JOSEPH, federal judge; b. Norristown, Pa., Dec. 16, 1940; s. A. Benjamin and Anna (Sclafani) S.; m. Susan Morgan, May 6, 1966; children—Benjamin, Sara. B.A., Wesleyan U., 1962; J.D., U. Mich., 1965; postgrad., Central U., Caracas, Venezuela, 1966. Bar: Pa., 1966, U.S. Dist. Ct. (ea. dist.) Pa., 1984, U.S. Ct. Appeals (3d cir.), 1987. Ptnr. McGrory, Scirica, Wentz & Fernandez, Norristown, Pa., 1966-80; asst. dist. atty. Montgomery County, Pa., 1967-69; mem. Pa. Ho. of Reps, Harrisburg, 1971-79; judge Montgomery County Ct. Common Pleas, Pa., 1980-84, U.S. Dist. Ct. (ea. dist.) Pa., Phila., 1984-87, U.S. Ct. Appeals (3d cir.), 1987—; chmn. Pa. Sentencing Commn., 1980-85. Fulbright scholar Central U., Caracas, Venezuela, 1966. Mem. Montgomery Bar Assn., Pa. Bar Assn., ABA. Roman Catholic. Office: US Courthouse Independence Mall W #22614 601 Market St Philadelphia PA 19106-1713*

SCISM, DANIEL REED, lawyer; b. Evansville, Ind., Aug. 27, 1936; s. Daniel William and Ardath Josephine (Gibbs) S.; m. Paula Anne Sedgwick, June 21, 1958; children: Darby Claire, Joshua Reed. BA, DePauw U., 1958; JD, Ind. U., 1965. Bar: Ind. 1965, U.S. Dist. Ct. (so. dist.) Ind. 1965, U.S. Ct. Appeals (7th cir.) 1967, U.S. Supreme Ct. 1976. Reporter Dayton (Ohio) Jour.-Herald, 1958-59; editor Mead Johnson & Co., Evansville, 1962; first assoc., then ptnr. Roberts, Ryder, Rogers & Scism and predecessor firms, Indpls., 1965-86; ptnr. Barnes & Thornburg, Indpls., 1987—; cons. Ind. Personnel Assn., 1984—. Treas. Marion County chpt. Myasthenia Gravis Found., Indpls., 1970; v.p. Marion County Mental Health Assn., Indpls., 1970-71; pres. The Suemma Coleman Agy., Indpls., 1973-74; bd. dirs. Ind. Humanities Coun., 1995—, chmn. bd., 1997. Edwards fellow Ind. U., 1964. Mem. ABA, Ind. Bar Assn., Indpls. Bar Assn., Ind. State C. of C. (social legis. com. 1970-80). Methodist. Clubs: Indpls. Athletic; Woodland Country (bd. dirs. 1984-88) (Carmel, Ind.). Home: 11070 Winding Brook Ln Indianapolis IN 46280-1258 Office: Barnes & Thornburg 1313 Mchts Bank Bldg 11 S Meridian St Indianapolis IN 46204-3506

SCITOVSKY, ANNE AICKELIN, economist; b. Ludwigshafen, Germany, Apr. 17, 1915; came to U.S., 1931, naturalized, 1938; d. Hans W. and Gertrude Margarete Aickelin; 1 dau., Catherine Margaret. Student, Smith Coll., 1933-35; B.A., Barnard Coll., 1937; postgrad., London Sch. Econs., 1937-39; M.A. in Econs., Columbia U., 1941. Mem. staff legis. reference svc. Libr. of Congress, 1941-44; mem. staff Social Security Bd., 1944-46; with Palo Alto (Calif.) Med. Rsch. Found., 1963—, chief health econs. div., 1973-91, sr. staff scientist, 1992—; lectr. Inst. Health Policy Studies, U. Calif., San Francisco, 1975—; mem. Inst. Medicine of NAS, Nat. Acad. Social Ins., Pres.'s Commn. for Study of Ethical Problems in Medicine and Biomed. and Behavioral Rsch., 1979-82, U.S. Nat. Com. on Vital and Health Stats., 1975-78, Health Resources and Svcs. Adminstrn., AIDS adv. com., 1990-94; cons. HHS, Inst. Medicine Coun. on Health Care Tech. Assessment, 1986-90. Mem. Am. Assn. for Health Svc. Rsch., Am. Pub. Health Assn. Home: 161 Erica Way Menlo Park CA 94028-7439 Office: Palo Alto Med Found Rsch Inst 860 Bryant St Palo Alto CA 94301-2707

SCLAR, CHARLES BERTRAM, geology educator, researcher; b. Newark, Mar. 16, 1925; s. Norman and Dorothy (Botvinick) S.; m. Ruth E. Choyke, Feb. 10, 1946; children: David A., Philip J. BS, CCNY, 1946; MS, Yale U., 1948, PhD, 1951. Instr. dept. geology Ohio State U., 1949-51; research petrographer Battelle Meml. Inst. (Minerals Processing div.), Columbus, Ohio, 1951-53, prin. research geologist, 1953-57, asst. tech. cons., 1957-59, asst. tech. cons. chem. physics div., 1959-62, research fellow, 1962-65, assoc. chief, dir. high pressure lab., 1965-68; prof., dept. geol. scis. Lehigh U., Bethlehem, Pa., 1968-90; prof. emeritus Lehigh U., Bethlehem, 1990—; chmn. dept. geol. scis. Lehigh U., Bethlehem, Pa., 1976-85; prin. investigator Apollo program NASA, 1968-78. Contbr. articles to profl. jours.; patentee in field. William E. Ford scholar Yale U., 1947-48, James Dwight Dana fellow, 1948-49. Fellow Mineralogical Soc. Am., Geol. Soc. Am., Soc. Econ. Geol. Home: 2075 Pleasant Dr Bethlehem PA 18015-5134 Office: Lehigh U Dept Earth and Environ Scis 31 Williams Dr Bethlehem PA 18015-3126

SCOATES, WESLEY MARVIN, mining company executive; b. Jacksonville, Fla., Apr. 21, 1938; s. Harry William and Orlene (Buffkin) S.; m. Patty Ann Flora, 1958 (div. 1969); children: Teresa, Lesa, Leslie, Randall; m. Anneliese Marie Knorlein, May 11, 1970; children: Stephen, Cherry. B in Mech. Engring., U. Dayton, 1962; MBA, Fla. Internat. U., 1983. Commd. 2d lt. U.S. Army, 1962, advanced through grades to lt. col., 1982; artillery officer U.S. Army, Ft. Sill, Okla., 1962-65; mech. engr. U.S. Army Corps of Engrs., Jacksonville, 1965-66; artillery officer U.S. Army, Republic of Vietnam, Republic of Korea, Federal Republic of Germany, 1968-76, refrad, 1975; project engr. U.S. Gypsum Co., Jacksonville, 1966-67; div. chief City of Jacksonville, 1976-78; asst. equipment supt. Metro Dade County, Miami, Fla., 1978-79; asst. service mgr. Kelly Tractor Co., Miami, 1979-81; maintenance supt. Vulcan Materials Co., Miami, 1981-87, area mgr., 1987-91; equipment mgr. Lowell Dunn Co., Miami, 1991-92; ops. mgr. Ind. Aggregates, Inglis, Fla., 1992-93; dir. mining ops. Marcona Ocean Industries Ltd., Jacksonville, Fla., 1993—; CGSOC instr. USAR Sch., 1979-88. Contbr. articles to army logistician mag. With USAR, 1975-90. Decorated Bronze Star with oak leaf cluster, Air medal, Army Commendation medal with oak leaf cluster, Meritorious Svc. medal. Mem. Acad. Polit. Sci., Coun. on Fgn. Rels., Am. Def. Preparedness Assn., Am. Assn. Individual Investors, Sunshine Via De Cristo (lay dir.). Republican. Methodist. Avocations: fishing, singing, photography. Office: Marcona Ocean Ind Ltd 2101 State Road 434 W Ste 103 Longwood FL 32779-4958

SCOFIELD, DAVID WILLSON, lawyer; b. Hartford, Conn., Oct. 17, 1957; s. Leslie Willson and Daphne Winifred (York) S. AB, Cornell U., 1979; JD, U. Utah, 1983. Bar: Utah 1983, U.S. Dist. Ct. Utah 1983, U.S. Dist. Ct. Ariz. 1993, U.S. Dist. Ct. Hawaii 1995, U.S. Ct. Appeals (10th cir.) 1990, U.S. Ct. Appeals (9th cir.) 1995, U.S. Supreme Ct. 1996. Assoc. Parsons & Crowther, Salt Lake City, 1983-87; assoc. Callister, Duncan & Nebeker, Salt Lake City, 1987-89, ptnr., 1989-92; founding ptnr. Parsons, Davies, Kinghorn & Peters, Salt Lake City, 1992-96, pres., 1996—. Author: Trial Handbook for Utah Lawyers, 1994; mem. Utah Law Rev., 1981-83; contbr. articles to legal jours. Bd. dirs. Westminster Coll. Found., 1994-96, chmn. cultivation com., 1995-96. Named to Outstanding Young Men of Am., 1986. Mem. ABA, Assn. Trial Lawyers Am., Utah Trial Lawyers Assn., Salt Lake County Bar Assn., Zeta Psi. Congregationalist. Avocations: American history, writing, sports. Home: 2331 Scenic Dr Salt Lake City UT 84109 Office: Parsons Davies Kinghorn & Peters 185 S State St Ste 700 Salt Lake City UT 84111-1550

SCOFIELD, GORDON LLOYD, mechanical engineer, educator; b. Huron, S.D., Sept. 29, 1925; s. Perry Lee and Zella (Reese) S.; m. Nancy Lou Cooney, Dec. 27, 1947; children: Cathy Lynn, Terrence Lee. B.M.E., Purdue U., 1946; M.M.E., U. Mo., Rolla, 1949; Ph.D. in M.E, U. Okla., 1968. Instr. mech. engring. S.D. State Coll., Brookings, 1946-47; successively grad. asst., instr., asst. prof., asso. prof., prof. U. Mo., Rolla, 1947-69; prof., head mech. engring.-engring. mechs. dept. Mich. Technol. U., Houghton, 1969-81; disting. prof. mech. engring. S.D. Sch. Mines and Tech., Rapid City, 1981-88; asst. v.p. for acad. affairs S.D. Sch. Mines and Tech., 1981-83, v.p., dean engring., 1984-86; pres. S.D. Sch. Mines and Tech. Found., 1982-90; cons. U.S. Naval Ordnance Test Sta., China Lake, Calif., 1956-71; bd. dirs. Accreditation Bd. for Engring. and Tech., 1994—; cons. to industry. Served with USNR, 1943-46. NSF sci. faculty fellow, 1966-67; recipient alumni achievement award U. Mo., Rolla, 1975. Mem. Soc. Automotive Engrs. (pres. 1977), ASME, Am. Soc. Engring. Edn., AIAA, Sigma Xi, Tau Beta Pi, Pi Tau Sigma, Phi Kappa Phi. Home: PO Box 1085 Rapid City SD 57709-1085 *Satisfaction comes from sharing achievements. By acknowledging and sharing the importance of others in our success it is possible to accomplish more that is worth remembering.*

SCOFIELD, JOHN, jazz guitarist; b. Wilton, Conn., Dec. 26, 1951; s. Leavitt and Anne Fay S.; m. Susan Scofield, 1978; children: Jean, Evan. Student, Berklee Sch. Music, 1970-73. Profl. musician, 1974—; with Billy Cobham George Duke Band, 1974-77; with Dave Liebman quintet, 1978-82; with Miles Davis Band, 1983-85, soloist, collaborating musician, group leader, 1986—; with Enja/rec. artist, 1977-82; Grammavision rec. artist, 1984-89, Blue note rec. artist, 1990—; adv. bd. Guitar Player Mag. Albums include Live, 1977, Rough House, 1978, Shinola, 1982, Still Warm, 1985, Blue Matter, 1986, Loud Jazz, 1987, Pick Hits, 1987, Flat Out, 1989, Slo Sco, 1990, Time on My Hands, 1990, Meant to Be, 1991, Grace Under Pressure, 1992, What We Do, 1993, (with Pat Metheney) I Can See Your House From Here, 1994, Hand Jive, 1994. Recipient numerous Down Beat Mag. Internat. Critic/ Reader Polls. Office: Ted Kurland Asso Inc 173 Brighton Ave Boston MA 02134-2003*

SCOFIELD, LOUIS M., JR., lawyer; b. Brownsville, Tex., Jan. 14, 1952; s. Louis M. and Betsy Lee (Aiken) S.; children: Christopher, Nicholas. BS in Geology with highest honors and high distinction, U. Mich., 1974; JD with honors, U. Tex., 1977. Bar: Tex. 1977, U.S. Dist. Ct. (ea. and so. dists.) Tex., U.S. Ct. Appeals (5th cir.) 1981, U.S. Supreme Ct. 1984. Ptnr. Mehaffy & Weber, Beaumont, Tex.; spkr. Jefferson County Ins. Adjusters, S.E. Tex. Ind. Ins. Agts., Gulf Ins. Co., Dallas, Employers Casualty Co., Beaumont, Tex. Employment Commn., Jefferson County Young Lawyers Assn., Jefferson County Bar Assn., South Tex. Coll. of Law, John Gray Inst., Lamar U., 1991, Tex. Assn. Def. Counsel, 1991; cert. arbitrator Nat. Panel of Consumer Arbitrators; arbitrator BBB; presenter Forest Park H.S., Martin Elem. Sch., St. Anne's Sch. Contbr. articles to profl. jours.; columnist Jefferson County Bar Jour. Patron Beaumont Heritage Soc., John J. French Mus.; bd. dirs. Beaumont Heritage Soc., 1983-84, mem. endowment fund com., 1988; chmn. lawyers divsn. United Appeals Campaign, 1984; grand patron Jr. League of Beaumont, 1989, 90. Fellow Tex. Bar Found., State Bar of Tex. (mentors com. 1995); mem. ABA (contbg. editor newsletter products, gen. liability and consumer law com., vice chmn. of com.), Tex. Assn. Def. Counsel (dir. at large 1986-87, v.p. 1987-89, adminstrv. v.p. 1989-90, program chmn. San Diego 1989), Assn. Def. Trial Attys., Def. Rsch. Inst., Am. Judicature Soc., Jefferson County Bar Assn. (disaster relief project 1979, outstanding young lawyer's com. 1980), Beaumont Country Club, Tower Club of Beaumont, Phi Beta Kappa. Democrat. Episcopalian. Avocations: golf, reading, fishing. Home: 4790 Littlefield St Beaumont TX 77706 Office: Mehaffy & Weber PO Box 16 Beaumont TX 77704

SCOFIELD, PAUL, actor; b. Jan. 21, 1922; m. Joy Parker; 2 children. Trained London Mask Theatre Drama Sch., Birmingham Repertory Theatre 1941, 43-46; Stratford-on-Avon Shakespeare Meml. Theatre, 1946-48, Arts Theatre, 1946, Phoenix Theatre, 1947. With H.M. Tennent, 1949-56; assoc. dir. Nat. Theatre, 1970-71; has appeared in Adventure Story, Chekhov's Seagull, Anouilh's Ring Round the Moon, Gielgud's prodn. Much Ado About Nothing, Charles Morgan's The River Line, Richard II, The Way of the World, Venice Preserved, Time Remembered, A Question of Fact, Hamlet, Power and the Glory, Family Reunion, A Dead Secret, Expresso Bongo, The Complaisant Lover, A Man for All Seasons, Stratford Festival, Ont., Can., 1961, Coriolanus, Don Armado, New York, 1961-62, A Man for All Seasons, London, 1962-63, King Lear, N.Y.C, Moscow and Ea. Europe, 1964, Timon, 1965, Staircase, 1966, The Government Inspector, 1967, Macbeth, 1968, The Hotel in Amsterdam, 1968, Uncle Vanya, 1970, The Captain of Kopenik, 1971, Rules of the Game, 1971, Savages 1973, The Tempest, 1974, 75, Dimetos, 1976, Volpone, 1977, The Madras House, 1977, The Family, 1978, Amadeus 1979, Othello, 1980, Don Quixote, 1982, A Midsummer Night's Dream, 1982, I'm Not Rappaport, 1986-87, Heartbreak House, 1992, John Gabriel Borkman, 1996; films: The Train, 1963, A Man for All Seasons (Oscar and N.Y. Film Critics award Moscow Film Festival and Brit. Film Acad. awards), King Lear, 1970, Scorpio, 1972, Bartleby, 1980, A Delicate Balance, A Potting Shed, 1981, If Winter Comes, 1981, Song at Twilight 1982, Come into the Garden Maud, 1982, 1919, 1985, Anna Karenina, 1984, Mr. Corbett's Ghost, 1986, The Attic, 1987, Why The Whales Came, 1989, Henry V, 1990, Hamlet, 1990, UTZ, 1991, Quiz Show, 1994, Martin Chuzzlewit, 1994, The Little Riders, 1995, The Crucible, 1996. Decorated comdr. Brit. Empire. Address: The Gables, Balcombe Sussex RH17 6ND, England

SCOFIELD, THOMAS CAREY, retired army officer; b. Opp, Ala., Nov. 3, 1940; s. Waylon Dalton and Belva Ann (Williams) S.; m. Judy Lee Jackson, Dec. 19, 1964; children: Carey Leigh Scofield Long, Kimberly Lee, Seth Thomas. BS in Math., Troy State U., 1963; diploma, Acad. Health Scis., 1964, Acad. Health Scis., 1970; diploma R&D mgmt., U.S. Army Logistic Ctr., Ft. Lee, Va., 1972; diploma in rotary wing instrument flight examiner, U.S. Army Aviation Ctr., 1972; M in Mil. Arts and Scis., Command and Gen. Staff Coll., Ft. Levenworth, Kans., 1977; postgrad., Army War Coll., 1983-85, Nat. Def. U., 1985. FAA cert. comml. pilot, flight instr. With U.S. Army, advanced through grades to col.; exec. officer Co. B, 3d Bn. U.S. Army Med. Ctr., Ft. Sam Houston, Tex., 1964-65; med. evacuation pilot 498th Med. Co., Vietnam, 1966-67; med. evacuation pilot crash rescue U.S. Army Aviation Ctr., Ft. Rucker, Ala., 1967-68; med. evacuation pilot, maintenance officer 68th Med. Detachment, Ft. Bragg, N.C., Vietnam, 1968-69; comdr. 15th Med. Bn., 1st Cav. Divsn. Air Ambulance Co., Vietnam, 1969-70; chief instrumentation and methodology br., ops. divsn. U.S. Army Aviation Test Bd., Ft. Rucker, 1970-73; chief aviation and environ. medicine br., dir. environ. medicine U.S. Army Med. R&D Command, Washington, 1973-76; chief ops. divsn. office of asst. chief staff 7th Med. Command, Europe, 1977-78, comdr. 421st Med. Bn., 1978-80, asst. chief staff ops. plans and security, 1989-90, chief staff, 1990-92; chief aviation and ops. br., dir. ops. Dept. Army Office Surgeon Gen., Washington, 1980-84, dir., dep. dir. task force on health care Dept. Army, 1985-87; comdr. 44th Med. Brigade, 1st Corps Support Command XVIII Airborne Corps, Ft. Bragg, N.C., 1987-89; devel. dir. Henry M. Jackson Found. for the Advancement of Military Medicine. Decorated Legion of Merit with two oak leaf clusters, D.F.C. with three oak leaf clusters, Soldier's medal, Bronze Star with one oak leaf cluster, Air Medal with "V" device for valor and 39 oak leaf clusters, Army Commendation medal with one oak leaf cluster; Cross of Gallantry with silver star (Vietnam), with palm (Vietnam). Mem. Order Mil. Med. Merit, Army War Coll. Alumni Assn., Indsl. Coll. Armed Forces Alumni Assn., Assn. U.S. Army, Army Aviation Assn. Am., DUSTOFF Assn. Home: 11958 Cotton Mill Dr Woodbridge VA 22192

SCOGIN, MARTHA ADUDDELL, public information officer; b. Brice, Tex., Jan. 16, 1933; d. Jeff and Elizabeth Dale Aduddell; m. Andrew J. Scogin Jr., May 3, 1977; childern: Jerry Don Taylor, Sherri Carol Drobil, Charlotte Jean Taylor, Sherry Denise Stewart. BA, Tarleton State U.; MA, PhD, Tex. Women's U., 1986. Lic. profl. counselor, marriage & family therapist, chem. dependency specialist. Pvt. practice Granburg, Tex.; affiliate Psychiat. Inst.; advt. and pub. rels. cons., instr. in psychology Hill Jr. Coll.; cons. Johnson County Ctrs.; pub. info. coord. City of Dallas. Speaker in field; creator (workshops) on motivational topics. Named Profl. Woman of Yr., Bus. & Profl. Women, Granbury, 1992. Mem. Am. Assn. Counseling Devel., Nat. Coun. Family Rels., Tex. Coun. Family Rels., Tex. Assn. Family Rels., Tex. Mental Health Assn. Home: 8609 Westover Ct Granbury TX 76048-7900

SCOGLAND, WILLIAM LEE, lawyer; b. Moline, Ill., Apr. 2, 1949; s. Maurice William and Harriet Rebecca (Lee) S.; m. Victoria Lynn Whitham, Oct. 9, 1976; 1 child, Thomas. BA magna cum laude, Augustana Coll., 1971; JD cum laude, Harvard U., 1975. Bar: Ill. 1975, U.S. Dist. Ct. (no. dist.) Ill. 1975. Assoc. Wildman, Harrold, Allen & Dixon, Chgo., 1975-77, Hughes Hubbard & Reed, Milw., 1977-81; from assoc. to ptnr. Jenner & Block, Chgo., 1981—. Author: Fiduciary Duty: What Does It Mean?, 1989; co-author Employee Benefits Law, 1987. Mem. Phi Beta Kappa, Omicron Delta Kappa. Republican. Office: Jenner & Block 1 E Ibm Plz Chicago IL 60611-3586

SCOGNO, STACIE JOY, financial services company executive; b. Camden, N.J., Dec. 5, 1957; d. Albert Joseph Scogno and Josephine Geovanni Fiorello. AAS, Bay State Coll., Boston, 1978; BS in mgmt., Boston Coll., 1986; cert. of mgmt. and spl. scis., Harvard Ext. Sch., 1994. Software sys. cons., owner North Shore Svcs., Boston, 1984-88; tech. cons. Lotus Devel. Corp., Boston, 1988-90; mgr. MIS Blackwell Sci. Publs., Boston, 1990-93; product design analyst Thomson Fin. Corp., Boston, 1993-95; sr. cons. The Hunters Group, Boston, 1995-96; N.E. regional mgr. nat. fin. systems Coopers & Lybrand, Boston, co-dir. Natl. PeopleSoft Ctr. of Excellence, 1996—; notary pub. Commonwealth of Mass., 1980—. Trustee Action Dance Theater, treas., 1980-91; bd. dirs. Friends of City Sq., Charlestown, Mass., 1996—. Avocations: triathlons, body building. Office: 144 Middlesex Tpke Burlington MA 01803-4403

SCOLES, CLYDE SHELDON, library director; b. Columbus, Ohio, Apr. 14, 1949; s. Edward L. and Edna M. (Ruddock) S.; m. Diane Francis, July 14, 1976; children: David, Kevin, Karen, Stephen. BS, Ohio State U., 1971; MLS, U. Mich., 1972. Librarian Columbus Pub. Library, 1972-74; library dir. Zanesville (Ohio) Pub. Library, 1974-78; asst. dir. Toledo-Lucas County Pub. Library, 1978-85, dir., 1985—; adj. lectr., libr. bldg. cons. U. Mich.; v.p. bd. dirs. Read for Literacy. Mem. ALA, Ohio Libr. Assn., Ohio Libr. Coun., Toledo C. of C., Com. of 100, Maumee Hist. Soc. Club: Torch (Toledo). Lodge: Rotary.

SCOLES, EUGENE FRANCIS, law educator, lawyer; b. Shelby, Iowa, June 12, 1921; s. Sam and Nola E. (Leslie) S.; m. R. Helen Glawson, Sept. 6, 1942; children—Kathleen Elizabeth, Janene Helen. A.B., U. Iowa, 1943, J.D., 1945; LL.M., Harvard U., 1949; J.S.D., Columbia U., 1955. Bar: Iowa 1945, Ill. 1946. Assoc. Seyfarth-Shaw & Fairweather, Chgo., 1945-46; asst. prof. law Northeastern U., 1946-48, assoc. prof., 1948-49; assoc. prof. U. Fla., 1949-51, prof., 1951-56; prof. U. Ill., Champaign, 1956-68; Max Rowe prof. law U. Ill., 1982-89, prof. emeritus, 1989—; vis. prof. McGeorge Law Sch. U. Pacific, Sacramento, 1989-92; prof. U. Oreg., 1968-82, dean Sch. Law, 1968-74, disting. prof. emeritus, 1982—; vis. prof. Khartoum U., Sudan, 1964-65. Author: (with H.F. Goodrich) Conflict of Laws, 4th edit., 1964, (with R.J. Weintraub) Cases and Materials on Conflict of Laws, 2d edit., 1972, (with E.C. Halbach, Jr.) Problems and Materials on Decedents' Estates and Trusts, 5th edit., 1993, Problems and Materials on Future Interests, 1977, (with P. Hay) Conflict of Laws, 2d edit., 1992; contbr. articles to profl. jours.; notes and legislation editor Iowa Law Rev., 1945; reporter Uniform Probate Code Project, 1966-70; mem. joint editorial bd. Uniform Probate Code, 1972—. Mem. ABA, Soc. Pub. Tchrs. Law, Am. Law Inst., Ill. Bar Assn., Assn. Am. Law Schs. (pres. 1978), Order of Coif. Home: 1931 Kimberly Dr Eugene OR 97405-5849 Office: U Oreg Sch of Law 11th And Kincaid Eugene OR 97403-1221

SCOLLARD, DIANE LOUISE, retired elementary school educator; b. Seattle, Mar. 12, 1945; d. James Martin and Viola Gladys (Williams) S. BA in Edn., Wash. State U., 1967; 5th yr. cert. in edn., U. Wash., 1970; cert. edn., Oakland U., 1977. Tchr. Battle Ground (Wash.) Sch. Dist., 1967-70, Lapeer (Mich.) Cmty. Schs., 1970-95; ret. Mem. AAUW, NEA, NAFE, Nat. Assn. Career Women, Am. Bus. Women's Assn., Mich. Edn. Assn., Lapeer Edn. Assn. (bldg. rep. 1985, 89), Beta Sigma Phi. Democrat. Episcopalian. Avocations: travel, cooking, movies, collecting thimbles, bowling.

SCOLLARD, PATRICK JOHN, hospital executive; b. Chgo., Apr. 20, 1937; s. Patrick J. and Kathleen (Cooney) S.; m. Gloria Ann Carroll, July 1, 1961; children: Kevin, Maureen, Daniel, Thomas, Brian. B.S. in Econs., Marquette U., 1959; grad. sr. exec. devel. program, MIT, 1976. With Equitable Life Assurance Soc. U.S., N.Y.C., 1962-79, asst. v.p., 1969-71, v.p., personnel dir., 1971-75, v.p. corp. adminstrv. svcs., 1975-79; sr. v.p. Chem. Bank, N.Y.C., 1979-80, exec. v.p., 1980-87, chief adminstrv. officer, 1987-92; pres., CEO St. Francis Hosp., Roslyn, N.Y., 1992—; bd. dirs. Work in Am.; met. regional adv. bd. Chase Manhattan Corp. Bd. dirs. Cath. Charities, St. Francis Hosp., Woodstock Theol. Ctr. Office: St Francis Hosp 100 Port Washington Blvd Roslyn NY 11576-1353

SCOLNICK, EDWARD MARK, science administrator; b. Boston, Aug. 9, 1940; s. Barbara (Chasen) Scolnick; m. Barbara Bachrach; children: Laura, Jason, Daniel. AB, Harvard U., 1961; MD, Harvard U. Med. Sch., 1965. Intern Mass. Gen. Hosp., 1965-66, asst. resident internal medicine, 1966-67; research assoc. USPHS, 1967-69; sr. staff fellow lab. biochem. genetics NIH, 1969-70; instr. NIH Sem., 1970; sr. staff fellow viral leukemia and lymphoma br. Nat. Cancer Inst., 1970-71, spl. advisor to spl. virus cancer program, 1973-78, mem. coordinating com. for virus cancer program, 1975-78, chief. lab. tumor virus genetics, head. molecular virology sect., 1975-82; exec. dir. basic research virus and cell biology research Merck Sharp & Dohme Rsch. Labs., West Point, Pa., 1982-83, v.p. virus and cell biology research, 1983-84, sr. v.p., 1984, pres., 1985-93; sr. v.p. Merck & Co., Inc., 1991-93, exec. v.p., pres. rsch., 1993—; adj. prof. microbiology Sch. Medicine U. Pa., 1983-86. Editor-in-chief Jour. Virology; mem. editorial bd. Virology; contbr. numerous articles to profl. jours.;. Served with USPHS, 1965-67. Recipient Arthur S. Fleming award, 1976, PHS Superior Svc. award, 1978, Eli Lilly award, 1980, Indsl. Rsch. Inst. medal, 1990. Mem. NAS, Am. Soc. Biol. Chemists, Am. Soc. Microbiologists. Home: 811 Wickfield Rd Wynnewood PA 19096-1610 Office: Merck Rsch Labs PO Box 2000 Rahway NJ 07065-0900*

SCOMMEGNA, ANTONIO, physician, educator; b. Barletta, Italy, Aug. 26, 1931; came to U.S., 1954, naturalized, 1960; s. Francesco Paola and Antonietta (Maresca) S.; m. Lillian F. Sinkiewicz, May 3, 1958; children: Paola, Frank, Roger. B.A., State Lyceum A. Casardi, Barletta, 1947; M.D., U. Bari (Italy), 1953. Diplomate: Am. Bd. Obstetrics and Gynecology, also sub-bd. endocrinology and reprodn. Rotating intern New Eng. Hosp., Boston, 1954-55; resident obstetrics and gynecology Michael Reese Hosp. and Med. Center, Chgo., 1956-59; fellow dept. research human reprodn. Michael Reese Hosp. and Med. Center, 1960-61, research asso., 1961; fellow steroid tng. program Worcester Found. Exptl. Biology, also Clark U., Shrewsbury, Mass., 1964-65; asso. prof. obstetrics and gynecology Chgo. Med. Sch., 1965-69; mem. staff Michael Reese Hosp. and Med. Center, 1961—, attending physician obstetrics and gynecology, 1961—, dir. sect. gynecologic endocrinology, 1965-81; dir. ambulatory care obstetrics and gynecology Mandel Clinic, 1968-69, chmn. dept., 1969-89; attending, chief svc. U. Ill. Chgo. Hosp. and Med. Ctr., 1989—; trustee Mandel Clinic, 1977-80; prof. dept. ob-gyn. Pritzker Sch. Medicine U. Chgo., 1969-89; prof., head dept. ob-gyn. Coll. Medicine U. Ill. Chgo., 1989—. Author numerous articles in field. Fulbright fellow, 1954-55. Fellow Am. Coll. Obstetricians and Gynecologists, Endocrine Soc., Chgo. Inst. Medicine, Am. Gynecol. and Obstet. Soc.; mem. AMA, Ill., Chgo. med. socs., Am. Fertility Soc., Chgo. Gynecol. Soc. (sec. 1976-79, pres. 1981-82), Soc. Study Reprodn., AAAS, Soc. for Gynecologic Investigation. Home: 1023E W Vernon Park Pl Chicago IL 60607-3400

SCONYERS, RONALD T., career officer; m. Amber Sconyers; children: Adrienne, Michael. BS in Internat. Affairs, USAF Acad., 1970; MA in Comm., St. Louis U., 1974; PhD in Comm., Denver U., 1977. Commd. 2d lt. USAF, 1970; dep. dir., dir. info. Hdqs. Aerospace Rescue and Recovery Svc., advanced through grades to brig. gen., 1995; pub. info. officer Hdqs. Mil. Airlift Command; mil. fellow Continental Broadcast Co., Chgo., 1973-74; chief advt. and publicity divsn., chief ops. divsn. 356th USAF Recruiting Squadron, Lowry AFB, Colo., 1974-77; mgm. cons., exec. asst. to comdr. USAF Recruiting Svc., Randolph AFB, Tex., 1977-81; comdr. 3544th USAF Recruiting Squadron, Arlington, Tex., 1982-84; chief tng. and analysis divsn. Hdqs. USAF Recruiting Svc., Randolph AFB, Tex., 1984-86; dir. pub. affairs U.S. So. Command, Quarry Heights, Panama, 1987-90, Hdqs. Tactical Air Command, Hdqs. Air Combat Command, Langley AFB, Va., 1990-92; comdr. 363d Support Group, Shaw AFB, S.C., 1992-94; dep. dir. pub. affairs Office Sec. Air Force, Washington, 1994, dir. pub. affairs, 1994—. Contbr. articles to profl. jours. Decorated Legion of Merit; recipient Golden Trumpet award Publicity Club Chgo., 1995. Mem. Pub. Rels. Soc. Am. (Silver Anvil award 1989, 95, cert. excellence 1995), Nat. Assn. Govt. Communicators. Office: Pub Affairs 1690 Air Force Pentagon Washington DC 20330*

SCOPES, GARY MARTIN, professional association executive; b. St. Petersburg, Fla., July 16, 1947; s. Louis Martin and Eleanor Beebe (Kurkjian) S.; m. Connie Joy Kowalski, Sept. 16, 1967; children: Darryl, Sandra, Adrian. BA in Rhetoric, U. South Fla., 1971; postgrad., La. State U. Cert. assn. exec. (nationally). Lobbyist La. Mcpl. Assn., Baton Rouge, 1972-74; exec. dir. Soc. La. CPAs, Metairie, 1974-84, Tex. Soc. CPAs, Dallas, 1984-87, Inst. Mgmt. Accts. (formerly Nat. Assn. Accts.), Montvale, N.J., 1987—; pres. La. Soc. Assn. Execs., 1980-81, CPA Soc. Execs. Assn., 1982-83, Kaypro Computer Users Group, 1979. 1st lt. U.S. Army, 1966-69. Mem. N.J. Soc. Assn. Execs. (pres. 1995), Ethics Officer Assn. Avocations: tennis, skiing, golf, fishing, guitar. Home: 1 Van Wyck St Montvale NJ 07645-1025 Office: Institute of Mngmt Accountants 10 Paragon Dr Montvale NJ 07645-1718

SCOPP, IRWIN WALTER, periodontist, educator; b. N.Y.C., Dec. 8, 1909; s. Leon and Anne S.; B.S., CCNY, 1930; DDS, Columbia U., 1934; m. Edith Halprin, Dec. 25, 1941; 1 son, Alfred. Pvt. practice periodontics, N.Y.C., 1934-42; chief dental service VA Med. Center, N.Y.C., 1945-80; prof. periodontics N.Y.U. Coll. Dentistry, 1945-80, dir. continuing dental edn., 1980-85, dir. course in medicine Coll. Dentistry, 1982-90, clin. prof. periodontics, 1980—. Bd. govs. div. oral hygiene N.Y.C. Tech. Coll., 1960-79, chmn., 1979. Served to capt. Dental Corps, AUS, 1942-45. Recipient Disting. Profs. award N.Y.U., 1981. Mem. Northeastern Soc. Periodontics (sec.-treas. 1955-90), ADA (chmn. research 1978), Am. Acad. Periodontology, Am. Acad. Oral Medicine, Am. Coll. Dentists, Am. Acad. Sci., Internat. Assn. Dental Research, Am. Pub. Health Assn., Assn. Mil. Surgeons, Research Soc. Am., Hosp. Dental Chiefs Assn., Am. Acad. Sci. Author: Oral Medicine - A Clinical Approach with Basic Science Correlation, 1969, 2d edit., 1973. Contbr. chpts. to books.

SCORDELIS, ALEXANDER COSTICAS, civil engineering educator; b. San Francisco, Sept. 27, 1923; s. Philip Kostas and Vasilica (Zois) S.; m. Georgia Gumas, May 9, 1948; children: Byron, Karen. B.S., U. Calif., Berkeley, 1948; M.S., M.I.T., 1949. Registered profl. engr., Calif. Structural designer Pacific Gas & Electric Co., San Francisco, 1948; engr. Bechtel Corp., San Francisco, summer 1951, 52, 53, 54; instr. civil engring. U. Calif., 1949-50, asst. prof., 1951-56, assoc. prof., 1957-61, prof., 1962-89, asst. dean Coll. Engring., 1962-65, vice chmn. div. structural engring. structural mechanics, 1970-73, Nishkian prof. emeritus, 1990—; cons. engring. firms, govt. agys. Contbr. articles on analysis and design of complex structural systems, reinforced and prestressed concrete shell and bridge structures to profl. jours. Served to capt., C.E. U.S. Army, 1943-46, ETO. Decorated Bronze star, Purple Heart; recipient Western Electric award Am. Soc. Engring. Edn., 1978; Axion award Hellenic Am. Profl. Soc., 1979; Best paper award Canadian Soc. Civil Engring., 1982, K.B. Woods award NAS Transp. Rsch. Bd., 1983, Citation U. Calif. Berkeley, 1989, Disting. Engring. Alumnus award Berkeley Engring. ALumni Soc., 1993, Leadership award Am. Segmental Bridge Inst., 1993, Freyssinet medal Internat. Fedn. for Prestressed Concrete, 1994. Fellow ASCE (hon. mem. 1989, Moissieff award 1976, 81, 92, Howard award 1989), Am. Concrete Inst.; mem. Internat. Assn. Shell and Spatial Structures (hon., Torroja medal 1994), Internat. Assn. Bridge and Structural Engring., Structural Engrs. Assn. Calif., Nat. Acad. Engring. Home: 724 Gelston Pl El Cerrito CA 94530-3045 Office: U Calif 729 Davis Hall Berkeley CA 94720

SCORGIE, GLEN GIVEN, religious organization leader; b. Mar. 29, 1952; married; 3 children. BTh, Can. Bible Coll., 1973; MA, Wheaton Grad. Sch., 1974; MCS, Regent Coll., 1982; postgrad., Cambridge U., 1983; PhD, U. St. Andrews, 1986. Data-processing mktg. asst. IBM Can., Toronto, 1974-76; dir. admissions Can Bible Coll., Regina, 1976-79, asst. prof. theology, 1984-88, acting dean faculty, 1989, assoc. prof. theology, 1988-91; dean, v.p. N.Am. Bapt. Coll., 1991-96; prof. systematic theology Bethel Seminary West, San Diego, 1996—; adj. prof. theology Can. Theol. Sem., 1984-91; speaker in field. Author: A Call for Continuity: The Theological Contribution of James Orr, 1988; contbr. articles to profl. jours. British Govt. Overseas Rsch. scholar, 1981-84, Ont. scholar, 1969; recipient Regent Coll. Ch. History prize, 1981. Mem. Can. Theol. Soc., Can. Soc. Ch. History, Can. Evang. Theol. Assn., Conf. Faith and History, Delta Epsilon Chi. Office: Bethel Theol Seminary 6116 Arosa St San Diego CA 92115-3902

SCORSESE, MARTIN, film director, writer; b. Flushing, N.Y., Nov. 17, 1942; s. Charles and Catherine (Cappa) S.; m. Laraine Marie Brennan, May 15, 1965 (div.), 1 daughter: Catherine Terese Glinora Sophia; m. Julia Cameron, 1975 (div.), 1 daughter: Dominica Elizabeth; m. Isabella Rosellini, Sept. 29, 1979 (div. 1983); m. Barbara DeFina, Feb. 9, 1985. BS in Film Communications, NYU, 1964, MA in Film Communications, 1966. Faculty asst., then instr. film NYU, N.Y.C., 1963-70. Films include: (dir.): The Big Shave, 1968 (also writer), Who's That Knocking at My Door?, 1968 (also writer, assoc. prodr., actor), Boxcar Bertha, 1972 (also actor), Mean Streets, 1973 (also co-writer, actor), Alice Doesn't Live Here Anymore, 1975, Taxi Driver, 1976 (also actor, Palme d'Or Cannes Internat. Film Festival), New York, New York, 1977, The Last Waltz, 1978, Raging Bull, 1980, The King of Comedy, 1983 (also actor), After Hours, 1985, The Color of Money, 1986, The Last Temptation of Christ, 1988, New York Stories (Life Lessons), 1989, GoodFellas, 1990 (also co-writer), Cape Fear, 1991, The Age of Innocence, 1993 (also co-writer), Casino, 1995 (also writer); (prodr.): The Grifters, 1990, Mad Dog and Glory, 1993, Clockers, 1995 (also exec. prodr.), Casino, 1995; (exec. prodr.): Naked in New York, 1994, Grace of My Heart, 1996; documentaries include: (editor): Woodstock, 1970 (also asst. dir.), Elvis on Tour, 1973; (assoc. prodr.): Medicine Ball Caravan, 1971; (dir.): Street Scenes 1970, 1970, Italianamerican, 1974, American Boy: A Profile of Steven Price, 1979, Man in Milan, 1990; other film appearances include: Cannonball, 1976, Pavlova: A Woman for All Seasons, 1983, 'Round Midnight, 1986, Akira Kurosawa's Dreams, 1990, Guilty by Suspicion, 1991, Quiz Show, 1994, Search and Destroy, 1995 (also prodr.), (TV film) La Memoire retrouvee, 1996. Recipient Edward L. Kingsley Found. award, 1963-64, 1st prize Rosenthal Found. awards Soc. Cinemetologists, 1964, 1st prize Screen Producer's Guild, 1965, 1st prize Brown U. Film Festival, 1965, also others; named Best Dir. Cannes Film Festival, 1986. Office: Jeff Dooley Starr & Co 350 Park Ave Fl 9 New York NY 10022-6022 also: care CAA 9830 Wilshire Blvd Beverly Hills CA 90212-1804

SCORZA, SYLVIO JOSEPH, religion educator; b. Zürich, Switzerland, Mar. 21, 1923; came to U.S., 1929; s. Joseph Peter and Helena Christina (Kopp) S.; m. Phyllis Joan VanSetters, June 6, 1952; children: Christine Marie, Philip Joseph, John Forrest. AA, Woodrow Wilson Jr. Coll., 1942; AB, Hope Coll., 1945; BD, Western Theol. Sem., Holland, Mich., 1953; ThD, Princeton Theol. Sem., 1956; PhD, U. Ill., 1972. Ordained to ministry Ref. Ch. in Am., 1955. Stated supply pastor Hickory Bottom Charge, Loysburg, Pa., 1957-58; prof. religion Northwestern Coll., Orange City, Iowa, 1959-90, prof. emeritus, 1990—; vis. prof. Lancaster (Pa.) Theol. Sem., 1956-57, Western Theol. Sem., Holland, Mich., 1958-59; v.p. Ref. Ch. in Am., N.Y.C., 1988-89, pres., 1989-90, moderator, exec. com., 1990-91. Co-editor: Concordance to the Greek and Hebrew Text of Ruth, The Computer Bible, Septuagint series, Vols. XXX, XXX-B, 1988-89; contbr. articles to profl. jours. County del. Iowa Dems., Ft. Dodge, 1984. Recipient Disting. Alumnus award Hope Coll., 1989, Homecoming Honors award Northwestern Coll. N Club, 1990, Handicapped Person of Siouxland award Siouxland

Com. for the Handicapped, 1990, Gov.'s award Iowa Commn. of Persons with Disabilities, 1990, Victory award Nat. Rehab. Hosp., 1991. Mem. Internat. Orgn. for Septuagint and Cognate Studies, Smithsonian Instsn., Nat. Geog. Soc., Iowa State Chess Assn. (v.p. 1984-85, dir. postal tournament 1987—). Avocations: chess, bridge. Home: 520 2nd St SW Orange City IA 51041-1728 Office: Northwestern Coll Orange City IA 51041

SCOTCH, BARRY MARTIN, lawyer; b. Newark, Aug. 2, 1939; s. Philip and Clara (Blecher) S.; m. Barbara Katz, May 2, 1970; children: Adam Michael, Matthew Laurence, Molly Claire. AB, Columbia U., 1961, JD, 1964. Bar: N.J. 1965, U.S. Ct. Mil. Appeals 1967, U.S. Supreme Ct. 1969, N.H. 1974, U.S. Ct. Appeals (1st cir.) 1982. Assoc. atty. Teltser, Byrne & Greenberg, East Orange, N.J., 1965-66, Baker, Garber, Chazen & Duffy, Hoboken, N.J., 1966-69, Canter & Chazen, Jersey City, 1969-70; atty. Barry M. Scotch, Esq., Hackensack, N.J., 1970-74, Scotch Law Office, Manchester, N.H., 1974-84; atty., ptnr. Scotch & Zalinsky, Manchester, N.H., 1984—. Pres. Cystic Fibrosis Found., Manchester, 1977-78; pres., bd. dirs. Temple Adath Yeshurun, Manchester, 1986-93; judge advocate Merrimack Valley Naval League, Manchester, 1984—; sec., bd. dirs. N.H. Assn. Blind, Concord, 1982-93. Lt. comdr. USNR, 1965. Mem. ATLA, N.H. Bar Assn., N.H. Trial Lawyers Assn., Def. Rsch. Inst. Republican. Jewish. Home: 21 Garrison Dr Bedford NH 03110-5911 Office: Scotch & Zalinsky 1650 Elm St Manchester NH 03101-1217

SCOTT, A. HUGH, lawyer; b. Auckland, New Zealand, Jan. 10, 1947; came to U.S., 1957; s. John E. and Leona (Lacey) S.; m. Susan Campbell, Dec. 3, 1946; 1 child, Matthew Campbell. BA, Williams Coll., 1968; JD, Columbia U., 1974. Bar: Mass. 1974, U.S. Dist. Ct. Mass 1975, U.S. Ct. Appeals (1st cir.) 1975, U.S. Supreme Ct. 1982. Asst. U.S. atty. U.S. Atty.'s Office, Boston, 1978-83; assoc. Choate, Hall & Stewart, Boston, 1975-78, 83-85, ptnr., 1986—. Lt. (j.g.) USNR, 1968-71. Democrat. Unitarian. Home: 10 Cazenove St Boston MA 02116-6205 Office: Exchange Pl 53 State St Boston MA 02109-2804

SCOTT, A. TIMOTHY, lawyer; b. Natchez, Miss., Feb. 16, 1952; s. John William and Patricia (O'Reilly) S.; m. Nancy E. Howard, June 7, 1976; children: Kevin Howard, Brian Howard. BA in Psychology, Stanford U., 1974, JD, 1977. Bar: Calif. 1977, U.S. Tax Ct. 1978. Assoc. then ptnr. Agnew, Miller & Carlson, L.A., 1977-83; assoc. Greenberg, Glusker, Fields, Claman & Machtinger, L.A., 1983; ptnr. Sachs & Phelps, L.A., 1983-91; mem. Heller, Ehrman White & McAuliffe, L.A., 1991-96, of counsel, 1996—; sr. v.p., tax counsel Pub. Storage, Inc., Glendale, Calif., 1996—; speaker in field. Note editor Stanford Law Rev., 1976-77; contbr. article to profl. publs., chpt. to book. Mem. ABA, L.A. County Bar Assn. (chmn. real estate taxation com. 1988-91, exec. com., taxation sect. 1989-91), Order of Coif. Democrat. Avocations: volleyball, gardening, Calif. wine, contemporary art. Office: Heller Ehrman White & McAuliffe 601 S Figueroa St Fl 40 Los Angeles CA 90017-5704 Office: Pub Storage Inc 701 Western Ave Glendale CA 91201-2349

SCOTT, ADRIENNE, social worker, psychotherapist; b. N.Y.C.; d. William and Anne Scott; m. Ross F. Grumet, 1957 (div. 1969). BA, Finch Coll., 1957; postgrad., NYU, 1958-62, MA in English, 1958; MSW, Adelphi U., 1988. Mem. English faculty Fordham U., N.Y.C., 1966-68; editor Blueboy Mag., Miami, Fla., 1974, "M" Mag., N.Y.C., 1976; freelance writer N.Y.C., 1958—; mem. English faculty NYU, 1958-65; pres. Googolplex Video, N.Y.C., 1981-86; clin. social worker Mt. Sinai Hosp., N.Y.C., 1988-93, Stuyvesant Polyclinic, N.Y.C., 1993-95; presenter Nat. Methadone Conf., 1992. Author: Film as Film, 1970; contbg. editor Menstyle Mag., 1995; contbr. articles to numerous mags., including Vogue, Interview, N.Y. mag.; pioneer in fashion video; videographer documentaries; performance artist in Robert Wilson's King of Spain, 1973. Mem. exec. com. Adopt-An-AIDS Rschr. Program Rockefeller U.; nat. co-chairperson Gay Rights Nat. Lobby, 1976. Mem. NASW (cert.), AAUW (co-chmn.), Assn. for Psychoanalytic Self Psychology. Home: 165 E 66th St New York NY 10021-6132 Office: 7 Patchin Pl New York NY 10011-8341

SCOTT, ALASTAIR IAN, chemistry educator; b. Glasgow, Scotland, Apr. 10, 1928; came to U.S., 1968; s. William and Nell (Newton) S.; m. Elizabeth Wilson Walters, Mar. 4, 1950; children: William Stewart, Ann Walker. BSc, Glasgow U., 1949, PhD, 1952, DSc, 1964; MA (hon.), Yale U., 1968; DSc (hon.), U. Coimbra, Portugal, 1990, U. Pierre & Marie Curie, Paris, 1992. Lectr. organic chemistry Glasgow U., 1957-62; prof. U. B.C., Vancouver, 1962-65, Sussex (Eng.) U., 1965-68, Yale U., 1968-77; disting. prof. Tex. A&M U., 1977-80, Davidson prof. sci., 1982—; prof. dept. chemistry U. Edinburgh, Scotland, 1980-82; cons. in field. Author: Interpretations of Ultraviolet Spectra of Natural Products, 1964; contbr. articles to profl. jours. Recipient rsch. achievement award Am. Soc. Pharmacognosy, 1993. Fellow Royal Soc. (Bakerian lectr. 1996), Royal Soc. Edinburgh; mem. Am. Chem. Soc. (Ernest Guenther award 1976, A.C. Cope scholar 1992), Chem. Soc. (Corday-Morgan medal 1964, Centenary lectr. 1994, Tetrahedron prize for creativity in organic chemistry 1995, Natural Products Rsch. award 1996), Biochem. Soc., Japan Pharm. Soc. (hon.). Office: Tex A&M U Chemistry Dept College Station TX 77843

SCOTT, ALEXANDER ROBINSON, engineering association executive; b. Elizabeth, N.J., June 15, 1941; s. Marvin Chester and Jane (Robinson) S.; m. Angela Jean Kendall, July 17, 1971; children: Alexander Robinson, Jennifer Angela, Ashley Kendall. B.A. in History, Va. Mil. Inst., 1963; M.A. in Personnel and Counseling Psychology, Rutgers U., 1965. Sales mgr. Hilton Hotels, 1967-70; meetings mgr. Am. Inst. Mining Engrs., N.Y.C., 1971-73; exec. dir. Minerals, Metals and Materials Soc., 1973—. Served with U.S. Army, 1965-67. Decorated Bronze Star. Mem. Am. Soc. Assn. Execs. Republican. Baptist. Home: 107 Staghorn Dr Sewickley PA 15143-9506 Office: TMS 420 Commonwealth Dr Warrendale PA 15086-7511

SCOTT, ALICE H., librarian; b. Jefferson, Ga.; d. Frank D. and Annie D. (Colbert) Holly; m. Alphonso Scott, Mar. 1, 1959; children—Christopher, Alison. A.B., Spelman Coll., Atlanta, 1957; M.L.S., Atlanta U., 1958; Ph.D., U. Chgo., 1983. Librarian Bklyn. Pub. Library, 1958-59; br. librarian Chgo. Pub. Library, 1959-72, dir. Woodson Regional Library, 1974-77, dir. community relations, 1977-82, dep. commr., 1982-87, asst. commr., 1987—. Doctoral fellow, 1973. Mem. ALA (councilor 1982-85), Ill. Library Assn., Chgo. Spelman Club, DuSable Mus., Chgo. Urban League. Democrat. Baptist. Office: Chgo Pub Library 400 S State St Chicago IL 60605-1203

SCOTT, ALLEN JOHN, public policy and geography educator; b. Liverpool, England, Dec. 23, 1938; came to U.S., 1980; s. William Rule and Nella Maria (Pieri) S.; m. Nga Thuy Nguyen, Jan. 19, 1979. BA, Oxford (Eng.) U., 1961; PhD, Northwestern U., 1965. Prof. geography UCLA, 1980—, dir. Lewis Ctr. for Regional Policy Studies, 1990-94, assoc. dean Sch. Pub. Policy and Social Rsch., 1994-97; Professeur associé U. Paris, 1974. Author: Combinatorial Programming, 1971, Urban Land Nexus, 1980, Metropolis, 1988, New Industrial Spaces, 1988, Technopolis, 1993. Fellow Com. on Scholarly Communication with People's Republic China, 1986. Croucher fellow U. Hong Kong, 1984; Guggenheim fellow, 1986-87. Office: UCLA Sch Pub Policy/Social Rsch Los Angeles CA 90095

SCOTT, ANDREW, retired corporate executive; b. St. Paul, Apr. 5, 1928; s. Ulric and Annamay (Gorry) S.; m. Kathleen Kennedy, May 7, 1960; children: Andrea Kennedy Scott, Lucia Scott Duff. BS, U. Minn., 1950, LLB, 1952. Bar: Minn. 1952. Ptnr. Doherty, Rumble & Butler, Mpls. and St. Paul, 1952-77; chmn. Andrew Scott Ltd., Mpls., 1978-81; founder, vice chmn. Cray Rsch. Inc., Mpls., 1972-93, also bd. dirs. Bd. dirs. Minn. Orchestral Assn., Mpls., 1961-78, First Trust Co., Inc., St. Paul, 1981-90; trustee Mpls. Soc. Fine Arts, 1966-78, Twin City Area Pub. TV Corp., St. Paul, 1967-74, St. Paul Acad./Summit Sch., 1972-75. Roman Catholic. Avocations: gardening, tai chi, megalithic cave art, skiing, zazen. Home: Winslow House 100 SE 2nd St Minneapolis MN 55414-2129 also: The Rookery 1370 Hwy 61E Little Marais MN 55614

SCOTT, ANNA MARIE PORTER WALL, sociology educator; b. South Fulton, Tenn.; d. Thomas Madison and Jevvie Roggie (Patton) P.; m. John T. Scott Sr. (dec.); 1 child, Harvey G. BA, U. Ill., MEd, MSW. Cert. tchr. and social worker, Ill. Caseworker Dept. Pub. Aid, Champaign, Ill., 1961-63; psychiat. social worker Vets. Hosp., Danville, Ill., 1964-68; prof. sociology Parkland Coll., Champaign, Ill., 1968—. Mem. Dem. Ctrl. Com., 1974-78; head Dem. 21st Congl. Dist., 1974-78; del. Nominating Conv./Mini Conv., 1975, 76; vol. Nominating Com., 1988; commr. Ill. Banking Bd.; mem. AME Ch., Hadassah; mem. Vet. of Armed Svcs. Named Outstanding Black Alumni, U. Ill., Urbana, 1977. Mem. LWV, NAACP, Nat. Coun. Negro Women (past pres.), Am. Legion (post adjutant), AMVETS, Champaign-Urbana Symphony Guild, Order Ea. Star (grand organist Eureka Grand chpt.). Avocations: pub. speaking, piano, baking, gardening, politics. Home: 309 W Michigan Ave Urbana IL 61801-4945 Office: Parkland Coll 2400 W Bradley Ave Champaign IL 61821-1806

SCOTT, ANNE BYRD FIROR, history educator; b. Montezuma, Ga., Apr. 24, 1921; d. John William and Mary Valentine (Moss) Firor; m. Andrew Mackay Scott, June 2, 1947; children: Rebecca, David MacKay, Donald MacKay. AB, U. Ga., 1941; MA, Northwestern U., 1944; PhD, Radcliffe Coll., 1958; LHD (hon.), Lindenwood Coll., 1968, Queens Coll., 1985, Northwestern U., 1989, Radcliffe Coll., 1990, U. of the South, 1990, Cornell Coll., 1991. Congressional rep., editor LWV of U.S., 1944-53; lectr. history Haverford Coll., 1957-58, U. N.C., Chapel Hill, 1959-60; asst. prof. history Duke U., Durham, N.C., 1961-67; assoc. prof. Duke U., 1968-70, prof., 1971-80, W.K. Boyd prof., 1980-91, W.K. Boyd prof. emerita, 1992—, chmn. dept., 1981-85; Gastprofessor Universität, Bonn, Germany, 1992-93; vis. prof. Johns Hopkins U., 1972-73, Stanford U., 1974, Harvard U., 1984, Cornell U., 1993, Williams Coll., 1994; Times-Mirror scholar Huntington Libr., 1995; vice chmn. Nat. Humanities Ctr., 1991—; mem. adv. com. Schlesinger Libr.; Fulbright lectr., 1984, 92-93. Author: The Southern Lady, 1970, 25th anniversary edit., 1995, (with Andrew MacKay Scott) One Half the People, 1974, Making the Invisible Woman Visible, 1984, Natural Allies, 1991; editor: Jane Addams, Democracy and Social Ethics, 1964, The American woman, 1970, Women in American Life, 1970, Women and Men in American Life, 1976, Unheard Voices, 1993; mem. editl. bd. Revs. in Am. History, 1976-81, Am. Quar., 1974-78, Jour. So. History, 1978-84; contbr. articles to profl. jours. Chmn. Gov.'s Commn. on Status of Women, 1963-64; mem. Citizens Adv. Council on Status of Women U.S., 1964-68; trustee Carnegie Corp., 1977-85, W.W. Ctr. for Scholars, 1977-84; chmn. bd. dirs. Nat. Cmty. Investment Fund, 1996—. AAUW fellow, 1956-57; grantee NEH, 1967-68, 76-77, Nat. Humanities Ctr., 1980-81; grad. medal Radcliffe Coll., 1986, Duke U. medal, 1991, John Caldwell medal N.C. Humanities Coun., 1994; fellow Ctrl. Advanced Study in Behavioral Sci., 1986-87; Fulbright scholar, 1984, 92-93. Mem. Am. Antiquarian Soc., Orgn. Am. Historians (exec. bd. 1973-76, pres. 1983), So. Hist. Assn. (exec. bd. 1976-79, pres. 1989), Soc. Am. Historians, Phi Beta Kappa. Democrat. Office: Duke U Dept History Durham NC 27708

SCOTT, BILL, advertising agency executive; b. Phila., Sept. 1, 1949; s. Norris A. and Jean (Satterthwaite) S. BA in Writing, West Chester U., 1971; BS in Radio-TV-Film, Temple U., Phila., 1974. Advt. coord. S.M.S., Malvern, Pa., 1978-81; dir. pub. rels. Thomas R. Sundheim Inc., Jenkintown, Pa., 1981-88; v.p., creative dir. Kingswood Advt., Inc., Ardmore, Pa., 1988—; cons. Yonex USA, Torrance, Calif., 1990—, Peco Energy Corp., Phila. Author: Chinese Kung-Fu, 1976; creator, writer comic strip Latchkids, 1995—. Republican. Avocations: tennis, running, weightlifting, writing. Home: 77 Croton Rd Strafford PA 19087-2663 Office: Kingswood Advt Inc Cricket Ter Ardmore PA 19003

SCOTT, CAMPBELL, artist; b. Milngavie, Scotland, Oct. 5, 1930; s. Robert and Catherine S. Apprentice woodcarver, Glasgow, Scotland, 1946-51; student, Royal Acad. Art, Copenhagen, 1965-66; studies with, S.W. Hayter, Paris, 1966. Exhbns. include 1st Biennial Internat. Graphics, Krakow, Poland, 1966, 1st Brit. Internat. Prin Biennale, Eng., 1969, traveling exhbn., Nat. Gallery Can., Ottawa, 1969, 4th Am. Biennial Engraving, Santiago, Chile, Can. Embassy, Washington, 1971, Pratt Inst., N.Y.C., 1971; represented in permanent collections, Brit. Mus., Bibliotheque Nat., Paris, Scottish Nat. Gallery Modern Art, Montreal Mus. Art, Victoria and Albert Mus., London, Art Gallery of Ont., Toronto, Can., Hart House Collection, U. Toronto; commd. works include: bronze sculpture, Pub. Libr. Niagara Falls, Can., wood sculpture, Pub. Libr., St. Catharines, Can.; mural, The Pumphouse Art Ctr. Niagara on the Lake, Can. Mem. Print and Drawing Council Can. Address: 89 Byron, Niagara on the Lake, ON Canada L0S 1J0

SCOTT, CATHERINE DOROTHY, librarian, information consultant; b. Washington, June 21, 1927; d. Leroy Stearns Scott and Agnes Frances (Meade) Scott Schellenberg. AB in English, Cath. U. Am., 1950, MS in Library Sci., 1955. Asst. Librarian Export-Import Bank U.S.A., Washington, 1951-55; asst. librarian Nat. Assn. Home Builders, 1955-62, reference librarian, 1956-62; founder, chief tech. librarian, Bellcomm, Inc., subs. AT&T, Washington, 1962-72; chief librarian Nat. Air and Space Mus., Smithsonian Instn., Washington, 1972-82, chief librarian Mus. Reference Ctr., 1982-88, sr. reference librarian, 1989-95; info. cons., 1995—; bd. visitors Cath. U. Am. Library Sci. Sch. and Libraries, 1984-93; apptd. by Pres., mem. Nat. Commn. Libraries and Info. Sci., 1971-76. Editor International Handbook of Aerospace Awards and Trophies, 1980, 81; guest editor Aeronautics and Space Flight Collections, 1985, in Spl. Collections, 1984. Vice-chmn. D.C. Rep. Com., 1960-68; mem. platform com. Rep. Nat. Com., 1964, sec., 1968; del. Rep. Nat. Conv., San Francisco, 1964, Miami, Fla., 1968. Recipient Sec.'s Disting. Service award Smithsonian Instn., 1976, Alumni Achievement award Cath. U. Am., 1977, Disting. Fed. Svc. Nat. Commn. Libr. and Info. Sci. medal, 1985. Mem. Spl. Librs. Assn. (pres. Washington chpt. 1973-74, cons. 1976-89, chmn. cons. com. 1994—, chmn. aerospace div. 1980-81, aerospace divsn. 30th anniversary com. 1995, Disting. Svc. award 1982, 96, 97, Mem. of Yr. Washington chpt. 1994, nat. dir. 1986-89, bd. dirs. 1986-89, 91-94, Washington chpt. awards com. 1990-91, assn. pres.-elect 1991-92, pres. 1992-93, immediate past pres. 1993-94, chair assn. awards and honors 1994-95, Hall of Fame award 1996), Am. Soc. Assn. Execs. (internat. roundtable), Internat. Fedn. Library Assns. (del. 1976, 83, 85, 88, 89), Friends of Cath. U. Libraries (founder, pres. 1984-88, exec. coun. 1984—), Nat. Fedn. Rep. Women, League Rep. Women D.C. (dir. mem. 1995—, mem. nominating com. 1996—), Capital Yacht Club (Washington). Roman Catholic.

SCOTT, CHARLES DAVID, chemical engineer, consultant; b. Chaffee, Mo., Oct. 24, 1929; s. Charles Perry and Alma Gertrude (Kendall) S.; m. Alice Reba Bardill, Feb. 11, 1956; children—Timothy Charles, Mary Alice, Lisa Ann. B.S. in Chem. Engring., U. Mo., 1951; M.S. in Chem. Engring., U. Tenn., 1961, Ph.D., 1966. Registered profl. engr., Tenn. Devel. engr. Union Carbide Corp., Oak Ridge, 1953-57; research engr. Oak Ridge Nat. Lab., 1957-73, sect. chief, 1973-76, assoc. div. dir., 1976-83, research fellow, 1983-86, sr. research fellow, 1987-94; dir. bioprocessing rsch. and devel. ctr., 1991-94; engring. R & D cons., Oak Ridge, 1994—; adj. prof. chem. engring. U. Tenn., Knoxville. Served to 1st lt. AUS, 1951-53. Recipient U.S. Dept. Energy E.O. Lawrence award, 1980, U. Tenn. Nathan W. Doughtery award, 1987, U. Mo. Honor award, 1988, David Perlman award Am. Chem. Soc., 1994; Union Carbide Corp. fellow, 1983; Martin Marietta Sr. Corp. fellow, 1987. Mem. AAAS, Am. Chem. Soc. (chmn. separation sci. subdiv.), Am. Assn. Clin. Chemistry (chmn. com. advanced analytical concepts, nat. award 1980), Am. Inst. Chem. Engrs. (bd. dirs.), Nat. Acad. Engring., Sigma Xi, Alpha Chi Sigma. Lutheran. Contbr. articles to profl. jours.; patentee in field.

SCOTT, CHARLES FRANCIS, health facility administrator; b. Phila., Mar. 21, 1950; married. BS, Princeton U., 1972; M in Bus. Adminstrn., U. Chgo., 1975. Diplomate Am. Coll. Health Care Execs. Adminstrv. intern Med. Coll. Pa. and Hosp., Phila., 1974; adminstrv. asst. Reading (Pa.) Hosp. & Med. Ctr., 1975-78; asst. adminstr. ops. Mercy Hosp., Council Bluffs, Iowa, 1979-82; assoc. exec. dir. ops. Tampa (Fla.) Gen. Hosp., 1982-84; v.p. St. Joseph's Hosp., Tampa, 1984-88, COO, adminstr., 1988-94, pres. hosp. ops., 1994—. Office: St Josephs Hosp 3001 W Martin King Luther Tampa FL 33677-4227

SCOTT, CHARLES LEWIS, photojournalist; b. Grayville, Ill., Aug. 18, 1924; s. Marvin Joseph and Prudence (Blood) S.; m. Jane Turner, Jan. 14, 1945 (dec. 1983); children—Lyntha Ann, Thomas Marvin; m. Martha McDonald, Aug. 23, 1986. B.S. in Journalism, U. Ill., 1948; M.S., Ohio U., 1970. Photographer Champaign-Urbana (Ill.) Courier, 1946-50, chief photographer, 1953-56; photographer Ill. Natural History Survey, 1946-51, Binghamton (N.Y.) Press, 1951-53; asst. picture editor Milw. Jour., 1956-58; picture editor, 1958-66; graphics dir. Chgo. Daily News, 1966-69; instr. Sch. Journalism, Ohio U., Athens, 1969-70; asst. prof. Sch. Journalism, Ohio U., 1971-72, asso. prof., 1972-74, 76-77, prof., 1977—; dir. Sch. Visual Communication, 1978-95; picture editor Chgo. Tribune, 1974-76; dir. photography Rocky Mountain News, Denver, 1987-88; ret., 1995. Served with U.S. Navy, 1942-45. Decorated D.F.C., Air medal (3); recipient numerous awards in regional and nat. news photo contests. Mem. Nat. Press Photographers Assn. (charter mem., Newspaper Photographer of Yr. 1952, Editor of Yr. 1966, Joseph Sprague Meml. award 1975, Robin F. Garland Educator award 1979), Soc. Profl. Journalists, Ohio News Photographers Assn. (Lifetime Achievement award 1995). Presbyterian. Home: 8559 Lavelle Rd Athens OH 45701-9190

SCOTT, CHARLOTTE H., business educator; b. Yonkers, N.Y., Mar. 18, 1925; d. Edgar B. and Charlotte Agnes (Palmer) Hanley; m. Nathan Alexander Scott, Jr., Dec. 21, 1946; children: Nathan Alexander Scott, Leslie Kristin Scott Ashamu. A.B., Barnard Coll., 1947; postgrad., Am. U., 1949-53; M.B.A., U. Chgo., 1964; LL.D., Allegheny Coll., 1981. Research asso. Nat. Bur. Econ. Research, N.Y.C., 1947-48; economist R.W. Goldsmith Assos., Washington, 1948-55, U. Chgo., 1955-56, Fed. Res. Bank, Chgo., 1956-71; asst. v.p. Fed. Res. Bank, 1971-76; prof. bus. adminstrn. and commerce, sr. fellow Tayloe Murphy Inst., U. Va., Charlottesville, 1976-86; prof. commerce and edn. U. Va., Charlottesville, 1986—; bd. dirs. Atlantic Rural Expn., Inc.; mem. adv. bd. NationsBank Charlottesville, 1991-93; mem. nat. adv. bd. coun. SBA, 1979-82; mem. consumer adv. coun. bd. govs. FRS, 1979-82, vice chmn., 1980-81, chmn., 1981-82. Mem. editorial bd. Jour. Retail Banking, 1978-85, Jour. Internat. Assn. Personnel Women, 1981-85; contbr. articles to profl. jours. Pres. women's bd. Chgo. Urban League, 1967-69; mem. Va. Commn. on Status of Women, 1982-85, Gov.'s Commn. on Va.'s Future, 1982-85, Gov.'s Commn. on Efficiency in Govt., 1985-87; treas. Va. Women's Cultural History Project, 1982-85; bd. dirs. Boys and Girls Club of Charlotteville/Albemarle; governing bd. Charlottesville/Albemarle Found., 1993—; mem. adv. bd. Ash Lawn-Highland Mus. Mem. Internat. Assn. Personnel Women (v.p. mems.-at-large 1980-82), Am. Edn. Fin. Assn., Va. Assn. Econs., Acad. Mgmt., Barnard Coll./Columbia U. Alumnae Assn. (bd. dirs. 1977-81, trustee 1977-81). Episcopalian. Home: 1419 Hilltop Rd Charlottesville VA 22903-1226 Office: U Va McIntire Sch Commerce Monroe Hall Charlottesville VA 22903

SCOTT, DALE ALLAN, major league umpire; b. Springfield, Oreg., Aug. 14, 1959; s. Jesse Lee and Betty Ann (Potts) S. AS, Lane C.C., 1979. Radio disc jockey Sta. KBDF, Eugene, Oreg., 1976-81; minor league umpire various orgns., 1981-85; umpire Am. League, 1986—; ofcl. H.S. basketball Portland Basketball Ofcls. Assn., 1986-96; ofcl. H.S. football Portland Football Ofcls. Assn., 1989—; instr. Golden State Umpire Camp, 1991—. Democrat. Office: Am League Profl Baseball 350 Park Ave New York NY 10022-6022

SCOTT, DARREL JOSEPH, healthcare executive; b. Indpls., Sept. 12, 1947; s. Hubert Norris and Beverly June (Hiatt) S.; m. Janice L. Meredith, June 21, 1969; children: Andrew, Brennan. BA, Ind. U., 1969, MHA with high honors, 1971; JD, U. Louisville, 1990. Planning assoc. Ind. Hosp. Assn., Indpls., 1970-72; asst. dir. Welborn Bapt. Hosp., Evansville, Ind., 1972-77, AMA, Chgo., 1977-78; pres., chief exec. officer King's Daus. Hosp., Madison, Ind., 1978-90; v.p. legal svcs. Sisters St. Francis Health Svcs., Mishawaka, Ind., 1990-94, sr. v.p. corp. affairs, 1994—; mem. Ind. Emergency Med. Services Commn., 1974-75. Bd. dirs. Jefferson County United Way, 1979-85; chair coms. Trinity United Methodist Ch., Madison, 1982, Clay United Meth. Ch., 1992-95. Fellow Am. Coll. Healthcare Execs. Republican. Home: 51563 Fox Pointe Ln Granger IN 46530-8473 Office: Srs of St Francis Hlth Servs PO Box 1290 Mishawaka IN 46546-1290

SCOTT, DAVID KNIGHT, physicist, university administrator; b. North Ronaldsay, Scotland, Mar. 2, 1940; married, 1966; 3 children. BSc, Edinburgh U., 1962; DPhil in Nuclear Physics, Oxford U., 1967. Rsch. officer nuclear physics lab. Oxford U., 1970-73; rsch. fellow nuclear physics Balliol Coll., 1967-70, sr. rsch. fellow, 1970-73; physicist Lawrence Berkeley Lab. U. Calif., 1973-75, sr. scientist nuclear sci., 1975-79; prof. physics, astronomy and chemistry Nat. Superconducting Cyclotron Lab. Mich. State U., East Lansing, 1979-93; Hannah disting. prof. physics, astronomy and chemistry Mich. State U., East Lansing, 1979-86, assoc. provost, 1983-86, provost, v.p. acad. affairs, 1986-92; Hannah Disting. prof. learning, sci. and soc. Nat. Superconducting Cyclotron Lab. Mich. State U., East Lansing, 1992-93; chancellor U. Mass., Amherst, 1993—. Fellow Am. Phys. Soc. Office: U Mass Office of Chancellor 374 Whitmore Adminstrn Bldg Amherst MA 01003

SCOTT, DAVID MICHAEL, pharmacy educator; b. St. Paul, July 5, 1949; s. David Marvin and Cecelia (Ventura) S.; m. Patti L. Anderson, May 1, 1976; children: Michael, Justin, Nathan. BS, U. Minn., 1972, MPH, 1982, PhD, 1987. Lic. pharmacist, Minn. Pharmacy intern United Hosps., St. Paul, 1972-73, staff pharmacist, 1973-75; pharmacy dir. Cmty.-Univ. Health Care Ctr., Mpls., 1975-84; clin. instr. pharmacy U. Minn., Mpls., 1975-86; assoc. dir. orthop. rsch. St. Paul Ramsey Med. Ctr., 1984-86; assoc. prof. U. Nebr. Med. Ctr., Omaha, 1986—; project epidemiologist Toward a Drug-Free Nebr., Nebr. Dept. Edn., Lincoln, 1989-94; mem. Springville Elem. Sch. Drug Abuse, Omaha, 1988-97; faculty advisor Acad. Student Pharmacists, Omaha, 1994—. Contbr. articles to sci. jours. Coach Keystone Little League, Omaha, 1991-94; bd. dirs. Butler-Gast YMCA, Omaha, 1992-96; vice chmn. bd. dirs., 1994-95; chmn. Nebr. PACT (Pulling Am. Cmtys. Together) Sch. Truancy Task Force, Lincoln, 1994-97. Grantee Am. Assn. Colls. Pharmacy, Alexandria, Va., 1995-97, U.S. Dept. Edn., Washington, 1996-97. Mem. APHA (mem. program com. 1991-93), Am. Ednl. Rsch. Assn., Nat. Assn. Retail Pharmacists (faculty liaison 1987—), Am. Assn. Colls. of Pharmacy (mem. program com. 1990-92, grant 1995-97), Internat. Soc. Pharmacoepidemiology (mem. program com. 1992-97). Avocations: jogging, softball, golf, reading, children's sports. Home: 5305 Raven Oaks Dr Omaha NE 68152-1750 Office: U Nebr Med Ctr Coll Pharmcy 600 S 42nd St Omaha NE 68198-1002

SCOTT, DAVID RODICK, lawyer, legal educator; b. Phila., Dec. 30, 1938; s. Ernest and Lydia Wister (tunis) S.; m. Ruth Erskine Wardle, Aug. 20, 1966; children: Cintra W., D. Rodman. AB magna cum laude, Harvard U., 1960, JD, 1965; MA, Cambridge U., 1962. Bar: Pa. 1966, D.C. 1977, U.S. Dist. Ct. (ea. dist.) Pa. 1966, U.S. Ct. Appeals (3rd cir.) 1966, U.S. Ct. Appeals (D.C. cir.) 1977, U.S. Supreme Ct. 1977. Law clk. to assoc. justice Supreme Ct. Pa., Phila., 1965-66; assoc. Pepper, Hamilton & Scheetz, Phila., 1966-69, 72-76; asst. dist. atty. City of Phila., 1970-72; sr. trial atty. criminal div. U.S. Dept. Justice, Washington, 1976-80; chief counsel, acting dir. Office Govt. Ethics, Washington, 1980-84; univ. counsel Rutgers U., New Brunswick, N.J., 1984—; acting dir. U.S. Office Govt. Ethics, 1982-83; tchr., lectr. in law Cath. U. Am., Washington, 1977-81, Inst. Paralegal Tng., Phila., 1970-74; lectr. in field. Contbr. chpts. to textbooks, articles to profl. jours. Trustee United Way Greater Mercer County, 1990—, Princeton Area Cmty. Found., Inc.; bd. mgrs. Episc. Acad., Merion, Pa., 1970-74. Keasbey Found. fellow, 1960-62. Mem ABA, Pa. Bar Assn., Nat. Assn. Coll. and Univ. Attys. (bd. dirs. 1993-96), Am. Friends Cambridge U. (head N.J. chpt. 1987-93). Home: 255 Russell Rd Princeton NJ 08540-6733 Office: Rutgers U Office of Univ Counsel Winants Hall New Brunswick NJ 08901

SCOTT, DAVID WARREN, statistics educator; b. Oak Park, Ill., July 16, 1950; s. John V. and Nancy (Mellers) S.; m. Jean Charlotte Madera, June 15, 1974; children: Hilary Kathryn, Elizabeth Alison, Warren Robert. BA, Rice U., 1972, MA, 1976, PhD, 1976. Asst. prof. Baylor Coll. Medicine, Houston, 1976-79; asst. prof. Rice U., Houston, 1979-80, assoc. prof., 1980-85, chmn. statistics dept., 1990-93; vis. prof. Stanford U., Palo Alto, Calif., 1985-86; vis. prof. Dept. Def., Ft. Meade, Md., 1993-94. Co-editor: jour. Computational Stats. and jour. Stat. Scis.; contbr. articles to profl. publs.; author: Multivariate Density Estimation, 1992. Grantee NASA, 1982-84, Office Naval Rsch., 1985-93, NSF, 1993—. Fellow Internat. Stats. Inst., Inst. Math. Stats., Am. Statis. Assn.; mem. Am. Status Soc. (assoc. editor jour. 1983-94), Inst. Math. Statis. (cons.). Avocations: woodworking, hiking, family. Home: 4143 Marlowe St Houston TX 77005-1953 Office: Rice U Dept Stats 6100 Main St # 138 Houston TX 77005-1827

SCOTT, DEBORAH EMONT, curator; b. Passaic, N.J.; d. Rhoda (Baumgarten) Emont; m. George Andrew Scott, June 4, 1983; children: Meredith Suzanne, Diana Faith. BA, Rutgers U., 1973; MA, Oberlin Coll., 1979. Asst. curator Allen Meml. Art Mus., Oberlin, Ohio, 1977-79; curator collections Memphis Brooks Mus. Art, 1979-83; curator The Nelson-Atkins Mus. Art, Kansas City, 1983—; project dir. Kansas City Sculpture Pk., 1986—. Author: (catalogue) Alan Shields, 1983, (essay) Jonathan Borofsky, 1988, (essay) Judith Shea, 1989, (interview) John Ahearn, 1990, (essay) Gerhard Richter, 1990, (essay) Kathy Muehlemann, 1991, (essay) Nate Fors, 1991, (essay) Julian Schnabel, 1991, (essay) Louise Bourgeois, 1994, (essay) Joel Shapiro, 1995, (essay) Lewis deSoto, 1996. Office: Nelson-Atkins Mus Art 4525 Oak St Kansas City MO 64111-1818

SCOTT, DONALD ALLISON, lawyer; b. Phila., Oct. 7, 1929; s. Garfield and Grace Louise (Nevin) S.; m. Jeanne Marie Cooper, June 25, 1955; children: Allison Cooper, Andrew Garfield, John Wallace, Lindsay Nevin. A.B., Princeton U., 1951; J.D., Harvard U., 1956. Bar: Pa. 1958. Law clk. Judge Learned Hand, U.S. Ct. Appeals, 2d Circuit, 1956-57; assoc. Morgan, Lewis & Bockius, LLP, Phila., 1957-64, ptnr., 1964—. Served with USNR, 1951-53. Mem. ABA, Pa. Bar Assn., Phila. Bar Assn., Am. Law Inst., Merion Cricket Club, Paupack Hills Golf Club. Presbyterian. Home: 714 W Mt Airy Ave Philadelphia PA 19119-3326 Office: Morgan Lewis & Bockius LLP 2000 One Logan Sq Philadelphia PA 19103

SCOTT, DONALD MICHAEL, educational association administrator, educator; b. L.A., Sept. 26, 1943; s. Bernard Hendry and Barbara (Lannin) S.; m. Patricia Ilene Pancoast, Oct. 24, 1964 (div. June 1971); children: William Bernard, Kenneth George. BA, San Francisco State U., 1965, MA, 1986. Cert. tchr. Calif. Tchr. Mercy High Sch., San Francisco, 1968-71; park ranger Calif. State Park System, Half Moon Bay, 1968-77; tchr. adult div. Jefferson Union High Sch. Dist., Daly City, Calif., 1973-87; dir. NASA-NPS Project Wider Focus, Daly City, 1983-90; dir. Geo.S. Spl. Projects Wider Focus, San Francisco, 1990—; also bd. dirs. Wider Focus, Daly City; nat. park ranger/naturalist Grant-Kohrs Ranch Nat. Hist. Site, Deer Lodge, Mont., 1987-88; nat. park ranger pub. affairs fire team Yellowstone Nat. Park, 1988; nat. park ranger Golden Gate Recreation Area, 1988-92; rsch. subject NASA, Mountain View, Calif., 1986-90; guest artist Yosemite (Calif.) Nat. Park, 1986; nat. park ranger Golden Gate Nat. Recreation Area, Nat. Park Svc., San Francisco, 1986, nat. park svc. history cons. to Bay Dist., 1988-94; adj. asst. prof. Skyline Coll., 1989-94, Coll. San Mateo, 1992-94; aerospace edn. specialist NASA/OSU/AESP, 1994—. Contbr. articles, photographs to profl. jours., mags. Pres. Youth for Kennedy, Lafayette, calif., 1960; panelist Community Bds. of San Francisco, 1978-87; city chair Yes on A com., So. San Francisco, San Mateo County, Calif., 1986; active CONTACT Orgn., 1991—, bd. dirs. 1995—. Mem. Yosemite Assn. (life), Wider Focus, Friends of George R. Stewart, Nat. Sci. Tchrs. Assn., Nat. Coun. of Tchrs. of Math., Internat. Tech. Edn. Assn., Smithsonian Air and Space (charter mem.), Planetary Soc. (charter mem.), Indep. Scholar, 1982—. Democrat. Avocations: photography, hiking, camping, travel. Home and Office: MS 253-2 NASA Ames Rsch Ctr Moffett Field CA 94035-1000

SCOTT, EDWARD PHILIP, lawyer; b. Somers Point, N.J., Dec. 17, 1937; s. Harry Edward and Gladys Louise (Atkinson) s.; m. Jane Anne Wilby, June 6, 1961; children: Young-Joon, Edward P. Jr., Lauren, Tracey. BA, Rutgers U., 1959; JD, U. Pa., 1963. Bar: N.J. 1963, D.C. 1968. Assoc. Arnold & Porter, Washington, 1967-68; atty./advisor Peace Corps, Washington, 1968-69, dep. gen. counsel, 1970; dep. dir. Peace Corps, Seoul, Korea, 1971-72; dir. Peace Corps, Korea, 1972-73; staff atty. Mental Health Law Project, Washington, 1973-77; minority gen. counsel U.S. Senate Com Vets. Affairs, Washington, 1981-86, gen. counsel, 1977-80, 87-90; chief counsel, staff dir. U.S. Senate on Com. Vets. Affairs, Washington, 1990-93; asst. sec. for Congressional affairs Dept. Vets. Affairs, Washington, 1993—; legis. asst. Sen. Alan Cranston, D.C. 1981-88. Author: Mental Health Issues in State Law, 1976. Capt. USAF, 1964-67. Mem. ABA, D.C. Bar Assn., Audubon Naturalist Soc., Montgomery County Road Runners. Democrat. Avocations: running, birding, scuba diving. Home: 3703 Inverness Dr Chevy Chase MD 20815-5660 Office: Dept Vets Affairs Asst Sec Congl Affairs 810 Vermont Ave NW Washington DC 20420-0001

SCOTT, EDWARD WILLIAM, JR., computer software company executive; b. Panama City, Panama, May 25, 1938; s. Edward William and Janice Gertrude (Grimison) S.; m. Cheryl S. Gilliland, apr. 23, 1988; children: Edward William, Heather Yolanda Deirdre, Reece Donald. BA, Mich. State U., 1959, MA, 1963; BA, Oxford (Eng.) U., 1962. Personnel specialist Panama Canal Co., 1962-64, staff asst. to dir. personnel, 1964-66; personnel officer IRS, Detroit, 1966-68; staff personnel mgmt. specialist U.S. Dept. Justice, Washington, 1968-69; chief personnel systems and evaluation sect. U.S. Dept. Justice, 1970-72; dir. U.S. Dept. Justice (Office Mgmt. Programs), 1972-74; asso. dep. commr. planning and evaluation U.S. Dept. Justice (U.S. Immigration and Naturalization Service), 1974-75, dep. asst. atty. gen. adminstrn., 1972-75; asst. sec. for adminstrn. (Transp. Dept.), 1977-80; pres. Office Power, Inc., Washington, 1980-81; dir. mktg. Computer Consoles, Inc., 1981-84; v.p. mktg. Dest Systems, 1984-85; dir. govt. mktg. Sun Microsystems, Mountain View, Calif., 1985-88; exec. v.p. Pyramid Tech., Mountain View, 1988-95; founder, exec. v.p. worldwide ops. BEA Sys., Inc., Sunnyvale, Calif., 1995—; pres. U.S. Dept. Justice Fed. Credit Union, 1970-73. Recipient Presdl. Mgmt. Improvement certificate, 1971; Spl. Commendation award Dept. Justice, 1973; also Spl. Achievement award, 1976; William A. Jump Meml. award, 1974; presdl. sr. exec. service rank of Disting. Exec., 1980; Mich. State U. scholar, 1957-60. Mem. Phi Eta Sigma, Phi Kappa Phi. Democrat. Office: BEA Sys Inc 385 Moffett Park Dr Sunnyvale CA 94089-1214

SCOTT, EUGENIE CAROL, science foundation director, anthropologist; b. LaCrosse, Wis., Oct. 24, 1945; d. Allen K. and Virginia Meliss (Derr) S.; m. Robert Abner Black, Oct. 18, 1965 (div. 1970); m. Thomas Charles Sager, Dec. 30, 1971; 1 child, Carrie Ellen Sager. BS, U. Wis., Milw., 1967, MS, 1968; PhD, U. Mo., 1974. Asst. prof. anthropology U. Ky., Lexington, 1974-82; postdoctoral fellow U. Calif., San Francisco, 1983-84; asst. prof. U. Colo., Boulder, 1984-86; exec. dir., pub. newsletter NCSE Reports, Nat. Ctr. Sci. Edn., Berkeley, Calif., 1987—; bd. dirs. Nat. Pub. Edn. and Religious Liberty, Washington; pub. Bookwatch Revs., 1988-92. Author, editor: Biology Textbooks, The New Generation, 1990; prodr. videotape series How Scientists Know About...; featured guest as sci. authority on creationism and/or pseudosci. Recipient Disting. Alumnus award U. Mo. Arts & Scis., 1993. Fellow Com. for Sci. Investigation Claims of Paranormal (Sci. and Edn. award 1991), Calif. Acad. Scis. (elected 1994); mem. Am. Assn. Phys. Anthropology (bd. dirs., exec. com. 1988-93, sec.-treas. 1993-97). Office: Nat Ctr Sci Edn PO Box 9477 Berkeley CA 94709-0477

SCOTT, FRED DACON, surgeon; b. Folsom, Calif., Mar. 12, 1962; s. Winfield Morrill and LaRee (Taggart) S.; m. Deborah Lynn Weese, May 16, 1986; children: Emily Diane, Dacon Spencer, Andrew Tucker, Peter Allen. BS in Biology, Phillips U., Enid, Okla., 1986; DO, Okla. State U., Tulsa, 1990. Diplomate Nat. Bd. Osteo. Med. Examiners. Intern Mt. Clemens (Mich.) Gen. Hosp., 1990-91, resident in gen. surgery, 1991-95, chief resident in gen. surgery, 1994; mem. gen. surgery staff Passavant Area Hosp., Jacksonville, Ill., 1995-97; second counselor to bishop, 1997—. Stake missionary Ch. of Jesus Christ of Latterday Saints, 1992-96, Sunday Sch. tchr., 1991-96, deacon, tchrs. quorums instr., 1986-89, elders quorum/1st counselor, sec., 1989-90, 92-95, 2d counselor to bishop, 1997; mem. U.S. rifle team U.S. Olympic Com., 1980-81. Named to Outstanding Young Men of Am., 1988; named All-Am. Coll. Rifle, NRA, 1981. Mem. AMA, Am. Osteo. Assn., Ill. Med. Assn., Ill. Assn. Osteo. Physicians and Surgeons, Morgan-Scott County Med. Soc., Atlas Frat. Republican. Avocations: gardening, bonsai, photography, camping. Home: 2 Collins Pl Jacksonville IL 62650-1032 Office: Passavant Area Hosp 800 W State St Jacksonville IL 62650-1910

SCOTT, FREDERICK ISADORE, JR., editor, business executive; b. Balt., Oct. 27, 1927; s. Frederick Isadore and Rebecca Esther (Waller) S.; m. Viola Fowlkes, Feb. 4, 1949. B.E. in Chem. Engring, Johns Hopkins, 1950; M.S. in Mgmt. Engring, Newark Coll. Engring., 1956. Chem. process engr. in research and devel. RCA, Harrison, N.J., 1951-59; with Kearfott div. Gen. Precision Aerospace, Little Falls, N.J., 1960-62; asst. sales mgr. Isotopes, Inc., Westwood, N.J., 1964-66; mgr. capacitor sect. Wellington Electronics, Inc., Englewood, N.J., 1967-68; owner F.I. Scott & Assos. (med. equipment), Montclair, N.J., 1968-80; tech. product mktg. and editorial svcs. F.I. scott & Assocs., Check, Va., 1980-86; editor instrumentation publ. Am. Lab. and Internat. Lab., Fairfield, Conn., 1968-80, cons. editor, 1980—; pres. Group Tech., Ltd., 1979—; editor Am. Clin. Lab., 1990—. Served with AUS, 1946-47. Mem. Am. Chem. Soc. (sr.), AAAS, N.Y. Acad. Sci., IEEE (editor newsletter No. N.J. sect. 1957-58, chmn. publs. com. 1958-59), N.Y. Micros. Soc. Home and Office: 1 E Chase St Apt 410 Baltimore MD 21202-2557 *Perhaps the most significant aspect of my life is a long-felt realization that each person is ultimately responsible for his or her condition in life. Application of this principle continually requires that the individual assess a failure in such a way as to determine how his or her actions might have avoided it or, if unavoidable, how its recurrence can be obviated. Accepting responsibility in this manner can, I believe, lead the way toward a society based on a federation of autonomous individuals delegating authority to units of government when appropriate but clearly retaining the capability to recall that delegated authority should it be abused.*

SCOTT, FREDRIC WINTHROP, veterinarian; b. Greenfield, Mass., Nov. 22, 1935; s. Clifton William and Mildred E. (Bradford) S.; m. Lois Ellen Williams, May 26, 1957; children: Duane Douglas, John Gardner, Raymond Clifton. BS in Chemistry, U. Mass., 1958; DVM, Cornell U., 1962, PhD in Virology, 1968. Veterinarian Rutland (Vt.) Vet. Clinic, 1962-64; rsch. veterinarian USDA, Plum Island Animal Disease Ctr., Greenport, N.Y., 1964-65; NIH postdoctoral fellow Cornell U., Ithaca, N.Y., 1965-68, asst. prof. vet. microbiology, 1968-73, assoc. prof. vet. microbiology, 1973-79, prof. microbiology and immunology, 1979-96, prof. emeritus, 1997—; dir. Cornell Feline Health Ctr., 1974-96; mem. bd. comparative virology WHO/FAO; mem. vet. med. adv. com. Ctr. for Vet. Medicine, FDA, Rockville, Md., 1984-86; mem. vet. sci. tech. adv. coun. Agrl. and Tech. Coll., SUNY, Delhi, 1972-75; cons., rschr. in field. Editor-in-chief Feline Practice Jour.; co-author: Infectious Diseases Domestic Animals, 1988, Infectious Diseases, 1986; contbr. articles to profl. publs.; inventor vaccines. Bd. elders Bethel Grove Bible Ch., 1979-91, 93—; faculty advisor Christian Vet. Fellowship; coach youth baseball and hockey; mem. Town of Ithaca Planning Bd.; mem. troop com. Boy Scouts Am., Ellis Hollow. Nat. Acads. Practice disting. scholar in vet. medicine, 1991—; NIH grantee, 1970-83. Fellow Acad. Feline Practice (bd. dirs. 1991—); mem. AVMA (sci. program com. 1973-81, coun. on biologic and therapeutic agts. 1986-92, chmn. 1987-89), Am. Coll. Vet. Microbiologists (diplomate, examinations com. 1975-79), Am. Soc. Virology, N.Y. State Vet. Med. Soc. (com. on small animal practice 1985-90), So. Tier Vet. Med. Assn., Am. Assn. Feline Practitioners (pres. 1976-78, adv. bd. past pres. 1990—, rsch. award 1975), Am. Animal Hosp. Assn. (Carnation award 1990), Conf. Rsch. Workers on Animal Diseases. Republican. Mem. Evangelical Ch. Avocations: golf, archery, gardening, basketball. Office: Cornell U Coll Vet Medicine Feline Health Ctr Ithaca NY 14853

SCOTT, GARY KUPER, retired academic administrator; b. Jefferson City, Mo., Jan. 3, 1933; s. Ralph Elmer and Lillian Rachel (Kuper) S.; children—Tina Marie, Lisa René, Corey Kuper. A.A., Jefferson City Jr. Coll., 1953; B.Ed., Western Wash. State Coll., 1960, M.Ed., 1962; Ph.D., U. Minn., 1965. Dir. student counseling center Minot (N.D.) State Coll., 1965-67; faculty, head dept. psychology Lincoln U., Jefferson City, 1967-77, chmn. dept. edn. and psychology, 1979-83, dean Sch. Edn. and Grad. Studies, 1983-85, dir. grad. and continuing edn., 1985-88, dean grad. and continuing edn., 1988-95; ret., 1995. Pres. Cole County Mental Health Assn., 1969-70; Bd. dirs. YMCA.; mem. Jefferson City Sch. Bd., 1985-87; mem. Cole County Democratic Com., 1968-70. Mem. Am., Mo. psychol. assns. Club: Rotary. Home: 1002 Roseridge Cir Jefferson City MO 65101-3640

SCOTT, GARY LEROY, photographic manufacturing executive, photographer; b. Portland, Oreg., May 14, 1954; s. Glenn Howard and Esther Ruth (Robinson) S. Grad., USN Sch. Photography, Pensacola, Fla., 1974; BS, U. Oreg., 1979, MS, 1982. Freelance photographer and filmmaker Scott Cinema and Visual, Inc., various locations, 1969—; computer traffic operator Burlington No. R.R., Portland, 1979-81; instr. U. Oreg., Eugene, 1981-82; S.E. dist. sales mgr. E. Leitz, Inc., 1984-87; mgr. profl. products Fla. div. Fuji Photo Film USA, Inc., Lake Mary, Fla., 1987—; freelance media cons., advt. copywriter, TV and film script writer, 1984—; lectr. in field. Served with USN, 1972-76. U. Oreg. Sch. Journalism research grantee, 1981. Mem. Am. Soc. Mag. Photographers, Profl. Photographers of Am. Republican. Avocations: photography exhibitions, outdoor activities, history. Home and Office: PO Box 952619 Lake Mary FL 32795-2619

SCOTT, GARY THOMAS, historian; b. Wichita Falls, Tex., Mar. 9, 1944; s. Thomas Clifford, Jr. and Lillian (Hanks) Fecher. BA, Southwestern U., Georgetown, Tex., 1966; MA, U. N.C., 1969. History instr. Tusculum Coll., Greeneville, Tenn., 1969-70, Herringswell Manor Sch., Bury St. Edmunds, UK, 1970-71; hist. rschr. Washington Nat. Cathedral, 1971-75; archtl. historian Nat. Park Svc., Washington, 1976-82, regional historian, 1982-95, historian Nat. Capital area, 1995—; chief historian Nat. Capital Region, 1996—; lectr., tour leader Smithsonian Inst., Washington, 1981—; prin. N.Am. rep. in course on archtl. conservation hist. bldgs. Property Svcs. Agy. and English Heritage of Brit. Govt., West Dean Coll., Chichester, Sussex, Eng., 1982-90. Author: The Kappa Alpha Order-1865-1897, 1994. Rep. Nat. Park Svc., D.C. Bicentennial, Washington, 1991-93; mem. Committee of One Hundred, Washington, 1993—, U.S. Capitol Cornerstone Bicentennial, Washington, 1993; active Hist. Soc. Washington, 1977—, So. Hist. Assn., 1980—; mem. Friends Attingham Summer Sch., N.Y.C., 1981—, Preservation Roundtable, Washington, 1989—; preservation officer, Victorian Soc., Washington, 1990—. Recipient Disting. Pub. Svc. award, Kappa Alpha Order, 1988. Mem. Scottish Rite (K.C.C.H. award 1993), Masons (Master 1996), Kappa Alpha Order (chief alumnus 1991-95). Episcopalian. Avocations: book and antique collector. Office: Nat Park Svc National Capital Region 1100 Ohio Dr SW Washington DC 20242-0001

SCOTT, GEORGE ERNEST, publisher, writer; b. Detroit, Sept. 12, 1924; s. George Ernest and Ruth Janet (Moffett) S.; m. Lois Aurlie Brown, Mar. 28, 1953; m. Elaine Lorraine Phillips, Feb. 14, 1982. Student, U. Detroit, 1946-47, Woodbury Coll., Los Angeles, 1947-48. With advt. prodn. dept. D.P. Brother Advt., Detroit, 1947-49, Ruthrauff & Ryan Advt., Detroit, 1950-51; advt. account exec. Betteridge & Co. Advt., Detroit, 1951-53; founder, 1954; pub., pres. Scott Advt. & Pub. Co., Livonia, Mich.; owner, pub. Ceramic Arts & Crafts mag., 1955—, Ceramic Teaching Projects and Trade News, quar., 1965—. Songwriter: (words and music) I Want A Lovin' Man, Tropic Memories, A Second Chance at Love, I Think I'm Falling in Love With You, Sing, Sing, Sing at Christmas, Boomerang Lovin' You's the Best Thing Tthat I Do and Over 100 More. With USNR, 1942-46. Mem. Nat. Ceramic Mfrs. Assn. (past dir.), Mich. Ceramic Dealers Assn. (past pres.). Home: 574 Herald St Plymouth MI 48170-1537

SCOTT, GREGORY KELLAM, state supreme court justice; b. San Francisco, July 30, 1943; s. Robert and Althea Delores Scott; m. Carolyn Weatherly, Apr. 10, 1971; children: Joshua Weatherly, Elijah Kellam. BS in Environ. Sci., Rutgers U., 1970, EdM in Urban Studies, 1971; JD cum laude, Ind. U., Indpls., 1977. Asst. dean resident instrn. Cook Coll. Rutgers U., 1972-75; trial atty. U.S. SEC, Denver, 1977-79; gen. counsel Blinder, Robinson & Co., Inc., Denver, 1979-80; asst. prof. coll. law U. Denver, 1980-85, assoc. prof., 1985-93, prof. emeritus, 1993—, chair bus. planning program, 1986-89, 92-93; justice Colo. Supreme Ct., Denver, 1993—; of counsel Moore, Smith & Bryant, Indpls., 1987-90; v.p., gen. counsel Comml. Energies, Inc., 1990-91; presenter in field. Author: (with others) Structuring Mergers and Acquisitions in Colorado, 1985, Airport Law and Regulation, 1991, Racism and Underclass in America, 1991; contbr. articles to profl. jours. Mem. ABA, Nat. Bar Assn., Nat. Assn. Securities Dealers, Inc., Nat. Arbitration Panel (arbitrator), Colo. Bar Found., Sam Cary Bar Assn., Am. Inn Ct. (founding mem. Judge Alfred A. Arraj inn). Avocations: golfing, reading, traveling.

SCOTT, HAL S., law educator; b. 1943. AB, Princeton U., 1965; MA, Stanford U., 1967; JD, U. Chgo., 1972. Law clk. to judge U.S. Ct. Appeals D.C. Cir., Washington, 1972-73, to assoc. justice White, U.S. Supreme Ct., Washington, 1973-74; acting prof. law U. Calif.-Berkeley, 1974-75; asst. prof. law Harvard U. Sch. Law, Cambridge, Mass., 1975-79, prof., 1980-90, Nomura prof. internat. fin. systems, 1990—; cons. IBM, N.Y.C., 1977. Contbr. articles to legal jours. Dir. Program on Internat. Fin. Systems. Mem. Internat. Acad. of Consumer and Comml. Law (past pres.). Office: Law Sch Harvard U Cambridge MA 02138

SCOTT, HANSON LEE, airport executive; m. Laraine Newman; children: Craig, Randy. Student, N.Mex. State U.; BS in Engring. Scis., USAF Acad., 1961; MBA, Auburn U.; grad., Air Force Air Command and Staff Coll., Dept. Def. Indsl. Coll. of the Armed Forces; postgrad., St. Louis U. Commd. 2d lt. USAF, advanced through grades to brigadier gen.; vice-comdr., dir. ops. 314th Tactical Airlift Wing, Little Rock AFB, 1982-85; comdr. 463rd Tactical Airlift Wing, Dyess AFB, Abilene, Tex., 1985-86; comdr., installation comdr. 1st Spl. Ops. Wing, Hurlburt Field, Fla., 1986-87, vice-comdr. Air Force spl. ops. command, 1987-89; comdr. spl. ops. command Pacific Camp H. M. Smith, Hawaii, 1989-91; ret. USAF, 1991; prin., sr. mktg. dir. Quatro Corp., Albuquerque, 1992-93; dir. aviation Albuquerque Internat. Airport, 1994—, Albuquerque's Double Eagle II Airport, 1994—. Decorated Def. Disting. Svc. medal, Legion of Merit with oak leaf cluster, Disting. Flying Cross, Meritorious Svc. medal with 3 oak leaf clusters, Air medal with 8 oak leaf clusters. Mem. Am. Assn. Airport Execs. Office: Albuquerque Internat Airport 2200 Sunport Blvd PO Box 9022 Albuquerque NM 87106

SCOTT, HELEN CECILE, critical care nurse; b. Paragould, Ark., Apr. 30, 1929; d. Cecil Lloyd and Ora Elvie (Gatlin) Cox; m. Benjamin J. Scott, Dec. 19, 1948; children: Sharon J. Yarbrough, Susan Cecile. ADN, So. State Coll., Magnolia, Ark., 1970; BSN, Graceland Coll., Lamoni, Iowa, 1986. Staff nurse Independence (Mo.) Regional Hosp., clin. care coord.; short-course instr. Jennie Lund Sch. Nursing, Independence; CVI specialist Wellness div. Independence Regional Health Ctr.; part-time critical care staff nurse. Home: 808 N Cherokee St Independence MO 64056-1959

SCOTT, HELEN KINARD, corporate executive; b. Washington, July 3, 1943; d. David and Helen (Young) Madison; m. Victor F. Scott; children: Lenise Sharon, Monique Sherine. B in Med. Tech., Washington Sch. of Med. Tech., 1963; BA, Howard U., 1971, MSW, 1973, postgrad., 1976-78; D in Pub. Adminstrn., Grant U., 1994. Lic. clin. social worker, real estate broker. Asst. to mgr. Cramton Auditorium Howard U., Washington, 1968-70, asst. prof., 1972-73, asst. to adminstrv. asst. to prof., 1973-75; writer, co-star Family Counselor Sta. WJZ-TV, Balt., 1971-73; dir. asst. prof. social work Howard U. Children's Concern Ctr., Washington, 1973-74; conf. coord. World Peace Through Law Ctr., Washington, 1974-75; chairperson social planning sequence, asst. prof. U. D.C., Washington, 1974-76; v.p. Roy Littlejohn Assocs., Inc., Washington, 1975-95, also bd. dirs.; exec. dir. Assn. Black Psychologists, Washington, 1995—; bd. dirs. Caribbean Festivals, Inc., Washington; project dir. The Zambia Hird Project, U.S. Agy. Internat. Devel., Usaba. Author: (poems) To Life-To Love, 1983; editor: (report) Desegregation in Pub. Higher Edn., 1975. Bd. dirs. Washington Parent-Child Ctr., 1983—, Big Sisters of Washington Met. Area. Grantee NIMH, 1971-73; recipient EMMY award AFTRA, 1973. Contbr. to Human Rights award UN, N.Y.C., 1974. Mem. NASW, Am. Planning Assn. (assoc.), Assn. Black Psychologists (bd. dirs.), Howard U. Nat. Alumni Assn. (pres., bd. dirs.), Howard U. Alumni Club of D.C. (pres. 1983-88), Freedom Bowl Alumni Com. (bd. dirs.), Caribbean-Am. Intercultural Orgn. (bd. dirs.), Phi Delta Kappa (charter), Delta Sigma Theta. Home: 10 Travilah Ter Potomac MD 20854 Office: Assn Black Psychologists 821 Kennedy St NW Washington DC 20011-2913

SCOTT, H(ERBERT) ANDREW, retired chemical engineer; b. Marion, Va., Mar. 29, 1924; s. Charles Wassum and Carolyn Enyde (Snider) S.; widowed; children: Mark Andrew, Paul Ethan; m. Helen R. LaFollette, July 21, 1984. BSChemE, Va. Tech. Inst. and State U., 1944, MSChemE, 1947. Registered profl. engr., Tenn. Chem. engr. Tenn. Eastman Co., Kingsport, 1947-55, asst. to works mgr., 1955-60, supt. glycol dept., 1960-64, supt. polymers dept., 1964-67; plant mgr. Holston Def. Corp., Kingsport, 1967-70, dir. systems devel., 1970-73, dir. engring. dvsn., 1974-87; vis. prof. U. Alaska, Fairbanks, 1988-89; mem. standards com. Eastman Kodak Co., Rochester, N.Y., 1982-87. Mem. mayor's adv. com. City of Kingsport, 1971-76; chmn. Kingsport Park Commn., 1976-80. Sgt. AUS, 1944-46. Named Engr. of yr., Tenn. Soc. Profl. Engrs., 1984. Fellow AIChE (mem. Inst. Chem. Process Safety 1984-87, vocat. guidance com. 1960-64, chmn. local sect. 1956); mem. Am. Soc. Engring. Edn., Am. Soc. Engring. Mgmt., Kiwanis. Republican. Presbyterian. Achievements include patent in process for manufacture of acetic anhydride, implement pioneering quality management for knowledge workers, design for manufacturing chemicals from coal. Home: 4512 Chickasaw Rd Kingsport TN 37664-2110 *Being born of honest, ambitious and loving religious parants in a small town in the mountains of the USA was a great start. Work was a virtue, wages in a depression-a life saver! Successfully practicing chemical engineering in one of America's great companies complete the image.*

SCOTT, HOWARD WINFIELD, JR., temporary help services company executive; b. Greenwich, Conn., Feb. 24, 1935; s. Howard Winfield and Janet (Lewis) S.; B.S., Northwestern U., 1957; m. Joan Ann MacDonald, Aug. 12, 1961; children: Howard Winfield III, Thomas MacDonald, Ann Elizabeth. With R.H. Donnelly Corp., Chgo., 1958-59; sales rep. Masonite Corp., Chgo. also Madison, Wis., 1959-61; sales rep. Manpower Inc., Chgo., 1961-63, br. mgr., Kansas City, Mo., 1963-65, area mgr., Mo. and Kans., 1964-65, regional mgr. Salespower div., Phila., 1965-66; asst. advt. mgr. soups Campbell Soup Co., Camden, N.J., 1966-68; pres. PARTIME, Inc., Paoli, Pa., 1968-74; dir. marketing Kelly Services Inc., Southfield, Mich., 1974-78; pres. CDI Temporary Services, Inc., 1978-91; pres. Dunhill Pers. System, Inc., Woodbury, N.Y., 1991-94; v.p. SOS Temporary Svcs., Salt Lake City, 1994; pres., chief operating officer SOS Staffing Svcs., Salt Lake City, 1995—. Served with AUS, 1957-58. Mem. Nat. Assn. Temporary Services (sec. 1970-71, pres. 1971-73, bd. dirs. 1982-91), Kappa Sigma. Republican. Home: PO Box 980142 Park City UT 84098-0142 also: 1204 Annapolis Sea Colony E Bethany Beach DE 19930 Office: SOS Staffing Svcs 1415 S Main St Salt Lake City UT 84115-5313

SCOTT, HUGH PATRICK, physician, naval officer; b. Phila., Feb. 12, 1938; s. Hugh Patrick and Martha (Papiana) S.; m. Diane Marie Lopatzie, July 1, 1961; children: Karen, Brendan, Catherine. BA, LaSalle Coll., 1960; DO, Phila. Coll. Osteo. Medicine, 1964, LLD (hon.), 1991. Diplomate Am. Osteo. Bd. Ophthalmology and Otolaryngology. Intern Detroit Osteo. Hosp., Highland Park, Mich., 1964-65, resident otorhinolatyngology, 1965-68; lt. med. corps USNR, 1967, advanced through grades to rear adm., 1991; naval med. officer U.S. Naval Dispensary N.O.B., Norfolk, Va., 1968-70, Submarine Squadron 10, Groton, Conn.; Submarine Group 2; naval med. officer Naval Submarine Med. Ctr., New London, Conn., 1975-83; dir. undersea medicine and radiation health Naval Med. Command, Washington, 1983-86; comdg. officer Naval Hosp., Groton, 1986-88, Camp Lejeune, N.C., 1988-90; fleet surgeon Comdr. in Chief, U.S. Pacific Fleet, Pearl Harbor, Hawaii, 1990-91; asst. chief for operational medicine and fleet support Bur. Medicine and Surgery, Washington, 1991-92; dir. med. resources, plans and policy Office Chief of Naval Ops., Washington, 1992-94; asst. clin. prof. medicine Mich. State U., Lansing, Mich., 1970-75; pvt. practice, Madison Heights, Mich., 1970-75; cons. Am. Coll. Undersea and Hyperbaric Medicine, Washington, 1985-86; cons., 1994-96; sr. program mgr. Grumman Data Sys. Corp., Northrop Grumman Corp., 1996—. Decorated Legion of Merit, Gold Star (3). Fellow Osteo. Coll. Ophthalmology and Otolaryngology, Am. Acad. Otolaryngology and Head and Neck Surgery; mem. Am. Osteo. Coll. Otolaryngology--Head and Neck Surgery (past pres.), Assn. Mil. Osteopathic Physicians and Surgeons (2nd v.p.). Republican. Roman Catholic. Home: 3707 Merlin Way Annandale VA 22003-1326

SCOTT, IRENE FEAGIN, federal judge; b. Union Springs, Ala., Oct. 6, 1912; d. Arthur H. and Irene (Peach) Feagin; m. Thomas Jefferson Scott, Dec. 27, 1939 (dec.); children: Thomas Jefferson, Irene Scott Carroll. A.B., U. Ala., 1932, LL.B., 1936, LL.D., 1978; LL.M., Catholic U. Am., 1939. Bar: Ala. 1936. Law libr. U. Ala. Law Sch., 1932-34; atty. Office Chief Counsel IRS, 1937-50, mem. excess profits tax coun., 1950-52, spl. asst. to head appeals div., 1952-59, staff asst. to chief counsel, 1959-60; judge U.S. Tax Ct., 1960-82, sr. judge serving on recall, 1982—. Contbr. articles to Women Lawyers Jour. Bd. dirs. Mt. Olivet Found., Arlington. Mem. ABA (taxation sect.), Ala. Bar Assn., Fed. Bar Assn., D.C. Bar Assn. (hon.), Nat. Assn. Women Lawyers, Nat. Assn. Women Judges, Kappa Delta, Kappa Beta Pi. Office: US Tax Ct 400 2nd St NW Washington DC 20217-0001

SCOTT, ISADORE MEYER, former energy company executive; b. Wilcoe, W.Va., Nov. 21, 1912; s. David and Libby (Roston) S.; m. Joan Rosenwald, Feb. 14, 1943; children: Betsy Scott Kleeblatt, Peggy, Jonathan D. A.B., W.Va. U., 1934, M.A., 1938; J.D., Washington and Lee U., 1937; LLD, West Va. U., 1983. Bar: Va. 1937. Practiced law Richmond, Va., 1937-38; v.p. Lee I. Robinson Hosiery Mills., Phila., 1938-42; with Winner Mfg. Co., Inc., Trenton, 1947-61, v.p., 1947-51, pres., 1951-61; chmn. bd. Tri-Instl. Facilities, Inc., Phila., 1962-78; chmn. bd. TOSCO Corp., Los Angeles, 1976-83, vice-chmn. bd., 1983-87; bd. dirs., chmn. Univ. City Assocs., Inc.; founder, mem. U.S. Adv. Bd. Brit.-Am. Project. Bd. dirs. S.E. Pa. chpt. ARC, Internat. Rescue Com., Univ. City Sci. Ctr., Phila.; mem. adv. com. Urban Affair Partnership; bd. dirs. emeritus, former mem. exec. com., vice-chmn. Phila. Mus. Art; former chmn. World Affairs Council Phila.; mem. Phila. Com. Fgn. Rels.; trustee emeritus Washington and Lee U.; emeritus trustee George C. Marshall Found.; former chmn. Christ Ch. Preservation Fund, Phila., Jefferson House Restoration, Phila. With inf. U.S. Army, 1942-46, NATOUSA, ETO. Decorated Legion of Merit, Silver Star, Purple Heart, Bronze Star (U.S.); Crown of Italy; medal of merit Czechoslovakia; Mentioned-in-dispatches, Eng.; fellow Mus. Am. Jewish History. Mem. Va. State Bar, Phila. Club, Gulph Mills Golf, Anglers of Phila., Masons, Phi Beta Kappa, Omicron Delta Kappa, Order of Coif. (hon.). Republican. Jewish. Clubs: Phila.; Gulph Mills Golf, Anglers of Phila. Lodge: Masons.

SCOTT, JACQUELINE DELMAR PARKER, educational association administrator, business administrator, consultant, fundraiser; b. L.A., May 18, 1947; d. Thomas Aubrey and Daisy Beatrice (Singleton) Parker (div.); children: Tres Mali, Olympia Ranee, Stephen Thomas. AA in Theatre Arts, L.A. City Coll., 1970; BA in Econs., Calif. State U., Dominquez Hills, Carson, 1973; MBA, Golden Gate U., 1979; postgrad., Pepperdine U., 1997—. Cert. parenting instr. 1994. Sales clk. Newberry's Dept. Store, L.A., 1963-65; long distance operator Pacific Telephone Co., L.A., 1965-66; PBX operator Sears, Roebuck & Co., L.A., 1966-68; retail clk. Otey's Grocery Store, Nashville, 1968-69; collector N.Am. Credit, L.A., 1970-71; office mgr. Dr. S. Edward Tucker, L.A., 1972-74; staff coord. sch. edn. dept. Calif. State U., 1973-74; bank auditor Security Pacific Bank, L.A., 1974-76, corp. loan asst., 1976-77; dist. credit analyst Crocker Nat. Bank, L.A., 1977-78, asst. v.p., 1978-80; capital planning adminstr. TRW, Inc., Redondo Beach, Calif., 1980-82, ops. bus. adminstr., 1982-84, lab. sr. bus. adminstr., 1984-86, project bus. mgr., 1986-87, div. sr. bus. adminstr., 1987-92; ptnr., co-author, co-facilitator, cons. Diversified Event Planners, Inc., L.A., 1990-93; asst. area devel. dir. United Negro Coll. Fund, L.A., 1993—, cons., 1996—. Co-founder career growth awareness com. TRW Employees Bootstrap, Redondo Beach, Calif., 1980, pres., 1983-84; role model Inglewood High Sch., TRW Youth Motivation Task Force, Redondo Beach, 1981-83, Crozier Jr. High Sch., 1981-83, Monroe Jr. High Sch., Redondo Beach, 1981-83, Frank D. Parent Career Day, TRW Affirmative Action Com., Redondo Beach, 1987, St. Bernard's Career Day, 1991; chairperson community involvement com., 1981, chairperson disaster com., 1989-90; chairperson gen. and local welfare com. TRW Employees Charitable Orgn., 1989-90, disaster com. chair, 1988-89, bd. dirs. 1987-89; pres. Mgmt. Effectiveness Program Alumnae, L.A., 1982-83, TRW Employees Bootstrap Program Alumnae, 1983-84; group leader Jack & Jill of Am., Inc., South L.A., 1980-81, parliamentarian, 1986-87, v.p., 1981-82, chpt. pres., 1984-86, regional dir., 1987-89, nat. program dir., 1992-96, liaison to Young Black Scholars Program, 1986—; bd. dirs. Adolescent Pregnancy Child Watch, 1993—; nat. program dir., bd. dirs. Jack & Jill Am. Found., 1992-96; L.A. mem. Nat. Black Child Devel. Inst., 1994—; vol. ARC, 1994—; parenting instr. Am. Red Cross, 1994—; founder Jack & Jill of Am. Leadership Devel. Program, 1993. Recipient commendation NAACP, 1985, United Negro Coll. Fund, 1986, United Way, 1988, Austistic Children's Telephon, 1980, Inglewood Sch. Dist., 1981, Pres. award Harbor Area Chpt. Links, Inc., 1985, Women of Achievement award City of L.A., Black Pers. Assn., 1994. Mem. Black Women's Forum (sponsor), Delta Sigma Theta. Avocations: reading, dancing.

SCOTT, JAMES ARTHUR, radiologist, educator; b. Cleve., Aug. 23, 1950; s. Robert James and Margaret Emma (Hinz) S.; m. Phyllis Virginia Gauthier, Oct. 3, 1981. S.B., MIT, 1972; M.D., Boston U., 1976. Diplomate Am. Bd. Radiology, Am. Bd. Nuclear Medicine. Resident Harvard U. Med. Sch.-Mass. Gen. Hosp., Boston, 1976-80, fellow, 1980-81, instr., 1982-83, asst. prof., 1984-93, assoc. prof. 1994—. Recipient New Investigator Research award NIH, 1984-87. Mem. Am. Fedn. Clin. Research, Sigma Xi, Am. Coll. Radiology, N.Y. Acad. Scis., AAAS, Phi Lambda Upsilon, Theta Xi. Lutheran. Avocations: writing, meditation, golf. Office: Div Nuclear Medicine Mass Gen Hosp Boston MA 02114

SCOTT, JAMES J., retired mining engineer; b. Wiota, Wis., Apr. 22, 1928; m. Edna M. Kettler, 1947 (dec. May 1995); 5 children; m. Ingeborg Kalinski, June 6, 1996. BS, Mo. Sch. of Mines, 1950; MS, U. Wis., 1959, PhD in Mining Engring., 1962. Mine engr. Bethlehem (Pa.) Steel Co., 1950-53, mine foreman, 1953-57; from instr. to asst. prof. mining U. Wis., 1957-63; assoc. prof. U. Mo., Rolla, 1963-65, prof. mining, 1965-80, chmn. depts. mining & petroleum, 1970-76; gen. mgr. Black River Mine, Marble Cliff Quarries Co., 1967; asst. dir. mining rsch. US Bur. Mines, 1970—; adj. prof. mining engring. U. Mo., Rolla, 1980—; pres. Scott Mine Tech. Svc. Inc. Recipient Rock Mechanics award Soc. Mining Engrs. Mem. Am. Inst. Mining, Metall. and Petroleum Engrs. (Daniel C. Jackling award 1990), Can. Inst. Mining and Metallurgy. Achievements include research in field rock mechanics, mine operational problems, experimental stress analysis, photoelasticity, model studies, stress distribution problems, mine and research management; patentee in field. Home: 16720 State Rt O Rolla MO 65401 Office: Scott MTS Inc 16720 State Rt 0 Rolla MO 65401

SCOTT, JAMES MARTIN, state legislator, healthcare system executive; b. Fairfax County, Va., June 11, 1938; s. Fred Sharp and Mary Ruth (Bishop) S.; m. Nancy Virginia Cromwell, Nov. 27, 1976; children: Catherine Virginia, Mary Alice. BA in English, U. N.C., 1960, MA in English, 1965; MPA, George Mason U., 1982. Tchr. Edison High Sch., Fairfax, Va., 1963-64; exec. dir. Fairfax Community Action Program, 1966-69, Washington Suburban Inst., Fairfax, 1969-72; bd. suprs. Fairfax County, 1972-86; dir. comminuty affairs Inova Health System, Springfield, Va., 1986-90, asst. v.p., 1990—; mem. Va. Ho. Dels., Richmond, 1992—; pres. Va. Assn. Counties, Richmond, 1978-79; chair No. Va. Transp. Commn., Arlington, 1982. Pres. Fairfax Fair, 1988-90; bd. dirs. Washington Area Housing Partnership, 1990—, Washington Met. Coun. Govts., 1993—. Recipient David and Betty Scull Pub. Svc. award Washington Met. Coun. Govts., 1983; named Fairfax County Citizen of Yr., Washington Post, 1991. Democrat. Methodist. Avocation: sports. Office: PO Box 359 Merrifield VA 22116-0359

SCOTT, JAMES MICHAEL, research biologist; b. San Diego, Sept. 20, 1941; m. 1966; 2 children. BS, San Diego State U., 1966, MA, 1970; PhD in Zoology, Oreg. State U., 1973. Biol. aide U.S. Bur. Comml. Fisheries, 1966-68; asst. curator vertebrates Nat. Hist. Mus., Oreg. State U., 1969-73; rschr. Dept. Fisheries & Wildlife, 1973-74; biologist in charge Mauna Loa Field Sta. U.S. Fish & Wildlife Svc., 1974-84, dir. Condor Field Sta., 1984-86; instr. ornithology Malheur Environ. Field Sta., Pacific U., 1972, 73; leader Fish & Wildlife Rsch. Unit U. Idaho, Moscow, 1986—; leader Maui Forest Bird Recovery Team, 1975-79, Hawaii Forest Bird Recovery Team, 1975; mem. Palila Recovery Team, 1975; mem. Am. Ornithologists Union Conservation Com., 1974-75, 75-76, sci. adv. bd. Nature Conservancy Hawaii Forest Bird Project, 1981; Richard M. Nixon scholar Whittier Coll. Fellow Am. Ornithologists Union; mem. Nature Conservancy, Ecol. Soc. Am., The Wildlife Soc., Soc. Conservation Biology, Inst. Biol. Sci., Cooper Ornithol. Soc. (pres. 1997—). Office: U Idaho Fish & Wildlife Rsch Unit 1130 Kamiaken St Moscow ID 83843-3855

SCOTT, JIM, sound recording engineer. Recipient Grammy award for Best Engineered Album, Non Classical ("Wildflowers" by Tom Petty), 1996. Office: Warner Brothers Records 3300 Warner Blvd Fl 2 Burbank CA 91505-4632*

SCOTT, JOANNA JEANNE, writer, English language educator; b. Rochester, N.Y., June 22, 1960; d. Walter Lee and Yvonne (de Potter) S.; m. James Burton Longenbach; children: Kathryn Scott Longenbach, Alice Scott Longenbach. BA, Trinity Coll., Hartford, 1983; MA, Brown U., 1985. Asst. prof. English U. Md., College Park, 1987-88; from asst. to prof. U. Rochester, N.Y., 1988-95, prof., 1995—. Author: (novels) Fading, My Parmacheese Belle, 1987, The Closest Possible Union, 1988, Arrogance, 1990, (collection of stories) Various Antidotes, 1994 (PEN/Faulkner award nomination 1995), The Manikin, 1996. Recipient Richard and Hinde Rosenthal award Am. Acad.-Inst. Arts and Letters, 1991, finalist Pulitzer Prize, 1997; fellow Guggenheim Found., 1988, MacArthur Found., 1992—; PEN faulkner nomination, 1991, 95. Mem. PEN (chair women's com.), Writers and Books (bd. dirs. 1993-97). Office: U of Rochester Dept of English Rochester NY 14627-0451

SCOTT, JOHN BROOKS, research institute executive; b. Morenci, Ariz., Aug. 8, 1931; s. Brooks and Lucile (Slagle) S.; m. Jo Ann Rohrbach, June 5, 1987; children from previous marriage: Janice, Steven, Sarah. B.S., U. Ariz., 1957, M.A., 1959. Asst. prof. systems engring. U. Ariz., Tucson, 1959-61; mgr. Bell Aerosystems Co., Tucson, 1961-62; sr. v.p. IIT Research Inst., Annapolis, Md., 1962-90; pres. IIT Research Inst., Chgo., 1990—. Author papers on computer software, electromagnetic compatibility. Past pres. bd. dirs. Md. Hall for Creative Arts, Inc.; past chmn. Md. Hall Found.; mem. bd. govs. IIT Rsch. Inst.; trustee Ill. Inst. Tech. Sr. mem. IEEE, Greater Annapolis C. of C. (pres. 1987); mem. University Club Chgo., Phi Kappa Phi, Sigma Pi Sigma, Pi Mu Epsilon. Home: Apt 605 2937 S Atlantic Ave Daytona Beach Shores FL 32118 Office: 10 W 35th St Chicago IL 60616-3703

SCOTT, JOHN BURT, life insurance executive; b. St. Louis, July 25, 1944; s. Conley J. and Margaret (Dowdy) S.; m. Darlene Kuhnen Lady, Nov. 18, 1967; children: Kristen, Kathryn. BA in English, U. of South, 1966; MBA in Fin., Loyola U., 1971. Fin. analyst Kemper Nat. Property and Casualty Cos., Chgo., 1967-73; fin. officer Kemper Life, Long Grove, Ill., 1973-77, v.p. ops., 1977-86, pres., chief exec. officer, 1986-87, chmn., pres., chief exec. officer, 1987—; bd. dirs. Fed. Kemper Life Long Grove, Fidelity Life Assn., Long Grove, Kemper Investors Life, Long Grove, Kemper Fin. Cos., Chgo., Am. Coun. Life Insurers, Washington, Ill. Life Ins. Coun., Springfield, Nat. Orgn. Life and Health Guaranty Assn. Bd. dirs., exec. com. Omni Youth Svcs., Buffalo Grove, Ill., 1989—; bd. dirs. Lake County United Way, Life & Health Med. Rsch. Fund. Fellow Life Mgmt. Inst. Episcopalian. Avocations: golf, tennis.

SCOTT, JOHN CARLYLE, gynecologist, oncologist; b. Mpls., Sept. 24, 1933; s. Horace Golden and Grace (Melges) S.; m. Beth Krause, 1958 (div. 1977); m. Paola Maria Martini, Feb. 8, 1986; children: Jeff, David, Suzanne, Danielle. AB, Princeton U., 1956; BS, MD, U. Minn., 1961. Diplomate Am. Coll. Ob-gyn., Pan Am. Ob-gyn. Soc. Intern Sch. Medicine Marquette U., Milw., 1961-62, resident Sch. Medicine, 1962-66; resident Harvard Med. Sch., Boston, 1965; Am. Cancer fellow Marquette Med. Sch., Milw., 1966-67, instr. ob-gyn., 1966-67; clin. instr. ob-gyn. U. Wash. Med. Sch., Seattle, 1968-75, clin. asst. prof., 1975-85, clin. assoc. prof., 1985—; mem. faculty adv. com. dept. ob-gyn. U. Wash., Seattle, 1973—. Author: First Aid for N.W. Boaters, 1977; author Am. Jour. Ob-Gyn., 1970, 75, 77. Bd. dirs. Renton (Wash.) Handicapped Ctr., 1968-70, March of Dimes, 1974-79; bd. dirs. enabling sys. U. Hawaii, Honolulu, 1977-80. Capt. U.S. Army, 1950-52, Korea. Decorated U.S. Senate Medal of Freedom, Bronze and Silver Stars, Pres. Ronald Reagan's Task Force Medal of Merit and Eternal Flame of Freedom. Fellow Royal Soc. Medicine (gynecology and oncology sects.), Am. Coll. Ob-Gyn, Internat. Coll. Surgeons (pres. elec. 1997—, v.p., N.Am. Fedn. sec. 1997—); mem. Pan Am. Ob-Gyn Soc., S.W. Oncology Group, N.W. Oncology Group, Puget Sound Oncology Group, Seattle Gynecol. Soc. (pres. 1978), Baker Channing Soc., Sigma Xi. Avocations: photography, constrn., ornithology, sailing, skiing. Home: 726 16th Ave E Seattle WA 98112-3916 Office: 9730 4th Ave NE Ste 202 Seattle WA 98115-2143

SCOTT, JOHN CONSTANTE, marketing company executive; b. Charleston, S.C., Jan. 31, 1941; s. John C. and Annabelle (Holmes) S.; m. Mary Frances Turner. BS in Psychology, St. Joseph's U., Phila., 1975; JD, Temple U., 1979. Commd. USAF, 1962, advanced through grades to lt. col.; served in Vietnam; resigned, 1972; personnel mgr. Campbell Soup Co., Camden, N.J., 1972-79, corp. mgr. employee relations, 1980-84; v.p. ops. Insilco Corp., Meriden, Conn., 1984-89; v.p. human resources Howmet Corp., Greenwich, Conn., 1989-92; pres. StarMedia, Inc., Greenwich, 1992—. Mem. pres.'s coun. St. Joseph's U., 1985-90. Mem. ABA, N.J. Bar Assn., Pa. Bar Assn., Res. Officers Assn. (life), Greater Meriden C. of C. (bd. dirs. 1986-89). Roman Catholic. Avocations: mountain hiking, flying. Office: 15 E Putnam Ave Ste 320 Greenwich CT 06830-5424 *Peace: The product of justice; politics: the major subset of religion; law (human) rules that institutionalize political power (often as not related to justice).*

SCOTT, JOHN EDWARD, librarian; b. Washington, Ga., Aug. 12, 1920; s. John Edward and Martha Heard (Williams) S.; m. Dorris Louise Webb, Jan 28, 1948; children—Patricia Louise, Clifford Allen, Martha Ellen. A.B., Morehouse Coll., 1948; B.L.S., Atlanta U., 1949; M.L.S., U. Ill., 1955. Librarian Kans. Tech. Inst., Topeka, 1949-55; circulation librarian Va. State Coll., Petersburg, 1955-56; asst. reference librarian U. Kans., 1956-57; dir. library resources W. Va. State Coll., 1957—. Served with USNR, 1942-46. Mem. AAUP, ALA (councilor 1964—, chmn. coll. libraries sect. 1969-70), Southeastern Library Assn. (treas. 1979—), W.Va. Library Assn. (chmn coll. library sect. 1958-60, pres. 1961-62), Tri-State Assn. Coll. and Research Libraries, Middle Atlantic Regional Library Fedn. (exec. bd.), Kappa Delta Pi, Beta Phi Mu, Alpha Phi Alpha. Home: PO Box 303 Institute WV 25112-0303

SCOTT, JOHN EDWARD SMITH, lawyer; b. St. Louis, Aug. 6, 1936; s. Gordon Hatler and Luella Margarite (Smith) S.; m. Beverly Joan Phillips, Dec. 17, 1960; 1 dau., Pamela Anne. AB, Albion Coll., 1958; JD, Wayne State U., 1961. Bar: Mich. 1961, U.S. Dist. Ct. (ea. dist.) Mich. 1962, U.S. Dist. Ct. (we. dist.) Mich. 1970, U.S. Tax Ct. 1979, U.S. Ct. Appeals (6th cir.) 1964, U.S. Supreme Ct. 1966. Law clk. Supreme Ct. Mich., Lansing, 1961-62; assoc. Dickinson, Wright, Moon, Van Dusen & Freeman, Detroit, 1962-69, ptnr., 1970—; adj. prof. U. Detroit Law Sch., 1967-71. Supreme Ct. appointee State Bar Rep. Assembly, Detroit, 1972-77; mayor City of Pleasant Ridge, Mich., 1973-81; commr. Mich. Appellate Defender Commn., Detroit, 1979—, chmn., 1992—; hearing referee Mich. Civil Rights Commn., Detroit, 1974-80; chmn. Detroit Legal Aid & Defender Commn., 1972-77; chmn. case flow mgmt. com. Mich. Supreme Ct., 1989-90. Fellow Am. Coll. Trial Lawyers, Internat. Soc. Barristers; mem. ABA (chmn. trial evidence com. sect. litigation 1988-91), Am. Bd. Advs., Internat. Assn. Def. Counsel, Am. Bar Found., Mich. Bar Found., Detroit Golf Club. Office: Dickinson Wright Moon Van Dusen & Freeman 500 Woodward Ave Ste 4000 Detroit MI 48226-3423

SCOTT, JOHN ROLAND, lawyer, oil company executive; b. Wichita Falls, Tex., May 13, 1937; s. John and Margaret S.; m. Joan Carol Redding, Sept. 5, 1959; 1 child, John Howard. LLB, Baylor Sch. Law, Waco, Tex., 1962. Bar: Tex. 1962, Alaska 1970, U.S. Dist. Ct. (we. dist.) Tex. 1965, U.S. Dist. Ct. Alaska 1975. Assoc. litigation sect Lynch & Chappell, Midland, Tex., 1962-65; regional atty. Atlantic Richfield Co., Midland, 1965-79; sr. atty., Anchorage, 1969-77, sr. atty., Dallas, 1977-80; v.p., assoc. gen. counsel Mitchell Energy & Devel. Corp., Houston, 1980-82; asst. gen. counsel Hunt Oil Co., Dallas., 1982-84, v.p., chief counsel, 1984-91; v.p. gen. counsel, 1991—; bar examiner in Alaska, 1974-77. Mem. State Bar Tex. (lectr.), Dallas Bar Assn., ABA, Phi Alpha Delta. Republican. Clubs: Petroleum (Dallas). Office: Hunt Oil Co 1445 Ross Ave Dallas TX 75202-2812

SCOTT, JOHN WALTER, chemical engineer, research management executive; b. Berkeley, Calif., May 27, 1919; s. John Walter and Cora Viola (Wampfler) S.; m. Jane Ellen Newman, June 27, 1942; children—Nancy, Barbara, Charles, James, Richard. B.S. in Chemistry, U. Calif.-Berkeley, 1941, M.S. in Chem. Engring., 1951. Registered profl. chem. engr., Calif. Process and catalyst research and devel. Chevron Research, Richmond, Calif., 1946-67, v.p., 1967-84, cons., 1985—. Contbr. articles to profl. jours.; patentee in field. Trustee U. Calif.-Berkeley Found., 1985-91; adv. coun. Lawrence Hall of Sci., 1990-97; mem. coun. Town of Ross, Calif., 1992-96. Capt. U.S. Army, 1941-46. Fellow Am. Inst. Chem. Engrs. (awards com. 1979-84, award 1978), AAAS; mem. Nat. Acad. Engring., Am. Chem. Soc., Am. Petroleum Inst. (chmn. research data info. services 1971-73, 77-80, cert. of appreciation 1983). Avocations: history; travel. Home: PO Box 2004 Ross CA 94957-2004

SCOTT, JOHN WILLIAM, food processing executive; b. Okamoto, Hyogo-Ken, Japan, July 12, 1935; s. John William and Alice Cunningham (Harrison) S.; m. Marilyn Merrill Ackland, July 20, 1962; children: John William, Matthew Thompson, Julia Leigh Harrison, Robert Augustine Thornton. AB, Princeton U., 1958. With CPC, Chgo. and Mexico, 1957-63; ops. mgr. Maizena (CPC), Cali, Colombia, 1964-65; mng. dir. PROMASA (CPC), Guatemala City, Guatemala, 1965-69, IMSA (CPC), Montevideo, Uruguay, 1969-70, Productos Knorr (CPC), Caracas, Venezuela, 1971-75; v.p. consumer div. Refinacoes de Milho (CPC), Sao Paulo, Brazil, 1975-79; mng. dir. Refinerias de Maiz (CPC), Buenos Aires, Argentina, 1979-83; asst. to pres. CPC Internat., Englewood Cliffs, N.J., 1983-84, v.p., 1985—. Bd. dirs. ACCION Internat., Boston, 1986—; bd. dirs. Dwight Englewood (N.J.) Sch., 1990-96, pres. bd. trustees, 1992-95; pres. Englewood Cmty. Chest, 1988. With AUS, 1954-56. Mem. Princeton Club (N.Y.C.), Englewood Field Club. Democrat. Episcopalian. Avocation: squash, sailing. Home: 40 Lydecker St Englewood NJ 07631-3005 Office: CPC Internat Inc International Plaza PO Box 8000 Englewood Cliffs NJ 07632-9976

SCOTT, JOSEPH C., professional hockey team executive; m. Pat Scott; children: Joe Jr., Greg, Jeff, Trent, Linda. Owner Phila. Flyers, now chmn. emeritus; lifetime mem. NHL Bd. Govs., 1985—. Bd. dirs. Jr. Baseball Fedn., Big Bros Am., Police Athletic League, Little Quakers, Pop Warner Little Scholars, Inc., Pa. Sports Hall of Fame, Maxwell Club, IVB Golf Classic; mem. John Wanamaker awards com. and boys work com. Union League of Phila. Named to Pa. Sports Hall of Fame, 1974; co-recipient Pop Warner award for youth activities, 1960. Office: Phila Flyers Core States Spectrum 3601 N Broad St Philadelphia PA 19140-4107*

SCOTT, JOYCE ALAINE, university official; b. Long Beach, Calif., May 21, 1943; d. Emmett Emery Scott and Grace (Evans) Wedum. B.A., U. Conn., 1964; M.A., U. Va., 1966; Ph.D., Duke U., 1973. From instr. to assoc. prof. U. Wyo., Laramie, 1971-74, asst. dean, 1974-78, asst. v.p. acad. affairs, 1976-81, assoc. v.p. acad. affairs, 1981-84; provost, v.p. SUNY-Potsdam, 1984-86; exec. v.p. Wichita State U., Kans., 1986-90, v.p. on spl. assignment, 1990-91; sr. cons. Am. Assn. State Colls. and Univs., 1991-92, v.p. acad. and internat. programs, 1992—; mem. Commn. on Edal. Credit and Credentials of Am. Council on Edn., Washington, 1982-87; cons. faculty Am. Open U., Lincoln, Nebr., 1981-82. Contbr. articles to profl. jours. Trustee Internat. U. Jones Intercable. Mem. MLA, AAUW, AAHE, Am. Assn. Tchrs. French, Phi Beta Kappa, Phi Sigma Iota. Republican. Presbyterian. Office: AASCU 1 Dupont Cir NW Ste 700 Washington DC 20036-1133

SCOTT, JUDITH MYERS, elementary education educator; b. Loredo, Mo., Dec. 29, 1940; d. Wilbur Charles and Dora Emma (Frazier) Myers; m. David Ronald Scott, Dec. 18, 1965; children: Russell Myers, Geoffrey Douglas. BA in Edn., Ariz. State U., 1962, MA in edn., 1970. Cert. tchr., Ariz. Tchr. 2d grade Scottsdale (Ariz.) Elem. Dist., 1962-64; tchr. 1st grade Cahuilla Sch., Palm Springs, Calif., 1965, Palm Crest Sch., La Canada, Calif., 1968-69; tchr. Ak Chin Community Sch., Maricopa, Ariz., 1969-70; grad. asst. Ariz. State U., Tempe, 1970-71; pvt. tutor Tempe, 1970-77; tchr. Dayspring Presch., Tempe, 1978-83; tchr. 3d grade Waggoner Elem. Sch., Kyrene, Ariz., 1984-86; reading specialsit Tempe Elem. Sch. Dist., 1986-90, tchr., trainer collaborative literacy intervention project, 1990—; exec. dir. Beauty for All Seasons, Tempe, 1982-86; presenter in field. Coord. New Zealand Tchr. Exch., Tempe Sister Cities, 1992—. Mem. NEA, ASCD, IRA, ARA, Ariz. Sch. Adminstrs., Ariz. Edn. Assn. Methodist. Avocations: Painting, reading, hiking. Home: 1940 E Calle De Caballos Tempe AZ 85284-2507 Office: Tempe Elem Sch Dist 3205 S Rural Rd Tempe AZ 85282-3853

SCOTT, KELLY, newspaper editor. Mng. editor sunday calendar The L.A. Times. Office: LA Times Times Mirror Sq Los Angeles CA 90012-3816*

SCOTT, KENNETH ELSNER, mechanical engineering educator; b. Webster, Mass., May 18, 1926; s. Henry Anderson and Amanda (Elsner) S.; m. Elizabeth Ann Oldham, June 21, 1952; children—Kenneth Elsner, Cynthia Lynne, Jeffrey Alan, Donald Leighton. B.S. in Mech. Engring, Worcester Poly. Inst., 1948, M.S., 1954. Registered profl. engr., Mass. Mem. faculty Worcester Poly. Inst., 1948-91, prof. mech. engring., 1966-91, prof. emeritus, 1991—, George I. Alden prof. engring., 1971-75, inst. dir. audio-visual devel., 1971-74, dir. instructional TV, 1974-90, dir. CAD Lab., 1981-93, acting head dept. mech. engring., 1988-89. Mem. bd. health, Holden, Mass., 1963-70. Served with AUS, 1944-46. Recipient Trustees' award for Outstanding Tchr. of Year, 1971, Western Electric Fund award for excellence in instrn. New Eng. sect. Am. Soc. Engring. Edn., 1972, Teaching Excellence and Campus Leadership award Sears-Roebuck Found., 1990-91. Fellow ASME (exec. com. Worcester sect. 1952-57, sec.-treas. 1955-56, chmn. 1956-57, region I chmn. profl. divs. com. 1957-59, chmn. agenda, audit, budget and nominating com. Worcester 1957-58, chmn. symposium lubrication Worcester sect. 1957-58, chmn. Adm. Earle award com. 1958-59, chmn. devel. com. 1960-61); mem. Am. Soc. Engring. Edn. (sec.-treas. New Eng.), Sigma Xi, Pi Tau Sigma, Tau Beta Pi. Home: 9750 Cypress Lake Dr Fort Myers FL 33919-6064

SCOTT, KENNETH EUGENE, lawyer, educator; b. Western Springs, Ill., Nov. 21, 1928; s. Kenneth L. and Bernice (Albright) S.; m. Viviane H. May, Sept. 22, 1956 (dec. Feb. 1982); children: Clifton, Jeffrey, Linda; m. Priscilla Gay, July 30, 1989. BA in Econs., Coll. William and Mary, 1949; MA in Polit. Sci., Princeton U., 1953; LLB, Stanford U., 1956. Bar: N.Y. 1957, Calif. 1957, D.C. 1967. Assoc. Sullivan & Cromwell, N.Y.C., 1956-59, Musick, Peeler & Garrett, L.A., 1959-61; chief dep. savs. and loan commr. State of Calif., L.A., 1961-63; gen. counsel Fed. Home Loan Bank Bd., Washington, 1963-67; Parsons prof. law and bus. Stanford (Calif.) Law Sch., 1968-95, emeritus, 1995—; sr. rsch. fellow Hoover Instn., 1978-95, emeritus, 1995—; mem. Shadow Fin. Regulatory Com., 1986—, Fin. Economists Roundtable, 1991—; bd. dirs. Benham Capital Mgmt. Mut. Funds, Mountain View, Calif., RCM Capital Funds, San Francisco. Author: (with others) Retail Banking in the Electronic Age, 1977; co-editor: The Economics of Corporation Law and Securities Regulation, 1980. Mem. ABA, Calif. Bar Assn., Phi Beta Kappa, Order of Coif, Pi Kappa Alpha, Omicron Delta Kappa. Home: 610 Gerona Rd Stanford CA 94305-8453 Office: Crown Quadrangle Stanford Law Sch Stanford CA 94305-8610

SCOTT, KENNETH R., transportation executive; b. Iowa City. BCE, U. Iowa, 1960; MCE, U. Mo., Rolla, 1966. Commd. U.S. Army, 1961, advanced through grades, 1970; airport project engr. Norfolk (Va.) Airport Authority, 1970-72, asst. airport mgr., 1971-72, exec. dir., 1972—; adj. prof. Embry-Riddle Aero. U. at Norfolk Naval Air Sta. and Langley AFB. Bd. dirs. Norfolk Cmty. Promotion Corp., Va. Aviation and Space Edn. Forum. Mem. Am. Assn. Airport Execs., Va. Airport Operators Coun. Office: Norfolk Airport Authority Norfolk Intl Airport Norfolk VA 23518-5897

SCOTT, LAWRENCE VERNON, microbiology educator; b. Anthony, Kans., Jan. 28, 1917; s. Lawrence Garfield and Mable Grace (Madden) S.; m. Elizabeth Buchanan Rowe, Jan. 28, 1945; children: James Robert, Jean Elizabeth, Lawrence Rowe. B.A., Phillips U., 1940; M.S., U. Okla., Norman, 1947; Sc.D., Johns Hopkins U., 1950. Asst. prof. bacteriology, assoc. prof., 1950-58; prof. microbiology and immunology Sch. Medicine, U. Okla. Health Sci. Center, Oklahoma City, 1958-83, prof. emeritus, 1983—; chmn. dept. microbiology and immunology Sch. Medicine, U. Okla. Health Sci. Center, 1961-83; fellow in tropical medicine La. State U., 1967; cons. microbiologist St. Anthony and VA Hosps., 1957—; vis. prof. U. Otago, Dunedin, N.Z.; condr. microbiol. rsch. South Pole Sta., Antarctica, 1974, 75; participant People to People program to China, 1983, med. missions to Jamaica, 1988-93; invited participant reconciliation trip to Vietnam, 1993. Contbr. writings to profl. publs.; author: Medical Microbiology, 1982. Served to lt. USNR, 1942-46. Recipient Disting. Alumnus award Phillips U., 1968, Superior and Profl. Univ. Svc. award U. Okla., 1984. Mem. Am. Soc. Microbiology, Am. Acad. Microbiology, Assn. Med. Sch. Microbiologists (chmn.), N.Y. Acad. Scis., Okla. Acad. Scis., Am. Soc. Tropical Medicine and Hygiene, Sigma Xi. Democrat. Mem. Christian Church (Disciples of Christ). Condr. research. Home: 4125 NW 61st Ter Oklahoma City OK 73112-1346 Office: PO Box 26901 Oklahoma City OK 73126-0901 *Through hard work and education, my goal was to repay society. Thus, it* *has been important to make a contribution. In all activities, honesty and integrity are central.*

SCOTT, LEE HANSEN, retired holding company executive; b. Atlanta, Sept. 25, 1926; s. Elbert Lee and Auguste Lillian (Hansen) S.; m. Margaret Lee Smith, July 20, 1951; children: Bradley Hansen, Randall Lee. B.E.E., U. Fla., 1949. With Fla. Power Corp., St. Petersburg, 1949-94; dir. constrn., maintenance and operating Fla. Power Corp., 1968-71, v.p. customer ops., 1971-77, sr. v.p. ops., 1977-83, pres., 1983-88, chmn. bd., 1988-90, also bd. dirs.; also bd. dirs. Fla. Progress Corp.; ret., 1994; bd. dirs. Sun Banks; cons. in field. Pres. St. Petersburg chpt. ARC, 1977, Pinellas Com. of 100, 1980, Community Services Council, 1970, St. Petersburg Progress, 1983, Bus. and Industry Employment Devel. Council, 1983; chmn. bd. United Way. Served with USAF, 1944-46. Named Mr. Sun of St. Petersburg, 1990. Mem. Fla. Engring. Soc., IEEE, Elec. Council Fla. (pres. 1979), St. Petersburg C. of C. (v.p. 1980), Fla. C. of C. (pres. 1987-88), Pinellas Suncoast C. of C. (past chmn., chmn. bd. trustees). Presbyterian. Home: 601 Apalachee Dr NE Saint Petersburg FL 33702-2766

SCOTT, LINDA ANN, assistant principal, elementary education educator; b. St. Louis, Jan. 21, 1955; d. Jay R. and Bernadette (Hogan) S. BS, Youngstown State U., Ohio, 1979; MS, Gov.'s State U., Park Forest, Ill., 1991. Tchr. Bishop Blanchette, Joliet, Ill., 1981-85, St. Joseph's, Joliet, Ill., 1985-86, Hufford Jr. H.S., Joliet, Ill., 1986-92; asst. prin. Washington Jr. H.S., Joliet, 1992—; edni. coord. Warren-Sharpe Community Ctr., Joliet, 1990—. Mem. life PTA, 1990—. No. Ill. U. grantee, 1990, Argonne Nat. Lab. grantee, 1990, U. Ill. grantee, 1991. Mem. Ill. Coun. Tchrs. of Math. Home: 7324 Heritage Ct Frankfort IL 60423-9587 Office: Washington Jr HS 402 Richards St Joliet IL 60433-2218

SCOTT, LORRAINE ANN, fraternal organization executive; b. Cleve., Dec. 14, 1947; d. Harry F. and Ann Mae (Dolecek) Dufek; m. John William Scott, Jan. 4, 1969; 1 son, Bruce. BBA, Dyke Coll., Cleve., 1967. Acct., Fulton, Reid & Staples, Cleve., 1967-69; acct., data control Nat. City Bank, Cleve., 1969-70; asst. treas. Independence (Ohio) Bd. of Edn. 1978-80; exec. dir. Nat. Frat. of Phi Gamma Nu, Cleve., 1980—; owner, pres. L.A. Comics and Collectibles, Inc., 1988—. Mem. Am. Soc. Assn. Execs., Coll. Fraternities Editors Assn., Profl. Fraternity Execs.

SCOTT, LOUIS EDWARD, advertising agency executive; b. Waterbury, Conn., June 17, 1923; s. Louis Arthur and Ellen (Eckert) S.; m. Phyllis Corrine Denker, Jan. 27, 1942; children: Susan Louise, Eric Richard, Jane Lynn. BS, U. Calif., Berkeley, 1944. Sr. account exec. McCarty Co., L.A., 1946-50; with Foote, Cone & Belding, L.A., 1950-87; v.p. Foote, Cone & Belding, 1956, gen. mgr., 1959, became sr. v.p., 1963, dir., 1961—, chmn. exec. com., 1970-82; chmn. ops. com., pres. Foote, Cone & Belding/Honig, 1975-82; bd. dirs. Smart and Final Corp., Casino Internat., True North Comm.. Chmn. publicity com. Los Angeles Community Chest, 1960; patron mem. Los Angeles YMCA; mem. Freedoms Found.; chmn. So. Calif. advisory bd. Advt. Council; mem. exec. advisory bd. Art Center Coll. Design. Served with U.S. Maritime Service, also USNR, World War II. Named Western Advt. Man of Year, 1972. Mem. Am. Assn. Advt. Agys. (dir., past chmn. Western region), L.A. Advt. Club (dir.), L.A. C. of C., L.A. World Affairs Coun., Town Hall Club, Rio Verde Country Club, Seattle Yacht Club, Cruising Club Am. Home: PO Box 65079 Port Ludlow WA 98365-0079 Winter Home: 19119 E Tonto Tr Rio Verde AZ 85263 Office: 101 E Erie St Chicago IL 60611

SCOTT, LOUYSE HULSEY, school social worker; b. Toccoa, Ga., Feb. 20, 1952; d. William Floyd Hulsey Sr. and Doris Elaine (Smith) Carter; m. Roy Leon Scott, Jan. 11, 1975. AA, Emmanuel Coll., Franklin Spring, Ga., 1974; BSW, North Ga. Coll., Dahlonega, 1979; MSW, U. Ga., 1983. Lic. master social worker; cert. sch. social worker, pupil pers. dir. Social worker Alpine Psychoeducational Ctr., Gainesville, Ga., 1978-84; sch. social worker Stephens County Schs., Toccoa, Ga., 1984-96. Author: (poetry) Poetry for Everyday People, 1994. Mem. Stephens County Child Abuse Protocol Com., 1992—, Stephens County Domestic Violence Task Force, 1995—, Interagy. Staffing Com., 1994—; chairperson, past treas. Action Cmty. Team for A Drug Free Stephens County, 1990—; vol. Hand-in-Hand Hospice, Toccoa, 1995, Hospice of the Upstate, Anderson, S.C., 1989-90, Stephens County Red Ribbon Campaign, Toccoa. Mem. NASW (Sch. Social Work Specialist credentials), Sch. Social Workers Assn. Ga., Inc. (past membership chair, 9th Dist. Sch. Social Worker of Yr. 1992), Ga. Assn. Educators (sec. local chpt. 1994-96). Baptist. Avocations: writing, travel, collecting, music, politics. Home: PO Box 202 Carnesville GA 30521-0202 Office: Stephens County Pub Schs Rt 1 Box 75 Toccoa GA 30577

SCOTT, MARIANNE FLORENCE, librarian, educator; b. Toronto, Dec. 4, 1928; d. Merle Redvers and Florence Ethel (Hutton) S. BA, McGill U., Montreal, Que., Can., 1949, BLS, 1952; LLD (hon.), York U., 1985, Dalhousie U., 1989; DLitt (hon.), Laurentian U., 1990. Asst. librarian Bank of Montreal, 1952-55; law librarian McGill U., 1955-73, law area librarian, 1973-75, dir. libraries, 1975-84, lectr. legal bibliography faculty of law, 1964-75; nat. librarian Nat. Library of Can., Ottawa, Ont., 1984—. Co-founder, editor: Index to Can. Legal Periodical Lit, 1963—; contbr. articles to profl. jours. Decorated officer Order of Can., 1995; recipient IFLA medal, 1996. Mem. Internat. Assn. Law Libraries (dir. 1974-77), Am. Assn. Law Libraries, Can. Assn. Law Libraries (pres. 1963-69, exec. bd. 1973-75, honored mem. 1980—), Can. Library Assn. (council and dir. 1980-82, 1st v.p. 1980-81, pres. 1981-82), Corp. Profl. Librarians of Que. (v.p. 1975-76), Can. Assn. Research Libraries (pres. 1978-79, past pres. 1979-80, exec. com. 1980-81, sec.-treas. 1983-84), Ctr. for Research Libraries (dir. 1980-83), Internat. Fedn. Library Assns. (honor com. for 1982 conf. 1979-82), Conf. of Dirs. of Nat. Libraries (chmn. 1988-92). Home: 119 Dorothea Dr, Ottawa, ON Canada K1V 7C6 Office: Nat Libr Can, 395 Wellington St, Ottawa, ON Canada K1A 0N4

SCOTT, MARK ALDEN, hospital network executive; b. Chattanooga, Dec. 4, 1959; s. Dewey Alden and Rowena (Lowery) S.; m. Donna Ruth Kibble, Sept. 11, 1982; children: Matthew, Jacob. Student, Tenn. Tech. U., Cookeville, 1978-80, Chattanooga State U., 1981, 93—. Cert. network engr. Programmer Jerry Bell Constrn., Chattanooga, 1986-88; PC specialist Siskin Steel & Supply, Chattanooga, 1988-89; support and network mgr. Tiger Data Systems, Chattanooga, 1989-90, programmer, 1990; system cons. Data Concepts, Chattanooga, 1990—; microcomputer specialist Meml. Hosp., Chattanooga, 1991-93, network mgr., 1993-96, mgr. network svcs., 1996—; programmer Candlelighters, Chattanooga. Mem. Netware Users Internat., Chattanooga Area Netware Users Group (pres.). Republican. Baptist. Avocations: photography, volleyball, computers, music. Home: 8411 Forrest Breeze Dr Harrison TN 37341-6903 Office: Meml Hosp 2525 Desales Ave Chattanooga TN 37404-1161

SCOTT, MARY CELINE, pharmacologist; b. Los Angeles, July 14, 1957; d. Walter Edward and Shirley Jean (Elvin) S. BS in Biol. Sci., U. Calif., Irvine, 1978; MS in Biology, Calif. State U., Long Beach, 1980; PhD in Pharmacology, Purdue U., 1985; MBA in Pharm.-Chem. Studies, Fairleigh Dickinson U., 1995. Teaching asst. Calif. State U., Long Beach, 1979-80; teaching asst. Purdue U., West Lafayette, Ind., 1980-82, grad. instr., 1982-83, rsch. fellow, 1983-85, 1988-89; rsch. fellow Mayo Found., Rochester, Minn., 1985-87; sr. scientist Schering-Plough, Bloomfield, N.J., 1989-92; assoc. prin. scientist Schering-Plough, Kenilworth, N.J., 1993—. Contbr. articles to profl. jours. Mem.-at-large, bd. dirs. Washington Rock Girl Scout Coun. Mem. AAAS, Am. Chem. Soc., Am. Soc. Pharm. and Exptl. Therapeutics, Internat. Soc. for Study Xenobiot, Soc. Electroanalytical Chemistry, Soc. Neurosci., Sigma Xi, Delta Mu Delta. Democrat. Office: Schering-Plough Rsch Inst Dept Drug Metabolism & PK 2015 Galloping Hill Rd Kenilworth NJ 07033-1310

SCOTT, MICHAEL DENNIS, lawyer; b. Mpls., Nov. 6, 1945; s. Frank Walton and Donna Julia (Howard) S.; m. Blanca Josefina Palacios, Dec. 12, 1981; children: Michael Dennis, Cindal Marie, Derek Walton. B.S., MIT, 1967; J.D., UCLA, 1974. Bar: Calif. 1974, U.S. Dist. Ct. (no., so. and cen. dists.) Calif. 1974, U.S. Patent Office 1974, U.S. Ct. Appeals (9th cir.) 1974, U.S. Supreme Ct. 1978, U.S. Ct. Appeals (fed. cir.) 1989. Systems programmer NASA Electronics Research Lab., Cambridge, Mass., 1967-69, Computer Sciences Corp., El Segundo, Calif., 1969-71, Univac, Valencia, Calif., 1971; from assoc. to ptnr. Smaltz & Neelley, Los Angeles, 1974-81; exec. dir. Ctr. for Computer/Law, Los Angeles, 1977-94; sole practice Los Angeles, 1981-86, 88-89; pres. Law and Tech. Press, 1981-94; ptnr. Scott & Roxborough, Los Angeles, 1986-88, Graham & James, 1989-93; v.p., gen. counsel Sanctuary Woods Multimedia, Inc., San Mateo, Calif., 1993-94; of counsel Steinhart & Falconer, San Francisco, 1995-97; pvt. practice L.A., 1997—; adj. assoc. prof. law Southwestern U., L.A., 1975-80; chmn. World Computer Law Congress, L.A., 1991, 93. Author: (with David S. Yen) Computer Law Bibliography, 1979, The Scott Report, 1981-86, Computer Law, 1984, Scott on Computer Law, 1991, Law of Online Commerce, 1996, Scott on Multimedia Law, 1996, Multimedia: Law and Practice, 1993; editor in chief: Computer/Law Jour., 1978-94, Software Protection, 1982-92, Software Law Jour., 1985-94, Internat. Computer Law Adviser, 1986-92, The Cyberspace Lawyer, 1996—. Mem. Computer Law Assn. (bd. dirs. 1994—), Calif. State Bar Assn. Office: 32nd Fl 4 Arboldo Cir Manhattan Beach CA 90266-4937

SCOTT, MICHAEL LESTER, artist, educator; b. Lawrence, Kans., Sept. 24, 1952; s. Lester F. and Robbie (Guthrie) S.; m. Cheryl Ann Scott, May 24, 1982 (div.); children: Erik, Maxfield. BFA, Kans. City Art Inst., 1976; MFA, U. Cin., 1978. instr. Baker Hunt Found., Covington, Ky., 1986-93, Art Acad. of Cin. Work represented in pub. collections Butler Mus. Art, Youngstown, Ohio, New Orleans Mus. Art, Cin. Art Mus., Mus. Acquisitions of Chgo., J.B. Speed Mus., Bronnin-Foreman, Louisville, Owensboro (Ky.) Mus. Art, Hunter Mus. Art, Chattanooga, Phila. Mus. Art, Manhattan Life, N.Y.C. Mem. Sierra Club, Wilderness Soc., Green Peace, Nature Conservancy, Redwood League, Oxbow Found. Avocation: canoeist. Home and Studio: 2477 Country Pl New Richmond OH 45157-9511

SCOTT, MIMI KOBLENZ, psychotherapist, actress, publicist, journalist; b. Albany, N.Y., Dec. 15, 1940; d. Edmund Akiba and Tillie (Paul) Koblenz; m. Barry Stuart Scott, Aug. 13, 1961 (dec. Nov. 1991); children: Karen Scott Zantay, Jeffrey B. BA in Speech, English Edn., Russell Sage Coll., 1962; MA in Speech Edn., SUNY, Albany, 1968; M in Social Welfare, SUNY, 1985; PhD in Psychology, Pacific Western U., Encino, Calif., 1985. Cert. tchr., social worker. Tchr. English, speech Albany Pub. Schs., 1961-63; hostess, producer talkshow Sta. WAST-TV 13, Albany, 1973-75; freelance actress N.Y.C., 1975-77; producer, actress Four Seasons Dinner Theater, Albany, 1978-82; instr. of theatre Albany Jr. Coll., 1981-83; pvt. practice psychotherapy Albany, N.Y., 1985-92; exec. producer City of Albany Park Playhouse, 1989-92; actor self-employed N.Y.C., 1992—; actor Off Broadway show Grandma Sylvia's Funeral, 1996—; guest psychotherapist Sally Jessy Raphael Show, 1992, 93, Jane Whitney Show, 1994, A Current Affair, 1995, News Talk TV, 1995. Scriptwriter, dir., actress TV movie, 1985; feature writer Backstage, 1995-96, (off-Broadway) Grandma Sylvia's Funeral; featured in ind. film Mt. Vincent. Event organizer AmFar, 1985; co-chmn. March of Dimes Telethon, 1985-86; fundraiser Leukemia Found., 1987, Aids Benefit, N. Miami Beach, Fla., 1988; elected to SUNY Albany U. Found., 1990. Recipient FDR Nat. Achievement award March of Dimes, 1985, Recognition Cert. Capital Dist. Psychiat. Ctr., 1983, 84, 85; named Woman of Yr. YWCA, 1986, Commr. Albany Tricentennial Celebration, 1986; Mimi Scott Day proclaimed by Mayor of Albany, 1989. Mem. AEA, SAG, AFTRA, NASW. Jewish. Avocations: horseback riding, boating, golf, tennis. Home and Office: 211 West 71st # 6C New York NY 10023

SCOTT, NATHAN ALEXANDER, JR., minister, literary critic, religion educator; b. Cleve., Apr. 24, 1925; s. Nathan Alexander and Maggie (Martin) S.; m. Charlotte Hanley, Dec. 21, 1946; children: Nathan Alexander III, Leslie K. AB, U. Mich., 1944; BD, Union Theol. Sem., 1946; PhD, Columbia U., 1949; LittD, Ripon Coll., 1965, St. Mary's Coll., Notre Dame, Ind., 1969, Denison U., 1976, Brown U., 1981, Northwestern U., 1982, Elizabethtown Coll., 1989; LHD, Wittenberg U., 1965; DD, Phila. Div. Sch., 1967; STD, Gen. Theol. Sem., 1968; LHD, U. D.C., 1976; DD, The Protestant Episcopal Theological Seminary in Va., 1985; HumD, U. Mich., 1988; LHD, Wesleyan U., 1989, Bates Coll., 1990; STD, Univ of the South, 1992; DD, Kenyon Coll., 1993, Wabash Coll., 1996; Ordained priest Episcopal Ch., 1960; canon theologian Cathedral St. James, Chgo., 1967-76. dean of chapel, Va. Union U., 1946-47; instr. humanities, Howard U., 1948-51, asst. prof., 1951-53, assoc. prof., 1953-55; asst. prof. theology and literature, U. Chgo., 1955-58, assoc. prof., 1958-64, prof., 1964-72, Shailer Mathews prof. of theology and lit., 1972-76, prof. English, 1967-76; Commonwealth prof. religious studies, U. Va., 1976-81, William R. Kenan prof. religious studies, 1981-90, prof. English, 1976-90, prof. emeritus, 1990—. Author: Rehearsals of Discomposure: Alienation and Reconciliation in Modern Literature, 1952, The Tragic Vision and the Christian Faith, 1957, Modern Literature and the Religious Frontier, 1958, Albert Camus, 1962, Reinhold Niebuhr, 1963, The New Orpheus: Essays toward a Christian Poetic, 1964, The Climate of Faith in Modern Literature, 1965, The Broken Center: Studies in the Theological Horizon of Modern Literature, 1966, Ernest Hemingway, 1966, The Modern Vision of Death, 1967, Adversity and Grace: Studies in Recent American Literature, 1968, Negative Capability: Studies in the New Literature and the Religious Situation, 1969, The Unquiet Vision: Mirrors of Man in Existentialism, 1969, The Wild Prayer of Longing: Poetry and the Sacred, 1971, Nathanael West, 1971, Three American Moralists: Mailer, Bellow, Trilling, 1973, The Poetry of Civic Virtue: Eliot, Malraux, Auden, 1976, Mirrors of Man in Existentialism, 1978, The Poetics of Belief: Studies in Coleridge, Arnold, Pater, Santayana, Stevens and Heidegger, 1985, Visions of Presence in Modern American Poetry, 1993; co-editor Jour. Religion, 1963-77, (with Ronald Sharp) Reading George Steiner, 1994; adv. editor Religion and Lit., Literature and Theology, Callaloo. Fellow Am. Acad. of Arts and Scis.; mem. Soc. Arts, Religion and Contemporary Culture, Soc. for Values in Higher Edn. (Kent fellow), MLA., Am. Acad. Religion (pres. 1986), Century Assn. (N.Y.C.), Quadrangle Club, Arts Club (Chgo.), Greencroft Club (Charlottesville, Va.). Office: U Va Dept Religious Studies Charlottesville VA 22903

SCOTT, NINA OGLE, nurse; b. Pulaski, Va., Feb. 4, 1954; d. Willie James and Oletha (Horton) Ogle; m. Willard Montie Newman, Aug. 29, 1981 (div. 1983); 1 child, Travis Willard Newman; m. Jerry Wayne Scott, Nov. 23, 1995. LPN magna cum laude, New River C.C., 1977; AA, Wytheville C.C., 1985. RN, Va.; cert. Am. Bd. Quality Assurance and Utilization Rev. Physicians. Charge nurse Pulaski Cmty. Hosp., 1977-85; case mgr. Home Link Home Health Agy., Radford, Va., 1985-86; personal care coord. Carroll County Health Dept., Hillsville, Va., 1986-87; performance improvement coord. Twin County Regional Home Health, Galax, Va., 1987-97; dir. quality mgmt. Columbia St. Luke's Hosp., Bluefield, W.Va., 1997—; total quality mgmt. facilitator Twin County Regional Hosp., 1995-97. Mem. Nat. Assn. Healthcare Quality, Va. Assn. Healthcare Quality, S.W. Va. Assn. Healthcare Quality. Democrat. Methodist. Avocations: music, dancing. Home: 308 Parkdale St Bluefield VA 24605 Office: Columbia St Lukes Hosp 1333 Southview Dr Bluefield WV 24701-4317

SCOTT, NORMAN LAURENCE, engineering consultant; b. Meadow Grove, Nebr., Oct. 17, 1931; s. Laurence Ray Scott and Ruth Louise Braun; m. Joan Culbertson, Jan. 21, 1956; 1 child, Douglas Jay. BS in Civil Engring., U. Nebr., 1954. Registered prof. engr., Ill., Fla., Md., Minn., Va., Tex.; registered structural engr., Ill. Sales engr. R.H. Wright & Son, Ft. Lauderdale, Fla., 1956-58; mgr. Wright of Palm Beach, West Palm Beach, Fla., 1958-59; exec. sec. Prestressed Concrete Inst., Chgo., 1959-63; gen. mgr. Wiss, Janney, Elstner & Assoc., Northbrook, Ill., 1963-66; pres., chmn. The Consulting Engrs. Group Inc., Mt. Prospect, Ill., 1966—. 1st lt. USAF, 1954-56. Mem. ASCE (life), Am. Concrete Inst. (hon., pres. 1983-84, Henry C. Turner medal 1993), Ill. Soc. Profl. Engrs. (pres. North Shore chpt. 1962). Republican. Home: 701 Chatham Dr Glenview IL 60025-4403 Office: The Consulting Engrs Group 55 E Euclid Ave Mount Prospect IL 60056-1287

SCOTT, NORMAN ROSS, electrical engineering educator; b. N.Y.C., May 15, 1918; s. George Norman and Lillias B.H. (Ogg) S.; m. Marjorie M. Fear, Apr. 6, 1950; children: Mari, George, Ian, Charles. BS, MS, MIT, 1941; PhD, U. Ill., 1950. Asst. prof. elec. engring. U. Ill., Urbana, 1946-50; asst. prof. to prof. elec. engring. U. Mich., Ann Arbor, 1951-87, assoc dean Coll. Engring., 1965-68; dean Dearborn Campus U. Mich., 1968-71, prof. emeritus of elec. engring. and computer sci., 1987—; cons. Nat. Cash Register Co., Dayton, 1956-65; mem. math. and computer sci. rsch. adv. com. AEC, Washington, 1961-63. Editor-in-chief IEEE Trans. on Computers, N.Y.C., 1961-65; author: Analog and Digital Computer Technology, 1959, Electronic Computer Technology, 1970, Computer Number Systems and Arithmetic, 1985. Maj. U.S. Army, 1941-46. Fellow IEEE. Home: 2260 Gale Rd Ann Arbor MI 48105-9512 Office: U Mich Eecs Dept Ann Arbor MI 48109

SCOTT, NORMAN ROY, academic administrator, agricultural engineering educator; b. Spokane, Wash., Sept. 6, 1936; s. Roy Samuel and Agnes Sarafia (Lilljegren) S.; m. Sharon R. Cogley, June 17, 1961; children: Robin, Nanette, Shirlene. BS in Agrl. Engring., Wash. State U., 1958; PhD, Cornell U., 1962. Mem. faculty agrl. engring dept. Cornell U., Ithaca, N.Y., 1962—, chmn. agrl. engring. dept., 1978-84, dir. office for rsch. agrl. experimentation sta., 1984-89, v.p. rsch. and advanced studies, 1989—; mem. bd. on agriculture NRC, Nat. Acad. Scis., 1993-96. Contbr. articles to profl. jours.; patentee in field. Recipient Alumni Achievement award Wash. State U., 1995. Fellow ASHRAE, Am. Inst. for Med. and Biol. Engring. (founding 1991), Am. Soc. Agrl. Engrs. (tech. v.p. 1989-92, pres. elect 1992-93, pres. 1993-94, Henry Giese award 1989); mem. AAAS, N.Y. Acad. Scis., Nat. Acad. Engring., Am. Soc. for Engring. Edn., Instrument Soc. Am. (sr.). Democrat. Methodist. Avocations: sailing, golf. Home: 1662 Taughannock Blvd Trumansburg NY 14886-9120 Office: Cornell U Rsch and Advanced Studies 314 Day Hall Ithaca NY 14853-2801

SCOTT, OLOF HENDERSON, JR., priest; b. Phila., May 13, 1942; s. Olof Henderson and Julia Irene (Rutroff) S.; m. Eva Jakowenko, Sept. 13, 1969; children: Lisa Ann, Christopher Olof, Timothy Nicholas. BA in Physics, Franklin and Marshall Coll., 1964; MS in Nuclear Engring., Pa. State U., 1966; postgrad., St. Vladimir's Orthodox Theol. Sem., 1975-76. Ordained deacon Antiochian Orthodox Christian Ch., 1975, priest, 1976, archpriest, 1988. Ops. engr. S3G ops. Knolls Atomic Power Lab., GE Co., Schenectady, N.Y., 1966-68; project engr. S3G ops. Knolls Atomic Power Lab., GE Co., 1968-69; lead nuclear engr. Seabrook Nuclear project Pub. Svc. Co. of N.H., Manchester, 1969-70; project engr. VEPCO projects Nuclear Energy Sys. divsn. Westinghouse Elec. Co., Monroeville, Pa., 1970-72; project mgr. VEPCO projects Nuclear Energy Sys. divsn. Westinghouse Elec. Co., 1972-74, regional sales mgr. mktg., 1974-75; pastor St. George Orthodox Ch., Charleston, W.Va., 1976—; dean of clergy Appalachian-Ohio Valley Deanery, 1976—; spiritual advisor NAC-SOYO of Archdiocese, 1977-82, vice-chmn. inter-orthodox and inter-faith rels., 1987—; mem. exec. bd. W.Va. Coun. Chs., 1977—; bd. govs. Nat. Coun. Chs., 1977—, mem. nominating com., 1979-81, exec. com., 1985-96, membership com., 1988-91, unity and rels., 1989-92; mem. West Va. Ecumenical Coalition on Infant Mortality, 1992—. Contbr. articles to profl. jours. Bd. dirs. Religious Coalition for Cmty. Renewal in Charleston, 1987-95; bd. dirs. Kanawha Home for Children, 1986-89, pres., 1989; long-range planning com. W.Va. State Rep. Exec. Com., 1985-87; adv. bd. Nat. Ctr. for Human Rels. Mem. Acad. Parish Clergy (pres. W.Va. chpt. 1983-85), Am. Nuclear Soc., St. Vladimir's Theol. Found., Charleston Ministerial Assn., Order of St. John of Jerusalem-Knights Hospitellers (chaplain 1985—), Order of St. Ignatius of Antioch, Soc. for Preservation and Encouragement Barbershop Quartet Singing in Am. Inc. (v.p. 1984-85), Pa. State Club W.Va. (pres. 1984-88), Alden Kindred of Am., Sigma Pi Sigma, Delta Sigma Phi. Avocations: camping, barbershop quartet, motorcycling. Home: 4409 Staunton Ave SE Charleston WV 25304-1743 Office: St George Orthodox Ch PO Box 2044 Charleston WV 25327-2044 *My thoughts on life are but mere recitations of the Holy Scripture and my feeble attempts at making Those words and Thoughts my own.*

SCOTT, OTTO, writer; b. N.Y.C., May 26, 1918; s. Otto Felix and Katherine (McGivney) S.; m. Rose Massing (div. 1952); 1 child, Katherine; m. Nellie Mouradian (div. 1963); children: Mary, Philipa; m. Anna Barney Scott, Apr. 29, 1963; 1 child, Ann Elizabeth. MA in Polit. Sci., Valley Christian U., Fresno, Calif., 1985. Mem. staff United Features Syndicate, N.Y.C., 1939-40; v.p. Globaltronix de Venezuela, Caracas, 1954-56, Mohr Assocs., N.Y.C., 1957-59, Becker, Scott & Assocs., N.Y.C., 1960-63; editor Bill Bros., N.Y.C., 1964-67; asst. to chmn. Ashland (Ky.) Oil, Inc., 1968, 69; edn. writer, reviewer San Diego Union Tribune, 1970; sr. writer Chalcedon Found., Vallecito, Calif., 1982-94; cons. Ashland Oil, Inc., 1972—; editor, pub. Otto Scott's Compass, Seattle, 1990—. Author: History Ashland Oil (The Exception) 1968, Robespierre: Voice of Virtue (History French Revolution), 1974, The Professional: Biography of J.B. Saunders, 1976, The Creative Ordeal: History of Raytheon Corporation, 1976, James I: The Fool as King, 1976, 86, Other End of the Lifeboat (History of South Africa), 1985, Buried Treasure: The Story of Arch Mineral, 1987, The Secret Six: The Fool as Martyr, 1987, The Great Christian Revolution, 1991, The Powered Hand, History of Black and Decker, 1994. With U.S. Merchant Marine, 1941-47. Mem. Author's Guild, Overseas Press Club, Com. for Nat. Policy, Com. for Monetary Rsch. and Edn. Presbyterian. Office: Otto Scotts Compass Uncommon Books 828 S 299th Pl Federal Way WA 98003-3749

SCOTT, OWEN MYERS, JR., nuclear engineer; b. Birmingham, Ala., Oct. 15, 1952; s. Owen Myers and Sarah (Watson) S.; m. Eleanor Eason, July 15, 1978; 1 child, Owen Myers III. BCE, Auburn U., 1977; MBA, U. Ala., Birmingham, 1981; MS Nuclear Engring., Ga. Inst. Tech., 1986. Registered profl. engr., Ala., Fla., Ga., Miss. Physics lab. instr. Auburn (Ala.) U., 1977; civil/structural design engr. So. Co. Svcs., Inc., Birmingham, 1977-84, nuclear analysis engr., 1984-90; sr. nuclear engr. So. Nuclear Co., Birmingham, 1991—; pres. So. Investors, Birmingham, 1994—. Co-author (computer program) radiol. shielding analysis, 1986. Instr., advisor Jr. Achievement/Project Bus., Birmingham, 1982. Recipient Tech. award Electric Power Rsch. Inst., 1995. Mem. Am. Nuclear Soc., ASCE, Nat. Mgmt. Assn., Omicron Delta Epsilon. Methodist. Avocations: golf, music, computer programming, clockmaking, woodworking. Home: 3876 Timberline Way Birmingham AL 35243-2452 Office: So Nuclear Co 40 Inverness Center Pkwy PO Box 1295 Birmingham AL 35201

SCOTT, PAMELA MOYERS, physician assistant; b. Clarksburg, W.Va., Jan. 5, 1961; d. James Edward and Norma Lee (Holbert) Moyers; m. Troy Allen Scott, July 19, 1986. BS summa cum laude, Alderson-Broaddus Coll., 1983. Cert. physician asst. Physician asst. Weston (W.Va.) State Hosp., 1983-84, Rainelle (W.Va.) Med. Ctr., 1984—; support faculty physician asst. program Coll. W.Va., 1994—, mem. physician asst. adv. coun. 1993—, physician asst. program admission selection com., 1994—; keynote spkr. Alderson-Broadous Coll. Ann. Physician Assn. Banquet, 1992; presenter civa. Task Force on Adolescent Pregnancy and Parenting State Meeting, Charleston, 1992, W.Va. Primary Care Assn. Ann. Conf., Beckley, W.Va., 1994, W.Va. State Rural Health Conf., Morgantown, 1992, Chinese Med. Soc., Beijing, 1992; guest Lifetime TV med. program Physician Jour. Update, 1993; adv. coun. W.Va. Rural Health Networking, 1994-95, W.Va. Rural Networking Managed Care Policy Group, 1996. Mem. edtl. bd. Jour. Am. Acad. Physician Assts., dept. editor Procedures in Family Practice Dept., 1996; contbr. articles to profl. jours. Mem. W.Va. State Task Force on Adolescent Pregnancy and Parenting, 1992—, sec., 1996—; W.Va. Rural Networking Managed Care Study Group, 1995, W.Va. Rural Networking Managed Care Policy Group, 1996. Named Young Career Woman of Yr. Rainelle chpt. and Dist. V of W. Va., Citation of Honor at State Level of Competition, Bus. and Profl. Women's Club, 1986, Nominee for W. Va. Women's Commn. Celebrate Women award, 1996, 97. Fellow Am. Acad. Physician Assts. (del. to People's Republic China 1992, W.Va. chief del. Ho. of Dels. Nat. Conv. 1992, 94, 95, 96, W.Va. del. 1993, mem. rural health caucus 1991—, mem. pub. edn. com. 1992—, chair pub. edn. com. 1996—, presenter ann. CME conf. San Antonio 1994, Las Vegas 1995), W.Va. Assn. Physician Assts. (chair membership com. 1989-91, nominations and elections com. 1990-91, pres. 1991-94, immediate past pres. 1994-95, presenter Continued Med. Edn. Conf. 1993). Republican. Baptist. Avocations: reading, handicrafts, shopping. Home: PO Box 43 Williamsburg WV 24991-0043 Office: Rainelle Med Ctr 645 Kanawha Ave Rainelle WV 25962-1013

SCOTT, RALPH MASON, physician, radiation oncology educator; b. Leemont, Va., Nov. 23, 1921; s. Benjamin Thomas and Marion Hazel (Mason) S.; m. Alice Latine Francisco, Dec. 21, 1946; children: Susan Taylor, Ralph Mason, John Thomas. BA, U. Va., 1947; MD, Med. Coll. Va., 1950. Diplomate Am. Bd. Radiology (trustee 1965-76, treas. 1969-70, v.p. 1970-72, pres. 1972-74). Intern Robert Packer Hosp., Sayre, Pa., 1953-54, resident, 1954-57, dir. radiation therapy and nuclear medicine sect., 1957-59; with Christie Hosp. and Holt Radium Inst., Manchester, England, 1956-57; asst. prof. radiology U. Chgo. Med. Sch., 1959-60; assoc. prof. radiology, dir. radiation therapy and radioisotopes U. Louisville Med. Sch., 1960-64, prof., dir. radiation therapy, 1964-77, prof. radiation therapy, 1981-82; prof. emeritus U. Louisville, 1995; dir. J. Graham Brown Regional Cancer Ctr., Health Scis. Ctr. U. Louisville Med. Sch., 1981-82; dir. dept. radiation medicine Christ Hosp., Cin., 1982-93; ret.; clin. prof. radiology U. Cin. Coll. Medicine, 1982-93; prof., chmn. dept. therapeutic radiology U. Md. Sch. Med., 1977-80; dir. radiation therapy program div. cancer rsch. resources and ctrs., Nat. Cancer Inst. (on leave from U. Louisville), 1976-77. Pres. Ky. divsn. Am. Cancer Soc., 1972-73; bd. dirs. LADD, 1993-95, NKAR, 1993-95, Day Spring Inc., 1993-95, United Health Care, 1994-95, Seven Counties Svcs., Inc., 1997—. Lt. (j.g.) USNR, 1943-45. Fellow Christie Hosp. and Holt Radium Inst., Manchester, Eng., 1956-57. Mem. Am. Roentgen-Ray Soc. (exec. coun. 1968—, chmn. exec. coun. 1972-73), AMA, Am. Coll. Radiology (vice chmn. commn. on cancer 1968-69), Am. Radium Soc., Am. Soc. Therapeutic Radiologists, Assn. U. Radiologists, Radiol. Soc. N.Am., Pi Kappa Alpha, Phi Chi. Home: 5516 Tecumseh Cir Louisville KY 40207-1692

SCOTT, RAYMOND PETER WILLIAM, chemistry research educator, writer; b. Erith, Eng., June 20, 1924; came to U.S., 1969; s. Ronald and Annie (Hoadley) S.; m. Barbara Winifred Doreen Strange, Apr. 20, 1946; children: Kerry Raymond, Kevin Francis. B.Sc., U. London, 1946, D.Sc., 1958. Lab. leader Burroughs Welcome, Dartford, Eng., 1946-48; chief chemist APCM, 1948-52; research mgr. Benzole Producers, Watford, Eng., 1952-60; divisional mgr. Unilever, Sharnbrook and Bedfordshire, Eng., 1960-69; dir. phys. chemistry Hoffman La Roche, Nutley, N.J., 1969-80; dir. applied rsch. Perkin-Elmer, Norwalk, Conn., 1980-86; research prof. chemistry Georgetown U., Washington, 1986—; rsch. prof. dept. chemistry Birkbeck Coll., London. Author: Liquid Chromatography Detectors, 1977, 3d edit., 1987, Contemporary Liquid Chromatography, 1976, Liquid Chromatography Column Theory, 1991, Silica Gel and Bonded Phases, 1993, Liquid Chromatography for the Analyst, 1994, Chromatography Techniques, 1995, Chromatography Detectors, 1996, Tandem Techniques, 1996; editor: Gas Chromatography, 1960, Small Bore Columns in Liquid Chromatography, 1983. Recipient Tswett medal Am. Internat. Symposia on Chromatography, 1978; recipient Tswett award USSR Tech. Inst. Moscow, 1978, Martin medal in chromatography Chromatography Group Gt. Britain, 1982. Fellow Royal Soc. Chemistry (chartered, Analysis and Instrumentation award 1988), Am. Inst. Chemists (cert.), Am. Chem. Soc. (Chromatography award 1977). Office: Chemistry Dept Georgetown U Washington DC 20057 also: Birkbeck Coll, Chemistry Dept, London England

SCOTT, REBECCA ANDREWS, biology educator; b. Sunny Hill, La., June 4, 1939; d. Hayward and Dorothy (Nicholson) Andrews; m. Earl P. Scott, June 8, 1957; children: Stephanie Scott Dilworth, Cheryl L. BS, So. U., 1962; MS, Eastern Mich. U., 1969. Biology tchr., Detroit, 1966-68; sci. tchr. Ann Arbor (Mich.) Pub. Schs., 1968-69; biology tchr. North High Sch., Mpls., 1972—, coord. math., sci. tech. magnet, 1986—, advisor Jets Sci. Club. Mem. LVW (pres. 1981-83, 87-89, treas. 1989-94), Nat. Sci. Tchrs. Assn., Minn. Sci. Tchrs. Assn., Minn. Acad. Sci., Nat. Assn. Biology Tchrs., Iota Phi Lambda (pres. 1995—). Democrat. Presbyterian. Home: 3112 Wendhurst Ave Minneapolis MN 55418-1726 Office: 1500 James Ave N Minneapolis MN 55411-3161

SCOTT, RICHARD G., church official; b. Pocatello, Idaho, Nov. 7, 1928; s. Kenneth Leroy and Mary Whittle S.; m. Jeanen Watkins, July 16, 1953; 7 children. Degree in mech. engring., George Washington U.; postgrad. in nuclear engring. Mem. staff naval and land based power plants, 1953-65; head North Mission LDS Ch., Cordoba, Argentina, 1965-69; regional rep. in Uruguay, Paraguay, N.C., S.C., Va., Washington LDS Ch., 1969-77, mem. 1st Quorum of Seventy, 1977-83, mem. presidency of 1st Quorum of Seventy, 1983-88, apostle, 1988—. Avocations: jazz and classical music, hiking, birding, painting. Office: LDS Ch 50 E North Temple Salt Lake City UT 84150-0002*

SCOTT, RICHARD KEVIN, army officer; b. N.Y.C., Apr. 6, 1971; s. Richard Nathaniel and Edith Magdaline (Taylor) S. BSBA, BS in Am. Politics, Bucknell U., 1993. Commd. 2nd lt. U.S. Army, 1993, advanced through grades to 1st lt.; exec. officer 194th Mil. Police Co., Ft. Campbell, Ky., 1994-95; advanced party comdr. 194th Mil. Police Co., Panama, 1994-95; exec. officer Hdqs. Law Enforcement Command, Ft. Campbell, 1995-96; plans officer Hdqs. and Hdqs. Co. 101st Corps Support Group, Ft. Campbell, 1996—. Active Combined Fed. Campaign, 1993-96. Mem. Assn. U.S.Army, Ft. Campbell Officer's Club, Kappa Alpha Psi. Episcopalian. Avocations: investments, real estate, exercise. Home: 11150 Homewood Rd Ellicott City MD 21042

SCOTT, RICHARD L., health and medical products company executive; b. Kansas City, Mo., 1953. BSBA, U. Mo.; JD, So. Meth. U. Bar: Tex. Pvt. practice, until 1987; chmn., CEO, Columbia/HCA Healthcare Corp., Nashville, 1987—; bd. dirs. Banc One Corp. Recipient silver award as CEO of Yr. Fin. World mag.; named One of Top 25 Performers, U.S. News & World Report, 1995. Mem. Healthcare Leadership Coun., Bus. Roundtable, Bus. Coun. Office: Columbia/HCA Healthcare Corp 1 Park Plz St Nashville TN 37203*

SCOTT, RICHARD THURSTON, publishing executive; b. Glens Falls, N.Y., Apr. 28, 1936; s. Richard T. and Yvonne M. (Roulier) S.; m. Jeanne M. DeFilippo, Sept. 27, 1959; children: Kimberly Ann, Debra Lynne. BA, Colgate U., 1958; MS, Coll. St. Rose, Albany, N.Y., 1962. Supr., tchr. Glens Falls City Schs., 1962-66; reading coordinator pub. schs. Kingston, N.Y., 1966-68; div. mgr. Reader's Digest, Pleasantville, N.Y., 1968-84; pres., pub. David McKay Co., Inc., N.Y.C., 1985-86; pres. pub. Fodor's Travel Guides, N.Y.C., 1986-87; pub. Bantam Travel Books Bantam, Doubleday Dell Pub. Group, N.Y.C., 1987—; mng. editor Am. Bookseller Mag., Tarrytown, N.Y., 1993—; co-host In Conversation, radio talk show, Sta. WOR, N.Y.C., 1975-76. Author short stories, 1972; contbr. articles to profl. jours. pres. Mahopac (N.Y.) Pub. Library, 1975-80. Home: 18 Mekeel St Katonah NY 10536 Office: Am Bookseller Mag Managing Editor 828 S Broadway Tarrytown NY 10591-6603

SCOTT, RIDLEY, film director; b. South Shields, Northumberland, Eng., Nov. 30, 1939. Ed., Royal Coll. Art, London. Dir.: (films) Boy on Bicycle, The Duellists, 1978, Alien, 1978, Blade Runner, 1982, Legend, 1986, Someone to Watch Over Me (also exec. prodr.), 1987, Black Rain, 1989, Thelma & Louise (also co-prodr.), 1991, 1492: Conquest of Paradise (also co-prodr.); co-prodr.: The Browning Version, 1994, White Squall, 1996; exec. prodr.: Monkey Trouble, 1994; co-and exec. prodr. G.I. Jane, 1997; dir. more than 3,000 TV commls.; set designer Z-Cars, The Informers series (BBC, London). Winner Design scholarship, N.Y. Office: CAA 9830 Wilshire Blvd Beverly Hills CA 90212-1804

SCOTT, ROBERT ALLYN, academic administrator; b. Englewood, N.J., Apr. 16, 1939; s. William D. and Ann F. (Waterman) S.; m. Phyllis Virginia Brice, Mar. 23, 1963; children: Ryan Keith, Kira Elizabeth. BA, Bucknell U., 1961; PhD, Cornell U., 1975. Mgmt. trainee Procter & Gamble Co., Phila., 1961-63; asst. dir. admissions Bucknell U., Lewisburg, Pa., 1965-67; asst. dean Coll. Arts and Scis. Cornell U., Ithaca, 1967-69, assoc. dean, 1969-79, anthropology faculty, 1978-79; dir. acad. affairs Ind. Commn. for Higher Edn., Indpls., 1979-84, asst. commr., 1984-85; pres. Ramapo (N.J.) Coll., 1985—; cons. Sta. WSKG Pub. TV and Radio, 1977-79, also to various colls. and univs., pubs., 1966—; mem. curriculum adv. com. Ind. Bd. Edn., 1984-87, Lilly Endowment Think Tank, 1984-86; mem. nat. adv. panel Ind. 21st Century Schooling Project, 1990-92; U.S. rep. to creation of U. Mobility Asia-Pacific, 1993—; U.S. rep. to meetings of Coun. European Rectors, 1991—; sr. cons., chair N.J. Higher Edn. Restructuring Team, 1994; bd. dirs. World Trade Coun., Hackensack Univ. Med. Ctr.; chmn. bd. Am. Ednl. Products, Inc. Author books and monographs; editorial bd. Cornell Rev., 1976-79; book rev. editor Coll. and Univ., 1974-78; cons. editor Change mag., 1979—; cons. editor Jour. Higher Edn., 1985—; exec. editor Saturday Evening Post book div. Curtis Pub. Co., 1982-85; contbr. articles to sociols., ednl. and popular publs. Trustee Bucknell U., 1976-78, First Unitarian Ch., Ithaca, 1970-73, 78-79, chmn., 1971-73, Unitarian Universalist Ch. of Indpls., 1980-85. With USNR, 1963-65. Spencer Found. rsch. grantee, 1977; recipient Sagamore of the Wabash award, 1986, Prudential Found. Leader of Yr. award, 1987, Disting. Svc. award West Bergen Mental Health Ctr., 1991, NYU Presdl. medal, 1994, Sci. and Edn. award Boy Scouts Am., 1993. Fellow Am. Anthrop. Assn.; mem. Assn. Study Higher Edn., Am. Sociol. Assn., Am. Assn. Higher Edn., Am. Assn. State Colls. and Univs. (Coll. and Univ. Satellite Ednl. Sys. chair, coun. on Liberal Arts and Scis., chair 1990-93), O.E.C.D. (higher edn. program Paris), Am. Coun. on Edn. Commn. On Internat. Edn. (chair), Am. Forum Higher Edn. Colloquium (chmn. 1982-84, 96—), N.J. Assn. of Coll. and Univs. (chair 1991-92), Bucknell U. Alumni Assn. (bd. dirs. 1971-80, pres. 1976-78, Outstanding Achievement 1991), Indian Trail Club, Phi Kappa Psi, Phi Kappa Phi. Office: Ramapo Coll 505 Ramapo Valley Rd Mahwah NJ 07430-1623

SCOTT, ROBERT CORTEZ, congressman, lawyer; b. Washington, Apr. 30, 1947; s. Charles Waldo and Mae (Hamlin) S. BA, Harvard U., 1969; JD, Boston U., 1973; LLD (hon.), Commonwealth Coll., Hampton, Va., 1988. Pvt. practice Newport News, 1973—; del. Va. Ho. Dels., Richmond, 1978-83, senator, 1983-92; mem. 103rd-105th Congresses from 3rd Va. dist., Washington, D.C., 1993—; mem. econ. & ednl. opportunity com., judiciary com., edn. and workforce com., judiciary com. Br. pres. NAACP, Newport News, 1974-80; pres. bd. Peninsula Legal Aid Ctr., Hampton, 1977-81; mem. state exec. bd. March of Dimes, Va., 1987—; chmn. 1st dist. Dem. Party Va., 1980-85; bd. dirs. Hampton Roads March of Dimes; adv. com. Peninsula Boy Scouts Am. Recipient Brotherhood Citation award Nat. Conf. Christians & Jews, 1985, Child Adv. award Va. Acad. Pediatrics, 1987, Disting. Svc. award Va. State Fraternal Order Police, 1987, Outstanding Legislator award So. Health Assn., 1989. Mem. Peninsula C. of C., Alpha Phi Alpha, Sigma Pi Phi. Democrat. Office: US House of Reps 2464 Rayburn Bldg Washington DC 20515-0003*

SCOTT, ROBERT EDWARD, JR., lawyer; b. Washington, Oct. 1, 1945; s. Robert Edward Sr. and Helen (Jackson) S.; m. Carolyn Damron, Oct. 14, 1977; children: Kathryn Damron, Elizabeth Carolyn. BS in Econs., U. Md., 1967; JD, Georgetown U., 1970. Bar: Md. 1970, U.S. Dist. Ct. Md. 1971, U.S. Ct. Appeals (4th cir.) 1971, U.S. Supreme Ct. 1974, U.S. Ct. Appeals D.C. 1980. Law clk. Chief Judge Edward S. Northrop U.S. Dist. Ct. Md., Balt., 1970-71; assoc. Semmes, Bowen & Semmes, Balt., 1971-77, ptnr., 1978—. Contbr. articles to profl. jours. Bd. dirs. Ruxton, Riderwood, Lake Roland Area Community Assn. (pres. 1988-89), Ruxton, Md., Shock Trauma Bd. Visitors, Balt.; pres. Murray Hill Improvement Assn., Balt., 1985-87. Mem. ABA, Fed. Bar Assn., Internat. Assn. Def. Counsel, Def. Rsch. Inst. (bd. dirs., pres.-elect 1997-98, regional v.p. 1989-92, Md. State chmn. 1984-89), D.C. Bar Assn., Md. Assn. Def. Trial Counsel (pres. 1983-84), 4th Cir. Jud. Conf., Md. Bar Assn., Balt. City Bar Assn. (libr. com., bd. dirs.). Avocations: golf, reading, gardening. Home: 6409 Murray Hill Rd Baltimore MD 21212-1028

SCOTT, ROBERT EDWIN, law educator; b. Nagpur, India, Feb. 25, 1944; came to U.S., 1955; s. Roland Waldeck and Carol (Culver) S.; m. Elizabeth (Loch) Shumaker, Aug. 14, 1965; children: Christina Elaine, Robert Adam. BA, Oberlin (Ohio) Coll., 1965; JD, Coll. of William and Mary, 1968; LLM, U. Mich., 1969, SJD, 1973. Bar: Va. 1968. From asst. to assoc. prof. Law Sch. Coll. of William and Mary, Williamsburg, Va., 1969-74; prof. law Sch. of Law U. Va., Charlottesville, 1974-82, Lewis F. Powell, Jr. prof. Sch. of Law, 1982—, dean and Arnold H. Leon prof., 1991—. Author: Commercial Transactions, 1982, 91, Sales Law and the Contracting Process, 1982, 91, Contract Law and Theory, 1988, 93. Fellow Am. Bar Found.; mem. Va. Bar Assn. Democrat. Methodist. Home: 1109 Hilltop Rd Charlottesville VA 22903-1220 Office: U Va Sch of Law Charlottesville VA 22903

SCOTT, ROBERT HAL, minister; b. Floydada, Tex., Apr. 2, 1930; s. Samuel Price and Fannie (Miller) S.; m. Carolyn Weaver, July 31, 1950; children: Vicki Lynette Reese, Steven Robert Scott. BA, Pasadena Coll., 1950; DD, Point Loma Coll., 1983. Ordained to ministry Ch. of the Nazarene, 1953. Pastor various Chs. of the Nazarene, Calif., 1950-75; dist. supt. Ch. of the Nazarene/So. Calif. Dist., Orange, Calif., 1975-86; dir. internat. missions Ch. of the Nazarene, Kansas City, Mo., 1986-94, dir. 21st Century Rsch. Inst., 1994—; trustee Pasadena (Calif.) Coll., 1964-75, Point Loma Coll., San Diego, Calif., 1975-86, Nazarene Bible Coll., Colorado Springs, 1976-80. Author: All Over the World, Our Family, 1994; contbr. articles to World Mission mag., 1986—.

SCOTT, ROBERT HAYWOOD, JR., lawyer; b. Hazelton, Pa., Mar. 27, 1941; s. Robert Haywood and Marjorie Jane (Briggs) S.; m. Sandra Lou Carroll, June 6, 1966; children: Paige Carroll, Robert Haywood. AB magna cum laude, Kenyon Coll., 1963; JD with distinction, Duke U., 1966. Bar: Mo. 1969, Kans. 1966, Ohio 1972. Assoc. Hoskins King Springer McGannon and Hahn, Kansas City, Mo., 1970-72; operating v.p., sr. counsel Federated Dept. Stores, Cin., 1972-83; ptnr. Roberts Fleischaker & Scott, Joplin, Mo., 1983-88; chief exec. officer W&S Mfg., Inc., Joplin, 1988-92, also chmn. bd. dirs.; CEO Robert Scott Investment Banking, 1988—; chmn. Deep Sea Archaeology Rsch. Coun., 1994—. Contbr. articles to profl. jours. Served to capt. USAF, 1966-70. Mem. Mo. Bar Assn., Order of the Coif, Phi Beta Kappa. Republican. Episcopalian. Home: 1330 Valle Dr Joplin MO 64801-1074

SCOTT, ROBERT LANE, chemist, educator; b. Santa Rosa, Calif., Mar. 20, 1922; s. Horace Albert and Maurine (Lane) S.; m. Elizabeth Sewall Hunter, May 27, 1944; children: Joanna Ingersoll, Jonathan Armat, David St. Clair, Janet Hamilton. S.B., Harvard U., 1942; M.A., Princeton U., 1944, Ph.D., 1945. Sci. staff Los Alamos Lab., 1945-46; Frank B. Jewett fellow U. Calif., Berkeley, 1946-48; faculty UCLA, 1948—, prof. chemistry, 1960-92, prof. emeritus, 1993—, chmn. dept., 1970-75. Author: (with J.H. Hildebrand) Solubility of Nonelectrolytes, 3d edit, 1950, rev., 1964, Regular Solutions, 1962, Regular and Related Solutions, 1970; contbr. articles to profl. jours. Guggenheim fellow, 1955; NSF sr. fellow, 1961-62; Fulbright lectr., 1968-69. Fellow AAAS, Am. Phys. Soc.; mem. Am. Chem. Soc. (Joel Henry Hildebrand award 1984), Royal Soc. Chemistry (London), Sigma Xi. Home: 11128 Montana Ave Los Angeles CA 90049-3509

SCOTT, ROBERT LEE, speech educator; b. Fairbury, Nebr., Apr. 19, 1928; s. Walter Everett and Ann Maria (Jensen) S.; m. Betty Rose Foust, Sept. 13, 1947; children—Mark Allen, Janet Lee, Paul Matthew. B.A., U. No. Colo., 1950; M.A., U. Nebr., 1951; Ph.D., U. Ill., 1955. Asst. prof. speech U. Houston, 1953-57; asst. prof. U. Minn., 1957-59, assoc. prof., 1959-63, prof., 1963—, chair dept. speech communication, 1971-89, chair dept. Spanish and Portuguese, 1992-94. Author: Rhetoric of Black Power, 1969, Moments in the Rhetoric of the Cold War, 1970; contbr. articles to profl. jours. Recipient Teaching award Coll. of Liberal Arts, U. Minn., 1981. Mem. Speech Comm. Assn. (editor Quar. Jour. Speech 1971-74, Winans-Wichelns Rsch. award 1970, Charles H. Woolbert Rsch. award, 1981, Douglas-Ehninger Disting. Scholar award 1989, Disting. Scholar of Assn. 1992), Ctrl. States Speech Assn., Internat. Soc. for Study of Rhetoric. Office: U Minn Dept Speech Communication Minneapolis MN 55455-0194

SCOTT, ROBERT MONTGOMERY, museum executive, lawyer; b. Bryn Mawr, Pa., May 22, 1929; s. Edgar and Helen Hope (Montgomery) S.; m. H. Gay Elliot, June 30, 1951 (separated); children: Hope Tyler Scott Rogers, Janny Scott Ritter, Elliot Montgomery. AB, Harvard U., 1951; LLB, U. Pa., 1954; DHL (hon.), Thomas Jefferson U., 1996. Ptnr. Montgomery McCracken Walker & Rhoads, Phila., 1961-82, of counsel, 1982-88; spl. asst. to U.S. Amb. to Ct. of St. James, London, 1969-73; hon. Brit. consul Phila., 1979-83; pres., chief exec. officer Phila. Mus. Art, 1992-96, hon. chmn., 1997—; pres. Acad. Music of Phila., 1973-80; mem. adv. bd. First Union Bancorp. No. Trustee Phila. Mus. Art, 1965—, Royal Oak Found., 1978-86, Inst. Cancer Rsch., Fox Chase Cancer Ctr., 1960-86, Lankenau Hosp., 1959-86, William Penn Found., 1986-91; pres. Mary Louise Curtis Book Fedn., 1989—, Curtis Inst. of Music, 1994—; bd. dirs. Glyndebourne Assn. Am., Inc. Recipient Superior Honor award Dept. State, 1973, Gov. of Pa. award for Leadership in the Arts, 1996, Citizen of Yr. award Penjerdel Coun., 1996, Hospitality City U.S.A. Grand award Greater Phila. Hotel Assn., 1996. Fellow Am. Bar Found.; mem. Am. Assn. Mus., Greater Phila. Cultural Alliance, Phila. Club, Knickerbocker Club, Locust Club, White's Club. Republican. Home: Ardrossan 807 Newtown Rd Villanova PA 19085-1031

SCOTT, RONALD, lawyer; b. Lexington, Mich., Aug. 31, 1947. BA, Baylor U., 1969; JD, U. Tex., 1975. Bar: Tex. 1975. Mem. Bracewell & Patterson, Houston. Mem. State Bar Tex., Tex. Bar Found., Houston Bar Found., Houston Bar Assn., Order of Barristers, Phi Delta Phi. Office: Bracewell & Patterson South Tower Pennzoil Pl 711 Louisiana St Ste 2900 Houston TX 77002-2721

SCOTT, RONALD CHARLES, lawyer; b. Greenville, S.C., Jan. 8, 1948; s. Robert Claude and Louise Helen (Tinsley) S.; m. Debra Whaley, Aug. 11, 1973; children: Robert Marion, Jordan Whaley, Carter Whaley. BBA cum laude, The Citadel, 1970; MBA, U. S.C., 1972, M in Acctg., JD, 1976. Bar: S.C. 1976, U.S. Dist. Ct. S.C. 1977, U.S. Tax Ct. 1977. Pres. Scott & Mathews P.A., Columbia, S.C., 1978-92, Scott Law Firm, P.A., Columbia, S.C., 1993—; pres. Heritage Title, Columbia, 1980—. Bd. of visitors, pres.'s adv. council Med. U. S.C.; past state pres. Nat. Soc. to Prevent Blindness, past state sec.; state fundraising chmn. Arthritis Found. Served to capt. (adj. gen. corps.) USAR, 1970-76. Named Outstanding Young Man of Columbia Jaycees, 1982; recipient State Dist. Svc. award U.S. Jaycees, 1982, Leadership S.C. award Office of the Gov., 1986; recipient Fellowship Regional Finalist award White House, 1984. Mem. ABA (past state rep., significant legis. com., real property com.), S.C. Bar Assn. (sec. subcom. model corp. act panel), Columbia C. of C. (com. of 100, Leadership Columbia award 1981), Summit Club, Palmetto Club (Columbia), DeBordieu Club (Georgetown, S.C.), Capital City Club. Office: Scott & Scott Law Firm PA 1331 Laurel St # 2065 Columbia SC 29201-2513

SCOTT, ROSA MAE, artist, educator; b. East Hampton, N.Y., Apr. 12, 1937; d. James Alexander and Victoria (Square) Nicholson; m. Frank Albert Hanna, Apr. 1, 1957 (div. Mar. 1985); 1 child, Frank Albert Hanna III; m. Warner Bruce Scott, Aug. 3, 1985; children: Bernadine, John, Patricia, Charlene, Lawrence. AA, Dabney Lancaster, 1989; BA, Mary Baldwin, 1992. Cosmetologist Rosa's Beauty Shop, East Hampton, 1962-68; sec. Frank Hanna's Cleaning Co., East Hampton, 1962-77; cashier, clk. Brook's Pharmacy, East Hampton, 1992; lead tchr. East Hampton Day Care, 1992-94; substitute tchr. Lexington (Va.) Schs., 1994—; sec. Lylburn Downing Cmty. Ctr., Inc., Lexington, 1985-92; arts and crafts tutor, supr. E. Hampton Town Youth After Sch. Program, 1996—. Acrylic painter. Pres. Rockbridge Garden Club, Lexington, 1996; co-organizer Va. Co-op. Ex. Garden Clubs, Lexington, 1995; bd. dirs. Rockbridge Area Pres. Homes, 1996, Fine Arts of Rockbridge, 1985-92, Friends of Lime Kiln, Lexington, 1985-92. Mem. Rockbridge Arts Guild. Avocations: collecting Emmett Kelly clowns, art, reading, theater, tennis. Address: PO Box 1265 154 Springs Rd East Hampton NY 11937

SCOTT, RUTH LOIS, dental hygiene educator; b. Chanute, Kans., Aug. 28, 1934; d. Walter Roy and Ruth Lois (Cunningham) Harder; m. Charles Calvin Scott, July 3, 1956 (div. July 1963); children: Valerie Elizabeth, Matthew Stuart, David Bruce. BA in Psychology and Theatre with honors, U. Kans., 1958; Cert., U. Mo., Kansas City, 1954, MS in Dental Hygiene Edn., 1972. Asst. prof. U. Iowa Coll. Dentistry, 1972-73; from instr. to clin. instr. dept. dental hygiene U. Mo.-Kansas City Sch. Dentistry, 1969-71; asst. prof. dept. preventive dentistry U. Mo. Kansas City Sch. Dentistry, asst. prof. comprehensive dentistry for adults, 1975-77, asst. prof. div. dental hygiene, 1977-81, assoc. prof., 1981—; pvt. practice dentistry Kansas City, 1954-90. Contbr. articles to profl. jours. Charter mem. Kansas City chpt. Parents Without Ptnrs., 1973—; mem. Ch. Without Walls. Recipient Dental Hygiene Alumni Svc. award U. Mo.-Kansas City, 1992. Mem. Am. Dental Hygienists Assn., Mo. Dental Hygienists Assn., Greater Kansas City Dental Hygiene Component Soc., Am. Assn. Dental Schs., Am. Assn. Dental Rsch., U. Mo.-Kansas City Dental Hygiene Alumni Assn., Phi Beta Kappa, Sigma Phi Alpha (exec. sec. 1990-96), Phi Beta Kappa, Phi Psi, Phi Kappa Phi. Unitarian-Universalist. Office: U Mo-Kansas City 650 E 25th St Kansas City MO 64108-2716

SCOTT, STANLEY DEFOREST, real estate executive, former lithography company executive; b. Hudson County, N.J., Nov. 2, 1926; s. Stanley DeForest and Anne Marie (Volk) S.; B.A., U. So. Calif., 1950; m. Mary Elizabeth Hazard, Dec. 30, 1953. Gen. mgr. Alfred Scott Publishers, N.Y.C., 1951-56; chmn., pres. S.D. Scott Printing Co., Inc., N.Y.C., 1956-92; gen. ptnr. 145 Hudson St. Assocs. Art mus. hist. socs.; past co-chmn. Fraunces Tavern Mus. com., 1973-87; assoc. J. Carter Brown Libr.; former mem. Mayor's Industry Adv. Com.; former bd. dirs., Bus. Relocation Com. With USNR, 1944-46. Frick Collection fellow. Mem. Soc. Mayflower Descs., Soc. Colonial Wars, Pilgrims U.S., S.R. (bd. mgrs., 1969—, treas. 1972-73, 3d v.p. 1975-77, 2d v.p. 1977-79, 92-94, 96—, chmn. museum and art com. 1987), Am. Numismatic Soc., English-Speaking Union U.S. (patron), Royal Oak Found., Am. Assocs. Royal Acad. Arts, Am. Friends English Heritage, Sir John Soane's Museum Found. (patron), Met. Mus. Art, Mus. Modern Art, Morgan Libr., rare book librs., Am. Mus. in Britain (coun. 1986—), Mt. Vernon (Va.) Ladies Assn. (adv. com.), Grolier Club, Knickerbocker Club, Union Club, Downtown Athletic Club, The Church Club of N.Y., Merchants Club (v.p. 1985-94). Republican. Episcopalian. Home: 1 Sutton Pl S New York NY 10022-2471 Office: 145 Hudson St New York NY 10013-2103

SCOTT, STEPHEN BRINSLEY, theater producer; b. Pitts., Aug. 27, 1950; s. Robert Crawford and Lucille (Hendrickson) S. BS in Edn., U. Kans., 1972; MA, U. Denver, 1973. Artistic dir. Creede (Colo.) Repertory Theatre, 1976-78; chair dept. theatre Baker U., Baldwin, Kans., 1978-80; dir. edn. and cmty. svcs. Goodman Theatre, Chgo., 1980-84, dir. arts in edn., 1986-88, artistic assoc., 1988-94, assoc. producer, 1994—; dir. ednl. programs Chgo. Internat. Theatre Festival, 1985-86; spl. instr. Loyola U. Chgo., 1987-95; instr. Columbia Coll., Chgo., 1981-85, 92-97, Latin Sch. Chgo., 1984-86; mem. arts in edn. panel Nat. Endowment for Arts, Washington, 1990-91. Mem. adv. panels Ill. Arts Coun., Chgo., 1984-87; mem. com. League Chgo. Theatres, 1990—; cmty. rep. local sch. coun. Franklin Sch., Chgo., 1990-94. pres. Chgo. Coalition for Arts in Edn., 1983-85. Mem. Ill. Theatre Assn. (exec. com. 1987-97), Soc. Stage Dirs. and Choreographers, Ill. Alliance for Arts in Edn., Ill. Arts Alliance, Phi Beta Kappa. Democrat. Home: 124 W Polk St Apt 207 Chicago IL 60605-2069 Office: Goodman Theatre 200 S Columbus Dr Chicago IL 60603-6402

SCOTT, STEPHEN CARLOS, academic administrator; b. Greenville, S.C., Sept. 20, 1949; s. Carlos O'Dell and Christina (Nikitas) S.; m. Patsy Jordan, Apr. 13, 1968; children: Stephanie Christina, Lance Stephen. BA, Clemson (S.C.) U., 1971, MEd, 1975, EdD, 1987. Owner, mgr. Scotty's Inc., restaurant, Clemson, 1967-71; tchr. math. Pickens (S.C.) Sr. High Sch., 1972-74; instr. bus. Tri-County Tech. Coll., Pendleton, S.C., 1974-76, head dept., 1976-78; dir. br. campus Tri-County Tech. Coll., Easley, S.C., 1978-80; dean bus. Greenville Tech. Coll., 1980-85, assoc. v.p., 1985-88; pres. Southeastern C.C., Whiteville, N.C., 1988—; cons. P.C.E. Fed. Credit Union, Liberty, S.C., 1975-88, Jacobs Mfg. Co., Clemson, 1979-80, Flat Rock Shelter Ctr., Easley, 1980-85. Contbr. articles to profl. jours. and mags. Pres. So. Shelter Ctr., Greenville, 1986—, Good Shepherd Found., Whiteville, 1990-92; bd. dirs. Good Shepherd, 1988-91; chmn. Columbus County Sch. Bond Dr., 1989, Am. Heart Fund Drive Columbus County, 1992; co-chmn. Columbus County Long Range Planning Com., 1989-91; vice chmn. Pvt. Industry Coun. Region O, 1992—; founding dir. Habitat for Humanity Columbus County, 1992; co-chmn. bd. dirs. Columbus County Rural Health Ctr., 1994. Recipient award for patriotism U.S. Savs. Bonds Program, 1987. Mem. Am. Assn. Community and Jrs. Colls. (Pres.'s Acad.), Rotary (bd. dirs. Whiteville 1990-92, pres. 1992-93). Presbyterian. Avocations: running, chess, numismatics, reading. Office: Southeastern CC RR 1, Hwy 74-76 Box 151 Whiteville NC 28472*

SCOTT, STUART, sports anchor; b. July 19, 1965. BA in Speech Comms. and Radio/TV/Film, U. N.C., 1987. News reporter, weekend anchor WPDE-TV, Florence, S.C., 1987-88; news reporter WRAL-TV, Raleigh, N.C., 1988-90; sports reporter, sports anchor WESH-TV, Orlando, Fla., 1990-93; anchor SportSmash, sports anchor, sports reporter ESPN, 1993—; anchor reporter SportsNight: College Football Edition, 1995—, co-host SportsNight, 1994. Office: ESPN ESPN Plaza Bristol CT 06010

SCOTT, SUSAN, lawyer; b. Orange, N.J., July 25, 1943; d. Bailey Bartlett and Regina Margaret (Butler) S.; m. Robert John Gillispie, Aug. 20. 1966 (div. 1979); children: Robert John Jr., Megan Anne. BA in Math, Catholic U. Am., 1965; JD, Rutgers U., 1975. Bar: N.J. 1975, U.S. Dist. Ct. N.J. 1975, U.S. Ct. Appeals (3d cir.) 1988, U.S. Supreme Ct. 1993. Applied math. CIA, Washington, 1965-68; assoc. Pitney, Hardin, Kipp & Szuch,

Morristown, N.J., 1975-76; corp. counsel Allied-Signal, Inc., Morristown, 1977-78; with Riker, Danzig, Scherer, Hyland & Perretti, Morristown, 1979—; mem. Child Placement Rev. Bd., Morristown,1992—; commr. Morris County Bd. Condemnation, Morristown, 1989—. Mem. ABA, N.J. Bar Assn., Morris County Bar Assn. Democrat. Roman Catholic. Avocations: tennis, photography. Home: 362 South St Morristown NJ 07960 Office: Riker Danzig Scherer Hyland & Perretti Headquarters Plz 1 Speedwell Ave Morristown NJ 07960-6838

SCOTT, SUZANNE, writer, artist; b. Athens, Ga., Mar. 1, 1940; d. Jane Scott (Terrell) Overby; divorced; children: Elizabeth Atwell, William F. Atwell Jr., Stephanie Atwell Zehr, David Allan Atwell; life ptnr. Lynne Mary Constantine. BA in English, Eastern Mennonite Coll., 1979; MA in English Lit., James Madison U., 1986. Continuity writer WSVA TV-AM-FM, Harrisonburg, Va., 1966-68, 71-72, WBTX-FM, Broadway, Va., 1972; instr. English as 2d lang. Eastern Mennonite Coll., Harrisonburg, 1977-78, instr. English, 1979; teaching asst. English James Madison U., Harrisonburg, 1979-81; writer Psychiatric Insts. Am., Washington, 1981-84; founding ptnr. Community Scribes, Arlington, Va., 1984—; founding ptnr., mng. editor Womans Monthly, 1992—; v.p., artist Arts & Space, Inc., Arlington, 1995—. Co-author: Migraine: The Complete Guide, 1994; contbr. articles to profl. jours. Mem. Nat. Gay & Lesbian Journalist Assn., Washington, 1995—. Meth. Ch. Coll. scholar, 1958; Teaching fellow James Madison U., 1979, 80. Mem. Arlington C. of C., Arlington Arts Ctr. Democrat. Methodist. Office: Community Scribes 1001 N Highland St Arlington VA 22201-2142

SCOTT, TERRY LEE, communications company executive; b. Rockford, Ill., Oct. 21, 1950; s. Wilson C. and Marie G. (Bunger) S.; divorced; 1 child, Andrea; m. Jenny Scarborough, Aug. 1, 1981; children: Brady, Tiffany. BS in Acctg. magna cum laude, Bradley U., 1972. CPA, Ill., Tex. Audit prin. Arthur Young and Co., Dallas, 1972-82; v.p. fin. and adminstrn., treas. Paging Network Inc., Dallas, 1982-90; sr. v.p. Paging Network, Inc., Dallas, 1990-92, pres., CEO, bd. dirs., 1993-95; pres., CEO, bd. dirs. Flash Comm., Inc., 1995—; ptnr. Players Comm. Network, Dallas, 1996—; bd. dirs. XY Point Corp., People's Choice TV Corp. Mem. AICPA, Tex. Soc. CPAs, Phi Kappa Phi, Zeta Pi. Methodist. Home: 1704 Riviera Dr Plano TX 75093-2910 Office: Players Comm Network 17101 Preston Rd Ste 180 Dallas TX 75248-1331

SCOTT, THEODORE R., lawyer; b. Mount Vernon, Ill., Dec. 7, 1924; s. Theodore R. and Beulah (Flannigan) S.; m. Virginia Scott, June 1, 1947; children: Anne Laurence, Sarah Buckland, Daniel, Barbara Gomon. AB, U. Ill., 1947, JD, 1949. Bar: Ill. 1950. Law clk. to judge U.S. Ct. Appeals, 1949-51; pvt. practice Chgo., 1950—; assoc. Spaulding Glass, 1951-53, Loftus, Lucas & Hammand, 1953-58, Ooms, McDougall, Williams & Hersh, 1958-60; ptnr. McDougall, Hersh & Scott, Chgo., 1960-87; of counsel Jones, Day, Reavis & Pogue, 1987—. 2nd lt. USAAF, 1943-45. Decorated Air medal. Fellow Am. Coll. Trial Lawyers; mem. ABA, Ill. Bar Assn., Chgo. Bar Assn., 7th Cir. Bar Assn. (past pres.), Legal Club Chgo., Law Club Chgo., Patent Law Assn. Chgo. (past pres.), Union League Club, Exmoor Country Club (Highland Park, Ill.), Phi Beta Kappa. Home: 1569 Woodvale Ave Deerfield IL 60015-2350 Office: Jones Day Reavis & Pogue 77 W Wacker Dr Chicago IL 60601

SCOTT, THOMAS CLEVENGER, lawyer; b. Columbus, Ohio, May 16, 1936; s. Willard Baldwin and Elizabeth (Clevenger) S.; m. Nancy Jo Tiberi, Nov. 11, 1961; children: Amy J., Molly M. BA, Ohio State U., 1958, JD, 1961. Bar: Ohio 1961. Ptnr. McLeskey & McLeskey, Columbus, 1961-79, Loveland, Callard, Clapham & Scott, Columbus, 1979-80, Scott, Kuehnle, Grace & Mills (and predecessor firm Scott, Walker & Kuehnle), Columbus, 1980-86; ptnr. Thompson, Hine & Flory, Columbus, 1986—, ptnr. in charge, 1992-97, chair banking bankruptcy and comml. fin., 1997—; adj. prof. Ohio State U., Columbus; mem. bd. advisors North Ctrl. Bankruptcy Inst. Capital U. Law Ctr., 1987-90, Midwest Regional Bankruptcy Seminar, 1990—; mem. standing local rules adv. com. U.S. Bankruptcy Ct., 1987—. Contbr. articles to profl. jours., outlines for confs. and seminars. Mem. ABA, Columbus Bar Assn. (chmn. bankruptcy com. 1986-88), Ohio State Bar Assn., Lawyers Club (pres.). Office: Thompson Hine & Flory LLP One Columbus 10 W Broad St Columbus OH 43215-3418

SCOTT, THOMAS JEFFERSON, JR., lawyer, electrical engineer; b. Montgomery, Ala., Dec. 30, 1943; s. Thomas Jefferson Sr. and Irene (Feagin) S.; m. Betsy Sue Mackta, Apr. 25, 1981; children: Elspeth Watts, Margherita Taylor, Thomas Jefferson III. BEE, Yale U., 1966, BA in Econs., 1967; JD, Vanderbilt U., 1974. Bar: Va. 1974, D.C. 1975, N.Y. 1980, U.S. Dist. Ct. D.C. 1986, U.S. Dist. Ct. (ea. dist.) Va. 1993, U.S. Tax Ct. 1981, U.S. Ct. Fed. Claims, 1982, U.S. Ct. Appeals (fed. cir.) 1982, U.S. Ct. Appeals (4th cir.) 1993, U.S. Supreme Ct. 1984. Trial atty. civil div. U.S. Dept. of Justice, Washington, 1974-78; assoc. Cooper & Dunham, N.Y.C., 1978-80, sr. trial counsel civil div., 1980-85; ptnr. Pennie & Edmonds, Washington, 1985-90, Howrey & Simon, Washington, 1990-97, Hunton & Williams, Washington, 1997—. Capt. USNR, 1966-71. Decorated D.F.C. Mem. ABA, Am. Intellectual Property Law Assn. Office: Hunton & Williams 1900 K St NW Washington DC 20006-1109

SCOTT, TOM, musician. Albums include New York Connection, Tom Cat, Bluestreak, Streamlines, 1988, GRP All Star Band, 1992, Born Again, 1992, Reed My Lips, 1994, Night Creatures, 1995, Tome Scot & The L.A. Express, 1996. Recipient Grammy award for Best Large Jazz Ensemble Performance ("All Blues"), 1996. Office: GRP Records Inc 555 W 57th St New York NY 10019-2925*

SCOTT, TOM KECK, biologist, educator; b. St. Louis, Aug. 4, 1931; s. George Drake and Mary Ann (Keck) S.; children: David Seymour, Stephen Arthur, John Warner, Cynthia Keck; m. Margaret Ray, Apr. 7, 1990. AB, Pomona Coll., Calif., 1954; MA, Stanford U., 1959, PhD, 1961. Rsch. prof. Princeton U., 1961-63; from asst. prof. to assoc. prof. biology Oberlin Coll., Ohio, 1963-69; faculty U. N.C., Chapel Hill, 1969—; prof. botany U. N.C., 1972-82, prof. biology, 1982—, chmn. biology curriculum, 1970-75, chmn. dept. botany, 1972-82, dir. rsch., 1985-90; sr. scientist div. life scis. divsn. NASA, 1994-96, program scientist, 1996—; vis. rsch. prof. U. Nottingham, Eng., 1967-68; Fulbright sr. lectr. Ege U., Izmir, Turkey, 1972-73; chmn. space biology panel NASA, 1984-89, chmn. plant growth working group, 1989-93, cons. space sta. freedon, 1984-88. Author: Plant Regulation and World Agriculture, 1979, The Functions of Hormones from the Level of the Cell to the Whole Plant, 1984, Plant Gravitational and Space Research, 1984. Served with AUS, 1954-56. Danforth assoc., 1974; NATO grantee, 1978; Japanese Soc. for Promotion of Sci. fellow, 1985. Fellow AAAS; mem. Am. Inst. Biol. Scis., Am. Soc. Plant Physiologists (trustee 1979-88, chmn. 84-86), Bot. Soc. Am., NAS (com. on space biology and medicine 1986-92), Am. Soc. Gravitational and Space Biology (bd. govs. 1985-88), Internat. Plant Growth Substance Assn. (bd. govs. 1985-88), Sigma Xi. Achievements include research on characteristics of growth development and hormone translocation in higher plants and gravitational plant biology. Home: 800 E Rosemary St Chapel Hill NC 27514-3722 Office: U NC Dept Biology Coker Hall CB # 3280 Chapel Hill NC 27599

SCOTT, VICKI SUE, school system administrator; b. Pine Bluff, Ark., Feb. 16, 1946; d. John Wesley and Ruby Gray (Whitehead) and Hannah (Lewis) S. BA, Hendrix Coll., 1968; MS in Edn., U. Cen. Ark., 1978, postgrad., 1979-84; postgrad., U. Ark., 1983-85, Ark. State U., 1993-94. Cert. adminstrn., secondary sch. prin., middle sch., secondary health and phys. edn. Tchr., coach Brinkley (Ark.) Pub. Schs., 1968-76, Lonoke (Ark.) Jr. and Sr. High Schs., 1976-77; tchr., coach S.E. Jr. High Sch., Pine Bluff, 1978-92, asst. prin., 1992—, dir. summer sch., 1991, 92; AIDS educator Arkansas River Edn. Svc. Coop., Pine Bluff, 1989-92. Active Leadership Pine Bluff, 1993-94. Scholar Assn. Women Ednl. Suprs., 1985; named Outstanding Young Women of Am., 1974. Mem. ASCD, DAR, Ark. Assn. Ednl. Adminstrs., Nat. Assn. Secondary Prins., Order Ea. Star, Delta Kappa Gamma (scholar 1984, Epsilon chpt. pres.), Phi Delta Kappa. Baptist. Avocations: tennis, reading, hiking, travel, golf. Home: 3215 S Cherry St Pine Bluff AR 71603-5983 Office: SE Mid Sch 20001 S Ohio St Pine Bluff AR 71601-6901

SCOTT, W. PETER, bishop. Bishop London (Ont.) Synod United Ch. Can. Office: United Church of Canada, 359 Windermere Rd, London, ON Canada N6G 2K3*

SCOTT, WALDRON, mission executive; b. Kansas City, Kans., July 14, 1929; s. Waldron and Audrean (Spurgeon) S.; m. Georgia Dyke; children by previous marriage—Melody, Cheryl, Gregory, Douglas, Linda. B.A., Am. U., Beirut, 1953. Dir. The Navigators, Washington, 1954-59, Middle East and Africa, 1960-66, Asia/Australia, 1967-72; internat. field dir. The Navigators, Colorado Springs, Colo., 1973-74; gen. sec. World Evang. Fellowship, Colorado Springs, 1975-80; pres. Am. Leprosy Missions, Elmwood Park, N.J., 1981-84, Holistic Ministries Internat., Paterson, N.J., 1985—; chairman emeritus Holistic Ministries Internat., 1994—; chair Greater Paterson YMCA, 1995—; adj. prof. world mission Eastern Bapt. Sem., Phila., 1995—; bd. dirs. Passaic County Cultural and Heritage Coun., Paterson Habitat for Humanity, Christian Leadership in Higher Edn.; adv. coun. Passaic County Human Svcs., Paterson YMCA, Scheffelin Rsch. and Tng. Ctr., Ch. World Svc., Divsn. Overseas Ministries' Nat. Coun. Chs., Vellore Christian Med. Coll., Paterson Cmty. Health Ctr., Jubilee Svc. Author: Karl Barth's Theology of Mission, 1978, The Paterson Paradigm; Bring Forth Justice, 1980; editor: Serving our Generation, 1980. Chmn. Greater Paterson YMCA, Paterson Coun. Social Svcs., Citizens Alliance for a Drug Free Paterson. Mem. Leadership Paterson Alumni Assn., Am. Soc. Missiology (v.p. ea. br.), Nat. Assn. Evangelicals, Evangelicals for Social Action. Mem. Christian Reformed Ch.

SCOTT, WALTER, JR., construction company executive; b. 1931. BS, Colo. State U., 1953. With Peter Kiewit Sons, Inc., Omaha, 1953—, mgr. Cleve. dist., 1962-64, v.p., 1964, exec. v.p., 1965-79, chmn. bd. dirs., pres., CEO, 1979—; also pres. Joslyn Art Mus., Omaha. Served with USAF, 1954-56. Office: Peter Kiewit Sons Inc 1000 Kiewit Plz Omaha NE 68131-3302 also: Joslyn Art Mus 2200 Dodge St Omaha NE 68102-1208*

SCOTT, WALTER COKE, retired sugar company executive, lawyer; b. Norfolk, Va., July 20, 1919; s. Walter Coke and Rosemary (White) S.; m. Virginia Kemper Millard, May 14, 1949; children: Mary Lyman (Mrs. K. Logan Jackson), Roberta (Mrs. Frederick Warth), Alexander McRae, Buford Coke. B.S., Hampden-Sydney Coll., 1939; J.D., U. Va., 1948. Bar: Va. 1947, Ga. 1954. Atty. U.S. Dept. Justice, Jacksonville, Fla., 1948; commerce atty. S.A.L. Ry., Norfolk, 1948-54; commerce counsel, gen. solicitor Central of Ga. Ry., Savannah, 1954-60; v.p. Cen. of Ga. Ry., (Norfolk Southern), 1960-62, dir., 1960-88; ptnr. law firm Hitch, Miller & Beckmann, Savannah, 1956-60; sr. v.p., sec. Savannah Foods & Industries, Inc. (formerly Savannah Sugar Refining Corp.), 1962-72, exec. v.p., mem. exec. com., 1972-87, also dir.; exec. v.p., sec. mem. exec. com., dir. Everglades Sugar Refinery, Inc., Clewiston, Fla., 1964-87; sec., mem. exec. com., dir. The Jim Dandy Co., Birmingham, Ala., 1968-81; bd. dirs. 1st Union Nat. Bank Savannah, Atlanta, 1975-91. Pres., chmn. exec. com. Historic Savannah Found., 1963-64; bd. dirs. United Community Services, 1965-68, pres., 1967; gen. chmn. United Community Appeal, 1966; mem. Chatham-Savannah Met. Planning Commn., 1963-68; trustee, chmn. finance com. Telfair Acad. Arts and Scis., 1964-67; trustee, vice chmn. Savannah Country Day Sch., 1967-69, chmn., 1970-72; Bd. dirs., chmn. finance com. Savannah Speech and Hearing Center, 1967-70; bd. dirs. Savannah Symphony Soc., Inc. Mem. Va. State Bar, Ga. State Bar, St. Andrews Soc., Savannah Benevolent Assn. (pres. 1990-92), Kappa Sigma, Omicron Delta Kappa, Phi Alpha Delta, Chi Beta Phi, Pi Delta Epsilon. Episcopalian. Clubs: Chatham, Oglethorpe, Savannah Golf; Farmington Country (Charlottesville, Va.). Home: 3710 Abercorn St Savannah GA 31405-3314

SCOTT, WALTER DILL, management educator; b. Chgo., Oct. 27, 1931; s. John Marcy and Mary Louise (Gent) S.; student Williams Coll., 1949-51; BS, Northwestern U., 1953; MS, Columbia, 1958; m. Barbara Ann Stein, Sept. 9, 1961; children: Timothy Walter, David Frederick, Gordon Charles. Cons. Booz, Allen & Hamilton, N.Y.C., 1956-58; assoc. Glore, Forgan & Co., N.Y.C., 1958-63, ptnr., Chgo., 1963-65; ptnr. Lehman Bros., Chgo., 1965-72, sr. ptnr., 1972-73, also bd. dirs.; assoc. dir. econs. and govt. Office Mgmt. and Budget, Washington, 1973-75; sr. v.p. internat. and fin. Pillsbury Co., Mpls., 1975-78, exec. v.p., 1978-80, also bd. dirs.; pres., chief exec. officer Investors Diversified Services, Inc., Mpls., 1980-84, group mng. dir. Grand Met. PLC, 1984-86, also bd. dirs.; chmn. Grand Met U.S.A., 1984-86; prof., sr. Austin fellow Kellogg Grad. Sch. Mgmt., Northwestern U., 1988—; bd. dirs. Chgo. Title and Trust, Intermatic, Inc., Ill. Power Co., Illinova Corp, Orval Kent Food Co. Bd. dirs. Chgo. Communities in Schs., Internat. Urban Assocs., Leadership for Quality Edn. Lt. (j.g.) USN, 1953-56. Home: 55 Meadowview Dr Northfield IL 60093-3547 Office: Northwestern U J L Kellogg Grad Sch of Mgmt Leverone Hall Evanston IL 60208

SCOTT, WILLARD HERMAN, radio and television performer; b. Alexandria, Va., Mar. 7, 1934; s. Willard Herman and Thelma Matti (Phillips) S.; m. Mary Ellen Dwyer, Aug. 7, 1959; children: Mary Phillips, Sally W. B.A. in Philosophy and Religion, Am. U., 1955. With NBC, 1950—; formerly staff announcer children's TV shows Voice of NASA radio show; weather reporter, performer Today Show and NBC Radio, N.Y.C., 1980—; host Willard Scott's Home and Garden Almanac (Cable TV); free-lance comml. actor, narrator. Active March of Dimes, Easter Seals, ARC, Am. Cancer Soc., Nat. Symphony of Washington, Nat. Park Service, Alzheimer's Found. Served with USN, 1956-58. Episcopalian. Club: De Molay. Office: NBC Today Program 30 Rockefeller Plz # 374E New York NY 10112

SCOTT, WILLIAM CLEMENT, III, entertainment industry executive; b. N.Y.C., Apr. 25, 1934; s. William Clement and Susan L. (Cameron) S.; m. Cindy L. Taylor, Dec. 5, 1981; children by previous marriage: Katherine Louise, David Campbell. A.B., Coll. William and Mary, Williamsburg, Va., 1956. Self-employed, 1956-64; v.p. Booz-Allen & Hamilton, N.Y.C., 1964-69; group v.p. Cordura Corp., Los Angeles, 1969-72; exec. v.p. Western Pacific Industries, N.Y.C., 1972-76; pres., chief operating officer Western Pacific Industries, 1976-87; pvt. investor N.Y.C., 1987-88; chmn, CEO Panavision Inc., N.Y.C., 1988—. Bd. dirs., pres. Opera Orch. of N.Y. Republican. Episcopalian. Clubs: Racquet and Tennis, Met. Opera (N.Y.C.); Hay Harbor; Fishers Island Country; Coral Beach (Bermuda). Office: Panavision Inc 140 E 45th St New York NY 10017-3144

SCOTT, WILLIAM CORYELL, medical executive; b. Sterling, Colo., Nov. 22, 1920; s. James Franklin and Edna Ann (Schillig) S.; m. Jean Marie English, Dec. 23, 1944 (div. 1975); children: Kathryn, James, Margaret; m. Carolyn Florence Hill, June 21, 1975; children: Scott, Amy Jo, Robert. AB, Dartmouth Coll., 1942; MD, U. Colo., 1944, MS in OB/GYN, 1951. Cert. Am. Bd. Ob-Gyn., 1956, 79, Am. Bd. Med. Mgmt., 1991. Intern USN Hosp., Great Lakes, Ill., 1945-46, Denver Gen. Hosp., 1946-47; resident Ob-Gyn St. Joseph's Hosp., Colo. Gen. Hosp., Denver, 1946-51; practice medicine specializing in Ob-Gyn Tucson, 1951-71; assoc. prof. emeritus U. Ariz. Med. Sch., Tucson, 1971-94, 1994; v.p. med. affairs U. Med. Ctr., Tucson, 1984-94. Contbr. articles to med. jours. and chpt. to book. Pres. United Way, Tucson, 1979-80, HSA of Southeastern Ariz., Tucson, 1985-87; chmn. Ariz. Health Facilities Authority, Phoenix, 1974-83. Served to capt. USNR, 1956-58. Recipient Man of Yr. award, Tucson, 1975. Fellow ACS, Am. Coll. Ob-Gyn, Pacific Coast Ob-Gyn Soc., Ctrl. Assn. of Ob-Gyn; mem. AMA (coun. on sci. affairs 1984-93, chmn. 1989-91), Am. Coll. Physician Execs., Am. Coll. Health Care Execs., Ariz. Med. Assn., La Paloma Country Club. Republican. Episcopalian. Avocations: golf, gardening, photography. Home: PO Box 805 Sonoita AZ 85637-0805

SCOTT, WILLIAM FRED, cultural organization administrator; b. Thomasville, Ga., 1953. B cum laude, Sch. Fgn. Svc., Georgetown U., 1974. Formerly assoc. condr., artistic adminstr. Opera Co. of Boston; artistic dir. The Atlanta Opera, 1985—; prin. condr. Opera New England; asst. condr. Atlanta Symphony Orch., 1981—, assoc. condr., 1987—; guest condr. various orgns. including Opera Co. of Boston, Wolf Trap Opera Co., N.Y.C. Opera at Lincoln Ctr., Boston Pro Arte Chamber Orch.; conducted opera workshop in Tel Aviv at request of Israeli Govt., 1983. Operatic debut as condr. Opera Company of Boston, 1975. Office: Atlanta Opera 1800 Peachtree St NW Ste 620 Atlanta GA 30309-2507*

SCOTT, WILLIAM HERBERT, state agency administrator; b. Estancia, N.Mex., Mar. 19, 1925; s. Chester Ray and Elizabeth Bryan (McNama) S.; m. Maryann Mavis Munro, Dec. 26, 1952 (div. 1980); children: Jean Ann, Megan Lynne; m. Dorothy Caroline Caster, Apr. 16, 1980. BS in Civil Engring., U. N.Mex., 1949, BBA in Acctg., 1949. CPA, Alaska. Field engr., office mgr. Kincaid & King Constrn., Anchorage, 1949-50; office mgr. M-B Contracting Co., Inc., Anchorage, 1951-52; staff acct. R.L. Rettig, CPA, Anchorage, 1952-54; ptnr. Rettig, Scott & Co., CPAs, Anchorage, 1955-60; mng. ptnr. Scott, McMahon & Co., CPAs, Anchorage, 1960-61, Peat, Marwick Mitchell & Co., Anchorage, 1961-83; cons., 1983-91; exec. dir. Alaska Indsl. Devel., Anchorage, 1991-92, Alaska Permanent Fund Corp., Juneau, 1992-94; sec. Alaska Bd. Pub. Accountancy, 1963-65. Mem. Com. on Operation U.S. Senate, Washington, 1976; honorary consul Denmark, Anchorage, 1963-88. Lt. j.g. USNR, 1942-46, PTO. Named Knight of Dannebrog Queen of Denmark, 1973, 83. Mem. Am. Arbitration Assn. (panel 1984—), Alaska Soc. CPAs (pres., founder 1961-62), AICPA (coun. 1961-62), Anchorage C. of C. (pres. 1966), Alaska State C. of C. (pres. 1968), Alaskan Air Command Civilian Affairs, Sigma Chi. Avocations: tennis, alpine skiing.

SCOTT, WILLIAM PAUL, lawyer; b. Staples, Minn., Nov. 8, 1928; A.L.A., U. Minn., 1949; B.S.L., St. Paul Coll. Law, 1952, J.D., 1954; m. Elsie Elaine Anderson, Feb. 7, 1968; 1 son, Jason Lee; children: William P., Mark D., Bryan D., Scott; stepchildren: Thomas J. (dec.), Terri L. Weeding-Berg. Bar: Minn. 1954. Atty. right of way div. Minn. Hwy. Dept., 1954-52, civil engr. traffic and safety div., 1953-55; practice law Arlington, Minn., 1955-61, Gaylord, Minn., 1963-67; sr. partner firm Scott Law Offices and predecessors, Pipestone, Minn., 1967—; probate, juvenile judge Sibley County, Minn., 1956-61; Minn. pub. examiner, 1961-63; county atty. Sibley County, 1963-68, city atty., Pipestone, 1978—. Formerly nat. committeeman Young Rep. League; Sibley County Rep. chmn., 1961-67. Served with USMCR, 1946-50; from 2d lt. to lt. col. USAF Res., 1950-77; ret. Recipient George Washington Honor medal Freedoms Found., 1970, 72. Mem. Minn. Bar Assn., TROA, Mensa, V.F.W., DAV, Am. Legion, Res. Officers Assn. Home: PO Box 689 Pipestone MN 56164-0704 Office: Park Plz Offices Pipestone MN 56164

SCOTT, WILLIAM PROCTOR, III, lawyer; b. Berkeley, Calif., Dec. 1, 1946; s. William Proctor Jr. and Marcia (Wood) S.; m. Helen Elizabeth Hiller, June 16, 1968; children: William Proctor IV, Jennifer Anne. BS, MIT, 1968; JD cum laude, U. Pa., 1975. Assoc. Ballard, Spahr, Andrews & Ingersoll, Phila., 1975-82, ptnr., 1982—; regional chmn. MIT Ednl. Coun., 1988—. Lt. (j.g.) USNR, 1969-72. Mem. ABA, Pa. Bar Assn., Phila. Bar Assn., MIT Club of Delaware Valley (mem. exec. com. 1991—). Office: Ballard Spahr Andrews & Ingersoll 1735 Market St Philadelphia PA 19103-7501

SCOTT, W(ILLIAM) RICHARD, sociology educator; b. Parsons, Kan., Dec. 18, 1932; s. Charles Hogue and Hildegarde (Hewit) S.; m. Joy Lee Whitney, Aug. 14, 1955; children: Jennifer Ann, Elliot Whitney, Sydney Brooke. AA, Parsons Jr. Coll., 1952; AB, U. Kans., 1954, MA, 1955; PhD, U. Chgo., 1961. Asst. prof. to assoc. prof. sociology Stanford (Calif.) U., 1960-69, prof., 1969—, chair dept. sociology, 1972-75; courtesy prof. Sch. Medicine, Stanford U., 1972—, Sch. Edn., Grad. Sch. Bus., 1977—; fellow Ctr. for Advanced Study in Behavioral Scis., 1989-90; dir. Orgns. Rsch. Tng. Program, Stanford U., 1972-89, Ctr. for Orgns. Rsch., 1988-96; mem. adv. panel Sociology Program NSF, Washington, 1982-84; mem. epidemiol. and svc. rsch. rev. panel NIMH, Washington, 1984-88; mem. Commn. on Behavioral and Social Scis. and Edn., NAS, 1990-96; vis. prof. Kellogg Grad. Sch. Mgmt., Northwestern U., winter 1997. Author: (with O.D. Duncan et al) Metropolis and Region, 1960, (with P.M. Blau) Formal Organizations, 1962, Social Processes and Social Structures, 1970, (with S.M. Dornbusch) Evaluation and the Exercise of Authority, 1975, Organizations: Rational, Natural and Open Systems, 1981, rev. edit., 1992, (with J.W. Meyer) Organizational Environments: Ritual and Rationality, 1983, edit., 1992, (with A.B. Flood) Hospital Structure and Performance, 1987, (with J.W. Meyer), Institutional Environments and Organizations: Structural Complexity and Individualism, 1994, Institutions and Organizations, 1995, (with S. Christinsen) The Institutional Construction of Organization, 1995; editor Ann. Rev. of Sociology, 1986-91. Fellow Woodrow Wilson, 1954-55; mem. Nat. Commn. Nursing, 1980-83; chair Consortium Orgns. Rsch. Ctrs., 1989-91; elder First Presby. Ch., Palo Alto, Calif., 1977-80, 83-86. Social Sci. Rsch. Coun. fellow, U. Chgo., 1959; named Edmund P. Learned Disting. Prof., Sch. Bus. Adminstrn., U. Kans, 1970-71; recipient Cardinal Citation for Disting. Svc. Labette C.C., Parsons, 1981, Disting. Scholar award Mgmt. and Orgn. Theory divsn. Acad. Mgmt., 1988, Richard D. Irwin award for scholarly contbns. to mgmt. Acad. Mgmt., 1996. Mem. Inst. Medicine, Am. Sociol. Assn. (chmn. sect. on orgns. 1970-71, mem. coun. 1989-92), Acad. Mgmt., Sociol. Rsch. Assn., Macro-Organizational Behavior Soc., Phi Beta Kappa. Democrat. Presbyterian. Home: 940 Lathrop Pl Stanford CA 94305-1060 Office: Stanford U Dept Sociology Bldg 120 Stanford CA 94305

SCOTT-FINAN, NANCY ISABELLA, government administrator; b. Canton, Ohio, June 13, 1949; d. Milton Kenneth and Gertrude (Baker) Scott; m. Robert James Finan II, Aug. 23, 1986. Student, Malone Coll., 1970-73; BA magna cum laude, U. Akron, 1976, postgrad., 1976; postgrad., Kent State U., 1977; MA in Internat. Transactions, George Mason U., 1995. Legal sec. Krugliak, Wilkins, Griffiths & Dougherty, Canton, 1969, Amerman, Burt & Jones, Canton, 1970-77; legal sec., paralegal Black, McCuskey, Souers & Arbaugh, Canton, Ohio, 1977-81; adminstrv. staff mem. com. on judiciary U.S. Senate, Washington, 1981-86; adminstrv. asst. to counsel to Pres., The White House, Washington, 1986-89; adminstrv. asst. to former counsel to pres. O'Melveny & Myers, Washington, 1989; asst. dir. congl. rels. Office Legis. Affairs U.S. Dept. Justice, Washington, 1989-91; spl. asst. to asst. atty. gen. U.S. Dept. of Justice, Washington, 1991—; substitute tchr. North Canton City Sch. System, 1979-80; residential tutor Canton City Sch. System, 1980-81, Fairfax (Va.) County Sch. System, 1983;instr. dance and exercise Siffrin Home for Developmentally Disabled, Canton, 1980. East coast regional v.p. for spl. projects Childhelp U.S.A., Washington, 1988-90; mem. Rep. Women of Capitol Hill, Washington, 1984-95; bd. mem. Have a Heart Homes for Abused Children, Washington, 1990-91. Mem. AAUW, Women of Washington. Presbyterian. Avocations: skiing, cooking, reading, music. Office: US Dept Justice 10th and Constitution Washington DC 20530

SCOTTI, DENNIS JOSEPH, educator, researcher, consultant; b. N.Y.C., Apr. 20, 1952; s. Joseph Charles and Theresa (Giancola) S. BS, Stony Brook U., 1974; MBA, Adelphi U., 1977; MS, Temple U., 1980, PhD, 1982. Cert. healthcare fin. profl., managed care profl. Dep. chief adminstr. Dept. Mental Health Devel. Ctr., Suffolk, N.Y., 1975-77; asst. prof. Rutgers U., N.J., 1980-83; assoc. prof. Fairleigh Dickinson U., N.J., 1983-88; prof. Fairleigh Dickinson U., 1989—; exec. v.p. Presscott Associates, Ltd., Avon, Conn., 1989—; bd. dirs. Rsch. Fuels Corp.; citizens com. biomed. ethics N.J. Health Decision Assembly. Author: Strategic Management in the Health Care Sector, 1988; contbr. articles to profl. jours. Recipient Acad. Excellence award EMBA, 1997. Fellow Healthcare Financial Mgmt. Assn.; mem. Am. Coll. Healthcare Execs., Assn. for Health Svcs. Rsch., Health Planning and Mktg. Soc., Acad. Mgmt., Peoples Med. Soc., Health Decisions Assembly, Phi Theta Kappa, Delta Mu Delta. Office: Fairleigh Dickinson U 1000 River Rd Teaneck NJ 07666-1914

SCOTTI, JAMES VERNON, astronomer; b. Bandon, Oreg., Aug. 22, 1960; s. Paul Carl and Elizabeth Louise (Garoutte) S.; m. Karriaunna K.-R. Harlan, May 15, 1983; children: Jennifer Anne, Christopher James. BS, U. Ariz., 1983. Planetarium asst. Flandrau Planetarium, Tucson, 1979-82; student rsch. asst. Lunar and Planetary Lab., Tucson, 1982-83, rsch. asst., 1983-93, sr. rsch. specialist, 1993—. Mem. Am. Astron. Soc. (assoc.), Div. for Planetary Scis., Assn. Lunar and Planetary Observers (asst. comets recorder). Achievements include being a leading observer of faint comets, being heavily involved in observing comet P/Shoemaker-Levy 9 before and during its impact on Jupiter in July 1994. Office: U Ariz Lunar and Planetary Lab Tucson AZ 85721

SCOTTI, MICHAEL JOHN, JR., medical association executive; b. N.Y.C., Oct. 30, 1938; s. Michael John and Florence (Ellis) S.; m. Susan Faye Suit, Aug. 25, 1961; children: Michael John III, Pamela Anne, Jennifer Beth. BS, Fordham Coll., 1960; MD, Georgetown U., 1965; postgrad., Indsl. Coll., Washington, 1982-83. Diplomate Am. Bd. Internal Medicine, Am. Bd.

Family Practice; CAQ Geriat. Commd. 2d lt. U.S. Army, 1963, advanced through grades to maj. gen., 1990; dir. residency program Dept. Family Practice, Ft. Gordon, Ga., 1976-79; family practice cons. Surgeon Gen., Washington, 1979-80; dir. Grad. Med. Edn. U.S. Army, Washington, 1980-82; comdr. army hosp. Ft. Polk, La., 1983-86; dir. quality assurance Army Med. Dept., Washington, 1986-88; dir. profl. svcs. Army Med. Dept., 1988-90; comdg. gen. European 7th Med. Comd, Heidelberg, Fed. Republic Germany, 1990-95; ret. maj. gen., 1995; v.p. AMA, Chgo., 1996—; assoc. prof. Georgetown U. Sch. Medicine, 1986; chmn. Def. Med. Standardization, Ft. Detrick, Md., 1988-90; prof. Uniformed Svcs. U., Bethesda, Md., 1990. Health cons. Nat. PTA, Chgo., 1976-79. Named Person of Yr. Phi Delta Kappa, 1976. Fellow Am. Acad. Family Physicians (vice speaker 1988-90, speaker, bd. dirs. 1990-92), ACP; mem. AMA, Acad. Medicine. Office: AMA 515 N State St Chicago IL 60610-4325

SCOTT MORTON, MICHAEL STEWART, business management educator; b. Mukden, Manchuria, Peoples Republic of China, Aug. 25, 1937; came to U.S., 1958; s. William and Alice (Gleysteen) S.M.; m. Mary Louise Mansell, June 20, 1964; children: Fiona Margaret, Lesley Elizabeth. Student, Glasgow U., Scotland, 1957-58; BS, Carnegie Mellon, 1961; DBA, Harvard U., 1967. Asst. prof. Sloan Sch. MIT, Cambridge, 1966-69, assoc. prof., 1969-75, Jay W. Forrester prof. mgmt., 1989—; bd. dirs. Sequent Computer Sys.; trustee Met. Life-State St., State St. Rsch. and Mgmt. Author: Decision Support System, 1978, Strategic Control, 1986, Management in the 1990s, 1991, Information Technology and the Corporation, 1994; contbr. articles to profl. jours. Mem. Assn. for Computing Machinery, Inst. Mgmt. Sci., Handel and Haydn Soc. (gov.), Fidelco Guide Dog Found. (dir.), Somerset Club, Harvard Club (Boston). Avocations: sailing, walking. Home: 31 Somerset Rd Lexington MA 02173-3519 also: Ledgrianach, Appin, Argyll Scotland Office: MIT Sloan Sch Mgmt 50 Memorial Dr Cambridge MA 02142-1347

SCOTTO, RENATA, soprano; b. Savona, Italy, Feb. 24, 1935; m. Lorenzo Anselmi. Studied under, Ghirardini, Merlino and Mercedes Llopart, Accademia Musicale Savonese, Conservatory Giuseppe Verdi, Milan. Debut in La Traviata, Teatro Nuevo, Milan, 1954; then joined La Scala Opera Co.; appeared with Met. Opera, N.Y.C., 1965, Convent Garden, Hamburg (Fed. Republic of Germany) State Opera, Vienna (Austria) State Opera, Nat. Theatre Munich, San Francisco Opera, Chgo. Lyric Opera, 1988; roles include: Ballo in Maschera, La Sonnambula, I Puritani, L'Elisir d'amore, Lucia di Lammermoor, La Boheme, Turandot, Otello (Verdi), Trovatore, Le Prophete, Madama Butterfly, Adriana Lecouvreur, Norma, Tosca, Manon Lescaut, Rosenkavalier (Marschallin), La Voix Humaine, Pirata, Italy; dir. Madama Butterfly, N.Y. Met. Opera, 1986; recordings include Christmas at St. Patrick's Cathedral, French Arias with Charles Rosekrans, Live in Paris with Ivan Davis, Great Operatic Scenes with Jose Carreras, various recitals and concerts. Office: care Robert Lombardo Assocs One Harkness Plaza 61 W 62nd St Apt 6F New York NY 10023-7017 also: care Il Teatro la Scala, via Filodrammatici 2, Milan Italy

SCOTT-WABBINGTON, VERA V., elementary school educator; b. Holland, Tex., Jan. 17, 1929; d. John Leslie Scott and Willie Mattie (Dickson) Stafford. BA, Huston-Tillotson Coll., 1950; MA, Roosevelt U., 1965. Cert. elem. tchr., Tex. Tchr. Ft. Hood/Killeen (Tex.) Ind. Sch. Dist., 1951-58, Gary (Ind.) Sch. Dist., 1958-83; tchr. Ft. Worth Pub. Schs., 1983—, key tchr. minority math. and sci. edn. coop., 1989-92; mem. mentorship program Ft. Worth Ind. Sch. Dist.; mem. Nat. Rev. Panel to Review Nat. Coun. of Social Studies Curriculum Stds., 1993; adj. prof. Tex. Weslyan U., Ft. Worth. Active in several polit., civic and social orgns. Recipient Outstanding Achievement in Edn. award Baker Chapel African Meth. Episc. Ch., 1991, NAACP Edn. award, 1992. Mem. Nat. Alliance Black Sch. Educators (tchr. 1991), Am. Fedn. Tchrs., Tex. Fedn. Tchrs., Tex. Alliance Black Educators. Avocations: reading, live theater, museums, shopping. Home: 7212 Misty Meadow Dr S Fort Worth TX 76133-7117

SCOULAR, ROBERT FRANK, lawyer; b. Del Norte, Colo., July 9, 1942; s. Duane William and Marie Josephine (Moloney) S.; m. Donna V. Scoular, June 3, 1967; children—Bryan T., Sean D., Bradley R. B.S. in Aero. Engring., St. Louis U., 1964, J.D., 1968. Bar: Mo. 1968, Colo. 1968, N.D. 1968, U.S. Supreme Ct. 1972, Calif. 1979. Law clk. to chief judge U.S. Ct. Appeals (8th cir.), 1968-69; ptnr. Bryan, Cave, McPheeters & McRoberts, St. Louis, 1969-89; mng. ptnr. Bryan, Cave, McPheeters & McRoberts, Los Angeles, 1979-84, exec. com., 1984-85, sect. leader tech., computer and intellectual property law, 1985-89; ptnr. Sonnenschein, Nath, Rosenthal, Chgo., 1990—; mng. ptnr. Sonnenschein, Nath, Rosenthal, L.A., 1990—, mem. policy and planning com., 1995—; co-leader intellectual property practice, dir. Mo. Lawyers Credit Union, 1978-79. Contbr. articles to profl. jours. Bd. dirs. St. Louis Bar Found., 1975-76, 79; Eagle Scout, bd. dirs. L.A. Area Coun. Boy Scouts Am.; league commr. Am. Youth Soccer Orgn.; mem. alumni council St. Louis U., 1979-82. Mem. ABA (nat. dir. young lawyers div. 1977-78), Am. Judicature Soc., Bar Assn. Met. St. Louis (v.p. 1978-79, sec. 1979, chmn. young lawyers sect. 1975-76), Los Angeles County Bar Assn., Assn. Bus. Trial Lawyers, Calif. Bar. Assn., Mo. Bar (chmn. young lawyers sect. 1976-77, disting. svc. award), Computer Law Assn., Fed. Bar Assn. Home: 1505 Lower Paseo La Cresta Pls Vrds Est CA 90274-2066 Office: Sonnenschein Nath & Rosenthal 601 S Figueroa St Ste 1500 Los Angeles CA 90017-5720

SCOUTEN, REX W., curator. Curator White House, Washington, D.C.; ex officio mem., Comm. for the Preservation of the White House. Office: White House 1600 Pennsylvania Ave NW Washington DC 20500-0005*

SCOUTEN, WILLIAM HENRY, chemistry educator, academic administrator; b. Corning, N.Y., Feb. 12, 1942; s. Henry and M. Anna (Kimble) S.; m. Nancy Jane Coombs, July 16, 1965; children: Lisa, Linda, Michael, William Jr., Thomas, David. BA, Houghton Coll., 1964; PhD, U. Pitts., 1969. NIH postdoctoral fellow SUNY, Stony Brook, 1969-71; asst. prof. Bucknell U., Lewisburg, Pa., 1971-77; assoc. prof. Bucknell U., Lewisburg, 1977-83, prof., 1983-84; prof., chmn. dept. chemistry Baylor U., Waco, Tex., 1984-93; dir. biotech. ctr. Utah State U., Logan, 1993—; vis. scientist for minority inst. Fedn. Am. Socs. Exptl. Biology, Washington; adj. prof. U. of Utah, 1996, mem. Ctr. for Biopolymers at Interfaces, 1996; chmn.-elect Ctrs. of Biotech. Cos., 1997; mem. govt. rels. coms. Coun. Chem. Rsch., 1996; bd. dirs. emerging cos. sect. BIO, 1997. Author: Affinity Chromatography, 1981; editor: Solid Phase Biochem., 1983; assoc. editor Internat. Jour. Bio-Chromatography, 1994—; mem. editl. bd. Bioconjugate Chemistry, 1994—, Jour. Molecular Recognition, 1994—, Bioseparation, 1995. Fulbright fellow, 1976; Dreyfus Tchr. scholar, Dreyfus Found., 1976; NSF Sci. Devel. NSF, 1978; Lindbach Disting. Tchr. Bucknell U., 1975. Mem. Am. Soc. Biol. Chemists, Am. Chem. Soc., Internat. Soc. for Biorecognition Tech., Coun. for Biotech. Ctrs. (bd. dirs. 1996—), Internat. Soc. for Molecular Recognition (pres. 1990-93), Assn. for Internat. Practical Tng. (bd. dirs. 1991—). Republican. Baptist. Office: Biotechnology Ctr Utah State U Logan UT 84322

SCOVIL, LARRY EMERY, minister; b. Conneaut, Ohio, Dec. 1, 1950; s. Lynn Edgar and Shirley Jean (Cook) S.; m. Kristine Adell Schulz, Dec. 19, 1970; children: Jennifer, Jarin, Lindsay. B. Music Edn., U. Wis., Oshkosh, 1972; MDiv, Bethel Theol. Sem., 1987. Ordained to ministry Conservative Congl. Christian Conv., 1976. Pastor Zoar Congl. Ch., Mott, N.D., 1975-81, Calvary Evang. Congl. Ch., St. Paul, 1981-86, Emmanuel Congl. Ch., Scottsbluff, Nebr., 1986—; bd. dirs. Conservative Congl. Christian Conf., St. Paul, 1988-91, rec. sec., 1991—, Rocky Mountain area rep., 1989—. Writer, arranger musical: Joy to the World, 1990, Christmas Carol, 1992, Little Town of Bethlehem, 1995. Mem. Panhandle Evang. Ministerial Assn. (pres. 1990-92). Republican. Office: Emmanuel Congl Ch 317 W 40th St Scottsbluff NE 69361-4634

SCOVIL, ROGER MORRIS, engineering company executive; b. Greenville, S.C., Apr. 23, 1929; s. Roger Peniston and Sophia Rose (Herbert) S.; m. Mary Earle Nock; children: Randolph, Frances, Elizabeth. Student, Davidson Coll., 1946-48; BS in Civil Engring., N.C. State U., 1951. Registered profl. engr., Ga., S.C., P.R. Project mgr. McKoy-Helgerson Co., Greenville, 1953-63; v.p., maintenance div. mgr. Daniel Constrn. Co., Greenville, 1963-66; v.p., Caribbean div. mgr. Daniel Internat. Corp., San Juan, P.R., 1966-74; v.p. Europe and Middle East Daniel Internat. Corp., Brussels and Jeddah, Saudi Arabia, 1974-79; v.p. internat. mkgt. Daniel Constrn. Co., Greenville, 1980; pres. Polysius Corp., Atlanta, 1981-88; sr. v.p., dir. Lockwood Greene Systems Corp., Atlanta, 1988—; sr. v.p., dir. Lockwood Greene Internat., Atlanta, 1991-95, pres., 1995—; mem. operating bd. Lockwood Greene Engrs., Inc., 1995—; bd. dirs. GLG Ingenieria Internacional, Mex.; chmn. bd. dirs. Alternica Lockwood Greene, Argentina. Mem. Atlanta Dist. Export coun., 1996—, So. Ctr. for Internat. Studies, 1996—. Capt. U.S. Army, 1951-53. Mem. Atlanta World trade Ctr. (bd. dirs.), Internat. Club Atlanta, Brazilian Am. C. of C. of Ga. (bd. dirs. 1997—), Tau Beta Pi, Chi Epsilon, Sigma Phi Epsilon. Episcopalian. Home: 6025 Riverwood Dr Atlanta GA 30328-3732 Office: Lockwood Greene Engrs 250 Williams St NW Ste 4000 Atlanta GA 30303-1032

SCOVILLE, GEORGE RICHARD, marketing professional; b. Ashtabula, Ohio, May 18, 1954; s. George Rueben and Lois Jean (Prince) S.; m. Cindy Leah Thayer, Aug. 2, 1975; children: Kimberly Michelle, Karolyn Marie, Richard Michael. Cert. indsl. engr., Lakeland Coll., 1979. Quality mgr. Geneva (Ohio) Rubber Co., 1974-81, dir. quality, 1982-84; quality mgr. Mich. Rubber Co., Cadillac, 1981-82; tech. sales rep. Whittaker Corp., West Alexandria, Ohio, 1984-90; product mgr. Morton Internat., West Alexandria, 1990-93, nat. accounts mgr., 1993-97, market mgr., 1997—. Mem. Am. Chem. Soc., Boston Rubber Group, N.E. Ohio Rubber Group, West Mich. Rubber Group, Ft. Wayne Rubber & Plastics Group, Detroit Rubber Group. Republican. Methodist. Avocations: golf, precision model cars. Home: 248 Porter Dr Englewood OH 45322-2452 Office: Morton Internat 10 Electric St West Alexandria OH 45381-1212

SCOVILLE, JAMES GRIFFIN, economics educator; b. Amarillo, Tex., Mar. 19, 1940; s. Orlin James and Carol Howe (Griffin) S.; m. Judith Ann Nelson, June 11, 1962; 1 child, Nathan James. B.A., Oberlin Coll., 1961; M.A., Harvard U., 1963, Ph.D., 1965. Economist ILO, Geneva, 1965-66; instr. econs. Harvard U., Cambridge, Mass., 1964-65; asst. prof. Harvard U., 1966-69; assoc. prof. econs. and labor and indsl. relations U. Ill.-Urbana, 1969-75, prof., 1975-80; prof. indsl. rels. Indsl. Rels. Ctr., U. Minn., Mpls., 1979—, dir., 1979-82, dir. grad. studies, 1990—; cons. ILO, World Bank, U.S. Dept. Labor, Orgn. for Econ. Cooperation and Devel., AID; labor-mgmt. arbitrator. Author: The Job Content of the US Economy, 1940-70, 1969, Perspectives on Poverty and Income Distribution, 1971, Manpower and Occupational Analysis: Concepts and Measurements, 1972, (with A. Sturmthal) The International Labor Movement in Transition, 1973, Status Influences in 3rd World Labor Markets, 1991. Mem. Am. Econ. Assn., Indsl. Rels. Rsch. Assn., Internat. Indsl. Rels. Assn. Home: 4849 Girard Ave S Minneapolis MN 55409-2214 Office: U Minn Ind Rels Ctr 271 19th Ave S Minneapolis MN 55455-0430

SCOWCROFT, BRENT, retired air force officer, government official; b. Ogden, Utah, Mar. 19, 1925; s. James and Lucile (Ballantyne) S.; m. Marian Horner, Sept. 17, 1951 (dec. 1995); 1 dau., Karen. B.S., U.S. Mil. Acad., 1947; M.A., Columbia U., 1953, Ph.D., 1967; postgrad., Georgetown U., 1958. Commd. 2d lt. USAF, 1947, advanced through grades to lt. gen., 1974; asst. prof. dept. social sci. U.S. Mil. Acad., 1953-57; asst. air attache Am. Embassy, Belgrade, Yugoslavia, 1959-61; assoc. prof. dept. polit. sci. U.S. Air Force Acad., Colo., 1962-63; prof., head dept. U.S. Air Force Acad., 1963-64; mem. staff long range planning div. Office Dep. Chief Staff Plans and Ops., Washington, 1964-67; assigned Nat. War Coll., 1967-68; staff asst. Western Hemisphere region Office Asst. Sec. Def. Internat. Security Affairs, Washington, 1968-69; dep. asst. dir. plans for nat. security matters office Dep. Chief Staff Plans and Ops., 1969-70; spl. asst. to dir. Joint Staff, Joint Chiefs of Staff, 1970-71; mil. asst. to Pres., 1972-73, dep. asst. to Pres. for nat. security affairs, 1973-75, asst. to Pres. for nat. security affairs, 1975-77; mem. Pres.'s Gen. Adv. Com. on Arms Control, 1977-80; vice chmn. Kissinger Assocs., Inc., 1982-89; asst. to Pres. Nat. Security Coun., Washington, 1989-93; pres. Forum for Internat. Policy, Washington, 1993—; bd. dirs. Nat. Bank of Washington; chmn. Pres.' Commn. on Strategic Forces; mem. Pres.' Commn. on Def. Mgmt., Pres. Spl. Rev. Bd. on the Iran/Contra Affair; pres. The Scowcroft Group, 1994—. Bd. dirs. Atlantic Council U.S.; Bd. visitors U.S. Air Force Air U., 1977-79; mem. adv. bd. Georgetown Center for Strategic and Internat. Studies. Decorated D.S.M. with two oak leaf clusters, Legion of Merit with oak leaf cluster, Air Force Commendation medal, D.S.M. Dept. Def., Nat. Security medal; recipient Medal of Freedom, 1991; named Hon. Knight Brit. Empire, 1993. Mem. Council Fgn. Relations (bd. dirs.), UN Assn. U.S. (vice chmn.), Am. Polit. Sci. Assn., Acad. Polit. Sci. Mem. Ch. Jesus Christ of Latter-day Saints. Office: 1750 K St NW Ste 800 Washington DC 20006-2318*

SCOWCROFT, JOHN MAJOR, petroleum refinery process development executive; b. Ogden, Utah, June 19, 1924; s. John William and Charlene (Major) S.; m. Barbara Marie Caine, Mar. 12, 1951; children: Charlene, John Arthur, Barbara Ann, Sally Caine. BS, U. Utah, 1951; MBA, Northwestern U., 1952. Served in U.S. Army, 1942-45; various mgmt. positions Standard Oil Co. (Ind.), Chgo., N.Y.C., 1952-74; gen. mgr. Deseret Mgmt. Corp., Salt Lake City, 1974-84; founder Utah Tech. Fin. Corp., Salt Lake City, 1984; exec. v.p. Utah Innovation Ctr., Salt Lake City, 1984-86; founder Utah Ventures, Salt Lake City, 1985; pres. Process Innovators, Inc., Salt Lake City, 1986—, bd. dirs.; bd. dirs., cons. small bus. devel. various orgns., Salt Lake City, 1984—; bd. dirs. Maverik Country Stores, Afton, Wyo., IMPETUS, Inc., Spl. Ltd. Ptnr. of Utah Ventures; founding bd. dirs. Geneva Steel, Salt Lake Bd. First. Security Corp., Salt Lake City; mem. Mountain West Venture Group, past pres., chmn. Mem. nat. adv. coun. David Eccles Sch. Bus., U. Utah; regional rep. LDS Ch., 1973-79; mem. Utah Gov.'s Health Care Options Commn. With U.S. Army, 1942-45. Cash Rsch. grantee U.S. Dept. Energy, 1989, Utah Dept. Energy, 1990, Utah Ctrs. of Excellence, 1989, Utah Tech. Fin. Corp., 1989. Mem. Salt Lake Area C. of C. (chmn. 1983), Alta Club (bd. dirs.), Rotary Club Salt Lake (treas. 1988-89, pres. 1993-94). Avocations: amateur radio, computers, skiing, hiking. Home: 1292 Federal Heights Dr Salt Lake City UT 84103-4326 Office: Utah Ventures 423 Wakara Way Ste 206 Salt Lake City UT 84108-3532

SCOZZIE, JAMES ANTHONY, chemist; b. Erie, Pa., Nov. 3, 1943. AB, Gannon Coll., 1965; MS, Case Western Res. U., 1968, PhD in Chemistry, 1970. Jr. rsch. chemist ctrl. rsch. dept. Lord Corp., 1965; rsch. chemist Diamond Shamrock Corp., 1970-72, sr. rsch. chemist, 1972-76, rsch. supr. pharmaceutics, 1976-78, group leader agrl. chemistry, 1978-81, assoc. dir. agrl. chemistry rsch., 1981-83; dir. agrl. chemistry rsch. SDS Biotech Corp., 1983-85, dir. corp. rsch., 1985—; pres. Ricerca, Inc., Painesville, Ohio, 1986—. Chmn. bd. trustees State of Ohio Edison Biotechnology Ctr.; bd. governance Edison Biotechnology Inst., Ohio Technology Network. Mem. Am. Chem. Soc. Achievements include research in structure and chemistry of peptide antibiotics, synthesis of biologically active compounds, pesticides, process studies of organic compounds, commercial evaluation, nutrition and animal health, herbicides, plant growth regulants, cardiovascular agents and anti-inflammatory agents. Office: Ricerca Inc PO Box 1000 7528 Auburn Rd Painesville OH 44077

SCRABECK, JON GILMEN, dental eductor; b. Rochester, Minn., Dec. 6, 1938; s. Clarence and Nancy Alma (Brown) S.; m. DeAnn Louise Jacks, June 16, 1962; children: Joan Louise, Erik Jon. Student, Contra Costa Coll., San Pablo, Calif., 1964-66, U. Calif., Berkeley, 1966-67; DDS, UCLA, 1971; MA in Edn., U. Colo., 1985. Pvt. practice, Santa Rosa, Calif., 1971-78; sr. instr. U. Colo. Sch. Dentistry, Denver, 1978-79, asst. prof., 1980-86, dir. patient care, 1979-80, acting dir. clin. affairs, 1980-81; acting assoc. dean U. Colo. Sch. Dentistry, Denver, 1983-84; acting div. chmn. U. Colo. Sch. Dentistry, Denver, 1984-85; dept. chmn. Marquette U. Sch. Dentistry, Milw., 1986-90, assoc. prof., 1986—, assoc. prof. tenure, 1989, curricular head, 1990—; cons. Dental Student mag.,1983-86, Colo. Bd. Dentistry, Denver, 1985-86, Dentist mag., 1986-90, VA, Milw., 1987-90. Editor Jour. Colo. Dental Assn., 1980-86; contbr. articles and abstracts to dental jours. mem. vol. staff Morey Dental Clinic, Denver, 1982-85, Health Fair, Denver, 1983-85; ofcl. judge S.E. Wis. Sci. Fair, Milw., 1988—. Fellow Internat. Coll. Dentists, Acad. Dental Materials, Am. Coll. Dentists, Pierre Fauchard Acad.; mem. ADA (coun. on journalism 1984-86, coun. on dental rsch. 1986-88, manuscript reviewer 1988—), Acad. Operative Dentistry, Wis. Dental Assn. (assoc. editor Jour. 1987—), Omicron Kappa Upsilon, Alpha Gamma Sigma. Roman Catholic. Avocations: foreign and domestic travel, photography, boating, fishing, water skiing. Home: W349s10140 Bittersweet Ct Eagle WI 53119-1851 Office: Marquette U Sch Dentistry 604 N 16th St Milwaukee WI 53233-2117

SCRAIRE, JEAN-CLAUDE, lawyer, investment company executive; b. Montreal, Que., Can., Aug. 25, 1946; s. Paul and Constance (Beaulac) S.; children: Louis-Marrin, Jean-François, Valérie. Diploma, Coll. St. Laurent, 1966; Law Degree, U. Montreal, 1969. Bar: Que. 1970. Assoc. in comml. law Beaulé et Assocs., Montreal, 1970-74; various mgmt. positions Quebec Govt., Quebec City, 1974-81; minister Dept. of Justice; legal advisor Caisse de dépôt et placement du Que., Montreal, 1981-82, legal affairs dir., 1982-83, sr. v.p. legal and corp. affairs, 1983-86, sr. v.p. legal, corp. affairs, real estate investments, 1986-93, sr. v.p. Caisse Real Estate Group, 1993-95, CEO, 1995, chmn. bd., CEO, 1995—. Mem. Bd. of Trade of Met. Montreal; mem. Montreal Coun. for Internat. Rels.; mem. Leaders' Networking group of Que.; participant Que.-Japan Bus. Forrum; gov. Jr. C. of C. of Que.; mem. sponsoring com. of employment forum and hon. chmn. 10th fundraising campaign Que. Red Cross. Mem. French C. of C. in Can., Amnesty Internat., St. Jérôme C. of C., Laval C. of C., Mount Stephen Club (Montreal). Office: Caisse De Depot et Placement, 900-1981 Ave McGill College, Montreal, PQ Canada H3A 3C7

SCRASE, DAVID ANTHONY, German language educator; b. Upton, Dorset, Eng., Nov. 27, 1939; came to U.S., 1969; s. Robert Stanley and Dorothy Adelaide (Ridgewell) S.; m. Mary Ellen Martin, May 5, 1973 (div. Apr. 1985); 1 child, Anna Rachel Martin-Scrase; m. Mary McNeil, July 15, 1995. BA, Bristol U., 1962; PhD, Ind. U., 1972. Lectr. Zurich U., Switzerland, 1964-68; asst. prof. Oxford Poly., Eng., 1968-69; prof. U. Vt., Burlington, 1971—. Author: Wilhelm Lehmann, A Critical Biography, 1984, Understanding Johannes Bobrowski, 1995 (with W. Mieder) The Holocaust: Introductory Essays, 1996; contbr. articles, translations. Fellow Brit. Acad., London, 1973, Humboldt Found., Bonn, Germany, 1974, 79. Avocations: reading, music, woodwork, sport. Office: U Vt Dept German Waterman Bldg Burlington VT 05405

SCREPETIS, DENNIS, nuclear engineer, consultant; b. Hoboken, N.J., Feb. 12, 1930; s. George and Athanasia (Stasinos) S.; m. Betty Pravasilis, Sept. 17, 1960. Student, Stevens Inst. Tech., Bklyn. Poly. Inst., Cooper Union, Rutgers U. Registered profl. engr., N.J., N.Y. Nuclear engr. Vitro Corp. Am., N.Y.C., 1957-60; project engr. Gen. Cable Corp., Bayonne, N.J., 1960-63; project mgr. AMF Atomics, York, Pa., 1963-65; sr. staff engr. nuclear div. Combustion Engring. Corp., Windsor, Conn., 1965-66; corp. engr. Standard Packaging Corp., N.Y.C., 1966-68; v.p. engring. Eastern Schokbeton, Bound Brook, N.J., 1968-74; cons. engr., Ft. Lee, N.J., 1974—. Patentee in nuclear sci. Mem. Soc. of Am. Mil. Engrs., Am. Biog. Inst. Rsch. Assn. (bd. dirs.), Internat. Biog. Ctr. (bd. dirs.). Greek Orthodox. Home and Office: 2200 N Central Rd Fort Lee NJ 07024-7557

SCRIBNER, BARBARA COLVIN, museum administrator; b. Bangor, Maine, Dec. 18, 1926; d. Howard Morton and May Josephine (Tierney) Colvin; m. Harold B. Scribner, Mar. 10, 1956 (dec. June, 1982); 1 child, Scott Colvin. Student Pratt Inst., 1945-46. Assoc. editor McCall's Mag., N.Y.C., 1950-59; assoc. editor Am. Home, N.Y.C., 1960-64, contbg. editor, 1964-67; free-lance writer-editor, N.Y.C., 1968-77; dir. pub. info. Stamford Mus. and Nature Ctr., Conn., 1978—, curator Going to Blazes exhbn., 1988-89, Music Mania exhbn., 1988-89, Antique Toy Banks exhbn., 1990-91, Antique Bottles exhbn., 1992-93, Toy Bldg. Sets Exhbn., 1994—, Bendel Estate Exhibit, 1994—, Puzzling Challenges Exhibit, 1997-98; mem. attractions com. State of Conn., 1982—. Mem. product com. New Eng. U.S.A. Found., 1989-90; American Trail, 1990, Tourism Network Conn., 1992-94; exec. bd. Council Darien Sch. Parents, Conn., 1974-82; cons. Conn. Humanities Coun., 1997—, Episcopal Ch. Women, Darien, 1970-78, Darien High Sch. Parents Assn., 1980-82. Republican. Lodge: Order Eastern Star. Home: 40 Maple St Darien CT 06820-5209 Office: Stamford Mus & Nature Ctr 39 Scofieldtown Rd Stamford CT 06903-4023

SCRIBNER, BELDING HIBBARD, medical educator, nephrologist; b. Chgo., Jan. 18, 1921; s. Carleton Spear and Mary Elizabeth (Belding) S.; m. Elizabeth F. Browne, Dec. 28, 1942 (div. Dec. 1965); children—Peter B., Robert R., Thomas B., Elizabeth A., m. Ethel Victoria Hackett, Jan. 28, 1966. A.B., U. Calif.-Berkeley, 1941; M.D., Stanford U., 1945; M.A., U. Minn., 1951; D. (hon.), U. Goteborg, 1981; postgrad., Med. Sch. London, 1985. Asst. to staff Mayo Clinic, Rochester, Minn., 1950-51; instr. medicine U. Wash., Seattle, 1951-55, asst. prof. medicine, 1955-58, assoc. prof. medicine, 1958-64, prof. medicine, 1964—. Patentee med. device. Served with U.S. Navy, 1941-44. Recipient Gaindner Found. award, Toronto, 1969, David Hume award Nat. Kidney Found., 1975, Mayo Soley award Western Soc. Clin. Investigation, 1982, Jean Hamburger award Internat. Soc. Nephrology, 1987, Gov.'s medal State of Wash., 1989; Markle Found. scholar, 1954-59. Mem. Am. Soc. Clin. Investigation, Am. Soc. Artificial Organs (pres. 1963-64), Am. Soc. Nephrology (pres. 1978-79, John P. Peters award 1986), Assn. Am. Physicians, Inst. Medicine. Office: Univ Wash Divsn Nephrology Mail Stop Box 356521 Seattle WA 98195

SCRIBNER, CHARLES, III, publisher, art historian, lecturer; b. Washington, May 24, 1951; s. Charles and Joan (Sunderland) S.; m. Ritchie Harrison Markoe, Aug. 4, 1979; children: Charles IV, Christopher Markoe. AB, Princeton U., 1973, MFA, 1975, PhD, 1977. Editor Charles Scribner's Sons, N.Y.C., 1975—, dir. subs. rights, 1978-82, pub. paperback div., 1982-83, exec. v.p., 1983-84; v.p. Macmillan Pub. Co., N.Y.C., 1984-94; instr. dept. art and archaeology Princeton U., 1976-77; mem. adv. council Princeton U. Library, 1981-90; mem. adv. council dept. art and archaeology Princeton U., 1983-91; trustee Princeton U. Press, 1984-90, Homeland Found., 1987—; bd. advisors Wethersfield Inst., 1985—; bd. dirs. Met. Opera Guild, 1990-92. Author: The Triumph of the Eucharist - Tapestries by Rubens, 1982, Rubens, 1989, Bernini, 1991. Trustee St. Paul's Sch., Concord, N.H., 1994—. Mem. Assn. Princeton U. Press. Roman Catholic. Clubs: Racquet and Tennis (N.Y.C.); Ivy (Princeton); Piping Rock (N.Y.). Avocations: music, art, opera. Office: Charles Scribners Sons 14th Fl 1230 Avenue of the Americas New York NY 10020

SCRIBNER, RODNEY LATHAM, former state official; b. Rumford, Maine, May 6, 1935; s. Dwight Latham and Evaline May (House) S.; m. Evelyn Jean Sanborn, Feb. 28, 1963. B.S. in Marine Sci., Maine Maritime Acad., 1956. C.P.A., Maine. With Mobil Oil Co., N.Y.C., 1958-62; acct. Staples & Boyce, Portland, Maine, 1962-68; mem. Maine Ho. of Reps., 1967-68; dep. commr. Maine Dept. Fin. and Adminstrn., 1968-69, state controller, 1971-72, state budget officer, 1972-73; with Maine Leg. Fin. Office, 1973-74; treas. State of Maine, 1975-76, auditor, 1977; dep. dir. Office Revenue Sharing, U.S. Treas. Dept., Washington, 1977-79; commr. Dept. Fin. and Adminstrn., State of Maine, 1979-87; auditor State of Maine, 1987-96; instr. U. Maine, 1971. Treas., United Way of Kennebec County; mem. Augusta Housing Authority, Maine, 1979-89; mem. planning com. Colby Coll. Mgmt. Inst., Waterville, Maine, 1973-89; past treas. Augusta Salvation Army; chmn. Maine Mcpl. Bond Bank, Augusta, 1976-77. Served to lt. (j.g.) USNR, 1956-58. Mem. AICPA, Maine Soc. CPAs (gov. 1983-84, 89—), Am. Soc. Pub. Adminstrn. (pres. Maine chpt. 1972-73), Rotary (treas. 1986-89). Democrat. Baptist. Home: 150 Green St Augusta ME 04330-5427 Office: State of Maine Dept Audit Station #66 Augusta ME 04333

SCRICCA, DIANE BERNADETTE, principal; b. Flushing, N.Y., Mar. 18, 1951; d. Dominic John (Scricca) and Anne (Quinterno) Freohlich; m. Mark Scheinbart, Jan. 19, 1975 (div. Dec. 1988); 1 child, Mark Anthony. BA in Social Studies, St. John's U., 1973, MS in Curriculum and Teaching, 1977, D of Adminstrn. and Supervision, 1980. Tchr., social studies various high schs., N.Y.C., 1973-78; coord. spl. edn. Jamaica (N.Y.) High Sch., 1979-81, asst. prin., 1981-87; asst. prin. Ft. Hamilton High Sch., Bklyn., 1987-90; prin. Elmont (N.Y.) Meml. High Sch., 1990—; cons. in field; instr. new tchr., N.Y.C. Bd. Edn., 1982-90, instr., new suprs., 1988-90. Mem. ASCD, Nat. Assn. Secondary Sch. Prins. Roman Catholic. Avocations: tennis, travel, mus., reading. Home: 53 Corwin Ave New Hyde Park NY 11040-3953 Office: Elmont Meml High Sch 555 Ridge Rd Floral Park NY 11003-3524

SCRIGGINS, ALAN LEE, developmental pediatrician; b. Englewood, N.J., Jan. 16, 1940; s. Thomas Dalby and Patricia (Fowler) S.; m. Geneva M. Brown, June 5, 1965; children: Jennifer A., Elizabeth B. AB, Middlebury Coll., 1961; MD, McGill U., Montreal, Que., Can., 1965. Diplomate Am.

Bd. Pediatrics. Resident in pediats. U. Vt. Hosp., 1968-70; pvt. practice St. Albans, Vt., 1970-79; commd. maj. USAF, 1979, advanced through grades to col., 1988; pediatrician USAF Hosp., Plattsburg AFB, N.Y., 1979-86, USAF Med. Ctr., Andrews AFB, Md., 1986-89; pediat. devel. USAF Hosp./RAF, Lakenheath, Eng., 1989-91; fellow devel. pediats. Georgetown U. Hosp., Washington, 1991-93; devel. pediatrician USAF Med. Ctr., Wright-Patterson AFB, Ohio, 1993-97; ret. USAF, 1997. Fellow Am. Acad. Pediatrics, Soc. Devel. Pediats.; mem. Am. Assn. Mental Retardation, Learning Disabilities Assn. Avocation: fishing. Office: Wright-Patterson USAF Med Ctr Pediat Specialty Clinic Wright Patterson Med Ctr Wright Patterson AFB OH 45433

SCRIGGINS, LARRY PALMER, lawyer; b. Englewood, N.J., Nov. 27, 1936; s. Thomas Dalby and M. Patricia (Fowler) S.; m. Victoria Jackola, Feb. 17, 1979; children: Elizabeth J., Thomas P. AB, Middlebury Coll., 1958; JD, U. Chgo., 1961. Bar: Md. 1962. Law clk. to chief judge Md. Ct. Appeals, 1962; assoc. Piper & Marbury L.L.P., Balt., 1962-69, ptnr., 1969—, vice chmn. 1988-93, mem. exec. com., CFO, 1993—; mem. legal adv. com. N.Y. Stock Exchange, 1992—; bd. dirs. USF & G Corp., 1979—, Center Stage Assocs., 1979-89, Balt. Choral Arts Soc., 1979—, Balt. Conv. Bur., 1982-95, YMCA of Greater Balt., 1987-94, Fund for Ednl. Excellence, 1990—, chmn. bd. trustees, 1993—; bd. dirs. Nat. Aquarium in Balt., bd. govs. 1987-93. Fellow Am. Bar Found.; mem. Md. Bar Assn. (coun. 1976-78, chmn. 1977-78, chmn. com. on corp. laws 1981-84), ABA (sect. on bus. law, council 1972-76, chair 1991-92, vice-chair and editor in chief The Bus. Lawyer 1989-90, chmn. law and acctg. com. 1985-88), Internat. Bar Assn., Am. Judicature Soc., Am. Law Inst., Task Force on Fin. Instruments, Fin. Acctg. Standards Bd., Am. Inst. CPAs Planning Com. (pub. mem. 1989-92). Contbr. articles to profl. jours. Home: 13 E Eager St Baltimore MD 21202-2513 Office: Piper & Marbury LLP 36 S Charles St Baltimore MD 21201-3020

SCRIMSHAW, NEVIN STEWART, physician, nutrition and health educator; b. Milw., Jan. 20, 1918; m. Mary Ware Goodrich, 1941; 5 children. B.A. with honors, Ohio Wesleyan U., 1938; M.A. in Biology, Harvard U., 1939, Ph.D. in Physiology, 1941; M.D. with honors, U. Rochester, 1945; M.P.H. with honors, Harvard U., 1959. Diplomate Am. Bd. Med. Examiners. Intern Gorgas Hosp., C.Z., 1945-46; Rockefeller postdoctoral fellow U. Rochester, N.Y., 1946-47, Merck NRC fellow, 1947-49; asst. resident in ob-gyn Strong Meml. Hosp., Genesee Hosp., N.Y., 1948-49; cons. nutrition Pan-Am. San. Bur. WHO, 1948-49, regional advisor on nutrition, 1949-53; dir. Inst. Nutrition C.Am. and Panama, Guatemala, 1949-61, cons. dir., 1961-65, cons. 1965—; dir. Clin. Research Ctr., MIT, 1962-66, 79-85, dir. internat. food and nutrition program, 1976-88, prof. human nutrition, 1961-76, head dept. nutrition and food sci., 1961-79, inst. prof. emeritus, 1988—; vis. prof. Columbia U., N.Y., 1976-88; vis. lectr. 1961-66; vis. lectr. Harvard U., 1968-85; vis. prof. Tufts U; mem. govt. adv. com. NIH; chmn. internat. com. NRC; dir. devel. studies div. U.N. U., 1985-86, food nutrition program 1975—. mem. adv. com. WHO, Nutrition Found., others. Contbr. articles to profl. jours.; editor: (with others) Amino Acid Fortification of Protein Foods, 1971, Nutrition, National Development and Planning, 1973, The Economics, Marketing and Technology of Fish Protein Concentrate, 1974, Nutrition and Agricultural Development: Significance and Potential for the Tropics, 1976, Single-Cell Protein: Safety for Animal and Human Feeding, 1979, Nutrition Policy Implementation: Issues and Experience, 1983, Diarrhea and Malnutrition: Interactions, Mechanisms and Interventions, 1983, Chronic Energy Deficiency, 1987, Acceptability of Milk and Milk Products in Populations With Lactose Intolerance, 1988, Nutrition in the Elderly, 1989, Activity, Energy Expenditure and Energy Requirements of Infants and Children, 1990, RAP: Rapid Assessment Procedures: Qualitative Methodologies for Planning and Evaluation of Health Related Programs, 1992, Protein-energy Interactions, 1992, Community-based Longitudinal Nutrition and Health Studies: Classical Examples from Guatemala, Haiti, and Mexico, 1995, The Effects of Improved Nutrition in Early Childhood: The Institute of Nutrition of Central America and Panama Follow-up Study, 1995, The Nutrition and Health Transition of Democratic Costa Rica, 1995. Recipient Osborne and Mendal award, 1960, Internat. award Inst. Food Technologists, 1969, medal of honor Fundacion F. Cuenca Villoro, Spain, 1978, Bristol-Myers prize, 1988, Alan Shawn Feinstein award, 1991, World Food prize, 1991, also others. Trustee Rockefeller Found., 1971-83, Pan-Am. Health and Edn. Found., 1986-92; pres. Internat. Nutrition Found. for Developing Countries, 1982—. Fellow Am. Inst. Nutrition, Royal Soc. Health, AAAS, Am. Soc. Clin. Nutrition, Am. Pub. Health Assn. (v.p. 1978 award of excellence in promoting and protecting health of people 1974); mem. Am. Coll. Nutrition, NAS (ch. applied biol. section, 1973-76, 88-91), Inst. of Medicine, Am. Acad. Arts Scis., Am. Coll. Preventive Medicine, Am. Bd. Nutrition, Mass. Pub. Health Assn., New Eng. Pub. Health Assn., Mass. Med. Soc., Am. Physiol. Soc., Am. Epidemol. Soc., Internat. Union Nutritional Scis. (pres. 1978-81), Internat. Epidemol. Assn., also others. Home: Sandwich Mountain Farm PO Box 330 Campton NH 03223-0330 Office: Charles St Sta PO Box 500 Boston MA 02114-0500

SCRIMSHAW, SUSAN, dean. PhD in Anthropology, Columbia U., 1974. Dean U. Ill. Sch. Pub. Health, Chgo., 1995—. Recipient Margaret Mead award, 1985. Fellow AAAS; mem. Inst. Medicine-Nat. Acad. Sci., Am. Anthropology Assn., Soc. Applied Anthropology, Nat. Soc. Med. Anthropology (pres. 1985). Office: Sch of Pub Health(M/C 922) U Ill Chicago 2121 W Taylor St Chicago IL 60612-7260*

SCRIPPS, EDWARD WYLLIS, newspaper publisher; b. San Diego, May 21, 1909; s. James G. and Josephine (Stedem) S.; m. Betty Jeanne Knight McDonnell, Jan. 31, 1950; children: Edward Wyllis III, Barry Howard. Student, Pomona Coll. Chmn. bd. Scripps Enterprises, Inc., 1931—. Mem. St. Francis Yacht Club, Lyford Cay (Nassau, Bahamas), Boars Head Sports Club, Farmington Country Club, Everglades Club, Bath and Tennis Club, Colony Club, Mrs. Club (N.Y.C.). also: 947 N Ocean Blvd Palm Beach FL 33480-3325 Office: Dulles Corner Park 2411 Park S Ste 250 Herndon VA 22071

SCRIPTER, FRANK C., manufacturing company executive; b. Dansville, Mich., June 21, 1918; s. Edgar and Maggie Alice (Havens) S.; student Warren's Sch. of Cam Design, 1946. Lic. firmarms mfg.; m. Dora Maebelle Smalley, Nov. 2, 1940 (dec. Sept. 1945); 1 child, Karen Scripter Allen; m. Elvira Elaine Taylor, Aug. 6, 1951; children: James Michael, Mark Lee, Anita Elaine, Warren Arthur, Charles Edward. Apprentice, Lundberg Screw Products Co., 1940-41; set-up man Reo Motors, Inc., 1942-43; night supt. Manning Bros. Metal Products Co., 1943; with McClaren Screw Products Co., 1946-47; ptnr. Dansville Screw Products Co., 1946-54, pres., dir. Scripco Mfg. Co., Laingsburg, Mich., 1954-88, ret. 1988; mfg. of ASP Pistol, 1980-81. Chmn., Citizens Com. Laingsburg, 1956-58; mem. Laingsburg Community Schs. Bd. Edn., 1971-75, sec., 1973-74, pres., 1974-75. With USNR, 1944-45. Mem. Nat. Rifle Assn. (life), Mich. Antique Arms Collectors (life), The Am. Leopard Horse Assn. (founder 1967), N.Am. Hunting Club (life), Am. Legion (life mem.). Republican. Methodist. Patentee in field. Home: 9701 Round Lake Rd Laingsburg MI 48848-9404

SCRIVEN, L. E.(DWARD), II, chemical engineering educator, scientist; b. Battle Creek, Mich., Nov. 4, 1931; s. L. Edward and Esther Mabel (Davis) S.; m. Dorene Bates Hayes, June 19, 1952; children: Ellen Dorene, Teresa Ann, Mark Hayes. BS, U. Calif., Berkeley, 1952; PhD, U. Del., 1956. Rsch. engr. Shell Devel. Co., Emeryville, Calif., 1956-59; asst. prof. chem. engring. and fluid mechanics U. Minn., Mpls., 1959-62, assoc. prof., 1962-66, prof., 1966-89, Regents' prof., 1989—, assoc. dept. head, 1975-78, program dir. Ctr. Interfacial Engring., 1988—; cons. in fields; advisor to Humboldt Found., Fed. Republic of Germany; vis. com. to chem. engring. MIT, sci. assoc. Jet Propulsion Lab., 1977, 79; tech. expert UN Indsl. Devel. Orgn., Vienna, Austria, 1979-88; exec. com. on chem. engring. frontiers NRC, 1984-87; mem. NRC Bd. on Chem. Scis. and Tech., 1987-92, chmn., 1992; mem. NRC Commn. on Phys. Scis., Math. and Applications, 1994—; sci. adv. com. Packard Found., 1988—. Editor: Physico-chemical Hydrodynamics (V.G. Levich), 1992; assoc. editor Jour. Fluid Mechanics, 1970-75; adv. editor Jour. Coll. Interfluid Sci., Physics of Fluids, L.Am. Jour. Chem. Engring. and Applied Chemistry, Internat. Jour. Numerical Methods in Fluid Mechanics; contbr. numerous articles to sci. jours.; patentee in field. Recipient chem. engring. award Am. Soc. Engring. Edn., 1968, Minn. Achievement award, 1989, Murphree award Am. Chem. Soc., 1990; named Fairchild disting. scholar Calif. Inst. Tech., 1989; Guggenheim fellow, 1969-70, fellow Minn. Supercomputer Inst., 1984—. Mem. NAE, Am. Inst. Chem. Engrs. (mem. nat. program. com. 1964-69, Colburn award 1960, Walker award 1977, Tallmadge award 1992), Am. Phys. Soc., Soc. Petroleum Engrs., Gordon Rsch. Confs., Chem. Soc. (Faraday div.), Soc. Indsl. and Applied Math., Soc. Rheology. Research in capillarity, fluid mechanics and coating processes, porous media, cold-stage electron microscopy, microstructured fluids and interfaces, origins of pattern and form, supercomputer-aided analysis. Office: Univ Minn 151 Amundson Hall 421 Washington Ave SE Minneapolis MN 55455-0373

SCRIVER, CHARLES ROBERT, medical scientist, human geneticist; b. Montreal, Que., Can., Nov. 7, 1930; s. Walter deM. and Jessie (Boyd) S.; m. E.K. Peirce, Sept. 8, 1956; children: Dorothy, Peter, Julie, Paul. B.A. cum laude, McGill U., Montreal, 1951, M.D.C.M. cum laude, 1955; DSc (hon.), U. Man., 1992, U. Glasgow, 1993, U. Montreal, 1993. Intern Royal Victoria Hosp., Montreal, 1955-56; resident Royal Victoria and Montreal Children's hosps., 1956-57, Children's Med. Center, Boston, 1957-58; McLaughlin travelling fellow Univ. Coll., London, 1958-60; chief resident pediatrics Montreal Children's Hosp., 1960-61; asst. prof. pediatrics McGill U., 1961, prof. biology Faculty of Sci., prof. pediatrics Faculty of Medicine, 1969—; Alva prof. human genetics, 1994—; mem. med. adv. bd. Howard Hughes Med. Inst., 1981-88; dir. Med. Rsch. Coun. Group in Genetics, 1972-94; assoc. dir. Can. Genetic Diseases Network, 1989—. Co-author: Amino Acid Metabolism and Its Disorders, 1973, Garrod's Inborn Factors in Disease, 1989; sr. editor Metabolic and Molecular Bases Inherited Disease, 1986—; contbr. more than 500 rsch. publs. in field. Decorated Order of Can., Que.; recipient Wood Gold medal McGill U., 1955, Gairdner Internat. award Gairdner Found., 1979, Ross award Can. Pediatric Soc., 1990, Award of excellence Genet Soc. Can., 1992, Prix d'Excellence Inst. Rsch. Clin. de Montreal, 1993, Prix du Quebec, Wilder Penfield, 1995, Medal of Merit Can. Med. Assn., 1996, Lifetime Achievement award March of Dimes Birth Defect Found., 1997; Royal Coll. lectr., 1992, Markle scholar, 1962-67; Med. Rsch. Coun. assoc., 1968-95, Disting. Scientist, 1995—. Fellow AAAS, Royal Soc. Can. (McLaughlin medal 1981), Royal Soc. London (Can. Rutherford lectr. 1983); mem. Can. Soc. Clin. Investigation (pres. 1974-75, G. Malcolm Brown Meml. award 1979), Soc. Pediat. Rsch. (pres. 1975-76), Am. Soc. Human Genetics (dir. 1971-74, pres. 1986-87, William Allan award 1978), Am. Pediat. Soc. (pres. 1994-95), Am. Soc. Clin. Investigation, Assn. Am. Physicians, Brit. Pediat. Assn. (50th Anniversary lectr. 1978), Soc. Francaise de Pediat., Am. Acad. Pediat. (Mead Johnson award for rsch. in pediat. 1968). Office: McGill Univ-Montreal, Childrens Hosp Rsch Inst, 2300 Tupper St, Montreal, PQ Canada H3H 1P3

SCRIVNER, THOMAS WILLIAM, lawyer; b. Madison, Wis., Sept. 10, 1948; s. William H. and Jane (Gehrz) S.; m. Meredith Burke, Aug. 16, 1980; children: Allison, David. AB, Duke U., 1970, MAT, 1972; JD, U. Wis., 1977. Assoc. Michael, Best & Friedrich, Milw., 1978-85, ptnr., 1985—. Mem. ABA, Wis. Bar Assn., Milw. Bar Assn. (labor sect.), Corp. Practice Inst. (pres. 1989-92). Episcopalian. Home: 4626 N Cramer St Milwaukee WI 53211-1203 Office: Michael Best & Friedrich 100 E Wisconsin Ave Milwaukee WI 53202-4107

SCROGGS, DEBBIE LEE, communications professional; b. Norton, Va., Sept. 27, 1953; d. Jennings Eugene and Edith Marie (Harris) S.; m. John L. Price, Apr. 1, 1984. AAS in Acctg., C.C. of Denver, 1981; BSBA magna cum laude, Regis Coll., 1987; MSS in Applied Comms., U. Denver, 1992. Bookkeeper Am./Trayer, Inc., Bristol, Va., 1972-74; assessment transcriber Dept. of Interior, Bristol, 1974-78; supr. computer asst. Dept. of Labor, Mine Safety and Health Adminstrn., Lakewood, Colo., 1978-82; lead tech. writer OAO Corp., Lakewood, 1982-83; tech. writer, editor Tele-Communications, Inc., Denver, 1984-85, Integrated Svcs., Inc., Aurora, Colo., 1985-87; sr. documentation specialist AT&T Customer Edn. Tng., Denver, 1988-89; sr. project mgr. AT&T Customer Edn. and Tng., Denver, 1989-94; tng. facilitator AT&T Customer Edn. Tng., Denver, 1993-94; resource/dept. mgr. AT&T Customer Edn. & Tng., Whippany, N.J., 1994-96; customer tng. and info. products dept. mgr. Lucent Technologies, Whippany, N.J., 1996—. Contbr. articles to profl. jours., publs. Vol. Art Reach of Denver, 1988-94, Channel 6 TV, Denver, 1989-94, Jersey Cares, 1996-97; team mem. Citizen Amb. Program for Tech. Comm. Delegation to China, 1997. Mem. AAUW, Internat. Soc. for Performance Improvement, Soc. Tech. Comm. (Achievement award for user manual 1986, Achievement award for mktg. brochure 1986, Merit award for user manual 1988, spk. nat. conf. 1991, 93, 95-96, networking lunch coord./nat. conf. 1992-95). Avocations: weight training, jogging, golf, tai chi, reading. Office: Lucent Tech 67 Whippany Rd Rm 14J-323 Whippany NJ 07981-1406

SCRUGGS, CHARLES G., editor; b. McGregor, Tex., Nov. 4, 1923; s. John Fleming and Adeline (Hering) S.; m. Miriam June Wigley, July 5, 1947; children—John Mark, Miriam Jan. B.S., Tex. A&M U., 1947. Assoc. editor Progressive Farmer, Dallas, 1947-61, editor, 1962—, v.p., 1964—, exec. editor, 1972, editorial dir., 1973—, editor-in-chief, 1982-87; editorial chmn. So. Progress Pubs., 1987-89; pres. Torado Land and Cattle Co., pres. Tex. Comml. Agr. Council 1953-54; chmn. bd. Sunlean Foods, Inc., 1989—. Author: The Peaceful Atom and the Deadly Fly, 1975, American Agricultural Capitalism. Founding gen. chmn. Chancellors' Century Coun., Tex. A&M U. System, 1987-90; Mem. Gov.'s Com. for Agr., 1950, Tex. Animal Health Council, 1955-61; chmn. So. Brucellosis Com., 1956; pres. Tex. Rural Safety Com., 1957-59; chmn. Nat. Brucellosis Com., 1958-59, 71-72; del. World Food Congress, 1963; pub. mem. U.S. del. 17th Biennial Conf. of FAO, UN, Rome, 1973; chmn. Joint Senate-House Interim Com. Natural Fibers, Tex. Legislature, 1971; mem. coordinating bd. Tex. Coll. and Univ. System, 1965-69; bd. regents Tex. Tech U., 1971-78; founding pres. S.W. Animal Health Research Found. 1961-63, trustee, 1961—. Served to lt. col. U.S. Army; Res., ret. Recipient Christian Svc. Mass Media award, 1995, Abilene Christian U., Southwestern Cattle Raisers award, 1962, Am. Seed Trade Assn. award, 1963, award of honor Am. Agrl. Editors Assn., 1964, Reuben Brigham award Am. Assn. Agrl. Coll. Editors, 1965, Disting. Svc. award Tex. Farm Bur., 1966, Journalistic Achievement award Nat. Plant Food Assn., 1967, Nat. award for agrl. excellence Nat. Agri-Mktg. Assn., 1983, Agrl. Vision award Nat. Forum for Agr., 1994; named Disting. Alumnus Tex. A&M U., 1982. Mem. Am. Agrl. Editors Assn. (pres. 1963), Am. Soc. Mag. Editors, Tex. Assn. Future Farmers Am. (pres. 1940-41), Dallas Agrl. Club (pres. 1951), Nat. Livestock Confedn. Mexico (hon.), The Austin Club, Headliners Club, Alpha Zeta, Sigma Delta Chi.

SCRUGGS, EARL EUGENE, entertainer; b. Cleveland County, N.C., Jan. 6, 1924; s. George Elam and Georgia Lula (Ruppe) S.; m. Anne Louise Certain, Apr. 18, 1948; children: Gary Eugene, Randy Lynn, Steven Earl. HHD in Folk Music (hon.), Gardner-Webb Coll., 1986. Banjo player, 1945—; formed Earl Scruggs Revue, 1969—; major performances include Carnegie Hall, N.Y.C., Wembley Festival, London, Washington Moratorium for Peace, 1969, also rock festivals, coll. concerts; TV appearances include NET-TV Spl. Earl Scruggs: His Family and Friends, 1971, Midnight Spl., NBC-Harper Valley U.S.A. Spl., NBC Country Music Awards Show, Phil Donahue Show, Mike Douglas Show, Austin City Limits, 1977, The Grand Ole Opry's 60th Anniversary Show, 1985, The Nashville Network spl. The American Music Shop, 1990, The Grand Ole Opry's 65th Anniversary Show, 1991, Country Music Assn. Awards Show, 1991, Country Music Assn. Hall of Fame 25th Anniversary TV show, 1992, The Legend of The Beverly Hillbillies, CBS-TV, 1993, Folk Sound USA-Revlon Revue, The Tonight Show, Les Crane Show, Mac Davis Special, The Johnny Cash Show, The Hootenanny Show, Frank McGee's Here and Now, Ernie Ford Show, Jimmy Dean Show, The Anatomy of Pop, Kraft's American Profile, The Roots of Country, CBS-TV, 1994, Red Hot and Country, TNN-TV, 1995, A Night at the Ryman, TNN-TV, 1995; rec. artist: Columbia Records, 1950—; albums include: Nashvilles Rock, Dueling Banjos, Kansas State, I Saw the Light, Earl Scruggs Revue, Rockin' Cross the Country, Family Portrait, Top of the World, Anniversary Special Vol. I and Vol. II, Live! At Austin City Limits, Earl Scruggs: His Family and Friends Soundtrack, Today and Forever, Bold and New, American-Made, World-Played, others; recorded theme song for TV series The Beverly Hillbillies, 1962, also made guest appearances; composer (with others) movie score Where The Lilies Bloom, 1973, also Earl Scruggs Revue rec. music soundtrack for movie; composer instrumental Foggy Mountain Breakdown (used in movie Bonnie and Clyde, Grammy award 1968, Broadcast Music, Inc. award 1969); star: (movie) Banjo Man, 1975; guest appearance (TV movie) Return of the Beverly Hillbillies, 1981; author: (book) Earl Scruggs and the 5-String Banjo, 1968. Apptd. hon. mem. Lt. Gov.'s Staff, State of Tenn., 1987. Named Artist of Yr. Hi-Fi Inst., 1975, Best Country and Bluegrass Banjoist, Frets mag., 1980; recipient Country Music award best instrumental group Billboard Mag., 1975, Cert. of Merit Internat. Bluegrass Music Assn., 1988, Order of the Long Leaf Pine award Gov. State of N.C., 1988, cert. appreciation Tenn. Gov. Ned McWherter, 1990, Spl. Citation of achievement recognition of nat. popularity over 1 million broadcasts of Foggy Mountain Breakdown, Broadcast Music, Inc., 1993, N.C. Folk Heritage award, N.C. Arts Coun. Dept Cultural Resources, others; inducted into Gibson Hall of Fame, 1981, Country Music Assn. Hall of Fame, 1985, Internat. Bluegrass Music Assn. Hall of Honor, 1991; Nat. Heritage fellow NEA, 1989; Nat. Medal of Arts presented by Pres. George Bush at White House, 1992; recipient N.C. Heritage award N.C. Arts Coun. Dept. Cultural Resources, 1996. Developer Scruggs style of banjo playing; inventor Scruggs Tuning Pegs.

SCRUGGS, JACK GILBERT, retired chemical executive; b. Cullman County, Ala., Sept. 9, 1930; s. Carlton Vann and Grace Blanche (Thoroman) S.; m. Anna Faye Thomas, Aug. 21, 1954; children: Pamela Ann, Linda Dianne. BS in Pharmacy, U. Mich., 1952, MS in Pharm. Chem., 1953, PhD in Organic Chem., 1956. Research and devel. mgr. Monsanto Fibers Div., Durham, N.C., 1956-66; tech. v.p. Phillips Fibers Corp., 1966-94. Patentee in polymers and fibers. Pres. Jr. Achievement, Greenville, 1985-86; active Boy Scouts Am.; coach, umpire Little League Baseball, Cary, N.C., 1963-65. Mem. Am. Chem. Soc., Phi Beta Kappa, Sigma Xi, Phi Eta Sigma, Rho Chi, Phi Lambda Upsilon. Republican. Mem. Ch. of Christ. Avocations: golf, racquetball, softball. Home: 614 Devenger Rd Greer SC 29650-3715

SCUDDER, EDWARD WALLACE, JR., newspaper and broadcasting executive; b. Newark, Dec. 8, 1911; s. Edward Wallace and Katherine (Hollifield) Scudder; m. Louise Bagby Fry, Jan. 19, 1945; children: Katherine Allison Tiballi, Mary Gale Doe, Edward, Robert. AB, Princeton, 1935. Treas. Newark Evening News, 1950-70; pres. Evening News Pub. Co., 1955-72, Newark Broadcasting, operating Sta. WVNJ, Newark, to 1978; chmn. of bd. Orange Mountain Comm., West Orange, N.J., 1971—. Trustee Paper Mill Playhouse, Millburn, N.J., Newark Mus.; treas. Lake Placid (N.Y.) Edn. Found. Lt. (j.g.) to lt. comdr. USNR Air Force, 1942-46. Mem. Short Hills Club, Gulfstream Golf Club, Gulfstream Bath and Tennis Club, Delray Beach Yacht Club. Home: 1171 N Ocean Blvd Delray Beach FL 33483-7273 Office: PO Box 79 Summit NJ 07902-0079 Summer home: Birchgate Lake Placid NY 12946

SCUDDER, RICHARD B., newspaper executive; b. Newark, May 13, 1913; s. Edward W. and Katherine (Hollifield) S.; m. Elizabeth A. Shibley, June 24, 944; children: Elizabeth H. (Mrs. Philip Difani), Charles A., Carolyn (Mrs. Peter M. Miller), Jean (Mrs. Joseph Fulmer). AB, Princeton U., 1935; LHD (hon.), Mon Coll. Reporter Newark News, 1935-37, v.p., 1941-51, pub., 1951-72; reporter Boston Herald, 1937-38; chmn. MediaNews Group, Gloucester County Times, Inc., Garden State Newspapers, Inc., Garden State Paper Co., Denver Newspapers, Inc. Trustee Riverview Hosp., N.J. Conservation Found., Monmouth County Conservation Found.; former trustee Rutgers U.; adv. com. Princeton (N.J.) Environ. Inst. Served from pvt. to maj. AUS, 1941-45. Decorated bronze star; recipient TAPPI award, 1971; Nat. Recycling award Nat. Assn. Secondary Materials Industries, 1972; Nat. Resource Recovery Man of Year award, 1978; Papermaker of Yr. award Paper Trade Jour., 1978; named to Paper Industry Hall of Fame, 1995. Mem. N.J. Audobon Soc. Clubs: Rumson Country, Seabright Beach, Seabright Lawn Tennis, Mill Reef, Adirondack League. Office: Denver Post 1560 Broadway Denver CO 80202-6000 Address: 309 S Broad St Woodbury NJ 08096

SCUDDER, ROBERT, minister, youth home administrator; b. Monroe, LA., May 1, 1926; s. Lee and Aldyth (Flenniken) S.; m. Mary Nichols, Oct. 28, 1967; children: Lee, Doug, Vicki, Dana. BA in Human Behavior, Newport U., Newport Beach, Calif., 1983. Ordained to ministry So. Bapt. Conv., 1979. Min., tchr. Books 'n Tapes, Shreveport, La., 1974—; counselor Shreveport Counsel Ctr., 1975-80; asst. pastor Woodlawn Bapt. Ch., Shreveport, 1976; exec. dir., adminstr. Joy Home for Boys, Greenwood, La., 1979—; bd. dirs. Johnny Robinson Youth Shelter, Monroe, 1980—; mem. licensing bd. Dept. Health and Hosps. for Group Homes and Adoptions, State of La., 1986-88, 89—. Author: Genesis, 1976, Cults Exposed, 1981, Customs and Prayer, 1983; also child care pamphlet. Served with USN, 1941-43, PTO. Mem. Am. Assn. on Mental Deficiency (religious v.p. 1984-86, Kiwanis (pres. 1971-72, Child Care award 1984). Home: PO Box 550 Greenwood LA 71033-0550 Office: Joy Home for Boys PO Box 550 Greenwood LA 71033-0550

SCUDDER, THAYER, anthropologist, educator; b. New Haven, Aug. 4, 1930; s. Townsend III and Virginia (Boody) S.; m. Mary Eliza Drinker, Aug. 26, 1950; children: Mary Eliza, Alice Thayer. Grad., Phillips Exeter Acad., 1948; A.B., Harvard U., 1952, Ph.D., 1960; postgrad., Yale U., 1953-54, London Sch. Econs., 1960-61. Research officer Rhodes-Livingstone Inst., No. Rhodesia, 1956-57; sr. research officer Rhodes-Livingstone Inst., 1962-63; asst. prof. Am. U., Cairo, 1961-62; research fellow Center Middle East Studies, Harvard U., 1963-64; asst. prof. Calif. Inst. Tech., Pasadena, 1964-66; assoc. prof. Calif. Inst. Tech., 1966-69, prof. anthropology, 1969—; dir. Inst. for Devel. Anthropology, Binghamton, N.Y., 1976—; cons. UN Devel. Program, FAO, IBRD, WHO, Ford Found., Navajo Tribal Coun., AID, World Conservation Union, Lesotho Highlands Devel. Authority, South China Electric Power Joint Venture Corp., U.S. Nat. Rsch. Coun., Que.-Hydro, Environ. Def. Fund. Author: The Ecology of the Gwembe Tonga, 1962; co-author: Long-Term Field Research in Social Anthropology, 1979, Secondary Education and the Formation of an Elite: The Impact of Education on Gwembe District, Zambia, 1980, No Place to Go: The Impacts of Forced Relocation on Navajos, 1982, For Prayer and Profit: The Ritual, Economic and Social Importance of Beer in Gwembe District, Zambia, 1950-1982, 1988, The IUCN Review of the So. Okavango Integrated Water Development Project, 1993. John Simon Guggenheim Meml. fellow, 1975. Mem. Am. Anthrop. Assn. (1st recipient Solon T. Kimball award for pub. and applied anthropology 1984, Edward J. Lehman award 1991), Soc. Applied Anthropology, Am. Alpine Club. Office: Calif Inst Tech # 228-77 Pasadena CA 91125

SCULLIN, FREDERICK JAMES, JR., federal judge; b. Syracuse, N.Y., Nov. 5, 1939; s. Frederick James and Cleora M. (Fellows) S.; m. Veronica Terek Sauro, Aug. 31, 1984; children: Mary Margaret, Kathleen Susan, Kellie Anne, Rebecca Rose; 1 stepchild, Angel Jenette Sauro. B.S. in Econs., Niagara U., 1961; LL.B., Syracuse U., 1964. Bar: N.Y. 1964, Fla. 1976, U.S. Dist. Ct. (no. dist.) N.Y. 1967, U.S. Supreme Ct. 1971. Assoc. Germain & Germain, Syracuse, 1967-68; asst. dist. atty. Onondaga County, Syracuse, 1968-71; asst. atty. gen. N.Y. State Organized Crime Task Force, 1971-78; dir. regional office N.Y. State Organized Crime Task Force, Albany, 1974-78; chief prosecutor, dir. Gov.'s Council on Organized Crime State of Fla., Tallahassee, 1978—; sole practice Syracuse, 1979-82, U.S. atty. for No. Dist. N.Y., 1982-92; judge U.S. Dist. Ct. (no. dist.) N.Y., 1992—. With U.S. Army, 1964-67, Vietnam; col. USAR. Decorated Air medal, Bronze Star; Cross of Gallantry (Vietnam). Mem. Am. Judicature Soc., Fla. Bar Assn., Fed. Bar Assn., Fed. Bar Coun., Onon City Bar Assn. Office: US Dist Ct US Courthouse 100 S Clinton St Syracuse NY 13261-9211

SCULLION, ANNETTE MURPHY, lawyer, educator; b. Chgo., Apr. 6, 1926; d. Edmund Patrick and Anna (Nugent) Murphy; 1 son, Kevin. B.Ed., Chgo. Tchrs. Coll., 1960; J.D., DePaul U., 1964, M.Ed., 1966; M.Ed., Loyola U., Chgo., 1970; Ed.D., No. Ill. U., 1974. Bar: Ill. 1964, U.S. Dist. Ct. (no. dist.) Ill. 1965, U.S. Ct. Appeals (D.C. cir.) 1978. Lectr. Chgo. Community Coll., 1964-68; pvt. practice law, Chgo., 1964—; asst. prof. bus. edn. Chgo. State U., 1966-69, assoc. prof., 1970-73, prof., 1974—. Club founder, adviser Bus. Edn. Students Assn., Chgo. State U., 1976—; sch. law workshop coordinator Ill. Div. Vocat. and Tech. Edn., 1981. Mem. Nat. Bus. Edn. Assn., Women's Bar Assn. Ill., ABA, Am. Tchr. Edn., Beta Gamma Sigma Home: 386 Muskegon Ave Calumet City IL 60409-2347 Office: Chgo State U 95 And King Dr # 203 Chicago IL 60601

SCULLION, TSUGIKO YAMAGAMI, non-profit organization executive; b. China, June 30, 1946; d. Hajime and Akemi (Murazumi) Yamagami; m. William James Scullion, Nov. 26, 1971; 1 child, James. BA, Baldwin-Wallace Coll., 1970; MA, Sch. Internat. Tng., 1971. Area cons. Conn. AFS Internat./Intercultural Programs, N.Y.C., 1972-73, regional mgr. for Asia and Pacific, 1973-78, dir. internat. ops., 1978-81, v.p. Europe, Africa, Middle East, 1981-83, v.p. program svcs., 1083-85, exec. v.p., 1985-87; exec. v.p. U.S. Com. UNICEF, N.Y.C., 1988-95; mgmt. cons. strategic planning, mktg. and fundraising, 1995-96; chief oper. officer Synergos Inst., 1996—. Bd. dirs. Oberlin Shansi Meml. Assn., Whitby Sch. Avocations: golf, classical music, ballet. Home: 7 Chasmar Rd Old Greenwich CT 06870-1404

SCULLY, JOHN CARROLL, life insurance marketing research company executive; b. Springfield, Mass., Mar. 16, 1932; s. James and Frances (Carroll) S.; m. Barbara A. Fougere, Sept. 7, 1953; children: Kathleen, Margaret, John, James, Patricia, Mary Ellen, Susan. B.A., Holy Cross Coll., 1953; C.L.U., Boston U., 1963; postgrad., Dartmouth Inst., 1977. With John Hancock Mut. Life Ins. Co., 1953-92; gen. agent John Hancock Mut. Life Ins. Co., Indpls., 1966-75; sr. v.p. agency dept. John Hancock Mut. Life Ins. Co., Boston, 1975-80; pres. retail sector John Hancock Mut. Life Ins. Co., 1980-92; pres., chief. exec. officer Life. Ins. Mktg. Rsch. Assoc., Windsor, Conn., 1992—. Bd. dirs. Greater Boston YMCA, 1975-91; chmn. Mass. campaign Holocaust Meml. Mus., 1985—; div. chmn. United Way, 1985—; bd. dirs. Cath. Charities, 1986—; trustee Springfield Coll., 1986, Suffolk U., 1986. With U.S. Army, 1954-56. Mem. Am. Coll. Life Underwriters, Nat. Assn. Life Underwriters (v.p. Ind. 1973-75), Life Ins. Mktg. and Rsch. Assn. (past chmn.), Gen. Agts. and Mgrs. Assn. (past pres. Indpls. Nat. Mgmt. award 1973-75), Life Underwriter Tng. Coun. (past chmn.), Greater Boston C. of C. (bd. dirs. 1985—), Wellesley Club, Executives Club (past pres.), Algonquin Club (bd. dirs.), Farmington Country Club, Hartford Club, KC. Roman Catholic. Home: 2 Shibah Dr Bloomfield CT 06002-1527 Office: Limra Internat PO Box 208 Hartford CT 06141-0208

SCULLY, JOHN THOMAS, obstetrician, gynecologist, educator; b. N.Y.C., Mar. 11, 1931; s. John Thomas and Mildred Frances (Dunstrop) S.; children: John, Helen Mary, Thomas, Nora, James, Sara, Megan, Devin. B.S., Georgetown U., 1952; M.D., U. Mex., 1959. Diplomate Am. Bd. Ob-Gyn. Intern, Nassau Hosp., 1959-60, resident, 1960-63; practice medicine specializing in ob-gyn, 1963—; sr. attending dept. ob-gyn St. Peter's Med. Center, Robert Wood Johnson U. Hosp.; clin. prof. ob-gyn Rutgers U. Med. Sch., 1971—. Fellow ACS, Am. Coll. Ob-Gyn; mem. N.J. Med. Soc., Middlesex County Med. Soc., N.J. Ob-Gyn Soc., N.J. Right to Life (charter). Republican. Roman Catholic. Office: 23 Duke St New Brunswick NJ 08901-1738

SCULLY, MALCOLM GRIFFIN, editor, writer; b. Pitts., Nov. 25, 1941; s. Cornelius Decatur and Elinor Hilliard (Tucker) S.; m. Jane Carney, Sept. 11, 1965; children: Randolph Ferguson, Allen Tucker. BA in English, U. Va., 1963; MA in English, Cornell U., 1965. Reporter Norfolk Virginian-Pilot, 1963-64, The Charlotte (N.C.) Observer, 1965-67; asst. editor The Chronicle of Higher Edn., Washington, 1967-71, sr. editor, 1973-76, internat. editor, 1976-87, mng. editor, 1987—; freelance writer, Susan, Va., 1971-73; contbg. editor Saturday Review, San Francisco, 1972-73. With U.S. Coast Guard Reserve, 1964-70. Recipient 1st Prize Reporting award Edn. Writers Assn., 1969. Avocation: ornithology, tennis. Home: 321 Forest Dr Falls Church VA 22046 Office: The Chronicle of Higher Edn 1255 23rd St NW Washington DC 20037-1125

SCULLY, MARTHA SEEBACH, speech and language pathologist; b. S.I., Nov. 1, 1951; d. Henry F. and Rose Anne (Callahan) Seebach; m. Roger Tehan Scully, Dec. 29, 1979; 1 child, Roger Tehan. BA, Trinity Coll., 1972; MS, George Washington U., 1974; postgrad., Syracuse (N.Y.) U., 1976-79. Lic. speech-lang. pathologist, Md. Clin. supr. Syracuse U., 1976-79; speech-lang. pathologist Fairfax (Va.) County Pub. Schs., 1979—. Bd. dirs. Trinity Coll., Washington, Nat. Children's Choir, 1987-91; trustee Davis Meml. Goodwill Industries, 1994-96, bd. dirs. Goodwill Guild, 1990—, chair ball; docent Folger Shakespearean Libr.; chmn. Nat. Challenge Com. of Disabled, 1985; mem. Ear Ball, 1988, 89; mem. Internat. Children's Festival, 1990, 91; co-chmn. Jr. League of Washington Capital Collection, 1990; chmn. Salvation Army Garden Party, 1992, Washington Embassy Tour, 1993. Recipient First Order Affiliation Order of Franciscans mirror, 1985; named Outstanding Woman in Am., 1987, 88. Mem. Am. Biog. Inst., Am. Speech-Lang.-Hearing Assn., Coun. for Exceptional Children, Montgomery County Assn. for Hearing Impaired Children. Home: 10923 Wickshire Way Rockville MD 20852-3220

SCULLY, MICHAEL ANDREW, pharmaceutical company executive, writer, editor; b. Bridgeport, Conn., Apr. 26, 1949; s. Michael Richard and Mary-Louise (McQueeney) S.; m. Mary Agnes Tortora, July 29, 1995; 1 child, Grace Mary. BA, Colgate U., 1971; MA, Boston Coll., 1977. Legis. aide U.S. Senate Staff, Washington, 1975-77; mng. editor The Pub. Interest, N.Y.C., 1978-81; editor This World mag., N.Y.C., 1981-86; asst. to amb. U.S. Embassy, London, 1989-91; sr. advisor to dir. U.S. Info. Agy., Washington, 1991-92; dir. policy comms. Pfizer Inc., N.Y.C., 1992—; speechwriter, editl. cons. Fortune 500 cos. including Contel, Pfizer, also presdl. cabinet secs., 1978-89. Editor: Best of This World, 1986; contbr. articles and revs. to popular mags. and newspapers. Recipient Meritorious Honor award U.S. Dept. State, 1991. Mem. Nat. Press Club, Reform Club (London). Republican. Roman Catholic. *Died Dec. 17, 1996.*

SCULLY, PAULA CONSTANCE, journalist; b. Carlisle, Pa., Nov. 7, 1948; d. Alfred Albert and Concetta (Rosati) Sanelli. BA in Anthropology, U. Wis., 1970. Pub. rels. writer Valley Forge Mil. Acad., Wayne, Pa., 1977-79; reporter Main Line Times, Ardmore, Pa., 1979-81; mng. editor Kane Communications, Phila., 1981-82; publicist Running Press Book Publishers, Phila., 1982-84; sr. writer Paolin & Sweeney Advt., Cherry Hill, N.J., 1984-87; free-lance pub. rels., 1987; reporter Beach Haven Times, Manahawkin, N.J., 1989—. Mem. Beach Haven WWII Commemorative Com., 1992-95. Mem. Mystery Writers Am., Romance Writers Am. Home: 331 Mcmull Dr Wayne PA 19087-2025 Office: Beach Haven Times 345 E Bay Ave Manahawkin NJ 08050-3314

SCULLY, ROGER TEHAN, lawyer; b. Washington, Jan. 10, 1948; s. James Henry and Marietta (Maguire) S.; m. Martha Anne Seebach, Dec. 29, 1979. BS, U. Md., 1977; JD, Cath. U., 1980. Bar: Md. 1980, D.C. 1981, U.S. Tax Ct. 1982, U.S. Supreme Ct. 1988. V.p. Bogley Related Cos., Rockville, Md., 1971-75; law clk. to presiding justice Superior Ct. of D.C., Washington, 1979-81; assoc. Lerch, Early & Roseman, Bethesda, Md., 1981-82; gen. counsel Laszlo N. Tauber, M.D. & Assocs., Bethesda, 1982-94, Jefferson Meml. Hosp., Alexandria, Va., 1982-94; spl. counsel Venable, Baetjer, Howard & Civiletti, Washington, 1991-96; cons. in real estate Order of Friar Minor, N.Y.C., 1977—; lectr. Mortgage Bankers Assn., Washington, 1984—; bd. dirs. Nozzoli Constrn. Co., Washington; exec. com., spl. counsel to bd. dirs., bd. dirs. Chromachron Technology Corp., Toronto; bd. dirs. MusicWorks, N.Y.C.; vice chair Sayett Tech., Inc., Rochester, N.Y.; vice chair, bd. dirs., exec. com. MediaShow, Inc., Rochester. Author: (with Quarles & Howard) Summary Adjudication Dispositive Motions and Summary Trials, 1991. Mem. pres.'s coun. St. Bonaventure U., Olean, N.Y., 1995—, chmn. pres.'s coun., 1986-95; trustee Belmont Abbey Coll., Charlotte, N.C., 1993-95, Edmund Burke Sch., Washington, 1984—; bd. dirs. Nat. Children's Choir, Washington, 1980-94. Recipient First Order Affiliation Order of Friars Minor, 1985; named one of Outstanding Young Men in Am., 1982. Fellow D.C. Bar Assn.; mem. ABA, ATLA, FBA, Md. Bar Assn. (chmn. corp. counsel sect.), Am. Judicature Soc., Assn. Governing Bd. of Univs. and Colls., Am. Inns of Ct., Irish Legal Soc., Selden Soc., U.S. Jud. Conf. of 4th Cir. (permanent mem.), U.S. Jud. Conf. Fed. Cir. (del.), Jud. Conf. of D.C. (del.). Republican. Roman Catholic. Home: 10923 Wickshire Way Rockville MD 20852-3220 Office: 7201 Wisconsin Ave Ste 450 Bethesda MD 20814-4847

SCULLY, STEPHEN J., plastic surgeon; b. Lawrence, Mass., Jan. 29, 1937; s. Joseph A. and Frances M. (Hart) S.; m. Diane Loretta Lizotte, Apr. 22, 1967; children: Stephen, Christopher, Caroline, Jacqueline. AB summa cum laude, Merrimack Coll., 1958; MD cum laude, Georgetown U., 1962. Surg. resident Tufts New Eng. Med. Ctr., Boston, 1962-67; plastic surg. resident NYU, N.Y.C., 1969-72. Trustee Holy Family Hosp., Methuen, Mass., 1993, Merrimack Coll., North Andover, Mass., 1993. Lt. comdr. USNR, 1967-69. Fellow ACS; mem. Am. Soc. Reconstructive Surgeons, Am. Soc. Aesthetic Plastic Surgery. Roman Catholic. Avocations: photography, skiing. Office: Plastic Cosmetic Reconstr Surgery Inc 451 Andover St North Andover MA 01845-5044

SCULLY, VINCENT EDWARD, sports broadcaster; b. Bronx, N.Y., Nov. 29, 1927; s. Vincent Aloysius and Bridget (Freehill) S.; m. Sandra Hunt, Nov. 11, 1973; children: Michael, Kevin, Todd, Erin, Kelly, Catherine Anne. B.A., Fordham U., 1949. Sports announcer Bklyn. Dodgers Profl. Baseball Team, 1950-57, L.A. Dodgers Profl. Baseball Team, 1957—, CBS-TV, 1975-82, NBC-TV, 1982-89. Served with USNR, 1944-45. Recipient TV award Look mag., 1959; named Sportscaster of Year in Calif., 1959, 60, 63, 69, 71, 73-75; Nat. Sportscaster of Year, 1966, 78, 82; named to Fordham U. Hall of Fame, 1976. Mem. AFTRA, Screen Actors Guild, Catholic Actors, TV Acad. Arts and Scis. Roman Catholic. Clubs: Lambs (N.Y.C.); Bel Air Country, Beach. Office: LA Dodgers 1000 Elysian Park Ave Los Angeles CA 90012-1112*

SCURLOCK, ARCH CHILTON, chemical engineer; b. Beaumont, Tex., Jan. 29, 1920; s. Marvin and Mary (Chilton) S.; m. Maurine Spurbeck, Nov. 27, 1945 (div.); children: Arch, Susan, Marvin Curtis; m. Nancy Morrison Yonick, Nov. 16, 1962; children: Mary, Nancy, Margaret Ann. B.S. in Chem. Enging, U. Tex., 1941, A.B. in Physics, 1941; M.S., Mass. Inst. Tech., 1943, Sc.D., 1948; spl. course meteorology, U. Chgo., 1944. Research asso. chem. enging. dept. Mass. Inst. Tech., 1946-48; asst. dir. chemistry Enging. Research Assocs., 1948-49; pres. Atlantic Research Corp., Alexandria, Va., 1949-62; chmn. bd. Atlantic Research Corp., 1962-65; pres., dir. Research Industries Inc., Alexandria, 1968—; chmn. TransTechnology Corp., 1969-92, Halifax Corp. Served to lt. (s.g.) USNR, 1943-46. Mem. AAAS, AIAA, Am. Inst. Chem. Engrs., Am. Chem. Soc., Am. Phys. Soc., Am. Meteorol. Soc., Am. Def. Preparedness Assn., Combustion Inst., Univ. Club (Washington), Belle Haven (Va.) Country Club, Army Navy Country Club (Va.), Mid-Ocean Club (Tuckers Town, Bermuda), Phi Beta Kappa, Sigma Xi, Tau Beta Pi. Home: 1753 Army Navy Dr Arlington VA 22202-1633 Office: 123 N Pitt St Alexandria VA 22314-3133

SCURRY, BRIANA COLLETTE, amateur soccer player; b. Mpls., Sept. 7, 1971. BS in Polit. Sci., U. Mass., 1995. Goalkeeper U.S. Women's Nat. Soccer Team, Chgo. Named Nat. Goalkeeper of Yr. Mo. Athletic Club Sports Found., 1993, 2d Team All-Am., 1993, Gold medal Atlanta Olympics, 1996. Office: US Soccer Fedn US Soccer House 1801 S Prairie Ave Chicago IL 60616-1319*

SCURRY, RICHARDSON GANO, JR., investment management company financial executive; b. Dallas, June 7, 1938; s. Richardson Gano and Josephine (DuVall) S.; m. Pamela Ruth Edith McGinley, Oct. 11, 1975; children: Richardson, Kristina. BA, U. Tex., 1961; MBA, Stanford U., 1963. Mktg. rep. DP div. IBM, Dallas, 1963-68; mgr. fin. planning, DP group IBM, Harrison, N.Y., 1968-72; exec. asst., group exec. IBM, Armonk, N.Y., 1973; mgr. fin. planning office products div. IBM, Franklin Lakes, N.Y., 1974; mgr. fin. analysis, antitrust litigation IBM, N.Y.C., 1975; controller system communication div. IBM, White Plains, 1976-80; dir. plans, controls internal info. systems & communications IBM Corp., Purchase, N.Y., 1981-84; sr. v.p. fin. Chem. Bank, N.Y.C., 1985-89; pres., chief exec. officer Pearce, Mayer & Greer Realty Corp., N.Y.C., 1989-94; fin. advisor Sanford C. Bernstein & Co., Inc., N.Y.C., 1994—; v.p. fin., ptnr. Wicker Garden's Children, 1984—; bd. dirs. Info. Mart, Dallas, Firecom, Woodside, N.Y.; treas., bd. dirs. 1158 Fifth Ave. Corp., N.Y.C., 1985-90; mem. real estate coms. Lincoln Ctr., N.Y.C., 1990—. Mem. bus. com. Met. Mus. Art, N.Y.C., 1986—. Mem. Fin. Exec. Inst. (com. info. mgmt. 1979—, dir. N.Y.C. chpt. 1988-90), Salesmanship Club of Dallas, Union League Club of N.Y.C., Phi Delta Theta. Republican. Home: 1158 Fifth Ave New York NY 10029-6917 Office: Sanford C Bernstein & Co Inc 767 5th Ave Fl 22 New York NY 10153-0001

SCUSERIA, GUSTAVO ENRIQUE, theoretical chemist; b. San Fernando, Buenos Aires, Argentina, July 30, 1956; came to U.S., 1985; s. Eraldo L. and Alicia (Capitanelli) S.; m. Ana Inés Ilvento, Apr. 17, 1982; children: Ignacio, Tomás. BS, MS, U. Buenos Aires, 1979, PhD in Physics, 1983. Grad. asst. U. Buenos Aires, 1979-83, asst. prof., 1983-85; rsch. assoc. U. Calif., Berkeley, 1985-87; sr. rsch. assoc. U. Ga., Athens, 1987-89; asst. prof. Rice U., Houston, 1989-93, assoc. prof., 1993-95, prof., 1995—. Camille and Henry Dreyfus Teacher scholar Camille and Henry Dreyfus Found., 1992. Mem. AAAS, Am. Chem. Soc., Am. Phys. Soc., Materials Rsch. Soc., Electrochemical Soc. Office: Rice U Dept Chemistry 6100 Main St # S60 Houston TX 77005-1827

SCUTT, CHERYL LYNN, communications executive; b. Columbus, Ind., Dec. 7, 1948; d. Russell O. and Hazel Jeannette (Gordon) S. BA in Journalism, Ind. U., 1971. Freelance writer various nat. orgns. various orgns., Bloomington, Ind., 1971—; feature writer, columnist The Herald-Telephone, Bloomington, Ind., 1971-80, asst. lifestyles editor, 1980-83; comm. assoc. United Way of Mid. Tenn., Nashville, 1983-85, asst. comm. dir., 1985-88, v.p. comm., 1988-94; pres. Scutt Comm. Svcs., Antioch, Tenn., 1994—; instr. Ind. U. H.S. Journalism Inst., Bloomington, 1981, 82; presenter in field United Way Am., 1988-93. mem. Nat. Profl. Adv. Mktg. Com./United Way of Am., 1990-92; comm. coun. mem. Nashville Area C. of C., 1993-94; pub. rels. and devel. comm. cons. Adolescent Pregnancy and Prevention Coun., Nashville, 1992-93; pub. rels. com. ARC, Nashville, 1994—; pub. rels. com. League for Hearing Impaired, 1995-96. Recipient Gold award United Way Am., 1984, Silver award, 1984, 85, 87, Spl. Recognition award, 1985, Second Century Initiative award, 1988, 90, 90, 91, 1st Pl. award UPI, 1975, 1st Pl. award Women's Press Club Ind., 1976, 77, 78, 79, 83, Edn. award Am. Lupus Soc., 1981, Diamond award Nashville Advt. Fedn., 1984, 86, 87, 88, 89, Merit award, 1984, 87, 88, 1st Pl. award 7th Dist. Advt. Fedn., 1984, Merit award Nashville chpt. Pub. Rels. Soc. Am., 1988, numerous others. Mem. ASCAP, Soc. Profl. Journalists, N.Am. Assn. Ventriloquists. Avocations: songwriting, boating, reading, ventriloquism, guitar.

SCUTT, ROBERT CARL, lawyer; b. Newark, N.Y., Dec. 24, 1950; s. Charles E. and Lois L. (Armstrong) S. BA, Union Coll., 1973; JD, Duke U., 1976. Bar: N.Y. 1977, U.S. Dist. Ct. (we. dist.) N.Y. 1977, U.S. Tax Ct. 1978. Assoc. Harris, Beach & Wilcox, Rochester, N.Y., 1976-83, ptnr., 1984—. Mem. N.Y. State Bar Assn., Nat. Assn. Health Lawyers. Office: Harris Beach & Wilcox Granite Buiding 130 Main St E Rochester NY 14604-1620

SCZUDLO, RAYMOND STANLEY, lawyer; b. Olean, N.Y., July 5, 1948; s. Raymond Stanley and Ann Marie (Frisina) S.; children: Gregory Martin, Edward James. BChemE, U. Detroit, 1971; JD, Georgetown U., 1974. Bar: D.C., 1975., U.S. Dist. Ct. (fed. dist.) D.C. 1975, U.S. Ct. Appeals (D.C. cir.) 1975, U.S. Ct. Appeals (5th cir.) 1980, U.S. Supreme Ct. 1981. Assoc. Martin, Whitfield, Thaler & Bebchick, Washington, 1974-78, Verner, Liipfert, Bernhard & McPherson, Washington, 1978-80; ptnr. Verner, Liipfert, Bernhard, McPherson & Hand, Washington, 1981-87, Weil, Gotshal & Manges, Washington, 1987—; bd. dirs. Benlink, Inc., Washington, 1984—; adj. prof. banking law George Washington U. Nat. Law Ctr., 1991—. Contbr. articles on banking to profl. jours. Bd. dirs. Children's Nat. Med. Ctr., Washington, 1985—, chmn. fin. com., 1988-92, vice chmn. bd., 1989-92, chmn-elect, 1992, chmn. bd., 1993-95; chmn. bd. Children's Hosp. Found., 1996—; trustee Monsignor Smyth Endowment Fund, Washington, 1994—, Fedn. Am. Scientists Fund, 1994—. Mem. ABA, D.C. Bar Assn., Am. Coll. Investment Coun., Univ. Club. Office: Weil Gotshal & Manges 1615 L St NW Ste 700 Washington DC 20036-5621

SEAB, CHARLES GREGORY, astrophysicist; b. Ft. Benning, Ga., May 26, 1950; s. James A. and Ruby (Jones) S.; m. Peggy R. McConnell, May 9, 1979; 1 child, Jenna R. McConnell-Seab. BS in Physics, La. State U., 1971, MS in Physics, 1974; PhD in Astrophysics, U. Colo., 1982. Enging. analyst, programmer Mid. South Svcs., New Orleans, 1974-77; NRC rsch. assoc. NASA Ames Rsch. Ctr., Mountain View, Calif., 1983-85; rsch. scientist U. Calif., Berkeley, 1985, Va. Inst. Theoretical Astronomy, Charlottesville, 1985-87; vis. asst. prof. U. New Orleans, 1987-89, asst. prof., 1989-91, assoc. prof. astrophysics, 1991-96; prof., 1996—; bd. dirs. Freeport McMoran Obs., New Orleans, 1991—. Author: Astronomy, 1994; contbr. articles to profl. jours., chpts. to books. Capt. USAR, 1971-80. Nat. Merit scholar, 1967-71. Mem. Am. Astron. Soc., Pontchartrain Astronomy Soc., Phi Kappa Phi. Avocations: amateur astronomy, tennis. Office: U New Orleans Physics Dept Lakefront New Orleans LA 70148

SEABOLT, RICHARD L., lawyer; b. Chgo., Aug. 28, 1949; *Wife, Kathleen Hallissy, also graduated with a Juris Doctor from Hastings College of the Law, University of California, in 1975, and was a Contra Costa County district attorney from 1975 to 1993. Sons, Jack Seabolt, 9, and Will Seabolt, 7, are students at Wildwood Elementary School, Piedmont, California. Father, Lee Seabolt, before retirement was President and Chairman of Selz Seabolt Associates, a public relations firm located in Chicago, Illinois.* BGS with distinction, U. Mich., 1971; JD, U. Calif., Hastings, 1975. Bar: Calif. 1975. Ptnr. Hancock, Rothert & Bunshoft, San Francisco. Author: (with others) Insuring Real Property, 1988, Construction Litigation: Representing the Contractor, 1992; editorial adv. Construction and Environmental Insurance Case Digests, 1991; contbr. articles to profl. jours. Mem. ABA, State Bar Calif., Bar Assn. San Francisco. Office: Hancock Rothert & Bunshoft 10th Flr 4 Embarcadero Ctr Fl 10 San Francisco CA 94111-4106 *Hancock Rothert & Bunshoft has offices in San Francisco, Los Angeles, Tahoe City, and London, England, and focuses its practice on complex business and insurance litigation. Lead defense lawyer, representing certain Underwriters' at Lloyd's, London in an environmental insurance coverage trial between Aerojet-General Corporation and approximately forty of its liability insurers. After approximately ten months of trial, the jury rendered a verdict for the defendants. The defense verdict in that case was featured in 1992 articles in California Law Business and the National Law Journal as among the largest cases tried to a defense verdict in California and in the United States for that year.*

SEABORG, DAVID MICHAEL, evolutionary biologist; b. Berkeley, Calif., Apr. 22, 1949; s. Glenn Theodore and Helen Lucille (Griggs) S.; m. Adele Fong Yee, June 17, 1990. BS, U. Calif., Davis, 1972; MA, U. Calif., Berkeley, 1974. Biology tchr. U. Calif., Berkeley, 1972-73; biol. rschr., photographer Trans Time Labs., Berkeley, 1978; self-employed, 1974—; hypnosis and self-hypnosis tchr. Open Edn. Exchange, Oakland, Calif., 1978-81; biol. tchr. Oakland Mus., Calif., 1983-87, rsch. biologist, dept. ecology and evolutionary biology U. Calif., Irvine, 1987; pres., dir. rsch. Found. for Biol. Conservation and Rsch., Lafayette, Calif., 1983—; radio talk show host Sta. KPFA, Berkeley, 1996; biology and life sci. tchr. Phillip and Sala Burton Acad. High Sch., San Francisco; vol. asst. to curator Smithsonian Instn., 1966-67, Lab. Chem. Biodynamics, U. Calif., Berkeley, 1975; comedian, 1969—; lectr. sci., philos., environ. issues, 1974—. Contbr. articles to profl. jours. Inventor game, Sum-It, 1981. Chmn. Com. for Arts and Lectures, U. Calif., Berkeley, 1974-75; chmn., master of ceremonies, Bastille Day, Lafayette (Calif.)-Langeac Soc., 1982-86. Recipient Meritorious Service award Smithsonian Inst., 1967, Animal Photography award Soc. Photographic Scientists and Engrs., 1967. Democrat. Mem. Calif. Acad. Scis., World Wildlife Fund, Earth Island Inst., Greenpeace, Nat. Resources Def. Coun., Desert Tortise Preserve Com., Rainforest Action Network, Save the Bay Assn., Sierra Club, Nature Conservancy, Zero Population Growth, Calif. Alumni Assn., Calif. Aggie Alumni Assn., Lafayette Langeac Soc., Club of Rome-USA (bd. dirs.), Lafayette gen. plan adv. com. Address: 1888 Pomar Way Walnut Creek CA 94598-1424

SEABORG, GLENN THEODORE, chemistry educator; b. Ishpeming, Mich., Apr. 19, 1912; s. H. Theodore and Selma (Erickson) S.; m. Helen Griggs, June 6, 1942; children: Peter, Lynne Seaborg Cobb, David, Stephen, John Eric, Dianne. AB, UCLA, 1934; PhD, U. Calif.-Berkeley, 1937; numerous hon. degrees; LLD, U. Mich., 1958, Rutgers U., 1970; DSc, Northwestern U., 1954, U. Notre Dame, 1961, John Carroll U., Duquesne U., 1968, Ind. State U., 1969, U. Utah, 1970, Rockford Coll., 1975, Kent State U., 1975; LHD, No. Mich. Coll., 1962; DPS, George Washington U., 1962; DPA, U. Puget Sound, 1963; LittD, Lafayette Coll., 1966; DEng, Mich. Technol. U., 1970; ScD, U. Bucharest, 1971, Manhattan Coll., 1976, U. Pa., 1983; PhD, U. Paris S., 1996. Rsch. chemist U. Calif., Berkeley, 1937-39, instr. dept. chemistry, 1939-41, asst. prof., 1941-45, prof., 1945-71, univ. prof., 1971—, leave of absence, 1942-46, 61-71, dir. nuclear chem. research, 1946-58, 72-75, asso. dir. Lawrence Berkeley Lab., 1954-61, 71—; chancellor Univ. (U. Calif.-Berkeley), Berkeley, 1958-61; dir. Lawrence Hall of Sci. U. Calif., Berkeley, 1982-84, chmn. Lawrence Hall of Sci., 1984—; sect. chief metall. lab. U. Chgo., 1942-46; chmn. AEC, 1961-71, gen. adv. com., 1946-50; research nuclear chemistry and physics, transuranium elements.; chmn. bd. Kevex Corp., Burlingame, Calif., 1972-87, Advanced Physics Corp., Irvine, Calif., 1988-94; mem. Pres.'s Sci. Adv. Com., 1959-61; mem. nat. sci. bd. NSF, 1960-61; mem. Pres.'s Com. on Equal Employment Opportunity, 1961-65, Fed. Radiation Council, 1961-69, Nat. Aeros. and Space Council, 1961-71, Fed. Council Sci. and Tech., 1961-71, Nat. Com. Am.'s Goals and Resources, 1962-64, Pres.'s Com. Manpower, 1964-69, Nat. Council Marine Resources and Enging. Devel., 1966-71; chmn. Chem. Edn. Material Study, 1959-74, Nat. Programming Council for Pub. TV, 1970-72; dir. Ednl. TV and Radio Center, Ann Arbor, Mich., 1958-64, 67-70; pres. 4th UN Internat. Conf. Peaceful Uses Atomic Energy, Geneva, 1971, also chmn. U.S. del., 1964, 71; U.S. rep. 5th-15th gen. confs. IAEA, chmn., 1961-71; chmn. U.S. del. to USSR for signing Memorandum Cooperation Field Utilization Atomic Energy Peaceful Purposes, 1963; mem. U.S. del. for signing Limited Test Ban Treaty, 1963; mem. commn. on humanities Am. Council Learned Socs., 1962-65; mem. sci. adv. bd. Robert A. Welch Found., 1957—; mem. internat. Orgn. for Chem. Scis. in Devel., UNESCO, 1981-92, pres., 1981-92, pres. emeritus, 1992—; mem. Nat. Commn. on Excellence in Edn., Dept. Edn., 1981-83; co-discoverer elements 94-102 and 106: plutonium, 1940, americium, 1944-45, curium, 1944, berkelium, 1949, californium, 1950, einsteinium, 1952, fermium, 1953, mendelevium, 1955, nobelium, 1958, seaborgium, 1974; co-discoverer nuclear energy isotopes Pu-239, U-233, Np-237, other isotopes including I-131, Fe-59, Te-99m, Co-60; originator actinide concept for placing heaviest elements in periodic system. Author: (with Joseph J. Katz) The Actinide Elements, 1954, The Chemistry of the Actinide Elements, 1957, (with Joseph J. Katz and Lester R. Morse) 2d ed. Vols. I & II, 1986, The Transuranium Elements, 1958, (with E.G. Valens) Elements of the Universe, 1958 (winner Thomas Alva Edison Found. award), Man-Made Transuranium Elements, 1963, (with D.M. Wilkes) Education and the Atom, 1964, (with E.K. Hyde, I. Perlman) Nuclear Properties of the Heavy Elements, 1964, (with others) Oppenheimer, 1969, (with Ben Loeb) Stemming the Tide, 1987, (with W.R. Corliss) Man and Atom, 1971, Nuclear Milestones, 1972, (with Ben Loeb) Kennedy, Khruschev and the Test Ban, 1981, (with Walt Loveland) Elements beyond Uranium, 1990, (with Ben Loeb) The Atomic Energy Commission Under Nixon, 1992, (with Ray C. Colvig) Chancellor at Berkeley, 1994, (with Ronald L. Kathren, Jerry B. Gough, Gary T. Benefiel) The Plutonium Story: The Journals of Professor Glenn T. Seaborg 1939-1946, 1994; editor: Transuranium Elements: Products of Modern Alchemy, 1978, (with W. Loveland) Nuclear Chemistry, 1982, Modern Alchemy: The Selected Papers of Glenn T. Seaborg, 1994, A Scientist Speaks Out: A Personal Perspective on Science and Society, 1996; assoc. editor Jour. Chem. Physics, 1948-50; mem. editorial adv. bd. Jour. Inorganic and Nuclear Chemistry, 1954-82, Indsl. Rsch., Inc, 1967-75; mem. adv. bd. Chem. and Enging. News, 1957-59; mem. editorial bd. Jour. Am. Chem. Soc., 1950-59, Ency. Chem. Tech., 1975—, Revs. in Inorganic Chemistry, 1977—; mem. hon. editorial adv. bd. Internat. Ency. Phys. Chemistry and Chem. Physics, 1957—, Nuclear Sci. and Techniques, Chinese Nuclear Soc., 1989—; mem. panel Golden Picture Ency. for Children, 1957-61; mem. cons. and adv. bd. Funk and Wagnalls Universal Standard Ency, 1957-61; mem. Am. Heritage Dictionary Panel Usage Cons., 1964-80; contbr. articles to profl. jours. Trustee Pacific Sci. Ctr. Found., 1962-77, Sci. Svc., 1965, pres., 1966-88, chmn., 1988-95; trustee Am.-Scandinavian Found., 1968—, Ednl. Broadcasting Corp., 1970-72; bd. dirs. Swedish Coun. Am., 1976—, chmn. bd. dirs., 1978-82; bd. dirs. World Future Soc., 1969—, Calif. Coun. for Environ. and Econ. Balance, 1974-83; bd. govs. Am. Swedish Hist. Found., 1972—; sr. tech. rev. group Amarillo Nat. Resource Ctr. for Plutonium, 1995—. Decorated officier Legion of Honor (France); recipient John Ericsson Gold medal Am. Soc. Swedish Engrs., 1948; Nobel prize for Chemistry (with E.M. McMillan), 1951, John Scott award and medal City of Phila., 1953, Perkin medal Am. sect. Soc. Chem. Industry, 1957, U.S. AEC Enrico Fermi award, 1959, Joseph Priestley Meml. award Dickinson Coll., 1960, Sci. and Enging. award Fedn. Enging. Socs., Drexel Inst. Tech., Phila., 1962; named Swedish Am. of Year, Vasa Order of Am., 1962; Franklin medal Franklin Inst., 1963; 1st Spirit of St. Louis award, 1964; Leif Erikson Found. award, 1964; Washington award Western Soc. Engrs., 1965; Arches of Sci. award Pacific Sci. Center, 1968; Internat. Platform Assn. award, 1969; Prometheus award Nat. Elec. Mfrs.

Assn., 1969; Nuclear Pioneer award Soc. Nuclear Medicine, 1971; Oliver Townsend award Atomic Indsl. Forum, 1971; Disting. Honor award U.S. Dept. State, 1971; Golden Plate award Am. Acad. Achievement, 1972, Daniel Webster medal, 1976, John R. Kuebler award Alpha Chi Sigma, 1978; Founders medal Hebrew U. Jerusalem, 1981; Great Swedish Heritage award, Swedish Coun. Am., 1984, Ellis Island Medal of Honor, 1986, Swedish Coun. Am. Seaborg medal UCLA, 1987, Vannevar Bush award NSF, 1988, Nat. Medal of Sci. NSF, 1991, Royal Order of the Polar Star Sweden, 1992, Profl. Fraternity Assn. Career Achievement award, 1993; Minor Planet 4856-Asteroid Seaborg named in his honor, 1995. Fellow Am. Phys. Soc., Am. Inst. Chemists (Pioneer award 1968, Gold medal award 1973), Chem. Soc. London (hon.), Royal Soc. Edinburgh (hon.), Am. Nuclear Soc. (hon. chair Spl. Panel on Protection and Mgmt. of Plutonium 1994-95, Henry DeWolf-Smyth award 1982, Seaborg award 1984, 85, Am. Nuclear Soc., Calif. Acad. Scis., N.Y. Acad. Scis., Washington Acad. Scis., AAAS (pres. 1972, chmn. bd. 1973), Royal Soc. Arts (Eng.); mem. Am. Chem. Soc. (award in pure chemistry 1947, William H. Nichols medal N.Y. sect. 1948, Charles L. Parsons award 1964, Gibbs medal Chgo. sect. 1966, Madison Marshall award No. Ala. sect. 1972, Priestley medal 1979, pres. 1976, George C. Pimentel award in chem. edn., 1994), Am. Philos. Soc., Royal Swedish Acad. Engring. Scis. (adv. council 1980), Am. Nat., Argentine Nat., Bavarian, Polish, Royal Swedish, USSR acads. scis., Royal Acad. Exact, Phys. and Natural Scis. Spain (acad. fgn. corr.), Soc. Nuclear Medicine (hon.), World Assn. World Federalists (v.p. 1980), Fedn. Am. Scis. (bd. sponsors 1980—), Deutsche Akademie der Naturforscher Leopoldina (East Germany), Nat. Acad. Pub. Adminstrn., Internat. Platform Assn. (pres. 1981-86), Am. Hiking Soc. (bd. dirs. 1979-84, v.p. 1980, adv. com. 1984—), Royal Soc. of Edinburgh, Phi Beta Kappa, Sigma Xi, Pi Mu Epsilon, Alpha Chi Sigma (John R. Kuebler award 1978), Phi Lambda Upsilon (hon.); fgn. mem. Royal Soc. London, Chem. Soc. Japan, Serbian Acad. Sci. and Arts. Clubs: Bohemian (San Francisco); Chemists (N.Y.C.); Cosmos (Washington), University (Washington); Faculty (Berkeley). Office: Mailstop 70A-3307 1 Cyclotron Rd Berkeley CA 94720

SEABROOK, JOHN MARTIN, retired food products executive, chemical engineer; b. Seabrook, N.J., Apr. 16, 1917; s. Charles Franklin and Norma Dale (Ivins) S.; m. Anne Schlaudecker, Apr. 5, 1939 (div. 1951); children: Carol Ormsby (Mrs. Jacques P. Boulanger), Elizabeth Anne; m. Elizabeth Toomey, 1956; children: John Martin, Bruce Cameron. B.S. in Chem. Engring, Princeton, 1939; LL.D. (hon.), Gettysburg Coll., 1974. Registered profl. engr., N.J., Del. Engr. Deerfield Packing Corp., 1939-41; v.p. Seabrook Farms Co., 1941-50, exec. v.p., 1950-54, dir., 1941-59, pres., 1954-59, chief exec. officer, 1955-59; cons. IU Internat. Corp., Wilmington, Del., 1959; v.p. IU Internat. Corp., 1960-65, dir., 1963-87, pres., 1965-73, 74-78, chief exec., 1967-80, chmn. bd., 1969-82, chmn. exec. com., 1982-87; pres., bd. dirs. Cumberland Automobile & Truck Co., 1954-59, Cumberland Warehouse Corp., 1954-59, Salem Farms Corp, N.J., 1948—; chmn. bd. dirs. Frick Co., Waynesboro, Pa., 1959-68; chmn., bd. dirs. S.W. Fabricating & Welding Co., Inc., Houston, 1964-68; chmn. Divcon, Inc., Houston, 1967-69; pres. bd. dirs. Internat. Utilities Overseas Capital Corp., Wilmington, 1966-82, chmn., 1970-80; v.p. Gen. Waterworks Corp., Phila., 1959-66, pres., 1966-68, chmn., 1968-71; chmn. bd. dirs. GWC Inc., Phila., 1971-73; pres. Brown Bros. Contractors, Inc., Phila., 1960, chmn. bd. dirs., 1965-67; pres. Am. Portable Irrigation Co., Eugene, Oreg., 1961, chmn. bd. dirs., 1966-68; chmn. bd. dirs. Gotaas-Larsen Shipping Corp., 1963, chmn., 1979, pres., CEO, 1982-88; chmn. bd. dirs. Amvit Corp., Cleve., 1964-68; bd. dirs. Echo Bay Mines Ltd., South Jersey Gas Co., Folsom, N.J., South Jersey Industries, Inc., Folsom, Bell Atlantic Corp.; dir. emeritus Bell Atlantic-N.J., Inc. Mem. N.J. Migrant Labor Bd., 1945-67, chmn., 1955-67; mem. N.J. Bd. Higher Edn., 1967-70, Pres.' Air Quality Adv. Bd., 1968-70; bd. dirs. Brandywine Conservancy, Inc., 1972-95, pres., 1992-93, hon. dir., 1997—; trustee Eisenhower Exch. Fellowships, 1974-85; trustee Hitchcock Found., 1991-96, chmn., 1993-96. Mem. Phi Beta Kappa. Clubs: Racquet and Tennis (N.Y.C.), The Philadelphia, Wilmington (Del.), Coaching (N.Y.C., U.K.). Home and Office: 55 Nimrod Rd Salem NJ 08079-4323

SEADEN, GEORGE, civil engineer; b. Cracow, May 26, 1936; s. Simon and Mary (Guttman) S.; m. Linda Helen Mutch, Mar. 18, 1978; children: Amy Elisabeth, Maia Claire. BE, McGill U., Montreal, Que., Can., 1958; MS, Harvard U., 1968; postgrad., Northwestern U., 1992. Engr. Gatineau Power, Hull, Que., 1958-59, Ent. Fougerolle, Paris, 1960-62; mgr. Warnock Hersey Ltd., Montreal, 1959-60; assoc. Cartier, Coté, Piette, Montreal, 1962-67; sr. advisor Ministry Urban Affairs, Ottawa, Ont., Can., 1969-71; pres. Archer, Seaden & Assoc., Inc., Montreal, 1971-84; dir. gen. Inst. Rsch. in Constrn. Nat. Rsch. Coun., Ottawa, 1985—; chief Constrn. Tech. Group NRC, 1995—; vis. prof. U. Ottawa, 1968-73; mem. Can. Constrn. Rsch. Bd., 1985-91, Constrn. Industry Devel., Can., 1988-93, Civil Engring. Rsch. Found., 1993—, Rsch. Bd. Am. Pub. Works Assn., 1994—; dir. Conf. Automated Bldg. Assn., Can. Rsch. Mgrs. Assn., CERIU; pres. Conseil Internat. du Batiment, Rotterdam, The Netherlands, 1989-92; vice chair Constrn. for Sustainable Devel. in the Twenty First Century Conf., Washington, 1996; mem. jury to select best Can. Constrn. projects and engring. design; lectr. numerous univs. and rsch. ctrs. Co-editor: Trends in Building Construction Worldwide, 1989; mem. editl. bd. Bldg. Rsch. and Practice, 1990-94, Constrn. Bldg. Rev., 1991—; contbr. numerous articles to profl. publs. Chmn. bd. dirs. St. Andrew's Sch., Westmount, Que., 1975-82. Home: 80 Lyttleton Gardens, Rockcliffe Park, ON Canada K1L 5A6 Office: Inst for Rsch in Construction, Montreal Rd Bldg M-20, Ottawa, ON Canada K1A 0R6

SEADER, JUNIOR DEVERE, chemical engineering educator; b. San Francisco, Aug. 16, 1927; s. George Joseph and Eva (Burbank) S.; m. Sylvia Bowen, Aug. 11, 1961; children: Steven Frederick, Clayton Mitchell, Gregory Randolph, Donald Jeffrey, Suzanne Marie, Robert Clark, Kathleen Michelle, Jennifer Anne. BS, U. Calif., Berkeley, 1949, MS, 1950; PhD, U. Wis., 1952. Instr. chem. engring. U. Wis., Madison, 1951-52; group supr. chem. process design Chevron Rsch. Corp., Richmond, Calif., 1952-57; group supr. engring. rsch. Chevron Rsch. Corp., 1957-59; prin. scientist heat transfer and fluid dynamics rsch. Rocketdyne div. N.Am. Aviation, Canoga Park, Calif., 1959-65, sr. tech. specialist, summer 1967; prof. chem. engring. U. Idaho, 1965-66; prof. chem. engring. U. Utah, Salt Lake City, 1966—, chmn. dept. chem. engring., 1975-78; tech. cons.; trustee CACHE Corp., Austin, Tex.; inst. lectr. Am. Inst. Chem. Engrs., 1983, also dir., 1983-85. Author 5 books; assoc. editor IEC Rsch. jour.; contbr. articles to profl. jours. Served with USNR, 1945-46. Recipient Disting. Teaching award U. Utah, 1975, Donald L. Katz lectureship, 1990. Fellow Am. Inst. Chem. Engrs. (Computing in Chem. Engring. award 1988); mem. ACS, Sigma Xi, Phi Lambda Upsilon. Heat transfer rsch. connected with the devel. of rocket engines associated with the Apollo and Space Shuttle projects, 1960-65; rsch. on tar sands, process synthesis, catalyst effective factors, finding all roots to system of nonlinear equations. Home: 13696 Vestry Rd Draper UT 84020 Office: U Utah Dept Chem Engring Meb # 3290 Salt Lake City UT 84112-1180

SEADLER, STEPHEN EDWARD, business and computer consultant, social scientist; b. N.Y.C., 1926; s. Silas Frank and Deborah (Gelbin) S.; AB in Physics, Columbia U., 1947, postgrad. in atomic and nuclear physics, 1947; postgrad. with George Gamow in relativity, cosmology and quantum mechanics, George Washington U., 1948-50; m. Ingrid Linnea Adolfsson, Aug. 7, 1954; children: Einar Austin, Anna Carin. Legal rsch. asst., editor AEC, Washington, 1947-51; electronic engr. Cushing & Nevell, Warner, Inc., N.Y.C., 1951-54; seminar leader, leader trainer Am. Found. for Continuing Edn., N.Y.C. 1955-57; exec. dir. Medimetric Inst., 1957-59; mem. long range planning com., chmn. corporate forecasting com., mktg. rsch. mgr. W. A. Sheaffer Pen Co., Ft. Madison, Iowa, 1959-65; founder Internat. Dynamics Corp., Ft. Madison and N.Y.C., 1965, pres., 1965-70; orginator DELTA program for prevention and treatment of violence, 1970; founder ID Ctr., Ft. Madison, now N.Y.C., 1968, pres., 1968—; mgmt. cons. in human resources devel. and conflict reduction, N.Y.C., 1970-73; pres. UNICONSULT computer-based mgmt. and computer scis., N.Y.C., 1973-96; speaker on decision support systems, internat. affairs and ideological arms control; author/speaker (presentation) Holocaust, History and Arms Control; originator social sci. of ideologics and computer based knowledge systems sci. of ideotopology; spl. works collection accessible via On-line Computer Libr. Ctr. Instr. polit. sci. Ia. State Penitentiary, 1959-62. Served with AUS, 1944-46. Recipient 20th Century Achievement award, Internat. Biographical Ctr., 1995. Mem. Am. Phys. Soc., Am. Statis. Assn., Acad. Polit. Sci., Am. Sociol. Assn., IEEE, N.Y. Acad. Sci., Am. Mgmt. Assn. (lectr. 1963-68), Foreign Policy Assn., Lib. Congress Assocs., Internat. Platform Assn. Unitarian. Lodges: Masons (32 deg.), Shriners. Author: Holocaust, History and Arms Control II, 1990; contbr. Ideologics and ideotopology sects. to Administrative Decision Making, 1977, Societal Systems, 1978; Management Handbook for Public Administrators, 1978; also articles profl. jours. Statement on ideological arms control in Part 4 of Senate Fgn. Relations Com. Hearings on Salt II Treaty, 1979. Ideologics extended to treat ethnic, racial, religious conflict, 1992, with first call for Western Ecumenical Reformation at Morristown, N.J., Unitarian Ch., 1993. Guest speaker on radio and television. Achievements include complementing interdisciplinary and mathematical developments, operational milestones on the trail to ideologics include: being Charge-of Quarters of a camp holding thousands of Afrika Corps PWs; leading adult-education seminars developed by the Chicago Council on Foreign Relations, and successfully transforming rigid, stereotypical thinking into critical, independent thinking; designing/conducting a popular course at Iowa State Penitentiary that was credited with breaking the criminal subculture; leading and reporting a highly acclaimed anti-racism project at Xerox Corp; leading a major project for the U.S. Postal Service that resolved widespread workforce conflicts, and healthfully reconstituted an alleged psychopath in a one-hour unscheduled session. Office: 521 5th Ave Ste 1700 New York NY 10175 *In retrospect, a single, predominant thread has woven through my entire life since childhood, sometimes as primary track, sometimes as parallel, but always as relentless destiny; to gain such learning and skills as to enable me to revolutionize mankind's thinking, slay the dragons of racism, religionism, ethnicism and other ideologies of malevolence, oppression and war, and bring true peace for the first time. To accomplish that mission requires development of a single comprehensive framework, which has become the new field of ideologics, and a single comprehensive, revolutionary work employing that framework, to appear at the foothills of the new millennium. That work, it is now clear, shall be the book on which I have been laboring for several years: Principia Ideologica.*

SEAGAL, STEVEN, actor; b. Lansing, Mich., Apr. 10, 1951; m. Kelly LeBrock; children: Anna Aliza, Dominick, Arissa. Studied martial arts under masters, Japan. Founded Aikido Ten Shin Dojo, L.A. Martial arts choreographer The Challenge, 1982; actor, prodr., martial arts choreographer Above the Law, 1988, Marked for Death, 1990; actor, martial arts choreographer Hard to Kill, 1990; actor, prodr. Out for Justice, 1991, Under Siege, 1992, Under Siege 2, 1995; actor, dir., co-prodr. On Deadly Ground, 1994; fight scene choreographer various films; appeared in films The Glimmer Man, 1996, Executive Decision, 1996, Fire Down Below, 1997. First non-Asian to open martial arts acad. in Japan; black belt numerous martial arts. Office: ICM 8942 Wilshire Blvd Beverly Hills CA 90211*

SEAGER, DANIEL ALBERT, university librarian; b. Jacksonville, Fla., Jan. 1, 1920; s. Harry James and Albertina Adeline (Klarer) S.; m. Helen Ruthe Medearis, Mar. 6, 1943; children: Mary Adele, Susan Kathleen, Dana Ruthe. AA, St. John's Coll., Winfield, Kans., 1941; AB, Okla. Bapt. U., 1948; BA in L.S, U. Okla., 1950, MA, 1953; postgrad., Colo. State Coll. (now U. No. Colo.), 1956-59. Head librarian, prof. English Southwest U., Bolivar, Mo., 1949-53; head librarian, asst. prof. library sci., chmn. dept. Ouachita U., Arkadelphia, Ark., 1953-56; head librarian, head library sci. edn., assoc. prof. library sci. U. No. Colo., Greeley, 1956-66; dir. library services U. No. Colo., 1966-71, coordinator library research and devel., 1971—, prof. library sci., 1984—, chief bibliographer/editor library publns., cons., instr. edml. media program, 1968-71; libr. cons., 1968—; cons. Ency. Brit. ultramicrofiche project, 1967-69; lectr. in field. Contbr. articles to profl. jours. Mem. book adv. coun. Edn. for Freedom Found.; mem. Com. library standards Colo. pub. schs., 1960-62; mem. exec. bd. Rocky Mountain Bibliog. Ctr. Research, 1959-60, 65-74, sec., 1961-63; sec. Colo. Council Librarians State-Operated Instns., 1966, chmn., 1968-70; mem. exec. bd. Weld County Assn. Mental Health, 1966, mem. library com., 1969; mem. Colo. Civil Service Examining Bd., 1961—; mem. U. N.C. Friends Libr., 1984—; Rep. com. chmn., Weld County, 1985-86; deacon, elder Christian Ch. With U.S. Army Signal Corps, WWII, 1942-44, ETO, 1944-45. Recipient several citations of merit profl. orgns. Fellow Intercontinental Biog. Assn.; mem. NEA, AAUP, Am. Library Assn. (library recruitment com. 1957—), Nat., Colo. assns. higher edn., United Profs. for Acad. Order Nat. Hist. Soc., Colo. Assn. Sch. Librarians (cons.), Spl. Libraries Assn., ALA (region recruitment rep. 1958—), Utah Library Assn., Kans. Library Assn., Wyo. Library Assn., Nebr. Library Assn., N.D. Library Assn., S.D. Library Assn., Nev. Library Assn., Mountain Plains Library Assn. (treas. 1959-63, exec. sec. 1963-76, spl. hons. plaque 1968, archivist 1974-84, constitution com. 1979, 83, chmn. nominating com. 1980, awards com. 1984, bylaws and amendments coms. 89-91, Pres.'s and Assn.'s Spl. award 17 Years Service award, Spl. Presdl. award 1994), Colo. Library Assn. (auditor), Tex. Library Assn., Southwestern Library Assn., Ill. Library Assn., Calif. Library Assn., Cath. Library Assn., Mich. Library Assn., Ohio Library Assn., N.Y. Library Assn., Pa. Library Assn., Midcontinent Med. Library Assn., Library Automation Research and Cons. Assn., U N.C. Friends of the Libr., 1984, Intercollegiate Studies Inst., Am. Security Council, Alumni Assn. U. No. Colo., Black Silent Majority Com. (hon.), Colo. Council Higher Edn., Colo. Edn. Assn. (mem. coms., del. to convs.), U. No. Colo. Edn. Assn. (treas. 1980-84, sec.-treas. 1984-85), U. Colo. Safety Com., Assn. Coll. and Reference Libraries, Colo. Hist. Soc., Assn. Research Libraries, Colo. Audiovisual Assn., Air Force Assn., Internat. Platform Assn., Acad. Polit. Sci. Columbia, Nat. Geog. Soc., Weld County Assn. Mental Health (mem. bd., chmn. library com.), Am. Judicature Soc., Emeritus Faculty Assn. U. No. Colo., Am. Numis. Assn., Am. Sci. Affiliation, Council on Consumer Info., Smithsonian Assocs., Chem. Abstracts Service Panel, Colo. Gerontol. Soc., Western Gerontol. Soc., Am. Assn. Retired Persons (vote com.), Audubon Nature Program, Forest History Soc., Journalism Edn. Assn., Greeley Numis. Club, Greeley C. of C., U. No. Colo. Emeritus Faculty Assn., Nat. Travel Club, Civitan (lt. gov. Mountain Plains dist. 1960-62), Knife and Fork Club, Rep. Club (Washington), Rep. Congl. Club (Washington), Eagles Club, Phi Delta Kappa. Mem. Reformed Christian Ch. Am. Home: 1230 24th Ave Greeley CO 80631-3516

SEAGER, STEVEN ALBERT, small business owner, accountant; b. Phelps, N.Y., Oct. 17, 1958; s. Harold John and Eleanor Ruth (Vogel) S.; m. Linda Ann Lee, Oct. 11, 1980 (div. Nov. 1991); children: Anna M., Ashley I., Amy E.; m. Nataliya Aslanyan, Oct. 14, 1994; 1 child, Yevgeniya A. AA in Acctg., C.C. of Finger Lakes, 1978; postgrad., SUNY, Geneseo, 1978, 89. Bookkeeper Exxon Co. USA, Clifton Springs, NY, 1977-79; acct. MXR Innovations, Inc., Rochester, N.Y., 1980-81, credit mgr., 1981-83, asst. controller, 1983-84; mgr.-cost and gen. acctg. Nat. Brands Beverage, Rochester, N.Y., 1984-87; owner/propr. Reader's Rendezvous Bookstore, Phelps, 1987-90; acctg. mgr. Almor Corp., Warsaw, N.Y., 1990-92, mgr. fin., 1992-94; owner, operator La Mancha Prodns., 1993—; ptnr. A A A Store Signage, Geneseo, N.Y., 1993-95; registered rep. MetLife, Rochester, 1995—. Author: Songs From the Heart, 1988 (Golden Poet award 1989, 90), Thirteenth at Love's Table, 1992 (Poet of Merit award 1992), Diamonds in The Rough, 1993 (Poetry Acad. award, 1993). Mem. Phelps-Clifton Springs Sch. Bd., Clifton Springs, 1989-90, Phelps Hist. Dist. Com., 1990, Phelps Comty. Theater, 1978-87, Geneseo Comty. Theatre, 1993—. Recipient Rep. Senatorial Medal of Freedom, 1993, Rep. Legion of Merit medal, 1993. Roman Catholic. Avocations: poetry, chess, reading, theatre. Office: MetLife 200 Canal View Blvd Ste 220 Rochester NY 14623-2809

SEAGLE, EDGAR FRANKLIN, environmental engineer, consultant; b. Lincolnton, N.C., June 27, 1924; s. Franklin Craig and Lillie Mae (James) S.; m. Doris Elaine Long, Mar. 23, 1958; children: Rebecca Jane, Mary Elaine, James Craig, William Franklin. AB in Chemistry, U. N.C., 1949, MS in Pub. Health, 1954; BCE, U. Fla., 1961; DPH, U. Tex., 1974. Registered profl. engr., Ala. Sr. sanitarian Health Dept., City of Charlotte, N.C., 1950-52, chief indsl. hygiene sect., 1956-59; sanitation cons. N.C. State Bd. Health, Raleigh, 1954-56; engr. dir. USPHS, Rockville, Md., 1961-78; asst. dir. Fellowship Office Nat. Acad. Scis., Washington, 1978-83; pub. health engr. Dept. of Environ., State of Md., Balt., 1985-88; ind. engring. cons. Rockville, 1984-85, 88—. Contbr. articles to profl. publs. With USN, 1943-46, PTO. Mem. ASCE, APHA, Am. Acad. Environ. Engrs. (diplomate). Methodist. Home and Office: 14108 Heathfield Ct Rockville MD 20853-2760

SEAGRAM, NORMAN MEREDITH, corporate executive; b. Toronto, Ont., Can., July 10, 1934; s. Norman Oliver and Constance Beatrice (Mills) S.; m. Joyce Elizabeth McMackon, Aug. 21, 1958; children: Susan Elizabeth, Norman Philip, Joseph Frederick, Samantha. Student, Trinity Coll., Port Hope, Ont.; BASc, U. Toronto, 1958; MSc, U. Birmingham, Eng., 1964. Cons. Associated Indsl. Cons. Ltd. and Mgmt. Scis. Ltd., London, Nairobi, Kenya, Moshi, Tanzania, Harari, Zimbabwe, Halifax, N., S., Can., Toronto, Ont., Can., 1960-68; various mktg. and planning positions The Molson Cos., Molson Breweries of Can. Ltd., 1968-78; pres. Seaway/Midwest Ltd., Toronto, 1978-82, Molson Western Breweries Ltd., Calgary, Alta, Can., 1983-85, Molson Ont. Breweries Ltd., Toronto, 1985-86; exec. v.p. The Molson Cos., Toronto, 1986-92; chmn., CEO Can. Liquid Air, Toronto, 1993—; chmn. Molson Breweries Can. Ltd., Club de Hockey Can. Inc., Vancouver (Can.) Baseball Ltd., Santa Fe Beverage Co., 1986-88; bd. dirs. Harbourfront Ctr., VitalAire Co. Mem. Bus. Coun. on Nat. Issues, Coun. for Can. Unity, Coun. for Bus. and Arts in Can., Can. Found. for Internat. Mgmt., Inst. Corp. Dirs., Olympic Trust Can., Trinity Coll. Sch. Mem. Assn. Profl. Engrs. Ont., Alpha Delta Phi, Toronto Club, Toronto Badminton and Racquet Club, Montreal Badminton and Squash Club, Hillside Tennis Club, Empire Club, The Mount Royal Club. Conservative. Anglican. Avocations: tennis, squash, golf, skiing, hockey. Office: 20 York Mills Rd Ste 400, Toronto, ON Canada M2P 2C2

SEAGREN, ALICE, state legislator; b. 1947; m. Fred Seagren; 2 children. BS, SE Mo. State U. Mem. Minn. Ho. of Reps., 1993—. Active Bloomington (Minn.) Sch. Bd., 1989-92. Mem. Bloomington C. of C. (bd. dirs. 1990-92), Phi Gamma Nu, Alpha Chi Omega. Republican. Home: 9730 Palmer Cir Bloomington MN 55437-2017 Office: Minn Ho of Reps State Capital Building Saint Paul MN 55155-1606*

SEAGREN, STEPHEN LINNER, oncologist; b. Mpls., Mar. 13, 1941; s. Morley Raymond and Carol Christine (Linner) S.; m. Jill Garrie; 1 child, Sean Garrie. AB, Harvard U., 1963; MD, Northwestern U., 1967. Diplomate Am. Bd. Internal Medicine, Am. Bd. Med. Oncology, Am. Bd. Radiology. From asst. prof. to assoc. prof. radiology and medicine U. Calif., San Diego, 1977-88, prof., 1988—, chief divsn. radiology and oncology. Contbr. over 80 articles to profl. jours. Bd. dirs. Wellness Cmty., San Diego, 1988—, chair profl. adv. com., 1988—; chair radiol. oncology com. Cancer and Acute Leukemia Group, Chgo., 1986—. Lt. comdr. USNR, 1971-73. Fellow ACP. Avocations: physical fitness, bridge, skiing, golf, tennis. Office: U Calif San Diego Med Ctr 200 W Arbor Dr San Diego CA 92103-1911

SEAL, popular musician; b. London. Albums include Seal, 1994; singles include Crazy, 1991, Killer, 1991; song included in Batman Forever, 1995. Recipient Song of Yr. Grammy award, 1996, Record of Yr. Grammy award, 1996, Best Male Pop Vocal Performance Grammy award, 1996. Office: Warner Bros Records Inc 75 Rockefeller Plz New York NY 10019-6908*

SEALE, JAMES MILLARD, religious organization administrator, clergyman; b. Middlesboro, Ky., Oct. 4, 1930; s. Albert Tyler and Edith Josephine (Buchanan) S.; m. Mary Dudley Harrod; children: William Alan, Ann Lynn Seale Hazelrigg. BA, Transylvania U., 1952; BD, Lexington Theol. Sem., 1955, MDiv, 1963, D Ministry, 1981. Ordained to ministry Christian Ch. (Disciples of Christ), 1951. Student pastor various Christian Chs., Ky., 1949-54; pastor 1st Christian Ch., Pikeville, Ky., 1954-58, Erlanger (Ky.) Christian Ch., 1958-61; sr. minister 1st Christian Ch., Mt. Sterling, Ky., 1961-70, Paris, Ky., 1978-82; stewardship sec. Gen. Office Christian Ch., Indpls., 1970-74; adminstr. Christian Ch. Home of Louisville, 1974-78; dir. devel. Christian Ch. Homes Ky., Louisville, 1978; pres. Disciples of Christ Hist. Soc., Nashville, 1983-95. Author: A Century of Faith and Caring, 1983, Forward From The Past, 1991; editor jour. Discipliana, 1983-92. Pres. Kiwanis Club, Pikeville, 1957, Mt. Sterling, 1963, lt. gov., Ctrl. Ky., 1965. Avocations: writing, photography, golf, fishing.

SEALE, JOHN CLEMENT, director, cinematographer; b. Warwick, Queensland, Australia, Oct. 5, 1942; s. Eric Clement and Marjorie Lyndon (Pool) S.; m. Louise Lee Mutton, Sept. 23, 1967; children: Derin Anthony, Brianna Lee. Grad. high sch., Sydney, Australia. Camera asst. film dept. Australian Broadcasting Com., 1962-68; freelance technician, camera operator various films, series, commls., 1968-76, dir. photography various film cos., 1976; dir. feature film, Till There Was You, 1989-90. Dir. photography: Goodbye Paradise (Golden Tripod 1982), Careful, He Might Hear You (Best Cinematography 1983), Witness, 1984 (Golden Tripod 1984, Oscar nomination 1986, Brit. Acad. award nomination 1986), The Hitcher, 1985, Children of a Lesser God, 1985 (Golden Tripod 1985), The Mosquito Coast, 1986, Stakeout, 1987, Gorillas in the Mist (Brit. Acad. award nomination 1989, Premier Mag. Cinematographer of the Yr. 1989), Rainman, 1988 (Acad. award nomination 1988, Artistic Achievement award 1989), Dead Poets Society, 1989, The Doctor, 1991, Lorenzo's Oil, 1992, The Firm, 1993, The Paper, 1993, Beyond Rangoon, 1994, The American President, 1995, The English Patient, 1995-96 (Best Cinematography award L.A. Film Critics Assn., Acad. award Cinematography, 1996, Brit. Acad. award 1996, Best Cinematrography award Am. Soc. Cinematographers 1996, Chgo. Film Critics award, Fla. Film Critics award), Ghosts of Mississippi, 1996, City of Angels, 1997. Recipient Film Critics Cir. Australia 1990 Tribute. Mem. Australian Cinematographers Soc. (named Cinematographer of Yr. 1982, 84, Inaugural mem. Hall of Fame 1997), Am. Soc. Cinematographers. Avocations: building boats, sailing.

SEALE, ROBERT ARTHUR, JR., lawyer; b. Shreveport, La., July 17, 1942; s. Robert Arthur Sr. and Lucille (Frank) S.; m. Virginia Meyers, Feb. 16, 1944; children: Robert A. III, John Meyers. BBA, La. State U., 1964, JD, 1967. Bar: La. 1967, Tex. 1969. Rsch. asst. La. Law Inst., Baton Rouge, 1967; law clk. U.S. Dist. Ct. (we. dist.) La., Shreveport, 1967-68; atty./ptnr. Vinson & Elkins, Houston, 1968-97; bd. dirs. Post Oak Bank, Houston; trustee, legal counsel The Mus. of Fine Arts, Houston, 1981-89, The Creel Found., Augusta, Ga., 1989—; pres., trustee The Lyons Found., Houston, 1986—. Mem. La. Law Rev., 1965-67. Sr. Warden St. Martin's Episcopal Ch., Houston, 1990; pres. Pine Shadows Civic Assn., Houston, 1991; trustee Episcopal High Sch., Houston, 1985-88; bd. dir. Boys' and Girls' Country, Houston, 1990-94. Fellow Houston Bar Found.; mem. ABA, Houston Bar Assn., Houston Country Club (bd. dir. 1985-88), Corondo Club (pres. 1991), Bob Smith Yacht Club (bd. dir. 1980-90), Omicron Delta Kappa. Avocations: civic and charitable activities, golf. Office: PO Box 27356 Houston TX 77227

SEALE, ROBERT L., state treasurer; b. Inglewood, Calif., Oct. 4, 1941; m. Judy Seale (dec.). BSA, Calif. Poly. U. Former contr. and sr. fin. officer Rockwell Internat.; sr. accountant Ernst & Ernst, L.A.; mng. ptnr. Pangborn & Co., Ltd. CPA's, 1985-88; now state treas. State of Nev. Former treas. Nev. Rep. Com. Mem. Nat. Assn. State Treas. (past pres.). Office: Office of State Treas Capital Bldg Carson City NV 89710

SEALE, WILLIAM EDWARD, finance educator; b. Lynchburg, Va., Feb. 10, 1941; s. Frank Earl and Viola Elizabeth (Parks) S.; m. Patricia Jeanette Marquart, 1962 (div. 1990); children: William E. Jr., James Anthony, Patricia Jeanette; m. Marguerite E. Pelissier, 1992. A.B. in Chemistry, U. Ky., 1963, M.S. in Agrl. Econs., 1969, Ph.D. in Agrl. Econs., 1975. Farm mgmt. specialist U. Ky., Lexington, 1969-74; legis. asst. U.S. Senate, Washington, 1975-79; v.p. Commodity Exchange Inc., N.Y.C., 1979-83; commr. Commodity Futures Trade Commn., Washington, 1983-88; prof. fin., chmn. dept. Sch. Bus. and Pub. Mgmt. George Washington U., Washington, 1988—. Contbr. articles to profl. jours. and mags. Mem. So. Agrl. Econs. Assn., Am. Agrl. Econs. Assn., Am. Fin. Assn., Fin. Mgmt. Assn. Democrat. Roman Catholic. Avocations: yachting, amateur radio. Home: 1936 Franklin Ave Mc Lean VA 22101-5307 Office: George Washington U Dept Fin Washington DC 20052

SEALL, STEPHEN ALBERT, lawyer; b. South Bend, Ind., Oct. 24, 1940; s. Stephen Henry and Mildred Rita (MacDonald) S.; m. Barbara Ann Halloran, June 25, 1966; children: John Paul, Edward Andrew, Ann Marie. BA, Purdue U., 1963; postgrad., Cornell U. Grad. Sch. Bus. Adminstrn., 1963; LLB, U. Notre Dame, 1966. Bar: Ind. 1966, U.S. Claims Ct. 1973, U.S. Tax Ct. 1968, U.S. Ct. Appeals (6th cir.) 1980, U.S. Ct. Appeals (7th cir.) 1969, U.S. Supreme Ct. 1973. Assoc. Thornburg, McGill, Deahl, Harman, Carey & Murray, South Bend, 1966-71; ptnr. Barnes & Thornburg and predecessor firm Thornburg, McGill, Deahl, Harman, Carey & Murray, 1972—, vice chmn. exec. and mgmt. coms., 1985—; speaker in field. Mem. editorial bd. Notre Dame Law Rev., 1964-66. Mem. Mayor's Com. on Downtown Devel., South Bend, 1975-77, Mayor's Com. on Utilization of Downtown Bldgs., South Bend, 1988—; trustee Project Future,

South Bend, 1986—; dir. Meml. Health Found., 1992—, United Way of St. Joseph County, Inc., 1992—. Fellow Am. Coll. Tax Counsel, Ind. Bar Found.; mem. ABA (taxation sect.), Ind. State Bar Assn. (chmn. taxation sect. 1977-78), Summit Club (chmn. 1976-77), Morris Park Country Club. Democrat. Roman Catholic. Avocations: weightlifting, softball, golf. Home: 17705 Waxwing Ln South Bend IN 46635-1328 Office: Barnes & Thornburg 600 1st Source Bank Ctr 100 N Michigan St South Bend IN 46601-1610

SEALS, DAN WAYLAND, country music singer; b. McCarney, Tex., Feb. 8, 1948. With England Dan & John Ford Coley, 1969-80; recording artist A&M, 1971-80, EMI Records, 1985-86, Liberty Records, 1988-92, Warner Bros., 1992—. Albums (with John Ford Coley) Nights are Forever Without You, 1976, Dowdy Ferry Road, 1977, Dr. Heckle & Mr. Jive, 1979; solo albums Won't Be Blue Anymore, 1985, The Best, 1988, Rage On, 1988, On Arrival, 1990, The Songwriter, 1992, Walking the Wire, 1992, Best of Dan Seals, 1994, Fired Up, 1994; gold #1 single (with John Ford Coley) I'd Really Love To See You Tonight, 1976. Recipient Duet of Yr. award (with Marie Osmond) for Meet Me in Montana from Country Music Assn., 1985, Single of Yr. award for Bop from Country Music Assn., 1988. Office: Warner Bros Records 3300 Warner Blvd Burbank CA 91505-4632*

SEALS, MARGARET LOUISE, newspaper editor; b. Buckhannon, W.Va., Oct. 27, 1944; d. James Richard and Helen Margaret (Brown) Crumrine; m. Harry Eugene Seals, Jan. 10, 1975. BS in journalism, W. Va. U., 1966; MS in mass. comm., Va. Commonwealth U., 1983. Reporter, copy editor Democrat & Chronicle, Rochester, N.Y., 1966-67, Dayton (Ohio) Daily News, 1967-68; copy editor Richmond (Va.) Times-Dispatch, 1968-75, copy desk slot editor, 1975-81, exec. news editor, 1981, asst. mng. editor, 1982-92, deputy mng. editor, 1992-93, mng. editor, 1994—; adv. bd. Sch. Mass. Comms., Va. Commonwealth U., 1988-93. Named Outstanding Woman in Comms. YWCA Met. Richmond, 1989. Mem. Am. Soc. Newspaper Editors, Nat. Fedn. Press Women (bd. dirs. 1990-92), Soc. Profl. Journalists, Va. Press Women Inc. (pres. 1990-92, 2d v.p. 1988-90, treas. 1986-88, Press Woman of Yr. 1986), Assn. Press Mng. Editors (dir. 1993-95, editor APME News 1993-94, treas. 1996), Phi Kappa Phi. Avocations: history, historical fiction, jazz, walking. Office: Richmond-Times Dispatch PO Box 85333 Richmond VA 23293

SEALY, ALBERT HENRY, lawyer; b. Columbus, Ohio, Oct. 23, 1917; s. Albert H. and Lillian E. (Stock) S.; m. Flora Kinkel, Aug. 23, 1947; children: Catherine Ann, Thomas P., Joan Deborah. BA summa cum laude, Ohio State U., 1938; LLB (JD), Harvard Coll., 1941; DL (hon.), Wright State U., 1982. Bar: N.Y. 1942, Ohio 1955. With Simpson, Thacher & Bartlett, N.Y.C., 1941-43, 46-55, Smith and Schnacke, Dayton and Columbus, Ohio, 1955-89; sec. Mead Corp., 1964-75. Author: Macro Blueprint, 1986; contbr. articles to profl. jours. Mem. Ohio Ho. Reps., 1966-68; chmn. Ohioans for Fair Taxation, 1972—, Ohio Inst. on Pub. Fin., 1973—; chmn. bd. trustees Wright State U., 1977—; exec. dir. Inst. Nat. Econ. and Social Dialogue, 1982-87. Lt. USNR, 1943-46. Mem. ABA, Assn. of Bar of City of N.Y., Phi Beta Kappa, Sigma Chi. Home: 3105 Burr St Fairfield CT 06430-1853

SEAMAN, ALFRED BARRETT, journalist; b. Rockville Ctr., N.Y., July 4, 1945; s. Alfred Jarvis and Mary Margaret (Schill) S.; m. Laura Powers Maxwell, Apr. 25, 1970; children: Katherine Maxwell, Margaret Elise, Elizabeth Barrett. BA, Hamilton Coll., 1967; MBA, Columbia U., 1971. Reporter Life mag., N.Y.C., 1971-72, Fortune mag., N.Y.C., 1972; corr. Time mag., N.Y.C., 1973, Chgo., 1973-76, Bonn, Germany, 1976-78; bur. chief Time mag., Detroit, 1978-81; dep. bur. chief Time mag., Washington, 1981-83, White House corr., 1984-88; dep. chief corrs. Time mag., N.Y.C., 1988-91, sr. editor, 1991-94, spl. projects editor, 1994—. Co-author: Going for Broke: The Chrysler Story, 1981. Alumni trustee Hamilton Coll., Clinton, N.Y., 1990-93, 94-95, charter trustee, 1997—; trustee Village of Irvington, N.Y., 1992-94. With USNR, 1969-71. Mem. Ardsley County Club. Episcopalian. Avocations: squash, tennis, golf. Home: Ardsley Ave W Ardsley On Hudson NY 10503 Office: Time Mag Rockefeller Ctr New York NY 10020

SEAMAN, ALFRED JARVIS, retired advertising agency executive; b. Hempstead, L.I., N.Y., Sept. 17, 1912; s. Alfred J. and Ellen (Delaney) S.; m. Mary M. Schill, Sept. 26, 1937 (dec. June 1975); children: Marilyn Hollingsworth, Susan, Barry, Deborah; m. Honor S. Mellor, July 16, 1977. BS, Columbia U., 1935; LittD, L.I. U., 1987. Account exec. Fuller & Smith & Ross, Inc., N.Y.C., 1937-41; partner Knight & Gilbert. Inc., Boston, 1941-43; with Compton Advt., Inc., N.Y.C., 1946-59; exec. v.p., creative dir., dir. Compton Advt., Inc., 1954-59; vice chmn. bd., chmn. exec. com. SSC & B, Inc., 1959-60, pres., chief exec. officer, 1960-79, chmn., chief exec. officer, 1979-81; dir., mem. exec. com. Interpublic Group of Cos., Inc. Hon. bd. dirs., adv. council, founding chmn. Advt. Ednl. Found.; bd. dirs., hon. dir. com. Advt. Council.; chmn. planning bd., 1962—, mayor Village Upper Brookville, 1966—; chmn. emeritus Samuel Waxman Cancer Research Found. Lt. USNR, 1943-46. Named to Advt. Hall of Fame, 1983. Clubs: U.S. Sr. Golf Assn., Creek (Locust Valley, L.I.) (pres.), Piping Rock (Locust Valley, L.I.), Racquet and Tennis (N.Y.C.), Links (N.Y.C.), Brook (N.Y.C.), Jupiter Island (Fla.), Nat. Golf Links Am. (Southampton, N.Y.), Seminole (Fla.), Hobe Sound Yacht (Fla.). Home: Wolver Hollow Rd Upper Brookville Oyster Bay NY 11771 also: Jupiter Island 126 Gomez Rd Hobe Sound FL 33455-2424 Office: 220 E 42nd St New York NY 10017-5806

SEAMAN, BARBARA (ANN ROSNER), author; b. N.Y.C., Sept. 11, 1935; d. Henry Jerome and Sophie Blanche (Kimels) Rosner; m. Gideon Seaman, Jan. 13, 1957 (div.); children: Noah Samuel, Elana Felicia, Shira Jean. B.A. (Ford Found. scholar), Oberlin Coll., 1956, L.H.D. (hon.), 1978; cert. in advanced sci. writing (Sloan-Rockefeller fellow), Columbia U. Sch. Journalism, 1968. Columnist Brides Mag., N.Y.C., 1964-68; columnist, contbg. editor Ladies' Home Jour., N.Y.C., 1965-69; editor child care and edn. Family Circle, N.Y.C., 1970-73; contbg. editor Omni mag., 1978; cons. FYI, ABC-TV, 1979-80; v.p. for devel. David Brooks Prodns., 1990-94; contbg. editor MS Mag., 1993—; cons. U.S. Senate subcom. on monopoly: Nelson pill hearings, 1970; presented testimony to Senate and Congl. coms., 1970—; lectr. in field; participant TV discussion shows; tchr. Coll. New Rochelle, 1975, Sagaris Inst., 1975, CUNY, 1993; founding mem. N.Y. Women's Forum, 1973—; co-founder Nat. Women's Health Network, 1975—, Comm. Consultants for Choice, 1985-86, Nat. Task Force Sexual Malpractice, 1985-86, Families Against Sexually Abusive Therapists and Other Profls., 1992—; v.p. Women's Med. Ctr., N.Y.C., 1971-73; mem. ERA Emergency Task Force, 1979; mem. adv. coun. Feminist Press, Old Westbury, N.Y., 1975; mem. adv. bd. Feminist Ctr. for Human Growth and Devel., 1979, Women's History Libr., Berkeley, Calif., 1973-75; mem. steering com. Women's Forum, 1974; mem. adv. bd. NOW, N.Y., 1973, Women's Guide to Books, 1974, Jewish Women for Affirmative Action, Evanston, Ill., 1973—, Jour. Women and Health, 1975, Jewish Feminist Orgn., N.Y.C., 1975; chair com. domestic violence Nat. Coun. Women's Health, 1993—; judge for various journalism awards. Author: The Doctors' Case Against the Pill, 1969, rev. edit., 1980, 25th anniversary edit., 1995, Free and Female, 1972, (with G. Seaman) Women and the Crisis in Sex Hormones, 1977, Lovely Me: The Life of Jacqueline Susann, 1987, 10th anniversary edit., 1996; contbg. author: foreword to Lunaception, 1975; The Bisexuals, 1974, Career and Motherhood, 1979, The Menopause Industry, 1994; author (play) I Am a Woman, 1972; contbr. various anthologies including Rooms with No View, 1974, Women and Men, 1975, Seizing Our Bodies, 1978, Encyclopaedia of Childbirth, 1992, The Conversation Begins, 1996, Real Majority Media Minority, 1997, The Reader's Companion to U.S. Women's History, 1997, Jewish Women in America: An Historical Encyclopedia, 1997; narrator (film) Taking Our Bodies Back, 1974; contbr. editorials and revs. to newspapers, popular mags.; books and articles translated into Spanish, German, Dutch, Turkish, Japanese, Hebrew, French, Italian. Alumni cons. women's studies program Oberlin Coll., 1975; mem. motivation com. Am. Cancer Soc., 1973; mem. adv. com. Older Women's Health Project, NYU Med. Ctr., 1980; bd. dirs. Safe Transp. of People, N.Y.C., 1975, Women's Health Newsletter, 1983; adv. bd. DES Action, 1977; cons. Nat. Task Force on DES, 1978; contraceptive research br. HEW, 1980; v.p., bd. dirs. ARM (Abortion Rights Moblzn.), 1981—; mem. hon. bd. Carcinogen Info. Program, St. Louis, 1981; trustee Nat. Coun. on Women in Medicine, 1990—; chmn. adv. bd. Coalition for Family Justice, 1991—; co-chair Domestic Violence com. N.Y. Women's Agenda, 1992-93, del. Canada-USA Women's Health Forum, 1996. Recipient citation for books as first to raise issue of sexism in health care as world-wide issue Libr. of Congress, 1973, citation as author responsible for patient package inserts on prescriptions HEW, 1970, Matrix award, 1978, Pioneer Woman award Resources Divsn. of Am. Assn. Retired Persons, 1986, Athena award Nat. Coun. Women's Health, 1992, Health Advocacy award Health Policy Adv. Ctr., APHA, 1994, Project Censored award, 1996; inviting com. Am. Writers Congress. Mem. PEN, Internat. Women's Forum, Authors League, Nat. Assn. Sci. Writers. Address: 110 West End Ave Apt 5D New York NY 10023-6348

SEAMAN, DARYL KENNETH, oil company executive; b. Rouleau, Sask., Can., Apr. 28, 1922. BSME, U. Sask., 1948, LLD (hon.), 1982; LLD (hon.), U. Calgary, 1993. Cert. mech. engr. CEO Bow Valley Industries Ltd., Calgary, Alta., Can., 1962-70, 85-91, chmn., chief exec. officer, 1970-82; chmn. Box Valley Industries Ltd., Calgary, Alta., Can., 1982-85; pres. Bow Valley Industries Ltd., Calgary, Alta., Can., 1985-87; chmn. Bow Valley Industries Ltd., 1991-92; bd. dirs. Renaissance Energy Ltd., Calgary, Potash Corp. Sask. Inc., Encal Energy Ltd., Can. Chem. Reclaiming Ltd., Abacan Resource Corp., Basic Industries Corp., Bow Valley Energy Ltd.; co-owner, bd. dirs. Calgary Flames Hockey Club; chmn., pres. Dox Investments, Inc. Mem. Royal Commn. Econ. Union and Devel. Prospects for Can., 1982-85; active numerous coms. for fundraising U. Sask.; hon. chmn. The Western Heritage Centre Soc.; chmn. nat. adv. com. Banff Sch. Mgmt. Served with RCAF, 1941-45, North Africa, Italy. There is no repetition since it is indicated as an award you received and as a membership. Mem. Assn. Profl. Engrs., Geologists and Geophysicists (hon. life, Frank Spragins award, 1985, McGill Mgmt. Achievement award, 1979), Order of Canada 1993, Western Heritage Centre Soc., Ranchmen's Club, RAF Club, Earl Grey Golf Club, Calgary Petroleum Club, Calgary Golf and Country Club, U. Calgary Chancellor's Club. Progressive Conservative. Mem. United Ch. Can. Avocations: ranching, golf, hunting, skiing. Home and Office: Dox Investments Inc, 500 333 5th Ave SW, Calgary, AB Canada T2P 3B6

SEAMAN, DONALD ROY, investment company executive; b. b., Rouleau, Sask., Can., July 26, 1925; s. Byron Luther and Letha Mae (Patton) S.; m. Eleanor Victoria Lee, Nov. 4, 1950; children: Victoria Anne, Donna Jane, Lauraine Suzanne (dec.), Marilou Kathleen. B.S.M.E., U. Sask., 1947. Indsl. engr. Canadian Industries Ltd., Kingston, Ont., Can., 1947-50; v.p. Bow Valley Industries, Calgary, Alta., Can., 1950-75, dir., 1950-89, sr. v.p., 1986-87; pres. Bow Valley Resource Services, Calgary, 1976-86; bd. dirs. NuGas Ltd., Northstar Energy Corp., Artisan Corp., Best Pacific Resources Ltd., Can. Chem. Reclaiming Ltd., Ryan Energy Techs., Inc. Mem. Profl. Engrs. Alta. Clubs: Petroleu, Glencoe, Earl Grey Golf (dir. 1966-72), Calgary Golf. Office: D R S Resource Investments Inc, 333-5 Ave SW # 500, Calgary, AB Canada T2P 3B6

SEAMAN, EMMA LUCY, artist, poet; b. West Freedom, Pa., Dec. 5, 1932; d. Roger Leslie and Lillian Emeline (Phillips) Eddinger; m. Roger John Seaman, Sept. 14, 1958; 1 child, Roger Kent. Grad. H.S., Seneca, Pa. Sec. to supt. Cranberry H.S., Seneca, 1951-56; flight attendant, hostess Trans World Airlines, Newark, 1956-57; copy writer Radio St. WFRA, Franklin, Pa., 1957-58. Works have been exhibited at Art League of Marco Island, Fla., 1985-93, Sussex County Arts and Heritage Coun. Fine Arts Exhbns., Newton, 1990-94, N.J. Herald Art Show, Newton, 1990, Annual Sparta (N.J.) Day Event, 1990, St. Mary's Art Festival, Sparta, 1991-94, Hilltop Art Exhibit, Sparta, 1991-94, Edison Festival of Light, Ft. Myers, Fla., 1992; represented in permanent collection of Fame Mus. Teterboro (N.J.) Airport; one woman show: Sparta Libr., N.J., 1994; contbr. numerous poems to pubIs. Sunday sch. tchr., Sparta, 1965-74; organizer, operator Paper Drives, Sparta, 1965-74. Recipient First Pl. Beginners Oils award Creative Canvas Art Assn., Newton, 1982, Purchase award St. Mary's Art Festival, Sparta, N.J., 1991, honorable mention, 1993. Mem. ASPCA, AARP, People for the Ethical Treatment Animals, Art League Marco Island, Sussex County Arts and Heritage Coun., Sussex County Artists Assn., Studio A Art Assn., Edison Festival of Light, Nat. Humane Edn. Soc., Human Soc. U.S., Doris Day Animal League, Animal Legal Def. Fund, Women's Mus. Art, Smithsonial Assn., Antique Airplane Assn., Newton (N.J.) Meml. Hosp. Aux., Sparta (N.J.) Woman's Club, Lake Mohawk Country Club. Avocations: flying, reading, cooking, sewing, traveling. Home: 54 Alpine Trl Sparta NJ 07871-1509

SEAMAN, IRVING, JR., public relations consultant; b. Milw., July 14, 1923; s. Irving and Anne (Douglas) S.; m. June Carry, June 24, 1950; children: Peter Stewart, Marion Carry, Irving Osborne, Anne Douglas. B.A., Yale U., 1944. With Continental Ill. Nat. Bank & Trust Co., Chgo., 1947-61; v.p. Continental Ill. Nat. Bank & Trust Co., 1959-61; pres., chief exec. officer, dir. Nat. Boulevard Bank, Chgo., 1961-65; chmn. exec. com., chief exec. officer, dir. Nat. Boulevard Bank, 1966-76; vice chmn. bd., dir. Sears Bank and Trust Co., Chgo., 1976-77; pres., chief operating officer, dir. Sears Bank and Trust Co., 1977-82; sr. cons. Burson-Marsteller, Chgo., 1982-94; chmn. bd. Associated Bank Chgo., 1985—. Mem. Northwestern U. Assn.; life mem. bd. dirs. Lake Forest Hosp.; bd. dirs. United Way of Chgo., 1975-89, pres., 1979; bd. dirs. United Way/Crusade of Mercy, 1980-89, 94-95, vice chmn., 1980-81; trustee Chgo. Symphony Orch., 1987—. Lt. (j.g.) USNR, WWII. Mem. Commonwealth Club, Econ. Club, Chgo. Club, Comml. Club, Racquet Club, Onwentsia Club, Winter Club, Old Elm Club (Highland Park, Ill.), Shoreacres Club (Lake Bluff, Ill.), Augusta Nat. Golf Club (Ga.), Marsh Landing Club (Fla.). Home: 946 Elm Tree Rd Lake Forest IL 60045-1410 Office: 1 E Wacker Dr Chicago IL 60601-1802

SEAMAN, JEFFREY RICHARD, academic administrator; b. Roslyn, N.Y., Feb. 22, 1949; s. Richard MacAvoy and Jane Louise (Decker) S.; m. I. Elaine Allen, Jan. 21, 1978; children: Christopher, Julia. BS, Cornell U., 1971, MA, MS, 1977, PhD, 1984. Lectr. Cornell U., Ithaca, N.Y., 1976-77; rsch. assoc. U. Pa., Phila., 1978-86, lectr. stats., 1979-84, dir. rsch. project, 1982-84, dir. microcomputer svcs., 1984-85, dir. computing resource, 1985-92, assoc. vice provost, 1990-92; pres. Pond View Assocs., Dover, Mass., 1992—; exec. dir. tech. Lesley Coll., Cambridge, Mass., 1994—; cons. Schuykill Twp., Valley Forge, Pa., 1990-92; mem. adv. bd. Apple Computer, 1985-90, Word Perfect, Orem, Utah, 1989-91, IBM, 1984-86. Office: Lesley Coll 29 Everett St Cambridge MA 02138-2702

SEAMAN, JEROME FRANCIS, actuary; b. Oak Park, Ill., Nov. 4, 1942; s. William Francis and Bernice Florence (Haughey) S.; m. Jacquelyn Ann Robinson, Aug. 22, 1970; children: Carolyn, John. BA, U. Notre Dame, 1964; MA, Northwestern U., 1991. Asst. actuary Combined Ins. Co. of Am., Chgo., 1966-73; v.p., actuary United Equitable Life Ins. Co., Skokie, Ill., 1975-77; mgr. Peat Marwick Mitchell & Co., Chgo., 1973-75, 77-78; nat. dir. actuarial svcs. Arthur Young & Co., Chgo., 1978-83; pres., cons. actuary Jerome F. Seaman & Assocs., Northfield, Ill., 1983—; dir. Polysystems, Inc., Chgo., 1987-91. Contbr. articles to profl. jours. Recipient Commendation for Svc. Pres. Ronald Reagan, 1982. Fellow Soc. of Actuaries, Conf. of Cons. Actuaries; mem. Am. Acad. Actuaries (task force on risk based capital health orgns. 1993-95). Democrat. Unitarian Universalist. Avocations: golf, classical music, opera, baseball. Home: 1864 Sherman Ave 1SE Evanston IL 60201 Office: Jerome F Seaman & Assocs 550 W Frontage Rd Northfield IL 60093-1202

SEAMAN, PEGGY JEAN, lawyer; b. New Orleans, Nov. 21, 1949; d. William David and Leah Catherine (Bourdet) Smith; m. Terry Noako Seaman, Dec. 22, 1970; children: Vanya Lianne, Ember Catherine. BA, Rutgers U.-Camden, 1974; JD, N.Y. Law Sch., 1978. Bar: N.Y. 1978, Va. 1980, U.S. Dist. Ct. Va., 1980, U.S. Dist. Ct. (so. and ea. dists.) N.Y. 1978. Pvt. practice, N.Y.C., 1978-79; gen. atty. Merit Systems Protection Bd., Office of Appeals, Washington, 1980-82, presiding ofcl., Washington regional office, Falls Church, Va., 1982-85, adminstrv. judge St. Louis regional office, 1985-87; atty. Office of Dep. Exec. Dir. for Regional Ops., Washington, 1987-89; gen. atty. Office of Appeals Counsel, Washington, 1989-95; adminstrv. judge Denver Field Office, 1995—. Recipient Sustained Superior Performance awards Merit Systems Protection Bd., Spl. Act award, 1988, Chmn.'s Honor award, 1991). Mem. ABA, Athenaeum Honor Soc., Mensa. Democrat. Home: 383 Van Gordon St Apt 11-357 Denver CO 80228 Office: Denver Field Office 12567 W Cedar Dr Denver CO 80228-2009

SEAMAN, ROUAL DUANE, data processing company executive; b. East Chicago, Ind., Apr. 25, 1930; s. Elmer Earl and Roxanna Isabelle (Bennett) S.; m. Sadako Itabashi, July 29, 1957; 1 child, Victor Shayne. Student, U. Mo., 1950-51, Jochi Daigaku, Tokyo, 1956, U. Houston, 1966-69. Mgmt. trainee GE Corp., Atomic Energy Commn., Richland, Wash., 1951-52; project mgr. Dynalectron Corp., Ft. Worth, 1952-63; project supr. Apollo Test Facility N.Am. Rockwell Project Apollo, NASA, Houston, 1964-69; mktg. mgr. Gen. Space Corp., Houston, 1969-70; pres. AIM Fin. Systems Group, Inc., Houston, 1970—; bd. dirs. Am. Credit Control; ptnr. Automated Info. Mgmt., 1984—; ptnr. CA$SH Enterprises, 1989—. Author software. Pres. Tex. Intercity Football, Inc., Harris/Galveston County, 1971, League City (Tex.) Little League, 1972; mem. S.W. Football Ofcls. Assn., 1976; mem. Better Bus. Bur., Houston, 1982—. With USAF, 1947-50. Recipient Recognition award Greater Houston Partnership, 1990. Mem. Am. Guild of Patient Mgmt., Houston C. of C., Nat. Fedn. Ind. Businesses, Nat. Assn. Pvt. Enterprise, Tex. Hosp. Assn., Tex. Hosp. Info. Systems Soc., Healthcare Fin. Mgrs. Assn., 100 Club of Houston, Smithsonian Instn., Am. Mus. Natural History. Republican. Christian/Bhuddist. Avocations: golf, baseball, football, gardening, travel. Office: AIM Fin Systems Group Inc 7015 Gulf Fwy Ste 145 Houston TX 77087-2538

SEAMAN, TONY, university athletic coach. Head coach NCAA Divsn. 1A lacrosse Johns Hopkins Blue Jays, Balt., 1990—. Office: Johns Hopkins U Charles And # 34th Sts Baltimore MD 21218*

SEAMAN, WILLIAM BERNARD, physician, radiology educator; b. Chgo., Jan. 5, 1917; s. Benjamin and Dorothy E. S.; m. Veryl Swick, February 26, 1944; children—Cheryl Dorothy, William David. Student, U. Mich., 1934-37; M.D., Harvard U., 1941. Diplomate: Am. Bd. Radiology. Intern Billings Hosp., U. Chgo., 1941-42; asst. radiology Yale U. Sch. Medicine, 1947-48, instr., 1948-49; instr. radiology Washington U. Sch. Medicine, St. Louis, 1949-51, assoc. prof., 1951-55, prof., 1955-56; prof. radiology, chmn. dept. Coll. Phys. and Surg., Columbia U., 1956-82; James Picker prof. emeritus Columbia U., 1982—; dir. radiology service, trustee Presbyn. Hosp., N.Y.C. Served as maj. USAAF, 1942-46; flight surgeon. Recipient W.B. Cannon medal Soc. Gastro-intestinal Radiologists, 1979, Gold medal Am. Coll. Radiology, 1983. Mem. Radiol. Soc. N.A., Am. Roentgen Ray Soc. (pres. 1973-74, gold medal 1988), Am. Coll. Radiology (pres. 1980-81), Assn. U. Radiologists (pres. 1955-56, Gold medal 1979), N.Y. Roentgen Soc. (pres. 1961-62), N.Y. Gastroent. Soc. (pres. 1965-66), Soc. Chmn. Academic Radiology Depts. (pres. 1967-68), Eastern Radiol. Soc. (pres. 1985-86). Presbyterian. Home: Olympic K 9129 SE Riverfront Ter Tequesta FL 33469-1159

SEAMAN, WILLIAM CASPER, retired news photographer; b. Grand Island, Nebr., Jan. 19, 1925; s. William H. and Minnie (Cords) S.; m. Ruth Witwer, Feb. 14, 1945; 1 son, Lawrence William. Grad. high sch. Photographer Leschinsky Studio, Grand Island; news photographer Mpls. Star & Tribune, 1945-82; ret., 1982. Recipient Pulitzer prize, 1959; also awards Nat. Headliners Club; also awards Nat. Press Photographers Assn.; also awards Inland Daily Press Assn.; also awards Kent State U.; also awards Mo. U.; also awards Local Page One; State A.P. contest; Silver Anniversary award Honeywell Photog. Products, 1975. Mem. Nat. Press Photographers Assn., Sigma Delta Chi. Home: 8206 Virginia Cir S Minneapolis MN 55426-2458

SEAMANS, ANDREW CHARLES, editorial and public relations consultant, columnist, author; b. Hillside, N.J., Sept. 10, 1937; s. Thomas Randall and Marie Josephine (Mazur) S.; m. Marion Gloria Lufbery, Aug. 25, 1956 (div. June 1986); children: Andrew Charles, Darryl Wayne, Marion Gloria Seamans Raynor, Dawn Louise Seamans Wheeler. AS cum laude, No. Va. Community Coll., Annandale, 1989. Lic. real estate salesman, Va. Editorial writer U.S. Press Assn., McLean, Va., 1968-70; pub. rels. asst. Nat. Right to Work Com., Washington, 1970; assoc. editor Human Events, Washington, 1970-81; mng. editor Heritage Features Syndicate, Washington, 1981-91; syndicated columnist The Answer Man Creators Syndicate, L.A., 1985—; chief copy editor The Hill Newspaper, Washington, 1996—; bd. dirs., pub. rels. cons. Marine Learning Inst., St. Louis, 1980—. Author: Who, What, When, Where, Why In the World of American History, 1991, Who, What, When, Where, Why In the World of World History, 1991, Who, What, When, Where, Why In the World of Nature, 1992; co-author: Whose FBI?, 1974. Bd. dirs. McLean Little League Baseball, Inc., 1975-83, pres., 1982-83; pres. Rahway (N.J.) Young Rep. Club, 1964-66; chmn. platform com. Union County Young Reps., N.J. Young Reps., various other Rep. orgns. Recipient cert. of appreciation McLean Little League Baseball, 1978, named to Hall of Fame, 1985. Mem. Pub. Rels. Soc. Am., Soc. Profl. Journalists (bd. dirs. D.C. chpt. 1986-87, membership dir. 1986-87, 89-90, dir. pub. info. 1988), No. Va. Assn. Historians, Va. Hist. Soc., Internat. Platform Assn., Nat. Press Club. Episcopalian. Home and Office: Horizon House #603 1300 Army-Navy Dr Arlington VA 22202

SEAMANS, ROBERT CHANNING, JR., astronautical engineering educator; b. Salem, Mass., Oct. 30, 1918; s. Robert Channing and Pauline (Bosson) S.; m. Eugenia Merrill, June 13, 1942; children: Katherine (Mrs. Louis Padulo), Robert Channing III, Joseph, May (Seamans Baldwin), Daniel M. BS, Harvard U., 1939; MS, MIT, 1942, ScD, 1951; grad. exec. program bus. adminstrn., Columbia U., 1959; DSc, Rollins Coll., 1962, NYU, 1967; DEng, Norwich Acad., 1971, Notre Dame U., 1974, Rensselaer Poly. Inst., 1974, U. Wyo., 1975, George Washington U., 1975, Lehigh U., 1976, Thomas Coll., 1980, Curry Coll., 1982. Successively instr. dept. aero. engring., staff engr. instrumentation lab., asst. prof., project leader instrumentation lab., asso. prof. Mass. Inst. Tech., 1941-55; chief engr. Project Meteor, 1950-53, dir. flight control lab., 1953-55; mgr. airborne systems lab., chief systems engr. airborne systems dept. RCA, 1955-58, chief engr. missile electronics and controls div., 1958-60; asso. adminstr. NASA, 1960-68, dep. adminstr., 1965-68, cons., 1968-69; vis. prof. MIT, 1968, Hunsaker prof., 1968-69; sec. air force, 1969-73; pres. Nat. Acad. Engring., 1973-74; adminstr. ERDA, Washington, 1974-77; Henry R. Luce prof. environment and pub. policy MIT, 1977-84, sr. lectr. dept. aeros. and astronautics, 1984-96, dean Sch. Engring., 1978-81; mem. sci. adv. bd. USAF, 1957-62, assoc. adviser, 1963-67. Bd. overseers Harvard U., 1968-74; trustee Mus. Sci., Boston, Sea Edn. Assn.; trustee emeritus Nat. Geog. Soc., Carnegie Inst., Washington, Woods Hole Oceanographic Inst. Recipient naval ordnance devel. award 1945, Godfrey L. Cabot award Aero Club New Eng., 1965, disting. svc. medal NASA, 1965, 69, Robert H. Goddard meml. trophy, 1968, disting. pub. svc. medal Dept. Def., 1973, exceptional civilian svc. award Dept. Air Force, 1973, Gen. Thomas D. White U.S. Air Force Space Trophy, 1973, Ralph Coats Roe medal ASME, 1977; achievement award Nat. Soc. Profl. Engrs., Thomas D. White Nat. Def. award, 1980, exceptional svc. award Dept. Air Force, 1985. Fellow Am. Acad. Arts and Scis., Am. Astron. Soc., IEEE, AIAA (hon., Lawrence Sperry award 1951); mem. Internat. Acad. Astronautics, Am. Soc. Pub. Adminstrn., Nat. Acad. Engring. (Arthur M. Bueche Award, 1994, Daniel Guggenheim award 1996), AAAS, Air Force Acad. Found., Fgn. Policy Assn., Coun. on Fgn. Rels., Sigma Xi. Clubs: Harvard (Boston); Manchester Yacht (Mass.); Essex County (Mass.); Chevy Chase, Metropolitan (Washington); Cruising of Am. (Boston Sta.).

SEAMANS, WARREN ARTHUR, museum director; b. Loveland, Colo., Aug. 8, 1935; s. James Lamott and Eleanor Caroline (Baechler) S. BS, Colo. State U., 1957. Pers. officer Stone & Webster Engring. Co., Boston, 1963-64; pers. officer MIT, Cambridge, 1964-66, adminstrn. officer dept. humanities, 1966-71, founding dir. mus., 1971-96; mus. cons., 1996—. Capt. USAF, 1958-63. Mem. Am. Mus. Assn. Democrat. Avocations: theatre, musical theatre recordings, history, gardening. Home: 1401 Quincy Rd Rumney NH 03266-3545 Office: MIT Mus 265 Massachusetts Ave Cambridge MA 02139-4109

SEAMANS, WILLIAM, writer, commentator, former television and radio journalist; b. Providence, July 8, 1925; s. William and Mary Seamans; m. Jane Kingsbury, Sept. 15, 1951; children: Laurie, Jonathan, Adam. AB, Brown U., 1949; MS, Columbia U., 1952. Freelance journalist, 1952-53; journalist CBS News, 1953-63; producer evening news ABC News, 1963-65; European producer ABC News, London, 1965-70; field producer ABC News, N.Y.C., 1970-72; corr., bur. chief ABC News, Tel Aviv, 1972-92; commentator Vt. Pub. Radio, lectr., freelance writer, 1992—. Producer

Nightline in Israel Week (including Palestinian-Israeli town meeting) (Emmy award, Dupont award). Served with inf. AUS, 1942-45. Decorated Bronze Star medal; CBS Murrow News fellow Columbia U., 1961-62. Mem. Writers Guild Am., Nat. Acad. TV Arts and Scis. (Emmy award 1961, 89), Overseas Press Club Am. (award for best radio reporting invasion of Cyprus 1974, award for best fgn. affairs documentary Yitzhak Rabin biography 1975), Nat. Press Club (Washington), Fgn. Corrs. Assn. in Israel.

SEAPKER, JANET KAY, museum director; b. Pitts., Nov. 2, 1947; d. Charles Henry and Kathryn Elizabeth (Dany) S.; m. Edward F. Turberg, May 24, 1975. BA, U. Pitts., 1969; MA, SUNY, Cooperstown, 1975. Park ranger Nat. Park Svc., summers 1967-69; archtl. historian N.C. Archives and History, Raleigh, 1971-76, hist. preservation adminstr., 1976-77, grant-in-aid adminstr., 1977-78; dir. Cape Fear Mus. (formerly New Hanover County Mus.), Wilmington, N.C., 1978—; bd. dirs. Bellamy Mansion Found., Wilmington, 1986-89, 91—, Lower Cape Fear Hist. Soc., Wilmington, 1985-88; N.C. rep. S.E. Mus. Conf., 1986-90; field reviewer Inst. Mus. Svcs., 1982—. Contbr. articles to profl. jours. Bd. dirs. Downtown Area Revitalization Effort, Wilmington, 1979-81, Thalian Hall Ctr. for Performing Arts, 1996—; bd. dirs. Hist. Wilmington Found., 1979-84, pres., 1980-81; mem. Cmty. Appearance Commn., Wilmington, 1984-88, 250th Anniversary Commn., Wilmington, 1986-90. Grad. program fellow SUNY, Cooperstown, 1969-70; recipient Profl. Svc. award N.C. Mus. Coun., 1982, Woman of Achievement award YWCA, 1994. Mem. Am. Assn. Mus. (accreditation vis. com. 1983—, reviewer mus. assessment program 1982—), Nat. Trust Hist. Preservation, Southeastern Mus. Conf. (N.C. state rep. 1986-90), N.C. Mus. Coun. (sec.-treas. 1978-84, pres. 1984-86), Hist. Preservation Found N.C. (sec. 1976-78). Democrat. Presbyterian. Home: 307 N 15th St Wilmington NC 28401-3813 Office: Cape Fear Mus 814 Market St Wilmington NC 28401-4731

SEAQUIST, ERNEST RAYMOND, astronomy educator; b. Vancouver, B.C., Can., Nov. 19, 1938; s. Egron Emanuel and Sigrid Alice (Back) S.; m. Gloria Stewart Jenkins, June 11, 1966; children: Jonathan William, Carolyn Suzanne. BASc, U. B.C., Vancouver, 1961; MA, U. Toronto, Ont., Can., 1962, PhD, 1966. Lectr. astronomy U. Toronto, 1965-66, asst. prof., 1966-72, assoc. prof., 1972-78, prof., 1978—, assoc. chmn. dept., 1974-88, chmn., 1988—; dir. David Dunlap Obs. U. Toronto, Richmond Hill, Ont., 1988—. Contbr. author: Classical Novae, 1989; also over 150 articles. Rsch. grantee Natural Scis. and Engring. Rsch. Coun. Can., 1967—. Mem. Internat. Astron. Union, Am. Astron. Soc., Can. Astron. Soc. (pres. 1986-88). Avocations: painting and sketching, collecting antiques. Office: U Toronto Dept Astronomy, 60 St George St, Toronto, ON Canada M5S 1A7

SEAR, MOREY LEONARD, federal judge, educator; b. New Orleans, Feb. 26, 1929; s. William and Yetty (Streiffer) S.; m. Lee Edrehi, May 26, 1951; children: William Sear II, Jane Lee. J.D., Tulane U., 1950. Bar: La. 1950. Asst. dist. atty. Parish Orleans, 1952-55; individual practice law Stahl & Sear, New Orleans, 1955-71; spl. counsel New Orleans Aviation Bd., 1956-60; magistrate U.S. Dist. Ct. (ea. dist.) La., 1971-76, judge, 1976—, chief judge, 1992—; judge Temp. Emergency Ct. of Appeals, 1982-87; adj. prof. Tulane U. Coll. Law; former chmn. com. on adminstrn. of bankruptcy sys., former chmn. adv. com. on bankruptcy rules, former mem. com. on adminstrn. of fed. magistrate sys. Jud. Conf. U.S.; former mem. Jud. Conf. of U.S. and Its Exec. Com.; mem. cir. coun. 5th Cir. of U.S.; founding dir. River Oaks Pvt. Psychiat. Hosp., 1968. Pres. Congregation Temple Sinai, 1977-79; bd. govs. Tulane Med. Ctr., 1977—; former chmn. Tulane Med. Ctr. Hosp. and Clinic, 1980-85. Mem. ABA, La. Bar Assn., New Orleans Bar Assn., Order of Barristers, Order of the Coif (hon.). Office: US Dist Ct C-256 US Courthouse 500 Camp St New Orleans LA 70130-3313

SEARCY, ALAN WINN, chemist, educator; b. Covina, Calif., Oct. 12, 1925; s. Claude Winn and Esther (Scofield) S.; m. Gail Vaught, Oct. 30, 1945; children: Gay, William, Anne. A.B., Pomona Coll., 1946; Ph.D., U. Calif. at Berkeley, 1950. Faculty Purdue U., 1949-54, asst. prof. chemistry, 1950-54; faculty U. Calif., Berkeley, 1954—, prof., 1958-91, prof. materials sci., 1960-91, prof. emeritus, 1991—, assoc. div. head inorganic materials div. Lawrence Radiation Lab., 1961-64, asst. to chancellor, 1963-64, vice-chancellor, 1964-67, chmn. faculty Coll. Engring., 1969-70, Miller rsch. prof., 1970-71, acting chmn. dept. materials sci. and engring., 1973; assoc. dir. Lawrence Berkeley Lab., head materials and molecular research div., 1980-84; Fulbright lectr. phys. chemistry Inst. Physics, Bariloche, Argentina, 1960; cons. Gen. Motors Tech. Center, 1956-64, Union Carbide, 1956-72, Gen. Atomic, 1957-72; Mem. com. high temperature chemistry NRC, 1961-70. Editor: (with D.V. Ragone, U. Colombo) Chemical and Mechanical Behavior of Inorganic Materials, 1970; assoc. editor Jour. Am. Ceramic Soc., 1996—; editl. adv. bd. High Temperature High Pressure, 1969-93, High Temperature Sci., 1969-94, Advanced in High Temperature Chemistry, 1971-75, Materials Chemistry and Physics, 1976-87, Reactivity of Solids, High Temperature and Materials Science, 1994—; contbr. numerous articles to profl. jours. Served with AUS, 1944-46. Recipient citation for distinction in rsch. U. Calif., Berkeley, 1991; Guggenheim fellow, 1967-68. Fellow Am. Ceramic Soc., AAAS; mem. Am. Chem. Soc., Acad. of Ceramics (charter), Materials Rsch. Soc., Phi Beta Kappa, Sigma Xi. Home: 24 Northampton Ave Berkeley CA 94707-1715

SEARCY, JARRELL D. (JAY), sportswriter; b. Stevenson, Ala., Mar. 26, 1934; s. Harley Johnson and Dovie Mae (Ryan) S.; m. Jackie Lou Hildebrand, Nov. 17, 1957; children—Michael Jarrell, Mark William. Student, U. Tenn., 1953-54, East Tenn. State U., 1956-57. Reporter Kingsport Times-News, Tenn., 1956-57; reporter Chattanooga Times, 1958-64, sports editor, 1964-71; editor/reporter N.Y. Times, N.Y.C., 1972-75; exec. sports editor Phila. Inquirer, 1975-86, sr. writer, 1986—. Author: (with Sam Goldaper) Golden State Warrior, 1975. Mem. Nat. Turf Writers' Assn., Nat. Boxing Writers Assn., Nat. Sportswriters and Broadcasters Assn., AP Sports Editors Assn. (pres. 1984-85), Quality Life Assn. (pres. 1990). Avocations: tennis; golf; gardening. Office: Phila Inquirer 400 N Broad St Philadelphia PA 19130-4015

SEARIGHT, PATRICIA ADELAIDE, retired radio and television executive; b. Rochester, N.Y.; d. William Hammond and Irma (Winters) S. BA, Ohio State U. Program dir. Radio Sta. WTOP, Washington, 1952-63, gen. mgr. info., 1964; radio and TV cons., 1964-84; ret., 1984; producer, dir. many radio and TV programs; spl. fgn. news corr. French Govt., 1956; v.p. Micro Beads, Inc., 1955-59; sec. dir. Dennis-Inches Corp., 1955-59; exec. dir. Am. Women in Radio and TV, 1969-74; fgn. service officer U.S. Dept. State, ret., AEC, ret. Mem. pres.'s coun. Toledo Mus. Art. Recipient Kappa Kappa Gamma Alumna achievement award. Mem. Am. Women in Radio and TV (program chmn.; corrs. sec.; dir. Washington chpt.; pres. 1958-60, nat. membership chmn. 1962-63, nat. chmn. Industry Info. Digest 1963-64, Mid-Eastern v.p. 1964-66), Soc. Am. Travel Writers (treas. 1957-58, v.p. 1958-59), Nat. Acad. TV Arts and Scis., Women's Advt. Club (Washington, pres. 1959-60), Nat. Press Club, Soroptimist, Kappa Kappa Gamma. Episcopalian. Home: 9498 E Via Montoya Dr Scottsdale AZ 85255-5074 *Personal philosophy: "There is no such word as can't."*

SEARING, MARJORY ELLEN, government official, economist; b. N.Y.C., Mar. 29, 1945; d. William Edgar Searing and Jean Frances (Smith) Searing Fusaro; 1 child, Stephanie Anne Lane. B.A. in Econs., SUNY-Binghamton, 1966; M.A. in Econs., Georgetown U., 1969, Ph.D. in Econs., 1972. Economist Bur. Econs. Analysis U.S. Dept. Commerce, Washington, 1967-73, internat. economist Bur. East-West Trade, 1973-74, dir. Office Internat. Sector Policy, 1980-84, dir. Office Industry Assessment, 1984-86, acting dep. asst. sec. sci. and electronics, 1984-85, dir. Office Multilateral Affairs, 1986-90; dep. asst. sec. for Japan U.S. Dept. Commerce, 1991—; sr. internat. economist Office Trade Policy U.S. Dept. Treasury, Washington, 1974-76, dir. Office East-West Econ. Policy, 1976-79. Contbr. numerous articles to profl. publs. N.Y. State Regents scholar, 1962-65; Georgetown U. fellow, 1966-71. Office: US Dept Commerce 14th Pl SE Rm 2320 Washington DC 20230

SEARLE, ELEANOR MILLARD, history educator; b. Chgo., Oct. 29, 1926; married. BA, Harvard U., 1948; Licentiate Medieval Studies, Pontifical Inst. Medieval History, 1961, D Medieval Studies, 1972; D honoris causa, Pontifical Inst., 1994. Lectr. history Calif. Inst. Tech., Pasadena, 1962-63, prof. history, 1979-87, Edie and Lou Wasserman prof. history, 1987—; rsch. fellow Rsch. Sch. Social Sci., Australian Nat. U., 1963-65, fellow, 1965-68; assoc. prof. UCLA, 1969-72, prof., 1972-79; vis. fellow Cambridge U., 1976, 81; sr. rsch. fellow Hungtington Libr., 1986—; cons. Huntington Libr., 1980-82. Author: Lordship and Community: Battle Abbey and Its Banlieu, 1066-1538, 1974; editor: The Chronicle of Battle Abbey, 1980; co-editor: Accounts of the Cellarers of Battle Abbey, 1967, Predatory Kinship and the Creation of Norman Power, 840-1066, 1988; contbr. articles to profl. jours. Fellow Royal Hist. Soc., Royal Soc. Antiquaries of London; mem. Am. Hist. Soc., Medieval Acad. Am. (pres. 1985-86), Econ. History Soc., Am. Soc. Legal History, Haskins Soc. (bd. dirs. 1982—, pres. 1990-96). Office: Calif Inst Tech Dept History Pasadena CA 91125*

SEARLE, PHILIP FORD, bank executive; b. Kansas City, Mo., July 23, 1924; s. Albert Addison and Edith (Thompson) S.; m. Jean Adair Haneman, Nov. 22, 1950 (dec. Nov. 1990); 1 child, Charles Randolph; m. Jean Walker, Oct. 4, 1992 (dec. Oct. 1993); m. Elizabeth Gordon, Nov. 4, 1994. AB, Cornell U., 1949; grad. in banking, Rutgers U., 1957, 64. With Geneva (Ohio) Savs. and Trust Co., 1949-60, pres., 1959-60; pres., sr. trust officer Northeastern Ohio Nat. Bank, Ashtabula, 1960-69; pres., chief exec. officer BancOhio Corp., Columbus, 1969-75; chmn., chief exec. officer Flagship Banks, Inc., Miami, Fla., 1975-84; chmn. bd. Sun Banks, Inc., Orlando, Fla., 1984-85, cons., 1986-94; mem. faculty Sch. Banking, Ohio U., 1959-70, Nat. Trust Sch., Northwestern U., Evanston, Ill., 1965-68; mem. corp. adv. com. Nat. Assn. Securities Dealers, 1981-83; v.p., mem. fed. adv. coun. to bd. govs. FRS, 1983-85; chmn. Nat. Adv. Bd. to Oversight Bd. for Resolution Trust Corp., 1991-92 . Co-author: The Management of a Trust Department, 1967. Past chmn. bd. regents Stonier Grad. Sch. Banking, Rutgers U., 1974-76, past mem. faculty; trustee Fin. Acctg. Found., Norwalk, Conn., 1989-93. Capt. AUS, 1943-46, 51-52, ETO. Decorated Bronze Star; named Outstanding Citizen in Ashtabula County, 1967. Mem. Am. Bankers Assn. (bd. dirs. 1972-74, governing coun.), Bank Adminstrn. Inst. (nat. chmn. 1987-88, bd. dirs. Chgo., Ill. 1985-89), Fla. Bankers Assn. (bd. dirs. 1979-81, coun. 1981), Ohio Bankers Assn. (pres. 1970-71), Assn. Bank Holding Cos. (bd. dirs. 1979-81, exec. com. 1981), Fla. Assn. Registered Bank Holding Cos. (pres. 1979-81), Fla. C. of C. (bd. dirs. 1978-82), Royal Poinciana Golf Club (Naples, Fla.), Naples Yacht Club, Catawba Island Club (Port Clinton, Ohio), Phi Kappa Tau.

SEARLE, ROBERT FERGUSON, minister; b. Auburn, N.Y., July 13, 1951; s. Loren Rawson and Esther Lucille (Ferguson) S. BS, Cornell U., 1973; MDiv, Princeton Theol. Sem., 1977; DMin, Asbury Theol. Sem., 1997. Cert. clin. pastoral edn., pastoral care; ordained deacon United Meth. Ch., 1978, ordained elder, 1980. Pastor of Blodgett Mills Freetown and McGraw (N.Y.) United Meth. Ch., 1978-84; pastor Pennsylvania Ave. United Meth. Ch., Pine City, N.Y., 1984—; mem. dist. bd. Ordained Ministry, Syracuse, N.Y., 1980-84, mem. conf. bd., 1980-85, dist. youth dir., Syracuse, 1981-84; spiritual dir. Walk to Emmaus, Rome, N.Y., 1993. Bd. dirs. Meals on Wheels, Elmira, 1985-88; bd. dirs. CPC, Elmira, 1985-93; mem. edn. and rsch. instl. rev. bd. Arnot Ogden Hosp., Elmira, 1995; mem. cmty. bd. Southport Correctional Facility, 1987—. Mem. Am. Assn. Christian Counselors, Marathon Lodge, Royal Arch Mason, Knight Templar. Republican. Avocations: reading, exercise, travel, music. Home: 1240 Pennsylvania Ave Pine City NY 14871 Office: Pa Ave United Meth Ch 1238 Pennsylvania Ave Pine City NY 14871-9251

SEARLE, RODNEY NEWELL, state legislator, farmer, insurance agent; b. Camden, N.J., July 17, 1920; s. William Albert and Ruby Marie (Barrus) S.; m. Janette Elizabeth Christie, May 17, 1941; children: R. Newell Jr., Linda Jennison, Alan John. B.A., Mankato State U., 1960. Prodn. coordinator Johnson & Johnson, New Brunswick, N.J., 1940-47; farmer Waseca, Minn., 1947—; spl. agt. John Hancock Mut. Ins. Co., Waseca, Minn., 1961-84; mem. Minn. Ho. of Reps., St. Paul, 1957-80, speaker, 1979—. Author: Minnesota Standoff—The Politics of Deadlock, 1990. Lay reader St. John's Episcopal Ch., 1952—; chmn. Upper Mississippi River Basin Commn., 1981-82; pres. Minn. State U. Bd., 1981-92; chmn. Minn. Higher Edn. Bd., 1991-92; bd. dirs. Minn. Wellsprings, 1984-90; emeritus mem. adv. bd. Hubert H. Humphrey Inst.; emeritus mem. coun. Minn. Hist. Soc.; bd. dirs. Minn. Agrl. Interpretive Ctr., 1983—. Named Minn. State Tree Farmer of Yr., 1978. Mem. Am. Tree Farm System, Nat. Conf. State Legislators, Minn. Forestry Assn. (bd. dirs. 1991—), Masons, Rotary (pres. club 1968). Republican.

SEARLE, RONALD, artist; b. Cambridge, Eng., Mar. 3, 1920; s. William James and Nellie (Hunt) S.; m. Monica Koenig, 1967. Ed., Cambridge Sch. Art. Author: pub. in U.S. The Female Approach, 1954, Merry England, 1957; (with Kaye Webb) Paris Sketchbook, 1958, The St. Trinian's Story, 1959, Refugees, 1960, (with Alex Atkinson) The Big City, 1958, U.S.A. for Beginners, 1959, Russia for Beginners, 1960, Escape from the Amazon, 1964, Which Way Did He Go?, 1962, From Frozen North to Filthy Lucre, 1964, Those Magnificent Men in Their Flying Machines, 1965, (with Heinz Huber) Haven't We Met Before Somewhere?, 1966, Searle's Cats, 1968, The Square Egg, 1969, Hello: Where Did All the People Go?, 1970, (with Kildare Dobbs) The Great Fur Opera, 1970, The Addict, 1971, More Cats, 1975, Zoodiac, 1978, Ronald Searle Album, 1979, The Situation is Hopeless, 1981, The Big Fat Cat Book, 1982, Winespeak, 1983, Ronald Searle in Perspective, 1985, To the Kwai-- and Back, 1986, Something in the Cellar, 1988, Ah Yes, I Remember It Well: Paris 1961-75, 1988, Ronald Searle's Non-Sexist Dictionary, 1989, Slightly Foxed- But Still Desirable, 1989, The Curse of St. Trinian's, 1993, Marquis de Sade Meets Goody Two-Shoes, 1994; contbr. to New Yorker; 1st pub. work appeared in Cambridge Daily News, 1935-39; subject of Ronald Searle: a biography by Russell Davies, 1992; one-man shows include Leicester Galleries, London, 1948, 50, 54, 57, Kraushaar Gallery, N.Y.C., 1959, Blanchini Gallery, N.Y.C., 1963, city mus. Bremen, Hannover, Dusseldorf, Stuttgart, Berlin, 1965, 3d Biennale, Tolentino, Italy, 1965, Galerie Pro Arte, Delmenhorst, Germany, Mus. Art, Bremerhaven, Germany, Galerie Münsterberg, Basle, Switzerland, Galerie Pribaut, Amsterdam, Holland, Wolfgang-Gurlitt Mus., Linz, Austria, Galerie La Pochade, Paris, 1966-71, Art Alliance Gallery, Phila., 1967, Galerie Gurlitt, Munich, 1967-76, Grosvenor Gallery, London, 1968, Galerie Obere Zaune, Zurich, 1968, Galerie Hauswedell, Baden-Baden, 1968, Galerie Brumme, Frankfurt, 1969, Konsthallen, Södertälje, Sweden, 1969, Rizzoli Gallery, N.Y.C., 1969-81, Kunsthalle, Konstanz, 1970, Würzburg, 1970, Galerie Welz, Salzburg, 1971, Galerie Rivolta, Lausanne, 1972, Galerie Gaëton, Geneva, 1972, Bibliothèque Nationale, Paris, 1973, Galerie Würthle, Vienna, 1973, Kulterhaus Graz, Austria, 1973, 79, Galerie Rivolta, Lausanne, 1974, 78, Galerie l'Angle Aigu, Brussels, 1974, 77, Galerie Carmen Casse, Paris, 1975-77, Staatliche Museen Preussicher Kulturbesitz, Berlin, 1976, Galerie Bartsch and Chariau, Munich, 1981, Neue Galerie Wien, Vienna, 1985, 1988, Imperial War Mus., London, 1986, British Mus., London, 1986, Fitzwilliam Mus., Cambridge, 1987, Fine Arts Mus., San Francisco, 1987, Heineman Galleries, N.Y., 1994, Wilhelm Busch Mus., Hannover, 1996, Stadtmus., Munich, 1996, others; contbr. to nat. publs., 1946—; theatre artist: Punch, 1949-61; created series of cartoons on fictitious girls sch., 1941, which became a film series called Belles of St. Trinian's, 1954, Blue Murder at St. Trinian's, 1957, The Pure Hell of St. Trinian's, 1960, The Great St. Trinian's Train Robbery, 1965, Wildcats of St. Trinian's, 1980; films designs include John Gilpin (Brit. Film Inst.), 1951, On the Twelfth Day, 1954 (nominated Acad. award), Energetically Yours, 1957, The Kings Breakfast, 1963, Those Magnificent Men in Their Flying Machines, 1965, Monte Carlo or Bust, 1969, Scrooge, 1970, Dick Deadeye, or Duty Done, 1975. Recipient medal Art Dirs. Club Los Angeles, 1959, medal Art Dirs. Mem. Club Phila., Pa., 1959, gold medal 3d Biennale, Tolentino, Italy, 1965, Prix de la Critique Belge, 1968, medaille de la ville d'Avignon, 1971, Prix de l' Humour S.P.H. Festival d' Avignon, 1971, Prix de l' Humour Noir Grandville France, 1971, Prix Internationale Charles Huard France, 1972, Best Advt. Illustration award Nat. Cartoonists Soc., 1988. Club: The Garrick (London). Home: care Tessa Sayle, 11 Jubilee Pl, London SW 3-3TE England Office: care Eileen McMahon Agy PO Box 1062 Bayonne NJ 07002

SEARLES, ANNA MAE HOWARD, educator, civic worker; b. Osage Nation Indian Terr., Okla., Nov. 22, 1906; d. Frank David and Clara (Bowman) Howard; A.A., Odessa (Tex.) Coll., 1961; BA, U. Ark., 1964; M.Ed., 1970; postgrad. (Herman L. Donovan fellow), U. Ky., 1972—; m. Isaac Adams Searles, May 26, 1933; 1 dau., Mary Ann Rogers (Mrs. Herman Lloyd Hoppe). Compiler news, broadcaster sta. KJBC, 1950-60; corr. Tulsa Daily World, 1961-64; tchr. Rogers (Ark.) H.S., 1964-72; tchr. adult class rapid reading, 1965, 80; tchr. adult edn. Learning Center Benton County (Ark.), Bentonville, 1973-77, supr. adult edn., 1977-79; tchr. North Ark. C.C., Rogers, 1979-90, CETA, Bentonville, 1979-82; tchr. Joint Tng. Partnership Act, 1984-85; coordinator adult edn. Rogers C. of C. and Rogers Sch. System, 1984—. Sec. Tulsa Safety Council, 1935-37; leader, bd. dirs. Girl Scouts U.S.A., Kilgore, Tex., 1941-44, leader, Midland, Tex., 1944-52, counselor, 1950-61; exec. sec. Midland Community Chest, 1955-60; gray lady Midland A.R.C., 1958-59; organizer Midland YMCA, Salvation Army; dir. women's div. Savings Bond Program, Midland; mem. citizens com. Rogers Hough Meml. Library, women's aux. Rogers Meml. Hosp.; vol. tutor Laubach literacy orgn., 1973—; tutor Laubach Lit. Orgn., 1973-96; sec. Beaver Lake Literacy Council, Rogers, 1973-83, Little Flock Planning Commn., 1975-77, Benton County Hist. Soc., 1981—; pub. relations chmn. South Central region Nat. Affiliation for Literacy Advance, 1977-79; bd. dirs. Globe Theatre, Odessa, Tex., Midland Community Theatre, Tri-County Foster Home, Guadalupe, Midland youth centers, DeZavala Day Nursery, PTA, Adult Devel. Center, Rogers CETA, 1979-81; vol. recorder Ark. Hist. Preservation Program, 1984—; docent Rogers Hist. Mus., 1988—, vol. tutor; with Ptnrs. in Edn., 1995-96. Recipient 21 yr. pendant Benton Hist. Soc., Nice People award Rogers C. of C., 1987, Thanks badge Midland Girl Scout Assn., 1948, Appreciation Plaque award Ark. Natural Heritage Commn., 1988; Cert. of recognition, Rogers Pub. Schs., 1986, Cert. of Recognition, Beaver Lake Literacy Coun., 1993; Instr. of Yr. award North Ark. Community Coll. West Campus, Conservation award Woodmen of the World Life Ins. Soc., 1991, Vol. of Yr. award Rogers Hist. Mus., 1993, 95. Mem. NEA (del. conv. 1965), Ark. Assn. Public Continuing and Adult Edn. (pres. 1979-80), South Central Assn. for Lifelong Learning (sec. 1980-84), PTA (life), Future Homemakers Am. (life; sec. 1980—), Benton County Hist. Soc. (life, pub. rels. chmn. 1990-96, recording sec. 1990-96), Delta Kappa Gamma (Disting. Acheivement award Beta Pi chpt. 1992). Episcopalian. Clubs: Altrusa (pres. 1979—), Apple Spur Community (Rogers), Garden Club Rogers (publicity chmn. 1994-95, garden therapy 1994-96). Home: 2808 N Dixieland PO Box 03319400 Rogers AR 72756

SEARLES, DEWITT RICHARD, retired investment firm executive, retired air force officer; b. Birmingham, Ala., Aug. 7, 1920; s. DeWitt Richard and Miriam (Hostetler) S.; m. Barbara Elizabeth Brown, Jan. 28, 1949; children: Ann Hampton, DeWitt Richard III, Elizabeth Alison. Student, Coll. William and Mary, 1939-41; B.A., U. Md., 1949; M.A., George Washington U., 1964; grad., Army Command and Gen. Staff Sch., Ft. Leavenworth, Kans., 1945, USAF Command and Gen. Staff Coll., Maxwell AFB, Ala., 1956, Nat. War Coll., Washington, 1964. Commd. 2d lt. USAAF, 1942; advanced through grades to maj. gen. USAF, 1971; fighter pilot and squadron comdr. New Guinea and Philippines, 1943-45; wing comdr. 81st Tactical Fighter Wing, Eng., 1965-67; insp. gen. Tactical Air Command, Langley AFB, Va., 1967-69; comdr. 327th Air Div., Taiwan, Republic of China, 1969-71; dep. comdr. 7/13 Air Force, Udorn AFB, Thailand, 1971-72; dep. insp. gen. Hdqrs. USAF, Washington, 1972-74, ret.; asst. v.p. Merrill Lynch, Pierce, Fenner & Smith, Washington, 1974-87, ret., 1987. Decorated D.S.M. with 2 oak leaf clusters, Legion of Merit with oak leaf cluster, D.F.C., Air medal with 7 oak leaf clusters. Home: 1605 Dunterry Pl Mc Lean VA 22101-4318

SEARLES, RICHARD BROWNLEE, botany educator, marine biology researcher; b. Riverside, Calif., June 19, 1936; s. Nathan Francis and Margaret Louise (Ashbrook) S.; m. Georgiana Elizabeth Miller, June 11, 1957; children: Timothy Edward, Andrew Nathan, Elizabeth Louise. AB, Pomona Coll., Claremont, Calif., 1958; PhD, U. Calif., Berkeley, 1965. Asst. prof. botany Duke U., Durham, N.C., 1965-69, assoc. prof., 1969-83, prof., 1983—, chmn. dept., 1991-97. Co-author: Seaweeds of the Southeastern U.S., 1991. Served to 2d lt. U.S. Army, 1961-63, capt. Res. ret. Mem. Internat. Phycol. Soc., Phycol. Soc. Am. (Gerald W. Prescott award, 1993), Brit. Phycol. Soc., Oceanographic Soc. Am., Phi Beta Kappa, Sigma Xi. Unitarian. Home: 1800 Woodburn Rd Durham NC 27705-5725 Office: Duke Univ Dept Botany Durham NC 27706-0338

SEARLS, EILEEN HAUGHEY, lawyer, librarian, educator; b. Madison, Wis., Apr. 27, 1925; d. Edward M. and Anna Mary (Haughey) S.; BA, U. Wis., 1948, JD, 1950, MS in LS, 1951. Bar: Wis. 1950. Cataloger Yale U., 1951-52; instr. law St. Louis U., 1952-53, asst. prof., 1953-56, assoc. prof., 1956-64, prof., 1964—, law librarian, 1952—; chmn. Coun. Law Libr. Consortia, 1984-90; sec. Bd. of Conciliaton and Arbitration, Archdiocese of St. Louis, 1986—. Named Woman of Yr., Women's Commn., St. Louis U., 1986—. Mem. ABA, ALA, Wis. Bar Assn., Bar Assn. Met. St. Louis, Am. Assn. Law Librs., Mid-Am. Assn. Law Librs. (pres. 1984-86), Mid Am. Law Sch. Libr. Consortium (chmn. 1980-84), Southwestern Assn. Law Librs., Altrusa Club. Office: 3700 Lindell Blvd Saint Louis MO 63108-3412

SEARS, ALAN EDWARD, lawyer; b. Chattanooga, Oct. 31, 1951; s. Edward Lee and Anna Maria (Shepperd) S.; m. Paula Scott Lebeau, Nov. 11, 1988; children: Kelley, Shelby, Anna Marie, Rebecca, Isaiah, Isabella. BA, U. Ky., 1974; JD, U. Louisville, 1977. Bar: Ky. 1977, U.S. Supreme Ct. 1980, Ariz. 1987, D.C. 1989, Calif. 1990, U.S. Dist. Ct. (we. and ea. dists.) Ky., U.S. Dist. Ct. Ariz., U.S. Dist. Ct. D.C., U.S. Ct. Appeals (D.C., 4th, 5th, 6th, 7th, 9th, 11th and D.C. cirs.), U.S. Tax Ct., U.S. Dist. Ct. (ctrl. & so. dists.) Calif. Asst. corp. counsel City of Ashland, Ky., 1977-78; assoc. Johnson, Dunnagan & Martin, Ashland, 1977-79, Amshoff & Amshoff, Louisville, 1979-81; chief criminal div., asst. U.S. atty. U.S. Dept. Justice, Louisville, 1981-85; exec. dir. atty. gens. commn. on pornography U.S. Dept. Justice, Washington, 1985-86; assoc. solicitor U.S. Dept. Interior, Washington, 1986-87; exec. dir. Children's Legal Found., Phoenix, 1987-90; assoc. Snell & Wilmer, Phoenix, 1990; exec. dir., gen. counsel Nat. Family Legal Found., Phoenix, 1990-91; asst. U.S. atty. U.S. Dept. Justice, 1991-93; pres., gen. counsel Alliance Def. Fund, 1993—; cons. and pub. speaker to numerous organizations. Co-author: Time, Place & Manner Regulation, 1989, Prosecution & Trial of Obscenity Case, 1988; contbr. chpts. to books. Bd. dirs. Ariz. Family Rsch. Inst. Phoenix, 1988-92, Lincoln Caucus Ednl. Corp., Phoenix, 1990—, Nat. Family Legal Found., Phoenix, 1991—; precinct capt. Rep. Party, 1979-81, legis. dist. chmn., 1980-81; mem. campaign staff Gov. Louie Nunn, 1979, and Senator Cook for U.S. Senate, 1974, other party activities. Mem. ABA, Ariz. Lawyers Div. Federalist Soc. (dir. 1988—), Calif. Bar Assn., Ariz. Bar Assn., Ky. Bar Assn., D.C. Bar Assn. Office: Alliance Def Fund 7819 E Greenway Rd Ste 8 Scottsdale AZ 85260-1719

SEARS, BRADFORD GEORGE, landscape architect; b. Philmont, N.Y., June 21, 1915; s. Russell Lockwood and Alla (Scutt) S.; m. Ruth Ellen Fox, July 5, 1936; children—Bradford Alan, Brian Scutt, Patricia Ruth. B.S., N.Y. State Coll. Forestry, 1939, M.S., 1948. With State U. N.Y., Syracuse, 1941-76; prof. landscape architecture State U. N.Y., 1950-76, dean landscape architecture, 1968-76, dean emeritus, 1976—; pvt. practice landscape architecture, 1945—; vis. lectr. Sch. Design, N.C. State U., 1978-83; mem. bd. landscape architecture N.Y. State Dept. Edn., 1967-79. Contbr. articles to profl. jours. and manuals. Fellow Am. Soc. Landscape Architects; mem. (past pres. N.Y. Upstate chpt., past chmn. nat. accreditation bd. for profl. programs), Am. Camping Assn. Methodist. Address: 116 Wellwood Dr Fayetteville NY 13066-2353

SEARS, CURTIS THORNTON, JR., educational administrator; b. Wareham, Mass., Aug. 3, 1938; s. Curtis Thornton Sr. and Ruth (Blake) S.; m. Martha Wilda Colvin, July 5, 1960 (div. May 1977); children: Amy Elizabeth, Leslie Edward; m. Ronnie Spilton, Mar. 23, 1980. AB, W.Va. Wesleyan U., 1961; PhD, U. N.C., 1966. NATO postdoctoral fellow Bristol (Eng.) U., 1966-67; asst. prof. chemistry U. S.C., Columbia, 1967-71; from asst. to assoc. prof. Ga. State U., Atlanta, 1977, assoc. chmn. chemistry dept., 1986-91, assoc. v.p. rsch. and info. tech., 1993-94; reviewer NSF, Washington, 1975—, vis. scientist, 1991-92, 94. Author: Inquiries in Chemistry, 1977, Chemistry for the Health Sciences, 1976, 2d edit., 1982, Aspects of Chemistry, 1979. NATO fellow NSF, 1966; Recipient Teaching award Nat. Sci. Tchrs. Assn., 1973, Arts and Scis. Teaching award Ga. State U., 1977. Mem. Am. Chem. Soc., Royal Soc. Chemistry, Exams. Inst. of Am. Chem. Soc. (chair commn. 1986-91). Methodist. Avocations: cooking, gardening. Office: Ga State U Atlanta GA 30303

SEARS, DONNA MAE, technical writer and illustrator; b. St. Paul, Oct. 23, 1951; d. Raymond and Shirley Marie (Dupre) Waldoch; m. Mark D. Sears, Sept. 4, 1993. BA in Art and Edn., Cardinal Stritch Coll., Milw.,

1969-73; postgrad., Rock Valley Coll., Rockford, Ill., 1985, 87, 89-90, So. Ill. U., 1983; cert. of tng., Computervision Tech. Ctr., Itasca, Ill., 1986, 88. Electronic assembler Warner Electric Co., Marengo, Ill., 1973-75, machine hand, 1976-78, quality assurance lead insp., 1978-80, draftswoman, 1980-86, CAD-sr. draftswoman, 1986-87; tchr. art Stephen Mack Sch. Dist., Rockford, 1975, Harrison Sch. Dist., Wonder Lake, Ill., 1975-76; CAD specialist Greenlee Textron Inc., Rockford, 1988-89, resigned, 1989; asst. buyer Ingersoll Milling, Rockford, 1989-90; asst. office mgr. and sign maker Shake-A-Leg Signs, Rockford, 1990-92; tech. writer and illustrator Mathews Co., Crystal Lake, Ill., 1992; tech. writer and CAD support Clinton Electronics, Loves Park, Ill., 1993—. Author: (with others) Treasured Poems of America, 1990, Poetic Voices of America, spring 1992, Anthology of American Poetry, fall 1991 (awards of Poetic Excellence 1992), Distinguished Poets of America, spring 1993, The Sound of Poetry, spring 1993. Vol. Boone County Conservation Dist., 1990-92; mem. choir St. James Ch., Belvidere, Ill., 1985-93; assoc. mem. Spl. Olympics. Recipient Leadership award YWCA, Rockford, 1988. Mem. Internat. Soc. Poets, Exptl. Aircraft Assn., Nat. Right to Life Assn., Macktown Restoration Found. Roman Catholic. Avocations: bicycling, art, gardening, fishing.

SEARS, EDWARD L., English language educator; b. Pratt, Kans., Jan. 27, 1954; s. Melvin Leroy and Deloris Fay (Owens) S. BA in English, West Tex. State U., 1990; MA in English, Tex. Tech. U., 1993. Firefighter Dodge City (Kans.) Fire Dept., 1981-83, Amarillo (Tex.) Fire Dept., 1983-86; tutor Writing Ctr. West Tex. State U., Canyon, 1987-90; tutor Writing Ctr. Tex. Tech. U., Lubbock, 1990-92, tchg. asst., 1990-92; writing lab. super. South Plains Coll., Levelland, Tex., 1992—, asst. prof. English, 1993—; coord. computer-assisted writing South Plains Coll., Levelland, 1995—, mem. technology task force, 1994-95, mem. non-faculty recognition process action team, 1996-97. Ssgt. USAF, 1977-81. Democrat. Office: South Plains Coll 1401 College Ave Levelland TX 79336-6503

SEARS, EDWARD MILNER, JR., newspaper editor; b. Bluefield, W.Va., Dec. 28, 1944; s. Edward Milner and Helene (Stras) S.; m. Jo Ann Langworthy, May 15, 1971; 1 child, Helene Mateer. B.S. in Journalism, U. Fla., 1967. Makeup editor Atlanta Constn., 1970, news editor, 1971-73, feature editor, 1974, city editor, 1975-76, asst. mng. editor, 1977, mng. editor, 1978-80; mng. editor Atlanta Jour., 1980-82, Atlanta Jour. and Atlanta Constn., 1982-85; editor Palm Beach Post, 1985—. Served with U.S. Army, 1968-69. Mem. Fla. Soc. Newspaper Editors, Am. Soc. Newspaper Editors, Sigma Delta Chi. Home: 230 Dyer Rd West Palm Beach FL 33405-1218 Office: Palm Beach Post 2751 S Dixie Hwy West Palm Beach FL 33405-1233

SEARS, GEORGE AMES, lawyer; b. Chehalis, Wash., Oct. 17, 1926; s. Briton Wallis and Merle (Kelso) S.; m. Mary Ann Deggeller, May 5, 1951; children: Kathrin Elizabeth, Geoffrey John. BA, Yale U., 1949; JD, Stanford U., 1952. Bar: Calif. 1952. Assoc. Pillsbury, Madison and Sutro, San Francisco, 1952-58, ptnr., 1959—, chmn. firm, 1984-89. Bd. dirs. Bay Area Coun., San Francisco, 1984-89, Invest-in-Am. No. Calif. Coun., San Francisco, 1988-90, Marin Conservation League, 1992—, Buck Ctr. for Rsch. in Aging, 1996—; trustee Marin Country Day Sch., Corte Madera, Calif., 1961-65; mem. exec. com. bd. visitors Stanford (Calif.) U. Law Sch., 1982-86; mem. bd. visitors Brigham Young U. Law Sch., Provo, Utah, 1986-88; pres. Stanford U. Law Fund, 1985-86; pres. Legal Aid Soc., San Francisco, 1969-70; mem. Coun. Friends of Bancroft Libr., 1993—. With USN, 1945-46. Fellow Am. Coll. Trial Lawyers, Am. Bar Found.; mem. ABA, Calif. Bar Assn. (chmn. adminstrn. of justice com. 1973-74), San Francisco Bar Assn., Pacific-Union Club, Belvedere Tennis Club. Avocations: reading, music, hiking, tennis. Home: 161 Harrison Ave Sausalito CA 94965-2043 Office: Pillsbury Madison & Sutro 225 Bush St San Francisco CA 94104-4207

SEARS, JOHN PATRICK, lawyer; b. Syracuse, N.Y., July 3, 1940; s. James Louis and Helen Mary (Fitzgerald) S.; m. Carol Jean Osborne, Aug. 25, 1962; children: James Louis, Ellen Margaret, Amy Elizabeth. B.S., Notre Dame U., 1960; LL.B., J.D., Georgetown U., 1963. Bar: N.Y. bar 1963. Clk. N.Y. Ct. Appeals, 1963-65; asso. firm Nixon, Mudge, Rose, Guthrie, Alexander & Mitchell, 1965-66; mem. staff Richard M. Nixon, 1966-69; dep. counsel to Pres. Nixon, 1969-70; ptnr. Gadsby & Hannah, Washington, 1970-75, Baskin & Sears, Washington, 1977-84; pvt. practice Washington, 1984—; mgr. Ronald Regan's Presdl. Campaign, 1975-76, 79-80; polit. analyst NBC Today Show, 1984-89; mem. Wall Street Jour. bd. of polit. experts, 1984—; columnist LA Times, Newsday, 1992—. Sr. advisor Jack Kemp for V.P. Campaign, 1996. Fellow Kennedy Inst. Politics, Harvard, 1970. Home: 2801 New Mexico Ave NW Washington DC 20007-3921 Office: 2021 K St NW Washington DC 20006-1003

SEARS, MARVIN, ophthalmologist, educator; b. N.Y.C., Sept. 16, 1928; s. Louis and Blanche Sears; children: Anne, David, Jonathan, Edward, Benjamin. AB, Princeton U., 1949; MD, Columbia U., 1953. Intern Bellevue Hosp., N.Y.C., 1954; resident in ophthalmology Johns Hopkins Hosp., 1954-61; fellow NIH, 1959-60; chmn. sect. ophthalmology Yale-New Haven (Conn.) Hosp., 1961-71; asst. prof. dept. ophthalmology and visual sci. Yale U. Sch. Medicine, 1961-64, assoc. prof., 1964-69, prof., 1969—, chmn., 1971-93; cons. Vets. Meml. Med. Ctr., Meriden, Conn., 1986—, Princess Margaret Hosp., Nassau, 1982—, Waterbury (Conn.) Hosp., 1975—, William W. Backus Hosp., Norwich, Conn., 1974—, Hosp. Albert Schweitzer, Des Chapelles, Haiti, 1968-83, Jenkins (Ky.) Clinic Hosp., 1968, Hosp. St. Raphael, New Haven, New Britain (Conn.) Gen. Hosp.; chief cons. VA Med. Ctr., West Haven, Conn., 1961—; instr. Johns Hopkins Hosp., 1959-61; vis. prof. dept. ophthalmology U. Puerto Rico; mem. numerous adv. coms. Editorial bd.: Am. Jour. Ophthalmology, 1967-82, Investigative Ophthalmology, 1968-78, Jour. Ocular Pharmacology, 1985—; contbr. articles to profl. jours. Recipient McKosh prize/Epistemology, Princeton U., 1949, Schwentker medal Johns Hopkins Hosp., 1958, Alcon Rsch. Inst. award, 1985, Method to Extend Rsch. in Time award Nat. Eye Inst., 1990—; named Gifford lectr. Chgo. Ophthal. Soc., 1985; endowed professorship established in Sears' name Yale U., 1993. Fellow ACS, Pierson Coll. Yale U.; mem. Am. Acad. Ophthalmology, Am. Ophthal. Soc., Assn. for Rsch. in Vision and Ophthalmology (Jonas S. Friedenwald award 1977), Assn. Univ. Profs. Ophthalmology, Conn. State Med. Soc., Internat. Agy. for Prevention Blindness, Internat. Soc. for Eye Rsch., New England Ophthal. Soc. (award 1969), Pan Am. Assn. Ophthalmology, Soc. Eye Surgeons, Wilmer Residents Assn., Appalachian Mountain Club, Audubon Soc., Lions (Melvin Jones fellow). Jewish. Avocation: mountaineering. Office: Yale Eye Ctr PO Box 208061 330 Cedar St New Haven CT 06520-8061

SEARS, MARY HELEN, lawyer; b. Syracuse, N.Y.; d. James Louis and Helen Mary (Fitzgerald) Sears. AB, Cornell U., 1950; JD with honors, George Washington U., 1960. Bar: Va. 1960, D.C. 1961, U.S. Supreme Ct. 1963. Chemist Allied Chem. and Dye Corp., Syracuse, 1950-52, Hercules Powder Co., Wilmington, Del., 1952-55; patent examiner U.S. Patent Office, Washington, 1955-60; pvt. practice Washington, 1960-61; assoc. Irons, Birch, Swindler & McKie, Washington, 1961-69; mem. firm Irons and Sears, Washington, 1969-84; chmn. trade regulation practice dept. Memel, Jacobs, Pierno, Gersh & Ellsworth, Washington, 1984-87; ptnr., chmn. intellectual property and unfair competition practice dept. Ginsburg, Feldman & Bress, Washington, 1987-91; ptnr., chmn. intellectual property and telecomm. practice group Reid & Priest, Washington, 1991-94; founder, chmn. M. H. Sears Law Firm, 1994—; mem. adv. bd. Boardroom Reports, Inc., N.Y.C., 1980-85; mem. Cornell U. Coun., 1981-87, 89-93, life mem., 1995—, mem. adminstrv. bd., 1984-86. Contbr. articles to various publs. Recipient Outstanding Performance award U.S. Dept. Commerce, 1957. Mem. ABA (co-chmn. appellate practice com., litigation sect. 1989-92), Am. Intellectual Property Law Assn., Am. Chem. Soc., Am. Soc. Internat. Law, Licensing Execs. Soc., Internat. Trademark Assn., Va. State Bar Assn., D.C. Bar Assn., George Washington U. Law Alumnae Assn. (bd. dirs. 1995—), Order of Coif, Phi Alpha Delta. Republican. Office: M H Sears Law Firm Chartered 2300 N St NW Washington DC 20037-1122

SEARS, ROBERT LOUIS, industrial engineer; b. Oakland, Calif., Jan. 28, 1927; s. Louis Francis and Lucille (Hargreaves) S.; m. Phyllis Ann Barnes, Apr. 30, 1955; children: Stephen A., Jeffrey R., Garth E. BS, U.S. Mil. Acad., 1952; MS in Indsl. Engring., Ariz. State U., 1968. Registered profl. engr., Ariz. Commd. 2d lt. U.S. Army, 1952, advanced through grades to col., 1972, ret. 1973; supt. emergency med. services State of Ariz., 1973-75; gen. mgr. Behavior Modification Clinic, Inc., Phoenix, 1975-78; pres., dir. Indsl. Systems Assocs., Phoenix, 1978-80; assoc. dir. Ariz. Solar Energy Commn., Phoenix, 1980-87; program dir. Cogeneration Research Ctr. for Energy Systems Research Coll. Engring. and Applied Scis. Ariz. State U., Tempe, 1987-89, assoc. dir. program devel., adj. prof., 1990-97, prof. emeritus, 1997—; pres. Robert Sears and Assocs., 1985—. Decorated Legion of Merit (2). Mem. Nat. Soc. Profl. Engrs., Am. Inst. Indsl. Engrs. (sr.), Assn. Energy Engrs. (cert., pres. Ariz. chpt. 1986-87, bd. dirs., 1987-95), Am. Solar Energy Soc., Am. Cogeneration Assn. (dir. 1990-94), Am. Cogeneration Assn., Ariz. Cogeneration Assn. (pres. 1988-90). Republican. Episcopalian. Club: Triathlon Fedn./USA, U.S. Masters Swimming. Contbr. articles to profl. jours.

SEARS, ROBERT STEPHEN, finance educator; b. Odessa, Tex., May 27, 1950; s. William Bethel and Leola Vernon (Little) S.; Reva Dana Flournoy, Aug. 17, 1973; children: Matthew Stephen, Elizabeth Rea. AAS, Odessa Jr. Coll., 1970; BA summa cum laude, Tex. Tech. U., 1973, MS, 1976; PhD, U. N.C., 1980. Supr. Bethel Enterprises, Odessa, Tex., 1973-74; tchg. asst. Tex. Tech. U., Lubbock, 1974-76, dir. Inst. Banking and Fin. Studies, 1988-97; tchg. asst. U. N.C., Chapel Hill, 1976-79; asst. prof. U. Ill., Champaign, 1979-85, assoc. prof., 1985-88; rsch. prof. Bur. Econ. and Bus., Champaign, 1984; tchg. asst. Lubbock Bankers Assn., 1990—; chmn. dept. fin. Tex. Tech. U., 1997—; cons. Cameron Brown Mortgage Co., Raleigh, N.C., 1978-80, Howard Savings Bank, Livingston, N.J., 1980; asset mgr., trustee, pvt. investors, 1984—. Author: Investment Management, 1993, (chpt) Modern Real Estate, 1980, 84; assoc. editor Rev. of Bus. Studies, 1989-95, Jour. Fin. Rsch., 1990-96, Internat. Chmn. fin. com. Temple Bapt. Ch., Champaign, Ill., 1982, bd. deacons, 1982-88, chmn. deacons, lay leader, 1983; Sunday sch. tchr. Carrboro (N.C.) Bapt. Ch., 1977-79; bd. deacons Ind. Ave. Bapt. Ch., Lubbock, 1989—, Sunday sch. tchr., 1991-92, master design com., 1993—; trustee All Saints Episcopal Sch., 1995—. Rsch. grantee Cameron Brown Mortgage Co., Raleigh, N.C., 1978-80, U. Ill, Champaign, 1980-84, 86-87, Investors in Bus. Edn., Champaign, 1980-81, 84. Mem. Am. Fin. Assn., Southwestern Fin. Assn. (pres. 1989-90, v.p., program chmn. 1988-89, sec., treas. 1986-88, bd. dirs. 1984-86, mem. program com. 1985-86, 89—), Fin. Mgmt. Assn. (mem. program com. 1986, 89-94, 97), So. Fin. Assn. (mem. program com. 1986), Western Fin. Assn. (mem. program com. 1986), Ea. Fin. Assn., Lake Ridge Country Club. Republican. Baptist. Avocations: golf, walking, participating in sports with my children. Office: Tex Tech U COBA PO Box 4320 Lubbock TX 79409-4320

SEARS, ROLLIN GEORGE, wheat geneticist, small grains researcher; b. Salem, Oreg., Dec. 15, 1950; s. George Lestor and Margret (Mead) S.; m. Donna Jean DeNoma, Sept. 12, 1971; children: Stephanie L., Mark C., Scott N. BS, Montana State U., 1972, MS, 1974; PhD, Oreg. State U., Corvallis, 1979. Asst. prof. N.D. State U., Fargo, 1979-80; asst. prof. Kansas State U., Manhattan, 1980-84, assoc. prof., 1984-89, prof., 1989—; chmn. Nat. Wheat Improvement Com., 1991-97. Vestry Episc. Ch., Manhattan, Kans., 1982-85, sr. warden, 1985-87; pres. Manhattan Marlins, 1986-90. Fellow Am. Soc. Agronomy (bd. rep. 1992-95), Crop Sci. Soc. Am.; mem. Internat. Soc. Plant Molecular Biology, Sigma Xi, Alpha Zeta. Avocations: reading, fishing, golf. Office: Kansas State U Agronomy Dept TH Hall Manhattan KS 66506-5501

SEARS, WILLIAM REES, engineering educator; b. Mpls., Mar. 1, 1913; s. William Everett and Gertrude (Rees) S.; m. Mabel Jeannette Rhodes, Mar. 20, 1936; children—David William, Susan Carol. BS in Aero. Engring, U. Minn., 1934; Ph.D., aeronautics, Calif. Inst. Tech., 1938; DSc (hon.), U. Ariz., 1987. Asst. prof. Calif. Inst. Tech., 1939-41; chief aerodynamics Northrop Aircraft, Inc., 1941-46; dir. Grad. Sch. Aero. Engring., Cornell U., Ithaca, N.Y., 1946-63; dir. Center Applied Math., 1963-67, J.L. Given prof. engring., 1962-74; prof. aerospace and mech. engring. U. Ariz., Tucson, 1974-88, prof. emeritus, 1988—; F. W. Lanchester lectr. Royal Aero. Soc., 1973, Gardner lectr. MIT, 1987, Guggenheim lectr. Internat. Congress Aero. Scis., 1988; cons. aerodynamics. Author: The Airplane and its Components, 1941, Stories from a 20th-Century Life, 1994; editor: Jet Propulsion and High-Speed Aerodynamics, vol. VI, 1954, Jour. Aerospace Scis., 1956-63, Ann. Revs. of Fluid Mechanics, Vol. I. Recipient Vincent Bendix award Am. Soc. Engring. Edn., 1965, Prandtl Ring Deutsche Gesellschaft für Luft- und Raumfahrt, 1974, Von Karman medal AGARD (NATO), 1977, ASME medal, 1989, NAS Award in Aeronautical Engrng Nat. Acad of Sciences, 1995, Daniel Guggenheim medal, 1996; named to Ariz. Aviation Hall of Fame, 1996. Fellow AIAA (hon., G. Edward Pendray award 1975, S.A. Reed Aeros. award 1981, Von Karman lectr. 1968); mem. Nat. Acad. Engring. Mex. (fgn.), Am. Phys. Soc. (Fluid Dynamics prize 1992), NAS (award in aero. engring. 1995), Sigma Xi. Home: Santa Catalina Villas 8202 7500 N Calle Sin Envidia Tucson AZ 85718

SEASE, GENE ELWOOD, public relations company executive; b. Portage, Pa., June 28, 1931; s. Grover Chauncey and Clara Mae (Over) S.; m. Joanne D. Cherry, July 20, 1952; children: David Gene, Daniel Elwood, Cheryl Joanne. A.B., Juniata Coll., 1952; B.D., Pitts. Theol. Sem., 1956, Th.M., 1959; Ph.D., U. Pitts., 1965, M.Ed., 1958; LL.D., U. Evansville, 1972, Butler U., 1972; Litt.D., Ind. State U., 1974; DD, U. Indpls., 1989. Ordained to ministry United Methodist Ch., 1956; pastor Grace United Meth. Ch., Wilkinsburg, Pitts., 1952-63; conf. dir., supt. Western Pa. Conf. United Meth. Ch., Pitts., 1963-68; lectr. grad. faculty U. Pitts., 1965-68; mem. staff U. Indpls., 1968-89, asst. to pres., 1968-69, pres., 1970-88, chancellor, 1988-89, pres. emeritus, 1989—; chmn. Sease, Gerig & Assocs., Indpls., 1989—; bd. dirs. Indpls. Life Ins. Co., Nat. City Bank of Ind., Bankers Life Ins. Co. of N.Y., Ctrl. Newspapers Fedn. Author: Christian Word Book, 1968; also numerous articles. Pres. Greater Indpls. Progress Com., 1972-75; pres. Marion County Sheriff's Merit Bd.; mem. Ind. Scholarship Commn.; cons. Am. Cablevision Indpls.; bd. dirs. Indpls. Conv. Bur., Ind. Law Enforcement Tng. Acad., 500 Festival, Crossroads coun. Boy Scouts Am., Community Hosp. Indpls., St. Francis Hosp. Mem. Internat. Platform Assn., English Speaking Union, Japan-Am. Soc. Ind., Ind. C. of C. (bd. dirs.), Indpls. C. of C. (bd. dirs.), Ind. Schoolmen's Club, Econ. Club of Indpls. (bd. dirs.), Phi Delta Kappa, Alpha Phi Omega, Alpha Psi Omega. Clubs: Mason (Indpls.) (33 deg., Shriner), Kiwanian. (Indpls.), Columbia (Indpls.).

SEASE, JOHN W(ILLIAM), chemistry educator; b. New Brunswick, N.J., Nov. 10, 1920; s. Virgil Bernard and Rosalyn (Summer) S.; m. Mary Lieurance, June 5, 1943; children—Margaret, Catherine, Ann, John Lieurance. A.B., Princeton U., 1941; Ph.D., Calif. Inst. Tech., 1946. Research asst. Nat. Def. Research Com., Calif. Inst. Tech., Pasadena, 1942-45; instr. chemistry Wesleyan U., Middletown, Conn., 1946-48, asst. prof. chemistry, 1948-52, assoc. prof. chemistry, 1952-58, prof. chemistry, 1958-82, E.B. Nye prof. chemistry, 1982-88, prof. emeritus, 1988—. Mem. Portland Sch. Bd., Conn., 1959-65. Mem. AAAS, Am. Chem. Soc. (councilor, sec., chmn. Conn. Valley sect.), Phi Beta Kappa, Sigma Xi. Office: Wesleyan U Dept Chemistry Middletown CT 06459

SEASHORE, MARGRETTA REED, physician; b. Red Bank, N.J., June 20, 1939; d. Robert Clark Reed and Lillie Ann (Heaviland) R.; m. John Seashore, Dec. 26, 1964; children: Robert H., Carl J., Carolyn L. BA, Swarthmore Coll., 1961; MD, Yale U., 1965. Diplomate Am. Bd. Pediatrics, Am. Bd. Med. Genetics, Nat. Bd. Med. Examiners. Intern in pediatrics Yale U. Sch. Medicine, Haven, Conn., 1965-66, asst. resident in pediatrics, 1966-68; postdoctoral fellow in genetics and metabolism, depts. of pediatrics and medicine Yale U. Sch. Medicine, 1968-70; clin. asst. prof. pediatrics U. Fla. Coll. Medicine, Gainesville, 1970-71; attending physician Hope Haven Children's Hosp., Jacksonville, Fla., 1970-73; asst. prof. pediatrics Duval Med. Ctr., Jacksonville, Fla., 1970-71; attending physician Duvall Med. Ctr. U. Hosp. Jacksonville, 1970-73; asst. prof. pediatrics U. Fla. Coll. Medicine, 1971-73; attending physician Shands Teaching Hosp., Gainesville, Fla., 1971-73; asst. clin. prof. human genetics and pediatrics Yale U. Sch. Medicine, 1974-78; attending physician Yale-New Haven Hosp., 1974—; cons. physician Bridgeport (Conn.) Hosp., 1974—; attending physician Danbury (Conn.) Hosp., 1977—; dir. Genetic Consultation Svc. Yale-New Haven Hosp., 1977-86; from asst. prof. to assoc. prof. human genetics and pediatrics Yale U. Sch. Medicine, 1978-90; cons. physician Lawrence and Meml. Hosp., New London, Conn., 1979—, Norwalk (Conn.) Hosp., 1981—; dir. Genetic Consultation Svc. Yale-New Haven Hosp., 1989—; prof. genetics and pediatrics Yale U. Sch. Medicine, 1990—. Contbr. chpts. to books. Fellow Am. Acad. Pediatrics (chair com. on genetics 1990-94, mem. screening com. Conn. chpt. 1977—, mem. genetics com. 1989—), Am. Coll. Med. Genetics (founder, mem. screeing subcom. 1993—); mem. AMA, AAAS, Am. Soc. Human Genetics (mem. genetic svcs. com. 1986-91), Soc. Inherited Metabolic Disorders (bd. dirs. 1989—, sec. 1991-96, pres.-elect 1996), Soc. for Study of Inborn Errors of Metabolism, New Eng. Genetics Group (co-dir. 1992-95, chmn. outreach com. 1979-89, chmn. screening com. 1989-93, mem. steering com. 1979—). Avocations: music, gardening, sewing, computers. Office: Yale U Sch Med Dept Genetics 333 Cedar St New Haven CT 06510-3206

SEASTRAND, ANDREA H., former congresswoman; b. Chgo., Aug. 5, 1941; m. Eric Seastrand (dec.); children: Kurt, Heidi. BA in Edn., DePaul U., 1963. Prof. religion U. Santa Barbara; mem. Calif. Assembly, 1990-94, U.S. Ho. of Reps., 1995-96; asst. Rep. leader; mem. Rep. caucus; mem. edn. com., agr. com., consumer protection com., new tech. com., govtl. efficiency com., and ways and means com.; mem. rural caucus and select com. on marine resources. Mem. Calif. Fedn. Rep. Women (past pres.). *

SEATON, ALBERTA JONES, biologist, consultant; b. Houston, Dec. 31, 1924; d. Charles Alexander and Elizabeth (Polk) Jones; m. Earle Edward Seaton, Dec. 24, 1947 (dec. Aug. 1992); children: Elizabeth Wamboi, Dudley Charles. BS in Zoology and Chemistry, Howard U., 1946, MS in Zoology, 1947; DSc in Zoology, U. Brussels, 1949. Asst. prof. Spelman Coll., Atlanta, 1953-54; assoc. prof. biology Tex. So. U., Houston, 1954-60, prof. biology, 1960-72, 91-95; adminstr. Ministry Edn., Bermuda, 1973-76; lectr. biology Bermuda Coll., Devonshire, 1976-78; prof. anatomy Sch. Allied Health U. Tex. Health Ctr., Houston, 1979-80; cons. sci. sect. Nat. Inst. Pedagogy Ministry of Edn. Sci., Victoria, Seychelles, 1980-89; head dept. biology Wiley Coll., Marshall, Tex., 1950-51; dir. NSF Summer Sci. Inst. Tex. So. U., 1957-59, gen. studies program, 1970-72, undergrad. and grad. rsch. in biology, 1954-72; mem. Univ. Honors Program Com., Tex. So. U., 1960-70; chair self-study com., Tex. So. U., 1969-71, ednl. policies com., 1968-72; lectr. biology U. Md., USN Air Sta., Bermuda, 1972-78; supr. adminstrn. and budget Office of the Minister Ministry Edn., Bermuda, 1973-76; lectr. in field. Author, editor: Conserving the Environment, Part 1, 1984; editor: Reprints of Agrinews, 1982; co-author, co-editor: Conserving the Environment, Part 2, The Seychelles, 1986, Conserving the Environment, Part 3, Focus on Aldabra, 1991; contbr. articles to profl. jours. Evaluator grant proposals NSF, 1957-72; active regional meetings Com. on Undergrad. Edn. in Biol. Sci., 1967-72, AAC-AAUP confs. on curriculum improvement, 1970-72; chair nurses licensing bd., Hamilton, Bermuda, 1973-75; mem. Endangered Species Com., Hamilton, 1974-77. Postdoctoral fellow Calif. Inst. Tech., Pasadena, 1959-60, NSF postdoctoral fellow Roscoe B. Jackson Lab., Bar Harbor, Maine, 1959, U. Brussels, 1965-66. Mem. AAAS, AAUP (apptd. to ad hoc coms. 1968-71, sec.-treas. Tex. State Conf. 1968-70), AAUW, Am. Assn. Zoologists, Assn. des Anatomistes, Assn. Women in Sci., Tex. Acad. Sci., Beta Kappa Chi, Beta Beta Beta. Episcopalian. Home and Office: 3821 Gertin St Houston TX 77004

SEATON, EDWARD LEE, newspaper editor and publisher; b. Manhattan, Kans., Feb. 5, 1943; s. Richard Melvin and Mary (Holton) S.; m. Karen Mathisen, Sept. 4, 1965; children: Edward Merrill, John David. AB cum laude, Harvard U., 1965; postgrad., U. Cen., Quito, Ecuador, 1965-66, U. Mo., 1966-67. Staff writer Courier-Jour., Louisville, 1968-69; editor-in-chief, pub. Manhattan Mercury, 1969—; bd. dirs., officer 9 other newspaper and broadcasting affiliates; mem. adv. com. Knight Internat. Press Fellowship Program; mem. Pulitzer Prize bd. Contbr. articles to profl. jours. Chmn. Alfred M. Landon lecture patrons Kans. State U.; chmn. Latin Am. Scholarship Program Am. Univs., Cambridge, Mass., 1986-87. Decorated comendador Order of Christopher Columbus (Dominican Republic); Fulbright scholar, 1965; recipient Cabot prize Columbia U., 1993. Mem. Am. Soc. Newspaper Editors (v.p., pres. found.), Inter-Am. Press Assn. (pres. 1989-90), Internat. Ctr. Journalists (bd. dirs.), Internat. Press Inst., Kans. C. of C. and Industry (pres. 1987), Fly Club (Harvard U.). Avocations: tennis, cooking. Office: Manhattan Mercury 318 N 5th St Manhattan KS 66502-5910

SEATON, RICHARD MELVIN, newspaper and broadcasting executive; b. Washington, Jan. 25, 1913; s. Fay Noble and Dorothea Elizabeth (Schmidt) S.; m. Mary Holton, June 1, 1936 (dec. 1989); children: Richard H., Frederick D., Elizabeth, Edward L.; m. Eva Lee Sanborn, May 18, 1991. B.S. in Journalism, Kans. State U., 1934. Officer and dir. various cos. comprising Seaton News Media Group, 1937—. Trustee William Allen White Found., Kans. State U., Found.; mem. initial Kans. State Water Resources Bd., 1954-61, initial Kans. Cultural Arts Commn., 1965-67; founder Coffeyville Hist. Mus. Mem. Kans. Press Assn. (pres. 1949), Kans. AP (chmn. 1953), Am. Soc. Newspaper Editors, Internat. Press Inst., Coffeyville C. of C. (pres. 1950-51), Kans. State Hist. Soc. (dir. 1979—), Sigma Delta Chi, Phi Kappa Phi, Beta Theta Pi. Republican. Unitarian. Established R.M. Seaton profl. journalism chair Kans. State U., 1978, Dalton Defenders Meml. Mus., Coffeyville, Kans., 1953, Brown Mansion Mus., Coffeyville, 1973. Office: 218 W 8th St Coffeyville KS 67337-5808

SEATON, ROBERT FINLAYSON, retired planned giving consultant; b. Hancock, Mich., Nov. 28, 1930; s. Donald W. and Mary Lucille (Finlayson) S.; m. Helen Jean Robarts, Apr. 18, 1954; children: Scott, Sandy. BS, Mich. Technol. U., 1952; MBA, Stanford, 1956; postgrad., Ind. U., 1966, U. So. Calif., 1973. Asst. sec. Palo Alto (Calif.) Mut. Savs. and Loan Assn., 1956-60; asst. v.p. Am. Savs. and Loan Assn. No. Calif., 1960-63; v.p. 1st Western Savs. and Loan Assn., Las Vegas, 1963-67; v.p., sec. Fed. Home Loan Bank, Cin., 1967-72; pres., chief exec. officer 2d Fed. Savs. and Loan Assn., Cleve., 1973; pres., chief exec. officer Cardinal Fed. Savs. Bank, Cleve., 1973-87, chmn., 1987-88; sr. v.p. Planned Giving Systems, Inc., Cleve., 1989—, pres., 1990-94. Pres. The Orange Schs. Edn. Found.; trustee Univ. Circle, Inc.; v.p. Luth. Housing Corp., N.E. Ohio Coun. Higher Edn.; trustee, exec. com. Clean-Land-Ohio. Lt. USNR, 1952-54. Republican. Methodist. Home: 16 Pepper Creek Dr Cleveland OH 44124-5248

SEATON, VAUGHN ALLEN, veterinary pathology educator; b. Abilene, Kans., Oct. 11, 1928; m. Clara I. Bertelrud; children: Gregory S., Jeffrey T. BS, Kans. State U., 1954, DVM, 1954; MS, Iowa State U., 1957. Pvt. practice Janesville, Wis., 1954; instr. pathology Vet. Diagnostic Lab. Iowa State U., Ames, 1954-57, from asst. to assoc. prof. pathology Vet. Diagnostic Lab., 1957-64, prof., head Vet. Diagnostic Lab., 1964—; lab. coord. regional emergency animal disease eradication orgn. Animal and Plant Health Inspection Svc. USDA, 1974—; mem. rsch. com. Iowa Beef Industry Coun., 1972-85; mem. adv. bd. Iowa State Water Resources Rsch. Inst., 1973-80; cons. several orgns. Co-author: (monographs) Feasibility Study of College of Veterinary Medicine, 1972, Veterinary Diagnostic Laboratory Facilities-State of New York, 1970; bd. dirs. Iowa State U. Press, 1985-88, mem. manuscript com., 1982-85; contbr. articles to profl. jours. Trustee Ames Pub. Libr., 1979-85; mem. Iowa State Bd. Health, 1971-77, v.p., 1976-77. Mem. AVMA, Am. Assn. Vet. Lab. Diagnosticians (bd. govs. 1973-88, pres. 1968, E.P. Pope award 1980), Am. Coll. Vet. Toxicologists, U.S. Animal Health Assn., Iowa Vet. Med. Assn. (pres. 1971), North Cen. Assn. Vet. Lab. Diagnosticians, Western Vet. Conf. (exec. bd. 1986-90, v.p. 1994, pres.-elect 1995, pres. 1996), World Assn. Vet. Lab. Diagnosticians (pres. 1980-86), masons (bd. dirs. 1985-88), Ames C. of C. (bd. dirs. 1970-73), Phi Kappa Phi, Phi Zeta (pres. 1964), Alpha Zeta, Gamma Sigma Delta. Office: Iowa State U Coll Vet Medicine Vet Diagnostic Lab Ames IA 50011

SEATS, PEGGY CHISOLM, marketing executive; b. Lisman, Ala., Oct. 12, 1951; d. William H. and Bernice (Berry) Chisolm; m. Melvin Seats (div.). BA in Communications cum laude, Lewis U., 1974; grad. cert. in event mgmt., George Washington U., 1995; MA in Pub. Comm., Am. U., 1997. Account exec. Globe Broadcasting, Chgo., 1976-78, Merrill Lynch, Chgo., 1978-79, Transp. Displays, Inc., Chgo., 1979-81; with Reverie, Inc., 1981—; nat. accounts mgr. Soft Sheen Products Co., Chgo., 1981-83; mktg. cons. Reverie, Inc., Chgo., 1983-85; pres., mktg. cons. Reverie, Inc., Washington, 1987—; pub. rels., mktg. mgr. Proctor & Gardner Advt., Chgo., 1985-86; dir. pub. rels., mktg. Morris Brown Coll., Atlanta, 1986-87; mgr. mktg. Howard U. Press, Washington, 1989-90; cons. White House Initiative on Historically Black Colls., Univs., 1990-92; founder Black Pub. Rels. Soc., Atlanta, 1987. Contbr. numerous articles to newspapers and mags. Bd. dirs

Congl. Award; state advisor U.S. Congl. Adv. Bd., Ill. 1982; founder Benjamin Banneker Overlook Meml. Fund, WDC. Recipient Kizzie award Black Women Hall of Fame, Chgo., 1981, Svc. award Nat. Assn. Women in Media, Chgo., 1982. Mem. Internat. Platform Assn., Internat. Assn. Bus. Communicators, Internat. Spl. Events Soc., Pub. Rels. Soc. Am., Black Pub. Rels. Soc. (Atlanta chpt. pres. emeritus), Nat. Assn. Market Developers, World Affairs Coun., Lewis U. Alumni Assn. (bd. dirs. Ill. 1979). Democrat. Baptist. Avocations: music, art collecting, reading. Home: 2020 Pennsylvania Ave NW Washington DC 20006-1846

SEAU, JUNIOR (TIANA SEAU, JR.), professional football player; b. Samoa, Jan. 19, 1969. Student, U. So. Calif. Linebacker San Diego Chargers, 1990—; player Super Bowl XXIV, 1994. Named to Sporting News Coll. All-Am. Team, 1989, to Pro Bowl Team, 1991-93, 96, to Sporting News NFL All Pro Team, 1992, 93. Office: San Diego Chargers PO Box 609609 San Diego CA 92160-9609*

SEAVER, FRANK ALEXANDER, III, retired medical center administrator; b. Detroit, Aug. 13, 1940; s. Frank A. Jr. and Emily Eugenia (Stafford) S.; m. Ellison Murton, Aug. 1967 (div. Jan. 1979); children: Frank A. IV, Dean, Claire; m. Robin Millan, May 17, 1980. BA cum laude, Mich. State U., 1965, MA, 1967. Pers. adminstr. Ford Motor Co., Mt. Clemens, Mich., 1965-67; pers. mgr. Allied Supermarkets, Detroit, 1967-76; dir. human resources Harper-Grace Hosps., Detroit, 1976-85; v.p. human resources Detroit Med. Ctr., 1985-92. Contbr. articles to profl. jours. Mem. vocat. edn. adv. bd. Detroit Pub. Schs., 1976-92. Sgt. USMC, 1958-61. Mem. Am. Soc. Human Resource Adminstrs. (pers. rsch. com. 1980-86), Mich. Hosp. Assn. (ins. com. 1984-88), Hosp. Pers. Assn. SE Mich. (President's citation 1983, Profl. Achievement award 1984). Avocations: golf, model railroading, strategy computer games, tennis, reading.

SEAVER, JAMES EVERETT, historian, educator; b. Los Angeles, Oct. 4, 1918; s. Everett Herbert and Gertrude Lillian (Sharp) S.; m. Virginia Stevens, Dec. 20, 1940; children—Richard Everett, William Merrill, Robert Edward. A.B., Stanford U., 1940; Ph.D., Cornell U., 1946. Asst. instr. history Cornell U., 1940-42, 44-46; instr. Mich. State U., 1946-47; mem. faculty U. Kans., Lawrence, 1947—; prof. history U. Kans., 1960—; prof. emeritus, 1989—; pres. faculty U. Kans., 1972-74, 82-83. Author: The Persecution of the Jews in the Roman Empire, 313-438 A.D, 1952, also articles. Fulbright-Hays grantee Italy, 1953-54; Fulbright-Hays grantee Israel, 1963-64; Carnegie grantee Costa Rica, 1966-67. Mem. Am. Hist. Assn., Am. Philol. Assn., Archaeol. Inst. Am., Am. Numismatic Soc., AAUP, Am. Acad. Rome, U.S. Archives of Recorded Sound. Democrat. Episcopalian. Clubs: Alvamar Tennis, Alvamar Country. Home: 600 Louisiana St Lawrence KS 66044-2336 Office: U Kans Dept History Lawrence KS 66045

SEAVER, ROBERT LESLIE, law educator; b. Brockton, Mass., June 13, 1937; s. Russell Bradford and Lois (Marchant) S.; m. Marjorie V. Rote, Aug. 21, 1960 (div. 1974); children: Kimberly, Eric, Kristen; m. Elizabeth A. Horwitz, May 22, 1984. AB cum laude, Tufts U., Medford, Mass., 1958; JD, U. Chgo., 1964. Bar: Ohio 1964, U.S. Ct. Appeals (6th cir.) 1964, U.S. Dist. Ct. (so. dist.) Ohio 1965. Assoc. Taft, Stettinius and Hollister, Cin., 1964-66; v.p., sec., gen. counsel IDI Mgmt. Inc., Cin., 1966-74; pvt. practice Cin., 1974-75; prof. law No. Ky. U. Salmon P. Chase Coll. Law, Highland Heights, 1975—; of counsel Cors & Bassett, Cin., 1993—; cons. in field, 1975—. Author/editor: Ohio Corporation Law, 1988; contbr. chpts. to books. Advisor subcom. on pvt. corps of Ky. Commn. on Constl. Rev., 1987. With USMC, 1958-61. Recipient Justice Robert O. Lukowsky award of Excellence Chase Law Sch. Student Bar Assn., 1986. Mem. ABA, Ohio Bar Assn., Cin. Bar Assn., No. Ky. Bar Assn., U. Chgo. Law Sch. Alumni Assn. (regional v.p. 1976—). Republican. Unitarian. Avocations: duplicate bridge, history. Home: 826 Woodscene Ct Cincinnati OH 45230-4334 Office: Northern Kentucky U Salmon Chase Coll Law Newport KY 41099

SEAVER, TOM (GEORGE THOMAS SEAVER), former professional baseball player; b. Fresno, Calif., Nov. 17, 1944; s. Charles H. and Betty Lee (Cline) S.; m. Nancy Lynn McIntyre, June 9, 1966; children: Sarah, Anne Elizabeth. Student, Fresno City Coll., 1964, U. So. Calif., 1965-68. Pitcher Jacksonville (Fla.) Suns, 1966; pitcher N.Y. Mets, 1967-77, 83-84, 87, mem. World Series Championship team, 1969; pitcher Cin. Reds, 1977-82, Chgo. White Sox, 1984-86, Boston Red Sox, 1986; announcer N.Y. Yankees WPIX-TV, N.Y.C. Author: (with Lee Lowenfish) The Art of Pitching, 1984, (with Alice Seigel) Tom Seaver's Baseball Card Book, 1985, (with Herb Resnicow) novel Beanball, 1989. Served with USMCR, 1963. Recipient Cy Young award Nat. League, 1969, 73, 75; named Rookie of Yr. Baseball Writers Assn. Am., 1967, Nat. League Pitcher of Yr. Sporting News, 1969, 73, 75, Sportsman of Yr. Sports Illustrated, 1969; named to Nat. League All-Star team, 1969-73, 75-78, to Baseball Hall of Fame Baseball Writers Assn. Am., 1992. Credited with more than 300 career victories; pitched over 3,000 career strikeouts. Office: care Matt Mendola 185 E 85th St Apt 18G New York NY 10028-2146*

SEAVEY, WILLIAM ARTHUR, lawyer, vintner; b. Los Angeles, Aug. 28, 1930; s. Arthur Jones and Dorothy (Keyes) S.; m. Mary van Beuren, June 25, 1955; children: Dorothy K., Arthur V.B., William G., Frederic A., Charles K. AB, Princeton U., 1952; LLB, Harvard U., 1955; grad. Inst. Internat. Studies, U. Geneva, Switzerland, 1956, D in Polit. Sci., 1970. Bar: Calif. 1957, U.S. Dist. Ct. (so. and no. dist.) Calif. 1957, U.S. Ct. Appeals (9th cir.) 1957. Assoc. Luce, Forward, Kunzel & Scripps, San Diego, 1956-57; asst. U.S. atty. U.S. Dist. Ct. (so. dist.) Calif., 1957-59; with Noon & Seavey, San Diego, 1959-65; lectr. in internat. law and econ., asst. to pres. Mills Coll., Oakland, Calif., 1968-74; ptnr. Richards & Seavey, San Francisco, 1974-76, Davis, Stafford, Kellman & Fenwick, San Francisco, 1976-78; of counsel Friedman, Olive, McCubbin, Spalding, Bilter, Roosevelt etal, San Francisco, 1987—; proprietor Seavey Vineyard, Napa County, 1981—. Author: Dumping Since the War: The Gatt and National Laws, 1970. Councilman City of Coronado, Calif., 1960-62, mayor 1962-64; trustee French-Am. Internat. Sch., San Francisco, 1968-96; pres. English Speaking Union, San Francisco, 1982-85, Alliance Francaise, San Francisco, 1979-81; chair Javits Fellowship Bd., Washington, 1989-92; mem. Columbus Fellowship Found. Bd., Washington, 1993—; dir. San Francisco Com. on Fgn. Rels., 1995—. Mem. ABA, Calif. Bar Assn., San Francisco Bar Assn., Am. Soc. Internat. Law. Republican. Clubs: Pacific Union, Cercle de l'Union, World Trade (San Francisco), The Met. (Washington). Avocation: skiing, jazz piano. Home: 303 Pacific Ave Piedmont CA 94611-3432 Office: 425 California St Fl 22 San Francisco CA 94104-2102 also: 1310 Conn Valley Rd Saint Helena CA 94574

SEAWELL, THOMAS ROBERT, artist, retired educator; b. Balt., Mar. 17, 1936; s. Robert James and Cynthia Edith (Bass) S.; m. Barbara Louise Frey, Nov. 30, 1985; children: James Bradford, Lee Thomas, Gustin Charles, Jay Turner Frey. B.F.A., Washington U., 1958; M.F.A., Tex. Christian U., 1960. Mem. faculty dept. art SUNY-Oswego, 1963-91, prof., 1973-91; vis. artist Ox Bow Print Symposium, 1985, Ann. Matrix Artist, U. Dallas, 1989, Midwestern State U., 1993, East Tenn. State U., 1997, Henderson State U., 1997; juror 50th Cooperstown Nat., 1985, Nat. Print Exhbn., Minot State U., N.D., 1985., Rochester Print Club Annual, Meml. Art Gallery U. Rochester, 1988. One-man exhbns. include retrospective U. Md., Baltimore County, 1983, Schoharie County Arts Ctr., 1991, Tyler Art Gallery, SUNY, Oswego, 1991, Univ. Gallery, Tex. A&M U., Commerce, 1995; group exhbns. include Contemporary Am. Prints in Leningrad, USSR, 1983-84, The Collagraph, U. Mont., 1987, SUNY, Oswego, 1988, DeCordova Mus., 1991; traveling exhbn. So. Arts Fedn. Traveling Exhbn. "A Sense of Place," 1986—, St. Angelo Mus., 1996, Columbia Coll., 1996-97; represented in permanent collections Bklyn. Mus., DeCordova Mus. Art, Rochester Meml. Art Gallery, Pushkin Mus., USSR, Brit. Mus., Munson-Williams-Proctor Inst., Library of Congress, Portland Art Mus.; commd. print editions: Geldermann Securities Ltd., 1985-92. Mem. Boston Printmakers, Phila. Water Color Club, Soc. Am. Graphic Artists. Home (summer): PO Box 14 Sterling NY 13156-0014

SEAWELL, WILLIAM THOMAS, former airline executive; b. Pine Bluff, Ark., Jan. 27, 1918; s. George Marion and Harriet (Aldridge) S.; m. Judith Alexander, June 12, 1941; children: Alexander Brooke, Anne Seawell Robinson. B.S., U.S. Mil. Acad., 1941; J.D., Harvard U., 1949. Commd. 2d lt. U.S. Army, 1941; advanced through grades to brig. gen. USAF, 1959; comdr. 401st Bombardment Group, ETO, World War II, 11th Bomb Wing SAC, 1953-54; dep. comdr. 7th Air Div., 1954-55; mil. asst. to sec. USAF, 1958-59, to dep. sec. def., 1959-61; comdt. cadets U.S. Air Force Acad., 1961-63; ret., 1963; v.p. operations and engring. Air Transport Assn. Am., Washington, 1963-65; sr. v.p. ops. Am. Airlines, N.Y.C., 1965-68; pres. Rolls Royce Aero Engines Inc. U.S. subsidiary Rolls Royce, Ltd., 1968-71; pres., chief operating officer Pan Am. World Airways Inc., N.Y.C., 1971-72; chmn. bd. Pan Am. World Airways Inc., 1972-81. Decorated Silver Star, D.F.C. with three oak leaf clusters, Air medal with three oak leaf clusters; Croix de Guerre with palm France). Clubs: Wings (N.Y.C.), Pine Bluff Country. Home: 21 Westridge Dr Pine Bluff AR 71603-7149

SEAWRIGHT, JAMES L., JR., sculptor, educator; b. Jackson, Miss., May 22, 1936; s. James L. and Josephine (Power) S.; m. Mabelle M. Garrard, June 22, 1960; 1 child, James Andrew. Student, U. of South, 1953-54, Delta State Coll., 1954-55; BA in English, U. Miss., 1957; postgrad., Art Students League of N.Y., 1961-62. Tech. supr. Columbia-Princeton Electronic Music Center, N.Y.C., 1963-69; tchr. Sch. Visual Arts, 1967-69; dir. visual arts program Princeton U., 1972—, prof. coun. of humanities and visual arts, 1992—. Asst. to choreographer, Henry St. Playhouse, N.Y.C., 1962-63, spl. effects, tech. cons., Mimi Garrard Dance Co., N.Y.C., 1964—; sculptor represented in permanent collections, Mus. Modern Art, N.Y.C., Whitney Mus., N.Y.C., N.J. State Mus., Trenton, Guggenheim Mus., N.Y.C., Wadsworth Atheneum, Hartford, Conn., others; pub. commns. for SEA-TAC Internat. Airport, Seattle, Logan Internat. Airport, Boston; also pvt. collections. Served with USN, 1957-61. Recipient Theodoron award Guggenheim Mus., 1969; Graham Found. Advanced Study in Arts fellow, 1970. Mem. Am. Abstract Artists, Am. Acad. Arts and Letters (Art award 1996), Phi Delta Theta. Democrat. Episcopalian. Office: 185 Nassau St Princeton NJ 08544-2003

SEAY, FRANK HOWELL, federal judge; b. Shawnee, Okla., Sept. 5, 1938; s. Frank and Wilma Lynn Seay; m. Janet Gayle Seay, June 2, 1962; children: Trudy Alice, Laura Lynn. Student, So. Meth. U., 1956-57; B.A., U. Okla., 1960, LL.B., 1963. Bar: Okla. 1963. Atty. Seminole County, 1963-66; asst. dist. atty., 1967-68, assoc. dist. judge, 1968-74; judge Okla. Dist. Ct. 22, 1974-79; judge ea. dist. U.S. Dist. Ct., Okla., 1979—, now chief judge. Mem. ABA, Okla. Bar Assn., Seminole County Bar Assn. Democrat. Clubs: Masons, Elks, Lions. Office: US Dist Ct PO Box 828 Muskogee OK 74402*

SEBASCO, SALVADOR MONASTRA, safety engineer; b. Phila., Mar. 13, 1961; s. Sal Monastra and Elizabeth Sebasco Bauer; m. Berta J. Monastra, Oct. 13, 1983 (div. July 1994); children: Anthony, Samantha. BS in Occupl. Safety and Health, Mont. Tech., 1984. Registered profl. engr., Mass.; bd. cert. safety profl. Sr. safety engr. Lockheed Idaho Inc., Idaho Falls, 1991-95, Sci. Applications Internat. Corp., Pleasanton, Calif., 1995-97, Sebasco & Assocs., Livermore, Calif., 1997—; engring. adv. bd. N.Mex. Highlands U., Las Vegas, 1994—. Co-author: Bloodbourne Pathogens (booklet), 1993. Bd. dirs. Bonneville County Crime Stoppers, Idaho Falls, 1992-95. Mem. ASME (nat. nominating com.), Am. Soc. Safety Engrs. (pub. rels. chair 1992—), Soc. Hispanic Profl. Engrs. (bd. dirs. 1993-95), Internat. Conf. Bldg. Code Ofcls. Ch. of the Nazarene. Avocations: chess, hiking, swimming, theatre, cooking. Office: Sebasco & Assocs PO Box 725 Livermore CA 94551

SEBASTIAN, MICHAEL JAMES, retired manufacturing company executive; b. Chgo., July 8, 1930; s. Michael and Larraine (DeAmicis) S.; m. Sally Ervin, Nov. 29, 1953; children: Michael, Mark, Lisa. B.S. in M.E., Santa Clara U., 1952; A.M.P., Harvard U., 1972. Div. mgr. FMC Corp, Indpls., 1953-77; pres. Rotek, Aurora, Ohio, 1977-78; v.p. Gardner-Denver, Dallas, 1978-79; group pres. Cooper Industries, Dallas, 1979-81; v.p. Cooper Industries, Houston, 1981-82, exec. v.p., 1982—; bd. dirs. Cooper Cameron Corp., Quanex Corp., Gardner Denver Machinery, Inc. Past dir. Weatherford Internat.; mem. adv. bd. U. Houston Ctr. Pub. Policy. Mem. Lakeside Country Club (Houston). Republican. Roman Catholic. Avocations: golf, gardening, travel. Home: 11511 Shadow Way Houston TX 77024-5216 Office: Cooper Industries Inc 600 Travis St Ste 5800 Houston TX 77002

SEBASTIAN, PETER, international affairs consultant, former ambassador; b. June 19, 1926; m. Harvel Huddleston, Dec. 11, 1951; 1 child, Christopher. B.A., U. Chgo., 1950; postgrad., U. d'Aix-Marseille, Nice, France, 1949, New Sch. for Social Research, N.Y.C., 1950, Nat. War Coll., 1969-70. Dir., owner cons. co., N.Y.C., 1950-57; U.S. Fgn. Service officer Dept. State, Washington, 1957-76, dep. exec. sec., 1976-77, sr. seminar, 1977-78; U.S. consul gen. Casablanca, Morocco, 1978-80; minister, counselor Am. embassy, Rabat, Morocco, 1980-82; dir. for North Africa Dept. State, Washington, 1982-84; ambassador to Tunisia Tunis, 1984-87; ambassador-in-residence Ctr. for Strategic Internat. Studies, Georgetown U., Washington, 1987-88; cons in fgn. affairs to the public and pvt. sector, lectr., 1988—. Contbr. poems to Osmose, 1949; author studies for U.S. Dept. State and other U.S agys. Served to sgt. AUS, 1944-46. Decorated Ouissam Alaouite (Morocco), numerous U.S. mil. decorations; recipient Presdl. Meritorious Service award, 1985. Mem. Am. Fgn. Svc. Assn., Nat. Geog. Soc., Mid. East Inst. Episcopalian. Avocations: painting; drawing; photography.

SEBASTIAN, RICHARD LEE, physicist, executive; b. Hutchinson, Kans., June 22, 1942; s. Leroy Clarence and Marion Alta (Brown) S.; m. Judy Ann French, Dec. 29, 1964; children: Todd Winslow, Alison Louise. A.B. in Math, Princeton U., 1964; Ph.D. in Physics, U. Md., 1970. Staff scientist ENSCO, Inc., Springfield, Va., 1969-72; chief scientist ENSCO, Inc., 1972-73, v.p. research, 1973-83; pres. Wackenhut Research Corp., Springfield, 1980-81; pres., chmn. Digital Signal Corp., Springfield, 1983-91; corp. v.p., gen. mgr. Digital Signal div. Coleman Rsch. Corp., Springfield, 1991-95; pres. Digital Forecasting Corp., 1996—. Mem. Am. Phys. Soc., IEEE, Soc. Exploration Geophysicists. Home: 6128 River Dr Mason Neck VA 22079-4124 Office: Coleman Rsch Corp Digital Signal Div 6551 Loisdale Ct Springfield VA 22150-1808

SEBASTIAN, SANDRA MARY THOMPSON, mental health counselor, social worker; b. Moncton, Can., June 14, 1943; came to U.S., 1965; d. Alan G. E. Thompson and Jean Glenn Hyde Thompson Hart; m. John Francis Sebastian, Jr., Aug. 12, 1967; children: Byron David, Colin Alan. Diploma, Queen Elizabeth's Coll., Surrey, Eng., 1962, Morley Coll, London, 1965; BA in Sociology, Miami U., 1986; MS in Mental Health Counseling, Wright State U., 1995. Rsch. sec. St. Thomas' Hosp. Med. Sch., London, 1962-65; prodn. editor Ency. Britannica, Chgo., 1966-67; sec. Miami U., Oxford, Ohio, 1980-86; social worker Butler CY.CSB, Hamilton, Ohio, 1987-95, Family Preservation, 1992-95; mental health counselor, child/adolescent, adult therapist Hamilton Counseling Ctr., 1995—; Spkr. in field. Apptd. commr. on volunteerism State Ohio, 1986-87; mem. Conflict Resolution Svcs., 1991—, Oxford Citizens for Peace & Justice, 1988—, Butler County AIDS Task Force, 1990; v.p. McGuffey Sch. PTA, Oxford, 1978. Mem. ACA, Am. Mental Health Counselors Assn., Internat. Assn. Play Therapy, NAACP (Oxford chpt.), UN Assn. USA, Miami U. Women's Club (v.p. 1980), Sigma Chi Iota. Democrat. Unitarian. Avocations: traveling, classical music, reading, writing. Home: 220 Mckee Ave Oxford OH 45056-9060 Office: Hamilton Counseling Ctr 111 Buckeye St Hamilton OH 45011-1645

SEBASTIANELLI, CARL THOMAS, clinical psychologist; b. Jessup, Pa., Dec. 12, 1943; s. Carlo and Antonia (Antonelli) S.; B.S. magna cum laude in Psychology, U. Scranton, 1965; M.A. in Psychology, Temple U., Phila., 1967; postgrad. in clin. psychology L.I.U., 1968-70; Ph.D. in Psychopathology/Psychotherapy, Clayton U., 1983. Psychologist, Farview State Hosp., Waymart, Pa., 1967-68; clin. psychology doctoral intern N. Dauphin Mental Health/Mental Retardation Ctr., 1970-71; clin. psychology doctoral intern family therapy center and psychology lab. Harrisburg (Pa.) State Hosp., 1970-71, clin. psychologist, 1971-77, chmn. psychology forum, 1974-76, clin. psychologist, psychiat. treatment center, 1977-79; pvt. practice clin. psychology Comprehensive Health Svcs. Ctr., Dunmore, Pa., 1979-90; ind. pvt. practice clin. psychology, Dunmore, 1990—; mem. adj. faculty U. Scranton, 1979-86, Pa. State U., 1973-86; mem. state bd. Pa. Social Services Union, 1974-75; media commentator psychopathology topics, 1979—. Pa. Profl. Edn. Program scholar L.I.U.; recipient award N.E. Pa. chpt. Am. Diabetes Assn., 1980. Lic. psychologist, Pa. Mem. Am. Psychol. Assn., Internat. Acad. Behavioral Medicine Counseling and Psychotherapy, Anxiety Disorders Assn. Am., Acad. Psychologists Marital, Sex and Family Therapy, Pa. Psychol. Assn. (chmn. public info. com. 1981-83), Northeastern Pa. Psychol. Assn. (sec. 1981, exec. council 1982-83), Nat. Register Health Service Providers in Psychology. Contbr. articles to profl. jours, UPI; interviewed for articles in newspapers and nat. mags.; featured in Pa. Dept. Welfare publ. on subject of family therapy tng. Home: 1224 Monroe Ave Scranton PA 18509-2808

SEBELA, VICKI D., association executive, freelance writer; b. Des Plaines, Ill., Mar. 7, 1964; d. James Edward and Mary Nell (Davis) S.; m. Julius Michael Colangelo, Oct. 8, 1988. AA, AS, Harper Coll., 1984; BS, Roosevelt U., 1986; student, Inst. Orgnl. Mgmt., Boulder, Colo., 1991-93. Adminstrv. asst. McDonald's Corp., Rolling Meadows, Ill., 1979-83; info. specialist William Rainey Harper Coll., Palatine, Ill., 1983-84; teller Arlington Fed. Savs. and Loan, Arlington Heights, Ill., 1984-85; asst. to the pres. Ill. Women's Agenda, Chgo., 1984-85; student outreach coord. William Rainey Harper Coll., Palatine, 1985-86; adminstrv. asst. women's affairs Office of the Gov., Chgo., 1986-88; exec. adminstr. Social Engring. Assocs., Inc., Chgo., 1988-89; exec. dir. Greater Wheaton (Ill.) C. of C., 1989-94; internat. conf. dir. Environ. Planning Group, Barrington, Ill., 1994-95; pres. SEBCO Enterprises, Wheaton, Ill., 1995—; freelance writer, 1992—; founder Wheaton Womens Bus. Coun., Greater Wheaton Cycle Classic, Do it Yourself Messiah, Wheaton Criterium. Columnist Daily Herald, 1992—; corr. Wheaton Leader, Warrenville Post, Winfield Estate, 1996—; contbr. articles to Ency. Brit. Cert. paraprofl. Talk Line/Kids Line Crisis Hot Line, Elk Grove Village, Ill., 1983; plan commr. City of Wheaton, 1994—, vice chair plan commn., 1995, chair, 1996—; mem. Wheaton History Ctr., chair Silver and Gold Ball Auction, 1995, publicity coord. Heritage Tour, 1996, bd. dirs. 1996, membership com. chair protem, 1996. Harper Coll. scholar, 1982, Roosevelt U. scholar, 1984. Mem. APA, Chgo. Women in Govt. Rels. (membership chair, bd. dirs. 1988-89), Women's Opportunity Internat., Greater Wheaton C. of C. (hon. life, chair clubs and orgn. autumn fest 1995), South Wheaton Bus. Assn., Phi Theta Kappa. Republican. Avocations: travel, gardening, photography, nature studies, piano.

SEBELIUS, KATHLEEN GILLIGAN, state commissioner; b. Cin., May 15, 1948; d. John J. and Mary K. (Dixon) Gilligan; m. Keith Gary Sebelius, 1974; children: Edward Keith, John McCall. BA, Trinity Coll., 1970; MA in Pub. Adminstrn., U. Kans., 1977. Cert. ins. agt., Kans. Dir. planning Ctr. for Cmty. Justice, Washington, 1971-74; spl. asst. Kans. Dept. Corrections, Topeka, 1975-78; mem. Kans. Ho. of Reps., 1987-95; ins. commr. State of Kans., 1995—. Founder Women's Polit. Caucus; mem. Friends of Cedar Crest, Florence Crittendon Svcs.; precinct committeewoman, 1980-86; mayor-elect, Potwin, 1985-87; exec. com. NAIC, Kans. Health Care Commn.; appointed Presdl. adv. commn. consumer protection and quality in Health Care Industry, 1997. Mem. Common Cause (state bd., nat. gov. bd. 1975-81), Nat. Assn. Ins. Commrs. (chair), Kans. Trial Lawyers Assn. (dir. 1978-86). Democrat. Roman Catholic. Home: 224 SW Greenwood Ave Topeka KS 66606-1228

SEBEOK, THOMAS ALBERT, linguistics educator; b. Budapest, Hungary, Nov. 9, 1920; came to U.S., 1937, naturalized, 1944; s. Dezso and Veronica (Perlman) S.; m. Eleanor Lawton, Sept. 1947; 1 child, Veronica C.; m. Jean Umiker, Oct. 1972; children: Jessica A., Erica L. B.A., U. Chgo., 1941; M.A., Princeton, 1943, Ph.D., 1945; PhD honoris causa, U. Budapest, Hungary, 1990; Dr. honoris causa, U. Nacional de Rosario, Argentina, 1991; DSc honoris causa, U. So. Ill., 1991. Mem. faculty Ind. U., Bloomington, 1943—, Disting. prof. linguistics, 1967-78, Disting. prof. linguistics and semiotics, 1978-91, Disting. prof. emeritus, 1991—, prof. anthropology, prof. Uralic and Altaic studies, fellow Folklore Inst., mem. Russian and East European Inst., chmn. Research Center for Lang. and Semiotic Studies, 1956-91, chmn. emeritus Grad. Program in Semiotic Studies, 1991—; mem.-at-large NAS-NRC, also mem. various coms.; lectr. various acads. and univs., U.S. and abroad; vis. prof. U. Mich., 1945, 58, U. P.R., 1949, U. N.Mex., 1953, U. Ariz., 1958-59, U. Vienna, 1963, U. Besançon, 1965, U. Hamburg, 1966, U. Bucharest, 1967, 69, U. Ill., 1968, U. Colo., 1969, Stanford U., 1971, U. South Fla., 1972, Linguistic Soc. Am. prof., 1975, Internat. Christian U., Tokyo, 1985, U. Quebec, 1985, El Colegio de Mexico, 1987, U. of Republic, Montevideo, Uraguey, 1987, others; Disting. vis. prof. Internat. Summer Inst. for Semiotic and Structural Studies, 1980-88; cons. Ford Found., Guggenheim Found., Wenner-Gren Found. for Anthrop. Research, U.S. Office Edn., NSF, fellowship div. Nat. Acad. Scis., Can. Council; panel mem. for linguistics Nat. Endowment for Humanities, 1966-67; mem. U.S. del. to permanent council Internat. Union Anthrop. and Ethnol. Scis., 1970-73; U.S. del. Comité International Permanent des Linguistes, 1972—; mem. internat. sci. council Royaumont Center for Sci. of Man, 1973—; exch. prof. NAS-USSR Acad. Scis., 1973; Regents fellow Smithsonian Instn., 1983-84; adj. fellow Woodrow Wilson Internat. Ctr. for Scholars, 1983-84, mem. program on history, culture and soc., 1986-87. Author: Perspectives in Zoosemiotics, 1972, Structure & Texture: Selected Essays in Cheremis Verbal Art, 1974, The Play of Musement, 1981, others; editor-in-chief: Semiotica, 1968—, Current Trends in Linguistics, 1963—, Approaches to Semiotics, 1968-74; editor: Studies in Semiotics, 1974—, others; gen. editor: Advances in Semiotics, 1974—, others; contbr. numerous articles to profl. and scholarly jours. Mem. vis. com. Harvard U., 1973, Simon Fraser U., 1975, Georgetown U., 1977, Vanderbilt U., 1977-78. Recipient Pres.'s medal of excellence Ind. U., 1991, Profl. Achievement citation U. Chgo., 1992; John Simon Guggenheim Meml. Found. fellow, 1958-59, 81-82, Ctr. for Advanced Study in Behavioral Scis. fellow, 1960-61, 66-67, 71, NSF sr. postdoctoral fellow, 1966-67, NEH fellow, 1973-74, 80-81, Netherlands Inst. for Advanced Study fellow, 1973-74, Nat. Humanities Ctr. fellow, 1980-81, Smithsonian Instn. Regents fellow, 1983-84, Rsch. Assoc., 1984-87, Woodrow Wilson Internat. Ctr. for Scholars adj. fellow, 1983-84, Com. for Sci. Investigation of Claims of Paranormal fellow, 1983—; Fulbright grantee Germany, 1966, 71, Italy, 1969, 71, 87, Argentina, 1987, Uruguay, 1987, Am., Am. Coun. Learned Socs. grantee, Ford Found., Wenner-Gren Found. Anthrop. Rsch., USIA, other fed. agys. Fellow Am. Anthrop. Assn. (disting. service award 1984), Am. Folklore Soc., Soc. Cultural Anthropology, AAAS, Explorers Club, also fgn. linguistic socs.; mem. Internat. Assn. Semiotic Studies (editor-in-chief 1968—, exec. com. 1969—), Linguistic Soc. Am. (sec.-treas. 1969-73, v.p. 1974, pres. 1975, asso. dir. Linguistic Inst. 1958, 75, dir. 1964), Central States Anthrop. Soc. (pres. 1956), Am. Assn. Machine Translation and Computational Linguistics (exec. bd. 1964-66), Animal Behavior Soc. (exec. bd. 1968—), Semiotic Soc. Am. (sec.-treas. 1975, exec. dir. 1976-85, pres. 1984), Sigma Xi, others. Clubs: Cosmos (Washington); University (Chgo.); Princeton (N.Y.C.) ; Internat. House (Tokyo). Home: 1104 S Covenanter Dr Bloomington IN 47401-6043 Office: Indiana U PO Box 10 Bloomington IN 47402-0010

SEBOK, GYORGY, pianist, educator; b. Szeged, Hungary, Nov. 2, 1922; came to U.S., 1962; s. Vilmos and Klara (Krausz) S.; m. Eva Mandel, Jan. 29, 1957. Ed., Franz Liszt Acad. Music, Budapest, Hungary. Prof. piano Bela Bartok Conservatory, Budapest, 1949-56; prof. piano Ind. U., Bloomington, 1962—, disting. prof., 1985—; guest prof. Hochschule der Künste, Berlin; hon. life mem. Toho Gakuen Sch. Music, Tokyo; founder, dir. Festival der Zukunft, Ernen, Switzerland. First pub. appearance, 1936, concerts throughout Europe, N.Am., Japan, Africa, 1957—; rec. artist for, Erato, Mercury, Philips records. Recipient Internat. Prize Berlin, Germany, 1951, Liszt Prize, Budapest, 1952, Grand Prix du Disque, Paris, 1958, Gold medal City of Paris, 1995, Prix de Consécration of the Canton Wallis, Switzerland, 1996; named hon. citizen City of Ernen, 2d Order of Merit, Republic of Hungary, Chevalier de l'Ordre des Arts et des Lettres, Paris, 1997. Home: Woodcrest Ct 2610 E 2nd St Bloomington IN 47401-5349

SEBOLD, DUANE DAVID, food manufacturing executive; b. Dorchester, Wis., Mar. 25, 1945; s. Louis J. and Geraldine M. (Herman) S.; m. Kathrin Saunders, June 6, 1970 (dec. Sept. 1973); m. Marcia K. Church, Mar. 19, 1989. BS, U. Wis., Stevens Point, 1967; degree advanced mgmt., Wharton Bus. Sch., 1989. Salesman Ciba-Geigy Corp., San Diego, 1970-73, sales mgr., 1973-76; dir. sales and mktg. Tombstone Pizza Corp., Medford, Wis., 1976-77, v.p. mktg., 1977-80, exec. v.p., gen. mgr., 1980-86, pres., chief exec. officer, 1986-89; chief exec. officer Sebold Enterprises, Medford, 1990—; pres. Nat. Frozen Pizza Inst., McLean, Va., 1985-87; chmn. Tombstone Pizze Found., Medford, 1983—; chmn. policy adv. coun. Marshfiel Med. Rsch. Found.; chmn. Tombstone Pizze Exec. Com., Medford, 1986-89; dir. Accrediting Commn. on Edn. for Health Svcs. Adminstrn., Marshfield Med. Rsch. Found., U. Wis.-Stevens Point Found. Bd. dirs. Arthritis Found., Milw., 1985-86; guest spkr. U. Wis.-Madison Exec. Program, 1984-90. With USN, 1967-70. Recipient Disting. Alumni award U. Wis., 1994. Mem. Am.

Mktg. Assn., Am. Mgmt. Assn., Nat. Mgmt. Assn. (Marketer of Yr. 1979, Gold Knight award of Mgmt. 1988), Safari Club Internat., Ducks Unltd., Found. for N.Am. Wild Sheep, Toastmasters. Roman Catholic. Avocations: hunting, fishing, golf. Home and Office: 5369W N Chelsea Ave Medford WI 54451

SEBOLD, RUSSELL PERRY, III, Romance languages educator, author; b. Dayton, Ohio, Aug. 20, 1928; s. Russell Perry and Mary (Kiger) S.; m. Jane Norvell Hale, Nov. 24, 1955; children: Mary Norvell, Alice Hale. Student, U. Chgo., 1945-47; B.A., Ind. U., 1949; M.A. (Woodrow Wilson fellow), Princeton U., 1951, Ph.D., 1953; D.Phil. and Letters (hon.), U. Alicante, Spain, 1984. Instr. Spanish, Duke U., 1955-56; instr. Spanish, U. Wis., 1956-58, asst. prof., 1958-62, assoc. prof., 1962-66; prof. Spanish, chmn. dept. fgn. langs. and lits. U. Md., 1966-68; prof. Spanish, U. Pa., 1968-88, chmn. dept. Romance langs., 1968-78, Edwin B. and Leonore R. Williams prof. Romance langs., 1988—; mem. adv. coun. Soc. Ibero-Am. Enlightenment, 1968—, treas., 1969—; steering com. Am. Soc. Eighteenth Century Studies, 1970—; corresponding academician Royal Spanish Acad., 1993—, Royal Acad. Humane Letters of Barcelona, 1993—. Author: Tomás de Iriarte: poeta de rapto racional, 1961, El rapto de la mente, 1970, 2nd edit., 1989, Colonel Don José Cadalso, 1970, Cadalso: el primer romántico europeo de España, 1974, Novela y autobiografía en la Vida de Torres Villarroel, 1975, Trayectoria del romanticismo español, 1983, Descubrimiento y fronteras del neoclasicismo español, 1985, Bécquer en sus narraciones fantásticas, 1989, De Ilustrados y románticos, 1992; author, editor: Fray Gerundio de Campazas (José Francisco de Isla), 4 vols, 1960-64, 2d edit., 1992, Visiones y visitas de Torres con don Francisco de Quevedo por la Corte (Diego de Torres Villarroel), 1966, 2d edit., 1991, Numancia destruida (Ignacio López de Ayala), 1971, Poética (Ignacio de Luzán), 1977, Comedias (Tomás de Iriarte), 1978; Gustavo Adolfo Bécquer (antologia crítica), 1985, Vida (Diego de Torres Villarroel), 1985, Rimas (Gustavo Adolfo Bécquer), 1991, (with David T. Gies) Ilustración y neoclasicismo, 1992, Noches lúgubres (José de Cadalso), 1993, (with Jesus Perez Magallon) El hombre practico (Conde de Fernán Núñez), 1996 ; gen. editor: Hispanic Rev.; adv. editor Eighteenth Century Studies, 1983, Cuadernos para Investigación de la Literatura Hispánica, 1987—, Discurso Literario, 1987—, El Gnomo, 1992—, Dieciocho, 1994—, Siglo XIX, 1995; columnist ABC newspaper, Madrid, 1985—; contbr. articles to profl. jours. Served with AUS, 1953-55. Guggenheim fellow, 1962-63; Am. Philos. Soc. grantee, 1971, 76, 82; Am. Council Learned Socs. fellow, 1979-80. Mem. Am. Assn. Tchrs. Spanish and Portuguese, Am. Assn. Tchrs. French, Ctr. 18th Century Studies (Oviedo, Spain), Sociedad de Literatura Española del Siglo XIX, Hispanic Soc. Am. (corr. mem.), Phi Beta Kappa, Phi Gamma Delta, Sigma Delta Pi. Episcopalian. Home: 16 Flintshire Rd Malvern PA 19355-1108 Office: U Pa Dept Romance Langs Philadelphia PA 19104-6305

SEBOROVSKI, CAROLE, artist; b. San Diego, June 16, 1960; d. Stanley and Eleanor Frances (Ononska) S. BFA, Calif. Coll. Arts and Crafts, 1982; MFA, Hunter Coll., 1987. Artist: solo exhibitions include: Damon Brandt Gallery, N.Y.C., 1986, Hunter Coll. Art Gallery, N.Y.C., 1986, Lorence-Monk Gallery, N.Y.C., 1988, 89, Galerie Karsten Greve, Paris, 1991, 94, Cologne, 1992, Milan, 1995, Angles Gallery, Santa Monica, Calif., 1991, 92, 93, 96, Betsy Senior Contemporary Prints, N.Y.C., 1993, John Weber Gallery, N.Y.C., 1993, 95, John Berggruen Gallery, San Francisco, 1994, Locks Gallery, Phila., 1997, Karsten Greve, Koln, 1997; group exhbns. at: Willard Gallery, N.Y.C., 1984, Nora Haime Gallery, N.Y.C, 1985, 86, 93, 95, Manhattan Arts Ctr., N.Y.C., 1985, Hillwood Art Gallery L.I. Univ., Brookville, N.Y., 1985, Damon Brandt Gallery, 1985, 86 (2), 87, Mus. de Arte, La Tertuila, Columbia, 1986, Weatherspoon Gallery, Greensboro, N.C., 1986, Barbara Krakow Gallery, Boston, 1986, 88, 90 (travels to John C. Stoller & Co., Mpls.), Anne Plumb Gallery, N.Y.C., 1987, Am. Acad. and Inst. Arts and Letters, 1987, Bklyn. Mus., 1987, Lorence-Monk Gallery, 1987, 89 (3), 90, 91 (2), Carnegie Mellon U. Art Gallery, Pitts., 1988, Reynolds/ Minor Gallery, Richmond, Va., 1988, John Good Gallery, N.Y.C., 1988, 92, Pamela Auchincloss Gallery, N.Y.C., 1988, Dart Gallery, Chgo., 1988, Angles Gallery, 1989, Persons & Lindell Gallery, Helsinki, Finland, 1989, Anderson Gallery Va. Commonwealth U., Richmond, 1989, Baxter Gallery, Richmond, 1989, Hillwood Art Gallery, Brookville (travels through 1991 to Blum Helman Gallery, N.Y.C., Richard F. Brush Gallery, Canton, N.Y., Contemporary Mus. Art, Caracas, Venezuela), Cheryl Haines Gallery, San Francisco, 1989, 94, 96, Security Pacific Corp. Gallery, Santa Monica, 1990, Meml. Art Gallery U. Rochester, N.Y., 1990, Hood Mus. Art Dartmouth Coll., Hannover, N.H., 1990, San Francisco Mus. of Art, 1991, Pfizer, Inc. (Mus. Modern Art, N.Y. Collection), 1991, John Berggruen Gallery, 1991, travelling exhbn. to Anthony Ralph Gallery at Earl McGrath, L.A., Mars Gallery, Tokyo, Katonah Mus. Art, N.Y., Ind. U. Fine Arts Gallery, Kerr Gallery, Alberta Coll. of Art, Can., Huntsville Mus. Art, Ala., Worcester Art Mus., Mass., Lamont Gallery N.H., San Diego State U. Gallery, 1992, Barbara Mathes Gallery, N.Y.C., 1993, Transamerica Pyramid Lobby, San Francisco, 1993, travelling exhbn. to The Drawing Ctr., N.Y., Corcoran Gallery Art, Washington, Santa Monica Mus., L.A., The Forum, St. Louis, Am. Ctr., Paris, 1993, Addison Gallery, Andover, Mass., 1994, John Weber Gallery, 1994, 96, Huntington Gallery Mass. Coll. Art, Boston, 1995, Rice U. Art Gallery, Houston, 1995, The Altered Stages, N.Y., 1995, Brooke Alexander Gallery, N.Y.C., 1995, Thread Waxing Space, N.Y., 1996, Duchess County C.C., N.Y., 1996, Gallery 7, Hong Kong, 1996, Century Club, N.Y.C., 1996, Dutchess Coll., N.Y., 1997; represented in permanent collections including Whitney Mus. Art, N.Y., Paine Webber, N.Y., Weatherspoon Art Gallery, Greensboro, N.C., J. Walter Thompson, N.Y., Refco Collection, Chgo., Panza Collection, Italy, San Francisco Mus. Modern Art, Mus. Modern Art, N.Y., Mus. Cantonale d'Arte, Lugano, Switzerland, Met. Mus. Art, N.Y., Merril Lynch Inc., N.Y., MIT Visual Ctr., Hood Mus. Art, Hanover, N.H., Fogg Art Mus., Harvard U., Cambridge, Mass., Cleve. Ctr. Contemporary Art, Chase Manhattan Bank, N.Y., Carnegie Mus. Art, Pitts., Bklyn. Mus., Balt. Mus., Anderson Collection, Calif., Addison Gallery, Phillips Acad., Andover, Mass. Grantee Pollock-Krausner Found., 1986, NEA, 1991, Art Devel. Com., 1997; named Artist in Residence, Villa Monalvo, Saratoga, Calif., 1989, Djerassi Found., Calif., 1990; Agnes Bourne fellow in visual arts, 1990. Achievements include works in permanent collections of: Weatherspoon Art Gallery, Greensboro, N.C., Whitney Mus. of Art, N.Y.C., Refco Collection, Chgo., Met. Mus. of Art, MIT Visual Ctr., Fogg Art Mus., Harvard U., Cleve. Ctr. for Contemporary Art, Carnegie Mus. of Art, Pitts., Bklyn. Mus., Balt. Mus., Addison Gallery, Phillips Acad., Andover, Mass. Home: Box 171 S Anson Rd Stanfordville NY 12581

SEBRIS, ROBERT, JR., lawyer; b. N.Y.C., May 20, 1950; s. Robert and Ruth (Kagis) S.; m. S. Lawson Hollweg, Sept. 8, 1973; children: Jared Matthew, Bryan Taylor. BS in Indsl. Labor Rels., Cornell U., 1972; JD, George Washington U., 1978. Bar: D.C. 1978, Wash. 1980. Labor rels. specialist Onondaya County Office labor rels., Syracuse, N.Y., 1973-74, U.S. Dept. Labor, Washington, 1972-75; labor rels. mgr. U.S. Treasury Dept., Washington, 1975-78; employee rels. mgr. Washington, 1978-80; assoc. Davis, Wright, Todd, Riese & Jones, Seattle, 1980-84; ptnr. Davis, Wright, Tremain, Bellevue, Wash., 1985-92, Sebris Busto, P.S., Bellvue, Wash., 1992—; expert witness T.E.A.M. Acd. Amendments NLRA hearing, 1997. Co-Author: Employer's Guide to Strike Planning, 1985; contbr. articles to profl. jours. Pres. Bellevue C.C. Found., 1988-95; co-chair employment law cert. program U. Wash. Law Sch., 1996. Mem. ABA (health law forum, labor and employment law sect., com. on employee rights), Wash. Bar Assn., D.C. Bar Assn., Seattle/King County Bar Assn. (chmn. 1991-92, labor law sect.), Pacific Coast Labor Law Conf. (planning com. 1980-93, chmn. 1991-92), Nat. Acad. Hosp. Attys., Soc. Human Resource Mgmt. Avocations: golf, soccer, coaching youth sports. Home: 16301 Mink Rd NE Woodinville WA 98072-9463 Office: Sebris Busto PS 1500 Plaza Center 10900 NE 8th St Bellevue WA 98004-4405

SECADA, JON, musician; b. Cuba, 1962. Albums include Otro dia Mas Sin Verte, 1992, Jon Secada, 1992, Hear, Soul & A Voice, 1994, Si Te Vas, 1994, Amor, 1995; soundtrack include Pochahontas, 1995. Recipient Music award for Best Latin Pop Performance, 1996. Office: Capitol Records Inc EMI Latin 1750 Vine St Hollywood CA 90028-5209*

SECHRIST, CHALMERS FRANKLIN, JR., electrical engineering educator; b. Glen Rock, Pa., Aug. 23, 1930; s. Chalmers F. and Lottie V. (Smith) S.; m. Lillian Beatrice Myers, June 29, 1957; children: Jonathan A., Jennifer N. BEE, Johns Hopkins U., 1952; MS, Pa. State U., 1954, PhD in Elect. Engring., 1959. Sr. engr. Bendix Corp., summers 1952, 53, 54; instr. elec. engring. Pa. State U., 1954-55; staff engr. HRB-Singer, Inc., State College, Pa., 1959-65; from asst. prof. to prof. elec. engring. U. Ill., Urbana, 1965-96, assoc. head instructional programs dept. elec. and computer engring., 1984-86, asst. dean engring., 1986-96, prof. Emeritus, 1996—; program dir. divsn. undergrad. edn. NSF, Washington, 1992-96; acting sci. sec. Sci. Com. on Solar-Terrestrial Physics, 1981; chmn. publs. com. Middle Atmosphere Program, 1980-86, editor handbook, 1981-86. Editor: Proc. Aeronomy Confs, 1965, 69, 72; contbr. articles to profl. jours. NSF grantee. Mem. Edn. Soc. of IEEE (v.p. 1989-90, pres. 1991-92, edn. activities bd. 1990, 92-93, 97, tech. activities bd. 1991-92, life), Am. Geophys. Union, Am. Meteorol. Soc., Am. Soc. for Engring. Edn. Home: 12767 Yacht Club Cir Fort Myers FL 33919-4589

SECK, MAMADOU MANSOUR, ambassador, career officer; b. Dakar, Senegal, July 3, 1935. Attended, St. Cyr Milit. Acad., France, Salon Air Force Acad., French Air War Coll., Institut des Hautes Etudes de la Def. Nat. Commanding officer 1st Senegalese Air Force Squad, 1966; comdr. 1st Senegalese Air Force, 1972; dep. chief gen. staff, 1980-84, spl. chief of staff to Pres. of Republic of Senegal, chief of staff of Sene-Gambia Confedn., 1984, gen. chief of staff, gen. chief Confedn., 1988; amb. to U.S. Govt. of Republic of Senegal, 1993-97; amb. to Mex., Arbentina, Jamaica, Haiti, Trinidad and Tobago, Barbados, 1997—. Decorated Senegal, France, Gabon, Hollan, Luxembourg. Office: Embassy of Republic of Senegal 2112 Wyoming Ave NW Washington DC 20008-3926

SECOR, DONALD TERRY, JR., geologist, educator; b. Oil City, Pa., Nov. 22, 1934; s. Donald Terry and Mary Elizabeth (LaRue) S.; m. Dorothy Eisenhart, June 15, 1959; children: Beth Ann, Jane Marie, Carol Lynn. B.S., Cornell U., 1957, M.S., 1959; Ph.D., Stanford U., 1963. Asst. prof. geology U. S.C., Columbia, 1962-66, assoc. prof., 1966-79, prof., 1979—, chmn. dept., 1966-68, 77-81. Am. Assn. Petroleum Geologists Disting. lectr., 1978-79; recipient U. S.C. Ednl. Found. award, 1991; NSF grantee, 1966-70, 76-94, U.S. Geol. Survey grantee, 1979-82. Fellow Geol. Soc. Am.; mem. Am. Geophys. Union, AAAS. Home: RR 1 Box 251 Newberry SC 29108-9738 Office: U SC Dept Geol Scis Columbia SC 29208

SECORD, LLOYD DOUGLAS, healthcare administrator; b. Lachine, Que., Can., Nov. 22, 1946; s. George William and Gladys Mable (Wilson) S.; m. Louise Margaret Morrison, Dec. 21, 1966; children: Steven Lloyd, Gordon Arthur, Mary Elizabeth. BS in Chemistry, U. New Brunswick, 1968; M of Adminstrn., U. Toronto, Ont., Can., 1970. Cert. accreditation surveyor Can. Coun. on Health Facilities, 1990-92. Adminstrv. resident Toronto East Gen. and Orthopaedic Hosp., 1969-70; adminstrv. asst. Moncton Hosp., summer 1968, asst. adminstr., 1970-75; exec. dir. Kiwanis Nursing Home Inc., 1975—; facility adminstr. Region 2 Hosp. Corp., Sussex, N.B., Can., 1975—; sec. Sussex Health Ctr. Svcs. Inc., Bryant Dr. Holdings Inc., 1975—, CEO, adminstr. hosp., 1975—; chmn. adv. com. Min. Health; mem. Fundy Linen Svcs. Inc., 1976-92; mem. regional hosp. planning com. Health Region II, 1974-76; commr. of oaths, 1975—. Bd. dirs. Atlantic Bapt. Sr. Citizen's Home Inc., 1973-79, original bldg. com., 1971-74, rec. sec., 1971-74, chmn. bldg. com.; founding chmn. Comty. Based Svcs. Coord. Com. for Sussex, 1981; founding pres. Sussex Sr. Housing Inc., 1981, 82; established Sussex Health Ctr. Svcs. Inc., 1991, Bryant Dr. Holdings Inc., 1992-93; founding sec. Kings County Wellness Ctr., 1997; bd. trustees, bd. deacons Sussex United Bapt. Ch.; dir. Sussex br. Order of St. John, 1976-78, 90-92; trombonist Sussex Comty. Adult Band, 1989—. Lord Beaverbrook scholar, Leonard Found. scholar. Fellow Can. Coll. Health Svc. Execs., Soc. Mgmt. Accountants Can., Am. Coll. Health Care Execs. (affiliate, regent for Atlantic provinces 1992—, membership oral examiner 1984, 85, 86, 88, 93, 95, 96, mem. ethics com. 1985-88), Can. Coll. Health Svc. Execs. (various provincial coms.), Soc. Mgmt. Accts. Can. (cert., mem. provincial coun. 1977-88, provincial sec.-treas. 1982, provincial chmn. 1987, nat. edn. svcs. com. 1985, 86, nat. bd. dirs. 1986, 87, nat. strategic planning com. 1986); mem. New Brunswick Hosp. Assn. (numerous provincial coms.), New Brunswick Assn. Nursing Homes (numerous provincial coms.), Northeastern Can./Am. Health Coun. (Can. co-chmn. 1991-94, co-chair internat. mini conf. on rural health care New London, N.H. 1988, chair bi-ann. conf. Montreal 1991), Provincial Ambulance Operators Assn. (exec. com. 1990-96), Sussex and Dist. C. of C. (pres. 1985), Kiwanis Club Sussex Inc. (pres. 1985). Avocations: band, golf, gardening, painting, education. Office: Sussex Health Ctr, PO Box 5006/Leonard Dr, Sussex, NB Canada E0E 1P0

SECULAR, SIDNEY, federal agency administrator, procurement analyst; b. N.Y.C., Dec. 20, 1940; s. Benjamin and Mollie (Stern) S.; m. Mildred Lucille Vance, Nov. 1, 1969. BA, SUNY, Stony Brook, 1962. Cert. high sch. tchr. Contract asst. U.S. Army, Bklyn., 1962-66; contract specialist USN, Washington, 1966-67, FDA, Washington, 1967-68; contracting officer Dept. Justice, Washington, 1968-81; procurement ctr. rep., counselor to small bus. SBA, Washington, 1986—; mem. consumer bd. Giant Food Corp., WSSC Water Utility; freelance writer Silver Spring, Md., 1985-86, 89—; weather forecaster Washington Weatherline, Bethesda, Md., 1982-91, Comprehensive Weather Svcs., 1982-85, Bell Atlantic Telephone Co., 1991—. Activist Citizens to Preserve Old Silver Spring, 1981—, East Silver Spring Citizens Assn., 1981—; vice chmn. Md. Libertarian Party, 1977-78. With U.S. Army, 1963-69. Recipient performance and suggestion awards U.S. DEA and SBA. Mem. Am. Soc. Pub. Adminstrn., Nat. Contract Mgmt. Assn., Am. Meteorol. Soc., Am. Numis. Assn., Area Small and Disadvantaged Bus. Coun., Ctr. Hiking Club (trails dir. 1975), Masons. Avocations: natural health studies and counseling, meteorology, American history, environmental improvement, entrepreneurial activities. Home: 740 Silver Spring Ave Silver Spring MD 20910-4661 Office: US SBA Code SBA Arlington VA 22245-5200

SECUNDA, EUGENE, marketing communications executive, educator; b. Bklyn., June 15, 1934; s. Sholom and Betty (Almer) S.; m. Shirley Carol Frummer, Sept. 23, 1961; children—Ruthanne, Andrew. Comml. degree, N.Y. Inst. Photography, 1955; B.S., NYU Sch. Bus., 1956; M.S., Boston U., 1962; PhD, NYU, 1988. News editor Sta.-WBMS, Boston, 1956-57; reporter New London (Conn.) Daily Day, 1958-59; publicist various Broadway shows, 1959-62; sr. publicist 20th Century Fox Film Corp., N.Y.C., 1962-65; with J. Walter Thompson Co., N.Y.C., 1965-73; dir. corp. and public affairs J. Walter Thompson Co., 1974-78, sr. v.p., dir. entertainment group, 1974-80; dir. entertainment div. J. Walter Thompson Co., N.Y.C., 1978-80; sr. v.p., dir. communications services N.W. Ayer Internat., N.Y.C., 1980-82; pres. Barnum/Secunda Assocs., N.Y.C., 1982-85, Secunda Mktg. Communications, N.Y.C., 1985—; adj. prof. advt. NYU, N.Y.C., 1972-85; prof. mktg. and advt. NYU Grad. Sch. Bus., N.Y.C., 1985-88, Baruch Coll., CUNY, 1988-93; prof. mktg. Adelphi U., Garden City, N.Y., 1993-96, N.Y.U., 1993—; guest lectr. FBI Acad., 1993-96; Columbia U., UCLA; pres. Secunda Mktg. Communication, N.Y.C., 1985—. Contbr. articles to profl. jours. Mem. Greenwich Village Trust. Served with USAR, 1957-63. Mem. NATAS, Internat. Comm. Assn., Internat. Advt. Assn., Am. Acad. Advt., Mcpl. Arts Soc., Am. Mktg. Assn. Address: 30 Fifth Ave New York NY 10011-8859

SEDACCA, ANGELO ANTHONY, financial executive; b. Bronx, N.Y., Mar. 14, 1971; s. Joseph and Marie Ann (Rella) S. BA in French Studies, Fordham U., 1993, BA in Italian Studies, 1993; MA in French Lang. and Civilization, NYU, 1995; postgrad. Inst. Religious Studies, St. Joseph's Sem. Asst. martial arts instr. U.S.A. Martial Arts Ctr., 1991-94; tchr. Italian, St. Raymond's H.S., Bronx, 1994; Italian-English and French-English translator Legal Lang. Svcs., N.Y.C., 1994-97; tchr. theology and Italian Salesian H.S., New Rochelle, N.Y., 1995-96; tchr. Latin, Our Lady of Solace Sch., Bronx, 1996; fin. officer A.I. Credit Corp., N.Y.C., 1996—. Mem. bd. govs. Fordham Prep. Sch. Alumni Assn., 1995—; mem. young alumni com. Fordham U.; eucharistic min., 1990—. Mem. Cath. League, K.C. (4th degree), N.Y. Bartenders' Assn., Secular Franciscan Order, Knights of Pythias, Knights of Malta Aux., Knights of Immaculata. Avocations: martial arts, theology, philosophy, canon law, country music, opera. Home: Apt 5C 1650 Hutchinson River Pky E Bronx NY 10461

SEDAKA, NEIL, singer, songwriter; b. Mar. 13, 1939; s. Mac and Eleanor (Appel) S.; m. Leba Margaret Strassberg, Sept. 11, 1962; children: Dara Felice, Marc Charles. Grad., Juilliard Sch. Music. Composer numerous popular songs including Breaking Up Is Hard to Do, Stupid Cupid, Calendar Girl, Oh! Carol, Stairway to Heaven, Happy Birthday Sweet Sixteen, Laughter in the Rain, Bad Blood, Love Will Keep Us Together, Solitaire, The Hungry Years, Lonely Night (Angel Face); solo performer worldwide, 1959—; appeared in NBC-TV Special, 1976; recorded numerous albums including In the Pocket, Sedaka's Back, The Hungry Years, Steppin' Out, A Song, All You Need Is the Music, Come See About Me, Greatest Hits, 1988, Oh! Carol and Other Hits, 1990, Timeless, 1992 (Platinum LP). Recipient numerous gold records and industry awards; named to Songwriters' Hall of Fame, 1980; received star on Hollywood Walk of Fame. Mem. AGVA, Am. Fedn. Musicians, AFTRA. Office: care Neil Sedaka Music 201 E 66th St Apt 3N New York NY 10021-6454

SEDARES, JAMES L., conductor; b. Chgo., Jan. 15, 1956. BMusEd, Webster U., 1977; MMusEd, Washington U., St. Louis, 1979. Assoc. condr. San Antonio Symphony, 1979-89; music dir. Phoenix Symphony Orch., 1989-96, also prin. condr. Office: Herbert Barrett Mgmt 1776 Broadway Ste 1610 New York NY 10019-2002*

SEDDON, JOHANNA MARGARET, ophthalmologist, epidemiologist; b. Pitts.; m. Ralph Hingson, 1974. BS, U. Pitts., 1970, MD, 1974; MS in Epidemiology, Harvard U., 1976. Intern Framingham (Mass.) Union Hosp., 1974-75; resident Tufts New Eng. Med. Ctr., Boston, 1976-80; fellow ophthalmic pathology Mass. Eye and Ear Infirmary, Boston, 1980-81, clin. fellow vitreoretinal Retina Svc., 1981-82; instr. clin. ophthalmology Harvard Med. Sch., Boston, 1982-84, asst. prof., asst. surgeon ophthalmolgy, 1984, assoc. prof., 1989—; assoc. surgeon, dir. ultrasound svc. Mass. Eye and Ear Infirmary, Boston, 1989—, orgn. epidemiology rsch. unit, 1984-85, dir. epidemiology unit, 1985—, surgeon in ophthalmology, 1992—; assoc. prof. faculty dept. epidemiology Harvard Sch. Pub. Health, Boston, 1992—; mem. com. vision Commn. Behavioral and Social Scis. and Edn., NRC, NAS, Washington, 1984; mem. divsn. rsch. grants NIH, 1987-89, 94—; mem. sci. adv. bd. Found for Fighting Blindness, 1994—, Macular Internat., 1994—. Author books and articles in field; mem. editl. staff ophthalmic jours. Recipient NIH Nat. Svc. Rsch. awards, 1975, 80-81, Lewis R. Wasserman merit award Rsch. to Prevent Blindness for contbns. to ophthalmic rsch., 1996; grantee, prin. investigator Nat. Eye Inst., 1984-96, Nat. Cancer Inst., 1986; med. sch. scholar, 1970-74, Henry H. Clark Med. Edn. Found. scholar, 1973. Mem. AMA, APHA, Am. Acad. Ophthalmology (Honor award 1990), Am. Med. Women's Assn., Assn. Rsch. in Vision and Ophthalmology (elected, chair epidemiology sect. 1990, trustee clin. vision epidemiology sect. 1992-97. v.p. 1996-97), Soc. Epidemiologic Rsch., New Eng. Ophthal. Soc., Am. Coll. Epidemiology, Retina Soc., Macula Soc. Home: 4 Louisburg Sq Boston MA 02108-1203

SEDDON, JOHN THOMAS, III, theologian, business consultant, educator; b. Yonkers, N.Y., Aug. 9, 1945; m. Anne Christine Iversen, June 29, 1968; 2 children. BA in Govt. and Internat. Rels., U. Notre Dame, 1967, MA in Edn., 1969; MA in Theology, Maryknoll Sch. Theology, 1980; PhD in Theology, Fordham U., 1989. Cert. tchr., N.Y. Asst. prof. theology Maryknoll (N.Y.) Sch. Theology, 1982-83; dir. fgn. affairs divsn. NYANG/USAF, Newburgh, N.Y., 1983-89; adj. prof. religious studies Sacred Heart U., Fairfield, Conn., 1990—, Ctrl. Conn. State U., New Britain, 1992—; adj. prof. mgmt. Sacred Heart U., Fairfield, Conn., 1993—; adj. prof. philosophy U. Hartford/Albertas Magnus Coll. Grad. Sch., Conn., 1993—; owner Overlooked Concepts, Newington, Conn., 1995—; adj. prof. mgmt. grad. program Albertus Magnas Coll., New Haven, Conn., 1997—; tutor, 1990—; creator of seminar series God in the Market Place, 1989—, The Five Pillars of Christian Living, 1994—, Middle Religion and Peace, 1995—, EMS: Ethical Mgmt. Sys., 1995—. Author: When Saints are Lovers, 1997. Maj. USAF, 1968-72. Mem. Am. Acad. Religion, Soc. Bibl. Lit., Coll. Theol. Soc., Soc. Christian Ethics, Am. Polit. Sci. Assn., Am. Phil. Assn., Orton Dyslexia Soc. Office: Overlooked Concepts 135 Day St Newington CT 06111

SEDELMAIER, JOHN JOSEF, film director, cinematographer; b. Orrville, Ohio, May 31, 1933; s. Josef Heinrich and Anne Isabel (Baughman) S.; m. Barbara Jean Frank, June 6, 1965; children: John Josef, Nancy Rachel, Adam Frederich. BFA, Art Inst. Chgo. at U. Chgo., 1955. Dir. art Young and Rubicam, Chgo., 1955-61; dir. art, assoc. creative dir. Clinton E. Frank, Chgo., 1961-64; dir. art, producer J. Walter Thompson, Chgo., 1964-67; pres. Sedelmaier Film Prodns., Chgo., 1967—. Retrospective exhibits Mus. Broadcast Communications, Chgo., 1988, Mus. Broadcasting, L.A., 1991, Mus. TV and Radio, N.Y.C., 1992. Recipient Golden Ducat award for short film MROFNOC Mannheim Film Festival, 1968, Golden Gate award for short film Because That's Why, San Francisco Film Festival, 1969, 82 Clio awards, 1968-92, numerous Gold, Silver and Bronze Lion awards Cannes Film Festival, 1972-90, Gold Hugo award Chgo. Film Festival, 1976, 91, 2d Ann. IDC Creative award, Chgo., 1980, Internat. Broadcasting award for world's best TV comml., 1980, 86, Clio award for dir. of yr., 1981, London Internat. Advt. awards, 1986-88, numerous awards Internat. Festival of N.Y., 1984-93, Ann. Achievement award Assn. Ind. Comml. Producers, 1988, British Design and Art Direction silver pencils, 1989; named Advt. Person of Yr., Chgo. Advt. Club, 1984, Jewish Communicator of Yr., 1985; named one of 50 Pioneers & Visionaries Who Made TV America's Medium, Advt. Age Mag., 1995; profiled in Communication Arts mag., Mar. 1976, Print mag., Jan. 1982, Fortune mag., June 1983, Newsweek mag., Nov. 1986, numerous others; featured on 60 Minutes, 48 Hours; subject of cover story Esquire mag., Aug. 1983. Office: Sedelmaier Film Prodns Inc 858 W Armitage Ave # 267 Chicago IL 60614-4329

SEDER, ARTHUR RAYMOND, JR., lawyer; b. Oak Park, Ill., Apr. 20, 1920; s. Arthur Raymond and Mary Aline (Grantham) S.; m. Marion Frances Heltzel, Feb. 28, 1942; children: James A., Susan J., Elizabeth A. Student, U. Minn., 1938-39; BSL, Northwestern U., 1946, LLB, 1947. Bar: Ill. 1948, Mich. 1961. Law clk. to Justice Vinson U.S. Supreme Ct., 1948-50; mem. Sidley & Austin., Chgo., 1950-72; pvt. practice Washington, 1985—; pres. Am. Natural Resources Co., Detroit, 1973-76; chmn., chief exec. officer, dir. Am. Natural Resources Co., 1976-85; bd. dirs. EnviroSource, Inc. Life trustee Northwestern U., Evanston, Ill. Mem. ABA, Ill. Bar Assn., Mich. Bar Assn. Home: 11221 Crest Hill Rd Marshall VA 22115-2713

SEDERBAUM, ARTHUR DAVID, lawyer; b. N.Y.C., Sept. 14, 1944; s. William and Harriet (Warschauer) S.; m. Francine Haba, Dec. 30, 1967 (div. Aug. 1982); children: Rebecca, David; m. Phyllis Padow, Jan. 18, 1986; 1 child, Elizabeth. AB cum laude, Columbia U., 1965, JD, 1968; LLM, NYU, 1972. Bar: N.Y. 1968, Fla. 1980, U.S. Dist. Ct. (so. and ea. dists.) N.Y. 1972. Assoc. Zissu, Halper & Martin, N.Y.C., 1968-70, Berlack, Israels & Liberman, N.Y.C., 1970-72, Rubin Baum Levin Constant & Friedman, N.Y.C., 1972-76; ptnr. Certilman, Haft, Balin, Buckley, Kremer & Hyman, N.Y.C., 1976-88, Olshan, Grundman, Frome, Rosenzweig & Orens, N.Y.C., 1988-92, Patterson, Belknap, Webb & Tyler, L.L.P., 1992—. Mem. adv. bd. NYU Inst. Fed. Taxation, CCH Fin. and Estate Planning. Author: Setting Up and Executing Trusts, 1988. Recipient J.K. Lasser Tax prize NYU Inst. Fed. Taxation, 1968. Fellow Am. Coll. Trusts and Estates Coun.; mem. ABA, N.Y. State Bar Assn. (vice-chmn. com. on estate planning trusts and estates law sect.), Assn. Bar City N.Y. (com. surrogates cts.), Practicing Law Inst. (chmn. income taxation of estates and trusts program). Home: 5 Pheasant Dr Armonk NY 10504-1321 Office: Patterson Belknap Webb & Tyler LLP 1133 Avenue Of The Americas New York NY 10036-6710

SEDERBAUM, WILLIAM, marketing executive; b. N.Y.C., Dec. 22, 1914; s. Harry and Sarah (Steingart) S.; m. Harriet Warschauer, Aug. 29, 1940; children: Arthur David, Caroline Joan. B.S., NYU, 1936, M.A., 1943, Ph.D. Assoc. Sigmund Pines Co., Pub. Accts., 1935-38; tchr. N.Y.C. pub. schs., 1935-39; restaurant propr., 1939-41; v.p. Schenley Distillers Co., N.Y.C., 1941-61; pres. Distbrs. New Eng., 1956-61, Melrose Distillers Co., 1959-60, Park & Tilford Distillers Co., 1959-61; exec. v.p. Meade & Co., 1961-62; v.p., mktg. dir. J. T. S. Brown Distillers Co., 1962-65; mktg. cons., 1965-67; exec. v.p., gen. mgr. Fulton Distbg. Co., 1967-77; asst. gen. mgr., dir. spl. projects Am. Distbrs. Fla., 1977—; instr. acctg. Fla. Jr. Coll., 1984-89. Mem. Eleanor Roosevelt Cancer Com.; mem. U.S. Olympic Games Com.; exec. com. Fedn. Jewish Charities, March of Dimes; bd. dirs. Jacksonville Urban League, 1975-87; mem. Com. of 100; bus. cons. Jr. Achievement Project, Jacksonville; chmn. bd. trustees, pres. men's club Reform Cong. of Merrick, L.I. Recipient Arch award NYU; named Chevalier,

Confrerie de la Chaine des Rotisseurs, Bailliage de Jacksonville, Fla. Mem. Jacksonville Wholesale Liquor Assn. (pres. 1970-76), Jacksonville Symphony Assn., Jacksonville Civic Music Assn., Jacksonville C. of C. (econ. edn. com., airline svc. com., hon. adm. of flag ship Am. Airlines), Kappa Phi Kappa. Clubs: River, Carriage (N.Y.C.); NYU, Playboy, Key. Home: 4305 Plaza Gate Ln Apt 201 Jacksonville FL 32217-4439 Office: Am Distbrs Fla 6867 Stuart Ln S Jacksonville FL 32254-3438 *Live life the way it should be-not the way it is.*

SEDGWICK, ALEXANDER, historian, educator; b. Boston, June 8, 1930; s. William Ellery and Sarah (Cabot) S.; m. Charlene Mary Maute, June 24, 1961; children—Catherine Maria, Alexander Cameron. BA, Harvard U., 1952, PhD in History, 1963. Asst. prof. history Dartmouth Coll., 1962-63; assoc. prof. U. Va., Charlottesville, 1963-66, 1966-74, prof., 1974—; chmn. history dept. U. Va., 1979-85, dean Coll. Arts and Scis., 1985-90; dean grad. studies U. Va., Charlottesville, 1990-95, univ. prof., 1995—; mem. adv. com. in history Sr. Fulbright Awards Council for Internat. Exchange of Scholars. Author: The Ralliment in French Politics 1890-98, 1965, The Third French Republic, 1870-1914, 1968, Jansenism in Seventeenth Century France, Voices in the Wilderness, 1977, The Travails of Conscience. The Arnauld Family in Early Modern France, 1997; co-author: Church, State and Society Under the Bourbon Kings of France, 1982, For Want of a Horse, 1985, That Gentle Strength, 1980, Les Discour sur les Révolutions, 1991, History Today, 1991, Chroniques de Port-Royal, 1993, 95. Served with U.S. Army, 1952-54. Fulbright fellow, 1960-62; recipient Am. Coun. Learned Socs. grant-in-aid, 1967-68, Am. Philos. Soc. grant-in-aid, 1971. Mem. AAUP (nat. council 1976-79), Soc. French Hist. Studies (sec. 1979-83, pres. 1983-84), Am. Hist. Assn., Century Assn. Home: 1409 Rugby Rd Charlottesville VA 22903-1240 Office: U Va Dept History Randall Hall Charlottesville VA 22903

SEDGWICK-HIRSCH, CAROL ELIZABETH, financial executive; b. Cin., Apr. 16, 1922; d. Howard Malcolm Sedgwick and Lucile Alleen (Willard) Sedgwick-Schenk; m. Donald Sebastian Freeman, Nov. 25, 1944 (div. July 1968); children: Elizabeth P. Freeman Closson, Lucy S. Freeman; m. William Christian Hirsch, June 16, 1983. BS, U. Cin., 1944, postgrad., 1972; postgrad., Art Acad. of Cin., 1953-56; MEd, Xavier U., 1966; MS in Criminal Justice, Xavier U., Cin., 1990. Dir., head tchr. Sacred Heart Acad. PreSch., Cin., 1952-53; caseworker dependent children Hamilton County Welfare Dept., Cin., 1959-62; instr. ednl. psychology and child devel. Wright State U., Fairborn, Ohio, 1970-71, 71-72; pres., chief exec. officer Joseph England Hutton Enterprises, Cin., 1979-97. Mem. Cin. Women's Club, Cin. Club of Cin., Kappa Alpha Theta. Avocations: golf, swimming, needlework, creative writing. Home: 9092 Lake St Alanson MI 49706-9733 also: 605 E Epworth Ave Cincinnati OH 45232-1705 Office: Joseph England Hutton Enterprises 605 E Epworth Ave Cincinnati OH 45232-1705 Mailing Address: PO Box 72 Conway MI 49722

SEDLAK, JAMES WILLIAM, organization administrator; b. Tarrytown, N.Y., Nov. 17, 1943; s. Jacob Frank and Catherine Eva (Sedlak) S.; m. G. Michaeleen Bizub, June 17, 1967; children: Frank George, Jeanette Michele Sedlak Veltri, Terri Lynn Rose. BS in Physics, Manhattan Coll., 1967; MS in Indsl. Adminstrn., Union Coll., Schenectady, 1975. Customer engr. IBM, N.Y.C., 1963-67; semicondr. engr. IBM, East Fishkill, N.Y., 1967-80; sr. engr. IBM, Harrison, N.Y., 1980-92; co-founder, nat. dir. Stop Planned Parenthood, La Grangeville, N.Y., 1986-93; pres., writer, editor The Ryan Report, STOPP (Stop Planned Parenthood) Internat., La Grangeville, 1994—; former guest lectr. med. ethics Mt. St. Mary's Coll., Newburgh, N.Y.; guest lectr. ethics Vassar Coll., Poughkeepsie, N.Y., 1986-92. Author: Quarterly Dividends, 1975, Parent Power!!, 1990, Deadly Deception, 1996; contbr. to pro-life publs. Past pres. PTO; mem. bd. advisors Am. Life League, Inc.; mem. faculty Apostles of Life Leadership Acad., Human Life Internat.; cons. to nat. and internat. pro-life groups; speaker numerous statewide pro-life convs. and events, U.S., Can., Mex., Italy, Australia, No. Ireland and New Zealand; workshop presenter nat. convs. Concerned Women for Am., Human Life Internat., Am. Life League; numerous appearances on radio and TV. Recipient Dutchess County Right to Life Pro-Lifer of Yr. award, 1984, Expectant Mother Care N.Y. Pro-Life Champion award, 1987, family life award Parent's Roundtable, 1987, Unsung Hero award Am. Life League, 1988, Disting. Svc. to Life award Grand Haven (Mich.) Pro-Lifers, 1993, also others. Mem. KC (3d degree). Roman Catholic. Office: STOPP Internat PO Box 8 Lagrangeville NY 12540

SEDLAK, S(HIRLEY) A(GNES), freelance writer; b. Chgo., Sept. 6; d. Frederick Jesse and Agnes (Baum) Machacek; m. Harold Otto Sedlak; 1 child, Linda Carol. Student, Morton Jr. Coll., Cicero, Ill. Editor children's books Benefic Press subs. Harcourt Brace Jovanovich, Westchester, Ill., 1973-75; publicity and pub. rels. The Nat. League of Am. Pen women, Inc., Chgo. br., 1987-89. Home: 2226 S 9th Ave North Riverside IL 60546-1110

SEDLAK, VALERIE FRANCES, English language educator, university administrator; b. Balt., Mar. 11, 1934; d. Julian Joseph and Eleanor Eva (Pilot) Sedlak; 1 child, Barry. AB in English, Coll. Notre Dame, Balt., 1955; MA, U. Hawaii, 1962; PhD, U. Pa., 1992. Grad. teaching fellow East-West Cultural Ctr. U. Hawaii, 1959-60; adminstrv. asst. Korean Consul Gen., 1959-60; tchr. Boyertown (Pa.) Sr. High Sch., 1961-63; asst. prof. English U. Balt., 1963-69; assoc. prof. Morgan State U., Balt., 1970—, asst. dean Coll. Arts and Scis., 1995—, sec. to faculty, 1981-83, faculty research scholar, 1982-83, 92-93, communications officer, 1989-90, dir. writing for TV program, 1990—; cons. scholar Md. Humanities Coun., 1992—. Author poetry and lit. criticism; exec. assoc. editor Middle Atlantic Writer's Assn. Rev., 1989—; assoc. editor Md. English Jour., 1994—, Morgan Jour. Undergrad. Rsch., 1995—; editor Arts and Scis. Rev., 1996—. Coord. Young Reps., Berks County, Pa., 1962-63; chmn. Md. Young Reps., 1964; election judge Baltimore County, Md., 1964-66; regional capt. Am. Cancer Soc., 1978-79; mem. adv. bd. Md. Our Md. Anniversary, 1984, The Living Constitution: Bicentennial of the Fed. Constitution, 1987. Morgan-Penn Faculty fellow, 1977-79, Nat. Endowment Humanities, 1984; named Outstanding Teaching Prof., U. Balt. Coll. Liberal Arts, 1965, Outstanding Teaching Prof. English, Morgan State U., 1987. Mem. MLA, South Atlantic MLA, Coll. Lang. Assn., Coll. English Assn. (v.p. Mid-Atlantic Group 1987-90, pres. 1990-92, exec. bd. 1992—), Women's Caucus for Modern Langs., Md. Coun. Tchrs. English, Md. Poetry and Lit. Soc., Md. Assn. Depts. English (bd. dirs. 1992—), Mid. Atlantic Writers' Assn. (founding 1981, exec. assoc. editor Mid. Atlantic Writers' Assn. Rev. 1989—), Delta Sigma Epsilon (v.p. 1992-94, pres. 1994-96). Roman Catholic. Home: 102 Gorsuch Rd Lutherville Timonium MD 21093-4318 Office: Morgan State U Coll Arts & Scis Dean Baltimore MD 21239

SEDLER, ROBERT ALLEN, law educator; b. Pitts., Sept. 11, 1935; s. Jerome and Esther (Rosenberg) S.; m. Rozanne Friedlander, Jan. 24, 1960; children: Eric, Beth. BA, U. Pitts., 1956, JD, 1959. Bar: D.C. 1959, Ky. 1968, Mich. 1979; U.S. Supreme Ct. 1969. Asst. prof., assoc. prof. law St. Louis U., 1961-65; assoc. prof. law, asst. dean Addis Ababa U., Ethiopia, 1963-66; assoc. prof. to prof. law U. Ky., Lexington, 1966-77; prof. law Wayne State U., Detroit, 1977—. Author: American Constitutional Law, 1994, Across State Lines, 1989: Applying the Conflict of Law to Your Practice, 1989 (with R. Cramton) The Sum and Substance of Conflict of Laws, 1987, Ethiopian Civil Procedure, 1968; contbr. articles to profl. jours. Gen. counsel ACLU Ky., 1971-76. Gershenson Disting. Faculty fellow, Wayne State Univ., 1985-87. Mem. ABA, AAUP, Phi Beta Kappa, Order of the Coif. Democrat. Jewish. Home: 18851 Capitol Dr Southfield MI 48075-2680 Office: Wayne State U 468 Ferry Mall Detroit MI 48202-3620

SEDLIN, ELIAS DAVID, physician, orthopedic researcher, educator; b. N.Y.C., Jan. 21, 1932; s. Arnold Boris and Sonia Lipschitz Sedlin; m. Barbara Sue Zidell, July 9, 1960; children: Faith Avril, Adrian. BS in Biology, U. Ala., 1951; MD, Tulane U., 1955; D.Med. Sci., U. Gothenburg, Sweden, 1966. Diplomate: Am. Bd. Orthopedic Surgery. Intern Mobile (Ala.) Gen. Hosp., 1955-56; resident Charity Hosp., New Orleans, 1956-57; chief resident Bronx (N.Y.). Mcpl. Hosp., 1959-60; sr. resident Henry Ford Hosp., Detroit, 1960-61, rsch. assoc., emergency room lectr., 1961-63, NIH fellow, 1963-64; jr. attending physician Detroit Receiving Hosp., 1962-63; spl. NIH fellow dept. orthopedic surgery Sahlgrenska Sjukhuset, Gothenburg, 1964-66; asst. prof. dept. orthopaedic surgery Albert Einstein Coll. Medicine, 1966-69, assoc. prof., 1969-75, prof., 1975—, dir. orthopaedic surgery, 1969-79; prof. orthopaedic surgery Mt. Sinai Sch. Medicine, 1980—, dir. orthopaedic edn. Contbr. to multiple symposia, profl. meetings, also articles to profl. jours. Served to capt. AUS, 1957-59. Fulbright scholar, 1962; NSF postdoctoral fellow, 1964; recipient P.D. McGehee award Mobile Gen. Hosp., 1956; Ludvic Hektoen gold medal AMA, 1963; Nicholas Andry award Assn. Bone and Joint Surgeons, 1964. Fellow ACS, AAAS, Am. Acad. Orthopaedic Surgeons; mem. Orthopaedic Rsch. Soc., Phi Beta Kappa. Office: 5 E 98th St New York NY 10029-6501

SEDRA, ADEL SHAFEEK, electrical engineering educator, university administrator; b. Assuout, Egypt, Nov. 2, 1943; arrived in Can., 1966; s. Chafik and Hélène (Monsour) S.; m. Doris M. Barker, May 5, 1973; children: Paul Douglas, Mark Andrew. BSEE, Cairo U., 1964; MASc in Elec. Engring., U. Toronto, Ont., Can., 1968, PhDEE, 1969. Registered profl. engr., Ont. Instr. Cairo U., 1964-66; asst. prof. elec. engring. U. Toronto, 1969-72, assoc. prof., 1972-78, prof., 1978—, chmn. dept., 1986-93, v.p., provost, chief acad. officer, 1993—; pres. Elec. Engring. Consociates Ltd., Toronto, 1979-81; bd. dirs. Info. Tech. Rsch. Ctr., Toronto, 1988-93. Coauthor: Filter Theory and Design, 1978, Microelectronic Circuits, 1982, 4th edit., 1998 (also Spanish, Korean, Greek, Italian, Portuguese, Chinese and Hebrew transls.), SPICE, 1997; contbr. over 120 articles to sci. jours. Operating grantee Nat. Scis. and Engring. Rsch. Coun. Can., 1970—; Ryerson Poly. Inst. fellow, 1988. Fellow IEEE (Darlington best paper award 1984, Edn. medal 1996, Cir. and Sys. Soc. Edn. award 1994, Guillemin Cauer paper award 1987); mem. Am. Soc. Engring. Edn. (Terman award 1988), Info. Tech. Assn. Can. (Tech. Achievement award 1993), Assn. Profl. Engrs. Ont. Home: 18 High Park Blvd, Toronto, ON Canada M6R 1M4 Office: U Toronto Simcoe Hall, 27 Kings College Cir, Toronto, ON Canada M5S 1A1

SEDWICK, JOHN W., judge; b. Kittanning, Pa., Mar. 13, 1946; s. Jack D. and Marion (Hilton) S.; m. Deborah Brown, Aug. 22, 1966; children: Jack D. II, Whitney Marie. BA summa cum laude, Dartmouth Coll., 1968; JD cum laude, Harvard U., 1972. Bar: Alaska 1972, U.S. Dist. Ct. Alaska 1972, U.S. Ct. Appeals (9th cir.) 1973. Lawyer Burr, Pease and Kurtz, Anchorage, 1972-81, 1982-92; dir. div. lands State of Alaska, Anchorage, 1981-82; judge U.S. Dist. Ct. Alaska, Anchorage, 1992—. Mem. Commonwealth North, Anchorage, 1985; bd. dirs. South Addition Alaska R.R. Com., Anchorage, 1984. Sgt. USNG, 1969-72. Mem. ABA, Alaska Bar Assn. (chmn. environ. law sect. 1984, law examiners com. 1986-89, civil rules com. 1990-92, fee arbitration com. 1991-92). Episcopalian. Office: US Dist Ct Box 32 222 W 7th Ave Anchorage AK 94513*

SEE, CAROLYN, English language educator, novelist, book critic; b. Pasadena, Calif., Jan. 13, 1934; d. George Newton Laws and Kate Louise (Sullivan) Daly; m. Richard Edward See, Feb. 18, 1955 (div. June 1959); 1 child, Lisa Lenine; m. Tom Sturak, June 11, 1959; 1 child, Clara Elizabeth Marya. BA, Calif. State U., L.A., 1958; PhD, UCLA, 1963. Prof. English, Loyola Marymount Coll., L.A., 1970-85, UCLA, L.A., 1985—; book critic L.A. Times, 1981-93, Washington Post, 1993—. Author: (novels) Rhine Maidens, 1980, Golden Days, 1986, Making History, 1991, Dreaming: Hard Luck and Good Times In America, 1995, The Handyman, 1998, also 3 others. Bd. dirs. Calif. Arts Coun., L.A., 1987-91, Day Break, for homeless, Santa Monica, Calif., 1989—, Friends of English, UCLA, 1990—; buddy for life AIDS Project Los Angeles, AIDS relief, L.A., 1990—. Recipient award Sidney Hillman Found., 1972, Robert Kirsch award L.A. Times, 1994; grantee Nat. Endowment for Arts, 1980, Guggenheim fellow, 1990-91. Mem. Writers Guild Am., Libr. Found. Calif., PEN Ctr. USA West (pres. 1990-91), Nat. Book Critics Cir. (bd. dirs. 1986-90). Democrat. Avocations: gardening, sailing, dancing, brush clearing. Home: PO Box 107 Topanga CA 90290-0107 Office: UCLA Dept English 405 Hilgard Ave Los Angeles CA 90095-9000

SEE, EDMUND M., lawyer; b. Marietta, Ohio, Oct. 9, 1943; s. Edgar Thorpe and Katherine M. (Merriam) S.; m. Ellen Engler, June 5, 1976; children: Kevin, Gregory, Tyler. BA, Wesleyan U., Middletown, Conn., 1965; JD, Harvard U., 1971. Bar: Conn. 1971. Assoc. Day, Berry & Howard, Hartford, Conn., 1971-77; ptnr. Day, Berry & Howard, Hartford, 1978—. Vol. Peace Corps, Gabon, 1965-67, Vista, 1968-69; trustee St. Joseph Coll., 1991—. Mem. Nat. Assn. Bond Lawyers, Conn. Govtl. Fin. Officers Assn. Office: Day Berry & Howard Cityplace 25th Fl Hartford CT 06103-3499

SEE, ROBERT FLEMING, JR., lawyer; b. Kansas City, Mo., Apr. 23, 1942; s. Robert Fleming and Betty (Conard) S.; m. Leslie, Apr. 26, 1985. BA with honors, U. Tex., 1964, JD with honors, 1966. Bar: Tex. 1966. Assoc. Locke, Purnell, Rain, Harrell and predecessor, Dallas, 1966, ptnr., 1972, pres., 1989-96; spkr. in field. Contbg. author: Loan Documentation Guide, 1990. Mem. bd. commrs. Dallas Housing Authority; bd. dirs., chair affordable housing com. Dallas Citizens Coun. Mem. ABA, Tex. Bar Assn., Dallas Bar Assn., Greater Dallas C. of C., North Dallas C. of C., Salesmanship Club Dallas. Office: Locke Purnell Rain Harrell 2200 Ross Ave Ste 2200 Dallas TX 75201-2748

SEE, SAW-TEEN, structural engineer; b. Georgetown, Penang, Malaysia, Mar. 23, 1954; came to U.S., 1974; d. Hock-Eng and Ewe-See (Lim) S.; m. Leslie Earl Robertson, Aug. 11, 1982; 1 child, Karla Mei. BSc in Civil Engring., Cornell U., 1977, M in Civil Engring., 1978. Registered profl. engr., N.Y., Calif., Conn., Fla., Md., N.J., Ohio, Pa., Wash. Design engr. Leslie E. Robertson Assocs., R.L.L.P., N.Y.C., 1978-81, assoc., 1981-85, ptnr., 1986—, mng. ptnr., 1990—; profl. cons. M of Engring. class Cornell U., 1994-95; project dir., project mgr. Shinji Shumeikai Mus., Kyoto, Japan, West Side H.S., N.Y.C., Jr. H.S. 234, Bklyn., Jewelry Trade Ctr., Bangkok, Bilbao (Spain) Emblematic bldgs., Internat. Trade Ctr., Barcelona, Spain, Seattle Art Mus., San Jose (Calif.) Convention Ctr., San Jose Arena; project dir. Balt. Conv. Ctr., Rock 'N Roll Hall of Fame and Mus., Cleve., Pontiac Marina Hotel and Retail, Singapore, acad. bldgs. and greenhouse, SUNY, Binghamton, N.Y.; project mgr. Coll. of Law bldg. U. Iowa, Iowa City, Neiman-Marcus store, San Francisco, AT&T Exhbn. bldg., N.Y.C., Bank of China Tower, Hong Kong, PPG Hdqs., Pitts., AT&T Corp. Hdqs., N.Y.C. Contbr. articles to profl. jours. Named to Those Who Made Marks in the Constrn. Industry in 1988, Engring. News Record, N.Y.C., 1989. Mem. ASCE, Archtl. League, Coun. on Tall Bldgs. and Urban Habitat (past chairperson com. on gravity loads and temperature effects 1982-85), Architects, Designers, Planners for Social Responsiblity, N.Y. Assn. Cons. Engrs. (dir. 1989-93, structural codes com. 1991—). Avocations: sailing, skiing, reading, photography. Home: 45 E 89th St Apt 25C New York NY 10128-1230 Office: Leslie E Robertson Assocs RLLP 211 E 46th St New York NY 10017-2935

SEEBACH, LYDIA MARIE, physician; b. Red Wing, Minn., Nov. 9, 1920; d. John Henry and Marie (Gleusen) S.; m. Keith Edward Wentz, Oct. 16, 1959; children: Brooke Marie, Scott. BS, U. Minn., 1942, MB, 1943, MD, 1944, MS in Medicine, 1951. Diplomate Am. Bd. Internal Medicine. Intern Kings County Hosp., Bklyn., 1944; fellow Mayo Found., Rochester, Minn., 1945-51; pvt. practice Oakland, Calif., 1952-60, San Francisco, 1961—; asst. clin. prof. U. Calif., San Francisco, 1981—; mem., vice chmn. Arthritis Clinic, Presbyn. Hosp., San Francisco, 1961-88, pharmacy com., 1963-78; chief St. Mary's Hosp. Arthritis Clinic, San Francisco, 1968-72; exec. bd. Pacific Med. Ctr., San Francisco, 1974-76. Contbr. articles to med. jours. Fellow ACP; mem. AMA, Am. Med. Womens Assn. (pres. Calif. chpt. 1968-70), Am. Rheumatism Assn., Am. Soc. Internal Medicine, Pan Am. Med. Womens Assn. (treas.), Calif. Acad. Medicine, Calif. Soc. Internal Medicine, Calif. Med. Assn., San Francisco Med. Soc., San Francisco Med. Assn., San Francisco Soc. Internal Medicine, No. Calif. Rheumatism Assn., Internat. Med. Women's Assn., Mayo Alumni (bd. dirs. 1983-89), Iota Sigma Pi. Republican. Lutheran. Avocations: music, cooking, gardening, needlepoint. Office: 490 Post St Ste 939 San Francisco CA 94102-1410

SEEBASS, ALFRED RICHARD, III, aerospace engineer, educator, university dean; b. Denver, Mar. 27, 1936; s. Alfred Richard Jr. and Marie Estelle (Wright) S.; m. Nancy Jane Palm, June 20, 1958; children: Erik Peter, Scott Gregory. BS in Engring. magna cum laude, Princeton U., 1958, MS in Engring., 1961; PhD, Cornell U., 1962. Rsch. asst. Cornell U., Ithaca, N.Y., 1960-62, asst. prof. aerospace engring., 1962-64, assoc. prof., 1964-72, prof. aerospace engring., assoc. dean, 1972-75; hdqrs. staff rsch. divsn. NASA, 1966-67; prof. aerospace engring., mech. engring. and math. U. Ariz., Tucson, 1975-81; dean Coll. Engring. & Applied Sci. U. Colo., Boulder, 1981-94, prof. aerospace engring. scis., 1994—, also chair, 1995—; faculty assoc. Boeing Sci. Rsch. Labs., 1970; cons. in field; mem. coms. NAE, NAS, NRC, NASA, Dept. Transp., sci. adv. bd. Air Force, Aeros. and Space Engring. Bd., Los Alamos Nat. Lab; grant investigator NASA, Office Naval Rsch., Air Force Office Sci. Rsch., 1966—; mem. univ. com. on applied math. U. Ariz., 1976-81; mem. aeronautics and space engring. bd. NRC, 1977-84, vice-chmn., 1979-81, chmn., 1981-83, mem. Commn. on Engring. and Tech. Sys., 1982-83; mem. Numerical Aerodynamics Simulator Adv. Group, 1978—; chmn. Air Force Office Scientific Rsch. rev. panel Flight Dynamics Lab., Wright-Patterson AFB, 1979; mem. NASA adv. coun., 1981-83; mem. survey com. on plasma physics and fluids, subcom. on fluids NRC, 1983-84; mem. engring. rsch. bd. Panel on Transp. Sys. Rsch., 1984-85; mem. sci. adv. bd. USAF, 1984-88, chmn. Air Force Operational Test & Evaluation Ctr. Divsn. Adv. Group, 1986-88, mem. Arnold Engring. & Devel. Ctr. Divsn. Adv. Group, 1984-88, mem. aerospace vehicles panel, 1984-88; mem. adv. coun. univ. study planning group NASA, 1988-89; bd. dirs. Boulder Tech. Incubator; mem. mech. and electronic external adv. com. Los Alamos (N.Mex.) Nat. Lab., 1991-93, chair divsn. rev. com. Engring. Scis. & Applications, Los Alamos, 1995; mem. NASA Adv. Coun. U. Rels. Task Force, 1991-93; mem. Commn. on Phys. Scis., Math. & Applications NRC, 1992-95. Editor: Sonic Boom Research, 1967, Nonlinear Waves 1974, Russian, 1977; assoc. editor: Physics of Fluids, 1978-80; mem. editl. bd. Ann. Rev. Fluid Mechanics, Phys. Fluids, AIAA Jour.; editor-in-chief (book series) Progress Astronautics and Aeronautics, 1990-95; contbg. author: Handbook of Applied Mathematics, 1974; contbr. articles to profl. jours., chpts. to books; reviewer Jour. Fluid Mechanics, Physics of Fluids, Jour. Acoustical Soc. Am., AIAA Jour., Jour. Aircraft, Jour. Applied Mechanics, NSF, others. Recipient Daniel and Florence Guggenheim fellow Princeton U., 1958-59, Woodrow Wilson fellow Cornell U., 1959-60, Disting. Engring. Alumni award U. Colo., 1983, Meritorious Civilian Svc. award Dept. Air Force, 1988, (with H. Sobieczky) Max Planck Rsch. prize, Germany, 1991, Internat. Astro. Fed. Frank J. Malina Astronautics medal 1994, U. Colo. medal 1994, U. Colo. Coll. of Engring. Centennial medal 1994, Frank J. Malina medal Internat. Astronautics Fedn., 1994. Fellow AAAS (mem. engring. sect. nominating com. 1987-90, chair 1990, coun. del. engring. sect. 1991-94, vice chair, chair engring. sect. 1995-97), AIAA (mem. fluid mechanics tech. com. 1977-80, tech. dir. bd. dirs. 1978-81, exec com. 1980-81, assoc. editor jour. 1981-83, Biannual Durand lecturer and medalist 1994); mem. Nat. Acad. Engring. (aerospace peer com. 1987-90, chair 1990, mem. com. on membership 1991-93, vice chmn. 1991, chair 1992, acad. adv. bd. 1997—), Am. Soc. Engring. Edn. (mem. sr. rsch. award com. 1990-93, chair 1993), Sigma Xi, Tau Beta Pi. Office: U Colo Campus Box 429 Coll Aerospace Engring Sci Boulder CO 80309

SEED, ALLEN H., elementary and secondary education educator, science educator; b. Lakewood, Ohio, June 9, 1953; s. Hugh A. and Patricia (Peattie) S.; m. Laura Seed, Aug. 11, 1979; children: David, Vicki. BS, Miami U., Oxford, Ohio, 1975; MEd, Miami U., 1980, PhD, 1994. Tchr. Hamilton (Ohio) city schs., Summit County Day Sch., Cin.; sci. curriculum coord. Maderia City Schs., Cin.; tchr. Maderia City Schs.; mem. adj. faculty Bowling Green State U., Miami U.; asst. prof. mid. grades edn. No. Ky. U. Greater Cin. Found. grantee; recipient Ohio Gov.'s award for sci., 1987, 88. Mem. ASCD, Nat. Staff Devel. Coun., Nat. Sci. Tchrs. Assn., Staff Devel. Coun. Ohio, Nat. Mid. Sch. Assn., Am. Ednl. Rsch. Assn., Ky. Mid. Sch. Assn. Home: 151 Hidden Hills Dr Fairfield OH 45014-8607

SEEDLOCK, ROBERT FRANCIS, engineering and construction company executive; b. Newark, Feb. 6, 1913; s. Frank Andrew and Mary Elizabeth (Prosner) S.; m. Hortense Orcutt Norton, Sept. 1, 1937; children: Robert Francis, Elizabeth Munsell Seedlock Morrissette, Walter Norton, Mary Marion. Student Case Inst. Tech., 1931-33; BS, U.S. Mil. Acad., 1937; MS in Civil Engring., MIT, 1940; grad. Armed Forces Staff Coll., 1948, Nat. War Coll., 1958. Registered profl. engr., D.C., Pa. Commd. 2d lt. U.S. Army, 1937, advanced through grades to maj. gen., 1963; asst. to dist. engr., Pitts., 1937-39, Tulsa Aircraft Assembly Plant, 1941; regtl. exec. bn. comdr. Engr. Unit Tng. Ctr., Camp Claiborne, La., 1942; asst. theatre engr., CBI, also comdr. Burma Road Engrs., also chief engr. Shanghai Base Command, 1943-45; mem. Gen. Marshall's Mediation Mission, Peking, 1946-47; mem. gen. staff U.S. Army, Mem. Am. del. Far Eastern Commn., 1948-49; aide to chief staff U.S. Army, 1949-54; mem. U.S. del. NATO Ministerial Conf., 1952-53; dep. div. engr. Mediterranean div., 1954-57; mil. asst. to asst. sec. def. for pub. affairs, 1958-62; div. engr. Missouri River, Omaha, 1962-63; sr. mem. UN Mil. Armistice Commn., Korea, 1963-64; dir. mil. personnel Office dep. chief of staff for personnel Dept. Army, 1964-66; dir. mil. constrn. Office Chief of Engrs., 1966; comdg. gen. U.S. Army Engr. Center and Ft. Belvoir, Va., and comdt. U.S. Army Engr. Sch., Ft. Belvoir, 1966-68, ret., 1968; pres. Yuba Industries, 1968-69, v.p. Standard Prudential Corp. (merged with Yuba Industries), 1969-70; v.p., dir. Petro-Chem. Devel. Co., Inc., N.Y.C., 1968-70, Petchem Constrn. Co., N.Y.C., 1968-70, Petrochem. Isoflow Furnaces, Ltd. (Can.), 1968-70; dir. constrn. and devel. Port Authority of Allegheny County, Pitts., 1970-73; assoc. Parsons, Brinckerhoff, Quade & Douglas, N.Y.C., 1973-75, mgr. So. region, 1975-77; dep. project dir. Parsons, Brinckerhoff-Tudor-Bechtel, Atlanta, 1973-77; program dir. Ralph M. Parsons Co., Pasadena, Calif., Phila. and Washington, 1977-83; cons. engr. 1983—; dir. T.Y. Lin Intl., 1985-89; chief liaison, cons. Chinese Acad. Sci. for Beijing Inst. Mgmt., 1985-89; U.S. rep. to Permanent Tech. Com. Number 1 of Permanent Intl. Assn. of Navigation Congresses, 1984-93; pres. First Am. chapt. Burma Star Assn., 1984—; chmn. Sino-Am. Ventures, Inc., 1987—; cons. The Knowledge Co., 1989—, Dove & Assocs., 1990; mem. radio engring. adv. com. Voice of Am., 1990-93. Contbr. to mil. and engring. jours. Bd. dirs. Army and Air Force Exchange and Motion Picture Svc., 1964; mem. Miss. River Commn., 1962-63, Bd. Engrs. Rivers and Harbor, 1962-63, Def. Adv. Commn. Edn., 1964; chmn. Mo. Basin Inter-Agy. Com., 1962-63; fed. rep., chmn. Big Blue River Compact Commn., 1962-63; mem. U.S. Com. on Large Dams, 1962-82; exec. bd. Nat. Capital Area council Boy Scouts Am., 1967-68, Atlanta Area council, 1975-77. Decorated DSM, Legion of Merit with oak leaf cluster; chevalier Legion of Honor (France); 1st class, grade A medal Army, navy, air force, also spl. breast order Yun Hui (China); named Engr. of Yr., Met. Atlanta Engring. Soc., 1976; Ga. Engr. of Yr. in Govt., Ga. Soc. Profl. Engrs., 1976; recipient Silver Beaver award Boy Scouts Am., 1977, Case Alumni Assn. Gold medal, 1985. Fellow Soc. Am. Mil. Engrs. (nat. dir., Cathedral Latin Alumni Assn. Man of the Yr. award 1992); mem. ASCE (hon., aerospace div. program com. 1980-82, sec. exec. com. 1982-83, chmn. 1984-85, editor Jour. Aerospace Engring., 1986-93), Assn. U.S. Army, West Point Soc. N.Y. (life), West Point Soc. Atlanta (pres. 1976), Burma Star Assn. (pres. 1st Am. chpt., 1982—), Sigma Xi, Tau Beta Pi. Roman Catholic. Clubs: Army-Navy Country (sec., chmn. bd. govs. 1952-54, 61-62) (Arlington, Va.); MIT (pres. Shanghai 1946); Met. (N.Y.C.); Oglethorpe (Savannah, Ga.), Ansley Golf (Atlanta). Home and Office: 3 Plantation Ct Savannah GA 31419-2731 *Live by Duty, Honor and Country and you will live forever.*

SEEFELDT, CAROL, education educator; b. St. Louis, May 3, 1935; d. George and Mary (Reznicek) Wohanka; m. Eugene Seefeldt; children: Paul, Andrea. BA, U. Wis., Milw., 1956; MA, U. South Fla., 1968; PhD, Fla. State U., 1971. Reg. tng. officer Fla. Project Head Start, Tallahassee, 1968-71; prof. U. Md., College Park, 1971—. Author: Social Studies for the Preschool and Primary Child, 1997, Continuing Issues in Early Childhood Education, 1990, Early Childhood Education, 1994. Bd. dirs. Md. Com. for Children, Balt., 1988-90. Named Disting. Scholar/Tchr., U. Md., 1983—. Mem. Nat. Assn. for Edn. of Young Children (tchr. edn. commn. 1986—), Assn. for Childhood Edn. Internat., Am. Ednl. Research Assn., Phi Delta Kappa. Home: 881 Mt Airy Rd Davidsonville MD 21035-2225 Office: U Md Inst for Child Study College Park MD 20742

SEEGAL, HERBERT LEONARD, department store executive; b. Brookline, Mass., Aug. 13, 1915; s. Morris and Rose (Beerman) S.; m. Dorothy Goldstein, June 27, 1941 (div. June 1954); children: Jane Laura, Norma Ann; m. Juanita C. Steele, Feb. 4, 1987. AB, U. Mich., 1937. With R.H. White's, Boston, 1937-41; with Thalhimer's, Richmond, Va., 1941-53, v.p. charge gen. merchandising, 1949-53; sr. v.p. merchandising, dir. Macy's N.Y., N.Y.C., 1953-62; pres. Bamberger's N.J., Newark, 1962-71; dir. R.H. Macy & Co., Inc., 1965—, vice chmn. bd. dirs., 1971-72, pres., 1972-80. Mem. Princeton Club (N.Y.C.), Century Country Club (Purchase, N.Y.). Home: 128 Central Park S New York NY 10019-1565 also: 2451 Windsor Way Ct West Palm Beach FL 33414-7035

SEEGAL, JOHN FRANKLIN, lawyer; b. Newton, Mass., May 21, 1946; s. Samuel Melbourne and Martha (Lewenberg) S.; m. Barbara Ellen Wayne, Apr. 2, 1982; children: Sarah Rachel, Laura Rose.B.A., Harvard U., M.B.A., 1973, J.D., 1973. Assoc. Orrick, Herrington & Sutcliffe, San Francisco, 1973-78, ptnr., 1979—. Mem. ABA, Calif. Bar Assn. Republican. Jewish. Office: Orrick Herrington & Sutcliffe 400 Sansome St San Francisco CA 94111-3304

SEEGER, LEINAALA ROBINSON, law librarian, educator; b. Wailuku, Hawaii, July 2, 1944; d. John Adam and Anna Hiilani (Leong) Robinson; 1 child, Maile Lea. BA, U. Wash., 1966; JD, U. Puget Sound, 1977; M in Law Librarianship, U. Wash., 1979. Bar: Wash. 1977. Reference librarian U. Puget Sound Sch. Law., Tacoma, 1977-79, assoc. law librarian, 1981-86; asst. librarian McGeorge Sch. Law, U. of Pacific, Sacramento, 1979-81; assoc. librarian pub. svc. Harvard Law Sch., Cambridge, Mass., 1986-89; dir. law library, assoc. prof. law U. Idaho Coll. Law, Moscow, 1989-97, U. Hawaii Sch. of Law, Honolulu, 1997—. Mem. Palouse Asian-Ams. Assn., Moscow, 1989-96. Mem. Assn. Am. Law Schs. (mem. librs. and technol. com.), Wash. state Bar Assn., Am. Assn. Law Librs. (chmn. minority com. 1990-91, v.p., pres.-elect Western Pacific chpt. 1985-86, 90-91, pres. 1991-92, vice chmn. edn. com. 1991-92, chmn. 1992-93), Idaho Coun. Acad. Librs. Avocations: scuba, snorkeling, wine education, flying, aerobics.

SEEGER, MICHAEL, musician, singer, folklorist; b. N.Y.C., Aug. 15, 1933; s. Charles Louis and Ruth Porter (Crawford) S.; m. Marjorie L. Ostrow, Dec. 20, 1960 (div. 1968); children: Kim, Arley, Jeremy; m. Alice L. Gerrard, Aug. 16, 1970 (div.); m. Alexia Smith, Aug. 27, 1995. guest lectr. English dept. U. Calif., Fresno, 1974; mem. jazz/folk/ethnic music sect. Nat. Endowment for Arts, 1973-77; dir. Am. Old Time Music Festival, 1975-78, Rockbridge Mountain Music Conv., Buena Vista, Va., 1986-92. Performs Appalachian vocal and instrumental music in a variety of styles at concerts, folk festivals, on radio and TV in U.S. and abroad; also numerous record albums and documentary recordings from traditional folk musicians and dancers; founding mem. New Lost City Ramblers, 1958—, Strange Creek Singers, 1968-76, Bent Mountain Band, 1981. Trustee John Edwards Meml. Found., UCLA, 1962—; bd. dirs. Newport (R.I.) Folk Festival, 1963-71, Nat. Folk Festival, Washington, 1972-78, Smithsonian Am. Folklife Co., 1970-76. Recipient 1st prize banjo category Galax Va. Old Time Fiddlers conf., 1975, Ralph J. Gleason Meml. award Rex Found., 1994; award of merit Internat. Bluegrass Music Assn., 1995; Grammy nominee for best traditional folk album, 1986, 91, 94; Nat. Endowment Arts grantee, 1975, 82, 84, 87; vis. scholar Smithsonian Instn., 1983; Guggenheim fellow, 1984. Home: PO Box 1592 Lexington VA 24450-1592

SEEGER, PETE, folk singer, songwriter; b. N.Y.C., May 3, 1919; s. Charles Louis and Constance de Clyver (Edson) S.; m. Toshi-Aline Ohta, July 20, 1943; children: Daniel Adams, Mika Salter, Tinya. Student, Harvard U., 1936-38. Teamed with Woody Guthrie, toured south and southwest; an organizer, Almanac Singers, 1940, toured U.S. with group, 1941-42; collaborated on writing labor and anti-Fascist songs; sang on overseas broadcasts, OWI; became nat. dir., People's Songs, Inc., 1946; performed: motion picture film To Hear My Banjo Play, 1946; toured with Progressive Party candidate Henry Wallace; helped organize the Weavers, 1948; appeared nat. radio and TV shows until blacklisted from networks, night clubs and theaters; rec. for, Decca, 1949-52, Folkways, 1953-80, Columbia, 1961-73 toured schs., summer camps, colls., univs. U.S.A. and 35 other countries; assisted orgn., Newport (R.I.) Folk Festivals; songwriter: Where Have All the Flowers Gone, 1961, If I Had a Hammer, (in collaboration with Lee Hays) Kisses Sweeter than Wine, (in collaboration with Weavers) Turn, Turn, Turn, 1959; recent albums include Sing Along, 1980, (with John Hammond) Waist Deep in the Big Muddy and other Love Songs, 1994; TV series Rainbow Quest, 1965; producer ednl. short subjects, Folklore Research Films; performed global singing tour including 24 countries, 1963-64; appeared: Smothers Bros. Show, as network blacklist was lifted, 1967; appeared in: film Tell Me That You Love Me, Junie Moon, 1970; author: American Favorite Ballads, 1961, The Bells of Rhymney, 1964, How To Play The Five-String Banjo, Henscratches and Flyspecks, 1973, The Incompleat Folksinger, 1973, (with Charles Seeger) The Foolish Frog, 1973, Abiyoyo, 1983, (with Robert Reiser) Carry It On, 1986, (with Robert Reiser) Everybody Says Freedom., 1990, Where Have All the Flowers Gone, 1993. Served with U.S. Army, 1942-45. Recipient: Nat. Medal of the Arts, 1994, Kennedy Center Honor, 1994. Pioneered the appreciation of Southern folk music through over 45 years of concerts, recordings and writings, interested many others in the idea of making their own music, revived old music of many types and used music as a means of speaking out against war, racism, poverty, pollution, etc. Office: care Harold Leventhal 250 W 57th St New York NY 10107

SEEGER, RONALD L., lawyer; b. Prairie Farm, Wis., June 10, 1930; s. John M. and Mildred G. (Moen) S.; m. Theresa A. Seeger, Sept. 3, 1955; children—Mark, Scott, John, Lynn, Eric. B.A., U. Wis., 1951; J.D., U. Minn., 1956. Bar: Minn. 1956, U.S. Dist. Ct. 1957, U.S. Supreme Ct. 1983. Pres. Dunlap & Seeger (formerly Michaels, Seeger, Rosenblad & Arnold), Rochester, Minn., 1956—. Counsel, City of Rochester Charter Commn., 1962-74, chmn., 1971-72; pres. Legal Assistance of Olmsted County, 1973-76; bd. dirs., v.p. Legal Assistance of Minn., 1972-74; chmn. Gamehaven area Boy Scout Found., 1974-76, now trustee; dir. Minn. Lawyers Mutual. Served with U.S. Army, 1951-53; Korea. Fellow Am. Bar Found.; mem. ABA (ho. of dels. 1974-80, 92-96, bd. govs. 1991-95), Minn. State Bar Assn. (bd. govs. 1974-85, pres. 1983-84, lifetime svc. award 1997), Minn. Bar Found. (dir.), Minn. Legal Cert. Bd. (chmn. 1985-90). Home: 524 9th Ave SW Rochester MN 55902-2910 Office: PO Box 549 505 Marquette Bank Bldg Rochester MN 55903

SEEGER, SONDRA JOAN, artist; b. L.A., May 27, 1942; d. Reinhold Josheph and Bertha Catherine (Monese) S.; m. Richard John Pahl, Aug. 18, 1961 (div. 1974); children: Catherine Marie, Douglas Richard, Angela Gay, Susan Joan; m. David Ernest Matteson, Apr. 25, 1990. Student, Marylhurst Coll., 1960. Pvt. practice musician various locations, 1973-81; security guard MGM Hotel, Las Vegas, 1981-82; real estate salesperson Century 21, Kent, Wash., 1983-85; mgr. Viera Land & Cattle, Inc., La Grande, Oreg., 1984-92; freelance artist, Casper, Wyo., 1991—; ptnr. Old West Saddle Shop, Casper, 1989-93, Casper, Wyo., 1993—; com. mem. Oreg. State Forest Practices Com., N.E. Region, 1990-91. Named Union Co. Tree Farmer of Yr., Am. Tree Farm System, 1987. Mem. NRA, Nat. Soc. Artists, Women Artists of the West, Allied Artists, Cider Painters of Am., Australian Soc. of Miniature Art, Small Woodlands Assn., Knickerbocker Artists (assoc.), United Pastelists of Am. (signature), Nat. Soc. Artists (signature), Women Artists of the West, Pacific Art League, The Art League of Alexandria, Va., Miniature Art Soc. Fla., Oil Painters Am., Wyo. Artists Assn., Cody Country Art Guild, Am. Soc. Classical Realism, Gen. Artist Mem., Internat. Platform Assn., Oreg. Forest Resources Inst., Am. Artists' Profl. League. Republican. Avocations: dog obedience tng., hunting, wildlife habitat enhancement. Home and Office: Old West Saddle Shop PO Box 4300 Casper WY 82604-0300

SEEGMILLER, JARVIS EDWIN, biochemist, educator; b. St. George, Utah, June 22, 1920; m. Roberta Eads, 1950; children: Dale S. Maudlin, Robert E., Lisa S. Taylor, Richard L. (dec. 1992); m. Barbara A. Ellertson, 1995. AB, U. Utah, 1942; MD, U. Chgo., 1948. Asst. U.S. Bur. Mines, Utah, 1941; asst. nat. def. rsch. com. Northwestern Tech. Inst., 1942-44; asst. medicine U. Chgo., 1948-49; intern Johns Hopkins Hosp., 1948-49; biochemist Nat. Inst. Arthritis and Metabolic Diseases, 1949-51; rsch. assoc. Thorndike Meml. Lab. Harvard Med. Sch., 1952-53; vis. investigator Pub. Health Rsch. Inst., N.Y.C., 1953-54; chief sect. human biochemistry, genetics, asst. sci. dir. Nat. Inst. Arthritis and Metabolic Diseases, 1954-69; prof. dept. medicine, dir. divsn. rheumatology U. Calif., San Diego, 1969-90, founding dir. Stein Inst. Rsch. Aging, 1983-90, prof. emeritus medicine, assoc. dir. Stein Inst. Rsch. Aging, 1990—; vis. scientist U. Coll. Hosp. Sch. Medicine, London, 1964-65; Harvey Soc. lectr., 1970. Contbr. numerous articles to profl. jours. Macy scholar Basel Inst. Immunology; Guggenheim fellow Swiss Inst. Exptl. Cancer Rsch., Lausanne, 1982-83, John Simon Guggenheim Meml. Found. fellow, 1982, Fogarty Internat. fellow Oxford U., 1989. Mem. Nat. Acad. Sci., Harvey Soc. (hon.), Am. Soc. Biol. Chemists, Am. Rheumatism Assn., Am. Fedn. Clin. Rsch., Am. Soc. Human Genetics, Am. Soc. Clin. Investigation, AAAS, Assn. Am. Physicians, Am. Acad. Arts and Sci. Office: U Calif at San Diego 9500 Gilman Dr La Jolla CA 92093-5003

SEEHRA, MOHINDAR SINGH, physics educator, researcher; b. Panjab, Pakistan, Feb. 14, 1940; came to U.S., 1963; s. Bakhshish Singh and Rattan (Kaur) S.; m. Harbhajan Kaur, May 12, 1963; children: Jasmeet, Parveen. BS, Panjab U., 1959; MS, Aligarh (India) U., 1962; PhD, U. Rochester, 1969. Instr. chemistry Arya Coll., Nawanshahr, India, 1959-60; lectr. physics Jain Coll., Ambala City, India, 1962-63; asst. prof. physics W.Va. U., Morgantown, 1969-73, assoc. prof., 1973-77, prof., 1977-91, Eberly disting. prof. physics, 1992—. Contbr. numerous articles to profl. jours. Rsch. fellow A.P. Sloan Found., 1973-75, ORAU Summer fellow, 1976, 77, 84, 85; recipient Outstanding Rsch. award Coll. Arts and Scis., U. W.Va., 1985. Fellow Am. Phys. Soc., Materials Rsch. Soc., ASM Internat. Office: WVa State U Dept Physics PO Box 6315 Morgantown WV 26506-6315

SEELBACH, WILLIAM ROBERT, management executive; b. Lakewood, Ohio, Apr. 26, 1948; s. William Fowler and Carolyn (Paisley) S.; m. Nancy Chockley, June 28, 1969; children: Scott, Ryan. BS, Yale U., 1970; MBA, Stanford U., 1972. Assoc. Intasa, Menlo Park, Calif., 1972-74; sr. assoc. Griffenhagen-Kroeger, San Francisco, Calif., 1974-75; assoc. to ptnr. McKinsey & Co., Cleve., 1975-86; pres. Parkwood Corp., 1986-88; chmn. Inverness Ptnrs. and Inverness Castings Group, Cleve., 1988—; bd. dirs. Lumitex, Inc., Cleve. Trustee Work in N.E. Ohio Coun., Cleve., 1984—, Enterprise Devel. Inc., Cleve., 1985—, Playhouse Sq. Found., Cleve., 1986—, Univ. Sch., Cleve. Office: Inverness Ptnrs 25700 Science Park Dr Beachwood OH 44122-7312 also: Inverness Castings Group Inc 65059 M 43 Bangor MI 49013-9674

SEELENFREUND, ALAN, distribution company executive; b. N.Y.C., Oct. 22, 1936; s. Max and Gertrude (Roth) S.; m. Ellyn Bolt; 1 child, Eric. BME, Cornell U., 1959, M. in Indsl. Engring., 1960; PhD in Mgmt. Sci., Stanford U., 1967. Asst. prof. bus. adminstrn. Grad. Sch. Bus. Stanford U., Palo Alto, Calif., 1966-71; mgmt. cons. Strong, Wishart and Assocs., San Francisco, 1971-75; various mgmt. positions McKesson Corp., San Francisco, 1975-84, v.p., chief fin. officer, 1984-86, exec. v.p., chief fin. officer, 1986-89, chmn., CEO, 1989-97, chmn., 1997—, also bd. dirs., chmn., 1997—; bd. dirs. Pacific Gas and Electric Co. Bd. dir. Golden Gate Nat. Park Assn. Mem. World Affairs Coun. No. Calif., Bay Area Coun., Calif. Bus. Roundtable, Bankers Club, St. Francis Yacht Club, Villa Taverna Club, Pacific Union Club. Avocations: sailing, skiing. Office: McKesson Corp 1 Post St San Francisco CA 94104-5203

SEELER, RUTH ANDREA, pediatrician, educator; b. N.Y.C., June 13, 1936; d. Thomas and Olivia (Patten) S. BA, U. Vt., 1959, MD, 1962. Diplomate Am. Bd. Pediatrics, Am. Bd. Pediatric Hematology/Oncology. Intern Bronx (N.Y.) Mcpl. Hosp., 1962-65; pediats. hematology/oncology fellow U. Ill., 1965-67; dir. pediatric hematology/oncology Cook County Hosp., 1967-84; prof. pediatrics, dir. pediatric edn. coll. medicine U. Ill., Chgo., 1984—; assoc. chief pediatrics Michael Reese Hosp., Chgo., 1990—; course coord. pediatrics Nat. Coll. Advanced Med. Edn., Chgo., 1987-96; mem. subboard Pediatric Hematology/Oncology, Chapel Hill, 1990-95. Mem. editl. bd. Am. Jour. Pediatric Hematology/Oncology, 1985-95. Jr. and sr. warden, treas. Ch. Our Saviour, Chgo., 1970-92; founder camp for hemophiliacs Hemophilia Found., Ill., 1973—, current med. dir.; pres. Hemophilia Found. Ill., 1981-85. Mem. Gamma Phi Beta Found. (trustee 1994—), Phi Beta Kappa. Avocations: triathalons, biking. Office: Columbia Michael Reese Hosp Dept Pediat 2929 S Ellis Ave Chicago IL 60616-3302

SEELEY, HARRY WILBUR, JR., microbiology educator; b. Bridgeport, Conn., Mar. 5, 1917; s. Harry W. and Genevieve (Quinlan) S.; m. Margaret Johnson, Dec. 21, 1940; children: Gail Seeley Fox, Beth (dec.), Carol Seeley-Teboe. B.S., U. Conn., 1941, M.S., 1942; Ph.D., Cornell U., 1947. Mem. faculty Cornell U., 1947—, prof. bacteriology, 1955—, chmn. sect. microbiology, 1964-68, prof.-in-charge microbiology, 1974-77, acting chmn. dept. microbiology, 1977-78, ret., 1979. Author: Microbes in Action, 1962, 4th edit., 1991, Microbes and Man, 1974. Guggenheim fellow, 1958. Mem. Soc. Gen. Microbiology, Am. Soc. Microbiology, Am. Acad. Microbiology, Soc. Applied Bacteriology, Internat. Oceanographic Found., AAAS, Am. Inst. Biol. Scientists, AAUP, Sigma Xi, Phi Kappa Phi. Home: Park Ln Jacksonville NY 14854-0001 Office: Cornell U Dept Microbiology Wing Hall Ithaca NY 14853

SEELEY, JOHN GEORGE, horticulture educator; b. North Bergen, N.J., Dec. 21, 1915; s. Howard Wilson and Lillian (Fiedler) S.; m. Catherine L. Cook, May 28, 1938; children: Catherine Ann, David John (dec.), Daniel Henry, George Bingham, Thomas Dyer. B.S., Rutgers U., 1937, M.S., 1940; Ph.D., Cornell U., 1948. Research asst. N.J. Agrl. Exptl. Sta., 1937-40, foreman ornamental gardens, 1940-41; instr. floriculture Cornell U., Ithaca, N.Y., 1941-43, 45-48, asst. prof., 1948-49, prof. floriculture, 1956-83, prof. emeritus, 1983—, head dept. floriculture, 1956-70; prof. floriculture Pa. State U., 1949-56; D.C. Kiplinger chair floriculture, prof. horticulture Ohio State U., 1984-85; asst. agronomist Bur. Plant Industry Dept. Agr., 1943-44; chemist Wright Aero. Corp., Paterson, N.J., 1944-45. Trustee Kenneth Post Found., 1956-84, Fred. C. Gloeckner Found., 1970—, pres., 1993—. Recipient S.A.F. Found. for Floriculture Rsch. & Edn. award, 1965, Cornell Edgerton Career Teaching award, 1983. Fellow AAAS, Am. Soc. Hort. Sci. (pres. 1982-83, chmn. bd. 1983-84, Leonard H. Vaughn rsch. award 1950, Bittner Extension award 1982); mem. Internat. Soc. for Horticultural Scis.(hon. mem award, 1992), mem. Am. Acad. Floriculture (hon.), Soc. Am. Florists (Hall of Fame 1979), Mass. Hort. Soc. (Silver medal 1980), Internat. Soc. Hort. Sci., Am. Carnation Soc., Ohio Florists' Assn. (hon.), N.Y. Flower Growers Assn., Pa. Flower Growers Assn., Sigma Xi, Phi Kappa Phi, Alpha Zeta, Pi Alpha Xi (pres. 1951-53), Epsilon Sigma Phi, Phi Epsilon Phi. Presbyterian. Lodge: Rotary Internat. (dist. gov. 1973-74). Home: 403 Savage Farm Dr Ithaca NY 14850-6506

SEELEY, ROD RALPH, physiology educator; b. Rupert, Idaho, Dec. 29, 1945; s. Earl W. Seeley and Alice E. (Hall) Walker; m. Jeanette Brady, Aug. 27, 1965; children: Teri, Alicia, Christopher, Kara. BS, Idaho State U., 1968; MS, Utah State U., 1971, PhD, 1973. Asst. prof. dept. biol. scis. Idaho State U., Pocatello, 1973-78, assoc. prof., 1978-83, prof., 1983—, chmn. dept., 1986—. Author: Human Anatomy and Physiology, 1989, 4th edit., 1997, Essentials of Anatomy and Physiology, 1991, Understanding Anatomy and Physiology, 1994; contbr. articles on reproductive physiology to profl. jours. Mem. bd. Sch. Dist. 25, Pocatello, 1982-88, chmn. bd., 1985-87. Recipient Disting. Tchr. award Idaho State U., 1986. Mem. AAAS, Idaho Acad. Sci., Human Anatomy and Physiology Soc., Soc. Study Reproduction, Sigma Xi. Avocations: running, fishing, backpacking, hunting. Office: Idaho State U Dept Biol Scis PO Box 8007 Pocatello ID 83209-8007

SEELIG, GERARD LEO, management consultant; b. Schluchtern, Germany, June 15, 1926; came to U.S., 1934, naturalized, 1943; s. Herman and Bella (Bach) S.; m. Lorraine Peters, June 28, 1953; children: Tina Lynn, Robert Mark and Carol Ann (twins). BEE, Ohio State U., 1948; MS in Indsl. Mgmt, N.Y. U., 1954. Registered profl. engr., Ohio. Electronics engr. Martin Corp., Balt., 1948-50; sr. engr. Fairchild Aircraft Co., Farmingdale, N.Y., 1950-54; program mgr. RCA, Moorestown, N.J., 1954-59, Van Nuys, Calif., 1959-61; div. mgr. Missile & Space Co. div. Lockheed Aircraft Corp., Van Nuys, 1961-63; v.p., gen. mgr. Lockheed Aircraft Corp. (Lockheed Electronics div.), Los Angeles, 1963-68; exec. v.p. Lockheed Electronics Co., Inc., Plainfield, N.J., 1968-69; pres. Lockheed Electronics Co., Inc., 1969-71; group exec., exec. asst. to office of pres. ITT, N.Y.C., 1971-72; corp. v.p. ITT, 1972-79, sr. v.p., 1979-81, exec. v.p., 1981-83; pres. indsl. and tech. sector Allied Corp.; exec. v.p. Allied Corp., Morristown, N.J., 1983-87; disting. exec. lectr. Rutgers Grad. Sch. Mgmt.; exec.-in-residence, vis. prof. Columbia U. Grad. Sch. Bus.; bd. dirs. 5 corps.; cons. various investment firms. Served with AUS, 1944-46. Recipient Disting. Alumnus award Ohio State U., 1987. Fellow AIAA (assoc.); mem. IEEE (sr.).

SEELIN, JUDITH LEE, rehabilitation specialist; b. Bklyn., Feb. 22, 1941; d. Sidney and Helene Agnes (Minkowitz) S.; m. Mel Schwartz, Sept. 30, 1965 (div. 1983); children: Jeffrey, Robin; m. Arnold Seelin, Oct. 16, 1983. AAS, SUNY, Farmingdale, 1972; BSN, SUNY, Stony Brook, 1973. CRRN, CIRS, CCM. Staff nurse surg. unit L.I. Jewish Med. Ctr., New Hyde Park, N.Y., 1962-67; DON Home Health Aids, Inc., Hempstead, N.Y., 1973-78, Able Home Health Care, Wantagh, N.Y., 1978-84; nursing adminstr. Aides at Home, Inc., Hicksville, N.Y., 1984-86; asst. ADON Savana Cay Manor, Port Saint Lucie, Fla., 1986; Fla. state supr. CCM, Hollywood, Fla., 1987-93; med. team leader Resource Opportunities, Fort Lauderdale, Fla., 1993-95; ind. med. case mgr., 1993-95; Workers Compensation resource nurse Humana Health Care Plan, Mirama, Fla., 1995-97; Medicaid outreach mgr. Humana Health Care Plan, Mirama, 1997—; spkr. Am. Inst. Med. Law; adv. bd. mem. Whithal, Boca Raton. Mem. AARN, CMSA. Avocations: painting, sculpting, reading, antiquing. Home: 857 Tanglewood Cir Weston FL 33327

SEELY, ELLEN WELLS, endocrinologist; b. N.Y.C., Sept. 25, 1955; d. Robert Daniel and Marcia (Wells) S.; m. Jonathan David Strongin, June 11, 1983; children: Jessica, Matthew. BA magna cum laude, Brown U., 1977; MD, Columbia U., 1981. Diplomate Am. Bd. Internal Medicine, Endocrinology and Metabolism. Residency internal medicine Brigham & Women Hosp., Boston, 1981-84, fellow in endocrinology, 1984-87; rsch. fellow medicine Harvard U., Boston, 1984-87; dir. clin. rsch. endocrine hypertension divsn. Brigham & Women's Hosp., Boston, 1987—, dir. ambulatory clin. rsch. ctr., 1995—; instr. medicine Harvard Medical Sch., Boston, 1987-91; asst. prof. medicine Harvard Med. Sch., Boston, 1991-95; assoc. physician Brigham & Women's Hosp., 1987-95, physician, 1996—; assoc. physician Beth Israel Hosp., Boston, 1988—; med. internship selection com. Brigham and Women's Hosp., 1983-94, co-dir. endocrinology fellowship tng. program, 1993-95, dir. Pregnancy-Related Endocrine and Hypertensive Disorders Clinic, 1988—; coord. Diabetes and Pregnancy Clinic, 1988—, coord. osteoporosis program Harvard Pilgrim Health Plan, Boston, 1995—. Contbr. articles to profl. jours. Capps scholar in diabetes Harvard Med. Sch., 1994-96. Mem. ADA, Endocrine Soc., Am. Fedn. Clin. Rsch., Internat. Soc. Study of Hypertension in Pregnancy, Coun. for High Blood Pressure Rsch., Am. Heart Assn., Sigma Si. Office: Brigham & Women's Hosp 221 Longwood Ave Boston MA 02115-5822

SEELY, JAMES MICHAEL, defense consultant, retired naval officer, small business owner; b. Los Angeles, Oct. 15, 1932; s. Louis K. and Mary Edith (Gleason) S.; m. Gail Margaret Deverman, July 13, 1957; children: Ted Andrew, Nina Marie. BS, UCLA, 1955; MS, George Washington U., 1976. Commd. ensign USN, 1955, advanced through grades to rear adm.; student pilot, 1955-56, attack pilot, 1957-75; comdg. officer Attack Squadron 165, Naval Air Sta. Whidbey Island, Wash., 1972-73; comdr. Carrier Air Wing 9, Naval Air Sta. Lemoore, Calif., 1974-75; comdg. officer U.S. Naval Air Sta., Whidbey Island, 1977-79; dep. dir. DCNO (Air Warfare, OP-50), Pentagon, Washington, 1979-82; dir. Joint Analysis Directorate, Office Joint Chiefs Staff, Washington, 1982-84; comdr. Medium Attack Tactical Electronic Warfare Wing, Pacific Fleet, Naval Air Sta. Whidbey Island, 1984-86; dir. DCNO (Air Warfare, OP-50), Pentagon, 1986-88; dep. comptr. of Navy, Pentagon, 1988-89; ret. Pentagon, 1989; with RRP Def. Cons. Assocs., Arlington, Va., 1989—; Vietnam combat duty with Attack Squadrons 93, 152, 165 flying from aircraft carriers USS Enterprise, Hancock, Bon Homme Richard, Shangri-La and Constellation; 447 combat missions. Decorated Defense Superior Service, Legion of Merit (2), D.F.C. (4), Bronze Star, Air Medal (43). Mem. Naval Inst., Tailhook Assn., Assn. Naval Aviation, Marine Corps Aviation Assn., Red River Valley Fighter Pilots Assn., Navy League, Am. Legion, Am. Def. Preparedness Assn., Assn. Old Crows. Republican. Roman Catholic. Avocations: sports, automobiles. Home: 5730 Shropshire Ct Alexandria VA 22315-4027 Office: RRP Def Cons Assocs 2171 Crystal Dr Arlington VA 22202-3705

SEELY, JOHN F., dean. Dean faculty medicine U. Ottawa, Ont., Can. Office: U Ottawa Faculty Medicine, 451 Smyth Rd, Ottawa, ON Canada K1H 8M5 also: U Ottawa Faculty Med, 43 Bruyere St, Ottawa, ON Canada K1N 5C8*

SEELY, ROBERT DANIEL, physician, medical educator; b. Woodmere, N.Y., Nov. 4, 1923; s. Harry and Ethel (Weil) S.; m. Marcia Ann Wells, June 19, 1953; children: Ellen Wells, Anne Wells. B.S., NYU, 1943; M.D., Columbia U., 1946. Intern Mt. Sinai Hosp., N.Y.C., 1946-47, asst. resident in medicine, 1950-51, resident in pathology, 1951-52, chief resident in medicine, 1952-53; Sara Welt fellow in cardiovascular research Presbyn. Hosp., N.Y.C., 1953-54; instr. dept. physiology, cardiovascular research Western Res. U., Cleve., 1947-48; chief rheumatic heart disease clinic Mt. Sinai Hosp., N.Y.C., 1961-70, attending physician medicine and cardiology, 1978—, chief of service dept. medicine, 1979—, clin. prof. medicine, cardiology Sch. Medicine, 1970—; practice medicine specializing in cardiovascular disease N.Y.C., 1953—. Contbr. articles to profl. jours. Served to capt. M.C. AUS, 1948-50. Recipient Solomon Berson Meml. award Mt. Sinai Hosp., 1977. Fellow Am. Coll. Cardiology, ACP; mem. N.Y. Heart Assn., AMA, N.Y. County Med. Soc., Soc. Cert. Internists N.Y., Phi Beta Kappa, Alpha Omega Alpha, Beta Lambda Sigma. Office: 994 5th Ave New York NY 10028-0100

SEEMAN, MELVIN, sociologist, educator; b. Balt., Feb. 5, 1918; s. Morris and Sophie (Kostman) S.; m. Alice Ruth Zerbola, June 30, 1944; children—Teresa E., Paul D. B.A., Johns Hopkins U., 1944; Ph.D., Ohio State U., 1947. Asst. prof. sociology Ohio State U., 1947-52, assoc. prof., 1953-59; prof. UCLA, 1959-88, prof. emeritus, 1988—. Mem. Am. Social. Assn. Home: 21532 Paseo Serra St Malibu CA 90265-5112 Office: Dept Sociology UCLA 405 Hilgard Ave Los Angeles CA 90095-9000

SEEMANN, ROSALIE MARY, international business association executive; b. St. Louis, July 30, 1942; d. Ulysses Sylvester and Helen Marie (Hootselle) Simon; ed. Lindenwood Colls., St. Charles, Mo., 1973-76, Harris Tchrs. Coll., St. Louis, 1961, U. Fla., Gainesville, 1964; m. Richard Vaughn, Jan 20, 1968 (dec.); 1 child, Heather Elizabeth. Vol. U.S. Peace Corps, Brazil, 1964-66; tech. analyst, group leader Conductron-Mo., St. Charles, 1966-71; bus. mgr., 1971-77; maintenance engr. McDonnell Douglas Astronautics, St. Louis, 1977-78; mgr. supply support Northrop Def. Systems Div., Rolling Meadows, Ill., 1978-80; logistics mgmt. cons., Logistic Support Svcs., Spring Grove, Ill., 1980-85; mgr. reliability, maintainability, integrated logistic support Recon/Optical, Inc., Barrington, Ill., 1985-90, v.p. exec. dir. Mid-America Com. for Internat. Bus. and Govt. Coop., Chicago, 1991—; bd. dirs. Libr. Internat. Rels., Chgo.- Kent Coll. Law, Prime Med. Products. Bd. dirs. Women For Leadership, Mid.-Am. Found., Ill. Coordinating Coun. Exports; mem. women's bd. Goodman Theatre, Chgo.; commr. ways and means St. John the Bapt. Cath. Ch.; active Girl Scouts U.S.A. Recipient commendation Conductron-Mo., 1967, Pres. award Recon/Optical, 1989. Mem. Am. Soc. Assn. Execs. (internat. sect. coun. 1996—), Am. Women Internat. Understanding, Soc. Logistics Engrs. (Mem. of Yr. award, sr. mem.), Japan Am. Soc., Chgo. Coun. Foreign Rels. (Chgo. com.), Assn. Old Crows, Coun. Women Leaders, Execs. Club Chgo., Arts and Bus Coun. Chgo., Internat. Trade Assn., Lindenwood Colls. Assocs. Fine Arts. Home: PO Box 3547 Barrington IL 60011-3547 Office: 150 N Michigan Ave Chicago IL 60601-7524

SEESE, WILLIAM SHOBER, chemistry educator; b. Meyersdale, Pa., June 13, 1932; s. Carmon Doyle and Florence Evelyn (Shober) S.; m. Ann Reeves, July 25, 1958; children: David Scott, John Steven. BS in Pharmacy, U. N.Mex., 1954, MS in Chemistry, 1959; PhD in Chemistry, Wash. State U., 1965. Instr. Ft. Lewis Coll., Durango, Colo., 1958-61; research chemist Internat. Minerals and Chem. Corp., Wasco, Calif., 1965-66; instr. Casper (Wyo.) Coll., 1966-87, emeritus; instr. U. Petroleum and Minerals, Dhahran, Saudi Arabia, 1973-76, U. N.Mex., Gallup, 1976-77; Fulbright lectr., Sudan, 1987-88, Oman, 1993-94; prof. chemistry alice Lloyd Coll., Pippa Passes, Ky., 1989-91. Author: (with G. William Daub) Basic Chemistry, 1972, 7th edit., 1996, In Preparation for College Chemistry, 1974, 5th edit., 1994. Recipient Regional award Chem. Mfrs. Assn. for Outstanding Teaching, 1981. Mem. Am. Chem. Soc. Democrat. Presbyterian. Lodge: Masons. Avocations: fishing, jogging. Home: 2915 Ridgecrest Dr Casper WY 82604-4619

SEESSEL, THOMAS VINING, nonprofit organization executive; b. Chattanooga, Nov. 16, 1937; s. Ben Adolph and Dorothy Anne (Parham) S.; m. Diane Farnham Wiener, Jan. 26, 1963; children: Adam Humphreys, Jessica Parham, Ben Vining. BA, Dartmouth Coll., 1959; MPA, Princeton U.,

1964. Asst. to dir. Community Progress, Inc., New Haven, 1964-67; exec. dir. N.J. Housing Fin. Agy., Trenton, 1967-70; sr. program officer The Ford Found., N.Y.C., 1970-74; dep. commr. N.J. Dept. Environ. Protection, Trenton, 1974-75; exec. v.p. Manpower Demonstration Res. Corp., N.Y.C., 1975-78; owner, mgmt. cons. T.V. Seessel Assocs., Hopewell, N.J., 1979-85; exec. dir. Nat. Coun. on Alcoholism, N.Y.C., 1985-88, pres., 1988; pres. Seedco, N.Y.C., 1988—, treas., 1986-88; vis. lectr. Cornell U., Ithaca, N.Y., 1966-68, Princeton (N.J.) U., 1968-69; adj. prof. New Sch. Social Rsch., N.Y.C., 1978-79; mem. tech. adv. com. Adolescent Sch.-based Health Care Svcs. program Robert Wood Johnson Found., Princeton, 1986-91, and nat. adv. com. "Fighting Back" program to combat substance abuse, 1989—. Author numerous articles, speeches and reports on alcoholism, and other health topics and community devel. Mem. bd. edn. Hopewell Valley Regional Sch. Dist., Pennington, N.J., 1971-74; trustee Thomas Edison Coll. N.J., 1979-92, chmn. bd. trustees, 1987-89; bd. trustees Thomas Edison Coll. N.J. Found., 1992—; bd. dirs. Bus. Employment Found., Paterson, N.J., 1979-87, Freedom Inst., N.Y.C., 1988-91, Nat. Neighborhood Coalition, 1995—; bd. dirs. Ctr. for Sci. in Pub. Interest, 1990-93, treas., 1991-93. Assoc. fellow Branford Coll., Yale U., 1965-70. Mem. Princeton Grad. Alumni (chmn. nominating and awards com. 1978-80), Phi Beta Kappa. Democrat. Club: N.Y. Princeton. Office: Seedco 915 Broadway New York NY 10010-7108

SEEVERS, CHARLES JUNIOR, foundation executive, psychologist; b. Seward, Nebr., May 13, 1925; s. Ferdinand Carl and Hilda Anna (Schultz) S.; m. Florine Marie Viets, June 5, 1949 (dec. 1991); children: Steven, Roger, Sandra, Jane; m. Ruth Ann Krohn Rehschuh, Aug. 28, 1993. AA, St. John's Coll., 1945; BA, Concordia Sem., St. Louis, 1949; MS magna cum laude, St. Francis Coll., Ft. Wayne, Ind., 1965, postgrad., 1966; PhD, U. Notre Dame, 1970. Ordained to ministry Lutheran Ch., 1949; asst. pastor Immanuel Luth. Ch., Balt., 1949-50; pastor St. Paul's Luth. Ch., Kingsville, Md., 1950-57, Bethlehem Luth. Ch., Richmond, Va., 1957-63; sr. pastor Zion Luth. Ch., Ft. Wayne, 1963-66; exec. dir. Assn. for Disabled of Elkhart County, Ind., 1966-82; exec. dir. Aux Chandelles Found., 1982-93, exec. dir. emeritus, 1993; adj. prof. psychology and spl. edn. Ind. U., South Bend, 1972-76; speaker Pres.'s Com. on Mental Retardation 3d Internat. Congress on Prevention of Mental Retardation, Buenos Aries, Argentina, 1986; apptd. del. health psychologist Ind. People to People Internat. Study Mission to Russia, People's Republic China, 1987; l cons. Kans. Developmental Disabilities Div., 1972-79, Accreditation Council for Facilities for the Mentally Retarded, Chgo., 1972-80; cons. on assessment of developmentally disabled in various states, 1974—, cons. Leicester, Eng., 1974-75; mem. Ind. Gov.'s Planning and Adv. Bd. for Mental Retardation and Other Developmental Disabilities, 1973-78, chmn., 1976-78; mem. Gov.'s Preventive Health and Handicap Services Coordination Study Commn., 1987-90, Devel. Disabilities Planning Council on Child Health, 1987-90, No. Ind. Health Systems Agy. Central Sub-Area Adv. Council, 1976-78, vice chmn., 1977-78; cons. psychonutrition, 1981-93, emeritus 1993—; regional psychologist Youth for Understanding, 1985-87. Contbr. articles to profl. publs. Chmn. United Way Execs., Elkhart, 1971-73; bd. dirs. Mill Neck Manor Sch. for the Deaf, L.I., N.Y., 1950-57, Assn. for Retarded Citizens Ind., 1983-89, No. Ind. Health Found., 1981-87; charter mem. Area Vocat. Edn. Adv. Bd., 1973-76; mem. state adv. bd. Prevention: To Be Born Well Curriculum Project, 1977-80; mem. residential services and facilities com. Nat. Assn. Retarded Citizens, 1973-78; mem. No. Ind. Developmental Disabilities Adv. Council, 1977-81, chmn., 1980-81; mem. Dept. Mental Health Multi-Disciplinary Screening Team, 1983-84; mem. bd. teenage parents adv. bd. Elkhart Community Schs., 1984-87; chmn. state policy Ind. Healthy Mothers/Healthy Babies Coalition, 1986-87; hon. chmn. Michiana Fetal Alcohol Syndrome Week, 1986. Recipient United Way Exec. of Yr. award, 1979; Eli Lilly fellow in religion and mental health Ind. U. Med. Center, Indpls., 1964-65; Recipient Liberty Bell award Elkhart Bar Assn., 1974, Outstanding Kindness award Elkhart County Assn. for Retarded, 1974, Concerned for Mankind in Our Nation award Jaycees, 1975, State of Ind. Citizen Participation award Gov.'s Voluntary Action Program, Sagamore of Wabash award Gov. of State of Ind., 1990; elected to Wall of Fame Assn. for Disbaled Elkhart County, Ind., 1985. Mem. Nat. Conf. Execs. of Assns. for Retarded Children (chmn. 1974-75), Am. Psychol. Assn., Soc. Behavioral Medicine, Am. Pub. Health Assn., Nat. Fedn. Parents for Drug Free Youth, Luth. Acad. for Scholarship, Internat. Psychol. Assn., United Cerebral Palsy Am., Luth. Human Relations Assn. Am., Ctr. for Sci. in Pub. Interest, Am. Orthopsychiat. Assn., Elkhart C. of C. (bd. dirs. 1974-76), Am. Council on Drug Edn., Assn. Birth Defect Children, Healthy Mothers/Healthy Babies Coalition, Internat. Council Psychologists. Lodge: Rotary (v.p. 1986, chmn. world affairs conf. dist. 654, 1985-87, pres.-elect 1987-88, gen. chmn. dist. assembly conf. 1986-87, Gov.'s award 1987, Chmn. of Yr. 1987). Home: 2103 Norwood Dr Mountain Home AR 72653 *I believe I am a uniquely individual child of God, born to fulfill a purpose for which God continues to give me life each new day. We are joined together in a common effort to fulfill the purpose for which each of us is given life.*

SEFCIK, JOHN DELBERT, financial services executive; b. Temple, Tex., Jan. 21, 1921; s. John J. and Annie (Chaloupka) S.; m. Norma Marie Kuzel, May 22, 1942 (div. Sept. 1985); children: John D. Jr., Camille Freitas; m. Christine Gajdica Goodlett, Dec. 13, 1987. Student, Temple Jr. Coll., 1938-39; acctg. grad., Four C. Bus. Coll., 1948-50; A in Mgmt., Brewster Coll., 1956-59; student, So. Meth. U., 1958-70; grad., Civil Def. Staff Coll., Assn. Logistics Ex Sch., Command & Gen. Staff Coll., Indsl. Coll. Armed Forces, Arty. and Civil Affairs Mil. Govt. Sch. Cert. Army logistician. Placement mgr., tax auditor Tex. Employment Commn., 1945-51; with Phoenix Life Ins. Co., 1951-53; mktg. and dist. mgr. Armour Pharm. Co., Inc., 1953-86; regional mgr. ins. and investments, real estate broker Primerica Fin. Svcs., 1987-96. Bd. dirs., gen. chmn. 1st Dallas Mil. Ball, 1965, past pres., 1992-93, mem. to date. Master sgt. U.S. Army, 1940-45; col. USAR, 1948-78. Decorated Legion of Merit, Bronze Star. Mem. 102d Inf. Divsn. Assn. (life, pres., v.p., bd. dirs., reunion gen. chmn. 1983-89), Res. Officers Assn. (life, nat. chmn. civil preparedness com. 1989-94, numerous other coms., Brigade of Vols., Wall of Gold, Waco chpt. pres. 1951-53, Dallas chpt. pres. 1963-65, Army Tex. dept. v.p. 1963-67, 90th divsn. arty. chpt. pres. 1965-66, pres. 1967-68, Tex. dept. nat. councilman 1968-69, Tex. ROA Conv. Gen. chmn. 1981), Mil. Order World Wars (life), Am. Legion (life), Ret. Officers Assn. (life), 2d INF Indian Head Divsn. Assn., KC (4th degree, Sir Knight Abram J. Ryan Assembly Coun. No 799).

SEFF, LESLIE S., securities trader; b. N.Y.C., Oct. 3, 1950; s. Fredric and Dorothy (Jacobson) S.; children: Dylan, Cortney, Blake, Matthew. BBA in Fin. cum laude with high honors, Hofstra U., Hempstead, N.Y., 1971; MBA, Baruch Coll., N.Y.C., 1980. Co-mgr. Muller & Co., N.Y.C., 1974-88; dir. over-the-counter trading Gruntal & Co., N.Y.C., 1988-92; dir. over-the-counter trading dept. Wagner Stott Mercator Ptnrs., N.Y.C., 1992-96, trading mgr. Fidelity Capital Markets NASDAQ/OTC trading, 1996—. Trustee Saddle River (N.J.) Recreation Commn., 1988; active Rep. Eagles, Washington, 1986-87. allied mem. N.Y. Stock Exch. Avocations: tennis, bicycling, playing the harmonica. Office: Fidelity Capital Markets 14 Wall St New York NY 10005-2101

SEFFRIN, JOHN REESE, health science association administrator, educator; b. Hagerstown, Ind., May 19, 1944; s. Theodore H. and Mary Ellen (Reese) S.; m. Carole Sue Washburn, Apr. 16, 1966; 1 child, Mary. BS in Edn., Ball State U., 1966, DSc (hon.), 1994; MS, U. Ill., 1967; PhD in Health Edn., Purdue U., 1970. Asst. prof. health edn. Purdue U., West Lafayette, Ind., 1970-76, assoc. prof., 1976-79; prof., chmn. dept. applied health sci. Ind. U., Bloomington, 1979-92; CEO Am. Cancer Soc., Atlanta, 1992—; cons. Ind. Dept. Public Instrn., 1979-81, ADA, 1972—; guest lectr. various public health orgns. and schs., 1970—. Contbr. numerous articles on health edn. to profl. publs.; chmn. editorial bd.: Jour. Sch. Health, 1982-85, Smoking and Health Reporter, 1983-88; mem. editorial bd.: Health Edn., 1981-85; cons. editor: Jour. ADA, 1980—. Pres. State Welfare Bd., Dept. Public Welfare, Ind., 1979-80, 83-85; treas. Midwest Nuclear Bd., 1973-76; bd. dirs. Wabash Center for the Mentally Retarded, 1970-73; chmn. community edn. com. Am. Lung Assn., 1981-83, v.p., 1986-88, nat. bd. dirs., 1980-92; treas. Partnership for Prevention...of Premature Death, Disease and Disability, 1991—, Acordia Small Bus. Benefits, Inc., 1992-96. Recipient Cert. of Recognition, ADA, 1975, Cert. Appreciation Surgeon Gen. of Pub. Health Svc., 1992; named Sagamore of Wabash, State of Ind., 1980, 88; Outstanding Alumnus award Ball State U., 1982. Fellow Am. Sch. Health Assn. (mem. governing coun. 1978-81, 82-89, pres. 1987-88, Howe award 1991); mem. AMA, Nat. Assn. State Bds. of Edn. (commn. on the sch. community role in improving adolescent health 1989-90), Assn. for Advancement Health Edn. (bd. dirs. 1989-92), Ind. Assn. Health Educators (pres. 1975-76), Ind. Family Health Coun. (dir. 1979-81, v.p. 1980-81, pres. 1981), Ind. Thoracic Soc. (mem. governing coun. 1977-84), Am. Cancer Soc. (dir. Ind. Div. 1977-92, chmn. nat. bd. dirs. 1989-91, dir.-at-large to nat. bd. dirs., chmn. nat. pub. edn. com. 1984-87, nat. v.p. 1986-87), Ind. Assn. for Health, Phys. Edn. and Recreation (pres. 1976, Cert. of Appreciation 1977, Honor award 1982), Nat. Interagy. Coun. on Smoking and Health (bd. dirs. 1979—), Phi Delta Kappa, Eta Sigma Gamma. Roman Catholic. Office: Am Cancer Soc 1599 Clifton Rd NE Atlanta GA 30329-4250

SEGAL, BERNARD GERARD, lawyer; b. N.Y.C., June 11, 1907; s. Samuel I. and Rose (Cantor) S.; m. Geraldine Rosenbaum, Oct. 22, 1933; children: Loretta Joan Segal Cohen, Richard Murry. A.B., U. Pa., 1928, LL.B., 1931, LL.D., 1969; LL.D., Franklin and Marshall Coll., 1953, Temple U., 1954, Dropsie U., 1966, Jewish Theol. Sem. Am., 1977, Vt. Law Sch., 1978, Villanova U., 1980, Georgetown U., 1983; J.S.D., Suffolk U., 1969; D.H.L., Hebrew Union Coll., 1970. Bar: Pa. 1932, D.C. 1976. Mem. faculty U. Pa., 1928-35, 45-47; Am. reporter on contracts Internat. Congress of Law, The Hague, The Netherlands, 1932; asst. dep. atty. gen. Commonwealth of Pa., 1932-33, dep. atty. gen., 1933-34; co-founder Schnader Harrison Segal & Lewis, Phila., 1935—; instr. grad. bus., govt. Am. Inst. Banking, 1936-39; chmn. Schnader Harrison Segal & Lewis, Phila., 1968-86, sr. ptnr., 1986-88, of counsel, 1988-94; mem. Bd. Law Examiners, Phila., 1940-46; chmn. Commn. Jud. and Congl. Salaries, U.S. Govt., 1953-55; mem. Atty. Gen.'s Nat. Com. to Study Antitrust Laws, 1953-55; mem. exec. com. Atty. Gen.'s Nat. Conf. on Ct. Congestion, 1958-61; mem. standing com. on rules of practice and procedure Jud. Conf. U.S., 1959-76; co-chmn. Lawyers Com. on Civil Rights Under Law, 1963-65 (Founder award, 25th Anniversary, 1988); chmn. Pa. Jud. Nominating Commn., 1964-66; mem. Nat. Citizens Com. on Community Rels., 1964-74; mem. adv. com. U.S. mission to UN, 1967-68; mem. adv. panel internat. law U.S. Dept. State, 1967-79; mem. Adminstrv. Conf. U.S., 1968-74; chmn. nat. adv. com. on legal svcs. U.S. OEO, 1968-76, chmn. exec. com., 1971-74; chmn. bd. Coun. Legal Edn. Opportunities, 1968-71; mem. Jud. Coun. Pa., 1968-71; coun. World Peace Through Law Ctr., chmn. 1st demonstration trial, Belgrade, Yugoslavia, 1971, coun., 1973-94, participant world confs., Athens, Greece, Washington, Geneva, Bangkok, Abidjan, Ivory Coast, Manila and Cairo, chmn. com. on internat. communications, world chmn. World Law Day, Madrid, 1979, Berlin, 1985; mem. U.S. Commn. on Exec., Legis. and Jud. Salaries, 1972-73, 76-77; mem. Appellate Ct. Nominating Commn., 1973-79; mem. U.S. Commn. Revision Fed. Ct. Appellate System, 1974-75; chmn. World Conf. on Peace and Violence, Jerusalem, 1979. Editor-in-chief: Pennsylvania Banking and Building and Loan Law, 3 vols., 1941; editor: The Belgrade Spaceship Trial, 1972; mem. internat. hon. bd. Ency. Judaica; contbr. articles to law revs., other publs. Life trustee, mem. exec. bd. U. Pa., 1959-77, life trustee emeritus, 1977—; emeritus mem. bd. overseers U. Pa. Law Sch., 1959—; mem. Commn. on Anti-Poverty Program for Phila., 1967-71, Bus. Leadership Organized for Cath. Schs., 1979-92, Commonwealth Commn. on Bicentennial of U.S. Constn., 1986-87; chmn. bd. Coun. Advancement Legal Edn., 1972-77; coun. trustees Hebrew U. Jerusalem; bd. dirs. So. Africa Legal Svcs. and Legal Edn. Project, 1979—, NAACP Legal Def. and Ednl. Fund, Found. Fed. Bar Assn.; bd. govs. emeritus, past. v.p., past treas. Dropsie Coll.; trustee emeritus, former exec. com. Albert Einstein Med. Ctr.; trustee Phila. Martin Luther King, Jr. Ctr. Nonviolent Social Change (Drum Major award for legal justice, 1984), 1984—, Found. for the Commemoration of the U.S. Constn., 1986-88, Found. for U.S. Constn., 1988—, bd. dirs. Chapel of Four Chaplains; mem. planning comm. Miracle at Phila., 1986-87. Recipient Arthur von Briesen medal Nat. Legal Aid and Defender Assn., 1970, Nat. Human Rels. award NCCJ, 1972, Herbert Lewis Harley award, Am. Judicature Soc., 1974, World Lawyer award World Peace through Law Ctr., 1975, Judge William H. Hastie award NAACP Legal Def. Fund, 1986, Legion Honor Gold Medallion award Chapel of Four Chaplains, 1988, Nat. Civil Rights award U.S. Atty. Gen. and Lawyers Com. for Civil Rights Under Law, 1969, Ford Found. award to our Counselor on Pub. Interest, 1979, Nat. Award of Merit Fed. Adminstrv. Law Judges Conf., 1984, Pa. Bar Assn. award for Dedicated and Disting. Service, Field of Jurisprudence and Admin. of Justice, 1962, 10th Anniversary award Pub. Interest Law Ctr. Phila., 1984; co-recipient Nat. Neighbors Disting. Leadership in Civil Rights award, 1988, ACLU Civil Liberties award, 1991, U. Pa. Law Alumni award of Merit, 1991. Fellow Am. Coll. Trial Lawyers (pres. 1964-65), ABA (pres. 1969-70, Gold medal 1976), Inst. Jud. Adminstrn. (bd. dirs. 1968-86), Am. Bar Found. (pres. 1976-78); mem. Jewish Fed. Greater Phila. (mem. emeritus exec. com.), Pa. Bar Assn., Phila. Bar Assn. (chancellor 1952, 53), Pa. Urban Affairs Partnership, Fed. Bar Assn. (nat. coun.), Assn. of Bar of City of N.Y., D.C. Bar Assn., Am. Arbitration Assn. (former dir.), Am. Law Inst. (1st v.p. 1976-86, 2nd v.p. 1970-75, treas. 1955-69, counselor emeritus 1987—), Am. Judicature Soc. (chmn. 1958-61, bd. dirs. 1956—), Coun. Legal Edn. for Profl. Responsibility (dir.), Fed. Jud. Conf. 3d Cir. (life), World Assn. Lawyers (pres. for Ams. 1976-86), Nat. Conf. Bar Pres., Taxpayers Forum Pa. (past pres.), Allied Jewish Appeal (past pres., hon. pres.), Legal Aid Soc. Phila.)bd. dirs.), Jewish League Israel (nat. bd.), Jewish Pub. Soc. Am. (life trustee, mem. exec. com.), Jewish Family Svc. (hon. dir.), Order of Coif, Tau Epsilon Rho, Delta Sigma Rho. Republican. Clubs: Locust, Union League, Faculty, Metropolitan (Washington). Office: Schnader Harrison Segal & Lewis 1600 Market St Ste 3600 Philadelphia PA 19103-7286

SEGAL, BERNARD LOUIS, physician, educator; b. Montreal, Que., Can., Feb. 13, 1929; came to U.S., 1961, naturalized, 1966; s. Irving and Fay (Schecter) S.; m. Idajane Fischman, Feb. 17, 1963; 1 dau., Jody Segal. BSc cum laude, McGill U., 1950, postgrad., 1950-51, MD, C.M. high standing, 1955. Diplomate Am. Bd. Internal Medicine. Intern Jewish Gen Hosp., Montreal, 1955-56; resident Balt. City Hosp., 1956-57, Beth Israel Hosp., Boston, 1957-58, Georgetown Med. Ctr., Washington, 1958-59, St. George's Hosp., London, Eng., 1959-61; practice medicine specializing in internal medicine and cardiology Phila., 1961—; prof. medicine Med. Coll. Pa., Hahnemann U., 1996—; prof., sr. attending physician med. Hahnemann Med. Coll., Phila., 1964—; dir. Phila. Heart Inst., 1987; prof. med. Allegheny Univ. Hosp.; sr. v.p. Allegheny Integrated Health Group-Cardiology. Author: Auscultation of the Heart, 1965; Editor: Theory and Practice of Auscultation, 1964, Engineering in the Practice of Medicine, 1966, Your Heart, 1972, Arteriosclerosis and Coronary Heart Disease, 1972; mem. editl. bd. Am. Jour. Cardiology, 1970—, Clin. Echocardiography, 1978; contbr. numerous articles on cardiology to med. jours. Fellow ACP, Am. Coll. Cardiology (chmn. scholar-trainee com., trustee 1969-71), Am. Coll. Chest Physicians; mem. N.Y. Acad. Scis., Alpha Omega Alpha. Home: 1156 Red Rose Ln Villanova PA 19085-2121 Office: 1320 Race St Philadelphia PA 19107-2046 also: 401 City Line Ave Ste 610 Bala Cynwyd PA 19004

SEGAL, CHARLES PAUL, classics educator, author; b. Boston, Mar. 19, 1936; s. Robert and Gladys (Barsky) S.; m. Esther Rogers, Dec. 20, 1961 (div. June, 1979); children: Joshua H., Thaddeus G.; m. Nancy Ann Jones, Jan. 9, 1988; 1 child, Cora M. A.B., Harvard U., 1957, Ph.D., 1961; A.M. (hon.), Brown U., 1969. teaching fellow, classics tutor Harvard U., Cambridge, Mass., 1959-61, instr., 1963-64; asst. to assoc. prof. classics U. Pa., Phila., 1964-67; assoc. prof. to prof. Brown U., Providence, 1968-78; prof. classics and comparative lit., 1978-86; chmn. classics dept., 1978-81; Benedict prof. classics, prof. comparative lit., 1980-86; prof. classics, comparative lit. Princeton U., 1987-90; prof. Greek and Latin, Harvard U., Cambridge, Mass., 1990-96, Walter C. Klein Prof. of the Classics, 1996—. chmn. classics grad. studies U. Pa., 1967; jr. fellow Ctr. for Hellenic Studies, 1967-68; vis. prof. Intercollegiate Ctr. for Classical Studies, Rome, 1970-72; vis. prof. Brandeis U., 1974; vis. dir. Ecole des Hautes Etudes, Paris, 1975-76; Fulbright exchange lectr. U. Melbourne, Australia, 1978; vis. prof. Greek Columbia U., N.Y.C., 1979; participant 1st and 2d Soviet/Am. Semiotics Colloquia, Am. Council Learned Socs./USSR Acad. Sci., 1980, 83; cons. in field; mem. jury Classical Sch. Am. Acad. Rome, 1972-74, resident in classics, spring 1986; mem. exec. council Ctr. Semiotics, Brown U., 1979-85; chmn. curriculum revision com. Brown U., 1982-84. Author: Landscape in Ovid's Metamorphoses, 1969, The Theme of Mutilation in the Iliad, 1971, Tragedy and Civilization: An Interpretation of Sophocles, 1981, Poetry and Myth in Ancient Pastoral: Essays on Theocritus and Virgil, 1981, Dionysiac Poetics and Euripides' Bacchae, 1982, Pindar's Mythmaking, 1986; Language and Desire in Seneca's Phaedra, 1986; Interpreting Greek Tragedy, 1986, La Musique du Sphinx, 1987, Orpheus: The Myth of the Poet, 1989, Italian translation 1995, Lucretius on Death and Anxiety, 1990, Ovidio e la poesia del mito, 1991, Oedipus Tyrannus: Tragic Heroism and the Limits of Knowledge, 1993, Euripides and the Poetics of Sorrow, 1993, Singers, Heroes and God in the Odyssey, 1994, Sophocles' Tragic World, 1995; editor: The Heroic Paradox, 1982, The Rhetoric of Imitation, 1986, Roads to Paradise: Reading the Lives of the Early Saints, 1987; editorial bd. Am. Jour. Semiotics, 1985, Scholars Press, 1982-90, Helios, 1984—, MD, 1985—, Lexis, 1987—, Harvard Studies in Classical Philology, 1994—; contbr. articles to profl. jours. Am. Council Learned Socs. fellow, 1975; NEH grantee, 1977, fellow 1985-86; Guggenheim fellow, 1981-82; sr. fellow Ctr. Hellenic Studies, 1987-92; fellow Ctr. for Advanced Study in Behavioral Scis., 1989-90, fellow Nat. Humanities Center, 1993-94; Stanford Humanities Ctr. fellowr, 1997—; recipient Prix de Rome Am. Acad. in Rome, 1961-63. Fellow Am. Acad. Arts and Scis.; mem. Am. Philol. Assn. (bd. dirs. 1982-86, pres. 1994), Societa Italiana per lo Studio dell' Antichita Classica (hon.), Virgilian Soc., Classical Assn. New Eng., Internat. Ovid Soc. Office: Harvard U Dept Classics 319 Boylston Hall Cambridge MA 02138

SEGAL, DONALD E., lawyer; b. Houston, Nov. 13, 1947. BA with honors, Brandeis U., 1969; JD, Boston Coll., 1972. Bar: Mass. 1972, D.C. 1973, U.S. Supreme Ct. 1976, U.S. Dist. Ct. (D.C. dist.) 1976. Assoc. chief counsel FDA, Washington, 1979-91; ptnr. Baker & Hostetler, Washington, 1991-93, Akin, Gump, Strauss, Hauer & Feld, Washington, 1993—. Editor law review; mem. Law Rev. Boston Coll. Mem. ABA, FBA, Food and Drug Inst. Office: Akin Gump Ste 1100 1333 New Hampshire Ave NW Washington DC 20036-1510

SEGAL, GEORGE, sculptor; b. N.Y.C., Nov. 26, 1924; s. Jacob and Sophie (Gerstenfeld) S.; m. Helen Steinberg, Apr. 7, 1946; children—Jeffrey, Rena. BS in Art Edn., N.Y. U., 1950; MFA, Rutgers U., 1963, PhD in Fine Art (hon.), 1970; PhD in Fine Art (hon.), SUNY, Purchase, 1992. One man shows include Hansa Gallery, N.Y.C., 1956-59, Rutgers U., 1958, 63, Green Gallery, N.Y.C., 1960-62, 64, Sonnabend Gallery, Paris, 1963, Schmela Gallery Dusseldorf, 1963, Janis Gallery, N.Y.C., 1965, 67, 68, 70, 71, 73-74, 77, 78, 80, 82, 84, 88, 89, 91, 93, Mus. Contemporary Art, Chgo., 1968, Galerie Speyer, Paris, 1969, 71, Princeton U., 1969, Western Gallery Western Wash. State Coll., 1970, Onnasch Galerie, Cologne, 1971, also European mus. tour, 1971-73, U. Wis., Milw., 1973, Onnasch Galerie, Switzerland, 1974, Andre Emmerich, Zurich, 1975, Dartmouth Coll., 1975, Inst. Contemporary Art, 1976, Nina Freudenheim Gallery, Buffalo, 1976, Art Assn. Newport, R.I., 1976, Suzette Schochet Gallery, 1976, Santa Barbara Mus. Art, 1976, Whitney Mus. Am. Art, N.Y.C., 1979, Jacksonville Art Mus., 1982, U. Miami, 1983, Jewish Mus., N.Y.C., Makler Gallery, Phila., 1983, 84, Galleria Il Ponte, Rome, 1984, Evelyn Aimis Fine Art, Toronto, 1984, Galerie Esperanza, Toronto, 1985, 87, Galerie Brusberg, Berlin, 1986, Richard Gray Gallery, Chgo., 1987, Riva Yares Gallery, Scottsdale, Ariz., 1988, Casino Knokke, Belgium, 1989, Galerie Tokoro, Tokyo, 1990, Marguiles/Taplin Gallery, Bay Harbor, Fla., 1990, Art Gallery U. Rochester, N.Y., 1991; retrospective group shows include Sao Paulo Bienal, Janis Gallery, Jewish Mus., N.Y.C., Carnegie Internat., Whitney Mus., others; represented in permanent collections including Mus. Modern Art, Whitney Mus., Mint Mus., Charlotte, N.C., Albright-Knox Mus., Mus. Modern Art, Stockholm, Sweden, Met. Mus. Art, N.Y.C., Guggenheim Mus., N.Y.C., Bklyn. Mus., Art Inst. Chgo., Cleve. Mus. Art, Detroit Mus. Art, Modern Art Mus., Ft. Worth, Newark Mus., Weisman Mus. Contemporary Art, L.A., Pa. Acad. Fine Arts, Phila., Carnegie Mus. Art, Pitts., Portland (Oreg.) Mus. Art, San Francisco Mus. Modern Art, Hirschorn Mus. & Sculpture Garden, Washington, Libr. Congress, Washington, Nat. Gallery Art, Washington, Nat. Mus. Am. Art, Washington, Nat. Portrait Gallery, Washington, Musee d'Art Contemporain, Montreal, Nat. Gallery Art, Ottawa, Can., Art Gallery Ontario, Can., Vancouver Art Gallery, Can., Tamayo Mus., Mexico, Museo de Arte Contemporaneo, Caracas, Venezuela, Musees Royaux des Beaux-Arts, Brussels, Art Mus. of Atenaeum, Helsinki, Finland, Centre Nat. d'Art Contemporain, Paris, Neue Galerie der Stadt Aachen, Germany, Kolnisches Stadtsmuseum, Cologne, Germany, Stadtische Kunsthalle Mannheim, Germany, Staatsgalerie Moderner Kunst, Munich, Germany, Museum Boymans-van Beuningen, The Netherlands, Mus. Modern Art, Teheran, Iran, Israel Mus., Jerusalem, Kunsthaus Zurich, Switzerland, Fukuoka Mcpl. Mus. Art, Japan, Hiroshima (Japan) City Mus. Contemporary Art, Mus. Modern Art, Seibu Takanawa, Karuizawa, Japan, Nat. Mus. Art, Osaka, Japan, Tokyo Ctrl. Mus., Shiga Mus. Art, Japan, and numerous others. Recipient 1st prize Art Inst. Chgo., 1966, award Walter H. Gutman Found., 1962. Office: care Sidney Janis Gallery 110 W 57th St New York NY 10019-3319

SEGAL, GERALDINE ROSENBAUM, sociologist; b. Phila., Aug. 26, 1908; d. Harry and Mena (Hamburg) Rosenbaum; m. Bernard Gerard Segal, Oct. 22, 1933; children: Loretta Joan Cohen, Richard Murry. BS in Edn., U. Pa., 1930, MA in Human Rels., 1963, PhD in Sociology, 1978; MS in Libr. Sci., Drexel U., 1968; Dr. Letters (Hon.), Franklin & Marshall Coll., 1990. Social worker County Relief Bd., Phila., 1931-35; sociologist, Phila., 1935—; cons. and lectr. in field. Author: In Any Fight Some Fall, 1975; Blacks in the Law, 1983. Bd. dirs. NCCJ, 1937-47, 82—, sec., 1983-91; bd. overseers U. Pa. Sch. Social Work, 1983—; bd. dirs., Juvenile Law Ctr., 1984—; chair Phila. Tutorial Project, 1966-68; 1st v.p. U. Pa. Alumnae Assn., 1967-70. Co-recipient Nat. Neighbors Disting. Leadership in Civil Rights award, 1988; recipient Drum Major award for Human Rights, Phila. Martin Luther King, Jr. Assn. for Nonviolence, 1990, Brotherhood Sisterhood award NCCJ, 1994. Democrat. Jewish. Home: 2401 Pennsylvania Ave Apt 19-C-44 Philadelphia PA 19130-3001

SEGAL, HELENE R., editor; b. L.A., Jan. 31, 1955; d. Alan and Lila E. Segal; m. David Scott Wright, May 6, 1979. Student, Calif. State U., Fullerton, 1973-75; BA in English, U. Calif., Santa Barbara, 1978. Library asst. ABC-CLIO, Santa Barbara, 1979-80, editorial asst., 1980-81, asst. editor, 1981-83; mng. editor ABC POL SCI, ABC-CLIO, Santa Barbara, 1983—. Mem. Am. Polit. Sci. Assn., Current World Leaders (adv. bd. 1989—). Avocations: reading, collecting, swimming. Home: 142 La Vista Grande Santa Barbara CA 93103-2817 Office: ABC-CLIO 130 Cremona Dr Santa Barbara CA 93117-5599

SEGAL, IRVING EZRA, mathematics educator; b. N.Y.C., Sept. 13, 1918; s. Aaron and Fannie Segal; m. Osa Skotting, 1955 (div. 1977); children: William, Andrew, Karen; m. Martha Fox., 1985; 1 child, Miriam Elizabeth. A.B., Princeton U., 1937; Ph.D., Yale U., 1940. Instr. Harvard U., 1941; research asst. Princeton U., 1941-42, assoc., 1942-43; asst. to O. Veblen, Inst. for Advanced Study, 1945-46; asst. prof. to prof. U. Chgo., 1948-60; prof. MIT, Cambridge, 1960—; vis. assoc. prof. Columbia U., 1953-54; vis. fellow Insts. Math. and Theoretical Physics, Copenhagen, 1958-59; vis. prof. Sorbonne, Paris, France, 1965, U. Lund, Sweden, 1971, Coll. de France, 1977. Author: Mathematical Problems of Relativistic Physics, 1963, (with R.A. Kunze) Integrals and Operators, 1968, Mathematical Cosmology and Extragalactic Astronomy, 1976, (with J.C. Baez and Z. Zhou) Introduction to Algebraic and Constructive Quantum Field Theory, 1992; editor: (with W.T. Martin) Analysis in Function Space, 1964, (with Roe Goodman) Mathematical Theory of Elementary Particles, 1988; contbr. articles to profl. jours. Served with AUS, 1943-45. Recipient Humboldt award, Germany, 1982-83; Guggenheim fellow, 1947, 51-52, 67-68. Mem. Am. Math. Soc., Am. Phys. Soc., Am. Acad. Arts and Sci., Royal Danish Acad. Scis., Am. Astron. Soc., Nat. Acad. Sci. Home: 25 Moon Hill Rd Lexington MA 02173-6139 Office: MIT Rm 2-244 Cambridge MA 02139

SEGAL, IRVING RANDALL, lawyer; b. Allentown, Pa., Oct. 15, 1914; s. Samuel I. and Rose (Kantor) S.; m. Eleanor F. Smolens, Dec. 26, 1943; children: Betsy A. Segal Carter, Kathy J., Robert J. BA, U. Pa., 1935; LLB, 1938. Bar: Pa. 1938. Instr. polit. sci. U. Pa., 1938-42; law clk. Ct. Common Pleas No. 4, Phila. County, Pa., 1938-39; assoc. Schnader, Harrison, Segal & Lewis, Phila., 1939-49, ptnr., 1949-92, sr. counsel, 1993—; Permanent mem. Jud. Conf. 3d Circuit U.S. Ct. Appeals; regional rationing atty. OPA, 1942. V.p. Nat. Kidney Disease Found., 1954-59, hon. life del., 1959-64; pres. Nephrosis Found., Phila., 1953-56; bd. mgrs. Woman's Hosp. Phila., 1957-64, v.p., 1962-63; bd. Jewish Edn., Phila., 1948-72; trustee YMHA, YWHA, 1954-58. Served to capt. Judge Adv. Gen. Dept. AUS, 1942-46. Decorated Mil. Commendation medal. Fellow Am. Coll. Trial Lawyers (regent 1976-79, sec. 1979-80); mem. ABA (corrections com. 1980-87, jud. selection tenure and compensation com. 1988-93), Pa. Bar Assn., Phila. Bar Assn. (chmn. sr. lawyer 1996—), Am. Law Inst., Am. Bar Found., Am. Judicature Soc.,

World Peace Through Law, Am. Acad. Polit. and Social Sci., Order of Coif, Phi Beta Kappa, Pi Gamma Mu (pres., 1934-35), Delta Sigma Rho. Jewish (dir., v.p. temple). Clubs: Phila. Lawyers, Art Alliance, Locust, Army and Navy of Washington. Home: 210 W Rittenhouse Sq Apt 2306 Philadelphia PA 19103-5726

SEGAL, JACK, mathematics educator; b. Phila., May 9, 1934; s. Morris and Rose (Novin) S.; m. Arlene Stern, Dec. 18, 1955; children: Gregory, Sharon. B.S., U. Miami, 1955, M.S., 1957; Ph.D., U. Ga., 1960. Instr. math. U. Wash., Seattle, 1960-61; asst. prof. U. Wash., 1961-65, assoc. prof., 1965-70, prof., 1970—, chmn. dept., 1975-78. Author: Lecture Notes in Mathematics, 1978, Shape Theory, 1982. NSF postdoctoral fellow Inst. Advanced Study, Princeton, N.J., 1963-64; Fulbright fellow U. Zagreb, Croatia, 1969-70, U. Coll. London hon. rsch. fellow, 1988; Nat. Acad. Sci. exch. prof. U. Zagreb, Croatia, 1979-80. Mem. Am. Math. Soc. Home: 8711 25th Pl NE Seattle WA 98115-3416 Office: U Washington Dept Mathematics Seattle WA 98195

SEGAL, JOAN SMYTH, library consultant, business owner; b. Bklyn., Sept. 14, 1930; d. John Patrick and Anna Catherine (Green) Smyth; m. William Segal, June 25, 1955; children: Harold M., Nora A. BA, Douglass Coll., Rutgers U., 1951; MS in LS, Columbia U., 1955; PhD, U. Colo., 1978. Cert. assn. exec., 1988. Librarian, Math Inst., NYU, 1955-58, Western Interstate Commn. for Higher Edn., Boulder, Colo., 1970-76; libr. cons., Boulder, 1976-78; resource sharing program mgr. Bibliog. Ctr. for Rsch., Denver, 1978-80, exec. dir., 1980-84; exec. dir. Assn. of Coll. and Rsch. Librs., ALA, Chgo., 1984-90; assoc. exec. dir. programs ALA, 1990-93; owner Vintage Ventures, 1993—; trainer library automation, group devel., resource sharing; cons. in field. Contbr. articles to profl. publs. Named Colo. Librarian of Yr., Colo. Library Assn., 1984; named to Douglass Soc. Mem. ALA, Spl. Libraries Assn. (chmn. edn. divsn. 1981-82, pres. Rocky Mountain chpt. 1981-82, 1994-95, bd. dirs. 1983-86, chair mus., arts and humanities divsn. 1998—), OCLC Network Dirs. (chmn. 1983), Mountain Plains Library Assn., Am. Soc. Assn. Execs.

SEGAL, JOEL MICHAEL, advertising executive; b. N.Y.C., Sept. 2, 1933; s. Michel M. and Ethel (Meshaloff) S.; m. Alix Hegeler, Aug. 9, 1968; children: Mark J., Gregg F.; 1 grandchild, Nina. B.A., Cornell U., 1954; M.B.A., Columbia U., 1960. Media supr. Benton & Bowles, 1960-63; dir. network TV presentations NBC, 1963-65; successively network negotiator, network supr. and v.p., sr. v.p. then exec. v.p. network cable and syndicated broadcasting and dir. Ted Bates & Co., Inc., N.Y.C., 1965-87; exec. v.p. nat. broadcasting McCann-Erickson, N.Y.C., 1988—; bd. dirs. Rigel Inc. Served with AUS, 1956-58. Office: McCann-Erickson USA 750 3rd Ave New York NY 10017-2703

SEGAL, JONATHAN BRUCE, editor; b. N.Y.C., May 12, 1946; s. Clement and Florence Lillian (Miller) S.; m. Haidi Kuhn, June 30, 1974. B.A., Washington Coll., 1966. Writer, editor N.Y. Times, N.Y.C., 1966-73; editor Quadrangle/N.Y. Times Book Co., N.Y.C., 1974-76; sr. editor Simon & Schuster, N.Y.C., 1976-81; exec. editor, editor-in-chief, editorial dir., v.p. Times Books, N.Y.C., 1981-89; editor-at-large Random House, N.Y.C., 1985-89; v.p., sr. editor Alfred A. Knopf, N.Y.C., 1989—. Contbr. articles to popular jours. Democrat. Jewish. Home: 115 E 9th St Apt 12E New York NY 10003-5428 Office: Alfred A Knopf 201 E 50th St New York NY 10022-7703

SEGAL, LORE, writer; b. Vienna, Austria, Mar. 8, 1928; came to U.S., 1951, naturalized, 1956; d. Ignatz and Franzi (Stern) Groszmann; m. David I. Segal, Nov. 3, 1960 (dec.); children: Beatrice Ann, Jacob Paul. B.A. in English, Bedford Coll., U. London, Eng., 1948. Prof. writing div. Sch. Arts, Columbia U., also Princeton U., Sarah Lawrence Coll., Bennington Coll.; prof. English U. Ill., Chgo., 1978-92, Ohio State U., 1992—. Author: Other People's Houses, 1964; Lucinella, 1976, Her First American, 1985; (children's book) Tell Me A Mitzi, 1970, All the Way Home, 1973, Tell Me a Trudy, 1977; The Story of Mrs. Brubeck and How She Looked for Trouble and Where She Found Him, 1981, The Story of Mrs. Lovewright and Purrless Her Cat, 1985; translator: (with W.D. Snodgrass) Gallows Songs, 1968, The Juniper Tree and Other Tales from Grimm, 1973, The Book of Adam to Moses, 1987, The Story of King Saul and King David, 1991; contbr. short stories, articles to N.Y. Times Book Rev., Partisan Rev., New Republic, The New Yorker, others. Guggenheim fellow, 1965-66; Council Arts and Humanities grantee, 1968-69; Artists Public Service grantee, 1970-71; CAPS grantee, 1975; Nat. Endowment Arts grantee, spring 1982, 1987; NEH grantee, 1983; Acad. Arts and Letters award, 1986. Address: 280 Riverside Dr New York NY 10025-9010

SEGAL, MARTIN ELI, retired actuarial and consulting company executive; b. Vitebsk, Russia, Aug. 15, 1916; came to U.S., 1921, naturalized, 1928; s. Isidor and Anna (Title) S.; LHD (hon.), Pratt Inst., 1976; MusD (hon.), Mannes Coll. Music, 1976; LHD (hon.), Grad. Center CUNY, 1979; LHD (hon.) L.I. U., 1986, NYU, 1988; m. Edith Levy, June 17, 1937; children: Susan Segal Rai, Paul. Various positions ins. industry, 1935-39; founder The Segal Co., consultants and actuaries, N.Y.C., 1939, pres., chief exec. officer, 1939-67, chmn. bd., 1967-91, chmn. emeritus, 1991—; pres. Wertheim Asset Mgmt. Svcs., Inc., N.Y.C., 1972-75, chmn., bd., 1975-82; ptnr. Wertheim & Co., investment bankers, N.Y.C., 1967-82. Bd. dirs. Helena Rubinstein Found., 1972-95; founding chmn. The N.Y. Internat. Festival of the Arts, Inc., 1985—; chmn. bd. Lincoln Ctr. Performing Arts, Inc., 1981-86, chmn. emeritus, 1986—; bd. dirs. Pub. Radio Internat., 1981-94, dir. emeritus, 1994—; co-chmn. Conf. on Intellectual Property The Arts and Tech., 1994; chmn. arts and culture com., N.Y. 92, N.Y. 93, N.Y. 94, N.Y. 95; mem., bd. dirs. Nat. Bldg. Mus., 1983-91; bd. advisers Libr. of Am., 1984—; trustee Am.-Scandinavian Found., 1986-91, adv. trustee, 1991—; bd. visitors Grad. Sch. and Univ. Ctr., CUNY, 1983-96; bd. dirs. The Grad. Ctr. Found., Inc., 1996—; bd. trustees, chmn. exhibitions com. Mus. Modern Art, 1978-81; trustee Inst. for Advanced Study, Princeton, N.J., 1972-91, trustee emeritus, 1991—; pres. Cultural Assistance Ctr., Inc., 1977-82, chmn., 1982-84; founding pres. Film Soc. of Lincoln Ctr., 1968-78, pres. emeritus, 1978—; mem. adv. bd. The Alliance for New Am. Musicals, 1991—; mem. adv. coun. Theatre Devel. Fund, 1992—; bd. dirs. N.Y. Conv. and Visitors Bur., Inc., 1981—; mem. Nat. Bd. of Young Audiences, Inc., 1979—; founding mem. publs. com. The Pub. Interest, 1965—; mem. vis. com., Harvard U. Sch. Pub. Health, 1979-92, dean's coun. Sch. Pub. Health, 1990—; chmn. mayor's Com. on Cultural Policy, 1974; founding chmn. Commn. for Cultural Affairs City of N.Y., 1975; chmn. pub. svc. awards com. Fund for City of N.Y., 1978, 79, bd. dirs, 1978-87; mem. leadership Coun. Nat. Cultural Alliance, 1993—. Decorated Royal Swedish Order of Polar Star, 1984; officer of Arts and Letters, Ministry of Culture of French Govt., 1985; recipient cert. of merit Mcpl. Art Soc., 1974; spl. award Internat. Film Importers and Distbrs. Am., 1973; N.Y.C. Mayor's award of honor for arts and culture, 1982; Ann. award of distinction Mus. City of N.Y., 1982; Concert Artists Guild award, 1983; Disting. Am. of Fgn. Birth award Internat. Ctr. N.Y.C., 1985; John H. Finley medal Alumni Assn. CCNY, 1985; Town Hall Friend of the Arts award, 1987; Dirs. Emeriti award Lincoln Ctr. for Performing Arts, Inc., 1987; N.Y. State Gov.'s Arts award, 1989; Pres.'s award Grad. Sch. and Univ. Ctr. of City of N.Y., 1990; City of N.Y. Edn. Fund award LWV, 1984; Songwriter's Hall of Fame Patron of the Arts award, 1988; Nat. Fedn. Music Clubs Presdl. Citation award, 1989; Creative Arts Rehab. Ctr. Pub. Spirit award, 1989; Honor medal The Nat. Arts Club, 1992; Ellis Island medal of honor, 1996; Lincoln Ctr. Laureate, 1997. Mem. Century Assn., Players Club. Democrat. Jewish. Office: 375 Park Ave Ste 2602 New York NY 10152

SEGAL, ROBERT MANDAL, lawyer; b. Worcester, Mass., Mar. 21, 1915; s. Abe Charles and Bella (Perry) S.; m. Sharlee Mysel, June 17, 1941; children: Terry P., Ellen Huvelle. AB, Amherst Coll., 1936; postgrad., U. Chgo., 1936-38; JD, Harvard U., 1942. Bar: Mass. 1942, U.S. Dist. Ct. Mass. 1946, U.S. Supreme Ct. 1952. Economist U.S. Steel Corp., 1939; sr. ptnr. Segal & Flamm, Boston, 1955-72; New Eng. counsel AFTRA, 1948-86; sr. ptnr. Segal, Roitman & Coleman, Boston, 1972—; lectr. labor law Harvard U. Bus. Sch., 1962-82, Boston Coll. Law Sch., 1979-81, Northeastern U. Labor Inst., U.S. State Dept., 1971, 73; trustee Mass. Continuing Legal Edn., 1970-83; counsel Mass. State Labor Coun., AFL-CIO, 1948-85. Co-author: History of Labor and Employment Section of the ABA, 1946-86, 1986; contbr. articles to profl. jours. Chmn. Harvard U. Law Sch. Rec. Alumni Com., 1973-93; pres. Jewish Cmty. Coun. of Boston, 1975; mem. film Commn. Mass., 1990—; mem. adv. coun. Mass. Prepaid Legal Svcs., 1984—; life trustee Combined Jewish Appeal. With U.S. Army, 1943-45. Recipient Cushing-Gavin Labor award, 1986; Brookings Instn. fellow, 1938-39. Fellow Coll. Labor and Employment Lawyers Inc. (emeritus); mem. ABA (ho. of dels. 1957-58, mem. consortium 1975-80, chmn. labor and employment sect. 1957, co-chmn. membership and fin. com. labor sect. 1978-96, forum com. 1984-86), AFTRA (New Eng. counsel 1947-85), Am. Guild of Musical Artists (N.E. counsel 1970—), Screen Actors Guild (New Eng. counsel 1955-88), Mass. Bar Assn., Boston Bar Assn. (mem. coun. 1960-84, co-chmn. labor law sect. 1957-85), Mass. Adv. Bd. of Film Bur., Mass. Prepaid Legal Svcs. Inst. (adv. bd. 1980—), Indsl. Rels. Assn., Mass. Ams. for Dem. Action (chmn. 1960), Harvard U. Law Sch. Alumni Assn. (mem. coun. 1970-73), Phi Beta Kappa, Delta Sigma Rho. Jewish. Home: 50 Longwood Ave Apt 1112 Brookline MA 02146-5227 also: 6750 Gulf Mexico Dr Longbeach Key FL 34228 Office: Segal Roitman & Coleman 11 Beacon St Boston MA 02108-3002

SEGAL, ROBERT MARTIN, lawyer; b. Atlantic City, N.J., Apr. 7, 1935; s. Nathan Albert and Edna (Dutkin) S.; m. Rhoda Sue Luber, June 8, 1958; children—Deborah Ann, William Nathan, Elizabeth Ann. Student, Cornell U., 1953-54; B.S. in Econs., U. Pa., 1957; LL.B. cum laude, Harvard Law Sch., 1960. Bar: Pa. 1961. Assoc. Wolf, Block, Schorr & Solis-Cohen, Phila., 1960-69, ptnr., 1969—, chmn., exec. com., 1978-79, 82-83, 86-87, 89—; hon. pres. Jewish Employment and Vocat. Svc. Contbr. articles to profl. jours. and mags. Constable of elections Lower Merion Twp., Pa., 1970-72; mem. Rep. Jewish Coalition, 1984-85; bd. dirs. Jewish Family and Children's Agy., Am. Jewish Com., Rosenbach Mus. and Libr., Greater Phila. Urban Affairs Coalition; bd. govs. Nat. Jewish Coalition. Mem. ABA, Pa. Bar Assn., Phila. Bar Assn., Internat. Coun. Shopping Ctrs., Urban Land Inst. (assoc.), Am. Coll. Real Estate Lawyers, Phila. Bar Found. (trustee 1981-87), Am. Law Inst., Harvard Law Sch. Assn. Phila., The Federalist Soc. (bd. advisors Phila. chpt.), Atlantic City C ountry Club, Gov.'s Club, Chaine des Rotisseurs, Sunday Breakfast Club, La Coquille Club, Harvard Club, Beta Gamma Sigma. Avocations: golf, swimming. Office: Wolf Block Schorr & Solis-Cohen 12th Fl Packard Bldg SE Corner 15th and Chestnut Philadelphia PA 19102-2678

SEGAL, SANFORD LEONARD, mathematics educator; b. Troy, N.Y., Oct. 11, 1937; s. Joseph and Bessie (Katz) S.; m. Rima Maxwell, Sept. 3, 1959; children: Adam, Joshua, Zoë. BA, Wesleyan U., 1958; PhD, U. Colo., 1963. Instr. U. Rochester, N.Y., 1963-64, asst. prof., 1964-70; rsch. fellow U. Vienna, Austria, 1965-66; assoc. prof. U. Rochester, N.Y., 1970-77, assoc. chmn., maths., 1969-79; vis. lectr. U. Nottingham, Eng., 1972-73; prof. U. Rochester, N.Y., 1977—, chmn. maths., 1979-87. Author: (book) Nine Introductions in Complex Variables, 1981; contbr. numerous articles to profl. jours. Fulbright fellow, Mainz, Germany, 1958-59, Fulbright Rsch. fellow, Vienna, Austria, 1965-66; fellow Inst. Math. Para e Applicada, Brazil, 1982, Alexander Von Humboldt Found., Fed. Rep. Germany, 1988. Mem. Am. Maths. Soc., Math. Assn. Am. (various coms. and chmn.), History Scis. Soc. Democrat. Avocations: gardening, chess, reading. Home: 511 Rockingham St Rochester NY 14620-2519 Office: U Rochester Wilson Blvd Rochester NY 14627

SEGAL, SHELDON JEROME, biologist, educator, foundation administrator; b. N.Y.C., Mar. 15, 1926; s. Morris M. and Florence (Bogan) S.; m. Harriet Ellen Feinberg, May 22, 1961; children: Amy Robin, Jennifer Ann, Laura Jane. BA, Dartmouth Coll., 1947; postgrad., U. Geneva, 1947-48; MS, U. Iowa, 1951, PhD, 1952; MD (hon.), U. Tampere, Finland, 1984, U. Upssala, Sweden, 1985. Rsch. scientist William S. Merrill Co., Cin., 1952-53; rsch. assoc., asst. prof. U. Iowa, 1953-56; asst. med. dir. Population Coun., N.Y.C., 1956-63, med. dir., 1963-78, v.p., 1969-76, sr. v.p., 1976-78; affiliate Rockefeller U., N.Y.C., 1956-76, adj. prof., 1977-87; dir. population scis. Rockefeller Found., 1978-91; disting. scientist Population Coun., N.Y.C., 1991—; lectr. Columbia U., 1959-61; vis. prof. All-India Inst. Med. Scis., New Delhi, 1962-63, Amir Chand lectr., 1975; mem. Marine Biol. Lab, Woods Hole, Mass.; cons. World Bank, WHO, NIH, Ford Found., Indian Govt., UN Office Sci. and Tech., UN Fund Population Activities; mem. com. on contraceptive tech. NAS, 1977-80, com. on health effects of marijuana Inst. Medicine, 1981-82, NAS com. on demographic impact of contraceptive tech., 1988-89, nat. rsch. con., overview com. for Indo-U.S. sci. initiative, 1985—; adv. com. on human reproduction FDA; cons. to dir. Nat. Inst. Child Health and Human Devel., 1978-80; plenary lectr. 3d World Congress Endocrinology, 1968, Upjohn lectr. Am. Fertility Soc., 1971, plenary lectr. World Fertility Congress, 1975, Sigma Xi lectr. U. Idaho, 1976, plenary lectr. World Congress on Ob-Gyn., 1976, lectr. Chinese Acad. Scis., 1977, Carl Gemzell lectr. U. Upssala, 1982, Pierre Soupart lectr. Axel Munthe Found., 1988, Alpha Omega Alpha lectr. U. Pa. Coll. Medicine, 1989, plenary lectr. World Congress on Human Reproduction, 1990; hon. prof. Peking Union Med. Coll., Beijing, 1987, Chinese Acad. Scis., 1988; trustee Marine Biol. Lab., 1985—, chmn. bd. trustees, 1991—. Co-editor 8 books; contbr. numerous articles to profl. jours. Trustee Rye Country Day Sch., 1979—, pres. bd. trustees, 1981-85; trustee Ctr. for Reproductive Law and Policy, 1992—. Lt. (j.g.) USNR, 1943-45. Decorated Order Comdr. of Lion (Finland); recipient Honor award Innsbruck U., Austria, hon. citation Pres. of India, 1978, Clarence J. Gamble award World Acad. Arts and Scis., 1980, Joseph C. Wilson award Rochester Assn. for UN, 1981, UN Population award, 1984, Axel Munthe award in medicine Axel Munthe Found., Italy, 1985, Sci. award Planned Parenthood Fedn. Am., 1990, Dmitirus N. Chorafas award in medicine Swiss Acad. Scis., 1995. Fellow AAAS; mem. Royal Coll. Obstetricians and Gynecologists (hon.), Am. Fertility Soc. (hon. v.p. 1975-76, trustee found. 1975-77), Endocrine Soc., Am. Assn Anatomists, Internat. Soc. for Study Reprodn. (pres. 1968-72), Internat. Inst. Embryology, Am. Soc. Zoologists, Coun. Fgn. Rels., Mexican Acad. Medicine (hon.), Inst. Medicine, Dartmouth Club N.Y., Woods Hole Yacht Club. Home: 9 Topland Rd Hartsdale NY 10530-3001 Office: Population Coun One Dag Hammarskjold Plz New York NY 10017

SEGALAS, HERCULES ANTHONY, investment banker; b. N.Y.C., Mar. 21, 1935; s. Anthony Spiros and Katherine A. (Michas) S.; m. Margaret Wharton, Sept. 18, 1956; children: Donnell Anthony, Stephen Wharton, Katherine Lacy Devlin. BS, Yale U., 1956. Various engring. and mfg. positions Procter & Gamble Co., Cin., 1956-65; pres. for Latin Am., mgr. Internat. Flavors and Fragrances, N.Y.C., 1965-68; exec. v.p., mem. bd. dirs. William D. Witter Inc., N.Y.C., 1969-76; sr. v.p. Drexel Burnham Lambert Inc., N.Y.C., 1976-87, mng. dir., 1987-88, also bd. dirs., 1976-88; mng. dir. head consumer products investment banking group PaineWebber Inc. Investment Banking Group, N.Y.C., 1988—, also bd. dirs. Bd. dirs. Nantucket Land Coun., Mass., 1982-85; mem. corp. Nantucket Cottage Hosp., 1984-85. Mem. Morristown Field Club, Nantucket Yacht Club (bd. govs. 1987-93, mem. exec. com. 1988-93), The Windsor Club. Republican. Avocations: tennis, sailing, languages, woodworking. Home: 17 Hilltop Cir Morristown NJ 07960-6312 Office: Paine Webber Inc 1285 Avenue Of The Americas New York NY 10019-6028

SEGALL, HAROLD ABRAHAM, lawyer; b. N.Y.C., May 22, 1918; s. Morris and Mildred (Borkan) S.; m. Edith S. Besser, Jan. 27, 1952; children—Mark E., Grant D., Bruce K. BA with distinction, Cornell U., 1938; LLB cum laude, Yale U., 1941. Bar: N.Y. 1941. Practiced in N.Y.C., 1946—; assoc. mem. firm Gilbert, Segall and Young, 1946-49, ptnr., 1949-93, sr. counsel, 1994—; vis. lectr. Yale U. Law Sch., 1974-75, Yale U. Sch. Orgn. and Mgmt., 1983-85. Author: (with R.B. Kelley) Estate Planning for the Corporate Executive, 1971, Representing the Seller of a Closely-Held Business, 1973, reprint, 1976; (with J.A. Arouh) How to Prepare Legal Opinions-Boldness and Caution, 1979, reprint, 1990; (with M.S. Sirkin) Providing for Withdrawal from a Joint Venture, 1982, Seventeen Suggestions for Improving Communications with Clients and Colleagues, 1994, reprint, 1995, How to Keep Improving a Highly Successful Law Firm, 1994, An Executive's Lesson in the Law from a Typical Business Encounter, 1996; contbr. articles to profl. jours. Mem. council State U. N.Y. at Purchase, 1974-79; Counsel United Republican Finance Com., N.Y. State, 1955-61, Rep. City Com., N.Y.C., 1961, Nat. Rep. Citizens Com., 1962, Keating for Senator Com., 1964, Eisenhower 75th Birthday Com., 1965, Friends of the Gov. Wilson Team, 1974, Gov.'s Club, N.Y., 1965-75; trustee, v.p., treas. Philip D. Reed Found. Inc., 1989-96; bd. dirs. Oneita Knitting Mills, 1973-83. Served to maj. AUS, World War II, ETO and PTO. Recipient Edgar M. Cullen prize, 1939. Mem. ABA, Bar City N.Y. (com. on trademark and unfair competition 1967-69, chmn. subcom. legislation 1968-69), Jewish Community Center, Order of Coif, Phi Beta Kappa, Phi Kappa Phi, Phi Sigma Delta. Clubs: University (N.Y.C.); Elmwood Country (gov. 1966-70, 73-75). Home: 60 Woodlands Rd Harrison NY 10528-1419 Office: 430 Park Ave New York NY 10022-3505

SEGARD, HUBERT J., international marketing company executive, consultant; b. Tourcoing, Nord, France, Apr. 24, 1930; s. Jacques and Marguerite (Prouvost) S.; m. Diane du Luart, Jan. 21, 1969 (div.); children: Elodie, Stanislas; m. Wendy C. Collassard, June 6, 1986. BSc, St. Louis, Paris, 1949; postgrad., Harvard U., 1949-50. Pres., CEO H&H Segard, Tourcoing, 1965-77; ptnr. Jacques Segard & Co., Paris, 1963-77; founder, owner Souffle de Paris, Laguna Beach, Calif., 1977—; pres., CEO, CFO Napoleon Gourmet Foods Inc., Laguna Beach, 1986—; sr. ptnr. Am. EC Mktg. Assocs., Laguna Beach, 1989—; pres. FFINTEL, Paris, 1975-77; v.p. Comite Central de la Laine, Paris, 1975-77; mem. adv. bd. CNEP Bank, Paris, 1970-74. Gen. consul Republic of San Marino, 1973. Capt. French Army, 1950-54. Mem. Global League (O.C. chpt., assoc.), World Trade Coun. Paris (assoc.), Sr. Exec. Network Asns. Corp. Growth. Roman Catholic. Avocations: sociology, art, wine, sailing, travel. Office: Am EC Mktg Assocs PO Box 1833 Laguna Beach CA 92652-1833

SEGARRA, TYRONE MARCUS, pharmacist, medicinal chemist; b. N.Y.C., Oct. 6, 1959; s. Saris Enrique and Delia Esther (Medina) S. BS in Pharmacy, U. P.R., 1982; MS in Medicinal Chemistry, U. Iowa, 1984, PhD in Medicinal Chemistry, 1988; MBA in Health Care Mgmt. and Mktg., SUNY, Buffalo, 1994. Staff relief pharmacist Ross Rexall Pharmacy, Belle Plaine, Iowa, 1983-87; postdoctoral rsch. assoc. SUNY, Buffalo, 1987-88; staff pharmacist Rite Aid Corp., Buffalo, 1988-89, Cy's Elma (N.Y.) Pharmacy, 1989-90, Fay's Drugs, Buffalo, 1990—; part-time asst. prof. in chemistry Erie C.C., SUNY, 1994—. Vol. City Mission, Buffalo, 1993. Mem. Am. Chem. Soc. (mem. organic divsn., medicinal chemistry, chemistry and th e law, mktg. and bus. econs.). Democrat. Roman Catholic. Avocations: guitarist, editl. writing, reading, baseball, photography. Office: Fays Drugs 214 Elmwood Ave Buffalo NY 14222-2202

SEGEL, JOSEPH M., broadcasting executive; b. Phila., Jan. 9, 1931; s. Albert M. and Fannie B. (Scribner) S.; m. Renee A., June 1, 1951 (div. 1960); 1 child, Marvin; m. Doris Usem, Dec. 20, 1963; 1 child, Alan; 1 stepchild, Sandy Stern. BS in Econs., U. Pa., 1951. Chmn. Nat. Bus. Services, Inc., Phila., 1950-63; chmn., cons. Franklin Mint Corp., Franklin Center, Pa., 1963-85; chmn. Presdl. Airways Corp., Phila., 1975-79; chmn. QVC Network Inc., West Chester, Pa., 1986-93, chmn. emeritus, 1993—; chmn. Software Digest, Inc., Wynnewood, Pa., 1983-86, Nat. Software Testing Labs., Inc., Phila., 1984-86. Editor The Counselor mag., 1951-61. Chmn. UN Assn. U.S.A., N.Y.C., 1973-75; mem. U.S. delegation UN Gen. Assembly, , 1974. Republican. Jewish. Club: LeMirador Country (Switzerland) (chmn. 1974-89). Office: QVC Inc Goshen Pk 1365 Enterprise Dr West Chester PA 19380-5959*

SEGELMAN, ALLYN EVAN, dentist, researcher; b. Boston, July 25, 1947; s. Edward David John and Harriett Sylvia (Shuman) S.; m. Sandra Ruth Steiman, June 17, 1973 (div. Aug. 1995); children: Tovah Chanah, Rayna Devorah. AB in Biology, Boston U., 1969; DMD, Tufts U., 1973; SM in Epidemiology, Harvard U., 1997. Diplomate Am. Bd. Oral and Maxillofacial Surgery, Am. Bd. Oral Medicine. Intern Tufts-New Eng. Med. Ctr., 1973-74, fellow in oral cancer, 1974-75; resident Boston City Hosp., 1975-77, chief resident, 1976-77; pvt. practice oral and maxillofacial surgery Mass., 1977-95; asst. clin. prof. oral and maxillofacial surgery Tufts U. Sch. of Dental Medicine, Boston, 1980—; rsch. fellow in dental care adminstrn. Harvard Sch. of Dental Medicine, Harvard Sch. Pub. Health, Boston, 1996-97; dental ops. and policy dir. Blue Cross Blue Shield, N. Quincy, Mass., 1997—; dir. dental consultative svcs. New Eng. Area Comprehensive Hemophilia Care Ctr., Worcester, Mass., 1977-78; cons. managed care benefit sys. Blue Cross Blue Shield of Mass., Boston, 1984—; cons. Ctrl. Mass. Healthcare Inc., Worcester, 1992, Mass. Pro Inc. and Nat. Quality Health Coun., Waltham, 1995. Editor: Procedural Terminology for Oral and Maxillofacial Surgery, 1985, Procedural Terminology with Glossary, 1985; contbr. articles to profl. jours. Gov.'s appointee Legis. Spl. Commn. on Sch. Bus Safety, Boston, 1985-88; bd. registration in dentistry appointee Mass. Dept. Pub. Health Prescription Monitoring Program, Boston, 1994—; chmn. sch. com. Congregation Mishkan Tefila, Newton, Mass., 1993-95, bd. trustees, 1983-95. Recipient Brotherhood award Mass. Com. of Catholics, Protestants and Jews, 1965. Fellow Am. Acad. Oral Medicine (pres. 1996—), Am. Assn. Oral and Maxillofacial Surgeons (chmn. spl. com. coding and nomenclature 1991-94), Mass. Dental Soc. Anesthesiology (pres. 1987-88); mem. Tufts U. Dental Alumni Assn. (exec. coun., pres. 1985-86), Omicron Kappa Upsilon. Democrat. Jewish. Avocations: photography, theology, nosology. Home: 19 Westgate Rd Apt 4 Chestnut Hill MA 02167-3429 Office: Blue Cross Blue Shield Mass Dental Ops and Policy 100 Hancock St North Quincy MA 02171-1745

SEGER, LINDA SUE, script consultant, writer; b. Peshtigo, Wisc., Aug. 27, 1945; d. Linus Vauld and Agnes Katherine Seger; m. Theodore Newton Youngblood, Jr., Aug. 28, 1968 (div. Jan. 1970); m. Peter Hazen LeVar, April 12, 1987. BA in English, Colo. Coll., Colorado Springs, 1967; MA in theatre arts, Northwestern U., Evanston, 1968; MA in religion and arts, Pacific Sch. of Religion, Berkeley, 1973; ThD in drama and theology, Graduate Theological U., Berkeley, 1976; postgrad., Immaculate Heart Coll. Ctr., L.A., 1994—. Instr. drama Grand Canyon Coll., Phoenix, 1969-71; instr. drama and theology McPherson (Kans.) Coll., 1976-77; instr. drama and humanities LaVerne (Calif.) U., 1977-79; asst. Provisional Theatre, L.A., 1979-80, Tandem/TAT, L.A., 1980-81; story analyst EMI Films, L.A., 1982-83; pvt. practice script cons. L.A., 1981—, pvt. practice lectr., author, 1984—. Author: Making a Good Script Great, 1988, Creating Unforgettable Characters, 1990, The Art of Adaptation, 1992, When Women Call the Shots, 1996; co-author: From Script to Screen, 1994. Mem. NOW, Women in Film, Acad. of TV Arts and Scis., Ind. Feature Project-West. Democrat. Mem. Soc. of Friends. Avocations: horseback riding, piano, travel. Home and Office: 2038 Louella Ave Venice CA 90291-4015

SEGERSTEN, ROBERT HAGY, lawyer, investment banker; b. Boston, June 24, 1941; s. Wendell C. and Claire H. S.; m. Marie E. Makinen, Feb. 13, 1965; children: Amanda Beth, Vanessa Bryce. A.B., Bates Coll., 1963; J.D., Boston U., 1970. Bar: Mass. 1970. Assoc. Nessen & Csaplar, Boston, 1970-75; v.p. March Co., Boston, 1975-77; pres. March-Eton Corp., Concord, Mass., 1977-82; ptnr. Nessen, Goodwin & Segersten, Concord, 1977-82, Kane & Segersten, Dedham, Mass., 1983-85; pres. Woodbine Optical Corp., Braintree, Mass., 1990—; adj. prof. Sch. Am. Studies, Boston U.; adj. prof. real estate law Bentley Coll. Officer, bd. dirs. Friends of The Jimmy Fund, Boston. Served to lt. USN, 1963-67. Mem. ACLU, Mass. Bar Assn. Democrat. Episcopalian. Home: 64 Folsom Ave Hyannis MA 02601-4823 Office: 41 Brooks Dr Braintree MA 02184-3809

SEGESVÁRY, VICTOR GYÖZÖ, retired diplomat; b. Miskolc, Hungary, Feb. 20, 1929; came to U.S., 1984; s. Viktor and Margit (Kovács) S.; m. Andrea Bárczay, Jan. 20, 1955 (div. Nov. 1957); 1 child, Gábor; m. Monika Schwarz, Dec. 28, 1968. PhD in Polit. Sci., Grad. Inst. Internat. Studies, Switzerland, 1968; DD, U. Geneva, 1973. Asst., libr. Reformed Theol. Acad., Budapest, Hungary, 1953-56; sec. gen. African Inst., Geneva, 1961-63; asst. editor, market rsch. officer Bus. Internat. S.A., Geneva, 1963-66; market rsch. officer SESAF S.A., Geneva, 1967-68; chief rsch. dept. Henry Dunant Inst. Internat. Red Cross, Geneva, 1968-71; cons. Internat. Trade Ctr., UNCTAD/GATT, Geneva, 1969-71; tech. advisor market rsch.-market study Internat. Trade Ctr., Algiers, Algeria, 1971-72; sr. trade promotion advisor, project mgr. UNCTAD/GATT/ITC, Algiers, 1973-74; chief advisor in internat. econ. rels., project mgr. UNCTAD/GATT/ITC, Kabul, Afghanistan, 1975-79, Bamako, Mali, 1979-83; sr. advisor, cons. UN Devel. Programme, African countries, 1984-93; sr. advisor, cons. dept. for tech. cooperation for devel. UN, N.Y.C., 1985-88. Author: Le réalisme khrouchtchevien-Politique soviétique au Proche-Orient, 1968, La Réforme et l'Islam, 1500-1550, 1973, A Raday Könyvtár 18. századi története, 1992, Inter-Civilizational Relations and the Destiny of the West: Dialogue or Confrontation?, 1997. Sec.-gen. Internat. Fedn. Students in Polit. Sci., Geneva, 1958-59. Home: 330 E 39th St Apt 21/e New York NY 10016-2123

SEGGER, MARTIN JOSEPH, museum director, art history educator; b. Felixtowe, Eng., Nov. 22, 1946; s. Gerald Joseph and Lillian Joan (Barker-Emery) S.; m. Angele Cordonier, Oct. 4, 1968; children: Cara Michelle, Marie-Claire, Margaret Ellen. B.A., U. Victoria, 1969, Diploma in Edn., 1970; M. in Philosophy, U. London, 1973. Prof. art history U. Victoria, B.C., 1970-74; museologist Royal B.C. Mus., Victoria, 1974-77; dir. Maltwood Art Mus., prof. art history U. Victoria, B.C., 1977—; cons. Nat. Mus. Corp., Ottawa, 1977, UNESCO, O.E.A., Cairo, 1983. Author: exhbn. catalogue House Beautiful, 1975, Arts of the Forgotten Pioneers, 1971, Victoria: An Architectural History, 1979, (commendation Am. Assn. State and Local History 1980), This Old House, 1975, This Old Town, 1979, British Columbia Parliament Buildings, 1979, The Heritage of Canada, 1981, Samuel Maclure: In Search of Appropriate Form, 1986 (Hallmark award 1987), (a guide) St. Andrew's Cathedral, 1990, The Development of Gordon Head Campus, 1988, An Introduction to Museum Studies, 1989, An Introduction to Heritage Conservation, 1990, Botswana Live, 1994, Exploring Victoria's Architecture, 1996. Bd. govs. Heritage Can. Found., 1979-83; chmn. City of Victoria Heritage Adv. Com., 1975-79; bd. dirs. Heritage Trust, 1977-86, B.C. Touring Coun., Sta. CFUV Radio, B.C. Govt. House Found., 1987-93, Royal Brit. Columbia Mus.; mem. B.C. Heritage Adv. Bd., 1973-83; councillor City of Victoria, 1987-93; vice-chair Provincial Capital Commn., 1991—; pres. Assn. Vancouver Island Municipalities, 1993-94. Decorated knight Equestrian Order of Holy Sepulchre of Jerusalem; recipient award Heritage Can. Communications, 1976, Heritage Conservation award Lt. Gov. B.C., 1989, Harley J. McKee award Assn. Preservation Technology, 1994. Fellow Royal Soc. Arts; mem. Can. Mus. Assn. (counsellor 1975-77), Internat. Coun. Mus. (chair internat. com. for tng. of pers. 1995—), Internat. Coun. Monuments and Sites (bd. dirs. 1980-92), Soc. Study Architecture Can. (bd. dirs. 1979-81), Authors Club (London), Can Mus. Dirs. Orgn., Carnavon Club. Roman Catholic. Avocations: travel, motor mechanics, walking. Home: 1035 Sutlej St, Victoria, BC Canada V8V 3P2

SEGGERMAN, ANNE CRELLIN, foundation executive; b. Los Angeles, May 13, 1931; d. Curtis Vergil and Yvonne (LaGrave) Crellin; m. Harry G.A. Seggerman, Apr. 14, 1951; children: Patricia, Henry, Marianne, Yvonne, Suzanne, John. Studies with Albert Levesque, Paris, 1948-50; Student, Sch. Decorative Arts, Paris, 1950, Sch. of the Louvre, Paris, 1950, Albertus Magnus Coll., 1951; D.H.L. (hon.), Sacred Heart U., 1980. French tchr. Beverly Hills, Calif., 1958-60; translator World Affairs Council, Los Angeles, 1958-60; staff mem. West Side Sch. Gifted Children, Beverly Hills, 1958-60; pres. Huxley Inst. for Bio-Social Research, Fairfield, Conn., 1972—, 4th World Found. Interfaith Media Action, Fairfield, 1977—, Steiner Prodns., Fairfield, 1981—; founder The Com. for Guadalupe Research, Fairfield, 1982—; bd. dirs. Anuk, Inc. co-founder Christian/Jewish Ctr. Understanding Sacred Heart U., Fairfield, Conn.; active Pres. Reagan's Health Task Force Resources Com. on Health Adv. Couns. of U.S. Dept. Health and Human Svcs.; mem. Pres.'s Com. Mental Retardation, 1981-86, Com. Housing Handicapped Families, 1989; mem. Nat. Coun. on Disability, 1992-95; bd. dirs. Easter Seal Rehab. Ctr., Fairfield, Internat. Coll. Applied Nutrition, World Health Med. Group, Cath. League for Religion and Civil Rights. Recipient Am. Assn. Sovereign Mil. Order of Malta, 1991, Lady of Equestrian Order of Holy Sepulchre of Jerusalem, 1991. Mem. Nat. Health Fedn., The Inst. for Study of Human Knowledge, Am. Holistic Med. Inst., Internat. Acad. Preventive Medicine, Calif. Orthomolecular Soc., Am. Phys. Rsch., Fairfield County Organic Gardeners.

SEGIL, LARRAINE DIANE, materials company executive; b. Johannesburg, South Africa, July 15, 1948; came to U.S., 1974; d. Jack and Norma Estelle (Cohen) Wolfowitz; m. Clive Melwyn Segil, Mar. 9, 1969; 1 child, James Harris. BA, U. Witwatersrand, South Africa, 1967, BA with honours, 1969; JD, Southwestern U., L.A., 1979; MBA, Pepperdine U., 1985. Bar: Calif. 1979, U.S. Supreme Ct. 1982. Cons. in internat. transactions, L.A., 1976-79; atty. Long & Levit, L.A., 1979-81; chmn., pres. Marina Credit Corp., L.A., 1981-85; pres., chief exec. officer Electronic Space Products Internat., L.A., 1985-87; mng. ptnr. The Lared Group, L.A., 1987—. Author: (novel) Belonging, 1994, Intelligent Business Amaries, 1996. Bd. govs. Cedars Sinai Med. Ctr., L.A., 1984—; bd. dirs. So. Calif. Tech. Execs. Network, 1984-86. Mem. ABA (chmn. internat. law com. young lawyers div. 1980-84), Internat. Assn. Young Lawyers (exec. coun. 1979-81, coun. internat. law and practice 1983-84), World Tech. Execs. Network (chmn.). Avocations: piano, horseback riding. Office: The Lared Group 1901 Avenue Of The Stars Los Angeles CA 90067-6001

SEGNER, EDMUND PETER, III, natural gas company executive; b. Dallas, Oct. 23, 1953; s. Edmund Peter Jr. and Martha Fairfax (Smith) S.; m. Kathryn Louise Daily, July 10, 1976; children: Peter Michael, Christian James. BSCE, Rice U., 1976; MA in Econs., U. Houston, 1980. CPA, Tex. Acct. Touche Ross & Co., Houston, 1976-78; asst. v.p. planning United Gas Pipe Line Co., Houston, 1978-86; asst. v.p. rsch. Drexel Burnham Lambert, N.Y.C., 1986-88; v.p. pub. and investor rels. Enron Corp., Houston, 1988-90; sr. v.p. pub. and gov. rels., investor Enron Corp, Houston, 1990-92, exec. v.p., chief staff, 1992—; lectr. civil engring. Rice U., Houston, 1982-84, 97. Bd. dirs. Zool. Soc. Houston, 1992-95, Greater Houston Partnership for Ednl. Excellence, 1991-93, Rice U. Fund Coun., 1992—, Sam Houston Area coun. Boy Scouts Am.; treas. Tex. Nature Conservancy, 1992—; chmn. Cmty. Ptnrs., 1993-95. Mem. Houston Soc. Fin. Analysts, Houston City Club, Briar Club, Braeburn Country Club, Coronado Club, Old Baldy Club. Republican. Lutheran. Home: 4130 Tennyson St Houston TX 77005-2750 Office: Enron Corp 1400 Smith St Houston TX 77002

SEGUIN, DAVID GERARD, community college official; b. Fulton, N.Y., Apr. 17, 1943; s. Leonell Joseph and Jasmine (Dumany) S.; m. Katherine Shiely (div. Oct. 1977); m. Brenda G. Eastman, Sept. 17, 1983; 1 child, Shivani. AA, Onondaga Community Coll., Syracuse, N.Y., 1964; BA in Psychology, Trinity U., 1967, MS in Psychology, 1970; PhD in Psychology, U. Toledo, 1985. Instr., prof. Jamestown (N.Y.) C.C., 1970-86, ad hoc assoc. dean, 1986-88, assoc. dean, 1988—, dir. instnl. rsch., 1991—, chmn. div. behavioral scis., 1975-77; instr. stop shoplifting program Better Bus. Bur., Jamestown, 1988-92. Contbr. articles to profl. jours. Bd. mem. Chautauqua County (N.Y.) Tchrs. Resource Ctr., 1987-88. Mem. Am. Psychol. Soc., Assn. Instl. Rsch., North Ea. Assn. Instl. Rsch. Democrat. Roman Catholic. Avocations: jazz, golf. Office: Jamestown Community Coll 515 Falconer St Jamestown NY 14701-1920

SEHN, SUSAN CLEARY, psychiatrist; b. Denver, Feb. 2, 1943; d. Herbert J and Helen (Wetherill) Cleary; m. George James Sehn, Jan. 23, 1965 (div. 1985); children: Natalie, Michael. BA, U. Colo., 1965; MS, Pa. State U., 1974; MD, Med. Coll. Pa., 1978. Diplomate in gen. psychiatry and child and adolescent psychiatry Am. Bd. Psychiatry and Neurology. Intern in pediatrics Hahnemann U. Hosp., Phila., 1978-79; resident in gen. psychiatry Med. Coll. Pa., Phila., 1979-81, fellow in child psychiatry, 1981-83; attending physician Horsham Clinic, Ambler, Pa., 1984-89; dir. adolescent psychiatry Eugenia Hosp., Lafayette Hill, Pa., 1988-90; attending physician Northwestern Inst., Ft. Washington, Pa., 1983-93; dir. adolescent psychiatry Warminster (Pa.) Psychiat. Ctr., 1990-91; attending psychiatrist Phila. Child Guidance Ctr., 1992—; v.p., treas. Askelpios Ltd., Levittown, Pa., 1990-91; sec. bd. dirs. United Psychiat. Svc., Lafayette Hill, 1988-90; mem. bd. med. dirs. Guillain Barré Found., Wynnewood, Pa., 1983—. Mem. Psyciat. Physicians Pa. (co-chair com. on women 1988-94), Regional Coun. Child and Adolescent Psychiatry (treas. 1993-95), Phila. Adolescent Soc. (v.p. 1988-93). Avocations: personal computing, singing, music, birding. Home: 4005 Fairway Rd Lafayette Hill PA 19444-1303

SEIBEL, ERWIN, oceanographer, educator; BS, CCNY, 1965; MS, U. Mich., 1966, PhD, 1972. Asst. research oceanographer U. Mich., Ann Arbor, 1972-75, assoc. research oceanographer, 1975-78, asst. dir. sea grant, 1975-78; environ. lab dir. San Francisco State U., 1978-81, chmn. dept. geoscis., 1981-88, dean undergraduate studies, 1988—. commr. Calif. Commn. on Tchr. Credentialing; sr. scientist cruises U. Mich., 1971-78; mem. sea grant site rev. teams Nat. Sea Grant Program, Washington, 1978—; bd. govs. Moss Landing Marine Labs., Calif., 1981—; mem. adv. com. Ctr. Advancement Mercantile Spacefaring; coord. Biology Forum Calif. Acad. Scis., 1988-89; exec. sec. Oceans 83 Marine Tech. Soc., IEEE, San Francisco, 1982-83; coord. Symposium for Pacific AAAS El Nino Effect, 1983-84; dir. environ. monitoring nuclear power plant, 1972-78; mem. sci. adv. panel Calif. Commn. Tchr. Credentialing, 1988-93; mem. steering com. Pacific Basin Studies Ctr., 1990-93; commr. Calif. Commn. on Teaching Credentialing, 1993—, fiscal planning & policy com., 1994—, performance stds. com., 1995—, appeals & waivers com., 1996—. Contbr. articles to profl. jours.; developer photogrammetric technique for continuous shoreline monitoring. Advisor MESA program for Minority Students, San Francisco area, 1981-88; vol. San Francisco Bay Area council Girl Scouts U.S., 1982-86. Served to capt. U.S. Army, 1967-71, Vietnam. Grantee Am. Electric Power Co., 1972-78, Gt. Lakes Basin Commn., 1975-76, Calif. Div. Mines and Geology, 1986-88, Am. Coun. Edn. and Ford Found., 1990-94. Recipient Exceptional Merit Service award San Francisco State U., 1984. Fellow AAAS, Calif. Acad. Scis., Geol. Soc. Am.; mem. N.Y. Acad. Scis., Am. Geophys. Union, Marine Tech. Soc. (pres. San Francisco Bay chpt. 1982-83), Western Assn. Schs. and Colls. (mem. student learning and teaching effectiveness task force 1994-95), U. Mich. Alumni Assn., Gold Key (hon.), Sigma XI (pres. San Francisco State U. chpt. 1982-84, 90-92, Chautauqua coord, 1989-96, faculty athletic rep. NCAA, NCAC, 1991-93). Office: San Francisco State U Dean of Undergrad Studies 1600 Holloway Ave San Francisco CA 94132-1722

SEIBER, WILLIAM JOSEPH, financial and insurance consultant; b. Huntington, W.Va., Dec. 24, 1943; s. Charles Joseph Jr. and Esther (Huddleston) S.; m. Ruby Mae Smith, Mar. 3, 1973 (div. June 1985); children: William Joseph, Scott Joseph; m. Nancy Jeanne Toothman Manfredi, Aug. 3, 1990; stepchildren: Maria C. Manfredi, Anthony C. Manfredi. BBS in Chemistry, Marshall U., 1966, MBA in Fin., 1972, BBA in Acctg., 1973. CLU, CHFC, RHU. Analytical chemist Houdaille Industries, Inc., Huntington, W.Va., 1966-67; real estate office mgr. Fla. Tradewinds, Inc., Columbus and Savannah, Ga., 1969-70; asst. prodn. mgr. Chemetron Corp., Huntington, 1970-71; grad. teaching asst. Marshall U., Huntington, 1972-73, instr. acctg., 1977-80; acctg. systems analyst Ashland Oil, Inc., Ashland, Ky., 1973; asst. prof. bus. W.Va. State Coll., Institute, 1980-81, W.Va. U. Grad. Studies, 1981-85; fin. and ins. cons. The Paul Revere Ins. Group, Worcester, Mass., 1973—; mem. Nat. Multistate Ins. Licensing Com., Ednl. Testing Svc., Princeton, N.J., 1983-90; mem. W.Va. Ins. Commrs. Agts. Licensing Adv. Com., Charleston, 1981-92, also past chmn.; R&D in field. Fund raiser Salvation Army, Charleston, 1987—; mem. fin. and planned giving com. Cath. Charities, Charleston, 1984—; mem. W.Va. U. Found. Planned Giving Com., 1991—; coach Little League and Sr. League Baseball. 1st lt. U.S. Army, 1967-69. Acad. scholarship and Benedum grantee Marshall U., 1961-66, 70-72; Million Dollar Round Table, 1985-89, 92, 93, 96, 97. Mem. Am. Soc. CLU and ChFC (sec.-treas., pres. Charleston chpt. 1989-91, Pres.'s award 1991), Nat. Assn. Life Underwriters (Charleston chpt.), Nat. Assn. Health Underwriters, Am. Sternwhell Assn., Charleston Estate Planning Coun., Cross Lanes Recreation Assn. (bd. dirs. 1986-90). Republican. Roman Catholic. Avocations: tennis, boating, fishing, travel. Home: 17 Hidden Cv Cross Lanes WV 25313-1171 Office: 910 Quarrier St Ste 307 Charleston WV 25301-2613

SEIBERLICH, CARL JOSEPH, retired naval officer; b. Jenkintown, Pa., July 4, 1921; s. Charles A. and Helen (Dolan) S.; m. Trudy Germi, May 29, 1952; children: Eric P., Heidi M., Curt A. B.S., U.S. Mcht. Marine Acad., 1943; grad., Armed Forces Staff Coll., 1959. Commd. ensign U.S. Navy, 1943, advanced through grades to rear adm., 1971; designated naval aviator, 1947; comdg. officer Airship ZPM-1, 1949, Air Anti-Submarine Squadron 26, 1961, U.S.S. Salamonie, 1967, U.S.S. Hornet, 1969; dir. recovery astronauts Apollo 11 and 12 lunar missions, 1969; comdr. anti-submarine warfare group 3 Flagship U.S.S. Ticonderoga, 1971; comdr. task force 74 Viet Nam Ops., 1972; asst. dep. chief naval ops. for air warfare Navy Dept., 1975-77; dep. chief naval personnel, 1977-78; comdr. Naval Mil. Personnel Command, 1978-80; with VSE Corp., 1980-82; pres. U.S. Maritime Resource Ctr.; dir. mil. program Am. Pres. Lines, 1983-95, VZM/TranSystems Corp., Reston, Va., 1996—; co-chmn. intermodal task force Nat. Rsch. Coun., Transp. Bd.; mem. NAFTA Info. Exch. & Automation working group. Vice pres. Naval Aviation Mus. Found.; active Boy Scouts Am. Decorated Legion of Merit (6), Air medal; recipient Harmon Internat. trophy for devel. 1st variable depth towed sonar, 1951. Mem. VFW, AIAA, Am. Soc. Naval Engrs., Am. Helicopter Soc., U.S. Naval Inst., U.S. Naval Sailing Assn. (commodore 1979), Am. Angus Assn., Tailhook Assn., Navy Helicopter Assn., Naval Airship Assn., Early and Pioneer Naval Aviators Assn., Nat. Def. Transp. Assn., Am. Def. Preparedness Assn., Navy League U.S. (maritime affairs com.), Propeller Club, Order of Daedalians, U.S. Mcht. Marine Acad. Alumni Assn., Assn. Naval Aviation, Am. Legion, N.Y. Yacht Club, Nat. Space Club, Delta Sigma Pi. Clubs: N.Y. Yacht, Nat. Space. Home: Seagate Farm 1510 Loudoun Dr Haymarket VA 20169-1120 Office: VZM/Tran Systems Corp 2100 Reston Pkwy Ste 202 Reston VA 20191-1218 *Maintain a clear set of moral values, prepare yourself professionally, maintain physical fitness, persevere as you move toward your goal. Value personal relationships. Never give less than your best; never accept less than the best. Don't trade on the accomplishments of yesterday. Have fun and at times pause and admire the flowers.*

SEIBERLING, JOHN FREDERICK, former congressman, law educator, lawyer; b. Akron, Ohio, Sept. 8, 1918; s. J. Frederick and Henrietta (Buckler) S.; m. Elizabeth Pope Behr, June 4, 1949; children—John B., David P., Stephen M. AB, Harvard U., 1941; LLB, Columbia U., 1949. Bar: N.Y. 1950, Ohio 1955. Assoc. mem. firm Donovan, Leisure, Newton, Lumbard & Irvine, N.Y.C., 1949-53; atty. Goodyear Tire & Rubber Co., Akron, 1954-71; mem. 92d-99th Congresses from 14th Ohio Dist.; mem. com. on judiciary, com. on interior and insular affairs, chmn. subcom. on public lands; vis. prof. law U. Akron, 1987, 90, dir. Ctr. for Peace Studies, 1991-96; ptnr. Goldman, Seiberling, Davis & Tsarnas, Akron, 1988-89. Served to maj. AUS, 1942-46. Mem. United Ch. of Christ. Home: 154 Tecumseh Ln Akron OH 44321-2753

SEIBERT, RUSSELL JACOB, botanist, research associate; b. Shiloh Valley, Ill., Aug. 14, 1914; s. Erwin W. and Helen A. (Renner) S.; m. Isabelle L. Pring, Dec. 26, 1942; children: Michael, Donna, Lisa. A.B., Washington U., St. Louis, 1937, M.S., 1938, Ph.D., 1947. With U.S. Dept. Agr., 1940-50; botanist-geneticist rubber plant investigations U.S. Dept. Agr., Haiti, 1941-42; botanist-geneticist U.S. Dept. Agr., Peru, 1943-46, Costa Rica, 1947-49; dir. Los Angeles State and County Arboretum, Arcadia, Calif., 1950-55, Longwood Gardens, Kennett Square, Pa., 1955-79; adj. curator tropical horticulture Marie Selby Bot. Garden, Sarasota, Fla., 1979-96; adj. prof. bot. garden mgmt. U. Del., 1967-79; head dept. arboreta and bot. gardens, Los Angeles County, 1952-55; alt. del. Internat. Soc. Hort. Sci., 1960-70; chmn. Am. Hort. Council-U.S.A. (hort. exhbn.), 1960; (floriade), Rotterdam, Holland; v.p. XVII Internat. Hort. Congress, 1966; chmn. Am. Hort. Film Festival, 1964-69. Recipient Frank N. Meyer Meml. medal Am. Genetic Soc., 1966, Arthur Hoyt Scott Garden and Horticulture medal Swarthmore Coll., 1975, Disting. Svc. awrd Hort. Soc. N.Y., 1969, award of merit Am. Assn. Bot. Gardens and Arboreta, 1982. Mem. AAAS, Am. Hort. Soc. (pres. 1964-65, Liberty Hyde Bailey medal 1975), Am. Inst. Biol. Scis., Rotary, Sigma Xi, Phi Sigma, Gamma Sigma Delta. Home: 1613 Caribbean Dr Sarasota FL 34231-5305

SEIBOLD, JAMES RICHARD, physician, researcher; b. Washington, Apr. 5, 1950; s. Herman Rudolph and Clara Bond (Taylor) S.; m. Margaret Frances Bennett, Jan. 20, 1968; children: Jon Drew, Zachary Bennett. BS, La. State U., 1972; MD, SUNY, Stony Brook, 1975. Diplomate Am. Bd. Internal Medicine, Am. Bd. Rheumatology. Intern in medicine L.I. Jewish Hosp., New Hyde Park, N.Y., 1975-76, resident in medicine, 1976-78; fellow in rheumatology U. Pitts., 1978-80; asst. prof. medicine Robert Wood Johnson Med. Sch. U. Medicine and Dentistry of N.J., New Brunswick, 1980-86, assoc. prof. medicine Robert Wood Johnson Med. Sch., 1986-92, chief rheumatology Robert Wood Johnson Med. Sch., 1986-91, dir. clin. rsch. ctr. Robert Wood Johnson Med. Sch., 1989-95; mem. adv. bd. Ctr. for Advanced Biotech. and Medicine, Piscataway, N.J., 1989-95, dir. Scleroderma program 1995—; W.H. Conzen chair clin. pharmacology Schering-Plough Found., Inc., 1989. Author: (chpt.) Rheumatology, 1988, 91, 94, 95; contbr. over 200 articles to profl. jours. Fellow ACP, Am. Coll. Rheumatology (regional coun. 1985). Mem. Soc. of Friends. Home: 16 Durham Rd Skillman NJ 08558-1805 Office: U Medicine & Dentistry NJ Robert Wood Johnson Med Sch 1 Robert Wood Johnson Pl # 19cn New Brunswick NJ 08901-1928

SEIBOLD, RONALD LEE, sociologist, writer; b. Kansas City, Mo., May 8, 1945; s. Dean Phillip and Helen H. (Haney) S.; m. Christine Herbst, June 23, 1971 (div. July 1975). BS, Emporia State U., 1967; MA, Colo. State U., 1969. Dir. chpt. services Alpha Kappa Lambda, Ft. Collins, Colo., 1969-71; v.p. Siever & Assocs., Ft. Collins, 1971-72; pvt. practice sociology research Colo., 1972-75; coodinator Pines Internat., Lawrence, Kans., 1975—, sec., treas., 1976-87, pres., 1987—; pres. Live Foods Co., Lawrence, 1978—. Author: AKL Manual, 1969, Pines...The Wheat Grass People, 1982, Condominium Farming, 1986; editor: Cereal Grass: What's in it for You, 1990, Cereal Grass: Nature's Greatest Health Gift, 1993; contbr. articles to profl. mags. Founder, pres. Midwestern Interfraternity Coun., Emporia, Kans., 1966; pres. Interfraternity Coun., Emporia, 1965; v.p. Collegiate Young Reps., Emporia, 1965; mem. Kans. Organic Producers, 1978—, Organic Crop Improvement Assn., 1990—; pres. Wilderness Cmty. Edn. Found., 1989—. George Meredith scholar Emporia State U., 1963. Mem. Nat. Nutritional Foods Assn., Nutritional Products Quality Assurance Assn. (co-chmn. green foods group 1992—), Organic Crop Improvement Assn., Lawrence C. of C., U.S. C. of C., Kappa Mu Epsilon, Xi Phi. Presbyterian. Home: 1992 E 1400 Rd Lawrence KS 66044-9803 Office: Pines Internat Inc PO Box 1107 Lawrence KS 66044-8107

SEIDE, PAUL, civil engineering educator; b. N.Y.C., July 22, 1926; s. Julius David and Sylvia (Eiler) S.; m. Joan Cecilia Matalka, Jan. 7, 1951; children: Richard Laurence, Wendy Jane Seide Kielsmeier. B.C.E., CCNY, 1946; M. Aero. Engring, U. Va., 1952; Ph.D., Stanford U., 1954. Aero. research scientist Nat. Adv. Commn. for Aeros., Langley AFB, Va., 1946-52; research asst. Stanford Calif. U., 1952-53; research engr. Northrop Aircraft Co., Hawthorne, Calif., 1953-55; head methods and theory sect. TRW Inc., Los Angeles, 1955-60; head methods and research sect. Aerospace Corp., El Segundo, Calif., 1960-65; prof. civil engring. U. So. Calif., L.A., 1965-91, prof. emeritus, 1991—, assoc. chmn. dept. civil engring., 1971-73, 81-83; Albert Alberman vis. prof. Technion-Israel Inst. Tech., Haifa, 1975; vis. prof. U. Sydney, Australia, 1986, U. Canterbury, N.Z., 1986; cons. Northrop Inc., 1972-77, Aerospace Corp., 1966-68, Rockwell Inc., El Segundo, 1982-85. Author: Small Elastic Deformations of Thin Shells, 1975; contbr. numerous articles to profl. jours. NSF fellow, 1964-65. Fellow ASME, Am. Acad. Mechanics; mem. ASCE (life), Tau Beta Pi, Sigma Xi. Democrat. Jewish. Home: 300 Via Alcance Palos Verdes Peninsula CA 90274-1105 Office: U So Calif University Park Civil Engring Dept Los Angeles CA 90089-2531

SEIDEL, FREDERICK LEWIS, poet; b. St. Louis, Feb. 19, 1936; s. Jerome Jay and Thelma (Cartun) S.; children: Felicity, Samuel. AB, Harvard U., 1957. occasional lectr., Rutgers U., New Brunswick, 1964—; Paris editor, Paris Review, 1961, advisory editor, 1962. Author: (poetry) Final Solutions, 1963, Sunrise, 1979 (Lamont Poetry prize Acad. Am. Poets 1980, Am. Poetry Rev. prize 1980, Nat. Book Critics Circle award for poetry 1981), Men and Woman: New and Selected Poems, 1984, Poems 1959-1979, 1989, These Days, 1989, My Tokyo, 1993. Guggenheim Fellow, 1993.

SEIDEL, GEORGE ELIAS, JR., animal scientist, educator; b. Reading, Pa., July 13, 1943; s. George E. Sr. and Grace Esther (Heinly) S.; m. Sarah Beth Moore, May 28, 1970; 1 child, Andrew. BS, Pa. State U., 1965; MS, Cornell U., 1968, PhD, 1970; postgrad., Harvard U. Med. Sch., Boston, 1970-71. Asst. prof. physiology Colo. State U., Ft. Collins, 1971-75, assoc. prof., 1975-83, prof., 1983—; vis. scientist Yale U., 1978-79, MIT, 1986-87; mem. bd. on agr. NRC. Co-editor: New Technologies in Animal Breeding, 1981; contbr. articles to profl. jours. Recipient Alexander Von Humboldt award, N.Y.C., 1983, Animal Breeding Research award Nat. Assn. Animal Breeders, Columbia, Mo., 1983, Clark award Colo. State U., 1982, Upjohn Physiology award, 1986; Gov's. award for Sci. and Tech., Colo., 1986. Mem. AAAS, NAS, Am. Dairy Sci. Assn., Am. Soc. Animal Sci. (Young Animal Scientist award 1983), Soc. for Study of Reprodn., Internat. Embryo Transfer Soc. (pres. 1979). Home: 3101 Arrowhead Rd Laporte CO 80535-9374 Office: Colo State U Biotechnol Lab Animal Reproduction Fort Collins CO 80523

SEIDEL, MILTON JOSEPH, government administrator; b. Milw., July 3, 1931; s. Lawrence John and Anna (Norville) S.; m. Katherine Vukelic, Aug. 18, 1956; 1 child, Joseph Lawrence. BS cum laude, St. Louis U., 1956; MS, Washington U., St. Louis, 1963, postgrad., 1963-64. Spl. project engr. Alton (Ill.) Box Bd. Co., 1960-68; dir. mfg. engring. Colt Industries, St. Louis, 1968-71, Kuhlman Corp., Lexington, Ky., 1971-72; mgr. engring. edn. program U.S. Postal Service, Washington, 1972-74; chief Bur. Engraving and Printing, Office of Engring., Washington, 1974-79, asst. dir. research and engring., 1979-88, asst. dir. tech., 1988-96, assoc. dir. tech., 1996—; assoc. prof. Grad. Sch. Engring., George Washington U., Washington, 1973—; author, chmn. proceedings Internat. Conf. Machine Inspection Printed Security Documents, 1986, Internat. Conf. on Security Documents in 21st Century, 1987. Author: Economic Analysis for Capital Investment, 1972, Volume Forecasting, 1973, Network Analysis, 1973, Manpower Scheduling, 1974, Electronics Scanning, 1981, Electronic Quality Examination, 1981, Progress of Manufacturing Operation, 1985, Technology Innovation and Development Program, 1987. Served with U.S. Army, 1948-52. Mem. ASME, Ops. Research Soc. Am., Tech. Assn. Graphic Arts, Am. Soc. Pub. Adminstrn., Sigma Xi, Alpha Eta Rho. Home: 14412 Ansted Rd Silver Spring MD 20905-4410 Office: Bur Engraving and Printing 14th C St SW Washington DC 20228

SEIDEL, ROBERT WAYNE, science historian, educator, institute administrator; b. Kansas City, Mo., June 9, 1945; s. Wayne Herman and Harriet Anita (Day) S.; m. Alison Publicover, Aug. 26, 1972 (div. 1989); 1 child, Mary Ruth; m. Christine Ruth Stack, July 1, 1993. BA, Westmar Coll., 1967; MA, U. Calif., Berkeley, 1968, PhD, 1978. Exhibit designer Lawrence Hall Sci., Berkeley, 1970-72; specialist Poland 4-city tour USIA, Warsaw, 1971-72; grad. rsch. and teaching asst. U. Calif., 1972-78; asst. prof. Tex. Tech U., Lubbock, 1978-83, dir. rsch. history of enginrg. program, 1979-83; rsch. historian U. Calif., Berkeley, 1980-82, Laser History Project, Albany, Calif., 1983-85; adminstr. Bradbury Sci. Mus., Los Alamos, N.Mex., 1985-90, project leader, 1990-92; sr. staff mem. Ctr. Nat. Security Studies, Los Alamos, N.Mex., 1992-94; dir. Charles Babbage Inst., U. Minn., Mpls., 1994—; ERA Land Grant prof. History of Tech. U. Minn., Mpls., 1994—. Author: Lawrence and His Laboratory: A History of the Lawrence Berkeley Laboratory, 1989, Los Alamos and the Making of the Atomic Bomb, 1995. Mem. N.Mex. Sci. Ctr. Commn., 1989-92; mem. adv. com. County Cultural Ctr., Los Alamos, 1986-89; bd. dirs. The Bakken Mus., 1994—. Woodrow Wilson fellow, 1967, U. Calif. Regent's fellow, 1968, German Marshall Fund fellow, Grenoble, France, 1975. Mem. History Sci. Soc., Soc. for History Tech. Democrat. Avocations: hiking, chess. Home: 5625 Woodlawn Blvd Minneapolis MN 55417-2667 Office: Charles Babbage Inst 103 Walter Libr, U Minn Minneapolis MN 55455

SEIDEL, SELVYN, lawyer, educator; b. Long Branch, N.J., Nov. 6, 1942; s. Abraham and Anita (Stoller) S.; m. Deborah Lew, June 21, 1970; 1 child, Emily. BA, U. Chgo., 1964; JD, U. Calif., Berkeley, 1967; Diploma in Law, Oxford U., 1968. Bar: N.Y. 1970, U.S. Dist. Ct. (so. and ea. dists.) N.Y. 1970, D.C. Ct. Appeals, 1982. Ptnr. Latham & Watkins, N.Y.C., 1984—; adj. prof. Sch. Law, NYU, 1974-85; instr. Practicing Law Inst., 1980-81, 84. Mem. ABA, New York County Bar Assn., N.Y.C. Bar Assn. (mem. fed. cts. com. 1982-85, internat. law com. 1989-92, 95-96), Boalt Hall Alumni Assn. (bd. dirs. 1980-82), Contbr. articles to profl. jours. Office: Latham & Watkins 885 3rd Ave New York NY 10022-4834

SEIDELMAN, ARTHUR ALLAN, director; b. N.Y.C.; s. Theodore and Jeanne (Greenberg) S. BA, Whittier (Calif.) Coll., 1958; MA, UCLA, 1960. Adminstr. Forum Theater, Lincoln Ctr., N.Y.C., 1970-72; pres. LSV Prodns., N.Y.C., 1972-76; v.p. Golden Eagle Prodns., N.Y.C., 1977-79; pres. Entertainment Profls., Inc., L.A., 1980-92, Entpro, Inc., L.A., 1992—. Dir.: (feature films) Rescue Me, The Caller, Children of Rage, Echoes; (TV episodes) Hill Street Blues (Emmy, Humanitas awards for "Doris in Wonderland"), Murder She Wrote, Magnum, P.I., Knots Landing, Trapper John, M.D., Fame, A Year in the Life, L.A. Law, Capital News, WIOU, F.B.I. The Untold Stories, Sweet Justice, Amazing Grace, others; (TV movies) Which Mother is Mine? (Emmy award, Christopher award, Golden Halo award), I Love Liberty (Writer's Guild award), Schoolboy Father, Having a Baby, Look Away (Emmy nomination), Macbeth, Matter of Time (Emmy award, Chgo. Film Festival Silver plaque, N.Y. Internat. Film Festival Silver plaque), She Drinks a Little (Emmy award, Golden Halo award), Strange Voices, A Place at the Table, An Enemy Among Us (Nancy Susan Reynolds award), Poker Alice, Sin of Innocence, Kate's Secret, A Friendship in Vienna (Grand prize N.Y. Internat. Film Festival), The People Across the Lake, Addicted to His Love, The Glory Years, False Witness, The Kid Who Loved Christmas, Body Language, Dying to Remember, Trapped in Space, The Secrets of Lake Success, Amazing Grace (pilot), Harvest of Fire (Movie Guide award), The Summer of Ben Tyler, Deep Family Secrets, Miracle in the Woods; dir. broadway and off-broadway plays Hamp. Ceremony of Innocence, Awake and Sing, Billy, Inherit the Wind, Justice Box, Vieux Carrè, The Most Happy Fella for the N.Y.C. Opera, Gypsy Princess for Opera Pacific, The Sisters at the Pasadena Playhouse, others; host TV series Actors on Acting (Emmy award). Bd. dirs. ACLU So. Calif., L.A., 1986-94. Democrat. Office: Entpro, Inc 1015 Gayley Ave # 1149 Los Angeles CA 90024-3424

SEIDELMAN, SUSAN, film director; b. Pa., Dec. 11, 1952. Student, Drexel U., NYU. Dir. films, including: Smithereens, 1982, Desperately Seeking Susan, 1985, Making Mr. Right, 1987, Cookie, 1989, She-Devil, 1990, The Dutch Master (nominee Acad. award in dramatic short category), 1994, The Barefoot Executive, 1995; directorial debut with short film: You Act Like One, Too (Student Film award AMPAS). Office: care Michael Shedler 225 W 34th St Ste 1012 New York NY 10122-1099 also: William Morris Agy 151 El Camino Los Angeles CA 90048*

SEIDEMANN, ROBERT SIMON, manufacturing company executive; b. Cleve., Jan. 25, 1938; s. Hans and Ilse (Cohn) S.; m. Anita Claire Rudolph, Dec. 27, 1959; children: Lisa Eiduson, Teri Robbins. AB, U. Mich., 1959; MA, Ohio State U., 1962. CPA, Ohio. Staff acct. Soloway & von Rosen, Cleve., 1962-68; controller, v.p. fin. Hunting Oil Co., Lakewood, Ohio, 1968-72; dir. devel. Second Fed. Savs. & Loan, Cleve., 1972-74; v.p. Fin. Am., Inc., Cleve., 1974-76; v.p. fin., CFO Tokyo Shapiro Inc., Cleve., 1976-80; chmn. bd., CEO Seidemann & Assoc., Inc., Cleve., 1980-88; dir. Price Waterhouse, Cleve., 1988-92; nat. ptnr. Arthur Andersen, Cleve., 1992-94; chmn., CEO Vicon Fabricating Co., 1994—. Co-author: Workouts and Turnarounds, 1991. Bd. trustees Fairmont Temple, Beachwood, 1980—. Mem. Turnaround Mgmt. Assn. (bd. dirs. 1985-93), Assn. Insolvency Accts. (bd. dirs. 1984-88). Home: 3122 Bremerton Rd Pepper Pike OH 44124-5345 Office: Vicon Fabricating Co 150 Parker Ct Chardon OH 44024-1112

SEIDEN, ANDY, lawyer; b. N.Y.C., Sept. 16, 1956; s. Stanley and Dorothy Rose. BS in Indsl. and Labor Rels., Cornell U., 1978; vis. student, Harvard Law Sch., 1980-81; JD, U. Calif., Berkeley, 1981. Bar: Calif. 1981, N.Y. 1993. Assoc. Donovan Leisure Newton & Irvine, L.A., 1981-85, Curtis Mallet-Prevost Colt & Mosle, N.Y.C., 1987-89, Pettit & Martin, San Francisco, 1989-91; pvt. practice San Francisco, 1991-93; ptnr. Whitehead & Porter, San Francisco, 1993-95; v.p. bus. devel. and bus. affairs, gen. counsel Big Top Prodns., San Francisco, 1995-96; v.p. bus. and legal affairs Walt Disney Feature Animation, Burbank, Calif., 1997—. Bd. dirs. L.A. League of Conservation Voters, L.A., 1983-85. Mem. ABA (com. on negotiated acquisitions 1994-96), Phi Kappa Phi. Democrat. Avocations: world travel, skiing, cultural anthropology, computers. Office: Walt Disney Co 500 S Buena Vista St Burbank CA 91521-0001

SEIDEN, HENRY (HANK SEIDEN), advertising executive; b. Bklyn., Sept. 6, 1928; s. Jack S. and Shirley (Berkowitz) S.; m. Helena Ruth Zaldin, Sept. 10, 1949; children: Laurie Ann, Matthew Ian. BA, Bklyn. Coll., 1949; MBA, CCNY, 1954. Trainee Ben Sackheim Advt. Agy., 1949-51; nat. promotion mgr. N.Y. Post Corp., 1951-53; promotion mgr. Crowell-Collier Pub. Co., Inc., 1953-54; copy group head Batten, Barton, Durstine & Osborn, Inc., 1954-60; v.p., creative dir. Keyes, Madden & Jones, 1960-61; sr. v.p., assoc. creative dir. McCann-Marschalk, Inc., 1961-65, chmn. plans bd., 1964-65; creative dir., dir., prin. Hicks & Greist, Inc., N.Y.C., 1965—, sr. v.p., 1965-74, exec. v.p., 1974-83, COO, 1983—, pres., 1986—; CEO Ketchum/Hicks & Greist Inc., 1987-89; chmn., CEO Ketchum Advt., 1989-91; exec. v.p. Ketchum Comm. Inc., also bd. dirs.; vice chmn. Jordan, McGrath, Case & Taylor, Inc., 1992—; chmn., CEO The Seiden Group, Inc.; bd. dirs. Ketchum Internat. Inc.; guest lectr. Bernard M. Baruch Sch. Bus. and Pub. Adminstrn., CCNY, 1962—, Baruch Coll., 1969—, New Sch. Social Scis., 1968, 72,73, Sch. Visual Arts, 1979, 80—, Lehman Coll., CCNY, 1980—, Ohio U., 1981, Newhouse Grad. Sch., Syracuse U., 1981, NYU, 1983; cons. pub. rels. and comm. to mayor City of New Rochelle, N.Y., 1959—; cons. mktg. dept. Ohio State U.; cons. to pres. N.Y.C. City Coun., 1972-73; cons. Postmaster Gen. U.S., 1972-74; comm. advisor to commr. N.Y.C. Police Dept., 1973—, hon. dept. commr., 1991—, spl. cons. to commr., 1992—. Author: Advertising Pure and Simple, 1976, Advertising Pure and Simple: The New Edition, 1990; contbg. editor: Madison Ave. mag, 1966—, Advt. Age, Mag. Age; guest columnist: N.Y. Times, 1972. Vice commr. Little League of New Rochelle; bd. dirs. Police Res. Assn. N.Y.C., 1973—, pres. exec. com.; bd. dirs. Cancer Rsch. and Treatment Fund, Inc., pres., 1992—, Transmedia Network, Inc.; bd. dirs., pres. New York's Finest Found., 1975—, pres., 1996; bd. dirs., sr. v.p. Drug Enforcement Agy. Found., 1995—. Recipient award Four Freedoms Found., 1959, award Printers Ink, 1960, promotion award Editor and Pub., 1955, Am. TV Commls. Festival award, 1963-69, Effie award Am. Mktg. Assn., 1969, 70, award Art Dirs. Club N.Y., 1963-70, award Am. Inst. Graphic Arts, 1963, Starch award, 1969, spl. award graphic art lodge B'nai B'rith Greater N.Y., 1971, 87, award of highest honor FBI Nat. Acad., 1994. Mem. NATAS, Am. Inst. Mgmt. (assoc.), Drug Enforcement Agts. Found. (sr. v.p. 1995), Advt. Club N.Y. (exec. judge Andy awards, award 1963-65), Advt. Writers Assn. N.Y. (Gold Key award for best newspaper and mag. advts. 1962-640, Copy Club (co-chmn. awards com., Gold Key award for best TV comml. 1969), Alpha Phi Omega. Home: 1056 Fifth Ave New York NY 10028-0112 Office: The Seiden Group 445 Park Ave New York NY 10022-2606 *Be yourself but don't take yourself too seriously.*

SEIDEN, STEVEN ARNOLD, executive search consultant; b. N.Y.C., Feb. 18, 1936; s. Leon and Eleanor (Troy) S.; m. Katherine Cohen, June 8, 1965; children: Lisa Brooke, Hilary Anne. AB, Yale U., 1958. Pres. Seiden Krieger Assocs., 1984—; mem. N.Y. Stock Exchange Regulatory Adv. Com., 1981-83, policy com. Am. Council for Capital Formation, 1982-87. Mem. adv. bd. Registered Rep. Mag., 1982-84. Served with U.S. Army, 1961-62. Mem. Wall St. Tax Assn. (bd. dirs. 1981-83), Assn. Corp. Growth (bd. dirs., asst. v.p. 1987-88), Securities Industry Assn. (bd. dirs. 1981-83), N.Y. Soc. Security Analysts, Turnaround Mgmt. Assn. (program co-chair N.Y. chpt. 1991-92), Internat. Assn. Corp. and Profl. Recruiters (editorial bd. 1993-95), U.S. C. of C. (small bus. coun. 1985-89), Century Country Club, Bond Club. Republican. Office: Seiden Krieger Assocs 375 Park Ave New York NY 10152-0002

SEIDENBERG, IVAN G., telecommunications company executive; b. N.Y.C., Dec. 10, 1946; s. Howard and Kitty (Zaretsky) S.; m. Phyllis A. Maisel, Dec. 13, 1969; children: Douglas, Lisa. BS in Math., CUNY, 1972; MBA in Mktg. Mgmt., Pace U., 1980. Various engring. positions N.Y. Tel., 1966-74; dist. mgr. transmission design AT&T, Basking Ridge, N.J., 1974-76; dist. mgr. tech. planning AT&T, Basking Ridge, 1976-78; div. mgr. fed. regulatory AT&T, N.Y.C., 1978-81, asst. v.p. mktg., 1981-83; v.p. fed. relations Nynex Corp., Washington, 1983-86, former v.p. external affairs, former pres. and vice chmn., chmn., 1995—. Served as sgt. U.S. Army, 1966-68, Vietnam. Mem. U.S. Telephone Assn. (bd. dirs. 1985—), Rockland Bus. Council (trustee 1987). *

SEIDENBERG, RITA NAGLER, education educator; b. N.Y.C., Mar. 24, 1928; d. Jack and Anna (Weiss) Nagler; m. Irving Seidenberg, Apr. 10, 1949; children: Jack, Melissa Kolodkin. BA, Hunter Coll., 1948; MS, CCNY, 1968; PhD, Fordham U., 1985. Cert. reading tchr., specialist, N.Y. Reading tchr. East Ramapo (N.Y.) Sch. Dist., 1967-68, clinician reading ctr., 1968-83, reading diagnostician, 1983-85, student support specialist, 1985-94; instr. N.Y. State Dept. Edn., 1978; presenter Northeastern Rsch. Assn., 1978, 85, N.Y. State Reading Assn., 1986-94, N.Y. State Reading Assn., 1996; adj. asst. prof. Fordham U. Grad. Sch. Edn., 1986-89, adj. assoc. prof., 1989—. Mem. Internat. Reading Assn., N.Y. State Reading Assn., Phi Delta Kappa, Kappa Delta Pi. Avocations: reading, art mus., opera, travel. Office: Fordham U Grad Sch Edn 113 W 60th St New York NY 10023-7404

SEIDENSTICKER, EDWARD GEORGE, Japanese language and literature educator; b. Castle Rock, Colo., Feb. 11, 1921; s. Edward George and Mary Elizabeth (Dillon) S. B.A., U. Colo., 1942; M.A., Columbia U., 1947; postgrad., Harvard U., 1947-48; LittD (hon.), U. Md., 1991. With U.S. Fgn. Service, Dept. State, Japan, 1947-50; mem. faculty Stanford U., 1962-66, prof., 1964-66; prof. dept. Far Eastern langs. and lit. U. Mich., Ann Arbor, 1966-77; prof. Japanese Columbia U., 1977-85, prof. emeritus, 1986—. Author: Kafu the Scribbler, 1965, Japan, 1961, Low City, High City, 1983, Tokyo Rising, 1990, Very Few People Come This Way, 1994; transl.: (by Murasaki Shikibu) The Tale of Genji, 1976. Served with USMCR, 1942-46. Decorated Order of Rising Sun Japan; recipient Nat. Book award, 1970; citation Japanese Ministry Edn., 1971; Kikuchi Kan prize, 1977; Goto Miyoko prize, 1982; Japan Found. prize, 1984; Tokyo Cultural award, 1985; Yamagata Banto prize, 1992. *"Make yourself a routine and stick to it," said my childhood piano teacher when I went off to college. I have never had, as some people seem to have, great plans for my future; but if a person has a serious routine and sticks resolutely with it, something is bound to get accomplished.*

SEIDERMAN, ARTHUR STANLEY, optometrist, consultant, author; b. Phila., Nov. 28, 1936; s. Morris and Anne (Roseman) S.; m. Susan Levin, Aug. 19, 1965; children: David, Leeann, Scott. Student, U. Vienna (Austria) Med. Sch., 1965; OD, Pa. Coll. of Optometry, 1963; AB, W.Va. Wesleyan Coll., 1959; MA, Fairleigh Dickinson U., 1973. Pvt. practice Elkins Park, Pa., 1971-94, Plymouth Meeting, Pa., 1994—; vision cons. U.S. Olympic Teams, Phila. Flyers Hockey Team. Co-author: The Athletic Eye, 1983, 20/20 Is Not Enough, 1990; mem. editoral adv. bd. Jour. of Learning Disabilities, 1979—. Vice pres. Jewish Nat. Fund, Phila., 1988—. Capt. U.S. Army, 1963-68. Fellow Am. Acad. Optometry, Coll. of Optometrists in Vision Devel.; mem. Multidisciplinary Acad. of Clin. Edn. (pres.), Internat. Reading Assn. (pres. disabled group 1987-89). Home: 155 Sawgrass Dr Blue Bell PA 19422 Office: 919 E Germantown Pike Ste 4 Norristown PA 19401-2442

SEIDERS, JOSEPH ROBERT, service company corporate executive, lawyer; b. Reading, Pa., Oct. 21, 1948; s. Harry Robert and Evelyn Kathryn (Knauer) S.; m. Sharon Ann Hunter, Aug. 21, 1976. BA, LaSalle Coll., Phila., 1970, MBA, 1982; JD, Temple U., Phila., 1974. Bar: Pa. 1974, U.S. Dist. Ct. (ea. dist.) Pa. 1974. Sole practice, Horsham, Pa., 1974-78; corp. counsel CDI Corp., Phila., 1978-80, v.p., sec., 1980-87, sr. v.p., sec., 1987—. Pres., bd. dirs. Lafayette Place Homeowners Assn., 1986-88. Mem. ABA, Pa. Bar Assn., Phila. Bar Assn., Nat. Tech. Services Assn. (pres., chmn. legal and legis. com. 1984-97). Republican. Home: 11 Bunker Hill Dr Washington Crossing PA 18977-1415 Office: CDI Corp 1717 Arch St Fl 35 Philadelphia PA 19103-2713

SEIDL, FREDRICK WILLIAM, dean, social work educator; b. Buffalo, Sept. 29, 1940; s. Wolfgang and Anna Clara (Schneider) S.; m. Ann Jane Hazlewood, Apr. 19, 1963; children: Andrew, Barbara. AB, Ohio U., 1962; MSW, SUNY, Buffalo, 1964; PhD, U. Wis., 1970. Asst. prof. U. Minn., Morris, 1964-68; assoc. prof. Wilfred Laurier U., Waterloo, Ont., Can., 1970-72; assoc. prof. U. Wis., Madison, 1972-78, prof., 1978-84, dir. Sch. Social Work, 1980-82; dean, prof. Sch. Social Work SUNY, Buffalo, 1985—; resident Toynbee Hall, London, England, 1991. Author: The Wisconsin Experiment, 1984; contbr. articles on social issues, edn., to jours., 1964—; author, performer: (musical) Hull House: A Folk Music Celebration, 1988, Songs of New Horizons, 1989, Letter From America, 1992, 3 albums of Folk Revival music, 1990-92. Bd. dirs. Child and Family Svcs., Buffalo, 1989—, Gateway Youth and Family Svcs., Williamsville, N.Y., 1989—, United Way, Buffalo, 1989—, Urban League, Buffalo, 1989—; bd. visitors Ohio U., Athens; chair edn. div. Buffalo Philharm. Ann. Appeal; mem. editorial com. Social Work Encyclopedia. Recipient Alumnus of Yr. award SUNY, Buffalo, 1985. Mem. Nat. Assn. Social Workers, Nat. Assn. Deans and Dirs. Social Work Schs., Coun. Social Work Edn. Democrat. Avocations: folk music, canoeing. Office: SUNY Buffalo Sch Social Work 359 Baldy Hall Buffalo NY 14260-2203*

SEIDL, JANE PATRICIA, lawyer; b. Stamford, Conn., June 9, 1958; d. Francis Xavier and Frances (Nizolek) S. BA magna cum laude, Boston Coll., 1980; JD, U. Conn., 1985. Bar: Conn. 1985, U.S. Dist. Ct. Conn. 1985. Fin. editor Fin. Acctg. Standards Bd., Stamford, 1980-82; assoc. Schatz & Schatz, Ribicoff & Kotkin, Hartford, Conn., 1985-92; sr. counsel Northeast Utilities, Hartford, Conn., 1992—. Mem. ABA, Conn. Bar Assn., Hartford County Bar Assn., Hartford Assn. Women Attys. (pres. dir 1992—). Avocations: photography, water sports, literature. Office: Northeast Utlities PO Box 270 Hartford CT 06141-0270

SEIDLER, B(ERNARD) ALAN, lawyer; b. N.Y.C., Nov. 26, 1946; s. Aaron H. and Ethel T. (Berkowitz) S.; m. Lynne Aubrey, Jan. 21, 1978; children—Jacob A., Morgan H., Lily R. B.A., Colgate U., 1968; J.D., Seton Hall U., 1972. Bar: N.Y. 1973, U.S. Dist. Ct. (ea. and so. dists.) N.Y. 1975, U.S. Ct. Appeals (2d cir.) 1976, U.S. Supreme Ct. 1977, U.S. Ct. Appeals (3rd cir.) 1984. Staff atty. N.Y. Legal Aid Soc., N.Y.C., 1972-75; sole practice, N.Y.C. and Nyack, N.Y., 1975—. Mem. ABA. Club: Snedens Landing Tennis Assn. (Palisades, N.Y.). Office: 127 S Broadway Nyack NY 10960-4433

SEIDLER, DORIS, artist; b. London, Nov. 26, 1912; m. Bernard Seidler, Sept. 5, 1935; 1 son, David. Group exhbns. include Bklyn. Mus. Bi-Ann., Vancouver Internat., Honolulu Acad. Arts, Pa. Acad. Fine Arts, Phila., Soc. Am. Graphic Artists, Assoc. Am. Artists Gallery, Jewish Mus., N.Y.C., Bklyn. Mus., Albright-Knox, 1994; represented in permanent collections Libr. of Congress, Smithsonian Instn., Washington, Phila. Mus. Art, Bklyn. Mus., Seattle Mus. Art, Whitney Mus., Nat. Gallery Art, Nassau County (N.Y.) Mus. Fine Arts, Brit. Mus., London, Victorial and Albert Mus. London, Pallant House Coll., Eng., Portland Mus. Art, Oreg. Mem. Soc. Am. Graphic Artists (rec. sec. 1964-71, past v.p.). Address: 14 Stoner Ave Great Neck NY 11021-2101

SEIDMAN, DAVID N(ATHANIEL), materials science and engineering educator; b. N.Y.C., July 5, 1938; s. Charles and Jeanette (Cohen) S.; m. Shoshanah Cohen-Sabban, Oct. 21, 1973; children: Elie, Ariel, Eytan. BS, NYU, 1960, MS, 1962; PhD, U. Ill., Urbana, 1965. Postdoc. assoc. Cornell U., Ithaca, N.Y., 1964-66, asst. prof. materials sci. and engring., 1966-70, assoc. prof. materials sci. and engring., 1970-76, prof. materials sci. and engring., 1976-85; prof. materials sci. and engring. Northwestern U., Evanston, Ill., 1985-96, Walter P. Murphy prof. materials sci. and engring., 1996—; vis. prof. Technion, Haifa, 1969, Tel-Aviv U., Ramat-Aviv, 1972; Lady Davis vis. prof. Hebrew U., Jerusalem, 1978, 80-81, prof. materials sci., 1983-85; vis. scientist C.E. de Grenoble, 1981, C.N.E.T.-Meylan, 1981, C.E. de Scalay, 1989, U. Goettingen, 1989, 92; sci. cons. Argonne (Ill.) Nat. labs., 1985-94. Spl. issues editor, editl. bd. Interface Sci., 1993—; contbr. numerous articles on internal interfaces, atomic-scale imperfections in metals and semicondrs., radiation effects, field-ion, atom-probe and electron microscopy, 1964—; mem. editl. bd. Materials Sci. Forum, 1996. Recipient Max Planck Rsch. prize Max-Planck-Gesellschaft and the A. von Humboldt-Stiftung, 1993; Guggenheim fellow, 1972-73, 80-81, Humboldt fellow, 1989, 92; named chair for phys. metallurgy Gordon Conf., 1982. Fellow Am. Phys. Soc., TMS (Hardy Gold medal 1967); mem. AAAS, Am. Ceramic Soc., Materials Rsch. Soc., Microscopy Soc. Am., A. von Humboldt Soc. Am. Democrat. Jewish. Avocations: reading history and novels, travel. Home: 9056 Tamaroa Ter Skokie IL 60076-1928 Office: Northwestern U Engring Dept MLSF Bldg Evanston IL 60208-3108

SEIDMAN, ELLEN SHAPIRO, lawyer, government official; b. N.Y.C., Mar. 12, 1948; d. Benjamin Harry Shapiro and Edna (Eysen) Stern; m. Walter Becker Slocombe, June 14, 1981; 1 child, Benjamin William. AB, Radcliffe Coll., 1969; JD, Georgetown U., 1974; MBA, George Washington U., 1988. Bar: D.C., 1975. Law clk. U.S. Ct. of Claims, Washington, 1974-75; assoc. Caplin & Drysdale, Washington, 1975-78; atty., advisor U.S. Dept. of Transportation, Washington, 1978-79, dep. asst. gen. counsel, 1979-81; assoc. gen. counsel Chrysler Corp Loan Guaranty Bd., Washington, 1981-84; atty., advisor U.S. Dept. of Treasury, Washington, 1981-86, spl. asst. to the Under Sec. Fin., 1986-87; dir. strategic planning Fed. Nat. Mortgage Assn., Washington, 1987-88, v.p., asst. to chmn., 1988-91, sr. v.p. regulation rsch. and econs., 1991-93; spl. asst. to the pres. for econ. policy The White House, Washington, 1993—. Office: Nat Econ Coun 3900 Wisconsin Ave NW Washington DC 20016-2806

SEIDMAN, L(EWIS) WILLIAM, television commentator; b. Grand Rapids, Mich., Apr. 29, 1921; s. Frank E. and Esther (Lubetsky) S.; m. Sarah Berry, Mar. 3, 1944; children: Thomas, Tracy, Sarah, Carrie, Meg, Robin. A.B., Dartmouth Coll., 1943; LL.B., Harvard U., 1948; M.B.A., U. Mich., 1949. Bar: Mich. 1949, D.C. 1977. Spl. asst. fin. affairs to gov. of Mich., 1963-66; nat. mng. partner Seidman & Seidman C.P.A.s, N.Y.C., 1969-74; asst. for econ. affairs to Pres. Gerald R. Ford, 1974-77; dir., chief fin. officer Phelps Dodge Corp., N.Y.C., 1977-82; vice chmn. Phelps Dodge Corp., 1980-82; dean Coll. Bus. Adminstrn. Ariz. State U., Tempe, 1982-85; chmn. FDIC, Washington, 1985-91; chief commentator Sta. CNBC-TV, 1991; pub. Bank Dir. Mag., 1992; chmn. Detroit Fed. Res. Bank Chgo., 1970, RTC, 1989-91; co-chair White House Conf. on Productivity, 1983-84. Lt. USNR, 1942-46. Decorated Bronze Star. Mem. D.C. Bar Assn., Chevy Chase Club (Md.), Univ. Club (N.Y.C.), Crystal Downs Club (Mich.), Nantucket Yacht Club. Home: 1694 31st St NW Washington DC 20007-2924 Office: CNBC 1825 K St NW Washington DC 20006-1202

SEIDMAN, MARIAN TAYLOR, adult education educator; b. Montclair, N.J., Oct. 25, 1954; d. John Albert and Virginia Anne (Cooney) Taylor; m. Stephen Michael Seidman, Aug. 17, 1979; 1 child, Julie Anne. BS in Elem. Edn., U. Hartford, West Hartford, Conn., 1976; MEd, West Chester (Pa.) U., 1990. Cert. reading specialist, elem. edn. tchr. Tchr. Our Lady of Mt. Carmel Sch., Boonton, N.J., 1977-79, Catawba County Schs., Hickory, N.C., 1980-82, St. Joseph Sch., Big Bend, Wis., 1982-87; tchr., evaluator, asst. coord. Del. County Lit. Coun., Chester, Pa., 1991—. Author: Study Guide for the Pennsylvania Driver's Manual, 1996. Mem. Internat. Reading Assn., Del. Valley Reading Assn., Keystone State Reading Assn., Laubach Lit. Action, Kappa Delta Pi. Avocations: gardening, crafts, baking, reading. Office: Del County Lit Coun Chester PA 19013

SEIDMAN, SAMUEL NATHAN, investment banker, economist; b. N.Y.C., Mar. 31, 1934; s. Hyman and Pauline (Seidman) S.; m. Herta Lande, Sept. 4, 1964. B.A., Bklyn. Coll., 1955; Ph.D., NYU, 1964. Instr. Douglass Coll., Rutgers U., New Brunswick, N.J., 1960-62; v.p. Lehman Bros. Internat., N.Y.C., 1962-70; pres. Seidman & Co. Inc., N.Y.C., 1970—; pres., dir. Productivity Techs. Corp.; dir. Amrep Corp., N.Y.C., Harken Oil Corp., Dallas; dir., chmn. Victoria Station Corp., San Francisco, 1985-87. Trustee Mental Health Assn. N.Y., N.Y.C. 1980—. Served to pfc. U.S. Army, 1954-56. Univ. fellow Inst. Labor Relations, NYU, N.Y.C., 1957-58; Fulbright scholar U. Philippines, 1959-60. Mem. Am. Econ. Assn., Univ. Club (N.Y.C.), Lake Waramug Country Club (Conn.). Avocations: music; history of Asia. Office: 520 Madison Ave New York NY 10022-4213

SEIFER, JUDITH HUFFMAN, sex therapist, educator; b. Springfield, Ill., Jan. 18, 1945; d. Clark Lewis and Catherine Mary (Fisher) Huffman; married; children: Christopher, Patrick, Andrea. RN, St. John's Hosp./Quincy Coll., 1965; MHS, Inst. Advanced Study Human Sexuality, 1981, PhD, 1986. RN, Ohio; Diplomate Am. Bd. Sexology. Charge nurse Grandview Hosp., Dayton, Ohio, 1967-70; v.p. Sego, Inc., Dayton, 1970-84, pres., 1984—; marital and sex therapist Grandview Ob-Gyn., Inc., Dayton, 1975-87; asst. clin. prof. psychiatry and ob-gyn Wright State U. Sch. Medicine, Dayton, 1985-93; edn. cons., screenwriter The Learning Corp., Ft. Lauderdale, Fla., 1990—; COO Am. Sex Inst., Hillsborough Beach, Fla., 1995—; CEO In Good Co., Inc., Lewisburg, W.Va., 1995—; adj. prof. psychology U. Dayton, 1985-93; profl. spkr. The Upjohn Co., Kalamazoo, 1986—, CIBA-GEIGY Co., 1987-90; chmn. tech. adv. com. Mercari Comm., Inc., Englewood, Colo., 1988-89; cons. dept. psychology VA Hosp., Dayton, 1990-93. Author, screenwriter film script: Mercari Communications, 1988; editor: Jour. Sexuality and Relationships, 1995—; author, screenwriter film script: In Good Co., Inc., 1994—; guest editor: The D.O., 1985; contbr. articles to profl. jours. Pres. Dayton Osteopathic Aux., 1974-75, Aux. Ohio Osteopathic Assn., Columbus, 1981-82, Sister City Assn., Oakwood, Ohio, 1985-86; bd. dirs. Grace House Sexual Abuse Resource Ctr., Dayton, 1987-89, Planned Parenthood Miami Valley, Ohio, 1985-86, Social Health Assn., Dayton, 1976-87. Grantee Dayton Found., 1980-82; fellow Masters and Johnson Inst., 1984. Fellow Internat. Coun. Sex Educators, Am. Acad. Clin. Sexologists; mem. Am. Assn. Sex Educators, Counselors and Therapists (cert., rec. sec. 1986-91, pres. 1994—), Am. Coll. Sexologists. Roman Catholic. Avocation: public speaking. Office: Sego Corp 2 Deerfield Rd PO Box 426 Lewisburg WV 24901-0426

SEIFER, MARC JEFFREY, psychology educator; b. Far Rockaway, N.Y., Feb. 17, 1948; s. Stanley Cyclone and Thelma (Imber) S. BA, U. R.I., 1970; postgrad., New Sch. for Social Rsch., 1970-72, Sch. Visual Arts, 1971; MA, U. Chgo., 1974; PhD, Saybrook Inst., 1986. Cert. handwriting expert. Investigator neurol. study hand writing of schizophrenics Billings Hosp., Chgo., 1972-73; coll. instr. Providence Coll. Sch. of Continuing Edn., 1975-90, U. R.I. Extension, Providence, 1975-80, Bristol C.C., Fall River, Mass., 1980—, C.C. of R.I., Warwick, 1988—; expert handwriting neurol. investigation epileptic split brain writers UCLA, 1986; handwriting expert U. R.I. Crime Lab, Kingston, 1974-75; assoc. editor Jour. of Occult Studies, Providence, 1977-79; editor MetaScience, Kingston, 1979—, Jour. Am. Soc. Profl. Graphologists, Bethesda, Md., 1989—; dir. MetaSci. Found., Kingston, 1979—; handwriting expert Dept. Social Svcs. and R.I. Atty. Gen.'s Office, Providence, 1990—; lectr. on Tesla, U.S. Mil. Acad., West Point, N.Y., 1982, Colo. Coll., Colorado Springs, 1984, CCNY, 1984, Zagreb, Yugoslavia, 1986, Colorado Springs, 1992, 96; lectr. on graphology, Jerusalem, Israel, 1985, U. Vancouver, B.C., Can., 1986, Oxford (Eng.) U., 1987, Santa Fe, 1991, Cambridge (Eng.) U., 1992, Ann Arbor, Mich., 1994, N.Y.C., 1997; lectr. on consciousness U. Ariz., Tucson, 1996; cons. Inventors Series Discover Channel and Koch TV, 1994, The American Experience, PBS and Elevator Pictures, 1995, BBC, 1995. Author: Startez Encounter, 1988, The Man Who Harnessed Niagara Falls, 1991, Handwriting and Brainwriting, 1992, (screenplay) Tesla: The Lost Wizard (performed at Producer's Club Theater, 1996), 1992, video, 1984, Hail to the Chief, 1991, Mr. Rhode Island: The Stephen Rosati Story, 1994, Wizard: The Life and Times of Nikola Tesla, 1996 (designated as a book of unusual interest and merit, Publishers Weekly, 1996, designated as serious piece of scholarship, Sci. Am., 1997); contbr. chpts. to books; contbg. editor: Extraordinary Science, 1996, The Tesla Journal, 1997. Fellow Am. Coll. Forensic Examiners (bd. dirs. 1992-93); mem. APA, Am. Soc. Profl. Graphologists (bd. dirs. 1989—), Tesla Soc., Nat. Bur. Document Examiners, Nat. Soc. for Graphology. Avocations: snorkeling, bridge. Home: PO Box 32 Kingston RI 02881-0032

SEIFERT, BLAIR WAYNE, clinical pharmacist; b. Regina, Sask., Can., June 5, 1955; s. John Martin and Lottie P. S. (Murray) S. BS in Pharmacy, U. Sask., Saskatoon, 1977; PharmD, U. Tex., 1981. Hosp. pharmacy resident Regina Gen. Hosp., 1977-78; clin. pharmacy resident Bexar County Hosp., San Antonio, 1978-81; asst. dir. pharmacy Thomason Gen. Hosp., El Paso, 1981-83; perinatal clin. pharmacist Victoria (B.C.) Gen. Hosp., 1983-84; pediat. clin. pharmacist Health Scis. Centre, Winnipeg, Man., Can., 1984—; asst. prof. pharmacy U. Man., Winnipeg, 1984—, asst. prof. pediat., 1994—; reviewer Am. Jour. Hosp. Pharmacy, 1988—, Clin. Pharmacy, 1988—, Can. Jour. Hosp. Pharmacy, 1989—; mem. panel examiners Pharmacy Examining Bd. Can., 1992-94; reviewer ind. learning material panel Can. Coun. on Continuing Edn. in Pharmacy, 1994—; lectr. family asthma program Man. Lung Assn., 1985—; spkr. KNOW Drug Program, Man. Pharm. Assn., 1989—; presenter in field. Vol. Man. Riding for the Disabled, Winnipeg, 1987-89, Teddy Bears' Picnic, Children's Hosp. Rsch. Found., 1987-90 92—, Children's Miracle Network Telethon, Children's Hosp. Rsch. Found., 1987—, Can. Nat. Inst. for the Blind, 1990—. Fellow Can. Soc. Hosp. Pharmacists (jr. chmn. Man. chpt. 1987-88, sr. chmn. com. 1988-89, v.p. 1989-90, pres. 1990-91, past pres. 1991-92, mem. corr. edn. com. 1988-89, host com. 1990 ann. gen. meeting 1989-90, stds. com. 1990-91, clin. pharmacy adv. com. 1991-93, chmn. intravenous admixture revision task force 1993-95), Man. Pharm. Assn. (edn. com. 1988-89, 91—, planning com. 1989-92). Avocations: reading, horseback riding, figure skating. Office: Health Scis Ctr Dept Pharm Svcs, 820 Sherbrook St, Winnipeg, MB Canada R3A 1R9

SEIFERT, LUKE MICHAEL, lawyer; b. Smyrna, Tenn., Apr. 8, 1957; s. Donald R. and Joan (Clemas) S.; m. Kathleen Louise Schaffer, Aug. 1, 1980; children: Joseph, Nicholas, Peter, Rachel. BA, Creighton U., 1979; JD,

William Mitchell Sch. of Law, St. Paul, 1983. Bar: U.S. Dist. Ct. Minn., Minn. Page Minn. Ho. of Reps., St. Paul, 1980, com. adminstr., 1981-82; assoc. Holmen Law Office, St. Cloud, Minn., 1983-87; pvt. practice St. Cloud, 1987—. Mem. ABA, Minn. Bar Assn., Minn. Trial Lawyers Assn., Stearns Benton Bar Assn. (sec., treas. 1986-87, v.p. 1987-88, pres. 1988-89), K.C. (guard 1986-87, advocate 1987-90), Delta Theta Phi. Home: 1305 W Oakes Dr Saint Cloud MN 56303-0741 Office: 125 11th Ave N Saint Cloud MN 56303-4643

SEIFERT, THOMAS LLOYD, lawyer; b. Boston, June 6, 1940; s. Ralph Frederick and Hazel Bell (Harrington) S.; m. Ann Cecelia Berg, June 19, 1965. BS cum laude, Ind. U., 1962, JD cum laude, 1965. Bar: Ill. 1965, Ind. 1965, N.Y. 1979. Assoc. law firm Keck, Mahin & Cate, Chgo., 1965-67; atty. Essex Group, Inc., Ft. Wayne, Ind., 1967-70, Amoco Corp., Chgo., 1970-73; assoc. gen. counsel, asst. sec. Canteen Corp., Chgo., 1973-75; sec., gen. counsel The Marmon Group, Inc. (and predecessor cos.), Chgo., 1975-78; v.p., gen. counsel, sec. Hanson Industries, Inc., N.Y.C., 1978-82; sr. v.p. law, chief fin. officer Petrie Stores Corp., N.Y.C., 1982-83; mem. Finley, Kumble, Wagner, Heine, Underberg, Manley, Myerson & Casey, N.Y.C., 1983-87, Paul, Weiss, Rifkind, Wharton & Garrison, N.Y.C., 1987-91; gen. counsel, chief legal officer Sterling Grace Capital Mgmt., L.P. and affiliated cos., N.Y.C., 1991—. Note editor Ind. Law Jour., 1964-65. Named to Ind. Track and Cross Country Hall of Fame, 1993. Mem. ABA, N.Y. State Bar Assn., Order of Coif, The Creek, Beta Sigma Gamma. Home: Museum Tower 15 W 53rd St Apt 31 E New York NY 10019-5410 Office: Sterling Grace Capital Mgmt 515 Madison Ave Rm 2000 New York NY 10022-5403

SEIFF, ALVIN, planetary, atmospheric and aerodynamics scientist; b. Kansas City, Mo., Feb. 26, 1922; s. Harry Louis and Sara Dorothy (Silverstone) S.; m. Robbye Walker, Mar. 27, 1948 (div. Oct. 1959); children: David Wilson, Deborah Ellen Seiff Hedgecock; m. Julia Gwynne Hill, June 23, 1968; children: Michael Harry, Geoffrey Bernard. BS ChemE, U. Mo., 1942; postgrad., U. Tenn., 1946-48, Stanford U., 1959-60. Chem. engr. TVA, Florence, Ala., 1942-43; tech. supr. uranium isotope separ. Tenn. Eastman Corp., Oak Ridge, 1944-45; instr. physics U. Tenn., Knoxville, 1945-48; aero. rsch. scientist NACA Ames Aero. Lab., Moffett Field, Calif., 1948-57; chief supersonic free flight rsch. br. NACA, Moffett Field, 1952-63; chief vehicle environment div. NASA Ames Rsch. Ctr., Moffett Field, 1963-72, sr. staff scientist dir.'s office, 1972-77, sr. staff scientist space sci. div., 1977-86; sr. rsch. assoc. San Jose (Calif.) State U. Found., 1987—; mem. entry sci. team Viking Mars Mission Langley Rsch. Ctr., NASA, Hampton, Va., 1972-77, mem. sci. steering group Pioneer Venus Project Ames Rsch. Ctr., Moffett Field, 1972-82, Galileo Project, sci. group Jet Propulsion Lab., Pasadena, 1979—, mem. sci. team Soviet-French Vega Venus Balloon Mission, 1984-87, chmn. sci. adv. team atmosphere structure and meteorology Mars Pathfinder Mission, 1993—; mem. basic Rsch. Coun., NASA, Washington, 1973-76; Von Karman lectr., 1990; prin. investigator structure of Jupiter's atmosphere, Galileo entry probe, 1995. Author and editor: Ballistic Range Technology, 1972; (with others) Venus, 1983; contbr. articles to profl. jours. Recipient Exceptional Scientific Achievement medals NASA, 1978, 81, 97, H. Julian Allen award Ames Rsch. Ctr., 1982; named to Space Hall of Fame Mus., 1997. Fellow AIAA (assoc.); mem. Am. Astron. Soc. (div. planetary sci.), Am. Geophys. Union. Avocations: music, piano, gardening, home design and construction. Office: Ames Rsch Ctr Mail Stop 245-2 Moffett Field CA 94035

SEIFF, ERIC A., lawyer; b. Mt. Vernon, N.Y., Apr. 25, 1933; s. Arthur N. and Mathilde (Cohen) S.; m. Sari Ginsburg, June 26, 1960 (div. Oct. 1983); children: Judith C., E. Kenneth, Dean A.; m. Meredith Feinman, Jan. 15, 1984; children: Abigail, Sarah. BA, Yale U., 1955; LLB, Columbia U., 1958. Bar: N.Y. 1958, U.S. Dist. Ct. (so. dist.) N.Y. 1960, U.S. Dist. Ct. (ea. dist.) N.Y. 1981, U.S. Ct. Appeals (2d cir.) 1965, U.S. Supreme Ct. 1967. Assoc. Bower and O'Connor, N.Y.C., 1959-60, Yellin, Kramer & Levy, N.Y.C., 1961; asst. dist. atty. N.Y.C. Dist. Atty.'s Office, 1962-67; asst. counsel Agy. for Internat. Devel., Washington, 1967-70; counsel Agy. for Internat. Devel., Rio de Janeiro, 1970-72; gen. counsel N.Y. State Divsn. Criminal Justice Svcs., 1972-74; dep. chief atty. Legal Aid Soc. Criminal Def., N.Y.C., 1974-75; first dep. commr. N.Y. State Investigation Commn., 1975-77; chmn. N.Y. State Investigation Commn., N.Y.C., 1977-79; ptnr. Seiff & Kretz (formerly Scoppetta & Seiff), N.Y.C., 1981—; spl. dist. atty. Bronx County, 1986-89; spl. asst. atty. gen. State of N.Y., Gov.'s Task Force Investigating Conduct of Attica Prosecutions, 1975. Bd. dirs. Legal Aid Soc., N.Y.C., 1994—; Prisoners' Legal Svcs., N.Y.C., 1989—, Lawyers Fund for Client Protection, N.Y., 1980—. Recipient Frank S. Hogan Meml. award Frank S. Hogan Assn., 1994. Mem. N.Y. Criminal Bar Assn. (bd. dirs. 1980—, past pres.). Office: Seiff & Kretz 645 Madison Ave New York NY 10022-1010

SEIFFER, NEIL MARK, photographer; b. Bklyn., July 18, 1960; s. Martin Henry and Eileen S. AAS in Bus. Adminstrn., County Coll. Morris, 1980; BS, Montclair State Coll., 1984. Photo asst. Lewis Studios, Fairfield, N.J., 1980-82; photographer B & E Prodns., West Paterson, N.J., 1982-84; celebrity/entertainment photographer West Paterson, N.J., 1984—, N.Y.C., 1995—; official photographer 1st annual Touchstone Awards for Women in Music, 1997. Author: Photographic Guidelines for Performing and Recording Artists, 1987, Model's Guide/What You Need to Know About a Modeling Career, 1994, Neil Seiffer's Photographic Guidelines for the Performing Artist, 1995, Neil Seiffer's Photo Tips for Actors, 1996. Home: 147 Overmount Ave Apt A West Paterson NJ 07424-3221

SEIGEL, JERROLD EDWARD, historian, writer; b. St. Louis, June 9, 1936; s. William and Katherine (Ginsberg) S.; m. Jayn Rosenfeld, Aug. 28, 1966; children: Micol, Jessica. A.B., Harvard U., 1958; Ph.D., Princeton U., 1963. Instr. Princeton (N.J.) U., 1962-65, asst. prof., 1965-68, assoc. prof., 1968-78, prof. history, 1978-88; prof. history NYU, N.Y.C., 1988—; Kenan prof., 1994—; vis. prof. history Maitre d'Etudes, Ecoles des hautes études, Paris, 1988-94; finalist Nat. Book Critics Cir., 1987. Author: Rhetoric and Philosophy, 1968, Marx's Fate, 1978, Bohemian Paris, 1986, Private Worlds of Marcel Duchamp, 1995. Fulbright fellow Inst. Internat. Edn., 1961-62; NEH fellow, 1979-80, 87-88. Mem. N.Y. Inst. for Humanities, Phi Beta Kappa. Home: 48 Horatio St New York NY 10014-1614 Office: NYU History Dept 53 Washington Sq S New York NY 10012-1018

SEIGEL, STUART EVAN, lawyer; b. N.Y.C., Mar. 25, 1933; s. Philip Herman and Betty Sarah (Leventhal) S.; m. Joyce Roberta Meyers (div.); children: Charles Meyers, Lee Bennett, Suzanne Marcie; m. Sherry Diane Jackson,Sept. 24, 1989. BS, N.Y. U., 1953, LLB, 1957; LLM in Taxation, Georgetown U., 1960. Bar: N.Y. 1958, D.C. 1958. Atty. Office Chief Counsel, IRS, Washington, 1957-65, Office Tax Legis. Counsel, Dept. Treasury, Washington, 1965-69; assoc. tax legis. counsel Office Tax Legis. Counsel, Dept. Treasury, 1968-69; ptnr. firm Cohen and Uretz, Washington, 1969-77; chief counsel IRS, Washington, 1977-79; ptnr. firm Williams and Connolly, Washington, 1979-89, Arnold and Porter, N.Y.C., 1989—; lectr. George Washington U. Sch. Law, 1970-73; adj. prof. law Antioch Sch. Law, 1973-76, Georgetown U. Sch. Law, 1981. Mem. ABA, Am. Law Inst., Am. Judicature Soc., Am. Coll. Tax Counsel, N.Y. State Bar Assn., Assn. of Bar of City of N.Y. Club: Metropolitan (Washington). Office: Arnold and Porter 399 Park Ave New York NY 10022

SEIGLER, DAVID STANLEY, botanist, chemist, educator; b. Wichita Falls, Tex., Sept. 11, 1940; s. Kenneth R. and Floy M. (Wilkinson) S.; m. Janice Kay Cline, Jan. 20, 1961; children: Dava, Rebecca. BS in Chemistry, Southwestern (Okla.) State Coll., 1961; PhD in Organic Chemistry, U. Okla., 1967. Postdoctoral assoc. USDA No. Regional Lab., Peoria, Ill., 1967-68; postdoctoral fellow dept. botany U. Tex., Austin, 1968-70; asst. prof. botany U. Ill., Urbana, 1970-76, assoc. prof., 1976-79, prof. botany, 1979—, head dept. plant biology, 1988-93; curator U. Ill. Herbarium, 1993—. Editor: Crop Resources, 1977, Phytochemistry and Angiosperm Phylogeny, 1981; contbr. numerous articles to profl. jours. Recipient Fulbright Hays Lecturer award Fulbright Commn., Argentina, 1976, (alternate) Germany, 1995-96, study award Deutsche Akademischer Austauschdienst, Germany, 1995. Mem. Phytochem. Soc. N.Am. (pres. 1988-89), Bot. Soc. Am., Am. Chem. Soc., Am. Soc. Plant Taxonomists, Internat. Soc. Chem. Ecology (pres. 1990-91). Mem. Assembly of God Ch. Avocation: genealogy. Home: 510 W Vermont Ave Urbana IL 61801-4931 Office: U Ill Dept Plant Biology 265 Morrill Hall 505 S Goodwin Ave Urbana IL 61801-3707

SEIL, FREDRICK JOHN, neuroscientist, neurologist; b. Nove Sove, Yugoslavia, Nov. 9, 1933; s. Joseph and Theresa (Krieger) S.; m. Daryle Faith Wolfers, July 2, 1955; children: Jonathan Fredrick, Joel Philip Timothy. BA, Oberlin Coll., 1956; MD, Stanford U., 1960. Intern Kaiser Found. Hosp., San Francisco, 1960-61; resident in neurology Stanford (Calif.) U., 1961-64, fellow in neurology, 1964-66; staff neurologist VA Med. Ctr., Palo Alto, Calif., 1969-76; clin. investigator VA Med. Ctr., Portland, Oreg., 1976-79, staff neurologist, 1979-81, dir. VA office regeneration research programs, 1981—; asst. prof. neurology Stanford U., 1969-75, assoc. prof. neurology Oreg. Health Sci. U., Portland, 1976-78, prof. neurology, 1978—, prof. cell and devel. biology, 1990—. Editor: Nerve, Organ and Tissue Regeneration: Research Perspectives, 1983, Neural Regeneration, 1987, 94, Current Issues in Neural Regeneration and Transplantation, 1989, Advances in Neural Regeneration Research, 1990, Neural Injury and Regeneration: 1993, Multiple Sclerosis: Current Status of Research and Treatment, 1994, Neural Regeneration, Reorganization, and Repair, 1997; contbr. articles to profl. jours. Served to capt. U.S. Army, 1966-68. Grantee VA, 1970—, NIH, 1986-95. Mem. Internat. Brain Rsch. Orgn., Internat. Soc. Develop. Neurosci., Am. Neurol. Assn., Am. Assn. Neuropathologists, Soc. Neurosci., Soc. Exptl. Neuropathology. Democrat. Home: 10306 SW Radcliffe Rd Portland OR 97219-7956 Office: VA Med Ctr Office Regeneration Rs Portland OR 97201

SEILER, FRITZ ARNOLD, physicist; b. Basel, Switzerland, Dec. 20, 1931; came to U.S., 1980; s. Friedrich and Marie (Maibach) S.; m. Mary Catherine Coster, Dec. 22, 1964; children: Monica, Simone, Daniel. BA in Econs., Basel Sch. of Econs., 1951; PhD in Physics, U. Basel, 1962. Rsch. assoc. U. Wis., Madison, 1962-63; scientific assoc. U. Basel, 1963-69, privat dozent, 1969-75, dozent, 1975-80; sr. scientist Lovelace Inhalation Toxicology Inst., Albuquerque, 1980-90; sr. tech. assoc. IT Corp., Albuquerque, 1990-92, disting. tech. assoc., 1992-96; v.p. Inst. Regulatory Sci., Albuquerque, 1996—; cons. Swiss Dept. Def., 1968-74; vis. scientist Lawrence Berkeley Labs., 1974-75. Contbr. numerous articles to profl. jours. With Swiss Army staff, 1964-75. Fellow Am. Phys. Soc., Health Physics Soc., Soc. for Risk Analysis, Fachverband fuer Strahlenschutz, Am. Stats. Assn., Am. Nat. Stds. Inst. (mgmt. coun. 1987—, com. N14 1986—). Office: Inst Regulatory Sci Western Office PO Box 14006 Albuquerque NM 87191 also: Inst Regulatory Sci 5457 Twin Knolls Rd Columbia MD 21045

SEILER, JAMES ELMER, judge; b. LaCrosse, Wis., Sept. 2, 1946; s. Elmer Bernard and Margaret Theresa (Mader) S.; m. Sonia Gonzales, Feb. 9, 1968; children: Rebecca, Cristina. BA, U. Wis., LaCrosse, 1968; JD, U. Wis., 1973. Bar: Wis. 1973, Minn. 1981, U.S. Supreme Ct. 1985, Mo. 1986. Pvt. practice Balsam Lake, Wis., 1973-81; in-house counsel Farm Credit Banks, St. Paul, 1981-85; corp. counsel Hussmann Corp., St. Louis, 1985-94; adminstrv. law judge Social Security, Evansville, Ind., 1994-95, Office of Hearings and Appeals, Creve Coeur, Mo., 1995—. Candidate Dist. Atty., Polk County, Wis., 1980. With U.S. Army, 1969-71. Avocations: soccer coach, swimming, water skiing, running. Home: 18 Harbor Point Ct Lake Saint Louis MO 63367-1336 Office: 11475 Olde Cabin Rd Saint Louis MO 63141-7130

SEILER, STEVEN LAWRENCE, health facility administrator; b. Chgo., Dec. 30, 1941; married. B, U. Ariz., 1963; M, U. Iowa, 1965. Adminstrv. resident Rush-Presbyn.-St. Luke's Med. Ctr., Chgo., 1965, adminstrv. asst., 1965-68; asst. adminstr. Lake Forest (Ill.) Hosp., 1968-71, adminstr., 1971-73, pres., 1973-86; exec. v.p Voluntary Hosps. Am., Park Ridge, Ill., 1987-89, sr. v.p., 1986-92; CEO Good Samaritan Regional Med. Ctr., Phoenix, 1992—; adj. prof. Contbr. articles to profl. jours. Mem. AHA (svc. com.), Ill. Hosp. Assn. (chair 1980-81). Home: 3930 E Rancho Dr Paradise Valley AZ 85253-5025 Office: Good Samaritan Regional Med Ctr 1111 E Mcdowell Rd Phoenix AZ 85006-2612*

SEILHAMER, RAY A., bishop. Bishop United Brethren in Christ. Office: United Brethren in Christ 302 Lake St Huntington IN 46750-1264*

SEILS, WILLIAM GEORGE, lawyer; b. Chgo., Aug. 9, 1935; s. Harry H. and Hazel C. (Sullivan) S.; m. Evelyn E. Oliver, Sept. 8, 1956; children: Elizabeth Ann, Ellen Carol, Eileen Alison. A.B., J.D., U. Mich., 1959. Bar: Ill. bar 1959. Since practiced in Chgo.; ptnr. Arvey, Hodes & Costello & Burman, 1968-87; gen. counsel, sec., sr. v.p. Richardson Electronics, Ltd., LaFox, Ill., 1986—. Contbr. articles to profl. jours.; asst. editor: Mich. Law Rev, 1958-59. Mem. Ill. Bar Assn., Order of Coif. Office: Richardson Electronics Ltd 40w267 Keslinger Rd Lafox IL 60147

SEINFELD, JERRY, comedian; b. Bklyn., Apr. 29, 1955; s. Kal and Betty S. Grad. with degree in theatre communications, Queens (N.Y.) Coll., 1976. Former salesman. Stand-up comedian, 1976—; joke-writer (TV series) Benson, ABC, 1980; actor, co-writer, prod. (TV series) Seinfeld, NBC-TV, 1989— (Emmy award Outstanding Comedy Series, 1993, Emmy nomination, Lead Actor - Comedy Series, 1994); writer Jerry Seinfeld-Stand-Up Confidential, 1987; author: Sein Language, 1993. Recipient Am. Comedy award funniest male comedy stand-up, 1988, funniest actor in a TV series, 1992. Jewish. Avocations: Zen, yoga. Office: care Lori Jonas Pub Rels 417 S Beverly Dr Ste 201 Beverly Hills CA 90212-4401

SEINFELD, JOHN HERSH, chemical engineering educator; b. Elmira, N.Y., Aug. 3, 1942; s. Ben B. and Minna (Johnson) S. BS, U. Rochester, 1964; PhD, Princeton U., 1967. Asst. prof. chem. engring. Calif. Inst. Tech., Pasadena, 1967-70, assoc. prof., 1970-74, prof., 1974—, Louis E. Nohl prof., 1980—, exec. officer for chem. engring., 1973-90, chmn. engring. and applied sci. div., 1990—; Allan P. Colburn meml. lectr. U. Del., 1976; Camille and Henry Dreyfus Found. lectr. MIT, 1979; mem. coun. Gordon Rsch. Confs., 1980-83; Donald L. Katz lectr. U. Mich., 1981; Reilly lectr. U. Notre Dame, 1983; Dean's Disting. lectr. U. Rochester, 1985; Katz lectr. CUNY, 1985; McCabe lectr. N.C. State U., 1986; Lewis lectr. MIT, 1986; Union Carbide lectr. SUNY, Buffalo; Van Winkle lectr. U. Tex., 1988; Bicentennial lectr. La. State U., 1988; Ida Beam lectr. U. Iowa, 1989, David Mason lectr. Stanford U., 1989; Julian Smith lectr. Cornell U., 1990; Merck lectr. Rutgers U., 1991; Henske Disting. lectr. Yale U., 1991; mem. sci. adv. bd. EPA; lectr. AIChE, 1980; Centennial lectr. U. Pa., 1993; Miles Disting. lectr. U. Pitts., 1994; Kelly lectr. Purdue U., 1996. Author: Numerical Solution of Ordinary Differential Equations, 1971, Mathematical Methods in Chemical Engineering, Vol. III, Process Modeling, Estimation and Identification, 1974, Air Pollution: Physical and Chemical Fundamentals, 1975, Lectures in Atmospheric Chemistry, 1980, Atmospheric Chemistry and Physics of Air Pollution, 1986, Fundamentals of Air Pollution Engineering, 1988, Distributed Parameter Systems - Theory and Applications, 1989; assoc. editor Environ. Sci., Tech., 1981—; mem. editorial bd. Computers, Chem. Engring, 1974—, Jour. Colloid and Interface Sci, 1978—, Advances in Chem. Engring, 1980—, Revs. in Chem. Engring, 1980—, Aerosol Sci. and Tech., 1981—, Large Scale Systems, 1982—; assoc. editor: Atmospheric Environment, 1976—. Recipient Donald P. Eckman award Am. Automatic Control Coun., 1970, Pub. Svc. medal NASA, 1980, Disting. Alumnus award U. Rochester, 1989; Camille and Henry Dreyfus Found. Tchr. Scholar grantee, 1972. Fellow Japan Soc. Promotion Sci., AIChE (bd. dirs. 1988-91, mem. editl. bd. jours. 1985—, Allan P. Colburn award 1976, William H. Walker award 1986); mem. NAE, Am. Assn. Acad. Sci., Am. Soc. Engring. Edn. (Curtis W. McGraw Rsch. award 1976, George Westinghouse award 1987), Assn. Aerosol Rsch. (bd. dirs. 1983—, v.p. 1988-90, pres. 1990-92), Am. Acad. Arts and Scis., Air Waste Mgmt. Assn., Am. chem. Soc. (Svc. through Chemistry award 1988, Creative Advances in Environ. Sci. and Tech. award 1993), Sigma Xi, Tau Beta Pi. Home: 525 S Catalina Ave Pasadena CA 91106 Office: Calif Inst Tech Div Engring and Applied Sci Pasadena CA 91125

SEIPLE, ROBERT ALLEN, Christian relief organization executive; b. Harmony, N.J., Dec. 6, 1942; s. Chris and Gertrude (Crozier) S.; m. Margaret Ann Goebel, May 14, 1965; children: Chris, Amy, Jesse. AB, Brown U., 1965; LHD (hon.), Alderson-Broaddus, 1986, Sioux Falls Coll., 1986, Azusa Pacific U., 1993, Gordon Coll., 1995, Lawrence U., 1996. Sales rep. Boise Cascade, Mich., 1969-71; dir. athletics Brown U., Providence, 1972-79, v.p. devel., 1979-83; pres. Eastern Coll. and Eastern Bapt. Theol. Sem., St. Davids, Pa., 1983-87, World Vision, Inc., Monrovia, Calif., 1987—; bd. dirs. Stop Cancer, One to One Found.; bd. advisors World Impact, Young Life-Urban Phila., Opportunity Internat. Contbr. articles to mags. Capt. USMC, 1966-69, Vietnam. Decorated D.F.C., 28 Air medals, Vietnam Campaign medal with 5 Battle Stars, Navy Commendation award. Presbyterian. Avocations: deer hunting, trout fishing. Office: World Vision Inc 34834 Weyerhaeuser Way S Federal Way WA 98001-9520

SEIREG, ALI A(BDEL HAY), mechanical engineer; b. Arab Republic of Egypt, Oct. 26, 1927; came to U.S., 1951, naturalized, 1960; s. Abdel Hay and Aisha Seireg; m. Shirley Marachowsky, Dec. 24, 1954; children: Mirette Elizabeth LaFollette, Pamela Aisha. B.Sc. M.E., U. Cairo, 1948; Ph.D., U. Wis., 1954. Lectr. Cairo U., 1954-56; staff adv. engr. Falk Corp., Milw., 1956-59; assoc. prof. theoretical and applied mechanics Marquette U., 1959-64, prof., 1964-65; prof. (Kaiser chair) mech. engring. U. Wis., Madison, 1965—; Ebaugh Prof. U. Fla., Gainesville, 1986—; cons. industry, ednl. and govt. agys.; chmn. U.S. council Internat. Fedn. Theory of Machines, 1974-94; co-chmn. 5th World Congress of Theory of Machines, 1979, 1st USSR-USA Conf. on Composite Materials, 1989. Author: Mechanical Systems Analysis, 1969, Biomedical Analysis of Musculoskeletal Structure for Medicine and Sports, 1989, Optimized Motion Planning, 1994, The Kinematic Geometry of Gearing, 1995, Optimizing the Shape of Mechanical Elements, 1997; editor Computers in Mechanical Engineering; editor in chief SOMA, Engineering for the Human Body, 1986-90; contbr. numerous articles to profl. jours. Recipient Kuwait prize for sci., 1987. Fellow ASME (Richards Meml. award 1973, Machine Design award 1978, Design Automation award 1990, chmn. div. design engring. 1977-78, chmn. computer tech. 1978-81, mem. policy bd. communications 1978-80, mem. policy bd. gen. engring. 1979-80, chmn. Century II Internat. Computer Tech. Conf. 1980, founding chmn. computer engring. div. 1980-81, v.p. systems and design 1981-85, sr. v.p., chmn. council on engring. 1985-90, pres. Gen. Research Inst. 1984—), Am. Soc. Engring. Edn. (George Westinghouse award 1970), Soc. Exptl. Stress Analysis, Am. Inst. Med. and Biol. Engring. (founding fellow), Am. Gear Mfg. Assn. (E. P. Connell award 1974), Automation Research Council; mem. Chinese Mech. Engring. Soc. (hon.), USSR Acad. Sci. (fgn.), Russian Acad. Sci. (fgn.). Home: 2670 SW 14th Dr Gainesville FL 32608-2049 Office: 1513 University Ave Madison WI 53706-1539 *I have always tried my best to look beyond what I hear, to think beyond what I see, to give more than I receive, and to do good as its own reward.*

SEITEL, FRASER PAUL, public relations executive; b. Jersey City, June 6, 1946; s. Robert and Helen (Barmad) S.; m. Rosemary Kierstein, Dec. 20, 1969; children: Raina, David. BJ, U. Mo., 1964; MA, U. N.D., 1970; MBA, NYU, 1977. Pub. rels. officer Chase Manhattan Bank, N.Y.C., 1970-73, v.p., 1974-85, sr. v.p., dir. pub. affairs, 1985-92; mng. ptnr. Emerald Ptnrs., Ft. Lee, N.J., 1992—; sr. counselor Burson Marsteller, N.Y.C., 1992—; sr. counselor investor rels. and mktg. communications Greater N.Y. Savs. Bank, 1994—; pub. rels. cons. Hill and Knowlton, N.Y.C., 1973; instr. Profl. Devel. Inst., N.Y.C., Ragan Communications, Chgo., Estes Park Inst., Colo. Author: The Practice of Public Relations, 6th edit., 1995; pub., editor The Public Relations Strategist, 1995—; columnist U.S. Banker, 1989-94, Profit Mag., 1993-95; columns editor PRSA Tactics mag., 1994-95. Col. USAR, 1969-76. Mem. Pub. Rels. Soc. Am., Bank Mktg. Assn. Avocations: baseball, football, basketball, tai chi, rugby. Home: 12 King Pl Closter NJ 07624-2936 Office: 177 Main St Ste 215 Fort Lee NJ 07024-6936

SEITELMAN, MARK ELIAS, lawyer; b. N.Y.C., Apr. 14, 1955; s. Leo Henry and Pearl (Elias) S. BA, Bklyn. Coll., 1976; JD, Bklyn. Law Sch., 1979. Bar: N.Y. 1980, U.S. Dist. Ct. (ea., so., and we. dists.) N.Y. 1980, U.S. Supreme Ct. 1995, U.S. Ct. Mil. Appeals, 1995. Law asst. Criminal Ct., Bklyn., 1979; law clk. to Hon. Justice Aaron D. Bernstein N.Y. Supreme Ct., Bklyn., 1980; assoc. Lester, Schwab, Katz & Dwyer, N.Y.C., 1981-87, Weg and Myers, 1987-88, Kroll & Tract, 1988-90; pvt. practice N.Y.C., 1990—. Mem. ABA, ATLA (sustaining mem. motor vehicle and small practice sect.), N.Y. State Bar Assn., N.Y. County Bar Assn. (ins. and supreme ct. coms.), N.Y. State Trial Lawyers Assn. (sustaining mem., bd. dirs., mem. spkrs. bur., conv. com., legis. com., contbg. editor Trial Lawyers Quar.), Bklyn. Bar Assn. (legis. com.). Office: 233 Broadway Rm 901 New York NY 10279-0999

SEITMAN, JOHN M., lawyer; b. Bloomington, Ill., Feb. 9, 1942. BS, U. Ill., 1964, JD, 1966. Bar: U.S. Dist. Ct. (so., cen., no. and ea. dists.) Calif., U.S. Ct. Appeals (9th cir.), Calif. Supreme Ct. Prin. Lindley, Lazar & Scales, San Diego; mediator, Arbitrator, mem. Calif. adv. coun. for large, complex case panel Am. Arbitration Assn.; lectr. in continuing legal edn. Bd. dirs. San Diego County Bar Found., 1983-89, treas., 1983-84, pres., 1988-89; del. to 9th Cir. Jud. Conf., 1986, 88. Fellow Am. Bar Found.; mem. ABA, State Bar Calif. (pres. 1991-92), San Diego County Bar Assn. (pres. 1986), Lawyers Club San Diego. Office: Lindley Lazar & Scales 600 W Broadway Ste 1400 San Diego CA 92101-3355

SEITZ, COLLINS JACQUES, federal judge; b. Wilmington, Del., June 20, 1914; s. George Hilary and Margaret Jane (Collins) S.; m. Virginia Anne Day; children: Virginia Anne, Collins Jacques, Mark, Stephen. A.B., U. Del., 1937, LL.D., 1962; LL.B., U. Va., 1940; LL.D., Widener Coll., 1975, Villanova U. Sch. Law, 1983, Cath. U., 1985, Dickinson Sch. of Law, 1988. Bar: Del. 1940. Vice chancellor Del., 1946; chancellor, 1951-66; judge U.S. Ct. Appeals, 3d Circuit, 1966-71, chief judge, 1971-84, judge, 1984-89, sr. judge, 1989—. Recipient James J. Hoey award, 1954, award NCCJ, 1957, Pro Ecclesia et Pontifice (papal award), 1965, award in law Thomas Jefferson Meml. Found., 1990. Mem. Am., Del. bar assns. Democrat. Roman Catholic. Club: Wilmington. Office: US Ct Appeals 844 N King St Ste 32 Wilmington DE 19801-3519*

SEITZ, FREDERICK, former university administrator; b. San Francisco, July 4, 1911; s. Frederick and Emily Charlotte (Hofman) S.; m. Elizabeth K. Marshall, May 18, 1935. AB, Leland Stanford Jr. U., 1932; PhD, Princeton U., 1934; Doctorate Hon. Causa, U. Ghent, 1957; DSc (hon.), U. Reading, 1960, Rensselaer Poly. Inst., 1961, Marquette U., 1963, Carnegie Inst. Tech., 1963, Case Inst. Tech., 1964, Princeton U., 1964, Northwestern U., 1965, U. Del., 1966, Poly. Inst. Bklyn., 1967, U. Mich., 1967, U. Utah, 1968, Brown U., 1968, Duquesne U., 1968, St. Louis U., 1969, Nebr. Wesleyan U., 1970, U. Ill., 1972, Rockefeller U., 1981; LLD (hon.), Lehigh U., 1966, U. Notre Dame, 1962, Mich. State U., 1965, Ill. Inst. Tech., 1968, N.Y. U., 1969; LHD (hon.), Davis and Elkins Coll., 1970, Rockefeller U., 1981, U. Pa., 1985, U. Miami, 1989. Instr. physics U. Rochester, 1935-36, asst. prof., 1936-37; physicist research labs. Gen. Electric Co., 1937-39; asst. prof. Randal Morgan Lab. Physics, U. Pa., 1939-41, assoc. prof., 1941-42; prof. physics, head dept. Carnegie Inst. Tech., Pitts., 1942-49; prof. physics U. Ill., 1949-57, head dept., 1957-64, dir. control systems lab., 1951-52, dean Grad. Coll., v.p. research, 1964-65; exec. pres. Nat. Acad. Scis., 1962-69; pres. Rockefeller U., N.Y.C., 1968-78; U. Miami (Fla.), 1989; trustee Ogden Corp., 1977—; dir. tng. program Clinton Labs., Oak Ridge, 1946-47; chmn. Naval Rsch. Adv. Com., 1960-62; vice chmn. Def. Sci. Bd., 1961-62, chmn., 1964-68; sci. adviser NATO, 1959-60; mem. nat. adv. com. Marine Biomed. Inst. U. Tex., Galveston, 1975-77; mem. adv. group White House Conf. Anticipated Advances in Sci. and Tech., 1975-76; mem. adv. bd. Desert Rsch. Inst., 1975-79, Ctr. Strategic and Internat. Studies, 1975-81; mem. Nat. Cancer Adv. Bd., 1976-82; dir. Akzona Inc. Author: Modern Theory of Solids, 1940, The Physics of Metals, 1943, Solid State Physics, 1955, The Science Matrix, 1992, On the Frontier: My Life in Science, 1994, Stalin's Captive: Nikolaus Riehl and the Soviet Race for the Bomb, 1995. Trustee Rockefeller Found., 1964-77, Princeton U., 1968-72, Lehigh U., 1970-81, Rsch. Corp., 1966-82, Inst. Internat. Edn., 1971-78, Woodrow Wilson Nat. Fellowship Found., 1972-82, Univ. Corp. Atmospheric Rsch., Am. Mus. Natural History, 1975—; trustee John Simon Guggenheim Meml. Found., 1973-83, chmn. bd., 1976-83; mem. Belgian Am. Edn. Found.; bd. dirs. Richard Lounsberry Found., 1980—. Decorated Order of the Brilliant Star (Republic of China); recipient Franklin medal Franklin Inst. Phila., 1965, Hoover medal Stanford U., 1968, Nat. Medal Sci., 1973, James Madison award Princeton U., 1978, Edward R. Loveland Meml. award ACP, 1983, Vannevar Bush award Nat. Sci. Bd., 1983, J. Herbert Holloman award Acta Metallurgica, 1993, Von Hippel award Materials Rsch. Soc., 1993. Fellow Am. Phys. Soc. (pres. 1961); mem. NAS, Am. Acad. Arts and Scis., AIME, Am. Philos. Soc., Am. Inst. Physics (chmn. governing bd. 1954-59), Inst. for Def. Analysis, Finnish Acad. Sci. and Letters (fgn. mem.), Phi Beta Kappa Assos. Address: Rockefeller U 1230 York Ave New York NY 10021-6307

SEITZ, KARL RAYMOND, editor; b. Corpus Christi, Tex., Sept. 26, 1943; s. Kerlin McCullough and Martha Elisabeth (Tillman) S.; m. Patricia Jean Floyd, June 13, 1970; 1 child, Lee Kerlin. BA, Birmingham So. Coll., 1970. Copy editor Birmingham (Ala.) Post-Herald, 1967-70, asst. news editor, 1970-73, chief editorial writer, 1973-78, editor editorial page, 1978—; dir. Birmingham Post-Birmingham Typographical Union Pension Plan, 1983-90, chmn., 1986-90; dir. Goodfellow Fund, Inc., Birmingham, 1983—, v.p., 1986—. Active exec. in residence Birmingham So. Coll., 1987, Leadership Birmingham, 1986—. With USN, 1961-64. Mem. Am. Acad. Polit. and Social Sci., Nat. Conf. Editorial Writers, Acad. Polit. Sci. Home: 1212 30th Street S Birmingham AL 35205-1910 Office: Birmingham Post Herald PO Box 2553 Birmingham AL 35202-2553

SEITZ, MARY LEE, mathematics educator. BS in Edn. summa cum laude, SUNY, Buffalo, 1977, MS in Edn., 1982. Cert. secondary tchr., N.Y. Prof. math. Erie C.C.-City Campus, Buffalo, 1982—; Reviewer profl. jours. and coll. textbooks. Reviewer profl. jours. Mem. Nat. Coun. Tchrs. Maths., N.Y. Maths. Assn. Two Yr. Colls., Assn. Maths. Tchrs. N.Y., N.Y. Assn. Two Yr. Colls., Inc., Pi Mu Epsilon. Avocations: gardening, photography, bird watching. Office: Erie C C-City Campus 121 Ellicott St Buffalo NY 14203-2601 *Ad Astra per Aspera - To the Stars Through Difficulties.*

SEITZ, MELVIN CHRISTIAN, JR., distributing company executive; b. Indpls., Aug. 9, 1939; s. Melvin Christian and Francis Sue (Lee) S.; m. Bette Louise Pierson, May 5, 1941; children: David, Mark, Keith, Cindy. Student Butler U., 1957-60. Salesman, Service Supply Co., Inc., Indpls., 1963-71, sec.-treas., 1971-74, v.p., 1974-81, exec. vp., 1981-83, pres., 1983-94, COO, 1995, dir. corporate rels. Home: 4716 Northeastern Ave Indianapolis IN 46239-1665 Office: Svc Supply Co Inc Ind 603 E Washington St Indianapolis IN 46204-2620

SEITZ, NICHOLAS JOSEPH, magazine editor; b. Topeka, Kans., Jan. 30, 1939; s. Frank Joseph and Lydia Natalie (Clerico) S.; m. Velma Jean Pfannenstiel, Sept. 12, 1959; children: Bradley Joseph, Gregory Joseph. BA, U. Okla., 1966. Sports editor Manhattan (Kans.) Mercury, 1960-62, Norman (Okla.) Transcript, 1962-64, Okla. Jour., Oklahoma City, 1964-67; mem. staff Golf Digest mag., Norwalk, Conn., 1967—; editor Golf Digest mag., 1973-82; editorial dir. Golf Digest and Tennis, 1982-90; editorial dir. Sports/Leisure div. N.Y. Times Co. Mag. Group, 1991-92, sr. v.p., editor in chief, 1992—; syndicated golf instrn. and commentary CBS Radio Network; commentary ESPN TV Network. Author: Superstars of Golf, 1978, (with Dave Hill) Teed Off, 1977, (with Tom Watson) Getting Up and Down, 1983, Getting Back to Basics, 1991, Tom Watson's Strategic Golf, 1993; contbr. articles to profl. jours.; anthologized in: Best Sports Stories. Named Okla. Sports Writer of Year Nat. Sportswriters and Sportscasters Assn., 1965; winner contests Nat. Basketball Writers Assn.; winner contests Golf Writers Assn.; recipient Lincoln A. Werden award for outstanding contbn. to golf journalism, 1993. Home: 36 Hunt St Norwalk CT 06853-1015 Office: 5520 Park Ave Trumbull CT 06611-3426

SEITZ, PATRICIA ANN, lawyer; b. Washington, Sept. 2, 1946; d. Richard J. and Bettie Jean (Merrill) S.; m. Alan Graham Greer, Aug. 14, 1981. BA in History cum laude, Kans. State U., 1968; JD, Georgetown U., 1973. Bar: Fla. 1973, D.C. 1975, U.S. Dist. Ct. (no., mid., so. dists., trial bar) Fla., U.S. Ct. Appeals (5th and eleventh cir.), U.S. Supreme Ct. Reporter Dallas Times Herald, Washington, 1970-73; law clk. to Hon. Charles R. Rickey U.S. Dist. Ct., Washington, 1973-74; assoc. Steel, Hector & Davis, Miami, Fla., 1974-79, ptnr., 1980-96; dir. office legal counsel Office of Nat. Drug Control Policy, Exec. Office of Pres., Washington, 1996—; adj. faculty U. Miami Law Sch., Coral Gables, Fla., 1984-88; faculty Nat. Inst. Trial Advocacy, Boulder, Colo., 1982, 83, 95, Chapel Hill, N.C., 1984, 87. Fla. region, 1989; lectr. in field. Contbr. numerous articles to law jours. Mem. Dade Munroe Mental Health Bd., Miami, 1982-84, United Way of Greater Miami comty. devel. com., 1984-87; chmn. family abuse task force United Way of Greater Miami, 1986; chmn. devel. com. Miami City Ballet, 1986-87, bd. dirs., 1986-90. Fellow Am. Bar Found., Am. Bd. Trial Advocacy, Internat. Soc. Barristers; mem. ABA (chmn. various coms. 1979-85, Ho. Dels. 1992-96), Am. Arbitration Assn. (nat. bd. dirs. 1995-97, complex case panel arbitrator), The Fla. Bar Assn. (bd. govs. young lawyer divsn. 1981-82, bd. govs. 1986-92, pres. 1993-94, bd. cert. civil trial), Fla. Assn. Women Lawyers, Dade County Bar Assn. (pub. interest law bank). Democrat. Roman Catholic. Avocations: travel, art. Home: 224 Ridgewood Rd Miami FL 33133-6614 Office: Exec Office of the Pres Policy Office of Nat Drug Control Washington DC 20503

SEITZ, WALTER STANLEY, cardiovascular research consultant; b. L.A., May 10, 1937; s. Walter and Frances Janette (Schleef) S. BS in Physics and Math., U. Calif., Berkeley, 1959; PhD in Biophysics, U. Vienna, 1981, MD, 1982. Health physicist U. Calif. Radiation Lab., 1959-61; rsch. assoc. NIH at Pacific Union Coll., 1961-63; physicist Lockheed Rsch. Labs., Palo Alto, Calif., 1961-63; staff scientist Xerox Corp., Pasadena, Calif., 1963-66; sr, scientist Applied Physics Cons., Palo Alto, 1966-75; instr. clin. sci. U. Ill Coll. Medicine, Urbana, 1983-84; cons. cardiology Cardiovascular Rsch. Inst. U. Calif. Sch. Medicine, San Francisco, 1987—; sr. scientist Inst. Med. Analysis and Rsch., Berkeley, 1987—. Contbr. articles to profl. jours. Postdoctoral Rsch. fellow, U. Calif. San Francisco, 1984. Fellow Am. Coll. Angiography; mem. AAAS, Royal Soc. Medicine London, N.Y. Acad. Scis., Physicians for Social Responsibility. Avocations: reading, music, hiking. Office: IMAR Cons Inc 38 Panoramic Way Berkeley CA 94704-1828

SEITZER, KEVIN LEE, professional baseball player; b. Springfield, Ill., Mar. 26, 1962; m. Lisa Seitzer; 1 child, Brandon. BS in Indsl. Electronics, Ea. Ill. U., 1984. Baseball player Kansas City (Mo.) Royals, 1986-91, Milw. Brewers, 1992, 93-96, Oakland (Calif.) Athletics, 1993, Cleve. Indians, 1996—. Mem. Am. League All Star Team, 1987, 95. Office: Cleve Indians 2401 Ontario St Cleveland OH 44115*

SEKANINA, ZDENEK, astronomer; b. Mlada Boleslav, Czechoslovakia, June 12, 1936; came to U.S., 1969; s. Frantisek Sekanina and Hedvika (Kolarikova) Sekaninova; m. Jana Soukupova, Apr. 1, 1966; 1 child, Jason. Diploma, Charles U., Prague, Czechoslovakia, 1959, PhD in Astronomy, 1963. Astronomer Stefanik Obs., Prague, 1959-66, Ctr. for Numerical Math., Charles U., Prague, 1967-68; vis. scientist Inst. d'Astrophysique, Univ. de Liege, Cointe-Ougree, Belgium, 1968-69; physicist Smithsonian Astrophys. Obs., Cambridge, Mass., 1969-80; mem. tech. staff Jet Propulsion Lab., Pasadena, Calif., 1980-81, rsch. scientist, 1981-84, sr. rsch. scientist, 1984—; assoc. Harvard Coll. Obs., Cambridge, 1969-80; mem. NASA Comet Sci. Working Group, 1977-80; cons. Jet Propulsion Lab., 1977-80; prin. U.S. co-investigator Particulate Impact Analyzer Experiment, Dust Impact Detector Sys. Experiment, European Space Agy.'s Giotto Mission to Comet Halley, 1980-89; mem. NASA-European Spacy Agy. Comet Halley Environ. Working Group, 1980-89; discipline specialist Near Nucleus Studies Network, Internat. Halley Watch, 1982-90; mem. imaging sci. subsys. team Comet Rendezvous Asteroid Flyby Mission, 1986-92; mem. sci. definition team ESA/NASA Comet Nucleus Sample Return Mission, 1988—; co-investigator STARDUST Discovery Mission, 1994—. Editor Comet Halley Archive, 1982-91; mem. editorial bd. Kosmicke Rozhledy, 1963-69. Recipient Exceptional Sci. Achievement medal NASA, 1985; minor planet named Sekanina, 1976. Mem. Internat. Astron. Union (mem. commns. 15, 10, 22, mem. organizing commn. 22 1976-82, organizing commn. 15 1979-85, mem. working group on comets 1988—, assoc. dir. Ctrl. Bur. for Astron. Telegrams 1970-80), COSPAR (working group 3, panel C, exec. mem. 1980-82), Learned Soc of Czech Republic (hon.). Roman Catholic. Office: Jet Propulsion Lab 4800 Oak Grove Dr Pasadena CA 91109-8001

SEKERKA, ROBERT FLOYD, physics educator, scientist; b. Wilkinsburg, Pa., Nov. 27, 1937; s. John Jacob and Vivian Mae (Smith) S.; m. Dianne Thompson, Apr. 30, 1960 (div. Apr. 1981); children: Lee Ann, Robert Thompson; m. 2d Carolyn Lee Confer, May 24, 1981. BS in Physics, U. Pitts., 1960; AM, Harvard U., 1961, PhD, 1965; PhD (hon.), U. Timisora, Romania, 1996. Engr. Westinghouse Rsch. Labs., Pitts., 1965-68, mgr. materials growth and properties dept., 1968-69; lectr. Carnegie-Mellon U., Pitts., 1967-69, assoc. prof., 1969-72, prof. metallurgy and materials sci., 1972-82, dept. head, 1976-82, prof. physics and math., dean Mellon Coll. Sci., 1982-91, Univ. Prof., 1991—; mem. space studies bd. NRC, 1989-91. Assoc. editor Jour. Crystal Growth, 1971-94; Metallurgical Trans., 1970-76; editorial bd. Applied Microgravity Tech., 1987-90. Past bd. dirs. Forbes Health Sys., Pitts., Pitts. Regional Ctr. for Sci. Tchrs.; past vice chmn. bd. dirs. NMR Inst.; past mem. rsch. com. Allegheny Singer Rsch. Inst., Pitts. Recipient A.G. Worthing award U. Pitts., 1959, Philip M. McKenna Meml. award, 1980; Woodrow Wilson fellow, 1960, NSF fellow, 1962-65. Fellow Am. Soc. Metals, Am. Phys. Soc.; mem. Minerals Metals Materials Soc., Am. Assn. Crystal Growth (mem. exec. com.), Internat. Assn. Crystal Growth (co-v.p., Frank prize 1992), Edgewood Country Club, Phi Beta Kappa, Sigma Xi, Omicron Delta Kappa. Home: 307 S Dithridge St Apt 407 Pittsburgh PA 15213-3514 Office: Carnegie Mellon U Dept Physics 6319 Wean Hall Pittsburgh PA 15213-3890

SEKINE, DEBORAH KEIKO, systems analyst, programmer; b. Honolulu, Dec. 1, 1952; d. Yoshiteru and Yaeko (Matsuda) Isa; m. Andrew K. Sekine, May 8, 1993. BA in Math. with distinction, U. Hawaii, 1974, BEd with distinction, 1974, MS in Computer Sci., 1976, MBA, 1987. Data analyst, engr. in-charge Kentron, Honolulu, 1977-81; sys. analyst Am. Savs., Honolulu, 1981-82; analyst, programmer City and County of Honolulu, 1982—; cons. Am. Savs., Honolulu, 1982. Contbr. articles to profl. jours. Vol. Hawaii Dem. Conv., Honolulu, 1984, Mayoral campaign, 1988, 92; com. co-chair Hui Makaala, Honolulu, 1989—; caregiver Makiki Christian Ch., Honolulu, 1991—. Mem. IEEE, Assn. for Computing Machinery, Am. Fedn. State County Mcpl. Employees, U. Hawaii MBA Alumni Assn., Phi Kappa Phi. Mem. United Ch. of Christ. Avocations: jogging, reading, writing, tennis, listening to gospel music. Home: 3322 George St Honolulu HI 96815-4319

SEKITANI, TORU, otolaryngologist, educator; b. Kochi, Japan, May 5, 1932; s. Fusaharu and Miyoko (Tokushige) S.; m. Miyoko Uejo, Dec. 26, 1960; children: Miwako, Yoshiko, Tetsuko. MD, Yamaguchi Med. Sch., 1957. Intern Yamaguchi Med. Sch. Hosp., Ube, Japan, 1957-58, asst. prof., 1962, assoc. prof., 1971, prof., chmn. dept. otolaryngology, 1976-93; resident USAF Hosp., Fukuoka, 1959; emeritus prof. Yamaguchi U., Japan, 1993—; dir. Nat Shimonoseki Hosp, Japan; rsch. assoc. Univ. Iowa, Iowa City, 1969-71; vis. scholar U. Wash., Seattle, 1983-84. Author: (with others) Vertigo: Basic and Clinic, 1976, Vastbular Mechanism in Health and Disease, 1978; editor: Vestibular Ganglia and Vastbular Neuronitis, 1988, Fundamentals of Galvanic Body Sway Test for Dizziness, 1995. Mem. Barany Soc. (Sweden), Prosper Meniere Soc. (U.S.A.), Otorhinolaryngological Soc. Japan, Japan Soc. Equilibrium and Rsch., Brian F. McCabe Soc. (U.S.A.).

SEKLER, EDUARD FRANZ, architect, educator; b. Vienna, Austria, Sept. 30, 1920; came to U.S., 1954; s. Eduard Jakob and Elisabeth (Demmel) S.; m. Mary Patricia May, July 21, 1962. Dipl. Ing., Tech. U., Vienna, 1945; student, Sch. Planning and Regional Research, London, 1947; Ph.D., London U., 1948; A.M. (hon.), Harvard U., 1960; D Tech. Scis. (hon.), Fed. Inst. Tech., Zurich, Switzerland, 1988. Ptnr. archtl. firm Prehsler and Sekler, Vienna, 1945-95; teaching asst., lectr. faculty architecture Tech. U., Vienna, 1945-54; vis. prof. architecture Harvard U., Cambridge, Mass., 1955-56, assoc. prof., 1956-60, prof., 1960-91, 93-97, Osgood Hooker prof. visual art, 1970-91, prof. emeritus, 1991-93, prof., 1993—; Beinecke-Reeves Disting. chair in archtl. preservation U. Fla., 1995-96; coord. studies Carpenter Ctr. Visual Arts, 1962-65, dir., 1966-76, chmn. dept. visual and environ. studies, 1968-70; expert mem. internat. com. hist. monuments UNESCO, 1951-54; UNESCO advisor to planning and archeology depts. Govt. of Nepal, 1972-94; cons. Hist. Monuments Office, Vienna, 1975, 89, 91-96; head UNESCO team for masterplan for Conservation Cultural Heritage of Kathmandu Valley, 1975; UNESCO cons. masterplan for Sukothai Hist. Park, Thailand, 1978, 84. Author: Point-houses in European Housing, 1952, Wren and His Place in European Architecture, 1956, Proportion, a Measure of Order, 1965, Historic Urban Spaces I-IV, 1962-71, Proposal for the Urbanistic Conservation of Patan Durbar Square, 1980, Jos. Hoffmann, The Architectural Work, 1982, Die Architektur und die Zeit, 1988; co-author: Kathmandu Valley, The Preservation of Physical Environment and Cultural Heritage, 2 vols., 1975, Le Corbusier at Work: The Genesis of the Carpenter Center for the Visual Arts, The Building and The Town: Essays for E. Sekler, 1994, Das Semperdepot, 1997, Form, Modernism, and History, 1997; archtl. works include restoration ch., Leopoldsberg, nr. Vienna, urban redevel., Alt Erdberg, 1956, Austrian Cultural Inst., N.Y.C., 1962, several housing schemes, Vienna, 1948-68, Telephone Exchange, Vienna, 1970. Mem. Cambridge Arts Council, 1975-84; bd. dirs. Archtl. Heritage, Inc., 1969-75; chmn. Kathmandu Valley Preservation Trust. Decorated Cross of Honor for Scis. and Art (Austria); recipient prize for humanities City of Vienna, 1983, Inst. honors AIA, 1989, Jean Tschumi prize Internat. Union Architects, 1990, Prechtl medal Vienna Tech. U., Gold medal City of Vienna, 1995, Medal of Honor, Austrian Soc. Archtl. Conservation, 1995; Guggenheim fellow, 1961-63. Fellow Am. Acad. Arts and Scis., U.S. Nat. Com. for Internat. Council of Monuments and Sites, Academia Scientiarum et Artium Europea; mem. Internat. Council Monuments and Sites, Soc. Archtl. Historians (dir. 1963-66, 70-73), Archtl. Assn. London, Austrian Chamber Architects, Royal Town Planning Inst. (hon. corr. mem. London), Signet Soc. Office: Grad Sch Design Gund Hall 48 Quincy St Cambridge MA 02138-3804

SEKO, MOBUTU SESE, President Zaire; b. Lisala, Belgian Congo, Oct. 30, 1930; m. Bobi Ladaw. Student, Inst. d'Etudes Sociales l'Etat, Brussels, 1948-49. Form asst. editor to editor in chief L'Avenir, 1958; mem. Congolese Nationalist Party; sec. state nat. def. Dem. Rep. Congo, 1960; chief staff to comdr. in chief Congolese Army. Sgt. maj. Belgian Colonial Army, 1956. Office: Presidence Repulique Zaire, Mont Ngaliema Kinshasa Zaire*

SEKOWSKI, CYNTHIA JEAN, corporate executive, contact lens specialist; b. Chgo., Feb. 14, 1953; d. John L. and Celia L. (Matusiak) S. PhD in Health Svcs. Adminstrn., Columbia Pacific U., 1984, PhD in Health Scis., 1984. Chief contact lens dept. Lieberman & Kraff, Chgo., 1974-87; pres., CEO Seko Eye Care, Inc., Chgo., 1988—; realtor Country Club Realty Group, Naples, Fla., 1995—; researcher, technologist U. Ill., Chgo., 1976-78. Mem. Chgo. Zool. Soc., 1984—, Little City Inner Circle, 1991—; sponsor Save the Children Orgn., 1983—; asst. to campaign mgr. Rep. state senatorial candidate, Chgo., 1972; pres. Compass Point Condo Assn., Naples, Fla., 1996—; mem. budget com. Windstar Masters Assn., Naples. Fellow Contact Lens Soc. Am.; mem. Ill. Soc. Opticianry, Opticians Assn. Am., Better Vision Inst., Nat. Contact Lens Examiners, Fla. Assn. Realtors, Nat. Assn. Realtors, Naples Area Bd. of Realtors, Women's Coun. of Realtors, Nat. Geographic Soc., Columbia Pacific U. Alumnae Assn., Nat. Wildlife Fedn. Roman Catholic. Avocations: gardening, reading, photography, writing poetry, golf. Office: Country Club Realty Ste 105 2640 Golden Gate Pkwy Naples FL 34105-3200

SEKULA, EDWARD JOSEPH, JR., financial executive; b. Brandonville, Pa., Sept. 2, 1937; s. Edward Joseph and Dorothy May (Fritz) S.; m. Carol Lee Helton, July 13, 1963; 1 child, David. BSBA, Pa. State U., 1961. Dep. fin. officer Aberdeen Proving Ground, Md., 1961-63; with Peat, Marwick, Mitchell & Co., N.Y.C., 1963-77; corp. cont. N.Y.C. Health & Hosp. Corp., 1977-78; dir. fin. Mt. Sinai Med. Ctr., N.Y.C., 1979-82; CFO Vis. Nurse Svc. N.Y., N.Y.C., 1982-86, Wallkill Valley Gen. Hosp., 1986-94; pres. EJ Sekula Ent. Inc.; sec.-treas. Planning Assistance Inc., N.Y.C., 1978—. Mem. parish coun. of deacons Abiding Peace Luth. Ch., 1972-89; cubmaster, com. chmn., Webelos leader Cub Scouts Am., 1974-78; scoutmaster Troop 186, Boy Scouts Am., 1978-85, asst. dist. commr.; vol. fireman Netcong Fire Co. 1, 1974—; co-treas. Lenape Valley Regional H.S. Band Parents Assn., 1981-83; chmn. environ. commn. Borough of Netcong, 1988—, Lake Musconetcong Regional Planning Bd., 1989—. With U.S. Army, 1961-63; capt. Res. (ret.). Recipient Dist. Award of Merit, Boy Scouts Am., Silver Beaver Mem. AICPA, Hosp. Fin. Mgmt. Assn., Home Care Assn., N.Y. Soc. CPAs, Musconetcong Club, Beta Alpha Psi, Phi Kappa Tau. Republican. Lutheran. Fishing, Trout Unltd., Rotary (Paul Harris fellow). Home: 39 Amendola Dr Netcong NJ 07857-1401

SEKULER, ROBERT WILLIAM, psychology educator, scientist; b. Elizabeth, N.J., May 7, 1939; s. Sidney and Mary (Siegel) S.; m. Susan Pamela Nemser, June 25, 1961; children: Stacia, Allison, Erica. A.B., Brandeis U., 1960; Sc.M., Brown U., 1963, Ph.D., 1964; postgrad. (NIH postdoctoral fellow), M.I.T., 1964-65. Prof. psychology Northwestern U., Evanston, Ill., 1973-89, chmn. dept., 1975-79, prof. ophthalmology Med. Sch., 1978-89, prof. neurobiology and physiology, 1982-89, assoc. dean Coll. Arts and Scis., 1985-89, John Evans prof. neurosci., 1986-89; v.p. Optronix, Inc., 1980-82; provost, dean of faculty Brandeis U., Waltham, Mass., 1989-91, Louis and Frances Salvage prof. psychology, 1989—; mem. Ctr. for Complex Systems, 1990—; rsch. prof. biomed. engring. Boston U., 1992—; adj. prof. cognitive and neural systems Boston U., 1994—; cons. NSF, NIH, AAAS, USAF, U. Calif, Am. Psychol. Assn.; chmn. NRC-Nat. Acad. Sci. Vision Com.; chmn. NRC working Group on Visual Function and Aging; chmn. NRC Working Group on Aging Workers and Visual Impairment. Author: (with D. Kline and K. Dismukes) Aging and Human Visual Function, 1981, (with R. Blake) Perception, 1985, 2d edit., 1990, 3d edit., 1994; editor: Perception & Psychophysics, 1971-86, Jour. Exptl. Psychology, 1973-74, Vision Rsch. Jour., 1974-79, 80-92, Optics Letters, 1977-79, Am. Jour. Psychology, Ophthalmic and Physiol. Optics, 1986—, Intelligent Systems, 1986-92, Psychology and Aging, 1987-92; contbr. Handbook of Geriatric Medicine, 1992; contbr. articles to profl. jours. Grantee Nat. Inst. Neurol. Diseases and Stroke, USAF, NSF, Nat. Eye Inst., Nat. Inst. Aging, USN, James McDonnell Found. Fellow AAAS, Optical Soc. Am., Am. Psychol. Soc.; mem. Assn. Rsch. in Vision and Ophthalmology, Neurosci. Soc., Internat. Neural Network Soc., Psychonomic Soc., Knowles Inst. for Hearing Rsch. (bd. dirs. 1988-90), Sigma Xi. Home: 64 Strawberry Hill Rd Concord MA 01742-5502 Office: Brandeis U Ctr for Complex Systems Waltham MA 02254

SEKULOVICH, MALDEN See MALDEN, KARL

SEKULOW, JAY ALAN, lawyer; b. 1956. BA, JD, Mercer U. Bar: Ga. 1980. Chief counsel Am. Ctr. for Law and Justice, Virginia Beach; adj. prof. law Regent U. Author: From Intimidation to Victory, 1990, Knowing Your Rights, 1993, Students Rights and the Public School, And Nothing But The Truth, 1996. Office: Am Ctr for Law & Justice PO Box 64429 Virginia Beach VA 23467-4429

SELANNE, TEEMU, hockey player; b. Helsinki, Finland, July 3, 1970. Hockey player Winnipeg Jets Nat. Hockey League, 1992-95, hockey player Phoenix Coyotes, 1995—; played in All-Star Game, 1996, 94, 93. Named Rookie of Yr. Sporting News, 1992-93, All Rookie team, 1992-93; Recipient Calder Meml. Trophy, 1992-93. Office: Phoenix Coyotes One Renaissance Sq Ste 1930 Phoenix AZ 85004

SELBIN, JOEL, chemistry educator; b. Washington, Aug. 20, 1931; s. Abram Jacob and Rose (Aronson) S.; m. Marion F. Kilsheimer, Aug. 28, 1955; children: Eric Allyn, Jeffrey Lynn, Deborah Lyn, Jonathan David. BS, George Washington U., 1953; PhD, U. Ill., 1957. Asst. prof. chemistry La. State U., Baton Rouge, 1957-61, assoc. prof., 1961-67, prof., 1967-91, also dir. Summer Inst. for High Sch. Tchrs., 1984—; spl. vis. prof. U. Colo., Denver, 1991—; speaker Union of Concerned Scientists, 1980—. Author: Theoretical Inorganic Chemistry, 2d edit., 1969; patentee in field; contbr. articles to profl. jours. Grantee Am. Chem. Soc., NSF, Rsch. Corp. Fellow AAAS; mem. Am. Chem. Soc. (Charles E. Coates award 1973), Phi Beta Kappa, Sigma Xi. Office: U Colo Dept of Chemistry Denver CO 80304

SELBY, CECILY CANNAN, dean, educator, scientist; b. London, Feb. 4, 1927; d. Keith and Catherine Anne Cannan; m. Henry M. Selby, Aug. 11, 1951 (div. 1979); children: Norman, William, Russell; m. James Stacy Coles, Feb. 21, 1981. A.B. cum laude, Radcliffe Coll., 1946; Ph.D. in Phys. Biology, MIT, 1950. Teaching asst. in biology MIT, 1948-49; adminstrv. head virus study sect. Sloan-Kettering Inst., N.Y.C., 1949-50; asst. mem. inst. Sloan-Kettering Inst., 1950-55; research assoc. Sloan-Kettering div. Cornell U. Med. Coll., N.Y.C., 1953-55; instr. microscopic anatomy Cornell U. Med. Coll., 1955-57; tchr. sci. Lenox Sch., N.Y.C., 1957-58; headmistress Lenox Sch., 1959-72; nat. exec. dir. Girl Scouts U.S.A., N.Y.C., 1972-75; adv. com. Simmons Coll. Grad. Mgmt. Program, 1977-78; mem. Com. Corp. Support of Pvt. Univs., 1977-83; spl. asst. acad. planning N.C. Sch. Sci. and Math., 1979-80, dean acad. affairs, 1980-81, chmn. bd. advisors, 1981-84; cons. U.S. Dept. Commerce, 1976-77; dir. Avon Products Inc., RCA, NBC, Loehmanns Inc., Nat. Edn. Corp. pres. Am. Energy Ind., 1976; co-chmn. commn. pre-coll. math. and sci. Nat. Sci. Bd., 1982-83; adj. prof. NYU, 1984-86, prof. sci. edn., 1986-94; mem. policy steering com. Gov. Cuomo's Conf. on Sci. and Engring., 1989-90. Contbr. articles to profl. jours., chpt. to book. Founder, chmn. N.Y. Ind. Schs. Opportunity Project, 1968-72; mem. invitational workshops Aspen Inst., 1973, 75, 77, 79; trustee MIT, Bklyn. Law Sch., Radcliffe Coll., Woods Hole Oceanographic Instn., Women's Forum N.Y., Skin Disease Found., N.Y. Hall of Sci., 1982—, vice chmn., 1989—, trustee Girls Inc., 1992—, Nat. Coun. Women in Medicine, 1990-94; mem. Yale U. Peabody Mus. Adv. Coun., 1981-89. Recipient Woman Scientist of Yr. award N.Y. chpt. Am. Women in Sci., 1992. Mem. Headmistresses of East (hon., pres. 1970-72), Sigma Xi, Phi Delta Kappa. Clubs: Century Assn., Woods Hole Golf, Cosmopolitan Club. Home and Office: 1 E 66th St New York NY 10021 also: 100 Ransom Rd Falmouth MA 02540-1652

SELBY, CLARK LINWOOD, JR., sales executive; b. Miami, Okla., Sept. 20, 1936; s. Clark Linwood and Edith Opal (Clark) S.; m. Patricia Ann Hayes, Dec. 22, 1952; children: Michael Lynn, Robert Clark. Sales engr. Carl Evans Co., Kansas City, Mo., 1962-70; asst. dir. traffic and parking U. Iowa, Iowa City, 1970-72; parking cons. De Leuw and Cather & Co., Chgo., 1972-77; pres. Enterprising Am. Corp., Hutchinson, Kans., 1978-82; dir. mfg. Duncan Industries, Harrison, Ark., 1982-85, dir. internat. sales, 1985-86, v.p. internat. sales, 1987-88, pres., 1988-90, v.p. sales and mktg., 1991-94; pres. Annell Corp., Wichita, Kans., 1991-95, bd. dirs., 1991-95; instr. free trade mktg. Kiev (USSR) Inst., 1991; chmn., sec. Florentine Corp., Flippin, Ark., 1994—; pres., CEO Worldwide Parking, Rockville, Md., 1994—; dir. Eyewear Shoppe, Inc., Hutchinson; chmn. Florentine Corp., Flippin, Ark., 1994. Inventor in field. Served with USNG, 1955-60. Recipient Presdl. E award for excellences in exporting, 1988. Methodist. Home: 1801 Par Ln Harrison AR 72601-6708 Office: 6000 Executive Blvd Ste 700 Rockville MD 20852-3803

SELBY, DIANE RAY MILLER, fraternal organization administrator; b. Lorain, Ohio, Oct. 11, 1940; d. Dale Edward and Mildred (Ray) Miller; m. David Baxter Selby, Apr. 14, 1962; children: Elizabeth, Susan, Sarah. BS in Edn., Ohio State U., 1962. Sec. Kappa Kappa Gamma Frat., Columbus, Ohio, 1962-63, editor, 1972-86; tchr. Hilliard (Ohio) High Sch., 1963-65; exec. dir. Mortar Bd., Inc. Nat. Office, Columbus, Ohio, 1986—. Editor The Key of Kappa Kappa Gamma Frat, 1972-86 (Student Life award, 1983, 84, 85). Founding officer Community Coordinating Bd., Worthington, Ohio, 1983; pres. PTA Coun., Worthington, 1984, Worthington Band Boosters, 1985; sec., treas. Sports and Recreation Facilities Bd., Worthington, 1986—; mem. sustaining com. Jr. League Columbus, 1991-93, docent Kelton House, 1979—. Mem. Mortar Bd., Inc., Twig 53 Children's Hosp. (assoc.), Assn. Coll. Honor Soc., Ladybugs and Buckeyes, Kappa Kappa Gamma (House Bd. vp. 1997-98). Republican. Lutheran. Home: 6750 Merwin Pl Columbus OH 43235-2838 Office: Mortar Bd Inc 1250 Chambers Rd Ste 170 Columbus OH 43212-1754

SELBY, HUBERT, JR., writer; b. N.Y.C., July 23, 1928; s. Hubert and Adalin (Layne) S.; m. Inez Taylor, Apr. 23, 1955 (div. 1960); children: Claudia, Kyle; Suzanne Schwartzman, Dec. 26, 1969; children: Rachel, William. Student public schs., Bklyn. Author: Last Exit to Brooklyn, 1964, The Room, 1971, The Demon, 1976, Requiem for a Dream, 1978, Song of the Silent Snow, 1986; screenwriter: Day and Night, 1986, Remember the Sabath Day, 1974, Love Your Buddy Week, 1978, Solder of Fortune, 1990. Served with U.S. Mcht. Marine, 1944-46. Mem. Writers Guild Am. (West chpt.), Authors Guild.

SELBY, JEROME M., mayor; b. Wheatland, Wyo., Sept. 4, 1948; s. John Franklin and Claudia Meredith (Hudson) S.; m. Gloria Jean Nelson, June 14, 1969; children: Tyan, Cameronn, Kalen. BS in Math., Coll. Idaho, 1969, MA in Ednl. Adminstrn., 1974; MPA, Boise State U., 1978. Assoc. engr. Boeing Co., Seattle, 1969-71; dir. evaluation WICHE Mountain States Regional Med. Program, Boise, 1971-74; dir. rsch., evaluation Mountain States Health Corp., Boise, 1974-76, with health policy analysis and accountability, 1976-78; dir. health Kodiak (Alaska) Area Native Assn., 1978-83; mgr. Kodiak Island Borough, 1984-85, mayor, 1985—; proprietor Kodiak Tax Svc., 1978—, Registered Guide, Kodiak, 1987—; cons. Nat. Cancer Inst., Washington, 1973-78, others. Contbr. articles to profl. jours. Treas. ARC, Kodiak, 1978-93, bd. dirs., 1978-95, chmn., 1989-90, mem. western ops.

hdqrs. adv. bd., 1986-92, mem. group IV and V nat. adv. coj., 1986-89, nat. bd. govs., 1989-95, chmn. chpt. rels. com., 1994-95; pres. S.W. Alaska Mcpl. Conf., Anchorage, 1988-89, v.p., 1986-87, treas., 1996—, bd. dirs., 1986—; pres. Alaska Mcpl. League Investment Pool, Inc., 1992—; v.p. Alaska Mcpl. League, 1988-90, pres., 1990-91, bd. dirs., 1988—; bd. dirs. Alaska Mcpl. League Jt. Ins. Assn. Bd., 1995—, v.p., 1996—; mem. Alaska Resource Devel. Coun., 1987—, exec. com., 1989—; mem. policy com. of outer continental shelf adv. bd. U.S. Dept. Interior, 1990—, v.p., 1996—; co-chair Alaska Task Force, 1995—; mem. Com. on Oil Pollution Act, 1995; mem. Nat. Assn. Counties, Cmty. and Econ. Devel. Steering Com., 1990—, Alaska govtl. roles task force, 1991-92; mem. Alaska state/local govt. task force, 1996; chmn. Kodiak Island Exxon Valdez Restoration Com., 1991-95; dir. Kodiak Health Care Found., 1992—; co-chmn. Arctic Power, 1993—; mem. bd. dirs. Western Interstate Region Nat. Assn. of Counties, 1993—. Paul Harris fellow, 1987, 88, 91, 92, 96; recipient Outstanding Contbn. award Alaska Mcpl. League, 1994. Mem. Alaska Conf. Mayors, Nat. Soc. Tax Profls., Acad. Polit. Sci., Alaska Mcpl. Mgrs. Assn., Kodiak C. of C. (dir. 1983—), Rotary (bd. dirs. 1989—, treas. 1989-93, v.p. 1993-94, pres.-elect 1994-95, pres. 1995-96). Office: Kodiak Island Borough 710 Mill Bay Rd Kodiak AK 99615-6340

SELBY, ROY CLIFTON, JR., neurosurgeon; b. Little Rock, Sept. 28, 1930; s. Roy Clifton Sr. and Annie Mae (Bular) S.; m. Marilyn Triffler, May 12, 1960; children: Brian M.T., Bretta L.T. BSc, MSc, La. State U., 1952; MD, U. Ark., Little Rock, 1956. diplomate Am. Bd. Neurol. Surgery. Intern Montreal Gen. Hosp., 1956-57; resident VA Hosp., Little Rock, Ark., 1957-58, U. Ill. Depart. Neurology and Neurosurgery, Chgo., 1958-61; sr. fellow Neurosurgery Lahey Clinic, Boston, 1961-62; dir. dept. neurosurgery Ministry Health Gen. Hosp., Kuala Lumpur, Malaysia, 1963-70; chmn. dept. neurosurgery Cook County Hosp., Chgo., 1970-74; practice medicine specializing in neurosurgery Texarkana, Tex., 1974-86; assoc. clin. prof. neurosurgery U. Ill., Chgo., 1970-74; prof. Cook County Postgrad. Sch. Med., 1970-74; vis. assoc. prof. Rush Presbyn. Med. Ctr., 1970-74; lectr. dept. psychology E. Tex. U., Texarkana, 1986—. Author short stories; contbr. chpts. to books. Fellow Royal Soc. Medicine; mem. Am. Assn. Neurol. Surgeons, N.Y. Acad. Scis., Soc. Neurol. Lange Francaise, N.Y. Acad. Medicine, French Soc. History of Medicine, Acad. Medicine (Paris), Internat. Soc. Surgery, Am. Osler Soc., Ark. Hist. Soc., Soc. Neurosci., Cen. Neuropsychiat. Soc., Inst. Charles DeGaulle, Ala. Hist. Soc., La. Hist. Soc., Sigma Xi, Alpha Omega Alpha. Avocations: reading, writing, gardening. Home: 7 Sweetbrush Ave Texarkana TX 75503-9999 Office: 1903 Mall Dr Texarkana TX 75503-2641 *The more I learn, the less I feel separated from all creatures; believing in all forms of life highly specialized, though greatly diverse, require respect and reverence.*

SELDEN, ROBERT WENTWORTH, physicist, science advisor; b. Phoenix, Aug. 11, 1936; s. Edward English and Mary Priscilla (Calder) S.; m. Mary Tania Hudd, June 1958 (div. 1976); 1 child, Ian Scott; m. Marjorie Anne Harmon, Feb. 20, 1977; children: Brock, Thane, Shawna, Kirsten. BA in Physics cum laude, Pomona Coll., 1958; MS in Physics, U. Wis., 1960, PhD in Physics, 1964. Rsch. assoc. Lawrence Livermore (Calif.) Nat. Lab., 1965-67, staff mem., 1967-73, group leader, 1973-78, asst. assoc. dir., 1978-80; div. leader applied theoretical physics Los Alamos (N.Mex.) Nat. Lab., 1980-83, dep. assoc. dir. strategic def. rsch., 1983-84, assoc. dir. theoretical and computational physics, 1984-86, dir. Ctr. for Nat. Securities Studies, 1986-88, assoc. dir. for lab. devel., 1991-94; chief scientist USAF, Washington, 1988-91, panel chmn. sci. adv. bd., 1984-88, 91—; cons. Los Alamos, 1994—; chmn. study group on reactor materials and nuclear explosives U.S. Dept. Energy, 1976-78; mem. ballistic missile def. techs. adv. panel U.S. Congress Office Tech. Assessment, 1984-85, The Pres.'s Defensive Tech. Study Team, Washington, 1983; strategic adv. group U.S. Air Command, 1996—. Editor Rsch. Jour. Lawrence Livermore Nat. Lab., 1976-77; contbr. sci. and tech. papers to profl. jours. Pres. Livermore Cultural Arts Coun., 1969-72; chmn. Livermore Sister City Orgn., 1973, Planning Commn. City of Livermore, 1971-76; bd. dirs. Orch. of Santa Fe, 1986-88. Capt. U.S. Army, 1964-67. Grad. fellow Edward John Noble Found., 1958-62; recipient Theodore von Karman award for outstanding contbn. to def. sci., 1989, medal for outstanding pub. svc. U.S. Sec. Def., 1996; decorated for exceptional civilian svc. USAF, 1996. Mem. AAAS, Am. Phys. Soc., N.Y. Acad. Sci., Air Force Assn. Avocations: tennis, hiking, music. Office: 624 La Bajada Los Alamos NM 87544-3805

SELDEN, WILLIAM KIRKPATRICK, retired educational administrator; b. Oil City, Pa., Nov. 11, 1911; s. Edwin van D. and Cornelia Fuller (Earp) S.; m. Virginia Barr, June 25, 1938; children: Edwin van Deusen, II, Joseph Barr. A.B., Princeton U., 1934; LL.D., Carthage Coll., 1954; Litt.D., Jacksonville U., 1964; L.H.D., Scholl Coll. Podiatric Medicine, 1984. Asst. to faculty dean, coll. dean Princeton U., 1934-37; clk. Eastman Kodak Co., Rochester, N.Y., 1937-38; asst. dir. admissions, admissions officer, asst. coll. dean Brown U., Providence, 1938-43; asst. to pres. Brown U., 1943-45; asst. dean students, dir. admissions Northwestern U., Evanston, Ill., 1945-52; univ. recorder Northwestern U., 1952-53; pres. Ill. Coll., 1953-55; exec. dir. Nat. Commn. on Accrediting, 1955-65; v.p. The Am. Assembly, 1965-66; former mem. various bds. and coms. concerned with issues in edn., mil., professions, and polit. affairs. Author: Accreditation--A Struggle Over Standards in Higher Education, 1960, Woodrow Wilson School, Princeton University, 1984, Princeton Summer Camp, 1987, Vignettes of Princeton University, 1987, Legacy of John Cleve Green, 1988, Its First 100 Years--Nassau Club of Princeton, 1989, From These Roots: The Creation of Princeton Day School, 1991, The Heritage of Isabella McCosh: A History of the Health Service at Princeton University, 1991, History of Princeton Theological Seminary, 1992, Drumthwaltet, The Governors Mansion, 1993, Club Life at Princeton, An Historical Account of the Eating Clubs at Princeton University, 1995, Nassau Hall, Princeton University's National Historic Landmark, 1995. Home: Loe 105 Pennswood Village Newtown PA 18940-2401

SELDES, MARIAN, actress; b. N.Y.C.; d. Gilbert and Alice (Hall) S.; m. Julian Claman, Nov. 3, 1953 (div.); 1 child, Katharine; m. Garson Kanin, June 19, 1990. Grad., The Dalton Sch., N.Y.C., 1945, Neighborhood Playhouse, N.Y.C., 1947; DHL, Emerson Coll., 1979. Mem. faculty drama and dance div. Juilliard Sch. Lincoln Center, N.Y.C., 1969-91. Appeared with Cambridge (Mass.) Summer Theatre, 1945, Boston Summer Theatre, 1946, St. Michael's Playhouse, Winooski, Vt., 1947-48, Bermudiana Theatre, Hamilton, Bermuda, 1951, Elitch Gardens Theatre, Denver, 1953; Broadway appearances include Medea, 1947, Crime and Punishment, 1948, That Lady, 1949, Tower Beyond Tragedy, 1950, The High Ground, 1951, Come of Age, 1952, Ondine, 1954, The Chalk Garden, 1955, The Wall, 1960, A Gift of Time, 1962, The Milk Train Doesn't Stop Here Any More, 1964, Tiny Alice, 1965, A Delicate Balance, 1967 (Tony award for best supporting actress), Before You Go, 1968, Father's Day, 1971 (Drama Desk award), Mendicants of Evening (Martha Graham Co.), 1973, Equus, 1974-77, The Merchant, 1977, Deathtrap, 1978; off-Broadway appearances include Diff'rent, 1961, The Ginger Man, 1963 (Obie award), All Women Are One, 1964, Juana LaLoca, 1965, Three Sisters, 1969, Am. Shakespeare Festival, Stratford, Conn., Mercy Street at Am. Place Theater, N.Y.C., 1969, Isadora Duncan, 1976 (Obie award), Painting Churches, 1983, 84 (Outer Critics Circle award 1984), Other People, Berkshire Theatre Festival, 1969, The Celebration, Hedgerow Theater, Pa., 1971, Richard III, N.Y. Shakespeare Festival, 1983, Remember Me, Lakewood Theatre, Skowhegan, Maine, Gertrude Stein and a Companion, White Barn Theatre, Westport, Conn., 1985, Lucile Lortel Theatre, N.Y.C., 1986, Richard II, N.Y. Shakespeare Festival, 1987, The Milk Train Doesn't Stop Here Anymore, WFA Theatre, N.Y.C., 1987, Happy Ending, Bristol (Pa.) Riverside Theatre, 1988, Annie 2 John F. Kennedy Ctr., Washington, 1989-90, Goodspeed Opera House, Chester, Conn., 1990, A Bright Room Called Day, N.Y. Shakespeare Festival, 1991, Three Tall Women, River Arts, Woodstock, N.Y., 1992, Another Time, Am. Jewish Theatre, 1993, Breaking the Code, Berkshire Theatre Festival, 1993, Three Tall Women, Vineyard Theatre, N.Y.C., 1994, Promenade Theatre, 1994-95, nat. tour, 1995-96, The Royal Family, Williamstown Theatre, Mass., 1996, Boys From Syracuse, City Ctr., N.Y.C., 1997; engaged in nat. tour Medea, 1947, U.S. entry Berlin Festival, 1951, nat. tour Three Tall Women, 1995-96; motion picture appearances include The Greatest Story Ever Told, Gertrude Stein and a Companion, 1988, In a Pig's Eye, 1988, The Gun in Betty Lou's Handbag, 1992, Tom and Huck, 1995, Digging to China, 1997, Home Alone 3, 1997, Affliction, 1997; (ABC series) Good and Evil, 1991, Murphy Brown, 1992, Truman, 1995, Cosby, 1996; also appeared on CBS Radio Mystery Theater, 1976-81, Theatre Guild on The Air; author: The Bright Lights, 1978, Time Together, 1981. Bd. dirs. Neighborhood Playhouse, The Acting Co., nat. repertory theatre. Winner Ovation award Theater L.A. for Three Tall Women, 1996, Connecticut Critics award for Three Tall Women, 1996. Mem. Players Club, Century Assn. Home: Apt 19 D 210 Central Park S New York NY 10019

SELDIN, DAVID, professional sports team executive; b. Henderson, Nev., Oct. 24, 1961; m. Judy Seldin; children: Abigail, Hannah, Sarah. BS in Econs. summa cum laude, U. Pa., 1982; MBA in Fin. and Mktg., U. Chgo., 1983. With Boston Consulting Group, Chgo., 1983-87; With Pritzker Orgn., Chgo., 1987-91; pres. Touchdown Jacksonville, Ltd., 1991-93; pres., COO Jacksonville (Fla.) Jaguars, 1993—; point man on constrn. of Jacksonville Mcpl. Stadium. Avocation: marathon runner (participated in 1992 Boston Marathon to support Dana-Farber Cancer Inst.).

SELDMAN, NEIL NORMAN, cultural organization administrator; b. Bklyn., Aug. 2, 1945; s. Fred Herman and Sylvia (Flaster) S.; m. Laura Jane Klugherz, Feb. 22, 1968; children: Oliver, Chloe. BS in Indsl. and Labor Rels., Cornell U., 1966; MS in Internat. Communism, George Washington U., 1968, PhD in Internat. Rels., 1974. Asst. to pres. B.H. Krueger Co., Bklyn., 1969-72; assoc. prof., lectr. George Washington U., Washington, 1974-76, asst. dir. exptl. program, 1976-77; founder Inst. for Local Self-Reliance (ILSR), Washington, 1974—, pres., 1980—; cons. World Bank/UN Environ. Program, Washington, 1980-81, City Coun., Phila., 1984-90. Author: Common Sense Radicalism, 1976, Waste to Wealth: A Guide for Community Enterprise, 1985; co-author: Integrated Resource Recovery-Recycling from Municipal Refuse: A State-of-the-Art Review and Annotated Bibliography, 1985, Proven Profits from Pollution Prevention, 1986, Garbage in Europe: Economics, Technologies, Trends, 1987; contbr. article to Ency. of Energy Tech. and the Environment, 1995. Fabrangen Cheder Jewish Community Orgn.; elected chair Neighborhood Planning Coun., Washington, 1976-82; co-founder D.C. Interracial Coalition for Environ. Equity, Washington, 1989, Nat. Recycling Coalition, 1980, Grass Roots Recycling Network, 1996. With NG, 1968-74. Grantee Moriah Fund, 1990-95, Pew Charitable Trusts, 1991, NSF, 1979-80, H. Heinz Endowment, 1995-96, U.S. EPA, 1993-96, Turner Found., 1995-96. Jewish. Avocations: fast pitch softball, nineteenth-century literature, French and Russian revolutions. Office: Inst Local Self-Reliance 2425 18th St NW Washington DC 20009-2003

SELDNER, BETTY JANE, environmental engineer, consultant, aerospace company executive; b. Balt., Dec. 11, 1923; d. David D. and Miriam M. (Mendes) Miller; m. Warren E. Gray, June 20, 1945 (div. 1965); children: Patricia, Deborah; m. Alvin Seldner, Nov. 15, 1965; children: Jack, Barbara. BA in Journalism, Calif. State U., Northridge, 1975, MA in Communications, 1977. Dir. pub. info. United Way, Van Nuys, Calif., 1958-63; dir. edn. United Way, Los Angeles, 1963-68; dir. pub. relations, fin. San Fernando Valley Girl Scout Council, Reseda, Calif., 1968-73; asst. dir. pub. info. Calif. State U., Northridge, 1973-75; dir. environ. mgmt. HR Textron Corp., Valencia, Calif., 1975-87; environ. engr. Northrop Aircraft, Hawthorne, Calif., 1987-88, EMCON Assocs., Burbank, Calif., 1988-92, Atkins Environ., 1992-93, Seldner Environ., Valencia, Calif., 1993—; prin. Seldner Environ. Svcs., 1993—. Author non-fiction. Mem. Santa Clarita Valley Environ. Mgrs. Soc. (chmn. bd. dirs. 1984), San Fernando Valley Round Table (pres. 1971-72), Hazardous Materials Mgrs.' Assn., Zonta Internat. Republican. Jewish. Avocation: sailing.

SELES, MONICA, tennis player; b. Novi Sad, Yugoslavia, Dec. 2, 1973; came to U.S., 1986; d. Karol and Esther Seles. Profl. tennis player, 1989—. Winner Houston, 1989, 91, 92, Oakland, 1990, 92, L.A., 1990, 91, Tampa, 1990, 91, U.S. Hardcourts, 1990, Lipton, 1990, 91, Roland Garros, 1990, 91, 92, Italian Open, 1990, German Open, 1990, French Open, 1990, 91, 92, Va. Slims, 1990, 91, 92, Phila., 1991, Milan, 1991, Tokyo Nichirie, 1991, 92, U.S. Open, 1991, 92, Australian Open, 1991, 92, 93, 96, Italian Open Doubles (with Kelesi) 1990, (with Capriati) 1991, (with Sukova), 1992, Essen, 1992, Indian Wells, 1992, Barcelona, 1992, Chgo., 1993, Can. Open, 1995, 96; finalist Dallas, 1989, Brighton, 1989, Palm Springs, 1991, U.S. Hardcourts, 1991, Hamburg, 1991, Italian Open, 1991, San Diego, 1991, Oakland, 1991, Wimbledon, 1992, Italian Open, 1992, L.A., 1992, Can. Open, 1992, Paris indoors, 1993, U.S. Open, 1995; singles semifinalist , New Orleans, 1988, Roland Garros, Washington, 1989, European indoors, 1989, Washington, 1990; doubles semifinalist (with A. Smith) Australian Open, 1991, (with Nagelsen), Chgo., 1993; named Yugoslavia's sportwoman of yr., 1985, World #1 ranked player, 1991, 92, #3 players in terms of career titles as a teenager, 1993; recipient 1990 Rado Topspin award, Ted Tinling Diamond award Va. Slims, 1990, Grand Slam Title, 1996; named Tennis Mag./Rolex Watch Female Rookie of Yr., 1989, World Champion, 1991, 92, Comeback Player of Yr. Tennis mag., 1995, Profl. Female Athlete by Yr., 1995. 3rd player in the Open-era to capture the Australian and Roland Garros in same calendar year; named youngest #1 ranked player in tennis history for women and men at 17 years, 3 months, 9 days. Office: care Internat Mgmt Group 1 Erieview Plz Cleveland OH 44114-1715

SELESKY, DONALD BRYANT, software developer; b. Englewood, N.J., Jan. 7, 1948; s. Harold Francis and Bernice Evelyn (Deacon) S.; m. Janet Borna (div.); m. Sandy Lynn Berke, Sept. 11, 1983. BA in Econ., Cornell U., 1970; MBA in Mktg., Columbia U., 1977; MS in Computer Sci., Boston U., 1990. Sr. Arthur Andersen & Co., N.Y.C., 1971-75; bus. sys. analyst Nabisco Inc., East Hanover, N.J., 1975-77; cons., 1977-81, 82-83; mgr. data processing Kings Dept. Stores, Watertown, Mass., 1981-82; sys. analyst The Analytical Scis. Corp., Reading, Mass., 1983-84; prin. software engr. Lotus Devel. Corp., Cambridge, Mass., 1984-86; prin. Ksoft, Westford, Mass., 1986—; sr. software engr. Kurzweil Applied Intelligence, Waltham, Mass., 1995—, product mgr., 1997; co-owner Pet Project, Westford, Mass., 1996—. Author (software program) @BASE, 1987; co-author (software program) Look and Link, 1988, Monarch, 1991, Monarch for Windows, 1994. Mem. Nashoba Valley Photo Club (pres.), Appalachian Mountain Club. Avocations: backpacking, photography, kayaking, shooting, biking. Home and Office: Ksoft 15 Bradley Ln Westford MA 01886-2544

SELF, CHARLES EDWIN, financial consultant, retail company executive; b. Roanoke, Va., June 6, 1934; s. Loy Evry and Louzelle (Childers) S.; m. Phyllis Ann Stevens, Sept. 2, 1961; children: Tim, Randy, Betsy. BA, Randolph Macon Coll., 1956. Budget specialist Gen. Electric Co., Schenectady, N.Y., 1960-64; merchandise contr. Montgomery Ward & Co., N.Y.C., 1964-67; contr. The Hecht Co., Washington, 1967-70; v.p., fin. contr. Zayre Corp., Framingham, Mass., 1970-79; v.p. fin. Wal-Mart Stores, Inc., Bentonville, Ark., 1979-87; pvt. practice fin. cons. Bellingham, Wash., 1987—; mem. fin. steering com. Nat. Mass Retail Inst., N.Y.C., 1980-86; chmn. Nat. Capital Group of Contrs., Washington, 1969; chmn., bd. dirs. Consumers' Choice Inc., Bellingham, Wash., 1990-94; bd. dirs. Bank of Bellingham, No. Automotive Corp., Phoenix. Commr. Conservation Commn., Mass., 1976-79; bd. dirs. Am. Field Svc., Ark., 1984, Whatcom Mus. History and Art, Bellingham, 1990-95, pres., 1994-95; trustee Western Found., Western Wash. U., 1991—, St. Luke's Found., 1994—, chm. bd., dirs., Bellingham Festival of Music, 1997—. Lt. USNR, 1956-60. Mem. B'Ham (Wash.) Yacht Club. Republican. Episcopalian. Avocations: boating, fishing, stained glass, woodwork. Home and Office: 324 Bayside Rd Bellingham WA 98225-7802

SELF, JAMES REED, librarian; b. Greeneville, Tenn., May 14, 1944; s. Rex Clive and Ethel (Reed) S.; m. Charlotte Clifford, Mar. 18, 1967; children—Jennifer Reed, Abigail Clifford. B.S., U. Tenn., 1967, M.A. in History, 1970; M.A. in Librarianship, U. Denver, 1971. Reference librarian Ind. U., Bloomington, 1971-78, head undergrad. library, 1978-81; dir. Clemons Library U. Va., Charlottesville, 1982—. Contbr. articles to profl. jours. Mem. ALA, Va. Library Assn. Office: University of Virginia Clemons Library Charlottesville VA 22904

SELF, LARRY DOUGLAS, architectural firm executive; b. Cleburne, Tex., Aug. 14, 1943. BArch, Tex. Tech U., 1968. Registered arch., Mo., Tex.; cert. Nat. Coun. Archtl. Registration Bds. Project designer Hellmuth, Obata & Kassabaum, Inc., St. Louis, 1968—; overseas dir. Hellmuth, Obata & Kassabaum, Inc., Riyadh, Saudi Arabia; dir. design, mng. prin. Hellmuth, Obata & Kassabaum, Inc., Dallas, 1980-91; exec. dir. Europe, bd. dirs. Hellmuth, Obata & Kassabaum, Inc., London, 1992-95, dir. corp. ops., 1995-96; exec. v.p. Hellmuth, Obata & Kassabaum, Inc., St. Louis, 1996—. Prin. works include Am South/Harbert Plz., Birmingham, Ala., Zale Corp. World Hdqrs., Dallas, Arco Exploration & Prodn., Rsch. Ctr., Plano, Tex., Collin County C.C., Plano, Cmty. Fedn. Ctr., St. Louis, Plano Civic Ctr., Xerox Rsch. Ctr., Palo Alto, Calif., Tuscon Mall, Aetna Life & Casualty Group Benefits Divsn. Hdqrs., Middletown, Conn., Albuquerque Plz. Hyatt Hotel, Riverchase Galleria Wyndham Hote, Birmingham, King Saud Univ., Riyadh, Saudi Arabia, others. Fellow AIA. Office: Hellmuth Obata & Kassabaum 211 N Broadway Saint Louis MO 63102-2733 Home: 7057 Kingsbury Blvd Saint Louis MO 63130-4305

SELF, MADISON ALLEN, chemical company executive; b. Ozawkie, Kans., June 30, 1921; s. Benjamin B. and Margaret E. (Allen) S.; m. Lila M. Reetz, Sept. 1, 1943; 1 son, Murray A. B.S. in Chem. Engring, U. Kans., 1943. Engr. York Corp., 1943-44; salesman and researcher Sharples Chems., Inc., 1944-47; with Bee Chem. Co., Lansing, Ill., 1947-84; chmn. bd., chief exec. officer Bee Chem. Co., until 1984; pres. Allen Fin., Inc., 1984—; chmn. bd. dirs. Tioga Internat., Inc., 1989—. Life trustee Ill. Inst. Tech. Mem. Chief Exec. Orgn., World Pres.'s Orgn., Hinsdale Golf Club. Office: Allen Fin Inc 1440 Huntington Dr Calumet City IL 60409-5464

SELF, PHYLLIS C., library director; b. Moline, Ill., Dec. 5, 1946; d. Charles Arthur and Henrietta Mary (Youngvorst) K.; m. David Alfred Self, June 22, 1968; 1 child, Linnea Christine. A.S., Black Hawk Coll., 1966; B.S., U. Ill., 1969, M.L.S., 1974, PhD, 1990. Jr. librarian R.I. Pub. Library, Rock Island, Ill., 1969-70; unit librarian Rockridge Sch. Unit, Edgington, Ill., 1970-71; biology tchr. Northwestern High Sch., Sciota, Ill., 1971-73; asst. phys. sci. librarian U. Ill., Urbana, 1974-75, asst. health scis. librarian, 1975-77, health scis. librarian, 1977-87, asst. dir. pub. services, 1980-84; health scis. libr., vis. instr. U. N.C., Chapel Hill, 1987-89; dir. Health Scis. Libr., U. Cin., Cin., 1989-91; head Tompkins-McCaw Libr., Va. Commonwealth U., Richmond, 1991—; cons. in Sudan WHO, Alexandria, Egypt, 1982. Editor: Physical Disabilities, 1984 (Presdl. commn. award 1985); contbr. articles to profl. jours. Mem. Med. Library Assn. (com. chmn. 1979—, pres. 1980 Midwest chpt.), Internat. Fedn. Librarians. Methodist. Avocations: travel; cooking; golf. Home: 320 Farnham Dr Richmond VA 23236-4025 Office: Va Commonwealth U - Med Coll Va Campus Tompkins McCaw Libr 509 N 12th St Richmond VA 23298-5015

SELF, W. M., textile company executive. Pres. Greenwood (S.C.) Mills. Inc., also bd. dirs. Office: Greenwood Mills Inc PO Box 1017 Greenwood SC 29648-1017*

SELFE, EDWARD MILTON, lawyer; b. St. Paul, Sept. 26, 1921; s. Edward Milton and Eleanor (Moen) S.; m. Rena Hill McMurry, July 10, 1950 (div. Oct. 1979); children: Murry, Edward, James; m. Jane Comer Bowron, Dec. 31, 1979. BA, Presbyn. Coll., Clinton, S.C., 1943; LLB, U. Va., 1950. Bar: N.Y., Va., Ala. Asst. prof. law Law Sch., U. Va., Charlottesville, 1950-51; assoc. Shearman & Sterling, N.Y.C., 1951-52; assoc. Bradley Arant Rose White, Birmingham, Ala., 1952-57, ptnr., 1957—; vice chmn. Secor Bank, Birmingham, 1988-91, gen. counsel, 1991-93. Chmn. Birmingham-Jefferson County Transit Authority, 1972-82. Served to capt., inf. U.S. Army, 1943-47, ETO. Decorated Silver Star, Bronze Star (V), Purple Heart. Fellow Am. Coll. Tax Counsel; mem. ABA, Ala. Bar Assn., Birmingham Bar Assn. Democrat. Avocation: tennis (ranked 22d nationally in men's singles-age 75). Home: Arlington Crest 84 2600 Arlington Ave Birmingham AL 35205-4164 Office: Bradley Arant Rose & White PO Box 830709 Birmingham AL 35283-0709

SELFRIDGE, CALVIN, lawyer; b. Evanston, Ill., Dec. 20, 1933; s. Calvin Frederick and Violet Luella (Bradley) S. BA, Northwestern U., 1956; JD, U. Chgo., 1960. Bar: Ill. 1961. Trust officer Continental Ill. Nat. Bank & Trust Co. Chgo., 1961-71; pvt. practice, Chgo., 1972-76, 79—; mem. Howington, Elworth, Osswald & Hough, Chgo., 1976-79; pres., dir. Northwest Newspapers Corp., Des Plaines Pub. Co., 1977-90. Pres., bd. dirs. Scholarship Fund Found., 1965—; trustee, corp. sec. Lawrence Hall Youth Svcs., 1982—; mem. Soc. Colonial Wars. With AUS, 1959. Mem. Chgo., Am., Ill. Bar Assn., Law Club Chgo., Legal Club Chgo., Chi Psi, Phi Delta Phi, Attic Club (gov., past pres.), Univ. Club, Racquet Club (Chgo.), Balboa Club (Mazatlan, Mex.), Indian Hill Country Club (Winnetka, Ill.). Republican. Congregationalist. Home: 4 Indian Hill Rd N Winnetka IL 60093 Office: 135 S La Salle St Ste 2145 Chicago IL 60603-4401

SELFRIDGE, GEORGE DEVER, dentist, retired naval officer; b. Pitman, N.J., Sept. 24, 1924; s. William John and Edith (Gorman) S.; m. Ruth Motisher, 1948; children: Pamela Ruth, Kimberly Dawn, Cheryl Beth. Student, Gettysburg Coll., 1942-43, Muhlenburg Coll., 1943-45; DDS, U. Buffalo, 1947; MA, George Washington U., 1974. Commd. lt. (j.g.) USN, 1948, advanced through grades to rear adm., 1973; intern Naval Dental Sch., Bethesda, Md., 1948-49, Naval Hosp., St. Albans, N.Y., 1949-50; various dental positions USN, 1951-64; sr. dental officer U.S.S. Cadmus, 1964-65, U.S.S. Vulcan, 1965-66, Svc. Force, 1964-66, Submarine Force, Atlantic Fleet, 1967-69; asst. dir. grad. edn. Navy Grad. Dental Sch., Bethesda, 1969-72, comdg. officer, 1973-76; exec. officer Norfolk (Va.) Navy Dental Clinic, 1972-73; ret. USN, 1976; dean Dental Sch., Washington U., St. Louis, 1976-86; dir. dental services Barnes Hosp., St. Louis, 1976-87, Children's Hosp., St. Louis, 1976-87; exec. dir. Am. Bd. Orthodontics, 1986—; mem. adv. bd. VA Hosp., St. Louis, 1977-79; mem. exec. coun. Cen. Region Testing Svc., 1976-86; mem. adv. com. St. Louis Jr. Coll. Dist., 1976-86. Contbr. articles to med. jours. Decorated Legion of Merit; recipient commendation medals, Greater St. Louis Gold Medallion award, 1995, Spl. Recognition award Am. Bd. Orthopedics, 1996. Mem. ADA, Am. Coll. Dentists, Internat. Coll. Dentists (dep. registrar, sec. U.S. sect.), Assn. Mil. Surgeons U.S., Omicron Kappa Upsilon. Republican. Home: 14545 Foxham Ct Chesterfield MO 63017-5620 Office: Am Bd Orthodontics 401 N Lindbergh Blvd Ste 308 Saint Louis MO 63141-7839

SELIG, ALLAN H. (BUD SELIG), professional baseball team executive; b. Milw., July 30, 1934; s. Ben and Marie Selig; m. Suzanne Lappin Steinman, Jan. 18, 1977; children: Sari, Wendy. Grad., U. Wis., Madison, 1956; LHD (hon.), Lakeland Coll., 1989. With Selig Ford (became Selig Chevrolet 1982), West Allis, Wis., 1959-90, pres., owner, 1966-90; with Selig Exec. Leasing Co., West Allis, 1959—, pres., owner, 1977—; part owner Milw. Braves (became Atlanta Braves 1965), 1963-65; co-founder Teams, Inc., 1964; co-owner, pres., chief exec. officer Milw. Brewers Baseball Club, Inc., 1970—; interim commr. Maj. League Baseball, 1991—; bd. dirs. Green Bay Packers Profl. Football Team. bd. dirs. Marcus Corp., Robert W. Baird & Co., Oil-Dri Corp. Am. Co-founder Child Abuse Prevention Fund, 1988. With U.S. Army, 1956-58. Recipient Major League Exec. of Yr. award UPI, 1978, Internat. B'nai B'rith Sportsman of Yr. award 1981, Sportsman of Yr. award U.S. Olympic Com., 1988, August A. Busch, Jr. award for long and meritorious svc. to baseball, 1989, Ellis Island Congl. medal of honor, 1993, Anti-Defamation League's "A World of Difference Award" 1994. Office: Milw Brewers Milw County Stadium PO Box 3099 Milwaukee WI 53201-3099

SELIG, KARL-LUDWIG, language and literature educator; b. Wiesbaden, Germany, Aug. 14, 1926; naturalized, 1948; s. Lucian and Erna (Reiss) S. B.A., Ohio State U., 1946, M.A., 1947; postgrad., U. Rome, Italy, 1949-50; Ph.D., U. Tex., 1955. Asst. prof. Romance langs. and lit. Johns Hopkins U., Balt., 1954-58; assoc. prof. U. N.C., Chapel Hill, 1958-61, U. Minn., Mpls., 1961-63; vis. prof. U. Tex., Austin, 1963-64, prof. Romance langs. and lit., 1964-65; Hinchliff prof. Spanish lit. Cornell U., Ithaca, N.Y., 1965-69; dir. grad. studies in Romance lit. Cornell U., Ithaca, 1966-69; prof. Spanish lit. Columbia U., N.Y.C., 1969—; Brown Found. fellow, vis. prof. Spanish and comparative lit. U. of the South, Sewanee, Tenn., 1990; vis. prof. U. Munich, 1963-64, U. Berlin, 1967, U. Greifswald, Germany, 1992—; hon. prof. U. Greifswald, 1996—; cons. prof. Ohio State U., Columbus, 1967-69; vis. lectr. U. Zulia, Maracaibo, Venezuela, 1968; dir. summer seminar NEH, 1975, cons., 1975-77; vis. scholar Ga. U. Sys., 1977; vis. rsch. scholar Fondation Hardt, Vandoeuvres, Switzerland, 1959, Herzog August Bibliothek Wolfenbüttel, Fed. Repubic Germany, 1979—; mem. com. grants-in-aid Am. Coun. Learned Soc., 1969-73; chmn. Comparative Lit. Program and Colloquia, Columbia Coll., 1976-88. Author: The Library of Vincencio Juan de Lastanosa, Patron of Gracián, Geneva, 1960, Studies on Alciato in Spain, 1990, Studies on Cervantes, 1992; also numerous articles, revs.; editor:

(Thomas Blundeville) of Councils and Counselors, 1963, (with A. G. Hatcher) Studia Philologica et Litteraria in Honorem L. Spitzer, 1958, (with J. E. Keller) Essays in Honor of N. B. Adams, 1966, (with R. Brinkmann) Theatrum Europaeum. Festschrift E. M. Szarota, 1982, (with S. Neumeister) Theatrum Mundi Hispanicum, 1986, (with R. Somerville) Florilegium Columbianum: Essays in Honor of Paul Oskar Kristeller, 1987, (with E. Sears) The Verbal and the Visual: Essays in Honor of William Sebastian Heckscher, 1990, Polyanthea Essays on Art and Literature in Honor of William Sebastian Heckscher, 1993; assoc. editor Modern Lang. Notes, 1955-58; mng. editor Romance Notes, 1959-61; editor: U. N.C. Studies in Comparative Lit, 1959-61, Bull. Comediantes, 1959-64, assoc. editor 1964-68, 79—; co-editor Yearbook of Comparative Lit., Vol. IX, 1960; editorial bd. Colección Támesis, London, 1962-79, Romanic Rev., 1969-89, Teaching Lang. Through Lit, 1978-88; assoc. editor Hispania, 1969-74, Ky. Romance Quar, 1973-85; gen. editor Revista Hispánica Moderna, 1971-86; mem. nat. adv. bd. MLA Internat. Bibliography, 1978-88; editorial bd. Yale Italian Studies, 1976-80. Recipient Mark Van Doren award Columbia, 1974, spl. citation Columbia Coll. Alumni Assn., 1991; fellow Fulbright Found., Rome, 1949-50, Newberry Library, 1958, Folger Shakespeare Library, 1959, 63, Belgian Am. Ednl. Found., 1961, 62; sr. fellow Mediaeval and Renaissance Inst. Duke U., 1978; Fulbright research scholar Utrecht, The Netherlands, 1958-59. Mem. MLA (sec., then chmn. Romance sect. 1965-66, chmn. comparative lit. 1973, James Russell Lowell prize com. 1989-90, chmn. 1990), Am. Friends of Herzog August Bibliothek (bd. dirs.), Internat. Assn. Hispanists, Am. Comparative Lit. Assn., Coll. Art Assn., Acad. Lit. Studies, Phi Beta Kappa (hon.). Home: 30 E 37th St New York NY 10016-3019

SELIG, WILLIAM GEORGE, university official; b. Prince Rupert, B.C., Can., Sept. 25, 1938; s. George Oliver Selig and Minerva Junuetta (Brand) Goodale; m. Judith Margaret Sprague, June 20, 1964; children: Cheryl, Cynthia. BA, Cen. Washington State Coll., 1961, MA, 1968; CAGS, U. Mass., 1972, EdD, 1973. Tchr. Sharon (Mass.) High Sch., 1963-64, Hydaburg (Alaska) Grade Sch., 1964-65, W. Puyallup (Wash.) Jr. High Sch., 1966-69; dir. spl. edn. Northampton (Mass.) Schs., 1969-73, 1974-76; asst. prof. Westfield (Mass.) State Coll., 1973; dir. pupil svcs. Longmeadow (Mass.) Pub. Schs., 1976-80; prof. Regent U., Virginia Beach, Va., 1980-83, dean, prof., 1984-89, provost, 1989—; bd. dirs. Set Net, Virginia Beach; pres. Motivational Teaching Systems, Inc.; spl. edn. adv. bd. dirs. Virginia Beach Pub. Schs.; bd. trustees Klingberg Family Ctrs., New Britain, Conn., 1991—. Author: Training for Triumph, 1984, Loving Our Differences, 1989, Handbook of Individualized Strategies for Classroom Discipline, 1995. Episcopalian. Avocations: skiing, tennis. Office: Regent University 1000 Regent University Dr Virginia Beach VA 23464-5037

SELIGER, MARK ALAN, photographer; b. Amarillo, Tex., May 23, 1959; s. Maurice and Carol Lee (Singer) S. BS, East Tex. State U., 1981. Contbg. photographer Rolling Stone Mag., N.Y.C., 1989-93, chief photographer, 1993—. Recipient Excellence in Journalism award Page One, 1988, Excellence awards Comm. Arts, 1988, 89, 90, 91, 92, 93, Creativity certs. Distinction Art Direction Mag., 1989, 93, Merit award Art Dirs. Club, 1991, Distinctive Merit award 1991, 92, Excellence certs. Am. Photography, 1991, 92, Distinctive Merit awards Soc. Pub. Designers, 1992, Distinguished Alumni award East Tex. State U., 1993; Mark Seliger Photography Scholarship named in his honor East Tex. State U., 1994. Mem. Am. Soc. Mag. Photographers. Office: Rolling Stone Mag 1290 Avenue Of The Americas New York NY 10104-0199

SELIGMAN, DANIEL, editor; b. N.Y.C., Sept. 25, 1924; s. Irving and Clare (O'Brien) S.; m. Mary Gale Sherburn, May 23, 1953; children: Nora, William Paul. Student, Rutgers U., 1941-42; A.B., NYU, 1946. Editl. asst. New Leader, 1946; asst. editor Am. Mercury, 1946-50; assoc. editor Fortune, 1950-59, editl. bd., 1959-66, asst. mng. editor, 1966-69, exec. editor, 1970-77, assoc. mng. editor, 1977-87, contbg. editor, 1988-97; contbg. editor Forbes, 1997; sr. staff editor all Time, Inc. (publs.), 1969-70; contbg. editor Forbes, 1997—. Author: A Question of Intelligence: The IQ Debate in America, 1992. Home: 190 E 72nd St New York NY 10021-4370

SELIGMAN, FREDERICK, lawyer; b. Bklyn.; s. Martin and Florence (Alperin) S.; m. Delice Felice. AB, Clark U., 1957; JD, N.Y. Law Sch., 1972. Bar: N.Y. 1973, U.S. Dist. Ct. (so. and ea. dists.) N.Y. 1974, U.S. Tax Ct. 1974, U.S. Ct. Appeals (2d cir.) 1975, U.S. Supreme Ct. 1979. Atty. N.Y.C. (N.Y.) Police Dept., 1972-73; asst. dist. atty. N.Y. County, N.Y.C., 1973-79; pvt. practice N.Y.C., 1980-85; ptnr. Seligman & Seligman, N.Y.C., 1986—. Mem. N.Y. Criminal Bar Assn., N.Y. State Defenders Assn. Home: Runge Rd Shokan NY 12481 Office: Seligman & Seligman 26 Broadway New York NY 10004-1703

SELIGMAN, GEORGE BENHAM, mathematics educator; b. Attica, N.Y., Apr. 30, 1927; s. George Frederick and Florence Rose (Benham) S.; m. Irene Alice Schwieder, July 31, 1959; children: Barbara, Karen. AB, U. Rochester, 1950; MA, Yale U., 1951, PhD, 1954. Instr. math. Princeton (N.J.) U., 1954-56; instr. math. Yale U., New Haven, 1956-57, asst. prof., 1957-60, assoc. prof., 1960-65, prof., 1965-82, James E. English prof., 1982-97, prof. emeritus, 1997—. Author: Modular Lie Algebras, 1967, Rational Methods, 1976, Constructions of Lie Algebras and Their Modules, 1988; mem. editorial bd. Am. Scientist, 1980-90. With USNR, 1945-46. Mem. AAUP, Am. Math. Soc. (con. mem.), Math. Assn. Am. Democrat. Avocation: gardening. Home: 143 Woodlawn St Hamden CT 06517-1341 Office: Yale U Dept Math PO Box 208283 New Haven CT 06520-8283

SELIGMAN, JOEL, law educator; b. N.Y.C., Jan. 11, 1950; s. Selig Jacob and Muriel (Bienstock) S.; m. Friederike Felber, July 30, 1981; children: Andrea, Peter. AB magna cum laude, UCLA, 1971; JD, Harvard U., 1974. Bar: Calif. 1975. Atty., writer Corp. Accountability Rsch. Group, Washington, 1974-77; prof. law Northeastern U. Law Sch., 1977-83, George Washington U., 1983-86, U. Mich., Ann Arbor, 1986-95; dean law U. Ariz., Tucson, 1995—; cons. Fed. Trade Commn., 1979-82, Dept. Transp., 1983, Office Tech. Assessment, 1988-89. Author (with others) Constitutionalizing the Corporation: The Case for the Federal Chartering of Giant Corporations, 1976, The High Citadel: The Influence of Harvard Law School, 1978, The Transformation of Wall Street: A History of the Securities and Exchange Commission and Modern Corporate Finance, 1982, The SEC and the Future of Finance, 1985, (multi-volume) Securities Regulation; contbr. articles to profl. jours. Mem. State Bar Calif., Am. Law Inst. (adv. com., advisor corp. governance project). Office: The U Ariz Coll Law Speedway & Mountain Tucson AZ 85721-0176

SELIGMAN, MARTIN E. P., psychologist; b. Albany, N.Y., Aug. 12, 1942; s. Adrian and Irene Seligman; A.B., Princeton U., 1964; Ph.D. in Psychology, U. Pa., 1967; PhD (hon.) Uppsala U., Sweden, 1989, Mass. Coll. Profl. Psychology, 1997; m. Mandy M. Seligman; children—Amanda, David, Lara, Nicole, Darryl. Asst. prof. Cornell U., 1967-70; assoc. prof. psychology U. Pa., 1972-76, prof., 1976—, dir. clin. program, 1980-94; vis. fellow Maudsley Hosp. Inst. Psychiatry, U. London, 1975; hon. prof. psychology U. Wales, Cardiff. Recipient MERIT award, 1991, James McKeen Cattell Fellow award Am. Psychol. Soc., 1995; NIMH grantee, 1969—; NSF fellow, 1963-64, Woodrow Wilson fellow, 1964-65, Guggenheim fellow, 1974-75; Center Advanced Study in Behavioral Scis. fellow, 1978-79; lic. psychologist, Pa. Fellow AAAS, Am. Psychol. Assn. (pres. divsn. clin. psychology 1993-95, William James Fellow award 1992, pres. 1997-99); mem. Ea. Psychol. Assn. (bd. dirs.), Psychonomic Soc., Assn. Advancement Behavior Therapy, Am. Psychopathol. Assn., Am. Psychosomatic Soc., Phi Beta Kappa, Sigma Xi. Author: Helplessness, 1975, Learned Optimism, 1991, What You Can Change & What You Can't, 1993, The Optimistic Child, 1995; contbr. numerous articles to profl. jours. Office: 3815 Walnut St Philadelphia PA 19104-3604

SELIGMAN, THOMAS KNOWLES, museum administrator; b. Santa Barbara, Calif., Jan. 1, 1944; s. Joseph L. and Peggy (Van Horne) S.; children: Christopher, Timothy, Dylan. BA, Stanford U., 1965; BFA with honors, San Francisco Acad. Art, 1967; MFA, Sch. Visual Art, N.Y.C., 1968. Tchr., mus. dir. Peace Corps, Liberia, 1968-70; curator dept. Africa, Oceania and Ams. Fine Arts Museums, San Francisco, 1971-88; dep. dir. edn. and exhbns. Fine Arts Museums, 1972-88, dep. dir. ops. and planning, 1988-91; dir. Stanford (Calif.) U. Mus. Art, 1991—; mem. cultural property adv. com. USIA, 1988-92, Nat. Endowment for Art Indemnity Panel, 1992-95. Author mus. catalogues, articles in field. Trustee Internat. Coun. Mus./Am. Assn. Mus., 1990-94, Am. Fedn. Arts; mem. adv. coun. Acad. Art Coll. Grad. Program. Fellow Nat. Endowment Arts, 1974-75, 87. Mem. Assn. Art Mus. Dirs., Am. Assn. Mus., Leaky Found. Address: Stanford U Mus Art Stanford CA 94305-5060

SELIGMANN, WILLIAM ROBERT, lawyer, author; b. Davenport, Iowa, Oct. 10, 1956; s. William Albert and Barbara Joyce (Carmichael) S.; m. Carole Lee Francis; children: D Anna, Matthew. BA, U. Calif., Santa Barbara, 1979; JD, Santa Clara U., 1982. Bar: Calif. 1983, U.S. Dist. Ct. (no. dist.) Calif. 1983. Assoc. Office of J.R. Dempster, Cupertino, Calif., 1983-85; city atty. City of Campbell, Calif., 1985—; ptnr. Dempster, Seligmann & Raineri, Los Gatos, Calif., 1985—; pro tem Mcpl. Ct. Calif., Los Gatos, 1992—. Bd. dirs. Los Galos C. of C. Mem. ABA, Santa Clara County Bar Assn., Am. Trial Lawyers Assn., Better Bus. Bur. Avocations: cross country skiing, scuba diving, swimming, writing, Aikido. Office: Dempster Seligmann & Raineri 3 1/2 N Santa Cruz Ave # A Los Gatos CA 95030-5916

SELIGSON, CARL HAROLD, management consultant; b. N.Y.C., Feb. 25, 1935; s. Harold P. and Lilian (Yohalem) S.; m. Joan Escott, May 19, 1957 (div. Nov. 1969); children: Susan S. Pattenaude, Barbara C.; m. Bonnie Laskin, Mar. 6, 1983. AB, Brown U., 1956; postgrad., NYU Grd. Sch. Bus. Adminstrn., 1961-63. Textile salesman Cohn, Hall, Marx Co., Montreal, Can., 1958-61; security analyst Burnham & Co., N.Y.C., 1961-67, Kuhn, Loeb & Co, N.Y.C., 1967-71; mng. dir. Merrill Lynch Capital Markets, N.Y.C., 1971-87, Kidder, Peabody & Co., N.Y.C., 1987-90; sr. exec. cons. regulated industries Deloitte & Touche, N.Y.C., 1990-92; mng. dir. Prudential Securities, N.Y.C., 1992-95; sr. advisor Andersen Consulting, N.Y.C., 1996—. Contbr. articles to profl. jours. including Pub. Utilities Fortnightly, Telephony, Fin. Exec., The Southern Banker, Coal Monthly and Energy News. Bd. dirs. Nuclear Energy Inst., Washington, 1988-95. With U.S. Army Counter Intelligence Corps. Fellow Fin. Analysts Fedn.; mem. Brown U. Club. Avocations: water sports, travel, theatre. Home: 40 E 94th St New York NY 10128-0709

SELIGSON, MITCHELL A., Latin American studies educator; b. Hempstead, N.Y., Nov. 12, 1945; s. Morris and Ethel (Finkel) S.; m. Susan Berk, June 18, 1967; 1 child, Amber Lara. BA, Bklyn. Coll., 1967; MA, U. Fla., 1968; PhD, U. Pitts., 1974. Vol. U.S. Peace Corps, Costa Rica, 1968-70; asst. prof./assoc. prof. U. Ariz., Tucson, 1974-85; prof. U. Pitts., 1986-93, Daniel H. Wallace prof. polit. sci., 1994—, dir. Latin Am. studies, 1986-92, rsch. prof., 1992—; cons. to U.S. AID, Guatemala, Honduras, Nicaragua, Costa Rica, Ecuador, Jamaica, Panama, El Salvador, Peru, Paraguay, 1980—. Author, editor: Peasants of Costa Rica and the Development of Agrarian Capitalism, 1980, The Gap Between Rich and Poor, 1984, Authoritarians and Democrats, 1987, Elections and Democracy in Central America, 1989, rev. edit. 1995, Development and Underdevelopment, 1993. Fulbright fellow, Costa Rica, 1986, Rockefeller Found. fellow, 1985-86; grantee Social Sci. Rsch. Coun., Ford Found., NSF, Mellon Found., Heinz Endowment. Mem. Am. Polit. Sci. Assn., Latin Am. Studies Assn. (chmn. fin. com. 1991). Office: U Pitts Dept Polit Sci Pittsburgh PA 15260

SELIGSON, THEODORE H., architect, interior designer, art consultant; b. Kansas City, Mo., Nov. 10, 1930; s. Harry and Rose (Haith) S.; m. Jacqueline Rose, Dec. 27, 1964 (div. 1976). BArch, Washington U., St. Louis, 1953. Registered architect, Mo., Kans. Intern Marshall & Brown, Kansas City, Mo., 1949-54; designer, head design Kivett & Myers, Kansas City, Mo., 1954-62; prin. Design Assocs., 1955—, Atelier Seligson, Kansas City, Mo., 1962-64; pres. Seligson, Eggen, Inc., Kansas City, 1964-73, Seligson Assocs., Inc., Architects Planners, Kansas City, 1973—; Seligson Assocs., Inc., Archs. Planners, Kansas City, 1973-97; prin. Foss, Seligson, Lafferty, 1997—; vis. lectr. adult edn. U. Mo.-Kansas City, 1958-61, vis. prof. arch., 1989-97; tchr., critic Kansas City Art Inst., Mo., 1961-64, 71-72, adj. prof., 1986, 89, 91, 92; adj. prof. Kansas State U., 1991-92, 97; vis. prof. Washington U., St. Louis, 1975, 77, 78, 81, 86, 91, U. Kans., Lawrence, 1978, 79, 80, 91, 92; art cons. Design Assocs., Kansas City, Mo., 1955—. Projects pub. in archtl. jours. V.p. Friends of Art Nelson-Atkins Mus. Art, Kansas City, bd. dirs. 1963-67, chmn. selections com., 1981, vis. curator, 1972, 87; chmn. Capitol Fine Arts Commn. Mo., 1983-90, Kansas City Worlds Fair goals and themes subcom., 1985-90; bd. dirs. Westport Tomorrow, Kansas City, 1980-87, Hist. Kansas City Found., 1984-90; pres. Native Sons of Kansas City, 1989, bd. dirs. 1978-94, Westport Cmty. Coun., 1973-75. Recipient Urban Design award Kansas City Mcpl. Art Commn., 1968, 74, 78; Nat. Archtl. award Am. Inst. Steel Constrn., 1970; Nat. award ASID/DuPont Corian, 1989. Fellow AIA, Kansas City chpt. AIA (pres. 1983, bd. dirs. 1979-84, Design Excellence award 1966, 68, 70, 74, Cen. States Regional award 1974, 78, Honor award for outstanding svc. to chpt. and profession 1982-83); mem. Mo. Coun. Archs., Am. Soc. Interior Designers, Nat. Coun. Archtl. Registration Bds. (task analysis adv. com. 1988-90), Soc. Archtl. Historians (pres. 1973-75, bd. dirs. 1994-97). Jewish. Office: Foss Seligson Lafferty 106 W 14th St Kansas City MO 64105-1906

SELIN, IVAN, entrepreneur; b. N.Y.C., Mar. 11, 1937; s. Saul and Freda (Kuhlman) Selin; m. Nina Kallet, June 8, 1957; children: Douglas, Jessica. B.E., Yale U., 1957, M.E., 1958, Ph.D., 1960; Dr. es Sciences, U. Paris, 1962. Rsch. engr. Rand Corp., Santa Monica, Calif., 1960-65; systems analyst Dept. Def., Washington, 1965-67, dep. asst. sec. def., 1967-69, acting asst. sec. for systems analysis, 1969-70; founder, chmn. bd. Am. Mgmt. Systems, Inc., Arlington, Va., 1970-89; undersec. state Dept. State, Washington, 1989-91; chmn. NRC, Washington, 1991-95; chmn., CEO Phoenix Internat., Washington, 1995—; lectr. UCLA, 1961-63; chmn. mil. econ. adv. panel to CIA, 1978-89. Author: Detection Theory, 1964; contbr. articles to profl. jours. Pres. Corp. Against Drug Abuse, 1988-95; bd. dirs., gov. UN Assn. U.S., 1979-89; mem. exec. com. Greater Washington Research Ctr., Fed. City Council; trustee Asia Soc., 1996—; chmn., bd. dirs. Smithsonian Nat. Mus. of Am. History, 1996—. Decorated Disting. Civilian Svc. medal, 1970; recipient Disting. Svc. medal Sec. of State, 1991; Fulbright scholar, 1959-61; Ford Found. grantee, 1952-54. Mem. Council Fgn. Relations, Fed. City Council Washington (trustee), IEEE (editor Trans. on Ifo. Theory 1960-65), Sigma Xi, Tau Beta Pi. Clubs: Yale, Cosmos. Home: 2905 32nd St NW Washington DC 20008-3526 Office: Phoenix Internat Inc 1050 17th St NW Washington DC 20036-5503

SELINGER, JERRY ROBIN, lawyer; b. Peekskill, N.Y., Nov. 3, 1947; s. Philip R. and Helen D. (Klein) S.; m. Barbara D. Wax, Aug. 2, 1969; children—Elise, Scott. B.S. in Engr. Sci., SUNY-Buffalo, 1969; M.S., Columbia U., 1971; J.D., George Washington U., 1975. Bar: Md. 1975, D.C. 1976, U.S. Ct. Appeals (fed. cir.) 1977, U.S. Supreme Ct. 1978, Tex. 1980, U.S. Ct. Appeals (5th and 11th cirs.) 1981, U.S. Ct. Appeals (3d cir.) 1982. Atty. firm Arent, Fox, Kintner, Plotkin & Kahn, Washington, 1975-79, Richards, Harris & Medlock, Dallas, 1979-82; mem., dir. Baker, Mills & Glast, Dallas, 1982-90; ptnr. Vinson & Elkins L.L.P., Dallas, 1990; shareholder Jenkens & Gilchrist, Dallas, 1990—. Contbr. articles to profl. jours. Mem. ABA, Tex. Bar Assn. (chair intellectual property law sect. 1996-97), Dallas Bar Assn. (bd. dirs. 1995-96), Tex. Young Lawyers Assn. (bd. dirs. 1984-86, Pres.'s award 1986), Am. Patent Law Assn., Dallas Assn. Young Lawyers (sec. 1983, treas. 1984), Order of Coif, Phi Delta Phi. Home: 10414 Woodford Dr Dallas TX 75229-6317 Office: Jenkens & Gilchrist 1445 Ross Ave Dallas TX 75202-2812

SELKE, OSCAR O., JR., physiatrist, educator; b. Houston, Mar. 13, 1917; s. Oscar Otto and Orile Mollie (Medlenka) S.; m. Edith Hicks Hardey, July 10, 1943; children: Charles Richard, Carolyn Selke Brophy, Barbara Selke-Kern, Bruce Hardey. BA, U. Tex., 1938; MD, U. Tex., Galveston, 1941; postgrad., U. Pa., 1945-46. Diplomate Am. Bd. Phys. Medicine and Rehab. Intern, resident Hermann Hosp., Houston, chief phys. medicine and rehab., 1946-76, chief emeritus, 1977—, med. dir. sch. phys. therapy, 1947-65; mem. clin. faculty phys. medicine and rehab. Baylor U. Coll. of Medicine, 1950—, emeritus, 1985—; chief phys. medicine and rehab. Methodist Hosp., 1952-60, St. Luke's Hosp., 1953-63, Tex. Children's Hosp., 1953-63, Ctr. Pavilion Hosp., 1966-77, Park Plaza Hosp., 1975—; mem. clin. faculty phys. medicine and rehab. U. Tex. Post-grad. Sch. of Medicine, 1952-63, U. Tex. Med. Sch., Houston, 1972—; area cons. VA in Phys. Medicine and Rehab., 1950-66; med. adv. bd. United Cerebral Palsy of Tex., 1959-73, bd. dirs., 1967-70, Gulf Coast, 1971-74; bd. dirs. Harris County Cerebral Palsy Treatment Ctr., 1947-50, 68-71, pres., 1952, med. adv. bd., 1947-70; bd. dirs. Muscular Dystrophy Assn. Gulf Coast, pres., 1953; med. adv. bd. Muscular Dystropy Assn. Am., 1972-76; bd. dirs. Child Guidance Ctr. of Houston, 1949-55, Soc. Crippled Children and Adults, Houston, 1958-62; mem. adv. bd. Harris County Muscular Dystrophy Assn., 1950-76, Harris County Multiple Sclerosis Soc., 1958-60, Am. Rehab. Found., 1961-66; mem. bd. Am. Registry of Phys. Therapists, 1957-71. Mem. editorial bd. Archives of Phys. Medicine and Rehab., 1957-72. Capt. USAF, 1942-45. Mem. AMA (residency rev. com. phys. medicine and rehab. 1970-75, past chmn. phys. medicine and rehab sect., Cert. of Appreciation 1975), Am. Assn. Electromyography and Electrodiagnosis, Am. Acad. Phys. Medicine and Rehab., Am. Congress Rehab. Medicine, Tex. Phys. Medicine and Rehab. Soc. (past pres.), Tex. State Med. Assn., Harris County Med. Assn., Houston Phys. Medicine and Rehab. Soc. (past pres.). Presbyterian. Avocations: writing, growing orchids. Home: 3646 Olympia Dr Houston TX 77019-3028

SELKIRK, JAMES KIRKWOOD, biochemist; b. N.Y.C., Dec. 3, 1938; s. James Kirkwood and Doris (Schuler) S.; m. Carole Ann Bozzone, Sept. 16, 1961; children: James Kirkwood, David Edward. BS, Coll. Environ. Sci. and Forestry, Syracuse (N.Y.) U., 1964; PhD, Syracuse U. Upstate Med. Ctr., Syracuse, 1969. Postdoctoral fellow McArdle Lab. Cancer Rsch., U. Wis., Madison, 1969-72; staff fellow Nat. Cancer Inst., NIH, Bethesda, Md., 1972-74, sr. staff fellow, 1974-75; sr. staff scientist unit leader chem. carcinogenesis biology divsn. Oak Ridge (Tenn.) Nat. Lab., 1975-85; chief carcinogenesis and toxicology evaluation br. nat. toxicology program Nat. Inst. Environ. Health Scis., 1985—, assoc. dir. divsn. toxicology rsch. and testing, 1989-92, chmn. carcinogen mechanism group Lab. Molecular Carcinogenesis, 1992—; adj. prof. Oak Ridge Biomed. Grad. Sch., U. Tenn., 1975-85; mem. breast cancer task force NIH, 1979-82; mem. com. on pyrenes and analogs NAS, 1981-83; chmn. Interagy. Testing Commn., 1986-90. Author rsch. articles, chpts. in books; mem. editorial bd. Carcinogenesis Jour., 1984-87, 91—, Cancer Rsch., 1981-86, Environ. Perspectives, 1993—. Mem. Orange County Planning Bd., 1997—; chmn. Weaver Dairy Precinct, Dem. Party Orange County, 1996—. With AUS, 1959-61. Recipient U.S. Interagy. Testing Com. Exemplary Svc. award, 1992. Mem. Am. Cancer Soc. (carcinogenesis study sect. 1992-96). Home: 113 Basswood Ct Chapel Hill NC 27514-1610 Office: Nat Inst Environ Health Scis PO Box 12333 Research Triangle Park NC 27709

SELKOE, DENNIS JESSE, neurologist, researcher, educator; b. N.Y.C., Sept. 25, 1943; mem. neurosci. adv. com. Howard Hughes Med. Inst., 1996—; s. Herbert E. and Mary P. (Lille) S.; m. Polly Ann Strasser, June 24, 1967; children: Gregory, Kimberly. BA, Columbia U., 1965; MD, U. Va., 1969. Diplomate Am. Bd. Psychiatry and Neurology, Nat. Bd. Med. Examiners. Intern in medicine Hosp. U. Pa., Phila., 1969-70; rsch. assoc. NIH, Bethesda, Md., 1970-72; resident in neurology Peter Bent Brigham/Children's Hosp., Boston, 1972-74, chief resident in neurology, 1974-75; rsch. assoc. Harvard U. Med. Sch., Boston, 1975-78, asst. prof. neurology, 1978-82, assoc. prof., 1982-85, assoc. prof. neurology and neurosci., 1985-90, faculty mem. div. on aging, 1980—, prof. neurology and neurosci., 1990—; co-dir. Ctr. Neurologic Diseases Brigham and Women's Hosp., Boston, 1985—; mem. sci. adv. bd. Alzheimer's Disease Assn., Chgo., 1983-89; mem. Gov.'s Commn. on Alzheimer's Disease, Mass., 1985-87. Author over 200 articles, book chpts. on biochemistry and molecular biology of Alzheimer's Disease. Asst. surgeon USPHS, 1970-72. Recipient Wood-Kalb Found. prize Alzheimers Disease Assn., 1984, Med. Rsch. award Met. Life Found., 1986, LEAD award Nat. Inst. on Aging, 1988, NIH Merit award, 1991—, Arthur Chertin award UCLA, 1995; grantee Bristol-Myers Squibb Neurosci., 1990. Fellow Am. Acad. Neurology (Potamkin prize 1989); mem. Am. Neurol. Assn., Soc. for Neurosci., Am. Assn. Neuropathologists, World Fedn. Neurologists, AAAS. Office: Harvard Med Sch Brigham & Womens Hosp 221 Longwood Ave Boston MA 02115-5822

SELKOWITZ, ARTHUR, advertising agency executive; b. N.Y.C., May 26, 1943; s. Harry and Anne (Lichten) S.; m. Betsey Wattenberg, Apr. 15, 1967; children: Adam, Jed. AB, Syracuse (N.Y.) U., 1965. Account exec. Dancer Fitzgerald Sample, 1969-71; with Benton & Bowles, Inc., N.Y.C., 1971-82; v.p., account supr. Benton & Bowles, Inc., 1972-75, sr. v.p., mgmt. supr., 1975-81, sr. v.p., account dir., 1981-82; founder, pres. Penchina, Selkowitz Inc., N.Y.C., 1982-90; exec. v.p. internat. D'Arcy, Masius, Benton & Bowles, N.Y.C., 1990-94, pres. Asia and Pacific, 1995-96, pres. N.Am., 1996-97, chmn., CEO, 1997—, also bd. dirs.; bd. dirs. Medicus Group Internat., Manning Selvage & Lee Pub. Rels. Dancer Fitzgerald Sample, N.Y.C., 1966-71. Office: 1675 Broadway New York NY 10019-5820

SELKOWITZ, LUCY ANN, security officer; b. Pitts., Oct. 15, 1956; d. Thomas Francis and Matilda Margaret (Carlini) Donato; m. Jeremiah Anthony Barry, Jan. 10, 1976 (div. July 1979); 1 child, Jeremiah; m. Stanley Irwin Selkowitz, Aug. 19, 1987; children: Lori, Lee, Mattie. Grad., William Boyd, 1974. Cert. EMT, Pa. Owner, buyer Tillie's Antiques, Pitts., 1972-86; legal aide Selkowitz & Assoc., Pitts., 1986-94; armed security officer Wackenhut Corp., Pitts., 1994—. Dance performer Shade Sisters, 1992—. Counselor troubled youths, Clairton, Pa., 1986—; active PTA, chair 1995—. Mrs. Am. Finalist, 1990-91. Avocations: jet skiing, camping, animal care, on-stage dance performer. Home: 100 Farm Ln Jefferson Boro PA 15025 Office: Wackenhut Inc Rt 88 Castle Shannon PA 15234

SELL, EDWARD SCOTT, JR., lawyer; b. Athens, Ga., Mar. 13, 1917; s. Edward Scott and Nettie Ruth (Whatley) S.; m. Mary Deupree Eckford, Sept. 14, 1940; 1 son, Edward Scott. A.B., U. Ga., 1937, J.D. cum laude, 1939. Bar: Ga. bar 1938. Ptnr. firm Lewis & Sell, 1940-55, Lane & Sell, 1955-56, Sell & Comer, Macon, Ga., 1956-69, Sell, Comer & Popper, Macon, 1969-80, Sell & Melton, 1980—; city atty., Macon, 1947-53; atty. Macon-Bibb County Planning & Zoning Commn., 1953-65; county atty. Bibb County, Ga., 1965—; lectr. law Mercer U., 1958-60. Trustee Wesleyan Coll., Macon, 1973-96, emeritus, 1997—. Served with U.S. Army, 1942-46. Decorated Bronze Star, Army Commendation medal. Fellow Am. Bar Found.; mem. State Bar Ga. (bd. govs. 1947-50), Macon Bar Assn. (past pres.), Macon Cir. Bar Assn. (past pres.), City Club of Macon, River North Club, Lions, Shriners, Masons, Phi Beta Kappa, Phi Kappa Phi, Phi Delta Phi. Clubs: City Club of Macon, Lions, Shriners, Masons, River North. Home: 1644 Hawthorne Rd Macon GA 31211-1213 Office: PO Box 229 Macon GA 31202-0229

SELL, ROBERT EMERSON, electrical engineer; b. Freeport, Ill., Apr. 23, 1929; s. Cecil Leroy and Ona Arletta (Stevens) S.; m. Ora Lucile Colton, Nov. 7, 1970. B.S., U. Nebr., 1962. Registered profl. engr., Nebr., Mo., Ill., Ind., Ohio, W.Va., Ky., Ark., Tex., Oreg., Wash., Calif. Chief draftsman Dempster Mill Mfg. Co., Beatrice, Nebr., 1949-53; designer-engr. U. Neb., Lincoln, 1955-65; elec. design engr. Kirkham, Michael & Assos., Omaha, 1965-67; elec. design engr. Leo A. Daly Co., Omaha, St. Louis, 1967-69; mech. design engr. Hellmuth, Obata, Kassabaum, St. Louis, 1969-70; chief elec. engr. Biagi-Hannan & Assos., Inc., Evansville, Ind., 1971-74; elec. project engr. H.L. Yoh Co., under contract to Monsanto Co., Creve Coeur, Mo., 1974-77; elec. project engr. Dhillon Engrs., Inc., Portland, Oreg., 1978-85; project coordinator Brown-Zammit-Enyeart Engring., Inc., San Diego, 1985-88; elec. engr. Morgen Design, Inc., San Diego, 1988; lead elec. engr. Popov Engrs., Inc., San Diego, 1988-89; mech. and elect. specialist Am. Engring. Labs., Inc. div. Prof. Svc. Industries, Inc., San Diego, 1990—; instr. Basic Inst. Tech., St. Louis, 1971. Mem. ASHRAE, IEEE. Home: PO Box 261578 San Diego CA 92196-1578 Office: AEL/PSI 7940 Arjons Dr Ste A San Diego CA 92126-6303

SELL, WILLIAM EDWARD, legal educator; b. Hanover, Pa., Jan. 1, 1923; s. Henry A. and Blanche M. (Newman) S.; m. Cordelia I. Fulton, Aug. 20, 1949; 1 son, Jeffrey Edward. AB, Washington and Jefferson Coll., 1944, LHD, 1973; JD, Yale U., 1947; LLD, Dickinson Sch. Law, 1968. Bar: D.C. 1951, Pa. 1952. Instr. law U. Pitts., 1947-49, asst. prof. law, 1949-51, assoc. prof. law, 1953-54, prof. law, 1954-77, assoc. dean, 1957-63, dean, 1966-77, disting. svc. prof. law, 1977-94; emeritus dean, disting. svc. prof. law, 1994—; sr. counsel firm Meyer, Unkovic & Scott, Pitts., 1977-94; vis. prof. U. Mich. Law Sch., 1957; past pres. Pa. Bar Inst.; bd. dirs. St. Clair Health Corp. Author: Fundamentals of Accounting Lawyers, 1960, Pennsylvania Business Corporations, 3 vols., 1969, revised, 1991, Sell on Agency, 1975, also articles; editor: Pennsylvania Keystone Lawyers Desk Library. Past pres., bd. dirs. St. Clair Meml. Hosp.; past chmn. St. Clair's Health Corp.

With USAAF, WWII. Fellow Am. Bar Found. (life); mem. ABA, Pa. Bar Assn., Allegheny County Bar Assn., Assn. Am. Law Schs., Am. Law Inst. (life), Univ. Club, Phi Beta Kappa, Order of Coif, Pi Delta Epsilon, Phi Gamma Delta, Phi Delta Phi, Omicron Delta Kappa. Presbyterian (elder, deacon). Home: 106 Seneca Dr Pittsburgh PA 15228-1029 Office: U Pitts Sch Law 531 Law Bldg Pittsburgh PA 15260

SELLER, ROBERT HERMAN, cardiologist, family physician; b. Phila., Mar. 21, 1931; s. David and Elsie (Straussman) S.; m. Maxine Schwartz, June 3, 1956; children: Michael, Douglas, Stuart. A.B., U. Pa., 1952, M.D., 1956. Intern. Grad. Hosp. of U. Pa., Phila., 1956-57; research asst. dept. pharmacology U. Pa., 1953-55; resident in cardiology, research fellow Am. Heart Assn., Phila. Gen. Hosp., 1957-58; resident in internal medicine Albert Einstein Med. Ctr., Phila., 1958-59; chief resident Albert Einstein Med. Ctr., 1959-60; instr. medicine Hahnemann Med. Coll. and Hosp., Phila., 1960-64; asst. prof. Hahnemann Med. Coll. and Hosp., 1964-69, assoc. prof., 1969-72, dir. Service F, 1962-67, asst. coordinator mil. edn. for nat. def., 1961-64, dir. div. family medicine, 1967-72, acting chmn. dept. family medicine and community health, 1972-74, prof. medicine, family medicine and community health, 1973-74; practice medicine, specializing in cardiology Buffalo, 1974—; prof., chmn. dept. family medicine, prof. medicine SUNY-Buffalo, Deaconess Hosp., 1974-82, chmn. dept. family practice and dir. family practice residency program, 1974-82; prof. medicine and family medicine SUNY-Buffalo, 1974—. Author: Differential Diagnosis of Common Complaints, 1986, 3d edit., 1996; contbr. articles to profl. jours. NIH grantee, 1972-75; Deaconess Hosp. family practice resident tng. grantee, 1975—; health professions spl. projects grantee, 1975—. Fellow ACP, Am. Coll. Cardiology, Am. Acad. Family Physicians, Phila. Coll. Physicians; mem. AMA, N.Y. Med. Soc., Erie County Med. Soc., Am. Fedn. Clin. Research, Am. Heart Assn., Soc. of Tchrs. of Family Medicine, N.Y. Acad. Sci., N.Y. Acad. Family Physicians. Home: 125 Crestwood Ln Buffalo NY 14221-1462 Office: 1542 Maple Rd Buffalo NY 14221-3625

SELLERS, BARBARA JACKSON, federal judge; b. Richmond, Va., Oct. 3, 1940; m. Richard F. Sellers; children: Elizabeth M., Anne W., Catherine A. Attended, Baldwin-Wallace Coll., 1958-60; BA cum laude, Ohio State U., 1962; JD magna cum laude, Capital U. Law Sch., Columbus, Ohio, 1979. Bar: Ohio 1979, U.S. Dist. Ct. (so. dist.) Ohio 1981, U.S. Ct. Appeals (6th cir.), 1986. Jud. law clk. Hon. Robert J. Sidman, U.S. Bankruptcy Judge, Columbus, Ohio, 1979-81; assoc. Lasky & Semons, Columbus, 1981-82; jud. law clk. to Hon. Thomas M. Herbert, U.S. Bankrupcty Ct., Columbus, 1982-84; assoc. Baker & Hostetler, Columbus, 1984-86; U.S. bankruptcy judge So. Dist. Ohio, Columbus, 1986—; lectr. on bankruptcy univs., insts., assns. Recipient Am. Jurisprudence prize contracts and criminal law, 1975-76, evidence and property, 1976-77, Corpus Juris Secundum awards, 1975-76, 76-77. Mem. ABA (corp., litigation sect. 1986—, banking and bus. law sect. 1981-94, jud. adminstrv. sect. 1983-84), Columbus Bar Assn., Comml. Law Leage of Am., Am. Bankruptcy Inst., Nat. Conf. Bankruptcy Judges, Order of Curia, Phi Beta Kappa. Office: US Bankruptcy Ct 170 N High St Columbus OH 43215-2421

SELLERS, FRED WILSON, banker; b. Alexander City, Ala., Apr. 29, 1942; s. Fred Wilson and Helen (Hagan) Sellers); m. Nancy Wilbanks, July 11, 1964; children: Fredrick Hagan, Robert Wilbanks. BS, U. Ala., 1964; MBA, L.I. U., 1966; postgrad., U. Wis., Madison, 1974. CPA, N.C., Ala.; cert. fraud examiner. Staff acct. Ernst & Young, Winston-Salem, N.C., 1966-69; comptr. Citibanc Group, Inc., Andalusia, Ala., 1969-73; various positions, then sr. v.p., gen. auditor AmSouth Bank, Birmingham, Ala., 1973—; bd. dirs. Better Bus. Bur., Mobile, Ala., 1984-86. Mem. budget com. United Way, Birmingham, 1982-83. Mem. AICPA, N.C. Assn. CPAs, Ala. Assn. CPAs, Ala. United States Air Force Acad. Parents Club (pres. 1993-94, 94-95), Vestavia Country Club, The Club, Univ. Club (Tuscaloosa). Avocations: travel, photography. Home: 2112 Viking Cir Birmingham AL 35216-3325 Office: AmSouth Bankcorporation PO Box 11007 Birmingham AL 35288

SELLERS, LUCIA SUNHEE, marketing professional; b. Taegu, Korea, Mar. 26, 1949; came to U.S., 1965; d. Chongin and Elizabeth (Min) Kim; m. Gregory J. Sellers, Nov. 26, 1983; 1 child, Kristin. BS, Rutgers U., 1973; MBA, Keller Grad. Sch. of Mgmt., 1995. With MIS dept. N.J. Bell, Madison, 1972-84; with computer systems AT&T, Lisle, Ill., 1985-90; with govt. markets group AT&T Bell Labs., Naperville, Ill., 1991-95; mktg. profl. PCS Market Planning group Lucent Techs., Naperville, 1996—. Home: 7S 515 Oak Trails Dr Naperville IL 60540

SELLERS, PETER HOADLEY, mathematician; b. Phila., Sept. 12, 1930; s. Lester Hoadley and Therese (Tyler) S.; m. Lucy Bell Newlin, June 21, 1958; children—Mortimer, Therese, Mary, Lucy Bell. B.A., U. Pa., 1953, M.A., 1958, Ph.D., 1965. Math. tchr. Kangaru Sch., Embu, Kenya, 1961-63; programmer U. Pa., Phila., 1958-61; mem. faculty Rockefeller U., N.Y.C., 1966—; Johnson Found. postdoctoral fellow, 1963-65. mem. editorial bd. Genomics, 1986—; author: Combinatorial Complexes, 1979; contbr. articles to profl. jours. Trustee Coll. of the Atlantic, Bar Harbor, Maine, 1985—. Served to lt (j.g.) USNR, 1953-55. Mem. Am. Math. Soc., Math. Assn. Am., Soc. Indsl. and Applied Math. Democrat. Episcopalian. Avocation: boat building. Home: 413 W Stafford St Philadelphia PA 19144-4407 Office: Rockefeller Univ 1230 York Ave New York NY 10021-6307

SELLERY, J'NAN MORSE, English, Canadian and American literature educator; b. Oakland, Calif., Jan. 3, 1928; d. Raymond Stephen and Minna Esther (Bourus) Morse; m. Austin R. Sellery, Aug. 30, 1947; children: Stephen Brooke, Edward Austin, Margaret Joan, John Merritt. BA, U. Calif., Riverside, 1965; MA, U. Calif., 1967, PhD, 1970. Asst. prof. Harvey Mudd Coll., Claremont, Calif., 1970-74, assoc. prof. Claremont grad. sch., 1974-80, prof. English Claremont grad. sch., 1980—, Louisa & Robert Miller chair prof. humanities, 1989—; coord. women's studies Claremont Coll., 1988-91; cons. UMI Press, 1989, Conn. Rev., 1988. Co-editor: Faust Part I, 1969, The Scapegoat, 1972, Bibliography of Elizabeth Bowen, 1981; editor (jours.) Women's Voices, 1986, Gender, 1990; sr. editor Psychol. Perspectives, 1969-95; contbr. articles and poetry to mags. and profl. jours. NDEA fellow U. Calif., 1967-70; rsch. grantee Harvey Mudd Coll., 1971-90, NEH summer grantee Yale U., 1979, Mellon grantee in curriculum Claremont Colls., 1989; vis. humanities scholar U. Calgary, Can., 1992. Mem. AAUW (nat. bd. mem. 1982-83, mem. fellowship panel 1989-93), MLA, Nat. Women's Studies Assn. (coord. coun. 1989-92, cons. jour. and book awards 1991—). Office: Harvey Mudd Coll Humanities Dept Parsons Hall Claremont CA 91711

SELLES, ROBERT HENDRIKUS, actuary, consultant; b. Amsterdam, Netherlands, Nov. 8, 1938; came to U.S., 1969; s. Albertus Hendrikus and Jansje Suzanna (Cordes) S.; m. Manuela Ioana Cazaban Sava-Goiu Comnene, Aug. 27, 1966 (div. Mar. 1978); 1 child, Melina Joanna. B.Commerce with honors, U. Man., 1961. Actuarial asst. Can. Premier Life Ins. Co., Winnipeg, Man., 1961-62; asst. actuary Sun Life Assurance Co. Can., Montreal, Que., 1962-69; sr. v.p. Hay/Huggins Co., Inc., Phila., 1969-75, 77-79, 91—, Boston, 1975-77, San Francisco, 1979-84, 87-91, N.Y., 1984-87. Mem. nat. com. Republican party, 1980—. Fellow Soc. Actuaries; mem. Conf. of Cons. Actuaries, Am. Acad. Actuaries, Internat. Benefits Found., Western Pension and Benefits Conf., Actuaries Club San Francisco, Netherlands Soc. Phila. (pres. 1993-96), Netherlands Am. Assn. Delaware Valley (bd. dirs. 1993-96), Gavel Soc., Rainbow River Inc. (pres. 1995—). Home: 1420 Locust St # 24-N Philadelphia PA 19102-4223

SELLIN, ERIC, linguist, poet, educator; b. Phila., Nov. 7, 1933; s. Thorsten and Amy (Anderson) S.; m. Birgitta Sjöberg, Jan. 25, 1958; children: Frederick, Christopher. BA, U. Pa., 1955, MA, 1958, PhD, 1965. Asst. instr. French U. Pa., Phila., 1955-56, 1957-58, 1959-60; lectr. Am. lit. U. Bordeaux, France, 1956-57; instr. French Clark U., Worcester, Mass., 1958-59; lectr. creative writing U. Pa., 1960-62; instr. French Temple U., Phila., 1962-65; asst. prof. Temple U., 1965-67, assoc. prof., 1967-70, prof., 1970-91, chmn. dept. French and Italian, 1970-73, founder, dir. Center for Study of Francophone Lit. of North Africa, 1981—; prof. French Tulane U., New Orleans, 1991—, chmn. dept. French and Italian, 1995-97; USIS lectr., Africa and Near East, 1981-83, 85, 88-91, manuscript reader, cons. to various profl. jours., univ. presses, and founds.; sr. Fulbright-Hays lectr., Algiers, Algeria, 1968-69, Dakar, Senegal, 1978-79. Author: The Dramatic Concepts of Antonin Artaud, 1968, The Inner Game of Soccer, 1976, Soccer Basics, 1977, Reflections on the Aesthetics of Futurism, Dadaism and Surrealism-a Prosody Beyond Words, 1993, (poetry) Night Voyage, 1964, Trees at First Light, 1973, Tanker Poems, 1973, Borne Kilométrique, 1973, Marginalia, 1979, Crépuscule prolongé à El Biar, 1982, Nightfall over Lubumbashi, 1982, Night Foundering, 1985, Dead of Noon, 1992; editor: Africana Jour., 1983-87, CELFAN Edit. Monographs, 1987—, CELFAN Rev., 1981—; contbr. over 150 articles to profl. jours. and anthologies. Recipient faculty prize in Romance langs. U. Pa., 1955; Am. Philos. Soc. fellow, 1970, 82, NEH sr. fellow, 1973-74; Temple U. rsch. grantee, 1970, 82; sr. Fulbright-Hays Rsch. scholar Francophone Lit., Rabat, Morocco, 1989. Mem. Am. Assn. Tchrs. French, African Lit. Assn., Phi Beta Kappa. Office: Tulane U Dept French New Orleans LA 70118

SELLIN, IVAN ARMAND, physicist, educator, researcher; b. Everett, Wash., Aug. 16, 1939; s. Petrus and Amelia Fanny (Josephson) S.; m. Helen Kathleen Gill, June 16, 1962; children: Peter Bennington, Frank Erick. Student, Harvard U., 1956-59; MS, U. Chgo., 1960, PhD, 1964. Instr., rsch. assoc. U. Chgo., 1960-65; asst. prof. NYU, 1965-67; rsch. physicist Oak Ridge (Tenn.) Nat. Lab., 1967-70; assoc. prof. U. Tenn., Knoxville, 1970-74, prof., 1974-83, dist. prof., 1983—; adj. rsch. physicist Oak Ridge Nat. Lab., 1970—; program dir. NSF, Washington, 1988-89; mem. com. on atomic and molecular sci. NAS-NRC, 1973-76, chmn., 1980-83, mem. panel on accelerator related atomic and molecular sci., 1978-80; mem. panel on atomic, molecular and optical physics NAS-NRC Physics Survey, 1983-86; Orgn. Am. States vis. prof. Centro Atomico, Bariloche, Argentina, 1972, 81-82, Inst. für Kernphysik der Univ. Frankfurt, Germany, 1977, Rsch. Inst. for Physics, Stockholm, 1977-78, 83; invited visitor Harvard Smithsonian Instn. Astrophys. Obs., 1995; spkr., presenter in field; invited rsch. scholar, prof. Mann Siegbahn Lab., Stockholm U., Sweden, 1996-97. Editor, co-author: (with others) Advances in Atomic and Molecular Physics, 1976, McGraw-Hill Annual Yearbook of Science and Technology, 1978, McGraw-Hill Encyclopedia of Science and Technology, 5th edit., 1982, 7th edit., 1992, Beam Foil Spectroscopy: Vol 1, Atomic Structure and Lifetimes Vol. 2, Collisional and Radiative Processes, 1976, Structure and Collisions of Ions and Atoms, 1978, Forward Electron Ejection in Ion Collisions, 1984, Physics Through the 1990's; Atomic, Molecular and Optical Physics, 1986; contbr. more than 200 articles to profl. jours. Concert mgr. Oak Ridge Civic Music Assn., 1973. Grantee Office of Naval Rsch., 1972-82, NASA, 1972-73, 73-78, NSF, 1973—, Internat. Union Pure and Applied Physics, 1975, Dept. Energy, 1979-83, Oak Ridge Nat. Lab., 1980-82, NSF Divsn. Internat. Programs, 1986-92, 96—; recipient Sr. U.S. Scientist award Alexander von Humboldt Found., 1977, 86, 88; Fulbright scholar, 1977; rsch. scholar Japan Ministry of Edn., Sci. and Culture, 1994, Manne Siegbahn Nat. Lab., Stockholm, 1996-97. Fellow Am. Phys. Soc. (vice chmn. 1981, chmn. 1982-83, mem. com. on constn. and bylaws, mem. com. on meetings 1991-93, coun. advisor 1989-93, councillor 1979-83, chmn. publs. com. divsn. electron and atomic physics 1974-76, mem. program com. 1976-78, mem. nominating com. 1979-83, mem. fellowship com. 1979-83, mem. exec. com. 1979-83, mem. exec. com. S.E. sect. 1979-93, vice chmn. 1990-91, program chmn. 1990-91, chmn. 1991-92, Jesse Beams medal 1983), Acad. European, Cosmos Club. Achievements include research on highly ionized heavy ions, modes of formation and destruction in collisions with target atoms and molecules, and the excitations they induce in dilute gas and dense solid media; use of synchrotron radiation to form and study cold, multiply ionized ions using heavy ion accelerators, synchrotron storage rings, electron spectrometers, x-ray, soft x-ray, and extreme ultra-violet spectrometers, heavy particle spectrometers, and two-dimensional position-sensitive detectors.

SELLIN, THEODORE, foreign service officer, consultant; b. Phila., June 17, 1928; s. Thorsten and Amy (Anderson) S.; m. Taru Jarvi, July 10, 1965; 1 child, Derek. Student, U. Uppsala, Sweden, 1946-48; BA, U. Pa., 1951, MA, 1952. Joined Fgn. Svc., Dept. State, 1952; vice consul Copenhagen, 1952-56; rsch. analyst Dept. State, Washington, 1956-58; program officer Office Internat. Confs., 1965-67; acad. tng. staff U. Ind., 1958-59; 2d sec. Am. Embassy, Helsinki, Finland, 1959-64, 1st sec., polit. officer, 1971-73; 1st sec., labor-polit. officer Am. Embassy, Oslo, 1967-71; polar affairs officer Dept. State, 1975; consul gen. Goteborg, Sweden, 1978-80; fgn. rels. cons. Dept. State, Washington, 1980—. Office: Dept State IS/FPC/CDR Washington DC 20520

SELLMYER, DAVID JULIAN, physicist, educator; b. Joliet, Ill., Sept. 28, 1938; s. Marcus Leo and Della Louise (Plumhoff) S.; m. Catherine Joyce Zakas, July 16, 1962; children: Rebecca Ann, Julia Maryn, Mark Anthony. BS, U. Ill., 1960; PhD, Mich. State U., 1965. Asst. prof. MIT, Cambridge, 1965-72, assoc. prof., 1972; assoc. prof. U. Nebr., Lincoln, 1972-75, prof., 1975—, chmn. dept. physics, 1978-84, George Holmes disting. prof., 1987, dir. Ctr. Materials Rsch., 1988—; cons. Dale Electronics, Norfolk, Nebr., 1980—. Contbr. articles, book revs. to refereed jours. Recipient tech. award NASA, 1972; disting. vis. prof. S.D. Sch. Mines and Tech., Rapid City, 1981. Fellow Am. Phys. Soc. Office: U Nebr Ctr Materials Rsch 112 Brace Lab Lincoln NE 68588-0113

SELLO, ALLEN RALPH, forest products executive; b. Winnipeg, Man., Can.; m. Mary Lou Sello, June 3, 1972; children: Clint, Monique, Daren. B of Commerce (hon)., U. Man., 1963; MBA, U. Toronto, Ont., Can., 1964. Mgr. mktg. analysis Ford Motor Co. of Can., Oakville, Ont., Can., 1972-75, mgr. product plans, 1975-78, asst. treas., 1978-79; dir. acctg. Gulf Can. Ltd., Toronto, 1979-81, dir. fin. planning, 1981-82, contr., 1982-85; v.p., contr. Gulf Can. Corp., Calgary, Alta., Can., 1985-86; v.p. fin. Gulf Can. Resources, Ltd., Calgary, 1986-88, v.p. fin., chief fin. officer, 1988-95; v.p., CFO Internat. Forest Products Ltd., 1996—. Mem. Fin. Execs. Inst., Glencoe Golf and Country Club. Avocations: squash, skiing, tennis, golf.

SELLS, BOAKE ANTHONY, private investor; b. Ft. Dodge, Iowa, June 24, 1937; s. Lyle M. and Louise (Gadd) S.; m. Marian S. Stephenson, June 20, 1959; children: Damian, Brian, Jean Ann. BSC, U. Iowa, 1959; MBA, Harvard U., 1969. Bus. office mgr. Northwestern Bell Tel., Des Moines, 1959-63; salesman Hydraulic Cos., Ft. Dodge, 1964-67; pres. Cole Nat. Corp., Cleve., 1969-83; vice chmn. Dayton Hudson Corp., Mpls., 1983-84, pres., 1984-87; chmn., pres., chief exec. officer Revco D.S., Inc., Twinsburg, Ohio, 1987-92; bd. dirs. Promus Cos. (name changed to Harrah's Entertainment, Inc.), NCS Healthcare. Trustee Cleve. Ctr. for Contemporary Art, Cleve. Play House.

SELLS, BRUCE HOWARD, biomedical sciences educator; b. Ottawa, Ont., Can., Aug. 15, 1930; s. Charles Henry and Nell (Worth) S.; m. Bernice May Romain, Sept. 19, 1953; children: Jennifer, Monica, David, Lisa. B.S., Carleton U., 1952; M.A., Queen's U., 1954; Ph.D., McGill U., 1957. Demonstrator McGill U., Montreal, Ont., Can., 1954-57; research assoc. Columbia U., N.Y.C., 1961-62; asst. prof. St. Jude Children's Hosp.-U. Tenn., Memphis, 1962-64; assoc. prof. St. Jude Children's Hosp., Memphis, 1964-72, staff, 1968-72; prof., dir. molecular biology Meml. U. Nfld., St. John's, Can., 1972-83, assoc. dean, 1979-83; prof. molecular biology U. Guelph, Ont., Can., 1983-96, dean biol. sci., 1983-95; univ. prof. emeritus, 1997—; mem. adv. com. Ont. Health Rsch. Coun., 1992. Contbr. numerous articles to various publs. Adv. Com. Ont. Health Rsch. Coun., 1992—. Research fellow Damon Runyon Meml. Fund, Brussels, 1957-59; research fellow Damon Runyon Meml. Fund, Copenhagen, 1959-60; Killam sr. research fellow U. Paris, 1978-79; grantee NIH, 1963-72, NSF, 1965-69, Med. Research Council Can., 1972, Damon Runyon Meml. Fund for Cancer Research, 1962-76, Nat. Found.-March of Dimes, 1974-78, Muscular Dystrophy Assn. Can., 1974, Nat. Cancer Inst. Can., 1979, Vis. Prof. award Institut Pasteur, Paris, 1989; Exchange fellow Natural Scis. and Engring. Rsch. Coun. of Can., 1994. Fellow Royal Soc. Can. (rapporteur microbiology and biochemistry divsn. 1985-87, convenor 1987-89); mem. Acad. Sci. of Royal Soc. Can. (life scis. divsn. fellowship rev. com. 1990-92), Am. Soc. Microbiologists, Can. Assn. Univ. Tchrs., Am. Soc. Biol. Chemists, Am. Soc. Cell Biology, Can. Biochemistry Soc. (Ayerst award selection com. 1990, pres. 1981-82), Med. Rsch. Coun. (Centennial fellowships com., chmn. com. on biotech. devel. grants 1983-85, standing com. for Can. Genetic Disease Network 1991-92, chmn., 1992—), Nat. Rsch. Coun. Can. (biol. phenomena subcom. 1983-86, chmn. steering group, sci. criteria for environ. quality com. 1986, E.W.R. Steacie Prize com. 1986-88), Assn. Can. Deans of Sci. (co-founder 1989). Home: Rural Rte 6, Guelph, ON Canada N1H 6J3 Office: U Guelph, 577 Gordon St, Guelph, ON Canada N1G 2W1

SELMAN, ALAN LOUIS, computer science educator; b. N.Y.C., Apr. 2, 1941; s. Dan and Rose (Grass) S.; m. Sharon Jevotovsky, July 7, 1963; children: Jeffrey, Heather. BS in Math. cum laude, City Coll., CUNY, 1962; MA, U. Calif., Berkeley, 1964; PhD, Pa. State U., 1970. Asst. prof. computer sci. Fla. State U., Tallahassee, 1972-77; assoc. prof. Iowa State U., Ames, 1977-82; prof. Fern U., Hagen, Germany, 1982, Iowa State U., 1982-86; prof. Northea. U., Boston, 1986-90, acting dean, 1988-89; prof., chmn. dept. computer sci. SUNY, Buffalo, 1990-96, prof. dept. computer sci., 1990—. Editor: Complexity Theory Retrospective, 1990; assoc. editor Jour. Computer and Sys. Scis.; mem. edit. bd. Theory Computing Sys., Chgo. Jour. Theoretical Computer Sci. NSA grantee, 1987-90; Fulbright award, 1981-82. Mem. IEEE, Assn. Computing Machinery. Office: SUNY Dept Computer Sci 226 Bell Hall Buffalo NY 14260-2000

SELMAN, JAN COLLINS, artist; b. Boston, Apr. 4, 1945; d. James George and Dorothy Margarite (Euscher) Collins; m. Edwin Selman, Dec. 16, 1965 (div. June 1979); children: Jodie Michelle Selman, Stacey Elaine Kean. Student, Sch. of Mus. Fine Arts, 1962-64; AS, Cape Code C.C., 1981. Fine artist, owner Selman Studio, Avon, Mass., 1966-78, Falmouth, Mass., 1978—; cons. Emerson House Womans Program, Falmouth, 1980. Contbr. (landscape paintings) Am. Artist Mag., 1991, Nantucket Jour., 1991, Cap Cod Life Mag., 1992-93; permanent collections include Duxbury Mus. Complex, Cape Mus. of Fine Arts, Provincetown Art Mus. Juror awards for h.s. students Congrl. Arts Competition, Duxbury, 1990. Recipient 3rd Prize internat. competition Corel Systems Corp., 1991, 92. Mem. The Pastel Soc. of Am., Copley Soc. of Boston, Provinceton Art Assn., Cape Code Art Assn. Baptist. Avocations: filming documentaries on contemporary Cape Cod artists to donate to local museums, writing childrens short stories. Office: Selman Studio 79 Pinecrest Beach Dr East Falmouth MA 02536-4725

SELMAN, MINNIE CORENE PHELPS, elementary school educator; b. Freedom, Okla., Mar. 25, 1947; d. Maxwell Jack and Mary Elizabeth (Mountain) Phelps; m. Thomas O. Selman, Aug. 8, 1966; children: T. Justin, Jeffrey L. BS in Elem. Edn., Northwestern Okla. State U., 1969; diploma in aerospace sci. and tech. edn., Okla. City U./Internat. Space Academy, 1996. Cert. elem. tchr., early childhood edn. tchr., elem. sci. tchr., Okla.; cert. early experiences insci., Okla. Tchr. Woodward (Okla.) Pub. Sch., 1969-72; pre-sch. tchr. Free Spirit Pre-sch., Woodward, 1974-75; tchr. Montessori Discovery World Pre-sch., Woodward, 1975-78; tchr. kindergarten Woodward Pub. Sch., Woodward, 1978—; host Leaderhip Okla. in the Classroom, 1991; tng. tchr. Okla. State U., Stillwater, 1987, 90. Benefit vol. Western Plains Shelter Orgn., Woodward, 1990, 91; life mem. Plains Indians and Pioneers Hist. Found., Woodward. Woodward Pub. Schs. Ednl. Found. grantee, 1990, 91, 92, NASA/NSTA grantee, 1995. Mem. NEA, Okla. Edn. Assn., Woodward Edn. Assn. (pub. rels. com. 1990—), Nat. Sci. Tchr. Assn. (cert. in elem. sci., presenter convs.), Nat. Earth Sci. Tchrs. Assn., Okla. Sci. Tchrs. Assn. Democrat. Home: 318 Spruce Park Dr Woodward OK 73801-5945

SELMAN, ROLAND WOOTEN, III, lawyer; b. Kansas City, Mo., Aug. 16, 1941; s. Roland Wooten Jr. and Dixie R. (Chambliss) S.; m. Jean Calder; 1 child, Kellee Harris. Student, U. Kans., 1959-61, Stetson U., 1961-62; BA, U. Mo., Kansas City, 1963; JD, U. Calif., Hastings, 1971. Bar: Calif. 1972, U.S. Ct. Appeals (9th cir.) 1975, U.S. Supreme Ct. 1975, D.C. 1979, U.S. Ct. Appeals (D.C. cir.) 1980, U.S. Ct. Appeals (Fed. cir.) 1983. Assoc. Pillsbury, Madison & Sutro, San Francisco, 1971-79, gen. ptnr., 1979-95; commn. counsel Calif. Commn. on Jud. Performance, San Francisco, 1995—; judge pro tem Mcpl. Ct., San Francisco, 1984-95. Bd. dirs. Marin Svcs. for Women; planning commr. City of Sausalito, Calif., 1991-93; chmn. Sausalito Planning Commn., 1992-93. Lt. USN, 1963-68. Decorated D.F.C. (2), Air medals (9), Navy Commendation medals with combat V (3). Mem. San Francisco Bar Assn., Aircraft Owners and Pilots Assn., Harley Owners Group (life), Silver Wings Fraternity (life), Order of Coif. Mem. Christian Ch. Avocations: flying, scuba diving. Home: 28 Greenwood Bay Dr Belvedere Tiburon CA 94920-2252 Office: Commn on Jud Performance 101 Howard St Ste 300 San Francisco CA 94105-1619

SELMI, WILLIAM, JR., lawyer; b. Phila., June 18, 1937; s. William and Eleanor (Mishler) S.; m. Joan H. Silver, Dec. 4, 1966 (div. 1976); children: William III, Richard Kern; m. Patricia Ann Cantrell, Dec. 29, 1989 (div. 1995). AB, U. Miami, Coral Gables, Fla., 1969, JD, 1972. Bar: Fla. 1972, U.S. Dist. Ct. (so. dist.) Fla. 1973, U.S. Supreme Ct., 1976. Ptnr. Peer & Selmi, Jensen Beach, Fla., 1972-79; pvt. practice law Okeechobee, Fla., 1979—. Pres. Kiwanis Club, Jensen Beach, 1978; bd. dirs. Jensen Beach C. of C., 1977-78, Martin County Dem. Com., Stuart, Fla., 1977, Okeechobee br. ARC, 1990-95, Okeechobee United Way, 1993—. Avocations: military history, fishing. Home: 136 SW 85th Ave Okeechobee FL 34974-1554 Office: 306 NW 5th St Okeechobee FL 34972-2565

SELMON, LEE ROY, retired football player; b. Eufala, Okla., Oct. 20, 1954. Defensive right end Tampa Bay Buccaneers, 1976. Recipient Lombardi Trophy, 1975, Outland Trophy, 1975; named four time Defensive Lineman of Yr., NFL Players Assn., NFL Defensive Player of Yr., AP, 1979. Achievements include All-Am., 1975, three time All-Pro, All-NFC Choice, 1978, 79, 80, 82, 84, Pro-Bowl, 1979-84, co-Most Valuable Player Pro Bowl, 1981. Office: c/o Football Hall of Fame 2121 George Halas Dr NW Canton OH 44708-2630

SELOVER, WILLIAM CHARLTON, corporate communications and governmental affairs executive; b. Long Beach, Calif., Dec. 12, 1938; s. John Jesse and Myrtis Charlton (Holmes) S.; m. Mary-Louise Hutchins, Jan. 5, 1963 (div. 1985); children: Victoria, Edward. BA, Principia Coll., 1960; MA, U. Va., 1962. Editl. staff Christian Sci. Monitor, from congl. corr. to diplomatic corr., 1964-71; spl. asst. to sec. of the navy USN, 1971; mem. White House Coun. on Internat. Econ. Policy, Washington, 1971-72; history and archives divsn. chief Cost of Living Coun., Exec. Office of the Pres., Washington, 1973-74; asst. to adminstr. U.S. EPA, Washington, 1974-75, 77-78; from staff mem. White House Domestic Coun. to asst. to V.P. Nelson Rockefeller White House, Washington, 1975-76; speechwriter Pres. Gerald R. Ford, Washington, 1976; pub. affairs exec. Ford Motor Co., Detroit, 1978-88; pub. affairs mgr. diversified products ops. Ford Motor Co.; regional pub. affairs mgr. Ford Motor Co., L.A., 1988-91; v.p. corp. comms. and govtl. affairs USL Capital Corp. (subs. Ford Fin. Svcs. Group), 1991-96; prin. The Chaparral Working Group, San Francisco, 1997—. Speechwriter for chmn. and CEO of Ford Motor Co., Henry Ford II; editor autobiography former Pres. Richard M. Nixon, 1977. Helen Dwight Reid Found. fellow, Carnegie Found./Maxwell Grad. Overseas fellow, 1962. Mem. Conference Bd. (coun. corp. comm. execs.), Nat. Press Club, Press Club Detroit, Press Club L.A., Motor Press Guild, Internat. Motor Press Assn., Leadership Detroit Alumni Assn., Am. Polit. Sci. Assn. Address: 1257 Union St San Francisco CA 94109-1922

SELTSER, RAYMOND, epidemiologist, educator; b. Boston, Dec. 17, 1923; s. Israel and Hannah (Littman) S.; m. Charlotte Frances Gale, Nov. 16, 1946; children: Barry Jay, Andrew David. MD, Boston U., 1947; MPH, Johns Hopkins U., 1957. Diplomate Am. Bd. Preventive Medicine (trustee, sec.-treas. 1974-77), Am. Bd. Med. Specialties (mem. exec. com. 1976-77). Asst. chief med. info. and intelligence br. U.S. Dept. Army, 1953-56; epidemiologist div. internal health USPHS, 1956-57; from asst. prof. to prof. epidemiology Johns Hopkins U. Sch. Hygiene and Pub. Health, 1957-81, assoc. dean, 1967-77, dep. dir. Oncology Ctr., 1977-81; dean U. Pitts. Grad. Sch. Pub. Health, 1981-87, prof. epidemiology, 1981-88, emeritus dean, prof. epidemiology, 1988—; assoc. dir. USPHS Ctrs. for Disease Control, Rockville, Md., 1988-90; assoc. dir. Ctr. for Gen. Health Svcs. Extramural Rsch. Agy. for Health Care Policy and Rsch., Rockville, 1990—; cons. NIMH, 1958-70, also various govtl. health agys., 1958-79; expert cons. Pres.'s Commn. on Three Mile Island, 1979-80; mem. Three Mile Island Adv. Panel Health, Nat. Cancer Inst. Cancer Control Grant Rev. Com., Pa. Dept. Health Preventive Health Service Block Grant Adv. Task Force, Gov.'s VietNam Herbicide Info. Commn. Pa.; chmn. Toxic/Health Effects Adv. Com., 1985-87. Trustee, mem. exec. com., chmn. profl. adv. com. Harmarville Rehab. Ctr., Pitts., 1982-87; bd. dirs. Health Edn. Ctr., Media Info. Service. Served to capt. AUS, 1951-53, Korea. Decorated Bronze Star; recipient Centennial Alumni citation Boston U. Sch. Medicine, 1973; elected to Johns Hopkins Soc. of Scholars, 1986. Fellow AAAS, APHA (mem. governing coun. 1975-77, chmn. EPI sect. coun. 1979-80), Pa. Pub. Health

Assn. (bd. dirs. 1985-88, pres.-elect 1986-88), Am. Coll. Preventive Medicine, Am. Heart Assn.; mem. Am. Epidemiol. Assn., Internat. Epidemiol. Assn., Am. Soc. Preventive Oncology, Am. Cancer Soc. (bd. dirs. Pa. divsn. 1985-87, mem. exec. com. 1986-87), Assn. Schs. Pub. Health (sec. 1969-71, mem. exec. com., chmn. edn. com. 1983-87), Soc. Med. Cons. Armed Forces, Soc. Epidemiologic Rsch., Nat. Coun. Radiation Protection and Measurements (consociate), Johns Hopkins Alumni Coun. (mem. exec. com. 1994—), Sigma Xi, Delta Omega. Office: Agy Health Care Policy Rsch 2101 E Jefferson St Rockville MD 20852-4908

SELTZER, LEO, documentary filmmaker, educator, lecturer; b. Montreal, Que., Can., Mar. 13, 1910; came to U.S., 1916; s. Boris and Atalia (Gerowitz) S.; m. Elaine Basil, Apr. 15, 1941 (div. 1950); children: Janzie, John; m. Dicky Ransohoff, 1951 (div. 1963). BA, U. Mass., 1979. Faculty CCNY, 1949-54, New Sch. Social Rsch., 1949-51; pres. Leo Seltzer Assocs., Inc., N.Y.C., 1950-90; faculty Columbia U., 1954-60, Phila. Coll. Art, 1955-56, NYU, N.Y.C., 1966-67; dir. audio-visual therapy program pediatrics ward Univ. Hosp., N.Y.C., 1970-76; instr. film prodn. workshop Sch. Visual Arts, N.Y.C., 1969-84; adj. prof. performing and creative arts Coll. S.I., N.Y., 1977-78; prof. film Bklyn. Coll., 1978-83, prof. emeritus film, 1983—; lectr. in U.S. and abroad, including Mus. Modern Art, N.Y.C., Marymount Coll., Ghent U., Belgium, others. Prodr., dir. over 60 social documentary, informational, theatrical and TV films in 35 countries, including First Steps, UN Divsn. Social Affairs, 1947 (Acad. award for best documentary 1948), Fate of a Child, 1949, For the Living, City of N.Y., 1952, (with Walter Cronkite) Conquest of Aging, 1958, All the Years, 1959, Jacqueline Kennedy's Asian Journey, 1962, Progress through Freedom (pres. Kennedy's visit to Mex.), 1962, (with Edward R. Murrow) The American Commitment, USIA, 1963, Report on Acupuncture, 1977, (with John Huston) Let There Be Light; prodr., dir.: Nat. Film Bd. Can., 1941; chief cons. visual aids City of N.Y., 1941-42; prodr.: N.Y.C. Mcpl. Film and TV Unit Sta. WNYC, 1949-50; film biographer to White House for Pres. Kennedy; exec. prodr. Quadrant Comms., Inc., 1973-75 (7 citations Cannes and Edinburgh Film Festivals 1948-63); films are in Nat. Archives, Libr. of Congress, in collection and distributed by Mus. Modern Art; photographs are in Houston Mus. Fine Arts collection, Nat. Gallery Can., Visual Studies Workshop, Rochester, N.Y.; reconstructed 6 Am. social documentary films of 1930's for Mus. Modern Art Film Collection, 1976-77; subject of TV program by Bill Moyers, A Walk Through the Twentieth Century, CBC, BBC TV and Blackside Prodns.; contbr. film footage to Nat. Geographic, Blackside Prodns., CBC, BBC, History Channel (66 NY); prodr. TV series The Great Depression. 1st lt. Signal Corps. U.S. Army, 1943-46, ETO. Recipient Acad. award for best documentary, 1948, Silver medals Venice Film Festival, 1949, 63, Freedom's Found. award, 1953, Golden Reel award Scholastic Mag., 1955, Robert Flaherty award CCNY, 1956, Silver medal Atlanta Internat. Film Festival, 1977; honored in Leo Seltzer tribute Mus. Modern Art, 1990. Mem. Dirs. Guild Am. (charter). Achievements include research on Early American social documentary films. Home and Office: 368 E 69th St New York NY 10021-5706

SELTZER, PHYLLIS ESTELLE, painter, printmaker; b. Detroit, May 17, 1928; d. Max and Lillian (Weiss) Finkelstein; m. Gerard Seltzer, May 31, 1953; children: Kim, Hiram. BFA, U. Iowa, 1949, MFA, 1952; postgrad., U. Mich., 1953-55, Case Western Res. U., 1966-70. Faculty U. Iowa, 1950-52, U. Mich., Ann Arbor, 1954-55, Case Western Res. U., Cleve., 1966-70; program coord. arts and humanities Cleve. State U., 1969-71, Lake Erie Coll., Painesville, Ohio, 1970-72; art interior designer Dalton, VanDijk, Johnson, Cleve., 1973-74; pvt. practice as designer Cleve., 1975-87; lectr. Scuola di Grafica, Venice, Italy, 1994. Designer poster Cleve. Bicentennial, 1975; executed elevator murals Stouffer Inn on Sq. Cleve, wall murals Bistrot des Artistes, Cleve., 1987, Highland Grill, Chgo., 1990, Indian's Administration Bldg. Gateway Commn., Cleve., 1994; 3 commd. paintings for Soc. Nat. Bank, Cleve.; 4 commns. on video for New Cleve. Campaign, 1994-95; one-person shows include Vixseboxse Gallery, 1983, Old Detroit Gallery, 1985, Women's City Club, 1987, Bonfoey's, Cleve., 1989, 91, Jane Haslem Gallery, Washington, 1990, Galerie Bubaco, Venice, Italy, 1993, Bonfoey Gallery, Cleve., 1994, SG Gallery, Venice, Italy, 1994, 1995; group shows include Mitchell Mus., Mt. Vernon, Ill., 1979, Associated Am. Artists, N.Y.C., 1986, Nat. Print Exhbn., Trenton, N.J., 1988, Butler Inst. Am. Art, Youngstown, Ohio, 1989, S.W. Tex. State U., San Marcos, 1989, Cleve. Mus. Art, 1990, 93, Art Expo, N.Y.C., 1990, Artlink Contemporary Art Space, Ft. Wayne, Ind., 1990, Jan Cicero Gallery, Chgo., 1991, Bolton Gallery, Cleve. Playhouse, 1992, Wasmer Gallery, Ursuline Coll., Cleve., 1992, N.D. Print and Drawing Annual, U. N.D., 1992, 93, Mansfield Art Center, Ohio, 1992, Americana '92, Hong Kong, 1992, N.Y. Print Fair, 1992, 94, The Hammond Galleries, Lancaster, Ohio, Urban-Suburban, Bonfoey Co., Cleve., Great No. Corp. Ctr., Cleve., Dutchess County Art Assn., Poughkeepsie, N.Y., 1992, Michael Ingbar Gallery of Architecture, N.Y.C., 1992, Jane Haslem, Washington, 1993, Hunterton Art Ctr., Clinton, N.J., 1993, Ctrl. Pa. Festival of Arts, 1993, Northeastern Ohio Art Dealers Assn. Fine Arts Expo., 1993, Fla. Printmakers Soc., 1993, Cleve. Ctr. Contemporary Arts, 1993, 94, 95, Alexandria Mus. Art, 1993, Cleve. Mus. Art, 1993, Ctrl. Pa. Festival of Arts, 1993, Jan Cicero Gallery, Chgo., 1993, Trenton (N.J.) State Coll., 1993, Bonfoey Co., Cleve., 1993, Hunterdon Art Ctr., Clinton, N.J., 1993, Nat. Printmaking Exhibition, 1993, Jan Cicero Gallery, Chgo., 1994, Hunterdon Art Ctr., Clinton, N.J., 1994, NOADA Expo., Tower City, Ohio, 1994, 95, Art Multiple Dusselfof, Germany, 1994, Jane Haslem Gallery, Washington, Palm Springs (Calif.) Desert Mus., 1995, Jayson Gallery, Chgo., 1995, Citysights, 1995, Cleve. Play House, 1996, Print Biennial, Silvermine Guild Arts Ctr., New Canaan, Conn., 1996, The Park Synagogue, Cleveland Heights, Oh., 1996, Hunterdon Art Ctr., Clinton, N.J., 1996. Sec. Edgewater Homeowners Assn., Cleve., 1976-78. Tiffany fellow, 1952; recipient Cleve. Health Dept. award, 1975, Print Exhbn. award Hudson River Mus., 1987, Printmaking award Nat. Congress Art and Design, 1988, Juror's Merit award Chattahoochee Valley Art Mus., 1991, Purchase award Cleve. Mus. Art, 1993, Internat. award Find Arts divsn. N.Y. TV and Film Festival, 1996. Mem. Am. Soc. Aesthetics, New Orgn. Visual Arts Cleve. (v.p. 1974), Cleve. Soc. Contemporary Art, Print Club of Cleve. Mus. Art. (pres. 1983-84), New Orgn. Visual Arts Cleve. Studio: 7431 Detroit Ave Cleveland OH 44102-2862 *I am guided mainly by a need to make a visual contribution to society by adding innovative ways of seeing, as well as by utilizing the new techniques and technologies that are available to the visual artist. In my particular area this means the utilization of new printing processes-e.g. the mylar print, the 2080 Xerox print and the 6500 color Xerox and the laser Canon copier (with heat transfer printing). These new media also lend themselves to the continuance of painting in traditional methods, nevertheless expanding the horizon of surface and color on a single plane.*

SELTZER, RICHARD C., lawyer; b. N.Y.C., Sept. 3, 1943; s. Edward and Beatrice (Fishman) S.; m. Carol Reische, Aug. 31, 1969; children: Wendy, Mark. BA, Harvard U., 1965; JD, Columbia U., 1968. Bar: N.Y. 1969, U.S. Dist. Ct. (so. and ea. dists.) N.Y. 1969, U.S. Ct. Appeals (5th cir.) 1978, U.S. Ct. Appeals (2nd cir.) 1987, U.S. Supreme Ct. 1995. Ptnr. Kaye Scholer Fierman Hays and Handler LLP, N.Y.C., 1969—. Mem. ABA, Assn. of Bar of City of N.Y. Office: Kaye Scholer Fierman Hays and Handler LLP 425 Park Ave New York NY 10022-3506

SELTZER, RONALD, retail company executive; b. Boston, Nov. 16, 1931; s. Harold and Molly (Scheinberg) S.; m. Leila Podell, Feb. 24, 1957; children: Marjory, Michael, Barbara, Janet. B.B.A., Boston U., 1953. Asst. employment mgr. Gilchrist Co., Boston, 1956-59; personnel mgr. Bamberger's, Plainfield, N.J., 1959-61; employment and employee relations mgr. Bamberger's, Newark, 1961-66, v.p., store mgr., 1966-67, dir. sales promotion, 1967-70, sr. v.p., dir. stores, 1970-71; exec. v.p. Bamberger's, 1971-81, dir., 1969—; chmn. bd. R.H. Macy, N.Y.C., 1971-81; exec. v.p. ops. Macy N.Y., 1979-80; pres., chief exec. officer Lionel Leisure Inc., 1981-82; Louis Dryfus Retail Inc., 1981-90, bus. cons., 1990—; DWS. Retail Mgmt., Toronto; dir. Bradford Nat. Corp.; cons., pres. R & L Seltzer Assocs. Trustee Urban Coalition, N.J. Safety Council Inc., Garden State Ballet. Served with USNR, 1950-53; Served with AUS, 1953-55. Mem. Greater Newark C. of C. (dir. 1970—, mem. tax task force 1970—). Home: 278 Garfield Ave Oakhurst NJ 07755-1734

SELTZER, RONALD ANTHONY, radiologist, educator; b. Washington, Mar. 7, 1935; s. Lawrence H. and Sarah (Levin)S.; m. Adele Wishnow, June 25, 1961; children: Jeffrey David, Lauren Jill. AB with distinction, U. Mich., 1956; MD with high distinction, Wayne State U., 1960. Diplomate Am. Bd. Radiology. Resident in radiology Mass. Gen. Hosp., Boston, 1961-62, 64-66; asst. prof. radiology Stanford (Calif.) U. Med. Sch., 1966-67, asst. clin. prof., 1967-73, assoc. clin. prof., 1974-89; pvt. practice San Mateo, Redwood City,, Calif., 1967; mem. med. staff Mills Meml. Hosp., San Mateo, Calif., 1967-69; mem. med. staff Sequoia Hosp., Redwood City, 1969—, pres., 1986-88; cons. on radiation exposure divsn. radiol. health USPHS, 1964-67; cons. on nuclear medicine Palo Alto VA Hosp., 1967-75; cons. on computerized reporting in radiology GE, 1975-78; cons. advanced imaging divsn. Xerox Corp., 1978-82; cons. on electronic imaging Stanford Rsch. Internat., 1980-84; bd. dirs. Hosp. Consortium San Mateo County, 1986-88. Contbr. articles on biol. behavior and radiation dosimaty of radioactive materials, diagnostic radiology and uses of computers in medicine to med. jours. Sr. asst. surgeon USPHS, 1962-64. Fellow Inst. Cardiology Gt. Britain; mem. AMA, Calif. Med. Assn., Radiol. Soc. N.Am., Am. Roentgen Ray Soc., Western Angiography Soc. (pres. 1976-78), San Mateo County Ind. Practice Assn. (bd. dirs. Bay Pacific Health Plan 1979-84), Alpha Omega Alpha. Home: 140 Degas Rd Portola Valley CA 94028-7709 Office: Sequoia Hosp Med Staff Redwood City CA 94062

SELTZER, VICKI LYNN, obstetrician-gynecologist; b. N.Y.C., June 2, 1949; d. Herbert Melvin and Marian Elaine (Willinger) S.; m. Richard Stephen Brach, Sept. 2, 1973; children: Jessica Lillian, Eric Robert. BS, Rensselaer Poly. Inst., 1969; MD, NYU, 1973. Diplomate Am. Bd. Ob-Gyn. Intern Bellevue Hosp., N.Y.C., 1973-74, resident in ob-gyn, 1974-77; fellow gynecol. cancer Am. Cancer Soc., N.Y.C., 1977-78, Meml. Sloan Kettering Cancer Ctr., N.Y.C., 1978-79; assoc. dir. gynecol. cancer Albert Einstein Coll. Medicine, N.Y.C., 1979-83; assoc. prof. ob-gyn., SUNY, Stony Brook, N.Y.C., 1983-89; prof. ob-gyn. Albert Einstein Coll. Medicine, 1989—; chmn. ob-gyn. L.I. Jewish Med. Ctr., 1993—; dir. ob-gyn., Queens Hosp. Ctr., Jamaica, N.Y., 1983-93, pres. med. bd., 1986-89. Author: Every Woman's Guide to Breast Cancer, 1987; editor-in-chief: Primary Care Update for the Ob-Gyn, 1993—; editor: Women's Primary Health Care, 1995; mem. editorial bd. Women's Life mag., 1980-82, Jour. of the Jacobs Inst. Women's Health, 1990-95; contbr. over 75 articles to profl. jours.; host Weekly Ob-Gyn. TV Program, Lifetime Med. TV. Chmn. health com. Nat. Coun. Women, N.Y.C., 1979-84; mem. Mayor Beame's Task Force on Rape, N.Y.C., 1974-76; bd. govs. Nat. Coun. Women's Health, 1985-94; chmn. Coun. on Resident Edn. in Ob-Gyn., 1987-93. Galloway Fund fellow 1975; recipient citation Am. Med. Women's Assn., 1973, Nat. Safety Coun., 1978, Achiever award Nat. coun. Women, 1985, Achiever award L.I. Ctr. Bus. and Profl. Women, 1987. Fellow N.Y. Obstet. Soc., Am. Coll. Ob-Gyn (v.p. 1993-94, pres.-elect 1996—, gynecol. practice com. 1981, examener Am. Bd. Obstetrics and Gynecology 1988—); mem. Women's Med. Assn. (v.p. N.Y. 1974-79, editorial bd. jour. 1985—, resident review com. for obstetrics and gynecology 1993—), Am. Med. Women's Assn. (com. chmn. 1975-77, 78-79, editorial bd. jour. 1986—), N.Y. Cancer Soc., NYU Sch. Med. Alumni Assn. (bd. govs. 1979—, v.p. 1987-91, pres. 1992-93), Alpha Omega Alpha. Office: LI Jewish Med Ctr New Hyde Park NY 11040

SELTZER, WILLIAM, statistician, social researcher, former international organization director; b. N.Y.C., Sept. 22, 1934; s. William B. Seltzer and Edith S. (Goldman) Alt.; m. Jane E. Berger, Nov. 20, 1970; children: Benjamin, Ezra. BA, U. Chgo., 1956. Rsch. asst. Health Info. Found., N.Y.C., 1957-60; statistician U.S. Bur. Census, Suitland, Md., 1960-64; advisor Pakistan Inst. Devel., Econs. and Cen. Statis. Office, Karachi, 1964-68; staff assoc. Population Coun., N.Y.C., 1968-74; br. chief UN Statis. Office, N.Y.C., 1974-86, dir., 1986-94; sr. advisor to under-sec.-gen. Dept. Econ. and Social Info. and Policy Analysis, N.Y.C., 1993-94; sr. rsch. schlar Fordham U., N.Y.C., 1995—; mem. com. on population and demography, chair panel on data collection NAS, Washington, 1977-82; cons. UN Population Fund, 1995—, Internat. Criminal Tribunal for Rwanda, 1996. Author: Poems, 1960, Politics and Statistics, 1994; co-author: Population Growth Estimation, 1973; also various UN documents, jour. articles, reports. Fellow Am. Statis. Assn. (chair social stats. sect. 1983-84, chair com. on internat. rels. 1986-87), Royal Statis. Soc. (hon.); mem. Population Assn. Am., Internat. Statis. Inst., Internat. Assn. Official Statisticians. Mem. Soc. of Friends. Office: Fordham U Dept Sociology and Anthropology Dealy Hall Rm 522 441 E Fordham Rd Bronx NY 10458-5149

SELVADURAI, ANTONY PATRICK SINNAPPA, civil engineering educator, applied mathematician, consultant; b. Matara, Sri-Lanka, Sept. 23, 1942; arrived in Can., 1975; s. Kanapathiyar Sinnappa and W. Mary Adeline (Fernando) S.; m. Sally Joyce; children: Emily, Paul, Mark, Elizabeth. Diploma in Engring., Brighton Poly., U.K., 1964; Diploma, Imperial Coll./London U., 1965; MS, Stanford U., 1967; PhD in Theoretical Mechanics, U. Nottingham, 1971; DSc, U. Nottingham, Eng., 1986. Registered profl. engr., Can.; chartered mathematician, U.K. Staff rsch. engr. Woodward Clyde Assocs., Oakland, Calif., 1966-67; rsch. assoc. dept. theoretical mechanics U. Nottingham, 1969-70; lectr. dept. civil engring. U. Aston, Birmingham, Eng., 1971-75; asst. prof. civil engring. Carleton U., Ottawa, Ont., Can., 1975-76, assoc. prof., 1976-81, prof., 1982-93, chmn. dept., 1982-90, Davidson Dunton Rsch. lectr., 1987; prof., chmn. dept. civil engring./applied mechanics McGill U., Montreal, 1993-96; vis. rsch. scientist Bechtel Group, Inc., San Francisco, 1981-82; vis. prof. U. Nottingham, 1986, Inst. de Mécanique de Grenoble, France, 1990; cons. Atomic Energy of Can. Ltd., Pinawa, Man., 1983—, Ministry of Transp. Ont., Toronto, 1984—, Fleet Tech., Ottawa, 1988—, Atomic Energy Control Bd., 1987—. Author: Elastic Analysis of Soil Foundation Interaction, 1979, (with R.O. Davis) Elasticity and Geomechanics, 1996; editor: Mechanics of Structured Media, 1981, (with G.Z. Voyiadjis) Mechanics of Material Interfaces, 1986, Developments of Mechanics, 1987, (with M.J. Boulon) Mechanics of Geomaterial Interfaces, 1995, Mechanics of Poroelastic Media, 1996. King George VI Meml. fellow English Speaking Union of Commonwealth, 1965, rsch. fellow SRC, U.K., 1969, Erskine fellow U. Canterbury, New Zealand, 1992, Humboldt rsch. award, 1997. Fellow Am. Acad. Mechanics, Can. Soc. Civil Engring. (Leipholz medal 1991), Assoc. Prof. Engrs. of Ont. (Engring. medal for rsch. 1993), Engring. Inst. Can., Inst. Math. and Its Applications; mem. Internat. Assn. for Computer Methods and Advances in Geomechanics (award for significant paper in the category theory computational analytical 1994). Roman Catholic. Office: McGill U, Dept Civil Engring, Montreal, PQ Canada H3A 2K6

SELVER, PAUL DARRYL, lawyer; b. N.Y.C., May 28, 1947; s. Rene T. Selver and Marilyn (Steiner) Pomerance; m. Ellen J. Roller, Jan. 22, 1984; children: Adam, Max, Katelyn. BA magna cum laude, Harvard U., 1969, JD, 1972. Bar: N.Y. 1973. Assoc. Hale Russell & Gray, N.Y.C., 1972-74; ptnr. Brown and Wood (formerly Tufo and Zuccotti), N.Y.C., 1974-94, Battle Fowler, N.Y.C., 1994—; lectr. of law Columbia U. Law Sch., 1994—; assoc. adj. prof. Sch. Architecture, Planning and Preservation Columbia U., N.Y.C., 1986-88. Author: (N.Y. practice guide book) Real Estate: Land Use Regulations, 1986; edit. bd. Metroplis Mag., 1983-86. Mem. Manhattan Cmty. Bd. #6, N.Y.C., 1974-76, Westside Transit Com., N.Y.C., 1987; bd. dirs. Manhattan Bower Corp., N.Y.C., 1983—; mem. Sch. Facilities Planning Commn., Mountain Lakes, N.J., 1996-97. Mem. ABA, Assn. of Bar of City of N.Y., Am. Planning Assn. Office: Battle Fowler 75 E 55th St New York NY 10022-3205

SELVY, BARBARA, dance instructor; b. Little Rock, Jan. 20, 1938; d. James Oliver and Irene Balmat Banks; m. Franklin Delano Selvy, Apr. 15, 1959; children: Lisa Selvy Yeargin, Valerie Selvy Miros, Lauren, Franklin Michael. Student, U. Ctrl. Ark., 1955-57. Founder, dir. Carolina Ballet Theater, Greenville, S.C., 1973—; pres. Dance Arts Inc. and Incentives, Inc.; Advisory bd. dirs. Met. Arts Council and S.C. Governors Sch. Appeared in numerous TV commls., on Goodson-Toddman game show Play Your Hunch, 1958-59; toured Far East with TV show Hit Parade, 1958; named Miss Ark., 1956, Mrs. S.C., 1981; dir. and staged Mrs. Va., Mrs. N.C., Mrs. S.C. pageants; choreographed Little Theater prodns., Furman U. Opera. Mem. So. Assn. Dance Masters (ballet adviser, regional dir.), Dance Educators Am., Dance Masters of Am., Profl. Dance Tchrs. Home: 206 Honey Horn Dr Simpsonville SC 29681-5814 Office: Carolina Ballet Theatre 872 Woodruff Rd Greenville SC 29607-3538

SELWOOD, PIERCE TAYLOR, lawyer; b. Evanston, Ill., July 31, 1939; s. Pierce Wilson and Alice (Taylor) S.; m. Alexis Fuerbringer, June 8, 1964; children: Allison, Jonathan. AB, Princeton U., 1961; JD, Harvard U., 1964. Bar: Calif. 1965, U.S. Dist. Ct. (cen. dist.) Calif. 1965, U.S. Dist. Ct. (no. dist.) Calif. 1966, US. Dist. Ct. (ea. dist.) Calif. 1989, U.S. Ct. Appeals (9th cir.) 1970. Assoc. Sheppard, Mullin, Richter & Hampton, L.A., 1964-70, ptnr., 1971—, chmn. litigation dept., 1986-91; lectr. Calif. Continuing Edn. Bar, Berkley, 1970-84, Practicing Law Inst., N.Y.C., 1980s, ABA Nat. Inst., Chgo., 1986. Mem. ABA (chmn. various subcoms. 1984-89), Calif. Bar Assn., L.A. County Bar Assn., Assn. Bus. Trial Lawyers (bd. gov.s 1977-79), Jonathan Club (L.A.), Princeton Club So. Calif. (pres. 1970-72). Republican. Episcopalian. Avocations: tennis, hiking, camping, travel. Office: Sheppard Mullin Richter & Hampton 333 S Hope St Fl 48 Los Angeles CA 90071-1406

SELWYN, DONALD, engineering administrator, researcher, inventor, educator; b. N.Y.C., Jan. 31, 1936; s. Gerald Selwyn and Ethel (Waxman) Selwyn) Moss; m. Delia Nemec, Mar. 11, 1956 (div. Mar. 1983); children—Laurie, Gerald, Marcia; m. Myra Rowman Markoff, Mar. 17, 1986. BA, Thomas A. Edison Coll. N.J., 1977. Svc. engr. Bendix Aviation, Teterboro, N.J., 1956-59; svc. mgr. Bogue Electric Mfg. Co., Paterson, N.J., 1959; proposal engr. advanced design group Curtiss-Wright Corp., East Paterson, N.J., 1960-64; ind. bioengr., rehab. engring. cons. N.Y.C., 1964-67; pres. bd. trustees, exec. tech. and tng. dir. Nat. Inst. for Rehab. Engring., Hewitt, N.J., 1967—; cons. N.Y. State Office Vocat. Rehab., 1964—, Pres.'s Com. on Employment of Handicapped, 1966—, bus. and industry and for Am. with Disabilities Act compliance, also numerous state rehab. agys., health depts., vol. groups, agys. for handicapped in fgn. countries; cons., trainer computer applications. Contbr. articles on amateur radio, rehab. of severely and totally disabled to profl., gen. mags. Trustee Nat. Inst. for Rehab. Engring., Rehab. Research Center Trust. Decorated Knight of Malta; recipient Humanitarian award U.S. Ho. of Reps., 1972, Bicentennial Pub. Service award, 1975. Mem. Am. Acad. Consultants, I.E.E.E. (sr.), Soc. Tech. Writers and Pubs. (sr.), Nat. Rehab. Assn., N.Y. Acad. Scis., Mensa. Achievements include being the developer or co-developer field-expander glasses for hemianopsia, tunnel and monocular vision, electronic speech clarifiers, electronically guided wheelchairs, off-road vehicles and cars for quadriplegics, others; patentee indsl., mil. and handicapped rehab. inventions; expert, cons. on handicapped employment, handicapped product safety including design, manufacture, labelling and user instrnl. material, 1990—. Office: Nat Inst Rehab Engring PO Box T Hewitt NJ 07421-1020 *As I travel the road of life, it becomes more and more evident to me that people matter most, and technology is useful and good only so long as it serves man, and man is not made to serve technology. From technician I have evolved to humanist, using technology only as a tool. Always think positive. Don't waste your time or emotional energy on people who do not appreciate your good will. Think only about those who do, and you'll achieve more and enjoy life.*

SELYA, BRUCE MARSHALL, federal judge; b. Providence, May 27, 1934; s. Herman C. and Betty (Brier) S.; m. Ellen Hazel Barnes, Feb. 27, 1965; children: Dawn Meredith Selya Sherman, Lori Ann. BA magna cum laude, Harvard U., 1955, JD magna cum laude, 1958. Bar: D.C. 1958, R.I. 1960. Law clk. U.S. Dist. Ct. R.I., Providence, 1958-60; assoc. Gunning & LaFazia, Providence, 1960-62; ptnr. Gunning, LaFazia, Gnys & Selya, Providence, 1963-74, Selya & Iannuccillo, Providence, 1974-82; judge U.S. Dist. Ct. R.I., Providence, 1982-86, U.S. Ct. Appeals (1st cir.), Providence, 1986—; judge Lincoln Probate Ct., R.I., 1965-72; mem. R.I. Jud. Council, 1964-72, sec., 1965-70, chmn., 1971-72; mem. Gov.'s Commn. on Crime and Adminstrn. Justice, 1967-69; del. Nat. Conf. on Revisions to Fed. Appellate Practice, 1968-82; mem. various spl. govtl. commns. and adv. groups. Chmn. bd. trustees Bryant Coll., Smithfield, R.I., 1986-92; bd. dirs. Lifespan Health Sys., chmn. bd. dirs., 1994—, mem. bd. trustees R.I. Hosp. subs. Recipient Louis Dembitz Brandeis medal for disting. legal svc. Brandeis U., 1988, Neil Houston award Justice Assistance of Am., 1992. Mem. ABA, FBA, Fed. Judges Assn., R.I. Bar Assn. (chmn. various coms.), R.I. Bar Found., U.S. Jud. Conf. (mem. com. on jud. br.), Am. Arbitration Assn., Am. Judicature Soc. (bd. dirs.). Jewish. Home: 137 Grotto Ave Providence RI 02906-5720 Office: US Ct Appeals 311 Fed Bldg & US Courthouse Providence RI 02903 also: 1704 McCormack Boston MA 02109

SELZ, PETER HOWARD, art historian, educator; b. Munich, Germany, Mar. 27, 1919; came to U.S., 1936, naturalized, 1942; s. Eugene and Edith S.; m. Thalia Cheronis, June 10, 1948 (div. 1965); children: Tanya Nicole Eugenia, Diana Gabrielle Hamlin; m. Carole Schemmerling, Dec. 18, 1983. Student, Columbia U., U. Paris; MA, U. Chgo., 1949, PhD, 1954; DFA, Calif. Coll. Arts and Crafts, 1967. Instr. U. Chgo., 1951-56; asst. prof. art history, head art edn. dept. Inst. Design, Ill. Inst. Tech., Chgo., 1949-55; chmn. art dept., dir. art gallery Pomona Coll., 1955-58; curator dept. painting and sculpture exhbns. Mus. Modern Art, 1958-65; dir. univ. art mus. U. Calif., Berkeley, 1965-73, prof. history of art, 1965—; Zaks prof. Hebrew U., Jerusalem, 1976; vis. prof. CUNY, 1987; mem. pres.'s council on art and architecture Yale U., 1971-76. Author: German Expressionist Painting, 1957, New Images of Man, 1959, Art Nouveau, 1960, Mark Rothko, 1961, Fifteen Polish Painters, 1961, The Art of Jean Dubuffet, 1962, Emil Nolde, 1963, Max Beckmann, 1964, Alberto Giacometti, 1965, Directions in Kinetic Sculpture, 1966, Funk, 1967, Harold Paris, 1972, Ferdinand Holder, 1972, Sam Francis, 1975, The American Presidency in Political Cartoons, 1976, Art in Our Times, 1981, Art in a Turbulent Era, 1985, Chillida, 1986, Twelve Artists from the GDR, 1989, Max Beckmann: The Self Portraits, 1992, William Congdon, 1992, Beckmann, 1996; co-author: Theories and Documents of Contemporary Art, 1996; editor: Art in Am., 1967—, Art Quar., 1969-75, Arts, 1981-92; contbr. articles to art publs. Trustee Am. Crafts Coun., 1985-89, Creators Equity Found., 1980-97, Marin Mus. Assn., 1993—, Marin County Art Assn. 1993—; pres. Berkeley Art Project, 1988-93; mem. adv. coun. archives Am. Art, 1971—; project dir. Christo's Running Fence, 1973-76; commr. Alameda county Art Commn., 1990-95; mem. acquisitions com. Fine Arts Mus. San Francisco, 1993—; chair Berkeley Art Festival, 1997—. With OSS AUS, 1941-46. Decorated Order of Merit Fed. Republic Germany; Fulbright grantee Paris, 1949-50; fellow Belgian-Am. Ednl. Found.; sr. fellow NEH, 1972; resident Rockefeller Found. Study Ctr., Bellagio, 1994. Mem. Coll. Art Assn. Am. (dir. 1959-64, 67-71), AAUP, Internat. Art Critics Assn. Office: U Calif Dept Art History Berkeley CA 94720

SEMAK, MICHAEL WILLIAM, photographer, educator; b. Welland, Ont., Can., Jan. 9, 1934; s. John and Lena (Roketsky) S.; m. Annette Antoniuk, Jan. 30, 1960; children: James, Arlene. Student archtl. tech., Ryerson Poly. Inst., 1956-58. Freelance photographer Toronto-Pickering, 1961—; mem. faculty York U., Toronto, 1971—, assoc. prof. photography, 1977—. Exhibitor one-man shows, Image Gallery, N.Y.C., 1972, Il Diaframma Canon Gallery, Milan, Italy, 1976, Enjay Gallery, Boston, 1977, Ukraina Soc., Kiev, U.S.S.R., 1980, 81, group shows, Ont. Art Gallery, 1967, Expo '67 Internat. Exhbn., Montreal, 1967, Neikrug Gallery, N.Y.C., 1971; represented in permanent collections, Nat. Film Bd. Can., Ottawa, Nat. Gallery Can., Ottawa, Mus. Modern Art, N.Y.C., UN, Geneva. Recipient Photo Excellence Gold medal Nat. Film Bd., 1969; recipient Excellence award Pravda newspaper, Moscow, 1970, 71, Excellence diploma Fedn. Intenationale de l'art Photographique, Switzerland, 1972. Home: 1796 Spruce Hill Rd, Pickering, ON Canada L1V 1S4 Office: Dept Photography York U, 4700 Keeles St, Toronto, ON Canada M3J 1P3 *I see many contradictions around us, social realities which I believe rob us of our self-esteem and individuality. Must we continually accept and succumb to the never-ending hot baths for the mind society offers us? I wish my photography and words to disturb the complacent and the sleeper. I offer you cold showers for the mind.*

SEMAN, CHARLES JACOB, research meteorologist; b. Ripon, Wis., May 5, 1960; s. Leon Charles and Loretta Marie (Soda) S. BS in Meteorology, U. Wis., 1982, MS in Meteorology, 1985, PhD in Meteorology, 1991. Vis. scientist Nat. Meteorol. Ctr., Washington, 1991-93; rsch. assoc. Geophys. Fluid Dynamics Lab., Princeton, N.J., 1993—. Mem. Am. Meteorol. Soc. (Howard T. Orville award 1982), Geophys. Fluid Dynamics Lab. Employees Assn. (sec. 1994-95, treas. 1995—), Phi Beta Kappa. Avocations: music, travel. Home: 2-08 Fox Run Dr Plainsboro NJ 08536 Office: Geophys Fluid Dynamics Lab Forrestal Campus Rt 1 S Princeton NJ 08542

SEMANIK, ANTHONY JAMES, university program administrator; b. Cleve., Mar. 2, 1942; s. Anthony Joseph and Angela Theresa (Peters) S.; m.

Elaine Maria Christian, Apr. 20, 1968. BS in Edn., Kent State U., 1965, MEd, 1969. TV coord. Kent (Ohio) State U., 1967-71; TV producer/dir. High/Scope Ednl. Rsch. Found., Ypsilanti, Mich., 1971-72; dir. learning resource ctr. Mercy Coll. of Detroit, 1972-78; ind. media designer/cons. Detroit, 1972—; pub. affairs specialist Detroit bn. recruiting command U.S. Army, 1980-84; pub. affairs specialist tank-automotive command U.S. Army, Warren, Mich., 1984-85; dir. learning resource ctr. U. Detroit Mercy, 1985-96; dir. media svcs. Wayne State U., 1996—; chair Detroit Ednl. Cable Consortium, 1992—. Producer, designer, dir., editor instructional-educational multimedia and video programs-series for univ. and cable TV, 1985—; editor: (video programs) Elders in the New Japan, 1987, China and its Elders, 1989. Chmn. Detroit Ednl. Cable Consortium, 1992—. With U.S. Army, 1965-67. Mem. Consortium of Coll. and Univ. Media Ctrs., Assn. for Ednl. Comms. and Tech., Mich. Assn. Media in Edn., Phi Delta Kappa. Avocations: photography, videography, music, reading. Home: 7176 Green Farm Rd West Bloomfield MI 48322-2824 Office: Wayne State U 159 Purdy/Kresge Libr Detroit MI 48202

SEMANS, MARY DUKE BIDDLE TRENT, foundation administrator; b. N.Y., Feb. 21, 1920; d. Anthony Joseph Drexel and Mary (Duke) B.; m. Josiah Trent; m. James H. Semans. Attended, Hewitt Sch., N.Y.; AB in History, Duke U.; LLD (hon.), N.C. Cen. U., 1963; HHD (hon.), Elon Coll., 1965; degree (hon.), Davidson Coll., N.C. Wesleyan Coll., 1982, U.N.C. at Chapel Hill, Duke U., 1983; LLD (hon.), Furman U., 1993. trustee emeritus Duke U., 1961-81; chmn. The Duke Endowment, 1960—; various positions N.C. Sch. Arts, 1981—; former trustee Davidson Coll., N.C. Mus. Art, 1961-83, Shaw U., Converse U., Lincoln Hosp.; vice chmn. The Mary Duke Biddle Found., 1960—; chmn. Angier B. Duke Meml., Exec. Mansion Fine Arts Com., 1965—, Friends of Duke U. Library; pres. Durham Homes, Inc., 1968; mem. bd. dirs. Goodwill Industries of the Rsch. Triangle Area, 1964—, First Union Corp., 1980-82, N.C. State Library, 1958-61, Durham Pub. Library; numerous other positions. mem. Durham City Coun., 1951-55; mayor pro-tem City of Durham, 1953-55; commencement speaker Duke U., 1983. Recipient Merit award Duke U. Health and Hosp. Adminstrn. Alumni Assn., 1989, Giannini medal for meritorious svc. to N.C. Sch. of the Arts, 1990, Alan Keith-Lucas Friend of Children award N.C. Childcare Assn., 1991, Elna Spaulding award Women-in-Action, 1993, Outstanding Philanthropist award Triangle Chpt. Nat. Soc. Fund Raising Execs., 1993, Sam Ragan award St. Andrews Coll., 1993. Mem. LWV, Bus. and Profl. Women's Club, Altrusa Club, Half Century Club, Rotary Club. Democrat. Methodist. Home: 1415 Bivins St Durham NC 27707-1519 Office: The Mary Duke Biddle Found 1044 W Forest Hills Blvd Durham NC 27707-1678*

SEMANS, TRUMAN THOMAS, investment company executive; b. Oct. 27, 1926; s. William Ritchie and Ann (Thomas) S.; AB, Princeton U., 1949; postgrad. U. Va. Law Sch., 1950; m. Nellie Merrick, Dec. 14, 1961; children: Truman Thomas, Jr., William Merrick. Chmn. bd., pres. Robert Garrett & Sons, Balt., 1951-74; ptnr. Alex Brown & Sons, Balt., 1974—, mem. exec. com., 1979—, mng. dir., vice chmn. bd., 1987—; exec. com. Duke U. Investment Mgmt. Corp. V.p. bd. Md. Mus. and Hist. Soc., Balt., 1982—; trustee Chesapeake Bay Found., Annapolis, Md., Lawrenceville (N.J.) Sch., chair fin. com., exec. com., Eaton Found., Mercy Hosp., Balt., Duke U., 1993—; mem. fin. com. Roman Cath. Archdiocese Md.; exec. com. Duke U.; chmn. Duke U. Investment Corp. Served with USN, 1944-46; PTO. Mem. The Brook Club, Green Spring Valley Hunt Club, Hamilton St. Club, Va. Hot Springs Golf and Tennis Club, Ivy Club, Seminole Golf Club (West Palm Beach, Fla.), Jupiter Island Club (Hobe Sound, Fla.), Knights of St. Gregory, Knights of Malta. Democrat. Office: Alex Brown & Sons 19-21 South Rd Baltimore MD 21202

SEMAYA, FRANCINE L., lawyer; b. N.Y.C., Mar. 26, 1951; d. Julie and Ann (Tannenbaum) Levitt; m. Richard Semaya, Aug. 3, 1975; children: Stefanie Rachel, David Steven, Scott Brian. BA magna cum laude, Bklyn. Coll., 1973, MS magna cum laude, 1975; JD, N.Y. Law Sch., 1982. Bar: N.Y. 1983, U.S. Dist. Ct. (ea. and so. dists.) N.Y. 1983. Sr. legal analyst, atty. Am. Internat. Group, Inc., N.Y.C., 1977-83; assoc. counsel, asst. v.p. Beneficial Ins. Group, Inc. (formerly Benico, Inc.), Peapack, N.J., 1983-87; v.p., counsel Am. Centennial Ins. Co., Peapack, 1985-87; legal/reins. cons. Peapack, 1987; counsel reins. Integrity Ins. Co. in Liquidation, Paramus, N.J., 1988-91; ptnr. Werner & Kennedy, N.Y.C., 1991—; frequent author and spkr. on ins. regulatory, insolvency and reins. law. Editor: Law and Practice of Insurance Insolvency Revisited, 1989; contbg. editor Reference Handbook Ins. Co. Insolvency, 3rd edit., 1993. Mem. ABA (TIPS coun. 1994-97, chair TIPS task force on ins. insolvency 1995—, chmn. pub. regulation of ins. law com. 1990-91, chair ABA/TIPS pub. rels. com. 1993-94, co-editor State Regulation Ins. 1991), N.Y. State Bar (Practicing Law Inst. ins. law adv. com. 1995—), Phi Beta Kappa. Avocations: reading, travel. Office: Werner & Kennedy 1633 Broadway New York NY 10019-6708

SEMEGEN, PATRICK WILLIAM, lawyer; b. Akron, Ohio, Dec. 23, 1946; s. Stephen T. and Jane F. (Schmiedel) S.; m. Joann Kucharski, Jan. 10, 1975; children: Michael, Peter. B.S. in Econs., U. Pa., 1968; J.D., U. Mich., 1971. Bar: Ohio 1971, Calif. 1974. Chief crim. div. Summit County Prosecutor, Akron, Ohio, 1972-74; sole practice, Akron and San Diego, 1974-77; litigation counsel Beneficial Corp., Peapack, N.J., 1977-81; v.p. gen. counsel, sec. Western Auto Supply Co., Kansas City, Mo., 1981-96. Contbr. articles to profl. jours. Served to capt. USAR, 1968-71. Mem. ABA, Internat. Franchise Assn., Am. Fin. Services Assn., Am. Corp. Counsel Assn. Home: 6604 W 132 St Overland Park KS 66209 Office: 7300 W 110th St #230 Overland Park KS 66210

SEMEL, TERRY, entertainment company executive; b. N.Y.C., Feb. 24, 1943; s. Ben and Mildred S.; m. Jane Bovingdon, Aug. 24, 1977; children: Eric Scott, Courtenay Jane, Lily Bovingdon Semel, Kate Bovingdon Semel. BS in Acctg., L.I.U., 1964; postgrad. in market research, CCNY, 1966-67. Domestic sales mgr. CBS Cinema Center Films, Studio City, Calif., 1970-72; v.p., gen. mgr. Walt Disney's Buena Vista, Burbank, Calif., 1972-75; pres. W.B. Distbn. Corp., Burbank, 1975-78; exec. v.p., chief operating officer Warner Bros., Inc., Burbank, 1979-80, pres., chief operating officer, from 1980;, 1980-94, chmn., co-CEO, 1994—; chmn., co-CEO Warner Music Group, 1995—; bd. dirs. Revlon. Vice chmn. Pres.'s Com. for the Arts and Humanities; vice chair San Diego Host Com. for 1996 Rep. Nat. Conv.; bd. dirs. Solomon R. Guggenheim Mus., Edn. First, Cedars Sinai Med. Ctr., Environ. Media Assn. Pioneer of the Year, 1990, Found. of Motion PicturesPioneers. Office: Warner Bros Inc 4000 Warner Blvd Burbank CA 91522-0001*

SEMERARO, MICHAEL ARCHANGEL, JR., civil engineer; b. Paterson, N.J., Dec. 15, 1956; s. Michael Archangel and Ann Ruth (Windish) S.; m. Diane Cathleen Hartley, Oct. 12, 1986; children: Michael Archangel III, Laura Nicole, Chelsea Brooke, Julia Megan. BCE, Lehigh U., 1979; MCE, MIT, 1982; MBA, Rutgers U., 1989. Registered profl. engr., N.J., N.Y., Pa., Conn., Va.; registered profl. planner, N.J. Engr. DeGrace and Assocs., Wayne, N.J., 1978; prin., v.p. Langan Engrng. and Environ. Svcs., Elmwood Park, N.J., 1979—; Presenter in field. Pres. Passaic County (N.J.) 4-H Assn., 1992-94; chmn. exploring com. Passaic County Boy Scouts Am., 1986-89; leader Preakness Aggies 4-H Club, Wayne, 1977—; founding chmn. Passaic County Fair, 1988. Mem. ASCE, AAAS, N.Am. MOSS Users Group (founding pres. 1989-91), GDS Nat. Users Group (chmn. civil engrng. spl. interest group 1990-93, dir. 1995—), MIT Club No. N.J. (pres. 1992-94), Chi Epsilon. Roman Catholic. Home: 2 Warner Way Wayne NJ 07470-4161 Office: Langan Engrng Environ Svcs River Drive Ctr # 1 Elmwood Park NJ 07407

SEMERJIAN, HRATCH GREGORY, research and development executive; b. Istanbul, Turkey, Oct. 22, 1943; came to U.S., 1966; s. Krikor and Diruhi (Semerciyan) S.; m. Sona Kohar Kurkciyan, July 12, 1969 (dec. 1983); children: Tamar, Ara; m. Ayda Karabal, Feb. 8, 1986 (div. 1994). BSME, Robert Coll., Istanbul, 1966; MSc in Engrng., Brown U., 1968, PhD in Engrng., 1972. Rsch. asst. dir. engrng. Brown U., Providence, 1966-70; lectr. chemistry U. Toronto, Ont., Can., 1971-73; rsch. engr. Pratt & Whitney Aircraft United Technologies Corp., East Hartford, Conn., 1973-77; group leader Ctr. for Chem. Tech. Nat. Bur. Standards (now Nat. Inst. Standards and Tech.), Gaithersburg, Md., 1977-87, divsn. chief Chem. Sci. and Tech. Lab., 1987-92, dir. Chem. Sci. and Tech. Lab., 1992—; organizer tech. sessions, confs. and symposiums for various profl. orgns., 1978—. Contbr. rsch. articles to profl. publs.; editor numerous conf. procs. Mem. parish coun. St. George Armenian Apostolic Ch., Hartford, Conn., 1975-77; chmn. parish coun., dir. choir St. Mary Armenian Apostolic Ch., Washington, 1977—; coach youth soccer Montgomery Soccer Inc., Rockville, Md., 1978-81; mem. Ani Armenian Choral Group, Washington, 1988—. Hagopian scholar Robert Coll., 1961-64, A.M.&F. corp. fellow, 1965, C.B. Keen fellow Brown U., 1969; recipient Silver medal Dept. Commerce, Washington, 1984, Gold medal Dept. Commerce, Washington, 1995; named Fed. Engr. of Yr., NSPE, Washington, 1991. Fellow ASME; mem. AAAS, AIAA, AIChE, Am. Chem. Soc., Combustion Inst. Avocations: soccer, singing, boating. Office: Nat Inst Standards and Tech Bldg 222 Rm A317 Gaithersburg MD 20899

SEMION, A. KAY, editor; b. New Castle, Ind., July 27, 1944; d. Lowell Ernest and T. Byrneta (Byrne) Hooker; m. William Alexander Semion, June 21, 1969; children: Justin Alexander, Sonja Katherine. BA, Purdue U., 1966; AA, Delta Coll., 1974; MA, Wayne State U., 1981. Reporter The Flint (Mich.) Jour., 1966-70, The Daily Eagle, Wayne, Mich., 1970-71, The Bay City (Mich.) Times, 1971-72; copy editor The Ann Arbor (Mich.) News, 1979-83, editl. page editor, 1983-97; editl. writer The Tallahassee Dem., 1997—. Newsletter chmn. Lamaze Wayne County, Canton, Mich., 1977-80; leader La Leche League, Canton, 1978-81. Recipient Orthy awards Ch. 19 PBS, Bay City, 1973, 74. Mem. Soc. Profl. Journalists, Nat. Conf. Editl. Writers (chair mgmt. com., 1993-95, co-chair, mem. svcs. com. 1995-96, chmn. site selection com. 1996—, bd. dirs. 1997—). Home: 41629 Larimore Ln Canton MI 48187-3921 Office: The Tallahassee Democrat PO Box 9900 Tallahassee FL 32302-0990

SEMLER STRONG, MARGOT, association administrator; b. N.Y.C., June 26, 1933; d. Philip Grandin and Margot Violet (Berglind) Strong; m. Ralph Semler, Feb. 19, 1955; children: Ralph Parker, Christopher Strong, Michael. Student, Nat. Cathedral Sch., Bryn Mawr Coll., 1954. Exec. dir. Nat. Cathedral Assn., Washington Nat. Cathedral, 1974-95, canon, exec. dir. for nat. outreach, 1995—; comdr. sister Order of St. John of Jerusalem, 1983—. Mem. Alumnae Assn. Nat. Cathedral Sch. (pres., trustee 1994-96). Episcopalian. Office: Massachusetts & Wisconsin Aves NW Washington DC 20016

SEMLYEN, ADAM, electrical engineering educator; b. Gherla, Romania, Jan. 10, 1923; came to Can., 1969; naturalized, 1974; s. Aurel and Anna (Gyorgy) S.; m. Mary Semlyen; 1 dau., Georgeta. Dipl. Ing., Poly. Inst. Timisoara, Romania, 1949; Ph.D., Poly. Inst. Iasi, Romania. Engr. Regional Power Authority, Timisoara, Romania, 1949-51; mem. faculty Poly. Inst. Timisoara, 1949-69, prof., 1968-69; prof. elec. engring. U. Toronto, Ont., Can., 1969-88, prof. emeritus, 1988—. Fellow IEEE. Home: 65 High Park Ave # 2203, Toronto, ON Canada M6P 2R7 Office: U Toronto Dept Elec & Computer Engring, 10 King's College Rd, Toronto, ON Canada M5S 3G4

SEMM, KURT KARL, obstetrics & gynecology researcher/department head; b. 1927. MD, U. Munich. Prof. ob-gyn. univ. clinic U. Munich, 1953-70; dir. dept. ob-gyn. Michaelis Midwifery Sch., Christian Albrechts U., Kiel, Germany, 1970-95; ret., 1995. Mem. German-French Soc. for Ob-Gyn. (pres. 1976-88), Internat. Fed. of Fertility Socs. (sec.-gen. 1976-84, v.p. 1984—), European Sterility Congress Orgn. (sec.-gen. 1965—), Internat. Fedn. of Gynaecologic Endoscopists (v.p. 1984—). Home: Perlacher Str 24, D-82031 Grunwald Germany

SEMMEL, BERNARD, historian, educator; b. N.Y.C., July 23, 1928; s. Samuel and Tillie (Beer) S.; m. Maxine Loraine Guse, Mar. 19, 1955; 1 child, Stuart Mill. B.A., CCNY, 1947; M.A., Columbia U., 1951, Ph.D., 1955; postgrad., London Sch. Econs., 1959-60. With Nat. Citizens Commn. for Pub. Schs. and Coun. for Fin. Aid to Edn., N.Y.C., 1951-55; asst. prof. history Park Coll., Parkville, Mo., 1956-60; mem. faculty SUNY, Stony Brook, 1960-91; prof. history SUNY, 1964-91, chmn. dept., 1966-69; Disting. prof. Grad. Sch. CUNY, 1991-96; vis. prof. Columbia U., 1966-67. Author: Imperialism and Social Reform, 1960, Jamaican Blood and Victorian Conscience, 1963, The Rise of Free Trade Imperialism, 1970, The Methodist Revolution, 1973, John Stuart Mill and the Pursuit of Virtue, 1984, Liberalism and Naval Strategy, 1986, The Liberal Ideal and The Demons of Empire, 1993, George Eliot and the Politics of National Inheritance, 1994; editor: Occasional Papers of T.R. Malthus, 1963; editor, translator: Halévy's The Birth of Methodism in England, 1971; editor Jour. Brit. Studies, 1969-74, Marxism and the Science of War, 1981. Rockefeller Found. grantee, 1959-60; Am. Council Learned Socs. fellow, 1964-65; Guggenheim fellow, 1967-68, 74-75; Nat. Humanities Ctr. fellow, 1986-87. Fellow Royal Hist. Soc.; mem. Am. Hist. Assn. (profl. divsn. 1984-86), Conf. Brit. Studies, Phi Beta Kappa. Club: Cosmos. Home: PO Box 1162 Stony Brook NY 11790-0749

SEMMEL, JOAN, artist, educator; b. N.Y.C., Oct. 19, 1932; d. Lawrence and Sarah (Zucker) Alperstein; children; Patricia, Andrew. Diploma, Cooper Union Art Sch., N.Y.C., 1952; student, Art Students League, N.Y.C., 1958-59; BFA, Pratt Inst., 1963, MFA, 1972. Teaching positions Md. Inst. Art, Balt., 1973, Rutgers U., Livingston, N.J., 1974-75, Bklyn. Mus. Art Sch., 1976-78, Mason Gross Sch. Arts, Rutgers U., New Brunswick, N.J., 1978—; mem. jury Nat. Endowment for Arts, Washington, 1983, N.J. State Coun. on the Arts, 1990, 93. Solo exhbns. include Ateneo de Madrid, 1966, Mus. Plastic Arts, Montevideo, Uruguay, 1968, Juana Mordo Gallery, Madrid, 1969, Pratt Inst., N.Y.C., 1972, Lerner-Heller Gallery, N.Y.C., 1975, 78, 79, 81, Manhattanville Coll., Purchase, N.Y., 1985, BentonGallery, Southampton, N.Y., 1987, Skidmore Coll., Saratoga Springs, N.Y., 1992, SUNY Albany, 1992, SUNY Oswego, 1992, Pratt Manhattan Ctr., N.Y.C., 1993, Brenda Taylor Gallery, N.Y.C., 1996; exhibited in group shows at Mus. Modern Art, Barcelona, Salon Nacional, Madrid, Concurso Nacional, Madrid, Moravian Coll., Bethlehem, Pa., Bronx Mus., Whitney Mus., N.Y.C., Bklyn. Mus., Mus. of U. Tex., Chrysler Mus., Norfolk, Va., Henry St. Settlement, N.Y.C., Ball State U. Art Gallery, Ft. Wayne (Ind.) Art Mus., Indpls. Art League, Hudson Ctr. Gallery, N.Y.C., Mint Mus., Charlotte, N.C., L.I. U., Brookville, N.Y., Tampa (Fla.) Mus. Art, Richard Anderson Gallery, N.Y.C., David Zwirmer Gallery, N.Y.C., N.J. State Mus., Trenton, numerous others; represented in collections at Mus. Contemporary Art, Houston, Tex., Mus. of Univ. Tex., Austin, Chrysler Mus., Norfolk, Va., N.J. State Mus. Art, Mus. of Women in the Arts, Greenville County Mus., Greenville, S.C., numerous others; numerous commns, especially for portraits; subject of articles and book chpts. Grantee Nat. Endowment for the arts, 1980, 85, Yaddo Colony, 1980, MacDowell Colony, 1977, others. Address: 109 Spring St New York NY 10012-5219

SEMMLER, CARYL J., occupational therapist; b. Portland, Oreg., Sept. 15, 1949; d. Hardie Justus Sickles and Elna Gertrude (Kohlstedt) Linville; m. Maynard Jonathan Semmler, Aug. 22, 1970; children: Emma, Desireé, Kristoffer, Damon, Shane, Micah. BS, U. Kans., 1972; MS, Boston U., 1975; PhD, U. Tex., Dallas, 1984. Lic. occupational therapist, Tex. Occupational therapist St. Frances Hosp., Tulsa, 1972-74; instr. occupational therapy Tex. Women's U., Dallas, 1975-76; asst. prof. pediatrics U. Tex. Southwestern Med. Sch., Dallas, 1976-90; pvt. practice Dallas, 1990—; occupl. therapist ICU Medical City, Dallas, 1995-96; cons. phys. mgmt. adv. com. Tex. Dept. Mental Health/Mental Retardation, Austin, 1989-94; adj. prof. occupl. therapy Tex. Women's U., 1991-94; ind. contractor Comprehensive Home Health Svcs., Leisure Lodge Nursing Home; vol. occupl. therapist Children's Rehab. Clinic, Ryazan, Russia, 1994; guest workshop co-presenter Nat. Cheng Kung U. Med. Coll., Tainan, Taiwan, 1995. Author: Handle with Care, 1990, Early O.T. Intervention, 1991; author, editor: A Guide to Care and Management of Very Low Birth Weight Infants, 1989; contbr. numerous articles to profl. jours. Flutist Mesquite (Tex.) Symphony Orch., 1986—, North Dallas Symphony, 1993—; v.p. Mesquite Symphony Orch. Assn., 1989-91; bd. dirs. Mesquite Arts Coun., 1991-93. Grantee Maternal Child Health divsn. Boston U., 1974-75, North Ctrl. Tex. March of Dimes, 1983-85, NIH, 1986, Ronald McDonald Charities, 1989. Mem. Am. Occupl. Therapy Assn. (pediatric splty. cert. exam. com. 1990-97, Svc. award 1997), World Fedn. Occupl. Therapists. Office: 12820 Hillcrest Rd Ste C205 Dallas TX 75230-1526

SEMON, WARREN LLOYD, retired computer sciences educator; b. Boise, Ida., Jan. 17, 1921; s. August and Viola Lorreta (Eastman) S.; m. Ruth Valerie Swift, Dec. 1, 1945; children—Warren Lloyd, Nolan David, Jonathan Richard, Sue Anne. Student, Hobart Coll., 1940-43; S.B., U. Chgo., 1944; M.A., Harvard, 1949, Ph.D., 1954. Lectr. applied math. Harvard U., Cambridge, Mass., 1956-61, asst. dir. computation lab., 1954-61; head applied math. dept. Sperry Rand Research Ctr., Sudbury, Mass., 1961-64; mgr. computation and analysis lab. Burroughs Research Ctr., Paoli, Pa., 1964-67; prof. computer sci. Syracuse (N.Y.) U., 1967-84, prof. emeritus, 1984—, dir. system and information sci., 1968-76, dean Sch. Computer and Info. Sci., 1976-84; cons. USAF, 1957, NSA, 1957, Lockheed Electronics Corp., 1967, Monsanto Co., 1972. Contbr. profl. jours. Served to 1st lt. USAAF, 1943-46, MTO. Fellow IEEE; mem. Assn. Computing Machinery, Math. Assn. Am., IEEE Computer Soc. (chmn. publs. com. 1972-74, bd. govs. 1973-74, editor-in-chief 1975-76), Sigma Xi. Address: F54807 PO Box 44209 Cincinnati OH 45244-0209

SEMONIN, RICHARD GERARD, retired state official; b. Akron, Ohio, June 25, 1930; s. Charles Julius and Catherine Cecelia (Schooley) S.; m. Lennie Stuker, Feb. 3, 1951; children: Cecelia C., Richard G. Jr., James R., Patricia R. BS, U. Wash., 1955. With Ill. State Water Survey, Champaign, 1955-91, chief, 1986-91, chief emeritus, 1991—; adj. prof. U. Ill., 1975-91; chmn. Ill. Low-Level Radioactive Waste Task Group, 1994-96. Contbr. chpts. to books and articles to profl. jours.; co-editor: Atmospheric Deposition, 1983. Staff sgt. USAF, 1948-52. Grantee NSF, 1957-76, U.S. Dept. Energy, 1965-90. Fellow AAAS, Am. Meteorol. Soc. (councilor 1983-86); mem. Nat. Weather Assn. (councilor 1978-81), Weather Modification Assn., Ill. Acad. Scis., Sigma Xi. Roman Catholic. Avocations: Civil war, golf, fishing, geneology. Home: 1902 Crescent Dr Champaign IL 61821-5826 Office: Ill State Water Survey 2204 Griffith Dr Champaign IL 61820-7463

SEMORE, MARY MARGIE, abstractor; b. Cowlington, Okla., Feb. 11, 1920; d. William Leonard and Bessie Mae (Bellah) Barnett; m. Jack Sanford Semore, Mar. 3, 1940 (dec. Jan. 1985). Grad. high sch., Wagoner, Okla., 1938. Legal sec. W.O. Rittenhouse, Wagoner, Okla., 1938-40; abstractor Wagoner County Abstract Co., 1941—. Mem. Am. Legion Women's Aux., Wagoner Hist. Soc. Mem. Okla. Land Title Assn., Am. Land Title Assn., Wagoner C. of C., DAR, Daus. Am. Colonists. Democrat. Methodist. Avocations: photography, hunting, fishing, golf, swimming. Home: 902 S White Ave Wagoner OK 74467-7239 Office: Wagoner County Abstract Co 219 E Cherokee PO Box 188 Wagoner OK 74477

SEMOWICH, CHARLES JOHN, art historian, art dealer and appraiser, curator, artist; b. Binghamton, N.Y.; s. Zeekie and Alice (Osgood) S. BA, SUNY, Binghamton, 1971; MFA, Cath. U., 1972; PhD, Internat. Coll., L.A., 1981. Owner, operator Semowich Fine Arts, Albany, N.Y., 1982—; adj. prof. Empire State Coll., Albany, Saratoga Springs, N.Y., 1987—; cons. LePetit Musée, 1994—, Van Stedman Fine Arts, 1995—; instr. Chautauqua (N.Y.) Instn., 1988-90; curator Susquehanna County Hist. Soc., Montrose, Pa., 1976; guest curator SUNY-Albany, 1991; chmn. 19th nat. print exhbn., 1995; spkr. N.Y. State Coun. on the Humanities, 1996—. Exhibiting (mural) artist Rensselaer River Park; author: Am. Furniture, 1984; co-editor : Dorothy Lathrop-A Centenary Celebration, 1991, William Buttre: Furniture History, 1993; contbr. articles Dictionary of Art and profl. jours. V.p. Rensselaer City Arts Coun., 1995—; chair art com. Empire State Aeroscis. Mus., Schenectady, N.Y., 1991-93; mem. Chenango Town Bicentennial Commn., Chenango Bridge, N.Y., 1976, Mayor's Task Force for Arts, Albany, 1990; mem. visual arts com. Albany-Tula Alliance, 1992—; chmn. composition competition Ea. N.Y. Organist Guild, 1996, Albany Carillon 70th Anniversary Com., 1996; Rep. committeeman Rensselaer, N.Y., 1996-97; juror Kingston N.Y. Area Children's Art Exhibit, 1996; bd. dirs. Eastern N.Y. Am. Guild Organists, 1996—; mem. Rensselaer City Centennial Com., 1996-97; mem. bicentennary com. City of Albany, 1997. Recipient 1st place award Regina Bell Ringers, 1987, 2d and 3d art prizes N.Y. State Fair, 1970, hon. mention Rensselaer Movement Exhbn., 1997. Mem. Am. Guild Organists (historian Ea. N.Y. chpt. 1986—, bd. dirs. 1996—), Soc. Am. Graphic Artists (adv. coun. 1993—), Pub. Employees Fedn. (steward 1991-95, chair membership com. 1992-93), Guild Carollonneurs N.Am. (assoc.), Soc. Historians Am. Art, Coll. Art Assn., Assn. Ind. Historians Art, N.Y. State Archaeol. Assn. (officer Triple Cities chpt. 1977-81), Artist Action Group (co-chairperson 1975-76), Print Club Albany (pres. 1989—), Capital Area Archivists (sec. 1993-94, bd. dirs. 1994), Mus. Prints and Printmaking (pres. 1990—), Broome County Landmark Soc. (pres. 1975-76), Syracuse Printmakers, Masons (Most Wise Master Rose Croix chpt. 1995, sr. warden 1997), Shriners (organist 1992—). Avocations: organist, airplane pilot, motorcyling, archaeology. Home: 242 Broadway Rensselaer NY 12144-2705

SEMPLE, CECIL SNOWDON, retired manufacturing company executive; b. Assam, India, Aug. 12, 1917; came to U.S., 1927, naturalized, 1948; s. Fordyce B. and Anne (Munro) S. B.A., Colgate U., 1939. Buyer R.H. Macy & Co., 1939-42, 46-48; buyer, div. supt. Montgomery Ward, 1948-50; v.p. Nachman Corp., Chgo., 1950-55; sales mgr. radio receiver dept. Gen. Elec. Co., Bridgeport, Conn., 1955-60; mktg. cons. merchandising Gen. Elec. Co., N.Y.C., 1966-67, gen. mgr. audio products dept., 1967-68, dep. div. gen. mgr. housewares div., 1968-69, gen. mgr. housewares div., 1969, v.p., 1969-71, v.p. corp. customer relations, 1971-85; v.p. Rich's Inc., Atlanta, 1960-62, sr. v.p., dir., 1962-66; trustee Peoples Bank., Bridgeport, 1975-89, trustee emeritus. Bd. dirs. Nat. Jr. Achievement Inc., 1974-86, Bridgeport Area Found., 1970-91, dir. emeritus, 1991—; bd. dirs. Bridgeport Hosp., 1970-93, chmn., 1983-89, dir. emeritus, 1993—; bd. trustees Colgate U., 1970-84, vice chmn. 1978-84; trustee emeritus, past pres., bd. dirs. Alumni Corp.; chmn. So. Conn. Health Svc. Inc., 1990-93. Served to maj. USAAF, 1942-46. Mem. St. Andrews Soc. State N.Y. (chmn. bd. mgrs. 1968-70), Delta Kappa Epsilon. Clubs: Brooklawn Country (Fairfield, Conn.), Fairfield Country. Home: 25 Cartright St Bridgeport CT 06604

SEMPLE, JAMES WILLIAM, lawyer; b. Phila., Nov. 18, 1943; s. Calvin James and Marie (Robinson) S.; m. Ellen Burns, Nov. 26, 1966; children: Megan Ward, Luke Robinson. AB, St. Josephs U., Phila., 1965; JD, Villanova U., 1974. Bar: Del. 1974, U.S. Dist. Ct. Del. 1974, D.C. 1975, U.S. Ct. Appeals (3d cir.) 1982, U.S. Tax Ct. 1996. Ptnr. Morris, James, Hitchens & Williams, Wilmington, 1983—; lectr. numerous seminars; mediator Superior Ct. Voluntary Mediation Program. Mem. ABA (bus. law sect., litigation sect., torts and ins. practice sect.), Del. Bar Assn. (mem. exec. com. 1978, 80, 81, asst. sec. 1980, sec. 1981, chmn. torts and ins. practice sect. 1982-84, long range planning com. 1997—), Am. Bd. Trial Advs., Fedn. Ins. and Corp. Counsel, Am. Judicature Soc., Am. Soc. Law and Medicine, Assn. Internat. de Droit d'Assurance, Am. Inns of Ct. (Richard Rodney chpt.). Democrat. Roman Catholic. Clubs: Wilmington Country (Greenville, Del.). Home: 103 Brookvalley Rd Wilmington DE 19807-2003 Office: Morris James Hitchens & Williams PO Box 2306 Wilmington DE 19899-2306

SEMPLE, LLOYD ASHBY, lawyer; b. St. Louis, June 7, 1939; s. Robert B. and Isabelle A. S.; m. Cynthia T. Semple, Aug. 26, 1961; children: Whitney, Sarah, Lloyd Jr., Terrell. BA, Yale U., 1961; JD, U. Mich., 1964. Bar: Mich. 1964. Assoc. Dykema Gossett, Detroit, 1964-70, ptnr., 1971-94; chmn., 1994—; gen. counsel Daedalus Enterprises, Inc., Ralph Wilson Enterprises, Copper & Bass Sales; bd. dirs. Interface Sys., Inc. Councilman, mayor pro tem City of Grosse Pointe Farms, Mich, 1975-83; chmn. bd., trustee Harper Hosp.; vice chmn. bd. trustees Detroit Med. Ctr. Corp.; chmn. bd. dirs. Detroit Zool. Soc.; dir., trustee, sec. Karmanos Cancer Inst. Mem. ABA, Mich. Bar Assn., Detroit Bar Assn., Country Club, Yondotega Club, Detroit Athletic Club, Yale Club (N.Y.C.), Bohemian Club (San Francisco). Episcopalian. Home: 57 Cambridge Rd Grosse Pointe MI 48236-3004 Office: Dykema Gossett 400 Renaissance Ctr Detroit MI 48243

SEMPLE, ROBERT BAYLOR, JR., newspaper editor, journalist; b. St. Louis, Aug. 12, 1936; s. Robert B. and Isabelle Ashby (Neer) S.; m. Susan Riker Kirk, Aug. 19, 1961 (div. Feb. 1980); children: Robert Baylor III, Elizabeth, William, Mary; m. Lisa Pulling, Jan. 10, 1981. Grad., Phillips Acad., 1954; B.A., Yale U., 1959; M.A., U. Calif., Berkeley, 1961. Reporter Nat. Observer, 1961-63; corr. N.Y. Times, 1963-68, White House corr., 1968-72, dep. nat. editor, 1973-75, London bur. chief, 1975-77; fgn. editor N.Y. Times, N.Y.C., 1977-82, op-ed page editor, 1982-88, assoc. editor editorial page, 1988—. Recipient Pulitzer prize for editorial writing, 1996; Carnegie fellow, 1959-60; Woodrow Wilson fellow, 1960-61. Mem. Coun. Fgn. Rels., Century Assn. (N.Y.C.), Yale Club (N.Y.C.). Episcopalian. Office: 229 W 43rd St New York NY 10036-3913

SEMROD, T. JOSEPH, banker; b. Oklahoma City, Dec. 13, 1936; s. L.J. and Theda Jo (Hummel) S.; m. Janice Lee Wood, June 1, 1968 (div. 1988); children: Ronald, Catherine, Christopher, Elizabeth; m. Jaye Patricia Hewitt, May 27, 1989; 1 child, Kelsey. B.A. in Polit. Sci., U. Okla., 1958, LL.B., 1963. Bar: Okla. 1963. With Liberty Nat. Bank, Oklahoma City, 1963-81; v.p. Liberty Nat. Bank, 1967-69, sr. v.p., 1969-71, exec. v.p., 1971-73, pres., 1973-81; pres. Liberty Nat. Corp., Oklahoma City, 1976-81; chmn. bd., pres., chief exec. officer United Jersey Banks (name now UJB Fin. Corp.), Princeton, N.J., 1981-96; chmn., CEO, Summit Bancorp. (merged with UJB Fin. Corp.), Princeton, 1996—; chmn., bd. dirs., CEO Summit Bank, Princeton, N.J., 1981—; bd. dirs. Internat. Fin. Conf., chmn., 1994, bd. dirs. Fed. Reserve Bank of N.Y., 1983-86. Trustee, mem. exec. com. Nat. Urban League, 1963-95; mem. bd. advisors Outward Bound, Inc., 1984—, Ind. Coll. Fund N.J., 1986-90; commr. Citizens Commn. on Aids, 1988-90; chmn. bd. regents Stonier Grad. Sch. Banking, Rutgers U., 1983; mem. N.J. Transp. Trust Fund Authority, 1985-87; chmn. The Partnership for N.J., 1989-90, trustee; mem. N.J. Com.-U.S. Savings Bonds com.; chmn. banking industry U.S. Savs. Bonds campaign, 1992-93. 1st lt. U.S. Army, 1958-60. Mem. Am. Bankers Assn., N.J. Bankers Assn., N.J. Bar Assn., Okla. Bar Assn., Baankers Roundtable (bd. dirs. 1995—), Regional Plan Assn. (bd. dirs. 1989-91), Young Pres. Orgn., Am. Running and Fitness Assn. (bd. dirs. 1983-86), N.J. C. of C. (bd. dirs., vice chmn.), Drumthwacket Found. (chmn. 1990-94), Bedens Brook Club (Skillman, N.J.), River Club (N.Y.C.), Metedoconk Club (Jackson, N.J.), Coral Beach Club (Bermuda), Nassau Club, Tournament Players Club, Adirondack League Club (Old Forge, N.Y.). Democrat. Roman Catholic. Office: Summit Bancorp PO Box 2066 301 Carnegie Ctr Princeton NJ 08543-2066

SEN, ASHISH KUMAR, urban planner, educator; b. Delhi, India, June 8, 1942; came to U.S., 1967, naturalized, 1985; s. Ashoka Kumar and Arati Sen; m. Colleen Taylor. BS with honors, Calcutta U., 1962; MA, U. Toronto, Ont., Can., 1964, PhD, 1971. Research assoc., lectr. dept. geography Transp. Center, Northwestern U., 1967-69; mem. faculty Center Urban Studies, U. Ill., Chgo., 1969—; prof. Center Urban Studies, U. Ill., 1978—, dir. Sch. Urban Planning, 1991; dean Center Urban Studies, U. Ill. (Sch. Urban Scis.), 1977-78, acting dir., 1992; pres. Ashish Sen. and Assocs., Chgo., 1977—. Author: Regression Analysis: Theory, Methods and Applications, 1990, Gravity MOdels of Spatial Interaction Behavior, 1995; also articles. Mem. Chgo. Bd. Edn., 1990-95; chmn. budget com. 1992-94; bd. trustees Asian Inst., 1993-95. Fellow Royal Statis. Soc.; mem. Am. Statis. Assn., Inst. Math. Stats., Am. Soc. Planning Ofcls., Regional Sci. Assn., Transp. Rsch. Forum, Transp. Rsch. Bd., Cliffdwellers. Hindu. Home: 2557 W Farwell Ave Chicago IL 60645-4617

SEN, CHANDAN KUMAR, physiologist, scientist, educator; b. Chinsurah, India, Aug. 5, 1966; s. Dulal Chandra and Sankari (Gupta) S. BS in Physiology with honors, U. Calcutta, India, 1987, MS in Physiology, 1989; PhD in Physiology and Exercise Medicine, U. Kuopio, Finland, 1994. Resident expert physiology. Prin. investigator Finnish Ministry of Edn., 1993—; PhD program supr. faculty of medicine U. Kuopio, 1994—; rsch. biochemist U. Calif., Berkeley, 1995—; organizer internat. symposia and congresses on physiology; sec.-gen. III Internat. Congress on Pathophysiology, Finland, 1998; rsch. coord. dept. physiology U. Kuopio, 1994—. Editor: Exercise and Oxygen Toxicity, 1994; peer reviewer sci. jours. including Jour. Applied Physiology, Am. Jour. Applied Physiology, Jour. Immunology, Jour. Clin. Investigation, Jour. Nutrition, others; mem. editl. bd. Indian Jour. Physiology and Allied Scis.; contbr. over 65 articles to profl. jours. Recipient Jogue Jr. Scientist award, New Orleans, 1997; named to Order of Horse Collar Knight, U. Kuopio, 1994. Fellow Am. Coll. Sports Medicine; mem. Am. Physiol. Soc., Physiol. Soc. India (life, S.R. Moitra Gold medal 1991), Scandinavian Physiol. Soc. Avocations: teaching, philosophy, literature, wild life. Office: Univ Kuopio Dept Physiology, Savilahdentie 9, 70211 Kuopio Finland also: U Calif Dept Molecular Cell Biology 251 Life Scis Addition Berkeley CA 94720-3200

SEN, PARESH CHANDRA, electrical engineering educator; b. Patiya, Chittagong, Bangladesh, June 30, 1938; arrived in Can., 1963; s. Judhistir and Jaya Sen; m. Maya Dey, July 21, 1968; children: Sujit, Priya, Debashis. BSc with honors, Calcutta (India) U., 1958, MSc Tech., 1961; MASc., U. Toronto, Ont., Can., 1965; PhD, U. Toronto, 1967. Registered profl. engr., Ont. Elec. engr. TISCO, Dhanbad, India, 1961-62, DVC, Maithon, India, 1962-63; teaching asst. U. Toronto, 1963-65, 65-67; rsch. asst. Northern Electric Co., Ottawa, Ont., 1965; profl. assoc. Queen's U., Kingston, Ont., 1967-68; asst. prof. elec. engring. Queen's U., Kingston, 1968-73, assoc. prof., 1973-79, prof., 1979—; cons. Urban Transp. Devel. Corp., Alcan Ltd., Kingston, 1975-80; sr. indsl. fellow Inverpower Control Ltd., Toronto, 1985-86. Author: Thyristor DC Drives, 1981, Principles of Electric Machines and Power Electronics, 1989. Fellow IEEE (prize paper award indsl. drive com. 1986). Hindu. Avocations: oil painting, reading novels. Office: Queens Univ, Dept Elec Engring, Kingston, ON Canada K7L 3N6

SENA, JOHN MICHAEL, insurance agent; b. Santa Fe, Aug. 1, 1950; s. John Campos and Mary Sena; m. Dolores Ann Hockhalter, June 19, 1979; children: Johnny Ray, Beth Ann. AA in Bus., Catonsville C.C., Balt., 1978. CLU, ChFC. Agt. Nationwide Ins. Co., Balt., 1977-79; dist. mgr. Nationwide Ins. Co., Greenbelt, Md., 1979-81; advisor fin. plans Nationwide Ins. Co., Annapolis, Md., 1981-84, San Antonio, 1984-88; agt. Nationwide Ins. Co., Boca Raton, Fla., 1988—. With USN, 1971-75. Fellow Life Underwriters Tng. Coun. (moderator San Antonio, 1987-88, Deerfield Beach, Fla., 1989-92, committeeman contents and techniques Washington 1990-93); mem. Nat. Assn. Life Underwriters (pres. Boca Raton chpt. 1996-97). Avocations: golf, travel, weight lifting. Office: John Sena Ins Agy 190 Glades Rd Ste F Boca Raton FL 33432-1642

SENAHA, EIKI, English literature educator, university dean; b. Nago, Okinawa, Japan, Nov. 20, 1928; s. Eiko and Kami (Toguchi) S.; m. Shizu Kishimoto, Feb. 15, 1954; children: Yoko Shayesteh, Eijun, Tatsuko, Sawada. BS, Ctrl. Mo. State U., 1959, MA, 1959; MPhil, U. Kans., 1971, PhD, 1977. Asst. prof. Okinawa (Japan) U., 1959-65; prof. U. Ryukyus, Japan, 1965-94, dir. libns., 1983-85, dean edn., 1985-89, chair internat. programs, 1991-94; prof., dean Meio (Japan) U., 1994—; interviewer Soc. for Testing English Proficiency, Japan, 1978—; examiner Okinawa Human Resources Devel. Found., Japan, 1982—; screener Fulbright Found., Japan, 1986—; sec. gen. VII Pacific Sci. Inter-Congress, Japan, 1990-94. Author: (book) Essays for Professor Genshu Asato, 1972, Japanese Responses to Wordsworth's Concept of Nature, 1976; contbr. articles to profl. jours. Scholar Govt. of U.S., 1957-59, 67-71; rsch. grantee Govt. of Japan, 1976-77. Mem. English Lit. Soc. Japan, English Romantic Soc. Japan, English Romantic Soc. Okinawa (pres. 1994—), Pacific Sci. Assn. (Japan nat. com. 1990—, coun. 1990—). Avocations: sports, travel. Office: Meio U, 1220-1 Biimata, Nago 905, Japan

SENDAK, MAURICE BERNARD, writer, illustrator; b. Bklyn., June 10, 1928; s. Philip and Sadie (Schindler) S. Student, Art Students League, N.Y.C., 1949-51; LHD, Boston U., 1977; hon. degree, U. So. Miss., 1981, Keene State Coll., 1986. Window display artist Timely Svc., N.Y.C., 1946; display artist FAO Schwartz, N.Y.C., 1948-51; co-founder, artistic dir. The Night Kitchen, 1990—. One-man shows include Gallery Sch. Visual Arts, N.Y.C., 1964, Rosenbach Found., Phila., 1970, 75, Trinity Coll., 1972, Galerie Daniel Keel, Zurich, 1974, Ashmolean Mus., Oxford, 1975, Am. Cultural Center, Paris, 1978, Pierpont Morgan Library, N.Y.C., 1981; author, illustrator: Kenny's Window, 1956 (Spring Book Fesitval honor book 1956), Very Far Away, 1957, The Acrobat, 1959, The Sign on Rosie's Door, 1960, The Nutshell Library (contains Chicken Soup with Rice, One Was Johnny, Alligators All Around, Pierre: A Cautionary Tale), 1962, Where The Wild Things Are, 1963 (N.Y. Times Best Illustrated Book award 1963, Caldecott medal 1964, Lewis Carroll Shelf award 1964, Internat. Bd. on Books for Young People award 1966, Art Books for Children award 1973, 74, 75, Best Young Picture Books Paperback award Redbook Mag. 1984, Children's Choice award 1985), Hector Protector and As I Went Over the Water: Two Nursery Rhymes, 1965, Higglety, Pigglety, Pop!; or, There Must Be More to Life, 1967 (Am. Book award nomination 1980), In the Night Kitchen, 1970 (N.Y. Times Best Illustrated Book award 1970, Caldecott medal nomination 1971, Art Books for Children award 1973, 74, 75, Redbook Mag. award 1985), Ten Little Rabbits: A Counting Book with Mino the Magician, 1970, Pictures by Maurice Sendak, 1971, Maurice Sendak's Really Rosie, 1975, Some Swell Pup; or, Are You Sure You Want A Dog, 1976, Seven Little Monsters, 1977, Outside Over There, 1981 (N.Y. Times Best Illustrated Book award 1981, Boston Globe/Horn Book award 1981, Caldecott medal nomination 1982, Am. Book award 1982), We Are All in the Dumps with Jack and Guy, 1993, Tsippi, 1994, Moishe, 1994, Max, 1994; illustrator: Atomics for the Millions, 1947, Good Shabbos, Everybody!, 1951, The Wonderful Farm, 1951, A Hole is to Dig, 1952 (N.Y. Times Best Illustrated Book award 1952), Maggie Rose: Her Birthday Christmas, 1952, The Giant Story, 1953, Hurry Home Candy, 1953, Shadrach, 1953, A Very Special House, 1953 (Caldecott medal nomination 1954), I'll Be You and You Be Me, 1954 (N.Y. Times Best Illustrated Book award 1954), Happy Hanukkah, Everybody, 1954, The Tin Fiddle, 1954, Magic Pictures, 1954, Mrs. Piggle-Wiggle's Farm, 1954, The Wheel on the School, 1954, Charlotte and the White Horse, 1955, The Little Cow and the Turtle, 1955, Singing Family of the Cumberlands, 1955, What Can You Do With a Shoe?, 1955, Happy Rain, 1956, The House of Sixty Fathers, 1956, I Want to Paint My Bathroom Blue, 1956 (N.Y. Times Best Illustrated Book award 1956), Birthday Party, 1957 (N.Y. Times Best Illustrated Book award 1957), Circus Girl, 1957, You Can't Get There From Here, 1957, Little Bear, 1957, Along Came a Dog, 1958, No Fighting, No Biting!, 1958, Somebody Else's Nut Tree, 1958, What Do You Say, Dear?, 1958 (N.Y. Times Best Illustrated Book award 1958, Caldecott medal nomination 1959), The Moon Jumpers, 1959 (Caldecott medal nomination 1960), Father Bear Comes Home, 1959 (N.Y. Times Best Illustrated Book award 1959), Seven Tales, 1959, Dwarf Long-Nose, 1960, Little Bear's Friend, 1960, Open House for Butterflies, 1960 (N.Y. Times Best Illustrated Book award 1960), Let's Be Enemies, 1961, The Tale of Gockel, Hinkel and Gackeliah, 1961, What Do You Do, Dear?, 1961, Little Bear's Visit, 1961 (Caldecott medal nomination 1962), Schoolmaster Whackwell's Wonderful Sons, 1962, Mr. Rabbit and the Lovely Present, 1962 (Caldecott medal nomination 1963), The Singing Hill, 1962 (N.Y. Times Best Illustrated Book award 1962), Nikolenka's Childhood, 1963, She Loves Me, She Loves Me Not, 1963, The Bat-Poet, 1964 (N.Y. Times Best Illustrated Book award 1964), How Little Lori Visited Times Square, 1964, Pleasant Fieldmouse, 1964, Lullabies and Night Songs, 1965, The Animal Family, 1965 (N.Y. Times Best Illustrated Book award 1965), Zlateh the Goat, 1966 (N.Y. Times Best Illustrated Book award 1966), The Golden Key, 1967, Poems from William Blake's Songs of Innocence, 1967, The Big Green Book, 1968, Griffin and the Minor Canon, 1968, A Kiss for Little Bear, 1968 (N.Y. Times Best Illustrated Book award 1968), The Light Princess, 1969 (N.Y. Times Best Illustrated Book award 1969), The Bee-Man of Orn, 1971, Sarah's Room, 1971, The Juniper Tree and Other Tales from Grimm, 1973 (N.Y. Times Best Illustrated Book award 1973), Fortunia: A Tale by Mme. D'Aulnoy, 1974, Fly by Night, 1976 (N.Y. Times Best Illustrated Book award 1976), King Grisly-Beard: A Tale from the Brothers Grimm, 1978, The Nutcracker, 1984 (N.Y. Times Best Illustrated Book award 1984), In Grandpa's House, 1985, The Children's Books of Randall Jarrell, 1988, Dear Mili, 1988, I Saw Esau, 1992, The Ubiquitous Pig, 1992; author: Fantasy Sketches, 1970, Collection of Books, Posters, and Original Drawings, 1984, The Love for Three Oranges: The Glyndebourne Version, 1984, Posters, 1986, Caldecott & Co.: Notes on Books and Pictures, 1988, Maurice Sendak Book and Poster Package: Wild Things, 1991; editor: Maxfield Parrish Poster Book, 1974, The Disney Poster Book, 1977; contbr.: The Publishing Archive of Lothar Meggendorfer, 1975, Babar's Anniversary Album, 1981, Masterworks of Children's Literature, Vol. 7, 1984, Victorian Color Picture Books, 1985, Winsor McCay: His Life and Art, 1987, Mickey Mouse Movie Stories, 1988; dir., lyricist: Really Rosie, 1975; lyricist, set designer: Really Rosie, 1978; lyricist, set designer, costume designer: Where the Wild Things Are, 1980, Higglety, Pigglety, Pop!, 1984; set designer, costume designer: The Magic Flute, 1980, The Cunning Little Vixen, 1981, Love for Three Oranges, 1982, The Goose of Cairo, 1984, Idomeneo, 1988, L'Enfant et les Sortileges, 1989, L'Heure Espagnol, 1989, It's Alive!, 1994, So, Sue Me, 1994; photographer: The Cunning Little Vixen, 1985; designer: (film) The Nutcracker, 1986. Recipient Chandler Book Talk Reward of Merit, 1967, Hans Christian Andersen Internat. medal, 1970, Laura Ingalls Wilder award Assn. Libr. Svc. to Children, 1983, Nat. Medal Arts, 1997. Office: Harper & Row 10 E 53rd St New York NY 10022-5244

SENDAX, VICTOR IRVEN, dentist, educator, dental implant researcher; b. N.Y.C., Sept. 14, 1930; s. Maurice and Molly R. S.; m. Deborah deLand Cobb, Dec. 17, 1969 (div. June 1976); 1 child, Jennifer Reiland; m. Marcia Ayer Pearson, Dec. 13, 1986; children: Anneliese Chase, Cordelia Ayer. G-rad., Tanglewood Music Ctr., 1953; BA, NYU, 1951, DDS, 1955; postgrad., Harvard U. Sch. Dental Medicine, 1969-72. Diplomate Am. Bd. Oral Implantology/Implant Dentistry (pres. 1996). Commr. N.Y. State Dental Svc. Corp., 1969-73; pres., dir. BioDental Rsch. Found., Inc., N.Y.C., 1975—; pres. Victor I. Sendax, D.D.S., P.C., N.Y.C., 1972—, Mini Dental Implant Ctrs. Mgmt., Inc., 1985—; assoc. attending implantologist St. Lukes-Roosevelt Hosp. Dental Implant Ctr., N.Y.C., 1979—; vol. attending implantologist Beth Israel Hosp., N.Y.C., 1991—, Beth Israel North Hosp., N.Y.C., 1991—; adj. assoc. prof. implant prosthodontics Columbia U. Sch. Dental and Oral Surgery, N.Y.C., 1974-92; vis. lectr. dept. implant dentistry NYU Coll. Dentistry; faculty 1st Dist. Dental Soc. Sch. for Continuing Dental Edn.; mem. dental implant rsch. programs adv. com. Nat. Inst. Dental Rsch., HHS; cons. Julliard Sch. Voice and Drama, N.Y.C., 1972—, Vocal Dynamics Lab. Dept. Otolaryngology, Lenox Hill Hosp., N.Y.C., 1970-90; founder Sendax Seminars; 1st dir. implant prosthodontics resident program Columbia U. Sch. Dental and Oral Surgery and Columbia Presbyn. Hosp. Editor: Dental Clinics of North America: HA-Coated Dental Implants, 1992; mem. editl. bd. Oral Implantology, 1979—; patentee in oral implant magnetics, mini-implants, implant abutments and sinus graft implant stabilizers. Bd. dirs. City Ctr. Music and Drama, Inc. divsn. Lincoln Ctr. Performing Arts, N.Y.C., 1966-75; mem. adv. bd. Amagansett (N.Y.) Hist. Assn., 1969-89; trustee Leukemia Soc. Am., N.Y.C., 1967; bd. dirs. Schola Cantorum, 1980-90, Soc. Asian Music, 1965-76. Capt. Dental Corps USAF, 1955-57. Recipient Cert. of Honor, Brit. Dental Implant Assn., 1988., Aaron Gershkoff Meml. award for Outstanding Contbns. and Dedication to Oral Implantology Am. Acad. f Implant Dentistry, 1996. Fellow Am. Coll. Dentists, Internat. Coll. Dentists, Am. Acad. Implant Dentistry (nat. pres. 1981), Royal Soc. Medicine Gt. Britain; mem. ADA (ho. of dels. 1969), Am. Assn. Dental Schs. (chmn. interdisciplinary group on dental implant edn.), Acad. of Osseointegration, Am. Prosthodontic Soc., Am. Equilibration Soc., Am. Analgesia Soc., Fedn. Dentaire Internat., Am. Assn. Dental Rsch. (implant group), Internat. Assn. Dental Rsch., N.Y. Acad. Scis., Japan Soc., Century Assn., Players Club (N.Y.C.), Sigma Epsilon Delta. Home: 70 E 77th St Apt 6A New York NY 10021-1811 Office: Mini Dental Implant Ctr Ste 14B 30 Central Park S Rm 14B New York NY 10019-1628 *I stand in awe of mankinds' eternal need to innovate and push back the frontiers of knowledge, while tempering the harsher realities of existence with a perspective born of our cultural heritage.*

SENDERLING, JON TOWNSEND, journalist, public affairs specialist; b. Phila.; s. John Chester and Elizabeth (Nogle) S.; m. Elizabeth Marie Broadbent, Mar. 27, 1965; children: Jon, Tracy. Student, Ursinus Coll., 1960, Temple U., 1961-64; student (fellow), Stanford U., 1970. Reporter Bucks County Courier Times, Levittown, Pa., 1966-68, Wilmington (Del.) News-Jour., 1968-70; reporter, mag. writer, columnist, spl. projects editor Trenton (N.J.) Times, 1970-76; gen. assignments editor, state editor, nat.-fgn. editor Dallas Times Herald, 1976-80, editorial page dir., 1981-86; dep. fgn. editor Newsday, Melville, L.I., N.Y., 1987-89; pub. affairs mgr. EDS Corp., Dallas, 1989—. Author: play The Trashman, 1970. Recipient disting. service award for editorial writing Sigma Delta Chi, 1982, also 16 awards state press assns. Office: 5400 Legacy Dr Plano TX 75024-3105

SENDLEIN, LYLE V. A., geology educator; b. St. Louis, May 11, 1933; s. Lyle Vernon and Bernice Kathrine (Le Fevre) S.; m. Louise Pauline Darr; children: Lyle Scott, Todd Lockard, Erik Le Fevre. BS in Geol. Engring., Washington U., St. Louis, 1958, AM in Geology, 1960; PhD Geology-Soil Engring., Iowa State U., 1964. From instr. to prof. geology Iowa State U., Ames, 1960-77; prof. civil engr. Middle East Tech. U., Ankara, Turkey, 1973-74; assoc. div. chief Ames Lab. Iowa State U., Ames, 1974-77; prof., dir. Coal Rsch. Ctr., So. Ill. U., Carbondale, 1977-82; prof. geology U. Ky., Lexington, 1982—, acting chmn. dept. geol. scis., 1989-91, dir. Inst. Mining and Minerals Rsch., 1982-94; dir. Ky. Water Resources Rsch. Inst., 1991—; pres. Forest Ridge Maintenance Assocs. Inc., Lexington, 1989-90. Author: Introduction to Geology, 1970; editor: Surface Mining Handbook, 1983; mem. editorial bd. Groundwater, 1977-80. With U.S. Army, 1953-55. Recipient best paper award Nat. Water Well Assn., 1971, 75. Fellow Geol. Soc. Am.; mem. Am. Geophys. Union, Assn. Groundwater Scientists and Engrs. Avocations: scuba diving, sailing. Home: 108 South Dr Key Largo FL 33037 Office: Water Resources Rsch Inst 233 Mining & Mineral Bldg Lexington KY 40506

SENDLER, DAVID ALAN, magazine editor; b. White Plains, N.Y., Dec. 12, 1938; s. Morris and Rose Sendler; m. Emily Shimm, Oct. 17, 1965; 2 children. BA, Dartmouth Coll., 1960; MS, Columbia U., 1961. Assoc. editor Sport mag., 1964-65; editorial Pageant mag., 1965-71, exec. editor, 1969-71; editor Today's Health, 1971-74; sr. editor Parade, N.Y.C., 1974-75; articles editor Ladies Home Jour., 1975-76; mng. editor TV Guide mag., Radnor, Pa., 1976-79, exec. editor, 1979-80, co-editor, 1981-89; exec. editor Rediscover America Project Time Inc., 1990-91; editor-in-chief New Choices Mag., N.Y.C., 1992—. With U.S. Army, 1961-63. Named editor of yr. 1996 Am. Soc. Journalists and Authors. Mem. Am. Soc. Mag. Editors. Avocations: movies, public affairs, tennis, fitness.

SENDO, TAKESHI, mechanical engineering educator, researcher, author; b. Ena City, Japan, Aug. 5, 1917; s. Shigeyoshi and Michie (Yamamoto) S.; m. Hide Okamoto, Apr. 16, 1945; children: Mitsuyoshi, Sachiko, Kazuyasu. B of Engring., Tokyo U., 1941. Prof. mech. engring. Meijo U., Nagoya City, Japan, 1959-90, hon. prof., 1990—; curator libr. Meijo U., Nagoya City, 1975-80. Author: Treatise of High Speed Deformation of Metal, 1993, 2nd edit., 1994, Experiment: Behavior of Al Column by Drop Hammer Test, 1959-90; contbr. over 60 articles to profl. jours. Mem. cmty. activity com. Local Self-Governing Orgn., Moriyama City, Japan, 1990, 91. Served to lt. comdr. Japanese Navy, 1941-45. Fellow Japan Soc. Mech. Engring., Japan Soc. Precision Engring. Avocations: composing Haiku and Tanka, trying essay, jogging. Home: 21-8 Choei Moriyama-ku, Nagoya 463, Japan

SENECAL, CONNIE MONTOYA, special education educator; b. Iloilo, Panay, Philippines, Oct. 23, 1945; came to U.S., 1968; d. Pedro Altaya Montoya and Esperanza Canoy Tupino; m. William S. Goodyear Jr., Oct. 26, 1968 (div. Nov. 1981); children: Stacy, Katie; m. John Joseph Senecal, Dec. 31, 1982; 1 child, Amy. BA, U. Guam, Agana, 1967; MA, U. No. Colo., 1970. Cert. tchr., Colo., Tex. Med. social worker Dept. Pub. Health and Welfare, Agana, 1967-68; tchr. emotionally disturbed-behavior disordered students Boulder (Colo.) Valley Pub. Schs., 1970-83, Dept. of Def. Dependents Schs., Mannheim, Germany, 1989; cons., behavior mgmt. specialist Dept. of Def. Dependents Schs., Heidelberg, Germany, 1986-89; resource tchr. Ft. Campbell (Ky.) Schs., 1983-86; tchr. Northside Ind. Schs., San Antonio, 1990-95, N.E. Ind. Sch., San Antonio, 1995—; presenter workshops. Recording sec. Panay/Negros Filipino Assn., Agana, 1967; sec. AAUW, Agana, 1968. Mem. NEA, Coun. Exceptional Children. Democrat. Roman Catholic. Avocations: collecting Russian lacquer boxes, fairy tale plates, German tins. Office: Stahl Elem Sch 5222 Stahl Rd San Antonio TX 78247-1713

SENECHAL, ALICE R., judge, lawyer; b. Rugby, N.D., June 25, 1955; d. Marvin William and Dora Emma (Erdman) S. BS, N.D. State U., 1977; JD, U. Minn., 1984. Bar: Minn. 1984, U.S. Dist. Ct. Minn. 1984, N.D. 1986, U.S. Ct. Appeals (8th cir.) 1987. Law clk. U.S. Dist. Judge Bruce M. Van Sickle, Bismarck, N.D., 1984-86; with Robert Vogel Law Office, Grand Forks, N.D., 1986—; U.S. magistrate judge, 1990—. Office: Robert Vogel Law Office 106 N 3rd St Ste 202 Grand Forks ND 58203-3700

SENEFF, MICHAEL GEREN, anesthesiologist; b. Grand Rapids, Mich., Aug. 15, 1955; s. William Mabrey and Shirley Mae (Geren) S.; m. Marilyn E. Giles, Jan. 3, 11981; children: Alexis, Taylor, Spencer. BS in Chemistry magna cum laude, U. Mo., Columbia, 1977, MD cum laude, 1981. Diplomate Am. Bd. Internal Medicine, Am. Bd. Critical Care; cert. BLS, ATLS instr. House officer, resident in internal medicine U. Mass. Med. Ctr., Worcester, 1981-84; staff internist dept. internal medicine Naval Hosp. San Diego, 1984-86; clin. instr. U. Calif.-San Diego Med. Sch., 1985-86; staff physician Office Attending Physician U.S. Congress, Washington, 1986-88; fellow critical care medicine George Washington U. Med. Ctr., Washington, 1988-90, assoc. prof. anesthesiology/critical care, 1992—, dir. ICU, 1994—; staff physician critical care medicine, co-dir. ICU Nat. Naval Med. Ctr., Bethesda, Md., 1990-92, acting dept. head, 1990-91; asst. prof. medicine Uniformed Svcs. U. Health Scis., Bethesda, 1990-92; presenter, rschr. in field. Contbr. numerous articles to profl. jours. Mo. Curators scholar, 1973-77; recipient Epstein Rsch. award, 1990; grantee Bristol-Myers Squibb Cefpime, 1993, Synergen Inc., 1994, Cortech Inc., 1994, Liposome Co., Inc., Wallace Labs., RxTrials. Fellow ACP, Am. Coll. Chest Physicians; mem. Soc. Critical Care Medicine, Phi Beta Kappa, Phi Lambda Upsilon, Alpha Omega Alpha. Office: George Washington U Med Ctr 901 23rd St NW Washington DC 20037-2327

SENEFF, SMILEY HOWARD, business owner; b. Odon, Ind., June 28, 1925; s. Smiley and Ada Fern (Howard) S.; m. Barbara Jean Daum, July 17, 1950 (div. 1966); children: Nancy Kay Secrest, Cheryl Evans; m. Mary Ann Beeler, Mar. 12, 1966; children: Jill Midtbo, Judy Hiland, Jacalyn Harness, Jennifer Sillery, Donald. Student, Duke U., 1945; BS, Ind. U., 1950. Mem. acctg. staff Armour and Co., Indpls., 1950-52, Chevrolet Comml. Body Co., Indpls., 1952-54; owner, mgr. Seneff Hardware and Appliance, Plainfield, Ind., 1955-66, Catalina Motel, Indpls., 1966-73, Smiley's Pancake and Steak, Indpls., 1972—, Smiley's Car Wash, Indpls., 1972—. Mem. County Zoning Bd., 1959-63; Rep. precinct committeeman, del. to state Rep. conv., 1959-63. Mem. Elks, Rotary (pres.), Masons, Scottish Rite, Shriners. Avocations: golf, swimming, walking. Home: 6002 W Mount Auburn Dr Indianapolis IN 46224-6126 Office: Seneff Inns Inc 1307 S High School Rd Indianapolis IN 46241-3128

SENEKER, CARL JAMES, II (KIM SENEKER), lawyer; b. San Jose, Calif., Oct. 12, 1942; s. Carl James and Beth D. (Hearn) S.; m. Julie Marie Pardee, June 17, 1967; children: Mark Gwynn, Todd Christian. AB, Stanford U., 1964; JD, U. Calif., Berkeley, 1967. Bar: Calif. 1969, U.S. Dist. Ct. (no. dist.) Calif. 1973. Law clk. to Hon. William O. Douglas U.S. Supreme Ct., Washington, 1967-68; ptnr. Morrison & Foerster, San Francisco, 1971-84, 96—, L.A., 1984-96; adj. prof. law, lectr. law sch. Stanford U., Palo Alto, Calif., 1982-83. Co-editor: California Real Estate Law and Practice, Vols. 12 & 13, 1983-96; contbr. articles to profl. jours. Bd. dirs. L.A. Hdqs. City Assn., 1988-93. Capt. USAF, 1968-71. Mem. Am. Coll. Real Estate Lawyers (bd. govs. 1989-97, pres.-elect 1996-97), State Bar Calif. (real property law sect., vice-chair exec. com. 1987-90). Roman Catholic. Avocations: golf, travel, music. Office: Morrison & Foerster 425 Market St Fl 35 San Francisco CA 94105

SENER, JOSEPH WARD, JR., securities company executive; b. Balt., June 30, 1926; s. Joseph Ward and Clara (Hodshon) S.; m. Ann Clark TenEyck, May 3, 1952 (dec. Oct. 1967); children: J. TenEyck, Beverley T., Joseph Ward III; m. Jean Eisenbrandt-Johnston, Feb. 6, 1971. A.B., Haverford (Pa.) Coll., 1950; diploma, Inst. Investment Banking, U. Pa., 1954. With John C. Legg & Co., Balt., 1950-70; gen. partner John C. Legg & Co., 1961-70; exec. v.p., dir. Legg, Mason & Co., Inc., Balt., 1970-72; vice chmn. bd. dirs., chief adminstrv. officer Legg Mason Wood Walker, Inc., Balt., 1976-80; chmn. bd. dirs. Chesapeake Bank and Trust, Chestertown, Md. Trustee Boys' Latin Sch., Balt., pres. bd. trustees, 1980-82; chmn. bd. govs. Chesapeake Bay Maritime Mus. Served with USAAF, 1944-46. Mem. Nat. Assn. Securities Dealers (past dist. chmn.), Balt. Security Analysts Soc. (past pres.), Md. Club (Balt.). Republican. Episcopalian. Office: PO Box 511 Chestertown MD 21620-0511

SENERCHIA, DOROTHY SYLVIA, urban planner, author; b. Warwick, R.I.; d. Vincenzo Ralph and Theresa Felicia (Petrarca) S. BA, Pembroke Coll., Brown U., 1955; Cert., U. Florence, Italy, 1956. Cert. urban planner, N.Y.C. Tchr. Berlitz Sch. Langs., Florence, 1955-56; adminstrv. asst. Sheraton Corp. Am., N.Y.C., 1956-57, Inter-Am. Coun., N.Y.C., 1958-59, Roger Stevens Devel. Corp., N.Y.C., 1960-61; urban planner N.Y.C. Dept. City Planning, 1962-96. Author: Silent Menace, 1990; co-producer, co-star film The Funeral, 1980; solo concert violinist, 1945-62; co-founder singing group The Chattertocks of Brown U., 1952. One of the pioneers in cmty organization in the Urban Planning Process, N.Y.C., 1962-68; one of the early pioneers in women's movement, N.Y.C., 1969; mem. planning com. 1970

Women's March, N.Y.C., 1970; counselor Big Sisters Orgn., N.Y.C., 1969-82. Mem. Vet. Feminists Am. (co-founder, mem. founding bd.), The French Round Table (founder), Life-Affirming Group (founder). Democrat. Avocations: foreign languages, music, travel, flower gardening.

SENESE, DONALD JOSEPH, former government official; b. Chgo., Apr. 6, 1942; s. Leo Carl and Joan (Schaffer) S.; m. Linda Faye Wall, Dec. 29, 1973; 1 dau., Denise Nicole. B.S. in History, Loyola U., 1964, M.A., 1966; PhD, U. S.C., 1970; postgrad., Sophia U., Tokyo, 1970, Nat. Chengchi U., Taipei, Taiwan, 1971; cert. in adminstrv. procedures, U.S. Dept. Agr. Grad. Sch., 1976. Assoc. prof. history Radford (Va.) U., 1969-72; legis. asst. to senator from Va. Senator from Va., 1973; legis. dir. to Rep. from Tex., 1973-76; sr. research assoc. House Republican Study Com., U.S. Ho. of Reps., Washington, 1976-81; asst. sec. for ednl. research and improvement U.S. Dept. Edn., Washington, 1981-85; pres. Senese Edn. Enterprises, Inc., 1985—; dep. asst. sec. to asst. sec. Office Territorial and Internat. Affairs, Dept. Interior, Washington, 1989-93; writer, cons. SEE, Inc., Alexandria, Va.; instr. U.S.Dept. of Agrl. Grad. Sch., 1995-96; mem. child care liability task force study, Dept. Labor, 1989; instr. U.S. Dept. Agrl. Grad. Sch., 1995—. Author: Indexing the Inflationary Impact of Taxes, 1978, Modernizing the Chinese Dragon, 1980, Asianomics: Challenge and Change in Northeast Asia, 1981; editor: Ideas Confront Reality, 1981, Sweet and Sour Capitalism, 1985, Democracy in Mainland China, 1986; co-author: Can The Two Chinas Become One?, 1989; editor: George Mason and The Legacy of Constitutional Liberty, 1989. Vice chmn. Alexandria (Va.) Rep. Com., 1976-78, staff Rep. Nat. Com., 1987-89; mem. Alexandria Hist. Records Commn., 1979-84; mem. Fairfax County History Commn., 1985—, chmn., 1990-91; Fairfax County Bicentennial of U.S. Constn. Com., 1986-91; dir. Nat. Ctr. for Presdl. Rsch., 1987—; dir. opposition rsch. Rep. Nat. Com., 1995-96; dir. of rsch Co-Chairman Rep. Nat. Com., 1996—. Recipient William P. Lyons Master Essay award, 1967; Freedoms Found. award, 1981, 85, 90; named Outstanding Man of Yr. Jaycees, 1976, 78, Sec. Labor Exceptional Achievement award, 1990. Mem. Univ. Profs. for Acad. Order, Order Sons of Italy, Pi Gamma Mu, Phi Alpha Theta, Delta Sigma Rho-Tau Kappa Alpha. Roman Catholic. Office: PO Box 6886 Alexandria VA 22306-0886 *It has been important to have a philosophy of government which emphasizes honesty, integrity, a Ciceronian concept of duty, cost-effective public service, and a committment to the American heritage and traditions. These views have been reinforced by the support of family, friends, and a spiritual faith.*

SENGBUSCH, HOWARD GEORGE, biology, parasitology educator; b. Buffalo, Dec. 14, 1917; s. Howard Clarence and Blanche Anita (Foreman) S.; m. Beatrice Ardell Ebling, July 2, 1942; children: Craig Howard, Lee Ardell. BS in Edn., Buffalo State Tchrs. Coll., 1939; EdM, U. Buffalo, 1947; MS in Zoology, NYU, 1951, PhD in Parasitology, 1951. Tchr. Lockport (N.Y.) Sch. Dist., 1939-41; mem. faculty SUNY, Buffalo, 1951-81, prof. biology, 1957-81, prof. emeritus biology, 1981—, dean arts and scis., 1965-70; dir. Gt. Lakes Lab., Buffalo, 1965-66; vis. scientist Max Planck Inst. Meeresbiologie, Wilhelmshaven, Germany, 1957-58; Fulbright prof. Cen. Philippine U., Iloilo, 1962-63; vis. prof. parasitology U. Mysore, India, 1969-70; cons. in parasitology Roswell Park Meml. Inst., Buffalo, 1963—; adj. prof. biology Inst. Arthropodology and Parasitology, Ga. So. U., Statesboro, 1982—; courtesy prof. biology Fla. State U., Tallahassee, 1986—. Bd. dirs. Buffalo Zool. Soc., Buffalo Mus. Natural Sci. 1st lt. AUS, 1941-46, scientist dir. USPHS inactive res., 1956—. Fellow AAAS, Indian Acad. Zoology; mem. Acarological Soc. Am. (charter), Entomol. Soc. Am., Ga. Entomol. Soc., Hawaiian Entomol. Soc., Izaak Walton League (bd. dirs.), Rotary, Sigma Xi, Phi Delta Kappa, Kappa Delta Pi. Presbyterian. Home: 2112 Skyland Dr Tallahassee FL 32303-4324

SENGUPTA, DIPAK LAL, electrical engineering and physics educator, researcher; b. Bengal, India, Mar. 1, 1931; came to U.S., 1959; s. Jayanta Kumar and Pankajini Sengupta; m. Sujata Basu, Aug. 31, 1962; children: Sumit, Mita. BSc in Physics with honors, Calcutta U., India, 1950, MSc in Radio Physics, 1952; PhD, U. Toronto, Ont., Can., 1958. Assoc. rsch. physicist dept. elec. engring. U. Mich., Ann Arbor, 1959-63, rsch. physicist, 1965-75, rsch. scientist, prof. dept. elec. engring., 1975-86; asst. prof. dept. elec. engring. U. Toronto, 1963-64; asst. dir. Cen. Electronics Engring. Rsch. Inst., Pilani, India, 1964-65; prof., chmn. dept. elec. engring. and physics U. Detroit Mercy, 1986-95; prof. elec. engring. U. Detroit, Mercy, 1996—; Fulbright vis. lectr. in India, 1992-93; cons. Ford Motor Co., Dearborn, Mich., 1976-77, Battelle Pacific N.W. Labs., Richland, Wash., 1978. Author: Radar Cross Section Analysis and Control, 1991; contbr. articles to profl. jours. Fellow IEEE (Contbn. award 1969, recognition awards 1978-79); mem. Internat. Radio Scientists Union (sec. commn. B 1976-78), Sigma Xi, Eta Kappa Nu. Office: U Detroit Mercy Dept Elec Engring 4001 W Mcnichols Rd Detroit MI 48221-3038

SENGUPTA, MRITUNJOY, mining engineer, educator; b. Cuttack, Orissa, India, Oct. 24, 1941; came to U.S., 1968; s. Chandi P. and Bani S.; m. Nupur Bagchi, Jan. 15, 1981; children: Shyam S. ME, Columbia U., 1971, MS, 1972; PhD, Colo. Sch. of Mines, 1983. Mining engr. Continental Oil Co., Denver, 1977-78, United Nuclear Corp., Albuquerque, 1978-80, Morrison-Knudson Co., Boise, Idaho, 1975-77, 80-82; assoc. prof. U. Alaska, Fairbanks, 1983-88, prof., 1989-95; cons. UN Devel. Program, 1987. Author: Mine Environmental Engineering, vols. I and II, 1989, Environmental Impacts of Mining, 1992; contbr. articles to profl. publs. Recipient Gold medal Mining Metall. Inst. of India, 1976, Nat. Merit scholarship Govt. of India, 1959-63. Mem. NSPE, So. Mining Engrs. Achievements include development of new concepts for mine design in oilshale in Colo. Home: C102 20520 Bothel-Everett Hwy Bothell WA 98012

SENHAUSER, DONALD A(LBERT), pathologist, educator; b. Dover, Ohio, Jan. 30, 1927; s. Albert Carl and Maude Anne (Snyder) S.; m. Helen Brown, July 22, 1961; children: William, Norman. Student, U. Chgo., 1944-45; BS, Columbia U., 1948, MD, 1951; grad. with honors, U.S. Naval Sch. Aviation Medicine, 1953. Diplomate Am. Bd. Pathology. Intern Roosevelt Hosp., N.Y.C., 1951-52; resident Columbia-Presbyn. Hosp., N.Y.C., 1955-56, Cleve. Clinic, 1956-60; instr. in pathology Columbia U., 1955-56; fellow in immuno-pathology Middlesex Hosp. Med. Sch., London, 1960-61; mem. dept. pathology Cleve. Clinic Found., 1961-63; assoc. prof. pathology U. Mo., 1963-65; prof., asst. dean Sch. Medicine U. Mo., 1969-70, dir. teaching labs., 1968-70, prof., vice-chmn. dept. pathology, 1965-75; prof., chmn. dept. pathology Coll. Medicine Ohio State U., 1975-92, chair emeritus, 1992, prof. Sch. Allied Med. Professions, 1975-95; prof. emeritus, 1995—; dir. labs. Ohio State U. Hosps., 1975-92; pres. Univ. Reference Lab., Inc., 1984-86, CEO, 1986-92; bd. dirs. Columbus area chpt. ARC, 1978-82; cons. in field; WHO-AMA Vietnam med. edn. project mem. U. Saigon Med. Sch., 1967-72; vis. scientist HEW, 1972-73; acting dir. Ctrl. Ohio Regional Blood Ctr., 1976-79. Mem. editorial bd. Am. Jour. Clin. Pathology, 1965-76. With USN, 1945-46; lt. M.C. USNR, Korea, China; now capt. USNR ret. Served with USN, 1945-46; served as lt. M.C. USNR, Korea, China; now capt. USNR, Ret. Recipient Lower award Bunts Ednl. Found., 1960-61. Mem. AAAS, Coll. Am. Pathologists (bd. govs. 1980-86, v.p. 1989-90, pres.-elect 1990-91, pres. 1991-93, immediate past pres. 1993—, Pathologist of Yr. 1994), Am. Soc. Clin. Pathologists, Assn. Pathology Chmn., Am. Assn. Pathology, Internat. Acad. Pathology, Assn. Am. Med. Colls., Am. Assn. Blood Banks, Ohio Soc. Pathologists (gov. 1979, pres. 1987-89), Ohio Hist. Soc., Columbus Art League, Masons, Sigma Xi. Lutheran. Home: 1256 Clubview Blvd N Columbus OH 43235-1226 Office: 333 W 10th Ave Columbus OH 43210-1239

SENHAUSER, JOHN CRATER, architect; b. New Philadelphia, Ohio, Apr. 7, 1947; s. Edwin Crater and Margaret Jean (Huffman) S.; m. Teri A. Schleyer, June 25, 1988. BS in Architecture, U. Cin., 1971. Registered architect, Ohio, Ky. Designer Jones, Peacock, Garn & Ptnrs., Cin., 1971-72; project architect Smith Stevens Architects, Cin., 1972-76; project mgr. Herlringer Enterprises, Cin., 1976-79; prin., owner John C. Senhauser, Architect, Cin., 1979—; adj. assoc. prof. Sch. Architecture and Interior Design, U. Cin., 1992—. Exhibited in group shows at Toni Birckhead Gallery, 1990, Contemporary Arts Ctr., Cin., 1993, Canton (Ohio) Art Inst., 1993; prin. works include residences. Mem. historic conservation bd. City of Cin., 1986—; mem. dean's adv. coun. Coll. Design Architecture Art and Planning U. Cin., 1990; mem. design rev. com. U. Cin. Recipient Merit award Builder mag., 1985, 88, 94, Grand award, 1990, Grand Best in Region award Profl. Builder, 1988, 90, Grand award for Best Overall Design, Custom Home Mag., 1996, 97, other awards. Fellow AIA (pres. 1991, Honor award Cin. chpt. 1983, 85, 90, 91, 92, 93, 94, 95, 96, Merit award 1990, 93, 94); mem. AIA Ohio (bd. dirs., sec. 1997—, Honor award 1985, 90, 91, 93, 94). Office: 1118 Saint Gregory St Cincinnati OH 45202-1724

SENHOLZI, GREGORY BRUCE, secondary school educator; b. Amityville, N.Y., Apr. 16, 1952; s. Joseph Bruce and Beverly Ann (Sullivan) S.; m. Rochelle Ann Birnbaum, Nov. 20, 1976; children: David, Vicki. BA, Iona Coll., 1974; MLS, SUNY, Stony Brook, 1976. Salesman, printer R.H. Macy's, Huntington, N.Y., 1967-74; math. and computer tchr. Sachem Sch. Dist., Lake Ronkonkona, N.Y., 1974—; computer specialist Tex. Instruments, N.Y., 1982-84; audio video specialist Dart Audio Video, Centereach, N.Y., 1984-88; consulate, curriculum specialist Sachem Sch. Dist., 1978—. Deacon local Roman Cath. ch., Wading River, N.Y., 1989—. Mem. Adoptive Parents Com. (bd. dirs., workshop leader 1984—), K.C. (treas. 1988—). Avocations: swimming, acting, skiing, singing, travel. Home: 129 Gregory Way Calverton NY 11933 Office: Sachem Sch Dist Main St Holbrook NY 11742

SENIOR, ENRIQUE FRANCISCO, investment banker; b. Havana, Cuba, Aug. 3, 1943; came to U.S., 1960; s. Frank and Dolores (Hernandez) Senior; m. Robin Suffern Gimbel, Sept. 7, 1977; children: Tailer, Heather, Fern, Seanna. BA in Architecture, Yale U., 1964, BS in Elec. Engring., 1967; MBA, Harvard U., 1969. Corp. fin. exec. White, Weld & Co., N.Y.C., 1969-73; v.p. Allen & Co., Inc., N.Y.C., 1973-80, exec. v.p., mng. dir., 1980—; bd. dirs. Allen & Co., Inc., Dick Clark Prodns., Inc., Burbank, Calif. Mem. The Brook Club, Piping Rock Club, Farmington Country Club, Phi Beta Kappa, Tau Beta Pi. Avocations: flying, fishing, hunting, skiing, woodworking. Office: Allen & Co Inc 711 5th Ave New York NY 10022-3111

SENIOR, THOMAS BRYAN A., electrical engineering educator, researcher, consultant; b. Menston, Yorkshire, Eng., June 26, 1928; came to U.S., 1957; s. Thomas Harold and Emily Dorothy (Matthews) S.; m. Heather Margaret Golby, May 4, 1957; children—Margaret, David, Hazel, Peter. B.Sc., Manchester U., 1949, M.Sc., 1950; Ph.D., Cambridge U., 1954. Sr. sci. officer Royal Radar Establishment, Malvern, Eng., 1952-57; rsch. scientist U. Mich., Ann Arbor, 1957-69, prof. elec. engring., 1969-84, prof. elec. and computer sci., 1984—, Arthur F. Thurnau prof., 1990—, dir. radiation lab., 1975-87, assoc. chmn. elect. engring. & computer sci. dept., 1984-90, acting chmn., 1987-88, assoc. chmn. acad. affairs, 1991—; cons. in field. Author: (with Bowman and Uslenghi) Electromagnetic and Acoustical Scattering by Simple Shapes, 1969; Mathematical Methods in Electrical Engineering, 1986; (with Volakis) Approximate Boundary Conditions in Electromagnetics, 1995; contbr. articles to profl. jours. Fellow IEEE: mem. Internat. Sci. Radio Union (chmn. U.S. nat. com. 1982-84, vice chmn. Com. B. 1985-87, chmn. 1988-90, pres. 1996—, Van der Pol Gold medal 1993). Home: 1919 Ivywood Dr Ann Arbor MI 48103-4527 Office: U Mich Dept Elec Engring Comp S Ann Arbor MI 48109

SENN, RICHARD ALLAN, environmental safety professional; b. LaCrosse, Wis., Dec. 20, 1946; s. Hugo and Evelyn Ruth (Winters) S.; m. Denise Marie Corriveau, May 6, 1989; 1 stepchild, Danelle Marie Wiersma. BS in Chemistry and Bus., U. Wis., 1970, BS in Environ. Scis., 1975; MBA in Mgmt., U. Wis., Whitewater, 1980. Cert. hazardous materials mgr., 1990. Analytical chemist Warf Inst., Madison, Wis., 1970-75; scientist Warf Inst., Madison, 1975-77; scientist II Raltech Scientific Svcs., Madison, 1977-78, herbicide sect. leader, 1978-82; environ. chemist III U. Wis., Madison, 1982-84; pres. 4 Lakes Volleyball Assn., Madison, 1981-83; owner Sports Mgmt. Svcs., Madison, 1981-83; lab/safety mgr. Madison, 1984-86; environ. health safety mgr. Agracetus, Inc. sub. Monsanto, Middleton, Wis., 1984—; pres. 4 Lakes Enterprises (formerly 4 Lakes Recreation Inc.), Verona, Wis., 1984—; gen. ptnr., mgmt. com. Kidztime TV, Balt. affiliate, 1996—; instr. U. Wis. Ext. Engring., 1993—; owner Howling at the Moon, 1996—. Author: (with others) Waste Minimization in Research and Academic Institutions, 1995. Vol. WHA-Pub. TV, Madison, 1991—. Mem. Fedn. Environ. Techs. (Madison chpt. program chmn. 1986—, pres., founder 1990-92), Nat. Safety Coun., Acad. Cert. Hazardous Materials Mgrs. (bd. dirs. Greater Wis. chpt. 1993—, pres. 1996), Am. Biol. Safety Assn., Monsanto Sustainablility Com., U.S. Wis. Madison Volleyball Booster Club (bd. dirs. 1987-95). Avocations: photography, camping, travel, volleyball, investments. Home: 6066 Whalen Rd Verona WI 53593-9274 Office: Agracetus 8520 University Grn Middleton WI 53562-2508

SENNEMA, DAVID CARL, museum consultant; b. Grand Rapids, Mich., July 6, 1934; s. Carl Edward and Alice Bertha (Bieri) S.; m. Martha Amanda Dixon, Feb. 22, 1958; children—Daniel Ross, Julia Kathryn, Alice Dixon. B.A., Albion Coll., 1956. Mgr., Columbia Music Festival Assn., 1964-67; exec. dir. S.C. Arts Commn., Columbia, 1967-70; assoc. dir. Federal-State Partnership and Spl. Projects programs Nat. Endowment for the Arts, Washington, 1971-73; prof. arts adminstrn., dir. community arts mgmt. program Sangamon State U., Springfield, Ill., 1973-76; dir. S.C. Mus. Commn. Columbia, 1976-85; bus. mgr. Palmetto Mastersingers, 1986—; cons. in field. Mem. adv. panel Nat. Endowment for the Arts Music, 1968-70. Chmn. Springfield Arts Commn., 975-76. Served with U.S. Army, 1957-58. Lodge: Rotary (chmn. cultural affairs com. 1978-80).

SENNET, CHARLES JOSEPH, lawyer; b. Buffalo, Aug. 7, 1952; s. Saunders M. and Muriel S. (Rotenberg) S. AB magna cum laude, Cornell U., 1974; JD with high honors, George Washington U., 1979. Bar: Ill. 1979, U.S. Dist. Ct. (no. dist.) Ill. 1979, U.S. Ct. Appeals (7th cir.) 1982, U.S. Ct. Appeals (D.C. cir.) 1993. Assoc. Reuben & Proctor, Chgo., 1979-83; assoc. counsel Tribune Co., Chgo., 1984-91, sr. counsel, 1991—; adj. faculty Medill Sch. Journalism, Northwestern U., 1991—; co-chair Television Music Lic. Com., 1995—. Contbr. articles to profl. jours. Mem. ABA (spkr. 1984-88, 91-97, mem. gov. bd. Forum on Comms. Law 1995—), NATAS, Ill. Bar Assn. (chmn. media law com. 1989-91), Chgo. Bar Assn., Fed. Comms. Bar Assn. Office: Tribune Co 435 N Michigan Ave Chicago IL 60611

SENNETT, HENRY HERBERT, JR., theatre arts educator and consultant; b. Atlanta, Feb. 28, 1945; s. Henry Herbert and Betty Ruth (Wilson) S.; m. Beverly Ann Rodgers, Dec. 9, 1967; children: Cristie Aline, Herbert Alan. BS in Edn., Ark. State U., Jonesboro, 1968; MA, Memphis State U., 1971; MDiv, So. Bapt. Sem., Louisville, 1978; DMin, Midwestern Bapt. Sem., Kansas City, Mo., 1988; MFA, Fla. Atlantic U., 1989. Cert. tchr. Tchr. speech and English Covington (Tenn.) High Sch., 1971-72; freelance designer Lighting by Herb, Memphis, 1972-73; tchr. speech and English Augusta (Ark.) High Sch., 1973-76; instr. drama Jefferson Community Coll., Louisville, 1977-78; pastor Dublin (Ohio) Bapt. Ch., 1979-83, Trinity Bapt. Ch., Searcy, Ark., 1983-85; asst. prof. theatre arts, dept. chair Palm Beach Atlantic Coll., West Palm Beach, Fla., 1985-96; stress mgmt. cons. Palm Beach County Bd. Edn., West Palm Beach, 1988-94; freelance cons. theatrical lighting and design, West Palm Beach, 1986—; cons. drama edn. Fla. Dept. Edn., 1991-94; vis. prof. Midwestern Bapt. Sem., Kansas City, Mo., 1988; pres. S & R Prodns., Inc., 1995—; pres., dept. coord., assoc. prof. Commn. Arts, La. Coll. Author: Theatre in the Church, 1992, Religion and Dramatics: Essays on the Relationship Between Christianity and Theatrical Arts, 1994, author: (play) Stars, 1989. 1st lt. U.S. Army, 1968-70, Vietnam; chaplain USAR, 1984—. Mem. Nat. Assn. Schs. Theatre, Fla. Theatre Edn., Fla. Theatre Conf., South Western Theatre Conf., Assn. Theatre Higher Edn., Blue Key Nat. Honor Soc., Theatre Comm. Group, Pi Kappa Phi (pres. 1965-66). Republican. Baptist. Avocations: pastor, author. Office: Louisiana College 1140 College Dr Pineville LA 71359-0001

SENNETT, RICHARD, sociologist, writer; b. Chgo., Jan. 1, 1943; s. Maurice and Dorothy S. B.A. in History summa cum laude, U. Chgo., 1964; Ph.D., Harvard U., 1969. Asst. prof. Yale U., 1967-68; dir. Urban Family Study, Cambridge, Mass., 1969-71; mem. faculty NYU, 1971—, Univ. prof. of the humanities, 1984—; founder, dir. N.Y. Inst. Humanities, 1976-79, 81-84; chmn. adv. com. on urban studies UNESCO, 1988-93; chmn. Am. Coun. on Work and Society, 1997—; Sigmund Freud Meml. lectr. U. London, 1977; disting. vis. prof. Coll. de France, Paris, 1980; Henry Luce lectr. Yale U., 1986; vis. prof. humanities Harvard U., 1984; Goethe lectr. U. Frankfurt, Germany, 1991-92; scholar-in-residence Am. Acad., Rome, 1992; rep. Internat. Social Sci. Coun. to UN, 1992—. Author: Families Against the City, 1970, The Uses of Disorder, 1970, The Hidden Injuries of Class, 1972, The Fall of Public Man, 1977, Authority, 1980, The Frog Who Dared to Croak, 1982, An Evening of Brahms, 1984, Palais Royal, 1986, The Conscience of the Eye, 1990, Flesh and Stone, 1994, The Darwin Lectures, 1996. Fellow Guggenheim Found., 1973, Inst. Advanced Study, 1973-74, 79-80, Nat. Endowment for the Humanities, 1976, Woodrow Wilson Ctr.-Smithsonian Instn., Washington, 1993. Fellow Royal Soc. Lit. (Gt. Britain), Am. Sociol. Assn., Nat. Acad. Arts and Scis.; mem. Internat. Sociol. Assn., Nat. Coun. Family Rels., PEN (dir. 1977—, v.p. 1979-82). Clubs: Century Assn. (N.Y.C.); Signet Soc. (Harvard). Office: 26 Washington Pl Rm 777 New York NY 10003-6638

SENSE, KARL AUGUST, physicist, educator; b. Kiel, Schleswig-Holstein, Germany, Mar. 6, 1917; came to U.S., 1929; s. Carl Richard and Charlotte Irma (Neuenfeldt) S.; m. Rita Evelyn Sharp, June 5, 1948 (div. Jan. 1971); children: Karl D., Nancy C., Kurt A., Janet E., Eric M. BA, SUNY, Albany, 1939; MS, U. Minn., 1951. Asst. div. cons. Battelle Meml. Inst., Columbus, Ohio, 1951-58; sr. physicist Atomics Internat. (Rockwell), Canoga Park, Calif., 1958-61; rsch. scientist Astropower subs. Douglas Aircraft, Newport Beach, Calif., 1961-64; project mgr., staff engr. TRW Systems Group, Redondo Beach, Calif., 1964-69; pvt. practice cons. Garden Grove, Calif., 1969-80; engring. specialist satellite systems div. Rockwell Internat., Seal Beach, Calif., 1981-84, ret., 1984; lectr. in physics Calif. State U., Long Beach, 1986. Author: Theory on Determination of Molecular Complexes of Vapors of Binary Systems, 1957, Power Failure Analysis of Satellites in GPS Orbit, 1981; mgr., author: Nuclear-Magnetohydrodynamic Power Systems, 1967; patentee thermionic emitter. Comdr. Am. Legion Post # 286, Garden Grove, 1977; pres. Worthington (Ohio) Luth. Ch., 1957; co-chmn., bd. dirs. Luth. High Sch. Assn. of Orange County, Calif., 1968. 2d lt. USAAF, 1943-45. Fellow AIAA (assoc., Membership award 1991); mem. Am. Phys. Soc. (sr.). Avocations: eschatology, music. Home: 37 Marion Hts Galax VA 24333-4500

SENSEMAN, RONALD SYLVESTER, architect; b. Collingswood, N.J., Oct. 19, 1912; s. Raphael and Louise (Tanner) S.; m. Lois Hatt, Aug. 18, 1935 (dec. Aug. 1979); children: Marilyn Louise (Mrs. John Whitson Rogers), Peggy June (Mrs. James Orvil Hutchinson); m. Claire M. Stoehr, Sept. 8, 1980; children: Deborah Stoehr (Mrs. Tim Darrin), Darice (Mrs. Kevin Lang), Darla (Mrs. Jeffrey Schultz), D'Lynn Stoehr (Mrs. Shean Phelps). Student, Columbia Union Coll., 1931-34, Cath. U. Am., 1934-36. Pvt. practice architecture Met. Washington area, 1935-89; ret.; cons. architect Silver Spring, 1989—; dir. Park Motels Inc., Manor Care, Inc.; pres. Reef Properties Inc., St. Croix, V.I.; lectr. Columbia Union Coll., Seventh Day Adventist Theol. Sem. Archtl. works include: Nat. Indsl. Coll., Army War Coll., Ft. McNair, Washington, Naval War Coll., Newport, R.I., Atlantic Union Coll., South Lancaster, Mass., Columbia Union Coll., Takoma Park, Md., Shady Grove Adventist Hosp., Gaithersburg, Md., others. Republican candidate Md. State Legislature, 1958; Mem. univ. councillors Loma Linda U.; trustee Atlantic Union Coll. Fellow AIA (pres. Md. div. met. Washington chpt. 1947-49, pres. Potomac Valley chpt.); mem. Guild Religious Architecture, Washington Bd. Trade, Washington Building Congress, Prince George's County C. of C., Cath. U. Alumni Assn. (Archtl. Achievement award 1967). Lodge: Rotary. Home: 10718 Gatewood Ave Silver Spring MD 20903-1013

SENSENBRENNER, FRANK JAMES, JR., congressman, lawyer; b. Chgo., June 14, 1943; s. Frank James and Margaret Anita (Luedke) S.; m. Cheryl Lynn Warren, Mar. 26, 1977; children: Frank James III, Robert Alan. AB in Polit. Sci., Stanford U., 1965; JD, U. Wis., 1968. Bar: Wis. 1968, U.S. Supreme Ct. 1972. Mem. firm McKay and Martin, Cedarburg., Wis., 1970-75; mem. Wis. Assembly, 1969-75; mem. Wis. State Senate, 1975-79, asst. minority leader, 1977-79; mem. 96th-105th Congresses from 9th Wis. dist., Washington, 1979—; mem. House jud. com., chmn. House sci. com. Mem. Am. Philatelic Soc. Republican. Episcopalian. Club: Capitol Hill. Office: US Ho of Reps 2332 Rayburn House Bldg Washington DC 20515-4909

SENSENICH, ILA JEANNE, magistrate judge; b. Pitts., Mar. 6, 1939; d. Louis E. and Evelyn Margaret S. BA, Westminster Coll., 1961; JD, Dickinson Sch. Law, 1964, JD (hon.), 1994. Bar: Pa. 1964. Assoc. Stewart, Belden, Sensenich and Herrington, Greensburg, Pa., 1964-70; asst. pub. defender Westmoreland (Pa.) County, 1970-71; U.S. magistrate judge for We. Dist. Pa., Pitts., 1971—; adj. prof. law Duquesne U., 1982-87, vis. fellow Daniel & Florence Guggenheim program in criminal justice Yale Law Sch., 1976-77. Trustee emeritus Dickinson Sch. Law. Mem. ABA, Fed. Magistrate Judges Assn. (sec. 1979-81, sec. 1988-89, treas. 1989-90, 2d v.p. 1990-91, pres.-elect 1992-93, pres. 1993-94), Pa. Bar Assn., Allegheny County Bar Assn. (fed. ct. sect.), Nat. Assn. Women Judges, Westmoreland County Bar Assn., Allegheny Bar Assn. (civil litigation sect., com. women in law), Womens Bar Assn. of We. Pa., Am. Judicature Soc. Democrat. Presbyterian. Avocations: skiing, sailing, bicycling, classical music, cooking. Author: Compendium of the Law of Prisoner's Rights, 1979; contbr. articles to profl. jours. Office: 518B US PO And Courthouse Pittsburgh PA 15219

SENSIPER, SAMUEL, consulting electrical engineer; b. Elmira, N.Y., Apr. 26, 1919; s. Louis and Molly (Pedolsky) S.; m. Elaine Marie Zwick, Sept. 10, 1950; children—Martin, Sylvia, David. B.S.E.E., M.I.T., 1939, Sc.D., 1951; E.E., Stanford U., 1941. Asst. project engr. to sr. project engr., cons. Sperry Gyroscope, Garden City, Great Neck, N.Y., 1941-51; sect. head and sr. staff cons. Hughes Aircraft, Culver City, Malibu, Calif., 1951-60; lab. div. mgr. Space Gen. Corp., Glendale, Azusa, Los Angeles, 1960-67; lab. mgr. TRW, Redondo Beach, Calif., 1967-70; cons. elec. engr., Los Angeles, 1970-73; dir. engring. Transco Products, Venice, Calif., 1973-75; cons. elec. engr. in pvt. practice, Los Angeles, 1975—; faculty U. So. Calif., Los Angeles, 1955-56, 79-80. Contbr. articles to profl. jours. Recipient Cert. of Commendation U.S. Navy, 1946; indsl. electronics fellow M.I.T., 1947-48. Fellow IEEE, AAAS; mem. Calif. Soc. Profl. Engrs., Fedn. Am. Scientists, M.I.T. Alumni Assn., Stanford Alumni Assn., Electromagnetics Acad., Sigma Xi, Eta Kappa Nu. Patentee in field. Home: 6011 S Holt Ave Los Angeles CA 90056-1415 Office: PO Box 3102 Culver City CA 90231-3102

SENSKE, MARLOWE ORLYN, healthcare executive, hospital administrator; b. Perham, Minn., Feb. 23, 1948; s. William E. and Orline (schmidt) s.; m. Myrle M. Richter, Apr. 8, 1967 (div. 1978); children: Kim, Gina; m. Betty Ann Babbitt, June 27, 1987; children: Danielle Drummond, Shelly Drummond. B in Hosp. Adminstrn., Concordia Coll., 1969; M in Hosp. Adminstrn., U. Minn., 1972; BBA, Moorhead State U. Adminstrv. trainee Fairview Community Hosp., Mpls., 1969-70; resident St. Luke's Hosp., Kansas City, Mo., 1971-72; asst. adminstr. Abbott-Northwestern Hosp., Mpls., 1972-75, assoc. adminstr., 1975-79, adminstr., 1979-81; pres. Minn. Vol. Hosps. of Am., Mpls., 1982-84; pres. for North Cent. region Voluntary Hosps. of Am. (name now VHA Inc.), Mpls., 1984-85; sr. v.p. Vol. Hosps. of Am., Dallas, 1985-92; exec. v.p. Voluntary Hosps. of Am. (name now VHA Inc.), Dallas, 1992—; VHA Inc.; Dir. Multi Mutual Ins. Co./Bermuda, Cayman, 1978-82; bd./exec. com. Voluntary Hosps. of Am., 10 regions, 1985-92. Pres. Mpls. Jaycees, 1977; bd. mem. Downtown Coun., Mpls., 1978-79, C. of C., 1978-80; Mpls. War Meml. Blood Bank, 1980-85; founder Exec. Forum, Las Colinas, Tex., 1988. Recipient Stephen L. Collins Meml. Lectr. award Concordia Coll., Morehead, Minn., 1985. Mem. Am. Hops. Assn., Am Coll. Healthcare Execs. Avocations: atheletics, pilot, travel, reading.

SENTELLE, DAVID BRYAN, federal judge; b. Canton, N.C., Feb. 12, 1943; s. Horace Richard, Jr., and Maude (Ray) S.; m. Jane LaRue Oldham, June 19, 1965; children: Sharon Rene, Reagan Elaine, Rebecca Grace. AB, U. N.C., 1965, JD with honors, 1968. Bar: N.C. 1968, U.S. Dist. Ct. (we. dist.) N.C. 1969, U.S. Ct. Appeals (4th cir.) 1970. Assoc. Uzzell & Dumont, Asheville, N.C., 1968-70; asst. U.S. atty. City of Charlotte, N.C., 1970-74, dist. judge, 1974-77; ptnr. Tucker, Hicks, Sentelle, Moon & Hodge, P.A., Charlotte, 1977-85; judge U.S. Dist. Ct. (we. dist.) N.C., Charlotte, 1985-87, U.S. Ct. Appeals D.C., 1987—; adj. prof. Fla. State U. Coll. Law; presiding judge Spl. Divsn. for Appointment of Ind. Counsels, 1992—. Contbr. articles to profl. jours. Chmn. Mecklenburg County Rep. Com., 1978-80; chmn. N.C. State Rep. Conv., 1979-80. Dameron fellow, 1967. Mem. ABA, Fed. Bar Assn. (chpt. pres. 1975), Mecklenburg County Bar Assn. Baptist. Lodges: Masons, Scottish Rite, Shriners. Office: US Court of Appeals 333 Constitution Ave NW Washington DC 20001-2802

SENTENNE, JUSTINE, corporate ombudsman; b. Montreal, Que., Can.; d. Paul Emile and Irene Genevieve (Laliberte) S. MBA, U. Que., Montreal, 1993, postgrad. McGill U., Ecole Nat. d'Adminstrn. Publique, 1989-91. Fin. analyst, assoc. mgr. portfolio Bush Assocs., Montreal, 1970-82; city councillor, mem. exec. com. City of Montreal and Montreal Urban Com., 1978-82; adminstrv. asst. Montreal Conv. Ctr., 1983; dir. sponsorship Cen. Com. for Montreal Papal Visit, 1984; dir. pub. rels. Coopers & Lybrand, Montreal, 1985-87; exec. dir. Que. Heart Found., 1987-89; corp. ombudsman Hydro-Que., Montreal, 1991—; tchr. DSA program Concordia U.; v.p., bd. dirs. Armand Frappier Found., Can., Chateau Dufresne Mus. Decorative Arts, Montreal, 1985-90; chmn. bd. Wilfrid Pelletier Found., Montreal, 1986-91; bd. dirs. St. Joseph's Oratory, 1979-92, Caisse Populaire Desjardins Notre Dame de Grace, Montreal, 1980-96; mem. jury John Labatt Ltd., London, Ont., 1982-86. Notre Dame de Grace v.p. riding assoc. Liberal Party of Can., chairperson Women's Commn.; mem. bd. govs. Youth and Music Can., Montreal, 1981-86; chmn. bd. The Women's Ctr., Montreal, 1986-88, Vol. Bur. Montreal, 1986-87; bd. dirs. Palais des Congres de Montreal, 1981-89, Port of Montreal, 1983-84, Can. Ctr. for Ecumenism, Montreal, 1968-85, Villa Notre-Dame de Grace, Montreal, 1979-87, Montreal Diet Dispensary, 1989— (chairperson 1996), Pathways to Faith, 1990—, The Ombudsman Assn., 1996—; bd. mgmt. Saidye Bronfman Ctr. for Arts, 1994—. Named Career Woman of Yr., Sullivan Bus. Coll., 1979; recipient Silver medal Ville de Paris, 1981, Women's Kansas City Assn. for Internat. Rels. and Trade medal, 1982. Fellow Fin. Analysts Fedn. N.Y., Inst. Fin. Analysts, Montreal Soc. Investment Analysts; mem. The Ombudsman Assn. Roman Catholic.

SENTER, ALAN ZACHARY, communications company executive; b. N.Y.C., Nov. 8, 1941; s. Hyman B. and Reva (Cooperwasser) S.; m. Karen G. Yellin, Dec. 26, 1965; children: Marc G., Elise J. BS, U. R.I., 1963; MBA, U. Chgo., 1965. Dir. internat. fin. Xerox Corp., Stamford, Conn., 1975-77; v.p. fin. Latin Am. Xerox Corp., Greenwich, Conn., 1977-79; v.p. fin. bus. products Xerox Corp., Rochester, N.Y., 1979-80; asst. contr. Xerox Corp., Stamford, 1981-85, v.p., treas., 1985-90, v.p. fin., 1990-92; exec. v.p., CFO, Internat. Specialty Products/GAF Corp., Wayne, N.J., 1992-94, Nynex Corp., N.Y.C., 1994-96; ind. investor, advisor N.Y., 1996—; bd. dirs. Exel Ins., Bermuda, Advanced Radio Telecom, Spectragraphics, Inc. Bd. dirs. Theater Devel. Fund. Capt. USAR, 1966-68, Vietnam. Jewish. Avocations: skiing, tennis.

SENTER, JACK, art director, production designer. Art dir.: (TV movies) Kung Fu, 1972, The Execution, 1985, Desperate, 1987, Nutcracker: Money, Madness, and Murder, 1987, (films) No Deposit, No Return, 1976, Obsession, 1976, Freaky Friday, 1976, Oh, God!, 1977, Greased Lightning, 1977, Return from Witch Mountain, 1978, Go Tell the Spartans, 1978, Love and Bullets, 1979, The Man Who Loved Women, 1983, Micki & Maude, 1984, Far and Away, 1992; prodn. designer: (films) Modern Problems, 1981, The New Adventures of Pippi Longstocking, 1988. Office: care Tom Miller The Miller Agency 23236 Lyons Ave Ste 219 Santa Clarita CA 91321-5009*

SENTER, LYONEL THOMAS, JR., federal judge; b. Fulton, Miss., July 30, 1933; s. L. T. and Eva Lee (Jetton) S.; married. B.S., U. So. Miss., 1956; LL.B., U. Miss., 1959. Bar: Miss. 1959. County pros. atty., 1960-64, U.S. commr., 1966-68; judge Miss. Circuit Ct., Circuit 1, 1968-80, U.S. Dist. Ct. (no. dist.) Miss., 1980—. Mem. Miss. State Bar. Democrat. Office: US Dist Ct PO Box 925 Aberdeen MS 39730-0925

SENTER, MERILYN P(ATRICIA), former state legislator and freelance reporter; b. Haverhill, Mass., Mar. 17, 1935; d. Paul Barton and Mary Etta (Herrin) Staples; m. Donald Neil Senter, Apr. 23, 1960; children: Karen Anne Hussey, Brian Neil. Grad., McIntosh Bus. Coll., 1955. Sec. F.S. Hamlin Ins. Agy., Haverhill, Mass., 1955-60; free lance reporter Plaistow-Hampstead News, Rockingham county newspapers, Exeter and Stratham, N.H., 1970-89; mem. N.H. Gen. Ct., Rockingham Dist. 9, 1988-96. Vice-chmn. Hwy. Safety Com., Plaistow, N.H., 1976—; sec., bd. dirs. Region 10 Commn. Support Svcs. Inc., Atkinson, N.H., 1982-88; chmn. Plaistow Area Transit Adv. Com., 1990-93; active Devel. Disabilities Coun., 1993—; mem. Plaistow Bd. Selectmen, 1996-99. Named Woman of Yr., N.H. Bus. and Profl. Women, 1983, Nat. Grange Citizen of Yr., 1992. Republican. Avocations: nature, grandchildren, handicapped issues. Home and Office: 11 Maple Ave Plaistow NH 03865-2221

SENTER, WILLIAM JOSEPH, publishing company executive; b. N.Y.C., Dec. 4, 1921; s. Joseph and Sarah (Greenglass) S.; m. Irene Phoebe Marcus, Aug. 3, 1952; children: Adam Douglas, Caren Amy. B.B.A., CCNY, 1947. Chmn. bd., mng. editor Deadline Data, Inc., N.Y.C., 1962-66; pres. Unipub, Inc. (merged with Xerox Corp. 1971), N.Y.C., 1966-72; v.p. planning and devel. Xerox Info. Resources Group (includes AutEx Systems, R.R. Bowker Co., Ginn & Co., Univ. Microfilms Internat., Unipub Inc., Xerox Edn. Publs., Xerox Learning Systems, Xerox Computer Services), Greenwich, Conn., 1973-74; v.p. info. pub. Xerox Info. Resources Group, Greenwich, 1974-75; pres. Xerox Info. Resources Group, 1976-80, chmn., 1980-86; v.p. Xerox Corp., Stamford, Conn., 1978-86; pres. R.R. Bowker Co., N.Y.C., 1974-75. Served with U.S. Army, 1942-46. Mem. Assn. Am. Pubs. (dir. 1978-81), Info. Industry Assn. (dir. 1980-83). Office: PO Box 364 Cos Cob CT 06807-0364 *Always remember that life, in all its many stages, is truly a continuous series of adventures into the unknown and unexpected. Accordingly, the key to the fullness of life is each person's ability to daily generate a sense of excitement and discovery that one is able to overcome fears and the rebuffs of occasional failure.*

SENTER, WILLIAM OSCAR, retired air force officer; b. Stamford, Tex., June 15, 1910; s. William Oscar and Mary Ellen (Futrell) S.; m. Ruth Jane Tinsley, Apr. 10, 1937 (dec. Apr. 1967); children: Suellen, Ruth Jane; m. Carolyn C. Fallon, Jan. 2, 1973. Student, Hardin-Simmons U., 1929; BS, U.S. Mil. Acad., 1933; postgrad., Mass. Inst. Tech., 1938, Air War Coll., 1948-49; Aero. Engr., U. Okla., 1957. Commd. 2d lt. Coast Arty. Corps U.S. Army, 1933, attached to air corps and apptd. student officer, 1933; advanced through grades to lt. gen. USAF, 1963; comdr. Oklahoma City Air Material Area, 1954-57; dir. Procurement and Prodn. Hdqrs., Air Materiel Command Wright-Patterson AFB, 1957-59; asst. dep. chief staff materiel Hdqrs. USAF, 1959-63; dir. petroleum logistics policy Dept. Def., 1963-66, ret., 1966; exec. v.p. Natural Gas Supply Assn., 1966-74. Decorated D.S.M., Legion of Merit with oak leaf cluster. Mem. Air Force Assn., Assn. Grads. U.S. Mil. Acad., Air Force Hist. Found., Order Daedalians, Monarch Country Club. Roman Catholic. Home: 1100 SW Shoreline Dr Apt 200 Palm City FL 34990-4543

SENTURIA, YVONNE DREYFUS, pediatrician, epidemiologist; b. Houston, Jan. 16, 1951. BA in Biology and Sociology, Rice U., 1973; MD, U. Tex., San Antonio, 1977; MSc in Epidemiology, London Sch. Hygiene and Tropical Medicine, 1985. Diplomate Am. Bd. Pedias. Pediat. resident Shands Tchg. Hosp., Gainesville, Fla., 1977-79, Tex. Children's Hosp., Houston, 1979-80; instr., asst. prof. Coll. Medicine, Baylor U., Houston, 1980-82; sr. clin. med. officer Hammersmith and Fulham Health Authority, London, 1982-83; cons. pediatrician Kingston (Eng.) Hosp., 1983, Northwick Park Hosp., London, 1983; rsch. pediatrician Charing Cross Hosp. Med. Sch., London, 1984-85; clin. lectr. Inst. Child Health, London, 1985-88; attending pediatrician and epidemiologist Children's Meml. Hosp., Chgo., 1989-96; attending pediatrician Jacobi Hosp., Bronx, N.Y., 1996—. Fellow Am. Acad. Pediats.; mem. Ambulatory Pediat. Assn., Midwest Soc. Pediat. Rsch. Office: Jacobi Hosp Nurses Residence 7 S 12 Pelham Pkwy at Eastchester Bronx NY 10461

SENZEL, ALAN JOSEPH, analytical chemistry consultant, music critic; b. Los Angeles, May 26, 1945; s. Bernard and Esther Mildred (Shykin) S.; m. Phyllis Sharon Abt, June 22, 1969; children—Richard Steven, Lisa Beth. B.S. in Chemistry, Calif. State U.-Long Beach, 1967; M.S., UCLA, 1969, Ph.D., 1970. Assoc. editor Am. Chem. Soc., Washington, 1970-74; methods editor Assn. Ofcl. Analytical Chemists, Washington, 1974-78; info. dir. Chem. Industry Inst. Toxicology, Research Triangle Park, N.C., 1978-79; pvt. cons., Raleigh, N.C., 1978—; cons. Engring.-Sci., Cary, N.C. and Fairfax, Va., 1978—, Corning Glass Works, Raleigh, 1979-85, Research Triangle Inst., Research Triangle Park, 1983—, Combustion Engring., Chapel Hill, N.C., 1984-89, KilKelly Environ. Assocs., Raleigh, 1985—, Integrated Lab. Systems, Durham, 1987—, Technical Resources, Inc., Rockville, Md., 1987—, Am. Petroleum Inst., Washington, 1990—, Sanford Cohen & Assocs., Inc., McLean, Va., 1993—, Glaxo Pharmaceuticals, 1993—, Stewart Pesticide Registration Assocs., Inc., 1993—, Spray Drift Task Force, 1993—, Am. Agrl. Svcs., Inc., Cary, N.C., 1994—, Entropy, Inc., 1995—, Enthalpy Analytical Lab., Inc., 1996—; music critic Raleigh News & Observer, 1982-90, Spectator Mag., 1990—; dep. mgr. Environ. Systems Group, Environ. Resources Mgmt. Inc., Exton, Pa., 1988; project sci. Agrl. Div. Residue Chem. dept. CIBA-GEIGY Corp., Greensboro, N.C., 1989-93. Editor: Instrumentation in Analytical Chemistry, 1973, Newburger's Manual of Cosmetic Analysis, 1977 (FDA award 1978), Safety in the Laboratory, 1984 (STC award 1985); assoc. editor: Official Methods of Analysis, 1975; editor Inclusions Quar., 1993-94. Pres. Congregation Sha'arei Israel, 1981-83. Mem. Soc. Tech. Communication (treas. 1983-85, v.p. 1985-87, achievement award 1985), Am. Chem. Soc., Assn. Official Analytical Chemists. Republican. Jewish. Club: Bridge-Raleigh, Capitol, Vanderbilt. Lodge: B'nai Brith. Avocations: music; tennis; basketball; bridge. Home and Office: 7704 Audubon Dr Raleigh NC 27615-3403

SENZEL, MARTIN LEE, lawyer; b. Rochester, N.Y., June 21, 1944; s. Albert Benjamin and Besse (Lipson) S.; m. Dagni Maren Belgum, Feb. 17, 1979; 1 child, Whitney. BA, Yale U., 1966, LLB, 1969. Bar: N.Y. 1971, U.S. Dist. Ct. (so. dist.) N.Y., U.S. Ct. Appeals (2nd cir.) 1973. Assoc. Cravath, Swaine & Moore, N.Y.C., 1969-77; ptnr. Cravath, Swaine & Moore, 1977—. Mem. ABA, N.Y. State Bar Assn., Assn. Bar City N.Y. Home: 101 Central Park W New York NY 10023-4204 Office: Cravath Swaine & Moore Worldwide Plaza 825 8th Ave New York NY 10019-7416

SEPAHPUR, HAYEDEH C(HRISTINE), investment executive; b. Lincoln, Nebr., Dec. 8, 1958; d. Bahman and Marylin Lou (Duffy) S.; m. Bahman Robert Kosrovani, May 2, 1992; 1 child, Cyrus Thomas Simonson Kosrovani. BS, Lehigh U., 1983. V.p. Drexel Burnham Lambert Inc., N.Y.C., 1982-90, Donaldson, Lufkin & Jenrette, New York City, 1990-92, Lehman Bros., Inc., N.Y.C., 1992—. Sponsor Jr. Statesmen of Am. Found., Washington, 1976—; charter mem. Nat. Mus. Women in the Arts, Washington, 1985—; bd. dirs. Coll. Express Project, Bronx, N.Y., 1987-95; mem. Inst. Asian Studies, St. Thomas Episc. Ch. Mem. Nat. Trust Hist. Preservation, Ctrl. Park Playground Ptnrs., Women's Campaign Fund, N.Y. Soc. Libr., French Inst., WISH List, Parents League, N.Y. Women's Found., Fin. Women's Assn. (N.Y. chpt.), Persian Heritage Found., Mensa, Gamma Phi Beta. Club: Downtown Athletic (N.Y.C.). Home: 254 E 68th St 6D New York NY 10021-6013 Office: Lehman Bros Inc 3 World Fin Ctr 200 Vesey St Fl 6 New York NY 10281-1009

SEPPALA, KATHERINE SEAMAN (MRS. LESLIE W. SEPPALA), retail company executive, clubwoman; b. Detroit, Aug. 22, 1919; d. Willard D. and Elizabeth (Miller) Seaman; B.A., Wayne State U., 1941; m. Leslie W. Seppala, Aug. 15, 1941; children: Sandra Kay, William Leslie. Mgr. women's bldg. and student activities adviser Wayne State U., 1941-43; pres. Harper Sports Shops, Inc., 1947-85, chmn. bd., treas., sec., v.p. 1985—; ptnr. Seppala Bldg. Co., 1971—. Mich. service chmn. women grads. Wayne State U., 1962—, 1st v.p., fund bd., Girl and Cub Scouts; mem. Citizen's adv. com. on sch. needs Detroit Bd. Edn., 1957—, mem. high sch. study com., 1966—; chmn., mem. loan fund bd. Denby High Sch. Parents Scholarship; bd. dirs., v.p. Wayne State U. Fund; precinct del. Rep. Party, 14th dist., 1956—, del. convs.; mem. com. Myasthenia Gravis Support Assn. Recipient Ann. Women's Service award Wayne State U., 1963. Recipient Disting. Alumni award Wayne State U., 1971. Mem. Intercollegiate Assn. Women Students (regional rep. 1941-45), Women Wayne State U. Alumni (past pres.), Wayne State U. Alumni Assn. (dir., past v.p.), AAUW (dir. past officer), Council Women as Public Policy Makers (editor High lights) Denby Community Ednl. Orgn. (sec.), Met. Detroit Program Planning Inst. (pres.), Internat. Platform Assn., Detroit Met. Book and Author Soc. (treas.), Mortar Bd. (past pres.), Karyatides (past pres.), Anthony Wayne Soc., Alpha Chi Alpha, Alpha Kappa Delta, Delta Gamma Chi, Kappa Delta (chmn. chpt. alumnae adv. bd.). Baptist. Clubs: Zonta (v.p., dir.); Les Cheneaux. Home: 22771 Worthington Ct Saint Clair Shores MI 48081-2603 Office: Harper Sport Shop Inc 23208 Greater Mack Ave Saint Clair Shores MI 48080-3422 *Being successful has made it possible for me to help so many others along the way.*

SEQUEIRA, LUIS, plant pathology educator; b. San Jose, Costa Rica, Sept. 1, 1927; s. Raul and Dora (Jenkins) S.; m. Elizabeth Steinvorth, May 27, 1954; children: Anabel, Marta, Robert, Patricia. AB, Harvard U., 1949, AM, 1950, PhD, 1952. Plant pathologist United Fruit Co., Coto, Costa Rica, 1953-60; research assoc. N.C. State U., Raleigh, 1960-61; prof. plant pathology U. Wis., Madison, 1961-82, J.C. Walker prof. of plant pathology and bacteriology, 1982—; cons. Agracetus, Madison, 1982-93; mgr. competitive grants program USDA, Washington, 1984-85, chief scientist, 1987-88. Contbr. numerous articles to profl. jours. Recipient E. C. Stakman award U. Minn., 1992. Fellow Am. Phytopathological Soc. (editor-in-chief jour. 1979-81, St. Paul sect. v.p. 1984, pres. elect 1985, pres. 1986, Award of Distinction 1994), Am. Acad. Microbiology; mem. Nat. Acad. Scis., Linnean Soc. London. Democrat. Roman Catholic. Home: 10 Appomattox Ct Madison WI 53705-4202 Office: U Wis Dept Plant Pathology 1630 Linden Dr Madison WI 53706-1520

SEQUIN, CARLO H., computer science educator; b. Winterthur, Switzerland, Oct. 30, 1941; came to U.S., 1970; s. Carl R. and Margrit (Schaeppi) S.; m. Margareta Frey, Oct. 5, 1968; children: Eveline, Andre. B.S., U. Basel, Switzerland, 1965, Ph.D., 1969. Mem. tech. staff Bell Labs., Murray Hill, N.J., 1970-76; vis. Mackay lectr. U. Calif.-Berkeley, 1976-77, prof. elec. engring. computer scis., 1977—, assoc. chmn. computer sci., 1980-83. Contbr. 150 articles to profl. jours.; author first book on charge-coupled devices; patentee integrated circuits. Fellow IEEE; mem. Assn. Computing Machinery, Swiss Acad. Engring. Scis. Office: U Calif Dept EECS Computer Scis Divsn Berkeley CA 94720-1776

SERAFIN, BARRY D., television news correspondent; b. Coquille, Oreg., June 22, 1941; s. Peter B. and Ina V. Serafin; m. Lynn Van Camp, Aug. 24, 1963; children—Lisa Marie, Sandra Lynn. B.A., Wash. State U., 1964. Producer, dir. Sta. KOAP-TV, Portland, Oreg., 1964-65; reporter Sta. KOIN-TV, Portland, 1965-68, Sta. KMOX-TV, St. Louis, 1968-69; corr. CBS News, Washington, 1969-79; nat. corr. ABC News, Washington, 1979—. (Recipient Emmy award 1974). Office: ABC News Washington Bureau 1717 Desales St NW Washington DC 20036-4401

SERAFIN, DONALD, plastic surgeon; b. N.Y.C., Jan. 18, 1938; s. Stephen Michael and Julia (Sopko) S.; A.B., Duke U., 1960, M.D., 1964; m. Patricia Serafin; children: Allison Elizabeth, Christina Julia, Donald Stephen, Lara Leigh. Surg. intern Grady Meml. Hosp., Atlanta, 1964-65; resident in surgery Emory U. Hosp., Atlanta, 1965-69; asst. resident in plastic and reconstructive surgery Duke U. Med. Center, Durham, N.C., 1971-73, chief resident, 1973-74; Christine Kleinert fellow in hand surgery U. Louisville Hosp., 1972-73; practice medicine specializing in plastic surgery, Durham; mem. staff Durham County Gen. Hosp.; asst. prof. plastic, reconstructive and maxillofacial surgery Duke U., 1974-77, assoc. prof., 1977-81, prof., 1981-95, chief divisn. plastic reconstructive and maxillofacial and oral surgery, 1985-95, chmn. Plastic Surgery Rsch. Council, 1983. Assoc. editor Jour. Reconstructive Microsurgery. Contbr. articles to profl. jours. Served to maj. M.C., USAF, 1969-71, col. M.C., USAR. Diplomate Am. Bd. Surgery, Am. Bd. Plastic Surgery. Recipient Air Force commedation medal, 1971, U.S. Army commendation medal, 1990. Fellow ACS; mem. Internat. Soc. Reconstructive Microsurgery, Am. Soc. Plastic and Reconstructive Surgeons, Am. Assn. Plastic Surgeons, Am. Burn Assn., AMA, Plastic Surgery Research Council, N.C. Soc. Plastic, Maxillofacial and Reconstructive Surgeons, Southeastern Soc. Plastic and Reconstructive Surgeons, Southeastern Med. Dental Soc., Sigma Xi. Office: Duke U Med Ctr PO Box 3708 Durham NC 27710

SERAFIN, JOHN ALFRED, art educator; b. Washington, Nov. 3, 1942; s. John Bernard and Elizabeth (Pichette) S.; m. Josephine Azzarello, Apr. 12, 1969 (div. 1990); children: John Calvin, Michael Joseph, Mary Elizabeth. Student, Syracuse U., 1967-69, MS, 1974; BFA, U. Utah, 1971. Cert. tchr., N.Y. Graphic artist Sears, Roebuck and Co., Syracuse, 1967-68; dir. advt. Around the Town mag., Syracuse, 1969; tchr. art Blodgett Jr. High Sch., Syracuse, 1971-76, Roberts Elem. Sch., Syracuse, 1986-87, Fowler High Sch., Syracuse, 1976—; yearbook adviser Blodgett Jr. High Sch., 1971-75, coach track, 1971-74, coach cross-country, 1972-74; jr. class adviser Fowler High Sch., 1977-78. Artist mag. cover design U. Utah Pharmacy Mag., 1970, Fine Art Index Internat., 1995 edit., Chgo.; group exhbns. include Syracuse Stage, 1989-92, N.Y. State Fair, 1977, 89, 90, Everson Mus., Syracuse, 1985, Cooperstown (N.Y.) Nat. Show, 1991, Westmoreland Nat. Art Show, Latrobe, Pa., 1995, Nat. Design Congress of Art & Design Exhbn. Art Reach '95, Salt Lake City, Tex. Nat. Show, Stephen Austin State U., 1996, Stad Diksmuide World Show, Brussels, 1996; represented by Montserrat Art Gallery, N.Y.C., Limner Gallery, N.Y.C., Agora Gallery, N.Y.C.; painting included in Mut. of N.Y. M.O.N.Y. Art Collection, N.Y.C. Recipient award of Excellence, Manhattan Arts Mag., N.Y.C. Mem. N.Y. State United Tchrs., Syracuse Tchrs. Assn. (rep. 1972-75), Associated Artists Galleries, Allied Artists of N.Y., Nat. Art Educators Assn., Syracuse U. Orange Pack and Alumni Assn., Crimson Club U. Utah Alumni Assn., N.Y. State Art Tchrs. Assn., Cooperstown Art Assn., Elks, Moose. Democrat. Avocations: Syracuse University sports, brewing, blues music, working out, travel. Home: 1205 Teall Ave Syracuse NY 13206-3467 Office: Fowler H S 227 Magnolia St Syracuse NY 13204-2707 *The artist can turn the not yet into reality.*

SERANGELI, DEBORAH S., health care facility administrator; b. Ft. Madison, Iowa, Oct. 14, 1949; d. Ettore A. and Ann Eileen (Flynn) S.; m. Theodore Evans, Feb. 5, 1972 (div. Feb. 1975). Diploma, St. Francis Sch. Nursing, Peoria, Ill., 1970; BA, St. Joseph's Coll., Portland, Maine, 1993; BS in Health Care Mgmt., LaSalle U., 1997. ICU charge nurse St. Francis Hosp., Peoria; staff nurse Meth. Hosp., Fundren Brown Hosp., Houston; head nurse catheterization lab. Meml. City Hosp., Houston; dir. surg. svcs. Women's Hosp., Houston, Del Oro Hosp., Houston; adminstrv. dir. Columbia West Fla. Regional Med. Ctr., Pensacola. Mem. Greater Pensacola Tennis Assn. (sec./treas. 1993-96). Republican. Roman Catholic. Avocations: gourmet cooking, tennis, skiing. Office: Columbia W Fla Regional Med Ctr 8383 N Davis Hwy Pensacola FL 32514-6048

SERBAROLI, FRANCIS J., lawyer, educator, writer; b. N.Y.C., Feb. 8, 1952. AB, Fordham U., 1973, JD, 1977. Bar: N.Y. 1978, U.S. Dist. Ct. (ea. and so. dists.) N.Y. 1978, U.S. Ct. Appeals (2d and D.C. cirs.) 1979, U.S. Supreme Ct. 1983. Asst. atty. gen. N.Y. State Dept. Law, 1978-80; ptnr. Cadwalader Wickersham & Taft, N.Y.C.; vice chmn. N.Y. State Pub. Health Coun., 1995—; health law columnist The N.Y. Law Jour. Trustee Loyola Sch., N.Y.C. Fellow N.Y. Acad. Medicine; mem. Nat. Health Lawyers' Assn., N.Y. State Bar Assn., Assn. Bar City N.Y. Office: Cadwalader Wickersham Taft 100 Maiden Ln New York NY 10038-4818

SERBEIN, OSCAR NICHOLAS, business educator, consultant; b. Collins, Iowa, Mar. 31, 1919; s. Oscar Nicholas and Clara Matilda (Shearer) S.; m. Alice Marie Bigger, Sept. 16, 1952; children: Mary Llewellyn Serbein Parker, John Gregory. BA with highest distinction, U. Iowa, 1940, MS, 1941; PhD, Columbia U., 1951. Grad. asst. math. U. Iowa, Iowa City, 1940-41; clk. Met. Life Ins. Co., N.Y.C., 1941-42; lectr. U. Calif., Berkeley, summer 1948, 50; lectr., asst. prof., assoc. prof. Columbia U., N.Y.C., 1947-59; prof. ins. Stanford (Calif.) U., 1959-89, dir. doctoral program Grad. Sch. Bus., 1960-64, prof. emeritus ins., 1989—; cons. Ins. Info. Inst., N.Y.C., 1971-78, N.Am. Re-Assurance Life Service Co., Palo Alto, 1973, SRI Internat., Menlo Park, Calif., 1980-81, other bus.; cons., expert witness various law firms. Author: Paying for Medical Care in the U.S., 1953, Educational Activities of Business, 1961; co-author: Property and Liability Insurance, 4 ed., 1967, Risk Management: Text and Cases, 2 ed., 1983; also articles. Bd. dirs. Sr. Citizens Coord. Coun., Palo Alto, 1986-89, dir. emeritus, 1990—. Maj. USAF, WWII. Decorated Bronze Star, 1944. Mem. Am. Risk and Ins. Assn., Western Risk and Ins. Assn., Phi Beta Kappa, Sigma Xi, Beta Gamma Sigma. Democrat. Methodist. Club: Stanford Faculty. Avocation: gardening. Home: 731 San Rafael Ct Stanford CA 94305-1007 Office: Stanford U Grad Sch Business Stanford CA 94305

SERBUS, PEARL SARAH DIECK, former freelance writer, former editor; b. Riverdale, Ill.; d. Emil Edwin and Pearl (Kaiser) Dieck; m. Gerald Serbus, Jan. 26, 1946 (dec. Aug. 1969); children—Allan Lester, Bruce Alan, Curt Lyle. Mem. home econs. staff, writer Chgo. Herald Examiner, 1934-39; operator test kitchen Household Sci. Inst., Mdse. Mart, Chgo., 1940-45; free-lance writer grocery chains, Chgo., 1945-49; Riv.-Dolton corr. Calumet Index, Chgo., 1953-58, editorial asst., 1958-60, asst. editor, 1960-68, editor, 1968-72; with Suburban Index, Chgo., 1959-72, editor, 1960-72; mng. editor Index Publs., 1972-74; free lance writer, 1974-94, ret., 1994. Public relations vol. New Hope Sch., 1959-67; bd. dirs. United Fund of Riverdale, Roseland Mental Health Assn., Thornton chpt. Am. Field Service; cmty. rels. vol. Ctrl. Ark. Therapy Inst. Recipient Disting. Service Meml. scroll PTA, 1959, Sch. Bell award Ill. Edn. Assn., 1965, Outstanding Citizen award Chgo. South C. of C., 1972. Named Outstanding Civic Leader Am.; recipient Vol. citation Ctrl. Ark. Radiation Therapy Inst., 1994. Mem. Ill. Woman's Press Assn. (past pres. Woman of Distinction 1968, recipient 46 state awards, 3 nat. awards), Ark. Press Women (Communicator of Achievement award 1991, honored 50 Yr. member 1994), Nat. Fedn. Press Women (past pres. parley past presidents 1981, past dir. protocol, Honors 50 Yrs. Membership 1994), Riverdale (v.p. 1966-68), Chgo. South (v.p., dir.) chambers commerce. Home: 1421 N University Ave Apt 215N Little Rock AR 72207-5241

SERCHUK, IVAN, lawyer; b. N.Y.C., Oct. 13, 1935; s. Israel and Freda (Davis) S.; children: Camille, Bruce Mead, Vance Foster. BA, Columbia U., 1957, LLB, 1960. Bar: N.Y. 1961, U.S. Dist. Ct. (so. dist.) N.Y. 1963, U.S. Ct. Appeals (2d cir.) 1964, U.S. Tax Ct. 1966. Law clk. to judge U.S. Dist. Ct. (so. dist.) N.Y., 1961-63; assoc. Kaye, Scholer, Fierman, Hays & Handler, 1963-68; dep. supt., counsel N.Y. State Banking Dept., N.Y.C. and Albany, 1968-71; mem. Berle & Berle, 1972-73; spl. counsel N.Y. State Senate Banks Com., 1972; mem. Serchuk & Zelermyer LLP, White Plains, 1976—; lectr. Practising Law Inst., 1968-71. Mem. Assn. of Bar of City of N.Y., N.Y. State Bar Assn. Home: Mead St Waccabuc NY 10597 Office: Serchuk & Zelermyer LLP 81 Main St White Plains NY 10601-1711

SEREBRIER, JOSÉ, musician, conductor, composer; b. Montevideo, Uruguay, Dec. 3, 1938; came to U.S., 1956; s. David and Frida (Wasser) S.; m. Carole Farley, Mar. 29, 1969; 1 child, Lara Adriana Francesca. Diploma, Nat. Conservatory, Montevideo, 1956, Curtis Inst. Music, 1958; BA, U. Minn., 1960; studied with Aaron Copland, Anatal Dorati, Pierre Monteux. Ind. composer, condr., 1955—; apprentice condr. Minn. Orch., 1958-60; assoc. condr. Am. Symphony Orch., N.Y.C., 1962-66; music dir. Am. Shakespeare Festival, 1966; composer-in-residence Cleve. Orch., 1968-71; artistic dir. Internat. Festival of Ams., Miami, 1984—, Festival Miami, 1985—; guest condr. numerous orchs. including London Symphony, London Philharm., Paris Radio, Cleve. Symphony Orch., Phila. Symphony Orch., Pitts. Symphony Orch.; founder, artistic dir. Festival Miami (internat. arts festival), 1984. Composer: (for orch.) Variations on a Theme from Childhood, (for chamber) Symphony for Percussion, Concerto for Violin and Orch. (recorded by Royal Phila. Orch. on ASV), also works for chorus, voice, keyboard; recs. for RCA, CRI, ASV, KEM, Disc, Trax Classique, EMI, Tioch, Chandos, Varese-Sarabande Decca, IMG, Pickwick, BGM, Conifer Classics, with various orchs.; condr. for many recs. including Sibelius Symphony No. 1, Holst's The Planets, Carmen, Poulenc's opera La Voix Humaine, Shostakovich Film Suites vol. 1 (Deutsche Schallplatten award 1988), Carole Farley Sings French Songs (Deutsche Schallplaten award 1988), (home video) Kultur, Prokoviev's Alexander Nevsky, Beethoven's Eroica and Tchaikovsky Symphony No. 1 with Sydney and Melbourne Symphony Orch., Mendelssohn Symphonies, Beethoven Symphonies, Bloch's Violin Concerto and Serebrier's Poema Elegiaco CD, 1992, Laserdisc of Operas The Telephone by Menotti and La Voix Humaine by Poulenc with Scottish Chamber Orch., 1992, Royal Philharm. Orch., 1992, Dvôrak Symphonies with Czech State Philharm. for Conifer/BMG, Music of Janacek and Chadwick (4 CDs) for R.R., Hindemith CD with Philharmonia Orch. for ASV. Recipient Ford Found. Condr.'s award, Alice M. Ditson award, 1976, commn. award Nat. Endowment Arts, 1978, Deutsche Schall Platten Critics award, Music Retailers Assn. award for Best Symphony Rec., 1991; Guggenheim fellow, 1958-60; Rockefeller Found. grantee, 1968-70. Mem. Am. Symphony Orch. League, Am. Music Ctr., Am. Fedn. Musicians. Home: 270 Riverside Dr New York NY 10025 *A composer has the duty to communicate with his audience. The academic-intellectual composer of the 50's has become obsolete. Writing just for one's colleagues has fortunately been proven a dead-end.*

SERENBETZ, ROBERT, manufacturing executive; b. Rockville Centre, N.Y., Apr. 18, 1944; s. Raymond Robert Serenbetz and Mildred (Egner) Clapp; m. Karen Jeanne Jackson, Dec. 30, 1967; children: Todd, Gregg, Kathryn. AB, Dartmouth Coll., 1966; MBA, Harvard U., 1968. Mktg. staff asst. to group product mgr. Colgate-Palmolive Co., N.Y.C., 1968-75; dir. mktg. Colgate-Palmolive Colombia, Cali, Colombia, 1975-77; v.p. mktg. Colgate-Palmolive Canada, Toronto, Ont., Can., 1977-81; v.p. mktg. western hemisphere Warner-Lambert Co., Morris Plains, N.J., 1981; pres. Warner-Lambert Can., Toronto, 1981-85; pres. Latin Am., Asia, Australia Warner-Lambert Co., Morris Plains, 1986-89; pres. Am. Chicle, Morris Plains, 1989-91; pres., COO DNA Plant Tech. Corp., Cinnaminson, N.J., 1991-92; pres., CEO DNA Plant Tech. Corp., Oakland, Calif., 1992-94; chmn., CEO DNA Plant Tech. Corp., Cinnaminson, N.J., 1994-96; COO DNAP Holding Corp., Oakland, Calif., 1996—; mem. adv. bd. Coun. Ams., N.Y.C., 1987-89; mem. steering com. Pharm. Mfrs. Assn., Washington, 1987-89; bd. dirs. Caribbean/Cen. Am. Com., Washington, 1989; mem. adv. bd. Coun. for Internat. Unity, N.Y.C., 1987-89. Bd. dirs. Notch Brook Resort Gen. Ptnrs. Condominium Assn., Stowe, Vt., 1988-94; active U.S. Postal Svc. Mktg. Adv. Bd., 1990—. Mem. Nat. Candy Wholesalers Assn. (bd. dirs. 1989-91), Morris County C. of C. (bd. dirs. 1989-91), Leadership Inc. (bd. dirs. Phila. br. 1993-94), Union League (Phila.), Wild Dunes Club (Isle of Palms, S.C.). Republican. Episcopalian. Avocations: golf, stamp collecting, photography, tennis. Office: DNA Plant Tech Corp 6701 San Pablo Ave Oakland CA 94608-1239

SERENBETZ, WARREN LEWIS, financial management company executive; b. N.Y.C., Mar. 27, 1924; s. Lewis E. and Estelle (Weygand) S.; m. Thelma Randby, Apr. 10, 1948; children: Warren Lewis, Paul Halvor, Stuart Weygand, Clay Raymond. B.S., Columbia U., 1944, M.S., 1949. Cons. Emerson Engrs., N.Y.C., 1949-51; with Oliver Corp., 1951-53; with REA Express, 1953-68, sr. v.p., 1966-68; v.p., dir. REA Leasing Corp., 1961-68; chmn. exec. com., chief exec. officer Interpool, Ltd., 1968-86; pres., chief exec. officer Radcliff Group, Inc., 1986—; pres. Containerization and Intermodal Inst., 1986-87; bd. dirs. Containerization and Intermodal Inst., Interpool Ltd., Interpool Inc., Microtech Corp.; co-founder Inst. Internat. Container Lessors, pres., 1983-85. Trustee St. Cabrini Nursing Home. Served to lt. (j.g.) USNR, World War II. Named CEO of Yr., Fin. World, 1976; recipient key to city Savannah, Ga., Italy award Container Pioneer, 1978, Connie award Container and Intermodal Inst., 1983. Mem. Am. Mgmt. Pres. Assn., Larchmont Yacht Club, Univ. Club Larchmont, Union League Club, Bonnie Briar Country Club. Presbyterian. Home: Hunter Hill West St Harrison NY 10528 Office: Radcliff Group Inc 695 West St Harrison NY 10528-2508

SERETEAN, MARTIN B. (BUD SERETEAN), carpet manufacturing company executive; b. N.Y.C., 1924; married. B.S., Okla. A&M Coll., 1949; M.S., NYU, 1950. With Abraham & Straus Inc., 1950-51, Allied Stores Corp., 1951-53; sales mgr. Katherine Rug Mills, Inc., 1953-56; with Coronet Industries, Inc., Dalton, Ga., 1956—, pres., chief exec. officer, 1962-72, chmn. bd., chief exec. officer, 1972-80, chmn. bd., from 1980, also bd. dirs.; bd. dirs. Atlanta Hawks. Office: Atlanta Hawks One CNN Ctr South Tower Ste 405 Atlanta GA 30303

SERFAS, RICHARD THOMAS, architecture educator, urban planner, county official; b. Reading, Pa., Nov. 24, 1952; s. Clifford Donald and Helen Catherine (McGovern) S. Student, Jacksonville U., 1970-72; BA, Colo. State U., 1974; MPA, Pa. State U., 1977; MS in Real Estate Devel., Columbia U., 1995. Project coord. ACTION Peace Corps, VISTA, Gary, Ind., 1974-75; city adminstr. City of Beverly Hills, Mo., 1975; grad. rsch. asst. dept. pub. adminstrn. Pa. State U., Middletown, 1976-77; community planner St. Louis County Dept. Planning, 1977-78; mgmt. analyst Clark County Sanitation Dist., Las Vegas, Nev., 1978-79; environ. planner Clark County Dept. Comprehensive Planning, Las Vegas, 1979-80, prin. planner, 1980-84, asst. coord. planning, 1984-85, coord. advance planning, 1985-89, asst. dir., 1989-94; project mgr. Focus 2000, Las Vegas, 1996—; instr. U. Nev. Sch. Architecture, Las Vegas, 1989—; student advisor Las Vegas chpt. AIA, 1989—. Staff advisor Clark County Comprehensive Plan Steering Com., 1980—, Environ. Task Force, Las Vegas, 1984—, Archtl. Design Task Force, Las Vegas, 1984—, Devel. Sector Task Force, Las Vegas, 1984—; mem. Transit Tech. Com., Las Vegas, 1989—. Recipient achievement award Nat. Assn. Counties, 1983-90. Mem. Am. Inst. Cert. Planners, Urban Land Inst., Nat. Assn. Corp. Real Estate Execs., Nat. Coun. for Urban Econ. Devel., Am. Planning Assn. (treas. Nev. chpt. 1979-91, pres. 1992—, Appreciation award 1981, 83, 85, 87, 89, 91, Outstanding Pub. Sector Planning Accomplishment award 1987, 88, 90, 91), Cmty. Assns. Inst. So. Nev. (bd. dirs. 1990-92, sec. 1993—). Democrat. Roman Catholic. Avocations: tennis, skiing, hiking, photography. Home: 2129 Stone Croft St Las Vegas NV 89134

SERGEY, JOHN MICHAEL, JR., manufacturing company executive; b. Chgo., Nov. 17, 1942; s. John Michael and Helen Ann (Bruchan) S.; m. Sharon Lee Ourada (div. 1982); children: John Michael III, Elisabeth Ann, Mark William, Tanya Ruth; m. Pamela Lynne Murphy, Aug. 8, 1987; children: Brian M., Sarah L. BA in Bus., Northwestern U., 1968; MBA, U. Chgo., 1976. Mgr. rolled products A. M. Castle, Chgo., 1959-74; v.p. Dietzgen Corp., Chgo., 1974-78; dir. sales and mktg. Avery Label, Azusa, Calif., 1978-80; v.p., gen. mgr. Fasson Roll div. Avery, Painesville, Ohio, 1980-84; group v.p. Soabar Products Group div. Avery, Phila., 1984-87, Materials Group div. Avery, Painesville, 1987-89; pres., CEO GAF Materials Corp., Wayne, N.J., 1989-96, Strategic Distgn., Inc., Feasterville, Pa., 1996—. Office: Strategic Distbn Inc 1615 Bustleton Pike Fstrvl Trvose PA 19053-7305

SERI, ISTVAN, physician, researcher; b. Szombathely, Hungary, Apr. 15, 1951; came to U.S., 1986; s. Istvan and Katalin (Orszagh) S.; m. Eva Novoszel, Oct. 11, 1975; children: David, I. Adam. MD, Semmelweis Med. Sch., Budapest, 1976; PhD, Hungarian Acad. Scis., Budapest, 1985. Resident in pediatrics Semmelweis Med. Sch., Budapest, 1976-79, instr. in pediatrics, 1979-84, asst. prof. in pediatrics, 1984-91; rsch. fellow Karolinska Inst., Stockholm, Sweden, 1984-86; rsch. fellow in nephrology Harvard Med. Sch., Boston, 1986-88, fellow in neonatology, 1988-91, instr. in pediatrics, 1991-94; asst. prof. in pediatrics U. Pa., Phila., 1994—; clin. dir. neonatal svcs. Children's Hosp. Phila., U. Pa., 1994—. Contbr. over 40 articles to profl. jours. Recipient Janeway award Children's Hosp. Boston, 1991-92, CHRC award NIH, Washington, 1991-92, Clin. Investigator award NIH, 1992-94. Fellow Am. Acad. Pediatrics; mem. Am. Heart Assn., Hungarian Med. Assn., Soc. Pediat. Rsch. Avocations: soccer, tennis, bridge. Office: Children's Hospital Phila 34th St & Civic Ctr Blvd Philadelphia PA 19104

SERKIN, PETER, pianist; b. N.Y.C., July 24, 1947; s. Rudolf and Irene (Busch) S. Student, Curtis Inst. Music, 1958-64. Instr. piano Curtis Inst. Music, N.Y.C., Juilliard Sch. Music, N.Y.C. Debut in, N.Y.C., 1959, appearances including with, Phila., Cleve., N.Y.C., London (Eng.), Zurich (Switzerland), Paris (France), Casals Festival orchs., recitals in, N.Y.C., London, Japan, maj. European and Am. cities; premiered works composed for him by Takemitsu, Berio, Knussen, Goehr, Henze, and Lieberson; appearances including with benefit performances for pacifism, aid to victims of war; rec. artist for, RCA, ProArte, New World Records, CBS records, Boston Records. Recipient prize Premio Accademia Musicale Chigian Siena, 1983. also: Juilliard Sch Music New York NY 10000

SERNA, JOE, JR., mayor; b. Stockton, Calif.; m. Isabel Serna; children: Phillip, Lisa. BA in Social Sci., Govt., Sacramento State Coll., 1966; postgrad., U. Calif., Davis. Vol. Peace Corps, Guatemala, 1966; edn. advisor Lt.-Gov. Mervyn Dymally, 1975-77; prof. govt. Calif State U., Sacramento, 1969—; mayor City of Sacramento, 1992—. Mem. Sacramento City Coun. 5th Dist., 1981-92, law and legis. com., 1989-92, Housing & Devel. Commn., Sacramento, chmn. budget and fin. com., 1981-89, transp. and cmty. devel. com., 1989-92; dir. United Farmworkers Am.'s Support Com. in Sacramento County, 1970-75; co-trustee Crocker Art Mus. Assn.; founder Thursday Night Market, Mayor's Summer Reading Camp; mem. Sacramento Housing & Devel. Commn.; bd. dirs. Regional Transit. Office: Office of the Mayor 915 I St Sacramento CA 95814-2608*

SERNETT, RICHARD PATRICK, lawyer; b. Mason City, Iowa, Sept. 8, 1938; s. Edward Frank and Loretta M. (Cavanaugh) S.; m. Janet Ellen Ward, Apr. 20, 1963; children: Susan Ellen, Thomas Ward, Stephen Edward, Katherine Anne. BBA, U. Iowa, 1960, JD, 1963. Bar: Iowa 1963, Ill. 1965, U.S. Dist. Ct. (no. dist.) Ill. 1965, U.S. Supreme Ct. 1971. House counsel, asst. sec. Scott, Foresman & Co., Glenview, Ill., 1963-70; sec., legal officer Scott, Foresman & Co., Glenview, 1970-80; v.p., law sec. SFN Cos., Inc., Glenview, 1980-83, sr. v.p., sec., gen. counsel, 1983-85, exec. v.p., gen. counsel, 1985-87; pvt. practice Northbrook, Ill., 1988-90; v.p., sec., gen. counsel Macmillan/McGraw-Hill Sch. Pub. Co., 1990-92; v.p. Bert Early Assoc., Chgo., 1992-93; ptnr. Sernett & Blake, Northfield, Ill., 1993-95; ret., 1995; mem. U.S. Dept. State Adv. Panel on Internat. Copyright, 1972-75. Chmn. bd. dirs. Iowa State U., Broadcasting Co., 1987-94. Mem. ABA (chmn. copyright div. 1972-73, com. on copyright legis. 1967-68, 69-70, com. on copyright office affairs 1966-67, 79-81, com. on program for revision copyright law 1971-72), Am. Intellectual Property Law Assn., Am. Soc. Corp. Secs., Ill. Bar Assn. (chmn. copyright com. 1971-72), Chgo. Bar Assn., Patent Law Assn. Chgo. (bbd. mgrs. 1979-82, chmn. copyright law com. 1972-73, 77-78), Copyright Soc. U.S.A. (trustee 1972-75, 77-80), North Shore Country Club (Glenview, Ill.), Eagle Ridge Country Club (Galena, Ill.), Wyndemere Country Club (Naples, Fla.), Met. Club Chgo. Home: 2579 Fairford Ln Northbrook IL 60062-8101

SEROKA, JAMES HENRY, social sciences educator, university administrator; b. Detroit, Mar. 5, 1950; s. Henry S. and Mary (Wyoral) S.; m. Carolyn Marie White, June 27, 1970; children: Mihail, Maritsa. BA, U. Mich., 1970; MA, Mich. State U., 1972, PhD, 1976. Labor mkt. analyst U.S. Dept. of Labor, Washington, 1970-71; asst. prof. U. N.C., Greensboro, 1976-77, Appalachian State U., Boone, N.C., 1977-79, So. Ill. U., Carbondale, 1979-81; assoc. prof. So. Ill. U., 1981-87, prof., dir., 1987-88; prof., head div. humanities and social scis. Pa. State U., Erie, 1988-90; prof. U. North Fla., Jacksonville, 1990—; also dir. Ctr. for Pub. Leadership, Jacksonville; dir. Master of Pub. Affairs Program Soc. Ill. U., 1987-88, Rural and Small Town Adminstrn. Project, 1980-85; asst. dir. Appalachian Regional Bur. Govts., Boone, N.C., 1977-79; manpower planning analyst U.S. Dept. Labor, Washington, 1970-71; exchange prof. Fakultet Politickih Nauka, Univerzitet u Beogradu, Yugoslavia, 1986; sr. researcher Coun. for the Internat. Exchange Scholars Yugoslavia, 1980; mem. state adv. com. Gov.'s Rural Affairs Coun. for State of Ill., 1988. Co-author: Political Organizations in Social Yugoslavia, 1986 (Choice award 1987); editor Rural Public Adminstration, 1986; co-editor: Developed Socialism, 1982, Comparative Political Systems, 1990, Yugoslavia: The Failure of Democratic Transformation, 1992; contbr. numerous articles to profl. jours. Recipient Akademischer Austausch Dienst Lang. scholar Fed. Republic of Germany, 1988 and numerous other grants, traveling fellows. Mem. Am. Soc. Pub. Adminstrn. (so Ill. chpt. 1982-83), Nat. Civic League, Am. Polit. Sci. Assn., Internat. Polit. Sci. Assn., Midwest Polit. Sci. Assn., So. Polit. Sci. Assn., Southwestern Polit. Sci. Assn., Western Polit. Sci. Assn., Policy Studies Orgn., Acad. Polit. Sci., Rural Sociol. Assn., Internat. Studies Assn., Am. Assn. Advancement of Slavic Studies, Western Social Sci. Assn., Cmty. Devel. Soc. Office: U North Fla Ctr for Public Leadership 4567 Saint Johns Bluff Rd S Jacksonville FL 32224-2646

SEROTA, JAMES IAN, lawyer; b. Chgo., Oct. 20, 1946; s. Louis Henry and Phyllis Estelle (Horner) S.; m. Susan Perlstadt, May 7, 1972; children: Daniel Louis, Jonathan Mark. AB, Washington U., St. Louis, 1968; JD cum laude, Northwestern U., 1971. Bar: Ill. 1971, U.S. Dist. Ct. (no. dist.) Ill. 1972, D.C. 1978, U.S. Supreme Ct. 1978, U.S. Ct. Appeals (D.C. cir.) 1978, U.S. Dist. Ct. (D.C. dist.), U.S. Ct. Claims 1980, N.Y. 1981, U.S. Dist. Ct. (so. dist.) N.Y. 1981, (ea. dist.) N.Y. 1981, U.S. Ct. Appeals (2d cir.) 1983. Trial atty. Antitrust div. U.S. Dept. Justice, Washington, 1971-77; assoc. Bell, Boyd & Lloyd, Washington, 1977-81; ptnr. Werner, Kennedy & French, N.Y.C., 1982-85, Levitsky & Serota, 1985-86, Huber, Lawrence & Abell, N.Y.C., 1987—. Recipient Spl. Achievement award U.S. Dept. Justice, 1976. Mem. ABA (chmn. ins. industry com. 1987-90, vice chair program com. 1990-91, chair annual mtg. program 1991-94, chair fuel & energy com. 1994-97, coun. 1997—), N.Y. State Bar Assn., Assn. of Bar of City of N.Y. (antitrust and trade regulations com. 1988-91), Fed. Bar Council. Contbr. articles to profl. jours. Editor Law Rev. Northwestern U.

SEROTA, SUSAN PERLSTADT, lawyer; b. Chgo., Sept. 10, 1945; d. Sidney Morris and Mildred (Penn) Perlstadt; m. James Ian Serota, May 7, 1972; children: Daniel Louis, Jonathan Mark. AB, U. Mich., 1967; JD, NYU, 1971. Bar: Ill. 1971, D.C. 1972, N.Y. 1981, U.S. Dist. Ct. (no. dist.) Ill. 1971, U.S. Dist. Ct. (so. dist.) N.Y. 1981, U.S. Dist. Ct. (ea. dist.) N.Y. 1985, U.S. Ct. Claims 1972, U.S. Tax Ct. 1972, U.S. Ct. Appeals (D.C. cir.) 1972. Assoc. Gottlieb & Schwartz, Chgo., 1971-72, Silverstein & Mullens, Washington, 1972-75, Cahill Gordon & Reindel, N.Y.C., 1975-82; assoc. Winthrop, Stimson, Putnam & Roberts, N.Y.C., 1982, ptnr., 1983--; adj. prof. Sch. Law, Georgetown U., Washington, 1974-75; mem. faculty Practicins Law Inst., N.Y.C., 1983—. Editor: ERISA Fiduciary Law, 1995; assoc. editor Exec. Compensation Jour., 1973-75; dep. editor Tax Mgmt., Estate and Gift Taxation and Exec. Compensation, 1973-75; mem. editl. adv. bd. Benefits Law Jour., 1988—, Tax Mgmt. Compensation Jour., 1993—; mem. bd. editor ERISA and Benefits Law Jour., 1992—; contbr. articles to profl. jours. Fellow Am. Coll. Tax Counsel; mem. ABA (chmn. joint com. employee benefits taxation sect. 1991-92, coun. mem. taxation sect. 1994—), Internat. Pension and Employee Benefits Lawyers Assn. (co-chair 1993-95), N.Y. State Bar Assn. (exec. com. tax sect. 1988-92), Am. Bar Retirement Assn. (dir. 1994—). Democrat. Office: Winthrop Stimson Putnam & Roberts One Battery Park Pla New York NY 10004-1490

SEROW, WILLIAM JOHN, economics educator; b. N.Y.C., Apr. 8, 1946; s. William John and Dorothea (Goyette) S.; m. Elizabeth Goetz, Aug. 24, 1968; 1 child, Erika. BA, Boston Coll., 1967; MA, Duke U., 1970, PhD, 1972. Rsch. dir. Univ. Va., Charlottesville, 1970-81; prof., dir. Fla. State U., Tallahassee, 1981—. Editor: Handbook of International Migration, 1990; author: Population Aging in the United States, 1990. Capt. U.S. Army, 1967-73. Recipient grants Fla. Health Care Cost Containment Bd., 1988-90, Nat. Instn. Aging, 1983-89, Nat. Inst. Mental Health, 1984-86, Govt. Indonesia, 1992-97. Mem. Internat. Union for Scientific Study of Population, Population Assn. Am., Am. and So. Econ. Assns., So. Demographic Assn. (pres. 1986-87), So. Regional Sci. Assn. (pres. 1982-83), Gerontol. Soc. Am. Avocations: railroads, Sherlock Holmes, baseball rsch. Office: Fla State U Ctr for Study of Population Tallahassee FL 32306-4063

SERPE-SCHROEDER, PATRICIA L., elementary education educator; b. La Porte, Ind., Feb. 1, 1949; d. Fred J. and Priscilla (Nowak) Serpe; children: Matthew Aaron, Scott Allan. BA, Purdue U., 1971, MS in Edn., 1976. Cert. tchr., administr., Ind. Tchr., grades 1-2 Westville (Ind.) Sch.; tchr., grade 2 Lincoln Sch., Highland, Ind.; tchr. grades 1, 2, 4 Iddings Sch., Merrillville, Ind., 1985-92; prin. Hudson Lake Elem. Sch., New Carlisle, Ind., 1992-94; title I coord. New Prairie Sch. Corp., New Carlisle, 1994—; mem. drug-free, sci. textbook, elem. computer coms. New Prairie United Sch. Corp.; presenter in field; com. of practitioners for title I Ind. State Dept. of Edn. Recipient Ind. State grant. Mem. NEA, ASCD, Ind. Tchrs. Assn., Merrillville Tchrs. Assn. (sec., membership chmn., mem. computer and tech. coms. for sch. corp., bldg. adv. com.), Nat. Assn. Sch. Prins., Ind. Assn. Sch. Prins., Ind. Prins. Leadership Acad., New Prarie Classroom Tchrs. Assn. (sec.), Kappa Delta Pi, Delta Kappa Gamma, Pi Delta Phi. Home: PO Box 1076 New Carlisle IN 46552-1076 Office: Olive Twp Elem Sch 300 W Ben St New Carlisle IN 46552-9650

SERRAGLIO, MARIO, architect; b. Bassano, Veneto, Italy, Apr. 13, 1965; came to U.S., 1972; s. Luciano G. and Maria P. (Bellon) S. BS in Architecture, Ohio State U., 1988. Real estate agent Four Star Realty, Columbus, Ohio, 1984—; treas. Columbus Masonry, Inc., 1985-86; v.p. Serraglio Masonry, Inc., Columbus, 1986-87; pres. Serraglio Constrn., Columbus, 1987—; residential designer Gary A. Bruck, SGR, Inc., Columbus, 1988-89, Sullivan Gray Ptnrs., Columbus, 1989-92; project mgr. John Regan Archs., Columbus, 1992-93. Mem. AIA, Columbus Bd. Realtors. Office: Architettura Serraglio 7400 E Main St Reynoldsburg OH 43068-2166

SERRANI, THOM, contracting trade association executive; b. Glens Falls, N.Y., Nov. 5, 1947; s. Italo N. and Florence Rosemary (LaPointe) S.; m. Beth Burgeson, June 24, 1978. B.A. in Liberal Arts, Sacred Heart U., Bridgeport, Conn., 1970; postgrad., Fairfield U., 1970-72. Mem. Stamford Bd. Reps., Conn., 1973-75; mem. Conn. Ho. of Reps., 1975-81, Conn. Senate, 1981-84; mayor City of Stamford, Conn., 1983-91; bus. cons. Ludlow Assocs., Stamford, 1991-95; exec. v.p. Associated Gen. Contractors of Vt., Montpelier, 1995—; mem. Nat. Conf. State Legislators, 1975-83, vice chmn. transp. com., 1981-83. Mem. Springdale Vol. Fire Co., Stamford, 1973—; apptd. mem. Gov.'s Task Force on Safety in Pub. Spaces, Hartford, 1986, Gov's. Fire Marshall Tng. Council, Hartford, 1986; chmn. Met. Planning Orgn., Conn., 1986; vice chmn. Stamford Econ. Assistance Corp., Conn., 1986; del. Dem. Nat. Conv., N.Y., 1976, San Francisco, 1984; chmn. bd. (ex officio) Stamford Ctr. Arts. Recipient legis. award State Firemen's Assn., Conn., 1976, Community Svc. award Sacred Heart U., 1984, Outstanding Svc. award Easter Seal Rehab. Ctr., 1987, Equal Opportunity award NAACP, 1989, Aid for Retarded Recognition award, Disting. Community Svc. award B'nai Brith, 1988, Pitney Bowes Foreman's Club Merit award, 1987; named Legislator of Yr., Conn. Caucus of Dems., 1980, Downtown Man of Yr., 1985. Mem. Piedmont Assocs., Glenbrook Athletic Assn. Avocations: cross country skiing, construction, gardening. Home: 112 Ellison Rd Ludlow VT 05149 Office: Assoc Gen Contractors Vt 47 Court St Montpelier VT 05602-2813

SERRANO, JOSE E., congressman; b. Mayaguez, P.R., Oct. 24, 1943; s. Jose E. and Hipolita (Soto) S.; m. Mary Serrano; children: Lisa Marie, Jose Marco, Justine, Jonathan, Benjamin. With Mfrs. Hanover Trust Co., 1961-69; mem. Bd. Edn. N.Y., 1969-74; former N.Y. State Assemblyman Albany, from 1975; mem. 102nd-105th Congresses from 18th (now 16th) N. Y. dist.N.Y., Washington, D.C., 1991—; mem. appropriations com., subcom. fgn. ops., export financing and related programs, subcom. labor, health, human svcs. and edn., 1993-94, mem. subcom. constitution, judiciary com., 1995-96; chmn. Congl. Hispanic Caucus, 1993-94; mem. appropriations com., 1996—. Roman Catholic. Office: 2342 Rayburn Hob Washington DC 20515 also: 890 Grand Concourse Bronx NY 10451-2828*

SERRIE, HENDRICK, anthropology and international business educator; b. Jersey City, July 2, 1937; s. Hendrick and Elois (Edge) S.; m. Gretchen Tipler Ihde, Sept. 3, 1959; children: Karim Jonathan, Keir Ethan. BA with honors, U. Wis., 1960; MA, Cornell U., 1964; PhD with distinction, Northwestern U., 1976. Dir. Solar Energy Field Project, Oaxaca, Mex., 1961-62; instr. U. Aleppo, Syria, 1963-64; asst. prof. Beloit (Wis.) Coll., 1964-69, Calif. State U., Northridge, 1969-70, Purdue U., West Lafayette, Ind., 1970-72, New Coll./U. South Fla., Sarasota, 1972-77; tchr. Pine View Sch., Sarasota, 1978; prof. anthropology, internat. bus. Eckerd Coll., St. Petersburg, Fla., 1978—; dir. internat. bus. overseas programs Eckerd Coll., 1981—; sr. rsch. assoc., Human Resources Inst., St. Petersburg, 1988—. Author, editor: Family, Kinship, and Ethnic Identity Among the Overseas Chinese, 1985, Anthropology and International Business, 1986, What Can Multinationals Do for Peasants, 1994; writer, dir. films: Technological Innovation, 1962, Something New Under the Sun, 1963; contbr. articles to Wall Street Jour. and Wall Street Jour. Europe. Tchr. Sunday sch., North United Methodist Ch., Sarasota, 1977—. Exxon scholar, So. Ctr. for Internat. Issues, Atlanta, 1980-81; Presdl. fellow Am. Grad. Sch. Internat. Mgmt., 1991; recipient Leavy award, Freedoms Found., Valley Forge, Pa., 1989. Fellow Am. Anthropol. Assn., Soc. Applied Anthropology; mem. So. Ctr. Internat. Issues, Acad. Internat. Bus., Tampa Bay Internat. Trade Coun., Internat. Soc. Intercultural Edn., Tng. and Rsch. Democrat. Avocations: singing, drawing, beach walking, cycling, sailing. Home: 636 Mecca Dr Sarasota FL 34234-2713 Office: Eckerd Coll Dept Internat Bus Saint Petersburg FL 33733

SERRIN, JAMES BURTON, mathematics educator; b. Chgo., Nov. 1, 1926; s. James B. and Helen Elizabeth (Wingate) S.; m. Barbara West, Sept. 6, 1952; children: Martha Helen Stack, Elizabeth Ruth, Janet Louise Sucha. Student, Northwestern U., 1944-46; BA, Western Mich. U., 1947; MA, Ind. U., PhD, 1951; DSc, U. Sussex, 1972; DSc in Engring., U. Ferrara, Italy, 1992; DSc in Math., U. Padova, Italy, 1992. With MIT, Cambridge, 1952-54; mem. faculty U. Minn., Mpls., 1955—, prof. math., 1959-95, Regents prof., 1968—, head Sch. Math., 1964-65; emeritus, 1995; vis. prof. U. Chgo., 1964, 75, Johns Hopkins U., 1966, U. Sussex, 1967-68, 72, 76, U. Naples, 1979, U. Modena, 1988, Ga. Inst. Tech., 1990. Author: Mathematical Principles of Classical Fluid Mechanics, 1957. Mem. Met. Airport Sound Abatement Council, Mpls., 1969—. Recipient Disting. Alumni award Ind. U., 1979. Fellow AAAS; mem. NAS, Am. Math. Soc. (G.D. Birkhoff prize 1973), Math. Assn. Am., Soc. for Natural Philosophy (pres. 1969-70), Finnish Acad. Sci. and Letters. Home: 4422 Dupont Ave S Minneapolis MN 55409-1739

SERRITELLA, JAMES ANTHONY, lawyer; b. Chgo., July 8, 1942; s. Anthony and Angela (Deleonardis) S.; m. Ruby Ann Amoroso, Oct. 3, 1981. B.A., SUNY-S.I., 1965, Pontifical Gregorian U., Rome, 1966; postgrad., DePaul U., 1966-67; M.A., U. Chgo., 1968, J.D., 1971. Bar: Ill. 1971, U.S. Supreme Ct. 1976, U.S. Tax Ct. 1985. Ptnr. Kirkland & Ellis, Chgo., 1978; ptnr. Reuben & Proctor, Chgo., 1978-86, Mayer, Brown & Platt, Chgo., 1986—; lectr. in field. Contbr. articles to profl. jours. Mem. exec. bd. govt. rels. com. United Way of Chgo., 1979-84; bd. dirs. Child Care Assn. Ill., 1975-79, Lyric Opera Guild, 1979-84; v.p. Comprehensive Community Svcs. of Met. Chgo., 1976-81; chmn. adv. bd. DePaul U. Coll. Law Ctr. Ch./State Studies, 1982—, mem. dean's vis. com., 1982—; trustee Mundelein Coll., 1982-86, St. Xavier Coll., St. Mary of the Lake Sem., 1982-83, Sta. WTTW Chgo. Pub. TV, 1978-81, Loretto Hosp., 1989-91; mem. geriatrics/gerontology steering com. McGaw Med. Ctr. Northwestern U., 1981-82; mem. adv. bd. N.Am. Coll., 1990—; mem. Bus. Execs. for Econ. Justice, 1988—, State wide citizens com. on Child Abuse and Neglect, 1988—; mem. bd. advisors Alzheimer's Ctr. Rush-Presbyn.-St. Luke's Med. Ctr., 1990—; founder, chmn. bd. Chgo. Ctr. for Peace Studies, 1990—; mem. adv. coun. Charitable Trust div. Ill. Atty. Gen., 1991—; cons. Union of Bulgarian Founds., 1992, Internat. Acad. for Freedom of Religion and Belief, Budapest, Hungary, 1992; active Ill. State Hist. Soc. Coun. for Ill. History, 1994—. Fellow Am. Bar Found.; mem. ABA, FBA, NCCJ (adv. com. on ch., state and taxation), Am. Assn. homes for Aging, Nat. Health Lawyers Assn., Ill. State Bar Assn. (bd. govs., spl. com. on jud. redistricting), Ill. Bar Found. (charter), Chgo. Bar Assn. (com. on evaluation of jud. candidates), Cath. Lawyers Guild (bd. govs.), Canon Law Soc. Am. (active mem.), Diocesan Attys. Assn. (exec. com.), Nat. Cath. Cemetery Conf., Cath. Health Assn., The Park Ridge Ctr., The Chgo. Club, Econ. Club, Tavern Club. Office: Mayer Brown & Platt 190 S La Salle St Chicago IL 60603-3410

SERRITELLA, WILLIAM DAVID, lawyer; b. Chgo., May 16, 1946; s. William V. and Josephine Dolores (Scalise) S. J.D., U. Ill., Champaign, 1971. Bar: Ill. 1971, U.S. Dist. Ct. (no. and cen. dists.) Ill. 1972, U.S. Dist. Ct. (ea. and we. dists.) Wis. 1995, U.S. Ct. Appeals (7th cir.) 1974, U.S. Supreme Ct. 1979, U.S. Dist. Ct. (so. dist.) Ind. 1997. Law clk. U.S. Dist. Ct., Danville, Ill., 1971-72; ptnr. Ross & Hardies, Chgo., 1972—; arbitrator Am. Arbitration Assn. Mem. ABA, Ill. Bar Assn., Chgo. Bar Assn., Nat. Assn. R.R. Trial Counsel (Ill.), Soc. Trial Lawyers, Defense Rsch. Inst., Legal Club, Trial Lawyers Club (Chicago). Office: Ross & Hardies 150 N Michigan Ave Ste 2500 Chicago IL 60601-7524

SERTNER, ROBERT MARK, producer; b. Phila., Oct. 7, 1955; s. Morton I. Sertner and Laurie (Hymes) Blicker. BBA, U. Tex., 1977. Ptnr. von Zerneck/Sertner Films, Los Angeles, 1985—. Prodr. over 80 TV movies, including Hostage Flight, Too Young To Die? (INH Best Movie award), The Courtmartial of Jackie Robinson, Combat High, To Heal A Nation, 1987 (Best Picture Internat. TV Movie awards), Trouble in City of Angels, Celebration Family, Proud Men. Gore Vidal's Billy the Kid (winner Houston Film Festival), Man Against the Mob, Maybe Baby, Robin Cook's Mortal Fear, Take Me Home Again, Outbreak, (mini series) The Big One: The Great Los Angeles Earthquake, Queenie, Jackie Collins' Lady Boss, The West Side Waltz, TNT's Native American Miniseries, including Geronimo, 1993, The Broken Chain, 1993, Lakota Woman, 1994, Crazy Horse, 1995, (theater) Living in Oblivion (Best Picture award Sundance Film Festival), 1994, God's Lonely Man (Sundance Film Festival nomination 1996). Mem. Acad. TV Arts and Scis., Hollywood Radio and TV Soc., Nat. Acad. Cable Programming, Mus. of Broadcasting Creative Coun., Caucus for Producers, Writers and Dirs. Office: von Zerneck/Sertner Films 12001 Ventura Pl Ste 400 Studio City CA 91604-2629

SERVAAS, BEURT RICHARD, corporate executive; b. Indpls., May 7, 1919; s. Beurt Hans and Lela Etta (Neff) S.; m. Cory Jane Synhorst, Jan. 7, 1950; children: Eric, Kristin, Joan, Paul, Amy. Student, U. Mex., Mexico

City, 1938-39; AB, Ind. U., 1940, MD, 1970; postgrad., Purdue U., 1941; D Bus. Mgmt., Ind. Inst. Tech.; LHD (hon.), Butler U. Agt. CIA, China, 1946; v.p. constrn. Vestar Corp., N.Y.C., 1948; founder, chief exec. officer No. Vernon Forge, Inc. Rev. Pub. Co., SerVaas Labs., Indpls., 1949—; chmn. bd. SerVaas, Inc., Indpls. and affiliated cos. Curtis Pub. Co., Forge Mexicana, Edgerton Tool, Dependable Engring., SerVaas Mgmt., SerVaas Rubber, Premier, Indpls. Rubber Co., Bridgeport Brass Co.; bd. dirs. Bank One Ind. Pres. City-County Coun., Indpls.; chmn. Ind. State Commn. Higher Edn.; chmn. Kirksville Coll. Osteopathic Medicine; bd. dirs. Coll. Univ. Corp., Ind. Pub. Health Found., Robert Schuller Ministries; past bd. dirs. Indt. State Bd. Health, Nat. Fgn. Rels. Commn. With USNR, 1941-45. Decorated Bronze Star; recipient Horatio Alger award, 1980. Mem. NAM, Am. Acad. Achievement (Golden Plate award 1973), Assn. Am. Med. Colls., Ind. C. of C., Indpls. C. of C., Marion County Hist. Soc., Ind. Hist. Soc., Newcomen Soc. N.Am., U.S. Naval Res. Assn., World Future Soc., Am. Legion, Columbia Club, Econ. Club, Indpls. Athletic Club, Indpls. Press Club, Meridian Hills Country Club, Phi Delta Kappa. Presbyterian. Home: 2525 W 44th St Indianapolis IN 46228-3249 Office: Office of the City County Coun 241 City-County Bldg 200 E Washington St Indianapolis IN 46204-3307 Office: SerVaas Inc 1000 Waterbury Blvd Indianapolis IN 46202*

SER VAAS, CORY, health sciences association administrator. Pres., CEO Benjamin Franklin Literary Soc., Indpls. Office: BFLMS PO Box 567 Indianapolis IN 46206-0567

SERVER, RONALD DOUGLAS, criminologist, political scientist, lawyer, educator; b. Fort Worth, Oct. 19, 1950; s. Frederick Douglas and Mabel Marie (Brown) S. BA, Prairie View A&M U., 1974; MPA, Tex. Christian U., 1976; JD, South Tex. Coll. of Law, 1984. Bar: Tex. 1985. Adminstrv. intern Tarrant County Hosp. Dist., Fort Worth, 1975-76; asst. city mgr. City of Weatherford, Tex., 1976-77; asst. prof. Prairie View (Tex.) A&M U., 1977-88, coord. criminal justice program, 1989—, interim head social and polit. sci. dept., 1994—; assoc. Glenn Taylor & Assocs., Hempstead, Tex., 1992—. Author: Houston Defender, 1993. Vol. adv. coun. Atty. Gen. Office-CS, Houston, 1992—; parliamentarian Faculty Senate-Prairie View A&M U., 1991—. Named Advisor of the Yr., Prairie View A&M U., 1992. Mem. Tex. Bar Assn., Nat. Acad. Advisement Assn., Southwestern Pre Law Advisors Assn. (v.p. 1996—), So. Assn. Pre Law Advisors, Nat. Assn. Blacks in Criminal Justice. Democrat. Avocations: tennis, photography, travel. Office: Prairie View A&M U PO Box 748 Prairie View TX 77446-0748

SERVERIAN, HEIDI SUE WHITAKER, accountant, systems developer; b. Framingham, Mass., Sept. 21, 1964; d. Charles Harvey and Judith R. (Reich) Whitaker; m. Raymond Serverian, Oct. 8, 1988; 1 child, William Michael. BS in Acctg., BS in Mgmt. Info. Sys., U. Ariz., 1987. Acctg. clk. Inventory Auditors, Inc., Denver, 1984; leasing and adminstrv. asst. James Presley Co., Tucson, 1985-86; office mgr. Sid's Appliance and TV, Tucson, 1986; assoc. acct., acct. GTE Calif., Thousand Oaks, Calif., 1987-89; auditor I and II GTE Svc. Corp., Westlake Village, Calif., 1989-91, sr. auditor, 1991-94; staff acct., staff adminstr. regulatory acctg. GTE Telephone Ops., Irving, Tex., 1994-96; bus. process specialist sys. GTE Long Distance, Irving, 1996-97; mem. Project Mgmt. Inst., 1996—. Mem. Inst. Mgmt. Accts. (CMA), Inst. Internal Auditors, Lions Club Internat. (Lionette 1990-95, Flower Mound Lions Tail Twister 1996-97). Avocations: word puzzles, animals, gardening, reading. Office: GTE Long Distance PO Box 152211 Irving TX 75015-2211

SERVICE, ROBERT E., ambassador; b. Beijing, 1937; m. Karol Kleiner; children: Jennifer, John. BA, Oberlin Coll., 1958; MA, Princeton U., 1960; postgrad., Stanford U., Nat. War Coll. Head office so. cone affairs Dept State, Washington, 1980-82; polit. counselor Am. Embassy, Madrid, Spain, 1982-87; dep. chief of missions Am. Embassy, Buenos Aires, 1987-89, Brasilia, Brazil, 1989-92; coun. to asst. sec. fin. and mgmt. policy, under sec. mgmt. Am. Embassy, Brasilia, 1992; head reinventing govt. task force Dept. State, 1993; amb. to Parguay Am. Embassy, Asuncion, 1994—. Office: Am Embassy Paraguay Unit 4711 APO AA 34036-4711 also: US Dept State Paraguay Washington DC 20521-3020

SERVISON, ROGER THEODORE, investment executive; b. Columbus, Ohio, June 6, 1945; s. Theodore Calvin and Hilda Augusta (Longmack) S.; m. Kristin Landsteiner, Jan. 8, 1972. BA, U. Iowa, 1967; MBA, Harvard U., 1972. Chmn. Tax Man, Inc., Cambridge, Mass., 1970-72; v.p. Continental Investment Corp., Boston, 1972-75, Phoenix Investment Counsel, Boston, 1975-76; mng. dir. Fidelity Investments, Boston, 1976—; bd. dirs. Tax Man, Cambridge, Boston Fin. Group, Longwood Covered Coats, Brookline. Dir. First Night, Inc., Boston, 1985; overseer Boston Symphony Orch. Mem. Longwood Cricket Club, Sippican Club, Federal Club, City Club, Piney Point Beach Club. Avocations: art, antiques, tennis, aerobics.

SERVODIDIO, PAT ANTHONY, broadcast executive; b. Yonkers, N.Y., Nov. 9, 1937; s. Pasquale and Catherine (Verdisco) S.; children: Christian, Alexa. BS, Fordham U., 1959; postgrad., St. John's U., N.Y.C., 1960-63. Asst. to bus. mgr. Sta. WCBS-TV, N.Y.C., 1960-64; account exec. Sta. WTNH-TV, New Haven, 1964-66; account exec., N.Y. sales mgr. RKO TV Reps., N.Y.C., 1967-74; v.p., N.Y. sales mgr. Sta. WOR-TV, N.Y.C., 1974-79, v.p., gen. sales mgr., 1979-81; v.p., gen. mgr. Sta. WNAC-TV, Boston, 1981-82; pres. RKO TV, N.Y.C., 1982-87; pres. RKO Gen., Inc., N.Y.C., 1987-91, also bd. dirs.; v.p., gen. mgr. Sta. WKYC-TV, Cleve., 1991-92; pres. Multimedia Broadcasting Co., Cin., 1992-94; broadcast cons., 1995—. Bd. regents St. Peter's Coll., 1983—; mem. com. future financing Rutgers U., New Brunswick, N.J., 1983-85; dir. TV bur. Advt. Bd., 1993-94; bd. dirs. Internat. Radio and TV Found., 1983-93, Assn. for Maximum Svc. TV, Inc., 1993-95. With U.S. Army, 1959-62. Office: 380 Lexington Ave Ste 1700 New York NY 10168

SERWATKA, WALTER DENNIS, publishing executive; b. Irvington, N.J., July 19, 1937; s. Walter F. and Grace R. (Sheehan) S.; m. Beverly M. Farrell, Aug. 10, 1963 (div. Feb. 1988); children: David, Nora, Nancy; m. Constance L. Holcomb, May 10, 1991. BBA in Acctg., Upsala U., 1959; MBA in Fin., Fairleigh Dickinson U., 1966; postgrad., Harvard U., 1978, Columbia U., 1979, Stanford U., 1985. With treas.'s dept. WESTVACO, N.Y.C., 1964-68; dir. fin. analysis Random House Co., N.Y.C., 1968-72; with McGraw-Hill Info. Systems Co., 1972-83; from contr. Sweet's divsn. to asst. contr. McGraw-Hill, Inc., N.Y.C., 1972-76, sr. v.p., contr., 1976-79, group v.p. real estate info. svcs., 1979-83, sr. v.p. group mfg. and circulation svcs., 1985, exec. v.p., CFO, 1985-88, exec. v.p. ops., 1989—; exec. v.p. fin. and svcs. McGraw-Hill Publs. Co., N.Y.C., 1983-84; pres. McGraw-Hill Info. Svcs., N.Y.C., 1988-89. Trustee Upsala Coll., East Orange, N.J. Served with U.S. Army, 1959-62. Mem. Fin. Exec. Inst., Mag. Pubs. Assn., Am. Inst. Accts., Planning Execs. Inst., Pvt. Sector Council.

SERWER, ALAN MICHAEL, lawyer; b. Detroit, Aug. 31, 1944; s. Bernard Jacob and Marian (Borin) S.; m. Laurel Kathryn Robbert, June 6, 1968; children: David Matthew, Karen Anne. BA in Econs., U. Mich., 1966; JD, Northwestern U., 1969. Bar: Ill. 1969, D.C. 1980, U.S. Dist. Ct. (no. dist.) Ill. 1970, U.S. Ct. Appeals (7th cir.) 1979, U.S. Supreme Ct. 1979, U.S. Ct. Appeals (6th cir.) 1982, U.S. Ct. Appeals (5th cir.) 1983, U.S. Ct. Appeals (11th cir.) 1984, U.S. Ct. Appeals (9th cir.) 1986. Trial atty. U.S. Dept. Labor, Chgo., 1969-78, counsel safety and health, 1978-79; assoc. Haley, Bader & Potts, Chgo., 1979-82, ptnr., 1983-87; ptnr. Bell, Boyd & Lloyd, Chgo., 1987—. Mem. Ill. Bar Assn., Chgo. Bar Assn., Assn. Trial Lawyers Am., Fed. Bar Assn. (recipient Milton Gordon award 1977). Home: 233 Woodland Rd Highland Park IL 60035-5052 Office: Bell Boyd & Lloyd 70 W Madison St Ste 3200 Chicago IL 60602-4244

SESONSKE, ALEXANDER, nuclear and chemical engineer; b. Gloversville, N.Y., June 20, 1921; s. Abraham and Esther (Kreitzer) S.; m. Marjorie Ann Mach, Apr. 17, 1952 (dec. Jan. 1995); children: Michael Jan, Jana Louise. B.Chem. Engring., Rensselaer Poly. Inst., 1942; M.S., U. Rochester, 1947; Ph.D., U. Del., 1950. Engr. Chem. Constrn. Corp., N.Y.C., 1942; chem. engr. Manhattan Project, 1943-45, Columbia-So. Chem. Corp., 1945-46; staff Los Alamos Sci. Lab., 1950-54, 60-61, cons., 1961-63; faculty Purdue U., Lafayette, Ind., 1954; prof. nuclear and chem. engring. Purdue U., 1959-86, prof. emeritus, 1986—, asst. chmn. dept. nuclear engring., 1966-73; Cons. Oak Ridge Nat. Lab., 1963-67, Electric Power Research Inst., 1974; mem. rev. com. Argonne (Ill.) Nat. Lab., 1965-67, 75-81; ind. cons. 1986—. Author: (with Samuel Glasstone) Nuclear Reactor Engineering, 1963, 4th edit., 1994, Nuclear Power Plant Design Analysis, 1973; mem. editorial bd. Advances in Nuclear Sci. and Tech., 1972—; contbr. numerous articles to profl. jours. Recipient Wall of Fame award U. Del., 1988. Fellow Am. Nuclear Soc. (Arthur H. Compton award 1987); mem. Am. Inst. Chem. Engrs., Am. Soc. Engring. Edn., Sigma Xi, Omega Chi Epsilon. Research on nuclear fuel mgmt., liquid metal heat transfer and nuclear reactor engring. Home and Office: 16408 Felice Dr San Diego CA 92128-2804

SESSA, TODD RAYMOND, marketing executive; b. Phila., Jan. 7, 1963; s. Raymond Vincent and Nancy Joy (Robinson) S. BS, Bentley Coll., 1987; MBA, Coll. William and Mary, 1989. Merchandise mgr. Boston Trading Ltd., Inc., 1983-87; v.p. sales and mktg. John Widdicomb Co., Grand Rapids, Mich., 1989-95; v.p., nat. sales mgr. Henredon Furniture Industries, Inc., Morganton, N.C., 1995—; rep. Industry Found. Am. Soc. Interior Designers, Washington, 1990—. Mem. U.S. Rowing Assn., Grand Rapids Rowing Club, Peninsular Club, Kentree Polo Club. Republican. Episcopalian. Avocations: rowing, squash, polo, sailing. Home: 110 Pearson Dr Morganton NC 28655 Office: Henredon Furniture Indsl Inc 400 Henredon Rd Morganton NC 28655-4536

SESSER, GARY DOUGLAS, lawyer; b. Malden, Mass., June 4, 1950; s. Ralph and Esther Anne (Chalfen) S.; m. Rachel Wolkin, June 22, 1979; children: Michael, Benjamin, Anne. BA, Cornell U., 1972; JD, U. Mich., 1975. Bar: Mass. 1975, U.S. Dist. Ct. Mass. 1976, N.Y. 1977, U.S. Dist. Ct. (so. and ea. dists.) N.Y. 1977, U.S. Ct. Appeals (2d cir.) 1978, D.C. 1980, U.S. Supreme Ct. 1980, U.S. Ct. Appeals (D.C. cir.) 1987, U.S. Ct. Appeals (11th cir.) 1990. Assoc. H.M. Kaufman, Boston, 1976; assoc. Haight, Gardner, Poor & Havens, N.Y.C., 1976-84, ptnr., 1984-97; ptnr. Carter, Ledyard & Milburn, N.Y.C., 1997—. Fellow Am. Bar Found.; mem. ABA, Assn. of Bar of City of N.Y. (transp. com.), Maritime Law Assn., Fed. Bar Coun. Home: 520 Upper Mountain Ave Montclair NJ 07043-1507 Office: Carter Ledyard & Milburn 2 Wall St New York NY 10005

SESSIONS, JEFFERSON BEAUREGARD, III, senator; b. Selma, Ala., Dec. 24, 1946; s. Jefferson Beauregard and Abbie (Powe) S.; m. Mary Montgomery Blackshear, Aug. 9, 1969; children: Mary Abigail, Ruth Blackshear, Samuel Turner. B.A., Huntingdon Coll., Montgomery, Ala., 1969; J.D., U. Ala., 1973. Bar: Ala. 1973. Assoc. Guin, Bouldin & Porch, Russellville, Ala., 1973-75; asst. U.S. atty. U.S. Dept. Justice, Mobile, Ala., 1975-77, U.S. atty., 1981-93; assoc., ptnr. Stockman & Bedsole Attys., Mobile, Ala., 1977-81; ptnr. Stockman, Bedsole & Sessions, Mobile, 1993-94; atty. gen. State of Ala., 1996; U.S. senator from Ala., 1996—; mem. U.S. atty's. com. on legis. and rules, 1983-85; mem. U.S. atty. gen's. adv. com., 1987-89, vice chmn. 1989; chmn. controlled substances subcom. U.S. atty. gen's. adv. com., 1992-93; mem. environment and pub. works com., judiciary com. Presdl. elector State of Ala., 1972; mem. bd. trustees, exec. com. Mobile Bay Area Partnership for Youth, 1981—; chmn. adminstrv. bd. Ashland Pl. United Meth. Ch., Mobile, 1982; mem. bd. dirs. Mobile Child Advocacy Ctr., 1988—; chmn. com. on govt., judiciary and law enforcement Coalition for a Drug Free Mobile, 1990-93; 1st v.p. Mobile Lions Club, 1993-94. Capt. USAR, 1975-85. Recipient U.S. Atty. Gen.'s award for significant achievements in the war against drug trafficking U.S. Atty. Gen. William P. Barr, 1992. Mem. ABA, Ala. Bar Assn., Mobile Bar Assn., Omicron Delta Kappa. Home: 16 S Lafayette St Mobile AL 36604-1714 Office: US Senate B34 Dirksen Senate Office Bldg Washington DC 20510*

SESSIONS, JUDITH ANN, librarian, university library dean; b. Lubbock, Tex., Dec. 16, 1947; d. Earl Alva and Anna (Mayer) S. BA cum laude, Cen. Fla. U., 1970; MLS, Fla. State U., 1971; postgrad., Am. U., 1980, George Washington U., 1983. Head libr. U. S.C., Salkehatchie, 1974-77; dir. Libr. and Learing Resources Ctr. Mt. Vernon Coll., Washington, 1977-82; planning and systems libr. George Washington U., Washington, 1981-82, asst. univ. libr. for adminstrn. svcs., acting head tech. svcs., 1982-84; univ. libr. Calif. State U., Chico, 1984-88; univ. libr., dean of libr. Miami U., Oxford, Ohio, 1988—; cons. Space Planning, S.C., 1976, DataPhase Implementation, Bowling Green U., 1982, TV News Study Ctr., George Washington U., 1981; asst. prof. Dept. Child Devel., Mt. Vernon Coll., 1978-81; mem., lectr. U.S.-China Libr. Exch. Del., 1986, 91; lectr., presenter in field; mem. coord. com. OhioLink Adv. Coun., 1995—, v.p., 1996. Contbr. articles, book revs. to profl. jours. Trustee Christ Hosp., Cin., 1990-94, Deaconness Gamble Rsch. Ctr., Cin., 1990-94; bd. dirs. Hamilton (Ohio) YMCA, 1994-97, pres., 1995-96, v.p., 1996-97, 97-98; v.p. Ohio Link Co-ordinating Coun., 1995-97, pres., 1998. Recipient award for outstanding contbn. D.C. Libr. Assn., 1979; rsch. grantee Mt. Vernon Coll., 1980; recipient Fulbright-Hayes Summer Travel fellowship to Czechoslovakia, 1991. Mem. ALA (Olofson award 1978, councillor-at-large policy making group 1981-94, coun. com. on coms. 1983-84, intellectual freedom com. 1984-88, directions and program rev. com. 1989-91, fin. and audit subcom. 1989-90, mem. exec. bd. 1989-94), Assn. Coll. and Rsch. Librs. (editorial bd. Coll. and Rsch. Librs. jour. 1979-84, nominations and appointments com. 1983-85, faculty status com. 1984-86), Libr. and Info. Tech. Assn. (chair legis. and regulation com. 1980-81), Libr. Adminstrn. and Mgmt. Assn. (bd. dirs. libr. orgn. and mgmt. sect. 1985-87), Calif. Inst. Librs. (v.p., pres. elect 1987-88), Mid-Atlantic Regional Libr. Fedn. (mem. exec. bd. 1982-84), Jr. Mems. Round Table (pres. 1981-82), Intellectual Freedom Round Table (sec. 1984-85), Freedom to Read Found. (trustee 1984-88, v.p. 1985-86, treas. 1986-87, pres. 1987-88), Rotary, Beta Phi Mu. Home: 45 Waters Way Hamilton OH 45013-6324 Office: Miami U Edgar W King Oxford OH 45056

SESSIONS, PETE, congressman; b. Mar. 22, 1955; m. Juanita; children: Bill, Alex. Grad., Southwestern U., 1978. Mem. 105th Congress from 5th Tex. dist., 1996—; with Southwestern Bell Telephone Co., Southwestern Com. Rsch.; v.p. pub. policy Nat. Ctr. Policy Analysis; mem. govt. reform and oversight com., banking and fin. svcs. com., sci. com. Bd. mem. YMCA; active United Meth. Ch. Mem. Rotary Club. Avocations: hiking, mountain climbing, running.

SESSIONS, ROY BRUMBY, otolaryngologist, educator; b. Houston, July 28, 1937; s. Roy Brumby and Elizabeth (Compton) S.; m. Mary Cousart, Aug. 28, 1976: children: Kate, Elizabeth, Abigail, Matthew. BS, La. State U., Baton Rouge, 1958; MD, La. State U., New Orleans, 1962. Resident gen. surgery and otolaryngology Washington U. Sch. Medicine, St. Louis, 1965-69; asst. prof. Baylor Coll. Medicine, Houston, 1969-73, assoc. prof., 1973-83; prof. head and neck surgery Meml. Sloan Kettering Cancer Ctr., N.Y.C., 1983-89; prof., chmn. dept. otolaryngology, head and neck surgery Gerogetown U. Med. Sch., Washington, 1989—. Contbr. articles to profl. jours., chpts. to books. Lt. comdr. USN, 1962-65. Roman Catholic. Office: Georgetown U 3800 Reservoir Rd NW Washington DC 20007-2113*

SESSIONS, WILLIAM LAD, philosophy educator, administrator; b. Somerville, N.J., Dec. 3, 1943; s. William George and Alice Edna (Billhardt) S.; m. Vicki Darlene Thompson, Aug. 28, 1965; children: Allistair Lee, Laura Anne. BA magna cum laude, U. Colo., 1965; MA in Comparative Study of Religion, Union Theol. Sem., N.Y.C., 1967; postgrad., Oxford (Eng.) U., 1967-68; PhD, Yale U., 1971; postdoctoral studies, Stanford U., 1976, Harvard U., 1977-78. Tchg. fellow Yale U., 1969; instr. U. Conn., Waterbury, 1970-71; asst. prof. philosophy Washington and Lee U., 1971-77, assoc. prof., 1977-83, prof., 1983—; instr. So. Sem., 1972, vis. prof. St. Olaf Coll., 1985-86, assoc. dean Coll. Washington and Lee U., 1992-95, acting dean, 1995-96, head philosophy dept., 1996—. Author: The Concept of Faith, 1994; contbr. articles to religious and philos. jours. Ruling elder Lexington (Va.) Presbyn. Ch., 1983-89, tchr. Sunday sch., 1984-97. Glenn grantee Washington and Lee U., 1975—, Babcock Found. grantee, 1976, NEH grantee, 1977, 83, 86, Mellon Found. grantee, 1978-79, Mellon East Asian Studies grantee, 1990. Mem. Am. Philos. Assn., Va. Philos. Assn., Soc. for Philosophy of Religion (exec. coun. 1988-94, v.p. 1991, pres. 1992), Soc. Christian Philosophers (steering com. ea. region 1986-90, 92-95, 97—, exec. com. 1987-90), Phi Beta Kappa (exec. com. W&L chpt. 1986-95, v.p. 1989-91, pres. 1991-93). Office: Washington & Lee U Dept of Philosophy Lexington VA 24450

SESSIONS, WILLIAM STEELE, former government official; b. Ft. Smith, Ark., May 27, 1930; s. Will Anderson and Edith A. (Steele) S.; m. Alice Lewis, Oct. 5, 1952; children: William Lewis, Mark Gregory, Peter Anderson, Sara Anne. BA, Baylor U., 1956, JD, 1958; hon. degree, John C. Marshall Law Sch., St. Mary's U. Sch. of Law, Dickinson Sch. of Law, Flager Coll., Davis & Elkins Coll. Bar: Tex. 1959. Ptnr. McGregor & Sessions, Waco, Tex., 1959-61; assoc. Tirey, McLaughlin, Gorin & Tirey, Waco, 1961-63; ptnr. Haley, Fulbright, Winniford, Sessions & Bice, Waco, 1963-69; chief govt. ops sect. criminal divsn. U.S. Dept. Justice, Washington, 1969-71; atty. U.S. Dist. Ct., San Antonio, 1971-74; dist. judge U.S. Dist. Ct. (we. dist.) Tex., San Antonio, 1974-87, chief judge, 1980-87; dir. FBI, Washington, 1987-93; ptnr. Sessions & Sessions, San Antonio, 1995—; bd. dirs. Fed. Jud. Ctr., Washington, chmn. bench book com., 1981—; mem. Tex. Commn. on Judicial Efficiency, 1995. Contbr. articles to profl. jours. Mem. Dr. Martin Luther King Jr. Fed. Holicy Commn., 1991-93, 94-96, hon. bd. dirs., 1993-94. Lt. USAF, 1951-55; capt. USAFR,. Recipient Rosewood Gavel award St. Mary's U. Sch. Law, San Antonio, 1982, Disting. Alumni award Baylor U., Golden Plate award Am. Acad. Achievement, 1988, Law Enforcement Leadership award Assn. Fed. Investigators, 1989, medal of honor DAR, 1989, Disting. Eagle Scout award Boy Scouts Am., 1990, Person of Yr. award Am. Soc. for Indsl. Security, 1990, Magna Charta award Baronial Order of Magna Charta, 1990; named Lawyer of Yr., Baylor Law Sch., 1988, Father of Yr., Nat. Fathers Day Com., 1988, Ellis Island Congl. Medal of Honor, 1992. Mem. ABA, Jud. Conf. U.S. (com. on ct. adminstrn., chmn. jud. improvements subcom. 1983-85, ad hoc com. on automation to subcom. 1984-87, mem. ad hoc ct. reporter com. 1984-87), San Antonio Bar Assn. (bd. dirs. 1973-74), Fed. Bar Assn. (pres. San Antonio sect. 1974), Am. Judicature Soc. (exec. com. 1982-84), Dist. Judges Assn. of 5th Cir. (pres. 1982-83), State Bar of Tex. (chmn. com. to develop procedures for cert. state law questions to Supreme Ct. by Fed. Cts. 1983-85), Waco McLennan County Bar Assn. (pres. 1968), San Antonio Inns of Ct. (pres. 1986), William S. Sessions Inns of Ct. Republican. Methodist. Avocations: hiking, climbing, canoeing. Office: Sessions & Sessions 112 E Pecan St Ste 29 San Antonio TX 78205-1516

SESSLE, BARRY JOHN, university administrator, researcher; b. Sydney, NSW, Australia, May 28, 1941; immigrated to Can., 1971; s. Frederick George and Sadie Isobel (Lawson) S.; m. Mary Baldwin; children from previous marriage: Erica Jane, Claire Marie. BDS, Sydney U., New South Wales, 1963, MDS, 1965, MSc, 1965; PhD, U. New South Wales, 1969. Scholar Dental Found. Sydney U., 1963-64; teaching fellow U. New South Wales, 1965-68; vis. assoc. U.S. Nat. Inst. Dental Research, Bethesda, Md., 1968-70; assoc. prof. U. Toronto Dental Sch., Ont., Can., 1971-76, prof., 1976-85, chmn. div. biol. scis., 1978-84, assoc. dean research, 1985-90, dean, 1990—; mem. com. on dental scis. Can. Med. Research Council, Ottawa, 1979-82. Author: The Neural Basis of Oral and Facial Function, 1978; editor: Mastication and Swallowing, 1976, Oro-facial Pain and Neuromuscular Dysfunction, 1985, Effects of Injury of Trigeminal and Spinal Somatosensory Systems, 1987, Trigeminal Neuralgia: Current Concepts Regarding Pathogenesis and Treatment, 1991, Temporomandibular Joint and Masticatory Muscle Disorders, 1994, Temporomandibular Disorders and Related Pain Conditions, 1995; mem. editl. bd. Arch. Oral Biol. Jour., 1988—, Pain Jour., 1986-90, assoc. editor, 1990-93, Dysphagia Jour., 1990—, Pain Rsch. and Mgmt. Jour., 1995—. Recipient Tchr. award Can. Fund for Dental Edn., 1977; grantee Canadian Med. Research Council, 1971—, NIH, 1974—. Fellow Royal Soc. Can., Can. Acad. Sci., Internat. Coll. Dentists; mem. Internat. Assn. Study Pain (sec. Can. chpt. 1982-87, mem. coun. 1993—), Soc. Neurosci. (pres. South Ont. chpt. 1982-83), Internat. Assn. Dental Rsch. (pres. Can. divsn. 1977-78, sec.-treas. 1976-79, pres. neurosci. group 1985-86, pres. 1994-95, Oral Sci. award 1976, Pindborg Oral Biol. prize 1994), Internat. Union Physiol. Sci. (sec. oral physiology commn. 1983—). Office: Faculty Dentistry U Toronto, 124 Edward St, Toronto, ON Canada M5G 1G6

SESSLER, ANDREW MARIENHOFF, physicist; b. Bklyn., Dec. 11, 1928; s. David and Mary (Baron) S.; m. Gladys Lerner, Sept. 23, 1951 (div. Dec. 1994); children: Daniel Ira, Jonathan Lawrence, Ruth. BA in Math. cum laude, Harvard U., 1949; MA in Theoretical Physics, Columbia U., 1951, PhD in Theoretical Physics, 1953. NSF fellow Cornell U., N.Y., 1953-54; asst. prof. Ohio State U., Columbus, 1954, assoc. prof., 1960; on leave Midwestern Univs. Research, 1955-56; vis. physicist Lawrence Radiation Lab., 1959-60, Niels Bohr Inst., Copenhagen, summer 1961; rschr. theoretical physics U. Calif. Lawrence Berkeley Lab., Berkeley, 1961-73, rschr. energy and environment, 1971-73, dir., 1973-80, sr. scientist plasma physics, 1980-94, disting. sr. staff scientist, 1994—; U.S. advisor Panjab U. Physics Inst., Chandigarh, India; mem. U.S.-India Coop. Program for Improvement Sci. Edn. in India, 1966, high energy physics adv. panel to U.S. AEC, 1969-72, adv. com. Lawrence Hall Sci., 1974-78; chmn. Stanford Synchrotron Radiation Project Sci. Policy Bd., 1974-77, EPRI Advanced Fuels Adv. Com., 1978-81, BNL External Adv. Com. on Isabelle, 1980-82; mem. sci. pol. bd. Stanford Synchrotron Radiation Lab., 1991-92; L.J. Haworth dist. scientist Brookhaven Nat. Lab., 1991-92. Mem. editl. bd. Nuclear Instruments and Methods, 1969—; correspondent Comments on Modern Physics, 1969-71; contbr. articles in field to profl. jours. Mem. hon. adv. bd. Inst. Advanced Phys. Studies, LaJolla Internat. Sch. Physics, 1991—; mem. Superconducting Super Collider Sci. Policy Com., 1991-93. Recipient E.O. Lawrence award U.S. Atomic Energy Commn., 1970, U.S. Particle Accelerator Sch. prize, 1988, Nicholson medal for Humanitarian, APS, 1994, Wilson prize, 1997; fellow Japan Soc. for Promotion Sci. at KEK, 1985. Fellow AAAS (nominating com. 1984-87), Am. Phys. Soc. (chmn. com. internat. freedom scientist 1982, study of directed energy weapons panel 1985-87, chmn. panel pub. affairs 1988, chmn. divsn. physics of beams 1990, chmn. com. applications of physics 1993, v.p. 1996); mem. NAS, IEEE, Fedn. Am. Scientists Coun. (vice chmn. 1987-88, chmn. 1988-92), N.Y. Acad. Sci., Assoc. Univ. Inc. (bd. dirs. 1991-94). Office: U Calif Lawrence Berkeley Lab 1 Cyclotron Rd M/S 71-259 Berkeley CA 94720

SESSOMS, ALLEN LEE, academic administrator, former diplomat, physicist; b. N.Y.C., Nov. 17, 1946; s. Albert Earl and Lottie Beatrice (Leff) S.; m. Csilla Manette von Csiky, Apr. 18, 1990; children: Manon Elizabeth, Stephanie Csilla. BS, Union Coll., Schenectady, N.Y., 1968; PhD, Yale U., 1972. Sci. assoc. CERN, Geneva, Switzerland, 1973-78; asst. prof. physics Harvard U., Cambridge, Mass., 1974-81; sr. tech. advisor OES, State Dept., Washington, 1980-82; dir. Office Nuclear Tech. & Safeguards, State Dept., Washington, 1982-87; counselor for sci. and tech. U.S. Embassy, Paris, 1987-89; polit. minister, counselor U.S. Embassy, Mexico City, 1989-91, dep. chief of mission, 1991-93; exec. v.p., v.p. for acad. affairs U. Mass. Sys., Boston, 1993-95; pres. CUNY Queens Coll., Flushing, N.Y., 1995—; mem. adv. com. U.S. Sec. Energy; mem. NCAA Pres.'s Commn. Contbr. articles to profl. jours. Adv. com. mem. U.S. Sec. of Energy. Ford Found. travel/study grantee, 1973-74; Alfred P. Sloan Found. fellow, 1977-81. Mem. AAAS, NCAA (pres.'s commn.), Am. Phys. Soc., N.Y. Acad. Sci., Cosmos Club.

SESSOMS, STEPHANIE THOMPSON, accountant; b. Norton, Va., June 17, 1963; d. Lowell Prentice and Elizabeth Claudine (Steffey) Thompson; m. Wesley Ray Sessoms, Dec. 18, 1988. BS in Bus. and Pub. Adminstrn., Va. Commonwealth U., 1983; postgrad., U. Va., Wise, 1983-85. CPA, Tenn. Account clk. Sterchi Bros. Stores, Inc., Lexington, Ky., 1985-86; asst. office mgr. Ky.-Ind. Lumber, Inc., Lexington, 1986-87; acct. Kennedy's Piggly Wiggly Stores, Coeburn, Va., 1987-88; programs asst., acct. Mountain Empire Older Citizens, Big Stone Gap, Va., 1988-94; sr. fin. acct. Wellmont Health Sys., Bristol, Tenn., 1994—; acct. Holston Valley Hosp. and Med. Ctr. (name change toWellmont Health Sys.), Kingsport, Tenn., 1994-97, sr. acct., 1997—; mem. adj. acctg. faculty Mountain Empire C.C. Rschr. (handbook) Guide for Increasing Sales, 1985. Chmn. bd. dirs. Family Crisis Support Svcs., 1989-94; cert. vol. income tax preparer IRS Vol. Income Tax Assistance Program. Mem. AAUW, AICPA, Inst. Mgmt. Accts., U. Va. Alumni Assn. Baptist. Home: 909 Sherbrooke Circle Mount Carmel TN 37645 Office: Wellmont Health Sys 1 Medical Park Blvd Bristol TN 37620-7430

SESSOMS, STUART MCGUIRE, physician, educator, retired insurance company executive; b. Autryville, N.C., July 16, 1921; s. Edwin Tate and Lillian Olive (Howard) S.; m. Thelma Ernestine Call, June 21, 1944; children: Stuart McGuire, Cristi Kay. B.S., U. N.C., 1943; M.D., Med. Coll. Va., 1946; postgrad., Johns Hopkins U. Diplomate: Am. Bd. Internal Medicine. Intern U.S. Marine Hosp., Balt., 1946-47; resident internal medicine U.S. Marine Hosp., 1947-50, asst. chief med. service, charge med. outpatient dept., 1950-52; asst. resident medicine Meml. Center Cancer and Allied

Diseases, N.Y.C., 1952-53; with NIH, Bethesda, Md., 1953-68; mem. clin. medicine, surgery Nat. Cancer Inst., 1953-54, acting chief gen. medicine, 1954, asst. dir., 1958, asso. dir. collaberative research, 1961-62; chief cancer chemotherapy Nat. Service Center, 1958-62; asst. dir. clin. center NIH, 1955-57, dep. dir., 1962-68; clin. instr. medicine George Washington U., 1953-54; asso. dean, prof. medicine Duke Sch. Medicine, Durham, 1968-75; dir. Duke U. Hosp., 1968-75, prof. health adminstrn., 1973-75; sr. v.p. Blue Cross and Blue Shield of N.C., 1976-87. Contbr. articles to profl. jours. Active PTA. Recipient Distinguished Service award U.S. Jr. C. of C., 1957. Mem. AMA, Assn. Mil. Surgeons U.S., Am. Hosp. Assn., Am., N.C. hosp. assns., Am. Pub. Health Assn., N.Y. Acad. Sci., Phi Delta Chi, Rho Chi, Alpha Kappa Kappa. Presbyterian. Home: 3432 Dover Rd Durham NC 27707-4520

SESTINI, VIRGIL ANDREW, biology educator; b. Las Vegas, Nov. 24, 1936; s. Santi and Merceda Francesca (Borla) S. BS in Edn., U. Nev., 1959; postgrad., Oreg. State U., 1963-64; MNS, U. Idaho, 1965; postgrad., Ariz. State U., 1967, No. Ariz. U., 1969; cert. tchr., Nev. Tchr. biology Rancho High Sch., 1960-76; sci. chmn., tchr. biology Bonanza High Sch., Las Vegas, 1976-90; ret., 1990; co-founder, curator exhibits Meadows Mus. Nat. History, 1993-94; part-time tchr. Meadows Sch., 1987-94; ret., 1994; edn. specialist, cell biologist SAGE Rsch., Las Vegas, 1993; founder Da Vinci Enterprises, Las Vegas, 1995. Served with USAR, 1959-65. Recipient Rotary Internat. Honor Tchr. award, 1965, Region VIII Outstanding Biology Tchr. award, 1970, Nev. Outstanding Biology Tchr. award Nat. Assn. Biology Tchrs., 1970, Nat. Assn. Sci. Tchrs., Am. Gas Assn. Sci. Teaching Achievement Recognition award, 1976, 1980, Gustov Ohaus award, 1980, Presdl. Honor Sci. Tchr. award, 1983; Excellence in Edn. award Nev. Dept. Edn., 1983; Presdl. award excellence in math. and sci. teaching, 1984, Celebration of Excellence award Nev. Com. on Excellence in Edn., 1986, Hall of Fame award Clark County Sch. Dist., 1988, Excellence in Edn. award, Clark County Sch. Dist., 1987, 88, Spl. Edn. award Clark County Sch. Dist., 1988, NSEA Mini-grants, 1988, 89, 92, World Decoration of Excellence medallion World Inst. Achievement, 1989, Cert. Spl. Congl. Recognition, 1989, Senatorial Recognition , 1989, mini-grant Jr. League Las Vegas., 1989, Excellence in Edn. award, Clark Country Sch. Dist., 1989; named Nev. Educator of Yr., Milken Family Found./Nev. State Dept. Edn., 1989; grantee Nev. State Bd. Edn., 1988, 89, Nev. State Edn. Assn., 1988-89. Author: Lab Investigations For High School Honors Biology, 1989, Microbiology: A Manual for High School Biology, 1992, Laboratory Investigations in Microbiology, 1992, Genetics Problems for High School Biology, 1995, Science Laboratory Report Data Book, 1995, Field and Museum Techniques for the Classroom Teacher, 1995, Selected Lab Investigations and Projects for Honors and AP Biology, Vol. I Microbiology, 1995, Telecommunications: A Simulation for Biology Using the Internet, 1995; co-author: A Biology Lab Manual For Cooperative Learning, 1989, Metrics and Science Methods: A Manual of Lab Experiments for Home Schoolers, 1990, Experimental Designs in Biology I: Botany and Zoology, 1993, Designs in Biology: A Lab Manual, 1993, Integrated Science Lab Manual, 1994; contbr. articles to profl. jours. Mem. AAAS, NEA, Nat. Assn. Taxidermists, Nat. Sci. Tchrs. Assn. (life, Nev. State chpt. 1968-70), Nat. Assn. Biology Tchrs. (life, OBTA dir. Nev. State 1991-93), Am. Soc. Microbiology, Coun. for Exceptional Children, Am. Biographic Inst. (rsch. bd. advisors 1988), Nat. Audubon Assn., Nat. Sci. Suprs. Assn., Am. Inst. Biol. Scis., Internat. Plastic Modelers Soc., So. Nev. Scale Modelers (Las Vegas coord. Modeloberfest, 1995). Avocations: scale models, military figures, scale model circus, photography, chess.

SESTRIC, ANTHONY JAMES, lawyer; b. St. Louis, June 27, 1940; s. Anton and Marie (Gasparovic) S.; student, Georgetown U., 1958-62; JD, Mo. U., 1965; m. Carol F. Bowman, Nov. 24, 1966; children: Laura Antonette, Holly Nicole, Michael Anthony. Bar: Mo. 1965, U.S. Ct. Appeals (8th cir.) 1965, U.S. Dist. Ct. Mo., 1966, U.S. Tax Ct. 1969, U.S. Supreme Ct. 1970, U.S. Ct. Appeals (7th cir.) 1984, U.S. Dist. Ct. (no. dist.) Tex. 1985, U.S. Claims Ct. 1986. U.S. Dist. Ct. Ill., 1994, Minn. 1996. Law clk. U.S. Dist. Ct., St. Louis, 1965-66; ptnr. firm Sestric, McGhee & Miller, St. Louis, 1966-77; spl. asst. to Mo. atty. gen., St. Louis, 1968; ptnr. Fordyce and Mayne, 1977-78, Sestric & Garvey, St. Louis, 1978-96, Sestric Law Firm, 1996—; hearing officer St. Louis Met. Police Dept.; active Fed. Jud. Selection Commn., 1993; bd. dirs. Marquett Learning Ctr.; gen. chmn. 22nd jud. cir. bar com., 1995. Contbr. articles to profl. jours. Mem. exec. com. Nat. Caucus of Met. Bar Leaders, 1987-90; mem. Fed. Judicial Commn., 1993, mem. St. Louis Air Pollution Bd. Appeals and Varience Rev., 1966-73, chmn., 1968-73; mem. St. Louis Airport Commn., 1975-76; dist. vice chmn. Boy Scouts Am., 1970-76; bd. dirs. Full Achievement, Inc., 1970-77; bd. dirs. Legal Aid Soc. of St. Louis, 1976-77, Law Library Assn. St. Louis, 1976-78; v.p. bd. St. Elizabeth Acad., 1985-86; bd. dirs. Thomas Dunn Memls., 1995—, Marquette Learning Ctr., 1995—; mem. U.S. Judicial Selections Commn., 1993—. Mem. ABA (state chmn. judiciary com. 1973-75, cir. chmn. com. condemnation, zoning and property use 1975-77, standing com. bar activities 1982-88), Nat. Conf. Bar Pres.'s (exec. coun. 1987-90), Mo. Bar (vice chmn. young lawyers sect. 1973-76, bd. govs. 1974-77), Bar Assn. Met. St. Louis (chmn. young lawyers sect. 1974-75, exec. com. 1974-83, 94-95, pres. 1981-82, bd. govs. 1995—). Home: 3967 Holly Hills Blvd Saint Louis MO 63116-3135 Office: The Sestric Law Firm 801 N 2nd St Saint Louis MO 63102-2560

SETHI, SHYAM SUNDER, management consultant; b. Rawalpindi, Pakistan, July 11, 1942; s. Balraj and Shakuntala (Sawhney) S.; m. Kiran Nair, Oct. 17, 1972; children: Seema, Shana. B.E. in Mech. Engring., Birla Inst. Tech., Ranchi, India, 1964; M.S.I.E., U. Wis., 1970. Cert. mgmt. cons. V.p. Drake Sheahan/Stewart Dougall, N.Y.C., 1970-80; pres., ptnr. Distbn. Mgmt. Assocs., Inc., Princeton, N.J., 1980-96; exec. dir. Dechert-Hampe & Co./DMA, Princeton, 1996—; cons. in supplu chain, logistics, inventory mgmt., ops. for maj. consumer goods, indsl. and retail cos., Europe, S.Am. and U.S.; spkr. internat. logistics conf. Contbr. articles to profl. jours. Pres. N.J. chpt. Coun. Logistics Mgmt., 1987-88, N.J. chpt. Inst. Mgmt. Consultants, 1987-88. Mem. Yacht Assn. India. Hindu. Avocations: tennis, sailing. Home: 4 Haelig Ct Bridgewater NJ 08807-2377 Office: Dechert-Hampe & Co/DMA 22 Wall St Princeton NJ 08540-1513

SETHNA, BEHERUZ NARIMAN, university president, marketing, management educator; b. Bombay, July 31, 1948; came to U.S., 1973; s. Nariman Dhanjishaw and Mithu Nariman (Mistry) S.; m. Madhavi Kaji, May 25, 1974; children: Anita B., Shaun B. B in Tech. with honors, Indian Inst. Tech., Bombay, 1971; MBA, Indian Inst. Mgmt., Ahmedabad, 1973; MPhil, Columbia U., 1975, PhD in Bus., 1976; cert., Ind. U., 1986, Harvard U. Inst. Educ. Mgmt., 1991. Engring. and mgmt. trainee various corps., Bombay, 1968-69, 70-72; case writer, trainee Clarion Advt., Bombay, 1973; project mgr., cons. Lever Bros. Co., N.Y.C., 1974-76; prof., chair mktg. and mgmt. info. systems Clarkson U., Potsdam, N.Y., 1976-89, dir. grad. programs, 1978-80; mktg., rsch. and strategic planning mgr. Procter & Gamble (India)/Richardson Hindustan (Vicks), Bombay and Westport, Conn., 1980-81; interim exec. v.p. acad. and student affairs; interim exec. v.p. ASA; dean Coll. of Bus., chief acad. officer Lamar (Tex.) U., 1989-94, Gulf States Utilities prof. bus., 1991-94; pres. State U. W. Ga., Carrollton, 1994—; mem. adv. coun. SUNY-Canton (N.Y.) Coll., 1975-89; cons. in field. Author: Research Methods in Marketing, 1984; contbr. articles to profl. jours. Scoutmaster Boy Scouts Am., Potsdam, 1987-89, pack com. chair, den leader, 1987-89, mem. dist. bd., 1991-94, Pres.'s Scout Gold Cord, 1966; leader Girl Scouts U.S., Beaumont, 1989-94. Recipient Instrl. Innovation award Decision Scis. Inst., 1984, 85, 86, 87, 88, 89, Minority Achiever's award Role Model award, 1991, Dean's Leadership award Acad. Bus. Adminstrn., 1993, Nat. Svc. award, 1996; Fulbright scholar U.S. Info. Agy., 1986-87; U.S. Dept. Energy grantee, 1980, IBM Corp. grantee, 1984, AT&T grantee, 1985. Mem. Decision Scis. Inst., Rotary (polio plus edn. chair, Paul Harris fellow 1997). Avocations: family, scouting. Home: 107 Wind Song Ct Carrollton GA 30117-4122 Office: Office of Pres State U W Ga Carrollton GA 30118-4500

SETHNESS, CHARLES OLIN, international financial official; b. Evanston, Ill., Feb. 24, 1941; s. Charles Olin and Alison Louise (Burge) S.; 1 son, Peter Worcester; m. Geraldine Greene, June 25, 1977; stepchildren: John, Carla, Sarah Houseman. A.B., Princeton U., 1963; M.B.A. with high distinction (Baker scholar), Harvard U., 1966. Sr. credit analyst Am. Nat. Bank & Trust Co., Chgo., 1963-64; research asst. Harvard Bus. Sch., 1966-67; assoc. Morgan Stanley & Co., N.Y.C., 1967-71; v.p. Morgan Stanley & Co., 1972, mng. dir., 1975-81; mgr. Morgan & Cie Internat., S.A., Paris, 1971-73; U.S. exec. dir. World Bank; and spl. asst. to sec. treasury Washington, 1973-75; assoc. dean for external relations Harvard U. Bus. Sch., Boston, 1981-85; asst. sec. treasury for domestic fin. Dept. Treasury, Washington, 1985-88; dir. capital markets dept. Internat. Fin. Corp., 1988-89; chief fin. officer Inter-Am. Devel. Bank, 1990—. Home: 6219 Garnett Dr Chevy Chase MD 20815-6617 Office: Inter-Am Devel Bank 1300 New York Ave NW Washington DC 20577-0001

SETIAN, NERSES MIKAIL, bishop, former apostolic exarchate; b. Zara, Turkey, Oct. 18, 1918; s. Nishan and Bayzar (Deveciyan) S. B. in Philosophy, U. Gregoriana, Rome, 1937, L.Theology, 1942, J.C.D., 1945. Ordained priest Armenian Catholic Ch., 1941. Ordained titular bishop of Ancira at the Armenians and 1st exarch of the apostolic exarchate for Armenian-Rite Catholics in Can. and U.S.A. Armenian Catholic Ch., N.Y.C., 1981—. Home and Office: Our Lady Queen of Martyrs 1327 Pleasant Ave Los Angeles CA 90033-2328

SETLOW, JANE KELLOCK, biophysicist; b. N.Y.C., Dec. 17, 1919; d. Harold A. and Alberta (Thompson) Kellock; m. Richard Setlow, June 6, 1941; children—Peter, Michael, Katherine, Charles. B.A., Swarthmore Coll., 1940; Ph.D. in Biophysics, Yale U., 1959. With dept. radiology Yale U., 1959-60; with biology div. Oak Ridge Nat. Lab., 1960-74; biophysicist Brookhaven Nat. Lab., Upton, N.Y., 1974—; mem. recombinant DNA molecule program adv. com. NIH, chmn., 1978-80. Author articles; mem. editorial bd. jours. Predoctoral fellow USPHS, 1957-59; postdoctoral fellow, 1960-62. Mem. Biophys. Soc. (pres. 1977-78), Am. Soc. Microbiology. Democrat. Home: 57 Valentine Rd Shoreham NY 11786-1243 Office: Biology Dept Brookhaven Nat Lab Upton NY 11973

SETLOW, RICHARD BURTON, biophysicist; b. N.Y.C., Jan. 19, 1921; s. Charles Meyer and Elsie (Hurwitz) S.; children: Peter, Michael, Katherine, Charles; m. Neva Delihas, Mar. 3, 1989. AB, Swarthmore Coll., 1941; PhD, Yale U., 1947; DSc, U. Toronto, 1985; MD, U. Essen, 1993. Assoc. prof. Yale U., 1956-61; biophysicist Oak Ridge (Tenn.) Nat. Lab., 1961-74, sci. dir. biophysics and cell physiology, 1969-74; dir. U. Tenn.-Oak Ridge Grad. Sch. Biomed. Scis., 1972-74; sr. biophysicist Brookhaven Nat. Lab., Upton, N.Y., 1974—, chmn. biology dept., 1979-87, assoc. dir. life scis., 1985—; prof. biomed. scis. U. Tenn., 1967-74; adj. prof. biochemistry SUNY, Stony Brook, 1975—. Author: (with E.C. Pollard) Molecular Biophysics, 1962; editor: (with P.C. Hanawalt) Molecular Mechanisms for Repair of DNA, 1975. Recipient Finsen medal Internat. Assn. Photobiology, 1980, Enrico Fermi award U.S. Dept. Energy, 1988. Mem. NAS, Am. Acad. Arts and Scis., Biophys. Soc. (pres. 1969-70), Internat. Com. Photobiology (pres. 1972-76), Radiation Rsch. Soc., Am. Soc. Photobiology, Am. Soc. Biochemistry and Molecular Biology, Am. Soc. Cancer Rsch., Environ. Mutagen Soc., 11th Internat. Congress on Photobiology (hon. pres. 1992), Phi Beta Kappa. Home: 4 Beachland Ave East Quogue NY 11942-4941 Office: Brookhaven Nat Lab Dept Biology Upton NY 11973

SETO, WILLIAM RODERICK, public accounting company executive; b. N.Y.C., July 2, 1954; s. James and Dorothy (Tsang) S. BS, U. Pa., 1976; JD, Cornell Law Sch., 1979. Bar: N.Y. 1980; CPA. Ptnr. Ernst & Young, Atlanta; S.E. area dir. internat. tax, 1986—; mem. bd. advisors Fgn. Sales Corp./Domestic Internat. Sales Corp. Taxx Assn., 1994-95; lectr. in field. Mem. editl. bd. Atlanta Internat. Mag., 1992-94. Mem. Leadership Atlanta. Named one of Top Tax Advisors in U.S., Internat. Tax Rev. mag., 1995. Mem. ABA, AICPA, N.Y. Bar Assn., Soc. Internat. Bus. Fellows, Internat. Fiscal Assn. Office: Ernst & Young 2800 Nations Bank Plz 600 Peachtree St Atlanta GA 30308

SETON, CHARLES B., lawyer; b. Bridgeport, Conn., Oct. 1, 1910; s. Charles Hillison and Stella (Rosen) Shapiro; m. Suzanne Alexia Maimin, Mar. 7, 1948; children: Pam Elinor Seton Lorenzo, Charles B. B.A., Yale U., 1931, LL.B., 1934. Bar: N.Y. 1934. Pvt. practice N.Y, 1934-55, Larchmont, N.Y., 1955—; assoc. firm Rosenman, Goldmark, Colin & Kaye (and predecessors), 1935-51; partner Rosen & Seton, 1955-58, 74-79, Rosen, Seton & Sarbin, 1958-74; sec. Ziff-Davis Pub. Co., 1974-77, gen. counsel, 1958-79; sec. Ziff Corp., 1976-77; ann. guest lectr. Advanced Copyright Seminar, N.Y. U. Law Sch., 1953-76, Practising Law Inst., 1955-74; past chmn. bd. trustees Fed. Bar Coun.; mem. Consular Law Soc., 1959-91. Participating author: The Business and Law of Music, 1965, Internat. Music Industry Conference, 1969; contbr. articles to profl. jours. V.p., founding dir. Music for Westchester, Inc., 1962-75, Arthur Judson Found., Inc., 1959-96; founding trustee Copyright Soc. U.s., v.p., chmn. Copyright Luncheon Circle (co-chmn. 1952-82). Lt. comdr. USNR, 1942-45. Mem. ABA, Westchester County Bar Assn. (atty./client econ. dispute com.), Assn. of Bar of City of N.Y., Guadalcanal Campaign Vets. (N.Y. state rep. 1987-92), Mory's Club, Yale Club. Home: 33 W Putnam Ave Greenwich CT 06830-5333 Office: 1890 Palmer Ave Ste 403 Larchmont NY 10538-3031

SETON, FENMORE ROGER, manufacturing company executive, civic worker; b. Bridgeport, Conn., Nov. 27, 1917; m. Phyllis Winifred Zimmerman, Apr. 5, 1942; 1 child, Diana Seton Adams Wakerley. BA in English, Yale U., 1938; EdM, So. Conn. State Coll./Yale U., 1956; LLD (hon.), U. New Haven, 1990; DHL (hon.), Albertus Magnus Coll., 1994. Asst. prof. air sci. and tactics Yale U., New Haven, 1952-56; pres., chief exec. officer Seton Name Plate Corp., New Haven, 1956-81; pres. Nat. Assn. Metal Etchers, Washington, 1968-69, Internat. Mktg. Device Assn., Chgo., 1973-74, mfrs. div. New Haven C. of C., 1974-79; chmn. Am. Nat. Standards Com. A13, N.Y.C., 1972-82. Apptd. Pres.'s Com. on Employment of People With Disabilities, Washington, 1973—; world pres. Rehab. Internat., World Secretariat in N.Y.C., 1988-92; bd. govs. U. New Haven, 1979—; treas. Save the Children Fedn., Westport, Conn., 1984-88; assoc. fellow Calhoun Coll. Yale U., 1976—; bd. dirs. Gaylord Hosp., 1995—; trustee Albert B. Sabin Vaccine Found., 1994—. Recipient Citation of Honor Sec. HEW, Washington, 1976, Preminger medallion People-To-People program Com. for Handicapped, Washington, 1988, Elm and Ivy award Yale U., 1985, Pub. Svc.award Social Security Adminstrn., 1992, Yale medal Pres. Yale U. on behalf of Bd. Govs. Assn. Yale Alumni, 1992, Disting. Svc. award Pres. of U.S., 1992. Fellow Inst. Dirs. (U.K.); mem. Cercle de l'Union Interallié (Paris), Explorers Club (N.Y.C.), Circumnavigators Club (N.Y.C.), Elizabethan Club (New Haven), Mory's Assn. (New Haven), New Haven Country Club. Republican. Home: 2 Old Orchard Rd North Haven CT 06473-3022

SETRAKIAN, BERGE, lawyer; b. Beirut, Lebanon, Apr. 14, 1949; came to U.S. 1976; s. Hemayak and Arminee S.; m. Vera L. Nazarian, Nov. 22, 1975; children: Ani, Lara. Diplome d'Etudes de Doctorat, U. Lyons, France, 1973; Diplome d'Etudes de Doctorat Droit Compare, F.I.E.D.C., Strasbourg, France, 1974; Licence en Droit Francais, U. St. Joseph, Beirut, 1972, Licence en Droit Libanais, 1972. Bar: Beirut 1972, N.Y. 1983. Assoc. Tyan & Setrakian, Beirut, 1972-76; ptnr. Whitman & Ransom, N.Y.C., 1976-93, Whitman, Breed, Abbott & Morgan, N.Y.C., 1993—; bd. dirs. Cedars Bank, Calif., 1987—, Bank Audi, U.S.A., 1991; fgn. law cons., N.Y., 1978. Bd. dirs., v.p., sec. Armenian Gen. Benevolent Union, N.Y.C., 1977—; pres. Worldwide Youth orgns., 1978—; bd. dirs. Armenian Assy. of Am., Washington, 1978-87; bd. dirs. Am. Task Force for Lebanon, 1988—; bd. dirs. Am. U. Armenia, 1992—. Mem. ABA, N.Y. Bar Assn., Beirut Bar Assn., U.K. Law Soc., Am. Fgn. Law Assn., Englewood Field Club. Office: Whitman Breed Abbott Morgan 200 Park Ave New York NY 10166-0005

SETSER, DONALD WAYNE, chemistry educator; b. Great Bend, Kans., Jan. 2, 1935; s. Leo Wayne and Velma Irene (Hewitt) S.; m. Carole Sue Schulze, June 2, 1969; children: Bradley Wayne, Kirk Wesley, Brett Donald. BS, Kans. State U., 1956, MS, 1958; PhD, U. Wash., 1961. Asst. prof. Kans. State U., Manhattan, 1963-66, assoc. prof., 1966-68, prof. chemistry, 1968—, Alumni Disting. prof. chemistry, 1984—; vis. prof. U. Grenoble, France, 1981, 84, 87, 91. Editor Reactive Intermediates, 1976; contbr. 240 articles to profl. jours. Recipient Rank prize electro-optics divsn., 1992. Fellow Am. Phys. Soc.; mem. Am. Chem. Soc. (Midwest award St. Louis sect. 1984). Home: 414 Wickham Rd Manhattan KS 66502-3751 Office: Kans State U Dept Of Chemistry Manhattan KS 66506

SETTERHOLM, JEFFREY MILES, systems engineer; b. Rochester, N.Y., May 8, 1946; s. Vernon Miles and Grace Lorraine (Bogema) S.; m. Donna Jean Stollenwerk, July 6, 1974; children: Gregory Todd, Vincent Michael. BS in Engring., Applied Sci. cum laude, Yale U., 1968; MS in Sys. Sci. and Math., Washington U., 1976. Electronic engr. McDonnell Douglas Aircraft Divsn., St. Louis, 1974, sr. engr. flight simulation, 1976-78; prin. devel. engr. mil. avionics divsn. Honeywell Inc., Mpls., 1978-84; prin. engr. aerospace divsn. Rosemount, Inc., Burnsville, Minn., 1984-92; ind. software tech. cons. Lakeville, Minn., 1992-94; geodetic scientist Geospan Corp., Mpls., 1994—. Author: The Philosophy Works Manual, 1993. Capt. USAF, 1969-73. Decorated DFC. Mem. AIAA, Soc. Automotive Engrs. Lutheran. Achievements include patents in field; origination of the computer configurable six-axis hand controller concept; invention of surveying from non-coplanar images; research in virtual cockpit concepts. Home: 8095 230th St E Lakeville MN 55044-8287 Office: Geospan Corp 2905 Northwest Blvd Ste 60 Plymouth MN 55441-2644

SETTIPANI, FRANK G., news correspondent; b. Bklyn., July 18, 1948; s. Gaspare and Marion (Caronna) S.; m. Laura A. Czachor, Aug. 21, 1982; children: Cara, Paul. BA in Polit. Sci., Bklyn. Coll., 1968. Reporter UPI, N.Y.C., 1969-70; anchor, reporter Sta. WHLI Radio, L.I., N.Y., 1970-74, Sta. WNEW Radio, N.Y.C., 1975-80; anchor Sta. WGBB-Radio, L.I., 1974-75, Sta. WINS Radio, N.Y.C., 1980-81; reporter Dow Jones, N.Y.C., 1981; corr. CBS News, N.Y.C., 1982—. Trustee N.J. Ctr. for Outreach and Svcs. for Autism Cmty., Ewing, 1991-94. Recipient Champion-Tuck Econ. award for radio reporting Dartmouth Coll., 1984. Mem. AFTRA, TV and Radio Working Press Assn. Roman Catholic. Avocation: advocacy for handicapped and developmentally disabled. Office: CBS News 524 W 57th St New York NY 10019-2902

SETTLE, ERIC LAWRENCE, lawyer; b. N.Y.C., July 28, 1961; s. Elliott Titus and Thelma (Radzvill) S.; m. Robin Marks, Aug. 23, 1986; children: Adam Harrison, Alexander Howard. AB cum laude, Colgate U., 1983; JD with honors, George Washington U., 1986. Bar: Pa. 1986, U.S. Dist. Ct. (ea. dist.) Pa. 1987, U.S. Dist. Ct. (mid. dist.) Pa. 1995, U.S. Ct. Appeals (3d cir.) 1992, U.S. Supreme Ct. 1995. Assoc. Wolf, Block, Schorr & Solis-Cohen, Phila., 1986-90, Fox, Rothschild, O'Brien & Frankel, Phila., 1990-95; dep. gen. counsel to gov. Commonwealth of Pa., 1995—. Trustee Colgate U., Hamilton, N.Y., 1983-86, Bryn Mawr Rehab. Hosp., 1993-94; pres. Riverview Condominium Assn., Phila., 1991-93; counsel Craig Snyder for U.S. Congress, Phila., 1992. George Cobb fellow Colgate U., 1981, 82. Mem. ABA (young lawyers divsn., career issues com. 1992-93), Pa. Bar Assn. (exec. com. young lawyers divsn. 1992-93), Phila. Bar Assn. (young lawyers sect. exec. com. 1990-92, dir. bar edn. ctr. 1993-95, trustee Phila. Bar Found., 1994), Phi Alpha Delta (marshal 1984-85). Home: 1148 N Woodbine Ave Narberth PA 19072-1245 Office: Gov's Office of Gen Counsel Commonwealth of Pa 17th Fl 333 Market St Harrisburg PA 17101-2210

SETTLES, F. STAN, JR., manufacturing executive, educator; b. Denver, Oct. 3, 1938; s. Frank S. and Dorothy Marie (Johnson) S.; m. Evelyn Brown, June 10, 1961; children: Frank S. III, Richard, Charles, Michael. BS in Prodn. Tech., Indsl. Engring., LeTourneau Coll., Longview, Tex., 1962; MS in Indsl. Engring., Ariz. State U., 1967, PhD in Indsl. Engring., 1969. Sr. systems analyst AiResearch Mfg. Co., Phoenix, 1968-70, project mgr., 1970-74, mgr. operational planning, 1974-80; mgr. indsl. engrs. Garrett Pneumatic Systems, Phoenix, 1980-83; mgr. indsl. mfg. engring. Garrett Turbine Engring. Co., Phoenix, 1983-85; v.p. mfg. ops. AiResearch Mfg. Co., Torrance, Calif., 1985-87; dir. indusl. mfg. engring. The Garrett Corp., Phoenix, 1987-88; dir. planning Garrett Engine Div., Phoenix, 1988-92; asst. dir. White House Office of Sci. and Tech. Policy, 1992-93; program dir. NSF, 1992-94; prof., chmn. indsl. and systems enging. dept. U. So. Calif., L.A., 1994—; faculty assoc. Ariz. State U., Tempe, 1974-85, 90-92, rsch. prof., 1992-94. Mem. sch. bd. Tempe Elem. Sch. Dist., 1976-80; mem. YMCA Indian Guides, nat. chief, 1978-79. Fellow Inst. Indsl. Engrs. (pres. 1987-88, Ops. Rsch. award 1980); mem. Nat. Acad. Engrs., Soc. Mfg. Engrs. (sr.), Inst. Ops. Rsch. and Mgmt. Sci. (sr.), Am. Soc. Quality Control, Am. Soc. Engring. Edn. Republican. Presbyterian. Home: 1750 E Ocean Blvd Unit 713 Long Beach CA 90802-6019 Office: Univ So Calif Dept Indsl and System Engring Los Angeles CA 90089-0193

SETZEKORN, WILLIAM DAVID, retired architect, consultant, author; b. Mt. Vernon, Ill., Mar. 12, 1935; s. Merrett Everet and Audrey (Ferguson) S.; m. Georgia Sue Brown, Feb. 4, 1958 (div. 1968); children: Jeffrey Merle, Timothy Michael. BArch, Kans. State U., 1957; cert. in computer graphics, Harvard U., 1968; BA with MA equivalency in Humanities, Western Ill. U., 1982. Registered arch., Calif. Coord. design and constrn. Cal-Expo, Sacramento, 1968; pvt. practice, Los Altos and Redding, Calif., Seattle, 1968-85; cons. Contra Costa County, Martinez, Calif., 1985-89, El Dorado County, Placerville, Calif., 1985-89, Somerset, Calif., 1989—; cons. Fed. Emergency Mgmt. Agy., The Presidio, San Francisco, 1989-95, Gov. Keating's task force for disaster recovery, Oklahoma City, 1995; apptd. Calif. State Grand Jury, 1996—. Author: Formerly British Honduras: A Profile of the New Nation of Belize, 1975, 4 other titles; contbr. articles to mags. Recipient Ofcl. Commendation, State of Calif., 1968, U.S. Presdl. Medal of Merit, Ronald Reagan, 1988. Fellow Augustan Soc. (bd. dirs. 1994-96); mem. Noble Co. of the Rose (knight 1979, lt. magister rosae 1995—), Mil. and Hospitaller Order of St. Lazarus (comdr.), numerous other internat. orders of chivalry, Family Setzekorn Assn. (prin. officer 1979—), San Leandro (Calif.) Yacht Club (founding), Kiwanis. Republican. Unitarian. Avocations. Genealogy, medieval history, heraldry, travel. Home and Office: PO Box 706 Somerset CA 95684-0706

SETZER, HERBERT JOHN, chemical engineer; b. N.Y.C., Oct. 23, 1928; s. Leo and Barbara (Hafner) S. m. Elizabeth Bernadette Curran, May 30, 1957; children: Stephen Lawrence, Robert Drew, John Herbert, Brian Edmund. BChemE, CUNY, 1951; MChemE, NYU, 1958. Engr. U.S. Army Ordnance Corps Redstone Arsenal, Huntsville, Ala., 1955-57; rsch. asst. NYU, 1958-61; rsch. engr. Internat. Fuel Cells (joint venture United Techs. Corp., Hartford, Conn. and Toshiba Corp., Tokyo), 1962-92; vis. lectr. Am. Internat. Coll., Conn., 1993—. Holder 21 U.S. patents chem. processing and hydrogen generation, other patents in Can., Europe, Africa, Asia, Australia; contbr. tech. papers in field to publs. Chmn. troop com. Long Rivers coun. Boy Scouts Am., 1971-81, com. mem., 1973-81. With U.S. Army, 1951-56. Recipient Mason award, NYU, 1962, Spl. award United Techs. Corp., 1980. Mem. Catalyst Soc. New Eng., Sigma Xi, Elks. Roman Catholic. Office: 17 Virginia Dr Ellington CT 06029-3432

SETZER, KIRK, religious leader. Pres. Amana (Iowa) Ch. Soc. Office: Amana Ch Soc Box 103 Middle Amana IA 52307

SETZLER, EDWARD ALLAN, lawyer; b. Kansas City, Mo., Nov. 3, 1933; s. Edward A. and Margaret (Parshall) S.; m. Helga E. Friedemann, May 20, 1972; children: Christina, Ingrid, Kirstin. BA, U. Kans., 1955; JD, U. Wis., 1962. Bar: Mo. 1962, U.S. Tax Ct. 1962. Assoc. Spencer, Fane, Britt & Browne, Kansas City, 1962-67, ptnr., 1968—, mng. ptnr., 1974-77, 78-82, chmn. trust and estate sect., 1974—; lectr. U. Mo. and Kansas City Sch. Law Continuing Edn. programs, 1983-95; mem. Jackson County Probate Manual com., 1988—; Mo. State rep. Joint Editl. Bd./Uniform Probate Code, 1989—. Co-author: Missouri Estate Administration, 1984, supplements, 1985-93; co-author, co-editor, reviewer Missouri Estate Planning, 1986, supplements, 1987-93; contbg. editor: A Will Is Not The Way -- The Living Trust Alternative, 1988; contbg. editor: Understanding Living Trusts, 1990, expanded edit., 1994; bd. editors Wis. Law Rev., 1961-62. Amb., bd. govs., bd. dirs., chmn. found. com. Am. Royal, 1982—; mem. planning giving com., bus. coun. Nelson Atkins Mus. Art, 1984—; mem. deferred giving com. Children's Mercy Hosp., 1991—; mem. Kansas City Estate Planning Symposium Com., 1984-92, chmn., 1991. Fellow Am. Coll. Trust and Estate Counsel (state chmn. 1992-97); mem. ABA, Mo. Bar Assn. (lectr., vice chmn. probate and estate planning com. 1994—), Kansas City Met. Bar Assn. (lectr., chmn. probate and trust 1979, 92, vice chmn. 1983-85, 91, legis. rev. com. 1991-95), Estate Planning Soc. Kansas City (co-founder 1965, pres. 1983-84, dir. 1984-85, mem. social com. 1968—), Order of Coif, Sigma Chi, Phi Delta Phi. Office: Spencer Fane Britt & Browne 1000 Walnut St Ste 1400 Kansas City MO 64106-2123

SETZLER, WILLIAM EDWARD, chemical company executive; b. Bklyn., Dec. 20, 1926; s. William Edward and Gertrude A. (Seyer) S.; m. Dorothy C. Kress, Dec. 2, 1950 (dec. Mar. 1987); children: William John, Heather A.; m. Lenore Kelly, July 13, 1991. B of Chem. Engring., Cooper Union, 1950; MS in Liberal Studies, Columbia U., 1993. V.p. ops. Argus Chem. Corp., N.Y.C., 1950-66; v.p. engring., then group v.p. Witco Chem. Corp. (now Witco Corp.), N.Y.C., 1966-75, exec. v.p., 1975-90, ret., 1990, also bd. dirs.; chmn. and CEO Faimount Chem. Inc., 1993—. Author and patentee in field. Served with USAAF, 1945-46. Mem. Am. Inst. Chem. Engrs., Soap and Detergent Assn. (bd. dirs.). Home: 3921 Lincoln St Seaford NY 11783-2115

SEUFERT, EDWARD CECIL, librarian, retired military officer; b. Newark, Apr. 16, 1933; s. Edward William and Dorothy Marie (Mussehl) S.; m. Shirley Ann Pratt, Oct. 20, 1963; children: Edward Roy, Janet Arlene. BS in Forestry, U. Maine, 1955; Cert. in Teaching, Lambuth Coll., 1977; MLS, Vanderbilt U., 1979; MA in Edn., Western Ky. U., 1982. Commd. 2d lt. U.S. Army, 1955, advanced through grades to lt. col., 1970; infantry and field artillery unit leader U.S. Army, U.S. and Korea, 1955-62; mobile tng. team leader U.S. Army, Vietnam, 1962-63; instr. Artillery Sch. U.S. Army, Ft. Sill, Okla., 1964-66; officer-in-charge Range Control Element U.S. Army, Baumholder Tng. Area, Fed. Republic of Germany, 1967-69; faculty chmn. combat arms br. Ordnance Sch. U.S. Army, Aberdeen Proving Ground, Md., 1970-73; dean adminstrn. Judge Adv. Gen.'s Sch. U.S. Army, Charlottesville, Va., 1973-75; ret. U.S. Army, 1975; head libr. Lindsey Wilson Coll., Columbia, Ky., 1979—. Tchr. adult Sunday sch. United Meth. Ch.; vol. county vets. assistance officer Ky. Divsn. Vets. Affairs; vol. dist. commr. Boy Scouts Am. Decorated Army Commendation medals (2), Meritorious Svc. medal , Legion of Merit, Combat Infantryman badge. Mem. Ret. Officers Assn., Columbia Men's Club (pres.), Nat. Eagle Scout Assn. (Eagle Scout 1949), Xi Sigma Pi, Alpha Gamma Rho. Home: 452 Jack Smith Rd Fairplay KY 42735-8728 Office: Lindsey Wilson Coll Libr Columbia KY 42728

SEUNG, THOMAS KAEHAO, philosophy educator; b. Jungju, Korea, Sept. 20, 1930; m. Kwihwan Hahn, May 29, 1965; children: Hyunjune Sebastian, Kwonjune Justin, Haesue Florence. BA, Yale U., 1958, MA, 1961, PhD, 1965. Instr. Yale U., 1963-65; asst. prof. Fordham U., 1965-66; mem. faculty dept. philosophy U. Tex., Austin, 1966—; prof. in philosophy U. Tex., 1972—, prof. in govt., 1985—, prof. in law, 1993—, Jesse H. Jones prof. liberal arts, 1987—. Author: The Fragile Leaves of the Sybil, 1962, Kant's Transcendental Logic, 1969, Cultural Thematics, 1976, Structuralism and Hermeneutics, 1982, Semiotics and Thematics, 1982, Intuition and Construction, 1993, Kant's Platonic Revolution, 1994, Plato Rediscovered, 1996. Served as officer Korean Army, 1950-53. Recipient Wilbur Lucius Cross medal Yale Grad. Sch. Alumni Assn., 1988; Soc. Religion in Higher Edn. fellow, 1969-70; Am. Council Learned Soc. fellow, 1970-71; NEH fellow, 1977-78. Office: U Tex Dept Philosophy Austin TX 78712

SEVALSTAD, SUZANNE ADA, accounting educator; b. Butte, Mont., Mar. 26, 1948; d. John Cornelius and Ivy Jeanette (Cloke) Pilling; m. Nels Sevalstad, Jr., Mar. 11, 1975. BS in Bus. with high distinction, Mont. State U., 1970, MS in Bus., 1972. CPA, Mont. Internal auditor Anaconda Co., Butte, 1970-71; mgr. Wise River (Mont.) Club, 1976-79; instr. acctg. Bozeman (Mont.) Vocat./Tech. Ctr., 1970-72, Ea. Mont. Coll., Billings, 1972-73, Mont. State U., Bozeman, 1973-76, U. Nev., Las Vegas, 1979—. Recipient Women of Month award Freshman Class Women, 1976, Disting. Tchr. Coll. Bus. U. Nev., 1983, 86, 89, 93, Prof. of Yr. award Student Acctg. Assn. U. Nev., 1984, 87, 88, 90, 91, Outstanding Acctg. Prof. award Acctg. Students of U. Nev., 1987, 88, 89, Spanos Disting. Teaching award, 1989, 94. Mem. AICPA, Am. Acctg. Assn., Nat. Inst. Mgmt. Acctg. (campus coord. 1988—), Inst. Mgmt. Accts., Assn. for Female Execs., Golden Key Soc. (hon.). Avocations: horseback riding, hiking, tennis, golf. Office: U Nev Dept Acctg 4505 S Maryland Pky Las Vegas NV 89154-9900

SEVCENKO, IHOR, history and literature educator; b. Radosc, Poland, Feb. 10, 1922; came to U.S., 1949, naturalized, 1957; s. Ivan and Maria (Cherniatynska) S.; m. Oksana Draj-Xmara, Apr., 1945 (div. 1953); m. Margaret M. Bentley, July 16, 1953 (div. 1966); m. Nancy Patterson, June 18, 1966 (div. 1995); children: Catherine, Elisabeth. Dr.Phil., Charles U., Prague, Czechoslovakia, 1945; Doct. en Phil. et Lettres, U. Louvain, Belgium, 1949; PhD (hon.), U. Cologne, Germany, 1994. Fellow in Byzantinology Dumbarton Oaks, 1949-50, dir. studies, 1966, prof. Byzantine history and lit., 1965-75, sr. research assoc., 1975—; lectr. Byzantine and ancient history U. Calif., Berkeley, 1950-51; fellow Byzantinology and Slavic lit., research program USSR, 1951-52; instr., then asst. prof. Slavic langs. and lit. U. Mich., 1953-57; mem. faculty Columbia U., 1957-72, prof., 1962-65, adj. prof., 1965-72; vis. prof. Harvard U., 1973-74, prof., 1974-92, emeritus, 1992; vis. fellow All Souls Coll., Oxford U., 1979-80, Wolfson Coll., Oxford U., 1987, 93; vis. mem. Princeton Inst. for Advanced Study, 1956; vis. prof. Munich U., 1959, Coll. de France, spring 1985, Cologne U., fall 1992, 96, Ctrl. European U., Budapest, spring and fall 1995; treas., acting treas., bd. dirs. Am. Rsch. Inst. in Turkey, 1964-66, 67, 75—; assoc. dir. Harvard Ukrainian Rsch. Inst., 1973-89, acting dir., 1977, 85-86; chmn. Nat. Com. Byzantine Studies, 1966-77; mem. Internat. Com. for Greek Paleography, 1983—. Author: Etudes sur la polémique entre Théodore Métochite et Nicéphore Choumnos, 1962, Society and Intellectual Life in Late Byzantium, 1981, Ideology, Letters and Culture in the Byzantine World, 1982, Byzantium and the Slavs in Letters and Culture, 1991, Ukraine Between East and West, 1996; co-author: Der Serbische Psalter, 1978, Life of St. Nicholas of Sion, 1984; contbr. articles to profl. jours. Guggenheim fellow, 1963, Humboldt-Forschungspreistraeger, 1985. Fellow Mediaeval Acad. Am., Brit. Acad. (corr.); mem. Am. Philos. Soc., Am. Acad. Arts and Scis., Ukrainian Acad. Arts and Scis., Sci. Sevcenko Soc., Société des Bollandistes Belgium (adj.), Accademia di Palermo (fgn.), Internat. Assn. Byzantine Studies (v.p. 1976-86, pres. 1986-96, hon. pres. 1996—), Christian Archeological Soc. of Athens (hon.), Austrian Acad. Sci. (corr.), Accademia Pontaniana of Naples (fgn.), Acad. Sci. Ukrainian SSR (fgn.), Acad. Humanities Rsch. (Moscow), Cosmos Club (Washington), Harvard Club (N.Y.C.), Phi Beta Kappa (hon.). Office: Harvard Univ 319 Boylston Hall Cambridge MA 02138

SEVER, JOHN LOUIS, medical researcher and educator; b. Chgo., Apr. 11, 1932; s. John Louis and Harriet (Link) S.; m. Gerane Werle, Mar. 3, 1956; children: Kimberly, Beverly, Valerie. BA, U. Chgo., 1952; MD, Northwestern U., 1957, BS, MS, PhD, 1957. Head sect. infectious diseases NINDS, NIH, Bethesda, Md., 1960-71, chief infectious diseases, 1971-88; chmn. pediatrics Children's Nat. Med. Ctr., Washington, 1988-90, prof. pediatrics, ob-gyn. and microbiology/immunology, 1988—; bd. dirs. Bio Whitaker, Walkersville, Md.; pres. Pan Am. Soc. Rapid Viral Diseases, Western Hemisphere, 1992-94. Editor 10 med. books; contbr. more than 500 articles to profl. jours. Cons. NIH Bethesda, 1988—, Rotary Internat., Evanston, Ill., 1989—, WHO, Geneva, Switzerland, 1991—. Capt. USPHS, 1960-88. Recipient Wellcome Diagnostics award Pan Am. Med. Virology, 1989, Meritorious Alumni award Northwestern U., 1989, Pasteur award Microbiology Soc., 1987, Kimbel award Am. Soc. for Microbiology, 1979, Abbott award, 1996. Mem. Infectious Disease Soc. of Ob-Gyn. (pres. 1992-94), Assn. Med. Clin. and Lab. Immunologists (pres. 1992-94), Teratology Soc. (pres. 1976-77), Price Club, Country Glen Club. Avocation: gardening.

SEVER, TOM, labor union administrator; b. West Newton, Pa., Aug. 13, 1935; widowed; children: Margaret, Josephine, Thomas, Paul. Student, St. Vincent Coll., Latrobe, Pa. Trustee local 30 Internat. Brotherhood Teamsters, Jeanette, Pa., 1973-75, bus. agt. local 30, 1979-91, pres. local 30, 1985-93; gen. sec.-treas. Internat. Brotherhood Teamsters, Washington, 1992—. Mem. VFW, NRA, Eagles, Moose. Avocations: hunting, fishing. Office: Int Brotherhood Teamsters 25 Louisiana Ave NW Washington DC 20001-2130

SEVERANCE, CHRISTOPHER CHURCHILL, museum director; b. Sydney, N.S., Can., Aug. 12, 1943; s. Glenwood and Freda (Braye) S. BA, Univ. Kings Coll., 1965; BE, Dalhousie U., 1966; MA, St. Mary's U., 1972. Tchr. King's Coll., N.S., 1966-70; dir. Miners Mus., Glace Bay, N.S., 1971-74; curator London (Ont.) Historical Mus., 1974-88; gen. mgr. London Regional Art and Historical Mus., 1988-91; exec. dir. Prince Edward Island Mus. & Heritage Found., Charlottetown, 1991—. Home: 30 Rosebank Rd, Stratford, PE Canada C1B 1G2 Office: Museum & Heritage Foundation, 2 Kent St, Charlottetown, PE Canada C1A 1M6

SEVERANCE, HARRY WELLS, emergency medicine educator; b. Wilson, N.C.; s. Harry Wells Sr. and Harriet Lucille (Pripps) S. BA in Sociology, Duke U., 1970; BA in Biology, East Carolina U., 1976; MD, Duke U., 1981. Resident East Carolina U., Greenville, N.C., 1982-86; asst. prof. emergency medicine U. Miss. Sch. Medicine, Jackson, 1986-91, Duke U. Med. Ctr., Durham, N.C., 1991—. Contbr. articles to profl. jours. Cardiology rsch. fellow Duke U. Med. Ctr., 1981-82. Fellow Am. Coll. Emergency Physicians (chmn. sect. short term obs. svcs. 1994). Home: 404 Livingstone Dr Cary NC 27513-2919 Office: Duke U Med Ctr Divsn Emergency Medicine Box 3096 Durham NC 27710

SEVERDIA, ANTHONY GEORGE, chemistry research investigator; b. Sharon, Pa., Sept. 20, 1946; s. George Anthony and Angela Mary (Tomich) S. BS, Pa. State U., 1968; MS, Case Western Reserve U., 1971, PhD, 1974. Rsch., teaching assoc. Rensselaer Poly. Inst., Troy, N.Y., 1975-77; chemist N.Y. U., 1977-79, 82-83, Columbia U., N.Y.C., 1979-82; analytical chemist Mallinckrodt Group, Terre Haute, Ind., 1983-92; sr. chemist analytical sci. Sanofi Rsch., Gt. Valley, Pa., 1992—. Contbr. articles to profl. jours.; presenter in field. Recipient Summer fellowship NSF, Cleve., 1971. Mem. Am. Chem. Soc. (exec. com., treas. Terre Haute sect. 1991-92), Soc. Applied Spectroscopy, The Internat. Soc. for Optical Engring. Home: 301 Prichard Ln Wallingford PA 19086

SEVERINO, ROBERTO, foreign language educator, academic administration executive; b. Catania, Italy, July 19, 1940; s. Giuseppe and Alba (Scroppo) S. Student, State U. Catania, Italy, 1960-62; BA, Columbia Union Coll., 1967; MA, U. Ill., 1969, PhD, 1973. Head acct., pers. dir. Industria Nazionale Apparecchiature Scientifiche, Milan, 1961-63; teaching asst., lang. lab. supv. Columbia Union Coll., Takoma Park, Md., 1965-67; grad. teaching asst. U. Ill., Urbana, 1967-70, coord. Corr. Sch., 1970-71; instr. dept. French and Italian U. Mass., Amherst, 1971-73; prof. dept. Italian Georgetown U., Washington, 1973—, acting chmn., 1987, chmn. dept., 1988—; pres., co-founder Nat. Inst. Contemporary Italian Studies, 1986—; co-founder Associazione Internazionale del Diritto e dell'Arte, 1994—; pres. Am. U. of Rome, 1990-93; lit. dir. Georgetown U. Elec. Text Repository, Italian Archive, 1988—, Ultramarina, 1992—; mem. adv. bd. Nat. Italian Am. Found. Nat. Christopher Columbus 1992 Celebration; mem. U.S. delegation to 1st Conf. on Italian lang. and culture in U.S., 1987; lectr., speaker in field; pres. cultural assn. Res in Artibus, 1996—. Author: Le soluzioni immaginarie, 1985, The Signs and Sounds of Italian, 1985, A carte scoperte, 1990, Presente imperfetto ed altri tempi, 1992, The Battle for Humanism, 1994, A Dumas: Mariano Stabile Sindaco di Palermo, 1994; co-author: Periscopio, 1986, International Nuclear Agreements Multilingual Glossary, 1988, United Nations Organization Multilingual Glossary, 1988, Regularizing the Irregular Italian Verb, 1990; translator; The Next 6000 Days by Saverio Avveduto, 1987; editor: (serials) Segni, 1985-88, Hispano-Italic Studies, 1976, 79; mem. editorial bd. Educazione Comparata, 1993—; contbr. articles to profl. jours.; translator: Angelo Scandurra: The Hot-Tempered Musician and Other Poems, 1996; editor: Giuseppe Severino: Ricordi di Castelnuovo primi '900. Scene di vita paesana, 1992; U.S. editor: Colophon, An Internat. Lit. Jour., 1996—. Trustee Joel Nafuma Refugee Ctr., Rome, 1993—. Rsch. grantee Interuniversity Ctr. European Studies, 1977; recipient Accademia Internazionale di Lettere, Scienze, Arti medal, 1983, Internat. Poetry prize, 1986, Gold Cross Cavaliere dell'Ordine al Merito della Repubblica Italiana, 1983, Gold medal Italian Ministries of Univs. and Sci. Rsch., 1988, Marranzano d'Argento prize, 1989, Gold Commander class Cross al Merito della Repubblica Italiana, 1990, Georgetown U. Vicennial Disting. Svc. medal, 1994, Telamone prize, 1995. Mem. MLA, So. Atlantic Modern Lang. Assn., Nat. Assn. Secondary Sch. Prins. (mem. sch. partnerships internat. Italian adv. coun. 1988—), Italian Am. Cultural Found., Italian Cultural Soc. (pres. 1979-81, 83-85, Outstanding Svc. award 1983, chmn. acad. policy com. 1981—), Assn. Internationale Critiques Literaires and Associazione Italiana Critici Letterari, Greater Washington Assn. Tchrs. Fgn. Langs. (mem. award selection com. 1983-85), Manuscript Soc., Renaissance Soc. Am., Circolo Culturale Italiano (hon.), Am. Club (Rome), Touring Club Italiano (hon.), Gamma Kappa Alpha (v.p. 1990—, sec.-treas. and chpt. advisor 1985-90), World Jurist Assn. Ctr. Assocs. (U.S. pres. 1993—), Associazione Internazionale del Diritto e dell'Arte (v.p. 1994—), Nat. Italian Am. Found. Coun. of 1,000, Napoleonic Soc. Am., Istituto Internazionale di Epistemologia la Magna Grecia, Unione Nazionale per la lotta contro l'Analfabetismo, Sons of Italy. Home: 4949 Quebec St NW Washington DC 20016-3230 Office: Georgetown U Dept Italian 37th and O Sts NW Washington DC 20057

SEVERINSEN, DOC (CARL H. SEVERINSEN), conductor, musician; b. Arlington, Oreg., July 7, 1927; m. Emily Marshall, 1980; children—Nancy, Judy, Cindy, Robin, Allen. Ptnr. Severinsen-Akwright Co.; pops condr. The Phoenix (Ariz.) Symphony Orchestra. Mem., Ted Fio Rito Band, 1945, Charlie Barnet Band, 1947-49, then with, Tommy Dorsey, Benny Goodman, Norro Morales, Vaughn Monroe; soloist network band: Steven Allen Show, NBC-TV, 1954-55; mem., NBC Orch. Tonight Show, 1962-67 , music dir., 1967-92 ; past host of: NBC-TV show The Midnight Special; recs., RCA Records, including; albums: Brass Roots, 1971, Facets, 1988, The Tonight Show Band, Night Journey. Address: care Thomas Cassidy Inc 11761 E Speedway Blvd Tucson AZ 85748 also: care William Morris Agency 151 S El Camino Dr Beverly Hills CA 90212-2704 also: care The Phoenix Symphony Orch 455 N 3rd St Ste 390 Phoenix AZ 85004*

SEVERNS, PENNY L., state legislator; b. Decatur, Ill., Jan. 21, 1952. BS in Polit. Sci. and Internat. Relations, So. Ill. U., 1974. Spl. asst. to adminstr. AID, Washington, 1977-79; city councilwoman Decatur, 1983-87; mem. 51st dist. Ill. State Senate, 1987—, chief budget negotiator for Senate Dems., 1993-96, minority spokesperson appropriations com., 1994-96, senate minority whip, minority spokesperson revenue com., 1997—. Office: Ill State Senate State Capitol Springfield IL 62706

SEVERO, RICHARD, writer; b. Newburgh, N.Y., Nov. 22, 1932; s. Thomas and Mary Theresa (Farina) S.; m. Emöke Edith de Papp, Apr. 7, 1961. B.A., Colgate U., 1954; postgrad., NYU Inst. Fine Arts, 1955-56, Columbia U. Sch. Architecture and Urban Planning, 1964-65. News asst. CBS, N.Y.C., 1954-55; reporter Poughkeepsie (N.Y.) New Yorker, 1956-57, A.P., Newark, 1957-61, N.Y. Herald Tribune, 1961-63; writer TV news CBS, N.Y.C., 1963-66; reporter Washington Post, 1966-68; investigative reporter N.Y. Times, N.Y.C., 1968-71; fgn. corr. N.Y. Times, Mex., C. Am. and Caribbean, 1971-73; investigative and environ. reporter N.Y. Times, 1973-77, sci. and environ. reporter, 1979—; assoc. Seminar on the City, Columbia U., 1966-69; vis. lectr. Am. culture Vassar Coll., 1985—; bd. dirs. Colgate U. Alumni Corp., 1988-92. Author: Lisa H., 1985; (with Lewis Milford) The Wages of War, 1989 (Am. Legion Nat. Comdr.'s award 1990); contbr. articles to mags. Poynter fellow-in-residence Vassar Coll., 1974 75; CBS News fellow, 1964-65; Recipient Front Page award Washington-Balt. Newspaper Guild, 1967; Journalistic award H.A.V.E.N., 1969; Schaeffer Gold Typewriter award N.Y. Newspaper Reporters Assn., 1969; Page One award Newspaper Guild of N.Y., 1970; hon. mention Mike Berger award Columbia U., 1970; Leone di San Marco award Italian Heritage and Culture Com., 1982; George Polk Meml. award L.I. U. Sch. Journalism, 1975; Hudson River Fisherman's Assn. award, 1976; Mike Berger award Columbia U., 1976; James Wright Brown award Deadline Club, Sigma Delta Chi, N.Y.C., 1976; Feature award N.Y. Press Club, 1977; Page One award Newspaper Guild N.Y., 1977, 82; Media award Am. Cancer Soc., 1977; hon. mention Heywood Broun Meml. award Am. Newspaper Guild, 1977; Penney-Mo. Newspaper award U. Mo. Sch. Journalism, 1978; Media award Agt. Orange Victims Internat., 1982; Page One award N.Y. Newspaper Guild, 1982; Gift of Life award N.Y. Blood Ctr., 1991, Spl. Writing award Soc. of the Silurians, 1992. Home: 81 Balmville Rd Newburgh NY 12550-1917

SEVERS, CHARLES A., III, lawyer; b. N.Y.C., Sept. 16, 1942; s. Charles A. and Gertrude (O'Neill) S.; m. Regina Ferrone, Sept. 4, 1965; children: Charles A. IV, Cornelius Forsythe, Rudyard Pierrepont, Olivia Consuelo. BA, Georgetown U., 1964, JD, 1967. Bar: N.Y. 1968, D.C. 1985. Ptnr. Dewey Ballantine, N.Y.C., 1967-96; gen. counsel Nat. Madison Group, N.Y.C., 1996—; lectr. various continuing legal edn. programs. Contbr. articles to profl. jours. Dir., trustee various orgns. Fellow Am. Coll. Trust and Estate Counsel; mem. ABA, N.Y. State Bar Assn., Assn. of Bar of City of N.Y., D.C. Bar Assn., Union Club. Home: 1095 Park Ave New York NY 10128-1154 also: High Meadow Old Chatham NY 12136 Office: Nat Madison Group 355 Lexington Ave New York NY 10017-6603

SEVERS, WALTER BRUCE, pharmacology educator, researcher; b. Pitts., June 10, 1938; s. Walter Bruce and Pauline Marie (Sever) S.; m. Anne Elizabeth Daniels, Apr. 25, 1970; children—Mary, Jane, Steven, William, Katherine. B.S., U. Pitts., 1960, M.S., 1963, Ph.D., 1965. Postdoctoral fellow NIH, Bethesda, Md., 1966-68; asst. prof. pharmacology Coll. Medicine, Pa. State U., Hershey, 1968-71, assoc. prof., 1971-77, prof., 1977—; ad hoc grant cons. NIH, U.S. Army, NSF. Mem. editorial bd. Am. Jour. Physiology, 1978—, Pharmacology, 1978—. Contbr. numerous articles, chpts., revs. to profl. publs. Recipient Disting. Alumnus award U. Pitts., 1978, I.M. Setchenov medal Acad. Med. Sci. USSR, 1983, Blue medal for sci. Acad. Med. Sci., Bulgaria, Medal for Sci. U. Belgrade; NASA grantee, 1976—. Mem. Am. Physiol. Soc., Am. Soc. Pharmacology and Exptl. Therapeutics, Soc. for Neurosci., Pavlovian Soc. Am., Sigma Xi (pres. Pa. State U. chpt. 1981-82). Republican. Roman Catholic. Lodge: Kiwanis (pres. Hershey area 1980, bd. dirs.). Avocations: reading; camping; hiking; fishing. Home: 1011 Grubb Rd Palmyra PA 17078-3510 Office: Pa State U Coll Medicine Dept Pharmacology 850 University Dr Hershey PA 17033

SEVERS, WILLIAM, actor; b. Britton, Okla., Jan. 8, 1932; s. Harry Lysander Fletcher and Katherine Lucinda (McAuliffe) S.; m. Mary Anne Proctor, Jan. 18, 1964 (div. 1971); 1 child, Pilar; m. Barbara Alice Schonger, Sept. 9, 1978; children: Katherine Meghan, Erin Christine. AA, Pasadena Playhouse Coll., 1956. Appeared on Broadway in Cut of the Axe, 1959-60, On Borrowed Time, 1991-92, nat. tour Look Homeward, Angel, 1960; costar nat. tour Spoon River, 1964; actor Secret Storm, All My Children, One Life to Live, Guiding Light, Texas, Search for Tomorrow, Another World, Loving, 1963-93; other TV appearances include Armstrong Circle Theatre, 1963, The Defenders, 1964, World War II, A GI Diary, 1978, Nurse, 1980, Muggable Mary, 1986, Law and Order, recurring role as Hon. Henry Fillmore, 1990—; appeared in film Funny Farm, 1988, Regarding Henry, 1991; actor European tour West Side Story, 1990-91, 94; actor, voice artist numerous commls., 1964—. Staff sgt. USAF, 1946-53. Mem. Actors Equity Assn., Screen Actors Guild, Am. Fedn. Television and Radio Artists, Pasadena Playhouse Alumni Assn. Democrat. Avocations: reading, golf. Home: 92 Bibbins Ave Fairfield CT 06432 Office: Michael Hartig Agency Ltd 156 5th Ave New York NY 10010-7002

SEVERSON, ROGER ALLAN, bank executive; b. Thief River Falls, Minn., Sept. 2, 1932; s. Alfred Gerhard and Esther Olga (Landro) S.; m. Beverly Diane Hays, Aug. 30, 1953; children: Eric Hays, Holle Diane. BS, U. Minn., 1954. Group v.p. First Nat. Bank, Mpls., 1952-73; pres. FBS Fin., Inc., Mpls., 1974-77; exec. v.p. F&M Savs. Bank, Mpls., 1977-82; sr. v.p. First Nat. Bank, St. Paul, 1983-85; exec. v.p. Shelard Nat. Bank, Mpls., 1985-86, TCF Bank Savs., Mpls., 1986-92; ret., 1992; mem. Robert Morris Assocs., 1980-92; trustee Heitman Mortgage Investors, Chgo., 1970-71, Mass. Mut. Mortgage Realty Investors, Springfield, 1972-85. Vice chmn. bd. of trustees The Am. Luth. Ch., Mpls., 1976-81; trustee Children's Health Ctr., Mpls., 1971-72; bd. dirs. Goodwill Industries, Mpls., 1967-70. Fellow Versterheim Mus.; mem. Ethics in Pub. Policy Ctr., Ctr. for Am. Experiment, Sons of Norway. Home: 8321 Essex Rd Chanhassen MN 55317-8705

SEVERY, LAWRENCE JAMES, psychologist, educator; b. Detroit, Mar. 30, 1943; m. Linda Andrea Anstensen, Aug. 20, 1966; children: Beth Andrea, Lisa Ellen. BS in Psychology, Wayne State U., 1965; MA in Psychology, U. Colo., 1970, PhD in Psychology, 1970. Rsch. asst. Inst. Behavioral Sci., U. Colo., Denver, 1968-69; predoctoral trainee Inst. Genetics and Behavior for Psychologists, U. Colo., Denver, 1969; asst. prof. psychology, sr. rsch. scientist Ark. Rehab. Rsch. and Tng. Ctr., U. Ark., 1970-71; various positions to prof., dept. psychology U. Fla., Gainesville, 1971—, R. David Thomas Endowed Legis. prof. psychology, 1988, assoc. dean for student affairs Coll. Liberal Arts and Scis., 1990—; rsch. fellow Inst. Population Studies, U. Exeter, Devon, Eng., 1982, sr. rsch. assoc. Behavioral Rsch. Inst., 1976-77, postdoctoral trainee, U. N.C. Population Ctr.'s summer inst., 1973 and others; cons. in field. Author: A Contemporary Introduction to Social Psychology, 1976, Advances in Population: Psychosocial Perspectives, Vol. 1 1993, Vol. 2, 1994; contbr. articles, book chpts. and monographs to profl. publs. Recipient numerous grants in population and health fields. Fellow APA (numerous coms.); mem. Southeastern Psychol. Assn., Population Assn. Am. (psycho-social workshop program chmn. 1982, 92), Assn. Consumer Rsch., Internat. Assn. Applied Psychology. Home: 4242 SW 94th Dr Gainesville FL 32608-4164 Office: Coll Liberal Arts & Scis U Fla Gainesville FL 32611

SEVETSON, DONALD JAMES, retired minister, church administrator; b. Oak Park, Ill., Oct. 4, 1933; s. Earl Winfred and Lillian Ione (Anderson) S.; m. Mary Louise Frank, Nov. 30, 1957; children: Philip, Andrea, Erika. BA, Macalester Coll., 1954; BDiv, Chgo. Theol. Sem. and U. Chgo., 1957. Ordained to ministry Congl. Ch., 1958. Minister Raymond Congl. Ch., Franksville, Wis., 1959-62; assoc. minister 1st Congl. Ch., Mpls., 1957-59, Dekalb, Ill., 1962-65, Appleton, Wis., 1965-69; minister Parkview United Ch. of Christ, White Bear Lake, Minn., 1969-73; assoc. conf. minister Minn. Conf. United Ch. of Christ, Mpls., 1973-80; conf. minister Ctrl. Pacific Conf. United Ch. of Christ, Portland, Oreg., 1980-96; interim regional minister Conn. Conf. United Ch of Christ, 1996-97; ret., 1997; chairperson coun. conf. ministers United Ch. of Christ, Cleve., 1994-96, chairperson, bd. dirs. office of comm., 1989-93. Author: The First Century, 1994. Chair Oreg. Holocaust Resource Ctr., Portland, 1989-91, bd. dirs., 1984-91, 94-95; trustee Pacific U. Forest Grove, Oreg., 1989-96, Pacific U., Forest Grove, Oreg., 1989-96. Mem. Chgo. Theol. Sem. Alumni Assn. (pres. 1962-64). Democrat. Avocations: long distance running, golf, historical research. Office: United Ch of Christ Ctrl Pacific Conf 0245 SW Bancroft St Ste E Portland OR 97201-4258

SEVIER, ERNEST YOULE, lawyer; b. Sacramento, June 20, 1932; s. Ernest and Helen Faye (McDonald) S.; m. Constance McKenna, Apr. 12, 1969; children: Carolyn Stewart, Katherine Danielle. A.B., Stanford U., 1954, J.D., 1956. Bar: Calif. 1956, U.S. Supreme Ct. 1965. Asso. mem. firm Sedgwick, Detert, Moran & Arnold, San Francisco, 1958-62; mem. firm Severson & Werson, San Francisco, 1962—. Served with USAF, 1956-57. Fellow Am. Bar Found.; mem. ABA (chmn. tort and ins. practice sect. 1982-83, exec. coun. 1976-84, chmn. standing com. on assoc. comms. 1988-90, chmn. coord. com. on Outreach to Pub. 1989-90, chmn. standing com. on lawyers responsibility for client protection 1991-94, commn. on non-lawyer practice 1992-95), Calif. Bar Assn., Internat. Assn. Def. Counsel, Fedn. Ins. and Corp. Counsel. Office: Severson & Werson 1 Embarcadero Ctr Ste 2500 San Francisco CA 94111-3714

SEVIK, MAURICE, acoustical engineer, researcher; b. Istanbul, Turkey, Mar. 19, 1923; s. Benjamin and Esther (Barzilai) S.; m. Jacqueline Delannoy, June 2, 1953; children: Michele, Martine. DIC, Imperial Coll. Sci. Tech., London, 1946; PhD, Pa. State U., 1963. Registered profl. engr., Ont. With Bristol Aircraft Corp., U.K., 1946-51; sr. structures engr. Avro Aircraft Ltd., Can., 1952-59; prof. aerospace engring., dir. Garfield Thomas Water Tunnel, Pa. State U., University Park, 1959-72; mem. assoc. tech. dir. ship signatures directorate David Taylor Rsch. Ctr., Bethesda, Md., 1972—; vis. prof. Cambridge (Eng.) U., 1970; cons. USAF Office Sci. Rsch. 1965. Contbr. articles to profl. jours. Fellow Churchill Coll., Cambridge U., 1970; recipient Gold Medal award The Am. Soc. of Naval Engrs., 1990, Disting. Alumni award Central Pa. chpt. Acoustical Soc. of Am., Charles B. Martell Tech. Excellence award Nat. Security Indsl. Assn., 1992, Robert Dexter Conrad award Office Naval Rsch., 1996. Fellow ASME (Rayleigh lectr. 1995, Per Bruel Gold medal for noise control and acoustics 1996), Acoustical Soc. Am., Sigma Xi; mem. Nat. Acad. Engring. Home: 7817 Horseshoe Ln Rockville MD 20854-3828 Office: David Taylor Rsch Ctr Bethesda MD 20084

SEVILLA, STANLEY, lawyer; b. Cin., Apr. 3, 1920; s. Isadore and Dienna (Levy) S.; m. Lois A. Howell, July 25, 1948; children: Stanley, Susan, Donald, Carol, Elizabeth. BA in Econs. with high honors, U. Cin., 1942; J.D., Harvard U., 1948. Bar: Calif. 1949. Since practiced in Los Angeles; assoc. Williamson, Hoge & Curry, 1948-50; mem. firm Axelrod, Sevilla and Ross, 1950-75, Stanley Sevilla (P.C.), 1975—; gen. counsel La.-Pacific Resources, Inc., 1970-90. Bd. dirs. Caesars World, Inc., 1989-95. With USAAF, 1942-46. Mem. Los Angeles County Bar Assn., Beverly Hills Bar Assn., Phi Beta Kappa, Tau Kappa Alpha. Home: 16606 Merivale Ln

Pacific Palisades CA 90272-2236 Office: PO Box 308 Pacific Palisades CA 90272-0308

SEVY, ROGER WARREN, retired pharmacology educator; b. Richfield, Utah, Nov. 6, 1923; s. Carl Spencer and Maude (Malmquist) S.; m. Barbara Florence Snetsinger, Aug. 16, 1948; children—Pamela Jane, Jonathan Carl. Student, Utah State U., 1941-43, Harvard, 1943-45; M.S., U. Vt., 1948; Ph.D., U. Ill., 1951, M.D., 1954. Asst. physiology U. Ill., 1948-51, instr., 1951-54; asst. prof. pharmacology Temple U., Phila., 1954-56, prof., 1956-89, chmn. dept., 1957-73, dean Sch. Medicine, 1973-79, prof. emeritus, 1989—. Served with AUS, 1943-45. Mem. Am. Soc. Pharmacology and Exptl. Therapeutics, Am. Physiol. Soc., Endocrine Soc., AAAS, Sigma Xi., Alpha Omega Alpha. Research on hypertension and cardiovascular pharmacology. Home: 242 Mather Rd Jenkintown PA 19046-3129 Office: Temple U 3420 N Broad St Philadelphia PA 19140-5104

SEWARD, GEORGE CHESTER, lawyer; b. Omaha, Aug. 4, 1910; s. George Francis and Ada Leona (Rugh) S.; m. Carroll Frances McKay, Dec. 12, 1936 (dec. 1991); children: Gordon Day, Patricia McKay (Mrs. Dryden G. Liddle), James Pickett, Deborah Carroll (Mrs. R. Thomas Coleman). Grad., Louisville Male High Sch., 1929; BA, U. Va., 1933, LLB, 1936. Bar: Va. 1935, N.Y., Ky., D.C., U.S. Supreme Ct. With Shearman & Sterling, N.Y.C., 1936-53, Seward & Kissel, N.Y.C., 1953—; founder, hon. chmn. Internat. Capital Markets Group of Internat. Fedn. Accts., Fedn. Internat. des Bourses de Valeurs, Internat. Bar Assn.; legal adv. com. N.Y. Stock Exch., 1984-87; trustee Benson Iron Ore Trust; dir. Benson Mines, Inc., 1969-85, Chas. P. Young Co., 1965-72, Howmet Corp., 1955-57, pres., 1964-66; dir. Witherbee Sherman Corp., 1952-66. Author: Basic Corporate Practice, Seward and Related Families; co-author: Model Business Corporation Act Annotated, We Remember Carroll. Trustee Arts and Scis. Coun. U. Va., 1983-93, pres., 1991-93; trustee Edwin Gould Found. for Children, 1955-96; trustee Nature Conservancy of Ea. L.I., 1969-80, N.Y. Geneal. and Biog. Soc. Elected to Louisville Male High Sch. Alumni Assn. Hall of Fame, 1991; named Ky. Col., 1993. Fellow Am. Bar Found. (chmn. model corp. acts com. 1956-65), N.Y. State Bar Found.; mem. Internat. Bar Assn. (hon. life pres., hon. pres., founder sect. on bus. law, lectr. series named in his honor, New Delhi 1988, Lisbon 1992, Budapest 1993, Geneva 1994), ABA (chmn. bus. law sect. 1958-59, chmn. sect. com. corp. laws 1952-58, chmn. sect. banking com. 1960-61, mem. ho. of dels. 1959-60, 63-74, mem. joint com. with Am. Law Inst. on continung legal edn. 1965-74), Athenaeum Lit. Assn. (Louisville), Downtown Assn. (N.Y.C.), Knickerbocker Club, N.Y. Yacht Club, University Club (Chgo.), Met. Club (Washington), Bohemian Club (San Francisco), Shelter Island Yacht Club, Gardiner's Bay Country Club, Greencroft Club (Charlottesville, Va.), Cum Laude Soc., Raven Soc., Order of Coif, Phi Beta Kappa Assocs. (pres. 1969-75), Phi Beta Kappa, Theta Chi, Delta Sigma Rho. Home: 48 Greenacres Ave Scarsdale NY 10583-1436 Office: Seward & Kissel One Battery Park Plz New York NY 10004 also: Internat Bar Assn, 271 Regent St, London W1R 7PA, England

SEWARD, WILLIAM W(ARD), JR., author, educator; b. Surry, Va., Feb. 2, 1913; s. William Ward and Elizabeth (Gwaltney) S.; m. Virginia Leigh Widgeon, Dec. 27, 1941; children: Virginia R. Godwin, Leigh W. Huston. AB, U. Richmond, 1934, MA, 1935; grad. fellow, Duke U., 1938-39, 40-41. English tchr. pub. schs., 1935-38; instr. U. Richmond, 1939-40, summer 1944; head English dept. Greenbrier Mil. Sch., 1941-42; prof., head English dept. Tift Coll., 1942-45; faculty Old Dominion U., Norfolk, Va., 1945, 47—; prof. Old Dominion U., 1957-77, prof. emeritus, 1977—, head dept. English, 1947-61; lectr. U. Va. extension div., 1952-54. Author: The Quarrels of Alexander Pope, 1935; editor: The Longer Thou Livest the More Fool Thou Art (W. Wager), 1939, Literature and War, 1943, Skirts of The Dead Night, 1950, Foreword to Descent of the White Bird (Barbara Whitney), 1955, Contrasts in Modern Writers, 1963, My Friend Ernest Hemingway, 1969; contbr. to book: The True Gen: An Intimate Portrait of Hemingway by those Who Knew Him (Denis Brian), 1988; mem. editorial bd.: Lyric Virginia Today, 1956; contbr. articles to profl. jours. Recipient Charles T. Norman medal for best grad. in English U. Richmond, 1934. Mem. Poetry Soc. Va. (pres. 1952-55), Poetry Soc. Am., Hemingway Soc., Internat. Mark Twain Soc. (hon.), Va. Writers Club (emeritus), Princess Anne Country Club, Virginia Beach Sports Club, Phi Beta Kappa, Kappa Alpha, Pi Delta Epsilon. Methodist. Home: 701 Cavalier Dr Virginia Beach VA 23451-3837

SEWELL, CHARLES HASLETT, banker; b. Buford, Ga., Jan. 16, 1928; s. Grover C. and Jennie G. (Haslett) S.; m. Margaret Gillespie, Sept. 9, 1985; children: Anna E., William H., John L. BA, Emory U., 1951. Econs., mgmt. cons. Rsch. and Cons. Corp., Atlanta, 1952-72; sr. v.p. Deposit Guaranty Nat. Bank, Jackson, Miss., 1972-74, exec. v.p., 1974—; chmn., CEO Deposit Guaranty Mortgage Co., Jackson, Miss., 1976-91; acting dean Millsaps Coll. Grad. Sch. Mgmt., Jackson, 1993; cons. in field; chmn. Miss. Econ. Council, 1983—; chmn. Sml. Bus. Devel. Ctr. U. Miss, Oxford, 1979—. Contbr. articles to profl. jours. Trustee Miss. State Libr. Commn., 1983—; chmn. Miss. Com. for Humanities, 1983—; pres. Miss. Symphony Orch., 1988-89; chmn. Miss. internat. adv. bd. Emory U. Coll. Arts and Scis., 1992—; exec.-in-residence Else Sch. Mgmt., Millsaps Coll. Mem. University Club (Jackson). Republican. Presbyterian. Home: 25 Village Green Cir Jackson MS 39211-2927 Office: Millsaps Coll Grad Sch Mgmt Jackson MS 39210

SEWELL, ELIZABETH, author, English educator; b. Coonoor, India, Mar. 9, 1919; came to U.S., 1949; d. Robert Beresford Seymour and Dorothy (Dean) S. BA, Cambridge U., Eng., 1942, MA, 1945, PhD, 1949; LittD (hon.), Fordham U., N.Y.C., 1968, U. Notre Dame, 1984. Lectr. English Vassar Coll., Poughkeepsie, N.Y., 1951-52; vis. prof. Fordham U., 1954-55, 58-59, chair Bensalem Experimental Coll., 1967-69; lectr. Christian Gauss sem. Princeton U., N.J., 1957; vis. prof. English Bennett Coll., Greensboro, N.C., 1960-61, Tougaloo Coll., Miss., 1963-64; prof. English, Hunter Coll. CUNY, 1971-74; Rosenthal prof. humanities U. N.C., Greensboro, 1974-77. Author 4 novels, 1952, 55, 62, 95, 3 poetry collections, 1962, 68, 84 (nat. award AAAL 1981). Recipient Zoe Brockman Kincaid award N.C. Poetry Soc., 1985; fellow Howald Rsch., 1949-50, Sr. Simon, 1955-57, Ashley, 1979. Mem. Assn. Literary Scholars and Critics, The Polanyi Soc., Lewis Carroll Soc. N.Am., PEN Am. Ctr. Home: 854 W Bessemer Ave Greensboro NC 27408-8404

SEWELL, PHYLLIS SHAPIRO, retail chain executive; b. Cin., Dec. 26, 1930; d. Louis and Mollye (Mark) Shapiro; m. Martin Sewell, Apr. 5, 1959; 1 child, Charles Steven. B.S. in Econs. with honors, Wellesley Coll., 1952. With Federated Dept. Stores, Inc., Cin., 1952-88, research dir. store ops., 1961-65, sr. research dir., 1965-70, operating v.p., research, 1970-75, corp. v.p., 1975-79, sr. v.p., research and planning, 1979-88; bd. dirs. Lee Enterprises, Inc., Davenport, Iowa, Pitney Bowes, Inc., SYSCO Corp. Bd. dirs. Nat. Cystic Fibrosis Found., Cin., 1963—; chmn. divsn. United Appeals, Cin., 1982; mem. bus. adv. coun. Sch. Bus. Adminstrn., Miami U., Oxford, Ohio, 1982-84; trustee Cin. Cmty. Chest, 1984-94, Jewish Fedn., 1990-92, Jewish Hosp., 1990—; mem. bus. leadership coun. Wellesley Coll., 1990—, Fordham U. Grad. Sch. Bus., 1988-89. Recipient Alumnae Achievement award Wellesley Coll., 1979, Disting. Cin. Bus. and Profl. Woman award, 1981, Directors' Choice award Nat. Women's Econ. Alliance, 1995; named one of 100 Top Corp. Women Bus. Week mag., 1976, Career Woman of Achievement YWCA, 1983, to Ohio Women's Hall of Fame, 1982.

SEWELL, RALPH BYRON, investment broker, financial planner, manager; b. Oklahoma City, May 24, 1940; s. Ralph Llewellyn and Amy (Taylor) S.; m. Beverly Jean Bainbridge, Jan. 23, 1962; children: Michael Timothy, Pamela Jean. BS in Engring. Physics, U. Okla., 1963; MS in Fin. Planning, Coll. for Fin. Planning, 1994. Cert. fin. planner. Project engr. Kerr McGee Corp., Oklahoma City, 1969; sr. engr. Consumers Power Co., Charlevoix, Mich., 1969-70; nuclear licensing adminstr. Consumers Power Co., Jackson, Mich., 1970-77; ops. mgr. Plateau Resources Ltd., Grand Junction, Colo., 1977-80; investment broker Boettcher & Co., Grand Junction, 1980-83, spl. ptnr., 1983-87; v.p. investments A.G. Edwards & Sons, Inc., Grand Junction, 1987-90, assoc. v.p., 1990-94, v.p., 1994—. Lt. USN, 1963-68. Recipient Appreciation award Bus. Partnership Program Bd. Edn. Sch. Dist. #51, 1989, 90. Mem. Inst. of Cert. Fin. Planners, Lions. Republican. Avocations: tennis, fishing, cross country skiing. Home: 717 Wedge Dr Grand Junction CO 81506-1866 Office: AG Edwards & Sons Inc 501 Main St Grand Junction CO 81501-2607

SEWELL, RICHARD HERBERT, historian, educator; b. Ann Arbor, Mich., Apr. 11, 1931; s. Herbert Mathieu and Anna Louise (Broene) S.; m. Natalie Paperno, Jan. 13, 1971; 1 child, Rebecca Elizabeth. A.B., U. Mich., 1953; M.A., Harvard U., 1954, Ph.D., 1962. Asst. prof. No. Ill. U., DeKalb, 1962-64; asst. prof. history U. Wis., Madison, 1965-67, assoc. prof., 1967-74, prof, 1974-95, prof. emeritus, 1995—; vis. lectr. U. Mich., Ann Arbor, 1964-65; adv. bd. Lincoln and Soldiers Inst., Gettysburg Coll., Pa., 1990—. Author: John P. Hale and the Politics of Abolition, 1965, Ballots for Freedom, 1976, A House Divided, 1988; mem. editorial bd. Revs. in Am. History, 1981—; contbr. articles to profl. jours. Served to lt. (j.g.) USNR, 1954-57. Mem. Soc. Civil War Historians, So. Hist. Assn., Hist. Soc. Wis., Phi Beta Kappa, Phi Kappa Phi. Avocation: whitewater rafting. Home: 2206 Van Hise Ave Madison WI 53705-3822

SEWELL, ROBERT DALTON, pediatrician; b. Newman, Calif., Apr. 28, 1950; s. James Dalton and Mary Louise (Hartwell) S.; m. Esther Madiedo, Oct. 26, 1975; children: Kevin, David. BA magna cum laude, Pacific Union Coll., 1972; MD, Loma Linda U., 1975. Diplomate Am. Bd. Pediatrics. Pediatric intern and resident White Meml. Med. Ctr., L.A., 1975-77; pediatric resident, chief resident Milton S. Hershey Med. Ctr., Pa. State U., Hershey, 1977-80; pediatrician Children's Med. Ctr. Asheville, N.C., 1980-81, Lincoln City Med. Ctr. P.C., Lincoln City, Oreg., 1982-95; examining physician C.A.R.E.S. Ctr. Emanuel Hosp. & Health Ctr., Portland, Oreg., 1988-90; asst. prof. Loma Linda (Calif.) U. Sch. Medicine, 1995—; chmn. child protection team North Lincoln Hosp., Lincoln City, 1983-89, sec. med. staff, 1990-92, pres. med. staff, 1992-94; mem. Citizens' Rev. Bd. Lincoln County, Newport, Oreg., 1986-92, Early Intervention adv. com., Newport, 1986-90. Mem. North Lincoln Local Sch. Com., Lincoln City, 1983-94, chmn., 1986-90; bd. dirs. Lincoln Shelter and Svcs., Inc., Lincoln City, 1983-89, chmn., 1987-89; mem. North Lincoln divsn. Am. Heart Assn., Lincoln City, 1986-89, v.p., 1987-89; mem. Drug and Alcohol Task Force, Lincoln City, 1988; mem., 2d vice-chmn. Yr. 2000 Plan housing com. Lincoln City Planning Commn., 1987-88; mem. AIDS task force Lincoln County Sch. Dist., 1987-89; mem. Lincoln County Children's Agenda Taskforce, 1988; mem. med. rev. com. Oreg. Med. Assn., 1990-95, mem.-at-large med. staff sect. gov. bd., 1993-95. Named Citizen of Yr. child protection com. Lincoln County, 1984, Man of Yr. Lincoln City C. of C., 1988. Mem. Am. Acad. Pediatrics (sect. on child abuse), Am. Profl. Soc. of Abuse of Children (charter mem.), Nat. Assn. Counsel for Children, Internat. Soc. for Prevention Child Abuse and Neglect, N.Am. Oreg. Profl. Soc. on Abuse of Children (founding pres. 1992-94), Calif. Profl. Soc. on Abuse of Children. Democrat. Seventh-day Adventist. Avocations: music, sports, boating, auto racing. Office: Loma Linda U Med Ctr Dept of Pediatrics 11262 Campus St Loma Linda CA 92354-3204

SEWELL, ROBERT TERRELL, JR., executive search company owner; b. Gainesville, Ga., Nov. 7, 1932; s. Robert Terrell Sr. and Maude (Stradley) S.; divorced; children: Robert T. III, Teresa J., Melanie A., Walter E., James A. Student, Clemson U., 1950-53; BSc in Physics, Furman U., 1954. Office and rsch. signal engr. Western Pacific R.R., Sacramento, 1969-70; product mgr. Western Cullen, Chgo., 1970-72; sales mgr. midwest Erico Electronics, Bolingbrook, Ill., 1975-76; signal engr. Harmon Industries, Inc., Grain Valley, Mo., 1976-78; v.p. mktg. Electro Pneumatic Corp., Independence, Mo., 1978-84; dir. mktg. Harmon Industries Inc., Grain Valley, Mo., 1984-86, Knit Rite, Inc., Kansas City, Mo., 1987; pres. Detroit First Aid Co., Inc., Southgate, Mich., 1988-91; pres., owner Mgmt. Recruiters of Monroe (Mich.), Inc., 1991-94; mgr. contracts and projects Safetran Systems Corp., 1994—. 1st lt. AUS, 1955-57. Fellow Instn. Ry. Signal Engrs.; mem. IEEE, ASME, Am. Soc. Quality Control. Republican. Presbyterian. Avocations: study of economics, archeology and ancient history, travel. Home: 6617 Canary Pine Ave Alta Loma CA 91737-4249 Office: Mgmt Recruiters Monroe Inc 1505 Dixie Dr Ste 2 Monroe MI 48162-2598

SEWELL, WILLIAM HAMILTON, sociologist; b. Perrington, Mich., Nov. 27, 1909; s. Will H. and Lulu (Collar) S.; m. Elizabeth Shogren, June 13, 1936; children: Mary, William, Robert. A.B., Mich. State U., 1933, A.M., 1934, D.Sc. (hon.), 1973; Ph.D., U. Minn., 1939. Instr. U. Minn., 1934-37; asst. prof. sociology Okla. State U., 1937-38, assoc. prof., 1938-40, prof., 1940-44; prof. sociology, rural sociology U. Wis., 1946-64, Vilas research prof. sociology, 1964—, chmn. dept., 1951-53, chmn. social sci. research com., 1952-55, social sci. div., 1950-53, chmn. dept. sociology, 1958-63, univ. chancellor, 1967-68; vis. scholar Russell Sage Found., 1968-69; Walker-Ames vis. prof. U. Washington, 1954; vis. prof. U. Tex., 1941, U. P.R., 1949, Garrett Inst., 1950, Columbia U., 1952; Ford Found. vis. prof. Delhi, Bombay, Poona univs., 1956-57; cons. human resources Sec. War, Research and Devel. Bd., Dept. Def., 1946-54; cons. Nat. Inst. Mental Health, USPHS, 1957-80; chmn. behavioral scis. study sect., 1959-63; chmn. behavioral scis. tng. com. NIH, 1962-67, mem. metal health research adv. com., 1968-70; exec. com. behavioral sci. div. NRC, 1966-70; chmn. Nat. Commn. on Research, 1978-80; Trustee Chatham Coll., Am. Coll. Testing Program Reseach Inst., Nat. Opinion Research Center; bd. dirs. Social Sci. Research Council. Author: Construction and Standardization of a Scale for the Measurement of Farm Family Socioeconomic Status, 1941, (with others) Scandinavian Students on An American Campus, 1961, Attitudes and Facilitation in Status Attainment, 1972, Education, Occupation and Earnings: Achievement in the Early Career, 1975; co-editor: Uses of Sociology, 1967, Schooling and Achievement in American Society, 1976; assoc. editor: Am. Sociol. Rev, 1954-57, Sociometry, 1955-58, Human Resources, 1967-83, Sociology of Edn., 1983-87; contbr. articles, monographs on sociology to profl. jours. Served as lt. USNR, 1944-46. Recipient Outstanding Achievement award U. Minn., 1972, Disting. Rsch. award Am. Ednl. Rsch. Assn., 1975, Commonwealth award for disting. contbns. to sociology, 1983; fellow Center for Advanced Study in Behavioral Scis., 1959-60; rsch. fellow East-West Population Inst. Fellow AAAS (chmn. sect. 1975-76), Am. Sociol. Assn. (chmn. social psychology sect. 1960-61, v.p. 1961-62, pres. 1970-71, Cooley-Mead award in social psychology 1988, Willard Waller award in sociology edn. 1990), Am. Acad. Arts and Scis., Am. Philos. Soc.; mem. NAS (chmn. social and polit. scis. sect. 1981-84), Am. Statis. Assn., Rural Sociol. Soc. (pres. 1955), Southwestern Sociol. Soc. (pres. 1941), Midwestern Sociol. Soc. (pres. 1954), Sociol. Rsch. Assn. (pres. 1954), Soc. Rsch. in Child Devel. Clubs: Blackhawk Country, University. Home: 1005 Merrill Springs Rd Madison WI 53705-1314

SEWELL, WINIFRED, pharmaceutical librarian; b. Newport, Wash., Aug. 12, 1917; d. Harold Arthur and Grace (Vickerman) S. BA, State Coll. Wash., Pullman, 1938; BS in LS, Columbia U., 1940; DSc (hon.), Phila. Coll. Pharmacy and Sci., 1979. Asst. Columbia U. Library, N.Y.C., 1938-42; asst. librarian Wellcome Research Labs., Tuckahoe, N.Y., 1942-43; librarian Wellcome Research Labs., 1943-46, Squibb Inst. Med. Research, 1946-61; subject heading specialist Nat. Library of Medicine, 1961-62, dep. chief bibliog. services div., 1962-65, head drug literature program, 1965-70; adj. asst. prof. U. Md. Sch. Pharmacy, 1970-85; adj. lectr. U. Md. Coll. Libr. and Info. Svcs., 1969-92; cons. Nat. Health Planning Info. Ctr., 1975-81; instr. pharm. lit. and librarianship Columbia U., summer 1959; mem. com on modern methods for handling chem. info. Nat. Acad. Scis.-NRC; mem. Martindale Databank Adv. Panel, 1981-82. Editor: Unlisted Drugs, 1949-59, 62-64; author: Guide to Drug Information, 1976 (Ida and George Eliot award Med. Library Assn. 1977), (with Merle Harrison) Using MeSH for Effective Searching: a Programmed Guide, 1976, (with Sandra D. Teitelbaum) Micromanual for Casual Users of National Library of Medicine Databases, 1986, Reader in Medical Librarianship, 1973; editor: Health Affairs Series, Gale Info. Guides, 1971-80; mem. editorial bd.: Drug Info. Jour. Active Excerpta Medica adv. com., 1985-88. Fellow AAAS; mem. ALA, Am. Soc. for Info. Sci. (chmn. spl. interest group/classification rsch. 1974-75), Med. Libr. Assn. (chmn. Rittenhouse award com. 1975-76, chmn. recert. com. 1979-80, chmn. pub. health and health adminstrn. sect. 1979-80, chmn. med. librs. edn. sect. 1981-82), Spl. Librs. Assn. (chmn. pharm. sect., sci.-tech. divsn. 1952-53, pres. 1960-61, publs. award sci. and tech. divsn. 1966), Drug Info. Assn. (v.p. 1966-67, pres. 1970-71), Am. Assn. Colls. Pharmacy (chmn. librs./edn. resources sect. 1979-80, del. coun. on sects. adv. bd. 1980-83). Home and Office: 6513 76th Pl Cabin John MD 20818-1413

SEWER, DORIS E., critical care nurse, educator; b. Charlotte, St. Thomas, V.I., Oct. 23, 1934; d. Richard and Rachel (Callwood) Donovan; m. Edmundo Valerius Sewer, Mar. 19, 1959; children: Milagros Holden, Melinda Muganzo Mignel Sewer, Maria Vantine. Diploma, Bella Vista Sch. Nursing, Mayaguez, P.R., 1969; BSN, Andrews U., 1975; MA in Edn., Counseling, Calif. State U., San Bernardino, 1979; cert. in clin. pastoral edn., Loma Linda U., 1989; PhD, Walden U., 1997. Staff nurse ICU Lincoln (Nebr.) Gen. Hosp., 1969-72; charge nurse ICU Loma Linda (Calif.) Community Hosp., 1974-75; staff nurse ICU Loma Linda U. Med. Ctr., 1975-77; dir. nursing Mountain View Child Care Ctr., Loma Linda, 1977-79; asst. prof. nursing Chaffey Coll., Ont., Calif., 1979-82; nursing instr., missionary nurse Antillian Coll., Mayaguez, P.R., 1982—; counselor, lectr. Suicide and Crisis Intervention, San Bernardino, Calif., 1977-80; part-time clin. instr. psychiat. nursing Riverside (Calif.) City Coll., 1976-78; instr. ICU course Bella Vista Hosp., Mayaguez, 1984, 86, 88, 89; participating instr. Intensive Care Course Antillian Coll., Mayaguez, 1989; mem. San Bernardino Adv. Com. Drug Abuse, 1979-82; vis. prof. nursing U. V.I., St. Thomas, 1991; pres. Tutorial Nursing and Edn. Unlimited. Mem. Nat. League Nursing.

SEWITCH, DEBORAH E., health science association administrator, educator, sleep researcher; b. Perth Amboy, N.J., Nov. 21, 1954; d. Myron David and Barbara A. (Werner) S. BA, Duke U., 1976; MA, CCNY, 1980; MPhil and PhD in Psychology, CUNY, 1982. Diplomate Am. Bd. Sleep Medicine, Am. Bd. Forensic Examiners. Assoc. dir. Sleep Disorders Ctr. Columbia-Presbyn. Med. Ctr., N.Y.C., 1980-81; sr. clinician Sleep Evaluation Ctr. Western Psychiat. Inst. & Clinic, Pitts., 1982-84; assoc. dir. Sleep Evaluation Ctr. U. Pitts., 1985, instr. in psychiatry Sch. of Medicine, 1984-85; dir. Sleep Disorders Ctr. The Griffin Hosp., Derby, Conn., 1985-89; asst. clin. prof. psychiatry Sch. of Medicine Yale U., New Haven, 1987-89; rsch. dir. unit for exptl. thermoregulation Inst. of Pa. Hosp., Phila., 1989-91; clin. asst. prof. psychology U. Pa., Phila., 1990-91; dir. Sleep Disorders Ctr. Hampstead (N.H.) Hosp., 1991—; chair PhD part II exam. subcom. for bd. certification in clin. sleep disorders Am. Bd. Sleep Medicine, Rochester, Minn., 1989-92; cons. reviewer Jour. Sleep, Jour. Psychophysiology, Jour. Biol. Psychiatry; cons. in clin. sleep disorders and rsch. dept. psychiatry U. Pa., 1990-91. Mem. APA, Am. Sleep Disorders Assn., Am. Coll. Forensic Examiners, Internat. Brain Rsch. Orgn., Soc. for Neurosci., Sleep Rsch. Soc. Jewish. Avocations: singing, horseback riding, antique collector. Office: Hampstead Hosp Sleep-Wake Disorders Ctr 218 East Rd Hampstead NH 03841-2305

SEXSON, WILLIAM R., pediatrician, educator; b. Washington, Dec. 3, 1945; children: Sara Kristen, Ryan William. BS, USAF Acad., 1967; MD, U. Miss., 1971. Staff neurologist Crawford Long Hosp., Atlanta, 1984—, Egleston's Children's Hosp., Atlanta, 1984—; dir. nurseries Grady Meml. Hosp., Atlanta, 1987-94; vice chair dept. pediatrics Sch. Medicine Emory U., Atlanta, 1984—; chief pediatrics Grady Health Sys., Atlanta, 1994—. Mem. Ga. Policy Coun. for Children and Pediatrics, 1995—; co-chair Children's Health Coun., Ga. Dept. Med. Assts. Col. USAF. Named Outstanding Citizen of Ga., 1990. Mem. Am. Acad. Pediatrics (v.p. Ga. chpt. 1990-92, pres. 1993-96, chair com. on bioethics for Ga.), Coun. on Maternal and Infant Health (chair 1993-95), Ga. Perinatal Assn. Home: 804 Springdale Rd NE Atlanta GA 30306 Office: Grady Health Sys 68 Armstrong St SE Atlanta GA 30303-3040

SEXTER, DEBORAH RAE, lawyer; b. Bklyn., May 28, 1939; d. Benjamin and Minnie (Popkewitz) Rochkin; m. Jay Sexter, Apr. 14, 1957; children: David, Michael. BBA, CCNY, 1961; AAS, Bergen C.C., 1975; MS, Fordham U., 1978, JD, 1987; profl. diploma, United Hosps. Sch. Nurse Anesthesia, 1980. Bar: N.J. 1987, U.S. Dist. Ct. N.J. 1987, N.Y. 1988; RN, N.J., N.Y.; cert. RN anesthetist, Am. Assn. Nurse Anesthetists; cert. fraud examiner, Assn. Cert. Fraud Examiners. Community organizer N.Y.C., 1965-70; staff nurse community hosps., Bergen County, N.J., 1975-78; staff anesthetist Columbia-Presbyn. Med. Ctr., N.Y.C., 1980-83, Manhattan Eye, Ear, Throat Hosp., N.Y.C., 1983-84; chief nurse anesthetist Anesthesia Assocs., Nyack, N.Y., 1984-87; pvt. practice law Grand View-on-Hudson, N.Y., 1987-90; sr. asst. gen. counsel, inspector gen. Met. Transp. Authority, N.Y.C., 1990-94; pvt. practice Irvington, N.Y., 1994—; dir. paralegal studies cert. prog. Mercy Coll., White Plains, N.Y., 1997—; adj. asst. prof. law and govt. John Jay Coll., CUNY, N.Y.C., 1987-90; dir. Paralegal Studies Cert. program Mercy Coll., White Plains, N.Y., 1997—. Village justice Village of Grand View-on-Hudson, 1986-92; vice chmn. ethics com. Village of Irvington, N.Y., 1992—; mem. ethics com. Cmty. Hosp., Dobbs Ferry, N.Y., 1995—; ombudsman Long Term Program, N.Y. State, 1994—. Mem. Nat. Assn. Scholars, Fedn. Am. Immigration Reform, N.Y. State Magistrates Assn. Home and Office: 2 Hudson Rd E Irvington NY 10533-2612

SEXTON, DONALD LEE, business administration educator; b. New Boston, Ohio, June 14, 1932; s. Benjamin Franklin and Virgie Marie (Jordan) S.; m. Levonne Bradley, June, 1954 (div. June 1964); 1 child, Rhonda Jane; m. Carol Ann Schwaller, Dec. 18, 1965; children: David Lee, Douglas Edward. BS in Math. and Physics, Wilmington Coll., 1959; MBA, Ohio State U., 1966, PhD in Mgmt., 1972. Indsl. engr. Detroit Steel Corp., Portsmouth, Ohio, 1959-61; sr. rsch. engr. Rockwell Internat., Columbus, Ohio, 1961-68; v.p. merchandising R.G. Barry Corp., Columbus, 1968-74; v.p., gen. mgr. Henri Fayette, Inc., Chgo., 1976; gen. mgr. M.H. Mfg. Co., Jackson, Miss., 1976-77; assoc. prof. Sangamon State U., Springfield, Ill., 1977-79; Caruth prof. entrepreneurship Baylor U., Waco, Tex., 1979-86; Davis prof. free enterprise Ohio State U., Columbus, 1986-94; dir. Nat. Ctr. for Entrepreneurial Rsch. Kauffman Found., Kansas City, Mo., 1994—; mem. adv. bd. SBA, Columbus, 1986-94; rsch. adv. bd. U. So. Calif., L.A., 1986-90. Co-author: Entrepreneurship Educatoin, 1981, Experiences in Small Business, 1982, Starting A Business in Texas, 1983; co-editor: Encyclopedia of Entrepreneurship, 1981, Art and Science of Entrepreneurship, 1986, Women Owned Business, 1989, Entrepreneurship: Creativity and Growth, 1990, The State of the Art of Entrepreneurship, 1991, Leadership and Entrepreneurship, 1996, Entrepreneurship: 2000, 1996. Served to staff sgt. USAF, 1951-55. Recipient Leavy Free Enterprise award Freedoms Found. Valley Forge, 1985, Cert. Appreciation SBA, Washington, 1984, 85, Outstanding Contbn. to Entrepreneurship Edn. award Assn. Coll. Entrepreneurs, 1991, Disting. Alumni award Wilmington Coll., 1993; named Adv. of Yr.-Innovation SBA, Dallas, 1982, 83, 84. Mem. Internat. Coun. for Small Bus. (sr. v.p. 1986), U.S. Assn. for Small Bus. (v.p. pub. rels. 1987), Acad. Mgmt. (chmn. entrepreneurship com. 1981, mem. adv. bd. 1984-85), Masons, Shriners, Eagles, Am. Legion, Alpha Tau Omega. Republican. Baptist. Avocation: golf. Home: 12760 Cody Overland Park KS 66213-3418 Office: Kauffman Found 4900 Oak St Kansas City MO 64112-2702

SEXTON, JEAN ELIZABETH, librarian; b. Boone, N.C., June 24, 1959; d. Warren G. and Carol Jean (Smith) S. AA, Chowan Coll., Murfreesboro, N.C., 1979; AB, U. N.C., 1981, MS in Libr. Sci., 1983. Cataloging libr. Pembroke (N.C.) State U., 1983-89, coord. tech. svcs., 1989-92, asst. dir., coord. tech. svcs., 1992—; cons. Whitaker Libr. Chowan Coll., 1989—. Editor Libr. Lines, 1992; contbr. articles to profl. jours. Order of Silver Feather. Mem. AAUW, N.C. Libr. Assn., Southeastern Libr. Assn., Dickens Fellowship, N.C. Zool. soc., N.C. Aquarium Soc., Nat. Trust for Historic Preservation. Democrat. Baptist. Avocations: science fiction/fantasy reading, collecting estate jewelry, needlework. Home: 118 Charles St Apt 3 Lumberton NC 28358 Office: U NC Pembroke Livermore Libr Pembroke NC 28372

SEXTON, OWEN JAMES, vertebrate ecology educator, conservationist; b. Phila., July 11, 1926; s. Gordon and Elizabeth May (Evans) S.; m. Mildred Lewis Bloomsburg, Apr. 5, 1952; children: Kenneth, Jean, Ann, Carolyn. Student, Sampson Coll., 1947-48; BA, Oberlin Coll., 1951; MA, U. Mich., 1953, PhD, 1956. Sr. teaching fellow Washington U., St. Louis, 1955-56, instr., 1956-57, asst. prof., 1957-62, assoc. prof., 1962-68, prof. vertebrate ecology, 1968—, dir. Tyson Rsch. Ctr., 1996—; vis. prof. U. Mich. Biol. Sta., Pellston, 1975-83; cons. UNESCO, 1974-75; adj. curator St. Louis Sci. Ctr., 1986-88. Pres., bd. dirs. Mo. Prairie Found., Columbia, 1968—; pres. Wild Canid Survival and Research Ctr., St. Louis, 1971-73; sec. Contemporary Art Soc., 1972-73; bd. dirs. Creve Coeur Figure Skating Club, 1982-89; mem. membership com. U.S. Figure Skating Assn., 1987-90. NSF fellow, 1966-67; vis. research fellow U. New Eng., 1984. Fellow Herpetologists League; mem. Am. Soc. Icthyologists and Herpetologists, Ecol. Soc. Am., Soc. Study of Amphibians and Reptiles, Orgn. Tropical Studies (bd. dir. 1976-85).

Democrat. Home: 13154 Greenbough Dr Saint Louis MO 63146-3622 Office: Washington Lindell & Skinker Dept Biology Saint Louis MO 63130

SEXTON, ROBERT FENIMORE, educational organization executive; b. Cin., Jan. 13, 1942; s. Claude Fenimore and Jane (Wisenall) S.; m. Pam Peyton Papka, Sept. 15, 1985; children: Rebecca, Robert B., Ouita Papka, Paige Papka, Perry Papka. BA, Yale U., 1964; MA in History, U. Wash., Seattle, 1968, PhD in History, 1970; DHL (hon.), Berea Coll., 1990, Georgetown Coll., Ky., 1993. Asst. prof. history Murray (Ky.) State U., 1968-70; dir. Office Acad. Programs, Commonwealth of Ky., Frankfort, 1970-73; assoc. dean, exec. dir. Office Exptl. Edn. U. Ky., Lexington, 1973-80; dep. exec. dir. Ky. Coun. Higher Edn., Frankfort, 1980-83; exec. dir. Prichard Com. for Acad. Excellence, Lexington, 1983—; founder, pres. Ky. Ctr. Pub. Issues, Lexington, 1988—; vis. scholar Harvard U., Cambridge, Mass., 1992, 94; chair Nat. Ctr. for Internships, Washington, 1973-80, Coalition for Alternatives in Post-Secondary Edn., Washington, 1977-80; bd. dirs. Editl. Projects in Edn., Ky. Long Term Policy Rsch. Ctr., Coun. for Advancement Exptl. Learning, 1976-80, Edn. Commn. of the States; adv. bd. Consortium for Prodn. in Schs., 1992—. Pub. The Ky. Jour., 1988—; editor book series: Public Papers of Governors of Kentucky, 1973-86; author reports in field. Co-chair Carnegie Ctr. for Literacy, Lexington, 1990-93; mem. Gov.'s Task Force on Health Care, Frankfort, 1992—; bd. dirs. Ky. Inst. Edn. Rsch. Fund for Improvement in Postsecondary Edn., 1993—; chair Bluegrass Edn. Work Coun., Lexington, 1978-80; founder, mem. steering com. Gov.'s Scholars Program, Frankfort, 1983-85. Recipient Charles A. Dana award for pioneering achievement, 1994. Mem. Am. Assn. Higher Edn. (bd. dirs. 1979-83). Democrat. Avocations: fishing, travel. Office: Prichard Com Acad Excell 167 W Main St Ste 310 Lexington KY 40507-1702

SEYBERT, JOANNA, federal judge; b. Bklyn., Sept. 18, 1946; married; 1 child. BA, U. Cin., 1967; JD, St. John's U., 1971. Bar: N.Y. 1972, U.S. Dist. Ct. (ea. and so. dists.) N.Y. 1973, U.S. Ct. Appeals (2d cir.) 1973. Trial staff atty. Legal Aid Soc., N.Y.C., 1971-73; sr. staff atty. Legal Aid Soc., Mineola, N.Y., 1976-80; sr. trial atty. Fed. Defender Svc., Bklyn., 1973-75; bur. chief Nassau County Atty's Office, Mineola, 1980-87; judge Nassau County Dist. Ct., Hempstead, N.Y., 1987-92, Nassau County Ct., Mineola, 1992-94, U.S. Dist. Ct. (ea. dist.) N.Y., Bklyn., 1994—. Past mem. environ. bd. Town of Oyster Bay; mem. Rep. com. Nassau County, 1979-87. Recipient Norman F. Lent award Criminal Cts. Bar Assn., 1991. Mem. ABA, N.Y. State Bar Assn., Bar Assn. Nassau County, Nassau County Women's Bar Assn., Theodore Roosevelt Am. Inns of Ct., Fed. Judges Assn., Nassau Lawyer's Assn. (past pres.), Nat. Assn. Women Judges. Office: 2 Uniondale Ave Uniondale NY 11553-1259*

SEYFERTH, DIETMAR, chemist, educator; b. Chemnitz, Germany, Jan. 11, 1929; came to U.S., 1933; s. Herbert C. and Elisabeth (Schuchardt) S.; m. Helena A. McCoy, Aug. 25, 1956; children—Eric Steven, Karl Dietmar, Elisabeth Mary. B.A. summa cum laude, U. Buffalo, 1951, M.A., 1953; Ph.D., Harvard, 1955; Dr. honoris causa, U. Aix-Marseille, 1979, Paul Sabatier Univ., Toulouse, France, 1992. Fulbright scholar Tech. Hochschule, Munich, Germany, 1954-55; postdoctoral fellow Harvard U., 1956-57; faculty MIT, 1957—, prof. chemistry, 1965—, Robert T. Haslam and Bradley Dewey prof., 1983—; cons. to industry, 1957—. Author: Annual Surveys of Organometallic Chemistry, 3 vols, 1965, 66, 67; regional editor: Jour. Organometallic Chemistry, 1963-81; coordinating editor revs. and survey sects., 1964-81; editor: Organometallics, 1981—; contbr. research papers to profl. lit. Recipient Disting. Alumnus award U. Buffalo, 1964, Alexander von Humboldt Found. sr. award, 1984, Clifford C. Furnas Meml. award SUNY-Buffalo, 1987; Guggenheim fellow, 1968. Fellow AAAS, Am. Inst. Chemists, Inst. Materials, Am. Acad. Arts and Scis.; mem. Am. Chem. Soc. (Frederic Stanley Kipping award in organosilicon chemistry 1972, disting. svc. award advancement inorganic chemistry 1981, award in organometallic chemistry, 1996), Materials Rsch. Soc., Am. Ceramic Soc., Royal Soc. Chemistry, Gesellschaft Deutscher Chemiker, German Acad. Scientists-Leopoldina, Phi Beta Kappa, Sigma Xi. Office: MIT 77 Massachusetts Ave Rm 4-382 Cambridge MA 02139-4301

SEYFFARTH, LINDA JEAN WILCOX, corporate executive; b. Montour Falls, N.Y., May 10, 1948; d. Maurice Roscoe and Theodora (Van Tassell) Wilcox; m. P. Tomlin Agnew, June 29, 1991; 1 child by previous marriage, Kristin. BA magna cum laude, Syracuse (N.Y.) U., 1970; MBA with honors, NYU, 1977. Programmer Prudential Ins. Co., Newark, 1970-73; with Hoffmann-La Roche Inc., Nutley, N.J., 1973—, corp. controller, 1985-88, v.p., contr., 1989-95; v.p. fin. Roche Labs., 1995—. Bd. dirs. St. Barnabas Burn Found., West Orange, N.J., Ind. Coll. Fund, Summit, N.J.; bd. dirs., treas. Glen Ridge (N.J.) Ednl. Found. Mem. Nat. Assn. Accts., Fin. Execs. Inst., Leadership N.J., Phi Beta Kappa, Beta Gamma Sigma. Office: Hoffmann-LaRoche Inc 340 Kingsland St Nutley NJ 07110-1150

SEYMORE, JAMES W., JR., magazine editor. Mng. editor Entertainment Weekly, N.Y.C. Office: Entertainment Weekly 1675 Broadway New York NY 10019-5820

SEYMOUR, BRIAN RICHARD, mathematics educator, researcher; b. Chesterfield, Derby, Eng., Sept. 25, 1944; came to U.S., 1968, Can., 1973; s. Douglas and Hilda (Ball) S.; m. Rosemary Jane Pembleton, Sept. 23, 1943; children—Mark, Jane, Richard. B.Sc. with honors, U. Manchester, 1965; Ph.D., U. Nottingham, 1968. Asst. prof. Lehigh U., 1969-70, N.Y. U., 1970-73, U. B.C., 1973-76; assoc. prof. U. B.C., 1976-81, Vancouver, Can., prof. math., 1981—, dir. inst. applied math, 1986-93; vis. prof. Ctr. Water Rsch. U. Western Australia, 1993-94. Contbr. research papers to profl. jours. Sci. Research Council sr. research fellow Oxford U., 1978; Killam sr. fellow Killam Trust, Monash U., 1984. Mem. Can. Applied Math. Soc., Soc. Indsl. & Applied Math. Avocation: field hockey. Office: U BC, 222-1984 Mathematics Rd, Vancouver, BC Canada V6T 1Z2

SEYMOUR, JEFFREY ALAN, governmental relations consultant; b. L.A., Aug. 31, 1950; s. Daniel and Evelyn (Schwartz) S.; m. Valerie Joan Parker, Dec. 2, 1973; 1 child, Jessica Lynne. AA in Social Sci., Santa Monica Coll., 1971; BA in Polit. Sci., UCLA, 1973, MPA, 1977. Councilmanic aide L.A. City Coun., 1972-74; county supr.'s sr. dep. L.A. Bd. Suprs., 1974-82; v.p. Bank of L.A., 1982-83; prin. Jeffrey Seymour & Assocs., L.A., 1983-84; ptnr. Morey/Seymour & Assocs., 1984—; mem. comml. panel Am. Arbitration Assn., 1984—. Chmn. West Hollywood Parking Adv. Com., L.A., 1983-84; chmn. social action com. Temple Emanuel of Beverly Hills, 1986-89, bd. dirs. 1988-93, v.p. Congregation N'vay Shalom, 1990-93; mem. Pan Pacific Park Citizens Adv. Com., L.A., 1982-85; bd. dirs. William O'Douglas Outdoor Classroom, L.A., 1981-88; exec. sec. Calif. Fedn. Young Dems., 1971; mem. Calif. Dem. Cen. Com., 1979-82; pres. Beverlywood-Cheviot Hills Dem. Club, L.A., 1978-81; co-chmn. Westside Chancellor's Assocs. UCLA, 1986-88; mem. L.A. Olympic Citizens Adv. Com.; mem. liaison adv. commn. with city and county govt. for 1984 Olympics, 1984; v.p. cmty. rels. metro region, Jewish Fedn. Coun. of L.A., 1985-87, co-chmn. urban affairs commn., 1987-89, vice chmn., 1989-90, subcom. chmn. local govt. law and legislation commn., 1990—, chmn. campus outreach task force, 1994—; mem. adv. bd. Nat. Jewish Ctr. for Immunology & Respiratory Medicine, 1991—; bd. dirs. Hillel Coun. of L.A., 1991—; mem. platform on world peace and internat. rels. Calif. Dems., 1983; pres. 43d Assembly Dist. Dem. Coun., 1975-79; arbitrator BBB, 1984—; trustee UCLA Found., 1989—; pres. UCLA Jewish Alumni, 1992-95; mem. Santa Monica Mountains Conservancy, 1995-96, adv. com., 1996—; mem. cabinet Jewish Cmty. Rels. Com. Greater L.A., 1994—, chair campus outreach task force, 1994-95, govtl. rels. commn., 1995-96; mem. adv. bd. L.A. Peace Now. Recipient Plaques for services rendered Beverlywood Cheviot Hills Dem. Club, L.A., 1981, Jewish Fedn. Coun. Greater L.A., 1983; Certs. of Appreciation, L.A. Olympic Organizing Com., 1984, County of L.A., 1984, City of L.A., 1987; commendatory resolutions, rules com. Calif. State Senate, 1987, Calif. State Assembly, 1987, 96, County of L.A., 1987, City of L.A., 1987. Mem. Am. Soc. Pub. Adminstrn., Am. Acad. Polit. and Social Scis., Town Hall of Calif., So. Calif. Planning Congress, Urban Land Inst., UCLA Alumni Assn. (mem. govtl. steering com. 1983—, bd. dirs. 1995—, chair bd. dirs. 1995-97, pres.-elect 1997—). Office: Morey/Seymour and Assocs 233 Wilshire Blvd Ste 290 Santa Monica CA 90401-1206

SEYMOUR, JEFFREY L., hotel executive. Dir. franchise svcs. Knights Franchise Sys., Inc., Parsippany, N.J. Office: Knights Franchise Sys Inc 339 Jefferson Rd Parsippany NJ 07054-3707

SEYMOUR, JOYCE ANN, elementary school educator; b. Lafayette, Ind., Nov. 24, 1947; d. Richard Max and Helen Lois (North) Taylor; m. Timothy Joe Seymour, Dec. 27, 1969; children: Christy Nicole, Chad Richard. BS, Purdue U., 1970; MA, Wright State U., 1974. Cert. tchr. elem. edn.; cert. counselor. Tchr. grade 5 Fairborn (Ohio) City Schs., 1970-84, elem. guidance counselor, 1984-94, tchr. grade 6, 1994-95, elem. guidance counselor, 1995—; adv. com. Sch. Counseling, Wright State U., Dayton, 1986—. Mem. NEA, Ohio Sch. Counselor Assn., Phi Delta Kappa. Lutheran. Avocations: flying (pvt. pilot), water skiing. Home: 1100 Medway-Carlisle Rd Medway OH 45341 Office: Palmer-South Elementary 1020 S Maple Fairborn OH 45324-3735

SEYMOUR, MARY FRANCES, lawyer; b. Durand, Wis., Oct. 20, 1948; d. Marshall Willard and Alice Roberta (Smith) Thompson; m. Marshall Warren Seymour, June 6, 1970; 1 foster child, Nghia Pham. BS, U. Wis., LaCrosse, 1970; JD, William Mitchell Coll., 1979. Bar: Minn. 1979, U.S. Dist. Ct. Minn. 1979, U.S. Ct. Appeals (8th cir.) 1979, U.S. Supreme Ct. 1986. With Cochrane and Bresnahan, P.A., St. Paul, 1979-94, Loper & Seymour, P.A., 1994—. Mem. ATLA, Minn. Bar Assn., Ramsey County Bar Assn., Minn. Trial Lawyers Assn., Assn. of Cert. Fraud Examiners. Office: Loper & Seymour PA 24 4th St E Saint Paul MN 55101-1002

SEYMOUR, MCNEIL VERNAM, lawyer; b. St. Paul, Dec. 21, 1934; s. McNeil Vernam and Katherine Grace (Klein) S.; children—Margaret, McNeil Vernam, James, Benjamin; m. Mary Katherine Velner, May 15, 1993. A.B., Princeton U. 1957; J.D., U. Chgo., 1960. Bar: Minn. 1960, U.S. Dist. Ct. Minn. 1960. Mem. Seymour & Seymour, St. Paul, 1960-71; mem. firm Briggs & Morgan, St. Paul, 1971—, ptnr., 1976—. Trustee Oakland Cemetery Assn.; pres., treas. White Bear Unitarian Ch., 1964-65; sec., bd. dirs. Ramsey County Law Library, 1972-76. Served with U.S. Army, 1960-62. Mem. Ramsey County Bar Assn., Minn. Bar Assn. Republican. Unitarian. Clubs: Somerset Country Club. Home: 886 S Highview Cir Mendota Heights MN 55118-3686 Offices: Briggs & Morgan 2200 First National Bank Bldg Saint Paul MN 55101-1319

SEYMOUR, MICHAEL, production designer. Prodn. designer: (films) Robbery, 1967, Entertaining Mr. Sloane, 1970, Gumshoe, 1971, Theatre of Blood, 1973, Rosebud, 1975, Alien, 1979 (Academy award nomination best art direction 1979), Ghost Story, 1981, Eureka, 1984, The Bride, 1985, Mr. Destiny, 1990, (with Benjamin Fernandez) Revenge, 1990, Gunmen, 1992, The Thing Called Love, 1993, Beverly Hills Cop III, 1994. Recipient Brit. Acad. award for Art Direction, 1979. Office: 7917 Selma Ave Apt 207 Los Angeles CA 90046-2669*

SEYMOUR, RICHARD BURT, health educator; b. San Francisco, Aug. 1, 1937; s. Arnold Burt-Oakley and Florence Marguerite (Burt) S.; m. Michelle Driscoll, Sept. 15, 1963 (div. 1972); children: Brian Geoffrey, Kyra Daleth; m. Sharon Harkless, Jan. 5, 1973. BA, Sonoma State U., 1969, MA, 1970. Freelance writer Sausalito, Calif., 1960—; coord., adminstr. Coll. of Mendocino, Boonville, Calif., 1971-73; bus. mgr. Haight Ashbury Free Clinics, San Francisco, 1973-77; exec. adminstr., dir. tng. and edn. projects Height Ashbury Free Clinics, San Francisco, 1977-87; instr. John F. Kennedy U., Orinda, Calif., 1986—; asst. prof. Sonoma State U., Rohnert Park, Calif., 1985—; pres., chief exec. officer Westwind Assocs., Sausalito, Calif., 1988—; cons. Haight Ashbury Free Clinics, San Francisco, 1987—, treas., bd. dirs.; chmn. World Drug Abuse Treatment Network, San Francisco, 1988—; bd. dirs. Slide Ranch. Author: Physician's Guide to Psychoactive Drugs, 1987, Drug Free, 1987, The New Drugs, 1989, The Psychedelic Resurgence, 1993; editor-in-chief Internat. Addictions Infoline, 1995; mng. editor Jour. of Psychoactive Drugs, 1996; contbr. articles to profl. jours. Mem. Calif. Health Profls. for New Health Policy, Washington, 1976-80; chmn. Marin Drug Abuse Adv. Bd., San Rafael, Calif., 1979-81, CalDrug Abuse Svcs. Assn., Sacramento, 1975-79; mem. Alcohol and Drug Counselors Edn. Project, 1985—, San Francisco Delinquency Prevention Commn., 1981—, Calif. Primary Prevention Network, 1980—. Grantee NIMH, 1974—, Nat. Inst. on Drug Abuse, 1974—. Mem. Internat. Platform Assn., Commonwealth Club of Calif. Democrat. Episcopalian. Avocations: travel, writing, landscape painting, camping. Office: Westwind Assocs 90 Harrison Ave Apt C Sausalito CA 94965-2240

SEYMOUR, RICHARD DEMING, technology educator; b. Shelby, Ohio, Oct. 3, 1955; s. G. Deming and Elizabeth (Peterson) S.; m. Vicki Stebleton; 1 child, Ryan. BS in Edn., Ohio State U., 1978; MA, Ball State U., 1982; EdD, W.Va. U., 1990. Tchr. Crestview Sr. High Sch., Ashland, Ohio, 1978-81; from instr. to assoc. prof. Ball State U., Muncie, Ind., 1982—; vis. instr. W.Va. U., Morgantown, 1985, Oreg. State U., 1990-91. Co-author: Exploring Communications, 1987, rev. edit., 1996; co-editor: Manufacturing in Technology Education, 1993. Advisor 4-H Clubs, Richland County, Ohio, 1978-81; dir. tech. in-svc. workshops Ind. Dept. Edn., Indpls., 1988-97. Mem. Internat. Tech. Edn. Assn. (bd. dirs. 1992-94), Soc. Mfg. Engrs., Coun. on Tech. Tchr. Edn., Ind. Math., Sci., Tech. Alliance (bd. dirs. 1994—), Tech. Educators Ind. (pres. 1995-96), Am. Soc. Engring. Edn., Tech. Edn. Collegiate Assn. (internat. advisor 1990-92), Epsilon Pi Tau, Phi Delta Kappa. Methodist. Avocations: model railroads, sports, travel. Office: Ball State U Dept Industry/Tech Muncie IN 47306

SEYMOUR, RICHARD KELLOGG, linguist, educator; b. Hinsdale, Ill., June 21, 1930; s. William and Katharine (Fifield) S.; m. Nancy Ann Nutt, June 23, 1951; children: Michael Bradley, William David. B.A., U. Mich., 1951, M.A., 1952; cert., U. Tübingen, Tübingen, Germany, 1953; Ph.D., U. Pa., 1956, postgrad. linguistics, 1957. Asst. instr. U. Pa., 1952-55; instr. Princeton U., 1954-58; linguist NDEA Summer Inst., 1963; asst. prof. Duke U., 1958-63, assoc. prof., 1963-67, endowment fellow, 1966; prof., chmn. dept. European langs. and lit. U. Hawaii, Honolulu, 1967-75, prof., 1977-95; ret., 1995; dean Coll. Langs., Linguistics and Lit. U. Hawaii, Honolulu, 1981-95; prof. German dept. Pa. State U., University Park, 1975-77; vis. prof. Cologne (Germany) U., 1974. Author: A Bibliography of Word Formation in the Germanic Languages, 1968; asst. editor Unterrichtspraxis, 1969-80; editor Am. Jour. Germanic Linguistics and Lit., 1989-95; co-editor: Interdisciplinary Jour. for Germanic Linguistics and Semiotic Analysis, 1995—; contbr. articles to profl. jours. Princeton Research Council grantee, 1958; Am. Council Learned Socs. grantee, 1957; Fulbright travel award, 1981. Mem. Linguistic Soc. Am., Internat. Linguistic Assn., Am. Dialect Soc., Am. Assn. Tchrs. German, MLA, S. Atlantic MLA (exec. sec. 19662-67), Delta Phi Alpha (nat. sec.-treas. 1968-95). Congregationalist (bd. deacons, sec. 1970-71).

SEYMOUR, STEPHANIE KULP, federal judge; b. Battle Creek, Mich., Oct. 16, 1940; d. Francis Bruce and Frances Cecelia (Bria) Kulp; m. R. Thomas Seymour, June 10, 1972; children: Bart, Bria, Sara, Anna. BA magna cum laude, Smith Coll., 1962; JD, Harvard U., 1965. Bar: Okla. 1965. Practice Boston, 1965-66, Tulsa, 1966-67, Houston, 1968-69; assoc. Doerner, Stuart, Saunders, Daniel & Anderson, Tulsa, 1971-75, ptnr., 1975-79; judge U.S. Ct. Appeals (10th cir.) Okla., Tulsa, 1979—, now chief justice; assoc. bar examiner Okla. Bar Assn., 1973-79; trustee Tulsa County Law Library, 1977-78; mem. U.S. Jud. Conf. Com. Defender Svcs., 1985-91, chmn., 1987-91. Mem. various task forces Tulsa Human Rights Commn., 1972-76, legal adv. panel Tulsa Task Force Battered Women, 1971-77. Mem. Am. Bar Assn., Okla. Bar Assn., Tulsa County Bar Assn., Phi Beta Kappa. Office: US Courthouse 333 W 4th St Rm 4-562 Tulsa OK 74103-3839*

SEYMOUR, THADDEUS, English educator; b. N.Y.C., June 29, 1928; s. Whitney North and Lola Virginia (Vickers) S.; m. Polly Gnagy, Nov. 20, 1948; children—Elizabeth Halsey, Thaddeus, Samuel Whitney, Mary Duffie, Abigail Comfort. A.B., U. Calif., 1950; M.A., U. N.C., 1951, Ph.D., 1955; D.H.L. (hon.), Wilkes Coll., 1968; LL.D. (hon.), Butler U., 1971, Ind. State U., 1976; LLD (hon.), Wabash Coll., 1984, U. Cen. Fla., 1990, Stetson U., 1990; DHL (hon.), Rollins Coll., 1990. Mem. faculty Dartmouth Coll., 1954-69, prof. English, dean coll., 1959-69; pres. Wabash Coll., Crawfordsville, Ind., 1969-78; pres. Rollins Coll., Winter Park, Fla., 1978-90, prof. English, 1978—; pres. Ind. Conf. Higher Edn., 1977; v.p. Assoc. Colls. Ind., 1978; vice-chmn. Fla. Ind. Colls. Fund. Past mem. Ind. Bicentennial Commn.; del. N.H. Republican Conv., 1958, 64; vice-chmn. N.H. Rep. Com., 1967-68; trustee Park-Tudor Sch., 1970-78, Bach Festival Soc.; chmn. Fla. selection com. Rhodes Scholarship Trust, 1983-88. Mem. Nat. Rowing Found. (dir.), Ring 219 (charter), Internat. Brotherhood Magicians, Ind. Colls. and Univs. Fla. (sec.), Fla. Assn. Colls. and Univs., Century Assn., Omicron Delta Kappa. Home: 1350 College Pt Winter Park FL 32789-5700

SFAT, MICHAEL RUDOLPH, retired biochemical engineer; b. Timisoara, Romania, Oct. 28, 1921; came to U.S., 1924; s. Peter and Emilia (Iovin) S.; m. Jane Buckridge, Nov. 24, 1948; children: Gail Buckridge Sergent, Mary Anne Bauer. B Chem. Engring., Cornell U., 1943, M Chem. Engring., 1947; postgrad., Princeton U., 1949-50. Registered profl. engr., Wis. Rsch. assoc. Cornell U., Ithaca, N.Y., 1943-44; asst. microbiologist Merck & Co., Inc., Rahway, N.J., 1947-51, sr. microbiologist, 1951-52; dir. devel. pilot plant Pabst Brewing Co., Milw., 1952-54; rsch. dir. Rahr Malting Co., Manitowoc, Wis., 1954-58, coord. R&D, 1958-60, v.p. R&D, 1960-69; pres. Bio-Tech. Resources, Manitowoc, 1962-89, pres. emeritus, 1989-96; ret., 1997; mem. Gov.'s Counl on Biotech., Wis., 1990. Contbr. articles to profl. jours.; patentee in field. 2nd lt. U.S. Army, 1944-46. Recipient Schwarz prize for brewing tech., 1966, Disting. Svc. award Coll. Engring., U. Wis., 1993. Fellow Nat. Acad. Engring., Am. Acad. Microbiology, Am. Inst. Med. and Biol. Engrs.; mem. Am. Chem. Soc., Am. Inst. Chem. Engrs., Am. Soc. Brewing Chemists (pres. 1974-75), Am. Soc. Microbiology, Inst. Food Technologists, Master Brewers Assn. Am., Soc. Indsl. Microbiology, Manitowoc-Two Rivers C. of C. (dir. 1970-78), Branch River Country Club (dir. 1972-78), Elks. Republican. Presbyterian. Avocations: golf, tennis, skiing, windsurfing, barn restoration. Home: 1030 W Crescent Dr Manitowoc WI 54220-2420 Office: Bio-Technical Resources 1035 S 7th St Manitowoc WI 54220-5301

SFEKAS, STEPHEN JAMES, lawyer, educator; b. Balt., Feb. 12, 1947; s. James Stephen and Lee (Mesologites) S.; m. Joanne Lorraine Murphy, May 27, 1973; children: James Stephen, Andrew Edward Stephen, Christina Marie. BS in Fgn. Svc., Georgetown U., 1968; MA (Danforth fellow, Woodrow Wilson fellow) Yale U., 1972; JD, Georgetown U., 1973. Bar: Md. 1973, U.S. Dist. Ct. Md. 1974, U.S. Ct. Appeals (4th cir.) 1974. Law clk. U.S. Dist. Ct., Balt., 1973-74; assoc. firm Frank, Bernstein, Conaway & Goldman, Balt., 1974-75; asst. atty. gen. State of Md., Balt., 1975-81; assoc. firm Tydings & Rosenberg, Balt., 1981-82, ptnr., 1983-86, with firm Miles & Stockbridge, 1986-90; ptnr. Weinberg & Green, 1991—; instr. legal writing Community Coll. Balt., 1976-79; instr. legal ethics Goucher Coll., Balt., 1979; adj. prof. adminstrv. law U. Md., Balt., 1981-93, health, 1993—, law sch., 1993—. Editor Georgetown Law Jour., 1972-73; contbr. articles to legal publs. Bd. dirs. Md. region NCCJ, 1981-89, co-chmn. Md. region, 1986-89; mem. Piraeus Sister City Com., City of Balt., 1983-89; mem. parish council Greek Orthodox Cathedral of Annunciation, Balt., 1981-84; mem. internat. com. Balt. region ARC, 1984-85; mem. adv. com. on bread for the world, Dept. Ch. and Soc., Greek Orthodox Archdiocese N. and S.Am., 1984—; pres. Greek Orthodox Counseling and Social Services of Balt., 1984-88; bd. dirs. Orthodox Christian Laity, 1990—, Cen. Md. Ecumenical Coun., 1991—; mem. bylaw com. Girl Scouts of Cen. Md., 1989-91, Md. Leadership Program, 1997. WHO fellow, London, 1979. Fellow Soc. for Values in Higher Edn.; mem. ABA (Grant Morris fellow 1979, forum com. on health law), Md. Bar Assn., Bar Assn. Balt. City, Nat. Health Lawyers Assn., Am. Soc. Hosp. Attys. Democrat. Office: Weinberg & Green 100 S Charles St Baltimore MD 21201-2725

SFIKAS, PETER MICHAEL, lawyer, educator; b. Gary, Ind., Aug. 9, 1937; s. Michael E. and Helen (Thureanos) S.; m. Freida Platon, Apr. 24, 1966; children—Ellen M., Pamela C., Sandra N. BS, Ind. U., 1959; JD, Northwestern U., 1962. Bar: Ill. 1962, U.S. Dist. Ct. (no. dist.) Ill. 1963, U.S. Ct. Appeals (7th cir.) 1963, U.S. Supreme Ct. 1970, U.S. Ct. Appeals (9th cir.) 1976, U.S. Ct. Appeals (3d cir.) 1981, U.S. Ct. Appeals (D.C. cir.) 1984, U.S. Dist. Ct. (cen. dist.) Ill. 1988. Atty. Legal Aid Bur., United Charities Chgo., 1962-63; sr. ptnr. Peterson & Ross, Chgo., 1970-95; gen. counsel, assoc. exec. dir. div. legal affairs ADA, Chgo., 1995—; sr. ptnr. Bell, Boyd & Lloyd, Chgo., 1996—; prosecutor Village of LaGrange Park, Ill., 1969-74; mem. rules com. Ill. Supreme Ct., 1975-95, mem. spl. joint com. on discovery rules, 1995; arbitrator Nat. Panel Arbitrators, 1972—; adj. prof. Loyola U. Sch. Law, 1978—; guest lectr. U. Ill. Coll. Dentistry, 1988—; lectr. 23d ann. corp. counsel inst. Northwestern U. Sch. Law, 1984, lectr. 16th ann. Ray Garret Jr. Corp. and Securities Law Inst., 1996. Contbr. articles to profl. jours. Mem. Ill. steering com. Ct. Watching Project, LWV, 1975-77; pres. Holy Apostles Greek Orthodox Ch. Parish Coun., 1987-89; co-pres. Oak Sch. PTO, 1989-90; mem. com. to select sch. supr., dist. 86, DuPage County, Ill., 1993-94. Recipient Chgo. Bar Found. Maurice Weigle award 1973. Fellow Am. Bar Found., Am. Coll. Trial Lawyers, Chgo. Bar Found. (life); mem. ABA (editor in chief Forum Law Jour. sect. ins., negligence and compensation law 1972-76), Ill. Bar Found. (bd. dirs.), Northwestern U. Law Alumni Assn. (1st v.p. 1985-86, pres. 1986-87, Svc. award 1990), Ill. State Bar Assn. (bd. govs. 1970-76, chmn. antitrust law sect. coun. 1986-87), Chgo. Bar Assn. (editl. bd. Chgo. Bar Record 1973-84), Bar Assn. 7th Fed. Cir., Ill. Inst. Continuing Legal Edn. (chmn. profl. antitrust problems program 1976, author program on counseling corps., antitrust and trade regulation), Legal Club Chgo. (sec.-treas. 1984-86, v.p. 1989-90, pres. 1990-91), Law Club. Office: Bell Boyd & Lloyd 70 W Madison St Ste 3300 Chicago IL 60602-4243

SGANGA, JOHN B., furniture holding company executive; b. Bronx, N.Y., Nov. 21, 1931; s. Charles and Marie (Crusco) S.; B.S. in Acctg. cum laude, Bklyn. Coll., 1961; postgrad. Bernard Baruch Coll.; m. Evelyn Joan Battilana, Jan. 19, 1957; children: Mark, John B. Jr., Matthew. Systems analyst DIVCO, Wayne, N.Y., 1965-67; mgr. mgmt. cons. services Coopers & Lybrand, C.P.A.s, N.Y.C., 1967-74; sr. v.p. fin. and adminstrn. Aurora Products Co. subs. RJR Nabisco, West Hempstead, N.Y., 1974-79; controller Gt. Lakes Carbon Corp., N.Y.C., 1979-80, v.p., 1980-81, sr. v.p. fin., CFO, 1981-86; v.p. Cunard Line, Ltd., N.Y.C., 1988; exec. v.p., CFO Consolidated Furniture Corp. (formerly Mohasco Corp.), Wilmington, Del., 1989—, also bd. dirs. Served with USNR, 1950-54. Mem. Inst. Cert. Mgmt. Cons. (a founder), Inst. Mgmt. Accts., Fin. Execs. Inst. (past chmn. com. M.I.S.). Clubs: Treas.'s, Brookside Racquet and Swim. Contbr. articles to jours. in field; editl. adv. to Financial Management mag. Home: 255 Davidson Ave Ramsey NJ 07446-1003 Office: Consolidated Furniture Corp One Commerce Ctr 1201 N Orange St Ste 790 Wilmington DE 19801-1155

SGARAMELLA, PETER, chemical products executive, technical consultant; b. Molfetta, Bari, Italy, Jan. 6, 1928; came to U.S., 1954; s. Riccardo and Maria (Masta) S.; m. Mary Caputi, Aug. 3, 1953; children: Richard, Robert, Maria. PhD, U. Bari, Italy, 1951. Chief chemist Aerosol Techniques, Bridgeport, Conn., 1955-61; lab. mgr. Beecham Products, Clifton, N.J., 1961-67; dir. rsch. Shulton/Am.-Cyanamid, Clifton, N.J., 1967-93; tech. dir. Fluid Packaging, Lakewood, N.J., 1993—; Spkr. seminars and tech. presentations in U.S. and internat. Contbr. articles to profl. jours.; prin. author several patents. Leader Boy Scouts Am., 1964-70; mem. com. Knights of Columbus, 1984-90; chmn., moderator several trade assn. ann. meetings. Mem. ICA Fellowship Soc. (adminstrn.), FMA Native Town Fedn. (trustee), Soc. Cosmetic Chemists. Roman Catholic. Avocations: travel, reading, photography. Home: 54 3rd St Apt 4 Hoboken NJ 07030-4718

SGARLAT, MARY ANNE E. A., public relations professional, entrepreneur; b. Boston, Apr. 5, 1958; d. Francis Abbott and Elizabeth Maria (Paragallo) S. Diploma, Milton Acad., 1974; student, Roedean Sch., Brighton, Eng., 1975; BA, Bennington Coll., 1979. Adminstr. Harvard U., Cambridge, Mass., 1979-86; pub. rels. dir. Graham Gund Architects, Cambridge, 1986-89; mktg. and comms. mgr. Elkus/Manfredi Architects, Boston, 1989-90; comms. mgr. Turan Corp., Boston, 1990-92; mktg. dir. The Design Partnership of Cambridge, 1992-97; entrepreneur, 1997—. Mem. LWV, Bennington Coll. Alumni Assn. (regional dir. 1993—, exec. com. 1986-93). Avocations: politics, music, dancing, skiing, collecting rare books. Home and Office: 1214 Brook Rd Milton MA 02186-4136 also: The Sloane Club, 52 Lower Sloane St, London SW1 8BS, England

SGRO, BEVERLY HUSTON, state official, educator; b. Ft. Worth, Jan. 12, 1941; d. James Carl and Dorothy Louise (Foster) Huston; m. Joseph Anthony Sgro, Feb. 1, 1964; children: Anthony, Jennifer. BS, Tex. Woman's

U., 1963; MS, Va. Poly. Inst. and State U., 1974, PhD, 1990. Cert. tennis teaching profl. Instr. of deaf Midland (Tex.) Ind. Sch. System, 1963-64; speech pathologist Arlington (Tex.) Pub. Sch. System, 1964; rsch. asst. Tex. Christian U., 1964-65; tennis profl. Blacksburg (Va.) Country Club, 1977-81; from coord. for Greek affairs to exec. asst. to v.p. student affairs Va. Poly. Inst. and State U., Blacksburg, 1981-89, dean of students, 1989-93; sec. of edn. Commonwealth of Va., Richmond, 1994—; adj. faculty Coll. Edn., Va. Poly. Inst. and State U.; lectr., presented papers at numerous symposia and convs., 1983—. Trustee Foxcroft Sch., Middleburg, Va., 1989—, pres. bd. trustees, 1993-96. Mem. AACD, Nat. Assn. Student Pers. Adminstrs., Am. Coll. Pers. Assn. (sec., com. mem. 1986-88), Omicron Delta Kappa, Phi Kappa Phi, Phi Upsilon Omicron, Pi Lambda Theta, Sigma Alpha Eta, Zeta Phi Eta. Avocations: reading, travel, theatre. Home: 1324 Maple Ave Richmond VA 23216

SGRO, JOSEPH ANTHONY, psychologist, educator; b. New Haven, Conn., Nov. 22, 1937; s. Fred and Tullia (Francesconi) S.; m. Beverly Ann Huston, Feb. 1, 1964; children: Anthony, Jennifer. BA, Trinity Coll., 1959; MS, Lehigh U., 1961; PhD, Tex. Christian U., 1966. Asst. prof. Old Dominion U., Norfolk, Va., 1965-67; asst. prof. Va. Poly. Inst. & State U., Blacksburg, 1967-71, assoc. prof., 1971-79, prof., 1979—, dept. head psychology, 1982-96, mem. exec. bd., sec.-treas. coun. grad. dept. psychology, 1990-92, chmn., 1992-93; vice-chmn. Va. Bd. Psychologists Examiners, Richmond, 1970-75. Editor: Virginia Tech Symposium on Applied Behavioral Science, 1980. Mem. Am. Psychol. Assn., Am. Psychol. Soc., Psychonomic Soc., Southeastern Psychol. Assn. (chmn. assn. heads depts. psychology 1987-89), Ea. Psychol. Assn., So. Soc. for Philosophy & Psychology, Va. Psychol. Assn. (pres. 1974-76), Omicron Delta Kappa, Psi Chi, Sigma Xi. Avocations: golf, cooking. Home: 4185 Pearman Rd Blacksburg VA 24060-8549 Office: Va Poly Inst & State U Dept Psychology Blacksburg VA 24061

SHAAR, H. ERIK, academic administrator. V.p. acad. affairs Shippensburg U. of Pa., until 1986; pres. Lake Superior State U., Sault Sainte Marie, Mich., 1986-92, Minot (N.D.) State U., 1992—. Office: Minot State U Office of Pres 500 University Ave W Minot ND 58707-0001

SHABAZZ, AIYSHA MUSLIMAH, social work administrator; b. Columbia, S.C., Aug. 9, 1942; d. Jerry James Gadson and Edna Louise (Bellinger) Gadson Smalls; m. Abdullah Muslim Shabazz, July 28; children: Ain, Wali. BA, Fed. City Coll., Washington, 1973; MSW with honors, U. S.C., 1994, postgrad., 1994-97. Cert. child protective svcs. investigator, S.C., adoption investigator, S.C.; lic. social worker and ACBSW; cert. AIDS instr. ARC; lic. notary pub., S.C. Social work asst. Family Service Ctr., Washington, 1966-68; admission counselor Washington Tech. Inst., Washington, 1968-70; program dir. Park Motor Community Ctr., Washington, 1970-75; adminstrv. asst. Neighborhood Planning Council, Washington, 1974-75; substitue tchr. D.C. Pub. Sch. System, Washington, 1974-75; substitute tchr. Dist. I Pub. Schs., Columbia, 1977; home sch. program dir. Community Care, Inc., Columbia, 1977-81; monitor summer program U. S.C., Columbia, 1982; program dir. Dept. Social Services, Columbia, 1984—, case auditor, 1987-88, social worker supr., 1988—, project adminstr. for a alcohol and drug abuse program, 1994—; writer Acad. of Bacholu-Social Workers Exam, 1991; cons. substance abuse resch. program evaln., 1994—. substance abspeaker in field. Bd. dirs. Frederick Douglas Inst., Washington, 1968-69; pres. Park Motor Resident Coun., Washington, 1972-75; expert witness Family Ct.; bd. dirs. Coun. on Child Abuse and Neglect; adv. com., v.p. Benedict Coll. Sch. Social Work, S.C. Protection and Advocacy Handicapped Children; vol. AIDS instr. ARC, 1994; chairperson coordinating com. Voice of the Customer, 1995—. Mem. NASW (bd. dirs. 1993-95), S.C. Child Abuse and Neglect Task Force, AIDS Task Force (chmn. 1987-89). Democrat. Office: Dept Social Services 3220 Two Notch Rd Columbia SC 29204-2826

SHABICA, CHARLES WRIGHT, geologist, earth science educator; b. Elizabeth, N.J., Jan. 2, 1943; s. Anthony Charles and Eleanor (Wright) S.; m. Susan Ewing, Dec. 30, 1967; children: Jonathan, Andrew, Dana. BA in Geology, Brown U., 1965; PhD, U. Chgo., 1971. Prof. earth sci. Northeastern Ill. U., Chgo., 1971—; disting. prof., 1991; pres. Shabica & Assocs., Inc., Northfield, Ill., 1985—; chmn. bd. dirs. Aesti Corp.; rsch. collaborator Nat. Park Svc., 1978-82, 89—; adj. prof. Coll. V.I., St. Thomas, 1980; Kellogg fellow Northeastern Ill. U., 1979—; chmn. Task Force on Lake Michigan, Chgo., 1986-89; mem. Chgo. Shoreline Protection Commn., 1987-88; cons. Shedd Aquarium, Chgo., 1991; mem. Ft. Sheridan Commn., 1989-90. Commr., packmaster Boy Scouts Am., Winnetka, Ill., 1984-88. Coop. Inst. for Limnology and Ecosystems Rsch. Lab. fellow. Mem. Internat. Assn. for Great Lakes Rsch., Am. Shore and Beach Preservation Assn. (bd. dirs.), Sigma Xi. Home: 326 Ridge Ave Winnetka IL 60093-3842 Office: 345 Walnut St Northfield IL 60093-4127

SHACK, R. BRUCE, plastic surgeon; b. Vernon, Tex., Oct. 7, 1947; s. Nathan Lee and Patsy Lee (Holliday) S.; m. Sharon Summers Frazier, Aug. 16, 1969 (div. 1982); children: Robert David, Nathan Andrew; m. Wanda Kaye, Nov. 11, 1984; children: Jerion Elizabeth, Austin Ryan. BS, Midwestern U., 1969; MD, U. Tex., 1973. Diplomate Am. Bd. Plastic Surger. Resident in gen. surgery Vanderbilt U. Med. Ctr., Nashville, 1973-78, resident in plastic surgery, 1978-80; asst. prof. surgery Johns Hopkins Med. Sch., Balt., 1980-82; from asst. prof. to prof., chmn. plastic surgery Vanderbilt U. Med. Ctr., 1982—. Fellow Am. Coll. Surgeons; mem. AMA, Am. Assn. Plastic Surgeons, Am. Soc. Maxillofacial Surgeons, Am. Soc. Plastic and Reconstructive Surgeons, Am. Soc. Reconstructive Microsurgery, Am. Soc. Aesthetic Plastic Surgery, H. William Scott, Jr. Soc., John B. Lynch Soc., John Staige David Soc. Plastic Surgeons Md., Nashville Acad. Medicine, Nashville Surg. Soc., Southeastern Soc. Plastic and Reconstructive Surgeons, So. Med. Assn., Tenn. Soc. Plastic Surgeons. Republican. Methodist. Avocations: golf, travel, shooting. Office: Vanderbilt U Med Ctr 2100 Pierce Ave # 230 Mcs Nashville TN 37212-3162

SHACK, WILLIAM ALFRED, anthropology educator, researcher, consultant; b. Chgo., Apr. 19, 1923; s. William and Emma (McAvoy) S.; m. Dorothy Nash, Sept. 1, 1960; 1 child, Hailu A. B.A.E., Sch. of the Art Inst., Chgo., 1955; M.A., U. Chgo., 1957; Ph.D., London Sch. Econs., 1961. Asst. prof. sociology and anthropology Northeastern Ill. State Coll., Chgo., 1961-62; asst. prof. sociology Haile Selassie I Univ., Addis Ababa, Ethiopia, 1962-65; assoc. prof. anthropology U. Ill., Chgo., 1966-70; prof. anthropology U. Calif.-Berkeley, 1970-91, dean, grad. div., 1979-85. Author: The Gurage, 1966, The Central Ethiopians, 1974; co-author: Gods and Heroes, 1974; co-editor: Strangers in African Societies, 1979. Trustee, bd. dirs. World Affairs Council of No. Calif., San Francisco. Served with USCG, 1943-46; PTO. Fellow AAAS, Calif. Acad. Scis. (trustee, v.p. 1993-97), Am. Anthrop. Assn., Royal Anthrop. Inst. (pres. N.Am. com. 1983-86), Internat. African Inst. (econ. coun. 1984—, vice chmn. 1985-87, chmn. 1987-97, Chevalier l'Ordre Nationale du Merite 1987), Athenaeum (London); mem. Faculty Club U. Calif.-Berkeley (pres. 1991-94). Avocation: vintage motor racing. Home: 2597 Hilgard Ave Berkeley CA 94709-1104 Office: U Calif-Berkeley Dept Anthropology 232 Kroeber Hall Berkeley CA 94720-3711

SHACKELFORD, GEORGE GREEN, historian; b. Orange, Va., Dec. 17, 1920; s. Virginius Randolph and Peachy Gascoigne (Lyne) S.; m. Grace Howard McConnell, June 9, 1962. B.A., U. Va., 1943, M.A., 1948, Ph.D., 1955; postgrad., Columbia U., 1949-51; cert., Attingham, Eng., 1957. Asst. prof. history Birmingham (Ala.) So. Coll., 1948-49; rsch. fellow Va. Hist. Soc., Richmond, 1951-53; instr. Va. Poly. Inst. and State U., Blacksburg, 1954-55; asst. prof. history Va. Poly. Inst. and State U., 1955-58, assoc. prof., 1958-68, prof., 1968-90, prof. emeritus, 1990—; cons. hist. mgmt. Westmoreland Davis Meml. Found., Leesburg, Va., 1967-73, 77-81; vis. scholar Am. Acad., Rome, 1996. Author: George Wythe Randolph and the Confederate Elite, 1988, Jefferson's Adoptive Son: William Short, 1993, Jefferson's Travels in Europe, 1995; editor: Monticello Assn. Collected Papers Vol I., 1965, Vol II, 1984; co-editor Va. Social Sci. Jour., 1967-68; contbr. articles to profl. jours. Mem. Va. Commn. on Bicentennial of The U.S. Constitution, 1987-92. Lt. USNR, 1943-49. Recipient award Va. soc. Am. Inst. Architects for Hist. Preservation, 1985. Mem. Am. Hist. Assn., English Speaking Union (pres. S.W. Va. br. 1979), Nat. Trust for Hist. Preservation (bd. advisors 1976-79), Assn. Inst. Early Am. History and Culture, Attingham Assocs., Assn. Preservation Va. Antiquities (bd. dirs. 1960-64, 67-77), Monticello Assn. (pres. 1969-71), So. Hist. Assn., Va. Hist. Assn., Soc. Archl. History, Farmington Country Club. Democrat. Episcopalian. Home and Office: Westminster Canterbury 250 Pantops Mount Rd 55 Charlottesville VA 22911

SHACKELFORD, MARTIN ROBERT, social worker; b. Boonville, Mo., May 22, 1947; s. Hugh and Carol Lois (Schoene) S. BA in History, U. Mich., 1969. Driver Yellow Cab, Saginaw, Mich., 1969-70; sales clk. Waldenbooks, Saginaw, Mich., 1972; eligibility worker Saginaw County Dept. Social Svcs., 1972-73, employment worker, 1973-77, delinquency svcs. worker, 1977—; charter mem. social work adv. com. Saginaw Valley State U., 1981—. Contbr. articles on JFK assassination to profl. jours. Bd. dirs. Valley Film Soc., Saginaw, 1978—, ACLU, Cen. Mich. Br., 1978—; vice chmn. Lone Tree Coun. Avocations: film, photography, reading, writing, creative experimentation. Home: 216 N Webster St # 2 Saginaw MI 48602-4243

SHACKLEFORD, WILLIAM ALTON, SR., minister; b. Red Springs, N.C., Aug. 5, 1947; s. Purcell and Pearl (Walton) S.; m. Rebecca Belsches, Dec. 2, 1972; children: Kristal Lynn, William Alton Jr. Student, Hampton U., 1965-67, U. Richmond, 1969, 70; DD (hon.), Va. Sem. and Coll., 1990. Ordained to ministry Unity Bapt. Mins.' Conf., 1977. Pastor Cedar Grove Bapt. Ch., Charles City, Va., 1979-82, St. Paul High Street Bapt. Ch., Martinsville, Va., 1986—; past pres. Bapt. Sunday sch. and Bapt. Tng. Union Congress of Va., Sunday sch. Union of Hampton and Adjoining Cities, Unity Bapt. Min.'s Conf., Newport News, Va.; corr. sec. Va. Bapt. State Conv., 1986-96; sr. technician tech. svc. Badishe Corp., Williamsburg, Va., 1967-81, asst. supr. corp. office svcs., 1981-86. Contbr. articles to Martinsville Bull. Apptd. supt. Schs. Adv. Coun.; mem. Child Abuse and Neglect Multidiscipline Team; mem. exec. bd. Martinsville Voter's League, 1987—; mem. overall econ. devel. com., ad hoc drug and alcohol abuse com., past mem. adminstrv. bd. Martinsville Dept. Social Svcs.; mem. adv. coun. Good News Jail and Prison Ministries; past chmn. bd. dirs., mem. adv. com., mem. editl. bd. Patrick Henry Drug and Alcohol Coun.; vice chmn. Martinsville City Sch. Bd., 1991—; past chmn. bd. trustees Va. Sem. and Coll., Lynchburg, Va., 1992-96; v.p. Va. One Ch. One Child, 1992—; mem. edn. com. Va. Mcpl. League, 1993-95. Named Outstanding Min. Nat. Hairston Clan, 1988; recipient Dedicated Svc. award Va.'s One Ch. One Child Program, 1989, numerous others. Mem. NAACP, Smith River Bapt. Assn. (vice moderator), Martinsville and Henry County Ministerial Alliance (various positions). Home: 405 3rd St Martinsville VA 24112-3416 Office: St Paul High Street Bapt Ch PO Box 1003 401 Fayette St Martinsville VA 24114 *I live with the assurance that the invisible hand of God works to bless and exalt those who commit the totality of their existence to serve God and benefit humanity.*

SHACKMAN, DANIEL ROBERT, psychiatrist; b. N.Y.C., Nov. 15, 1941; s. Nathan H. and Dorothy K. Shackman. BA, Columbia U., 1962, MD, 1966. Diplomate Am. Bd. Psychiatry and Neurology. Intern Mount Sinai Hosp., N.Y.C., 1966-67, resident, chief resident, fellow, 1967-70; psychiatrist USAF, Spokane, Wash., 1970-72; clin. and adminstrv. staff Brentwood VA Hosp., L.A., 1972-79; pvt. practice psychiatry L.A., 1975-87, Santa Barbara, Calif., 1984—; asst. clin. prof. UCLA Sch. Medicine, L.A., 1975-87; psychiat. cons. Calif. Dept. Rehab., L.A., 1975-87; cons. psychiatrist Sanctuary Psychiat. Ctrs., Santa Barbara, 1984—; chmn. dept. psychiatry Santa Barbara (Calif.) Cottage Hosp., 1990-92. Bd. dirs. Family Counseling Svc., Spokane, 1971-72. Maj. USAF, 1970-72. Mem. Am. Psychiat. Assn., Am. Acad. Child/Adolescent Psychiatry, So. Calif. Psychiat. Soc. (dist. councillor 1989-92). Avocations: music appreciation and performance, computer science. Office: 924 Anacapa St Santa Barbara CA 93101-2115

SHACTER, DAVID MERVYN, lawyer; b. Toronto, Ont., Can., Jan. 17, 1941; s. Nathan and Tillie Anne (Schwartz) S. BA, U. Toronto, 1963; JD, Southwestern U., 1967. Bar: Calif. 1968, U.S. Ct. Appeals (9th cir.) 1969, U.S. Supreme Ct. 1982. Law clk., staff atty. Legal Aid Found., Long Beach, Calif., 1967-70; asst. city atty. City of Beverly Hills, Calif., 1970; ptnr. Shacter & Berg, Beverly Hills, 1971-83, Selwyn, Capalbo, Lowenthal & Shacter Profl. Law Corp., 1984—; del. State Bar Conf. Dels., 1976—; lectr. Calif. Continuing Edn. of Bar, 1977, 82, 83, 86; judge pro tem L.A. and Beverly Hills mcpl. cts.; arbitrator L.A. Superior Ct., 1983—, also judge pro tem; disciplinary examiner Calif. State Bar, 1986. Bd. dirs. and pres. Los Angeles Soc. Prevention Cruelty to Animals, 1979-89. Mem. Beverly Hills Bar Assn. (bd. govs. 1985—, editor-in-chief jour., sec. 1987-88, treas. 1988-89, v.p. 1989-90, pres.-elect 1990-91, pres. 1991-92), Am. Arbitration Assn. (nat. panel arbitrators, NASD arbitration panel), City of Hope Med. Ctr. Aux., Wilshire C. of C. (bd. dirs., gen. counsel 1985-87). Office: Selwyn Capalbo Lowenthal & Shacter Profl Law Corp 8383 Wilshire Blvd Ste 510 Beverly Hills CA 90211-2404

SHADBOLT, DOUGLAS, architecture educator, administrator; b. Victoria, B.C., Can., Apr. 18, 1925; s. Edmund and Alice Mary Maude (Healy) S.; m. Sidney Osborne Craig, June 29, 1960; stepchildren: James Osborne Craig, Catherine Shand Craig. B. Arch., U. Oreg., 1957; D. Eng. (hon.), N.S. Tech. Coll., 1969, Carleton U., 1982. Archtl. asst. Montreal, Que., Can., Ottawa, Ont., Vancouver, B.C., Victoria, B.C., Seattle, Boston, 1942-58; lectr. U. Oreg., 1955-57; asst. prof. McGill U., Montreal, 1958-60, assoc. prof., 1960-61; prof., founding dir. Sch. Architecture N.S. Tech. Coll., Halifax, Can., 1961-68; founding prof., dir. Sch. Architecture Carleton U., Ottawa, 1968-77, dir. Archtl. Research Group, 1977-79; prof., dir. Sch. Architecture, U. B.C., Vancouver, 1979-90, prof. emeritus, 1990—; pvt. practice cons. architect, 1961—. Author: Ron Thom, The Shaping of an Architect, 1995. Recipient Disting. Prof. award AIA Collegiate Schs. Architecture, 1987. Fellow Royal Archtl. Inst. Can. (Gold medal 1992); mem. Archtl. Inst. B.C.

SHADDOCK, CARROLL SIDNEY, lawyer; b. Beaumont, Tex., July 7, 1940; s. Carroll Bitting Jr. and Hulda Martha (Gaertner) S.; m. Dorothea Schulze, Nov. 30, 1963; children: Carroll Christian, Peter Eric, Matthew Nolan. BA, Rice U., 1962; JD, Yale U., 1965. Ptnr. Liddell, Sapp, Zivley, Hill & LaBoon L.L.P., Houston, 1967—. Chmn. Scenic Am., Washington, 1985-92, Scenic Tex., 1992—, Trees for Houston, 1982—, Billboards Limited, Houston, 1982-92. Republican. Lutheran. Avocations: church music, golf, travel. Home: 1715 South Blvd Houston TX 77098-5419 Office: Liddell Sapp Zivley Hill & LaBoon LLP Tex Commerce Tower 600 Travis St Ste 3200 Houston TX 77002-3004

SHADDOCK, PAUL FRANKLIN, SR., human resources director; b. Buffalo, Apr. 7, 1950; s. William Edmund and Rhea (Riester) S.; m. Linda Jeannine Bauer, July 19, 1980; children: Paul Jr., Jessica. BS, State U. Coll. N.Y., Buffalo, 1973; MBA, SUNY, Binghamton, 1975. Warehouse mgr. Ralston Purina Co., Denver, 1976-77; prodn. supr. Samsonite Corp., Denver, 1978-79, labor rels. rep., 1979-83; dir. human resources NBI, Inc., Denver, 1984-89, United Techs. Corp., Colorado Springs, Colo., 1990-95, Rockwell Semiconductor Sys., Newport Beach, Calif., 1995-96; v.p. human resources CSG, Systems, Inc., Denver, Colo., 1996—. Mem. Colo. Alliance of Bus., Denver, 1983-85, 90—, exec. com. U. Colo., Colorado Springs, 1990—. Mem. Assn. of Quality Participation, Am. Personnel Assn., Colo. Human Resource Assn., Human Resource Electroncis Group, Mountain States Employers Coun., Rocky Mountain Human Resources Group, Colorado Springs C. of C. Republican. Roman Catholic. Avocations: swimming, tennis, skiing. Home: 5400 S Park Terr # 11-103 Greenwood Village CO 80111

SHADDOCK, WILLIAM EDWARD, JR., lawyer; b. Lake Charles, La., Jan. 18, 1938; s. William Edward Shaddock and Edith (Burton) Plauche; m. Winifred Craig Gorham, Aug. 2, 1958; children: Stephen Gorham, Mary Craig, Nancy Edith. BS, La. State U., 1960, JD, 1963. Bar: La. 1963, U.S. Dist. Ct. (we. dist.) La. 1964, U.S. Supreme Ct. 1968, U.S. Ct. Appeals (5th cir.) 1981; cert. specialist in estate planning and adminstrn. La. Bd. Legal Specialization. Assoc. Plauche & Stockwell, Lake Charles, La., 1963-66; ptnr. Stockwell, Sievert, Viccellio, Clements & Shaddock, L.L.P., Lake Charles, 1966—. Fellow Am. Coll. Trusts and Estates Counsel (state chmn. 1994—). Republican. Methodist. Avocations: fishing, hunting, photography. Office: Stockwell Sievert Viccellio Clements & Shaddock PO Box 2900 One Lakeside Plz 4th Fl Lake Charles LA 70602

SHADEGG, JOHN B., congressman; b. Phoenix, Oct. 22, 1950; s. Stephen and Eugenia Shadegg; m. Shirley Shadegg; children: Courtney, Stephen. BA, U. Ariz., 1972, JD, 1975. Advisor U.S. Sentencing Commn.; spl. asst. atty. gen. State of Ariz., 1983-90; spl. counsel Ariz. Ho. Rep. Caucus, 1991-92; pvt. practice; mem. 104th-105th Congresses from 4th Ariz. dist., 1995—; mem. budget com., govt. reform and oversight com.; asst. whip 104th Congress from 4th Ariz. dist.; mem. Victims Bill of Rights Task Force, 1989-90; mem. Fiscal Accountability and Reform Efforts Com., 1991-92; counsel Arizonian's for Wildlife Conservation, 1992; chmn. Proposition 108-Two-Thirds Tax Limitation Initiative, 1992. Rep. Party Ballot Security chmn., 1982; active Corbin for Atty. Gen., 1982-86; Rep. Precinct committeeman; chmn. Ariz. Rep. Caucus, 1985-87; chmn. Ariz. Lawyers for Bush-Quayle, 1988; mem. steering com., surrogate spkr. Jon Kyl for Congress, 1988-92; former pres. Crime Victim Found.; founding dir. Goldwater Inst. Pub. Policy; chmn. Ariz. Juvenile Justice Adv. Coun.; mem. adv. bd. Salvation Army; mem. vestry Christ Ch. of Ascension, 1989-91; mem. class II Valley Leadership; bd. dirs. Ariz. State U. Law Soc. Office: US House Reps 430 Cannon Bldg Ofc Bldg Washington DC 20515-2215*

SHADEK, ARTHUR JOSEPH, radio station executive; b. Jersey City, Apr. 24, 1924; s. Arthur Joseph and Wilhelmina Elizabeth (Uhlenbush) S.; m. Katherine Flint, Feb. 2, 1949; children: Larry, Tom, Jim, Kit. BSME, Stevens Inst. Tech., 1946; JD, Columbia U., 1948. Bar: N.Y. 1949. Dir., prin. stockholder various cos. and radio stas., 1960-90; chmn. Oak Point Corp., Vero Beach, Fla., 1994—; dir. Jefferson Savs. & Loan Assn., Warrentown, Va., 1992-95; ptnr. Lompoc Gala Farm, Santa Barbara County, Calif., 1992—; chmn., CEO WADB radio sta., South Belmar, N.J., 1992-96; trustee emeritus Franklin and Marshall Coll., Lancaster, Pa., 1995—, vice chmn. bd. trustees, 1973-94; pres. Seaquay Condominium Assn., Vero Beach, 1991-95. Bd. trustees mem. Stevens Inst. Tech., Hoboken, N.J., 1989—, chmn. fin. and investment com., 1993—; bd. mgrs. mem. Dag Hammarskjold Condominium Assn., N.Y.C., 1983—, pres. 1983-95; treas. bd. dirs. 400 Beach Rd. Condominium Assn., Vero Beach, 1995—. Republican. Episcopalian. Avocations: gardening, bike riding. Home and Office: 688 Ocean Rd Vero Beach FL 32963

SHADER, RICHARD IRWIN, psychiatrist, educator; b. Mt. Vernon, N.Y., May 27, 1935; s. Myer and Beatrice (Epstein) S.; m. Aline Brown, Sept. 21, 1958; children: Laurel Beth, Jennifer Robin, Robert Andrew. Student, Harvard U., 1952-56; M.D., NYU, 1960; grad., Boston Psychoanalytic Inst., 1970. Diplomate Am. Bd. Psychiatry and Neurology (dir. 1977-84, treas. 1982-83, pres. 1984). Intern Greenwich Hosp., Conn., 1960-61; resident in psychiatry Mass. Mental Health Ctr., Boston, 1961-62, 64-65, NIMH, Bethesda, Md., 1962-64; asso. prof. psychiatry Harvard Med. Sch., 1970-79; prof. dept. psychiatry Tufts U. Med. Sch., Boston, 1979—, chmn. dept., 1979-91; psychiatrist in chief New Eng. Med. Ctr. Hosp., Boston, 1979-91; prof. pharmacology Tufts U. Med. Sch., Boston, 1989—, chmn. dept. pharmacology and exptl. therapeutics, 1991-93. Author: (with A. DiMascio) Psychotropic Drug Side Effects, 1970, (with D.J. Greenblatt) Benzodiazepines in Clinical Practice, 1974, Manual of Psychiatric Therapeutics, 1975, 2d edit., 1994; editor: Psychiatric Complications of Medical Drugs, 1972, (with A. DiMascio) Clinical Handbook of Psychopharmacology, 1970, (with D.J. Greenblatt) Pharmacokinetics in Clinical Practice, 1985, (with A. DiMascio) Butyrophenones in Psychiatry, 1972; MAOI Therapy, 1988, (with J.P. Tupin and D.S. Harnett) Handbook of Clinical Psychopharmacology, 1988, (with others) Drug Interactions in Psychiatry, 1989, 2d edit., 1995, Clinical Manual of Chemical Dependence, 1991; editor-in-chief Jour. Clin. Psychopharmacology, 1980—. Bd. dirs. Med. Found., Inc., 1980-87. Served with USPHS, 1962-64. Joseph J. Michaels merit scholar, 1968-69; fellow Ctr. for Advanced Study in Behavioral Scis., Stanford, Calif., 1990-91; recipient Seymour Vestermark award Am. Psychiat. Assn., 1988, 90. Mem. AMA, Mass. Med. Soc., Am. coll. Neuropsychopharmacology (v.p. 1984, pres. 1990), Am. Soc. Clin. Pharmacology & Therapeutics, Am. Soc. Pharmacology and Exptl. Therapeutics. Democrat. Jewish. Office: Tufts U Sch Medicine 136 Harrison Ave Boston MA 02111-1817

SHADEROWFSKY, EVA MARIA, photographer, writer; b. Prague, Czechoslovakia, May 20, 1938; came to U.S., 1940; d. Felix Resek and Gertrude (Telatko) Frank; children: Tom, Paul. Student, Oberlin Coll., 1955-56; BA, Barnard Coll., 1960. Women's channel coord., moderator America Online: Evenings with Eva. Exhibited in one-person shows at The Left Bank Gallery, Wellfleet, Mass., 1974, Art Ctr. No. N.J., Tenafly, 1975, Soho Photo, N.Y., 1974, 80, Esta Robinson Gallery, 1982, Fairleigh Dickinson U., 1983, Donnell Libr., N.Y.C., 1985, Piermont (N.Y.) Libr., 1987, The Turning Point, Piermont, N.Y., 1988, Hopper House, Nyack, N.Y., 1989, Puchong Gallery, N.Y., 1991, Rockland Ctr. for Arts, 1992; group shows include Soho Photo Gallery, N.Y., 1974, Fashion Inst. Tech., N.Y.C., 1975, Portland (Maine) Mus. Art, 1977, Maine Photog. Workshop, Rockport, 1978, Marcuse Pfeifer, N.Y., 1977, 78, Chrysler Mus., Norfol,, Va., 1978, Exposure Gallery Wellfleet, 1978, 79, The Art Ctr. No. N.J., Tenafly, 1980, Neuberger Mus., Purchase, N.Y., 1982, Hudson River Mus., 1982, Foto, N.Y., 1982, Barnard Coll., N.Y.C., 1983, Rockland Ctr. for Arts, 1978, 87, 89, 96, Print Club, Phila., 1988; represented in collections at Bklyn. Mus., Portland (Maine) Mus. Art, Met. Mus. Art, N.Y.C.; author and photographer (book) Suburban Portraits, 1977; photographer Women in Transition, 1975, (book) Earth Tones, 1993, The Womansource Catalog and Review: Tools for Connecting the Community of Women, 1996; poetry critic/essayist Contact II, 1980-93; contbr. story to anthology, 1980-93, Touching Fire, 1989, Sexual Harassment: Women Speak Out, 1992, Lovers, 1992, The Time of Our Lives, 1993; contbr. photography to Camera 35 mag., Shots mag., Shutterbug. Recipient Photography award Rockland Ctr. for Arts, 1978, Gt. Am. Photo Contest, 1981, Demarais Press, 1982, Harrison Art Coun., SUNY-Purchase, 1982, The Cape Codder, 1976, 79-82. Home and Office: 265 Maple Rd Valley Cottage NY 10989-1426

SHADID, RANDEL COY, lawyer; b. Dallas, Sept. 28, 1947; s. Coy Constant and Jimmie Lee (Burrow) S.; m. Dana Hieronymus, Mar. 9, 1996; children from previous marriage: Jerame Scott, Jerod Ryan. BBA, U. Okla., 1969, JD, 1972. Bar: Okla. 1973, U.S. Dist. Ct. (we. dist.) Okla. 1973. Researcher Okla. Employment Security Commn., Oklahoma City, 1969-72; pvt. practice Edmond, Okla., 1973—; adj. prof. Ctrl. State U., Edmond, 1975-78, 94-96. Mayor pro tem Edmond City Coun., 1979—, mayor, 1991-95; deacon First Christian Ch.; mem. Edmond Econ. Devel. Authority. Named to Edmond Hall of Fame, 1995. Mem. Okla. County Bar Assn., Edmond C. of C. (pres. 1984, Citizen of Yr. 1986)), Ambucs, Rotary (treas. 1978), Delta Theta Phi, Delta Sigma Pi, Omicron Delta Kappa, Beta Gamma Sigma. Avocations; tennis, skiing, fishing, gardening, art & antique collecting. Home: 507 Timberdale Ter Edmond OK 73034-4215 Office: 19 N Broadway St # 100 Edmond OK 73034-3732

SHADLE, DONNA A. FRANCIS, principal; b. Canton, Ohio, Oct. 29, 1944; d. Gerald W. and Virginia M. (Kerker) Francis; m. Joseph E. Shadle, Apr. 24, 1965; children: Joseph, Paul, Ann, Mary. Student, Walsh Coll., 1964; BS in Edn., Kent State U., 1980, MS in Edn., 1989. Cert. early childhood, kindergarten, elementary edn., Ohio. Tchr. grade 4 St. Joseph's Elem., Canton, Ohio, 1964-65; dir., adminstr. Community Pre-sch., Canton, 1969-79; substitute tchr., K-8 Diocese of Youngstown, Canton, 1965-80; tchr. kindergarten St. Paul's Elem., North Canton, Ohio, 1980-95; prin. Sacred Heart of Mary Elem. Sch., Harrisburg, Ohio, 1995—; reading pubs. cons.; tchr. rep. Home & Sch. Assn., North Canton, 1985; tech. com., 1992—; dir. drama Ctrl. Cath. H.S., Canton, 1987—; workshop presenter various ednl. conventions, 1989—; adv. bd. ADD Partnership of Ohio, North Canton, 1992—; invited to participate in various dept. projects Ohio State Dept. Edn.; cons. Sadlier Pub. editor, pub. (newsletter) KinderKindlings, 1989—, pub. cons., 1994. Troop Leader Girl Scouts Am., North Canton, 1977-93; dir. Mime Easter drama, North Canton, 1983-89; vol. United Way, March of Dimes, Heart Fund Canton, Canton, 1965—. Recipient spl. recognition award for Ohio Tchr. of Yr. Ashland Oil, 1989. Mem. ASCD, Assn. Childhood Edn. Internat., Nat. Assn. Edn. Young Children, Nat. Cath. Ednl. Assn. (regional rep. to exec. bd.), Nat. Assn. Elem. Sch. Prins., Ohio Assn. Edn. Young Children, Canton Area Assn. Edn. Young Children. Home: 5544 Frazer Ave NW North Canton OH 44720-4040 Office: Sacred Heart of Mary 8276 N Nickelplate St Louisville OH 44641-9543

SHADOAN, GEORGE WOODSON, lawyer; b. Galesburg, Ill., July 4, 1933; s. William Parker and Hortense (Lewis) S.; m. June Faith Spiegelman, May 16, 1969; 1 child, Jesse; 1 stepchild, Jenny Ducaud. B.S., U. Ky., 1958,

LL.B., 1960; LL.M., Georgetown U., 1961. Bar: Ky., 1960, D.C. 1960, Md. 1963. Ptnr. Shadoan and Michael, LLP, Rockville, Md.; prof. law Georgetown U. Law Ctr., 1962-66. Author, editor: Law and Tactics in Federal Criminal Cases, 1964; Maryland Tort Damages, 1983, 85, 90, 94. Named Lawyer of Yr., Assn. Plaintiffs Trial Attys. of D.C., 1974. Fellow Am. Bar Found., Am. Bd. Trial Advocates, Am. Bd. Profl. Liability Attys.; mem. ATLA (gov. 1982-85), Md. Bar Assn. (chmn. civil pattern jury instrns. subcom.), D.C. Bar Assn. (Young Lawyer of Yr. award 1963), Inner Circle of Advocates (pres. 1983-85), Trial Lawyers Pub. Justice (pres. 1984, Pub. Justice award 1994), Md. Trial Lawyers Assn. (pres. 1978-79), Internat. Soc. Barristers, Internat. Acad. Trial Lawyers, Am. Law Inst. Home: 4445 29th St NW Washington DC 20008-2307 Office: 108 Park Ave Rockville MD 20850-2619

SHADRACH, (MARTHA) JEAN HAWKINS, artist; b. La Junta, Colo., Nov. 7, 1926; d. Lloyd Marion Hawkins and Martha May (Hawkins) Sudan; widowed, 1987; children: John M., Karolyn Sue Shadrach Green. BA, U. Colo., 1948. Owner Artique, Ltd. Gallery, Anchorage, Alaska, 1971-87; instr. Foothills Art Ctr., Golden, 1988-89, Prince William Sound C.C., Homer, Alaska, 1993, Kachemak Bay C.C., Homer, 1994, 97, VAA, 1996; facilitator mktg. art seminars; guest lectr. Cunard Cruise Lines, 1988-90, 95. Bd. dirs. Bird Treatment and Learning Ctr., Anchorage, 1994, Anchorage Art Selection Com., 1984. Recipient gov.'s award for excellence in art, Anchorage, 1970, drawing award All Alaska Juried Show, 1970, 1st prize Fairbanks Watercolor Soc., 1987, Paul Schwartz Meml. award Sumi-e Soc. Am., 1993. Mem. Alaska Watercolor Soc. (v.p. 1994—, award 1988). Home and Studio: 3530 Fordham Dr Anchorage AK 99508-4558

SHADUR, ROBERT H., lawyer; b. Chgo., June 17, 1947. Upper 2d degree, U. Birmingham, Eng., 1968; BA magna cum laude, UCLA, 1969; JD, U. Chgo., 1972. Bar: Ill. 1973. Former ptnr. Winston & Strawn, Chgo. Mem. ABA, Ill. State Bar Assn., Chgo. Bar Assn., Phi Beta Kappa. Office: Shadur and Assocs 333 W Wacker Dr Ste 1650 Chicago IL 60606-1226

SHADWELL, WENDY JOAN, curator, writer; b. N.Y.C., Feb. 5, 1942; d. Howard and Phyllis Lilian (Jenner) S. BA with honors, Mary Washington Coll., 1963; postgrad. dept. art and archeology Columbia U., 1963-66. Curator Middendorf Collection, N.Y.C., 1966-73; cons. N.Y. Hist. Soc., N.Y.C., 1971-73, asst. editor, 1973-74, curator of prints, 1974—. Author: American Printmaking: The First 150 Years, 1969; Prized Prints, 1986. Contbr. articles to profl. jours. Sec. collections com. S.I. Hist. Soc., 1983—; v.p. Friends of Alice Austen House, S.I., 1983-85. Mem. Print Council Am., Am. Hist. Print Collectors Soc. (1st v.p.), Archivists Round Table, N.Am. Print Conf., Grolier Club, Phi Beta Kappa. Republican. Episcopalian. Office: NY Hist Soc 170 Central Park W New York NY 10024-5102

SHAEFFER, CHARLES WAYNE, investment counselor; b. Bridgeton, Pa., Dec. 12, 1910; s. Bartram Augustus and Carolyn I. (Morton) S.; m. Ruth S. Smyser, Oct. 2, 1937; children—Charles Wayne, Ann B. (Mrs. Clark F. MacKenzie), Julia P. B.A., Pa. State U., 1933; M.B.A., Harvard, 1935; LL.D., Loyola Coll., 1974. Investment counselor Mackubin Legg & Co., Balt., 1935-37; with T. Rowe Price Assos., Inc. (formerly T. Rowe Price & Assos., Inc.), Balt., 1938—; chmn. bd. T. Rowe Price Assos., Inc. (formerly T. Rowe Price & Assos., Inc.), 1966-76, pres., 1963-74, cons., 1976—; pres. T. Rowe Price Growth Stock Fund, Inc., 1968-74, chmn. bd., 1974-76; chmn. bd. Rowe Price New Income Fund, 1973—; dir. Rowe Price New Horizons Fund, Inc., 1966—, Rowe Price New Era Fund, Inc., Rowe Price Prime Res. Fund; trustee Monumental Properties Trust; lectr. investment mgmt. Balt. Coll. Commerce, 1938-70, Johns Hopkins, 1960-72. Trustee Pa. State U., Franklin Sq. Hosp.; bd. mgrs. Bryn Mawr Sch., U. Balt.; bd. dirs. Md. chpt. Nature Conservancy; chmn. bd. dirs. Md. Shock-Trauma Found. Recipient Distinguished Alumni award Pa. State U. Coll. Bus. Adminstrn., 1971-72. Mem. Investment Counsel Assn. Am. (pres. 1970-73, gov. 1965—), No-Load Mut. Fund Assn. (pres. 1972-75), Investment Co. Inst. (gov. 1968—, chmn. 1975-76), Alpha Sigma Phi, Pi Gamma Mu, Delta Sigma Pi. Episcopalian. Clubs: Maryland (Balt.), L'Hirodelle (Balt.), Merchants (Balt.), Center (Balt.), Elkridge (Balt.); Green Spring Valley Hunt (Garrison, Md.); Laurel Fish and Game Assn. (York, Pa.), Lafayette (York, Pa.); Seaview Country (Absecon, N.J.); Farmington Country (Charlottesville, Va.). Home: 603 Brightwood Club Dr Lutherville Timonium MD 21093-3632 Office: 100 E Pratt St Baltimore MD 21202-1009

SHAEFFER, THELMA JEAN, primary school educator; b. Ft. Collins, Colo., Feb. 1, 1949; d. Harold H. and Gladys June (Ruff) Pfeif; m. Charles F. Shaeffer, June 12, 1971; 1 child, Shannon Emily. BA, U. No. Colo., 1970, MA, 1972. Cert. profl. tchr., type B, Colo. Primary tchr. Adams County Dist #12 Five Star Schs., Northglenn, Colo., 1970-84; title I (lang. arts) tchr. Adams County Dist #12 Five Star Schs., Northglenn, 1984-97, title I, read succed tchr., 1992-97; mem. policy coun. Adams County Dist. # 12 Five Star Schs., Northglenn, 1975-79, dist. sch. improvement team, 1987-89; presenter Nat. Coun. Tchrs. of English, 1990. Vol. 1992 election, Denver, alumni advisor for Career Connections U. No. Colo., 1993-97. Mem. Colo. Tchrs. Assn. (del. 1992), Dist. Tchrs. Edn. Assn. (exec. bd. mem. 1991-93), Internat. Reading Assn. (pres. Colo. coun. 1988), Internat. Order of Job's Daughters (coun. mem.), Order of Eastern Star, Delta Omicron. Episcopalian. Home: 6502 Perry St Arvada CO 80003-6400 Office: Hulstrom Elem Sch 10604 Grant Dr Northglenn CO 80233-4117

SHAEVSKY, MARK, lawyer; b. Harbin, Manchuria, China, Dec. 2, 1935; came to U.S., 1938, naturalized, 1944; s. Tolio and Rae (Weinstein) S.; m. Lois Ann Levi, Aug. 2, 1964; children: Thomas Lyle, Lawrence Keith. Student, Wayne State U., 1952-53; BA with highest distinction, U. Mich., 1956, JD with highest distinction, 1959. Bar: Mich. 1959. Law clerk to presiding judge U.S. Dist. Ct., Detroit, 1960-61; assoc. Honigman Miller Schwartz & Cohn, Detroit, 1961-64; ptnr. Honigman, Miller, Schwartz & Cohn, Detroit, 1965-69, sr. ptnr., 1969—; instr. law Wayne State U. Law Sch., Detroit, 1961-64; comml. arbitrator Am. Arbitration Assn., Detroit; bd. dirs. Charter One Fin. Inc., Charter One Bank. Contbr. Wayne State U. Law Rev., U. Mich. Law Rev., 1957-59, asst. editor, 1958-59. Dir. Detroit Mens Orgn. of Rehab. through Tng., 1969-79; mem. exec. bd. Am. Jewish Com., Detroit, 1965-74; trustee Jewish Vocat. Svcs., Detroit, 1973-76; sec., dir. Am. Friends Hebrew Univ., Detroit, 1976-84; mem. capital needs com. Jewish Welfare Fedn., Detroit, 1986—. With U.S. Army, 1959-60. Burton Abstract fellow, 1959. Mem. ABA, Mich. Bar Assn., Franklin Hills Country Club, Order of the Coif, Phi Beta Kappa. Home: The Hills of Lone Pine 4750 N Chipping Gln Bloomfield Hills MI 48302-2390 Office: Honigman Miller Schwartz & Cohn 2290 First National Bldg Detroit MI 48226

SHAFER, ERIC CHRISTOPHER, minister; b. Hanover, Pa., Apr. 10, 1950; s. B. Henry and Doris M. (Von Bergen) S.; m. Kristi L. Owens, Nov. 24, 1973. BA, Muhlenberg Coll., 1972; MDiv, Hamma Sch. Theology, 1976. Ordained to ministry Luth. Ch. Am., 1976. Pastor Holy Trinity Meml. Luth. Ch., Catasauqua, Pa., 1976-83; asst. to Bishop Northeastern Pa. Synod, Wescosville, Pa., 1983-92; staff commn. for fin. support Evang. Luth. Ch. in Am., Chgo., 1988-92, asst. dir. dept. for comm., 1992-93, dir. dept. for comm., 1993—. Contbg. editor The Lutheran mag., 1989-92. Trustee Muhlenberg Coll., Allentown, Pa., 1972-83; chmn. Luth. Film Assn., 1995—; bd. govs. Religious Pub. Rels. Coun., Inc., 1993—; chmn. Comm. Commn., Nat. Coun. Chs. in USA, 1996—, mem. exec. bd., 1996—. Democrat. Avocations: running, computers, photography, travel. Office: Evang Luth Ch in Am 8765 W Higgins Rd Chicago IL 60631-4101

SHAFER, EVERETT EARL, business administration educator; b. Oelwein, Iowa, Apr. 19, 1925; s. Paul Emerson and Maude Blanche (Lovell) S.; m. Kathryn Elaine Rose, Sept. 4, 1949. B.S., Iowa State U., 1948; J.D., U. Iowa, 1951; M.B.A., U. Chgo., 1960. Bar: Iowa bar 1951, Ill. bar 1952. Mem. legal staff Motorola, Inc., Chgo., 1951-54; fin. adminstr. Motorola Fin. Corp., Chgo., 1954-60; asst. treas., credit mgr. Motorola Consumer Products, Inc., Chgo., 1960-68; assoc. prof. bus. adminstrn. Buena Vista Coll., Storm Lake, Iowa, 1968-72; chmn. faculty senate Buena Vista Coll., 1970-71; treas. Admiral Corp., Chgo., 1972-74; asst. treas. Addressograph Multigraph Corp., Cleve., 1975-76; pres., treas. Addressograph Multigraph Finance Corp., 1976-80; prof. bus. adminstrn. Buena Vista Coll., Storm Lake, Iowa, 1980-92, ret., 1992. Trustee Upper Iowa U. Served with USAAF, 1943-45. Decorated D.F.C., Air medal; recipient Outstanding Tchr. award Buena Vista Coll., 1972. Methodist. Home: 314 Forest Dr Bellevue NE 68005-2044 Office: Buena Vista Coll Off Bus Adminstrn Storm Lake IA 50588

SHAFER, JEFFREY RICHARD, federal official, investment banker; b. Lake Forest, Ill., Sept. 10, 1944; s. William McKinley and Betty (Schuchert) S.; m. Mary Louise Terenzio, Sept. 7, 1968; 2 children. AB cum laude, Princeton U., 1966; MPhil, Yale U., 1972, PhD, 1976. Economist internat. fin. divsn. bd. govs. Fed. Res. System, 1972-77, dep. assoc. dir., 1978-81; sr. internat. staff economist Pres.'s Coun. Econ. Advisers, 1977-78; v.p. rsch. function Fed. Res. Bank N.Y., 1981-84; dep. dir. econs. dept. Orgn. Econ. Cooperation and Devel., 1984-93; asst. sec. internat. affairs Dept. of Treasury, Washington, 1993-95; undersec. Internat. Affairs, 1995-97; mng. dir., vice chmn. Solomon Bros. Internat. Ltd., N.Y.C., 1997—. 1st lt. U.S. Army, 1966-68, Vietnam, capt. USAR. Decorated Bronze Star with oak leaf cluster. Office: Solomon Bros Inc 7 World Trade Ctr New York NY 10048-1102

SHAFER, RAYMOND PHILIP, lawyer, business executive; b. New Castle, Pa., Mar. 5, 1917; s. David Philip and Mina Belle (Miller) S.; m. Jane Harris Davies, July 5, 1941; children: Diane Elizabeth, Raymond Philip, Jane Ellen. AB cum laude, Allegheny Coll., 1938, LLD, 1963; LLB, Yale, 1941; numerous hon. LLD degrees. Bar: N.Y., Pa. Asso. firm Winthrop, Stimson, Putnam & Roberts, N.Y.C.; practice law Meadville, Pa., 1945-63; counsel Shafer, Swick, Bailey, Irwin and Stack; dist. atty. Crawford County, 1948-56; mem. Pa. Senate from 50th Dist., 1959-63; lt. gov. Pa., 1963-67; gov. Commonwealth Pa., 1967-71; vis. prof. U. Pa., 1973—; counselor to v.p. of U.S., 1975-77; ptnr., sr. counselor Coopers & Lybrand, 1977-88; former pres. and chmn. bd. trustees Allegheny Coll., Meadville, Pa. Chmn. Nat. Commn. on Marijuana and Drug Abuse; chmn. Nat. Com. U.S.-China Rels.; chmn. Nat. Coun. on Pub. Svc.; world bd. govs. USO; mem. adv. bd. Am. Enterprise Inst.; active charitable, cmty. drives; bd. dirs., vice chmn. Atlantic Coun. U.S., Am.-China Soc.; trustee Cleve. Clinic Found., Freedoms Found; vice chmn. Nat. Legal Ctr. Pub. Interest. With USNR, 1942-45, PTO. Recipient Gold Medal award Soc. Family of Man, 1972, numerous humanitarian and civic awards. Mem. ABA, Pa. Bar Assn., Crawford County Bar Assn. (pres. 1961-63), Council Fgn. Relations, Phi Beta Kappa, Phi Kappa Psi. Republican. Club: Mason (33 deg.). Office: Dunaway & Cross 1146 19th St NW Washington DC 20036-3703 *One makes a living by what one gets. One makes a life by what one gives.*

SHAFER, ROBERT TINSLEY, JR., judge; b. Cin., Sept. 11, 1929; s. Robert Tinsley and Grace Elizabeth (Welsh) S.; m. Barbara Jean Hough, Dec. 27, 1950; children: Richard Hough, Janet Lee Shafer Davis, Charles Welsh. BA, Coll. of Wooster, 1951; JD, U. Cin., 1956. Bar: Fla. 1956, U.S. Ct. Appeals (5th cir.) 1963, U.S. Dist. Ct. (so. dist.) Fla. 1961, U.S. Supreme Ct. 1965. Asst. trust officer 1st Nat. Bank, Ft. Myers, Fla., 1956-57; ptnr. Henderson, Franklin, Starnes & Holt, P.A., Ft. Myers, 1957-77; cir. judge 20th Jud. Cir. State of Fla., Ft. Myers, 1977-92, chief cir. judge, 1985-89, sr. judge, 1992—. Contbr. article to Corp. Law, 1955-56 (Goldsmith Corp. Law prize, 1956). Elder Covenant Presbyn. Ch., 1982-85; mem. jud. commn. Fla. Presbyn. Synod, 1960-63; chmn. Lee County chpt. Red Cross, Ft. Myers, 1963. 2nd lt. USMCR, 1951-53, PTO, Korea. Mem. ABA, Fla. Conf. Cir. Judges (exec. com. 1986-88), Fla. Bar Assn. (bd. govs. Jr. Bar sect. 1961-64), Lee County Bar Assn. (pres. 1968), Am. Judges Assn., Am. Judicature Soc., Nat. Conf. Met. Cts. Calusa Inn of Ct. Republican. Avocations: running races, bicycle racing, bicycle touring, travel, reading. Home: 2704 Shriver Dr Fort Myers FL 33901-5931

SHAFER, SUSAN WRIGHT, retired elementary school educator; b. Ft. Wayne, Dec. 6, 1941; d. George Wesley and Bernece (Spray) Wright; 1 child, Michael R. BS, St. Francis Coll., Ft. Wayne, 1967, MS in Edn., 1969. Tchr. Ft. Wayne Community Schs., 1967-69, Amphitheatre Pub. Schs., Tucson, 1970-96; ret., 1996; Odyssey of the Mind coord. Prince Elem. Sch., Tucson, 1989-91, Future Problem Solving, 1991-95. Tchr. Green Valley (Ariz.) Cmty. Ch., Vacation Bible Sch., 1987-89, dir. vacation bible sch., 1989-93. Mem. AAUW, NEA (life), Delta Kappa Gamma (pres. Alpha Rho chpt.), Alpha Delta Kappa (historian Epsilon chpt. 1990—), Phi Delta Kappa (life, Tucson chpt.). Republican. Methodist. Avocations: reading, traveling, walking. Home: 603 W Placita Nueva Green Valley AZ 85614-2827

SHAFFER, ALFRED GARFIELD (TERRY), service organization executive; b. Sunbury, Pa., Jan. 5, 1939; d. Alfred G. and Betty Marjorie (Vogel) S.; m. Nancy Jane Dawson, Aug. 29, 1976. BS, Susquehanna U., 1961. Cert. tchr., Pa. Tchr., Danville Sch. Dist. (Pa.), 1962-69; mgr. club service Kiwanis Internat., Chgo., 1969-74, dir. program devel., 1974-81, dir. program services, Indpls., 1982-85, dir. spl. services, 1985-87, asst. sec. for spl. svcs., 1987-88, asst. to internat. sec., 1988-94, internat. sec. 1994—; corp. affairs cons. Nat. Easter Seal Soc., Chgo., 1981-82; adminstr. Circle K Internat., Chgo., 1982; mem. Pres.'s Com. on Employment of Handicapped, 1983-86. Chmn. adv. council 70001 Ltd., Indpls., 1984-86; mem. adv. bd. Salvation Army, Indpls, 1996—. Recipient Gold Key of Svc., Pa. Dist. Key Clubs, 1964. Lutheran. Mem. Ind. Assn. Event Profls., Indpls. Athletic Club, 500 Festival Assocs., Kiwanis (pres. Selinsgrove, Pa. 1964, lt. gov. Pa. 1966-67, pres. Chgo. 1970-72, pres. Northwest Indpls. 1991-92, Outstanding Svc. award 1981, Kiwanian of Yr. 1966, 85). Home: 5688 Broadway St Indianapolis IN 46220-3073 Office: Kiwanis International 3636 Woodview Trce Indianapolis IN 46268-1168

SHAFFER, BERNARD WILLIAM, mechanical and aerospace engineering educator; b. N.Y.C., Aug. 7, 1924; s. Abraham and Eva (Ellinsky) S.; m. Florence Solow, Feb. 23, 1947 (dec. Oct. 29, 1986); children: Janet Ilene, Roberta Franceen. B in Mech. Engring., CCNY, 1944; MS in Mech. Engring., Case Inst. Tech., 1947; PhD, Brown U., 1951. Registered profl. engr., N.Y., R.I. Aero. rsch. scientist Flight Propulsion Rsch. NACA (now NASA), Cleve., 1944-47; spl. lectr. applied mechanics Case Inst. Tech., Cleve., 1946-47; rsch. assoc., grad. div. applied math. and engring., instr. Brown U., Providence, 1947-50; asst. prof. mech. engring. NYU, N.Y.C., 1950-53, assoc. prof., 1953-58, prof., project dir. rsch. div., 1958-73; prof. dept. mech. and aerospace engring. Poly. U., Bklyn. and Farmingdale, N.Y., 1973-93; prof. emeritus Poly. U., Bklyn. and Farmingdale, 1993—; cons. in field; mem. adv. coun. Coll. Aeros., N.Y.C., 1982—; vis. rsch. prof. mech. engring. Fla. Atlantic U., Boca Raton, 1992, Disting. vis. rsch. prof., 1993-95. Contbr. articles to profl. jours. Bd. dirs. Harbor Hills Civic Assn., Great Neck, N.Y., 1968-71. With USAAF, 1944-47. Recipient various govt. grants. Fellow ASME (Richards Meml. award 1968), AIAA (assoc.); mem. Sigma Xi, Tau Beta Pi, Pi Tau Sigma. Avocations: golf, swimming. Home and Office: 18 Old Field Ln Great Neck NY 11020-1265

SHAFFER, DAVID JAMES, lawyer; b. Springfield, Ohio, July 30, 1958; s. Frank James Shaffer and Martha Isabelle (Hardman) Matthews; m. Julie Renee Cohen, Oct. 8, 1995; 1 child, Brynn Danielle. BA, Wittenberg U., 1980; JD, Stanford U., 1983. Bar: Calif. 1984, U.S. Dist. Ct. (no. and ea. dists.) Calif. 1984, U.S. Ct. Appeals (9th cir.) 1984, U.S. Dist. Ct. (so. dist.) Calif. 1985, U.S. Dist. Ct. (we. dist.) Wash. 1986, D.C. 1988, U.S. Dist. Ct. D.C. 1988, U.S. Ct. Appeals (D.C. cir.) 1988, U.S. Dist. Ct. (no. dist.) Tex. 1991, U.S. Supreme Ct. 1993, Md. 1994, U.S. Dist. Ct. Md. 1997. Supr. field ops. U.S. Census Bur., Columbus, Ohio, 1980; legal intern Natural Resources Def. Coun., Inc., San Francisco, 1982-83; assoc. Gibson, Dunn & Crutcher, San Jose, Calif., 1983; law clk. to Judge Betty B. Fletcher, U.S. Ct. Appeals for 9th Cir., Seattle, 1983-84; assoc. Gibson, Dunn & Crutcher, San Jose, 1984-87, Arnold & Porter, Washington, 1987-92; ptnr. Semmes, Bowen & Semmes, Washington, 1992-94, Arter & Hadden, Washington, 1995—. Campaign mgr. Clark County Dem. Party, Springfield, 1978-80; organizer Citizens for Sensible County Planning, Fairfax, Va., 1989-94. Alumni scholar Wittenberg U., 1976. Mem. ABA, FBA (chmn. EEO com. 1992-94, individual rights and responsibilities 1994-95, co-chmn. alt. dispute resolution 1995—, mem. governing bd. labor law and labor rels. sect., editor newsletter Labouring Oar, Outstanding Svc. award 1992), D.C. Bar Assn., Calif. Bar Assn., Order of Coif. Avocations: music, hiking, nature study. Office: Arter & Hadden 1801 K St NW Ste 400K Washington DC 20006-1301

SHAFFER, DEBORAH, nurse; b. Tampa, Fla., Jan. 20, 1954; d. Frank Solomon and Mary Louise (Swann) Shaffer; children: Danny, Dionne. LPN, Suwanee-Hamilton Nursing Sch., Live Oak, Fla., 1984; student, Hillsborough CC, 1992—. LPN, Fla. Author (short stories) Skippy Goes to Ybor Square, Danny's Journey; also poems and songs. Active Neighborhood Crime Watch, Parents Without Ptnrs., The Spring, Literacy Vols. Am. Avocations: writing, painting, photography, gardening, guitar.

SHAFFER, DOROTHY BROWNE, retired mathematician, educator; b. Vienna, Austria, Feb. 12, 1923; d. Hermann and Steffy (Hermann) Browne; arrived U.S., 1940; m. Lloyd Hamilton Shaffer, July 25, 1943 (dec. 1978); children: Deborah Lee, Diana Louise, Dorothy Leslie. AB, Bryn Mawr Coll., 1943; MA, Harvard U., 1945, PhD, 1962. Mathematician, MIT, Cambridge, 1945-47; tchg. fellow, research asso., Harvard U., Cambridge, 1947-48; asso. mathematician Cornell Aeronautical Lab, Buffalo, N.Y., 1952-56; mathematician Dunlap & Assoc., Stamford, Conn., 1958-60; lectr. grad. engring. U. of Conn. at Stamford, 1962; prof. math Fairfield (Conn.) U., 1963-92, prof. emeritus, 1992—; vis. prof. Imperial Coll. Sci. and Tech., London, fall 1978, U. Md., College Park, spring 1981; vis. prof. U. Calif.-San Diego, summer 1981; vis. scholar, 1986; NSF faculty fellow IBM-T.J. Watson Research Center, Yorktown Heights, N.Y., 1979. Contbr. numerous papers in math. analysis. Mem. Am. Math. Soc., Math. Assn. of Am., Assn. for Women in Math., London Math. Soc. Achievement include patent in Viscosity Stabilized Solar Pond. Home: 156 Intervale Rd Stamford CT 06905-1311 Office: Fairfield U Dept Math & Computer Sci Fairfield CT 06430

SHAFFER, GAIL DOROTHY, secondary education educator; b. Summit, N.J., May 7, 1936; d. Franklin Clifford Jr. and Mildred Edna (Burgmiller) S. AB, Hood Coll., 1958. Tchr. Sherman Sch., Cranford, N.J., 1959-60, Gov. Livingston High Sch., Berkeley Heights, N.J., 1960—. Vol. intake worker Covenant House, N.Y.C., 1982-92, spkrs. bur., 1986—, bd. dirs., Newark, 1993—; mem. juvenile conf. Family Ct. Union County, Elizabeth, N.J., 1968—; project dir. Berkeley Heights (N.J.) Alliance Against Drugs and Alcohol, 1990-95; active Berkeley Heights Youth Com., 1960-65. Named Berkeley Heights Citizen of Yr. by Jr. C. of C., Speaker of Yr. by Covenant House Corp., Vol. of Yr. by Covenent House, Union County Tchr. of Yr., 1992-93, N.J. State Tchr. of Yr., 1992-93. Mem. DAR (Beacon Fire chpt.), ASCID, NEA, N.J. Edn. Assn., N.J. State Tchrs. of the Yr. (pres.), Union County Edn. Assn. Republican. Methodist. Avocations: reading, travel, U.S. history, needlework, Victoriana. Home: 522 Plainfield Ave Berkeley Heights NJ 07922-1919 also: 7 Embury Ave Ocean Grove NJ 07756-1354 Office: Gov Livingston High Sch 175 Watchung Blvd Berkeley Heights NJ 07922-2726

SHAFFER, JAMES BURGESS, communications executive; b. Boston, May 6, 1945; s. Robert Howard and Marjorie Jane (Fitch) S.; m. Lynn Elliott Eitzen, June 3, 1967; children: Derek Bruce, Ryan Brooke. B.S. in Mech. Engring, Purdue U., 1967; M.B.A., Ind. U., 1969. Staff engr. Aerospace Research Applications Center, Bloomington, Ind., 1967-69; ops. analyst Mpls. Star & Tribune Co., 1970-71, research planning analyst, 1972-73, research planning mgr., 1974, dir. acctg., 1975-77; pres., pub. Stromberg Publs., Inc. subs., Ellicott City, Md., 1977-79; sr. v.p., assoc. pub. Buffalo Courier-Express Co., Inc. subs., 1979-82; v.p., chief fin. officer L.A. Times, 1983-84, v.p. fin. and planning, 1985-89; exec. v.p. The Sun-Times Co., 1989-91; pres., chief exec. officer Guy Gannett COmmunications, Portland, Maine, 1991—; vice-chmn. bd. dirs. Better Bus. Bur. Western N.Y., 1980. Trustee Wildwood Sch., Santa Monica, Calif., 1987; mem. bd. trustees Portland (Maine) Symphony , 1993-95; bd. dirs. Maine Coalition Excellence in Edn., 1993—, Conf. & Visitors Bur., 1993—. Home: 12 Russell Rd Cumb Foreside ME 04110-1430 Office: Guy Gannett Comm Box 15277 1 City Ctr Portland ME 04112-5277

SHAFFER, JAY CHRISTOPHER, lawyer; b. Brookville, Pa., Sept. 18, 1947; s. John Rienard and Laverne (Berding) S.; m. Janice Rita McKenney, May 24, 1972; 1 child, Justin. BA, Ohio State U., 1969; JD, Harvard U., 1974. Bar: Ohio 1974, U.S. Supreme Ct. 1978. Atty. office gen. counsel FTC, Washington, 1974-77; counsel subcom. on oversight, interstate and fgn. com. U.S. Ho. of Reps., Washington, 1977-79; atty. antitrust div. U.S. Dept. of Justice, Washington, 1979-82, dep. dir. policy planning antitrust div., 1982-84, chief legal adv. unit antitrust div., 1984-86; dep. dir. bur. competition FTC, Washington, 1986-88; dep. gen. counsel Office of Gen. Counsel FTC, Washington, 1988—. Served to sgt. U.S. Army, 1970-72, Korea. Mem. ABA, Fed. Bar Assn. Home: 7016 Leewood Forest Dr Springfield VA 22151-3930 Office: FTC Rm 564 Washington DC 20580

SHAFFER, JEROME ARTHUR, philosophy educator; b. N.Y.C., Apr. 2, 1929; s. Joseph and Beatrice (Leibowitz) S.; m. Olivia Anne Connery, Sept. 3, 1960 (div. 1985); children: Diana, David; m. Eliana Bar-shalom, Aug. 7, 1994. BA, Cornell U., 1950; PhD, Princeton U., 1952; MA in Marital and Family Therapy, U. Conn., 1996. Prof. philosophy Swarthmore (Pa.) Coll., 1955-67; prof. U. Conn., Storrs, 1967-94, prof. emeritus, 1994—, head dept. philosophy, 1976-94; individual, marital, and family therapist, 1995—; exec. sec. Council Philos. Studies, 1965-72. Author: The Philosophy of Mind, 1968, Violence, 1970, Reality, Knowledge, and Value, 1971; contbr. articles to profl. jours. Served with U.S. Army, 1953-55. Fulbright fellow, 1952-53, fellow Ctr. for Advanced Study Behavioral Scis., 1963-64, NEH sr. fellow, 1973-74, Cambridge Clare Hall vis. fellow, 1987. Mem. Am. Philos. Assn., Phi Beta Kappa, Phi Kappa Phi. Home: 36 Clear View Dr Mansfield Center CT 06250-1608 Office: U Conn Dept Philosophy # U-54 Storrs CT 06268

SHAFFER, OREN GEORGE, manufacturing company executive; b. Sharpsville, Pa., Aug. 13, 1942; s. Oren G. and Alice Marie (Miller) S.; m. Evelyne Soussan, Oct. 2, 1965; children: Kathleen R., Oren O. BSBA, U. Calif., Berkeley, 1968; MS, MIT, 1985. Mem. internal tng. squad Goodyear Tire and Rubber Co., Akron, Ohio, 1968-69, asst. comptr., 1983-84, v.p., treas., 1985-87, exec. v.p., chief fin. officer, 1987—; mem. fin. staff Goodyear SA, Diegem, Belgium, 1969-70, fin. mgr. Benelux, 1970-75; chief fin. officer Goodyear France, Paris, 1975-80, pres., 1981-83; chief fin. officer Goodyear Tyre and Rubber Co., Wolverhampton, Eng., 1980-81. bd. dirs. Akron Priority Corp., pres. 1987. Mem. Nat. Assn. Accts., Fin. Execs. Inst., Officer's Conf. Group. Clubs: Firestone Country, Portage Country (Akron). Office: Goodyear Tire & Rubber Co 1144 E Market St Akron OH 44316-1000 Address: 2409 5th St Boulder CO 80304-3904

SHAFFER, PAUL, musician, bandleader; b. Thunder Bay, Ont., Can., Nov. 28, 1949; m. Cathy Vasapoli; 1 child, Victoria Lily. Mem. band Fabulous Fugitives, Thunder Bay, 1964-68; keyboardist NBC's Saturday Night Live, 1975-80; musical dir. Blues Bros. Band, 1978-79; leader, keyboardist The World's Most Dangerous Band NBC's Late Night with David Letterman, 1982-1993; music director The Late Show with David Letterman (CBS), 1993—. Mus. dir. (Toronto, Ont. prodn.) Godspell, 1972; musician: (N.Y.C. prodn.) The Magic Show, 1974, (Gilda Radner's mus. revue, also co-composer) Live in New York, 1979, (off-Broadway prodn.) Leader of the Pack, 1984; rec. artist, keyboardist: (with Barry Manilow) This One's For You, 1976, (with National Lampoon) Good-Bye Pop, 1976, (with the Jeff Healey Band) Feel This, 1977, (Blues Bros.) Briefcase Full of Blues, 1978, Made in America, 1980, (with Jaon Armatrading) Me Myself, 1980, (with Nina Hagen) Nunsexmonkrock, 1980, (with Diana Ross) Silk Electric, 1981, (with Yoko Ono) It's Alright, 1982, (Honey Drippers) The Honey Drippers, 1985, (film soundtrack) The Karate Kid II, 1986, (with Dion, Ben. E. King, Bobby Womack and Wilson Pickett) Coast to Coast, 1991, (with Blues Traveler) Save His Soul, 1993, (with the Party Boys of Rock 'n' Roll) The World's Most Dangerous Party, 1993; regular mem. cast (TV series) A Year at the Top, 1977; film appearances include This Is Spinal Tap, 1984; solo album Coast to Coast, 1989 (2 Grammy nominations). Office: Late Show w/ David Letterman CBS 530 W 57th St New York NY 10019-2902*

SHAFFER, PAUL E., retired banker; b. Rockford, Ohio, Aug. 3, 1926; s. Randall J. and Zelah V. (Alspaugh) S.; m. Dorothy L. Schumm, June 26, 1951; children: Paula Kay, Patti Lee. Grad., U. Wis. Sch. Banking, 1954; cert., Am. Inst. Banking; DHL (hon.), Purdue U., 1985. With Rockford Nat. Bank, 1945-48; asst. nat. bank examiner Treasury Dept., 1948-52; with Ft. Wayne (Ind.) Nat. Bank, 1952-65, from exec. v.p. to chmn., CEO, 1965-70, chmn., CEO, 1970-92, chmn. emeritus, 1993-95, ret., 1995; ret., 1996; bd. dirs. Old First Nat. Bank, Bluffton, Ind. Pres. Downtown Fort Wayne Assn., 1965, Credit Bur., Fort Wayne, 1962, Jr. Achievement, 1967-69; treas. Fort Wayne Better Bus. Bur., 1968, Ind.-Purdue Devel. Fund; mem. regional adv. com. Comptroller Currency, 1968-70; commr. Ft. Wayne Conv. and Tourism Authority.; past bd. dirs. Fort Wayne Conv. Bur., Fort Wayne

Philharmonic Orch., Parkview Meml. Hosp.; bd. dirs. Caylor-Nickel Hosp., Ft. Wayne campus Ind. U., Ind.-Purdue Found., Taxpayers Research Assn.; past bd. dirs. United Community Services, chmn. drive, 1970-71; past bd. dirs. Fort Wayne YMCA, v.p., 1964-67; bd. adviser Ind. U.-Purdue U., Ft. Wayne; mem. fin. adv. bd. Luth. Social Services; bd. govs. Assn. Colls. Ind.; chmn. vol. com. U.S. Savs. Bonds, Allen County, Ind., numerous other civic activities. Served with USAAF, 1945. Mem. Am. Inst. Banking (past pres. Ft. Wayne chpt.), Am. Bankers Assn. (governing coun. 1978-79), Ind. Bankers Assn. (past pres., bd. dirs.), Ft. Wayne C. of C. (past v.p., bd. dirs.), Ind. C. of C. (state dir.), Execs. Club (past pres.), Ft. Wayne Country Club, Summit Club, Quest Club, Ft. Wayne Press Club, Mad Anthonys Club, Sycamore Hills Country Club, Masons, Shriners. Home: 11132 Carnoustie Ln Fort Wayne IN 46804-9014

SHAFFER, PETER LEVIN, playwright; b. Liverpool, Eng., May 15, 1926; s. Jack and Reka (Fredman) S. BA, Cambridge U., Eng., 1950. Conscript coal mines, Eng., 1944-47; with N.Y. Pub. Libr., N.Y.C., 1951-54, Bosey & Hawkes, London, 1954-55; lit. critic Truth, 1956-57; music critic Time and Tide, 1961-62; vis. prof. contemporary drama Oxford (Eng.) U., 1994-95. Author: (plays) Five Finger Exercise, 1958 (Evening Standard Drama award 1958, N.Y. Drama Critics Cir. award 1960), The Private Ear, 1962, The Public Eye, 1962, It's About Cinderella, 1963, The Royal Hunt of the Sun, 1964, Black Comedy, 1965, The White Liars, 1967, The Battle of Shrivings, 1970, Equus, 1973 (Best Play Tony award 1975, Outer Critics Cir. Best Play award 1975), Amadeus, 1979 (Evening Standard Drama award 1979, London Drama Critics award 1979, Best Play Tony award 1980, Plays and Players Best Play award 1980), Yonadab, 1985, Lettice and Lovage, 1987 (Evening Standard Drama award 1988), The Gift of the Gorgon, 1992, (screenplays) Follow Me!, 1971, Equus, 1977 (Acad. award nomination for best screenplay adaptation 1977), Amadeus, 1984 (Acad. award for best screenplay adaptation 1984), (TV plays) The Salt Land, 1955, Balance of Terror, 1957, (radio plays) The Prodigal Father, 1955, Whom Do I Have the Honor of Addressing?, 1989, (novels, with Anthony Shaffer) The Woman in the Wardrobe, 1951, How Doth the Little Crocodile?, 1952, Withered Murder, 1955. Decorated comdr. Order Brit. Empire, 1987; recipient Hamburg Shakespeare prize, 1987, William Inge award for disting. achievement in Am. theatre, 1992. Fellow Royal Soc. Lt. (London chpt.). Address: The Lantz Office 888 7th Sve Ste 2500 New York NY 10010-6000*

SHAFFER, RICHARD JAMES, lawyer, former manufacturing company executive; b. Pe Ell, Wash., Jan. 26, 1931; s. Richard Humphrys and Laura Rose (Faas) S.; m. Donna M. Smith, May 13, 1956; children: Leslie Lauren Shaffer Litsinger, Stephanie Jane Athenton. B.A., U. Wash.; LL.B., Southwestern U. Bar: Calif. Vice pres., gen. counsel, sec. NI, Inc., Long Beach, Calif., 1974-89; gen. counsel Masco Bldg. Products Corp., Long Beach, 1985-89; pvt. practice Huntington Beach, Calif., 1989—; mem. ltd. liability co. drafting com. and task force Calif. State Bar, 1992-94; lectr. on ltd. liability cos. Trustee Ocean View Sch. Dist., 1965-73, pres., 1966, 73; mem. fin. adv. com. Orange Coast Coll., 1966; mem. Long Beach Local Devel. Corp., 1978-89, Calif. Senate Commn. on Corp. Governance, Shareholders' Rights and Securities Transactions, 1986—, chmn. drafting com. ltd. liability co. act for senate com., 1991-93; mem. City of Huntington Beach Pers. Commn., 1996—. Mem. ABA, Nat. Assn. Securities Dealers (bd. arbitrators), Calif. Bar Assn. (exec. com. corp. law dept. com. bus. sect. 1981-88, mem. drafting com. ltd. liability co. act), Orange County Bar Assn., Huntington Harbour Yacht Club, Wanderlust Skiers of Huntington Harbour, Huntington Harbour Ski Club.

SHAFFER, RUSSELL K., advertising agency executive; b. N.Y.C., Apr. 12, 1933; s. Russell Parl and Alice (Cole) S.; m. Leslie Van Nostrand, July 28, 1956; children—Cole Van Nostrand, Wendel L., Daniel W., Russell W. A.B., Brown U., 1954; M.B.A., Harvard U., 1958. Account exec. McCann-Erickson, N.Y.C., 1958-62; account supr. Grey Advt., N.Y.C., 1962-66; exec. v.p. Richard K. Manoff, Inc., N.Y.C., 1966-71; pres. Richard K. Manoff, Inc., 1971-77, also dir.; pres. David H. Mann, Inc., 1977-80; exec. v.p. F.W. Free Inc. (now Laurance, Charles & Free, Inc.), N.Y.C., 1980-86; sr. v.p. SSC&B, N.Y.C., 1986—. Served to lt. USNR, 1954-56. Home: 2 Richards Ave Norwalk CT 06854-2318 Office: One Dag Hammarskjold Pla New York NY 10017

SHAFFER, SHEILA WEEKES, mathematics educator; b. Syracuse, N.Y., Oct. 20, 1957; d. Carroll Watson and Reina Lou (Yonkers) Judd; m. Jason Craig Shaffer, June 4, 1983 (div. Sept. 1994). BA, SUNY, Albany, 1979, MS, 1983. Cert. tchr. English/Math., N.Y.; cert. advanced prof. in English and Math, Md. English tchr. Cortland (N.Y.) HS, 1979-81; English tchr. Prince George's County, Upper Marlboro, Md., 1984-86, math. tchr., 1986-87, math. tchr./coord., 1990-95, 1996—; math./English tchr. Camden HS, St. Mary's, Ga., 1988-90; math tchr. Frederick County, Va., 1995-96; mem. SAT com. The Coll. Bd., N.Y.C., 1993-96. Mem. Nat. Coun. Tchrs. Math. Avocations: reading, hiking, gardening. Office: Potomac High Sch 5211 Boydell Ave Oxon Hill MD 20745-3718

SHAFFER, SHERRILL LYNN, economist; b. Tyler, Tex., Aug. 1, 1952; s. Douglas Marsene and Ethel Elizabeth (Green) S.; m. Margaret Jane Ahrens, Jun 20, 1987; 1 child, David Carsten. BA, Rice U., 1974; MA, Stanford U., 1978, PhD, 1981. Rsch. asst. Stanford (Calif.) U., 1976-79, instr., 1979-80; from economist to chief Fed. Res. Bank N.Y., N.Y.C., 1980-88; from rsch. officer/economist to asst. v.p./discount officer Fed. Res. Bank Phila., 1988-97; John A. Guthrie disting. prof. banking and fin. svcs. U. Wyo., 1997—; violinist solo and with orchs., Calif., N.Y., 1976-88; cons. asst. Rosse & Olszewski, Palo Alto, Calif., 1978-80. Assoc. editor to editor Jour. Econs. and Bus., 1993—; contbr. numerous articles to profl. jours. Sec. bd. dirs. N.Y. Arts Group, N.Y.C., 1982-83; mem. program com. So. Fin. Assn., 1996; exec. adv. coun. mem. dept. fin. Temple U.; bd. dirs. artist selection com. Tri-County Concerts Assn., 1996-97. Recipient Messier cert. Astronomical League, 1993. Mem. AAAS, Am. Econ. Assn., Am. Math. Soc., Math. Assn. Am., N.Am. Econs. and Fin. Assn., Indsl. Orgn. Soc., N.Y. Acad. Scis., Fin. Mgmt. Assn. (program com. 1991), So. Fin. Assn. (program com. 1996), Delaware Valley Amateur Astronomers (observing chmn. 1993, publicity chmn. 1994, 95, 96). Episcopalian. Avocations: hiking, theology, number theory, astronomy, computer programming. Home: 30 Silver Spur Rd Laramie WY 82070 Office: Dept Econs and Fin U Wyo PO Box 3985 Laramie WY 82071-3985

SHAFFER, THOMAS LINDSAY, lawyer, educator; b. Billings, Mont., Apr. 4, 1934; s. Cecil Burdette and Margaret Jeanne (Parker) S.; m. Nancy Jane Lehr, Mar. 19, 1954; children: Thomas, Francis, Joseph, Daniel, Brian, Mary, Andrew, Edward. B.A., U. Albuquerque, 1958; J.D., U. Notre Dame, 1961; LL.D., St. Mary's U., 1983. Bar: Ind. 1961. Assoc. Barnes, Hickam, Pantzer, & Boyd, Indpls., 1961-63; prof. law U. Notre Dame, Ind., 1963-80, assoc. dean, 1969-71, dean, 1971-75, Robert and Marion Short prof., 1988—; supervising atty. Notre Dame Legal Aid Clinic, 1991—; prof. law Washington and Lee U., 1980-87, Robert E.R. Huntley prof. law, 1987-88; vis. prof. UCLA, 1970-71, U. Va., 1975-76, U. Maine, 1982, 87, Boston Coll., 1992; bd. dirs. Cornerstone Found.; mem. Ind. Constl. Revision Commn., 1969-70, Ind. Trust Code Study Commn., 1968-71; reporter Ind. Jud. Conf., 1963, 67. Author: Death, Property, and Lawyers, 1970, The Planning and Drafting of Wills and Trusts, 1972, 3d edit., 1991, Legal Interviewing and Counseling, 1976, 2d edit., 1987, On Being a Christian and a Lawyer, 1981, American Legal Ethics, 1985, Faith and the Professions, 1987, American Lawyers and Their Communities, 1991; co-author: Lawyers, Law Students, and People, 1977, Cases in Legal Interviewing and Counseling, 1980, Property Cases, Materials and Problems, 1992, Lawyers, Clients, and Moral Responsibility, 1994; co-editor: The Mentally Retarded Citizen and the Law, 1976; contbr. articles to legal jours. Served with USAF, 1953-57. Frances Lewis scholar Washington and Lee U., 1979; recipient Emil Brown Found. Preventive Law prize, 1966, Presdl. citation U. Notre Dame, 1975, St. Thomas More award St. Mary's U., 1983, Law medal Gonzaga U., 1991, Jour. Law and Religion award, 1993. Mem. Ind. State Bar Assn., Soc. Christian Ethics, Jewish Law Assn., Nat. Lawyers Assn. Roman Catholic. Home: 1865 Champlain Dr Niles MI 49120-8935 Office: Notre Dame Legal Aid Clinic 725 Howard St South Bend IN 46617-1529

SHAFFNER, PATRICK NOEL, architectural engineering executive; b. Burlington, N.C., Nov. 1, 1939; s. Samuel Hubert and Martha Jane (Noel) Shaffner; m. Patricia Anne Anders, June 12, 1961; children: Scott Anders, Kimberly Page, Melissa Hope. BS, Va. Poly. and State U., 1961. Registered profl. engr., Va. and others. Structural engr. Hayes, Seay, Mattern & Mattern, Roanoke, Va., 1963-68; sr. structural engr. Sherertz & Franklin, Roanoke, 1968-72; ptnr. Sherertz, Franklin, Crawford, Shaffner, Roanoke, 1972-87; chmn., CEO Sherertz, Franklin, Crawford, Shaffner, Inc., Roanoke, 1988—. Bd. dirs. Delta Dental, Mill Mt. Theatre, Va. Tech. Coll. Engring. Com. 100, Am. Heart Assn.; with ARC. Capt. Corps. Engrs., U.S. Army, 1961-63. Paul Harris fellow. Fellow ASCE; mem. AIA (assoc.), Soc. Am. Mil. Engrs., Roanoke Regional C. of C. (Small Bus. Person of Yr. 1991), Rotary (pres. Roanoke club 1986). Republican. Baptist. Lodge: Rotary (Roanoke) (pres. 1986). Home: 2635 Turnberry Rd Salem VA 24153-7483 Office: Sherertz Franklin Crawford Shaffner Inc 305 S Jefferson St Roanoke VA 24011-2003

SHAFRAN, HANK, public relations executive; b. Boston, Nov. 13, 1945; s. Milton and Pauline (Hoffman) S.; m. Jane D. Shafran, Aug. 11, 1969 (div. Apr. 1982); children: Michael, Debra; m. Antoinette M. Delisi, July 26, 1987. BS, Boston U., 1968. Account exec. Burson-Marsteller, N.Y.C., 1968-71; exec. asst. to dir. Gov.'s Com. on Criminal Justice, Boston, 1971-77; dir. communications Computer Libr. Systems Inc., Newton, Mass., 1977-78; dir. pub. rels. Arnold & Co., Boston, 1979-83; dep. commr. Mass. Dept. Commerce, Boston, 1983-84; exec. v.p., ptnr. Cone Comms., Boston, 1984-91; comms. and pub. rels. cons., 1991—; dir. mktg. Bingham, Dana & Gould, LLP, Boston, 1995—. V.p. Ronald McDonald House, Brookline, Mass., 1979—. Mem. Counselors Acad. Pub. Rels. Soc. Am., New England Broadcasting Assn., Advt. Club of Greater Boston, Publicity Club New England. Democrat. Jewish. Avocation: music.

SHAFRITZ, DAVID ANDREW, physician, research scientist; b. Phila., Oct. 5, 1940; s. Saul and Ethel (Kohn) S.; m. Sharon C. Klemow, Aug. 16, 1964; children: Gregory S., Adam B., Keith M. AB in Chemistry with honors, U. Pa., 1962, MD, 1966. Diplomate Nat. Bd. Med. Examiners, Am. Bd. Internal Medicine. Intern, then asst. resident U. Md. Hosp., Balt., 1966-68; rsch. assoc. NIH, Bethesda, Md., 1968-71; clin. and rsch. fellow Mass. Gen. Hosp., Boston, 1971-73; instr. Harvard Med. Sch., Boston, 1971-73, asst. prof. medicine, 1973; asst. prof. medicine and cell biology Albert Einstein Coll. Medicine, Yeshiva U., Bronx, N.Y., 1973-76, assoc. prof., 1976-81, prof. medicine and cell biology, 1981—, dir. Marion Bessin Liver Rsch. Ctr., 1985—, Herman Lapota prof. liver disease rsch., 1992—; cons. integrated Genetics, Inc., Framingham, Mass., 1981-86, Immuno, Vienna, Austria, 1986-91, Innovir, Inc., N.Y.C., 1991—, Eugenetech Internat., Inc., Ramsey, N.J., 1991-93; temp. advisor WHO, Geneva, 1983; mem. Nat. Com. for Clin. Lab. Stds., Villanova Pa., 1983—, Renaissance Techs., 1996—, Affymetrix, Inc., 1997—; sci. adv. bd. com. liver cancer program Inst. for Cancer Rsch., Fox Chase and Phila., 1987—, mem. rev. panel C. study sect. Nat. Inst. Diabetes and Digestive Kidney Diseases, 1988-92; mem. cen. coord. com. Liver Tissue Procurement and Distbn. Sys., 1986—, Nat. Inst. Health Metabolic Pathology Study sect., 1995—; mem. Nat. Bd. Med. Examiners and U.S. Med. Exam. Com., 1996—. Co-author: The Liver: Biology and Pathobiology, 1982, 3rd edit., 1993, Hepatobiliary Diseases, 1991; assoc. editor Hepatology, 1981-86; mem. editl. bd. Jour. Med. Virology, 1982-93, Hepatology, 1990—, Jour. Virology, 1992—; contbr. numerous rsch. articles and revs. to profl. publs.; contbr. chpts. to books; patentee in field. Trustee Westchester Jewish Ctr., Mamaroneck, N.Y., 1980-86. Lt. comdr. USPHS, 1968-71. Recipient Merck award U. Pa., 1962, Morton McCutcheon Meml. Rsch. prize Sch. Medicine, 1966, Career Scientist award Irma T. Hirschl Trust, N.Y.C., 1974-79, NIH Merit award, 1994; European Molecular Biology Orgn. fellow, 1978; recipient Rsch. Career Devel. award NIH, 1975-80, spl. rsch. fellow, 1971-73, rsch. grantee, 1974—. Mem. Am. Assn. for Study of Liver Diseases, Internat. Assn. for Study of Liver, Am. Gastroenterol. Assn., Am. soc. Biochemistry and Molecular Biology, Am. Soc. Investigative Pathology, Am. Soc. Clin. Investigation, Assn. Am. Physicians, N.Y. Acad. Scis., Harvey Soc., Interurban Clin. Club (sec./treas. 1996—). Democrat. Jewish. Avocations: jogging, tennis. Home: 4 Pheasant Run Larchmont NY 10538-3423 Office: Yeshiva U Albert Einstein Coll Med Marion Bessin Liver Rsch Ctr 1300 Morris Park Ave Bronx NY 10461-1926

SHAFTMAN, FREDRICK KRISCH, telephone communication executive, lawyer; b. Roanoke, Va., Apr. 9, 1948; s. Sydney and Rosalie (Krisch) S.; m. Diane Hasson, Dec. 27, 1970; children: Stephanie, Emily. BSBA, U. Ala., 1970, JD, 1973. Bar: Va. 1973. Gen. counsel Bell South Communication Systems (formerly Universal Communication Systems, Inc.), Roanoke, 1973-74, v.p., gen. counsel, 1974-79, pres., 1979-84, chief exec. officer, 1984—, also bd. dirs.; v.p. Am. Motor Inns, Inc. Bd. dirs. United Way of Roanoke Valley, Roanoke Mill Mountain Zoo; trustee North Cross Country Day Sch., Roanoke, Roanoke Valley Sci. Mus., Roanoke Valley Red Cross. Recipient Pres.'s Disting. Service award N.Am. Telecommunication Assn., 1985, Achievement award United Jewish Assn., 1989. Mem. N.Am. Telephone Assn. (bd. dirs.), Western Va. Better Bus. Bur. (bd. dirs.), ABA, Va. State Bar Assn. Lodge: Rotary. Office: Bellsouth Comm Systems 1936 Blue Hills Dr NE Roanoke VA 24012-8608

SHAFTO, ROBERT AUSTIN, insurance company executive; b. Council Bluffs, Iowa, Sept. 15, 1935; s. Glen Granville and Blanche (Radigan) S.; m. Jeanette DeFino, Dec. 17, 1954; children: Robert, Dennis, Teri, Shari, Michael. BS in Actuarial Sci., Drake U., Des Moines, 1959. Mgr. computer svcs. Guarantee Mut. Life Ins. Co., Omaha, 1959-65; v.p. Beta div. Electronic Data Systems, Dallas, 1965-71; from 2d v.p. to v.p. for computer systems devel. and info. svcs. New England Mutual Life Ins. Co., Boston, 1972-75, sr. v.p. policy holder and computer svcs., 1975-81, adminstrv. v.p., 1981-82, exec. v.p. individual ins. ops., 1982-86, exec. v.p. ins. and employee benefits ops., 1986-88, pres. ins. and personal fin. svcs., 1988-90, pres., chief oper. officer, 1990-92, pres., CEO, 1992-93, pres., CEO, chmn., 1993—, also bd. dirs.; bd. dirs., pres. New Eng. Variable Life, Fleet Bank of Mass., Am. Coun. Life Ins. Bd. overseers Children's Hosp., Boston, 1989—; mem. corp. Dana Farber Cancer Inst., Northwestern U.; bd. dirs. United Way of Mass; trustee Am. Coll. Mem. Greater Boston C. of C. (bd. dirs.). Roman Catholic. Avocations: tennis, golf, scuba diving, jogging. Office: New Eng Mut Life Ins Co 501 Boylston St Boston MA 02116-3706*

SHAGAM, MARVIN HÜCKEL-BERRI, private school educator; b. Monongalia, W.Va.; s. Lewis and Clara (Shagam) S. AB magna cum laude, Washington and Jefferson Coll., 1947; postgrad., Harvard Law Sch., 1947-48, Oxford (Eng.) U., 1948-51. Tchr. Mount House Sch., Tavistock, Eng., 1951-53, Williston Jr. Sch., Easthampton, Mass., 1953-55, Westtown (Pa.) Sch., 1955-58, The Thacher Sch., Ojai, Calif., 1958—; English dept. head Kurasini Internat. Edn. Centre, Dar-es-Salaam, Tanzania, 1966-67; dept. head Nkumbi Internat. Coll., Kabwe, Zambia, 1967-68; vol. visitor Prisons in Calif., 1980-95, Calif. Youth Authority, 1983-93; sr. youth crisis counsellor InterFace, 1984-94. 1st lt. M.I. res. U.S. Army, 1943-56. Danforth Found. fellow, 1942; Coun. for the Humanities fellow, Tufts U., 1983. Mem. Western Assn. Schs. and Colls. (accreditation com.), Great Teaching (Cooke chair 1977—), Phi Beta Kappa, Delta Sigma Rho, Cum Laude Soc. Republican. Avocations: hiking, camping, travel.

SHAGAN, BERNARD PELLMAN, endocrinologist, educator; b. Bklyn., Sept. 29, 1935; s. Samuel David and Pearl (Pellman) S.; m. Maureen Helen Oshever Amster, June 24, 1957 (div. 1970); children: Ellen Ruth Basch, Brian Ross; m. Phoebe Orange, Aug. 24, 1972; 1 child, Adam Irwin. AB, Harvard U., 1956; MD, NYU, 1960. Diplomate Am. Bd. Internal Medicine; bd. cert. endocrinology and metabolism. Chief sect. endocrinology Coney Island Hosp., Bklyn., 1968-79; chief sect. endocrinology, assoc. prof. medicine East Tenn. State U. Quillen Dishner Coll. Medicine, Johnson City, 1979-84; assoc. chmn., then acting chmn. dept. medicine Nassau County Med. Ctr., East Meadow, N.Y., 1984-87; assoc. prof. clin. medicine SUNY, Stony Brook, 1985-87; chmn., program dir. dept. medicine Monmouth Med. Ctr., Long Branch, N.J., 1987-96; prof. clin. medicine Hahnemann U., Med. Coll. Pa., Phila., 1988—; pvt. practice in endocrinology and metabolism Shrewsbury, N.Y., 1997—. Contbr. articles to med. jours. Capt. M.C., U.S. Army, 1966-68. Fellow ACP (gov. N.J. 1996-2000), Am. Coll. Endocrinologists; mem. Am. Assn. Clin. Endocrinologists, Am. Diabetes Assn., Endocrine Soc. Jewish. Avocations: music, singing, piano. Office: Ste 205 59 Ave at the Common Shrewsbury NJ 07702

SHAGAN, STEVE, screenwriter, novelist, film producer; b. N.Y.C., Oct. 25, 1927; s. Barnet Harry and Rachel (Rosenzweig) S.; m. Elizabeth Leslie Florance, Nov. 18, 1956; 1 son, Robert William. Grad. high sch. Film technician Consol. Film, Inc., N.Y.C., 1952-56, RCA, Cape Canaveral, Fla., 1956-59; asst. to publicity dir. Paramount Pictures, Hollywood, Calif., 1962-63. Prodr.: (TV series) Tarzan, 1966; prodr., writer movies for TV, Universal and CBS, Hollywood, Calif., 1968-70; writer original screenplay: Save the Tiger, 1972 (Writers Guild award, Acad. award nominee 1973); prodr. film, author screenplay: City of Angels (produced as movie Hustle), 1975, novel, screenplay The Formula, 1979, screenplay Voyage of the Damned, 1976 (Acad. award nominee); writer, prodr. film The Formula, 1980; author: (novels) Save the Tiger, 1972, City of Angels, 1975, The Formula, 1979, The Circle, 1982, The Discovery, 1985, Vendetta, 1986, Pillars of Fire, 1989, A Cast of Thousands, 1993, (screenplays) Primal Fear, 1996, Gotti, 1996. Served with USCG, 1944-46. Mem. Writers Guild Am. (bd. dirs. West chpt. 1978-82).

SHAGHOIAN, CYNTHIA LYNNE, accountant; b. Niagara Falls, N.Y., Apr. 23, 1962; d. Ralph and Joanne Lynne (Ishman) S. AAS in Acctg. with merit, Niagara County C.C., Sanborn, N.Y., 1982; BBA in Acctg. magna cum laude, Niagara U., 1984. CPA, N.Y. Staff acct. Salada Wynne Kling and Co. CPAs, Niagara Falls, 1985-88; fin. analyst Lockport (N.Y.) Meml. Hosp., 1988-90; acctg. mgr. Brown & Co. CPAS, Niagara Falls, 1990-96; pvt. practice Niagara Falls, 1996—; fundraising com. Lockport Meml. Hosp., 1990. Vol. United Way of Niagara, 1991, Arthritis Found., Tonawanda, N.Y., 1992—; membership subcom. Niagara Falls Area C. of C., 1994—; mem. Campaign Com. to Elect Greg Danoian to Niagara Falls City Coun., 1994. Mem. AICPA, N.Y. State Soc. CPAs, Inst. Mgmt. Accts. Democrat. Avocations: softball, basketball, reading, writing, continuing edn. Home: 504 22nd St Niagara Falls NY 14301

SHAH, BIPIN CHANDRA, banker; b. Bombay, July 23, 1938; s. Manilal and Keshar Shah; m. Fay Shah, 1962 (div. 1985); m. Ellen T. Dever, Sept. 20, 1985 (div. 1992); children: Nelie, Sarah Lynn, Genevieve. BA, Baldwin-Wallace Coll., 1962; MA, U. Pa., 1965. Pres. Vertex Systems, Inc., King of Prussia, Pa., 1970-74; sr. v.p. Fed. Res. Bank, Phila., Pa., 1974-78, Am. Express, N.Y.C., 1979-80; exec. v.p. Phila. Nat. Bank, 1980-84; exec. v.p. CoreStates Fin. Corp., Phila., 1984-86, vice chmn., 1986-89, COO, 1990-91; pres., CEO Gensar Holdings, Inc., Ft. Washington, Pa., 1991—; bd. dirs. VISA, USA, San Matteo, Calif., Franklin Inst., Phila., Phila. Internat. Bank, N.Y.C., U.S. Pro Indoor Tennis, Phila.; chmn. bd. dirs. CoreStates Bank Del., Wilmington. Fund raiser Phila. Indoor Tennis, 1985-88. Mem. Union League. Republican. Avocations: reading, golf, tennis, fishing. Office: Gensar Holdings Inc Highland Office Ctr 550 Pinetown Rd Fort Washington PA 19034-2605

SHAH, DEVANG KUNDANLAL, software engineer; b. Mombasa, Kenya, Oct. 2, 1963; s. Kundan B. and Saryu K. (Mehta) S. B Tech Electronics Engring. with honors, Inst. Tech. Banaras Hindu U., Varanasi, India, 1985; MA in Computer Sci., U. Tex., 1989; MBA, U. Calif., 1995. Software engr. Tata Consultancy Svcs., Bombay, India, 1985-86; staff engr. SunSoft, Inc. subs. Sun Microsystems, Inc., Mountain View, Calif., 1990—; Sun Microsystems rep. to Unix Internat. multiprocessor working group, Parsippany, N.J., 1990. Co-author: Programming with Threads, 1996; author tech. papers in field. Mem. IEEE (tech. com. on oper. systems & stds. 1990-91, stds. com. on threads ext. for portable oper. systems), Assn. for Computing Machinery. Avocations: reading, windsurfing, sailing, swimming, tennis. Home: 1031 Foster City Blvd Apt B Foster City CA 94404-2328 Office: SunSoft Inc M/S MPK17-301 2550 Garcia Ave Mountain View CA 94043-1109

SHAH, HARESH C., civil engineering educator; b. Godhra, Gujarat, India, Aug. 7, 1937; s. Chandulal M. and Rama Shah; m. Mary-Joan Dersjant, Dec. 27, 1965; children: Hemant, Mihir. BEngring., U. Poona, 1959; MSCE, Stanford U., 1960, PhD, 1963. From instr. to assoc. prof. U. Pa., Phila., 1962-68; assoc. prof. civil engring. Stanford (Calif.) U., 1968-73, prof., 1973—, chmn. dept. civil engring., 1985-94, John A. Blume prof. engring., 1988-91, Obayashi prof. engring., 1991—, dir. Stanford Ctr. for Risk Analysis, 1987-94; bd. dirs. 1st Indo Am. Bank, San Francisco, Stanford Mgmt. Group, Inc., Risk Mgmt. Solutions, Inc.; cons. in field; pres. World Seismic Safety Initiative, 1994—. Author 1 book; contbr. over 250 articles to profl. jours. Mem. ASCE, Am. Concrete Inst., Earthquake Engring. Rsch. Inst., Seismol. Soc. Am., Sigma Xi, Tau Beta Pi. Avocations: hiking, climbing, travel. Office: Stanford U Dept Civil Engring Stanford CA 94305

SHAH, JAMES M., actuarial consultant; b. Amadhara, India, Feb. 4, 1943; came to U.S., 1980; s. Manekchand Keshrichand and Kamuben Manekchand Shah; m. Urmila Jashwantlal Shah, May 16, 1966; children: Meeta, Keena, Jatin. BS, Gujarat U., India, 1965; MS, Gujarat U., 1969; MA, Georgetown U., 1983; MS, U. Nebr., 1986. Sr. rsch. asst. Nat. Inst. Rural Devel., Hyderabad, India, 1972-74; rsch. officer Population Ctr. World Bank Population Project, Bangalore, India, 1974-77; actuarial analyst Shelby (Ohio) Ins. Co., 1987-90; actuary ins. dept. State of N.D., Bismarck, 1990-91; pres. A S D Consulting Svcs., Mansfield, Ohio, 1991—. Contbr. articles to profl. jours. UN fellow Ministry of Fgn. Affairs, 1978; recipient Outstanding Young Person award Garden City Jaycees, 1977, 7th Summer Seminar award U. Hawaii, 1976. Mem. Internat. Actuarial Assn. (cert. 1996), Internat. Union for Sci. Study of Population, Soc. Actuaries (cert. 1994), Am. Acad. Actuaries (cert. 1994). Avocations: travel, reading, table tennis. Home: 3381 Clearview Ave Columbus OH 43221-1623 Office: ASD Consulting Svcs 91 S Ireland Blvd Mansfield OH 44906-2220

SHAH, MANU HIRACHAND, civil and structural engineer; b. Bardoli, Gujrat, India, May 14, 1936; came to U.S., 1959; s. Hirachand N. and Gulabben H. Shah; m. Ila M. Shah, Dec. 14, 1962; children: Paras, Pamona, Punam. BE Civil, Victoria Jubilee Tech. Inst., Bombay, 1958; MS Structural, U. Ill., 1960. Registered structural engr., Ill; registered profl. engr., 16 states. Design engr. Patel Engring., Bombay, 1958-59; project engr. Skidmore Owings & Merril, Chgo., 1960-73, Alfred Benesch & Co., Chgo., 1974-75; owner, pres. Shah Engring., Inc., Chgo., 1976—; pres. Chgo. Archtl. Assistance Ctr., 1985, bd. dirs., 1976-85. Mem. Zoning Bd. of Appeal, Village of Oak Brook, 1992—; pres. India Assn. Met. Chgo., 1965. Mem. ASCE, NSPE, Am. Concrete Inst. (bd. dirs. Chgo. chpt. 1984-85), Structural Engrs. Assn. Ill. (bd. dirs. 1982-85), Jain Soc. (coord. Chgo. 1986-88?), Jain Social Group (pres. Chgo. 1986-87), Midwest Club (Oak Brook) (trustee, chmn. archtl. com. 1986-90, 1993—), Toastmasters (pres. Speakers Forum 1976-77). Achievements include constrn. inspection of Kennedy Expressway and Lake Shore Dr., design and constrn. mgmt. of Metra's Kensington Yard facility, design of improvements on CTA Lake St. and North Main Line, rehab. of high rise bldg. at Cabrini Green. Home: 1510 Midwest Club Pky Oak Brook IL 60521-2521 Office: Shah Engring Inc 1 E Ibm Plz Ste 3200 Chicago IL 60611-7610

SHAH, NANDLAL CHIMANLAL, physiatrist; b. Sadra, Gujarat, India, July 3, 1933; came to U.S., 1969; s. Chimanlal D. and Dahiben C. (Shah) S.; m. Indira N. Shah, May 15, 1990; children: Sandip N., Tushar N. Student, M.G. Sci. Inst., Ahmedabad, India, 1952; MB, BS, B.J. Med. Coll., Ahmedabad, India, 1957. Diplomate Am. Bd. Phys. Medicine and Rehab., Am. Bd. Quality Assurance and Utilization Review Physicians. Intern Yonkers (N.Y.) Gen. Hosp., 1970; resident in internal medicine St. Barnabas Hosp., Bronx, N.Y., 1971; resident in phys. medicine and rehab. Albert Einstein Coll. Medicine, Bronx, 1971-74; staff physiatrist, dir. med. svcs. Inst. Phys. Medicine and Rehab., Peoria, Ill., 1974-79; med. dir. Thomas Rehab. Hosp., Asheville, N.C., 1979-81; staff physiatrist phys. medicine and rehab. Charlotte (N.C.) Inst. Rehab. (formerly Charlotte Rehab. Hosp.), 1981; pvt. practice Carolina Rehab. Clinic, Charlotte, 1981—. Mem. Masons. Hindu. Avocations: Indian classical music, social, cultural and religious programs. Office: Carolina Rehab Clinic 230 Baldwin Ave Charlotte NC 28204-3110

SHAH, RAMESH KESHAVLAL, engineering educator, researcher; b. Bombay, India, Sept. 23, 1941; came to U.S., 1963; s. Keshvlal M. and Hiraben K. (Kothari) S.; m. Rekha R. Maniar, Jan. 22, 1968; children: Nilay R., Nirav R. BME, Gujarat U., Ahmedabad, Gujarat, 1963; MS, Stanford U., 1964, ME, 1970, PhD in Mech. Engring., 1972. Project engr. Air Preheater Co., Wellsville, N.Y., 1964-66, Avco-Lycoming, Charleston, S.C., 1968-69; rsch. engr. Harrison Radiator Divsn. GM, Lockport, N.Y., 1971-75, tech. dir. rsch. Harrison Radiator Divsn., 1976-88, sr. staff rsch. scientist

Delphi Harrison Thermal Systems, 1989-95; chmn. dept. mech. engring. U. Ky., Lexington, 1995—; tchr. short courses, presenter keynote lectrs., seminars on heat exchanger design at various univs. and rsch. insts. in U.S., India, Can., U.K., Turkey, Yugoslavia, Fed. Republic of Germany, China, Japan, Australia, Argentina, Brazil, Portugal, Czechoslovakia, Hungary, Taiwan, South Korea, Israel, Belgium, Sweden, Lithuania, Russia, Greece, Italy, Malta, Singapore, Ukraine, France, Poland. Author: (with A.L. London) Laminar Flow Forced Convection in Ducts, Suppl. 1 to Advances in Heat Transfer, 1978; editor: (with S. Kakac and A.E. Bergles) Low Reynolds Number Flow Heat Exchangers, 1983, (with S. Kakac and W. Aung) Handbook of Single-Phase Convective Heat Transfer, 1987, (with E.C. Subbarao and R.A. Mashelkar) Heat Transfer Equipment Design, 1988, (with E.N. Ganic and K.T. Yang) Experimental Heat Transfer, Fluid Mechanics and Thermodynamics, 1988, (with A.D. Kraus and D.E. Metzger) Compact Heat Exchangers: A Festschrift for Professor A.L. London, 1990, (with H. Md. Roshan, V.M.K. Sastri and K.A. Padmanabhan) Thermomechanical Aspects of Manufacturing and Materials Processing, 1991, (with J.F. Keffer and E.N. Ganic) Experimental Heat Transfer, Fluid Mechanics and Thermodynamics, 1991, (with A. Hashemi) Aerospace Heat Exchanger Technology, 1993, (with M.D. Kelleher, K.R. Sreenivasan and Y. Joshi) Experimental Heat Transfer, Fluid Mechanics and Thermodynamics, 1993, (with S.P. Sukhatme, V. Venkat Raj and V.M.K. Sastri) Heat and Mass Transfer, 1994, (with G.P. Celata) Two-Phase Flow Modelling and Experimentation, 1995, Compact Heat Exchangers for the Process Industries, 1997; editor 12 symposium vols.; founding co-editor, editor-in-chief Exptl. Thermal and Fluid Sci., 1987-95; tech. papers reviewer ASME Jour. Heat Transfer, Internat. Jour. Heat and Mass Transfer, Jour. Numerical Heat Transfer, AIChE Jour., ASME Jour. Fluids Engring., Heat Transfer Engring. Jour., numerous fgn. jours. NSF grantee (9), 1981-95, NATO grantee (4), 1980-87, 96-97, UN grantee, 1985-86, 88-89. Fellow ASME (Region III Tech. Achievement award 1979, Valued Svc. award 1986, 87, 92, 50th Anniversary award of Heat Transfer Divsn. 1988, Charles Russ Richards Meml. award 1989); mem. Soc. Automotive Engrs., Indian Soc. Heat and Mass Transfer (life), Am. Soc. Engring. Edn., Niagara Frontier Assn. R&D Dirs. Jain. Avocations: travel, reading, bridge. Office: University of Kentucky Dept Mechanical Engineering Lexington KY 40506-0108

SHAH, SHIRISH ANANTLAL, pharmacist; b. Bombay, India, Apr. 26, 1938; s. Anantlal T. and Lilavati A. (Choksi) S.; m. Portia Rose Dahling, Apr. 30, 1966; children: Sanjay, Kishan, Kinnari. BS in Pharmacy, U. Bombay, 1961; MS, U. Conn., 1964; PhD, U. Iowa, 1975. Scientist product devel. Armour Pharm. Co., Kankakee, Ill., 1963-69; head pharm. product devel. sect. Pennwalt Corp., Rochester, N.Y., 1969-72; sr. pharm. scientist USV Pharm. Corp., Tuckahoe, N.Y., 1975-76; asst. mgr. pharm. research Johnson & Johnson Baby Products Co., Piscataway, N.J., 1976-79; dir. research and tech. services Zenith Labs., Inc., Northvale, N.J., 1979-85; v.p. devel. and tech. affairs Lemmon Co., Sellersville, Pa., 1985-87; dir. product devel. Ciba Consumer Pharm., Edison, N.J., 1988-89; mgr. R&D DuPont Pharm., Garden City, N.Y., 1990-91; mgr. new product devel. Perrigo Co., Allegan, Mich., 1992—. Mem. Am. Assn. Pharm. Scientists, Am. Pharm. Assn., Drug Info. Assn., Am. Chem. Soc., Rho Chi, Phi Lamda Upsilon. Hindu. Lodge: Masons. Home: 607 Springwood Dr Kalamazoo MI 49009-9390

SHAH, SHIRISH KALYANBHAI, computer science, chemistry and environmental science educator; b. Ahmedabad, India, May 24, 1942; came to U.S., 1962, naturalized, 1974; s. Kalyanbhai T. and Sushilaben K. S.; B.S. in Chemistry and Physics, St. Xavier's Coll., Gujarat U., 1962; PhD in Phys. Chemistry, U. Del., 1968; cert. in bus. mgmt. U. Va., 1986; PhD in Cultural Edn. (hon.) World U. West, 1986; m. Kathleen Long, June 28, 1973; 1 son, Lawrence. Asst. prof. Washington Coll., Chestertown, Md., 1967-68; dir. quality control Vita Foods, Chestertown, 1968-72; asst. prof., assoc. prof. sci., adminstr. food, marine sci. and vocat. programs Chesapeake Coll., Wye Mills, Md., 1968-76; assoc. prof., prof. sci., chmn. dept. tech. studies Community Coll. of Balt., 1976-91; assoc. prof. chemistry Coll. Notre Dame of Md., 1991—; advisor to Young Republicans, 1992—; chmn. computer systems and engring. techs., 1982-89, project facilitator telecomm. curriculum and lab., 1985-89, coord. tech. studies, 1989-91; adj. prof. Phys. Sci. Coppin State Coll., 1996-97; mem. Balt. City Adult Edn. Adv. Com., 1982-89; chmn. Coll. wide computer user com., 1985-91; coun. mem. Faculty Rsch. and Devel., 1994—; permanent mem. Rep. Senatorial Com.; charter mem. Rep. Presdl. Task Force. Mem. com. Am. Lung Assn., 1971-80; mem. Congl. Adv. Com., 1983—. Fellow Am. Inst. Chemists; mem. IEEE, APHA, Am. Chem. Soc., (chmn.-elect Md. sect. 1995-96, chmn. 1996-97, chair kids and chemistry program of Md. sect. 1997), Assn. Indsl. Hygiene, Data Processing Mgmt. Assn., Nat. Environ. Tng. Assn., Nat. Sci. Tchrs. Assn., Nat. Assn. Indsl. Tech. (dir. local region, bd. accreditors), Am. Vocat. Assn., Am. Tech. Edn. Assn., Am. Fedn. Tchrs., Md. State Tchrs. Assn., Md. Assn. Community and Jr. Colls. (v.p. 1977-78, pres. 1978—), Sigma Xi, Epsilon Pi Tau, Iota Lambda Sigma Nu. Jain, Roman Catholic. Contbr. articles on sci. and tech. to profl. jours. Home: 5605 Purlington Way Baltimore MD 21212-2950 Office: Coll Notre Dame Dept Chem 4701 N Charles St Baltimore MD 21210-2404

SHAH, SURENDRA POONAMCHAND, engineering educator, researcher; b. Bombay, Aug. 30, 1936; s. Poonamchand C. and Maniben (Modi) S.; m. Dorothie Crispell, June 9, 1962; children: Daniel S., Byron C. BE, B.V.M. Coll. Engring., India, 1959; MS, Lehigh U., 1960; PhD, Cornell U., 1965. Asst. prof. U. Ill., Chgo., 1966-69, assoc. prof., 1969-73, prof., 1973-81; prof. civil engring Northwestern U., Evanston, Ill., 1981—, dir. Ctr. for Concrete and Geomaterials, 1987—; dir. NSF Sci. and Tech. Ctr. for Advanced Cement-Based Materials Northwestern U., 1989—, Walter P. Murphy prof. of engring., 1992—; cons. govt. agys. and industry, U.S.A., UN, France, Switzerland, People's Republic China, Denmark, The Netherlands; vis. prof. MIT, 1969, Delft U., The Netherlands, 1976, Denmark Tech. U., 1984, LCPC, Paris, 1986, U. Sidney, Australia, 1987; NATO vis. sci. Turkey, 1992. Co-author: Fiber Reinforced Cement Composites, 1992, High Performance Concrete and Applications, 1994, Fracture Mechanics of Concrete, 1995; contbr. more than 400 articles to profl. jours.; editor 12 books; mem. editorial bds. 4 internat. jours.; editor-in-chief Jour. Advanced Based Materials. Recipient Thompson award ASTM, Phila., 1983, Disting. U.S. Vis. Scientist awrd Alexander von Humboldt Found., 1989, Swedish Concrete award, Stockholm, 1993, Engring. News Record award of Newsmaker, 1995. Fellow Am. Concrete Inst. (chmn. tech. com., Anderson award 1989), Internat. Union Testing and Rsch. Labs. Materials and Structures (chmn. tech. com. 1989—, Gold medal 1980); mem. ASCE (past chmn. tech. com., mem. exec. com.). Home: 921 Isabella St Evanston IL 60201-1773 Office: Northwestern U Tech Inst Rm A130 2145 Sheridan Rd Evanston IL 60208-0834

SHAH, VINOD PURUSHOTTAM, research scientist; b. Baroda, Gujarat, India, Sept. 2, 1939; came to U.S., 1960; s. Purushottam and Taraben Shah.; m. Manjula Shah, Feb. 18, 1965; children: Manish, Sujata. B in Pharmacy, U. Madras, 1959; PhD in Pharm. Chemistry, U. Calif., San Francisco, 1964. Pharm. R & D chemist Sarabhai Chems., Baroda, India, 1964-69; postdoctoral rsch. fellow U. Calif., San Francisco, 1969-75; sr. rsch. chemist, tech. coord. FDA, Washington, 1975-81; pharmaconkinetic reviewer FDA, Rockville, Md., 1981-84, br. chief, 1984-88, asst.. dir., 1988-90, assoc. dir., 1990-94, sr. rsch. scientist, 1994—. Editor: Integration of Pharmocokinetics, Pharmacodynamics and Toxicokinetics in Rational Drug Development, 1993, Topical Drug Bioavailability, Bioequivalence and Penetration, 1993; contbr. articles to profl. jours.; adv. bd. Skin Pharmacology Jour., 1987-92. Recipient Gold medal U. Madras, 1959. Fellow Am. Assn. Pharm. Scientists (co-chair sci. workshops 1986—), Am. Assn. Pharm. Scientists. Achievements include development of invitro release/dissolution methodology for topical, transdermal and water insoluble drug dosage forms for use as a quality control test. Home: 11309 Dunleith Pl North Potomac MD 20878 Office: FDA 7500 Standish Pl Rockville MD 20855-2764

SHAHAM, GIL, violinist; b. 1971. Student, Columbia U., Julliard Sch. Performed with Juilliard Orch., Avery Fisher Hall, London Symphony Orch.; albums include Paganini For Two, Barber and Korngold Violin Concertos. Avery Fisher Career grantee. Office: ICM 8942 Wilshire Blvd Beverly Hills CA 90211

SHAHEEN, MICHAEL EDMUND, JR., lawyer, government official; b. Boston, Aug. 5, 1940; s. Michael Edmund and Dorothy Wallace (Cameron) S.; m. Polly Adair Dammann, Sept. 11, 1976; children: Michael Edmund, Timothy Andrew. B.A., Yale U., 1962; LL.B., Vanderbilt U., 1965. Bar: Tenn. 1968. Dir. ann. capital support fund, instr. physics Memphis Univ. Sch., 1965-66; law clk. Judge Robert M. McRae, Jr., Memphis, 1966-68; individual practice law Tenn., Miss., 1968-73; dep. chief voting and public accomodations sect. Dept. Justice, Washington, 1973-74, dep. chief fed. programs sect., civil rights div., 1974-75; counsel to Atty. Gen. for Intelligence, 1975; spl. adv. to atty. gen., counsel, dir. Office Profl. Responsibility, 1975—; mayor, Como, Miss., 1970-73; pres. Como Resources, Inc., 1971-72; mcpl. judge, Como, 1970-73; chmn. Como Indsl. Devel. Commn., 1970-73. Mem. Phi Delta Phi, Zeta Psi. Office: Dept Justice 10th Constitution Ave NE Washington DC 20530-0001

SHAHIN, THOMAS JOHN, dry cleaning wholesale supply company executive; b. Buffalo, July 30, 1943; s. Thomas Mark and Marie (Colletto) S.; m. Laraine Edna Clements, Feb. 25, 1967; 1 child, Lori Lynn. BSBA, Calif. State U., L.A., 1966. Asst. v.p. stock brokerage div. United Calif. Bank, L.A., 1969-76; v.p., gen. mgr., treas. Newhouse Splty. Co. Inc., Santa Ana, Calif., 1976—, also bd. dirs. Patentee belt buckle. Officer USN, 1966-69, Vietnam. Mem. Textile Care Allied Trade Assn., Laundry and Drycleaners Suppliers, Internat. Fabricare Inst., Internat. Drycleaners Congress, Calif. Fabricare Inst., Beta Gamma Sigma. Republican. Roman Catholic. Avocations: new product research, reading, travel, golf, tennis. Office: Newhouse Splty Co Inc 2619 Oak St Santa Ana CA 92707-3720

SHAH-JAHAN, M. M., economist; b. Dhaka, Bangladesh, June 30, 1943; came to U.S., 1975; s. M.M. Serajul Hoq and Ayesha A. Khaton; m. Mahmuda Khatun, Aug. 15, 1972; children: Al M., Nydia. BA in Bus., Dacca U., 1963, MA in Bus., 1964; MA in Econs., Georgetown U., 1982; PhD in Econs., Georgetown-Pacific Western U., 1987. Asst. prof. edn. dept. Dacca Coll., 1965-75, sec. gen. prof. staff coun., 1971-75; audit supr. Marriott Corp., Arlington, Va., 1975-81; economist Potomac Electric Power Co., Washington, 1981—; cons. economist World Bank, Washington, 1988—. Author: (with M.R. Khan) Principles of Income Tax, 1970, Principles of Banking, 1974, An Econometric Forecasting Model, 1987, Jordan: A Macroeconomic Projection, 1988, U.S. Macroeconomic Outlook, 1989, The Open Economy Macro Model for Policy and Planning in the Developing Economies, 1993, Twenty-Five Year Macroeconomic Outlook for Bangladesh, 1994. Govt. of Pakistan scholar, 1964. Mem. Am. Econ. Assn., Soc. Govt. Economies, Nat. Economists Club, Swimming Club. Democrat. Islam. Avocations: tennis, swimming, movies, travel, photography. Home: 1223 S Buchanan St Arlington VA 22204-3407 Office: Potomac Electric Power Co 1900 Pennsylvania Ave NW Washington DC 20068-0001

SHAIKH, NAIMUDDIN, medical physicist; b. Khurda, Orissa, India, Feb. 10, 1951; s. Nasibuddin Shaikh and Mahemuda Bibi; m. Najmul Akhtar, Oct. 29, 1978; children: Arif, Alim, Amin. MS, Utkal U., 1974; MA, CCNY, 1981; MS, U. Wis., 1983, PhD, 1986. Diplomate Am. Bd. Radiology, Am. Bd. Med. Physics. Lectr. in physics Govt. Orissa, Bhubaneswar, Orissa, 1974-79; rsch. asst. U. Wis., Madison, 1986-87; chief diagnostic physicist Lahey Clinic Med. Ctr., Burlington, Mass., 1987—; mem. Lahey Clinic Radiation Safety Com., Burlington, 1987—; nat. examiner Am. Bd. Med. Physics, Reston, Va., 1990—; diagnostic imaging standards com. Am. Coll. Med. Physics, 1994. Recipient Nat. scholarship Govt. of India, 1968-74; CCNY fellow, 1980-81. Mem. Am. Assn. Physicists in Medicine (task group on high dose rate fluoroscopy 1995), Am. Coll. Med. Physicists, Am. Coll. Radiology, Internat. Orgn. Med. Physicists (working group for funding 1995). Home: 67 Tyngsboro Rd Westford MA 01886-1111 Office: Lahey Clinic Med Ctr 41 Mall Rd Burlington MA 01805-0001

SHAIMAN, MARC, composer, arranger, orchestrator; b. Newark, Oct. 22, 1959; s. William Robert and Claire (Goldfein) S. Composer (films) Misery, 1990, City Slickers, 1991, The Addams Family, 1991, Father of the Bride, 1991, Sister Act, 1992, A Few Good Men, 1992, Mr. Saturday Night, Sleepless in Seattle, 1992 (Acad. award nominee for best song), A Wink and a Smile, City Slickers II, 1994, Heart and Souls, 1993, Addams Family Values, 1993, North, Speechless, The American President, 1995 (Acad. award nominee for best achievement in music 1996); (Broadway and off Broadway shows) Bette Midler's Divine Madness, Harry Connick Jr. in Concert, Peter Allen in Concert, Leader of the Pack, Legends with Mary Martin and Carol Channing; record producer, arranger Bette Midler's Thighs and Whispers, Divine Madness, Beaches, When Harry Met Sally, We Are in Love, Some Peoples Lives; producer various concerts by artists including Barbara Streisand, Billy Crystal, Barry Manilow, Luther Vandross, Raquel Welch; film music adaptations, supervision include When Harry Met Sally, Beaches, Scenes from a Mall, For the Boys; composer, arranger (TV shows) Saturday Night Live, various Acad., Grammy, and Emmy awards shows, (HBO spls.) Martin Short, Robin Williams, Bette Midler, Billy Crystal; actor (films) Broadcast News, Hot Shots. Address: Kelly Bush Pub Rels 2047 Glencoe Way Los Angeles CA 90068-3129 also: The Kraft-Benjamin Agency 345 N Maple Dr Ste 385 Beverly Hills CA 90210*

SHAIN, IRVING, retired chemical company executive and university chancellor; b. Seattle, Jan. 2, 1926; s. Samuel and Selma (Blockoff) S.; m. Mildred Ruth Udell, Aug. 31, 1947; children: Kathryn A., Steven T., John R., Paul S. BS in Chemistry, U. Wash., 1949, PhD in Chemistry, 1952. From instr. to prof. U. Wis., Madison, 1952-75, vice chancellor, 1970-75, chancellor, 1977-86; provost, v.p. acad. affairs U. Wash., Seattle, 1975-77; v.p. Olin Corp., Stamford, Conn., 1987-92, ret., 1992, also bd. dirs.; mem. tech. adv. bd. Johnson Controls, Inc., Milw., 1980—; trustee Univ. Rsch. Park, Inc., Madison, pres., 1984-86, v.p., 1987—; mem. Nat. Commn. on Superconductivity, 1989-90. Contbr. articles on electroanalytical chemistry to profl. jours. Bd. dirs. Madison Gen. Hosp., 1972-75; v.p. Madison Cmty. Found., 1984-86. With U.S. Army, 1943-46, PTO. Fellow AAAS, Wis. Acad. Scis., Arts and Letters; mem. Am. Chem. Soc., Electrochem. Soc., Conn. Acad. Sci. and Engring., Phi Beta Kappa, Sigma Xi, Phi Kappa Phi. Home: 2820 Marshall Ct # 8 Madison WI 53705-2270 Office: Univ Wis Univ Rsch Park 610 Walnut St Madison WI 53705-2336

SHAIN-ALVARO, JUDITH CAROL, physician assistant; b. Bronx, N.Y., Aug. 13, 1953; d. Frank and Pearl (Crausman) Shain; m. Virgilio S. Alvaro, May 13, 1990; 1 child, Jessica Blaire. BS in Biology, Fairleigh Dickinson U., 1975; cert. physician asst., BS, Baylor Coll. Medicine, 1978. Cert. physician asst. Nat. Commn. Cert. Physician Assts.; lic. physician asst., N.Y., N.J.; BLS, ACLS, Am. Heart Assn. Resident surg. Montefiore Med. Ctr. and Albert Einstein Coll. Medicine, Bronx, 1979-81; physician asst. dept. cardiothoracic surgery N. Shore U. Hosp., Manhasset, N.Y., 1981-84; lic. med. officer Passenger Cruise Ships, Miami, Fla., 1984-88; med. cons. The Floating Hosp., Bankers Trust Co., N.Y.C., 1988-89; sr. physician asst. Pers. Health Svcs. St. Vincent's Hosp. and Med. Ctr., N.Y.C., 1990-93; sr. physician asst. N.J. Med. Sch. Nat. Tuberculosis Ctr., Newark, 1993—; physician asst. rep. N.J. AIDS Edn. Tng. Ctr., Newark, 1995—; mem. physician asst. work group Nat. AIDS Edn. Tng. Ctr., 1995—; lectr. in field; adj. med. staff U. Medicine and Dentistry of N.J. Fellow Am. Acad. Physician Assts., N.J. State Soc. Physician Assts., N.Y. State Soc. Physician Assts.; mem. Sisterhood Congregation Bnai Israel, Filipino Am. Assn. Fair Lawn. Democrat. Jewish. Avocations: travel, theater, reading. Home: 0-80 27th St Fair Lawn NJ 07410 Office: Univ Medicine Dentistry NJ 65 Bergen St Newark NJ 07107-3001

SHAINESS, NATALIE, psychiatrist, educator; b. N.Y.C., Dec. 2, 1915; d. Jack and Clara (Levy-Hart) S.; div.; children: David Spiegel, Ann Spiegel. BA in Chemistry, NYU, 1936; MD, Va. Commonwealth U., 1939. Diplomate in psychiatry; cert. in psychoanalysis. Pvt. practice N.Y.C., 1955—; faculty William Alanson White Inst. Psychiatry, Psychoanalysis, N.Y.C., 1961-81; asst. clin. prof. psychiatry N.Y. Sch. Psychiatry, N.Y.C., 1964-67; faculty med. edn. div. N.Y. Acad. Medicine, 1966-67; lectr. psychiatry Columbia U. Coll. Physicians and Surgeons, N.Y.C., 1966-80; faculty, supervising analyst L.I. Inst. Psychoanalysis, N.Y., 1980—; invited participant 1st and 2nd Internat. Conf. on Abortion, 1967, 68; research project on menstruation. Editorial bd. Jour. of the Am. Women's Med. Assn., 1985—; author: Sweet Suffering: Woman as Victim, 1984; contbr. over 100 articles to profl. jours. and over 90 profl. book revs. Mem. Physicians for Social Responsibility, Nuclear Freeze, several other anti-nuclear orgns. Recipient Silver medal Women's Soc. N.Y.C., 1967, 1st Presdl. award Women's Med. Assn., N.Y.C., 1990, Disting. Svc. award Am. Women's Med. Assn., several 1st and 2d pl. awards for poetry APA Arts Assn., honored by Soc. Med. Psychoanalysis, 1993. Fellow Am. Acad. Psychoanalysis (past trustee, organizer several panels), Am. Psychiat. Assn. (life mem., organizer several panels), N.Y. Acad. Medicine (hon.), Soc. Med. Psychoanalyst. Avocations: music, the arts. Home and Office: 140 E 83rd St New York NY 10028-1931

SHAINMAN, IRWIN, music educator, musician; b. N.Y.C., June 27, 1921; s. Samuel and Gussie (Pollack) S.; m. Bernice Cohen, Aug. 29, 1948; children—Joan, Jack. B.A., Pomona Coll., 1943; M.A., Columbia, 1948; Premier Prix, Conservatoire Nat. de Musique de Paris, France, 1950. Prof. music, curator Paul Whiteman collection Williams Coll., Williamstown, Mass., 1948-91, prof. emeritus, 1991—; chmn. music dept., 1971-77, dean faculty, 1972-73, coordinator performing arts, 1973-76, Class of 1955 prof. music, 1980-91; tchr. ext. U. Mass., 1952-55, Mass. State Coll., North Adams, 1957, also Bennington Coll. Composer's Conf. and Chamber Music Ctr.; cons. advanced placement program Coll. Entrance Exam. Bd., 1969-75; mem. edn. com. Saratoga Performing Arts Ctr., 1967-68; pres. Williamstown Theatre Found., 1972-77, South Mountain Concert Assn., 1980-96. Condr., Berkshire Symphony, 1950-65, also Williams Coll. band, brass ensemble and woodwind ensemble, 1st trumpet, Albany (N.Y.) Symphony Orch., 1960-65, Vt. Symphony Orch., 1954-58; contbr. articles to profl. jours.; columnist: Berkshire Eagle; author: Avoiding Cultural Default and Other Essays, 1991. Mem. merit aid panel Mass. Arts Council, 1984. Served with AUS, 1942-45. Decorated Purple Heart, Combat Inf. badge.; N.Y. Philharmonic scholar, 1934-35; Recipient Danforth Found. Tchrs. award, 1957-58. Mem. Am. Musicological Soc., Coll. Music Assn., Music Critics Assn. Home: 88 Baxter Rd Williamstown MA 01267-2111

SHAIR, DAVID IRA, human resources executive; b. N.Y.C., May 1, 1921; s. Henry and Jessie (Brinn) S.; m. Hortense Spitz, Oct. 18, 1947. BA, CUNY, 1940; MBA, NYU, 1950. Assoc. Benj. Werne Assocs., N.Y.C., 1952-70; dir. labor relations London Records, Inc., N.Y.C., 1970-80; v.p. personnel Carl Fischer, Inc., N.Y.C., 1980-92; mgmt. cons., freelance writer, 1993—. Author various articles on personnel and labor relations. Served with inf. U.S. Army, 1942-45, ETO. Decorated Purple Heart. Mem. Soc. Adminstrv. Mgmt. (v.p. 1986-87, exec. v.p. 1987-90), Indsl. Rels. Rsch. Assn., Soc. Human Resource Mgmt. (bd. dirs. 1996-98, treas. 1994-95, chair newsletter com., Dirs. Forum), N.Y. Pers. Mgmt. Assn. Jewish. Avocation: photography. Home: 6 Peter Cooper Rd New York NY 10010-6701 also: 7 Rosemaries Ln PO Box 3099 East Hampton NY 11937

SHAKESPEARE, FRANK, ambassador; b. N.Y.C., Apr. 9, 1925; s. Francis Joseph and Frances (Hughes) S.; m. Deborah Anne Spaeth, Oct. 9, 1954; children: Mark, Andrea, Fredricka. BS, Holy Cross Coll., 1945; D.Eng. (hon.), Colo. Sch. Mines, 1975; DCS (hon.), Pace U., 1979; LLD (hon.), Del. Law Sch., 1980, Sacred Heart U., 1985, U. Dallas, 1987, Pepperdine U., 1990, Nichols Coll., 1991, Marquette U., 1993; D of Pub. Svc. (hon.), Hillsdale Coll., 1996. Formerly pres. CBS-TV Services; exec. v.p. CBS-TV Stas.; dir. USIA, 1969-73; exec. v.p. Westinghouse Electric Corp., 1973-75; pres. RKO Gen. Inc., N.Y.C., 1975-85, vice chmn., 1983-85; U.S. ambassador to Portugal Lisbon, 1985-87; U.S. ambassador to The Holy See Vatican City, 1987-89. Chmn. Heritage Found., 1975-85, dir., 1989—; chmn. Radio Free Europe/Radio Liberty, Inc., 1976-85; dir. Bradley Founhd., 1989—. Served to lt. (j.g.) USNR, 1945-46. Club: Union League. Home: 303 Coast Blvd La Jolla CA 92037-4630

SHAKNO, ROBERT JULIAN, hospital administrator; b. Amsterdam, Holland, Aug. 15, 1937; came to U.S., 1939, naturalized, 1944; s. Rudy C. and Gertrude (Loeb) S.; m. Elka Linda Baum, June 10, 1962; children: Steven Lee, Deborah Sue. B.B.A. (scholar 1955), So. Methodist U., 1959; M.H.A., Washington U., St. Louis, 1961. Adminstrv. asst. Mt. Sinai Hosp., Chgo., 1961-63; asso. adminstr. Tex. Inst. Rehab. and Research, Houston, 1963-65; asst. adminstr. Michael Reese Hosp., Chgo., 1965-70; v.p., hosp. dir. Michael Reese Hosp., 1970-73; asso. exec. dir. Cook County Hosp., Chgo., 1973-75; pres. Hackensack Med. Center, N.J., 1975-85, Mt. Sinai Med. Ctr., Cleve., 1985-96; dir. nat. strategy practice KPMG Peat Marwick, 1996—; oper. trustee, sec. LAurelwood Hosp., Willoughby, Ohio; clin. instr. Washington U., St. Louis, U. Chgo., Northwestern U., Columbia U.; bd. dirs. Ohio Hosp. Ins. Co. Mem. editorial bd. Mgmt. Series, Am. Coll. Healthcare Execs. Mem. Leadership Cleve.; bd. dirs. Premier Hosp. alliance, chmn., 1994—; bd. dirs. The New Cleve. Inc., Univ. Circle Inc., Cleve., Cleve. Sight Ctr.; trustee Hope Lodge, Cleve. chpt. Am. Cancer Soc., Jewish Family Svcs.; chmn. social svcs. divsn. United Jewish Appeal, Cleve., 1987-88, chmn. health cabinet, 1990, gen. co-chmn., 1990—; chmn. Hosp. Pacesetter campaign United Way, chmn. health svcs. portfolio, 1988-89, oversight commn., 1992-93. Served to 1st lt. USAR, 1960-66. Named Young Adminstr. of Yr., Washington U., 1968. Fellow Am. Coll. Hosp. Adminstrs.; mem. Am. Hosp. Assn. (coun. urban hosps., del. coun. on met. hosps., rep. regional policy bd.), Washington U. Alumni Assn. (past pres.), Greater Cleve. Hosp. Assn. (bd. dirs.), Ohio Hosp. Assn. (bd. dirs.), Cleve. Sight Ctr. (trustee, bd. dirs.), Sigma Alpha Mu (past pres.). Home: 32050 Meadow Lark Way Pepper Pike OH 44124-5508 Office: Mt Sinai Med Ctr 1 Mount Sinai Dr Cleveland OH 44106-4191

SHAKOW, DAVID JOSEPH, law educator; b. 1945. BA, Harvard U., 1967, JD, 1970; LLM, NYU, 1976. Bar: N.Y. 1971. Law clk. to Hon. William H. Hastie Phila., 1970-71; assoc. Davis, Polk & Wardwell, N.Y.C., 1971-77; atty., adviser Office Tax Legis. Counsel U.S. Treasury, D.C., 1977-79, assoc. tax legis counsel, 1979-80, dep. tax legis. counsel, 1980-81; assoc. prof. U. Pa., Phila., 1981-87, prof. law, 1987—. Author: The Taxation of Corporation and Their Shareholders, 1991. Office: U Pa Law Sch 3400 Chestnut St Philadelphia PA 19104-6204

SHALALA, DONNA EDNA, federal official, political scientist, educator, university chancellor; b. Cleve., Feb. 14, 1941; d. James Abraham and Edna (Smith) S. AB, Western Coll., 1962; MSSC, Syracuse U., 1968, PhD, 1970; 24 hon degrees, 1981-91. Vol. Peace Corps, Iran, 1962-64; asst. prof. polit. sci. CUNY, 1970-72; assoc. prof. politics and edn. Tchrs. Coll. Columbia U., 1972-79; asst. sec. for policy devel. and research HUD, Washington, 1977-80; prof. polit. sci., pres. Hunter Coll., CUNY, 1980-88; prof. polit. sci., chancellor U. Wis., Madison, 1988-93; sec. Dept. HHS, Washington, 1993—. Author: Neighborhood Governance, 1971, The City and the Constitution, 1972, The Property Tax and the Voters, 1973, The Decentralization Approach, 1974. Bd. govs. Am. Stock Exch., 1981-87; trustee TIAA, 1985-89, Com. Econ. Devel., 1981-93; bd. dirs. Inst. Internat. Econs., 1981-93, Children's Def. Fund, 1980-93, Am. Ditchley Found., 1981-93, Spencer Found., 1988-93, M&I Bank of Madison, 1991-93, NCAA Found., 1991; mem. Trilateral Commn., 1988-93, Knight Commn. on Intercollegiate Sports, 1990-93; trustee Brookings Inst., 1989-93. Ohio Newspaper Women's scholar, 1958, Western Coll. Trustee scholar, 1958-62; Carnegie fellow, 1966-68; Guggenheim fellow, 1975-76; recipient Disting. Svc. medal Columbia U. Tchrs. Coll., 1989. Mem. ASPA, Am. Polit. Sci. Assn., Nat. Acad. Arts and Scis., Nat. Acad. Pub. Adminstrn., Coun. Fgn. Rels., Nat. Acad. Edn. (Spencer fellow 1972-73). Office: Dept Health and Human Svcs Office of Sec 200 Independence Ave SW Rm 615F Washington DC 20201-0004

SHALEK, JAMES ARTHUR, JR., insurance agent, financial consultant; b. Chgo., May 3, 1947; s. James Arthur and Evelyn Pearl (Kubitz) S.; m. Susan Ellen Keto, Feb. 12, 1977; 1 child, Stephanie Catherine. BA, Hope Coll., Holland, Mich., 1969. CLU, ChFC. Instr. 7th and 8th grade. Big Hollow Grade Sch., Ingleside, Ill., 1970-73; agt. Penn Mut. Life Ins. Co., Oak Brook, Ill., 1973-75; sr. agt. The Prin. Fin. Group, Oakbrook Terrace, Ill., 1975—. Fin. sec. First Congl. Ch. United Ch. of Christ, Geneva, Ill., 1991-94; pres. Midwest Epilepsy Ctr., Lombard, Ill., 1982-83. Mem. Am. Soc. CLU and ChFC, Nat. Assn. Life Underwriters (Nat. Quality award 14 yrs., nat. Sales Achievement award 15 yrs.) Ill. Life Underwriters Assn. (nominating com. 1992), DuPage Life Underwriters Assn. (nat. com. 1992-95, pres. 1990-91, bd. dirs. 1980-95), Million Dollar Round Table. Republican. Avocations: biking, swimming, golf, weight training. Home: ON 648 Lancaster Dr Winfield IL 60190 Office: The Prin Fin Group 1 Lincoln Ctr Ste 1450 Oakbrook Ter IL 60181-4271

SHALES, THOMAS WILLIAM, writer, journalist, television and film critic; b. Elgin, Ill., Nov. 3, 1953; s. Clyde LeRoy and Hulda Louise (Reko)

S. BA, Am. U., 1973. Entertainment editor Washington Examiner, 1968-71; arts reporter Washington Post, 1971-77, TV editor and chief TV critic, 1977—; film critic, modular arts service Nat. Public Radio, 1970-79, film critic, Morning Edit., 1979—; adj. prof. Am. U., 1978; syndicated columnist On the Air, Washington Post Writers Group, 1979—. Author: The American Film Heritage, 1972, On the Air!, 1982, Legends, 1989. Recipient Disting. Alumnus award Am. U., 1978. Recipient Pulitzer Prize, 1988. Office: Washington Post Co 1150 15th St NW Washington DC 20071-0001

SHALIKASHVILI, JOHN MALCHASE, military career officer; b. Warsaw, Poland, June 27, 1936; s. Dimitri and Maria (Ruediger) S.; m. Gunhild Bartsch, Apr. 18, 1963 (dec. Aug. 1965); m. Joan E. Zimpelman, Dec. 27, 1966; 1 child, Brant. BSME, Bradley U., 1958; attended, Naval War Coll., 1969-70, U.S. Army War Coll., 1977-78; MA in Internat. Affairs, George Washington U., 1970; LLD (hon.), U. Md., 1993, Bradley U., 1994. Joined U.S. Army, 1958, advanced through grades to gen., 1992—, various troop and staff assignments Alaska, U.S., Fed. Republic of Germany, Vietnam, Korea, 1959-75; battalion comdr. 9th infantry div. U.S. Army, Ft. Lewis, Wash., 1975-77; asst. chief of staff ops. So. European Task Froce U.S. Army, Vicenza, Italy, 1978-79; comdr. div. arty., 1st Armored Div. U.S. Army, Nuernberg, Fed. Republic of Germany, 1979-81; chief., politico-mil div. U.S. Army, Washington, 1981-84; asst. div. comdr. 1st. Armored div. U.S. Army, Nuernberg, Fed. Republic of Germany, 1984-86; dir. strategy, plans, policy U.S. Army, Washington, 1986-87; comdg. gen. 9th inf. div. Ft. Lewis, Wash., 1987-89; dep. comdr.-in-chief Hdqrs. USAREUR and 7th Army, Heidelberg, Fed. Republic of Germany, 1989-91; asst. to chmn. Joint Chiefs of Staff, Washington, 1991-92; Supreme Allied Comdr. Europe, Comdr.-in-Chief U.S. Forces Europe, 1992-93; chmn. Joint Chiefs of Staff, 1993—. Bd. govs. ARC; bd. trustees Bradley U. Decorated Def. D.S.M. with two oak leaf clusters, D.S.M., Legion of Merit with two oak leaf clusters, Bronze Star with V device, Meritorious Svc. medal with three oak leaf clusters, Air medal, Joint Svc. Commendation medal, Army Commendation medal, Nat. D.S.M. with bronze svc. star, Armed Forces Expeditionary medal, Humanitarian Svc. medal, Army Svc. ribbon, Order of Combat Infantry badge, Parachutist badge, Army Staff Identification badge, Overseas Svc. ribbon with bronze Arabic numeral 5, Inter-Am. Def. Bd. medal, Vietnam Svc. medal with silver svc. star, S.W. Asia Svc. medal with bronze svc. star, Republic of Vietnam Gallantry Cross with two silver and one bronze stars, Republic of Vietnam Armed Forces Honor medal 1st class, Republic of Vietnam Campaign medal; grand cordon Order of Leopold (Belgium), (2) Order of the Mil. Merit (Brazil), grand cross with star and sash Order of Merit (Germany), grand officer Nat. Order of Merit (France), grand cordon Order of Rising Sun (Japan), May Decoration of Mil. Merit (Argentina), Nat. Security Merit Tongil (Korea); recipient Disting. Alumni Achievement award George Washington U., 1994. Mem. Assn. U.S. Army, Field Arty. Assn., Ret. Officers Assn., Coun. Fgn. Rels., Am. Acad. Achievement. Home: 110 Grant Ave Arlington VA 22211-1204

SHALITA, ALAN REMI, dermatologist; b. Bklyn., Mar. 22, 1936; s. Harry and Celia; m. Simone Lea Baum, Sept. 4, 1960; children: Judith and Deborah (twins). AB, Brown U., 1957; BS, U. Brussels, 1960; MD, Bowman Gray Sch. Medicine, 1964; DSc (hon.), L.I. U., 1990. Intern Beth Israel Hosp., N.Y.C., 1964-65; resident dept. dermatology NYU Med. Ctr., 1967-68, NIH tng. grant fellow dept. dermatology, 1968-70, instr. dermatology, 1970-71; asst. prof. NYU, 1971-73, Columbia U., N.Y.C., 1973-75; assoc. prof. medicine, head divsn. dermatology SUNY Downstate Med. Ctr., Bklyn., 1975-79, prof., 1979—, head divsn. dermatology, 1979-80, chmn. dept. dermatology, 1980—, asst. dean, 1977-83; acting dean Queens campus SUNY Downstate Med. Ctr., 1983-84; assoc. dean clin. affairs SUNY Health Sci. Ctr., Bklyn., 1989-92, assoc. provost for clin. affairs, 1992-93, assoc. v.p. clin. affairs, 1993—; disting. tchg. prof. SUNY Health Sci. Ctr., Bklyn., 1996—; asst. attending in dermatology Univ. Hosp., N.Y.C., 1970-73, Bellevue Hosp. Ctr., 1970-73, Manhattan VA Hosp., 1971-73, Presbyn. Hosp., 1973-75; mem. med. bd. Kings County Hosp. Ctr.; cons. dermatology Bklyn. VA Hosp., 1975—; chief dermatology Brookdale Med. Ctr., 1977-90; chief dermatology Univ. Hosp. of Bklyn., 1975—; chief dermatology Kings County Hosp. Ctr., Bklyn., 1975—, acting med. dir., 1989-92; med. dir. Univ. Hosp. Bklyn., 1992-96. Pres. Temple Shaaray Tefila, N.Y.C., 1982-86, chmn. bd. trustees, 1987-95. Lt. M.C. USNR, 1965-67. Recipient Torch of Liberty award Anti-Defamation League, 1987, Surg. and Pediatric awards Beth Israel Hosp., N.Y.C., 1965; spl. fellow NIH, 1970-73. Dem. AMA, AAAS, Am. Acad. Dermatology (bd. dirs. 1983-87, v.p. 1995-96), Soc. Investigative Dermatology, Dermatology Found. (past trustee), Am. Dermatol. Assn. (asst. sec.-treas. 1995-96, sec.-treas. 1996—), Am. Soc. Dermatol. Surgery (past bd. dirs.), Soc. Cosmetic Chemists, Assn. Profs. of Dermatology (sec.-treas. 1988-94, pres.-elect 1994-96, pres. 1996—), Internat. Soc. Dermatology, N.Y. Acad. Scis., N.Y. State Med. Soc., N.Y. Acad. Medicine, N.Y. State Dermatol. Soc., Dermatol. Soc. Greater N.Y. (pres. 1980-81), N.Y. Dermatol. Soc. (pres. 1989-90), Brit. Assn. Dermatologists, Societe Francaise de Dermatologie et Syphilagraphie, Spanish Acad. Dermatology (hon.), Argentina Dermatology Soc., Venezuelan Dermatology Soc. Republican. Home: 70 E 77th St New York NY 10021-1811 Office: 450 Clarkson Ave Brooklyn NY 11203-2012 *Treat others with compassion, dignity and respect, add a little humor to everyone's life. Speak up for what you truly believe, be charitable.*

SHALKOP, ROBERT LEROY, retired museum director; b. Milford, Conn., July 30, 1922; s. Bertram Leroy and Dorothy Jane (Boardman) S.; m. Antoinette Joan Benkowsky, Dec. 7, 1963; 1 son, Andrew Goforth. Student, Maryville (Tenn.) Coll., 1940-42; M.A., U. Chgo., 1949; postgrad., Sorbonne, 1951-52. Dir. Rahr Civic Center, Manitowoc, Wis., 1953-56, Everhart Mus., Scranton, Pa., 1956-62, Brooks Meml. Art Gallery, Memphis, 1962-64; assoc. dir. Colorado Springs (Colo.) Fine Arts Center, also curator Taylor Mus., 1964-71; dir. Anchorage Mus. History and Art, 1972-87; pvt. practice mus. cons. Salisbury, N.C., 1987-94; archaeologist Smithsonian Instn., 1948, 50, Am. Found. Study Man, 1951, U. Wash., 1953, State U. Idaho, 1960. Author: Wooden Saints, the Santos of New Mexico, 1967, A Comparative View of Spanish Colonial Sculpture, 1968, Arroyo Hondo, the Folk Art of a New Mexican Village, 1969, A Comparative View of Spanish Colonial Painting, 1970, A Show of Color: 100 Years of Painting in the Pike's Peak Region, 1971, Russian Orthodox Art in Alaska, 1973, Sydney Laurence, an Alaskan Impressionist, 1975, Eustace Ziegler, 1977, Contemporary Native Art of Alaska, 1979, Henry Wood Elliott, 1982; Editor: An Introduction to the Native Art of Alaska, 1972; assoc. editor: Exploration in Alaska, 1980. Served with USAAF, 1942-45. Mem. Am. Assn. Museums. Home and Office: 309 W Marsh St Salisbury NC 28144-5345

SHALLENBERGER, GARVIN F., lawyer; b. Beloit, Wis., Jan. 7, 1921; s. Garvin D. and Grace (Hubbell) S.; m. Mary L., May 5, 1945; children: Diane, Dennis Clark. BA in Pre-law, U. Mont., 1942; JD, U. Calif., Berkeley, 1949; LLD (hon.), Western State U., Fullerton, Calif., 1988. Bar: Calif. 1949, U.S. Dist. Ct. (cent. dist.) Calif. 1949, U.S. Ct. Appeals (9th cir.) 1949, U.S. Supreme Ct. 1961, U.S. Dist. Ct. (no. and so. dists.) Calif. 1963. Rutan & Tucker, Costa Mesa, Calif.; chmn. spl. adv. com. state bar legal svcs. program, 1979-89, pub. law ctr Orange County, 1979-90. Recipient distinguished svc. award Boalt Hall (U. Calif. Berkeley); Judge Learned Hand Human Rel. award Nat. Jewish Com., 1990. Fellow Am. Coll. Trial Lawyers; mem. Am. Bd. Trial Advs. (founder and 1st sec.),Calif. Bar Assn. (bd. govs. 1975-76, pres. 1977-78; mem. com. on jud. nominees 1978-79, pres. 1980), mem. Orange County Bar Assn. (bd. dirs. 1970-71, pres. 1972, Franklin West award 1979). Democrat. Avocations: tennis, writing. Office: Rutan & Tucker 611 Anton Blvd PO Box 1950 Costa Mesa CA 92626

SHALOWITZ, ERWIN EMMANUEL, civil engineer; b. Washington, Feb. 13, 1924; s. Aaron Louis and Pearl (Myer) S.; m. Elaine Mildred Langerman, June 29, 1952; children—Ann Janet, Aliza Beth, Jonathan Avram. Student, U. Pa., U. Notre Dame, 1944-45; B.C.E., George Washington U., 1947, postgrad., 1948-49; grad. soil mechanics, Cath. U., 1951; M.A. in Pub. Adminstrn. (fellow U.S. Civil Service Commn.), Am. U., 1954. Registered profl. engr., Washington. Engr. Klemitt Engring. Co., N.Y.C., 1947; with cons. firm Whitman, Requardt & Assos., Balt., 1947-48; chief structural research engr., head def. research sect., project officer and tech. adviser for atomic tests Bur. Yards and Docks, Dept. Navy, Washington, 1948-59; supervisory gen. engr. spl. asst. for protective constrn. programs, project mgr. for bldg. systems, chief research br., chief mgmt. information, chief contracting procedures and support, chief contract evaluation and analysis, Pub. Bldgs. Service, Gen. Services Adminstrn., Washington, 1959—; also team leader/project mgr. Electronic Acquisition Sy. Pub. Bldgs. Service, Gen. Services Adminstrn., Washington; chmn. fed. exec. tng. program U.S. Civil Service Commn., 1950; fallout shelter analyst Dept. Def.; chmn. GSA Fire Safety Com., GSA Fallout Protection Com., GSA Bldg. Evaluation Com.; mem. Interagy Com. on Housing Rsch. and Bldg. Tech.; mem. Nat. Evaluation Bd. Architect-Engr. Selections; mem. standing com. on procurement policy Nat. Acad. Sci. Bldg. Research Adv. Bd. and Interagency Com. on Procurement Curriculum Rev.; coordinator pub. bldgs. design and constrn. Small Bus. Program and Minority Enterprise and Minority Subcontracting Programs. Contbr. articles profl. jours. Served to engring. officer USNR, 1944-46. Recipient Commendable Svc. award GSA, 1968, Outstanding Performance recognition, 1976, 77, 79, 83, 87, 93-96, Superior Accomplishment award, 1995, others; Engr. Alumni Achievement award George Washington U., 1985. Fellow ASCE, Am. Biog. Inst.; mem. Soc. Advancement Mgmt., Am. Biog. Inst. (nat. bd. advisors), Soc. Am. Mil. Engrs., Sigma Tau, Pi Sigma Alpha. Jewish. Home: 5603 Huntington Pky Bethesda MD 20814-1132 Office: 19th and F Sts NW Washington DC 20405 *PRINCIPLES: Look beyond the material for lasting values and meaning, optimize managerial effectiveness by creating an objective and challenging climate in an organization, delve into the underlying causes of problem areas for meaningful solutions, and persevere in spite of obstacles. IDEAS: Cultural pluralism; the intrinsic potential of each individual; and love, appreciation, and support of one's family as indispensable for real accomplishment. GOALS: To attain the highest level of professional accomplishment within my capabilities and to continue to have a rich, happy, and fulfilling family life. STANDARDS OF CONDUCT: To be fair, consistent, and straightforward; and to avoid over-reacting.*

SHAM, LU JEU, physics educator; b. Hong Kong, Apr. 28, 1938; s. T.S. and Cecilia Maria (Siu) Shen; m. Georgina Bien, Apr. 25, 1965; children: Kevin Shen, Alisa Shen. GCE, Portsmouth Coll., Eng., 1957; BS, Imperial Coll., London U., Eng., 1960; PhD in Physics, Cambridge U., Eng., 1963. Asst. rsch. physicist U. Calif. at San Diego, La Jolla, 1963-66, assoc. prof., 1968-75, prof., 1975—, chair dept. physics, 1995—, dean div. natural scis., 1985-89; asst. prof. physics U. Calif. at Irvine, 1966-67; rsch. physicist IBM Corp., Yorktown Heights, N.Y., 1974-75; reader Queen Mary Coll., U. London, 1967-68. Assoc. editor Physics Letters A., 1992—; contbr. sci. papers to profl. jours. Recipient Churchill Coll. studentship, Eng., 1960-63, Sr. U.S. Scientist award Humboldt Found., Stuttgart, Germany, 1978; fellow Guggenheim Found., 1984, Chancellor Assocs. award for Excellence in Rsch., 1995. Fellow Am. Phys. Soc.; mem. AAAS. Democrat. Avocation: tennis, folk dancing. Office: U Calif San Diego Dept Physics 0319 La Jolla CA 92093-0319

SHAMANSKY, ROBERT NORTON, lawyer; b. Columbus, Ohio, Apr. 18, 1927; s. Harry Solomon and Sarah (Greenberg) S. BA Polit. Sci. cum laude, Ohio State U., 1947; JD, Harvard U., 1950. Bar: Ohio 1950, U.S. Supreme Ct. 1963. Ptnr. Feibel, Feibel, Shamansky & Rogovin, Columbus, 1954-81; mem. U.S. House Reps., Washington, 1981-83; ptnr. Guren, Merritt, Sogg & Cohen, Columbus, Ohio, 1981-84; ptnr. Benesch, Friedlander, Coplan & Aronoff, Columbus, Ohio, 1984-93, of counsel, 1993; mem. Nat. Security Edn. Bd., 1994—; pres., founder Legal Aid and Defender Soc., Columbus, 1955-58; spkr. in field. Contbr. articles to newspapers. Mem. Rickenbacker Port Authority, Franklin County, Ohio, 1983-86; chmn. Indsl. Tech. and Enterprise adv. bd. State Ohio, Columbus, 1983-89. With U.S. Army, 1950-52. Mem. ABA, Ohio State Bar Assn. (chmn. legal ethics and profl. conduct com. 1970-73), Columbus Bar Assn., Columbus Housing Partnership, Inc. (sec. 1987-91, bd. dirs. 1987-96), Coun. Ethics in Econs. (bd. dirs. 1983-93), Phi Beta Kappa. Democrat. Jewish. Avocations: fgn., domestic travel, pub. policy. Home: 678 Mohawk St Columbus OH 43206-2109 Office: Benesch Friedlander Coplan & Aronoff 88 E Broad St Columbus OH 43215-3506

SHAMASH, YACOV, dean, electrical engineering educator; b. Iraq, Jan. 12, 1950; m. Linda Shamash, June 21, 1976; children: Aharon, Hela. BSEE, Imperial Coll., London, 1970; PhD in Control Systems, Imperial Coll., 1973. Postdoctoral fellowin elec. engring. Tel-Aviv U., 1973-75, from lectr. elec. engring. to sr. lectr. elec. engring., 1975-78; prof. elec. engring. Fla. Atlantic U., Boca Raton, 1977-85; prof., chair dept. elec. engring. dept. Wash. State U., Pullman, 1985-92; dean engring. SUNY, Stony Brook, 1992—; bd. dirs. KeyTronics, Spokane, Wash., 1990—; vis. asst. prof. U. Pa., Phila., 1976-77. Contbr. over 100 articles to profl. jours., book chpts. Fellow IEEE (sr.). Office: SUNY Coll Engring & Applied Sci Stony Brook NY 11790-2200

SHAMBAUGH, GEORGE ELMER, III, internist; b. Boston, Dec. 21, 1931; s. George Elmer and Marietta Susan (Moss) S.; m. Katharine Margaret Matthews, Dec. 29, 1956 (dec.); children: George, Benjamin, Daniel, James, Elizabeth; m. Martha Repp Davis, Jan. 3, 1987 (dec.). B.A., Oberlin Coll., 1954; M.D., Cornell U., 1958. Diplomate Am. Bd. Internal Medicine. Gen. med. intern Denver Gen. Hosp., 1958-59; research fellow physiologic chemistry U. Wis.-Madison, 1968-69; asst. prof. medicine Northwestern U. Med. Sch., Chgo., 1969-74, assoc. prof., 1974-81, prof., 1981—; mem. Ctr. for Endocrinology, Metabolism and Molecular Medicine, 1969—; chief endocrinology and metabolism VA Lakeside Med. Ctr., Chgo., 1974—; attending physician Northwestern Meml. Hosp., Chgo., 1969—. Contbr. articles to text books and profl. jours. Served with M.C., U.S. Army, 1959-67. NIH spl. postdoctoral fellow, 1967-69; Schweppe Found. fellow, 1972-75. Fellow ACP; mem. Am. Fedn. Clin. Rsch., Sci. Rsch. Soc., am. Endocrine Soc., Am. Thyroid Assn., Am. Inst. Nutrition, Am. Soc. Clin. Nutrition, Am. Physiol. Soc., Ctrl. Soc. Clin. Rsch., Inst. Medicine Chgo., Taipei Internat. Med. Soc. (pres. 1960), N.Y. Acad. Sci., Euro Diabetes Assn., Am. Men and Women of Sci., Sigma Xi, Nu Sigma Nu. Home: 530 S Stone Ave La Grange IL 60525-2720 Office: Northwestern Med Faculty Found Inc 303 E Ohio St Fl 460 Chicago IL 60611 also: VA Lakeside Med Ctr 333 E Huron St Chicago IL 60611-3004

SHAMBUREK, ROLAND HOWARD, physician; b. Adell, Wis., June 7, 1928; s. William and Catherine (Illig) S.; m. Gladys Irene Gibbons, June 21, 1952; children: Steven J., Robert D., Daniel J. BS, U. Wis., 1950, MD, 1953; MPH, Harvard U., 1960. Diplomate: Am. Bd. Preventive Medicine. Commd. 1st lt. M.C., U.S. Army, 1953, advanced through grades to col., 1968; intern St. Joseph's Hosp., Marshfield, Wis., 1953-54; grad. U.S. Naval Sch. of Aviation Medicine, Pensacola, Fla., 1957; resident in preventive medicine USAF Sch. Aerospace Medicine, Brooks AFB, 1960-63; service in Europe, 1955-56, 63-66; comdr. 67th EVAC Hosp., Vietnam, 1970-71, U.S. Army Med. Pers. Support Agy., 1975-77; ret., 1977; exec. v.p. Aerospace Med. Assn., 1977-79; clin. practice Pentagon Health Clinic, Washington, 1981-85; med. researcher Office of Army Surgeon Gen., 1985-87. Contbr. papers in field. Decorated Legion of Merit with oak leaf cluster, Commendation medal, Meritorious Service medal. Mem. AMA (del. 1978), Assn. Mil. Surgeons (John Shaw Billings award 1968), Am. Coll. Preventive Medicine (v.p. 1968-69), Aerospace Med. Assn. (v.p. 1968-69), Soc. Med. Cons. Armed Forces, Soc. U.S. Army Flight Surgeons, Soc. NASA Flight Surgeons, Internat. Acad. Aviation and Space Medicine, Internat. Health Soc. Address: 3700 Moss Dr Annandale VA 22003-1915

SHAMES, HENRY JOSEPH, lawyer; b. Milw., Jan. 20, 1921; s. Aron and Jennie (Greenberg) S.; m. Beverly Cleveland Van Wert, June 9, 1972; children: Stephen H., Suzanne Shames Sattelmeyer, Sarah Shames Phillips, Diana Shames Strandberg. A.B., U. Chgo., 1942; J.D., Harvard U., 1948. Bar: Ill. 1949, Calif. 1962. Mem. firm Arvey, Hodes & Mantynband, Chgo., 1949-61; partner Pacht, Ross, Warne, Bernhard & Sears, Los Angeles, 1962-75, Grossman & Shames, Los Angeles, 1975-83, Rosenfeld, Parnell & Shames Inc., Los Angeles, 1984-86; counsel Patterson, Belknap, Webb and Tyler, Los Angeles, 1986-87; chmn. bd. Switzer Center, Los Angeles, 1966-73. Served with USNR, 1943-46. Mem. Assn. Bus. Trial Lawyers (bd. govs. 1973-76, v.p. 1973-76), Calif. State Bar Assn., So. Def. Counsel, Los Angeles County Bar Assn., Phi Beta Kappa. Home: 4906 La Ramada Dr Santa Barbara CA 93111-1518 Office: 1875 Century Park E Los Angeles CA 90067-2501

SHAMES, IRVING HERMAN, engineering educator; b. Oct. 31, 1923; married; 2 children. BSME, Northeastern U., 1948; MS in Applied Mechanics, Harvard U., 1949; PhD in Applied Mechanics, U. Md., 1953. Instr. U. Md., College Park, 1949-53, asst. prof. mech. engring., 1953-55; asst. prof. Stevens Inst. Tech., Hoboken, N.J., 1955-57; prof., chmn. dept. engring. sci. Pratt Inst., Bklyn., 1957-62, acting chmn. dept. physics, 1960-61; prof., chmn. div. interdisciplinary studies and research Sch. Engring. SUNY, Buffalo, 1962-70, faculty prof. engring., applied sci., 1970-73, 79—, prof., chmn. dept. engring. scis., aerospace engring. and nuclear engring., 1973-83, disting. teaching prof., 1980—; prof. George Washington U., Washington, 1995—; lectr. Naval Ordnance Lab, 1952-55; vis. prof. materials dept. Technion, Israel, 1969, mech. engring. dept., 1976; Disting. vis. prof. George Washington U., 1993. Author: Engineering Mechanics: Statics, 1959, 3d rev. edit., 1980, Engineering Mechanics: Dynamics, 1959, 3d rev. edit., 1980, Mechanics of Fluids, 1962, rev. edit., 1982, 3d edit., 1992, Mechanics of Deformable Solids, 1964, (with C. Dym) Solid Mechanics- A Variational Approach, 1973, Introduction to Statics, 1971 Introduction to Solid Mechanics, 1975, (with C. Dym) Energy and Finite Elements in Structural Mechanics, 1985, (with F. Cozzarelli) Elastic and Inelastic Stress Analysis, 1992; editor McGraw-Hill Series in Advanced Engineering; contbr. numerous articles to profl. jours.; several books translated in Portuguese, Spanish, Japanese, Korean, Chinese, Arabic. Mem. Sigma Xi, Tau Beta Pi, Phi Eta Sigma, Pi Tau Sigma, Golden Key. Home: 1113 Fairview Ct Silver Spring MD 20910-4148

SHAMMAS, NAZIH KHEIRALLAH, environmental engineering educator, consultant; b. Homs, Syria, Feb. 18, 1939; came to U.S., 1991; s. Kheirallah Hanna and Nazha Murad (Hamwi) S.; m. Norma Massouh, July 28, 1968; children: Sarmed Erick, Samer Sam. Engring. degree with distinction, Am. U., Beirut, Lebanon, 1962; MS in Sanitary Engring., U. N.C., 1965; PhD in Civil Engring., U. Mich., 1971. Instr. Civil Engring. Am. U., Beirut, Lebanon, 1965-68; asst. prof. Civil Engring. Am. U., Beirut, 1972-76; tchg. fellow U. Mich., Ann Arbor, 1968-71; asst. prof. Civil Engring. King Saud U., Riyadh, Saudi Arabia, 1976-78; assoc. prof. King Saud U., Riyadh, 1978-91; prof. Environ. Engring. Lenox (Mass.) Inst. Water Tech., 1991—, dean edn., 1992-93; sr. prof. Sr. U., 1994—; adj. prof. environ. sci., Berkshire C.C., 1995—; cons., ptnr. Cons. and Rsch. Engrs., Beirut, 1973-76; advisor, cons. Riyadh Water and Sanitary Drainage Authority, 1979-83; Ar-Riyadh Devel. Authority, 1977-93, Associated Consulting Engring. Team, 1994—; assoc. cons. Vakakis Internat., 1995—. Co-author: Environmental Sanitation, 1988, Wastewater Engineering, 1988; contbr. over 30 articles to profl. jours. and confs. Recipient block grant U. Mich., 1968-70, Excellence in Teaching award King Saud U., 1981, 84. Mem. ASCE, Water Environ. Fedn., Am. Water Works Assn., New Eng. Water Environ. Assn., New Eng. Water Works Assn., Internat. Assn. Water Quality, Assn. Environ. Engring. Profs. Achievements include research on biological and physicochemical remediation processes, math. modeling of nitrification process, water and wastewater mgmt. in developing countries, water conservation, wastewater treatment and reuse, appropriate tech. for developing countries, multidisciplinary studies in environmental management and planning. Home: 14 Joan Dr Pittsfield MA 01201-8417 Office: Lenox Inst Water Tech 101 Yokun Ave Lenox MA 01240-2032

SHAMMAS, NICOLAS WAHIB, internist, cardiologist; b. Amyoun, El-Koura, Lebanon, Jan. 31, 1963; came to U.S., 1988; s. Wahib Nicolas and Vera Yousuf (El-Helou) S.; m. Gail Ann Hanson, Feb. 22, 1991; children: Waheeb John, Andrew Nicolas. BSc with distinction, Am. U. Beirut, Lebanon, 1983, MD, 1987, MSc in Physiology, 1987, Diploma in Computer Programming, 1985. Diplomate internal medicine, cardiology. Postdoctoral rsch. fellow Am. U. Beirut, 1987-88; resident in internal medicine U. Iowa Hosps., Iowa City, 1988-91; instr. medicine, clin. fellow cardiology U. Rochester (N.Y.) Med. Ctr., 1991-94; fellow assoc. in cardiology U. Iowa Hosps., Iowa City, 1995—; mem. staff Genesis Med. Ctr., Davenport, Iowa, 1995; founder Mastermind Pub., Phenix Realty Co., 1997. Author: (with others) Flavors of Lebanon, 1995; contbr. articles to profl. jours. Am. U. Beirut Univ. Rsch. Bd. awardee, 1986-87, John C. Sable Meml. Heart award J.C. Sable Fund, 1993, Trainee Investigator award for clin. rsch. meeting, Balt., 1994. Fellow Am. Coll. Cardiology; mem. AMA, ACP, Am. Fedn. Clin. Rsch., Am. Soc. Internal Medicine, Iowa Med. Soc. Achievements include research in basic cardiology: prostacyclin inhibits aminoacid transport in myocardial cells and modulates transmembrane calcium movements; dopamine binding sites are increased in hypertrophied rat hearts induced by renovascular hypertension; myocardial viability in hybernating myocardium cannot be predicted by clinical and exercise hemodynamic criteria; coronary flow reserve is underestimated if blood flow changes are assessed using flow velocity measurements alone; pretreatment with intracoronary nitroglycerin corrects this problem. Office: Cardiovasc Medicine PC 1230 E Rusholme St Ste 305 Davenport IA 52803-2400

SHAMOO, ADIL ELIAS, biochemist, biophysicist, educator; b. Baghdad, Iraq, Aug. 1, 1941; came to U.S., 1964, naturalized, 1973; s. Elias M. and Mariam T. (Mansour) S.; m. Joan Hutchison, Dec. 16, 1967; children: Abraheem, Zachary, Jessica. B.Sc. in Physics, U. Baghdad, 1962; M.S. in Physics (grad. fellow), U. Louisville, 1966; Ph.D. in Biophysics, CUNY, 1970. Instr. engring. physics Speed Sch., U. Louisville, 1965-68; asst. prof. physiology City U. N.Y., 1971-73; guest worker Lab. Biophysics and Neurochemistry, NIH, Bethesda, Md., 1972-73; asst. prof. radiation biology and biophysics U. Rochester, 1973-75; guest prof. Max-Planck Inst. Biophysics, Frankfurt, West Germany, 1977-78; assoc. prof. radiation biology and biophysics U. Rochester, 1975-79; prof., chmn. dept. biol. chemistry U. Md., Balt., 1979-82, head membrane biochemistry research lab., 1982-90, prof. dept. biochemistry and molecular biology, 1982—; cons. div. biol. scis. Kodak Co., Rochester, 1976-77; NIH tng. fellow U. Louisville, 1967; investigator Am. Heart Assn., 1976-79; Neurosci. Rsch. Program fellow, Boulder, Colo., summer 1977; pres. Sci. Profls. Inc., 1985-95; chmn. symposia, various coms. in field; mem. organizing coms. workshops in field; adj. profl. dept. physics East Carolina U., Greenville, N.C., 1996—. Editor (with M.W. Miller) Membrane Toxicity, 1977, Carriers and Channels in Biological Systems, 1975, Carriers and Channels in Biological Systems-Transport Proteins, 1980, Regulation of Calcium Transport Across Muscle Membranes, 1985, Principles of Research Data Audit, (with R. Verna) Biotechnology Today, 1995; editor in chief Membrane Biochemistry, 1977-93, Accountability in Research: Policies and Quality Assurance, 1988—; mem. editl. bd. Molecular and Cellular Biochemistry, 1987-94, Quality Assurance: Good Practice Regulation and Law, 1991—; contbr. articles and abstracts to profl. jours., chpts. to books. Bd. dirs. Alliance for Mentally Ill of Md., 1990-93, Friends Med. Rsch. Ctr., Inc., 1994-97; mem. rsch. monitoring com. Nat. Alliance for Mentally Ill, bd. dirs. 1994-97; pres. faculty senate U. Md., Balt., 1993-94; mem. coun. univ. systems U. Md., 1994—; mem. adv. com. Vantage Pl., 1995—; bd. dirs. Howard County Mental Health Authority, 1997—, Citizens for Responsible Care in Psychiatry and Rsch., 1996—. Recipient Advocacy award Mental Health Assn. Md., 1994, Disting. Svc. award Alliance for Mentally Ill of Md., 1994. Mem. AAAS, AAUP (chpt. sec. 1971-72), Basic Sci. Council of Am. Heart Assn., Am. Soc. Biol. Chemists and Mol. Biol., Am. Coll. Sports Medicine, Am. Assn. Physics Tchrs., Am. Physiol. Soc., Biophys. Soc. (Cole Membrane Award Com. 1983-84, chmn. biophysics subgroup 1982-83, council 1986-89), Membrane Biophys. Group (chmn. 1982-83, sec.-treas. 1983-85, co-chmn. U.S. bioenergetics group 1979-80), Md. Acad. Scis. (chmn. com. programs and exhbns. 1986-87, sci. council 1985-89), N.Y. Acad. Scis., Coun. of Biology (editor 1989—), Soc. Quality Assurance. Achievements include patents for liquid scintillators. Office: 108 N Greene St Baltimore MD 21201-1503

SHAMOS, MORRIS HERBERT, physicist educator; b. Cleve., Sept. 1, 1917; s. Max and Lillian (Wasser) S.; m. Marion Jean Cahn, Nov. 26, 1942; 1 son, Michael Ian. AB, NYU, 1941, MS, 1943, PhD, 1948; postgrad., MIT, 1941-42. Faculty NYU, 1942—, prof. physics, 1959-83, prof. emeritus, 1983—; chmn. dept. Washington Sq. Coll., 1957-70; sr. v.p. research and devel. Technicon Corp., 1970-75, chief sci. officer, 1975-83, also dir., prin. sci. cons., 1983-92; pres. M.H. Shamos & Assocs., 1983—; chmn. Protein Databases, Inc., 1985-90, Sci. Imaging Corp., 1985-88; Med. Mktg. Internat., 1992-94; dir. Anagen Ltd., 1989-92, Nat. Assn for Sci., Tech. & Soc., 1990-91, Anagen Holdings, Ltd., 1992-97, Xsirius, Inc., 1993-96; chmn. Med. Mktg. Internat., 1992-94; Cons. pvt. industry; cons. Armament Center, USAF, 1955-57, Tung-Sol Electric, Inc., 1949-65, Office Pub. Information, UN, 1958, NBC, 1957-67, AEC, 1957-70, N.Y. Eye and Ear Infirmary, 1961-64, 79—, L.I. Jewish Hosp., 1962—, N.Y.C. Health Dept., 1961-70, Technicon Instruments Corp., 1964-70, U.S. Office Edn., 1964-72. Author: Great Experiments in Physics, 1959, The Myth of Scientific Literacy, 1995 (Ness award 1995); co-editor: Recent Advances in Science, 1956, Industrial and Safety Problems of Nuclear Technology, 1950; cons. editor Addison-Wesley Pub. Co., 1965-69; adv. bd. Jour. Coll. Sci. Teaching, 1971-80, Clin

Lab. Guide Am. Chem. Soc., 1972-76. Dir. tng., N.Y.C. Office Civil Def., 1950-54; subscribing mem. N.Y. Philharmonic Soc.; mem. adv. council Pace U., 1971—, N.Y. Poly. Inst., 1980—; trustee Hackley Sch., 1971-80, Westchester Arts Council. Poly. U. fellow. Fellow N.Y. Acad. Scis. (past chmn. phys. sci., bd. govs. 1977-83, rec. sec. 1978-80, v.p. 1980-81, pres. 1982), AAAS; mem. IEEE, AAUP, AFTRA, NSTA (pres. 1967), Am. Chem. Soc., Nat. Assn. Ednl. Broadcasters, Am. Phys. Soc., Assn. Physics Tchrs. Britain, Chemist's Club, Am. Assn. Clin. Chemists, Cosmos Club, Phi Beta Kappa, Sigma Xi, Pi Mu Epsilon, Sigma Pi Sigma. Clubs: Cosmos, Chemists. Spl. research atomic and nuclear physics, biophysics. Home: 3515 Henry Hudson Pky Bronx NY 10463-1326

SHANAFELT, NANCY SUE, quality consultant, career consultant; b. Northampton, Mass., Nov. 21, 1947; m. John D. Shanafelt; children: Amy, Nicholas. BS, U. Mass., 1969; MA in Human Resources/Orgnl. Devel., U. San Francisco, 1991. Tchr. Southwick (Mass.) Pub. Schs., 1969-70; acctg. asst. Maricopa County Schs., Phoenix, Ariz., 1973-74; tax auditor to br. chief IRS, San Jose, 1974-89; enrolled agt., 1984-85; OD specialist IRS, San Jose, 1991-93; creator IRS Women's Network, San Francisco, 1981—. Leader Girl Scouts U.S., Santa Clara, 1980-96, Golden Valley, 1996—, cons., 1981-82, 96—, svc. mgr., 1982-84, trainer, 1982-84; leader Boy Scouts Am., 1992-96; facilitator Unwed Parents Anonymous, 1992—; master catechist Diocese of San Jose, 1992-96. Recipient Disting. Performance award IRS, 1993, 95. Mem. AAUW, NAFE, ASTD, Calif. Assn. for Counseling and Devel., Federally Employed Women, Commonwealth Club Am., Italian Cath. Fedn. (sec. 1991—), Bay Area Orgnl. Devel. Network, Medugorje PGL. Avocations: antique cars, travel. Office: Mail Stop FR4300 821 M St Fresno CA 93721-2716

SHANAHAN, BRENDAN FREDERICK, professional hockey player; b. Mimico, Ont., Canada, Jan. 23, 1969. Formerly with St. Louis Blues; with Hartford Whalers, 1995—. Played in NHL All-Star Game, 1994, 96; named to NHL All-Star First Team, 1993-94. Office: care Hartford Whalers 242 Trumbull St 8th Fl Hartford CT 06103

SHANAHAN, EILEEN FRANCES, secondary education educator; b. Bethlehem, Pa., Sept. 10, 1949; d. Edward Vincent and Geraldine Mary (Gilligan) S. BA, Moravian Coll., 1971. Cert. secondary tchr. in Spanish, English, N.J. Tchr. Kingsway Regional High Sch. Dist., Swedesboro, N.J., 1971—. Mem. NEA, N.J. Edn. Assn., Gloucester County Edn. Assn., Fgn. Lang. Educators N.J., Kingsway Edn. Assn. (sec. membership), Hellertown Hist. Soc. Democrat. Roman Catholic. Avocations: archaeology, historical research, genealogy.

SHANAHAN, ELIZABETH ANNE, art educator; b. High Point, N.C., Apr. 5, 1950; d. Joe Thomas and Nancy Elizabeth (Moran) Gibson; m. Robert James Shanahan, Aug. 31, 1969 (div. Mar. 1987); children: Kimberly Marie Shanahan Conlon, Brigette Susanne. Student, Forsyth Tech. Coll., 1974-83, Tri-County Tech. Coll., 1989, Inst. of Children's Lit., 1989. Owner cleaning bus. Winston-Salem, N.C., 1985-86, 87; instr. Anderson (S.C.) Arts Coun., 1987—, Tri-County Tech. Coll., Pendleton, S.C., 1987—. Artist Wild Geese, 1985 (Best in Show). Active Libr. of Congress, 1994. Mem. Anderson Art Assn. (con. 1987—), Met. Arts Coun. (Upstate Visual Arts divsn.), Triad Art Assn. (pres. Kernersville, N.C. chpt. 1984-85), Nat. Mus. Women in Arts (charter), Libr. of Congress (charter). Avocations: writing, sewing, traveling, decorating. Home: 7 Woodbridge Ct Anderson SC 29621-2260 Office: Tri County Tech Coll PO Box 587 Pendleton SC 29670-0587

SHANAHAN, EUGENE MILES, flow measurement instrumentation company executive; b. Great Falls, Mont., Sept. 18, 1946; s. Raymond Eugene and Helen Marjorie (Graham) S.; m. Beverly Ann Braaten, Sept. 8, 1967; children—Bret Allen, Shaun Eugene, Shae Erin. B.S. in Mech. Engring., Mont. State U., 1968; M.S., Mont. State U., 1969; M.B.A., Portland State U., 1976. Registered profl. engr., Oreg. Mech. engr. Tektronix, Beaverton, Oreg., 1968-71; mech. engr. Shell Oil Co., Martinez, Calif., 1967; chief mech. project engr. Mears Controls, Beaverton, 1971-76; mktg. mgr. Mears Controls, 1976-79; v.p., gen. mgr. Eaton Corp., Beaverton, 1979-87; pres. Dieterich Standard (a Fisher-Rosemount Co.), Boulder, Colo., 1987—. Served with N.G., 1969-75. NSF trainee, 1969. Mem. ASME, Instrumentation Soc. Am., Tau Beta Pi, Phi Kappa Phi, Pi Tau Sigma. Home: 8417 Sawtooth Ln Niwot CO 80503-7281 Office: Dieterich Standard PO Box 9000 Boulder CO 80301-9000

SHANAHAN, MICHAEL GEORGE, police officer; b. Seattle, Oct. 14, 1940; s. Raymond Roderick and Carletta (Anderson) S.; m. Jo-Anne Genevieve David, Sept. 16, 1961; children: Patrick, Matthew, Raymond. BA in Psychology, Stanford U., 1962. Asst. police chief U. Wash., Seattle, 1971-75, vol. police cons. and mgmt. pvt. sector issues, 1995—; mem. law enforcement task force interim mcpl. com. Wash. State Legis., 1970-71, campus law enforcement task force-higher edn. com., 1970-71; co-chmn. Wash. Law Enforcement Standards Task Force; founding chmn. Washington Law Enforcement Exec. Forum, 1981, Operation Bootstrap, 1985, others. Author: Private Enterprise and the Public Police: The Professionalizing Effects of a New Partnership, 1985; contbr. articles to profl. jours. Mem. nat. exploring com. Boy Scouts Am., 1977, exec. bd., chief Seattle council, 1984-88; mem. Blanchet High Sch. Bd., Seattle, 1978-79, Gov.'s Coun. on Criminal Justice, 1980-81, Gov.'s Coun. Food Assistance, 1983-86. Major U.S. Army, 1963-70, Vietnam. Decorated Bronze Star; recipient award for pub. svc. U.S. Dept. Transp., 1984, Humanitarian award Seattle chpt. NCCJ, 1985, Silver Beaver award Boy Scouts Am., 1986, St. Matthew award Northwest Harvest, 1987, Paul J. Breslin award Internat. Security Mgrs. Assn., 1990, Criminal Justice award of excellence Wash. State U., 1989. Mem. FBI Nat. Acad. Assocs., Nat. Inst. Justice (peer rev. program), Internat. Assn. Chiefs of Police (life, bd. officers 1983-84, gen. chmn. divsn. state assns. 1983-84, co-chmn. pvt. sector liaison com.), Police Exec. Rsch. Forum, Wash. Assn. Sheriffs and Police Chiefs, Rotary Internat. (pres. Univ. Rotary Club Seattle 1985-86, founding chmn. Rotary Op. First Harvest, Svc. Above Self award 1988). Roman Catholic. Avocations: fishing, gardening.

SHANAHAN, MIKE, professional football coach; b. Oak Park, Ill., Aug. 24, 1952; m. Peggy, children: Kyle, Krystal. BS Phys. Edn., Eastern Illinois U., Charleston, Ill., 1974; MS Phys. Edn., 1975. Student coach Eastern Illinois U.; asst. coach U. Oklahoma, 1975-76; offensive coord., No. Ariz. U., 1976-77, Ea. Ill. U., 1977-78, U. Minn., 1979-80, offensive coord., U. Fla., 1980-84, asst. head coach, 1983-84; receivers coach Denver Broncos, 1984-87; head coach Los Angeles Raiders, 1988-89; asst. coach Denver Broncos, NFL, 1989-91; offensive coordinator San Francisco 49ers, 1992-94; head coach Denver Broncos, 1995—. Golf, travel. Office: care Denver Broncos 13655 Broncos Pkwy Englewood CO 80112-4150*

SHANAHAN, ROBERT B., banker; b. Buffalo, Jan. 8, 1928; s. Bart J. and Florence (Dietrich) S.; m. Janet I. Mulholland, Feb. 6, 1954; children: Maureen Shanahan DeRose, Timothy, Karin Halpern, Molly Healy, Colleen Collins, Mark, Ellen Becker. BS in Econs., U. Pa., 1951. New bus. rep. Assocs. Discount Corp., Buffalo, 1951-55; pres. Universal Time Plan, Inc., Buffalo, 1956-67; v.p. Norstar Bank, Buffalo, 1967-69, sr. v.p., 1969-72, exec. v.p., dir., 1972-91; bd. dirs. Eastern States Bankcard Assn., Lake Success, N.Y., Chase Fed. Bank, Miami, Fla. Contbg. author: The Bankers Handbook, 1978; mem. adv. coun. Banking Mag., 1978-84; contbr. articles to profl. jours. Pres. Multiple Sclerosis Assn. Western N.Y., Buffalo, 1982-86; trustee Theodore Roosevelt Inaugural Site, Inc., Buffalo, 1983—; pres. Buffalo Council on World Affairs, 1984-86; chmn. Catholic Charities Buffalo, 1986-87, 89-90. Served with U.S. Army, 1944-46. Decorated Knight of Holy Sepulchre Order, 1991, Knight Commdr., 1996; recipient Past Pres.'s award Multiple Sclerosis Assn., 1985. Mem. Am. Bankers Assn. (bd. dirs. 1977-84, chmn. installment lending divsn. 1978-79, edn., policy and devel. coun. 1983-84, Eagle award 1978), N.Y. State Bankers Assn. (mem. exec. com. consumer divsn. 1988-90), Buffalo Area C. of C., U. Pa. Club Western N.Y. (bd. dirs.), Buffalo Club, Cherry Hill Club (Ridgeway, Ont., Can.) (pres. 1992-93). Republican. Roman Catholic. Home: A-3 109 Half Moon Cir Lantana FL 33462

SHANAHAN, SHEILA ANN, pediatrician, educator; b. N.Y.C., July 1, 1943; d. James Patrick and Eleanor Margaret (Breslin) S.; m. Justin Laurence Cashman Jr., Sept. 14, 1968; children: Justin III, Gillis. BA, Trinity Coll., 1963; MD cum laude, Med. Coll. Pa., 1969. Diplomate Nat. Bd. Med. Examiners, Am. Bd. Pediats. Intern Presbyn. Hosp., N.Y.C., 1969-70, resident in pediats., 1970-72, asst. in clin. pediats., 1972-75, assoc. clin. pediats., 1975-78; pvt. practice specializing in pediats. Greenwich, Conn., 1972-78; asst. attending Greenwich Hosp., 1972-73, assoc. attending, 1973-78; from instr. to assoc. Columbia Coll. Physicians and Surgeons, N.Y.C., 1972-78; asst. prof. pediats. George Washington U. Sch. Medicine, Washington, 1980—, Georgetown U. Sch. Medicine, Washington, 1984—; pvt. practice specializing in pediats. Washington, 1984—; attending dept. ambulatory medicine Children's Hosp. Nat. Med. Ctr., Washington, 1980-84; courtesy staff Georgetown U. Hosp., Washington, 1984—, George Washington U. Hosp., 1984—, Sibley Meml. Hosp., Washington, 1984—, Columbia Hosp. for Women, 1984—, Children's Hosp. Nat. Med. Ctr., 1984—. Fellow Am. Acad. Pediats.; mem. Am. Women's Med. Assn. Office: 4900 Massachusetts Ave NW Washington DC 20016-4358

SHANAHAN, THOMAS M., judge; b. Omaha, May 5, 1934; m. Jane Estelle Lodge, Aug. 4, 1956; children: Catherine Shanahan Trofholz, Thomas M. II, Mary Elizabeth, Timothy F. A.B. magna cum laude, U. Notre Dame, 1956; J.D., Georgetown U., 1959. Bar: Nebr., Wyo. Mem. McGinley, Lane, Mueller, Shanahan, O'Donnell & Merritt, Ogallala, Nebr.; assoc. justice Nebr. Supreme Ct., Lincoln, 1983-93; judge U.S. Dist. Ct. Nebr., Omaha, 1993—. Office: US Dist Ct PO Box 457 Omaha NE 68101-0457

SHANAS, ETHEL, sociology educator; b. Chgo., Sept. 6, 1914; d. Alex and Rebecca (Rich) S.; m. Lester J. Perlman, May 17, 1940; 1 child, Michael Stephen. AB, U. Chgo., 1935, AM, 1937, PhD, 1949; LHD (hon.), Hunter Coll., N.Y.C., 1985. Instr. human devel. U. Chgo., 1947-52, rsch. assoc. prof., 1961-65; sr. rsch. analyst City of Chgo., 1952-53; sr. study dir. Nat. Opinion Rsch. Ctr., Chgo., 1956-61; prof. sociology U. Ill., Chgo., 1965-82, prof. emerita, 1982—; vice chmn. expert com. on aging UN, 1974; mem. com. on aging NRC, Washington, 1978-82, panel on statistics for an aging population, 1984-86; mem. U.S. Com. on Vital and Health Stats., Washington, 1976-79. Author: The Health of Older People, 1962; (with others) Old People in Three Industrial Societies, 1968; editor: (with others) Handbook of Aging and the Social Sciences, 1976, 2d edit., 1985. Bd. govs. Chgo. Heart Assn., 1972-80; mem. adv. council on aging City of Chgo., 1972-78. Keston lectr. U. So. Calif., 1975; recipient Burgess award Nat. Council on Family Relations, 1978; Disting. Chgo. Gerontologist award Assn. for Gerontology in Higher Edn., 1988. Fellow Gerontol. Soc. Am. (pres. 1974-75, Kleemeier award 1977, Brookdale award 1981), Am. Sociol. Assn. (chmn. sect. on aging 1985-86 Disting. Scholar award, 1987); mem. Midwest Sociol. Soc. (pres. 1980-81), Inst. Medicine of Nat. Acad. Scis. (sr. mem.). Home: 222 Main St Evanston IL 60202

SHANDLING, GARRY, comedian, scriptwriter, actor; b. Chgo., Nov. 29, 1949; s. Irving and Muriel S. Grad., U. Ariz. TV screenwriter: Sanford and Son, Welcome Back Kotter, Three's Company; guest host The Tonight Show, 1986-88; host Emmy Awards 1987, 88, Grammy Awards 1990, 91, 92; writer, prodr. Garry Shandling: Alone in Las Vegas, 1984; exec. prodr., writer It's Garry Shandling's Show 25th Anniversary Special, 1986, It's Garry Shandling's Show, 1986-90 (Ace award best comedy series 1989, 90, Ace award best actor in a comedy seires 1990), Garry Shandling: Stand-Up, 1991, The Larry Sanders Show, 1992— (CableAce award, Writing in a Comedy Series, 1994); actor: (film) Love Affair, 1994, Mixed Nuts, 1994. Office: Brillstein/Grey 9150 Wilshire Blvd Ste 350 Beverly Hills CA 90212-3430*

SHANDS, COURTNEY, JR., lawyer; b. St. Louis, Mar. 17, 1929; s. Courtney and Elizabeth W. (Jones) S.; m. Frances Jean Schellfeffer, Aug. 9, 1952 (div. 1976); children: Courtney III, E.F. Berkley, Elizabeth V.; m. Nancy Bliss Lewis, Oct. 25, 1980. AB, Washington U., St. Louis, 1951; LLB, Harvard U., 1954. Assoc. Thompson and Mitchell, St. Louis, 1954-62, ptnr., 1962-63; ptnr. Thompson, Walther and Shewmaker, St. Louis, 1963-69, Kohn, Shands, Elbert, Gianoulakis & Giljum, St. Louis, 1970—. Trustee Frank G. and Florence V. Bohle Scholarship Found., Edward Chase Garvey Meml. Found., L.F. Jones Charitable Trust, 1958-60; bd. dirs. St. Louis Fund, 1972—, Law Libr. St. Louis, 1988—, pres. 1995—; bd. dirs. Hope Ednl. & Rsch. Found., 1989—, pres. 1995—, Citizenship Edn. Clearing House, St. Louis, 1985-87, pres. 1986-87, Mark Twain Summer Inst., St. Louis, 1968-89, pres., 1974-79; Andrews Acad., 1989—, v.p., 1989—; pres. com. Goldwater for Pres., Met. St. Louis, 1964, Ea. Mo. chpt. ACLU, 1966-69, nat. bd. dirs. 1969-72. Mem. ABA, Mo. Bar Integrated, Bar Assn. of Met. St. Louis, Selden Soc., Law Libr. Assn. (Mo. sect.), Noonday Club, Racquet Club, St. Louis Club. Republican. Episcopalian. Office: Kohn Shands Elbert 1 Mercantile Ctr Fl 24 Saint Louis MO 63101-1643

SHANDS, HENRY LEE, plant geneticist, administrator; b. Madison, Wis., Aug. 30, 1935; s. Ruebush George and Elizabeth (Henry) S.; m. Catherine Miller, Nov. 20, 1962; children: Deborah A., Jeanne A., James L. BS, U. Wis., 1957; MS, Purdue U., 1961, PhD, 1963. NSF fellow Swedish Seed Assn., Svalov, 1962-63; asst. prof. Purdue U., West Lafayette, Ind., 1963-66, asst. prof. botany and plant pathology, 1965-66; rsch. agronomist, leader ea. wheat project Dekalb Hybrid Wheat, Inc., Lafayette, 1966-79; rsch. agronomist, dir. sunflower rsch. Dekalb-Pfizer Genetics and predecessor firms, Glyndon, Minn., 1979-86; nat. program leader for plant germplasm USDA Agrl. Rsch. Svc., Beltsville, Md., 1986-92, assoc. dep. adminstr. for genetic resources, 1992-97, asst. adminstr. genetic resources, 1997—; mem. AID Project, Minas Gerais, Brazil, 1963-65. 1st lt. U.S. Army, 1957-59. Recipient 1st Victor M. Bendelow Meml. Lectr. award U. Man., 1992. Fellow AAAS, Am. Soc. Agronomy, Crop Sci. Soc. Am. (Frank N. Meyer medal for plant genetic resources 1992); Am. Genetic Assn., Genetics Soc. Can., Am. Phytopath. Soc. Office: USDA-ARS Bldg 005 BARC-W Beltsville MD 20705-2350

SHANDS, WILLIAM RIDLEY, JR., lawyer; b. Richmond, Va., Nov. 23, 1929; s. William Ridley and Josephine (Winston) S.; m. Lynneth Williams, May 31, 1958; children: William Tyler, Laura Sawyer. B.A., Hampden-Sydney Coll., 1952; LL.B., U. Va., 1958. Bar: Va. 1958. Atty., asso. firm Christian, Barton, Epps, Brent & Chappell, Richmond, 1958-61; counsel The Life Ins. Co. of Va., Richmond, 1961-66; asst. gen. counsel The Life Ins. Co. of Va., 1966-68, asso. gen. counsel, 1968-71, gen. counsel, 1971-73, v.p., gen. counsel, 1973-78, sr. v.p., gen. counsel, 1978-79; sr. v.p. law and public affairs Continental Fin. Services Co., Richmond, 1980-85; sr. v.p., sec. Life Ins. Co. Va., Richmond, 1985-88; counsel Sands, Anderson, Marks & Miller, Richmond, 1988—. Chmn. Eastern Appeal Bd. Selective Svc. System, 1969; pres., chmn. bd. dirs. Trinity Episcopal High Sch., 1971-72; bd. dirs. Richmond Area Heart Assn., 1965-71, Southampton Cotillion, 1970-72; vestryman St. Michael's Episc. Ch., 1965-68, sr. warden, 1968. Served with AUS, 1952-55, Philippines. Mem. Va. Bar Assn., Richmond Bar Assn., Assn. Life Ins. Counsel (pres. 1987-88), Am. Coun. Life Ins. (chmn. legal sect. 1982-83), Commonwealth Club, Country Club Va. Home: 3811 Darby Dr Midlothian VA 23113-1318 Office: Sands Anderson Marks & Miller 801 E Main St # 1998 Richmond VA 23219-2901

SHANE, JOHN MARDER, endocrinologist; b. Kansas City, Mo., Oct. 5, 1942; s. Henry Kamsler and Ruth (Marder) S.; m. Eileen Goodart, June 18, 1967; children: Robert M., Edward G. BS, U. Okla., 1964, MD, 1967. Diplomate Am. Bd. Ob-Gyn., Am. Bd. Reproductive Endocrinology. Resident Harvard Med. Sch., Boston, 1970-73, fellowship, 1973-75, instr., 1970-75, asst. prof., 1975-78; pvt. practice Tulsa, 1978—; lectr., cons. Tutorial Svcs. Internat., England, 1984—; bd. dirs. St. Francies G.I.F.T. Lab., Tulsa; cons. to preimplantation genetics project Chapman Genetics Inst., Children's Med. Ctr., Tulsa. Author: CIBA Symposium Infertility: Diagnosis and Treatment; contbr. articles to profl. jours. and publs. Mem. Tulsa Garden Ctr., 1988—; bd. dirs. Temple Israel, Tulsa, 1985-86, cited in The Best Doctor's in Am.:Ctrl. Region. Captain USAF, 1967-69. Recipient Annual award Boston Obstet. Soc., 1977. Mem. ACS, Tulsa Gynecol. Soc. (past pres. 1986-87), Soc. Reproductive Endocrinologists, Tulsa bonsai Soc. (bd. dirs. 1988—), Am. Coll. Ob-Gyn. (v.p. 1971-92, pres. New England Jr. divsn. 1972-73), Am. Bonsai Soc. (nat. bd. dirs.), Chanie des Rotisseurs (l'Ordre Mondial, Tulsa v.p.), Southside Rotary of Tulsa (bd. dirs., pres. 1997—), Nat. Arboretum (nat. bd. dirs.). Republican. Jewish. Avocations: bonsai, collector oriental arts. Office: 1705 E 19th St Ste 703 Tulsa OK 74104-5418

SHANE, PETER MILO, law educator; b. Oceanside, N.Y., July 12, 1952; s. Albert and Ann (Semanoff) S.; m. Martha Elisabeth Chamallas, June 27, 1981; 1 child, Elisabeth Ann. AB, Harvard U., 1974; JD, Yale U., 1977. Bar: N.Y. 1978, U.S. Ct. Appeals (5th cir.) 1978, D.C. 1979, U.S. Ct. Appeals (8th cir.) 1983, U.S. Supreme Ct. 1984, Pa. 1995. Law clk. to judge U.S. Ct. Appeals (5th cir.), New Orleans, 1977-78; atty., advisor office of legal counsel, U.S. Dept. Justice, Washington, 1978-81; asst. gen. counsel Office of Mgmt. and Budget, Washington, D.C., 1981; assoc. prof. law U. Iowa, Iowa City, 1981-85, prof., 1985-94; dean, prof. law U. Pitts., 1994—; adj. lectr. Am. U., Washington, D.C., 1979-80; vis. prof. law Duke U., Durham, N.C., 1986; cons. U.S. Dept. Edn., Washington, D.C., 1980, MacArthur Justice Found., Chgo., 1987; active Adminstrv. Conf. U.S., 1991, pub. mem. 1995; cons. Nat. Commn. Jud. Discipline and Removal, 1992-93; cooperating atty. Iowa Civil Liberties Union, Des Moines, 1982-94, bd. dirs., 1987-89; active Coun. on Legal Edn. Opportunity, 1996—; reporter Civil Justice Adv. Group, U.S. Dist. Ct. we. dist. Pa. Author: (with H.H. Bruff) The Law of Presidential Power: Cases and Materials, 1988, (with J. Mashaw and R. Merrill) Administrative Law: The American Public Law System, 1992, (with H.H. Bruff) Separation of Powers Law, 1996. Mem. Dem. cen. com. Johnson County, Iowa, 1982-88. Old Gold Summer fellow U. Iowa, 1981-84, Mellon Found fellow, 1982. Mem. ABA (coun. sect. adminstrv. law and regulatory practice 1993-96, chmn. com. on govt. orgn. and separation of powers 1987-91), Assn. Am. Law Schs. (chair adminstrv. law 1990, chair remedies 1992, chair law sch. deans 1997). Jewish. Office: U Pitts Sch Law 3900 Forbes Ave Pittsburgh PA 15213

SHANE, RITA, opera singer, educator; b. N.Y.C.; d. Julius J. and Rebekah (Milner) S.; m. Daniel F. Tritter, June 22, 1958; 1 child, Michael Shane. BA, Barnard Coll., 1958; postgrad., Santa Fe Opera Apprentice Program, 1962-63, Hunter Opera Assn., 1962-64; pvt. study with, Beverly Peck Johnson, Elizabeth Schwartzkopf, Bliss Hebert. Adj. prof. voice Manhattan Sch. of Music, 1993-95; prof. voice Eastman Sch. Music Rochester U., 1989—; pvt. teachng, N.Y.C., 1978—; judge Richard Tucker Music Found. Performer with numerous opera cos., including profl. debut, Chattanooga Opera, 1964, Met. Opera, San Francisco Opera, N.Y.C. Opera, Chgo. Lyric Opera, San Diego Opera, Santa Fe Opera, Teatro alla Scala, Milan, Italy, Bavarian State Opera, Netherlands Nat. Opera, Geneva Opera, Vienna State Opera, Phila., New Orleans, Balt. Opera, Opera du Rhin, Strasbourg, Scottish Opera, Teatro Reggio, Turin, Opera Metropolitana, Caracas, Portland Opera, Minn. Opera, also others; world premiere Miss Havisham's Fire, Argento; Am. premieres include Reimann-Lear, Schat-Houdini, Henze-Elegy for Young Lovers; participant festivals, including Mozart Festival, Lincoln Center, N.Y.C., Munich Festival, Aspen Festival, Handel Soc., Vienna Festival, Salzburg Festival, Munich Festival, Perugia Festival, Festival Canada, Glyndebourne Festival, performed with orchs. including Santa Cecilia, Rome, Austrian Radio, London Philharmn., Louisville, Cin., Cleve., Phila., RAI, Naples, Denver, Milw., Israel Philharm., rec. artist, RCA, Columbia, Louisville, Turnabout labels, also radio and TV. Recipient Martha Baird Rockefeller award, William Matheus Sullivan award. Mem. Am. Guild Mus. Artists, Screen Actors Guild. Office: care Daniel F Tritter 330 W 42nd St New York NY 10036-6902

SHANE, RONALD, financial company executive; b. Chgo., May 9, 1953. A.A., Miami Dade Jr. Coll., 1972; B.A., Fla. Internat. U., 1974. Pres. Trans Leasing of Fla., Ft. Lauderdale, 1976-77; co-founder, pres. Assoc. Leasing Internat. Corp., Ft. Lauderdale, 1977—; v.p., dir. Assoc. Fin. Internat. Corp., Ft. Lauderdale, 1977—, Assoc. Mortgage Internat. Corp., Ft. Lauderdale, 1980—. Contbr. articles to fin. trade jours. Sec., mem. bd. dirs. Manors of Inverrary CondoAssn., Lauderhill, Fla., 1971, 72; mem. archtl. com. San Simeon Homeowners Assn., Boca Raton, Fla., 1984—. Recipient Personalities of Am. award, 1986. Mem. Internat. Machine Tool Assn. (assoc.), Graphic Arts and Printing Soc. (assoc.), Radiol. Soc. N.Am. (assoc.), Roll Royce Owners Cub Club, Antique Automobile Club, Classic Car Club, Riviera Owners Club, Fraternal Order of Police (assoc. Nat. Grand Lodge, chartered), Woodlands Country Club (Tamarac, Fla., jr. mem.). Avocations: collecting and restoring classic cars, power boating, golf, travel. Office: Assoc Leasing Internat Corp 1489 W Palmetto Park Rd Ste 475 Boca Raton FL 33486-3326

SHANE, SANDRA KULI, postal service administrator; b. Akron, Ohio, Dec. 12, 1939; d. Amiel M. and Margaret E. (Brady) Kuli; m. Fred Shane, May 30, 1962 (div. 1972); 1 child, Mark Richard; m. Byrl William Campbell, Apr. 26, 1981 (dec. 1984). BA, U. Akron, 1987, postgrad., 1988-90. Scheduler motor vehicle bur. Akron Police Dept., 1959-62; flight and ops. control staff Escort Air, Inc., Akron and Cleve., 1972-78; asst. traffic mgr. Keen Transport, Inc., Hudson, Ohio, 1978-83; mem. ops. and mktg. staff Shawnee Airways and Essco, Akron, 1983-86; in distbn. U.S. Postal Svc., Akron, 1986—; rec. sec. Affirmative Action Coun., Akron, 1988-90. Asst. art tchr. Akron Art Mus., 1979; counselor Support, Inc., Akron, 1983-84; com. chmn. Explorer post Boy Scouts Am., Akron, 1984-85. Mem. Bus. and Profl. Women's Assn. (pres.), Delta Nu Alpha. Democrat. Roman Catholic. Avocations: painting, sculpting, fabric design. Home: 455 E Bath Rd Cuyahoga Falls OH 44223-2511

SHANE, WILLIAM WHITNEY, astronomer; b. Berkeley, Calif., June 3, 1928; s. Charles Donald and Mary Lea (Heger) S.; BA, U. Calif., Berkeley, 1951, postgrad., 1953-58; ScD, Leiden (The Netherlands) U., 1971; m. Clasina van der Molen, Apr. 22, 1964; children: Johan Jacob, Charles Donald. rsch. assoc. Leiden U., 1961-71, sr. scientist, 1971-79; prof. astronomy, dir. Astron. Inst., Cath. U. Nijmegen, The Netherlands, 1979-88; guest prof. astronomy Leiden U., 1988-93; C.H. Adams fellow Monterey (Calif.) Inst. Rsch. Astronomy, 1994—. With USN, 1951-53. Fellow AAAS; mem. Internat. Astron. Union (commns. 33, 34), Am. Astron. Soc., Astron. Soc. Netherlands, Astron. Soc. of the Pacific, Phi Beta Kappa. Achievements include research on structure and dynamics of galaxies, observational astronomy. Home: 9095 Coker Rd Prunedale CA 93907-1401 Office: Monterey Inst Rsch Astronomy 200 8th St Marina CA 93933-6002

SHANEFIELD, DANIEL JAY, ceramics engineering educator; b. Orange, N.J., Apr. 29, 1930; s. Benjamin and Nan (Leichter) S.; m. Elizabeth Davis, June 28, 1964; children: Alison, Douglas. BS in Chemistry, Yale U., 1952; PhD in Chemistry, Rutgers U., 1962. Sr. project engr. ITT Group, Nutley, N.J., 1962-67; sr. mem. tech. staff AT&T Bell Labs., Princeton, N.J., 1967-86; disting. prof. Rutgers U., New Brunswick, N.J., 1986—; adv. panel NSF, 1990—; course dir. Ctr. for Profl. Advancement, U.S. and The Netherlands, 1993—; cons. in field; presenter at profl. confs. Author: Organic Additives and Ceramic Processing, 1995; co-author: Defects in Gold Plating, 1981; contbr. 4 chpts. to tech. books, articles to profl. jours.; co-inventor 17 patents; assoc. editor Jour. Am. Ceramic Soc., 1987—. With U.S. Army, 1952-54, Korea. Fellow Am. Inst. Chemists, Am. Ceramic Soc. (Best Paper award); mem. IEEE (chmn. standards com. 1984—), Am. Chem. Soc., Ceramic Assn. of N.J. (Man of Yr. award 1996). Republican. Avocations: modifying sports cars, writing audio, stereo articles. Home: 119 Jefferson Rd Princeton NJ 08540-3373 Office: Rutgers U Ceramics Engring Dept PO Box 909 Piscataway NJ 08855-0909

SHANG, CHARLES YULIN, medical physicist; b. Shanghai, May 6, 1956; came to U.S., 1987; s. Jian and Ming Shang; m. Monica Jinhong Meng, Aug. 1, 1985; children: Stephen, Michael. MD, 2nd Med. Coll., Shanghai, China, 1983; postdoctoral cert., Chgo. Med. Sch., North Chgo., Ill., 1988; MS in Radiation, Health/Med. Physics, U. Pitts., 1990. Diplomate in Radiological Physics, Am. Bd. Radiology. Resident 301 Gen. Hosp., Beijing, China, 1983-85; radiologist 301 Gen. Hosp., Beijing, 1985-87; vis. radiologist Evanston (Ill.) Univ. Hosp., 1988, Allegheny Gen. Hosp., Pitts., 1988-89; grad. student rschr. Presbyn. Univ. Hosp., Pitts., 1989-90; med. physicist St. Mary's Hosp., Waterbury, Conn., 1991-93; sr. med. physicist Boca Raton (Fla.) Comty. Hosp., 1993—. Contbr. articles to profl. jours. including Radiology, Neurosurgery, Annals N.Y. Acad. Scis., IEEE Transactions on Biomed. Engring. Recipient grad. scholarship U. Pitts., 1989-90. Mem. Am. Assn. Physicists in Medicine, Am. Coll. Radiology. Achievements include patents on a handheld body stereotactic guider for interventional radiology, China and U.S. Office: Boca Raton Cmty Hosp Lynn Regional Cancer Ctr 16313 Military Trl Delray Beach FL 33484-6628

SHANG, ER-CHANG, acoustician; b. Sheng Yain, Liaonin, China, Feb. 5, 1932; came to U.S., 1986.; BS in Theoretical Physics, Peking U., Beijing, China, 1958; PhD equivalent, Inst. Acoustics, Acad. Sinica, Beijing, 1982. Asst. prof. Inst. of Acoustics, Beijing, 1958-62, assoc. prof., 1962-75, prof., 1975-82, dep. dir., 1982-86; sr. rsch. assoc. AOML/NOAA, Miami, Fla., 1983-84, Wave Propagation Lab./NOAA, Boulder, Colo., 1987-88; NRC postdoctoral advisor Wave Propagation Lab./NOAA, 1991—; rsch. assoc. CIRES/U. Colo./NOAA, Boulder, 1988-91, rsch. prof., supervisor, 1991—; vis. scientist Scripps Inst. Oceanography, U. Calif. San Diego, La Jolla, 1982-83; vis. prof. U. Wis., Madison, 1983, Yale U., New Haven, 1986-87. Author: Underwater Acoustics, 1981. Recipient Nat. award for sci. Nat. Com. of Sci, Beijing, 1982, 89. Fellow Acoustical Soc. Am. Achievements include new method of source localization in ocean waveguides--matched mode processing; modal ocean acoustic tomography and applied for El Nino monitoring; impact of mode-coupling on modal travel time in ocean waveguide; modal theory in shallow water acoustics. Office: ETL/NOAA 325 Broadway St Boulder CO 80303-3337

SHANGE, NTOZAKE (PAULETTE WILLIAMS), playwright, poet; b. Trenton, N.J., Oct. 18, 1948; d. Paul T. and Eloise Williams; m. David Murray, July 4, 1977 (div.); 1 child: Savannah. BA in Am. Studies cum laude, Barnard Coll., 1970; MA in Am. Studies, U. So. Calif., 1973. mem. faculty Sonoma State U., 1973-75, Mills Coll., 1975, CCNY, 1975, Douglass Coll., 1978; lectr. in field. Author: (plays) for colored girls who have considered suicide/when the rainbow is enuf, 1975 (Obie award for best play 1977, Outer Critics Circle award for best play 1977, Audelco award 1977, Tony award nomination for best play 1977, Grammy award nomination for best spoken word rec. 1977), Melissa and Smith, 1976, A Photograph: A Study of Cruelty, 1977, (with Thulani Nkabinde and Jessica Hagedorn) Where the Mississippi Meets the Amazon, 1977, Boogie Woogie Landscapes, 1978, From Okra to Greens, 1978, Spell #7: A Geechee Quick Magic Trance Manual, 1979, Black and White Two Dimensional Planes, 1979, Mouths, 1981, A Photograph: Lovers in Motion, 1981, Three For a Full Moon, 1982, Bocas, 1982, Three Views of Mt. Fuji, 1987; (adaptations) Mother Courage and Her Children (Brecht), 1980 (Obie award for best play 1981), Educating Rita, 1982; (operetta) Carrie, 1981; (novels) Sassafrass, 1976, Sassafrass, Cypress and Indigo, 1982, Betsey Brown, 1985, Liliana: Resurrection of the Daughter, 1994; (poems) Natural Disasters and Other Festive Occasions, 1977, Nappy Edges, 1978, Three Pieces, 1981 (L.A. Book prize for poetry 1981), A Daughter's Geography, 1983, From Okra to Greens, 1984, The Love Space Demands, 1991, I Live in Music, 1994; (non-fiction) See No Evil: Prefaces, Essays and Accounts 1976-1983, 1984, Ridin' the Moon in Texas: Word Paintings, 1987; contbr. poetry, essays and short stories to numerous mags. and anthologies, including Third World Women, Chgo. Rev., Am. Rag, Sojourner, Womansports; actress: For Colored Girls Who Have Considered Suicide/When the Rainbow is Enuf, 1976, Where the Mississippi Meets the Amazon, 1977; dir.: The Mighty Gents, 1979, A Photograph: A Study in Cruelty, 1979, The Issue, 1979, The Spirit of Sojourner Truth, 1979; writer: An Evening with Diana Ross: The Big Event, 1977 (Emmy award nomination 1977); performing mem.: Sounds in Motion Dance Co.; performed in various jazz/poetry collaborations; dancer with Third World Collective, Raymond Sawyer's Afro-American Dance Co., Sound in Motion, West Coast Dance Works; founder, dancer For Colored Girls Who Have Considered Suicide. Recipient Frank Silvera Writer's Workshop award, 1978, Excellence medal Columbia U., 1981, Taos World Poetry Heavyweight Champion, 1992, 93, 94; NDEA fellow, 1973, Guggenheim fellow, 1981. Mem. Actors Equity, Nat. Acad. TV Arts and Scis., Acad. Am. Poets, Dramatist's Guild, PEN Am Center, Poets and Writer's, Inc., N.Y. Feminist Art Guild. Office: care St Martins Press 175 5th Ave New York NY 10010-7703*

SHANIES, HARVEY MICHAEL, pulmonologist, medical educator; b. N.Y.C., Nov. 17, 1944; s. William and Helen (Friedman) S.; children: Tabitha Amity, David Bradley. BS, George Washington U., 1966; MS, NYU, 1968, PhD, 1970, MD, 1973. Diplomate Am. Bd. Med. Examiners, Am. Bd. Internal Medicine, Am. Bd. Critical Care Medicine, Subspecialty Bd. in Pulmonary Diseases. Intern Bronx (N.Y.) Mcpl. Hosp. Ctr., 1973-74, med. resident, 1974-75, resident chest medicine, 1975-76, chief resident chest medicine, 1976-77; med. dir. respiratory care svcs. San Dimas (Calif.) Community Hosp., 1977-88, Foothill Prebyn. Hosp., Glendora, Calif., 1983-88; dir. respiratory ICU Mt. Sinai Svcs., Elmhurst (N.Y.) Hosp. Ctr., 1988-93, chief pulmonary medicine, 1993—; asst. prof. medicine Mt. Sinai Sch. Medicine, N.Y.C., 1988—, clin. assoc. prof. medicine, 1997—. Author: Pulmonary Emergencies, 1993; editor: Medicine Stat! Cards, 1992. Fellow NSF, 1961, NIH, 1968-70. Fellow Am. Coll. Chest Physicians, Am. Coll. Angiology; mem. Am. Thoracic Soc. (bd. dirs. joint rev. com. for respiratory therapy edn. 1996—). Office: Elmhurst Hosp Ctr 79-01 Broadway Elmhurst NY 11373-1329

SHANK, FRED ROSS, federal agency administrator; b. Harrisonburg, Va., Oct. 11, 1940; m. Peggy Anne Westbrook, June 1967; children: Virginia Anne, Fred Ross III. BS in Agriculture, U. Ky., 1962, MS in Nutrition, 1964; PhD, U. Md., 1969. Dep. dir. Office Nutrition and Food Sci. FDA, Washington, 1979-86, dir. Office Phys. Sci., 1986-87, dep. dir. Ctr. for Food SAfety and Applied Nutrition, 1987-89, dir., 1989—. Fellow Inst. Food Technologists; mem. Am. Assn. Cereal Chemists, Am. Inst. Nutrition, Am. Soc. for Clin. Nutrition, Assn. Food and Drug Ofcls. Home: 2621 Steeplechase Dr Reston VA 20191-2130 Office: FDA Ctr Food Safety & Applied Nutrition 200 C St SW Washington DC 20204-0001

SHANK, MAURICE EDWIN, aerospace engineering executive, consultant; b. N.Y.C., Apr. 22, 1921; s. Edwin A. and Viola (Lewis) S.; m. Virginia Lee King, Sept. 25, 1948; children: Christopher K., Hilary L. Shank-Kuhl, Diana L. Shank. B.S. in Mech. Engring., Carnegie-Mellon U., 1942; D.Sc., MIT, 1949. Registered profl. engr., Mass. Assoc. prof. mech. engring. MIT, Cambridge, 1949-60; with Pratt & Whitney, East Hartford, Conn., 1960-87, dir. engine design and structures engring., 1980-81, dir. engring. tech., 1981-85, dir. engring. tech. assessment, 1985-86; v.p. Pratt Whitney of China, Inc., East Hartford, 1986-87; pvt. exec. cons. to industry and govt., 1987—; cons. editor McGraw-Hill Book Co., N.Y.C., 1960-80; adv. com. to mechanics div. Nat. Bur. Standards, Washington, 1964-69; vis. com. dept. mech. engring. Carnegie-Mellon U., Pitts., 1968-78; corp. vis. coms. depts. materials sci. and engring., dept. aeros. and astronautics MIT, 1968-74, 79-92; mem. rsch. and tech. adv. coun. com. on aero. propulsion NASA, Washington, 1973-77, mem. aero. adv. com., 1978-86; mem. aero. and space engring. bd. NRC, 1989-92; lectr. in field. Contbr. articles to profl. jours. Served to maj. U.S. Army, 1942-46. Fellow AIAA, ASME, AIME, Am. Soc. Metals; mem. Nat. Acad. Engring., Conn. Acad. Sci. and Engring. Episcopalian. Club: Cosmos. Avocations: boating; fishing.

SHANK, ROBERT ELY, physician, preventive medicine educator emeritus; b. Louisville, Sept. 2, 1914; s. Oliver Orlando and Isabel Thompson (Ely) S.; m. Eleanor Caswell, July 29, 1942; children: Jane, Robert Oliver, Bruce. A.B., Westminster Coll., 1935; M.D., Washington U., 1939. Diplomate: Am. Bd. Nutrition. Intern, house physician Barnes Hosp., 1939-41; asst. resident physician, asst. in research Hosp. Rockefeller Inst. Med. Research, 1941-46; research assoc. div. nutrition and physiology Pub. Health Research Inst. City N.Y., 1946-48; prof. preventive medicine Washington U. Sch. Medicine, 1948-55, Danforth prof. preventive medicine, 1955-83, prof. emeritus preventive medicine, 1983—; Cutter lectr. preventive medicine Harvard, 1964; Mem. food and nutrition bd. NRC, 1949-69; spl. cons. nutrition USPHS, 1949-53; chmn. adv. bd. health and hosps., St. Louis County, 1949-54; med. adv. bd. St. Louis Vis. Nurses Assn., 1950-86; mem. com. food and nutrition nat. adv. bd. health services A.R.C., 1950-53; mem. adv. com. metabolism Office Surgeon Gen., 1956-60, mem. adv. com. on nutrition, 1964-72; mem. Am. Bd. Nutrition, 1955-64, sec., treas., 1958-64; mem. Nat. Bd. Med. Examiners, 1957-58; co-dir. nutrition survey NIH, Peru, 1959, N.E. Brazil, 1963; mem. sci. adv. bd. Nat. Vitamin Found., 1958-61; mem. nutrition study sect. NIH, 1964-68, chmn. sect., 1966-68; mem. gastroenterology and nutrition tng. com., 1968-69, mem. nat. adv. child health and human devel. council, 1969-73; mem. clin. application and prevention adv. com. Nat. Heart, Lung and Blood Inst., 1976-80. Author sects. in med. textbooks, sci. papers relating to nutritional, metabolic disorders.; Asso. editor: Nutrition Revs, 1948-58; editorial adv. bd.: Nutrition Today, 1966-76, Hepatology, 1980-85. Served as lt. comdr. M.C. USNR, 1942-46. Recipient Alumni Achievement award Westminster Coll., 1970, Alumni Faculty award Washington U., 1989. Fellow Am. Pub. Health Assn. (governing council 1955-56), Am. Inst. Nutrition; mem. N.Y. Acad. Scis., Harvey Soc., Am. Soc. Biol. Chemists, Soc. Exptl. Biology and Medicine (council 1952-54), Central Soc. Clin. Research, Am. Soc. Clin. Investigation, Assn. Tchrs. Preventive Medicine (v.p. 1955-57, pres. 1957-58), A.M.A. (council on foods and nutrition 1960-69, chmn. 1963-66), Gerontological Soc., Assn. Am. Physicians, Am. Soc. Clin. Nutrition (council 1963-65, pres. 1967-68), Am. Dietetic Assn. (hon.), Am. Soc. for Study Liver Diseases (council 1963-66, pres. 1966), Am. Heart Assn. (chmn. nutrition com. 1973-76, award of merit 1981), Sigma Xi, Alpha Omega Alpha. Presbyterian. Home: 1325 Wilton Ln Saint Louis MO 63122-6940 Office: Wash U Sch Medicine 4566 Scott Ave Saint Louis MO 63110-1031

SHANK, RUSSELL, librarian, educator; b. Spokane, Wash., Sept. 2, 1925; s. Harry and Sadie S.; m. Doris Louise Hempfer, Nov. 9, 1951 (div.); children: Susan Marie, Peter Michael, Judith Louise. B.S., U. Wash., 1946, B.A., 1949; M.B.A., U. Wis., 1952; Dr.L.S., Columbia U., 1966. Reference libr. U. Wash., Seattle, 1949; asst. engring. libr. U. Wis.-Madison, 1949-52; chief pers. Milw. Pub. Libr., 1952; engring.-phys. scis. libr. Columbia U., N.Y.C., 1953-59; sr. lectr. Columbia U., 1964-66, assoc. prof., 1966-67; asst. univ. libr. U. Calif.-Berkeley, 1959-64; dir. sci. libr. N.Y. Met. Reference and Rsch., 1966-68; dir. librs. Smithsonian Instn., Washington, 1967-77; univ. libr. prof. UCLA, 1977-89, asst. vice chancellor for libr. and info. svcs. planning, 1989-91, univ. libr., prof. emeritus, 1991—; cons. Indonesian Inst. Sci., 1970; bd. cons. Pahlavi Nat. Library, Iran, 1975-76; pres. U.S. Book Exchange, 1975; bd. trustees Freedom to Read Found., 1989—. Trustee OCLC, Inc., 1978-84, 87, chmn., 1984; mem. library del. People's Republic of China, 1979; bd. dirs. Am. Council on Edn., 1980-81. Served with USNR, 1943-46. Recipient Disting. Alumnus award U. Wash. Sch. Librarianship, 1968, Role of Honor award Freedom to Read Found., 1990, Disting. Alumnus award Columbia U. Sch. Libr. Sci., 1992; fellow Coun. on Libr. Resources, 1973-74. Fellow AAAS; mem. ALA (pres. 1978-79, coun. 1961-65, 74-82, exec. bd. 1975-80, chmn. internat. rels. com. 1980-83, pres. info. sci. and automation div. 1968-69), Assn. Coll. and Rsch. Librs. (pres. 1972-73, Hugh Atkinson award 1990), Assn. Rsch. Librs. (bd. dirs. 1974-77). Home: 12919 Montana Ave Apt 101 Los Angeles CA 90049-4843 *Intellectual freedom is the paramount human right. It is the American's premier heritage. Without it the claim to democracy is a sham. Should the principles of our society fade or perish, the survival of this freedom alone would justify the nation's experience. The freedom to think, to read, and to speak will be our enduring monument. Their diffusion throughout the world must be our unending crusade.*

SHANK, WILLIAM O., lawyer; b. Hamilton, Ohio, Jan. 11, 1924; s. Horace Cooper and Bonnie (Winn) S.; m. Shirleen Allison, June 25, 1949; children—Allison Kay, Kristin Elizabeth. BA, Miami U., Oxford, O., 1947; JD, Yale, 1950. Bar: Ohio, Ill. bars, also U.S. Supreme Ct. bar. Pvt. practice Hamilton, Ohio, 1951-55, Chgo., 1955—; mem. firm Shank, Briede & Spoerl, 1951-55; assoc. Lord, Bissell & Brook, 1955-58; atty. Chemetron Corp., 1958-60, sr. atty., 1960-61, gen. atty., asst. sec., 1961-71, sec., gen. counsel, 1971-78; v.p., gen. counsel, sec. Walgreen Co., Deerfield, Ill., 1978-89; ptnr. Burditt & Radzius, Chartered, Chgo., 1989—; exec. v.p. Internat. Bus. Resources, Inc., Chgo., 1993—; mem. bus. adv. coun. Miami U., Oxford, Ohio, 1975—. Bd. dirs. Coun. for Cmty. Svcs. Met. Chgo., 1973-77; trustee Libr. Internat. Rels., 1971-78; bd. dirs. Chgo. Civic Fedn., 1984-89, Walgreen Drug Stores Hist. Found., 1990—; mem. Chgo. Crime Commn., 1985-89. 1st lt., pilot 8th Air Force, USAAF, World War II, ETO. Fellow Am. Bar Found. (life); mem. ABA (com. corp. gen. counsel), Ill. Bar Assn., Chgo. Bar Assn. (chmn. com. on corp. law depts. 1971-72, 89-90), Am. Soc. Corp. Secs. (pres. Chgo. regional group 1983-84, nat. bd. dirs. 1984-87), Yale U. Law Sch. Assn. (pres. Ill. Alumni, formerly exec. com. New Haven), Walgreen Alumni Assn. (pres. 1992-94), Legal Club (pres. 1979-80), Law Club, Univ. Club, Econ. Club, Yale Club of Chgo., Omicron Delta Kappa, Phi Delta Phi, Sigma Chi. Home: 755 S Shore Dr Crystal Lake IL 60014-5530 Office: Burditt & Radzius Chartered 333 W Wacker Dr Ste 2600 Chicago IL 60606-1227

SHANKEL, DELBERT MERRILL, microbiology and biology educator; b. Plainview, Nebr., Aug. 4, 1927; s. Cecil Wilfred and Gladys Dalton (Dodd) S.; m. Carol Jo Mulford, Sept. 10, 1962; children: Merrill, Jill, Kelley. BA, Walla Walla Coll., 1950; PhD, U. Tex., 1959. Tchr. Walla Walla Coll. Acad., College Place, Wash., 1950-51; instr. San Antonio Coll., 1954-55; asst. prof., assoc. prof. microbiology and biology U. Kans., Lawrence, 1959-68, prof., 1968—, asst. dean, assoc. dean arts and sci., 1966-72, acting dean, 1973, exec. vice chancellor, 1974-80, 86, 90-92, acting chancellor, 1980-81, chancellor, 1994-95, prof. and chancellor emeritus, 1996; cons., evaluator, commr. North Cen. Assn. Colls. and Schs., Chgo., 1969-96. Editor: (conf. procs.) Antimutagenesis and Anticarcinogenesis: Mechanisms, Vols. 1-3, 1986, 89, 93; assoc. editor Mutation Rsch., 1992-95. Active numerous civic orgns. With U.S. Army, 1952-54. Named Outstanding Educator award Mortar Bd., U. Kans., 1982, 85, 90, Disting. Alumnus of Yr., Walla Walla Coll., 1989; recipient numerous grants for sci. rsch. Fellow Am. Acad. Microbiology; mem. Am. Soc. for Microbiology (past chmn. edn. com., mem., chmn. numerous coms.), Environ. Mutagen Soc. (chmn. pub. policy com. 1991-93, mem., chmn. numerous coms.), Genetics Soc. Am. (nat. coun. 1994-97), Soc. Gen. Microbiology (Gt. Britain), Radiation Rsch. Soc., Sigma Xi (pres. U. Kans. chpt. 1967). Republican. Unitarian. Avocations: sports, music, theater, reading. Office: U Kans 7035 Haworth Hall Lawrence KS 66045

SHANKEL, GERALD MARVIN, professional society administrator; b. Alma, Mich., Jan. 1, 1943; s. Marvin A. Shankel and Ruth E. (Walworth) Heppner; m. Lois M. Herzberg, June 22, 1963; children: Cheryl A., Jill M., Steven G. BA, Alma Coll., 1965; MBA, U. Mich., 1966. Auditor Ernst & Ernst, Detroit, 1966-68; mng. dir. fin. and adminstrn. Soc. Mfg. Engrs., Dearborn, Mich., 1968-87; assoc. exec. dir. fin. and adminstrn. ASME, N.Y.C., 1988-92; exec. dir. Nat. Assn. Corrosion Engrs. Internat., Houston, 1992—; bd. dirs. Greater Houston (Tex.) Visitors & Conv. Bur., 1994—. Mem. Am. Soc. Assn. Execs. (cert. assn. exec.), Coun. Engring. and Sci. Soc. Execs. (treas. 1978-86). Avocations: swimming, reading, traveling. Home: 3414 Cinco Lakes Dr Katy TX 77450-5775 Office: NACE Internat PO Box 218340 1440 S Creek Dr Houston TX 77218*

SHANKER, MORRIS GERALD, lawyer, educator; b. Cleve., Aug. 23, 1926; s. Hyman and Anna (Kaplan) S.; m. Bernice Jacobs, Dec. 16, 1956; children: Chari, Jaymie Ann. BSEE, Purdue U., 1948; MBA, JD, U. Mich., 1952. Bar: Ohio 1952. Assoc. Grossman, Schlesinger & Carter, Cleve., 1952-61; prof. law Case Western Res. U., Cleve., 1961—, acting dean Law Sch., 1972—, John Home Kapp prof. law, 1975—; vis. prof. law U. Mich., 1964, U. Calif., Berkeley, 1966, Wayne State U., 1969, U. London, 1971, 87; cons., asst. reporter adv. com. on bankruptcy rules U.S. Supreme Ct., 1965-68, mem. com., 1969-77; mem. Nat. Bankruptcy Conf., 1966—; comml. and labor arbitrator; spl. master R.R. reorgn. procedures; lectr. comml. and bankruptcy law throughout U.S., Can. and U.K., 1961—. Contbr. articles to profl. jours. With USNR, 1944-46. Fellow Am. Coll. Bankruptcy; mem. ABA, Ohio Bar Assn., Cleve. Bar Assn., Am. Law Inst., Nat. Bankruptcy Conf., Order of Coif, Tau Beta Pi, Eta Kappa Nu. Home: 15712 Chadbourne Rd Cleveland OH 44120-3334 Office: Sch Law Case Western Res U Cleveland OH 44106

SHANKLIN, DOUGLAS RADFORD, physician; b. Camden, N.J., Nov. 25, 1930; s. John Ferguson and Muriel (Morgan) S.; student Wilson Tchrs. Coll., 1949; A.B. in Chemistry, Syracuse U., 1952; M.D., SUNY, Syracuse, 1955; m. Virginia McClure, Apr. 7, 1956; children—Elizabeth, Leigh, Lois Virginia, John Carter, Eleanor. Intern in pathology Duke U., 1955-56, resident, 1958; resident in pathology SUNY, Syracuse, 1958-60; practice medicine specializing in pathology, Gainesville, Fla., 1960-67, 78-83; mem. faculty U. Fla., 1960-67; prof. pathology, ob-gyn U. Chgo., 1967-78; pathologist-in-chief Chgo. Lying-In Hosp., 1967-78; prof. dept. pathology U. Tenn.-Memphis, 1983—, prof. obstetrics, 1986—, vice chmn. dept. pathology, 1983-90; vis. prof. U. Okla., 1967, Duke U., Mich. State U., 1969, Leeds U., Dundee U., Karolinska, 1974, Leeds U., 1978, 85, Emory U., 1980, London U., Edinburgh U., 1981, 85, U. Brit. Coll., 1987; jr. investigator Marine Biol. Lab., Woods Hole, Mass., 1951-54, sr. investigator, 1966—, mem. corp., 1970—; parliamentarian, 1990-94; mem. Marine Resources Adv. Com., 1988-90, mem. election com., 1994—; chmn. nat. adv. com. W-I-C evaluation U.S. Dept. Agr., 1979-86; lectr. Coll. Law U. Fla., 1963-67, 77-83; cons. Pan Am. Health Orgn., 1973-89; sr. cons. Santa Fe Found., 1976-79, exec. dir., 1979-83; course dir. Center Continuing Edn., U. Chgo., 1980-82. Trustee Coll. Light Opera Co., Falmouth, Mass., 1970—, Hippodrome Theatre, Gainesville, 1975-83, Opera Memphis, 1989-92. With M.C., USNR, 1956-58. Recipient Best Basic Sci. Teaching award U. Fla., 1967; named freeman citizen of Glasgow, 1981. Fellow Royal Soc. Medicine (London); mem. AAAS, Am. Soc. Exptl. Pathology, Am. Soc. Molecular Marine Biology and Biotech., Am. Chem. Soc., Astronom. Soc. Pacific Am. Hosp. Assn., Am. Coll. Rheumatology (spl. study com. 1995-96), Soc. Pediat. Rsch., Internat. Acad. Pathologists, So. Soc. Pediatric Research, So. Med. Assn., N.Y. Acad. Scis., Am. Coll. Ob-Gyn, Physicians Social Responsibility, Internat. Physicians for Prevention Nuclear War, Coll. Physicians and Surgeons Costa Rica, Pediatric Pathology Club (sec.-treas. 1970-75, pres. 1981-82), Navy League, Cosmos Club, Phi Beta Kappa. Sigma Xi. Author: Syllabus for Study of Gynecologic-Obstetric-Pediatric Disease, 1961, Diseases of Woman, Pregnancy, Child, 1964, Maternal Nutrition and Child Health, 1979, 2nd edit., 1996, Tumors of Placenta and Umbilical Cord, 1990; editor: Interscience Devel. Disorders, 1971-80; assoc. editor Jour. Reproductive Medicine, 1968-70, 79-85, editor in chief, 1970-75; contbr. articles to profl. jours. Home: 1238 NW 18th Ter Gainesville FL 32605-5370 Office: 134 Grove Park Cir Memphis TN 38117-3115

SHANKLIN, RICHARD VAIR, III, mechanical engineer; b. Bklyn., Feb. 12, 1937; s. Richard Vair and Sue Hall (Morfit) S.; m. Margaret Krogstad Courtney, July 3, 1981; children by previous marriage: Carolyn Dennett Shanklin Payne, Anne Landon Scott Weaver. B.S.M.E., Duke U., 1959; M.S., U. Tenn., 1965, Ph.D., 1971. Engring. asst. Phillips Petroleum Co., Tex., 1959-60; assoc. engr. Boeing Co., Seattle, 1960-62; design engr. Aro Inc., Arnold Air Force Sta., Tenn., 1962-64; chief engr. J.B. Dicks & Assos., Inc., Tullahoma, Tenn., 1967-70; assoc. prof. mech. engring. technology Nashville State Tech. Inst., 1971-72; asst. prof. U. Tenn., Tullahoma, 1972-73; sr. scientist Systems Research Labs., Dayton, Ohio, 1973-75; asst. dir. MHD div. ERDA, Washington, 1975-77; sr. staff engr. Energy Systems Group, TRW Inc., Morgantown, W.Va., 1977-78; dir. MHD div. Dept. Energy, Washington, 1978-79; mgr. combustion programs Energy Systems Group, TRW, Inc., Redondo Beach, Calif., 1979-80; asst. ops. mgr. for process devel. Energy Systems Group, TRW, Inc., McLean, Va., 1980-82; project officer U.S. Synthetic Fuels Corp., Washington, 1982-86; cons. to industry, 1986-89; dir. planning and facility transition BDM Fed., Inc., McLean, Va., 1989-95; cons. to industry, 1995—. Author papers and reports in field. Recipient Spl. Achievement awards ERDA, 1976, 77. Mem. ASME (George Westinghouse silver medal 1976), Cosmos Club Washington, Sigma Xi. Episcopalian. Home: 6206 Hardy Dr Mc Lean VA 22101-3113

SHANKS, ANN ZANE, filmmaker, producer/director, photographer, writer; b. N.Y.C.; d. Louis and Sadye (Rosenthal) Kushner; m. Ira Zane (dec.); children—Jennifer, Anthony; m. Robert Horton Shanks, Sept. 25, 1959; 1 child, John. Student, Carnegie-Mellon U., Columbia U., 1949. tchr., moderator spl. symposiums Mus. Modern Art, N.Y.C.; tchr. New Sch. for Social Research. Photographer, writer for numerous mags. and newspapers; producer, dir.: (movie shorts) Central Park, 1969 (U.S. entry Edinburgh Film Festival, Cine Golden Eagle award, Cambodia Film Festival award), Denmark... A Loving Embrace (Cine Golden Eagle award 1973), Tivoli, 1972-79 (San Francisco Film Festival award, Am. Film Festival award), (TV series) American Life Style (Silver award, 5 Gold medal awards Internat. TV and Film Festival N.Y., 2 Cine Golden Eagle awards), He's Fired, She's Hired; producer CBS TV Drop-Out Mother; producer, dir., writer (TV short) Mousie Baby; dir. (TV movie) Friendships, Secrets and Lies, NBC; producer: (TV movie) Drop-out Father, CBS, (video spl.) The Avant-Garde in Russia 1910-1930, Arts and Entertainment channel, ABC Morning Show, Good Afternoon Detroit; producer, dir. (TV spl.) A Day in the Country, PBS, (Emmy award nomination); producer, dir. play S.J. Perelman in Person; producer Broadway play, Lillian; exec. producer Gore Vidal's Am. Pres. series Channel Four, London, Discovery channel, U.S.; exhibited photographs Mus. Modern Art, Mus. City N.Y., Transit Mus., Brooklyn Heights, N.Y., Met. Mus. Art, Jewish Mus.; author: (photographs and text) The Name's the Game, New Jewish Ency; author, photographer, writer Old Is What You Get, Busted Lives...Dialogues with Kids in Jail, 1983; writer, photographer Garbage and Stuff. Recipient awards from internat. photography competitions. Mem. Am. Soc. Mag. Photographers (bd. govs.), Overseas Press Club Am., Women in Film (v.p.), Dirs. Guild Am. *I guess I have "adolescent enthusiasm" for most of my work. It gives me infinite pleasure to be alive and have the chance to take an idea and see it through to its final form on the screen, or on the television set...savoring all the headaches, joys and the working together— step-by-step. I seek responsibility for my work , my family, and those I love.*

SHANKS, DAVID, publishing executive. Pres. Berkley Pub. Co., N.Y.C. Office: Berkley Pub Group 200 Madison Ave New York NY 10016-3903*

SHANKS, EUGENE BAYLIS, JR., banker. BA, Vanderbilt U., 1969; MA, PhD, Stanford U., 1974. With Bankers Trust Co., N.Y.C., 1973-95, pres., dir., 1992-95; pres. NetRisk, Inc., Greenwich, Conn., 1995—. Office: NetRisk Inc 81 Holly Hill Ln Greenwich CT 06830-6071

SHANKS, HERSHEL, editor, writer; b. Sharon, Pa., Mar. 8, 1930; s. Martin and Mildred (Freedman) S.; m. Judith Alexander Weil, Feb. 20, 1966; children: Elizabeth Jean, Julia Emily. BA, Haverford (Pa.) Coll., 1952; MA, Columbia, 1953; LLB, Harvard, 1956. Bar: D.C. 1956. Trial atty. Dept. Justice, 1956-59; pvt. practice Washington, 1959-88; ptnr. Glassie, Pewett, Beebe & Shanks, 1964-88; editor Bibl. Archaeology Rev., Washington, 1975—; pres. Bibl. Archaeology Soc., 1974—, Jewish Ednl. Ventures Inc., 1987—. Author: The Art and Craft of Judging, 1968, The City of David, 1973, Judaism in Stone, 1979, Jerusalem--An Archaeological Biography, 1995, also articles; co-editor: Recent Archaeology in the Land of Israel, 1984; editor: Ancient Israel, A Short History, 1988, Christianity and Rabbinic Judaism, 1992, Understanding the Dead Sea Scrolls, 1992; editor Bible Rev., 1985—, Moment mag., 1987—. Mem. ABA, D.C. Bar Assn., Am. Schs. Oriental Rsch., Nat. Press Club, Phi Beta Kappa. Home: 5208 38th St NW Washington DC 20015-1812 Office: Bibl Archaeology Soc 4710 41st St NW Washington DC 20016-1700 *I try to take time to identify what is important in my life, to focus on that and ignore the rest when it conflicts. It takes conscious effort not to dissipate energy on activities and attitudes that don't matter in the big picture of my priorities. Free to concentrate on what I value most, I try to accomplish something each day in a regular, habitual way.*

SHANKS, JUDITH WEIL, editor; b. Montgomery, Ala., Nov. 2, 1941; d. Roman Lee and Charlotte (Alexander) Weil; m. Hershel Shanks, Feb. 20, 1966; children: Elizabeth Jeannette, Julia Emily. BA in Econs., Wellesley Coll., 1963; MBA, Trinity Coll., 1980. Econs. asst. Export-Import Bank, Washington, 1963-68; cons. econs. and social sci., 1968-76; researcher Time-Life Books, Alexandria, Va., 1976-80, prin. researcher, 1980-83, illustrations editor, 1983, adminstrv. editor, 1984-95, dir. editl. adminstrn., 1996. Vol. Mentors, Inc. Democrat. Jewish. Avocations: dancing, scuba diving, hiking, gardening, research on women in finance and business area. Home: 5208 38th St NW Washington DC 20015-1812

SHANKS, KATHRYN MARY, health care administrator; b. Glens Falls, N.Y., Aug. 4, 1950; d. John Anthony and Lenita (Combs) S. BS summa cum laude, Spring Hill Coll., 1972; MPA, Auburn U., 1976. Program evaluator Mobile Mental Health, Ala., 1972-73; dir. spl. projects Ala. Dept. Mental Health, Montgomery, 1973-76; dir. adminstrn. S.W. Ala. Mental Health/Mental Retardation, Andalusia, Ala., 1976-78; adminstr. Mobile County Health Dept., 1978-82; exec. dir. Coastal Family Health Ctr., Biloxi, Miss., 1982-95; cons. med. group practice, 1995—; ptnr. Shanks & Allen, Mobile, 1979—; healthcare consulting pvt. practice, 1995—; cons. S.W. Health Agy., Tylertown, Miss., 1984-86; instr. U. South Ala., 1997—; preceptor Sch. Nursing, U. So. Miss., Hattiesburg, 1983, 84; advisor Headstart Program, Gulfport, Miss., 1984-95; LPN Program, Gulf Coast C.C., 1984-95; lectr. Auburn U., Montgomery, 1977-78. Bd. dirs. Mobile Cmty. Action Agy., 1979-81, Moore Cmty. House; mem. S.W. Ala. Regional Goals Forum, Mobile, 1971-72, Cardiac Rehab. Study Com., Biloxi, Miss., 1983-84, Mothers and Babies Coalition, Jackson, Miss., 1983-95, Gulf Coast Coalition Human Svcs., Biloxi, Miss., 1983-95; exec. dir. Year for Miss., 1993-94. Spring Hill Coll. Pres.'s scholar, 1972. Mem. Miss. Primary Health Care Assn. (pres.), Med. Group Mgmt. Assn., ACLU, Soc. for Advancement of Ambulatory Care, Spring Hills Alumni Assn. Avocations: tennis, home restoration, golf.

SHANKS, PATRICIA L., lawyer; b. Salt Lake City, Apr. 3, 1940. BA in Microbiology with honors, Stanford U., 1962; JD, U. Colo., 1978. Bar: Calif. 1978. Mng. ptnr. McCutchen, Doyle, Brown & Enersen, L.A. Recipient West Publishing award; Stork scholar. Mem. Order of the Coif. Office: McCutchen Doyle Brown & Enersen 355 S Grand Ave Ste 4400 Los Angeles CA 90071-3106

SHANKS, WILLIAM ENNIS, JR., lawyer; b. Jackson, Miss., Sept. 5, 1950; s. William Ennis and Alice Josephine (Crisler) S.; m. Jean F. Steinschneider, Sept. 7, 1974; 1 child, William E. III. B.A., Harvard U., 1972; J.D. cum laude, Emory U., 1976; LL.M. with highest honors in Taxation, Ala. U., 1979. Bar: Ga. 1976, Ala. 1976. Ptnr. Balch & Bingham, Birmingham, Ala., 1976—. Bd. dirs. Birmingham Festival Theatre, 1980—, treas., 1980-84; trustee Creative Montessori Bd. Dirs.. Mem. Birmingham Estate Planning Council, Birmingham Employee Benefit Forum, Birmingham Profit Sharing Group, ABA (tax sect.), Order of Coif. Presbyterian. Clubs: Summit, Exchange (bd. dirs. 1984-85, sec. 1985-86, v.p. 1985-86, pres. 1986-87). Home: 4516 Old Leeds Rd Birmingham AL 35213 Office: Balch & Bingham 600 18th St N Birmingham AL 35203-2206

SHANMAN, JAMES ALAN, lawyer; b. Cin., Aug. 1, 1942; s. Jerome D. and Mildred Louise (Bloch) S.; m. Marilyn Louise Glassman, June 11, 1972; 1 child, Ellen Joan. BS, U. Pa., 1963; JD, Yale U., 1966. Bar: N.Y. 1967, U.S. Ct. Mil. Appeals 1971, U.S. Supreme Ct. 1971, U.S. Ct. Appeals (2d cir.) 1972, U.S. Dist. Ct. (so. and ea. dists.) N.Y. 1972, U.S. Ct. Internat. Trade 1976, U.S. Ct. Appeals (fed. cir.) 1987, U.S. Dist. Ct. (ea. dist.) Mich. 1989. Assoc. Cahill Gordon & Reindel, N.Y.C., 1971-74, Freeman, Meade, Wasserman, Sharfman & Schneider, N.Y.C., 1974-76; mem. firm Sharfman, Shanman, Poret & Siviglia, P.C., N.Y.C., 1976-95; ptnr. Camhy Karlinsky & Stein LLP, N.Y.C., 1995-96; mem. firm Sharfman, Siviglia, Poret, Kook, Ross & Shanman, P.C., N.Y.C., 1996—; speaker on reins. law topics. Capt. USAF, 1966-71. Mem. ABA, N.Y. State Bar Assn., Assn. of Bar of City of N.Y. (com. ins. law 1985-88, 90-92, com. profl. liability ins. 1988-92, com. on assn. ins. plans 1989—), Am. Arbitration Assn. (comml. panel arbitrators 1980—). Office: Sharfman Siviglia Poret Kook Ross & Shanman P C 750 Lexington Ave New York NY 10022-1200

SHANNAHAN, JOHN HENRY KELLY, energy consultant; b. Sparrows Point, Md., Nov. 1, 1913; s. John Henry Kelly and Beulah Williams (Day) S.; m. Mary Reynolds Kline, Apr. 22, 1939 (dec. Mar. 1995); children: John H.K., James R., Jennifer K. (Mrs. Bernard R. Koerner, Jr.). AB, Princeton U., 1934; postgrad., U. Mich., 1954. Sr. exec. program Mass. Inst. Tech., 1959; Comml. mgr. Ind.-Mich. Electric Co., 1955-59; asst. v.p. Am. Electric Power Service Corp., 1959-61; asst. to pres. Kans. Power & Light Co., 1961-63; v.p., exec. dir. Electric Heating Assn., 1964-72; pres. Electric Energy Assn., 1972-75; sr. v.p. Edison Electric Inst., N.Y.C., 1975—; cons. energy matters, 1975-80. Trustee Suttons Bay Congl. Ch. Maj. F.A., AUS, 1942-45, ETO. Decorated Bronze Star with oak leaf cluster; recipient Trend Maker award Elec. Info. Publs. Inc., 1967. Presbyterian (elder). Club: Marines Memorial (San Francisco), Suttons Bay Rotary. Home: 2393 N Lake Leelanau Dr Lake Leelanau MI 49653-9707

SHANNAHAN, WILLIAM PAUL, lawyer; b. Detroit, Mich., Nov. 21, 1934; s. William and Jean (Boyle) S.; m. Saracia L. Price, Sept. 24, 1983; children: MeglynAnne, Michael-Padraic. AB, U. Detroit, 1956; JD, Georgetown U., 1958. Bar: D.C. 1958, Mich. 1958, Calif. 1962. Ptnr. Higgs, Fletcher & Mack, La Jolla, Calif., 1967-81, Aylward, Kintz, et al.2, La Jolla, Calif., 1981-87, pvt. practice, La Jolla, Calif., 1987—. with U.S. Army, 1959-60. Democrat. Roman Catholic. Office: 1200 Prospect St Ste 425 La Jolla CA 92037-3608

SHANNON, ALBERT JOSEPH, educator; b. Pitts., Apr. 12, 1949; s. William Park and Dorothea B. (Brown) S.; m. Mary Jean Boblick, May 22, 1971; children: Erica Lynne, Sean Paul. BA summa cum laude, Marquette U., 1971; MEd, Boston U., 1972; PhD, Marquette U., 1978; grad. mgmt. devel. program Harvard U., 1989. Tchr. reading North Div. High Sch., Milw., 1972-76; reading cons. sch. dists. Wis., 1976-78; mem. faculty St. Mary's Coll., Notre Dame, Ind., 1978-83, asst. prof. dir. edn., 1978-83; assoc. prof. Sch. Edn., Rider U., Lawrenceville, N.J., 1983-86; chmn. dept. edn., dir. grad. edn. St. Joseph's U., Phila., 1986-88, chmn., grad. dir. edn. and health svcs., 1988-92; v.p. acad. affairs St. Joseph's Coll., Rensellaer, 1992-93, pres. 1993—; cons. on reading edn., 1978—; cons. computer edn., N.J.; mem. presdl. leadership commn. Am. Coun. Edn.; mem. pres. commn. NCAA. Contbr. articles to profl. jours. Recipient Outstanding Secondary Teaching award, 1975; Nat. Endowment for Humanities fellow Middlebury Coll., 1987-88, Am. Coun. on Edn. fellow U. Pa., 1990-91; named Sagamore of the Wabash, Gov. Office in Ind., 1995. Mem. ACE, Nat. Collegiate Athletics Assn. (presdl. commn.), Ind. Coll. Found. (dir.), Phi Beta Kappa, Phi Delta Kappa. Roman Catholic. Home: 215 E Thompson St Rensselaer IN 47978-3133 Office: St Joseph's Coll Box 869 Rensselaer IN 47978

SHANNON, CYNTHIA JEAN, biology educator; b. Phila., Feb. 19, 1961; d. Foster Lloyd and Nancy Ellen (Chapman) S.; ptnr. Gerald Thomas Braden. AA, Fullerton (Calif.) Coll., 1981; BA in Psychology, Calif. State U., Fullerton, 1986; BS in Zoology, Calif. Poly. State U., 1985, MS in Biology, 1991. Biology instr. Calif. State Poly. U., Pomona, Calif., 1986-91, Mt. San Antonio Coll., Walnut, Calif., 1986—; chair biology dept. Mt. San Antonio Coll., Walnut, 1996-97. Mem. AAAS, Ornithological Soc. N.Am., So. Assn. Naturalists, Golden Key, Phi Kappa Phi. Democrat. Avocations: bird watching, hiking, dogs, food and wine, reading. Office: Mt San Antonio Coll 1100 N Grand Ave Walnut CA 91789-1341

SHANNON, DAVID THOMAS, SR., academic administrator; b. Richmond, Va., Sept. 26, 1933; s. Charlie Lee and Phyllis (Gary) S.; m. Shannon P. Averett, June 15, 1957; children—Vernitia Averett, Davine Belinda S. Sparks, David Thomas Jr. B.A., VA. Union U., 1954, B.D., 1957; S.T.M., Oberlin Grad. Sch. Theology, 1959; D. Min., Vanderbilt U., 1974; D.D. (hon.), U. Richmond, 1983; Ph.D., U. Pitts., 1975; LHD (hon.), Interdenominational Theol. Ctr., 1992; LLD (hon.), Tuskegee U., 1993. Pastor Fair Oaks (Va.) Bapt. Ch., 1954-57; student asst. Antioch Bapt. Ch., Cleve., 1957-59; grad. asst. Oberlin (Ohio) Grad. Sch. Theology, 1958-59; univ. pastor Va. Union U., Richmond, 1960-61, lectr. humanities and history, 1959-69; pastor Ebenezer Bapt. Ch., Richmond, 1960-69; eastern dir. Christian Higher Edn. Services Am. Bapt. Bd. Edn. and Publ., Valley Forge, Pa., 1969-71; vis. prof. St. Mary's Sem. Urban Tng. Program, Cleve., 1969-72; assoc. prof. religion and dir. minority studies Bucknell U., Lewisburg, Pa., 1971-72; dean faculty Pitts. Theol. Sem., 1972-79; Bibl. scholar Hartford (Conn.) Sem. Found., 1979; pres. Va. Union U., Richmond, 1979-85; vice pres. for acad. services, dean faculty Interdenominational Theol. Ctr., Atlanta, 1985-91; pres. Andover Newton Theol. Sch., Newton Centre, Mass., 1991-94, Allen U, Columbia, S.C., 1994—; co-chmn. internat. dialogue Secretariat of Roman Catholic Ch. Bapt., Rome and Washington, 1985-90; co-chmn. task force on witnessing apostolic faith World Council of Chs., Geneva, 1984—; mem. faith and order commn. Nat. Council of Chs., N.Y.C., 1984; mem. commn. on doctrine and inter-ch. cooperation Bapt. World Alliance, Washington, 1980—; active Faith and Order Commn. World Coun. Chs. Author: Studies in the Life and Works of Paul, 1961, Old Testament Experience of Faith, 1977; co-editor: (with G. Wilmore) Black Witness to the Apostolic Faith, 1985; contbr. articles to profl. jours., chpts. to books. Life mem. NAACP, N.Y., 1950. Recipient Nat. Clergy award Opportunities Industrialization Ctrs. Am., 1993; named Man of Yr., NCCJ, 1981. Mem. Am. Assn. Higher Edn., Am. Acad. Religion, Soc. for Study of Black Religion, Soc. Bibl. Lit., S.C. Rotary Club, Columbia Rotary Club, Alpha Kappa Mu, Phi Beta Sigma, Theta Phi. Home: 1825 Saint Julian Pl Apt 15-L Columbia SC 29204-2423 Office: Allen U 1530 Harden St Columbia SC 29204-1057

SHANNON, DONALD HAWKINS, retired newspaperman; b. Auburn, Wash., Feb. 1, 1923; s. Ernest Victor and Fern (McConville) S.; m. Sally van Deurs, June 13, 1952; children—John McConville, Susanna Shepard. B.A., Stanford, 1944; postgrad., Law Sch., 1946-47. Reporter Brazil Herald, Rio de Janeiro, 1947-48; Reporter UPI, London, 1949-51, Western Reporters, Washington, 1951-53; mem. staff L.A. Times, 1954-92; bur. chief L.A. Times, Paris, 1962-65; bur. chief for Africa, L.A. Times, 1965-66; bur. chief L.A. Times, Tokyo, 1966-71, UN, N.Y.C., 1971-75, UN (Washington bur.), 1975-92; sr. editor Georgetown and Country, Washington, 1996—. Served with AUS, 1944-46, PTO. Mem. Nat. Press Club, Fed. City Club, City Tavern Club, Overseas Press Club (N.Y.C.), Phi Gamma Delta. Address: 1068 30th St NW Washington DC 20007-3822

SHANNON, EDGAR FINLEY, JR., English language educator; b. Lexington, Va., June 4, 1918; s. Edgar Finley and Eleanor (Duncan) S.; m. Eleanor H. Bosworth, Feb. 11, 1956; children—Eleanor, Elizabeth, Lois, Susan, Virginia. A.B., Washington and Lee U., 1939, Litt.D., 1959; A.M., Duke U., 1941, Harvard U., 1947; Rhodes scholar, Merton Coll., Oxford, 1947-50; D.Phil., Oxford U., 1949, D.Litt., 1996; LL.D., Rhodes Coll., 1960, Duke U., 1964, Hampden-Sydney Coll., 1971; H.H.D., Wake Forest U., 1964; D.H.L., Thomas Jefferson U., Phila., 1967, U. Hartford, 1981, Ohio State U., 1981; Litt.D., Centre Coll., 1968, Coll. William and Mary, 1973; L.H.D., Bridgewater Coll., 1970. Assoc. prof. naval. sci. and tactics Harvard U., 1946, instr. English, 1950-52, asst. prof. English, 1952-56; assoc. prof. English U. Va., Charlottesville, 1956-59; prof. English U. Va., 1959-74, pres., 1959-74, pres. emeritus, 1988—, Commonwealth prof. English, 1974-86, Linden Kent Meml. prof. English, 1986-88, prof. emeritus, 1988—, chmn. dept. English, 1980-81; mem. state and dist. selection coms. Rhodes scholars; pres. Council So. Univs., 1962-64, 71-72; pres. State Univs. Assn., 1963-64; exec. com. Nat. Assn. State Univs. and Land-Grant Colls., 1964-67, chmn. exec. com., 1966-67, pres., 1965-66; mem. So. Regional Edn. Bd., 1963-71; bd. govs. Nat. Commn. on Accrediting, 1961-67; mem. U.S. Nat. Commn. for UNESCO, 1966-67, Pres.'s Commn. on CIA Activities within U.S., 1975. Author: Tennyson and the Reviewers, 1952; editor: (with Cecil Y. Lang) The Letters of Alfred, Lord Tennyson, vol.I, 1981, vol. II, 1987, vol. III, 1990; contbr. articles to various jours. Bd. visitors U.S. Naval Acad., 1962-64, USAF Acad., 1965-67; bd. cons. Nat. War Coll., 1968-71; bd. dirs. Am. Council on Edn., 1967-70, vice chmn., 1971-72; trustee Thomas Jefferson Meml. Found., 1973-88, hon. trustee, 1988—, pres., 1980-83, chmn. 1987-88; trustee Washington and Lee U., 1973-85, Darlington Sch., 1966-76, Mariners Mus., 1966-75, Colonial Williamsburg Found., 1975-88; chmn. Va. Found. Humanities and Pub. Policy, 1973-79; v.p. Oceanic Edn. Found., 1968-83; bd. adminstrs. Va. Inst. Marine Sci., 1963-71; hon. v.p. Tennyson Soc., 1960—; mem. council White Burkett Miller Center for Pub. Affairs, 1975—; mem. Gov. Va.'s Task Force on Sci. and Tech., 1982-83. Served from midshipman to lt. comdr. USNR, 1941-46; capt. Res. ret. Decorated Bronze Star, Meritorious Service medal; Distinguished Eagle Scout, 1973; named Va. Cultural Laureate, 1987; recipient Distinguished Service award Va. State C. of C., 1969; Medallion of Honor Virginians of Md., 1964; Thomas Jefferson award U. Va., 1965; Algernon Sydney Sullivan award Washington and Lee U., 1939; Algernon Sydney Sullivan award U. Va., 1975; Jackson Davis award Va. chpt. AAUP, 1977, Disting. Alumnus award Darlington Sch., 1986; Guggenheim fellow, 1953-54; Fulbright research fellow Eng., 1953-54. Mem. MLA, Assn. Va. Colls. (pres. 1969-70), Raven Soc., Signet Soc., Jefferson Soc., Soc. Cin., Am. Soc. Order of St. John of Jerusalem, Phi Beta Kappa (senator 1967-85, vis. scholar 1976-77, v.p. 1976-79, pres. 1979-82, chmn. Coun. Nominating Com. 1988-94), Omicron Delta Kappa (Laurel Crowned Cir. award 1980), Phi Eta Sigma, Beta Theta Pi, Century Assn. Club, University Club (N.Y.C.). Presbyterian. Home: 250 Pantops Mountain Rd # 3 Charlottesville VA 22911-8600

SHANNON, JAMES PATRICK, foundation consultant, retired food company executive; b. South St. Paul, Minn., Feb. 16, 1921; s. Patrick Joseph and Mary Alice (McAuliffe) S.; m. Ruth Church Wilkinson, Aug. 2, 1969. B.A. in Classics, Coll. St. Thomas, St. Paul, 1941; M.A. in English, U. Minn., 1951; Ph.D., Yale U., 1955; J.D., U. N.Mex., 1973; LL.D., U. Notre Dame, 1964, Macalester Coll., 1964, Lora Coll., 1964, DePaul U., 1965, St. Mary's Coll., 1965, Carleton Coll., 1965, Creighton U., 1966, Northland Coll., Ashland, Wis., 1979, William Mitchell Coll. Law, 1980; Litt.D., Seton Hall, 1965, Coe Coll., Cedar Rapids, Iowa, 1966, U. Minn., 1966; J.U.D., Lawrence U., 1969. Ordained priest Roman Catholic Ch., 1946; asst. prof. history Coll. St. Thomas, 1954-56, pres., 1956-66; aux. bishop Archdiocese of St. Paul, 1965-68; pastor St. Helna Parish, Mpls., 1966-68; tutor Greek St. John's Coll., Santa Fe, 1969-70; v.p. St. John's Coll., 1969-70; mem. firm Sutin, Thayer & Browne, Albuquerque, Santa Fe, 1973-74; exec. dir. Mpls. Found., 1974-78; v.p. Gen. Mills, Inc., 1980-88; columnist, writer, found. cons., 1970-79, 88-90; dir. Midwest Importers, Inc., 1988-96. Author: Catholic Colonization on the Western Frontier, 1957. Bd. dirs. James H. Hill Libr., St. Paul, 1985-94, Inst. Ecumenical and Cultural Rsch., Collegeville, Minn., 1985—, chmn., 1990-94; bd. dirs. Ind. Sector, Washington, 1988-94, N.Mex. Cmty. Found., 1991-95, Gen. Svc. Found., 1991-94; coun. Conf. Bd., 1982-88; chmn. Rhodes Scholarship Selection Com. for Upper Midwest Selection Com., 1976-86; chmn. coun. founds., Washington, 1984-85; vice chmn. Found. Ctr., N.Y.C.; sr. cons. Coun. on Founds. Mem. D.C. Bar Assn., N.Mex. Bar Assn., Minn. Bar Assn., Mpls. Club (bd. govs. 1989-96, pres. 1994-95). Democrat. Address: PO Box 112 Wayzata MN 55391-0112

SHANNON, JOHN SANFORD, retired railway executive, lawyer; b. Tampa, Fla., Feb. 8, 1931; s. George Thomas and Ruth Evangeline (Garrett) S.; m. Elizabeth Howe, Sept. 22, 1962; children: Scott Howe, Elizabeth Garrett, Sandra Denison. AB, Roanoke Coll., 1952; JD, U. Va., 1955. Bar: Va. 1955. Assoc. Hunton Williams Gay Powell & Gibson, Richmond, Va., 1955-56; solicitor Norfolk & Western Ry., Roanoke, Va., 1956-60, asst. gen. solicitor, 1960-64, gen. atty., 1964-65, gen. solicitor, 1965-68, gen. counsel, 1968-69, v.p. law, 1969-80, sr. v.p. law, 1980-82; exec. v.p. law Norfolk (Va.) So. Corp., 1982-96, ret., 1996; bd. dirs. Norfolk So. Ry. Co., Pocahontas Land Corp., Va. Holding Corp., Norfolk and Western Ry. Co. Editor-in-chief: Va. Law Rev, 1954-55. Chancellor Episcopal Diocese Southwestern Va., 1974-82; pres. bd. trustees North Cross Sch., Roanoke, 1973-82; trustee, past chmn. exec. com. Roanoke Coll., Salem, Va.; bd. dirs. Legal Aid Soc., Roanoke Valley, 1969-80, pres., 1970-79; trustee Chrysler Mus., Norfolk, 1982-94, Norfolk Acad., 1987—. Mem. ABA, Va. Bar Assn., Norfolk and Portsmouth Bar Assn., Shenandoah Club, Roanoke Country Club, Norfolk Yacht and Country Club, Harbor Club, Order of Coif, Sigma Xi, Omicron Delta Kappa, Phi Delta Phi. Home: 7633 Argyle Ave Norfolk VA 23505-1701

SHANNON, LARRY REDDING, administrative assistant; b. St. Joseph, Mo., Apr. 5, 1949; s. Charles R. Jr. and Dorothy May (Dunham) Redding. Student, U. Tex., Arlington, 1967-69. Announcer Sta. KVIL, Dallas, 1968, Sta. KFJZ, Ft. Worth and Dallas, 1968-78; pvt. practice pub. rels. and advt., Ft. Worth, 1978-85; pvt. practice pub. rels., advt. and mgmt., N.Y.C., 1985-86; adminstrv. asst. to former spkr. Jim Wright, U.S. Ho. of Reps., Ft. Worth, 1986—. Democrat. Avocations: reading, travel. Office: PO Box 17563 Fort Worth TX 76102-0563

SHANNON, LYLE WILLIAM, sociology educator; b. Storm Lake, Iowa, Sept. 19, 1920; s. Bert Book and Amy Irene (Sivits) S.; m. Magdaline W. Shannon, Feb. 27, 1943; children: Mary Shannon Will, Robert William, John Thomas, Susan Michelle. BA, Cornell Coll., Mount Vernon, Iowa, 1942; MA, U. Wash., 1947, PhD, 1951. Acting instr. U. Wash., 1950-52; mem. faculty dept. sociology U. Wis., Madison, 1952-62, assoc. prof., 1958-62; prof. sociology U. Iowa, Iowa City, 1962—, chmn. dept. sociology and anthropology, 1962-70, dir. Iowa Urban Community Research Ctr., 1970—, prof. emeritus, 1991—; vis. prof. Portland State U., Wayne State U., U. Wyo., U. Colo. Author: Underdeveloped Areas, 1957, Minority Migrants in the Urban Community, 1973, Criminal Career Continuity: Its Social Context, 1988, Changing Patterns of Delinquency and Crime: A Longitudinal Study in Racine, 1991, Developing Areas, 1995, Socks and Cretin: Two Democats Helping Bill with the Presidency, 1995; editor: Social Ecology of the Community series, 1974-76. With USNR, 1942-46. Mem. AAAS, Am. Sociol. Assn., Midwest Sociol. Soc., Urban Affairs Assn., Population Assn. Am., Soc. Applied Anthropology, Am. Soc. Criminology, Phi Beta Kappa. Democrat. Lodge: Kiwanis. Home: River Heights Iowa City IA 52240 Office: Univ Iowa Iowa Urban Cmty Rsch Ctr 170W Seashore Hall Iowa City IA 52242-1402

SHANNON, MARGARET ANNE, lawyer; b. Detroit, July 6, 1945; d. Johannes Jacob and Vera Marie (Spade) Van De Graaf; m. Robert Selby Shannon, Feb. 4, 1967. Student Brown U., 1963-65; B.A. in History, Wayne State U., 1966, J.D., 1973. Bar: Mich. 1973. Housing aide City of Detroit, 1967-68; employment supr. Sinai Hosp., Detroit, 1968-69; assoc. gen. counsel regulatory affairs Blue Cross Blue Shield of Mich., Detroit, 1969-80; ptnr. Honigman Miller Schwartz and Cohn, Detroit, 1980-95, of counsel, 1996—. Nat. Merit scholar, 1963-66. Mem. Detroit Bar Assn., Mich. State Bar (chmn. health care com. 1991, 92, co-chmn. payor subcom. health law sect.), Nat. Health Lawyers Assn., ABA (vice chmn. pub. regulation of ins. law com. 1981-82), U. Liggett Sch. Alumni (bd. govs.). Home: 2003 Shorepointe Grosse Pointe MI 48236 Office: Honigman Miller Schwartz and Cohn 2290 First National Bldg Detroit MI 48226-3583

SHANNON, MARGARET T., nursing administrator, educator; b. New Haven, June 23, 1939; d. Michael Joseph and Ellen (McNamara) S. MS in Chemistry, St. Louis U., 1967; BSN, Northwestern State U. of La., Nachitoches, 1978; MN, La. State U., New Orleans, 1981; PhD., U. New Orleans, 1987. Staff nurse Touro Infirmary, New Orleans, 1978-80; instr. nursing Touro Infirmary Sch. Nursing, New Orleans, 1980-85; asst. prof. nursing La. State U. Med. Ctr., New Orleans, 1985-87; dean divsn. nursing Our Lady of Holy Cross Coll., New Orleans, 1988—. Author: Giovani & Hayes Drugs and Nursing Implications, 8th edit., 1995, (with B.A. Wilson and C. Stang) Nurses' Drug Guide (Annual), 1993, 94, 95, 96, 97, 98. Mem. ANA, NLN, La. League for Nursing, La. State Nurses Assn., Sigma Theta Tau, Phi Kappa Phi, Phi Delta Kappa.

SHANNON, MARY LOU, adult health nursing educator; b. Memphis, Apr. 4, 1938; d. Sidney Richmond Shannon and Lucille (Gwaltney) Cloud. BSN, U. Tenn., 1959; MA, Columbia U., 1963, MEd, 1964, EdD, 1972. Staff nurse City of Memphis Hosps., 1959-60, instr. Sch. Nursing, 1960-62; asst. prof. U. Tenn., Memphis, 1964-70, assoc. prof., 1970-73, prof., 1973-89; prof., chair adult health dept. Sch. Nursing U. Tex., Galveston, 1989—; bd. dirs. Nat. Pressure Ulcer Adv. Panel, Buffalo, 1987-96; vis. prof. U. Alta., Edmonton, Can., 1982; mem. project adv. bd. RAND, Santa Monica, Calif., 1994. Contbr. chpts. to books in field and to periodicals; mem. editl. bd. Advances in Wound Care, 1987—. Trustee Nurses Edn. Funds, N.Y.C., 1972-86. Mem. ANA, Nat. League Nursing (bd. of rev. 1983-86), Orthopedic Nurses Assn., So. Nursing Rsch. Soc., Am. Assn. for History of Nursing. Avocations: travel, reading. Office: U Tex Sch Nursing 301 University Blvd Galveston TX 77550-2708

SHANNON, MICHAEL EDWARD, specialty chemical company executive; b. Evanston, Ill., Nov. 21, 1936; s. Edward Francis and Mildred Veronica (Oliver) S.; m. A. Laura McGrath, July 4, 1964; children: Claire Oliver Mary, Kathryn Ann Elizabeth. BA, U. Notre Dame, 1958; MBA, Stanford U., 1960. With Continental Oil Co., Houston, 1960-62; with Gulf Oil Corp., 1962-75, asst. treas., 1970-75; treas. Gulf Oil Co. U.S., Houston, 1970-72, Gulf Oil Co.-Ea. Hemisphere, London, 1972-75; treas. Republic Steel Corp., Cleve., 1975-84, v.p., 1978-82, exec. v.p., 1982-84; exec. v.p., chief fin. officer Ecolab Inc., St. Paul, 1984, chief fin. and adminstrv. officer, 1984-90; pres. ChemLawn Svcs. Corp., Columbus, Ohio, 1988-90; CFO Ecolab Inc., 1990-92, pres. Residential Svcs. Group, 1990-92, vice chmn., chief fin. and adminstrv. officer, 1992-95, chmn. bd., chief fin. and adminstrv. officer, 1996—; bd. dirs. Minn. Pub. Radio, St. Paul, Minn. Orchestral Assn., Mpls., chair. Bd. dirs. Minn. Pub. Radio, St. Paul, Minn. Orchestral Assn., Mpls., chair. Mem. Fin. Execs. Inst., Nat. Assn. Mfrs. (bd. dirs.), Univ. Club, Rolling Rock Club, Mpls. Club, Minikahada Club, Minn. Club. Roman Catholic. Office: Ecolab Inc 370 Wabasha St N Saint Paul MN 55102-1306

SHANNON, PETER MICHAEL, JR., lawyer; b. Chgo., Oct. 13, 1928; s. Peter Michael Sr. and Marian (Burke) S.; m. Anne M. Mueller, April 3, 1969; children: Peter III, Stephen, Heather, Eamon. BA, St. Mary of the Lake, Mundelein, Ill., 1949, MA, 1952, STL, 1953; JCL, Gregorian U., Rome, 1958; JD, U. Calif., Berkeley, 1971. Bar: Calif. 1972, D.C. 1972, Ill. 1988, U.S. Dist. Ct. Md. 1972, U.S. Dist. Ct. D.C. 1972, U.S. Dist. Ct. (no. dist.) Ill. 1988, U.S. Ct. Appeals (1st, 2d, 3d, 4th, 5th, 6th, 7th, 8th, 9th, 10th and D.C. cirs.) 1972-75, U.S. Supreme Ct. 1975. Supervisory atty. litigation U.S. Dept. of Justice, Washington, 1971-75; sr. appellate atty. ICC, Washington, 1975-77, dir. enforcement, 1977-80; ptnr. Shannon, et al, Washington, 1980-82, Keck, Mahin & Cate, Chgo., 1982-96, Arnstein & Lehr, Chgo., 1996—. Author: Energy and Transportation Implications of Ratemaking Policy Concerning Sources of Energy, 1980, Disposition of Real Estate by Religious Institutions, 1987, The Dual Approach of Civil Law Courts to Ecclestical Related Disputes, 1988. Mem. ABA (chmn. transp. com., adminstrv. law and regulatory practice sect. 1984-87, coun. mem. 1988-91), Am. Acad. Hosp. Attys., Assn. Transp. Law, Logistics and Policy, Canon Law Soc. (pres. 1965-66). Office: Arnstein & Lehr 120 S Riverside Plz Rm 1200 Chicago IL 60606-3910

SHANNON, ROBERT RENNIE, optical sciences center administrator, educator; b. Mt. Vernon, N.Y., Oct. 3, 1932; s. Howard A. and Harriebell S.; m. Helen Lang, Feb. 13, 1954; children: Elizabeth, Barbara, Jennifer, Amy, John, Robert. B.S., U. Rochester, 1954, M.A., 1957. Dir. Optics Lab., ITEK Corp., Lexington, Mass., 1959-69; prof. Optical Scis. Ctr., U. Ariz., 1969—, dir., 1983-92, prof. emeritus, 1992—; cons. Lawrence Livermore Lab., 1980-90; trustee Aerospace Corp., 1985-94, 96—; mem. Air Force Sci. Adv. Bd., 1986-90; mem. NRC Commn. on Next Generation Currency, 1992-94, NRC Commn. on Optical Sci. and Engring., 1996-97; mem. com. on def. space tech. Air Force Studies Bd., 1989-93, com. on optical sci. and engring, 1996-97, Hubble Telescope recovery panel, 1990; bd. dirs. Precision Optics Corp. Editor: Applied Optics and Optical Engineering, Vol. 7, 1980, Vol. 8, 1981, Vol. 9, 1983, Vol. 10, 1987, Vol. 11, 1992, Art and Science of Optical Design, 1997; editor Engring. and Lab. Notes, 1995—. Fellow Optical Soc. Am. (pres. 1985, mem. engring. coun. 1989-91), Soc. Photo-Optical Instrumentation Engrs. (pres. 1979-80, recipient Goddard award 1982, Gold medal, 1996); mem. NAE, Tucson Soaring Club (past pres.), Sigma Xi. Home: 7040 E Taos Pl Tucson AZ 85715-3344 Office: U Ariz Optical Scis Ctr Tucson AZ 85721

SHANNON, THOMAS ALFRED, retired educational association administrator emeritus; b. Milw., Jan. 2, 1932; s. John Elwood and Eleanor Ann (Mitchell) S.; m. Barbara Ann Weidner, June 26, 1954; children: Thomas Alfred, Paul J., Suzanne L., Terrence D. BS, U. Wis, 1954; JD, U. Minn., 1961. Bar: Minn. 1961, Calif. 1963, U.S. Supreme Ct. 1965, D.C. 1977, Va. 1984; Life cert. as sch. adminstr., Calif.; cert. assoc. exec. Am. Soc. Assn. Execs. Pvt. practice law Mpls., 1961-62; schs. atty. San Diego City Schs., 1962-73; dept. supt., gen. counsel, 1973-77; exec. dir. Nat. Sch. Bds. Assn., Washington, 1977-97, ret., 1997; adj. prof. law and edn. U. San Diego; vis. prof. edn. U. Va.; adv. mem. Edn. Commn. of States; prof. Nat. Acad. Sch. Execs., 1971—; legal counsel Am. Assn. Sch. Adminstrs., 1973-77; adj. prof. ednl. adminstrn. George Washington U., 1996—. Exec. pub. The American School Board Jour, 1977—, Exec. Educator, 1978—, Sch. Bd. News, 1981—. Chmn. San Diego County Juvenile Justice Commn., 1973-74; mem. nat. coun. Boy Scouts Am., 1979—; bd. dirs. Found. for Teaching Econ., San Francisco, 1993—. With USN, 1954-59. Mem. VFW (life), Am. Bar Assn. (chmn. com. public edn. 1978-82), Nat. Orgn. on Legal Problems of Edn. (pres. 1973), Nat. Sch. Bds. Assn. (chmn. council sch. attys. 1967-69). Home: 3811 26th St N Arlington VA 22207-5241

SHANNON, THOMAS FREDERIC, German language educator; b. Cambridge, Mass., Mar. 16, 1948; m. Christine D. Höner. BA in German summa cum laude, Boston Coll., 1969; MA in German Lit., SUNY, Albany, 1973; MA in Theoretical Linguistics, Ind. U., 1975, PhD in Germanic Linguistics, 1982. Instr. in German Boston Coll., 1969-70; teaching fellow in German SUNY, Albany, 1971-73; univ. fellow Ind. U., Bloomington, 1973-74, assoc. instr., 1974-76, 79-80; acting asst. prof. in Germanic linguistics U. Calif., Berkeley, 1980-82, asst. prof., 1982-87, assoc. prof., 1987-94, prof., 1994—, dir. lang. lab., 1989-92, assoc. dir. Berkeley Lang. Ctr., 1994-95; co-organizer Berkeley Confs. on Dutch Lang. and Lit., 1987, 89, 91, 93, 95, 97; econs. presenter and spkr. in field. Contbr. articles to profl. jours. With USAR, 1970-76. Grantee Fulbright Found., 1976-78, U. Calif. Berkeley, 1983-84, 94-95, ACLS, 1987, Internat. Assn. Netherlandic Studies, 1988, 91, 94, 97, German Acad. Exch. Svc., summer 1996; NDEA fellow, 1969; Fulbright rsch./lectr. grantee Rijksuniversiteit Groningen, Netherlands, 1992-93; Inst. fuer deutsche Sprache summer rsch. grantee, Mannheim, Germany, 1997. Mem. MLA (exec. com. discussion group in Germanic philology 1989-94, discussion group for Netherlandic Studies 1995—, divsn. on lang. change 1995—), Am. Assn. Netherlandic Studies (exec. com. 1988—, editor newsletter 1989-95, series editor publs. 1994—), Am. Assn. Tchrs. German, Internat. Assn. Netherlandic Studies, Internat. Assn. Germanistik, Internat. Soc. Hist. Linguistics, Linguistic Soc. Am., Netherlands Am. U. League, Pacific Ancient & Modern Lang. Assn., European Linguistic Soc., Soc.

Germanic Philology (v.p. 1991-92, 95—), Interna. Cognitive Linguistics Soc., Alpha Sigma Nu. Home: 770 Rose Dr Benicia CA 94510-3709 Office: U Calif Dept German 5317 Dwinelle Hall Berkeley CA 94720-3243

SHANNON, WILLIAM NORMAN, III, marketing and international business educator, food service executive; b. Chgo., Nov. 20, 1937; s. William Norman Jr. and Lee (Lewis) S.; m. Bernice Urbanowicz, July 14, 1962; children: Kathleen Kelly, Colleen Patricia, Kerrie Ann. BS in Indsl. Mgmt., Carnegie Inst. Tech., 1959; MBA in Mktg. Mgmt., U. Toledo, 1963. Sales engr. Westinghouse Electric Co., Detroit, 1959-64; regional mgr. Toledo Scale, Chgo., 1964-70; v.p. J. Lloyd Johnson Assoc., Northbrook, Ill., 1970-72; mgr. spl. projects Hobart Mfg., Troy, Ohio, 1972-74; corp. v.p. mktg. Berkel, Inc., La Porte, Ind., 1974-79; gen. mgr. Berkel Products, Ltd., Toronto, Can., 1975-78; chmn. Avant Industries, Inc., Wheeling, Ill., 1979-81; chmn., pres. Hacienda Mexican Restaurants, South Bend, Ind., 1978—; chmn. Ziker Shannon Corp., South Bend, 1982-88, Hacienda Franchising Group, Inc., South Bend, Ind., 1987—; assoc. prof. mktg. and internat. bus. St. Mary's Coll., Notre Dame, Ind., 1982—; chmn. Hacienda Franchise Group, Inc., 1987—, Hacienda Mex. Restaurants Mgmt., Inc., 1994—; mem. London program faculty, 1986, 89, 92, 94, coord. internat. bus. curriculum, 1989—, mktg. curriculum, 1983, 88, 95—; advisor Coun. Internat. Bus. Devel., Notre Dame, 1991—; mng. dir. Alden & Torch Lake Railway, 1995—. Co-author: Laboratory Computers, 1971; columnist small bus. Bus. Digest mag., 1988—; bd. editors Jour. Bus. and Indsl. Mktg., 1986—; mem. bd. editorial advisors South Bend Tribune Business Weekly, 1990—; contbr. articles to profl. jours. V.p. mktg. Jr. Achievement, South Bend, Ind., 1987-90; pres. Small Bus. Devel. Coun., South Bend., 1987-90; bd. dirs. Ind. Small Bus. Coun., Indpls., 1986—, Mental Health Assn., South Bend, 1987-90, Michiana World Trade Orgn., Internat. Bus. Edn., 1989-91; Entrepreneurs Alliance Ind., 1988-92, Nat. Small Bus. United, Washington, 1989-92, Women's Bus. Initiative, 1986-90, dir. ednl. confs., 1986-90; chmn. bd. trustees, Holy Cross Coll., Notre Dame, Ind., 1987—, chmn. edn. com., 1993—; chmn. St. Joseph County Higher Edn. Coun., 1988-91, Nat. Coun. Small Bus., Washington, 1988—; Midwest region adv. coun. U.S. SBA, 1988-91; at-large mem. U.S. Govt. Adv. Coun. on Small Bus., Washington, 1988-90, 1994—, chmn. Bus. and Econ. Devel. Com., 1988-90, 1994—; vice chmn. Internat. Trade Com., 1994—; mem. nat. adv. coun. Women's Network for Entrepreneur Tng., 1991—; mem., vice chmn. State of Ind. Enterprise Zone Bd., 1991—; elected del. White House Conf. Small Bus., Washington, 1986; bd. dirs. Ind. Small Bus. Devel. Ctrs. Adv. Bd. Named Small Bus. Person of the Yr., City of South Bend, 1987, Small Bus. Advocate of the Yr., State of Ind., 1987, Ind. Entrepreneur Advocate of the Yr., 1988. Mem. Am. Mktg. Assn. (chmn. Mich./Ind. chpt., pres. 1985-86), U.S. Assn. Small Bus. and Entrepreneurship (nat. v.p. for entrepreneurship edn. 1991-92, nat. v.p. entrepreneurship devel. 1992—), Ind. Inst. New Bus. Ventures (mktg. faculty 1987-91), Michiana Investment Network (vice chmn. 1988-91), SBA (adminstrn. adv. coun. 1988—, contbg. editor Our Town Michiana mag. 1988-91), U.S. C. of C., Nat. Coun. Small Bus. (Washington), South Bend C. of C. (bd. dirs. 1987—, vice chmn. membership 1993—), Assn. for Bus. Communications (co-chmn. Internat. Conf. 1986), Univ. Club Notre Dame (vice chmn.), Shamrock Club Notre Dame (exec. dir., trustee 1993—), Rotary. Roman Catholic. Home: 2920 S Twyckenham Dr South Bend IN 46614-2116 Office: Saint Mary's Coll Dept Bus Adminstrn Eco Notre Dame IN 46556 *Enjoy good fortune resulting from LUCK, an acronym for (L) Learning how to (U)Use your talents with genuine (C) Concern on how your (K) Knowlege can benefit others.*

SHANOR, CLARENCE RICHARD, clergyman; b. Butler, Pa., Dec. 26, 1924; s. Paul L. and Marion (McCandless) S.; B.A., Allegheny Coll., 1948; S.T.B., Boston U., 1951, Ph.D., 1958; m. Anna Lou Watts, June 23, 1948; 1 son, Richard Watts. Ordained to ministry Methodist Ch., 1950; pastor Meth. Ch., South Hamilton, Mass., 1951-54; research asso. Union Coll., Schenectady, 1954-55; prof. Christian edn. Nat. Coll., Kansas City, Mo., 1956-58; asso. minister First United Meth. Ch., St. Petersburg, Fla., 1958-61, First United Meth. Ch., Fullerton, Calif., 1961-66; coord. Metro dept. San Diego dist. United Meth. Union, San Diego, 1966-87, ret., 1987; pres. Human Svcs. Corp., 1972-77. Treas. San Diego County Ecumenical Conf., 1970-71, pres., 1975-77; chmn. Coalition Urban Ministries, 1970-71, Cultural and Religious Task Force Rancho San Diego, 1970-74; chmn. western jurisdiction Urban Network United Meth. Ch., 1978. Chmn. San Diego Citizens Com. Against Hunger, 1969-72; bd. dirs. Interfaith Housing Found., chmn., 1979, pres. 1988—; v.p. North County Interfaith Coun., 1987—; mem. Gaslamp Quarter Project Area Com., San Diego, 1978, mem. coun., 1980-84; chmn. bd. Horton House Corp., 1978; mem. Mayor's Task Force on the Homeless, 1983-84; chmn. Downtown Coordinating Coun., 1983-84; mem. regional Task Force on Homeless, 1986-87; vice-chmn. Community Congress, 1987, ret., 1987; bd. dirs. North County Interfaith Coun., 1987-92, Redwood Town Ct., 1995, v.p. 1996; pres., bd. dirs. North County Housing Found., 1987-96. Recipient San Diego Inst. for Creativity award, 1969, Boss of Yr. award Am. Bus. Women's Assn., 1972, Christian Unity award Diocesan Ecumenical Commn., 1984, Congl. Disting. Svc. award, 1984, Helen Beardsley Human Rights award, 1986, Mayor O'Connor's Seahorse award 1989, Ecumenical Conf. award San Diego County, 1991, Vol. Extraordinaire award No. County Interfaith Coun., 1993. Home: 1636 Desert Gln Escondido CA 92026-1849

SHANSTROM, JACK D., federal judge; b. Hewitt, Minn., Nov. 30, 1932; s. Harold A. and Willian (Wendorf) S.; m. June 22, 1957; children: Scott S., Susan K. BA in Law, U. Mont., 1956, BS in Bus., 1957, LLB, 1957. Atty. Park County, Livingston, Mont., 1960-65; judge 6th Jud. Dist. Livingston, 1965-82; U.S. magistrate Billings, Mont., 1983-90, U.S. Dist. judge, 1990—. Capt. USAF, 1957-60. Office: US Dist Ct Federal Bldg 316 N 26th St Ste 5405 Billings MT 59101-1362*

SHAO, OTIS HUNG-I, retired political science educator; b. Shanghai, China, July 18, 1923; came to U.S., 1949, naturalized, 1956; s. Ming Sun and Hannah (Chen) S.; m. Marie Sheng, Apr. 2, 1955. B.A., St. John's U., 1946; M.A., U. Colo., 1950; Ph.D., Brown U., 1957. From instr. to prof. polit. sci. Moravian Coll., Bethlehem, Pa., 1954-62; assoc. prof., then prof. polit. sci. Fla. Presbyn. Coll., St. Petersburg, 1962-68; prof. internat. politics, dean (Grad. Sch., U. Pacific), 1968-74; dir. Pub. Affairs Inst., 1969-74; provost Callison Coll., 1974-76; dean faculty, v.p. Occidental Coll., 1976-78; asso. exec. dir. sr. commn. Western Assn. Schs. and Colls., 1978-80; v.p., dean Hawaii Loa Coll., 1980-85; pres. Sheng Shao Enterprises Calif., 1985-92; CEO, chmn. D.S. Capital Internat., Calif., 1993-94; Mem. grad. students relations com. Council Grad. Schs. U.S., 1970-73; mem. exec. council undergrad. assessment program Ednl. Testing Service, 1978-80. Contbr. articles to profl. jours. Chmn. bd. dirs. Fgn. Policy Assn. Lehigh Valley, 1961-62; bd. dirs. World Affairs Council, San Joaquin County, 1969-77; trustee Inst. Med. Scis., Pacific Med. Center, San Francisco, 1968-72, optical scis. group of Profl. and Pub. Service Found., 1969-72; Resident fellow Harkness House, Brown U., 1953-54, Danforth Assn., 1958-85. Recipient Distinguished Service award Fgn. Policy Assn. Lehigh Valley, 1962. Mem. AAUP (pres. Fla. Presbyn. Coll. chpt. 1965-66), Am. Assn. Higher Edn., Rho Psi, Tau Kappa Epsilon. Democrat. Presbyn. Home: 6218 Embarcadero Dr Stockton CA 95219-3824

SHAPAZIAN, ROBERT MICHAEL, publishing executive; b. Fresno, Calif., Nov. 3, 1942; s. Ara Michael and Margaret (Azhderian) S. BA, U. Calif., 1964; AM, Harvard U., 1965, PhD in Renaissance English and Fine Arts, 1970. Design assoc. Arthur Elrod Assocs., L.A., 1971-73; v.p. El Mar Corp., Fresno, Calif., 1973-87; dir., art dir. The Lapis Press, Venice, Calif., 1987—; mem. photographic forum San Francisco Mus. Art, 1982-85, Mus. Modern Art, N.Y.C., 1985; mem. photographic com. Met. Mus. Art, N.Y.C., 1994; assoc. Gagosian Gallery, N.Y.C. Author: Metaphorics of Artificiality, 1970, Maurice Tabard, 1985; editor: Surrealists Look at Art, 1991 (AIGA award 1991, N.Y. Art Dirs. award 1991), A Witch, 1992 (AIGA award 1992, N.Y. Art Dirs. award 1992, L.A. Art Dirs. award 1992), Pacific Wall (AIGA award 1993), Albucius (We. Art Dirs. award 1993, N.Y. Art Dirs. award 1994), Sam Francis: Saturated Blue, Writings from the Notebooks, 1996. Bd. dirs. Big Brothers/Big Sisters, Fresno, Calif., 1980-82, Film Forum, L.A., 1984-86, Grunwald Ctr. for Graphic Arts, UCLA, 1996—. Recipient Individual Achievement award Lit. Market Pl., N.Y.C., 1992, 23 awards for art direction and design; named Chevalier in Order of Arts and Letters, Govt. of France. Mem. Harvard Club (N.Y.C.). Avocations: twentieth century art, illustrated books, experimental photography. Office: PO Box 36821 Los Angeles CA 90036-0821

SHAPELL, NATHAN, financial and real estate executive; b. Poland, Mar. 6, 1922; s. Benjamin and Hela S.; m. Lilly Szenes, July 17, 1948; children: Vera Shapell Guerin, Benjamin (dec.). Co-founder Shapell Industries, Inc., Beverly Hills, Calif., 1955; now chmn. bd. Shapell Industries, Inc.; mem. adv. bd. Union Bank, Beverly Hills; mem. residential bldgs. adv. com. Calif. Energy Resources Conservation and Devel. Commn.; speaker in field. Mem. Calif. Commn. Govt. Reform, 1978; Atty. Gen. Calif. Adv. Council, Dist. Atty. Los Angeles County Adv. Council; chmn. Calif. Govt. Commn. Orgn. and Economy, 1975—, Gov.'s Task Force on Affordable Housing, 1980—; mem. adv. council Pres.'s Commn. on the Holocaust, 1979; pres. Am. Acad. Achievement, 1975—; mem. deans council UCLA Sch. Architecture and Urban Planning, 1976—. Author: Witness to the Truth, 1974. Trustee U. Santa Clara, Calif., 1976—; bd. councillors U. So. Calif. Med. Sch., 1973—. Recipient Golden Plate award Am. Acad. Achievement, 1974, Fin. World award, 1977. Jewish. Club: Hillcrest Country (Los Angeles). Prisoner in Auschwitz, 1943-45. Address: Shapell Industries Inc 8383 Wilshire Blvd Ste 700 Beverly Hills CA 90211*

SHAPERE, DUDLEY, philosophy educator; b. Harlingen, Tex., May 27, 1928; s. Dudley and Corinne (Pupkin) S.; m. Hannah Hardgrave; children—Hannah Elizabeth, Christine Ann; children by previous marriage: Alfred Dudley, Catherine Lucretia. B.A., Harvard U., 1949, M.A., 1955, Ph.D., 1957. Instr. philosophy Ohio State U., 1957-60; asst. prof. U. Chgo., 1960-65, asso. prof., 1965-67, prof., 1967-72, mem. com. on evolutionary biology, 1969-72, chmn. undergrad. program in history and philosophy of sci., 1966-72, chmn. com. on conceptual founds. sci., 1970-72; prof. U. Ill., Urbana, 1972-75; chmn. program in history and philosophy of sci. U. Ill., 1972-75; prof. U. Md., College Park, 1975-84; Z. Smith Reynolds prof. philosophy and history of sci. Wake Forest U., 1984—; mem. com. on history and philosophy of sci. U. Md., 1975-84; chmn. program in history and philosophy of sci. U. Md., 1983-84.; vis. prof. Rockefeller U., 1965-66, Harvard U., 1968; mem. Inst. Advanced Study, Princeton, N.J., 1978-79, 81, 89; spl. cons. (program dir.) program in history and philosophy of sci. NSF, 1966-75; Sigma Xi nat. biocentennial lectr., 1974-77. Author: Philosophical Problems of Natural Science, 1965, Galileo: A Philosophical Study, 1974, Reason and the Search for Knowledge, 1984; editorial bd.: Philosophy of Sci., Studies in History and Philosophy of Sci.; rev. bd.: Philosophy Research Archives; contbr. articles to profl. jours. Served with AUS, 1950-52. Recipient Quantrell award for excellence in undergrad. teaching U. Chgo., 1968; Disting. Scholar-Tchr. award U. Md., 1979-80. Fellow AAAS (sec. sec. 1972); mem. APA, Philosophy of Sci. Assn., History of Sci. Soc., Am. Philos. Assn., Acad. Internat. de Philosophie des Scis. Home: 3125 Turkey Hill Ct Winston Salem NC 27106-4951 Office: Wake Forest U PO Box 7229 Winston Salem NC 27109-7229

SHAPERO, HARRIS JOEL, pediatrician; b. Winona, Minn., Nov. 22, 1930; s. Charles and Minnie Sara (Ehrlichman) S.; m. Byong Soon Yu, Nov. 6, 1983; children by previous marriage: Laura, Bradley, James, Charles. AA, UCLA, 1953; BS, Northwestern U., 1954, MD, 1957. Diplomate and cert. specialist occupational medicine Am. Bd. Preventive Medicine; qualified med. evaluator, Indsl. Med. Coun.; ind. med. examiner, Calif.; cert. aviation medicine FAA. Intern, L.A. County Harbor Gen. Hosp., 1957-58, resident in pediatrics, 1958-60, staff physician, 1960-64; attending physician Perceptually Handicapped Children's Clinic, 1960-63; disease control officer for tuberculosis, L.A. County Health Dept., 1962-64; pvt. practice medicine specializing in pediatrics and occupational medicine, Cypress, Calif., 1965-85; pediatric cons. L.A. Health Dept., 1983-85, disease control officer sexually transmitted diseases, 1968-78; emergency room dir. AMI, Anaheim, Calif., 1968-85; mem. med. staff Anaheim Gen. Hosp., Beach Cmty. Hosp., Norwalk Cmty. Hosp.; courtesy staff Palm Harbor Gen. Hosp., Bellflower City Hosp.; pediatric staff Hosp. de General, Ensenada, Mex., 1978—; primary care clinician Sacramento County Health, 1987-88; pvt. practice medico-legal evaluation, 1986-92; founder Calif. Legal Evaluation Med. Group; apptd. med. examiner in preventive and occupational medicine State of Calif. Dept. of Indsl. Rels., 1989; health care provider, advisor City of Anaheim, City of Buena Park, City of Cypress, City of Garden Grove, Cypress Sch. Dist., Magnolia Sch. Dist., Savanna Sch. Dist., Anaheim Unified Sch. Dist., Orange County Dept. Edn.; pediatric and tuberculosis cons. numerous other orgns.; FAA med. examiner, founder Pan Am. Childrens Mission. Author: The Silent Epidemic, 1979. Named Headliner in Medicine Orange County Press Club, 1978. Fellow Am. Coll. Preventive Medicine; mem. L.A. County Med. Assn., L.A. County Indsl. Med. Assn., Am. Pub. Health Assn., Mex.-Am. Border Health Assn. Republican. Jewish. Avocations: antique books and manuscripts, photography, graphics, beekeeper. Home: PO Box 228 Wilton CA 95693-0228 Office: Molina 2920 Arden Way Sacramento CA 95825-1377

SHAPEY, RALPH, composer, conductor, educator; b. Phila., Mar. 12, 1921; s. Max and Lillian (Paul) S.; m. Vera Shapiro, Oct. 28, 1957; 1 child, Max Klement; m. Elsa Charlston, Oct. 12, 1985. Student violin with, Emanuel Zetlin; composition with, Stefan Wolpe. Prof. music U. Chgo., 1964-85, Disting. prof., 1985-91; ret., 1991; vis. prof. Queens Coll., 1973; chmn. admissions com. MacDowell Colony. Dir. Contemporary Chamber Players, Chgo., ret. 1994; asst. condr., Phila. Nat. Youth Adminstrn. Symphony Orch., 1938-42; guest condr., Phila. Symphony Orch. at Robin Hood Dell, 1942 (winner Phila. Finds Contest); condr. 1st performance saxophone quartet by Wolpe, McMillan Theatre, N.Y.C., 1950, repeat performance, Times Hall, N.Y.C., 1950; condr. clarinet concerto, N.Y. Philharmonic Chamber Soc., 1955, Internat. Soc. Contemporary Music, N.Y.C., 1961, 62, Phila., 1961-63, Fromm Found. Concert, N.Y.C., 1962; guest condr., London Symphony Orch. for BBC, mus. dir. orch. and chorus, U. Pa., 1963-64, mus. dir., Contemporary Chamber Players, U. Chgo., 1964—; Composer: Challenge-The Family of Man, for symphony orchestra, 1955, Mutations, for piano, 1956, Duo for Viola and Piano, 1957, Ontogeny for symphony orchestra, 1958, Form for piano, 1959, Rituals for symphony orchestra, 1959, Dimensions for soprano and 23 instruments, 1960, Incantations for soprano and 10 instruments, 1961, Convocation for chamber group, 1962, Birthday Piece for piano, 1962, Brass Quintet, 1963, String Quartet VI, 1963, VII, Sonance for carillon, 1964, Configurations for Flute and Piano, Praise, oratorio, Variations for piano, O Jerusalem, for soprano and flute, Songs of Eros, for soprano, orch. and tape, Covenant for Soprano, 16 players and tape, 1977, 21 Variations for Piano, 1978, Song of Songs 1, 1979, II, 1980, III, 1980, Evocation for cello, piano and percussion, 1979, Evocation III for viola and piano, 1981, Fanfare for 2 trumpets, horn, trombone and tuba, Concerto Grosso for woodwind quintet, 1981, Songs for Soprano and Piano, 1982, Passacaglia for Piano, 1982, Double Concerto for Violin, Cello and Orchestra, 1983, Discourse II for Violin, Clarinet, Cello, and Piano, 1983, Fantasy for Violin and Piano, 1983, Mann duo for Violin and Viola, 1983, Songs for Soprano and Four Instruments, 1984, Gottlieb Duo for Piano and Percussion, 1984, Variations for Organ, 1985, Duo Variations for Violin and Cello, 1985, Psalm I for Soprano and Piano, 1986, Psalm II for Baritone and Piano, 1986, Duo Variations for violin and cello, 1985, Soli for percussion, 1985, Kroslish Sonata for cello and piano, 1985, Symphonie Concertante for symphony orch. (commd. Phila. Orch.), 1986, Songs of Love (I am My Beloved's) for baritone and piano, 1986, Songs of Love (And My Beloved is Mine) for baritone and piano, 1986, Concerto for cello, piano and string orch., 1986, In Memorium for soprano,baritone and 9 players, 1987, Theme and Variations for harpsicord, 1987, Concertante #II for alto saxophone and 14 players, 1987, Songs of Joy for soprano and piano, 1987, Variations on a Cantus for piano, 1987, Kroslish Sonate for cello and piano, 1987, Concertante #1 for trumpet and 10 players, 1987, Variations for Viola and 9 Players, 1987, 2 For 1 Solo for Snare Drum, 1988, Concerto Fantastique for Symphony Orch., 1989, Chgo. Symphony Orch., Intermezzo for Dulceme & piano/Celesta, 1990, Duo for 6 Winds, Two Players, 1991, Centennial Celebration for soprano, mezzo soprano, tenor, baritone and 12 players, 1991, Movement of VariedMoments for Two-flute and vibraphone, 1991, Trio 1992 for violin, cello, piano,1992, Trio Concertant for Violin, Piano and Percussion, 1992, Inventions for Clarinet and Percussion, 1992, Dinosaur Annex for Violin, Vibraphone & Marimba/Glock, 1993, String Quartet VIII, Naumberg, 1993, Constellations for Bang on the Can All-Stars, 1993, Rhapsody for Cello and Piano, 1993, Evocations # IV for Violin, Cello, Piano & Percussion, others: Recs. include: Music for a 20th Century Violinist, Fromm Variation: 31 Variations for Piano, 1973, Three for Six, 1980, 21 Variations for Piano. "Sonata Appassionata", "Sonata Profondo", 1995, String Quartet # IX, 1995, Goethe Songs for Soprano & Piano, 1995, Discourse Encore for Violin Cello, Clarinette & Piano, 1996; "Stony Brook Concerto", Woodwinds brass, percussion, violin, 1996—, Interchange in Four Movements for Percussion Quartet, 1996. Served with AUS, 1942-45. Mac Arthur fellow, 1982, Inst. of Arts and Letters fellow, 1989; grantee Italian govt., 1959-60; recipient Creative Arts award Brandeis U., 1962, Nat. Found. Arts and Letters award, 1966, Norlin Found. award, 1978, 1st prize Friedheim award, 1990, Fromm award Outstanding contbn. 20th century Music, 1993. Mem. ASCAP, AAAL, Am. Acad. Arts and Scis., Internat. Soc. Contemporary Music (dir.). Office: U Chgo Dept Music 1010 E 59th St Chicago IL 60637-1512 *My credo: Great art is a miracle! The music must speak for itself.*

SHAPIRA, DAVID S., food chain executive; b. 1942; married. B.A., Oberlin Coll., 1964; M.A., Stanford U., 1966. V.p. Giant Eagle, Inc. (formerly Giant Eagle Markets, Inc.), Pitts., 1974-81, pres., 1981-1994, chief exec. officer, also bd. dirs.; chmn. & CEO Giant Eagle, Youngstown; chmn. bd. Phar-Mor Inc., Youngstown. Office: Giant Eagle Inc 101 Kappa Dr Pittsburgh PA 15238-2809 Office: Tamarkin Company PO Box 1588 Youngstown OH 44501-1588*

SHAPIRA, EMMANUEL, clinical geneticist, biochemical geneticist, educator; b. Kovno, Lithuania, Nov. 22, 1933. MD, Hebrew U., Jerusalem, 1959; PhD in Immunochemistry, Weizmann Inst. Sci., Rehovot, Israel, 1968. Diplomate Am. Bd. Clin. Genetics, Am. Bd. Clin. Biochem. Genetics. Intern Kaplan Hosp., Rehovot, 1958-59, resident in pediatrics, 1962-66; with Tulane U. Med. Ctr., New Orleans; assoc. prof. pediatrics Med. Sch. Northwestern U., New Orleans, 1973; prof. pediatrics and pathology Med. Sch. Tulane U., 1978-83, prof. pediatrics and biochemistry Med. Sch., 1984, dir. human genetics program Hayward Genetics Ctr. Sch. Medicine, 1984—. Mem. AAAS, AMA, Assn. Am. Physicians, Am. Coll. Med. Genetics, Am. Pediatric Soc., Am. Soc. Human Genetics, Am. Soc. Pediatric Rsch., La. State Med. Soc., N.Y. Acad. Sci., Midwestern Soc. Pediatric Rsch., Southern Soc. Pediatric Rsch., Israel Immunol. Soc., European Soc. Pediatric Rsch., Internat. Soc. Newborn Screening, Soc. Inherited Metabolic Disease (bd. dirs.), Assn. Profs. Human & Med. Genetics (sec./treas.). Office: Tulane U Sch Med Human Genetics Prog 1430 Tulane Ave New Orleans LA 70112-2699

SHAPIRO, ALVIN PHILIP, physician, educator; b. Nashville, Dec. 28, 1920; s. Samuel and Mollie (Levine) S.; m. Ruth Thomson, 1951; children: Debra, David. A.B., Cornell U., 1941; M.D., L.I. Coll. Medicine, Bklyn., 1944. Diplomate Nat. Bd. Med. Examiners.; cert. Am. Bd. Internal Medicine. Intern L.I. Coll. Hosp., Bklyn., 1944-45; asst. resident internal medicine Goldwater Meml. Hosp., N.Y.C., 1945-46; asst. resident psychiatry L.I. Coll. Hosp. and Kings County Hosp., 1947-48; practice acad. medicine specializing in internal medicine Cin., 1948-51, Dallas, 1951-56, Pitts., 1956—; research fellow Cin. Gen. Hosp., 1948-49; med. teaching fellow Commonwealth Fund Psychosomatic Program, 1949-51, attending physician, 1949-51; attending physician Parkland, VA hosps., Dallas, 1951-56, Presbyn.-Univ. Hosp., Pitts., 1957-61; sr. staff Presbyn.-Univ. Hosp., 1962—; attending physician VA Hosp., Pitts., 1960-66; cons. VA Hosp., 1967—; attending physician Shadyside Hosp., 1986—; co-dir. hypertension-renal clinic Falk Clinic U. Pitts., 1956-65, dir. hypertension clinic, 1965-86; instr. dept. internal medicine U. Cin. Coll. Medicine, 1949-51; asst. prof. Southwestern Med. Sch., U. Tex., 1951-56; asst. prof. depts. clin. sci. and medicine U. Pitts. Sch. Medicine, 1956-60, assoc. prof. dept. medicine, 1960-67, prof., 1967-93, prof. emeritus, 1993—, dir. psychosomatic program dept. medicine, 1960-71, interim chief renal sect., 1962-65, chief clin. pharmacology-hypertension sect., 1960-71, assoc. dean acad. affairs, 1971-75, vice-chmn. dept. medicine, 1975-79, interim chmn. dept. medicine, 1977-79; dir. Internal Medicine Residency program, Shadyside Hosp., 1986-93; cons. AMA Council on Drugs, 1959, Med. Letter of Drugs and Therapy, 1960; Fulbright vis. prof. U. Utrecht, The Netherlands, 1968; chmn. spl. projects study com. Nat. Heart Inst., 1970, chmn. policy adv. bd. nat. hypertension study, 1972-82. Author: (with S.O. Waife) Clinical Evaluation of New Drugs, 1959, Hypertension-Current Management, 1963, 77, Hypertension in Renal Disease, 1969, Pharmacologic Mechanisms in Control of Hypertension, 1971, Hypertension and Stress, 1996; assoc. editor: Psychosomatic Medicine, 1963-92; ass. editor Integrative Physiol. and Behavioral Sci., 1990; contbr. articles to profl. jours. Served as capt. M.C. AUS, 1946-47. Co-recipient Alfred Lasker Spl. Pub. Health award, 1980; named Honored Mem. of Yr., Minute Men of U. Pitts., 1995. Fellow ACP (Laureate award for teaching excellence Pa. chpt. 1988), AAAS (elected fellow 1989); mem. Am. Fedn. Clin. Rsch., Am. Psychosomatic Soc. (sec.-treas. 1969-73, pres. 1975), AMA, Am. Heart Assn. (med. adv. bd. coun. high blood pressure, coun. on circulation, coun. on epidemiology), Pa. County Med. Soc., Allegheny County Med. Soc., N.Y. Acad. Sci., Am. Diabetes Assn., Am. Soc. Clin. Investigation, Soc. for Exptl. Biology and Medicine, Am. Soc. for Pharmacology and Exptl. Therapeutics, Cen. Soc. Clin. Rsch., Internat. Soc. Hypertension, Acad. Behavioral Medicine (coun. 1986, pres. 1987), Alpha Omega Alpha. Achievements include research in hypertension and related diseases and in behavioral sciences. Office: Shadyside Hosp Pittsburgh PA 15232

SHAPIRO, ASCHER HERMAN, mechanical engineer, educator, consultant; b. Bklyn., May 20, 1916; s. Bernard and Jennie (Kaplan) S.; m. Sylvia Charm, Dec. 24, 1939 (div. 1959); children: Peter Mark, Martha Ann, Bernett Mary; m. Regina Julia Lee, June 4, 1961 (div. 1972); m. Kathleen Larke Crawford, Sept. 6, 1985. Student, CCNY, 1932-35; SB, MIT, 1938, ScD, 1946; DSc (hon.), Salford U., Eng., 1978, Technion-Israel Inst. Tech., 1985. Asst. mech. engring. MIT, 1938-40, faculty, 1940—, prof. mech. engring., 1952—, prof. charge fluid mechanics divsn., mech. engring. dept., 1954-65, Ford prof. engring., 1962-75, chmn. faculty, 1964-65, head dept. mech. engring., 1965-74, inst. prof., 1975-86, inst. prof. emeritus, sr. lectr., 1986—; vis. prof. applied thermodynamics U. Cambridge, Eng., 1955-56; Akroyd Stuart Meml. lectr. Nottingham (Eng.) U., 1956; editor Acad. Press, Inc., 1962-65; cons. United Aircraft Corp., M.W. Kellogg Co., Arthur D. Little, Inc., Hardie-Tynes Mfg. Co., Carbon & Carbide Chems. Corp., Oak Ridge, Rohm & Haas Co., Ultrasonic Corp., Jackson & Moreland (Engrs.), Stone & Webster, Bendix Aviation, Oak Ridge Nat. Lab., Acushnet Processing Co., Kennecott Copper Co., Welch Sci., Sargent-Welch, Bird Machine Co., Organogenesis, Inc., CARR Separations, Inc., others; served on subcoms. on turbines, internal flow, compressors and turbines NACA; mem. Lexington Project to study and report on nuclear powered flight to AEC, summer 1948; dir. Project Dynamo to study and report to AEC on technol. and econs. nuclear power for civilian use, 1953, Lamp Wick study Office Naval Research, 1955; mem. tech. adv. panel aeronautics Dept. Def.; cons. ops. evaluation group Navy Dept.; sci. adv. bd. USAF, 1964-66; founder, mem. Nat. Com. for Fluid Mechanics Films, 1962—, chmn., 1962-65, 71—; chmn. com. on ednl. films Commn. on Engring. Edn., 1962-65; dir. lab. for devel. power plants for use in torpedoes Navy Dept., 1943-45; mem. ad hoc med. devices com. FDA, HEW, 1970-72; mem. com. Nat. Council for Research and Devel., Israel, 1971—; mem. com. sci. and pub. policy Nat. Acad. Scis., 1970-74. Author: The Dynamics and Thermodynamics of Compressible Fluid Flow, vol. 1, 1953, vol. 2, 1954 (with Chinese translation), Shape and Flow, 1961 (Japanese, Italian, German and Spanish translations); also 3 ednl. films, 39 videotape lecture series: Fluid Dynamics, 1984; contbr. over 130 articles to sci. jours.; mem. editl. bd. Applied Mechanics, 1955-56; mem. editl. com. Ann. Rev. Fluid Mechanics, 1967-71; mem. editl. bd. MIT Press, 1977-87, chmn., 1982-87. Mem. Town Meeting Arlington, Mass.; chmn. 1st Mass. chpt. Atlantic Union Com., 1951-52, mem. council, 1954—; bd. govs. Technion, Israel Inst. Tech., 1968-89. Recipient Naval Ordnance Devel. award, 1945; joint certificate outstanding contbn. War and Navy depts., 1947; Richards Meml. award ASME, 1960; Worcester Reed Warner medal, 1965; Fluids Engring. award, 1981; Townsend Harris medal Coll. City N.Y., 1978. Fellow AIAA, Am. Acad. Arts and Scis. (councillor 1967-71), ASME (hon.); mem. Am. Sci. Films Assn., Nat. Acad. Scis. (com. on sci. and pub. policy 1973-77), Nat. Acad. Engring. (adv. com. on edn. 1985-89), Am. Inst. Med. and Biol. Engring. (founding fellow), Biomed. Engring. Soc. (charter mem. 1968), AAAS, Am. Soc. Engring. Edn. (Lamme medal 1977), MIT Faculty Club, Cavendish Club (Brookline, Mass.), Sigma Xi, Tau Beta Pi, Pi Tau Sigma. Patentee fluid metering equipment, combustion chamber, propulsion apparatus, gas turbine aux., magnetic disc, magnetic disc storage device, vacuum pump, low-density wind tunnel, recipe calculator, decanter centrifuges (6). Home: 111 Perkins St Apt 86 Jamaica Plain MA 02130-4321

SHAPIRO, BARRY ROBERT, lawyer; b. Bklyn., Apr. 10, 1947; s. Sam and Jean (Moak) S.; m. Marjorie Spiegelman, Dec. 24, 1968; children: Andrew, Daniel. BA, Hofstra U., 1968; JD, Columbia U., 1973. Bar: N.Y., U.S. Dist. Ct. (so. dist.) N.Y., U.S. Ct. Appeals (2d cir.). Assoc. Shereff, Friedman et al, N.Y.C., 1973-74; v.p., gen. counsel Avis, Inc., Garden City, N.Y., 1974-83; ptnr. Farrell, Fritz, Caemmerer, Cleary, Barnosky & Armentano P.C., Uniondale, N.Y., 1983-88; sr. ptnr. Rivkin, Radler & Kremer, 1988—. Contbr. article to profl. jours. Chmn. bd. dirs. L.I. Philharmonic, Melville, N.Y., 1986—; bd. dirs. L.I. Coalition Fair Broadcasting, 1989—, Inst. Cmty. Devel., 1992-94, New Ctr. Wholistic Health Edn. Rsch., 1992—. Mem. ABA, N.Y. State Bar Assn., Nassau County Bar Assn. (lectr. 1985-86, 93), Hofstra Club (Hempstead, N.Y.). Avocations: sports, music. Office: Rivkin Radler & Kremer EAB Plz Uniondale NY 11556

SHAPIRO, BENNETT MICHAELS, biochemist, educator; b. Phila., July 14, 1939; s. Simon and Sara (Michaels) S.; m. Fredericka Foster, Mar. 13, 1982; children: Lisa, Lise, Jonathan. BS, Dickinson Coll., 1960; MD, Jefferson Med. Coll., 1964. Research assoc. NHLI, NIH, 1965-68, med. officer, 1970-71; vis. scientist Inst. Pasteur, Paris, 1968-70; from assoc. prof. to full prof. biochemistry U. Wash., 1971-90, chmn. biochemistry dept., 1985-90; exec. v.p. for worldwide basic rsch. Merck Rsch. Labs., Rahway, N.J., 1990—. Contbr. articles to profl. jour. Served as surgeon USPHS, 1968-70. John S. Guggenheim fellow, 1982; Japan Soc. for Promotion Sci., 1984. Mem. Am. Soc. Biol. Chemists, Am. Soc. Cell Biology, Am. Soc. Devel. Biology, Phi Beta Kappa, Alpha Omega Alpha. Office: Merck Rsch Labs PO Box 2000 Rahway NJ 07065-0900

SHAPIRO, BURTON LEONARD, oral pathologist, geneticist, educator; b. N.Y.C., Mar. 29, 1934; s. Nat Lazarus and Fay Rebecca (Gartenhouse) S.; m. Eileen Roman, Aug. 11, 1958; children—Norah Leah, Anne Rachael, Carla Faye. Student, Tufts U., 1951-54; D.D.S., NYU, 1958; M.S., U. Minn., 1962, Ph.D., 1966. Faculty U. Minn. Sch. Dentistry, Mpls., 1962—; assoc. prof. div. oral pathology U. Minn. Sch. Dentistry, 1966-70, prof., chmn. div. oral biology, 1970-79, prof., chmn. dept. oral biology, 1979-88, prof. dept. oral pathology and genetics, 1979-88, dir. grad. studies, mem. grad. faculty genetics, 1966—, prof. dept. oral sci., 1988—, mem. grad. faculty pathobiology, 1979; prof. dept. lab. medicine and pathology U. Minn. Sch. Medicine, 1985—, mem. Human Genetics Inst., 1988—, univ. senator, 1968-72, 88-93; also mem. med. staff U. Minn. Health Scis. Center; exec. com. Grad. Sch. U. Minn., chmn. health scis. policy rev. council, chmn. univ. faculty consultative com., 1988-92; chmn. univ. fin. and planning com. Grad. Sch. U. Minn., 1988; hon. research fellow Galton Lab. dept. human genetics Univ. Coll., London, 1974; spl. vis. prof. Japanese Ministry Edn., Sci. and Culture, 1983. Mem. adv. editorial bd.: Jour. Dental Research, 1971—; Contbr. articles to profl. jours. Served to lt. USNR, 1958-60. Am. Cancer Soc. postdoctoral fellow, 1960-62; advanced fellow, 1965-68; named Century Club Prof. of Yr., 1988. Fellow Am. Acad. Oral Pathology, AAAS; mem. Internat. Assn. Dental Research (councilor 1969), Am. Soc. Human Genetics, Craniofacial Biology Soc. (pres. 1972), Sigma Xi, Omicron Kappa Upsilon. Home: 148 Nina St # 2 Saint Paul MN 55102-2160 Office: U Minn Sch Dentistry Dept Oral Sci Minneapolis MN 55455

SHAPIRO, CARL, economics educator and consultant; b. Austin, Tex., Mar. 20, 1955; s. Sherman and Ellen S.; m. Dawn Boyer, Apr. 16, 1978; children: Eva, Benjamin. BS, MIT, 1976, PhD, 1981; MA, U. Calif., 1977. Prof. econs. and pub. affairs Princeton (N.J.) U., 1981-90; prof. bus. and econs. Univ. Calif., Berkeley, 1990—; dep. asst. atty. gen. U.S. Dept. Justice, 1995-96; founder The Tilden Group, 1996. Assoc. editor Rand Jour. Econs., 1984-85, Quar. Jour. Econs., 1984-87; co-editor Jour. Econ. Perspectives, 1986-93, editor, 1993-95. NSF grantee, 1982, 84, 86, 88, 91; Sloan Found. fellow, 1984. Mem. Am. Econ. Assn., Econometric Soc. Avocations: frisbee, camping, bicycling. Office: U Calif Haas Sch Bus 350 Barrows Hall Berkeley CA 94720-1901

SHAPIRO, CHERYL BETH, lawyer; b. Neptune, N.J., July 11, 1962; d. Bernard D. and Marcia K. (Goldstein) S.; m. David B. Lebowitz, Nov. 22, 1992. BA, George Washington U., 1983; JD, Widener U., 1986. Bar: Pa. 1986, N.J. 1986. Law clk. Samuel Shevlin, Phila., 1986; coord. planning & devel. Goldco Devel. C., Lakewood, N.J., 1986-87; law clk. Ct. Common Pleas, Phila., 1988-89; corp. atty. CSS Industries, Inc., Phila., 1989-96; corp. counsel Copelco Fin. Svcs. Group Inc., Mt. Laurel, N.J., 1997—. Pa. Bar Assn., Phila. Bar Assn., Phi Delta Phi. Avocations: theatre, travel. Office: Copelco Fin Svcs Group 700 E Gate Dr Mount Laurel NJ 08054-3803

SHAPIRO, DAVID, artist, art historian; b. N.Y.C., Aug. 28, 1916; s. Jacob and Ida (Katz) S.; m. Cecile Peyser, June 18, 1944; children: Deborah Jane, Anna Roberta. Student, Ednl. Alliance Art Sch., 1933-35, Am. Artists Sch., 1936-39. Instr. Smith Coll., 1946-47, Bklyn. Coll., summer, 1947; asst. prof. art U. B.C., 1947-49; mem. faculty dept. art Hofstra U., 1961-81, prof. emeritus, 1981—; prof. fine art New Coll., 1972-81; prof. fine art, artist-in-residence U. Belgrade, Yugoslavia, 1981; vis. critic Vt. Studio Ctr., Johnson, Vt., 1990. Author: Social Realism: Art as a Weapon, 1973, Abstract Expressionism: A Critical Record, 1989; one-man shows include Ganso Gallery, N.Y.C., 1955, Milch Gallery, N.Y.C., 1958, 61, 63, Galleria Dell'Orso, Milan, 1971, Tweed Art Mus., Duluth, Minn, 1978, U. Belgrade Gallery, 1981; 50 yr. retrospective T.W. Wood Art Gallery, Vt. Coll. Arts Ctr., 1987; represented in permanent collections Bklyn. Mus., Met. Mus., Libr. Congress, Nat. Mus., Smithsonian Instn., Phila. Mus. Art. Fulbright grantee, 1951-52, 52-53; MacDowell fellow, 1976; Tamarind fellow, 1976; Nat. Endowment Arts, grantee, 1978; Fulbright grantee, 1980-81. Mem. Soc. Am. Graphic Artists (pres. 1968-70), Coll. Art Assn. Home: RR 1 Box 77 Cavendish VT 05142-9711 *My work and my family are the main interests in my life. Both make it very worthwhile.*

SHAPIRO, DAVID L., lawyer; b. Corsicana, Tex., May 19, 1936; s. Harry and Alice (Laibovitz) S. BA, U. Tex., 1967; JD, St. Mary's U., 1970. Bar: Tex. 1970, U.S. Dist. Ct. (we. dist.) Tex. 1972, U.S. Supreme Ct. 1975, U.S. Ct. Appeals (5th cir.) 1981. Assoc. Law Office Jim S. Phelps, Houston, 1971; pvt. practice Austin, 1972—; spl. counsel com. human resources Tex. Ho. Reps., Austin, 1973-74; counsel subcom. health svcs. Tex. Senate, Austin, 1983-87. With U.S. Army, 1959-61. Mem. State Bar Tex. (chmn. lawyer referral svc. com. 1980-82, adminstrn. of justice com. 1990-93, contbr. Media Law Handbook supplement 1986), Travis County Bar Assn. (sec.-treas. 1977-78, dir. 1979, pres. family law sect. 1980-81), Coll. of State Bar of Tex., Austin Criminal Def. Lawyers Assn. Democrat. Avocations: automobiles, reading. Home: 920 E 40th St #106 Austin TX 78751-4821 Office: 1200 San Antonio St Austin TX 78701-1834

SHAPIRO, DAVID LOUIS, lawyer, educator; b. N.Y.C., Oct. 12, 1932; s. Louis and Sara (Grabelsky) S.; m. Jane Wilkins Bennett, June 19, 1954; 1 child, Lynn Mayson. Grad., Horace Mann Sch., 1950; A.B. magna cum laude, Harvard U., 1954, LL.B. summa cum laude, 1957. Bar: D.C. 1957, Mass. 1964. Assoc. atty. firm Covington & Burling, Washington, 1957-62; law clk. Supreme Ct. Justice John M. Harlan, 1962-63; faculty Harvard Law Sch., 1963—, prof. law, 1966—, William Nelson Cromwell prof. law, 1984—, assoc. dean, 1971-76; dep. solicitor gen. U.S. Dept. Justice, 1988-91; mem. labor arbitration and comml. arbitration panels Am. Arbitration Assn., 1966-89; reporter, adv. com. on fair trial and free press ABA, 1965-68. Author: Federalism: A Dialogue, 1995, (with others) The Federal Courts and the Federal System, 1973, 88, 96; editor: The Evolution of a Judicial Philosophy: Selected Opinions of Justice John M. Harlan, 1969; directing editor Found. Press, Univ. Casebook Series, 1980—; contbr. articles to profl. jours. Mem. Am. Law Inst. (asst. reporter study of div. of jurisdiction 1963-65, reporter Restatement of Judgments 2d 1970-74). Home: 17 Wendell St Cambridge MA 02138-1816 Office: Law Sch Harvard U Cambridge MA 02138

SHAPIRO, EDWARD MURAY, dermatologist; b. Denver, Oct. 6, 1924; s. Isador Benjamin and Sara (Berezin) S.; student U. Colo., 1941-43; m. Ruth Young, Oct. 14, 1944; children: Adrian Michael, Stefanie Ann; m. Dorothy Rosmarin, July 22, 1990. AB with honors, U. Tex., 1948, MD, 1952. Intern, Jefferson Coll. Medicine Hosp., Phila., 1952-53; resident in dermatology U. Tex. Med. Br., Galveston, 1953-55; resident in dermatology Henry Ford Hosp., Detroit, 1955-56, asso. in dermatology div. dermatology, 1956-57; clin. instr. dermatology Baylor U. Coll. Medicine, Houston, 1957-68, assoc. clin. prof., 1968—; staff Ben Taub Gen. Hosp., Houston, 1958—; active staff Columbia Bayshore Hosp., 1962—, Meml. Pasadena Hosp., 1958—. Served with USAAF, 1943-46. Henry J. N. Taub research grantee, 1958-60; diplomate Am. Bd. Dermatology. Fellow Am. Acad. Dermatology; mem. AMA, Tex. Med. Assn., Tex. Dermatol. Soc. (pres.-elect 1988, pres. 1989-90), South Cen. Dermatol. Assn. (bd. dirs. 1987-88), Harris County Med. Assn. (pres. S.E. br. 1968-69), Houston Dermatology Assn., Houston Art League, Gulf Coast Art Soc., Am. Physicians Art Assn. (v.p. 1993). Jewish. Clubs: B'nai B'rith, Rotary Internat. (Paul Harris fellow 1995, 97). Contbr. articles in field to med. jours. Home: 2506 Potomac Dr Houston TX 77057-4548 Office: 1020 Pasadena Blvd Pasadena TX 77506-4700

SHAPIRO, EDWARD ROBERT, psychiatrist, educator, psychoanalyst; b. Boston, Sept. 13, 1941; s. Jacob and Ruth (Yankelovich) S.; m. Donna Elmendorf; 1 child, Joshua Jackson; 1 child from previous marriage, Jacob Matthew; 1 stepchild, Zachary Andrew Robbins. BA magna cum laude, Yale U., 1962; MA in Anthropology, Stanford U., 1966; MD, Harvard U., 1968. Diplomate Am. Bd. Psychiatry and Neurology. Intern in medicine Beth Israel Hosp., Boston, 1968-69; resident in psychiatry Mass. Mental Health Ctr., Boston, 1969-72, chief resident in psychiatry, 1971-72; clin. assoc. NIMH, Bethesda, Md., 1972-74; dir. Adolescent and Family Treatment and Study Ctr. McLean Hosp., Belmont, Mass., 1974-89, dir. Psychosocial Tng. and Consultation, 1989-91; bd. dirs. Ctr. for Study of Groups and Social Systems, Boston, 1983-90; bd. dirs. A.K. Rice Inst., Washington, 1983-90, dir. Nat. Group Rels. Conf., 1989-91; faculty mem. Boston Psychoanalytic Inst., 1978—; assoc. clin. prof. psychiatry Harvard Med. Sch., Boston, 1982—; med. dir., CEO The Austen Riggs Ctr., Stockbridge, Mass., 1991—. Co-author: (with A.W. Carr) Lost in Familiar Places: Creating New Connections Between the Individual and Society, 1991; editor: The Inner World in the Outer World: Psychoanalytic Perspectives, 1997; mem. editorial bd. Jour. Adolescence, 1977-82, Psychiatry, 1988—; assoc. editor Jour. Adolescence, 1982-84; contbr. articles to profl. jours. Mem. Yale Russian Chorus. With USPHS, 1972-74. Recipient Isenberg Teaching award McLean Hosp., 1980, Rsch. prize Soc. for Family Therapy and Rsch., 1984, Felix and Helen Deutsch Sci. prize Boston Psychoanalytic Inst., 1980. Fellow Am. Psychiat. Assn., Am. Coll. Psychoanalysis, A.K. Rice Inst.; mem. Am. Psychoanalytic Assn., Am. Family Therapy Assn. Avocation: music. Office: The Austen Riggs Ctr PO Box 962 25 Main St Stockbridge MA 01262-0962

SHAPIRO, ELI, business consultant, educator, economist; b. Bklyn., June 13, 1916; s. Samuel and Pauline (Kushel) S.; m. Beatrice Ferbend, Jan. 18, 1946; 1 child, Laura J. A.B., Bklyn. Coll., 1936; A.M., Columbia U., 1937, Ph.D., 1939. Instr. Bklyn. Coll., 1936-41; rsch. assoc. Nat. Bur. Econ. Rsch., 1938-39; cons. Nat. Bur. Econ. Research, 1939-42; mem. rsch. staff Nat. Bur. Econ. Rsch., 1955-62; asst. prof. fin. U. Chgo., 1946-47, asso. prof., 1948-52, prof., 1952; prof. fin. Mass. Inst. Tech., 1952-61; assoc. dean Mass. Inst. Tech. (Sch. Indsl. Mgmt.), 1954-58, Alfred P. Sloan prof. mgmt., 1976-84, Alfred P. Sloan prof. emeritus, 1984—; prof. fin. Harvard Bus. Sch., 1962-72, Sylvan C. Coleman prof. fin. mgmt., 1968-72; chmn. fin. com., dir. Travelers Ins. Cos., Hartford, Conn., 1971-78; vice chmn. bd., dir. Travelers Ins. Cos., 1976-78; chmn. bd. Mass. Co., 1971-72; pres. Nat. Bur. Econ. Research, 1982-84; chmn. bd. Fed. Home Loan Bank Boston, 1970-89; econ. analyst div. monetary rsch. U.S. Dept. Treasury, 1941-42; economist rsch. div. OPA, 1941-42; staff cons. Com. Econ. Devel., 1950-51, mem. rsch. adv. com., 1961-64, 69—, project dir., 1966-69; cons. to sec. treasury; mem. enforcement commn. WSB, 1952-53; cons. Inst. Def. Analyses; dep. dir. Rsch. Com. on Money and Credit, 1959-61. Author: (with others) Personal Finance Industry and Its Credit Standards, 1939, (with Steiner) Money and Banking, 1941, Development of Wisconsin Credit Union Movement, 1947, Money and Banking, 1953, (with others), 1958, (with D. Meiselman) Measurement of Corporate Sources and Uses of Funds, 1964, (with others) Money and Banking, 1969, (with Wolf) The Role of Private Placement in Corporate Finance, 1972; Editor: (with W.L. White) Capital for Productivity and Growth, 1977. Served from ensign to lt. USNR, 1942-46. Recipient Econ. Dept. award Bklyn. Coll., 1936, Honors Day award for distinguished alumni, 1949. Fellow Am. Acad. Arts and Scis.; mem. Nat. Bur. Econ. Research (pres.), Am. Econ. Assn., Council Fgn. Relations, Am. Fin. Assn. Home and Office: 180 Beacon St Boston MA 02116-1401

SHAPIRO, ELLEN MARIE, graphic designer, writer; b. L.A., June 26, 1948; d. Leon E. and Elizabeth (Nussbaum) S.; m. Jerry Miller, Oct. 10, 1980 (div. 1986); 1 child, Alex Miller; m. Julius Rabinowitz, Sept. 6, 1992. BA, UCLA, 1970. Art dir. UCLA Alumni and Devel. Ctr., 1970-72; sr. designer Lubalin Smith Carnase, Inc., N.Y.C., 1972-74; art dir. Barton-Gillet Co., N.Y.C., 1974-76; ptnr. Design Concern, N.Y.C., 1976-78; pres. Shapiro Design Assocs. Inc., N.Y.C., 1978—, Shapiro Communications, Inc., 1992—; mem. faculty dept. communication design, Parsons Sch. Design, N.Y.C., 1986—; judge design and advt. shows, U.S. and Can. Art dir., Upper & Lower Case, 1988; author: Clients and Designers, 1989; contbr. numerous articles to mags. Recipient over 60 awards from profl. orgns. Mem. Am. Inst. Graphic Arts (v.p. N.Y. chpt. 1987-89), N.Y. Art Dirs. Club (Gold and Silver awards), N.Y. Type Dirs. Club. Avocations: cooking, gardening, tennis, swimming. Office: Shapiro Design Assocs Inc 10 E 40th St New York NY 10016-0200

SHAPIRO, FRED DAVID, lawyer; b. Cleve., Nov. 10, 1926; s. Isadore R. and Lottie (Turetsky) S.; m. Helen Solomon, Sept. 5, 1948; children—Gary N., Ira R., Diane S. B.A. cum laude, Ohio State U., 1949; LL.B., Harvard U., 1954. Bar: Ohio 1954. Since practiced in Cleve.; sr. partner firm Shapiro, Turoff & Belkin, 1976-94; prin. Fred D. Shapiro Co., L.P.A., 1994—. Served with USNR, 1945-46. Mem. Ohio Bar Assn., Greater Cleve. Bar Assn., Cuyahoga County Bar Assn., The Rowfant Club, Phi Beta Kappa. Jewish. Home: 29226 S Woodland Rd Cleveland OH 44124-5737

SHAPIRO, FRED LOUIS, physician, educator; b. Mpls., Aug. 18, 1934; s. Ralph Samuel and Dora (Cullen) S.; m. Merle Sandra Rosenzweig, June 23, 1957; children: Wendy Judith, Richard Scott. BA magna cum laude, U. Minn., 1958, BS, 1961, MD, 1961. Intern Hennepin County Med. Ctr., Mpls., 1961-62, resident in internal medicine, 1962-65, instr., 1965-68, chief nephrology, 1965-84; med. dir. Regional Kidney Disease Program, 1966-84; asst. prof. U. Minn., Mpls., 1968-71, assoc. prof., 1971-75, prof., 1975—; pres. Hennepin Faculty Assocs., 1983-95. Contbr. articles to profl. jours. With USNR, 1953-55. Mem. Phi Beta Kappa, Sigma Xi, Alpha Omega Alpha. Home: 3490 Fairway Ln Minnetonka MN 55305-4451 Office: Hennepin Facility Assocs 600 HFA Bldg 914 S 8th St Minneapolis MN 55404-1204

SHAPIRO, GARY MICHAEL, philosophy educator; b. St. Paul, June 17, 1941; s. Irving H. and Florence Beverly (Gleckman) S.; m. Anne Goll, 1961 (div. 1966); 1 child, Marya Suzanne; m. Lynne Margolies, 1968 (div. 1991); children: David Benjamin, Rachel Shulamith. B.A. magna cum laude, Columbia U., 1963, Ph.D., 1970; postgrad., Yale U., 1963-64. Instr. Columbia U., N.Y.C., 1967-70; asst. prof. U. Kans., Lawrence, 1970-75, assoc. prof., 1975-81, prof., 1981-91; prof. philosophy, Tucker Boatwright prof. in humanities U. Richmond, Va., 1991—. Author: Nietzschean Narratives, 1989, Alcyone, 1991, Earthwards: Robert Smithson and Art after Babel, 1995; editor: After the Future, 1990; mem. editl. adv. bd. Philosophy and Literature, 1982-96, Contemporary Studies in Philosophy and Literature, Jour. History of Philosophy, Clio; co-editor: Hermeneutics: Questions & Prospects, 1984; contbr. articles to profl. jours. Woodrow Wilson fellow. Am. Coun. Learned Socs. fellow, 1978, U. Calif., Irvine Sch. of Criticism and Theory fellow, 1976; sr. rsch. fellow Wesleyan U. Ctr. for the Humanities, 1985, Nat. Humanities Ctr. fellow, 1993-94. Mem. Internat. Assn. for Philosophy and Lit. (exec. com. 1984-89), N. Am. Nietzsche Soc. (exec. com. 1983-89), Am. Philo. Assn. (com. on lectrs. pub. and research 1985-88), Phi Beta Kappa. Office: U Richmond Dept Philosophy Richmond VA 23173

SHAPIRO, GEORGE HOWARD, lawyer; b. St. Louis, Nov. 10, 1936; s. Isadore T. and Alice (Schucart) S.; m. Mary Kenney Leonard, 1977 (div. 1994); 1 child, Ellen. BA, Harvard U., 1958, LLB, 1961; postgrad., London Sch. Econs., 1961-62. Bar: Ga. 1960, D.C. 1963. Atty. U.S. Dept. Labor, Washington, 1962-63; assoc. Arent Fox Kintner Plotkin & Kahn, Washington, 1963-69, ptnr., 1970—. Co-author: 'Cable Speech' The Case for First Amendment Protection, 1983; editor: New Program Opportunities in the Electronic Media, 1983, Current Developments in CATV, 1981. Served with USAR, 1962-68. Frank Knox Meml. fellow Harvard U., 1961-62. Mem. D.C. Bar Assn., Fed. Communications Bar Assn., Fed. Bar Assn. (dep. chmn. communications law com. 1970-71), ABA (vice chmn. cable TV com. 1982-83). Democrat. Jewish. Avocation: skiing. Home: 3249 Sutton Pl NW # D Washington DC 20016-3507 Office: Arent Fox Kintner Plotkin & Kahn 1050 Connecticut Ave NW Washington DC 20036

SHAPIRO, GEORGE M., lawyer; b. N.Y.C., Dec. 7, 1919; s. Samuel N. and Sarah (Milstein) S.; m. Rita V. Lubin, Mar. 29, 1942; children: Karen Shapiro Spector, Sanford. BS, LIU, 1939; LL.B. (Kent scholar), Columbia U., 1942; LL.D. (hon.), L.I. U., 1986. Bar: N.Y. 1942. Mem. staff gov. N.Y., 1945-51, counsel to gov., 1951-54; ptnr. Proskauer, Rose, Goetz & Mendelsohn, N.Y.C., 1955—, mem. exec. com., mng. ptnr., 1974-84, co-chmn. corp. dept., 1980-90; pres. Edmond de Rothschild Found., 1964-92; dir. Bank of Calif., 1973-84; counsel, majority leader N.Y. Senate, 1955-59; counsel N.Y. Constl. Revision Commn., 1960-61. Chmn. council State U. Coll. Medicine, N.Y., 1955-71; mem. Gov.'s Com. Reapportionment, 1964, Mayor's Com. Jud. Selection, 1966-69; chmn. Park Ave. Synagogue, 1973-81; mem. Coun. on Fgn. Rels., 1974-92. Served with USAAF, 1943-45. Club: Harmonie. Home: 1160 Park Ave New York NY 10128-1212 Office: Proskauer Rose Goetz & Mendelsohn 1585 Broadway New York NY 10036-8200

SHAPIRO, GILBERT LAWRENCE, orthopedist; b. Lewiston, Maine, June 14, 1931; s. Samuel and Freda (Meyer) S.; m. Frima Lee Goldman, Aug. 28, 1955; children: Beth S. Lewyckyi, Karen S. Goldaber, Ruth A. BA, Dartmouth Coll., 1953; MD, Tufts U., 1957. Diplomate Am. Bd. Orthopaedic Surgery. Pvt. practice orthopaedic surgery New Bedford, Mass., 1963—. Bd. dirs. NBIS Savings Bank, New Bedford, 1982-95; trustee St. Luke's Hosp., New Bedford, 1989-96; pres. bd. trustees. Pilgrim Health-care (HMO), Norwell, Md., 1991-95, Old Dartmouth Hist. Soc. (whaling mus.), New Bedford, 1991—; trustee Southcoast Health Sys., 1996—; co-pres. bd. Harvard-Pilgrim Health Care, 1996, chair fin. com., 1996—, bd. dirs., 1997—. Mem. ACS, Am. Acad. Orthopaedic Surgeons, New England Orthopaedic Soc. (pres. 1988-90), Ea. Orthopaedic Soc. Office: 84 Grape St New Bedford MA 02740-2143 also: New Bedford Whaling Mus 18 Johnny Cake Hl New Bedford MA 02740-6317

SHAPIRO, HAROLD DAVID, lawyer, educator; b. Chgo., Apr. 15, 1927; s. Charles B. and Celia (Nierenberg) S.; m. Beatrice Cahn, June 6, 1950; children: Matthew D., Michael Ann, Nicholas J. BS, Northwestern U., Chgo., 1949, JD, 1952. Adminstrv. asst. State of Ill. Dept. Fin., Springfield, 1952; assoc. Sonnenschein Nath & Rosenthal, Chgo., 1953-59; ptnr. Sonnenschein Nath & Rosenthal, 1959—; Edward A. Harriman adj. prof. law Northwestern U., Chgo., 1970—; sec., bd. dirs. West Side Affordable Housing, Inc., West Side Village, Inc. Trustee, mem. exec. com., sec. Jr. Achievement of Chgo.; bd. dirs. Schwab Rehab. Ctr., Chgo.; pres. Homan & Arthington Found., 1995-96; pres. Northwestern U. Law Sch. Alumni Assn., Chgo., 1984-85. Served with Seabees, USNR, 1945-50, PTO. Recipient Merit award Northwestern U., 1988. Mem. Ill. Bar Assn., ABA, Chgo. Bar Assn., Chgo. Council Lawyers, Legal Club of Chgo. (pres.), Law Club of Chgo., Order of Coif, Wigmore Key, Standard Club, Met. Club, Cliff Dwellers, Chicago Club, Lake Shore Country Club. Democrat. Jewish. Home: 34 Linden Ave Wilmette IL 60091-2837 Office: Sonnenschein Nath & Rosenthal 8000 Sears Tower 233 S Wacker Dr Chicago IL 60606-6306

SHAPIRO, HAROLD TAFLER, academic administrator, economist; b. Montreal, Que., Can., June 8, 1935; s. Maxwell and Mary (Tafler) S.; m. Vivian Bernice Rapoport, May 19, 1957; children: Anne, Marilyn, Janet, Karen. BComm, McGill U., Montreal, 1956; PhD in Econs. (Harold Helm fellow, Harold Dodds sr. fellow), Princeton U., 1964. Asst. prof. econs. U. Mich., 1964-67, assoc. prof., 1967-70, prof., 1970-76, chmn. dept. econs., 1974-77, prof. econs. and pub. affairs, from 1977, v.p. acad. affairs, 1977-79, pres., 1980-87; research adv. Bank Can., 1965-72; prof. econ. and pub. affairs, pres. Princeton U., 1988—; bd. dirs. Dow Chem.; trustee Univs. Rsch. Assn., 1988—; mem. exec. com. Assn. Am. Univs., 1985-89, N.J. Commn. on Sci. and Tech., 1988-91; mem. Pres.'s Coun. Advisors on Sci. and Tech., 1990-92; chmn. com. on employer-based health benefits Inst. Medicine, 1991. Trustee Alfred P. Sloan Found., 1980—, Interlochen Ctr. for Arts, 1988-95, U. Pa. Med. Ctr., 1992—, Ednl. Testing Svc., 1994—; dir. Am. Coun. Edn., 1989-92; chmn. Spl. Presdl. Com., The Research Libraries Group, 1980-91; mem. Gov.'s High Tech. Task Force, Mich., 1980-87; mem. Gov.'s Commn. on Jobs and Econ. Devel. (Mich.), 1983-87; mem. Carnegie Commn. on Coll. Retirement, 1984-86. Recipient Lt. Gov.'s medal in commerce McGill U., 1956. Fellow Am. Acad. Arts and Scis., Mich. Soc. Fellows (sr.); mem. Inst. Medicine of NAS, Am. Philos. Soc., Nat. Bur. Econ. Rsch. (bd. dirs.). Office: Princeton U 1 Nassau St Princeton NJ 08542-4502

SHAPIRO, HARRY DEAN, lawyer; b. Louisville, June 21, 1940; s. Herman Shapiro and Toby (Spector) Levy; m. Linda Siegel, Dec. 19, 1970; 1 child, Deborah Anne. BS, U. Louisville, 1962, JD, 1964. Bar: Ky. 1964, D.C. 1968, Md. 1970. Trial and appellate atty. U.S. Dept. Justice, Washington, 1964-70; assoc. Venable, Baetjer & Howard, Balt., 1970-74, ptnr., 1975-87; sr. ptnr., head of tax practice Weinberg & Green, Balt., 1987—, chmn. corp. dept., 1993-95; transaction group coord., 1995—. Author: Federal Tax Liens, 1981; contbr. articles to profl. jours. Mem. Md. State Bd. Edn., 1990—; v.p. Assoc. Jewish Charities of Balt., Inc. 1991-94; vice chmn. The Assoc. Jewish Cmty. Fedn. Balt. 1987-89, asst. treas., 1989-91, mem. exec. com., 1993—; trustee Sinai Hosp., Balt., 1987-90; counsel Balt. Mus. Art, 1984—, trustee, 1984-96, sec., 1985-92, v.p., sec., 1992-94, v.p., 1994-96; dir., 1989—; chmn. Joint Budgeting Coun., 1993-96, Coun. Jewish Fedns. Capt. USAR, 1967-70. Mem. ABA (tax sect.), Md. State Bar Assn., Ky. Bar Assn., D.C. Bar Assn., Md. Club, Center Club. Home: 7903 7 Mile Ln Baltimore MD 21208-4306 Office: Weinberg & Green 100 S Charles St Baltimore MD 21201-2725 *Our country is at a crossroads in its history, and it is becoming clear that a sea change is necessary. Basic reforms must occur in our governmental and educational structures. The question is whether we have the intelligence to reject the cries for bigger government and more taxes to solve these problems when fundamental action is required.*

SHAPIRO, HARVEY, poet; b. Chgo., Jan. 27, 1924; s. Jacob J. and Dorothy (Cohen) S.; m. Edna Lewis Kaufman, July 23, 1953; children—Saul, Dan. B.A., Yale U., 1947; M.A., Columbia U., 1948. Instr. English Cornell U., 1949-50, 51-52; creative writing fellow Bard Coll., 1950-51; mem. editorial staff Commentary, New Yorker, 1955-57; editorial staff N.Y. Times Mag., N.Y.C., 1957; asst. editor N.Y. Times Mag., 1964-75; editor N.Y. Times Book Rev., 1975-83; dep. editor N.Y. Times Mag., 1983-96, sr. editor, 1996—. Author: The Eye, 1953, The Book and Other Poems, 1955, Mountain, Fire, Thornbush, 1961, Battle Report, 1966, This World, 1971, Lauds, 1975, Nightsounds, 1978, The Light Holds, 1984, National Cold Storage Company, 1988, A Day's Portion, 1994, Selected Poems, 1997. Served with USAAF, World War II. Decorated D.F.C., Air medal with 3 oak leaf clusters.; Rockefeller Found. grantee in poetry, 1967. Club: Elizabethan (New Haven), Century (N.Y.). Office: NY Times 229 W 43rd St New York NY 10036-3913

SHAPIRO, HOWARD, newspaper editor. Travel editor The Phila. Inquirer. Office: The Philadelphia Inquirer 400 N Broad St Philadelphia PA 19130-4015

SHAPIRO, HOWARD ALAN, lawyer; b. Albany, N.Y., May 12, 1932; s. Ralph and Estelle (Warshak) S.; m. Eleanor Siegel, June 20, 1954; children: David Todd, Andrew Neil, Diane Graser. A.B. magna cum laude, Harvard U., 1953, LL.B. magna cum laude, 1956. Bar: N.Y. 1956. Assoc. Proskauer Rose Goetz & Mendelsohn, N.Y.C., 1956-65, ptnr., 1965—; lectr. Practicing Law Inst., 1971-79. Editor Harvard Law Rev., 1954-56, note editor, 1955-56. Mem. Assn. of Bar of City of N.Y. (com. on corp. law 1971-74, com. on banking law 1978-81, 86-89), N.Y. State Bar Assn., ABA, N.Y. County Lawyers' Assn. Home: 140 E 72nd St New York NY 10021-4243 Office: Proskauer Rose et al 1585 Broadway New York NY 10036-8200

SHAPIRO, IRVING SAUL, lawyer; b. Mpls., July 15, 1916; s. Sam I. and Freda (Lane) S.; m. Charlotte Farsht, Mar. 1, 1942; children: Stuart Lane, Elizabeth Irene. B.S., U. Minn., 1939, LL.B., 1941. Bar: Minn. 1941, Del. 1958. Atty. criminal div. Dept. Justice, 1943-51; with E.I. duPont de Nemours & Co., Inc., 1951-81; v.p. E.I. du Pont de Nemours & Co., Inc., 1970-73, vice chmn. bd., 1973, chmn., chief exec. officer, 1974-81, also dir., chmn. exec. com., chmn. pub. affairs com., until 1981; ptnr. firm Skadden, Arps, Slate, Meagher & Flom, N.Y.C., 1981-89, of counsel, 1990; bd. dirs. AEA Investors Inc., J.P. Morgan Fla. Fed. Savs. Bank. Chmn. bd. trustees

Howard Hughes Med. Inst., Pediat. Scvs. of Am. Inc., Sola Internat. Inc. Office: Skadden Arps Slate Meagher & Flom 1 Rodney Sq Wilmington DE 19801 Office: Skadden Arps Slate Meagher Flom PO Box 636 Wilmington DE 19899

SHAPIRO, IRWIN IRA, physicist, educator; b. N.Y.C., N.Y., Oct. 10, 1929; s. Samuel and Esther (Feinberg) S.; m. Marian Helen Kaplun, Dec. 20, 1959; children: Steven, Nancy. A.B., Cornell U., 1950; A.M., Harvard U., 1951, Ph.D., 1955. Mem. staff Lincoln Lab. MIT, Lexington, 1954-70; Sherman Fairchild Distinguished scholar Calif. Inst. Tech., 1974; Morris Loeb lectr. physics Harvard, 1975; prof. geophysics and physics MIT, 1967-80, Schlumberger prof., 1980-84; Paine prof. practical astronomy, prof. physics Harvard U., 1982—; sr. scientist Smithsonian Astrophys. Obs., 1982—; dir. Harvard-Smithsonian Ctr. for Astrophysics, 1983—; cons. NSF, NASA. Contbr. articles to profl. jours. Recipient Albert A. Michelson medal Franklin Inst., 1975, award in phys. and math. scis. N.Y. Acad. Scis., 1982, Einstein medal Einstein Soc. Bern, 1994; Guggenheim fellow, 1982. Fellow AAAS, Am. Geophys. Union (Charles A. Whitten medal 1991, William Bowie medal 1993), Am. Phys. Soc.; mem. AAAS, NAS (Benjamin Apthorp Gould prize 1979), Am. Astron. Soc. (Dannie Heineman award 1983, Dirk Brouwer award 1987, Gerard Kuiper award 1997), Internat. Astron. Union, Phi Beta Kappa, Sigma Xi, Phi Kappa Phi. Home: 17 Lantern Ln Lexington MA 02173-6029 Office: Harvard-Smithsonian Ctr Astrophysics 60 Garden St Cambridge MA 02138-1516

SHAPIRO, ISAAC, lawyer; b. Tokyo, Jan. 5, 1931; s. Constantine and Lydia (Chernetzky) S.; m. Jacqueline M. Weiss, Sept. 16, 1956; children: Tobias, Alexandra, Natasha. A.B., Columbia U., 1954, LL.B., 1956; postgrad., Inst. de Droit Compare, U. Paris, 1956-57. Bar: N.Y. 1957, U.S. Supreme Ct. 1971, Paris 1991. Assoc. Milbank, Tweed, Hadley & McCloy, N.Y.C., 1956-65, ptnr., 1966-86; resident ptnr. Milbank, Tweed, Hadley & McCloy, Tokyo, 1977-79; ptnr. Skadden Arps Slate Meagher & Flom, LLP, N.Y.C., 1986—; resident ptnr. Skadden Arps Slate Meagher & Flom, Hong Kong, 1989-90, Paris, 1990—; tchg. fellow comparative law NYU, 1959-61; lectr. Soviet law, 1961-67; adj. asst. prof. NYU, 1967-69, adj. assoc. prof., 1969-71, 74-75; bd. dirs. Bank of Tokyo Mitsubishi Trust Co., N.Y.C., Carl Zeiss, Inc., Thornwood, N.Y., PRT Group, Inc., N.Y.C. Author: (with Hazard and Maggs) The Soviet Legal System, 1969; author: Japan: The Risen Sun (in Japanese), 1982; editor: The Middle East Crisis-Prospects for Peace, 1969; contbr. articles to periodicals. Mem. Joint Com. U.S.-Japan Cultural and Ednl. Cooperation, Washington, 1972-78; mem. Japan-U.S. Friendship Commn., 1975-78; trustee Nat. Humanities Ctr., Triangle Park, N.C., 1976-89, Bank of Tokyo Mitsubishi Trust Co. Found., 1996—; trustee, v.p. Chamber Music Soc. Lincoln Ctr., 1980-86; trustee, pres. Isamu Noguchi Fedn., 1985—; trustee, chmn. Ise Cultural Fedn., 1984—; bd. dirs. Bus. Coun. for Internat. Understanding, 1989-95, Nat. Com. for U.S.-China Rels., 1989-95, Asian Cultural Coun., 1980—. Fulbright scholar, 1956-57. Mem. ABA, N.Y. State Bar Assn., Assn. Bar City N.Y., Japan Soc. (pres. N.Y. 1970-77), Coun. Fgn. Rels. Home: 6 rue Goethe, 75116 Paris France Office: Skadden Arps Slate et al, 105 rue faubourg St Honore, 75008 Paris France

SHAPIRO, ISADORE, materials scientist, consultant; b. Mpls., Apr. 25, 1916; s. Jacob and Bessie (Goldman) S.; m. Mae Hirsch, Sept. 4, 1938; children: Stanley Harris, Jerald Steven. BChemE. summa cum laude, U. Minn., 1938, PhD, 1944. Asst. instr. chemistry U. Minn., 1938-41, rsch. fellow, 1944-45; rsch. chemist E. I. duPont de Nemours and Co., Phila., 1946; head chem. lab. U.S. Naval Ordnance Test Sta., Pasadena, Calif., 1947-52; dir. rsch. lab. Olin-Mathieson Chem. Corp., 1952-59; head chemistry Hughes Tool Co., Aircraft div., Culver City, Calif., 1959-62; pres. Universal Chem. Systems Inc. 1962—, Aerospace Chem. Systems, Inc., 1964-66; dir. contract rsch. HITCO, Gardena, Calif., 1966-67; prin. scientist Douglas Aircraft Co. of McDonnell Douglas Corp., Santa Monica, Calif., 1967; prin. scientist McDonnell Douglas Astronautics Co., 1967-70; head materials and processes AiResearch Mfg. Co., Torrance, Calif., 1971-82, cons., 1982—; inaugurated dep. gov. Am. Biog. Inst. Rsch. Assn., 1988; dep. dir. gen. Internat. Biog. Ctr., 1989, Eng. Rater U.S. Civil Svc. Bd. Exam., 1948-52. Served 1st lt. AUS, 1941-44. Registered profl. engr., Calif. Fellow Am. Inst. Chemists, Am. Inst. Aeros and Astronautics (assoc.); mem. AAAS, Am. Ordnance Assn., Am. Chem. Soc., Soc. Rheology, Soc. Advancement Materials and Process Engring., Am. Inst. Physics, AIM, Am. Phys. Soc., N.Y. Acad. Sci., Am. Assn. Contamination Control, Am. Ceramic Soc., Nat. Inst. Ceramic Engrs., Am. Powder Metallurgy Inst., Internat. Plansee Soc. for Powder Metallurgy, Sigma Xi, Tau Beta Pi, Phi Lambda Upsilon. Author articles in tech. publs. Patentee, discoverer series of carborane compounds; created term carborane; formulator of universal compaction equation for powders (metals, ceramics, polymers, chemicals). Home: 5624 W 62nd St Los Angeles CA 90056-2009

SHAPIRO, IVAN, lawyer; b. N.Y.C., Nov. 11, 1928; s. Archie M. and Auguste (Reiff) S.; m. Florence Goodstein, June 24, 1951 (div. Oct. 1958); 1 child, Lisa J. Kubiske; m. Maria Schaffner, Sept. 16, 1960; 1 child, Alexandra. B.S.S., CCNY, 1948; J.D., Harvard U., 1951. Bar: N.Y. 1952. Assoc. Wien, Lane, Klein & Purcell, N.Y.C., 1954-59; ptnr. Wien, Lane & Klein, 1959-74, Greenbaum, Wolff & Ernst, N.Y.C., 1974-81, Willkie Farr & Gallagher, N.Y.C., 1981-91; lectr. Real Estate Inst., NYU Sch. Continuing Edn., N.Y.C., 1978-81. Author: Case Studies in Real Estate Finance, 1980; author pamphlets on ethical issues, 1973-80, articles on civil liberties issues, 1966-80. Trustee Ethical Culture Soc., N.Y.C., 1970—, pres., 1972-78; pres. Ethical Culture Schs., N.Y., 1976-82; bd. visitors Grad. Sch., Univ. Ctr. CUNY, 1986—, vice chmn., 1992—; mem. Asia Watch Com. Human Rights Watch, 1990-95; bd. dirs., pres. Urban Pathways, Inc. (formerly West Side Cluster Inc.), 1991-95; bd. dirs. Bklyn. Navy Yard Devel. Corp., 1991-95, chmn. bylaws com., 1992-94; bd. dirs. Abortiion Rights Assn. N.Y., 1970-71, Nat. Assn. for Repeal of Abortion laws, 1971-74. Mem. ACLU (bd. dirs. N.Y. chpt. 1966-80, 87—, treas. 1989-95), Assn. Bar of City of N.Y., Phi Beta Kappa. Democrat.

SHAPIRO, JAMES EDWARD, judge; b. Chgo., May 28, 1930; s. Ben Edward and Rose (Slate) S.; m. Rhea Kahn, Dec. 28, 1958; children—Jeffrey Scott, Steven Mark. B.S., U. Wis., 1951; J.D., Harvard U., 1954. Bar: Wis. 1956, U.S. Dist. Ct. (ea. dist.) Wis. 1956, U.S. Ct. Appeals (7th cir.) 1962, U.S. Supreme Ct. 1971. Sole practice, Milw., 1956-57; resident house counsel Nat. Presto Industries, Eau Claire, Wis., 1957-60; ptnr. Bratt & Shapiro, Milw., 1960-64; sole practice, Milw., 1964-74; ptnr. Frank, Hiller & Shapiro, Milw., 1974-82; judge U.S. Bankruptcy Ct., Milw., 1982-96, chief judge, 1996—. Mem. Bayside Bd. Appeals, Wis., 1969-77; Milw. county ct. commr., 1969-78; dir. Milw. Legal Aid Soc., 1969-77. Served to 1st lt. U.S. Army, 1954-56. Mem. State Bar Assn. Wis. (chmn. bankruptcy, insolvency, creditors rights sect.), Milw. Bar Assn. (past chmn., past vice chmn. bankruptcy sect.). Jewish. Office: US Courthouse 140 Fed Bldg 517 E Wisconsin Ave Milwaukee WI 53202-4504

SHAPIRO, JEROME GERSON, lawyer; b. N.Y.C., May 12, 1924; s. Joseph Louis and Beatrice Rebecca S.; m. Marjorie Kemble Mackay, Dec. 31, 1959; children—Jeffrey Kemble, Jill Dara, Eric Paul. A.B. summa cum laude, N.Y. U., 1946; LL.B. magna cum laude, Harvard U., 1948. Bar: N.Y. State bar 1949, U.S. Supreme Ct. bar 1955. Asso. mem. firm Hughes Hubbard & Reed, N.Y.C., 1949-51, 52-57; spl. asst. atty. gen., sr. asst. counsel N.Y. State Crime Commn., 1951-52; ptnr. firm Hughes Hubbard & Reed, N.Y.C., 1957-95; chmn. Hughes Hubbard & Reed, 1975-90; counsel, 1995—; prof. law N.Y. Law Sch., 1951-53. Vice chmn. trustees James W. Johnson Community Centers, Inc., N.Y.C., 1975-78; trustee Lawyers Com. for Civil Rights Under Law, 1976—. Served with AUS, 1943-45. Decorated Purple Heart, Bronze Star. Fellow Am. Coll. Trial Lawyers; mem. Assn. of Bar of City of N.Y. (exec. com. 1967-73), Am. Bar Found. (rsch. com.), Harvard Club, Phi Beta Kappa. Jewish. Office: Hughes Hubbard & Reed 1 Battery Park Plz New York NY 10004-1405

SHAPIRO, JEROME HERBERT, radiologist, educator; b. Cleve., Aug. 5, 1924; s. Louis and Rose (Hamburgher) S.; m. Amy Elizabeth Alderman, June 16, 1948 (dec. Jan. 1991); children: Nancy Lee, Mathew Paul, Wendy Jane, Deborah Gail; m. Meredith Pearlstein, Dec. 16, 1993. Student, Western Res. U., 1942-44; MD, Yale U., 1948. Intern Mt. Sinai Hosp., Cleve., 1948-49; resident in radiology Montefiore Hosp., N.Y.C., 1949-52; fellow X-ray diagnosis Meml. Center, N.Y.C., 1952; attending radiologist Montefiore Hosp., 1952-63; assoc. clin. prof. radiology NYU, 1960-63; prof. radiology Boston U. Sch. Medicine, 1963—, chmn. dept. radiology, 1963-92; dir. radiology Boston City, Univ. hosps., 1963-92; Lectr. radiology Harvard, Tufts med. schs., 1963—. Sr. author: Cardiac Calcifications, 1963; Contbr. numerous articles to profl. jours. Vice pres. Wellesley (Mass.) Symphony Orch., 1980-82, pres., 1982-86. Fellow Am. coll. Radiology (chancellor 1973-79, 89-90, v.p. 1980-81, pres. 1989-90, gold medal 1992), Coun. Med. Splty. Socs. (pres. 1992-93); mem. AMA, Radiol. Soc. N.Am. (Gold medal 1996), Am. Roentgen Ray Soc. (pres. 1974-75), Assn. Univ. Radiologists, Am. Soc. Neuroradiology, Mass. Radiol. Soc. (pres. 1970-71). Jewish (pres. temple 1968-72). Home: 416 Commonwealth Ave Apt 505 Boston MA 02215-2810 Office: Univ Hosp Dept Radiology 88 E Newton St Boston MA 02118-2308

SHAPIRO, JOAN ISABELLE, laboratory administrator, nurse; b. Fulton, Ill., Aug. 26, 1943; d. Macy James and Frieda Lockhart; m. Ivan Lee Shapiro, Dec. 28, 1968; children: Audrey, Michael. RN, Peoria Methodist Sch. Nursing, Ill., 1964. Nurse, Grant Hosp., Columbus, Ohio, 1975-76; nurse Cardiac Thoracic and Vascular Surgeons Ltd., Geneva, Ill., 1977—, mgr. non-invasive lab., 1979—; owner, operator Shapiro's Mastiff's 1976-82; sec.-treas. Sounds Svcs., 1976—, Mainstream Sounds Inc., 1980-84; co-founder Cardio-Phone Inc., 1982—, Edgewater Vascular Inst., 1987-89, Associated Profls., 1989-92; v.p., bd. dir. Computer Specialists Inc., 1986-89; founder, pres. Vein Ctr., Edema Ctr. Ltd. Mem. Soc. Non-invasive Technologists, Soc. Peripheral Vascular Nursing (community awareness com. 1984—), Oncology Nursing Soc., Internat. Soc. Lymphology, Kane County Med. Soc. Aux. (pres. 1983-84, adviser, 1984-85). Lutheran. Office: Cardiac Thoracic and Vascular Surgeons Ltd PO Box 564 Geneva IL 60134-0564

SHAPIRO, JOEL ELIAS, artist; b. N.Y.C., Sept. 27, 1941; s. Joseph and Anna (Lewis) S.; m. Ellen Phelan; 1 dau., Ivy Bess. BA, NYU, 1964, MA, 1969. One-person shows include Paula Cooper Gallery, N.Y.C., 14 shows 1970-89, 90-92, Inst. Art and Urban Resources, N.Y.C., 1973, Mus. Contemporary Art, Chgo., 1976, Albright-Knox Art Gallery, Buffalo, 1977, Gallery M. Bochum, W. Ger., 1977, Galerie Mukai, Tokyo, 1980, 81, 88, Asher/Faure, L.A., 1980, 89, Whitechapel Gallery, London, 1980, Hans Lange, Krefeld, W. Ger., 1980, Moderna Museet, Stockholm, 1980, Brown U., 1980, Ackland Art Mus., Chapel Hill, N.C., 1981, Contemporary Arts Ctr., Cin., 1981, Israel Mus., Jerusalem, 1981, Portland Ctr. Visual Arts, Oreg., 1982, Whitney Mus. Am. Art, N.Y.C., 1982, Galerie Aronowitsch, Stockholm, 1983, Delahunty Gallery, Dallas, 1983, Donald Young Gallery, Chgo., 1984, Stedelijk Mus., Amsterdam, 1985, Kunstmuseum, Dusseldorf, 1985, Staatliche Kunsthalle, Baden-Baden, 1985, Seattle Art Mus., 1986, Galerie Daniel Templon, Paris, 1986, 88, The John and Mable Ringling Mus., Sarasota, 1986, John Berggruen Gallery, San Francisco, Hirshhorn Mus. and Sculpture Garden, Washington, 1987, Hans Strelow, Dusseldorf, Germany, 1988, Toledo Mus. Art, 1989, Waddington Gallery, London, 1989, Museet I Varberg, Sweden, 1990, Balt. Art Mus., 1990, Des Moines Art Ctr., 1991, Ctr. for Fine Arts, Miami, 1991, IVAM Centre Julio Gonazlez, Valencia, Spain, 1990, Ctr. for the Fine Arts, Miami, 1991, Asher-Faure, L.A., 1991, Gallery Mukai, Tokyo, 1991, John Berggruen Gallery, San Francisco, 1991, Pace Gallery, 1993, Galerie Karsten Greve, Cologne, Germany, 1993, Gallery Seomi, Seoul, 1994, 96, Glerie Aronowitsch, Stockholm, 1995, Karsten Greve, Paris, 1995, Pace Gallery, N.Y., 1995, Walker Art Ctr./Mpls. Sculpture Garden, 1995, Nelson-Atkins Mus. Art/Kansas City Sculpture Park, 1996, Pace Wildenstein Gallery, N.Y., 1996, Addison Gallery, Andover, Mass., 1997, Haus der Kunst, Munich, 1997, Galerie Jamileh Weber, Zurich, Switzerland, 1997; numerous group exhibits; permanent collections and commns. include Mus. Modern Art, N.Y.C., Whitney Mus. Art, N.Y.C., Walker Art Center, Mpls., Met. Mus. Art, N.Y.C., Albright Knox Art Gallery, Buffalo, Detroit Inst. Art, Stedelijk Mus., Amsterdam, Moderna Museet, Stockholm, Dallas Mus. Art, Centre Pompidou, Paris, Nat. Gallery Art, Washington, Brit. Mus., London, Bklyn. Mus., Cocoran Gallery, Washington, Fogg Art Mus. at Harvard U., Cambridge, Mass., High Mus. Art, Atlanta, Hirshhorn Mus. and Sculpture Garden at Smithsonian Instn., Washington, Israel Mus., Jerusalem, Kunsthaus Zürich, Switzerland, Mus. Contemporary Art, L.A., Mus. Fine Arts, Boston, Mus. Modern Art, Friuli, Italy, Parrish Art Mus., Southampton, N.Y., Phila. Mus. Art, Tate Gallery, London, commissions include Cigna Corp., Phila., 1983-84, Fukuoka (Japan) Sogo Bank, 1988, Creative Artists Agy., L.A., 1988-89, Kawamura Meml. Mus. Art, Chiba, Japan, 1988-89, Govt. Svc. Adminstrn., L.A., 1988-90, Hood Mus. Art at Dartmouth Coll., Hanover, N.H., 1989-90, U.S. Holocaust Meml. Mus., Washington, 1993, Sony Music Entertainment, N.Y.C., 1994-95, Friedrichstadt Passagen, Berlin, 1994-95, Kansas City (Mo.) Internat. Airport, 1995-96; represented by Pace Gallery, N.Y.C., Cleve. Mus. Art, N.C. Mus. Art, Raleigh, Des Moines Art Ctr., Pace Gallery, N.Y.C. Recipient Nat. Endowment for Arts award, 1975, Brandeis award, 1984, Skowhegan medal, 1986, Award of Merit, Am. Acad. and Inst. of Arts and Letters, 1990. Mem. Swedish Royal Acad. Art. Office: care Pace Gallery 32 E 57th St New York NY 10022-2513

SHAPIRO, JUDITH R., anthropology educator, university official; b. N.Y.C., Jan. 24, 1942. Student Ecole des Haute Etudes Institut d'Etudes Politiques, Paris, 1961-62; BA, Brandeis U., 1963; PhD, Columbia U., 1972. Asst. prof. U. Chgo., 1970-75; postdoctoral fellow U. Calif.-Berkeley, 1974-75; Rosalyn R. Schwartz lectr., asst. prof. anthropology Bryn Mawr Coll., Pa., 1975-78, assoc. prof., 1978-85, prof., 1985—, chmn. dept., 1982-85, acting dean undergrad coll., 1985-86, provost, 1986-94; pres. Barnard Coll., N.Y., 1994—; contbr. articles to profl. jours., chpts. to books. Fellow Woodrow Wilson Found., 1963-64, Columbia U., 1964-65, NEH Younger Humanist, 1974-75, Am. Coun. Learned Socs., 1981-82, Ctr. for Advanced Study in the Behavioral Scis., 1989; grantee NSF summer field tng., 1965, Ford Found. 1966, NIMH, 1974-75, Social Sci. Rsch. Coun., 1974-75. Mem. Phila. Anthrop. Soc. (pres. 1983), Am. Ethnol. Soc. (nominations com. 1983-84, pres. elect 1984-85, pres. 1985-86), Am. Anthrop. Assn. (ethics com. 1976-79, bd. dirs. 1984-86, exec. com. 1985-86), Social Sci. Rsch. Coun. (com. social sci personnel 1977-80), mem. bd. dirs. Consortium on Financing Higher Edn.; dir. Fund for the City of N.Y.; mem. exec. com. Women's Coll. Coalition; mem. nat. adv. com. Woodrow Wilson Nat. Fellowship Found., Women's Forum, Phi Beta Kappa, Sigma Xi. Office: Barnard Coll Office of the Pres 3009 Broadway New York NY 10027-6501

SHAPIRO, KARL JAY, poet, former educator; b. Balt., Nov. 10, 1913; s. Joseph and Sarah (Omanski) S.; m. Evalyn Katz, Mar. 25, 1945 (div. Jan. 1967); children: Katharine, John J., Elizabeth (dec. Jan. 1993); m. Teri Kovach, July 31, 1967 (dec. July 1982); m. Sophie Wilkins, Apr. 25, 1985. Student, Johns Hopkins U., 1937-39; PhD (hon.), Bucknell U. Cons. poetry Library of Congress, 1946-47; assoc. prof. writing Johns Hopkins U., 1947-50; editor Poetry: A Magazine of Verse, 1950-56; prof. English U. Nebr., Lincoln, 1956-66, U. Ill. Circle Campus, Chgo., 1966-68, U. Calif. at Davis, 1968-85; now ret. Author: Poems, 1935, New and Selected Poems, 1940-46, Person, Place and Thing, 1942, The Place of Love, 1942, V-Letter and Other Poems, 1944, Essay on Rime, 1945, Trial of a Poet, 1947, Bibliography of Modern Prosody, 1948, Poems, 1942-53, 1953, Beyond Criticism, 1953, Poems of a Jew, 1958, In Defense of Ignorance, 1960, (with James E. Miller, Jr. and Bernice Slote) Start with the Sun, 1960, Prose Keys to Modern Poetry, 1962, The Bourgeois Poet, 1964, A Prosody Handbook, 1964, (with Robert Beum) Selected Poems, 1968, To Abolish Children, 1968, White-Haired Lover, 1968, The Poetry Wreck, Selected Essays 1950-70, 1975, Adult Bookstore, 1976, Love & War, Art & God, 1984, Collected Poems 1940-1978, 1978, New and Selected Poems, 1940-86, 1987, The Younger Son, 1988, Reports of My Death, 1990, The Old Horsefly, 1993; (novel) Edsel, 1971: (film) Karl Shapiro's America, 1976. Served with AUS, 1941-45. Recipient Jeanette S. Davis prize, 1942, Levinson prize, 1943, Contemporary Poetry prize, 1943, Pulitzer prize for poetry, 1945, Shelley Meml. prize, 1945, Bollingen prize for poetry, 1969, Robert Kirsch award L.A. Times, 1989, Charity Randall citation, 1990; grantee Am. Acad. Arts and Letters, 1944; fellow Kenyon Sch. Letters, 1956, 57, Guggenheim fellow, 1953-54, fellow Libr. of Congress. Mem. PEN, Nat. Acad. Arts and Letters, Am. Acad. Arts and Scis.

SHAPIRO, LARRY JAY, pediatrician, scientist, educator; b. Chgo., July 6, 1946; s. Philip and Phyllis (Krause) S.; m. Carol-Ann Uetake; children: Jennifer, Jessica, Brian. A.B., Washington U., St. Louis, 1968, M.D., 1971. Diplomate Am. Bd. Pediatrics, Am. Bd. Med. Examiners, Am. Bd. Med. Genetics. Intern St. Louis Children's Hosp., 1971-72, resident, 1971-73; research assoc. NIH, Bethesda, Md., 1973-75; asst. prof. Sch. Medicine, UCLA, 1975-79, assoc. prof., 1979-83, prof. pediatrics and biol. chemistry, 1983-91; investigator Howard Hughes Med. Inst., 1987-91, W.H. and marie Wattis Disting. Prof.; prof., chmn. dept. pediat. U. Calif.-San Francisco Sch. Medicine, 1991—, chief pediat. svcs. U. Calif. San Francisco Med. Ctr., 1991—. Contbr. numerous articles to profl. publs. Served to lt. comdr. USPHS, 1973-75. Fellow AAAS, Am. Acad. Pediatrics (E. Mead Johnson award in rsch. 1982); mem. Inst. Medicine-NAS, Soc. Pediatric Rsch. (coun. 1984-87, pres. 1991-92), Western Soc. for Pediatric Rsch. (coun. 1983-87, Ross award in rsch. 1981, pres. 1989-90), Soc. for Inherited Metabolic Disease (coun. 1983-88, pres. 1986-87), Assn. Am. Physicians, Am. Soc. Human Genetics (council 1985-88, pres. elect 1995, pres. 1997), Am. Soc. Clin. Investigation, Am. Pediatric Soc., Am. Acad. Arts & Scis. Office: U Calif Third Ave & Parnassus San Francisco CA 94143

SHAPIRO, LEO J., social researcher; b. N.Y.C., July 8, 1921; m. Virginia L. Johnson, Feb. 9, 1952; children: David, Erik, Owen, Amy. BA, U. Chgo., 1942, PhD, 1952. Survey specialist Fed. Govt. Agy., Washington, 1941-45, Sci. Rsch. Assn., Chgo., 1948-52; prin., founder Leo J. Shapiro and Assocs., Chgo., 1952-91; pres. Greenhouse, Inc., 1991—; bd. dirs. CM Ptrns. Mktg. Mem. vis. com. bd. trustees U. Chgo. Fellow U. Chgo., 1949. Fellow Social Sci. Research Council; mem. Am. Sociol. Assn., Phi Beta Kappa.

SHAPIRO, LEONARD, immunologist, allergist; b. Phila., Apr. 11, 1941; s. Nathan and Lottie (Ginsberg) S.; m. Linda Carol Adelman, June, 1964 (div. 1986); children: Lauren, Jonathan, Brett; m. Janet Susan Rubenstein, Nov. 7, 1987; 1 child, Eliana. AB, Temple U., 1963, MD, 1967. Diplomate Am. Bd. Allergy and Immunology, Am. Bd. Pediat. Intern Pa. Hosp., Phila., 1967-68; resident Children's Hosp., Phila., 1968-70; pvt. practice Reno, 1974—; fellow Nat. Jewish Hosp./Univ. Colo. Med. Sch., 1972-74; assoc. clin. prof. pediat. U. Nev. Med. Sch., 1974—; cons. VA Hosp., Reno, 1974—. Pres. Temple Emanu El, Reno, 1980, 81, 93, Jewish Cmty. Coun. No. Nev., 1982, 83. Major USAF, 1970-72. Recipient Maimonides award State of Israel, 1982. Fellow Am. Acad. Pediat., Am. Coll. Allergy Asthma Immunology, Am. Acad. Allergy Astmha Immunology; mem. Alpha Omega Alpha. Republican. Jewish. Avocations: jogging, theology. Office: Allergy Asthma Assocs 2005 Silverada Blvd Ste 250 Reno NV 89512-2057

SHAPIRO, LUCILLE, molecular biology educator; b. N.Y.C., July 16, 1940; d. Philip and Yetta (Stein) Cohen; m. Roy Shapiro, Jan. 23, 1960 (div. 1977); 1 child, Peter; m. Harley H. McAdams, July 28, 1978; stepchildren: Paul, Heather. BA, Bklyn. Coll., 1961; PhD, Albert Einstein Coll. Medicine, 1966. Asst. prof. Albert Einstein Coll. Medicine, N.Y.C., 1967-72, assoc. prof., 1972-77, Kramer prof., chmn. dept. molecular biology, 1977-86, dir. biol. scis. div., 1981-86; Eugene Higgins prof., chmn. dept. microbiology, Coll. Physicians and Surgeons Columbia U., N.Y.C., 1986-89; Joseph D. Grant prof. devel. biology Stanford U. Sch. Medicine, 1989—, chmn. dept. devel. biology, 1989-97; bd. dirs. Silicon Graphics, SmithKline Beecham; bd. sci. counselors NIH, Washington, 1980-84, DeWitt Stetten disting. lectr., 1989; bd. sci. advisors G.D. Searle Co., Skokie, Ill., 1984-86; sci. adv. bd. Mass. Gen. Hosp., 1990-93, SmithKline Beecham, 1993—, PathoGenesis, 1995—; bd. trustees Scientists Inst. for Pub. Info., 1990-94; lectr. Harvey Soc., 1993; commencement address U. Calif., Berkeley, 1994. Editor: Microbiol. Devel., 1984; mem. editorial bd. Jour. Bacteriology, 1978-86, Trends in Genetics, 1987—, Genes and Development, 1987-91, Cell Regulation, 1990-92, Molecular Biology of the Cell, 1992—, Molecular Microbiology, 1991-96, Current Opinion on Genetics and Devel., 1991—; contbr. articles to profl. jours. Mem. sci. bd. Helen Hay Witney Found., N.Y.C., 1986-94; co-chmn. adv. bd. NSF Biology Directorate, 1988-89; vis. com., bd. overseers Harvard U., Cambridge, Mass., 1987-90; mem. sci. bd. Whitehead Inst., MIT, Boston, 1988-93; mem. sci. rev. bd. Howard Hughes Med. Inst., 1990-94, Cancer Ctr. of Mass. Gen. Hosp., Boston, 1994; mem. Presidio Coun. City of San Francisco, 1991-94; mem. Pres. Coun. U. Calif., 1991—. Recipient Hirschl Career Scientist award, 1976, Spirit of Achievement award, 1978, Alumna award of honor Bklyn. Coll., 1983, Excellence in Sci. award Fedn. Am. Soc. Exptl. Biology, 1994; Jane Coffin Child fellow, 1966; resident scholar Rockefeller Found., Bellagio, Italy, 1996. Fellow AAAS, Am. Acad. Arts and Scis., Am. Acad. Microbiology; mem. NAS, Inst. Medicine of NAS, Am. Soc. Biochemistry and Molecular Biology (nominating com. 1982, 87, coun. 1990-93), Am. Heart Assn. (sci. adv. bd. 1984-87). Avocation: watercolor painting. Office: Stanford U Sch Medicine Beckman Ctr Dept Devel Biology Stanford CA 94305

SHAPIRO, MARCIA HASKEL, speech and language pathologist; b. N.Y.C., Nov. 6, 1949; d. Ben and Edna Haskel; m. Louis Shapiro, Aug. 1, 1981. BA, Hunter Coll., 1982; MA, NYU, 1983; MA in Speech Pathology, U. Cen. Fla., 1991. Cert. deaf educator, Fla. Tchr. deaf Pub. Sch. 47, N.Y.C., 1983-84; speech pathologist St. Francis Sch. for the Deaf, Bklyn., 1984-86, Seminole County Schs., 1986-87, Lake County Schs., 1987-89, Orange County Schs., Orlando, Fla., 1989-91, West Volusia Meml. Hosp., Deland, Fla., 1991-93, Orlando Regional Med. Ctr., 1993, Sand Lake Hosp., 1993—; staff head swallowing dept. Leesburg Regional Med. Ctr., 1994; dir. speech pathology Fla. Hosp., Waterman, 1995—. Mem. ASHA, AFTRA, EQITY, Annals of Deaf, CAID, Alexander Graham Bell Assn. for Deaf.

SHAPIRO, MARIAN KAPLUN, psychologist; b. N.Y., July 13, 1939; d. David and Bertha Rebecca (Pearlman) Kaplun; m. Irwin Ira Shapiro, Dec. 20, 1959; children: Steven, Nancy. BA, Queens Coll., 1959; MA in Teaching, Harvard U., 1961, EdD, 1978. Cert. psychologist. Tchr. North Quincy High Sch., Quincy, Mass., 1962-64; instr. Carnegie Inst., Boston, 1968-74; staff psychologist South Shore Counselling Assn., Hanover, Mass., 1978-80; pvt. practice psychologist Lexington, Mass., 1980—; adj. instr. Mass. Sch. Profl. Psychology, Dedham, 1985—. Author: 2nd Childhood: Hypnoplay Therapy with Age--Regressed Adults, 1989; contbr. articles on teaching reading, hypnotherapy, multiple personality and other clin. issues to profl. jours. Fellow Am. Orthopsychiat. Assn.; mem. APA, Mass. Psychol. Assn., N.E. Soc. Group Psychotherapy, Am. Soc. Group Psychotherapy (clin.), Am. Soc. Clin. Hypnosis (cert. cons.), New Eng. Soc. for the Study of Multiple Personality Disorders, Internat. Soc. for the Study of Multiple Personality Disorders, New Eng. Soc. Clin. Hypnosis, Sigma Alpha, Pi Lambda Theta. Jewish Quaker. Avocations: music, singing, piano, violin. Home and Office: 17 Lantern Ln Lexington MA 02173-6029

SHAPIRO, MARK HOWARD, physicist, educator, academic dean, consultant; b. Boston, Apr. 18, 1940; s. Louis and Sara Ann (Diamond) S.; m. Anita Rae Lavine, June 8, 1961; children: David Gregory, Diane Elaine, Lisa Michelle. A.B. with honors, U. Calif., Berkeley, 1962; M.S. (NSF coop. fellow), U. Pa., 1963, Ph.D., 1966. Research fellow Kellogg Radiation Lab., Calif. Inst. Tech., Pasadena, 1966-68; vis. assoc. Kellogg Radiation Lab., Calif. Inst. Tech., 1976—; research assoc. Nuclear Structure Research Lab. U. Rochester (N.Y.), 1968-70; mem. faculty Calif. State U., Fullerton, 1970—, prof. physics, 1978—, acting assoc. dean Sch. Math., Sci. and Engring., 1985-86, acting dir. Office Faculty Research and Devel., 1986-87, chmn. physics dept., 1989-96; dir. tchr. enhancement program NSF, Washington, 1987-88; tour speaker Am. Chem. Soc., 1983-85. Contbr. over 125 articles to profl. jours. Pres. Pasadena Young Democrats, 1967-68; mem. pub. info. and edn. com. Calif. Task Force on Earthquake Preparedness, 1981-85; bd. dirs. Calif. State U. Fullerton Found., 1982-85. Grantee Research Corp., 1971-74, Calif. Inst. Tech., 1977-78, U.S. Geol. Survey, 1978-85, Digital Equipment Corp., 1982, NSF, 1985-87, 90—. Mem. AAAS, Am. Phys. Soc., Am. Assn. Physics Tchrs. (profl. concerns com. 1990-93, chmn. 1991-93), Am. Geophys. Union, N.Y. Acad. Scis., Materials Rsch. Soc., Coun. on Undergrad. Rsch. (physics/astronomy councillor 1993—). Achievements include research in experimental nuclear physics, experimental nuclear astrophysics, geophysics and atomic collisions in solids. Office: Calif State Univ Physics Dept Fullerton CA 92834-6866

SHAPIRO, MARTIN, law educator; b. 1933. B.A., UCLA, 1955; Ph.D., Harvard U., 1961. Instr. polit. sci. Harvard U., Cambridge, Mass., 1960-62; prof. Harvard U., 1971-74; asst. prof. Stanford U., Calif., 1962-65; assoc. prof. U. Calif.-Irvine, 1965-70, prof. law, 1970; prof. law U. Calif.-Berkeley, 1977—, U. Calif.-San Diego, 1974-77; bd. dirs. Nat. Bank N.E., Pa., 1982-85; dir. N.E. Bancorp; musician throughout U.S., 1956—; permanent guest condr. to Shandong Provincial Symphony Orch., Jinan, China; mem. Erie Philharm. Author: Law and Politics in the Supreme Court, 1964, Freedom of Speech, The Supreme Court and Judicial Review, 1966, Supreme Court and

Administrative Agencies, 1968, Courts, 1981, Who Guards the Guardians, 1987. Mem. Law and Soc. Assn. (trustee 1992-95), Western Polit. Sci. Assn. (pres. 1978), Am. Acad. Arts and Scis., Am. Polit. Sci. Assn. (v.p. 1988). Office: U Calif Law Sch 225 Boalt Hall Berkeley CA 94720-7201

SHAPIRO, MARVIN LINCOLN, communications company executive; b. Erie, Pa., Feb. 12, 1923; s. Hyman and Flora (Burstein) S.; m. B. Gertrude Berkman, Oct. 25, 1946; children: Susan Jo, Barbara Ann, Jonathan David. BS, Syracuse U., 1948; postgrad., Williams Coll., 1966, Columbia U., 1975. Account exec. WSYR, Syracuse, 1948-50; account exec. sta. WCAU-TV, Phila., 1950-55; nat. sales mgr. sta. WCAU-TV, 1956-58; account exec. CBS TV Spot Sales, Chgo., 1955-56, N.Y.C., 1958-60; with TV Advt. Reps., Inc., N.Y.C., 1961-66; exec. v.p. TV Advt. Reps., Inc., 1965-66, pres., 1968-69, dir., vice chmn., 1969-77, chmn., 1978; pres. Radio Advt. Reps., Inc., N.Y.C., 1966-68; dir., vice chmn. Radio Advt. Reps., Inc., 1969-77; exec. v.p., COO, pres. sta. group Westinghouse Broadcasting Co., Inc., N.Y.C., 1969-77; sr. v.p. Westinghouse Broadcasting Co., Inc., 1978-83, also dir., 1969-83; pres., dir. Foxwood Comm. Inc., N.Y.C., 1983—; mng. dir. Veronis, Suhler & Assocs., N.Y.C., 1983—; pres., dir. Farragut Comm., Inc., Yakima, Wash., 1992—, Columbia Empire Broadcasting Corp., Yakima, 1992-96; bd. dirs. Broadcasting Ptnrs. Holdings, L.P., 1997—; chmn. bd. Micro-Relay, Inc., 1974-83; chmn. bd., pres. CATV Enterprises, Inc., 1970-83. Boxing official Pa. Athletic Commn., 1952-55; Bd. dirs. TV Bur. Advt., 1974-81, chmn., 1977-79; bd. dirs. Radio Advt. Bur., 1970-77; With USAAF, 1942-45. Decorated Air medal with 9 oak leaf clusters.; recipient Communications Alumni award Syracuse U., 1960. Mem. Internat. Radio and TV Soc., DAV, Alpha Epsilon Rho (hon.). Clubs: Long Ridge (Stamford). Home: 26 Foxwood Rd Stamford CT 06903-2207 Office: Foxwood Communications Inc 866 United Nations Plz New York NY 10017-1822

SHAPIRO, MARVIN SEYMOUR, lawyer; b. N.Y.C., Oct. 26, 1936; s. Benjamin and Sally (Book) S.; m. Natalie Kover, July 12, 1959; children: Donna, Meryl. AB, Columbia U., 1957, LLB, 1959. Bar: D.C. 1959, Calif. 1962. Atty. appellate sect. Civil Div. U.S. Dept. Justice, Washington, 1959-61; ptnr. Irell & Manella, L.A., 1962—, mng. ptnr., 1992-97; lectr. U. So. Calif. Tax Inst., Calif. Continuing Edn. of the Bar, Practising Law Inst. Articles editor Columbia Law Rev., 1958-59. V.p., bd. dirs. Jewish Fedn. Coun., L.A., 1985-95; treas. Alan Cranston Campaign, 1974, 80, 86; chmn. credentials com. Dem. Nat. Com., 1972-76. Mem. L.A. County Bar Assn., Beverly Hills Barristers (pres. 1970). Avocations: travel, golf. Home: 432 N Cliffwood Ave Los Angeles CA 90049-2620 Office: Irell & Manella 1800 Avenue Of The Stars Los Angeles CA 90067-4212

SHAPIRO, MATTHEW DAVID, economist; b. Mpls., Apr. 11, 1958; s. Irving and Janet (Reinstein) S.; m. Susan L. Garetz, Oct. 21, 1989; 1 child, Benjamin Avigdor Shapiro. BA summa cum laude, Yale U., 1979, MA, 1979; PhD, MIT, 1984. Jr. staff economist Coun. Econ. Advisers, Washington, 1979-80, sr. economist, 1993-94; asst. prof. Yale U., New Haven, 1984-89; assoc. prof. U. Mich., Ann Arbor, 1989-95, prof., 1995—; rschr. Nat. Bur. Econ. Rsch., Cambridge, 1986—. Bd. editors Am. Econ. Rev., 1993-96, co-editor, 1997—; contbr. articles to profl. jours. Olin fellow Nat. Bur. Econ. Rsch., Cambridge, 1986-87, Alfred P. Sloan fellow Sloan Found., 1991-93. Mem. Am. Econ. Assn., Econometric Soc., Phi Beta Kappa. Office: U Mich Dept Econs 611 Tappan Ave Ann Arbor MI 48109-1220

SHAPIRO, MAURICE MANDEL, astrophysicist; b. Jerusalem, Israel, Nov. 13, 1915; came to U.S., 1921; s. Asher and Miriam R. (Grunbaum) S.; m. Inez Weinfield, Feb. 8, 1942 (dec. Oct. 1964); children: Joel Nevin, Elana Shapiro Ashley Naktin, Raquel Tamar Shapiro Kislinger. B.S., U. Chgo., 1936, M.S., 1940, Ph.D., 1942. Instr. physics and math. Chgo. City Colls., 1937-41; chmn. dept. phys. and biol. scis. Austin Coll., 1938-41; instr. math. Gary Coll., 1942; physicist Dept. Navy, 1942-44; lectr. physics and math. George Washington U., 1943-44; group leader, mem. coordinating council of lab. Los Alamos Sci. Lab., U. Calif., 1944-46; sr. physicist, lectr. Oak Ridge Nat. Lab., Union Carbon and Carbide Corp., 1946-49; cons. div. nuc. energy for propulsion aircraft Fairchild Engine & Aircraft Corp., 1948-49; head cosmic ray br. nucleonics div. U.S. Naval Research Lab., Washington, 1949-65, supt. nucleonics div., 1953-65, chief scientist Lab. for Cosmic Ray Physics, 1965-82, apptd. to chair of cosmic ray physics, 1966-82, chief scientist emeritus, 1982—; lectr. U. Md., 1949-50, 52—, assoc. prof., 1950-51, vis. prof. physics and astronomy, 1986—; vis. prof. physics and astronomy U. Iowa, 1981-84; vis. prof. astrophysics U. Bonn, 1982-84; vis. scientist Max Planck Inst. für Astrophysik, W. Ger., 1984-85; cons. Argonne Nat. Lab., 1949; cons. panel on cosmic rays U.S. nat. com. IGY; lectr. physics and engring. Nuclear Products-Erco div. ACF Industries, Inc., 1956-58; lectr. E. Fermi Internat. Sch. Physics, Varenna, Italy, 1962; vis. prof. Weizmann Inst. Sci., Rehovoth, Israel, 1962-63, Inst. Math. Scis., Madras, India, 1971; Inst. Astronomy and Geophysics Nat. U. Mex., 1976; vis. prof. physics and astronomy Northwestern U., Evanston, Ill., 1978, exec. dir.Astrophysics assocs.(non profit corp.) 1995—; cons. space rsch. in astronomy Space Sci. Bd., Nat. Acad. Scis., 1965; cons. Office Space Scis., NASA, 1965-66, 89; prin. investigator Gemini S-9 Cosmic Ray Expts., NASA, 1964-69, Skylab, 1967-76, Long Duration Exposure Facility, 1977—; mem. Groupe de Travail de Biologie Spatiale, Council of Europe, 1970—; mem. steering com. DUMAND Consortium, 1976—, mem. exec. com., 1979-82, mem. sci. adv. com., 1982—; lectr. Summer Space Inst., Deutsche Physikalische Gesellschaft, 1972; dir. Internat. Sch. Cosmic-Ray Astrophysics, Ettore Majorana Centre Sci. Culture, Erice, Italy, 1977—, also sr. corr., 1977—; chmn. U.S. IGY com. on interdisciplinary research, mem. nuclear emulsion panel space sci. bd.; Nat. Acad. Scis., 1959—; chief U.S. rep., steering com. Internat. Coop. Emulsion Flights for Cosmic Ray Research; cons. CREI Atomics, 1959—; vis. com. Bartol Research Found., Franklin Inst., 1967-74; mem. U.S. organizing com. 13th and 19th Internat. Confs. on Cosmic Rays; mem. sci. adv. com. Internat. Confs. on Nuclear Photography and Solid State Detectors, 1966—; mem. Com. of Honor for Einstein Centennial, Acad. Naz. Lincei, 1977; mem. Internat. Organizing com. Tex. Symposia on Relativistic Astrophysics, 1976—; Regents lectr. U. Calif. Riverside, 1985; Edison lectr. Naval Rsch. Lab award, 1990; Victor Hess Meml. lectr., Rome, 1995. Mem. editorial bd. Astrophysics and Space Sci., 1968-75; assoc. editor: Phys. Rev. Letters, 1977-84; editor (NATO) ASI Series on Cosmic-Ray Astrophysics; contbr. to Am. Inst. Handbook of Physics, various encys. Mem. exec. bd. Cong. Beth Chai, Washington, 1987—; trustee Nat. Capital Astronomers, Washington, 1989—; mem. internat. panel Chernobyl World Lab., 1988. Recipient Disting. Civilian Svc. award Dept. Navy, 1967, medal of honor Soc. for Encouragement au Progrés, 1978, publs. award Naval Rsch. Lab., 1970, 74, 76, Dir.'s Spl. award, 1974, Sr. U.S. Scientist award Alexander von Humboldt Found., 1982, Profl. Achievement citation U. Chgo., 1992. Fellow Am. Phys. Soc. (chmn. organizing com. div. cosmic physics, chmn. 1971-72, com. on publs. 1977-79), AAAS, Washington Acad. Scis. (past com. chmn., Disting. Career in Scis. award, 1993); mem. Am. Astron. Soc. (exec. com. div. high-energy astrophysics 1978—, chmn. 1982), Philos. Soc. Washington (past pres.), Am. Technion Soc. (Washington bd.), Assn. Los Alamos Scientists (past chmn.), Assn. Oak Ridge Engrs. and Scientists (past chmn.), Fedn. Am. Scientists (past mem. exec. com., nat. council), Internat. Astron. Union (organizing com. commn. on high-energy astrophysics), Internat. Conf. on Cosmic Rays (Victor Hess Meml. lectr., 1995), Phi Beta Kappa, Sigma Xi (Edison lectr. 1990). Club: Cosmos (Washington). Achievements include patents in field; discovery of first definitive evidence for production of cosmic ray secondaries in the interstellar medium; research in cosmic radiation, composition, origin, propagation, and nuclear transformations; in high-energy astrophysics; in particles and fields; in nuclear physics, neutron physics and fission reactors; in hydrodynamics and gamma-ray and neutrino astronomy. Office: 205 S Yoakum Pky Ste 1514 Alexandria VA 22304-3838 *In scientific achievement, good judgement (e.g., in choice of research problems)is sometimes more important than brilliance.*

SHAPIRO, MEL, playwright, director, drama educator; b. Bklyn., Dec. 16, 1935; s. Benjamin Shapiro and Lillian (Lazarus) Bestul; m. Jeanne Elizabeth Shapiro, Feb. 23, 1963; children: Joshua, Benjamin. BFA, Carnegie-Mellon U., 1961, MFA, 1961. Resident dir. Arena Stage, Washington, 1963-65; producing dir. Tyrone Guthrie Theater, Mpls., 1968-70; master tchr. drama NYU, N.Y.C., 1970-80; guest dir. Lincoln Ctr. Repertory, N.Y.C., 1970; dir. N.Y. Shakespeare Festival, N.Y.C., 1971-77; prof. Carnegie Mellon U., Pitts., 1980-90, head. dept., 1980-87; head acting UCLA Sch. Theatre, Film & TV, L.A.; bd. dirs. Pitts. Pub. Theater, 1982—; head acting UCLA Sch. Theater, Film and TV, 1990—; founder Onstage Co., L.A., 1993. Dir. N.Y.C. prodns. The House of Blue Leaves, 1970, Bosoms and Neglect, 1978; co-adaptor mus. Two Gentlemen of Verona, 1971 (Tony award); author: (plays) The Price of Admissions, 1984 (Drama-Logue mag. award), The Lay of the Land (Joseph Kesselring award 1990), A Life of Crime, 1993, (book) An Actor Performs, 1996. With U.S. Army, 1955-57. Recipient N.Y. Drama Critics award, 1971, 72, Obie award Village Voice, 1972, Drama Desk award, 1973, Drama-logue award, 1993. Mem. Soc. Stage Dirs. and Choreographers (founder, editor The Jour. 1978). Office: UCLA Sch Theatre Film & TV 405 Hilgard Ave Los Angeles CA 90095-9000

SHAPIRO, MICHAEL, supermarket corporate officer; b. N.Y.C., Mar. 3, 1942; s. Jack and Celia (Schwartzbaum) S.; m. Sara Louise Ress, Mar. 22, 1964; children: Jeffrey, Lisa, Kenneth. B.S., CCNY, 1962. CPA, N.Y., N.J. Acct. Sidney Kaminsky & Co., N.Y.C., 1964-68; supr. Hurdman Cranston, Penney & Co. (C.P.A.s), N.Y.C., 1968-71; with Mayfair Super Markets Inc., Elizabeth, N.J., 1971-87; v.p. fin. and adminstrn. Mayfair Super Markets Inc., 1978-80, sr. v.p. fin. and adminstrn., 1980-86, exec. v.p. fin. and corp. devel., 1986-87, also dir.; self employed ins. cons., 1988-89; v.p. Fin. Fidelity Land Devel. Corp., Chatham, N.J., 1989-92; v.p. fin. and ops. Apex One Inc., Piscataway, N.J., 1992-94; sr. v.p., CFO, treas. Foodarama Supermarkets, Inc., Freehold, N.J., 1994—. Mem. AICPA, N.Y. State Soc. CPAs. Office: Foodarama Supermarkets Inc 922 Hwy 33 Bldg 6 Ste 1 Freehold NJ 07728

SHAPIRO, MICHAEL B., lawyer; b. Akron, Ohio, 1947. BBA summa cum laude, Kent State U., 1969; JD magna cum laude, U. Mich., 1972. Bar: Mich. 1972. Ptnr. Honigman, Miller, Schwartz & Cohn, Detroit; mem. citizens property tax commn. Mich. Senate, 1986-87. Mem. ABA, Am. Property Tax Counsel, State Bar of Mich., Inst. Property Taxation, Order of the Coif, Beta Alpha Psi, Pi Sigma Alpha, Beta Gamma Sigma. Office: Honigman Miller Schwartz & Cohn 2290 1st Nat Bldg Detroit MI 48226

SHAPIRO, MICHAEL EDWARD, museum administrator, curator, art historian; b. N.Y.C., Nov. 15, 1949; s. Edward Aaron and Sylvia (Fishman) S.; m. Elizabeth Harvey, 1977; 2 children. BA, Hamilton Coll., 1972; MA, Williams Coll., 1976, Harvard U., 1978; PhD, Harvard U., 1980. Asst. prof. dept. art history Duke U., Durham, N.C., 1980-84; curator 19th-20th century art St. Louis Art Mus., 1984-92, chief curator, 1987-92; dir. Los Angeles County Mus. Art, 1992-93; dir. mus. programs, chief curator High Mus. Art, Atlanta, 1994-95, dep. dir., chief curator, 1996—. Author: Bronze Casting and American Sculpture, 1985; contbg. author: Frederic Remington: The Masterworks, 1988, George Caleb Bingham, 1990; mng. curator, editor Rings: Five Passions in World Art, 1996.

SHAPIRO, MICHAEL HENRY, government executive; b. Bayonne, N.J., Sept. 23, 1948; s. William and Sophie (Slotkin) S. BS, Lehigh U., 1970; MS, Harvard U., 1972, PhD, 1976. Assoc. prof. Harvard U., Cambridge, Mass., 1976-82, analyst, 1980-81, br. chief, 1981-83, dir. econs. and tech. divsn., 1983-89; dep. asst. adminstr., air and radiation EPA, Washington, 1989-93; dir. Office of Solid Waste, Washington, 1993—. Office: EPA # 5301 401 M St SW # 5301 Washington DC 20460-0001

SHAPIRO, MURRAY, structural engineer; b. N.Y.C., July 5, 1925; s. Samuel and Fannie (Korman) S.; m. Florence Morrison, June 16, 1951; children: Fred Richard, Alan Neil. BCE, CCNY, 1947. Registered profl. engr., N.Y., N.J., Pa., Md., Ga., N.C., Mass., Conn. Steel detailer Knopf & Amron, N.Y.C., 1947-48; asst. engr. N.Y.C. Bd. Transp., 1948-50; designer James Ruderman cons. engrs., N.Y.C., 1950-53, sr. engr., 1953-58, assoc., 1958-65; jr. ptnr. Office of James Ruderman, N.Y.C., 1965-66, sr. ptnr., 1966—. Structural designer many highrise office buildings, including GM Bldg., N.Y.C., Pan Am Bldg., N.Y.C., also schs., apartment houses, theaters. With U.S. Army, 1943-45, ETO. Decorated Purple Heart, Bronze Star. Mem. N.Y. Cons. Engrs. Assn. (trustee 1972-77, sec. 1974-76), Am. Concrete Inst., N.Y. Acad. Scis., Fresh Meadow Country Club. Republican. Jewish. Home: 170 West End Ave Apt 15D New York NY 10023-5448 Office: Office of James Ruderman 15 W 36th St New York NY 10018-7910

SHAPIRO, NELLA IRENE, surgeon; b. N.Y.C., Nov. 13, 1947; d. Eugene and Ethel (Pearl) S.; m. Jack Schwartz, Oct. 16, 1977; children: Max, Molly. BA, Barnard Coll., 1968; MD, Albert Einstein Coll., 1972. Resident in gen. surgery Montefiore Hosp., N.Y.C., 1972-76; mem. staff North Cen. Hosp., Bronx, N.Y., 1976-77, Bronx Mcpl. Hosp., 1977-87; chief gen. surgery Bronx Mcpl. Hosp. Ctr., 1983-87; mem. staff in gen. surgery Albert Einstein Coll. Hosp., Bronx, 1977-93, chief gen. surgery, 1991-93; atty. Lear Surg. Assocs., 1993-94; pvt. solo practice Bronx, 1994—; asst. prof. surgery Albert Einstein Coll., Bronx, 1980—; assoc. dir. gen. surgery Weiler Hosp., Bronx, 1991-93; co-founder Whaecom Breast Ctr., Bronx, 1991—. Fellow Am. Coll. Surgeons. Avocations: travel, skiing. Office: 1695 Eastchester Rd Apt 304 Bronx NY 10461-2332

SHAPIRO, NORMA SONDRA LEVY, federal judge; b. Phila., July 27, 1928; d. Bert and Jane (Kotkin) Levy; m. Bernard Shapiro, Aug. 21, 1949; children: Finley, Neil, Aaron. BA in Polit. Theory with honors, U. Mich., 1948; JD magna cum laude, U. Pa., 1951. Bar: Pa. 1952, U.S. Supreme Ct. 1978. Law clk. to presiding justice Pa. Supreme Ct., 1951-52; instr. U. Pa. Law Sch., 1951-52, 55-56; assoc. Dechert Price & Rhoads, Phila., 1956-58, 67-73; ptnr. Dechert Price & Rhoads, 1973-78; judge U.S. Dist. Ct. (ea. dist.) Pa., 1978—; assoc. trustee U. Pa. Law Sch., 1978-93; former trustee Women's Law Project, Albert Einstein Med. Ctr.; v.p. Jewish Pub. Soc.; trustee Fedn. Jewish Agys., 1980-83; mem. lawyers adv. panel Pa. Gov.'s Commn. on Status of Women, 1974; legal adv. regional Coun. Child Psychiatry, bd. dirs. Women Judges' Fund for Justice. Guest editor: Shingle, 1972. Mem. Lower Merion County (Pa.) Bd. Sch. Dirs., 1968-77, pres., 1977, v.p., 1976; v.p. Jewish Community Relations Council of Greater Phila., 1975-77; chmn. legal affairs com., 1978; pres. Belmont Hills Home and Sch. Assn., Lower Merion Twp.; legis. chmn. Lower Merion Sch. Dist. Intersch. Council; mem. Task Force on Mental Health of Children and Youth of Pa.; treas., chmn. edn. com. Human Relations Council, Lower Merion; v.p., parliamentarian Nes Ami Penn Valley Congregation, Lower Merion Twp. Named Woman of Yr., Oxford Circle Jewish Community Center, 1979, Woman of Distinction, Golden Slipper Club, 1979; Gowen fellow, 1954-55; recipient Hannah G. Solomon award Nat. Coun. Jewish Women, 1992. Mem. Am. Law Inst., Am. Bar Found., ABA (ho. dels. 1990-96, coun./chmn. conf. fed. judges 1986-87, chmn. Judical Divsn., 1996—, Pa. Bar Assn. (ho. of dels. 1979-81), Phila. Bar Assn. (chmn. com. women's rights 1972, 74-75, chmn. bd. govs. 1977-78, chmn. pub. rels. com. 1978), Fed. Bar Assn. (Bill of Rights award 1991), Nat. Assn. Women Lawyers, Phila. Trial Lawyers Assn., Am. Judicature Soc., Phila., Nat. Assn. Women Judges, Fellowship Commn., Order of Coif (chpt. pres. 1973-75), Tau Epsilon Rho, Jurisprudence. Office: US Dist Courthouse Independence Mall West 601 Market St Rm 10614 Philadelphia PA 19106-1774

SHAPIRO, NORMAN RICHARD, Romance languages and literatures educator; b. Boston, Nov. 1, 1930; s. Harry Alexander and Eva (Goldberg) S. BA, Harvard U., 1951, MA, 1952, PhD, 1958; Diplôme de Langue et Lettres Françaises, Université d'Aix-Marseille, 1956, BA (hon.), 1972. Instr. French Amherst Coll., 1958-60; asst. prof. romance langs. and lits. Wesleyan U., 1960-65, assoc. prof., 1965-71, prof., 1971—. Editor: Echos, 1965, Palabres, 1973; translator, editor: Négritude, 1971; translator: Four Farces by Georges Feydeau, 1970, Comedy of Eros, 1971, Kamouraska by Anne Hébert, 1973, Virginie, or the Dawning of the World by Joseph Majault, 1974, The Camp of The Saints by Jean Raspail, 1975, Feydeau, First to Last, 1982, Fables from Old French: Aesop's Beasts and Bumpkins, 1983, A Fitting Confusion by Georges Feydeau, 1985, The Pregnant Pause, or Love's Labor Lost, by Georges Feydeau, 1987, The Brazilian by Henry Meilhac and Ludovic Halévy, 1987, A Slap in the Farce by Eugène Labiche, 1988, A Matter of Wife and Death by Eugène Labiche, 1988, Fifty Fables of La Fontaine, 1988, The Fabulists French: Verse Fables of Nine Centuries, 1992, La Fontaine's Bawdy: Of Libertines, Louts and Lechers, 1992, A Flea in Her Rear, or Ants in Her Pants, and Other Vintage French Farces, 1994; composer: Three Songs, 1961; contbr. articles, transls. and revs. to profl. jours. Mem. African Studies Assn., Am. Assn. Tchrs. French, Universala Esperanto-Asocio, Esperanto League N.Am., Judezmo Soc., Am. Lit. Transl. Assn. (Disting. Translation award 1992), Am. Translators Assn., Dramatists Guild, Beast Fable Soc. (editorial bd. Bestia), Signet Soc. of Harvard, Delta Kappa Epsilon. Jewish. Home: 214 High St Middletown CT 06457-3242

SHAPIRO, PAUL SAUVEUR, chemical engineer, researcher; b. Pitts., Dec. 4, 1942; s. Carl Lynwood and Lillian Ruth (Simon) S.; m. Melissa Friedland, Jan. 19, 1986; 1 child, Felix Benjamin. SB in Chem. Engring., MIT, 1963, SM in Chem. Engring., 1965, postgrad., 1967-71; EdM in Edn. Planning, Harvard U., 1966. Expert cons. HEW and Action, Washington, 1972-76; sr. staff officer NRC, Washington, 1976-77; cons. Office Sci. and Tech. Adviser World Bank, Washington, 1977-80; cons. on nat. and internat. sci. and tech. AID, NSF and other agys., Washington, 1980-81; cons. Office Toxic Substances EPA, Washington, 1981-82, environ. engr. Office of Solid Waste, 1983-84, program mgr. Office R&D, 1985-94, CSI coord. Office R&D, 1994—; vis. sr. rschr. Tel Aviv (Israel) U., 1979. Contbr. over 20 articles to profl. publs. Vol., advisor Vols. in Tech. Assistance, Arlington, Va., 1978-81; chmn. career edn. adv. coun. Washington Pub. Schs.; vice chmn. Early Environs., Inc. Fellow NDEA, NDFL, 1967, 70. Mem. AIChE (program coord.), Fed. Water Quality Assn. (sec.), Air and Waste Mgmt. Assn. (work group leader), MIT Club of Washington (pres.), MIT Luncheon Club (pres.), Sigma Xi, Phi Delta Kappa. Democrat. Jewish. Achievements include development of mitigation research programs for radon, indoor air pollution, stratospheric ozone protection, global climate change, and mixed hazardous and radioactive wastes; development of pollution prevention research programs with metal finishing and electronics industries; development with SBA and DOC of cooperative technical assistance programs for small business; co-development and implementation of EPA's highest priority program, The Common Sense Initiative including development of the first national sectoral environmental R&D plan. Avocations: mysteries, swimming, singing, computers. Home: 1312 4th St SW Washington DC 20024 Office: EPA Office R&D (8722) 401 M St SW Washington DC 20460-0001

SHAPIRO, PERRY, economics educator; b. Los Angeles, Jan. 15, 1941; s. Abraham and Ann (Warshaw) S.; m. Jody Silverstein, June 25, 1994; children: Elizabeth Naomi, Samuel Robert, Sarah Gertrud. BA in Econs., U. Calif.-Berkeley, 1962, PhD in Econs., 1968. Postdoctoral fellow in urban econs. Washington U., St. Louis, 1967-68; lectr. London Sch. Econs., 1968-69; asst. prof. econs. U. Calif.-Santa Barbara, 1969-74, assoc. prof., 1974-78, prof., 1978—, chair dept. econs., 1987-93; vis. prof. U. Mich., Ann Arbor, 1979-80; vis. scholar Federalism Rsch. Ctr. Australian Nat. U., 1992, adj. prof. Rsch. Sch. Social Scis., 1994—. Author: An Analytical Framework for Regional Policy, 1970. Vis. scholar U.S. Bur. Labor Stats., Washington, 1975-76; grantee NSF, 1979—, Nat. Inst. Justice, 1980-85; Fulbright sr. rsch. scholar Australia Nat. U., 1990-91. Mem. Am. Econs. Assn., Econometric Soc., Nat. Tax Assn. Office: U of Calif Dept Econs Santa Barbara CA 93016

SHAPIRO, RAYMOND L., lawyer; b. N.Y.C., Aug. 1, 1934; s. Alexander and Sadye (Morrison) S.; m. Judith Manis, Dec. 23, 1956; children: Joel, Todd, Lisa. BS, Temple U., 1956, LLB, 1959. Ptnr. Wexler, Weisman, Forman & Shapiro, Phila., 1959-84, Blank, Rome, Comisky & McCauley, Phila., 1984—. Author: Dunlap-Hanna Pa. Forms, 1963-83, Pa. Civil Practice Handbook, 1973-83; contbg.-author: Business Workouts Manual. Trustee Phila. Fedn. Jewish Agys., 1979—, treas., 1984-87, v.p., 1987-90; pres. Jewish Pub. Group, 1992-95. Fellow Am. Coll. Bankruptcy (v.p., chmn. bd. dirs. 1997—); mem. ABA, Nat. Bankruptcy Conf., Pa. Bar Assn., Phila. Bar Assn., Locust Club (bd. dirs. 1990). Office: Blank Rome Comisky & McCauley 4 Penn Ctr Plz 10-13 4th Fl Philadelphia PA 19103-2599

SHAPIRO, RICHARD CHARLES, sales and marketing executive; b. Bklyn., May 28, 1936; s. Isidore and Sylvia (Rappaport) S.; m. Marilyn Joyce Bialy, Feb. 17, 1957 (div. 1974); children: Joseph, Scott; m. Francine L. Shaw, Sept. 19, 1975. BS in Edn., Golden State U., 1978, MBA, 1981; PhD in Bus. Adminstrn., Honolulu U., 1987. Lic. real estate broker, Ill. Affiliate Effective Motivation Assocs./Success Motivation inst., Bethpage, N.Y., 1965-68; v.p. sales Field Enterprises, Chgo., 1962-78; pres., CEO Snack-In, Inc., Detroit, 1978-82; sr. ptnr. Directions Growth and Strategy Cons., Chgo., 1982-95; v.p. domestic & internat. mktg. & sales Ency., oper. officer Ency. Brit.-Compton's Learning Co., 1991-93, specialist network mktg. & relationship mktg., pres., bd. dirs.; CEO Am.'s Home Detailing Corp., 1995, 1995—; pres., COO Am.'s Deep Clean Divsn., Deerfield, Ill., 1995—; instr. planning Life Underwriter Tng. Coun., L.I., 1965-66; assoc. editor Media Technics Pub. Assn., Lake Forest, 1988; bd. dirs. Master Deep Clean Co., Nat. Video Libr.; spkr. on mktg., sales and leadership; cons. in field. Author various self-improvement cassettes; contbr. articles to profl. jours. Active Explorers, high schs., youth clubs, 1965-74; founder, pres. Abundance and Goodwill Soc., 1968—. Served with USAF, 1957-60. Recipient Leadership award Am. Sales Masters, 1968; named Sales/Mktg. Execs. Leadership Recruiter/Trainer of Decade award. Mem. Salesmen With a Purpose, Chgo. Computer Soc., Effective Motivation Assocs. Avocations: wild-water rafting, white-water canoeing, camping, tennis, writing.

SHAPIRO, RICHARD GERALD, retired department store executive, consultant; b. N.Y.C., Apr. 24, 1924; s. David and Sophie (Hayflich) S.; m. Lila Eig, July 27, 1951; children—Judith, Amy, Donald. B.A., U. Mich., 1946; M.B.A., Harvard, 1948. With Lord & Taylor, N.Y.C., 1948-64; v.p. Lord & Taylor, 1959-63, sr. v.p., 1963-64; also mem. adv. bd.; pres. Wm. Filene's Sons Co., Boston, 1965-68; chief exec. officer, chmn. bd. Wm. Filene's Sons Co., 1968-73; pres. Gimbel Bros. Corp., N.Y.C., 1973-76; v.p. W.R. Grace & Co., pres. sporting goods div., 1977-79, pres. splty. store div., 1979-84; pres. Richard Shapiro Assocs., 1979—; sr. v.p. Montgomery Ward, Inc., 1986-88; bd. dirs. Assoc. Merchandising Corp., Nitrotec Corp., Capital Market Fund; retail chmn. Greater N.Y. Fund, 1963; chmn. merc. div. Mass. Bay United Fund, 1967. Mem. corp. Simmons Coll., Boston Mus. Fine Arts (permanent); bd. dirs. Mass. Mchts.; bd. dirs Family Counseling and Guidance Centers, 1969-72, v.p., 1970; trustee Brandeis U. Served with AUS, 1942-46. Mem. Harvard Bus. Sch. Assn. (gov.). Home: 10019 Gable Manor Ct Potomac MD 20854-5000

SHAPIRO, RICHARD STANLEY, physician; b. Moline, Ill., June 11, 1925; s. Herbert and Esther Dian (Grant) S.; BS, St. Ambrose Coll., 1947; BS in Pharmacy, U. Iowa, 1951, MS in Preventive Medicine and Environ. Health, 1951, M.D., 1957; m. Arlene Blum, June 12, 1949; children: Michele Pamela, Bruce Grant, Gary Lawrence; m. Merry Lou Cook, Oct. 11, 1971. Pharmacist, Rock Island, Ill., 1951-53; research asst. U. Iowa Coll. Medicine, Iowa City, 1950-51, 53-57; practice medicine specializing in allergy, Beverly Hills, Calif., 1958-62, Lynwood, Calif., 1962—; attending physician Good Hope Found. Allergy Clinic, Los Angeles, 1958-62, Cedars of Lebanon Hosp., Hollywood, Calif., 1959-68, U. So. Calif.-Los Angeles County Med. Center, 1962—; physician St. Francis Hosp., Lynwood, 1962—; assoc. clin. prof. medicine U. So. Calif., 1978-84, emeritus, 1984—. Bd. dirs. Westside Jewish Community Center, 1961-65, Camp JCA, 1964-65. Served with USNR, 1943-45; PTO. Diplomate Am. Bd. Allergy and Immunology. Fellow Am. Geriatric Soc., Am. Coll. Allergy, Am. Assn. Clin. Immunology and Allergy; mem. Am. Soc. Tropical Medicine and Hygiene, Am. Acad. Allergy, Los Angeles Allergy Soc., AMA, Calif., Los Angeles County med. assns., West Coast Allergy Soc., AAAS, Am., Calif. socs. internal medicine, Calif. Soc. Allergy, Am. Heart Assn., Sierra Club, Sigma Xi. Jewish. Mason; mem. B'nai B'rith. Contbr. articles to profl. jours. Office: 8301 Florence Ave Ste 104 Downey CA 90240-3946

SHAPIRO, ROBERT ALAN, retail executive; b. Denver, Dec. 24, 1946; s. George and Ruth Bearnice (Horn) S.; m. Jan Laurelle Tilker, Nov. 8, 1980; children: Aaron Phillip, Michael Samuel. BA, U. Denver, 1968; student, Northwestern U. Law Sch, 1968-70. V.p. Draper and Kramer, Inc., Chgo., 1970-73; asst. v.p. Urban Investment & Devel. Co., Chgo., 1973-75; dir. real estate The Limited, Columbus, Ohio, 1975-78; pres. Robert A. Shapiro & Assocs., Chgo., 1978-85; sr. v.p., corp. ops. asst. sec. County Seat Stores, Inc., Dallas, 1985-97; v.p. real estate Eddie Bauer, 1997—; lectr. Northwestern U., Evanston, Ill., Ohio State U., Columbus, 1976-78; mem. retail adv. bd. Shopping Ctr. Bus. mag.; originator Old Farmer's Almanac Gen. Stores. Mem. Internat. Coun. Shopping Ctrs. (tenant com. 1975-78), Nat. Retail Fedn. (splty. store task force com.). Jewish. Avocations: swimming, reading, skiing. Office: County Seat Stores 17950 Preston Rd Dallas TX 75252-5793

SHAPIRO, ROBERT B., manufacturing executive; b. N.Y.C., Aug. 4, 1938; s. Moses and Lilly (Langsam) S.; m. Berta Gordon, Mar. 27, 1964; children: James Gordon, Nina Rachel. A.B., Harvard U., 1959; LL.B., Columbia U., 1962. Bar: NY. 1963. Assoc. in law Columbia U., 1962-63; atty. firm Poletti Freidin Prashker Feldman & Gartner, N.Y.C., 1963-67; spl. asst. to gen. counsel and undersec. U.S. Dept. Transp., Washington, 1967-69; assoc. prof. law Northeastern U., Boston, 1969-71; asst. prof. law U. Wis., Madison, 1971-72; v.p., gen. counsel Gen. Instrument Corp., N.Y.C., 1972-79, G.D. Searle & Co., Skokie, Ill., 1979-82; pres. NutraSweet Group div. G.D. Searle & Co., Skokie, Ill., 1982-85; chmn., pres., chief exec. officer Nutra Sweet Co. subs. Monsanto, Skokie, Ill., 1985-95, also bd. dirs; now chmn., CEO Monsanto Co., St. Louis, 1995—. Mem. Mass. Gov.'s Transp. Task Force, 1970-71; mem. com. on procedure CAB, 1975-76; mem. bus. adv. com. White House Domestic Policy Rev. on Indsl. Innovation, 1978-79; Nat. Bd.. Trustees Boys Clubs of Am. Recipient John R. Miller award as outstanding corporate mktg. exec., 1984; Outstanding Achievement award Sales and Mktg. Mgmt. Mag., 1984. Mem. Am. Bar Assn. (vice chmn. com. on corp. counsel 1981-82), U.S. C. of C. (council on antitrust policy 1981-82), N.Y. State Bar Assn. Home: 20 E Cedar St Chicago IL 60611-1149 Office: Monsanto Co 800 N Lindbergh Blvd Saint Louis MO 63141-7843*

SHAPIRO, ROBERT FRANK, investment banking company executive; b. St. Louis, Dec. 19, 1934; s. Eugene J. and Clara (Katz) S.; m. Anna Marie Susman, Dec. 21, 1960; children: Albert Andrew, Robert Jr., Jeanne Savitt. Grad., St. Louis Country Day Sch., 1952; BA, Yale U., 1956. Assoc. Lehman Bros., N.Y.C., 1956-67, ptnr., 1967-73, dir., sr. mng. dir., 1970-73; ptnr. Wertheim & Co., 1974; exec. v.p. Wertheim & Co., Inc., N.Y.C., 1974-75, pres., 1975-86; co-chmn. Wertheim Schroder & Co., Inc., 1986-87; chmn. RFS and Assocs., Inc., N.Y.C., 1988—, New Street Capital Corp., 1992-94; bd. dirs. TJX Cos., Inc., The Burnham Fund, Am. Bldgs. Co., Magainin Pharms., Inc.; ind. gen. ptnr. Equitable Capital Ptnrs.; chmn. nominating com. N.Y. Stock Exch., 1980, mem. regulatory adv. com., 1988—, surveillance com., 1989—; bd. govs. Am. Stock Exch., 1970-76. Trustee Lenox Hill Hosp., Skowhegan; mem. gov. bd. Yale U. Art Gallery, New Haven, 1993—. Mem. Securities Industry Assn. (chmn. 1985, Bond Club N.Y. (pres. 1987-88, Yale Club, Rockefeller Ctr. Club, Century Country Club, Knickerbocker Club. Office: RFS & Assocs 787 7th Ave New York NY 10019-6018

SHAPIRO, ROBERT LESLIE, lawyer; b. Plainfield, N.J., Sept. 2, 1942. BS in Fin., UCLA, 1965; JD, Loyola U., L.A., 1968. Bar: Calif. 1969, U.S. Ct. Appeals (9th cir.) 1972, U.S. Dist. Ct. (cen., no. & so. dists.) Calif. 1982. Dep. dist. atty. Office of Dist. Atty., L.A., 1969-72; sole practice L.A., 1972-87, 88—; of counsel Bushkin, Gaims, Gaines, Jonas, L.A., 1987-88; Christensen, White, Miller, Fink & Jacobs, L.A., 1988-95; ptnr. Christensen, Miller, Fink, Jacobs, Glaser, Weil & Shapiro, L.A., 1995—. Author: Search for Justice, 1996. Recipient Am. Jurisprudence award Bancroft Whitney, 1969. Mem. Nat. Assn. Criminal Def. Lawyers, Calif. Attys. for Criminal Justice, Trial Lawyers for Pub. Justice (founder 1982), Century City Bar Assn. (Best Criminal Def. Atty. 1993). Office: 2121 Avenue Of The Stars Fl 19 Los Angeles CA 90067-5010

SHAPIRO, ROBYN SUE, lawyer, educator; b. Mpls., July 19, 1952; d. Walter David and Judith Rae (Sweet) S.; m. Charles Howard Barr, June 27, 1976; children: Tania Shapiro-Barr, Jeremy Shapiro-Barr, Michael Shapiro-Barr. BA summa cum laude, U. Mich., 1974; JD, Harvard U., 1977. Bar: D.C., 1977, Wis., 1979, U.S. Supreme Ct., 1990. Assoc. Foley & Lardner, Washington, 1977-79; ptnr. Barr & Shapiro, Menomonee Falls, Wis., 1980-87; assoc. Quarles & Brady, Milw., 1987-92; ptnr. Michael Best & Friedrich, Milw., 1992—; adj. asst. prof. law Marquette U., Milw., 1979-83; assoc. dir. bioethics ctr. Med. Coll. Wis., Milw., 1982-85, dir., 1985—; asst. prof. bioethics Med. Coll. Wis., 1984-89, assoc. prof. bioethics, 1989—; dir. Wis. Ethics Com. Network, 1987—; bd. mem. Wis. Health Decisions, 1990-93. Editorial bd. mem: Cambridge Quarterly, 1991—, HEC Forum, 1988-91; contbr. articles to profl. jours. Mem. ethics com. St. Luke's Hosp., Milw., 1983—, Elmbrook Meml. Hosp., Milw., 1983-86, Cmty. Meml. Hosp., Menomonee Falls, 1984—, Sinai Samaritan Hosp., Milw., 1986—, Milw. County Med. Complex, 1984—, Froedtert Meml. Luth. Hosp., 1985—; mem. subcom. organ transplantation Wis. Health Policy Coun., Madison, 1984, bioethics com., 1986-89; mem. com. study on bioethics Wis. Legis. Coun., Madison, 1984-85; bd. dirs. Jewish Home and Care Ctr., 1994—, chair ethics com., 1994—; chair Bayside Ethics Bd., 1994—; bd. dirs. Milw. area chpt. Girl Scouts U.S., Am. Bioethics Assn., 1995—, Wis. Perinatal Found., 1996—. James B. Angell scholar, 1971-72. Mem. ABA (forum com. health law, individual rights and responsibilities sec., health rights com. chair 1994—, mem. coordinating com. on bioethics and law, chair 1995—), Nat. Health Lawyers Assn., Am. Soc. Law & Medicine, Am. Hosp. Assn. (bioethics tech. panel 1991-94, spl. com. HIV & practitioners 1991-93), Wis. Bar Assn. (coun. Wis. health law sect. 1988-89, individual rights sect. coun. 1987-90), Assn. Women Lawyers, ACLU, Wis. Found. (Atty. of Yr. 1988), Milw. Acad. Medicine (coun. 1992—, chair bioethics com. 1992—), Wis. AIDS Coalition (steering com. 1988-91), Internat. Bioethics Assn. (chair task force on ethics coms.), Profl. Dimensions (Golden Compass award 1994), Phi Beta Kappa, others. Home: 9474 N Broadmoor Rd Milwaukee WI 53217-1309 Office: Med Coll Wis Bioethics Ctr 8701 W Watertown Plank Rd Milwaukee WI 53226-3548

SHAPIRO, SAM, health care analyst, biostatistician; b. N.Y.C., Feb. 12, 1914; married, 1938; 2 children. BS, Bklyn. Coll., 1933. Chief natality analysis br. Nat. Office Vital Stats., USPHS, 1947-54; sr. study dir. Nat. Opinion Rsch. Ctr., 1954-55; assoc. dir. div. rsch. and stats. Health Ins. Plan Greater N.Y., 1955-59, v.p., dir., 1959-73; dir. Health Svc. R & D Ctr., Balt., 1973-83; prof. health policy and mgmt. Johns Hopkins Sch. Hygiene and Pub. Health, Balt., 1973-85; emeritus prof. Johns Hopkins Sch. Hygiene and Pub. Health, 1985—; lectr. in pub. health Columbia U. Sch. Pub. Health and Adminstrv. Medicine, 1961-80; adj. prof. medicine Mt. Sinai Sch. Medicine, N.Y.C., 1972-78. Recipient prize GM Cancer Rsch. Found., 1988, Disting. Achievement award Am. Soc. Preventive Oncology, 1985. Fellow AAAS, APHA (award for excellence 1977), Am. Statis. Assn., Am. Coll. Radiology (hon.); mem. Inst. Medicine, Assn. for Health Svcs. Rsch. (Disting. Career in Health Svcs. Rsch. award 1985). Office: Johns Hopkins U Sch Hygiene and Pub Health 624 N Broadway Baltimore MD 21205-1900

SHAPIRO, SAMUEL BERNARD, management consultant; b. Chgo., Nov. 15, 1909; s. Bernard and Ida (Schwartz) S.; m. Mary Heller, Dec. 24, 1933; children: Judith Shapiro DeGraff, Richard B. B.S., U. Chgo., 1935. Asst. to mgr. Greater Chgo. Safety Council, 1928-33; exec. sec. Authorized Ford Dealers Assn., 1933-38; mgr. Chgo. Automobile Trade Assn. and Chgo. Auto Shows, 1938-43; chief research and planning, automobile rationing br. (OPA), 1943; exec. dir. Linen Supply Assn. Am., 1946-75; pres. Samuel B. Shapiro Cons. Inc., 1975—; v.p. Seminars, Speakers, Travel, Inc., Washington, 1976-82; Sr. v.p., treas., dir. Am. Soc. Assn. Execs., 1958-62, pres., 1962-63; chmn. bd. trustees CAE-ASAE, 1972; pres. Assn. Execs. Forum Chgo., 1956-57; chmn. exec. operating council Insts. Orgn. Mgmt., Mich. State U., 1957; mem. exec. adv. council Fla. Atlantic U., 1974-84. Co-author: textbook Association Management, 1958, Forward Planning, 1969, Future Perspectives, 1985, Handbook for Corporate Directors, 1985; author: The Whys of Association Executive Success (and Failure), 1977, Before and After Retirement, 1978, Financial Incentives for Association Executives, 1983, From the Past Comes the Future, 1986, Coming of Age of the Association Profession, 1987; mem. adv. bd.: Adult Edn. mag, 1956-58; contbr. articles and monographs to profl. lit.; lectr. in field. Served with AUS, 1943-45. Recipient Key award Cert. Assn. Exec.-Am. Soc. Assn. Execs., 1960. Mem. ACLU, Am. Soc. Assn. Execs. (1st hon. mem. 1988), Internat. Soc. Gen. Semantics (charter mem., v.p. 1969-82), Am. Vets. Com., Phi Beta Kappa. Home: 5945 N Bay Rd Miami FL 33140

SHAPIRO, SANDER WOLF, lawyer; b. St. Louis, Sept. 24, 1929; s. Robert and Bess (Fisher) S.; m. Lottie F. Frankel, Aug. 14, 1955; children: Julie A. Shapiro Schechter, Susan B. Shapiro Schmitz. BA, Rice U., 1951; postgrad., Columbia U., 1951-52; JD, U. Tex., 1954. Atty. tax div. Dept. Justice, Washington, 1955-57; atty. advisor U.S. Tax Ct., Washington, 1957-58; ptnr. Clark, Thomas, Winters & Shapiro, Austin, 1958-84; sr. prtnr. Shapiro, Edens & Cook, Austin, 1984-91; of counsel Jenkens & Gilchrist, P.C., Austin, 1991—; adj. prof. law U. Tex., 1975—; lectr. in tax field. Author, editor Tex. Franchise Earned Surplus and Tax, 1985—, Family Solutions to Family Concerns, 1991—, A Walk Through Form 706, 1991—; co-editor Tex. Tax Svc., 1986-94. Bd. dirs. Austin Symphony Orch. Soc., 1974-97, fin. v.p., 1980-95; bd. dirs. U. Tex. Coll. Fine Arts Adv. Coun., 1987-95, pres., 1991-94; bd. dirs. Capital of Tex. Pub. Telecomm. Coun., 1988—, pres., 1994-95; bd. dirs. Ronald McDonald House of Ctrl. Tex., Austin, 1990—, pres., 1994-95; bd. dirs. Capital Met. Transit Authority, 1988-91, chair, 1990; bd. dirs. Austin Cmty. Found., 1985-92, pres., 1991. Sander W. Shapiro Presdl. Scholarship in Law at U. Tex. endowed in his honor by Jenkens & Gilchrist, 1992. Fellow Am. Bar Found. (life), Am. Coll. Trust and Estate Counsel, Am. Coll. Tax Counsel, Tex. Bar Found. (sustaining life); mem. ABA, State Bar Assn. Tex., Am. Law Inst., Internat. Acad. Estate and Trust Law (academician), Nat. Assn. State Bar Tax Sects. (bd. dirs., chair 1997), Tex. Law Rev. Assn. (pres. 1992-93). Avocations: reading, music, golf. Office: Jenkens & Gilchrist 600 Congress Ave Ste 2200 Austin TX 78701-3248

SHAPIRO, SANDOR SOLOMON, hematologist; b. Bklyn., July 26, 1933. BA, Harvard U., 1954, MD, 1957. Intern Harvard med. svc. Boston City Hosp., 1957-58, asst. resident, 1960-61; asst. surgeon divsn. biol. std. NIH, USPHS, 1958-60; NIH spl. fellow MIT, 1961-64; from instr. to assoc. prof. Cardeza found. Jefferson Med. Coll., Phila., 1964-72, prof. medicine, 1972—, assoc. dir., 1978-85, dir., 1985—; mem. hematology study sect. NIH, 1972-76, 78-79; mem. med. adv. coun. Nat. Hemophilia Found., 1973-75; chmn. Pa. State Hemophilia Adv. Com., 1974-76. Mem. Am. Soc. Clin. Investigation, Am. Soc. Hematology, Am. Assn. Immunologists, Assn. Am. Physicians, Internat. Soc. Thrombosis and Hemostasis. Achievements include research in hemostasis and thrombosis, prothrombin metabolism, hemophilia, lupus anticoagulants, endothelial cells. Office: Thomas Jefferson U Cardeza Found Hematologic Rsch 1015 Walnut St Philadelphia PA 19107-5005

SHAPIRO, SANDRA, lawyer; b. Providence, Oct. 17, 1944; d. Emil and Sarah (Cohen) S. AB magna cum laude, Bryn Mawr Coll., Pa., 1966; LLB magna cum laude, U. Pa., 1969. Bar: Mass. 1970, U.S. Dist. Ct. Mass. 1971, U.S. Ct. Appeals (1st cir.) 1972, U.S. Supreme Ct. 1980. Law clk. U.S. Ct. Appeals (1st cir.), Boston, 1969-70; assoc. Foley, Hoag & Eliot LLP, Boston, 1970-75; ptnr. Foley, Hoag & Eliot, Boston, 1976—; mem. Bd. Bar Overseers Mass. Supreme Judicial Ct., 1988-92, Gender Bias Study Com., 1986-89. Contbr. articles to profl. jours. Bd. dirs. Patriots' Trail coun. Girl Scouts U.S., 1994—; mem. bd. overseers Boston Lyric Opera, 1993—, New England Conservatory of Music, 1995—. Woodrow Wilson fellow, 1966. Mem. ABA (ethics, professionalism and pub. edn. com. 1994—), Women's Bar Assn. of Mass. (prs. 1985-86), New Eng. Women in Real Estate, Nat. Women's Law Ctr. Network, Mass. Bar Assn. (chmn. real property sect. coun., com. on profl. ethics), Boston Bar Assn. (mem. coun.), U. Pa. Law Sch. Alumni Assn. (bd. mgrs. 1990—), Order of Coif, Boston Club. Office: Foley Hoag & Eliot LLP 1 Post Office Sq Boston MA 02109

SHAPIRO, STEPHEN MICHAEL, lawyer; b. Chgo., May 3, 1946; s. Samuel H. and Dorothy A. (D'Andrea) S.; m. Joan H. Gately, Oct. 30, 1982; children: Dorothy Henderson, Michael Clifford. BA magna cum laude, Yale U., 1968, JD, 1971. Bar: Ill. 1971, Calif. 1972, D.C. 1991, U.S. Dist. Ct. (no. dist. trial bar) Ill. 1992, U.S. Ct. Appeals (all cirs.), U.S. Supreme Ct. 1975. Law clk. U.S. Ct. Appeals (9th cir.), San Francisco, 1971-72; ptnr., sr. mem. appellate practice Mayer, Brown & Platt, Chgo., 1972-78, 83—; asst. to solicitor gen. U.S. Dept. Justice, Washington, 1978-80, dep. solicitor gen., 1981-82; trustee Product Liability Adv. Found. Co-author: Supreme Court Practice, 1993; contbr. articles to profl. jours. Mem. ABA, Am. Law Inst., Am. Acad. Appellate Lawyers, Supreme Ct. Hist. Soc., Phi Beta Kappa. Republican. Jewish. Office: Mayer Brown & Platt 190 S La Salle St Chicago IL 60603-3410

SHAPIRO, STEPHEN RICHARD, retired air force officer, physician; b. Bklyn., Dec. 30, 1934; s. George Daniel and Bertha Brinna (Bazerman) S.; m. Myrna Farber, May 28, 1960; children: David C., Robert S., Marc E. BA, Bklyn. Coll., 1956; MD, SUNY Downstate Med. Ctr., 1960. Diplomate Am. Bd. Internal Medicine, Am. Bd. Allergy and Immunology, Am. Bd. Med. Mgmt. Commd. 2nd lt. USAF, 1960, advanced through grades to brig. gen., 1987; intern, then resident and fellow Walter Reed Gen. Hosp., Washington, 1960-65; asst. chief allergy Wilford Hall USAF Med. Ctr., San Antonio, 1965-73; chief clin. svc. Ramstein (Germany) Clinic, 1973-74; chief divsn. clin. medicine Hdqrs. USAFE/SG, Ramstein, 1974-76; comdr. USAF Hosp. RAF, Upper Heyford, Eng., 1976-80; dep. surgeon Hdqrs. AFSC/SG, Andrews AFB, Md., 1980-82; surgeon Hdqrs. AFRES/SG, Robins AFB, Ga., 1982-84; command surgeon Hdqrs. AFSC/SG, Andrews AFB, Md., 1984-87; comdr. Malcolm Grow USAF Med. Ctr., Andrews AFB, 1987-89; command surgeon Hdqrs. AFLC/SG, Wright-Patterson AFB, Ohio, 1989-92, Hdqrs. AFMC, 1991-92; chief of staff VA Health Care Ctr., El Paso, Tex., 1992—. Fellow Aerospace Med. Assn. (assoc.); mem. Am. Coll. Physician Execs., Am. Acad. Allergy and Immunology, Air Force Soc. Flight Surgeons, Air Force Soc. Physicians, Alpha Omega Alpha. Jewish. Avocations: gardening, reading, travel. Office: 5001 N Piedras St El Paso TX 79930-4210

SHAPIRO, STEVEN DAVID, dermatologist; b. Oakhurst, N.J., Oct. 15, 1961; s. Alfred J. and Marilyn G. S.; m. Lynn A. Shapiro Feb. 6, 1993. BA cum laude, Vanderbilt U., 1984; MD, N.J. Med. Sch., 1988. Diplomate Nat. Bd. Med. Examiners, Am. Bd. Dermatology; lic. MD N.J., Fla. Intern internal medicine Hahnemann Univ. Hosp., Phila., 1988-89; resident in dermatology Mt. Sinai Med. Ctr. Greater Miami, Miami Beach, Fla., 1989-90; chief resident in dermatology U. Miami Sch. of Medicine, VA Med. Ctr., Mt. Sinai Med. Ctr., Miami, Fla., 1991-92; dermatologist pvt. practice Long Branch, N.J., 1992-95; dermatologist Dermatology Specialists of Palm Beach County P.A., Boca Raton, Fla., 1995—, Steven B. Rosenberg MD P.A., W. Palm Beach, Fla., 1995—; affiliate St. Mary's Hosp, Good Samaritan Hosp., W. Palm Beach, Jackson Meml. Hosp., VA Med. Ctr., Miami; clin. instr. dept. dermatology and cutaneous surgery, U. Miami Sch. of Medicine. Contbr. articles to profl. jours. including Internat. Jour. Dermatology, Cutaneous Pathology and others. Chmn. profl. edn. com. Monmouth County chpt. Am. Cancer Soc., 1992-94, vol. coord. skin cancer screenings, 1992-95, chmn. task force on skin cancer, 1994-95, v.p. 1995; presenter workshops to Am. Acad. Dermatology, San Francisco, 1989, Dermatology Nurses Assn., Atlanta, 1990, Skin Signs of Internal Disease Conf., Neptune, N.J., 1991. Finalist Marion Merrel Dow Pharm. Clin. Cases in Dermatology, 1991; named Physician of Yr. Monmouth County Chpt. Am. Cancer Soc., 1994. Fellow Am. Acad. Dermatology; mem. AMA (Physician's Recognition award 1991), Am. Soc. Dermatologic Surgery, Am. Soc. Dermatology, Am. Soc. Moh's Surgery, Phi Eta Sigma, Alpha Lambda Delta. Avocations: golf, water sports, weight tng. Home: 11 Via Verona Palm Beach Gardens FL 33418

SHAPIRO, STUART CHARLES, computer scientist, educator; b. N.Y.C., Dec. 30, 1944; s. Louis M. and Bertha (Rubinstein) S.; m. Caren Dee Knight, July 16, 1972. BS, MIT, 1966; MS, U. Wis., 1968, PhD, 1971. Lectr. computer scis. dept. U. Wis., Madison, 1971; vis. asst. prof. Ind. U., Bloomington, 1971-72, asst. prof., 1972-77, assoc. prof., 1977-78; asst. prof. SUNY, Buffalo, 1977-78, assoc. prof., 1978-83, prof., 1983—, chmn., 1984-90, 96—; cons. Calspan UB Rsch. Ctr., Buffalo; rsch. scientist Nat. Ctr. for Geographic Info. and Analysis, 1989—. Author: Techniques of Artificial Intelligence, 1979, LISP: An Interactive Approach, 1986, Common Lisp: An Interactive Approach, 1992; editor: Encyclopedia of Artificial Intelligence, 1987, paperback edit., 1990, 2d edit., 1992; contbr. articles to profl. jours. Grantee NSF, 1971—; recipient numerous grants for computer sci. research, 1971—. Fellow Am. Assn. Artificial Intelligence; mem. IEEE (sr.), Assn. Computing Machinery (chmn. spl. interest group on artificial intelligence 1991-95), Assn. Computational Linguistics, Cognitive Sci. Soc., Sigma Xi. Home: 142 Viscount Dr Buffalo NY 14221-1770 Office: SUNY at Buffalo Dept of Computer Sci 226 Bell Hall Buffalo NY 14260-2000

SHAPIRO, SUMNER, retired naval officer, business executive; b. Nashua, N.H., Jan. 13, 1926; s. Maurice David and Hannah (Goodman) S.; m. Eleanor S. Hymen, June 14, 1949; children: Martha, Steven, Susan. B.S., U.S. Naval Acad., 1949; M.S., George Washington U., 1966; postgrad., Naval War Coll., 1966, U.S. Army Inst. Advanced Soviet and Eastern European Studies, 1961. Commd. ensign U.S. Navy, 1949; advanced through grades to rear adm.; asst. naval attache U.S. Navy (Am. embassy), Moscow, 1963-65; dep. asst. chief of staff for intelligence U.S. Naval Forces Europe, London, 1967-69; comdg. officer Naval Intelligence Processing System Support Activity, Washington, 1969-72; asst. chief staff for intelligence U.S. Atlantic Command and U.S. Atlantic Fleet, Norfolk, Va., 1972-76; dep. dir. naval intelligence, 1976-77; comdr. Naval Intelligence Command, Washington, 1977-78; dir. naval intelligence Washington, 1978-82; ret., 1982; v.p. for advanced planning BDM Internat., 1983-89; pres. The Sumner Group Inc., 1989—. Pres. Naval Intelligence Found. Decorated D.S.M., Legion of Merit and others., Nat. Intelligence D.S.M., Netherlands Order Orange-Nassau, Brazil Order Naval Merit, French Nat. Order Merit, others. Mem. Naval Intelligence Found. (pres.), Naval Intelligence Profls. (bd. dirs.), U.S. Naval Inst., Assn. Former Intelligence Officers, Nat. Mil. Intelligence Assn., Nat. Security Industries Assn., U.S. Naval Acad. Alumni Assn., Naval Submarine League.

SHAPIRO, THEODORE, psychiatrist, educator; b. N.Y.C., Feb. 26, 1932; s. Herman Alexander and Nettie (Rosenblatt) S.; m. Joan May Itkin, June 26, 1955; children: Susan, Alexander Herman. BA, Wesleyan U., 1953; MD, Cornell U., 1957. Diplomate Am. Bd. Psychiatry and Neurology, Am. Bd. Child Psychiatry, Am. Psychoanalytic Assn. Intern Montefiore Hosp., N.Y.C., 1957-58; resident in psychiatry NYU-Bellevue Hosp., 1958-61, rsch. assoc. child psychiatry, 1961-65; instr. to prof. NYU Sch. Medicine, 1960-76; prof. psychiatry and pediatrics Cornell U. Med. Coll., N.Y.C, 1976—; vice chair for child and adolescent psychiatry, 1995—; asst. lectr. N.Y. Psychoanalytic Inst., N.Y.C., 1970-86, tng. and supervising analyst, 1986—; cons. Alcohol, Drug Abuse and Mental Health Adminstrn., WHO, Washington, Geneva, Copenhagen, 1980-82, Am. Acad. Child and Adolescent Psychiatry, Washington; chair com. on stewardship Task Force Future, 1980-82, acad. sec., 1981-83, chair work group on sci. issues, 1988-89, chair com. editorship and stewardship of jour., 1984-86, 90-92; participant in APA bilateral exch. in Ea. Europe, 1992; reviewer child psychopathology and treatment rev. com. NIMH, 1994—. Author: Clinical Psycholinguistics, 1979; co-editor: Infant Psychiatry, 1976; editor: Psychoanalysis and Contemporary Science, 1976, Structure in Psychoanalysis, 1991, Affect: Psychoanalytic Perspectives, 1992; co-author: Manual of Panic-Focused Psychodynamic Psychotherapy, 1996; editor Jour. Am. Psychoanalytic Assn., 1984-93; book rev. editor Internat. Jour. Psychoanalysis, 1993—; co-editor Research in Psychoanalysis, 1995; contbr. articles to profl. jours. Recipient Sandor Rado lectureship Columbia Psychoanalytic Clinic, 1991, Prager lectureship George Washington U. Sch. Medicine, Exie Welsch lectureship N.Y. Coun. on Child and Adolescent Psychiatry, 1995; NIMH residency tng. grantee, 1976-86; recipient Wilfred C. Hulse N.Y. Coun. Child Psychiatry, 1982, Harry Bakwin Meml. NYU, 1982, Maurice Laufer lectureship E.P. Bradley Hosp., 1982. Fellow Am. Acad. Child Psychiatry (sec. 1981-83), Am. Psychiat. Assn.; mem. Soc. Profs. Child Psychiatry (chmn. com. on edn. 1982—), Group for Advancement of Psychiatry (chmn. com. on child psychiatry 1985-90), Am. Bd. Psychiatry & Neurology (com. on child and adolescent psychiatry 1987-93, chmn. 1992-93), N.Y. Psychoanalytic Soc. Jewish. Office: Cornell U Med Coll Payne Whitney Clinic Box 147 525 E 68th St New York NY 10021-4873

SHAPIRO, VICTOR LENARD, mathematics educator; b. Chgo., Oct. 16, 1924; s. Joseph E. and Anna (Grossman) S.; m. Florence Gilman, Mar. 21, 1948; children—Pamela Sue Shapiro Baer, Laura Fern Shapiro Young, Charles R., Arthur G. B.S., U. Chgo., 1947, M.S., 1949, Ph.D., 1952. Mem. faculty Rutgers U., 1952-60, prof. math., 1959-60; mem. Inst. Advanced Studies, Princeton, N.J., 1953-55, 58-59; mem. faculty U. Oreg., Eugene, 1960-64; prof. math. U. Calif., Riverside, 1964—; faculty research lectr. U. Calif., 1978. Author: Topics in Fourier and Geometric Analysis, 1961, Conpemproary Mathematics, vol. 208, 1997, also articles. Served with AUS, 1943-46. NSF postdoctoral fellow, 1954-55. Mem. Am. Math. Soc., Math. Assn. Am., Am. Soc. Indsl. and Applied Math. Office: U Calif Math Dept Riverside CA 92521

SHAPIRO, WALTER ELLIOT, political columnist; b. N.Y.C., Feb. 16, 1947; s. Salem Seeley and Edith Geraldine (Herwitz) S.; m. Meryl Gordon, Aug. 24, 1980. BA, U. Mich., 1970, postgrad., 1970-71. Reporter Congl. Quarterly, Washington, 1969-70; editor Washington Monthly, 1972-76; spl. asst. U.S. Sec. Labor, Washington, 1977-78; Presdl. speechwriter The White House, Washington, 1979; reporter Washington Post, 1979-83; gen. editor Newsweek, N.Y.C., 1983-87; sr. writer Time Mag., N.Y.C., 1987-93; White House corr. Esquire mag., 1993-97; polit. columnist USA Today, 1995—; Contbg. editor Washington Monthly, 1976—. Leadership fellow Japan Soc., U.S.-Japan, 1991. Mem. Judson Welliver Soc. Jewish. Avocations: standup comedy, rotisserie baseball. Home: 201 W 86th St Apt 1105 New York NY 10024-3351 Office: 3133 Connecticut Ave NW Apt 315 Washington DC 20008-5105

SHAPLEY, LLOYD STOWELL, mathematics and economics educator; b. Cambridge, Mass., June 2, 1923; s. Harlow and Martha (Betz) S.; m. Marian Ludolph, Aug. 19, 1955; children—Peter, Christopher. A.B., Harvard U., 1948; Ph.D., Princeton U., 1953; PhD (hon.), Hebrew U., Jerusalem, 1986. Mathematician Rand Corp., Santa Monica, Calif., 1948-50; 54-81; prof. depts. math. and econs. UCLA, 1981—; instr. Princeton U., 1952-54; sr. research fellow Calif. Inst. Tech., 1955-56; fellow Inst. Advanced Studies, Hebrew U., Jerusalem, 1979-80; mem. faculty Rand Grad. Inst. for Policy Studies, 1970-86. Author: (with S. Karlin) Geometry of Moment Spaces, 1953, (with R. Aumann) Values of Non-Atomic Games, 1974; editor: (with others) Advances in Game Theory, 1964; mem. editorial bd. Internat. Jour. Game Theory, 1970—, Math. Programming, 1971-80, Jour. Math. Econs, 1973—, Math. Ops. Research, 1975—, Games and Econ. Behavior, 1988—. Served with AC U.S. Army, 1943-45. Decorated Bronze Star. Fellow Econometric Soc., Am. Acad. Arts and Scis.; mem. Nat. Acad. Scis., Ops. Research Soc. Am., Am. Math. Soc., Math. Programming Soc. Research in game theory, math., econs., polit. sci. Office: UCLA Dept Math Los Angeles CA 90024

SHAPO, MARSHALL SCHAMBELAN, lawyer, educator; b. Phila., Oct. 1, 1936; s. Mitchell and Norma (Schambelan) S.; m. Helene Shirley Seidner, June 21, 1959; children: Benjamin, Nathaniel. AB summa cum laude, U. Miami, 1958, JD magna cum laude, 1964; AM, Harvard U., 1961, SJD, 1974. Bar: Fla. 1964, Va. 1977. Copy editor, writer Miami (Fla.) News, 1958-59; instr. history U. Miami, 1960-61; asst. prof. law U. Tex., 1965-67, assoc. prof., 1967-69, prof., 1969-70; prof. law U. Va., 1970-78, Joseph M. Hartfield prof., 1976-78; Frederic P. Vose prof. Northwestern U. Sch. Law, Chgo., 1978—; of counsel Sonnenschein, Nath & Rosenthal, Chgo., 1991—; vis. prof. Juristisches Seminar U. Gottingen (Fed. Republic Germany), 1976; cons. on med. malpractice and tort law reform U.S. Dept. Justice, 1978-79; mem. panel on food safety Inst. Medicine, NAS, 1978-79; vis. fellow Centre for Socio-legal Studies, Wolfson Coll., Oxford, vis. fellow of Coll., 1975, Wolfson Coll., Cambridge, 1992; mem. Ctr. for Advanced Studies, U. Va., 1976-77; cons. Pres.'s Commn. for Study of Ethical Problems in Medicine and Biomed. and Behavioral Rsch., 1980-81; reporter Spl. Com. on Tort Liability System Am. Bar Assn., 1980-84; del. leader People to People Citizen Amb. program delegation to East Asia Tort and Ins. Law, 1986; lectr. appellate judges' seminars ABA, 1977, 83, 90; reporter symposium on legal and sci. perspectives on causation, 1990; advisor Restatement of the Law, Third, Torts: Products Liability, 1992—. Author: Towards a Jurisprudence of Injury, 1984, Tort and Compensation Law, 1976, The Duty to Act: Tort Law, Power and Public Policy, 1978, A Nation of Guinea Pigs, 1979, Products Liability, 1980, Public Regulation of Dangerous Products, 1980, The Law of Products Liability, 1987, Tort and Injury Law, 1990, The Law of Products Liability, 2 vols., 2d edit., 1990, 3d edit., 1994, supplements, 1991, 92, 93, 95, 96, Products Liability and the Search for Justice, 1993, (with Helene Shapo) Law School Without Fear, 1996, (with Page Keeton) Products and the Consumer: Deceptive Practices, 1972, Products and the Consumer: Defective and Dangerous Products, 1970; mem. editl. bd. Jour. Consumer Policy, 1980-88, Products Liability Law Jour.; author: A Representational Theory of Consumer Protection: Doctrine, Function and Legal Liability for Product Disappointment, 1975; mem. adv. bd. Loyola Consumer Law Reporter; contbr. articles to legal and med. jours. NEH sr. fellow, 1974-75. Mem. Am. Law Inst., Am. Assn. Law Schs. (chmn. torts compensation systems sect. 1983-84, torts round table coun. 1970). Home: 1910 Orrington Ave Evanston IL 60201-2910 Office: Northwestern U Sch Law 357 E Chicago Ave Chicago IL 60611-3008

SHAPOFF, STEPHEN H., financial executive; b. N.Y.C., Nov. 1, 1944; s. Barney and Freda Shapoff; m. Andrea Dorin, May 30, 1967; 1 child, Matthew F. BBA, Pace U., 1967. CPA, N.Y. With audit dept. Ernst & Young, N.Y.C., 1967-72; asst. controller Seeburg Industries, Inc., 1972-74, 1967-72; with Estee Lauder, Inc., N.Y.C., 1974-78; controller Coleco Industries, Inc., Hartford, Conn., 1978-79; sr. v.p. fin. Ivy Hill Corp. subs. of Time

Warner Inc., N.Y.C., Conn., 1979-85; exec. v.p. Ivy Hill Corp., N.Y.C., 1985—; adj. asst. prof. Pace U., N.Y.C., 1971—. Mem. AICPA, Fin. Exec. Inst. (pres. L.I. chpt. 1988, 92-94, chair nat. membership com., nat. dir. 1996), N.Y. Soc. CPAs, Nat. Assn. Accts. Office: Ivy Hill Corp 375 Hudson St New York NY 10014-3658

SHAPPIRIO, DAVID GORDON, biologist, educator; b. Washington, June 18, 1930; s. Sol and Rebecca (Porton) S.; m. Elvera M. Bamber, July 8, 1953; children: Susan, Mark. B.S. with distinction in Chemistry, U. Mich., 1951; A.M., Harvard U., 1953, Ph.D. in Biology, 1955. NSF postdoctoral fellow in biochemistry Cambridge U., Eng., 1955-56; research fellow in physiology Am. Cancer Soc.-NRC, U. Louvain, Belgium, 1956-57; mem. faculty U. Mich., Ann Arbor, 1957—, prof. zool. and biology, 1967—, Arthur F. Thurnau prof., 1989—; assoc. chair div. biol. scis. U. Mich., 1976-83, acting chair, 1978, 79, 80, 82, coordinator NSF undergrad. sci. edn. program, 1962-67, dir. honors program Coll. Lit. Sci. and Arts, 1983-91; vis. lectr. Am. Inst. Biol. Scis., 1966-68; reviewer, cons. to pubs. on textbook devel.; reviewer rsch. and ednl. tng. grant proposals NSF, NIH, mem. program site visit teams. Author rsch. on biochemistry and physiology growth, devel., dormancy; invited spkr., rsch. symposia of nat. and internat. orgns. in field. Recipient Disting. Teaching award U. Mich., 1967, Excellence in Edn. award, 1991, Bausch & Lomb Sci. award, 1974; Lalor Found fellow, 1953-55; Danforth Found. assoc. Fellow AAAS; mem. Am. Inst. Biol. Scis. (vis. lectr. 1966-68), Am. Soc. Cell Biology, Biochem. Soc., Am. Soc. Zoologists, Soc. Exptl. Biology, Assn. Biol. Lab. Edn., Xerces Soc., Assn. Biol. Computing, Phi Beta Kappa (v.p. U. Mich. chpt. 1995—). Office: U Mich Dept Biology 1121 Natural Sci Bldg Ann Arbor MI 48109-1048

SHARBONEAU, LORNA ROSINA, artist, educator, author, poet, illustrator; b. Spokane, Wash., Apr. 5, 1935; d. Stephen Charles Martin and Midgie Montana (Hartzel) Barton; m. Thomas Edward Sharboneau, Jan. 22, 1970; children: Curtis, Carmen, Chet, Cra, Joseph. AA in Arts, Delta Coll., 1986; studies with Steve Lesnick, Las Vegas, Nev.; studies with Bette Myers/Zimmerman, Phoenix and Bonners Ferry, Idaho. Prin. Sharboneau's Art Gallery, Spokane, 1977-80; tchr. art Michell's Art Gallery, Spokane, 1978-79; art therapist Vellencino Sch. Dist., Calif., 1981-83; ind. artist Lind, Wash., 1948—; dir., producer, stage designer Ch. of Jesus Christ of LDS, San Jose, Sonora, Modesto, Calif., 1978 (1st. place road show San Jose); dir. Sharboneau's Art Show, Spokane, 1979, Hands On-Yr. of the Child; platform spkr., poet, fundraiser, libr., 1984-87; asst., apprentice to Prof. Rowland Cheney, Delta Coll., Stockton, Calif., 1985, 86, 87; demonstrated drip oil technique, Bonners Ferry, Idaho, Spokane, Wash., Stockton, Calif., Delta Coll. Author, illustrator: Through the Eyes of the Turtle Tree, The One-Armed Christmas Tree, The Price of Freedom, William Will, Bill Can, Song of the Turtle Tree, Chet's Ottle-Bottle: The Unbreakable Bottle, One Drop of Water and a Grain of Sand; poet; prolific artist completed over 4000 paintings and drawings, displayed works in galleries through western states; featured in Magnolia News, Seattle, Delta Coll. Impact, Stockton, Calif., Stockton Record, Union Democrat, Sonora, Calif., Lincoln Center Chronicle, Stockton, Calif., Spokesman Rev., Spokane, Wash., Modesto (Calif) Bee, Angels Camp, Calif., Union Democrat, Sonora, Calif., New-Letter, Ch. of Jesus Christ of L.D.S 1st ward, Sonora; artist mixed media, oil, drip oil works, sculptures, pastel, watercolor; illustrations pen and ink, acrylic; sculptor bronze, lost wax method, ceramic art, soap stone, egg-tempra, original techniques, collage, variation on a theme. Dir., programmer, fundraiser Shelter Their Sorrows, Sonora, Calif., 1989-92, vol. Cmty. Action Agy. and Homeless Shelter; fundraiser for Homeless Flood Victims of No. Calif., 1997. Recipient Golden Rule award J.C. penny, 1991, Recognition award Pres. George Bush, cert. Spl. Congl. Recognition Congressman Richard H. Lehman, 3rd Pl. Best Show East Valley ARtists/Pala Show, 1973, 74, 75, 3d Pl. Artist of Yr., 1974, Valley Fair, Santa Clara, Calif., 1974, 1st and 2d Pl. Spokane County Fair, 1978, 3 honorable mentions, 4 premiums, 1979, 3 1st Pl., 3 2d Pl., 2 3rd Pl., honorable mention Calaveras County Fair/Angels Camp, Calif., 1983, 1st and 3rd Pl. Unitarian Art Festival, Stockton, Calif., 1984, 2d Pl., 1985, 3d Pl., 1986, 1st Pl. Lodi Art Ann., 1985, 3rd Pl., 1986, 1st Pl. 1987, 1st Pl., 1988, honorable mental SJCAC Junque Art Show, Stockton, 1985, 1st Pl Ctrl. Calif. Art League, Modesto, 1986, 88, 2d Pl. 1995; 3d Pl. Camilla Art Show, San Jose, Calif., 1974, and numerous others; 1st, 2d, and 3d Pl., Spokane County Fair, 1978; 4 honorable mentions, Sonora, Calif., 1993, 2nd Pl. Ctrl. Calif. Art Show, 1996. Mem. Ctrl. Sierra Arts Coun., Mother Lode Artists Assn., Sacramento Fine Arts Ctr., Inc., Internat. Platform Assn. (Judges Choice conv. arts competition 1993), The Planetary Soc., The Nat. Mus. of Women of Arts. Mem. Ch. of Jesus Christ of LDS. Achievements include: homeless shelter kitchen named in her honor, Sonora. Avocations: mathematics, astronomy, baseball, archeology. Office: Internat Platform Assn PO Box 250 Winnetka IL 60093-0250

SHARER, JOHN DANIEL, lawyer; b. Bklyn., Sept. 19, 1950; s. Albert Robert and Alda Loretta (Tapiro) S.; m. Kathleen Gail Donaldson, Feb. 14, 1981; 1 child, Stephanie Erin. AB, Dartmouth Coll., Hanover, N.H., 1972; JD, U. Pa., 1975. Bar: Pa. 1975, N.J. 1975, D.C. 1976, N.Y. 1989, Va. 1994. Law clk. Superior Ct. Pa., Hon. Edmund B. Spaeth, Jr., Phila., 1975-76; assoc. Sutherland, Asbill & Brennan, Washington, 1976-82, ptnr., 1982-94; counsel Christian & Barton, L.L.P., Richmond, Va., 1994-95; ptnr. Christian % Barton, L.L.P., Richmond, Va., 1996—. Bd. dirs. Wakefield Sch., Marshall, Va., 1990-94; pres., dist. enrollment dir. Dartmouth Club of Cen. Va. Mem. Phi Beta Kappa. Republican. Avocations: classical music, computers, dogs. Home: 12317 Northlake Ct Richmond VA 23233-6635 Office: Christian & Barton LLP 909 E Main St Ste 1200 Richmond VA 23219-3013

SHARETT, ALAN RICHARD, lawyer, environmental litigator, mediator, and arbitrator, law educator; b. Hammond, Ind., Apr. 15, 1943; s. Henry S. and Frances (Givel) Smulevitz; children: Lauren Ruth, Charles Daniel; m. Cherie Ann Vick, Oct. 15, 1993. Student Ind. U., 1962-65; J.D., DePaul U., 1968; advanced postgrad. legal edn. U. Mich. and U. Chgo., 1970-71. Bar: N.Y. 1975, Ind. 1969, U.S. Ct. Appeals (2d cir.) 1975, U.S. Ct. Appeals (7th cir.) 1974, U.S. Supreme Ct. 1973. Assoc. Call, Call, Borns & Theodoros, Gary, Ind., 1969-71; judge protem Gary City Ct., 1970-71; environ. dist. atty. 31st Jud. Cir., Lake County, Ind., 1971-75; counsel Dunes Nat. Lakeshore Group, 1971-75; mem. Cohan, Cohan & Smulevitz, 1971-75; town atty., Independence Hill, Ind., 1974-75; judge pro tem Superior Ct., Lake County, Ind., 1971-75; professorial dir. NYU Pub. Liability Inst., N.Y.C., 1975-76; speaker, guest lectr., adj. faculty ATLA, Purdue U., N.Y. U., Ind. U., De Paul U., Valparaiso U., St. Joseph Coll., U. Miami; Coll. paralegal instr., 1970-89; adj. faculty prof. constl. law Union Inst., Miami, Cin., 1990-92; adj. prof. environ. litigation and alternative dispute resolution Ward Stone Coll., Miami, 1994; guest prof. internat. environ. law Dept. Internat. and Comparative Law, U. Miami, 1992—; mem. adv. panel, seminar speaker on internat. issues Interamerican Dialogue on Water Mgmt., 1993; spkr. on environ. transactions and litigation North Dade County Fla. Bar Assn., 1995—; seminar spkr. on environ. politics U. Miami Dept. Environ. Sci., 1995—; gen. counsel Marjory Stoneman Douglas Friends of Everglades, 1992-93; asst. atty. gen., chair fed. and constnl. practice litigation group, N.Y. State, N.Y.C., 1976-78; pvt. practice, Flushing, N.Y., 1980-82, Miami Beach, Fla., 1988—, lead trial counsel, chmn. lawyers panel for No. Ind., ACLU, 1969-71; liaison trial counsel Lake County and Ind. State Health Depts. and Atty. Gen., 1971-75; mem. Nat. Dist. Attys. Assn., 1972-75, mem. environ. protection com; pres. ESI Group, Nat. Environ. Responsibility Cons, Inc.; spkr. in field. Editor in chief DePaul U. The Summons, 1967-68; mem. staff DePaul Law Rev., 1968; jud. clerkship Superior Ct. 31st Ind. Jud. Cir., 1971-73; contbr. articles to profl. jours. Mem. coalition Fla. Save Our Everglades Program. Recipient Honors award in forensic litigation Law-Sci. Acad. Am., 1967. Mem. ABA (nat. article editor law student div. 1967-68, nat. com. environ. litigation, com. fed. procedure, com. toxic torts, hazardous substances and environ. law, com. energy resources law, com. internat. environ. law, com. internat. litigation, environ. interest group, sect. natural resources, energy and environ. law, judge negotiation competition championship round, law student divsn., midyear meeting 1995, sect. sci. and tech., biotech. com., environ. law and pub. health com., standing com. sci. evidence, spl. com. legal edn., nat. toxic and hazardous substances and environ. law com., sect. tort and ins. practice, corp. gen. counsel com., non-profit orgns. com., media law and defamation torts com., tort and hazardous substances and environ. law com.), Am. Arbitration Assn., Soc. Profls. in Dispute Resolution, Assn. Bar of City of N.Y., N.Y. County Lawyers Assn. (com. on fed. cts. 1977-82), Am. Judicature Soc., ATLA (nat. coms. toxic, environ. and pharm. torts, environ. litigation), Environ. Law Inst., Am. Immigration Lawyers Assn., Ill. State Bar Assn. (staff editor 1967-68), N.Y. State Bar Assn. (environ. law sect., family law sect.), Ind. State Bar Assn. (environ. law sect., internat. law sect., trial practice sect.), Nat. Fla. Assn. Environ. Profls., Greater Miami C. of C. (coms. on environ. awareness, environ. econs., biomedical exch., planning and zoning growth mgmt., internat. econ. devel., bus. and industry econ. devel., govtl. affairs, ins., internat. banking, Europe/Pacific rim), AAAS (physics, math., astronomy), Am. Acad. Poets. Office: ESI Group Nat Environ Responsibility Cons Inc 6421 Cow Pen Rd Apt M 107 Miami Lakes FL 33014-6655

SHARF, STEPHAN, automotive company executive; b. Berlin, Dec. 30, 1920; came to U.S., 1947; s. Wilhelm and Martha (Schwartz) S.; m. Rita Schantzer, June 17, 1951. Degree in Mech. Engring., Tech. U., Berlin, Fed. Republic Germany, 1947. Tool and die maker Buerk Tool & Die Co., Buffalo, 1947-50; foreman Ford Motor Co., 1950-53; gen. foreman Ford Motor Co., Chgo., 1953-58; with Chrysler Corp., Detroit, 1958-86, master mechanic Twinsburg stamping plant, 1958-63, mfg. engring. mgr., 1963-66, mrg. prodn. Twinsburg stamping plant, 1966-68, plant mgr. Warren stamping plant, 1968-70, plant mgr. Sterling stamping plant, 1970-72, gen. plants mgr. stamping, 1972-78, v.p. Engine and Casting div., 1978-80, v.p. Power Train div., 1980-81, exec. v.p., mfg., dir., 1981-85, exec. v.p. internat., 1985-86, also bd. dirs.; pres. SICA Corp., Troy, Mich., 1986—; bd. dirs. Medar, Inc. Columnist Ward's Auto World Common Sense mag., 1987—. Bd. dirs. Jr. Achievement, Detroit council Boy Scouts Am.; trustee, v.p. Oakland U. Mem. Soc. Auto Engrs., Detroit Engring. Soc. Club: Wabeek Country. Home: 966 Adams Castle Dr Bloomfield Hills MI 48304-3713 Office: SICA Corp PO Box 623 Troy MI 48099-0623

SHARFSTEIN, STEVEN SAMUEL, health care executive, medical director; b. N.Y.C., July 2, 1932; s. Sidney J. and Beverly (Zevie) S.; m. Margaret Shiling, June 13, 1965; children: Joshua, Daniel, Sarah. BA magna cum laude, Dartmouth Coll., 1964; MD, Albert Einstein Coll. Medicine, 1968; MPA, Harvard U., 1973. Diplomate Nat. Bd. Med. Examiners. Intern in pediatrics Bronx (N.Y.) Mcpl. Hosp. Ctr., 1968-69; jr. resident Mass. Mental Health Ctr., Boston, 1969-70, sr. resident, 1970-71, chief resident, 1971-72; dir. mental health svcs. Brookside Park Family Life Ctr., Jamaica Plain, Mass., 1972-73; spl. asst. to dir. Office Planning & Evaluation Nat. Inst. Mental Health, 1973-74, dir. program analysis and evaluation Office Program Devel. and Analysis, 1974-76, dir. divsn. mental health svc. programs, 1976-80, attending psychiatrist clin. ctr., 1980-82, assoc. dir. behavioral medicine, 1980-82; dep. med. dir. Am. Psychiat. Assn., 1983-86; exec. v.p., COO, med. dir. The Sheppard & Enoch Pratt Hosp., Balt., 1986-91, pres., CEO, med. dir., 1992—; lectr. in psychiatry Johns Hopkins U., Balt., 1987—; professorial lectr. in psychiatry dept. psychiatry Georgetown U., Washington, 1984—; clin. prof. U. Md., College Park, 1986—; cons. Neighborhood Employment Ctr. and Barbara Street Welfare Office, 1970-71, Allegheny County Mental Health/Retardation Bd., Pitts., 1973-74; examiner Am. Bd. Psychiatry and Neurology, 1979—; active Gov. Adv. Coun. on Mental Hygiene, 1987—, Inst. Medicine Bd. on Biobehavioral Scis. & Mental Disorders, 1993—. Co-author: Madness and Government: Who Cares for the Mentally Ill, 1983, Maintaining and Improving Psychiatric Insurance Coverage: An Annotated Bibliography, 1983, Coverage for Mental and Nervous Disorders, 1983, Health Insurance and Psychiatric Care, 1984; author chpts. to books; co-editor: Neighborhood Psychiatry, 1977, The New Economics and Psychiatric Care, 1985, Prospective Payment & Psychiatric Care, 1988; assoc. editor Am. Jour Psychiatry, 1993; mem. ednl. adv. bd. Cmty. Mental Health Jour., 1980—; mem. editl. bd. Jour. Mental Health Adminstrn., 1989—, Relapse, 1993; contbr. articles to profl. jours. Served with USPHS, 1970-73. Recipient Andrew Edison prize in govt. Dartmouth Coll., 1964; Harry C. Solomon prize Harvard U. Med. Sch., 1974; Adminstr.'s award for meritorious achievemnet Alcohol, Drug Abuse and Mental Health Adminstrn., 1980; Sr. Exec. Service Bonus award, 1981. Fellow Am. Psychiat. Assn. (mem. commn. on stds. and third party payments 1976-82, chmn. budget com. 1987-90, chmn. com. on managed care 1990—, sec. 1991—), Am. Coll. Psychiatrists (mem. pubs. com. 1984-87, mem. budget com. 1987-89, chair Dean award com. 1990—), Am. Orthopsychiat. Assn., Am. Coll. Mental Health Adminstrn.; mem. AMA, AAAS, Am. Assn. Gen. Hosp. Psychiatrists, Am. Assn. Psychiat. Adminstrs. (Significant Contbns. in Adminstrn. award 1987), Am. Psychosomatic Soc., Washington Psychiat. Soc. (mem. coun. 1982—, Outstanding Svc. award 1984), Md. Assn. Private Practicing Psychiatrists, Md. Psychiat. Soc., Balt.-Washington Soc. for Psychoanalysis (affiliate), Washington Psychoanalytic Soc. (hon.), Med. Soc. D.C. Office: Sheppard and Enoch Pratt Hosp 6501 N Charles St Baltimore MD 21204-6819

SHARICK, MERLE DAYTON, JR., mortgage insurance company executive; b. Bloomington, Ill, May 5, 1946; s. Merle Dayton and Joyce Madeline (Reed) S.; m. Cheryl Jean Easterday, Dec. 28, 1966; children: Amber Dawn, Cami Nicole. BA, Southwestern Coll., Winfield, Kans., 1968; MS in Edn., U. Kans., 1970. Tchr., coach Kans. High Schs., Lawrence, Hutchinson, 1968-73; asst. prin., prin. Kans. High Schs., Buhler, Inman, Leoti, 1973-77; auctioneer, real estate salesman R.E.I.B., Inc., Hutchinson, Kans., 1977-78; account exec. Mortgage Guaranty Ins. Co., Hutchinson, 1978-81; regional sales mgr. Mortgage Guaranty Ins. Co., Shawnee Mission, Kans., 1981-83, Houston, 1983-86; div. risk mgr. Mortgage Guaranty Ins. Co., Atlanta, 1986-90; regional dir. Mortgage Guaranty Ins. Co., Charlotte, N.C., 1990-93; v.p., mgr. risk mgmt. Republic Mortgage Ins. Co., Winston-Salem, N.C., 1993—; sports editor Winfield (Kans.) Daily Couier, 1966-68; grad. asst. U. Kans., Lawrence, 1968-70; owner, operator Riverside Home Style Laundry, South Hutchinson, Kans., 1975-79, founder, owner, The Sport Shack, Hutchinson, Kans., 1977-79; guest speaker various orgns. Active in Rep. support groups, Houston, Atlanta, 1983—. Fellow Inst. for Devel. Ednl. Adminstrs.; mem. Nat. Assn. Rev. Appraisers and Mortgage Underwriters (bd. dirs. 1989-93, Ark. Traveler award 1995), Mortgage Bankers Am., Ga. Mortgage Bankers, Mortgage Bankers Carolinas, N.C. Alliance Cmty. Fin. Instns., S.C. League Savs. Instns., Fla. Mortgage Bankers, Tex. Mortgage Bankers, Charlotte Mortgage Bankers, The Housing Roundtable, The Piedmont Club. Baptist.

SHARIFY, NASSER, educator, librarian, author; b. Tehran, Iran, Sept. 23, 1925; came to U.S., 1953, naturalized, 1972; s. Ebrahim and Eshrat (Saghafy) S.; m. Homayoun Taslimy, June 14, 1950 (div. 1978); children: Sharareh, Shahab. Licencie es Lettres, U. Tehran, 1947; M.S., Columbia U., 1954, Dr. L.S., 1958. Editorial staff Teheran jours. Rah-e Now, Jahan-e Now, Saba, Jonb va Jush, 1943-51; translator, announcer All India Radio, 1948-49; librarian, dep. dir. Library of Parliament Iran, Tehran, 1949-53; cataloger Library of Congress, 1954-55; program asst. libraries devel. sect. UNESCO, Paris, 1959-61; acting chief servicing sect. Dept. Edn., 1962-63; dir. gen. Ministry Edn., Tehran, 1961-62; asst. prof. library and info. scis. and internat. edn. U. Pitts., 1963-66; founder, dir. Internat. Library Info. Center, 1964-66; vis. lectr. SUNY Albany Sch. Library Sci., summer, 1966; dir. internat. librarianship and documentation, internat studies and world affairs SUNY, Oyster Bay, 1966-68; dean, prof. grad. sch. library and info sci. Pratt Inst., Bklyn., 1968-87, chmn. inst. research council, 1971-89, disting. prof., dean emeritus sch. computer, info. and library scis., 1987—; pres. B.E.L.T., Inc., internat. planning cons., 1981—; Dir. Grad. Library Tng. Program, UNESCO Mission, Nat. Tchrs. Coll., Tehran, 1960; Iran's Ofcl. del. to UNESCO Conf. Ednl. Pubs., Geneva, 1961, SE Asia Edn. Secs. Conf., Murree, Pakistan, 1961, Internation Conf., on Cataloging Prins., Paris, 1961, CENTO Libr. Devel. Conf., Ankara, Turkey, 1962; chmn. standing com. for preparation reading materials for new literates UNESCO, Tehran, 1961-62; mem. U.S. AID Mission, Turkey, Iran, Pakistan, 1966; dir. Conf. on Internat. Responsibility Coll. and Univ. Librarians, Oyster Bay, 1967; U.S. del. 33d Conf. and Internat. Congress on Documentation, Tokyo, 1967; ALA del. UN Conf. on Non-Govtl. Orgn., 1969; cons. U.S. AID, Conf. on Book Devel., 1967; mem. adv. bd. Ency. Libr. and Info. Scis., 1969—; chmn. Pre-Am. Library Assn. Conf. Inst. on Internat. Libr. Manpower, Edn. and Placement in N.Am., Detroit, 1970; mem. Am. del. Internat. Fedn. Libr. Assn. Conf., Liverpool, Eng., 1971, Budapest, 1972, Grenoble, France, 1973, Washington, 1974, Brussels, 1977, Montreal, 1982, Chgo., 1985, Barcelona, 1992; bldg. cons. Learning Resources Center, Nat. Tchrs. Coll., Iran, 1972-73, cons. campus planning, 1972-73; UNESCO cons. missions to plan and evaluate Nat. Sch. Info. Sci., Morocco, 1973-74, 79-81, 89; cons. U.S. Info. Agy., Morocco, 1991, 92, 95; chmn. Conf. on Orgn. and Control of Info for Islamic Research, 1982; chmn. bd. cons. to Nat. U. Iran, 1974-75, Pahlavi Nat. Library of Iran, 1975-77; speaker Symposium Internat. sur l' information Economique, Casablanca, Morocco, 1990; inaugural speaker Ctr. Documentation et D'Information Multimedia, Rabat, Morocco, 1995. Author: cataloging of Persian works Including Rules for Transliteration Entry and Description, 1959, Book Production, Importation and Distribution in Iran, Pakistan and Turkey, 1966; Beyond the National Frontiers: The International Dimension of Changing Library Education for a Changing World, 1973; The Pahlavi National Library of the Future, 17 vols., 1976, other books; contbr. to Ency. of Library and Info. Sci., 1969, ALA World Ency. Library and Info. Services, 1980, 86, library jours., 1973—, Bookmark, 1972, Library Education in the Middle East, 1991, Remembering Rangathan: A Sentimental Reflection, 1992; contbr. poetry to various jours. and anthologies, 1947-51, 67, 91-93 lyrics to Iranian motion pictures and recs., 1948-52; works on display at Archieves of Hoover Inst. on War Revolution and Peace, Stanford U.; Contbr. to: film script for motion picture Morad, 1951-52. Trustee Bklyn. Public Library, 1970-82; pres. Maurice F. Tauber Found., 1981—. Recipient Taj (crown) medal and citation for disting. svc. Mohammad Reza Shah Pahlavi, Shah of Iran, 1978, Kaula Gold medal and citation for disting. svc. to internat. librarianship, 1985; named for Annual Nasser Sharify Lecture Series, Sch. of Computer Info. and Libr. Scis., Pratt Inst., 1988—; writings by and about Nasser Sharify are preserved at Archives of Hoover Instn. on wars, revolutions and peace., Stanford U., Stanford, Calif. Mem. ALA (chmn. com. equivalencies and reciprocity 1966-71, mem. UNESCO panel, mem. nominating com. 1970-71, chmn. Pakistan, Iran, Turkey, Morocco, and Middle East Resource panels, internat. library edn. com. 1973—, mem. com. internat. library schs. div. library edn. 1968-72, coordinator country resources panels, internat. library edn. com. library edn. div. 1973-78), N.Y. Library Assn. (dir. library edn. sect. 1969-72), Pub. Library Assn. (task force on internat. relations 1981-86), Am. Assn. Library Schs. (chmn. govtl. relations com., 1984-88), Am. Soc. Info. for Sci., Spl. Librarian Assn., Internat. Fedn. Library Assns. (adv. group library edn. 1971-73, v.p. library schs. sect. 1973-77). Home: 252 Jericho Tpke Westbury NY 11590-1213 Office: Pratt Inst Sch Info and Libr Sci 200 Willoughby Ave # 4 Brooklyn NY 11205-3817 *If I am asked to wash a car, I try to make it spotless. If I am to write a book, I try to make it faultless. But it seems that I always find spots on the shining surface of the car, and faults in many well-written pages of the book. This gives me another reason to live for another day.*

SHARIK, TERRY L., forest resources educator. BS in Forestry and Wildlife Mgmt., W.Va. U., 1964; MF in Forest Recreation, U. Mich., 1966, PhD in Forest Botany, 1970. Tchg. fellow biology of woody plants U. Mich., Ann Arbor, 1964-68, NSF rsch. trainee in systematic and evolutionary biology, 1967-69, rsch. asst. Sch. Natural Resources, instr. adult edn., 1967-70, tchg. asst. forest genetics, 1970; asst. prof. biology Oberlin Coll., 1971-73; biologist ecol. scis. divsn., sect. mgr., project mgr. NUS Corp., Pitts., 1973-75; rsch. faculty Sch. Forestry and Wildlife Resources Va. Poly. Inst. and State U., Blacksburg, 1975-82, asst. prof. forest biology, 1975-82; rsch. faculty Sch. Forestry and Wood Products Mich. Tech. U., Houghton, 1986-93, assoc. prof., prof. forest ecology, 1986-93, rsch. faculty Lake Superior Ecosys. Rsch. Ctr., 1989-93; rsch. faculty dept. forest resources, prof. forest ecology Utah State U., Logan, 1993—, head dept. forest resources, 1993—, dept. coord. internship program, 1995—, dean's coun. Coll. Natural Resources, 1993—; peer reviewer grad. degree program in environ. sci., policy and mgmt. U. Calif., Berkeley, 1995; rev. team chair Soc. Am. Foresters' accreditation rev. of undergrad. degree programs U. Tenn., Knoxville, 1995; plant com. Va. Endangered Species Program, 1977-86; sec. Betula uber Protection, Mgmt. and Rsch. Coordinating Com., 1986-89, 93—; mem. sci. adv. com. Mich. chpt. Nature Conservancy, 1991-93; co-organizer, moderator tech. session on endangered species and ecosystems Soc. Am. Foresters Ann. Conv., 1992; mem. organizing com. Lake Superior Biol. Conf., 1992; bd. mem. Teton Sci. Sch., Kelly, Wyo., 1994—; mem. steering com. 1st Biennial Conf. in Natural Resources Edn. Pa. State U., 1994-95; chair Utah Natural Resources Coordinating Coun., Ecosys. Classification and Mapping Working Group, 1995—; bd. mem. Canyonlands Field Inst., Moab, Utah, 1996—; chair 2nd Biennial Conf. in Natural Resources, 1996—; mem. steering com. 1st N.Am. Forest Ecology Workshop, 1996—. Peer reviewer Forest, Jour. Forestry, Can. Jour. Forest Rsch., No. Jour. Applied Forestry, Jour. Ecology, Am. Jour. Botany, Jour. Mammalogy, Am. Midland Naturalist, South African Jour. Botany, Internat. Jour. Remote Sensing, Bull. Torrey Bot. Club, S.W. Naturalist, Mich. Botanist, NatureScope, Ranger Rick Mag., Forest Ecology, Environ. Conservation, Management Options for the Rehabilitation of Damaged Ecosystems, Biogeography and Ecology of the Lake Erie Islands, NSF rsch. proposals U.S. Dept. Agr. rsch. proposals, U.S. Forest Svc.; contbr. articles to profl. jours., chpts. to books. Recipient Carleton Macarron scholarship U. Mich., 1966-67; grantee Oberlin Coll., 1972, Ohio Edison, 1974-75, Houston Lighting and Power, 1975-76, Gulf Std., 1975-77, U.S. Forest Svc., 1976-84, 90-94, 95, Va. Agrl. Found., 1976-78, Am. Elec. Power Svc. Corp., 1978-79, 80, U.S. Fish and Wildlife Svc., 1978-79, 81-91, U.S. Army C.E., 1979-81, EPA and U.S. Forest Svc., 1985-88, NASA, 1988-93, Mich. Dept. Natural Resources, 1988-93, USDA, 1988-93, NASA, 1990-93, U.S. Dept. Def., 1994—, U.S. AID, 1995—; univ. disting. tchg. fellow U. Mich., 1968, Disting. Tchr. of Yr. Sch. of Forestry and Wood Products, Mich. Tech. U., 1993. Mem. Soc. Am. Foresters (natural areas coun. 1975-82), Forest Ecology Working Group (chair elect, chair 1992-96, editl bd. Jour. Forestry 1995—), Ecol. Soc. Am., Am. Inst. Biol. Scis., Soc. Conservation Biology, Alpha Zeta (chancellor 1964), Gamma Sigma Delta, Phi Epsilon Phi, Phi Sigma, Sigma Xi, Xi Sigma Pi (ranger 1964, forester 1966). Office: U State U Coll Natural Resources Dept Forest Resources Logan UT 84322-5215

SHARIR, YACOV, artistic director, choreographer; b. Casablanca, Morocco, Aug. 22, 1940; came to U.S., 1978; s. Simon and Rene Sharir. Student, Jerusalem Acad. Music, 1962-65, Bat-Sheva Dance Co. Sch., 1965-67; grad., Jerusalem Besalel Acad. F.A., 1966. Instr. Bat-Sheva Dance Co., 1966-74; ballet instr. Israeli Ballet Co. & Kibbutz Dance Co., 1970-73; founder, artistic dir. Am. Deaf Dance Co., Austin, Tex., 1977-82, Sharir Dance Co., Austin, 1982—; sr. lectr. U. Tex., Austin, 1977—; faculty dance Jerusalem Rubin Acad. Music & Dance, 1988—; arts fellow for dance & virtual reality project Banff Ctr. For the Arts, 1992-94; choreographer over 70 pieces for various dance companies. Choreographer Homage to Jerome Robbins, Mechanical Doll, Quadroped, Right to Left, others. Choreography fellow NEA, 1989, 89-90.. Avocations: ceramics, sculpting, gardening. Home: 5406 Mt Bonnell Rd Austin TX 78731-4610 Office: U Tex Dept Theatre & Drama Austin TX 78712*

SHARITS, DEAN PAUL, motion picture company executive; b. Mankato, Minn., Feb. 6, 1944; s. Loran Ross and June Banita (Timmerman) S.; m. Patricia Ann Taylor, June 14, 1966 (div. 1973); 1 child, James Dean; m. Adela Zamora, July 23, 1988.. AS in Engring., L.A. Trade Tech., 1974; BS in Bus., Calif. State U., Northridge, 1979; MBA, Mankato State U., 1980. Prodn. mgr. Walt Disney Imagineering, Glendale, Calif., 1980-84; gen. mgr. Recreation Entertainment Comml., Burbank, Calif., 1984-85; pres., CEO Apogee Prodns., Inc., Van Nuys, Calif., 1985-90; sr. v.p. Landmark Entertainment Group, L.A., 1990-92; pres., CEO Gold Springs Enterprises, Inc., San Diego, 1992-93; exec. v.p. Scenic Techs., Las Vegas, 1994—; pres. Sharits & Assocs., Las Vegas, 1995—; dir. Internat. Kinetics Corp., Altadena, Calif., 1990—, Concerned Calif. for Motion Pictures and TV, Hollywood, Calif., 1986-88; cons. Technifex, Inc., Sun Valley, Calif., 1989-91, Water Entertainment Tech., Universal City, Calif., 1989-91. Contbr. articles to profl. jours. With USN, 1961-65. Republican. Avocations: golf, tennis, skiing, running. Home and Office: 3827 Arroyo de Viejas Alpine CA 91901

SHARKEY, COLLEEN MARY, sports association administrator; b. Jersey City, Sept. 26, 1950; d. Martin and Helen (Sirangelo) Powers; 1 child, Jessica; stepchildren: Matthew, Debra, Janet. BA, U. Ctrl. Fla., Orlando, 1986; MBA, Crummer Grad. Sch. Bus., Winter Park, Fla., 1995. Keypunch supr. Alpha Metals, Inc., Jersey City, 1969-71, computer operator, 1971-73, computer programmer, 1973-75; computer lab. trainer Seminole C.C., Sanford, Fla., 1982-86; litigation support paralegal Rumberger, Kirk, Caldwell, Cabaniss, Burke & Wechsler, PA, Orlando, 1986-91; law firm adminstr. Cabaniss & Burke, PA, Orlando, 1991-96; asst. dir. adminstrn. RDV Sports, Orlando Magic, 1996—; adj. prof. U. Ctrl. Fla. Author seminar Keeping the Good Ones, 1995. Recipient Nat. Collegiate award U.S. Achievement Acad., 1986. Mem. NAFE, AAUW, Assn. Legal Adminstrs. Republican. Roman Catholic. Avocations: computers, meditation, golf, tennis, NBA Basketball. Office: RDV Sports Orlando Magic One Magic Place Orlando Arena Orlando FL 32801-1114

SHARKEY, KATHLEEN, accountant; b. Phila., Jan. 25, 1951; d. Joseph Philip and Florence Veronica (Noykoff) Sharkey; m. Joel David Delpha, Sept. 24, 1977; children: Daniel Joseph, Madeleine Day. BA, John Carroll U., 1973. Tchr. St. Michael's Sch., St. Louis, 1976-79; acct. Citicorp Acceptance, St. Louis, 1986-89; fin. dir., adminstr. Women's Self Help Ctr., St. Louis, 1989—. Bd. dirs. Mo. Religious Coalition for Reproductive Choice, St. Louis, 1992—; co-chair St. Louis Caths. for a Free Choice, 1992—; treas. Shaw Neighborhood Improvement Assn., 1994—, Mo. Coalition Against Domestic Violence, 1995—. Democrat. Roman Catholic. Home: 4047 Magnolia Pl Saint Louis MO 63110-3914 Office: Women's Self Help Ctr Inc 2838 Olive St Saint Louis MO 63103-1428

SHARKEY, LEONARD ARTHUR, automobile company executive; b. Detroit, May 21, 1946; s. Percy and Lillian (Peros) S.; m. Irene Johnson, Aug. 9, 1969 (div. Nov. 1991); children: Michelle, Wesley Tucker (step-son). Cert. pvt. pilot. Tool and diemaker Ford Motor Co., Dearborn, Mich., 1965-85; indsl. hazardous substance educator Ford Motor co., Dearborn, Mich., 1985-86, indsl. health, safety and energy control educator, 1987-88, tool and diemaker leader, 1989—; non-fiction author Individual Initiative, Brighton, Mich., 1989—. Author: Journey Into Fear (reprinted title Split Decision, 1997), 1995, Hidden Shadows - An Opening to the Windows of the Mind, 1996. Mem. Nat. Geog. Soc., Livingston Players, Nat. Rifle Assn., Boat U.S., Drummond Island Sportsman's Club, Mich. United Conservation Clubs. Avocations: boating, shooting sports, political awareness studies, Biblical prophetic studies, theater.

SHARKEY, RICHARD DAVID, product designer, architect, musician; b. Columbus, Ohio, May 8, 1957; s. John David and Beatrice Diane (Ziesler) S.; m. Melissa Duke Smith, Dec. 21, 1980 (div. 1995); children: Flax Allistair Linden, Ambrosia Rose Ashley. Student, U. No. Colo., 1975-77, Emporia State U., 1977-78, U. Denver, 1978-81. Music tchr., pvt. studio, piano, cello, composition theory Evergreen, Colo., 1978-82; pvt. bus., period residential restoration Sharkey and Assocs., Evergreen and Denver, 1978-86; stair apprentice Denver Stair Co., 1985-86; stair master Heidelberg Stair Co., Evergreen, 1986; pvt. bus., designer period staircases, millwork O'Searcaigh, Ltd., Evergreen and Denver, 1986-90; with Archtl. Artworks, Englewood, Colo., 1993-95, Form & Structure Ltd., Denver, 1995-96; prin. Adobe Homes, Denver, 1996—; cons. archtl. product design and devel. Heidelberg Stair, Evergreen, Frank's Woodworking, Lyons, Colo., Pierce Segerberg & Spaeh Architects, Vail, Colo., Charles Cunnifree & Assoc., Apsen, Colo., numerous manufacturers, contractor, architecture, design firms, 1987—; cons. archtl. design period features. Composer numerous piano compositions, 1972—; designer, inventor numerous archtl. products, machines, tools and accessories. Recipient scholarship Outward Bound Colo., Optimist Club of Evergreen, 1973, music grant, U. No. Colo., Greeley, 1975-76, Emporia (Kans.) U., 1977; scholar U. No. Colo., 1976. Mem. Internat. Soc. Archtl. Artisans (pres., founder 1988—), Denver Cherry Creek Club (charter mem.), Rotary. Mem. Christian Science Ch. Avocations: art history, architecture history, collecting and designing of architectural products, musician, ballroom dancing. Home and Office: 3975 Zenobia St Denver CO 80212

SHARKEY, ROBERT EMMETT, lawyer; b. Chgo., Oct. 21, 1942; s. Edward Francis and Catherine Christine (Grundhoefer) S.; m. Phoebe Dadakis, July 28, 1963; children: Siobhan, Edward, Catherine, James. BA, Georgetown U., 1964, JD, 1967. Bar: Md. 1967, U.S. Dist. Ct. Md. 1967, U.S. Ct. Appeals (4th cir.) 1972, U.S. Ct. Appeals (2nd cir.) 1973, U.S. U.S. Supreme Ct. 1973, U.S. Ct. Appeals (fed. cir.) 1986, U.S. Ct. Fed. Claims 1986, D.C. 1995, U.S. Dist. Ct. D.C. 1996. Mem. staff subcom. fed., state, local rels. Commn. for Re-orgn. Exec. Branch Md. Govt., College Park, 1967; law clerk for Chief Judge Edward S. Northrop U.S. Dist. Ct. Md., Balt., 1967-68; assoc. Gordon, Feinblatt, Rothman, Hoffberger & Hollander, Balt., 1968-74, ptnr., 1974—. Mem. Md. State Bar Assn. (profl. ethics 1987—, vice chmn. com. profl. ethics 1991-93, chmn. com. profl. ethics 1993), Bar Assn. Balt. City (com. profl. ethics 1984-86), St. Thomas More Soc. Md. (pres. 1982-83), Georgetown U. Alumni Assn. (law alumni rep. 1992), Ice Club Balt. (v.p. 1981-83), Phi Delta Phi. Avocation: figure skating. Office: Gordon Feinblatt Rothman Hoffberger & Hollander 233 E Redwood St Baltimore MD 21202-3306

SHARKEY, THOMAS DAVID, educator, botanist; b. Detroit, Jan. 28, 1953; s. Robert Hugh and Patricia June (Elliot) S.; m. Paulette Marie Bochnig June 21, 1974; 1 child, Jessa Sung. BS in Biology, Mich. State U., 1974, PhD in Botany and Plant Pathology, 1980. Postdoctoral fellow Australian Nat. U., Canberra, 1980-82; assoc. rsch. prof. Desert Rsch. Inst., Reno, Nev., 1982-87; asst. prof. U. Wis., Madison, 1987-88, assoc. prof., 1988-91, prof., 1991—; assoc. dir. Biolog. Scis. Ctr., Reno, Nev., 1983-87; chmn. dept. botany U. Wis., Madison, 1992-94; dir. Biotron, U. Wis., Madison, 1993—. Editor: (book) Trace Gas Emissions from Plants, 1991; contbr. more than 80 articles to profl. peer-reviewed jours. Mem. AAAS, Am. Soc. Plant Physiologists, Internat. Photosynthesis Soc. Home: 5901 S Highlands Ave Madison WI 53705-1108 Office: Univ Wis Dept Botany 430 Lincoln Dr Madison WI 53706-1313

SHARKEY, VINCENT JOSEPH, lawyer; b. Newport, R.I., May 25, 1944; s. Vincent Joseph and Dorothy (Auvil) S.; m. Joyce Toomey, Dec. 27, 1969; children: Alison, Christina, John, Julia. BA in Econs., Yale U., 1966; JD, U. Va., 1971. Bar: N.J. 1971, U.S. Ct. Appeals (3d cir.) 1985. Asst. prosecutor Bergen County Prosecutor's Office, Hackensack, N.J., 1971-72; pvt. practice, Bergen County, 1972-75; ptnr. Riker, Danzig, Scherer, Hyland & Perretti, Morristown, N.J., 1975—. Lt. U.S. Army, 1966-68. Mem. ABA, N.J. Bar Assn., Bergen County Bar Assn., Yale U. Alumni Assn. (pres. Bergen County chpt. 1986-88). Office: Riker Danzig Scherer 1 Speedwell Ave Morristown NJ 07960-6838

SHARMA, ARJUN DUTTA, cardiologist; b. Bombay, June 2, 1953; came to U.S., 1981; s. Hari D. and Gudrun (Axelsson) S.; m. Carolyn D. Burleigh, May 9, 1981; children: Allira, Eric, Harisson. BSc, U. Waterloo, Ont., Can., 1972; MD, U. Toronto, Ont., 1976. Intern Toronto Gen. Hosp., 1976-77, resident in medicine, 1978-80; resident in medicine St. Michael's Hosp., Toronto, 1980-81; residency medicine Toronto Gen. Hosp., 1977-78; Rsch. assoc. Washington U., St. Louis, 1981-83; asst. prof. pharmacy and toxicology U. Western Ont., London, 1985-89, asst. prof. medicine, 1983-89, assoc. prof. medicine, 1989-90; dir. interventional electrophysiology Sutter Meml. Hosp., Sacramento, 1990-95; abstract reviewer, faculty of ann. sci. sessions N.Am. Soc. for Pacing and Electrophysiology, 1993-94; assoc. clin. prof. U. Calif., Davis, 1990—; cons. Medtronic Inc., Mpls., 1985—, Telectronics Pacing Sys., Inc., 1990-94; mem. rsch. com. Sutter Inst. Med. Rsch., 1991—; mem. exec. com. Sutter Heart Inst., 1992; program dir. Update in Tachyarhythmia Mgmt., Palm Springs, 1996, Pacing Defibrillation and Electrophysiology, Squaw Valley, 1997. Reviewer profl. jours., including Circulation, Am. Jour. Cardiology; contbr. articles to profl. publs. Mem. coun. for basic sci. Am. Heart Assn., chmn. ann. sci. session, 1989. Recipient John Melady award, 1972, Dr. C.S. Wainwright award, 1973-75, Rsch. prize Toronto Gen. Hosp., 1979, 80, Ont. Career Scientist award Ont. Ministry of Health, 1983-89; Med. Rsch. Coun. Can. fellow, 1981-83. Fellow ACP, Am. Coll. Cardiology; mem. Am. Fedn. Clin. Rsch., Canadian Cardiovasc. Soc., N.Y. Acad. Scis., Sacramento Eldorado Med. Soc. Avocations: skiing, tennis, philately. Office: 3941 J St Ste 260 Sacramento CA 95819-3633

SHARMA, BRAHAMA D., chemistry educator; b. Sampla, Punjab, India, June 5, 1931; naturalized Am. citizen; s. Des Raj and Kesara Devi (Pathak) S.; m. Millicent M. Hewitt, Dec. 22, 1956 (div. 1996); children: Nalanda V. Sharma Bowman, Renuka D. BS with honors, U. Delhi, India, 1949, MS, 1951; PhD, U. So. Calif., 1961. Chemist Govt. Opium Factory, Ghazipur, India, 1951-52; lab. assoc., sci. asst. Nat. Chem. Lab., Poona, India, 1952-55; lab. assoc. U. So. Calif., L.A., 1955-61; research fellow Calif. Inst. Tech., Pasadena, 1961-65; asst. prof. chemistry U. Nev., Reno, 1963-64, Oreg. State U., Corvallis, 1965-70; asst. prof. chemistry Calif. State U., Northridge, 1973-75, assoc. prof., 1975-76; prof. L.A. Pierce Coll., Woodland Hills, Calif., 1976-96; part-time assoc. prof. chemistry Calif. State U., L.A., 1973-85, prof., 1985—; vis. assoc. Calif. Inst. Tech., 1979, 82; pres. L.A. Pierce Coll. Senate, 1981-82, chmn. profl. and acad. stds., 1989-92. Contbr. articles to profl. jours. Grantee E.I. duPont de Nemours, L.A., 1961, NSF, 1967-69. Mem. Am. Chem. Soc. (chmn. edn. com. So. Calif. chpt. 1981-82, rsch. grantee 1965-69), Royal Soc. Chemistry (chartered chemist), Am. Inst. Parliamentarians (sec., adminstr., lt. gov. region VII, exec. lt. gov.), Nat. Assn. Parliamentarians, Calif. Assn. Parliamentarians (pub. rels. chmn., statewide edn. chmn. So. area, pres. Calif. Sigma unit). Avocations: playing bridge, reading, history, classical music, crystal models. Office: LA Pierce Coll Chem Dept Woodland Hills CA 91371

SHARMA, DHARMENDRA K., federal agency administrator , electrical engineer. BTech with honors, Indian Inst. Tech., Kharagpur; MEE, U. Windsor, Ont., Can.; M and PhD in Electric Power Engring., Rensselaer Poly. Inst. Registered profl. engr., Mass. With Heavy Elecs. Ltd., Bhopal, India, Gen. Electric Co., Calif., N.Y., Mass., EPRI, Palo Alto, Calif.; IEEE Congl. fellow U.S. Senate, 1992; tech. liaison with Congress and industry Electric power Rsch. Inst., Washington, 1993-94; adminstr. rsch. and spl. programs adminstrn. U.S. Dept. Transp., 1994—. Pres. bd. edn. Morgan Hill Unified Sch. Dist., 1984-85. Fellow IEEE; mem. various profl. engring. socs. Office: US Dept Transp Rsch & Spl Prog Adminstrn 400 7th St SW Washington DC 20590-0001

SHARMA, MARILYN I., economist; d. Leonard and Lily (Rampersad) Sagar; m. Ramesh Sharma, Mar. 16, 1971; children: Khushee, Shiva. BA, York U., 1978, MA, 1981; BEd, U. Toronto, 1986. Mem. Soc. Ont. Adjudicators & Regulars (edn. adv. com.). Home: 135 Pemberton Rd, Richmond Hill, ON Canada L4C 3T6

SHARMA, SANTOSH DEVRAJ, obstetrician, gynecologist, educator; b. Kenya, Feb. 24, 1934; came to U.S., Jan. 1972; d. Devraj Chananram and Lakshmi (Devi) S. BS, MB, B.J. Medical Sch., Pune, India, 1960. House surgeon Sasson Hosp., Poona, India, 1960-61; resident in ob-gyn. various hospitals, England, 1961-67; house officer Maelor Gen. Hosp., Wrexham, U.K., 1961-62; asst. prof. ob-gyn. Howard U. Med. Sch., Washington, 1972-74; assoc. prof. John A. Burns Sch. Med., Honolulu, 1974-78, prof., 1978 --. Fellow Royal Coll. Ob-Gyn., Am. Coll. Ob-Gyn. Avocations: travel, photography, environmental protection. Office: 1319 Punahou St Rm 824 Honolulu HI 96826-1032

SHARMA, SHIV KUMAR, geophysicist; b. India, July 2, 1946; came to U.S., 1977; m. Madhu Malaviya, Aug. 10, 1974; 2 children. BSc, Jiwaji U., 1968; MSc, Jiwaji (India) U., 1973; PhD, Indian Inst. Tech., Delhi, 1980. Rsch. fellow IIT, Delhi, India, 1969-74; rsch. assoc. U. Leicester, 1974-77; with Geophysics Lab., Washington, 1977-80; with Hawaii Inst. Geophysics & Planet U. Hawaii, 1980—. Contbr. over 150 rsch. papers to profl. jours; patentee in field. Carnegie Postdoctoral fellow; rsch. grantee. Fellow Nat. Acad. Sci.; mem. Am. Geophys. Union, Am. Ceramic Soc., Am. Electrochem. Sco., Mineral Soc. Am., Optical Soc. Am., Pacific Congress, Soc. for Applied Spectroscopy. Avocations: reading, writing, travel. Office: U Hawaii Sch Ocean & Earth Sci & Tech Hawaii Inst Geophys & Planet 2525 Correa Rd Honolulu HI 96822-2219

SHARMAN, RICHARD LEE, telecommunications executive, consultant; b. Warren, Pa., Oct. 23, 1932; s. Scott Albert Sr. and Viola Lena Marie (Kittner) S.; m. Diane Lee Van Patten, Nov. 3, 1973; children: Daria Lee, Deedra Lee; children by previous marriage, Suzanne Annette, Cynthia Lee. BS in Engring. Physics, U. Toledo, 1959; MS in Elec. Engring., Cornell U., 1961. Project engr. advanced electronics ctr. GE, Syracuse, N.Y., 1965-68, mgr. infrared and optics, electronics lab., 1965-68; mgr. info. networks, info. systems div. GE, Bethesda, Md., 1968-73; mgr. comml. analysis Xerox Corp., Rochester, N.Y., 1973-78; mgr. mktg. systems Xerox Corp., Rochester, 1978-80; v.p. bus. sector GTE Corp., Stamford, Conn., 1980-84; v.p. mktg. GTE Mobilnet Inc., Houston, 1984-87, gen. mgr. Tex. region, 1987-90; v.p. ops. GTE Mobilnet Inc. Hdqrs., Houston, 1990-92; pres., COO Guidry Group, Houston, 1992-93; pres., owner Mgmt. Consulting Svcs. Co., The Woodlands, Texas, 1993—; pres., founder Mgmt. Cons. Svcs., The Woodlands, Tex., 1993—; bd. dirs. Cellular Communications Corp., Irvine, Calif., 1985-87. Contbr. articles profl. jours. Bd. dirs. Houston unit ARC. With USCG, 1951-54. Mem. Am. Mktg. Assn. (exec. mem.), Houston C. of C. (mem. region mobility com.), Houston Grand Opera (patron 1990—), Tau Beta Pi, Forum Club (Houston), Cornell Alumni Assn. Republican. Episcopalian. Avocation: photography. Home and Office: 26 Fernglen Dr The Woodlands TX 77380-3968

SHARMAN, WILLIAM, professional basketball team executive; b. Abilene, Tex., May 25, 1926; m. Joyce Sharman; children by previous marriage: Jerry, Nancy, Janice, Tom. Student, U. So. Calif. Basketball player Washington Capitols, 1950-51, Boston Celtics, 1951-61; coach Los Angeles/Utah Stars, 1968-71; coach Los Angeles Lakers, 1971-76, gen. mgr., 1976-82, pres., 1982-88, spl. cons., 1991—. Author: Sharman on Basketball Shooting, 1965. Named to Nat. Basketball Assn. All Star First Team, 1956-59, 2d Team, 1953, 55, 60, All League Team, 7 times; named Coach of Year Nat. Basketball Assn., 1972, Naismith Basketball Hall of Fame, 1976. Home: 27996 Palos Verdes Dr E Rancho Palos Verdes CA 90275 Office: LA Lakers PO Box 10 3900 W Manchester Blvd Inglewood CA 90306

SHARON, NATHAN, biochemist; b. Brisk, Poland, Nov. 4, 1925; arrived in Israel, 1934; m. Rachel Itzikson, 1948; children: Esther, Osnat. MS, Hebrew U., Jerusalem, 1950, PhD, 1953; Dr. (hon.), U. Rene Descartes, Paris, 1990. Rsch. asst. Agrl. Rsch. Sta., Rehovot, Israel, 1949-53; rsch. asst. dept. biophysics Weizmann Inst. Sci., Rehovot, Israel, 1954-57, rsch. assoc. dept. biophysics, 1957-60, sr. scientist dept. biophysics, 1960-65, assoc. prof. dept. biophysics, 1965-68, prof. dept. biophysics, 1968—; vis. scientist numerous univs. and colls. Author: Complex Carbohydrates: Their Chemistry, Biosynthesis and Functions, 1975; co-editor: Biotechnological Applications of Proteins and Enzymes, 1977, The Lectins: Properties, Functions and Applications in Biology and Medicine, 1986; co-author: Lectins, 1989; contbr. over 400 articles to profl. jours. Recipient Laundau prize Mifal Hapyis, Israel, 1973, Weizmann prize in exact scis. City of Tel Aviv, 1977, Olitzki prize Israel Soc. Microbiology, 1989, Datta lectureship award Fedn. European Biochem. Socs., 1987, Bijvoet medal Utrecht U., 1989, Israel Prize in Biomedical and Medical Research, 1994. Mem. Am. Chem. Soc., Biochem. Soc. Eng., Am. Soc. Biol. Chemists (hon.), European Molecular Biology Orgn., Israel Acad. Scis. and Humanities, Internat. Sci. Writers Assn., Israel Biochem. Soc. (pres. 1969-70), Soc. for Complex Carbohydrates, Fedn. European Biochem. Socs. (chmn. 1980-81), Internat. Glycoconjugate Orgn. (pres. 1989-91). Avocation: swimming. Home: 77 Mishmeret, Afeka Tel Aviv 69012, Israel Office: Weizmann Inst Sci, Dept Membrane Rsch Biophysics, Rehovot 76100, Israel

SHARON, YITZHAK YAAKOV, physicist, educator; b. Tel Aviv, Feb. 29, 1936; came to U.S., 1948; s. Abraham Sharon-Schwadron and Dina Freidenberg; m. Sandra Brook, Jan. 13, 1991; 1 child, Dina Avrahama. AB with highest honors, Columbia U., 1958; MA in Physics, Princeton U., 1960, PhD in Physics, 1966. Asst. Inst. for Advanced Study, Princeton, N.J., 1965-66; asst. prof. Northeastern U., Boston, 1966-72; assoc. prof. Stockton State Coll., Pomona, N.J., 1972-75; prof. physics Richard Stockton Coll. N.J., Pomona, 1975—; cons. Ednl. Svcs., Inc. Phys. Sci. Study Commn., 1962-63; vis. prof. Temple U., Phila., 1970-71, U. Montreal, 1970; vis. fellow Princeton U., 1980-82, 91-92; summer physicist Nat. Bur. Standards, Washington, 1971, Oak Ridge (Tenn.) Nat. Lab., 1969, Lawrence Radiation Lab., Berkeley, Calif., 1968; visitor Rutgers U., 1995-96. Contbr. articles to profl. jours. Grantee NSF, N.J. Dept. Higher Edn. Mem. Am. Phys. Soc., Am. Assn. Physics Tchrs., Sigma Xi, Phi Beta Kappa. Jewish. Home: 19 James Ave Kendall Park NJ 08824-1620 Office: Richard Stockton Coll NJ Dept Physics Pomona NJ 08240

SHARP, AARON JOHN, botanist, educator; b. Plain City, Ohio, July 29, 1904; s. Prentice Daniel and Maude Katharine (Herriott) S.; m. Cora Evelyn Bunch, July 25, 1929; children: Rosa Elizabeth, Maude Katharine, Mary Martha (dec.), Fred Prentice, Jennie Lou. AB, Ohio Wesleyan U., 1927, DSc, 1952; MS, U. Okla., 1929; PhD, Ohio State U., 1938. Instr. botany U. Tenn., Knoxville, 1929-37, asst. prof., 1937-40, assoc. prof., 1940-46, prof., 1946-65, Disting. Service prof., 1965-74, prof. emeritus, 1974—, curator herbarium, 1949-68, assoc. curator herbarium, 1968-80, head dept. botany, 1951-61; assoc. editor The Bryologist, 1938-42, 45-53, acting editor, 1943-44; assoc. editor Castanea, 1947-66; trustee Highlands (N.C.) Biol. Lab., 1934-38, 48-64, bd. mgrs., 1946-52; Cecil Billington lectr. Cranbook Inst. Sci., 1947; sec. sect. Inter-Am. Conf. on Conservation of Renewable Natural Resources, Denver, 1948; vis. prof. Stanford U., 1951, U. Mich. Biol. Sta., 1954-57, 59-64, U. Minn. Biol. Sta., 1971, U. Mont. Biol. Sta., 1972, Nat. U. Taiwan, 1965, Instituto Universitario Pedagógico Experimental, Maracay, Venezuela, 1976, U. Va. Biol. Sta., 1980; mem. staff Hattori (Japan) Bot. Lab., 1956—; vis. lectr. Am. Inst. Biol. Scis., 1967-70; mem. nat. adv. bd. Ministry of Ecology, 1975-81; cons. Time-Life Books, 1975, Brit. Broadcasting Corp., 1984, Nat. Geog. Books, 1985; hon. curatorship in the Inst. of Systematic Botany of the N.Y. Bot. Garden, 1994; hon. life mem. Save-the-Redwoods League, 1995. Assoc. editor: Hattori Bot. Jour., Nichinan, Japan, 1961—; contbr. articles to sci. jours. and Ency. Britanica. Bd. dirs. Nature Conservancy, 1955-61, Gt. Smoky Mountains Nat. Hist. Assn., 1979-81. Decorated officer Order of Rising Sun (Japan); Guggenheim Found. fellow, 1944-46; recipient Merit award Tenn. Environ. Edn. Assn., 1991, Disting. Achievement award Ohio Wesleyan U., 1992, Eloise Payne Luquer medal Garden Club Am., 1983, Appreciation cert. Great Smoky Mountains Nat. Park, 1994. Fellow AAAS (v.p. 1963), Linnean Soc. London; mem. AAUP, New Eng. Bot. Club, Internat. Soc. Phytomorphologists, Internat. Assn. Plant Taxonomy, So. Appalachian Bot. Club (pres. 1946-47), Sullivant Moss Soc. (pres. 1935), Am. Bryol. and Lichen. Soc., Am. Fern Soc., Bot. Soc. Am. (editorial com. 1948-53, treas. 1957-62, v.p. 1963, pres. 1965, Merit award 1972), Soc. for Study Evolution, Soc. Botánica de México (hon.), Soc. Mexicana de Historia Natural, Tenn. Acad. Sci. (exec. com. 1943-44, v.p. 1952, pres. 1953), Am. Soc. Plant Taxonomists (pres. 1961), Assn. Southeastern Biologists (v.p. 1956, Meritorious Tchr. award 1972, Bartholomew award 1989), Ecol. Soc. Am. (v.p. 1958-59), Torrey Bot. Club, Nature Conservancy (gov. 1955-61), Am. Soc. Naturalists, Bot. Brit. Bryol. Soc., Internat. Soc. Tropical Ecology, Internat. Phycolog. Soc., Nat. Assn. Biology Tchrs., Palynolog. Soc. India, Phycolog. Soc. Am., Systematics Assn., Am. Assn. Stratigraphic Palynol., Soc. Latino-Americano de Briologia (hon.), Tenn. Nat. Plant Soc. (hon.), Gt. Smoky Mountains Conservation Assn., (bd. dirs. 1960—), U. Tenn. Arboretum Soc. (bd. dirs. 1979—), Explorers Club, Phi Beta Kappa, Phi Kappa Phi, Sigma Xi, Phi Sigma, Phi Epsilon Phi, Sigma Delta Pi. Home: 1105 Tobler Rd Knoxville TN 37919-8164 Office: U Tenn Dept Botany Knoxville TN 37996 *The Universe is so constructed that for every error committed someone must pay a penalty now or in the future.*

SHARP, ALLEN, chief federal judge; b. Washington, D.C., Feb. 11, 1932; s. Robert Lee and Frances Louise (Williams) S.; children: Crystal Catholyn, Scarlet Frances. Student, Ind. State U., 1950-53; AB, George Washington U., 1954; JD, Ind. U., 1957; MA, Butler U., 1986. Bar: Ind. 1957. Practiced in Williamsport, 1957-68; judge Ct. of Appeals Ind., 1969-73; judge U.S. Dist. Ct. (no. dist.) Ind., South Bend, 1973—, now chief judge. Bd. advisers Milligan (Tenn.) Coll. Served to JAG USAFR. Mem. Ind. Judges Assn., Blue Key, Phi Delta Kappa, Pi Gamma Mu, Tau Kappa Alpha. Republican. Mem. Christian Ch. Club: Mason. Office: US Dist Ct 124 Fed Bldg 204 S Main St South Bend IN 46601-2122*

SHARP, ANNE CATHERINE, artist, educator; b. Red Bank, N.J., Nov. 1, 1943; d. Elmer Eugene and Ethel Violet (Hunter) S. BFA, Pratt Inst., 1965; MFA (teaching fellow 1972), Bklyn. Coll., 1973. tchr. art Sch. Visual Arts, 1978-89, NYU, 1978, SUNY, Purchase, 1983, Pratt Manhattan Ctr., N.Y.C., 1982-84, Parsons Sch. Design, N.Y.C., 1984-90, Visual Arts Ctr. of Alaska, Anchorage, 1991, Anchorage Mus. Hist. and Art, 1991, 93, 94, 95, U. Alaska, Anchorage, 1994-96, Fashion Inst. Tech., SUNY, 1997—; lectr. AAAS, The 46th Arctic Divsn. Sci. Conf., U. Alaska, Fairbanks, 1995. One-person shows Pace Editions, N.Y.C., Ten/Downtown, N.Y.C., Katonah (N.Y.) Gallery, 1974, Contemporary Gallery, Dallas, 1975, Art in a Public Space, N.Y.C., 1979, Eatontown Hist. Mus., N.J., 1980, N.Y. Pub. Library Epiphany Br., 1988, Books and Co., N.Y., 1989, The Kendall Gallery, N.Y.C., 1990, Alaska Pacific U., Carr-Gottstein Gallery, Anchorage, 1993, Internat. Gallery Contemporary Art, Anchorage, 1993, Art Think Tank Gallery, N.Y.C., 1994, U.S. Geol. Survey, Reston, Va., 1994, Stonington Gallery, Anchorage, 1994; group shows include Arnot Art Mus., Elmira, N.Y., 1975, Bronx Mus., 1975, Mus. Modern Art, N.Y.C., 1975-76, Nat. Arts Club, N.Y.C., 1979, Calif. Mus. Photography, Riverside, 1983-92, Jack Tilton Gallery, N.Y.C., 1983, Lincoln Ctr., N.Y.C., 1983, Cabo Frio Print Biennale, Brazil, 1983, Pratt Graphic Ctr., N.Y.C., 1984, State Mus. N.Y., Albany, 1984, Kenkeleba Gallery, N.Y.C., 1985, Hempstead Harbor Art Assn., Glen Cove, N.Y., 1985, Mus. Mod. Art, Weddel, Fed. Republic of Germany, 1985, Kenkeleba Gallery, N.Y.C., 1985, Paper Art Exhbn. Internat. Mus. Contemporary Art, Bahia, Brazil, 1986, Mus. Salon-de-Provence, France, 1987, Mus. Contemporary Art, Sao Paulo, Brazil, 1985-86, Salon de Provence, France, 1987, Adirondack Lakes Ctr. for Arts, Blue Mountain Lake, N.Y., 1987, Kendall Gallery, N.Y.C., 1988, Exhibition Ctr. Parsons Sch. Design, N.Y.C., 1989, F.M.K. Gallery, Budapest, Hungary, 1989, Galerie des Kulturbundes Schwarzenberg, German Dem. Republic, Q Sen Do Gallery, Kobe, Japan, 1989, Anchorage Mus. History and Art, 1990-91, 94, U. Alaska, Anchorage, 1990, 91, Coos Art Mus., Coos Bay, Oreg., 1990, Spaceship Earth, Mus. Internat. de Neu Art, Vancouver, Can., 1990, Councourse Gallery, Emily Carr Coll. Art and Design, 1990, Nat. Mus. Women in the Arts, Washington, 1991, Visual Arts Ctr. Alaska, 1991, 92, Nomad Mus., Lisbon, Portugal, 1991, Mus. Ostdeutsche Gallery, Regensberg, Germany, 1991, Mcpl. Mus. Cesley Krumlov (So. Bohemia) CSFK, Czechoslovakia, 1991, Böltmiche Dörter Exhbn. Hochstrass 8, Munich, 1992, BBC-TV, Great Britain, U.K., Sta. WXXI-TV, Rochester, N.Y., 1992-93, Site 250 Gallery Contemporary Art., Fairbanks, 1993, Santa Barbara (Calif.) Mus. Art, 1993, The Rochester (N.Y.) Mus. and Sci. Ctr., 1990-94, Space Arc: The Archives of Mankind, Time Capsule in Earth Orbit, Hughes Comm., Divec TV Satellite Launch, 1994, Stonington Gallery, Anchorage, 1994, 95, UAA Art Galley U. Alaska, 1995, Arctic Trading Post, Nome, Alaska, 1995, Lawrenceville (N.J.) Sch., 1996; represented in permanent collections Smithsonian Instn., Nat. Air and Space Mus., Washington, Albright Knox Gallery, Buffalo, St. Vincent's Hosp, N.Y.C., N.Y. Pub. Libr., N.Y.C., U.S. Geol. Survey, Reston, Va., White House (Reagan, Bush adminstrns.), Site 250 Gallery Contemporary Art, Anchorage Mus. History and Art, others; Moon Shot series to commemorate moon landing, 1970-76, Cloud Structures of the Universe Painting series, 1980-86, Am. Landscape series, 1987-89, Thoughtlines, fall 1986, Swimming in the Mainstream with Her, U. Va., Charlottesville; author: Artist's Book - Travel Dreams U.S.A., 1989, Artworld-Welt Der Kunst, Synchronicity, 1989—, Art Think Tank: Projects in Art and Ecology, 1990—, The Alaska Series, 1990—, Potraits in the Wilderness, 1990—; columnist: Anchorage Press, 1995—. Sponsor Iditorod Trail Com., Libby Riddles. Artist-in-residence grantee Va. Center for Creative Arts, 1974, Artpark, Lewiston, N.Y., 1980, Vt. Studio Colony, 1989; recipient Pippin award Our Town, N.Y.C., 1984, certificate of Appreciation Art in Embassy program U.S. Dept. State, 1996. Mem. Nat. Space Soc., Nat. Mus. Women in Arts, Alaska Photography Ctr., Pratt Inst. Alumni Assn., The Planetary Soc., Internat. Assn. Near-Death Studies, Art and Sci. Collaborations, The Internat. Gallery of Contemporary Art. Address: Murray Hill Station PO Box 1776 Murray Hill Sta New York NY 10156-1776 Gallery: Decker Morrys Gallery 621 W 6th Ave Anchorage AK 99501 also: Fine Art Gallery Site 250 Custaman St Ste 2A Fairbanks AK 99701 *As an active painter I explore the mysteries of the 20th century space adventure in my American landscapes, painted directly from nature and in planetary landscapes, fantastic pictures of the cosmos. I believe it is in the reconciliation between inner and outer experience, through a personal sense of humor and use of universal symbols that a mystical or cosmic harmony can be expressed in art.*

SHARP, BERT LAVON, retired education educator, retired university dean; b. Philadelphia, Miss., Nov. 4, 1926; s. Bert L. and Louie (McBeath) S.; m. Mary Warren, Dec. 24, 1948; children—Kenneth, Richard. B.S., Miss. Coll., Clinton, 1949; M.Ed., U. Fla., Gainesville, 1953, D.Ed., 1960. Tchr., dir. guidance Miss. and Fla., 1945-55; dir. ednl. research Pinellas County, Fla., 1955-56; dir. secondary curriculum and ednl. services, 1958-61; assoc. prof., chmn. counselor edn. Auburn (Ala.) U., 1961-63; mem. faculty U. Fla., Gainesville, 1956-58, prof. edn., 1963-85, prof. emeritus, 1985—, dean Coll. Edn., 1968-78, dean emeritus, 1978—; cons. in field. Contbr. articles to profl. jours. Mem. Am. Assn. Colls. Tchr. Edn. (dir. 1973-76, exec. com. 1974-76, 78-81, pres. 1979), Assn. Colls. Schs. Edn. in State Univs. and Land-Grant Colls (pres. 1976), Am. Personnel and Guidance Assn., Am. Assn. Counselor Edn. and Supervision, Fla. Council Deans, Am. Sch. Counselor Assn., Assn. Deans Edn. Land Grant Coll. and State Univs., Fla. Council Tchrs. Edn., Am. Assn. Sch. Adminstrs., Gov. Fla. Council Tchr. Edn. Centers, Internat. Council for Edn. of Tchrs. (bd. dirs. 1980—), Phi Kappa Phi, Phi Delta Kappa, Alpha Kappa Delta. Home: 500 Elmington Ave Nashville TN 37205-2513

SHARP, DANIEL ASHER, foundation executive; b. San Francisco, Mar. 29, 1932; s. Joseph C. and Miriam (Asher) S.; m. Jacqueline Borda, 1967 (div. 1975); 1 son, Benjamin Daniel; m. Revelle Pergament Allen, 1989. B.A., U. Calif.-Berkeley, 1954; J.D., Harvard U., 1959. Bar: Calif. 1959. Dep. atty. gen. State of Calif., San Francisco, 1959-61; with U.S. Peace Corps, 1961-68; asst. dir. internat. programs U.S. Peace Corps, Washington, 1961-62; assoc. dir. U.S. Peace Corps, Cuzco, Peru, 1962-64; acting dir. Peace Corps, La Paz, Bolivia, 1964; creator, dir. Staff Tng. Ctr. Peace Corps, Washington, 1965-68; dir. div. edn. resources U.S. Peace Corps, 1966;, 1988—; dir. edn. and Latin Am. programs, asst. dir. Adlai Stevenson Inst. Internat. Affairs, U. Chgo., 1968-70; dir. tng. ITT, Latin Am., 1970-72; mgr. mgmt. devel. ITT World Hdqrs., N.Y.C., 1973; with Xerox Corp., 1973-88; dir. human resources devel. Xerox Corp. (Xerox LatinAm. group), 1973-75, chmn. overhead value analysis task force, 1975-76; dir. ops. support Xerox Corp. (Xerox Latinam. group), 1976, dir. Inter-Am. affairs, 1977-79; dir. internat. affairs Xerox Corp. Hdqrs., 1979-85, dir. internat. and pub. affairs, 1985-87, internat. cons., 1988-93, sr. internat. advisor InterMatrix Group, 1990—; pres. Am. Assembly Columbia U., 1987—; adj. prof. internat. and pub. affairs Columbia U., 1991—; faculty Aspen Inst., 1995—; cons. U.S. Dept. State, fgn. govts., corps., founds.; mem. U.S. del. to UN Econ. and Social Coun., Geneva, 1961; mem. U.S. del. to OAS, San Juan, 1986; negotiated 6 treaties U.S. Govt.; U.S. rep. Internat. Conf. on Vol. Programs, The Hague, Netherlands, 1961; mem. outside bd. adv. coun. Macmillan Ltd. (U.K.), 1982; rep. U.S. bus. cmty. nat. task force on Europe Bus. and Industry Adv. Com., regional trade blocs, Paris, 1989. Editor: United States Foreign Policy and Peru, 1972, Los Estados Unidos y La Revolucion Peruaña, 1972, U.S. editor European Business Journal, 1988-95; contbr. articles to N.Y. Times, Wall St. Jour., Internat. Herald Tribune, and chapters in several books. Chmn. adv. bd. Coun. of Ams., 1978-85; bd. dirs. Overseas Devel. Coun., 1980-96, Internat. Ctr. of N.Y., 1980-88, Fund for Multinat. Mgmt. Edn., 1979-85, Accion, 1980-88, World Press Inst., 1986-89, Forum for World Affairs, 1987-95, Stamford Symphony, 1987-91; bd. advs. Landegger Program in Internat. Bus. Diplomacy, Sch. Fgn. Svc., Georgetown U., 1981-92, Econ. Growth Ctr., Yale U., 1987, Consortium on Competitiveness and Coop., U. Calif., 1987-90, Fletcher Sch. Law and Diplomacy, 1984-89; bd. visitors Duke U. Inst. of Policy Scis. and Pub. Affairs, 1988-91; mem. U.S./Mex. Bus. Coun., 1981-87. Served with U.S. Army, 1954-55; capt. Res. Recipient Medalla de Oro y Diploma de Honor del Consejo Provincial del Cuzco, 1963, Manchester Leadership award, 1992; Woodrow Wilson fellow Princeton, N.J., 1981-85. Mem. State Bar Calif., Coun. on Fgn. Rels., Century Assn., Mid-Atlantic Club (bd. dirs.). Home: 94 Campbell Dr Stamford CT 06903-4032 Office: Am Assembly Columbia U 475 Riverside Dr Ste 456 New York NY 10115-0499 *Changing careers frequently keeps life exciting, as one must constantly learn new roles and ideas and organizations. Public service and the not-for-profit sector are ultimately more satisfying, but the management skills learned in the private sector are practically indispensable.*

SHARP, DONALD EUGENE, bank consultant; b. Chgo., Nov. 4, 1929; s. Arthur Eugene and Alma (Melchior) S.; m. Phyllis Stevens, Sept. 11, 1954; 1 child, John Stevens. BA in Polit. Sci., Denison U., 1952; MA in History, Columbia U., 1959. Cert. econ. developer. With Chem. Bank, 1962-86, v.p. regular credit com., 1976-86; v.p. N.Y. Job Devel. Authority, 1986-91; lending cons. Community Mutual Savings Bank, 1992-96, The Merchants Bank of N.Y., 1996—. Contbr. articles to profl. jours. Trustee Village of Bronxville, N.Y., 1989-91. Sgt. U.S. Army, 1952-54, Korea. Mem. Am. Econ. Devel. Coun., Northeastern Indsl. Devel. Assn., Acad. Polit. Sci., Shenorock Shore Club, Skytop Club, Rotary. Democrat. Episcopalian. Home: 66 Avon Rd Bronxville NY 10708-1721

SHARP, DOUGLAS ANDREW, secondary school educator; b. Austin, Tex., July 19, 1945; s. Jack Weston and Jean Ernestine (Beeman) S.; m. Marylin Gene Martin, Jan. 20, 1977. BA in Math., Tex. A&M U., 1967, MS in Math., 1970, postgrad., 1969-71; EdD, La Salle U., Mandville, La., 1993. Teaching fellow dept. math. Tex. A&M U., College Station, 1967-71; chmn. math. dept., asst. coach/coach athletics dept. Southfield Sch., Shreveport, La., 1972-73; coach athletics dept. St. John's Sch., Houston, 1975, chmn. math. dept., 1981-93, master teaching chair math., 1987-89; disting. vis. lectr. U. Houston, 1989-90, adj. prof., 1990. Contbr. articles to profl. jours. Recipient Excellence in Teaching award Fin. Dept. U. Houston, 1993, Outstanding Tchr. award Tandy Technol. Scholars, 1993-94. Mem. Am. Math. Soc., Am. Soc. Composer, Authors and Pubs., Am. Statistical Assn., Math. Assn. Am. (Edyth May Sliffe award 1991), Calculus and Elem. Analysis Tchrs. Houston, Nat. Coun. Tchrs. Math., Cum Laude Soc. Office: St John's Sch 2401 Claremont St Houston TX 77019-5811

SHARP, ELAINE CECILE, obstetrician, gynecologist; b. Hoven, S.D., Feb. 19, 1952; d. Lewis Ralph and Bernadette Teresa (Bastien) Arbach; m. Walton H. Sharp, Oct. 26, 1979 (div.); m. Shane Daigle, Nov. 1991; 1 child, Sean Patrick Daigle. BA, No. State U., 1974, BS, 1976; MD, U. Tex., Houston, 1985. Diplomate Am. Bd. Ob-Gyn. Pvt. practice Pensacola, Fla., 1989—; speaker, chmn. Body Talk, Milton, Fla., 1989—. Mem. Am. Med. Womens' Assn., Am. Diabetes Assn., Am. Bus. Womens' Assn., Am. Coll. Ob-Gyn, Soc. Laparoendoscopic Surgeons, Fla. Ob-Gyn Soc., Exec. Club (asst. chmn. cancer com.). Republic. Roman Catholic. Avocations: biking, running, swimming, boating, racquetball. Office: PO Box 17062 Pensacola FL 32522-7062 also: Elaine Sharp MD PA 1717 N E St # 436 Pensacola FL 32501-6339

SHARP, GEORGE KENDALL, federal judge; b. Chgo., Dec. 30, 1934; s. Edward S. and Florence S.; m. Mary Bray; children: Florence Kendall, Julia Manger. BA, Yale U., 1957; JD, U. Va., 1963. Bar: Fla. 1963. Atty. Sharp, Johnston & Brown, Vero Beach, Fla., 1963-78; pub. defender 19th Cir. Ct., Vero Beach, 1964-68; sch. bd. atty. Indian River County, Fla., 1968-78; Fla. circuit judge 19th Cir., 1978-83; judge U.S. Dist. Ct. (mid. dist.) Fla., Orlando, 1983—. Office: US Dist Ct 635 US Courthouse 80 N Hughey Ave Orlando FL 32801-2231*

SHARP, GLENN (SKIP SHARP), technical education administrator; b. Stroud, Okla., Nov. 19, 1938; s. Charles W. and Adeline M. Sharp; m. Sherry Caroline Waddle, Aug. 29, 1959; children: Stephanie, Patricia, Nancy, Christopher. BS, Emporia State U., 1960, MS, 1966. Bus. educator Windthorst High Sch., Spearville, Kans., 1960-64; Bus. educator Northwest Kans. Tech. Coll., Goodland, 1964-66, asst. dir., 1966—. Commr. Goodland City Commn., 1986-87; mem. State Scholar Com., Topeka, 1984-85; county chmn. Am. Cancer Soc., Sherman County, Kans., 1981-82; bloodmobile chmn. ARC, Sherman County, 1978-80; cubmaster Boy Scouts Am., Goodland, 1976— (Silver Beaver award 1992, Award of Merit 1989, James E. West Fellowship 1995); bd. dirs. Goodland Regional Med. Ctr., 1993—. Recipient Outstanding Svc. award Kans. Jaycees, 1972, Silver Beaver award Boy Scouts Am., 1992, Award of Merit, 1989, named Eagle Scout, 1952, Employee of Yr. Goodland C. of C., 1988. Mem. Nat. Assn. Fin. Aid (bd. dirs. 1988-91), Am. Vocat. Assn. (life, Nat. Leadership award 1995), Rocky Mountain Assn. Fin. Aid (pres., bd. dirs. 1985-91, Disting. Svc. awards 1985, 87, Hall of Fame 1992), Kans. Vocat. Assn. (life), Kans. Assn. Fin. Adminstrs. (pres., bd. dirs. 1983-93, Outstanding Svc. award 1986, Hall of Fame 1996, Meritorious Achievement award 1995, 30 Yr. award 1997), Kiwanis (pres. 1968-69, 92-93, Outstanding Kiwanian 1968, 94, 95), Phi Delta Kappa (life, pres. 1983-84, Outstanding Educator 1985-86, Svc. Key 1991). Democrat. Christian. Avocations: camping, collecting, travel. Home: 702 Walnut St Goodland KS 67735-2048

SHARP, J(AMES) FRANKLIN, finance educator, academic administrator; b. Johnson County, Ill., Sept. 29, 1938; s. James Albert and Edna Mae (Slack) S. B.S. in Indsl. Engring., U. Ill., 1960; M.S., Purdue U., 1962, Ph.D., 1966, cert. mgmt. acctg., 1979. Chartered fin. analyst, 1980; cert. in fin. mgmt. Asst. prof. enging., econs. Rutgers U., New Brunswick, N.J., 1966-70; assoc. prof. NYU Grad. Sch. Bus., N.Y.C., 1970-74; supr. bus. research AT&T, N.Y.C., 1974-77, dist. mgr. corp. planning, 1977-81, dist. mgr. fin. mgmt. and planning, 1981-85; prof. fin. Grad. Sch. Bus. Pace U., N.Y.C., 1975-91; chmn. Sharp CFA Rev. & Inst. for Investment Edn., 1987-96, Sharp Seminars, 1996—; speaker, moderator meetings, 1965—; cons. Sharp Investment Mgmt., 1967—. Contbr. numerous articles to profl. publs.; corr.: Interfaces, 1975-78; fin. editor: Planning Rev., 1975-78. Mem. N.Am. Soc. Corp. Planning (treas. 1976-77, bd. dirs. at large 1977-78), Inst. Mgmt. Sci. (chpt. v.p. acad. 1972-74, chpt. v.p. program 1974-75, chpt. v.p. membership 1975-76, chpt. pres. 1976-77), Internat. Affiliation Planning Socs. (coun. 1978-84), N.Y. Soc. Security Analysts (CFA Rev. 1985-87), Ops. Rsch. Soc. Am. (pres. corp. planning group 1976-82), AAUP (v.p. Pace U. chpt. 1980-83), Theta Xi. Republican. Office: 315 E 86th St # 7H New York NY 10028-4714

SHARP, JOHN LEWIS, oil industry executive, geologist; b. Warren, Ark., Nov. 1, 1959; s. Billy Ray and Jerry Lynn (Lewis) S.; m. Kyoung Sun Kim, June 20, 1981; 1 child, Alex Lewis. BS in Geology with high hons., U. Ark., Fayetteville, 1981, MS in Geology, 1983. Exploration geologist Marathon Oil Co., Houston, 1983-88; ops. geologist Marathon Petroleum Korea, Ltd., Houston, 1988-90; sr. geologist ArkLa Exploration Co., Houston, 1990-93; geol. cons. Houston, 1993; exploration mgr. Transfuel Resources, Inc., Houston, 1993-94, v.p. exploration, 1994-95; co-owner Praxis resources LLC, Houston, 1996-97; project geologist Exxon Oil and Gas Co., Corpus Christi, Tex., 1997—. Mem. Am. Assn. Petroleum Geologists (cert. petroleum geologist), Houston Geolog. Soc. Republican. Avocation: golf. Office: Exxon Oil and Gas 539 N Carancahua St Ste 800 Corpus Christi TX 78401-2401

SHARP, M. RUST, lawyer; b. 1941. Student, Hotchkiss Sch.; AB, U. N.C., 1962; postgrad., U.S. Naval Justice Sch., 1963; JD, Temple U., 1968. Bar: Pa. 1968, U.S. Patent and Trademark Office. Counsel Pepper, Hamilton & Scheetz, Phila.; lectr. Temple U., 1990-92. Mem. staff, editor Temple Law Quar., 1967-68. Office: Pepper Hamilton & Scheetz LLP 1 Commerce Sq 1235 Westlakes Dr Ste 400 Philadelphia PA 19312-2401

SHARP, MARSHA, basketball coach. Bachelor's, Wayland Bapt. U., 1974; Master's, West Tex. State U., 1976. Grad. asst. basketball coach The Flying Queens Wayland Bapt. U., 1974-75; asst. basketball coach Lockney U., 1976-82; head coach Lady Raiders basketball Tex. Tech. U., Lubbock, 1982—. Led Lady Raiders basketball to NCAA Championship, 1993, 5 S.W. Conf. titles, 3 post-season crowns; named Nat. Coach of Yr. Women's Basketball News Svc., Ohio Touchdown Club, 1993, Nat. Coach of Yr. Women's Basketball Coaches Assn., 1994. Office: Tex Tech Box 43021 Lubbock TX 79409

SHARP, MITCHELL WILLIAM, advisor to prime minister; b. Winnipeg, Man., Can., May 11, 1911; s. Thomas and Elizabeth (Little) S.; m. Daisy Boyd, Apr. 23, 1938 (dec.); 1 son, Noel; m. Jeannette Dugal, Apr. 14, 1976. B.A., U. Man., 1934, LL.D. (hon.), 1965; postgrad., London Sch. Econs., 1937-38; hon. Dr. Social Sci., U. Ottawa, 1970; LLD (hon.), U. Western Ont., 1977, Carleton U., 1994, McMaster U., 1995. Statistician Sanford Evans Statis. Service, 1926-36; economist James Richardson & Sons, Ltd., 1936-42; officer Canadian Dept. Fin., Ottawa, 1942-51; dir. econ. policy div. Canadian Dept. Fin., 1947-51; assoc. dep. minister Canadian Dept. Trade and Commerce, 1951-57, dep. minister, 1957-58; v.p. Brazilian Traction, Toronto, Can., 1958-62; mem. Can. Ho. of Commons, from 1963; minister trade and commerce, 1963-65, minister fin., 1965-68, sec. state external affairs, 1968-74, pres. Privy Council, house leader, 1974-76, resigned, 1978; commr. No. Pipeline Agy., 1978-88. Decorated officer Order of Can. Address: 33 Monkland Ave, Ottawa, ON Canada K1S 1Y8

SHARP, PAUL DAVID, institute administrator; b. Youngstown, Ohio, Nov. 3, 1940; s. Robert Henderson and Kathryn (Tadsen)S.; m. Carole G. Graff, Sept. 16, 1967; children: David Allen, Kathryn Sharp Snyder. BA cum laude, Kenyon Coll., Gambier, Ohio, 1962; MPA, Auburn U., 1974. Commd. 2d lt. USAF, 1962, advanced through grades to col., 1983, intelligence officer, 1962-80; comdr. Detachment 1, 7450th Intelligence Squadron USAF, Neubruecke, Germany, 1980-83; comdr. 480th Reconnaissance Tech. Group USAF, Langley AFB, Va., 1983-85, dir. intelligence systems HQ Tactical Air Command, 1985-86, dep. chief intelligence Tactical Air Command, 1986-88; mgr. operational intelligence group Battelle Meml. Inst., Columbus, Ohio, 1988-89, mgr. fgn. tech. assessment group, 1989-91, mgr. intelligence projects/programs, 1991-92, v.p. bus. devel. fgn. sci. and tech., 1992-95; dir. fgn. sci. and tech. programs Batelle Meml. Inst., Columbus, Ohio, 1995—; mem. student career coun. Kenyon Coll., Columbus, 1992—. Trustee Brandywine Assn., Yorktown, Va., 1987, Chase Assn., Powell, Ohio, 1991. Decorated Legion of Merit, Meritorious Svc. medals. Mem. Nat. Mil. Intelligence Assn., Armed Forces Communications and Electronics Assn., Air Force Assn., Retired Officers Assn., Sigma Pi (pres. Lambda chpt. 1961-62). Republican. Episcopalian. Avocations: golf, woodworking, photography, music. Office: Battelle Meml Inst 505 King Ave Columbus OH 43201-2696

SHARP, PAUL FREDERICK, former university president, educational consultant; b. Kirksville, Mo., Jan. 19, 1918; s. Frederick J. and L. Blanche (Phares) S.; m. Rosella Ann Anderson, June 19, 1939; children: William, Kathryn, Paul Trevor. AB, Phillips U., 1939; PhD, U. Minn., 1947; LLD (hon.), Tex. Christian U., 1961, Austin Coll., 1978, Drake U., 1980; LHD (hon.), Buena Vista Coll., 1967, U. Nev., Towson State U., 1980, Oklahoma City U., 1996, U. Okla., 1997; LittD (hon.), Limestone Coll., 1971; HHD, Okla. Christian U. Sci. & Arts, 1992. Instr. U. Minn., 1942, 46-47, vis. lectr., 1948; asso. prof. Am. history Iowa State U., 1947-54; prof. Am. history, chmn. Am. Instns. program U. Wis., 1954-57, vis. lectr., 1953; vis. lectr. San Francisco State Coll., 1950, U. Oreg., 1955; Fulbright lectr. Am. Instns., univs. Melbourne, Sydney, 1952; pres. Hiram Coll., 1957-64; chancellor U. N.C., Chapel Hill, 1964-66; pres. Drake U., Des Moines, 1966-71; pres. U. Okla., Norman, 1971-78, pres. emeritus, Regents' prof., 1978-88, pres. emeritus, Regents' prof. emeritus, 1988—; disting. prof. history U. Sci. and Arts, Okla., 1990—; dir. Am. Coun. on Edn. Insts. for Coll. and Univ. Presidents, 1977-79; vis. lectr. Harvard U. Bus. Sch. summer session, 1970-72. Author: Agrarian Revolt in Western Canada, 1948, Old Orchard Farm, Story of an Iowa Boyhood, 1952, Whoop-Up Country, Canadian American West, 1955; cons. author: Heritage of Midwest, 1958; editor: Documents of Freedom, 1957; contbr. articles to profl. jours. Pres. Norman Cmty. Found., 1995—. USN liaison officer His Majesty's Australian Ship, Hobart, 1943-46. Recipient Iowa State U. Alumni Fund award, 1952, award of merit Am. Assn. State and Local History, 1955, Silver Spur award Western Writers Am., 1955, Fulbright award to Australia, 1952; named to Okla. Higher Edn. Hall of Fame, 1995; Minn. Hist. Soc. grantee, 1947, 48, Social Sci. Rsch. Coun. grantee, 1949, 51; Ford Faculty fellow, 1954, Guggenheim fellow, 1957. Mem. Phi Beta Kappa, Phi Kappa Phi, Phi Delta Kappa, Pi Gamma Mu, Phi Alpha Theta. Mem. Disciples of Christ Ch. Home: 701 Mockingbird Ln Norman OK 73071-4829 Office: U Okla 630 Parrington Oval Rm 105 Norman OK 73019-4032

SHARP, PHILLIP ALLEN, academic administrator, biologist, educator; b. Ky., June 6, 1944; s. Joseph Walter and Katherin (Colvin) S.; m. Ann Christine Holcombe, Aug. 29, 1964; children: Christine Alynn, Sarah Katherin, Helena Holcombe. BA, Union Coll., Barbourville, Ky., 1966, LHD (hon.), 1991; PhD, U. Ill., 1969; DSc (hon.), U. Ky., 1994, Bowdoin Coll., 1995, U. Tel Aviv, Israel, 1996, Albright Coll., 1996. NIH postdoctoral fellow Calif. Inst. Tech., 1969-71; sr. research investigator Cold Spring Harbor (N.Y.) Lab., 1972-74; assoc. prof. MIT, Cambridge, 1974-79, prof. biology, 1979—, head dept. biology, 1991—, dir. Ctr. Cancer Rsch., 1985-91; co-founder, mem. sci. bd., dir. BIOGEN, 1978—; chmn. sci. bd., 1987—; mem. Pres.' Adv. Coun. on Sci. and Tech., 1991—; mem. bd. trustees Alfred P. Sloan Found., 1995—; mem. presdl. appt. Nat. Cancer Adv. Bd., NIH, 1996—; chmn. GM Cancer Rsch. Found. Awards Assembly, 1994—; pres. com. of advisors on sci. and tech. Mem. editl. bd. Cell, 1974-95, Jour. Virology, 1974-86, Molecular and Cellular Biology, 1974-85. Co-recipient Nobel Prize in Physiology or Medicine, 1993; recipient awards Am. Cancer Soc., 1974-79, awards Eli Lilly, 1980, awards Nat Acad. Sci./U.S. Steel Found., 1980, Howard Ricketts award U. Chgo., 1985, Alfred P. Sloan Jr. prize Gen. Motors Research Found., 1986, award Gairdner Found. Internat., 1986, award N.Y. Acad. Scis., 1986, Louisa Horwitz prize, 1988, Albert Lasker Basic Med. Rsch. award, 1988, Dickson prize U. Pitts., 1990; awarded Class of '41 chair, 1986-87, John D. MacArthur chair, 1987-92, Salvador E. Luria chair, 1992—. Fellow AAAS; mem. Am. Chem. Soc., Am. Soc. Microbiology, NAS (councilor 1986), Am. Acad. Arts and Scis, European Molecular Biology Orgn. (assoc.), Am. Soc. Biochemistry and Molecular Biology (elected mem. coun.), Am. Philos. Soc. (elected mem.), Inst. of Medicine of NAS (elected mem.). Home: 36 Fairmont Ave Newton MA 02158-2506 Office: MIT Ctr for Cancer Rsch 40 Ames St Rm E17 529B Cambridge MA 02142-1308

SHARP, RICHARD L., retail company executive; b. Washington, Apr. 12, 1947. Student, U. Va., 1965-66, Coll. of William and Mary, 1968-70. Programmer Group Health Inc., Washington, 1970-75; founder, pres. Applied Systems Corp., Washington, 1975-81; with Circuit City Stores, Inc., Richmond, Va., 1982—, exec. v.p., 1982-84, pres., 1984-86, pres., CEO, 1986-94, chmn. pres., CEO, 1994—; bd. dirs. Flextronics Internat., James River Corp. With USAF, 1967-70. Office: Circuit City Stores Inc 9950 Mayland Dr Richmond VA 23233-1463

SHARP, ROBERT PHILLIP, geology educator, researcher; b. Oxnard, Calif., June 24, 1911; s. Julian Hebner Sharp and Alice Sharp Darling; m. Jean Prescott Todd, Sept. 7, 1938; adopted children—Kristin Todd, Bruce Todd. B.S., Calif. Inst. Tech., Pasadena, 1934, M.S., 1935; M.A., Harvard U., Cambridge, Mass., 1936, Ph.D., 1938. Asst. prof. U. Ill., Urbana, 1938-43; prof. U. Minn., Mpls., 1946-47; prof. Calif. Inst. Tech., Pasadena, 1947-79, chmn., 1952-67, prof. emeritus, 1979—. Author: Glaciers, 1960, Field Guide-Southern California, 1972, Field Guide-Coastal Southern California, 1978, Living Ice-Understanding Glaciers and Glaciation, 1988, (with A.F. Glazner) Geology Under Foot in Southern California, 1993. Served to capt. USAF, 1943-46. Recipient Exceptional Sci. Achievement medal NASA, 1971, Nat. Medal Sci., 1989, Charles P. Daly medal Am. Geog. Soc., 1991; Robert P. Sharp professorship Calif. Inst. Tech., 1978. Fellow Geol. Soc. Am. (councillor, Kirk Bryan award 1964, Penrose medal 1977, G.K. Gilbert and Disting. Career award 1996), Am. Geophys. Union; hon. fellow Internat. Glaciological Soc.; mem. NAS. Republican. Avocations: flyfishing, snorkeling, camping. Home: 1901 Gibraltar Rd Santa Barbara CA 93105-2326 Office: Calif Inst Tech 1200 E California Blvd Pasadena CA 91106

SHARP, ROBERT WEIMER, lawyer; b. Cleve., Feb. 12, 1917; s. Isaac Walter and Ruth (Weimer) S.; m. Norine Wines, Nov. 13, 1948; children: Kathleen L. Sharp Samuel, Pamela J. Sharp Adamson, Janet E. Sharp Schoon, Andrea S. Sharp Bobak, Gail N. Sharp Henderson. A.B. magna cum laude, Oberlin Coll., 1939; LL.B., Harvard U., 1942. Bar: Ohio 1944. Practiced in Cleve; ptnr. Gallagher, Sharp, Fulton & Norman and predecessors, 1958-92; pres. Bulkley Bldg. Co., 1966-70. Trustee emeritus St. Luke;s Hosp. Assn.; trustee emeritus, hon life mem. Ohio divsn. Am. Cancer Soc.; trustee emeritus Ohio East Area United Meth. Found., 1974—, sec., 1967-74, 83-86, pres., 1974-80. Mem. ABA, Ohio Bar Assn., Cleve. Bar Assn., Phi Beta Kappa. Republican. Methodist. Home: 3090 Fairmount Blvd Cleveland OH 44118-4129 Office: Gallagher Sharp Fulton & Norman 600 Bulkley Bldg Cleveland OH 44115

SHARP, RONALD ALAN, English literature educator, author; b. Cleve., Oct. 19, 1945; s. Jack Trier and Florence (Tenenbaum) S.; m. Inese Brutans, June 22, 1968; children: Andrew Janis, James Michael. BA, Kalamazoo Coll., 1967; MA, U. Mich., 1968; PhD, U. Va., 1974. Instr. in English Western Mich. U., Kalamazoo, 1968-70; instr. Kenyon Coll., Gambier, Ohio, 1970-72, asst. prof. English, 1974-78, assoc. prof., 1978-85; prof. Kenyon Coll., 1985-90, John Crowe Ransom prof. English, 1990—, chmn. dept. English, 1984-86, co-editor Kenyon Rev., 1978-82; dir. Keats Bicentennial Conf., Harvard U., 1995. Author: Keats, Skepticism and the Religion of Beauty, 1979, Friendship and Literature: Spirit and Form, 1986; translator: Teatro Breve (Garcia Lorca), 1979, editor (with Eudora Welty) The Norton Book of Friendship, 1991, (with Nathan Scott) Reading George Steiner, 1994; contbr. articles to profl. jours. Recipient award for editl. excellence Ohioana Assn., 1980; fellow Nat. Humanities Ctr., 1981, 86, NEH, 1981, 84-87, 93, 94, 96, Ford Found., 1971, Mellon Found., 1980, Danforth Found., 1971, English Speaking Union, 1973, Am. Coun. Learned Socs., 1986. Mem. MLA, NEH (chmn's. adv. group humanities edn. 1987), Wordsworth-Coleridge Assn., Keats-Shelley Assn. Jewish. Home: 11671 Kenyon Rd Mount Vernon OH 43050-8578 Office: Kenyon Coll Dept English Gambier OH 43022

SHARP, RONALD ARVELL, sociology educator; b. Vivian, La., Sept. 29, 1941; s. Walter Arvell and Virginia (Refield-King) S.; m. Imelda Idalia Pena, Sept. 16, 1967; children: Ronald Arvell II, Donald Allen. BS in Edn., Cameron U., 1976; BA in Sociology, SUNY, Albany, 1977; MEd in Counseling Psychology, U. Okla., 1978; PhD in Sociology, Clayton U., 1985. Ret. U.S. Army, 1960-82; radiologic technologist VA Hosp., Temple, Tex., 1983-84; vets. counselor Vets. Outreach Program, San Antonio, Tex., 1982-83; dir. personnel & mktg. Heran Pharms., San Antonio, Tex., 1988-91; prof. sociology Ctrl. Tech. Coll., Killeen, 1991-95; instr. sociology Tex. State Tech. Coll., Waco, 1995-96, Academia Assocs., 1996—; part-time instr. Ctrl. Tex. Coll., 1980-82, City Coll. Chgo., 1981, Big Bend C.C., Mannheim, Germany, 1981-82; instr. Acad. Health Scis., 1977-79. Contbr. articles to profl. jours. Coach Youth Soccer Orgns., San Antonio and Mannheim, 1976-82. Nat. Coll. Radiology Technologists fellow, 1968. Mem. AAUP, Am. Sociol. Assn., Soc. Applied Sociology, La. Archeol. Soc., Choctaw Nation of Okla., Okla. Anthrop. Soc., Okla. Hist. Soc., La. Archeol. Conservancy, Caddoan Hist. Soc., Okla. Archeol. Survey, Okla. Hist. Soc., Okla. Anthropol. Survey, Okla. Archeol. Soc., Order of Alhambra, KC, Masons, Soc. for the Study of Social Problems, Psi Beta (chpt. sponsor), Alpha Kappa Delta, Psi Chi, Sigma Eta Sigma (nat. dir.). Roman Catholic. Avocations: soccer, golf, paleo-historic anthropology. Home: 9310 Oak Hills Dr Temple TX 76502-5272 Office: Academia Assocs Waco TX 76705

SHARP, SHARON LEE, gerontology nurse; b. Beatrice, Nebr., Jan. 14, 1939; d. Clarence Alfred and Edna Clara (Grosshuesch) Wolters; m. Philip Butler, June 27, 1959 (div. 1964); m. Ted C. Sharp, Sept. 21, 1966 (div. 1988); children: Sheryl Butler, Philip Butler. Diploma, Lincoln Gen. Hosp., 1959. RN Nebr. Charge nurse Mary Lanning Meml. Hosp., Hastings, Nebr., 1960-61; asst. head nurse Ingleside State Hosp., Hastings, Nebr., 1961-62; charge nurse Rio Hondo Meml. Hosp., Downey, Calif., 1969-71, Santa Barbara (Calif.) Cottage Hosp., 1974-78; supr. Marlora Manor Convalescent Hosp., Long Beach, Calif., 1979-80; supr. Marlinda Nursing Home, Lynwood, Calif., 1982-84, dir. nursing, 1984-89; dir. nursing Ramona Care Ctr., El Monte, Calif., 1989-90, Oakview Convalescent Hosp., Tujunga, Calif., 1990-91, North Valley Nursing Ctr., Tujunga, Calif., 1992—; asst. dir. nursing Skyline Health Care Ctr. (Gran Care), L.A., 1993-94; resident assessment coord. Country Villa Rehab. Ctr., L.A., 1994-95; case mgr. Vitas Innovative Hospice Care, West Covina, Calif., 1996—; mem. adv. bd. Regional Occupational Program, Downey, 1985-86. Avocations: metaphysics, paranormal experiences, reading, alternative ways of healing, healing touch practitioner. Home: 2875 E Del Mar Blvd Pasadena CA 91107-4314

SHARP, VERNON HIBBETT, psychiatrist; b. Nashville, Apr. 6, 1932; s. Vernon Hibbett Sr. and Sarah McDonald (Robinson) S.; m. Valeria Nell Parker Storms, Aug. 17, 1956 (div. July 1975); children: Mark, Christopher, Daniel; m. Alix Ingrid Weiss, Nov. 17, 1979; 1 child, Monica Elena. BA, Vanderbilt U., 1953, MD, 1957. Diplomate Am. Bd. Psychiatry and Neurology. Intern internal medicine Washington U., St. Louis, 1957-58; resident psychiatry Yale U., New Haven, 1958-61; asst. prof. dept. psychiatry Cornell U. Med. Ctr., N.Y.C., 1963-66, SUNY, Downstate Med. Ctr., Bklyn., 1966-69; pvt. practice adults, adolescents and families Scarsdale, N.Y., 1969-83; pvt. practice Nashville, 1983-93; clin. asst. prof. psychiatry Vanderbilt U. Sch. Medicine, Nashville, 1983-86, clin. assoc. prof., 1986—; chief dept. psychiatry St. Thomas Hosp., Nashville, 1985-87; dir. family treatment tng. program Vanderbilt Med. Sch., Nashville, 1990—; founding mem. bd. dirs. Ctr. for Family, Nashville, 1985-93; vis. lectr. adolescent psychiatry Columbia U. Sch. Social Work, 1979-81; asst. attending psychiatrist Cornell U. Med. Coll., 1982-83; adj. assoc. prof. human resources Peabody Coll., Vanderbilt U., 1994-95; mem. attending staff various hosps. Contbr. articles to profl. jours. Lt. comdr. USN, 1961-63. Recipient Career Tchr. award NIMH, Downstate Med. Ctr., Bklyn., 1967-69. Mem. Am. Psychiat. Assn., Soc. for Adolescent Psychiatry, Am. Assn. Marriage and Family Therapy, Am. Family Therapy Acad., Coffee House Club (pres. 1985). Democrat. Episcopalian. Avocations: sailing, caving, hiking, geology. Home and Office: 215 Leonard Ave Nashville TN 37205-2425

SHARP, WILLIAM LESLIE, performing arts educator; b. Chgo., Sept. 3, 1924; s. Arthur Eugene and Alma (Melchior) S.; m. Shirley Vanderwalker, Dec. 27, 1949 (div. 1977); children: Katherine, Arthur, Elizabeth. BA, U. Chgo., 1948, MA, 1949; PhD, Stanford U., 1957. Prof. U. Calif., Riverside, 1957-64, Stanford (Calif.) U., 1964-69; prof. Emerson Coll., Boston, 1969—, chmn. drama dept., 1969-82. Author: The Language in Drama, 1970. With U.S. Army, 1943-46, ETO. Home: 151 Tremont St Apt 21C Boston MA

02111-1119 Office: Emerson Coll Dept Performing Arts 100 Beacon St Boston MA 02116-1501

SHARP, WILLIAM WHEELER, geologist; b. Shreveport, La., Oct. 9, 1923; s. William Wheeler and Jennie V. (Benson) S.; m. Rubylin Slaughter, 1958; children: Staci Lynn, Kimberly Cecile; 1 child from previous marriage, John E. BS in Geology, U. Tex., Austin, 1950, MA, 1951. Lic. pvt. pilot. Geol. Socony-Vacuum, Caracas, Venezuela, 1951-53; surface geol. chief Creole, 1953-57; dist. devel. geologist, supr. exploration, devel., and unitization of 132 multi-pay oil and gas fields, expert geol. witness, coll. recruiter, research assoc. ARCO, 1957-85; discovered oil and gas at Bayou Boullion, Bayou Sale, Jeanerette, La.; petroleum exploration in Alaska, Aus., Can., U.S. and S.A. Contbr. articles to profl. jours. Past dir. and chmn. U.S. Tennis Assn. Tournaments, 12th Nat. Boys Tournament; pres. Lafayette Tennis Adv. Com., 1972; past dir. Jr. Achievememt and United Fund Programs. Served as sgt. USAF, 1943-46, PTO. Winner and finalist more than 75 amateur tennis tournaments including Confederate Oil Invitational, Gulf Coast Oilmen's Tournament, So. Oilmen's Tournament, Tex.-Ark.-La. Oilmen's Tournament; named Hon. Citizen of New Orleans, 1971, recipient Key to New Orleans. Mem. Dallas Geol. Soc., Lafayette Geol. Soc. (bd. dirs. 1973-74), Am. Assn. Petroleum Geologists (co-author Best of SEG conv. 1982), VFW, Am. Legion, Appaloosa Horse Club. Republican. Methodist. Avocations: sports, music, reading history. Home: 7312 Mimosa Ln Dallas TX 75230-5446

SHARPE, AUBREY DEAN, college administrator; b. Miami, Fla., Oct. 4, 1944; s. William Gibson and Ila-Mae (Albritton) S.; m. Linda Lee Rush, Dec. 22, 1973. BA, E. Tex. Bapt. U., 1967; MDiv, Southwestern Bapt. Theol. Sem., Ft. Worth, 1970; MA, southwestern Bapt. Theol. Sem., Ft. Worth, 1972; EdD, U. No. Tex., 1993. Assoc. pastor edn. Trinity Bapt. Ch., Ft. Worth, Tex., 1970-72; minister edn. Polytechnic Bapt. Ch., Ft. Worth, Tex., 1972-73; dean community svcs. Tarrant County Jr. Coll., Ft. Worth, Tex., 1973-84; religion inst. Tarrant County Jr. Coll., Ft. Worth, 1976-78; nat. dir. tng. Presbyn. Ministers Fund, Phila., 1984-89; v.p. The Pat Petersen Collection, Ft. Worth, 1984-91; owner ADS Investments, Ft. Worth, 1984—; dean continuing studies, Regional Tng. and Devel. Complex Tyler (Tex.) Jr. Coll., 1989—. Pres. Ft. Worth Boys Club, 1979; allocations chmn. United Way Tarrant County, Ft. Worth, 1981-87, Sr. Citizens, Inc., Ft. Worth, 1985-86, Tyler Metro YMCA, 1992-93; bd. dirs. United Way Tyler and Smith County, 1991-96, v.p. allocations/funding, trainer for loaned exec. program, 1991-95, Pacesetter Campaign chair 1996, campaign chair, 1997; adv. bd. North Tex. Small Bus. Devel. Ctr., 1995-96. Recipient Nat. Sales Achievement award Nat. Assn. Life Underwriters, 1987, Nat. Sales Leader award 1987; recipient Achievers award Presbyn. Ministers Fund, 1987, Vol. Svc. Award, United Way of Tarrant County, 1987. Mem. ASTD (pres.-elect 1991, pres. 1992-93), Tex. Assn. Community Svcs. and Continuing Edn., Tex. Jr. Coll. Tchrs. Assn., Nat. Coun. for Community Svcs./Continuing Edn., Tex. Adminstrs. Continuing Edn., Tyler Area C. of C., Phi Delta Kappa. Republican. Baptist. Avocations: reading, collecting old books, landscaping. Home: 503 Towne Oaks Dr Tyler TX 75701-9536 Office: Tyler Jr Coll Regional Training Complex 1530 S Southwest Loop 323 Tyler TX 75701

SHARPE, DONALD EDWARD, lawyer; b. Edmonton, Alta., Can., Oct. 24, 1937; came to U.S., 1945; s. Eldon Durwood Sharpe and Bertha Evelyn (Johnston) Skinner; m. JoAnn Firth; children: Jennifer, William, Gregory. BA, U. Md., 1960, LLB, 1963. Bar: Md. 1963, U.S. Dist. Ct. Md. 1964, U.S. Ct. Appeals (4th cir.) 1964, U.S. Dist. Ct. D.C. 1981. Law clk. to presiding judges U.S. Dist. Ct. Md., Balt., 1963-64; assoc. Piper & Marbury, Balt., 1964-67, 69-71, ptnr., 1971—; asst. U.S. atty. U.S. Atty.'s Office, Balt., 1967-69. Recent Decisions editor Md. Law Rev., 1963. Mem. ABA (chmn. products-torts and ins. practice sect. 1985-86, membership com. 1988-89, task force on selection and performance standards of counsel 1988-89), Order of Coif. Democrat. Presbyterian. Avocations: golf, volleyball, woodworking, gardening, fishing. Office: Piper & Marbury LLP 36 S Charles St Baltimore MD 21201-3020

SHARPE, HENRY DEXTER, JR., retired manufacturing company executive; b. Providence, May 5, 1923; s. Henry Dexter and Mary Elizabeth (Evans) S.; m. Peggy Plumer Boyd, Aug. 1, 1953; children: Henry Dexter, Douglas, Sarah. Grad., Brown U., Providence, 1945. With Brown & Sharpe Mfg. Co., Providence, 1946-96, v.p., 1950-51, pres., 1951-76, chmn., chief exec. officer, 1976-80, chmn., 1980-96, ret., 1996; bd. dirs., mem. exec. com. Providence Jour. Co.; vice chancellor Brown U., 1986-87. Bd. dirs. R.I. Pub. Expenditure Coun.; trustee, fellow Brown U.; trustee Coll. of the Atlantic, 1992—. Lt. (j.g.) USNR, 1943-46. Mem. Nat. Machine Tool Builders Assn. (pres. 1969-70), Machinery and Allied Products Inst. (ret. mem. exec. com.). Office: Pojac Point Rd North Kingstown RI 02852-1031

SHARPE, JAMES SHELBY, lawyer; b. Ft. Worth, Sept. 11, 1940; s. James Henry and Wanzel (Vanderbilt) S.; m. Martha Moudy Holland, June 9, 1962; children: Marthanne Freeman, Caren Roark, Stephen. BA, U. Tex., 1962, JD, 1965. Bar: Tex. 1965, U.S. Dist. Ct. (no. dist.) Tex. 1966, U.S. Dist. Ct. (ea. dist.) Tex. 1993, U.S. Ct. Appeals (5th and 6th cirs.) 1982, U.S. Ct. Appeals (fed. cir.) 1983, U.S. Ct. Appeals (10th cir.) 1992, U.S. Supreme Ct. 1972. Briefing atty. for chief justice Supreme Ct. of Tex., Austin, 1965-66; ptnr. Brown, Herman, Scott, Dean & Miles, Ft. Worth, 1966-84, Gandy Michener Swindle Whitaker & Pratt, Ft. Worth, 1984-87; shareholder Sharpe & Tillman, Ft. Worth, 1988—; adj. prof. polit. sci. Tex. Christian U., Ft. Worth, 1969-79, Dallas Bapt. U., 1987, 1992-94; gen. counsel U.S.A. Radio Network, Internat. Christian Media, Denton Pub. Co. Pres. Ft. Worth-Tarrant County Jr. Bar, 1969-70, bd. dirs., 1968, sec., 1968, v.p., 1968-69; head marshal USA-USSR Track and Field Championships, Ft. Worth, USA-USSR Jr. Track and Field Championships, Austin, Tex., Relays, Austin, 1963—, NCAA Nat. Track and Field Championships, 1976, 80, 85, 92, 95, S.W. Conf. Indoor Track and Field Championships, 1987-96, Olympic Festival, San Antonio, 1993, Colorado Springs, 1995; 12 time head marshall S.W. Conf. Track and Field Championships, Big 12 Outdoor Conf. Track and Field Championship. USA/Mobil Track Championship, 1994, 95; USA Nat. Jr. Track Championship, 1994, 95, USA Track and Field Track championship, 1997. Mem. ABA, State Bar of Tex. (dist. 7-A grievance com. 1983-85, com. adminstrn. of justice 1985-92, com. on ct. rules 1992—, chmn. 1992-93, 93-94). Baptist. Home: 8304 Crosswind Dr Fort Worth TX 76179-3003 Office: Sharpe & Tillman 500 Throckmorton St Ste 2706 Fort Worth TX 76102-3814

SHARPE, KEITH YOUNT, retired lawyer; b. Hiddenite, N.C., July 11, 1930; s. Ruel Yount and Eileen Lois (Lackey) S.; m. Margaret Joyce Land, Aug. 27, 1955 (div.); children: Jonathan, Matthew, Leonora, Felicia. A.B., Duke U., 1952; J.D., Wake Forest U., 1957, M.B.A., 1982. Bar: N.C. 1957. Practiced law Winston-Salem, N.C., 1957-62, 82-94; asst. solicitor Mcpl. Ct. of Winston-Salem, 1958-60; with Pilot Freight Carriers Inc., Winston-Salem, 1962-82; sr. v.p. Pilot Freight Carriers Inc., 1967-76, v.p., 1976-82; also dir.; v.p., dir. Comml. Automotive Co., 1967-76, Terminal Warehouse Corp., 1967-82; bd. govs. So. Motor Carriers Rate Conf., 1977-81. Served with inf. U.S. Army, 1952-54. Mem. Assn. Transp. Practitioners, Phi Alpha Delta, Theta Chi. Democrat. Episcopalian. Home: Box 19633 Asheville NC 28815

SHARPE, MYRON EMANUEL, publisher, editor, writer; b. Chester, Pa., Sept. 10, 1928; s. Abraham Maxwell and Emma (Friedman) S.; m. Jacqueline Steiner, 1959 (div.); children: Susanna, Matthew; m. Carole S. Brafman, 1983; children: Elizabeth, Hannah. B.A., Swarthmore Coll., 1950; M.A., U. Mich., 1951, postgrad., 1951-54. Pres. Modern Factors Corp., Phila., 1957; founder, chmn. bd., pres. M.E. Sharpe, Inc. (Pub.), Armonk, N.Y., 1958—, writer, editor, 1955—; founder, exec. dir. Com. to Save the Life of Henry Spetter, 1974; co-founder, coord. Initiative Com. for Nat. Econ. Planning, 1974-76; participant in drafting Full Employment and Balanced Growth Act of 1978; co-founder, pres. M.E. Sharpe, Ltd. (Arts and Antiques), New Canaan, Conn., 1981-83. Author: John Kenneth Galbraith and the Lower Economics, 1973. Chmn. Pro Arte Chamber Singers of Conn., 1982-83; pres. Waveny Chamber Music Soc., 1987—; econ. advisor to Senator Birch Bayh for presdl. campaign, 1975. Office: M E Sharpe Inc 80 Business Park Dr Armonk NY 10504-1710

SHARPE, RICHARD SAMUEL, architectural company executive; b. New Haven, Conn., Aug. 7, 1930; s. Herman and Betty (Silberman) S.; m. Anne Johnson; children: Peter, Andrew, Rebecca. BArch, U. Pa., 1953; postgrad., U. Liverpool, Eng., 1953-54. Registered architect, Conn., N.Y., R.I., Mass. Prin. Richard Sharpe Assocs. P.C., Norwich, Conn., 1957—; v.p. Pan-Am. Fedn. Architects, 1972-78. Bd. dirs. Conn. Humanities council, 1974-78; pres. Conn. Habitat, 1978-79; pres. Thames River Devel. Corp., 1982-83. Recipient Ann. award Producers Council, 1974-78, Ann. Craft award Slater Mus., Norwich, 1986, spl. citation AIA, 1978. Fellow Am. Inst. Archs.; mem. Conn. Soc. Archs. (v.p. 1963, pres. 1966), Hist. Dist. Conn. (com. chmn.), S.E. Conn. Grievence Comm., Rotary. Avocations: wood pottery, photography, pre-Columbian art collecting, sailing. Office: Richard Sharpe Assocs PC 30 Connecticut Ave Norwich CT 06360-1502

SHARPE, ROBERT F., SR., writer, lecturer, educator, consultant, publisher; b. Florence, Ala., Sept. 8, 1926; s. Thomas Leslie and Lida (Gammill) S.; m. Jane A. Sharpe, Dec. 28, 1948; children: Susan, Robert Jr., Paul, Timothy. BS, Memphis State U., 1957. Life ins. agt. Pilot Life Ins. Co., Greensboro, N.C., 1950-54; agt., supr. Vol. Life Ins. Co., Chattanooga, 1954; agt. Crown Life Ins. Co., Toronto, Ont., Can., 1954-59; sec. stewardship Good News Broadcasting Assn., Lincoln, Nebr., 1959-63; exec. dir. Reformed Presbyn. Found., St. Louis, 1963-65; founder Robert F. Sharpe & Co. Inc., Memphis, 1963-93, sr. cons., 1993—; founder, exec. dir. Nat. Planned Giving Inst. at Coll. William and Mary, 1967-93, Nat. Planned Giving Assn., 1985. Author: The Planned Giving Idea Book, Before You Give Another Dime, 27 Plus Ways to Increase Giving to Your Church; pub. monthly newsletter Give and Take; contbr. articles to publs. Trustee Memphis Symphony Orch., Ch. Health Ctr., Memphis, Endowment Assn. Coll. William and Mary, Williamsburg, Va.; chmn. bd. dirs. Wesley Housing Ministries Found., Memphis; pres. Memphis Mus. Inc., 1994-95. With USN, 1944-47, PTO. Recipient Disting. Svc. award Memphis State U., 1970. Mem. Soc. Entrepreneurs. Methodist. Avocations: sailing, music. Office: 5050 Poplar Ave Fl 7 Memphis TN 38157-0101 Office: College of William and Mary 519 Richmond Rd Williamsburg VA 23185-3537

SHARPE, ROBERT FRANCIS, equipment manufacturing company executive; b. Buffalo, Mar. 29, 1921; s. Bertram Francis and Agnes (Coppinger) S.; m. Audrey Rembe, July 10, 1943; 1 son, Robert Francis. B.S. in Chem. Engring, Rensselaer Poly. Inst., 1942. With Duriron Co., 1946—; mgr. pump sales Duriron Co., Dayton, 1955-58; dir. research, devel. Duriron Co., 1958-63, v.p. plastics ops., 1963-65, exec. v.p., 1967-68, pres., chief operating officer, 1968-69, pres., 1969-76, chief exec. officer, 1969-79, chmn. bd., 1978-83. Served with USAAF, 1943-46. Mem. Am. Inst. Chem. Engrs., Hydraulic Inst. Home: 15520 Whitney Ln Naples FL 34110-7611 also: PO Box 8820 Dayton OH 45401-8820

SHARPE, ROCHELLE PHYLLIS, journalist; b. Gary, Ind., Apr. 27, 1956; d. Norman Nathaniel and Shirley (Kaplan) S. BA, Yale U., 1978. Reporter Concord (N.H.) Monitor, 1979-81; statehouse rep. Wilmington News Jour., Dover, Del., 1981-85; statehouse corr. Gannett News Svc., Albany, N.Y., 1985; nat. reporter Gannett News Svc., Washington, 1986-93; staff reporter social issues The Wall St. Jour., Washington, 1993—. Contbr. articles to profl. jours. Recipient Pulitzer prize for series in child abuse, Columbia U., 1991. Home: 2500 Q St NW Apt 315 Washington DC 20007-4360 Office: Wall St Jour Washington Bur 1025 Connecticut Ave NW Ste 800 Washington DC 20036-5419*

SHARPE, ROLAND LEONARD, engineering company executive, earthquake and structural engineering consultant; b. Shakopee, Minn., Dec. 18, 1923; s. Alfred Leonard and Ruth Helen (Carter) S.; m. Jane Esther Steele, Dec. 28, 1946; children: Douglas Rolfe, Deborah Lynn, Sheryl Anne. BS in Civil Engring., U. Mich., 1947, MSE, 1949. Registered civil engr. and structural engr., Calif. Designer, Cummins & Barnard, Inc., Ann Arbor, Mich., 1947-48; instr. engring. U. Mich., 1948-50; exec. v.p. John A. Blume & Assocs., engrs., San Francisco, 1950-73; chmn., founder Engring. Decision Analysis Co., Inc., Cupertino, 1974-87; cons. earthquake engr., 1987—; mng. dir. EDAC, GmbH, Frankfurt, Germany, 1974-82; dir. EDAC; pres. Calif. Devel. & Engring. Co., Inc., Las Vegas, Nev., 1973-81; mem. nat. earthquake hazard reduction program adv. com. overviewing Fed. Emergency Mgmt. Agy., U.S. Geol. Survey, NSF and Nat. Inst. Stds. and Tech., 1990-93. Author: (with J. Blume, E.G. Kost) Earthquake Engineering for Nuclear Facilities, 1971. Mem. Planning Commn., Palo Alto, 1955-60; mng. dir. Applied Tech. Coun., Palo Alto, 1973-83; dir. Earthquake Engring. Rsch. Inst., 1972-75, now mem.; project dir., editor Tentative Provisions for Devel. of Seismic Regulations for Buildings, 1978; tech. mgr., contbr., editor Data Processing Facilities: Guidelines for Earthquake Hazard Mitigation, 1987. Served with USMC, 1942-46. Author, co-author over 200 engring. papers and reports; author of chpts.: (with others) DOE Seismic Safety Manual, 1996. Fellow ASCE (hon. mem. 1994, chmn. dynamic effects com., 1978-80, exec. com. structural div. 1980-84, 89-93, chmn. 1983, mgmt. group B 1989-93, Earnest E. Howard award 1994); mem. Japan Structural Cons. Assn. (hon. mem. 1992), Structural Engrs. Assn. Calif. (dir. 1971-73, chmn. seismology com. 1972-74), Structural Engrs. No. Calif. (dir. 1969-71, life mem.), Am. Concrete Inst. (life), Structural Engrs. World Congress (pres. 1995—). Recipient citation for contbn. to constrn. industry Engring. News Record, 1978-79, 86-87; chmn. U.S. Joint Com. on Earthquake Engring., 1982-88. Home: 10320 Rolly Rd Los Altos CA 94024-6520 Office: Sharpe Struct Engrs 10320 Rolly Rd Ste 1 Los Altos CA 94024-6520 *Personal philosophy: One's conduct should be beyond reproach both morally and ethically and I should serve each of my clients to the best of my ability.*

SHARPE, SHANNON, professional football player; b. Chgo., June 26, 1968. Student, Savannah State U. Tight end Denver Broncos, 1990—; player AFC Championship Game, 1991. Named to Pro Bowl Team, 1992, 93, 96, Sporting News NFL All-Pro Team, 1993. Office: Denver Broncos 13655 Broncos Pkwy Englewood CO 80112-4150*

SHARPE, STERLING, former professional football player, sports commentator; b. Chgo., Apr. 6, 1965. BA, U. S.C., 1987. With Green Bay Packers, 1988-95; analyst, broadcaster ESPN, Bristol, Conn., 1995—. Named to Sporting News Coll. All-Am., 1987; named receiving leader NFL, 1989, 92, wide receiver All-Pro Team NFL, 1989. Played in Pro Bowl, 1989, 90, 92; named to Pro Bowl, 1993. *

SHARPE, WILLIAM FORSYTH, economics educator; b. Cambridge, Mass., June 16, 1934; s. Russell Thornley Sharpe and Evelyn Forsyth (Jillson) Maloy; m. Roberta Ruth Branton, July 2, 1954 (div. Feb. 1986); children: Deborah Ann, Jonathan Forsyth; m. Kathryn Dorothy Peck, Apr. 5, 1986. AB, UCLA, 1955, MA, 1956, PhD, 1961. Economist Rand Corp., 1957-61; asst. prof. econs. U. Wash., 1961-63, assoc. prof., 1963-67, prof., 1967-68; prof. U. Calif., Irvine, 1968-70; Timken prof. fin. Stanford U., 1970-89, Timken prof. emeritus, 1989-92; prin. William F. Sharpe Assocs., 1986-92; prof.fin. Stanford U., 1993-95, STANCO 25 prof. of fin., 1995—. Author: The Economics of Computers, 1969, Portfolio Theory and Capital Markets, 1970; co-author: Fundamentals of Investments, 1989, 2d edit., 1993, Investments, 5th edit., 1995. With U.S. Army, 1956-57. Recipient Graham and Dodd award Fin Analysts' Fedn., 1972, '73, '86-88. Nicholas Molodovsky award, 1989. Nobel prize in econ. scis., 1990. Mem. Am. Fin. Assn. (v.p. 1979, pres. 1980), Western Fin. Assn. (Enduring Contbn. award 1989), Ea. Fin. Assn. (Disting. Scholar award 1991), Am. Econ. Assn., Phi Beta Kappa.

SHARPE, WILLIAM NORMAN, JR., mechanical engineer, educator; b. Chatham County, N.C., Apr. 15, 1938; s. William Norman and Margaret Horne (Womble) S.; m. Margaret Ellen Strowd, Aug. 21, 1959; children: William N., J. Ashley. BS, N.C. State U., 1960, MS, 1961; PhD, Johns Hopkins U., 1966. Registered profl. engr., Mich., La., Md. Assoc. prof. Mich. State U., East Lansing, 1970-75, prof., 1975-78; prof., chmn. dept. mech. engring. La. State U., Baton Rouge, 1978-83; prof., dept. mech. engring. Johns Hopkins U., Balt., 1983—, Decker prof. mech. engring., 1985—. Recipient Alexander von Humboldt award, Fed. Republic Germany, 1989. Fellow ASME (Nadai award 1993), Soc. Exptl. Mechanics (Tatnall award, exec. bd. 1979-81, pres. 1984-85); mem. ASTM, Am. Soc. Engring. Edn. Home: 220 Ridgewood Rd Baltimore MD 21210-2539 Office: Johns Hopkins U Dept Mech Engring Latrobe Hall Rm 126 Baltimore MD 21218

SHARPLES, D. KENT, college administrator; b. Swanton, Ohio, May 26, 1943; s. Morrill and Doris Elizabeth (Saeger) S.; m. Linda Mancini Sharples; children: Dawn, Steven. BS, Bowling Green State U., 1965, MEd, 1966; PhD in Ednl. Adminstrn., Ohio U., 1973. Tchr. Maumee (Ohio) Jr. High. Sch., 1966-67; instr. dept. engring. graphics Coll. Engring. and Tech., Athens, Ohio, 1967-73; project dir. S.C. State Bd. for Tech. and Comprehensive Edn., West Columbia, 1973-76; v.p. for edn., dean of instrn. Tri-County Tech. Coll., Pendleton, S.C., 1976-80; pres. Horry-Georgetown Tech. Coll., Conway, S.C., 1980—. Mem. Am. Assn. Community and Jr. Colls. (chair small/rural coll. commn. 1983-87, bd. dirs. 1987), Assn. Community Colls Trustees, So. Assn. of Colls. and Schs., Council for Occupational Edn., Am. Tech. Edn. Assn., Myrtle Beach C. of C. Episcopalian. Lodge: Rotary. Office: Horry-Georgetown Tech Coll PO Box 261966 Highway 501 Conway SC 29528

SHARPLES, WINSTON SINGLETON, automobile importer and distributor; b. Springfield, Mass., Oct. 24, 1932; s. Winston Singleton and Carmela (Parrino) S.; m. Jeanette Williams, July 1961 (div. Apr. 1981); children: John, Hadley, Gillian; m. Ruth Emily Lissak, June 26, 1981. BA, Harvard Coll., 1953; postgrad. drama, Yale U., 1956-57; MFA, Carnegie Mellon U., 1959; postgrad., Univ. Md., 1978-80. Freelance writer, 1959—; producer, dir. Mon. Valley Playhouse, Charleroi, Pa., 1959, Robin Hood Theater, Arden, Del., 1960-61; pres., film and music editor Synchro-Sound Inc., N.Y.C., 1961-71; prof. CUNY, N.Y.C., 1969-74, Temple Univ., Phila., 1974-76, U. Md., College Park, 1978-79; adminstr. film preservation and documentation Am. Film Inst., Washington, 1976-78; prof. Howard Univ., Washington, 1978-80; pres. Cantab Motors, Ltd., Round Hill, Va., 1984—. Author: (with others) A Primer for Film-Making, 1971—; supr. Am. Film Inst. Catalog of Feature Films, 1960-69, 77; editor, music editor films and cartoons; contbr. articles to profl. jours. and mags. With U.S. Army, 1953-56. Nat. Endowment for the Humanities grantee, 1977. Mem. ASCAP, Archeol. Soc. Va., Am. Studies Assn., Univ. Film Assn. (v.p. 1975-76), Soc. for Cinema Studies, Soc. Automotive Engrs., Washington Automotive Press Assn., Morgan Car Club, Land Rover Owners Assn. Va., British Automobile Mfrs. Assn., Harvard Club (N.Y.C.). Democrat. Avocations: forestry, archeology. Home: 16657 Tree Crops Ln Round Hill VA 20141-9310 Office: Cantab Motors Ltd Valley Indsl Park 12 E Richardson Ln Purcellville VA 20132-3500

SHARPLESS, JOSEPH BENJAMIN, former county official; b. Takoma Park, Md., Feb. 4, 1933; s. William Raiford and Julia Maude (Rouse) S.; m. Nancy Kathleen Steffen, July 28, 1962 (dec. Feb. 1988); 1 child, Carole Marie. BA, Earlham Coll., 1955; MS, Pa. State U., 1960. Instr. recreation Montgomery County Recreation Dept., Rockville, Md., 1957-58; from program supr. to dir. Recreation and Parks Dept., Livingston, N.J., 1959-70; chief recreation svc. Md.-Nat. Capital Park and Planning Commn. Prince George's County, Riverdale, Md., 1970-77, parks and recreation div. chief, 1977-95; ret., 1995—. Contbr. articles to profl. jours. V.p. Montpelier Cmty. Assn., South Laurel, Md., 1983-84, pres., 1985; mem. Md. Sports Adv. Com., 1988-92; Md. State Games Commr., 1986-91; bd. regents, instr. Sch. Sports Mgmt., N.C. State U., 1989-92; nat. volleyball chmn. AAU, 1966-69, 72, volleyball chmn. N.J. chpt. 1961-70, volleyball chmn. Potomac Valley chpt., 1971-73; mem. volleyball games staff 1996 Olympic Games, Atlanta; dir. volleyball Spl. Olympics Internat., 1994—; sec. U.S. Volleyball Edn. Found., 1996—. Fellow Nat. Recreation Parks Assn. (Disting. Svc. award Mid-Atlantic Coun.); mem. U.S. Volleyball Assn. (bd. dirs. 1973—, mem. exec. com. 1976-80, 85-89, 92-96, v.p. 1973-90, 96—, regional commr. 1965-78, nat. ofcl. 1967-96, exec. cons. 1989-91, corp. sec. 1992-96, mng. editor pubs. 1994—, numerous awards), Nat. Intercollegiate Soccer Ofcls. Assn. (sec. 1966-68, treas. 1968-70), Am. Park and Recreation Soc. (bd. dirs. 1977-80, nat. coun., coun. affiliate pres.), N.J. Recreation and Pks. Assn. (sec. 1965, v.p. 1965, pres. 1967), Md. Recreation and Pk. Assn. (v.p. 1975-77, pres. 1977-78, Mem. of Yr. 1975, Citation 1985), Ret. Life Profl. (Disting. Fellow award 1996), N.J. Soccer Ofcls. Assn. (sec. 1966-70), Nat. Capitol Area Bd. Volleyball Ofcls. (sec. 1985-89), U.S. Volleyball Edn. Found. (sec. 1996—). Republican. Mem. Soc. of Friends. Home: 8754 Oxwell Ln Laurel MD 20708-2469

SHARPLESS, RICHARD KENNEDY, lawyer; b. Springdale, Pa., Mar. 30, 1911; s. Charles Thomas and Luella Lincoln (Kennedy) S.; m. Eleanor Ridgway Crowther, Mar. 4, 1946; m. Nancy Jean Sleight, July 23, 1948; children: Kendall Deborah, Richard Kennedy, Lincoln Kennedy. AB, Boston U., 1932; LLB, Harvard U., 1935, JD, 1969. Bar: Pa. 1936, Calif. 1947, Hawaii 1949, U.S. Ct. Appeals (9th dist.) 1964, U.S. Supreme Ct. 1960. With firm Dalzell, McFall & Pringle, Pitts., 1936-42; mem. legal sect. trust dept. Bank of Am., Los Angeles, 1946-48; atty. Office Dist. Engr., Honolulu, 1948-49; with Office Atty. Gen., T.H., 1949-55, atty. gen., 1956-57; mem. Lewis, Saunders & Sharpless (and predecessor firm), 1957-68; mng. dir. City and County of Honolulu, 1968-72, 75-78, corp. counsel, 1973-75, 78-80; of counsel firm Case, Kay & Lynch, Honolulu, 1980-81. Mem. Planning Commn. City and County of Honolulu, 1966-68, chmn., 1968; asst. to Town Atty. of Chapel Hill, 1984-93; bd. dirs. United Way, 1982-85, Pub. Sch. Found., 1984-89, Village Cos. Found., 1987-89; mem. exec. com. PTA Thrift Show, 1986-90. Capt. C.E., AUS, 1942-46. Mem. Bar Assn. Hawaii (pres. 1960-61), Chapel Hill-Carrboro C. of C. (v.p. 1982-85), SAR (pres. Hawaii 1961), Kiwanis. Episcopalian. Home: 134 Berry Patch Ln Chapel Hill NC 27514

SHARPTON, ALFRED CHARLES, minister, political activist. Founder, pres. Nat. Action Network, Inc., Bklyn., 1991—. Office: Nat Action Network Inc 1941 Madison Ave Ste 2 New York NY 10035-1801*

SHARPTON, THOMAS, physician; b. Augusta, Ga., July 15, 1949; s. Thomas and Elizabeth (Dozier) S. BA, Northwestern U., 1971; MS, Stanford U., 1973, MD, 1977. Intern Martinez (Calif.) VAMC, 1977-78, resident, 1978-80; mem. staff Kaiser Permanente Med. Group, Oakland, Calif., 1980—; asst. clin. prof. medicine U. Calif., San Francisco, 1994—; cons. Berkeley (Calif.) Free Clinic, 1977—; chmn. peer review Kaiser Permanente Med. Group, Oakland, 1985-86; clin. mem. faculty U. Calif., San Francisco, 1992, asst. clin. prof., 1994; chair AIDS therapeutics com. No. Calif. Kaiser Hosps., 1996—. Mem. Alameda County Profl. Adv. Com., Oakland, 1984-88, Alameda County AIDS Task Force, Oakland, 1985-88. Fellow ACP; mem. Calif. Med. Assn., Alameda-Contra Costa Med. Assn., Mensa, Sigma Pi Sigma, Phi Beta Kappa. Democrat. Club: Phi Beta Kappa of No. Calif. Avocations: classical piano. Office: Kaiser PMG 280 W Macarthur Blvd Piedmont CA 94611-5642

SHARROW, LEONARD, musician, educator; b. N.Y.C., Aug. 4, 1915; s. Saul and Sonia (Berson) S.; m. Emily M. Kass, Oct. 22, 1942; 1 son, Neil Jason. Grad., Juilliard Sch. Music, 1935. Prin. bassoonist Nat. Symphony Orch., Washington, 1935-37; bassoonist NBC Symphony, N.Y.C., 1937-41; prin. bassoonist NBC Symphony, 1947-51, Detroit Symphony, 1946-47, Chgo. Symphony Orch., 1951-64, Pitts. Symphony Orch., 1977-87; mem. faculty Juilliard Sch. Music, 1949-51; mem. faculty, performer Gunnison Music Camp, Western State Coll., Colo., 1962-63; pvt. teaching, 1946—; tchr. bassoon Ind. U. Sch. Music, Bloomington, Ind., part-time 1963-64; prof. music (bassoon) Ind. U. Sch. Music, 1964-77; assoc. prof. Indiana U. of Pa., 1979-80; part-time faculty Pa. State U., 1979-80, 80-81; adj. prof. Sch. of Music, Carnegie Mellon U., 1981-86; mem. bassoon faculty New Eng. Conservatory Music, Boston, 1986-89; faculty, performer New Coll. Summer Music Festival, 1976, 77, 79-86, Aspen Music Festival, 1967—, Waterloo Music Festival, 1979, 80, 83, 86, Banff Ctr. for Arts, Can., 1982, Johannesen Internat. Sch. Arts Summer Festival, Victoria, B.C., Can., 1984; solo bassoonist World Philharm. Orch., Stockholm, 1985; Alan R. Rose fellow, guest artist, lectr., performer Victorian Coll. Arts, Melbourne, Canberra, Sydney, Australia, 1989; mem. faculty, performer Nagano Aspen Music Festival, Japan, 1990-94; mem. faculty Marrowstone Music Festival, Port Townsend, Wash., 1995-96. Mem. Am. Woodwind Quintet, 1964-77; Editor: major works for bassoon; performances chamber music groups, Washington, N.Y.C., Chgo. others; participant, Pablo Casals Festival, Prades, France, 1953, soloist, NBC Symphony, Chgo. Symphony Orch., Pitts. Symphony, Aspen Festival Orch.; TV concerts, Chgo. and Pitts. symphonies; solo recs.: Mozart Bassoon Concerto in B flat Major, with Arturo Toscanini and NBC Symphony, Vivaldi Concerti for Bassoon with Max Goberman and N.Y. Symphonietta, Leonard Sharrow Plays Bassoon Solos, with piano, Concerto da Camera for Bassoon and Orch. (Dan Welcher), Concerto for bassoon and orch. (Ray Luke); assisting artist: A Baroque Trumpet recital with Gerard Schwarz. Served with AUS, 1941-45. Recipient award Toscanini Collection Assn., 1985. Mem. AAUP, Pi Kappa Lambda. Office: 3153 Coppertree Dr Bloomington IN 47401-9699

SHARROW, MARILYN JANE, library administrator; bd. Oakland, Calif.; d. Charles L. and H. Evelyn S.; m. Lawrence J. Davis. BS in Design, U. Mich., 1967, MALS, 1969. Librarian Detroit Pub. Libr., 1968-70; head fine arts dept. Syracuse (N.Y.) U. Librs., 1970-73; dir. libr. Roseville (Mich.) Pub. Libr., 1973-75; asst. dir. librs. U. Wash., 1975-77, assoc. dir. librs., 1978-79; dir. libraries U. Man., Winnipeg, Can., 1979-82; chief libr. U. Toronto, Can., 1982-85; univ. libr. U. Calif., Davis, 1985—. Recipient Woman of Yr. in Mgmt. award Winnipeg YWCA, 1982; named Woman of Distinction, U. Calif. Faculty Women's Rsch. Group, 1985. Mem. ALA, Assn. Rsch. Librs. (bd. dirs., v.p., pres-elect 1989-90, pres. 1990-91, chair sci. tech. work group 1994—, rsch. collections com. 1993-95, preservation com. 1997—), Online Computer Libr. Ctr.-Rsch. Librs. Adv. Com. (vice chmn. 1992-93, chair 1993-94), Calif. State Network Resources Lib. Com. Office: U Calif Libr Adminstrn Davis CA 95616

SHARTLE, KEITH ROBERT, producer. BA, UCLA, 1974. Purchasing agt. Profl. Photosystems Corp., 1970, v.p., gen. mgr. retail and photo supply div.; with client rels. and contracts, photography and film editing depts. Dream Quest Images, Simi Valley, Calif., 1982, bus. mgr., 1987, exec. producer Film divsn., 1987-94, pres. Film Group, 1994-96; sr. v.p. Dream Quest Images subs. Walt Disney Co., Simi Valley, 1996—. Exec. producer of visual effects for films including The Abyss, Total Recall, Jungle 2 Jungle, Con Air, George of the Jungle, The Lost Boys, Crimson Tide; overseer prodn. of effects for feature films, TV episodes and movies, numerous film attractions worldwide theme parks. Office: Dream Quest Images 2635 Park Center Dr Simi Valley CA 93065-6209

SHARWELL, WILLIAM GAY, retired university president and company executive; b. Newark, July 26, 1920; s. William G. Sharwell and Lillian Kenny; m. Jacqueline Larocque, Oct. 22, 1960; children: William L., Paul L. BS, Seton Hall U., 1941, DBA (hon.), 1980; MBA, NYU, 1950, Harvard U., 1952; DCS, Harvard U., 1960; LLD (hon.), Pace U., 1979. V.p., comptr. N.Y. Tel., N.Y.C., 1967-68, exec. v.p. ops., 1968-76; sr. v.p. AT&T, N.Y.C., 1976-84; pres. Pace U., N.Y.C., 1984-90; ret., 1990; bd. dirs. Am. Biogenetic Scis., Inc., Copiague, N.Y., Associated Solo Artists, TII Industries, Inc., Toa Alta, P.R.; gen. ptnr. Equitable Capital Ptnrs., L.P. Mem. editorial bd. Ency. of Profl. Mgmt., 1978. Bd. dirs. Internat. House. Mem. Harvard Club (N.Y.C.). Avocations: tennis, kite flying, video editing.

SHASTEEN, DONALD EUGENE, government official; b. Englewood, Colo., Dec. 3, 1928; s. George Donald and Frances True (Meyers) S.; m. Shirley Mae Johnson, Aug. 8, 1954; children: Jon Randolph, Ron Winston, Sherilyn Sue. B.A. in Journalism, U. Colo., 1950. Reporter Omaha World-Herald, Des Moines, 1954-58, Lincoln, Nebr., 1958-66; exec. asst. to Senator Carl T. Curtis of Nebr., Washington, 1966-73, adminstrv. asst., 1973-78; adminstrv. asst. to Sen. Gordon J. Humphrey, 1979-80; with transition group Senate Republican Conf., 1980; dep. under sec. for legislation and intergovtl. affairs Dept. Labor, 1981-83, dep. asst. sec. for vets. employment, 1983-85, asst. sec. for vets. employment and tng., 1985-89; chmn. exec. com. Am. World Svcs., Inc.; v.p. Cocke & Phillips, Inc. Rep. nominee for U.S. Senate Nebr., 1978. Served with U.S. Army, 1951-52. Mem. Am. Legion, VFW, Am. Vets., Disabled Am. Vets., Phi Delta Theta. Republican. Lutheran.

SHASTID, JON BARTON, wine company executive; b. Hannibal, Mo., Nov. 21, 1914; s. Jon Shepherd and Mary (Barton) S.; m. Natalie Kiliani, Dec. 16, 1944; children—Lucinda, Jon G.H., Victoria A., Thomas Bartwyn. Bar: Calif. bar 1959; C.P.A., Calif., Kans. Pub. accountant Dodge City, Kans., 1938-42; v.p. finance Johnson Bronze Co., New Castle, Pa., 1946-54; exec. v.p., treas. E. & J. Gallo Winery, Modesto, Calif., 1954-88; pres. Gallo Wine Co. of La. at New Orleans, 1960-89. City councilman, Modesto, 1961-69. Served to capt. USAAF, 1942-46. Mem. State Bar of Calif., Am. Bar Assn., Calif. Soc. C.P.A.'s. Home and Office: PO Box 3808 Modesto CA 95352-3808

SHASTRI, RANGANATH KRISHNA, materials scientist; b. Gokarn, Mysore, India, Feb. 24, 1951; came to U.S., 1974; s. Krishna Ganesh and Radha K. (Kurse) S. B of Engring. in Chem. Engring., U. Mysore, Surathkal, India, 1973; MSChemE, U. Cin., 1976, PhD in Materials Sci., 1979. Rsch. assoc. dept. orthop. surgery/materials sci. U. Cin., 1979-81; polymer scientist Revere Rsch. Inc., Edison, N.J., 1981-82; v.p. J.R. Enterprises, Greenwich, Conn., 1983; sr. rsch. engr. Dow Chem. Co., Midland, Mich., 1983-86, project leader, 1986-89, project leader database devel. Materials Engring. Ctr., 1989-91, devel. leader, 1991—. Contbr. articles to profl. jours., chpt. in book; holds 13 patents. Bd. dirs. Voluntary Action Ctr. Midland County, 1986-88. NIH fellow, 1976-79. Mem. Am. Soc. Materials Internat. (chmn. polymer composites session Indpls. 1989, polymer composites com. of composites tech. divsn. 1987—, World Material Congress chmn. advanced composites tutorial/panel discussion session, engring. materials achievement award selection com. 1990-92), ASTM (chmn. task groups 1990—), Am. Chem. Soc. (chmn. materials sci. info. session Atlanta 1990), Internat. Orgn. Standardization (comm. com. U.S. del. tech. com. 61), Soc. Plastics Engrs. (sr. mem., bd. dirs. PD3), Soc. Automotive Engrs., N.Y. Acad. Scis., Soc. Plastics Industry (internat. tech. adv. com. divsn. polymeric material producers). Home: 2913 Jeffrey Ln Midland MI 48640-2472 Office: Dow Chem Co MEC 433 Bldg Midland MI 48667

SHATAN, CHAIM FELIX, psychiatrist, medical educator, expert on Vietnam veterans, traumatic stress pioneer; b. Wloclawek, Poland, Sept. 1, 1924; s. Morris Y. and Millie (Erdberg) S.; m. Norma Claire Altstedter, May 29, 1955; children: Gregory Samuel, Gabrielle Rebecca, Jessica Anne, Jeremy Daniel Irving. BSc. magna cum laude, McGill U., 1945, M.D., C.M., 1947. Cert. in psychoanalysis; cert. in hypnosis. Intern Montreal Gen. Hosp., 1947-48; resident in psychiatry Queen Mary Vets. Hosp., Montreal, 1948-50, Hillside Hosp., N.Y.C., 1950-52; cons. Children's Village, Dobbs Ferry, N.Y., 1953-55; supervising psychiatrist ednl. clinic CCNY, 1957-62; instr., adj. attending psychiatrist Presbyn. Hosp.-Columbia U. Coll. Physicians and Surgeons, 1962-65; tng., supervising analyst, co-dir. postdoctoral psychoanalytic tng. clinic, assoc. prof., then prof. psychoanalysis NYU Grad. Sch., N.Y.C., 1963-75; clin. prof., clinic supr., tng. analyst NYU Grad. Sch., 1975—; vis. lectr. post-Vietman syndrome Austen Riggs Found., Stockbridge, Mass., 1972; vis. lectr. post-Vietnam syndrome Middlebury Coll., Vt., 1973, U. Ill., Urbana, 1974, Dartmouth Coll. Med. Sch., Hanover, N.H., 1980, numerous other univs.; vis. lectr. hypnosis for stage fright Lowell U. Coll. Music, Mass., 1975-76, Boston U., Tanglewood Inst., 1980; co-founder, coordinator Vietnam Vets. Psychol. Service, 1970-75, Vietnam Vets. Working Group, 1975—; research assoc. Inst. Psychohistory, Inst. Research History; cons., participant radio and TV interviews on combat and other strss disorders, mercenaries, hostages, stage fright and hypnosis, speaker in field. Contbg. author rsch. papers to profl. lit., chpts. in books, articles on body lang., hypnosis, stagefright, cmty. psychiatry, vets. post-traumatic stress disorders, combat, enemies, war babies, psychoanalysis to newspapers, mags., convs., profl. jours. Presbyn. Ch. for Vietnam Vets. grantee; recipient 1st Nat. Holocaust Meml. award N.Y. Soc. Clin. Psychologists, 1974, Armstrong award for best pub. radio program, 1975, Haley award for Clin. Excellence Internat. Soc. Traumatic Stress Studies, 1994. Fellow Am. Orthopsychiat. Assn. (grantee), Am. Acad. Psychoanalysis, Am. Psychiat. Assn., Can. Psychiat. Assn., World Psychiat. Assn., Internat. Psychoanalytic Forum, Internat. Soc. Polit. Psychology (founder); mem. AMA, Group for Use of Psychology in History, Internat. Psychohist. Assn., Internat. Soc. Traumatic Stress Studies (founder, bd. dirs.), N.Y. State Med. Soc., N.Y. Coun. Child Psychiatry, N.Y. County Med. Soc., Montreal Med. Soc., W.A. White Psychoanalytic Soc., Lenstock Assn., Alpha Omega Alpha. Home: Beachwood Mahkeenac Rd Stockbridge MA 01262 Home and Office: 415 Central Park W New York NY 10025-4856 *I love uphill struggles. Disappointments rarely stop me. Persistence and knowledge overcome most obstacles. I am drawn to victims of uprooting and cruelty-survivors, Amerindians, combat vets, war babies-especially those ignored by society. Relief of such injustice and pain is central to my identity as physician, writer, psychoanalyst. I learn about human catastrophe from medicine, but also from artists (my spouse), poets, Scriptures and my children. I shall continue to learn and strive till I am 100.*

SHATIN, HARRY, medical educator, dermatologist; b. N.Y.C., July 7, 1910; s. Samuel and Hannah (Papish) Shatinsky; m. Vera Brusilowsky, Oct. 30, 1943; 1 dau., Beth. B.S., Coll. City N.Y., 1930; M.D., Strasbourg U., France, 1936; postgrad., N.Y. U., 1949-50. Intern Unity Hosp., N.Y.C., 1937-38; pvt. practice medicine, 1938-41; staff physician VA Hosp., Bronx, N.Y., 1946-51; chief sect. dermatology VA Hosp., 1951-74, sr. cons. dermatology, 1974—; prof. clin. medicine Mt. Sinai Sch. Medicine, City U. N.Y., 1969-74, prof. dermatology, chmn. dept., 1974-79, prof. emeritus, 1979—; dir. dermatology Mt. Sinai Hosp., N.Y.C., 1974-79, cons. dermatology, 1979—. Served from lt. to maj. AUS, 1942-46. Fellow Am. Acad. Dermatology, A.C.P. (asso.), N.Y. Acad. Medicine; mem. AMA, Soc. Investigative Dermatology, Manhattan Dermatol. Soc. (pres. 1967-68), Dermatol. Soc. Greater N.Y., Internat. Soc. Tropical Dermatology. Home: 3720 Independence Ave Bronx NY 10463-1429

SHATIN, JUDITH, music composing educator; b. Boston, Nov. 11, 1949; d. Leo and Harriet Evelyn (Sommer) S.; m. Michael Kubovy, June 28, 1992. AB, Douglass, Coll., 1971; MM, Julliard Sch., 1974; PhD, Princeton U., 1979. Asst. prof. U. Va., Charlottesville, 1979-85, assoc. prof., 1985-92, prof., 1992—, chair McIntire dept. music, 1995—; dir. Va. Ctr. Computer Music, 1988—. Composer (piano concerto) Passion of St. Cecilia, 1985, (flute concerto) Ruah, 1985, (piano trio) View from Mt. Nebo (commd. by Garth Newel Chamber Players), 1985, (piano trio) Ignoto Numine (commd. Monticello Trio), 1986, (flute, clarinet, violin, cello) Secret Ground, 1990, (soprano and tape) Three Summers Heat, 1989 (Barlow Found. Commn.), (orchestra) Piping the Earth (commd. by Women's Philharm.), 1990, (flute and electronics) Kairos, (commd. Va. Commn. for the Arts), 1991, (chorus, brass quintet, tympani) We Hold These Truths (commd. UVA), 1992, (string orchestra) Stringing the Bow (commd. Va. Chamber Orch.), 1992, COAL (commd. as part of 2-yr. retrospective of work, sponsored by Lila Wallace-Readers Digest Arts Ptnrs. Program), 1994, (piano and percussion) 1492 (commd. Arioso Ensemble), 1992, (piano) Chai Variations on Eliahu HaNavi, 1995, (flute and guitar) Dreamtigers (commd. Ekko!), 1996, (chorus) Adonai Ro'i, 1995; (string quartet) Janus Quartet (commd. Arcata Quartet), 1994, (string quartet and electronic playback) Elijah's Chariot, (commd. Kronos Quartet), 1995, Sea of Reeds (commd. F. Gerard Errante), 1997. Nat. Endowment for Arts Composer fellow, 1980, 85, 89, 92; recipient award Va. Commn. for the Arts, 1989. Mem. Am. Music Ctr., Am. Women Composers (pres. 1989-93), Am. Composers Alliance (bd. dirs. 1993—). Avocations: yoga.

SHATKIN, AARON JEFFREY, biochemistry educator; b. Providence, July 18, 1934; s. Morris and Doris S.; m. Joan A. Lynch, Nov. 30, 1957; 1 son, Gregory Martin. AB, Bowdoin Coll., 1956, DSc (hon.), 1979; PhD, Rockefeller Inst., 1961. Sr. asst. scientist NIH, Bethesda, Md., 1961-63; rsch. chemist NIH, 1963-68; vis. scientist Salk Inst., La Jolla, Calif., 1968-69; assoc. mem. dept. cell biology Roche Inst. Molecular Biology, Nutley, N.J., 1968-73, full mem., 1973-77, head molecular virology lab., 1977-86, head dept. cell biology, 1983-86; dir. N.J. Ctr. Advanced Biotech. Medicine, 1986—; prof. molecular genetics UMDNJ, 1986—; univ. prof. molecular biology Rutgers U., New Brunswick, N.J., 1986—; adj. prof. cell biology Rockefeller U.; vis. prof. molecular biology Princeton U. Mem. editl. bd. Jour. Virology, 1969-82, Archives of Biochemistry and Biophysics, 1972-82, Virology, 1973-76, Comprehensive Virology, 1974-82, Jour. Biol. Chemistry, 1977-83, 94—, RNA Jour., 1995-96, Procs. of NAS, 1997—; editor Advances in Virus Rsch., 1983—, Jour. Virology, 1973-77; editor-in-chief Molecular and Cellular Biology, 1980-95. Served with USPHS, 1961-63. Recipient U.S. Steel Found. prize in molecular biology, 1977, N.J. Sci. and Tech. Pride award, 1989, Thomas Edison Sci. award State of N.J., 1991; Rockefeller fellow, 1956-61. Fellow AAAS, Am. Acad. Microbiology, N.Y. Acad. Scis.; mem. NAS, Am. Soc. Microbiology, Am. Soc. Biol. Chemists, Am. Soc. Virology, Am. Chem. Soc., Am. Soc. Cell Biology, Harvey Soc. Home: 1381 Rahway Rd Scotch Plains NJ 07076-3452 Office: Ctr Advanced Biotech and Medicine 679 Hoes Ln Piscataway NJ 08854-5627

SHATNER, WILLIAM, actor; b. Montreal, Que., Can., Mar. 22, 1931; s. Joseph and Anne S.; m. Gloria Rand, Aug. 12, 1956 (div. Mar. 1969); m. Marcy Lafferty, Oct. 20, 1973; 3 daus. B.A., McGill U., 1952. Stage debut, 1952; appeared Montreal Playhouse, summers 1952, 53; played juvenile roles Canadian Repertory Theatre, Ottawa, 1952-53, 53-54; appeared Stratford Shakespeare Festival, Ont., 1954-56; Broadway appearances include Tamburlaine the Great, 1956, The World of Suzie Wong, 1958, A Shot in the Dark, 1961; films include The Brothers Karamazov, 1958, The Explosive Generation, 1961, Judgement at Nuremburg, 1961, The Intruder, 1962, The Outrage, 1964, Dead of Night, 1974, The Devil's Rain, 1975, Star Trek, 1979, The Kidnapping of the President, 1979, Star Trek: The Wrath of Khan, 1982, Star Trek III: The Search for Spock, 1984, Star Trek IV: The Voyage Home, 1986, (director) Star Trek V: The Final Frontier, 1989, Star Trek VI: The Undiscovered Country, 1991, National Lampoon's Loaded Weapon, 1992, Star Trek: Generations, 1994; also TV movies and appearances on The Andersonville Trial, The Bastard, 1978, Disaster on the Coastliner, 1979, Secrets of a Married Man, 1984, North Beach and Rawhide, 1985, Columbo, 1993; star of TV show Star Trek, 1966-69, animated series, 1973-75; TV series Barbary Coast, 1975-76, The Babysitter, 1979, T.J. Hooker; host (TV series) Rescue 911, CBS, 1989—; dir. TV movie TekWar; author: (novels) TekWar, 1989, TekLords, 1991, TekLab, 1991, Tek Vengeance, 1992, Tek Secret, 1993, (memoirs) Star Trek Memories, 1993, Star Trek Movie Memories, 1994, Tek Power, 1994, Tek Money, 1995, The Ashes of Eden, 1995, Man O' War, 1996, Tek Kill, 1996, The Return, 1996, Avenger, 1997, Delta Search: Quest for Tomorrow, 1997. Recipient Tyrone Guthrie award, 1956, Theatre World award, 1958. Mem. Actors Equity Assn., AFTRA, Screen Actors Guild, Dirs. Guild. Address: care of Lemli Prodns 760 N La Cienega Blvd Los Angeles CA 90069-5231

SHATTO, GLORIA MCDERMITH, academic administrator; b. Houston, Oct. 11, 1931; d. Ken E. and Gertrude (Osborne) McDermith; m. Robert J. Shatto, Mar. 19, 1953; children: David Paul, Donald Patrick. BA with honors in Econs., Rice U., 1954, PhD (fellow), 1966. Mkt. rsch. Humble Oil & Refining Co., Houston, 1954-55; tchr. pub. sch. C.Z., 1955-56; tchr. Houston Ind. Sch. Dist., 1956-60; asst. prof. econs. U. Houston, 1965-69, assoc. prof., 1969-72; prof. econs., assoc. dean Coll. Indsl. Mgmt., Ga. Inst. Tech., Atlanta, 1973-77; George R. Brown prof. bus. Trinity U., San Antonio, 1977-79; pres. Berry Coll., Mt. Berry, Ga., 1980—; sml. bus. adv. com. U.S. Treasury, 1977-81; trustee Joint Coun. Econ. Edn., 1985-88; dir. Ga. Power Co., So. Co., Becton Dickinson and Co., Tex. Instruments, Inc. Contbr. articles to profl. jours.; Editor: Employment of the Middle-Aged, 1972; mem. editorial bd.: Ednl. Record, 1980-82. Mem. Tex. Gov.'s Commn. on Status of Women, 1970-72, Gov.'s Commn. on Economy and Efficiency in State Govt., 1991; trustee Ga. Tech. Rsch. Inst., 1975-77, Berry Coll., Ga., 1975-79, Ga. Forestry Commn., 1987-95; mem. Ga. Gov.'s Commn. on Status of Women, 1975; mem. commn. on women in higher edn. Am. Coun. on Edn., 1980-82, chmn., 1982; mem. Ga. Study Com. on Pub. Higher Edn. Fin., 1981-82; v.p. Ga. Found. Ind. Colls., 1981, pres. 1982, 94; mem. adv. bd. to Sch. Bus. Adminstrn., Temple U., Phila., 1981-83; mem. Study Com. on Ednl. Processes, Soc. Assn. Colls. and Schs., 1981-82, Ga. United Meth. Commn. on Higher Edn. and Campus Ministry, 1981-82; trustee Redmond Park Hosp., Rome, Ga., 1981-87, 1st United Meth. Ch., 1986-89; alumni gov., bd. govs. Rice U., Houston, 1997. Recipient Disting. Alumni award Rice U., 1987; OAS fellow, summer 1968. Mem. Royal Econ. Assn., Am. Econ. Assn., So. Econ. Assn., Southwestern Econ. Assn. (pres. 1976-77), Am. Fin. Assn. (nominating com. 1976), Southwestern Social Scis. Assn., Fin. Execs. Inst. (chmn. Atlanta edn. com. 1977-78, nat. com. on profl. devel. 1981), AAUW (area rep. 1967-68, Tex. chmn. legis. program 1970-71, mem. internat. fellowships-awards com. 1970-76, chmn. 1974-76), Ga. Newcomen Soc. (chmn. 1991—), Newcomen Soc. U.S. (trustee), Phi Beta Kappa, Phi Kappa Phi, Omicron Delta Epsilon. Office: Berry Coll Office of the President PO Box 490039 Mount Berry GA 30149-0039

SHATTO, JOHN FREDERICK, court administrator; b. Frederick, Md., July 5, 1957; s. Paul Frederick and Dell (Napier) S.; m. Elizabeth Vandiver Scott, Aug. 16, 1980; children: Julia Reed, Scott Napier. BS in Psychology, Armstrong State Coll., 1985; MS in Adminstrn., Cen. Mich. U., 1988. Dep. ct. adminstr. County of Chatham, Savannah, Ga., 1986-91; ct. adminstr. Howard County Cir. Ct., Ellicott City, Md., 1991—. Fellow Inst. Ct. Mgmt.; mem. Nat. Assn. for Ct. Mgmt., Sigma Iota Epsilon. Episcopalian. Avocations: tennis, reading. Home: 9796 Chestnut Oak Ct Frederick MD 21701-6724 Office: Howard County Cir Ct 8360 Court Ave Ellicott City MD 21043-4550

SHATTUCK, CATHIE ANN, lawyer, former government official; b. Salt Lake City, July 18, 1945; d. Robert Ashley S. and Lillian Culp (Shattuck). B.A., U. Nebr., 1967, J.D., 1970. Bar: Nebr. 1970, U.S. Dist. Ct. Nebr. 1970, Colo. 1971, U.S. Dist. Ct. Colo. 1971, U.S. Supreme Ct. 1974, U.S. Ct. Appeals (10th cir.) 1977, U.S. Dist. Ct. D.C. 1984, U.S. Ct. Appeals (D.C. cir.) 1984. V.p., gen. mgr. Shattuck Farms, Hastings, Nebr., 1967-70; asst. project dir. atty. Colo. Civil Rights Commn., Denver, 1970-72; trial atty. Equal Employment Opportunity Commn., Denver, 1973-77; vice chmn. Equal Employment Opportunity Commn., Washington, 1982-84; pvt. practice law Denver, 1977-81; mem. Fgn. Svc. Bd., Washington, 1982-84, Presdl. Personnel Task Force, Washington, 1982-84; ptnr. Epstein, Becker & Green, L.A. and Washington, 1984—; lectr. Colo. Continuing Legal Edn. Author: Employer's Guide to Controlling Sexual Harrassment, 1992; mem. editorial bd. The Practical Litigator, 1988—. Bd. dirs. KGNU Pub. Radio, Boulder, Colo., 1979, Denver Exchange, 1980-81, YWCA Met. Denver, 1979-81. Recipient Nebr. Young Career Woman Bus. and Profl. Women, 1967; recipient Outstanding Nebraskan Daily Nebraskan, Lincoln, 1967. Mem. ABA (mgmt. chair labor and employment law sect. com. on immigration law 1988-90, mgmt. chair com. on legis. devels. 1990-93), Nebr. Bar Assn., Colo. Bar Assn., Colo. Women's Bar Assn., D.C. Bar Assn., Nat. Women's Coalition, Delta Sigma Rho, Tau Kappa Alpha, Pi Sigma Alpha, Alpha Xi Delta, Denver Club.

SHATTUCK, GEORGE CLEMENT, lawyer; b. Syracuse, N.Y., Sept. 2, 1927; s. Frank M. and Geneveive Mary (Hannon) S.; m. Sheila Eagan, Sept. 21, 1957 (div. 1985); children: Edward, George, Frank, Mark, Patrick; m. Carla A. Amussen, June 16, 1987; 1 child, Morgan. BS in Mgmt., Syracuse U., 1950, JD, 1953. Bar: N.Y. 1954, U.S. Supreme Ct. 1973. Ptnr., estate planning splty. practice group Bond, Schoeneck & King Law Firm, Syracuse, 1954—. Author: Oneida Land Claims, 1991, Estate Planning for the Small Business Owner, 1993. Mem. Syracuse Bd. Edn., 1968-75. Roman Catholic. Avocations: writing, reading history and philosophy, fishing, biking. Home: 5158 W Lake Rd Cazenovia NY 13035-9633 Office: Bond Schoeneck & King One Lincoln Ctr Syracuse NY 13202

SHATTUCK, JOHN, federal official; m. Ellen Hume; 4 children. BA magna cum laude, Yale U., JD; MA with 1st-class honors, Cambridge U., Eng. Law clk. to Hon. Edward Weinfeld U.S. Dist. Ct. (so. dist.) N.Y., 1970-71; nat. counsel ACLU, 1971-77, dir. Washington office, 1977-84; v.p. govt., community and pub. affairs Harvard U., 1984-93, sr. assoc. sci. tech. and pub. policy program John F. Kennedy sch. govt., 1984-93; asst. sec. of state bur. human rights and humanitarian affairs Dept. of State, Washington, 1993—; lectr. Harvard U.; vis. lectr. Princeton U. Editor Yale U. Law Jour.; contbr. articles to profl. jours. Recipient H.L. Mencken award Free Press Assn., Pub. Svc. award Yale U., Roger Baldwin medal. Mem. Leadership Conf. Civil Rights (mem. exec. com.). Office: Dept of State Office of the Secretary 2201 C St NW Rm 7802 Washington DC 20520-0001*

SHATTUCK, LAWRENCE WILLIAM, admissions director; b. Nashua, N.H., Aug. 24, 1951; s. Fred and Shirley (Lundeen) S. AS, Middlesex C.C., Mass., 1975; MEd, Cambridge (Mass.) Coll., 1990. Admissions officer Tufts U. Sch. Dental Medicine, Boston, 1976-90; dir. admissions New Eng. Coll. Optometry, Boston, 1990—. Mem. Nat. Assn. Grad. Admissions Profls. (mem. membership com.), Nat. Assn. Advisors for the Health Professions, N.E. Assn. Advisors to the Health Professions. Home: 278 Manning St Unit 904 Hudson MA 01749-1046 Office: New Eng Coll Optometry 424 Beacon St Boston MA 02115-1129

SHATTUCK, MAYO ADAMS, III, investment bank executive; b. Boston, Oct. 7, 1954; s. Mayo Adams Jr. and Jane (Bergwall) S.; children: Mayo Adams IV, Kathleen Elizabeth. BA, Williams Coll., 1976; MBA, Stanford U., 1980. Analyst Morgan Guaranty Trust Co., N.Y.C., 1976-78; mgr. Bain & Co., Menlo Park, Calif., 1980-83; v.p. to mng. dir. and head of corp. fin. Alex Brown & Sons, San Francisco, 1985-91; pres. and COO Alex Brown & Sons, Balt., 1991—; bd. dirs. Alex Brown, Inc., Balt., Constellation Holdings Inc. subs. Balt. Gas and Electric. Trustee Gilman Sch., Bryn Mawr Sch., Wellness Cmty., Balt., 1991—; chmn. bd. dirs. Columbus Ctr., Balt., 1992—; adv. dir. U. Md., Balt., 1992—. Mem. Am. Bus. Conf. Avocations: tennis, golf. Office: Alex Brown & Sons 1 South St Baltimore MD 21202-3298

SHATTUCK, ROGER WHITNEY, author, educator; b. N.Y.C., Aug. 20, 1923; s. Howard Francis and Elizabeth (Colt) S.; m. Nora Ewing White, Aug. 20, 1949; children—Tari Elizabeth, Marc Ewing, Patricia Colt, Eileen Shepard. Grad., St. Paul's Sch., Concord, N.H., 1941; B.A., Yale, 1947; Doctorat honoris causa, U. Orléans, France, 1990. Information officer UNESCO, Paris, France, 1947-48; asst. editor Harcourt, Brace & Co., 1949-50; mem. Soc. Fellows, Harvard, 1950-53, instr. French, 1953-56; faculty U. Tex., Austin, 1956-71; prof. English, French U. Tex., 1968-71, chmn. dept. French and Italian, 1968-71; Commonwealth prof. French U. Va., Charlottesville, 1974-88; univ. prof., prof. modern fgn. langs. Boston U., 1988-97; mem. adv. bd. Nat. Translation Center, 1964-69, chmn., 1966-69; provediteur gen. Coll. de Pataphysique, Paris, 1961—; Fulbright prof. U. Dakar, Senegal, 1984-85. Author: The Banquet Years, 1958; poems Half Tame, 1964, Proust's Binoculars, 1963, Marcel Proust, 1974 (Nat. Book award 1975), The Forbidden Experiment, 1980, The Innocent Eye, 1984, Forbidden Knowledge, 1996; editor or co-editor: Selected Writings of Guillaume Appollinaire, 1950, Mount Analogue, (René Daumal), 1959, The Craft and Context of Translation (with William Arrowsmith), 1961, Selected works of Alfred Jarry, 1965, Occasions by Paul Valèry, 1970; mem. editl. bd. PMLA, 1977-78. Served to capt. USAAF, 1942-45. Decorated Ordre Palmes Academiques (France).; Guggenheim fellow, 1958-59; Fulbright research fellow, 1958-59; Am. Council Learned Socs. research fellow, 1969-70. Fellow AAAS; mem. Assn. Literary Scholars and Critics (pres. 1995-96).

SHATZ, CARLA J., biology educator. Prof. neurobiology U. Calif., Berkeley. Recipient Charles A. Dana award for pioneering achievements in health NAS, 1995. Mem. AAAS, Nat. Acad. Scis., Am. Philos. Soc. Office: Univ California Dept Molec & Cell Bio Berkeley CA 94720

SHATZ, STEPHEN SIDNEY, mathematician, educator; b. Bklyn., Apr. 27, 1937; s. Nathan and Agusta S.; children: Geoffrey, Adria. A.B., Harvard U., 1957, A.M., 1958, Ph.D., 1962; A.M. (hon.), U. Pa., 1971. Instr. Stanford U., 1962-63, acting asst. prof., 1963-64; asst. prof. U. Pa., Phila., 1964-67; assoc. prof. U. Pa., 1967-69, prof. math., 1969—, chmn. dept. math., 1983-86; vis. prof. U. Pisa, 1966-67; mem. Math. Scis. Rsch. Inst., 1986-87, Inst. Advanced Study, 1997. Author: Profinite Groups, Arithmetic and Geometry, 1972; contbr. articles to profl. jours. Mem. Am. Math. Soc. (editor Trans. 1975-78, coun. 1975-80, exec. com. coun. 1979-80). Office: U Pa Dept Math Philadelphia PA 19104-6395

SHATZKIN, LEONARD, publishing consultant; b. Warsaw, Poland, July 16, 1919; came to U.S., 1920, naturalized, 1922; s. Isaac and Helen (Feiman) S.; m. Eleanor Oshry, Aug. 4, 1940; children: Michael, Karen, Nancy. Student, CCNY, 1935-38; B.S., Carnegie Inst. Tech., 1941. Prodn. mgr. House Beautiful Mag., N.Y.C., 1941-43; research scientist Manhattan Project, N.Y.C., 1943-45; prodn. mgr. Viking Press, N.Y.C., 1945-50; asst. to dir. mfg. Doubleday & Co., N.Y.C., 1950-55; dir. research Doubleday & Co., 1955-60; v.p. Crowell-Collier Macmillan Co., N.Y.C., 1960-63; dir. mfg. McGraw-Hill Book Co., N.Y.C., 1963-68; v.p. McGraw-Hill Book Co., 1968-70; pres. Planned Prodn., N.Y.C., 1970-78, Two Continents Pub. Group, Ltd., N.Y.C., 1972-78; prin. Shatzkin & Co. (Cons.), Croton-on-Hudson, N.Y., 1979—; instr. div. gen. studies NYU, 1948-53; bd. dirs. Yates Industries, 1965-72; instr. Pratt Inst., 1971-72; cons. George Banta Co., Avon Industries, Macmillan Co., Orbis Books, Doubleday & Co., Grove Press, St. Martin's Press, Thomas Nelson, Grolier, Inc., CBS Internat., Dodd Mead, N.Y. Bot. Garden, Pahlavi Nat. Libr., Teheran, Iran., Ford Found., Gen. Mills, USIA, Raben & Sjogren, Stockholm, Sweden, Nat. Endowment for Arts, John Wiley & Sons, Ediouro Pub. Co., Rio de Janeiro, Curio Bookstore, Rio de Janeiro, Internat. Trademark Assn., N.Y.; cons. to Christian Lit. Assn. of Malawi, Internat. Exec. Svc. Corps re-book distbn. in Russia. Editor and translator: The Stars Bear Witness, 1947; author: In Cold Type, 1982; contbr.: articles to Publishers Weekly, others. Mem. Am. Inst. Graphic Arts (treas. 1952-59), Trade Book Clinic, Christian Literature

Assn., Publishers Round Table, Tamiment Inst., Amnesty Internat. Mem. Democratic Socialists of Am. Patentee field of book binding. Home: 132 Old Post Rd N Croton On Hudson NY 10520-1934

SHAUGHNESSY, EDWARD LOUIS, Chinese language educator; b. Sewickley, Pa., July 29, 1952; s. James Francis and Marie Rosalie (Kraus) S.; m. Gina Lynn Look, May 15, 1976 (div. Sept. 1992); m. Elena Valussi, Sept. 6, 1997. BA, U. Notre Dame, 1974; MA, Stanford U., 1980, PhD, 1985. Asst. prof. U. Chgo., 1985-90, assoc. prof., 1990-96, prof., 1996—. Assoc. editor: Early China, 1985-88, editor, 1988-96; editor: New Sources of Earlys Chinese History: An Introduction to Reading Inscriptions and Manuscripts, 1997; author: Sources of Western Zhou History: Inscribed Bronze Vessels, 1991, I Ching, The Classic of Changes: The First English Translation of the Newly Discovered Second-Century B.C. Mawangdui Manuscripts, 1996, Before Confucius: Studies in the Creation of the Chinese Classics, 1997, (with Robert Poor and Harrie A. Vanderstappen) Ritual and Reverence: Chinese Art at the University of Chicago, 1989, (with Cai Fangpei and James F. Shaughnessy) A Concordance of the Xiaotun Nandi Oracle-Bone Inscriptions, 1988; contbr. essays to books. Andrew W. Mellon fellow for Chinese studies, 1984-85, divsn. of humanities jr. faculty fellow U. Chgo., 1986. Home: 711 S Dearborn St Apt 506 Chicago IL 60605-1823 Office: U Chgo East Asian Langs/Civilizat 1050 E 59th St Chicago IL 60637-1512

SHAUGHNESSY, THOMAS WILLIAM, librarian, consultant; b. Pitts., May 3, 1938; s. Martin T. and LaVerne (O'Brien) S.; m. Marlene D. Reuben, Aug. 11, 1968; 1 child, Mark Andrew. AB, St. Vincent Coll., 1961; MLS, U. Pitts., 1964; PhD, Rutgers U., 1970. Asst. dean Rutgers U., New Brunswick, N.J., 1969-71; libr. dir. Rutgers-Newark, 1971-74; assoc. dean U. So. Calif., L.A., 1974-78; asst. libr. dir. U. Houston, 1978-82; libr. dir. U. Mo.-Columbia, 1982-89; univ. libr. and dir. U. Minn., Mpls.-St. Paul, 1989—; rsch. dir. Chgo. Pub. Libr. Survey, 1968-69; cons. U. Tulsa Libr., 1982-83. Author: (with Lowell A. Martin) Library Response to Urban Change, 1969, Developing Leadership Skills: A Source Book for Librarians, 1990. U.S. Office Edn. grantee Rutgers U., 1971; fellow Coun. Libr. Resources, 1973, sr. fellow, 1985; recipient Hugh C. Atkinson Meml. award, 1996. Mem. ALA, Assn. Coll. and Rsch. Librs., Assn. Rsch. Librs. (cons. tng. fellow 1981, bd. dirs. 1989-92), Minn. Libr. Assn., Beta Phi Mu. Home: 5705 Wycliffe Rd Minneapolis MN 55436-2264 Office: U Minn Wilson Libr Minneapolis MN 55455-0414

SHAUL, ROGER LOUIS, JR., health care consultant, executive, researcher; b. Hartford, Conn., Jan. 12, 1948; s. Roger Louis Shaul Sr. and Margot (Bradley) Vinson; m. Michele Marie Morland, Dec. 21, 1974; children: Lisa Marie, John Benjamin, Robert Louis. AA, Palm Beach Jr. Coll., Lake Worth, Fla., 1968; BS, U. Fla., 1970, MBA, 1974; cert., Yale U. and U. N.C., 1981, 1984. Adminstrv. resident Univ. Hosp. of Jacksonville, Fla., 1974-79; dir. rev. svcs. Capital Health Systems Agy., Durham, N.C., 1979; dir. Sun Alliance, Charlotte, N.C., 1979-83; v.p. Sun Health, Inc., Charlotte, 1983-87; pres. Preferred Med. Mktg. Corp., Charlotte, 1987—; mem. adj. faculty, lectr. Duke U., Durham, 1974-78, U. N.C., Chapel Hill, 1974-78; cons. health seminars U. Tex., Am. Hosp. Assn., Am. Coll. Healthcare Execs., N.C. Hosp. Assn., Ga. Hosp. Assn., Fla. Hosp. Assn., Pa. Hosp. Assn., Va. Healthcare Fin. Mgmt. Assn., Fla. Healthcare Fin. Mgmt. Assn. Mem. com. Mecklenburg County chpt. ARC, Charlotte, 1985, bd. dirs. Durham County chpt., 1976-79, chmn. fin. com., 1979; mem. missions com. Myers Pk. United Meth. Ch., Charlotte, 1989-95. Mem. Am. Hosp. Assn., Am. Coll. Healthcare Execs., Am. Assn. Preferred Provider Orgn., Healthcare Fin. Mgmt. Assn., Mecklenburg Entrepreneurial Coun., Civitan (pres., v.p., sec. Durham chpt. 1976-79). Republican. Methodist. Avocations: boating, skiing. Office: Preferred Med Mktg Corp 7621 Little Ave Ste 218 Charlotte NC 28226-8162

SHAULL, RICHARD, theologian, educator; b. Felton, Pa., Nov. 24, 1919; s. Millard and Anna (Brenneman) S.; m. Mildred Miller, May 17, 1941 (div. May 1975); children: Madelyn, Wendy; m. Nancy Johns, Apr. 14, 1981. B.A., Elizabethtown Coll., 1938, D.D., 1958; B.Th., Princeton Theol. Sem., 1941, Th.M., 1946, Th.D., 1959. Ordained to ministry Presbyn. Ch., 1941; pastor in Wink, Tex., 1941-42; missionary in Colombia, 1942-50, U. Brazil, 1952-62; prof. ch. history Campinas (Brazil) Presbyn. Sem., 1952-60; v.p. Mackenzie Inst., São Paulo, Brazil, 1960-62; prof. ecumenics Princeton Theol. Sem., 1962-80, prof. emeritus, 1980—; cons. internat. programs, 1960—; chmn. N.Am. Congress Latin Am., 1966-89, World Student Christian Fedn., 1968-73; acad. dir. Instituto Pastoral Hispano, N.Y.C., 1983-89. Author: Encounter with Revolution, 1955, (with Carl Oglesby) Containment and Change, 1967, (with Gustavo Gutierrez) Liberation and Change, 1977, Heralds of a New Reformation, 1984, Naming the Idols, 1988, The Reformation and Liberation Theology, 1991, also 3 books in Portuguese. Home and Office: 46 Morgan Cir Swarthmore PA 19081-2214

SHAVELSON, MELVILLE, writer, theatrical producer and director; b. N.Y.C., Apr. 1, 1917; s. Joseph and Hilda (Shalson) S.; m. Lucille T. Myers, Nov. 2, 1938; children: Richard, Carol-Lynne. AB, Cornell U., 1937. Author: How to Make a Jewish Movie, 1970, Lualda, 1975, The Great Houdinis, 1976, The Eleventh Commandment, 1977, Ike, 1979, Don't Shoot, It's Only Me, 1990; writer Bob Hope Pepsodent Show, NBC radio, 1938-43; screenwriter The Princess and the Pirate, 1944, Wonder Man, 1944, Room for One More, 1951, I'll See You in My Dreams, 1952; screenwriter, dir. The Seven Little Foys, 1954, Beau James, 1956, Houseboat, 1957, The Five Pennies, 1958, It Started in Naples, 1959, On the Double, 1960, Yours, Mine and Ours, 1968, The War Between Men and Women, 1972, The Legend of Valentino, 1975, Deceptions, 1985; screenwriter, dir., producer The Pigeon That Took Rome, 1962, A New Kind of Love, 1963, Cast a Giant Shadow, 1966, Mixed Company, 1974, The Great Houdinis, 1976, Ike, 1979; dir. The Other Woman, 1983; creator TV shows including Danny Thomas Show, ABC-TV, 1953, My World—and Welcome To It, NBC-TV, 1969; author Broadway mus. Jimmy, 1969. Recipient Screen Writers Guild award, 1959, Christopher award, 1959, Sylvania TV award, 1953, Acad. Award nominations (screenplay), 1955, 58, Screen Writers Ann. award nominations (screenplay), 1952 (2), 58, 59, 62, 68, 72, 75, Screen Writers award (best written Am. mus.), 1959, Award of Merit United Jewish Appeal, 1966. Mem. Dirs. Guild Am., Writers Guild Am. (exec. bd. dirs 1960-75, 78, pres. screen writers br. 1967, pres. found. 1975-96, v.p. 1996—), Acad. Motion Picture Arts and Scis. (mem. bd. govs.), Writer Guild Am. West (pres. 1969-70, 79-81, 85-87, Valentine Davies award 1979, Laurel award 1984), Sigma Delta Chi. Home and Office: 11947 Sunshine Ter Studio City CA 91604-3708

SHAVER, CARL A., government official; b. St. Joseph, Mo., Feb. 11, 1939; s. Charley and Vera Lucille (Fry) S.; m. Marsha Ann Streeby, June 27, 1964; children: Christopher Bruce, Craig Anthony. Grad., Indsl. Coll. Armed Forces, Washington, 1980; BS in Agrl. Engrng., U. Mo., Columbia, 1961; MS in Mgmt., Naval Postgrad. Sch., Monterey, Calif., 1974. Commd. USMC, advanced through grades to col.; def. contractor cons. Engrng./Documentation Systems, Inc., Fallbrook, Calif., 1991-92; chief staff, program analyst, project mgr. Pacific Divsn. Naval Ordnance Ctr., Fallbrook, 1992—; pres. CAS & Assocs. Internat., Oceanside, Calif., 1991—. Mem. Rep. Nat. Com., 1994—. Decorated Silver Star, Bronze Star, Purple Heart, Disting. Svc. Medal. Mem. Armed Forces Electronics and Comm. Assn., Nat. Security Indsl. Assn., Pacific and Asian Affairs Coun., Marine Corps Assn., Naval Inst. Avocations: sailing, travel, astronomy. Home: 5886 Ranch View Rd Oceanside CA 92057 Office: Marine Corps Program Dept NOCPAC Divsn 700 Ammunition Rd Fallbrook CA 92028-3187

SHAVER, JAMES PORTER, education educator, university dean; b. Wadena, Minn., Oct. 19, 1933. BA magna cum laude, U. Wash., Seattle, 1955; MA in Teaching, Harvard U., 1957, EdD, 1961. Instr. Grad. Sch. Edn., Harvard U., 1961-62; assoc. prof., dir. Social Studies Curriculum Ctr., Ohio State U., Columbus, 1964-65; mem. faculty Utah State U. Coll. Edn., Logan, 1962-64, prof., 1965—, chmn. Bur. Rsch. Svcs., 1965-93, assoc. dean rsch., 1978-93, acting dean Sch. Grad. Studies, 1990-91, 92-93, dean, 1993—; mem. Commn. Youth Edn. for Citizenship, ABA, 1975-81; mem. edn. task force Am. Hist. Assn.-Am. Polit. Sci. Assn. Project '87, 1981-84; tech. advisor Nat. Ctr. on Effective Secondary Schs., 1988-91; mem. adv. bd. program in civic and moral edn. Inst. for Philosophy and Pub. Policy, U. Md., 1992—; mem. steering com. Nat. Assessment Ednl. Progress Civics Consensus Project, 1995-96. Co-author: Teaching Public Issues in the High School, 1966, 2d edit., 1974, Facing Value Decisions: Rationale-building For Teachers, 1976, 2d edit., 1982; editor: Building Rationales for Citizenship Education, 1977, Handbook of Research on Social Studies Teaching and Learning, 1991; co-editor: Democracy, Pluralism, and the Social Studies, 1968; also others. Mem. AAAS, AAUP, Nat. Coun. Social Studies (pres. 1976), Am. Ednl. Rsch. Assn. Home: PO Box 176 Hyrum UT 84319-0176 Office: Utah State U Main 132 Logan UT 84322-0900

SHAVER, KELLY G., psychology educator; b. Highland Park, Ill., Oct. 30, 1941. BS, U. Wash., 1963, MS, 1965; PhD, Duke U., 1969. Teaching asst. U. Wash., 1963-64, rsch. asst., 1964-65; rsch. asst. Duke U., 1965-68; asst. prof. Coll. William and Mary, Williamsburg, Va., 1968-73, assoc. prof., 1973-82, prof., 1982—, rsch. dir. Tech. Entrepreneurship Ctr., 1989-90; dir. social and devel. psychology program divsn. behavioral and neural scis. NSF, 1977-79; chair Hampton-Roads Innovation and Tech. Edn. Consortium, 1990-94; issues facilitator Va. sect. White House Conf. Small Bus., 1994; mem. adv. com. Va. Assembly on Adult Corrections, 1983-84; mem. oversight review com. programs in cognitive sci. divsn. behavioral and neural scis. NSF, 1984, mem. adv. panel social psychology divsn. social scis., 1973-75, mem. presdl. young investigator awards review panel divsn. behavioral and neural scis., 1989, mem. review panel undergrad. faculty enhancement program divsn. undergrad. sci., engrng. and math. edn., 1990, mem. rsch. tng. groups adv. panel for biol., behavioral and social scis., 1991, mem. rsch. experiences undergrads. adv. panel for biol., behavioral and social scis., 1991, mem. adv. panel undergrad. course and curriculum devel. program divsn. undergrad. sci., engrng., and math. edn. directorate for edn. and human resources, 1992, mem. small bus. innovation rsch. adv. panel, decision risk and mgmt. scis. program divsn. social and econ. sci., 1992, rep. to interagy. panel for rsch. adolescence, 1977-79, leader behavioral and neural scis. review panel, 1980, mem. adv. panel social and devel. psychology divsn. behavioral and neural scis., 1982; cons. Commonwealth Fund, 1986; lectr. Kendon Smith meml. lectrs. U. N.C., Greensboro, 1988; ad-hoc reviewer behavioral scis. rsch. review com. Nat. Inst. Mental, 1990; ad-hoc reviewer rsch. review com. on human devel., Nat. Insts. Health, 1990, human devel. and aging spl. study sect., 1990, 91, 92; chair social scis. review panel La. Ednl. Quality Support Fund, Bd. Regents, 1991-92, 94, 96; lectr. psychology seminar series Coll. Charleston, 1982; mem. program review com. dept. psychology Bucknell U., 1982; mem. editorial bd. Entrepreneurship and Regional Devel., 1992—, Entrepreneurship: Theory and Practice, 1989-92, Jour. Personality, 1983-87, Jour. Applied Social Psychology, 1983—, Jour. Personality and Social Psychology, 1977-88; proposal reviewer various orgns.; editor Entrepreneurship: Theory and Practice, 1994—; outside evaluator various colls. and univs.; presenter in field. Author: An Introduction to Attribution Processes, 1975, Principles of Social Psychology, 1977, Attribution of Blame: Causality, Responsibility, and Blameworthiness, 1985, (with E. Stotland and S. Sherman) Empathy and Birth Order: Some Experimental Explorations, 1971, (with R.M. Tarpy) Psychology, 1993; author: (with others) New Directions in Attribution Research, 1981, Life Crises and Experiences of Loss in Adulthood, 1992; contbr. 40 articles to profl. jours. Mem. Am. Psychol. Soc., Am. Psychology-Law Soc., Ea. Psychol. Assn. (program com. 1991-94), Capital Area Social Psychology Assn., Acad. Mtmg., Soc. Exptl. Social Psychology, Soc. Psychol. Study Social Issues, Soc. Advancement Social Psychology (steering com. 1984-85), Richmond Venture Capital Club (bd. dirs.), Small Bus. Devel. Ctr. Greater Hampton Rds. (bd. dirs.). Office: Coll William and Mary Williamsburg VA 23187-8795

SHAVIV, EDDIE, marketing and sales executive; b. Suceava, Romania, Oct. 24, 1940; s. Friedrich and Paula (Eidinger) Scherzer; m. Emanuela Drach, July 7, 1968; children: Bernard Daniel, Enid Naomi. MSME, Poly. Inst. Bucharest, Romania, 1962; MBA with distinction, N.Y. Inst. Tech., 1988. Engrng. mgr. Malaxa Engine Factory, Bucharest, 1962-73, Savkel, Tel Aviv, Israel, 1973-78; plant mgr. Sivaro, Carmiel, Israel, 1978-80; engrng. mgr. Tadiran Batteries, Rehovoth, Israel, 1980-84; mktg. & sales mgr. Tadiran Batteries, Port Washington, N.Y., 1984-90; nat. accounts mgr. Varta Batteries Inc., Elmsford, N.Y., 1990—, dir. nat. accounts OEM sales and mktg., 1992—, dir. OEM sales and mktg., 1988-90, v.p. sales and engrng., 1996—. Patentee for water pumps, rechargeable batteries; contbr. articles to profl. jours. Sgt. Israeli Def. Forces, 1975-80. Recipient Galil War award Israeli Def. Forces, 1979. Mem. Delta Mu Delta Nat. Honor Soc. Jewish. Home: 57 Netto Ln Plainview NY 11803-3129 Office: Varta Batteries 300 Executive Blvd Elmsford NY 10523-1200

SHAW, ALAN, lawyer, corporate executive; b. Long Branch, N.J., July 23, 1930; m. Margaret Knight, Oct. 15, 1959; children: Andrew Macbeth, Adriane Macbeth. AB, U. Mich., 1952; LLB, Harvard U., 1955. Bar: Mass. 1955, N.Y. 1958. Assoc. Skadden, Arps, Slate, Meagher & Flom, N.Y.C., 1958-65; v.p., gen. counsel, sec. Athlone Industries Inc., Parsippany, N.J., 1966-93, also bd. dirs.; Adjunct assoc. prof. of Law, Fordham U., 1996—. Served as cpl. U.S. Army, 1955-57. Mem. ABA (sect. on corps.), N.J. Gen. Counsel Group, Assn. Bar City N.Y., Morristown (N.J.) Club, Washington Assn. (Morristown), Morris County Golf Club (Convent Station, N.J.), Harvard Club (N.Y.C.). Home: 490 S Maple Ave Basking Ridge NJ 07920-1327 Office: 601 Jefferson Rd Parsippany NJ 07054-3790

SHAW, ALAN BOSWORTH, geologist, paleontologist, retired; b. Englewood, N.J., Mar. 28, 1922; s. Carroll Harper and Natalie Frederique (Howe) S.; m. Helen Louise Wilson, Nov. 2, 1945 (div. Apr. 1952); m. Marian Tavenner Stoll, Mar. 11, 1954 (dec. Apr. 1981); children: Nancy Jeanne, Sally Ann; m. Mary Elizabeth Merrem, Sept. 3, 1982. AB magna cum laude, Harvard Coll., 1946; AM, PhD, Harvard U., 1949. Asst. prof. geology U. Wyo., Laramie, 1949-55; paleontologist Shell Oil Co., Denver, 1955-60; owner Nat. Elec. Svc., N.Y.C., 1960-61; consulting geologist Denver, 1961; supr. Pan Am. Rsch. (currently Amoco), Tulsa, Okla., 1961-68; various positions Pan Am. Petroleum, Denver, 1968-76; chief paleontologist Amoco Prodn., Chgo., 1976-77, chief geologist, 1977-81; geol. rsch. cons. Amoco Rsch., Tulsa, 1981-85; ret., 1985; oil industry rep. NRC Com. on Paleontology, Washington, 1963-69; mem. Com. on Paleontology and Stratigraphy Deep Sea Drilling Program, 1973-75. Author: Time in Stratigraphy, 1964; contbr. numerous articles to profl. jours. Served to 1st lt., USAAF, 1943-45. Recipient Moore Paleontology medal Soc. Sedimentary Geology, 1996. Mem. Paleontol. Soc. (pres. 1968). Achievements include invention of graphic correlation system for use of fossils in making time correlations of sedimentary rocks. Home: 1315 Kamira Dr Kerrville TX 78028-8805

SHAW, ALAN ROGER, financial executive, educator; b. Bklyn., July 7, 1938; s. Sewall S. and Vera (Dimmick) S.; children: Stephen S., Todd J., Bradley C.; married 2d, Mary Elizabeth Hogg, May 30, 1987. Student, Susquehanna U., 1957, Adelphi U., 1963-66. Analyst Harris Upham & Co., N.Y.C., 1958-71, asst. v.p., 1971-73, v.p., 1973-75; 1st v.p. Smith, Barney, Harris, Upham & Co., N.Y.C., 1975-80; sr. v.p., mng. dir. Smith Barney, N.Y.C., 1980—; tchr. N.Y. Inst. Fin., 1966—. Mem. Market Technicians Assn. (pres. 1974), N.Y. Soc. Security Analysts, Securities Industry Assn. Inst. (trustee 1986-92), Southward Ho Country Club, Unqua Corinthian Yacht Club (commodore 1988-90). Home: 87 Wagstaff Ln West Islip NY 11795-5206 also: 322 W 57th St New York NY 10019-3701 also: 2111 Fisher Island Dr Fisher Island FL 33109-0052 Office: Smith Barney Inc 388 Greenwich St New York NY 10013-2375

SHAW, ANESTHER O(LIVE), university administrative staff member; b. Trinidad, West Indies, Aug. 3. AA in Bus., Caribbean Union Coll., Trinidad, West Indies; BSc in Bus. Adminstrn., Columbia Union Coll.; MEd in Adminstrn., Howard U., 1989, PhD Orgn. Communication, 1995. Sec. Bell Canada, Montreal, AT&T, N.Y.C.; adminstrv. sec. The World Bank, Washington; corp. banker Canadian Imperial Bank of Commerce, Toronto; adminstrv. asst. IBM, Canada, Toronto, 1979-80, Washington Hosp. Ctr., 1980-82; adminstrv. asst. Howard U., Washington, 1982—, rschr. orgn. com., 1994—; rschr. Organ Com., 1994—. Fund raiser community charities, Montgomery County, Md., 1980—; coord., Combined Fed. Campaign of Washington at Howard U., 1980—. Recipient Gov. Recognition cert. State of Md., 1988, Acad. Excellence award U. Md., 1993. Mem. State of Md. Real Estate Commn., Caribbean Union Coll. Alumni Assn. (sec., archivist 1982—). Avocations: travel, reading, ethics, international information, gardening. Home: 1105 Loxford Ter Silver Spring MD 20901-1130 Office: Howard U Office of Assoc VP for Info Sys and Svcs 2301 Georgia Ave NW Ste 334 Washington DC 20001-3000

SHAW, ANGUS ROBERTSON, III, minister; b. Charlotte, N.C., Oct. 7, 1932; s. Angus Robertson Jr. and Claudia (Morrison) S.; m. Carolyn Farmer, Aug. 14, 1965; children: Karen, Rob. BA, Bob Jones U., 1955; MDiv, Columbia Theol. Sem., 1958, DMin, 1989; DD (hon.), King Coll., 1965. Asst. pastor 1st Presbyn. Ch., Pulaski, Va., 1956-62; pastor Seagle Meml. Ch., Pulaski, 1956-62, Royal Oak Ch., Marion, Va., 1962-69; sr. pastor 1st Presbyn. Ch., Dothan, Ala., 1969-78, Johnson City, Tenn., 1978—; chmn. bd. Salvation Army, Johnson City, Tenn., 1986, Contact Teleministries, Johnson City, 1987-88. Trustee Lees-McRae Coll., Banner Elk, N.C., 1979-84; chmn. ch., coll. coun. Montreat (N.C.)-Anderson Coll., 1980; chmn. ann. fund King Coll., Bristol, Tenn., 1985-86; bd. trustees Tusculum Coll., 1993—, chair coun. on ch. rels., 1992, chair Ptnrs. in Ministry Drive, 1996; bd. dirs. United Way, 1991—. Mem. Watauga Mental Health Assn. (bd. dirs. 1990-96, chair 1992-93), Kiwanis (pres. 1990-91), Soc. Theta Pi. Home: 1013 Somerset Dr Johnson City TN 37604-2919 Office: 1st Presbyn Ch 105 S Boone St Johnson City TN 37604-6262

SHAW, ANTHONY, physician, pediatric surgeon; b. Shanghai, China, Oct. 31, 1929; s. Bruno and Regina (Hyman) S.; m. Iris Violet Azian, Mar. 12, 1955; children: Brian Anthony, Diana Shaw Clark, Daniel Aram. BA cum laude, Harvard Coll., 1950; MD, NYU, 1954. Diplomate Am. Bd. Surgery, Am. Bd. Pediat. Surgery. Intern and resident in surgery Columbia-Presbyn. Med. Ctr., N.Y.C., 1954-56, 58-62; resident in pediat. surgery Babies Hosp., N.Y.C., 1962; asst. prof. surgery Columbia U. Coll. Physicians and Surgeons, N.Y.C., 1965-70; chief pediat. surgery St. Vincent's Hosp., N.Y.C., 1963-70, Harlem Hosp. Ctr., N.Y.C., 1965-70; prof. surgery U. Va., Charlottesville, 1970-81, chief pediat. surgery Med. Ctr., 1970-81; prof. surgery UCLA, 1981—; chief pediat. surgery Olive View-UCLA Med. Ctr., Sylmar, 1986—; expert witness on child abuse L.A. Superior Ct., 1986—; chmn. gov.'s adv. com. child abuse and neglect Commonwealth of Va., 1975-80; vis. prof. pediat. surgery People's Republic of China, 1985. Contbr. more than 220 articles to profl. jours. Mem. Gov.'s Task Force on Child Abuse Va., 1973-74; bd. dirs. Nat. Burn Victim Found., Orange, N.J., 1996—. Capt. U.S. Army, 1956-58. Recipient Commrs. award Va. Dept. Social Svcs., 1980, award Gov.'s Adv. Bd., Cert. of Recognition HEW, 1978. Fellow Am. Pediat. Surg. Assn. (sec. 1982-85), ACS (v.p. 1987-89); mem. AMA, Pacific Coast Surg. Assn. (v.p. 1989-90), Am. Soc. Law, Medicine, and Ethics, Am. Profl. Soc. on Abuse of Children, Alpha Omega Alpha. Avocations: writing humor, grandchildren. Home: One S Orange Grove Blvd # 9 Pasadena CA 91105 Office: Olive View-UCLA Med Ctr 14445 Olive View Dr Sylmar CA 91342-1437

SHAW, ARTIE, musician, writer, lecturer; b. N.Y.C., May 23, 1910; s. Harry and Sarah Shaw; m. Margaret Allen; m. Lana Turner; m. Elizabeth Kern; 1 son, Steven Kern; m. Ava Gardner (div. Oct. 1946); m. Kathleen Winsor, Oct. 28, 1946; m. Doris Dowling (div.); 1 son, Jonathan; m. Evelyn Keyes, 1957 (div. June 1985). Extension work in lit., Columbia U.; MusD (hon.), U. Nebr., 1938, LittD (hon.); LHD (hon.), Calif. Luth. U., 1987; DFA (hon.), U. Ariz., 1995. former owner firm Shooters Svc. and Dewey (gun mfrs.); pres. Artixo Prodns., Ltd. (film distbn. co.); lectr. colls. and univs.; ann. lectr. U. Calif., Santa Barbara, Oxnard Coll., Camarillo, Calif., Yale U., U. Pa., Memphis U. Orch. leader, 1936-54; appeared in motion pictures Dancing Coed, Second Chorus; also engaged in film, theatrical prodn.; producer Broadway mus. The Great Gatsby; recipient Downbeat award best Am. swing band, Esquire Mag. Poll award as favorite band of armed services, Hall of Fame award for rec. Begin the Beguine; Stardust, Nat. Acad. Rec. Arts and Scis. 1977); condr., composer numerous songs and orchestral works including Concerto for Clarinet; author: A Clarinet Method; The Trouble with Cinderella; I Love You, I Hate You, Drop Dead! Three Variations on a Theme; The Best of Intentions, and Other Stories, 1989. Former mem. exec. council, bd. Hollywood Ind. Citizens Com. Arts, Scis. and Professions. Served with USNR, 1942-44. Recipient Presdl. award Am. Soc. Mus. Arrangers, 1990. Subject of film: Artie Shaw: Time is All You've Got (Acad. award Best Feature-length Documentary 1986). *I'm still trying to figure life out and will let you know when, as, or if I ever do. But don't hold your breath; I imagine it'll take some 80 years more for me to find an answer.*

SHAW, BERNARD, television journalist; b. Chgo., 1940; m. Linda Shaw; children: Anil, Amar. Corr. Washington bur. CBS News, 1971-77; fgn. corr., bur. chief ABC News, 1977-80; anchor Cable News Network, Washington, 1980—. Served with USMC. recipient, Cable Ace award: Best Newscaster, 1994. Office: CNN 820 1st St NE Washington DC 20002-4243*

SHAW, BRYAN P. H., retired investment company executive; b. Kwongtung, China, Aug. 16, 1921; came to U.S., 1947, naturalized, 1962; s. Ying-Chow (Chung-ching) and Sui-ming (Soo) S.; m. Linda L.T. Tan, Apr. 4, 1953 (dec. 1976). B.A., St. John's U., Shanghai, China, 1946; M.A., Fordham U., 1955. Vice pres., treas. Counselled Funds Distbr. Inc., N.Y.C., 1959-61, also dir.; sec., treas. Axe Sci. Mgmt. Co., Inc., Tarrytown, N.Y., 1960-74; treas. Axe Sci. Corp., Tarrytown, 1960-74, Axe-Houghton Found., Tarrytown, 1968-70, Axe-Houghton Income Fund, Inc., Tarrytown, 1968-86, Axe-Houghton Fund B, Inc., Tarrytown, 1969-86, Axe-Houghton Stock Fund, Inc., Tarrytown, 1970-86, Axe-Houghton Money Market Fund, Inc., Tarrytown, 1982-86; v.p. Axe-Houghton Mgmt., Inc., Tarrytown, 1977-86. Clubs: Fordham U. (Bronx); Fordham U. Wall Street (N.Y.C.). Home: Hermitage 3200 N Ocean Blvd Apt 807 Fort Lauderdale FL 33308

SHAW, BRYCE ROBERT, author; b. Mansfield, Pa., Feb. 22, 1930; s. Wilford Walter and Genevieve (Cox) S.; m. Sally Ruth Prutsman, June 29, 1952; children: David Bryce, Jody Lynn McMillin, Erin Suzanne Hunsinger. AB, Muhlenberg Coll., Allentown, Pa., 1952; MA, U. Mich., 1953, postgrad., 1959-64. Cert. secondary edn. tchr. Teaching fellow U. Mich., Ann Arbor, 1953-55; math. analyst Willow Run Rsch. Ctr., Ypsilanti, Mich., 1954-59; tchr. math. Mt. Morris (Mich.) Bd. Edn., 1959-60, Flint (Mich.) Bd. Edn., 1960-64; lectr. math. U. Mich, Flint, 1961-68; coord. math. Flint Bd. Edn., 1964-75, dir. math. and computer systems, 1975-77; author in residence Houghton Mifflin Co., Boston, 1977-81, sr. author, 1970—; rsch. mathematician sch. dists., univs., Houghton Mifflin, others, Flint, Boston, L.A., 1961—; math. cons. sch. bds., state edn. depts., univs., U.S., Can., Mex., 1965—, Am. Sch. Found., Mexico City, 1965-68; lectr. edn. Ea. Mich. U., Ypsilanti, 1964-67; lectr. math. Nat. and Regional Math. Couns., Mich. State U., East Lansing, 1965-67; chmn. math. dept. Flint Bd. Edn., 1960-64; lectr. math. curriculum Flint Bd. Edn., 1960-80; lectr. math. curriculum devel. bds. edn., sch. math. staffs. Author: (textbooks) General Math I, 2d edit., 1979, Mathematics Plus, 1980, Fundamentals of Mathematics, 2d edit., 1986, Personalized Computational Skills Program, Vol. I, 1980, vol. II, 1981, Personalized Computational Skills Program--Skills and Applications, 1982, Personalized Computational Skills Program: Module A, B, C, D, E, and F, 3d edit., 1982, Mathematics Plus!, 1982, Computer Math Program, Computational Skills Program, 1988, Brush-Up: Mathematics Program, 1995; contbr. articles to profl. jours. Recipient Citation of Meritorious Acheivement in laser rsch., Internat. Man of Yr. award, 1991-92, Key of Success; Profl. Performance Achievement Rsch. and Notable Author award Biog. Honor award in Math., Internat. Cultural Diploma of Honor, others; named Disting. Lectr. Coll. Mathematicians. Mem. Math. Assn. Am., Nat. Coun. Tchrs. Math., N.Y. Acad. Scis., Textbook Authors Assn., Phi Delta Kappa, Omicron Delta Kappa, Alpha Kappa Alpha. Avocations: music, chess. Home and Office: PO Box 531 Venice FL 34284-0531

SHAW, CAROLE, editor, publisher; b. Bklyn., Jan. 22, 1936; d. Sam and Betty (Neckin) Bergenthal; m. Ray Shaw, Dec. 27, 1957; children: Lori Eve Cohen, Victoria Shaw Locknar. BA, Hunter Coll., 1962. Singer Capitol Records, Hilton Records, Rama Records, Verve Records, 1952-65; TV appearances Ed Sullivan, Steve Allen, Jack Paar, George Gobel Show, 1957; owner The People's Choice, L.A., 1975-79; founder, editor-in-chief Big Beautiful Woman mag., Beverly Hills, Calif., 1979—; creator Carole Shaw and BBW label clothing line for large-size women. Author: Come Out, Come Out Wherever You Are, 1982. Avocations: piano, painting, swimming, travel. Office: BBW Mag PO Box K-298 Tarzana CA 91356

SHAW, CHARLES ALDEN, engineering executive; b. Detroit, June 8, 1925; s. Fred Alden and Amy (Ellis) S.; m. Barbara Loveland, Mar. 9, 1963 (div. 1979); children: Amy Elizabeth, Polly Nicole; m. Jeanne Steves Partridge, Apr. 22, 1989. BS, Harvard U., 1945; MSEE, Syracuse U., 1958. Test and design engr. G.E., Syracuse-Schenectady, N.Y., 1947-51; chief engr.

Onondaga Pottery Co., Syracuse, 1951-60; mgr. semiconductor div. G.E., Syracuse-Schenectady, 1960-66; cons. to gen. dir. Bull-G.E., Paris, 1966-69; mgr. CAD sect. integrated cir. product dept. G.E., Syracuse, 1969-71, mgr. CAD ctr. solid state applied ops., 1971-78, mgr. computer support solid state applied ops., 1978-81; dir. CAD G.E. Intersil, Cupertino, Calif., 1981-88; cons. in field Cupertino, 1988-89; mgr. tech. program Cadence Design Systems, Santa Clara, Calif., 1989—. Trustee Hidden Villa, Los Altos Hills, Calif., 1986-92; vol. tech. KTEH Channel 54 pub. TV, 1984—. With USN, 1942-45, PTO. Mem. IEEE, Assn. Computing Machinery (chmn. spl. interest group SIGDA 1986-91), Design Automation Conf. (exec. bd. 1985-95), Harvard Club of Peninsula. Democrat. Unitarian. Avocations: skiing, scuba diving, music. Home: 4925 Monaco Dr Pleasanton CA 94566-7671 Office: 555 River Oaks Pky San Jose CA 95134-1917

SHAW, CHARLES ALEXANDER, judge; b. Jackson, Tenn., Dec. 31, 1944; s. Alvis and Sarah S.; m. Kathleen Ingram, Aug. 17, 1969; 1 child, Bryan Ingram. BA, Harris Stowe State Coll., 1966; MBA, U. Mo., 1971; JD, Cath. U. Am., 1974. Bar: D.C. 1975, Mo. 1975, U.S. Ct. Appeals (8th and D.C. cirs.) 1975, U.S. Dist. Ct. (ea. dist.) Mo. 1976, U.S. Ct. Appeals (6th and 7th cirs.) 1976. Tchr. St. Louis Pub. Schs., 1966-69, D.C. Pub. Schs., Washington, 1969-71; law clk. U.S. Dept. Justice, Washington, 1972-73; law clk. NLRB, Washington, 1973-74, atty., 1974-76; assoc. Lashly, Caruthers, Theis, Rava & Hamel, St. Louis, 1976-80, asst. U.S. atty., 1980-87; judge Mo. Cir. Ct., St. Louis, 1987-94, asst. presiding judge, 1993-94; judge U.S. Dist. Ct., St. Louis, 1994—; hearing officer Office of the Mayor, Washington, 1973-74; instr. U. Mo., St. Louis, 1980-81. State bd. dirs. United Negro Coll. Fund, St. Louis, 1979-83; trustee St. Louis Art Mus., 1979-82, 89-96; bd. dirs. Arts and Edn. Coun., 1992-96, Metro Golf Assn., Landmarks Assn., St. Louis, 1980-82. Danforth Found. fellow, 1978-79; Cath. U. Am. scholar, 1971-74. Mem. D.C. Bar Assn., Mo. Bar Assn., Mound City Bar Assn., Bar Assn. Metro. St. Louis, Harris-Stowe State Coll. Alumni Assn. (bd. dirs., Disting. Alumni 1988), Phi Alpha Delta (Svc. award 1973-74). Avocations: golf, tennis. Office: 1114 Market St Saint Louis MO 63101-2043

SHAW, CHARLES RAYMOND, journalist; b. Phila., Feb. 2, 1951; s. Charles Raymond Sr. and Dorothy Blanche (Buckman) S.; m. Francine Ruth Pennock, Jan. 14, 1983. BS in Journalism, Temple U., 1972; MS in Journalism, Columbia U., 1973. Staff writer Intelligencer Jour., Lancaster, Pa., 1973-83, asst. news editor, 1983-88, news editor, 1989-97; editor Intelligencer Jour., Lancaster, 1997—. Mem. Pa. Soc. of Newspaper Editors, Am. Soc. Newspaper Editors. Office: Lancaster Newspapers Inc Intelligencer Jour 8 W King St Lancaster PA 17603-3824

SHAW, CHARLES RUSANDA, government investigator; b. Detroit, Aug. 17, 1914; s. Leonard George and Harriet (Kratzer) S.; m. Sally Madeline Jock, May 3, 1947 (dec. June 1996); children: Patrick R., Sandra L. Keding (dec.), Janice L., Lisa Keding; stepchildren: Lillian Genna, Ruth Czenkus. Cert., Wicker Sch. of Fine Arts, 1936, Mich. Acad. Advt. Art, 1937; student, Intelligence Corps Sch., 1947. Freelance artist Detroit, 1936-39; spl. agt. U.S. Army Counter Intelligence Corps, Washington, 1947-48, Office Spl. Investigations, USAF, Washington, 1948-66; pvt. investigator Charles Shaw Assocs., Mt. Clemens, Mich., 1966-84; contract investigator USAF & U.S. Customs Svc., Washington, 1984-94; entrepreneur-inventor neoteric products, patents pending, 1994—. Master sgt. U.S. Army, 1939-45, PTO, ETO. Mem. Assn. Former OSI Spl. Agts. (chartered). Democrat. Roman Catholic. Avocations: fine arts, photography, gardening, home improvements. Home and Office: 59295 Bates Rd New Haven MI 48048-1728

SHAW, DAVID ELLIOT, financial executive; b. Chgo., Mar. 29, 1951; s. Charles B. Jr. and Marilyn (Baron) S. BA, U. Calif., San Diego, 1972; MS, Stanford U., 1975, PhD, 1980. Pres. Stanford Systems Corp., Palo Alto, Calif., 1976-79; assoc. prof. Columbia U., N.Y.C., 1980-86; v.p. Morgan Stanley & Co., N.Y.C., 1986-88; chmn. D.E. Shaw & Co., Inc., N.Y.C., 1988—. Contbr. articles to profl. jours. Chmn. N.Y.C. Mayor's Panel on Tech. and Fin., 1987; mem. N.Y.C. Partnership Subcom. on Tech. and Fin., 1987; apptd. to Pres. Clinton's Com. of Advisors on Sci. and Tech., 1994; chmn. Pres. Clinton's Panel on Ednl. Tech., 1995. Mem. Am. Fin. Assn., N.Y. Acad. Scis. (bd. govs. 1993-95). Democrat. Jewish.

SHAW, DAVID LYLE, journalist, author; b. Dayton, Ohio, Jan. 4, 1943; s. Harry and Lillian (Walton) S.; m. Alice Louise Eck, Apr. 11, 1965 (div. Sept. 1974); m. Ellen Torgerson, July 17, 1979 (dec.); stepchildren: Christopher, Jordan; m. Lucy Stille, Apr. 14, 1988; 1 child, Lucas. BA in English, UCLA, 1965. Reporter Huntington Park Signal (Calif.), 1963-66, Long Beach Independent (Calif.), 1966-68; reporter L.A. Times, 1968-74, media critic, 1974—. Author: WILT: Just Like Any Other 7-Foot, Black Millionaire Who Lives Next Door, 1973, The Levy Caper, 1974, Journalism Today, 1977, Press Watch, 1984, The Pleasure Police, 1996; contbr. numerous articles to mags. including Gentlemen's Quar., Cigar Aficionado, Esquire, TV Guide, New York. Recipient Mellet Fund Nat. award, 1983, PEN West award, 1990, Calif. Bar Assn. Gold Medallion, 1990, Pulitzer Prize for disting. criticism, 1991. Office: LA Times Times Mirror Sq Los Angeles CA 90012

SHAW, DAVID TAI-KO, electrical and computer engineering educator, university administrator; b. China, Mar. 13, 1938; came to U.S., 1960, naturalized, 1972; m. Katharine Lin-Yee Yang; children: Albert, Stanley. B.S.M.E., Nat. Taiwan U., Taipei, 1959; M.S. in Nuclear Engring., Purdue U., 1961, Ph.D., 1964. Asst. prof. div. interdisciplinary studies and research Sch. Engring., SUNY-Buffalo, 1964-67, assoc. prof. faculty engring. and applied scis., 1967-74, prof. elec. engring. and nuclear engring., aerospace and engring. sci., 1974-77, prof. elec. and computer engring., 1974—, dir. lab. for power and environ. studies, 1978—; exec. dir. N.Y. State Inst. on Superconductivity, 1987—; vis. prof. U. Paris, 1976-77; vis. scientist Centre d'Etudes Nucleairs de Fontenay-aux-Roses (France) Commissariat a L'Energie Atomique, 1976-77; vis. assoc. dept. environ. health engring. Calif. Inst. Tech., 1970-71; mem. U.S. del. French Commissariat a L'energie ATomique, 1974, U.S. del. Joint Nuclear Energy Agy. IAEA Internat. Liaison Group on Thermionic Elec. Power Generation, Paris, 1974; mem. U.S. vis. team USSR Acad. Scis.;. Editor: Fundamentals of Aerosol Science, 1978, Recent Developments in Aerosol Science, 1978, Assessment of Airborne Radioactivity, 1978; editor-in-chief: Jour. Aerosol Sci. and Tech., 1982-93; contbr. numerous articles to profl. publs. Mem. IEEE, ASME, AAAS, Am. Assn. Aerosol Rsch. (pres. 1982-85, Assn. award 1984, Internat. Aerosol Fellow award 1994), Am. Nuclear Soc., Air Pollution Control Assn., Assn. Aerosol Rsch. (Germany), Sigma Xi, Sigma Pi Sigma. Office: SUNY-Buffalo NYS Inst Superconductivity 330 Boner Hall Buffalo NY 14260

SHAW, DEAN ALVIN, architect; b. El Paso, Tex., Jan. 22, 1954; s. Harold Alvin and Ann May (Glass) S.; m. Wendy June Hudgens, May 11, 1985; 1 child, Deanna Marie. BArch, Tex. Tech. U., 1979. Registered architect, Tex., Calif. Draftsman J.V. Scoggins Engring., Lubbock, Tex., 1978-79; intern R.S. Colley Architects, Corpus Christi, Tex., 1979-82, Campbell Taggart, Inc. subs. Anheuser-Busch Cos., Inc., Dallas, 1982-83; archtl. sec. leader Campbell Taggart, Inc., Dallas, 1983, dir. facilities design, 1983-94; project mgr. Anheuser-Busch Cos., Inc., St. Louis, 1994—. Chmn. youth edn. com. Wilshire Bapt. Ch., Dallas, 1990—. Named Best Citizen, Ozona Women's League, 1972, Outstanding Young Am., 1985. Mem. Constrn. Specifications Inst., AIA, Mo. Soc. of Architects, Nat. Coun. Archtl. Registration Bd.. Republican. Baptist. Avocations: photography, golf.

SHAW, DENIS MARTIN, university dean, former geology educator; b. St. Annes, Eng., Aug. 20, 1923; emigrated to Can., 1948; s. Norman Wade and Alice Jane Sylvia (Shackleton) S.; m. Pauline Mitchell, Apr. 6, 1946 (div. 1975); children—Geoffrey, Gillian, Peter; m. Susan L. Evans, Apr. 9, 1976. BA, Emmanuel Coll., Cambridge, Eng., 1943, MA, 1948; Ph.D., U. Chgo., 1951. Lectr. McMaster U., Hamilton, Ont., Can., 1949-51; asst. prof. McMaster U., 1951-55, asso. prof., 1955-60, prof. geology, 1960-89, prof. emeritus, 1989—, chmn. dept., 1953-59, 62-66, dean grad. studies, 1978-84; assoc. prof. Ecole nationale supérieure de géologie appliquée, U. Nancy, France, 1959-60; invited prof. Inst. de Minéralogie, U. Genève, 1966-67. Exec. editor: Geochimica et Cosmochimica Acta, 1970-88; asso. editor: Handbook of Geochemistry, 1966—; Author: Masson Et Cie, 1964. Served with RAF, 1943-46. Fellow Royal Soc. Can. (W.G. Miller medal 1981); mem. Geol. Assn. Can., Geochem. Soc., Mineral. Assn. Can. (pres. 1964, Past Pres.' medal 1985), Am. Geophys. Union, AAAS, Geol. Soc. of Am. Address: McMaster U, Dept Geology, Hamilton, ON Canada L8S 4M1

SHAW, DENNIS LEE, academic administrator; b. Beloit, Wis., Sept. 16, 1955; s. Glen Wellington and Mary Irene (Collier) S.; m. Mary Ann Baker, June 5, 1983 (div. Mar. 1990); 1 child, Michael Wellington; m. Dawn Marie Heinle, Feb. 13, 1993 (div. Aug. 1995). AS, U. Wis. Ctr. System, Rock County Campus, 1983; BBA, U. Wis., Whitewater, 1986, MBA, 1992; cert., CACUBO Mgmt. Inst., 1995. Cert. Cacubo Mgmt. Inst. Security supr. Martin Security, Inc., Beloit, 1974-78; security opns. mgr. Beloit Coll., 1978-89, security dir., 1989-93; coll. instr. (part-time) Blackhawk Tech. Coll., Janesville, Wis., 1987-93; dir., sec. & police svcs. U. Wis.-Stout, Menomonie, 1993—; mgmt. cons. Peripheral Visions, Ltd., Janesville, 1989-92; computer cons. Carlson & Shaw Mktg. Assocs., Beloit, 1988-89; owner-ptnr. Computer Odyssey, Janesville, 1990—. Author: (computer programs) Coresort, 1987, Key Sort I, 1985. Bd. dirs. The Bridge to Hope Domestic Abuse Program, Menomonie, 1997—. Mem. Am. Soc. Indsl. Security (bd. dirs. 1990-93, coord. No. Ill. chpt. Am. Soc. Indsl. Security Found., Rockford 1988-93), Assn. MBA Execs., Internat. Assn. Chiefs of Police, Internat. Assn. Campus Law Enforcement Adminstrs., Jaycees (pres. Menomonie area 1993-94). Republican. Avocations: play by mail computer gaming. Home: 2214 4th Ave N Apt 1 Menomonie WI 54751-2357 Office: U Wis-Stout Rm 113 817 Broadway St S Menomonie WI 54751-2473

SHAW, DONALD HARDY, lawyer; b. Oelwein, Iowa, June 1, 1922; s. John Hardy and Minnie (Brown) S.; m. Elizabeth Jean Orr, Aug. 16, 1946; children: Elizabeth Ann, Andrew Hardy, Anthony Orr. B.S., Harvard U., 1942; J.D., U. Iowa, 1948. Bar: Ill. 1949, Iowa 1948, cert. fin. planner 1983. With firm Sidley & Austin, Chgo., 1948-55; with Iowa-Ill. Gas & Electric Co., Davenport, Iowa, 1956-87; treas. Iowa-Ill. Gas & Electric Co., 1960-72, v.p. finance, 1973-87, also dir.; of counsel Walton, Creen, Curry and Robertson, Davenport, Iowa, 1987-88, Newpor, Bell, Leon & Martinez, Davenport, 1989—. Mem. Iowa State Bd. Regents, 1969-81, Iowa State TV-Radio Com., 1976-81; trustee St. Luke's Hosp., Davenport, 1966-91. Served to capt. USAAF, 1942-45. Recipient Philo Sherman Bennett award, 1942. Mem. Scott County Iowa Bar Assn., Rock Island Arsenal Club, Outing Club, Harvard Club N.Y.C., Order of Coif, Delta Thata Phi. Congregationalist. Home: 29 Hillcrest Ave Davenport IA 52803-3726 Office: Newport Bell Leon & Martinez 246 W 3rd St Davenport IA 52801-1902

SHAW, DONALD LESLIE, Spanish language educator; b. Manchester, Eng., Feb. 11, 1930; s. Stephen Leslie and Lily (Hughes) S.; m. Maria Concetta Cristini, June 30, 1958; children: Andrew Leslie, Sylvia Maria Pierina. BA, U. Manchester, Eng., 1952, MA, 1953; PhD, U. Dublin, Ireland, 1960. Asst. lectr. U. Dublin, 1955-57; lectr. U. Glasgow, Scotland, 1957-64, U. Edinburgh, Scotland, 1964-69, sr. lectr., 1969-72, reader, prof. Spanish, 1972-86; prof. Spanish, U. Va., Charlottesville, 1986—; vis. prof. Brown U., Providence, 1967, U. Va., Charlottesville, 1983. Author: Historia de la Literatura Española, 1973, La Generación del 98, 1977, Nueva Narrativa Hispanoamericana, 1981, Alejo Carpentier, 1985, Borges' Narrative Strategies, 1992, Antonio Skármeta and the Post-Boom, 1994. Served with RAF, 1953-55. Avocation: cycling. Home: 1800 Jefferson Park Ave Charlottesville VA 22903 Office: U Va 402 Cabell Hall Charlottesville VA 22903

SHAW, DORIS BEAUMAR, film and video producer, executive recruiter; b. Pitts., July 13, 1934; d. Emerson C. and Doris Llorene (Rees) Beaumar; m. Robert Newton Shaw, July 6, 1957. BA summa cum laude, Lindenwood Coll., St. Charles, Mo., 1955. Writer, asst. to pres. Baker Prodns., Benton Harbor, Mich., 1955; asst. prodn. mgr. Condor Films, Inc., St. Louis, 1955-57; chief editor, asst. to v.p. Frederick F. Watson Inc., N.Y.C., 1957-58; v.p. Gen. Pictures Corp., Cleve., 1958-71; dir., editor, unit mgr. Cinecraft Inc., Cleve., 1971-72; mgr. audio-visual dept. Am. Greetings Corp., Cleve., 1972-73; proprietor Script to Screen Svcs., Chagrin Falls, Ohio, 1973-76; pres. D & B Shaw, Inc., Chardon, Ohio, 1976-87, Hudson, Ohio, 1987—; pres. Execusearch, Inc., Hudson, 1987—, Infosearch Inc., Hudson, 1994—, Cybersearch, Inc., Hudson, 1995—; film festival judge, tchr. Martha Holden Jennings Found./Hawken Sch., Gates Mills, Ohio, 1970-85; advisor teenage film contests, seminars Cleve. Bd. Edn., 1970-88; contest judge/film and video WVIZ-TV, Channel 25, Parma, Ohio, 1971—; guest lectr. Lindenwood Coll., 1973-80; adj. prof. U. Akron, 1990—; cons. to bus. and industry regarding sales, mktg., bus. mgmt., info. and rsch. svcs. Writer, dir., editor, prodr. hundreds of film, video, multi-image, multi-media, audio/visual prodn., radio, TV commls. and programs; contbr. articles to profl. jours. Bd. trustees Ohio Boys Town, Cleve., 1957-68; mem. alumnae coun. Lindenwood Coll., 1973-77; publicity chmn. Geauga County Preservation Soc., 1984-91; active various charitable orgns. Named Outstanding Young Woman of Am., Fedn. of Women's Clubs, 1965, Alumna of Yr. Merit award Lindenwood Coll., 1971; recipient numerous awards and grants for film, video projects including Gold Camera Best Documentary award, 1979. Mem. Soc. Motion Picture and TV Engrs., Info. Film Prodrs. Am., Assn. for Multi Image (charter), Detroit Prodrs. Assn., Internat. TV and Video Assn. (charter), Internat. Comm. Industries Assn., Alpha Epsilon Rho. Republican. Avocations: computers, travel, physical fitness, environmental issues. Office: D & B Shaw Inc 118 W Streetsboro St Hudson OH 44236-2711

SHAW, E. CLAY, JR. (CLAY SHAW), congressman; b. Miami, FL, Apr. 19, 1939; s. E. Clay and Rita (Walker) S.; m. Emilie Costar, Aug. 22, 1960; children: Emilie, Jennifer, E. Clay, John C. B.S., Stetson U., 1961, J.D., 1966; M.B.A., U. Ala., 1963. Bar: Fla. 1967; CPA, Fla. Asst. city atty. City of Ft. Lauderdale, 1968, chief city pros., 1968-69, assoc. mcpl. judge, 1969-71, city commr., 1971-73, vice mayor, 1973-74, mayor, 1975-80; mem. 97th-105th Congresses from 15th Fla. dist., 1981—; mem. Ways and Means com. 97th-105th Congresses from 15th (now 22nd) Fla. dist.; chmn. Ways and Means subcom. on human resources; U.S. spl. ambassador to Papua New Guinea Independence; pres. U.S. Conf. Republican Mayors; mem. adv. and exec. bd. U.S. Conf. Mayors.; former chmn. mcpl. div. Ft. Lauderdale United Fund Campaign, 1971; former Young Rep. Club Broward County, Ft. Lauderdale Rep. Exec. Com.; past mem. exec. com. Rep. Nat. Com.; former mem. House Selects Com. Narcotics Abuse and Control; past bd. dirs. Broward County Traffic Assn.; mem judiciary com. Pub. Works and Transp. Bd. overseers Stetson Coll. Law. Home: 700 Coral Way Fort Lauderdale FL 33301-2532 Office: US Ho of Reps 2408 Rayburn Bldg Washington DC 20515-0005*

SHAW, ELEANOR JANE, newspaper editor; b. Columbus, Ohio, Mar. 23, 1949; d. Joseph Cannon and Wanda Jane (Campbell) S. BA, U. Del., 1971. With News-Jour. newspapers, Wilmington, Del., 1970-82, editor HEW desk, asst. met. editor, 1977-80, bus. editor, 1980-82; topics editor USA Today, 1982-83; asst. city editor The Miami Herald, 1983-85; projects editor The Sacramento Bee, 1985-87, news editor, 1987-91, exec. bus. editor, 1991-93, editor capitol bureau news, 1993-95, state editor, 1995—. Bd. dirs. Del. 4-H Found., 1978-83. Mem. Calif. Soc. Newspaper Editors (bd. dirs. 1990-96), No. Calif. Wine Soc. (v.p. 1987-93, pres. 1993—). Office: The Sacramento Bee PO Box 15779 Sacramento CA 95852-0779

SHAW, GAYLORD, newspaper executive; b. El Reno, Okla., July 22, 1942; m. Judith Howard, 1960; children: Randall, Kristine, Kelly. Attended, Cameron Coll., 1960-62, U. Okla., 1962-64. Night police reporter Lawton (Okla.) Constitution Press, 1960-62; Okla. City bur. night editor, statehouse correspondent AP, 1962-66, Washington bur. night editor, investigative reporter, spl. assignment team editor, White House correspondent, 1966-75; asst. mng. editor to mng. editor/news Dallas Times Herald, 1981-83; editor-in-chief Shaw Comms. Inc., Charlotte, N.C., 1983-85; correspondent Washington, Denver L.A. Times, 1975-81, correspondent, projects coord. Washington bur., 1985-88; Washington bur. chief Newsday, 1988-95; sr. corr. for projects Newsday, Washington, 1995—. Recipient Pulitzer Prize Nat. Reporting, 1978, Disting. Svc. award for Washington correspondence Sigma Delta Chi/Soc. Profl. Journalists, 1978, Loeb award Disting. Bus. Reporting, 1978, Disting. Reporting award Merriman Smith/White House Correspondents Assn., 1974, Worth Bingham Disting. Reporting award, 1968, Washington Correspondence award Nat. Press Club, 1991. Home: 2815 Otsego Dr Herndon VA 22071-2444 Office: Washington Bur Newsday 1730 Pennsylvania Ave NW Washington DC 20006-4717

SHAW, GEORGE BERNARD, consulting engineer, educator; b. Dayton, Ohio, Feb. 25, 1940; s. William E. and Edna E. (Hartley) S.; m. Carol M. Crawford, Aug. 6, 1966. A in Mech. Engring., U. Dayton, 1963, BCE, 1967, MSCE, 1971. Diplomate Am. Acad. Environ. Engrs.; registered profl. engr., Ohio, Va., Ind., Ky., Tenn., W.Va., Fla., Kans., Mich., Mo., Okla., Ill., Tex.; lic. profl. surveyor, Ohio. Asst. to chief engr. Northmont Engrs., Vandalia, Ohio, 1960-66; estimator Oberer Constrn., Dayton, 1966-67; sanitary engr. Alden E. Stilson & Assocs., Columbus, 1967-68; staff cons. Miami Conservancy Dist., Dayton, 1969-71; assoc. prof. civil and environ. engring. U. Dayton, 1967—; dir. environ. and engring. program; pres., CEO Shaw, Weiss & De Naples, Dayton, 1968—; pres., CEO GBS Environ., 1989—; chmn. Panterra Corp., 1990—. Contbr. articles to profl. jours. Pres. Engrs. Club Dayton Found.; v.p. Dayton chpt. United Cerebral Palsy; chmn. govt. affairs com. on transp. Dayton C. of C. Mem. NSPE, ASCE, Am. Consulting Engrs. Coun., Soc. Am. Mil. Engrs., Water Environment Fedn., Inter-Am. Assn. Sanitary Engring., Am. Water Works Assn. Avocation: travel. Office: Shaw Weiss & De Naples Corp 14 W 1st St Dayton OH 45402-1213

SHAW, (FRANCIS) HAROLD, performing arts administrator; b. Hebron, N.Y., June 11, 1923. Student, Ithaca Coll., 1942, Columbia, 1944, N.Y. U. Extension, 1948. Former assoc. Hurok Concerts, Inc., N.Y.C.; chmn., owner Shaw Concerts, Inc., N.Y.C., 1969—; performing arts dir. Seattle World's Fair, 1961-62; concert mgr. Nathan Milstein, Vladimir Horowitz, Dame Janet Baker, Jessye Norman, Helen Donath, Jacqueline duPre, Wolfgang Holzmair, Jard van Nes, Mitsuko Uchida, Garrick Ohlsson, Shura Cherkassky, Horacio Gutiérrez, Julian Bream, John Williams, Elmar Oliveira, Kyoko Takezawa, Robert Shaw, Andrew Davis, and over 100 artists and attractions; exec. dir. President's Shakespeare Ann. Com., 1964. Dir. exec. staff, mem. performing arts com. Cultural Commn., N.Y.C., 1966; nat. chmn. Performing Arts Energy Commn., 1974; chmn. bd. trustees Am. Shakespdare Theatre, Sfratford, Conn., 1974. With USAAF, 1942-43. Mem. Internat. Performing Arts Adminstrs., Am. Symphony Orch. League, Assn. Coll., Univ. and Community Arts Adminstrs., Actors Equity Assn., Am. Summer Stock Mgrs. Assn. (co-founder), Players Club, Bohemians, N.Y. Athletic Club, Phi Mu Allpha Sinfonia. Office: Shaw Concerts Inc 2211 Broadway New York NY 10024-6200

SHAW, HELEN LESTER ANDERSON, university dean; b. Lexington, Ky., Oct. 18, 1936; d. Walter Southall and Elizabeth (Guyn) Anderson; m. Charles Van Shaw, Mar. 14, 1988. BS, U. Ky., 1958; MS, U. Wis., 1965, PhD, 1969. Registered dietitian. Dietitian Roanoke (Va.) Meml. Hosp., 1959-60, Santa Barbara (Calif.) Cottage Hosp., 1960-61; dietitian, unit mgr. U. Calif., Santa Barbara, 1961-63; rsch. asst., NIH fellow U. Wis., Madison, 1963-68; from asst. prof. to prof. U. Mo., Columbia, 1969-88, assoc. dean, prof., 1977-84; prof., chair dept. food and nutrition U. N.C., Greensboro, 1989-94, dean Sch. Human Environ. Scis., 1994—; cluster leader Food for 21st Century rsch. program U. Mo., 1985-88. Contbr. articles to rsch. publs. Elder 1st Presbyn. Ch., Columbia, 1974-89, Greensboro, 1992—. Recipient Teaching award Home Econ. Alumni Assn., 1981, Gamma Sigma Delta, 1984; rsch. grantee Nutrition Found., 1971-73, NIH, 1972-75, NSF, 1980-83. Mem. Am. Soc. for Nutrition Scis., Am. Bd. Nutrition, Am. Soc. for Clin. Nutrition, Am. Dietetic Assn., Am. Family and Consumer Sci. Assn., Soc. for Nutrition Edn., Sigma Xi, Phi Upsilon Omicron, Kappa Omicron Nu. Democrat. Avocations: tennis, choral singing.

SHAW, HERBERT JOHN, physics educator emeritus; b. Seattle, June 2, 1918; s. Herbert John and Nell Grace (Cayley) S.; m. Francel Harper, Apr. 25, 1943; children: John Joseph, Kathleen, Karen. BA, U. Wash., 1941; MS, Stanford U., 1943, PhD, 1948. Test engr. GE, Schenectady, 1940-41; rsch. assoc. elec. engring. dept. Stanford (Calif.) U., 1948-50, rsch. assoc. Microwave Lab., 1950-57, sr. rsch. assoc., 1957-74, assoc. dir., 1968-77, adj. prof., 1974-83, rsch. prof. applied physics dept., 1983-88, prof. emeritus, 1989—; liaison scientist U.S. Office Naval Rsch., London, 1968-69; cons. to numerous electronics and optics cos. and govt. agys., 1950—. Fellow IEEE (Morris N. Liebmann Meml. award 1976, achievement award group on sonics and ultrasonics 1981); mem. NAE, Tau Beta Pi. Home: 719 Alvarado Row Stanford CA 94305-1037 Office: Stanford U Edward L Ginzton Lab Stanford CA 94305

SHAW, IAN ALEXANDER, accountant, mining company executive; b. Toronto, Feb. 28, 1940; m. JoAnne Millyard, Dec. 22, 1967; children: Julia, Martin, Laura. B.Comm., U. Toronto, 1964. Chartered acct. Deloitte Touche & Sells, Toronto, 1964-68; v.p. fin. A.G.F. Mgmt. Ltd., Toronto, 1968-75; treas. Sherritt Gordon Mines Ltd., Toronto, 1975-86; v.p., treas. Curragh Inc., Toronto, 1986-93; CFO Caribgold Resources, Inc., Metallica Resources, Inc., Pelangio-Larder Mines, Ltd., AMT Internat. Mining corp., Toucan Gold Corp., So. Cross Resources, Inc. Office: Ste 905 Box 22, 26 Wellington St E, Toronto, ON Canada M5E 1S2

SHAW, JACK ALLEN, communications company executive; b. Auburn, Ind., Jan. 1, 1939; s. Marvin Dale and Vera Lucille (Harter) S.; m. Martha Sue Collins, Aug. 24, 1963; 1 child, Mark Allen. BSEE, Purdue U., 1962, hon. doctorate Capitol Coll., 1994, DS (hon.), 1995. Project engr. Hughes Aircraft Co., El Segundo, Calif., 1962-69; dir. program mgmt. ITT Space Communications, Ramsey, N.J., 1969-74; v.p., corp. devel. Digital Communications Corp., Gaithersburg, Md., 1974-78, exec. v.p., COO, Germantown, Md., 1978-81, pres., CEO, 1981-84, pres., CEO M/A-com Telecom. divsn., 1984-87; chmn., CEO Hughes Network Systems Inc., 1988—; chmn. also bd. dirs. 1978—, Hughes Network Systems Inc., Germantown, 1987—; bd. dirs. DCC Ltd., Milton Keyes, Eng., Hughes Software Systems, Pvt. Ltd., New Delhi; sr. v.p., mem. office of chmn. Hughes Electronics; chmn. am. Mobile Satellite Corp.; co-chmn. U.S.-India Comml. Alliance. Vice chmn. United Fund Campaign Montgomery County, 1982. Named Disting. Engring. Alumni Purdue U., 1994, Outstanding Electrical Engr. Purdue U., 1994. Mem. IEEE (sr.), Radio Club of Am.(honored 1993). Republican. Clubs: Lakewood Country, Aspen Hill Racquet. Home: 11504 Lake Potomac Dr Potomac MD 20854-1223 Office: Hughes Network Systems Inc 11717 Exploration Ln Germantown MD 20876-2700

SHAW, JAMES, computer systems analyst; b. Salt Lake City, June 26, 1944; s. James Irvin and Cleo Lea (Bell) S. Student, San Antonio Coll., 1962-64; BA in History, St. Mary's U., San Antonio, 1966. With VA Automation Ctr., Austin, Tex., 1967—, sr. computer programmer analyst, 1984-87, supervisory computer programmer analyst, 1987-88, computer systems analyst, 1988-94, sr. computer systems analyst, 1994—; conversion team manual to computerized acctg. VA, 1974-76; participant conversion computerized acctg. sys. to database, 1984-88; participant complete replacement of VA computerized acctg. sys., 1989-95. Active Smithsonian Institution, Planned Parenthood, Met. Mus. Art, Austin Mus. Art. Mem. Am. Assn. Individual Investors. Democrat. Home: 11500 Jollyville Rd Apt 1312 Austin TX 78759-4070 Office: VA Automation Ctr 1615 Woodward St Austin TX 78741-7830

SHAW, JAMES ROBERT, broadcast executive; b. Brigden, Ont., Can., Aug. 14, 1934; s. Francis Earl and Lottie Myrtle (Gaw) S.; m. Carol Bulman, July 21, 1956; children: James Jr., Heather, Julie, Bradley. BA, Mich. State U., 1958; LLD (hon.), Graceland Coll., Lamoni, Iowa, U. (Can.) Alta. Various positions, pres. western cos. Shaw Industries, Calgary, Regina, Edmonton, Vancouver, Can.; founder, chmn., CEO Shaw Comm., Inc., Calgary, Can., 1966—; chmn. bd. govs. No. Alta. Inst. Tech.; operator 10 radio stas.; owner Shaw Fiberlink, Shaw Wave, video game svc. for Sega Channel, Shaw MobileComm., Inc., YTV, TreeHouse, country music video network CMT, others; bd. dirs., past chmn. Shaw Industries, Ltd., Can., U.S., England, Thailand, Saudi Arabia, Australia. Pres., bd. dirs. Shaw Family Found.; hon. life bd. dirs. Edmonton Northlands. Named to Honour List CCTA, 1992, Bus. Hall Fame Jr. Achievement No. Alta., 1993; recipient Velma Graham award contbns. Can. broadcasting sys. Ted Rogers Sr., 1992, Entrepreneur of Yr. award, 1993, Pinnacle award for bus. leadership So. Alta. Milner Fenerty, Friend Industry award Alta. Motion Picture Industries Assn., 1997. Mem. Rotary, Calgary Golf and Country, Mayfair Golf and Country, Edmonton Petroleum, Ranchmen's (Calgary). Protestant. Avocations: skiing, golf. Office: Shaw Comm Inc Ste 900, 630 3d Ave SW, Calgary, AB Canada*

SHAW, JAMES SCOTT, astronomy research administrator; b. Grand Junction, Colo., Oct. 13, 1942; 1 child. AB, Yale U., 1964; PhD in Astronomy, U. Pa., 1970. Asst. prof. U. Ga., Athens, 1970-77, assoc. prof. astronomy, 1977—. Mem. Internat. Astron. Union, Am. Astron. Soc., Sigma Xi. Office: Univ of Georgia Dept Physics & Astronomy Athens GA 30602*

SHAW, JEANNE OSBORNE, editor, poet; b. Stone Mountain, Ga., June 1, 1920; d. Virgil Waite and Daisy Hampton (Scruggs) Osborne; m. Harry B. Shaw, Dec. 10, 1982; children: Robert Allan Gibbs, Marilyn Osborne Gibbs Barry. BA, Agnes Scott Coll., 1942. Mem. editl. staff Atlanta Constitution, 1942; feature writer New London (Conn.) Day, 1943; book reviewer Atlanta Constitution, 1940-42, Atlanta Jour., 1945-48; poetry editor Banner Press, Emory U., 1957-59; book editor Georgia Mag., Decatur, 1957-73. Pres., Newton class Druid Hills Bapt. Ch., 1973-74, dir. ch. tng., 1978-79, ch. clk., 1995-97. Recipient Internat. Narrative Poem award Poets and Patrons, Inc., Chgo., 1992, Robert Martin, Burke, Otto, In Praise of Poetry awards N.Y. Poetry Forum, 1973, 79, 81; Westbrook award Ky. Poetry Soc., 1976; Ariz. award, 1981, Ind. State Fedn. of Poetry Clubs award, Ala. State Poetry Soc. award, 1990, Nat. Fedn. State Poetry Socs. Mem. Ga. Writers Assn. (lit. achievement award 1971), Poetry Soc. Ga. (John Clare prize 1955, Katharine H. Strong prize 1975, Eunice Thomson prize 1976, Jimmy Williamson prize 1977, Capt. Frank Spencer prize 1985, 88, Conrad Aiken prize, 1987, 88, Sarah Cunningham prize 1989, 94, 97, Soc. prize 1989, Lucy McEntire prize 1990, 94, Grace Schley Knight prize 1991, 93, Gerald Chan Sieg prize 1991, 95, Eunice Thompson prize 1992, Harriet Ross Colquitt prize 1994, 95, Eva Tennyson Forbes Meml. prize 1996), Atlanta Writers Club (pres. 1949-50, named Aurelia Austin Writer of Year in poetry 1971, Wyatt award 1986, 95, Light Verse award 1989, Edward Davin Vickers award, Light Verse award 1990, Daniel Whitehead Hicky award, 1991, 95, F. Levering Neely award 1991, Poet Laureate's award 1993, Ben Willingham award, Gerry Crocker award 1995), Ga. Poetry Soc. (Traditional award 1984, Cole and Ledford award 1986, Goreau award, 1987, 93, Melissa Henry award 1989, Charles and Virginia Dickson award 1990, Jo Ann Yeager Adkins award 1991, Poem About Atlanta award 1992, 14th Aniv. Free Verse award 1993, My Very Best Poem award 1995, Jabberwocky award 1997), Phi Beta Kappa. Author: The Other Side of the Water (Author of Year in Poetry award Dixie Coun. of Authors and Journalists), 1970; Unravelling Yarn, 1979; co-author: Noel! Poems of Christmas, 1979; They Continued Steadfastly, History of Druid Hills Baptist Church, 1987; author: Faithbuilders, 1982-84; contbr. poems, pen and ink sketches to mags. Home: 809 Pinetree Dr Decatur GA 30030-2332

SHAW, JIAJIU, chemist; b. Taichung, Taiwan, China, Jan. 21, 1950; came to U.S., 1979; s. Pei-Fan and Yu-Jane (Lin) S.; m. Shu-Chin, Mar. 5, 1982; children: Allen J., Cindy Y. BS in Chemistry, Tsing Hua U., Taiwan, 1972; PhD in Chemistry, U. Kans., 1984. Postdoctoral rsch. assoc. U. N.C., Chapel Hill, 1984-86; sr. chemist Nat. Analytical Labs., Rockville, Md., 1986-87; sr. rsch. scientist Ciba-Geigy Corp., Summit, N.J., 1987-89, staff scientist, 1990-93; dir. Lannett Co., Phila., 1993-94, Caraco Pharms., Detroit, 1994—; v.p. Unitech, Inc., Ann Arbor, Mich., 1996—; prin. Ann Arbor Chinese Sch., 1996—. Contbr. articles to profl. jours. Recipient Ray Q. Brewster award U. Kans., 1984. Mem. AAAS, Am. Chem. Soc., Am. Assn. Pharm. Scientists. Republican. Achievements include design of new pharmaceutical controlled release system, synthesis of new anti-cancer drugs. Avocation: painting. Office: 3166 Shamrock Ct Ann Arbor MI 48105-9675

SHAW, JIM, JR., broadcast executive; b. Ontario, Can., July 29, 1957; m. Wanda Shaw; children: Haley Morgan, Parker James. Various mgmt. positions Shaw Comm., Inc., Calgary, Alta., Can., 1982, past pres. cable TV, past sr. v.p. ops., pres., COO, 1995—; chmn. bd. dirs. Vision.com, Can.; bd. dirs. Microcell Telecomm., Montreal, CableLabs, Montreal; mem. adv. coun. faculty bus. U. Alberta; owner Shaw FiberLink, Shaw DBS Ventures, YTV, SEGA Channel, Digital Music Express, Microcell; operator 9 radio stas. Gov. Shawnigan Lake Sch., B.C.; active Young Pres. Orgn.; past bd. dirs. Cable TV Stds. Found. Office: Shaw Comm, 630 3d Ave SW, Calgary, AB Canada T2P 4Z4*

SHAW, JOHN, sports association administrator; 1 dau., Alexandra. BS in Acctg., U. San Diego; JD, NYU. Lawyer Calif.; acct. Arthur Andersen & Co.; pres. St. Louis Rams, 1980—; primary advisor to chmn. and owner St. Louis Rams; mem. NFL Mgmt. Coun. Exec. Com. Bd. dirs. Greater St. Louis United Way; mem. Coun. Trustees LEARN, St. Louis. Office: St Louis Rams 1 Rams Way Saint Louis MO 63045

SHAW, JOHN ARTHUR, lawyer; b. San Antonio, June 6, 1922; s. Samuel Arthur and Ellen Agnes (Lawless) S.; m. Margaret Louise Strudell, June 9, 1951; children: John Richard, Barbara Ann, David William. Student, Loyola U., Chgo., 1940-41, U. N.C., 1943-44; LL.B., St. Louis U., 1948, J.D., 1969. Bar: Mo. 1948. Assoc. firm Pollock, Tenney & Dahman, St. Louis, 1948-51; atty. St. Louis Probate Ct., 1951-53; ptnr. firm Pollock, Ward, Klobasa & Shaw, St. Louis, 1953-63; gen. counsel Reliable Life Ins. Co., Webster Groves, Mo., 1967-83, sr. v.p., 1969-80, sec., 1980-83, dir., 1968-83, also dir., officer, gen. counsel subs. cos., 1967-85. Contbg. author: Basic Estate Planning, 1957; editor: Missouri Probate Law and Practice, 1960. Bd. dirs., sec. Tatman Found., 1967-84; committeeman Boy Scouts Am., 1969-77; bd. dirs. Mo. Ins. Guaranty Assn., 1973-87, sec. 1983-87. Served as lt. AUS, 1943-46, ETO; maj. U.S. Army Res., (ret.). Mem. Mo. Bar, Met. St. Louis Bar Assn., Assn. Life Ins. Counsel, Nat. Lawyers Assn., St. Thomas More Soc., Lawyers for Life, Ret. Officers Assn., Mil. Order of the World Wars, Alpha Sigma Nu, Delta Theta Phi. Home and Office: 306 Luther Ln Saint Louis MO 63122-4647

SHAW, JOHN FIRTH, orchestra administrator; b. Chesterfield, U.K., June 28, 1948; s. Jack Firth and Mary Stuart (MacPherson) S.; m. Julia Valette Phillips, Dec. 29, 1973; children: Mary Valette, Mark Firth, Andrew Nicholas. Licentiate Royal Acad. Music, 1968; grad. Royal Schs. of Music, 1970. Freelance musician, 1966-70; prin. musician Calgary Philharm. Orch., 1970-77, asst. mgr., 1977-78, asst. gen. mgr., 1978-79, gen. mgr., 1979-93; mng. dir. Hamilton Philharm. Orch., 1993-95; pres., CEO Renaissance Arts Enterprises, 1996—. Bd. dirs. Calgary Philharm. Soc., 1974-77, Calgary Centre for Performing Arts, 1980-85, Choral Music Assn. Calgary, 1991-92; mem. adv. com. Mount Royal Coll. Conservatory of Music, 1990-93. Recipient Alta. Achievement award, 1991, Disting. Citizen Calgary award, 1993. Mem. Assn. Can. Orchs. (dir. 1982-84, 86—, pres. 1988-92, dir. 1992—). Home: 10 Lantern Ln, Dundas, ON Canada L9H 6N9

SHAW, JOHN FREDERICK, retired naval officer; b. Dallas, Oct. 14, 1938; s. John Frederick and Sarah E. (Crouch) S.; m. Janice Muren, July 14, 1962; children: Elizabeth Lee, Suzanne Michele. BS, U.S. Naval Acad., 1960; MS in Mgmt. with distinction, Naval Postgrad. Sch., Monterey, Calif., 1970; grad., Armed Forces Staff Coll., 1971. Commd. ensign USN, 1960, advanced through grades to rear adm., 1983; exec. officer USS Long Beach (CGN 9), 1978-79; comdg. officer USS Bainbridge (CGN 25), 1980-83; dir. guided missile destroyer 51, Arleigh Burke program Comdr. Naval Sea Systems Command, Washington, 1983-85, mgr. AEGIS shipbldg. program, 1985-87; comdr. Cruiser-Destroyer Group One, San Diego, 1987-88; dep. chief staff plans and policy Supreme Allied Comdr., Atlantic, Norfolk, Va., 1988-89, chief staff, 1989-91; ret., 1991; prof. joint mil. ops. Coll. Continuing Edn., Naval War Coll., San Diego, 1992-94; bd. advisors United Svc. Benefit Assn., Kansas City, Kans., 1987-93. Decorated Def. D.S.M., Legion of Merit with two gold stars, Meritorious Svc. medal with gold star, Navy Commendation medal with gold star. Mem. U.S. Naval Inst.(life), U.S. Naval Acad. Alumni Assn. (life, pres. Washington chpt. 1986, bd. govs. San Diego/Coronado chpt. 1996—), Surface Navy Assn. Avocations: golf, reading, economics, travel.

SHAW, JOHN W., lawyer; b. Mo., 1951. BA, U. Mo., 1973, MA, 1973, JD, 1977. Bar: Mo. 1977. Ptnr. Bryan Cave, Kansas City. Mem. ABA, Securities Industry Assn. (legal and compliance group), Mo. Bar, Def. Rsch. Inst. (chmn. firearms litigation subcom.), Order of Coif. Office: Bryan Cave LLP 3500 One Kansas City Pl 1200 Main St Kansas City MO 64105

SHAW, JOSEPH THOMAS, Slavic languages educator; b. Ashland City, Tenn., May 13, 1919; s. George Washington and Ruby Mae (Pace) S.; m. Betty Lee Ray, Oct. 30, 1942; children: David Matthew, Joseph Thomas, James William. AB, U. Tenn., 1940, AM, 1941; AM, Harvard, 1947, PhD, 1950. Asst. prof. Slavic langs. Ind. U., 1949-55, assoc. prof., 1955-61; prof. Slavic langs. U. Wis., 1961-89, prof. emeritus, 1989—, chmn. dept. Slavic langs., 1962-68, 77-86, chmn. div. humanities, 1964-65, 72-73, assoc. dean Grad. Sch., 1965-68. Author: The Letters of Alexander Pushkin, 1963, Pushkin's Rhymes: A Dictionary, 1974, Baratynskii: A Dictionary of the Rhymes and a Concordance to the Poetry, 1975, Batiushkov: A Dictionary of the Rhymes and a Concordance to the Poetry, 1975, Pushkin: A Concordance to the Poetry, 1985, American Association Teachers Slavic and East European Languages: The First Fifty Years 1941-91, 1991, Pushkin's Poetry of the Unexpected: The Nonrhymed Lines in the Rhymed Poetry and the Rhymed Lines in the Nonrhymed Poetry, 1994, Pushkin, Poet and Man of Letters, and His Prose (Collected works, vol. 1), 1995, Pushkin Poems and Other Studies (collected works vol. 2), 1996; editor: The Slavic and East European Jour., 1957-70; contbr. articles to profl. jours. Served to capt. USNR, 1942-46, 51-53. Mem. Am. Assn. Tchrs. Slavic and East European Langs. (mem. exec. council 1953-70, 73-80, pres. 1973-74). Home: 4505 Mineral Point Rd Madison WI 53705-5071

SHAW, (GEORGE) KENDALL, artist, educator; b. New Orleans, Mar. 30, 1924; s. George Kendall and Florence Gladys (Worner) S.; m. Frances Glenn Fort, Oct. 31, 1955. Student, Ga. Inst. Tech., 1944-46; B.S. in Chemistry, Tulane U., 1949, M.F.A. in Painting, 1959; postgrad., La. State U., 1950. instr. Columbia U., 1961-66, Hunter Coll., 1966-68, Parsons Sch. Design, N.Y.C., 1966-86, Lehman Coll., 1968-70, Bklyn. Mus. Art Sch., 1970-76. One-man shows include Columbia U., 1965, Bienville Gallery, New Orleans, 1968, Tibor de Nagy Gallery, N.Y.C., 1964, 65, 67, 68, Southampton Coll., 1969, John Bernard Myers Gallery, 1972, Alessandra Gallery, 1976, Lerner/Heller Gallery, N.Y.C., 1979, 81, 82, Bernice Steinbaum Gallery, N.Y.C., 1991, Artists Space, N.Y.C., 1992; group shows include P.S.I., N.Y.C., 1977, Gladstone-Villani Gallery, N.Y.C., 1978, Galerie Habermann, Cologne, 1979, Modern Art Gallery, Vienna, 1980, Jacksonville Art Mus. (Fla.), 1983, Hudson Guild, N.Y.C., 1997, others; represented in permanent collections Peter Ludwig, Aachen, Bklyn. Mus., Albright-Knox Gallery, Buffalo, Mus. Contemporary Art, Nagaoka, Japan, Everson Mus., Syracuse, Chase Manhattan Bank, N.Y.C., Chem. Bank, N.Y.C., N.Y. U., N.Y.C. Served with USN, 1943-46. Mem. Coll. Art Assn., Artists Equity Assn. Democrat. Address: 458 Broome St New York NY 10013-2651

SHAW, KENNETH ALAN, university president; b. Granite City, Ill., Jan. 31, 1939; s. Kenneth W. and Clara H. (Lange) S.; m. Mary Ann Byrne, Aug. 18, 1962; children: Kenneth William, Susan Lynn, Sara Ann. BS, Ill. State U., 1961, DHL, 1987; EdM, U. Ill., 1963; PhD, Purdue U., 1966, EdD (hon.), 1990; DHL, Towson State, 1979, Ill. Coll., 1986. Tchr. history, counselor Rich Twp. High Sch., Park Forest, Ill., 1961-63; residence hall dir., instr. edn. Ill. State U., 1963-64; counselor Office Dean of Men, Purdue U., 1964-65, Office Dean of Men, Purdue U. (Office Student Loans), 1965-66; asst. to pres., lectr. sociology Ill. State U., 1966-69; v.p. acad. affair, dean Towson State U., Balt., 1969-76; pres. So. Ill. U., Edwardsville, 1977-79; chancellor So. Ill. U. System, Edwardsville, 1979-86; pres. U. Wis. System, Madison, 1986-91; chancellor Syracuse U., 1991—. Trustee CICU, Albany, N.Y., 1993—, Am. Coll. Testing, 1990—; bd. dirs. Unity Mutual Life Ins. Co., 1992—, Syracuse (N.Y.) C. of C., 1991—, NCAA Pres. Commn., 1993—, Met. Devel. Assn., 1991—, Key Bank of Ctrl. N.Y., 1995—. Recipient Young Leader in Edn. award, 1980, Citizen of Yr. award So. Ill. Inc., 1985, Silver Anniversary award NCAA, 1986, Coaches Silver Anniversary award Nat. Assn. of Basketball, 1986; named to Ill. Basketball Hall of Fame, 1983. Mem. Am. Assn. State Colls. and Univs. (external rels. com. 1986-88), Am. Coun. Edn. (com. on minorities in higher edn. 1987-91), Am. Social. Assn., Am. Higher Edn. Assn., State Higher Edn. Exec. Officers Assn., Phi Delta Kappa, Pi Gamma Mu. Office: Syracuse Univ Off of Chancellor Syracuse NY 13244-1100*

SHAW, L. EDWARD, JR., lawyer; b. Elmira, N.Y., July 30, 1944; s. L. Edward and Virginia Anne (O'Leary) S.; m. Irene Ryan; children—Christopher, Hope, Hillary, Julia, Rory. B.A. in Econs., Georgetown U., Washington, 1966; J.D., Yale U., New Haven, 1969. Bar: N.Y. 1969. Assoc. Milbank, Tweed, Hadley & McCloy, N.Y.C., 1969-77, ptnr., 1977-83; sr. v.p., gen. counsel Chase Manhattan Corp., N.Y.C., 1983-85, exec. v.p., gen. counsel, 1985-96; vice chmn., gen. counsel Natwest Markets, N.Y.C., 1996—. Mem. Assn. Bar City N.Y., Winged Foot Golf Club, Phi Beta Kappa. Roman Catholic. Avocations: youth athletics; golf. Office: Natwest Market 175 Water St New York NY 10038-4918

SHAW, LAURIE JO, grant project director; b. Morris, Minn., Feb. 23, 1956; d. Edgar Allen and Dorothy Ruth (Harms) S.; m. Grant William Carlson, July 23, 1983 (div. Feb. 1986). Tchr. aide degree, Hutchinson Area Vocat. Tech., Minn., 1975; audio visual prodn., Hutchinson (Minn.) AVTI, 1976; BA in Psychology, S.W. State U., 1982; MA in Counseling, N.Mex. State U., 1987. Libr. tech. S.W. State U., Marshall, Minn., 1976-84; student svcs. coord. Mohave C.C., Bullhead City, Ariz., 1987-91; counselor, instr. Prestonsburg C.C., Pikeville, Ky., 1992-93; project dir. So. W.Va. C.C., Williamson, 1993—. Mem. AAUW (v.p. 1990-92), Nat. Assn. Student Pers. Adminstrs., Ky. Assn. Student Fin. Aid Adminstrs., Bus. and Profl. Women (pres. 1990-91, Young Career Woman award 1989), W.Va. Assn. Edn. Opportunity Program Pers., Mid.-East Assn. Edn. Opportunity Program Pers. Democrat. Methodist. Avocations: cross country skiing, oriental cooking, collecting Hummels. Office: So WV Community Coll Armory Dr Williamson WV 25661

SHAW, LEANDER JERRY, JR., state supreme court justice; b. Salem, Va., Sept. 6, 1930; s. Leander J. and Margaret S. BA, W.Va. State Coll., 1952, LLD (hon.), 1986; JD, Howard U., 1957; PhD (hon.) in Pub. Affairs, Fla. Internat. U., 1990; LLD (hon.), Nova Law Sch., 1991, Washington & Lee Law Sch., 1991. Asst. prof. law Fla. A&M U., 1957-60; sole practice Jacksonville, Fla., 1960-69, 72-74; asst. pub. defender Fla., 1965-69; asst. state's atty. Fla., 1969-72; judge Fla. Indsl. Relations Commn., 1974-79, Fla. Ct. Appeals (1st dist.), 1979-83; justice Fla. Supreme Ct., Tallahassee, 1983—, chief justice, 1990-92. Office: Fla Supreme Ct Supreme Ct Bldg Tallahassee FL 32399

SHAW, LEE CHARLES, lawyer; b. Red Wing, Minn., Feb. 17, 1913; s. Marvil Thomas and Bernice (Quinland) S.; m. Lorraine Schroeder, July 1, 1939; children—Lynda Lee, Robert, Candace Jean, Lee Charles. B.A., U. Chgo., 1936, J.D., 1938. Bar: Ill. 1938. Assoc. Pope & Ballard, Chgo., 1938-44, ptnr., 1944-45; founding ptnr. Seyfarth, Shaw, Fairweather & Geraldson, Chgo., 1945—; mem. arbitration svcs. adv. com. Fed. Mediation and Conciliation Svc. Contbr. articles on labor law to profl. jours. Mem. ABA, Chgo. Bar Assn. (bd. mgrs. 1956-57), U. Chgo. Alumni Assn., Tavern Club, Union League Club (Chgo.). Republican. Episcopalian. Home: Pacific Regent La Jolla 3890 Nobel Dr Apt 1702 San Diego CA 92122-5784 Office: Seyfarth Shaw Fairweather 55 E Monroe St Ste 4200 Chicago IL 60603-5803

SHAW, LEONARD GLAZER, electrical engineering educator, consultant; b. Toledo, Aug. 15, 1934; s. A. Daniel and Mary (Glazer) S.; m. Susan Gail Weil, Dec. 24, 1961; children: Howard Benjamin, Mitchell Bruce, Jenny Louise. BSEE, U. Pa., 1956; MSEE, Stanford U., 1957, PhD, 1961. From asst. prof. to assoc. prof. Polytech. U., N.Y., Bklyn., 1960-1975, prof., 1975—, head dept. elec. engring. and computer sci., 1982-90, dean sch. elec. engring. and computer sci., 1990-94; vice provost for undergraduate studies, 1995-96. vis. prof. Tech. U., Eindhoven, Netherlands, 1970, Ecole Nationale Superieure de Mecanique, Nantes, France, 1977; cons. Sperry Systems Mgmt. Div., Great Neck, N.Y.; mem. grant rev. panels NSF, 1986—. Author: (with others) Signal Processing, 1975. Contbr. articles to profl. jours. Research grantee NSF, 1973, 81. Fellow IEEE (various coms., editorial bd. 1961-92, editor-in-chief, IEEE Press 1988-91, gen. chmn. Conf. on Decision and Control, Dec. 1989, v.p. Fin. Control System Soc., 1992-93, chair Tech. Field Award Coun., 1995-97; mem. IEEE, Am. Soc. for Engring. Edn. Office: Polytech U Jacobs Coll Engring & Sci 6 Metrotech Ctr Brooklyn NY 11201-3840

SHAW, LILLIE MARIE KING, vocalist; b. Indpls., Nov. 27, 1915; d. Earl William and Bertha Louise (Groth) King; m. Philip Harlow Shaw, June 26, 1940. Student, Jordan Conservatory Music, Indpls., 1940-43; BA, Ariz. State U., 1959; MA, Denver U., 1962; pvt. vocal study, 1944-70. Educator, libr. Glendale (Ariz.) Schs., 1959-67; lectr. libr. sci. Ariz. State U., Tempe, 1962-68. Concertizing, oratorio, symphonic soloist, light opera, 1965-82; soloist First Ch. of Christ Scientist, Sun City West, Ariz., 1980—. Monthly lectr. Christian Women's Fellowship, Phoenix, 1989—; World Conf. del. Soc. of Friends, 1967. Mem. Nat. Soc. Arts and Letters (sec. 1990-94, nat. del. 1992), Am. Philatelic Assn. (life), Am. Topical Assn., Phoenix Philatelic Soc., Auditions Guild Ariz. (sec. 1989-92), Phoenix Opera League, Phoenix Symphony Guild, Sigma Alpha Iota Alumnae (Phoenix chpt., life, treas. 1988-96, Sword of Honor 1972, Rose of Honor 1982, Rose of Dedication 1995). Republican. Avocations: philately, gardening. Home: 6802 N 37th Ave Phoenix AZ 85019-1103

SHAW, M. THOMAS, III, bishop; b. Battle Creek, Mich., Aug. 28, 1945; s. M.T. and Wilma Jaynes Shaw. BA, Alma (Mich.) Coll.; MDiv, Cath. U.; DD (hon.), Gen. Theol. Sem. Ordained priest Episcopal Ch., 1971. Mem. Co. of Mission Priests, Eng., 1970-72, Milw., 1972-74; mem. Soc. St. John the Evangelist, Cambridge, Mass., 1974—; bishop Episcopal Diocese of Mass., 1994—. Address: 980 Memorial Dr Cambridge MA 02138-5717

SHAW, MARGERY WAYNE SCHLAMP, geneticist, physician, lawyer; b. Evansville, Ind., Feb. 15, 1923; d. Arthur George and Louise (Meyer) Schlamp; m. Charles Raymond Shaw, May 31, 1942 (div. Nov. 1972); 1 dau., Barbara Rae. Student, Hanover Coll., 1940-41; A.B. magna cum laude, U. Ala., 1945; M.A., Columbia U., 1946; postgrad., Cornell U., 1947-48; M.D. cum laude, U. Mich., 1957; J.D., U. Houston, 1973; D.Sc. (hon.), U. Evansville, 1977, U. So. Ind., 1986. Intern St. Joseph Mercy Hosp., Ann Arbor, Mich., 1957-58; practice medicine specializing in human genetics Ann Arbor, 1958-67; instr. dept. human genetics Med. Sch. U. Mich., 1958-61, asst. prof., 1961-66, assoc. prof., 1966-67; assoc. prof. dept. biology Grad. Sch. Biomed. Scis., U. Tex., Houston, 1967-69; prof. Grad. Sch. Biomed. Scis., U. Tex., 1969-88, dir. Med. Genetics Ctr., 1971-83, acting dean, 1976-78, prof. emeritus, 1988—; mem. genetics study sect. NIH, Bethesda, Md., 1966-70, mem. genetics tng. com., 1970-74, adv. com. to dir., 1979-82; chromosome studies astronauts NASA, 1970-71; mem. med. adv. bd. Nat. Genetics Found., 1972-88; rsch. adv. bd. Planned Parenthood, Houston, 1972-79; vis. scholar Yale Law Sch., 1974; Andrew D. White prof.-at-large Cornell U., 1982-88; vis. prof. U. Utah, 1983; adj. prof. U. Houston Law Ctr., 1986-88. Asso. editor: Am. Jour. Human Genetics, 1962-68; editorial bd.: Am. Jour. Med. Genetics, 1977-87, Am. Jour. Law and Medicine, 1977-88; contbr. articles to profl. jours. First aid instr. ARC, 1962-67; unit chmn. United Fund, 1966. Recipient Billings Silver medal AMA, 1966; Achievement award AAUW, 1970-71; Am. Jurisprudence award, 1973. Mem. Am. Soc. Human Genetics (past sec., dir., pres. 1982), Genetics Soc. Am. (sec. 1971-73, pres. 1977-78, Wilhelmene Key award 1977), Tissue Culture Assn. (trustee 1970-72), Environ. Mutagen Soc. (coun.), Am. Soc. Cell Biology, Am. Soc. Law Medicine (trustee 1980-88), Phi Beta Kappa, Alpha Omega Alpha. Home: 2617 Pine Tree Dr Evansville IN 47711-2117

SHAW, MARILYN MARGARET, artist, photographer; b. San Diego, Dec. 19, 1933; d. George Louis and Helen Frances (Wright) Mitchell; m. Robert Dale Shaw, Feb. 19, 1952; children: Austin Allen, Kenneth Duane, Frank Lloyd. BA in Fine Arts and Photography, Juniata Coll., 1989. Photographer The Daily News, Huntingdon, Pa., 1988-92; owner, tchr. Marilyn Shaw Studios, Tyrone, Pa., 1989—; photographer The Jamesyouth, St. James. Luth. Ch., Huntingdon, 1987-92; photojournalist Easter Seals Telethon, 1991-92; art dir. Allegheny Riding Camp-The GrierSch., Tyrone, Pa., 1992; art instr. The Pa. House, Tyrone, 1995—, Ben Franklin Crafts, Altoona, Pa., 1997—; art tchr. homeschooled students, 1994—. One-woman shows include Shoemaker Gallery, Huntingdon, 1989; group shows include Standing Stone Art League, Huntingdon, 1978-92, Washington St. Art Gallery, Huntingdon, 1991, 94; author, illustrator The Prize, 1989. Vol. The Huntingdon House, 1992—, Presbyn. Ch., Huntingdon, 1992-95, Tyrone Presbyn. Ch., 1995—. Recipient numerous ribbons Huntingdon County Fair, 1978, 90, 91, Sinking Valley Farm Show, 1992, 94, 95, 96, Huntingdon County Arts Coun., 1989, 90, 91, Merit Cert. Photographers Forum, 1989, Vila Gardner Metzger art award, 1989, others. Mem. Standing Stone Art League, Huntingdon County Arts Coun., Women's League Juniata Coll., Nat. Mus. of Women in the Arts (charter mem.). Avocations: hunting, fishing, needlecrafts, camping, travel. Home and Office: 104 W 12th St Tyrone PA 16686-1634

SHAW, MARY M., computer science educator; b. Washington, Sept. 30, 1943; d. Eldon Earl and Mary Lewis (Holman) Shaw; m. Roy R. Weil, Feb. 15, 1973. BA cum laude, Rice U., 1965; PhD, Carnegie Mellon U., Pitts., 1972. Asst. prof. to prof. computer sci. Carnegie Mellon U., Pitts., 1972—, assoc. dean computer sci. for profl. programs, 1992—, Alan J. Perlis chair computer sci.; chief scientist Software Engring. Inst., Carnegie Mellon U., Pitts., 1984-88; mem. Computer Sci. and Telecommunications Bd., NRC, Washington, 1986-93. Author: (with W. Wulf, P. Hilfinger, L. Flan) Fundamental Structures of Computer Science, 1981, The Carnegie Mellon Curriculum for Undergraduate Computer Science, 1985, (with David Garlan) Software Architecture: Perspectives on an Emerging Discipline, 1996; contbr. articles to profl. jours. Recipient Warnier prize, 1993; named Woman of Achievement, YWCA of Greater Pitts., 1973. Fellow AAAS, IEEE (disting. lectr.), Assn. for Computing Machinery (SIGPLAN exec. com. 1979-83, Recognition of Svc. award 1985, 90); mem. Sigma Xi. Office: Carnegie Mellon U Dept Computer Sci Pittsburgh PA 15213

SHAW, MELVIN PHILLIP, physicist, engineering educator, psychologist; b. Bklyn., Aug. 16, 1936; s. Harry and Yetta (Stutsky) S.; m. Carol Joan Phillips, Sept. 5, 1959 (div. Feb. 1987); children: Adam, Evan; m. Bernetta Berger, May 16, 1987. BS, Bklyn. Coll., 1959; MS, Case Western Res. U., 1963, PhD, 1965; MA, Ctr. for Humanistic Studies, 1988. Research scientist United Techs. Research Labs., E. Hartford, Conn., 1964-68, scientist-in-charge, 1966-70; prof. Wayne State U., Detroit, 1970-96; adminstrv. dir. Assocs. of Birmingham/Kingswood Hosp., 1991-93; cons. Energy Conversion Devices, Troy, Mich., 1970-92. Co-author: The Gunn-Hilsum Effect, 1979, The Physics and Applications of Amorphous Semiconductors, 1988, The Physics of Instabilities in Solid State Electron Devices, 1992, Creativity and Affect, 1994. Fellow Am. Phys. Soc.; mem. IEEE (sr.), Am. Psychol. Assn. (assoc.). Avocations: cooking, walking, travel.

SHAW, MICHAEL, biologist, educator; b. Barbados, W.I., Feb. 11, 1924; s. Anthony and Myra (Perkins) S.; m. Jean Norah Berkinshaw, Oct. 16, 1948; children—Christopher A., Rosemary E., Nicholas R., Andrew L. B. Sc., McGill U., 1946, M. Sc., 1947, Ph.D., 1949, D.Sc., 1975. Nat. Research Council Can. postdoctoral fellow Botany Sch., Cambridge U., 1949-50; Assoc. prof. biology U. Sask., 1950-54, prof., 1954-67, prof., head dept. biology, 1961-67; dean faculty agrl. scis. U. B.C., 1967-75, v.p. acad. devel., 1975-81, acad. v.p., provost, 1981-83, univ. prof., 1983-89, univ. prof. emeritus, 1989—; mem. Sci. Council Can., 1976-82, Natural Scis. and Engring. Research Council Can., 1978-80. Contbr. articles to profl. jours. Recipient Queen's Silver Jubilee medal, 1977, gold medal Biol. Coun. Can., 1983. Fellow Royal Soc. Can. (Flavelle medal 1976), Can. Phytopath. Soc., Am. Phytopath. Soc., N.Y. Acad. Scis.; mem. Can. Bot. Assn., Can. Soc. Plant Physiologists (gold medal 1971), Am. Soc. Plant Physiologists. Home: 1792 Western Pky, Vancouver, BC Canada V6T 1V3 Office: U BC, Dept Plant Sci, Vancouver, BC Canada V6T 1Z4

SHAW, MICHAEL ALLAN, lawyer, mail order company executive; b. Evanston, Ill., July 14, 1940; s. Frank C. and Mabel I. (Peacock) S.; m. Genevieve Schrodt, Aug. 16, 1964; children: M. Ian, Trevor A. BA, Colo. State U., 1962; JD, U. Denver, 1965; MBA, DePaul U., 1969; postgrad., Columbia U., 1970. Bar: Ill. bar 1965. Practiced in Chgo., 1965-83; asst. counsel, staff asst. to v.p. traffic Jewel Cos., Inc., Melrose Park, Ill., 1965-71; corp. sec., asst. treas., house counsel Wieboldt Stores, Inc., Chgo., 1972-83; pvt. practice law Naperville, Ill., 1983-89; pres. Kingston Korner, Inc., Naperville, Ill., 1983—, Aztec Corp., Naperville, Ill., 1989—. Pres. Folk Era Prodns., producers folk music concert series, records, 1985—; editor Folk Music Editor, 1984; contbr. articles to legal jours. Mem. Village Planning Commn., Itasca, Ill., 1973-77; bd. dirs. Crimestoppers, Naperville, 1984—, chmn., 1988-94; session mem. Naperville Lumen Christi United Presbyn. Ch., 1984-85; chmn. bldg. fin. com. Naperville Presbyn. Ch., 1989-93. Mem. Fox Valley Folklore Soc. (bd. dirs. 1991—). Home: 6 S 230 Cohasset Rd Naperville IL 60540 Office: Aztec Corp 705 S Washington St Naperville IL 60540-6654

SHAW, MILTON CLAYTON, mechanical engineering educator; b. Phila., May 27, 1915; s. Milton Fredic and Nellie Edith (Clayton) S.; m. Mary Jane Greeninger, Sept. 6, 1939; children—Barbara Jane, Milton Stanley. B.S. in Mech. Engring, Drexel Inst. Tech., 1938; M.Eng. Sci., U. Cin., 1940, Sc.D., 1942; Dr. h.c., U. Louvain, Belgium, 1970; D of Engring., Drexel U., 1996. Research engr. Cin. Milling Machine Co., 1938-42; chief materials br. NACA, 1942-46; with Mass. Inst. Tech., 1946-61, prof. mech. engring., 1953-61, head materials processing div., 1952-61; prof., head dept. mech. engring. Carnegie Inst. Tech., Pitts., 1961-75; univ. prof. Carnegie Inst. Tech., 1974-77; prof. engring. Ariz. State U., Tempe, 1977—; Cons. indsl. cos.; lectr. in, Europe, 1952; pres. Shaw Smith & Assos., Inc., Mass., 1951-61; Lucas prof. Birmingham (Eng.) U., 1961; Springer prof. U. Calif. at Berkeley, 1972; Distinguished guest prof. Ariz. State U., 1977; mem. Nat. Materials Adv. Bd., 1971-74; bd. dirs. Engring. Found., 1976, v.p. conf. com., 1976-78. Recipient Outstanding Research award Ariz. State U., 1981, Am. Machinist award, 1972, Schlesinger award German Govt., 1997; P. McKenna award, 1975; Guggenheim fellow, 1956; Fulbright lectr. Aachen T.H., Germany, 1957; OECD fellow to Europe, 1964—. Fellow Am. Acad. Arts and Scis., ASME (Hersey award 1967, Thurston lectr. 1971, Outstanding Engring. award 1975, ann. meeting theme organizer 1977, Gold medal 1985, hon. 1980), Am. Soc. Lubrication Engrs. (hon., nat. award 1964), Am. Soc. Metals (Wilson award 1971, fellow 1981); mem. Internat. Soc. Prodn. Engring. Research (pres. 1960-61, hon. mem. 1975), Am. Soc. for Engring. Edn. (G. Westinghouse award 1956), Soc. Mfg. Engrs. (hon. mem. 1970, Gold medal 1958, internat. edn. award 1980), Nat. Acad. Engring., Polish Acad. Sci., Am. Soc. Precision Engrs. (hon.). Home: C119 2625 E Southern Ave Tempe AZ 85282-7633 Address: Arizona State Univ Engring Dept Tempe AZ 85287-6106

SHAW, MILTON HERBERT, conglomerate executive; b. Phila., June 16, 1918; s. Milton Herbert and Ethel (Shane) S.; m. Rita P. Revins, Nov. 24, 1971. BS, U. Pa., 1949. cons. indsl. safety and workmen's compensation. Accountant Franklin Sugar Refinery, Phila., 1945-52; with Kaiser Metal Products, Inc., Bristol, Pa., 1952-61; mgr. ins. and taxes Kaiser Metal Products, Inc., 1955-61; with Kidde Consumer Durables Corp., Bala Cynwyd, Pa., 1961-88; asst. v.p. Kidde Consumer Durables Corp., 1968-88, dir. corp. svcs. and risk mgmt., 1977-88; cons. Indsl. Safety-Workmans Compensation, 1988; owner Golden Grain Goldens; co-owner Potpourri Promotions, Rita P. Shaw Porcelain Studio. Served with USNR, 1936-45. Mem. NRA, VFW (treas. home assn. post 9788), Nat. Wildlife Fedn., Sigma Kappa Phi. Home and Office: 2209 Blackhorse Dr Warrington PA 18976-2118

SHAW, MONTGOMERY THROOP, chemical engineering educator; b. Ithaca, N.Y., Sept. 11, 1943; s. Robert William and Charlotte (Throop) S.; m. Stephanie Habel, Sept. 5, 1966 (dec. 1989); 1 child, Steven Robert; m. Maripaz Nespral, June 25, 1994. BChemE, Cornell U., 1966, MS, 1966; MS, Princeton (N.J.) U., 1968, PhD, 1970. Engr., project scientist Union Carbide Corp., Bound Brook, N.J., 1970-76; assoc. prof. Dept. Chem. Engring., U. Conn., Storrs, 1977-83, prof., 1983—; sabbatical prof. Sandia Nat. Labs., Albuquerque, 1983-84; vis. scientist E.I. Dupont de Nemours and Co., Experimental Station, Wilmington, Del., 1991-92; adv. bd. Jour. of Applied Polymer Sci., 1984-89. Co-author: Polymer-Polymer Miscibility, 1977, Computer Programs for Rheologists, 1994. Grantee Alcoa Found., 1985, Exxon Edn. Found., 1986. Mem. IEEE (sr. mem., assoc. editor transactions on dielectrics and elec. insulation), Soc. Rheology (sec. 1977-81), Am. Chem. Soc., Am. Phys. Soc. Achievements include patents on rheological measurement method and apparatus and low density microcellular foams. Office: U Conn IMS 97 N Eagleville Rd Storrs CT 06269-3136

SHAW, NANCY RIVARD, museum curator, art historian, educator; b. Saginaw, Mich.; d. Joseph H. and Jean M. (O'Boyle) Marcotte; m. Danny W. Shaw, Feb. 29, 1980; 1 stepchild, Christina Marie. BA magna cum laude, Oakland U., 1969; MA, Wayne State U., 1973. Asst. curator Am. art Detroit Inst. Arts, 1972-75, curator, 1975—; adj. prof. art and art history Wayne State U., Detroit, 1991—. Contbg. author: American Art in the Detroit Institute of Arts, 1991; contbr. articles to exhbn. catalogues and profl. jours. Mem. Wayne State U. Alumni Assn. Roman Catholic. Avocations: knitting, painting, golf. Office: Detroit Inst Arts 5200 Woodward Ave Detroit MI 48202-4008

SHAW, SIR NEIL MCGOWAN, sugar, cereal and starch refining company executive; b. Montreal, Que., Can., May 31, 1929; s. Harold LeRoy and Fabiola Marie (McGowan) S; m. Frances Audrey Robinson, July 6, 1952; children: David, Michael, Cynthia, Andrea, Sonia; m. 2nd Elizabeth Mudge Massey, Sept. 15, 1985. Student, Lower Coll. With Tate & Lyle plc, London, 1986—, chmn., 1992-93; vice chmn. Redpath Industries Ltd., Toronto, 1981; bd. dirs. United Biscuits Holdings, plc, U.K., Alcantara, Portugal, Can. Imperial Bank of Commerce, Toronto, Tate & Lyle Mgmt. and Fin. Ltd., Bermuda, Tunnel Refineris, Inst. of Dirs., mem. adv. com., 1991; chmn. Tate & Lyle Holdings, London, 1981-91; mem. adv. coun. Prince's Youth Bus. Trust, 1990—; chmn. World Sugar Rsch. Orgn., U.K., 1994-96; dir. A.E. Staley, Decatur, 1988-91; dir. United World Coll. Atlantic, 1997. Gov. Reddy Meml. Hosp., Montreal Gen. Hosp., World Econ. Forum, World Food Argo Forum; mem. adv. coun. Youth Enterprise Scheme, 1986; chmn. Anglo Can. Support Group Care, 1989; mem. Can. Meml. Found., 1989; mem. adv. coun. London Enterprise Agy., 1986; chmn. Bus. in Cmty., 1991-94; trustee Royal Botanic Gardens Kew Found., 1990—; dir. World Coll. of the Atlantic, 1997. Created Knight Bachelor; honored at Queen of Eng. Birthday, 1994. Fellow Inst. Grocery Distbn.; mem. Food Assn. Can. Univs. Soc. Gt. Britain (adv. coun. 1989), Brit. N.Am. Com., Ptnrs. of the World, Brit. Inst. Mgmt. (companion 1981—), Home-Start Consultancy (v.p.), Toronto Golf Club, Brooks Club, Toronto Club, Wentworth Golf Club, Taymouth Estate Golf Club (Scotland), Per Cent Club (joint chmn.). Avocations: skiing, golf, sailing. Office: Tate & Lyle PLC, Sugar Quay Lower Thames St, London EC3R 6DQ, England

SHAW, RANDY LEE, human services administrator; b. Revenna, Ohio, Oct. 18, 1945; s. Robert and Dorothy Mae (Turner) S.; m. Terri Marie Richardson, July 4, 1988; 1 child, Garrett Samuel. BTh, Ridgedale Sem., 1975, ThM, 1977. Cert. social worker. Exec. dir. Boy's Recovery Home, Detroit, 1979; clin. dir. Boniface, Detroit, 1979-83; unit dir. Problem Daily Living, Detroit, 1983-84; clin. dir. Calvin Wells, Detroit, 1984-86; exec. dir. Children Youth Equal Rights Adv. House, Pontiac, Mich., 1986-87, Touch of Hope, Hartford, Mich., 1988-89; program supr. New Ctr. Community Mental Health, Detroit, 1989-91; exec. dir. Nat. Inst. Hypertension Studies, Detroit, 1979-88. Local rep., magician for Make-A-Wish Found.; exec. dir. Magicians Against Gangs, Ignorance, and Crime Intervention Program, M.A.G.I.C., 1991—. Mem. Soc. Am. Magicians (local pres. 1993-94), Magic Circle, Internat. Brotherhood of Magicians (local pres. 1993-94), Supreme Magic Club of U.K. Home and Office: 249 Lolly Pop St Westland MI 48186-6849

SHAW, RICHARD ALLAN, lawyer; b. Portland, Oreg., Oct. 14, 1937; s. Leland B. and Vena (Gaskill) S.; m. Jo-Ann O. Shaw, Mar. 23, 1959; 1 child, Kevin A. BS, U. Oreg., 1959, JD, 1962; LLM in Taxation, NYU, 1963. Bar: Oreg. 1962, Ariz. 1967, Calif. 1969. Assoc. Kramer, Roche, Burch, Streich & Cracchiolo, Phoenix, 1966-68, Hewitt & Greaves, San Diego, 1968-71; ptnr. Hewitt & Shaw, San Diego, 1971-72; pres. Shenas, Shaw & Spievak A.P.C., San Diego, 1978-96; ptnr. Shaw & O'Brien, LLP, San Diego, 1996—; teaching fellow NYU Sch. Law, N.Y.C., 1962-63; disting. adj. prof. advanced bus. planning and advanced corporate tax problems U. San Diego Sch. Law, 1978—; founding incorporator, dir. San Diego County Bar Found., 1979; lectr. insts. and programs nationally. Editor Oreg. Law Rev., 1961-62, The Fed. Bar Jour., 1964-68, The Tax Lawyer, 1973-74, Jour. of S Corp. Taxation, 1988—; contbr. articles in field to profl. jours. Pres. San Diego County Boy Scouts, 1982-84; chmn. Washington-Lincoln Laurels for Leaders, San Diego, 1986-87; chmn. Corp. Fin. Coun., 1993-94; chmn. Eagle Scout Alumni Assn., 1978. Capt. JAGC, U.S. Army, 1963-66. Recipient Silver Beaver award Boy Scouts Am., San Diego, 1979, Silver Antelope award, 1982, Disting. Eagle Scout award, 1988. Fellow Am. Coll. Tax Counsel, ABA (chmn. tax. com. on S corps. 1974-76, coun. dir. taxation sect. 1988-94, vice-chmn. taxation sect. 1991-94); chair Taxation Taskforce White House Conf. on Small Bus.; mem. Oreg. State Bar, Ariz. State Bar, Calif. State Bar (chmn. taxation sect. 1981-82, V. Judson Klien award 1985), Western Region Tax Bar Assn. (chmn. 1988), San Diego County Bar Assn. (chmn. bus. law sect. 1974), Am. Bar Retirement Assn. (bd. dirs. 1996—), Kiwanis (disting. past pres. 1985-86). Republican. Avocations: skiing, painting, stained glass. Office: Shaw & O'Brien 750 B St Ste 2850 San Diego CA 92101-8132

SHAW, RICHARD DAVID, marketing and management educator; b. Pitts., Kans., Aug. 25, 1938; s. Richard Malburn and Jessie Ruth (Murray) S.; m. Adolphine Catherine Brungardt, Aug. 21, 1965; children: Richard David Jr., John Michael, Shannon Kathleen. BSBA, Rockhurst Coll., 1960; MS in Commerce, St. Louis U., 1964. Claims adjuster Kemper Ins. Group, Kansas City, Mo., 1961; tchr. acctg. Corpus Christi High Sch., Jennings, Mo., 1961-63; assoc. prof. econs. Fontbonne Coll., St. Louis, 1963-70; chmn. social behavioral sci. dept. Fontbonne Coll., 1968-70; mem. faculty, chmn. bus. div. Longview Community Coll., Lee's Summit, Mo., 1970-81, coord. mktg., 1979-81; prof. mktg. Rockhurst Coll., Kansas City, 1981—, chmn. mgmt. and mktg., 1983-85, co-chair MBA program, 1996—; workshop leader Rockhurst Coll., 1975—, faculty moderator Jr. Execs. Assn., The Rock yearbook, Students in Free Enterprise, Rockhurst Coll. Reps., Rockettes; pvt. cons., 1981—, chmn. freshman seminar com., 1994; instr. principles of mktg. on The Learning Channel on Cable TV for the PACE Program, 1994; chmn. sch. mgmt. curriculum com., 1993—; co-chair Task Force on Diversity, 1997. Author: Personal Finance, 1983, Principles of Marketing Study Guide, 1993, Contemporary Marketing Study Guide, 1994, Consumer Behavior Study Guide, 1997, Instructor's Manual for Michael Solomon's Consumer Behavior; co-author: Instructor's Resource Manual and Video Guide for Philip Kotler's Marketing Management, 9th edit.; cooperating author: Philip Kotler's Marketing Management. Mem. alumni bd. assessment task force Rockhurst Coll., 1971-73, 78-80, chmn. 30 yr. reunion com., 1990, 35 yr. reunion com., 1995, chmn. curriculum com., curriculum task force; chmn. Eastwood Hills Coun., Kansas City, 1974-76, bd. dirs., 1988-91, co-chmn. of Solid Rocks Faculty-Staff Fund Raising Campaign, 1994; lead couple Marriage Preparation Classes, Kansas City St. Joseph Dioceses; co-chmn. Kansas City Vols. Against Hunger, 1975-80; campaign mgr. Larry Ferns for City Coun., Kansas City, 1975; bd. govs. Citizens Assn., 1976—. With USAR, 1960-64. Recipient Gov.'s Excellence in Teaching award, Mo., 1993, Harry B. Kies award, 1997; Hallmark fellow Rockhurst Coll.; faculty devel. grantee Sch. Mgmt., Rockhurst Coll., 1984, 93, 95. Mem. Am. Mktg. Assn., Soc. for Advancement of Mgmt., Mid-Am. Mktg. Assn., Alpha Sigma Nu. Roman Catholic. Avocations: gardening, photography. Home: 11014 Washington St Kansas City MO 64114-5177 Office: Rockhurst Coll 1100 Rockhurst Rd Kansas City MO 64110-2508

SHAW, RICHARD EUGENE, cardiovascular researcher; b. Springfield, Ohio, Jan. 20, 1950; s. Eugene Russell and Marjorie Catherine Shaw; m. Nov. 26, 1976; 2 children. BA, Duquesne U., 1972; MA, U.S. Internat. U., San Diego, 1977; PhD, U. Calif., San Francisco, 1984. Cert. nuc. med. technologist. Nuclear Medicine Tech. Cert. Bd. Staff nuc. med. technologist Scripps Meml. Hosp., La Jolla, Calif., 1975-79; rsch. asst. U. Calif. San Francisco Sch. Medicine, 1980-85; mgr. rsch. programs San Francisco Heart Inst., Daly City, Calif., 1985-87, dir. rsch., 1988-90, dir. rsch. and ops., 1991—; sr. advisor steering com. for databases Daus. of Charity Nat. Health Sys., St. Louis, 1993—; cons. comm. informatics project HealthLink SmartPhone, San Francisco, 1992—. Editor-in-chief Jour. Invasive Cardiology, King of Prussia, Pa., 1989—; contbr. more than 200 articles and book chpts. to med. lit. Coach Am. Youth Soccer Orgn. and Youth Baseball Assn. (bd. dirs.), Burlingame, Calif., 1990—. Fellow Am. Coll. Cardiology; mem. Am. Heart Assn., Soc. for Clin. Trials, N.Y. Acad. Scis., Am. Statis. Assn., Am. Med. Informatics Assn., Soc. Behavioral Medicine. Avocation: music. Office: San Francisco Heart Inst Seton Med Ctr 1900 Sullivan Ave Daly City CA 94015-2200

SHAW, ROBERT E., carpeting company executive; b. Cartersville, GA, 1931. Pres., chief exec. officer Star Finishing Co. Inc. (merged into Shaw Industries Inc.), Dalton, Ga., until 1969; now pres., chief exec. officer Shaw Industries Inc., Dalton, Ga., 1969—, also bd. dirs., 1969—. Office: Shaw Industries Inc 616 E Walnut Ave Dalton GA 30721-4409*

SHAW, ROBERT EUGENE, minister, administrator; b. Havre, Mt., Apr. 8, 1933; s. Harold Alvin and Lillian Martha (Kruse) S.; m. Marilyn Grace Smit, June 14, 1957; children—Rebecca Jean, Ann Elizabeth, Mark David, Peter Robert. B.A., Sioux Falls Coll., 1955; M.Div., Am. Baptist. Sem. of West, 1958; D.D. (hon.), Ottawa U., 1976, Judson Coll., 1984. Ordained to ministry Am. Bapt. Chs. U.S.A., 1958; pastor First Bapt. Ch., Webster City, Ia., 1958-63, Community Bapt. Ch., Topeka, Kans., 1963-68; sr. pastor Prairie Bapt. Ch., Prairie Village, Kans., 1968-78; pres. Ottawa U, Kans., 1978-83; exec. minister Am. Bapt. Chs. Mich., East Lansing, 1983—; mem. gen. bd. Am. Bapt. Chs. U.S.A., Valley Forge, Pa., 1972-80, nat. v.p., 1978-80; nat. v.p. Am. Bapt. Minister Council, Valley Forge, 1969-72, nat. pres., 1972-75; nat. chair Am. Bapt. Evang. Team, 1988—; mem. Internat. Commn. on Edn. and Evangelism, Bapt. World Alliance, 1990—; mem. nat. exec. com. Am. Bapt. Adminstrs. Colls. and Univs., 1980-82; bd. dirs. Kans. Ind. Colls. Assn., 1980-82. Trustee No. Bapt. Theol. Sem., Lombard, Ill., 1983—, Kalamazoo Coll., Mich., 1983—, Judson Coll, Elgin, Ill., 1983—; dir. Webster City C. of C., 1961-62, Ottawa C. of C., 1980-82. Office: Am Baptist Chs of Mich 4578 S Hagadorn Rd East Lansing MI 48823-5355

SHAW, ROBERT FLETCHER, retired civil engineer; b. Montreal, Que., Can., Feb. 16, 1910; s. John Fletcher and Edna Mary Baker (Anglin) S.; m. Johann Alexandra MacInnes, Dec. 24, 1935; 1 son, Robert Fletcher (dec.). B.C.E., McGill U., Montreal, 1933; D.Sc. (hon.), McGill U., 1985; Sc.D. (hon.), McMaster U., 1967, U. N.B., 1986; D.Eng. (hon.), Tech. U. of N.S., 1967. Registered profl. engr., Que. With Found. Co. Can. Ltd., Montreal, 1933-63; pres. Found. Co. Can. Ltd., 1962-63, dir., 1968-71; shipyard mgr. Found. Maritime Ltd., Pictou, N.S., 1943-45; on loan to Govt. Can. as v.p., chief engr. Def. Constrn. (1951) Ltd., 1951-52; on loan as mem. working party mil. airfields NATO, 1952; dep. commr. gen., also dir. Expo '67, Montreal, 1963-68; v.p. adminstrn. McGill U., 1968-71; chmn. bd., dir. Found. Can. Engring. Corp., 1968-71; dep. minister environment Govt. Can., 1971-75; pres., dir. Monenco Pipeline Cons. Ltd., 1975-78; adv. Nfld. Dept. Indsl. Devel., 1978-80; sr. cons. Montreal Engring. Co. Ltd., 1975-92; chmn. rsch. policy com. Ctr. Cold Ocean Resources Engring. Meml. U. Nfld., 1981-82. Bd. govs. McGill U., 1964-68; bd. govs. U. N.B., 1973-85, chmn., 1978-80; bd. govs. Montreal Gen. Hosp., 1963-94; pres. Can. Assn. Mentally Retarded, 1963-65; bd. dirs. Montreal Internat. Music Competition, 1967-87. Decorated companion Order Can., 1967; recipient Can. Centennial medal, 1967, citation Engring. News Record, 1967, Queen's Jubilee medal, 1977; named Hon. Chmn. Can. Engring. Centennial Bd., 1984-87. Fellow Engring. Inst. Can. (pres. 1975-76, Julian C. Smith award 1967, Keefer medal 1979), Can. Soc. Civil Engrs., Can. Acad. of Engring; mem. Order Engrs. Que. (pres. 1953), Can. Council Profl. Engrs. (v.p. 1954, gold medal 1979), Grads. Soc. McGill U. (pres. 1964-65, Gold medal 1968), Royal Montreal Golf. Home: Apt C29, 3980 Cote des Neiges Rd, Montreal, PQ Canada H3H 1W2 *Exploding population is creating a heavy demand on the world's resources. If species man is to survive and improve, he must innovate, mass produce, provide the additional energy required, enhance the environment, and learn the value of interdependence. So far we are losing ground. The human reaction to these problems seems to be confrontation, conflict, fragmentation and increased social and economic nationalism. I hope that I have made a contribution to increasing productivity, better management and more interdependent action.*

SHAW, ROBERT GILBERT, restaurant executive, senator; b. Erwin, N.C., Nov. 22, 1924; s. Robert Gilbert B. and Annie Elizabeth (Byrd) S.; m. Grace Lee Wilson, Jan. 29, 1951 (div. 1976); children: Ann Karlen, Barbara Jean; m. Linda Owens, May 27, 1982. AA, Campbell U., 1948; postgrad., U. N.C., 1948-50. Restaurateur, 1951—. County commr. County of Guilford, Greensboro, N.C., 1968-76; chair N.C. Rep. Party, Raleigh, 1975-77; minority leader N.C. Senate, Raleigh, 1984—; chair Guilford County Rep. Party, 1973-75; mem. Rep. Nat. Com., Washington, 1975-77. With USAAC, 1943-46. Named Legislator of Yr. Nat. Fedn. Wildlife, 1990. Mem. Elks (life, bd. govs. 1953—). Presbyterian. Avocations: fishing, hunting, politics. Home: 4901-E Tower Rd Greensboro NC 27410-5724 Office: NC Senate 1129 Legislative Bldg Raleigh NC 27611

SHAW, ROBERT LAWSON, symphony orchestra conductor; b. Red Bluff, Calif., Apr. 30, 1916; s. Shirley Richard and Nelle Mae (Lawson) S.; m. Maxine Farley, Oct. 15, 1939 (div. 1973); children: Johanna, Peter Thein, John Thaddeus; m. Caroline Sauls Hitz, Dec. 19, 1973; 1 child, Thomas Lawson. AB, Pomona Coll., 1938; hon. degree, Coll. of Wooster, 1951, Pomona Coll., 1953, St. Lawrence U., 1955, Mich. State U., 1960, Kenyon Coll., 1962, U. Alaska, 1963, Cleve. Inst. Music, 1966, Case Western Res. U., 1966, Emory U., 1967, Fla. State U., 1968, Westminster Choir Coll., 1975, U. Akron, 1976, Morehouse Coll., 1977, Oglethorpe U., 1977, Baldwin-Wallace Coll., 1980, Stetson U., 1983, New Eng. Conservatory, 1983, St. Olaf Coll., 1985, Duke U., 1988, Atlanta Coll. Art., 1988, Fla. So. Coll., 1989, Baylor U., 1990, Rhodes Coll., 1990, Johns Hopkins U., 1990, Eastman Sch. Music, 1991, State U. of N.Y., 1993, Ind. Univ., 1993, Boston U., 1994. Dir. choral music Juilliard Sch. Music, N.Y.C., 1945-48; founder, condr. Robert Shaw Chorale, 1948-65; condr. San Diego Symphony, 1953-57; music dir. Alaska Festival, Anchorage, 1956-75; assoc. condr., dir. choruses Cleve. Orch., 1956-67; condr., music dir. Atlanta Symphony Orch., 1967-88, music dir. emeritus and conductor laureate, 1988—; vis. prof. U. Tex, Austin, 1988. Dir. Fred Waring Glee Clubs, 1938-45; founder, condr. Collegiate Chorale, N.Y.C., 1941-60, choral dir.: Aquacades, 1942-43, Carmen Jones, 1943, Seven Lively Arts, 1944, Berkshire Music Ctr., Tanglewood, Mass., 1945-48; guest condr. numerous orchs. including, Chgo. Symphony, Cin. Symphony, Minn. Orch., N.Y. Philharm., Phila. Orch., Boston Symphony, NBC Symphony, Dallas Symphony, others; recs. on RCA Victor, Telarc, Vox (Turnabout), Pro Arte and New World labels including (with Robert Shaw Chorale) Mass in B Minor by Bach (Grammy award 1961), Ceremony of Carols by Britten (Grammy award 1964), Handel's Messiah (Grammy award 1966), Gloria by Poulenc (Grammy award 1965), Symphony of Psalms by Stravinsky (Grammy award 1965), (with Atlanta Symphony) Pellaes et Melisande by Faure (Grammy award 1986), Requiem by Berlioz (2 Grammy awards 1986), Verdi Requiem, 1989 (2 Grammy awards, Gramaphone award), Rorem String Symphony, 1989 (Grammy award). Recipient ASCAP award 1976, 81, 86, Alice M. Ditson award Columbia U., 1955, Govs. award in the arts, Ga., 1973, 75, Disting. Svc. award Atlanta Boys Club, 1975, Nat. Fedn. Music Clubs award, 1975, Samuel Simons Sanford medal Yale U., 1980, Am. Choral Dirs. Assn. award, 1981, Martin Luther King Jr. award for artistic achievement, 1982, Fulton County (Ga.) Arts Coun. award, 1985, Gold Baton award Am. Symphony Orch. League, 1988, George Peabody medal for outstanding contbn. to music in Am. Peabody Conservatory, 1990, Kennedy Ctr. Honors, 1991, Nat. Medal of Arts award White House, 1992, Theodore Thomas award Conductor's Guild, 1993; Guggenheim fellow, 1944, Ind. U. fellow, 1983; Housewright Eminent scholar Fla. State U., 1986; named Outstanding Am. Born Condr. of Yr., 1943, Musician of Yr. in Musical Am., 1992. Office: Atlanta Symphony Orch 1293 Peachtree St NE Atlanta GA 30309-3525*

SHAW, ROBERT WILLIAM, JR., management consultant, venture capitalist; b. Ithaca, N.Y., Aug. 10, 1941; s. Robert William and Charlotte G. (Throop) S.; m. Anne P. Meads, Aug. 29, 1964; children: Mark Andrew, Christopher Matthew. B of Engring. Physics, Cornell U., 1964, MSEE, 1964; PhD, Stanford U., 1968; MPA, Am. U., 1981. Postdoctoral fellow Cavendish Lab., Cambridge, Eng., 1968-69; mem. tech. staff Bell Tel. Labs., Murray Hill, N.J., 1969-72; with Booz Allen Hamilton, Bethesda, Md., 1972-83, sr. v.p. energy and environ. divsn., 1979-83, mem. oper. coun., 1981-83, also bd. dirs.; pres. Arete Ventures, Inc., 1983-97, Utech Venture Capital Corp., 1985—; gen. ptnr. Utech Venture Capital Corp. Fund I, 1985—, Utech Venture Capital Corp. Fund II, 1988—, Utech Venture Capital Corp. I Parallel Fund L.P., 1988—, Utech Venture Capital Corp. II Parallel Fund, L.P., Rockville, Md., 1991—, Utech Climate Challenge Fund, L.L.C., Rockville, Md., 1995—; v.p. Can. Energy and Environment Ventures, Inc., 1993-95; pres. Arete Corp., 1997—; mem. energy com. Aspen Inst. Humanistic Studies, Investor's Cir.; chmn. bd. dirs. Superconductivity, Inc., Evergreen Solar, Inc., Proton Energy Sys., Inc.; bd. dirs. Nanophase Tech. Corp. Contbr. articles to profl. jours. NASA trainee; Office Sci. rsch. fellow USAF, 1968-69. Mem. AAAS, Am. Phys. Soc. (mem. investment com.), Nat. Venture Capital Assn., Orgnl. Devel. Network, Assn. Humanistic Psychology, Inst. Noetic Scis., Internat. Transactional Analysis Assn., Sigma Xi, Tau Beta Pi, Phi Kappa Phi, Pi Alpha Alpha, Kappa Delta Rho. Home: PO Box 1664 Center Harbor NH 03226 Office: 6110 Executive Blvd Ste 1040 Rockville MD 20852-3903 also: PO Box 1299 Center Harbor NH 03226-1299

SHAW, RONALD AHREND, physician, educator; b. Toledo, July 20, 1946; s. Harold Michael and Eve Helen (Ganch) S.; m. Carol Ann Rapp, June 13, 1970; children: Robert, Benjamin, Daniel. BS, U. Toledo, 1968; MD, Washington U., 1972. Diplomate Am. Bd. Emergency Medicine. Intern, then resident in surgery St. Luke's Hosp., St. Louis, 1972-73, resident in surgery, 1973; mem. staff Bapt. Med. Ctr.-Montclair, Birmingham, Ala., 1976-81, chief emergency svc., 1979-81; assoc. dir. lifesaver flight ops. Caraway Meth. Med. Ctr., Birmingham, 1981-85; dir. emergency svc. sch. medicine U. Ala., 1985-89; asst. dir. emergency svc. R.I. Hosp., Providence, 1989-95; attending physician emergency dept. Bapt. Med. Ctr. and Jackson Hosp., Montgomery, Ala., 1996—; cons. U. Tex., Houston, 1986, Bell Helicopter, Ft. Worth, 1986, Mut. Assurance, Birmingham, 1986-89, NYU, 1988-89, R.I. State Med. Examiners Office, 1991-96, Fla. Dept. Health, EMS Office, 1991—, Joint Underwriters Assocs. of R.I., 1991-96; chmn. adv. bd. emergency svc. Ala. Dept. Pub. Health, 1986-89; med. dir. Emergency Med. Svcs. div. R.I. Dept. Health, 1990-95; med. dir. Health Care Rev., Inc., 1995-96. Bd. dirs. MADD, Ala., 1986, Univ. Emergency Medicine Found., 1995-96; mem. planning com. Youth Baseball, Vestavia Hills, ala., 1986, 87; mem. disaster com. City of Birmingham, 1984-89; mem. 911 Commn., State of R.I., 1991-96. Recipient Disting. Achievement award Birmingham Emergency Med. Svc., 1988. Fellow Am. Coll. Emergency Physicians (bd. dirs. Ala. chpt. 1984-89, steering com. EMS sect. 1991-94, sec.-treas. R.I. chpt. 1995-96); mem. AAAS, ACS (state com. on trauma R.I. chpt. 1990-96), N.Y. Acad. Sci., Med. Assn. Ala. (mem. coun. med. svc. 1985-86). Republican. Avocations: hunting, stamp and record collecting.

SHAW, ROSLYN LEE, elementary education educator; b. Bklyn., Oct. 1, 1942; d. Benjamin Biltmore and Bessie (Banilower) Deretchin; m. Stephen Allan Shaw, Feb. 1, 1964; children: Laurence, Victoria, Michael. BA, Bklyn. Coll., 1964; MS, SUNY, New Paltz, 1977, cert. advanced study, 1987; cert. gifted edn., Coll. New Rochelle, 1986. Cert. sch. adminstr., supr., sch. dist. adminstr., reading tchr., tchr. N-6. Tchr. Hillel Hebrew Acad., Beverly Hills, Calif., 1965-66, P.S. 177, 77, Bklyn., 1964-65, 66-67; tchr. Middletown (N.Y.) Sch. Dist., 1974-77, reading specialist, 1977—, compensatory edn. reading tchr., 1977—, tchr. gifted children, 1984-87, asst. project coord. pre-K, 1988-89, instrnl. leader, 1989-93. Pres. Middletown H.S. Parents' Club, 1983-86; bd. dirs. Mental Health Assn., Goshen, N.Y., 1980-81; mem. Middletown Interfaith Coun., 1983-85. Mem. ASCD, Amy Bull Crist Reading Coun. (pres. 1989-91, 93-95), N.Y. State Reading Assn. (Coun. Svc. award 1990, regional dir. 1991-94, bd. dirs. 1991—, chair reading tchrs. spl. interest group 1993-94, newsletter editor The Empire State Reading Scene), Internat. Reading Assn., Univ. Women's Club, Delta Kappa Gamma. Avocations: photography, walking, reading. Home: 133 Highland Ave Middletown NY 10940-4712 Office: Liberty St Sch 6 Liberty St Middletown NY 10940-5508

SHAW, RUSSELL BURNHAM, author, journalist; b. Washington, May 19, 1935; s. Charles Burnham and Mary (Russell) S.; m. Carmen Hilda Carbon, July 19, 1958; children: Mary Hilda, Emily Anne, Janet, Charles, Elizabeth. BA, Georgetown U., 1956, MA, 1960. Staff writer Cath. Standard, Washington, 1956-57; reporter Nat. Cath. News Svc., 1957-66; dir. publs., pub. info. Nat. Cath. Ednl. Assn., 1966-69; dir. Nat. Cath. Office for Info., 1969-73; assoc. sec. for communication U.S. Cath. Conf., 1973-74, sec. for pub. affairs Nat. Conf. Cath. Bishops, 1975-87; dir. pub. info. KC, 1987-97; Washington editor Our Sunday Visitor, 1997—; assoc. prof. Pontifical Atheneum of the Holy Cross, 1996—; consultor Pontifical Commn. for Social Communications, 1984-89. Author: The Dark Disciple, 1961, Abortion on Trial, 1968, Church and State, 1979, Choosing Well, 1982, Why We Need Confession, 1986, Renewal, 1986, Signs of the Times, 1986, Does Suffering Make Sense?, 1987, To Hunt, To Shoot, To Entertain, 1993, Understanding Your Rights, 1994; co-author: S.O.S. for Catholic Schools, 1970, Beyond the New Morality, 3d edit., 1988, Fulfillment in Christ, 1991, others; editor Ency. of Cath. Doctrine, 1997; columnist (monthly mag.) Washington Report, 1966—. Mem. Nat. Press Club, Equestrian Order of Holy Sepulchre of Jerusalem, Phi Beta Kappa. Roman Catholic. Home: 2928 44th Pl NW Washington DC 20016-3555 Office: Knights of Columbus 401 Michigan Ave NE Washington DC 20017-1557

SHAW, RUSSELL CLYDE, lawyer; b. Cleve., Mar. 19, 1940; s. Clyde Leland and Ruth Arminta (Williams) S.; BS, Ohio State U., 1962; JD, Ohio State U., 1965; m. Jane Ann Mohler, Feb. 15, 1969 (div. 1988); children: Christopher Scott, Robin Nicole, Curtis Russell; m. Lynn Baird Breuer, Oct. 21, 1989; stepchildren: Heather Shaw, Matthew Breuer, Russell Breuer. Bar: Ohio 1965, U.S. Supreme Ct. 1968. Assoc., Thompson, Hine & Flory, Cleve., 1965, 69-74, ptnr., 1979-93, chmn. area specialty group, 1988-90; ptnr. Walter & Haverfield P.L.L. (formerly Walter, Haverfield, Buescher & Chockley), Cleve., 1993—, chmn. area specialty group, 1993—. Mem. Geauga United Way Svcs. Council, 1980-87, officer, 1982-87, chmn. (chief vol. officer), 1984-87; trustee United Way Svcs. of Cleve., 1983-88, assoc. v.p., 1986-88; trustee Cleve. Community Fund, 1986-88, Ohio Citizen's Council; trustee Ohio United Way, 1986—, v.p., 1987-90, chmn., 1990-92, mem. exec. com., 1990-94; chmn. Ohio Citizen's Council Welfare Reform Task Force, 1987-90, mem. United Way of Am. Welfare Reform Task Force; mem. Ohio Adv. Coun. for the Aging, 1990—, vice chmn., 1992-93, chmn., 1993—; mem. Gov. Ohio's Ops. Improvement Task Force, 1991-93; Nat. Inst. for Responsible Fatherhood and Family Devel., 1990-95; mem. Cleve. adv. bd. Inst. for Responsible Fatherhood and Family Revitalization, 1995—; trustee, exec. com. mem. Fairmount Presbyn. Ch.; del. White House Conf. on Aging, Washington, 1995; trustee Univ. Settlement, 1996—. Served to capt. AUS, 1965-69. Recipient Harvey H. Hebert Meml. award Delta Sigma Phi, 1989; named to Honorable Order of Ky. Cols. Commonwealth of Ky. Mem. ABA (employee benefits com. taxation sect.), Def. Rsch. Inst. (employee benefits com.), Fed. Bar Assn., Ohio Bar Assn., Nat. Lawyers Club, Internat. Found. Employee Benefit Plans, Employee Benefits Attys. Forum Cleve., Old English Sheepdog Club Am. (nat. officer 1972-74), Fedn. Ohio Dog Clubs (pres. 1978-82), Sugarbush Kennel Club (pres. 1975-78, 81—), Midwest Pension Conf., Delta Sigma Phi (nat. officer 1975—, nat. officer Found. 1978—, trustee Found. 1983-95, Herbet Meml. award), Pres.'s (Ohio State U.). Presbyterian. Office: Walter & Haverfield 50 Public Sq 1300 Terminal Tower Cleveland OH 44113

SHAW, SAMUEL ERVINE, II, retired insurance company executive, consultant; b. Independence, Kans., Apr. 10, 1933; s. Samuel Ervine and Jessie Elizabeth (Guernsey) S.; m. Dale Foster Dorman, June 19, 1954; children: Samuel Ervine III, Christopher Atwood, Elizabeth Foster. BA, Harvard U., 1954; JD, Boston Coll., 1965. Bar: Mass. 1965, U.S. Supreme Ct. 1971; enrolled actuary 1976-93; cons. actuary, 1987. With John Hancock Mut. Life Ins. Co., Boston, 1957-87, group pension and ins. actuary, 2d v.p., 1979-85, v.p., group ins. actuary, 1985-87; dir. Health Reins. Assn. Conn., Hartford, 1980-87; cons. Internat. Exec. Service Corps, Guayaquil, Ecuador, 1973, Jakarta, Indonesia, 1988, Perm, Russia, 1994, Pension Benefit Guaranty Corp., Washington, 1974-75, Nat. Hosp. Ins. Fund, Nairobi, Kenya, 1990. Mem. Brookline Hist. Commn. (Mass.), 1981-88, Brookline Retirement Bd., 1985-90; chmn. Brookline Com. on Town Orgn. and Structure, 1975-79. Served to maj. USAF, 1954-57. Fellow Soc. Actuaries; mem. Am. Acad. Actuaries, Internat. Actuarial Assn., ABA, Mass. Bar Assn., Boston Bar Assn. Episcopalian. Home and Office: 131 Sewall Ave Brookline MA 02146-5314

SHAW, SCOTT ALAN, photojournalist; b. Danville, Ill., 1963. BS in Journalism, So. Ill. U., 1985. Formerly with The Comml. News, Danville; with The Paragould (Ark.) Daily Press, 1985-86; staff photographer The Odessa (Tex.) Am., 1986-89; with St. Louis Sun, 1989-90; now staff photographer The Plain Dealer, Cleve., 1990—. Recipient Pulitzer Prize for spot news photgraphy, 1988. Office: The Plain Dealer 1801 Superior Ave E Cleveland OH 44114-2107*

SHAW, STANLEY MINER, nuclear pharmacy scientist; b. Parkston, S.D., July 4, 1935; s. George Henry and Jensina (Thompson) S.; m. Excellda J. Watke, Aug. 13, 1961; children: Kimberly Kay, Renee Denise, Elena Aimee. BS, S.D. State U., 1957, MS, 1959; PhD, Purdue U., 1962. Instr. S.D. State U., 1960-62; asst. prof. bionucleonics Purdue U., West Lafayette, Ind., 1962-66; assoc. prof. Purdue U., 1966-71, prof. nuclear pharmacy, 1971—, head. Div. Nuclear Pharmacy, 1990—, acting head Sch. Health Scis., 1990-93; Mem. Bd. Pharm. Spltys., Splty. Council Nuclear Pharmacy, 1978-82. Contbr. sci. articles to profl. jours. Recipient Lederle Pharmacy faculty awards, 1962, 65, Parenteral Drug Assn. rsch. award, 1970, Henry Heine Outstanding Tchr. award Sch. Pharmacy Purdue U., 1989, 93, Disting. Alumnus award S.D. State U., 1991, Disting. Pharmacy Educator award AACP, 1994. Fellow Acad. Pharmacy Practice (chmn. sect. nuclear pharmacy 1979-80, historian 1981-85, mem.-at-large 1993-95, chair-elect 1995-96, chair 1996-97), Am. Soc. Hosp. Pharmacy; mem. Health Physics Soc., Am. Pharm. Assn. (ho. of dels. 1977, 79, 86, 92, Founder's award nuclear pharmacy sect.), Sigma Xi, Phi Lambda Upsilon, Phi Lambda Sigma, Rho Chi. Home: 7208 W Greenview Dr Battle Ground IN 47920-9732 Office: Purdue U Sch Pharmacy West Lafayette IN 47907-1333

SHAW, STEVEN JOHN, retired marketing educator, academic administrator; b. Hamilton, N.Y., Nov. 16, 1918; s. Constantine J. and Agnes (Tilicki) S.; m. Aracelis Goberna, June 8, 1952. B.S., N.Y. State U., 1941; M.S. in Retailing, N.Y. U., 1946, Ph.D., 1955. Instr. mktg. U. Miami, Coral Gables, Fla., 1948-52; asst. prof. Tulane U., New Orleans, 1954-55, U. Fla., Gainesville, 1955-57; assoc. prof., then prof. U. S.C., Columbia, 1957-89, Disting. prof. emeritus, 1989—, dir. dept. mktg., 1968-72; cons. Hoffman LaRoche, Nutley, N.J.; exec. dir. S.C.-Southwestern Colombia chpt. Ptnrs. of Ams., 1977-79, asst. exec. dir., 1987-91, also bd. dirs. Author: Salesmanship: Modern Viewpoints on Personal Communication, 1960, Marketing in Business Management, 1963, Cases in Marketing Management Strategy, 1971. Recipient N.Y. U. Founders Day award, 1956, Steven J. Shaw award for most scholarly article in Jour. Bus. Research. Mem. So. Marketing Assn. (pres. 1964), Beta Gamma Sigma (pres. 1965). Home and Office: 7600 Tryall Dr Hialeah FL 33015-2931

SHAW, TALBERT O., university president. BD, Andrews U., 1963; MA, U. Chgo., 1968, PhD, 1973. Dean of students Oakwood Coll., Huntsville, Ala., 1965-71; dean Howard U., Washington, 1971-76; dean Coll. Arts and Scis. Morgan State U., Balt., 1976-87; pres. Shaw U., Raleigh, N.C., 1987—. Office: Shaw U 118 E South St Raleigh NC 27601-2341

SHAW, THOMAS DOUGLAS, newspaper executive; b. Dixon, Ill., Jan. 2, 1948; s. Benjamin Douglas and Lucy Bates (Denny) S.; m. Tamsin Johanna Davis, May 9, 1971; children: Jesse Thomas, Benjamin Davis, John Peter Morgan, Katherine Johanna, Mary Alice Powell. BBA, Colo. Coll., 1970. Owner Dixon Cable TV, 1970-81; asst. gen. mgr. Dixon Telegraph, 1974-75, gen. mgr., 1975-86; chief ops. officer Shaw Newspapers, Dixon, 1986-93, pres., CEO, 1993—; owner Durango (Colo.) Stockman, 1976-87; bd. dirs. Amcore Bank Dixon. Bd. dirs., pres. Dixon Family YMCA, 1972-78; pres. Dixon Rural Fire Dist., 1972-76; pres. Katherine Shaw Bethea Hosp. Found., Dixon, 1985-86; bd. dirs. KSB Hosp., Dixon, 1979-85; Alternate del. Rep. Nat. Conv., Detroit, 1980, 84. Mem. Inland Daily Press Assn., Ill. Press Assn. Avocations: skiing, swimming, roller blading. Office: Shaw Newspaper 444 Pine Hill Dr Dixon IL 61021-8754

SHAW, TIMOTHY MILTON, political science educator; b. Frimley, Surrey, Eng., Jan. 27, 1945; came to Can., 1971; s. Arnold J. and Margaret E. (Milton) S.; m. Jane L. Parpart, Sept. 2, 1983; children—Laura, Lee Parpart; m. Susan M. Sturt, July 8, 1967 (div. 1980); children—Benjamin, Amanda. B.A., Sussex U., Brighton, Eng., 1967; M.A., East Africa U., Kampala, Uganda, 1969; M.A., Princeton U., 1971, Ph.D., 1975. Vis. faculty mem. Makerere U., Kampala, 1968-70, U. Zambia, Lusaka, 1973-74, Carleton U., Ottawa, Ont., Can., 1978-79, U. Ife, Nigeria, 1979-80, U. Zimbabwe, 1989, Rhodes U., South Africa, 1993; prof. polit. sci. Dalhousie U., Halifax, N.S., Can., 1971-73, 74-78, 80—; dir. Centre African Studies, Halifax, 1983-89, dir. Centre for Fgn. Policy Studies, Halifax, 1993—; dir. Internat. Devel. Studies Program, 1986-89; dir. Pearson Inst., Halifax, 1985-87, Canadian Internat. Devel. Agy., 1994-95; cons. UN Econ. Commn. for Africa, Addis Ababa, Ethiopia, 1983-88; editor Macmillan Press Internat. Polit. Economy Series, London, 1984—. Author: Reformism and Revisionism in Africa's Political Economy in the 1990s, 1993; co-editor (with Julius Nyang'oro) Beyond Structural Adjustment in Africa, 1992, Corporatism in Africa, 1988, Political Economy of NICs, 1988, (with Larry A. Swatuk) The South at the End of the Twentieth Century, 1994, (with Julius E. Okolo) The Politcal Economy of Foreign Policy in ECOWAS, numerous others. Mem. New Democratic party, Halifax, 1984—. Research grantee Social Scis. & Humanities Research Council of Can., Africa, 1981—. Mem. Internat. Polit. Sci. Assn. (chair study group # 3 on New World Orders?), Can. Assn. Devel. Studies (pres. 1993-94), Can. Assn. African Studies (pres. 1984-85), Internat. Studies Assn. (pres. global devel. sect. 1995-96), Waegwoltic Club (Halifax). Avocations: jogging; cooking; building; traveling. Home: 1143 Studley Ave, Halifax, NS Canada B3H 3R8 Office: Dalhousie University, Halifax, NS Canada B3H 4H6

SHAW, VIRGINIA RUTH, clinical psychologist; b. Salina, Kans., Dec. 10, 1952; d. Lawrence Eugene and Gladys (Wilbur) S.; m. Joseph Eugene Scuro Jr., July 14, 1990. BA magna cum laude, Kans. Wesleyan U., 1973; MA, Wichita State U., 1975; PhD, U. Southern Miss., 1984. Diplomate Am. Bd. Med. Psychotherapists (fellow). Rsch. fellow Wichita (Kans.) State U., 1973-75; rsch. fellow, teaching fellow U. So. Miss., 1978-79, 80-81; staff psychologist Big Spring (Tex.) State Hosp., 1976-78; predoctoral clin. psychology intern U. Okla. Health Scis. Ctr., Oklahoma City, 1981-82; postdoctoral fellow in neuropsychology Neuropsychiat. Inst., UCLA, 1982-83; rsch. psychologist, neuropsychologist L.A. VA Med. Ctr. Wadsworth Div., 1983-84; clin. neuropsychologist Patton (Calif.) State Hosp., 1984-85; clin. neuropsychologist Brentwood div. LA VA Med. Ctr., 1985; clinical, neuropsychologist Timberlawn Psychiatric Hosp., Dallas, 1985-87, Dallas Rehab. Inst., 1987-93; cons. clin. neuropsychology Dallas area hosps., Willowbrook Hosp., Waxahachie, Tex., Cedars Hosp., Waxahachie, 1988-96; br. chief, clin. psychologist Maui child and adolescent mental health team State of Hawaii Dept. Health, 1996—; presenter profl. meetings, 1975—. Contbr. articles to profl. jours. Mem. Dallas Mayor's Com. for Employment of the Disabled (cert. appreciation), 1987, 500 Inc., Dallas, 1988-96; mem. Maui Spl. Edn. Adv. Coun., 1996—, Maui Children's Coalition Coun., 1996—. Remiatte Meml. scholar Kans. Wesleyan U., 1970-73; recipient Nat. Disting. Svc. Registry award in rehab., 1989, Early Career Contbns. to Clin. Neuropsychology award candidate Nat. Acad. Neuropsychology, 1993, 94. Mem. AAUW (v.p. programs Maui chpt. 1996—, Maui Spl. Edn. adv. coun., 1996-97, Children's Coalition, 1996-97), APA Divsn. 35/Psychology of Women (student rsch. prize com. 1996), Internat. Neuropsychol. Soc., Nat. Head Injury Found., Assn. for Women in Psychology, Tex. Head Injury Found., Dallas Head Injury Found. (Vol. award, cert. appreciation 1991), Am. Congress Rehab. Medicine, Nat. Rehab. Assn., Nat. Acad. Neuropsychology (membership com. 1991-94, rsch. consortium 1991—, co-chair poster program com. 1994, 95). Avocations: coin collecting, skiing, gourmet cooking, travel, dancing. Office: 444 Hana Hwy Ste 202 Kahului HI 96732-2315

SHAW, WILLIAM FREDERICK, statistician; b. Bklyn., Feb. 24, 1920; s. Charles Peter and Josephine Veronica (Seusing) S.; m. Josephine Cannington Kerbey, Jan. 18, 1947; children—William Frederick, Teresa Anne. B.B.A., U. Miami, 1949; M.A., George Washington U., 1953; postgrad. studies in econometrics, math. and computer scis., U.S. Dept. Agr. Grad. Sch., 1964-74; Ph.D. (fellow), Walden U., 1977. Research asst. U. Miami, 1948-49; with Research and Stats. div. FHA, Washington, 1950-73; chief statistician Research and Stats. div. FHA, 1969—; chief statistician, dir. Advanced Statis. Analysis and Computer Applications Staff HUD, 1974-82, chief statistician, dir. housing stats. div., 1982-89, chief statistician, dir. info. systems div., 1990-91, chief statistician, dir. Office of Evaluation, 1991—; pres. Kerbey-Shaw Assos. Served with F.A. AUS, 1943-45. Decorated D.S.C., Silver Star and Bronze Star medals for heroism; recipient Superior Performance award HUD, 1977; named by Info. Resources Adminstrn. Council as Fed. Office Systems Profl. of Yr., 1983. Mem. AAAS, Am. Statis. Assn., Am. Risk and Ins. Assn., Western Fin. Assn., Am. Real Estate and Urban Econ. Assn., Am. Econ. Assn., Am. Fin. Assn., Assn. Computing Machinery, N.Y. Acad. Scis., Nat. Assn. Rev. Appraisers and Mortgage Underwriters, Soc. Cost Estimating and Analysis, Res. Officers Assn. U.S., 101st Airborne Divsn. Assn., Air Force Assn., Alpha Kappa Psi. Roman Catholic. Home: 6527 Byrnes Dr Mc Lean VA 22101-5227 Office: HUD 7th and D Sts SW Washington DC 20411

SHAW-COHEN, LORI EVE, magazine editor; b. Manhattan, N.Y., Apr. 22, 1959; d. Ray and Carole (Bergenthal) Shaw; m. Robert Mark Cohen, Sept. 20, 1981; children: Joshua Samuel, Drew Taylor, Logan Shaw. BA in Journalism, U. So. Calif., 1981. Editorial asst., writer BBW: Big Beautiful Woman Mag., Los Angeles, 1979-80; editorial asst., writer Intro Mag., Los Angeles, 1980-81; mng. editor 'Teen Mag., Los Angeles, 1981-86; writer, interviewer Stan Rosenfeld & Assocs. Pub. Relations, Los Angeles, 1980-81; cons. BBW: Big Beautiful Woman Mag., Los Angeles, 1981—, Media Research Group, Los Angeles, 1984; condr. seminars Women in Communication, Los Angeles, 1983, Pacific N.W. Writers Conf., Seattle, 1984. Patentee children's toy, 1971; lyricist for songs, 1977—; contbr. articles and poems to profl. jours. and mags. Avocations: travel; reading; photography; horseback riding. Office: BBW: Big Beautiful Woman Mag 19528 Ventura Blvd # 298 Tarzana CA 91356-2917

SHAWL, S. NICOLE, hypnobehavioral scientist; b. South Amboy, N.J., July 26, 1940; d. Michael Joseph and Kathleen Shawl; life ptnr. Donna J. Talcott. BA, Georgian Court Coll., 1971; MA, Kean Coll. of N.J., Union, 1975; PhD, Calif. Coast U., Santa Ana, 1992; postgrad., Saybrook Inst., San Francisco; postgrad. studies in hypno-behavioral psychology, The Union Inst., Cin. Joined Sisters of Mercy, 1958, left, 1966; cert. student pers. svcs., adminstr., prin., supr., dir. student pers. svcs., substance awareness coord. Georgian Ct. Coll., substance awareness corrd. State of N.J.; cert. hypnobehavioral scientist.; cert. tchr. of psychology, N.J. Tchr. pub. and parochial schs., Monmouth & Ocean Counties, N.J., 1960-79; interviewer, pub. rels. mgr. ARC, Toms River, N.J., 1980; editor, writer Prentice-Hall, Englewood Cliffs, N.J., 1980; counselor, asst. dir. coll. program Georgian Court Coll., Lakewood, N.J., 1980—; adj. instr. UCLA, 1975-76; owner, pres. Auntie Nuke Enterprises; substance awareness coord. State of N.J. Active NOW, Nat. Gay and Lesbian Task Force. Mem. AAUW, ACLU, ACA, NOW, So. Poverty Law Ctr., Mercy Higher Edn. Colliquium Assn., Nat. Guild Sypnotists, Am. Soc. Clin. Hypnosis, Nat. Psychology Adv. Assn., Nat. Bd. for Cert. Clin. Hypnotherapists, Ednl. Opportunity Assn. (nat. coun.) Assn., Union Inst. Ctr. for Women (rsch. fellow bd. advisors), Am. Biog. Inst., Internat. Platform Assn., Am. Biog. Inst. (rsch. fellow), National Gay and Lesbian Task Force. Democrat. Avocations: singing opera,. sailing, fishing and crabbing, gardening, carpentry. Office: Georgian Court Coll 900 Lakewood Ave Lakewood NJ 08701-2600

SHAWN, WALLACE, playwright, actor; b. N.Y.C., Nov. 12, 1943; s. William and Cecille (Lyon) S. BA, Harvard U., 1965; BA, Oxford U., Eng., 1968, MA, 1975. Instr. English Indore Christian Coll., Madhya Pradesh, India, 1965-66; tchr. English, Latin, drama Ch. of Heavenly Rest Day Sch., N.Y.C., 1968-70; shipping clk. Laurie Love Ltd., N.Y.C., 1974-75; machine operator Hamilton Copy Ctr., N.Y.C., 1975-76. Author: (plays) Our Late Night, 1975 (Obie award for disting. playwriting 1975), Summer Evening, 1976, The Youth Hostel, 1976, Mr. Frivolous, 1976, (libretto) In the Dark, 1976, (trans.) The Mandrake, 1977, Marie and Bruce, 1980, The Hotel Play, 1981, Aunt Dan and Lemon, 1985; (monologue) The Fever, 1990 (Obie award for best play 1991); (screenplay) My Dinner with Andre, 1981; actor: (theatre) The Mandrake, 1977, The Master and Margarita, 1978, Chinchilla, 1979, The First Time, 1983, Ode to Napoleon Bonaparte, 1984, Aunt Dan and Lemon, 1985, The Fever, 1991; (films) Manhattan, 1979, Starting Over, 1979, All That Jazz, 1979, Simon, 1980, Atlantic City, 1981, My Dinner with Andre, 1981, A Little Sex, 1982, The First Time, 1983, Deal of the Century, 1983, Lovesick, 1983, Strange Invaders, 1983, Saigon-Year of the Cat, 1983, Crackers, 1984, The Hotel New Hampshire, 1984, The Bostonians, 1984, Micki and Maude, 1984, Heaven Help Us, 1985, Head Office, 1986, Radio Days, 1987, The Bedroom Window, 1987, Nice Girls Don't Explode, 1987, Prick Up Your Ears, 1987, The Princess Bride, 1987, The Moderns, 1988, She's Out of Control, 1989, Scenes From the Class Struggle in Beverly Hills, 1989, We're No Angels, 1989, Shadows and Fog, 1992, Mom and Dad Save the World, 1992, Nickel and Dime, 1992, The Cemetary Club, 1993, Unbecoming Age, 1993, The Meteor Man, 1993, Vanya on 42nd Street, 1994, Mrs. Parker and the Vicious Circle, 1994, Canadian Bacon, 1995, Clueless, 1995; (TV) The Cosby Show, Taxi, How To Be Perfect In Three Days. Fulbright scholar, India, 1956-66. Office: care Rosenstone/Wender 3 E 48th St New York NY 10017-1027 Office: William Morris Agy 1350 Avenue Of The Americas New York NY 10019-4702*

SHAWSTAD, RAYMOND VERNON, business owner, retired computer specialist; b. Brainerd, Minn., Mar. 17, 1931; stepson Klaas Ostendorf, s. Ruth Catherine Hammond. Student, San Bernardino Valley Coll., 1959-60, 65, West Coast U., 1960-62, UCLA Extension, 1966-81, Liberal Inst. Natural Sci. and Tech., 1973-83, Free Enterprise Inst., 1973-83, Kingsway Christian Coll., 1994-96. Salesman Marshalltown, Iowa, 1952-53; asst. retail mgr. Gamble-Skogmo, Inc., Waverly, Iowa, 1953-54; retail mgr. Gamble-Skogmo, Inc., Iowa Falls, Iowa, 1954-57; sr. programmer County of San Bernardino (Calif.), 1958-64; info. systems cons. Sunkist Growers, Inc., Van Nuys, Calif., 1965-75, sr. systems programmer, 1975-92; univ. extension instr. UCLA, 1980-81; propr. artificial intelligence rschr. Lang. Products Co., 1980—; propr., fin. educator Pennyseed Mgmt. Co., 1987—; reader in geriatrics, propr., instr. econs. Liberal Pentagon, 1991-93, Liberal Propr., 1993-94; propr. Med. Investments, 1993—; distbn. specialist, propr. Networking Group Co., 1992—. Author numerous software programs; editor VM Notebook of GUIDE Internat. Corp., 1982-92. Vol. bedside music therapist VA Hosp., 1984—; musician Project Caring, 1984-87; mentor The Caring Connection; vol. Meals-on-Wheels; rep. U.S. Senatorial Bus. Adv. Bd., Calif., 1988-92; mem. data processing adv. bd. City of Marshalltown, Iowa, 1993—; vol. League of Mercy of Salvation Army; patron DAV. With Iowa N.G., 1948-57; 1st lt. USAR, 1957-63. Mem. Am. Def. Preparedness Assn., Res. Officers Assn., Am. Legion, U.S. Naval Inst., Assn. U.S. Army, Toastmasters, Kiwanis. Home and Office: 303 Sunset Ln Marshalltown IA 50158-5146 *Personal philosophy: To search for knowledge for the survival of the human species without initiating force or fraud.*

SHAY, DAVID E., lawyer; b. Scranton, Pa., Nov. 9, 1962; s. Howard E. Jr. and Arlene (Pace) S.; m. Kimberly R. Grow, June 22, 1985; children: Daniel E., Andrew W., Matthew D. BS in Journalism, Kans. U., 1984, JD, 1988. Bar: Mo. 1988, U.S. Dist. Ct. (we. dist.) Mo. 1988, U.S. Ct. Appeals (5th and 8th cirs.) 1991. Reporter KDXE, Sulphur Springs, Tex., 1984, KTTR/KZNN, Inc., Rolla, Mo., 1984-85; shareholder Shughart, Thomson & Kilroy, P.C., Kansas City, Mo., 1988—. Contbr. articles to profl. publs., chpt. to Mo. Bar Deskbook, 1991, 97. Chmn. gen. bd. Hillcrest Christian Ch., Overland Park, Kans., 1992. Mem. ABA, Mo. Bar Assn. (chair environ. and energy law com. 1995—), Lawyers Assn. Kansas City/Young Lawyers (bd. dirs. 1991-97, officer 1993-97, pres. 1996-97), Kansas City Met. Bar Assn., Order of Coif, Phi Kappa Phi. Republican. Mem. Christian Ch. (Disciples of Christ). Office: Shughart Thomson & Kilroy 120 W 12th St Ste 1500 Kansas City MO 64105-1917

SHAY, JOHN E., JR., academic administrator; b. Rochester, N.Y., July 29, 1933; m. Patricia Kopacz; children: Maria, John, David. B.A., U. Fla., 1955; M.A., Tchrs. Coll., Columbia U., 1960; Ph.D. in Higher Edn., U. Mich., 1966. Asst. dir. student activities Harpur Coll., SUNY, 1960-62; dean men Marshall U., 1964-65, dean student affairs, 1965-67; dean student Coll. Holy Cross, 1967-71, v.p. student affairs, 1969-71; v.p. student affairs U. R.I., 1971-80; pres. Marygrove Coll., Detroit, 1980—; v.p. student pers. adminstr. W.Va. Coll. and Univs., 1966-67. Contbr. articles to profl. jours. Trustee Detroit Symphony Orch. Hall; bd. dirs. Sta. WTVS-Pub. TV, Detroit, Greater Detroit Interfaith Roundtable NCCJ. Mem. NAACP, Nat. Assn. Student Pers. Adminstrs. (edn. bd. 1967-70, region I v.p. 1970-71), Mich. Colls. Found. (exec. com.), Nat. Assn. Ind. Colls. and Univs. (bd. dirs.), Assn. Ind. Coll. and Univs. Mich. (treas., exec. com.). Office: Marygrove Coll Office of the Pres 8425 W Mcnichols Rd Detroit MI 48221-2546*

SHAY, ROSHANI CARI, political science educator; b. Milw., Oct. 5, 1942; d. Walter John and Dorothee May (Dahnke) O'Donnell; 1 child, Mark Sather. Student, Willamette U., 1960-63; BA, U. Oreg., 1968, MA, 1971, PhD, 1974. Adminstrv. asst. Dept. of Youth Svcs., Lubbock, Tex., 1963; teaching asst., instr. U. Oreg., Eugene, 1969-72; vis. asst. prof. Oreg. State U., Corvallis, 1973-74, Willamette U., Salem, Oreg., 1973-79, Lewis and Clark Coll., Portland, Oreg., 1976, 78; from asst. prof. to prof. Western Oreg. State Coll., Monmouth, 1979—, chair history, polit. sci., pub. adminstrn. dept., 1991-94; chair social sci. divsn., 1994—. Author: (with others) The People of Rajneeshpuram, 1990, Annual Yearbook on the Sociology of Religion, 1995, (simulation) European Unity Project, 1982. Co-founder, v.p., sec.-treas Ind. Opportunities Unltd., Salem, 1986—; co-founder, sec. Inst. for Justice and Human Rights, San Francisco, 1988-94; bd. dirs. Oreg. UN Assn., Portland, 1982—, Salem UN Assn., 1982-91; v.p., pres., bd. dirs. Garten Found. for Disabled, Salem, 1989—; pres. Assn. Oreg. Faculties, 1989-91; mem. adv. bd. Connections Program for Disabled Deaf, Salem, 1989—; pres., bd. dirs. Model UN of the Far West, San Diego, 1981-84, 86-88, 95—; mem. Oreg. Women's Polit. Caucus. Danforth Found. fellow, 1968-74; named Woman of Achievement YMCA Tribute, Salem, 1990, Mem. of Yr., Oreg. Rehab. Assn., 1995. Mem. Am. Fedn. Tchrs. (v.p., legis. officer local 2278 1982-88), Western Polit. Sci. Assn., Communal Studies Assn., Mental Health Assn. Oreg., Oreg. Acad. Sci., Oreg. Internat. Coun., Phi Kappa Phi (hon.). Democrat. Avocations: volunteer work with multiply disabled deaf, reading, meditation. Home: 348 S Main St Falls City OR 97344-9763 Office: Western Oreg State Coll 345 Monmouth Ave N Monmouth OR 97361-1314

SHAYE, ROBERT KENNETH, cinema company executive; b. Detroit, Mar. 4, 1939; s. Max Mendle and Dorothy S.; m. Eva G. Lindsten, 1970; children: Katja, Juno. B.B.A., U. Mich., 1960; postgrad., Sorbonne, 1961; J.D., Columbia U., 1964. Bar: N.Y. 1967. Chmn. of the bd. New Line Cinema Corp., N.Y.C., 1967—; trustee Neurosci. Inst., Am. Film Inst.; dir. Mind, Body Found. Recipient 1st prize Rosenthal competition Soc. Cinematologists, 1964; recipient cert. of merit Inst. Copyrights and Patents, U. Stockholm, 1966; Recipient award ASCAP/Nathan Burkan Meml. competition, 1964; Fulbright scholar, 1964-66. Mem. Motion Picture Pioneers (bd. dirs.). Club: Friar's (N.Y.C.). Office: New Line Cinema 116 N Robertson Blvd West Hollywood CA 90048-3103 also: New Line Cinema Corp 888 7th Ave New York NY 10106 *Life is a lot tougher than television watching in the '50's led me to believe.*

SHAYKIN, LEONARD P., investor; b. Chgo., Nov. 17, 1943; s. Lawrence L. and Rose (Yaker) S.; m. Norah Josephine Kan, June 26, 1966 (div.) ; children: Benjamin, Gabriel, Rebecca. BA, U. Chgo., 1965, MA, 1966, MBA, 1973; postgrad., U. Sussex, Brighton, Eng., 1970. Investment officer First Capital Corp., Chgo., 1970-74; asst. to chmn. Apeco Corp., Chgo., 1975-76; div. pres. Brown Mfg. Co., Woodstock, Ill., 1976-78; v.p. Citicorp Venture Capital, N.Y.C., 1978-79; v.p., dir. Citicorp Capital Investors, N.Y.C., 1979-82; mng. ptnr. Adler & Shaykin, N.Y.C., 1983-94; chmn., dir. NaPro BioTherapeutics, Inc., Boulder, Colo., 1994—, Kimeragen, Inc., Newtown, Pa., 1995—; vice chmn., dir. To Life! LLC, Del Mar, Calif., 1996—; bd. dirs. Avigen, Inc., The Jerusalem Post; chmn. The Neuroblastoma Found.; governing trustee The Jackson Lab.; trustee U. Chgo. Grad. Sch. Bus. Chmn. Hebrew Arts Sch. and Merkin Concert Hall, N.Y.C., 1983-86. Avocations: sailing, skiing. Home: 166 W 66th St Apt 27G New York NY 10023 also: Chgo Sun-Times Inc 401 N Wabash Ave Rm 110 Chicago IL 60611-3532

SHAYMAN, JAMES ALAN, nephrologist, educator; b. Chgo., June 14, 1954; s. Benjamin and Chernie (Abrams) S.; children: Rebecca Lynn, David Aaron. AB, Cornell U., 1976; MD, Washington U., St. Louis, 1980. Intern and resident Barnes Hosp., St. Louis, 1980-83; instr. Washington U., St. Louis, 1985-86; asst. prof. U. Mich., Ann Arbor, 1986-92, assoc. prof., 1992—, assoc. chair rsch. programs dept. internal medicine, 1997—. Mem. Am. Soc. Nephrology, Internat. Soc. Nephrology, Am. Diabetes Assn., Am. Soc. Clin. Investigation, Am. Physiol. Soc., Phi Beta Kappa, Phi Kappa Phi, Alpha Omega Alpha. Achievements include research in renal inositol phosphate metabolism and renal glycolipid metabolism. Office: U Mich Med Ctr 1500 E Med Ctr Dr Ann Arbor MI 48109

SHAYS, CHRISTOPHER, congressman; b. Stamford, Conn., Oct. 18, 1945; m. Betsi deRaismes, 1968; 1 child. BA, Principia Coll.; MBA, MPA, NYU. Vol. U.S. Peace Corps, 1968-70; state rep. State of Conn. (Dist. 147), Stamford, 1974-87; mem. 100th-105th Congresses from 4th Conn. Dist., Washington, 1987—; mem. budget com., govt. reform and oversight com. Republican. Office: House of Reps 1502 Longworth Bldg Washington DC 20515-0704*

SHAYS, RONA JOYCE, lawyer; b. N.Y.C., July 16, 1928; d. Samuel and Beatrice (Fleischer) Eskin; children: Douglas, Sharon; m. Henry C. Shays, Sept. 15, 1974. Student, U. Mich., 1944-47; LLB, Bklyn. Law Sch., 1950; MA, Columbia U., 1968. Bar: N.Y. 1950, U.S. Dist. Ct. (so. and ea. dists) N.Y. 1952. Law clk., assoc. Arthur Bardack, Esquire, Bklyn., 1947-51; assoc. Legal Aid Soc., Mineola, N.Y., 1951-52; legal asst. Mut. Life Ins. Co., N.Y.C., 1959-63; assoc. Hays, Sklar & Herzberg, N.Y.C., 1963-68; from assoc. to ptnr. Mitchell Salem Fisher & Shays, N.Y.C., 1966-76; ptnr. Shersky, Kalman & Shays, N.Y.C., 1976-77, Rosenthal & Shays, N.Y.C., 1977-95, Shays Kemper, N.Y.C., 1995—. Named Matrimonial Law Arbitrator, Am. Acad. Matrimonial Lawyers, 1992. Fellow Am. Acad. Matrimonial Lawyers (sec. N.Y. state chpt. 1975-82, 90-91, v.p. N.Y. state chpt. 1984-85, 89-90, chair admissions com. N.Y. state chpt. 1986-91, counsel N.Y. state chpt. 1992-93, nat. co-chair interdisciplinary rels. com. 1990-94), Internat. Acad. Matrimonial Lawyers; mem. Assn. Bar City of N.Y. (matrimonial law com. 1982-85, 86-89, 92-95), Nat. Forum on Mental Health and Family Law (co-chair 1990-93), N.Y. State Interdisciplinary Forum on Mental Health and Family Law (co-chair 1986—). Office: Shays Kemper 276 5th Ave New York NY 10001-4509

SHEA, BERNARD CHARLES, retired pharmaceutical company executive; b. Bradford, Pa., Aug. 7, 1929; s. Bernard and Edna Catherine (Green) S.; m. Marilyn Rishell, Apr. 12, 1952; children—David Charles, Melissa Leone. BS in Biology, Holy Cross Coll., Worcester, Mass. Dir. mktg. Upjohn Co., Kalamazoo, Mich., 1954-80; pres. pharm. div. Pennwalt Corp., Rochester, N.Y., 1980-86; v.p. health div. Pennwalt Corp., Phila., 1986, sr. v.p. health div., 1987-88, sr. v.p. chemicals, 1988-89; group pres. Atochem N.Am., Inc., Phila., 1989-90, pharm. cons., 1990-93. Served to lt. (j.g.) USN, 1951-54, Korea.

SHEA, BRENT MACK, social science educator; b. Oneida, N.Y., June 3, 1946; s. Mack Evered and Alice May (Meeker) S. BA, SUNY, Binghamton, 1968, MA, 1972, PhD, 1977. Vis. instr. Harpur Coll. SUNY, Binghamton, 1975-76, resident dir. Coll.-in-the-Woods, 1976-78, rsch. assoc., 1977-78; asst. prof. Sweet Briar (Va.) Coll., 1978-84, assoc. prof., 1984-92, prof., 1992—, chmn. dept. anthropology and sociology, 1986-90, 96—; postdoctoral fellow Yale U., New Haven, 1985-86; vis. fellow Yale U., New Haven, 1984-85; sci. collaboarator Centro studi per l'Evoluzione Umana, Rome, Italy, 1990—; vis. scholar Summer Inst. for Survey Rsch. U. Mich., 1991; consulting prof. Emile Durkheim Inst., George Town, B.W.I., 1989-92; sec. of faculty Sweet Briar Coll., 1991-92; presenter, rschr. in field. Coeditor, contbg. author: Social Psychiatary Across Cultures, 1995; editor conf. procs. Work and Mental Health, 1996; contbr. articles to profl. jours., chpts. to books. Vis. fellow Yale U., New Haven, 1984-85, Sweet Briar faculty fellow Yale U., 1984-85, Centro studi per l'Evoluzione Umana Rome, 1992-93, NIMH postdoctoral rsch. fellow Instn. for Social and Policy Studies, Yale U., 1985-86; Regents scholar Harpur Coll. SUNY, 1964-68. Mem. AAUP (chpt. pres. 1996—), Internat. Sociol. Assn. (v.p. exec. bd. 1994—, mental health and illness rsch. com. 1994—), Ius Primi Viri Internat. Assn. Rome (vice pres. bd. govs. 1994—), Ea. Ednl. Rsch. Assn. (dir. rsch. ethics 1979-83, bd. dirs. 1979-85, gen. sec. 1983-85), Va. Sociol. Assn. (pres., mem. exec. com. 1980-81). Avocations: classical piano, classic cars. Home: PO Box 1 Sweet Briar VA 24595-0001 Office: Sweet Briar Coll Dept Anthropology & Sociology Sweet Briar VA 24595

SHEA, DANIEL BARTHOLOMEW, JR., English language educator, actor; b. Mpls., Oct. 29, 1936; s. Daniel Bartholomew and Dorothea (Lonergan) S.; m. Kathleen Anne Williams, June 3, 1978; children: Timothy, Matthew, Catherine, Daniel, Emily. B.A. summa cum laude, Coll. St. Thomas, 1958; M.A., Stanford U., 1962, Ph.D., 1966. Teaching asst. Stanford U., 1959-61; instr. to prof. English Washington U., St. Louis, 1962—; chmn. dept. Washington U., 1978-84, 95—; acting chair performing arts, prof. drama, 1995; Fulbright-Hays lectr. Univs. of Caen and Nice, France, 1968-69; vis. fellow Clare Hall, U. Cambridge, Eng., 1984-85. Author: Spiritual Autobiography in Early America, 1968, 2d edit., 1988; editorial bd.: Early Am. Lit, 1972-74; sect. editor: Columbia Literary History of the United States; contbr. chpts. to books. Woodrow Wilson fellow, 1958; NEH summer grantee, 1971. Mem. MLA (del. gen. assembly 1977-78), AFTRA, Equity. Home: 6138 Kingsbury Blvd Saint Louis MO 63112-1102 Office: Washington Univ Dept of English Saint Louis MO 63130

SHEA, DAVID MICHAEL, state supreme court justice; b. Hartford, July 1, 1922; s. Michael Peter and Margaret (Agnes) S.; m. Rosemary Anne Sasseen, Apr. 28, 1956; children—Susan, Kathleen, Margaret, Rosemary, Christina, Michael, Maura, Julie. B.A., Wesleyan U., 1944; LL.B., Yale U., 1948. Bar: Conn. 1948. Assoc. Tunick & Ferris, Greenwich, Conn., 1948-49; assoc. Bailey & Wechsler, Hartford, 1949-57; ptnr. Bailey, Wechsler & Shea, Hartford, 1957-65; judge Conn. Superior Ct., Hartford, 1966-81; justice Conn. Supreme Ct., Hartford, 1981-92, trial referee, 1992—. Served with U.S. Army, 1943-46. Democrat. Roman Catholic. Office: Conn Superior Ct 95 Washington St Hartford CT 06106-4406

SHEA, DION WARREN JOSEPH, university official, fund raiser; b. New London, Conn., June 10, 1937; s. Frank Steven and Violette Marie (Dion) S.; m. Elizabeth M. Siaba, Dec. 31, 1986; children from previous marriage: Dion Warren Joseph, Nancy Wallace. A.B., Sc.B. in Physics, Brown U., 1959; M.A. in Physics, Boston U., 1962; Ph.D., U. Colo., 1968. Mem. tech. staff RCA, 1959-62; asst. prof. physics Creighton U., 1967-68; NRC/Environ. Sci. Svcs. Adminstrn. fellow, rsch. assoc. Environ. Sci. Svcs. Adminstrn., Boulder, Colo., 1968-70; exec. dir. Soc. Physics Students, Am. Inst. Physics, 1970-87, mgr. edn. div., 1972-87; cons. ednl. and computer sytems, 1988—; dir. alumni affairs U.S. Merchant Marine Acad., Kings Point, N.Y., 1989-93; asst. dir. devel. CUNY Grad. Sch., 1993—. Author sci. articles. Fellow AAAS; mem. Am. Phys. Soc., Am. Assn. Physics Tchrs., Assn. Coll. Honor Socs. (exec. com. 1984-86), Am. Soc. Assn. Execs., N.Y. Soc. Assn. Execs., Nat. Soc. Fund Raising Execs. (greater N.Y. chpt.), Planned Giving Group Greater N.Y., Coun. Advancement and Support Edn., Sigma Xi, Sigma Pi Sigma, Sigma Chi, Huntington Bicycle Club, Appalachian Mountain Club, Port Dive Club (treas. 1980-83). Home: 1 Doone Dr Syosset NY 11791-6308 Office: CUNY Office of Devel Grad Sch & Univ Ctr 33 W 42nd St New York NY 10036-8003

SHEA, DONALD RICHARD, political science educator; b. Mpls., July 15, 1926; s. John James and Marjorie (Jennings) S.; m. Mary Patricia Donovan, June 4, 1948; children: Barbara, John, Marjorie, Kathleen. B.A., U. Minn., 1947, M.A., 1949, Ph.D., 1953. Prof. polit. sci. U. Wis., Milw., 1949-89, prof. emeritus, 1989—, chmn. dept. polit. sci., 1957-61, dir. Inst. for World Affairs, 1960-63, spl. asst. to chancellor, 1962-64, adminstr. Peace Corps Tng. Center, 1962-69, dean Internat. Studies and Programs, 1963-70, dir. Ctr. for Latin America, 1976-89, dir. Inst. World Affairs, Summer Fgn. Student Seminar, 1962, 63, 71, 72; cons. Ford Found., 1966-68. Author: The Calvo Clause: A Problem of Inter-American and International Law and Diplomacy, 1955; editor: Business and Legal Aspects of Latin America Trade and Investment, 1976; sr. editor: Reference Manual on Doing Business in Latin America, 1979; co-editor: Mass Communication in the Americas: Focus on the New World Information and Communication Order, 1985; contbr. to Ency. Americana, The Univ. of Wis.-Milw.: A Hist. Profile, 1992. Bd. dirs. World Affairs Council Milw., Inst. World Affairs, Milw. Internat. Student's Center. Served with USNR, 1944-46. Doherty fellow for rsch. in Latin Am., 1955-56; recipient Kiekhofer Meml. Tchg. award, 1975, Donald R. Shea scholarship in Latin Am. studies established in 1995. Mem. Am. Soc. for Internat. Law, Am. Polit. Sci. Assn., Latin Am. Studies Assn. Home: 3346 N Summit Ave Milwaukee WI 53211-2929

SHEA, DONALD WILLIAM, career officer; b. Butte, Mont., Apr. 15, 1936; s. Edward Joseph and Agnes C. (Stanton) S. BA, Carroll Coll., 1958; BTh, St. Paul (Minn.) Sem., 1962; MA in Human Rels., U. Okla., 1984; MEd, L.I. U., 1975; MA in Pers. Mgmt., Cen. Mich. U., 1981. Ordained priest Roman Cath. Ch., 1962. Commd. 1st lt. U.S. Army, 1966, advanced through grades to maj. gen.; student Basic Chaplain Officer Sch., Ft. Hamilton, N.Y., 1966, Airborne Sch., Ft. Bragg, N.C., 1966; with 3d Brigade, 5th Inf. Div. Dept. of the Army, Ft. Carson, Colo., 1966; student spl. forces officer course Ft. Bragg, N.C., 1967; chaplain 10th Spl. Forces Group Dept. of the Army, Bad Toelz, Germany, 1967; chaplain 5th Spl. Forces Group Dept. of the Army, Vietnam, 1968; chaplain 1st Brigade, 7th Inf. Div. Dept. of the Army, Republic of Korea, 1969; chaplain 15th Field Arty. Group Dept. of the Army, Vietnam, 1970; chaplain 4th Bn., 10th Inf. Dept. of the Army, Panama, 1972; chaplain 2d Brigade, 9th Inf. Div. Dept. of the Army, Ft. Lewis, Wash., 1975; chaplain 1st Brigade, 1st Armored Div. Dept. of the Army, Germany, 1977; student Command and Gen. Staff Coll., Ft. Leavenworth, Kans., 1978; div. chaplain 1st Armored Div. Dept. of the Army, Germany, 1978; with office Chief of Chaplains Dept. of the Army, Washington, 1979; student U.S. Army War Coll., Carlisle Barracks, Pa., 1984; chaplain VII Corps U.S. Army, Germany, 1984; staff chaplain U.S. Army Europe, 7th Army U.S. Army War Coll., Germany, 1986; exec. officer, chief of chaplains U.S. Army, Washington, 1989; dep. chief of chaplains U.S. Army War Coll., Washington, 1990-94; chief of chaplains U.S. Army, 1994—. Apptd. Domestic Prelate Pope John Paul II, 1992. Office: Office Chief of Chaplains US Army The Pentagon Washington DC 20310-2700

SHEA, EDWARD EMMETT, lawyer, educator, author; b. Detroit, May 29, 1932; s. Edward Francis and Margaret Kathleen (Downey) S.; m. Ann Marie Conley, Aug. 28, 1957; children: Michael, Maura, Ellen. AB, U. Detroit, 1954; JD, U. Mich., 1957. Bar: Mich. 1957, Fla. 1959, N.Y. 1961. Assoc. Simpson Thacher & Bartlett, N.Y.C., 1960-63, Dykema, Wheat, Spencer, Detroit, 1963-69, Cadwalader Wickersham & Taft, N.Y.C., 1969-71; v.p., gen. counsel, chmn. Reichhold Chems., White Plains, N.Y., 1971-81; adj. prof. Grad. Sch. Bus. Pace U., N.Y.C., 1982—; counsel, ptnr. Windels, Marx, Davies & Ives, 1982-84, ptnr., 1986—; sr. v.p., gen. counsel GAF Corp., 1984-86; sec. Peridot Chems., 1988—; lectr. N.Y. Inst. Fin., 1995—. Co-author: Acquisitions, Mergers, Sales, Buyouts and Takeovers, 1991; author: An Introduction to the U.S. Environmental Laws, 1995, The Lead Regulation Handbook, 1996; editor: The Acquisitions Yearbook, 1991, 92, 93; contbr. articles to profl. jours. Mem. adv. bd. N.Y. State Small Bus. Ctr. Program, 1988-93. 1st lt. JAGC, USAF, 1957-60. Mem. N.Y. Athletic Club, Chemist's Club. Office: Windels Marx Davies & Ives 156 W 56th St New York NY 10019-3800

SHEA, GERALD PATRICK, engineering executive; b. N.Y.C., May 10, 1935; s. William James and Mary M. (Fitzmaurice) S.; m. Joan Elaine Bergener, Mar. 3, 1938; children: Jerry, Kevin, Kathleen O'Connell, William, Brian. BSCE, U. Notre Dame, 1956; MCE, NYU, 1963. Registered profl. engr., N.Y., N.J., Conn., Pa., Fla., Ark., S.C., Va. Bridge design engr. Parsons Brinckerhoff, N.Y.C., 1956-58; bridge engr. Bur. Pub. Roads, Richmond, Va., 1958-62; assoc. TAMS Consultants, N.Y.C., 1963-78; v.p. Louis Berger Internat. Inc., East Orange, N.J., 1978—; bd. dirs. Internat. Road Fedn.; pres. Internat. Road Ednl. Found. Contbr. numerous articles to profl. jours. Fellow Inst. Transp. Engrs.; mem. ASCE, Soc. Am. Mil. Engrs., MOLES. Roman Catholic. Avocations: golf, walking, travel, sailing. Home: 5 Placid Lake Ln Westport CT 06880-2250 Office: Louis Berger Internat Inc 100 Halsted St East Orange NJ 07018-2612

SHEA, JAMES F., manufacturing executive. CEO Fairmont Homes, Nappanee, Ind. Office: Fairmont Homes 502 S Oakland Ave Nappanee IN 46550-2327*

SHEA, JAMES WILLIAM, lawyer; b. N.Y.C., July 10, 1936; s. William P. and Mildred E. (McCaffrey) S.; m. Ann Marie Byrne, June 6, 1964; children: James T., Kathleen A., Tracy A. BS, St. Peters Coll., 1957; JD, Fordham U., 1962; LLM in Taxation, NYU, 1965. Bar: N.Y. 1962, U.S. Dist. Ct. (so. and ea. dists.) N.Y. 1966, U.S. Supreme Ct. 1967. Revenue agent U.S. Treasury Dept., N.Y.C., 1961-63; tax atty. Kennecott Copper Corp., N.Y.C., 1963-67; tax counsel CBS Inc., N.Y.C., 1968-71; ptnr. Hunton & Williams and predecessor firm Conboy, Hewitt, O'Brien & Boardman, N.Y.C., 1971—; bd. dirs. Victory Van Lines Inc., N.Y.C. Rep. committeeman, Staten Island, N.Y., 1980; mem. adv. com. tax and fin. N.Y. State Charter Commn. City of S.I. Served to 1st lt. U.S. Army, 1957-61, to capt. USAR, 1962-72. Mem. ABA, N.Y. State Bar Assn., Richmond County Country Club (S.I., sec. 1993-96, v.p. 1996—). Republican. Roman Catholic. Home: 399 Tysens Ln Staten Island NY 10306-2844 Office: Hunton & Williams 200 Park Ave New York NY 10166-0005

SHEA, JOHN J., catalog and retail company executive; b. Newark, NJ, 1938. BS, La Salle Coll., 1959; MBA, U. Pitts., 1960. With John Wanamaker, Phila., 1953-80; pres., chief exec. officer Spiegel, Inc., Hinsdale, Ill., 1981—, now also vice chmn. Office: Spiegel Inc 3500 Lacey Rd Downers Grove IL 60515-5431*

SHEA, KEVIN MICHAEL, lawyer; b. Indpls., Dec. 23, 1951; s. James Louis and Elizabeth (Walker) S.; m. Marilyn Alkire, Nov. 27, 1985; children: Brendan Alkire, Maura Kathryn. BS, U. Colo., 1973; JD, U. Detroit, 1976. Bar: Colo. 1976, U.S. Dist. Ct. D.C. 1976, U.S. Ct. Appeals (10th cir. 1980), U.S. Supreme Ct. 1982. Dep. dist. atty. Boulder, Colo., 1976-79; shareholder, dir., assoc. Roath & Brega P.C., Denver, 1980-85; spl. counsel Holme Roberts & Owen, Denver, 1985-87, ptnr., 1987-94; ptnr. Ballard, Sphar, Andrews & Ingersoll, Denver, 1995—. Mem. ABA (vice chair environ. crime sect. 1991—), Colo. Bar Assn. (chair criminal law sect. 1990-91), Denver Country Club. Democrat. Avocation: ranching. Office: Ballard Sphar Andrews Inger 1225 17th St Ste 2300 Denver CO 80202-5534

SHEA, ROBERT MCCONNELL, lawyer; b. North Adams, Mass., May 28, 1924; s. Edward Michael and Margaret Frances (McConnell) S. AB cum laude, Harvard U., 1948, LLB, 1951; grad. sr. exec. program, MIT, 1962. Bar: Mass. 1951. With John Hancock Mut. Life Ins. Co., Boston, 1951-91, counsel, 1966-70, v.p., counsel, 1970-85; pvt. practice cons., 1986-91. Bd. trustees Labouré Coll., Boston, 1976-88, sec., 1981-88. Served with U.S. Army, 1943-46. Decorated Bronze Star; recipient Labouré medal Labouré Coll., 1989. Mem. Am., Boston Bar Assns., Assn. Life Ins. Co., Am. Life Ins. Assn., Health Ins. Assn. Am., Harvard Club of Boston, Harvard Faculty Club, Wellesley Coll. Club. Republican. Catholic. Club: Harvard. Home: 85 Grove St Apt 209 Wellesley MA 02181-7823

SHEA, ROBERT STANTON, retired academic administrator; b. Quincy, Mass., Oct. 15, 1928; s. Arthur Joseph and Isabella (Crowley) S.; m. Ruth Eva Summers, May 30, 1952; children: Robert S. Jr., Stephen D., Lisa A., Louise M., David R. BS in Math., Boston Coll., 1952; MBA, Calif. State U., Fullerton, 1969. CLU, Chartered Fin. Cons. Test equipment engr. Hughes Aircraft Co., El Segundo, Calif., 1952-56; rsch. engr., project engr. Rockwell Internat., Anaheim, Calif., 1956-70; acctg. systems analyst Safeguard Bus. Systems, Van Nuys, Calif., 1971-76; cons. Am. Grad. U., Covina, Calif., 1987-94; registered rep. Mut. of N.Y., Anaheim, Calif., 1987-94; fin. cons. Empcom Ins. Svcs., Inc., Long Beach, Calif., 1984-94, also bd. dirs.; dean Coll. of Bus. Adminstrn. Pacific States U., L.A., 1972-94; ret., 1994. Track and field official The Athletics Congress, L.A., 1958-88; mem. Anaheim East chpt. Rotary Internat., Anaheim, 1973-85, pres. 1980; patrol leader Boy Scouts Am., Anaheim, 1964-75. With USN, 1946-48. Recipient Merit award Rotary Internat., 1978, Award of Merit, The Athletics Congress, 1977. Mem. Beta Gamma Sigma. Republican. Roman Catholic. Avocations: bicycling, backpacking, fishing, electronics, amateur radio. Home: 43815 Pioneer Ave Hemet CA 92544-6662

SHEA, STEPHEN MICHAEL, physician, educator; b. Galway, Ireland, Apr. 25, 1926; came to U.S., 1956, naturalized, 1966; s. Stephen and Margaret Mary (Cooke) S. BSc in Anatomy and Pathology, Univ. Coll., Galway Nat. U. Ireland, 1948; MB, BChir in Medicine, 1950, MSc in Pathology, 1951, MD, 1959. Diplomate: Am. Bd. Pathology. Intern St. Vincent's Hosp., Dublin, Ireland, 1950-51; Dr. Keenan traveling scholar, dept. physiology Univ. Coll., London, 1951-53; asst. lectr. pharmacology Univ. Coll., Dublin, 1953-56; resident in pathology Mallory Inst. Pathology, Boston City Hosp., 1956-59, chief resident, 1958-59; asst. prof. pathology U. Toronto, Ont., Can., 1959-61; from instr. to assoc. prof. Harvard U. Med. Sch., 1961-73; assoc. pathologist Mass. Gen. Hosp. and Shriners Burns Inst., Boston, 1972-73; prof. pathology Robert Wood Johnson Med. Sch., U.M.D.N.J., 1973—. Contbr. articles to profl. publs. Fellow Royal Coll. Pathologists (U.K.), Royal Coll. Physicians (Can.); mem. Am. Soc. Invest Pathologists, Internat. Acad. Pathology, Am. Soc. Cell Biology, Soc. Math. Biology, Microcirculatory Soc., Harvard Club, Travellers Club, Harvard Club of Boston. Roman Catholic. Home: 1050 George St Apt 12L New Brunswick NJ 08901-1020 Office: UMDNJ-Robert Wood Johnson Med Sch Piscataway NJ 08854

SHEA, WILLIAM RENE, historian, science philosopher, educator; b. Gracefield, Que., Can., May 16, 1937; s. Herbert Clement and Jeanne (Lafreniere) S.; m. Evelyn Fischer, May 2, 1970; children: Herbert, Joan-Emma, Louisa, Cecilia, Michael. B.A., U. Ottawa, 1958; L.Ph., Gregorian U., Rome, 1959; L.Th., Gregorian U., 1963; Ph.D., Cambridge U., Eng., 1968. Assoc. prof. U. Ottawa, Ont., Can., 1968-73; fellow Harvard U., Cambridge, Mass., 1973-74; prof. history and philosophy of sci. McGill U., Montreal, 1974—; dir. d'etudes Ecole des Hautes Etudes, Paris, 1981-82; sec.-gen. Internat. Union of History and Philosophy of Sci., 1983-89, pres., 1990-93; mem. gen. com. Internat. Coun. of Sci. Union, Paris, 1983-89; cons. Killam Found., Ottawa, Ont., 1983-85; mem. McGill Centre for Medicine, Ethics and Law, 1990-95; Hydro Que. prof. environ. ethics, 1992—; vis. prof. U. Rome, 1992; dir. Inst. History of Sci., U. Louis Pasteur, Strasbourg, 1995—. Author: Galileo Intellectual Revolution, 1972, The Magic of Numbers and Motion, 1991; co-author: Galileo Florentine Residences, 1979; editor: Nature Mathematized, 1983, Otto Hahn and the Rise of Nuclear Physics, 1983, Revolutions in Science, 1988, Creativity in the Arts and Science, 1990, Persuading Science: The Art of Scientific Rhetoric, 1991, Interpreting the World, Science and Society, 1991, Energy Needs in the Year 2000: Ethical and Environmental Perspectives, 1994. Can. Coun. fellow, 1965-68, Can. Cultural Inst. fellow, Rome, 1973, Social Scis. and Humanities Rsch. Coun. Can., 1980-81, Inst. of Advanced Studies in Berlin fellow, 1988-89; recipient The Alexandre Koyre medal Internat. Acad. of History of Sci., 1993, Knight of the Order of Malta, 1993. Fellow Royal Soc. Can.; mem. Royal Swedish Acad. Scis., Acadmie D'Alsace, Academia Europaea, History of Sci. Soc. (coun. 1973-76), European Sci. Found. (standing com. for humanities 1989-95), Can. Nat. Com. of History and Philosophy of Sci. (coun. 1982-93), Can. Philos. Assn., Internat. Acad. History of Sci. (ordinary), McGill Faculty Club, Rotary. Home: 6 Rue Gottfired, 6700 Strasbourg France Office: Inst d'Histoire des Scis, 7 Rue de L'Universite, 6700 Strasbourg France

SHEAFF, RICHARD DANA, graphic designer; b. Winchester, Mass., Apr. 26, 1944; s. Harold Dana and Edna Mae (Mosher) S.; m. Cheryl Ann Barchard Ferguson, July 18, 1970 (div. Oct. 1984); 1 stepchild, Leonard Sean; m. Margaret Jean Reiley, Nov. 11, 1987; 1 child, Dana. AB in Biology, Dartmouth Coll., Hanover, N.H., 1966; MFA in Visual Comm./Design, Syracuse (N.Y.) U., 1977. Asst. media buyer Benton & Bowles Inc., N.Y.C., 1966; account exec. Donald W. Gardner, Inc., Boston, 1966-67; tech. cons. Internat. Pers. Cons., Hanover, N.H., 1968-69; ops. coord. N.H.-Tomorrow, Concord, 1969-71; cons. Dartmouth Coll., Hanover, 1972-73; design cons. U.S. Postal Svc., Washington, 1983—; sr. designer Gregory Fossell Assocs., Boston, 1977-78; pres., creative dir. Sheaff Design, Inc., Needham, Mass., 1978-89; creative cons. R. Dana Sheaff & Co., Norwood, Mass., 1989—; pres. Glass Art Ctr., Bradford Coll., 1996—; cons. in field. Author: Formation of Land Trusts, 1971; designer/dir.: (handbook) Varnish Techniques, 1984; contbr. articles to profl. jours.; designer and/or art dir. some 250 issued stamps. Adv. bd. Mt. Ida, Newton, Mass., 1992-95; chmn. bd. dirs. Upper Valley Children's Ctr., Lebanon, N.H., 1968-69; project coord. The Upper Valley Project, Hanover, N.H., 1972-73. With USAR, 1966-69. Mem. Soc. Printers (mem. coun. 1986-88), Nat. Early Am. Glass Club, Am. Inst. Graphic Arts, Am. Philatelic Soc., Am. Revenue Assn., Ephemera Soc. Am. (bd. dirs. 1996—), Soc. for Protection of N.H. Forests. Avocations: collecting early American glass, photography, antiques, postal history, ephemera.

SHEAHAN, JOHN BERNARD, economist, educator; b. Toledo, Sept. 11, 1923; s. Bernard William and Florence (Sheahan) S.; m. Denise Eugénie Morlino, Nov. 29, 1946; children: Yvette Marie, Bernard Eugene. BA, Stanford U., 1948; PhD, Harvard U., 1954. Econ. analyst Office Spl. Rep. in Europe, ECA, Paris, France, 1951-54; mem. faculty Williams Coll., 1954-94; prof. econs. Williams Coll., Williamstown, Mass., 1966-94, prof. emeritus; mem. devel. adv. service Colombia adv. group Harvard, 1963-65; nat. research prof. Brookings Instn., 1959-60; vis. prof. El Colegio de México, Mexico City, 1970-71; Fulbright research scholar Institut de recherche économique et de planification, Université de Grenoble, France, 1974-75; vis. scholar Inst. Devel. Studies, U. Sussex, 1981-82; vis. fellow Ctr. for U.S.-Mexican Studies, U. Calif. at San Diego, 1991. Author: Promotion and Control of Industry in Postwar France, 1963, The Wage-Price Guideposts, 1967, An Introduction to the French Economy, 1969, Patterns of Development in Latin America, 1987, Conflict and Change in Mexican Economic Strategy, 1992. Mem. Presdl. Price Adv. Com., 1979-80. Mem. Am. Econ. Assn., Latin Am. Studies Assn., New England Coun. Latin Am. Studies (pres. 1989-90), Phi Beta Kappa. Home: Syndicate Rd Williamstown MA 01267 Office: Williams Coll Dept Econs Williamstown MA 01267

SHEAHAN, ROBERT EMMETT, lawyer, consultant; b. Chgo., May 20, 1942; s. Robert Emmett and Lola Jean (Moore) S.; m. Pati Smith, Mar. 20, 1991. BA, Ill. Wesleyan U., 1964; JD, Duke U., 1967; MBA, U. Chgo., 1970. Bar: Ill. 1967, La. 1975, N.C. 1978. Vol. VISTA, N.Y.C., 1967-68; trial atty. NLRB, Milw. and New Orleans, 1970-75; ptnr. Jones, Walker, Waechter, Poitevent, Carrere & Denegre, New Orleans, 1975-78; pvt. practice, High Point, N.C., 1978—; bd. dirs. Inst. for Effective Mgmt., Bus. Publs. Inst. Author: Employees and Drug Abuse: An Employer's Handbook, 1994, The Encyclopedia of Drugs in the Workplace, Labor and Employment Law in North Carolina, 1991, Personnel and Employment Law in North Carolina, 1992, Desk Book of Labor and Employment Law for Healthcare Employers, 1995, North Carolina's Healthcare Employers' Desk Manual, 1995; contbg. author: The Developing Labor Law, 1975—; editor: The World of Personnel; contbg. editor: Employee Testing and the Law. Bd. dirs. High Point United Way, 1979-83; mem. congressional action com. High Point C. of C., chmn., 1991—, bd. dirs., 1996—. Mem. ABA, N.C. Bar Assn., High Point Bar Assn., Ill. Bar Assn., La. Bar Assn. Republican. Roman Catholic. Clubs: Sedgefield (N.C.) Country, String and Splinter (High Point), Bald Head (N.C.) Island Club. Home: 101 Bellwood Ct Jamestown NC 27282-9446 Office: Eastchester Office Ctr 603B Eastchester Dr High Point NC 27262-7634

SHEALY, CLYDE NORMAN, neurosurgeon; b. Columbia, S.C., Dec. 4, 1932; s. Clyde Lemuel and Palma Leona (Padget) S.; m. Mary-Charlotte Bayles, June 13, 1959; children: Brock Allison, Craig Norman, Laurel Elizabeth. B.S. in Medicine, Duke U., 1956, MD, 1956; PhD, Humanistic Psychology Inst., San Francisco, 1977; DSc (hon.), Ryodomaku Rsch. Inst., Kansas City, 1979. Intern Duke U. Hosp., Durham, N.C., 1956-57; resident in neurosurgery Mass. Gen. Hosp., Boston, 1958-63; sr. instr., then asst. prof. neurosurgery Western Res. U. Med. Sch., 1963-66; chief neurosurgery Gundersen Clinic, LaCrosse, Wis., 1966-71; assoc. clin. prof. neurosurgery U. Minn. Med. Sch., 1970-75; asst. clin. prof. U. Wis. Med. Sch., 1967-74; dir. Pain and Health Rehab. Center, S.C., LaCrosse, 1971-81; pres. Holos Insts. Health, 1981—; founder, dir. Shealy Pain and Health Rehab. Inst., Springfield, Mo.; clin. prof., prof. clin. research Forest Inst. Profl. Psychology; adj. prof. Columbia Pacific U. Author: Occult Medicine Can Save Your Life, 1975, The Pain Game, 1976, 90 Days to Self Health, 1977 (with Mary-Charlotte Shealy), To Parent or Not, 1981, SpeedyGourmet, 1985, AIDS: Pathway to Transformation, 1987, The Creation of Health, 1988, Third Party Rape: The Conspiracy to Rob You of Health Care, 1993, The Self-Healing Workbook, 1993, The Self-Healing Workbook, 1993, Miracles Do Happen, 1995; also articles. Served with USNR, 1956-63. Fellow ACS, Am. Coll. Preventive Medicine; mem. AMA, Am. Acad. Pain Medicine, Am. Acad. Pain Mgmt., Mo. State Med. Assn., Greene County Med. Soc., Harvey Cushing Soc., Am. Holistic Med. Assn. (founder, past pres., chmn. edn. com.), Am. Assn. Study Headache, Internat. Assn. Study Pain, Internat. Acad. Preventive Medicine, Phi Beta Kappa, Alpha Omega Alpha. Address: 1328 E Evergreen St Springfield MO 65803-4400 *Preventing illness is infinitely more important than treating it. My belief and practice has evolved from the treatment of illness to a major educational role. Most illnesses are the result of unhealthy habits. We need to teach people how to deal with those at all levels: physical, chemical, emotional, mental and spiritual.*

SHEALY, DAVID LEE, physicist, educator; b. Newberry, S.C., Sept. 16, 1944; s. William Elmer and Elizabeth (Plaxico) S.; m. Elaine Wohlford, June 17, 1969; children: Bridget McGill, David McElwee. BS, U. Ga., 1966, PhD, 1973. Prof., chmn. dept. physics, U. Ala., Birmingham, 1984—; cons. Motorola, Phoenix, 1978-84, Jet Propulsion Lab., Pasadena, Calif., 1980-82, Los Alamos Nat. Lab., 1989-91, NASA Marshall Space Flight Ctr., 1989—. Contbr. articles to profl. jours. Faculty fellow NASA, ASEE, 1980, 81;

recipient Silver Quill and Publ. award Motorola, 1982, 83. Mem. IEEE (adminstrv. com., 1988-90, research paper award Ala. Sect. 1984), Am. Assn. Physics Tchrs., Am. Physical Soc., Optical Soc. Am. (fellow 1988), Material Rsch. Soc., N.Y. Acad. Sci. Republican. Methodist. Avocations: running. Home: 2337 Morningstar Dr Birmingham AL 35216-2005 Office: U Ala-Birmingham Dept Physics CH-310 Birmingham AL 35294-1170

SHEALY, RALPH MCKEETHA, emergency physician, educator; b. Columbia, S.C., Oct. 31, 1948; s. Forrest Metz and Dorothy Elise Shealy; m. Lynn Merritt Mathias, Aug. 29, 1969; children: Kimberly Mathias, Kristen Merritt, Forrest Benson, Allison Christine. AB, Princeton U., 1970; MDiv, Union Theol. Sem., N.Y.C., 1974; MD, Med. U. S.C., 1978. Diplomate Am. Bd. Emergency Medicine. Emergency physician Roper Hosp., Charleston, S.C., 1981-94; ptnr. Roper Emergency and Trauma Group, Charleston, 1981-90; CEO Charleston Emergency Physicians, P.C., 1990-94; dir. dept. emergency svcs. Med. U. S.C., Charleston, 1994—; med. dir. Charleston County Emergency Med. Svcs., 1981—; rec. physician Charleston County Vol. Rescue Squad, 1981—. Fellow Am. Coll. Emergency Physicians; mem. S.C. Coll. Emergency Physicians (bd. dirs.). Lutheran. Avocations: third degree black belt, World Tae Kwon Do Assn. Office: Med U SC 171 Ashley Ave Charleston SC 29425-0001

SHEALY, Y. FULMER, medicinal and organic chemist; b. Chapin, S.C., Feb. 26, 1923; s. L. Yoder and L. Essie (Fulmer) S.; m. Elaine Curtis, Oct. 5, 1950; children: Robin T., Nancy G., Priscilla B. BS, U. S.C., 1943; PhD, U. Ill., 1949. Chemist Office of Sci. R&D, 1943-45; postdoctoral fellow U. Minn., Mpls., 1949-50; rsch. chemist Upjohn Co., Kalamazoo, 1950-56; asst. prof. U. S.C., 1956-57; sr. chemist So. Rsch. Inst., Birmingham, 1957-59, sect. head, 1959-66, head medicinal chem. div., 1966-90, disting. scientist, 1990—; speaker 12th Internat. Cancer Congress, 3d Internat. Conf. on Prevention of Cancer. Named to Hall of Fame, Chapin, S.C. U.S. and fgn. Patentee for medicinal agents; pioneer in carbocyclic analogs of purine and pyrimidine nucleosides including carbodine, 2'-CDG and aristeromycin; synthesized anti-cancer drugs dacarbazine, clomesone and BCTIC; synthesized antifungal and antibacterial agents including the first monocyclic 1,2,5-Selenadiazoles and triazenylimidazole esters; synthesized antiviral and anticancer agents including MCTIC and MTIC (which laid the foundations for mitozolomide and temozolomide) and chloroethylnitrosocarbamates; synthesized cancer chemopreventative retinoids such as retinoylamino acids, retinyl ethers and 4-oxoretinoic acid derivatives. Contbr. more than 140 articles to profl. jours.; awarded 19 patents. Fellow AAAS; mem. Am. Chem. Soc., Am. Assn. Cancer Rsch., Internat. Soc. Nutrition and Cancer, N.Y. Acad. Scis., Internat. AIDS Soc., Am. Pharm. Assn., Internat. Soc. Antiviral Rsch., European Retinoid Rsch. Group, Sigma Xi, Phi Beta Kappa, Phi Lambda Upsilon, Pi Mu Epsilon, Alpha Chi Sigma. Office: So Rsch Inst 2000 9th Ave S Birmingham AL 35205-2708

SHEAR, IONE MYLONAS, archaeologist; b. St. Louis, Feb. 19, 1936; d. George Emmanuel and Lella (Papazouglou) Mylonas; BA, Wellesley Coll., 1958; MA, Bryn Mawr Coll., 1960, PhD, 1968; m. Theodore Leslie Shear, June 24, 1959; children: Julia Louise, Alexandra. Research asst. Inst. for Advanced Study, Princeton, N.J., 1963-65; mem. Agora Excavation, Athens, 1967, 72-93; lectr. art and archaeology Princeton U., 1983-84; lectr. Am. Sch. Classical Studies, Athens, summers 1989—; also excavator various other sites in Greece and Italy. Mem. Archaeol. Inst. Am., Greek Archaeol. Soc. (hon.). Author: The Panagia Houses at Mycenae, 1987; contbr. articles to profl. jours. Address: 87 Library Pl Princeton NJ 08540-3015 also: Deinokratous 30, Athens 106-76, Greece

SHEAR, THEODORE LESLIE, JR., archaeologist, educator; b. Athens, Greece, May 1, 1938; s. Theodore Leslie and Josephine (Platner) S.; m. Ione Doris Mylonas, June 24, 1959; children: Julia Louise, Alexandra. AB summa cum laude, Princeton U., 1959, MA, 1963, PhD, 1966. Instr. Greek and Latin Bryn Mawr Coll., 1964-66, asst. prof., 1966-67; asst. prof. art and archaeology Princeton (N.J.) U., 1967-70, assoc. prof., 1970-79, chmn. program in classical archaeology, 1970-85, assoc. chmn. dept. art and archaeology, 1976-78, 82-83, prof. classical archaeology, 1979—; prof. archaeology Am. Sch. Classical Studies, Athens, 1988-94; mem. mng. com. Am. Sch. Classical Studies, Athens, 1972—; mem. archaeol. expdns. to Greece and Italy, including Mycenae, 1953-54, 58, 62-63, 65-66, Eleusis, 1956, Perati, 1956, Corinth, 1960, Morgantina, Sicily, 1962; mem. Ancient Agora of Athens, 1955, 67, field dir., 1968-94; trustee William Alexander Procter Found., 1982-89, Princeton Jr. Sch., 1983—, pres., 1994—. Author: Kallias of Sphettos and the Revolt of Athens in 286 B.C., 1978; contbr. articles to profl. jours. White fellow Am. Sch. Classical Studies, 1959-60. Mem. Archaeol. Inst. Am., Am. Philol. Assn., Coll. Art Assn., Archaeol. Soc. Athens (hon.), Phi Beta Kappa. Republican. Episcopalian. Clubs: Century Assn. (N.Y.C.); Nassau (Princeton); Princeton (N.Y.C.); Hellenic Yacht (Piraeus, Greece). Home: 87 Library Pl Princeton NJ 08540-3015

SHEARER, CHARLES LIVINGSTON, academic administrator; b. Louisville, Ky., Nov. 23, 1942; s. Guy Cooper and Kathryn (Aufenkamp) S.; m. Susan Pulling Shearer, Nov. 30, 1968; children: Todd A., Mark G., Scott B. BS, U. Ky., 1964, MA, 1967; MA, Mich. State U., 1973, PhD, 1981. Instr. Henderson (Ky.) Community Coll., 1967-69; asst. prof. Ferris State Coll., Big Rapids, Mich., 1969-71; grad. asst. Mich. State U., East Lansing, 1971-73; dir. mgmt. program Albion (Mich.) Coll., 1973-75, dir. ops., 1975-79; v.p. fin. Transylvania U., Lexington, Ky., 1979-83, pres., 1983—; bd. dirs. Ky. Utilities, Lexington. Bd. dirs. Lexington Philharmonic Soc., 1983-89; mem. adv. bd. Salvation Army, Lexington, 1983-87; mem. Henry Clay Meml. Found., Lexington, 1983-89. Capt. U.S. Army Nat. Guard, 1966-76. Named One of Outstanding Young Men in Am., 1978. Mem. Am. Econs. Assn., Lexington C. of C. (bd. dirs. 1985—). Mem. Christian Ch. (Disciples of Christ). Lodge: Rotary.

SHEARER, DEREK N., international studies educator, diplomat, administrator; b. L.A., Dec. 5, 1946; s. Lloyd and Marva (Peterson) S.; m. Ruth Y. Goldway, July 8, 1976; 1 child, Casey; stepchildren: Anthony, Julia. BA, Yale U., 1968; PhD, Union Grad. Sch., Yellow Springs, Ohio, 1977. Lectr. U. Calif., L.A., 1979-81; dir. internat. and pub. affairs ctr., prof. of pub. policy Occidental Coll., L.A., 1981-94; dep. under sec. U.S. Dept. Commerce, Washington, 1993; U.S. ambassadorto Finland U.S. Dept. State, Washington, 1994—; fellow Econ. Strategy Inst., Washington, 1993; policy adv. to Presidential Candidate Bill Clinton, 1990-92. Contbr. articles to profl. publs. Planning commr. City of Santa Monica (Calif.), 1984; bd. mem. Nat. Consumer Bank, Washington, 1991. Recipient Guggenheim Fellowship Guggenheim Found., 1984, U.S.-Japan Leadership fellow Japan Soc., 1991. Democrat. Avocations: basketball, tennis, travel, mysteries. Home: 12725 Sunset Blvd Los Angeles CA 90049

SHEARER, PAUL SCOTT, government relations professional; b. Clinton, Ill., Feb. 27, 1948; s. Lloyd Jr. and Pauline Lucille (Glosser) S.; m. Barbara Boston, July 3, 1981; children: Jason J., Carrie K. Brunk. BS, U. Ill., 1970, MS, 1975. Asst. dir. cash mgmt. State Treas. Ill., Springfield, 1973-74, asst. CFO, 1974-77, chief fiscal officer, 1977-78; dir. vehicle svc. State of Ill., Springfield, 1978-81; legis. asst. Senator Dixon U.S. Senate, Washington, 1981-84; exec. dir. Nat. Corn Growers Assn., St. Louis, 1984-90; dir. govt. rels. Halfpenny, Hahn, Roche & Marchese, 1990-93; dir. legis. affairs Zeneca Inc., Washington, 1993; dep. asst. sec. congl. rels. USDA, 1993-96; dir. nat. rels. Farmland Industries, Inc., Washington, 1996—; mem. adv. com. Ill. Atty.'s Gen. Agr. Law, State of Ill., 1985-91; dean Coll. Agriculture, U. Ill., 1989-90, U. Ill. Dept. Agrl. Econs., 1986-89. Del. Dem. Nat. Conv., 1978, Mo. Dem. State conv., 1988, Va. Dem. State Conv., 1992, 93, 94, 96, 97; mem. Police Bd. Commrs., Chesterfield, Mo., 1988-90; pres. Mo. river Dem. Club, 1987-89. Named to Hon. Order of Ky. Cols., 1990, Alpha Gamma Sigma nat. merit award, 1991. Mem. St. Louis Agr.-Bus. Club (sec.-treas. 1987-88, 2d v.p. 1988-89, v.p. 1989-90, pres. 1990), U. Ill. Alumni Assn., U. Ill. Coll. Agr. Alumni Assn. (dir. at large 1990), Ill. Group (chmn. 1993), Ill. State Soc. (bd. dirs. 1996-97), Alpha Zeta. Methodist. Home: 2744 Clarkes Landing Dr Oakton VA 22124-1120 Office: Farmland Industries Inc Ste 520 Ea 1100 New York Ave NW Washington DC 20005-3934

SHEARER, RICHARD EUGENE, educational consultant; b. Connellsville, Pa., Dec. 30, 1919; s. H.D. and Florence (Prinkey) S.; m. Ruth Mansberger, June 16, 1944 (dec. Mar. 1993); children: Patricia (Mrs. Richard Wilson), Suzanne (Mrs. Terry Jones), Richard J.; m. Marilyn Likeness Erdman, May 7, 1994. A.B., Eastern Bapt. Coll. and Sem., Phila., 1943, D.D., 1953; B.D., New Brunswick Theol. Sem., 1945; M.A., Columbia, 1948, Ed.D., 1959; LL.D., Denison U., 1958; H.H.D., Bishop Coll., 1977. Ordained to ministry Bapt. Ch., 1943; minister Atlantic Highlands, N.J., 1943-45, New Brunswick, N.J., 1945-50; pres. Alderson-Broaddus Coll., Philippi, W.Va., 1951-83; ind. cons., 1983—; cons., interim dir. W.Va. Found. Ind. Colls.; prin. resdl. devel. Bridgeport, W.Va., 1983—; v.p., exec. dir. United Health Found., Clarksburg, W.Va., 1987—; pres. R. Shearer & Assocs., Philippi, W.Va., 1984; lectr. Mex. Pastor's Conf., summer 1955; past pres. W.Va. Found. Ind. Colls.; mem. Commn. on Instnl. Funding, Am. Bapt. Chs., U.S.A.; coordinator (Central Europe Coll. Program); pres. Am. Bapt. Assn. Sch. and Coll. Adminstrs., 1977; mem. W.Va. Ednl. Found., W.Va. State Scholarship Commn. Bd. regents W.Va. Assn. Pvt. Colls.; bd. dirs. W.Va. Found. Independent Colls.; sr. min. Bridgeport (W.Va.) Bapt. Ch., 1988-93; bd. dirs. Eastern Bapt. Theol. Sem., Phila. Named Phi Delta Kappa Profl. Educator of Year, 1964. Mem. Am. Assn. Sch. Adminstrs., W.Va. Assn. Coll. and Univ. Presidents (sec. mem. exec. com. 1963—), Assn. Am. Colls. (commn. coll. and soc.), Kiwanis. Office: Alderson-Broaddus Coll RR 3 Box 27216 Philippi WV 26416-9803 *The joint impact of good religion and good education has been the dominant theme of my life and work. I feel that education is a powerful force which can be directed in either constructive or destructive directions. Good religion can assure that the power in education is constructive, and good education can assure that religion has depth.*

SHEARER, RICK LELAND, academic administrator; b. Wichita, Kans., Jan. 8, 1955; s. Jack Leland and Marjorie Louise (Pearson) S. BSc, U. Calgary, Alberta, Can., 1979; MBA in Fin., Nat. U., 1984; MA in Edn., San Diego State U., 1992. V.p., gen. mgr. Direction Holdings Ltd., Calgary, 1979-81; cons. Ethic Mgmt. Ltd., Calgary, 1981-82; from dir. computer based edn. to dir. rsch. and evaluation Nat. U., San Diego, 1985-92, dir. instl. rsch., founding assoc. distance edn. system, 1992-96, dir. rsch. and instrnl. systems, 1996—; presenter conf. procs. Distance Teaching and Learning, 1993-94, 95-96, 96-97, Ed Media 93, 1993. Author: Am. Jour. Distance Edn., 1994. Mem. Assn. Edn. Comm. & Tech., Am. Coun. Distance Edn. Avocations: fitness, skiing, sailing, skating. Office: Nat Univ 4141 Camino Del Rio S San Diego CA 92108-4103

SHEARER, RONALD ALEXANDER, economics educator; b. Trail, C., Can., June 15, 1932; s. James Boyd and Mary Ann (Smith) S.; m. Renate Elizabeth Selig, Dec. 20, 1956 (dec.); children: Carl, Bruce. B.A., U. B.C., 1954; M.A., Ohio State U., 1955, Ph.D., 1959. Asst. prof. econs. U. Mich., 1958-62; economist Royal Commn. Banking and Finance, Toronto, 1962-63; mem. faculty U. B.C., Vancouver, 1963—; prof. econs. U. B.C., 1970—, head dept., 1972-76. Co-author: Money and Banking, 1975, The Economics of the Canadian Financial System, 1994; editor: Trade Liberalization and a Regional Economy, 1971. Mem. Am., Canadian econs. assns. Office: Univ BC, Dept Economics, Vancouver, BC Canada

SHEARER, VELMA MILLER, clergywoman; b. Hines, Minn., Jan. 2, 1921; d. Floyd and Mary (Ross) M.; m. Byron C. Shearer, Nov. 3, 1946; 1 child, Mary Jane. RN, Rockford (Ill.) Meml. Hosp., 1944; BFA, U. Dayton, Ohio, 1968; MDiv, United Theol. Sem., Dayton, 1984, DMin, 1987. Ordained to ministry Ch. of the Brethren, 1987. Staff nurse, supr. Castaner (P.R.) Gen. Hosp., 1945-47; staff nurse, oper. rm. supr. Dettmer Hosp., Troy, Ohio, 1954-58; nursing instr. Miami Valley Hosp., Dayton, 1970-72; clergy So. Ohio dist. Ch. of the Brethren, 1983—, Neighbors in Need, 1990—; field edn. supervisor Bethany Theol. Sem., Richmond, Ind., 1994—; mem. issues caucus com. Ohio Coun. Chs., 1988-96. Author: Nuc Radiation and Cancer, 1981; artist numerous paintings and drawings. Mem. nuclear study com. Ch. of Brethren, So. Ohio, 1978-92; bd. dirs. Ohio Environ. Coun., 1994—; mem. adv. bd. Ohio Coalition, 1995—; mem. issues caucus com. Ohio Coun. Chs., 1988-96. Recipient Ann. Peace award Wright State U.; Ohio Humanities Coun. grantee, 1989-90. Mem. Internat. Assn. Women Mins. Home and Office: 124 Chestnut St Apt 210 Englewood OH 45322-1410

SHEARER, WILLIAM KENNEDY, lawyer, publisher; b. Marysville, Calif., Jan. 21, 1931; s. William and Eva (Kennedy) S.; m. Eileen Mary Knowland; Nov. 25, 1956; 1 child, Nancy Lorena. BA, San Diego State U., 1955; JD, Western State U., 1975. Bar: Calif. 1975, U.S. Dist. Ct. (so. dist.) Calif. 1975, U.S. Ct. Claims 1976, U.S. Supreme Ct. 1982, U.S. Ct. Appeals (fed. cir.) 1982, U.S. Ct. Appeals (9th cir.) 1983. Legis. asst. to Congressman James Utt, 1953, 55-56; exec. dir. San Diego County Rep. Cen. Com., 1956-58; pub. Oceanside-Carlsbad Banner, Oceanside, Calif., 1958-63; adminstrv. asst. Assemblyman E.R. Barnes, Sacramento, Calif., 1963-65; polit. campaign cons. Banner Advt., San Diego, Los Angeles, 1964-75; atty. Duke, Gerstel, Shearer & Bregante, San Diego, 1975—. Pub. newsletters Calif. Statesman, 1962—, Legis. Survey, 1963—, Fgn. Policy Rev., 1972—, Am. Ind., 1974—. Rep. nominee for State Assembly, San Diego County, 1956, 58; state chmn. Am. Ind. Party, Calif., 1967-70, nat. chmn. 1968-71, 73-77; nat. vice chmn. U.S. Taxpayers Party, 1992-96, chmn. 1996—; Am. Ind. nominee for Gov., 1970; adv. com. Elections Com., Calif. Legislature, Sacramento, 1971-76; mem. Blue Ribbon Task Force on Calif.'s Home Constrn. Industry; bd. dirs. San Diego Gilbert & Sullivan Co., 1984-90, pres. 1986-88, v.p., 1985-86, 88-90. With U.S. Army, 1953-55. Mem. ABA, Calif. Bar Assn., San Diego County Bar Assn., Consumer Attys. of Calif. (mem. legis. com.). Avocations: ancient Near Eastern history, gardening, music. Home: 8160 Palm St Lemon Grove CA 91945-3028 Office: Duke Gerstel Shearer & Bregante 101 W Broadway Ste 600 San Diego CA 92101-8207

SHEARER, WILLIAM THOMAS, pediatrician, educator; b. Detroit, Aug. 23, 1937. BS, U. Detroit, 1960; PhD, Wayne State U., 1966; MD, Washington U., St. Louis, 1970. Diplomate Am. Bd. Pediatrics, Am. Bd. Allergy and Immunology (chmn. 1994-95, dir. 1990-95, chair nominations com., clin. immunology soc.), Nat. Bd. Med. Examiners; cert. in diagnostic lab. immunology. Post-doctoral fellow in biochemistry dept. chem. Indiana U., Bloomington, 1966-67; intern in pediatrics St. Louis Children's Hosp., 1970-71, resident in immunology in pediatrics, 1971-72, dir. divsn. allergy and immunology, 1974-78; fellow in immunology in pediatrics Barnes Hosp., Washington U., St. Louis, 1972-74; spl. USPHA sci. rsch. fellow in medicine dept. medicine Washington U., 1972-74, assoc. prof., 1978, prof., 1978; prof. pediat., microbiology, immunology Baylor Coll. Medicine, Houston, 1978—, dir. AIDS rsch. ctr., 1991—; head sect. allergy & immunology Tex. Children's Hosp., Houston, 1978—; mem. ACTU Cmty. Adv. Bd., Tex. Children's Hosp., Houston, 1991—; chmn. pediat. core com. pediat. AIDS clin. trial group Nat. Inst. Allergy and Infectious Diseases NIH, Bethesda, Md., 1989—, ad hoc reviewer, 1991, mem. therapeutics subcom. AIDS rsch. adv. com., 1993—, chmn. pediat. AIDS clin. trial group immunology com., 1994—, mem. pediat. AIDS clin. trials group exec. com., 1991-95, mem. spl. rev. com. persons affected by chronic granulomatous disease, 1992; site visitor Gen. Clin. rsch. Ctr., NIH, Bethesda, 1993, vice chmn. pediat. AIDS clin. trials group exec. com., 1996—; chmn. study population/patient mgmt. com. Clin. Ctrs. for the Study of Pediat. Lung and Heart Complications of HIV Infection Nat. Heart, Lung and Blood Inst. NIH, Bethesda, 1989—, mem. AIDS ad hoc work group, 1991; dir. pediat. HIV/AIDS Clin. Rsch. Ctr., Houston, 1988—; chmn. exec. com. clin. trial intravenous gammaglobulin in HIV infected children Nat. Inst. Child and Health and Human Devel., Bethesda, 1989—; dir. Am. Bd. Allergy and Immunology, 1990-95, chair, 1994-95; vice-chair Pediatrics AIDS Clin. Trials Group Exec. com., 1996—. Editor: Pediatric Asthma, Allergy, and Immunology, 1989; editl. bd. Jour. of Allergy and Clin. Immunology, 1993—, Clin. and Diagnostic Lab. Immunology, 1994—; editor Pediatric Allergy and Immunology, 1995—, Allergy and Immunology Tng. Program Dir.; guest editor Seminar Pediatric Infectious Disease, 1990; contbr. intro.: Allergy: Principles and Practice, 1992; contbr. articles to profl. jours. including New Eng. Jour. Medicine. AIDS cons. Houston Ind. Sch. Dist., 1986—; med. adv. Spring Branch Ind. Sch. Dist., Houston, 1987—; chmn. community HIV/AIDS adv. group Tex. Med. Ctr., 1991—. Recipient faculty rsch. award Am. Cancer Soc., 1977-79, Myrtle Wreath award Hadassah, 1985, spl. recognition award Am. Acad. Allergy and Immunology, 1994; rsch. scholar Cystic Fibrosis Found., 1974-77; grantee NIH, 1988—. Mem. Am. Soc. Clin. Investigation, Am. Acad. Pediats. (mem. exec. com. sect. allergy and immunology 1991—), Tex. Allergy Soc. (exec. com. 1990—, Tex. Allergy and Immunology Soc. (chmn. nat. issues com. 1992-96, pres. 1994-96), Am. Acad. allergy and Immunology (chmn. clin. and lab. immunology com. 1994-96, chmn. tng. program dirs. nat. issues subcom. 1994-96), Am. Acad. Allergy, Asthma and Immunology (assoc. chmn. for planning of 1997-98 internat. meetings, profl. ednl. coun.), Clin. Immunology Soc. (chair Am. Bd. Allergy and Immunology nominations com. 1994-96). Achievements include research in half-matched T-cell-depleted bone marrow transplants, in membrane signal pathway of human B lymphcytes. Office: Tex Childrens Hosp A/I Svc 6621 Fannin St MC 1-3291 Houston TX 77030-2303

SHEARING, CLIFFORD DENNING, criminology and sociology educator; b. Durban, Natal, South Africa, Feb. 2, 1942; s. Cecil and Amy (Clifford) S.; children: Anthony Denning, Renée Anne. B Social Sci. in Psychology-nd Sociology, U. Natal, Durban, 1965, B Social Sci. in Sociology cum laude, 1967; MA in Sociology 1st class, U. Toronto, Ont., Can., 1968, PhD in Sociology, 1977. Assoc. Can. Inst. for Advanced Rsch., 1985-89; rsch. assoc. Ctr. Criminology U. Toronto, 1972-75, sr. rsch. assoc., 1976-83, coord. grad. studies, 1978-83, 89—, sr. fellow Woodsworth Coll., 1985—, assoc. prof. Ctr. Criminology, 1984-89, prof., 1989—, dir. Ctr. Criminology, 1993—, instr. Woodsworth Coll., 1976-81, assoc. prof., 1981-89, prof., 1989—, assoc. prof. dept. sociology, 1981-89, prof., 1989—; mem. bd. control Ctr. for Socio-Legal Studies, U. Natal, 1988-90, assoc. mem., 1990—; vis. rsch. prof. Cmty. Law Ctr., U. Western Cape, Cape Town, South Africa, 1991-93, dir., 1993—; vis. prof. faculty law U. Cape Town, 1992-93, vis. lectr., rsch. assoc. Inst. Criminology, 1992-93; vis. fellow dept. law Rsch. Sch. Social Sci., Australia Nat. U.; assoc. fellow Massey Coll.; reviewer, 1983-85; reviewer Can. Jour. Sociology, 1982—, Social Problems, 1982—, Law and Society Rev., 1983-85, Am. Bar Found. Rsch. Jour./Law and Social Inquiry, 1988—, Can. Jour. Criminology, 1988—, Criminology, 1989—, Jour. Contemporary Ethnography, 1990—, Law and Policy, 1991—; assoc. cons. Jour. Criminal Law and Criminology, 1991—; cons. Can. Police Coll., 1979-80, Met. Toronto Housing Authority, 1987-89, Toronto Transit Commn., 1987, Office Pub. Compaints Commr., Ont., 1986-87, Hoppo Valley Estates, Zimbabe, 1986, Ont. Waste Mgmt. Corp., 1986, Law Reform Commn. Can., 1979-80, 84-85, Nat. Mus. Can., 1983; advisor police powers project Can. Human Rights Found., 1983; advisor Commn. of Inquiry Concerning Activities of the Royal Can. Mounted Police, 1977-81; numerous others. Author: (with Hilstan L. Watts) Blood Donation: Attitudes and Motivation, 1966, (with Margaret B. Farnell) Private Security: An Examination of Canadian Statistics, 1961-71, (with Philip C. Stenning) Police Training in Ontario: An Evaluation of Recruit and Supervisory Course, 1980, (with Farnell and Stenning) Contract Security in Ontario, 1980, (with Michael Brogden) Policing for a New South Africa, 1993; editor: Organizational Police Deviance: Its Structure and Control, 1981, -a-Cop: A Study of Police Mobilization, 1984; co-editor: Private Security and Private Justice: The Challenge of the 80's, 1983, Private Policing, 1987, Criminology: A Readers Guide, 1991; assoc. editor Can. Jour. Sociology, 1975-78, Critical Arts, 1986-95; mem. editl. bd. Natal U. Law and Society Rev., 1985-95, Policing and Society, 1988—, Jour. Regulatory Law and Practice, 1992—; mem. internat. adv. bd. Brit. Jour. Criminology, 1996—; contbr. articles and revs. to profl. jours., chpts. to books. Office: U Toronto Ctr Criminology, 130 Saint George St Rm 8001, Toronto, ON Canada M5S 1A1

SHEARING, GEORGE ALBERT, pianist, composer; b. London, Aug. 13, 1919; came to U.S., 1947, naturalized, 1956; s. James Philip and Ellen Amelia (Brightman) S.; m. Beatrice Bayes, May 1, 1941 (div.); 1 child, Wendy Ann; m. Eleanor Geffert, July 28, 1984. Student, Linden Lodge Sch. for Blind, London; D Music (hon.), Westminster Coll., Salt Lake City, 1975, Hamilton Coll., 1994. Composer: Lullaby of Birdland, numerous other popular songs; recs. English Decca and Parlophone, Am. Savoy, London, MGM Capitol, Sheba Records, Concord Jazz, Telarc; albums include: An Evening with George Shearing and Mel Torme, 1982 (Grammy), Top Drawer, 1983 (Grammy), An Evening at Charlie's, 1984, Grand Piano, 1985, An Elegant Evening, 1986, George Shearing and Barry Tuckwell Play the Music of Cole Porter, 1986, More Grand Piano, 1987, (with Marian McPartland) Alone Together, 1981, George Shearing and Dakota Staton: In the Night, A Vintage Year, 1987, George Shearing and Hank Jones: The Spirit of 176, 1989, George Shearing In Dixieland, 1989, I Hear a Rhapsody: Live at the Blue Note, 1994, On a Clear Day, 1980, How Beautiful is Night, 1993, Best of George Shearing, 1993, That Shearing Sound, 1994, Walkin' - Live at the Blue Note, 1995, The George Shearing Quintet: By Request, 1995, Jazz Moments, 1995, Paper Moon: Music of Nat King Cole, 1996, George Shearing and Friends, 1996; appearances at: London Symphony Pops Concerts, 1986, 87, London Paladium, 1987, Concord Jazz Festival, Japan, 1987, Hong Kong Cultural Ctr., 1992, European Jazz Festivals, 1995, Birmingham (Eng.) Symphony with Sir Simon Rattle, 1995, Japan Tour, 1996, New Eng. Jazz Festival, 1996, Tanglewood, Mass., 1996, Can. Tour, 1995, US Tour, 1996, others. Bd. dirs. Guide Dogs for Blind, San Rafael, Hadley Sch. for Blind, Winnetka, Ill. Voted top English pianist, 1941-47; winner all Am. jazz polls, also many pvt. awards; recipient Golden Plate award Am. Acad. of Achievement, 1968, Helen Keller Achievement award, 1995. Mem. Broadcast Music Inc., Friars Club, Lotos Club (N.Y.), Bohemian Club (San Francisco). Avocations: long walks, listening to tennis and cricket matches, quiet dinners, bridge. Office: care Joan Shulman, 103 Avenue Rd Ste 301, Toronto, ON Canada M5R 2G9*

SHEARING, MIRIAM, justice; b. Waverly, N.Y., Feb. 24, 1935. BA, Cornell U., 1956; JD, Boston Coll., 1964. Bar: Calif. 1965, Nev. 1969. Justice of peace Las Vegas Justice Ct., 1977-81; judge Nev. Dist. Ct., 1983-92, chief judge, 1986; justice Nevada Supreme Ct., Carson City, 1993—. Mem. ABA, Am. Judicature Soc., Nev. Judges Assn. (sec. 1978), Nev. Dist. Ct. Judges Assn. (sec. 1984-85, pres. 1986-87), State Bar Nev., State Bar Calif., Clark County Bar Assn. Democrat.

SHEARON, FORREST BEDFORD, humanities educator; b. Bolivar, Tenn., Sept. 7, 1934; s. George W. and Carrie Mae (Shinault) S.; m. Jeannette Brooks, June 5, 1955 (div. 1972); children: Angelia J. Shearon Schulte, Michael F.; m. Lynn Britton, June 11, 1981. AB in History, Union U., 1956; postgrad., Northwestern U., 1962-63; MA in English, U. Louisville, 1965, PhD in English, 1973. English tchr. Halls (Tenn.) High Sch., 1956-58, Pleasure Ridge Park High Sch., Louisville, 1958-62, 63-65; asst. prof. English Ky. So. Coll., Louisville, 1965-68; instr. English U. Louisville, 1969-73; asst. prof., assoc. prof., prof. humanities Ea. Ky. U., Richmond, 1973—. Contbr. articles to profl. jours. Recipient Outstanding Grad. Student award U. Louisville, 1973; Ford Found. fellow, 1962-63, NEH fellow, 1979; Fulbright-Hays grantee, 1987. Mem. MLA, So. Humanities Coun. (co-chair 1995-96, sec. 1989—), Ky. Philological Assn. (exec. sec. 1983-84), South Atlantic MLA, South Asian Lit. Assn., Phi Kappa Phi. Democrat. Presbyterian. Avocations: travel, reading, writing. Home: 305 Summit St Richmond KY 40475-2133 Office: Ea Ky U Dept Humanities Case Annex 368 Richmond KY 40475-3140

SHEA-STONUM, MARILYN, judge; b. Anaconda, Mont., June 6, 1947. AB, U. Calif., Santa Cruz, 1969; JD, Case Western Res. U., 1975. Bar: Ohio 1975, Calif. 1976. Law clk. to Hon. Battisti U.S. Dist. Ct. (no. dist.), Ohio, 1975-76; ptnr. Jones, Day, Reavis & Pogue, Cleve., 1984-94; bankruptcy judge U.S. Bankruptcy Ct. (no. dist.) Ohio, Akron, 1994—. Office: US Bankruptcy Ct No Dist Ohio Ea Divsn 2 S Main St Rm 240 Akron OH 44308-1810

SHEBESTA, LYNN MARIE, school administrator; b. Manitowoc, Wis., Dec. 16, 1955; d. Joseph J. Shebesta and Shirley Ann (Pietras) Kent. BS, U. Wis., La Crosse, 1978; MS, Mankato State U., 1986; postgrad. study Admissions, Harvard Grad. Sch. Edn., 1992. Admissions counselor Silver Lake Coll., Manitowoc, Wis., 1980-83; asst. dir. admissions Mankato (Minn.) State U., 1983-88; dir. admissions Lakeland Coll., Sheboygan, Wis., 1988-90; dean of admissions and fin. aid Wayland Acad., Beaver Dam, Wis., 1990-95; econ. devel. profl. Northeast Wis. Tech. Coll., Green Bay, Wis., 1995—; cons. to admissions Northwestern Military/Naval Acad., Lake Geneva, Wis., 1992; adj. instr. N.E. Wis. Tech. Coll., Lakeland Coll.; presenter, workshop presenter in fiel. Editor, designer, publisher (ednl. insts. brochures, viewbooks), 1986-93. Bd. dirs., founder Civitan, Mankato, 1986-88; bd. dirs. Big Brothers/Big Sisters, Manitowoc, Wis., 1989, Girl Scouts, Green Bay, Wis., 1996. Mem. Rotary Internat. (bd. dirs. DePere, Wis.), Green Bay Area C. of C. (advance econ. devel. com., advance retention com.). Avocations: skiing, camping, motorcycling, gardening. Home: 448 N Good Hope Rd De Pere WI 54115-2405 Office: Northeast Wis Tech Coll PO Box 19042 2740 W Mason St Green Bay WI 54307-9042

SHECHTER, BEN-ZION, artist, illustrator; b. Tel Aviv, Aug. 7, 1940; s. Isaac and Elka (Demb) S.; m. Laura Judith Goldstein, Feb. 26, 1969; 1 child, Adam. B.F.A., Bezalel Acad. Fine Art, Jerusalem, 1966. Airplane mechanic Israeli aviation industry (Lod), 1961-62; free-lance comml. artist N.Y.C., 1966—, artist, illustrator, 1974—. Illustrator: Common Ground, 1980; one-man shows Martin Sumers Graphic, N.Y.C., 1983, Wustum Mus., Racine, Wis., 1982, Cayuga Community Coll., Auburn, N.Y., 1982, Suffolk County Community Coll., Selden, N.Y., 1984, Capricorn Gallery, Bethesda, Md., 1989, FDR Gallery, N.Y.C., 1993, Richmond Art Ctr., Windsor, Colo., 1997; exhibited in group shows U. Iowa Mus., 1983, Bklyn. Mus., 1980, 84, Minn. Mus. Art, St Paul, 1980, Elvchjem Mus., U. Wis.-Madison, 1983, Ark. Art Ctr., Little Rock, 1986, 92, Hunt Inst. (Carnegie Instn.), Pitts., 1988, Butlur Inst., Youngstown, Ohio, 1988, Kutztown (Pa.) U., 1989, Suffolk County C.C., Selden, N.Y., 1994; represented in permanent collections Bklyn Mus., U. Iowa Mus., Boston Mus. Fine Art, Israel Mus., Jerusalem. Served with Israeli Air Force, 1958-61. City of Jerusalem scholar, 1963, 64; Israeli Ministry Edn. scholar, 1965, 66. Jewish. Home: 429 4th St Brooklyn NY 11215-2901

SHECHTER, LAURA JUDITH, artist; b. Bklyn., Aug. 26, 1944; d. Philip and Jeannette (Newmark) Goldstein; m. Ben-Zion Shechter, Feb. 26, 1969; 1 son, Adam. B.A. with honors in Art, Bklyn. Coll., 1965. Case worker Dept. Social Service, N.Y.C., 1965-73; artist N.Y.C., 1965—; lectr., 1978—; curator Forum Gallery, N.Y.C., 1978; tchr. Parson Sch. Design, N.Y.C., 1984, Nat. Acad. Design, N.Y.C., 1985-88, 94—. Exhibited one-woman shows Forum Gallery, N.Y.C., 1976, 80, 83, Greenville County Mus. Art, 1982, Wustum Mus., Racine, Wis., 1982, Schoelkopf Gallery, N.Y.C., 1985, Staempfli Gallery, N.Y.C., 1987, 88, Rahr West Mus., Manitowoc, Wis., U. Richmond, 1991, Perlow Gallery, N.Y.C., 1992, 94, Pucker Gallery, Boston, 1996; group shows include Akron Art Inst., 1974, Minn. Mus. Art, St. Paul, 1981, Pa. Acad. Art, Phila., 1982, Boston Mus., 1982, Bklyn. Mus., 1980, 84, Nat. Mus. Am. Art, Washington, 1985, San Francisco Mus. Modern Art, 1985, Huntsville Mus., Ala., 1987, Butler Inst., Youngstown, Ohio, 1987, 88, Ind. U. Art Mus., Joplin, Mo., 1991, Ark. Art Ctr., 1992; represented in pub. collections including Boston Mus. Fine Art, Bklyn. Mus., Carnegie Inst., Indpls. Mus., Israel Mus., others. Recipient Creative Artist Pub. Service award N.Y. State, 1982. Mem. Artists Equity, Nat. Acad. Design. Home: 429 4th St Brooklyn NY 11215-2901 *I believe that my work is always slowly changing through hard and consistent effort. There was a strong idea that initiated this work. Although that idea has been completely altered, it still exists.*

SHECHTMAN, RONALD H., lawyer; b. Hartford, Conn., Sept. 26, 1946; s. Allen A. and Jean (Bernstein) S.; m. Carolyn Meadow, Dec. 11, 1982; 1 child, Jonathan. BA, Amherst Coll., 1968; JD, NYU, 1972. Bar: U.S. Dist. Ct. (so. dist.) N.Y. 1973, N.Y. 1973, U.S. Ct. Appeals (2d cir.), U.S. Supreme Ct. Ptnr. Gordon & Shechtman PC, N.Y.C., 1972-85, Pryor, Cashman, Sherman & Flynn, N.Y.C., 1985—; mem. free speech com. ACLU, 1972, labor & employment com. N.Y.C. Bar Assn., 1988-91. Office: Pryor Cashman Sherman & Flynn 410 Park Ave New York NY 10022-4407

SHEDD, DENNIS W., federal judge; b. 1953. BA, Wofford Coll., 1975; JD, U. S.C., 1978; M of Laws, Georgetown U., 1980. Bar: S.C. Mem. staff U.S. Senator Strom Thurmond, 1978-88; chief counsel U.S. Senate Jud. Com., Washington, 1985-86; of counsel Bethea, Jordan & Griffin, Columbia, S.C., 1988-90; pvt. practice, 1989-90; judge U.S. Dist. Ct. S.C., Greenville, 1990-91; adj. prof. U. S.C., 1989-90. Mem. S.C. Bar Assn., Richland County Bar Assn., Phi Beta Kappa. Office: US District Court 1845 Assembly St Columbia SC 29201-2455*

SHEDD, DONALD POMROY, surgeon; b. New Haven, Aug. 4, 1922; s. Gale and Marion (Young) S.; m. Charlotte Newsom, Mar. 17, 1946; children: Carolyn, David, Ann, Laura. B.S., Yale U., 1944, M.D., 1946. Diplomate Am. Bd. Surgery. Intern Yale New Haven Hosp., 1946-47, asst. resident, resident, 1949-53; instr. surgery Yale U. Med Sch., New Haven, 1953-54, asst. prof., 1954-56, assoc. prof., 1956-67; chief dept. head and neck surgery Roswell Park Cancer Inst., Buffalo, 1967-96, prof. emeritus, 1996—. Co-editor: Surgical and Prosthetic Speech Rehabilitation, 1980, Head and Neck Cancer, 1985; contbr. numerous articles to profl. jours. Founding bd. dirs. Hospice Buffalo, Inc., 1973-83. Served to capt. U.S. Army, 1947-49. Mem. Soc. Univ. Surgeons, Soc. Surg. Oncology, New Eng. Surg. Soc., Soc. Head and Neck Surgeons (pres. 1976-77). Avocations: sailing; windsurfing; tennis, history of medicine. Home: 671 Lafayette Ave Buffalo NY 14222-1435 Office: Roswell Park Cancer Inst Elm & Carlton Sts Buffalo NY 14263-0001

SHEDDEN, KENNETH CHARLES, fire department official, business owner; b. Everett, Mass., Feb. 18, 1953; s. Ernest Charles and Ethel Muriel (Jones) S.; m. Lynn Diane Barbas, Aug. 20, 1978; children: Tracy M., Matthew C., Laura A., Andrew F., Rebecca C. Student, USCG Acad., 1971-72; BA in Fire Sci. and Criminal Justice, U. Mass., 1982. EMT, Boston; lic. pilot; cert. scuba diver, USCG; cert. fire instr. Mass. Firefighting Acad. Program coord., mem. faculty fire sci. program Middlesex C.C., Bedford, Mass., 1987-96; staff instr. OSHA operational programs Inst. Environ. Edn., Woburn, Mass., 1993—; ops. officer Area I radiol. response team Mass. Emergency Mgmt. Agy., Tewksbury, 1990—, staff trainer, 1994—; chief Mansfield (Mass.) Fire Dept., 1988; aux. firefighter Everett (Mass.) Fire Dept., 1972-76, firefighter, 1976-85, dir. aux., 1976-86, intermittent acting lt., 1977-85, capt., 1985-89, dep. chief, 1989-96, chief, 1996—, mem. confined space rescue team, 1994—, infection control instr., 1995—; CEO, owner METRO Consus., Inc., Everett, 1985-96; instr., trainer CPR, ARC, 1977-90, first aid instr., 1985-90, CPR instr., 1976—, vol. CPR coord., 1978-80; instr. fire program Civil Def. Tng. Acad., Topsfield, Mass., 1987-90. Bd. dirs. Greater Boston EMT's, 1979; local emergency planning coord. City of Everett, 1991-96, emergency mgmt. dir., 1996—. With USCG, 1971-72. Recipient Cert. of Merit, ARC, 1977, Firefighter of Yr. award Elks Lodge 642, 1988, VFW Post 834, 1978, 91, citation City Govt., 1980, commendation Everett Fire Dept., 1981, Cert. of Merit Medic Alert, 1982, commendation Somerville Fire Dept., 1986. Mem. New Eng. Assn. Fire Chiefs, Internat. Assn. Fire Chiefs, Everett Aux. Fire Dept. Assn. (pres. 1975, 79), Masons. Avocations: pleasure flying, scuba, sports, computers, photography. Home: 59 School St South Hamilton MA 01982-2524 Office: Everett Fire Dept 384 Broadway Everett MA 02149-3427

SHEDLOCK, JAMES, library director, consultant; b. Detroit, Nov. 25, 1950. BA in English, U. Notre Dame, 1974; AM in LS, U. Mich., 1977. Reference and serials libr. St. Joseph Mercy Hosp., Pontiac, Mich., 1977-79; document delivery libr. Wayne State U. Med. Libr., Detroit, 1979-81; coord. online search svc. U. N.C. Health Scis. Libr., Chapel Hill, 1982-85; head pub. svcs. Med. Libr., Northwestern U., Chgo., 1985-88, assoc. dir., 1988-91, dir. Galter Health Scis. Libr., 1991—; cons. U.N. High Commr. for Refugees, Cyprus, 1993-94. Mem. ALA, Med. Libr. Assn., Am. Med. Informatics Assn., Assn. Acad. Health Scis. Libr. Dirs. (rep.), Acad. Health Info. Profls. (disting.). Offices: Northwestern U Galter Health Scis Libr 303 E Chicago Ave Chicago IL 60611-3008

SHEDLOCK, KATHLEEN JOAN PETROUSKIE, community health/research nurse; b. Victorville, Calif., Jan. 22, 1952; d. Frank A. and Joan O. (Bird) Petrouskie; m. Ronald Francis Shedlock, Dec. 1, 1973; children: Pamela, Alison. Diploma, York Hosp. Sch. Nursing, 1973; BSN, SUNY, Utica, 1978; MS in Cmty. Health Nursing, Syracuse U., 1991; MPA in Health Care, Maxwell Sch., 1991. Cert. adult practitioner ANCC, Am. Acad. Nurse Practitioners. Staff nurse, charge nurse emergency rm. Doctors' Hosp., Freeport, N.Y., 1973; staff nurse ICU SUNY Health Sci. Ctr., Syracuse, 1974-76; primary care nurse with pvt. practice ob.-gyn. physician Liverpool, N.Y., 1977-79; staff nurse post anesthesia care unit, diabetes educator Community Gen. Hosp., Syracuse, 1978-87; trainer, supr. home health aides Upjohn Health Care Svcs., Liverpool, 1986; staff nurse, health educator Syracuse U. Health Svcs., 1986-88; mem. faculty Crouse Irving Meml. Hosp. Sch. Nursing, Syracuse, 1987-93; rsch. coord. Hematology-Oncology Assocs. of Cen. N.Y., Syracuse, 1993—; Syracuse coord. Breast Cancer Prevention Trial; mem. clin. trials nurse com. Nat. Surg Adjuvant Breast and Bowel Project; mem. psycho-oncology core com. CALGB; cons., planner Oneida (N.Y.) Nation Healthcare Program, 1990; reviewer Mosby Year Book Med. Pub., St. Louis, 1991; presenter at profl. confs. workshops; cons. Ctrl. N.Y. Coun. Occupl. Safety and Health, Syracuse, 1987-90; childbirth educator Childbirth Edn. Assn., Greater Syracuse, 1976-81, consumer rep., 1977. Bd. dirs. Onondaga County chpt. Am. Cancer Soc., 1993—. Mem. Oncology Nursing Soc. (health policy contact person 1994-96, ethics regional cons. 1994—), N.Y. State Nurses Assn. (chair coun. on ethical practice 1990-94, dist. treas. 1990-94, chair nominating com. 1996-97, Excellence in Nursing award 1991), Internat. Soc. Nurses in Genetics, Syracuse U. Nursing Alumni Assn. (pres.-elect), York Hosp. Sch. Nursing Alumni Assn., Sigma Theta Tau, Omicron and Iota Delta, Omicron Alpha (nominating com., steering com. 1995-97). Avocations: running, swimming, biking. Home: 8544 E Seneca Tpke Manlius NY 13104-9763 Office: Hematology-Oncology Assocs Ctrl NY 1000 E Genesee St Ste 400 Syracuse NY 13210-1853

SHEEDY, PATRICK THOMAS, judge; b. Green Bay, Wis., Oct. 31, 1921; s. Earl P. and Elsie L. (Brauel) S.; m. Margaret P. Mulvaney, Sept. 6, 1952; children: Michael, Mary, Kathleen, Patrick Thomas, Ann, Maureen. BS in Bus. Adminstrn., Marquette U., 1943, JD, 1948; LLM in Taxation, John Marshall Law Sch., 1972. Bar: Wis. 1948. Pvt. practice Milw., 1948-80; judge Wis. Cir. Ct., Milw., 1980-90; chief judge 1st Jud. Dist., Milw., 1990—. Past vice chmn. Archdiocesean Sch. Bd., Milw., chairperson, 1986—. Served to col. USAR, 1942-73. Decorated Legion of Merit. Mem. ABA (state del. 1983-85, 89-92, bd. govs. 1985-88), Wis. Bar Assn. (pres. 1974-75, bd. govs., exec. com.). Roman Catholic. Club: Exchange (pres.).

SHEEHAN, CHARLES VINCENT, investment banker; b. London, Dec. 19, 1930; came to U.S., 1931; s. Charles Vincent and Mary Margaret (Stokes) S.; m. Susan Ellen Rosar, May 5, 1962. BS, Georgetown U., 1952. Chief fin. officer Gen. Electric Co., Tokyo, Sydney, Australia and Sao Paulo, Brazil, 1962-64, 64-66, 67-71; staff exec. Gen. Electric Co., Fairfield, Conn., 1972-83, v.p. corp. exec. office, 1983-87; sr. v.p., chief fin. and adminstrn. officer Kidder, Peabody Group, Inc., N.Y.C., 1987-90; bd. dirs. Fleet Trust Co. Chmn. Non-partisan Polit. Action Com. for Gen. Electric Co. employees, Fairfield, 1982-83. Served to lt. USN, 1952-54. Mem. Johns Island Club (Vero Beach, Fla.), Wildcat Cliffs Country Club (Highlands, N.C.). Republican. Roman Catholic. Avocations: golfing, surf fishing. Home: 884 Indian Ln Vero Beach FL 32963-1131

SHEEHAN, DANIEL EUGENE, bishop; b. Emerson, Nebr., May 14, 1917; s. Daniel F. and Mary Helen (Crahan) S. Student, Creighton U., 1934-36, LL.D. (hon.), 1964; student, Kenrick Sem., St. Louis, 1936-42; J.C.D., Cath. U. Am., 1949. Ordained priest Roman Cath. Ch., 1942; asst. pastor Omaha, 1942-46; chancellor Archdiocese Omaha, 1949-69; aux. bishop Archdiocese Omaha, Omaha, 1964-69; Archbishop of Omaha, 1969-93; Pres. Canon Law Soc. Am., 1953; chaplain Omaha club Serra Internat., 1950-64. Office: Chancery Office 100 N 62nd St Omaha NE 68132-2702

SHEEHAN, DENNIS WILLIAM, SR., lawyer; b. Springfield, Mass., Jan. 2, 1934; s. Timothy A. and H. Marjorie (Kelsey) S.; m. Elizabeth M. Hellyer, July 27, 1957; children: Dennis William Jr., Catherine Elizabeth, John Edward. BS, U. Md., 1957; JD, Georgetown U., 1960, LLM, 1962. Bar: D.C., Md. 1960, Mo. 1976, Ohio 1977. Legal asst. to chmn. NLRB, Washington, 1960-61; trial atty. U.S. SEC, Washington, 1962-63; corp. atty. Martin Marietta, Balt., N.Y.C., 1963-64; v.p., gen. counsel, sec. Bunker Ramo Corp., Oak Brook, Ill., 1964-73; exec. v.p., gen. counsel, dir. Diversified Industries, Inc., St. Louis, 1973-75; v.p., gen. counsel, dir. N-ReN Corp., Cin., 1975-77; v.p., gen. counsel, sec., dir. Axia, Inc., Lombard, Ill., 1977-84; chmn., pres., CEO Axia Corp., Lombard, Ill., 1984—; bd. dirs. Compagnie Fischbein (S.A.), Brussels, Greenfield Industries, Augusta, Ga., CST, Inc., Wheeling, Ill., Bradington-Young, Inc., Hickory, N.C.; chmn. Allied Healthcare Sys., St. Louis. Bd. dirs. St. Margaret's Sch. Found., Mgmt. Alliance, Washington, U.S. C. of C., Nat. Coun. on Crime and Delinquency. Mem. ABA, Chgo. Club, St. Louis Club, Econ. Club Chgo., Met. Club Washington, Downtown Club Richmond, Met. Club Chgo., Univ. Club Balt., Phi Delta Pi, Sigma Alpha Phi, Delta Sigma Phi. Republican. Home: Rte 1217 Box 2032 Tappaharrock VA 22560 Office: Axia Corp 100 22d St Lombard IL 60148

SHEEHAN, DONALD THOMAS, academic administrator; b. Winsted, Conn., Jan. 2, 1911; s. James J. and Louise (Coffey) S.; m. Betty Young, June 25, 1941; 1 son, Michael Terrence. Grad., Gilbert Sch., Winsted, 1931; B.S. in Edn, Syracuse U., 1935; student, Sch. Pub. Affairs, Am. U., 1936. Dir. health edn. D.C. Tb. Assn., 1937-39; dir. Washington office NCCJ, 1939-41; dir. Bur. Info. Nat. Cath. Welfare Conf., Washington, 1941-42; spl. cons. to U.S. Commr. Edn., 1946; staff mem. John Price Jones Co., Inc. (pub. relations cons.), 1946-51; cons. civil def. edn. program, asst. adminstr. charge vol. manpower FCDA, 1951-54, cons. vol. manpower, 1954—; dir. pub. relations U. Pa., 1954-76, sec. corp., 1975-76, sec., v.p. emeritus, 1976—; spl. lectr. pub. relations Drexel U., 1957-72; cons. Nat. Bd. Med. Examiners, 1964—, Coll. Physicians Phila., 1973—, Citizens' Action Com. to Fight Inflation, 1974-75, Wistar Inst. Anatomy and Biology, 1979, Univ. Mus., U. Pa., 1982—, Inst. Environ. Medicine, 1983—; Mem. adv. com. Nat. Trust for Hist. Preservation; cons. Am. Philos. Soc., 1988—. Served from 1st lt. to lt. col. USAAF, 1942-46. Decorated Bronze Star medal. Fellow Coll. Physicians Phila. (hon. assoc.), ; mem. Public Relations Soc. Am., Pi Gamma Mu. Roman Catholic. Club: Nat. Press. Home: 201 W Evergreen Ave Apt 310 Philadelphia PA 19118-3830

SHEEHAN, EDWARD JAMES, technical consultant, former government official; b. Johnstown, Pa., Dec. 31, 1935; s. Louis A. and Ethel F. (Schaefer) S.; m. Florence Ann Hartnett, June 17, 1958; children—Edward, James, John, William, Mary. B.S. in Physics, St. Francis Coll., 1959; M.S. (Sloan fellow), Mass. Inst. Tech., 1972. Project engr. Electronics Command, Dept. Army, 1959-61, project team leader electro-optic equipment for tanks, 1961-63, project team leader electro-optic equipment for infantry, 1963-65, tech. area dir. electro-optic night vision equipment, 1965-73, assoc. lab. dir. for devel. engring., 1973-76; lab. dir. Night Vision Lab., Fort Belvoir, Va., 1976-79; founder, pres. Sheehan Assos. Inc., Alexandria, Va., 1979-92; founder, CEO, chmn. Stardyne, Inc., Johnstown, 1990-96; chmn. Nat. and Internat. Symposia for Electro-Optical Tech. and Applications. Recipient numerous awards including Meritorious Civilian Svc. award Dept. Army, Disting. Alumnus award in sci. St. Francis Coll., 1989; named Man of Yr., Combined Svc. Clubs, Johnstown, Pa., 1993. Home: 8502 Crestview Dr Fairfax VA 22031-2803

SHEEHAN, JAMES JOHN, historian, educator; b. San Francisco, May 31, 1937; s. James B. and Sally W. (Walsh) S.; m. 1960; 1 child, Michael L.; m. Margaret L. Anderson, Sept. 2, 1989. BA, Stanford U., 1958; MA, U. Calif., Berkeley, 1959, PhD, 1964. From asst. to assoc. prof. Northwestern U., Evanston, Ill., 1964-79; prof. Stanford (Calif.) U., 1979-86, chmn. dept., 1982-89, Dickason prof. in humanities, 1986—. Author: Lujo Brentano, 1966, German Liberalism, 1978, German History 1770-1866, 1989, Der Ausklang des alten Reiches, 1994; editor: The Boundaries of Humanity, 1991; contbr. articles to profl. jours. Fellow Am. Council Learned Socs., 1981-82, NEH, 1985-86, Wissenschaftskolleg Berlin. Fellow AAAS (Humboldt Rsch. prize 1995); mem. Royal Hist. Soc. (corr.), Am. Hist. Assn. (nominating com. 1979-81, chmn. conf. group on Ctrl. European history 1985-86). Office: Stanford U Dept of History Stanford CA 94305

SHEEHAN, JOHN FRANCIS, cytopathologist, educator; b. Portsmouth, N.H., July 28, 1906; s. John Thomas and Ellen Agnes (Lynes) S.; m. Grace Anne O'Neil, Aug. 3, 1935; 1 child, John Thomas. B.S., U. N.H., 1928, M.S., 1930; Ph.D., State U. Iowa, 1945; postgrad., McGill U., 1949, Jefferson Med. Coll., 1951. Grad. asst. U. N.H., 1928-30; instr. biology Creighton U., 1930-38, asst. prof., 1938-44, assoc. prof., 1944-49, chmn. biology dept., 1949-58, prof. biology, 1949-67, prof. pathology Sch. Medicine, 1967-88, prof. ob-gyn, 1975-88, prof. emeritus pathology and gynecology, 1988—; attending staff AMI St. Joseph Hosp.; dir. cytopathology St. Joseph Hosp., Omaha, 1978-82; dir. cytopathology emeritus St. Joseph Hosp., 1982—; prof. emeritus biology and pathology Creighton U., 1989. Recipient Golden Jubilee Svc. award Creighton U., 1981, Certificate award AAUP, 1988; Dept. Biology Creighton U. lecture hall named in his honor, 1984. Fellow Am. Soc. Colposcopy and Cervical Pathology; mem. AAUP, Am. Soc. Cytopathology, Internat. Coll. Surgeons (vice regent for Nebr. 1984), Am. Inst. Biol. Scis., Am. Micros Soc., Am. Men and Women of Sci., Am. Soc. Clin. Pathologists, Nebr. Heart Assn., Nebr. Acad. Scis., Smithsonian Nat. Assocs., Sigma Xi, Alpha Omega Alpha, Alpha Sigma Nu, Phi Rho Sigma, Phi Sigma. Home: 7300 Graceland Dr Apt 307A Omaha NE 68134-4341 Office: St Joseph Hosp 601 N 30th St Omaha NE 68131-2137

SHEEHAN, JOHN J., career officer; b. Somerville, Mass., Aug. 23, 1940; m. Margaret M. Sullivan; children: Kristen, Catherine, Karen, John. BA in English, Boston Coll., 1962; MA in Govt., Georgetown U. Commd. 2d lt. USMC, 1962; advanced through rank to gen.; dir. ops. Joint Staff, Washington; Atlantic comdr. in chief U.S. Atlantic Command, 1994—. Decorated Silver Star medal, Bronze Star medal with Combat "V" and gold star, Purple Heart with gold star. Office: US Atlantic Command 2000 Navy Pentagon Washington DC 20350-2000*

SHEEHAN, LARRY JOHN, lawyer; b. N.Y.C., Apr. 14, 1955; s. James Albert and Hortense Rose (Carlo) S.; m. Sylvia Margaret Poschman, Apr. 30, 1978; children: Nicole, Kelly, Daniel. BA, St. John's U., 1978; JD, N.Y. Law Sch., 1983. Bar: N.Y. 1984, U.S. Dist. Ct. (so. and ea. dists.) N.Y. 1984. Asst. dist. atty. Bronx Dist. Atty., N.Y.C., 1984-89; atty. Alemany, Gonzalez, McLoone & Sheehan, Scarsdale, N.Y., 1989—; atty. N.Y.C. Assigned Counsel, N.Y.C., 1989—, Fed. Assigned Counsel Plan, So. Dist., N.Y., 1991—, Ea. Dist., N.Y., 1993—. Campaign mgr. Dem. Party, Yonkers, N.Y., 1989. Mem. N.Y. State Bar Assn., Bronx County Bar Assn., Westchester County Bar Assn., N.Y. State Criminal Trial Assn. Roman Catholic. Avocations: reading, brief writing, basketball, running. Home and Office: Alemany Laskorski & Sheehan 111 Brook St Scarsdale NY 10583-5149

SHEEHAN, LAWRENCE JAMES, lawyer; b. San Francisco, July 23, 1932. AB, Stanford U., 1957, LLB, 1959. Bar: Calif. 1960. Law clk. to chief judge U.S. Ct. Appeals 2d Cir., N.Y.C., 1959-60; assoc. O'Melveny & Myers, L.A., 1960-68, ptnr., 1969-94, of counsel, 1995—; bd. dirs. FPA Mut. Funds, TCW Convertible Securities Fund Inc., Source Capital, Inc. Mem. ABA, Los Angeles County Bar Assn., Calif. Bar Assn., Order of Coif. Office: O'Melveny & Myers 1999 Avenue Of The Stars Los Angeles CA 90067-6022 also: O'Melveny & Myers 400 S Hope St Los Angeles CA 90071-2801

SHEEHAN, LINDA SUZANNE, educational administrator; b. Dayton, Ohio, Aug. 1, 1950; d. Paul J. and Betty L. (Fowler) King; m. J. Scott Sheehan, Dec. 18, 1971. 1 child Amy Elizabeth. BS in Edn. with honors, Ohio State U., 1971; MEd, U. Tex., 1974; adminstrn. cert. Houston Bapt. U., 1983. Cert. tchr., Tex. Tchr. Upper Arlington Schs., Columbus, Ohio, 1971-72, Brown Sch., San Marcos, Tex., 1972-73, Comal Ind. Sch. Dist., New Braunfels, Tex., 1973-75, Alief Ind. Sch. Dist., Houston, 1975-79; asst. prin. Killough Mid. Sch., Houston, 1979-84; prin. Olle Mid. Sch., Houston, 1984-92, Holub Middle Sch., 1992—. Named Tchr. of Yr., Olle Mid. Sch., Houston, 1978. Mem. NEA, Nat. Mid. Sch. Assn., Nat. Assn. Secondary Sch. Prins., Tex. Assn. Secondary Sch. Prins., Tex. Mid. Sch. Assn. (dir. 1979-91, pres. 1991-92, state convention chair 1993-94), Houston Council Social Studies, Kappa Delta Pi (pres. 1984-85), Phi Delta Kappa. Roman Catholic. Home: 526 Nottingham Oaks Trl Houston TX 77079-6332 Office: Holub Mid Sch 9515 S Dairy Ashford St Houston TX 77099-4909*

SHEEHAN, MICHAEL JARBOE, archbishop; b. Wichita, Kans., July 9, 1939; s. John Edward and Mildred (Jarboe) S. MST, Gregorian U., Rome, 1965; D of Canon Law, Lateran U., Rome, 1971. Ordained priest Roman Cath. Ch., 1964. Asst. gen. sec. Nat. Coun. Cath. Bishops, Washington, 1971-76; rector Holy Trinity Sem., Dallas, 1976-82; pastor Immaculate Conception Ch., Grand Prairie, Tex., 1982-83; bishop Diocese of Lubbock, Tex., 1983-93; archbishop Archdiocese of Santa Fe, Albuquerqe, N.Mex., 1993—; past chmn. Am. Bd. Cath. Missions, 1989-91; trustee Cath. Relief Svcs., 1992—. Contbr. articles to New Cath. Ency. Trustee St. Mary Hosp., Lubbock, 1983-89; bd. dirs. Tex. Conf. of Chs. Mem. Serra Club (chaplain 1983-93). Avocations: snow skiing, racquetball. Office: Archdiocese of Santa Fe 4000 Saint Josephs Pl NW Albuquerque NM 87120-1714

SHEEHAN, MICHAEL TERRENCE, arts administrator, historian, consultant; b. Washington, Dec. 15, 1942; s. Donald Thomas and Betty (Young) S. BA, U. Pa., 1965, MA, 1968, PhD, 1974. House mgr. Annenberg Ctr., Phila., 1968-72; magr. Performing Arts Ctr. SUNY, Albany, 1972-76; mng. dir. Taconic Theatre Co., Spencertown, N.Y., 1973-77; exec. dir. Snug Harbor Cultural Ctr., N.Y.C., 1978-82; cons. Washington, 1984-87; pres. Oatlands Plantation, Leesburg, Va., 1987-89; dir. Woodrow Wilson House Nat. Trust for Historic Preserve, Washington, 1989—. Bd. dirs. Albany League of Arts, 1972-77, Loudon County League of Arts, Leesburg, 1988-89; mem. Loudon County Tourism Bd., 1987-89, chmn. profl. interest coun., 1995-97; consortium officer Historic House Museums of Met. Washington, 1992-97; mem. D.C. Heritage Tourism Coalition. Mem. Am. Assn. Mus., Nat. Press Club Washington, Nat. Trust Historic Preservation, Internat. Coun. Mus. Office: Woodrow Wilson House 2340 S St NW Washington DC 20008-4016

SHEEHAN, MONICA MARY, banker; b. New Milford, Conn., Apr. 27, 1955; d. Walter F. and Lillian S. BA cum laude, Williams Coll., 1977; MBA, NYU, 1984. Fl. dir. Sta. WVIT-TV, Hartford, Conn., 1977-78; cable franchise adminstr. Viacom Internat. Inc., N.Y.C., 1978-81, corp. fin. analyst, 1981-82, from mgr. fin. planning entertainment group to asst. to CFO, 1982-85; fin. analyst, chmn. bd. Citibank/Citicorp., N.Y.C., 1985-86; project dir. World Corp. Group/Citibank, N.Y.C., 1986-87; relationship banker NCD-East/Citibank, N.Y.C., 1987-88; v.p., area mgr. N.E. region The Mitsubishi Bank Ltd., N.Y.C., 1988-95; corp. fin. cons. MMS Enterprises, N.Y.C., 1995; v.p. specialized lending divsn. State St. Bank and Trust Co., Boston, 1995—. Founding mem. pres.'s coun. St. Vincent's Hosp., N.Y.C., 1986-95. Mem. NYU Stern Sch. Bus. Grad. Alumni Assn. (sec. 1994-95), Williams Club (bd. govs. 1979-84), U. Club Boston. Democrat. Roman Catholic. Avocations: tennis, golf, reading. Office: State St Bank and Trust Co 225 Franklin St Boston MA 02110-2804

SHEEHAN, NEIL, reporter, scholarly writer; b. Holyoke, Mass., Oct. 27, 1936; s. Cornelius Joseph and Mary (O'Shea) S.; m. Susan Margulies, Mar. 30, 1965; children—Maria Gregory, Catherine Fair. AB cum laude, Harvard, 1958; LittD (hon.), Columbia Coll., Chgo., 1972; LHD (hon.), Am. Internat. Coll., 1990, U. Lowell, 1991. Vietnam Bur. chief U.P.I., Saigon, 1962-64; reporter N.Y. Times, N.Y.C., Djakarta, Saigon, Washington, 1964-72. Author: The Arnheiter Affair, 1972, A Bright Shining Lie: John Paul Vann and America in Vietnam, 1988 (Nat. Book award 1988, Pulitzer Prize for gen. non-fiction 1989, Robert F. Kennedy book award 1989, Vetty award Vietnam Vets. Ensemble Theatre Co. 1989, Spl. Achievement award Vietnam Vets. Am. 1989, Outstanding Investigative Reporting award Investigative Reporters and Editors, Inc. of U. Mo. Sch. Journalism 1989, Amb. award English-Speaking Union 1989, John F. Kennedy award, Holyoke, Mass 1989), After the War Was Over: Hanoi and Saigon, 1992, also articles and book revs. for popular mags.; contbr. to The Pentagon Papers, 1971. Served with AUS, 1959-62. Recipient Louis M. Lyons award for conscience and integrity in journalism, 1964, Silver medal Poor Richard Club, Phila., 1964, certificate of appreciation for best article on Asia Overseas Press Club Am., 1967, 1st Ann. Drew Pearson prize for excellence in investigative reporting, 1971, Columbia Journalism awards, 1972, 89, Sidney Hillman Found. awards, 1972, 88, Page One award Newspaper Guild N.Y., 1972, Distinguished Service award and Bronze medallion Sigma Delta Chi, 1972, citation of excellence Overseas Press Club, 1972, Literary Lion award N.Y. Pub. Libr., 1992; Guggenheim fellow, 1973-74; Adlai Stevenson fellow, 1973-75; Lehrman Inst. fellow, 1975-76; Rockefeller Found. fellow in humanities, 1976-77; Woodrow Wilson Internat. Center for Scholars fellow, 1979-80. Mem. Soc. Am. Historians, Am. Acad. Achievement. Obtained Pentagon Papers, 1971. Home: 4505 Klingle St NW Washington DC 20016-3580

SHEEHAN, PATTY, professional golfer. 4th ranked woman LPGA Tour, 1992; winner U.S. Women's Open, 1992, 94, LPGA Championship, 1983-84, 93. Inductee LPGA Hall of Fame, 1993, Sports Illustrated Sportsman of the Yr., 1987. Winner 31 LPGA Tournaments including Mazda Japan Classic, 1981, 88, Inamori Classic, 1982-83, 86, Orlando Lady Classic, 1982, Safeco Classic, 1982, 90, 95, LPGA Corning Classic, 1983, LPGA Championship, 1983-84, 93, Henredon Classic, 1983-84, Elizabeth Arden Classic, 1984, McDonald's Kids Classic, 1984, 90, Sarasota Classic, 1985-86, 88, J&B Scotch Pro AM, 1985, Konica San Jose Classic, 1986, Rochester Internat.,

1989-90, 92, 95, Jamaica Classic, 1990, Ping-Cellular One Championship, 1990, Orix Hawaiian Ladies Open, 1991, Jamie Farr Toledo Classic, 1992, Weetabix Women's Brit. Open, 1992, U.S. Women's Open, 1992, 94, Mazda LPGA Championship, 1993. Office: LPGA 100 International Golf Dr Daytona Beach FL 32124-1082*

SHEEHAN, ROBERT C., lawyer; b. N.Y.C., Oct. 12, 1944; s. John Edward and Mary Elizabeth (Trede) S.; m. Elizabeth Mary Mammen, Aug. 17, 1968; children: Elizabeth, Robert, William. BA, Boston Coll., 1966; LLB, Univ. Pa., Phila., 1969. Bar: N.Y. 1970. Ptnr. Skadden, Arps, Slate, Meagher & Flom LLP, N.Y.C., 1978—, exec. ptnr., 1994—. Office: Skadden Arps Slate Meagher Flom LLP 919 3rd Ave New York NY 10022

SHEEHAN, STEPHEN DENNIS, airport commissioner; b. Oct. 29, 1942. BS, USAF Acad., 1965; M Aviation Mgmt. with honors, Embry Riddle Aero. U., 1979; postgrad., Air War Coll., 1982-83. Commd. officer USAF, 1965, advanced through grades to col., ret., 1992, chief test pilot, instr., flight examiner, 1965-75; chief Air Base Plans Divsn., Incirilik, Turkey, 1975-76; pilot, action officer, exec. officer, dept. chief staff Hdqrs. USAF Tact Air Command, 1977-80; pilot, chief air ops. tng., comdr. air support ops. squadron, 1980-82; asst. inspector gen. Unified Command Hdqrs., 1983-86; group comdr. USAF, 1986-89, base comdr., 1989-91; faculty mem., dir. Tactical Air Ops., U.S. Army War Coll., 1991-92; dep. commr. Ops., Safety and Security Cleve. Hopkins Internat. Airport, 1992-94; commr. Cleve. Hopkins Internat. Airport, 1994—. Decorated Legion of Merit, 3 Disting. Flying Crosses, 13 Air medals. Office: 5300 Riverside Dr Cleveland OH 44135-3145

SHEEHAN, SUSAN, writer; b. Vienna, Austria, Aug. 24, 1937; came to U.S., 1941, naturalized, 1946; d. Charles and Kitty C. (Herrmann) Sachsel; m. Neil Sheehan, Mar. 30, 1965; children—Maria Gregory, Catherine Fair. BA (Durant scholar), Wellesley Coll., 1958; DHL (hon.), U. Lowell, 1991. Editorial researcher Esquire-Coronet, N.Y.C., 1959-60; free-lance writer N.Y.C., 1960-61; staff writer New Yorker mag., N.Y.C., 1961—. Author: Ten Vietnamese, 1967, A Welfare Mother, 1976, A Prison and a Prisoner, 1978, Is There No Place on Earth for Me?, 1982, Kate Quinton's Days, 1984, A Missing Plane, 1986, Life For Me Ain't Been No Crystal Stair, 1993; contbr. articles to various mags., including N.Y. Times Sunday Mag., Washington Post Sunday Mag., Harper's, Atlantic, New Republic, McCall's, Holiday, Boston Globe Sunday Mag., Life. Judge Robert F. Kennedy Journalism awards, 1980, 84; mem. lit. panel D.C. Commn. on Arts and Humanities, 1979-84; mem. pub. info. and edn. com. Nat. Mental Health Assn., 1982-83; mem. adv. com. on employment and crime Vera Inst. Justice, 1978-86; chair Pulitzer Prize nominating jury in gen. non-fiction for 1988, 1994, mem., 1991. Recipient Sidney Hillman Found. award, 1976, Gavel award ABA, 1978, Individual Reporting award Nat. Mental Health Assn., 1981, Pulitzer prize for gen. non-fiction, 1983, Feature Writing award N.Y. Press Club, 1984, Alumnae Assn. Achievement award Wellesley Coll., 1984, Carroll Kowal Journalism award NASW, 1993, Disting. Grad. award Hunter Coll. H.S., 1995, Pub. Awareness award Nat. Alliance for Mentally Ill, 1995; fellow Guggenheim Found., 1975-76, Woodrow wilson Internat. Ctr. for Scholars, 1981. Mem. Soc. Am. Historians, Phi Beta Kappa, Authors Guild. Home: 4505 Klingle St NW Washington DC 20016-3580 Office: New Yorker Mag 20 W 43rd St New York NY 10036-7400

SHEEHY, BARRY M., management consultant. BA in History, Econs. cum laude, Loyola Coll.; MA in History, McGill U.; C.E.L.E., Can. Forces Sch. Comm. Electronic Engring. Prin. The Atlanta Consulting Group, Savannah, Ga.; mem. faculty Estes Pk.(Healthcare) Inst., Healthcare Governance Inst., Healthcare Forum; guest spkr. U.S. C. of C., Quality Coun. Can., Quality Coun. Mex., Microsoft Healthcare Forum, INC 500, Am. Express Bank Global Forum, others. Author: In Search of Quality: 4 Unique Perspectives, 43 Different Voices (Exec. Excellence 1995); (with others) Firing on All Cylinders, 1992, Economic Divide: Winners and Losers in an Age of Abundance, 1996, Winning the RAce, 1996; contbr. articles to profl. jours. Guest spkr. SCLC, Savannah Found. Officer Can. Armed Forces. Co-recipient Am. Soc. Indsl. Engrs. award, 1985. Office: The Atlanta Consulting Group 18 E Macon St Savannah GA 31401-4346

SHEEHY, GAIL HENION, author; b. Mamaroneck, N.Y., Nov. 27, 1937; d. Harold Merritt and Lillian Rainey (Paquin) Henion; m. Albert F. Sheehy, Aug. 20, 1960 (div. 1967); 1 dau., Maura; 1 adopted dau., Mohm; m. Clay Felker, Dec. 16, 1984. BS, U. Vt., 1958; fellow, Journalism Sch., Columbia U., 1970. Traveling home economist J.C. Penney & Co., 1958-60; fashion editor Rochester Democrat & Chronicle, 1961-63; feature writer N.Y. Herald Tribune, N.Y.C., 1963-66; contbg. editor New York mag., 1968-77. Contbr. to N.Y. Times Mag., Parade, New Republic, Washington Post; polit. contbg. editor Vanity Fair mag., 1988—; author: Lovesounds, 1970, Panthermania: The Clash of Black Against Black in One American City, 1971, Speed Is of the Essence, 1971, Hustling: Prostitution in Our Wide-Open Society, 1973, Passages: Predictable Crises of Adult Life, 1976, Pathfinders, 1981, Spirit of Survival, 1986, Character: America's Search for Leadership, 1988, Gorbachev: The Man Who Changed the World, 1990, The Silent Passage: Menopause, 1992, New Passages: Mapping Your Life Across Time, 1995; (plays) Maggie and Misha, 1991. Adv. bd. Women's Health Initiative, NIH; bd. dirs. Girls Inc., Poets and Writers; eminent citizen's com. UN Internat. Conf. on Population and Devel., 1994. Recipient 4 Front Page awards Newswomen's Club N.Y., Nat. Mag. award Columbia U., 1973, Penney-Mo. Journalism award U. Mo., 1975, Anisfield-Wolf Book award, 1986, Best Mag. Writer award Washington Journalism Rev., 1991, N.Y. Pub. Libr. Literary Lion, 1992; Columbia U. fellow, 1970; Alicia Patterson Found. grantee, 1974. Mem. PEN, NOW, Authors Guild.

SHEEHY, HOWARD SHERMAN, JR., minister; b. Denver, Mar. 19, 1934; s. Howard Sherman and Mildred Louise (Fishburn) S.; m. Thelma Fline Florine Clise, Sept. 4, 1954; children: John Robert, Lisa Florine, Michael Howard. A.A., Graceland Coll., 1953; B.S., Central Mo. State Coll., 1955; M.S., U. Kans., 1960, postgrad. Ordained to ministry Reorganized Ch. of Jesus Christ of Latter-Day Sts., 1954. Youth dir. Reorganized Ch. Jesus Christ Latter-day Saints, Independence, Mo., 1960-64; pastor Des Moines, 1964-68; church supr. Haiti, 1968-70, Canada, 1970-74, Australia, 1970-75, N.Z., 1970-75, India, 1970-78, Japan, Korea, Republic of China, Philippines, 1976-78; mem. Council of Twelve Apostles, 1968-78, mem. 1st presidency, 1978—; mem. corp. body Outreach Internat., Restoration Trail Found. Editor-in-chief: Saints Herald. Mem. nat. Protestant com. on scouting Boy Scouts Am., 1964-66; trustee Independence Regional Health Ctr., 1979-88, 90-95. Lt. USNR, 1955-59. Mem. Pi Omega Pi, Phi Delta Kappa, Phi Kappa Phi. Republican. Home: 3403 S Crane St Independence MO 64055-2532 Office: The Temple PO Box 1059 Independence MO 64051-0559

SHEEHY, JEROME JOSEPH, electrical engineer; b. Hartford, Conn., Dec. 3, 1935; s. Jeremiah and Anna (Foley) S.; m. Jean Ann Baldassari, Oct. 13, 1962; children: Caroline, Jerome, Daniel, Carlene. BSEE, U. Conn., 1962, MSEE, 1967. Electronic engr. USN Underwater Sound Lab., New London, Conn., 1962-69; mem. tech. staff Rockwell Internat., Anaheim, Calif., 1969-74; staff engr. Hughes Aircraft Co., Fullerton, Calif., 1974-83; systems engr. Norden Systems, Santa Ana, Calif., 1983-89; advanced engring. specialist Lockheed Martin Aircraft Svc., Ontario, Calif., 1990—. Contbr. articles to Jour. Acoustical Soc. Am. With USAF, 1954-57. Mem. Acoustical Soc. Am., Tau Beta Pi, Eta Kappa Nu. Achievements include research in detection and estimation theory for non-gaussian noise, non-normal statistics. Home: 22951 Belquest Dr Lake Forest CA 92630-4007

SHEEHY, JOAN MARY, nurse; b. Newton, Mass., Sept. 14, 1931; d. Daniel Joseph and Mary Frances (Herlihy) Welch; m. James E. Sheehy, Sept. 14, 1969; children: James M., Robert E., Patricia A., Julie M. Diplomate in nursing, St. Mgts. Sch. Nursing, Dorchester, Mass., 1952; student, Boston Coll., 1952-56; cert. x-ray technician, Northeastern U., 1962. RN, Mass.; cert. sch. nurse. Staff nurse St. Margaret's Hosp., Dorchester, 1952-53, Newton (Mass.) Vis. Nursing Assn., 1953-54, Cambridge (Mass.) Health Dept., 1954-56, John Hancock Mut. Life Ins., Boston, 1956-68, Boston Sch. Dept., 1969-93; mem. staff Deutsches Altenheim, Boston, 1993—; aides educator, Boston, 1985-93. Mem. alumni assn. Our Lady's H.S., Newton, 1989, 93; assoc. Human Rights, Newton, 1985—. Mem. Nat. Sch. Nursing Assn. Roman Catholic. Avocations: caring for grandchild, knitting, sewing, crocheting, plays. Home: 16 Lucille Pl Newton MA 02164-1211

SHEEHY, VINCENT, automotive executive; b. 1928. V.p. Sheehy-Manassas, Inc., Manassas, Va., 1991—; pres. Sheehy Ford, Inc., Suitland, Md., 1966—; CEO Sheehy Automotive, Fairfax, Va., 1988—. Office: 12450 Fair Lakes Cir Ste 380 Fairfax VA 22033-3810*

SHEELINE, PAUL CUSHING, hotel executive; b. Boston, June 6, 1921; s. Paul Daniel and Mary (Child) S.; m. Harriet White Moffat, May 23, 1948 (dec. 1962); children: Christopher White, William Emerson, Mary Child, Leonora Moffat; m. Sandra Dudley Wahl, July 24, 1965; 1 child, Abby Tucker. B.S., Harvard U., 1943, J.D., 1948. Bar: N.Y. 1949, D.C. 1986. Assoc. Sullivan & Cromwell, N.Y.C., 1948-54; with Lambert & Co., N.Y.C., 1954-65, gen. ptnr., 1958-65; chief fin. officer Intercontinental Hotels Corp., N.Y.C., 1966-71, pres., 1971-74, chief exec. officer, 1971-85, chmn. bd., 1972-87, cons., 1987-90; of counsel Verner, Liipfert, Bernhard, McPherson & Hand, Washington, 1986-93; bd. dirs. Resorts Internat., Inc., 1991-94; mem. Presdl. Bd. Advisors on Pvt. Sector Initiatives, Washington, 1987-89. Vice chmn. Community Service Soc. of N.Y., 1962-63; dir. Am. Assn. for UN, 1951-58; former mem. Harvard Overseers Com. to visit Center for Internat. Affairs and Dept. Romance Langs.; trustee East Woods Sch., Oyster Bay Cove, N.Y., 1959-68, Camargo Found., St. Luke's/Roosevelt Hosp. Ctr.; bd. dirs. Bus. Council for Internat. Understanding., 1975-88, Fgn. Policy Assn., 1981-90, Scientists' Inst. Pub. Info., 1984-91, Battle of Normandy Found., 1986-91; mem. bd. zoning appeals Village of Lloyd Harbor, N.Y., 1988—. Served to capt. USAAF, 1942-46. Decorated Silver Star medal, French Legion of Honor, Croix de Guerre with palm, Moroccan Ouissam Alaouite. Mem. Am.-Arab Assn. Commerce and Industry (chmn. bd. 1984-86), Phi Beta Kappa. Clubs: Cold Spring Harbor Beach; Harvard (N.Y.C.); Balsam Lake Anglers (N.Y.).

SHEEM, SANG KEUN, fiber optics engineering professional; b. Seoul, Korea, Mar. 20, 1944; s. Eung-Taek and Ki-Jik (Oh) S.; m. Susan Kim, Mar. 22, 1970; children: Edward J., Shana J. MS in Engring., U. Calif., 1973, PhD in Engring., 1975. Rsch. physicist U.S. Naval Rsch. Lab., Washington, 1976-81; mgr. Rockwell Internat., Dallas, 1981-86; mgr. sensor program Lawrence Livermore (Calif.) Nat. Lab., 1986—; mem. corp. optical panel Rockwell Internat., Dallas, 1982-86; cons. Kaptron Fiber Optic Co., Palo Alto, Calif., 1987-88, Amaco Rsch. Ctr., Naperville, Ill., 1986-87; pres. Berkeley Optics Co., Livermore, 1994—. Contbr. articles, referee to profl. jours. Mem. IEEE, Optical Soc. Am., Korean Scientist and Engr. Assn. (pres. No. Calif. chpt. 1990-91), Internat. Platform Assn., Calif. Commonwealth Club. Achievements include 20 patents in fiber optics and integrated optics; major inventions include single-mode fiber couplers and self-biased optical fiber gyroscope. Office: Lawrence Livermore Nat Lab 7000 East Ave L-156 Livermore CA 94550

SHEEN, ROBERT TILTON, manufacturing company executive; b. Phila., Dec. 10, 1909; s. Milton Roy and Emma Elizabeth (Tilton) S.; m. Dorothy Martha Dillenbeck, June 25, 1932; children—James D., Roberta Alace (Mrs. R. Donald Peterson); m. Mary Regina Orban, Aug 17, 1951; 1 dau., Regina Elizabeth (Mrs. Brian C. Ridgway); m. Frieda Marie Van Riter, July 19, 1972. B.S. in Chem. Engring, Lehigh U., 1931, Chem Engr., 1936. Registered profl. engr., Pa., N.J., Ohio, Ill. Chem. engr. Swann Chem. Co., Anniston, Ala., 1931-32; tech. dir., then dir. cons. div. W.H. & L.D. Betz Co., 1932-43; co-founder Milton Roy Co., Phila and St. Petersburg, Fla., 1946; pres., chmn. bd. Milton Roy Co., 1947-68, chmn. bd., chief exec. officer, 1968-72, chmn. bd., 1972-74, dir., chmn. exec. com., 1975-89. Author: Robert T. Sheen-His-Story, 1991; contbr. articles to profl. jours. Pres. Jr. Achievement of St. Petersburg, 1965-66; chmn. Bayfront Med. Center, Inc., St. Petersburg, 1968-72, hon. chmn. campaign for New Times, 1984-86; mem. Fla. Gov.'s Council on Productivity and Council on Profl. Regulation, 1980-83; bd. dirs. United Fund S. Pinellas, Fla., 1962; trustee Eckerd Coll., St. Petersburg, 1959—, chmn. bd., 1974-77, mem. Acad. Sr. Profls. Eckerd Coll., 1983—; hon. trustee Sci. Center Pinellas County; mem. Fla. Com. on Aging, 1984-86; hon. bd. dirs. Fla. Council on Econ. Edn., 1984—; mem. council advisers Fla. State U., Tallahassee, 1975-82; former dir., chmn. health care com. Fla. Council of 100, 1969-77, chmn. human affairs com., 1978-82. Recipient Diamond Jubilee award U.S. CSC, 1958, Outstanding Citizen award, 1967, West Coast Fla. Engr. of Yr. award, 1968, Silver Medallion Brotherhood award NCCJ, 1977, Top Mgmt. award Soc. Mfg. Engrs., St. Petersburg, 1981, Monroe J. Rathbone Alumni Achievement award Lehigh U., 1989, Robert T. Sheen award for Vol. Leadership, Bayfront Med. Ctr., 1993; Robert T. and Fran V.R. Sheen Conference Ctr., Bayfront Med. Ctr., named in his honor, 1995; inducted into Sr. Hall of Fame, City of St. Petersburg, Fla., 1996. Fellow Instrument Soc. Am. (pres. 1955-56); hon. mem. Am. Mgmt. Assn. (dir. 1962-67, 70-73, mem. exec. com. 1965-67, 70-73, life mem.); mem. Am. Chem. Soc., Nat. Soc. Profl. Engrs., Am. Inst. Chem. Engrs., Suncoasters Inc. (named Mr. Sun 1969, pres. 1974-75), Newcomen Soc. N.Am. Patentee chem. pumps, chem. feed systems. Home: 672 Boca Ciega Point Blvd N Saint Petersburg FL 33708-2730

SHEER, BARBARA LEE, nursing educator; b. Riverside, N.J., Dec. 16, 1946; d. David J. and Edna (Maher) Phelan; m. George W. Sheer, Nov. 15, 1969; 1 child, Jeffrey B. Grad., Phila. Gen. Hosp. Sch. Nursing, 1967; BSN, U. Pa., 1971; PNP, Rutgers U., 1976; MSN, SUNY, Binghamton, 1981; DNSc, Widener U., 1989. Cert. family nurse practitioner ANA, CRNP, Pa. Instr. Coll. Misericordia, Dallas, Pa.; asst. prof. U. Scranton (Pa.); nurse practitioner Maternal Health Svcs., Wilkes Barre, Pa.; assoc. prof. Wilkes U., Wilkes Barre; asst. prof. U. Del., coord. family nurse practitioner program. Author: Nurse Practitioners: A Review of the Literature. Recipient Del. C. of C. Superstar Educator of Yr., 1994; Pub. Health Svcs. Policy fellow, 1992. Mem. ANA, Nat. Alliance of Nurse Practitioners (mem. governing body 1990-94, chair 1994-95), Am. Acad. Nurse Practitioners (membership sec. 1987-90, pres. 1990-92, Outstanding Leadership and Svc. award 1994, State award for excellence 1995), Pa. Nurses Assn., Primary Health Care Nurse Practitioners N.E. Pa., Sigma Theta Tau. Home: Box 374 Grouse Hill Dalton PA 18414 Office: U Del McDowell Hall Newark DE 19716

SHEERAN, MICHAEL JOHN LEO, priest, college administrator; b. N.Y.C., Jan. 24, 1940; s. Leo John and Glenna Marie (Wright) S. AB, St. Louis U., 1963, PhL, 1964, AM in Polit. Sci., 1967, AM in Theology, 1971, STL, 1971; PhD, Princeton U., 1977. Joined Soc. Jesus, 1957; ordained priest Roman Catholic Ch., 1970. Exec. editor Catholic Mind, N.Y.C., 1971-72; assoc. editor Am. mag., N.Y.C., 1971-72; assoc. chaplain Aquinas Inst., Princeton, N.J., 1972-75; asst. dean Regis U., Denver, 1975-77, dean of Coll., 1977-82, v.p. acad. affairs, 1982-92, acting pres., 1987-88, pres., 1993—; retreat dir., cons. on governance for religious communities, 1970—. Author: Beyond Majority Rule, 1984. Contbr. articles and editorials to publs. Trustee Rockhurst Coll., Kansas City, Mo., 1982-91, Creighton U., Omaha, 1985-95, U. San Francisco, 1985-94, Loyola U., New Orleans, 1994-96, Rocky Mountain Coll. of Art and Design, 1994—; active Mile High United Way, 1995—. Ford Found. scholar, 1963. Democrat. Home: 3333 Regis Blvd Denver CO 80221-1099 Office: Regis U 3333 Regis Blvd Denver CO 80221-1154

SHEERAN, THOMAS JOSEPH, education educator, writer, consultant, judge; b. N.Y.C., Feb. 24, 1947; s. John Joseph and Dorothy (McAdams) S.; m. Maureen Elizabeth Flynn, June 27, 1970; children: Meaghan, Brendan. BS, Ithaca (N.Y.) Coll., 1968, MS, 1969; MEd, Niagara U., 1976; EdD, SUNY, Buffalo, 1976. Cert. tchr., N.Y. Teaching asst. Ithaca Coll., 1968-69; instr. Niagara U., Lewiston, N.Y., 1969-81, men's swimming coach, 1969-80, asst. prof., 1969—, women's swimming coach, 1969-74; prof., 1980—; chmn. dept. phys. edn. Niagara U., Lewiston, N.Y., 1980-82, chmn. dept. edn., 1988-91; tchr. Niagara U. Campus Sch., Lewiston, 1969-81; cons. various colls. and high schs., 1984-90. Mem. water safety com. ARC, Niagara Falls, N.Y., 1970-81; mem. planning bd. Town of Lewiston, 1982-84, zoning bd., 1986-92; mem. zoning bd. Town Justice, 1992—. Fellow Am. Coll. Sports Medicine; mem. ASCD, Am. Alliance Health and Phys. Edn. (rsch. fellow), Assn. Tchr. of Edn., N.Y. Assn. Coll. Tchr. Edn. (pres. 1992-93), N.Y. Magistrates Assn., Niagara County Magistrates Assn. (sec.), Niagara Falls Tchrs. Ctr. (policy bd. 1993—), N.Y. State Tchr. Edn. Cert. and Practices Bd., Am. Assn. Coll. Tchrs. Edn. (state rep. 1992-93), Niagara Falls Country Club (bd. govs., v.p.), Phi Delta Kappa, Pi Lambda Theta. Democrat. Roman Catholic. Avocations: golf, tennis. Home: 5230 Hewitt Pky Lewiston NY 14092-1923 Office: Niagara U Dept Edn Niagara Falls NY 14109

SHEERR, DEIRDRE MCCRYSTAL, architectural firm executive; m. Clinton Jay Sheerr. BA, Monmouth Coll., 1969; MArch, U. Colo., 1978; MA in Counseling Psychology, Antioch U., 1995. Registered architect, N.H., Colo. Computer systems and program analyst, 1970-75; pres. McCrystal Design & Devel., Inc., Denver, 1976-83; ptnr., head housing divsn. Sheerr & McCrystal, Inc., New London, N.H., 1983—; instr. passive solar design Denver Free U.; cons. solar and low income housing design Capitol Hill Architects and Planners; solar cons. Bros. Redevelopment, Inc. Prin. works include Lawrence Berkeley (Calif.) Lab., Solar Homestead, Boulder, Colo. (Nat. Passive Solar Design award HUD), 1515 South Pearl St., Curtis Pk. Face Block Renovation Project, Denver (Nat. Honor award AIA), St. Paul's Episcopal Ch. (Archtl. award Gov.'s Commn. Handicapped 1987). Mem. pres.'s adv. coun. Colby Sawyer Coll., 1987-91; mem. fundraising com. Ausbon Sargent Land Preservation Trust, 1989—; co-chair ski-a-thon, 1990—, trustee, 1991—; bd. dirs. 1992—, vice-chmn. 1996—; mem. affordable housing task force charrette for City of Laconia, N.H. Housing Authority, 1989; mem. bus. adv. coun. Town of New London, 1990—; life mem. Upper Valley Humane Soc.; active Nature Conservancy, Wilderness Soc., Greenpeace, Connecticut River Watershed Coun., Sierra Club, Nat. Audubon Soc. Recipient Main St. Comml. Beautification award New London Garden Club, Best Restoration of Yr. award Denver Mag., 1983, Heritage Concord Grand award 1994; Nat. Hist. Preservation grantee Sec. of Interior, 1980. Mem. AIA (bd. dirs. N.H. chpt. 1984-89, sec. 1985, pres.-elect 1986, pres. 1987, immediate past pres. 1988, mem. exec. bd. New Eng. regional coun., 1986-87, spkr. N.W. regional conf., Denver Housing Authority Law Income Housing Design co-winner 1976, Western Regional Merit award 1981, 11 awards for Excellence in Architecture N.H. chpt. 1983, 85, 86, 88, 90, 91, 92, 93, 94, 95, Nat. Honor award 1983), Nat. Trust Hist. Preservation, Nat. Pks. and Conservation Assn., Homebuilder's Assn. N.H. (SAM Silver award), N.H. Hist. Soc., Boston Computer Soc., New London Hist. Soc., Urban Design Forum, Appalachian Mountain Club. Office: Sheerr & McCrystal Inc PO Box 1500 177 Main St New London NH 03257-4551*

SHEETS, HERMAN ERNEST, marine engineer; b. Dresden, Germany, Dec. 24, 1908; s. Arthur Chitz and Gertrude (Stern) S.; m. Norma Sams, Oct. 17, 1942 (dec. Dec. 1970); m. Paulann Hosler, May 29, 1982; children: Lawrence S., Michael R., Arne H., Diana E., Elizabeth J., Karn N. M.E., U. Dresden, 1934; Dr. Tech. Scis. in Applied Mechanics, U. Prague, Czechoslovakia, 1936. Engr. Prvni Brněnska Strojima, Brno, 1936-39; Chief engr. Chamberlin Research Corp., East Moline, Ill., 1939-42; mgr. research St. Paul Engring. & Mfg. Co., 1942- 44; project engr. Elliott Co., Jeannette, Pa., 1944-46; engring. mgr. Goodyear Aircraft Corp., Akron, Ohio, 1946-53; v.p. Electric Boat div. Gen. Dynamics Corp., Groton, Conn., 1953-69; v.p. engring, and research; prof. dept. ocean engring. U. R.I., Kingston, 1969-80, dept. chmn., 1971-79; dir. engring. Analysis and Tech., North Stonington, Conn., 1979-84; cons. engr. Groton, 1980—. Author numerous articles in field. Recipient citation sec. war. Fellow AIAA (asso.), ASME, AAAS; mem. N.Y. Acad. Scis., Nat. Acad. Engring., Soc. Naval Architects and Marine Engrs., Am. Soc. Naval Engrs., Marine Tech. Soc., Pi Tau Sigma. Home and Office: Mumford Cove 87 Neptune Dr Groton CT 06340-5421

SHEETS, JOHN WESLEY, JR., research scientist; b. Jacksonville, Fla., Sept. 17, 1953; s. John Wesley and Alice Marie (Hagen) S.; m. Robin Adair Ritchie, June 27, 1987; 1 child, Camille Barbara. BS in Zoology, U. Fla., 1975, MS in Materials Sci., 1978, PhD in Materials Sci., 1983. Grad. rsch. asst. U. Fla., Gainesville, 1976-78, grad. rsch. assoc., 1978-82; biomaterials engr. Intermedics Intraocular, Pasadena, Calif., 1982-84, mgr. biomaterials rsch., 1984-87; dir. rsch. Pharmacia Ophthalmics, Pasadena, 1987-88; dir. new product and process devel. IOLAB Corp. Johnson & Johnson, Claremont, Calif., 1988-94; sr. dir. devel. Alcon Labs., Ft. Worth, 1994—; lectr. Calif. State Poly. U., Pomona, 1984; evaluator, chmn. subcom. Am. Nat. Standards Inst. Z80.7, Accreditation Bd. for Engring. and Tech.; instr. U. North Tex. Health Sci. Ctr., 1996. Contbr. articles to profl. jours. Mem. AAAS, Accreditation Bd. for Engring. and Technology, Am. Chem. Soc., Soc. Plastics Engrs., The Materials Soc., Soc. Biomaterials, Mensa, Sigma Xi, Tau Beta Pi, Alpha Sigma Mu. Avocations: weight training, swimming, cooking, backpacking. Home: 4001 Sarita Dr Fort Worth TX 76109-4740 Office: Alcon Labs 6201 S Freeway R5-12 Fort Worth TX 76134 *Personal philosophy: Build from basics: strength and personal integrity. Challenge the obvious and trivial solutions. Continuously seek improvements.*

SHEETZ, MICHAEL PATRICK, cell biology educator; b. Hershey, Pa., Dec. 11, 1946; s. David Patrick and Mary Patricia (Blumer) S.; m. Katherine Elliott, Jan. 25, 1968; children: Jonathon Patrick, Jennifer Mikaere, Courtney Elizabeth. BA, Albion Coll., 1968; PhD in Chemistry, Calif. Inst. Tech., 1972. Postdoctoral rsch. fellow U. Calif., San Diego, 1972-74; asst. prof. cell biology dept. physiology U. Conn. Health Ctr., Farmington, 1974-79, assoc. prof., 1980-85; prof. dept. cell biology and physiology Sch. Medicine, Washington U., St. Louis, 1985-90; prof., chmn. dept. cell biology Med. Sch., Duke U., Durham, N.C., 1990—; presenter profl. confs. Contbr. chpt. to Erythrocyte Mechanics and Blood Flow, 1980; co-contbr. chpt. to The Red Cell, 1978, Motility in Cell Function, 1979, White Blood Cell Mechanics, 1984, The Cytoskeleton, 1985, Protein-Membrane Interactions, Current Topics in Membranes and Transport, Vol. 36, 1989; co-contbr. chpts. to Cell Movement, Vol. 2, 1988; contbr. articles to sci. jours. Established investigator Am. Heart Assn., 1981-86. NIH trainee, 1969-72; Dernham jr. fellow Calif. div. Am. Cancer Soc., 1973-74. Office: Duke U Med Ctr Dept Cell Bi PO Box 3079 Durham NC 27710*

SHEETZ, RICHARD LATRELLE, retired association executive; b. Macon, Mo., Aug. 10, 1906; s. Robert Karl and Lena M. (Fetter) S.; m. Aagot Velline, Aug. 12, 1939; children: Robert K., Susan S. Laitsch, Timothy R.; stepchildren: Ferne D. Holmes, Harold S. Austin, Geraldine M. Beck. A.B., Westminster Coll., 1928. Asst. sales mgr. Lowe and Campbell Athletic Goods Co., Kansas City, Mo., 1928-33; officer mgr., campaign asst. Kansas City Charities Fund, 1933-36; exec. dir. N.D. Community Chest, Fargo, 1936-39, Tex. Community Chest and Planning Council, Austin, 1939-43, Va. United Communities Fund, Norfolk, 1943-71, The Norfolk Found.-Community Trust, 1971-86; ret., 1986; pres. S.E. region Community Chests and Councils of Am., 1948-49, Va. Fedn., 1949-59; nat. bd. dirs. Community Chests and Councils of Am., 1953-59. Author: Savannah, Georgia, A Study of Community Organization, 1950. Named Mr. Citizen of his generation Norfolk Union Labor Council, 1971; recipient citation for outstanding service City of Norfolk, 1970, Golden Legion award Westminster Coll., 1978. Mem. Nat. Conf. Social Welfare, Beta Theta Pi. Club: Virginia. Home: 2545 Murray Ave Norfolk VA 23518-4521

SHEETZ, STANTON R., retail executive. Student, Bentley Coll. With Colt Industries, 1977-81; CEO Sheetz Inc., 1981—. Office: 5700 6th Ave Altoona PA 16602-1111*

SHEFFEL, IRVING EUGENE, psychiatric institution executive; b. Chgo., July 5, 1916; s. Joseph and Jennie (Leibson) S.; m. Beth Silver, Aug. 2, 1942 (dec.); 1 child, Anita (dec.); m. Peggy Shelton, Apr. 6, 1996. A.B., U. Chgo., 1939; M.P.A., Harvard U., 1946; LHD (hon.), Washburn U., 1987. Insp., wage and hour div. Dept. Labor, Chgo., 1940-41; mgmt. and budget analyst VA, Washington, 1946-48; budget analyst U.S. Bur. of Budget, Washington, 1948-49; controller, treas. Menninger Found., Topeka, 1949-73; v.p. Menninger Found., 1973-93, v.p. emeritus, 1993—; instr. Menninger Sch. Psychiatry. Bd. dirs. Washburn U. Art Center, 1969—, pres., 1971-73; treas. Karl Menninger lect. series, 1983—. Served to maj. U.S. Army, 1942-45. Fellow Assn. Mental Health Adminstrs. (charter); mem. Am. Soc. Public Adminstrn. (charter), Topeka Opera Soc. (treas. 1985—). Jewish. Home: 1215 SW 29th Ter Topeka KS 66611-2192 Office: PO Box 829 Topeka KS 66601-0829

SHEFFIELD, GARY ANTONIAN, professional baseball player; b. Tampa, Fla., Nov. 18, 1968. Player Milw. Brewers, 1986-92, San Diego Padres, 1992-93, Florida Marlins, 1993—. mem. Nat. League All-Star Team, 1992-93, 96; Sporting News Player of the Year, 1992; Sporting News All-Star Team, 1992; recipient Silver Slugger award, 1992; named Minor League Co-Player of the Yr. Sporting News, 1988, Comeback Player of Yr., Sporting News, 1992. Nat. Batting League Champion, 1992. Office: Fla Marlins 2267 NW 199th St Miami FL 33056*

SHEFFIELD, LESLIE FLOYD, retired agricultural educator; b. Orafino, Nebr., Apr. 13, 1925; s. Floyd L. and Edith A. (Presler) S.; BS with high distinction in Agronomy, U. Nebr., 1950, MS, 1964; postgrad. U. Minn., summer 1965; PhD, U. Nebr., 1971; m. Doris Fay Fenimore, Aug. 20, 1947; children: Larry Wayne, Linda Faye (Mrs. Bernard Eric Hempelman), Susan Elaine (Mrs. Randy Thorman). County extension agt. Lexington and Schuyler, Nebr., 1951-52; exec. sec. Nebr. Grain Improvement Assn., 1952-56; chief Nebr. Wheat Commn., Lincoln, 1956-59; exec. sec. Great Plains Wheat, Inc., market devel., Garden City, Kans., 1959-61; asst. to dean Coll. Agr., U. Nebr. at Lincoln, 1961-66, supt. North Platte Expt. Sta., 1966-71, asst. dir. Nebr. Coop. Extension Service, Nebr. Agrl. Expt. Sta., Lincoln, 1971-75, asst. to vice chancellor Inst. Agr. and Natural Resources, 1975-84, also extension farm mgmt. specialist and assoc. prof. agrl. econs., 1975-94; ret. U. Nebr., Lincoln, 1994. v.p. U. Nebr. Found., 1982-86; sec.-treas. Circle 4S-L Acres, Wallace, Nebr., 1973-87; cons. econs. of irrigation in N.D., Minn., S.D. and Brazil, 1975, 88, Sudan, Kuwait and Iran, 1976, People's Republic of China, 1977, 81, Can., 1977, 78, 79, 80, Mex., 1978, 79, Argentina, 1978, Hong Kong, 1981, Japan, 1981, Republic of South Africa, 1985, Argentina, Brazil and Paraguay, 1992, Australia, 1994, New Zealand, 1994. Author: Economic Impact of Irrigated Agriculture, 1985; co-author: Flat Water-A History of Nebraska and Its Water, 1993; author chpt. to book; editor: Procs. of Nebr. Water Resources and Irrigation Devel. for 1970's, 1972; contbg. editor Irrigation Age Mag., St. Paul, 1974-86; contbr. articles to various publs. With U.S. Army, 1944-46; ETO. Recipient Hon. State Farmer award Future Farmers Am., 1955, Hon. Chpt. Farmer award, North Platte chpt., 1973; fellowship grad. award Chgo. Bd. Trade, 1964, Agrl. Achievement award Ak-Sar-Ben, 1969, Citizen award U.S. Dept. Interior Bur. Reclamation, 1984; Pub. Svc. award for contbns. to Nebr. agr. Nebr. Agribus. Club, 1984, Ditch Rider award Four States Irrigation Coun., 1988, Disting. Svc. award Am. Soc. Farm Mgrs. & Rural Appraisers Nebr. chpt., 1993, Alumnus of Yr. award U. Nebr.-Lincoln Coll. Agr. & Natural Resources Alumni Assn., 1993, Headgate award Four States Irrigation Coun., 1995, Pioneer Irrigation award Nebr. Water Conf. Coun. and U. Nebr. Lincoln, 1995 ; NASA Rsch. grantee, 1972-77; inducted Nebr. Hall of Agrl. Achievement, 1988; named Irrigation Man of Yr. Irrigation Assn., 1988; honoree Disting. Svc. Nebr. Hall Agrl. Achievement, 1996, Silver Eagle award Nebr. Farm Bur. Fedn., 1996. Mem. Am. Agrl. Econs. Assn., Am., Nat., Nebr. Water Resources Assns. (Pres.'s award 1979, award for Commitment to Irrigated Agriculture 1993, bd. dirs. 1995—), Nebr. Irrigation Assn., Nebr. Assn. Resource Dists., Am. Soc. Farm Mgrs. Rural Appraisers, Orgn. Profl. Employees of U.S. Dept. Agr., Lincoln C. of C. (chmn. agrl. com. 1974-77), Rotary (dir. 1965-66), Gamma Sigma Delta, Alpha Zeta (v.p. Nebr. agrl. rels. coun., 1993-94). Home: 3800 Loveland Dr Lincoln NE 68506-3842

SHEFFLER, DUDLEY, telecommunications industry executive. CEO Reltec Corp., Cleve. Office: Reliance Comm/Tec Corp 6065 Parkland Blvd Cleveland OH 44124-4186 Office: Reltec 5875 Landerbrook Dr Ste 250 Cleveland OH 44124-4069*

SHEFLIN, MICHAEL JOHN EDWARD, environment and transportation official; b. Toronto, Ont., Can., Dec. 27, 1938; s. John Edward and Marguerite Christine (MacKinnon) S.; m. Elizabeth Anne Taylor, Apr. 19, 1965; children: Sydney Michelle Taylor, Siobahn Morgan Taylor. Diploma in engring., St. Francis Xavier U., Antigonish, N.S., 1959; B of Civil Engring., Tech. U. N.S., 1962; diploma, Banff Sch. Advanced Mgmt., Alta., 1972. Engr. USAF, Harmon AFB, 1962-65; town mgr. Town of Stephenville, Nfld., 1965-66; sr. engr. ops. City of St. Catharines, Ont., 1966-70; dir. engring. and works City of Halifax, N.S., 1970-75; transp. commr. Regional Municipality of Ottawa-Carleton, Ont., 1975-95; environ. and transp. commr. Regional Municipality of Ottawa-Carleton, Ont., 1995—; gov. Internat. Pub. Works Fedn., Washington, 1989-92; eminent overseas speaker Instn. of Engrs., Canberra, Australia, 1989. Co-author: Management of Local Public Works, 1986; contbr. articles to jours. V.p. Liberal Party of Nfld., Stephenville, 1966; chmn. Econ. Affairs, Jaycees, Can., 1966, 67, Niagara Regional Sci. Fair, St. Catharines, 1969, United Way City of Halifax, 1973. Fellow Inst. Transp. Engrs. (Outstanding Svc. award 1991); mem. Internat. Fedn. Mcpl. Engrs. (life mem. Oslo, 1st v.p. 1991-94, 2d v.p. 1985-88, pres. 1988-91), Transp. Assn. Can. (v.p. 1989, treas. 1990-93, award of merit 1991, hon. life mem. Calgary), Inst. Mcpl. Engrs. (pres. 1976-77, hon. mem.), Am. Pub. Works Assn (Leader of Yr. 1981). Avocations: history, traveling, walking. Home: 35 3d Ave, Ottawa, ON Canada K15 2J5 Office: Regional Municipality, 111 Lisgar St Cartier Sq, Ottawa, ON Canada K2P 2L7

SHEFTEL, ROGER TERRY, merchant banking executive; b. Denver, Sept. 10, 1941; s. Edward and Dorothy (Barnett) S.; m. Phoebe A. Sherman, Sept. 7, 1968; children: Tisha B., Ryan B. BS in Econs., U. Pa., 1963. Comml. lending officer Provident Nat. Bank, Phila., 1963-65; asst. to pres. Continental Finance Corp., Denver, 1965-68; v.p. Eastern Indsl. Leasing Corp., Phila., 1968-71, exec. v.p., dir., 1971-73; exec. v.p., dir. HBE Leasing Corp., Phila., 1971-73; dir. Kooly Kupp, Inc., Boyertown, Pa., 1974-77, pres., dir., 1977; prin. Trivest, Phila., 1973-77; pres. Trivest, Inc., Phila., 1977-78, 1670 Corp., mgmt. cons.'s, 1978-82; pres. Am. Cons. Group, Inc., 1982-83; exec. v.p., dir. Argus Rsch. Labs., Inc., 1982-83; pres. Leasing Concepts, Inc., 1983-87, Brice Capital Corp., 1987-92; pres. Rhodes Fin., Inc., 1992—. Mem. Nantucket Yacht Club, Friars Club, Rotary. Home: 414 Barclay Rd Bryn Mawr PA 19010-1218 Office: Rhodes Fin Inc PO Box 7338 Saint Davids PA 19087-7338

SHEFTELL, FRED DAVID, psychiatrist, educator, writer; b. N.Y.C., Jan. 4, 1941; s. Joseph and Wilma Elizabeth (Schwartz) S.; m. Karen Ruth Rosenthal, June 13, 1942; children: Lauren Gale, Jason Howard. AB, NYU, 1962, MD, 1966. Diplomate Am. Bd. Psychiatry and Neurology. Resident N.Y. Med. Coll., N.Y.C., 1967-69; chief resident Met. Hosp., N.Y.C., 1969-70; med. dir. Drug Liberation Program, Stamford, Conn., 1972-79; clin. asst. prof. N.Y. Med. Coll., Valhalla, N.Y., 1972—; founder New Eng. Ctr. for Headache, Stamford, 1979—; clin. chief CMHC, Stamford, 1972-79; spkr. in field. Author 5 books on headache; contbr. articles on headache to profl. jours. Maj. U.S. Army, 1970-72. Decorated Army Commendation medal; recipient United Way Silver award, 1989; named on of Best Doctors in Am., Woodward & White, 1993. Mem. Am. Psychiat. Assn., Am. Assn. Study of Headache (program dir. 1988, bd. dirs.), Am. Pain Soc., Am. Coun. Headache Edn. (nat. pres. 1994—), Conn. State Med. Soc., Fairfield County Med. Soc. Avocations: playing and writing music, photography. Office: New Eng Ctr for Headache 9778 Longridge Ridge Rd Stamford CT 06902-1251

SHEFTMAN, HOWARD STEPHEN, lawyer; b. Columbia, S.C., May 20, 1949; s. Nathan and Rena Mae (Kantor) S.; m. Sylvia Elaine Williams, Nov. 30, 1974; children: Amanda Elaine, Emily Catherine. BS in Bus. Adminstrn., U. S.C., 1971, JD, 1974. Bar: S.C. 1974, U.S. Dist. Ct. 1975, U.S. Ct. Appeals (4th cir.) 1982. Assoc. Kirkland, Taylor & Wilson, West Columbia, S.C., 1974-75; ptnr. Sheftman, Oswald & Holland, West Columbia, 1975-77, Finkel & Altman, LLC, Columbia, 1977—. Mem. S.C. Bar Assn. (practice and procedure com. 1978—), S.C. Trial Lawyers Assn. (chmn. domestic rels. sect. 1982-83, bd. govs. 1987-93, 94—), Richland Bar Assn., Met. Sertoma Club (pres. 1986-87). Jewish. Office: Finkel & Altman LLC PO Box 1799 Columbia SC 29202-1799

SHEH, ROBERT BARDHYL, environmental management company executive; b. N.Y.C., July 29, 1939; s. Talat and Nedime (Karali) S.; m. Mary Cheney Fleming, Dec. 29, 1961; children—Andrea K., Jonathan C., Robert R., Elisabeth F., Theresa N. BS in Civil Engring, Rennselaer Poly. Inst., 1960; grad. program for Mgmt. Devel., Harvard U., 1974. With The Ralph M. Parsons Co., 1971—; sr. v.p., mgr. petroleum, chem., mining and metall. div. The Ralph M. Parsons Co., Pasadena, Calif., 1981-88, pres., 1989-92, also bd. dirs.; pres., CEO Internat. Tech. Corp., Torrance, Calif., 1992-96; mem. adv. bd. Sch. Chem. Engring., U. Calif., Berkeley, 1986—; bd. dirs. Davidson Assocs., 1993—; mem. adv. bd. Rensselaer Poly. Inst., 1995. Bd. regents Marymount Internat. Sch., London, 1979; bd. trustees Harvey Mudd Coll., 1992—. With USNR, 1960-64. Mem. Calif. Club (L.A.), Annandale Golf Club (Pasadena), L.A. Country Club.

SHEHADI, SAMEER IBRAHIM, plastic surgeon; b. Zahle, Lebanon, Mar. 3, 1931; came to U.S., 1984; s. Ibrahim A. and Mounira D. (Dumit) S.; m. Leila A. Nassif, June 18, 1960; children: Ramzi Richard, Kamal Sameer, Imad Edward. BA, Am. U. Beirut, 1952, MD, 1956. Diplomate Am. Bd. Surgery, Am. Bd. Plastic Surgery. Intern. Am. U. Hosp., Beirut, resident gen. surgery, 1956-59, chief resident gen. surgery, 1959-60; resident plastic surgery St. Louis U. Hosps., 1960-62; fellow hand surgery Pitts. U. Hosps., 1962; resident head and neck surgery Roswell Park Meml. Inst., Buffalo, N.Y., 1963; clin. asst. prof. Am. U. Beirut, 1963-79, clin. prof. surgery, 1979-84, chmn. dept. surgery, 1976-79, 81-84; prof., dir. div. plastic surgery St. Louis U., 1984—. Contbr. articles to profl. jours. Recipient Chevaliers award Order of the Cedars, Govt. Lebanon, 1968. Fellow ACS (gov. at large Lebanon chpt. 1981-84); mem. AMA, St. Louis Met. Med. Soc., St. Louis Surg. Soc., Mo. Med. Assn., Lebanese Order of Physicians, Am. U. Beirut Med. Alumni Assn., Am. Soc. Plastic and Reconstructive Surgeons, Am. Soc. Maxillofacial Surgeons, Am. Assn. Chmn. Plastic Surgery, Am. Assn. Plastic Surgeons, Am. Assn. Hand Surgeons, Lebanese Soc. Plastic and Reconstructive Surgeons (pres. 1974-84), Internat. Soc. Burn Injuries (Lebanon rep. 1968-84). Home: 12256 Ladue Woods Dr Saint Louis MO 63141-8159 Office: St Louis U Med Ctr PO Box 15250 Saint Louis MO 63110-0250

SHEHEEN, FRED ROUKOS, education agency administrator; b. Camden, S.C., July 7, 1936; s. Austin M. and Lucile (Roukos) S.; m. Rose Maria Serio, Nov. 26, 1966; children: Maria, Vincent, Margaret Rose. AB Polit. Sci., Duke U., 1958; postgrad., Harvard U., 1990; LLD (hon.), Claflin Coll., 1990; HHD, Lander Coll., 1992; AA honoris causa, Tech. Coll. Lowcountry, Beaufort, S.C., 1992. Bureau chief Charlotte (N.C.) Observer, Rock Hill, Columbia, S.C., 1958-63; press sec. to Gov. Donald Russell, Columbia, 1963-65; exec. asst. to Sen. Donald Russell, Washington, 1965-66; asst. to dir. S.C. State Devel. Bd., Columbia, 1967-68; v.p. & sec., pres. & publisher Banner Publishers Inc., Chronicle Publishers Inc., N.C., S.C., 1968-76; founder, pres., prin. owner Camden (S.C.) Co., 1976-87; commr. of higher edn. S.C. Commn. on Higher Edn., Columbia, 1987—; bd. dirs. S.C. Rsch. Authority, Columbia, 1983-86; mem. S.C. Commn. Human Affairs, 1971-72, S.C. Commn. Higher Edn., 1971-75, 79-86, (chmn. 1983-86), Edn. Improvement Act Selection com., 1983-86, Commn. Future S.C., Columbia, 1987-89. Contbr. chpt. to book, article to profl. jour. Pres. Kershaw County Mental Health Assn., Camden, S.C., 1971, 76; mem. S.C. Tuition Grants Commn., 1988—, Nat. Edn. Goals Panel task force Collegiate Attainment and Assessment, 1988—, S.C. Edn. Goals Panel, 1992—, So. Regional Coun. Coll. Bd., 1993—; adv. bd. Master Pub. Adminstrn. program U. S.C. Coll. Charleston, 1992—; trustee Springdale Sch., Camden, 1976-84, Boyland-Haven-Mather Acad., Camden, 1976-83, S.C. Gov's. Sch. Sci. and Mathematics, 1987—; bd. dirs. Kershaw County Cancer Soc. Recipient Sertoma Svc. to Mankind award Sertoma club, 1973; named Educator of Yr. S.C. Tech. Edn. Assn., 1990. Mem. State Higher Edn. Exec. Officers (exec. com. 1990—, Nat. Ctr. Edn. Statistics Network adv. com. 1990—), S.C. Agy. Dir's. Orgn. (pres. 1992). Roman Catholic. Avocations: racquetball, water sports, reading. Home: 2107 Washington Ln Camden SC 29020-1723 Office: SC Commn Higher Edn 1333 Main St Ste 200 Columbia SC 29201-3201

SHEIKH, SUNEEL ISMAIL, aerospace engineer, researcher; b. Bristol, Gloucester, Eng., Jan. 21, 1966; came to U.S., 1975, U.S. Citizen 1987; s. Hyder Ismail and Joan Mary (Duncan) S. BS in Aerospace Engring, Maths., U. Minn., 1988; MS in Aeronautics and Astronautics, Stanford U., 1990. Lic. pvt. pilot, U.S. Student intern Honeywell, Inc., Mpls., 1989-90; assoc. engr. Martin Marietta Corp., Denver, 1990-91; prin. rsch. scientist Honeywell, Inc., Mpls., 1991—; cons., engr. Honeywell, Inc., Mpls., 1991. Recipient Honorable Mention award NSF, 1988. Mem. AIAA, Inst. Navigation, Planetary Soc., Nat. Space Soc. Home: 1012 Thomas Ave S Minneapolis MN 55405-2113 Office: Honeywell Inc 3660 Technology Dr Minneapolis MN 55418-1006

SHEILS, DENIS FRANCIS, lawyer; b. Ridgewood, N.J., Apr. 7, 1961; s. Denis Francis and Anna Marie (Clifford) S.; m. Harriet A. Bonawitz, Sept. 17, 1988. BA, La Salle Coll., 1983; JD, Fordham U., 1986. Bar: N.Y. 1987, Pa. 1987, U.S. Dist. Ct. (ea. dist.) Pa. 1987, U.S. Ct. Appeals (3d cir.) 1987, U.S. Dist. Ct. (so. and ea. dists.) N.Y. 1992, U.S. Supreme Ct. 1994, U.S. Dist. Ct. (no. dist.) N.Y. 1997. Assoc. Kohn, Swift & Graf, P.C., Phila., 1987-97, shareholder, 1997—. Active Lower Makefield Twp. Cable TV Adv. Bd. Mem. ABA, N.Y. State Bar Assn., Phila. Bar Assn. Roman Catholic. Home: 2124 Ashley Rd Newtown PA 18940-3737 Office: Kohn Swift & Graf PC 2400 1 Reading Ctr 1101 Market St Philadelphia PA 19107-2934

SHEIN, JAY LESING, financial planner; b. Chgo., Jan. 27, 1951; s. Garrett Melchior and Evelyn (Blitt) Hamm; m. Val Margaret Rich, Dec. 14, 1984; children: Melissa Loree, Blair Charles, Christina Anne, Allison Marie, Lindsay Gayle. Student, Broward C.C., Davie, Fla., 1969-71; CFP, Coll. for Fin. Planning, Denver, 1990; MS in Taxation and Fin., LaSalle U., 1994, PhD, 1994. Tech. technician Broward County Sch. Bd., Ft. Lauderdale, Fla., 1973-76; owner, mgr. Bus. and Tax Consulting Firm, Ft. Lauderdale, 1976-83; dist. mgr. United Group and Group One, Ft. Lauderdale, 1983-84; from account exec. to v.p. Compass Fin. Group, Inc., Lighthouse Point, Fla., 1984-90; pres. Compass Fin. Group, Inc., Lighthouse Point, 1990—; adv. bd. devel. coun., mem. Highlands Christian Acad., Pompano Beach, Fla., 1992—; adj. prof. Nova Southeastern U. Grad. Sch. Bus., 1995-96; mem. adj. faculty Rollins Coll., 1996; adj. prof. La Salle U., 1994—, Nova Southeastern U. Sch. Bus., 1997—. Contbr. articles to newspapers and pubs. in field. Mem. Estate Planning Coun. of Broward County. Mem. Inst. CFP, Nat. Assn. Life Underwriters, Practising Law Inst. (assoc.), South Fla. Soc. of Inst. of CFPs (pres.-elect 1996, pres. 1997, edn. chmn. 1994, dir. ethics 1993-94), Broward County Assn. Life Underwriters (v.p. 1992-94), Greater Ft. Lauderdale Tax Coun., Marine Industries of South Fla. Republican. Baptist. Avocations: volleyball, racquetball, travel. Office: Compass Fin Group Inc 3050 N Federal Hwy Ste 208 Lighthouse Point FL 33064-6866

SHEINBAUM, GILBERT HAROLD, international management consultant; b. N.Y.C., Apr. 20, 1929; s. Herman and Selma (Klimberg) S.; m. Inger Fredebo Thomsen, Aug. 28, 1971; children: Neil, Britt. AB in History, NYU, 1950; postgrad., CUNY, 1954-55, New Sch. for Social Rsch., 1955-56. Various fgn. svc. posts Washington, Laos, France, Vietnam, 1957-68; polit. officer Am. Embassy, Copenhagen, 1968-72, U.S. Dept. of State, Washington, 1972-75; chargé d'affaires Am. Embassy, Antananarivo, Madagascar, 1975-77; dep. chief of mission Am. Embassy, Lilongwe, Malawi, 1977-79; Am. consul Am. Consulate, Cebu, Philippines, 1979-83; polit. counselor U.S. Mission to the UN, Geneva, 1983-86; dir. Colombo Plan (internat. orgn.), Colombo, Sri Lanka, 1986-91; assoc. Global Bus. Access, Ltd., Washington, 1991; cons. Nat. Security Edn. Program, Washington, 1992-95, Internat. Found. for Election Sys., Washington, 1995-96; internat. observor Sri Lankan elections, 1993, 94. Author and editor articles on econ. devel. in Asia. Co-founder, trustee George Keyt Cultural Found., Colombo, 1987-91; bd. chmn. Overseas Children's Sch., Colombo, 1987-90; commr. Boy Scouts Am., Geneva, 1984-86; stage mgr. Am. Light Opera Co., Washington, 1962-64. 1st lt. U.S. Army, 1951-53. Recipient Award of Recognition, Mindanao State U., Marawi, Philippines, 1983. Mem. Am. Fgn. Svc. Assn., World Affairs Coun. of Washingotn DC, World Affairs Coun. of No. Calif., Asia Soc., Vietnamese-Am. C. of C. (bd. dirs. 1992—), Diplomatic and Consular Officers Ret. (treas.). Avocations: tennis, jogging, touring, reading. Home: 407 East St NE Vienna VA 22180

SHEINBERG, ISRAEL, computer company executive; b. Fort Worth, Apr. 15, 1932; s. Samuel I. and Pauline C. (Fram) S.; m. Betty S. Topletz, Aug. 19, 1962; children—Amy, Karen, David, Paula. B.S. in Physics, U. Tex., 1953; student, UCLA, 1957-58, Arlington (Tex.) State Coll., 1960, Southwestern Med. Sch., 1961. Electronic engr. Hughes Aircraft Co., 1956-60, Nat. Data Processing Corp., 1961; also exec. v.p. and gen. mgr. European ops. Recognition Equipment Inc., 1961-90; pvt. cons. to industry Dallas, 1990—; bd. dirs. Tex. Commerce Bank, Balchem Corp.; mem. adv. coun. of engring. found., adv. coun. for natural scis. U. Tex., Austin; speaker on image technology, optical character recognition and related subjects. Contbr. articles to profl. jours. With AUS, 1954-56. Inducted into Assn. for Work Process Improvement Hall of Fame. Mem. Optical Soc. Am., Am. Mgmt. Assn. Jewish (bd. dirs. synagogue). Home: 5706 Watson Cir Dallas TX 75225-1653 Office: Sheinberg Assocs 5706 Watson Cir Dallas TX 75225-1653

SHEINBERG, SIDNEY JAY, producer, entertainment company executive; b. Corpus Christi, Tex., Jan. 14, 1935; s. Harry and Tillie (Grossman) S.; m. Lorraine Gottfried, Aug. 19, 1956; children: Jonathan J., William David. AB, Columbia Coll., 1955; LLB, Columbia U., 1958. Bar: Calif. 1958. Assoc. in law UCLA Sch. Law, 1958-59; with MCA, Inc., Universal City, Calif., 1959-95, pres. TV divsn., 1971-74, corp. exec. v.p., 1969-73, corp. pres., COO, 1973-95; ptnr. The Bubble Factory, Beverly Hills, CA, 1995—. Bd. dirs. Simon Wiesenthal Ctr., Human Rights Watch, Mus. TV and Radio, NCCJ, Am. Jewish Com. Mem. Assn. Motion Picture and Television Producers (chmn. bd.). Office: The Bubble Factory 8840 Wilshire Blvd Beverly Hills CA 90211-2606

SHEINFELD, DAVID, composer; b. St. Louis, Sept. 20, 1906; s. Joseph and Feige (Sandler) S.; m. Dorothy Jaffe, Apr. 12, 1942; children: Daniel, Paul. MusB, Am. Conservatory Music, Chgo., 1929; studies with Ottorino Respighi, Santa Cecilia Acad., Rome, 1929-31. Violinist, arranger various radio programs, Chgo., 1934-40; violist Pitts. Symphony, 1944-45; violinist San Francisco Symphony, 1945-71; ind. composer, tchr. San Francisco, 1971—. Composer orchestral and chamber music works including Adagio and Allegro, 1947, Patterns, 1962, Dualities, 1981, Dreams and Fantasies, 1982; commd. to compose work for San Francisco Symphony Assn. Orch.'s 60th anniversary, 1971 (Recipient Norman Fromm award for chamber music composition 1979), 2d string quartet Kronos Quartet, 1990; compositions performed by symphony orchs. in San Francisco, Chgo., Pitts., Phila., Phila. Chamber Symphony, chamber music performed, numerous cities in U.S., Can., Eng. Recipient Composer's award AAAL, 1993, award Koussevitzky Music Found., 1993; NEA grantee for orch. work, 1987-88. Mem. Broadcast Music, Inc. Avocations: astronomy, physics. Home and Office: 1458 24th Ave San Francisco CA 94122-3312 *Respect for the rights of others; respect for our cultural achievements and ideals; respect for the art of music; these principles have guided my life.*

SHEINFELD, MYRON M., lawyer, educator; b. Mass., Mar. 18, 1930; s. Robert and Sadye (Rosenberg) S.; m. Christina Trzcinski, Mar. 30, 1985; children: Scott, Tom. BA, Tulane U., 1951; JD, U. Mich., 1954. Bar: Mich. 1954, Tex. 1956. Researcher Legis. Research Inst. U. Mich., 1954; asst. U.S. atty. So. Dist. Tex., 1958-60; law clk. U.S. Dist. Judge, 1960-61; ptnr. Strickland, Gordon & Sheinfeld, Houston, 1961-68, Shareholder, Sheinfeld, Maley & Kay, P.C., Houston, 1968—; adj. prof. law U. Tex.; mem. Nat. Bankruptcy Conf.; chmn. Tex. Bankruptcy Adv. Commn.; bd. dirs. Nabors Industries, Third Ave. Value Fund, Inc., Am. Coll. Bankruptcy, v.p.. Bd. editors Practical Lawyer; contbr. articles to profl. jours. With JAG U.S. Army, 1955-58. Fellow Am. Coll. Bankruptcy; mem. State Bar Tex., Houston Ctr. Club (bd. dirs.), Ramada Tejas Club, Phi Beta Kappa, Phi Sigma Alpha. Office: Sheinfeld Maley & Kay PC 1001 Fannin St Ste 3700 Houston TX 77002-6797

SHEINGOLD, DANIEL H., electrical engineer; b. Boston, Sept. 26, 1928; s. Louis S. and Elsie (Frank) S.; m. Ann Silverman, Aug. 2, 1953 (dec. Feb. 1995); children: Mark J., Laura R. BSEE with distinction, Worcester Poly. Inst., 1948; MSEE, Columbia U., 1949. Engr. George A. Philbrick Rschs. Inc., Boston, 1949-55, application engring. mgr., 1957-63; v.p. George A. Philbrick Researches, Inc., Dedham, Mass., 1964-67; staff cons. Teledyne Philbrick, Dedham, 1967-68; tech. mktg. mgr. Analog Devices, Inc., Norwood, Mass., 1969—. Editor: Analog-Digital Conversion Handbook, 1972, 3d edit., 1986, Nonlinear Circuits Handbook, 1974, Transducer Interfacing Handbook, 1980; editor Analog Dialogue jour., 1969—, others. With AUS, 1955-57. Fellow IEEE; mem. IEEE Instrumentation and Measurement Soc. (sec.-treas. 1976, v.p. 1977, pres. 1978), AAAS. Jewish. Avocations: music, walking, crosscountry skiing, reading. Office: Analog Devices Inc PO Box 9106 3 Technology Way Norwood MA 02062-9106

SHEININ, ROSE, biochemist, educator; b. Toronto, Ont., Can., May 18, 1930; d. Harry and Anne (Szyber) Shuber; BA, U. Toronto, 1951, MA (scholar), 1953, PhD in Biochemistry, 1956, L.H.D., 1985; DHL (hon.), Mt. St. Vincent U., 1985; DSc (hon.) Acadia U., 1987, DSc (hon.) U. Guelph, 1991; m. Joseph Sheinin, July 15, 1951; children—David Matthew Khazanov, Lisa Basya Judith, Rachel Sarah Rebecca. Demonstrator in biochemistry U. Toronto (Ont., Can.), 1951-53, asst. prof. microbiology, 1964-75, asst. prof. med. biophysics, 1967-75, prof. microbiology, 1975-90, prof. med. biophysics, 1978-90, assoc. prof. med. biophysics, 1975-78, chmn. microbiology and parasitology, 1975-82, vice dean Sch. Grad. Studies, 1984-89; vice-rector acad., Concordia U., Montreal, Que., Can., 1989-94, prof. dept. biology, 1989—; mem. Health Scis. Com.; vis. rsch. assoc. chem. microbiology, Cambridge U., 1956-57, Nat. Inst. Med. Rsch., London, 1957-58; rsch. assoc. fellow div. biol. research Ont. Cancer Inst., 1958-67; sci. officer cancer grants panel Med. Research Council Can.; mem. Can. Sci. Del. to People's Republic of China, 1973; mem. adv. com. Provincial Lottery Health Research Awards; mem. adv. com. on biotech. NRC Can., 1984-87; mem. Sci. Council Can., 1984-87; adv. com. on sci. and tech. CBC, 1980-85; mem. bd. dirs. Can. Bacterial Disease Network, 1989-94; vis. prof. biochemistry U. Alta., 1971. Nat. Cancer Inst. Can. fellow, 1953-56, 58-61; Brit. Empire Cancer Campaign fellow, 1956-58; Recipient Queen's Silver Jubilee medal, 1978, Woman of Distinction award Health and Edn., YWCA, 1988; Josiah Macy Jr. Faculty scholar, 1981-82; fellow Ligue Contre le Cancer, France, 1981-82, Massey Coll. U. Toronto, 1981—, continuing sr. fellow, 1994—; hon. fellow Ryerson Polytech. U., 1993. Fellow Am. Acad. Microbiology, fellow Royal Soc. Can. (chair women in scholarship com. 1990-93); mem. Can. Biochem. Soc. (pres. 1974-75), Can. Soc. Cell Biology (pres. 1975-76), Am. Soc. Virology, Am. Soc. Microbiologists, Canadian Assn. Women in Sci., Internat. Assn. Women Bioscientists, Sigma Xi Rsch. Soc., Scitech, Soc. Complex Carbohydrates, Toronto Biochem. and Biophys. Soc. (pres. 1960-70, council 1970-74). Assoc. editor Can. Jour. Biochemistry, 1968-71, Virology, 1969-72, Intervirology, 1974-85; editorial bd. Microbiol. Revs., 1977-80; author, co-author various publs. Office: Concordia U Dept Biology, 1455 de Maisonneuve Rm H-1207-1, Montreal, PQ Canada H3G 1M8

SHEINKMAN, JACK, union official, lawyer; b. N.Y.C., Dec. 6, 1926; s. Shaia and Bertha (Rosenkrantz) S.; m. Betty Francis Johnson, May 31, 1954; children: Michael, Joshua, Mark. B.S., Cornell U., 1948, LL.B., 1952; cert. in econs., Oxford U., 1949. Bar: N.Y. 1952. Atty. NLRB, Washington, 1952-53; atty. Amalgamated Clothing Workers Am., N.Y.C., 1953-58, gen. counsel, 1958-72, v.p., 1968-72, sec.-treas., 1972-76; sec.-treas. Amalgamated Clothing and Textile Workers Union, N.Y.C., 1976-87, pres., 1987-95, pres. emeritus, 1995—; chmn. bd. Amalgamated Bank of N.Y.; mem. exec. coun., v.p. AFL-CIO, 1987-95; mem. indsl. union dept. Internat. Textile, Garment and Leather Workers Fedn., Brussels, 1972-95. Dir. internat. rescue com. N.Y. Hist. Soc.; bd. dirs. Martin Luther King Jr. Inst., Economists Allied Against Arts; vice chmn. Coun. Competitiveness United Housing Found.; trustee Aspen Inst.; mem. Pres.'s Adv. Com. on Trade Policy Negotiations, 1987-95; trustee emeritus Cornell U. Lt. (j.g.) USNR, 1944-46, PTO. Mem. Workers Def. League (dir.), Am. Arbitration Assn. (dir.) Coun. Fgn. Rels., UN Assn. U.S.A. (bd. govs.), Brit.-N.Am. Com. (exec. com.), Nat. Planning Com. (exec. com.). Democrat. Jewish. Home: 52 W 76th St New York NY 10023-1517 Office: Amalgamated Bank NY 11 Union Sq W # 15 New York NY 10003-3316

SHEINMAN, MORTON MAXWELL, editor, consultant, writer, photographer; b. N.Y.C., Oct. 7, 1933; s. Irving and Mollie (Feigenblatt) S.; m. Claire Rosenfeld, Aug. 27, 1967 (div.). BA in English, CCNY, 1954. Sports tabulator New York Daily News, 1956-58; reporter Women's Wear Daily, N.Y.C., 1960-69, news editor, 1970-71, mng. editor, 1971—; mng. editor W Mag., N.Y.C., 1972-82, assoc. editor, 1982—; cons., writer ATT Summer Olympics Exhibit, L.A., 1984, Cafe Concepts, N.Y.C., 1989—, Pru Ctr. Observatory, Boston, 1995; cons. Med. Mktg. Detailing, N.Y.C., 1990—. Contbr. articles and photographs to various publs. including Diverson mag., 1979—. With U.S. Army, 1954-56. Mem. Nat. ARts Club, CCNY Comm. Alumni. Home: 60 Gramercy Park N New York NY 10010-5423 Office: Women's Wear Daily 7 W 34th St New York NY 10001-8100

SHEKHAR, STEPHEN S., obstetrician, gynecologist; b. New Delhi, India, Jan. 13, 1944; s. S.P. Jain and Shakuntala Mithal; came to U.S., 1972; m. Claudette Dorita, Jan. 6, 1978; children—Sasha, Stephen. MB BS, Govt. Med. Coll., Punjabi U., Patiala, India, 1966. Intern Columbia U. Coll. Phys. and Surgeons-Roosevelt Hosp. N.Y.C., 1972-73; surgeon, Nat. Health Service U.K., 1966-72; resident in ob-gyn. St. Clare's Hosp.-Margaret Hauge Maternity Hosp., N.Y.C. and N.J., 1973-76, Columbia U., Harlem Hosp., N.Y.C., 1976-77; practice medicine specializing in ob-gyn., North Hollywood, Calif., 1977—; mem. staff Los Angeles County-U. So. Calif. Med. Sch.; assoc. clin prof. ob-gyn. and family medicine U. So. Calif. Sch. Medicine. Fellow ACS, Am. Coll. Ob-Gyn., L.A. Soc. Ob-Gyn.; mem. AMA, Calif. Med. Assn., Los Angeles County Med. Assn. Jain. Office: PO Box 40013 Studio City CA 91614-4013

SHELAN, DEBBIE LEVIN, travel agency administrator, school system administrator; b. Dallas, Sept. 27, 1951; d. Sol and Charlotte (Yonack) Levin; m. Evan B. Shelan, June 10, 1973; children: Erin N., Stephanie L. BS in Elem. Edn., U. Tex., 1973, MA in Early Childhood Edn., 1983. Tex. Teaching Cert. Kindergarten tchr. Dallas I.S.D., 1973-74; preschool tchr. Methods Inst., Sacramento, 1974-75, preschool dir., 1975; 2nd grade tchr. Gay Ave. Elem., Gladewater, Tex., 1976; kindergarten tchr. Longview (Tex.) I.S.D., 1976-80; v.p. Evan's World Travel, Inc., Longview, Tex., 1980—; elected sch. trustee Pine Tree I.S.D., Longview, Tex., 1991-97; chmn. Pine Tree Z Club, Longview Zenta Club, 1992—. Bd. mem. Longview (Tex.) Commn. on Arts and Culture, 1985-91; placement adv. Jr. League of Longview (Tex.), 1988-89; chmn. Gregg Co. Early Childhood Devel. Ctr. Enrichment Program, Longview, Tex., 1992, Longview (Tex.) Preschool Lang. and Devel. Program, 1991, Longview (Tex.) Preschcool Devel. Parenting and Curriculum Libr., 1992, Pine Tree Odyssey, 1992-97; vol. Junior Achievement, 1991-95; advisor Temple Emanu-El Youth Group, 1994—, chmn. 1995—. Named Best Chmn. Jr. League of Longview, Tex., 1991. Mem. Tex. Assn. Sch. Bds. Avocations: travel, reading.

SHELBURNE, JOHN DANIEL, pathologist; b. Washington, Aug. 27, 1943; s. Clarence Daniel and Edith (McDanel) S.; m. Katherine Howard Parrish, June 17, 1966; children: Mark, Kerri. BA, U. N.C., 1966; PhD, Duke U., 1971, MD, 1972. Intern, then resident Duke U. Med. Ctr., Durham, N.C., 1973-76; asst. prof. Duke U., Durham, 1973-78, assoc. prof., 1978-85, prof. pathology, 1985—; dir. electron microscopy lab. VA Med. Ctr., Durham, 1976—, chief lab. svc., 1983—; adv. WHO, Manila, 1990; panel mem. VA Program, Washington, 1987—; participant Nordrhein/Westfalen Exchange, Germany, 1988. Editor: Basic Methods in Biological X-Ray Microprobe, 1983; author, editor: Microprobe Analysis in Medicine, 1989. Mem. Appalachian Trail Conf., Harpers Ferry, West, Va., 1970—; bd. dirs. Cen. Carolina Youth Soccer, Durham, 1987-90; founding mem. N.C. Soc. for Electron Microscopy and Microprobe, Research Triangle Park, N.C., 1980—. Recipient Morehead scholarship, 1961-66, AOA Med. Honorary Duke Med. Sch., 1970; named Med. Scientist Tng. Program participant NIH, 1966-72, Shelley Meml. lectr., 1985, Florey Meml. lectr., 1988. Fellow Coll. Am. Pathologists; mem. Am. Assn. Pathologists, Microscopy Soc. Am., Microbeam Analysis Soc. Democrat. Episcopalian. Home: 4302 Malvern Rd Durham NC 27707-5451 Office: Duke U Dept of Pathology PO Box 3712 Durham NC 27710

SHELBY, BRYAN ROHRER, information systems consultant; b. Bryn Mawr, Pa., June 26, 1952; s. Albert Rohrer and Elizabeth Ellen (Griffinger) S.; m. Linda Yale Pole, Sept. 9, 1972; children: Caroline Belle, Christina Marie, Heather Lynn. AB in Math. cum laude, Harvard U., 1974. Programmer Litton Industries, Morris Plains, N.J., 1974-75; mgr. info. svcs. The Becker Co., East Orange, N.J., 1975-81; mgr. design and devel. Key Fin. Systems, Pine Brook, N.J., 1982-85; v.p., group project mgr. Bankers Trust Co., Jersey City, N.J., 1985-93; pres. Contek Systems, Inc., Madison, N.J., 1993—; process reengring. and project mgmt. cons. for maj. corps.; tech. advisor for venture capital investments. Designer/project mgr./sys. integrator fin./portfolio mgmt./trust acctg./telecom. computer sys. Mem. vestry St. Paul's Episcopal Ch., Chatham, N.J., 1988, chair fin. com., 1989-90, sr. warden, 1991-95. Mem. Am. Soc. Pension Actuaries. Democrat. Avocations: reading, building sandcastles. Office: Contek Systems Inc PO Box 292 Madison NJ 07940-0292

SHELBY, JAMES STANFORD, cardiovascular surgeon; b. Ringgold, La., June 15, 1934; s. Jesse Audrey and Mable (Martin) S.; BS in Liberal Arts La. Tech. U., 1956; MD, La. State U., 1958; m. Susan Rainey, July 15, 1967; children: Bryan Christian, Christopher Linden. Intern, Charity Hosp. La., New Orleans, 1958-59, resident surgery and thoracic surgery, 1959-65; fellow cardiovascular surgery Baylor U. Coll. Medicine, Houston, 1965-66; practice medicine specializing in cardiovascular surgery, Shreveport, La., 1967—; mem. staff Schumpert Med. Ctr., Highland Hosp., Willis-Knighton Med. Ctr.; assoc. prof. surgery La. State U. Sch. Medicine, Shreveport, 1967—. With M.C., AUS, 1961-62. Diplomate Am. Bd. Surgery, Am. Bd. Thoracic Surgery. Recipient Tower of Medallion award La. Tech. U., 1982. Mem. Am. Coll. Cardiology, AMA, Soc. Thoracic Surgeons, Am. Heart Assn., Southeastern Surg. Congress, So. Thoracic Surg. Assn. Home: 6003 E Ridge Dr Shreveport LA 71106-2425 Office: 3300 Virginia Ave Ste 7B Shreveport LA 71103-3948

SHELBY, JEROME, lawyer; b. N.Y.C., Mar. 17, 1930; s. Morris and Rose Shelby; m. Adrian Austin, Nov. 24, 1957; children: Karen A. Anderson, P. Austin. AB, NYU, 1950; LLB, Harvard U., 1953. Bar: D.C. 1953, N.Y. 1954. Assoc. Cadwalader, Wickersham & Taft, N.Y.C., 1953-63, ptnr., 1963-92, of counsel, 1993—; sr. v.p. Marine Transport Lines Inc., N.Y.C., 1958-74, also dir., 1989-92, adv. dir., 1993—; exec. v.p., dir. Energy Transp. Corp., N.Y.C., 1973—; dir. Astro Tankers Ltd.; trustee Seamen's Ch. Inst. Trustee Monclair (N.J.) Pub. Libr. Mem. Assn. Bar City N.Y., Montclair Golf Club, Palm Beach Polo Club (Fla.). Home: 74 Highland Ave Montclair NJ 07042-1910 Office: Cadwalader Wickersham & Taft 100 Maiden Ln New York NY 10038-4818

SHELBY, NINA CLAIRE, special education educator; b. Weatherford, Tex., Oct. 23, 1949; d. Bill Hudson and Roselle (Price) S.; m. Richard Dean Powell, May 29, 1971 (div. 1973); 1 child, Stoney Hudson. BA in English, Sul Ross State U., 1974, MEd, 1984; MA in English, U. Tex., 1995. Jr. high lang. arts educator Liberty Hill, Tex., 1974-75; H.S. resource educator Georgetown (Tex.) I. S. D., 1976-77; intermediate resource educator Raymondille (Tex.) I. S. D., 1977-81; educator of severe profound Napper Elem. Pharr (Tex.) San Juan Alamo Ind. Sch. Dist., 1981-90; H. S. life skills educator Pharr (Tex.) San Juan Alamo ISD North H.S., 1990-93; intermediate inclusion educator Carman Elem. Pharr (Tex.) San Juan Alamo Ind. Sch. Dist., 1993—; coach asst. Tex. Spl. Olympics, Pharr, 1981—, sponsor vocat. adj. club, 1990-93, adaptive asst. device team, Edinburg, Tex., 1993-95. Asst. den leader Cub Scouts of Am., 1994-95, parent vol. Boy's and Girl's Club of McAllen, 1992—. Mem. DAR, Assn. of Tex. Profl. Educators, Alpha Delta Kappa. Democrat. Mem. Ch. of Christ. Avocations: reading, horticulture, piano, opera. Home: 2501 Falcon Ave McAllen TX 78504-4315 Office: Pharr San Juan Alamo ISD Carman Elem 100 Ridge Rd San Juan TX 78589

SHELBY, RICHARD CRAIG, senator, former congressman; b. Birmingham, Ala., May 6, 1934; s. O.H. and Alice L. (Skinner) S.; m. Annette Nevin, June 11, 1960; children: Richard Craig, Claude Nevin. AB, U. Ala., 1957, LLB, 1963. Bar: Ala. 1961, D.C. 1979. Law clk. Supreme Ct. of Ala., 1961-62; practice law Tuscaloosa, Ala., 1963-79; prosecutor City of Tuscaloosa, 1964-70; spl. asst. atty. gen. State of Ala., 1969-70; U.S. magistrate No. Dist. of Ala., 1966-70; mem. Ala. State Senate, 1970-78, 96th-99th Congresses from 7th Ala. dist., 1979-87; mem. energy and commerce com., mem. vets. affairs com., U.S. senator from Ala., 1987—, mem. com. on appropriations, com. on banking, housing, and urban affairs, chmn. select com. on intelligence, spl. com. on aging. Active Boy Scouts Am.; pres. Tuscaloosa County Mental Health Assn., 1969-70; bd. govs. Nat. Legis. Conf., 1975-78. Mem. ABA, Ala. Bar Assn., Tuscaloosa County Bar Assn., D.C. Bar Assn., Exch. Club. Republican. Presbyterian. Home: 1414 High Forest Dr N Tuscaloosa AL 35406-2152 Office: US Senate 110 Hart Senate Bldg Washington DC 20510

SHELBY, RONALD VAN DORN, information systems executive; b. Covington, Ind., Jan. 14, 1948; s. Richard Van Dorn and Edna Belle (Sweet) S.; m. Susan Gail Bamford, Apr. 27, 1985; 1 child, Richard James Harold. BA, Wabash Coll., 1970; MAT, Ind. U., 1973; MBA, U. Toronto, 1984. Claims mgr. Travelers Ins. Co., Toronto, Ont., 1972-74, project leader, 1976-79, mgr. data adminstrn., 1979-82; asst. dir. data processing div. Travelers Can., Toronto, Ont., 1983-84; data adminstr. U.S. Dept. Interior, Washington, 1984-86; prin. Am. Mgmt. Sys., Arlington, Va., 1986-89; v.p. info. and tech. svcs. Conn. Mut. Life, Hartford, 1989-94; v.p. info. mgmt. divsn. USF & G Corp., Balt., 1994-96; v.p. tech. leader Am. Express Co., Phoenix, 1996—. Author: Selecting a DBMS, 1984, Project Manager's Guide to System Development, 1985, also chpts. to books; reviewing editor Data Resource Mgmt., 1989—. Mem. Data Adminstrn. Mgmt. Assn. (adv., bd. dirs., founder Washington chpt. 1988—, internat. pres. 1990). Episcopalian. Avocations: photography, baseball, jogging. Home: 5240 Hartford Ave Scottsdale AZ 85254 Office: Am Express Co 10010 N 25th Ave Phoenix AZ 85021-1660

SHELBY, TIM OTTO, secondary education educator; b. Longview, Wash., Mar. 23, 1965; s. William Richard and Ruth (Masser) S. BA in Edn., Eastern Wash. U., 1989. Cert. grades 4-12 English tchr., Wash. English tchr. Kahlotus (Wash.) H.S., 1989-90; tchr. various dists., 1990-92; Eng. tchr. Kalama (Wash.) H.S., 1992-95; tchr. English, head basketball coach Frazier Mountain H.S., Lebec, Calif., 1995—; founder, co-exec. dir. Evergreen Environ. Working Ctr., Frazier Park, Calif., 1997—; asst. basketball coach Kalama H.S., 1992-95; head basketball and football coach Kahlotus High Sch., 1989-90. Mem. ASCD, Nat. Coun. Tchrs. Eng., Internat. Reading Assn., Nat. Assn. Basketballs Coachs, So. Calif. Interscholastic Coaches Assn., Calif. Edn. Assn. (bldg. rep.). Roman Catholic. Avocations: traveling, reading, coaching sports, theatre, movies. Home: PO Box 113 Frazier Park CA 93225-0113 Office: El Tajon Unified Sch Dist Box 876 Lebec CA 93243

SHELDON, CHARLES HARVEY, political science educator; b. Jerome, Idaho, Aug. 2, 1929; s. Milo Francis and Martha Susan (McCorkle) S.; m. Patricia Ann Murphy, Dec. 31, 1970; children—Lee Ann, Christopher, Ross, Thomas. B.A., U. Wash., Seattle, 1952, M.A., 1957; Ph.D., U. Oreg., 1965. Instr. polit. sci. Boise (Idaho) Jr. Coll., 1958-61; asst. prof., chmn. dept., dir. Sch. Social Sci., U. Nev., Las Vegas, 1962-68; asso. prof., chmn. dept. Southampton (N.Y.) Coll., L.I. U., 1968-70; mem. faculty Wash. State U., Pullman, 1970—; prof. polit. sci. Wash. State U., 1974—, dir. div. govtl. studies and services, 1976, dept. chmn., 1993-94, Claudius O. and Mary W. Johnson disting. prof. polit. scis., 1994—. Author: The American Judicial Process: Models and Approaches, 1974, A Century of Judging: A Political History of the Washington Supreme Court, 1988, The Washington High Bench: A Biographical History of the State Supreme Court, 1992; co-author: Democracy at the Crossroads, 1978, Politicians, Judges and the People, 1980, Political Life in Washington, 1985, Government and Politics in the Evergreen State, 1992, Choosing Justice: The Recruitment of State and Federal Judges, 1997; editor: The Supreme Court: Politicians in Robes, 1969; co-editor: Postwar America: The Search for Identity, 1968, Government and Politics of Washington State, 1978; contbr. articles to profl. jours. and law revs. Served with AUS, 1952-55. Grantee Am. Philos. Soc., 1976; grantee Nat. Endowment Humanities, 1978; grantee NSF, 1982-83, 95-96. Mem. ACLU, Am. Polit. Sci. Assn., Am. Judicature Soc., Wash. State Com. Minority and Justice, Wash. State Hist. Soc., Western Polit. Sci. Assn., Law and Soc. Assn., Ea. Dist. Washington Hist. Soc., Ninth Judicial Ct. Hist. Soc., U.S. Masters Swimming, Alpha Delta Phi. Nationally ranked masters swimmer, 1975-80, 85, 87. Address: SE 905th Spring St Pullman WA 99163

SHELDON, ELEANOR HARRIET BERNERT, sociologist; b. Hartford, Conn., Mar. 19, 1920; d. M.G. and Fannie (Myers) Bernert; m. James Sheldon, Mar. 19, 1950 (div. 1960); children: James, John Anthony. AA, Colby Jr. Coll., 1940; AB, U. N.C., 1942; PhD, U. Chgo., 1949. Asst. demographer Office Population Rsch., Washington, 1942-43; social scientist USDA, Washington, 1943-45; assoc. dir. Chgo. Community Inventory, U. Chgo., 1947-50; social scientist Social Sci. Rsch. Coun., N.Y.C., 1950-51, rsch. grantee, 1953-55, pres., 1972-79; rsch. assoc. Bur. Applied Social Rsch. Columbia U., 1950-51, lectr. sociology, 1951-52, vis. prof., 1969-71; social scientist UN, N.Y.C., 1951-52; rsch. assoc., lectr. sociology UCLA, 1955-61; assoc. rsch. sociologist, lectr. Sch. Nursing U. Calif., 1957-61; sociologist, exec. assoc. Russell Sage Found., N.Y.C., 1961-72; vis. prof. U. Calif., Santa Barbara, 1971; dir. Equitable Life Assurance Soc., Mobil Corp., H.J. Heinz Co. Author: (with L. Wirth) Chicago Community Fact Book, 1949, America's Children, 1958, (with R.A. Glazier) Pupils and Schools in N.Y.C, 1965; editor: (with W.E. Moore) Indicators of Social Change, Concepts and Measurements, 1968, Family Economic Behavior, 1973; contbr. (with W.E. Moore) articles to profl. jours. Bd. dirs. Colby-Sawyer Coll., 1979-85, UN Rsch. Inst. for Social Devel., 1973-79; trustee Rockefeller Found., 1978-85, Nat. Opinion Rsch. Ctr., 1980-87, Inst. East-West Security Studies, 1984-88, Am. assembly, 1976-95. William Rainey Harper fellow U. Chgo., 1945-47. Fellow Am. Acad. Arts and Scis., Am. Sociol. Assn., Am. Statis. Assn.; mem. AAAS, U. Chgo. Alumni Assn. (Profl. Achievement award), Sociol. Rsch. Assn. (pres. 1971-72), Coun. on Fgn. Rels., Am. Assn. Pub. Opinion Rsch., Ea. Sociol. Soc., Internat. Sociol. Assn., Internat. Union Sci. Study of Population, Population Assn. Am. (2d v.p. 1970-71), Inst. of Medicine (chmn. program com. 1976-77), Cosmopolitan Club. Home and Office: 630 Park Ave New York NY 10021-6544

SHELDON, ERIC, retired physics educator; b. Pilsen, Bohemia, Oct. 24, 1930; s. Robert Bernard and Martha (Martin) S.; m. Sheila Harper, July 8, 1959; 1 child, Adrian. B.Sc., London (Eng.) U., 1951, B.Sc. in Physics, with honors, 1952, Ph.D., 1955, D.Sc., 1971. Chartered chemist; chartered physicist. Lectr., rsch. assoc. Acton Tech. Coll., London, 1952-55; assoc. physicist IBM Rsch. Lab., Switzerland, 1957-59; rsch. assoc. E.T.H., Zurich, Switzerland, 1959-62, lectr., 1962-64, prof., 1964-69; prof. physics and applied physics Lowell (Mass.) Technol. Inst. and U. Lowell, 1970-91, U. Mass. at Lowell, 1991-96; honors dir., 1994-96, emeritus prof., 1996—; Univ. prof. U. Lowell, 1985-88; vis. prof., NSF sr. fgn. sci. fellow U. Va., 1968-69; vis. prof. U. Tex., 1969-70, U. Oxford (Eng.), 1989. Author: (with R. Szostak and P. Marmier) Kernphysik I, 1960, Kernphysik II, 1961, (with P. Marmier) Physics of Nuclei and Particles, Vol. I, 1969, Vol. II, 1970; editor Procs. Internat. Conf. on Interactions of Neutrons with Nuclei, 1976; contbr. articles to books, encys. and profl. jours. Mem. Convocation London U., 1951—. Decorated Order of Merit (Poland). Fellow AAAS, Am. Phys. Soc. (chmn. New Eng. sect. 1985-86, mem. exec. com. 1983-87), Inst. Physics, Royal Soc. Chemistry, Royal Astron. Soc.; mem. Zurich Physical Soc. (life), Royal Instn. Gt. Britain (sr. assoc.), Mensa. Anglican/Episcopalian (lay reader). Home: 38 Cathy Rd Chelmsford MA 01824-2043 also: 56 Cunliffe Close, Oxford OX2 7BL, England *The benefits of happiness in my work and throughout my life, of health, contentment, fulfillment and zest for living, impose an obligation to repay this good fortune in some measure through direct service to the world around me. And still the wonder remains: Life has given me so much more than I ever could contribute—inspiration and love from family and friends, the grace of beauty in the world around me, vivacity and the radiant miracle of laughter. For all that is gentle, peaceful, wise, goodwilled, compassionate, spiritually inspiring and nobly idealistic in this wondrous universe, I feel deep reverence, appreciation and profound gratitude.*

SHELDON, GARY, conductor, music director; b. Bay Shore, N.Y., Jan. 21, 1953. Student, Wash. U., St. Louis, 1972; BMus, Juilliard Sch. Music, 1974; diploma, Inst. Hautes Etudes Musicales, Montreux, Switzerland, 1975. Prin. condr. Opera Theater, Syracuse, 1976-77; asst. condr. Syracuse Symphony Orch., 1976-77, New Orleans Symphony Orch., 1977-80; assoc. condr. Columbus (Ohio) Symphony Orch., 1982-89; music dir. Lancaster (Ohio) Festival, 1988—, Marin Symphony Orch., San Rafael, Calif., 1990—. Composer: Variations on a Theme of Handel, 1984, Mississippi River (for documentary film Miss. River Mus.), Memphis; rec. performances include Beauty and the Beast (with Frank DiGiacomo), 1977, Ballet Class with Karen Hebert, 1982. Recipient New Orleans Music and Drama Found. award, 1982, 3d prize Rupert BBC Symphony Found., London, 1982, 4th prize Leopold Stokowski Conducting Competition, 1986. Mem. Am. Symphony Orch. League (youth orch. div. bd. dirs. 1980—). Office: Marin Symphony Orchestra 4340 Redwood Hwy San Rafael CA 94903-2104*

SHELDON, GEORGE F., medical educator; b. Dec. 20, 1934; s. Richard Robert and Helen Irene (Zerzan) S.; m. Ruth Guy, Aug. 28, 1959; children: Anne Anderson, Elizabeth, Julia. BA, U. Kans., 1957, MD, 1961; postgrad., Mayo Clinic Grad. Sch., 1965. Intern Kans. U. Med. Ctr.; resident in surgery U. Calif., San Francisco, 1965-69; fellow in surg. biology Harvard Med. Sch. of Peter Bent Brigham Hosp., 1969-71; from asst. to full prof. U. Calif., 1971-82; Dr. Zack D. Owens Disting. prof. surgery, dept. chmn. U. N.C., Chapel Hill, 1984—; chmn. residency rev. com. accreditation Coun. for Grad. Med. Edn.; mem. Coun. Grad. Med. Edn. of Health and Human Svcs., 1986; mem. adminstrv. bd. Coun. Acad. Socs. Author: (with J.B. Runnell) Pictorial History of Kansas Medicine, 1961, (with Jill Ridky) Managing in Academics, 1993; editor: (with J.B. Davis) Clinical Surgery, 1995. With USPHS, 1962-64. Recipient Surgeon's award for Svc. to Safety, Nat. Safety Coun., 1993, Douglass Stubbs award Nat. Med. Assn., 1991. Hon. fellow Royal Coll. Surgeons of Edinburgh, European Surg. Assn., Assn. of Surgeons of Gt. Britain and Ireland; mem. ACS (sec. bd. govs., regent 1984-92), Am. Bd. Surgery (chmn. 1989-90), Nat. Bd. Med. Examiners (test com. 1981-84), Am. Assn. Surgery of Trauma (pres. 1984), Am. Surg. Assn. (sec. 1989-94, pres. 1994-95), Assn. Am. Med. Colls. (exec. com.), Coun. Acad. Socs. (com. on gender equity and com. on health workforce), Inst. Medicine (sec. com. on employer based health ins. and tech. assessment edn. bds., com. on Nation's Physician Workforce 1996), Merit Rev. Bd. for Surgery Va. (chmn.), Inst. Medicine NAS. Office: U NC at Chapel Hill 136 Burnett-Womack Bldg 229 Chapel Hill NC 27599

SHELDON, GILBERT IGNATIUS, clergyman; b. Cleve., Sept. 20, 1926; s. Ignatius Peter and Stephanie Josephine (Olszewski) S. Student, John Carroll U.; M.Div., St. Theol. Sem., 1970; D.Min., St. Mary Sem. and Ohio Consortium of Sems., 1974. Ordained priest Roman Cath. Ch., 1953, bishop, 1976. Assoc. pastor Cleve. Diocese, 1953-64, diocesan dir. propagation of faith, 1964-74; pastor, Episcopal vicar Lorain County, Ohio, 1974-76; aux. bishop Cleve., 1976—; vicar for Summit County, 1979-80, So. Region, 1980-92; bishop Steubenville, 1992—; bd. dirs. Soc. Propagation of Faith, 1968-74, Diocesan Presbyteral Coun.; instr. theology St. John Coll.; clergy adv. bd. econ. edn. Akron U.; mem. Bishop's Com. Latin Am.; bd. trustees St. Mary Seminary, Diocesan Health Ins. Adv. Bd., Cath. Charities Corp.; former mem. bd. trustees Borromeo Coll.; mem. acad. bd. St. Mary Seminary; bd. dirs. Bishops' Com. Latin Am., adminstrv. com. Nat. Conf. Cath. Bishops/USCC, Nat. Adv. Coun., Bishops' Com. for Missions, Nat. Bd. Soc. for Propagation of Faith; bd. trustees Pontifical Coll. Josephinum. Mem. adv. bd. Internat. Chem. Workers; mem. econ. adv. bd. Akron U. Clergy; mem. Summit Mental Health Adv. Bd.; mem. Summit chpt. Nat. Cancer Soc.; mem. Goals for Greater Akron. Served with USAAF, 1944-45. Mem. Nat. Conf. Cath. Bishops (adminstrv. bd. 1985—), Am. Legion, Cath. War Vets., Knights of Columbus, Order of Alhambra., Rotary Club Akron and Steubenville. Club: K.C. Lodge: Rotary (Akron). Avocations: golf, astronomy, photography, history, travel. Office: PO Box 969 Steubenville OH 43952-5969

SHELDON, INGRID KRISTINA, mayor; b. Ann Arbor, Mich., Jan. 30, 1945; d. Henry Ragnvald and Virginia Schmidt (Clark) Blom; m. Clifford George Sheldon, June 18, 1966; children: Amy Elizabeth, William David. BS, Eastern Mich. U., 1966; MA, U. Mich., 1970. Cert. tchr., Mich. Tchr. Livonia (Mich.) Pub. Schs., 1966-67, Ann Arbor Pub. Schs., 1967-68; bookkeeper Huron Valley Tennis Club, Ann Arbor, 1978—; acct. F.A. Black Co., Ann Arbor, 1984-88; coun. mem. Ward II City of Ann Arbor, 1988-92, mayor, 1993—; chair Housing Bd. Appeals, Ann Arbor, 1988-91; chair fin. and budget com. S.E. Mich. Coun. Govts. Mem. Huron Valley Child Guidance Clinic, Ann Arbor, 1984—, Ann Arbor Hist. Found., 1985—, Parks Adv. Commn., 1987-92, Ann Arbor Planning Commn., 1988-89; excellence com. Ann Arbor Pub. Schs. reorgn., 1985; treas. SOS Cmty. Crisis Ctr., Ypsilanti, Mich., 1987-93; precinct ward city vice-chair Ann Arbor Rep. City Com., 1978—. Recipient Cmty. Svc. award Ann Arbor Jaycees, 1980, DAR Cmty. Svc. award, 1997; AAUW fellow, 1982. Mem. Mich. Mcpl. League (del. 1989—), Ann Arbor Women's City Club (chair endowment com. 1989-90, fin. com. 1987-90, treas.), Rotary (dir. Ann Arbor chpt.), Kappa Delta Pi, Alpha Omnicron Pi. Republican. Methodist. Avocation: musical theatre. Home: 1416 Folkstone Ct Ann Arbor MI 48105-2848

SHELDON, JEFFREY ANDREW, college official; b. Northampton, Mass., Sept. 1, 1959; s. Wallace J. and Marilyn M. S. BS, Springfield (Mass.) Coll., 1981; postgrad., U. Va., 1981-83; EdM in Adminstrn., Harvard U., 1990. Mem. sci. faculty, chmn. dept. The Forman Sch., Litchfield, Conn., 1984-89; fin. mgr. and adminstrn. The Clin.-Devel. Inst., Belmont, Mass., 1989-90; owner, dir. Island Tutorials, Hilton Head Island, S.C., 1990-93; dir. instl. advancement Tech. Coll. of Lowcountry, Beaufort, S.C., 1993—; mgmt. team Acad. C.C. Leadership Advancement Innovation & Modeling (ACCLAIM), 1995—; presenter in field. Bd. dirs. Beaufort Chamber Orch. Guild, 1994-96, 2d v.p.; mem. Leadership Hilton Head, 1994, Nat. Coun. for Resource Devel., Beaufort County Human Svcs. Coun., 1996; v.p. bd. dirs. Hilton Head Choral Soc., 1992-93, tenor, 1991—; mem. core curriculum task force Beaufort 2000, 1992-93; candidate for Beaufort County Bd. Edn., Hilton Head, 1992, 94; bd. dirs. YMCA, Beaufort County, 1995, sec., 1996, 97; active ACCLAIM Project, Beaufort County, 1993—; co-team leader Rural C.C. Initiative (Ford Found.). Klingenstein Summer Inst. fellow Columbia U., 1988. Mem. Paris Island Masters Swim Team, Greater Beaufort C. of C. (govt. rels. com., edn. com.). Republican. Presbyterian. Avocations: swimming, rowing, community service. Home: PO Box 1788 Beaufort SC 29901 Office: Tech Coll Lowcountry 921 Ribaut Rd Beaufort SC 29902-5441

SHELDON, MICHAEL RICHARD, judge, law educator; b. Schenectady, Apr. 6, 1949; s. Richard Charles and Evelyn Marie (Delisle) S.; m. Diane Mary Micklos, May 29, 1971; children: Graham Andrew, Conor Michael, Rowan Richard, Cameron Ashleigh. AB, Princeton U., 1971; JD, Yale U., 1974; postgrad. Georgetown U., 1974-76. Bar: D.C. 1975, U.S. Dist. Ct. D.C. 1975, U.S. Ct. Appeals (D.C. cir.) 1975, U.S. Dist. Ct. (no. dist.) N.Y. 1976, Conn. 1976, U.S. Dist. Ct. Conn. 1976, U.S. Supreme Ct. 1978. Legal intern Georgetown U. Law Ctr., Washington, 1974-76; prof. law, dir. legal clinic U. Conn. Sch. Law, Hartford, 1976-91, adj. prof. law, 1991—; judge Conn. Superior Ct., 1991—; vis. scholar Yale U., New Haven, Conn., 1985-86; vis. prof. U. Aix-Marseille, 1986; bd. dirs. Conn. Civil Liberties Union, Hartford, 1979-83; ednl. cons. Office of Chief Pub. Defender, Hartford, 1978-91. Contbg. author: Handbook on the Connecticut Law of Evidence, 1982. Bd. dirs. Legal Aid Soc. of Hartford County, 1978-91; mem. Am. Leadership Forum, Hartford, 1988; mem. Dem. Town Com., Canton, Conn., 1988-91; mem. bd. fin., Canton, 1989-91; pres. Canton-Kuntsevo Exchange Com., Inc., 1990-92. Recipient Outstanding Faculty Mem. award Student Bar Assn. U. Conn. Sch. Law, 1979, 82, Alva P. Loiselle award Conn. Moot Ct. Bd., 1989; sr. fellow Am. Leadership Forum, 1989—. Mem. Conn. Bar Assn. (exec. com. sect. on human rights and responsibilities, exec. com. sect. on criminal justice 1978—), Conn. Prison Assn. (bd. dirs. 1993—, v.p. 1994—). Office: Litchfield Superior Ct 15 West St Litchfield CT 06759-3501

SHELDON, NANCY WAY, environmental management consultant; b. Bryn Mawr, Pa., Nov. 10, 1944; d. John Harold and Elizabeth Semple (Hoff) W.; m. Robert Charles Sheldon, June 15, 1968. BA, Wellesley Coll., 1966; MA, Columbia U., 1968, M in Philosophy, 1972. Cert. hazardous materials mgr., environ. auditor, Calif.; registered environ. profl., environ. assessor, Calif. Mgmt. cons. ABT Assocs., Cambridge, Mass., 1969-70; mgmt. cons. Harbridge House, Inc., 1970-79, L.A., 1977-79, v.p., 1977-79; mgmt. cons., pres. Resource Assessment, Inc., 1979—. Author: Social and Economic Benefits of Public Transit, 1973. Contbr. articles to profl. jours. Columbia U. fellow, 1966-68; recipient Nat. Achievement award Nat. Assn. Women Geographers, 1966. Mem. DAR, Nat. Environ. Health Assn., Air and Waste Mgmt. Assn., Nat. Ground Water Assn., Water Pollution Control Fedn., Water Environment Fedn., Fla. Pollution Control Assn., Grad. Faculties Alumni Assn. Columbia U. Office: Resource Assessment Inc 1192 Kittiwake Cir Sanibel FL 33957-3606

SHELDON, RICHARD ROBERT, Russian language and literature educator; b. July 12, 1932; s. Richard Robert and Helen Irene (Zerzan) S.; m. Karen Ryden Sears, Feb. 8, 1964; children: Katherine Palmer, John Ryden, Robert Charles, Rebecca Ann. BA, U. Kans., 1954; JD, U. Mich., 1960, MA, 1962; PhD, Mich. U., 1966. Chmn. Russian dept. Grinnell (Iowa) Coll., 1965-66; asst. prof. Dartmouth Coll., Hanover, N.H., 1966-70, assoc. prof., 1970-75, prof. Russian lang. and lit., 1975—, chmn. dept., 1970-81, 90-96, formerly dir. fgn. studies programs, chmn. com. on orgn. and policy, com. on admissions, com. on diversity, com. on off-campus study, dean of humanities, 1984-89, acad. dir. alumni coll., 1990; vis. prof. U. Calif. Berkeley, 1968, Stanford (Calif.) U., 1974; cons. Coun. Internat. Ednl. Exchange, N.Y.C., 1967-83, Dept. Edn., Washington, 1979—, Cornell U. Press, Ithaca, N.Y., 1970—; sr. assoc. mem. St. Antony's Coll., Oxford, Eng., 1983-

84. Translator, editor: (books by V. Shklovsky) A Sentimental Journey, 1970, Zoo or Letters Not About Love, 1971, Third Factory, 1977; compiler: Viktor Shklovsky: An International Bibliography of Works by and about Him, 1977; co-editor: Soviet Society and Culture, 1988; author articles, book revs., other transls. Chmn. bd. Norwich (Vt.) Day Care Ctr., 1980-81. Pfc. U.S. Army, 1955-57. Summerfield scholar, 1952-54; Nat. Def. Act fellow Dept. Edn., Washington, 1961-64, Alfred P. Lloyd fellow U. Mich., Ann Arbor, 1964-65, Ctr. Advanced Study fellow U. Ill., Urbana, 1969-70, Am. Coun. Learned Socs. fellow, 1970; Internat. Rsch. and Exchanges Bd. study grantee, USSR, 1964-65. Mem. Am. Assn. Advancement of Slavic Studies, Am. Assn. Tchrs. Slavic and East European Langs., Coun. of Mem. Instns. (exec. com., adv. com. to pres.), Phi Beta Kappa, Phi Alpha Theta, Phi Delta Theta (pres. 1953), Delta Sigma Rho. Democrat. Episcopalian. Home: 86 S Main St Hanover NH 03755-2029 Office: Dartmouth Coll Russian Dept 44 N College St Hanover NH 03755-1801

SHELDON, SIDNEY, author, producer; b. Chgo., Feb. 11, 1917; s. Otto and Natalie (Marcus) S.; m. Jorja Curtright, Mar. 28, 1951 (dec. 1985); 1 dau., Mary; m. Alexandra Kostoff, 1989. Ed., Northwestern U. Started as reader, Universal and 20th Century Fox Studios; author: novels The Naked Face, 1970, The Other Side of Midnight, 1975, A Stranger in the Mirror, 1976, Bloodline, 1977, Rage of Angels, 1980, Master of the Game, 1982, If Tomorrow Comes, 1985, Windmills of the Gods, 1987, The Sands of Time, 1988, Memories of Midnight, 1990, The Doomsday Conspiracy, 1991, The Stars Shine Down, 1992, Nothing Lasts Forever, 1994, Morning, Noon and Night, 1995, The Best Laid Plans, 1997; creator, writer, producer: Nancy, The Patty Duke Show, I Dream of Jeannie; created TV show Hart to Hart; author: plays including Roman Candle, Jackpot, Dream With Music, Alice in Arms, Redhead; writer: screenplays including Billy Rose's Jumbo, The Bachelor and the Bobby-Soxer, Easter Parade, Annie Get Your Gun; writer, dir.: screenplays including Dream Wife, Buster Keaton Story; writer: screenplays including Anything Goes, Never Too Young; recipient Acad. award for screenplay The Bachelor and the Bobby-Soxer 1947, Tony award for Redhead 1959, Writers Guild Am. Screen awards for Easter Parade, 1948, Annie Get Your Gun 1950, Edgar Allan Poe award Mystery Writers Am. for Naked Face, 1970. Served with USAAF, World War II. Inducted into the Guinness Book of Records as the Most Translated Author for 1997. Address: care William Morrow & Co Press Rels 1350 Ave of Americas New York NY 10019-4702

SHELDON, TED PRESTON, library director; b. Oak Park, Ill., July 5, 1942; s. Preston and Marjorie Sheldon; m. Beverly Stebel; children: Kathy, Mark. BA, Elmhurst (Ill.) Coll., 1964; MA, Ind. U., 1965, PhD, 1976; MLS, U. Ill., 1977. Asst. archivist U. Ill., Urbana, 1976-77; reference librarian U. Kans., Lawrence, 1977-79, head collection devel., 1979-81; assoc. dir. libraries SUNY, Binghamton, 1981-83; assoc. dir. libraries U. Mo., Kansas City, 1983-85, dir. libraries, 1985—; pres. Mo. Libr. Network Corp., 1991-95, bd. dirs. Author: Population Trends, 1976, Kans. Coll. Devel. Policy, 1978, History, Sources Social Science, 1985. Mem. ALA, Mus. Libr. Assn., Internat. Assn. Sound Archives, Assn. Recorded Sound Collection (mng. editor jour 1988-95, pres. 1996—). Office: U Mo Libraries 5100 Rockhill Rd Kansas City MO 64110-2446

SHELDON, TERRY EDWIN, lawyer, business consultant, advisor; b. Sacramento, June 22, 1945; s. Earl M. and Christine M. S.; m. Jan L. Winters, Aug. 26, 1966; children: Jeffrey, Tiffini, Melissa. BS magna cum laude, Abilene Christian U., 1967; JD, So. Meth. U., 1970. Bar: Calif. 1970. Assoc. Bronson, Bronson & McKinnon, San Francisco, 1970-74; gen. counsel, also dir. Consol. Capital Cos., Emeryville, Calif., 1974-83, exec. v.p., chief oper. officer, 1984-85, cons., advisor, 1986-87; pres., trustee Consol. Capital Spl. Trust, 1980-85; exec. v.p., trustee Consol. Capital Realty Investors, 1975-85, Consol. Capital Income Trust, 1978-85, Consol. Capital Income Opportunity Trust, 1983-85, Consol. Capital Income Opportunity Trust 2, 1985; chmn. Nat. Syndication Forum (a div. of RESSI), 1981-82; real estate securities specialist RESSI; v.p., prin. Alpha Venture Corp., Walnut Creek, Calif., 1987; bus. cons., 1988—. Chmn. bd. visitors adv. com. Coll. of Bus. Adminstrn. Abilene Christian U., 1990. Mem. ABA, Calif. Bar Assn., Nat. Assn. Securities Dealers (direct participation programs com., real estate com., standing adv. com. to bd. govs. 1980-83), Nat. Syndication Forum. Republican. Mem. Ch. of Christ.

SHELDON, THOMAS DONALD, academic administrator; b. Canastota, N.Y., July 15, 1920; s. Harry Ellsworth and Sadie Joyce (McNulty) S.; m. Helen Elizabeth Kyser, Aug. 29, 1941; children: Thomas, Paul, Edward, Patricia, Curtis, Roberta, Kevin, Kelly. B.S., Syracuse U., 1942, M.S., 1949, Ed.D., 1958; grad., USAF Air Command & Staff AirWar Coll., 1972. Tchr. sci., coach Split Rock (N.Y.) High Sch., 1942-43; tchr. sci., coach, vice prin., prin. Minoa (N.Y.) High Sch., 1946-59; prin., asso. supt. Hempstead (N.Y.) High Sch., 1959-63; supt. schs. Hempstead Public Schs., 1963-68; supt. Balt. City Schs., 1968-71; dep. commr. N.Y. State Edn. Dept., Albany, 1971-77; pres. Utica Coll. of Syracuse U., 1977-82; interim pres. Mohawk Valley Community Coll., 1983; then interim pres. Onondaga Community Coll., 1984, now hon. pres. emeritus; prof. ednl. adminstrn. Syracuse U., N.Y., 1984-85; supt. Sewanhaka Central High Sch. Dist., 1985-86; interim pres. Munson-Williams-Proctor Inst., 1990-91; exec. dir. Syracuse U. Relations, N.Y.C., 1987-93; chmn. Edn. Profls. Internat., 1977—. Co-author and editor various N.Y. State Regents publs., 1971-76. Served with U.S. Army, 1943-46; served to col. USAF, 1961-62, Berlin; to brig. gen. Air N.G. 1955-76. First recipient Outstanding Grad. award Syracuse U. Sch. Edn., 1977; recipient Outstanding Md. Educator award Md. State Council PTA's, 1969; Disting. Am. Educator award Freedoms Found., 1966; Conspicuous Service medal N.Y. State Gov., 1976; N.Y.C. PSAL medal, 1978; named to Balt. Afro-Am. Honor Roll, 1970. Mem. VFW, N.Y. State PTA (hon. life), N.Y. State Coaches Assn. (pres. 1957), Am. Legion, Lions (hon. life), Phi Delta Kappa. Clubs: Lions (hon. life). Home: 437 Fox Rd Bridgeport NY 13030 Office: Edn Profls Internat 437 Fox Rd Bridgeport NY 13030

SHELDRICK, GEORGE MICHAEL, chemistry educator, crystallographer; b. Huddersfield, Great Britain, Nov. 17, 1942; s. George and Elizabeth S.; m. Katherine E. Herford, 1968; 4 children. Student, Huddersfield New Coll., Jesus Coll., Cambridge. Lectr. Cambridge U., Eng., 1966-78; prof. inorganic chemistry U. Göttingen, Germany, 1978—; with Inst. Anorg Chemie, Göttingen, Germany. Contbr. numerous articles to profl. jours. Recipient Meldola and Corday-Morgan medals Royal Soc. Chemistry, Leibniz prize Deutsche Forschungsgemeinschaft, A.L. Patterson award Am. Crystallographic Assn., 1993. Achievements include authorship of widely used computer programs for crystal structure determination. Office: Institut für Anorganische Chemie, Tammannstrasse 4, D-37077 Gottingen Germany

SHELET, DAWN ARDELLE, financial analyst; b. Lac La Biche, Alberta, Can., Feb. 23, 1954; d. Laura Myrtle (Gould) Thacher; m. Paul Buettiker, Aug. 30, 1983. Student, McMaster U., Hamilton, Ontario, Can., 1976-78, B of Commerce (with honours), 1986; MBA, U. Miami, 1988. Mktg. rsch. asst. U. Miami Mktg. Dept., Coral Gables, Fla., 1986-87; fin. mgmt. intern Am. Express TRS Inc., Latin Am. Hdqrs., Coral Gables, Fla., 1987; internat. law rsch. asst. U. Miami Bus. Law Dept., Coral Gables, 1987-88; fin. analyst mktg. Eastern Air Lines Hdqrs., Miami, 1988-89; fin. planning systems analyst Am. Airlines Hdqrs., Dallas, 1989-90, fin. analyst internat., 1990-93, sr. bus. analyst, 1993—. Fund raising coord. United Way, Dallas-Ft. Worth Airport, 1989, 90, 91, 93, 94. Recipient U. Miami Grad. scholarship, 1986, 87, 88, Fees scholarship McMaster U., 1977; named to Dean's Honours list McMaster U., 1976, 77, 84, 85, 86. Mem. AMR Mgmt. Club (sec. 1991, treas. 1990-91, dir. 1992-93, v.p. 1994-95), Internat. Bus. Assn. (treas. 1986-87), Beta Gamma Sigma. Avocations: internat. travel, cookbook collection, fgn. lang. studies, wine tasting, classical music.

SHELL, ART, professional football team coach; b. Charleston, S.C.; m. Janice Shell; 2 children. Student, Md. State Coll. Player L.A. Raiders, 1968-83, coach, 1983-89, head coach, 1989-94; offensive line coach Kansas City Chiefs, 1995-96, Atlanta Falcons, 1997—. Inducted into Pro Football Hall of Fame, 1989; recipient, Jackie Robinson Award for Athletics (Ebony mag.), 1990; named N.F.L. Coach of Yr., 1991. Office: Atlanta Falcons 1 Falcon Pl Suwanee GA 30174*

SHELL, BILLY JOE, retired university president; b. Ecorse, Mich., Sept. 2, 1925; s. Millard Wootson and Flossie Mae (Evans) S.; m. Edythe Lorraine Roach, Dec. 25, 1948; children: Deborah Shell Zulkowski, Brian Jeffrey. B.S., Mich. State U., 1947, M.S., 1949, Ph.D., 1955. Registered profl. engr., Ariz., Miss., Tex. Faculty U. Ariz., 1949-53, Mich. State U., 1955; v.p., chief engr. San Xavier Rock & Sand Co., Tucson, 1956-66; asso. dean engrng. Miss. State U., 1966-70, acting v.p. for research, 1969-70; dean engrng. Calif. State Poly. U., Pomona, 1970-73, acting v.p. acad. affairs, 1971-72; pres. Northrop U., Inglewood, Calif., 1973-89, ret., 1989, also trustee; pres. Calif. Engrng. Found., 1982-85; vice chmn. Ariz. Bd. Tech. Registration, 1965-66; chmn. Calif. Council for Pvt. Postsecondary Ednl. Instns. Mem. Environ. Quality Control Com., Los Angeles County, 1971; chmn. bd. dirs. Tucson Boys Chorus, 1965-66. Served with USMCR, 1943-45. Recipient Engr. of Year award So. chpt. Ariz. Soc. Profl. Engrs., 1965, Outstanding Service award, 1966, Educator of Year award Region VII, Soc. Mfg. Engrs., 1973; Skill, Integrity and Responsibility award Asso. Gen. Contractors Calif., 1975. Fellow ASCE, Inst. for Advancement Engrng.; mem. NSPE, AAAS, AAUP, Calif. Soc. Profl. Engrs. (Outstanding Svc. award 1973, Edn. Achievement award 1975), Nat. Coun. Engrng. Examiners, Am. Water Works Assn., Water Pollution Control Fedn., Am. Soc. Engrng. Edn., Inglewood C. of C. (pres. 1986-87, bd. dirs.), Sigma Xi, Chi Epsilon, Sigma Pi Alpha, Delta Theta Phi, Tau Beta Pi. Clubs: Mason, Rotarian. Home: 1182 Steele Dr Brea CA 92821-2233

SHELL, KARL, economics educator; b. Paterson, N.J., May 10, 1938; s. Joseph J. and Grace (De Young) S.; m. Susan Witherow Schulze, Jan. 27, 1962; children: Stephanie Shell Read, Jason Anthony. AB in Math. with honors, Princeton U., 1960; PhD in Econs., Stanford U., 1965; MA (hon.), U. Pa., 1971. Asst. and assoc. prof. econ. MIT, Cambridge, 1964-68; assoc. prof. U. Pa., Phila., 1968-70, prof., 1970-87; Robert Julius Thorne Prof. Econs. Cornell U., Ithaca, N.Y., 1986—; vis. prof. Stanford U., Calif., 1972-73, Autonomous U. Barcelona, 1989, Bocconi Inst. Mgmt., Milan, Italy, 1990, U. Calif., San Diego, 1992, Doshisha U., Kyoto, Japan, 1995; adj. prof. U. Paris, 1979-81, 91; rschr. CEPREMAP, Paris, 1977-78; dir. Ctr. for Analytic Rsch. in Econs. and the Social Scis., Phila., 1975-86; Ctr. for Analytic Econs., Ithaca, 1986-92; pvt. practice econ., Ithaca, 1964—. Co-author: Economic Theory of Price Indices, 1972; editor: Optimal Economic Growth, 1967, Jour. Econ. Theory, 1968—; co-editor: Investment and Finance, 1972, Hamiltonians, 1976, Economic Complexity, 1989. Woodrow Wilson Found. fellow, 1960-61, 63-64; Ford Found. faculty rsch. fellow, 1967-68; Guggenheim fellow, 1977, Ctr. for Advanced Study in Behavioral Sci. fellow, 1984; Fulbright scholar, Barcelona, Spain, 1989. Fellow Econometric Soc.; mem. Am. Econ. Assn., European Econ. Assn., Econ. Study Soc., Soc. for Promotion of Econ. Theory, Elm Club (Princeton), Princeton Club (N.Y.C.), Statler Club (Ithaca), Sigma Xi. Republican. Episcopalian. Home: 917 Wyckoff Rd Ithaca NY 14850-2130 Office: Cornell U Dept Econs 402 Uris Hall Ithaca NY 14853-7601

SHELL, OWEN G., JR., banker; b. Greenville, S.C., June 19, 1936; s. Owen and Katherine S.; m. Mary Ruth Trammell, Aug. 9, 1980; children: Katherine Sloan, Mary Carroll, Robert Owen, James Walker. B.S., U. S.C., 1960; post grad., Stonier Grad. Sch. Banking, 1971; grad., Advanced Mgmt. Program, Harvard U., 1979. Tech. supt. Deering-Milliken, Inc., 1962-63; v.p. Citizens & So. Nat. Bank S.C., Columbia, 1968-71; sr. v.p. Citizens & So. Nat. Bank S.C., 1971-74, exec. v.p., 1974-79; pres., dir., chief exec. officer First Am. Nat. Bank, Nashville, 1979-86; vice chmn. bd., dir. First Am. Corp., 1979-86; chmn., pres., chief exec. officer Sovran Bank/Tenn., Nashville, 1986-91; pres. Nations Bank of Tenn. (formerly Sovran Bank), Nashville, 1992-96; pres. asset mgmt. group NationsBank Corp., St. Louis, 1997—; chmn. NationsBank of Ky.; bd. dirs. Nashville br. Fed. Res. Bank, Atlanta. Adv. bd. INROADS/Nashville; active Leadership Nashville, Tenn. Performing Arts Found., Mid. Tenn. coun. Boy Scouts Am., Vanderbilt U. Owen Grad. Sch. Mgmt.; trustee Met. Nashville Pub. Edn.; bd. dirs. Tenn. Bus. Roundtable, Tenn. Tomorrow. Mem. Assn. Res. City Bankers, Nashville Area C. of C., Kappa Alpha, Omicron Delta Kappa. Presbyterian. Clubs: Rotary, Cumberland, Belle Meade Country. Home: 4412 Chickering Ln Nashville TN 37215-4915 Office: NationsBank Corp 800 Market St Fl 13 Saint Louis MO 63101-2500

SHELL, ROBERT EDWARD LEE, photographer, writer; b. Roanoke, Va., Dec. 3, 1946; s. James Ralph and Mary (Terry) S.; m. Darlene Bridget. Student, Va. Poly. Inst. and State U., 1965-68, Elkins Inst., 1972, Nat. Camera Inst., 1973. Staff SMithsonian Inst., Washington, 1968-72; photographer Sta. WBRA-Pub. TV, Roanoke, 1972-74; owner Camera, Inc., Salem, Va., 1974-76; photographer, technician Gentry Studios, Blacksburg, Va., 1976-81; tech. editor Shutterbug Mag., Patch Communications, Radford, Va., 1984-91; editor Shutterbug Mag., Patch Communications, Titusville, Fla., 1991—; U.S. corr. Asahi Camera, Tokyo, 1986—, Color Foto, Munich, 1989—, Photo Answers, U.K.; pub. PIC Mag., U.K., 1994—. Author: Photography with Canon EOS System, 1990, Hasselblad Camera System Guide, 1991, Mamiya Camera System Guide, 1992, Photo Business Careers, 1992, Canon Compendium, 1994, Metz Flash System Handbook, 1994, Olympus IS System Handbook, 1994, Canon Rebel Handbook, 1994; tech. editor numerous publs; contbr. articles to profl. jours. Smithsonian Inst. grantee, Washington, 1968. Mem. Photo Mktg. Assn. Internat., German Photographers Soc., Megapress. Avocations: painting, drawing, classic automobiles. Home and Office: Bob Shell Photography 1601 Grove Ave Radford VA 24141-1624

SHELLEDY, JAMES EDWIN, III, editor; b. Spencer, Iowa, Nov. 11, 1942; s. James E. Jr. and Patricia L. (Cornwall) S.; m. Susan Emily Thomas, Mar. 7, 1986; 1 child, Ian Whittaker. BA, Gonzaga U., 1966. Reporter Spkesman-Rev., Spokane, Wash., 1963-66; tchr., coach Kootenai High Sch., Harrison, Idaho, 1967-71; reporter AP, Boise, Idaho, 1971-72; reporter, editor Lewiston (Idaho) Morning Tribune, 1973-80; editor, pub. Idahonian, Moscow, Idaho, 1981-91, Daily News, Pullman, Wash., 1981-91; editor The Salt Lake Tribune, Salt Lake City, 1991—; juror Pulitzer Prize Com., Columbia U., 1987-88; dir. Investigative Reporters and Editors, 1978-82; bd. dirs. New Directions for News, 1989—, Newspaper Agy. Corp., 1994—; mem. AP audit com., N.Y.C., 1982-91. Dir. Idaho Parks Found., Boise, 1976-78, Idaho-Washington Symphony, Pullman, Wash., 1986-89; commr. Idaho Lottery Commn., Boise, 1990-91; adv. bd. Utah YWCA, 1992—. Roman Catholic. Avocations: golf, sailing. Office: The Salt Lake Tribune 143 S Main St Salt Lake City UT 84111-1917*

SHELLER, JOHN WILLARD, lawyer; b. L.A., Oct. 29, 1950; s. Willard Newton and Barbara (Tremaine) S.; m. Mary Elizabeth Hodor, Aug. 9, 1975; children: Matthew John, James Henry. BA, Stanford U., 1972; JD, Loyola U., L.A., 1975. Bar: Calif. 1975. Ptnr. Haight, Brown & Bonesteel, Santa Monica, Calif., 1975—; pub. Melville Press, Pacific Palisades, Calif.; mem. Am. Bd. Trial Advs. Contbr. articles to profl. jours. Mem. Calif. State Bar Assn., Los Angeles County Bar Assn., So. Calif. Assn. Def. Counsel, Fedn. Ins. and Corp. Counsel, L.A. Country Club. Avocation: golf. Home: 15461 De Pauw St Pacific Palisades CA 90272-4370 Office: Haight Brown & Bonesteel PO Box 680 1620 26th St Santa Monica CA 90406-0680

SHELLEY, CAROLE, actress; b. London, Aug. 16, 1939; came to U.S., 1964; d. Curtis and Deborah (Bloomstein) S.; m. Albert G. Woods, July 26, 1967 (dec.). Student, Arts Ednl. Sch., 1943-56, Prepatory Acad. Royal Acad. Dramatic Art, 1956-57. Studied with Iris Warren and Eileen Thorndike; Trustee Am. Shakespeare Theatre., 1974-82. Appeared in revues, films, West End comedies, including Mary Mary at the Globe Theatre; first appeared as Gwendolyn Pigeon in stage, film and TV versions of The Odd Couple, Absurd Person Singular; The Norman Conquests (L.A. Drama Critics Circle award 1975); appeared as Rosalind in As You Like It, as Regan in King Lear, as Neville in She Stoops to Conquer, Stratford, Ont., Can., 1972, as Mrs. Margery Pinchwife in The Country Wife, Am. Shakespeare Festival, Stratford, Conn., 1973, as Nora in A Doll's House, Goodman Theatre, Chgo., as Ann in Man and Superman, Shaw Fest., 1977, as Lena in Misalliance, Zita in Grand Hunt,1980, Stepping Out, 1986 (Tony nomination 1986), Broadway Bound, 1987-88; appeared in: The Play's the Thing, Bklyn. Acad. Music, 1978; played Eleanore in stage prodn. Lion in Winter, 1987; other stage appearances include Nat. Co. of The Royal Family (L.A. Drama Citics Circle award 1977), The Elephant Man (Outer Critics Circle award 1978-79 season, Tony award for best actress 1978-79 season), What the Butler Saw, 1989; appeared inaugural season, Robin Phillips Grand Theatre Co., London, Ont., Can., 1983-84, Broadway and Nat. Co. of Noises Off, 1985, Waltz of the Toreadors, 1986, Oh Coward, 1986-87 ; appeared as Kate in Broadway Bound by Neil Simon The Nat. Co. and L.A. Premiere, 1987-88; played Lettice in Lettice and Lovage Globe Theatre, London, 1989-90, Frosine in The Miser, 1990, Cabaret Verboten, 1991, The Destiny of Me, 1992-93, Later Life, 1993 (Outer Critics nominee), Richard II, 1994, London Suite (Neil Simon) 1995, Show Boat, 1995-96; films include: The Boston Strangler, The Odd Couple, The Super, 1990, Devlin, 1991, Quiz Show, 1993, The Road to Wellville, 1993; created: voice characters in Walt Disney films Robin Hood, The Aristocats, Hercules. Recipient Obie Award for Twelve Dreams N.Y. Shakespeare Festival, 1982. Jewish. Office: care Duva-Flack Assocs Inc 200 W 57th St New York NY 10019-3211

SHELLEY, EDWARD HERMAN, JR., retired insurance company executive; b. Harrisburg, Pa., Oct. 14, 1919; s. E. Herman and Elizabeth (Workman) S.; m. Dorothy M. Treier, Feb. 14, 1942; children: David, Martha. A.B., Franklin and Marshall Coll., Lancaster, Pa., 1941. Office mgr. Nationwide Ins. Co., Harrisburg, Pa., 1941-50; head systems dept. Nationwide Ins. Co., Columbus, 1950-57, Agway, Ithaca, N.Y., 1958-60; v.p. data processing State Farm Ins. Co., Bloomington, Ill., 1960-83; bd. dirs. Bank One, Bloomington/Normal. Bd. dirs. Project Oz, Bloomington, 1980; with Vol. Income Tax Assistance, 1987-95; vol. Sr. Health Ins. Counselor, 1996—. Served with AUS, 1944-46. Mem. Nat. Office Mgmt. Assn., Assn. for Computing Machinery, Life Office Mgmt. Assn. (mem. property and casualty sys. com. 1981-83), Am. Legion, Phi Sigma Kappa, Pi Gamma Mu. Republican. Lutheran. Home: RR 2 Box 168 Lexington IL 61753-9548 Office: State Farm Ins Cos 1 State Farm Plz Bloomington IL 61701-4300

SHELLEY, ELBERT VERNELL, professional football player; b. Tyronza, Ark., Dec. 24, 1964. Student, Ark. State U. Cornerback Atlanta Falcons, 1987—. Named to Pro Bowl Team, 1992, 93. Office: Atlanta Falcons One Falcon Pl Suwanee GA 30174-2127*

SHELLEY, HERBERT CARL, lawyer; b. Stamford, Tex., Jan. 28, 1947; s. Carl B. and Lourena A. (Whitley) S.; m. Jerilyn S. Ray, Aug. 9, 1969; children: Megan, Caitlyn, Daniel. BA, Columbia Coll., 1969; JD, Vanderbilt U., 1972; LLM Internat. and Comparative Law magna cum laude, Vrije Universiteit Brussel, Brussels, Belgium, 1973. Bar: D.C. 1973, Md. 1985, U.S. Ct. Appeals (fed. cir.) 1981, U.S. Ct. Internat. Trade 1982, U.S. Supreme Ct. 1987. Atty./adv. U.S. Tariff Commn., Washington, 1973-74; Internat. trade specialist, asst. Office dir. Office Tariff Affairs U.S. Dept. Treasury, Washington, 1974-76; internat. trade negotiator Office Spl. Trade Reps., Geneva, Switzerland, 1976-79; ptnr. Plaia & Schaumberg, Washington, 1979-86, Howrey & Simon, Washington, 1986—. Mem. ABA, D.C. Bar Assn., Md. Bar Assn., City Club Washington. Avocations: skiing, golf, cooking, travel. Office: Howrey & Simon 1299 Pennsylvania Ave NW Washington DC 20004-2400

SHELLEY, JAMES LAMAR, lawyer; b. Joseph City, Ariz., Dec. 8, 1915; s. Thomas Heber and Eva (Tanner) S.; m. Virginia Rand, Nov. 21, 1942; children: Carol (Mrs. Danny Parker Boyle), Marlene (Mrs. J. Robert Tolman), Jana (Mrs. Gunn B. McKay), Mary (Mrs. Mark Hutchings), Gerald LaMar, James Rand. B.A., Ariz. State Coll., 1936; J.D., U. Ariz., 1949. Bar: Ariz. 1948. Asst. city atty. City of Mesa, Ariz., 1948-49, city atty., 1950-87; ptnr. Johnson & Shelley, Mesa, 1951-88; gen. counsel League Ariz. Cities and Towns, Phoenix, 1959—; ptnr. Shelley & Bethea, Mesa, 1988—. Adv. bd. Theodore Roosevelt coun. Boy Scouts Am., 1962-92, adv. coun. Grand Canyon coun., 1993—, Mesa Dist. chmn., 1967-68; v.p. Mesa United Fund, 1967-69, pres., 1970; pres. bd. mgmt. Mesa br. YMCA; pres. Mesa Christmas Basket Assn., Mesa Fine Arts Assn., 1978-80; mem. religious adv. com. Ariz. Dept. Corrections, 1981. Lt. USNR, 1942-45. Named Mesa Man of Year, 1965. Mem. Ariz. Acad., Nat. Inst. Mcpl. Law Officers (past pres.), Internat. Mcpl. Lawyers Assn. Republican. Mem. Ch. of Jesus Christ of Latter-day Saints (former regional rep.). Clubs: Exchange (past pres.), Southside Dinner (past pres. Mesa). Home: 550 N Emerson St Mesa AZ 85201-5516 Office: Shelley & Bethea 1201 S Alma School Rd Ste 3400 Mesa AZ 85210-2010

SHELLEY, WALTER BROWN, physician, educator; b. St. Paul, Feb. 6, 1917; s. Patrick K. and Alfaretta (Brown) S.; m. Marguerite H. Weber, 1942 (dec.); children: Peter B., Anne E. Kiselewich, Barbara A. (dec.); m. E. Dorinda Loeffel, 1980; children: Thomas R., Katharine D., William L. B.S., U. Minn., 1940, Ph.D., 1941, M.D., 1943; M.A. honoris causa, U. Pa., 1971; M.D. honoris causa, U. Uppsala, Sweden, 1977. Diplomate: Am. Bd. Dermatology (pres. 1968-69, dir. 1960-69). Instr. physiology U. Pa., Phila., 1946-47; asst. instr. dermatology and syphilology U. Pa., 1947-49, asst. prof. dermatology, 1950-53, assoc. prof., 1953-57, prof., 1957-80, chmn. dept., 1965-80; prof. dermatology U. Ill. Peoria Sch. Medicine, 1980-83; prof. medicine (dermatology) Med. Coll. Ohio, 1983—; instr. dermatology Dartmouth Coll., 1949-50; Regional cons. dermatology VA, 1955-59; mem. com. on cutaneous system NRC, 1955-59, Commn. Cutaneous Diseases, Armed Forces Epidemiological Bd., 1958-61, dep. dir., 1959-61; cons. dermatology Surgeon Gen. USAF, 1958-61, U.S. Army, 1958-61; mem. NRC, 1961-64. Author: (with Crissey) Classics in Clinical Dermatology, 1953, (with Pillsbury, Kligman) Dermatology, 1956, Cutaneous Medicine, 1961, (with Hurley) The Human Apocrine Sweat Gland in Health and Disease, 1960, (with Botelho and Brooks) The Endocrine Glands, 1969, Consultations in Dermatology with Walter B. Shelley, 1972, Consultations II, 1974 (with Shelley) Advanced Dermatologic Therapy, 1987, Advanced Dermatologic Diagnosis, 1992, A Century of International Dermatological Congresses, 1992; mem. editorial bd.: Jour. Investigative Dermatology, 1961-64, Archives of Dermatology, 1961-62, Skin and Allergy News, 1970-93, Excerpta Medica Dermatologica, 1960—, Cutis, 1972—, Jour. Geriatric Dermatol, 1993; assoc. editor: Jour. Cutaneous Pathology, 1972-81; editorial cons.: Medcom, 1972—. Served as capt. M.C. AUS, 1944-46. Recipient Spl. award Soc. Cosmetic Chemists, 1955, Hellerstrom medal, 1971, Am. Med. Writers Assn. Best Med. Book award, 1973, Dohi medal, 1981, Rothman medal Soc. for Investigative Dermatology, 1987, Rose Hirschler award, 1990. Master A.C.P.; fellow Assn. Am. Physicians, St. John's Dermatol. Soc. London (hon.); mem. AMA (chmn. residency rev. com. for dermatology 1963-67, chmn. sect. dermatology 1969-71), Assn. Profs. Dermatology (pres. 1972-73), Pacific Dermatol. Assn. (hon.), Am. Dermatol. Assn. (hon., dir., pres. 1975-76), Soc. Investigative Dermatology (hon. pres. 1961-62), Am., Phila. physiol. socs., Brit. Dermatol. Soc. (hon.), Phila. Dermatol. Soc. (pres. 1960-61), Mich. Dermatol. Soc., Ohio Dermatol. Soc. (hon.), Am. Acad. Dermatology (Gold medal 1992, hon. pres. 1971-72), Pa. Acad. Dermatology (pres. 1972-73), Am. Soc. for Dermatologic Surgery, North Am. Clin. Dermatol. Soc. (hon.), Noah Worcester Dermatological Soc., Royal Soc. Medicine; corr. mem. Nederlandse Vereniging Van Dermatologen, Israeli Dermatol. Assn., Finnish Soc. Dermatology, Swedish Dermatol. Soc., French Dermatologic Soc.; fgn. hon. mem. Danish Dermatol. Assn., Japanese Dermatol. Assn., Dermatol. Soc. S.Africa. Home: 21171 W River Rd Grand Rapids OH 43522-9703 Office: Med Coll Ohio PO Box 10008 3000 Arlington Ave Toledo OH 43614-2595

SHELLHASE, LESLIE JOHN, social work educator; b. Hardy, Nebr., Jan. 12, 1924; s. John Clayton and Sanna Belle (Muth) S.; m. Fern Eleanor Kleckner, June 8, 1948; children: Jeremy Clayton, Joel Kleckner. Student, U. Calif.-Berkeley, 1943-44; A.B., Midland Coll., 1947; M.S.W., U. Nebr., 1950; D.Social Work, Catholic U. Am., 1961. Lic. social worker, Ala. Parole supr. Child Welfare, Omaha, 1948-49; psychiat. social work intern Letterman Gen. Hosp. San Francisco, 1950-51; commd. 2d lt. U.S. Army, 1949, advanced through grades to lt. col., 1966; chief social worker (6th Inf. Div.), Ft. Ord, Calif., 1952-55; chief med. social worker Walter Reed Gen. Hosp. Washington, 1955-57, research investigator Walter Reed Inst. Research, 1957-63; head social work faculty Med. Field Service Sch., Ft. Sam Houston, Tex., 1963-66; chief sociologist U.S. Army, Washington, 1966-68; prof. Sch. Social Work, U. Ala., Tuscaloosa, 1968-89; prof. emeritus Sch. Social Work, U. Ala., 1989—; pvt. practice social work, 1968—; dir. tour, interpreter to surgeon gen. Belgium Armed Forces, 1961; lectr. Cath. U. Am., 1961-63, 66-68; rsch. dir. Jewish Social Svc. Fedn., San Antonio, 1963-66; rep. to internat. social and behavioral scis. cmty. Dept. Army, 1966-68; cons. Family Svc. Assn. Am., 1969—, Ala. Mental Health Dept., 1989—; mem. expert grop on social welfare UN, 1975—; mem. Internat. Rels. Forum, 1981—; rsch. fellow U. Exeter, 1981-82; mem. social work tng. com. NIMH, 1983—; mem. Interfaith Com. on AIDS, 1993; newscaster Radio Reading Svc., Ala. Pub. Broadcast, 1989—; condr. workshops; cons. on group psychotherapy Ala. Dept. Mental Health, 1989—. Author: The

Group Life of the Schizophrenic Patient, 1961, Bibliography of Army Social Work, 1962; book rev. editor Social Perspectives, 1979-83; editorial reviewer Social Work Papers, mem. editorial bd., 1986—; editorial reviewer Mac Millan Press, 1990—, Families in Society, 1992—, Oxford U. Press, 1994; internat. editorial bd. Internat. Abstracts Social Sci.; contbr. articles on social and behavioral sci. to nat. and internat. profl. jours., chpts. to books. Bd. dirs. Crisis Intervention Ctr.; bd. dirs., chmn. Soc. for Crippled Children and Adults. Served with inf. U.S. Army, 1942-46. Decorated Legion of Merit, Bronze Star, Purple Heart; recipient letter of commendation from Pres. of U.S., 1968, letter of commendation from Surgeon Gen., 1961. Fellow Am. Sociol. Assn.; mem. NASW (mem. nat. task force on ethics 1976-79, chmn. 1976-77, dir. 1963-66), Coun. social Work Edn., Acad. Cert. Social Workers, Brit. Sociol. Assn., Brit. Assn. Social Workers, Ret. Officers Assn., So. Sociol. Soc. Democrat. Home: 3823 Somerset Pl Tuscaloosa AL 35405-5436 Office: PO Box 870314 Tuscaloosa AL 35487-0154

SHELLHORN, RUTH PATRICIA, landscape architect; b. L.A., Sept. 21, 1909; d. Arthur Lemon and Lodema (Gould) S.; m. Harry Alexander Kueser, Nov. 21, 1940. Student dept. landscape architecture, Oreg. State Coll., 1927-30; grad. landscape architecture program, Cornell U. Coll. Architecture, 1933. Pvt. practice landscape architecture, various cities Calif., 1933—; exec. cons. landscape architect Bullocks Stores, Calif., 1945-78, Fashion Sqs. Shopping Ctrs., Calif., 1958-78, Marlborough Sch., L.A., 1968—, El Camino Coll., Torrance, Calif., 1970-78, Harvard Sch., North Hollywood, Calif., 1974-90; cons. landscape architect, site planner Disneyland, Anaheim, Calif., 1955, U. Calif., Riverside Campus, 1956-64, numerous others, also numerous gardens and estates; landscape architect Torrance (Calif.) City Goals Com., 1969-70; cons. landscape architect City of Rolling Hills (Calif.) Community Assn., 1973-93. Contbr. articles to garden and profl. publs.; subject of Oct. 1967 issue Landscape Design & Constrn. mag. Named Woman of Year, Los Angeles Times, 1955, Woman of Year, South Pasadena-San Marino (Calif.) Bus. Profl. Women, 1955; recipient Charles Goodwin Sands medal, 1930-33, Landscape Architecture award of merit Calif. State Garden Clubs, 1984, 86, Horticulturist of the Yr. award So. Calif. Hort. Inst., numerous nat., state, local awards for excellence. Fellow Am. Soc. Landscape Architects (past pres. So. Calif. chpt.), Phi Kappa Phi, Kappa Kappa Gamma (Alumni Achievement award 1960). Projects subject of Oct. 1967 issue of Landscape Design and Constrn. Mag. Home and Office: 362 Camino De Las Colinas Redondo Beach CA 90277-6435 *Integrity, honesty, dependability, sincerity, dedication, and a willingness to give more than is expected in service, are the basic principles which have guided my career. Never losing sight of the importance of the individual, I have tried to create total environments of harmony and beauty to which each individual can relate in a very personal and pleasureable way, and for a little while, can find a calm oasis in a busy and demanding world.*

SHELLMAN, EDDIE J., ballet dancer, teacher, choreographer; b. Tampa, Fla., May 10, 1956; s. Eddie J. and Elizabeth (Coleman-Smith) Lucas. Ed., High Sch. Performing Arts, N.Y.C. Dancer Pepsie Bethel Jazz Co., N.Y.C., 1972-73; dancer U.S. Terpisichore, N.Y. Sch. Ballet, N.Y.C., 1974-75; prin. dancer Dance Theatre Harlem, N.Y.C., 1975—, also choreographer, bd. dirs.; guest artist The Royal Ballet, London, Iowa U. Gala, Ballet New Eng. Performed in Internat. Ballet Festival of Havana, 1986, 66th Acad. Awards. Recipient Key to City, Birmingham, Ala., 1981, Resolution, City of Balt., 1981. Club: 4 Sevens (N.Y.C.). Avocations: Photography; cars; swimming; refinishing wood furniture. Office: Dance Theatre Harlem 466 W 152nd St New York NY 10031-1814*

SHELLMAN-LUCAS, ELIZABETH C., special education educator, researcher; b. Thomas County, Ga., Feb. 5, 1937; d. Herbert and Juanita (Coleman) Smith; m. John Lee Lucas, Jr. (div.); 1 child, Sandie Juanita Lucas Boyce; m. Eddie Joseph Shellman; 1 child, Eddie Joseph Shellman, Jr. MS in Edn., CUNY, 1990. Pvt. practice cosmetologist N.Y.C., 1959—; tchr. N.Y.C. Bd. of Edn. High Sch. Dist., 1984—. Vol. various community orgns.; citizen amb. del. People to People Internat., 1994. Mem. Coun. for Exceptional Children. Avocations: reading, music, dancing, jogging, languages.

SHELLOW, ROBERT, management service company executive, consultant; b. Milw., Sept. 22, 1929; s. Henry G. and Sadie (Myers) S.; m. Dorothea Laadt, Aug. 30, 1963; children: Sarah Katherine, Leslie Suzzane. BA, Reed Coll., 1951; MA, U. Mich., 1952, PhD, 1956. Commd. USPHS, Bethesda, Md., 1955, advanced through grades to commdr., Psychol. U.S. Bureau Prisons, 1955-58; asst. dep. dir. Nat. Adv. Commn. on Civil Disorders, 1967-68; dir. pilot programs D.C. Dept. Pub. Safety, 1968-70; prof. Carnegie-Mellon U., Pitts., 1970-76; pres. IMAR Corp., Washington, 1978—; cons. in field; expert witness psychol. deterence, security negligence cases, state and fed. cts., 1978—; mng. dir. Cross-Continent Assocs., Ltd., 1993—. Author: Issues in Law Enforcement, 1976; contbr. numerous articles to profl. jours. USPHS fellow U. Mich., 1953. Fellow Am. Psychol. Assn. ; mem. Nat. Bus. Aircraft Assn., Internat. Assn. Profl. Security Cons. (v.p. 1987-89, pres. 1989-91), Sigma Xi. Avocations: sailing; automobile and boat restoration. Office: IMAR Corp PO Box 34528 Bethesda MD 20827-0528

SHELLY, CHRISTINE DEBORAH, foreign service officer; b. Pontiac, Mich., May 1, 1951; d. Chester Price and Margaret Alice (Neafie) S. BA cum laude, Vanderbilt U., 1973; MA, Tufts U., 1974, MA in Diplomacy, 1975. Fgn. affairs analyst Intelligence and Rsch. Bur. Dept. State, Washington, 1975-77, desk officer Near Eastern Affairs, 1977-79; fin. attache Am. Embassy Dept. State, Cairo, 1979-81; asst. v.p. BankAmerica Internat., N.Y.C., 1981-82; spl. asst. Near Eastern Affairs Dept. State, Washington, 1982-83, econ., polit. officer Am. Embassy Dept. State, Lisbon, Portugal, 1983-87; dep. econ. advisor U.S. Mission to NATO, Brussels, 1987-90, dep. cabinet dir. Sec. Gen., 1990-93; dep. spokesman, dep. asst. sec. pub. affairs Dept. State, Washington, 1993-95; mem. Sr. Exec. Seminar U.S. State Dept., 1995-96; min. counselor polit. affairs Am. Embassy, Ottawa, Ont., Can., 1996—. Avocation: equestrian. Office: US Embassy Ottawa (POL), 100 Wellington St, Ottawa, ON Canada K1P 5T1

SHELNUTT, JOHN MARK, lawyer; b. Gainesville, Ga., Jan. 19, 1963; s. Dumas Broughton and Georgia Texana (Ruff) S.; m. Leila Christine Ricketson, June 24, 1989; children: John Mark Jr., Sarah. AA, Emory U., 1983, BA, 1985, JD, 1988. Bar: Ga. 1988, U.S. Dist. Ct. (mid. dist.) Ga. 1994. Asst. dist. atty. Dist. Atty.-Dougherty Jud. Cir., Albany, Ga., 1988, Dist. Atty.-Chattahoochee Jud. Cir., Columbus, Ga., 1989-94; ptnr. Berry and Shelnutt, Columbus, 1994—; faculty basic litigation course Prosecuting Atty.'s Coun., Forsyth, Ga., 1992—. Mem. ABA, State Bar Ga., Columbus Bar Assn., Ga. Trial Lawyers Assn., Ga. Assn. Criminal Def. Lawyers. Methodist. Home: 7802-4 Harpers Ferry Rd Upatoi GA 31829 Office: Berry & Shelnutt 1024 2nd Ave Columbus GA 31901-2406

SHELTON, BESSIE ELIZABETH, school system administrator; b. Lynchburg, Va.; d. Robert and Bessie Ann (Plenty) Shelton; B.A. (scholar), W.Va. State Coll., 1958; student Northwestern U., 1953-55, Ind. U., 1956; M.S., SUNY, 1960; diploma Profl. Career Devel. Inst., 1993. Young adult libr. Bklyn. Pub. Libr., 1960-62; asst. head cen. ref. div. Queens Borough Pub. Libr., Jamaica, N.Y., 1962-65; instructional media specialist Lynchburg (Va.) Bd. Edn., 1966-74; ednl. research specialist, 1974-77; ednl. media assoc. Allegany County Bd. Edn., Cumberland, Md., 1977—. Guest singer Sta. WLVA, 1966—, WLVA-TV Christmas concerts, 1966—;cons. music and market rsch. Mem. YWCA, Lynchburg, 1966—, Fine Arts Ctr., Lynchburg, 1966—; ednl. adv. bd., nat. research bd. Am. Biog. Inst.; mem. U.S. Congl. Adv. Bd., USN Nat. Adv. Coun.; amb. goodwill Lynchburg, Va., 1986. Named to Nat. Women's Hall of Fame. Mem. AAUW, NEA, NAFE, Md. Tchrs. Assn., Allegany County Tchrs. Assn., Va. Edn. Assn., State Dept. Sch. Librarians, Internat. Entertainers Guild, Music City Songwriters Assn., Vocal Artists Am., Internat. Clover Poetry Assn., Internat. Platform Assn., Nat. Assn. Women Deans, Adminstrs. and Counselors, Intercontinental Biog. Assn., World Mail Dealers Assn., N.Am. Mailers Exch., Am. Assn. Creative Artists, Am. Biog. Inst. Research Assn., Tri-State Community Concert Assn. Pi Delta Phi, Sigma Delta Pi. Contbr. poems to various publs. Democrat. Baptist. Clubs: National Travel, Gulf Travel. Home: PO Box 187 Cumberland MD 21501-0187

SHELTON, DAVID HOWARD, economics educator; b. Winona, Miss., Nov. 30, 1928; s. Tuttle M. and Kate (Moss) S.; m. Margaret Murff, Feb. 4, 1951; children: David Keith, Sarah Katherine, Susan Esther. B.A., Millsaps Coll., 1951; M.A., Ohio State U., 1952, Ph.D., 1958. Instr. Ohio State U., 1958; asst. prof. U. Del., 1958-63, asso. prof., 1963-65; prof. U. N.C., Greensboro, 1965—, head dept. econs., bus. adminstrn., 1967-70, dean Sch. Bus. and Econs., 1970-83, head dept. econs., 1988-93; Cons. Joint Council on Econ. Edn., 1969-72, N.C. Dept. Pub. Instrn., 1970-73. Trustee N.C. Council on Econ. Edn., 1971—, chmn., 1971-75, pres., 1975-85. Served with USNR, 1946-48. M.D. Lincoln fellow, 1956-57; H.L. and Grace Doherty fellow, 1957. Mem. Beta Gamma Sigma, Omicron Delta Kappa, Kappa Sigma. Episcopalian. Home: 3609 Dogwood Dr Greensboro NC 27403-1010 Office: U NC 462 Bryan Bldg Greensboro NC 27412

SHELTON, DOROTHY DIEHL REES, lawyer; b. Manila, Sept. 16, 1935; came to U.S., 1945; d. William Walter John and Hedwig (Glienecke) Diehl; m. Charles W. Rees, Jr., June 15, 1957 (div. 1971); children: Jane Rees Stebbins, John B., Anne Rees Slack, Esq., David C., Esq.; m. Thomas C. Shelton, Mar. 4, 1977 (dec.). BA in Music, Stanford Univ., 1957; JD, Western State Univ. Coll. Law, 1976. Bar: Calif. 1977, U.S. Dist. Ct. (so. dist.) Calif. 1977. Pvt. practice, San Diego, 1977—. Mem. ABA, Calif. State Bar, San Diego County Bar Assn., Consumer Attys. San Diego, Stanford U. Alumni Assn., Jr. League San Diego, Gt. Pyrenees Club Am., Dachshund Club Am., Nu Beta Epsilon. Avocations: gardening, reading, tennis, Great Pyrenees dogs. Office: 110 W C St Ste 812 San Diego CA 92101-3906

SHELTON, JODY, educational executive director; b. Norton, Kans., Aug. 4, 1944; d. James Pratt and Rita Merle (Thompson) Shelton. BA, Ottawa U., 1967; MEd, Emporia State U., 1977; EdD, Kans. U., 1991. Tchr. Belvoir Elem. Sch., Topeka, 1967-68, Ctrl. Elem. Sch., Olathe, Kans., 1968-77; prin. Westview Elem. Sch., Olathe, Kans., 1977-80, Tomahawk Elem. Sch., Olathe, Kans., 1980-88; exec. dir. human resources Olathe Dist. Schs., 1988—; cons. Master Tchr., Manhattan, Kans., 1981-86; adj. prof. Emporia (Kans.) State U., 1990—; chair North Ctrl. Edn. Team, 1984; mem. adv. coun. Sch. Edn., Kans. U., Lawrence, 1992—; mem. com. Five Yr. Tech. Plan, Olathe, 1991—. Contbr. articles to profl. jours. Recipient Outstanding Jayne award Jaycees, 1972, Outstanding Young Woman Kans., 1980. Mem. NAESP (Nat. Disting. Prin. award 1987-88), AASPA (affiliate), Kans. Career Devel. and Placement Assn., Kans. Assn. Elem. Sch. Prins. (pres., Nat. Disting. Prin. award 1987-88, Olathe C. of C., United Sch. Adminstrs. (bd. dirs.), Optimist. Avocations: theatre, reading, aerobics, bridge, dancing, traveling. Home: 11546 S Brentwood Dr Olathe KS 66061-9388 Office: Olathe Dist Schs 14160 S Black Bob Rd Olathe KS 66062-2024

SHELTON, KARL MASON, management consultant; b. Lincolnton, N.C., June 8, 1933; s. Karl and Annie (Grace) S.; m. Deloris Hundley, May 8, 1954; children: Melanie Dwain, Leslie Elaine, Kevin Karl. Grad., Am. Inst. Banking, 1960, Carolinas Sch. Banking, 1963, Stonier Grad. Sch. Banking, 1967. Vice pres. N.C. Nat. Bank, Charlotte, 1954-71; sr. v.p., treas. Seattle-First Nat. Bank, 1971-79; pres. Citizens Fidelity Corp., Louisville, 1979-82; exec. v.p. Southeast Bank, N.A., Miami, Fla., 1982-86; pres., chmn. bd. Shelton Mgmt. Services, Panama City, Fla., 1987-88, 89—; pres., chief operating officer Sec. Fed. Savs. Bank, Columbia, S.C., 1988-89. Contbg. editor: Bankers Handbook, 1978. Served with AUS, 1952-54. Methodist.

SHELTON, KEVIN L., geology educator. Prof. geology U. Mo., Columbia. Recipient Lindgren award Soc. Economic Geologists, 1991. Office: Univ of Missouri Columbia Dept of Geol Scis 101 Geol Scis Bldg Columbia MO 65211

SHELTON, LESLIE HABECKER, adult literacy program director; b. Lancaster, Pa., Feb. 15, 1948; d. William Powell and Mary Louise (Habecker) S. BS in Health and Phys. Edn., West Chester U., 1970; MA in Student Pers. Work, U. Iowa, 1972; cert. in graphic design, U. Calif., Santa Cruz, 1980; postgrad., Union Inst., 1997—. Cert. cmty. coll. instr., Calif., tchr., counselor, Iowa, tchr., Pa. Student devel. specialist U. Maine, Farmington, 1972-74; rsch. asst. career counseling U. Colo., Boulder, 1974-75; coord. student activities Iowa Lakes C.C., Estherville, 1975-76, coord. counseling svcs., 1976-78; career counselor, apt. mgr. Loyola Marymount U., L.A., 1978-79; exec. dir. Am. Cancer Soc. Monterey, Calif., 1979-82; patient svcs. coord. Am. Cancer Soc. San Mateo County, Calif., 1982-85; dir. Project READ South San Francisco Pub. Libr., 1985—. Author: Honoring Diversity: A Multidimensional Learning Model for Adults, 1991, The Dinner Buffet Approach to Learner Support, 1994; illustrator: The Tree Deva. Facilitator, moderator Nat. Issues Forums, South San Francisco, 1987-94; cons., co-creator Easy Reader Voter Guide New Reader Coun. San Francisco Bay Area, 1994; founding bd. dirs. Salinas Valley (Calif.) Hosp. Assn., 1979-81; c.c. rep. Iowa Alliance for Arts in Edn., 1977-78. Grant honoree AAUW, 1989; named one of Outstanding Young Women Am., 1979; Literacy Leader fellow Nat. Inst. Literacy, 1995-96. Mem. Calif. Libr. Assn. (coun. rep. 1991-94, chair literacy chpt. 1988-92), Bay Area Libr. Literacy Programs (chair 1987, 88, 92), New Reader Coun. Bay Area (staff coord. 1989-95), AAUW (chair edn. San Bruno br. 1988), North County Literacy Coun. (chair 1986-94, coord. Calif. statewide adult learner conf. 1996). Avocations: painting, photography, skiing, creating multimedia productions, writing. Office: Project Read South San Francisco Libr 840 W Orange Ave South San Francisco CA 94080-3125

SHELTON, MURIEL MOORE, religious education administrator; b. Freeport, N.Y., May 29, 1921; d. Samuel Talbott and Agnes Jerolean (Trigg) Payne; m. Ernest William Moore, May 29, 1944 (dec. Apr. 2, 1978); children: Diana Moore Williams, David E. Moore, Cathi Moore Mount, Douglas L. Moore; m. Malcolm Wendell Shelton, Aug. 9, 1987. AB, Eastern Nazarene Coll., 1942; MusM, U. Tex., 1966. Cert. educator gen. and choral music, English, Tex., Tenn., Ark., Kans. Music dir. Coll. Ave. United Meth. Ch., Manhattan, Kans., 1969-71, Cen. United Meth. Ch., Lawrence, Kans., 1971-75, First United Meth. Ch., Horton, Kans., 1975-78; dir. Christian edn. St. Mark's United Meth. Ch., Bethany, Okla., 1980—; chmn. bd. dirs. Northwest Food Pantry, Oklahoma City, 1987-88; rep. St. mark's United Meth. Ch. Labor Link Ctr., 1989—; lectr. in field. Contbr. articles to quar. mags.; author: Song of Joy, 1985, Promises of Good, 1989, Healing in His Wings, 1992. Mem. Christian Educators' Fellowship. Home: 6404 NW 35th St Bethany OK 73008-4136 Office: St Mark's United Meth Ch 8140 NW 36th St Bethany OK 73008-3526 *A life for God is eternally significant.*

SHELTON, PHILIP ANDERSON, criminal investigator, writer; b. Coeur d'Alene, Idaho, July 3, 1938; s. Philip Anderson and Mildred Evelyn (Wendt) S.; 1 child, Thane Kevit. Student, Chico (Calif.) State Coll., 1957, U. Calif., Davis, 1960-62, Sacramento State U., 1973-75; BS in Criminology, U. Ala., 1996; postgrad. in Writing, Norwich U., 1996—. Cert. criminal investigator, Calif.; lic. pvt. investigator, Calif. Fraud investigator Philip A. Shelton Profl. Investigations, Sacramento, 1960-64, owner, operator, 1964-77; chief investigator Yolo County Conflict Def., Woodland, Calif., 1966-69; investigator Fed. Pub. Defender, Sacramento, 1975; chief investigator Fed. Pub. Defender, Fresno, 1977-78, Santa Barbara (Calif.) County Pub. Defender, 1978-96; dir. Calif. Death Penalty Rev. and Re-investigation, Santa Barbara, 1996—. Author short stories and novella. Bd. dirs. Santa Barbara Mus. of Art, 1980-84; founding mem. G.A.T.E. Sch. Program, Santa Barbara, 1980-85; mem., group leader City/County Disaster Svcs., Santa Barbara, 1980-89. Recipient Honor for Bravery World Secret Svc. Orgn., 1960; grantee Calif. Cattlemen's Assn., 1956, Fed. Defender Program, Washington, 1978. Mem. World Assn. Detectives, Assn. Brit. Detectives, Coun. Internat. Investigators, Calif. Assn. Lic. Investigators (co-founder 1966, Svc. award 1969), Inst. Personal Injury Investigators (dir., co-founder 1966—), Def. Investigators Assn. Avocations: printing, designing, amateur radio, lecturing, acting.

SHELTON, RICKY VAN, country music singer, songwriter; b. Danville, Va., Jan. 12, 1952; s. Jenks Dewitt and Julia Eloise (Simpson) S.; m. Bettye Witt, Aug. 4, 1986. Grad. high sch., Gretna, Va., 1970. Various pipefitting and constrn. jobs various cos., 1970-86; car salesman Alta Vista (Va.) Ford Co., 1972-74; plumber J.H. Cothran Plumbing Co., Alta Vista, Va., 1980-84; country music singer Columbia Records, Nashville, 1985—. Albums: Wild-Eyed Dream, 1987, Loving Proof, 1988, Ricky Van Shelton Sings Christmas, 1989, RVS III, 1990, Backroads, 1991, Don't Overlook Salvation, 1992, Greatest Hits Plus, 1992, A Bridge I Didn't Burn, 1993, Love and Honor, 1994. Recipient TNN/Music City News Awards Entertainer of the Yr., 1990, 91. Mem. Country Music Assn. (Horizon award 1988, Male Vocalist of Yr. 1989), Acad. County Music. Recipient Male Vocalist of Yr. award, Album of Yr. award Nashville Network Viewer's Choice, 1989. Avocations: farming, fishing, raising beefalo. Office: care Michael Campbell & Assocs 40 Music Sq E Nashville TN 37203-4323 also: 34 Music Sq E Nashville TN 37203*

SHELTON, ROBERT NEAL, physics educator, researcher; b. Phoenix, Oct. 5, 1948; s. Clark B. and Grace M. (McLaughlin) S.; m. Adrian Ann Millar, Aug. 30, 1969; children: Christian, Cameron, Stephanie. BS, Stanford U., 1970; MS, U. Calif., San Diego, 1973, PhD, 1975. Postdoctoral researcher U. Calif.-San Diego, La Jolla, 1975-76, asst. rsch. physicist, 1976-78; asst. prof. Iowa State U., Ames, 1978-81, assoc. prof., 1981-84, prof. physics, 1984-87; prof. physics, chmn. dept. U. Calif.-Davis, 1987-90, vice chancellor for rsch., 1990-96, vice provost for rsch., 1996—. Contbr. over 200 articles to profl. jours. Fellow Am. Phys. Soc.; mem. Sigma Xi. Office: U Calif Dept Physics Davis CA 95616

SHELTON, ROBERT WARREN, marketing executive; b. Albuquerque, Apr. 26, 1943; s. Eugene and Rusty M. (Jentsch) S.; children: Elise Straus, Samantha; m. Ginger Lee Rapp, Feb. 14, 1984. BBA in Mktg., St. Mary's U., San Antonio, 1969; postgrad., Ga. State U., 1972-73, postgrad. in fin. and internat. bus., 1973. Field mgr. Ford Motor Co., Atlanta, 1969-78; dir. fleet ops. Rollins, Inc., Atlanta, 1978-81; v.p. sales and ops. Lease Plan U.S.A., Atlanta, 1981-85; v.p. mktg. Spencer Services, Inc., Roswell, Ga., 1985-87; v.p. FX-10 Corp., 1987-88; pres. Shiloh Capital Corp., 1989—; pres. Victory Svcs., Inc., 1998—, Shiloh Capital Corp., 1989, USA Calling, Inc., The Phone Co., Inc., 1993. Mem. Lost Forest Civic Assn. (pres. 1980-81). Mem. Nat. Assn. Fleet Adminstrs., Am. Fleet and Leasing Assn., NRA. Republican. Christian. Avocations: golf, racquetball, tennis, shooting. Office: 1201 Peachtree St NE Atlanta GA 30361-3500

SHELTON, SLOANE, actress; b. Hahira, Ga., Mar. 14, 1934; d. Clarence Duffie and Ruth Evangeline (Davis) S. Student, Berea Coll., 1955; honors diploma, Royal Acad. Dramatic Art, London, 1959. Mem. O'Neill Found., Waterford, Conn., 1981-83, 85, 89, 91, 94; mem. theater panel N.Y. State Coun. on the Arts, 1979-81. Producer: (with Kevin Brownlow and Norma Millay Ellis) (documentary film) Millay at Steepletop, 1976; appearances in Broadway plays include: I Never Sang for My Father, Sticks & Bones, The Runner Stumbles, The Shadow Box, Orpheus Descending, Passione, Open Admissions; films include: All That Jazz, All the President's Men, Tiger Warsaw, Running on Empty, Jacknife, Lean on Me. Pres. Berrilla Kerr Found., N.Y.C., 1993-96. Mem. SAG, AFTRA, Actors Equity Assn., Actors Fund Am. Democrat.

SHELTON, STEPHANI, broadcast journalist, consultant; b. Boston; d. Phil and Babette (Belloff) Saltman; m. Frank Herold. BS, Boston U. Reporter, news broadcaster Sta. WPAT, Paterson, N.J., 1972-73; corr. CBS News, N.Y.C., 1973-84; news corr. WWOR-TV, N.Y.C., 1984-88; corr., anchor Fin. News Network, N.Y.C., 1989-91; ind. broadcast journalist, producer, cons., 1991—; freelance reporter Sta. WPIX-TV, 1991-95, Sta. WNBC-TV, 1993-96; freelance radio documentary writer Westinghouse Group W Broadcasting, N.Y.C., 1970-73. Recipient Peabody award, 1972, N.J. Best Spot News award AP, 1987, 88, N.J. Working Press award, 1992, 93, 94; Emmy nominee, 1994-95. Mem. Radio and TV Working Press Assn. (v.p. 1985—), Soc. Profl. Journalists, Radio and TV News Dirs. Assn., N.Y.C. Press Club. *Guiding principles: a questioning mind, a refusal to take no for an answer and the memory of 28 marathons. Whatever happens the important thing is to survive.*

SHELTON, WAYNE VERNON, professional services and systems integration company executive; b. Mpls., Nov. 27, 1932; s. Olen George and Evelyn Ruth (Karpen) S.; m. Mary Kay Schwappach, Dec. 29, 1956; children: William David, Susan Evelyn. BS, U. Minn., 1954. Instr. U. Minn., Mpls., 1954-56; tchr. Mpls. Pub. Schs., 1956-57; mathematician Rand Corp., Santa Monica, Calif., 1957-62; sr. assoc. Planning Research Corp., Los Angeles, 1963-72; v.p. Planning Research Corp., McLean, Va., 1972-83, sr. v.p., 1983-85, pres., chief operating officer, 1985-87, chmn., pres. and chief exec. officer, 1987-90; v.p. Emhart Corp., Farmington, Conn., 1987-88; exec. v.p., pres. Emhart Info. and Electronics Systems, Towson, Md., 1988-90; v.p., sr. v.p. Hughes Aircraft Co., 1990—; pres. Hughes Info. Systems, Reston, Va., 1994—; instr. data processing Santa Monica (Calif.) Coll., 1960-62; pres. Assn. Ind. Software Cos., McLean, 1970-71; bd. dirs. Profl. Svcs. Coun., Washington, 1972—, vice chmn., 1993-95; bd. dirs. Security Affairs Support Assn., Annapolis, Md., 1983-85, chmn., 1983-84. Bd. dirs. No. Va. Tech. Coun., 1992—, Wolf Found., 1996—; mem. Va. Bus. Coun., 1996—. Mem. Armed Forces Comm. and Electronics Assn. (bd. dirs. 1987—, internat. v.p. 1994-96), Navy League (life), Assn. U.S. Army, Air Force Assn., Nat. Security Indsl. Assn., Am. Electronics Assn. (bd. dirs. 1988-89, 93—). Republican. Avocations: gardening, personal investments, personal computers, running. Home: 8578 Brickyard Rd Rockville MD 20854-4833

SHELTON, WILLIAM CHASTAIN, retired government statistician, investor; b. Athens, Ga., May 5, 1916; s. William Arthur and Effie Clyde (Landrum) S.; m. Helen Higgins, Dec. 17, 1938; children: Stuart H., Terry Ann Shelton Coble, Jean R. Shelton Jaffray, Alvin C. AB, Princeton U., 1936; postgrad. U. Chgo., 1937-38. Economist, statistician Fed. Govt., Washington, 1936-48; chief stats. sect. USRO-Marshall Plan, Paris, France, 1948-55; mgr. bus. research Fla. Devel. Com., Tallahassee, 1956-60; asst. com. foreign labor Bur. Labor Stats., Washington, 1960-75; spl. asst. statis. policy div. Office Mgmt. and Budget, 1975-77. Author: (with Joseph W. Duncan) Revolution in U.S. Government Statistics, 1926-76, 1978; contbr. articles to profl. jours. Mem. Am. Statis. Assn., Washington Soc. Investment Analysts, Nat. Economists Club, Sigma Xi, Phi Beta Kappa. Republican. Presbyterian. Home: 8401 Piney Branch Rd Silver Spring MD 20901-4353

SHELTON, WILLIAM EVERETT, university president; b. Batesville, Miss., Sept. 6, 1944; s. Loyd Taylor and Merle Golden (Barlow) S.; m. Sharon Nordengreen, Apr. 23, 1965; 1 child, William Bradley. BS, Memphis State U., 1967, MA, 1970; EdD, U. Miss., 1975. Tchr. Olive Branch (Miss.) High Sch., 1967-68; prin. Oakland (Tenn.) Elem. Sch., 1968-70; adminstr., instr. N.W. Miss. Jr. Coll., Senatobia, 1970-76; dean for student devel. Henderson State U., Arkadelphia, Ark., 1976-78, v.p., 1978-83; v.p. Kent (Ohio) State U., 1983-89; pres. Ea. Mich. U., Ypsilanti, 1989—. Vice chmn. Ohio Pub. TV, 1986-89. Mem. Am. Assn. for Higher Edn., Am. Assn. State Colls. and Univs., Kent Area C. of C. (pres. 1986). Avocations: flying, golf. Office: Ea Mich U 202 Welch Hall Ypsilanti MI 48197-2214*

SHEMANSKY, CINDY ANN, nursing educator; b. Mt. Holly, N.J., Sept. 27, 1959; d. Richard and Joan Mary (Schiehle) Wright; m Paul Joseph Shemansky, Feb. 14, 1981; 1 child, Craig Richard. RN, Mercer Med. Ctr., 1980; BA in Edn., St. Joseph's Coll., Maine, 1993; MEd, City U., Washington, 1997. Cert. in gerontology. Preceptor, staff nurse med.-surg. area Mercer Med. Ctr., Trenton, N.J.; dir. edn. Masonic Home N.J., Burlington; task force mem. N.J. Dept. of Health Nurse Aide Curriculum. Contbr. articles to profl. jours.; columnist Nat. Nursing Staff Devel. Orgn. Recipient Excellence in Nursing Practice cert. N.J. Dept. Health, 1991, N.J. Dirs. Nursing Excellence in LTC cert., 1992, RN Splty. award in edn. N.J. Dirs. Nursing Adminstrn., 1993, Nat. Recognition award Nat. Nursing Staff Devel. Orgn., 1994. Mem. ANA, Nat. Gerontol. Nurses Assn. (apptd. to edn. com.), N.J. State Nurses Assn., Nat. Nursing Staff Devel. Orgn. (Promoting Excellence in the Climate for Edn. award 1994, Belinda E. Puetz award 1995), Trenton Regional Assn. Insvc. Nurses (past pres., v.p.).

SHEMIN, BARRY L., insurance company executive; b. Bklyn., Dec. 17, 1942. AB magna cum laude, Brown U., 1963; MA, U. Mich., 1964. With John Hancock Mut. Life Ins. Co., Boston, 1968—, sr. v.p., corporate actuary; bd. dirs. John Hancock Property and Casualty Holding Co., Hancock Natural Resource Group. Bd. dirs. ARC of Mass. Bay, also vice chair. Fellow Soc. Actuaries; mem. Am. Acad. Actuaries, Internat. Actuarial Assn., Phi Beta Kappa, Sigma Xi. Club: Brown Univ. (Boston). Office: John Hancock Mut Life Ins Co PO Box 111 Boston MA 02117-0111

SHEN, BENJAMIN SHIH-PING, scientist, engineer, educator; b. Hangzhou, China, Sept. 14, 1931; s. Nai-cheng and Chen-chiu (Sun) S.; m.

Lucia Elisabeth Simpson, 1971; children: William, Juliet. AB, Assumption Coll., Mass., 1954, ScD (hon.), 1972; AM in Physics, Clark U., 1956; DSc d'Etat in Physics, U. Paris, 1964; MA (hon.), U. Pa., 1971. Asst. prof. physics SUNY, Albany, 1956-59; assoc. prof. space sci., dept. aeros. and astronautics Engring. Sch., NYU, 1964-66; assoc. prof. U. Pa., Phila., 1966-68, prof., 1968-72, Reese W. Flower prof. astronomy and astrophysics, 1972-96, Reese Flower prof. emeritus, 1996—, assoc. provost, 1979-80, chmn. coun. grad. deans, 1979-81, provost, 1980-81, chmn. dept. astronomy and astrophysics, 1973-79, dir. Flower and Cook Obs., 1973-79, mem. Ctr. for Energy and Environment, 1976-93, chmn. roundtable on sci., industry and policy, 1976-96, prof. Sch. Engring. and Applied Sci., 1980-85; mem. U.S. Nat. Sci. Bd., 1990-94, chmn. U.S. sci. and engring. indicators, 1990-92, chmn. task force on sci. literacy, 1992-94; mem. Nat. Coun. on Sci. and Tech. Edn., 1996—; cons. GE, 1961-68, Office Tech. Assessment, U.S. Congress, 1977-78; sci. and tech. adviser Budget Com., U.S. Senate, 1976-77; guest staff Brookhaven Nat. Lab., 1963-64, 65-70; chmn. commn. on pub. understanding on sci. N.Y. Acad. Scis., 1972-75; mem. adv. com. Mt. John Obs., New Zealand, 1978-84. Author: Nuclear Problems in Radiation Shielding in Space, 1963, Passage des Protons dans des Milieux Condenses, 1964; co-editor, co-author: High-Energy Nuclear Reactions in Astrophysics, 1967; Spallation Nuclear Reactions and Their Applications, 1976, Research in the Age of the Steady, 1982; mem. editorial bd. Earth and Extraterrestrial Scis., 1974-78, assoc. editor, 1978-79; assoc. editor: Comments on Astrophysics, 1979-85; contbr. articles to profl. jours. Mem. Hayden Planetarium com. of bd. trustees Am. Mus. Natural History, 1978—; mem. sci. adv. bd. Children's TV Workshop, N.Y.C., 1977, 79—; mem. ABA-AAAS Nat. Conf. Bd. Lawyers and Scientists, 1986-92; former trustee or bd. dirs. N.Y. Acad. Scis., University City Sci. Ctr. Rsch. Park, Phila., U. Pa. Rsch. Found., Morris Arboretum, Phila., Univ. Mus., Phila., Pa. Ballet Co. Decorated Ordre des Palmes Academiques (France); recipient Vermeil medal for sci. Soc. d'Encouragement au Progres, France, 1978. Fellow Am. Phys. Soc., AAAS (com. on sci. engring. and pub. policy 1978-84, Royal Astron. Soc. (U.K.); mem. Internat. Astron. Union. Office: U Pa Dept Physics & Astronomy Philadelphia PA 19104-6396

SHEN, CHIA THENG, former steamship company executive, religious institute official; b. Chekiang, China, Dec. 15, 1913; came to U.S., 1952, naturalized, 1964; s. Foo Sheng and Wen Ching (Hsai) S.; m. Woo Ju Chu, Apr. 21, 1940; children: Maria May Shen Jackson, Wilma Way Shen George, David Chuen-Tsing, Freda Foh. BEE, Chiao Tung U., 1937; LittD (hon.), St. John's U., 1973. With Central Elec. Mfg. Works, China, 1937-44; factory mgr. Central Elec. Mfg. Works, 1942-44; dep. coordinating dept. Nat. Resources Commn., Govt. of China, 1945-47; pres. China Trading and Indsl. Devel. Corp., Shanghai, 1947-49; mng. dir. China Trading & Indsl. Devel. Co. Ltd., Hong Kong, 1949-53; with TransAtlantic Financing Corp., 1954-62, pres., 1958-62; pres. Pan-Atlantic Devel. Corp., N.Y.C., 1955-70; with Marine Transport Lines Inc., N.Y.C., 1958-70; sr. v.p. Marine Transport Lines Inc., 1964-70; with Am. Steamship Co., Buffalo, 1967-80; chmn. bd., chief exec. officer Am. Steamship Co., 1971-80. Trustee Inst. Advanced Studies World Religions, N.Y., 1970—, chmn. bd., chief exec. officer, 1970-92, pres., 1970-84, 90—; trustee China Inst. in Am., N.Y.C., 1963-90, vice chmn., 1970-79, chmn., 1979-80, mem. exec. com., 1963-84; trustee, v.p. Buddhist Assn. U.S., N.Y.C., 1964—. Mem. Chinese Inst. Engring., Electronic Buddhadharma Soc. (dir.). Home and Office: RD 13 Rte 301 Carmel NY 10512-9802 *To benefit all human beings and to work toward freeing them from fear is my goal. The collective wisdom of all world religions furnishes us the direction and means to achieve that goal. To introduce such wisdom into the daily life of mankind in general and America in particular, is therefore what I devote my energy to.*

SHEN, EDWARD NIN-DA, cardiologist, educator; b. Hong Kong, July 3, 1950; came to U.S., 1979; s. Han-Ting and Yay-Wen (Tsu) S.; m. MaryRose Yung-Yung Wong, June 19, 1983; children: Erin Pey-Juan, Dylan Hua-Juan. BSc in Biochemistry with 1st class honors, McGill U., Montreal, Que., Can., 1972, MD, CM, 1976. Diplomate Am. Bd. Internal Medicine, Am. Bd. Cardiovascular Disease, Am. Bd. Electrophysiology, Am. Bd. Clin. Cardiac Electrophysiology. Resident in internal medicine McGill U., 1976-79; cardiology fellow U. Calif., San Francisco, 1979-81, electrophysiology fellow Cardiovascular Rsch. Inst., 1981-82, instr. in medicine Moffitt Hosp., 1982-83; assoc. chief cardiology Santa Clara Valley Med. Ctr., San Jose, Calif., 1983-85; clin. asst. prof. U. Calif., San Francisco, Stanford, 1983-85; dir. clin. electrophysiology Straub Clinic, Honolulu, 1986-93, chief of medicine, 1991-93; assoc. prof. medicine U. Hawaii, Honolulu, 1988-93, chief cardiology, 1993—, prof. medicine, 1994—; attending physician Moffit-Long Hosps., 1982-83; dir. electrocardiography, co-dir. noninvasive cardiac lab. Santa Clara Valley Med. Ctr., 1983-85; attending cardiologist Queen's Heart Inst., Straub Clinic & Hosp., St. Francis Hosp., Kuakini Hosp., 1993—; fellow Med. Rsch. Coun. Can., 1981-83; presenter in field. Contbr. over 90 articles to profl. jours. Bd. dirs. Am. Heart Assn., 1987-89, mem. peer rev. bd. for grant-in-aid applicants, 1987-89. Univ. scholar, 1968-75; recipient Charles E. Frosst prize and medal, Cushing Meml. prize Montreal Children's Hosp., John C. Milnor Profl. and Grey Champion Activities award Straub Found., 1990; Edward N. Shen scholar award in his honor U. Hawaii. Fellow ACP, Royal Coll. Physicians of Can., Am. Coll. Cardiology (gov. 1989-92), Am. Coll. Chest Physicians, Am. Heart Assn. Coun. Clin. Cardiology (Hawaii rep. 1991—); mem. Royal Coll Physicians and Surgeons Can. (cert. internal medicine, cardiology), N.Am. Soc. Pacing and Electrophysiology, Assn. Profs. of Cardiology, Mensa. Roman Catholic. Achievements include performance of first percutaneous transaluminal coronary angioplasty in Hong Kong, the first cases of automatic implantable cardiovertor-defibrillator, catheter ablation of arrhythmic circuits, coronary atherectomy, intracoronary stenting in Hawaii. Avocations: golf, classical guitar, Chinese poetry and literature. Office: 1380 Lusitana St Ste 701 Honolulu HI 96813-2443

SHEN, GENE GIIN-YUAN, organic chemist; b. Taipei, Taiwan, Apr. 12, 1957; came to U.S., 1981; s. Chi and Su-Chin Shen; m. Grace Hsiao-Fen Shen, July 31, 1982; 1 child, Jennifer Iting. BS in Chemistry, Nat. Taiwan U., 1979; PhD in Organic Chemistry, U. Calif., Riverside, 1986. Postdoctoral fellow U. Calif., Riverside, 1986-87; rsch. chemist Nucleic Acid Rsch. Inst. ICN, Costa Mesa, Calif., 1987-88; prin. investigator Pharm-Eco Labs., Inc., Simi Valley, Calif., 1988-91; staff scientist Beckman Instruments, Inc., Brea, Calif., 1991—. Contbr. articles to Jour. Am. Chem. Soc., Jour. Steroid Biochemistry and Molecular Biology, Tetrahetron Letters, Nucleosides and Nucleotides, others. Mem. Am. Chem. Soc., Phi Beta Kappa. Achievements include research in antisense oligonucleotides, near infrared fluorescent dyes and their applications to fluoroimmuno assay and DNA sequencing, dideoxynucleosides and deoxynucleosides as anti-AIDS drugs, avidin-biotin chemistry, turbidimetric and nephelometric immunoinhibition assay, Vitamin A and Vitamin D analogs as cancer chemopreventive and chemotherapeutic agents, sigmatropic rearrangement of vinylallenes. Office: Beckman Instruments Inc 200 S Kraemer Blvd Brea CA 92821-6208

SHEN, HUNG TAO, hydraulic engineering educator; b. Shanghai, China, May 4, 1944; s. Chin Mei and Ai-Yuan (Chen) S.; m. Hayley Hsi, May 26, 1973; children: Scott P., June P. BSCE, Chung Yuan U., Chungli, Taiwan, 1965; ME, Asian Inst. Tech., Bangkok, 1969; PhD in Mechanics and Hydraulics, U. Iowa, 1974. Engring. analyst Sargent & Lundy, Chgo., 1974-76; asst. prof. Clarkson U., Potsdam, N.Y., 1976-81, assoc. prof., 1981-83, prof. civil and environ. engring., 1983—, chair fluid mechanics and thermal sci. program, 1980-88; expert, cons. U.S. Army Cold Regions Rsch. and Engring., Hanover, N.H., 1984—; vis. prof. Lulea (Sweden) U., 1990-91; advisor China Inst. Water Resources and Hydropower Rsch., Beijing, 1994—. Editor: Frontiers in Hydraulic Engineering, 1983; assoc. editor Jour. Cold Regions ASCE, 1994—; mem. editorial bd. Jour. Hydraulic Rsch., 1993—; contbr. articles to Jour. Hydraulic Engring., Geophys. Rsch., Hydraulic Rsch., Fluid Mechanics. Bd. dirs. Asian Inst. Tech. Found., N.Y., 1984-90. U.S. Nat. Acad. Sci. vis. scholar, 1991; grantee NSF, U.S. Army Rsch. Office, NOAA, Dept. Transp., World Bank. Mem. ASCE (tech. coms. 1980—), Am. Geophys. Union, Internat. Assn. Hydraulic Rsch. (ice rsch. and engring. com. 1986-94, chair 14th Internat. Symposium on Ice), Internat. Assn. Great Lakes Rsch. Achievements include development of first comprehensive computer model on river ice, and theories on frazil jam evolution, and dynamic transport and jamming of surface ice in rivers; computer models on oil/chemical spills in rivers. Office: Clarkson U Dept Civil & Environ Engr Box 5710 Potsdam NY 13699-5710

SHEN, LIANG CHI, electrical engineer, educator, researcher; b. China, Mar. 17, 1939; came to U.S., 1962; s. Kuang Huai and Ting Chin (Yu) S.; m. Grace Liu, June 26, 1965; children: Michael, Eugene. BSEE, Nat. Taiwan U., Taipei, 1961; PhD, Harvard U., 1967. Registered profl. engr., Tex. Prof., chmn. electrical engring. dept. U. Houston, 1977-81, prof., dir. well logging lab., 1978—. Author: Applied Electromagnetism, 1987, 3d edit., 1995. Fellow IEEE. Office: U Houston Dept Elec Engring Houston TX 77204

SHEN, MASON MING-SUN, medical center administrator; b. Shanghai, Jiang Su, China, Mar. 30, 1945; came to U.S., 1969; s. John Kaung-Hao and Mai-Chu (Sun) S.; m. Nancy Hsia-Hsian Shieh, Aug. 7, 1976; children: Teresa Tao-Yee, Darren Tao-Ru. BS in Chemistry, Taiwan Normal U., 1963-67; MS in Chemistry, S.D. State U., 1971; PhD in Biochemistry, Cornell U., 1977; postgrad., U. Calif., Berkeley, 1977-79; MS in Chinese Medicine, China Acad., Taipei, Taiwan, 1982; OMD, San Francisco Coll Acupuncture, 1984; AMD (hon.), Asian Am. Acupuncture Coll., San Diego, 1985; MD (Medicina Alternativa), Internat. U., Colombo, Sri Lanka, 1988. Diplomate Nat. Commn. for Cert. of Acupuncturists; lic. acupuncturist. Rsch. assoc. Lawrence Livermore (Calif.) Lab., 1979-80; assoc. prof. Nat. Def. Med. Coll., Taipei, 1980-82; prof. Inst. of Chinese Medicine China Acad., Taipei, 1981-82, San Francisco Coll. Acupuncture, 1983-85, Acad. Chinese Culture & Health Scis., Oakland, Calif., 1985-86; pres. Florescent Inst. Traditional Chinese Medicine, Oakland, 1995—; adminstr. Am. Ea. Med. Inst., Pleasanton, 1993—; chmn. adminstrn. subcom., 1991-92, acupuncture com. State of Calif., 1988-92; dir. United Calif. Practitioners of Chinese Medicine, San Francisco, 1995—. Contbr. articles to profl. jours. Rep. Republican Party, Danville, 1988-93; bd. dirs. Asian Rep. Assembly, 1989—; mem. presdnl. adv. com. Republican Presdl. Task Force, 1992; mem. chmn's. adv. bd. Republican Nat. Com., 1993. Recipient Nat. Rsch. Svc. award NIH, 1977, Presdl. Order of Merit, Pres. of the U.S., 1991. Mem. AAAOM (pres.), N.Y. Acad. Sci., Calif. Cert. Acupuncturists Assn. (bd. dirs. 1984-88, pres. 1984-85, mem. polit. action com. 1995—), Acupuncture Assn. Am. (bd. dirs. 1986-90, v.p. 1987-89), Am. Assn. Acupuncture and Oriental Medicine (bd. dirs. 1987-92, pres. 1989-90), Nat. Acupuncture Detoxification Assn. (cons. 1987—), Presdl. Round Table (presdl. adv. com.), Hong Kong and Kowloon Chinese Med. Assn. (hon. life pres. 1985). Republican. Avocations: travel, horse back riding, rifles. Home: 3240 Touriga Dr Pleasanton CA 94566-6966 Office: Eastern Med Ctr 3510 Old Santa Rita Rd Ste D Pleasanton CA 94588-3466 also: 400 El Cerro Blvd Ste 105 Danville CA 94526

SHEN, MICHAEL, lawyer; b. Nanking, Jiangsu, Peoples Republic of China, Aug. 15, 1948; came to U.S. 1951; s. James Cheng Yee and Grace (Pai) S.; m. Marina Manese (div.); m. Pamela Nan Bradford, Aug. 12, 1983; 1 child, Jessica Li. BA, U. Chgo., 1969; MA, U. Pa., 1970; JD, Rutgers U., 1979. Bar: U.S. Dist. Ct. N.J. 1979, N.Y. 1980, U.S. Dist. Ct. (so., no. and ea. dists.) N.Y. 1980, N.J. 1981, U.S. Ct. Appeals (2d cir.) 1987, U.S. Supreme Ct. 1988, U.S. Ct. Appeals (3rd cir.) 1996. Staff atty. Bedford Stuyvesant Legal Svcs., Bklyn., 1979-80, Com. for Interns and Residents, N.Y.C., 1980-81; ptnr. Shneyer & Shen, P.C., N.Y.C. 1981—; pres. bd. dirs. Asian Am. Legal Def. and Edn. Fund, N.Y.c.; of counsel 318 Restaurant Workers Union, N.Y.C., 1984—. Bd. dirs. Nat. Asian Pacific Am. Legal Consortium, N.Y.C., Nat. Employment Law Project; bd. dirs. N.Y. Civil Liberties Union, N.Y.C., 1987—. Mem. Internat. Platform Assn., Nat. Employees Lawyers Assn., N.Y. State Bar Assn., N.Y. County Bar Assn., Nat. Lawyers Guild. Avocations: squash, reading. Office: Shneyer & Shen PC 2109 Broadway Ste 206 New York NY 10023-2106 also: 1085 Cambridge Rd Teaneck NJ 07666-1901

SHEN, SIN-YAN, physicist, conductor, acoustics specialist; b. Singapore, Nov. 12, 1949; came to U.S., 1969, naturalized, 1984; s. Shao-Quan and Tien-Siu (Chen) S.; m. Yuan-Yuan Lee, Aug. 4, 1973; children: Jia, Jian. BSc U. Singapore, 1969; MS Ohio State U. 1970, PhD, 1973. concert recitalist on Erhu fiddle, 1963—; instr. math. U. Singapore, 1969; asst. prof. physics Northwestern U., Evanston, Ill., 1974-77, assoc. prof., 1977-81; faculty assoc. Argonne Nat. Lab., Ill., 1974-77, scientist, 1977-83; sr. rsch. leader, 1983—; dir. rsch. Div. Natural Resource Mgmt., SUPCON Internat., 1988—; prof. Harvard U., 1989—; meeting series reviewer NSF, Washington, 1981—; coord. Tech. Rev., Argonne, Atlanta, Phoenix, Portland (Oreg.), 1983—; dir. Global Warming Internat. Ctr., 1991—, chmn. of Internat. Conference Chgo., 1990-93, San Francisco, 1994-95, Vienna, 1996, Columbia U., N.Y.C., 1997; Chinese Music Internat. Conf., 1991, 94; advisor Internat. Energy Agy, 1986—, Gas Rsch. Inst., 1984—, SUPCON Internat., 1986—, Nat. Geographic, 1986—, Internat. Boreal Forest Rsch. Assn., 1991—, Electric Power Rsch. Inst., 1992—, UN Devel. Program, 1993—, World Bank, 1994—, U.S. Dept. Energy and U.S. EPA, 1995—; prof. Chinese Acad. Forestry, 1986—; mem. panel on biol. diversity Nat. Acad. Scis., Smithsonian Instn., 1986; chmn. internat. program com. Austrian Acad. Scis., 1995-96; music dir. Orch. of Chinese Music Soc. of N.Am., 1976—, The Silk & Bamboo Ensemble, 1981—; delagation leader, UN Conference Environ. and Devel., Rio, 1992; panelist Nat. Endowment for Arts, 1981—, New England Found. for Arts, 1987—, Arts Midwest, 1985—, Ill. Arts Coun., 1982—, Chgo. City Arts, 1990—, Ill. Art's Alliance Found. (adv. coun. 1992—, bd. dirs., 1988—), mem. adv. coun. Mid-Am. Arts Alliance, 1992—; tech. adv. Shanghai Nat. Musical Instruments Co., 1985—; adv. West Lake Qin Soc., Hangzhou, China, 1991—. Author: Superfluidity, 1982, Chinese Music and Orchestration: A Primer om Principles and Practice, 1991, Global Warming Science and Policy, 1992, The Boreal Forests and Global Change, 1993; patentee molten liquids, 1974, 1980; editor-in-chief Chinese Music Internat. Jour., 1978—; mem. internat. editorial bd. World Resource Review, 1989—, Internat. Boreal Forest Rsch., 1992—, Ency. of Life Support Sys., 1994—; adv. Ency. Brit., 1983—; contbr. over 300 articles prof. jours. Fulbright scholar U.S. State Dept, 1969; merit scholar Govt. Singapore, 1967; recipient Mich. Heritage award, 1992. Mem. AAAS, Am. Phys. Soc., Ops. Rsch. Soc. Am., Acoustical Soc. Am., Chinese Music Soc. N.Am. Current work: Renewable energy and materials techs.; global change; indsl. sonic techs.; energy policy, planning and economics; acoustics; cultural acoustics. Office: Chinese Music Soc N Am 2329 Charmingfare Dr Downers Grove IL 60517-2910 also: SUPCON Internat PO Box 5275 Woodridge IL 60517-0275

SHEN, THEODORE PING, investment banker; b. N.Y.C., Feb. 18, 1945; s. Shih-Chang and Clara Grace (Low) S.; m. Carol Lee Wing, June 13, 1968; 1 child, Carla Patricia. B.A. in Econs., Yale U., 1966; M.B.A. in Fin., Harvard U., 1968. V.p., securities analyst Donaldson, Lufkin & Jenrette, N.Y.C., 1968-78, mng. dir. research, 1978-81, mng. dir. equities div., 1981-84, pres. DLJ Capital Markets Group, 1984-86, chmn. DLJ Capital Markets Group, 1986—; bd. dirs. Donaldson, Lufkin & Jenrette, Inc., N.Y.C., 1984—. Trustee Phillips Exeter Acad., The Packer Collegiate Inst.; chmn. The Packer Collegiate Inst., 1992-96. Mem. N.Y. Soc. Securities Analysts, The Bond Club of N.Y., Heights Casino Club (Brooklyn Heights, N.Y.). Office: Donaldson Lufkin & Jenrette Securities Corp 277 Park Ave New York NY 10172

SHEN, THOMAS TO, environmental engineer; b. Chia-Shing, Chekiang, China, Aug. 14, 1926; m. Cynthia Shen; children: Grace, Joyce. BS in Civil Engring., St. John's U., Shanghai, People's Rep. China, 1948; MS in Sanitary Engring., Northwestern U., 1960; PhD in Environ. Engring., Rensselaer Poly. Inst., 1971. Registered profl. engr., Wash., N.Y. Assoc. engr. Boeing Co., Renton, Wash., 1961-63; sanitary engr. Wash. State Health Dept., Seattle, 1963-66; sr. sanitary engr. N.Y. State Health Dept., Albany, 1966-70; sr. rsch. scientist N.Y. State Dept. Environ. Conservation, Albany, 1970-93; adj. prof. Columbia U., N.Y.C., 1981-93; mem. U.S. EPA Sci. Adv. Bd., 1987-90; cons. UN's Environ. Protection Program, various Asian cities, 1983—; lectr. various U.S. and fgn. univs., 1978—; cons. World Bank, 1990; tech. reviewer Annual Pres. Bush's Environ. and Conservation Challenge awards, 1991, 92. Author: Air Pollution and Its Control, 1985, Hazardous Waste Incineration, 1982, Assessment and Control of VOC Emissions from Waste Treatment and Disposal Facilities, 1993, Industrial Pollution Prevention, 1995; author: (with others) Electrostatic Precipitator, 1979, Air Quality Assessment, 1989; contbr. articles to profl. jours. Bd. dirs. Internat. Ctr. of the Capital Region, Albany, 1984-88, Am. Bur. Med. Advancement of China, N.Y.C., 1985—. Recipient Svc. award Phi Tau Phi, 1986, Nat. award Indsl. Wast. Minimization Taiwan Environ. Protection Adminstrn., Ministry Fgn. Affairs, 1993, Man of Yr. award N.Y. State Capital Region Chinese Am. Alliance, 1995; Named for Outstanding Editorial Contbn. on Pollution Engring., Chgo., 1978, 81. Fellow ASCE (chmn. N.Y. State Coun. 1979-80); mem. Am. Acad. Environ. Engrs. (diplomate 1973), Air and Waste Mgmt. Assn. (com. chmn. 1985—, Frank Chamber award for Outstanding Achievement in Sci. of Air 1993), Delmar Club (pres. 1979-80), Rotary. Avocations: travel, music appreciation. Home: 146 Fernbank Ave Delmar NY 12054-4215

SHEN, TSUNG YING, medicinal chemistry educator; b. Beijing, China, Sept. 28, 1924; came to U.S., 1950; s. Tsu-Wei and Sien-Wha (Nieu) S.; m. Amy T.C. Lin, June 20, 1953; children: Bernard, Hubert, Theodore, Leonard, Evelyn, Andrea. B.Sc., Nat. Ctrl. U., Chongqing, China, 1946; diploma, Imperial Coll. Sci. and Tech., London, 1948; Ph.D., U. Manchester, Eng., 1950, D.Sc., 1978. Research assoc. Ohio State U., Columbus, 1950-52, MIT, Cambridge, 1952-56; sr. research chemist Merck, Sharp & Dohme Research Labs., Rahway, N.J., 1956-65, dir. synthetic chem. research, 1966-76, v.p. membrane chem. research, 1976-77, v.p. membrane and arthritis research, 1977-86; A. Burger prof. medicinal chemistry U. Va., Charlottesville, 1986-96, emeritus and rsch. prof., 1996—; vis. prof. U. Calif., Riverside, 1973, U. Calif., San Francisco, 1985, Harvard Med. Sch., 1986; adj. prof. Stevens Inst. Tech., Hoboken, N.J., 1982-85; hon. prof. Beijing Med. U., Chinese Acad. Med. Sci., Inst. Material Medica, China Pharm. U.; mem. sci. bd. CytoMed, 1989—, T Cell Sci, 1988-93, Gene Labs., 1989-94, Osteo Arthritis Sci, 1993-95, Argonex, 1994—. Mem. editl. bd. Clinica Europa Jour., 1977, Prostaglandins and Medicine, 1978, Medicinal Rsch. Revs., 1979-94, Jour. Medicinal Chemistry, 1980-83, Medicinal Chem. Rsch., 1991; patentee in field. Recipient Outstanding Patent award N.J. Research and Devel. Council, 1975, Rene Descartes medal U. Paris, 1977, medal of Merit Giornate Mediche Internazionali del Collegium Biologicum Europea, 1977, cert. of merit Spanish Soc. Therapeutic Chemistry, 1983, achievement award Chinese Inst. Engrs.-U.S.A., 1984. Mem. AAAS, Am. Chem. Soc. (1st Alfred Burger award in medicinal chemistry 1980), N.Y. Acad. Scis., Acad. Pharm. Assn. (hon.), Chinese Am. Chem. Soc. (bd. dirs. 1995-97). Home: 10013 Park Royal Dr Great Falls VA 22066-1847 Office: Chem Dept U Va Charlottesville VA 22901

SHEN, YUEN-RON, physics educator; b. Shanghai, China, Mar. 25, 1935; came to U.S.,; BS, Nat. Taiwan U., 1956; MS, Stanford U., 1959; PhD, Harvard U., 1963. Rsch. asst. Hewlett-Packard Co., Palo Alto, Calif., 1959; rsch. fellow Harvard U., Cambridge, Mass., 1963-64; asst. prof. U. Calif., Berkeley, 1964-67, assoc. prof., 1967-70, full prof., 1970—; prin. investigator Lawrence Berkeley Nat. Lab., 1967—. Author: The Principles of Nonlinear Optics, 1984. Sloan fellow, 1966-68; recipient Guggenheim Found. fellowship, 1972-73, Charles Hard Townes award, 1986, Arthur L. Schawlow prize Am. Phys. Soc., 1992, Alexander von Humboldt award, 1984, Outstanding Rsch. award DOE-MRS Rsch., 1983, Sustained Outstanding Rsch. award, 1987, Max Planck Rsch. award, 1996. Fellow Am. Phys. Soc. (disting. traveling lectr. Laser Sci. Topical Group 1994-96), Optical Soc. Am., Photonics Soc. Chinese-Ams.; mem. AAAS, NAS, Academia Sinica, Chinese Acad. Scis. (fgn.). Achievements include research in nonlinear optics and condensed matter physics. Office: U Calif Berkeley Dept Physics Berkeley CA 94720

SHENEFIELD, JOHN HALE, lawyer; b. Toledo, Jan. 23, 1939; s. Hale Thurel and Norma (Bird) S.; m. Judy Simmons, June 16, 1984; children: Stephen Hale, Christopher Newcomb. AB, Harvard U., 1960, LLB, 1965. Bar: Va. 1966, D.C. 1966. Assoc. Hunton & Williams, Richmond, Va., 1965-77; dep. asst. atty. gen. antitrust div. Dept. Justice, Washington, 1977; asst. atty. gen. Dept. Justice, 1977-79, assoc. atty. gen., 1979-81; assoc. Milbank, Tweed, Hadley & McCloy, 1981-86, Morgan, Lewis & Bockius, Washington, 1986—; assoc. prof. law U. Richmond, 1975; prof. law Georgetown Law Ctr., 1981-83; chmn. Nat. Commn. for Rev. Antitrust Law and Procedures, 1978-79. Co-author The Antitrust Laws - A Primer, 2d edit., 1996; contbr. articles on law to profl. jours. Sec. Va. Dem. Com., 1970-72, treas., 1976-77; chmn. Richmond Dem. Party, 1975-77; bd. govs. St. Albans Sch., 1983-90, chmn. 1988-90; mem. chpt. Washington Cathedral, 1988—; pres. Nat. Cathedral Assn., 1993-96; chmn. Va. Racing Commn., 1989—. 2d lt. U.S. Army, 1961-62; to capt. Res., 1965. Mem. ABA, Va. Bar Assn. Home: 220 Carrwood Rd Great Falls VA 22066-3721 Office: Morgan Lewis & Bockius 1800 M St NW Ste 6 Washington DC 20036-5828

SHENG, TSE CHENG (TED C. SHENG), natural resources educator; b. Chia-Hsing, China, Oct. 16, 1924; came to U.S. 1984; s. Tsu Ming and Chen Hwa (Sze) S.; m. Chuan Shen, June 1, 1947; children: Tom Sze-Tsan, Richard Van. BSc, Nat. Chekiang U., 1947; MSc, Colo. State U., 1966. Soil conservation specialist Chinese-Am. Joint Commn. on Rural Reconstruction, Taipei, Republic of China, 1953-68; expert advisor Food and Agrl. Orgn. of UN, Rome, 1968-84; prof. watershed mgmt. Colo. State U., Ft. Collins, 1985-97; cons. Computer Assisted Devel. Inc., Ft. Collins, 1988—. Author: Watershed Conservation I & II, 1986-90, Soil Conservation for Small Farmers in the Humid Tropics, 1989, Watershed Survey and Planning, 1990; editor: Conservation Policies for Sustainable Hillslope Farming, 1992. Recipient award Crown Zellerbach Found., 1965, Hugh Hammond Bennett award, 1991. Mem. Soil and Water Conservation Soc. (life, vice chair internat. affairs com. 1994-97), World Assn. Soil and Water Conservation, Chinese Soil and Water Conservation Soc. (bd. dirs. 1966-68). Avocations: writing poems, prose, articles for newspapers and journals. Office: Computer Assisted Devel Inc. Fort Collins CO 80524

SHENG, YEA-YI PETER, oceanographic engineer, educator, researcher; b. Shanghai, Republic China, Aug. 3, 1946; came to U.S., 1969; s. Ting and Yu-Sen (Yuan) S.; m. Ruth Chou, Aug. 31, 1970; 1 child, David. BSME, Nat. Taiwan U., Taipei, 1968; MS, Case Western Res. U., 1972, PhD, 1975. Research assoc., then sr. research assoc. Case Western Res. U., Cleve., 1975-78; assoc. cons. Aero. Research Assocs. Princeton, N.J., 1978-80, cons., 1980-84, sr. cons., 1984-86, mgr. coastal oceanography, 1985-86; assoc. prof. engring. U. Fla., Gainesville, 1986-88, prof., 1988—; mem. Marine Resources Council, Melbourne, Fla., 1987—; invited prof. Inst. de Mecanique Grenoble, France, 1987; vis. prof. U. Western Australia, 1992-93. Grantee numerous govt. agys. and industries, 1979—. Mem. Am. Geophys. Union, ASCE, ASME, Am. Soc. Engring. Edn. Lutheran. Avocations: tennis, music. Office: U Fla Dept Coastan Ocean Engring 336 Weil Hall Gainesville FL 32611-6590

SHENK, GEORGE H., lawyer; b. N.Y.C., Sept. 10, 1943; BA, Princeton U., 1965; M in Internat. Affairs, Columbia U., 1967; JD, Yale U., 1970. Bar: N.Y. 1971, Calif. 1985. Assoc. Coudert Bros., Paris, 1970, N.Y.C., 1970-73, Hong Kong, 1973-75, Tokyo, 1975-78, ptnr., N.Y.C., 1978-91, San Francisco, 1991-94, ptnr. Heller Ehrman, White & McAuliffe, 1994—. Contbr. articles to publs. Bd. dirs. alumni council Columbia Sch. Internat. Affairs, N.Y.C., 1982-85, French-Am. C. of C. San Francisco, 1991-93, Internat. Ctr., N.Y.C., 1983-86. Mem. Bar Assn. City of N.Y., Calif. State Bar Assn., Council Fgn. Relations, San Francisco Tennis Club. Office: Heller Ehrman White & McAuliffe 333 Bush St San Francisco CA 94104-2806

SHENK, LOIS LANDIS, writer, caregiver; b. Ephrata, Pa., May 30, 1944; d. Raymond Earle and Esther May (Forry) L.; m. John Barge Shenk, June 12, 1965; children: Philip Jon, Matthew Alan. BA in English, Eastern Mennonite Coll., 1966; MSc in Edn., Temple U., 1984. English mistress Githumu Secondary Sch., Thika, Kenya, 1966-68; English tchr. Kraybill's Jr. High, Mount Joy, Pa., 1976-77; freelance writer, 1978—; religious news corr. Gospel Herald, Scottdale, Pa., 1978-82; observer, corr. The U.S. Senate, Washington, 1987—. Author: Out of Mighty Waters, 1982 (R.I.M. excellence award 1983), The Story of Ephrata Mennonite School, 1996; (one act play) A House for David in (anthology) Swords into Plowshares, 1983; (study guide for Christian edn.) Hebrews, 1988; contbr. poems, stories & features to jours.; editl. work Mennonite Ctrl. Com., Akron, Pa., 1977. Democrat. Avocations: reading, swimming, cooking, music, public service. Home and Office: 301 E Church St Stevens PA 17578

SHENK, RICHARD LAWRENCE, real estate developer, photographer, artist; b. Columbus, Ohio, Jan. 26, 1940. BBA, Tulane U., 1961, U. of Va., 1961-62, Ohio State U., 1962-65. Plant mgr. S.A. Shenk Co., 1962-65; v.p. Konter Corp., Cin., 1965-70; owner Richard L. Shenk Devel., Cin., 1970—; former bd. dirs. Consol. Stores Corp., Columbus; co-founder Images Photographic Gallery, Cin., 1980; past pres. Cmty. Improvement Corp., Springdale, Ohio, 1989-93; past. pres., bd. dirs., chmn. fin. com. Talbert

House, Inc., Cin. Author: Different Way of Seeing, 1989. Mem. program com. Judaic studies program U. Cin.; mem. bd. overseers Cin. Campus Hebrew Union Coll.; bd. dirs. Jewish Home of Cin., past campaign chmn., pres. Jewish Fedn. of Cin.; bd. dirs. Adath Israel Synagogue, Israil Ednl. Fund; bd. dirs. Simon Wiesenthal Ctr., L.A., chair fedn. rels. Mem. United Jewish Appeal (nat. vice chmn.), Rotary (past pres. Springdale chpt.), Cedar Village (bd. dirs.). Home: 2349 Grandin Rd Cincinnati OH 45208-3309

SHENK, WILLIS WEIDMAN, newspaper executive; b. Manheim, Pa., Nov. 2, 1915; s. John Horst and Amanda (Weidman) S.; m. Elsie Sherer, Aug. 31, 1940; 1 son, J. David. Acct. Raymond D. Shearer, Lancaster, Pa., 1937-39; sr. acct. Lancaster Newspapers, Inc., 1940-50, sec.-controller, 1950-61, v.p., sec., 1961-76, pres., 1977-83, chmn. bd., 1984—. Pres. United Way of Lancaster County, 1961; pres., bd. trustees Lancaster Country Day Sch., 1971-72; trustee Franklin and Marshall Coll., Lancaster, 1977-85; sec. Pequea Twp. Planning Commn., 1965-77. Mem. Nat. Assn. Accts., Pa. Inst. CPAs, Lancaster Country Club. Lutheran. Clubs: Hamilton, Masons. Office: Lancaster Newspapers Inc PO Box 1328 8 W King St Lancaster PA 17603-3824

SHENKER, IRA RONALD, physician; b. N.Y.C., July 8, 1934; s. Morris and Rose (Wilner) S.; m. Caroline Cabin, June 22, 1958; children: Diane Amy, Mitchell Steven. B.S., U. Wis., 1955, M.D., 1958. Diplomate Am. Bd. Pediatrics. Intern, L.I. Jewish Med. Ctr., New Hyde Park, N.Y., 1958-59; resident pediat., 1959-61; resident pub. health Nassau County Health Dept., N.Y., 1961-62; coll. health physician Mt. Holyoke Coll., 1962-64; chief adolescent medicine L.I. Jewish Med. Ctr., 1965—; assoc. prof. pediat. SUNY-Stony Brook, 1979—; prof. pediat. Albert Enstein Coll. Medicine, 1989—. Author: Human Figure Drawings in Adolescence, 1972. Editor: Adolescent Medicine, 1981, Clinical Monographs in Pediatrics: Adolescent Medicine, 1994. Contbr. articles to profl. jours. Bd. dirs. Roslyn Sr. Citizens, N.Y., 1975-78. USPHS grantee, 1965-82. Fellow Am. Acad. Pediat.; mem. Queens Pediat. Soc. (pres. 1981-82), N.Y. Pediat. Soc., Nassau Pediat. Soc., Soc. for Adolescent Medicine (pres. 1986), pres. N.Y. Pediatric Soc., 1996-97. Home: 5 Fairway Rd Roslyn NY 11576-1099 Address: 270-05 76th Ave New Hyde Park NY 11040-1433 Office: Schneider Children's Hosp of LI Jewish Med Ctr New Hyde Park NY 11042

SHENKER, JOSEPH, academic administrator; b. N.Y.C., Oct. 7, 1939; s. George and Isabelle (Schwartz) S.; m. Adrienne Green (div. 1979); children: Deborah, Karen; m. Susan Armiger, Jan. 2, 1988; children: Sarah Gabrielle, Jordan. BA in Psychology, Hunter Coll., 1962, MA in Econ., 1963; EdD in High Edn., Tchrs. Coll., 1969. Dean, community coll. affairs CUNY, 1967-69; acting pres. Kingsborough Community Coll., N.Y.C., 1969-70; chief negotiator for mgmt. CUNY, 1977; acting pres. Hunter Coll., N.Y.C., 1979-80; founding pres. LaGuardia Community Coll., N.Y.C., 1970-88; pres. Bank St. Coll. Edn., N.Y.C., 1988-95; provost C.W. Post Campus, L.I. U., 1995—; bd. dirs. Sch. & Bus. Alliance, N.Y.C.; ptnr. N.Y.C. Partnership, 1990—. chmn. Liberty Scholarship Adv. Com., Albany, N.Y., 1989—; co-chmn. Task Force on Early Childhood Edn., N.Y.C., 1989—, Agenda for Children Tomorrow, 1989—; chmn. Chancellor's Com. on U./Sch. Collaboratives, N.Y.C., 1988. Recipient Distinguished Alumni award Tchrs. Coll. Columbia, N.Y.C., 1990. Office: C W Post Campus Long Island U 720 Northern Blvd Greenvale NY 11548-1319

SHENKIR, WILLIAM GARY, business educator; b. Three Rivers, Tex., June 27, 1938; s. William and Lydia (Jancik) S.; m. Missy Smith, Jan 1, 1973. B.B.A., Tex. A & M U., 1960; postgrad. (Rockefeller Bros. Theol. fellow), Drew U. Sem., 1960-61; M.B.A., U. Tex., 1962, Ph.D., 1964. Asst. prof. McIntire Sch. Commerce, U. Va., Charlottesville, 1967-69; assoc. prof. McIntire Sch. Commerce, U. Va., 1969-72, prof., 1972-73, dean, 1977-92; William Stamps Farish prof. McIntire Sch. Commerce U. Va., 1982—; project dir. Fin. Acctg. Standards Bd., Stamford, Conn., 1973-76; vis. prof. NYU Grad. Sch. Bus., N.Y.C., 1976-77; bd. dirs. 1st Union Nat. Bank Va., Roanoke. Editor: Carman Blough: His Professional Career and Accounting Thought, 1978; co-editor: The University of Virginia's McIntyre School of Commerce: The First 75 Years, 1921-96, 1996; contbr. articles to profl. jours. Served to lt. USAF, 1964-67. Mem. AICPA, Am. Acctg. Assn. (former v.p.), Acctg. Edn. Change Commn., Am. Assembly Collegiate Schs. of Bus. (former bd. dirs., pres. 1990-91), Fin. Execs. Inst., Va. Soc. CPAs, Boar's Head Sports Club, Raven Soc., Landfall Club, Phi Delta Kappa, Beta Gamma Sigma, Phi Kappa Phi. Presbyterian. Home: 420 Rookwood Dr Charlottesville VA 22903-4732

SHENNUM, ROBERT HERMAN, retired telephone company executive; b. Scobey, Mont., Apr. 12, 1922; s. Joseph M. and Nellie M. Shennum; m. Doris Postlewait; children: Sharon, Keith, Marsha Shennum Burns. B.S.E.E., Mont. State U., 1944, M.S.E.E., 1948, D. Eng. (hon.), 1963; Ph.D. in Physics and Elec. Engring., Calif. Inst. Tech., 1954. Instr. engring. Mont. State U., Bozeman, 1946-50; rsch. assoc. engring. Calif. Inst. Tech., Pasadena, 1950-54; cons. Kelman Electric Co., Los Angeles, 1954; mem. tech. staff AT&T Bell Labs., Murray Hill, N.J., 1954-85; also dir. AT&T Bell Labs., Parsippany, N.J.; mem. adv. com. Internat. Telecommunications Energy Conf., 1974-87. Contbr. articles to profl. jours.; patentee pulse code modulation. Served to 1st lt. Signal Corps, U.S. Army, 1944-46, ETO. Recipient cert. of appreciation for patriotic services U.S. Army, 1975. Fellow IEEE (chmn. N.C. sect. 1973), Greensboro C. of C. (chmn. continuing edn. 1970-74). Republican. Home: 2888 Swan Hwy Bigfork MT 59911-6414

SHEON, AARON, art historian, educator; b. Toledo, Oct. 7, 1937; s. Benjamin William and Katherine (Rappoport) S.; m. Martine Bruel, Jan. 26, 1963 (div. 1986); children: Sandrine, Nicolas. B.A., U. Mich., 1959, M.A., 1960; M.F.A. (Wilson fellow), Princeton U., 1962, Ph.D., 1966; postgrad., U. Paris, 1962-63. Staff officer, dir. gen.'s cabinet UNESCO, Paris, 1963-66; asst. prof. U. Pitts., 1966-69, asso. prof., 1969-78, prof. art history, 1979—, acting chmn. dept. fine arts, 1969, 79-80; dir. univ. program U. Pitts., Rouen, France, 1974-75; vis. prof. Carnegie-Mellon U., 1981; Vis. exhbn. curator Mus. Art, Carnegie Inst., Pitts., 1977-81; program cons. Nat. Endowment Arts and Humanities, 1978-85; visual arts cons. Pa. Arts Council, 1981; vis. mem. Inst. for Advanced Study, Princeton, 1984-85. Author: The Gosman Collection, 1969, Monticelli, His Contemporaries, His Influence, 1978, Organic Vision, The Architecture of Peter Berndtson, 1980, Monticelli, 1986, Paul Guigou, 1987. Recipient Charles E. Merrill faculty award, 1968; Chancellor Bowman award, 1976; Honor award Pa. Soc. Architects, 1982; grantee Ford Found., 1967, NEH, 1979; Gould Arts Found. fellow, 1986. Mem. Coll. Art Assn., Société de l'histoire de l'art français, Am. Assn. of Mus. Office: U Pitts Dept History Arts & Arch Pittsburgh PA 15260

SHEPARD, ALAN BARTLETT, JR., former astronaut, real estate developer; b. East Derry, N.H., Nov. 18, 1923; s. Alan Bartlett and Renza (Emerson) S.; m. Louise Brewer, Mar. 3, 1945; children: Laura, Juliana. Student, Admiral Farragut Acad., 1940; B.S., U.S. Naval Acad., 1944; grad., Naval War Coll., 1958; M.S. (hon.), Dartmouth Coll.; D.Sc. (hon.), Miami U. Commd. ensign USN, 1944, advanced through grades to rear adm., 1971, designated naval aviator, 1947; assigned destroyer U.S.S. Cogswell, Navy Test Pilot Sch., Pacific, World War II, Fighter Squadron 42, aircraft carriers in Mediterranean, 1947-49; with USN Test Pilot Sch., 1950-53, 55-57, took part in high altitude tests, expts. in test and devel. in-flight refueling system, carrier suitability trials of F2H3 Banshee; also trials angled carrier deck ops. officer Fighter Squadron 193, Moffett Field (Calif.), carrier U.S.S. Oriskany, Western Pacific, 1953-55; test pilot for F4D Skyray, 1955, F3H Demon, F8U Crusader, F11F Tigercat, 1956; project test pilot F5D Skylancer, 1956; instr. Naval Test Pilot Sch., 1957; aircraft readiness officer staff Comdr.-in-Chief, Atlantic Fleet, 1958-59; joined Project Mercury man in space program NASA, 1959; first Am. in space, May 5, 1961, chief of astronaut office, 1965-74, selected to command Apollo 14 Lunar Landing Mission, 1971, became 5th man to walk on moon, hit 1st lunar golf shot; pres. Seven Fourteen Enterprises, 1986; presdl. appointee, del. 26th Gen. Assembly UN, 1971. Author: (with Deke Slayton) Moon Shot: The Inside Story of America's Race to the Moon, 1994. Decorated D.S.M., D.F.C., Presdl. unit citation, NASA Disting. Service medal, Congressional Space Medal of Honor, 1978; recipient Langley medal Smithsonian Instn., 1964. Fellow Soc. Exptl. Test Pilots; mem. Order Daedlians, Soc. Colonial Wars, Lions, Kiwanis, Rotary.

SHEPARD, EARL ALDEN, retired government official; b. Aurora, Ill., Sept. 30, 1932; s. Ralph George and Marcia Louise (Phelps) S.; m. Carolyn Mae Borman, Sept. 1, 1959; 1 son, Ralph Lyle. AS in Bus. Adminstrn. magna cum laude, Southea. U., 1967, BSBA magna cum laude, 1969; MBA, U. Chgo., 1974. Chief program budget divsn. U.S. Army Munitions Command., Joliet, Ill., 1971-73; comptr., dir. adminstrn. U.S. Navy Pub. Works Ctr., Gt. Lakes, Ill., 1973-77; dep. comptr. U.S. Army Electronics Command/U.S. Army Communications Electronics Materiel Readiness Command, Ft. Monmouth, N.J., 1977-79; dir. resource mgmt., comptr., dir. programs U.S. Army, White Sands Missile Range, N.Mex., 1979-92; bd. dirs. 1st Nat. Bank of Dona Ana County, 1987—; mem. adv. com. Rio Grande Bancshares/First Nat. Bank of Dona Ana County, 1983-84; founding mem. White Sands Missile Range Hist. Found., 1992—. Mem. bd. govs. Southea. U. Ednl. Found., 1969-71; chmn. fin. com. No. Va. Assn. for Children with Learning Disabilities, 1966-67, treas., 1968-70; pres. West Long Branch (N.J.) Sports Assn., 1979. Fed. and local govt. employee scholar, 1967, Ammunition Procurement Supply Agy. fellow, 1974. Republican. Home: 2712 Topley Ave Las Cruces NM 88005-1334

SHEPARD, ELAINE ELIZABETH, writer, lecturer; b. Olney, Ill.; d. Thomas J. and Bernice E. (Shadle) S.; m. Terry D. Hunt, Apr. 16, 1938; m. George F. Hartman, Oct. 1, 1943 (div. June 1958). Covered nat. polit. convs. for Stas. WTTG-TV and WINS, Chgo., 1952, 1956; polit. reporter for NANA and WINS, Chgo. and Los Angeles, 1960; reporter Congo rebellion for N.Am. Newspaper Alliance and N.Y. Mirror, 1960-61; corr. covering Pres. Eisenhower's Middle East, Far East and S. Am. tour, 1959-60; Vietnam corr. MBS, 1965-66; granted interviews with Khrushchev, Castro, Tito, Chou En-lai, Nasser, Shah of Iran, King Hussein, King Faisel, Duvalier, Lumumba, Chiang-Kai-Shek, Nehru, Menzies, John F. Kennedy, Richard M. Nixon, others; mem. White House Press Corps accompanying Pres. Nixon to, Austria, Iran, Poland, Moscow, 1972. Film and theater actress, Hollywood, N.Y.C., Europe, 1939-50, cover girl, John Robert Powers, 1939-43, under contract to, RKO and Metro-Goldwyn-Mayer, 1940-45, guest commentator for, Voice of Am.; contbr.: feature articles to various mags., including N.Y. News Sunday Mag, 1953—; columnist, contbg. editor: feature articles to various mags., including Nat. Cath. Press, 1969-74; author: Forgive Us Our Press Passes, 1962, The Doom Pussy, 1967, The Doom Pussy II, 1991. Recipient 2 citations for participating in armed helicopter assaults with 145th Aviation Bn. Vietnam. Mem. Screen Actors Guild, AFTRA, Actors Equity. Club: Overseas Press (N.Y.C.). Home: 12 E 62nd St New York NY 10021-7218 *Happiness is the full use of your powers along lines of excellence in a life affording hope.*

SHEPARD, GEOFFREY CARROLL, insurance executive; b. Santa Barbara, Calif., Nov. 7, 1944; s. James J. and Barbara (Hoose) S.; m. Saundra Gayle Carlton, Jan. 10, 1973; children: Jonathan Pettus, William Dabney. B.A., Whittier Coll., 1966; J.D., Harvard U., 1969. Bar: Wash. 1970, D.C. 1972, Pa. 1977, U.S. Supreme Ct. 1973. White House fellow, 1969-70; staff asst. to Pres. White House, 1970-72, assoc. dir. domestic coun., 1972-75; sr. assoc. Steptoe & Johnson, Washington, 1975-77; sr. v.p., assoc. gen. counsel CIGNA Corp., Phila., 1977-91; sr. v.p., gen. counsel, corp. sec. Reliance Ins. Group, Phila., 1991-94; pres. corp. divsn. Karr Barth Assocs., Phila., 1994—; mem. pvt. security adv. coun. Dept. Justice, 1975-77. Adv. coun. on gen. govt. Rep. Nat. Com., 1977-78; Phila. Cmty. Leadership Seminar, 1978-79, exec. com. Boy Scouts Am., Phila. 1981-83, exec. bd. Valley Forge Coun., 1994-96; mem. exec. bd. Cradle of Liberty Coun., 1996—; bd. dirs. Sacred Heart Med. Ctr., 1983-85, Swarthmore Presbyn. Ch., 1984-86, 97—, Wallingford Hills Civic Assn., 1983-85, Com. of 70, 1985-87, Acad. Natural Scis., Phila., 1987-93, Pub. Affairs Coun., Washington, 1986-89, Episc. Acad., 1987-90; mem. exec. com. White House Fellows Regional Selection Panel, 1987-93; prin. counsel Excellence in Govt., 1994-96; bd. dirs. White House Fellows Found., 1997—. Mem. ABA, Assn. for Advancement Life Underwriting, Pa. Bar Assn., Phila. Assn. of Life Underwriters, D.C. Bar Assn., White House Fellows Alumni Assn., Met. Club (Washington), Union League Club (Phila.), Harvard Club (N.Y.C.). Office: Karr Barth Assocs Inc Corp Divsn 40 Monument Rd Bala Cynwyd PA 19004-1735

SHEPARD, HENRY BRADBURY, JR., lawyer; b. Exeter, N.H., Oct. 29, 1927; s. Henry Bradbury and Frances Gardner (Dudley) S.; m. Klaudia Ockert Steidle, July 26, 1958; children: Katherine Shepard Alexander, Emily Perry, Julia Bradbury. BA with honors, Yale U., 1949; postgrad., U. Goettingen, Germany, 1951-52; LLB with honors, Harvard U., 1957. Instr. Am. U. in Cairo (Egypt), 1949-51; asst. dir. Fridtjof Nansen Internat. Student House, Goettingen, Germany, 1951-52; instr. Interpreters Inst., Goettingen, Germany, 1951-52; assoc. Goodwin, Procter & Hoar, Boston, 1957-64, ptnr., 1964-93, counsel, 1994—; dir. Mass. Venture Capital Corp., Boston, 1973-88, The C.T. Main Corp., Boston, 1975-85, Neworld Bancorp, Inc., Boston, 1986-92, Neworld Bank, Boston, 1968-92. Author: Handbook of Recent Developments in Massachusetts Banking Law, 1983, Obligations and Liabilities of Bank Directors and Trustees, 1990. Trustee George R. Wallace Found., Boston, 1978—, N.H. Hist. Soc., Concord, 1991—; hon. trustee Deree-Pierce Coll., Athens, Greece, 1970—. With U.S. Army, 1952-54. Mem. ABA (chmn. subcom. on regulatory liaison mut. savs. banks 1980-85), Mass. Bar Assn., Boston Bar Assn., Greater Boston C. of C. (bd. dirs. 1974-80, pres. 1979-80, hon. v.p. 1980-93), The Hamilton Trust (v.p. 1989, pres. 1990-91), New Bedford Yacht Club, The Country Club, Harvard Travellers Club, Phi Beta Kappa. Independent. Office: Goodwin Procter & Hoar Exch Pl Boston MA 02109

SHEPARD, JAMES EDWARD, physician; b. Laconia, N.H., Dec. 8, 1933; s. Robinson and Myra Ellen (Foster) S.; m. Sally-Jean Shupert, Oct. 4, 1958; children: Sandra Jean, Elizabeth Anne. BA, Wesleyan U., Middletown, Conn., 1955; MD, Cornell U., 1959. Diplomate Am. Bd. Nephrology, Am. Bd. Internal Medicine. Practice medicine specializing in internal medicine and nephrology Marin County, Calif., 1966—; chief medicine Marin (Calif.) Gen. Hosp., 1974-76; asst. clin. prof. medicine U. Calif., San Francisco, 1970—. Contbr. articles to profl. jours. Pres. Marin Heart Assn., 1969-71; active, founder Marin Kidney Assn., 1970-80; mem. San Francisco Graphic Arts Council, 1980-86. Fellow ACP; mem. Nat. Soc. Nephrology, Internat. Soc. Nephrology, Calif. Acad. Medicine, Sigma Xi. Club: Mill Valley (Calif.) Tennis. Office: Drs Shepard Lambert Hancock & Ley 5 Bar Ave Rd Ste 101 Larkspur CA 94939

SHEPARD, JEAN HECK, author, publishing company consultant, agent; b. N.Y.C., Feb. 2, 1930; d. Chester Reed and Anna S. (Charig) Heck; m. Lawrence Vaeth Hastings, Mar. 29, 1950 (div. 1953); 1 child, Lance Clifford Hastings; m. Daniel A. Shepard, July 26, 1954 (div. 1981); 1 child, Bradley Reed. BA, Barnard Coll., 1950; postgrad., Columbia U., 1952. Mem. sch. and libr. svc. Viking Press, N.Y.C., 1956-57; asst. dir. sch. and libr. promotion E.P. Dutton, N.Y.C., 1957-58; dir. advt. publicity and promotion Thomas Y. Crowell Co., N.Y.C., 1958-62; dir. advt. and promotion Charles Scribner's Sons, N.Y.C., 1962-67; cons. Stephen Greene Press, Brattleboro, Vt., 1970-73; mktg. mgr. A&W Publishers, N.Y.C., 1979-80, Franklin Watts Publ., N.Y.C., 1980-82; pub. mags., divsn. advt. & promotion mgr. McGraw Hill Book Co., N.Y.C., 1983-85; cons. Monitor Publ. Co., N.Y.C., 1988—. Author: Simple Family Favorites, 1971, Herb and Spice Sampler, 1972, Cook With Wine!, 1973, Earth Watch: Notes on a Restless Planet, 1973, Harvest Home Steak Cookbook, 1974, Fresh Fruits and Vegetables, 1974, Yankee Magazine, 1972. Mem. Authors Guild, Pub. Ad Club, Am. Libr. Assn., Women's Nat. Book Assn. Methodist. Avocations: the dance, reading, writing, travel, music. Home: 73 Kingswood Dr Bethel CT 06801 Office: The Shepard Agy Ste 3 Pawling Savs Bank Bld Southeast Plz Brewster NY 10509

SHEPARD, JON MAX, sociologist; b. Ashland, Ky., July 15, 1939; s. Maxwell Irwin and Mabel Louise S.; m. Virginia Kay Vogel, July 16, 1961; 1 son, Jon Mark. B.A., Georgetown (Ky.) Coll., 1961; M.A., U. Ky., 1963; Ph.D., Mich. State U., 1968. Rsch. assoc. MIT, 1968-69; from asst. prof. to prof. sociology U. Ky., 1969-78, prof. mgmt. and sociology, 1978-88; head dept. mgmt. and prof. mgmt. and sociology Va. Poly. Inst. and State U., Blacksburg, 1989—, head dept. mgmt. and Pamplin prof. mgmt. Author: Automation and Alienation, A Study of Office and Factory Workers, 1971, Organizational Issues in Industrial Society, 1972, (with H. Voss) Social Problems, 1978, Sociology, 1996; contbr. articles to profl. jours. Recipient Gt. Tchr. award U. Ky., 1978. Mem. Am. Acad. Mgmt., Am. Sociol. Assn. Home: 2817 Newton Ct Blacksburg VA 24060-4120 Office: Va Poly Inst & State U Pamplin Hall Blacksburg VA 24061

SHEPARD, JULIAN LEIGH, lawyer, humanitarian; b. St. Paul, Feb. 17, 1957; s. Frank and Beatrice (Getsug) S.; m. Jo Ellen Cartmell, Aug. 6, 1988. BS, Ind. U., 1980, JD, 1983; postgrad., Am. U., 1995—. Bar: Pa. 1985, Ind. 1984, D.C. 1987; U.S. Ct. Appeals (D.C. cir.) 1984; U.S. Dist. Ct. (so. dist.) Ind. 1984. Atty. Nat. Assn. Broadcasters, Washington, 1984-86, asst. gen. counsel, 1986-87; counselor at law Heron, Burchette, Ruckert & Rothwell, Washington, 1987-88; sr. policy adv. mass media Nat. Telecommunications & Info. Adminstrn./U.S. Dept. Comm., Washington, 1988-90; v.p., gen. counsel Assn. for Maximum Svc. TV, Inc., Washington, 1990-95; atty. Verner, Liipfert, Bernhard, McPherson & Hand, Washington, 1995—; mem. fed. spectrum planning and policy adv. com., U.S. Dept. Commerce, Washington, 1992—. Co-chmn. editorial adv. bd. Fed. Comms. Law Jour., Washington, 1992-94; contbr. articles to profl. jours. Bd. vis. Georgetown U. Inst. on Comparative Polit. and Econ. Systems, 1984-95; prin. Coun. for Excellence in Govt., Washington, 1990-. Mem. ABA (law practice mgmt. sect. leadership activities bd. 1995-96), Fed. Comms. Bar Assn. (law jour. com. 1992—), Ind. State Bar Assn., Phi Delta Phi (Nat. Belfour scholar 1983); fellow Bar Assn. of D.C. Avocations: visual arts, scuba diving, underwater photography, amateur radio and computer telecommunications. Office: Verner Liipfert Bernhard McPherson & Hand 901 5th St NW Ste 700 Washington DC 20001-2501

SHEPARD, KATHRYN IRENE, public relations executive; b. Tooele, Utah, Jan. 6, 1956; d. James Lewis and Glenda Verleen (Slaughter) Clark; m. Mark L. Shepard, June 5, 1976. BA in History, Boise State U., 1980. On-air writer Sta. KTTV, Channel 11, L.A., 1982-85; publicity dir. Hollywood (Calif.) C. of C., 1985-87; pres. Kathy Shepard Pub. Rels., Burbank and Portland, 1987-93; dir. public relations Las Vegas Hilton, 1993-94; dir. comms. Hilton Gaming, 1994-96; dir. corp. comms. Hilton Hotels Corp., 1996-97, v.p. corp. comms., 1997—; instr. pub. rels. ext. program UCLA, 1991-92. Contbr. articles to profl. publs. Mem. Publicity Club L.A. (pres. 1991-92, bd. dirs. 1987-91), Pub. Rels. Assn. Am., Women in Comms. Avocations: genealogy, film, travel. Office: Hilton Hotels Corp PR Dept 9336 Civic Center Dr Beverly Hills CA 90210-3604

SHEPARD, RANDALL TERRY, judge; b. Lafayette, Ind., Dec. 24, 1946; s. Richard Schilling and Dorothy Ione (Donlen) S.; m. Amy Wynne MacDonell, May 7, 1988; one child, Martha MacDonell. AB cum laude, Princeton U., 1969; JD, Yale U., 1972; LLM, U. Va., 1995; LLD (hon.), U. So. Ind., 1995. Bar: Ind. 1972, U.S. Dist. Ct. (so. dist.) Ind. 1972. Spl. asst. to under sec. U.S. Dept. Transp., Washington, 1972-74; exec. asst. to mayor City of Evansville, Ind., 1974-79; judge Vanderburgh Superior Ct., Evansville, 1980-85; assoc. justice Ind. Supreme Ct., Indpls., 1985-87, chief justice, 1987—; instr. U. Evansville, 1975-78, Indiana U., 1995. Author: Preservation Rules and Regulations, 1980; contbr. articles to profl. publs. Bd. advisors Nat. Trust for Hist. Preservation, 1980-87, chmn. bd. advisors, 1983-85, trustee, 1987-96; dir. Hist. Landmarks Found. Ind., 1983—, chmn., 1989-92, hon. chmn., 1992—; chmn. State Student Assistance Commn. on Ind., 1981-85; chmn. Ind. Commn. on Bicentennial of U.S. Constn., 1986-91; vice chmn. Vanderburgh County Rep. Ctrl. Com., 1977-80. Recipient Friend of Media award Cardinal States chpt. Sigma Delta Chi, 1979, Disting. Svc. award Evansville Jaycees, 1982, Herbert Harley award Am. Judicature Soc., 1992. Mem. ABA (coun. mem. sect. on legal edn. 1991—, chair-elect sect. on legal edn. 1997—, chair appellate judges conf. 1997—), Ind. Bar Assn., Ind. Judges Assn., Princeton Club (N.Y.), Capitol Hill Club (Washington), Columbia Club (Indpls.). Republican. Methodist. Home: 3644 Totem Ln Indianapolis IN 46208 Office: Ind Supreme Ct 304 State House Indianapolis IN 46204-2213

SHEPARD, ROBERT M., lawyer, investment banker, engineer; b. Amityville, N.Y., Feb. 15, 1932; s. Sidney M. and Undine L. (Lehmann) Shapiro; m. Barbara S. Stannard, June 25, 1955 (div. 1980); children: Karen Michele Shepard Sweer, Daniel Robert; m. Joanne E. Devlin, May 16, 1981 (div. 1993). B.C.E., Cornell U., 1954; M.B.A., Hofstra Coll., 1960; LL.B., Yale U., 1963; LLM, NYU, 1988. Bar: N.Y. 1964; registered profl. engr., N.Y., Conn. Project engr. Lockwood Kessler & Bartlett, Syosset, N.Y., 1956-60; assoc. atty. Cravath, Swaine & Moore, N.Y.C. and Paris, 1963-70; gen. ptnr. Kuhn, Loeb & Co., N.Y.C., 1970-77; sr. v.p. Donaldson, Lufkin & Jenrette, N.Y.C., 1977-83; gen. ptnr. Donovan Leisure Newton & Irvine, N.Y.C., 1983-89, Adler & Shepard, N.Y.C., 1989-91, Shepard & van Essche, N.Y.C., 1991, Ballon Stoll Bader & Nadler, P.C., N.Y.C., 1992—. Note and comment editor: Yale Law Jour., 1962-63. Bd. dirs. N.Y. Grand Opera, Regency Whist Club. Recipient Fuertes Medal Cornell U., 1953. Mem. ABA, Am. N.Y. State Bar Assn., Pub. Power Assn., Nat. Assn. Bond Lawyers, Order of Coif, Union League Club, Regency Whist Club, Inc., Tau Beta Pi, Chi Epsilon. Home: 750 Park Ave Apt 12C New York NY 10021-4252 Office: Ballon Stoll Bader & Nadler 1450 Broadway New York NY 10018-2201

SHEPARD, ROGER NEWLAND, psychologist, educator; b. Palo Alto, Calif., Jan. 30, 1929; s. Orson Cutler and Grace (Newland) S.; m. Barbaranne Bradley, Aug. 18, 1952; children: Newland Chenoweth, Todd David, Shenna Esther. B.A., Stanford U., 1951; Ph.D., Yale U., 1955; A.M. (hon.), Harvard U., 1966; ScD (hon.), Rutgers U., 1992. Rsch. assoc. Naval Research Lab., 1955-56; rsch. fellow Harvard, 1956-58; mem. tech. staff Bell Telephone Labs., 1958-66, dept. head, 1963-66; prof. psychology Harvard U., 1966-68, dir. psychol. labs., 1967-68; prof. psychology Stanford U., 1968—, Ray Lyman Wilbur prof. social sci., 1989—. Guggenheim fellow Center for Advanced Study in Behavioral Scis., 1971-72; recipient, N.Y. Acad. Scis. award, 1987, Nat. Medal of Sci., 1995. Fellow AAAS, Am. Psychol. Assn. (pres. exptl. div. 1980-81, Disting. Sci. Contbn. award 1976); mem. Am. Acad. Arts and Scis., Nat. Acad. Scis., Psychometric Soc. (pres. 1973-74), Psychonomic Soc., Soc. Exptl. Psychologists (Howard Crosby Warren medal 1981). Office: Stanford U Dept Psychology Bldg 420 Stanford CA 94305-2130

SHEPARD, SAM (SAMUEL SHEPARD ROGERS), playwright, actor; b. Ft. Sheridan, Ill., Nov. 5, 1943; s. Samuel Shepard and Jane Elaine (Schook) Rogers; m. O-Lan Johnson Dark, Nov. 9, 1969 (div.); 1 son, Jesse Mojo; children with Jessica Lange: Hannah Jane, Samuel Walker. Student, Mt. San Antonio Jr. Coll., Walnut, Calif., 1961-62. Playwright-in-residence Magic Theatre, San Francisco. Author: (plays) Cowboys, 1964, The Rock Garden, 1964, 4-H Club, 1965, Up to Thursday, 1965, Dog, 1965, Rocking Chair, 1965, Chicago, 1965 (Obie award 1966), Icarus's Mother, 1965 (Obie award 1966), Fourteen Hundred Thousand, 1966, Red Cross, 1966 (Obie award 1966), Melodrama Play, 1966 (Obie award 1968), La Turista, 1967 (Obie award 1967), Cowboys #2, 1967, Forensic and the Navigators, 1967 (Obie award 1968), The Holy Ghostly, 1969, The Unseen Hand, 1969, Operation Sidewinder, 1970, Shaved Splits, 1970, Mad Dog Blues, 1971, Terminal, 1971, (with Patti Smith) Cowboy Mouth, 1971, Black Bog Beast Bait, 1971, The Tooth of Crime, 1972 (Obie award 1973), Blue Bitch, 1973, (with Megan Terry and Jean-Claude van Itallie) Nightwalk, 1973, Geography of a Horse Dreamer, 1974, Little Ocean, 1974, Action, 1974 (Obie award 1975), Killer's Head, 1974, Suicide in B-Flat, 1976, Angel City, 1976, Curse of the Starving Class, 1977 (Obie award 1977), Buried Child, 1978 (Pulitzer Prize in drama 1979, Obie award 1979), Tongues, 1979, Savage/Love, 1979, Seduced, 1979, True West, 1981, Fool for Love, 1983 (Obie award 1984), Superstitions, 1983, The Sad Lament of Pecos Bill on the Eve of Killing his Wife, 1983, A Lie of the Mind, 1985 (New York Drama Critics' Circle award 1986), States of Shock, 1991, Simpatico, 1993; (collections of plays) Five Plays by Sam Shepard, 1967, The Unseen Hand and Other Plays, 1971, 2nd edit., 1986, Mad Dog Blues and Other Plays, 1972, The Tooth of Crime and Geography of a Horse Dreamer, 1974, Angel City, Curse of the Starving Class and Other Plays, 1976, Buried Child, Seduced, Suicide in B-Flat, 1979, Four Two-Act Plays by Sam Shepard, 1980, Chicago and Other Plays, 1981, Seven Plays, 1981, Fool for Love and The Sad Lament of Pecos Bill on the Eve of Killing His Wife, 1983, Fool For Love and Other Plays, 1984, 1986; contbr. to Oh! Calcutta, 1976; (screenplays) Me and My Brother, 1967, (with Michelangelo Antonioni, Tonino Guerra, Fred Graham, and Clare Peploe) Zabriskie Point, 1970, (with Murray Mednick) Ringaleevio, 1971, (with others) Oh! Calcutta!, 1972, (with Bob Dylan) Renaldo and Clara, 1978, Paris, Texas, 1984 (Golden Palm award Cannes Film Festival 1984), Fool for Love, 1985; (other writings) Rolling Thunder Logbook, 1977, Hawk Moon: A Book of Short Stories, Poems and

Monologues, 1981, Motel Chronicles, 1982; writer, dir.: (plays) Fool for Love, 1983, A Lie of the Mind, 1985, (screenplays) Far North, 1988, Silent Tongue, 1993; actor: (films) Renaldo and Clara, 1978, Days of Heaven, 1978, Resurrection, 1980, Raggedy Man, 1981, Frances, 1982, The Right Stuff, 1983 (Academy award nomination best supporting actor 1984), Country, 1984, Fool for Love, 1985, Crimes of the Heart, 1986, Baby Boom, 1987, Steel Magnolias, 1989, Hot Spot, 1990, Bright Angel, 1991, Defenseless, 1991, Thunderheart, 1992, The Pelican Brief, 1993, Safe Passage, 1994, The Good Old Boys, 1995, Curtain Call, 1997, The Only Thrill, 1997, (TV performances) Streets of Laredo, 1995, Lily Dale, 1996. Fellow U. Minn., 1966, Yale U., 1967; grantee Rockefeller Found., 1967, Guggenheim Found., 1968, 71; recipient Nat. Inst. and Am. Acad. Arts and Letters award for lit., 1974, Creative Arts award Brandeis U., 1975, Theater Hall of Fame, 1994. mem. Am. Acad. and Inst. of Arts and Letters, 92. Office: Internat Creative Mgmt 8942 Wilshire Blvd Beverly Hills CA 90211-1934*

SHEPARD, STEPHEN BENJAMIN, journalist, magazine editor; b. N.Y.C., July 20, 1939; s. William and Ruth Shepard; m. Lynn Povich, Sept. 16, 1979; children: Sarah, Ned. B.S., CCNY, 1961; M.S., Columbia U., 1963. Reporter, editor, writer Business Week, N.Y.C., 1966-75; asst. prof., dir. Walter Bagehot fellowship program econs. and bus. journalism Columbia U., N.Y.C., 1975-76; sr. editor Newsweek, N.Y.C., 1976-81; editor Saturday Rev., N.Y.C., 1981-82; exec. editor Business Week mag., N.Y.C., 1982-84, editor in chief, 1984—. Mem. Am. Soc. Mag. Editors (v.p. 1990-92, pres. 1992-94), Coun. Fgn. Rels., Century Assn. Home: 322 Central Park W New York NY 10025-7629 Office: Business Week McGraw Hill Inc 1221 Ave Of The Americas New York NY 10020-1001

SHEPARD, THOMAS AKERS, physician assistant; b. Buffalo, N.Y., Oct. 4, 1948; s. Richard Marvin and Mabel Elizabeth (McVicker) S.; m. Ruth Virginia Heffleger Zebarth, June 5, 1971 (div. Nov. 1980); 1 child, Jared Nathaniel; m. Denise Hazel Donaldson, Sept. 25, 1993. BA, Franklin & Marshall Coll., 1971; AS in sci., Arapahoe Cmty. Coll., Littleton, Colo., 1977. RN, Colo.; lic. physician asst., Colo. Physician asst. Buffalo Park Medical Assn., Evergreen, Colo., 1975-82, ClearCreek Medical Ctr., Idaho Springs, Colo., 1982-85; occupational health dir. AMAX Inc. Henderson Mine, Empire, Colo., 1985-93; physician asst. urgent care Kaiser Permanente, Denver, 1988-96; mgr. med. svcs. Colo. Compensation Ins. Authority, Denver, 1993—. Co-author (book chpt.): Pain Treatment Centers At a Crossroads, 1996. Rule making testimony Colo. Dept. Labor, Denver, 1993, 94, 95; managed care task force Colo. Div. Workers Comp. Colo. Dept. Labor, 1993-94; apportionment working group, 1994. With Army, 1966-68, Vietnam. Fellow Am. Acad. Physicans Assts., Colo. Acad. Physicians Assts. Avocations: sailing, hiking, horseback riding. Office: Colo Compensation Authority Ins 720 S Colorado Blvd Denver CO 80246-1904

SHEPARD, THOMAS HILL, physician, educator; b. Milw., May 22, 1923; s. Francis Parker and Elizabeth Rhodes (Buchner) S.; m. Alice B. Kelly, June 24, 1946; children: Donna, Elizabeth, Ann. A.B., Amherst Coll., 1945; M.D., U. Rochester, 1948. Intern Strong Meml. Hosp., Rochester, N.Y., 1948-49; resident Strong Meml. Hosp., 1950-52, Albany (N.Y.) Med. Center, 1949-50; pediatric endocrine fellow Johns Hopkins Hosp., 1954-55; pediatrician U. Wash., Seattle, 1955-61; embryologist dept. anatomy U. Fla., 1961-62; teratologist U. Wash., 1961—, prof. pediatrics, head central lab. for human embryology, 1961-93, prof. emeritus, 1993—; research assoc. dept. embryology Carnegie Inst., 1962, U. Copenhagen, 1963; cons. NIH, FDA, EPA, 1971—; vis. prof. pediatrics U. Geneva, 1972, 73-74. Author: A Catalog of Teratogenic Agents, 1973, 8th edit., 1995; contbr. articles to profl. jours. Served with U.S. Army, 1946-48; Served with USAF, 1952-54. Mem. Teratology Soc. (hon. mem. 1993, pres. 1968), Western Soc. Pediatric Rsch. (pres. 1970), Am. Pediatric Soc., Acad. Pediatrics. Home: 3015 98th Ave NE Bellevue WA 98004-1818 Office: U Wash Sch Medicine Dept Pediatrics Seattle WA 98195

SHEPARD, THOMAS ROCKWELL, JR., publishing consultant; b. N.Y.C., Aug. 22, 1918; s. Thomas Rockwell and Marie (Dickinson) S.; m. Nancy Kruidenier, Sept. 20, 1941; children: Sue Shepard Jaques, Molly Shepard Richard, Amy S. Knight, Thomas Rockwell III. B.A., Amherst Coll., 1940. Asst. sales promotion mgr. Vick Chemical Co., 1940-41; with Look mag., N.Y.C., 1946-72; advt. sales mgr. Look mag., 1961-64, advt. dir., 1964-67, pub., 1967-72; cons. Cowles Communications, Inc.; pres. Inst. Outdoor Advt., 1974-76. Co-author: The Disaster Lobby, 1973; contbr. articles to various publs. Pres. Greenwich Community Chest, 1964-65; chmn. Robert A. Taft Inst. Govt., 1978-81, Rep. Roundtable of Greenwich, 1981-85; bd. dirs. Advt. Coun., Lit. Vols. Am., 1989-91, Community Answers, 1988-91; chmn. Amherst Coll. Alumni Fund, 1986; mem. exec. com. alumni coun. Amherst Coll.; hon. pres. Soc. Amherst Coll. Alumni. Lt. comdr. USNR, 1941-45. Recipient George Washington honor medal for pub. address Freedoms Found., 1970, 73, Amherst Coll. medal for eminent svc., 1990. Mem. Princeton Club (N.Y.C.), Bird Key Yacht Club (Fla.), Belle Haven Club, Round Hill Club. Republican. Home: 44 Lismore Ln Greenwich CT 06831-3760

SHEPARD, THOMAS ROCKWELL, III, advertising sales executive; b. Greenwich, Conn., Apr. 21, 1951; s. Thomas Rockwell, Jr. and Nancy (Kruidenier) S.; m. Margaret O'Neal, Sept. 1, 1972; children—Amanda Marie, Thomas Rockwell IV, Brian Dickinson. B.A., Amherst Coll., Mass., 1973. Hockey player Calif. Golden Seals, Oakland, 1973-74; salesman Union Carbide Battery Products, N.Y.C., 1974-78; became mem. advt. sales staff Hearst Mags., N.Y.C., 1978, became advt. dir. Good Housekeeping mag., 1984; now pub. Redbook mag. Republican. Clubs: Manursing (Rye, N.Y.); N.Y. Athletic (N.Y.C.). Office: Redbook Hearst Magazines 224 W 57th St New York NY 10019-3212*

SHEPARD, WILLIAM SETH, government official, diplomat, writer; b. Boston, June 7, 1935; s. Robinson and Myra Ellen (Foster) S.; m. Lois Rosalie Burke, June 25, 1960; children—Stephanie Lee, Cynthia Robin, Warren Burke (dec.). A.B. cum laude, Wesleyan U., Middletown, Conn., 1957; J.D., Harvard U., Cambridge, Mass., 1961. Bar: N.H. 1961, U.S. Ct. Mil. Appeals 1962 U.S. Supreme Ct. 1970,. Aide to ambassadors Henry Cabot Lodge and Ellsworth Bunker U.S. embassy, Saigon, Vietnam, 1966-67; staff officer Exec. Secretariat Dept. of State, Washington, 1967-69; consul, polit. officer U.S. Embassy, Budapest, Hungary, 1970-73; desk officer Hungarian affairs Dept. State, Washington, 1973-75; desk officer Singapore and Malaysian affairs Dept. of State, Washington, 1975-77; dep. polit. counselor U.S. embassy, Athens, Greece, 1978-80; consul gen. consulate gen. U.S., Bordeaux, France, 1983-85; dir. office congressional affairs U.S. Arms Control and Disarmament Agy., 1987-89; cons. to the gen. counsel U.S. Dept. Agriculture, 1991-92; lectr. internat. law U. Singapore, 1965-66; CEO The Shepard Internat. Group, Inc., 1994—. Author: Au Revoir Bordeaux, Tales from the Consular Service, 1996, Vintage Murder, 1997; also articles. Candidate for Rep. nomination 8th Md. Congl. Dist., 1985-86, Rep. nominee for Gov. of Md., 1990, candidate, 1994; del. Rep. Nat. Conv., 1992; Md. co-chmn. Dole Presdl. Campaign, 1996. Recipient Pro Libertate Hungariae Commemorative medallion, 1981, Pub. Svc. Leadership award U.S.-Baltic Found., 1996; French Govt. teaching asst. and Fulbright travel grantee, 1957-58; Congl. fellow Am. Polit. Sci. Assn. and fgn. policy legis. asst. to Senator Robert Dole, 1982-83. Mem. Am. Fgn. Service Assn., SAR, Soc. Mayflower Desc., Gov. Bradford Compact, Soc. Desc. Colonial Govs. (chancellor gen. 1993-95), Soc. Desc. Colonial Wars; corr. mem. Montesquieu Acad. France. Republican. Unitarian. Clubs: City Tavern (Washington), Flagon and Trencher, Les Chevaliers de Bretvin, Ordre des Compagnons de Bordeaux, Connetablie de Guyenne, La Jurade de St. Emilion, Bontemps Medoc et des Graves, Commanderie de Bordeaux (Washington). Avocations: Plantagenet history, vintage Bordeaux wines, rose cultivation. Home: 8602 Hidden Hill Ln Potomac MD 20854-4225 *I remember Himalayan peaks, Asian sunsets, Greek islands and Bordeaux vineyards.Along the way, hard work in a principled cause is its own reward. In the end, family life and friends, a foyer, pets, a book worth reading, and a glass of wine matter most.*

SHEPHARD, MARK SCOTT, civil and mechanical engineering educator; b. Buffalo, Oct. 27, 1951; s. William N. and Beatrice (Hass) S.; m. Sharon L. Nirschel, Nov. 25, 1972; children: Steven W., Kari L. BS, Clarkson U., 1974; PhD, Cornell U., 1979. Asst. prof. civil engring. and mech. engring. Rensselaer Poly. Inst., Troy, N.Y., 1979-84, assoc. prof., 1984-87, prof., 1988—, dir. Sci. Computation Rsch. Ctr., 1990—, Samuel A. and Elisabeth C. Johnson Jr. prof. engring., 1993—; assoc. dir. Rensselaer Design Rsch. Ctr., Troy, N.Y., 1980-90; vis. rsch. fellow GE Corp., R & D Schenectady, 1985, cons., 1984-87; cons. GM Rsch. Lab., Detroit, 1980—, also other orgns.; mem. tech. adv. bd. Aries Tech., Lowell, Mass., 1987-89. Co-editor: Engring. with Computers; mem. editl. bd. Internat. Jour. Numerical Methods Engring., Engring. Applications of Artificial Intelligence, Internat. Jour. Engring. Analysis and Design, Computational Mechanics; contbr. articles to profl. jours., chpts. to books. Fellow AIAA (assoc.), U.S. Assn. for Computational Mechanics (v.p.); mem. ASCE, ASME, Am. Soc. Engring. Edn., Am. Acad. Mechanics, Internat. Assn. for Computational Mechanics (exec. bd.), Sigma Xi, Tau Beta Pi, Phi Kappa Phi. Home: 305 Algonquin Beach Rd Averill Park NY 12018 Office: Rensselaer Poly Inst 110 8th St Troy NY 12180-3590

SHEPHERD, ALAN J., construction executive, management consultant; b. Bklyn., Jan. 15, 1942; s. Morris Elijah and Jean (Birnbaum) Shapiro; children: Robin Elyse, Kevin Peter. B.S. in Mech. Engring., Mich. State U.; M.S. in Indsl. Engring., Wayne State U., 1966. Mgmt. trainee Chrysler Corp., Detroit, 1964-65, product engr., 1965-66; exec. v.p. Bruce Erts & Assocs., Southfield, Mich., 1966-70; pres. Creative Mgmt. Group, Inc., Southfield, Mich., 1970-76, chmn. bd., 1976, pvt. cons., 1976-79; dir. planning and coordination Mgmt. Support Assocs., Tel Aviv, Israel, 1979-81, gen. mgr., 1981-82; mgmt. cons. MSA Consortium, Washington, 1982-83; regional mktg. dir. Hill Internat., Washington, 1983-84; mng. v.p. spl. projects CRS Sirrine, Inc., Washington, 1984-85; dir. advanced mgmt. program BDM Corp., McLean, Va., 1986-89; v.p. Hill Internat., Inc., Willingboro, N.J., 1989-90; v.p. mktg. and bus. devel. AWD Techs., Inc., Rockville, Md., 1990-94; dir. bus. devel. Brown & Root, Inc., Washington, 1994—; instr. Lawrence Inst. Tech., 1971, 73. Mem. Am. Inst. Indsl. Engrs., Project Mgmt. Inst., Soc. Am. Mil. Engrs. Office: Brown & Root Inc 1150 18th St NW Ste 200 Washington DC 20036-3839

SHEPHERD, CYBILL, actress, singer; b. Memphis, Feb. 18, 1950; d. William Jennings and Patty Shobe (Micci) S.; m. David Ford, Nov. 19, 1978 (div.); 1 child, Clementine; m. Bruce Oppenheim, March 1, 1987; children: Molly Ariel and Cyrus Zachariah (twins). Student, Hunter Coll., 1969, Coll. of New Rochelle, 1970, Washington Sq. Coll., NYU, 1971, U. So. Calif., 1972, NYU, 1973. Appeared in motion pictures Last Picture Show, 1971, The Heartbreak Kid, 1973, Daisy Miller, 1974, At Long Last Love, 1975, Taxi Driver, 1976, Special Delivery, 1976, Silver Bears, 1977, The Lady Vanishes, 1978, Earthright, 1980, The Return, 1986, Chances Are, 1988, Texasville, 1990, Alice, 1990, Once Upon a Crime, 1992, Married to It, 1993; star TV series The Yellow Rose, 1983-84, Moonlighting, 1985-89, Cybill, 1994—; TV films include A Guide for the Married Woman, 1978, Secrets of a Married Man, 1984, Seduced, 1985, The Long Hot Summer, 1985, Which Way Home, 1991, Memphis, 1992 (also co-writer, co-exec. prodr.), Stormy Weathers, 1992, Telling Secrets, 1993, There Was a Little Boy, 1993, Journey of the Heart, 1997; record albums include Cybill Does It To Cole Porter, 1974, Cybill and Stan Getz, 1977, Vanilla with Phineas Newborn, Jr, 1978; appeared in stage plays A Shot in the Dark, 1977, Picnic, 1980, Vanities, 1981. Office: Rogers and Cowan care Carscal-Werner Prodns 4024 Radford Ave Studio City CA 91604*

SHEPHERD, DANIEL MARSTON, executive recruiter; b. Madison, Ind., Apr. 8, 1939; s. Marston Vincent and Edith America (Brunson) S.; m. Bonnie Lynn Brawley, June 27, 1970 (div. Nov. 1987); children: Vincent, David, Christopher, Megan; m. Gail Lenore Sanborn, Oct. 3, 1989; children: Heather, Shannon. BS in Civil Engring., U. Ky., 1962; MBA, Harvard Bus. Sch., 1964. Mfg. and distbn. mgr. Procter & Gamble Co., Staten Island, N.Y., 1966-70; distbn. and ops. mgr. Mattel, Inc., Gardenia, Calif., 1970-73; gen. mgr., dir. ops. Fuqua Industries, Inc., Atlanta, 1973-76; v.p. product/market mgmt. Masonite Corp., Chgo., 1976-78; v.p. Heidrick & Struggles, Chgo., 1978-82, Lamalie Assocs., Chgo., 1982-86; prin. Sweeney Shepherd Bueschel Provus Harbert & Mummert, Chgo., 1986-91, Shepherd Bueschel & Provus, Inc., Chgo., 1991—. Capt. U.S. Army, 1964-66. Decorated Army Commendation medal, 1966; recipient Am.'s Top 150 Recruiters award Harper Bus., N.Y.C., 1992. Mem. Assn. Exec. Search Cons., Inc., Union League Club, Harvard Bus. Sch. Club. Republican. Episcopalian. Avocations: coin and art collecting, skiing, baseball, food, wine. Home: 990 N Lake Shore Dr Apt 27E Chicago IL 60611-1345 Office: 401 N Michigan Ave Ste 3020 Chicago IL 60611-4257

SHEPHERD, GILLIAN MARY, physician; b. Belfast, U.K., Mar. 12, 1948; came to U.S., 1957; d. John Thompson and Helen (Johnston) S.; m. Eduardo Goar Mestre, Aug. 4, 1973; children: Laura Elena, Cristina Alicia., Eduardo Goar. BA, Wheaton Coll., Norton, Mass., 1970, postgrad. Tufts U., 1970-73; MD, N.Y. Med. Coll., 1976. Diplomate Am. Bd. Internal Medicine, Am. Bd. Allergy and Immunology. Intern, resident Lenox Hill Hosp., N.Y.C., 1976-79; fellow in allergy and immunology N.Y. Hosp./Cornell Med. Sch., N.Y.C., 1979-81; assoc. prof. medicine Cornell U. Med. Coll., N.Y.C., 1988—, clin. assoc. prof. medicine, 1995—; assoc. attending physician N.Y. Hosp., N.Y.C.; cons. allergy and immunology dept. medicine Meml. Sloan-Kettering Cancer Ctr., N.Y.C., 1982—. Contbr. articles in field to profl. jours. Fellow ACP, Am. Acad. Asthma, Allergy and Immunology; mem. AAAS, Am. Fedn. for Clin. Research, Joint Coun. Allergy and Immunology, N.Y. Allergy Soc. (exec. com. 1982-94, pres. 1991-92), N.Y. County Med. Soc. Office: 235 E 67th St Rm 203 New York NY 10021-6040

SHEPHERD, JOHN FREDERIC, lawyer; b. Oak Park, Ill., May 22, 1954; s. James Frederic Shepherd and Margaret Joanne (Crotchett) Woollen; children: Eliza Marion, Justine Catherine. AB magna cum laude, Dartmouth Coll., Hanover, N.H., 1976; JD, U. Denver, 1979. Bar: Colo. 1979, U.S. Dist. Ct. Colo. 1979, D.C. 1981, U.S. Dist. Ct. D.C. 1981, U.S. Ct. Appeals (10th cir.) 1981, U.S. Ct. Appeals (D.C. cir.) 1982, U.S. Ct. Appeals (9th cir.) 1990, U.S. Supreme Ct. 1984. Assoc. Holland & Hart, Denver, 1979-81; assoc. Holland & Hart, Washington, 1981-85, ptnr., 1985-87; ptnr. Holland & Hart, Denver, 1987—. Reporter Mineral Law Newsletter, 1985-92. Mem. 50 for Colo., Denver, 1989. Mem. ABA (chmn. pub. lands and land use com. 1991-93, mem. coun. for sect. of natural resources energy and environ. law 1993-96), Rocky Mountain Oil and Gas Assn. (mem. pub. lands com. 1987—), Rocky Mountain Mineral Law Found. (mem. long-range planning com. 1988—, bd. trustees 1993-95), Dartmouth Alumni Club (pres. Washington chpt. 1985-86), Denver Athletic Club. Avocations: flyfishing, basketball, running. Home: 848 Monroe St Denver CO 80206 Office: Holland & Hart 555 17th St Ste 3200 Denver CO 80202-5555

SHEPHERD, JOHN MICHAEL, lawyer; b. St. Louis, Aug. 1, 1955; s. John Calvin and Bernice Florence (Hines) S.; m. Deborah Tremaine Fenton, Oct. 10, 1981; children: Elizabeth White, Katherine Tremaine. BA, Stanford U., 1977; JD, U. Mich., 1980. Bar: Calif. 1981, D.C. 1991, U.S. Dist. Ct. (no. dist.) Calif. 1981. Assoc. McCutchen, Doyle, Brown & Enersen, San Francisco, 1980-82; spl. asst. to asst. atty. gen. U.S. Dept. Justice, Washington, 1982-84, dep. asst. atty gen., 1984-86; assoc. counsel to The President The White House, Washington, 1986-87; sr. dep. comptroller of the currency Dept. Treasury, Washington, 1987-91; spl. counsel Sullivan & Cromwell, N.Y.C., 1991-93, Washington, 1993; exec. v.p., gen. counsel Shawmut Nat. Corp., Boston, 1993-95; ptnr. Brobeck, Phleger & Harrison LLP, San Francisco, 1995—. Contbr. articles to profl. jours. Asst. dir. policy Reagan-Bush Presdl. Transition Team, Washington, 1980-81; bd. dirs. Reagan Dep. Asst. Secs., Washington, 1985-90; trustee New Eng. Aquarium, 1994-96. Named one of Outstanding Young Men Am., U.S. Jaycees, 1984; Wardack Research fellow Washington U., 1976. Mem. ABA, (chmn. fin. markets and ins. com., antitrust law sect. 1992-95, chmn. bank holding co. acquisitions and dispositions subcom. 1995—, banking law com. 1983—, bus. law sect., standing com. on law and nat. security 1984—), D.C. Bar Assn., New Eng. Legal Found., (bd. dirs. 1994-96), Chevy Chase Club, Univ. Club, Met. Club. Home: 2699 Filbert St San Francisco CA 94123-3215 Office: Brobeck Phleger & Harrison 1 Market St San Francisco CA 94105-1521

SHEPHERD, JOHN THOMPSON, physiologist; b. No. Ireland, May 21, 1919; s. William Frederick and Matilda (Thompson) S.; m. Helen Mary Johnston, July 28, 1945; children: Gillian Mary, Roger Frederick John; m. Marion G. Etzwiler, Apr. 22, 1989. Student, Campbell Coll., Belfast, No. Ireland, 1932-37; M.B., B.Ch., Queen's U., Belfast, 1945, M.Chir., 1948, M.D., 1951, D.Sc., 1956, D.Sc. (hon.), 1979; M.D. (hon.), U. Bologna, 1984, U. Gent, 1985. Lectr. physiology Queen's U., 1948-53, reader physiology, 1954-57; assoc. prof. physiology Mayo Found., 1957-62, prof. physiology, 1962—, chmn. dept. physiology and biophysics, 1966-74; bd. govs. Mayo Clinic, 1966-80; trustee Mayo Found., 1969-81, dir. research, 1969-77, dir. for edn., 1977-83, chmn. bd. devel., 1983-88; dean Mayo Med. Sch., 1977-83; assoc. dir. Gen. Rsch. Ctr. Mayo Clinic, Rochester, 1992-94. Author, editor: Physiology of the Circulation in Human Limbs in Health and Disease, 1963, Cardiac Function in Health and Disease, 1968, Veins and Their Control, 1975, Human Cardiovascular System, 1979, Handbook of Physiology, The Cardiovascular System Peripheral Circulation and Organ Blood Flow, 1983, Vascular Diseases in the Limbs, 1993, Nervous Control of the Heart, 1996; co-editor: Exercise: Rebulation and Integration of Mulqiple Systems. Handbook of Physiology, 1996; mem. editl. bd. Hypertension, 1973—, Am. Jour. Physiology, Am. Heart Jour., Microvascular Rsch.; editor Circulation Rsch., 1982; editor-in-chief News in Physiol. Sci., 1988-94; contbr. more than 590 sci. articles and 350 papers to profl. jours. Recipient NASA Skylab Achievement award, 1974, A. Ross McIntyre medal for achievement, 1991; Brit. Med. Assn. scholar, 1949-50, Fulbright scholar, 1953-54; Anglo-French Med. exchange bursar, 1957; Internat. Francqui chair, 1978; Einthoven lectr. 1981, Volhard lectr., 1990. Fellow Am. Coll. Cardiology (hon.), Royal Coll. Physicians (London), Royal Acad. Medicine (Belgium); mem. Am. Physiol. Soc. (Disting. Svc. award 1990), Louis Rapkine Assn., Am. Heart Assn. (dir. 1968—, pres. 1975-76, chmn. vascular medicine and biology task force 1990, hon. fellow council clin. cardiology), Physiol. Soc. Gt. Brit., Med. Research Soc. London, Nat. Acad. Scis. (space sci. bd. 1973-74, chmn. com. space biology and medicine 1973), Assn. Am. Physicians, Internat. Union of Angiology (hon.), Rappaport Inst. Israel (sci. adv. bd.), Sigma Xi. Home: 600 4th St SW Rochester MN 55902-3291 Office: Mayo Clinic 1043 Plummer Bldg Rochester MN 55905

SHEPHERD, KAREN, former congresswoman; b. Silver City, N.Mex., July 5, 1940; m. Vincent P. Shepherd. BA, U. Utah, 1962; MA, Brigham Young U., 1963. Former instr. Brigham Young U., Am. U., Cairo; former pres. Webster Pub. Co.; former adminstr. David Eccles Sch. Bus., U. Utah; former dir. Salt Lake County Social Svcs., Utah; former dir. continuing edn. Westminster Coll.; former mem. Utah Senate; mem. 103d Congress from 2d Utah dist., Washington, 1993-95, Nat. Common Cause Governing Bd., Washington, 1995—; founding mem. Utah Women's Polit. Caucus, Project 2000; mem. Internat. Delegation to Monitor Elections in West Bank and Gaza, Israel. Former mem. United Way, Pvt. Industry Coun.; former mem. adv. bd. U.S. West Grad. Sch. Social Work; trustee Westminster Coll. Recipient Women in Bus. award U.S. Small Bus. Assn., Woman of Achievement award, Pathfinder award, YWCA Leadership award, 1st place award Nat. Assn. Journalists, Disting. Alumni award U. Utah Coll. Humanities. Fellow Inst. Politics Kennedy Sch Govt., Internat. Women's Forum; Salt Lake Area C. of C. (pub. rels. com.). Home: PO Box 1049 Salt Lake City UT 84110 Office: 21 G St Salt Lake City UT 84103-2949

SHEPHERD, KATHLEEN SHEAREN MAYNARD, television executive; b. N.Y.C., June 14, 1950; d. Theodore E. and Phyllis (Wildman) Shearer; m. Charles Dix Shepherd; m. Joseph Ashton Maynard (div. June 1977); 1 child, Natasha Candice. Student, Tufts U., Medford, Mass., 1968-69, Duke U., Durham, N.C., 1972-73, Westchester Community Coll., White Plains, N.Y., 1974-75, NYU, 1975-77. From administrv. asst. to assoc. producer WCBS-TV, N.Y.C., 1973-74, producer, 1975-76; from program devel. supr., exec. producer to dir. pub. affai WPIX TV, N.Y.C., 1977-84, v.p. pub. affairs, prodn., exec. producer; tchr. Montclair State Coll., 1985-88. Bd. dirs. Nat. Coalitin of 100 Black Women, lower Fairfield chpt., Conn., 1987, Childrens Village, Dobbs Ferry, N.Y., 1988. Mem. Nat. Acad. TV Arts, Sciences, Pvt. Industry Council, Archdiocese Communications Com. Democrat. Episcopalian. Avocations: jogging, exercise. Office: WPIX Inc 220 E 42nd St New York NY 10017-5806

SHEPHERD, MARK, JR., retired electronics company executive; b. Dallas, Jan. 18, 1923; s. Mark and Louisa Florence (Daniell) S.; m. Mary Alice Murchland, Dec. 21, 1945; children: Debra Aline Shepherd Robinson, MaryKay Theresa, Marc Blaine. BSEE, So. Meth. U., 1942; MSEE, U. Ill., at Urbana, 1947. Registered profl. engr., Tex. With GE, 1942-43, Farnsworth TV and Radio Corp., 1947-48; with Tex. Instruments, Dallas, 1948-88, v.p., gen. mgr. semicondr.-components div., 1955-61, exec. v.p., chief operating officer, 1961-66, pres., chief operating officer, 1967-69, pres., chief exec. officer, 1969-76, chmn. bd. dirs., chief exec. officer, 1976-84, chmn. bd. dirs., chief corp. officer, 1984-85, chmn., 1985-88; ret. Hon. trustee Com. for Econ. Devel.; councillor conf. Bd.; mem. Bus. Coun. Lt. (j.g.) USNR, 1943-46. Fellow IEEE; mem. NAE, Sigma Xi, Eta Kappa Nu.

SHEPHERD, MORGAN, professional race car driver; b. Conover, N.C., Oct. 12, 1941; m. Cindy Shepherd; children: Debbie, Crystal, Terri, Morgan Jr., Shanda Renee. NASCAR Winston Cup race car driver, 1970—, with 414 races, 4 wins, 61 top 5s; winner NASCAR Late Model Sportsman (now NASCAR Busch Series) nat. championship, 1980; winner 1992 Daytona 500 by STP, 1993 Motorcraft 500, others. Office: care NASCAR PO Box 2875 Daytona Beach FL 32120-2875

SHEPHERD, PAUL H., elementary school educator; b. Salt Lake City, Sept. 6, 1955; s. Richard Lawrence and Janis (Hoskings) S.; m. Marlene Wade, Aug. 31, 1978; children: Janice, Faith, Matthew, Andrew, Luke, Christian. BS in Elem. Edn., U. Utah, 1981, MEd, 1985. Cert. elem. tchr., Utah. Printer Transamerica Film Svc., Salt Lake City, 1978-81; tchr. Granite Sch. Dist., Salt Lake City, 1981—; pres. Granite Fedn. Tchrs., 1985-87, treas., 1990-92. Active mem. State House of Reps., 1992-94; Bishop LDS Ch., West Jordan, Utah, 1988; mem. Oquivrh Shadows Community Coun., West Jordan, 1987; chmn. rels. com. Boy Scouts Am., 1972—. Recipient Outstanding Tchr. award Excel Found., 1985, Elem. Tchr. of Yr. award Utah Fedn. Tchrs., 1991. Mem. ASCD, Utah Assn Gifted Children. Democrat. Avocations: fishing, guitar. Home and Office: 6644 S 5095 W West Jordan UT 84084-6889

SHEPHERD, R. F., retired bishop; b. July 15, 1926; s. Herbert George and Muriel (Grant) S.; m. Ann Alayne Dundas, 1952; 6 children. BA with honors, U. B.C., 1948; postgrad., King's Coll., London; DD (hon.), St. John's Coll., Winnipeg, 1988. Curate St. Stephen's, London, 1952-57; rector St. Paul's, Glanford, Ont., 1957-59, All Sts., Winnipeg, 1959-65; dean, rector All Sts. Cathedral, Edmonton, Alta., 1965-69, Christ Ch. Cathedral, Montreal, 1970-83; rector St. Matthias, Victoria, B.C., 1983-84; Anglican Bishop of B.C., 1985-92. Fellow Coll. of Preachers. Home: 110 Ensilwood Rd, Salt Spring Island, BC Canada V8K 1N1

SHEPHERD, ROBERT JAMES, plant pathology researcher, retired educator; b. Clinton, Okla., June 5, 1930; s. Lee Fines and Ruby (Gilleland) S.; m. Shirley Ann Stuby, Sept. 6, 1955 (div. Sept. 1976); children: Steven L., Eudora Deidre, David A.; m. Mary Ann Sall, Mar. 18, 1978. Student, U. Okla., 1948-50; BS, Okla. State U., 1954, MS, 1955; PhD, U. Wis., 1959. Asst. prof. U. Wis., Madison, 1959-61; asst. prof. U. Calif., Davis, 1961-66, assoc. prof., 1966-72, prof. plant pathology, 1972-84; prof. plant pathology U. Ky., Lexington, 1984-96; ret., 1996; chmn. plant virus subcom. Internat. Com. Taxonomy of Viruses, 1971-76; mem. sci. bd. Calgene Inc., Davis, 1980-85; cons. Ohio Bd. Regents, 1985-86. Editor Virology jour., 1971-73; contbr. articles and revs. to profl. jours. With U.S. Army, 1950-52, Korea. Fulbright scholar, Cambridge, Eng., 1955-56. Fellow Am. Phytopathol. Soc. (Ruth Allen award 1981); mem. NAS. Democrat. Avocations: bird watching, gardening.

SHEPHERD, STEVEN STEWART, auditor, consultant; b. Pauls Valley, Okla., Aug. 7, 1956; s. Lloyd Thomas and Barbara Lou (Garton) S.; m. Dawn Rachelle Godwin, Aug. 22, 1981; children: Shane, Lauren. BBA, U. Tex., 1981, MBA, 1990. Internal auditor Ark-La. Gas Co., Shreveport, La., 1982-84; sr. constrn. auditor Cen. & S.W. Svcs., Inc., Dallas, 1984-87; constrn. audit supr. City of Ft. Worth, 1987-96; city auditor City of Garland, Tex., 1996—; cons. Constrn. Mgmt. Svcs., Arlington, Tex., 1990—, Eagle Tax Svcs., Arlington, 1990—; mem. adv. com. for acctg. program Tarrant County Jr. Coll., 1995-97; mem. internal audit adv. bd. U. North Tex., 1993-96. Contbr. articles to profl. jours. Mem. allocation com. Tarrant County United Way, Ft. Worth, 1991; bd. dirs. Charlotte Anderson Elem. Sch. PTA, Mansfield, Tex., 1990-91. Mem. Inst. Internal Auditors (bd. govs. Ft. Worth chpt. 1990-96, sec. 1990-91, treas. 1991-92, v.p. 1992-93, pres. 1993-94),

Mansfield Youth Baseball Assn. (bd. dirs. 1993-95), Delta Upsilon (bd. dirs. 1991-96, sec. 1994-95). Republican. Mem. Ch. of Christ. Avocations: little league coach, horseback riding, water skiing, snow skiing, scuba diving.

SHEPHERD, STEWART ROBERT, lawyer; b. Chgo., Sept. 9, 1948; s. Stewart and LaVina Beatrice (Nereim) S.; m. Margaret Brownell Shoop, Aug. 14, 1970; children: Elisabeth Ashby, Megan Brownell, Blair Stewart. BA, Rockford Coll., 1970; JD, U. Chgo., 1973. Bar: Calif. 1973, U.S. Dist. Ct. (no. dist.) Calif. 1973, Ill. 1976, U.S. Dist. Ct. (no. dist.) Ill. 1976. Assoc. Heller, Ehrman, White & McAuliffe, San Francisco, 1973-75; assoc. Hopkins & Sutter, Chgo., 1975-79, ptnr., 1979-96; ptnr. Sidley & Austin, 1996—. Mem. ABA, Order of Coif, Phi Beta Kappa. Office: Sidley & Austin One First National Plz Chicago IL 60603

SHEPLEY, HUGH, architect; b. Boston, Mar. 17, 1928; s. Henry Richardson and Anna Lowell (Gardiner) S.; m. Mary Waters Niles, Dec. 27, 1950; children: Hamilton Niles, Philip Foster. B.A., Harvard U., 1951; BArch., Boston Archtl. Ctr., 1958; postgrad., Mass. Inst. Tech., 1958-59. Mem. archtl. firm Shepley, Bulfinch, Richardson & Abbott, Boston, 1955-63; ptnr. Shepley, Bulfinch, Richardson & Abbott, 1963-91. Bd. dirs. Greater Boston Red Cross, 1967-73, mem. exec. com., 1968-69; bd. dirs. Cmty. Music Ctr., Boston, 1968-72, Boston Ctr. for Blind Children, 1979-87; trustee New Eng. Conservatory Music, 1978-83, overseer, 1983—; trustee Univ. Hosp., 1980-96, mem. exec. com., 1981-92, vice chmn. bd. dirs., 1985-89, chmn. bd. dirs., 1989-92; trustee Am. Coll. of Greece, 1983-92, treas., 1986-88; trustee, sec. Rotch Travelling Scholarship, 1987-93, v.p., 1993—; mem. adv. coun. Boston U. Med. Ctr., 1990-96, Corp. Old South Assn., 1993—; v.p. Manchester (Mass.) Hist. Soc., 1994—. Fellow AIA; mem. Mass. Assn. Architects (pres. 1972), Boston Soc. Architects (pres. 1974), Boston Archtl. Ctr. (pres. 1969-71). Republican. Episcopalian. Clubs: Tavern (Boston); Manchester Yacht (commodore 1985-87). Home: 18 Forster Rd Manchester MA 01944-1420 Office: S B R & A 40 Broad St Fl 6 Boston MA 02109-4307

SHEPP, BRYAN EUGENE, psychologist, educator; b. Cumberland, Md., Sept. 13, 1932; s. Bryan Evert and Dorothy Lorene (Stell) S.; m. June Lee Langeluttig, Jan. 31, 1953; children—Karen Suzanne, David Bryan. B.S., U. Md., 1954, M.S., 1956, Ph.D., 1960; M.S. (hon.), Brown U., 1966. Research prof. U. Conn., 1961-63; asst. prof. psychology George Peabody Coll., 1963-64; asst. prof. Brown U., 1964-66, assoc. prof., 1966-69, prof., 1969—, chmn. dept. psychology, 1983-88, assoc. dean of faculty, 1988-91, dean of faculty, 1991-96; cons. in field; vis. scientist Oxford (Eng.) U., 1970. Contbr. numerous articles to profl. publs.; ad hoc editor for several psychol. jours. Served with USN, 1955-59. Decorated letter of commendation Sec. of Navy; USPHS postdoctoral fellow, 1959-61; Nat. Inst. Child Health and Human Devel. grantee, 1965—. Fellow Am. Psychol. Assn.; mem. Psychonomic Soc., AAAS, AAUP. Club: Univ. Office: 89 Waterman St Providence RI 02912-9079

SHEPPARD, ALBERT PARKER, JR., mathematics educator; b. Griffin, Ga., June 6, 1936; s. Albert Parker and Cornelia (Cooper) S.; m. Judith Prosser, Sept. 9, 1957 (div. 1976); children: Albert Parker III, Frank Phillip; m. Eleanor C. Davis, Feb. 8, 1978 (dec. Oct. 1994); 1 stepchild, Phillip Hancock; m. Marjory W. Dewell, Nov. 18, 1995. B.S., Oglethorpe U., 1958; M.S., Emory U., 1959; Ph.D., Duke U., 1965. Sr. engr. Orlando (Fla.) rsch. div. Martin Marietta Co., 1960-63; physicist U.S. Army Rsch. Office, Durham, N.C., 1963-65; prin. rsch. engr., head spl. techniques br., electronics div. Ga. Inst. Tech., 1965-71, chief of chem. sci. lab., 1971-72, assoc. dean coll. engring., 1972-74, prof. elec. engring., 1972-89, assoc. v.p. for rsch., 1974-88, acting v.p. rsch., 1979-80, asst. to pres. info. tech., 1986, v.p. for interdisciplinary programs, 1988-89, acting v.p. info. tech., 1988-89; Charles and Mildred Jenkins prof. math. Fla. So. Coll., Lakeland, 1989—, dir. acad. computing, 1996—; mem. evening faculty DeKalb Coll., Clarkston, Ga., 1967-71; pres. APS Enterprises Corp., Lakeland, 1980—; cons. scholar IBM So. Area 8, 1990-93. Contbr. articles to profl. jours. Inventor linear down-draft biomass gasifier. Trustee Southeastern Univs. Research Assocs., 1983-86. Recipient Disting. Alumni award Oglethorpe U., 1974; Woodrow Wilson fellow, 1959. Mem. IEEE (sr.), Univ. Space Rsch. Assn. (vice chmn. coun. instns. 1980-81, chmn. 1981-82, trustee 1985-89, vice chmn. bd. dirs. 1986-87, chmn. 1987-88, chmn. engring. sci. coun. 1989-94), Ga. Tech. Rsch. Corp. (trustee), Lone Palm Golf Club, Sigma Xi, Sigma Pi Sigma, Kappa Mu Epsilon. Presbyterian. Home: 1240 Jefferson Dr Lakeland FL 33803-2300 Office: Fla So Coll Dept Math Lakeland FL 33801

SHEPPARD, CLAUDE-ARMAND, lawyer; b. Ghent, Belgium, May 26, 1935; m. Claudine Proutat; children—Jean-Pierre, Michel, Marie-Claude, Stephane, Annabelle. B.A., McGill U., 1955; B.C.L., 1958. Bar: Que. 1959. Partner firm Robinson, Sheppard & Shapiro, Montreal, 1965—; legal commentator for French and English radio and television networks in, Can.; lectr. various instns.; counsel various royal commns.; counsel to com. Canadian Ho. of Commons; legal supr. Que. Commn. of Inquiry Lang. Rights; dir. various orgns. and founds. Author: The Law of Languages in Canada, 1965, The Organization and Regulation of the Health and Social Welfare Professions in Quebec, 1970, Language Rights in Quebec, 1973, also numerous papers. Past pres. Canadian Civil Liberties Union; former mem. Canadian Adv. Council on Status of Women. Fellow C.B.A. Found. for Legal Rsch. Mem. ABA (assoc.), Can. Bar Assn., Internat. Inst. Comparative Linguistic Law (pres. 1987—), Que. Bar Found. (gov.), Found. André-Guerin (pres. 1991—), Found. Montreal 2000 (v.p. 1994—). Office: Robinson Sheppard & Shapiro, 800 Place Victoria Ste 4700, Montreal, PQ Canada H4Z 1H6

SHEPPARD, HAROLD LLOYD, gerontologist, educator; b. Balt., Apr. 1, 1922; s. Joseph and Anna Leslie (Levy) S.; children: Mark, Jenny. MA, U. Chgo., 1945; PhD, U. Wis., Madison, 1949. Assoc. prof. sociology Wayne State U., Detroit, 1947-59; rsch. and staff dir. spl. com. on aging U.S. Senate, Washington, 1959-61; asst. adminstr. area redevel. adminstrn. U.S. Dept. Commerce, Washington, 1961-63; staff social scientist W.E. Upjohn Inst. Employment Rsch., Washington, 1963-75; sr. rsch. fellow Am. Inst. Rsch., Washington, 1975-80; counselor on aging to Pres. Carter Washington, 1980-81; assoc. dir. Nat. Coun. on Aging, Washington, 1981-82; dir. Internat. Exchange Ctr. Gerontology U. South Fla., Tampa, 1983-91; prof. Dept. Gerontology U. South Fla., Tampa, 1983—; cons. U.S. Dept. Labor, Washington, Senate Com. on Unemployment and Poverty, Washington, ILO, Geneva, OECD, Paris. Author, editor: Towards an Industrial Gerontology, 1970; co-author: Where Have all the Robots Gone?, 1972, The Graying of Working America, 1979; editor: Poverty and Wealth in America, 1972, Future of Older Workers, 1990. Fulbright scholar, France, 1957-58. Fellow Gerontol. Soc. Am. Avocation: sailing.

SHEPPARD, JACK W., retired air force officer; b. Parkersburg, W.Va., Aug. 8, 1931; s. James Lee and Audrey Irene (Heiney) S.; m. Norma Ann Stutler, Sept. 4, 1953; children—Bradley, Gregory. B.A.C., U. Akron, Ohio, 1955; M.A. in Pub. Adminstrn., George Washington U., 1965. Commd. lt. U.S. Air Force, 1955, advanced through grades to maj. gen.; vice comdr. 60 Mil. Airlift Wing, USAF, Travis AFB, Calif., 1977-79; comdr. 1606 Air Base Wing, USAF, Kirtland AFB, N.Mex., 1979-81; dir. internat. staff Inter Am. Def. Bd., USAF, Washington, 1981-82; dep. chief staff for personnel USAF Mil. Airlift Command, Scott AFB, Ill., 1982-83, chief of staff, 1983-85; comdr. Twenty First Air Force, McGuire AFB, N.J., 1985-87; asst. dep. chief staff programs and resources Hdqrs. USAF, Washington, 1987-88, ret., 1988. Mem. Order of Daedalians, Air Force Assn., Airlift Assn., Armed forces Adv. Assn. (pres. elect), Theta Chi. Presbyterian. Home: PO Box 908 21 Beaver Ln Cedar Crest NM 87008-0908

SHEPPARD, JOHN WILBUR, computer research scientist; b. Pitts., Aug. 21, 1961; s. Harry Reid and Mary Jane (Amon) S.; m. Justine Anne Pape, Oct. 29, 1988; 1 child, Jesse Carl. BS, So. Meth. U., 1983; MS, Johns Hopkins U., 1989, PhD, 1996. Systems analyst Sheppard Internat., Inc., Hermitage, Pa., 1979-86; prin. rsch. analyst ARINC Inc., Annapolis, Md., 1986—. Co-author: System Test and Diagnosis, 1994; contbr. articles to profl. jours. Mem. YMCA, Hermitage, 1979-85, Md. Hall for the Creative Arts, Annapolis, 1988-90; pres. Univ. Chapel Campus Ministry, Dallas, 1982-83. Mem. IEEE, Am. Assn. for Artificial Intelligence, Internat. Neural Network Soc., Mensa, Kappa Mu Epsilon. Republican. Lutheran. Achievements include U.S. patent awarded and foreign patent awarded for methods and apparatus for diagnostic testing; development of explanation-based learning approach for fault diagnosis. Home: 1203 Will-O-Brook Dr Pasadena MD 21122 Office: ARINC Inc 2551 Riva Rd Annapolis MD 21401-7435

SHEPPARD, LOUIS CLARKE, biomedical engineer, educator; b. Pine Bluff, Ark., May 28, 1933; s. Ellis Allen and Louise (Clarke) S.; m. Nancy Louise Mayer, Feb. 8, 1958; children: David, Susan, Lisa. BS in Chem. Engring., U. Ark., 1957; PhD in Elec. Engring., U. London, 1976. Registered profl. engr., Ala., Tex. Devel. staff supr. Diamond Alkali Co., Deer Park, Tex., 1957-63; staff engr. IBM, Rochester, Minn., 1963-66; assoc. prof. surgery dept. U. Ala.-Birmingham, 1966-88, sr. scientist Cystic Fibrosis Research Ctr., 1981-87, prof., chmn. biomed. engring. dept., 1979-88; prof. phsiology and biophysics, asst. v.p. rsch. U. Tex., Galveston, 1988-90, assoc. v.p. rsch., 1990-92, assoc. v.p. bioengring. and biotech., 1992—, prof. biomed. engring., Austin; adj. prof. elec. engring. U. Houston; mem. med. adv. bd. Hewlett Packard, 1980-84; cons. IMED Corp., 1982-83, Oximetrix, 1982, 86-88, MiniMed, 1986-88; mem. sci. adv. bd. JJMI, 1992-94; dir. FBK Internat.; pres. S.E.A. Corp., 1984-94; mem. editorial bd. Med. Progress Through Tech., 1984-94, Springer-Verlag, Berlin; cons. Nat. Heart, Lung and Blood Inst. Bd. dirs. Birmingham Met. Devel. Bd. Served with AUS, 1958-66. Recipient Ayerton Premium award IEE (U.K.), 1984. Recipient Disting. Alumnus citation, U. Ark., 1987, Lifetime Achievement award M.D. Buyline, 1987. Fellow IEEE, Am. Inst. for Med. and Biol. Engring., Am. Coll. Med. Informatics; mem. Brit. Computer Soc., Biomed. Engring. Soc. (dir.), IEEE, Am. Inst. Chem. Engrs., Am. Med. Informatics Assn., Univ. Space Rsch. Assn. (bd. dirs. 1995—), Acad. Med. Arts and Scis., Blue Key, Sigma Xi, Tau Beta Pi, Alpha Pi Mu, Eta Kappa Nu, Theta Tau. Clubs: St. Andrews Soc. of Middle South, The Houstonian. Contbr. abstracts, chpts. to books, editorials; patentee method and system for estimation of arterial pressure. Home: 5 E Broad Oaks Ln Houston TX 77056-1218 Office: U Tex Med Br 626 Jennie Sealy Hosp Galveston TX 77555-0455

SHEPPARD, POSY (MRS. JEREMIAH MILBANK), social worker; b. New Haven, Aug. 23, 1916; d. John Day and Rose Marie (Herrick) Jackson; m. John W. Sheppard, May 16, 1936 (dec. Apr. 1990); children: Sandra S. (Mrs. Allan Gray Rodgers), Gail G. (Mrs. Gail Bidwell), Lynn S. (Mrs. William Muir Manger), John W.; m. Jeremiah Milbank, May 4, 1991. Student, Vassar Coll., 1938. Vol. field cons. Conn. A.R.C., 1955-60; vice chmn. bd. govs. Am. Nat. Red Cross, 1962-66; rep. League Red Cross Socs. to UN, 1957-80, Am. Nat. Red Cross to com. internat. social welfare Nat. Social Welfare Assembly, 1957-61; chmn. Non-Govtl. Orgn. Com. for UNICEF, 1963-64, 71-73; chmn. Non-Govtl. Orgn. Com. exec. com. for Office Pub. Information, UN, 1964-66; pres. conf. non-govtl. orgns. in consultative status with UN Econ. and Social Council, 1966-69. Mem. Am. Soc. Polit. and Social Sci., Soc. Internat. Devel., Nat. Soc. Colonial Dames, Descs. Signers of Declaration Independence, Round Hill Club, River Club (N.Y.). Home: 535 Lake Ave Greenwich CT 06830-3831

SHEPPARD, SCOTT, magazine publisher. Publisher Southern Living, Birmingham, exec. v.p., 1997—. Office: Southern Living 2100 Lakeshore Dr Birmingham AL 35209-6721*

SHEPPARD, WALTER LEE, JR., chemical engineer, consultant; b. Phila., June 23, 1911; s. Walter Lee and Martha Houston (Evans) S.; m. Dorothy Virginia Cosby Vanderslice, Oct. 17, 1942 (div. Mar. 1947); m. Boudinot Atterbury Oberge Kendall, Mar. 24, 1953 (dec. Feb. 1996); stepchildren: Charles H. Kendall Jr., John Atterbury Kendall. BChem, Cornell U., 1932; MS, U. Pa., 1933. Registered profl. engr., Del., Calif.; diplomate Am. Acad. Environ. Engrs.; ordained deacon Liberal Cath. Ch., 1954, priest, 1955. Control chemist various cos., 1933-35; advt. writer N.W. Ayer & Son, 1936-37; asst. to editor The Houghton Line (E.F. Houghton Co.), 1937-38; salesman Atlas Mineral Products, 1938-48; plant mgr., cons. engr. Tanks & Linings, Ltd., Droitwich, Eng., 1948-49; sales engr., dist. mgr. ElectroChem. Engring. & Mfg., and successor cos., 1949-68; nat. accounts mgr., field sales mgr. Corrosion Engring. div. Pennwalt Corp., Phila., 1968-76; pres. C.C.R.M., Inc.; cons. on chemically resistant masonry, 1976—; profl. genealogist, 1936—. Author: Ancestry and Descendants of Thomas Stickney Evans and Sarah Ann Fifield, His Wife, 1940, Chemically Resistant Masonry, 1977, 2d edit., 1982, Ancestry of Edward Carleton and Ellen Newton, His Wife, 1978, microfilm, 1982; author, editor: Corrosion and Chemical Resistant Masonry Materials Handbook, 1986; editor: Passengers and Ships Prior to 1684, 1965; successor editor: Ancestral Roots of 60 New England Colonists, 3rd to 7th edits., 1992, Magna Charta Sureties 1215, 2nd to 4th edits., 1991; contbg. editor Am. Genealogist, 1941-70, Nat. Geneal. Quar., 1961—; mem. publs. com. Pa. Geneal. Mag., 1960-76; contbr. articles on corrosion resistant masonry constrn. to profl. jours. Dir. displaced persons camps UNRRA, also d.p. specialist, staff Chief of Mission, Vienna, Austria, 1945-46; founding trustee, v.p. Bd. Cert. Genealogists, 1965-82, pres., 1969-78, chmn., 1978-79. Served to maj. U.S. Army, 1941-45, UNRRA, 1945-46; lt. col., Res., ret. 1960. Named Hon. Mem. Class of 1928 U.S. Naval Acad., 1976. Fellow Am. Soc. Genealogists (sec. 1958-61, 66-67, v.p. 1967-70, pres. 1970-73), Nat. Geneal. Soc., Pa. Geneal. Soc.; mem. ASTM (membership sec. 1975-83, C-3 com.), NSPE, Am. Acad. Environ. Engrs., Welcome Soc. (pres. 1969-76), Illegitimate Sons and Daus. of Kings and Queens of Britain (founder, sec. 1950-68, pres. 1968-88), Flagon and Trencher Soc. (co-founder, pres. 1967-73), Nat. Assn. Corrosion Engrs. (cert. competence in corrosion engring., chmn. Phila. sect. 1962), New Eng. Historic Geneal. Soc. (com. on Heraldry, 1991—), Nat. Geneal. Soc. Quar. (contbg. editor), Geneal. Soc. Pa., Soc. Genealogists (London), Yorkshire Archeol. Soc., Savoy Co., Gilbert and Sullivan Soc. (founder, pres. Phila. br. 1957-63), Sovereign Order St. John of Jerusalem, Mil. Order Fgn. Wars, Mayflower Descs., Order of Three Crusades, Order of the Crown of Charlemagne in Am. (3rd v.p. 1989—), Ret. Officers Assn., Phi Kappa Psi (nat. v.p. 1964-68, pres. 1968-70), Alpha Chi Sigma. Home and Office: 923 Old Manoa Rd Havertown PA 19083-2610

SHEPPARD, WILLIAM STEVENS, investment banker; b. Grand Rapids, Mich., Apr. 29, 1930; s. James Herbert and Emily Gilmore (Stevens) S.; m. Jane Steketee, 1956 (dec. 1975); children: Stevens C., Elizabeth W., Emily R.; m. Patricia Gillis Bloom, Dec. 2, 1978. B.A. in Econs, U. Va., 1953. Trainee J.P. Morgan & Co., Inc., N.Y.C., 1955-58; investment adv. Delafield & Delafield, N.Y.C., 1958-71; from salesman to sr. v.p. and dir. F.S. Smithers & Co., N.Y.C., 1971-76; sr. v.p., dir. successor Paine, Webber, Jackson & Curtis, Inc., 1976-81; pres., chief exec. officer, dir. Paine Webber Real Estate Securities Inc., 1980-85; mng. dir. Paine Webber Capital Markets, N.Y.C., 1985-88; adv. dir. Berkshire Capital Corp., N.Y.C., 1988—; adminstr. Pequot Investment Advisors, Inc. (Adv. Divsn. Putnam Trust), Southport, Conn., 1995—; chmn. bd. dirs. Ea. Bancorp. An editor: Ginny Mae Manual, 1979; contbr. to handbooks. Trustee, treas. Riot Relief Fund City N.Y., 1970—. Served to lt. USNR, 1953-55. Republican. Clubs: N.Y. Yacht; Country of Fairfield (Conn.); Pequot Yacht; Mashomack Fish and Game, North Haven Casino. Home: 405 Sasco Rd Southport CT 06490 Office: Pequot Investment Advisors Box 139 Southport CT 06490

SHEPPARD, WILLIAM VERNON, engineer and construction executive; b. Harlan, Ky., Apr. 18, 1941; s. Vernon L. and Margaret M. (Montgomery) S.; m. Charlotte A. McGehee, Nov. 6, 1981; children: W. Kevin, Candice Gaye. BCE, The Citadel, 1964. Registered profl. engr., Pa., Calif. and 10 other states. Hwy. engr. Howard Needles, Tammen & Bergendoff, Kansas City, Mo., 1964-65; with Wilbur Smith & Assos., Columbia, S.C., 1967-80, various positions to western regional v.p., so. regional v.p.; dir. transp. Post Buckley, Schuh & Jernigan, Inc., Columbia, 1980-85; sr. v.p., Sverdrup Civil, 1985-94; sr. v.p., chmn. Surface Transp., HNTB, 1994-97; v.p., transportation prin., DMJM, 1997—; guest lectr. U. So. Calif. Sch. Architecture and Urban Planning. Mem. engring. adv. bd. Clemson U., 1977-80. Served to capt. U.S. Army, 1965-67. Decorated AEM medal. Fellow ASCE, Inst. Transp. Engrs. (pres. S.C. div. 1979); mem. Nat. Soc. Profl. Engrs., S.C. Coun. Engring. Socs. (pres. 1978), Tau Beta Pi. Republican. Roman Catholic. Home: 1 Rue Montreaux Newport Beach CA 92660

SHEPPE, JOSEPH ANDREW, surgeon; b. Huntington, W.Va., Sept. 24, 1953; m. Kathy Chapman; children: Sheree Nicole, Natalee Marie, Brittany Lee. BS summa cum laude in Chemistry and Zoology, Marshall U., 1975; MD, W.Va. U., 1979. Diplomate Am. Bd. Surgery, Am. Bd. Colon and Rectal Surgery. Intern in gen. surgery Charleston (W.Va.) Area Med. Ctr., 1979-84; fellow in colon and rectal surgery William Beaumont Army Med. Ctr., Royal Oak, Mich., 1984-85; pvt. practice Columbia, S.C., 1985—; physician Bapt. Med. Ctr., Columbia, Providence Hosp., Columbia, Richland Meml. Hosp., Columbia, Lexington Med. Ctr., West Columbia, S.C.; clin. instr. in gen./colorectal surgery U. S.C. Med. Sch. Mem. ACS, Am. Soc. Colon and Rectal Surgery, S.C. Med. Soc., Columbia Med. Soc. Home: 204 Leaning Tree Rd Columbia SC 29223-3009 Office: 1333 Taylor St Ste 4-a Columbia SC 29201-2923

SHEPPERD, SUSAN ABBOTT, special education educator; b. Pekin, Ill., May 12, 1942; d. Robert Fred and Martha Mae (Abbott) Belville; m. Thomas Eugene Shepperd, Oct. 7, 1960; children: Scott Thomas, Allison Marie Shepperd-Henry, Michele Lea. BA, Maryville Coll., 1990; MEd, U. Mo., 1994. Cert. elem. edn. tchr. grades 1-8, spl. reading tchr. grades K-12. Resource tchr. reading grades K-8 St. Joseph Sch., Ardiocese of St. Louis, Cottleville, Mo., 1990—. Mem. Pi Lambda Theta (pres. 1992-94), Assn. in Edn. (Gamma Zeta chpt.), Phi Kappa Phi, Delta Epsilon Sigma. Episcopalian. Avocations: golfing, music, swimming. Home: 15977 Chamfers Farm Rd Chesterfield MO 63005-4717 Office: St Joseph Sch Motherhead Rd Cottleville MO 63304

SHEPPERD, THOMAS EUGENE, accountant; b. Pekin, Ill., Aug. 19, 1941; s. William Thomas and Marguerite Louise (Meisinger) S.; m. Susan Abbott Belville, Oct. 7, 1960; children: Scott Thomas, Allison Marie Shepperd-Henry, Michele Lea. BS in Acctg., U. Ill., 1964. CPA, Ill., Mo., Iowa, Ind. From jr. acct. to mgr. Haskins & Sells, St. Louis, 1964-74; mgr. Haskins & Sells, Washington, 1974-75, ptnr., 1975-77; ptnr. Deloitte Haskins & Sells (formerly Haskins & Sells), St. Louis, 1977-89, Deloitte & Touche (merger Deloitte Haskins & Sells and Touche Ross & Co.), St. Louis, 1989—. Treas. Shepley concert com. Christ Ch. Cathedral, St. Louis, 1989. Mem. AICPA (various coms.), Mo. Soc. CPAs (adminstrv. v.p., bd. dirs. 1988-92, treas. 1992-95, v.p. 1996-97, pres.-elect 1997—, chair long range fin. planning com. and the office location com., terms on the tech. standards peer review exec., profl. ethics coms., legislation com., acctg. and auditing procedures com.), U. Ill. Press. Coun., Noonday Club (treas., bd. dirs. 1977-81), Glen Echo Country Club. Republican. Episcopalian. Avocations: golf, travel, sports. Home: 15977 Chamfers Farm Rd Chesterfield MO 63005-4717 Office: Deloitte & Touche LLP 1 City Ctr Saint Louis MO 63101-1883

SHEPRO, RICHARD W., lawyer; b. Berwyn, Ill., May 9, 1953; s. Justice Warren and Inez Marjorie (McKillip); m. Lindsay Ellen Roberts, Sept. 5, 1981; children: Claire Willoughby, Warren Boyd. AB, Harvard U., 1975, JD, 1979; MSc, London Sch. Econs., Eng., 1976. Bar: Ill. 1979, Calif. 1981, U.S. Ct. Appeals (9th cir.) 1981, U.S. Dist. Ct. (no. dist.) Ill. 1982, U.S. Supreme Ct. 1993. Teaching fellow Harvard U., Cambridge, Mass., 1979; law clk. to chief judge U.S. Ct. Appeals (9th cir.), San Francisco, 1979-81; assoc. Mayer, Brown & Platt, Chgo., 1981-85, ptnr., 1986—; lectr. law U. Chgo., 1992—; staff mem. U.S. Senate Judiciary Com., 1979; spl. asst. atty. gen., Ill., 1981-82; corr. on bus. law The Fin. Times, London, 1986—. Co-author: Bidders & Targets: Mergers and Acquisitions in the U.S., 1990; contbr. numerous articles to profl. jours. Del. nat. conv. NOW, Ind., 1982; bd. govs. Kohl Children's Mus.; vestryman St. Chrysostom's Ch., Chgo. Recipient U.S. Presdl. scholar Pres. of U.S., Washington, 1971, Greenman Prize Harvard U., 1975; named Harvard Law Rev. Supreme Ct. Editor, Harvard Law Rev. Assn., 1977-79; named to Am. Law Inst., 1993. Fellow Chgo. Bar Found.; mem. ABA, Chgo. Coun. Lawyers (bd. govs. 1986-89, chmn. election law com. 1987-94), Chgo. Coun. Fgn. Rels., The Chgo. Ensemble (dir. and v.p.), Chgo. Club, LaSalle Club (dir. and mem. exec. com.). Home: 837 W Oakdale Ave Chicago IL 60657-5121 Office: Mayer Brown & Platt 190 S La Salle St Chicago IL 60603-3410

SHER, GEORGE ALLEN, philosophy educator; b. N.Y.C., Nov. 10, 1942; s. Daniel and Clara (Landesberg) S.; m. Emily Fox Gordon, July 10, 1972; 1 child, Sarah Landesberg. BA, Brandeis U., 1964; PhD, Columbia U., 1972. Instr. philosophy Fairleigh Dickinson U., Teaneck, N.J., 1966-72, asst. prof. philosophy, 1972-74; assoc. prof. philosophy U. Vt., Burlington, 1974-80, prof., 1980-91; Herbert S. Autrey prof. philosophy Rice U., Houston, 1991—, chmn. dept. philosophy, 1993—; mem. Inst. for Advanced Study, Princeton, N.J., 1987-88. Author: (book) Desert, 1987, Beyond Neutrality: Perfectionism and Politics, 1997; editor: (book) Moral Philosophy: Selected Readings, 1989; contbr. articles to profl. jours. Named fellow Nat. Humanities Ctr., Rsch. Triangle Park, N.C., 1980-81. Mem. Am. Philos. Assn. Home: 2425 Dryden Rd Houston TX 77030 Office: Rice U Dept Philosophy 6100 Main St Houston TX 77005-1827

SHER, PAUL PHILLIP, physician, pathologist; b. Bklyn., Oct. 25, 1939; s. Louis and Lottie (Kloner) S.; m. Joan E. Zeffren, June 9, 1964; children: Matthew, Andrew, Lawrence. BS cum laude, Hobart Coll., 1961; MD, Washington U., 1965. Diplomate Am. Bd. Pathology. Intern in pathology Columbia-Presbyn. Hosp., N.Y.C., 1965-66, resident in pathology, 1966-69; instr. pathology Columbia Presbyn. Hosp., N.Y.C., 1968-70; resident in pathology Englewood (N.J.) Hosp., 1969-70; dir. clin. chemistry Frances Delafeld Hosp., N.Y.C., 1970-71; dir. blood bank Bethesda Naval Hosp., Rockville, Md., 1971-72, dir. hematology, 1973; dir. clin. chemistry NYU Med. Ctr., Tisch Hosp., 1973, dir. clin. labs., 1980-93; clin. prof. pathology, prof. med. informatics Biomed. Info. Comm. Ctr. Oreg. Health Scis. U., Portland, 1993—. Editor Lab. Med.; contbr. articles, editorial, revs. to profl. jours.;. Lt. comdr. USN, 1971-73. Fellow Coll. Am. Pathologists, Am. Soc. Clin. Pathologists, Explorer's Club.

SHER, PHYLLIS KAMMERMAN, pediatric neurology educator; b. N.Y.C., Aug. 13, 1944; d. Seymour K. and Shirley (Parmit) Kammerman; m. Kenneth Swaiman, Oct. 6, 1985. BA, Brandeis U., 1966; MD, U. Miami, 1970. Diplomate Am. Bd. Psychiatry and Neurology. Pediatric intern Montefiore Hosp., Bronx, N.Y., 1970-71; resident in neurology U. Miami (Fla.) Med. Sch., 1971-73, fellow in pediatric neurology, 1973-75, asst. prof. neurology, 1975-80; rsch. assoc. NIH, Bethesda, Md., 1980-83; asst. prof. neurology and pediatrics U. Minn. Med. Sch., Mpls., 1983-86, assoc. prof., 1986—; mem. Hennepin Faculty Assocs., 1996—; dir. Ripple program United Cerebral Palsy Found., Miami, 1972-75; chmn. med. svcs. com. 5-yr. action plan State of Fla., 1975; cons. Minn. Epilepsy Program for Children, 1983-85; vis. prof. Japanese Soc. Child Neurology, 1985, Chinese Child Neurology Ctr., 1989, Hong Kong Soc. Child Neurology & Devel. Pediat., 1995. Mem. editl. bd. Pediatric Neurology, 1991—, Brain and Devel., 1994—; contbr. articles and abstracts to med. jours., chpts. to books. Comdr. USPHS, 1980-83. Fellow United Cerebral Palsy Found., 1972-73; rsch. grantee Gillette Children's Hosp., U. Minn. Grad. Sch., Viking Children's Fund, Minn. Med. Found. Fellow Am. Neurol. Assn., Am. Acad. Neurology; mem. Child Neurology Soc. (exec. com., councillor 1993-95), Upper Midwest Child Neurology Soc., So. Clin. Neurology Soc. Office: Pediatric Neurology 1821 University Ave W Ste N188 Saint Paul MN 55104-2803

SHERAK, THOMAS MITCHELL, motion picture company executive; b. Bklyn., June 22, 1945; s. Myer and Freida (Rosenthal) S.; m. Madeleine Frankfurter, Nov. 22, 1967; children: Barbra, Melissa, William. A.A. in Mktg., N.Y. Community Coll., Bklyn., 1965. Salesman Paramount Pictures, N.Y.C., Washington, St. Louis, 1970-74; booker film R/C Theatres, Balt., 1974-77; dist. film buyer Gen. Cinema, Cherry Hill, N.J., 1977-78; v.p. film Gen. Cinema, N.Y.C., 1978-82; v.p. head film buyer Gen. Cinema, Cherry Hill, N.J., 1982-83; pres. domestic distbn. and mktg. 20th Century-Fox Pictures, Beverly Hills, Calif., 1983-85, pres. domestic distbn., 1985—. Served with U.S. Army, 1967-69. Mem. Motion Picture Bookers Club (hon.), Motion Picture Pioneer, Will Rogers. Democrat. Home: 4041 Declaration Ave Calabasas CA 91302-5742 Office: 20th Century-Fox Film Corp 1211 Avenue Of The Americas New York NY 10036-8701 also: PO Box 900 Beverly Hills CA 90213-0900*

SHERBELL, RHODA, artist, sculptor; b. Bklyn.; d. Alexander and Syd (Steinberg) S.; m. Mervin Honig, Apr. 28, 1956; 1 child, Susan. Student, Art Students League, 1950-53, Bklyn. Mus. Art Sch., 1959-61; also; pvt. study art, Italy, France, Eng., 1956. cons., coun. mem. Emily Lowe Gallery, Hofstra U., Hempstead, N.Y., 1978, pres., 1989-81, instr., 1991—, life mem. bd. friends, pres. bd. trustees; tchr. instr. Mus. Modern Art, N.Y.C., 1959, NAD Art Sch., N.Y.C., 1985—, Art Students League, N.Y.C., 1980—; Nat. Portrait Gallery Mus. rep. to 150th anniversary Smithsonian Instn., Washington,

1996. Exhibited one-woman shows Country Art Gallery, Locust Valley, N.Y., Bklyn. Mus. Art Sch., 1961, Adelphi Coll., A.C.A. Galleries, N.Y.C., 1967, Capricorn Galleries, Rehn Gallery, Washington, 1968, Huntington Hartford Mus., N.Y.C., 1969, Morris (N.J.) Mus. Arts and Scis., 1980, Bergen Mus. Arts and Scis., N.J., 1984, William Benton Mus., Conn., 1985, Palace Theatre of the Arts, Stamford, Conn., Bronx Mus. Arts, 1986, Hofstra Mus. Art, L.I., N.Y., 1989, 90, County Art Gallery, N.Y.C., 1990; one-woman retrospective at N.Y. Cultural Ctr., 1970, Nat. Arts Collection, Washington, 1970, Montclair Mus. of Art, 1976, Nat. Art Mus. of Sport, 1977, Jewish Mus. of N.Y.C., 1980, Black History Mus., 1981, Queens Mus., 1981, 82, Nat. Portrait Gallery, Washington, 1981, 82, Bronx Mus., N.Y., Bklyn. Mus., Mus. Modern Art, N.Y.C., Country Art Gallery, 1990, Port Washington Library, Nat. Mus. Am. Art, The Smithsonian Instn., 1982, Nat. Acad. Design, N.Y.C., 1984, 89, Castle Gallery Mus., N.Y.C., 1987, Emily Lowe Mus., N.Y.C., 1987, Heckshire Mus., N.Y.C., 1989, Islip Art Mus., N.Y.C., 1989, Gallery Emanuel, N.Y.C., 1993, Sundance Gallery, Bridgehampton, N.Y., 1995, CASTIRON Gallery SoHo Show, 1995, Nat. Acad. Design Exhibition, 1995; exhibited group shows Heckscher Mus., 1989, Islip Mus., 1989, Nassau Dept. Recreation and Parks, 1989, Downtown Gallery, N.Y.C., Maynard Walker Gallery, N.Y.C., F.A.R. Gallery, N.Y.C., Provincetown Art Assn., Detroit Inst. Art, Pa. Acad. Fine Arts, Bklyn. and L.I. Artists Show, Old Westbury Gardens Small Sculpture Show, Audubon Artists, NAD, Allied Artists, Heckscher Mus., Nat. Art Mus. Sports, Mus. Arts and Scis., L.A., Am. Mus. Natural History, Post of History Mus., 1987, 88, Caslte Gallery Mus., N.Y.C., 1987, Emiloy Lowe Gallery Mus., N.Y., 1987, Bronx Mus. Arts, 1987, Chgo. Hist. Soc., Mus. of Modern Art, N.Y.C., 1988, Sands Point Mus., L.I., NAD, Hofstra Mus., 1990, Nat. Mus. Sports Art, 1991, Indpls. Art Mus., Phoenix Mus. Art, Corcoran Mus. Art, Washington, IBM, N.Y.C., Fire House Gallery Mus. Nassau Cmty. Coll., L.I., 1992, Nat. Arts Club Ann. Exhbn., 1992, Sports in Art From Am. Mus. at IBM, N.Y.C., 1992, Nat. Sculpture Soc. and The Regina A Quick Ctr. for The Arts Fairfield U.Centennial Anniversary Exbn., 1993, Mus. Modern Art, N.Y.C., Nat. Sculpture Soc. 100 Anniversary Exhbn., 1993, Italy, 1994, Provincetown Assn. and Art Mus., 1993, Kyoto (Japan) Mus. Sculpture Guild, 1993, Nat. Sculpture Soc. Exhbn. in Italy, Lucca, 1994, Sculptures Guild, N.Y.C., 1994-95, Cline Gallery, Santa Fe, 1995; represented permanent collections, Stony Brook Hall of Fame, William Benton Mus. Art, Colby Coll. Mus., Oklahoma City Mus., Montclair (N.J.) Mus., Schonberg Library Black Studies, N.Y.C., Albany State Mus., Hofstra U., Bklyn. Mus., Colby Coll. Mus., Nat. Arts Collection, Nat. Portrait Gallery, Smithsonian Instn., Baseball Hall of Fame Cooperstown, N.Y., Nassau Community Coll., Hofstra U. Emily Lowe Gallery, Art Students League, Jewish Mus., Queens Mus., Black History Mus., Nassau County Mus., Stamford Mus. Art and Nature Ctr., Jericho Pub. Library, N.Y., African-Am. Mus., Hempstead, N.Y., 1988, Stamford (Conn.) Mus. Art and Scis., Silvermine Artists North East exhibition, 1989, Nassau Community Coll. Fire House Gallery Exbn., 1992, Nat. Portrait Gallery Smithsonian Instn., 1996; also pvt. collections, TV shows, ABC, 1968, 81; ednl. TV spl. Rhoda Sherbell-Woman in Bronze, 1977; important works include Seated Ballerina, portraits of Aaron Copland (Bruce Stevenson Meml. Best Portrait award Nat. Arts Club 1989), Eleanor Roosevelt, Variations on a Theme (36 works of collaged sculpture), 1982-86; appeared several TV shows; guest various radio programs; contbr. articles to newspapers, popular mags. and art jours. Council mem. Nassau County Mus., 1978, trustee, 1st v.p. council; assoc. trustee Nat. Art Mus. of Sports, Inc., 1975—; cons., community liaison WNET Channel 13, cultural coordinator, 1975-83; host radio show Not for Artists Only, 1978-79; trustee Women's Boxing Fedn., 1978; mem. The Art Comm of The City of New York, 1993. Recipient Gold medal Allied Artists of Am., 1989, Alfred G. B. Steel Meml. award Pa. Acad. Fine Arts, 1963-64; Helen F. Barnett prize NAD, 1965, Jersey City Mus. prize for sculpture, 1961, 1st prize sculpture Locust Valley Art Show, 1966, 67, Ann. Sculpture prize Jersey City Mus., Bank for Savs. 1st prize in sculpture, 1950, Ford Found. purchase award, 1964, 2 top sculpture awards Mainstreams 77, Cert. of Merit Salmagundi Club, 1978, prize for sculpture, 1980, 81, award for sculpture Knickerbocker Artists, 1980, 81, top prize for sculpture Hudson Valley Art Assn., 1981, Sawyer award NAD, 1985, Gold medal of honor Audubon Artists, 1985, 39th Ann. Silvermine Exhbn. award, Gold medal Allied Artists Am., 1990, Pres' award Nat Arts Club N.Y.C.; MacDowell Colony fellow, 1976, Am. Acad. Arts and Letters and Nat. Arts and Letters grantee, 1960, Louis Comfort Tiffany Found. grantee, 1962, Ford Found. grantee, 1964, 67, also award; named one of top 5 finalist World Wide Competition to do Monument of Queen Catherine of England, 1991; named to represent Nat. Portrait Gallery at Smithsonian Mus. 150th Anniversary Party, 1996. Fellow Nat. Sculpture Soc.; mem. Sculpture Guild (dir.), Nat. Assn. Women Artists (Jeffery Childs Willis Meml. prize 1978), Allied Artists Soc. (dir., Gold medal 1990), Audubon Artists (Greta Kempton Walker prize 1965, Chaim Gross award, award for disting. contbr. to orgn. 1979, 80, Louis Weskeem award, dir.), Woman's Caucus for Art, Coll. Art Assn., Am. Inst. Conservation Historic and Artistic Works, N.Y. Soc. Women Artists, Artists Equity Assn. N.Y., Nat. Sculpture Soc. (E.N. Richard Meml. prize 1989), Internat. Platform Assn., Profl. Artists Guild L.I., Painters and Sculptors Soc. N.J. (Bertrum R. Hulmes Meml. award), Am. Watercolor Soc. (award for disting. contbn. to orgn.), Catharine Lorillard Wolfe Club (hon. mention 1968), Nat. Arts Club (N.Y.C., Stevenson Meml. award 1989, Pres. award 1992), NAD Design (Leila Gordon Sawyer prize 1989; The Dessle Green Prize 1993). Home: 64 Jane Ct Westbury NY 11590-1410

SHERBORNE, ROBERT, editor; b. Fairborn, Ohio, Mar. 26, 1950; s. Henry Hall and Lauramay (Rider) S.; m. Pamela Saunders, Apr. 16, 1988; children: Laura, Sophie. BS in Comms., U. Tenn., 1976. Reporter Clarksville (Tenn.) Leaf Chronicle, 1976, Tullahoma (Tenn.) News, 1976-77; reporter The Tennessean, Nashville, 1977-92, regional editor, 1993-94, special project editor, 1995—. Recipient Nat. Gold Mass Media award Nat. Conf. Christians & Jews, 1983; special citation Nat. Headliners award Press Club of Atlantic City, N.J., 1983. Office: The Tennessean 1100 Broadway Nashville TN 37203-3116

SHERBOURNE, ARCHIBALD NORBERT, civil engineering educator; b. Bombay, India, July 8, 1929; s. Manekji and Sarah Agnes (Sherbourne) Bulsara; m. Jean Ducan Nicol, Aug. 15, 1959; children: Mary, Sarah, Jeffrey, Nicolas, Jonathan, Simon. B.Sc., U. London, 1953, D.Sc., 1970; B.S., Lehigh U., 1955, M.S., 1957; M.A., Cambridge U., 1959, Ph.D., 1960. Registered profl. engr., Ont.; chartered engr. U.K., European Engr. Mem. faculty U. Waterloo, Ont., Can., 1961-96; prof. civil engring. U. Waterloo, 1963-96; dean U. Waterloo (Faculty Engring.), 1966-74; dir. Sherbourne Consultants Ltd.; vis. prof. U. W.I., Trinidad, 1969-70, Nat. C.E. Lab., Lisbon, Portugal, 1970, Ecole Polytechnique Federale, Lausanne, Switzerland, 1975-77; DAAD vis. fellow, W. Ger., 1975, NATO sr. scientist fellow, vis. lectr., 1975-76; advisor-cons. Commonwealth Africa study group on tech. edn. in industry Commonwealth Secretariat London, 1978; Gledden vis. sr. fellow U. Western Australia, Perth, 1978; acad. adviser Centre for Sci. and Tech., Fed. U. Paraiba, Campina Grande, Brazil, 1979; prin. cons. acad. planning Faculty Engring., U. Victoria, B.C., Can., 1979-80; advisor Tata Sons Ltd., Bombay, 1980; vis. prof. civil engring. Mich. Technol. U., Houghton, 1980-81, 82-83, U. Melbourne, 1983; spl. cons. technol. edn. for developing countries Can. Internat. Devel. Agy.; vis. prof. ocean engring. Fla. Atlantic U., Boca Raton, 1985, archtl. engring. N.C. A & T State U., Greensboro, 1987; vis. prof. aerospace engring. I.I. Sci., Bangalore, India, 1990. Contbr. articles to profl. jours.; visting prof. civil engineering, U. Cape Town, S. Africa, 1995—. OECD fellow Switzerland, 1964; recipient Engring. medal Assn. Profl. Engrs., Province Ont., 1975. Fellow Instn. Structural Engrs. (London), Royal Soc. Arts, Can. Soc. Civil Engring., Can. Acad. Engring. Home: 131 Keats Way Pl, Waterloo, ON Canada N2L 5H4 Office: U Waterloo Dept Civil Engring, Faculty Engring, Waterloo, ON Canada N2L 3G1

SHERBURNE, DONALD WYNNE, philosopher, educator; b. Proctor, Vt., Apr. 21, 1929; s. Hermon Kirk and Alma May (Bixby) S.; m. Elizabeth Statesir Darling, July 30, 1955; children—Kevin Darling, Nancy Elizabeth, Lynne Darling. A.B., Middlebury Coll., 1951; B.A., Balliol Coll., Oxford U., 1953; M.A., Yale U., 1958, Ph.D., 1960. Instr. philosophy Yale, 1959-60; asst. prof. Vanderbilt U., Nashville, 1960-64, asso. prof., 1964-68, prof. philosophy, 1968-95, chmn. dept., 1973-80, 90-94, prof. emeritus, 1995; Cowling vis. prof. philosophy Carleton Coll., 1990; chmn. editorial adv. com. Vanderbilt U. Press, 1991-95. Author: A Whiteheadian Aesthetic, 1961, A Key to Whitehead's Process and Reality, 1966; editor: Soundings—An Interdisciplinary Jour, 1980-85; co-editor: Corrected Edition of Whitehead's Process and Reality, 1978. Troop leader Cub Scouts, 1965-67. Served with U.S. Army, 1954-56. Recipient Jeffrey Nordhaus award for excellence in teaching., 1984; Dutton fellow Oxford U., 1951-53; sr. fellow NEH, 1977-78. Mem. AAUP (pres. Vanderbilt chpt. 1966-67), Metaphys. Soc. Am. (governing coun. 1969-73, 86-90, pres.-elect 1992-93, pres. 1993-94), So. Soc. Philosophy and Psychology (governing coun. 1971-74, treas. 1974-77, pres.-elect 1977, pres. 1978, Jr. award for Excellence 1961), Am. Philos. Assn. (program com. 1982, com. on status and future of profession 1989-92, nominating com. 1994-95), Am. Soc. Aestheti cs, Phi Beta Kappa (pres. Vanderbilt chpt. 1975-77). Home: 3 Jefferson Ct S Saint Petersburg FL 33711-5144

SHERBY, KATHLEEN REILLY, lawyer; b. St. Louis, Apr. 5, 1947; d. John Victor and Florian Sylvia (Frederick) Reilly; m. James Wilson Sherby, May 17, 1975; children: Michael R.R., William J.R., David J.R. AB magna cum laude, St. Louis U., 1969, JD magna cum laude, 1976. Bar: Mo. 1976. Assoc. Bryan Cave, St. Louis, 1976-85; ptnr. Bryan Cave LLP, St. Louis, 1985—. Contbr. articles to profl. jours. Bd. dirs Jr. League, St. Louis, 1989-90, St. Louis Forum, 1992—, pres., 1995—); vice chmn. Bequest and Gift Coun. of St. Louis U., 1995—. Fellow Am. Coll. Trust and Estate Coun., Estate Planning Coun. of St. Louis (pres. 1986-87), Bar Assn. Met. St. Louis (chmn. probate sect. 1986-87), Mo. Bar Assn. (chmn. probate and trust com. 1996—, chmn. probate law revision subcom. 1988-96). Episcopalian. Home: 47 Crestwood Dr Saint Louis MO 63105-3032 Office: Bryan Cave LLP 1 Metropolitan Sq Ste 3600 Saint Louis MO 63102-2733

SHERE, DENNIS, publishing executive; b. Cleve., Nov. 29, 1940; s. William and Susan (Luskay) S.; m. Maureen Jones, Sept. 4, 1965; children: Rebecca Lynn, David Matthew, Stephen Andrew. B.S. in Journalism, Ohio U., 1963, M.S. in Journalism, 1964. Staff writer Dayton (Ohio) Daily News, 1966-69; asst. prof. Sch. Journalism Bowling Green (Ohio) State U., 1969-70; fin. editor Detroit News, 1970-72, city editor, 1973-75; editor Dayton Jour. Herald, 1975-80; pub. Springfield (Ohio) Newspapers Inc., 1980-83, Dayton Newspapers, Inc., 1983-88; gen. mgr. Media Group Moody Bible Inst., 1989—. Served with AUS, 1964-66. Mem. Sigma Alpha Epsilon, Omicron Delta Kappa. Office: Moody Bible Inst 820 N La Salle Dr Chicago IL 60610-3214

SHERER, SAMUEL AYERS, lawyer, urban planning consultant; b. Warwick, N.Y., June 17, 1944; s. Ernest Thompson and Helen (Ayers) S.; m. Dewi Sudewinahidah, June 28, 1980. AB magna cum laude, Oberlin Coll., 1966; JD, Harvard U., 1970; M in City Planning, MIT, 1970. Bar: D.C. 1972, U.S. Supreme Ct. 1979. Atty., advisor HUD, Boston, 1970; sr. cons. McClaughry Assoc., Washington, 1970-71, 74-76; cons. Urban Inst., Washington, 1971-72; atty., urban planner IBRD Jakarta (Indonesia) Urban Devel. Study, 1972-74; atty., advisor Office Minority Bus. U.S. Dept. Commerce, Washington, 1976-77; ptnr. Topping & Sherer, Washington, 1977-90; pres. Sherer-Axelrod-Monacelli, Inc., Cambridge, Mass., 1978—; prin. The Washington Team, Inc., 1992—; bd. dirs. Optical Comm. Corp., EnviroClean Solutions, Inc., The Urban Agr. Network; rep. Internat. Devel. Law Inst., Washington, 1983-90; sr. fellow Climate Inst., 1988—; cons. in field. Co-author: Urban Land Use in Egypt, 1977; editor: Important Laws and Regulations Regarding Land, Housing and Urban Development in the Arab Republic of Egypt, 1977, Important Laws and Regulations Regarding Land, Housing and Urban Development in the Hashemite Kingdom of Jordan, 1981. Bd. dirs. MIT Enterprise Forum of Washington-Balt., 1980-82; mem. D.C. Rep. Cent. Com., 1984-88; mem. nat. governing bd. Ripon Soc., Washington, 1977-83. Urban Studies fellow HUD, 1969-70. Mem. ABA, D.C. Bar Assn., Am. Planning Assn., Asia Soc., Phi Beta Kappa. Avocations: tennis, reading. Home: 4600 Connecticut Ave NW Apt 205 Washington DC 20008-5702 Office: 316 Pennsylvania Ave SE Ste 202 Washington DC 20003-1177

SHERESKY, NORMAN M., lawyer; b. Detroit, June 22, 1928; s. Harry and Rose (Lieberman) S.; m. Elaine B. Lewis, Oct. 30, 1977; 1 child, from previous marriage, Brooke Hillary. A.B., Syracuse U., 1950; LL.B., Harvard U., 1953. Bar: N.Y. 1953. Assoc. Gold & Pollack, N.Y.C., 1954-60; sole practice, N.Y.C., 1960-72; ptnr. Sheresky & Kalman, N.Y.C., 1972-77; ptnr. Colton, Hartnick, Yamin & Sheresky, N.Y.C., 1977-93; ptnr. Baer, Marks & Upham, N.Y.C., 1993-95; ptnr. Sheresky, Aronson & Mayefsky, 1995—. adj. prof. matrimonial litigation N.Y. Law Sch., 1979-86; mem. judiciary com. N.Y.C. Bar Assn.; pres.-elect Am. Coll. Family Trial Lawyers. Mem. Internat. Acad. Matrimonial Lawyers (past treas., gov. N.Y. chpt.), Am. Acad. Matrimonial Lawyers (gov., past pres. N.Y. chpt., pres. elect.), N.Y. State Bar Assn., Assn. Trial Lawyers Am., Met. Trial Lawyers Assn., Internat. Acad. Matrimonial Lawyers (bd. govs. 1986—, com. to examine lawyer conduct in matrimonial actions 1992-95). Author: (with Marya Mannes) Uncoupling, 1972; On Trial, 1977; contbr. editor: Fairshare mag. Office: Sheresky Aronson & Mayefsky LLP 400 Park Ave New York NY 10022-4406

SHERF, SANDEE CROFT, real estate corporation executive; b. Okmulgee, Okla., Feb. 24, 1950; d. C. Don and Joyce Marie (Harris) Croft; m. Paul P. DiGeronimo, Nov. 4, 1970 (div. 1980); children: Shawn Dale, Aimee Vanessa; m. E.W. Sherf, May 15, 1983; 1 child, Summer Ashley. Student Maryville Coll., 1969. Flight attendant Piedmont Airlines, Salem, N.C., 1969-70; credit card mgr. Blount Nat. Bank, Maryville, Tenn., 1970-72; travel agt. AAA of Va., Lynchburg, 1972-76; real estate agt. Century 21, Houston, 1979-81; real estate developer E.W. Sherf Interests, Humble, Tex., 1981—; comml. property mgr. SCS Mgmt. Co., Inc., Spring, 1984-93; real estate acquisitions MRR, Inc., 1987-92; presenter real estate seminars Pegasus Power Prodn., Inc., 1996—, med. hardware and software cons., diagnostic code investigator, eletronic claims processor Med. Opportunities, Inc.; pres. Reid Rd. Mcpl. Utility Dist., Houston, 1983—. Leader San Jacinto coun. Girl Scouts U.S., 1983; mem. Champion Forest Civic Club, Houston, 1983, Mus. Fine Arts, Houston, Smithsonian Inst., Washington. Recipient Managerial Acctg. and Fin. Concepts award Bldg. Owners and Mgrs. Inst., 1983. Mem. Tex. Assn. Realtors, Nat. Assn. Realtors, Houston Bd. Realtors, Real Estate Securities and Syndications, Realtors Nat. Mktg. Inst., Inst. Real Estate Mgmt., Houston Apt. Assn., Internat. Coun. Shopping Ctrs., Toastmasters Internat., Writer's Guild. Republican. Presbyterian. Avocations: swimming, dressage, dancing, writing.

SHERIDAN, CHRISTOPHER FREDERICK, human resources executive; b. Syracuse, N.Y., June 7, 1953; s. Frederick John and Patricia Ann (McCormick) S.; m. Diane Marie Harman, Dec. 31, 1977; children: Ryan, Kelly. BS in Indsl. Relations, LeMoyne Coll., 1975. Employee rels. trainee Anaconda Co., Buffalo, 1975-76; employee rels. rep. Anaconda Co., Los Angeles, 1976-78; pers. mgr. HITCO, Gardena, Calif., 1978-80; labor rels. rep. Miller Brewing Co., Fulton, N.Y., 1980-82; labor rels. mgr. Miller Brewing Co., Los Angeles, 1982-90; employee rels. mgr. Ryder Distbn. Resources, Anaheim, Calif., 1990-91; dir. human resources Alta-Dena Cert. Dairy Inc., City of Industry, Calif., 1991—. Mem. Soc. Human Resources Mgmt., Am. Mgmt. Assn. Roman Catholic. Avocations: golf, basketball, reading, music. Office: Alta-Dena Cert Dairy Inc 17637 Valley Blvd La Puente CA 91744-5731

SHERIDAN, DANIEL JOSEPH, lawyer; b. Holyoke, Mass., June 29, 1961; s. Philip J. and Elizabeth A. (Cauley) S.; m. Kimberly A. Miller, May 21, 1988. BBA with honors, U. Mass., 1983; JD with honors, Western New Eng. Coll., 1986. Bar: Mass. 1986, U.S. Dist. Ct. Mass. 1987, U.S. Ct. Appeals (1st cir.) 1988, U.S. Supreme Ct. 1992. Labor rels. cons. Sheridan & Assocs., Inc., Holyoke, 1979-95; assoc. Powers & Bowler, Holyoke, 1986-87; prin. Law Offices Daniel J. Sheridan, Holyoke, 1987-88; ptnr. Sheridan & Sheridan, South Hadley, Mass., 1988—; Sheridan and Assocs., Inc., 1988-95. Mem. Mass. Bar Assn., Hampden County Bar Assn., Hampshire County Bar Assn., John Boyle O'Reilly Club (Springfield, Mass.). Home: 296 Brainerd St South Hadley MA 01075-1702 Office: Sheridan & Sheridan 660 Newton St South Hadley MA 01075-2020

SHERIDAN, DIANE FRANCES, public policy facilitator; b. Wilmington, Del., Mar. 12, 1945; d. Robert Kooch and Eileen Elizabeth (Forrest) Bupp; m. Mark MacDonald Sheridan III, Dec. 7, 1968; 1 child, Elizabeth Anne. BA in English, U. Del., 1967. Tchr. English Newark (Del.) Sch. Dist., 1967-68, Lumberton (Tex.) Ind. Sch. Dist., 1969-71, Crown Point (Ind.) Sch. Dist., 1972-75; sr. assoc. The Keystone (Colo.) Ctr., 1986—; environ. policy facilitator Taylor Lake Village, Tex., 1986—; chair Keystone Siting Process Local Rev. Com.; mem. pub. adv. panel Chem. Mfrs. Assn. Responsible Care, 1989-97. 1st v.p. LWV, Washington, 1992-94, sec. treas. voters edn. fund, sec. treas. Nat. LWV, 1994-96, bd. dirs. 1996-98; pres. LWV of Tex., 1987-91, chair edn. fund, 1987-91, bd. dirs., 1983-87; pres. LWV of the Bay Area, 1981-83; mem. adv. com. Ctr. for Global Studies of Houston Advanced Rsch. Ctr., The Woodlands, Tex., 1991-97, Ctr. for Conflict Analysis and Mgmt., bd. advisors Environ. Inst.; mem. U. Houston-Clear Lake Devel. Adv. Coun., 1989-95; mem. Bay Area Cmty. Awareness and Emergency Response Local Emergency Planning Com., 1988-92; active Tex. House-Senate Select Com. on Urban Affairs Regional Flooding Task Force, 1979-80, Congressman Mike Andrews Environ. Task Force, 1983-85, Gov.'s Task Force on Hazardous Waste Mgmt., 1984-85; dir. local PTAs, 1981-91; coord. Tex. Roundtable on Hazardous Waste, 1982-87; sec., v.p. Tex. Environ. Coalition, 1983-85; co-chair Tex. Risk Commn. Project, 1986-89; mem. Leadership Tex., Class of 1988. Mem. LWV (bd. dirs. Washington chpt. 1996—, trustee nat. edn. fund), Soc. for Profls. in Dispute Resolution, Internat. Assn. for Pub. Participation Practitioners, Mortarboard, Pi Sigma Alpha, Kappa Delta Pi.

SHERIDAN, EILEEN, librarian; b. N.Y.C., Jan. 11, 1949; d. Edward John and Florence Veronica (Glennon) S. BA in English, U. Bridgeport, Conn., 1972; MLS, So. Conn. State U., 1974. Children's libr. I, Bridgeport Pub. Libr., 1974-80, children's libr. II, 1980-82, coord. youth svcs., 1982—. Pres. Sch. Vol. Assn., Bridgeport, 1987-89; bd. dirs. Action for Bridgeport Cmty. Devel., 1989-90; pres. Conn. Zool. Soc., 1989-91, v.p., 1991—. Recipient vol. award for contbn. to children Mt. Aery Bapt. Ch., 1988, Champion of Children award South End Cmty. Ctr., 1992. Mem. LWV. Avocations: writing, travel, reading. Home: Unit 11 3300 Park Ave Bridgeport CT 06604-1144 Office: Bridgeport Pub Libr 925 Broad St Bridgeport CT 06604-4812

SHERIDAN, JAMES EDWARD, history educator; b. Wilmington, Del., July 15, 1922; s. Phillip Lambert and Ida Alverna (Green) S.; m. Sonia Landy, Sept. 27, 1947; 1 son, Jamy. B.S., U. Ill., 1949, M.A., 1950; Ph.D., U. Calif. at Berkeley, 1961. Lectr. Chinese history Stanford U., 1960; mem. faculty Northwestern U., 1961—, prof. history, 1968—, chmn. dept., 1969-74, assoc. dean Coll. Arts and Scis., 1985-89, prof. emeritus, 1992—. Author: Chinese Warlord: The Career of Feng Yu-hsiang, 1966, China: A Culture Area in Perspective, 1970, China in Disintegration: The Republican Era in Chinese History, 1912-1949, 1975; editor: The Transformation of Modern China series, 1975—. Served to ensign USN, 1941-46. Fulbright fellow France, 1950-51; Ford Found. fellow, 1958-60; grantee Am. Council Learned Socs.-Social Sci. Research Council, 1966-67, 71-72. Home: 80 Lyme Rd Apt 429 Hanover NH 03755-1236 Office: Northwestern Univ Dept History Evanston IL 60201

SHERIDAN, JIM, director, screenwriter; b. Dublin, Ireland, 1949. Student, Univ. Coll., Dublin, NYU. Dir., writer Lyric Theatre, Belfast, No. Ireland; artistic dir. Project Arts Theatre, 1976-80, N.Y. Irish Arts Ctr., 1982-87; founder Children's Theatre Co., Dublin, Ireland. Scripts include (plays) Mobile Homes, Spike in the First World War (Edinburgh Festival Fringe Best Play award 1983); (film) Into the West, 1993; screenwriter, dir.: My Left Foot, 1989 (Acad. award nomination best dir. 1989, Acad. award nomination best adapted screenplay 1989), The Field, 1990, In the Name of the Father, 1993 (Acad. award nomination best dir. 1993, Acad. award nomination best adapted screenplay 1993). Office: Hells Kitchen Inc All Hallows Coll, Grace Park Rd, Dublin Ireland also: CAA 9830 Wilshire Blvd Beverly Hills CA 90212*

SHERIDAN, MARK WILLIAM, mechanical engineer, strategic planner; b. Bryn Mawr, Pa., July 9, 1959; s. Phillip Frederick and Shirley (Fraser) S. BSME, Lafayette Coll., 1981; MBA, Cornell U., 1987, M. Engring. (Mech.), 1988. Registered profl. engr., Ohio. Project engr. Internat. Paper Co., Mobile, Ala., 1981-83, sr. process engr., 1983-85; assoc. Booz-Allen & Hamilton, Cleve., 1988-90; coord. long range planning appliance motor divsn. Emerson Electric Co., St. Louis, 1990-93, resident engr. Paragould Plant, 1993-95; dir. mfg. Thermodisc, Mansfield, Ohio, 1996—; summer intern Saturn Corp., Troy, Mich., 1986, 87. Bd. dirs. ABC Condominium Assn., St. Louis, 1992-94; chmn. JGSM Student Faculty Com./Quality of Life Com., Ithaca, N.Y., 1985-87; pres. Mobile Soap Box Derby, 1983-85; v.p. ways and means, bd. dirs. Mobile Jaycees, 1984-85. Lester B. Knight scholar Cornell U., 1986-88, J. Stanford Smith scholar Cornell U., 1985-87; named Outstanding Young Man of Am., 1984, 85, 87. Mem. ASME, Inst. Indsl. Engrs., The Planning Forum, Gateway Area Macintosh Users Group, Soc. Indsl. Archaeology, World Future Soc., St. Louis Jaycees (bd. dirs. 1992-94), Am. Mensa. Republican. Presbyterian. Avocations: biking, golf, reading, tennis, computing. Home: 2403 Ranchwood Dr Mansfield OH 44903 Office: Thermodisc 1320 S Main St Mansfield OH 44907-2516

SHERIDAN, PATRICK MICHAEL, finance company executive; b. Grosse Pointe, Mich., Apr. 13, 1940; s. Paul Phillip and Frances Mary (Rohan) S.; m. Diane Lorraine Tressler, Nov. 14, 1986; children: Mary, Patrick, Kelly, Kevin, James. BBA, U. Notre Dame, 1962; MBA, U. Detroit, 1975. Acct. Peat, Marwick, Mitchell & Co., Detroit, 1962-72, audit mgr., 1969-72; exec. v.p. fin. Alexander Hamilton Life Ins. Co., Farmington, Mich., 1973-76; sr. v.p. ops. Sun Life Ins. Co. Am., Balt., 1976-78, exec. v.p., 1978-79; pres. Sun Ins. Services, Inc., 1979-81; pres., chief exec. officer Am. Health & Life Ins. Co., Balt., 1981-85; chief exec. officer Gulf Ins. Co., 1985-86; sr. v.p., chief fin. officer Comml. Credit Co., 1985-86, sr. v.p. audit, 1987; exec. v.p., chief fin. officer Anthem, Inc., Indpls., 1987—. Rep. candidate for U.S. Congress, 1972; past pres. Charlesbrooke Cmty. Assn.; past. v.p. Jr. Achievement of Met. Balt., 1984-85; bd. dirs. Goodwill Industries of Balt., 1986, bd. govs. 1994; bd. dirs. Family Svcs. Assn., 1994, Goodwill Industries of Indpls., 1994; mem. adv. coun. Clowes Meml. Hall. Capt. AUS, 1963-65. Recipient various Jaycee awards. Fellow Life Mgmt. Inst.; mem. Am. Mgmt. Assn. (pres.'s assn.), AICPAs, Mich. Assn. CPAs, Md. Assn. CPAs, Am. Soc. CLUs, U.S. Jaycees (treas. 1973-74), Mich. Jaycees (pres. 1971-72), Detroit Jaycees (pres. 1968-69), Balt. C. of C. (bd. dirs.), Mensa, Notre Dame Club, Skyline Club.

SHERIDAN, PHILP HENRY, pediatrician, neurologist; b. Washington, June 29, 1950; s. Andrew James and Mildred Adele (Stohlman) S.; m. Margaret Mary Williams, Oct. 3, 1987; children: Gerard Andrew, Philip Henry, Kathleen Mary, Patrick Gerard, Mary Margaret Gerard, Mary Anne Gerard. BS magna cum laude, Yale U., 1972; MD cum laude, Georgetown U., 1976. Diplomate Am. Bd. Pediatrics, Am. Bd. Psychiatry and Neurology, Am. Bd. Qualification in Electroencephalography. Resident in pediatrics Children's Hosp. Phila., 1976-79; fellow in pediatric neurology Hosp. of U. Pa., Phila., 1979-82; med. staff fellow NIH, Bethesda, Md., 1982-84, neurologist, epilepsy br. Nat. Inst. Neurol. Disorders and Stroke, 1984—, health scientist adminstr., guest worker researcher, 1984-89, chief Devel. Neurology Br., 1989-95, chief Epilepsy Br. NIH, 1995—; cons., lectr. Nat. Naval Med. Ctr., Bethesda, 1984—; med. dir. U.S. Pub. Health Svc. Contbr. articles on clin. and rsch. neurology to med. jours. Neurologist Div. Children's Splty. Svcs., Fairfax, Va., 1984—. Mem. Am. Acad. Neurology, Child Neurology Soc. (invited reviewer), Soc. for Neurosci., Am. Epilepsy Soc., Alpha Omega Alpha. Roman Catholic. Current work: Planning and administering a comprehensive research program concerning epilepsy, pediatric neurology, developmental neurobiology, neuroimmunology and neuromuscular disorders. Subspecialties: Neurology, Pediatrics. Office: NIH 7550 Wisconsin Ave Bethesda MD 20814-3559

SHERIDAN, RICHARD BERT, economics educator; b. Emporia, Kans., Feb. 10, 1918; s. Bert and Olive Nancy (Davis) S.; m. Audrey Marion Porter, Oct. 18, 1952; children—Richard David, Margaret Anne. B.S., Emporia Kans. State U., 1940; M.S., U. Kans., 1947; Ph.D., London Sch. Econs. and Polit. Sci., 1951. Instr. to assoc. prof. U. Kans., Lawrence, 1947-62, prof. econs., 1963-88; emeritus prof. econs., 1988—; external examiner U. W.I., Kingston, Jamaica, 1964-74; vis. prof. Coll. V.I., St. Thomas, 1971, U. West Indies, St. Augustine, Trinidad, 1987. Author: Economic History of South Central Kansas, 1956, Chapters in Caribbean History, 1970, Sugar and Slavery, 1974, Doctors and Slaves, 1985; cons. editor: Jour. Caribbean History, 1971—; contbr. articles to profl. jours. Served to lt. USNR, 1942-46. Recipient Article award N.C. Bicentennial Contest, 1976, article award

Kans. State Hist. Soc., 1989; honored with a festschrift, 1996; Fulbright scholar U. W.I., 1962-63; grantee NIH, Nat. Libr. Medicine, 1973. Fellow Royal Hist. Soc.; mem. Soc. for Human Econs., Assn. Caribbean History. Democrat. Congregationalist. Home: 1745 Louisiana St Lawrence KS 66044-4055 Office: U Kans Dept of Econ Lawrence KS 66045

SHERIDAN, SONIA LANDY, artist, retired art educator; b. Newark, Ohio, Apr. 10, 1925; d. Avrom Mendel and Goldie Cornelia (Hanon) Landy; m. James Edward Sheridan, Sept. 27, 1947; 1 son, Jamy. A.B., Hunter Coll., 1945; postgrad., Columbia U., 1946-48; M.F.A. with high honors, Calif. Coll. Arts and Crafts, 1961. Tchr. art public high schs. Calif., 1951-57; chmn. dept. art Taipei Am. Sch., Taiwan, 1957-59; instr. Calif. Coll. Arts and Crafts, 1960-61; asst. prof. art Sch. Art Inst. Chgo., 1961-67, assoc. prof., 1968-75, prof., 1976-80, prof. emeritus, 1980—, founder, head generative systems program, 1970-80; artist-in-residence 3M Corp., 1970, 76; cons. French Ministry of Culture, 1986; artist-in-residence Xerox Corp., 1981; lectr., univs., museums, art schs., workshops; lectr. Hungarian Acad. Scis. Symposium Collected Essays & Exhbn., Budapest, 1989. One-woman shows include Rosenberg Gallery, Chgo., 1966, Visual Studies Workshop, Rochester, N.Y., 1973, Iowa Mus. Art, Iowa City, 1976, Mus. Sci. Industry, Chgo., 1978; two-person show Mus. Modern Art, N.Y.C., 1974; exhibited in group shows at Print Ann, Boston Mus., 1963, Software, Jewish Mus., N.Y.C., 1969-70, Photography into Art, London, 1972-73, Photokino, Cologne, Germany, 1974, San Francisco Mus. Art, 1975, U. Mich. Mus. Art, 1978, Toledo Mus. Art, 1982-83, Mus. Modern Art, Paris, 1983, Siggraph, U.S., Japan, France, 1982, 83, Reina Sofia Mus., Madrid, Spain, 1986, Smithsonian Instn., 1990, Tokyo Met. Mus. Photography, 1991, Madrid City Cultural Ctr., 1992, Karl Ernst Osthaus Mus., Hagen, Germany, 1992, Circulo des Belles Artes, Madrid, 1992, Yale U. Art Gallery, 1995, Tokyo Intercom. Ctr., 1995, U. Montreal, 1995; represented in permanent collections Art Inst. Chgo., San Francisco Mus. Art, Mus. Sci. and Industry, Chgo., U. Iowa Mus. Art, Nat. Gallery Art, Ottawa, Can., Visual Studies Workshop, Rochester, Tokyo Met. Mus. Photography, Fundacion Arte y Technologia, Madrid; author: Energized Artscience: Sonia Landy Sheridan, 1978; co-editor Leonardo jour.; contbr. articles, essay to profl. jours. Guggenheim fellow, 1973; Nat. Endowment for Arts workshop grantee 1974, pub. media grantee, 1976, artist grantee 1981; Union Ind. Colls. Art grantee 1975. Mem. Coll. Art Assn., Internat. Soc. for Interdisciplinary Study of Symmetry.

SHERIDAN, THOMAS BROWN, mechanical engineering and applied psychology educator, researcher, consultant; b. Cin., Dec. 23, 1929; s. Mahlon Brinsley and Esther Anna (Brown) S.; m Rachel Briggs Rice, Aug. 1, 1953; children: Paul Rice, Richard Rice, David Rice, Margaret Lenore. BS, Purdue U., 1951; MS, UCLA, 1954; ScD, MIT, 1959; Dr. (hon.), Delft U. Tech., The Netherlands, 1991. Registered profl. engr., Mass. Asst. prof. mech. engring. MIT, Cambridge, 1959-65, assoc. prof., 1965-70, prof., 1970-78, prof. engring. and applied psychology, 1978-94, prof. aeronautics and astronautics, 1994—, Ford prof., 1995—; lectr. U. Calif., Berkeley, Stanford U., 1968; vis. prof. U. Delft, The Netherlands, 1972, Stanford U., 1989, Ben Gurion U., Israel, 1995; chmn. com. human factors, mem. com. aircrew-vehicle interaction, com. on commercially developed space facility, com. on human factors in air traffic control, NRC; mem. adv. com. on applied phys., math. and biol. scis. NSF; mem. life scis. adv. com., study group on robotics, oversight com. flight telerobotic servicer NASA; mem. task force on appropriate tech. U.S. Congress Office Tech. Assessment; mem. study sect. accident prevention and injury control NIH; mem. Def. Sci. Bd. Task Force on Computers, Tng. and Gaming, Nuclear Regulatory Commn. on Nuclear Safety Rsch. Rev. Com. Author: Telerobotics, Automation and Human Supervisory Control, 1992; co-author: Man Machine Systems, 1974; editor: (with others) Monitoring Behavior and Supervisory Control, 1976; assoc. editor Automatica, 1982-94; co-editor: Perspectives on the Human Controller, 1997; mem. edtl. adv. bd. Tech. Forecasting and Social Change, Computer Aided Design, Advanced Robotics, Robotics and Computer Integrated Mfg.; sr. editor Presence: Telerobots and Virtual Environments, 1991—. Served to 1st lt. USAF, 1951-53. Recipient Nat. Engring. award Nat. Assn. Engring. Socs., 1997. Fellow IEEE (pres. Systems, Man and Cybernetics Soc. 1974-76, Centennial medal 1984, Norbert Wiener award 1993, Joseph G. Wohl award 1995), Human Factors Soc. (Paul M. Fitts award 1977, pres. 1990-91), Nat. Acad. Engring. Democrat. Mem. United Ch. of Christ. Office: MIT 77 Massachusetts Ave Cambridge MA 02139-4301

SHERIF, S. A., mechanical engineering educator; b. Alexandria, Egypt, June 25, 1952; came to U.S., 1978; s. Ahmed and Ietedal H. (Monib) S.; m. Azza A. Shamseldin, Feb. 6, 1977; children: Ahmed S., Mohammad S. BSME (hon.), Alexandria U., 1975, MSME, 1978; PhD in Mech. Engring., Iowa State U., 1985. Tchg. asst. mech. engring. Alexandria U., 1975-78; tchg. assoc. mech. and environtl. engring. U. Calif., Santa Barbara, 1978-79; rsch. asst. mech. engring. Iowa State U., Ames, 1979-84; asst. prof. No. Ill. U., Dekalb, 1984-87, mem. grad. faculty, 1985-87; mem. grad. faculty U. Miami, Coral Gables, Fla., 1987-91, asst. prof. civil, archtl. and mech. engring., 1987-91; assoc. prof. mech. engring. U. Fla., Gainesville, 1991—, mem. doctoral rsch. faculty, 1992—; cons. Solar Reactor Techs., Inc., Miami, Fla., 1988-91, Dade Power Corp., Miami, 1988-91, Ind. Energy Sys., Miami, 1988-91, Carey Dwyer Eckhart Mason Spring & Beckham, P.A. Law Offices, Miami, 1988-89, Michael G. Widoff, P.A., Attys. at Law, Ft. Lauderdale, Fla., 1989-93, Law Offices Pomeroy and Betts, Ft. Lauderdale, 1991-92, Ctr. for Indoor Air Rsch., 1994—; cons. Fla. Power and Light Co., 1996—; cons. U. Roorkee, 1994-95; adj. faculty cons. Kennedy Western U., Thousand Oaks, Calif., 1994—; resident assoc. Argonne (Ill.) Nat. Lab., Tech. Transfer Ctr., summer 1992; faculty fellow NASA Kennedy Space Ctr., Cape Canaveral, Fla., summer 1993; rsch. assoc. summer faculty rsch. program Air Force Office Sci. Rsch., Arnold Engring. Devel. Ctr., Arnold AFB, Tenn., 1994; faculty fellow NASA Marhsall Space Flight Ctr., Huntsville, Ala., 1996; reviewer 23 internal jours., 90 conf. procs. and several pub. cos. and rsch. svc. orgns. Co-editor: Industrial and Agricultural Applications of Fluid Mechanics, 1989, The Heuristics of Thermal Anemometry, 1990, Heat and Mass Transfer in Frost and Ice, Packed Beds, and Environmental Discharges, 1990, Industrial Applications of Fluid Mechanics, 1990, rev. edit., 1991, Mixed Convection and Environmental Flows, 1990, Measurement and Modeling of Environmental Flows, 1992, Industrial and Environment Applications of Fluid Mechanics, 1992, Thermal Anemometry-1993, 1993, Heat Transfer in Turbulent Flows-1993, 1993, Developments in Electroheological Flows and Measurement Uncertainty-1994, 1994, Heat, Mass and Momentum Transfer in Environmental Flows, 1995, Thermal Anemometry, 1996, Fluid Measurement Uncertainty Applications, 1996; contbr. numerous articles to profl. jours. NASA ambassador, 1996—; mem. environ. awareness adv. com., Dade County Pub. Schs., 1989-91, lab. dir. cmty. lab. rsch. program, 1989-91, also faculty liaison design svcs. dept.; active Com. for Nat. Inst. for Environ., 1992—; mem. senate U. Fla., 1994-95, mem. OUTREACH Spkrs. program, 1996—. Mem. ASME (mem. coord. group fluid measurements, fluids engring. divsn. 1987—, vice chmn. 1990-92, chmn. 1992-94, fluids engring. divsn. adv. bd. 1994—, honors and awards com. 1995—, mem. fluid mechs. tech. com. 1990—, fluid mech. com. 1987-90, environ. heat transfer com. heat transfer divsn. 1987—, mem. fluid applications and systems tech. com. 1990—, systems analysis tech. com. advanced energy sys. divsn., 1989—, newsletter editor advanced energy sys. divsn. 1995—, fundamentals and theory tech. com. solar energy divsn. 1990—, chmn. CGFM nominating com. 1992-94, mem. 1994—, chmn. profl. devel. com. Rock River Valley sect. 1987, tech. activities operating com. Gator sect. 1994-96, MFFCC subcom. 1 on uncertainties in flow measurements 1995—), ASHRAE (mem. heat transfer fluid flow com. 1988-92, 93-97, corr. mem. 1992-93, mem. thermodynamics and psychrometrics com. 1988-92, 96—, corr. mem. 1992-96, vice chmn. 1990-92, mem. liquid to refrigerant heat exchangers com. 1989-93, 96-97, sec. 1990-92, chmn. standards project com. on measurement of moist air properties 1989-95), AIAA (sr.), AIChE, Internat. Assn. Hydrogen Energy, Internat. Solar Energy Soc., Am. Solar Energy Soc., Internat. Energy Soc. (mem. sci. coun.), Assn. Energy Engrs. (sr.), European Assn. Laser Anemometry (ASME/FED rep., mem. steering com.), Internat. Inst. Refrigeration (U.S. nat. com.), ABI (hon. mem. rsch. bd. adv. 1994—), Sigma Xi. Moslem. Avocations: reading, soccer, basketball, history, astronomy. Home: 3301 SW 13th St Apt W-302 Gainesville FL 32608 Office: U Fla Dept Mech Engring 228 MEB Gainesville FL 32611-6300

SHERIFF, JIMMY DON, accounting educator, academic dean; b. Greenville, S.C., Dec. 8, 1940; s. James Donald and Gladys Ellie (Chapman) S.; BA, So. Wesleyan U., 1964; MBA, U. Ga., 1970, PhD, 1976; m. Gwen Anne Campbell, Aug. 31, 1969. Acct., Maremont Corp., Greenville, 1965-68; instr. U. Ga., Athens, 1970-73; asst. prof. Presbyn. Coll., Clinton, S.C., 1973-74; prof. Clemson (S.C.) U., 1974-87, assoc. dean, dir. rsch., 1987-92, acting dean, 1992-93, sr. assoc. dean, 1993—; chmn. Bus. Sch. Adv. Bd., 1995—. U.S. rep. Network Internat. Bus. Schs. Chmn. Pickens County Aeros. Commn., 1980-91; founding pres. Pickens County Property Owners Assn.; chmn. S.C. Nat. Guard Scholarship Found., 1990—. Home: 988 Old Shirley Rd Central SC 29630-9337 Office: Clemson U Coll Bus & Public Affairs Dean's Office 165 Sirrine Hall Clemson SC 29634-1301

SHERIN, EDWIN, theatrical and film director, actor; b. Danville, Pa., Jan. 15, 1930; s. Joseph and Ruth (Berger) S.; m. Jane Alexander, Mar. 29, 1975; children: Anthony J., Geoffrey B. (dec.), Jonathan E.; 1 stepchild, Jason E. AB in History and Polit. Sci., Brown U., 1952. Acting tchr. Am. Theatre Wing, N.Y.C., 1962-64; acting tchr. Am. Theatre Tng. Inst. Southeastern Mass. U., South Dartmouth, 1974; Lucille Lortel Disting. guest artist U. Bridgeport (Conn.), 1980; dir. Sch. Theatre Arts Boston U., 1981; acting tchr. Okla. Summer Arts Inst., 1985-86, One on One, L.A., 1989, 90; exec. v.p. Altion Prodns., L.A., 1985-93; pres. Pumpkin House Prodns., 1993—; mem. nat. adv. for Mus. Am. Theatre; instr. Okla. Summer Arts Inst., guest dir. Calif. Inst. Arts. Actor with Houseman's troupe Phoenix Theatre, N.Y.C., 1957-58, actor N.Y. Shakespeare Festival, 1956-60; appeared as: Octavius Caesar in, Anthony and Cleopatra, 1958; appeared in Broadway plays Come Blow Your Horn, 1960, Desert Incident, 1961, Romulus, 1962, Face of a Hero, 1963; TV films Playhouse 90, 1956-58, Studio One, 1956-58, Omnibus, 1957-60, East Side/West Side, 1960; dir. Broadway plays including The Great White Hope, 1968, Glory Hallelujah, 1969, 6 RMS RIV VU, 1973, Find Your Way Home, Of Mice and Men, 1974, Red Devil Battery Sign, 1975, Sweet Bird of Youth, 1976, Eccentricities of a Nightingale, 1976, The First Monday in October, 1978, Goodbye Fidel, 1980, The Visit, 1992; assoc. producing dir. Washington's Arena Stage, 1964-68; dir. Cosi Fan Tutte, N.Y. City Opera Co., 1972, A Streetcar Named Desire, Piccadilly Theatre, London, 1973, Semmelweiss, Studio Arena Theatre, Buffalo, N.Y., 1978, Outrage, Kennedy Ctr., Washington, 1982; films including Valdez is Coming, 1970, My Old Man's Place, 1971; producing artistic dir. Showdown at Adobe Hotel, Semmelweiss, Hedda Gabler, Night Must Fall, A Streetcar Named Desire, Hartman Theatre, Stamford, Conn., 1980-85; dir. Chelsea Walls, Naked Angels, N.Y.C., 1990, TV programs Hill Street Blues, Moonlighting, WIOU, L.A. Law, Tour of Duty, MEN; co-exec. prodr. Law and Order, 1993-94, exec. prodr., 1994—, (TV films) The Father Clements Story, Lena, My 100 Children, Daughter of the Streets, Getting Even, A Marriage: Georgia O'Keeffe and Alfred Stieglitz, 1991. With USN, 1952-56, Korea. Recipient Outer Circle award, 1969; New Eng. Theatre award, 1969; Recipient N.Y. Drama Critics award, 1969, Drama Desk award, 1969, L.A. Drama Circle award, 1971, Recipient Tony nomination, 1974, London Evening Standard citation, 1973, Joseph Jefferson award, 1976, Buffalo drama award, 1978; New Eng. Theatre Conf. award; Ford Found. grantee, 1965-66. Mem. AFTRA, SAG, Actors Equity Assn., Dirs. Guild Am. nat. v.p. 1997—), Dramatists Guild, Soc. Stage Dirs. and Choreographers (v.p. 1970-80), Lincoln Soc., Phi Gamma Delta.

SHERK, KENNETH JOHN, lawyer; b. Ida Grove, Iowa, Feb. 27, 1933; s. John and Dorothy (Myers) Sherk; m. Virginia Kay Taylor, June 28, 1958; children: Karin Fulton, Katrina, Keith, Kyle. BSC, U. Iowa, 1955; JD, George Washington U., 1961. Bar: Ariz. 1962, U.S. Dist. Ct. Ariz. 1962, U.S. Ct. Appeals (9th cir.) 1966, U.S. Supreme Ct. 1974. Assoc. Moore & Romley, Phoenix, 1962-67, ptnr., 1967-79; ptnr. Romley & Sherk, Phoenix, 1979-85; dir. Fennemore Craig, Phoenix, 1985—. Served as 1st lt. U.S. Army, 1955-58, Korea. Recipient Profl. Achievement Svcs. award George Washington Law Assn., 1986, Ariz. Judges Assn., 1989, Disting. Svc. award Phoenix Assn. Def. Counsel, 1990; named Mem. of Yr. State Bar of Ariz., 1994. Fellow Am. Coll. Trial Lawyers, Am. Acad. Appellate Lawyers, Am. Bar Found., Ariz. Bar Found.; mem. ABA (ho. of dels. 1990-93), Ariz. Bar Assn. (pres. 1985-86), Maricopa Bar Assn. (pres. 1978-79). Republican. Congregational. Avocations: fishing, hiking, bicycling. Home: 1554 W Las Palmaritas Dr Phoenix AZ 85012-2913 Office: Fennemore Craig 3003 N Central Ave Ste 2600 Phoenix AZ 85012-2913

SHERLINE, HAROLD ALBERT, adult education professional; b. Bklyn., July 8, 1925; s. Herman Milton and Margaret (Bisset) S.; m. Frances Aileen Mitchell, Aug. 3, 1956; children: Dixie Sherline McQuality, Lori Sherline Coady, Charles. BS, U. Md., 1952; MEd, U. Ill., 1959. Cert. tchr., adminstr., Ill. Tchr., coach Ea. Jr. High Sch., Silver Spring, Md., 1952-54; tchr., coach, adminstr. Williamsville (Ill.) High Sch., 1954-56; coach, dir. athletics Taylorville (Ill.) High Sch., 1956-62; tchr., coach Larkin High Sch., Elgin, Ill., 1962-67; dir. Mattoon (Ill.) Area Adult Edn. Ctr., 1967—; appointee State Adv. Coun. Adult, Vocat. and Tech. Edn., Ill., 1977-83; del. nat. forum Excellence in Edn., 1983. Coord. successful overrides of gov.'s veto of adult edn. funding, Ill., 1973, 88, 89, 90. Cpl. USMC, 1943-46, PTO. Recipient Nat. Literacy award Internat. Reading Assn./Ea. Ill. U., 1993; named Adult Educator of Yr. Pub. Adult and Continuing Educators Assn. Ill., 1973; coach of teams in State Basketball Finals, 1959, State Cross-Country Finals, 1964. Mem. Ill. Adult and Continuing Educators Assn. (pres. 1990-91, Pres.'s award 1988), Am. Assn. Adult and Continuing Edn., Phi Delta Kappa (Cmty. Svc. award 1993). Avocations: reading, athletics, recreational activities, political activism. Office: Mattoon Area Adult Edn Ctr 1617 Lakeland Blvd Mattoon IL 61938-5915

SHERLOCK, JOHN MICHAEL, bishop; b. Regina, Sask., Can., Jan. 20, 1926; s. Joseph and Catherine S. Student, St. Augustine's Sem., Toronto, Ont., Can., 1950; student canon law, Catholic U. Am., 1950-52; LLD (hon.), U. Windsor, 1986; DD (hon.), Huron Coll., London, Ont., 1986. Ordained priest Roman Catholic Ch., 1950, bishop, 1974; asst. pastor St. Eugene's, Hamilton, Ont., 1952-59, St. Augustine's, Dundas, Ont., 1959-63, Cathedral Christ the King, Hamilton, also, Guelph and Maryhill, Ont., 1950-52; pastor St. Charles Ch., Hamilton, 1963-74; aux. bishop London, Ont., 1974-78; bishop, 1978—; chaplain Univ. Newman Club, McMaster U., Hamilton, 1963-66; pres. Canadian Conf. Cath. Bishops, 1983-85, liaison with U. Chaplains Can. and Pres. Cath. Coll. and Univs.; chmn. social affairs com. commn. Ont. Conf. Cath. Bishops, edn. commn., family life com.; adv. judge for the Regional Marriage Truban, 1954-72. Mem. Wentworth County Roman Cath. Separate Sch. Bd., 1964-74, chmn., 1972-73; chmn. Nat. Cath. Broadcasting Found., 1995—. Fellow honoris cause U.St. Michael's Coll., Toronto, 1994. Address: Chancery Office, 1070 Waterloo St, London, ON Canada N6A 3Y2*

SHERMAN, ALAN ROBERT, psychologist, educator; b. N.Y.C., Nov. 18, 1942; s. David R. and Goldie (Wax) S.; m. Llana Helene Tobias, Aug. 14, 1966 (div. 1989); children: Jonathan Colbert, Relissa Anne. BA, Columbia U., 1964; MS, Yale U., 1966, PhD, 1969. Lic. psychologist, Calif. Faculty psychology U. Calif., Santa Barbara, 1969—; clin. psychologist in pvt. practice Santa Barbara, 1981—; cons. in field. Author: Behavior Modification, 1973; contbr. articles to profl. jours. and chpts. in books. Pres. Santa Barbara Mental Health Assn., 1978, 84-85, 91, Mountain View Sch. Site Coun., Santa Barbara, 1978-84. Recipient Vol. of Yr. award Santa Barbara Mental Health Assn., 1979, Tchg. Excellence awards Delta Delta Delta, Alpha Chi Omega, Gamma Phi Beta, Santa Barbara; NIMH predoctoral rsch. fellow, 1964-69; grantee in field. Fellow Behavior Therapy and Rsch. Soc.; mem. APA, AAUP (chpt. pres. 1978-79), Calif. Psychol. Assn., Assn. for Advancement of Behavior Therapy, Santa Barbara County Psychol. Assn. (pres. 1985), Phi Beta Kappa (chpt. pres. 1977-78), Sigma Xi, Psi Chi (chpt. faculty advisor, 1979—). Office: Univ of Calif Dept Psychology Santa Barbara CA 93106-9660 *Pursuing a creative profession which allows one to help improve the condition of others, provides intrinsic rewards that make the work process satisfying in itself. I am fortunate to be involved in two such professions, college teaching and psychotherapy. When you genuinely enjoy what you are doing, you are likely to be successful at it.*

SHERMAN, ARTHUR, theater educator, writer, actor, composer; b. Dec. 5, 1920; s. Herman and Fay (Epstein) S.; m. Margery Frost Sherman, Apr. 15, 1974 (div. Sept. 1989); children: Claudia, Andrew Jay. MusB, Juilliard Sch. Music, 1955; M in Music Edn., Manhattan Sch. Music, 1957; Doctoral Equivalency, CUNY, 1962. Dir. performing arts N.Y.C. (N.Y.) Tech. Coll., 1964-72; prof. speech and theatre John Jay Coll., N.Y.C., 1990—, Borough Man C.C., N.Y.C., 1990—; judge Film Award Com., Australia, 1972-89, Acad. Awards, 1990; cons. Min. for Edn., Tasmania, Australia, 1977; presenter in field. Author: (screenplays) Thistle and Thorn, 1982, Same Difference, 1983, (book and lyrics) Lenore and the Wonder House, (children's novel) Paradise Lagoon, (book) Songwriting Is Easy and Fun; composer: (ook, music lyrics) Prisms in the Looking Glass, Once Upon a Crime; actor, dir. films, TV, theater in U.S. and Australia; sculptures displayed YWCA, Hamilton, Ont., Can., 1967, Lincoln Ctr., N.Y.C., 1969, State Bank, Sydney, Australia, 1974. Pres. United Fedn. Coll. Tchrs., N.Y.C., 1971. With USN, 1943-46. Grantee Australian Film Commn., 1981. Mem. ASCAP, Australasian Performing Rights Assn., Actors' Equity U.S. and Australia. Home: 315 W 57th St New York NY 10019-3158 Office: John Jay Coll 58th St 10th Ave New York NY 10019

SHERMAN, BRADLEY JAMES, congressman; b. L.A., Oct. 24, 1954; s. Maurice H. and Lane (Moss) S. BA summa cum laude, UCLA, 1974; JD magna cum laude, Harvard U., 1979. Bar: Calif. 1979; CPA, Calif. Pvt. practice, L.A., 1980-91; chmn. Calif. Bd. Equalization, Sacramento, 1991-95; mem. 105th Congress from 24th Calif. dist., 1997—; lectr. on tax law and policy; mem. Calif. Franchise Tax Bd., 1991-95. Contbr. articles to legal jours. Bd. dirs., rep. on tax issues Calif. Common Cause, 1984-89; mem. exec. com. Calif. Dem. Com., 1991—. Mem. Calif. State Bar. Jewish. Office: 1524 Longworth Washington DC 20515-0524

SHERMAN, CHARLES DANIEL, JR., surgeon; b. Avon Park, Fla., Oct. 5, 1920; s. Charles Daniel and Mary Alice (Oliver) S.; m. Jean Riebling, Aug. 13, 1943; children: Rachel, Charles Daniel, Edward. B.S., U. Fla., 1942; M.D., Johns Hopkins U., 1945. Diplomate: Am. Bd. Surgery. Intern Duke U. Hosp., Durham, N.C., 1945-46; resident U. Rochester Med. Center, 1948-52, instr., 1952-56, asst. prof., 1956-64, clin. assoc. prof. surgery, 1964-70, clin. prof., 1970—; fellow Meml. Center for Cancer, 1951; practice medicine specializing in cancer surgery Rochester, 1953—; mem. staff Highland Hosp., Rochester, N.Y.; v.p. Redd Labs., Clearwater, Fla., 1961-70; advisor N.Y. State Bur. Cancer Control, 1964-75; sec.-treas. Monroe County Health Planning Coun., 1967-69; mem. Monroe County Bd. Health, 1966-79; advisor to WHO, 1971, dir. Internat. Network of WHO Collaborating Ctrs. for Cancer Edn., 1996—; mem. advisory com. Nat. Cancer Insts.; dir. Internat. Union Against Cancer Project to Survey Cancer Edn. in L.Am., 1976, Asia, 1977; mem. hosp. adv. com. to Joint Com. on Accreditation of Hosps., 1980-88; organizer WHO/Internat. Union Against Cancer European Congress on Cancer Edn., 1981; mem. Accreditation Coun. for Continuing Med. Edn., 1983-89, vice-chmn., 1988, chmn., 1989; organizer Coordinating Coun. on Cancer Edn. in L.Am., 1986, in Asian-Pacific region, 1987; chmn. Coordinating Coun. for Cancer Edn. in Europe, 1987-88; bd. dirs. Nat. Resident Matching Plan, 1988-92, treas., 1989-90; mem. organizing com. Internat. Med. Scholar Program, 1987-89; keynote spkr. Internat. Cancer Congress, 1992; lectr. in field. Author: Clinical Concepts in Cancer Management, 1976; co-author: Clinical Oncology, 1974; editor, pub.: Directory of U.S. Oncologists, 1983—; editor: (with others) Programmed Instruction in Medical Education; Newsletter in Cancer, 1968-80; chmn. editorial bd. for 2d , 3d and 4th edits. Clinical Oncology (monograph): (with others) Internat. Union against Cancer, 1978-86; mem. editorial bd. Jour. Cancer Edn., 1984—, Greek Jour. Continuing Med. Edn., 1986—; participant movie on esophogeal reconstrn., 1957; producer exhibits on cancer treatment and cancer edn.; co-contbr. articles to profl. jours. Mem. adv. com. on Continuing Edn. in Oncology of the European Community, 1993; advisor European Sch. Oncology, European Med. Student Assn.; mem. internat. adv. com. Asian Pacific Cancer Congress, Beijing, 1991, Bangkok, 1993, Singapore, 1995, Malaysia, 1996. Fulbright fellow Mendoza, Argentina, 1963; recipient Health Edn. award N.Y. State Pub. Health Assn., 1973; cert. of merit. Rochester Acad. Medicine, 1982. Mem. ACS, AMA (N.Y. state del. to Ho. of Dels., coun. on med. edn. 1983-92, com. on med. liability 1984-85, com. on fgn. grads. 1984, com. on cancer 1970-74, exec. com. 1989-90), Am. Radium Soc., Soc. Head and Neck Surgeons, Royal Soc. Medicine, Am. Assn. Cancer Edn. (pres. 1975-76), Am. Fedn. Clin. Oncologic Socs. (bd. govs. 1974-77), N.Y. State Med. Soc. (councillor 1973-79, asst. treas. 1980-83, treas. 1983-85, v.p. 1986, pres.-elect 1987, pres. 1988-89, trustee 1990-95, chair trustees 1994-95, liaison com. on med. edn. 1992-94, Fineburg award disting. svc. 1997, Sherman award as adv. to med. student sect. 1997), N.Y. Acad. Sci., N.Y. State Cancer Programs Assn. (pres. 1970-71, chmn. UICC prof. edn. program 1986-94, exec. coun. 1986-94), Monroe County Med. Soc. (pres. 1965, Edward Mott Moore award 1978), Monroe County Cancer and Leukemia Assn. (pres. 1962-66), European Assn. Cancer Edn. (bd. dirs. 1987-92), Soc. Surg. Oncology (chmn. residents award com. 1963-66), Am. Soc. Preventive Oncology, U.S. Squash Rackets Assn. (dir. 1963-65), Argentine Anti-Smoking Union (hon.), Blue Key Soc., Phi Beta Kappa, Alpha Phi Omega. Home: 127 Southern Pky Rochester NY 14618-1052

SHERMAN, CHARLES EDWIN, broadcasting executive, educator; b. Phila., Mar. 20, 1934; s. Abe and Rae (Ginsberg) S.; m. Elaine Landsburg, Sept. 11, 1960; children: Jean, Eric, David. BS, Temple U., Phila., 1960, MA, 1962; PhD, Wayne State U., Detroit, 1967. Announcer, program producer Sta. WHAT, Phila., 1957-62; mem. prodn. staff Sta. WFIL-TV, Phila., 1961; grad. asst. Temple U., 1960-62; TV producer-dir., prodn. supr. Wayne State U., 1962-64, instr. dept. speech, 1964-66, asst. to dir. div. mass communication, 1966-67; asst. prof. dept. speech U. Wis., 1967-70, assoc. prof. dept. communication arts, assoc. chmn., 1970-73, assoc. prof., acting chmn., 1974, prof., assoc. chmn. dept. communication arts, 1974-75; prof., chmn. dept. telecommunications Ind. U., Bloomington, 1975-79, adj. prof. telecommunications, 1980—; pres., gen. mgr. WTRF-TV, Wheeling, W.Va., 1979-84, WHOI-TV, Peoria, Ill., 1984-88; sr. v.p. TV Nat. Assn. of Broadcasters, Washington, 1988—; pres. Nat. Assn. of Broadcasters Edn. Found., Washington, 1996—; cons. Forward Communications, Inc., Wausaw, Wis., 1974-79; mem. CBS Network TV Affiliates Bd., 1982-84, ABC Network TV Affiliates Bd., 1986-88; bd. dirs. Bank of Wheeling, Nat. Assn. TV Program Execs. Ednl. Found., 1986—, Accreditating Council on Edn. in Journalism and Mass Communication, 1986—; chmn. Task Force on Citizens Rights and Access, Wis. Commn. on Cable TV, 1973; vice chmn. W.Va. Ednl. Broadcasting Authority, 1980-85. Contbr. articles on broadcasting to profl. jours. Bd. dirs. Upper Ohio Valley United Way, 1979-85, Heart of Ill. United Way, 1986-88, Peoria Human Services Ctr., 1986-88; bd. dirs., mem. exec. com. Wheeling Devel. Conf., 1980-85; trustee Ohio Valley Med. Ctr., 1980-85. With U.S. Army, 1955-57; pres. Nat. Assn. Broadcasters Edn. Found., 1997—. Recipient Communications award Temple U., 1960, Sigma Delta Chi award Temple U., 1960, Disting. Service award in broadcasting Wayne State U., 1966. Mem. Speech Communication Assn., Broadcast Edn. Assn. (chmn. Internat. Seminar 1974, chmn. Internat. Interest Group 1974, dir., sec., treas. 1983-85, chmn. 1985-86), Nat. Assn. Ednl. Broadcasters, Nat. Assn. Broadcasters (chmn. rsch. com.), Wheeling C. of C. (bd. dirs. 1979-85), Alpha Epsilon Rho, Sigma Delta Chi. Jewish. Office: Nat Assn Broadcasters 1771 N St NW Washington DC 20036

SHERMAN, CINDY, artist; b. Glen Ridge, N.J., 1954. Student, State Univ. Coll. Buffalo, 1972-76. One-woman exhbns. include Hallwalls Gallery, Buffalo, 1976, 77, Contemporary Arts Mus., Houston, 1980, The Kitchen, N.Y., 1980, Metro Pictures, N.Y., 1980, 83, Saman Gallery, Genoa, 1981, Young/Hoffman Gallery, Chgo., 1981, Chantal Crousel Gallery, Paris, 1982, Stedelijk Mus., Amsterdam, 1982, St. Louis Art Mus., 1983, Fine Arts Ctr. Gallery, SUNY-Stony Brook, 1983, Rhona Hoffman Gallery, Chgo., 1983, Douglas Drake Gallery, Kansas City, 1983, 84, Seibu Gallery Contemporary Art, Tokyo, 1984, Akron Art Mus., 1984, Linda Cathcart Gallery, Santa Monica, Calif., 1992, Museo de Monterrey, Mex., 1992; group exhbns. include Albright-Knox Art Gallery, Buffalo, 1975, Artists Space, N.Y., 1978, Max Protetch Gallery, N.Y., 1979, Castelli Graphics, N.Y., 1980, Lisson Gallery, London, 1980, Centre Pompidou, Paris, 1981; NIT, 1981, Renaissance Soc. U. Chgo., 1982, Metro Pictures, N.Y., 1982, La Ciennale de Venezia, Venice, Italy, 1982, Documenta 7, Kassel, West Germany, 1982, Chantall Crousel Gallery, Paris, 1982, San Francisco Mus. Modern Art, 1982, Inst. Contemporary Art, London, 1982, Grey Art Gallery, N.Y., 1982, Inst. Contemporary Art, Phila., 1982, Young Hoffman Gallery, Chgo., 1983, Hirshhorn Gallery, Washington, 1983, 1983, Whitney Mus. Am. Art, N.Y., 1983, 85, 91; represented in permanent collections Mus. Fine Arts, Houston, Albright/Knox Art Gallery, Buffalo, Dallas Mus. Fine Arts, Mus. Boymans-van Beuningen, Rotterdam, Akron Art Mus., Ohio, Mus. Modern Art, N.Y.C., Walker Art Ctr., Mpls., Tate Gallery, London, Rose Art Mus., Brandeis U., Centre Pompidou, Paris, Stedelijk Mus., Amsterdam, Met.

Mus. Art, N.Y., St. Louis Art Mus., San Francisco Mus. Modern Art. Office: care Metro Pictures 150 Greene St New York NY 10012-3202*

SHERMAN, DEMING ELIOT, lawyer; b. Providence, July 22, 1943; s. Edwin Fisk and Martha Amy (Parkhurst) S.; m. Jane Catherine Bauer, Dec. 20, 1966; children: Melissa Jane, Nicholas Deming. BA, Amherst (Mass.) Coll., 1965; JD, U. Chgo., 1968. Bar: R.I. 1968, U.S. Dist. Ct. R.I. 1970, U.S. Supreme Ct. 1974, Mass. 1985, U.S. Dist. Ct. Mass. 1985. Ptnr. Edwards & Angell, Providence, 1969—, mng. ptnr., 1986-94. Trustee First Night Providence, 1988-93, pres., 1991-93; bd. dirs. R.I. Philharm. Orch., 1985—, pres., 1993-95; trustee Providence Preservation Soc., 1990—, pres. 1996—; mem. R.I. Com. on Jud. Tenure and Discipline, 1992—; bd. dirs. Providence YMCA, 1975-85, Blackstone Pk. Improvement Assn., 1979—, Nopes Island Conservation Assn., 1992—, New Eng. Legal Found., 1994—; corporator R.I. Hosp., 1989—. Fellow R.I. Bar Found.; mem. ABA, R.I. Bar Assn., Amherst Alumni Assn. R.I. (pres. 1980-91), Greater Providence C. of C. (bd. dirs. 1991-94). Home: 254 Irving Ave Providence RI 02906-5544 Office: Edwards & Angell 2700 Hospital Trust Tower Providence RI 02903

SHERMAN, ELAINE C., gourmet foods company executive, educator; b. Chgo., Aug. 1, 1938; d. Arthur E. and Sylvia (Miller) Friedman; m. Arthur J. Spiegel, Jan. 1989; children: Steven J., David P., Jaime A. Student, Northwestern U., 1956-58; diploma in cake decorating, Wilton Sch. Profl. Cake Decorating, 1973; diploma, Dumas Pere, L'école de la Cuisine Française. Tchr. cooking and adult edn. Maine, Oakton, Niles Adult and Continuing Edn. Program, Park Ridge, Ill., 1972-82; corp. officer The Complete Cook, Glenview, Ill., 1976-82, Madame Chocolate, Glenview, 1983-87; food columnist Chgo. Sun Times, 1985-87; dir. mktg. Sue Ling Gin, Chgo., 1987-88; co-owner Critical Eye, Chgo., 1988—; v.p., dir. merchandising, gen. mgr. Foodstuffs, Inc., Evanston, Ill., 1990-91, food cons. mgmt. and mktg., 1991—. Author: Madame Chocolate's Book of Divine Indulgences, 1984 (nominated Tastemaker award 1984). Bd. dirs. Chgo. Fund on Aging and Disability, 1989—; co-chmn. Meals on Wheels, 1989-90, 91. Mem. Les Dames D'Escoffier (founding pres.), Women's Foodservice Network (pres.), Confrerie de la Chaine Des Rotisseurs (vice conselliere gastronomique), Am. Inst. Wine and Food (bd. dirs.). Home and Office: 1728 Wildberry Dr # D Glenview IL 60025-1748

SHERMAN, EUGENE JAY, marketing executive, economist, retired; b. N.Y.C., Jan. 10, 1935; s. Samuel and Sarah (Lavinsky) S.; m. Mary Eileen Van, Apr. 22, 1966; 1 child, Rebecca. BA, CCNY, 1956; MBA, NYU, 1959, postgrad., 1959-63. Economist Fed. Res. Bank N.Y., 1959-62, Chase Manhattan Bank, N.Y.C., 1962-65; v.p. Bank of N.Y., N.Y.C., 1965-72; sr. v.p., exec. dir., dir. rsch. Merrill Lynch and Co., N.Y.C., 1972-78; v.p., chief economist, mgr.internat. investment Internat. Gold Corp., N.Y.C., 1980-86; sr. v.p., chief economist Fed. Home Loan Bank N.Y., 1986-93; sr. v.p., dir. rsch. M.A. Schapiro & Co., Inc., N.Y.C., 1993-96; gold cons., N.Y.C., 1986—; adj. prof. Touro Coll., N.Y.C., 1997—. Author: Gold Investment: Theory and Application, 1986; contbr. articles to profl. jours. Mem. Money Marketeers (pres. 1971-72. honored fellow 1987), Downtown Economist Club (chmn. 1988-89), Forecasters (winner 1986, 95), Treasury Securities Luncheon (pres. 1995-96), Nat. Assn. Bus. Econs., N.Y. Assn. Bus. Econs. Avocations: mountaineering, performing arts. Home: 115 E 9th St New York NY 10003-5414

SHERMAN, FRED, biochemist, educator; b. Mpls., May 21, 1932; s. Harry and Ann (Kaufman) S.; m. Revina Freeman, July 25, 1958 (div.); children: Aaron, Mark, Rhea. B.A., U. Minn., Mpls., 1953; Ph.D., U. Calif., Berkeley, 1958. Postdoctoral fellow U. Wash., Seattle, 1959-60; postdoctoral fellow Lab. Genetique Physiol., Gif-sur-Yvette, France, 1960-61; sr. instr. U. Rochester, N.Y., 1961-62, asst. prof., 1962-66, assoc. prof., 1966-71, prof. dept. biochemistry Sch. Medicine & Dentistry, 1971—, chmn. dept. biochemistry, 1982—; instr. Cold Spring Harbor Lab., N.Y., 1970-87; Wander Meml. lectr., 1975; Wilson prof. U. Rochester, 1982. Co-author: Cold Spring Harbor Manual on Yeast Genetics and Molecular Biology, 1970-87; assoc. editor Genetics, 1975-82, Molecular Cell Biology, 1979-88. Fellow NIH, 1959-61, grantee, 1963—. Mem. NAS, Genetic Soc. Am. (bd. dirs. 1983-85), AAAS, Am. Soc. Microbiology. Home: 69 Westminster Rd Rochester NY 14607-2223 Office: U Rochester Med Sch Dept Biochemistry 601 Elmwood Ave Rochester NY 14642-0001

SHERMAN, FRIEDA FRANCES, writer; b. N.Y.C., Oct. 21, 1929; d. Benjamin and Anna (Brown) Jeffe; m. Alan Morton Sherman, Feb. 21, 1952; children: Steven, Daniel, Elizabeth, Richard. BA, Hunter Coll., 1951. Market researcher Am. Broadcasting Co., N.Y.C., 1953-55, Am. Inst. Mgmt., N.Y.C., 1955-56; tchr. dance Palo Alto (Calif.), 1960-70; co-founder Workshop Unltd., Palo Alto, 1970-74; dir. client support Prognostics, Palo Alto, 1982-85; dance therapist pvt. practice, Palo Alto, 1975-90; cons. Market Intelligence Rsch., Palo Alto, 1985. Author of poems and short stories. Coord. cmty. outreach Lively Arts Stanford (Calif.) U., 1990-92; bd. dirs. SPCA, Santa Cruz, Calif., 1994; judge Nat. Poetry Contest, Santa Cruz, 1994. Mem. Nat. Writers Union, Phi Beta Kappa. Avocations: dancing, hiking, music. Home: 900 Glen Canyon Rd Santa Cruz CA 95060-1619

SHERMAN, GERALD, nuclear physicist, financial estate adviser, financial company executive; b. Bklyn., Sept. 7, 1938; s. Saul and Claire S.; m. Annette Ellen Drasin, Aug. 29, 1965; children: Rochelle Heidi, Sondra Nicole. BA in Physics, UCLA, 1960, MS in Nuclear Physics, 1962; PhD in Physics, Columbia Pacific U., 1985. Cert. Nat. Assn. Securities Dealers, Series 6 and 63, Investment Co. Products/Variable Contracts, registered rep.; lic. in securities and health and life ins. Calif.; lic. Fed. Securities Series 7; cert. mutual funds specialist. Physics instr., lower divsn. Lab. UCLA, 1960-62, physics instr. upper divsn. nuclear physics, 1961-62; nuclear ion engine rocket physicist Rocketdyne, Canoga Park, Calif., 1961; sr. scientist Advanced Tech. Co., L.A., 1965-66; physicist, principle superconductivity investigator Northrop Space Sci. Lab., Hawthorne, Calif., 1966-70; pres. Sherman Ins. Agy., Inc., L.A., 1970-84; pres., CEO Sherman Fin. Svcs., Inc., Thousand Oaks, Calif., 1984—; cons. TRW, 1970; speaker scientific seminars for NASA, U.S. Air Force, Lockheed; speaker fin. seminars, 1972—; developer bus. plan between Bank of China and New USA-China Project. Author: Microwave Phenomenological Theory of Superconductivity, 1965, Superconductive Antennas, 1966, Estate Tax Savings of 90%, 1992, Financial Security for Life, 1993. Recipient Atomic Energy Commn. award Am. Electronics, 1960, Top Prodr. Nationwide award U.S. Life Ins. Co. Calif., 1978, Leading Disability Prodr. Nationwide award Chubb Life Ins. Co. Am., 1983-85, 90, Leading Combined Life and Disability Prodr. award Chubb, 1987, Leading Combined Disability and Life Ins. Producer award Chubb, 1989, Internat. Life and Health Ins. awards Chubb Corp./Summit Club Calif., 1979, 88, 89, 92, 94, Hawaii, 1982, 92, 94, Italy, 1984, 93, Greece, 1984, Bermuda, 1985, 72, 88, England, 1985, Scotland, 1985, Mex., 1986, Monaco, 1987, Switzerland, 1987, Hong Kong, 1988, Thailand, 1988, France, 1989, Africa, 1989, Puerto Rico, 1990, 95, Ariz., 1991, Australia, 1992, Fla., 1993, Austria, 1994, Securities Acad. Award, 1997; PhD Rsch. fellow UCLA, 1962-64. Mem. Calif. Assn. Life Underwriters, Westlake Art Guild, UCLA Physics Honor Soc. (v.p. 1959, exec. v.p. 1960), Sigma Pi Sigma. Avocations: landscape artist, gallery and bank exhibitions, 1991; played trumphet and drums, 1956-58, USAF ROTC marching band; arranger and composer of ballad/symphonic music; planetary astrophotography. One of the first to design the NASA crystal experiment for astronauts; originated and performed first superconductive non-destructive test to determine aircraft titanium alloy strength; created concept and experimentally performed the first superconductive short antenna for very low frequency communication. Office: Sherman Financial Svcs Inc 2158 Calle Riscoso Thousand Oaks CA 91362-1141

SHERMAN, GORDON RAE, computer science educator; b. Menomenee, Mich., Feb. 24, 1928; s. Gordon E. and Myrtle H. (Evenson) S.; m. Lois E. Miller, July 3, 1951; children—Karen Rae, Gordon Thorstein. B.S., Iowa State U., 1953; M.S., Stanford U., 1954; Ph.D., Purdue U., 1960. Instr. math. and research assoc. Statis and Computational Lab., Purdue U., Lafayette, Ind., 1956-60; dir. Computing Ctr., U. Tenn., Knoxville, 1960—, prof. computer sci., 1960-93, prof. emeritus dept. computer sci., 1993—; program dir. techniques and systems Office of Computing Activities, NSF, 1971-72; chmn. membership com. EDUCOM Council, 1983-85. Served with USAF, 1946-49, 50-51. Recipient Chancellor's citation U. Tenn., 1983; NSF grantee, 1974. Fellow Brit. Computer Soc.; mem. Am. Statis. Assn., Assn. for Computing Machinery, Dta Processing Mgmt. Assn. (internat. computer sci. Man of Yr. award S.E. Region VIII, 1973; Profl. of Yr. Region VIII 1979), Ops. Research Soc. Am., Soc. for Indsl. and Applied Math., Sigma Xi, Phi Kappa Phi. Republican. Lutheran. Contbr. articles on computer sci. to profl. jours. Home: 301 Cheshire Dr Apt 105 Knoxville TN 37919-5849 Office: U Tenn 209 Stokely Mgmt Ctr Knoxville TN 37996

SHERMAN, IRWIN WILLIAM, biological sciences educator; b. N.Y.C., Feb. 12, 1933; s. Morris and Anna (Ezaak) S.; m. Vilia Gay Turner, Aug. 25, 1966; children: Jonathan Turner, Alexa Joy. BS, CCNY, 1954; MS, Northwestern U., 1959, PhD, 1960. Asst. prof. U. Calif., Riverside, 1962-67, assoc. prof., 1967-70, prof. biology, 1970—, chmn. biology dept., 1974-79, dean Coll. Natural and Agrl. Scis., dir. agrl. expt. sta., 1981-88, exec. vice chancellor, 1993-94; instr. marine biol. lab., Woods Hole, Mass., 1963-68; mem. study sect. tropical medicine NIH, 1970-73; cons. Agy. Internat. Devel., 1978-90; mem. ad hoc study group U.S. Army, 1975-78. Author: (book) The Invertebrates: Function and Form, 1976, Biology: A Human Approach, 1989. Mem. steering com. World Health Orgn., 1978-87. Served with U.S. Army, 1954-56. USPHS fellow Rockefeller Inst., 1960-62, Guggenheim fellow, 1967, NIH/Nat. Inst. Med. Rsch. fellow 1973-74, Walter and Eliza Hall Inst. for Med. Rsch. fellow, 1986; Wellcome Trust lectr. Brit. Soc. Parasitology, 1987, Scripps Rsch. Inst. fellow 1991. Mem. AAAS, Am. Soc. Tropical Medicine and Hygiene, Soc. Protozoology, Soc. Parasitology, Sigma Xi. Democrat. Jewish. Avocations: painting, reading. Office: Univ of Calif-Riverside Dept Biology Riverside CA 92521

SHERMAN, JEFFREY ALAN, dentist; b. Bklyn., June 16, 1947; s. Joseph G. and Gertrude P. S.; m. Roslyn B. Tillis, Aug. 15, 1970; children: Jodi Heather, Brett Andrew. BA, Adelphi U., 1969; DDS, Howard U., 1973. Diplomate Am. Bd. Oral Electrosurgery. Resident in gen. dentistry Del. State Hosp., 1974; pvt. practice, Oakdale, N.Y., 1975—; mem. faculty Albert Einstein Coll. Medicine; vis. lectr. Tufts U.; dir. Greater L.I. Dental Meeting, 1990—. Author: Oral Electrosurgery: An Illustrated Clinical Guide, 1992, Oral Radiosurgery, 2d edit.; contbr. to profl. publs. Fellow Internat. Coll. Dentists; mem. ADA (lectr. ann. meetings 1978—), Suffolk County Dental Soc. (bd. dels. 1989—, dental lab and trades com. 1989—, edn. com. 1989-91, photographer dental meeting 1990—), Acad. Gen. Dentistry (membership com. 1992—, area v.p. 1991-92), Am. Acad. Dental Electrosurgery (co-editor, pres. 1987), N.Y. State Acad. Gen. Dentistry (pub. info. officer 1992). Office: 1237 Montauk Hwy Oakdale NY 11769-1434

SHERMAN, JOHN FOORD, biomedical consultant; b. Oneonta, N.Y., Sept. 4, 1919; s. Henry C. and Ruth (Foord) S.; m. Betsy Deane Murray, Feb. 8, 1944; children: Betsy Deane, Mary Ann. B.S., Albany Coll. Pharmacy of Union U., 1949, D.Sc., 1970; Ph.D., Yale U., 1953. With NIH, 1953-74; assoc. dir. extramural programs Nat. Inst. Neurol. Diseases and Blindness, 1961-62, Nat. Inst. Arthritis and Metabolic Disease, 1962-63; assoc. dir. for extramural programs Office Dir. NIH, 1964-68, dep. dir., 1968-74; v.p. Assn. Am. Med. Colls., Washington, 1974-91, exec. v.p., 1987-91, spl. cons., 1991-94; mem. bd. advisors Am. Bd. Internal Medicine, 1991—; sr. advisor Rsch!Am., 1994—. Asst. surgeon gen. USPHS, 1964-68; spl. rsch. chemotherapy and neuropharmacology; mem. panel on data and studies NRC, 1976-87; mem. biomed. libr. rev. com. NIH; bd. dirs. Spinal Cord Injury Edn. and Tng. Found., 1986-92, Musculoskeletal Transplant Found., 1987—. With U.S. Army, 1941-46. Decorated Bronze Star; recipient Meritorious Svc. award USPHS, 1965, Disting. Svc. award HEW, 1971, Sec.'s Spl. Citation award, 1973, award Nat. Civil Svc. League, 1973, Disting. Alumnus award Union U.-Pharmacy Coll. Coun., 1974, Lifetime Achievement award Nat. Assn. for Biomed. Rsch., 1990. Fellow AAAS; mem. Inst. Medicine NAS, Cosmos Club, Sigma Xi. Congregationalist.

SHERMAN, JONATHAN HENRY, lawyer; b. Washington, Jan. 4, 1963; s. Gerald Howard and Lola (Kay) S. BA in History magna cum laude, U. Rochester, 1984; MA in History, Yale U., 1989; JD, Stanford U., 1991. Bar: N.Y. 1992, U.S. Dist. Ct. (so. dist.) N.Y. 1992, U.S. Supreme Ct. 1995, U.S. Dist. Ct. (ea. dist.) N.Y. 1996, U.S. Ct. Appeals (11th cir.) 1996. Assoc. Cahill Gordon & Reindel, N.Y.C., 1991—; lectr. Stanford U., Palo Alto, Calif., 1991, Yale Coll., New Haven, 1993. Sponsor, mentor Student-Sponsor Partnership, N.Y.C., 1992—; contbr. The Cornerstone Sch., Jersey City, 1994. Mem. ABA, N.Y. State Bar Assn., Phi Beta Kappa. Democrat. Avocations: writing, reading, cycling. Home: 101 W 90th St Apt 19A New York NY 10024 Office: Cahill Gordon & Reindel 80 Pine St New York NY 10005-1702

SHERMAN, JOSEPH HOWARD, clergyman; b. Marion, S.C., June 14, 1923; s. Samuel and Alma (Cannon) S.; m. Daisy Lee Littles; children: Joseph Howard Jr., Beatrice Sherman Boone. D.D. (hon.), Trinity Hall Coll.; LL.D. (hon.), New Haven Theol. Appointed Jurisdictional Bishop of N.C., 2d Jurisdiction, 1963. Founder, pastor Pentecostal Temple Ch. of God in Christ, Charlotte, N.C.; pres. N.C. Youth Dept.; dist. supt. N.C. Jurisdiction, Wadesboro; chmn. Council of Bishops, Memphis, 1976—; pres. C. H. Mason System of Bible Colls., Charlotte, N.C., 1975; mem. Nat. Hymnal Com. Author: (book) Weapons of the Righteous; (phamplet) Witchcraft, The Work of the Devil; (album) Peace That Only Christ Can Give; editor The Mighty Voice That Crieth mag. pres., founder J. Howard Sherman Scholarship Fund, Charlotte, 1974—; bd. dirs. C. H. Mason Scholarship Found., Memphis, Saints Ctr.; mem. NAACP, Charlotte, Hiring of the Handicapped, Charlotte, 1984, Ch. of God in Christ Hosp. Fund; mem. grievance com. Housing Authority, Charlotte, 1983, 84; mem. steering com. Democratic Governorship, N.C., 1984. Named Knight of Queen City, Charlotte, 1976, hon. citizen City of Balt., 1981, hon. atty. gen. N.C., 1983; J.H. Sherman Day named in his honor, Charlotte, 1980-84. Mem. Ministerial Alliance (sec. Charlotte chpt. 1983—). *

SHERMAN, JOSEPH OWEN, pediatric surgeon; b. Chgo., Aug. 15, 1936; s. Joseph Owen and Mary Elizabeth (Kelly) S.; m. June Marie Martin, Mar. 16, 1963; children: Brian William, Lee Ann. Student, U. Ill., 1955-58; BS, Northwestern U., 1959, MD, 1962. Diplomate Am. Bd. Surgery, Am. Bd. Pediatric Surgery; lic. physician, Ill. Rotating intern Passavant Meml. Hosp., Chgo., 1963-64; resident in gen. surgery VA Rsch. Hosp., Chgo., 1964-65, 67-68; Am. Cancer Soc. clin. fellow Northwestern U. Med. Sch., Chgo., 1965-66; resident in pediatric surgery Children's Meml. Hosp., Chgo., 1966, 68-69; resident in thoracic surgery Mcpl. Tb San., Chgo., 1967; from instr. to assoc. prof. surgery Northwestern U. Med. Sch., 1967-86, prof. clin. surgery, 1986—; emeritus staff dept. surgery Children's Meml. Hosp., 1995—, Evanston (Ill.) Hosp., 1995—. Contbr. articles to profl. jours. Served with Ill. Army N.G., 1953-69, Ill. Air N.G., 1966-67. Fellow ACS, Inst. Medicine Chgo.; mem. AMA, Am. Pediat. Surg. Assn., Assn. for Acad. Surgery, Chgo. Med. Soc., Chgo. Surg. Soc., Ill. Pediat. Surg. Assn., Ill. State Med. Soc. Avocations: photography, computer programing, indoor and outdoor gardening.

SHERMAN, JUDITH DOROTHY, producer, recording company owner, recording engineer; b. Cleve., Nov. 12, 1942; d. William Paul and Laverne (Spoerke) Luekens; m. Kenneth Sherman, Aug. 1, 1964 (div. Aug. 1972); m. Max Wilcox, Jan. 1, 1981 (div. Jan. 1988); m. Curtis Macomber, Apr. 29, 1988. BA, Valparaiso U., 1964; MFA, SUNY-Buffalo, 1971. Rec. engr. Edward at the Moog, N.Y.C., 1971-72; producer-music dir. WBAI-FM, N.Y.C., 1972-76; owner-producer Judith Sherman Prodns., N.Y.C., 1976—; rec. engr. Marlboro (Vt.) Music Festival, 1976-94; adminstrv. dir. La Musica di Asolo, Sarasota, Fla., 1986-88; vocalist Steve Reich and Musicians, 1971-72. Recipient Corp. Pub. Broadcasting award, 1976, two Grammy award nominations, 1991, Grammy award, Classical Prodr. of Yr., 1993, Grammy award nominations, 1994, 95. Mem. NAFE, Chamber Music Am., NARAS. Democrat. Home and Office: 645 W 239th St Apt 6F and 2A Bronx NY 10463-1277

SHERMAN, KATHRYN ANN, communication professional; b. Phila., Mar. 12, 1964; d. Edward and Ann Elizabeth (Shields) S. AA, Bucks County C.C., Newtown, Pa., 1988; BBA, Temple U., 1993. Waitress Posh Nosh, Newtown, Pa., 1985-89, Blue Fountain Diner, Langhorne, Pa., 1989-93; comm. assoc. The Vanguard Group, Valley Forge, Pa., 1993—. Mem. Inst. Mgmt. Accts. (bd. dirs., dir. membership acquisition), Golden Key, Beta Alpha Psi, Phi Theta Kappa. Republican. Lutheran.

SHERMAN, LOUIS ALLEN, biology educator; b. Chgo., Dec. 16, 1943; s. Stanley E. and Sarah R. Sherman; m. Debra Meddoff, June 15, 1969; children: Daniel, Jeff. BS in Physics, U. Chgo., 1965, PhD in Biophysics, 1970. Postdoctoral fellow Cornell U., Ithaca, N.Y., 1970-72; asst. prof. U. Mo., Columbia, 1972-78, assoc. prof., 1978-83, prof., 1983-88, dir. biol. scis., 1985-88; prof., head dept. biol. scis. Purdue U., West Lafayette, Ind., 1989—. Contbr. articles to profl. jours. NIH fellow, 1965-72; Fulbright Hayes scholar, The Netherlands, 1979-80; NSF travel grantee, Fed. Republic Germany, Japan; grantee NIH, USDA, Dept. Energy. Fellow AAAS, Am. Acad. Microbiology; mem. AAUP, Am. Soc. Microbiology, Am. Soc. Plant Physiology, Biophys. Soc., Plant Molecular Biology Soc. Office: Purdue U Dept Biol Scis Lilly Hall West Lafayette IN 47907

SHERMAN, MARTIN, entomologist; b. Newark, Nov. 21, 1920; s. Louis and Anna (Norkin) S.; m. Ruth Goldsmith, Sept. 25, 1943 (div. Nov. 1975); children: Laurel Deborah Sherman Englehart, Susan Leslie Sherman Kitakis. B.S., Rutgers U., 1941, M.S., 1943; Ph.D., Cornell U., 1948. Research fellow in entomology Rutgers U., 1941-43; research asst. Cornell U., 1945-48; entomologist Beech-Nut Packing Co., Rochester, N.Y., 1948-49; mem. faculty U. Hawaii, Honolulu, 1949—; prof. entomology U. Hawaii, 1958-86, prof. emeritus entomology, 1986—; Fulbright scholar U. Tokyo, 1956-57, Royal Vet. and Agrl. Coll. of Denmark, 1966; vis. prof. Rutgers U., 1973. Editorial bd.: Pacific Sci, 1962-66, Jour. Med. Entomology, 1968-72. Served to 1st lt. USAAF, 1943-45. Fellow Am. Inst. Chemists; mem. Entomol. Soc. Am. (gov. bd. 1974-77, pres. Pacific br. 1970), Am. Chem. Soc., Soc. Toxicology, Soc. Environ. Toxicology and Chemistry, Am. Registry Profl. Entomologists, Japanese Soc. Applied Entomology and Zoology, Hawaiian Entomology Soc. (pres. 1969-70), Internat. Soc. for Study Xenobiotics, Sigma Xi, Delta Phi Alpha, Phi Kappa Phi, Gamma Sigma Delta. Club: Torch. Address: 1121 Koloa St Honolulu HI 96816-5103

SHERMAN, MARY ANGUS, public library administrator; b. Lawton, Okla., Jan. 3, 1937; d. Donald Adelbert and Mabel (Felkner) Angus; m. Donald Neil Sherman, Feb. 8, 1958; children: Elizabeth, Donald Neil II. BS in Home Econs., U. Okla., 1958, MLS, 1969. Br. head Pioneer Libr. System, Purcell, Okla., 1966-76; regional libr. Pioneer Libr. System, Norman, Okla., 1976-78, asst. dir., 1978-80, dir., 1987—. Named one of Distinguished Alumni Sch. Home Econs., U. Okla., 1980. Mem. ALA (councilor 1988-96, planning and budget assembly 1990-91, internat. rels. com. 1992-96), Pub. Libr. Assn. (divsn. of ALA, pres. pub. policy for pub. librs. sect. 1995-96), AAUW (pres. Okla. chpt. 1975-77, nat. bd. dirs. 1983-87, S.W. ctrl. region dir. 1983-85, v.p. nat. membership 1985-87, Woman of the Yr. Purcell chpt. 1982), Okla. Libr. Assn. (pres. 1982-83, interlibrary cooperation com. 1993-95, chair 1994-95, Disting. Svc. award 1986), Norman C. of C. (bd. dirs. 1988-96, pres. 1994-95), Rotary (program chair 1991-92, bd. dirs. 1993-97, pres. 1995-96. Paul Harris fellow), Norman Assistance League Club (cmty. assoc.), Norman, Okla. Sister City Com. 1994—, Delta Gamma Mothers (pres. 1978-79), Kappa Alpha Theta (pres. Alpha Omicron House Corp. 1984-87, nat. dir. house corps. 1987-88), Beta Phi Mu, Phi Beta Kappa. Democrat. Methodist. Office: Pioneer Libr System 225 N Webster Ave Norman OK 73069-7133

SHERMAN, MONA DIANE, school system administrator; b. N.Y.C., Aug. 28, 1941; d. Hyman and Lillian (Baker) Ginsberg; m. Richard H. Sherman, May 9, 1964; children: Holly Baker, Andrew Hunter. BS, Hunter Coll., CUNY, 1962; MS, CUNY, 1965. Cert. elem. tchr., K-12 reading endorsement specialist, ESL tchr., elem. adminstrn. and supervision, instrnl. supervision, spl. edn. learning disabilities and neurologically impaired edn., Ind. Elem. tchr. N.Y.C. Pub. Schs., 1962-77; team leader Tchr. Corps Potsdam (N.Y.) State Coll., SUNY, 1977-79; dir. Tchr. Ctr., Sch. City of Hammond, Ind., 1979-87; lab. coord. PALS, Gary (Ind.) Sch. Corp., 1987-93, mentor, 1988—, facilitator of staff devel., 1993—; instr. Tex. Instrument Computer Co., Lubbock, 1983-84, Performance Learning Sys., Emerson, N.J., 1984—; cons. in classroom discipline and computer instrn. Gary Staff Devel. Ctr., 1987—; mentor Urban Tchr. Edn. program Ind. U. N.W., Gary, 1991—; chair sch. improvement team, tchr. of yr. com., 1993-94; mem., grantswriter Gary Tech. Com., Gary Distance Learning Com. Mem. Lake Area United Way Lit. Coalition NW Ind., 1990, Gary Reading Textbook Adoption Com.; sec. Martin Luther King Jr. Acad. PTSA, mem. sch. improvement team. Recipient Recognition NW Ind. Forum, 1988, Tchr. of Yr. award Merrillville (Ind.) Lions Club, 1988, Outstanding Tchr. of Yr. award Inland Ryerson, East Chicago, Ind., 1989. Mem. Ind. Reading Assn., Gary Reading Assn., Phi Delta Kappa, Delta Kappa Gamma. Avocations: theatre, crafts, tennis. Home: 1112 Fran Lin Pky Munster IN 46321-3607

SHERMAN, NORMAN MARK, advertising agency executive; b. N.Y.C., June 19, 1948; s. Sol and Rhoda (Kaplan) S.; m. Michelle Petnov, Jan. 8, 1978; 1 child, Michael Isaac. BA, U. Buffalo, 1970; MBA, Columbia U., 1972. Cert. tchr., N.Y. Product mgr. RCA Records, N.Y.C., 1972-73; dir. mktg. Shelter Records, N.Y.C., 1973-74; account exec. Rosenfeld Sirowitz & Lawson, N.Y.C., 1974-76; account exec. Benton & Bowles, N.Y.C., 1976-78, v.p. account supr., 1978-81, sr. v.p., mgmt. supr., 1981-84; exec. v.p., dir. account mgmt. Avrett, Free & Ginsberg, N.Y.C., 1984-85; sr. v.p., group account dir. D'Arcy, Masius, Benton & Bowles, 1985-93, mng. dir., bd. dirs., 1993-96, corp. exec. v.p., 1996—. Home: 330 W 72nd St New York NY 10023-2641 Office: D'Arcy Masius Benton & Bowles 1675 Broadway New York NY 10019-5820

SHERMAN, RANDOLPH S., lawyer; b. New Rochelle, N.Y., Nov. 19, 1944; s. Julius and Selma (Goldstein) S.; m. Joan E. Lauterbach, May 28, 1967; children: Elissa, Stephanie. BS in Indsl. Labor, Cornell U., 1966; JD, NYU, 1969. Bar: N.Y. 1970, U.S. Ct. Appeals (2d cir.) 1980, U.S. Ct. Appeals (3d cir.) 1983, U.S. Ct. Appeals (4th cir.) 1994, U.S. Ct. Appeals (8th cir.) 1986, U.S. Supreme Ct. 1984. Ptnr. Kaye Scholer, Fierman, Hays & Handler, N.Y.C., 1969—. Mem. ABA (antitrust sect., litigation sect.), U.S. Trademark Assn., N.Y.C. Bar Assn. Office: Kaye Scholer Fierman Hays & Handler LLP 425 Park Ave New York NY 10022-3598

SHERMAN, RICHARD ALLEN, lawyer; b. Atlanta, Mar. 16, 1946; s. Robert Hiram and Olivia Mae (Latham) S.; m. Mary Margaret Sawyer, June 23, 1973 (div. June 1994); children: Richard A. Jr., Jill Mary, James Warren; m. Catherine Agnes Oakley, May 4, 1996. BA, Tulane U., 1968, JD, 1972. Bar: Fla. 1974, La. 1973, U.S. Ct. Appeals (5th cir.) 1978, U.S. Ct. Appeals (11th cir.) 1981, U.S. Supreme Ct. 1981. Ptnr., head appellate divsn. Wicker, Smith, Blomqvist, Davant, Tutan, O'Hara, McCoy et al, Miami, 1973-83; pvt. practice Ft. Lauderdale, Fla., 1983—, practice limited to handling appeals in Fla. Active Rep. Nat. Com. Mem. ABA (vice-chmn. U.S. Ct. Appeals 5th cir. com. 1981), Fla. Bar Assn. (appellate rules com. 1979-81), Dade County Bar Assn. (chmn. appellate cts. com. 1982-83), Mensa, Pres. Club, Lauderdale Yacht Club, Upper Keys Sailing Club (bd. dirs.). Avocations: yacht racing, boating, scuba diving, travel, theatre. Office: 1777 S Andrews Ave Ste 302 Fort Lauderdale FL 33316-2517

SHERMAN, RICHARD BEATTY, history educator; b. Somerville, Mass., Nov. 16, 1929; s. James Beatty and Hilda Louise (Ford) S.; m. Hanni Fey, June 13, 1952; children: Linda Caroline, Alan Theodore. AB, Harvard U., 1951, PhD, 1959; MA, U. Pa., 1952. Instr. history Pa. State U., State College, 1957-60; asst. prof. Coll. of William and Mary, Williamsburg, Va., 1960-65, assoc. prof., 1965-70, prof. 1970-87, chancellor prof., 1987-92, Pullen prof., 1992-94, prof. emeritus, 1994—; Fulbright prof. Am. history U. Stockholm, 1966-67. Served with U.S. Army, 1952-54. Am. Philos. Soc. grantee, 1964, 66; faculty rsch. grantee, Coll. of William and Mary, 1962, 63, 65, 80, 87. Mem. AAUP, Phi Beta Kappa. Democrat. Author: The Negro and the City, 1970; The Republican Party and Black America, 1973, The Case of Odell Waller, 1992; co-author: The College of William and Mary: A History, 1993; contbr. articles to profl. jours. Home: 205 Matoaka Ct Williamsburg VA 23185-2810 Office: Coll William and Mary Dept History Williamsburg VA 23185

SHERMAN, RICHARD H., education educator; b. Yonkers, N.Y., Jan. 5, 1941; m. Mona D. Sherman, May 9, 1964; children: Holly Baker, Andrew Hunter. BA, Hunter Coll., 1962; MA, Iowa U., 1965; MS, Queens Coll., 1970; EdD, Yeshiva U., 1977. Cert. tchr., Ind., Ill., N.Y. Asst. prof. edn. SUNY, Potsdam; instr. Herbert H. Lehman Coll., CUNY; asst. prof. edn. Purdue U., Hammond, Ind.; assoc. dean Ind. Vocat. Tech. Coll., Gary; chmn., assoc. prof. Calumet Coll. St. Joseph, Whiting, Ind.; edn. dir. Mus.

Broadcast Communications, Chgo.; dir. Zarem/Golde ORT TECH Inst., Chgo.; workshop leader; presenter and speaker in field; exec. dir. Allied Ednl. Svcs. Author, playwright, poet, critic. Bd. dirs. Jewish Fedn. N.W. Ind.; chmn. events "Walk for Israel", Lake Area United Way, v.p. mobilization and resources devel, needs and assessment priorities com., chmn. section campaign; active Lake County chpt. ARC, N.W. Ind. Film Commn. Recipient N.W. Ind. Forum Svc. Recognition award, Jewish Fedn. N.W. Ind. Young Leadership award, Harlem Arts Svc. award. Mem. Internat. Reading Assn., Am. Assn. Theatre Critics, Dramatists Guild, Ind. Reading Coun., Ind. Reading Profs. (treas.), Hammond Reading Coun. (pres.), Ind. State Coun., N.W. Ind. Arts Assn. (subcom.), Soc. Children's Writers and Illustrators, Rotary Club, Sigma Tau Delta, Phi Delta Kappa.

SHERMAN, ROBERT B(ERNARD), composer, lyricist, screenwriter; b. N.Y.C., Dec. 19, 1925; s. Al and Rosa (Dancis) S.; student UCLA, 1943; BA, Bard Coll., 1949; MusD (hon.) Lincoln U., 1990; m. Joyce Ruth Sasner, Sept. 27, 1953; children: Laurie Shane, Jeffrey Craig, Andrea Tracy, Robert Jason. Popular songwriter, 1950-60, including Tall Paul, Pineapple Princess, You're Sixteen (Gold Record); songwriter Walt Disney Prodns., Beverly Hills, Calif., 1960-68, for 29 films including The Parent Trap, 1961, Summer Magic, 1963, Mary Poppins, 1964, That Darn Cat, 1965, Winnie The Pooh, 1965, Jungle Book, 1967, Bedknobs and Broomsticks, 1971; co-composer song It's A Small World, theme of Disneyland and Walt Disney World, Fla.; composer, lyricist United Artists, Beverly Hills, 1969—, songs for film Chitty, Chitty, Bang, Bang, 1969, Snoopy, Come Home!, 1972; song scores Charlotte's Web, 1972, Cabbage Patch Kids, 1974, Little Nemo, 1992, The Mighty Kong, 1996; composer for Walt Disney's Wonderful World of Color, TV, 1961—; co-producer NBC-TV spl. Goldilocks, 1970; v.p. Musi-Classics, Inc.; co-producer, composer, lyricist stage musical Victory Canteen, 1971; composer-lyricist Broadway show Over Here, 1975, Busker Alley, 1995; screenplay and song score Tom Sawyer, United Artists, 1972, Huckleberry Finn, 1974, The Slipper and the Rose, 1977, The Magic of Lassie, 1978. Served with inf. AUS, 1943-45; ETO. Decorated Purple Heart; recipient 2 Acad. awards best score for Mary Poppins, 1964, best song for Chim Chim Cheree, 1964; Grammy award, 1965; Christopher medal, 1965, 74; nine Acad. award nominations; Acad. award nomination for song score Bedknobs and Broomsticks, 1971, for best song The Age of Not Believing, 1971, others; 16 golden, 4 platinum and one diamond record album, 1965-83; first prize best composer song score Tom Sawyer, Moscow Film Festival, 1973, B.M.I. Pioneer award, 1977; Golden Cassette awards for Mary Poppins, Jungle Book, Bed Knobs and Broomsticks, 1983, Mouscar award Disney Studios, Disney Legend award, 1990, BMI Richard Kirk Achievment award, 1991. Mem. Acad. Motion Picture Arts and Scis. (exec. bd. music br. 12 yrs.), AFTRA, Nat. Acad. Rec. Arts and Scis., Composers and Lyricists Guild (exec. bd.), Dramatists Guild, Authors League. Office: 9030 Harratt St West Hollywood CA 90069-3858

SHERMAN, ROGER, economics educator; b. Jamestown, N.Y., Sept. 10, 1930; s. Claire Blanchard and Margaret Gertrude (Burke) S.; m. Charlotte Ann Murphy, Apr. 4, 1953 (div. Feb. 1995); children: Claire Randall, Thomas Allen; m. Geraldine Szott Moohr, May 25, 1996. B.S. in Math., Grove City Coll., 1952; M.B.A. in Fin., Harvard U., 1959; M.S. in Econs., Carnegie-Mellon U., 1965, Ph.D., 1966. Mgr. mfg. control IBM Corp., N.Y.C., 1956-62; asst. prof., assoc. prof., prof. U. Va., Charlottesville, 1965-72, Brown Forman prof. econs., 1982—, chmn. dept. econs., 1982-90; vis. scholar Oxford U., 1987, Sydney U., 1988. Author: Oligopoly: An Empirical Approach, 1972, The Economics of Industry, 1974, Antitrust Policies and Issues, 1978, The Regulation of Monopoly, 1989; editor: Perspectives on Postal Service Issues, 1980; contbr. articles to profl. jours. Bd. dirs. McGuffey Art Ctr., Charlottesville, 1984-92. Lt. USNR, 1953-62. U. Bristol fellow, 1968-69; Fulbright lectr., Madrid, 1972; Sci. Ctr. Berlinfellow, 1975, 79, 80; Rockefeller Found. Vis. scholar, 1985. Mem. Am. Econ. Assn., Royal Econ. Soc., Econometric Soc. Home: 500 Court Sq Apt 807 Charlottesville VA 22902-5147 Office: U Va Rouss Hall Charlottesville VA 22903-3288

SHERMAN, ROGER TALBOT, surgeon, educator; b. Chgo., Sept. 30, 1923; s. Joseph Bright and Alice Elizabeth (Baur) S.; m. Ruth Kathryn Thieman, Aug. 23, 1952; children: Nann, Alice, Nina, John, Julie. A.B., Kenyon Coll., 1946; M.D., U. Cin., 1948. Diplomate Am. Bd. Surgery (mem.). Intern, fellow in pathology St. Luke's Hosp., Chgo., 1948-50; resident in surgery Cin. Gen. Hosp., 1950-56; chief dept. exptl. surgery Walter Reed Army Med. Center, 1956-59; asst. prof. to prof. surgery U. Tenn., Memphis, 1959-72; prof., chmn. dept. surgery U. South Fla., Tampa, 1972-82; prof. surgery Emory U. Sch. Medicine, Atlanta, 1983-93; chief surgery Grady Meml. Hosp., Atlanta, 1983-92; Whitaker prof. surgery Emory U. Sch. Medicine, Atlanta, 1993—; dir. surg. edn. Piedmont Hosp., Atlanta, 1993—; cons. Walter Reed Army Med. Center. Mem. editorial bd. Am. Surgeon, 1970-91, Jour. Trauma, 1970-93; contbr. articles to profl. jours., chpts. to books. Served to maj. M.C. AUS, 1956-59. Recipient Golden Apple Tchr. of the Yr. award, 1972, Williams Disting. Teaching award Emory U., 1984, Curtis P. Artz award, 1988. Fellow ACS (gov.); mem. Am. Assn. Surgery of Trauma (pres. 1979), Am. Surg. Assn., So. Surg. Assn., Southeastern Surg. Congress (pres. 1985), Internat. Surg. Soc., Soc. Surgery of Alimentary Tract, Am. Burn Assn., Shock Soc., Am. Trauma Soc., Ga. Surg. Soc. (pres. 1997), Sigma Xi, Psi Upsilon, Alpha Omega Alpha. Home: 1170 Woods Cir NE Atlanta GA 30324-2736 Office: Piedmont Hospital Department of Surgery 1984 Peachtree Rd NW Atlanta GA 30309-1231 *Surgery. The opening, exploration and repair of the living human body is an awesome responsibility afforded to only a few. To be privileged to be counted among those is a high honor, surpassed only by being trusted to teach others this demanding, and marvelous craft.*

SHERMAN, RON, photographer; b. Cleve., May 10, 1942; s. Hyman B. and Sheryl D. Sherman; m. Myra LeBell, Aug. 16, 1969; children: Scott Neal, Jonathan Harris, Hannah Beth. BFA in illustrative photography, Rochester Inst. Tech., 1964; MA in photographic commn., Syracuse U., 1971. Staff photographer Gannett Newspapers (Democrat, Chronicle and Times Union), Rochester, N.Y., 1961-64, U. Fla., Gainesville, 1964-66; photo-officer, military intelligence unit U.S. Army-Signal Corps, Vietnam, 1967-68; staff photographer Milw. Journal, Wis., 1969; photographer Syracuse (N.Y.) U., 1969-71; prin. Ron Sherman Photographer, Atlanta, 1971—, Computer Aided Photography, Inc., Atlanta, 1991—; adv. comml. photography Gwinett Tech. Inst., Lawrenceville, Ga., 1983—; cons. ABC TV, Alcoa, AT&T, CBS Sports, The Coca-Cola Co., Eastman Kodak, Ford Motor Co., IBM, TRW, Atlanta Com. for the Olympic Games, BellSouth, So. Bell, Atlanta Gas Light Co., Nat. Hockey League, Sonat, Gen. Mills, Ga. Power, So. Co., Phoenix Comms. Photographer; pub. in Life, Time, Newsweek, Inside Sports, Bus. Week, Forbes, Reader's Digest, Ford Times, America Illustrated, Med. World News, N.Y. Times, U. S. News and World Report, Venture; pub. works in Atlanta calendar, 1994, 95, 96, 97, 98; Atlanta photos used to illustrate Peter Max's Super Bowl XXVIII poster; (hard cover books) Greater North Fulton and Atlanta, A Vision for the New Millenium. 1st Lt. U.S. Army 1968-69, Vietnam. Mem. Nat. Press Photographers Assn., Am. Soc. Media Photographers (pres. Atlanta chpt. 1980-81). Avocations: gardening, reading, classical and jazz music. Office: PO Box 2268 Roswell GA 30077-2268

SHERMAN, RUTH TENZER, artist, fixtures company executive; b. Chgo., Sept. 11, 1920; d. Philip and Jennie (Greitzer) Tenzer; m. Samuel Sherman, May 18, 1946 (dec. Nov. 1974); children: Patricia (dec.), Randy Mitchell. Art student, Pratt Inst., 1938-42, Art Students League, N.Y.C., 1942-45; studies with Raphael Soyer, N.Y.C., 1943, studies with Harold Baumbach, 1947-49; studies with Ruth Connery, Mamaroneck, N.Y., 1955; studies with Rudolph Baranik, White Plains, N.Y., 1961-63, studies with George Koras, 1966. Cert. artist Dept. Cultural Affairs. Pres. Pioneer Fixture Corp., Paterson, N.J., 1975-86. Exhbns. include Mamaroneck Artists Guild, 1963, Jr. League Artists of North Westchester, 1964, Westchester C.C., Valhalla, N.Y., 1964, The New Rochelle (N.Y.) Art Assn., 1964, Silvermine Guild Artists, New Canaan, Conn., 1964-88, Westchester Art Soc., White Plains, 1964-72, Hudson River Mus., Yonkers, N.Y., 1965, First Westchester Nat. Bank, New Rochelle, 1967, Conn. Acad. Fine Arts, Hartford, 1967, Stern Bros., N.Y.C., 1967, Nat. Jewish Hosp. Denver, Woodmere, N.Y., 1968, Quaker Ridge Sch., Scarsdale, N.Y., 1970, Gallery Shop, Westport, Conn., 1978, Mari Gallery, Woodstock, N.Y., 1978, The Village Gallery, Ardsley, N.Y., 1979, Todd Gallery, Kiamesha Lake, N.Y., 1980, Norwalk Mchts. Bank, New Canaan, 1980, Mchts. Bank, Norwalk, 1980, Emery Air Freight Hdqrs., Conn., 1981, Mari Hube Gallery, N.Y., 1990, Helio Gallery, N.Y.C., 1991, Maska Gallery, Seattle, 1991, Rockefeller Town House, N.Y.C., 1992, Denise Bibro Fine Art Gallery, Shoho, N.Y., 1993, Museè D'Art Moderne, Tonniens, France, 1993, Salon du Vieux Colombier, Paris, 1993, Md. Fedn. Art, Cardinal Gallery Md. Hall, Annapolis, 1993, Mus. Modern Art, Coral Gables, Fla., 1994, Wirtz Gallery, South Miami, Fla., 1994, U.S. Dept. State-Art in Embassies, 1995. Recipient Merit award Westchester Art Soc., 1964, Cert. of Honor Museè d'Art Moderne, 1994, Disting. Visitor award Mayor of Miami, 1994, U.S. Dept. of State, Art in Embassies Program, 1995; FIBA fellow, Cambridge, Eng., 1995. Avocations: golf, opera, classical and contemporary music, travel. Home: 58 Village Dr Stroudsburg PA 18360-1566

SHERMAN, RUTH TODD, government advisor, counselor, consultant; b. Memphis, July 3, 1924; d. Robbie M. and Lillie M. (Shreve) Todd. BS, Memphis State U., 1972, MEd, 1975; MA, Western Mich. U., 1986. Cert. tchr., counselor. Youth leader Assembly of God Ch., Memphis, 1962-64, youth dir., 1964-66; counselor Teen Challenge, Memphis, 1973-74; marriage and family therapist Memphis, 1976-77; govt. tng. advisor Def. Logistics Agy., Battle Creek, Mich., 1982-87; advisor Def. Logistics Agy., Alexandria, Va., 1987-94, ret., 1994; Agy. to Mil. Svc. cons. Def. Logistics Agy., Oklahoma City, 1990-94. Author: Federal Catalog Training Books/Videos, 1987 (Sustained Superior Performance award 1987). Mem. Internat. Assn. Marriage and Family Counselors, Nat. Employment Counseling Assn., Am. Mental Health Counseling Assn. Avocations: drawing, creating computer animations, photography. Home: 257 Vista Dr Gahanna OH 43230

SHERMAN, SIGNE LIDFELDT, portfolio manager, former research chemist; b. Rochester, N.Y., Nov. 11, 1913; d. Carl Leonard Broström and Herta Elvira Maria (Thern) Lidfeldt; m. Joseph V. Sherman, Nov. 18, 1944 (dec. Oct. 1984). BA, U. Rochester, 1935, MS, 1937. Chief chemist Lab. Indsl. Medicine and Toxicology Eastman Kodak Co., Rochester, 1937-43; chief rsch. chemist Chesebrough-Pond's Inc., Clinton, Conn., 1943-44; ptnr. Joseph V. Sherman Cons., N.Y.C., 1944-84; portfolio strategist Sherman Holdings, Troy, Mont., 1984—. Author: The New Fibers, 1946. Fellow Am. Inst. Chemists; mem. AAAS, AAUW (life), Am. Chem. Soc., Am. Econ. Assn., Am. Assn. Ind. Investors (life), Fedn. Am. Scientists (life), Union Concerned Scientists (life), Western Econ. Assn. Internat., Earthquake Engring. Rsch. Inst., Nat. Ctr. for Earthquake Engring. Rsch., N.Y. Acad. Scis. (life), Internat. Platform Assn., Cabinet View Country Club. Office: Sherman Holdings Angel Island 648 Halo Dr Troy MT 59935-9415

SHERMAN, STUART, physician; b. New York, N.Y., Feb. 21, 1955; s. Sol and Rhoda (Kaplan) S.; m. Leslie Jane Derus, Oct. 5, 1991; children: Matthew, Benjamin. BA, SUNY, Binghampton, 1977; MD, Washington U., St. Louis, 1982. Diplomate Am. Bd. Internal Medicine. Resident in internal medicine U. Pitts., 1982-85, rsch. fellow, 1985-86; gastroenterology fellow Sch. of Medicine UCLA, 1986-89; therapeutic endoscopy fellow Sch. Medicine Ind. U., 1989-90; asst. prof. medicine and pancreaticobiliary endoscopy UCLA, 1990-92; assoc. prof. medicine Ind. U., 1992—; cons. Bard Interventional Products Adv. Panel, Tewksbury, Mass., 1994—. Contbr. articles to profl. jours. Recipient Glaxo Award for excellence in gastroenterology Midwest Am. Fedn. Clin. Rsch., 1993, Young Scholars Rsch. award World Congress of Gastroenterology, L.A., 1994. Mem. ACP, Am. Coll. Gastroenterology, (editl. bd. Gastrointestinal Endoscopy), Am. Soc. for Gastrointestinal Endoscopy, Am. Gastroent. Assn. Avocations: traveling, skiing, tennis, golf. Office: Ind U Med Ctr 550 University Blvd Ste 2300 Indianapolis IN 46202-5149

SHERMAN, SUSAN JEAN, English language educator; b. N.Y.C., Oct. 30, 1939; d. Monroe and Gertrude Jean (Horn) S. BA, Sarah Lawrence Coll., 1969, MA in Lit., 1971. Tchr. English Riverdale Country Sch., N.Y., 1972—. Author: Give Me Myself, 1961; editor: May Sarton: Among the Usual Days, 1993 (Huntington Hartford fellow 1961, Amy Loveman award 1960), (rec.) Promises to Be Kept, 1962, May Sarton: Selected Letters, 1997. Office: Riverdale Country Sch 5250 Fieldston Rd Bronx NY 10471-2935

SHERMAN, THOMAS FRANCIS, education educator; b. Salamanca, N.Y., Dec. 20, 1946; s. Harry and Ione (Schultz) S.; m. Janice Ann Wade, Aug. 17; children: Piper Lee, Wade Thomas. AA, Paul Smith's Coll., 1967; BA, SUNY, Buffalo, 1970; MEd, Colo. State U., 1975; EdD, U. Colo., 1980. Tchr. Buffalo Pub. Schs., 1970; tchr. Poudre R.I. Pub. Schs., Ft. Collins, Colo., 1971, tchr., reading specialist, 1973-80; sr. resident supr. Lookout Mountain Schs. for Boys, Golden, Colo., 1972; faculty, dir. reading ctr. Ea. N.Mex. U., Portales, 1981-84; faculty Bemidji (Minn.) State U., 1985-90, Winona State U., Rochester, Minn., 1990-92; interim asst. v.p. acad. affairs S.W. State U., Marshall, Minn., 1992-93; interim asst. vice chancellor acad. affairs Minn. State Univ. System, St. Paul, 1993; mem. system quality facilitator team Minn. State U.; chair Winona State Outcomes/Indicators, 1990-92; coord. WSU/Minn. High Success Consortium Grad. Program. Contbr. articles on reading edn. to profl. jours. Bd. mem. Dodge/Fillmore/Olmstead Counties Corrections Bd., 1990-93; elder Presbyn. Ch. Mem. Internat. Reading Assn. (pres. Minn. Coun., cert. of merit, sub chair evaluation team Nat. Coun. Accreditation Tchr. Edn., mem. nat. media award com.), Rochester Kiwanis (bd. dirs. 1992-95), Alpha Upsilon Alpha Internat. (chair steering com.). Democrat. Avocation: former profl. skier. Home: 1735 Walden Ln SW Rochester MN 55902-0901 Office: Winona State U Highway 14 E Rochester MN 55904

SHERMAN, WILLIAM COURTNEY, foreign service officer; b. Edmonton, Ky., Sept. 27, 1923; s. George Frederick and Katherine Courtney (Kinnaird) S.; m. Mary Jane Hazelip, Apr. 28, 1945; children—Katherine Courtney, John Justin, Roger Woodson. AB, U. Louisville, 1946; student, U. Colo., 1945, Okla. A&M Coll., 1945-46, Nat. War Coll., 1967-68. With Mil. Govt., in Korea, 1946-48; ECA mission to Korea, 1948-50; joined Fgn. Service, Dept. State, 1951; vice consul Yokohama, Japan, 1952-54; 3d sec. embassy Tokyo, Japan, 1954-56; assigned State Dept., 1956-60; 1st sec. embassy Rome, Italy, 1960-65; spl. asst. to dep. under sec. state for adminstrn., 1966-67; consul gen. Kobe-Osaka, Japan, 1968-70; counselor for polit. affairs Am. embassy, Tokyo, 1970-73; minister-counselor, dep. chief mission Am. embassy, 1977-81; dir. for Japanese affairs State Dept., Washington, 1973-77; dep. U.S. rep. (with rank of amb.) UN Security Coun., 1981-84; dep. asst. sec. state for East Asian and Pacific Affairs, 1984-86; diplomat in residence Sch. Advanced Internat. Studies, Johns Hopkins U., 1986-94, sr. advisor Reischaver Ctr., 1994—. Served to lt. (j.g.) USNR, 1943-46, 50-51. Mem. Omicron Delta Kappa. Home and Office: 1702 Beaver Cir Reston VA 22090-4407

SHERMAN, ZACHARY, civil and aerospace engineer, consultant; b. N.Y.C., Oct. 26, 1922; s. Harry and Minnie (Schulsinger) S.; m. Bertha Leikin, Mar. 23, 1947; children: Gene Victor, Carol Beth. BCE, CCNY, 1943; MCE, Polytech. U. N.Y., Bklyn., 1953, PhD in Civil Engring. & Mechanics, 1969; MME, Stevens Inst. Tech., 1968. Registered profl. engr., N.Y., N.J. Stress analyst Gen. Dynamics, San Diego, 1943-45; sr. stress analyst Republic Aviation, Farmingdale, N.Y., 1945-47, 59-62; prof. civil engring. U. Miss., Oxford, 1954-59; lectr. civil engring. Stevens Inst. Tech., Hoboken, N.J., 1962-67, CUNY, 1967-69; assoc. prof. aerospace engring. Pa. State U., State College, 1969-73; prin. Dr. Zachary Sherman Cons. Engrs., Long Beach, N.Y., 1973—; aerospace cons. engr. FAA, N.Y.C., 1980-86; designated cons. engr. rep., FAA. Contbr. articles to profl. jours. NSF grantee, 1972. Fellow ASCE; mem. AIAA (v.p. Western Conn. chpt. 1977-78), N.Y. Acad. Scis., Sigma Xi. Achievements include development of beam/beam-column deck suspension bridge, prestressed aircraft wing. Home and Office: 25 Neptune Blvd Apt 7H Long Beach NY 11561-4657

SHERNOFF, ELISE RUBIN, special education educator; b. Savannah, Ga., Aug. 16, 1951; d. Irving and Madeline (Sadler) Rubin; m. Victor Harvey Shernoff, June 4, 1972; children: Jason Noah, Heather Toby. BA in History, Armstrong State Coll., 1973, MEd in Spl. Edn., 1977. Cert. spl. edn. tchr., Ga. Tchr. Myers Mid. Sch., Savannah, 1973, Bartlett Mid. Sch., Savannah, 1973-74, Jenkins High Sch., Savannah, 1976-81, Beach High Sch., Savannah, 1986—; bd. dirs. Rambam Day Sch., Savannah; presenter CEC conf., Denver, 1994, Indpls., 1995, NEA so. regional conf., Biloxi, Miss., 1995. Mem. Coun. for Exceptional Children, Jewish Edn. Alliance (bd. dirs. 1992—), Agudath Achim Synagogue-Sisterhood (life), Hadassah (life), B'nai B'rith Women. Democrat. Jewish. Avocations: cooking, baking, fitness walking.

SHERRATT, GERALD ROBERT, university president; b. Los Angeles, Nov. 6, 1931; s. Lowell Heyborne and Elva Genevieve (Lamb) S. B.S. in Edn., Utah State U., 1953, M.S. in Edn. Adminstrn., 1954; Ph.D. in Adminstrn. Higher Edn., Mich. State U., 1975. Staff assoc. U. Utah, Salt Lake City, 1961-62; dir. high sch. relations Utah State U., Logan, 1962-64, asst. to pres., 1964-77, v.p. for univ. relations, 1977-81; pres. So. Utah U., Cedar City, 1982—; dir. Honeyville Grain Inc., Utah; mem. council pres. Utah System Higher Edn., 1982—; chmn. bd. Utah Summer Games, Cedar City, 1984—; chmn. pres.'s council Rocky Mountain Athletic Conf., Denver, 1984-85. Author hist. pageant: The West: America's Odyssey, 1973 (George Washington Honor medal 1973). Chmn. Festival of Am. West, Logan, Utah, 1972-82; chmn. bd. Utah Shakespearean Festival, Cedar City, 1982-86; chmn. bd. dirs. Salt Lake City Br. of the Fed. Res. Bank of San Francisco; bd. trustees Salt Lake Organizing Com. Winter Olympics 2002; chair bd. trustees Am. Folk Ballet; pres. Utah Higher Edn. Found. 1st lt. USAF, 1954-57. Recipient Editing award Indsl. Editors Assn., 1962, Robins award Utah State U., 1967, Disting. Alumnus award Utah State U., 1974, So. Utah U., 1991, Total Citizen award Cedar City C. of C., 1993; named to Utah Tourism Hall of Fame, 1989. Mem. Am. Assn. State Colls. and Univs., Cache C. of C. (bd. dirs. 1980-82), Phi Kappa Phi, Phi Delta Kappa, Sigma Nu (regent 1976-78). Mem. LDS Ch. Lodge: Rotary. Home: 331 W 200 S Cedar City UT 84720-3101 Office: So Utah U 351 W Center St Cedar City UT 84720-2470

SHERREN, ANNE TERRY, chemistry educator; b. Atlanta, July 1, 1936; d. Edward Allison and Annie Ayres (Lewis) Terry; m. William Samuel Sherren, Aug. 13, 1966. BA, Agnes Scott Coll., 1957; PhD, U. Fla.-Gainesville, 1961. Grad. teaching asst. U. Fla., Gainesville, 1957-61; instr. Tex. Woman's U., Denton, 1961-63, asst. prof., 1963-66; rsch. participant Argonne Nat. Lab., 1973-80, 93, 94; assoc. prof. chemistry N. Cen. Coll., Naperville, Ill., 1966-76, prof., 1976—. Ruling elder Knox Presbyn. Ch., 1971—, clk. of session, 1976-94. Mem. AAAS, AAUP, Am. Chem. Soc., Am. Inst. Chemists, Ill. Acad. Sci., Sigma Xi, Delta Kappa Gamma, Iota Sigma Pi (nat. pres. 1978-81, nat. dir. 1972-78, nat. historian 1989—). Presbyterian. Contbr. articles in field to profl. jours. Office: North Ctrl Coll Dept Chemistry Naperville IL 60566

SHERRER, CHARLES DAVID, college dean, clergyman; b. Marion, Ohio, Sept. 21, 1935; s. Harold D. and Catherine E. (Fye) S. A.B., U. Notre Dame, 1958, M.A., 1965; S.T.L., Gregorian U., 1962; Ph.D., U. N.C., 1969; HHD, King's Coll., 1997. Ordained priest Roman Cath. Ch., 1961. Instr. English U. Portland, Oreg., 1963-64, asst. prof., 1969-74, prof., 1990—, chmn. dept., 1970-74, dean Grad. Sch., 1982-87, mem. Bd. Regents, 1986-87, acad. v.p., 1987-96; pres. King's Coll., Wilkes Barre, Pa., 1974-81; bd. trustees Stonehill Coll., 1992—; dir. studies Holy Cross Fathers, Ind. Province, 1979-88. Office: U Portland Portland OR 97203

SHERRER, GARY, state official; b. Paris, Tex., Oct. 23, 1948; s. Leonard Franklin and Florida Miller S.; m. Judith Lynn McGue; children: Tori Beth, Camill Lynn. Student, Okla. State U., 1966-67; BA, Southeastern Okla. State U., 1973. Rep. Okla. State Dist. 19; dir. Dept. Agr.; Lt. Gov. State of Kans.; editor and pub. rels. supr. Northeast Electric Co., Vinita, Okla., 1974-77; tchr., coach Nashoba Elem. Sch., 1977-80; Please provide the dates for the career section. Pres. Snow Cmty., 1980—, Pushmataha Fair Bd., 1981—; active Jaycees (Outstanding Young Man award).With U.S. Army, 1968-71. Decorated Bronze Star. Baptist. *

SHERRICK, DANIEL NOAH, real estate broker; b. Greenup, Ill., Mar. 28, 1929; s. Conrad Donovan and Helen Lorene (Neeley) S.; m. Dora Ann Moore, Aug. 11, 1957; children: Renata Ann Sherrick McBride, Sherrie Dee Sherrick Sierra. B.S. in Edn., Eastern Ill. U., Charleston, 1956. Owner Midwest Ins. Agy., Greenup, 1956-60; supt. agys. Midwest Life Ins. Co., Lincoln, Nebr., 1960-62; asst. v.p. Gulf Life Ins. Co., Jacksonville, Fla., 1962-71; pres. Bank of Carbondale, Ill., 1971-74, Prescription Learning Corp., Springfield, Ill., 1974-76; exec. v.p. Imperial Industries, Inc., Miami Lakes, Fla., 1976-88, pres., chief exec. officer, 1988-90; broker, salesman Coldwell Banker Residential Real Estate, 1990-91, 93—; pres., bd. dirs. Palmer State Bank, Taylorville, Ill., 1991-93; broker-salesman Coldwell Banker Hunter Realty, 1993—. Pres. Alderman Park Civic Assn., Jacksonville, 1968, Heritage Hills Home Owners Assn., Carbondale, 1973. With USAF, 1948-52. Mem. Am. Legion, Greater Sebring C. of C., VFW, Internat. Torch Club, Masons, Elks. Presbyterian. Home: 6228 Aquavista Dr Sebring FL 33870-7409 Office: Coldwell Banker Hunter Realty 2617 Us Highway 27 S Sebring FL 33870-2127

SHERRIFFS, RONALD EVERETT, communication and film educator; b. Salem, Oreg., Apr. 10, 1934; s. Robert William and Margaret Kathleen (Tutt) S.; m. Mary Lona West, July 9, 1960; children: Ellen, Matthew. BA, San Jose State U., 1955, MA, 1957; PhD, U. So. Calif., 1964. Instr. theater Mich. State U., East Lansing, 1960-61; asst. prof. broadcasting Tex. Tech U., Lubbock, 1964-65; asst. prof. speech U. Oreg., Eugene, 1965-70, assoc. prof., 1970-79, prof. telecomm. and film, 1979-92, chmn. dept. speech, 1978-84, 88-90, prof. journalism and comm., 1993—. Author: (with others) Speech Communication via Radio and TV, 1971, TV Lighting Handbook, 1977, Small Format TV Production, 1985, 3d edit., Video Field Production and Editing, 1994, 4th edit., 1996; prodr., dir. TV programs, 1965—. Mem. Oreg. Pub. Broadcasting Policy Adv. Bd., 1980-88. Served to lt. comdr. USNR, 1957-68, PTO. Faculty enrichment program grantee Can., 1984, 91. Mem. Speech Communication Assn. Am., AAUP, Western States Communication Assn. Clubs: Oreg. Track; McKenzie Flyfishers (Eugene). Office: Univ Oreg Journalism Dept Eugene OR 97403

SHERRILL, H. VIRGIL, securities company executive; b. Long Beach, Calif., 1920. Grad., Yale U., 1942, JD, 1948. Sr. dir. Prudential Securities Inc., N.Y.C. Office: Prudential Securites 199 Water St Fl 34 New York NY 10292-0002

SHERRILL, THOMAS BOYKIN, III, retired newspaper publishing executive; b. Tampa, Fla., Nov. 19, 1930; s. Thomas Boykin Jr. and Mary Emma (Addison) S.; m. Sandra Louise Evans, Dec. 27, 1969; children: Thomas Glenn, Stephen Addison. Circulation dir. Tampa (Fla.) Tribune, 1962-67, Sarasota (Fla.) Herald-Tribune, 1967-75; v.p. circulation The Dispatch Printing Co., Columbus, Ohio, 1975-78, v.p. mktg., 1978-97, bd. dirs., 1977-97; v.p., bd. dirs. Ohio Mag., Inc., Columbus, 1979-97. Chmn. bd. dirs. Salvation Army; trustee, past chmn. bd. dirs. Better Bus. Bur. Ctrl. Ohio, Inc.; bd. dirs. Ctrl. Ohio Ctr. Econ. Edn.; v.p., trustee Columbus Dispatch Charities; exec. bd. mem. Simon Kenton coun. Boy Scouts Am.; past pres. Wesley Glen United Meth. Retirement Ctr.; pres.'s adv. bd. mem. Meth. Theol. Sch.. With USN, 1951-56. Recipient Disting. Svc. award Editor and Pub. Mag., 1978; named hon. pres. Troy State U., 1979, hon. Ky. Col., 1980, hon. lt. col. aide-to-camp to Gov. State of Ala., 1984. Mem. Internat. Circulation Mgrs. Assn. (pres. 1975, Pres's award 1989), Internat. Newspaper Mktg. Assn., Ohio Newspaper Assn. (bd. dirs., pres. 1986-88, Pres.'s award 1990), So. Circulation Mgrs. Assn. (pres. 1967-68, C.W. Bevinger Meml. award 1972), Audit Bur. Circulations (bd. dirs. 1980-90), Am. Advt. Fedn., Navy League, Ohio Newspapers Found., Ohio Circulation Mgrs. Assn (Pres.' award 1989), Columbus Area C. of C., SAR, Internat. Platform Assn., Columbus Met. Club, Athletic Club of Columbus, Muirfield Village Country Club, Kiwanis (pres. 1982). Republican. Home: 5215 Hampton Ln Columbus OH 43220-2270

SHERROD, LLOYD B., nutritionist; b. Goodland, Kans., Mar. 5, 1931; s. Charles and Helen S.; m. Judith Harms Sherrod, Dec. 21, 1963; children: Donna J., Barbara E. BS, S.D. State U., Brookings, 1958; MS, U. Ark., Fayetteville, 1960; PhD, Okla. State U., Stillwater, 1964. Rsch. assoc. Okla. State U., Stillwater, 1963; asst. prof. U. Hawaii, Hilo, 1964-67; from assoc. prof to prof. Tex. Tech. U. Ctr., Pantex, 1967-79; nutrition-chemistry instr. Frank Phillips Coll., Borger, Tex., 1979-88; part-time nutrition instr. Amarillo (Tex.) Coll., 1989-95; ret., 1995; rschr. in field. Contbr. articles to sci. jours. Served with U.S. Army, 1951-53. Mem. AAAS, Am. Soc. Animal Science, Am. Dairy Science Assn., Am. Soc. Agronomy, Am. Inst. Biol. Scis., Tex. Jr. Coll. Tchrs. Assn., Plains Nutrition Coun., Sigma Xi., Phi Kappa Phi, Gamma Sigma Delta. Home: Box 1017 Panhandle TX 79068

SHERROD, LONNIE RAY, foundation administrator, researcher, psychologist; b. Knoxville, Tenn., Sept. 7, 1950; s. Raymond O. and Jane L.

(Lambdin) S.; m. Barbara A. Cornblatt, Jan. 31, 1981; 1 child, Sara Raye. BS, Duke U., 1972; MA, U. Rochester, N.Y., 1974, Yale U., 1976; PhD, Yale U., 1978. Rsch. assoc. Yale U., New Haven, 1978; staff assoc. Social Sci. Rsch. Coun., N.Y.C., 1979-85; sr. program assoc. William T. Grant Found., N.Y.C., 1986-89, v.p. programs, 1990-94; exec. v.p., 1995—; asst. dean grad. faculty New Sch. for Social Rsch., N.Y.C., 1986-89; mem. adj. faculty psychology dept. NYU, N.Y.C., 1980-85, grad. faculty, 1986-91. Co-author: Infant Social Cognition, 1981, Late Adolescence and the Transition to Adulthood, 1993, Stress, Risk and Resiliency in Childhood, 1994; assoc. editor Human Nature, 1989—, Jour. Applied Devel. Sci.; contbr. articles to profl. jours. Mem. program com. Grantmakers of Children and Youth, 1990, N.Y. Regional Assn. of Grantmakers, 1991-94; evaluation com. Nat. Found. Collaboration on Violence Prevention, 1994—; mem. adv. bd. Ctr. Study of Child and Adolescent Devel., Pa. State U., 1992—; bd. dirs. Life Trends, Inc., 1992—, Timber Trails Comty. Assn., 1992—, v.p., 1994—. Mem. APA (co-chair internat. com. 1994—), Am. Psychol. Soc., Soc. Study of Social Biology (sec., treas. N.Y.C. chpt. 1984-90), Internat. Soc. for Study of Behavior Devel., Soc. Rsch. on Adolescence, Soc. for Rsch. in Child Devel. (mem. com. on pub. info. and child devel., chmn. 1993—, chmn. subcom. on pub. info. 1992-94). Office: William T Grant Found 515 Madison Ave New York NY 10022-5403

SHERRY, GEORGE LEON, political science educator; b. Lodz, Poland, Jan. 5, 1924; came to U.S., 1939, naturalized 1945; s. Leon G. and Henrietta (Mess) S.; m. Doris H. Harf, Mar. 6, 1947; 1 child, Vivien Gail Sherry Greenberg. BA summa cum laude, CCNY, 1944; MA, Columbia U., 1951, MA, cert. Russian Inst., 1955, PhM, 1959. Reporter, radio news writer The N.Y. Times, N.Y.C., 1944-46; editor, interpreter, then sr. interpreter UN, N.Y.C., 1946-59, from polit. officer to dir. and dep. to under sec.-gen. for spl. polit. affairs, 1959-84; polit. advisor to missions Congo, Cyprus, India and Pakistan, 1962-66; asst. sec.-gen. for spl. polit. affairs UN (office in charge peacekeeping forces which won Nobel Peace Prize, 1988), N.Y.C., 1984-85; Stuart Chevalier prof. diplomacy and world affairs Occidental Coll., Los Angeles, 1985—; dir. Occidental at-the-UN program, N.Y.C., 1986—; U.S. del. staff Dartmouth Soviet-Am. confs., 1961-94; assoc. seminar on problem of peace Columbia U., N.Y.C.; cons. UN dept. peacekeeping ops., 1992, 93; leader UN tech. mission to Ga., 1993; UN envoy to follow Russian elections, 1993; advisor Internat. Peace Acad., 1993—. Author: The United Nations Reborn: Conflict Control in the Post-Cold War World, 1990; editorial adv. bd. Polit. Sci. Quar., N.Y.C., 1973-89; contbr. articles and revs. to profl. jours. Recipient Townsend Harris medal CCNY, 1993; UN Inst. for Tng. and Rsch. sr. fellow, 1985-93. Mem. Coun. on Fgn. Rels., Internat. Studies Assn., Acad. Coun. on UN Sys., UN Assn.-USA. Democrat. Avocations: piano playing; skiing; sailing. Home: 185 E 85th St Apt 3-c New York NY 10028-2172

SHERRY, HENRY IVAN, marketing consultant; b. Chgo., Aug. 10, 1930; s. Emmanuel H. and Dorothy Harriet S.; B.S. in Bus. Adminstrn., U. Ala., 1952; m. Maxine Rae Gould, Aug. 7, 1955; children—Dale Sara, Michael Jay. Account exec. Jones, Frankel Co., Chgo., 1954-60; account exec., account supr., v.p., group supr. Edward H. Weiss & Co., Chgo., 1960-66; v.p., account supr., sr. mgmt. officer Interpub. Group of Cos.-McCann Erickson, Inc., Atlanta, dir. Communications Counselors Network, 1966-69; sr. v.p., dir., exec. policy com. The Marchalk Co., Atlanta, N.Y.C., 1969-71; pres. Henry Sherry Assocs., Inc., Atlanta, 1971-88; chmn. Sherry & Bellows, Inc., Atlanta, 1988-91; pres. Sherry & Mitchell Inc., 1991—. Mem. assoc. bd. Mt. Sinai Hosp., 1965-66; chmn. pub. info. United Way, 1970; dir. The Temple, 1982—; mem. exec. com. Coverdell for Congress, 1976. Served with U.S. Army, 1952-54. Club: Standard (dir. 1967-68, 84-86). Office: Sherry & Mitchell Inc 1100 Circle 75 Pky NW Ste 800 Atlanta GA 30339-3097

SHERRY, PAUL HENRY, minister, religious organization administrator; b. Tamaqua, Pa., Dec. 25, 1933; s. Paul Edward and Mary Elizabeth (Stein) S.; m. Mary Louise Thornburg, June 4, 1957; children: Mary Elizabeth, Paul David. BA, Franklin and Marshall Coll., 1955; ThM, Union Theol. Sem., N.Y.C., 1958, PhD, 1969; hon. doctorate, Ursinus Coll., 1981, Elmhurst Coll., 1990, Defiance Coll., 1991, Lakeland Coll., Sheboygan, Wis., 1991, Reformed Theological Acad., Debrecen, Hungary, 1994, United Theol. Sem. Twin Cities, 1995. Ordained to ministry United Ch. of Christ, 1958. Pastor St. Matthew United Ch. of Christ, Kenhorst, Pa., 1958-61, Community United Ch. of Christ, Hasbrouck Heights, N.J., 1961-65; mem. staff United Ch. Bd. Homeland Ministry, N.Y.C., 1965-82; exec. dir. Community Renewal Soc., Chgo., 1983-89; pres. United Ch. of Christ, Cleve., 1989—; mem. gen. bd. Nat. Coun. Chs., N.Y.C., 1989—; mem. cen. com. World Coun. Chs., Geneva, 1991—, del. 7th Assembly, Canberra, Australia, 1991; bd. dirs. Ind. Sector, Washington, 1991—. Editor: The Riverside Preachers; editor Jour. Current Social Issues, 1968-80; contbr. numerous articles to religious jours.; host weekly radio programs local sta., 1974-78, 84-85, 93—. Mem. Soc. Christian Ethics. Democrat. Avocations: reading, hiking, cultural events. Home: 13400 Shaker Blvd Cleveland OH 44120-1599 Office: United Ch of Christ 700 Prospect Ave E Cleveland OH 44115-1131

SHERRY, ROBERT JOSEPH, lawyer; b. East Liverpool, Ohio, Dec. 22, 1957; s. Arthur William Jr. and Lillian Ann (Gebauer) S. BA cum laude, Dickinson Coll., 1979; JD, Am. U., 1982. Bar: DC 1982, U.S. Ct. Appeals (D.C. cir.) 1983; U.S. Dist. Ct. (D.C. cir.) U.S. Ct. Claims 1985. Law clk. Hon. Oscar H. Davis U.S. Fed. Ct. of Appeals, Washington, 1982-83; atty McKenna, Conner & Cuneo, Washington, 1983—. Contbr. articles to profl. jours. Mem. ABA, (antitrust sect. and pub. contracts sects. 1983—, comml. products services com. 1984), D.C. Bar Assn. Democrat. Roman Catholic. Avocation: amateur hockey. Office: McKenna & Cuneo Steuart St Tower 1 Market St Flr 27 San Francisco CA 94105

SHERTZER, BRUCE ELDON, education educator; b. Bloomfield, Ind., Jan. 11, 1928; s. Edwin Franklin and Lois Belle S.; m. Carol Mae Rice, Nov. 24, 1948; children: Sarah Ann, Mark Eldon. B.S., Ind. U., 1952, M.S., 1953, Ed.D., 1958. Tchr., counselor Martinsville (Ind.) High Sch., 1952-56; dir. div. guidance Ind. Dept. Pub. Instrn., 1956-58; assoc. dir. project guidance of superior students North Central Assn. Coll. and Secondary Sch., 1958-60; asst. prof. Purdue U., 1960—, assoc. prof., 1962-65, prof., 1965-95, head dept. ednl. studies, 1989-95, prof. emeritus of counseling, 1995—; vis. prof. ednl. psychology U. Hawaii, 1967; Fulbright sr. lectr., Reading, Eng., 1967-68; vis. prof. U. So. Calif. Overseas Grad. Program, 1975, 82; chmn. Nat. Adv. Council for Career Edn., 1976. Author: Career Exploration and Planning 1973, 2d edit., 1976, Fundamentals of Counseling, 3d edit., 1980, Fundamentals of Guidance, 4th edit., 1981, Individual Appraisal, 1979, Career Planning, 3d edit., 1985, also articles. Chmn. bd. trustees Found. Am. Assn. of Counseling and Devel., 1986-87. With AUS, 1946-47. Mem. Am. Counseling Assn. (pres. 1973-74, Disting. Profl. Svc. award 1986). Home: 1620 Western Dr West Lafayette IN 47906-2236 Office: Purdue U Liberal Arts Edn Bldg West Lafayette IN 47907

SHERVA, DENNIS G., investment company executive; b. Mpls., Dec. 3, 1942; s. Garfield Theodore and Dorothy Genevive (Oberlander) S.; m. Cathleen Marybeth Tischer, Oct. 15, 1965. B.A., U. Minn., 1964; M.A., Wayne State U., 1965. Chartered fin. analyst. Fin. analyst 1st Nat. Bank, Mpls., 1965-67; fin. analyst Honeywell, Inc., Mpls., 1967; v.p. Smith, Barney & Co., N.Y.C., 1967-71, Baker, Weeks & Co., N.Y.C., 1971-77; mng. dir. Morgan Stanley & Co., Inc., N.Y.C., 1977—; bd. dirs. Morgan Stanley Ventures, San Francisco, Morgan Stanley Venture Capital, N.Y.C., Morgan Stanley Asset Mgmt. Inc., N.Y.C. Recipient All-Am. Research Team 1st place award Instl. Investor Mag., 1979, 81, 83, 84, 85, 87. Mem. Nat. Assn. Securities Dealers (instl. com. 1985—), N.Y. Athletic Club, Torrington Country Club. Home: 791 Park Ave New York NY 10021-3551 Office: Morgan Stanley & Co Inc 1221 Ave Of The Americas New York NY 10020-1001

SHERVHEIM, LLOYD OLIVER, insurance company executive, lawyer; b. Kensington, Minn., June 22, 1928; s. Lewis and Ruth Amanda (Thronson) S.; m. Ruth Elaine Rhodes, Oct. 29, 1950; children: Daniel, Anne, Heidi, Garold, Robette, Shanna, Bryce. Student, Gustavus Adolphus Coll., 1948-50, U. Minn., 1950-52; B.S., William Mitchell Coll. Law, 1958, LL.B., 1958. Bar: Minn. 1959. Supr., asst. to corp. sec. Investors Diversified Services, Inc., 1952-59; legal counsel Investors Syndicate Life Ins. Co., Mpls., 1959-66; gen. counsel Western Life Ins. Co., St. Paul, 1966-72; corporate sec. St. Paul Cos., Inc., 1969-82, chief legal officer, 1972-78, v.p. legal affairs, 1978-85, sr. v.p. law, corporate sec., 1985-89; corporate sec. St. Paul Fire and Marine Ins. Co., 1969-82; dir. St. Paul Ins. Co., Tex., St. Paul Surplus Lines Ins. Co., St. Paul Mercury Ins. Co., St. Paul Guardian Ins. Co., St. Paul Ins. Co., Ill. Charter patron Minn. Theatre Co., 1958; mem. Lake Elmo City Council, 1970-78; past chmn. protection open space task force Met. Open Space Adv. Bd., 1969-70; trustee William Mitchell Coll. Law, 1981-92, vice chmn., 1983-86, chmn., 1986-89; dir. Minn. Citizens Council on Crime and Justice, 1986-89. With U.S. Army, 1946-48. Mem. ABA, Minn. Bar Assn. (chmn. ins. com. 1964-65, gov. 1980-81), Fed. Bar Assn. (pres. Minn. chpt. 1978-79), Ramsey County Bar Assn. (ethics com. 1978-80), Assn. Life Ins. Counsel, Am. Soc. Corp. Secs., Am. Life Conv. (v.p. Minn. chpt. 1969-71), Am. Judicature Soc., Corp. Counsel Assn. Minn. (dir., pres. 1979-80), Pool and Yacht Club (St. Paul). Lutheran (chmn. bd. trustees). Home and Office: 2325 E Chelsea St Lake Havasu City AZ 86404-5911

SHERWIN, BYRON LEE, religion educator, college official; b. N.Y.C., Feb. 18, 1946; s. Sidney and Jean Sylvia (Rabinowitz) S.; m. Judith Rita Schwartz, Dec. 24, 1972; 1 child, Jason Samuel. BS, Columbia U., N.Y.C., 1966; B of Hebrew Lit., Jewish Theol. Sem. of Am., 1966, M of Hebrew Lit., 1968; MA, NYU, 1969; PhD, U. Chgo., 1978; DHL, Jewish Theol. Sem. Am., 1996. Ordained rabbi, 1970. Prof. Jewish philosophy and mysticism Spertus Coll. Judaica, Chgo., 1970—, v.p. acad. affairs, 1984—. Author: Judaism, 1978, Encountering the Holocaust, 1979, Abraham Joshua Heschel, 1979, Garden of the Generations, 1981, Jerzy Kosinski: Literary Alarm Clock, 1981, Mystical Theology and Social Dissent, 1982, The Golem Legend, 1985, Contents and Contexts, 1987, Thank God, 1989, In Partnership with God: Contemporary Jewish Law and Ethics, 1990, No Religion Is an Island, 1991, Toward a Jewish Theology, 1991, How To Be a Jew: Ethical Teachings of Judaism, 1992, The Theological Heritage of Polish Jews, 1995, Sparks Amongst the Ashes: The Spiritual Legacy of Polish Jewry, 1996, also articles. Recipient Man of Reconciliation award Polish Coun. Christians and Jews, 1992, Presdl. medal, Officer of Order of Merit, Republic of Poland, 1995. Mem. Midwest Jewish Studies Assn. (founding pres.), Am. Philos. Assn., Assn. for Jewish Studies, Rabbinical Assembly, Am. Acad. Religion, Religious Ednl. Assn. Republican. Avocations: cooking, book collecting. Office: Spertus Coll Judaica 618 S Michigan Ave Chicago IL 60605-1900

SHERWIN, JAMES TERRY, lawyer, window covering company executive; b. N.Y.C., Oct. 25, 1933; s. Oscar and Stella (Zins) S.; m. Judith Johnson, June 21, 1955 (div. Apr. 1984); children—Miranda, Alison, Galen; m. Hiroko Inouye, June 15, 1985. BA, Columbia U., 1953, LLB (Stone scholar), 1956. Bar: N.Y. 1956, U.S. Supreme Ct. 1963. Assoc. Kaye, Scholer, Fierman, Hays & Handler, N.Y.C., 1957-60; with GAF Corp., N.Y.C., 1960-83, 84-90, asso. counsel, gen. mgr. European ops., 1969-71, group v.p. photography, 1971-74, exec. v.p. fin. and adminstrn., legal and investment svcs., 1974-83; vice chmn., chief adminstrv. officer GAF Corp., Wayne, N.J., 1984-90; exec. v.p., chief fin. officer Triangle Industries, Inc., 1983-84, Hunter-Douglas N.V., 1991—; exec. v.p., CFO. Bd. dirs. Internat. Rescue Com., chmn. exec. com., v.p. to 1990. Lt. comdr. USCGR, 1956-57. U.S. intercollegiate chess champion, 1951-53, N.Y. State champion, 1951, U.S. speed champion, 1956-57, 59-60, internat. master. Mem. Am. Chess Found. (pres., bd. dirs. to 1990), Marshall (N.Y.) Chess Club (pres. 1967-69, gov. to 1990), Phi Beta Kappa. Home: Stegenhöhe 24, CH 6048 Horw Switzerland Office: Hunter Douglas Mgmt AG, Adligenswilerstrasse 37, 6006 Lucerne Switzerland

SHERWIN, MICHAEL DENNIS, government official; b. Decorah, Iowa, Dec. 29, 1939; m. Diann May, Feb. 6, 1965; children: Catherine, Jennifer, Carolyn, Elizabeth. B.A., Coll. St. Thomas, 1962. Intelligence analyst CIA, Washington, 1963-66; copy editor St. Paul Pioneer Press, 1966-67; personnel mgr. Office Personnel Mgmt. U.S. Civil Service Commn., Washington, 1967-79; dir. human resources CAB, Washington, 1979-81, mng. dir., 1981-84; dir. mgmt. systems FAA, Washington, 1985-91, dep. asst. adminstr. for info. tech., 1991-92, dir. civil aviation security program mgmt., 1992-93; dep. asst. adminstr. USAID, Washington, 1993-96; dir. strategic devel. Oracle Corp., Herndon, Va., 1996—. Recipient Commrs. award U.S. CSC 1978, Adminstr.'s Spl. Achievement award for EEO, FAA, 1986, Meritorious Svc. award Sec. of Transp., 1990, Top 100 award Fed. Computer Week, 1990. Roman Catholic. Office: Oracle Corp AID 196 Van Buren St Herndon VA 22070

SHERWOOD, AARON WILEY, aerodynamics educator; b. St. Louis, Jan. 13, 1915; s. Charles Vliet and Amelia Pauline (Kappler) S.; m. Helene M. Gysin, 1944; children—Susan Helene, Mark Wiley. M.E., Rensselaer Poly. Inst., 1935; M.S., U. Md., 1943. Exptl. engr. Wallace & Tiernan Co., Inc., 1936-38; devel. engr. Assoc. Engring., 1938-39; layout engr. Glenn L. Martin Co., 1939-40; instr. U. Md., 1940-44; aero. project engr. David Taylor Model Basin, 1944-46, prof. aerodynamics, 1946—, acting head dept. aero. engring., 1950-58, head dept. aerospace engring., 1958-67, prof. dept. aerospace engring., 1967-77; in charge wind tunnel lab. Glenn L. Martin Inst. Tech., 1946-55; owner, engring. cons. Aerolab. Author: Aerodynamics, 1946. Fellow ASME (chmn. Washington sect. 1954-55); mem. Am. Inst. Aeros and Astronautics (sect. chmn.), Am. Soc. Engring. Edn., Sigma Xi, Tau Beta Pi, Phi Kappa Phi, Phi Kappa Tau. Home: 3411 Chatham Rd Hyattsville MD 20783-1852 Office: Aerolab 9580 Washington Blvd N Laurel MD 20723-1372 *Instead of carefully planned progress toward long-term fixed goals, I advocate frequent modifications of both goals and access routes according to current circumstances. One should follow his interests, tempered only by the needs of his associates and by firm ethical standards —a sort of intelligent muddling along.*

SHERWOOD, ALLEN JOSEPH, lawyer; b. Salt Lake City, Sept. 26, 1909; s. Charles Samuel and Sarah (Abramson) Shapiro; m. Edith Ziff, Jan. 19, 1941; children—Mary (Mrs. John Marshall), Arthur Lawrence. Student, UCLA, 1927-30; AB, U. So. Calif., 1933, LLB, 1933. Bar: Calif. 1933, U.S. Supreme Ct. 1944. Pvt. practice law L.A., 1933-54, Beverly Hills, 1954-95; legal counsel Internat. Family Planning Rsch. Assn., Inc., 1970-76; bd. dirs. Family Planning Ctrs. Greater L.A., Inc., 1968-84, pres., 1973-76. Mem. editorial bd. So. Calif. Law Rev., 1932-33. Contbr. articles to profl. jours. Mem. Calif. Atty. Gen.'s Vol. Adv. Coun. and its legis. subcom., 1972-78. Mem. Med.-Legal Soc. So. Calif. (bd. dirs. 1966-74), ABA, L.A. County Bar Assn., Beverly Hills Bar Assn., State Bar of Calif., Am. Arbitration Assn. (nat. panel arbitrators 1965—), Order of Coif, Tau Delta Phi, Brentwood Country Club (L.A.), Masons. Home: 575 Moreno Ave Los Angeles CA 90049-4840

SHERWOOD, ARTHUR LAWRENCE, lawyer; b. L.A., Jan. 25, 1943; s. Allen Joseph and Edith (Ziff) S.; m. Frances Merele, May 1, 1970; children: David, Chester. BA magna cum laude, U. Calif.-Berkeley, 1964; MS, U. Chgo., 1965; JD cum laude, Harvard U., 1968. Bar: Calif. 1969, US. dist. cts. (cen. dist.) Calif. 1968 (no. dist.) Calif. 1971 (so. dist.) Calif. 1973 (ea. dist.) Calif. 1973, U.S. Ct. Appeals (9th cir.) 1973, U.S. Ct. Appeals (D.C. cir.) 1991, U.S. Supreme Ct., 1980. Instr. UCLA Law Sch., 1968-69; assoc. Gibson, Dunn & Crutcher, Los Angeles, 1968-75, ptnr., 1975—; judge pro tem Los Angeles Mcpl. and Superior Ct., 1980—; instr. law, UCLA, 1968-69, arbitrator N.Y. Stock Exchange., Nat. Futures Assn. Co-author: Civil Procedure During Trial, 1995, Civil Procedure Before Trial, 1990, contbr articles to profl. jours. NASA fellow U. Chgo., 1964-65; chmn. Far Ea. Art Coun., L.A. County Mus. Art, 1992—. Mem. ABA, L.A. County Bar Assn., Calif. Bar Assn., Phi Beta Kappa. Republican. Avocations include: art, 18th century Am. history. Office: Gibson Dunn & Crutcher 333 S Grand Ave Fl 45 Los Angeles CA 90071-1504

SHERWOOD, ARTHUR MORLEY, lawyer; b. Buffalo, Oct. 3, 1939; s. Frederick T. and Neva E. (Merrill) S.; m. Karen H. Hilstad, Apr. 2, 1964; children: Laurel Ann, Carolyn Margaret. BA, Harvard U., 1961; JD, U. Mich., 1964. Bar: Mich. 1965, N.Y. 1967, U.S. Supreme Ct. 1989. Law clk. to Hon. Ralph M. Freeman U.S. Dist. Ct. (ea. dist.) Mich., Detroit, 1964-66; pntr. Phillips, Lytle, Hitchcock, Blaine & Huber, Buffalo, 1971—. Contbr. articles to Trusts and Estates, N.Y. State Bar Jour. and N.Y. Tax Svc. Asst. chancellor Episcopal Diocese of Western N.Y., 1982—; mem. adv. com. N.Y. State Legislature on N.Y. Estates, Powers and Trusts Law, Surrogate's Ct. Procedure. Fellow Am. Coll. Trust and Estate Counsel, N.Y. Bar Found.; mem. N.Y. State Bar Assn. (chairperson trusts and estates law sect. 1987). Home: 3770 Windover Dr Hamburg NY 14075-6322 Office: Phillips Lytle Hitchcock Blaine & Huber 3400 Marine Midland Ctr Buffalo NY 14203-2887

SHERWOOD, JAMES ALAN, physician, scientist, educator; b. Oneida County, N.Y., Jan. 4, 1953; s. Robert Merriam and Sally (Trevett-Edgett) S. AB, Hamilton Coll., 1974; MD, Columbia U., 1978. Diplomate Nat. Bd. Med. Examiners, Am. Bd. Internal Medicine. Intern Duke U. Med. Ctr., Durham, N.C., 1978-79; resident physician Strong Meml. Hosp., Rochester, N.Y., 1979-81; fellow U. Rochester Sch. Medicine and Dentistry, 1981-83, NIH, Bethesda, Md., 1983-86; rsch. investigator Walter Reed Army Inst. Rsch., Washington, 1986-92; vis. scientist Clin. Rsch. Ctr. Kenya Med. Rsch. Inst., Nairobi, 1987-92; physician Saradidi Rural Health Programme, Nyilima, Kenya, 1987-92; rsch. cons. Rockville, Md., 1992-93; physician St. Mary's Hosp., Waterbury, Conn., 1993—; clin. instr. Sch. Medicine Yale U., 1994—. Contbr. chpt. to book, articles to profl. jours. Comty. svc. vol. The Door, N.Y.C., 1976-77; vol. physician Washington Free Clinic, 1985-87; charity Sisters of St. Joseph of Chambery. Lt. col. Med. Corps, USAR, 1986-92. Recipient Norton prize in chemistry, 1974, Underwood prize in chemistry, 1974. Fellow Am. Coll. Physicians; mem. Med. Soc. D.C., Am. Fedn. Clin. Rsch., Am. Soc. Tropical Medicine and Hygiene, Muthaiga Club, Phi Beta Kappa, Sigma Xi. Avocations: drawing, book collecting. Office: PO Box 112 Waterbury CT 06720-0112

SHERWOOD, JOAN KAROLYN SARGENT, career counselor; b. Wichita, Kans., July 11, 1934; d. James Wirth and Ann K. (Freeburg) Sargent; m. Howard Kenneth Sherwood, Jan. 26, 1956 (div. 1966); children: Diane Elizabeth, Karolyn Sherwood Krause, David Matthew. BS, Kans. State U., 1956; MA, Wichita State U., 1964; PhD, U. Kans., 1978. Asst. dir. student fin. aid U. Kans., Lawrence, 1973-78, asst. vice chancellor/student affairs, 1978-81; asst. vice chancellor/student affairs U. Mo., Kansas City, 1981-84; v.p. student affairs Western Wash. U., Bellingham, 1984-87; pres./owner Corp. Tng. Assurance, Kansas City, 1987-95; career coord. Park Coll., Parkville, Mo., 1995—; program chair Phi Delta Kappa, Lawrence, 1983-84; initiation chair Phi Kappa Phi, Kansas City, 1983-84; organizer Singles Connection, Kansas City, 1983-84; creator SummerStart, Bellingham, 1988-89. Contbr.: Theatre Companies of the World, 1986; female voice: (film) Junction City, 1973. Long range planning coord. Ch. Redeemer, Kansas City, 1994; workshop facilitator South Side Jr. C. of C., Kansas City, 1991; presenter Centurians, Kansas City, 1982; spkr. Pi Lambda Theta, 1983; vol., resident mgr. Hillcrest Ministries, 1996—. NDEA fellow, 1969. Mem. ASTD, Phi Kappa Phi. Democrat. Roman Catholic. Avocations: creative writing, reading, films. Home: 422 N Missouri #1 Liberty MO 64068 Office: Park Coll 8700 NW River Park Dr Kansas City MO 64152-4358

SHERWOOD, KENNETH WESLEY, information systems executive, consultant; b. Denver, Nov. 15, 1943; s. Richard Wesley Sherwood and Mary Ellen (Sorling) McClure; m. Virginia Kay Betts, June 24, 1966; children: Jeremy James, Pamela Ann. BS summa cum laude, Met. State Coll., Denver, 1971. Missile mechanic helper Martin Marietta, Littleton, Colo., 1963-64, electronics technician, 1964, communications ctr. operator, 1968-69; systems rep. Burroughs Corp., Denver, 1971-76; systems supr. Burroughs Corp., Las Vegas, Nev., 1976-79; dept. mgr. Burroughs Corp., Atlanta, 1979-83, mgr. support ctr., 1983-85; sr. mgr. profl. svcs. UNISYS, Atlanta, 1985—; cons. in pers. computer and check processing fields. Sgt. U.S. Army, 1964-68, Tokyo. Methodist. Avocations: computers, handyman activities, fishing. Home: 5271 Lanford Springs Ct SW Lilburn GA 30247-6551 Office: UNISYS 5550A Peachtree Pkwy Norcross GA 30092-2555

SHERWOOD, LILLIAN ANNA, librarian, retired; b. South Bend, Ind., Dec. 22, 1928; d. Julius Andrew and Mary (Kerekes) Takacs; m. Neil Walter Sherwood, May 31, 1953; children: Susan Kay Huff, Nancy Ellen Coney, James Walter. AB in Home Econs., Ind. U., 1951, postgrad., 1978-83. Cert. libr. IV, Ind., 1984. Lab. tech. Lobund Inst., Notre Dame (Ind.) U., 1951-53; substitute tchr. Plymouth (Ind.) Community Schs., 1969-73; bookkeeper, processing clk. Plymouth (Ind.) Pub. Libr., 1973-76, audio-visual coord., 1976-79, reference and genealogical libr., 1980-93; retired, 1994; project dir. Ind. Heritage rsch. grant, Ind. Humanities Coun. and Ind. Hist. Soc., 1992-93; orgn. and verification com. Geneal. Socs., Pioneer Soc., Marshall County, Ind., Plymouth, 1988—. Mem. bd. dirs. Child Day Care Ctr. of Plymouth, 1971-75, pres., 1974. Mem. AAUW (v.p. 1966-68, pres. 1971-73, 85-87, 91-93), Marshall County Geneal. Soc. (v.p. 1986-87, treas. 1997), Omicron Nu. Methodist. Avocations: genealogy, music appreciation, gardening, travel. Home: 808 Thayer St Plymouth IN 46563-2859

SHERWOOD, (PETER) LOUIS, retail executive; b. London, Oct. 27, 1941; came to U.S., 1979; s. Peter and Mervyn (De Toll) S.; m. Nicole Dina, Aug. 22, 1970; children: Christopher, Anne, Isabelle. BA, Oxford U., 1963, MA, 1966; MBA, Stanford U., 1965. Fin. planning officer Morgan Grenfell & Co. Ltd., London, 1965-68; gen. mgr. Melias Ltd., Welwyn Garden City, Eng., 1969-72; dir. Anglo-Continental Investment & Fin. Co. Ltd., London, 1973-79; chmn., chief exec. officer Maidenhead Investments, London, 1977-79; sr. v.p. Grand Union Co., Elmwood Park, N.J., 1979-85; pres. Gt. Atlantic & Pacific Tea Co. Inc., Montvale, N.J., 1985-88; chmn., chief exec. officer Gateway Foodmarkets, Bristol, Eng., 1988-89; chmn. Airedale Holdings plc, Keighley, Yorkshire, Eng., 1990-92, HTV Group plc, Cardiff, Wales, 1991—, New Look plc, Weymouth, Dorset, 1994-96; non-exec. dir. Halifax plc. Harkness fellow Stanford U., 1965.

SHERWOOD, LOUIS MAIER, physician, scientist, pharmaceutical company executive; b. N.Y.C., Mar. 1, 1937; s. Arthur Joseph and Blanche (Burger) S.; m. Judith Brimberg, Mar. 27, 1966; children: Jennifer Beth, Arieh David. AB with honors, Johns Hopkins U., 1957; MD with honors, Columbia U., 1961. Diplomate Am. Bd. Internal Medicine, Subsplty. Bd. in Endocrinology and Metabolism. Intern Presbyn. Hosp., N.Y.C., 1961-62, asst. resident in medicine, 1962-63; clin. assoc. research fellow Nat. Heart Inst., NIH, Bethesda, Md., 1963-66; NIH trainee endocrinology and metabolism Coll. Physicians and Surgeons, Columbia U., N.Y.C., 1966-68; assoc. medicine Beth Israel Hosp. and Harvard Med. Sch., Boston, 1968-69; chief endocrinology Beth Israel Hosp., 1968-72; asst. prof. medicine Harvard U., 1969-71, assoc. prof., 1971-72; physician-in-chief, chmn. dept. medicine Michael Reese Hosp. and Med. Ctr., Chgo., 1972-80; prof. medicine, div. biol. scis. Pritzker Sch. Medicine, U. Chgo., 1972-80; Ted and Florence Baumritter prof. medicine and biochemistry Albert Einstein Coll. Medicine, 1980-88, vis. prof. medicine, 1989—, chmn. dept. medicine, 1980-87; physician-in-chief Montefiore Hosp. and Med. Ctr., N.Y.C., 1980-87; adj. prof. medicine U. Pa., 1993—; sr. v.p. med. and sci. affairs Merck, Sharp & Dohme Internat., 1987-89; exec. v.p. worldwide devel. Merck, Sharp & Dohme Rsch. Labs., 1989-92, sr. v.p. U.S. Med. and Sci. Affairs Merck Human Health, 1992—; Josiah Macy Jr. Found. fellow and vis. scientist Weizmann Inst., Israel, 1978-79; assoc. mem. bd. on subcom. endocrinology and metabolism Am. Bd. Internal Medicine, 1977-83; bd. dirs. UROCOR Inc.; med. adv. bd. HPR, 1996—; pres., chief med. officer Bone Measurement Inst., 1996—. Editor: Beth Israel seminars New Eng. Jour. Medicine, 1968-71; mem. editorial bd. Endocrinology, 1969-73; assoc. editor Metabolism, 1970-85, Gen. Medicine B Study Sect., NIH, 1975-79; mem. editorial bd. Yr. in Endocrinology, 1976-86, Calcified Tissue Internat., 1978-80, Internal Medicine Alert, 1979-89; contbr. numerous articles on endocrinology, protein hormones, calcium metabolism and ectopic proteins to jours. Trustee Michael Reese Med. Ctr., 1974-77; mem. vis. council CUNY Med. Sch., 1986—; mem. alumni council Columbia Coll. Physicians and Surgeons, 1986—. Served as surgeon USPHS, 1963-66. Recipient Joseph Mather Smith prize for outstanding alumni research Coll. Physicians and Surgeons, Columbia U., 1972, Sr. Class Teaching award U. Chgo., 1976, 77; grantee USPHS, 1968-88. Fellow ACP (Outstanding Contbn. to Internal Medicine award 1987); mem. AAAS, Am. Fedn. Clin. Rsch. (bd. dirs. Found. 1989-92, Spl. Recognition award 1992), Am. Inst. Chemists, Am. Soc. Biol. Chemists, Am. Soc. Clin. Investigation (pres. 1982-83), Assn. Am. Physicians, Endocrine Soc., Am. Physicians Fellowship for Medicine in Israel (pres. 1993—), N.Y. Acad. Medicine (bd. dirs. 1991-95), Am. Soc. Hypertension (bd. dirs. 1992-97), Mass. Med. Soc., Ctrl. Soc. Clin. Rsch., Assn. Program Dirs. Internal Medicine (coun. 1979-85, pres. 1983-84), Assn. Profs. Medicine, Chgo. Soc. Internal Medicine, Assn. Prof. Med. Industry Roundtable, Interurban Clin. Club, Phi Beta Kappa, Alpha Omega Alpha. Achievements include research in protein and polypeptide hormones: structure, function and regulation of secretion; molecular studies of hormone biosynthesis; clinical pharmacology, new drug development, outcomes research and disease management. Office: Merck & Co US Human Health West Point PA 19486 *To be a successful leader, you must be willing to surround yourself with outstanding individuals, give them your full support and enjoy their growth.*

SHERWOOD, PATRICIA WARING, artist, educator; b. Columbia, S.C., Dec. 19, 1933; d. Clark du Val and Florence (Yarbrough) Waring; divorced; children: Cheryl Sherwood Kraft, Jana Sherwood Kern, Marikay Sherwood Taitt. BFA magna cum laude, Calif. State U., Hayward, 1970; MFA, Mills Coll., Oakland, Calif., 1974; postgrad., San Jose State U., 1980-86. Cert. tchr., Calif. Tchr. De Anza Jr. Coll., Cupertino, Calif., 1970-78, Foothill Jr. Coll., Los Altos, Calif., 1972-78, West Valley Jr. Coll., Saratoga, Calif., 1978—; artist-in-residence Centrum Frans Masereel, Kasterlee, Belgium, 1989. One-woman shows include Triton Mus., Santa Clara, Calif., 1968, RayChem Corp., Sunnyville, Calif., 1969, Palo Alto (Calif.) Cultural Ctr., 1977, Los Gatos (Calif.) Mus., 1992, Stanford U. faculty club, Palo Alto, 1993, d.p. Fong Gallery, San Jose, Calif., 1995, 97, Heritage Bank, San Jose, 1997, City Jr. Coll., d.p. Fong Gallery, San Jose, 1997; exhibited in group shows at Tressider Union Stanford U., 1969, Oakland (Calif.) Mus. Kaiser Ctr., 1969, Sonoma (Calif.) State Coll., 1969, Bank Am., San Francisco, 1969, San Francisco Art Festival, 1969, 70, U. Santa Clara, 1967, Charles and Emma Frye Mus., Seattle, 1968, Eufrat Gallery DeAnza Coll., Cupertino, 1975, San Jose Mus. Art, 1976, Lytton Ctr., Palo Alto, 1968 (1st award), Zellerbach Ctr., San Francisco, 1970, Works Gallery, San Jose, 1994; represented in permanent collections Mills Coll., Bank Am., San Francisco, Heritage Bank, San Jose. Art judge studnet show Stanford U., Palo Alto, 1977; mem. d.p. Fong Gallery, San Jose, Calif., 1994. Nat. Endowment for Arts/We. States Art Fedn. fellow, 1994. Mem. Calif. Print Soc., Womens Caucus for Arts, Internat. Platform Assn. Home: 1500 Arriba Ct Los Altos CA 94024-5941 Office: West Valley Jr Coll Art Dept 14000 Fruitvale Ave Saratoga CA 95070-5640

SHERWOOD, ROBERT PETERSEN, retired sociology educator; b. Black Diamond, Wash., May 17, 1932; s. James Brazier and Zina (Petersen) S.; m. Merlene Burningham, Nov. 21, 1951; children: Robert Lawrence, Richard William, Rolene, RaNae. BS, U. Utah, 1956, MS, 1957; EdD, U. Calif., Berkeley, 1965. Tchr. Arden-Carmichael Sch. Dist., Carmichael, Calif., 1957-59; vice prin. jr. high Arden-Carmichael Sch. Dist., 1960-61, prin. jr. high, 1962-65; v.p., prin. San Juan Unified Sch. Dist., Sacramento, 1966-70; assoc. prof. Calif. State U., Sacramento, 1966-71; dir. outreach progs. Am. River Coll., Sacramento, 1971-73; acting assoc. dean of instrn. Am. River Coll., 1973-74, prof. sociology, 1970-92, chmn. sociology/anthropology dept., 1980-86, retired, 1992; pres. acad. senate Am. River Coll., 1990-91. With USN, 1953-55. Recipient Merit Recognition award, Boy Scouts Am., 1989. Mem. NEA, Calif. Tchrs. Assn., Faculty Assn. Calif. Community Colls., Western Assn. Schs. and Colls., Calif. Fedn. Coll. Profs., Phi Delta Kappa (life). Mem. LDS Ch. Avocations: reading, writing, woodworking, travel. Home: 4053 Esperanza Dr Sacramento CA 95864-3069

SHERZER, HARVEY GERALD, lawyer; b. Phila., May 19, 1944; s. Leon and Rose (Levin) S.; m. Susan Bell, Mar. 28, 1971; children: Sheri Ann, David Lloyd. BA, Temple U., 1965; JD with honors, George Washington U., 1968. Bar: D.C. 1970, U.S. Ct. Appeals (D.C. cir.) 1970, U.S. Ct. Fed. Claims 1970, U.S. Ct. Appeals (fed. cir.) 1970, U.S. Supreme Ct. 1974. Law clk. to trial judges U.S. Ct. Fed. Claims, Washington, 1968-69; law clk. to chief judge U.S. Ct. Appeals for Fed. Cir., Washington, 1969-70; assoc. Sellers, Conner & Cuneo, Washington, 1970-75, ptnr., 1975-80; ptnr. McKenna, Conner & Cuneo, Washington, 1980-82, Pettit & Martin, Washington, 1982-85, Howrey & Simon, Washington, 1985—; adv. bd. The Govt. Contractor, 1996—. Author: (with others) A Complete Guide to the Department of Defense Voluntary Disclosure Program, 1996; contbr. articles to profl. jours. Office: Howrey & Simon 1299 Pennsylvania Ave NW Washington DC 20004-2400

SHESTACK, ALAN, museum administrator; b. N.Y.C., June 23, 1938; s. David and Sylvia P. (Saffran) S.; m. Nancy Jane Davidson, Sept. 24, 1967. BA, Wesleyan U., 1961, DFA (hon.), 1978; MA, Harvard U., 1963. Mus. curator graphic art Nat. Gallery Art, Washington, 1965-67; assoc. curator prints and drawings Yale Art Gallery, New Haven, 1967-68; curator prints and drawings Yale Art Gallery, 1968-71, dir., 1971-85; adj. prof. history of art Yale U., 1971-85; dir. Mpls. Inst. Art, 1985-87, Boston Mus. Fine Arts, 1987-93; dep. dir. Nat. Gallery of Art, Washington, 1994—; mem. adv. com. Art Mus., Princeton, 1972-75; mem. vis. com. Harvard U. Art Mus., 1990-95; mem. mus. panel Nat. Endowment for the Arts, 1974-77; mem. com. prints and illustrated books Mus. Modern Art, N.Y.C., 1972—; mem. Fed. Arts and Artifacts Indemnification Panel, 1979-83. Author: Fifteenth Century Engravings of Northern Europe, 1967, The Engravings of Martin Schongauer, 1968, Master LCZ and Master WB, 1971, Exhibitions Organized and Catalogued: Master E.S. 1967, The Danube School, 1969, Hans Baldung Grien, Prints and Drawings, 1981; contbr. articles to profl. jours. Woodrow Wilson fellow Harvard U., 1963, David E. Finley fellow, 1963-65. Mem. Print Coun. Am. (bd. dirs., v.p. 1970-71), Coll. Art Assn. (bd. dirs. 1972-76), Am. Assn. Mus., Am. Fedn. Arts (trustee 1981-94), Alpha Delta Phi, Phi Beta Kappa. Office: Nat Gallery of Art Washington DC 20565

SHESTACK, JEROME JOSEPH, lawyer; b. Atlantic City, N.J., Feb. 11, 1925; s. Isidore and Olga (Shankman) S.; m. Marciarose Schleifer, Jan. 28, 1951; children: Jonathan Michael, Jennifer. A.B., U. Pa., 1944; LL.B., Harvard U., 1949. Bar: Ill. 1950, Pa. 1952. Teaching fellow Northwestern U. Law Sch., Chgo., 1949-50; asst. prof. law, faculty editor La. State Law Sch., Baton Rouge, 1950-52; dep. city solicitor City of Phila., 1952, 1st dep. solicitor, 1952-55; ptnr. Schnader, Harrison, Segal & Lewis, Phila. and Washington, 1956-91, Wolf, Block, Schorr & Solis-Cohen, Phila., 1991—; adj. prof. law U. Pa., 1956; U.S. amb. to UN Human Rights Commn., 1979-80; U.S. del. to ECOSOC, UN, 1980; sr. U.S. del. to Helsinki Accords Conf., 1979-80; mem. U.S. Commn. on Improving Effectiveness of UN, 1989—; chmn . Internat. League Human Rights, 1973—, U.S. del. to CSCE Conf., Moscow, 1991; founder, chmn. Lawyers Com. Internat. Human Rights, 1978-80, Jacob Blaustein Inst. Human Rights, 1988-92; mem. nat. adv. com. legal svcs. OEO, 1965-72; bd. dirs., exec. com. Laywers Com. Civil Rights. Editor: (with others) Rights of Americans, 1971, Human Rights, 1979, International Human Rights, 1985, Bill of Rights: A Bicentennial View, 1991, Understanding Human Rights, 1992, Thomas Jefferson; Lawyer, 1993, Abraham Lincoln, Circuit Lawyer, 1994. Mem. exec. com. Nat. Legal Aid and Defender Assn., 1970-80; trustee Eleanor and Franklin Roosevelt Inst., 1986—; bd. govs. Tel Aviv U., 1983—; v.p. Am. Jewish Com., 1984-89; chmn. bd. dirs. Am. Poetry Ctr., 1976-91; trustee Free Libr. Phila., vice chmn., 1989—. With USNR, 1943-46. Rubin fellow Columbia U. Law Sch., 1984; hon. fellow U. Pa. Law Sch., 1980. Mem. ABA (ho. of dels. 1971-73, 77—, mem. jud. com. 1985-90, bd. govs. 1992-95, exec. com. 1994-95, pres. elect 1996, pres. 1997), Internat. Bar Assn. (chmn. com. on human rights 1990-94), Am. Soc. Internat. Law (exec. com. 1993-95), Am. Law Inst., Am. Coll. Trial Lawyers, Am. Acad. Appellate Lawyers, Order of Coif. Home: Parkway House 2201 Pennsylvania Ave Philadelphia PA 19130-3513 Office: Wolf Block Schorr & Solis-Cohen Packard Bldg 12th Fl SE Corner 15th & Chestnut Sts Philadelphia PA 19102-2678

SHESTACK, MELVIN BERNARD, editor, author, filmmaker, television producer; b. Bklyn., Aug. 18, 1931; s. David and Sylvia Pearl (Saffran) S.; m. Jessica Gifford, Feb. 13, 1965; 1 dau., Victoria J.; 1 dau. by previous marriage, Lisa F. A.B., U. So. Calif., 1953; postgrad., U. Rochester, N.Y. U., New Sch. Social Research. Assoc. editor Sat. Eve. Post, 1965-67; staff producer CBS-TV News, 1967-69; asso. producer Sta. WOR-TV, 1970; exec. editor True mag., N.Y.C., 1971-75, editor-in-chief, 1975; editor In The Know mag., N.Y.C., 1975—; exec. dir. Ponca Inst. Am. Studies, 1976-80; exec. editor Antelope Classics, Empire Edits., 1977—; v.p., dir. spl. projects Montcalm Pub. Co., 1980-85; pres. Gifford-Shestack Assocs., 1985-89; exec. v.p., dir. creative devel. Gt. Western Entertainment Corp., N.Y.C., 1989—. Producer, writer: (documentary) The Forgotten American, 1967, Changing Health Care, 1986; dir., producer: (PBS series) America's Challenge, 1990; author: The Country Music Encyclopedia, 1974; co-author: (filmscript) The Soul, 1978, Secrets of Success, 1980, "How'm I Doing?": The Wit and Wisdom of Ed Koch, 1981, New Country Encyclopedia, 1993, (screenplay) 5 Rooms, 1992; pub. Fresh Ayer, 1994; contbr. articles to profl. publs. Served with AUS, 1953-55. Recipient Brown-Nickerson award for best religious radio program, 1967. Mem. Pi Lambda Phi. Home: 247 Front St Brooklyn NY 11201 Office: Centuri Internat Prodns 1650 Broadway New York NY 10036 *I have been blessed by a spectacular marriage. My wife is my best friend and continues to prove her devotion. I am an enthusiast. I meet a great many successful people and they share two qualities. They are serious about what they do and they're enthusiasts. They also work to the very top of their ability and rarely procrastinate. I am enthusiastic and serious, but I am given to procrastination. When I conquer that problem, I believe there is no end to what I can accomplish.*

SHESTOCK, LINDA, community foundation executive. BA, Canisius Coll.; MBA, U. La Verne (Calif.). Asst. contr. Claremont (Calif.) Colls.; exec. v.p., CFO Calif. Cmty. Found., L.A. Office: Calif Cmty Found 606 S Olive St Ste 2400 Los Angeles CA 90014-1501

SHETH, JAGDISH NANCHAND, business administration educator; b. Rangoon, Burma, Sept. 3, 1938; came to U.S., 1961, naturalized, 1975; s. Nanchand Jivraj and Diwaliben Sheth; m. Madhuri Ratilal Shah, Dec. 22, 1962; children—Reshma J., Raju J. B.Com. with honors, U. Madras, 1960; M.B.A., U. Pitts., 1962; Ph.D., 1966. Research asso., asst. prof. Grad. Sch. Bus., Columbia U., 1963-65; asst. prof. M.I.T., 1965-66, Columbia U., 1966-69; asso. prof. bus. adminstrn. U. Ill., Urbana, 1969-71; acting head dept. U. Ill., 1970-72, prof. and research prof., 1971-73, I.B.A. Disting. prof. and research prof., 1973-79, Walter H. Stellner Disting. prof. and research prof., 1979-83; Robert E Brooker Disting. prof. mktg. and research U. So. Calif., Los Angeles, 1983-91; Charles H. Kellstadt prof. mktg. Emory U., Atlanta, 1991—; founder, dir. Ctr. for Telecommunications Mgmt. U. So. Calif, 1983—, Ctr. Relationship Mktg. Emory U.; vis. prof. Indian Inst. Mgmt., 1969; vis. lectr. Internat. Mktg. Inst., Harvard U., 1969; Albert Frey vis. prof. mktg. U. Pitts., 1974; condr. seminars for industry and govt.; cons. to industry. Author: (with John A. Howard) The Theory of Buyer Behavior, 1969, (with S.P. Sethi) Multinational Business Operations: Advanced Readings, 4 vols, 1973, (with A. Woodside and P. Bennett) Consumer and Industrial Buying Behavior, 1977; (with Bruce Newman): A Theory of Political Choice Behavior, 1986; (with Dennis Garrett) Marketing Theory, 1986; (with S. Ram) Bringing Innovation to Market; (with Gary Frazier) Theories of Marketing Practice; (with Milind Lele) The Customer is Key; editor: Models of Buyer Behavior, 1974, (with Peter L. Wright) Marketing Analysis for Societal Problems, 1974, Multivariable Methods for Market and Survey Research, 1977, Winning Back Your Market, 1984, (with David Gardener and Dennis Garrett) Marketing Theory: Evolution and Evaluation, 1988, also (with Abdol Reza and Goli Eslghi) 9 vols. on global bus., 1989-90, (with Bruce Newman and Barbara Gross) Consumption Values and Choice Behavior, 1990; series editor Research in Marketing, 1978—, Research in Consumer Behavior, 1984—; contbr. articles profl. jours. Recipient Viktor Mataja medal Austrian Rsch. Soc., 1976, Mktg. Educator award Sales and Mktg. Execs. Internat., 1991; Mgmt. Program for Execs. fellow, S & H Green Stamps fellow, 1963-64. Fellow APA, Acad. Mktg. Sci. (Disting. fellow 1996, Mktg. Educator award 1989); mem. Am. Mktg. Assn. (P.D. Converse award 1992). Home: 1626 Mason Mill Rd NE Atlanta GA 30329-4133

SHETLER, CHRISTOPHER DAVID, chiropractor; b. Oneida, N.Y., Apr. 8, 1960; s. Harold Henry and Theila Marie (Bowman) S. AAS, Ricks Coll., 1984; D of Chiropractic, Tex. Chiropractic Coll., 1987. Lic. chiropractic physician, Ill. Physician Head-to-Toe Chiropractic, Hillsboro, Ill., 1988-89, Shetler Health Ctr., Irving, Ill., 1991-93, Shetler Clinic, Johnston City, Ill., 1993-94; physician, ctr. dir. Shetler Chiropractic Ctr., Effingham, Ill., 1994—. Capt. CAP. With U.S. Army, 1989-91. Mem. Motion Palpation Inst., Zone Fitness Ctr., C&S Self Defense Assn., Rotary Internat. Avocations: martial arts, computers, weight tng., reading, movies. Home: 802 W Edgar Ave Effingham IL 62401 Office: Shetler Chiropractic Ctr 802 W Edgar Ave Effingham IL 62401-2525

SHETTLES, LANDRUM BREWER, obstetrician-gynecologist; b. Pontotoc, Miss., Nov. 21, 1909; s. Basil Manly and Sue (Mounce) S.; m. Priscilla Elinor Schmidt, Dec. 18, 1948; children—Susan Flora, Frances Louise, Lana Brewer, Landrum Brewer, David Ernest, Harold Manly and Alice Annmarie (twins). B.A., Miss. Coll., 1933, D.Sc. (hon.), 1966; M.S. (fellow 1933-34), U. N.M., 1934; Ph.D., Johns Hopkins, 1937, M.D., 1943. Diplomate: Am. Bd. Obstretrics and Gynecology, N. Am. sect. obstetrics and gynecology Pan Am. Med. Assn. Instr. biology Miss. Coll., 1932-33; biologist U.S. Bur. Fisheries, 1934; instr. biology Johns Hopkins, 1934-37, research fellow, 1937-38; research fellow Nat. Com. Maternal Health, N.Y.C., 1938-43; intern Johns Hopkins Hosp., 1943-44; resident Columbia-Presbyn. Med. Center, N.Y.C., 1947-51; attending obstetrician-gynecologist Columbia-Presbyn. Med. Center, 1951-73, Doctors, Polyclinic and Flower-Fifth Av hosps., N.Y.C., 1974-75; chief obstetrician-gynecologist Gifford Meml. Hosp., Randolph, Vt., 1975-81, Star Clinic, Las Vegas, Nev., 1981-82, Oasis Clinic, Las Vegas, Nev., 1982-85; attending gynecologist-obstetrician Women's Hosp., Las Vegas, Nev., 1981-94, Sunrise Hosp. and Med. Ctr., 1994—; Markle Found. scholar Columbia Coll. Phys. and Surg., 1951-56; assoc. prof. clin. obstetrics-gynecology Coll. Phys. and Surg., Columbia, 1951-73; individual practice, N.Y.C., 1951-75; dir. research N.Y. Fertility Research Found., 1974-75; Anglo-Am. lectr. Royal Coll. Obstetricians and Gynecologists, London, Eng., 1959; Research cons. Office Naval Research, Am. embassy, London, 1951-52. Author: Ovum Humanum, 1960, Your Baby's Sex, Now You Can Choose, 1970, From Conception to Birth, 1971, Choose Your Baby's Sex, 1976, The Rites of Life: The Scientific Evidence of Life Before Birth, 1983, How to Choose Your Baby's Sex, 1984, 89, 21st Century Edition: How To Choose the Sex of Your Baby, 1997; also numerous articles. Served to maj., M.C. AUS, 1944-46. Editorial bd. Infertility. Recipient Ortho medal and award Am. Soc. Study Fertility, Sterility and Allied Subjects, 1960, Order of the Golden Arrow award Miss. Coll., 1993, Disting. Alumnus award Miss. Coll., 1993. Fellow ACS, AAAS, Am. Coll. Obstetricians and Gynecologists, World Med. Assn., Royal Soc. of Health (London), Royal Soc. Medicine (London); mem. AMA, Am. Soc. Zoologists, Am. Physiol. Soc., Soc. Exptl. Biology and Medicine, Vt. Med. Soc., Soc. U. Gynecologists, N.Y. Obstet. Soc., Harvey Soc., Wisdom Soc., N.Y. State Med. Assn., N.Y. County Nev. Med. Assn., Clarke County Med. Assn., 50 Yr. Club of Miss. Coll., 50 Yr. Club of Johns Hopkins U., 50 Year Club of Vt. State Med. Soc., 25 Yr. Club of Columbia-Presbyn. Med. Ctr., Phi Beta Kappa, Sigma Xi, Omicron Delta Kappa, Gamma Alpha. Spl. rsch. fisheries biology, physiology, human reprodn., fertility and sterility, hemorrhagic disease in newborn infants, sperm biology; discovered, identified male and female producing sperms; achieved gamete intrafallopian transfer, 1978; human in vitro fertilization, 1951; method for chorionic villi sampling, 1979. Home and Office: 2209 Pardee Pl Las Vegas NV 89104-3424 Office: Columbia Sunrise Hosp 3186 S Maryland Pkwy Las Vegas NV 89109-2317

SHETTY, MULKI RADHAKRISHNA, oncologist, consultant; b. Hiriadka, Karnataka, India, July 10, 1940; came to U.S., 1974; s. Mulki Sunderram and Kusumavati Shetty. MBBS, Stanley Med. Coll., Madras, 1964; DTM, U. Liverpool, Eng., 1968; LMCC, Med. Coun., Can., 1975. House surgeon and physician Bombay Hosp., 1965-66; sr. house officer Manor Pk. Hosp., Bristol, Eng., 1966-67, Torbay Hosp., 1967-68, St. Lukes Hosp., Huddersfield, 1969-70; sr. resident Gen. Hosp. Meml. U., New Foundland, 1971-72; intern Ottawa Gen. Hosp., 1972-73; fellow in chemotherapy Ont. Cancer Found., Ottawa, Can., 1973-74; fellow in clin. oncology U. Fla., Gainesville, 1974-75; attending oncologist N.W. Community Hosp., Arlington Heights, Ill., 1975—; cons. N.W. Community Hosp., 1975—. Author: Lung Cancer, 1980, Recent Advances in Chemotherapy, 1985, Wildlife Adventures, 1997; contbr. numerous articles to profl. jours.; coined new word calcifectomy; writer words and music Love Can Make a Grown Up Cry. Recipient Cert. for Outstanding Svc., Am Cancer Soc., 1982. Fellow Royal Soc. Medicine; mem. Internat. Assn. for Study of Lung Cancer, Chgo. Med. Soc. Hindu. Office: NW Community Hosp 800 W Central Rd Arlington Heights IL 60005-2349

SHEVEL, WILBERT LEE, information systems executive; b. Monessen, Pa., Oct. 26, 1932; s. Wilbert Lee and Lillian Marie (Palomaki) S.; m. Faye Elizabeth Johnston, Aug. 20, 1954; children: Lynn, Laurel, Kathleen, Amy. BSEE, Carnegie-Mellon U., 1954, MSEE, 1955, PhDEE, 1956. With IBM Corp., White Plains, N.Y., 1956-73; v.p. consumer electronics Motorola Corp., Franklin Park, Ill., 1973-74; v.p., gen. mgr. home electronics Rockwell Internat., Schaumburg, Ill., 1974-76; pres., chief exec. officer OMEX Inc., Santa Clara, Calif., 1976-80, Barrington Inc., San Jose, Calif., 1980-82; sr. v.p. corp. ops. Burroughs Corp., Detroit, 1982-84; v.p. systems and tech. Unisys (formerly Systems Devel. Corp.) div. Burroughs Corp., McLean, Va., 1984-88; pres Paramax Def. Systems Can., 1988-92; v.p. corp. info. systems Unisys Corp., 1992-94; mng. dir. EIM, San Deigo, 1994—. Patentee in field. Mem. adv. bd. Carnegie Mellon U. Sch. Computer Sci., 1988-95. 1st lt. U.S. Army, 1957. Fellow IEEE. Office: EIM Ste 110B 16776 Bernardo Center Dr San Diego CA 92128-2558

SHEVIN, ROBERT LEWIS, judge; b. Miami, Fla., Jan. 19, 1934; s. Aaron and Pauline (Bott) S.; m. Myrna Bressack, Jan. 27, 1957; children: Laura Dawn, Hilary Beth, Harry Alan. BA, U. Fla., 1955; JD magna cum laude, U. Miami, 1957. Bar: Fla. 1957, U.S. Dist. Ct. (so. and mid. dists.) Fla. 1963, U.S. Supreme Ct. 1971, U.S. Ct. Appeals (5th cir.) 1971, U.S. Dist. Ct. (no. dist.) Fla. Ptnr. Shevin, Goodman and Holtzman, 1957-67, Shevin and Shevin, 1967-70; mem. Fla. Ho. of Reps., 1963-65, chmn. interim com. on crime and law enforcement, 1965; mem. Fla. State Senate, 1966-70, chmn. select com. to investigate organized crime and law enforcemnt, 1967, mem. interim study com. on urban affairs, 1968; atty. gen. State of Fla., 1971-79; ptnr. Sparber, Shevin, Rosen, Shapo & Heilbronner, Miami, 1979-87, Stroock & Stroock & Lavan, Miami, 1988—; judge Third Dist. Ct. Appeals, Miami; mem. Fla. Tax Reform Commn., 1968, Fla. Constl. Revision Commn., 1978; city atty. City of Miami Beach, Fla., 1979-80. Chmn. Housing Fin. Authority Dade County, Fla., 1980-82, Fla. State Athletic Commn., 1984-87; mem. exec. com. Miami Citizens Against Crime; bd. dirs. Fla. Citizens Against Crime, 1985—; pres. Fla. Senate's Sunshine Adv. Com., 1988; chmn. Ptnrs. for Safe Neighborhoods, 1994; vis. com. U. Miami Law Sch. Recipient Allen Morris award, 1969, Intergovtl. award HUD, 1969, Conservationist of Yr. awards Fla. Wildlife Fedn., 1973, Audubon Soc., 1974, Furtherance of Justice award Fla. Prosecuting Attys. Assn., 1974, Disting. Svc. award Fla. Sheriff's Assn., 1976, Peace award State of Israel, 1977; named one of 10 Most Valuable Mems. Fla. Legislature Capital Press Corps, 1965. Mem. ABA, Internat. Bar Assn., Fla. Bar Assn., Dade County Bar Assn., Am. Trial Lawyers Assn., Am. Judicare Soc., Nat. Assn. Attys. Gen. (chmn. So. region 1981), Iron Arrow, Fla. Blue Key, Sertoma, Phi Delta Phi, Pi Lambda Phi, Phi Kappa Phi, Omicron Delta Kappa. Democrat. Jewish. Home: 7171 SW 56th St Miami FL 33155-5616 Office: Third Dist Ct of Appeal 2001 SW 117 Ave Miami FL 33175-1716

SHEVY, ALLEN EARL, JR., publishing executive; b. Mar. 23, 1959; s. Allen Earl Shevy Sr. and Myra Lee (Cone) Muller. Sales rep. Police Benevolent Assn., Tampa, Fla., 1974-79, Fox and Fink Inc., Tampa, 1979-85; pub. World of Fandom Mag., Tampa, 1985—; sales and mktg. rep. Fla. Spl. Olympics, 1979-85, U. South Fla. Basketball, 1979-85, U. South Fla. Baseball, 1979-85, U. South Fla. Soccer, 1979-85, U. South Fla. Volleyball, 1979-85, U. South Fla. Student Calendar of Events, 1979-85, Internat. Motor Sports Assn., 1979-85, Sports Car Off Road Events, 1979-85, Gasperilla Distance Classic, 1979-85, Saint Pete Grand Prix, 1979-85, Bucaneer Mag., 1989-93; pub. Rat Fink Comics, 1989-91, Comic Collectors Guide, 1989-91. Office: World of Fandom Mag PO Box 9421 Tampa FL 33674-9421

SHEWARD, DAVID JOHN, newspaper editor and critic; b. Wilamatic, Conn., May 7, 1959; s. John Albert and Marjorie Patricia (Berry) S. Student, Carnegie-Mellon U., 1977-79; BA, Temple U., 1982. Actor, dir. stock and regional theatres, Phila., N.Y.C., 1982—; mng. editor, critic Back Stage newspaper, N.Y.C., 1984—. Author: It's A Hit: The Back Stage Book of Broadway's Longest Running Hits 1884 to the Present, 1994, The Big Book of Show Business Awards, 1997; contbr. articles to theatrical publs.; actor in Long Day's Journey into Night, The Crucible, A Midsummer Night's Dream; dir. As Is, Talking With, Plaza Suite. Mem. Drama Desk (treas. 1994-96, nominating com. 1995—, pres. 1996—), N.Y. Drama Critics Circle, Outer Critics Circle, Am. Theatre Critics Assn. Avocations: acting, directing, travel. Office: Back Stage 1515 Broadway New York NY 10036

SHEWMAKER, KENNETH EARL, history educator; b. L.A., June 26, 1936; s. James Virgil and Jeanette M. (Greenberg) S.; m. Elisabeth L. Spalteholz, June 12, 1960; children: Richard Glenn, Nancy Jeanette. BS, Concordia Tchrs. Coll., 1960; MA, U. Calif., Berkeley, 1961; PhD, Northwestern U., 1966. Instr. Northwestern U., Evanston, Ill., 1965-66; asst. prof. Coll. William and Mary, Williamsburg, Va., 1966-67; from asst. prof. to assoc. prof. Dartmouth Coll., Hanover, N.H., 1967-78, prof. history, 1978—, acting chair dept. history, 1985-86, chmn. dept. history, 1986-89. Author: Americans and Chinese Communists, 1927-45: A Persuading Encounter, 1971 (Stuart L. Bernath prize 1972); editor: Papers of Daniel Webster, Diplomatic Papers, Vol. 1, 1841-1843, 1983, Vol. 2, 1850-1852, 1987, Daniel Webster, The Completest Man, 1990; contbr. articles to profl. jours. Mem. Am. Hist. Assn., N.H. Hist. Soc., Orgn. Am. Historians, Soc. Historians Am. Fgn. Rels. Lutheran. Avocations: fly fishing, fly tying. Office: Dartmouth College Dept History Hanover NH 03755

SHI, FENG SHENG, mathematician; b. Shanghai, China, Sept. 28, 1935; came to U.S., 1990; s. Jing Long and Xu Wenzheng Shi; m. Dorothy Shi, May 30, 1992. Degree of engr., 1957. Prof. math. and physics U. Industry, Shanghai, 1961-64; ship designer Govt. of China, Shanghai, 1964; rschr., business liaison Hong Kong of U.S.A. Liaison for Bus. Investment; owner, editor Pendulum Math. Jour. in Libr. of Congress; trustee, founder, dir. Chinese Math. Students Orgn., Miami, Fla., 1993—; dir. Chinese Internat. Math. Students Orgn., 1994—; mem. bd. intellectuals, Oxford Internat. Dictionary. Author: (math. solutions) Exist, 1991 (Libr. of Congress), Solving the Fermat Problem and Goldbach's Conjecture, 1993. Recipient Son of Yr. award Son's & Daughter's Found., 1990. Mem. All Nations (trustee, bd. dirs. 1990-93, Internat. Man of Yr. 1991). Home and Office: 1000 8th St N Saint Petersburg FL 33701-1510

SHIBASAKI, YOSHIO, chemistry educator, researcher; b. Gyoda, Japan, Mar. 21, 1934; s. Reiji and Shige (Kobayashi) S.; m. Teiko Ishizuka Shibasaki, Apr. 15, 1967; children: Hideaki, Miki. BS, Saitama U., Japan, 1959; DSc, U. Tokyo, 1980. Tech. official U. Tokyo, Japan, 1960-63, asst., 1963-67; lectr. Saitama U., Urawa, Japan, 1967-70, assoc. prof., 1970-92, prof., 1992—. Inventor: Kobunshi Kagaku, 1964, J. Polymer Science, 1967, 1980. Trustee Saitama U., Internat. Conf. Thermal Analysis & Calorimetry, Japan Soc. Calorimetry & Thermal Analysis. Avocations: appreciation of pictures. Home: 1642 Tsutsumine, Gyoda 361, Japan Office: Saitama U Faculty Sci, 255 Shimo-okubo, Urawa 338, Japan

SHIDELER, ROSS PATRICK, foreign language and comparative literature educator, author, translator, poet; b. Denver, Apr. 12, 1936. B.A., San Francisco State U., 1958; M.A., U. Stockholm, 1963; Ph.D., U. Calif., Berkeley, 1968. Instr. in comparative lit. U. Calif., Berkeley, 1967-68; asst. prof. English Hunter Coll., N.Y.C., 1968-69; asst. prof. Scandinavian lang. and comparative lit. UCLA, 1969-73, assoc. prof., 1973-79, prof., 1979—; chmn. program in comparative lit., 1979-86, 92-96. Author: (monograph) Voices Under The Ground: Themes and Images in the Poetry of Gunnar Ekelof, 1973, Per Olov Enquist-A Critical Study, 1984; translator: (play) The Night of the Tribades (Per Olov Enquist), 1977, The Hour of the Lynx, 1990 (Per Olov Enquist), 1990; U.S. assoc. editor Swedish Book Rev., 1984—. Fellow NDFL, 1964; fellow NDEA, 1965; Fulbright-Hays fellow, 1966-67. Mem. MLA (exec. com. divsn. Scandinavian Langs. and Lits. 1993-97), Soc. Advancement Scandinavian Studies (exec. coun. 1985-89, v.p. 1997—), Am. Comparative Lit. Assn., Assn. Depts. and Programs Comparative Lit. (exec. com. 1993-94, 94—). Office: UCLA Dept Comparative Lit Los Angeles CA 90024

SHIDELER, SHIRLEY ANN WILLIAMS, lawyer; b. Mishawaka, Ind., July 9, 1930; d. William Harmon and Lois Wilma (Koch) Williams; 1 dau., Gail Shideler Frye. LLB, Ind. U., 1964. Bar: Ind. 1964. Legal sec. Barnes, Hickam, Pantzer & Boyd, Indpls., 1953-63; assoc. Barnes & Thornburg, 1964-70, ptnr., 1971-92, of counsel, 1993—. Participant fund drives Indpls. Symphony, 1968-81, Indpls. Mus. Art, 1969-79, Marion County Libr. Restoration, 1985-88, Goodwill Industries, 1988-89; bd. dirs. bus. unit gals Indpls. Mus. Art, 1973-80; bd. dirs. Indpls. Legal Aid Soc., 1982-93, Community Hosp. Found., 1986-94, Cen. Newspapers Found. Fellow Am. Coll. Trust and Estate Counsel; mem. ABA, Ind. Bar Assn. (sec. 1975-76, chmn. probate, trust and real property sect. 1982), Nat. Conf. Bar Founds. (trustee 1988-94), Indpls. Bar Assn. (bd. mgrs. 1968-72, v.p. charge affairs 1972), Ind. Bar Found. (bd. mgrs. 1980-92, sec. 1981-82, treas. 1981-86, v.p. 1986-

88, pres. 1988-90), Indpls. Bar Found. (bd. mgrs. 1970-82, sec. 1972-77), Women's Rotary (pres. Indpls. club 1969-71, dir. 1968-79). Home: 2224 Boston Ct Apt C Indianapolis IN 46228-3257 Office: Barnes & Thornburg 1313 Mchts Bank Bldg 11 S Meridian St Indianapolis IN 46204-3506

SHIEH, CHING-LONG, structural engineering executive; b. Tainan, Taiwan, Jan. 24, 1948; came to U.S., 1973, naturalized, 1983; s. Yen-Chy and Jean (Tsai) S.; m. Shu-Hui Chuang, June 24, 1978; 1 dau., Lisa. B.S. in Civil Engring., Cheng Kung U.-Taiwan, 1970; M.S. in Civil Engring., Nat. Taiwan U., 1973; Ph.D. in Structural Engring., U. Fla., 1975. Registered profl. civil engr., Republic of China; registered profl. structural engr., Ill. Fla. Research asst. U. Fla., Gainesville, 1973-75; vis. scholar Northwestern U., Evanston, Ill., 1976-77; structural engring. specialist Sargent & Lundy Engrs., Chgo., 1978-80, sr. structural engr., specialist, 1980-96, structural project engr., 1996—; project engr. Bei Lungang Thermal Power Plant, China. Designer YongGwang 3&4 Nuclear Power Plant, Korea, Hgang Thermal Power Plant, China. Mem. ASCE, Mid.-Am. Chinese Sci. and Tech. Assn. (bd. dirs.). Contbr. tech. papers and reports to internat. jours. Home: 305 W Happfield Dr Arlington Heights IL 60004-7102 Office: 55 E Monroe St Chicago IL 60603-5701

SHIEH, JOHN TING-CHUNG, economics educator; b. China. BS, Chunghsing U., Taiwan, 1956; MS, Kans. State U., 1960; MA, U. Calif., Riverside, 1970; D in Bus. Adminstrn., U. So. Calif., 1981. Asst. prof. Northwestern State Coll., Alva., 1964-67; asst. prof. econs. Calif. State Poly. U., Pomona, 1967-70, assoc. prof., 1970-81, prof., chmn. dept. econs., 1982-85, prof. 1981—; prof., dir. Inst. Mainland China Studies, Nat. Dong-hua U., Hwalian, Taiwan, 1994—; cons. to small bus., So. Calif., Taiwan, 1975—; vis. prof. Tax Inst., U. So. Calif., L.A., 1977-84, U. Calif., Irvine, 1978-79, U. So. Calif., 1978-81, UCLA, 1983—. Rsch., publs. in field. NSF fellow, 1965, 66, 67, 73; fellow seminars in econs. and math. U. Wyo., summer 1972. Mem. Am. Econ. Assn., Omicron Delta Epsilon, Omega Rho. Office: Calif State Poly U Dept Econs Pomona CA 91768 also: Inst Mainland China Studies, Nat Dong-hua U, Hualien Taiwan

SHIEKMAN, LAURENCE ZEID, lawyer; b. Phila., Feb. 13, 1947; s. Morton and Roberta (Zeid) S.; m. Marjorie Kershbaum, Dec. 25, 1970; children: Wendy K., Thomas K. BS in Econs., U. Pa., 1968, JD, 1971. Bar: Pa. 1971. Law clk. to Hon. A. Leon Higginbotham, Jr. U.S. Dist. Ct. (ea. dist.) Pa., 1971-73; asst. prof. Fla. State U. Coll. Law, Tallahassee, 1973-75; assoc. Pepper, Hamilton & Scheetz, Phila., 1975-78, ptnr., 1978—. Chmn. 20th Yr. reunion com. U. Pa. Law Sch., Phila., 1995. Mem. ABA, Pa. Bar Assn., Phila. Bar Assn. Office: Pepper Hamilton & Scheetz 3000 Two Logan Sq 18th & Arch Sts Philadelphia PA 19103-2799

SHIELDS, ALLAN EDWIN, writer, photographer, retired educator; b. Columbus, Ohio, July 3, 1919; s. Richard Edwin and Eloessa (Smith) S.; m. Bernice Clark, Aug. 2, 1941; children—Allan Oakley, Richard Minter, Larry Michael, Catherine Marie. A.B., U. Calif.-Berkeley, 1941; M.A., U. So. Calif., 1947, Ph.D., 1951. Prof. philosophy San Diego State U., 1949-68, 70-78; emeritus prof. San Diego State Coll., 1978—; dean Coll. Humanities and Fine Arts U. No. Iowa, 1968-70; owner, pub. Jerseydale Ranch Press, 1992—; seasonal ranger naturalist Nat. Park Service, Yosemite Nat. Park, 1955-60; freelance writer, photographer, 1978—; violinist-violist, frequent recitalist; mem., sometime concertmaster Merced Symphony Orch., Calif., 1979-91; founder, with wife, Jerseydale Ranch Press, 1992. Author: Guide to Tuolumne Meadows Trails, 1960, rev. edit., 1973, (with Herbert Searles) A Bibliography of the Works of F.C.S. Schiller, 1969, (with Richard Shields) Tuolumne Profile: Yosemite, 1967, (novella) The Tragedy of Tenaya, 1974, new version 1992, A Bibliography of Bibliographies in Aesthetics, 1974, (poetry) A Horse in the House, 1985, Mariposa Now and Then, 1993, Tuffy, an Angel Hid in a Cloud, 1994, What the Animals Taught Me, 1995, (with Bernice Shields) Into the Valley: A Brief History of Jerseydale Ranch, 1995, (with John Sharsmith) Climb Every Mountain: A Portrait of Carl Sharsmith, 1996, also numerous poems and articles; editor: A Yosemite Adventure in 1863, 1992, Wild Bill Neely and the Pagan Brothers' Golden Goat Winery, 1993, The Song of Sonora, 1993, O.S.S.: One Sad Sack—Pvt. Neely Disciplines the Military, 1994, A Yosemite Naturalist's Odyssey, 1994, Wilderness Treks by Foot, Canoe, and Adobe Rocket, and Father's Far-Flung Fables, 1995, Dream Temple and Other Visions, 1997; pub. various profl. jours. Bd. dirs. San Diego Symphony. Served with USAAF, 1942-45. Mudd fellow in philosophy U. So. Calif., 1948-49. Mem. Am. Soc. for Aesthetics (trustee), Phi Beta Kappa, Phi Kappa Phi, Phi Mu Alpha Sinfonia (hon.). Home: 6506 Jerseydale Rd Mariposa CA 95338-9638 *My greatest satisfactions have come with tasks completed to the best of my abilities. Whether raising children, building a building, nurturing a marriage, learning the violin, or writing, all have inherent standards demanding recognition. Though there is always joy in the process of doing, joy can be transformed into satisfaction only in completion evaluated against the standards of worth for that kind of undertaking.*

SHIELDS, BROOKE CHRISTA CAMILLE, actress, model; b. N.Y.C., May 31, 1965; d. Francis A. and Teri (Schmon) S.; m. Andre Agassi, April 19, 1997. BA, Princeton U., 1987. Model for Ivory Soap commls. starting in 1966, later for Calvin Klein jeans and Colgate toothpaste commls.; actress: (films) Alice, Sweet Alice, 1975, Pretty Baby, 1977, King of the Gypsies, 1978, Wanda Nevada, 1978, Just You and Me Kid, 1978, Blue Lagoon, 1979, Endless Love, 1980, Sahara, 1983, Backstreet Strays, 1989, Brenda Starr, 1992, Seventh Floor, 1993, Running Wild, 1993, Freaked, 1993, Freeway, 1996; (TV movies) The Prince of Central Park, 1977, After the Fall, Wet Gold, I Can Make You Love Me: The Stalking of Laura Black, 1993, Nothing Lasts Forever, 1995, (TV shows) The Tonight Show, Bob Hope spls., The Diamond Trap, 1988, Friends, 1996, Suddenly Susan, 1996; appeared on Broadway in Grease, 1994-95. Office: Christa Inc 2300 W Sahara Ave Ste 18 Las Vegas NV 89102-4354

SHIELDS, CAROL ANN, writer, educator; b. Oak Park, Ill., June 2, 1935; came to Can., 1957, naturalized, 1974; d. Robert Elmer and Inez Adelle (Sellgren) Warner; m. Donald Hugh Shields, July 20, 1957; children: John, Anne, Catherine, Margaret, Sara. BA, Hanover Coll., 1957, hon. degree, 1996; MA, U. Ottawa, Ont., Can., 1975, hon. degree, 1995; hon. degree Queen's U., 1996, U. Winnipeg, 1996, U. B.C., 1996. Editl. asst. Can. Slavonic Papers, Ottawa, 1972-74; lectr. U. Ottawa, 1976-77, U. B.C., Vancouver, Can., 1978-80; prof. U. Man., Winnipeg, Can., 1980—; chancellor U. Winnipeg, 1996—; mem. Can. Coun., 1994-97. Author: (poems) Others, 1972, Intersect, 1974, Coming to Canada, 1991; (novels) Small Ceremonies, 1976, The Box Garden, 1977, Happenstance, 1980, A Fairly Conventional Women, 1982; Various Miracles, 1985, Swann: A Mystery, 1987, The Orange Fish, 1989, The Republic of Love, 1992, The Stone Diaries, 1993 (Nat. Book Critics Circle award for fiction 1994, Pulitzer Prize for fiction 1995), Larry's Party, 1997; (play) Women Waiting, 1983, Departures and Arrivals, 1984, Thirteen Hands, 1993, (with Catherine Shields) Fashion Power Guilt. Grantee Can. Council, 1973, 76, 78, 86, Man. Arts Council, 1984, 85; recipient prize CBC, 1983, 84, Nat. Mag. award, 1985, Arthur Ellis award, 1987, Can. Book Sellers'award 1994, Manitoba Book of the Yr., 1994, Marian Engel award Writers' Devel. Trust, 1990, Gov. Gen.'s award Can. Coun., 1993. Mem. PEN, Writers Union Can., Writers Guild Man., Jane Austen Soc., Royal Soc. Can., N.Am. Can. Coun. Bd. Quaker. Home: 701 237 Wellington Crescent, Winnipeg, MB Canada R3M 0A1 Office: care Bella Pomer Agency Inc, 22 Shallmar Blvd Penthouse 2, Toronto, ON Canada M5N 2Z8

SHIELDS, H. RICHARD, tax consultant,business executive; m. Frances Augenstein; 1 dau., Eileen. A.B., Bklyn. Coll.; LL.B., J.D., NYU; M.B.A., Harvard U. Bar: N.Y. bar 1940. Corp. practice law, 1940-60; sec., treas. Forbes Realty Corp., 1960-70; exec. v.p. Forbes Industries, Ltd., 1965-70; exec. v.p. Am. Diversified Industries Corp., 1964-66, pres., chmn. bd., 1966-76; exec. v.p. Daily Mirror, Sunday Mirror, N.Y.C.; chmn., chief exec. officer, dir. TTC Industries (also subs. Armstrong Glass Mfg. Corp.), Erwin, Tenn., 1970-76; pres., dir. Euro Industries, Ltd.; and dir.; pres., chief exec. officer, dir. Dairene Industries, Ltd., 1971-80; tax cons. Regal Cons., Ltd., Great Neck, N.Y., 1974-85; dir. Blue Ribbon Mktg. Corp.; govt. appeal agt. U.S. Selective Service; mem. N.Y. State Commn. on Human Rights; referee, arbitrator Civil Ct., N.Y.C. Served to maj. USAAF, 1942-46, CBI. Decorated Commendation medal, Legion of Merit, China War Meml. medal. Mem. Am. Inst. Mgmt., Nat. Assn. Accts., Nat. Tax Assn. (com. fed. taxation), Tax Inst. Am., Tax Execs. Inst., Nat. Assn. Corp. Dirs., Assn. Bar City N.Y. (legis. com.). Club: Harvard.

SHIELDS, JAMES JOSEPH, educational administrator, educator, author; b. Phila., Feb. 11, 1935; s. James Joseph and Lena Josephine (Dyer) S. (dec.). BS in Polit. Sci., Saint Joseph's U., 1956; EdM, Temple U., 1959; EdD, Columbia U., 1963. Asst. to dir., internat. studies Tchrs. Coll., Columbia U., N.Y.C., 1961; rechr., Tchrs. for East Africa Program Tchrs. Coll., Columbia U., N.Y.C. and Kampala, Uganda, 1961-62; asst. prof. history and philosophy of edn. SUNY, New Paltz, 1962-64; asst. prof. comparative and politics of edn. CUNY, 1964-69; assoc. prof. comparative and politics of edn. CUNY, N.Y.C., 1969-75, prof. comparative and politics of edn., 1975—, head, Sch. Adminstrn. Program, 1983-85, chair, dept. social and psychol. founds., 1988-90; dir. Japan Initiative, N.Y.C., 1986—; cons. Inst. for Ednl. Devel., N.Y.C., 1968-71, Equitable Life Ins. Co., N.Y.C., 1961, N.Y.C. Bd. Edn. Dist. 4, 1996; vis. rsch. prof. Tokyo Met. U., 1986—; vis. prof. Tchrs. Coll., Columbia U., 1965-67, 93-95, Yale U., 1997; mem. evaluation bd. Nat. Coun. on Accreditation of Tchr. Edn., Washington, 1970-75; assoc. Columbia U., Univ. Seminar on Modern Japan, N.Y.C., 1987—, chair, 1990-91. Author: Education in Community Development: Its Function in Technical Assistance, 1967; editor: Problems and Prospects in International Education, 1968, Foundations of Education: Dissenting Views, 1974, Japanese Schooling: Patterns of Socialization Equality and Political Control, 1989 (nominated for Books on Japan award), rev. edit. 1993; author numerous book chpts., monographs and book reviews; contbr. numerous articles to profl. jours. Mem. Pub. Edn. Assn. Task Force on a Reconstructed Ednl. Sys., N.Y.C., 1977-78, Pub. Edn. Assn. Task Force on Tchr. Selection, N.Y.C., 1981; mem. N.Y. Urban Coalition, 1982-84, Alumni Coun., Tchrs. Coll. Columbia U., 1993—. With USAR, 1959-59. Grantee SUNY Rsch. Found., 1964, N.Y. State Edn. Dept., 1969-72, Rsch. Found. CUNY, 1980-81, Japan-U.S. Friendship Commn., 1986-89, The City Coll., Provost, 1988-89, 89-90; Fulbright travel grantee, 1964, 1964, Japan Found. Ctr. for Global Partnership, 1994, The U.S.-Japan Found., 1994-96; recipient Wyo. Gov.'s Youth Coun. award, 1974, Higher Edn. award Holy Family Coll., Phila., 1990, Ann. Gertrude Langsam Ednl. Reconstrn. award Adelphi U., 1992; postdoctoral fellow Yale U., New Haven, 1967-68. Hon. fellow Comparative and Internat. Edn. Soc. (N.E. region conf. coord. 1984, bd. dirs. 1992-95); mem. Am. Ednl. Studies Assn. (pres. 1973-74, exec. coun. 1970-75), Carnegie Coun. on Ethics and Internat. Affairs, Japan Soc. of N.Y., Internat. House of Japan, Soc. for Ednl. Reconstrn. (exec. com. 1973—), Am. Ednl. Rsch. Assn. Avocations: collecting Long Island painters (1850-1950), travel, gardening. Home: 562 W End Ave Apt 4D New York NY 10024-2718 Office: CUNY 138th St and Convent Ave New York NY 10031

SHIELDS, JAMES RICHARD, alcohol and drug counselor, consultant; b. Milw., Mar. 1, 1935; s. Edmund and Louise S.; m. Marlene Brietkreutz, Nov. 20, 1957. Grad. high sch., Hartford, Wis. Cert. alcohol and drug counselor, Wis.; nat. cert. addiction counselor, alcohol and drug counselor; cert. employee asst. profl.; cert. addictions specialist. Cons. Wis. Energy Corp., Milw., 1979—. With U.S. Army, 1959-66. Mem. Occupational Programing Cons. Assn., Employee Assistance Soc. N.Am., Employee Assistance Program Assn. (cert.). Home: 7230 Maple Ln Hartford WI 53027-9703 Office: Wis Energy Corp A-149 333 W Everett St Milwaukee WI 53203

SHIELDS, LAWRENCE THORNTON, orthopedic surgeon, educator; b. Boston, Oct. 2, 1935; s. George Leo and Catherine Elizabeth (Thornton) S.; AB, Harvard U., 1957; MD, Johns Hopkins U., 1961; m. Karen S. Kraus, Sept. 21, 1968; children: Elizabeth Coulter, Laura Thornton, Sarah Daly, Michael Lawrence. Intern, Barnes Hosp., Washington U., St. Louis, 1961-62, resident, 1962-63; resident orthopedic surgeon Children's Hosp. Med. Ctr., Boston, 1966-67, Mass. Gen. Hosp., Boston, 1967-68, Peter Bent Brigham, Robert Breck Brigham hosps., Boston, 1968-69; resident orthopedic surgeon Harvard Med. Sch., Boston, 1965-69, instr., 1969—; orthopedic surgeon Peter Bent Brigham & Women's Hosp., Children's hosps., 1969—; orthopedic surgeon Waltham (Mass.) -Weston Hosp. and Med. Ctr., 1969—, also chief orthopedic surgery, pres. med. staff; mem. Waltham-Weston Orthopedic Assos.; proprietor Boston Athenaeum; mem. staffs Hahnemann Hosp., Boston, Newton-Wellesley (Mass.) hosps.; cons. orthopedic surgeon VA Hosp., Boston; mem. faculty Harvard Med. Sch.; vis. scholar Cambridge U., 1987; hon. prof. New Eng. Coll, Henniker, N.H. and Sussex, Eng., 1995; bd. dirs. Wal-West Health Systems, 1986—; pres. Massachusetts Bay Investment Trust; dir. Waltham Investment Group. Bd. dirs. Mass. Acad. Emergency Med. Technicians, Waltham Boys' Club; bd. of overseers Boston Lyric Opera, 1993—; trustee, exec. com. Waltham-Weston Hosp. and Med. Ctr. Lt. M.C., USNR, 1963-65. Diplomate Am. Bd. Orthopedic Surgery. Fellow ACS, Am. Acad. Orthopedic Surgeons, Mass. Hist. Soc. Libr., Mass. Hist. Soc.; mem. N.Y. Acad. Scis., Royal Soc. Medicine, Mass. Orthopaedic Assn. (bd. dirs., sec. 1986—), New Eng. Orthopaedic Club, Boston Orthopedic Club, Charles River Dist. (treas., exec. com., pres. 1982-83) Mass. (councillor; v.p. 1982-83) med. socs., R. Austen Freeman Soc. (v.p.), Thomas B. Quigley Sports Medicine Soc., Titanic Hist. Soc., Boston Opera Assns. (bd. dirs.), Harvard Mus. Assn., Thoreau Soc., Emerson Soc., Trollope Soc. (founding mem., bd. dirs., London), Handel and Hayden Soc. (bd. overseers), Waltham Hist. Soc., St. Botolph Club (Boston), Les Amis d'Escoffier Soc., Confrerie de La Chaine des Rotisseurs (elected 1996), Harvard Club, Algonquin Club of Boston (bd. dirs., pres. 1990—), St. Crispin's Soc. Boston (founding mem., pres. 1991—), English Speaking Union (bd. dirs.), Union Club of Boston, St. Botolph Club of Boston, Clover Club of Boston, Boston Lyric Opera (bd. overseers 1993), Harvard Musical Assn., Rotary, Pi Eta (Harvard). Contbr. articles to med. jours. Home: 9 Beverly Rd Newton MA 02161-1112 Office: 721 Huntington Ave Boston MA 02115-6010 also: 20 Hope Ave Ste 314 Waltham MA 02154-2717

SHIELDS, PATRICIA LYNN, educational broker, consultant; b. Bklyn.. BS in Biology, Bucknell U., 1984; postgrad., Rutgers U., 1985—. Pres., CEO Buttercup's Internat., Inc., Middletown, N.J., 1988—. Author: Seeing with Others' Hearts, 1987; author ednl. literary essays. Lifetime mem. Nat. Coun. Sr. Citizens, Washington, 1990—; assoc. mem. Nat. Coun. La Raza, Washington, 1990; participating mem. Am. Mus. Natural History, N.Y.C., 1988—; nat. assoc. mem. Smithsonian Mus., Washington, 1992—; sustaining mem. Friends of the Middletown Pub. Libr., 1987—. Recipient Gold Card Honor Roll award Nat. Coun. Sr. Citizens, Washington, 1990, Citation of Leadership N.J. State Dept. Higher Edn., Jersey City State Coll. and Nat. Conf. Christians and Jews, 1990. Office: Buttercup's Internat Inc PO Box 148 Middletown NJ 07748-0148

SHIELDS, RANA COLLEEN, special education educator; b. Midland, Tex., Oct. 2, 1951; d. Robert Campbell and Edith Sue (Alexander) S.; m. Micheal Leggett; children: Daniel Robert Tilly, Casey Michelle Leggett; 1 stepchild, Laurie Ayn Leggett. B of Journalism, U. Tex., 1974; JD magna cum laude, South Tex. U., 1984; MEd in Spl. Edn., S.W. Tex. State U., 1993. Bar: Tex., 1985; cert. generic spl. edn., reading, Tex. City editor Huntsville (Tex.) Item, 1976-78; asst. county atty. Travis County Atty.'s Office, Austin, Tex., 1986-87; tchr. spl. edn. Liberty Hill (Tex.) H.S., 1990-91, Tex. Sch. for the Blind, Austin, 1991-93; grad. rsch. asst. in spl. edn. U. Tex., Austin, spring 1994, tchg. asst. spl. edn., 1995-96. Asst. casenotes editor: South Tex. Law Jour., 1983. Recipient 1st Pl. Spot News Photography award AP Mng. Editors, 1978, Am. Jurisprudence awards, 1979, 82, 83; named Outstanding Sophomore Journalist, Women in Comm., 1971; Univ. fellow, 1996-97. Mem. Assn. Tex. Profl. Educators, Kappa Delta Pi, Phi Kappa Phi.

SHIELDS, RICHARD OWEN, JR., emergency physician; b. Toledo, Sept. 26, 1949; s. Richard Owen and Doris Ann (Chambers) S.; m. Leslie Ann Sjogren, Sept. 8, 1971; children: Brent Alan, Erin Christine. BS, Mich. State U., 1974; MD, Wayne State U., 1979. Diplomate Nat. Bd. Med. Examiners. Intern in internal medicine Detroit Gen. Hosp., 1979-80; resident in emergency medicine Detroit Receiving Hosp., 1981-83, emergency physician, 1983-84; emergency physician Meml. Med. Ctr., Savannah, Ga., 1984—, dir. med. edn., 1986—, chmn. dept. emergency medicine, med. dir. Emergency Ctr., 1989-92; dir. Regional Poison Control Ctr., Savannah, 1985-90; oral examiner Am. Bd. Emergency Medicine, 1987—. Served with U.S. Army, 1971-72. Fellow Am. Coll. Emergency Physicians (bd. dirs. Ga. chpt. 1987—, pres. Ga. chpt. 1992-94); mem. Alpha Omega Alpha. Office: Meml Med Ctr Emergency Dept 4700 Waters Ave Savannah GA 31404-6220

SHIELDS, ROBERT EMMET, merchant banker, lawyer; b. Ridley Park, Pa., May 18, 1942; s. Joseph Leonard and Kathryn J. (Walsh) S.; m. Mary Katherine Reid, July 22, 1967; children: Christopher D., David R., Kevin M., Kathleen. AB, Coll. Holy Cross, 1964; LLB cum laude, NYU, 1967. Bar: Pa. bar 1968. Mem. faculty Boalt Hall Sch. Law U. Calif., Berkeley, 1967-68; assoc. Drinker Biddle & Reath, Phila., 1968-74; ptnr. Drinker Biddle & Reath, 1974-94, mng. ptnr., 1979-83, 85-94, head corp. and securities group, 1983-93, CFO, 1993-94; mng. dir., ptnr. Questor Gen. Ptnr., L.P., 1995—; mng. dir. Questor Ptnrs. Fund, L.P., 1995—; sec. Wallquest Inc. Author: (with Eliot B. Thomas) Federal Securities Act Handbook, 4th edit, 1977; (with Robert H. Strouse) Securities Practice Handbook, 1987. Mem. ABA, Am. Law Inst., Pa. Bar Assn., Phila. Bar Assn. Club: Union League (Phila.). Home: 206 Atlee Rd Wayne PA 19087-3836 Office: Questor Mgmt Co 4000 Town Ctr Ste 530 Southfield MI 48075-1406 also: 1100 Phila Nat Bank Bldg 1345 Chestnut St Philadelphia PA 19107

SHIELDS, THOMAS CHARLES, lawyer; b. Evergreen Park, Ill., Apr. 26, 1941; s. Thomas James and Adelaide (McElligott) S.; m. Nicoline M. Murphy, Sept. 14, 1974; children: Thomas James II, Nicoline Margaret, Suzanne Adelaide, Kerry Anne. AB, Georgetown U., 1963; JD cum laude, Northwestern U., 1966. Bar: Ill. 1966, U.S. Dist. Ct. (no. dist.) Ill. 1966, U.S. Ct. Appeals (7th cir.) 1966, U.S. Tax Ct. 1968, U.S. Supreme Ct. 1977. Assoc. Hopkins & Sutter, Chgo., 1966-73; ptnr. Hopkins & Sutter, 1973-93; ptnr., head health care law group Bell, Boyd & Lloyd, Chgo., 1994—; chief counsel Cath. Health Assn. U.S., St. Louis, 1994—; mem. adv. bd. Health Law Inst. Loyola U. Sch. Law, Chgo., 1984-89, Health Law Inst. DePaul U. Sch. Law, Chgo., 1985-96; lectr. Ill. Inst. Continuing Legal Edn., 1973. Contbr. articles to profl. pubs., chpt. to book; mng. editor Northwestern Law Rev., 1965-66. Bd. dirs. Cancer Rsch. Found., Chgo., 1987—, Brother Louie and Fannie Roncoli Found., 1994—, Chgo. Zool. Soc., Cath. Charities Chgo. Mem. Am. Acad. Healthcare Attys. (bd. dirs. 1983-91, pres. 1989-90), Am. Soc. Law and Medicine, Am. Hosp. Assn. (tax adv. group 1987-90), Ill. Bar Assn., Ill. Assn. Healthcare Attys. (bd. dirs. 1983-89, pres. 1987-88), Chgo. Bar Assn., Exec. Club Chgo., Law Club Chgo., Mid-Am. Club Chgo., Order of Coif. Avocations: skiing, bicycling, golf, tennis. Office: Bell Boyd & Lloyd 3 First Nat Plz Ste 3200 Chicago IL 60602

SHIELDS, THOMAS WILLIAM, surgeon, educator; b. Ambridge, Pa., Aug. 17, 1922; s. John Jr. and Elizabeth (Flanagan) S.; m. Dorothea Ann Thomas, June 12, 1948; children: Thomas William, John Leland, Carol Ann. BA, Kenyon Coll., 1943, DSc (hon.), 1978; MD, Temple U., 1947. Resident surgery Northwestern U. Med. Sch., Chgo., 1949-55; prof. surgery Northwestern U. Med. Sch., 1968-92, prof. Emeritus of surgery, 1992—; practice medicine specializing in surgery Chgo., 1956—; chief of surgery VA Lakeside Hosp., Chgo., 1968-87; chief thoracic surgery VA Lakeside Med. Ctr., Chgo., 1987-90. Editor: General Thoracic Surgery, 1972, 4th edit., 1994, Bronchial Carcinoma, 1974, Mediastinal Surgery, 1991; assoc. editor Surgery, Gynecology and Obstetrics, Annals of Thoracic Surgery, 1993—; mem. editorial bd. Annals of Thoracic Surgery, Lung Cancer; contbr. articles to profl. jours. Served with U.S. Army, 1951-53. Mem. ACS, AMA, Am. Assn. for Thoracic Surgery, Soc. Thoracic Surgery, Central, Western Surg. Assns., Société Internationale de Chirurgie, Soc. for Surgery of Alimentary Tract, Internat. Assn. for Study Lung Cancer, Pan Pacific Surg. Assn., Phi Beta Kappa, Sigma Xi, Alpha Omega Alpha. Home: 1721 Jenks St Evanston IL 60201-1528 Office: 250 E Superior St Ste 201 Chicago IL 60611-2914

SHIELDS, WILL HERTHIE, football player; b. Fort Riley, Kans., Sept. 15, 1971; m. Senia Shields; 2 children. Degree in comm., U. Nebr. Guard Kansas City Chiefs, 1993—. Named to Pro Bowl, 1996. Office: Kansas City Chiefs 1 Arrowhead Dr Kansas City MO 64129*

SHIELY, JOHN STEPHEN, company executive, lawyer; b. St. Paul, June 19, 1952; s. Vincent Robert and Mary Elizabeth (Hope) S.; m. Helen Jane Pauly, Aug. 29, 1981; children: Michael, Erin, Megan. BBA, U. Notre Dame, 1974; JD, Marquette U., 1977; M of Mgmt., Northwestern U., 1990. With Arthur Andersen & Co., Milw., 1977-79, Hughes Hubbard & Reed, Milw., 1979-83, Allen-Bradley Co., Milw., 1983-86, Rockwell Internat. Corp., Milw., 1985-86; with Briggs & Stratton Corp., Milw., 1986—, gen. counsel, 1986-90, v.p., gen. counsel, 1990-91, exec. v.p. adminstrn., 1991-94, pres., COO, 1994—. Dir. St. Charles, Inc., Milw., 1978—, Children's Hosp. of Wis., Inc., 1992—, M&I Marshall & Ilsley Bank, Milw., 1995—, Consolidated Papers, Inc., Wisconsin Rapids, 1996—, Quad/Graphics, Inc., Pewaukee, Wis., 1996—; mem. bd. regents Milw. Sch. Engring., 1995—. Mem. Am. Corp. Counsel Assn. (past pres., bd. govs., Wis. chpt. 1984-94), Assn. for Corp. Growth (past pres., bd. dirs. Wis. chpt. 1988—). Office: Briggs & Stratton Corp PO Box 702 Milwaukee WI 53201-0702

SHIENTAG, FLORENCE PERLOW, lawyer; b. N.Y.C.; d. David and Ester (Germane) Perlow; m. Bernard L. Shientag, June 8, 1938. BS, NYU, 1940, LLB, 1933, JD, 1940. Bar: Fla. 1976, N.Y. Law aide Thomas E. Dewey, 1937; law sec. Mayor La Guardia, 1939-42; justice Domestic Relations Ct., 1941-42; mem. Tchrs. Retirement Bd., N.Y.C., 1942-46; asst. U.S. atty. So. dist. N.Y., 1943-53; cir. ct. mediator Fla. Supreme Ct., 1992; pvt. practice N.Y.C., 1960—, Palm Beach, Fla., 1976—; lectr. on internat. divorce; mem. Nat. Commn. on Wiretapping and Electronic Surveillance, 1973—, Task Force on Women in Cts., 1985-86. Contbr. articles to profl. jours. Candidate N.Y. State Senate, 1954; bd. dirs. UN Devel. Corp., 1972-95, Franklin and Eleanor Roosevelt Inst., 1985—; bd. dirs., assoc. treas. YM and YWHA; hon. commr. commerce, N.Y.C. Mem. ABA, Fed. Bar Assn. (exec. com.), Internat. Bar Assn., N.Y. Women's Bar Assn. (pres., dir., Life Time Achievement award 1994), N.Y. State Bar Assn., N.Y.C. Bar Assn. (chmn. law and art sect.), N.Y. County Lawyers Assn. (dir.), Nat. Assn. Women LAwyers (sec.). Home: 737 Park Ave New York NY 10021-4256 *Success is a product of self respect and hard work at what you do well.*

SHIER, GLORIA BULAN, mathematics educator; b. The Philippines, Apr. 20, 1935; came to U.S., 1966.; d. Melecio Cauilan and Florentina (Cumagun) Bulan; m. Wayne Thomas Shier, May 31, 1969; children: John Thomas, Marie Teresita, Anna Christina. BS, U. Santo Tomas, Manila, Philippines, 1956; MA, U. Ill., 1968; PhD, U. Minn., 1986. Tchr. Cagayan (Philippines) Valley Coll., 1956-58, St. Paul Coll., Manila, 1959-62, Manila Div. City Schs., 1958-64; asst. prof. U. of East, Manila, 1961-66; rsch. asst. U. Ill., Urbana, 1968-69; instr. Miramar Community Coll., San Diego, 1974-75, Mesa Community Coll., San Diego, 1975-80, Lakewood Community Coll., St. Paul, 1984, U. Minn., Mpls., 1986-87, North Hennepin Community Coll., Brooklyn Park, Minn., 1987—; cons. PWS Kent Pub. Co., Boston, 1989—. Chairperson Filipino Am. Edn. Assn., San Diego, 1978-79. Fulbright scholar U.S. State Dept., U. Ill., 1966-70; fellow Nat. Sci. Found., Oberlin Coll., 1967; recipient Excellence in Teaching award UN Ednl. Scientific Cultural Organ., U. Philippines, 1960-62, Cert. Commendation award The Gov. of Minn., 1990, Outstanding Filipino in the Midwest Edn. Cat. award 1992, Cavite Assn. Mem. Am. Math. Soc., Math. Assn. Am., Phi Kappa Phi, Sigma Xi Rsch. Honor Soc., Nat. Coun. Tchrs. Math., Am. Math. Assn. for Two Yr. Colleges, Internat. Group for Psychology of Math. Edn., Minn. Coun. of Tchrs. Math., Minn. Math. Assn. of Two Yr. Colleges, Fil-Minnesotan Assn (bd.dirs. 1991—), Am. Statistical Assn. Roman Catholic. Avocation: piano. Home: 210 Wexford Heights Dr New Brighton MN 55112-3144

SHIER, SHELLEY M., production company executive; b. Toronto, Mar. 15, 1957; d. Harry Shier and Rosaline (Cutler) Sonshine; m. Hank O'Neal, May 14, 1985. Student, H.B. Studio, N.Y.C., 1975-76, Stella Adler Conservatory, N.Y.C., 1976-80. Company mem., actor Soho Artists Theater, N.Y.C., 1976-81; casting dir. Lawrence Price Prodns., N.Y.C., 1981-82; pres. Hoss, Inc., N.Y.C., 1983—; v.p. Chiaroscuro Records, N.Y.C., 1987—; cons. Peter Martin Assocs., N.Y.C., 1983, Kloster Cruise Ltd., Miami, Fla., 1983—, Floating Jazz Festival, Big Bands At Sea, Rhythm & Blues Cruise, Dixieland At Sea, Oslo (Norway) Jazz Festival, 1986—, New Sch. for Social Rsch., N.Y.C., 1989—, Beacons In Jazz Awards Ceremony, A Tribute to the Music of Bob Wills and The Texas Playboys, Mardi Gras at Sea. Talent acquisition agt. Save the Children, N.Y.C., 1986, Tomorrow's Children, N.Y.C., 1990, Royal Caribbean Cruise Ltd., Miami, 1994—, Ultimate Caribbean Jazz Spectacular, Country Music Festival in the Caribbean, CUNARD N.Y.C., 1994—, Barcelona Olympics, NBC, 1992, Broadway at Sea, 1996, others. Avocations: karate, photography, riding, fishing, weightlifting. Office: HOSS Inc 830 Broadway New York NY 10003-4827

SHIFF, ALAN HOWARD WILLIAM, judge; b. New Haven, June 2, 1934; s. Philip Robert and Harriet (Panikoff) S.; children: Daniel Stuart, Andrew Reuben; m. Carol Sweeterman Brumbaugh. BA, Yale U., 1957; LLB, U. Va., 1960. Bar: Conn. 1960, U.S. Dist. Ct. Conn. 1960, U.S. Ct. Appeals (2d cir.) 1969. Ptnr. Shiff, Shiff and Schancupp, New Haven, 1960-81; judge U.S. Bankruptcy Ct., Dist. Conn., Bridgeport, 1981—, chief judge, 1996—; mem. bankruptcy apppellate panel svc., 1996—; mem. internat. law rels. com. Nat. Conf. Bankruptcy Judges, 1996—; spl. counsel Conn. Gen. Assembly Energy and Pub. Utilities Com., 1979-80; lectr. to various bar assns. Mem. Conn. Bar Assn., Administrv. office of U.S. Cts. (adv. com. of bankruptcy judges 1991-96, task force official on forms 1984-88, elected to serve 2nd cir. gov. Nat. Conf. Bankruptcy Judges, 1995—). Office: US Bankruptcy Court 915 Lafayette Blvd Bridgeport CT 06604-4706

SHIFFER, JAMES DAVID, retired utility executive; b. San Diego, Mar. 24, 1938; s. Kenneth Frederick and Thelma Lucille (Good) S.; m. Margaret Edith Rightmyer, Sept. 5, 1959 (div. July 1986); children: James II, Elizabeth Gonzales, Russell; m. Esther Zamora, Sept. 13, 1986; stepchildren: Bryan Boots, Jeremy Hellier, Marisol Boots. BS ChemE, Stanford U., 1960, MS ChemE, 1961. Registered profl. engr., Calif. Nuclear engr. Pacific Gas & Electric Co., Humboldt Bay Power Plant, Eureka, Calif., 1961-71; tech. mgr. Pacific Gas & Electric Co., Diablo Canyon Power Plant, Avila Beach, Calif., 1971-80; mgr. nuclear ops. Pacific Gas & Electric Co., San Francisco, 1980-84, v.p. nuclear power generation, 1984-90, sr. v.p., gen. mgr. nuclear power generation bus. unit, 1990-91; exec. v.p. Pacific Gas & Electric, San Francisco, 1991-97; ret., 1997; pres., CEO PG&E Enterprises, San Francisco, 1994-95, also bd. dirs.; bd. dirs. Nuclear Energy Inst., U.S. Oper. Svcs. Co., Math., Engrng., Sci. Achievement. Mem. AIChE, Commonwealth Club of Calif. (bd. govs. 1992-97). Republican. Episcopalian. Avocations: golf, music. Home: 2550 Royal Oaks Dr Alamo CA 94507-2227

SHIFFMAN, BERNARD, mathematician, educator; b. N.Y.C., June 23, 1942; s. Max and Bella S.; m. Doris Judith Yaffe, July 11, 1965; children: Jonathan, Daniel. BS, MIT, 1964; PhD, U. Calif., Berkeley, 1968. C.L.E. Moore instr. MIT, 1968-70; asst. prof. math. Yale U., 1970-73; assoc. prof. Johns Hopkins U., Balt., 1973-77, prof., 1977—, chair dept. math., 1990-93; mem. Inst. Advanced Study, Princeton, N.J., fall 1975, Math. Scis. Rsch. Inst., Berkeley, Calif., spring 1996; series lectr. U. Kaiserslautern, West Germany, 1977, Inst. Math., Academia Sinica, Beijing, China, 1978, U. Paris VI, 1979, Nordic Summer Sch., Joensuu, Finland, 1981; mem. Inst. des Hautes Etudes Scientifiques, Bures-sur-Yvette, France, June 1979; vis. prof. U. Paris VI, 1981, 85, U. Grenoble, June 1992, Nov. 1995. Editor Forum Mathematicum, 1989-95; assoc. editor Am. Jour. Math., 1990-92, editor, 1992-93, editor-in-chief, 1993—; rschr. publs. in complex analysis. Hon. Woodrow Wilson fellow, 1964, NSF fellow, 1968, Alfred P. Sloan rsch. fellow, 1973-75; recipient Woodrow Wilson Faculty Devel. award, 1979. Mem. Am. Math. Soc. Office: Johns Hopkins U Dept Math Baltimore MD 21218

SHIGEMOTO, APRIL FUMIE, English educator secondary school; b. Lihue, Hawaii, Apr. 22, 1948; d. Warren Itaru and Edith Yuriko (Y-oshimura) Tanaka; m. Tom Hideo Shigemoto, July 21, 1973; children: Taylor, Tyron, Tryson, Thomas-Jay. BA in English, U. Hawaii Manoa, 1970, profl. diploma secondary, 1971. English tchr. Kapaa (Hawaii) H.S. and Intermediate Sch., 1971-81, Kauai H.S. and Intermediate Sch., Lihue, Hawaii, 1981-90; core curriculum coord. Kauai H.S. and Intermediate Sch., 1990—. Leader Boy Scouts of Am., Lihue, Hawaii, 1982—. Recipient one of seven Status of Women awards, Kauai, Lihue, Hawaii, 1988, Den Leader of the Yr. award Boy Scouts of Am., 1988, Milken Educator's award, Milken Found., L.A., 1992; named Outstanding Working Mother, Garden Island Newspaper, Lihue, Hawaii, 1989, Kauai Dist. Tchr. of Yr., State Dept. Edn., Hawaii, 1990, State Tchr. of Yr., Scottish Rite Order of Free Masons, Honolulu, 1991, one of Kauai's Outstanding Families, Garden Island Newspaper, Hawaii, 1992. Mem. Phi Delta Kappa, Delta Kappa Gamma. Democrat. Avocations: traveling, reading, golfing. Office: Kauai HS & Intermediate Sch 3577 Lala Rd Lihue HI 96766-9520

SHIH, JASON CHIA-HSING, biotechnology educator; b. Chien-Chen, Hunan, China, Oct. 8, 1939; came to U.S., 1969; m. Jane Chu-Huei Chien, Aug. 31, 1966; children: Giles C., Tim C. BS, Nat. Taiwan U., Taipei, 1963, MS, 1966; PhD, Cornell U., 1973. Lectr. Tunghai U., Taichung, Taiwan, 1966-69; rsch. asst. Cornell U., Ithaca, N.Y., 1969-73, sr. rsch. assoc., 1975-76; rshc. assoc. U. Ill., Urbana, 1973-75; asst. prof. N.C. State U., Raleigh, 1976-80, assoc. prof., 1980-88, prof., 1988—; vis. fellow U. Coll. Cardiff, Wales, 1983, Acad. Sinica, Taiwan, 1997; sci. advisor Shenyang Agrl. U., China, 1985-89; vis. prof. Nat. Taiwan U., 1986, spl. advisor to the pres., 1994; vis. specialist UNDP, China, 1987-93; vis. prof. Bowman Gray Sch. Medicine, 1991. Patentee in field. Exec. com. mem. Triangle Area Chinese Am. Soc., Raleigh, 1979-82, pres., 1982-83, chmn. bd., 1992-93; coord. N.C. State U. exch. programs with China and Taiwan, 1985-95; sci. exch. fellow to Spelderholt Poultry Rsch. Ctr., The Netherlands, USDA-Office of Internat. Coop. and Devel., 1994, 95; vis. fellow Acad. Sinica, Taiwan, 1997. Recipent numerous rsch. grants, 1977—; Pew Nat. fellow faculty scholar, 1990-91. Fellow Am. Heart Assn., Arteriosclerosis Rsch. Coun.; mem. Am. Instn. Nutrition (Travel award 1981, 89), Am. Soc. for Microbiology, Poultry Sci. Assn., Soc. Chinese Bioscientists in Am. (sec. and treas. 1985-86), Phi Kappa Phi, Sigma Iota Rho (J. Rigney award for Internat. Svc. 1994). Office: N C State U Dept Poultry Sci Raleigh NC 27695-7608

SHIH, TSO MIN, mining engineering educator; b. Ying-Chen, Shantung, China, Apr. 4, 1935; s. Ren Ying and Sun Sum S.; m. Ching Chi Hsia, June 1, 1961; children: Rosa Hung-Chen, Kim Hung-Wei, Sophia Hung-Ren. BS, Nat. Cheng-Kung U., Tainan, Taiwan, 1958; MS, McGill U., Montreal, Can., 1965; postgrad., U. B.C., Vancouver, 1966-68. Rsch. asst. Nova Scotia Tech. Coll., Halifax, N.S., Can., 1965-66; lectr. Nat. Cheng-Kung U., Tainan, Taiwan, 1968-72, assoc. prof., 1972-74, dept. chmn., 1974-80, prof., 1980—; dir. Chinese Inst. Mining and Metal Engrng., Taipei, 1976-78. 2d lt. ROTC, 1958-60. Recipient award Pi Epsilon Tao, 1989, award dept. reconstructions Govt. Taiwan, 1993. Mem. Chinese Inst. Mining and Metal. Engrng. (award 1972, 91), Mining Assn. Rep. of China (dir. 1988-94, 96—, award 1996), Chinese Inst. Engrs. Office: Nat Cheng-Kung U, Ta-Hsueh Rd, 700 Tainan Taiwan

SHIH, WEI, astrophysicist; b. Shanghai, China, May 5, 1943; came to U.S., 1959; s. Frank I. and Emily Kwong S.; m. Yen-Chi Cheng, July 1980; children: Fredrick Yu-Fun Shih, Edwin Shih. BS in Physics, Nat. Taiwan U., 1956; MS in Physics, U. Del., 1963; PhD in Physics, NYU, 1969. Rsch. assoc. Union Indsl. Rsch. Inst., Hsinchu, Taiwan, 1956-59; rsch. microwave physicist Frequency Engrng. Lab., Farmingdale, N.J., 1968-71; rsch. physicist Atomic Energy Coun., Taipei, Taiwan, 1972-74; prof. physics Soochow U., Taipei, 1972-78; adj. prof. physics Tam Kang U., Tamsui, Taiwan, 1972-78. Author: Accretion Power and Mechanism for Conversion of Gravitational Potential to Radiative Energy in Active Galactic Nuclei, 1980; co-author: Magnetohydrodynamics of Viscous Gas Accreting on Highly Magnetized Neutron Stars and White Dwarfs, 1974, Dynamics and Accretion Column Structure for Neutron Stars, 1989. Rsch. grantee NASA, Goddard Space Flight Ctr., Greenbelt, Md., 1968. Mem. Am. Assn. for Advancement of Sci., Am. Phys. Soc., Nat. Geographic Soc., N.Y. Acad. Scis. Avocations: piloting, boating, fishing, travel. Office: Fortuna-CRX Inc 50 Bayard St Apt 7K New York NY 10013-4918

SHIHATA, IBRAHIM FAHMY IBRAHIM, development banker, lawyer; b. Damietta, Egypt, Aug. 19, 1937; s. Ibrahim and Neamat (El Ashmawy) S.; m. Samia S. Farid, June 18, 1967; children: Sharif, Yasmine, Nadia. LL.B., U. Cairo, 1957, diploma in pub. law and fin., 1958, diploma in pvt. law, 1959; S.J.D., Harvard U., 1964, LLD (hon.), U. Dundee, Scotland, 1995. Mem. Conseil d'Etat, UAR, 1957-60; mem. Tech. Bur. of Pres., Egypt, 1959-60; from lectr. to assoc. prof. internat. law Ain-Shams U., Cairo, 1964-66, 70-72; legal adviser Kuwait Fund for Arab Econ. Devel., 1966-70, 72-76; dir. gen. OPEC Fund for Internat. Devel., Vienna, 1976-83; exec. dir. Internat. Fund for Agrl. Devel., Rome, 1977-83; sr. v.p., gen. counsel World Bank, Washington, 1983—; sec. gen. Internat. Centre for Settlement of Investment Disputes, Washington, 1983—; chmn. bd. Internat. Devel. Law Inst., Rome, 1983—; bd. dirs. Internat. Fertilizer Devel. Ctr., Muscle Shoals, Ala., 1979-84, Vienna Devel. Inst.; mem. exec.coun., Am. Soc. Internat. Law, Washington, 1984-87; adv. com. Rsch. Ctr. Internat. Law, Cambridge, Eng., 1985—; founding adv., bd. dir. Inst. Transnat. Arbitration, Houston, 1986—. Author: The Power of the International Court to Determine Its Own Jurisdiction, 1965, International Air and Space Law, 1966, International Economic Joint Ventures, 1969, International Guarantee for Foreign Investments, 1971, Treatment of Foreign Investments in Egypt, 1972, Secure and Recognized Boundaries, 1974, The Arab Oil Embargo, 1975, The Other Face of OPEC, 1982, The OPEC Fund for International Development-The Formative Years, 1983, A Program for Tomorrow-Challenges and Prospects of the Egyptian Economy in a Changing World, 1987, MIGA and Foreign Investment, 1988, The European Bank for Reconstruction and Development, 1990, The World Bank and the Arab World, 1990, The World Bank in a Changing World, vol. 1, 1991, Legal Treatment of Foreign Investment: The World Bank Guidelines, 1993, Towards a Comprehensive Reform, 1993, The World Bank Inspection Panel, 1994, The World Bank in a Changing World, vol. 2, 1995, My Will for My Country, vol. 1, 1995, vol. 2, 1995, vol. 3, 1996; editor ICSID Rev.-Fgn. Investment Law Jour. Decorated Grosses Silbernes Ehrenzeichen am Bande fuer Verdienste um die Republik Oesterreich (Austria), 1983; recipient Kuwait prize for sci. progress in social scis., 1983. Mem. Am. Soc. Internat. Law, Institut de Droit Internat. (Geneva). Office: IBRD General Counsel 1818 H St NW Washington DC 20433-0001

SHIH-CARDUCCI, JOAN CHIA-MO, cooking educator, biochemist, medical technologist; b. Rukuan, Chunghua, Republic of China, Dec. 21, 1933; came to U.S., 1955; d. Luke Chiang-hsi and Lien-chin (Chang) Shih; m. Kenneth M. Carducci, Sept. 30, 1960 (dec. July 1988); children: Suzanne R., Elizabeth M. BS in Chemistry, St. Mary Coll., Xavier, Kans., 1959; intern in med. tech., St. Mary's Hosp., Rochester, N.Y., 1960. Med. rschr. Strong Meml. Hosp. U. Rochester, 1960-61; pharm. chemist quality control Strasenburgh Labs., Rochester, 1961-62; cooking tchr. adult edn. Montgomery County Pub. Schs., Rockville, Md., 1973-79; tchr. The Chinese Cookery Inc., Rockville, 1975-86; tchr. The Chinese Cookery Inc., Silver Spring, Md., 1986—, pres., bd. dirs., 1975—; chemist NIH, Bethesda, 1987—; analytical chemist NIH/WRAIR, Rockville, Md., 1994-96. Author: The Chinese Cookery, 1981, Hunan Cuisine, 1984. Mem. Am. Chem. Soc., Internat. Assn. Cooking Profls. (Woman of Yr. 1994-97). Republican. Roman Catholic. Avocations: piano, music, dance, flowers, vegetables. Home and Office: The Chinese Cookery Inc 14209 Sturtevant Rd Silver Spring MD 20905-4448

SHIKUMA, EUGENE YUJIN, travel agency executive; b. Tokyo, Nov. 18, 1948; came to U.S., 1957; s. Mitsuo and Yukiko (Kanaoka) S. BSEE, U. Hawaii at Manoa, Honolulu, 1971, MS in Computer Sci., 1975. Lab. test engr. and scientist McDonnell Douglas Astronautics, Inc., 1971-72; systems engr. Lear Siegler Astronics, 1972-73; jr. coord. Japan Travel Bur. Hawaii, Inc., Honolulu, 1978-83, sr. coord., 1983-84, supr., 1984-89, mgr., 1989—. Bd. dirs. Maui United Way, Kahului, Hawaii, 1988-89, Maui Hui Malama, Waiulku, 1989-90; bd. dirs., sec. Kamoa Views Apt. Owners Assn., 1991-96; mem. Maui County Visitor Task Force, 1995—; adv. bd. mem. Maui Acad. Travel and Tourism. Mem. Maui C. of C., Maui Japanese C. of C. Avocations: swimming, coin collecting, fine art, antique prints.

SHILLESTAD, JOHN GARDNER, financial services company executive; b. Oak Park, Ill., Oct. 31, 1934; s. John Nelson and Isabel Blanche (Gardner) S.; m. Astri Cedervall; children—Christine C., Annette. B.B.A., Northwestern U., 1964, M.B.A., 1967. CLU; CPCU; ChFC. Mktg. dir. spl. plans CNA Ins., Chgo., 1958-66; asst. v.p. Montgomery Ward Life, Chgo., 1966-69; pres., chief exec. officer Fort Dearborn Life Ins. Co., Chgo., 1969-79; sr. v.p. Hartford Life Cos., Conn., 1979-85, also bd. dirs., 1985-87; pres. JGS Fin. Svcs., Inc., 1987—; pres., chmn. bd., CEO, Columbian Mut. Life Ins. Co., Binghamton, N.Y., 1987—; chmn., CEO Columbian Life Ins. Co.; chmn. bd. dirs., CEO Washington Nat. Life N.Y. Mem. Bd. Edn., Dist. 30, Northbrook, Ill., 1976-79; bd. dirs. Salvation Army, Binghamton; mem. adv. bd. SUNY Sch. Mgmt., Binghamton, Kellogg Sch. Bus., Northwestern U. With U.S. Army, 1954-56. Mem. C. of C. (bd. dirs.), Sunset Ridge Club (Northfield, Ill.), Binghamton Country Club, City Club of Binghamton, Sky Club (N.Y.C.). Republican. Congregationalist. Home: 25 Virginia Ave Binghamton NY 13905-4305 Office: Columbia Mut Life Ins Co Vestal Pkwy E Binghamton NY 13802

SHILLING, A. GARY, economic consultant, investment advisor; b. Fremont, Ohio, May 25, 1937; s. A. Vaughn and Lettie E. (O'Harrow) S.; m. Margaret E. Bloete, Dec. 22, 1962; children: Geoffrey B., Andrew J., Stephen E., Jennifer E. AB in Physics magna cum laude, Amherst (Mass.) Coll., 1960; MA in Econs., Stanford (Calif.) U., 1962, PhD in Econs., 1965. Economist Standard Oil Co. (N.J.), N.Y.C., 1963-67; chief economist Merrill Lynch, Pierce, Fenner & Smith, N.Y.C., 1967-71; rsch. dir. Estabrook & Co., N.Y.C., 1971-72; sr. v.p., chief economist White, Weld & Co., N.Y.C., 1972-78; chmn., pres., dir. A. Gary Shilling & Co., Inc., Springfield, N.J., 1978—; pres. Lakeview Econ. Svcs., Inc., Springfield, 1979—; owner Lakeview Svcs., Inc., Springfield, 1993—; bd. dirs. Nat. Life Vt., Montpelier, Am. Productivity and Quality Ctr., Houston; adv. dir. Austin (Tex.) Trust Co., 1988—; informal econ. advisor Former Pres. George Bush, 1978—; mem. Nat. Com. on Jobs and Small Bus., 1986-87; dir. The Heartland Group of Mutual Funds, 1995—, Palm. Harbor Homes, 1995—. Author: Is Inflation Ending? Are You Ready?, 1983, The World Has Definitely Changed: New Economic Forces and Their Implications for the Next Decade, 1986, After the Crash: Recession or Depression? Investment and Business Strategies for a Deflationary World, 1988; creator bd. game The Deflation Game, 1989; columnist Forbes, S&P Credit Week, Nihon Keizai Shimbun Jour. Bd. dirs. Aim Packaging Inc., 1986-89, Episcopal Ch. Found., N.Y.C., 1989—; chmn. Episcopal Evangelism Found., N.Y.C., 1988—; trustee Bates Coll., Lewiston, Maine, 1988-91, Kent Pl. Sch., Summit, N.J., 1983-89; bd. dirs. The Gen. Theol. Episcopal Sem., N.Y.C., 1988—, treas., 1994—; chmn. N.J. State Revenue Forecasting Adv. Commn., 1995—. Named Wall St. Top Economist, Instl. Investor Mag., 1975, 76, Top Commodity Trading Advisor, Futures Mag., 1993. Mem. Nat. Assn. Bus. Economists, N.Y. Soc. Security Analysts, Short Hills Club, Phi Beta Kappa, Sigma Xi. Republican. Episcopalian. Avocations: tennis, travel, gardening, hunting, fishing, beekeeping. Home: 33 Lakeview Ave Short Hills NJ 07078-2264 Office: A Gary Shilling & Co Inc 500 Morris Ave Springfield NJ 07081-1020

SHILLING, ROY BRYANT, JR., academic administrator; b. Enville, Okla., Apr. 7, 1931; s. Roy Bryant and Lila M. (Prestage) S.; m. Margaret Riddle, Oct. 16, 1952; children: Roy Bryant III, Nancy Gale. BA, McMurry U., 1951, HHD, 1982; BD, So. Meth. U., 1957; MS, Ind. U., 1966, PhD, 1967. Presdl. asst. McMurry U., Abilene, Tex., 1959-61; asst. to pres. Tenn. Wesleyan Coll., 1961-64; asst. in devel. Ball State U., 1964-65; rsch. assoc. Ind. U., 1965-67; dir. planning and rsch. Baldwin Wallace Coll., 1967-68; exec. v.p. Southwestern U., 1968-69, pres., 1981—; pres. Hendrix Coll., 1969-81; mem. Nat. Commn. on United Meth. Higher Edn., 1975-77. Mem. Ark. Arts and Humanities Coun., 1970-76, chmn., 1974-75; bd. dirs. Ark. Children's Hosp., 1981; mem. bd. higher edn. and ministry United Meth. Ch., 1972-80, mem. univ. senate, 1980-88, v.p. 1983-84, pres., 1984-88; chmn. Gulf dist. Rhodes Scholarship Selection Com., 1992, Ark. chmn., 1973-74, Tex. chmn., 1985-91; mem. Young Pres. Orgn., 1975-81; mem. bd. visitors Air U., 1991-94. With U.S. Army, 1952-54. Recipient Disting. Alumnus award McMurry U., 1980, Perkins Disting. Alumnus award So. Meth. U., 1987, Owen B. Sherrill award for leadership in econ. devel. Georgetown, 1988; named one of Top 100 Most Effective Coll. Pres. in Nation, Bowling Green State U./Exxon Edn. Found., 1988. Mem. North Ctrl. Assn. Colls. and Schs. (vice chmn., chmn. elect 1980-81), Nat. Assn Schs. and Colls. of United Meth. Ch. (v.p. 1975-76, pres. 1976-77), Nat. Coun. Ind. Colls. and Univs. (bd. dirs. 1984-88), So. U. Conf. (exec. com. 1974-78), 79-86, sec.-treas. 1979-86, v.p. 1991-92, pres. 1992-93), Am. Coun. Edn. (bd. dirs. 1989-91), Inst. for Humanities (bd. dirs. Salado, Tex. chpt. 1985-91, mem. internat. coun. advs. 1994), Philos Soc. Tex., Rotary, Masons, Alpha Chi, Phi Delta Kappa. Office: Southwestern U Office Pres Georgetown TX 78626

SHILLINGLAW, GORDON, accounting educator, consultant, writer; b. Albany, N.Y., July 26, 1925; s. James McCombe and Margaret Blanche (Stephens) S.; m. Barbara Ann Cross, June 24, 1950; children—James McCombe, Laura Cross. A.B. magna cum laude, Brown U., 1945; M.S., U. Rochester, 1948; Ph.D., Harvard U., 1952. Asst. prof. Hamilton Coll., Clinton, N.Y., 1951-52; cons. assoc. Joel Dean Assocs., Yonkers, N.Y., 1952-55; asst. prof. MIT, Cambridge, 1955-61; assoc. prof. Columbia U., N.Y.C., 1961-66, prof. acctg., 1966-90, prof. emeritus, 1991—; vis. prof. Mgmt. Devel. Inst., Lausanne, Switzerland, 1964-65, 67-69; mem. U.S. Cost Acctg. Stds. Bd., 1978-80, U.S. R.R. Acctg. Prin. Bd., 1985-87; trustee Scudder Latin Am. Fund, Scudder Pacific Opportunities Fund, Scudder Value Fund, Scudder Capital Growth Fund, Scudder Devel. Fund, Scudder Micro Cap Fund, Scudder 21st Century Fund, Am. Assn. Ret. Persons Growth Trust, Income Trust, Insured Tax Free Income Trust, Money Market Trust; dir. Scudder Internat. Fund, Scudder Small Co. Value Fund, Scudder Gold Fund; cons. in field. Author: Managerial Cost Accounting, 1961, 5th edit., 1982, Accounting: A Managment Approach, 1964, 9th edit., 1993, Financial Accounting: Concepts and Applications, 1989; contbr. articles to profl. jours. Mem. bd. advisors Fund Directions, 1990-96; bd. dirs., treas. Feris Found. Am., Stamford, Conn., 1970-94. Served with U.S. Navy. 1943-46. Recipient Disting. Teaching award Columbia U., 1970. Mem. Am. Acctg. Assn. (v.p. 1966-67), Inst. of Mgmt. Accts., Phi Beta Kappa, Beta Gamma Sigma. Avocations: tennis; travel; French and Italian language study. Home: 196 Villard Ave Hastings On Hudson NY 10706 also: 115 Live Oak Ln Largo FL 33770-4056

SHILLINGSBURG, MIRIAM JONES, English educator, academic administrator; b. Balt., Oct. 5, 1943; d. W. Elvin and Miriam (Reeves) Jones; BA, Mars Hill Coll., 1964; MA, U. S.C., 1966, PhD, 1969; m. Peter L. Shillingsburg, Nov. 21, 1967; children: Robert, George, John, Alice, Anne Carol. Asst. prof. Limestone Coll., Gaffney, S.C., 1969; asst. prof. Mississippi State (Miss.) U., 1970-75, assoc. prof., 1975-80, prof. English, 1980-96, assoc. v.p. for acad. affairs, 1988-96, dir. summer sch., 1991-96; dean arts and scis. Lamar U., Tex., 1996—; vis. fellow Australian Def. Force Acad., 1989; Fulbright lectr. U. New South Wales, Duntroon, Australia, 1984-85. Nat. Endowment Humanities fellow in residence, Columbia U., 1976-77. Mem. Soc. Study So. Lit., S. Ctrl. Modern Lang. Assn., Australia-New Zealand Am. Studies Assn., Phi Kappa Phi, Simms Soc. (pres.). Author: Mark Twain in Australasia, 1988; editor: Conquest of Granada, 1988, The Cub of the Panther, 1997; mem. editorial bd. Works of W.M. Thackeray; assoc. editor Miss. Quarterly; contbr. articles to profl. jours. and mags.

SHILLINGTON, EDWARD BLAIN, government official; b. Grayburn, Sask., Can., Aug. 28, 1944; s. Sterling Arthur and Dorothy Jessie (Henry) S.; m. Sonia Shirley Koroscil, Aug. 15, 1970; children: Ryan Sterling, Tara Dawn. BA, LLB, U. Sask., 1967. Mem. Sask. Legis. (Regina N.E.), 1975—, minister of coop. and coop. devel., 1975-77, minister of consumer affairs, 1975-76, minister of govt. svcs., 1976-78, minister of culture and youth, 1977-80, minister of edn., 1978-79, assoc. minister of fin., 1992, minister of labour, 1992-95, assoc. minister fin. and minister of crown investments, 1995, minister of justice and atty. gen., 1995, minister of intergovtl. affairs and provincial sec., 1995—, govt. house leader, 1995—; ptnr. Shillington-Doré Law Office, 1980-92. Avocations: reading, boating, fishing, flying. Office: Government of Saskatchewan, Rm 204 Legislative Bldg, Regina, SK Canada S4S 0B3

SHILLMAN, JEFFREY NATHANIEL, lawyer; b. Detroit, Nov. 9, 1945; s. Morris H. and Esther F. (Cantor) S.; m. Marlene R. Weinberger, May 29, 1969 (div. Oct. 1983); children: Randall, Tracey, Derek; m. Barbara Susan Feldman, Apr. 27, 1984. BA, Wayne State U., 1967, JD cum laude, 1969. Bar: Mich. 1969, U.S. Dist. Ct. (ea. dist.) Mich. 1976. Ptnr. Sommers, Schwartz, Silver & Schwartz, Southfield, Mich., 1981—; mediator Mediation Tribunal Assn., Detroit, Oakland County Circuit Court, Pontiac. Co-author: Michigan Civil Procedure Forms Practice, 1989, supplement, 1994. Mem. ABA, Met. Detroit Trial Lawyers Assn. (pres.), Oakland County Trial Lawyers Assn. (pres.), Mich. Trial Lawyers Assn. (pres. 1980-81), Southfield Bar Assn. (pres.), Assn. Trial Lawyers Am., Oakland County Bar Assn. Jewish. Home: 2000 Town Ctr Ste 900 Southfield MI 48075-1142

SHILS, MAURICE EDWARD, physician, educator; b. Atlantic City, Dec. 31, 1914; s. Samuel L. and Sarah (Harris) S.; m. Cylia Finkiel, Feb. 19, 1939 (dec. Sept. 1987); children: Loraine J., Jonathan R.; m. Betty Ann Bell, Sept. 24, 1988. BA, Johns Hopkins U., 1937, ScD, 1940; MD, NYU, 1958. Intern joint program Cornell divsn. Bellevue Hosp. and Meml. Hosp., N.Y.C., 1958-59; fellow in physiology Meml. Hosp., 1959-60; instr., asst. prof. nutrition Sch. Pub. Health Columbia U., N.Y.C., 1946-54; instr. biochemistry Sch. Hygiene Johns Hopkins U., Balt., 1940-42; head Ctrl. Metabolic Lab. Sloan Kettering Inst., N.Y.C., 1960-72; from asst. to assoc. attending physician Meml. Hosp., N.Y.C., 1962-72, attending physician, 1972-85; asst. prof. biochem. Sloan-Kettering divsn. Med. Coll. Cornell U., N.Y.C., 1959-62, from asst. prof. to prof. medicine Med. Coll., 1962-85, prof. emeritus, 1985—; adj. prof. nutrition dept. pub. health scis. Bowman Gray Sch. Medicine, Winston-Salem, N.C., 1989-94, cons., 1994—. Author, co-editor: Modern Nutrition in Health and Disease, 8th edit., 1994; contbr. more than 200 rsch. and review articles to profl. jours. Fellow Am. Inst. Nutrition, Am. Coll. Physicians, N.Y. Acad. Medicine (Acad. Plaque award 1987); mem. AMA (chmn. nutrition adv. group 1974-77, Goldberger award 1983), Am. Soc. Clin. Nutrition (pres. 1985-86, Excellence in Med. Sch. award 1994), Am. Bd. Nutrition, Phi Beta Kappa, Alpha Omega Alpha.

SHIM, SANG KOO, state mental health official; b. Tokyo, Japan, Oct. 1, 1942; came to U.S., 1968; s. Sang Taek and Kum Ryon (Bae) S.; m. Jae Hee Lee, July 12, 1972; children: Tammy, David. BS, Seoul Nat. U., Korea, 1967; MBA, No. Ill. U., 1970; MS, U. Wis., 1975. CPA, Ill., cert. govt. fin. mgr., Assn. Govt. Accts. Acct. Vaughn Mfg. Co., Chgo., 1970-72, Stewart-Warner Corp., Chgo., 1972-73; fin. cons. Cen. Acctg. Assn., New Baden, Ill., 1977-79; auditor Ill. Dept. Mental Health, Springfield, 1980-82, CFO, 1983—. Treas. Korean Assn. Greater St. Louis, 1982. Mem. Ill. CPA Soc., Assn. Govt. Accts. (cert. govt. fin. mgr.), Korean-Am. C. of C. (v.p. Greater St. Louis chpt. 1994-95). Home: 5 Settlers Ln Springfield IL 62707-7725 Office: Ill Dept Mental Health Bur Fin Svcs 401 S Spring St Springfield IL 62706-0002

SHIMA, HIROMU, management educator; b. Kyoto, Japan, June 20, 1929; s. Seitaro and Teru Shima; m. Atsuko Onogi, Mar. 26, 1961; children: Katsutoshi, Yukihiro. B in Commerce, Doshisha U., Kyoto, Japan, 1951, M in Commerce, 1953; D in Bus. Adminstrn., Kobe (Japan) U., 1982. Teaching asst. Doshisha U., Kyoto, 1953-55, lectr., 1955-58, assoc. prof., 1958-67, prof., 1967—. Author: The Research of Scientific Management, 1963, Personnel Management, 1981, Big Business and Management, 1991, Management in an International Economy, 1996. Libr. Doshisha U., 1989-91. Mem. Assn. for Study of Theory of Pers. Mgmt. (dir.), Am. Acad. Mgmt., Assn. for Study of Bus. Adminstrn., Japan Soc. for Pers. and Labor Rsch. Home: 26 Hiraki-machi, Uji-shi Kyoto 611, Japan Office: Doshisha U, Karasuma-Imadegawa Kamikyo-ku, Kyoto 602, Japan

SHIMA, LARRY MITSURU, health facility administrator; b. Tokyo, Nov. 17, 1958; came to U.S., 1970; s. Masa and Amy A. (Narisawa) S.; m. Fran T. Shinsato, July 14, 1991; 1 child, Austin Y. BS in Med. Tech., U. Hawaii, 1981; MS in Health Svcs. Adminstrn., Cen. Mich. U., 1994. Med. technologist Kuakini Med. Ctr., Honolulu, 1980-86; chemistry specialist Straub Clinic and Hosp., Honolulu, 1986-89; chemistry supr. Health Care Internat., Aiea, Hawaii, 1989; from ops. supr. to ops mgr. Pali Momi Med. Ctr., Aiea, Hawaii, 1990-94; ops. mgr. Clin. Labs. Hawaii, Honolulu, 1994-96; ops mgr. Singapore divsn. Clin. Labs. Hawaii, 1996—; quality assurance coun. mem. Kapiolani Health Systems, Honolulu, 1993-94, tissueand transfusion mem., 1992-94, cons. cholesterol testing, 1991-94; cons. lab. computer sys., 1990-91. Mem. Clin. Lab. Mgmt. Assn., Am. Assn. for Clin. Chemistry, Am. Soc. Clin. Pathologists, Acad. Med. Arts & Scis., John A. Burns Sch. Medicine Alumni Assn. Republican. Achievements include rsch. in HPLC applications in clin. toxicology, ethics and managed care, managed care and the lab. Home: 10 G Braddell Hill #02-25, Braddell View 579726, Singapore Office: Clins Labs Hawaii, 219 Henderson Rd #07-03, Henderson Industrial Park 159556, Singapore

SHIMADA, HARUO, physical chemistry educator; b. Himeji, Hyōgo, Japan, Mar. 27, 1935; s. Shigeyoshi and Shige (Okamoto) S.; m. Ikuko Tanaka, Sept. 21, 1968; children: Yōko, Kenichiro. Grad., U. Tokyo, 1958, doctorate, 1968. Rschr. Yawata (Japan) Iron & Steel Co., 1958-72; sr. rschr. Nippon Steel Corp., Kawasaki, Japan, 1973-80; chief rschr. Nippon Steel Corp., Kawasaki, 1980-90; prof. Sci. U. Tokyo, Shinjuku, Japan, 1990—. Editorial mem.: (monthly jour.) Chem. Industry, 1972—; contbr. articles to profl. jours. Mem. Nat. Assn. Corrosion Engrs., Internat. Tech. Inst. (life mem.). Avocations: jogging, swimming. Home: Chuō 5-3-5, ōta 143, Japan Office: Sci Univ Tokyo, 1-3 Kagurazaka, Shinjuku 162, Japan

SHIMADA, TOSHIYUKI, orchestra conductor, music director; b. Tokyo, Dec. 23, 1951; came to U.S., 1966; s. Ron and Matsue Shimada; m. Eva Virsik, 1987; 1 child, Matias. MusB, Calif. State U., Northridge, 1977. Dir. music, condr. Youth Musicians Found. Debut Orch., L.A., 1978-81; assoc. condr. Houston Symphony Orch., 1981-86; dir. mus., condr. Rice U. Symphony Orch., Houston, 1982-85, Nassau (N.Y.) Symphony Orch., 1987-88, Portland (Maine) Symphony Orch., 1986—; artist cons. Tex. Inst. for Aesthetic Study, Houston, 1984-86; artist in residence U. So. Maine, Portland, 1986-88. Trustee Japan Am. Soc. Maine, Portland, 1990-91. Recipient Condrs. award Young Musicians Found., 1977; finalist Herbert von Karajan Competition, Berlin, 1979; Toshiyuki Shimada Day proclaimed by City of Houston, 1986. Office: Portland Symphony Orch 477 Congress St Portland ME 04101-3406*

SHIMANSKI, CHARLES STUART, organization executive; b. Madison, Wis., Jan. 17, 1957; s. Stuart Thomas and Gloria Mae (Schindler) S.; m. Christiane Leitinger, May 30, 1992. BA in Econs., U. Wis., 1980. Float control mgr. United Bank of Denver, 1980-84; cash mgr. Oppenheimer, Denver, 1985-86, project mgr. office automation, 1987-93; sys. cons. Darlington Asset Mgmt., Geneva, Switzerland, 1986-87; exec. dir. Am. Alpine Club, Golden, Colo., 1993—; lectr. U. Colo., Boulder, U. Denver, Arapahoe C.C., Sierra Club, Denver Pub. Schs., Jefferson County Pub. Schs., Boy Scouts Am., Wilderness Med. Soc., Nat. Park Svcs., Nat. Ski Patrol, Nat. Forest Svc., Mountain Rescue Assn., Colo. Search and Rescue Bd., Colo. Mountain Club, Internat. Alpine Sch., also mountaineering outfitters and corps.; tech. cons., including Rescue 911, CBS, Unsolved Mysteries, NBC, Turning Point, Women of Valor, ABC, Tour de France, CBS, Emergency Call, others; published over 300 photographs in areas of alpine mountaineering, mountain rescue, med.-evacuation helicopter rescue, avalanche safety and rescue; EMT, State of Colo., 1985—; dir. Avalanche Awareness Week, Colo. Search and Rescue Bd., 1988-93, instr. Breckenridge Avalanche Sch., 1988—; mem. Alpine Rescue Team, Evergreen, Colo., 1983—. Author: Helicopters in Search and Rescue Operations—Basic, 1993, Intermediate, 1993, AVALANCHE!!!, 1993, General Back-Country Safety, 1993, Avalanche Rescue Operations, 1995, Risks in Mountain Rescue Operations, 1996. Mem. Am. Assn. Avalanche Profls., Mountain Rescue Asssn. (vice chmn., tng. dir. Rocky Mountain region 1989-92, chmn. 1992-94, nat. exec. officer 1992-94, chmn. edn. com. 1994—), Wilderness Med. Soc., Emergency Med. Svcs. Assn. Colo., Am. Alpine Club, Colo. Mountain Club, Alpine Club Can. Avocations: mountain climbing, including peaks in France, Italy, Switzerland, Canada and U.S., photography. Office: Am Alpine Club 710 10th St Ste 100 Golden CO 80401-1022

SHIMAZAKI, YOJI, civil engineering educator; b. Yokohama, Kanagawa, Japan, Dec. 5, 1948; s. Fumio and Fusae (Ishikawa) S.; m. Mitsuko Nagai, Feb. 17, 1980; children: Eriko, Yosuke. BS, Tokai U., Kanagawa, 1971, MS, 1973; PhD, Colo. State U., 1980; DEng, Tohoku U., Sendai, Japan, 1987. Lectr. civil engring. Tokai U., 1981-83, assoc. prof., 1983-93, prof., 1993—; cons. Idemitsu Petrochem. Co. Ltd., Chiba, Japan, The Yokohama Rubber Co. Ltd., Kanagawa. Contbr. articles to profl. jours. Mem. Japan Soc. Civil Engrs., Japan Soc. Mech. Engrs., Soc. Rheology. Avocations: skiing, tennis. Home: 2-2-25 Hiratsuka, Hinataoka 254, Japan Office: Tokai U, 1117 Kitakaname Hiratsuka, Kanagawa 259-12, Japan

SHIMER, DANIEL LEWIS, corporate executive; b. San Angelo, Tex., July 30, 1944; s. Lewis V. and Mary A. (Slick) S.; married. BS in Acctg. and Mktg., Ind. U., 1972; postgrad., Loyola U., New Orleans, 1977. CPA. Sr. acct. Peat, Marwick, Mitchell & Co., Indpls., 1973-75; asst. treas. LTV Corp., Dallas, 1975-79; v.p. fin. Stoller Chem. Co., Houston, 1979-81; v.p., CFO Petro-Silver, Inc., Denver, 1981-83; v.p., treas. FoxMeyer Corp., Denver, 1983-86; v.p., treas., sec. CoastAmerica Corp., Denver, 1986-88; exec. v.p. Bard & Co., Denver, 1989-90; pres. nat accounts divsn. I Can't Believe It's Yogurt/ Brice Foods, Inc., Dallas, 1991-93; exec. v.p., CFO COREStaff Inc., Houston, 1994-96; pres. Shimer Capital Ptnrs., Inc., Dallas, 1996—. Mem. AICPA, Nat. Assn. Corp. Treas. Methodist. Avocations: sailing, carpentry, snow skiing, fishing. Home: 6441 Norway Rd Dallas TX 75230-5146

SHIMER, ZACHARY, lawyer; b. Bklyn., Sept. 13, 1933; s. Nathan and Ida (Antonowsky) S.; m. Susan Rosenthal, Feb. 26, 1961; children—Jennifer Shimer Piper, Robert Jay. A.B., UCLA, 1955, LL.B., 1960. Bar: Calif., N.Y. Atty. Antitrust div. U.S. Dept. Justice, Washington, 1960-62; assoc. firm Chadbourne, Parke, Whiteside & Wolff (now Chadbourne & Parke), N.Y.C., 1962-70, ptnr., 1970—. Contbr. articles to profl. jours. Served with U.S. Army, 1955-57. Mem. State Bar of Calif., Assn. Bar City of N.Y., ABA, Order of Coif. Democrat. Jewish. Office: Chadbourne & Parke LLP 30 Rockefeller Plz New York NY 10112

SHIMIZU, REIJU, anesthesiology educator; b. Negi Misato-machi, Japan, Feb. 14, 1935; s. Kenju and Asayo (Yashiro) S.; m. Yukiko Sakae, May 25, 1964; children: Juichirou, Yumiko, Risaburou. Grad., Kyoto Univ., 1961; MD, Tokyo U., 1968. Asst. Tokyo U., 1968-73; assoc. prof. Kyoto U., 1973-80; prof., chmn. Jichi Med. Sch., Tochigi, Japan, 1980—. Grantee Ministry of Edn. Culture and Sci., 1990-92, 93-95, 94-95. Mem. Japan Soc. of Anesthesiology (editor jour. 1987-92, Astra Rsch. award 1996), Japan Soc. Clin. Anesthesiology, Japan Soc. Circulation Control in Medicine (pres. 1994). Avocations: gardening, classical music, cats. Home: 1-9-16 Nishibori 338, Urawa City 338, Japan Office: Jichi Med Sch, 3311-1 Yakushiji, Minamikawachi-machi, Kawachi Tochigi 329-04, Japan

SHIMIZU, YOSHIAKI, art historian, educator; b. Tokyo, Feb. 27, 1936; came to U.S., 1953, U.S. resident, 1976; s. Mamoru and Michiko (Hayasaka) S.; children: Karen Akiko Marie, Kenneth Cuyler Norio, Katherine Kimie, Kei Robert. BA, Harvard U., 1963; MA, U. Kans., 1968; MFA, Princeton U., 1971, PhD, 1974. Asst. prof. dept. art and archaeology Princeton (N.J.) U., 1973-75, prof., 1984—, chmn. dept. art and archaeology, 1990-92, Marquand prof. art & archaeology, 1992—; asst. prof. U. Calif., Berkeley, 1975-78, assoc. prof., 1978-79; curator Japanese art Freer Gallery, Smithsonian Instn., Washington, 1979-84; guest curator Nat. Gallery Art, Washington, 1982-89; guest prof. U. of Heidelberg, 1993; guest prof. Ritsumeikan U., 1996; vis. fellow Dept. Art History U. Tokyo, 1996; mem. art adv. com. Japan Soc. Gallery, 1984—, adv. com. The Asia Soc. Galleries, N.Y.C., 1992—; vis. fellow dept. Comparative Culture Sophia U., Tokyo, 1993. Author: (with Suzan Nelson) Genji: The World of a Prince, 1982; (with John M. Rosenfield) Masters of Japanese Calligraphy, 1984; editor: (with Carolyn Wheelwright) Japanese Ink Paintings, 1976; author, editor: Japan: The Shaping of Daimyo Culture 1185-1858, 1988; mem. editorial bd. Archives of Asian Art, 1979—. Adv. bd. Asian Art, Smithsonian Inst., 1985-93; mem. vis. com. Arthur M. Sackler Gallery, Washington, 1984-94. Smithsonian Inst. fellow, 1967, Social Sci. Rsch. Coun./Am. Coun. Learned Socs. fellow, 1977-78, Asian Cultural Coun. fellow, 1995. Mem. Coll. Art Assn. (bd. dirs. 1987—), Japan Art History Assn., Japan Soc. N.Y., Ctr. for the Study of Japanese Woodblock Prints (mem. internat. adv. bd. 1983—). Home: 2 College Rd Princeton NJ 08542-7007 Office: Dept Art & Archaeology Princeton U Princeton NJ 08540

SHIMKUS, JOHN MONDY, congressman; b. Collinsville, Ill., Feb. 21, 1958; s. Gene Louis and Kathleen (Mondy) S.; m. Karen Kay Muth; children: David, Joshua. BS, U.S. Mil. Acad., 1980. Advanced through grades to capt. U.S. Army, 1980-86; stationed at U.S. Army Base, Columbus, Ga., 1980-81, 85; served at U.S. Army Base, Bamberg, Germany, 1981-84; stationed at U.S. Army Base, Monterey, Calif, 1985-86; tchr. Metro East Luth. H.S., Edwardsville, Ill., 1986-90; treas. Madison County, Edwardsville, 1990-96; mem. 105th Congress from 20th Ill. dist., 1997—; liaison officer U.S. Mil. Acad., 1987—; treas. So. Ill. Law Enforcement Commn., 1990—. Bd. dirs. Sr. Citizen Companion Program, Belleville, Ill., 1991; trustee Collinsville Twp., Ill., 1989-93; Rep. precinct committeeman, Collinsville, 1988—. Maj. USAR. Rep Cand. for U.S. House 20th dist I.L., 1996. Mem. Nat. Assn. County Treas. and Fin. Officers (bd. dirs.), Ill. County Treas. Assn., Am. Legion Post 365. Lutheran. Home: 504 Sumner Blvd Collinsville IL 62234-1934 Office: 513 Cannon HOB Washington DC 20515-1320 also: 301 N Sixth St Ste 100 Springfield IL 62701

SHIMM, MELVIN GERALD, law educator; b. 1926; s. Joseph George and Sadie Rosalie (Rosenblatt) S.; m. Cynia Brown, Aug. 15, 1948; children: David Stuart, Jonathan Evan. AB, Columbia U., 1947; LLB, Yale U., 1950. Bar: N.Y. 1950. Assoc., Cahill, Gordon, Zachry & Reindel, N.Y.C., 1950-51; atty. Wage Stblzn. Bd., Washington, 1951-52; Bigelow fellow U. Chgo., 1952-53; asst. prof. Duke U. Law Sch., Durham, N.C., 1953-56, assoc. prof., 1956-59, prof., 1959-96, prof. emeritus, 1996—, assoc. dean, 1978-83; vis. prof. NYU, 1957, U. So. Calif., 1965, U. Mich., Ann Arbor, 1973, U. Tex.-Austin, 1976; chmn. Durham (N.C.) Bd. Adjustment, 1966-70; dir. Assn. Am. Law Schs. Orientation Program in Am. Law, 1968-70, Duke Inst. in Transnat. Law, 1987-92; cons. The Brookings Instn., 1965-67; mem. N.C. Gen. Statutes Commn., 1984-88. Bd. dirs., vice-chmn. Lucy Daniels Found., 1989—; pres. Beth El Congregation, Durham, N.C., 1967-70, 1975-78. Lt. U.S. Army. 1943-46. Mem. Order of Coif, Phi Beta Kappa. Editor-in-chief Law & Contemporary Problems, Jour. Legal Edn., Am. Editor Jour. Bus. Law; editor Yale Law Jour. Office: Duke U Sch Law PO Box 90360 Durham NC 27708-0360

SHIMMYO, THEODORE TADAAKI, seminary president; b. Shiokawa-machi, Japan, Aug. 13, 1944; came to U.S. 1973; s. Shizuo and Tomiko (Saito) S.; m. Sumie Kurihara, Oct. 21, 1970; children: Keijo, Tatenaga, Keishin, Keika. BS in Nuclear Engring., U. Tokyo, 1971; diploma in religious edn., Unification Theol. Sem., Barrytown, N.Y., 1977; MPhil in Christian Theology, Drew U., Madison, N.J., 1981, PhD in Christian Theology, 1984. Asst. prof. theology Unification Theol. Sem., Barrytown, N.Y., 1984-96, asst. dean faculty, 1987; asst. acad. dean Unification Theol. Sem., Barrytown, 1987-94, pres., 1994—, assoc. prof. theology, 1996—. Author: Addressing Some of the Criticisms About the Divine Principle, 1985, Explorations in Unificationism, 1997; translator: The Divine Principle Study Guide Part II, 1975; contbr. articles to profl. jours. Mem. Ctr. for Process Studies, Soc. for Study of Process Philosophies, New Ecumenical Rsch. Assn., Unification Thought Inst. Am. (sec. gen.), Assn. Governing Bds. of Univs. and Colls., Karl Barth Soc. of N.Am. Mem. Unification Ch. Avocations: harmonica, classical guitar. Home: 20 Browning Ln Tarrytown NY 10591 Office: Unification Theol Sem 10 Dock Rd Barrytown NY 12507-5000

SHIMODA, JERRY YASUTAKA, retired national historic park superintendent; b. Haleiwa, Hawaii, Mar. 21, 1930; s. Tamotsu and Sasai Shimoda; m. Clara H. Segawa, Aug. 7, 1954; children: Karen Marie K., Randall T., Shaun T., Teri Ellen H., Jacqueline Y., David Y. BA in Govt., U. Hawaii, 1952, MA in Far Ea. Area Studies, 1957; postgrad., St. Louis U., 1957-59. Historian Jefferson Nat. Expansion Meml. Nat. Hist. Site, St. Louis, 1957-60; chief historian, in charge hist. rsch. and visitor svcs. Saratoga Nat. Hist. Park, Stillwater, N.Y., 1960-66; chief historian Home of Franklin D. Roosevelt Nat. Hist. Site and Frederick Vanderbilt Nat. Hist. Site, Hyde Park, N.Y., 1966-69; instr. Nat. Park Svc. Stephen T. Mather Tng. Ctr., Harpers Ferry, W.Va., 1969-72; supt. Pu'uhonua o Honaunau (Hawaii) Nat. Hist. Park, 1972-96, Puukohola Heiau Nat. Hist. Site, Honaunau, 1972-96; ret., 1996; lectr. environ. edn. Pa. State U., U. W.Va., Shepherd Coll., 1969-72; acting supr. Kaloko-Honokohau Nat. Hist. Park, 1988-90; instr. environ. edn., interpretive and basic instructing techniques U. Hawaii, Hilo, Kapiolani C.C.; U.S. del. U.S.-Japan Panel on Nat. Parks and Equivalent Res., 1968—, World Conf. on Marine Parks, Tokyo, 1975; Japanese translator U.S. Nat. Park Svc.; mem. internat. bd. dirs. Heritage Interpretation Internat.; numerous presentations at confs. and tng. courses. Author booklets on nat. parks, mgmt. and history; contbr. numerous articles to profl. publs., mags. and newspapers. Bd. dirs. Volcano Art Ctr.; mem. adv. com. Wailoa State Ctr.; mem. Hawaii Gov.'s Task Force on Ocean and Recreation; chmn. restoration com. St. Benedict's Ch., Honounau, 1982-95; chmn. bd. dirs. Kahua Na'au 'Ao, 1996-97. Recipient spl. achievement award Nat. Park Svc., 1964, 68, 70, resolution W.Va. Senate, 1971, Hawaii Ho. of Reps., 1982, sec.'s cert. Dept. Interior, 1971, Exec. of Yr. award West Hawaii chpt. Profl. Secs. Internat., 1981, cert. Govt. of Japan, 1981, staff plaque Pu'uhonua o Honaunau Nat. Hist. Park, Puukohola Heiau Nat. Hist. Site and Kaloko-Honokohau Nat. Hist. Park, 1988, cert. Japan Nat. Parks Assn., 1989, cert. of appreciation South Kona Aloha Lions Club, 1990, Meritorious Svc. award Sec. Interior, 1996, also others. Mem. Hawaii Mus. Assn. (bd. dirs. 1988-92), Kona Hist. Soc. (bd. dirs. 1988-92), Big Island Ocean Recreation and Tourism Assn. (exec. com.), Kona Judo Club (pres. 1977—), Rotary (pres. Kona Nauka 1978-79, Paul Harris fellow 1991, Disting. Svc. award 1992). Avocations: writing, reading, travel, teaching.

SHIMP, ROBERT EVERETT, JR., academic administrator, historian; b. Phila., Mar. 1, 1942; s. Robert Everett Sr. and Vivian (Myrtetus) S.; m. Marilyn Hopkins, Aug. 3, 1963; children: Gregory, Cecily, Jennifer. BA, Thiel Coll., 1964; MA, Ohio State U., 1965, PhD, 1970. Instr. history Ohio Wesleyan U., Delaware, Ohio, 1968-70, asst. prof., 1970-76, assoc. prof., 1976-82, prof. history, 1982-84, dir. off campus program, 1979-84; acad. dean Ky. Wesleyan Coll., Owensboro, 1984-88; provost, v.p. for acad. affairs Millikin U., Decatur, Ill., 1988-93; pres. McMurry U., Abilene, Tex., 1993—; vis. assoc. prof. Ohio State U., Columbus, summer 1978, Coll. of V.I., St. Croix, fall 1982; mem. inst. for Ednl. Mgmt. Harvard U., 1985; reader and table leader European history AP, Princeton, N.J. 1976-83; dir. Newberry Libr. Program in the Humanities, Chgo., 1976-77. Contbr. articles to profl. jours. Mem. Leadership Owensboro, 1986-87; capt. drives United Way, Owensboro and Delaware, 1981-85, bd. dirs., Decatur and Abilene; trustee for Sears Retirement Systems and Abilene Higher Edn. Authority; bd. dirs. Abilene C. of C. Fellow Ohio State U., 1968, Newberry Libr., Chgo., 1976-77. Mem. Ohio Acad. History, Conf. on Brit. Studies. Democrat. Methodist. Avocations: fishing, reading. Office: McMurry U Office of Pres PO Box 98 Abilene TX 79604-0098

SHIMPFKY, RICHARD LESTER, bishop; b. Albuquerque, Oct. 18, 1940; m. Jamel Shimpfky, 1966; children: Trevor, Allison, Joshua. Grad., U. Colo., 1963, Va. Theol. Seminary, 1970. Ordained to diaconate Episc. Ch., 1970. With William L. Philips Found., Richmond, Va., 1963-67; curate St. Peter's Ch., Arlington, 1970-72; vicar All Saints' Sharon Chapel, Alexandria, Va., 1972-73, rector, 1973-77; rector Christ Ch., Ridgewood, N.J., 1977-90; bishop Diocese El Camino Real, Monterey, Calif., 1990—. Avocations: reading, traveling. Office: Diocese of El Camino Real PO Box 1903 Monterey CA 93942-1093*

SHIN, EDWARD SUNG-SHIK, bilingual education educator; b. Seoul, Aug. 26, 1960; Came to U.S., 1977; s. Hyun-Woo and Sai-Shin (Jahng) S.; m. Rachel Youn-Kyung, Apr. 11, 1992; children: Calvin Joon Ho, Sarah Yerin. BA, UCLA, L.A., 1986; MEd, Harvard U., 1990. Cert. tchr., adminstrv. svcs., bilingual instr., Calif. Site/program dir. YMCA, L.A., 1984-86; bilingual tchr. L.A. Unified Sch. Dist., 1986—; chair faculty Overland Ave. Sch., L.A., 1991-92; tchr. Korean lang. L.A. Christian Reformed Ch., 1987-90. Singer Olympic Honor Choir, L.A., 1984; group leader, counselor UCLA, 1985; vol. Neuropsychiatric Inst. UCLA, 1986. Chancellor's scholar UCLA, 1980; grantee Harvard Grad. Sch. Edn., 1989-90. Mem. ASCD, Assn. Calif. Sch. Adminstrs., United Teachers of L.A. Korean Presbyterian. Avocations: reading, singing, playing tennis.

SHINAGEL, MICHAEL, English literature educator; b. Vienna, Austria, Apr. 21, 1934; came to U.S., 1941; s. Emanuel and Lilly (Hillel) S.; m. Ann Birdsey Mitchell, Sept. 1, 1956 (div. 1970); children: Mark Mitchell, Victoria Stuart; m. Rosa Joanne Bonanno, Dec. 6, 1973 (div. 1993); m. Marjorie Lee North, May 26, 1995. A.B., Oberlin Coll., 1957; A.M., Harvard U., 1959, Ph.D., 1964. Teaching fellow Harvard U., Cambridge, Mass., 1958-59, tutor in English, 1962-64, assoc. dir. career office, 1959-64, dean continuing edn., 1975—, lectr. extension, 1976—, sr. lectr. English, 1983—, master Quincy House, 1986—; asst. prof. English, Cornell U., Ithaca, N.Y., 1964-67; prof., chmn. dept. English, Union Coll., Schenectady, 1967-75; bd. dirs. Harvard Coop. Soc., publ. Harvard Rev.; pres. bd. dirs. Ednl. Exch. Boston, 1982-87. Author: Defoe and Middle-class Gentility, 1968; co-author: (handbook) Summer Institutes in English, 1965; editor: Concordance to Poems of Swift, 1972, Critical Edition of Robinson Crusoe, 1975 (revised 1993); co-editor: Harvard Scholars in English (1890-1990), 1991. Served with U.S. Army, 1952-54, Korea. Woodrow Wilson fellow, 1957; NEH grantee, 1965. Mem. Nat. Univ. Continuing Edn. Assn., Assn. Continuing Higher Edn., Mass. Hist. Soc., Old South Meeting House, The Johnsonians, The Saturday Club, Harvard Faculty Club (pres. 1985-87), Phi Beta Kappa. Avocations: reading; cooking; music; tennis. Home: Master's Residence Quincy House 58 Plympton St Cambridge MA 02138-6604 Office: Harvard U Div Continuing Edn 51 Brattle St Cambridge MA 02138-3701

SHINDELL, SIDNEY, medical educator, physician; b. New Haven, May 31, 1923; s. Benjamin Abraham and Freda (Mann) S.; m. Gloria Emhoff, June 17, 1945; children: Barbara, Roger, Lawrence, Judith. BS, Yale U., 1944; MD, L.I. Coll. Medicine, 1946; postgrad., Emory U., 1948-49; LLB, George Washington U., 1951. Diplomate Am. Bd. Preventive Medicine, Am. Bd. Occupl. Medicine. With USPHS, 1947-52; med. dir. Conn. Commn. on Chronically Ill and Aged, 1952-57, Am. Joint Distbn. Com., 1957-59; asst. prof. preventive medicine U. Pitts., 1960-65; dir. Hosp. Utilization project Western Pa., 1965-66; prof. dept. preventive medicine Med. Coll. Wis., Milw., 1966-93, chmn. dept., 1966-89, dir. office internat. affairs, 1989-93, prof. emeritus, 1993—, gubernatorial appt. bd. trustees, 1996—; exec. dir. Health Svc. Data of Wis., 1967-73; mem. bd. sci. advisers Am. Coun. on Sci. and Health, 1978-87, 92—; mem. Nat. Adv. Com. on Occupl. Safety and Health, U.S. Dept. Labor, 1982-84; cons. Caribbean Epidemiology Ctr. Pan. Am. Health Orgn./WHO, 1988, field epidemiology tng. program, Thailand, 1989, Nat. Office Occupl. and Environ. Medicine Royal Thai Ministry of Pub. Health, 1990—; mem. gov's white paper com. on health care reform, Wis., 1993; acad. cons. Faculties of Medicine, Padjadjaran U., Bandung, Airlangga U., Surabaya, Indonesia, 1993, 94; bd. dirs. Am. Coun. of Sci. and Health, 1987-89, chmn. 1989-92. Author: Statistics, Science and Sense, 1964, A Method of Hospital Utilization Review, 1966, The Law in Medical Practice, 1966, A Coursebook on Health Care Delivery, 1976; contbr. 120 articles to profl. jours. Gubernatorial appointee to bd. trustees Med. Coll. Wis., 1996—; mem. Sch. Bd. Fox Point-Bayside (Wis.), Sch. Dist., 1970-71; vice-chmn. Citizens' Adv. Com. Met. Problems, 1971-72; bd. dirs. Med. Care Evaluation S.E. Wis., 1973-76. With AUS, 1943-46. Recipient Frank L. Babbott Meml. award SUNY Health Sci. Ctr., Bklyn., 1996. Fellow Am. Coll. Preventive Medicine (mem. bd. regents 1982-85), APHA, Am. Coll. Occupl. and Environ. Medicine, Am. Coll. Legal Medicine; mem. Am. Assn. Health Data Sys. (sec. 1972-73), Assn. Tchrs. Preventive Medicine (dir. 1973-74, pres. 1976-77, Spl. Recognition award 1992), Assn. Occupl. Health Profls. (pres. 1980-90), Wis. State Med. Soc. (mem. coun. on health care financing and delivery, mem. coun. on govt. affairs, mem. ho. of dels., 50 Yr. Recognition award 1996), Am. Coll. Physician Execs., Internat. Commn. on Occupl. Health, Aircraft Owners and Pilots Assn., Masons, CAP. Home: 929 N Astor St # 2507 Milwaukee WI 53202-3490 Office: PO Box 26509 Milwaukee WI 53226-0509

SHINDLEDECKER, J. GREGORY, programmer, analyst; b. Indiana, Pa., May 2, 1954; s. Robert F. and Joanne E. (Weigle) S.; m. Debra L. Caplan, Sept., 1976 (dec. Aug., 1984); children: Ian J., Eric M.; m. Angela J. Muscelli, Mar. 29, 1986. AA in Nuclear Medicine, Essex Community Coll., 1974; BS in Computer Sci., Towson State U., 1987. Staff, sr. staff tech. Johns Hopkins Hosp., Balt., 1974-78, chief tech. myocardial infarction rsch. unit, 1978-82; computer programmer/operator divsn. nuclear medicine St. Joseph Hosp., Towson, 1982-86; cons., prin. Med. Software Systems, Kingsville, Md., 1985-87; sr. software engr. Cricket Software, Malvern, Pa., 1987-89; sr. nuclear application specialist Centocor, Inc., Malvern, 1989-90, image processing scientist, mgr. image processing ctr., 1990-92; assoc. dir. computer info. mgmt. Bio-Imaging Techs., Inc., West Trenton, N.J., 1992-94; dir. clin. sys. devel. Bio-Imaging Techs., Inc., West Trenton, 1994—. Asst. scoutmaster troop 101 Boy Scouts Am., 1990-96, com. chair, 1996—. Democrat. Avocations: model railroading, camping, bicycling, hiking, backpacking. Office: Bio-Imaging Techs Inc 830 Bear Tavern Rd Trenton NJ 08628-1020

SHINDLER, DONALD A., lawyer; b. New Orleans, Oct. 15, 1946; s. Alan and Isolene (Levy) S.; m. Laura Epstein, 1969; children: Jay, Susan. BSBA, Washington U., St. Louis, 1968; JD, Tulane U., 1971. Bar: La. 1971, U.S. Dist. Ct. (ea. dist.) La. 1971, U.S. Tax Ct. 1974, Ill. 1975, U.S. Dist. Ct. (no. dist.) Ill. 1975; CPA, La.; lic. real estate broker, Ill. Assoc. Pope, Ballard, Shepard & Fowle, Chgo., 1975-78; assoc. Rudnick & Wolfe, Chgo., 1978-81, ptnr., 1981—; seminar lectr. Chgo. Bar Assn., Ill. Inst. CLE, Profl. Edn. Sys., Inc., Internat. Assn. Corp. Real Estate Execs., Urban Land Inst., Am. Corp. Counsel Assn., Bldg. Owners and Mgrs. Assn., 1980—. Contbr. articles on real estate to legal jours. Trustee Glencoe (Ill.) Pub. Libr., 1981-87, pres., 1986-87; alumni bd. govs. Washington U., 1992-93; mem. Glencoe Zoning Commn./Bd. Appeals, 1994—. Lt. JAGC, USNR, 1971-75. Mem. ABA, La. State Bar Assn., Chgo. Bar assn. (com. chmn. 1979-80, 83-84, 90-94, 96—, editor land trust seminars 1984—), Urban Land Inst. (mem. exec. com. Chgo. dist. coun.), Internat. Assn. Corp. Real Estate Execs. (pres. Chgo. chpt. 1997—, Internat. Assn. Attys. and Execs. in Corp. Real Estate, Union League Club (chair real estate group 1993-96), Order of Coif, Beta Gamma Sigma, Omicron Delta Kappa. Office: Rudnick & Wolfe 203 N La Salle St Ste 1800 Chicago IL 60601-1225

SHINDLER, MERRILL KARSH, writer, radio personality; b. N.Y.C., July 2, 1948; s. Joseph and Miriam (Karsh) S. BA, CCNY, 1970; MFA, NYU, 1971. Entertainment editor San Francisco Bay Guardian, 1972-75; music editor Rolling Stone mag., San Francisco, 1976-79; film critic Los Angeles mag., 1979-89; restaurant critic L.A. Examiner, 1979-88; editor Zagat Los Angeles Restaurant Survey, 1986—; restaurant critic Daily Breeze, 1990-96, L.A. Reader, 1990-96, Daily Breeze, 1990—, Daily News, 1989-94, San Gabriel Valley Newspapers, 1994—, The Voice, 1996—. Author: Best Restaurants of L.A., 1989, Zagat, L.A. Restaurant Survey, 1986—, American Dish, 1996; writer (radio shows) Am. Top 40, 1979-89, Casey's Top 40, 1989—, Casey's Biggest Hits, 1990—, USA Top 20, 1990—, (TV shows) Am. Top 10, 1980-93, Cinemattractions, 1990—, USA Music Today, 1990—; host radio show Dining Out with Merrill Shindler, 1988—; contr. to Gault-Millau Best of Los Angeles, 1988, Gault-Millau Best of Hong Kong, 1989; contbr. articles to jours. Avocations: restaurants, cooking, jogging, travel.

SHINE, DANIEL I., hospital administrator; b. N.Y.C., Dec. 24, 1947; s. Ezra and Muriel (Gruber) S.; m. Cynthia Ruiz, Apr. 18, 1980; 1 child, Zachary. BA, Trinity Coll., 1970, MA, 1974; MD, Georgetown U., 1976. Diplomate Am. Bd. Internal Medicine. Resident in medicine U. Mass., Worcester, 1976-78; fellow in pharmacology Harvard U., Boston, 1978-80; attending physician Boston City Hosp., Boston, 1980-81; med. dir. outpatient Montefiore Med. Ctr., N.Y.C., 1981-85; med. dir. N.Y. Healthcare, N.Y.C., 1985-87; chief divsn. gen. medicine Bronx Lebanon Hosp. Ctr., N.Y.C., 1987-94; chief of medicine Lincoln Hosp. and Med. Ctr., N.Y.C., 1994—; med. dir., co-founder Addiction Treatment Ctr., Boston, 1981; vice-chair dept. medicine N.Y. Med. Coll., Valhalla, 1994-97. Mem. Soc. for Gen. Internal Medicine. Avocations: poetry, running. Home: 35 Beach Rd Ossining NY 10562 Office: Lincoln Hosp and Med Ctr 234 E 149th St Bronx NY 10451-5504

SHINE, KENNETH IRWIN, cardiologist, educator; b. Worcester, Mass., 1935. Grad., Harvard Coll., 1957; MD, Harvard U., 1961. Diplomate Am. Bd. Internal Medicine. Intern Mass. Gen. Hosp., 1961-62, resident, 1962-63, 65-66, fellow in cardiology, 1966-68; surgeon USPHS, 1963-65; assoc. in medicine Beth Israel Hosp., Resont, Va., from 1969; instr. Harvard Med. Sch., from 1968; asst. prof. medicine UCLA Sch. Medicine, 1971-73, assoc. prof., 1973-77, prof., 1977-92, prof. emeritus, 1993—, dir. CCU, 1971-75, chief div. cardiology, 1975-79, vice chmn. dept. medicine, 1979-81, exec. chmn., 1981-86, dean, 1986-92; clin. prof. medicine Georgetown U. Med. Ctr., Washington, 1993—; provost for med. scis. UCLA Sch. Medicine, 1991-92; pres. Inst. Medicine, Washington, 1992—. Mem. Am. Heart Assn. (pres. 1986-87), Assn. Am. Med. Colls. (adminstrv. bd. coun. deans 1989-92, exec. bd. 1990-92, chmn. coun. deans 1991-92). Office: Institute of Medicine 2101 Constitution Ave NW Washington DC 20418-0007*

SHINE, NEAL JAMES, journalism educator, former newspaper editor, publisher; b. Grosse Pointe Farms, Mich., Sept. 14, 1930; s. Patrick Joseph and Mary Ellen (Conlon) S.; m. Phyllis Theresa Knowles, Jan. 24, 1953; children: Judith Ann, James Conlon, Susan Brigid, Thomas Patrick, Margaret Mary, Daniel Edward. BS in Journalism, U. Detroit, 1952; PhD (hon.), Cleary Coll., 1989, Siena Heights Coll., 1995, U. Mich., 1995, U. Detroit Mercy, 1996, Ctrl. Mich. U., 1996. Mem. staff Detroit Free Press, 1950-95, asst. city editor, 1963-65, city editor, 1965-71, mng. editor, 1971-82, sr. mng. editor, 1982-89, pub., 1990-95; prof. journalism Oakland U., Rochester, Mich., 1995—. Host, moderator Detroit Week in Rev., Sta. WTVS-TV, 1981-89, host Neal Shine's Detroit, 1989-91. Trustee, vice chmn. bd. trustees Youth for Understanding, 1973-75, chmn., 1975-78; mem. bd.

for student publs. U. Mich.; bd. dirs. Children's Hosp., Econ. Club Detroit, Detroit Renaissance, New Detroit, Inc., Detroit Symphony Orch., Detroit Inst. Arts, Detroit Hist. Soc., United Way of Southeastern Mich., Met. Detroit Conv. and Visitors Bur., Operation ABLE, Detroit Press Club Found. With U.S. Army, 1953-55. Inducted Mich. Journalism Hall of Fame, 1990. Mem. Am. Soc. Newspape Editors, Am. Newspapers Pubs. Assn., Mich. Press Assn. (bd. dirs. 1990-95), AP Mng. Editors, Sons of Whiskey Rebellion (comdr.-in-chief 1979—), Inc. Soc. Irish-Am. Lawyers, Detroit Press Club (charter, bd. govs. 1966-89, sec. 1957-68, v.p. 1969-71, pres. 1971-73). Home: 11009 Harbor Place Dr Saint Clair Shores MI 48080-1527 also: Rathclaire, Gen Delivery, Pointe aux Roches, ON Canada N0R 1N0

SHINEFIELD, HENRY ROBERT, pediatrician; b. Paterson, N.J., Oct. 11, 1925; s. Louis and Sarah (Kaplan) S.; m. Jacqueline Marilyn Walker; children: Jill, Michael, Kimberley Strome, Melissa Strome. B.A., Columbia U., 1945, M.D., 1948. Diplomate: Am. Bd. Pediatrics (examiner, 1975—, bd. dirs., 1979-84, v.p., 1981-84). Rotating intern Mt. Sinai Hosp., N.Y.C., 1948-49; pediatric intern Duke Hosp., Durham, N.C., 1949-50; asst. resident pediatrician N.Y. Hosp. (Cornell), 1950-51, pediatrician to outpatients, 1953-59, instr. in pediatrics, 1959-60, asst. prof., 1960-64, asso. prof., 1964-65, asst. attending pediatrician, 1959-63, asso. attending pediatrician, 1963-65; pediatrician to outpatients Children's Hosp., Oakland, Calif., 1951-53; chief of pediatrics Kaiser-Permanente Med. Center, San Francisco, 1965-89, chief emeritus, 1989—; co-dir. Kaiser-Permanente Pediat4ric Vaccine Study Ctr., San Francisco, 1984—; asso. clin. prof. pediatrics Sch. Medicine U. Calif., 1966-68, clin. prof. pediatrics, 1968—, clin. prof. dermatology, 1970—; asso. attending pediatrician Paterson (N.J.) Gen. Hosp., 1955-59; chief of pediatrics Kaiser Found. Hosp., San Francisco, 1965—; attending Moffitt Hosp., San Francisco, 1967—; practice medicine specializing in pediatrics Paterson, 1953-59; cons. San Francisco Gen. Hosp., 1967—, Childrens Hosp., San Francisco, 1970—, Mt. Zion Hosp., San Francisco, 1970—; mem. research grants rev. br. NIH, HEW, 1970-74; med. dir. USPHSR, 1969—; bd. dirs. San Francisco Peer Rev. Orgn., 1975-81, sec., exec. com., 1976-81; chmn. Calif. State Child Health Disability Bd., 1973-82; mem. Inst. of Medicine, Nat. Acad. Scis., 1980—; cons. Bur. Drugs FDA, 1970, NIH, HEW, 1974—. Editorial bds. Western Jour. of Medicine, 1968-80, American Jour. of Diseases of Children, 1970-82; contbr. writings to profl. publs. Chmn. San Francisco Med. Adv. Com. Nat. Found. March of Dimes, 1969-80. Served with USPHS, 1951-53. Fellow Am. Acad. Pediatrics (com. of fetus and newborn 1969-76, mem. com. on drugs 1978-82); mem. AMA, Soc. Pediatric Research, Infectious Diseases Soc. Am., Western Pediatric Soc., Western Soc. Clin. Research, Am. Pediatric Soc., Phi Beta Kappa. Home: 2705 Larkin St San Francisco CA 94109-1117 Office: 2200 Ofarrell St San Francisco CA 94115-3357

SHINEMAN, EDWARD WILLIAM, JR., retired pharmaceutical executive; b. Canajoharie, N.Y., Apr. 9, 1915; s. Edward W. and Bertelle H. (Shubert) S.; m. H. Doris Thompson, Apr. 15, 1939; children: Edward T., Alan B. AB, Cornell U., 1937. With apparatus dept., acctg. dept. Gen. Electric Co., 1938-46, line auditor, 1942-46; with Beech-Nut, Inc. and predecessor cos., 1946-68, asst. treas., 1948-63, contr., 1959-63, treas., 1963-68; asst. sec.-treas. Squibb Corp., 1968-81; bd. dirs. Fenimore Asset Mgmt., Inc., Taconic Farms, Inc. Trustee, pres. Arkell Hall Found.; mem. emeritus coun. Cornell U. Mem. Fin. Execs. Inst., Inst. Mgmt. Accts. Republican. Home: 420 E 51st St Apt 14E New York NY 10022-8022

SHINN, ALLEN MAYHEW, retired naval officer, business executive; b. Niles, Calif., June 6, 1908; s. Joseph Clark and Florence Maria (Mayhew) S.; m. Sevilla Hayden Shuey, June 20, 1936; children: Allen Mayhew, James Washburn, Jonathan Hayden. BS, U.S. Naval Acad., 1932; grad., Nat. War Coll., 1953. Commd. officer USN, 1932, advanced through grades to vice adm.; served in battleships, 1932-36; naval aviator, 1937, served in various fleet aircraft squadrons, comdr. 3, also comdr. attack carrier air group, 1944-45; served on various staffs; comdr. 2 carriers USS Saipan, 1956, USS Forrestal, 1958; comdt. midshipmen U.S. Naval Acad., Annapolis, Md., 1956-58; comdr. Anti-Submarine Warfare Carrier Task Group, 1960-61, Attack Carrier Task Force, 1963-64; chief Bur. Naval Weapons, Washington, 1964-66; comdr. Naval Air Force Pacific Fleet, 1966-70; ret., 1970; chmn. bd. Harvard Industries, Inc., 1970-71, All-Am. Industries, 1973-78; pres., CEO Internat. Controls Corp., 1973-78, dir. 1973-79; dir. Loral Corp., 1973-96, Pennzoil Co., 1970-94; bd. dirs. Navy Mut. Aid Assn., 1962-66; bd. mgrs. Navy Relief Soc., 1962-64; pres. Naval Acad. Athletic Assn., 1956-58, North Water St. Corp., Edgartown, Mass., 1948-50. Trustee Longfellow Sch. Boys, Bethesda, Md., 1950-53. Decorated D.S.M. Mem. Soc. Mayflower Descendants, Cosmos Club, N.Y. Yacht Club, Edgartown Yacht Club, Delta Tau Delta. Republican. Unitarian. Home: 3130 Roadrunner Dr Borrego Springs CA 92004

SHINN, CLINTON WESLEY, lawyer; b. Haworth, Okla., Mar. 7, 1947; s. Clinton Elmo and Mary Lucille (Dowdy) S.; m. Catherine Borne; children: Laura Kathryn, Clinton Wesley, Timothy Daniel. BS, McNeese State U., 1969; JD, Tulane U., 1972; LLM, Harvard U., 1973. Bar: La. 1972, U.S. Dist. Ct. (ea. dist.) La. 1975, U.S. Dist. Ct. (we. dist.) La. 1980, U.S. Ct. Appeals (5th cir.) 1981, U.S. Ct. Appeals (11th cir.) 1982, U.S. Tax Ct. (1982). Asst. prof. law Tulane U., New Orleans, 1973-75; assoc. Stone, Pigman et al, New Orleans, 1975-78, ptnr., 1979—; faculty advisor, 1974-75, editor in chief Tulane Law Rev., 1971-72. Editor in chief Tulane Law Rev., 1971-72. Co-founder, bd. dirs. Childhood Cancer Families Network, 1987-90; co-founder Camp Challenge, 1988; team leader Campaign for Caring, Children's Hosp., New Orleans, 1989-91; bd. dirs. Christ Episcopal Sch., Covington, 1988-91, chmn. long-range planning, 1990-91, exec. com., 1989-91, chmn. legal com., 1989-91, chmn. admissions/recruitment com., 1988-90, mem. headmaster search com., 1993; bd. dirs. Greater New Orleans YMCA, 1989—, exec. com., 1991—, asst. sec., 1994-95, sec., 1996—, mem. fin. com., 1994—, exec. dir. search com., 1996; mem. Leadership Coun., 1997—; active Indian Guides/Princesses; bd. dirs. West St. Tammany YMCA, 1987-95, exec. com., 1988-95, bd. chmn., 1989-90, 92-93; bd. dirs. Christwood, 1992—; bd. dirs. La. Air & Waste Mgmt. Assn., 1993—; chmn. corp. rels. com., 1992-93, vice-chmn., 1996-97, chair, 1997—. Co-recipient Pals of the Yr. award Greater New Orleans YMCA Indian Guides/Princesses, 1987-88; named Vol. of Yr. West St. Tammany YMCA, 1990, 92. Mem. ABA, Nat. Com. on Planned Giving (New Orleans chpt.), Nat. Assn. Securities Dealers (bd. arbitrators), Nat. Wildlife Fedn. (life), La. Bar Assn., La. Forestry Assn., New Orleans Bar Assn., New Orleans Estate Planning Coun., Assn. Henri Capitant, Air and Waste Mgmt. Assn., Order of Coif, Nat. Commn. for Planning Giving (New Orleans chpt.). Avocations: backpacking, gardening. Home: Dogwood Ridge Farm 20297 Brunning Rd Covington LA 70435-7579 Office: Stone Pigman Walther Wittman & Hutchinson 546 Carondelet St New Orleans LA 70130-3509 *In all things be firm but fair.*

SHINN, DAVID HAMILTON, diplomat; b. Yakima, Wash., June 9, 1940; s. Guy Wilson and Ada Louise (Gelvin) S.; m. Judy Karen Rolfe, Sept. 9, 1961; children: Steven Hamilton, Christopher Rolfe. AA, Yakima Valley Coll., 1960; BA, George Washington U., 1963, MA, 1964, PhD, 1980; cert. African studies, Northwestern U., Evanston, Ill., 1969. With U.S. State Dept., 1964—; rotational officer U.S. Embassy, Beirut, Lebanon, 1964-66; polit. officer Nairobi, Kenya, 1967-68; desk officer East African affairs Washington, 1969-72; polit. officer Dar es Salaam, Tanzania, 1972-74; dep. chief of mission Nouakchott, Mauritania, 1974-76, Office of Mayor, City of Seattle, 1977-78; dep. coord. state and local govt. U.S. Dept. State, Washington, 1978-81; dep. chief of mission Yaounde, Cameroon, 1981-83, Khartoum, Sudan, 1983-86; U.S. ambassador Ouagadougou, Burkina Faso, 1987-90; diplomat-in-residence Southern U., Baton Rouge, La., 1990-91; diplomat State Dept., Washington, 1991-96; U.S. Amb. Addis Ababa, Ethiopia, 1996—. Recipient Superior Honor award State Dept., 1980, 85, 94, Alumnus of Yr. award Am. Assn. Cmty. Colls., 1994, Phi Theta Kappa, 1995. Mem. Internat. Studies Assn., Am. Fgn. Service Assn., Am. Philatelic Soc. Methodist. Avocations: philately, skiing, softball, tennis, volleyball. Home: Addis Ababa US Embassy Addis Ababa (DOS) Washington DC 20521-2030

SHINN, GEORGE, professional sports team executive; b. Kannapolis, N.C.. Owner The Charlotte (N.C.) Hornets, Charlotte Knights Baseball. Recipient Horatio Alger award, 1975. Mem. Charlotte C. of C. (bd. dirs.). Office: Charlotte Hornets 100 Hive Dr Charlotte NC 28217-4524*

SHINN, GEORGE LATIMER, investment banker, consultant, educator; b. Newark, Ohio, Mar. 12, 1923; s. Leon Powell and Bertha Florence (Latimer) S.; m. Clara LeBaron Sampson, May 21, 1949; children: Deborah, Amy, Martha, Sarah, Andrew. AB, Amherst Coll., 1948; LLD (hon.), Denison U., 1975, Amherst Coll., 1982; MA, Drew U., 1990, PhD, 1992. Trainee Merrill Lynch, Pierce, Fenner & Beane, 1948-49; various exec. positions, 1949-75; pres. Merrill Lynch & Co., Inc., 1973-75; chmn. bd., chief exec. officer 1st Boston Corp., 1975-83; investment banking consultant, 1983—; adj. prof. philosophy Drew U., Madison, N.J., 1992—; mem. exec. com. President's Pvt. Sector Survey on Cost Control, 1982-84; exec.-in-residence Columbia U. Grad. Sch. Bus., 1983-85; bd. govs. Am. Stock Exch., 1970-74; bd. dirs., trustee Colonial Group Mut. Funds; bd. dirs. Kelso & Co., 1992—, N.Y. Stock Exchange, 1975-83, vice chmn., 1979-83; bd. dirs. N.Y. Times Co., 1978—, Philps Dodge Corp., 1983-95, N.Y. Life Ins. Co., 1983-94, Lehigh Prass, 1983-91, Superior Gill Co., 1984-87. Gen. chmn. United Hosp. Fund, N.Y.C., 1973-74; trustee Kent Pl. Sch., Summit, N.J., 1966-73, Carnegie Found. for Advancement Teaching, 1976-85, Pingry Sch., 1977-79, Lucille P. Markey Charitable Trust, 1985-97, Rockefeller Family Office Trust, 1989-97, N.J. Coun. for the Humanities, 1994—, Arts Coun. Morris Area, 1978-91, Philharmonic Symphony Soc. N.Y., 1983-91, Nat. Humanities Ctr., 1988-94; trustee emeritus Amherst Coll., 1968-82, chmn. bd. trustees, 1973-80; bd. dirs. Rsch. Corp., 1975-86. Capt. USMCR, 1943-52. Fellow Am. Acad. Arts and Scis., River Club, Century Assn., Morris County Golf Club. Office: CS First Boston 11 Madison Ave New York NY 10010-3629

SHINN, RICHARD RANDOLPH, former insurance executive, former stock exchange executive; b. Lakewood, N.J., Jan. 7, 1918; s. Clayton Randolph and Carrie (McGravey) S.; m. Mary Helen Shea, Nov. 8, 1941; children: Kathleen, Patricia, John; m. Marion Berenson Weitman, Nov. 30, 1985. B.S., Rider Coll., 1938. C.L.U., 1949. With Met. Life Ins. Co., 1939-83, 2d v.p., 1959-63, v.p., 1963-64, sr. v.p., 1964-66, exec. v.p., 1966-68, sr. exec. v.p., 1968- 69, pres., dir., 1969-83, chief exec. officer, 1973-83, chmn., 1980-83, ret., 1983; exec. vice chmn. NYSE, N.Y.C., 1986-91; chmn. Olympia & York USA, 1993; bd. dirs. Union Tex. Petroleum Co., Grey Advt. Bd. dirs. Lincoln Ctr. for the Performing Arts, Inc.; mem. Cardinal's Com. for the Laity. Mem. Met. Opera Assn., Knights of Malta. Clubs: The Blind Brook (Port Chester, N.Y.); Round Hill (Greenwich, Conn.); Riverside Yacht; Sky Club, Links (N.Y.C.); Gulfstream Golf (Fla.), Delray Yacht Club (Fla.). Home: 136 Parsonage Rd Greenwich CT 06830-3943 Office: MetLife Bldg 200 Park Ave Ste 5700 New York NY 10166-0005

SHINNAR, REUEL, chemical engineering educator, industrial consultant; b. Vienna, Austria, Sept. 15, 1923; came to U.S., 1962; s. Abraham Emil and Rosa (Storch) Bardfeld; m. Miryam Halpern, June 22, 1948; children—Shlomo, Meir. Diploma in Chem. Engring., Technion, Haifa, Israel, 1945, M.Sc. in Chem. Engring., 1954; Dr. Engring. Sci., Columbia U., 1957. Various position in chem. engring. Israel, 1945-58; adj. assoc. prof. Technion, Haifa, Israel, 1958-62; visiting research fellow Guggenheim Labs., Princeton (N.J.) U., 1962-64; prof. chem. engring. CCNY, 1964—, disting. prof., 1979—; Pinhas Naor lectr. Technion U., 1974; Wilhelm Meml. lectr. Princeton U., 1985, Kelly lectr. Purdue U., 1991; cons. to various oil and chem. cos. Contbr. numerous articles to profl. jours.; patentee in field. Fellow AICE (Founders award 1992, Alpha Chi Sigma award 1979), N.Y. Acad. Scis.; mem. AIAA, Am. Chem. Soc., Nat. Acad. Engring. Office: City Coll NY Dept Chem Engring 140th St and Convent Ave New York NY 10031

SHINNAR, SHLOMO, child neurologist, educator; b. Haifa, Israel, Nov. 11, 1950; s. Reuel and Miryam (Halpern) S.; m. Shoshana Ellen Cohen, Aug. 11, 1974; children: Ora Rivka, Aviva Batya, Avraham Ever. BA in Physics summa cum laude, Columbia Coll., 1971; PhD, Albert Einstein Coll. Medicine, 1977, MD, 1978. Diplomate Am. Bd. Pediat., Am. Bd. Psychiatry and Neurology, with spl. competence in child neurology. Intern, asst. resident in pediatrics, fellow Johns Hopkins Hosp., Balt., 1978-80, asst. resident, resident in neurology, fellow, 1980-83; from asst. prof. neurology and pediatrics to prof. neurology and pediatrics Albert Einstein Coll. Medicine, Bronx, 1983—; from asst. attending to attending neurology and pediatrics Montefiore Med. Ctr., Bronx Mcpl. & North Ctrl. Bronx Hosps., 1983—; dir. CERC Seizure Clinic R.K. Kennedy Ctr., Bronx, 1983—; co-dir. Epilepsy Mgmt. Ctr. Montefiore Med. Ctr. Albert Einstein Coll. Medicine, Bronx, 1983-86, dir., 1986—; mem. adv. bd. Epilepsy Inst., N.Y.C., 1984—, chair 1996—, instnl. rev. bd. protection of human subjects Montefiore Med. Ctr., Bronx, 1985—, vice-chmn., 1989—; adj. sch. scientist Gertrude Sergievsky Ctr. Columbia Coll. Physicians and Surgeons, N.Y.C., 1985—, Sergievsky Scholar, 1986—; cons. in field. Field editor Epilepsy Advances, 1987-93; editl. bd. The Neurologist, 1993—, Epilepsia, 1994—, Pediatric Neurology, 1996—; contbr. articles to profl. jours. N.Y. State Regents scholar, 1967-71; Martin and Emily L. Fisher fellow, 1991—. Fellow Am. Acad. Pediats.; mem. Am. Epilepsy Soc. (profl. adv. bd. chmn. childhood onset epilepsy com. 1993-95, councillor 1992-95, Rsch. Recognition award 1989), Am. Acad. Neurology, Child Neurology Soc., Eastern EEG Soc., Internat. Child Neurology soc., Nat. Assn. Epilepsy Ctrs., Soc. for Pediat. Rsch., Am. Neurol. Assn. Office: Montefiore Med Ctr 111 E 210th St Bronx NY 10467-2401

SHINNERS, STANLEY MARVIN, electrical engineer; b. N.Y.C., May 9, 1933; s. Earl and Molly (Planter) S.; m. Doris Pinsker, Aug. 4, 1956; children: Sharon Rose Cooper, Walter Jay, Daniel Lawrence. BEE, CCNY, 1954; MS in Elect. Engring., Columbia U., 1959. Equipment engr. Western Electric Co., N.Y.C., 1953-54; staff engr. electronics div. Otis Elevator Co., Bklyn., 1954-56; project engr. Consol. Avionics Corp., Westbury, N.Y., 1956-58; sr. rsch. sect. head fed. sys. sector Lockheed Martin Corp. (formerly Loral Corp., Unisys Corp.), Great Neck, N.Y., 1958—; adj. prof. engring. The Cooper Union, N.Y.C., 1966—, N.Y. Inst. Tech., Old Westbury, N.Y., 1972-92, Poly. Inst. Bklyn., 1959-72. Author: Control System Design, 1964, Techniques of Systems Engineering, 1967, A Guide to Systems Engineering and Management, 1976, Modern Control System Theory and Application, 1978, Modern Control System Theory and Design, 1992. Recipient Career Achievement medal CCNY Alumni Assn., 1980. Fellow IEEE; mem. Am. Soc. for Engring. Edn., Eta Kappa Nu, Tau Beta Pi. Home: 28 Sagamore Way N Jericho NY 11753-2358 *I was very poor financially as a child, but I received an abundance of love and encouragement from parents and family. I have always tried to succeed and to help others succeed. Above all, I have always tried to do what is right whether the decision had to be made in the business world or in private and family matters.*

SHINOLT, EILEEN THELMA, artist; b. Washington, May 18, 1919; d. Edward Lee and Blanche Addie (Marsh) Bennett; m. John Francis Shinolt, June 14, 1956 (dec. Aug. 1969). Student, Hans Hoffman Sch Art, 1949, Pa. Acad. Arts, 1950, Corcoran Sch. Art, 1945-51, Am. U., 1973-77. Sect. chief Dept. Army, Washington, 1940-73, retired, 1973. One-woman shows include various locations, 1982, 83, 85, 90, 94, 96; group shows include Perlmutter & Co., 1981, Fitch Fox and Brown, 1986, Foundry Gallery, 1987, Ann. Add Arts, 1986, Westminster Gallery, London, 1995; represented in permanent collections Women's Nat. Mus., Washington, Cameo Gallery, Columbia, S.C., others. Mem. Woman's Nat. Dem. Club, Washington, 1980—. Mem. Am. Art League (editor newsletter 1985-86, 1st pl. 1987, 2d pl. 1986), Arts Club Washington (exhbn. com. 1985—, admissions com. 1987-88), Miniature Painters, Sculptors & Gravers Soc. (historian 1989—, editor newsletter 1986-89). Roman Catholic. Avocations: reading, studying art periodicals, art galleries. Home: 4119 Davis Pl NW Apt 203 Washington DC 20007-1254

SHIPLER, DAVID KARR, journalist, correspondent, author; b. Orange, N.J., Dec. 3, 1942; s. Guy Emery Jr. and Eleanor (Karr) S.; m. Deborah S. Isaacs, Sept. 17, 1966; children: Jonathan Robert, Laura Karr, Michael Edmund. AB, Dartmouth Coll., 1964; LittD (hon.), Middlebury Coll., 1988, Glassboro (N.J.) State Coll., 1988; AM (hon.), Dartmouth Coll., 1994. News clk. N.Y. Times, 1966-67, news summary writer, 1968, reporter met. staff, 1968-73, fgn. corr. Saigon bur., 1973-75, fgn. corr. Moscow Bur., 1975—, bur. chief Moscow Bur., 1977-79, chief Jerusalem bur., 1979-84, corr. Washington bur., 1985-87, chief diplomatic corr., 1987-88; sr. assoc. Carnegie Endowment for Internat. Peace, Washington, 1988-90; guest scholar Brookings Instn., 1984-85; adj. prof. Am. U. Sch. Internat. Svc., Washington, 1990; Ferris prof. journalism and pub. affairs, Princeton U., 1990-91; Woodrow Wilson vis. fellow, 1990—. Author: Russia: Broken Idols, Solemn Dreams, 1983 (Overseas Press Club award), Arab and Jew: Wounded Spirits in a Promised Land, 1986 (Pulitzer prize for Gen. Nonfiction 1987), exec. producer, prin. writer, narrator documentary film made from book, 1989 (Alfred DuPont-Columbia U. award for Broadcast Journalism 1990); author: A Country of Strangers: Blacks and Whites in America, 1997; contbr. articles to nat. mags. Trustee Dartmouth Coll. With USNR, 1964-66. Recipient award for disting. reporting Soc. Silurians, 1971; award for disting. pub. affairs reporting Am. Polit. Scis. Assn., 1971; award N.Y. chpt. Sigma Delta Chi, 1973; co-recipient George Polk award, 1982. Mem. Human Rights Watch Middle East (adv. com.). Office: 4005 Thornapple St Chevy Chase MD 20815-5037 *I have been governed professionally by the conviction that an open society needs open examination of itself to survive. Defining problems, inspecting blemishes, probing wounds, and exposing injustice are the required pastimes of a free people. Nothing intelligent can come from ignorance. If information does not guarantee wisdom, it is at least a prerequisite, for the only wise course is through knowledge. To write about current affairs, then, is to play a small role in a great endeavor. It is to measure one's own performance continually against the highest standards of honesty, fairness, thoroughness, intelligence, to search every day for a bit of truth, then share it. These are the ingredients of happiness, for such a job involves a life of constant learning, perpetual self-education. It keeps a man whole.*

SHIPLEY, DAVID ELLIOTT, university dean, lawyer; b. Urbana, Ill., Oct. 3, 1950; s. James Ross and Dorothy Jean (Elliott) S.; m. Virginia Florence Coleman, May 24, 1980; 1 child, Shannon C. BA, Oberlin Coll., 1972; JD, U. Chgo., 1975. Bar: R.I. 1975. Assoc. Tillinghast, Collins & Graham, Providence, 1975-77; asst. prof. U. S.C. Sch. Law, Columbia, 1977-81, assoc. prof., 1981-85, prof., 1985-90, assoc. dean, 1989-90; dean U. Miss. Sch. Law, University, 1990-93, U. Ky. Coll. Law, Lexington, 1993—; vis. prof. Coll. William and Mary, Williamsburg, Va., 1983-84, Ohio State U. Coll. Law, Columbus, 1986-87. Author: South Carolina Administrative Law, 1983, 2d edit., 1989; co-author Copyright Law, 1992. Pres. Shandon Neighborhood Assn., Columbia, 1988-90. Named Prof. of Yr., U. S.C. Sch. Law, 1990, faculty scholar, 1989-90. Mem. ABA, R.I. Bar Assn., S.C. Bar Assn. (assoc.). Methodist. Avocations: running, yardwork, gardening, reading. Home: 827 Lakeshore Dr Lexington KY 40502-3125 Office: U Ky Coll Law Lexington KY 40506-0048

SHIPLEY, GEORGE CORLESS, political consultant; b. Houston, May 26, 1947; s. George Hale and Florence (Corless) S.; m. Donna West, June 2, 1972; children: George West Shipley, Andrew Corless Shipley. BA in Fgn. Affairs, U. Va., 1969; PhD, U. Tex., 1977; grad. study, Harvard U., 1968. Teaching asst. U. Tex., Austin, 1970-73; rsch. asst. U. Tex., 1971; spl. asst. U.S. Sen. Lloyd Bentsen, Austin, 1973-77; faculty mem. U. Tex. Govt. Dept., Austin, 1977-78; ptnr. Henson, Hopkins & Shipley, Austin, 1978-80; pres., CEO Shipley & Assocs., Inc., Austin, 1980—; vis. faculty LBJ Sch. Pub. Affairs, U. Tex. Contbr. articles to profl. jours. Communications dir. Gore for Pres., 1987-88; cons. Dem. Congl. Campaign Com., 1983-86. Named Congl. fellow Am. Polit. Sci. Assn., 1973, U. Tex. fellow, 1972. Mem. Dem. Leadership Coun., Congl. Fellows Assn., Internat. Assn. Polit. Cons., Am. Assn. Polit. Cons., Am. Polit. Sci. Assn., U. Va. Alumni Assn., Friends of LBJ Libr., Va. Club of N.Y.C. Democrat. Episcopalian. Avocations: offshore sailing, fishing. Office: Shipley & Assocs Inc 919 Congress Ave Ste 750 Austin TX 78701-2444

SHIPLEY, L. PARKS, JR., banker; b. Orange, N.J., Aug. 2, 1931; s. L. Parks and Emily Catherine (Herzog) S.; m. Micheline Genevieve Oltramare, Apr. 2, 1966; children—Christiane, Daniel, Alix. B.A., Yale U., 1953. Vol. Moral ReArmament, Europe, Africa, S.Am., 1954-64; participant in founding Up With People Inc., 1964-69; from internat. banking officer to v.p. Marine Midland Bank, N.Y.C., 1969-76; v.p. Irving Trust Co., N.Y.C., 1976-84, exec. v.p., 1984-89; exec. v.p. Bank of N.Y., N.Y.C., 1989-90; pres. Ultramar Assoc., Inc., N.Y.C., 1990-91, Ultramar Group, Inc., 1991-92; U.S. rep., bd. advisor Banco Credito Argentino; pres. Shipley Assocs.; bd. dirs. The Keimei Fund for Internat. Edn. Inc. Trustee Young Life, 1991; mem. adv. bd. Ams. Soc. Corp. Program. Mem. Argentine Am. C. of C. (bd. dirs.), Yale Club, Baltusrol Golf Club. Home: 77 Bellevue Ave Summit NJ 07901-2007 Office: 375 Park Ave Ste 1007 New York NY 10152-1099

SHIPLEY, LUCIA HELENE, retired chemical company executive; b. Boston, Oct. 26, 1920; d. Harry Jacob and Helen Merrill (Dillingham) Farrington; m. Charles Raymond Shipley, Oct. 11, 1941; children: Helen Merrill, Richard Charles. Student, Smith Coll., 1938-41. Chief exec. officer, treas. Shipley Co. Inc., Newton, Mass., 1957-92, also bd. dirs. Patentee for immersion tin, electroless copper. Recipient Winthrop Sears award Chem. Industry Assn., 1985, Semi award Semicon West, 1990, Dana Hall Sch. Disting. Alumna award. Mem. Garden Club (pres. 1954-56). Republican. Congregationalist. Avocations: gardening, shell collecting, dogs, cage birds.

SHIPLEY, SAMUEL LYNN, advertising and public relations executive; b. Marlborough, Mass., Nov. 14, 1929; s. Clifford Lynn and Esther (Jacobs) S.; m. Sue Finucan, Sept. 5, 1955; children—Jeffrey Lynn, Beth Ann, Amy. Student, Charles Morris Price Sch. Advt. and Journalism, U. N.H., 1948-50. Exec. dir. Democratic Party N.H., 1953-56; pres., chmn. Shipley Assos., Inc., Wilmington, Del., 1962—; pres. Cable TV Advt. Inc., 1982—; dir. Del. Devel. Dept., Dover, 1965-69; mem. bd. overseers Del. Coll. Art and Design. Nominee for U.S. Congress, 1976; pub. relations dir. Del. Democratic Com., 1964-68; chmn. Del. Dem. Com., 1982-90; bd. dirs. Blood Bank of Del., Jobs for Del. Grads.; mem. Del. Heritage Commn.; trustee Grand Opera House; former chair Dem. State Com. Served with U.S. Army, 1951-53. Recipient Freedoms Found. Honor medal, 1966, Outstanding Grad. award Charles Morris Price Sch., 1974. Mem. Am. Advt. Fedn., Wilmington Advt. Club, Masons. Home: 1196 Paper Mill Rd Newark DE 19711-2924 Office: 1300 Pennsylvania Ave Wilmington DE 19806-4311 *The ingredients for success are good health, average intelligence, a giving spirit, positive thinking, good imagination, self-discipline, hard work, and persistence.*

SHIPLEY, TONY L(EE), software company executive; b. Elizabethton, Tenn., July 19, 1946; s. James A. and Edith J. (Crowder) S.; m. Lynda Anne Jenkins, Nov. 19, 1971; children: Blake Alan, Sarah Robyn. BS in Indsl. Engring., U. Tenn., 1969; MBA, U. Cin., 1975. Indsl. engr. Monsanto Co., Pensacola, Fla., 1969-72; mktg. mgr. SDRC, Cin., 1972-76; v.p. sales and mktg. Anatrol Corp., Cin., 1977-81; pres. Entek Sci. Corp., Cin., 1981—; pres., CEO Entek IRO Internat. Corp. Named Small Bus. Person of Yr., Greater Cin. C. of C., 1994, Entrepreneur of Yr. in Cin., No. Ky. Region, 1996. Mem. ASME, The Exec. Com., Soc. Automotive Engrs., Vibration Inst., Greater Cin. Software Assn. (pres. 1996-97), Greater Cin. C. of C., Leadership Class XVIII, Terrace Park (Ohio) Country Club. Republican. Avocations: golf, family activities. Home: 7 Laurelwood Milford OH 45150-9748 Office: Entek IRO Internat Corp 1700 Edison Dr Milford OH 45150-2729

SHIPLEY, VERGIL ALAN, political science educator; b. Amber, Okla., June 25, 1922; s. Guy and Ida Jean (Grant) S.; m. Zannie May Manning, May 3, 1947; children—Douglass Manning, John Grant. B.A., U. Okla., 1947, M.A., 1948; postgrad., U. Tex., 1947; Ph.D., London (Eng.) Sch. Econs., 1950. Assoc. prof. polit. sci. Wichita State U., 1950-56; asst. prof. govt. U. Miami, Coral Gables, Fla., 1957-61; assoc. prof. U. Miami, 1962-68, prof. politics and pub. affairs, 1968-89, prof. emeritus, 1989—, chmn. dept., 1970-77; acting dean Sch. Bus. Adminstrn., 1968-69; Polit. election analyst WTVJ-CBS, 1962-84; cons. to study commn. on local govt., 1971-72. Served to capt. AUS, 1942-46, ETO. Mem. Am. Polit. Sci. Assn., Am. Soc. Pub. Adminstrn., Phi Beta Kappa, Phi Eta Sigma, Pi Sigma Alpha, Beta Gamma Sigma (pres. U. Miami chpt. 1969), Delta Sigma Pi (faculty adviser 1968-76). Democrat. Home: 1127 Alberca St Miami FL 33134-2446 Office: U Miami Dept Politics Pub Affa Coral Gables FL 33124

SHIPLEY, WALTER VINCENT, banker; b. Newark, Nov. 2, 1935; s. L. Parks and Emily (Herzog) S.; m. Judith Ann Lyman, Sept. 14, 1957; children: Barbara, Allison, Pamela, Dorothy, John. Student, Williams Coll., 1954-56; BS, NYU, 1961. With Chem. Bank, N.Y.C., 1956-96, pres., 1982-83, chmn. bd., 1983-91, pres., 1992-93, chmn., CEO, 1994-96; chmn., CEO Chase Manhattan Corp., N.Y.C., 1996—; Bd. dirs. Champion Internat. Corp., NYNEX Corp., Reader's Digest Assn., Inc. Bd. dirs. Lincoln Ctr.

for Performing Arts Inc., Goodwill Industries Greater N.Y. Inc., United Way Tri-State. Mem. The Bus. Coun., Bus Roundtable, Coun. Fgn. Rels., Links, Augusta Nat. Golf Club, Baltusrol Golf Club (Springfield, N.J.). Office: Chase Manhattan Corp 270 Park Ave New York NY 10017-2014

SHIPMAN, CHARLES WILLIAM, chemical engineer; b. Phillipsburgh, N.J., Aug. 29, 1924; s. George Funk and Elizabeth (Johnston) S.; m. Louise Jean Hendrickson, Aug. 31, 1946; children—Nancy Ruth, Jane Louise, Robert Walter George. SB, MIT, 1948, SM, 1949, ScD, 1952. Instr. chem. engring. MIT, 1949-50, research assoc., 1955-58; asst. prof. U. Del., 1952-55; mem. faculty Worcester (Mass.) Poly. Inst., 1958-74, prof. chem. engring., 1964-74, dean grad. studies, 1971-74; engr. Cabot Corp., Billerica, Mass., 1974-87; mgr. Carbon Black R/D, 1980-86; cons., 1953-74, 1987—; bd. dirs. Knox Dist. Housing, Bar Harbor, Maine, 1988—, MDI Helpers, Bar Harbor, 1988-90, treas. 1989-90. Contbr. articles to profl. jours. Trustee Monteux Meml. Found., 1994—. With USMCR, 1944-46. Mem. Combustion Inst. (recipient Silver Combustion medal 1964, bd. dirs. 1978-90), Am. Chem. Soc., Am. Inst. Chem. Engrs., Sigma Xi, Alpha Chi Sigma, Chi Phi. Home and Office: PO Box 32 Prospect Harbor ME 04669-0032

SHIPMAN, KEITH BRYAN, sportscaster; b. Puyallup, Wash., Apr. 26, 1961; s. Richard James and Carol Esther (Christianson) S.; m. Julie Anne Poppe, June 30, 1984; children, Alicia Bryanne, Gregory Dane. BA in Comms., Wash. State U., 1983. Sportscaster/producer KOMO Radio/TV, Seattle, 1983-85; sports/pub. affairs dir. KCPQ TV, Tacoma-Seattle, 1986—; AM drive sports host KJR Radio, Seattle, 1991-93; play by play announcer RayCom Sports, Charlotte, N.C., 1992-95; disc jockey KPUG AM/KNWR FM Radio, Belligham, Wash., 1978-81; play-by-play annoucer Turner Broadcasting System, Atlanta, 1990; host/prodr. "The Chuck Knox Show", Anderson/Baer Prodns., Bainbridge Island, Wash., 1987-88; host "The Chuck Knox Show", Andersen Ent., Bellevue, Wash., 1985-88, various other free-lance work; Edward R. Murrow Sch. of Comms. profl. adv. bd. Wash. State U., 1996—. Pres. bd. dirs. Plaza Hall, Tacoma, Wash., 1989-94; exec. com. Muscular Dystrophy Assn., Seattle, 1989-91; vol. Boys and Girls Club of King County, Seattle and Whatcom County, Bellingham, 1988—, Children's Hosp., Seattle, 1992—. Named Sportscaster of the Yr. for Wash., Nat. Sportscasters and Sportswriters Assn., 1986, 87, 88; recipient Emmy award NATAS, 1990, 92, 94. Mem. Nat. Sportscasters and Sportswriters Assn. (bd. dirs. 1989-96), NATAS, Radio TV News Dirs. Assn. Office: KCPQ TV 4400 Steilacoom Blvd SW Tacoma WA 98499-4002

SHIPMAN, LYNN KAREN, lawyer; b. N.Y.C., Oct. 21, 1950; d. Charles B. and Henrietta J. (Karsh) S.; m. Lawrence J. Meyer, Aug. 25, 1975; children: Michael Shipman-Meyer, Bethany Shipman-Meyer. BA, SUNY, Stony Brook, 1972; JD, St. John's U., 1975; LLM in Taxation, NYU, 1979. Bar: N.J. 1977, Pa. 1980, N.Y. 1980, U.S. Dist. N.J. 1977, U.S. Tax Ct. 1980. Sr. tax editor Prentice-Hall, Inc., Englewood Cliffs, N.J., 1975-79; assoc. Krekstein, Wolfson & Krekstein, P.C., Phila., 1979-86, shareholder, officer, 1986-92, also bd. dirs.; of counsel LaBrum & Doak, Phila., 1993; sr. counsel PNC Bank, Nat. Assn., Phila., 1993—; lectr. Fed. Tax Conf., 1986, 29th Ann. Wharton Sch. Tax Conf., 1989, 1996 N.J. Bankers Assn. Ann. Fin. Mgmt. and Trust Conf.; discussion leader, lectr. CPA socs., Mass., 1988, Pa., 1985-90, Va., 1988, Fla., 1988, 90, 91, Ky., 1990, Ill., 1991, N.C., 1991, AICPA, 1989. Converted AICPA course Coping with Problems in Pensions and Profit Sharing Plans to home study course. Trustee Tamarac Lakes Assn. Recipient Outstanding Instr. award Pa. Inst. CPAs for AICPA courses taught 1988-89. Mem. ABA (com. employee benefits tax sect. 1996—, com. affiliated corp. and related entities tax sect. 1981-90), Phila. Bar Assn. (lectr. tax lecture series 1988, com. on employee benefits tax sect.), Investment Co. Inst. (pension com.). Office: PNC Bank Nat Assn 1600 Market St Ste 28 Philadelphia PA 19103-7201

SHIPPEY, LYN, reading center director; b. Childress, Tex., Mar. 6, 1927; d. Robert Coke and Alta (Timmons) Elliott; m. James George Shippey, Mar. 29, 1947; children: James Robert, Deborah Shippey Meyer, Marilyn Shippey Buron. BS, U. Corpus Christi, 1963; MA in Edn., San Diego State U., 1977; EdD, U. San Diego, 1993. Cert. tchr., reading specialist, tchr. of learning handicapped, Calif. Substitute tchr. Dept. Edn., Guam, 1958-61; tchr. counselor Robstown Ind. Sch. Dist., Tex., 1964-65; elem. tchr. Cupertino Union Sch. Dist., Calif., 1965-68, tchr., secondary, 1968-71; dir. PIRK Reading Center, Poway, Calif., 1973—; cons., workshop presenter PIRK Reading Programs, Calif., Tex., 1974—. Author: Perceptual Integration Reading Kits, 1971, PIRK Reading Program, 1977, rev. 1987. Mem. Coun. for Exceptional Children, Alcala Soc. U. San Diego (scholar), Orton Dyslexia Soc. (bd. dirs. San Diego br.), Learning Disabilities Assn., Coun. for Learning Disabilities. Avocations: photography, gardening. Office: PIRK Reading Center 16957 Cloudcroft Dr Poway CA 92064-1306

SHIPPEY, SANDRA LEE, lawyer; b. Casper, Wyo., June 24, 1957; d. Virgil Carr and Doris Louise (Conklin) McClintock; m. Ojars Herberts Ozols, Sept. 2, 1978 (div.); children: Michael Ojars, Sara Ann, Brian Christopher; m. James Robert Shippey, Jan. 13, 1991. BA with distinction, U. Colo., 1978; JD magna cum laude, Boston U., 1982. Bar: Colo. 1982, U.S. Dist. Ct. Colo. 1985. Assoc. Cohen, Brame & Smith, Denver, 1983-84, Parcel, Meyer, Schwartz, Ruttum & Mauro, Denver, 1984-85, Mayer, Brown & Platt, Denver, 1985-87; counsel western ops. GE Capital Corp., San Diego, 1987-94; assoc. Page, Polin, Busch & Boatwright, San Diego, 1994-95; v.p., gen. counsel First Comml. Corp., San Diego, 1995-96; legal counsel Next Wave Telecom Inc., San Diego, 1996—. Active Pop Warner football and cheerleading. Mem. Phi Beta Kappa, Phi Delta Phi. Republican. Mem. Ch. of Christ. Avocations: tennis, photography. Home: 11878 Glenhope Rd San Diego CA 92128-5002 Office: NextWave Telecom Inc 6256 Greenwich Dr Ste 500 San Diego CA 92122-5941

SHIPULA, ANTHONY JAMES, II, church diocese administrator; b. Wilkes-Barre, Pa., Dec. 12, 1956; s. Anthony and Phyloretta (Horoshko) S.; m. Christine Hudak, June 16, 1979; children: Jennifer Ann, Anthony Joseph, Joseph James. BS in Commerce and Fin., Wilkes Coll., 1978; cert. Nat. Planned Giving Inst., Coll. of William and Mary, 1997. Life ins. salesman Home Life Ins. Co. Am., Wilkes-Barre, 1978-79; nat. acct. rep. underwriting/mktg. Aetna Life & Casualty, Phila. and Hartford, Conn., 1979-83; ins. salesman and svc. Chamberlin Ins., Scranton, Pa., 1983-84; corp. underwriter WVIA TV Channel 44, Wilkes-Barre and Scranton, Pa., 1984-85; alumni dir. Wilkes U., Wilkes-Barre, 1985-96; dir. devel. Diocese of Scranton, Pa., 1996—. Bd. dirs. Cystic Fibrosis Found., Allentown, 1987-95; mem. PARD com. United Way of Wyoming Valley, 1993-94; grad. Leadership Wilkes-Barre, 1993, bd. dirs., chmn. alumni com., 1994-95. Mem. Wyoming Valley Country Club (sec. 1990-91), Wyoming Valley "Mickey Noonan" Football chpt. (football ofcl.). Avocations: golf, travel, running, football officiating. Home: 19 Grandview Ave Wilkes Barre PA 18702-3104 Office: Diocese of Scranton Director of Development 300 Wyoming Ave Scranton PA 18503-1224

SHIRA, ROBERT BRUCE, university administrator, oral surgery educator; b. Butler, Pa., Dec. 2, 1910; s. Thomas Plummer and Erla (Brown) S.; m. Anne Eileen Anderson, Mar. 27, 1933; children: Sharon Lu, Mary Ann, Linda Kay. Student, Bartlesville (Okla.) Jr. Coll., 1927-28; D.D.S., U. Mo., Kansas City, 1932; D.Sc., Georgetown U., 1976, Tufts U., 1979, U. Mo., Kansas City, 1982, U. Detroit, 1987. Diplomate: Am. Bd. Oral and Maxillofacial Surgery (pres. 1974-75). Pvt. practice dentistry Pawhuska, Okla., 1932-38; commd. 1st lt., Dental Corps U.S. Army, 1938, advanced through grades to maj. gen., 1967; chief oral surgery Walter Reed Gen. Hosp., 1954-64; dir. dental activities Walter Reed Army Med. Center, 1966-67; dental surgeon Europe, 1964-66; asst. surgeon gen., chief Army Dental Corps, 1967-71; ret., 1971; prof. oral surgery Tufts U., Boston, 1971-93; dean Sch. Dental Medicine, Tufts U., Boston, 1972-78; sr. v.p., provost Tufts U., Boston, 1979-82, asst. to pres., 1982-93; vis. prof. U. of Pacific, 1954-71, U. Pa., 1956-71; professorial lectr. Georgetown U., 1955-71. Contbr.: chpts. Textbook of Oral Surgery, 1973, Management of Office Emergencies, 1979, Improving Dental Practice through Preventive Measures, 1965; contbr. articles to profl. jours. Decorated D.S.M., Legion of Merit with 2 oak leaf clusters, Army Commendation medal, Army Disting. Svc. medal, Army Disting. Svc. medal; recipient Sword of Hope award Am. Cancer Soc., 1959; named Man of Yr. U. Mo., Kansas City, 1960. Mem. ADA (pres. 1975-76, cons. Council on Therapeutics, Disting. Service award), Am. Assn. Oral and Maxillofacial Surgery (pres. 1965-66), Am. Acad. Oral Pathology. Republican. Presbyterian. Home: Ste 814 3310 N Leisure World Blvd Silver Spring MD 20906

SHIRAI, SCOTT, communications executive; b. Honolulu, June 5, 1942; s. George Yoshio and Thelma Takeko (Tominaga) S.; children: Todd, Kimberly, Lance, Lyle. MusB, U. Hawaii, 1983; exec. dir. news, reporter Sta. KHON-TV, Honolulu, 1974-81; asst. gen. mgr. Vanguard Investments, Berkeley, Calif., 1976-79; newscaster Sta. KPOI, Honolulu, 1979-80; news dir. Sta. KGU, Honolulu, 1981-82; owner Visual Perspectives, 1981—; dir. pub. rels. Hawaiian Electric Co., Honolulu, 1982-90; dir. cmty. rels., Hawaiian Electric Industries, 1990—; instr. U. Hawaii, 1984—; pres. Hawaii Cmty. TV, 1993—; dir. BBB of Hawaii, 1995, Hawaii Pub. Broadcasting, 1996—. Author: Karaoke: Sing Along Guide to Fun & Confidence, 1997. Bd. dirs., sec. Hawaii Com. For Freedom of Press, 1982—; bd. dirs. Mental Health Assn. in Hawaii, 1981—, Moanalua Gardens Found., 1981-84, Health and Cmty. Svcs. Coun., 1982-86, Friends of Father Damien, 1986; v.p. Mele Nani Singers, 1986—; mem. Mayors Adv. Com. on Mcpl. TV, 1987, Office of Hawaiian Affairs Pub. Rels. Adv. Com., 1987, (all Honolulu); sec., dir. Pro Geothermal Alliance, 1990-91. Recipient Jefferson award Honolulu Advertiser, 1985, Gold award Audio-Visual Producers Assn. Am., 1985, Audio-Visual Dept. of Yr. award Videography mag., 1986, Award of Excellence Nat. Hospice Orgn., 1987, Intre award Inst. Teleradial Atica Puerto Rico, Inc., 1988. Mem. ASTD, Internat. TV Assn. (pres. 1983—), Am. Film Inst., AFTRA (bd. dirs. 1980-83), Pub. Rels. Soc. Am. (immediate past pres. and del. 1995—), Hawaii Speakers Assn., Hawaii Film Bd., Honolulu Cmty. Media Council, Hawaii Cmty. TV Assn. (pres. 1990—). Clubs: Honolulu Press (bd. dirs. 1984—), Hui Luna (bd. dirs. 1986-90) (Honolulu). Avocations: martial arts, singing. Office: Hawaiian Electric Industries PO Box 730 1001 Bishop St Ste 811 Honolulu HI 96808

SHIRAI, SHUN, law educator, lawyer; b. Tokyo, June 18, 1942; s. Kyo and Tomi Shirai; m. Junko Matsushita, Apr. 10, 1969; children: Akiko, Yuko, Jin. LLB, Hitotsubashi U., Tokyo, 1966, LLM, 1969. Cert. atty. at law. Asst. prof. criminal law Kokugakuin U., Tokyo, 1974-81, prof., 1981—; atty. at law Tokyo (Japan) 2nd Bar Assn., 1992—. Author: Phenomenology of Crime, 1984, Thought on Criminal Law of Ancient India, 1985, Legal History on Criminal Law of Ancient India, 1990, Philosophy of Criminal Law in Ancient India, 1995. Mem. Indian History Congress. Buddhist. Home: 17-25 Matsudoshinden, Matsudo-shi Chiba Pref 271, Japan Office: Kokugakuin U, 4-10-28 Higashi Shibuya-Ku, Tokyo 150, Japan

SHIRBROUN, RICHARD ELMER, veterinarian, cattleman; b. Coon Rapids, Iowa, Oct. 22, 1929; s. Francis Clyde and Clara Mable (Bell) S.; m. Treva Margaret Teter (div.), Sept. 9, 1951; children: Randal Mark, Camille Leean, James Bradley; m. Wava Lynne Frank, Nov. 11, 1989. DVM, Iowa State U., 1952. Owner, vet. Shirbroun Vet. Med. Ctr., Coon Rapids, 1955—. Lt. USAF, 1952-55. Mem. AVMA (trustee 1982—), Am. Assn. Bovine Practitioners (bd. dirs. 1982—, Excellence Preventive Medicine award 1987), Am. Assn. Swine Practitioners, Iowa Vet. Med. Assn. (pres. 1981, Pres.' award 1985), Soc. for Theriogenology, N.Am. Limousin Found. (founding mem. 1968), Nat. Cattlemen Assn., Iowa Cattlemen Assn., Am. Legion, Rotary (pres. Coon Rapids 1965). Republican. Methodist. Home and Office: Shirbroun Vet Med Ctr 32284 Velvet Ave Coon Rapids IA 50058

SHIRE, DAVID LEE, composer; b. Buffalo, July 3, 1937; s. Irving Daniel and Esther Miriam (Sheinberg) S.; m. Talia Rose Coppola, Mar. 29, 1970 (div.); 1 child, Matthew Orlando; m. Didi Conn. Feb. 11, 1984; 1 child, Daniel Joshua. BA, Yale U., 1959. Film scores include The Conversation, 1974, The Taking of Pelham 1-2-3, 1974, Farewell, My Lovely, 1975, The Hindenburg, 1975, All the President's Men, 1977, Saturday Night Fever (adaptation and additional music), 1977, Norma Rae, 1979 (Acad. award for best original song It Goes Like It Goes), Only When I Laugh, 1981, The World According to Garp, 1982, Max Dugan Returns, 1983, 2010, 1984, Return to Oz, 1985, Short Circuit, 1986, 'Night, Mother, 1986, Vice Versa, 1988, Monkey Shines, 1988, Paris Trout, 1991, Bed and Breakfast, 1992, The Journey Inside (IMAX), 1993, One Night Stand, 1994; TV scores include Raid on Entebbe, 1977 (Emmy nomination), The Defection of Simas Kudirka, 1978 (Emmy nomination), Do You Remember Love?, 1985 (Emmy nomination), Promise, 1986, Echoes in the Darkness, 1987, The Women of Brewster Place, 1989, The Kennedys of Massachusetts, 1990 (Emmy nomination), Common Ground, 1990, Sarah Plain & Tall, 1991, Last Wish, 1992, Broadway Bound, 1992, Skylark, 1993, Remember, 1993, The Companion, 1994, My Brother's Keeper, 1995, Serving in Silence, 1995, The Heidi Chronicles, 1995, My Antonia, 1995, The Streets of Laredo, 1995, Last Stand at Saber River, 1997; theatre scores include The Sap of Life, 1961, Graham Crackers, 1962, The Unknown Soldier and His Wife, 1967, How Do You Do, I Love You, 1968, Love Match, 1970, Starting Here, Starting Now, 1977, Baby, 1983 (Tony nominee best mus. and best original score), Urban Blight, 1988, Closer Than Ever, 1989 (Outer Critics Circle award best off-Broadway musical and best score), Big, 1996 (Tony nominee best score); composer Sonata for Cocktail Piano, 1965; recorded songs include Autumn, 1959, Starting Here, Starting Now, 1965, What About Today?, 1969, Manhattan Skyline, 1977, The Promise, 1978 (Acad. award nomination), It Goes Like It Goes, 1979 (Acad. award), With You I'm Born Again, 1979; albums include Saturday Night Fever, 1977 (Grammy award 1978), Starting Here, Starting Now, 1977 (Grammy nomination 1977), Baby, 1984, Return to Oz, 1985, Closer Than Ever, 1990, David Shire at The Movies, 1991, Big, 1996. With Army N.G., 1960-66. Mem. Composers and Lyricists Guild Am., Am. Fedn. Musicians, Broadcast Music Inc., Acad. Motion Picture Arts and Scis., Nat. Acad. Rec. Arts and Scis., Nat. Acad. TV Arts and Scis., Dramatists Guild Am. (coun. mem.). Jewish. Office: Savitsky Satin & Geibelson Ste 1450 1901 Avenue Of The Stars Los Angeles CA 90067-6015

SHIRE, DONALD THOMAS, retired air products and chemicals executive, lawyer; b. Boston, Jan. 13, 1930; s. Thomas J. and Nellie M. S.; m. Anne Court Bither, Nov 21, 1953; children: Jennifer Anne, Andrew Carter, Daniel Orchard. B.S. in Bus. Adminstrn, Boston U., 1951, LL.B., 1953; postgrad., Harvard Bus. Sch., 1985. Atty. Air Products and Chems., Inc., 1957-64, sec., atty., 1964-75, sec., asst. gen. counsel, 1975-78, v.p. energy and materials, 1978-85, v.p. human resources, 1986-90, sr. v.p. human resources and adminstrn., 1990-91, sr. v.p. adminstrn., 1991-93; ret., 1993; also bd. dirs. Air Products and Chems., Inc.; chmn. Air Products Found., 1991-93; bd. dirs., chmn. Exec. Svc. Corps of Lehigh Valley; bd. dirs. Lehigh Valley Bus./Edn. Partnership. Trustee Muhlenberg Coll., 1976-95, Lehigh Valley Hosp. Lt. USNR, 1954-57. Mem. Am. Arbitration Assn. Episcopalian. Home: 1133 N Main St Allentown PA 18104-2913 Office: Air Products and Chems Inc 7201 Hamilton Blvd Allentown PA 18195-1526

SHIREMAN, JOAN FOSTER, social work educator; b. Cleve., Oct. 28, 1933; d. Louis Omar and Genevieve (Duguid) Foster; m. Charles Howard Shireman, Mar. 18, 1967; 1 child, David Louis. BA, Radcliffe Coll., 1956; MA, U. Chgo., 1959, PhD, 1968. Caseworker N.H. Children's Aid Soc., Manchester, 1959-61; dir. research Chgo. Child Care Soc., 1968-72; assoc. prof. U. Ill., Chgo., 1972-85; prof. Portland (Oreg.) State U., 1985—, dir. PhD program, 1992—; interim exec. dir. Partnership for Rsch., Tng. and Grad. Edn. in Child Welfare, 1994; research cons. child welfare orgns., Ill., 1968-85, Oreg. 1985—; lectr. U. Chgo., 1968-72. Co-author: Care and Commitment: Foster Parent Adoption Decisions, 1985, Adoption: Theory, Policy and Practice, 1996; mem. editl. bd. Jour. Sch. Social Work, 1978-81, Social Work Rsch. and Abstracts, 1990-93, Children and Youth Svcs. Rev., 1990-95, Jour. Social Work Edn., 1990-95; contbr. articles to profl. jours., chpts. to books. Bd. dirs. Oreg. chpt. Nat. Assn. for Prevention Child Abuse, 1985-87; bd. dirs. Friendly House, Portland, 1991—, pres., 1995-96; mem. adv. com. children's svcs. divsn. State of Oreg., 1985-95. Grantee HEW, 1980-82, Chgo. Community Trust, 1982-86, Oreg. Children's Trust Fund, 1991-96. Mem. NASW, AAUP, Am. Profl. Soc. Abuse of Children, Children First Oreg., Acad. Cert. Social Workers, Coun. on Social Work Edn., Phi Beta Kappa. Home: 2535 SW Sherwood Dr Portland OR 97201-1679 Office: Portland State U Grad Sch Social Work PO Box 751 Portland OR 97207-0751

SHIRER, BRUCE EDWARD, pathologist; b. Chgo., Sept. 22, 1941; s. Benjamin Franklin and Thelma Katherine (Borgstrom) S.; m. Janett Margaret Jurasek, Sept. 16, 1967 (div. Nov. 1982); m. Linda Locke Sevcik, July 7, 1984; children: Brandt Stephen, Benjamin Stuart. Student, North Ctrl. Coll., Naperville, Ill., 1958-61; MD, U. Wis., 1965. Diplomate Am. Bd. Pathology. Resident internal medicine Northwestern U., Chgo., 1968-69, resident in pathology, 1969-73; pathologist, co-dir. San Diego Inst. Pathology, 1973-82; locum tenens pathologist various labs., San Diego, 1982-84; med. dir. Lab. Corp. Am., San Diego, 1984—; assoc. pathologist Yuma (Ariz.) Regional Med. Ctr., 1986—. Lt. comdr. USNR, 1966-68, Vietnam. Fellow Coll. AM. Pathologists, Am. Soc. Clin. Pathologists; mem. AMA, Calif. Med. Assn., San Diego County Med. Soc. Republican. Avocations: travel, skiing, classical music, opera, reading. Home: 6037 Firwood Run La Jolla CA 92037 Office: Lab Corp Am 5601 Oberlin Dr San Diego CA 92121-3747

SHIRES, GEORGE THOMAS, surgeon, educator; b. Waco, Tex., Nov. 22, 1925; s. George Thomas and Donna Mae (Smith) S.; m. Robbie Jo Martin, Nov. 27, 1948; children: Donna Blain, George Thomas III, Jo Ellen. MD, U. Tex., Dallas, 1948. Diplomate Am. Bd. Surgery (dir. 1968-74, chmn. 1972-74). Intern Mass. Meml. Hosp., Boston, 1948-49; resident Parkland Meml. Hosp., Dallas, 1950-53; mem. faculty U. Tex. Southwestern Med. Sch. at Dallas, 1953-74, assoc. prof. surgery, acting chmn. dept., 1960-61, prof., chmn. dept., 1961-74; surgeon in chief surg. services Parkland Meml. Hosp., 1960-74; prof., chmn. dept. surgery U. Wash. Sch. Medicine, Seattle, 1974-75; chief of service Harborview Med. Center, Seattle, Univ. Hosp., Seattle, 1974-75; chmn. dept. surgery N.Y. Hosp.-Cornell Univ. Med. Coll., 1975-91; dean and provost for med. affairs Cornell U. Med. Coll., 1987-91; prof., chmn. surgery Tex. Tech. U., Lubbock, 1991-95, Canizaro disting. prof. surgery, 1995-97; prof. surgery U. Nev. Sch. Medicine, Las Vegas, 1997—; cons. Surgeon Gen., U.S. Army, 1965-75, Jamaica Hosp., 1978-91, Inst. Medicine Nat. Acad. Scis., 1975—; mem. com. metabolism and truama Nat. Acad. Scis.-NRC, 1964-71, com. trauma, 1964-71; mem. rsch. program evaluation com., reviewer clin. investigation applications career devel. program VA, 1972-76; mem. gen. med. rsch. program projects com. NIH, 1965-69; mem. Surgery A study sect., 1970-74, chmn., 1976-78; mem. Nat. Adv. Gen. Med. Scis. Coun., 1980-84; cons. editl. bd. Jour. Trauma, 1968-88. Mem. editl. bd. Year Book Med. Publs., 1970-92, Annals of Surgery, 1972—, Surg. Techniques Illustrated: An International Comparative Text, 1974-75, Am. Jour. Surgery, 1968—, Contemporary Surgery, 1973-89; assoc. editor-in-chief Infections in Surgery, 1981; mem. editl. coun. Jour. Clin. Surgery, 1980-82; editor Surgery, Gynecology and Obstetrics, 1982-93. Lt. M.C. USNR, 1949-50, 53-55. Life Ins. Med. Rsch. fellow, 1947. Mem. ACS (bd. regents 1971-82, chmn. bd. regents 1978-80, pres. 1981-82), AMA, Dallas Soc. Gen. Surgeons (pres.-elect, pres. 1972-74), Am. Assn. Surgery Trauma, Am. Surg. Assn. (sec. 1969-74, pres. 1980), Digestive Disease Found. (founding mem.), Halsted Soc., Internat. Soc. Burn Injuries, Internat. Surg. Soc. (sec. 1978-81, v.p. 1982-83, pres. U.S. chpt. 1984-85), Pan-Am. Med. Assn. (surgery council 1971—), Pan Pacific Surg. Assn., Soc. Clin. Surgery, Soc. Surgery Alimentary Tract, Soc. Surg. Chairmen (pres. 1972-74), Soc. Univ. Surgeons (chmn. publs. com. 1969-71), So. Surg. Assn., Surg. Biology Club (sec. 1968-70), Western Surg. Assn., Allen O. Whipple Surg. Soc., James IV Assn. Surgeons (bd. dirs. 1980-81, sec. 1981-87, pres. 1987-91), Alpha Omega Alpha, Alpha Pi Alpha, Phi Beta Pi. Office: U Nev Sch Medicine 2040 W Charleston Blvd Ste 304 Las Vegas NV 89102-2230

SHIREY, MARGARET (PEGGY SHIREY), elementary school educator; b. Sussex, N.J., Nov. 24, 1950; d. Steve and Grace (McGlew) Piniaha; children: Todd, Jessica. BS, Marymount Coll., Salina, Kans., 1972; M Elem. Edn., Ctrl. State U., 1985. Cert. elem. tchr., Okla. Tchr. Putnam City Sch. Dist., Oklahoma City, 1980—. Active Putnam City Reading Coun.; bargaining mem. Putnam City, 1993-95. Recipient Excellent Educator award; named One of Okla.'s Best Tchrs. Channel 5 Alive, Oklahoma City, 1991. Mem. NEA, ASCD, Okla. Edn. Assn., Putnam City Assn. Classroom Tchrs. (bldg. rep. 1983-86, legis. chairperson 1989-92). Democrat. Avocations: writing, reading, walking. Home: 3720 N Eagle Ln Bethany OK 73008-3542 Office: Putnam City Sch Dist 5401 NW 40th St Oklahoma City OK 73122-3302

SHIRILLA, ROBERT M., executive recruiter. BA in Econs. magna cum laude, UCLA, 1971; MBA with honors, Harvard U., 1975. Asst. product mgr. Gen. Foods Corp., White Plains, N.Y., 1975-76, assoc. product mgr., 1977; product mgr. Hunt Wesson Foods, Inc., Fullerton, Calif., 1977-78, mktg. mgr., 1978-79, sr. mktg. mgr., 1979-80, group mktg. mgr., 1980-81; dir. mktg. Citicorp, N.Y.C., 1981, v.p. mktg., 1982-84; v.p. mktg. Am. Savings Bank, L.A., 1984, sr. v.p. mktg., 1984-86; pres., co-founder Computerized Vehicle Registration, L.A., 1986-91; gen. mgr., mng. dir. Inst. Mgmt. Resources, L.A., 1991-93; exec. v.p. F.B. Schmidt Internat., L.A., 1993—. Contbr. articles to profl. jours. Mem. Pres.'s Commn. on White House Fellowships; chmn. Hugh O'Brian Youth Found. Calif. Leadership Seminar; chmn. adv. com. March of Dimes, bd. dirs.; bd. dirs. L.A. Jr. C. of C., Charity Found., Golf Found. 1st lt. U.S. Army, 1971-73, col. Res. Army ROTC scholar UCLA. Mem. Am. Mgmt. Assn. (bd. dirs.), World Affairs Coun., Acad. Polit. Sci., Rotary, Theta Chi (pres.), Pershing Rifles (pres.), Pi Mu Epsilon, Beta Alpha Psi, Psi Chi, Pi Gamma Mu, Phi Eta Sigma, Omicron Delta Epsilon, Pi Sigma Slpha, Alpha Kappa Psi (scholarship award). Home: 601 Hampshire Rd Unit 546 Thousand Oaks CA 91361

SHIRLEY, AARON, pediatrician; b. Gluckstadt, Miss., Jan. 3, 1933; married; 4 children. BS, Tougaloo Coll., 1955; MD, McHarry Med. Coll., 1959, U. Miss., 1968. Intern Herbert Hosp., Tenn., 1959-60; gen. practice Vicksburg, 1960-65; project dir. Jackson-Hinds Comprehensive Health Ctr., Jackson, Miss., 1980-96; dir. cmty. health svcs. Jackson (Miss.) Med. Mall, 1996—; mem. faculty medicine Tufts U. Medicine, Mass., 1968-73, U. Miss. Med. Sch., 1970—; head start cons. Am. Acad. Pediats., 1969-74; adv. bd. rural practice project Robert Wood Johnson Found., 1974-78; mem. Select Panel Prom. Child Health, Washington, 1979-81. Mem. Inst. Medicine-NAS (mem. coun. 1988—). Office: Jackson Med Mall 350 W Woodrow Wilson Ste 302 A Jackson MS 39213*

SHIRLEY, CHARLES WILLIAM, farm owner; b. Norfolk, Va., Jan. 28, 1954; s. Norris Winfred and Margorie Elizabeth (Whedbee) S.; m. Carol Ruth Montgomery, May 21, 1977; children: Sarah Ruth, Daniel Talmadge. Student, U. S.C., 1972-74; BS in Bus. and Journalism, Old Dominion U., 1977, cert. profl. fin. planner, 1986; cert. land use planner, Va. Polytech. Inst., 1987. Cert. profl. fin. planner Am. Express Fin. Planners, Inc.; cert. assoc. agt. Nationwide Ins.; security lic. series 6, 7, 63 and 65. Ptnr. N.W. Shirley Farms, Virginia Beach, Va., 1977-88; owner C.W. Shirley Farms, Chesapeake, Va., 1982—; dealer Northrup King, Chesapeake, Va., 1985-94; assoc. agt. Nationwide Ins., 1995—. Contbr. articles to newspapers and mags., 1985—. Planning commr. City of Chesapeake, 1986-94; chmn. Planning Commn., 1991-92; mem. Chesapeake Growth Commn., 1993; chmn. Virginia Beach Young Farmers Com., 1983-95; cmn. food com. S.E. Young Farmer's Tractor Pull, 1984; bd. dirs. Chesapeake Crime Line, 1985-93. Recipient Young Farmer award and Discussion Meet award Va. Farm Bur., 1984; named Young Farmer of Yr., Virginia Beach Jaycees, 1984; winner Va. corn yield contest, 1993. Mem. Nat. Assn. Profl. Fin. Planners, Va. Soybean Assn. (mem. com. chmn. 1991-92, v.p. 1992-93, pres. 1994, Young Leader Va. 1990), Virginia Beach Farm Bur. (v.p. 1990-92), Chesapeake Farm Bur. (v.p. 1994-95, pres. 1995), Creeds Ruritan Club (sec. 1987), Nat. Corn Growers Assn. (Va. Corn Contest winner 1993), Va. Small Grain Assn., Va. Citizen's Planners Assn., Va. Soybean Bd., Chesapeake Arboretum, Virginia Beach Bus. Exch. Baptist. Avocations: deer hunting, deep sea fishing, snow skiing. Home: 2420 Carolina Rd Chesapeake VA 23322-1428 Office: CW Shirley Farms 2424 Carolina Rd Chesapeake VA 23322-1428

SHIRLEY, DAVID ARTHUR, chemistry educator, science administrator; b. North Conway, N.H., Mar. 30, 1934; m. Virginia Schultz, June 23, 1956 (dec. Mar. 1995); children: David N., Diane, Michael, Eric, Gail; m. Barbara Cerny, Dec. 26, 1995. BS, U. Maine, 1955, ScD (hon.), 1978; PhD in Chemistry, U. Calif.-Berkeley, 1959; D honoris causa, Free U. Berlin, 1987. With Lawrence Radiation Lab. (now Lawrence Berkeley Lab.), U. Calif., Berkeley, 1958-92, assoc. dir., head materials and molecular research div., 1975-80, dir., 1980-89, lectr. chemistry, 1959-60, asst. prof., 1960-64, assoc. prof., 1964-67, prof., 1967-92, vice chmn. dept. chemistry, 1968-71, chmn. dept. chemistry, 1971-75; sr. v.p. rsch., dean grad. sch. Pa. State U., University Park, 1992-96; dir. emeritus Lawrence Berkeley Nat. Lab., 1997—. Contbr. over 400 rsch. articles. NSF fellow, 1955-58, 66-67, 70; recipient Ernest O. Lawrence award AEC, 1972, Humboldt award (sr. U.S. scientist); listed by Sci. Citation Index as one of the world's 300 most cited scientists for work published during 1965-78. Fellow Am. Phys. Soc.; mem. Nat. Acad. Scis., Am. Chem. Soc., AAAS, Am. Acad. Arts and Scis., Sigma Xi, Tau Beta Pi, Sigma Pi Sigma, Phi Kappa Phi.

SHIRLEY, DENNIS LYNN, education educator; b. Columbia, S.C., Feb. 28, 1955; s. Edward Lynn and Margaret Jane (Farnham) S.; m. Laura Shelley Cochran, Jan. 5, 1960; children: Syke Atla, Gabriel Delayne. BA, U. Va., 1977; MA in Sociology, New Sch. for Social Rsch., 1980; EdD, Harvard U., 1988. Tchr. Ecole D'Humanité, Goldern, Switzerland, 1980-83; prof. Rice U., Houston, 1988—. Author: The Politics of Progressive Education: The Odenwaldschule in Nazi Germany, 1992, Community Organizing for Urban School Reform, 1997. Fed. Chancellor's scholar Alexander von Humboldt Found., Bonn, Germany, 1990-91. Office: Rice Univ Dept Edn MS-146 6100 Main St Houston TX 77005-1827

SHIRLEY, GEORGE PFEIFFER, lawyer, educational consultant; b. Algood, Tenn., Dec. 12, 1939; s. Howard Dunbar and Maryhils Lewis (Pfeiffer) S.; m. Mary Ann Clawson, May 24, 1958 (div.); m. Susan Hawkins, July 24, 1971 (div.); m. Laura Gail Salmonsen, Feb. 29, 1992; children: Kathleen Underwood, Bryan, Andrew, Robert. BA, U. Denver, 1962, MA, 1963, JD, 1966. Tchr. various high schs., coll. and law schs., 1964—; adminstr. Pan Am Petrol, Denver, 1966-68; lobbyist Sacramento and Washington, 1968-72; lawyer, exec. dir. legal svcs. Calif., Fla. and Minn., 1972-80; trial and appellate lawyer in pvt. practice, Monterey, Calif., 1980-86; tchr. Alisal H.S., Salinas, Calif., 1984-86; pvt. ednl. cons. San Jose, Calif., 1986-92; CEO Edn. Reform for the 21st Century, Sacramento, 1997—; author and essayist Sacramento, 1994—; bd. dirs. Cal-Micro, Inc., San Jose, Am. Grinding Co., San Jose; lectr. various univs., 1986—. Screenwriter movie Brown Eyed Children of the Sun, 1997. Campaign coord. Dem. Party, Sacramento, 1972, 84, 92, 96. 1st lt. ROTC, USMC 1957-66. Mem. Internat. Platform Assn., Order of Coif, Pi Gamma Mu. Methodist. Avocation: baseball. Home: 8690 Cliffwood Way Sacramento CA 95826-3641

SHIRLEY, GLENN DEAN, writer; b. Payne County, Okla., Dec. 9, 1916; s. Ellis Dean and Effie Teresa (Knorr) S.; m. Carrie Mabel Jacob, 1946; children: Glenda Lea, Kenneth Ellis. Diploma, N.Y. Inst. Photography, 1941, Internat. Criminologist Sch., 1948, Delehanty Inst., 1949, Okla. Inst. Tech., 1950; LL.B., LaSalle U., Chgo., 1940. Capt., asst. chief Stillwater Police Dept., (Okla.), 1936-57; criminal dep. Payne County Sheriff's Office, 1957-59; asst. chief security Okla. State U., Stillwater, 1959-69; publs. specialist, asst. dir. Okla. State U. Press, 1969-79, ret., 1980; freelance writer Stillwater, 1980—; now hist. cons. Western Publs., pub. True West, Old West mags., Stillwater; lectr. in field. Author: books of western history and personalities, including Toughest of Them All, 1953; Six-Gun and Silver Star, 1955, Law West of Ft. Smith: A History of Frontier Justice in the Indian Territory,, 1834-1896/1957, 11th edit., 1996, Pawnee Bill: A Biography of Gordon W. Lillie, 1958, 4th edit., 1981, rev. 1993, Buckskin and Spurs: A Gallery of Frontier Rogues and Heroes, 1958, Outlaw Queen, 1960, Heck Thomas, Frontier Marshal: The Story of a Real Gunfighter, 1962, rev. edit., 1981, Born to Kill, 1963, Henry Starr, Last of the Real Badmen, 1965, 2d edit., 1976, Buckskin Joe: The Unique and Vivid Memoirs of Edward Jonathan Hoyt, Hunter-Trapper, Scout, Soldier, Showman, Frontiersman and Friend of the Indians, 1840-1918, 1966, 2d edit., 1988, Shotgun for Hire: The Story of Deacon "Jim Miller", Killer of Pat Garrett, 1970, 2d edit., 1980, The Life of Texas Jack: Eight Years a Criminal—41 Years Trusting in God, 1973, Red Yesterdays, 1977, West of Hell's Fringe: Crime, Criminals and the Federal Peace officer in Oklahoma Territory 1889-1907, 1978, Temple Houston, Lawyer with a Gun, 1980, Belle Starr and Her Times: The Literature The Facts and The Legends, 1982, Guardian of the Law, The Life and Times of William Matthew Tilghman, 1988, Purple Sage, The Exploits, Adventures and Writings of Patrick Sylvester McGeeney, 1989, Hello, Sucker! The Story of Texas Guinan, 1989, Gunfight at Ingalls, Death of an Outlaw Town, 1990, They Outrobbed Them All, The Rise and Fall of the Vicious Martins, 1992, The Fighting Marlows, Men Who Wouldn't Be Lynched, 1994, Marauders of the Indian Nations: The Bill Cook Gang and Cherokee Bill, 1994, 13 Days of Terror, The Rufus Buck Gang in Indian Territory, 1996; contbr. numerous short stories, novelettes and factual articles to Western pulps, fact-detective and men's mags. and gen. markets, to anthologies; former contbg. editor: Westerner, Old Trails, Oklahoma Monthly; collector Western Americana. Recipient Okla. Literary Endeavor award, 1960, Am.'s Star award U.S. Marshal Svc., 1989, Profl. Writing award U. Okla., 1990; inducted into Okla. Journalism Hall of Fame, 1981, Okla. Profl. Writers Hall of Fame, 1992;. Mem. Okla. Writers Fedn. (past pres., life mem.), Indian Ter. Posse Westerners (past pres.), Western Writers Am., Western History Assn., Nat. Assn. Outlaw and Lawman History, Oklahoma Heritage Assn., Inst. Great Plains, Assocs. Western History Collections (trustee), Okla. State Hist. Soc., Kans. State Hist. Soc., Mont. State Hist. Soc. Address: PO Box 824 Stillwater OK 74076-0824

SHIRLEY, GRAHAM EDWARD, management executive; b. Starkville, Miss., Jan. 4, 1943; s. Herman Milford and Helen (Lang) S.; m. Deborah Kay Long, 1996; children: Jennifer, Caryn; 1 stepchild, Tyler. BS, USAF Acad., 1966; MA, U. So. Calif., 1973. Commd. 2d lt. USAF, 1966, advanced through grades to brig. gen., 1988; ops. officer 393d Bomb Squadron, Pease AFB, N.H., 1977-78; comdr. 84th Fighter Interceptor Squadron, Castle AFB, Calif., 1978-80, 86th Tactical Fighter Wing, Ramstein Air Base, Germany, 1984-85, 20th Tactical Fighter Wing, RAF Upper Heyford, Eng., 1985-88; with Hdqrs. USAF, Washington, 1980-83, dir. regional plans, 1988-90; assigned to Air War Coll., Maxwell AFB, Ala., 1983-84; vice comdr. Air Force Intelligence Command, San Antonio, 1990-92; ret. brig. gen. USAF, 1992; v.p. Kasten & Co., Washington, 1992-94; pres. The Ettington Group, Inc., McLean, Va., 1994—. Decorated DSM, Legion of Merit, DFC, Air medal. Mem. Air Force Assn., Internat. Inst. for Strategic Studies (London), Air Force Acad. Assn. Grads., Daedalians. Avocations: flying, reading, hunting, fishing, travel. Office: 300 Convent St Ste 1250 San Antonio TX 78205-3710 *An enlightened and progressive society cannot exist unless the leadership at all levels has compassion, integrity and courage. Compassion for the less fortunate—integrity to know what is right—courage to do what is right regardless of the personal consequences.*

SHIRLEY, ROBERT CLARK, retired university president, strategic planning consultant, educator; b. Jacksonville, Tex., July 1, 1943; s. James Cullen and Mary Jim (Clark) S.; m. Terrie Thomas, June 17, 1967; children: Robin, Deron. B.B.A., U. Houston, 1965, M.B.A., 1967; Ph.D., Northwestern U., 1972. Asst. dean faculties U. Houston, 1974-76; asst. to pres. SUNY-Albany, 1976-77, assoc. v.p. acad. affairs, 1977-79; assoc. prof. Central U. Iowa, Pella, 1979-81; prof. Trinity U., San Antonio, 1981-84; pres. U. So. Colo., Pueblo, 1984-96, pres. emeritus, 1997—; cons. on strategic planning and mgmt. to numerous colls. and univs. Author: Strategy and Policy Formation, 1981; contbr. articles to profl. publs. Mem. Pueblo Econ. Devel. Bd. Bill Laufman Meml. scholar U. Houston, 1965-66; Northwestern U. fellow, 1969-71; HEW research asst. grantee, 1971, 72; La. State U. Found. grantee, 1972, 73. Mem. Acad. Mgmt., Soc. Coll. and Univ. Planning, Pueblo C. of C. Presbyterian. Lodge: Rotary. Office: U So Colo 2200 Bonforte Blvd Pueblo CO 81001-4901*

SHIRLEY, VIRGINIA LEE, advertising executive; b. Kankakee, Ill., Mar. 24, 1936; d. Glenn Lee and Virginia Helen (Ritter) S. Student, Northwestern U., 1960-61. With prodn. control dept. Armour Pharm., Kankakee, 1954-58; exec. sec. Adolph Richman, Chgo., 1958-61; mgr. media dept. Don Kemper Co., Chgo., 1961-63, 65-69; exec. sec. Playboy mag., Chgo., 1964-65; exec. v.p. SMY Media inc., Chgo., 1969-96, CEO, chmn. bd., 1996—. Mem. Pla. Club., Tavern Club. Home: 1502-J S Prairie Ave Chicago IL 60605-2856 Office: SMY Media Inc 333 N Michigan Ave Chicago IL 60601-3901

SHIRLEY-QUIRK, JOHN, concert and opera singer; b. Liverpool, Eng., Aug. 28, 1931; came to U.S., 1990; s. Joseph Stanley and Amelia (Griffiths) S.-Q.; m. Patricia May Hastie, July 1955 (dec. Feb. 1981); children: Kate, Peter; m. Sara Van Horn Watkins, Dec. 29, 1981; children: Benjamin, Emily, Julia. BSc, Liverpool U., 1953, MusD (hon.), 1977; D Univ., Brunel U., 1981. Asst. lectr. Acton Tech. Coll., London, 1956-60; vicar choral St. Paul's Cathedral, London, 1960-61; profl. singer, 1960—; joint artistic dir. Aldeburgh Festival, 1981-84; mem. voice faculty Peabody Conservatory, Balt., 1991—; vis. artist Carnegie-Mellon U., Pitts., 1994-97; vis. lectr. Acad. Vocal Arts, Phila., 1997—. Numerous recs. and 1st performances, especially works of Benjamin Britten. Mem. ct. Brunel U., 1977—. Flying officer RAF, 1952-55. Mem. Royal Acad. Music (hon.), Order of the British Empire (comdr. 1975).

SHIRTUM, EARL EDWARD, retired civil engineer; b. Montague, Mich., Feb. 20, 1927; s. Earl Willard and Elizabeth Caroline (Boelke) S.; m. Martha Louise Wright, June 19, 1953. BS in Civil Engring., Ind. Tech. Coll., Ft. Wayne, 1950. Bridge design squad leader Mich. Dept. Transp., Lansing, 1952-63, transp. planning engr., 1963-96; mem. Bridge Replacement and Rehab. Com., Lansing, 1967-94. With U.S. Army, 1945-46, ETO. Mem. Mich. Profl. Engring. Soc. (rep. engr. in govt. 1974-77), Lansing Engr. Club (bd. mem. 1980-84). Republican. Methodist. Avocations: fishing, bridge. Home: 1617 Victor Ave Lansing MI 48910-6511

SHIRVANI, HAMID, architect, educator, author, administrator; b. Tehran, Iran, Oct. 20, 1950; came to U.S., 1974, naturalized, 1986; s. Majid and Taji (Granpisheh) S. Diploma in architecture, Poly. of Cen. London, 1974; MArch, Pratt Inst., 1975; MS, Rensselaer Poly. Inst., 1977; MA, Harvard U., 1978, Princeton U., 1979; PhD, Princeton U., 1980. Project designer London Borough of Barnet, 1973-74; prin. Techonokam Inc., Tehran and N.Y.C., 1975-77; asst. prof. architecture Pa. State U., 1979-82; prof., dir. grad. studies SUNY, Syracuse, 1982-85; prof., dir. Sch. Urban Planning and Devel., U. Louisville, 1985-86; prof. architecture and urban design U. Colo., Denver, 1986-92, dean Sch. of Architecture and Planning, 1986-91; prof. philosophy, dean Coll. Arts and Scis. U. Mass., Lowell, 1992-95; v.p. grad. studies and rsch., prof. urban studies CUNY Queens Coll., Flushing, 1995—; mem. vis. faculty So. Calif. Inst. Architecutre, U. So. Calif.; lectr. numerous universities worldwide including U. Tex., San Antonio, Lehigh U., U. Waterloo (Can.), U. Sydney (Australia), Mo. State U., Columbia U., N.Y.C., Amsterdam Acad. Art, U. Venice (Italy), Chinese U. Hong Kong, So. China Inst. U., U. Calif., Irvine, Villanova U., Rutgers U., Ariz. State U., Duke U., U. Pa., Yale U., U. Colo., U. N.C. Author: Urban Design: A Comprehensive Reference, 1981, Urban Design Review, 1981, Urban Design Process, 1985, Beyond Public Architecture, 1990; editor Urban Design Rev., 1982-85, Urban Design and Preservation Quar., 1985-88; mem. editorial bd. Jour. Archtl. Edn., 1988-94, Avant Garde, 1988-93, Jour. Planning Edn. and Rsch., 1987-93, Art and Architecture, 1974-78, Jour. Am. Planning Assn., 1982-88. Recipient Gold Medal in Architecture and Urbanism, Faculty Honor award, Acad. Leadership award, Faculty Rsch. award. Fellow Soc. for Values in Higher Edn., Royal Geog. Soc., Royal Soc. Arts; mem. Am. Studies Assn., Am. Soc. Landscape Architects (recognition award), Am. Inst. Cert. Planners, Am. Planning Assn. (chmn. urban design divsn. 1987-89, Disting. award 1984, Urban Design award 1985), Sigma Xi, Omicron Delta Epsilon, Tau Sigma Delta (Silver medal in archtl. edn. 1988), Tau Beta Pi, Sigma Lambda Alpha. Office: Queens Coll CUNY Flushing NY 11367-1597

SHISTER, JOSEPH, arbitrator, educator; b. Montreal, Can., Nov. 27, 1917; came to U.S., 1939, naturalized, 1943; s. Eli Harry and Pearl (Millman) S.; m. Edna Louise Tuck, Dec. 28, 1941; children—Neil Barry, Jayne Ellen, Gail Marilyn, Diane Marjorie. B.S., U. Montreal, 1939; M.A., Harvard, 1941, Ph.D., 1943. Instr. econs. Cornell U., 1942-43; research assoc. study trade-unionism Rockefeller Found., 1944-45; asst. prof. econs. Syracuse U., 1945-46; asst. prof., dir. research, labor and mgmt. center Yale U., 1946-49; mem. faculty SUNY, Buffalo, 1949-83; prof. SUNY, 1950-83, prof. emeritus indsl. relations, 1983—, chmn. dept. indsl. relations, 1950-78; vis. prof. Tufts U., Wesleyan U., Montreal U., 1949-55; moderator U. Buffalo Round Table of the Air, WBEN, WBEN-TV, WBEN-FM, 1952-72; labor arbitrator, 1944—; Cons. economist Nat. War Labor Bd., 1944; pub. mem. constrn. commn. Nat. Wage Stblzn. Bd., 1951-52; referee System Boards of Adjustment, 1959—; chmn. Presdl. Emergency Dispute Bd., 1961, 62, 64; spl. adviser labor legislation Gov. Conn., 1948-50; mem. social stratification com. Social Sci. Research Council, 1952-53; mem. N.Y. State Mediation Bd., 1966-69; spl. cons. N.Y. State Med. Bd., 1968-72; also spl. Mayor's Office Settlement Emergency Labor Disputes, 1959-70; spl. cons. Buffalo Full Employment Com., 1958-60; chmn. Erie County Grievance Bd., 1963-70; mem. N.Y. State Minimum Wage Bd. in Amusement and Recreation Industry, 1957-59, White House Conf. on Nat. Econ. Issues, 1962, White House Conf. on Indsl. World Ahead, 1972, Nat. Acad. Arbitrators, 1950—; arbitration panel Fed. Mediation and Conciliation Svc., 1952—, Am. Arbitration Assn., 1955—; mem. labor dispute panels various bds. and commns. Author: Economics of the Labor Market, rev. edit 1956, Readings in Labor Economics and Industrial Relations, rev. edit, 1956; Co-author: Job Horizons, 1948, Conflict and Stability in Labor Relations, 1952; contbg. author: A Decade of Industrial Relations Research, 1958, Unions, Management and the Public, 1967, Problems de Planification, 1964, Economic Issues and Policies, 1965, Negotiation and Administration of Collective Bargaining Agreements, 1966, The Business World, 1967, Rights and Obligations of Parties Under Collective Agreements, 1967; Co-editor: Insight Into Labor Issues, 1948, Public Policy and Collective Bargaining, 1962; Contbr. articles to profl. jours. Served as pvt. AUS, 1943-44. Mem. Indsl. Rels. Rsch. Assn. (exec. bd. 1959-62), Phi Beta Kappa, Beta Gamma Sigma. Home: 2460 NW 15th St Delray Beach FL 33445-1359

SHIVE, PHILIP AUGUSTUS, architect; b. Luebo, Zaire, Apr. 14, 1938; came to U.S., 1955; s. Alexander M. and Jean B. (Setser) S.; m. Marilyn Ayce Miller, Aug. 3, 1968; children: Susannah, Heather. Student, Davidson Coll., 1956-58; BArch, N.C. State U., 1963; MArch, U. Pa., 1964. Registered architect, N.C., N.Y., Ga. Design architect I.M. Pei & Ptnrs., N.Y.C., 1964-68; ptnr. Gorman, Mixon & Shive, Atlanta, 1968-77; v.p. Wolf Assocs., Charlotte, 1977-83; v.p., dir. design J.N. Pease Assocs., Charlotte, 1983-88; pres. Shive/Bohm-NBBJ, Charlotte, 1988-91, Shive Assocs. Architects, Charlotte, 1991-95, Nix Mann Shive, 1995-96, Nix Mann Shive Perkins & Will, 1996—. Mem. citizen's adv. com. Charlotte-Mecklenburg Planning Commn., 1985-87. Fellow AIA (Kamphoefner prize 1992, 27 design awards); mem. Nat. Am. Inst. Architects (urban design com.), N.C. Arts Coun. Design (arts planning com.), Charlotte City Club. Democrat. Presbyterian. Office: Nix Mann Shive Perkins & Will 1130 E 3rd St Ste 200 Charlotte NC 28204-2624

SHIVE, RICHARD BYRON, architect; b. Cleve., Jan. 16, 1933; s. Roy Allen and Mary Elizabeth (Thompson) S.; m. Patricia Butler, Aug. 28, 1954; children: Lisa Ann, Laura Mary, John Thompson, Nancy Butler. BS, Rensselaer Poly. Inst., Troy, N.Y., 1954; postgrad., Newark (N.J.) Coll. Engring., 1957, Rutgers U., 1960-63. Registered architect, N.J., N.Y., Pa., Vt.; lic. profl. planner, N.J. Field engr. Wigton-Abbott Corp., Plainfield, N.J., 1954-55, The Glenwal Co., Rochelle Park, N.J., 1955; asst. supt. Wigton-Abbott Corp., Plainfield, 1955-57; archtl. draftsman Raymond B. Flatt, Architect, Bloomfield, N.J., 1957-58; chief draftsman Raymond B. Flatt, Architect, 1958-60; project architect Scrimenti/Swackhamer/Perantoni Architects, Somerville, N.J., 1960-66; assoc. Scrimenti/Swackhamer/Perantoni Architects, 1966-69; ptnr. Scrimenti, Shive, Spinelli, Perantoni Architects, Somerville, 1969-86, Shive/Spinelli/Perantoni & Assocs., Architects & Planners, Somerville, 1986—; adv. com. First Fidelity Bank, Bound Brook, N.J., 1989-91; chmn. bd. Somerset Health Care Corp., 1987-91. Contbr. articles to profl. jours. Bd. dirs., exec. com. N.J. Hosp. Assn., Princeton, 1986-92, 93-95; chmn. bd. trustees Somerset Med. Ctr., Somerville, 1973-96; mem. Nat. Trust for Hist. Preservation; bd. dirs. Ctr. for Health Affairs, Inc., 1992-93. Recipient award James F. Lincoln Arc Welding Found., 1973, President's award for outstanding svc. Rolling Hills coun. Girl Scouts U.S.A., 1988, Trustee of Yr. award N.J. Hosp. Assn., 1993, Outstanding Citizen of Yr. award Somerset County C. of C., 1993; Paul Harris fellow Bound Brook-Middlesex Rotary Club, 1993. Mem. AIA, ASTM, ASHRAE, ACI (chpt. bd. dirs. 1978-83), N.J. Soc. Architects, Illuminating Engring. Soc., Nat. Fire Protection Assn., Greater Somerset County C. of C. (v.p. 1985-86, 92-93, Outstanding Citizen of Yr. award 1993), Rotary (pres. 1969-70, Paul Harris fellow 1993), Wash. Campground Assn. (pres. 1975-76, v.p. 1977-78, sec. 1978—), Chi Phi (sec. 1973). Republican. Congregationalist. Avocations: fishing, photography, skiing, canoeing, backpacking. Home: 1001 N Mountain Ave Bound Brook NJ 08805-1451 Office: Shive Spinelli Perantoni & Assocs PO Box 758 148 W End Ave Somerville NJ 08876-0758

SHIVELY, JOHN ADRIAN, pathologist; b. Rossville, Ind., Oct. 29, 1922; s. Henry Adam and Lucy (Gascho) S.; m. Lois Lorene Faris, Aug. 26, 1945; children—David A., Ann M., Theodore J., Janet S. B.A., Ind. U., 1944, M.D., 1946. Intern Phila. Gen. Hosp., 1946-47; resident internal medicine Clinic Hosp., Bluffton, Ind., 1949-50; resident pathology South Bend Med. Found., 1950-52; asst. prof. clin. pathology Ind. U. Sch. Medicine, 1954-57; assoc. prof. pathology U. Ky. Med. Sch., 1962-63; prof. pathology, chief clin. pathology U. Tex. M.D. Anderson Hosp., 1963-68; prof. pathology U. Mo. Med. Sch., 1968-71; prof. pathology, chmn. dept. U. Tenn. Coll. Medicine, 1971-76; vice chancellor for acad. affairs U. Tenn. Ctr. for Health Scis., 1976-82; med. dir. SmithKline Clin. Labs., Tampa, Fla., 1983-88; prof. pathology U.S. Fla. Coll. Medicine, 1988-93, assoc. dean, 1990-93, interim chmn. pathology, 1993-94; prof. emeritus, 1993—; pathologist-in-chief City of Memphis Hosps., 1971-76. Served with AUS, 1947-49. Mem. Am. Soc. Clin. Pathologists, Coll. Am. Pathologists, ACP, Am. Soc. Hematology, Am. Assn. Blood Banks (pres. 1967-68), Phi Beta Kappa, Sigma Xi, Alpha Omega Alpha. Research on platelet physiology. Office: # 11 12901 N 30th St Tampa FL 33612-4742

SHIVELY, JUDITH CAROLYN (JUDY SHIVELY), office assistant, contract administrator; b. Wilkinsburg, Pa., Jan. 30, 1962; d. John Allen and Edith (Crowell) S. BA in English, U. Nev., Las Vegas, 1984. Circulation aide Charleston Heights Libr., Las Vegas, 1979-86; asst. food editor Las Vegas Sun Newspaper, 1985-88, asst. horse racing editor, 1985-90, features writer, page editor, 1988-89, editor youth activities sect., 1989-90; racebook ticket writer, cashier Palace Sta. Hotel Racebook, Las Vegas, 1989-92; contract adminstr., gen. office asst. Loomis Armored, Inc., Las Vegas, 1992—; propr. Creative Computing, Las Vegas, 1996—; horse racing historian, rschr., Las Vegas, 1985—; vol. rsch. asst. Dictionary of Gambling and Gaming, 1982-84; part-time clk. Hometown News, Las Vegas, 1994-96. Staff writer horse race handicaps, columns, articles, feature stories Las Vegas Sun Newspaper, 1985-90; freelance writer for monthly horse racing publ. Inside Track, 1992-94. Mem. Phi Beta Kappa. Republican. Avocations: collecting horse racing books, clippings, materials for personal library of horse racing, computers. Home: PO Box 26426 Las Vegas NV 89126-0426

SHIVELY, MERRICK LEE, pharmaceutical scientist, consultant; b. Alamagordo, N.Mex., Dec. 12, 1958; s. Milton Lee and Dorothy Jean (Garlock) S.; m. Maureen Lynch, Dec. 28, 1985; 1 child, Sierra Lange. BS in Pharmacy, U. Conn., 1982, PhD in Pharmaceutics, 1986. Registered pharmacist, Colo., Mass. Sr. rsch. assoc. Baxter Healthcare, Morton Grove, Ill., 1985-87; asst. prof. U. Colo., Boulder, 1987-93; sr. rsch. scientist Atrix Labs., Inc., Ft. Collins, Colo., 1993-94; sr. scientist Nexagen, Inc., Boulder, 1994-96; founder, mng. ptnr. Drug Delivery Solutions LLC, Louisville, Colo., 1996—; pharm. cons. Glaxo, Synergen, Chemex, Cell Tech., Lilly; del. U.S. Pharmacopeia, 1988-94. Contbr. articles to Pharm. Rsch., Jour. Colloid Interface Sci., Drug Devel. and Indsl. Pharmacy, Internat. Jour. Pharmaceutics, others. Mem. Denver Econ. Com., 1989. Richardson-Vicks fellow, 1982-85. Mem. Am. Assn. Pharm. Scientists, Soc. of Controlled Release, Am. Chem. Soc., Rocky Mountain Devel. Forum (treas. 1989—), Phi Kappa Phi, Rho Chi. Achievements include patents in field; discovery and method of manufacture of solid state emulsions; findings that the formation of multi-molecular inclusion compounds are responsible for unique properties. Home and Office: 10ll Turnberry Cir Louisville CO 80027-9594

SHIVELY, WILLIAM PHILLIPS, political scientist, educator; b. Altoona, Pa., Mar. 31, 1942; s. Arthur Willard and Ruth Phillips S.; m. Barbara Louise Shank, Aug. 29, 1964; children—Helen, David. B.A., Franklin and Marshall Coll., 1963; Ph.D., U. N.C., 1968. Mem. faculty U. Oreg., Eugene, 1967-68, Yale U., 1968-71; mem. faculty U. Minn., Mpls., 1971—; prof. polit. sci. U. Minn., 1979—, provost arts, scis. & engring., 1995-97. Author: Craft of Political Research, 1974, 4th edit., 1997, Research Process in Political Science, 1985, Power and Choice, 1986, rev. edit., 1989, 5th edit., 1997, Comparative Governance, 1995, Cross-Level Inference, 1995; editor Am. Jour. Polit. Sci., 1977-79; contbr. articles on elections and voting to profl. jours. Home: 1572 Northrop St Saint Paul MN 55108-1322 Office: U Minn Dept Polit Sci Minneapolis MN 55455

SHIVERS, JANE, corporate communications executive, director; b. Georgetown, Tex., June 29, 1943; d. Marvin Bishop and Jewell (Petrey) Edwards; m. Harold E. Shivers; children: Clay Houston, Will Davis; m. Don Evans Hutcheson. BA, U. Md., 1965. Reseacher Amex Broadcasting Co., San Francisco, 1965-67; pub. info. officer Semester at Sea, Orange, Calif., 1967-69; dir. pub. rels. Atlanta Arts Alliance, 1974-78, RSVT, Atlanta, 1978-82; pres. Shivers Communications, Atlanta, 1982-84; exec. v.p., dir. Ketchum Pub. Rels., Atlanta, 1985—; pres. Midtown Bus. Assocs., Atlanta, 1987-91; bd. dirs. Crown Crfts, Inc. Trustee Alliance Theatre Co., Atlanta, 1980-93, Care, Internat., Atlanta, 1988-89; bd. dirs. Piedmont Park Conservancy, Emory Sch. Pub. Health. Recipient Mgmt. Woman Achievement award Women in Communication, Atlanta, 1984. Mem. Pub. Rels. Soc. Am. (bd. dirs.), Cen. Atlanta Progress, Commerce Club, Peachtree Club, Crown Crafts, Inc. (bd. dirs.), Atlanta C. of C. (bd. dirs.), Woodbury Arts Ctr. (bd. dirs.). Episcopalian. Home: 238 15th St NE Atlanta GA 30309-3594 Office: Ketchum Pub Rels 999 Peachtree St NE Atlanta GA 30309-3964

SHIVLER, JAMES FLETCHER, JR., retired civil engineer; b. Clearwater, Fla., Feb. 17, 1918; s. James Fletcher and Estelle (Adams) S.; m. Katherine Lucille Howlett, Feb. 2, 1946; children: James Fletcher, Susan (Mrs. William J. Schilling). B.C.E., U. Fla., 1938, M.S., 1940. Registered profl. engr., Fla. Mem. engring. faculty U. Fla., 1940-41; with Reynolds, Smith & Hills Architects-Engrs.-Planners, Inc. (formerly Reynolds, Smith & Hills, architects and engrs.), Jacksonville, Fla., 1941-88, partner, 1950-69, pres., 1970-88, chmn. bd., 1983-88, ret.; ret., 1988; partner Lewis-Eaton Partnership (Architects-Engrs. & Planners), Jackson, Miss., 1969-88. Mem. Fla. Bd. Engr. Examiners, 1964-70, v.p., 1964-65, pres., 1965-70. Served to lt. j.g. USNR, 1943-46. Recipient Outstanding Service award Fla. Engring. Soc., 1971, Disting. Alumnus award U. Fla., 1972, citation for service to constrn. industry Engring. News Record, 1973. Fellow ASCE (pres. Fla. sect. 1952), Am. Cons. Engrs. Coun., Fla. Engring. Soc. (pres. 1960-61); mem. NSPE (pres. 1972-73, Meritorious Svc. award 1981), Am. Assn. Engring. Socs. (chmn. engring. affairs coun. 1982-83), Fla. C. of C. (dir.-at-large 1971-88), Jacksonville Exch. Club, Deerwood Club, Fla. Yacht Club, Tau Beta Pi. Presbyterian. Home: 8191 Hollyridge Rd Jacksonville FL 32256-7103

SHKLAR, GERALD, oral pathologist, periodontist, educator; b. Montreal, Que., Can., Dec. 2, 1924; came to U.S., 1950, naturalized, 1955; s. Louis and Ann (Schleifstein) S.; m. Judith Nisse, June 16, 1948 (dec. Sept. 18, 1992); children: David, Michael, Ruth. BS, McGill U., 1947, DDS, 1949; MS, Tufts U., 1952; MA (hon.), Harvard U., 1971. Diplomate Am. Bd. Oral Pathology, Am. Bd. Periodontology. Asst. prof. oral pathology Tufts U. Sch. Dental Medicine, Boston, Mass., 1953-59; assoc. prof. Tufts U. Sch. Dental Medicine, 1960-61, prof., 1961-71, research prof. periodontology, 1961-71, lectr. in oral pathology, 1971—; Charles A. Brackett prof. oral pathology Harvard U. Sch. Dental Medicine, Boston, 1971—, head dept. oral medicine and oral pathology, 1971-93; sr. clin. investigator Forsyth Dental Ctr., Boston, 1994—; cons. oral pathology Children's Hosp. Med. Ctr., Brigham and Women's Hosp., Mass. Gen. Hosp. Author 4 books, articles on oral diseases, oral cancer, exptl. pathology, exptl. oral cancer; contbr. numerous book chpts. Fellow Am. Acad. Dental Sci., AAAS, Am. Acad. Oral Pathology, Am. Coll. Dentists, Internat. Coll. Dentists; mem. ADA, Internat. Assn. Dental Rsch., Am. Acad. Periodontology, Am. Cancer Soc., Am. Assn. Cancer Rsch., Am. Assn. Cancer Edn., Am. Acad. Oral Medicine, Am. Acad. History Dentistry, History of Sci. Soc., Sigma Xi, Omicron Kappa Upsilon. Avocations: playing flute and harpsichord. Home: 7 Chauncy Ln Cambridge MA 02138-2401 Office: 188 Longwood Ave Boston MA 02115-5819

SHLAUDEMAN, HARRY WALTER, retired ambassador; b. L.A., May 17, 1926; s. Karl Whitman and Florence (Pixley) S.; m. Carol Jean Dickey, Aug. 7, 1948; children: Karl Frederick, Katherine Estelle, Harry Richard. BA, Stanford U., 1952. Joined U.S. Fgn. Svc., 1955; vice consul Barranquilla, Colombia, 1955-56; polit. officer Bogotá, Colombia, 1956-58; assigned lang. tng. Washington, 1958-59; consul Sofia, Bulgaria, 1960-62; chief polit. sect. Santo Domingo, Dominican Republic, 1962-64; officer charge Dominican Affairs State Dept., 1964-66; asst. dir. Office Caribbean Affairs, 1965-66; sr. seminar fgn. policy State Dept., 1966-67, spl. asst. to sec. state, 1967-69; dep. chief of mission Santiago, Chile, 1969-73; dep. asst. sec. state for Inter-Am. affairs Washington, 1973-75; amb. to Venezuela, 1975-76, asst. sec. state for Inter-Am. affairs, 1976-77, amb. to Peru, 1977-

80, amb. to Argentina, 1980-83; exec. dir. Nat. Bipartisan Commn. on Central Am., 1983-84; spl. amb. to Cen. Am., 1984-86; amb. to Brazil Brasilia, 1986-89; amb. to Nicaragua, 1990-92, ret., 1992. Served with USMCR, 1944-46. Recipient Disting. Honor award Dept. State, 1966, Pres. Disting. Svc. award, 1988, Pres. Medal Freedom, 1992. Mem. Am. Acad. Diplomacy, Bethesda Country Club, Phi Gamma Delta. Home: 3531 Winfield Ln NW Washington DC 20007-2378

SHMAVONIAN, GERALD S., entertainment executive; b. L.A., June 26, 1945; s. Sarkis Neshan and Berje-Lucia (der Hareutunyan) S. Student, U. Calif., Berkeley, 1964-70. Leader archaeol. excavation team Guatemala, Turkey, 1970-75; pub. City Mags., 1975-80; special advisor Bicentennial Commission, Washington, D.C., 1987; chmn. Am. Nationalities Coun., Stanford U., 1983-86; pres. L.A. Talent, 1986—. Mem. Calif. Scholarship Fedn. (life, pres. 1963), Nat. Forensic League (pres. 1963, degree of honor). Home: 6219 N Prospect Ave Fresno CA 93711-1658

SHMAVONIAN, NADYA KAY, administrative services administrator; b. Durham, N.C., Jan. 20, 1960; d. Barry M. and Verna M. (Andersen) S.; m. David Edwin Loder, Mar. 12, 1988. BA in U.S. History, U. Chgo., 1981; MBA Health Care Adminstrn, U. Pa., 1986. Intern Soc. for Health & Human Values, Phila., 1981-82; rsch. asst. Temple U. Hosp., Phila., 1982-83; vol. Internat. Rescue Com., Thailand, 1984; cons. Pa. Hosp., Phila., 1985; intern, cons. Prospective Payment Assessment Commn., Washington, 1985-86; cons. N.J. Dept. Health, Trenton, 1986; program officer health & human svcs. Pew Charitable Trusts, Phila., 1986-88; acting dir. health & human svcs. Pew Charitable Trusts, 1988-89, dir. admistrv. svcs., 1989—. Mem. Am. Pub. Health Assn., Pa. Pub. Health Assn. Democrat. Avocations: basketball, tennis, volleyball, running, handicrafts. Office: The Pew Charitable Trusts 3 Parkway Ste 501 Philadelphia PA 19102-1375

SHMUNES, EDWARD, dermatologist; b. Jacksonville, Fla., July 24, 1940; s. Nathan and Anne Lillian (Berg) S.; m. Barbara Sue Mayson Hagen, Apr. 17, 1996; children: Stephanie, Marjorie, Jennifer. MD, U. Fla., 1965. Diplomate Am. Bd. Dermatology. Intern U.S. Pub. Health Hosp., New Orleans, 1965-66; epidemic intelligence officer svc. Ctr. for Disease Control, Atlanta, 1966-68; resident in dermatology U. Pa., Phila., 1968-71; ptnr. Columbia (S.C.) Skin Clinic, 1973—, pres., 1991—. Grantee: NIH (2 Yr. grant) U. S.C., 1985. Mem. Greek Orthodox Ch. Office: Columbia Skin Clinic 3 Medical Park Rd Ste 500 Columbia SC 29203-6873

SHNAYERSON, ROBERT BEAHAN, editor; b. N.Y.C., Dec. 8, 1925; s. Charles and Madalene (Griffin) Beahan; m. Lydia Conde Todd, Dec. 23, 1950 (dec. Sept. 1973); children: Michael, Kate; m. Laurie Platt Winfrey, June 9, 1980; children: Maggie, Bonnie. AB, Dartmouth, 1950. Reporter N.Y. Daily News, 1946; reporter Life mag., N.Y.C., 1950-54; corr. Time-Life News Svc., 1954-56; contbg. editor Time mag., 1957-59, edn. editor, 1959-64, law editor, 1964-67, sr. editor, 1967-71; editor-in-chief Harper's Mag., N.Y.C., 1971-76; editor, pub. Quest mag., N.Y.C., 1976-81, Technology mag., N.Y.C., 1981-82; editorial dir. Sci. Digest mag., 1986-87; editl. cons. Lear's mag., 1987-90; cons. in mag. field; sr. advisor Travel Holiday mag., 1989-95. Author: Illustrated History of the Supreme Court, 1986; contbr. articles to various mags. With USNR, 1943-46. Home: 118 Riverside Dr New York NY 10024-3708

SHNEIDMAN, EDWIN S., psychologist, educator, thanatologist, suicidologist; b. York, Pa., May 13, 1918; s. Louis and Manya (Zukin) S.; m. Jeanne E. Keplinger, Oct. 1, 1944; children: David William, Jonathan Aaron, Paul Samuel, Robert James. A.B., UCLA, 1938, M.A., 1940; M.S., U. So. Calif., 1947, Ph.D., 1948. Diplomate: Am. Bd. Examiners Profl. Psychology (past v.p.). Clin. psychologist VA Center, Los Angeles, 1947-50; chief research VA Center, 1950-53; co-dir. Central Research Unit for Study Unpredicted Deaths, 1953-58; co.-dir. Suicide Prevention Center, Los Angeles, 1958-66; chief Center Studies Suicide Prevention NIMH, Bethesda, Md., 1966-69; vis. prof. Harvard U., 1969; fellow Ctr. Advanced Study in Behavioral Scis., 1969-70; clin. assoc. Mass. Gen. Hosp., 1969, Karolinska Hosp., Stockholm, 1978; prof. med. psychology UCLA, 1970-75, prof. thanatology, 1975-88, emeritus, 1988—; vis. prof. Ben Gurion U. of Negev, Beersheva, 1983. Author: Deaths of Man, 1973, Voices of Death, 1980; Definition of Suicide, 1985, Suicide as Psychache, 1993, The Suicidal Mind, 1996; editor: Thematic Test Analysis, 1951; editor: (with N.L. Farberow) Clues to Suicide, 1957, The Cry for Help, 1961, Essays in Self-Destruction, 1967, (with M. Ortega) Aspects of Depression, 1969, On the Nature of Suicide, 1969, (with N.L. Farberow, L.E. Litman) Psychology of Suicide, 1970, Death and the College Student, 1972, Death: Current Perspectives, 1976, 80, 84, Suicidology: Contemporary Developments, 1976, Endeavors in Psychology: Selections From The Personology of Henry A. Murray, 1981, Suicide Thoughts and Reflections, 1981. Served to capt. USAAF, 1942-45. Recipient Harold M. Hildreth award Psychologists in Pub. Service, 1966; Louis I. Dublin award Am. Assn. Suicidology, 1969; Disting. Profl. Contbn. to Pub. Service award Am. Psychol. Assn., 1987. Mem. Am. Assn. Suicidology (founder, past pres.), Am. Psychol. Assn. (past div. pres.), Soc. Projective Techniques (past pres.), Melville Soc. Office: UCLA Neuropsychiat Inst 760 Westwood Plz Los Angeles CA 90024-8300

SHNEIDMAN, J. LEE, historian, educator; b. N.Y.C., June 20, 1929; s. Bernard Wolf and Fannia Abramova (Raskin) S.; m. Conalee Levine, Sept. 3, 1961; children—Philip, Jack. B.A., NYU, 1951, M.A., 1952; Ph.D., U. Wis., Madison, 1957. Lectr. CCNY, 1956-57, U. Md. Overseas, 1957-58; asst. prof. Fairleigh Dickinson U., 1958-62; prof. history Adelphi U., 1963—; chmn. seminar on hist., legal, and polit. thought Columbia U., 1985—. Author: Rise of the Aragonese-Catalan Empire, 2 vols, 1970, Spain and Franco, 1949-59, 1973, John F. Kennedy, 1974. Democratic N.Y. County committeeman, 1970—. Mem. Am. Hist. Assn., Medieval Acad. Am., Am. Philatel. Soc., Internat. Psychohist. Assn. (editor bull.), Rossica Soc., China Soc. Jewish. Home: 161 W 86th St New York NY 10024-3411 Office: History Dept Adelphi University Garden City NY 11530 *Only by understanding from where we came can we understand where we are and where we are going.*

SHNEOUR, ELIE ALEXIS, biochemist; b. Neuilly-sur-Seine, France, Dec. 11, 1925; came to U.S., 1941, naturalized, 1944; s. Zalman and Salomea (Landau) S.; m. Polly H. Henderson, Sept. 7, 1990; children from previous marriage: Mark Zalman, Alan Brewster. B.A., Columbia U., 1947; DSc (hon.), Bard Coll., 1969; M.A., U. Calif., Berkeley, 1955; Ph.D., UCLA, 1958. Teaching., research fellowship U. Calif., Berkeley, 1953-55, Am. Heart Assn. research fellow, 1958-62; teaching., research fellowship U. Calif., L.A., 1958; research fellow Nat. Cancer Inst., 1956-57; Am. Heart Assn. research fellow N.Y.U., 1958-59; research assoc. genetics Stanford U., 1962-65; assoc. prof. biology and neurosciences U. Utah, 1965-69; research neurochemist City of Hope Nat. Med. Ctr., Duarte, Calif., 1969-71; dir. rsch. Calbiochem., 1971-75; pres. Biosystems Insts., Inc., 1975—; dir. Biosystems Rsch. Inst., 1979—; mem. exec. com. Nat. Acad. Sci. Study Group on Biology and the Exploration of Mars, 1964; chmn. Western Regional coun. Rsch. in Basic Bioscis. for Manned Orbiting Missions, Am. Inst. Biol. Scis., NASA, 1966-69; fellow Com. Sci. Investigation Claims of Paranormal, 1996—. Author: Extraterrestrial Life, 1965, (with Eric A. Ottesen) National Academy of Sciences, National Rsch. Coun., 1966, (with S. Moffat) Life Beyond the Earth, 1966, The Malnourished Mind, 1974; contbr. numerous articles to sci. and lay jours. Chmn. citizens adv. coun. San Diego Pub. Schs., 1971-72; mem. adv. coun. Cousteau Soc., 1977—; bd. dirs. Am.-Ukraine Trade Coun., 1991-96, Lunar Power System Coalition, 1993—, Transinnova S.A. France, 1996—; chmn. sci. adv. bd. County of San Diego, 1995—. With U.S. Army, 1944-45. Recipient William Lockwood prize, 1947. Mem. IEEE, AAAS (chmn. So. Calif. Skeptics soc. Pacific divsn. 1988-90), Am. Chem. Soc., N.Y. Acad. Scis., Am. Inst. Biol. Scis., Am. Soc. for Biochemistry and Molecular Biology (chmn. sci. advisors program 1973-75, mem. com. on pub. policy 1974-76, congl. liaison 1992—), Am. Soc. Neurochemistry (mem. coun. 1971-73), Soc. Neurosci., Internat. Soc. Neurochemistry, U.S.C. of C. (bd. dirs. 1993—), La Jolla Chamber Music Soc. (bd. dirs. 1994—), Internat. Coun. for Global Health Progress (N.Am. adv. bd. 1996—), Sigma Xi, Phi Sigma. Office: Biosystems Insts Inc 700 Front St # CDM-608 San Diego CA 92101-6009

SHNIDER, BRUCE JAY, lawyer; b. Lansing, Mich., Oct. 16, 1950; s. Harold A. and Raynor (Seidner) S.; m. Patricia Lynn Strandness, Dec. 28, 1973; 1 child, Ruth Strandness Shnider. AB magna cum laude, Dartmouth Coll., 1972; MPP, JD magna cum laude, Harvard U., 1977. Bar: Minn. 1977, U.S. Dist. Ct. Minn. 1977, U.S. Tax Ct., 1978, U.S. Ct. Appeals (8th cir.) 1980, U.S. Supreme Ct. 1981. Asst. to dir. Mich. Dept. Commerce, Lansing, 1972-73; law clk. United Mineworkers Am. Health/Retirement Funds, 1975; summer assoc. Robins, Davis & Lyon, Mpls., 1976; assoc. Dorsey & Whitney, Mpls., 1977-82, ptnr., 1983—; chmn. diversity com., 1990-93, chmn. tax practice group, 1994—; bd. dirs. Minn. Justice Found., Mpls., 1989-91. Mem. ABA, Minn. State Bar Assn., Hennepin County Bar Assn. Home: 1908 James Ave S Minneapolis MN 55403-2831 Office: Dorsey & Whitney 220 S 6th St Minneapolis MN 55402-4502

SHNIDERMAN, HARRY LOUIS, lawyer; b. Erie, Pa., Sept. 26, 1916; s. Frank and Sophie (Barber) S.; m. Lenore Hyman, Nov. 29, 1942; children—Craig Mitchell, Neal Barber. A.B., U. Mich., 1938; LL.B., Harvard U., 1941. Bar: D.C. bar 1941, Pa. bar 1945, U.S. Supreme Ct. bar 1945. With litigation div. OPA, 1941-44; law clk. to Justice Rutledge, U.S. Supreme Ct., 1944-45; firm Covington & Burling, Washington, 1945—; lectr. Continuing Legal Edn. Programs, 1955—. Author: Price Discrimination in Perspective, 1977, 2d edit., 1987; Contbr. articles to profl. jours. Mem. ABA, D.C. Bar Assn., Harvard Law Sch. Assn., Phi Beta Kappa, Phi Kappa Phi, Delta Sigma Rho. Clubs: Harvard, City Tavern. Office: Covington & Burling PO Box 7566 1201 Pennsylvania Ave NW Washington DC 20044

SHOAFF, THOMAS MITCHELL, lawyer; b. Ft. Wayne, Ind., Aug. 21, 1941; s. John D. and Agnes H. (Hanna) S.; m. Eunice Swedberg, Feb. 7, 1970; children: Andrew, Nathaniel, Matthew-John. BA, Williams Coll., 1964; JD, Vanderbilt U., 1967. Bar: Ind. 1968. Assoc. Isham, Lincoln & Beale, Chgo., 1967-68; ptnr. Baker & Daniels, Ft. Wayne, Ind., 1968—; bd. dirs. Ft. Wayne Nat. Bank, Ft. Wayne Nat. Corp., Weaver Popcorn Co., Inc., Ft. Wayne, Dreibelbiss Title Co., Inc., Ft. Wayne, Am. Steel Investment Corp., Ft. Wayne. Bd. dirs. McMillen Found., Ft. Wayne, Wilson Found., Ft. Wayne. Mem. ABA, Allen County Bar Assn., Ind. State Bar Assn. Presbyterian. Avocations: golf, sailing. Office: Baker & Daniels 111 E Wayne St Ste 800 Fort Wayne IN 46802-2603

SHOBE, NANCY, fundraising consultant, small business owner; b. Detroit, Oct. 3, 1961; d. Richard William and Barbara Ann (Williams) S.; 1 child, Allison Elizabeth Stelyn; m. William Wright Watling, Aug. 23, 1996. BA, Mich. State U., 1983. Copywriter Wickes Lumber Hdqr., Vernon Hills, Ill., 1983-85; asst. to prodr. Music Ctr. of L.A., 1985, mercado coord., 1985-86; dir. comms. Candlelight Pavilion, Claremont, Calif., 1987-88, corp. dir. mktg., 1988; asst. dir. devel. The Webb Schs., Claremont, Calif., 1988-90; dir. devel. Crane Sch., Santa Barbara, Calif., 1991-96; with Shobe Comms., Santa Barbara, Calif., 1996—. Contbr. chpts. to books. Mem. Coun. Advancement and Support of Edn. (heavy hitter spkr. 1993, cir. of excellence award for ednl. fund raising 1995). Democrat. Episcopalian. Avocations: antiques, travel, walking, swimming, reading. Office: Shobe Communications PO Box 41334 Santa Barbara CA 93140

SHOBER, EDWARD WHARTON, bioscience company executive; b. Bryn Mawr, Pa., Nov. 16, 1926; s. Edward Wharton and Catherine Mather S.; m. Sandra Metcalf, May 27, 1978; children: Jorie, Edward, Paula. Student, Princeton U., 1950; DSc, Wilkes U., 1975. Pres., CEO Atec Corp., N.Y.C., 1957-71; pres., CEO Hahnemann Med. Coll., Phila., 1971-77, pres. emeritus, 1977—; CEO, co-founder Gen. Arabian Medical, Riyadh, Saudi Arabia, 1978-88; chmn. Drexel, Hahnemann, Jefferson Med. Coll. Pa. Cancer Ctr., 1973-77l dir. Winfield Trust, 1996—. Author: Blood Lost, 1990, Royal Treachery, 1993. Dir. Old Phila. Devel. Corp., 1972-78, Bryn Mawr Hosp., Phila., 1965-72; hon. consul Nicaragua, Phila., 1960-75; dir. English Speaking Union, Newport, R.I., 1960-85; co-founder, chmn. Cubal Aide Relief, 1960. 1st lt. C.E. German mil., 1950-52. Home: Hankerton Field Farm, Crudwell Rd, Malmesbury SN16 9RY, England

SHOBERT, ERLE IRWIN, II, management consultant; b. DuBois, Pa., Nov. 19, 1913; s. Erle Irwin and Edna Mae (Gray) S.; m. Marjorie E. Sullivan, Apr. 6, 1939; children: Judith Ann (Mrs. Edward Marsden), Margaret (Mrs. William G. Hayes). AB summa cum laude, Susquehanna U., 1935, DSc, 1957; student, Georg August U., Goettingen, Germany, 1935-36; MA in Physics, Princeton, 1939. With Stackpole Carbon Co., St. Mary's, Pa., 1934-79, v.p. tech., 1971-79, cons., 1979—; bd dirs. Chemcut Corp., State College, Pa., 1968-83, chmn., 1978-80, Tech. Adv. Contact Tech., Inc., 1990—; mem. materials adv. panel Pa. Dept. Commerce, 1972; indsl. and adv. com. Pa. State U., 1968-71; adv. com. Am. Carbon Conf., 1967-73; bd. dirs. Engrs. Joint Council, 1969-72; exec. standards council Am. Nat. Standards Inst., 1973, bd. dirs., 1974-76; bd. dirs. Kaul Land Co. Author 3 books, tech. papers. Pres. Elk County Soc. Crippled Children and Adults; pres. St. Mary's Youth Council.; pres., bd. dirs. Susquehanna U., 1978—, chmn. 1978-86.; bd. dirs. Kaul Found., 1981—. Recipient Outstanding Alumni award Susquehanna U., 1969, named dormitory in honor of Mr. and Mrs. Shobert. Fellow ASTM (bd. dirs. 1966-74, pres. 1971-72), IEEE (Ragnar Holm Sci. Achievement award 1974, Armington Recognition award 1985, prize paper competition named in his honor, Outstanding Achievement award 1994), Soc. for Preservation of Old Tigers (sec.-treas. 1996—); mem. Masons, Sigma Xi, Omicron Delta Kappa. Patentee carbon products, electronic materials and applications. Home: PO Box 343 Saint Marys PA 15857-0343 *I am product of a Tom Sawyer youth and the scholarship and work opportunities of the American higher education system. My career was and continues to be with one organization, among people and work I liked and respected. My family, including my grandchildren and great grandchild, are my pride and joy. My wife and I try to repay some of the organizations and people who have helped us.*

SHOCHAT, STEPHEN JAY, pediatric surgeon; b. Balt., Dec. 17, 1938; s. Albert J. and Rose (Blechman) S.; m. Sheila Floam, July 1960 (div. July 1979); children: Francine Lynne, Alisa Joy; m. Carla Ann Centi, Jan. 26, 1980; children: David Robert, Sarah Elizabeth. BS, Randolph Mason Coll., 1959; MD, Med. Coll. Va., 1963. Surg. resident Washington U. Med. Ctr., St. Louis, 1963-68; pediatric surg. resident Boston Children's Hosp., 1968-70; thoracic surg. resident Queen Elizabeth Hosp., Birmingham, Eng., 1970, George Washington Hosp., Washington, 1972; chief pediatric surgery Hershey (Pa.) Med. Ctr., 1973-77, Stanford (Calif.) Med. Ctr., 1977-94; sr. surgeon Children's Hosp. Phila., 1994-96; surgeon-in-chief, chmn. dept. surgery St. Jude Children Rsch. Hosp., Memphis, 1996—; prof. pediats. and surgery U. Tenn., Memphis, 1996—. Lt. col. USAF, 1970-72. Office: St Jude Children Rsch Hosp Dept Surgery Memphis TN 38105

SHOCKEY, THOMAS EDWARD, real estate executive, engineer; b. San Antonio, Aug. 17, 1926; s. Verlie Draper and Margaret Ruth (Shuford) S.; BS (Davidson fellow Tau Beta Pi), Tex. A&M U., 1950; postgrad. St. Mary's U., 1964, San Antonio Coll., 1972, Pacific Western U., 1981; m. Jacqueline McPherson, June 4, 1949; children: Cheryl Ann, Jocelyn Marie, Valerie Jean. With Petty Geophys. Survey, 1947-49, J.E. Ingram Equipment Co., 1950-51; co-owner, archtl. engr., realtor Moffett Lumber Co., Inc., San Antonio, 1952-76; cons. gen. contracting, gen. real estate, 1944—, retailer wholesale bldg. material, 1951—, v.p., 1959—; real estate counselor, appraiser, 1972—; real estate appraiser Gill Appraisal Svc., San Antonio, 1977—; comml. loan appraiser, underwriter, analyst Gill Savs. Assn., Gill Cos., San Antonio, 1979; chief appraiser, underwriter, architect, engr., insp. Gill Cos., 1981, v.p., 1981-87, ret., 1987; v.p. La Hacienda Savs. Assn., 1988-91, ret., 1991. Fire chief Mico Vol. Fire Dept., 1993-95. With inf. Signal Corps, U.S. Army, 1944-46; ETO. Mem. San Antonio C. of C., Nat. Lumber Dealers, Nat. Home Builders, Nat. Real Estate Bd.. Nat. Inst. Real Estate Brokers, Internat. Soc. Real Estate Appraisers, Tex. Assn. Real Estate Insps., Real Estate Appraisers Tex., Nat. Assn. Rev. Appraisers and Mortgage Underwriters, Internat. Inst. Valuers, Internat. Platform Assn. Home: 126 County Road 2620 Mico TX 78056-5213

SHOCKLEY, CAROL FRANCES, psychologist, psychotherapist; b. Atlanta, Nov. 24, 1948; d. Robert Thomas and Frances Lavada (Scrivner) S. BA, Ga. State U., 1974, MEd, 1976; PhD, U. Ga., 1990. Cert. in gerontology; Diplomate Am. Bd. Forensic Examiners. Counselor Rape Crisis Ctr., Atlanta, 1979-80; emergency mental health clinician Gwinnett Med. Ctr., Lawrenceville, Ga., 1980-86; psychotherapist Fla. Mental Health Inst., Tampa, 1987-89, Tampa Bay Acad., Riverview, Fla., 1990-91; sr. psychologist State of Fla. Dept. of Corrections, Bushnell, 1991-92; ind. practice psychology Brunswick, Ga., 1992—; mem. Adv. Bd. for Mental Health/Mental Retardation, 1992-94. Author: (with others) Relapse Prevention with Sex Offenders, 1989. Vol. Ga. Mental Health Inst., Atlanta, 1972; leader Alzheimer's Disease Support Group, Athens, Ga., 1984; vol. therapist Reminiscence Group for Elderly, Athens, 1984-85. Recipient Meritorious Svc. award Beta Gamma Sigma, 1975. Mem. Am. Psychol. Assn., Ga. Psychol. Assn., Sigma Phi Omega, Psi Chi. Avocations: astronomy, archeology, music, travel. Office: 14 Saint Andrews Ct Brunswick GA 31520-6764

SHOCKLEY, EDWARD JULIAN, aerospace company executive; b. Augusta, Ga., Oct. 31, 1924; s. Julian P. and Margaret (Epps) S.; m. Dorothy Elizabeth Holley, Nov. 24, 1945; children: Edward J., Steven Holley. B.Aero. Engring., Ga. Inst. Tech., 1950; postgrad. (Sloan fellow), Stanford U. Grad. Sch. Bus., 1962-63. Flight test engr. Douglas Aircraft Co., 1950-53; with Lockheed-Ga. Co., 1953-80, dir. quality and safety, 1965-74, dir. mktg., 1974-78, v.p., 1978-80; pres. Lockheed Aircraft Service Co. div. Lockheed Corp., Burbank, Calif., 1980-86, sr. advisor to pres., 1986-87, ret., 1987; pres. Millimeter Wave Tech., Inc., Marietta, Ga., 1988-90, vice chmn. bd. dirs., 1991-92; dir. Aerosurge Mgmt. Cons., 1991-92; pres. Lockheed-Ga. Fed. Credit Union, 1971-74. Mem. bus. adv. coun. Ga. So. U.; mem. adv. coun. Sch. Bus. and Econs., Coll. of Charleston. Served with USN, 1941-46. Mem. Cherokee Town and Country Club. Republican. Methodist.

SHOCKLEY, W. RAY, travel trade association executive; b. Apalachee, Ga., Aug. 19, 1924; s. Benjamin Arthur and Sophie Sarah (Harris) S.; m. Virginia Nell Davis, Sept. 21, 1946; children—Lisa Wray, David Wray, Jenifer Wray. B.A. in Journalism, U. Ga., 1956. News editor Athens (Ga.) Banner Herald and, Gainesville (Ga.) Daily Times, 1948; sports news editor Augusta (Ga.) Chronicle, 1948-52; Sunday editor Atlanta Jour.-Constitution, 1952-54, 1954-56; field rep. pub. rels. Am. Textile Mfgs. Inst., Washington, 1956-58; asst. sec., treas. Am. Textile Mfgs. Inst., 1958-70, dep. exec. v.p., 1974-76, exec. v.p., 1976-84; exec. v.p. S.C. Textile Mfrs. Assn., Columbia, 1970-74; pres., chief oper. officer Am. Soc. Travel Agts., 1985-90; cons. pub. affairs, 1990-91; dir. industry and bus. affairs C. of C., Athens, 1991-95; ret., 1995. Served with USN, 1944-45, PTO. Mem. Am. Soc. Assn. Execs., Ga. Alumni Assn. (out-of-state v.p. 1967-69), Belle Haven Country Club (Alexandria, Va.), Athens C. of C. (dir. industry and small bus. affairs 1991—), Rotary (pres. Dilworth club 1964-65, Athens East 1991—). Methodist (treas. 1966-70). Home: 507 Cherokee Rd Winterville GA 30683-9566

SHOCKMAN, GERALD DAVID, microbiologist, educator; b. Mt. Clemens, Mich., Dec. 22, 1925; s. Solomon and Jennie (Madorsky) S.; m. Arlyne Taub, June 2, 1949; children—Joel, Deborah. B.S., Cornell U., 1947; Ph.D., Rutgers U., 1950; Docteur (hon.), U. Liege, 1991. Predoctoral fellow Rutgers U., 1947-50; research asso. U. Pa., 1950-51; research fellow, research asso. Inst. Cancer Research, Phila., 1951-60; asso. prof. Temple U. Sch. Medicine, Phila., 1960-66; prof. dept. microbiology and immunology Temple U. Sch. Medicine, 1966—, chmn. dept., 1974-90. Contbr. articles in field to profl. jours. Served with U.S. Army 1942-44. Recipient Research Career Devel. award NIH, 1965-70, Titular de la Chaire d'Actualité Scientifique U. Liège, Belgium, 1971-72; NRC fellow, 1954-55. Mem. Am. Soc. Biol. Chemists, Am. Acad. Microbiology, Am. Soc. Microbiology, AAAS, Sigma Xi. Home: 901 Rodman St Philadelphia PA 19147-1247 Office: Temple U Sch Medicine 3400 N Broad St Philadelphia PA 19140-5104

SHOCTOR, JOSEPH HARVEY, barrister, producer, civic worker; b. Edmonton, Alta., Can., Aug. 18, 1922. BA, LLB, U. Alta., 1946, LLD (hon.), 1981; diploma in theatre adminstrn. (hon.), Grant McEwan Coll., 1986. Named to Queens Counsel, 1960. Barrister, solicitor, sr. counsel Duncan & Craig, Edmonton, 1993—; bd. dirs. Saxony Investments, Inc., Desa Stores Ltd. Prodr. Broadway plays including Peter Pat, 1965, Henry, Sweet Henry, 1967, Billy, 1969, Hamlet, 1969; founder, pres., exec. producer, bldg. chmn., campaign chmn. Citadel Theater; producer Circle 8 Theatre, Civic Opera, Red Cross Entertainment; panelist pub. affairs talk show and sports forum. Active United Cmty. Fund, 1968—; chmn. Downtown Devel. Corp., Edmonton, 1986; mem. Edmonton Jewish Welfare Bd.; past pres. Edmonton Jewish Cmty. Coun.; past nat. sec. Federated Zionist Orgn.; past nat. v.p. United Israel Appeal, Inc.; past bd. dirs. Can. Coun. Jewish Welfare Funds; chmn. divsn. Brit. Commonwealth Games Found., 1978; bd. govs. Nat. Theatre Sch. of Can., officer Order of Can., 1986. Inducted into Cultural Hall of Fame, 1987; named Man of Hr., Sta. CFRN-TV, 1966, Citizen of Yr., B'nai B'rith, 1966, one of Twelve Top Albertans of the 70's, The Alberta Report, U. Alberta Alumni Wall of Recognition, 1995, Disting. Citizen Grant MacEwan C.C., 1995; recipient Performing Arts award City of Edmonton, 1972, Theatre Arts Achievement award Province of Alta., 1975, Prime Minister's medal State of Israel, 1978, Builder of Cmty. award City of Edmonton, 1979, Queen's Silver Jubilee medal, 1977, City of Edmonton Silver Ribbon award, 1985, Great Canadian award, 1992, Commemorative medal for 125th Anniversary Canadian Confederation, 1992; The Shoctor Theatre named in his honor, 1976; Alta. Order of Excellence. Mem. Edmonton C. of C. Clubs: The Edmonton, The Centre, Eskimo Football (founder, past sec.-mgr.). Office: Duncan & Craig, 10060 Jasper Ave 2800, Edmonton, AB Canada T5J 3V9

SHOEMAKER, BILL (WILLIAM LEE SHOEMAKER), retired jockey, horse trainer; b. Fabens, Tex., Aug. 19, 1931; s. B. B. and Ruby (Call) S.; 1 child, Amanda Elisabeth. Jockey, 1949-90, ret., 1990, trainer, 1990—. Author: Stalking Horse, 1994, Fire Horse, 1995, Dark Horse, 1996. Winner Ky. Derby, 1955, 59, 65, 86, Belmont Stakes, 1957, 59, 62, 67, 75, Preakness Stakes, 1963, 67; ret. with 8,833 wins, including over 1000 Stakes wins. Office: care Vincent Andrews Mgmt 315 S Beverly Dr Ste 208 Beverly Hills CA 90212-4310*

SHOEMAKER, CAROLYN SPELLMANN, planetary astronomer; b. Gallup, N.Mex., June 24, 1929; d. Leonard Robert and Hazel Adele (Arthur) Spellmann; m. Eugene Merle Shoemaker, Aug. 18, 1951; children: Christine Shoemaker Woodard, Patrick Gene, Linda Shoemaker Salazar. BA cum laude, Chico State Coll., 1949, MA, 1950; ScD (hon.), No. Ariz. U., 1990. Vis. scientist Br. astrogeology U.S. Geol. Survey, Flagstaff, Ariz., 1980—; rsch. asst. Calif. Inst. Tech., Pasadena, 1981-85; rsch. prof. astronomy No. Ariz. U., Flagstaff, 1989—; mem. staff Lowell Obs., Flagstaff, 1993—; guest observer Palomar Obs., Palomar Mountain, Calif., 1982-94; Ruth Northcott Meml. lectrs. R.A.S.C., 1995; co-McGovern lectr. Cosmos Club Found., 1995. Co-recipient Rittenhouse medal Rittenhouse Astron. Soc., 1988, Scientist of Yr. awrd ARCS Found., 1995; recipient Woman of Distinction award Soroptimists, 1994, 20th Anniversary Internat. Women's Yr. award Zonta and 99s, 1995, NASA Exceptional Scientific Achievement medal, 1996, Woman of Distinction award Nat. Assn. Women in Edn., 1996; named Disting. Alumna of the Calif. State U., Chico, 1996. Fellow Am. Acad. Arts and Scis.; mem. Astron. Soc. of Pacific. Achievements include discovery of 32 comets including Periodic Comet Shoemaker-Levy 9 which impacted Jupiter in July 1994, more than 500 asteroids including 44 Earth approachers and approximately 68 Mars crossers, meteorites at Veevers Crater, Australia and impactites at Wolfe Creek Crater, Australia. Home: RR 4 Box 998 Flagstaff AZ 86001-8346 Office: Lowell Obs 1400 W Mars Hill Rd Flagstaff AZ 86001-4470

SHOEMAKER, ELEANOR BOGGS, television production company executive; b. Gulfport, Miss., Jan. 20, 1935; d. William Robertson and Bessie Eleanor (Ware) Boggs; m. D. Shoemaker, April 9, 1955 (div. 1987); children: Daniel W. III, William Boggs. Student in protocol, Southeastern U., 1952-53; student, George Washington U., Washington, 1953-56; BA in Communications and Polit. Sci. with honrs, Goucher Coll., 1981; postgrad., Villanova U. Feature writer Washington Times Herald, 1951-54; dir. Patricia Stevens Modeling Agy., Washington, 1955-56; free-lance model Julius Garfinkel, Woodward & Lothrop, Washington, 1951-56; research analyst Balt. County Council, Towson, Md., 1980-81; feature news reporter Sta. WGCB-TV, Red Lion, Pa., 1980—; pub. speaker, protocol The Reliable Corp., Columbia, Md., 1982-86; media cons. The Enterprise Found., Columbia, Md., 1985-86; faculty, TV prodn. and communication St. Francis Prep Sch., Spring Grove, Pa., 1985-88; owner Windswept Prodns. Co., Felton, Pa., 1984—; mktg. svcs. coord. Yorktowne, Inc., Red Lion, Pa., 1993-95; mem. conservation bd. Pa. Parks and Recreation Soc., 1984—; prodr. The Pa. County TV Prodn., 1981; prodr., host Westar 4 Channel 9 half hour weekly news program Keystone Report. Prodr. The Pa. County TV Prodn., 1981, The Pa. County TV Prodn., 1981, documentary Human Rights: A Special Report, Sta. WGCB-TV, 1989; prodr., host Westar 4 Channel 9 half hour weekly news program Keystone Report, 1990. Bd. dirs. York (Pa.) County Parks and Recreation, 1972-87, YWCA, York, 1957-82, Hist. York, 1990—; mem. exec. com. York County Reps., 1972-82; accreditation adv. com. York Coll. of Pa.; instr. YWCA Women in Politics; founder, mem. Child Abuse Task Force, York, 1983—; mem. select com. Pa. Agrl. Zoning, 1988; mem. steering com. York Forum, 1989—; co-chmn. Cross Mill Restoration, 1987—; mem. Displaced Homemaker's Bd., 1989—, pres., 1993—; bd. dirs. Hist. York, 1990-95; founder, host Old Rose Tree Pony Club, 1967—; chmn. camp com. U.S. Pony Club Inc., 1973-75; chair Spring Valley County Pk. Task Force, 1972; master of fox hounds Mrs. Shoemaker's Hounds, 1969—; master of beagles Mrs. Shoemaker's Weybright Beagles, 1988-96. Recipient pro bono child legal representation grant Pa. Bar Assn., 1983, Pa. Tree Farmer of Yr. award, 1987, Outstanding Achievement in Broadcasting award Am. Women in Radio and TV, 1992, Lay Person of Yr. award Pa. Recreation and Parks Assn. and Gov. Thornburg, 1982, Jefferson award, 1992, Matrix award Ctrl. Pa. Women in Comm., 1993, First pl. corp. video prodn. Ctrl. Pa. Women in Comm., 1993; selected journalist for Novosti Press USSR-U.S. Press Exch. program, 1989. Mem. Am. Polled Hereford Assn., York Area C. of C., York County C. of C. (publicity com. 1985-90, agri. bus. com.), Masters of Foxhounds Assn. Episcopalian. Avocation: foxhunting, beagling. Home and Office: PO Box 167 Felton PA 17322-0167

SHOEMAKER, EUGENE MERLE, geologist; b. L.A., Apr. 28, 1928; s. George Estel and Muriel May (Scott) S.; m. Carolyn Jean Spellmann, Aug. 18, 1951; children: Christine Carol, Patrick Gene, Linda Susan. B.S., Calif. Inst. Tech., 1947, M.S., 1948; M.A., Princeton U., 1954, Ph.D., 1960; Sc.D., Ariz. State Coll., 1965, Temple U., 1967, U. Ariz., 1984. Geologist U.S. Geol. Survey, 1948-93, scientist emeritus, 1993—, exploration uranium deposits and investigation salt structures Colo. and Utah, 1948-50, regional investigations geochemistry, volcanology and structure Colorado Plateau, 1951-56, research on structure and mechanics of meteorite impact and nuclear explosion craters, 1957-60, with E.C.T. Chao, discovered coesite, Meteor Crater, Ariz., 1960, investigation structure and history of moon, 1960-73, established lunar geol. time scale, methods of geol. mapping of moon, 1960, application TV systems to investigation extraterrestrial geology, 1961—, geology and paleomagnetism, Colo. Plateau, 1969—, systematic search for planet-crossing asteroids and comets, 1973-94; with C.S. Shoemaker and D.H. Levy discovered Periodic Comet Shoemaker-Levy 9, 1993; with C.S. Shoemaker discovered 46 Trojan asteroids, 1985-94; geology of satellites of Jupiter, Saturn, Uranus and Neptune, 1978—, investigating role of large body impacts in evolution of life, 1981—, impact craters of Australia,, 1983—; organized br. of astrogeology U.S. Geol. Survey, 1961; co-investigator TV expt. Project Ranger, 1961-65; chief scientist, center of astrogeology U.S. Geol. Survey, 1966-68; prin. investigator geol. field investigations in Apollo lunar landing, 1965-70, also television expt. Project Surveyor, 1963-68; prof. geology Calif. Inst. Tech., 1969-85, chmn. div. geol. and planetary scis., 1969-72; sci. team leader Clementine Mission to the Moon, 1993-94; staff mem. Lowell Observatory, Flagstaff, Ariz., 1993—. Recipient (with E.C.T. Chao) Wetherill medal Franklin Inst., 1965, Arthur S. Flemming award, 1966, NASA medal for exceptional sci. achievement, 1967, 96, Honor award for meritorious svc. U.S. Dept. Interior, 1973, Disting. Svc. award, 1980, Disting. Alumni award Calif. Inst. Tech., 1986; co-recipient Rittenhouse medal, 1988, Nat. medal of Sci. Pres. Bush, 1992, McGovern award Cosmos Club Found., 1995. Mem. NAS, Internat. Astron. Union, Am. Acad. Arts and Scis., Geol. Soc. Am. (Day medal 1982, Gilbert award 1983), Mineral Soc. Am., Soc. Econ. Geologists, Geochem. Soc., Am. Assn. Petroleum Geologists (Spl. award 1997), Am. Geophys. Union (Whipple award 1993, Bowie medal 1996), Am. Astron. Soc. (Kuiper prize 1984), Meteoritical Soc. (Barringer award 1984, Leonard medal 1985). Home: RR 4 Box 998 Flagstaff AZ 86001-8346 Office: US Geol Survey 2255 N Gemini Dr Flagstaff AZ 86001-1637

SHOEMAKER, FORREST HILTON, JR., marketing and sales executive, consultant; b. Waycross, Ga., Sept. 2, 1953; s. Forrest Hilton Sr. and Flora Kay (Jacobs) S.; married 1974 (div. 1985) children: Thomas, Myriah; m. Corazon Betty Kendall, Dec. 18, 1982; children: Stephanie, Ryan. BA, Armstrong State Coll., 1975. Pres., mng. ptnr. Shoemaker Cons. Inc., Savannah, Ga., 1981-85, Hawaii Juice Co., Honolulu, 1986-87; gen. mgr. Island Liquid Sunshine, Honolulu, 1985-86, Barry Hall Sales/Banana Boat Hawaii, Honolulu, 1988-91; v.p. sales Practice Mgmt. Svcs., Honolulu, 1987-88; dir. mktg. and sales Webco Hawaii Inc.-Schering-Plough Healthcare Divsn., Honolulu, 1991—; pres. The Hilton Group, 1994—; v.p., mgmt. cons. Artistic Table Lighting Hawaii, 1992—. Avocations: surfing, running, playing tennis, diving, reading. Home: 5339 Poola St Honolulu HI 96821-1536

SHOEMAKER, FRANK CRAWFORD, physicist, educator; b. Ogden, Utah, Mar. 26, 1922; s. Roy Hopkins and Sarah Parker (Anderson) S.; m. Ruth Elizabeth Nelson, July 11, 1944; children—Barbara Elaine, Mary Frances. A.B., Whitman Coll., 1943, D.Sc. (hon.), 1978; Ph.D., U. Wis., 1949. Staff mem. Radiation Lab. MIT, 1943-45; instr. physics U. Wis., 1949-50; mem. faculty Princeton U., 1950-89, prof. physics, 1962-89, emeritus, 1989—; assoc. dir. Princeton U. Pa. Accelerator, 1962-66; vis. scientist Rutherford High Energy Lab., 1965-66; main accelerator sect. head Nat. Accelerator Lab., 1968-69; prin. investigator Dept. of Energy High Energy Physics Contract, 1972-85. Co-author proposal for 3 billion electron volt Princeton-Pa. Accelerator, 1955. Fellow Am. Phys. Soc.; mem. Phi Beta Kappa, Sigma Xi. Home: 361 Walnut Ln Princeton NJ 08540-3446

SHOEMAKER, GRADUS LAWRENCE, chemist, educator; b. Zeeland, Mich., Jan. 18, 1921; s. Corey and Hattie (Lubbers) S.; m. Florence Etta Wright, June 5, 1952; children—Robert Neil, Betty Lynn. A.B., Hope Coll., 1944; M.S., U. Ill., 1947, Ph.D., 1949. Mem. faculty U. Louisville, 1949—, prof. chemistry, 1965-88, prof. emeritus, 1988—, chmn. dept., 1963-64, 65-67, chmn. div. natural sci., 1967-79; mem. exec. bd. Covenant Housing, Inc., 1989-97. Served as ensign USNR, 1944-45. Mem. Am. Chem. Soc. (councillor 1968-80), AAUP, Ky. Acad. Sci., Blue Key, Sigma Xi, Alpha Epsilon Delta, Phi Kappa Phi, Phi Lambda Upsilon. Presbyn. Home: 2815 Meadow Dr Louisville KY 40220-2406

SHOEMAKER, HAROLD LLOYD, infosystem specialist; b. Danville, Ky., Jan. 3, 1923; s. Eugene Clay and Amy (Wilson) S.; A.B., Berea Coll., 1944; postgrad. State U. Ia., 1943-44, George Washington U., 1949-50, N.Y. U., 1950-52; m. Dorothy M. Maddox, May 11, 1947 (dec. Feb. 1991). Research physicist State U., Ia., 1944-45, Frankford Arsenal, Pa., 1945-47; research engr. N.Am. Aviation, Los Angeles, 1947-49, Jacobs Instrument Co., Bethesda, 1949-50; asso. head systems devel. group The Teleregister Corp., N.Y.C., 1950-53; mgr. electronic equipment devel. sect., head planning for indsl. systems div. Hughes Aircraft Co., Los Angeles, 1953-58; dir. command and control systems lab. Bunker-Ramo Corp., Los Angeles, 1958-68, v.p. Data Systems, 1968-69, corp. dir. data processing, 1969-75; tech. staff R & D Assocs., Marina Del Rey, Calif., 1975-85; info. systems cons., 1985—. Served with AUS, 1945-46. Mem. IEEE. Patentee elec. digital computer. Home: PO Box 3385 Granada Hills CA 91394-0385

SHOEMAKER, INNIS HOWE, art museum curator; b. Reading, Pa.; d. William Erety and Jean (Miller) S. AB, Vassar Coll., 1964; MA, Columbia U., 1968, PhD, 1975. Curator Vassar Coll. Art. Gallery, Poughkeepsie, N.Y., 1965-68, 73-76; asst. dir. Ackland Art Mus., U. N.C., Chapel Hill, 1976-82, dir., 1983-86; sr. curator prints, drawings and photographs Phila. Mus. Art, 1986—; fellow in art history Am. Acad. in Rome, 1971-73; adj. prof. U. N.C., Chapel Hill, 1983-86; bd. dirs. Conservation Ctr., Phila., 1987—; vis. com. Frances Lehman Lueb Art Ctr., Vassar Coll., 1993—. Co-author: The Engravings of Marcantonio Raimondi, 1981, Paul Cézanne: Two Sketchbooks, 1989. Mem. vis. com. Muscarelle Mus., Coll. of William and Mary, 1995—; mem. vis. com. Lehman Loeb Art Ctr., Vassar Coll., 1993—; bd. dirs. Conservation Ctr. for Art and Hist. Artifacts, Phila., 1987-97. Mem. Coll. Art Assn. Am., Am. Assn. Mus., Print Coun. Am. (bd. dirs. 1986-89). Office: Phila Mus Art PO Box 7646 Philadelphia PA 19101-7646

SHOEMAKER, RALEIGH A., lawyer; b. Charlotte, N.C., Aug. 24, 1945. AB magna cum laude, Duke U., 1967; JD with high honors, U. N.C., 1970. Bar: N.C. 1970. Ptnr. Kennedy Covington Lobdell & Hickman, Charlotte, N.C. Assoc. editor N.C. Law Review, 1969-70. Mem. ABA, Phi Beta Kappa, Order of Coif. Office: Kennedy Covington Lobdell & Hickman 100 N Tryon St Charlotte NC 28202-4000

SHOEMAKER, ROBERT MORIN, retired army officer, county government official; b. Almont, Mich., Feb. 18, 1924; s. Uriah Beebe and Pomala (Morin) S.; m. Mary Alice Rickard, July 17, 1948. BS, U.S. Mil. Acad., 1946; postgrad., U.S. Army Command and Gen. Staff Coll., 1959, Army War Coll., 1967. Commd. 2d lt. U.S. Army, 1946, advanced through grades to gen., 1978, platoon leader, bn. staff officer, co. comdr. 18th Inf., Fed. Republic Germany, 1947-50; co. comdr., regtl. S2, S3, 23d Inf. U.S. Army, Republic of Korea, 1953-54; staff officer inf. br. DA U.S. Army, 1954-56; student, faculty officer U.S. Army Aviation Sch. U.S. Army, Ft. Rucker, Ala., 1959-62; project officer Army Concept Team U.S. Army, Vietnam, 1962-63; bn. comdr., asst. chief of staff, G-3, 11th Air Assault Div. U.S. Army, Ft. Benning, Ga., 1963-65; bn. cmdr., squadron comdr. 1st Cav. Div., U.S. Army, Vietnam, 1965-66; chief plans and programs Army Aviation DA U.S. Army, 1967-69; chief of staff, asst. div. comdr. 1st Cav. U.S. Army, Vietnam, 1969-70; dep. comdr., chief. of staff III Corps and Ft. Hood, Tex. U.S. Army, 1970; dept. comdr. MASSTER U.S. Army, Ft. Hood, Tex., 1971-72; comdr. 1st Cav. U.S. Army, 1973-75; comdr. III Corps U.S. Army, Ft. Hood, 1975-77; dep. comdr. FORSCOM U.S. Army, Ft. McPherson, Ga., 1977-78; comdr. U.S. Army Forces Command, 1978-82; ret., 1982; county commr. Bell County, Tex., 1987-94. Decorated D.S.M., Silver Star medal with oak leaf cluster, Legion of Merit, D.F.C., Bronze Star, Air medal with 48 oak leaf clusters, Army Commendation medal with oak leaf cluster, Croix de Guerre (France), Gallantry Cross with palm (Republic of Vietnam), RVN Honor medal 1st class. Home: RR 4 Box 4510 K Belton TX 76513-9415

SHOEMAKER, SANDRA KAYE, aerospace executive; b. Dallas, July 13, 1954; d. Vondyl Claud and Billie Juanita (Pritchett) Willis; m. Carl Vernon Shoemaker, Aug. 16, 1975; children: Regan Amanda, Ryan Adam. BBA, Baylor U., 1975. Fin. coord. Tex. A&M U., College Station, 1975-77; from engrng. planner to mgr. adminstrv. support Gen. Dynamics Corp., Ft. Worth, 1977-90; dir. engrng. adminstrn. Lockheed Ft. Worth Co., 1990-94, dir. rsch. & engrng. svcs. & process support, 1994-96, dir. labs. and tech. support, 1996—. Republican. Baptist. Avocations: music, snow skiing, water skiing, racquetball, snorkeling and scuba diving. Home: 5100 Dewdrop Ln Fort Worth TX 76123-1931 Office: Lockheed Ft Worth Co PO Box 748 Fort Worth TX 76101-0748

SHOEMAKER, SYDNEY S., philosophy educator; b. Boise, Idaho, Sept. 29, 1931; s. Roy Hopkins and Sarah Parker (Anderson) S.; m. Molly McDonald, Oct. 1, 1960; 1 son, Peter William. B.A., Reed Coll., 1953; postgrad., Edinburgh Univ., Scotland, 1953-54; Ph.D., Cornell Univ., 1958. Instr. Ohio State Univ., Columbus, 1957-60; asst. prof. Cornell Univ., Ithaca, N.Y., 1961-64, assoc. prof., 1964-67, prof., 1970—, Susan Linn Sage prof. philosophy, 1978—; assoc. prof. Rockefeller Univ., N.Y.C., 1967-70; John Locke lectr. Oxford U., England, 1972; Josiah Royce lectr. Brown U., 1993. Author: Self-Knowledge and Self-Identity, 1963, Identity, Cause, and Mind, 1984; co-author: Personal Identity, 1984; co-editor: Knowledge and Mind, 1983, Philso. Rev., 1964—(intermittently); gen. editor: Cambridge Studies in Philosophy, 1982-90. Fulbright scholar Edinburgh, Scotland, 1953-54; Santayana fellow Harvard Univ., Cambridge, Mass., 1960-61; fellow Ctr. Advanced Study in Behavioral Scis., Stanford, Calif., 1973-74, Nat. Endowment for Humanities, 1980-81, Guggenheim Found., 1987-88, Nat. Humanities Ctr., 1987-88. Mem. AAUP, Am. Acad. Arts and Scis., Am. Philos. Assn. (mem. exec. com. ea. div. 1977-80, v.p. 1992-93, pres. 1993-94). Home: 104 Northway Rd Ithaca NY 14850-2241 Office: Cornell Univ Dept Philosophy 218 Goldwin Smith Hall Ithaca NY 14853-3201

SHOEMAKER, WILLIAM EDWARD, financial executive; b. Charleston, W.Va., Sept. 17, 1945; s. Robert Edward and Janet Elizabeth (Hoglund) S. BBA, U. Notre Dame, 1967. Assoc. buyer Proctor & Gamble, Cin., 1971; gen. mgr. Eastwind Inc., Anchorage, 1972-73; pres., operator Golden Horn Lodge, Inc., Bristol Bay, Alaska, 1973-79; treas. Hawley Resource Group, Inc., Anchorage, 1979-88; treas., chief fin. officer Golden Zone Resources, Inc., Campbell, Calif., 1988-90; ptnr. Resort Mgmt. Corp., Anchorage, 1987-90; pres. Discovery Holdings, Inc., Ft. Lauderdale, Fla., 1991—; bd. dirs. Pacific Art & Design Cons., Inc. Bd. dirs. Anchorage Econ. Devel. Corp., 1988-90. Served to lt. (j.g.) USN, 1967-71. Mem. Quarter Deck Club (Anchorage). Republican. Avocations: boating, skiing, fishing. Home: 2301 Solar Plaza Dr Fort Lauderdale FL 33301 Office: Discovery Holdings Inc 2400 E Las Olas Blvd Ste 173 Fort Lauderdale FL 33301-1529

SHOEMATE, CHARLES RICHARD, food company executive; b. LaHarpe, Ill., Dec. 10, 1939; s. Richard Osborne and Mary Jane (Gillette) S.; m. Nancy Lee Gordon, Sept. 16, 1962; children: Steven, Jeffrey, Scott. BS, Western Ill. U., 1962; MBA, U. Chgo., 1973. Supr. Corn Products Co., Summit, Ill., 1962-72; comptroller Corn Products Unit of CPC Internat., Englewood Cliffs, N.J., 1972-74; plant mgr. Corn Products Unit of CPC Internat., Corpus Christi, Tex., 1974-76; v.p. ops. Corn Products Unit of CPC Internat., Englewood Cliffs, 1976-81; pres. Can. Starch Co., Montreal, Que., 1981-83; v.p. Corn Refining div. CPC Internat., Englewood Cliffs, 1983-86, pres., 1986-88; corp v.p. CPC Internat., Englewood Cliffs, 1983-88, pres., 1988—, chmn., chief exec. officer, 1990—. Office: CPC Internat Inc Box 8000 Internat Plz Englewood Cliffs NJ 07632*

SHOENBERGER, ALLEN EDWARD, law educator; b. Waynesburg, Pa., Sept. 18, 1944; s. Allen Edward and Evelyn S.; m. Cynthia Grant (div. 1975); 1 child, Michael Grant; m. Caroline Orzac, Aug. 3, 1980; 1 child, Elisa Orzac. BA with honors, Swarthmore Coll., 1966; JD with honors, Columbia U., 1969; LLM, NYU, 1972. Bar: Ill. 1973, U.S. Dist. Ct. (no. dist.) Ill. 1973, U.S. Ct. Appeals (7th cir.) 1977, U.S. Supreme Ct. 1977. Vis. lectr. U. Nairobi, Kenya, 1969-71; fellow Internat. Legal Ctr., Nairobi, 1969-71; asst. prof. Loyola U., Chgo., 1972-77, assoc. prof., 1977-85, prof., 1985—, chmn. faculty coun., 1983—; cons. Adminstrv. Conf. U.S., Washington, 1988; mem. Ill. A.G. Task Force for Handicapped, 1982—; chmn. adv. bldg. com. Cir. Ct. of Cook County, Chgo., 1988-93. Editor Spina Bifida publ., 1985-93, East African Law Reports, 1969-71, Jour. Nat. Assn. Adminstrv. Law Judges, 1996—; contbr. articles to profl. publs. Mem. Ill. Spina Bifida Assn., Chgo., 1980-93; hearing officer Ill. Pollution Control Bd., 1974—, U.S. Dept. Energy, Ill., 1984-89. Recipient various grants, including NIE, 1973; fellow Ford Found., 1972, NEH, 1987. Mem. ABA, Fed. Bar Assn., Chgo. Bar Assn. (chmn. adminstrv. law com. 1985-86). Office: Loyola Sch of Law 1 E Pearson St Chicago IL 60611-2055

SHOFSTAHL, ROBERT MAXWELL, savings and loan executive; b. New Orleans, Feb. 8, 1942; s. Maxwell Frederick and Ellen Anna (Falkenstein) S.; m. Lois Alice Berrigan, June 6, 1964; children: Tyson Brahm, Elisia Ellette, Christian Aric. BA cum laude (scholar), Tulane U., 1964; postgrad., 1966. Mgr. So. Bell-South Central Bell, New Orleans, Baton Rouge, Shreveport, 1964-71; asst. to pres. Pelican Homestead Savs. & Loan, Metairie, La., 1971-73, exec. v.p., 1973-77, dir., 1973-92, pres., CEO, 1978-92; pres., COO, dir. AmWest Savs. Assn., Bryan, Tex., 1992-94, N.Y. Life, 1995-96; chief adminstrv. officer Adams and Reese, Registered Limited Liability Partnership, 1996—; dir. Eureka Homestead, 1996—, mem. exec. com., chmn. asset, liability com.; dir. Fed. Res. Bank of Atlanta, New Orleans br., 1986-88. Mem. future of industry task force U.S. League, 1987-88; mem. 9th dist. FHLB Com. on Mgmt. Consignment Program, 1985; mem. last carousel fin. com. Friends of City Park, 1986-87; bd. dirs. Neighborhood Housing Services of New Orleans, 1978-81, treas., 1979-81; trustee St. Martin Episcopal Sch., 1981-87, treas., 1984, v.p., 1985-86, capital funds tri-chmn., 1984, headmaster search com., 1985, bd. visitors, 1989—, chmn., 1996—; lectr. grad. bus. sch. Loyola U., 1982-91; mem. vis. com. Loyola U. Bus. Sch., 1991-92; speaker ann. conv. Deans So. Bus. Adminstn. Assn., 1989; apptd. to gov's. Thrift Industry Adv. Coun., 1981-84; mem. adv. bd. New Orleans Opera Ball, 1984; inaugural pres. New Orleans Aquatics, 1988; panelist New Orleans: The Decade Ahead, 1989; hon. econ. devel. ambassador State of La., 1985; La. Newsmaker of Yr., USA Today, 1983. Mem. U.S. League Savs. Instns. (vice chmn. ad hoc fl. ins. com., 1976-77, chmn. ins. and protective com., 1979-80), Assn. Legal Adminstrs., Nat. Law Firm Mktg. Assn., La. League Savs. Instns. (ins. com. 1974, exec. com. 1980-81, 87-89, legis. com. 1983-84), League Homestead/Savs. and Loan Assn. Greater New Orleans (pres. 1973), Nat. Assn. Bus. Economists (panelist nat. policy suvey 1989-92), New Orleans Coun. Bus. Economists, Bryan-College Station C. of C. (mem. inner circle 1993-94), Deutsches Haus, Bienville Club, Metairie Country Club, Phi Beta Kappa, Phi Eta Sigma, Eta Sigma Phi. Episcopalian. Home: 324 Homestead Ave Metairie LA 70005-3707 Office: Adams and Reese Ste 4500 One Shell Square New Orleans LA 70139

SHOGAN, ROBERT, news correspondent; b. N.Y.C., Sept. 12, 1930; s. Albert and Millie (Jacobs) S.; m. Ellen Shrewsbury, May 26, 1959; children: Cynthia Diane, Amelia Ford. B.A., Syracuse U., 1951; postgrad., U. Mich. Inst. Pub. Adminstrn., 1951, Columbia U. Grad. Faculty Polit. Sci., 1952. Reporter Detroit Free Press, 1956-59; telegraph editor Miami (Fla.) News, 1959-61; asst. editor Wall St. Jour., N.Y.C., 1961-65; evaluation officer Peace Corps, Washington, 1965-66; corr. Newsweek, Washington, 1966-73; nation polit. corr. Los Angeles Times, Washington, 1973—; profl.-in-residence Annenberg Sch. Communication, U. Pa., 1993. Author: Question of Judgement, 1972, Promises to Keep, 1977, None of the Above, 1982, The Riddle of Power, 1991, Hard Bargain, 1995; co-author: (with Tom Craig) The Detroit Race Riot, 1964. Served with U.S. Army, 1952-54. Recipient 1st prize Feature Writing, Mich. AP, 1959, Disting. Reporting Pub. Affairs award Am. Polit. Sci. Assn., 1969, Scribes Book award, 1972; rsch. grantee Harry S Truman Presdl. Libr., 1989, Lyndon B. Johnson Presdl. Libr., 1989, Gerald R. Ford Presdl. Libr., 1989; McCormick fellow Hoover Presdl. Libr., 1993. Mem. Phi Beta Kappa. Home: 3513 Raymond St Chevy Chase MD 20815-3227 Office: 1875 I St NW Washington DC 20006

SHOHEN, SAUNDRA ANNE, health care communications and public relations executive; b. Washington, Aug. 22, 1934; d. Aaron Kohn and Malvina (Kleiman) Kohn Blinder; children: Susan, Brian. BS, Columbia Pacific U., 1979, MS in Health Svcs. Adminstrn., 1981. Adminstr. social work dept. Roosevelt Hosp., N.Y.C., 1978-79; adminstr. emergency dept. St. Luke's-Roosevelt Hosp. Ctr., N.Y.C., 1979-83, assoc. dir. pub. rels., 1983-87; pres. Saundra Shohen Assocs., Ltd., N.Y.C., 1987-1992; v.p. Prism Internat., N.Y.C., 1988-91; bd. dirs. Tureck Bach Inst., N.Y.C., 1985—; panelist ann. Emmy awards NATAS, N.Y.C., 1983, 84; tchr. healthcare mktg. Baruch Coll., N.Y.C., 1994. Author: EMERGENCY!, 1989, (health scripts for radio) Voice of America, 1983 (Presdl. Recognition award 1984), (with others) AIDS: A Health Care Management Response, 1987. Mem. NATAS, Internat. Hosp. Fedn., Am. Soc. Hosp. Mktg. and Pub. Rels., Vols. in Tech. Assistance. Democrat. Jewish. Home: 240 Central Park S New York NY 10019-1413

SHOICHI, IDA, artist; b. Kyoto, Japan, Sept. 13, 1941; came to U.S., 1970; s. Ida Kikuji and Ida Yukie. BA, Kyoto Mcpl. U. Art, MFA, BA (hon.). Cert. mus. curator. lectr. dept. sculpture, printmaking Kyoto Mcpl. U. Art, 1965-68, 70-72, Ohio State U., Columbus, 1974, Columbus Inst. Printmaking, 1974, SUNY, New Paltz, 1974, Kala Art Inst., Berkeley, Calif. 1979, San Francisco Art Inst., 1979, Art Inst. Chgo., 1980, U. Alta., 1981, Calif. Coll. Art and Craft, 1986, Whitman Coll., Walla Walla, Wash., 1989, Art Mus. Cin., 1989, others; panelist in field. Solo exhbns. include Gallery Azuchi, Osaka, Japan, 1966, Dragon, Inc., Paris, 1970, Gallery Crews, N.Y.C., 1970, Himezi Gallery, Tokyo, 1974, 75, 76, Gallery Coco, Kyoto, Japan, 1976, Tokyo Gallery, 1977, 79, 82, 86, 92, Suzuki Gallery, N.Y.C., 1979, San Francisco Art Inst., 1979, Yoh Art Gallery, Osaka, 1979, 80, 82, 83, 84, 87, 88, 90, 92, Mary Baskett Gallery, Cin., 1981, 90, Gallery Ueda, Tokyo, 1983, 85, 87, 88, 89, 90, 92, Gallery 24, Osaka, 1983, 86, Chgo. Art Fair, 1993, Suzuki Gallery, N.Y., 1993, Life Gallery TEN, Fukuoka, Japan, 1994, Gallery Ueda, Tokyo, 1994, Perimeter Gallery, Chgo., 1994, Gallery Mori, Tokyo, 1994, many others; innumerable group exhbns. Japan, Europe, U.S, 1966—, include Kyoto Mcpl. Mus. Art, Mcpl. Mus. Mod. Art, Paris, Nat. Mus. Modern Art, Tokyo, Kyoto, San Jose (Calif.) Mus. Art, Mus. Modern Art, Chgo.; exhbns. Internat. Biennale Prints and Drawings; represented in collections Nat. Libr., Paris, Victoria and Albert Mus., London, MOMA, N.Y.C., Swedish Art Assn., Osaka (Japan) Contemporary Art Ctr., Museo de Arte Contemporaneo, Ibiza, Spain, Mus. Modern Art, Krakow, Poland, L.A. County Mus. Art, Art Acad. Cin., Smithsonian Internat.-Arthur M. Sackler Gallery, Deutsch Bank AG, Frankfurt, Ger., Hara Mus. Contemporary Art, Tokyo, numerous others. Recipient Peter Millard prize 7th Brit. Internat. Print Biennale, Bradford, Eng., 1982, (with Robert Rauschenberg) Award for Excellence Internat. Cultural Exchange NEA, Washington, 1986, Grand Priz Suntory Prize Suntory Found., 1989, Aequo Prize 12th Internat. Print Biennale, Krakow, Poland, 1988, The Suntry Grand prize, 1989, others; French Govt. grantee, 1968, Japan Soc. N.Y.C. grantee, 1974, Asian Cultural Coun. grantee, N.Y.C., 1986, Hitachi Found. grantee, Washington, 1986, Centrum Found. grantee, Commn. Centennial Wash. State, 1989. also: 2924 Russell St Berkeley CA 94705-2334*

SHOKEIR, MOHAMED HASSAN KAMEL, medical geneticist, educator; b. Mansoura, Egypt, July 2, 1938; emigrated to Can., 1969, naturalized, 1974; s. Hassan Sayed and Lolia Nora (Kira) S.; m. Donna Jean Nugent, Feb. 27, 1968; children: Marc Omar, Vanessa May. MB, BCh in Medicine and Surgery, Cairo U., 1960, ChD, 1963, ChD in Orthopedics, 1964; MS, U. Mich., 1965, PhD, 1969. Intern Cairo U. Hosps., 1960-61, resident, 1961-64; Fulbright rsch. scholar dept. human genetics U. Mich., 1964-69; asst. prof. pediatrics U. Sask., Saskatoon, 1969-71, assoc. prof., 1971-73, prof., 1977—, dir. div. med. genetics, 1975—, head dept. pediat., 1979-96; head dept. pediat. Saskatoon Dist. Health Bd., 1993-96; head sect. clin. genetics U. Man., Winnipeg, 1973-75; mem. staffs Univ. Hosp., Saskatoon City Hosp., St. Paul's Hosp.; cons. Winnipeg Health Scis. Centre, Regina Gen. Hosp. Contbr. articles to profl publs. Mem. Acad. Freedom and Tenure Com., Ottawa, Ont., Can., 1980-90, Queen Elizabeth II scientist, 1969-75. Med. Rsch. Coun. grantee, 1970-79; Canadian Coll. Med. Geneticists Found. fellow, 1975—. Fellow Can. Coll. Med. Geneticists, Can. Soc. Clin. Investigation (councillor 1974-76), Can. Med. Assn. (chmn., mem. adv. com. 1987—); mem. Assn. Med. Sch. Pediatric Dept. Chairmen, Assn. Canadian Univ. Dept. Chairmen, Am. Pediatric Soc., Soc. Pediatric Research, N.Y. Acad. Scis., Am. Geriatrics Soc., Am. Fedn. Clin. Research, Mid-Western Soc. Pediatric Research, Western Pediatric Soc., Am. Soc. Human Genetics, Genetics Soc. Am., Genetics Soc. Can., Am. Genetic Assn., Am. Pub. Health Assn. Home: 108 Riel Crescent, Saskatoon, SK Canada S7J OW8 Office: U Sask, Dept Pediatrics, Saskatoon, SK Canada S7N 0X0 *Never tried to imagine what the future will bring, found the present and its implications enough to occupy me. The overriding passions in my life have been the love of man and the pity for his suffering. I have come to accept the futility of eliminating bias, even prejudice—mine or others'; my hope now is to recognize it and shield one's actions from it. What the world needs is more tolerance. Always found praise a bit embarrassing, confusing and altogether inhibiting—the most lavish for the least deserved accomplishment. Always thought the world is, at best, approximate. I now realize that in life one cannot have all bases covered.*

SHOLES, DAVID HENRY, laywer, former state senator; b. Providence, June 1, 1943; s. Leonard and Anna S. BA, Brown U., 1965; JD, Boston U., 1968. Bar: R.I. 1968, Mass. 1968. Pvt. practice law, Providence and Warwick, R.I., 1969-72; sr. ptnr. Sholes & Sholes, Warwick, 1970—; former lectr. U. R.I. Extension; mem. R.I. State Senate, 1976-92, chmn. senate com. on health, edn. & welfare; state adv. com. U.S. Civil Rights Commn.; former mem. Def. Civil Preparedness Adv. Coun., Cranston Gen. Hosp. Mem. R.I. Bar Assn., R.I. Trial Laywers Assn., Cranston Hist. Soc., Phi Alpha Delta. Democrat. Jewish. Clubs: Elks, Masons, Kiwanis, Touro Fraternal Assn. Home: 32 Mauran St Cranston RI 02910-1818 Office: 1375 Warwick Ave Warwick RI 02888-5066

SHOLL, JOHN GURNEY, III, physician; b. Phila., Mar. 6, 1915; s. John Gurney Jr. and Helen (Hare) S.; m. Marjorie Louise Hill, June 27, 1942; children: John Douglas, Debora Sholl Humphreys, Robert Roy, David Gurney, Rebecca Sholl Baer. BS, Bucknell U., 1937; MD, Harvard U., 1941. Diplomate Am. Bd. Internal Medicine; cert. Nat. Bd. Med. Examiners. Intern Germantown Hosp., Phila., 1941-42; asst. resident in medicine Univ. Hosp., Cleve., 1942-43; pvt. practice in internal medicine, 1943-78; from demonstrator to assoc. clin. prof. medicine Case-Western Res. U., Cleve., 1943-78, assoc. prof. principles dental sch., 1965-76; dir. med. edn. U. Suburban Health Ctr., Cleve., 1973-78; chmn. edn. commn. Ohio Med. Assn., 1974-75; clin. prof. medicine U. Calif. San Diego, La Jolla, 1978-88, dir. internal medicine group, 1979-85; med. dir. E.F. Hutton Life

Ins. Co., La Jolla, 1978-82; vol. cons. to med. staff Maine Vets. Homes, 1990—. Mem. editoral bd. Consultant mag., Greenwich, Conn., 1980-84, San Diego Physician, 1986-87. Served to capt. U.S. Army, 1944-46, ETO. Fellow ACP; mem. AMA, Calif. Med. Assn. Republican. Baptist. Club: Rowfant (Cleve.). Avocation: boating, golf. Home: 11 Ross Rd Apt 200 Kennebunk ME 04043-1518

SHON, FREDERICK JOHN, nuclear engineer; b. Pleasantville, N.Y., July 24, 1926; s. Frederick and Lucy (Stelz) S.; m. Dorothy Theresa Patterson, June 8, 1946; 1 son, Robert Frederick. BS, Columbia U., 1946; postgrad., Ohio State U., U. Calif., Berkeley. With Publicker Alcohol Co., Phila., 1946-47, Thermoid Co., Trenton, N.J., 1947-48, Mound Lab., Miamisburg, Ohio, 1948-51; radiation chemist Atomics Internat., Canoga Park, Calif., 1951-52; physicist, reactor ops. supr. Lawrence Radiation Lab., Livermore, Calif., 1952-61; chief exam br., div. licensing and regulations U.S. AEC, Washington, 1961-62, chief reactor safety br., div. operational safety, 1963-67, asst. dir. nuclear facilities, 1967-72; dep. chief adminstrv. judge-tech., vice-chmn. tech., atomic safety and licensing bd. panel U.S. Nuclear Regulatory Commn., Washington, 1972—; cons. various nuclear firms including Danish AEC, Risoe, Atomics Internat., Spanish AEC, IAEA; lect. nuclear engring. U. Calif., Berkeley, 1955-63. Mem. Am. Nuclear Soc., Tau Beta Pi. Home: 4212 Flower Valley Dr Rockville MD 20853-1808 Office: US Nuclear Regulatory Commn Washington DC 20555

SHONK, ALBERT DAVENPORT, JR., advertising executive; b. L.A., May 23, 1932; s. Albert Davenport and Jean Spence (Stannard) S.; BS in Bus. Adminstrn., U. So. Calif., 1954. Field rep. mktg. div. Los Angeles Examiner, 1954-55, asst. mgr. mktg. and field supr. mktg. div. 1955-56, mgr. mktg. div., 1956-57; account exec. Hearst Advt. Svc., Los Angeles, 1957-59; account exec., mgr. Keith H. Evans & Assos., San Francisco, 1959-65; owner, pres. Albert D. Shonk Co., L.A., 1965—; gen. ptnr. Shonk Land Co. LTD, Charleston, W.Va., 1989—; pres. Signet Circle Corp., Inc., 1977-81, dir., 1962-81, hon. life dir., 1981—, treas., 1989—. Bd. dirs. Florence Crittenton Ctr., sec., 1978, 1st v.p., 1978-79, exec. v.p., 1979-81, pres., 1981-83, chmn. bd., 1983-85, hon. life dir., 1986—, treas., 1997—; co-chair centennial com., founding chmn. Crittenton Assocs. Recipient Medallion of Merit Phi Sigma Kappa, 1976, Founders award, 1961, NIC Interfraternal award, 1989 . Mem. Advt. Club Los Angeles, Pubs. Rep. Assn. of So. Calif., Nat. Assn. Pubs. Reps. (past v.p. West Coast 1981-83), Jr. Advt. Club L.A. (hon. life, dir., treas., 1st v.p.), Trojan Club, Skull and Dagger, U. So. Calif., U. S.C. Marshall Sch. Bus. Alumni Assn. (nat. bd. 1991-, treas. 1995—), U. S.C. Assocs., Inter-Greek Soc. (co-founder, hon. life mem. and dir., v.p. 1976-79, pres. 1984-86), Rotary, Phi Sigma Kappa (dir. grand council 1962-70, 77-79, grand pres. 1979-83, chancellor 1983-87, 90-91, recorder 1995—, v.p. meml. found. 1979-84, pres. 1984, trustee pres. Phi Sigma Kappa found. 1984-95, honorary and trustee emeritus 1995—), World Affairs Coun., Alpha Kappa Psi, Town Hall. Home: 3460 W 7th St Apt 806 Los Angeles CA 90005-2312 Office: Albert Shonk Co 3156 Wilshire Blvd Ste 7 Los Angeles CA 90010-1209

SHONS, ALAN RANCE, plastic surgeon, educator; b. Freeport, Ill., Jan. 10, 1938; s. Ferral Caldwell and Margaret (Zimmerman) S.; AB, Dartmouth Coll., 1960; MD, Case Western Res. U., 1965; PhD in Surgery, U. Minn., 1976; m. Mary Ella Misamore, Aug. 5, 1961; children: Lesley, Susan. Intern, U. Hosp., Cleve., 1965-66, resident in surgery, 1966-67; research fellow transplantation immunology U. Minn., 1969-72; resident in surgery U. Minn. Hosp., 1972-74; resident in plastic surgery NYU, 1974-76; asst. prof. plastic surgery U. Minn., Mpls., 1976-79, assoc. prof., 1979-84, prof., 1984; dir. div. plastic and reconstructive surgery U. Minn. Hosp., St. Paul Ramsey Hosp., Mpls. VA Hosp., 1976-84; cons. plastic surgery St. Louis Park Med. Center, 1980-84; prof. surgery Case Western Res. U., Cleve., 1984-93; dir. div. plastic and reconstructive surgery Univ. Hosps. Cleve., 1984-92; prof. surgery U. South Fla., H. Lee. Moffitt Cancer Ctr. and Rsch. Inst., Tampa, 1993—. Author: (with G.L. Adams and D. McQuarrie) Head and Neck Cancer, 1986; (with R. Jensen) Plastic Surgery Review, 1993. Served to capt. USAF, 1967-69. Diplomate Am. Bd. Surgery, Am. Bd. Plastic Surgery. Fellow ACS (chmn. Minn. com. on trauma 1978-84); mem. Am. Soc. Plastic and Reconstructive Surgeons, Am. Assn. Plastic Surgeons, Minn. Acad. Plastic Surgeons (pres. 1981-82), AMA, Soc. Head and Neck Surgeons, Am. Assn. Surgery Trauma, Transplantation Soc., Plastic Surgery Research Council, Am. Soc. Aesthetic Plastic Surgery, Am. Soc. Maxillofacial Surgeons, Am. Assn. Immunologists, Soc. Exptl. Pathology, Am. Burn Assn., Am. Cleft Palate Assn., Am. Soc. Craniofacial Surgery, Assn. Acad. Surgery, Central Surg. Assn., Fla. Soc. Plastic & Reconstructive Surgeons, Tampa Bay Soc. Plastic & Reconstructive Surgeons, Sigma Xi. Office: H Lee Moffitt Cancer Ctr & Rsch Inst 12902 Magnolia Dr Tampa FL 33612-9416

SHOOB, MARVIN H., federal judge; b. Walterboro, S.C., Feb. 23, 1923; s. Michael Louis and Lena (Steinberg) S.; m. Janice Paradies, Nov. 14, 1949; children: Michael, Wendy. J.D., U. Ga., 1948. Bar: Ga. 1948. Ptnr. Brown & Shoob, Atlanta, 1949-55; ptnr. Phillips, Johnson & Shoob, Atlanta, 1955-56, Shoob, McLain & Merritt, Atlanta, 1956-79; judge U.S. Dist. Ct., Atlanta, 1979—; chmn. Juvenile Ct. Com., 1964-70; mem. Ga. State Bar Grievance Tribunal, 1975-79; chmn. Ga. State Bar Fed. Legislation Com., 1977-79; guest lectr. Continuing Legal Edn., Athens, Ga., 1975-77. Chmn. 5th Dist. Democratic Exec. Com., 1974-76. Mem. Phi Eta Sigma, Phi Kappa Phi. Jewish. Office: US Dist Ct 1921 US Courthouse 75 Spring St SW Atlanta GA 30303-3309

SHOOK, ANN JONES, lawyer; b. Canton, Ohio, Apr. 18, 1925; d. William M. and Lura (Pontius) Jones; m. Gene E. Shook Sr., Nov. 30, 1956; children: Scott, William, Gene Edwin Jr. AB, Wittenberg U., 1947; LLB, William McKinley Law Sch., 1955. Bar: Ohio 1956, U.S. Dist. Ct. (no. dist.) Ohio 1961, U.S. Ct. Appeals (6th cir.) 1981. Cost acct. Hoover Co., North Canton, Ohio, 1947-51; asst. sec. Stark County Prosecutor's Office, Canton, Ohio, 1951-53; ins. adjuster Traveler's Ins. Co., Canton, 1953-56; ptnr. Shook & Shook Law Firm, Toledo, 1958-62, North Olmsted, Ohio, 1962—. Mem. at large coun. Olmsted Community Ch., Olmsted Falls, Ohio, 1987-90; chmn. ways and means com. North Olmsted PTA, 1968; area chmn. United Way Appeal, North Olmsted, 1963; v.p. LWV, Toledo, 1960-62. Mem. Cleve. Bar Assn. Avocations: reading, boating, dancing, fitness.

SHOOK, DONALD RAY, health care administrator; b. Detroit, Nov. 10, 1954; s. Donald Ray and Norma (Coquigne) S.; m. Pamela Jo Shook, Feb. 18, 1984; children: Patrick, Jennifer, Bradley, Spencer. BS, Lawrence Inst. Tech., 1978; MBA, Notre Dame U., 1990. Cost reimbursement analyst Henry Ford Hosp., Troy, Mich., 1979-81; dir. prospective payment sys. Mich. Hosp. Assn., Lansing, 1981-84; dir. fin. analysis Butterworth Hosp., Grand Rapids, Mich., 1984-86; CFO Cmty. Health Ctr. Branch County, Coldwater, Mich., 1986-89; dir. phys. svcs. St. Joseph Med. Ctr., Ft. Wayne, Ind., 1989-94; CEO Thomas Spann Clinic, Corpus Christi, Tex., 1994—. Chairperson Supershop Saturday, Ft. Wayne, 1993. Republican. Avocations: water skiing, running, swimming. Home: 15341 Key Largo Ct Corpus Christi TX 78418 Office: Thomas Spann Clinic PA 1533 S Brownlee Blvd Corpus Christi TX 78404-3131

SHOOK, ROBERT LOUIS, business writer; b. Apr. 7, 1938; m. Elinor Marks; children: Carrie, RJ, Michael. BSBA, Ohio State U., 1959. Chmn. bd. Shook Assocs. Corp.; co-founder, chmn. bd. Am. Exec. Corp., Am. Exec. Life Ins. Co.; bd. dirs. Value City Dept. Stores; appearances on over 600 radio and TV talk shows, including CNN, The David Susskind Show, The Sally Jessy Raphael Show, The Today Show, others. Author: Winning Images, 1977, 2d edit., 1978, The Greatest Salespersons, 1978, 2d edit., 1980, The Entrepreneurs, 1980, The Real Estate People, 1980, The Chief Executive Officers, 1981, Why Didn't I Think of That!, 1982, The Shaklee Story, 1982, The Book of Why, 1983, Survivors: Living with Cancer, 1983, The Healing Family, 1984, The IBM Way...Insights into the World's Most Successful Marketing Organization, 1986, The Perfect Sales Presentation, 1986, Wheel of Fortune, 1987, Honda: An American Success Story, 1988, All You Need to Know About Patents, Copyrights and Trademarks, 1989, How to Close Every Sale, 1989, Turnaround: The New Ford Motor Company, 1990, The Wall Street Dictionary, 1990, Hardball: Subtle High-Pressure Selling Techniques That Work, 1990, The Book of Odds, 1991, America's Best Kept Secret, 1991, The Name of the Game is Life, 1992, The Winner's Circle, 1992, It's About Time, 1992, Franchising: The Business Strategy That Changed the World, 1993; co-author: How to be the Complete Professional Salesman, 1974, Total Commitment, 1975, Successful Telephone Selling in the 90's, 1990, Joe Gandolfo's How to Make Big Money Selling, 1984, The Greatest Sales Stories Ever Told, 1995, I'll Get Back to You, 1996, (with C. Brett Beemer) Predatory Marketing, 1997. Past trustee Columbus Opera; chmn. bd., Franklin County Am. Cancer Soc., 1996. Home and Office: 261 S Columbia Ave Columbus OH 43209-1626

SHOOP, GLENN POWELL, investment consultant; b. Gracemont, Okla., Sept. 1, 1920; s. Roy Alonzo and Myrtle Nancy (Goodfellow) S.; m. Louise Wilhelmina Vollmer, Mar. 19, 1943; children: Merilou Love, Paul, Nancy Caver. Student, U. Okla., 1938-42. Pilot Braniff Internat. Airways, Dallas, 1946-80; cons. bd. dirs. Braniff Inc., 1984-88. Bd. dirs. 1st Bapt. Ch. Dallas, 1950-97; mem. devel. bd. Golden Gate Bapt. Sem., San Francisco, Southwestern Bapt. Sem., Fort Worth. Maj. USAF, 1942-46. Republican. Achievements include first U.S. pilot to fly Concorde in U.S. scheduled service. Avocations: farming, rebuilding and trading antique tractors.

SHOOTER, ERIC MANVERS, neurobiology educator, consultant; b. Mansfield, Eng., Apr. 18, 1924; came to U.S., 1964; s. Fred and Pattie (Johnson) S.; m. Elaine Staley Arnold, May 28, 1949; 1 child, Annette Elizabeth. BA, Cambridge (Eng.) U., 1945, MA, 1949, PhD, 1950, ScD, 1986; DSc, U. London, 1964. Sr. scientist biochemistry Brewing Industry Rsch. Fedn., 1950-53; biochemistry lectr. Univ. Coll., London, 1953-63; assoc. prof. genetics Stanford U., 1963-68, prof. genetics and biochemistry, 1968-75, prof., chmn. neurobiology dept., 1975-87, prof. neurobiology, 1987—, chmn. Neurosci. PhD Program, 1972-82; assoc. Neurosci. Rsch. Program, N.Y.C., 1979-89; teaching staff Internat. Sch. Neurosci., Praglia, Italy, 1987-93; sr. cons. Markey Charitable Trust, Miami, Fla., 1985—; chair sci. adv. bd., and dir. Regeneron Pharm., Inc., Tarrytown, N.Y., 1988—. Assoc. editor: (book series) Ann. Rev. Neuroscis., 1984—; contbr. numerous articles to profl. jours. Recipient Wakeman award Duke U., 1988; Faculty scholar Josiah Macy Jr. Found., N.Y.C., 1974-75. Fellow AAAS, Royal Soc. (London), Am. Acad. Arts and Scis.; mem. Inst. Medicine of NAS (fgn. assoc.), Biochem. Soc., Am. Assn. Biol. Chemists, Soc. for Neurosci. (Ralph W. Gerard prize 1995), Am. Soc. Neurochemistry, Internat. Soc. Neurochemistry, Internat. Brain Rsch. Orgn. Avocation: travel. Home: 370 Golden Oak Dr Portola Valley CA 94028-7757 Office: Stanford U Sch Medicine Dept Neurobiology Stanford CA 94305

SHOPE, ROBERT ELLIS, epidemiology educator; b. Princeton, N.J., Feb. 21, 1929; s. Richard Edwin Shope and Helen Madden (Ellis) Flemer; m. Virginia Elizabeth Barbour, Dec. 27, 1958; children—Peter, Steven, Deborah, Bonnie. BA, Cornell U., 1951, MD, 1954. Intern then resident Grace-New Haven Hosp., 1954-58; mem. staff Rockefeller Found., Belem, Brazil, 1959-65; dir. Belem Virus Lab., Brazil, 1963-65; from asst. to assoc. prof. epidemiology Yale Sch. Medicine, New Haven, 1965-75, prof., 1975-95; prof. pathology U. Tex. Med. Br., Galveston, 1995—; adv. bd. Gorgas Inst., Panema City, 1972-90; mem. WHO Expert Panel Arboviruses, Geneva, Switzerland, 1974—, U.S. del. U.S.-Japan Coop. Med. Scis. Program, Washington, 1977—, Pan Am. Health Orgn. Commn. for Dengue, Washington, 1980—. Served to capt. U.S. Army, 1955-57, Southeast Asia. Fellow Am. Acad. Microbiology; mem. Am. Soc. Tropical Medicine and Hygiene (pres. 1980, Bailey K. Ashford award 1974, Walter Reed award 1993), Am. Soc. Virology, Am. Soc. Epidemiology, Infectious Diseases Soc. Am. Democrat. Office: U Tex Med Br Dept Pathology 301 University Blvd Galveston TX 77555-5302

SHOR, GEORGE G., JR., geophysicist, oceanographic administrator, engineer; b. N.Y.C., June 8, 1923; s. George Gershon and Dorothy (Williston); m. Elizabeth Louise Noble, June 11, 1950; children: Alexander Noble, Carolyn Elizabeth, Donald Williston. B.S., Calif. Inst. Tech., 1944, M.S., 1948, Ph.D., 1954. Joined Seismic Explorations, Inc., Houston, 1948; party chief Seismic Explorations, Inc., 1949-50; asst. research geophysicist to research geophysicist Scripps Inst. Oceanography, La Jolla, Calif., 1953-69; prof. marine geophysics Scripps Inst. Oceanography, 1969-90, prof. emeritus, 1990—, assoc. dir., 1968-91; mgr. Calif. Sea Grant program, 1969-73; Mem. NAS-NRC panel on Mohole site selection, 1959; com. on underwater telecommunications, 1968, USN Marine Geophys. Survey Liaison Council, 1965-67; spl. adv. to Com. for Coordination of Joint Prospecting for Mineral Resources in Asian Offshore Areas, 1976-91; chmn. ship scheduling panel Univ. Nat. Oceanographic Lab. Systems, 1987-89; sci. leader oceanographic expdns. to various parts of Pacific and Indian oceans, 1955-82. Served to lt. (j.g.) USNR, 1943-46; now comdr. USNR Ret. Fellow Geol. Soc. Am., Am. Geophys. Union; mem. Soc. Exploration Geophysicists, Scholia Club, Am. Bamboo Soc. (pres. 1994-96). Home: 2655 Ellentown Rd La Jolla CA 92037-1147

SHOR, SAMUEL WENDELL WILLISTON, naval engineer; b. N.Y.C., June 25, 1920; s. George Gershon and Dorothy (Williston) S.; m. Joan Bopp, June 21, 1958; children: Peter Williston, Molly Hathaway. Student, Harvard U., 1937-39; B.S., U.S. Naval Acad., 1942; Naval Engr., MIT, 1949; M.S. in Math., NYU, 1963. Commd. ensign U.S. Navy, 1942, advanced through grades to capt., 1962; served in cruisers Chicago, St. Louis, and Quincy, Pacific and Atlantic, 1942-46; assigned San Francisco Naval Shipyard, 1949-52, naval reactors br. AEC, 1952-53; AEC rep. for initial test of submarine nuclear propulsion in U.S.S. Nautilus and U.S.S. Seawolf, 1953-57; AEC rep. for startup testing of Shippingport Atomic Power Sta., 1957-58; design supt., prodn. engring. officer N.Y. Naval Shipyard, 1958-63; dir. sonar systems office Naval Ship Systems Command, 1963-67, exec. dir. plans, 1967-69, dep. comdr. for engring., 1969-71; project mgr. electronic warfare Naval Electronic Systems Commd., 1971-73; with Bechtel Power Corp., San Francisco, 1973—. Author tech. papers. Mem. Soc. Naval Architects and Marine Engrs., Soc. Naval Engrs., Am. Math. Soc., Am. Phys. Soc., Sigma Xi. Home: 318 Montford Ave Mill Valley CA 94941-3313 Office: Bechtel Corp 50 Beale St San Francisco CA 94105-1813

SHORE, HARVEY HARRIS, business educator; b. Cambridge, Mass., Apr. 14, 1940; s. Jacob and Freda Edna (Pearlman) S.; m. Roberta Ann Rogers, Jan. 29, 1967; children: Nina Ellen, Elissa Amy. BA cum laude, Harvard U., 1961; MS, MIT, 1963; DBA, Harvard U., 1966. Asst. prof. indsl. adminstrn. U. Conn., Storrs, 1966-72; assoc. prof. indsl. adminstrn. U. Conn., 1972-77; dir. Hartford MBA prog. U. Conn., Hartford, 1977-82; assoc. prof. mgmt. U. Conn., Storrs, 1982-95, assoc. prof. emeritus, 1995—. Contbr. articles to profl. jours.; editor Cubic Rev., 1975-78; author: Arts Administration and Management, 1987. Chmn. bus. adv. com. Tunxis Community Coll., Farmington, Conn., 1983-85; bd. dirs. Temple Beth Sholom, Manchester, Conn., 1987-90. Mem. Employee Assistance Soc. N.Am., Coll. and Univ. Bus. Instrs. Conn. (pres. 1975-76), Greater Nashua Human Resources Assn. (treas. 1997—), Masons. Democrat. Jewish. Avocation: tennis.

SHORE, HERBERT, writer, poet, educator; b. Phila., June 6, 1924; s. Meyer and Frances (Smiler) S.; m. Yen Lu Wong, Dec. 23, 1977; children: Norman Jon, Pia Ilyen Wong. Maya Iming Wong. B.A., U. Pa., 1942; postgrad., Columbia U., 1946-48, Dramatic Workship New Sch., 1946-48; postgrad, Stanford U., 1948-53; M.A., Stanford U., 1958; Ph.D., Internat. Coll., 1983. Writer, poet, dramatist and dramaturg, 1956—; dir. Council Tech. and Cultural Transformation, UNESCO, 1974-88; prof., assoc. dean Sch. of Theatre U. So. Calif., 1979-93; prof. emeritus Sch. of Theatre, U. So. Calif., 1995; founding dir. TNR: The New Repertory, 1972—; cons. UNESCO, 1974—; provost Internat. Coll., 1983-86; writer-in-residence Blue Mountain Centre, 1985, 86; dir. plays for theatre and TV, author plays, also cantatas; disting. vis. fellow La Trobe U., Australia, 1990; artist in residence Eltham Coll., Australia, 1990; sr. affiliated scholar Ctr. for Multiethnic and Transnat. Studies, U. So. Calif., 1993—; fellow Mayibuye Ctr., South Africa, 1995; mentor global studies Immaculate Heart Coll. Ctr., 1993—; bd. dirs. Eduardo Mondlane Meml. Found., 1996; adj. prof. grad. program in profl. writing U. So. Calif., 1993—. Author: Come Back Africa, 1970, Ashes Dark Antigone, 1972, Toward the World of Tomorrow, 1978, Cultural Policy, 1981, Cicada Images, Moulting, 1983, No Future Wrapped in Darkness, 1984; Seek to Be Human, 1985, Beginnings are Born in Memory, 1986, Shime, 1986, Trees Die Standing, 1987, And the Dogs Are Silent, 1988, Should the Grain Perish, 1989, Namashawala, Santa Claus and the Bagamoyo Cock, 1990, South African Township Theatre, 1990, Southern Africa: A Dream Deferred, 1990, Apartheid's Waning and Dangerous Years, 1990, Sounds in the Wind, (poetry) 1991, Exile from El Salvador, Terra Infirma, 1992; co-author: (with George Houser) The Sisulu Tapes: Experiencing South African History Through the Life of Walter Sisulu, 1996, Sisulu: An Oral History for CD-Rom, 1997; also articles, short stories, poems. Adv. council Internat. Symposium on Arts, Banff Centre, 1984—; exec. com. Internat. Inst. Audio-Visual Media, Vienna, 1985—; assoc. scholar Ctr. for African Studies, Eduardo Mondlane U., 1988—. Served with USMC, 1943-46. Recipient Writers Digest prize for fiction, 1963, medal of Bagamoyo, Nat. Assembly, Mozambique, 1989; Herbert Shore Collection established Immaculate Heart Coll. Ctr., 1991, Jerome Lawrence Libr., 1995, Mayibuye Ctr., South Africa, 1995, Miebyl-Proctor Libr., Oakland, Calif., 1995; grantee Ford. Found., 1978-79, 96-97, Africa Fund, 1995-96, 97, Rockefeller Found., 1966-67, NEH, 1979-81, Helen Wurlitzer Found., 1958-60, Social Sci. Rsch. Coun., 1967-68, African and Am. Univs. Program, 1964-65, Kate Maremont Found., 1959-60, Centro Mexicano de Escritores, 1958. Mem. PEN Ctr. West, USA, LMDA, Assn. Theatre Higher Edn., Nat. Writers Union, Acad. Am. Poets, Soc. Writers and Poets, African Studies Assn. Office: U So Calif Ctr Multiethnic Transnat GFS 344 Los Angeles CA 90089-1694

SHORE, HOWARD LESLIE, composer; b. Toronto, Ontario, Canada, Oct. 18, 1946; s. Mac and Bernice (Ash) S.; m. Elizabeth Ann Cotnoir, Aug. 3, 1990; 1 child, Mae. Student, Berklee Sch. Music, 1965-67, Forest Hill Collegiate, Toronto, Ont., Can., 1961-64. Composer film scores including I Miss You, Hugs and Kisses, 1978, the Brood, 1979, Scaners, 1981, Videodrome, 1983, Nothing Lasts Forever, 1984, Places in the Heart, 1984, After Hours, 1985, Belizaire the Cajun, 1987, Fire with Fire, 1986, The Fly, 1986, Nadine, 1987, The Local Stigmatic, 1987, Heaven, 1987, Moving, 1988, Dead Ringers, 1988 (Genie award), Big, 1988, She-Devil, 1989, An Innocent Man, 1989, Signs of Life, 1989, Postcards from the Edge, 1990, The Silence of the Lambs, 1991, A Kiss Before Dying, 1989, Naked Lunch, 1990, Prelude to a Kiss, 1992, Single White Female, 1992, (TV score) Scales of Justice, 1990, Guilty as Sin, 1993, Sliver, 1993, M. Butterfly, 1993, Mrs. Doubtfire, 1993, Philadelphia, 1993, The Client, 1994, Ed Wood, 1994, Nobody's Fool, 1994, Moonlight and Valentino, 1995, White Man's Burden, 1995, Seven, 1995, Before and After, 1996, The Truth About Cats and Dogs, 1996, Looking for Richard, 1996, Crash, 1996; music dir. Saturday Night Live, 1975-80, Striptease, 1996. Mem. ASCAP, Lighthouse (founding mem.). Home: Wee Wah Lodge Tuxedo Park NY 10987 Office: The Kraft-Benjamin Agy 8491 Sunset Blvd Ste 492 Los Angeles CA 90069*

SHORE, JAMES H(ENRY), psychiatrist; b. Winston-Salem, N.C., Apr. 6, 1940; s. James Henry and Ellen Elizabeth (Hayes) S.; m. Christine Lowenbach, Aug. 24, 1963; children—Ellen Ottilie, James Henry. M.D., Duke U., 1965. Diplomate Am. Bd. Psychiatry and Neurology. Intern U. Utah Med. Center, 1965-66; resident in psychiatry U. Wash., 1966-69; chief mental health office Portland (Oreg.) Area Indian Health Service, 1969-73; assoc. prof. psychiatry, dir. community psychiatry tng. program U. Oreg. Health Scis. Center, 1973-75, prof., chmn. dept. psychiatry, 1975-85; chmn. dept. psychiatry U. Colo. Health Scis. Ctr., Denver, 1985—; interim chancellor, 1992-93; dir. Colo. Psychiatry Hosp., 1985—; interim dir. U. Colo. Hosp., Denver, 1987-88, interim exec. vice chancellor, 1995-97; mem. exptl. and spl. edn. com. NIMH-Internal Rev. Group, 1976-80; cons. in field. Contbr. numerous articles to profl. publs. Mem. Various community bds. Served with USPHS, 1969-73. Decorated USPHS Commendation medal; various grants. Fellow Am. Psychiat. Assn., Am. Coll. Psychiatry; mem. Am. Assn. Chmn. Depts. Psychiatry (pres. 1989), Am. Bd. Psychiatry and Neurology (dir. 1987—, pres. 1994), Residency Rev. Com. for Psychiatry (chmn. 1991-92). Office: U Colo Health Scis Ctr PO Box C-249 4200 E 9th Ave Denver CO 80262-0001

SHORE, MILES FREDERICK, psychiatrist, educator; b. Chgo., May 26, 1929; s. Miles Victor and Margaret Elizabeth S.; m. Eleanor M. Gossard, July 4, 1953; children: Miles Paul, Rebecca Margaret, Susanna Gladys. BA, U. Chgo., 1948; AB, Harvard U., 1950, MD, 1954. Intern U. Ill. Research and Edn. Hosp., Chgo., 1954-55; resident in psychiatry Mass. Mental Health Center, Beth Israel Hosp., Boston, 1956-61; asst. prof. psychiatry Tufts U. Sch. Medicine, Medford, Mass., 1964-68; assoc. prof. Tufts U. Sch. Medicine, 1968-71, prof., 1971-75, prof. community health, 1972-75; founder, dir. Tufts Community Mental Health Center, 1968-74, assoc. dean community affairs, 1972-75; mem. faculty Boston Psychoanalytic Inst., 1973—; Bullard prof. psychiatry Harvard Med. Sch., Boston, 1975—, dir. div. mental health systems, 1993—; supt. Mass. Mental Health Ctr., 1975-93; vis. scholar John F. Kennedy Sch. Govt. Harvard U., 1993—; dir. program for chronic mental illness Robert Wood Johnson Found., 1985-92. Editl. bd. Psychat. Svcs. Jour., 1990; bd. editors Jour. Interdisciplinary History, 1975, Psycho History Rev., 1978; column editor Harvard Rev. Psychiatry, 1993; contbr. articles to profl. jours. Bd. dirs. Federated Dorchester Neighborhood Houses, Boston, 1975-78, Med. Found., Boston, 1987—, Ctr. House, Boston, 1995—; mem. Blue Ribbon Commn., Mass. Dept. Mental Health, 1979-80. Capt. U.S. Army, 1956-58. Community Mental Health Center grantee, 1964-75. Fellow Am. Psychiat. Assn. (life, joint commn. on pub. affairs, adminstrv. psychiatry award 1987), Am. Coll. Psychiatrists (chmn. fin. com. 1983-89, bd. regents 1988-90, 1st v.p. 1994, pres. 1996-97, Bowis award for svc. 1990, Arthur P. Noyes award 1994); mem. Boston Psychoanalytic Soc. and Inst. (chmn. bd. trustees 1970-73), Mass. Psychiat. Soc. (pres. 1970-71), Mass. Hosp. Assn. (trustee 1980-85), Am. Hosp. Assn. (governing coun. mental health and psychiat. svcs. 1985-87, chmn. governing coun. for psychiat. and substance abuse svcs. 1992-93), Roxbury Clinic Record Club, Aesculapian Club, Mass. Hist. Soc. Office: JFK Sch Govt 79 Jfk St Cambridge MA 02138-5801

SHORE, RICHARD ARNOLD, mathematics educator; b. Boston, Aug. 18, 1946; s. Philip M. and Miriam (Krensky) S.; m. Naomi J. Spiller, Aug. 3, 1969; children—Deena A., Aviva R. B. Jewish Edn., Hebrew Coll., 1966; A.B., Harvard U., 1968; Ph.D., MIT, 1972. Instr. U. Chgo., 1972-74; asst. prof. Cornell U., Ithaca, N.Y., 1974-78, assoc. prof., 1978-83; asst. prof. U. Ill.-Chgo., 1977; vis. assoc. prof. MIT, Cambridge, 1980; vis. prof. Hebrew U., Jerusalem, 1982-83; prof. math. Cornell U., Ithaca, 1983—; organizing com. Logic Yr. at MSRI, 1989-90, other internat. meetings. Author: (with A. Nerode) Logic for Applications; editor North-Holland, Studies in Logic and the Fondations of Mathematics, 1996—; cons. editor Jour. Symbolic Logic, 1980-83, editor, 1984-93, coord. editor, 1989-91; mng. editor: Bull. Symbolic Logic, 1993—; contbr. articles to profl. jours. V.p. for edn. Hillel Acad. Broome County, Binghamton, N.Y., 1985-89; treas. Beth David Synagogue, 1993-96. NSF grantee, 1973—. Mem. Am. Math. Soc., Spl. Interest Group in Algorithms and Computation Theory, Assn. for Computing Machinery, Assn. for Symbolic Logic (coun. 1984—). Jewish. Home: 7 Avon Rd Binghamton NY 13905-4201 Office: Cornell U Dept Math White Hall Ithaca NY 14853

SHORE, STEPHEN, photographer; b. N.Y.C., Oct. 8, 1947; m. Ginger Cramer Seippel, 1980; 1 child, Nicholas; 1 stepchild, Alex Seippel. Student, Minor White, Workshop, 1970. Photographer, 1953—. One-man shows, Met. Mus. Art, N.Y.C., 1971, Light Gallery, N.Y.C., 1972, 73, 75, 77, 78, 80, Phoenix Gallery, San Francisco, 1975, Mus. Modern Art, N.Y.C., 1976, U. Akron, Ohio, 1978, Vision Gallery, Boston, 1978, La Photogaleria, Madrid, 1979, Ewing Gallery, Washington, 1979, Catskill Ctr. Photography, Woodstock, N.Y., 1980, Fraenkel Gallery, San Francisco, 1982, Mus. Arts and Scis., Daytona Beach, Fla., 1981, Polk Pub. Mus., 1982, ARCO Ctr. Visual Arts, L.A., 1982, N. Mex. State U. Art Gallery, Las Cruces, 1982, Art Inst. Chgo., 1984, Pace Wildenstein MacGill, N.Y.C., 1989, 95, Sprengel Mus., Hannover, 1995, Würt. Kunstverein, Stuttgart, 1995, Armerica Haus, Berlin, 1995, George Eastman House, Rochester, N.Y., 1996; group shows include, Met. Mus. Art, N.Y.C., 1973, 82, 97, Internat. Mus. Photography, George Eastman House, 1975, Documenta 6, Kassel, W. Ger., 1977, Art Inst. Chgo., 1977, 79, 89, Mus. Modern Art, N.Y.C., 1978, 91, Corcoran Gallery, Washington, 1979, Kunsthaus, Zurich, Switzerland, 1980, U. Ariz. Mus. Art, Tucson, 1981, Nat. Gallery, Washington, 1989, Getty Mus., 1992; represented in permanent collections, Met. Mus. Art, N.Y.C., Mus. Modern Art, N.Y.C., Internat. Mus. Photography, George Eastman House, Rochester, N.Y., Mus. Fine Arts, Boston, Library of Congress, Washington, Art Inst. Chgo., in Permanent collections, Ctr. Creative Photography, U. Ariz., Tucson, in permanent collections, Stedelijk Mus., Amsterdam, Netherlands, Neue Sammlung, Munich, W.Ger., Australian Nat. Gallery, Canberra; author: Andy Warhol, 1968, Uncommon Places, 1982, The Gardens at Giverny, 1983, Stephen Shore: Luzzara, 1993, Stephen Shore: Photographs 1973-1993, 1995, The Velvet Years, 1995; portfolio 12

Photographs, 1976; contbr. articles to profl. jours. Nat. Endowment Arts grantee, 1974, 79; Guggenheim fellow, 1975; Am. Acad. (Rome) spl. fellow, 1980; MacDowell Colony fellow, 1993.

SHORE, THOMAS SPENCER, JR., lawyer; b. Akron, Ohio, Jan. 1, 1939; s. T. Spencer and Harriet G. (Delicate) S.; m. Margaret F. Kudzma, Aug. 12, 1961; children—Thomas Spencer III, John Christopher, Daniel Andrew, Mary Margaret. B.A., Brown U., 1961; J.D., Northwestern U., 1964. Bar: Ohio 1964. Assoc. Taft, Stettinius and Hollister, Cin., 1964-69; asso. Rendigs, Fry, Kiely & Dennis, Cin., 1969-71; partner Rendigs, Fry, Kiely & Dennis, 1972—; adj. asst. prof. Chase Law Sch., U. No. Ky. Bd. dirs. United Cerebral Palsy of Cin., 1978—; bd. dirs., sec. Boys Club Am., Cin.; trustee emeritus Family Svc. of Cin. Area; past pres. Vis. Nurse Assn. of Cin., hon. trustee. Mem. Cin. Bar Assn., Ohio Bar Assn., Am. Bar Assn. Clubs: Cin. Country, Cin. Tennis, Queen City, Webhanet. Home: 3224 Columbia Pky Cincinnati OH 45226-1042 Office: 900 Central Trust Tower Cincinnati OH 45202

SHORENSTEIN, ROSALIND GREENBERG, physician; b. N.Y.C., Jan. 14, 1947; d. Albert Samuel and Natalie Miriam (Sherman) Greenberg; m. Michael Lewis Shorenstein, June 18, 1967; children: Anna Irene, Claire Beth. BA in Chemistry, Wellesley Coll., 1968; MA in Biochemistry and Molecular Biology, Harvard U., 1970, PhD in Biochemistry and Molecular Biology, 1973; MD, Stanford U., 1976. Diplomate Am. Bd. Internal Medicine. Resident in internal medicine UCLA Med. Ctr., 1976-79; pvt. practice internal medicine Santa Cruz, Calif., 1979—; mem. dept. internal medicine Dominican Hosp., Santa Cruz, 1979—; co-dir. med. svcs. Health Enhancement & Lifestyle Planning Systems, Santa Cruz, 1983—. Contbr. articles to profl. journals. Dir. Santa Cruz Chamber Players, 1993-94, pres., bd. dirs., 1994—. Recipient Charlie Parkhurst award Santa Cruz Women's Commn., 1989; NSF fellow, 1968-72, Sarah Perry Wood Med. fellow Wellesley Coll., 1972-76. Mem. Am. Soc. Internal Medicine (del. 1994, 95), Calif. Soc. Internal Medicine (trustee 1994—), Am. Med. Women's Assn. (Outstanding Svc. award 1987, br. #59 pres. 1986—), Calif. Med. Assn. (com. on women 1987-93), Santa Cruz County Med. Soc. (mem. bd. govs. 1993—), Phi Beta Kappa, Sigma Xi. Jewish. Office: 700 Frederick St Ste 103 Santa Cruz CA 95062-2239

SHORENSTEIN, WALTER HERBERT, commercial real estate development company executive; b. Glen Cove, N.Y., Feb. 23, 1915; m. Phyllis J. Finley, Aug. 8, 1945 (dec.); children: Joan (Dec.), Carole, Douglas. Student, Pa. State U., 1933-34, U. Pa., 1934-36; D in Econs. (hon.), HanYang U., Seoul, Republic of Korea, 1988. With property sales mgmt. depts. Milton Meyer & Co., San Francisco, 1946-51, ptnr., 1951-60, owner, chmn. bd. dirs., 1960—; owner, chmn. bd. dirs. Shorenstein Group, San Francisco, Shorenstein Co., San Francisco, 1960—. Past chmn. bd. trustees Hastings Law Ctr., U. Calif., San Francisco; founding mem. exec. adv. com. Hubert H. Humphrey Inst. Pub. Affairs, U. Minn.; founder Joan Shorenstein Barone Ctr. on Press, Politics and Pub. Policy, Harvard U. Kennedy Sch. Govt.; past pres., hon. life bd. dirs. San Francisco Park and Recreation Commn.; chmn. Vietnam Orphans Airlift; bd. dirs. San Francisco Performing Arts Ctr.; trustee Asia Found.; fin. chmn. Dem. Nat. Conv., 1984; apptd. by Pres. Clinton to Nat. Svc. Commn., 1994; chmn. San Francisco UN50 nat. com., 1995, also numerous polit. activities. Maj. USAF, 1940-45. Named Leader of Tomorrow, Time mag., 1953, Calif. Dem. of Yr., 1985; recipient Nat. Brotherhood award NCCJ, 1982, Disting. Svc. award Dem. Nat. Com., 1983, Golden Plate award Am. Acad. Achievement, Lifetime Achievement award Dem. Party, 1997. Mem. Calif. C. of C. (bd. dirs.), San Francisco C. of C. (past chmn. bd. dirs., life bd. dirs. Office: Shorenstein Co 555 California St Ste 4900 San Francisco CA 94104-1714

SHORES, JANIE LEDLOW, state supreme court justice; b. Georgiana, Ala., Apr. 30, 1932; d. John Wesley and Willie (Scott) Ledlow; m. James L. Shores, Jr., May 12, 1962; 1 child, Laura Scott. J.D., U. Ala., Tuscaloosa, 1959; AB, Samford U., 1968; LLM, U. Va., 1992. Bar: Ala. 1959. Pvt. practice Selma, 1959; mem. legal dept. Liberty Nat. Life Ins. Co., Birmingham, Ala., 1962-66; assoc. prof. law Cumberland Sch. Law, Samford U., Birmingham, 1966-74; assoc. justice Supreme Ct. Ala., 1975—; legal adviser Ala. Constn. Revision Commn., 1973; mem. Nat. Adv. Coun. State Ct. Planning, 1976—. Contbr. articles to legal jours. Mem. bd. dirs. State Justice Inst., 1995—. Mem. Am. Bar Assn., Am. Judicature Soc., Farrah Order Jurisprudence. Democrat. Episcopalian. Office: Ala Supreme Ct 300 Dexter Ave Montgomery AL 36104-3741

SHORS, CLAYTON MARION, cardiologist; b. Beemer, Nebr., June 10, 1925; s. Joseph Albert and Morva Edith (Clayton) S.; m. Arlene Towle, June 6, 1948; children—Susan Debra, Clayton Robert, Scott Towle. B.S., U. Nebr., 1950, M.D., 1952. Diplomate Am. Bd. Internal Medicine (subspecialty cardiovascular disease). Intern Detroit Receiving Hosp., 1952-53, resident, 1953-56; practice medicine specializing in cardiology Detroit; chief cardiology St. John Hosp., Detroit. Bd. dirs. Sedona Acad.; mem. Sedona 30. Served with U.S. Army, 1943-46. Fellow Am. Coll. Cardiology, Internat. Coll. Angiology, Am. Heart Assn. Council on Clin. Cardiology; mem. Alpha Omega Alpha. Home: 44 Rue De La Rose Sedona AZ 86336-5970 Office: 1785 W Us Highway 89A Sedona AZ 86336-5567

SHORS, JOHN D., lawyer; b. Ft. Dodge, Iowa, July 21, 1937; s. George A. and Catherine (Shaw) S.; m. Patricia Ann Percival, Oct. 7, 1967; children: John, Tom, Matt, Luke. BSEE, Iowa State U., 1959; JD, U. Iowa, 1964. Bar: Iowa, U.S. Supreme Ct. Assoc. then ptnr. Davis, Hockenberg, Wine, Brown, Koehn & Shors (now Davis, Brown, Koehn, Shors & Roberts, P.C.), Des Moines, 1964—. Co-author: Closely Held Corporations in Business and Estate Planning, 1982. Pres. Mercy Hosp. Found., Des Moines, 1981-84; chair Iowa State U. Found., Ames, 1989-92; bd. dirs. Mercy Housing, Denver, 1992—. Cpl. U.S. Army, 1960-61. Recipient Iowa State U. Alumni medal, Merit award Iowa State Bar Assn. Mem. Iowa State Bar Assn. (pres. 1992) Iowa Women Profl. Corp. (Good Guy award 1987), Iowa Rsch. Coun. (bd. dirs. 1994—), Am. Judicature Soc. (bd. dirs. 1974-79), Polk County Bar Assn. (pres. 1986), Rotary (Des Moines chpt.), DM Club, Glenoaks C.C. Republican. Roman Catholic. Office: Davis Brown Koehn Shors & Roberts PC 666 Walnut St Ste 2500 Des Moines IA 50309-3904

SHORT, ALEXANDER CAMPBELL, lawyer; b. Washington, July 26, 1940; s. Joseph Hudson and Beth (Campbell) S.; m. Patricia Graves Thompson, Aug. 24, 1968; children: Joseph Graves, Ashley Campbell, Justin Owen. BA, Amherst Coll., 1963; MA, U. Pa., 1968; JD, U. Va., 1972. Bar: Conn. 1972, Md. 1973. Field and site rep. U.S. Dept. of HUD, Phila., 1963-69; assoc. Reid & Riege P.C., Hartford, Conn., 1972-73, Piper & Marbury, Balt., 1973-79; assoc. Miles & Stockbridge, Balt., 1979-81, ptnr., 1981-94; pvt. practice Balt., 1994-95; ptnr. Hooper, Kiefer & Cornell, LLP, Balt., 1995-96, Eastman & Short, LLP, Balt., 1996—; bd. dirs., pres. Handel Soc. adv. bd. to Handel Choir, Balt., 1983-87; pres. Handel Choir, Balt., 1987-88. Bd. dirs. Homeland Assn., Balt., 1984-85, Kernewood Assn., Balt., 1995—; mem. bd. mgrs. Camp Dudley, YWCA, 1991-96; pres. North Baltimore Neighborhood Coalition, Balt., 1996—. Mem. Md. Bar Assn. (real property planning and zoning sect., coun. 1981-88, 96—, sec. 1982-84, chmn. elect 1984-86, chmn. 1986-88. Democrat. Presbyterian. Avocations: choral singing, scouting, gardening. Office: 201 N Charles St Ste 1640 Baltimore MD 21201-4120

SHORT, ANN MARIE HEROLD, library director; b. Richmond, Ind., June 15, 1957; d. Clarence Ferdinand and Dorothy Joyce (Holaday) H.; m. Michael Estill Short, May 7, 1977; 1 child, Wenona Jeannette. BFA, Ind. U., Indianapolis, 1979; MLS, Ind. U., Bloomington, 1986. Cert. libr. I, Ind. Libr. dir. Rauh Meml. Libr. Indpls. Children's Mus., 1980; children's libr. Shelbyville-Shelby County (Ind.) Pub. Libr., 1981-84, reference libr., 1987-88, libr. dir., 1988—; — Rushville (Ind.) Pub. Libr., 1984-87; mem. exec. com. Ind. Visual and Audio Network, Indianapolis, 1995—. Mem. Ind. Libr. Fedn., DAR, ACLU, Ind. Civil Liberties Union. Avocations: vegetarian cooking, herbs, painting, drawing, calligraphy. Office: Shelbyville-Shelby County Pub Libr 57 W Broadway St Shelbyville IN 46176-1255

SHORT, BETSY ANN, elementary education educator; b. Macon, Ga., Mar. 18, 1958; d. Garland Brooks Jr. and Mary Eleanor (Jordan) Turner; m. Lynn Robin Short, July 21, 1984. BS in Early Childhood Edn., Ga. Coll., Milledgeville, 1981, M in Early Childhood Edn., 1993, EdS, 1995. Cert. elem. tchr. and tchr. support specialist, Ga. Tchr. 3d grade Stockbridge (Ga.) Elem. Sch., 1983-84, tchr. kindergarten, 1984-93; tchr. augmented spl. instructional assistance Locust Grove (Ga.) Elem. Sch., 1993—. Author: Spinning Yarns, 1995; mem. editl. adv. bd. Ga. Jour. Reading; contbr. articles to profl. jours.; artist oil painting/pen and ink drawing. Mem. Profl. Assn. of Ga. Educators, Ga. Coun. Tchrs. Maths., Ga. Coun. Internat. Reading Assn., Ga. Coun. Social Studies, Ga. Sci. Tchrs. Assn., Henry Heritage Reading Coun. Baptist. Avocations: oil painting, cross-stitching, writing short stories, story telling. Office: Locust Grove Elem 1727 Griffin Rd Locust Grove GA 30248

SHORT, BOBBY See SHORT, ROBERT WALTRIP

SHORT, EARL DE GREY, JR., psychiatrist, consultant; b. Talladega, Ala., Jan. 11, 1933; s. Earl de Grey and Adeline Eugenia (McWilliams) S.; m. Martha Burt Rossiter, Oct. 12, 1963; children: Earl D III, Philip A., Catherine E., William R. BS, The Citadel, 1956; MD, Med. U. S.C., Charleston, 1959. Commd. 2d lt. USAR, 1956; entered active duty U.S. Army, 1961, advanced through grades to col., 1976; battalion surgeon 4th Armored BN, 8th Inf. div., Germany, 1961-62; resident psychiatry Walter Reed Army Med. Ctr., Washington, 1962-65; chief dept. psychiatry U.S. Army Hosp., Ft. Polk, La., 1965-68, U.S. Walson Army Hosp., Ft. Dix, N.J., 1968-70; student Command and Gen. Staff Coll., Ft. Leavenworth, Kans., 1970-71; divsn. surgeon, comdr. 2d Med. Bn., 2d Infantry divsn., Korea, 1971-72; chief psychiatry svc. Brooke Army Med. Ctr., Ft. Sam Houston, Tex., 1972-80; ret. U.S. Army, 1980; psychiatrist Mecklenburg County Mental Health Ctr., Charlotte, N.C., 1980-86; ret. Mecklenburg County, 1993; psychiatrist Carolinas Medical Ctr. Ctr. for Mental Health, Charlotte, N.C., 1986—; pvt. practice Carolinas Med. Group, Psychiat. and Psychol. Assocs., 1992—; psychiat. cons. Mecklenburg County, Charlotte, 1987—, Amethyst, Charlotte, 1993-95. Founder Philip Alexander Short Meml. Scholarship Fund, Wingate (N.C.) Coll., 1988, Short Endowment Fund, Wingate Coll., 1991, Philip Alexander Short Meml. Fund, Elon Homes for Children, Elon Coll., N.C., 1989. Decorated Meritorious Svc. medal with 1 oak leaf cluster, U.S. Army, 1972, 80, Army Commendation medal with 1 oak leaf cluster, U.S. Army, 1968, 70; recipient All Am. award The Citadel, 1956. Mem. AMA, Am. Psychiat. Assn., N.C. Med. Soc., N.C. Psychiat. Assn., Charlotte Psychiat. Soc., Assn. Mil. Surgeons, Mecklenburg County Med. Soc., Ret. Officers Assn., Am. Legion, VFW, Sons Am. Revolution, Nat. Assn. for Uniformed Svcs. Republican. Presbyterian. Avocations: genealogy, composing piano music, restoring ancestral homes, collecting stamps, books and coins. Office: PO Box 18773 Charlotte NC 28218-0773

SHORT, ELIZABETH M., physician, educator, federal agency administrator; b. Boston, June 2, 1942; d. James Edward and Arlene Elizabeth (Mitchell) Meehan; m. Herbert M. Short, Sept. 2, 1963 (div. 1969); 1 child, Timothy Owen; m. Michael Allen Friedman, June 21, 1976; children: Lia Gabrielle, Hannah Ariel, Eleanor Elana. BA Philosophy magna cum laude, Mt. Holyoke Coll., 1963; MD cum laude, Yale U., 1968. Diplomate Am. Bd. Internal Medicine, Am. Bd. Med. Genetics. Intern, jr. resident internal medicine Yale New Haven Hosp., 1968-70; postdoctoral fellow in human genetics Yale Med. Sch., 1970-72; postdoctoral fellow in renal metabolism U. Calif., San Francisco, 1972-73; sr. resident in internal medicine Stanford (Calif.) Med. Sch., 1973-74, chief resident in internal medicine, 1974-75; asst. prof. of medicine Stanford Med. Sch., 1975-83, asst. dean Student Affairs, 1978-80, assoc. dean Students Affairs/Medical Education, 1980-83; dep. dir. dept. acad. affairs Assn. Am. Med. Colls., Washington, 1983-88, dep. dir. biomedical rsch., 1987-88; dep. assoc. chief med. dir. for acad. affairs VA, Washington, 1988-92, assoc. chief medical dir. for acad. affairs, 1992-96; cons. DHHS Office Asst. Sec. Health, 1996—; vis. prof. human biology Stanford U., 1983-86; mem. resource allocation com. VA, 1989-91, mem. budget planning and policy rev. coun. 1991-96: mem. planning rev. com. VA, 1991-96; chmn. resident work limit task force 1991-96, mem. managed care task force, 1993-94; mem. numerous adminstrv. coms. Yale U. Med. Sch., Stanford U.; mem. Accreditation Coun. Grad. Med. Edn., 1988-97; mem. White House Task Force on Health Care Reform, 1993-94. assoc. editor Clin. Rsch. Jour., 1976-79, editor 1980-84; contbr. articles to profl. jours. Mem. nat. child health adv. coun. NIH, 1991—; mem. com. edn. and training Office Sci. and Tech. Policy, 1991—. Recipient Maclean Zoology award; Munger scholar, Markle scholar, Sara Williston scholar Mt. Holyoke Coll., 1959-63, Yale Men in Medicine scholar, 1964-68; Bardwell Meml. Med. fellow, 1963. Mem. AAAS, Am. Soc. Human Genetics (pub. policy com. 1984-95, chmn. 1986-94), Am. Fedn. Clin. Rsch. (bd. dirs. 1973-83, co-chmn. com. status women 1975-77, editor 1978-83, nat. coun., exec. com., pub. policy com. 1977-87), Western Soc. Clin. Investigation, Calif. Acad. Medicine, Phi Beta Kappa, Alpha Omega Alpha. Home: 6807 Bradley Blvd Bethesda MD 20817-3004

SHORT, GEORGE WILLIAM, financial executive; b. N.Y.C., Oct. 22, 1949; s. Robert Joseph and Marion Josephine (Roper) S.; m. Janet Tortorella, Oct. 6, 1973; children: Courtney, Matthew, Christopher. BBA, Ohio U., 1971; postgrad., NYU, 1973-77. CPA, N.Y. Staff acct. to mgr. Fox & Co., N.Y.C., 1971-81, ptnr., 1981-85; ptnr. Grant Thornton, N.Y.C., 1985-90; CFO, v.p. fin. Go America Tours, Inc., N.Y.C., 1990-93, Thomas Regional Directory Co., N.Y.C., 1993—. Treas. Am. Youth Soccer Orgn., Chappaqua, N.Y., 1990-96. Mem. AICPAs, N.Y. State Soc. CPAs, Fin. Execs. Inst., Mt. Kisco C.C. Avocations: gardening, carpentry, antiques. Home: 300 Roaring Brook Rd Chappaqua NY 10514-1712 Office: Thomas Regional Directory Co 5 Penn Plz New York NY 10001-1810

SHORT, JANET MARIE, principal; b. Boston, Sept. 18, 1939; d. Robert Emmet and Gertia Agnes (Mills) S. BS in Edn., Boston State Coll., 1962, MEd, 1967; LLD (hon.), Regis Coll., 1991. Tchr. Boston Pub. Schs., 1962-70, acting asst. dir. staff devel., 1970-71, tchr.-in-charge, 1971-75; prin. D.L. Barrett Sch., Boston, 1976-81; tchr. Boston Pub. Schs., 1981-82; prin. Maurice J. Tobin Sch., Boston, 1982—, lead cluster prin., 1995—; lectr. in field. Adv. bd. DiMaiti Stuart Found., Boston, 1990—; adv. bd. Mission Hill and Camp Mission Posible, 1984-87; community adv. bd. Harvard Sch. Pub. Health, Boston, 1990—; adv. bd. Boston Against Drugs, 1990-94. Recipient Women of Achievement award Big Sister Assn. of Greater Boston, 1994, Thankful Recognition award Channel 5, Boston, 1987, Recognition award Boston Women's Mag., 1988, Pub. Svc. award Henry L. Shattuck, Bus. Mcpl. Bur. Rsch. award, 1988, Freedom's Found. Honor medal, 1990, Annual Excellence in Edn. award Alpha Gamma chpt. Pi Lambda Theta, 1993 and others; movie based on J.M. Short, "A Matter of Principal", 1990. Mem. ASCD, Mass. Middle Level Adminstrs. Assn., Boston Assn. Sch. Adminstrs. (exec. bd. 1984-93), Boston Middle Sch. Assn., Boston Elem. Prins. Assn., MESPA, Delta Kappa Gamma (chpt. pres. 1978-80). Roman Catholic. Avocations: travel, bowling, reading. Home: 39 Ridgeway Dr Quincy MA 02169-2321 Office: Maurice Tobin Sch 40 Smith St Roxbury MA 02120-2702

SHORT, JOEL BRADLEY, lawyer, consultant, software publisher; b. Birmingham, Ala., Dec. 27, 1941; s. Forrest Edwin and Laura Elizabeth (Bradley) S.; m. Georgianna Pohl, June 5, 1965 (div. Apr. 1973); m. Nancy Ann Harty, Dec. 17, 1977; children: Christopher Bradley, Matthew Douglas. BA, U. Colo., 1963, LLB, 1966, JD, 1968. Bar: Kans. 1966, U.S. Dist. Ct. Kans. 1966, U.S. Ct. Appeals (10th cir.) 1975, U.S. Supreme Ct. 1976. Ptnr. Short & Short, Attys., Fort Scott, Kans., 1966-77, Nugent & Short, Overland Park, Kans., 1977-83; pvt. practice J. Bradley Short & Assoc., Overland Park, Kans., 1983-91; ptnr. Short & Borth, Overland Park, Kans., 1991—; owner Bradley Software; mem. tech. adv. com. Kans. Jud. Coun., Topeka, 1991-95. 1st lt. U.S. Army, 1967-73. Fellow Am. Acad. Matrimonial Lawyers; mem. Johnson County Bar Assn. (ethics and family law coms. 1983—). Avocation: sailing. Office: Short and Borth Attys 32/1111 Corporate Woods 9225 Indian Creek Pky Overland Park KS 66210-2009

SHORT, MARION PRISCILLA, neurology educator; b. Milford, Del., June 12, 1951; d. Raymond Calistus and Barbara Anne (Ferguson) S.; m. Michael Peter Klein; 1 child, Asher Calistus Klein. BA, Bryn Mawr Coll., 1973; diploma, U. Edinburgh (Scotland), 1975; MD, Med. Coll. Pa., 1978. Diplomate Am. Bd. Psychiatry and Neurology, Am. Bd. Internal Medicine. Intern in internal medicine Hahnemann Med. Coll. Hosp., Phila., 1978-79; med. resident in internal medicine St. Lukes-Roosevelt Hosp., N.Y.C., 1979-81; neurology resident U. Pitts. Health Ctr., 1981-84; fellow in med. genetics Mt. Sinai Med. Ctr., N.Y.C., 1984-86; fellow in neurology Mass. Gen. Hosp., Boston, 1986-90, asst. neurologist, 1990-95; asst. prof. dept. neurology Harvard Med. Sch., Boston, 1990-95; asst. prof. dept. neurology, pediat. and pathology U. Chgo., 1995—; dir. biomed. sci. and clin. rsch. AMA, Chgo., 1997—; cons. Spaulding Rehab. Hosp., Boston. Recipient Clin. Investigator Devel. award NIH, 1988-93. Mem. Am. Acad. Neurology, Am. Soc. for Human Genetics. Office: Am Med Assn WCHC 376 MC3055 515 N State St Chicago IL 60610

SHORT, RAY EVERETT, minister, sociology educator emeritus, author, lecturer; b. Coffeyville, Kans., Jan. 5, 1919; s. Franklin Marion and Jennie (Messersmith) S.; m. Jeannette Louise Stephens, June 12, 1954; children: Glenn Alan, Linda Louise, Kenneth Ray, Timothy Wesley, Karen Amy; 1 stepdau., Mary Jennings. AB, Willamette U., 1944; postgrad., U. Chgo., 1946; BD, Duke, 1948, PhD, 1961; postgrad., U. Idaho, 1950-51. Ordained to ministry Meth. Ch., 1946. Dir. Westminster Found., Duke, 1944-46; co-pastor Interracial Meth. Ch., Durham, N.C., 1947; asst. prof. religion, dir. chapel programs Fla. So. Coll., Lakeland, 1947-48; exec. dir. Fla. br. United World Federalists, 1948-51; dir. Intermountain Region, 1953-54, Wesley Found., U. Idaho, 1950-51; exec. dir. Student YMCA-YWCA, U. Denver, 1951-53; pastor Fairmont Meth. Ch., Lockport, Ill., 1954-56; grad. asst. sociology Duke, 1956-57; assoc. prof. religion, head divsn. religion and philosophy, chaplain Tenn. Wesleyan Coll., 1957-60; assoc. prof. sociology and religion, head dept. sociology U. Dubuque, Iowa, 1960-65, acting chmn. div. social sci., 1962-65; assoc. prof. sociology, head dept. sociology and anthropology U. Wis., Platteville, 1965-70, prof. sociology, 1966-87, prof. emeritus, 1987—; prof. sociology and anthropology Copenhagen Study Ctr. U. Wis., spring 1974, nat. lectr., 1975—; chmn. Peace and World Order divsn. North Iowa Meth. Conf., 1963-69; rep. U.S. Jr. C. of C. in testimony before U.S. Senate Com. on Fgn. Rels., 1950; Midwest region rep. Nat. Coun. World Federalist Assn., 1964-73, pres. Midwest region, 1967-69, chmn. nat. coun., 1971-72, nat. v.p., 1991—; (with wife) WFA dels. to NGO Forum and 4th UN Conf. on Women, Beijing, 1995; co-chmn. Grenville Clark Club; mem. spl. Wis. Conf. called with Pres.'s Commn. for Observance of 25th Anniversary of UN, 1970-87; mem. Wis. U. Meth. Bd. on Ch. and Soc., 1973-80, chmn. World Peace divsn., mem. exec. com., 1975-80. Author: Sex, Love or Infatuation: How Can I Really Know?, 1978, on videocassette, 1987, 2nd edit., 1990 (Augsburg Bestseller), Sex, Dating and Love: Questions Most Often Asked, 1984, 2nd edit., 1994 (Augsburg Bestseller); contbr. articles to profl. jours. Dem. candidate for Wis. 3rd Dist. Congl. Seat, 1970, 72; del. Dist. and State Convs., 1969-87, mem. state platform com., 1975-87; bd. dirs. Dubuque Salvation Army, 1961-65; mem. nat. bd. Am. Freedom Assn.; nat. v.p. Campaign for UN Reform, 1983-87, 1st v.p., 1989—; dir., founder Wis. Ann. High Sch. World Peace Study Program, 1975-87. Recipient NSF grant Anthropology Inst., Fairmont State Coll., W.Va., 1962. Fellow Am. Sociol. Assn.; mem. AAUP, Nat. Coun. on Family Rels., Fedn. Am. Scientists, Nat. United Meth. Men (mem. peace adv. task force 1990—). Home: 505 S Miller Ave Lafayette CO 80026-1545 *Nuclear and chemical weapons, crises of environments. While my life has largely been spent helping others have a better future, I now know we have to help assure that they have a future at all by establishing limited democratic enforcible world law.*

SHORT, ROBERT HENRY, retired utility executive; b. Klamath Falls, Oreg., Oct. 15, 1924; s. Judge Haywood and Henrietta Luella (Lyon) S.; m. Ruby Madalyn Rice, Aug. 1, 1946; children: Robert L., Victoria (Mrs. Gregory Baum), Casey. BS in Journalism, U. Oreg., 1950; PhD in Humane Letters (hon.), Linfield Coll., 1984. City editor Klamath Falls Herald and News, 1950-52; dir. pub. rels. Water and Elec. Bd., Eugene, Oreg., 1952-55; mgr. pub. info. Portland Gen. Electric Co., Oreg., 1955-57, asst. to chmn., 1957-62, v.p., 1962-71, sr. v.p., 1971-73, exec. v.p., 1973-77, pres., 1977-80, chmn. bd., chief exec. officer, 1980-88, ret., 1989; bd. dir. First Interstate Bank of Oreg. Bd. dirs. Oreg. Ind. Colls. Found., Oreg. Health Sci. U.; trustee Oreg. Grad. Inst. With USNR, 1942-45. Mem. Portland Golf Club, Arlington Club. Home: 1210 SW 61st Ct Portland OR 97221-1504 Office: 555 SW Columbia St Ste 1500 Portland OR 97201-5531

SHORT, ROBERT WALTRIP (BOBBY SHORT), entertainer, author; b. Danville, Ill., Sept. 15, 1924; s. Rodman Jacob and Myrtle (Render) S. Grad. high sch. Singing pianist as child and after high sch.; appeared in night clubs in U.S. and abroad, concerts in maj. cities; regular cabaret performer N.Y.C.; recordings include: Krazy for Gershwin, Live at Cate Carlyle, Loves Cole Porter, Short Celebrates Rodgers and Hart, Guess Who's in Town, 1987, 50 From Bobby Short, 1987. Late Night At The Cafe Carlyle, 1992, (with the Alden-Barret Quinlet) Swing That Music, 1993; appeared in TV movie Roots, The Next Generation, 1979; appeared in motion picture Splash, 1984; appeared in Broadway prodns., 1956—; appeared at White House for Duke and Duchess of Windsor at request of Pres. Nixon, 1970; Author: Black and White Baby, 1971; also articles. Grammy nomination, Best Jazz Vocal for "Swing That Music" (with the Alden-Barrett Quintet), 1994. Mem. NAACP (life). Address: care Cafe Carlyle Madison Ave at 76th St New York NY 10021*

SHORT, STEVE EUGENE, engineer; b. Crockett, Calif., Oct. 17, 1938; s. Roger Milton and Ida Mae (Mills) S.; B.S. in Gen. Engring. with honors, U. Hawaii, 1972, M.B.A., 1973; M.S. in Meteorology, U. Md., 1980; m. Yumie Sedaka, Feb. 2, 1962; children: Anne Yumie, Justine Yumie, Katherine Yumie. With Nat. Weather Service, NOAA, 1964—, tech. cons. 1994—; govt. exec. Silver Spring, Md., 1974-81, program mgr. ASOS, 1981—, transition dir. 1991—; ind. tech. cons., 1994—; pres. Short & Assocs., Inc.; cons. engring. and mgmt.; cons. SBA. Contbr. articles to sci. jours. Served with USMC, 1956-60. Registered profl. engr., Hawaii. Recipient Gold Medal award U.S. Dept. Commerce, 1992, Presdl. Meritorious Exec. award, 1992. Mem. VFW, Am. Meteorol. Soc., Japan-Am. Soc., Am. Soc. Public Adminstrn. Home: 3307 Rolling Rd Chevy Chase MD 20815-4033 Office: Nat Weather Svc 1325 E West Hwy Silver Spring MD 20910-3280

SHORTELL, STEPHEN M., medical educator; b. New London, Wis., Nov. 9, 1944. BBA, U. Notre Dame, 1966; MPH, UCLA, 1968; MBA, U. Chgo., 1970, PhD in Behavioral Sci., 1972. Rsch. asst. Nat. Opinion Rsch. Ctr., 1969; instr., rsch. assoc. Ctr. Health Adminstrv. Studies, 1970-72; acting dir. grad. program hosp. adminstrn. U. Chgo., 1973-74, from asst. prof. to assoc. prof., 1974-79; prof. Sch. Pub. Health & Comty. Medicine, Dept. Health Svc. U. Wash., 1979-82; A. C. Buehler Disting. prof. health svc. mgmt. Northwestern U., Evanston, Ill., 1982—; cons. VA, Robert Wood Found., Henry Keiser found.; asst. prof. Health Svcs. Orgn., U. Chgo., 1972-74; adj. asst. prof. dept. sociology U. Wash., 1975-76, dir. doctoral program dept. health svcs. Sch. Pub. Health & Comty. Medicine, 1976-78; prof. sociology dept. sociology Northwestern U., 1982, prof. comty. medicine dept. comty. health & preventive medicine Sch. Medicine. Contbr. numerous publs. to profl. jours. Mem. APHA, Inst. Med.-NAS. Office: Northwestern U J L Kellogg Grad Sch Mgmt 2001 Sheridan Rd Rm 3-076 Evanston IL 60208-0814*

SHORTER, JAMES RUSSELL, JR., lawyer; b. N.Y.C., June 10, 1946; s. James Russell and Helen (Ibert) S. AB, Columbia Coll., 1968; JD, Harvard U., 1975; LLM in Taxation, NYU, 1979. Bar: N.Y. 1976, U.S. Dist. Ct. (so. and ea. dists.) N.Y. 1976, U.S. Tax Ct. 1987. Assoc. Thacher Proffitt & Wood, N.Y.C., 1975-84, ptnr., 1984—. Capt. USNR, 1968—. Mem. ABA (tax, bus. law sect.). Republican. Club: Harvard (N.Y.C.). Home: 345 E 80th St Apt 26C New York NY 10021-0671 Office: Thacher Proffitt & Wood 2 World Trade Ctr Fl 39 New York NY 10048-3998

SHORTER, NICHOLAS ANDREW, pediatric surgeon; b. London, Oct. 14, 1953; came to the U.S., 1961; s. Roy Gerrard and Rhiannon (Morris) S.; m. Sally Jo Trued, Aug. 28, 1982; children: Timothy Anders, Brittain David, Jaime Elizabeth Rhiannon. AB, AM, Harvard U., 1975; MD, Johns Hopkins U., 1979. Bd. cert. in surgery and pediatric surgery. Intern in surgery The Johns Hopkins Hosp., Balt., 1979-80, jr. asst. resident in surgery, 1980-81, sr. asst. resident in surgery, 1981-82, 83-84, chief resident in surgery, 1984-85; rsch. fellow in surgery The Children's Hosp. Med. Ctr., Boston, 1982-83; asst. chief resident in pediatric surgery The Children's Hosp., Phila., 1985-86, chief resident in pediatric surgery, 1986-87; hosp. staff Duke U. Med. Ctr., Durham, N.C., 1987-91; dir. pediatric surg. svcs. Children's Hosp. at Dartmouth, Dartmouth-Hitchcock Med. Ctr., 1991—, exec. com., 1991—; teaching fellow biology Harvard U., Cambridge, Mass., 1974-75; asst. instr. pediatric surgery U. Pa., Phila., 1985-87, Duke U., Durham, 1987-91, asst. prof. pediatric surgery and pediatrics, 1987-91; asst. prof. pediatrics Dartmouth Med. Sch., Hanover, N.H., 1991-94, asst. prof. surgery, 1991-94, assoc. prof. pediatrics, 1994—, assoc. prof. surgery, 1994—; hosp. staff The Children's Hosp., Phila., 1986-87, Dartmouth-Hitchcock Med. Ctr., Lebanon, N.H., 1991—, Duke U. Med. Ctr., Durham, 1987-91; dir. Kiwanis Affiliated Pediatric Trauma Ctr., Children's Hosp. at Dartmouth, Lebanon, 1993—; others. Referee Jour. Pediatric Surgery; contbr. chpts. to books and articles to profl. jours. Recipient Regular Clin. fellowship Am. Cancer Soc., 1985-86. Fellow ACS, Am. Acad. Pediatrics, Southeastern Surg. Congress, Soc. Surg. Oncology; mem. Am. Pediatric Surg. Assn., Brit. Assn. Pediatric Surgeons, Internat. Soc. Pediatric Oncology, Internat. Pediatric Surg. Oncology, Pediatric Oncology Group (assoc.), Am. Assn. for Cancer Rsch., Assn. for Acad. Surgery, N.H. Med. Soc. (del. Grafton County), N.Y. Acad. Scis., N.H. Pediatric Soc., Kiwanis Club Lebanon, Cum Laude Soc., Phi Beta Kappa, Alpha Omega Alpha. Republican. Episcopalian. Avocation: collecting political memorabilia. Office: Dartmouth-Hitchcock Med Ctr Sect Gen Surgery One Med Ctr Dr Lebanon NH 03756

SHORTESS, EDWIN STEEVIN, marketing consultant; b. Cedar Rapids, Iowa, Oct. 31, 1920; s. Edwin Stephen and Rita (Clemente) S.; m. Jane Elizibeth Gallagher, Dec. 27, 1941 (div. Apr. 1970); children: E. Stephen, Richard J., Mark Andrew, Cathy Shortess Pool; m. Mary Francis Kerns, May 28, 1970; children: Dana Menshing, Emil Bartsche, Roger Bartsche, Lisa Bartsche, Vincent Bartsche, Kirsten Bartsche Chirico. Student, North Iowa U., 1938-39; BSEE, Chgo. Tech. Coll., 1942. Engring. rsch. analyst Douglas Aircraft Corp., El segundo, Calif., 1942-44; liaison engr. Martin Aircraft Corp., Omaha, 1944-45; chief engr., dir. Burlington (Iowa) Instrument co., 1945-53; adminstrv. engr., dir. Hickok Elec. Instrument Co., Cleve., 1953-59; ea. sales mgr. Hickok Elec. Instrument Co., Paramus, N.J., 1960-65; v.p., gen. mgr., dir. Wacline, Dayton, Ohio, 1959-60; v.p., gen. mgr. Colo. Hickok, Grand Junction, 1965-69; pres. Shortess Rawson & Assocs., Kenilworth, N.J., 1969-86; mktg. cons. Shortess Rawson & Assocs., Allenwood, N.J., 1986—; bd. dirs. Federated Purchasers Inc., Kenelworth, N.J. Author: Design and Application of Electrical Industrial Instruments, 1964. Mem. Instrument Soc. Engrs. (sr.). Republican. Methodist. Avocations: golf, bridge. Home and Office: 123 Everest Dr S Brick NJ 08724-0152

SHORTLIFFE, EDWARD HANCE, internist, medical informatics educator; b. Edmonton, Alta., Can., Aug. 28, 1947; s. Ernest Carl and Elizabeth Joan (Rankin) S.; m. Linda Marie Dairiki, June 21, 1970; children: Lindsay Ann, Lauren Leigh. AB, Harvard U., 1970; PhD, Stanford U., 1975, MD, 1976. Diplomate Am. Bd. Internal Medicine. Trainee NIH, 1971-76; intern Mass. Gen. Hosp., Boston, 1976-77; resident Stanford Hosp., Palo Alto, Calif., 1977-79; asst. prof. medicine Stanford U. Sch. Medicine, Palo Alto, 1979-85, assoc. prof., 1985-90, prof., 1990—, chief div. gen. internal medicine, 1988-95; assoc. dean info. resources and tech. Stanford U. Sch. Medicine, 1995—; pres. SCAMC, Inc. (Symposium on Computer Applications in Med. Care), Washington, 1988-89; assoc. chair medicine Primary Care, 1993-95; bd. dirs. Smart Valley, Inc.; advisor Nat. Bd. Med. Examiners, Phila., 1987-93; mem. Nat. Fed. Networking Adv. Coun., NSF, 1991-93; mem. computer sci. and telecomm. bd. NRC, 1991-96; bd. regents ACP, 1996—; mem. Presdl. Com. on High-Performance Computing and Comm., Info. Tech., and the Next Generation Internet, 1997—. Editor: Rule-Based Expert Systems, 1984, Readings in Medical Artificial Intelligence, 1984, Medical Informatics: Computer Applications in Health Care, 1990; developer several medical computer programs including MYCIN, 1976 (Grace M. Hopper award Assn. Computing Machinery). Recipient Young Investigator award Western Soc. Clin. Investigation, 1987, rsch. career award Nat. Libr. of Medicine, 1979-84; scholar Kaiser Family Found., 1983-88. Fellow Am. Assn. Artificial Intelligence, Am. Coll. Med. Informatics (pres. 1992-94); mem. Soc. for Med. Decisionmaking (pres. 1989-90), Inst. Medicine, Am. Soc. for Clin. Investigation, Am. Med. Informatics Assn., Assn. Am. Physicians, Am. Clin. and Climatol. Assn. Avocation: skiing. Office: Stanford U Sch Medicine Sect on Med Informatics 300 Pasteur Dr Palo Alto CA 94304-2203

SHORTRIDGE, DEBORAH GREEN, lawyer; b. Balt., Sept. 5, 1952; d. Harry Joseph Green and Dorothy Marie (Eser) Diamond; children: Bretton, Dana. BA magna cum laude, U. Balt., 1980, JD summa cum laude, 1982. Bar: Md. 1982, U.S. Dist. Ct. Md. 1983, U.S. Ct. Appeals (4th cir.), D.C. 1987. Assoc. prof. U. Balt., 1982-83; assoc. Weinberg and Green, Balt., 1982-89, adminstrv. ptnr., 1989-93; in-house counsel Weinberg & Green LLC, Balt., 1993—; mem. U. Balt. law adv. coun., 1993—. Bd. dirs., v.p. AIDS Interfaith Residential Svcs., Balt., 1991-96, pres. 1996—; bd. govs. U. Balt. Alumni Assn., 1985-91 (H. Melbane Turner Svc. award 1991); mem. bd. govs. ACLU of Md., 1983-90. Recipient Law Faculty award U. Balt. Law Sch., 1982. Mem. ABA (Ctr. for Profl. Responsibility, mem. Founders Cir.), Md. State Bar Assn. (pro bono sect.), Bar Assn. Balt. City. Office: Weinberg & Green LLC 100 S Charles St Baltimore MD 21201-2725

SHORTRIDGE, JUDY BETH, lawyer; b. Johnson City, Tenn., Feb. 17, 1954; d. George Edd and Anna Louise (Salmon) Copenhaver; m. Michael L. Shortridge, July 27, 1984; children: Sarah Elizabeth, Alexander Blake. BA, Va. Poly. Inst. and State U., 1976; MEd, U. Va., 1982; JD, U. Tenn., 1989. Bar: Va. 1990, U.S. Dist. Ct. (we. dist.) Va. 1990, Ea. Dist. Tenn., 1995. Tchr. Stafford County (Va.) Sch. System, 1976-84, Wise County (Va.) Sch. System, 1984-86; ptnr. Shortridge & Shortridge, P.C., Norton, Va., 1990—. Recipient Am. Jurisprudence award U. Tenn., 1989. Mem. Va. Bar Assn., Wise County Bar Assn., Nat. Orgn. Social Security Claimants Reps. Home: 325 Oakwood Ave SE Wise VA 24293-5470 Office: Shortridge & Shortridge PC 18 7th St NW Ste 300 Norton VA 24273-1946

SHORTS, GARY K., newspaper publisher; b. Grove City, Pa., Feb. 26, 1951; s. Leonard and Sarah Maxine (Young) S.; m. Karen Healy; children: Steven A., Elizabeth H., Daniel C. BA in Journalism, Economics, Ohio Wesleyan U., 1973; MBA, U. Pa., 1975. Circulation dir. News Democrat, Belleville, Ill., 1977-80; mktg. dir. Oakland Press, Pontiac, Mich., 1981-83; v.p., gen. mgr. Times Pub. Co., Wichita Falls, Tex., 1983-85; v.p. mktg. Harte-Hanks Comms., San Antonio, 1985-86; pres. So. Calif. Newspapers, Inc., San Diego, 1986-87; pub., chief exec. officer The Morning Call, Allentown, Pa., 1987—; dir. Pa. Newspaper Pubs. Assn., treas. 1991-92, v.p. daily newspapers 1992-93, pres. 1993-94; dir. Lehigh County Indsl. Devel. Corp., Allentown Econ. Devel. Corp., sec. 1988—. Chmn. United Way, Allentown, 1991; trustee Cedarcrest Coll. Mem. Allentown-Lehigh County C. of C. Office: Morning Call PO Box 1260 101 N 6th St Allentown PA 18105*

SHORTZ, RICHARD ALAN, lawyer; b. Chgo., Mar. 11, 1945; s. Lyle A. and Wilma Warner (Wildes) S.; m. Jennifer A. Harrell; children: Eric, Heidi. BS, Ind. U., 1967; JD, Harvard U., 1970. Bar: Calif. 1971, U.S. Supreme Ct. 1980. Assoc. Gibson, Dunn & Crutcher, L.A., 1970-73; sr. v.p., gen. counsel, sec. Tosco Corp., L.A., 1973-83; ptnr. Jones, Day, Reavis & Pogue, L.A., 1983-95, Rogers & Wells, L.A., 1995-97, Morgan Lewis & Bockius, L.A., 1997—. Mem. L.A. World Affairs Inst., 1983—, Town Hall L.A., 1983—. 2nd lt. U.S. Army, 1970-71. Mem. ABA, L.A. Bar Assn., Calif. Club, Beach Club (Santa Monica, Calif.), L.A. Country Club. Republican. Episcopalian. Home: 1343 Pavia Pl Pacific Palisades CA 90272-4047 Office: Morgan Lewis & Bockius 801 S Grand Ave Ste 2200 Los Angeles CA 90017-4649

SHORTZ, WILL, puzzle editor; b. Crawfordsville, Ind., Aug. 26, 1952; s. Lyle A. and Wilma Warner (Wildes) S. AB, Ind. U., 1974; JD, U. Va., 1977. Editor Penny Press, Stamford, Conn., 1977-78; assoc. editor Games Mag., N.Y.C., 1978-82, sr. editor, 1982-89, editor, 1989-93; crossword editor N.Y. Times, N.Y.C., 1993—; founder, dir. Am. Crossword Puzzle Tournament, Stamford, Conn., 1978—, World Puzzle Team Championship, N.Y.C., 1992; puzzlemaster Weekend Edit., Sunday NPR, Washington, 1987—; U.S. team capt. Internat. Crossword Marathon, Brno, Czechoslovakia, 1989, Bjelovar, Yugoslavia, 1990, World Puzzle Championship, Brno, 1993, Cologne, 1994, Brasov, Romania, 1995, Utrecht, The Netherlands, 1996; riddle writer Batman Forever, 1995. Author: Brain Games, 1979, The American Quiz Book, 1979, Grain Games 2, 1980, The Bantam Great Masters Winning Crossword Puzzles, vol. 1-3, 1980, World Class Ch ampionship Crosswords, 1982, Brain Games 3, 1983, Games Mag. Book of Crossword Puzzles, 1985, American Championship Crosswords, 1990, Games Mag. Giant Book of Games, 1991, Will Shortz's Best Brain Busters, 1991, Games Mag. Best Pencil Puzzles, 1992, The World's Most Ornery Crosswords, vol. 1, 1992, Brain Twisters from the First World Puzzle Championships, 1993, N.Y. Times Daily Crossword Puzzles, vol. 40-46, 1995—, The Puzzlemaster Presents, 1996; (with Ron Osher) Brain Twisters From the World Puzzle Championship, vol. 2, 1995. Mem. Am. Antiquarian Soc., Am. Cryptogram Assn., Authors Guild, Nat. Puzzlers' League (pres. 1977, 81, historian 1992—). Avocations: table tennis, book collecting. Office: NY Times 229 W 43rd St New York NY 10036-3913

SHORY, NASEEB LEIN, dentist, retired state official; b. Birmingham, Ala., Sept. 27, 1925; s. Lein George and Fomeyi (Buhana) S.; m. Mary Jo Howard, Sept. 8, 1951; children: Lawrence G., Richard L., Carl B., Celeste Marie. B.S., U. Ala., 1948; D.D.S., Loyola U., Chgo., 1952; M.P.H., U. Mich., 1962. Diplomate: Am. Bd. Dental Pub. Health. Pvt. practice dentistry Montgomery, Ala., 1952-60; dir. Bur. Dental Health, Ala. Dept. Pub. Health, 1961-68, 73-88; assoc. clin. prof. Med. Coll. Ala., 1966-68; assoc. prof., head dept. community and preventive dentistry La. State U. Sch. Dentistry, 1968-70; prof., chmn. dept. community dentistry Loyola U. of New Orleans, 1968-70; lectr. Tulane U. Sch. Pub. Health and Tropical Medicine, 1968-70; prof., dir. div. health services Sch. Dental Medicine, So. Ill. U., Edwardsville, 1970-72; asst. to dean Sch. Dental Medicine, So. Ill. U., 1972-73, chmn. dept. health ecology, 1970-73; mem. Ala. Bd. Dental Scholarships, 1965-68, 73-87; dir. Ala. Smile Keeper Program, 1976-87; mem. Ala. State Health Advisory Commn., 1977-79; Pres. Profl. Men's Credit Assn., Montgomery, 1960-61; mem. Montgomery Community Council, 1960-61, Youth Adv. Council, Montgomery Police Dept., 1960-61. Contbr. articles to profl. jours. Bd. dirs. Cath. Charities, 1959, 65, 66, New Orleans Area Health Planning Coun., 1968-70; mem. Montgomery Cath. High Sch. Bd., 1975-76, State Com. Pub. Health, Ala., 1988-92; chmn. Parish Coun., St. Joseph Cath. Ch., 1990-92. Served with AUS, 1943-45, ETO. Decorated Purple Heart; recipient Most Excellent Fellow award Ala. Dental Assn., 1968; D.G. Gill award Outstanding Contbn. to Pub. Health in Ala., 1982. Fellow Internat. Coll. Dentists (dep. regent for Ala. 1986-88, dist. V vice regent 1987-88); mem. ADA (chmn. nat. task force on prohibition confection sales in schs. 1978-79, mem. council dental health and health planning 1984-86; Council on Community Health, Hosps., Instns. and Med. Affairs 1986-88), Ill. Dental Assn., La. Dental Assn. (chmn. council on dental health 1969-70), Ala. Dental Assn. (ho. of dels., trustee), Am. Assn. Pub. Health Dentists, Assn. State and Territorial Dental Dirs. (pres. 1980-82, Outstanding Achievement award 1991), Ala. Pub. Health Assn. (pres. 1984-85), Council on Dental Health (state com. on pub. health 1988-92), Optimist Club (v.p. Perdido Bay chpt. 1991-92), Svc. Corps Ret. Execs. Home: 34090 Kathryn Dr Lillian AL 36549-5100

SHOSID, JOSEPH LEWIS, government official; b. Ft. Worth, Aug. 27, 1927; s. Samuel and Lilly Minna (Schneider) S.; children: Sharon Suzann, Steven Stanford; m. Linda D. Johnson, Oct. 8, 1994. BA, Tex. Christian U., 1950, MA, 1952; grad., Indsl. Coll. Armed Forces, Washington. Former exec. profl. baseball with L.A. (Bklyn.) Dodgers farm orgn.; bus. mgr. Ft. Worth Baseball Club, 1950-54; with various newspapers, radio & TV stas. as sportscasting and advt. exec.; pres. Advt. Unlimited, Inc., Ft. Worth, 1954-76; spl. asst. to U.S. Ho. of Reps. Speaker of Ho. Jim Wright 12th Dist. Tex., 1955-89; pres., CEO Shosid & Assocs., Ft. Worth and Washington, 1981—; chmn. Ft. Worth Airpower Coun., 1972-74; mem. adv. coun. Pres.'s Nat. Com. for Employer Support of Guard and Res., 1971—; spl. asst. to Vice Pres. Hubert H. Humphrey, 1966-69. Basketball and football ofcl. NCAA, 1953—, including 13 football bowl games, 21 basketball playoffs, 21 Aloha Classics, 1989-90, Japan Classics, Osaka and Tokyo; liaison officer USAFE-Sports, Ramstein AB, Feb. Republic of Germany, 1964—; referee NCAA Basketball Final Four game, 1973. With AUS, WWII; maj. gen. USAF Ret. Decorated D.S.M., Air Force Legion of Merit, Exceptional Service award USAF, 1975. Mem. Air Force Assn. (past nat. pres. and chmn. bd., Nat. Man of Yr. 1963, Medal of Merit 1962, Exceptional Svc. Plaque 1971, life mem., nat. bd. dirs.), S.W. Basketball Ofcls. Assn. (past pres.), Congl. Staff Club, Aerospace Edn. Found. (Dolittle fellow), Ft. Worth C. of C., Res. Officers Assn., Am. Basketball Assn., Air Force Pub. Affairs Alumni Assn. (life), Nat. Assn. Basketball Coaches, Fed. Internat. Basketball Assn., Naismith Basketball Hall of Fame, Am. Football Coaches Assn., Collegiate Sports Info. Dirs. Am., Atlantic Coast Football Ofcls. Assn. (life), Masons (32 degree), Shriners. Mem. Christian Ch. Home: 1612 Ems Rd W Fort Worth TX 76116-1828 *I had the good fortune of being schooled at an early age that a mind is a terrible thing to waste. And that every American has an obligation to serve his/her country in a constructive way, thus the inspiration for my interest in a military career. Parents who came to America from Lithuania, fleeing the Marxist Revolution didn't have to wait until post World War II to understand or be told about the "Soviet Threat." They saw it first hand. A major thesis of my life has been to be grateful that they had the great courage to immigrate to this great nation and thus allow me the freedom of thought and mind otherwise denied.*

SHOSKY, JOHN EDWIN, communications consultant, speechwriter; b. Colorado Springs, Colo., Nov. 1, 1955; s. Alexander Matthew and Barbara Marie (Middelkamp) S. BA in Polic. Sci., Colo. Coll., 1979; MA in Philosophy, U. Wyo., 1987; PhD in Philosophy, Am. U., 1992. Dep. dir. media and sports commns. White House Conf. for Drug Free Am., Washington, 1987-88; sr. policy analyst White House Office Pub. Affairs, 1988; cons. to sec. HHS, Washington, 1984-91, cons. to Surgeon Gen., 1991-92; cons. to office of nat. drug control policy Exec. Office of the Pres., Washington, 1992-93; pres., sr. writer Roncalli Comm., 1991—; asst. prof. philosophy Am. U., Washington, 1996-97; speech writer for govt. ofcls., corp. execs., profl. athletes, congressmen, senators; lectr. in philosophy Am. U., 1987—, asst. prof., 1996-97; lectr. No. Va. C.C., 1993-95; adj. prof. philosophy George Mason U., 1990-94; vis. sr. mem. Linacru Coll., Oxford, Eng., 1997. Contbr. numerous articles to acad. and profl. jours., trade publs., newsletters, regional and nat. newspapers. Mem. Nat. Assn. Advancement Sci., N.Y. Acad. Sci., Hume Assn., Russell Assn., Mind Assn., British Soc. for the History Philosophy, Colo. Coll. D.C. Alumni Assn., U. Wyo. Alumni Assn., Washington Philosophy Club. Republican. Roman Catholic. Home: 1806 Rollins Dr Alexandria VA 22307-1613 Office: Dept Philosophy & Religion American Univ Washington DC 20016

SHOSS, CYNTHIA RENÉE, lawyer; b. Cape Girardeau, Mo., Nov. 29, 1950; d. Milton and Carroll Jane (Duncan) S.; m. David Goodwin Watson, Apr. 13, 1986; 1 child, Lucy J. Watson. BA cum laude, Newcomb Coll., 1971; JD, Tulane U., 1974; LLM in Taxation, NYU, 1980. Bar: La. 1974, Mo. 1977, Ill. 1978, N.Y. 1990. Law clk. to assoc. and chief justices La. Supreme Ct., New Orleans, 1974-76; assoc. Stone, Pigman et al, New Orleans, 1976-77, Lewis & Rice, St. Louis, 1977-79, Curtis, Mallet-Prevost, et al, N.Y.C., 1980-82; ptnr. LeBoeuf, Lamb, Greene & MacRae, L.L.P., N.Y.C., 1982—; mng. ptnr. London office LeBoeuf, Lamb, Leiby & MacRae, 1987-89; assoc. editor Tulane Law Rev., 1972-74; frequent speaker before profl. orgns. and assns. Contbr. articles to profl. jours. Mem. ABA, Am. Mgmt. Assn. (ins. and risk mgmt. coun.), Corp. Bar Westchester and Fairfield, Lawyers Alliance N.Y. (chair, bd. dirs.). Office: LeBoeuf Lamb Greene Et Al 125 W 55th St New York NY 10019-5369

SHOSTAKOVICH, MAXIM DMITRIYEVICH, symphonic conductor; b. Leningrad, USSR, May 10, 1938; came to U.S., 1981; s. Dmitri Dmitriyevich and Nina (Varzar) S.; 1 child, Dmitri; m. Marina Tisie; children: Maria, Maxim. Student, Leningrad Conservatory, 1961-62, Moscow Conservatory, 1963; DFA, U. Md., 1982. Asst. condr. Moscow Symphony Orch., 1963-66, Moscow State Symphony Orch., 1966-69; prin. condr., artistic dir. Orch. Radio and TV USSR, Moscow, 1971-81; mus. advisor Hartford Symphony Orch., Conn., 1985; prin. guest condr. Hong Kong Philharm., 1982—; music dir. New Orleans Symphony Orch., 1986-91; hon. music dir. La. Philharmonic Orch., 1993-94. Debut London Philharm. Orch., 1968; toured Can., U.S., Mex. with USSR State Symphony Orch., 1969; guest condr., Europe, N.Am., Japan and Australia; pianist including Piano Concerto No. 2; rec. father's ballet compositions including Bolt, The Age of God, suites, music for films Zoya, Pirogov with Bolshoi Theater Orch., Shostakovich Symphonies; recs. EMI, Philips, Chandos including Shostakovich's Violin Concerto No. 1, Shostakovich's Symphony No. 5, Suite on Verses of Michelangelo, 1971, 77, Piano Concerti Nos. 1 and 2 rec. with Philips Shostakovich's Cello Concerti, 1984. Recipient Outstanding Performance for Arts award Combo Fund Campaign, 1982. Mem. Concert Artists Guild, Great Artists Series NYU (exec. bd. Gallatin div. N.Y.C.). Home: 173 Black Rock Tpke West Redding CT 06896-2519 Office: care Columbia Artists Mgmt Inc 165 W 57th St New York NY 10019-2201

SHOTTS, WAYNE J., nuclear scientist, federal agency administrator; b. Des Plaines, Ill., Mar. 20, 1945; s. Norman Russell Shotts and Winnifred Mae (Averill) Shotts Goeppinger; m. Melinda Maureen Antilla, June 24, 1967 (dec. Feb. 1975); children: Kenneth Wayne Shotts, Jeffrey Alan Shotts; m. Jacquelyn Francyle Willis, Aug. 11, 1979. BA in Physics, U. Calif., Santa Barbara, 1967; PhD, Cornell U., 1973. Rsch. physicist E.I. duPont deNemours & Co., Wilmington, Del., 1973-74; physicist U. Calif., Livermore, Calif., 1974—, Lawrence Livermore (Calif.) Nat. Lab., 1974-79; group leader, thermonuclear design divsn. Lawrence Livermore Nat. Lab., Livermore, Calif., 1979-85, divsn leader, nuclear chemistry, 1985-86, divsn. leader, prompt diagnostics, 1986-88, prin. dep. assoc. dir., military applications, 1988-92, prin. dep. assoc. dir. def. and nuclear techs., 1992-95, assoc. dir. nonproliferation arms control/internat. security, 1995—. Recipient Ernest Orlando Lawrence Meml. award U.S. Dept. Energy, Washington, 1990. Mem. Am. Phys. Soc., Am. Assn. Advancement Sci. Office: Lawrence Livermore Nat Lab PO Box 808 Livermore CA 94551-0808

SHOTWELL, CHERRIE LEIGH, speech and language pathologist; b. Munich, Nov. 15, 1950; parents Am. citizens; d. William Bedford and Pauline Leona (Bainbridge) S. BA with distinction, U. Redlands, 1973, MS, 1975. Cert. lang., speech and hearing tchr., Calif. Speech and lang. therapist Hawaii Dept. Edn., Wahiawa, 1976-86; lang. and speech specialist L.A. County Dept. Edn., Downey, Calif., 1986-87; day treatment instr. Assn. Retarded Citizens, Honolulu, 1987-88; speech and lang. pathologist Honolulu Cmty. Action Program, 1988-89, Hawaii Speech Pathology, Honolulu, 1989-90, Med. Pers. Pool, Honolulu, 1990-94, Hawaii Dept. Edn., Waipahu, 1994—. Mem. Hawaii Speech Lang. Hearing Assn. (com. chairperson Licensure and Ethics 1978-79). Democrat. Avocations: swimming, sailing, fashion design. Home: 1015 Laakea Pl Honolulu HI 96818-1987

SHOTWELL, MALCOLM GREEN, retired minister; b. Brookneal, Va., Aug. 14, 1932; s. John Henry and Ada Mildred (Puckett) S.; m. LaVerne Brown, June 19, 1954; children: Donna (dec.), Paula. BA in Sociology, U. Richmond, 1954; MDiv, Colgate Rochester Div. Sch., 1957; D Ministry, Ea. Bapt. Theol. Sem., 1990; DD (hon.), Judson Coll., 1990. Ordained to ministry Am. Bapt. Ch. in U.S.A., 1957. Student asst. Greece Bapt. Ch., Rochester, N.Y., 1954-57; pastor 1st Bapt. Ch., Cuba, N.Y., 1957-62; sr. pastor 1st Bapt. Ch., Galesburg, Ill., 1962-71, Olean, N.Y., 1971-81; area minister Am. Bapt. Chs. of Pa. and Del., 1981-90; regional exec. minister Am. Bapt. Chs. of Great Rivers Region, Ill. and Mo., 1990-96; ret., 1997; mem. Midwest Commn. on Ministry, Am. Bapt. Chs. U.S.A., 1990-96, mem. task force for So. Bapt.Am. Bapt. Chs. Relationships, 1990-96. Author: Creative Programs for the Church Year, 1986, Renewing the Baptist Principle of Associations, 1990-96. Trustee No. Bapt. Theol. Sem., Lombard, Ill., 1993-96, Judson Coll., Elgin, Ill., 1990—, mem. gen. bd. ABC, 1990-96, chmn. Junson Trustees, 1997—, mem. gen. exec. coun., 1990-96, regional exec. ministers coun., 1990-96, chmn. Judson trustees, 1997—; bd. dirs. Cen. Bapt. Theol. Sem., Kansas City, Kans., 1990-96; sec. bd. dirs. Shurtleff Fund, Springfield, Ill., 1990-96. Walter Pope Binns fellow William Jewell Coll., 1995. Mem. Ministers Coun. Ill. and Mo.

SHOUB, EARLE PHELPS, chemical engineer, educator; b. Washington, July 19, 1915; m. Elda Robinson; children: Casey Louis, Heather Margaret Shoub Dills. BS in Chemistry, Poly. U., 1938, postgrad. 1938-39. Chemist, Hygrade Food Products Corp., N.Y.C., 1940-41, Nat. Bur. Standards, 1941-43; regional dir. U.S. Bur. Mines, 1943-62, chief divsn. Accident Prevention & Health, 1962-70; dep. dir. Appalachian Lab. Occupational Respiratory Diseases, Nat. Inst. Occupational Safety and Health, Morgantown, W.Va., 1970-77, dep. dir. div. safety research, 1977-79; mgr. occupational safety, indsl. environ. cons., safety products div. Am. Optical Corp., Southbridge, Mass., 1979; cons., 1979—; assoc. clin. prof. dept. anesthesiology W.Va. U. Med. Center, Morgantown, 1977-82, prof. Coll. Mineral and Energy Resources, 1970-79. Recipient Disting. Service award Dept. Interior and Gold medal, 1959. Registered profl. engr.; cert. safety profl. Fellow Am. Inst. Chemists; mem. AIME, ASTM, NSPE, ANSI, Am. Indsl. Hygiene Assn. (emeritus mem.), Vets. of Safety, Am. Soc. Safety Engrs., Nat. Fire Protection Assn. (life), Am. Conf. Govtl. Indsl. Hygienists, Internat. Soc. Respiratory Protection (past pres., William H. Revoir award 1993), Am. Nat. Standards Inst., Sigma Xi. Methodist. Contbr. articles to profl. jours. and texts. Home: 5850 Meridian Rd Apt 202C Gibsonia PA 15044-9690

SHOULSON, BRUCE DOVE, lawyer; b. Phila., Feb. 12, 1940; s. I. Harry and Sonia (Rosen) S.; m. Robyn Winkler, June 16, 1963; children: Jeffrey S., Mark E., Adina L. AB, Columbia U., 1961; LLB, Harvard U., 1964. Bar: N.J. 1965, U.S. Dist. Ct. N.J. 1965, U.S. Ct. Appeals (3d cir.) 1967, U.S. Supreme Ct. 1977. Law sec. to hon. chief justice Joseph Weintraub N.J. Supreme Ct., Newark, 1964-65; assoc. Lowenstein, Sandler, Kohl, Fisher & Boylan, P.C., Newark, 1965-70; ptnr. Lowenstein, Sandler, Kohl, Fisher & Boylan, P.C., Roseland, N.J., 1970—. V.p. Daus. of Israel Geriatric Ctr., West Orange, N.J., 1988-90; pres., chair bd. Hebrew Youth Acad., West Caldwell, N.J., 1979-83; bd. dirs. Rabbi Isaac Elchanan Theol. Sem. of Yeshiva U., N.Y.C., 1986—. Recipient Young Leadership award Jewish Community Fedn. of Met. N.J., 1977, Community Leadership award Agudath Israel of Am., 1983. Mem. ABA, N.J. Bar Assn., Essex County Bar Assn. Office: Lowenstein Sandler Kohl Fisher & Boylan PC 65 Livingston Ave Roseland NJ 07068-1725

SHOUP, ANDREW JAMES, JR., oil company executive; b. Monroe, La., Mar. 26, 1935; s. Andrew James Sr. and Ruth (Landis) S.; m. Sue Cowles, Sept. 12, 1959; children: Catherine Shoup Collins, Andrew James III. BS in Petroleum Engring., La. State U., 1957; M in Indsl. Adminstrn., Yale U., 1959. Registered engr., Tex. Prodn. engr. Continental Oil Co., Houston, 1959-65; v.p. DeGolyer and MacNaughton, Dallas, 1965-74; chmn., chief exec. officer Sabine Corp., Dallas, 1974-89; pres. Pacific Enterprises Oil Co. U.S.A, Dallas, 1989-90; pres., chief exec. officer The Wiser Oil Co., Dallas, 1991—. 2nd lt. U.S. Army, 1959-60. Mem. Am. Petroleum Inst., Ind. Prodrs. Assn. Am., Soc. Petroleum Engrs. of AIME, Dallas Petroleum Club, Dallas Country Club. Avocations: skiing, jogging, tennis. Office: The Wiser Oil Co 8115 Preston Rd Ste 400 Dallas TX 75225-6311

SHOUP, CARL SUMNER, retired economist; b. San Jose, Calif., Oct. 26, 1902; s. Paul and Rose (Wilson) S.; m. Ruth Snedden, Sept. 27, 1924; children: Dale, Paul Snedden, Donald Sumner (dec.). AB, Stanford U., 1924; PhD, Columbia U., 1930; PhD (hon.), U. Strasbourg, 1967. Mem. faculty Columbia U., 1928-71; dir. Internat. Econ. Integration Program and Capital Tax Project, 1962-64; Editor Bull. Nat. Tax Assn., 1931-35; staff mem. N.Y. State Spl. Tax Commns., 1930-35; tax study U.S. Dept. Treasury, June-Sept. 1934, Aug.-Sept. 1937, asst. to sec. Treasury, Dec. 1937-Aug. 1938, research cons., 1938-46, 62-68; interregional adviser, tax reform planning UN, 1972-74; sr. Killam fellow Dalhousie U., 1974-75; staff Council of Econ. Advisers, 1946-49; dir. Twentieth Century Fund Survey of Taxation in U.S., 1935-37, Fiscal Survey of Venezuela, 1958, Shoup Tax Mission to Japan, 1949-50, Tax Mission to Liberia, 1969; co-dir. N.Y.C. finance study, 1950-52; pres. Internat. Inst. Pub. Finance, 1950-53; cons. Carnegie Ctr. for Transnat. Studies, 1976, Harvard Inst. for Internat. Devel., 1978-83, Venezuelan Fiscal Commn., 1980-83, Jamaica Tax Project, 1985, World Bank Value-Added Tax Study, 1986-87, Duke U. Tax Missions Study, 1987-88; vis. prof. Monash U., 1984. Author: The Sales Tax in France, 1930, (with E.R.A. Seligman) A Report on the Revenue System of Cuba, 1932, (with Robert M. Haig and others) The Sales Tax in the American States, 1934, (with Roy Blough and Mabel Newcomer) Facing the Tax Problem, 1937, (with Roswell Magill) The Fiscal System of Cuba, 1939, Federal Finances in the Coming Decade, 1941, Taxing to Prevent Inflation, 1943, Principles of National Income Analysis, 1947, (with others) Report on Japanese Taxation, 1949, (with others) The Fiscal System of Venezuela, 1959, Ricardo on Taxation, 1960,reprinted, 1992, The Tax System of Brazil, 1965, Federal Estate and Gift Taxes, 1966, Public Finance, 1969 (transl. into Japanese 1974, Spanish 1979), (with others) The Tax System of Liberia, 1970; Editor: Fiscal Harmonization in Common Markets, 1966. Decorated Order Sacred Treasure (Japan), Grand Cordon. Disting. fellow Am. Econ.

Assn.; mem. Nat. Tax Assn. (pres. 1949-50, hon. mem.), Phi Beta Kappa. Address: 21 Ledges Dr Laconia NH 03246

SHOUP, CHARLES SAMUEL, JR., chemicals and materials executive; b. Nashville, Dec. 10, 1935; s. Charles Samuel and Leola Ruth (Turner) S.; m. Frances Carolyn DiCarlo, June 7, 1958; children: Mark Steven, Elizabeth Ann Shoup Kehoe, Margaret Carol Shoup Meyer. AB, Princeton U., 1957; MS, U. Tenn., 1961, PhD, 1962. Rsch. chemist Oak Ridge (Tenn.) Natl. Lab., 1962-67; mgr. special projects Union Carbide Corp., N.Y.C., 1967-68; mgr. planning and controls Bell and Howell Co., Lincolnwood, Ill., 1968; v.p. Bell and Howell Sch. Inc., Chgo., 1968-69; mgr. tech. planning Cabot Corp., Boston and Cambridge, Mass., 1969-70, dir. corp. rsch., Mass., 1970-73, gen. mgr. E-A-R div., 1973-87, v.p., Indpls., 1984-87; pres. Alphaflex Ind. Inc., Indpls, 1987-88, bd. dirs., 1988, Cemkote Corp., Indpls., 1988-91; chmn. bd. dirs. Blasterz Corp., Carmel, Ind., 1992—; mem. adv. bd. Technalysis, Inc., Indpls., 1996—; bd. dirs. Exec. Svc. Corps, Indpls., 1993—, mem. exec. com., 1994—, v.p., 1997—; mem. bd. visitors Coll. Arts and Scis., U. Tenn., Knoxville, 1994—. Contbr. articles to profl. jours.; patentee in field. Treas. Oak Ridge Community Arts Ctr., 1965-67; pres. Sherborn Edn. Found., 1974-76; chmn. Met. Div. United Way, 1982; bd. trustees, Ind. Safety Equipment Assn. 1978-81. Fellow Am. Inst. Chemists; mem. AAAS, Am. Chem. Soc., Noise Control Products and Materials Assn. (trustee 1977-87, pres. 1982-84), Sigma Xi. Presbyterian. Home: 13019 Andover Dr Carmel IN 46033-2419

SHOUP, MICHAEL C., newspaper reporter, editor; b. Ringtown, Pa., July 17, 1940; s. Daniel George and Marie E (Fisher) S.; m. Mary Ellen Trimble, Jan. 2, 1965 (div. 1984); children: Rachael, Timothy; m. Mary Jo Crowley, July 22, 1988; stepchildren: David, Benjamin. BA, Moravian Coll., 1965; MS, Columbia U., 1966. Russian linguist intelligence svc. USAF, 1957-61; reporter, editor Phila. Bull., 1967-71; night city editor Phila. Inquirer, 1973, day city editor, 1974, mng. editor Phila. Inquirer Mag., 1975-79, travel editor, columnist, 1980-96; travel editor The Star-Ledger, Newark, 1996—; travel columnist for Knight-Ridder newspapers, 1980—. Avocations: bicycling, gardening. Home: 204 Totowa Rd Wayne NJ 07470 Office: The Star Ledger One Star Ledger Plz Newark NJ 07102

SHOVER, JOAN, secondary school educator; b. St. Joseph, Mo., Apr. 7, 1948; d. Jay S. and Clara Lillian (Burkett) Marquis; m. Rolland Craig Shover, May 31, 1975; children: Terra Jayne, Thomas Jay. BS in Edn., Ctrl. Mo. State U., 1971, MS in Edn., 1976, postgrad., 1989—. Cert. tchr., Mo. Phys. edn. tchr. Worth County H.S., Grant City, Mo., 1971-73, Blue Springs (Mo.) H.S., 1973—; mem. rev. com. Mo. Dept. Elem. and Secondary Edn., Jefferson City, 1993—. Named Am. Cancer Soc. Educator of Yr., 1989, Top 36 Am. Tchrs. award, Disney Corp., 1992, Mo. State Secondary Physical Educator of Yr., 1996. Mem. AAHPERD (ctrl. dist. secondary phys. educator of yr. 1997), NEA, Am. Coun. on Exercise, Internat. Dance Exercise Assn., Mo. Assn. Phys. Edn., Health, Recreation and Dance (Kansas City Dist. Phys. Educator asard 1989, Prewsl. award, Kansas City rep. 1988—), Mo. State Tchrs. Assn., Pilot Club. Avocations: reading, dancing, skiing, running. Home: 1418 NW A St Blue Springs MO 64015-3605 Office: 200 Ashton Dr Blue Springs MO 64015

SHOVLIN, JOSEPH PATRICK, optometrist. BA in Psychology, Gettysburg Coll., 1974; BS in Physiol. Optics, Pa. Coll. of Optometry, 1978, D of Optometry, 1980. Cert. optometrist Pa., N.Y., Va., Md. Assoc. Morrison Assocs., Harrisburg Pa., N.Y.C., 1980-85; clin. assoc. Northeastern Eye Inst., Scranton, Pa., 1985-91; sr. optometrist Northwestern Eye Inst., 1991—; cons. Lancaster County Blind Assn., Lancaster, Pa., 1980-85, State Bd. of Optometry, Commonwealth of Pa., 1988-90, Ophthalmic Devices' Adv. Panel, Ctr. for Devices and Radiological Health, Food and Drug Adminstrn., 1987-88, 1992-93; adj. faculty Pa. Coll. of Optometry, 1981—; cons. and expert witness Bur. of Profl. and Occupational Affairs, Commonwealth of Pa., 1983-85; voting mem. Ophthalmic Devices Adv. Panel, Ctr. for Devices and Radiological Health, Food and Drugs Administrn., 1988-92; presenter over 200 formal lectures to major internat., nat., regional and state ophthalmic groups. Author: (with others) Problems in Optometry, 1990, Clinical Contact Lens Practice, 1991, Optometric Pharmacology, 1992, Anterior Segment Complications of Contact Lens Wear, 1994; contbr. numerous articles to profl. jours. including: Review of Optometry (contbg. editor 1984-88, assoc. clin. editor 1988—), Metabolic, Pediatric and Systemic Ophthalmology, Contact Lens Forum, Focus on Product News, International Contact Lens Clinic (contbg. editor 1988-93), Primary Care Optometry News, (cons. editor, 1995—), Contemporary Optometry, Contact Lens Spectrum (consulting editor 1988—), Optometric Management (contbg. editor 1992-95), Practical Optometry, Review of Ophthalmology, American Acad. of Optometry Newsletter; assoc. editor Making Contact, 1982-88, 94—; editl. bd. Contacto; mem. jour. rev. bd. Optometry Clinics, 1991—; cons. editor Primary Care Optometry News, 1995—; referee, mem. jour. review bd. Jour. Am. Optometric Assn. and Optometry and Vision Sci. Mem. sci. adv. com. Pa. Lions' Sight Conservation and Eye Rsch. Found., nat. adv. eye coun. Nat. Eye Inst. Nat. Insts. Health, 1992-96. Fellow Am. Acad. Optometry (diplomate cornea and contact lens sect. 1985, mem. exec. bd., sec., spkrs. bur., bd. dirs. Pa. chpt. past mem., numerous other coms.); mem. APHA, Internat. Soc. Refractive Surgery (assoc.), Am. Optometric Assn. (sec. contact lens sect. 1988-89, vice chair 1989-90, chair elect 1990-91, chair 1991-92, immediate past chair 1992-93, mem. jour. rev. bd., numerous other coms. and offices, Am. Optometric Recognition award 1980—), Pa. Optometric Assn. (chmn. continuing edn. com. 1993, Keystone contact lens conf. 1987—, com. on contact lenses 1986-94, others), The Assn. for Rsch. in Vision and Ophthalmology, Nat. Eye Rsch. Found., Am. Optometric Found. (bd. dirs. 1988-90), The Prentice Soc., Adv. Bd. Eye Vision Assocs., The Optometric Coun. of the State of N.Y. (Disting. Svc. award 1984). Home: 1308 Oakmont Rd Clark's Summit PA 18411 Office: Northeastern Eye Inst 200 Mifflin Ave Scranton PA 18503-1907

SHOWALTER, BUCK (WILLIAM NATHANIEL SHOWALTER, III), major league baseball team manager; b. DeFuniak Springs, Fla., May 23, 1956. Student, Chipola Jr. Coll., Fla., Miss. State U. Player various minor league teams N.Y. Yankee orgn., 1977-83, minor league coach, 1984, minor league mgr., 1985-89; coach N.Y. Yankees, 1990-91, mgr., 1992-95; with Ariz. Diamondbacks, 1996—. Named N.Y.-Pa. League Mgr. of Yr., 1985, Eastern League Mgr. of Yr., 1989, Am. League Mgr. of Yr., 1994. Office: Arizona Diamondbacks PO Box 2095 Phoenix AZ 85001*

SHOWALTER, ELAINE, humanities educator; b. Cambridge, Mass., Jan. 21, 1941; d. Paul and Violet (Rotenberg) Cottler; m. English Showalter, June 8, 1963; children: Vinca, Michael. BA, Bryn Mawr Coll., 1962; MA, Brandeis U., 1964; PhD in English, U. Calif., Davis, 1970. Teaching asst. English U. Calif., 1964-66, from instr. to assoc. prof., 1967-78; prof. English Rutgers U., from 1978, Avalon Found. prof. humanities, Princeton (N.J.) U., 1984—; Avalon Found. prof. humanities Princeton (N.J.) U., 1987—; vis. prof. English and women's studies U. Del., 1976-77; vis. prof. Sch. Criticism and Theory, Dartmouth Coll., 1986; prof. Salzburg (Austria) Seminars, 1988; Clarendon lectr. Oxford (Eng.) U., 1989; vis. scholar Phi Beta Kappa, 1993-94; numerous radio and TV appearances. Author: A Literature of Their Own, 1977, The Female Malady, 1985, Sexual Anarchy, 1990, Sister's Choice, 1991, Hystories, 1997; co-author: Hysteria Beyond Freud, 1993; editor: These Modern Women, 1978, The New Feminist Criticism, 1985, Alternative Alcott, 1987, Speaking of Gender, 1989, Modern American Women Writers, 1991, Daughters of Decadence, 1993, Scribbling Women, 1997; also articles and revs. Recipient Howard Behrman humanities award Princeton U., 1989; faculty rsch. coun. fellow Ruthers U., 1972-73, Guggenheim fellow, 1977-78, Rockefeller humanities fellow, 1981-82, fellow NEH, 1988-89. Mem. MLA (v.p. 1996-97). Office: Princeton U Dept of English Princeton NJ 08544

SHOWALTER, ENGLISH, JR., French language educator; b. Roanoke, Va., May 14, 1935; m. 1963; 2 children. B.A., Yale U., 1957, Ph.D. in French, 1964. Asst. prof. French Haverford Coll., 1961-64, U. Calif.-Davis, 1964-66, Princeton U., N.J., 1966-74; assoc. prof. Rutgers U., Camden, N.J., 1974-78; prof. Rutgers U., 1978-83, disting prof., 1985—; dir. MLA, N.Y.C., 1983-85. Author: The Evolution of the French Novel, 1641-1782, 1972, Voltaire et ses Amis, D'apres la Correspondance de Mme De Graffigny, 1975, Rousseau and Mme De Graffigny, 1978, Exiles and Strangers: A Reading of Camus's Exile and the Kingdom, 1984, Humanity and the Absurd: Camus' The Stranger, 1989, My Night at Maud's, 1993. Fellow NEH, 1977-78; Guggenheim fellow, 1982-83. Mem. MLA, Am. Assn. Tchrs. French, Am. Soc. 18th Century Studies, French Soc. 18th Century Studies. Office: Rutgers Univ French Dept Camden NJ 08102

SHOWALTER, ROBERT EARL, banker; b. Vienna, W.Va., Feb. 16, 1937; s. Clay and Edna Melinda (Mahaney) S.; m. Shirley Anita Tessmer, June 24, 1961; children: Brent Alan, Lynn Allison, Eric Michael, Dean Edward. BS, Marietta Coll., 1959; MBA, Case Western Res. U., 1964; postgrad. Advanced Mgmt. Program, Harvard U., 1983. Mgmt. trainee Republic Steel, Cleve., 1959-60; sr. v.p. Fed. Res. Bank, Cin., 1960-84; pres., CEO Commerce Nat. Bank, Lexington, Ky., 1984-90; pres., CEO Nat. City Bank, Toledo, 1990-95, Akron, Ohio, 1996—; trustee Ohio Council Econ. Edn., 1980-83, Toledo C. of C., 1990-95, chmn., 1993-94. Trustee Good Samaritan Hosp., Cin., 1979-85, Rotary Found., 1982-84, ARC, 1981-85, Cardinal Hill Hops., 1985-90, sec., 1989-90, Med. Coll. Ohio, 1991-95; bd. dirs. United Way Bluegrass, 1985-90, campaign chmn., 1987, v.p., 1989. Named Disting. Alumnus, Marietta Coll., 1982. Mem. Thoroughbred of Am. Club, Firestone C. of C., Glenmoor C. of C., Wilderness C. of C., Portage C. of C., Akron City Club, Akron Regional Devel. Bd., Akron Tomorrow. United Methodist. Home: 6301 Bertram Ave NW Canton OH 44718-2261 Office: Nat City Bank 1 Cascade Plz Akron OH 44308

SHOWALTER-KEEFE, JEAN, data processing executive; b. Louisville, Mar. 11, 1938; d. William Joseph and Phyllis Rose (Reis) Showalter; m. James Washburn Keefe, Dec. 6, 1980. BA, Spalding U., 1963, MS in Edn. Adminstrn., 1969. Cert. tchr., Ky. Tchr., asst. prin. Louisville Cath. Schs., 1958-71; cons. and various editorial positions Harcourt Brace Jovanovich Co., Chgo. and N.Y.C., 1972-82; dir. editorial Ednl. Challenges, Alexandria, Va., 1982-83; mgr. project to cons. Xerox Corp., Leesburg, Va., 1983-88, mgr. systems edn., 1988-89; curriculum devel. mgr. corp. edn. and tng. Xerox Corp. Hdqrs., Stamford, Conn., 1989-94; mem. bd. Belcastle Cluster Assocs., Reston, Va., 1994—, pres. bd., 1995—, 1995—, mgmt. and sys. cons., 1995—; mem. adv. bd. Have a Heart Homes for Abused Children, 1991-93; instr. Sales Exec. Club N.Y., 1974-79; cons., Houston, 1980-83. Moderator Jr. Achievement, Louisville, 1968-70; cons. Future Bus. Leaders Am., Dade County, Fla. 1983. Named Outstanding Young Educator Louisville Jaycees, 1968. Mem. Nat. Assn. Female Execs., Am. Soc. Tng. and Devel., Am. Mgmt. Assn. Avocations: gardening, classical music. Home and Office: 1419 Belcastle Ct Reston VA 22094-1245

SHOWER, ROBERT WESLEY, financial executive; b. Harvey, Ill., Sept. 5, 1937; s. Glenn Wesley and Chrissie Irene (Ford) S.; m. Sandra Marie Stough, June 27, 1959; children: David Wesley, Lynece Marie. B.S., U. Tulsa, 1960; P.M.D., Harvard Business Sch., 1972. Sr. auditor Arthur Andersen & Co., Tulsa, 1960-64; with The Williams Cos., Tulsa, 1964-86; asst. v.p. The Williams Cos., 1968-69, v.p. adminstrn., 1969-71, v.p., treas., 1971, v.p. fin., 1971-73, sr. v.p. fin., 1973-77, exec. v.p. fin. and adminstrn., dir., 1977-86; mng. dir. Shearson, Lehman, Hutton, Dallas, 1986-90; v.p. fin. Ameriserv Food Co., Dallas, 1990-91; sr. v.p. fin., CFO Seagull Energy Co., Houston, 1992-94, exec. v.p., CFO, 1994-96. Mem. Okla. Soc. CPAs, Bent Tree Country Club (Dallas), Lambda Chi Alpha, Delta Sigma Pi. Home: 17224 Village Ln Dallas TX 75248-6047

SHOWERS, RALPH MORRIS, electrical engineer educator; b. Plainfield, N.J., Aug. 7, 1918; s. Ralph W. and Angelina (Jackson) S.; m. Beatrice Anne Cicko, July 11, 1944; children—Virginia Ann, Janet Lynne, Carolin Joan. B.S., U. Pa., 1939, M.S., 1941, Ph.D., 1950. Lab. asst. Farnsworth Radio & Television, 1939-40; test engr. Gen. Electric Co., Phila., Schenectady, 1940-41; lab. asst. U. Pa., Phila., 1941-43, instr. elec. engring., 1942-43, research engr., lab. supr., 1943-45, from asst. prof. elec. engring. to assoc. prof., 1945-58, prof., 1959-89, prof. emeritus, 1989—; v.p. Internat. Spl. Com. on Radio Interference, 1973-79, chmn., 1979-85; v.p. U.S. nat. com. Internat. Electrotech. Commn., 1975-94, chmn. accredited stds. com. C63, 1968—, chmn. com. of action adv. com. on electromagnetic compatibility, 1986-91; cons. Dept. Navy; cons. interference reduction panel R & D bd. Dept. Def., 1945; mem. spl. mission OSRD, Washington, 1945. Contbr. articles to profl. jours. Recipient Astin-Polk Internat. Standards medal Am. Nat. Standards Inst., 1991, meritorious achievement award 1995. Fellow IEEE (Charles Proteus Steinmetz award 1982, Centennial medal 1984, Standards medallion 1991); mem. EMC Soc. (life), Ops. Research Soc. Am., Am. Soc. Engring. Edn., Am. Nat. Standards Inst., AAUP, Sigma Xi. Home: 223 Oxford Rd Havertown PA 19083-3906 Office: U Pa Moore Sch Elec Engring Philadelphia PA 19104-6390

SHOWERY, CHARLES GEORGE, JR., financial services company executive, consultant; b. El Paso, Tex., Sept. 28, 1951; s. Charles George and Mildred Marie (Romeu) S.; 1 child, Raelene Marie. Degree in med. microbiology, U. Tex., El Paso, 1976. Lab. mgr. Glass-Columbia Med., Conn., 1976-82; agt. Transamerica Life Cos., L.A., 1982-84; pres. Chico Enterprises, El Paso, 1984—; instr. Life Underwriters Tng. Coun., L.A., 1982. Author: It's a Great Career But, 1974, (booklet) M.D. vs. M.T., 1974. Mem. Nat. Assn. Life Underwriters. Democrat. Roman Catholic. Office: Chico Enterprises PO Box 220217 El Paso TX 79913-2217

SHOWS, WINNIE M., speaker, author, consultant; b. L.A., Apr. 2, 1947; d. William Marion Arvin and Joan Catherine (Sperry) Wilson; m. George Albert Shows, Mar. 18, 1967 (div. May 1980); 1 child, Sallie; m. Michael P. Florio, Jan. 1, 1990 (div.). BA in English, UCLA, 1969; MEd, Calif. State U., Long Beach, 1976. Tchr. St. Joseph High Sch., Lakewood, Calif., 1969-71; tchr. high sch. Irvine (Calif) Unified Sch. Dist., 1972-79; freelance writer, 1979-80; mgr. pub. rels. Forth, Inc., Hermosa Beach, Calif., 1980-81; account mgr., account supr., dir. mktg. Franson & Assoc., San Jose, Calif., 1981-84; v.p., pres. Smith & Shows, Menlo Park, Calif., 1984-96. Author (newsletter) Smith & Shows Letter, 1989-94. Vol. Unity Palo Alto (Calif.) Cmty. Ch., 1989-94, Newcomers, Menlo Park, 1990-93, Kara, Palo Alto, 1991-94, Menlo Park Sch. Dist., 1993—. Named Woman of Vision, Career Action Ctr., 1994. Mem. Nat. Spkrs. Assn. (SRI Organon Toastmaster of the Yr. 1995, Karl Lind award 1996). Avocations: writing, reading, gardening. Home: PO Box 2796 Menlo Park CA 94026-2796 Office: Profl Speaker 872 Coleman Ave Menlo Park CA 94025-2408

SHPERLING, IRENA, internist; b. Tallin, Estonia, Sept. 20, 1938; came to U.S., 1976; d. Ber Epstein and Maria Minkov; m. Betsalel R. Shperling, June 16, 1960; 1 child, Elena. MD, First Pavlov's Med. Inst., Leningrad, Russia, 1961. Diplomate Am. Bd. Internal Medicine. Med. dr. City Hosp., Leningrad, USSR, 1961-75; resident in internal medicine Winthrop U. Hosp. SUNY, 1977-80; gen. practice medicine Mineola, N.Y., 1980—. Mem. Am. Soc. Internal Medicine, N.Y. State Soc. Internal Medicine, Nassau County Soc. Internal Medicine, Am. Coll. Physicians, Am. Coll. Physicians, Nat. Assn. Female Execs. Avocations: art, travel, music. Office: Nassau Internists 134 Mineola Blvd Mineola NY 11501-3959

SHRADER, CHARLES REGINALD, historian; b. Nashville, July 3, 1943; s. Reginald Woodrow and Freda Olene (Presley) S.; m. Carole Anne Analore, Aug. 17, 1963; children: Peter Reginald, Sheila Lynne Shrader Bixby. BA cum laude, Vanderbilt U., 1964; MA History, Columbia U., 1970, M Phil, 1974, PhD History, 1976; Grad., U.S. Army Command/Gen. Staff, Coll., 1978, U.S. Army War Coll., 1982, NATO Def. Coll., 1984. Commd. 2d lt. U.S. Army, 1964, advanced through grades to lt. col., retired, 1987; asst. prof. history U.S. Mil. Acad., 1971-74; instr. European Div. U. Md., Pirmasens and Landstuhl, Germany, 1974-77; instr. U.S. Army Command and Gen. Staff Coll., 1977-80, U.S. Army War Coll., 1980-84; mem. staff NATO Def. Coll., Rome, 1984-85; independent historian, 1987—; exec. dir. Soc. for Mil. History, Carlisle, Pa., 1992—; adj. instr. Elizabethtown Coll., 1988-89, Penn State U.-Harrisburg, 1988-90; lectr. various Army svc. schs., CIA, U. Kans., U. Victoria/B.C., NATO Def. Coll. Mem. Carlisle Mcpl. Authority, 1993—; pres. sch. bd. St. Patrick Sch., Carlisle. Mem. Army and Navy Club, Phi Kappa Psi, Phi Beta Kappa. Roman Catholic. Home and Office: 910 Forbes Rd Carlisle PA 17013

SHRADER, LYNNE ANN, secondary school educator, coach; b. Concord, Mass., May 13, 1955; d. Arthur E. Jr. and Helen Louise (Eaton) Fay; m. John Neal Shrader, Nov. 11, 1978; children: Kristen Michelle, Michael Aaron. BS in Phys. Edn. and Health, Fla. So. Coll., 1978; postgrad., U. Tex., 1984, Augusta (Ga.) Coll., 1989—. Cert. middle level sci., life phys. edn. and health tchr., Tex., health and phys. edn. tchr. (K-12), Ga. Tchr. sci. Copperas Cove (Tex.) Jr. High Sch., 1982-83; tchr., coach Manor Mid. Sch., Killeen, Tex., 1983-85; tchr. phys. edn. John Milledge Elem. Sch., Augusta, Ga., 1985-86, Blythe (Ga.) Elem. Sch., 1986-88, Terrace Manor Elem. Sch., 1988-90; tchr. phys. edn., health, coach, dept. chair Lakeside Mid. Sch., Evans, Ga., 1990—; recreation specialist Frankfurt (Germany) Mil. Comty. Recreation Svcs., 1978-80, Richmond County Recreation and Parks Dept., Augusta, 1986-91; dir. Spl. Edn. Summer Camp Free-To-Be-Me, 1995; dir. transp. Summer Olympics, Atlanta, 1996. Mem. exec. com. Lakeside Mid. Sch. Booster Club, 1990-93; pres. Lakeside Mid. Sch. Parent-Tchr.-Student Orgn., 1992-93. Recipient outstanding vol. award Hershey (Pa.) Track and Field Orgn., 1989, Tchr. of Month award Lakeside Mid. Sch., 1991. Mem. AAHPERD, Profl. Assn. Ga. Educators (bldg. rep. 1991-94). Republican. Congregationalist. Avocations: all sports, reading, sewing. Home: 432 Halifax Dr Martinez GA 30907-3349 Office: Lakeside Mid Sch 527 Blue Ridge Dr Evans GA 30809-3605

SHRADER, THOMAS HENRY, biologist; b. Marlinton, W.Va., July 12, 1943; s. George Henry and Lula Katherine (Wymer) S.; m. Michele H. Nguyen, Jan. 15, 1966; 1 child: Theodore Jack London. BS, U. Ariz., 1967, MS, 1972; postgrad., N.Mex. State U., 1972-77. Agronomist U.S. Bur. Reclamation, El Paso, Tex., 1972-73, conservation agronomist, 1974-77, ecologist, 1977-84, supervisory natural resource specialist, 1985-91; supervisory biologist U.S. Bur. Reclamation, Boulder City, Nev., 1991—; mem. Lower Colo. River Multi-Species Conservation Program, 1995—; lectr. in field. Contbr.: Herbicide Manual, 1983; contbr. articles to profl. jours. Dir. Celebrity Home Assn., Henderson, Nev., 1995; mem. Colo. River Work Group, 1993-95. Mem. Am. Soc. Agronomy, Weed Sci. Soc. Am., Ariz. Riparian Coun., Gamma Sigma Delta, Phi Kappa Phi. Avocations: civil war, rare books, photography. Home: 233 Jonquil Cir Henderson NV 89014-5244 Office: US Bureau of Reclamation PO Box 61470 Boulder City NV 89006-1470

SHRADER, WILLIAM KEATING, clinical psychologist, consultant; b. Quincy, Mass., Sept. 6, 1931; s. Eugene Royer and Florence Belle (Oakley) S.; m. Elizabeth Ann Grant, Sept. 12, 1959; children: Thomas, David (dec.). BA, U. Mass., Amherst, 1957, MS, 1960, PhD, 1963. Lic. psychologist, N.J.; cert. psychologist, N.Y. Staff clin. psychologist FDR, VAH, Montrose, N.Y., 1963-66; clin. rsch. psychologist Children's Psychiat. Ctr., Eatontown, N.J., 1967-68; dir. counseling ctr. Fairleigh Dickinson U., Madison, N.J., 1968-87; pvt. practice Madison, N.J., 1988-91; ret., 1993; part-time lectr. Monmouth Coll., Eatontown, 1967-68; part-time instr. in psychology Fairleigh Dickinson U., 1968-72; psychol. cons. Mendham (N.J.) H.S., 1979-88, Rossi Psychol. Group, Bound Brook, N.J., 1988-93. Author: Media Blight and the Dehumanizing of America, 1992; contbr. articles to profl. jours. Coord. of umpires Mendham (N.J.) Little League, 1972-76. With U.S. Army, 1953-55. Avocations: reading, skiing, tennis, aerobic exercise, biking. Home: 27 Mountainside Rd Mendham NJ 07945-2014

SHRADER, WILLIAM WHITNEY, radar consulting scientist; b. Foochow, China, Oct. 17, 1930; came to U.S., 1932; s. Ralph Raymond and Elizabeth Talmadge (Hand) S.; m. Natalie Lucinda Hutchinson, July 21, 1984. BSEE, U. Mass., 1953; MSEE, Northeastern U., 1961. Rsch. engr. Boeing Airplane Co., Seattle, 1953-56; cons. scientist, tech. dir. numerous radar systems developed Raytheon Co., Wayland, Mass., 1956-1994; pvt. practice radar cons. Stow, Mass., 1994—. Author: (with others) Radar Handbook, 1970, 2d edit., 1990; contbr. articles to profl. jours.; holder 10 U.S. patents, numerous fgn. patents. Fellow IEEE. Avocation: sports car rallying. Home and Office: 144 Harvard Rd Stow MA 01775-1070

SHRAUNER, BARBARA WAYNE ABRAHAM, electrical engineering educator; b. Morristown, N.J., June 21, 1934; d. Leonard Gladstone and Ruth Elizabeth (Thrasher) Abraham; m. James Ely Shrauner, 1965; children: Elizabeth Ann, Jay Arthur. BA cum laude, U. Colo., 1956; AM, Harvard U., 1957, PhD, 1962. Postdoctoral researcher U. Libre de Bruxelles, Brussels, 1962-64; postdoctoral researcher NASA-Ames Rsch. Ctr., Moffett Field, Calif., 1964-65; asst. prof. Washington U., St. Louis, 1966-69, assoc. prof., 1969-77, prof., 1977—; sabbatical Los Alamos (N.Mex.) Sci. Lab., 1975-76, Lawrence Berkeley Lab., Berkeley, Calif., 1985-86; cons. Los Alamos Nat. Lab., 1979, 84, NASA, Washington, 1980, Naval Surface Weapons Lab., Silver Spring, Md., 1984. Contbr. articles on transport in semiconductors, hidden symmetries of differential equations, plasma physics to profl. jours. Mem. IEEE (exec. com. of standing tech. com. on plasma sci. applications), AAUP (local sec.-treas. 1980-82), Am. Phys. Soc. (divsn. plasma physics, exec. com. 1980-82, 96—), Am. Geophys. Union, Univ. Fusion Assn., Phi Beta Kappa, Sigma Xi, Eta Kappa Nu, Sigma Pi Sigma. Home: 7452 Stratford Ave Saint Louis MO 63130-4044 Office: Washington U Dept Elec Engring 1 Brookings Dr Saint Louis MO 63130-4862

SHREEVE, JEAN'NE MARIE, chemist, educator; b. Deer Lodge, Mont., July 2, 1933; d. Charles William and Maryfrances (Briggeman) S. BA, U. Mont., 1953, DSc (hon.), 1982; MS, U. Minn., 1956; PhD, U. Wash., 1961; NSF postdoctoral fellow, U. Cambridge, Eng., 1967-68. Asst. prof. chemistry U. Idaho, Moscow, 1961-65; assoc. prof. U. Idaho, 1965-67, prof., 1967-73, acting chmn. dept. chemistry, 1969-70, 1973, head dept., and prof., 1973-87, v.p. rsch. and grad. studies, prof. chemistry, 1987—; Lucy W. Pickett lectr. Mt. Holyoke Coll., 1976, George H. Cady lectr. U. Wash., 1993; mem. Nat. Com. Standards in Higher Edn., 1965-67, 69-73. Mem. editl. bd. Jour. Fluorine Chemistry, 1970—, Jour. Heteroatom Chemistry, 1988-95, Accounts Chem. Rsch., 1973-75, Inorganic Synthesis, 1976—; contbr. articles to sci. jours. Mem. bd. govs. Argonne (Ill.) Nat. Lab., 1992—. Recipient Disting. Alumni award U. Mont., 1970; named Hon. Alumnus, U. Idaho, 1972; recipient Outstanding Achievement award U. Minn., 1975, Sr. U.S. Scientist award Alexander Von Humboldt Found., 1978, Excellence in Teaching award Chem. Mfrs. Assn., 1980; U.S. hon. Ramsay fellow, 1967-68, Alfred P. Sloan fellow, 1970-72. Mem. AAAS (bd. dirs. 1991-95), AAUW (officer Moscow chpt. 1962-69), Am. Chem. Soc. (bd. dirs. 1985-93, chmn. fluorine divsn. 1979-81, Petroleum Rsch. Fund adv. bd. 1975-77, women chemists com. 1972-77, Fluorine award 1978, Garvan medal 1972, Harry and Carol Mosher award Santa Clara Valley sect. 1992), Göttingen (Germany) Acad. Scis. (corr. mem.), Phi Beta Kappa. Office: U Idaho Rsch Office 111 Morrill Hall Moscow ID 83843

SHREINER, CURT, educational technologist, consultant; b. Ephrata, Pa., June 27, 1952; s. Paul H. and Grace B. BS in Edn., Millersville U., 1974; MS in Integrative Edn., Marywood Coll., 1977; MEd in Tech. and Media, Temple U., 1982; EdD in Tech. and Media, Columbia U., 1989. Tchr. Lebanon (Pa.) Sch. Dist., 1974-76; instr., researcher Millersville (Pa.) State U., 1976-77; writer, pub. Instrnl. Design Assocs., Lancaster, Pa., 1977-80; tchr. trainer Mainland (Pa.) Inst., 1980-81; videodisc designer WNET/THIRTEEN, Pub. TV, N.Y.C., 1981-82; computer software designer Academic Tech., Inc., Moorestown, N.J., 1982-86; audio scriptwriter Learn Inc., Mt. Laurel, N.J., 1986-87; CAI curriculum developer Constructive Alternatives, Inc., Phila., 1987-88; GUI designer Resolute, Ltd., Phila., 1988-91; multimedia designer Remtech Svcs. Inc., Newport News, Va., 1991-92; database design and info. mgmt. trainer The Work Group, Pennsauken, N.J., 1992; multimedia project dir. Vocat. Rsch. Inst., Phila., 1993-95; owner Curt Shreiner Prodns., 1995-96; multimedia designer Galaxy Scientific Corp., Warminster, Pa., 1996—; computer cons. Phila. Mayor's Commn. on Literacy, 1987-91; learning cons. for Pub. Health Videos, Phila. Dept. l.b. Health, 1989-90. Co-author: Straight Talk Parenting Series, 1988, Te.cner Revitalization, 1982, The Giggle Kids Present, 1978; designer: Ollie and Seymour, 1986 (Media and Materials Portfolio award); prodr., writer Maria's Story, 1995 (Telly award). Mem. Assn. of Ednl. Comm. and Tech., Soc. for Applied Learning Tech., World Future Soc., World Affairs Coun. Avocations: fine art, photography, travel.

SHREM, CHARLES JOSEPH, metals corporation executive; b. Cairo, May 9, 1930; came to U.S., 1959; s. Joseph C. and Paula (Cadranel) S.; m. Vivian L. Chalom, Jan. 30, 1955; children: Jeff, Leslie Allen. Degree in bus. and economy, Coll. Français, Cairo, 1951. Export mgr. Stanton Ironworks U.K., Middle East, 1950-57; comml. mgr. Soc. Sovibor, Paris, 1957-59; purchasing dir. Montanore, Inc., N.Y.C., 1959-65; exec. v.p. Commonwealth Metal Corp., Englewood Cliffs, N.J., 1965-85, pres., chief exec. officer, 1985—; bd. govs. Coll. Democracy, Arlington, Va. Bd. dirs. Adult Edn., Pequannock, N.J., 1970-80; bd. govs. Coll. Democracy, Arlington, Va.

Mem. U.S. C. of C. (econ. coun., exec. com. U.S. Polish Coun./U.S. C. of C.). Office: 560 Sylvan Ave Englewd Clfs NJ 07632-3104

SHRESTHA, BIJAYA, nuclear scientist; b. Kathmandu, Nepal, July 8, 1955; came to U.S., 1985; s. Kalidas and Kamala M. (Joshi) S.; m. Puja, May 7, 1975; children: Anjana, Anjaya, Srijana, Samjhana. MS in Plasma Physics, Tribhuvan U., Kathmandu, Nepal, 1978; MS in Nuclear Physics, La. State U., 1988; PhD, U. Mo., Rolla, 1995. Asst. lectr. Tribhuvan U., Kathmandu, Nepal, 1979-82, lectr., 1982-85; teaching asst. La. State U., Baton Rouge, 1985-88; rsch. teaching asst. U. Mo., Rolla, 1988-95, postdoctoral fellow, 1995-96, adj. faculty dept. elec. engring., 1996—. Author: Campus Physics, 1982. Treas. Univ. Tchrs. Assn., Kathmandu, 1982. Recipient Fulbright scholarship, 1985. Mem. Am. Phys. Soc., Am. Nuclear Soc., Nepal Phys. Soc., Am. Math. Soc., Sigma Pi Sigma, Alpha Nu Sigma (pres. U. Mo. at Rolla chpt.), Tau Beta Pi. Home: 1602 N Cedar St Rolla MO 65401-2335 Office: U Missouri Dept Nuclear Engring Rolla MO 65401

SHREVE, MICHAEL GERALD, computer consultant; b. La Porte, Ind., July 11, 1948; s. Russell Eugene and Elizabeth Ledeema (Masterson) S.; m. Virginia Louise Oliver, Apr. 13, 1950; children: Janine Marie Shreve Larkin, Michael Gerald II. BA in Psychology, Forensic Studies, Ind. U., 1974, MPA, 1988. Cert. law enforcement officer, Ind.; peace officer, Colo. Marshal Wanatah (Ind.) Police, 1974; police officer Purdue U., Ft. Wayne, Ind., 1975-76; dep. sheriff Gilpin County, Central City, Colo., 1977-79; dir. security Mark Resort, Vail, Colo., 1980; police officer Notre Dame (Ind.) Police, 1981-94; owner PC Fix, La Porte, Ind., 1989—. Sgt. USAF, 1968-72, Vietnam. Recipient Silver Safety Belt, Hoosiers for Safety Belts, 1988, 89. Mem. VFW, NRA, Law Enforcement Alliance, Mensa (coord. N.W. Ind. 1989—). Republican. Avocations: classic autos, shooting sports. Home: 2962 E 850 N La Porte IN 46350-8994

SHREVE, PEG, state legislator, retired elementary educator; b. Spencer, Va., July 23, 1927; d. Hubert Smith and Pearl (Looney) Adams; m. Don Franklin Shreve, June 17, 1950 (dec. Sept. 1970); children: Donna, Jennifer, John, Don. BA, Glenville State U., 1948. Cert. elem. tchr., Va., Wyo. Reading tchr. Wood County Bd., Parkersburg, W.Va., 1948-50; elem. tchr. Mt. Solon, Va., 1950-52, Bridgewater, Va., 1952-53, Cody, Wyo., 1970-86; mem. Wyo. Ho. of Reps., 1983—, chmn.. com. travel, recreation and wildlife, 1983-91, majority whip, 1992-94, speaker pro tem, 1995—. Mem. coun. Girl Scouts U.S.A., White Sulpher Springs, W.Va., 1962-65; co-chmn. Legis. Exec. Conf., Wyo., 1987; mem. Nat. Com. State Legislatures, 1982—; co-chair Select Com. Sch. Fin., 1996-99. Named Legislator of Yr., Wyo. Outfitters Assn., 1989, Ofcl. of Yr., Wyo. Wildlife Assn., 1990, Alumna of Yr., Glenville State Coll., 1994. Mem. AAUW (exec. bd.), Nat. Women Legislators, Soroptimists (Women Helping Women award 1985), Beta Sigma Phi (Lady of Yr. award 1986). Republican. Presbyterian. Avocations: golf, walking, needlepoint, knitting, bridge. Home: PO Box 2257 Cody WY 82414-2257

SHREVE, SUSAN RICHARDS, author, English literature educator; b. Toledo, May 2, 1939; d. Robert Kenneth and Helen (Greene) Richards; children—Porter, Elizabeth, Caleb, Kate. BA, U. Pa., 1961; MA, U. Va., 1969. Prof. English lit. George Mason U., Fairfax, Va., 1976—; vis. prof. Columbia U., N.Y.C., 1982—, Princeton U., 1991, 92, 93. Author: (novels) A Fortunate Madness, 1974, A Woman Like That, 1977, Children of Power, 1979, Miracle Play, 1981, Dreaming of Heroes, 1984, Queen of Hearts, 1986, A Country of Strangers, 1989, Daughters of the New World, 1992, The Train Home, 1993, Skin Deep: Women & Race, 1995, The Visiting Physician, 1995; (children's books) The Nightmares of Geranium Street, 1977, Family Secrets, 1979, Loveletters, 1979, The Masquerade, 1980, The Bad Dreams of a Good Girl, 1981, The Revolution of Mary Leary, 1982, The Flunking of Joshua T. Bates, 1984, How I Saved the World on Purpose, 1985, Lucy Forever and Miss Rosetree, Shrinks, Inc., 1985, Joshua T. Bates In Charge, 1992, The Gift of the Girl Who Couldn't Hear, 1991, Wait for Me, 1992, Amy Dunn Quits School, 1993, Lucy Forever & the Stolen Baby, 1994, The Formerly Great Alexander Family, 1995, Zoe and Columbo, 1995, Warts, 1996, Joshua Bates in Trouble Again, 1997, Jonah, The Whale, 1997; co-editor: Narratives on Justice, 1996, The Goalie, 1996, (with Porter Shreve) Outside the Law: Narratives on Justice, 1997. Recipient Jenny Moore award George Washington U., 1978; John Simon Guggenheim award in fiction, 1980; Nat. Endowment Arts fiction award, 1982. Mem. PEN/Faulkner Found. (pres.), Phi Beta Kappa.

SHRIBMAN, DAVID MARKS, editor; b. Salem, Mass., Mar. 2, 1954; m. Cynthia L. Skrzycki, Sept. 9, 1978; children: Elizabeth, Natalie. AB summa cum laude, Dartmouth Coll., 1976; LHD, Salem State Coll., 1995. Mem. city staff and Washington bur. Buffalo Evening News, 1977-80; mem. feature and nat. staff The Washington Star, 1980-81; with Washington bur. N.Y. Times, 1981-84; congl. reporter, nat. polit. corr. The Wall St. Jour., 1984-93; chief Washington bur., asst. mng. editor The Boston Globe, 1993—. Trustee Dartmouth Coll. James B. Reynolds scholar Jesus Coll.; recipient Pulitzer Prize for beat reporting, 1995. Mem. Phi Beta Kappa. Office: Globe Newspaper Co 1130 Connecticut Ave NW Washington DC 20036-3904

SHRIER, ADAM LOUIS, investment firm executive; b. Warsaw, Poland, Mar. 26, 1938; came to U.S., 1943, naturalized, 1949; s. Henry Leon and Mathilda June (Czamanska) S.; m. Diane Kesler, June 10, 1961; children: Jonathan, Lydia, Catherine, David. BS, Columbia U., 1959; MS (Whitney fellow), MIT, 1960; D.Engr. and Applied Sci. (NSF fellow), Yale U., 1965; postdoctoral visitor, U. Cambridge, Eng., 1965-66; J.D., Fordham U., 1976. With Esso Research & Engring. Co., Florham Park and Linden, N.J., 1963-65, 66-72; head. environ. scis. research area Esso Research & Engring. Co., 1969-72; coordinator pollution abatement activities, tanker dept. Exxon Internat. Co., N.Y.C., 1972-74; project mgr., energy systems Exxon Enterprises Inc., N.Y.C., 1974-75; gen. mgr. solar energy projects Exxon Enterprises Inc., 1975-77, pres. solar thermal systems div., 1977-81; corp. planning cons., sec. new bus. investments Exxon Corp., N.Y.C., 1981-82; div. mgr. supply and transp. Exxon Internat. Co., N.Y.C., 1983-86, mgr. policy and planning, 1986-88; mng. dir. Splty. Tech. Assocs., Washington, 1988-97; pres. Global Devel. Opportunities, LLC, Washington, 1997—; adj. lectr. chem. egnring. Columbia U., N.Y.C., 1967-69; industry adv. bd. Internat. Energy Agy., 1984-88, Energy and Environ. Policy Ctr., Harvard U., 1986-88, Internat. Energy Program, Johns Hopkins U., 1987-88; sr. assoc. Global Bus. Forum, 1988—, Cambridge Energy Rsch. Assocs., 1988—. Patentee in field; contbr. articles to profl. jours. Mem. AIChE, Am. Inst. Energy Economists, Cosmos Club, Sigma Xi, Tau Beta Pi, Phi Lambda Upsilon. Office: 4000 Cathedral Ave NW Washington DC 20016

SHRIER, DIANE KESLER, psychiatrist; b. N.Y.C., Mar. 23, 1941; d. Benjamin Arthur and Mollie (Wortman) Kesler; BS magna cum laude in Chemistry and Biology (Regents scholar 1957-61), Queen's Coll., CUNY, 1961; student Washington U. Sch. Medicine, St. Louis, 1960-61; M.D., Yale U., 1964; m. Adam Louis Shrier, June 10, 1961; children: Jonathan Laurence, Lydia Anne, Catherine Jane, David Leopold. Pediatric intern Bellevue Hosp., N.Y.C., 1964-65; psychiat. resident Albert Einstein Coll. Medicine-Bronx (N.Y.) Mcpl. Municipal Hosp. Center, 1966-68, child psychiatry fellow, 1968-70; staff cons. Family Service and Child Guidance Center of the Oranges, Maplewood, Milburn-Orange, N.J., 1970-73, cons., 1973-79; pvt. practice, Montclair, N.J., 1970-92, Washington, 1994—; cons. Community Day Nursery, E. Orange, 1970-79, Montclair State Coll., 1976-78; psychiat. cons. Bloomfield (N.J.) public schs., 1974-75; clin. instr. Albert Einstein Coll. Medicine, 1970-73; clin. asst. prof. psychiatry U. Medicine and Dentistry N.J., 1978-82, clin. assoc. prof., 1982-89, prof. clin. psychiatry, 1989-92; vice chmn., dir. clin. psychiat. svcs. Dept. Psychiatry Children's Nat. Med. Ctr., 1992-94, attending staff, 1994—; prof. psychiatry and pediatrics George Washington U. Med. Ctr., 1992-94, clin. prof. psychiatry and pediatrics, 1994—. cons. Walter Reed Med. Ctr., 1994—. Trustee, Montessori Learning Center, Montclair, 1973-75. Diplomate Am. Bd. Psychiatry and Neurology. Fellow Am. Psychiat. Assn., Acad. Child Psychiatry; mem. Tri-County Psychiat. Assn. (exec. com., rec. sec. 1977-78, 2d v.p. 1978-79, 1st v.p. 1979-80, pres. 1977-81), N.J. Psychiat. Assn. (councillor 1981-84), Am. Acad. Child and Adolescent Psychiatry (councillor at large 1992-95), Phi Beta Kappa. Contbr. articles to med. jours. Home: Apt 317B 4000 Cathedral Ave NW Washington DC 20016-5249 Office: 1616 18th St NW Apt 104 Washington DC 20009-2521

SHRIER, STEFAN, mathematician, educator; b. Mexico City, Nov. 7, 1942; s. Henry Leon Shrier and Mathilda June Czamanska; m. Helaine G. Elderkin, 1985. BS in Engring., Columbia U., 1964, MS in Ops. Rsch., 1966; PhD in Applied Math., Brown U., 1977. Chmn. computer sci. program Wellesley (Mass.) Coll., 1972-75; sr. engr. Booz, Allen and Hamilton, Bethesda, Md., 1977-79; dir. Latin Am. ops. SofTech, Inc., Springfield, Va., 1979-80; mem. rsch. staff Systems Planning Corp., Arlington, Va., 1980-83; tech. dir. Grumman-CTEC, Inc. subs. Grumman Data Systems, Inc. (absorbed by Grumman Data Systems, Inc. Jan. 1988), McLean, Va., 1983-85, dir. Lab. Machine Intelligence and Correlation, 1984-87, dir. R & D, 1985-87; asst. dir. tech. dept. Grumman Data Systems, Inc., McLean, Va., 1988-90, dep. dir. tech. dept. Washington ops., 1990-91; mem. tech. staff MRJ, Inc., Fairfax, Va., 1991-95; program mgr. MRJ, Inc., Fairfax, 1995-96; program dir. Crystal City Ops., 1997; chief scientist SeiCorp, Inc., Springfield, Va., 1997—; professorial lectr. statistics George Washington U., 1981-84, adj. prof. stats., 1984-85; adj. prof. computer sci. George Mason U., 1985-87; sec. New Eng. Regional Computing Program, Cambridge, Mass., 1973-75. Contbr. articles to profl. jours. Fellow Washington Acad. Sci.; mem. Sigma Xi, Tau Beta Pi. Office: SeiCorp Inc PO Box 19139 Alexandria VA 22320

SHRINER, THOMAS L., JR., lawyer; b. Lafayette, Ind., Dec. 15, 1947; s. Thomas L. Sr. and Margaret (Kamstra); m. Donna L. Galchick, June 5, 1971; children: Thomas L. III, John H. , Joseph P., James A. AB, Ind. U., 1969, JD, 1972. Bar: Wis. 1972, U.S. Ct. Appeals (7th cir.) 1972, U.S. Dist. Ct. (ea. dist.) Wis. 1973, U.S. Dist. Ct. (we. dist.) Wis. 1977, U.S. Supreme Ct. 1978, U.S. Ct. Appeals (8th cir.) 1989, U.S. Ct. Appeals (fed. cir.) 1990. Law clk to Hon. John S. Hastings U.S. Ct. Appeals (7th cir.), Chgo., 1972-73; assoc. Foley & Lardner, Milwaukee, Wis., 1973-79, ptnr., 1979—. Contbr. articles to profl. jours. Trustee Cath. Charities of Archdiocese of Milw. Fellow Am. Coll. Trial Lawyers; mem. 7th Cir. Bar Assn. (pres. 1993-94), Phi Beta Kappa. Republican. Roman Catholic. Office: Foley & Lardner 777 E Wisconsin Ave Milwaukee WI 53202-5302

SHRINSKY, JASON LEE, lawyer; b. Pitts., June 15, 1937; s. Abe and Sylvia S.; children: Jeffrey, Steven, Stacy. BA, U. Pitts., 1959; JD, George Washington U., 1962. Sr. ptnr. Shrinsky, Weitzman & Eisen, Washington, 1971-87; ptnr., exec. com. mem. Kaye, Scholer, Fierman, Hays & Handler, Washington, 1987—; mem. exec. com., 1993-97; panelist Paul Kagan Seminars on Radio and TV Acquisitions, Inst. Soc. Internat. Rsch.; atty.-advisor Complaints and Compliance Div. Broadcast Bur. FCC, Washington, 1961-64; bd. dirs. U.S. Com. Sports for Israel, Phila., FCC Bar Assn. Contbr. articles to Radio and Records mag., Broadcast Cable Fin. Jour. Presdl. del. Mt. Sinai transfer ceremonies, 1978; U.S. basketball chmn. 12th, 13th and 14th Maccabiah games, Israel; bd. dirs. Washington Hebrew Congregation, 1978-85. Mem. Internat. Radio and TV Soc., Nat. Broadcaster's Club (past pres.), U. Pitts. Alumni Assn. (bd. dirs.). Jewish. Office: Kaye Scholer Fierman 901 15th St NW Washington DC 20005-2327

SHRIVER, ALLEN KEITH, electrical engineer, contractor, executive; b. Grand Junction, Colo., Sept. 21, 1944; s. Herschel A. and Mable Alice (Thompson) S.; m. Lois R. Roy, Apr. 23, 1966 (div. Apr. 1982); m. Dorothy J. Pifer, July 1, 1982; children: Charlie C. Gilliam, Susan, Katheryn-Denise L., Kristin-Danielle L. AAS in Electronic Tech., Rangely (Colo.) Jr. Coll., 1964; BSEE, U. Colo., 1967. Assoc. engr. Convair div. Gen. Dynamics, San Diego, 1967; reliability engr. Electronics div. Gen. Dynamics, San Diego, 1967-70; apprentice electrician PreEngineered Bldgs., Grand Junction, 1970; elec. engr. Colo. Ute Electric Utility, Montrose, 1970-76; master electrician, contractor ALS Electric, Olathe, Colo., 1975-82; master electrician, contractor, chief exec. officer ALS Inc., Olathe, 1982—. Poet: Anthology of American Poets, 1968. Mem. Olathe Planning and Zoning Com., 1984-90, past sec., Montrose County Housing Authority 1984—, chmn., sub contract com. Montrose County Planning and Zoning, 1990-91; pub. housing commr. Nat. Assn. Housing, 1990; Rep. precinct chmn.; mem. Olathe town bd. trustees, 1996—; acting dir. daycare and preschool construction mgr. MCHA, 1997. Mem. Nat. Fedn. Ind. Bus., Odd Fellows (officer 1971-82, encampment officer 1976-82, col. to regimental comdr. 1976-82, decoration of chivalry 1981), Montrose Rod and Gun Club, Eta Kappa Nu, Tau Beta Pi. Baptist. Avocations: writing, fishing, hunting, carpentry and design, landscaping. Home and Office: ALS Inc 405 Colorado Hwy # 348 Olathe CO 81425

SHRIVER, DONALD WOODS, JR., theology educator; b. Norfolk, Va., Dec. 20, 1927; s. Donald Woods and Gladys (Roberts) S.; m. Peggy Ann Leu, Aug. 9, 1953; children: Gregory Bruce, Margaret Ann, Timothy Donald. B.A., Davidson Coll., 1951; B.D., Union Theol. Sem. Va., 1955; S.T.M., Yale U., 1957; Ph.D. (Rockefeller Doctoral fellow), Harvard U., 1963; L.H.D. (hon.), Central Coll., 1970, Davidson Coll., 1984, Union Medal, Union Theol. Sem. Am., 1991; D.D. (hon.), Wagner Coll., 1978, Southwestern Coll., Memphis, 1983, Colgate U., 1996; LHD (hon.), Jewish Theol. Sem., 1991; DD (hon.), Colgate U., 1996. Ordained to ministry Presbyterian Ch., 1955; pastor Linwood Presbyn. Ch., Gastonia, N.C., 1956-59; u. minister, prof. religion N.C. State U., Raleigh, 1963-72; dir. u. program on sci. and soc. N.C. State U., 1968-72; prof. ethics and soc. Emory U., Atlanta, 1972-75; William E. Dodge prof. applied Christianity Union Theol. Sem., N.Y.C., 1975-96, pres. faculty, 1975-91; adj. prof. bus. ethics Sch. Bus. Adminstrn., Columbia U., prof. ethics Sch. Internat. Affairs, 1995-98; sr. fellow freedom forum Sch. Journalism, Columbia U., 1992-93; adj. prof. ethics, 1994—; lectr. Duke U., Va. State U., Ga. State U., numerous colls. and univs. in Can., Kenya, India, Japan and Korea. Author: How Do You Do and Why: An Introduction of Christian Ethics for Young People, 1966, Rich Man Poor Man: Christian Ethics for Modern Man Series, 1972, (with Dean D. Knudsen and John R. Earle) Spindles and Spires: A Restudy of Religion and Social Change in Gastonia, 1976, (with Karl A. Ostrom) Is There Hope for the City?, 1977, The Social Ethics of the Lord's Prayer, 1980, The Gospel, The Church, and Social Change, 1980, The Lord's Prayer: A Way of Life, 1983, An Ethic for Enemies: Forgiveness in Politics, 1995; co-author: Redeeming the City, 1982, Beyond Success: Corporations and Their Critics in the Nineties, 1991; editor: The Unsilent South, 1965, Medicine and Religion: Strategies of Care, 1979. Dir. Urban Policy Study N.C. State U., 1971-73; precinct chmn. Democratic Party, Raleigh, N.C., del. to nat. conv., 1968; mem. Mayor's Com. on Human Relations, Raleigh, 1967-71; chmn. Urban Policy Seminar, Center for Theology and Public Policy, 1978-82. Served with Signal Corps U.S. Army, 1946-47. Recipient The Union medal, Union Theol. Sem., 1991; Kent fellow in religion, 1959. Mem. Am. Soc. Christian Ethics (pres. 1979-80), Soc. for Values in Higher Edn., Soc. for Health and Human Values, Soc. for Sci. Study of Religion, AAAS, Am. Sociol. Assn., Am. Soc. Engring. Edn. (chmn. liberal arts div. 1972-73), United Christian Youth Movement of Nat. Council of Chs. (nat. chmn. 1951-53), Council on Fgn. Relations. Home and Office: 440 Riverside Dr Apt 58 New York NY 10027-6830 *Modern people need to recover connections between memory and hope. The past we applaud pre-enacts the future we hope for, and the past we deplore forms our obligation, in the present, to make a different future. In a time when young people find it hard to envision a long human future, the connections of history and ethics are indispensable. The forging of such connections is my vocation as an educator.*

SHRIVER, DUWARD FELIX, chemistry educator, researcher, consultant; b. Glendale, Calif., Nov. 20, 1934; s. Duward Laurence and Josephine (Williamson) S.; m. Shirley Ann Clark; children: Justin Scott, Daniel Nathan. BS, U. Calif., Berkeley, 1958; PhD, U. Mich., 1961. From instr. to assoc. prof. chemistry Northwestern U., Evanston, Ill., 1961-70, prof., 1970-87, Morrison prof. of chemistry, 1987—, chmn. dept. chem., 1992-95; mem. Inorganic Syntheses Inc., 1974—, pres., 1982-85; vis. staff mem. Los Alamos (N.Mex.) Nat. Lab., 1976-85, cons., 1985-92; vis. prof. U. Tokyo, 1977, U. Wyo., 1978, U. Western Ont., Can., 1979. Author: The Manipulation of Air-Sensitive Compounds, 1969, edit., 1987; co-author: Inorganic Chemistry, 1990, 2d edit., 1994; editor-in-chief Inorganic Syntheses, vol. 19, 1979; co-editor: The Chemistry of Metal Cluster Complexes, 1990, Inorganic Synthesis, 1979—, Advances in Inorganic Chemistry, 1986—, Jour. Coordination Chemistry, Inorganic Chimca Acta, 1988—, Chemistry of Materials, 1988-90, 92—, Jour. Cluster Sci., 1990—, Organometallics, 1993-95; contbr. articles to profl. jours. Alfred P. Sloan fellow, 1967-69; Japan Soc. Promotion of Sci. fellow, 1977; Guggenheim Found. fellow, 1983-84. Fellow AAAS; mem. Am. Chem. Soc. (Disting. Svc. in Inorganic Chemistry award 1987), Royal Soc. Chemistry London (Ludwig Mond lectr. 1989), Electrochem. Soc., Materials Rsch. Soc. (medal 1990). Home: 1100 Colfax St Evanston IL 60201-2611 Office: Northwestern U Dept Chemistry Evanston IL 60208-3113

SHRIVER, GARNER EDWARD, lawyer, former congressman; b. Towanda, Kans., July 6, 1912; s. Edward Arthur and Olive (Glass) S.; m. Martha Jane Currier, June 4, 1941; children: Kay Kwon, David Garner, Linda Ann Breeding. A.B., U. Wichita, 1934; J.D., Washburn U., 1940; D. Pub. Service, Friends U., Wichita, 1970. Bar: Kans. 1940. Instr. English and speech South Haven (Kans.) High Sch., 1936-37; mem. firm Bryant, Cundiff, Shriver & Shanahan, Wichita, 1940-61; Mem. Kans. Ho. of Reps. from Sedgwick County, 1947-51; atty. Wichita Bd. Edn., 1951-60; mem. 87th-94th Congresses, 4th Kans. Dist.; Mem. Kansas Interstate Coop. Commn., 1953-55, Kans. Senate, 27th Dist., 1953-61; mem. Kan. Legis. Council, 1955-60; minority counsel Senate Vet. Affairs Com., 1975-80, gen. counsel, 1981-82; of counsel Johnson, Shriver & Kinzel, McPherson, Kans, 1983-86, Law Offices of David G. Shriver, McPherson, Kans., 1986—. Trustee Murdock Art Collection of Wichita Art Mus.; bd. dirs. Kans. Dialysis Assn., DeMolay Legion of Honor. Lt. USNR, World War II. Recipient U. Wichita Alumni Achievement award, 1961; recipient Washburn Alumni Disting. Service award, 1967. Mem. ABA, Kans. Bar Assn., Wichita Bar Assn., VFW, Am. Legion, Nat. Sorjourners, Masons (33d degree), Shriners. Republican. Methodist. Home: 15205 Timber Lake Cir Wichita KS 67230-9214 Office: Law Offices of David G Shriver 100 S Main St Mc Pherson KS 67460-4852

SHRIVER, PAMELA HOWARD, professional tennis player; b. Balt., July 4, 1962. Profl. tennis player, 1979—; winner 21 career singles, 112 career doubles titles 21 career singles, 92 career doubles titles; winner 7 Australian Opens (with Martina Navratilova), 4 French Opens (with Navratilova), 5 Wimbledons (with Navratilova), 6 U.S. Opens, French Open mixed doubles (with Emilio Sanchez); mem. U.S. Fedn. Cup Team, 1986-87, 89, 92, U.S. Wightman Cup Team, 1978-81, 83, 85, 87. V.P. Internat. Tennis Hall of Fame; pres. of Women's Tennis Association, 1991, 92, 93. Recipient Gold medal 1988 Olympic Games in doubles (with Zina Garrison). Mem. Women's Tennis Assn. Tour Players Assn. Address: care PHS Ltd Ste 902 401 Washington Ave Baltimore MD 21204

SHRIVER, PHILLIP RAYMOND, academic administrator; b. Cleve., Aug. 16, 1922; s. Raymond Scott and Corinna Ruth (Smith) S.; m. Martha Damaris Nye, Apr. 15, 1944; children: Carolyn (Mrs. Richard Helwig), Susan (Mrs. Lester LaVine), Melinda (Mrs. David Williams), Darcy, Raymond Scott II. BA, Yale U., 1943; MA, Harvard U., 1946; PhD, Columbia U., 1954; LittD, U. Cin., 1966; LLD, Heidelberg Coll., 1966, Eastern Mich., 1972, Ohio State U., 1973; DH, McKendree Coll., 1973; DPS, Albion Coll., 1974; LHD, Central State U., 1976, No. Ky. State U., 1980, Miami U., 1984, U. Akron, 1988. Mem. faculty Kent (Ohio) State U., 1947-65, prof. Am. history, 1960-65; dean Coll. Arts and Scis., 1963-65; pres. Miami U., Oxford, Ohio, 1965-81; pres. emeritus, prof. Am. history Miami U., 1981—; pres. Ohio Coll. Assn., 1974-75; chmn. coun. pres.'s Mid-Am. Conf., 1971-77; chmn. Ohio Bicentennial Commn. for NW Ordinance and U.S. Constn., 1985-89, Ohio Tuition Trust Authority, 1989-92; chmn. coun. pres.'s Nat. Assn. State Univs. and Land Grant Colls., 1975-76, mem. exec. coun., 1976-78. Author: The Years of Youth, 1960, George A. Bowman: The Biography of an Educator, 1963, (with D.J. Breen) Ohio's Military Prisons of the Civil War, 1964, A Tour to New Connecticut: The Narrative of Henry Leavitt Ellsworth, 1985. Bd. dirs. Cin. Ctr. Sci. and Industry, 1965-70; trustee Ohio Coll. Library Center, 1968-74; chmn. bd. Univ. Regional Broadcasting, 1975-76, 78-79. Served to lt. (j.g.) USNR, 1943-46, PTO. Decorated Order of Merit Grand Duchy of Luxembourg, 1976; recipient Disting. Acad. Svc. award AAUP, 1965, Gov.'s award 1969, A.K. Morris award, 1974, Ohioana Career medal, 1987, Converse award, 1990, Award of Merit, Am. Assn. for State and Local History, 1993. Mem. Orgn. Am. Historians, Ohio Acad. History (pres. 1983-84, Disting. Svc. award 1991), Archaeol. Inst. Am., Ohio Hist. Soc. (trustee 1982-91, v.p. 1983-84, pres. 1984-86), Ohio Humanities Council, Am. Studies Assn., Mortar Board, Phi Beta Kappa, Omicron Delta Kappa, Phi Alpha Theta, Alpha Kappa Psi, Kappa Delta Pi, Phi Eta Sigma, Phi Kappa Phi, Kappa Kappa Psi, Alpha Lambda Delta, Beta Gamma Sigma, Sigma Delta Pi, Alpha Phi Omega, Delta Upsilon (Disting. Alumni Achievement award 1985). Presbyterian. Club: Rotary. Home: 5115 Bonham Rd Oxford OH 45056-1428 Office: Miami U Oxford OH 45056

SHRIVER, ROBERT SARGENT, JR., lawyer; b. Westminster, Md., Nov. 9, 1915; s. Robert Sargent and Hilda (Shriver) S.; m. Eunice Mary Kennedy, May 23, 1953; children: Robert Sargent III, Maria, Timothy, Mark Kennedy, Anthony Paul Kennedy. Student, Canterbury Sch.; B.A. cum laude, Yale U., 1938, LL.B., 1941; LL.D., St. Procopius Coll., 1959, Notre Dame U., DePaul U., Seton Hall Coll., 1961, St. Louis U., Kansas State U., Brandeis U., 1962, St. Michael's Coll., Vt., Fordham U., Boston Coll., Yale U., Duquesne U., N.Y.U., Wesleyan U.; D.C.L., U. Liberia, 1963; H.H.D., Salem Coll., 1963, Bowling Green State U.; L.H.D., Springfield (Mass.) Coll., 1963, U. Scranton, Providence Coll.; Dr. Polit. Sci., Chulalongkorn U., Bangkok, Thailand. Bar: N.Y. State 1941, Ill. 1959, U.S. Supreme Ct. 1969, D.C. 1971. With Winthrop, Stimson, Putnam & Roberts, 1940-41; asst. editor Newsweek, 1945-46; assoc. Joseph P. Kennedy Enterprises, 1947-48; asst. gen. mgr. Merchandise Mart, Chgo., 1948-61; dir. Peace Corps., Washington, 1961-66, Office Econ. Opportunity, 1964-68; U.S. ambassador to France, 1968-70; spl. asst. to the Pres., 1965-68; sr. ptnr. law firm Fried, Frank, Harris, Shriver & Jacobson, N.Y.C., Washington, L.A., London, Eng., 1971-86; of counsel Fried, Frank, Harris, Shriver & Jacobson, 1986—; pres. Spl. Olympics, Washington, 1986-90, chmn., CEO, 1990-96, chmn. bd. dirs., 1996—; mem. Am. Com. on East-West Accord, 1978—, Ams. for SALT, 1979—. Author: Point of the Lance, 1964. Pres. Chgo. Bd. Edn., 1955-60; mem.-at-large Nat. Coun. Boy Scouts Am.; pres. Cath. Interracial Coun. Chgo., 1955-60; chmn. Internat. Orgn. Patrons of Israel Mus., 1972-75, Democratic candidate for v.p., 1972, ran for Dem. presdl. election, 1976; bd. dirs. The Arms Control Assn., 1983—. Lt. comdr. USNR, 1940-45. Recipient Yale U. medal, 1957, Chgo. medal of merit, 1957, James J. Hoey award Cath. Interracial Coun. N.Y., 1958, Franklin D. Roosevelt Freedom from Want award, 1991, Presdl. Medal of Freedom, 1994; named Lay Churchman of Yr. Religious Heritage Am., 1963; recipient Golden Heart Presdl. award Philippines, 1964, Laetare medal U. Notre Dame, 1968. Mem. Yale U. Law Sch. Assn. (exec. com.), Navy League (life), Chgo. Council Fgn. Relations (dir.), Delta Kappa Epsilon. Roman Catholic. Clubs: Serra, Economic, Racquet, Executives (Chgo.); Onwentsia (Lake Forest, Ill.); Yale (N.Y.C.); University (Washington); Chevy Chase (Md.). Extensive world travel to visit Peace Corps projects, 1961-66. Office: Spl Olympics Internat 1325 G St NW Ste 500 Washington DC 20005-3104

SHRODER, TOM, newspaper editor. Exec. editor sunday "tropic" sec. The Miami Herald, Fla. Office: The Miami Herald Pub Co One Herald Plz Miami FL 33132-1693

SHROFF, FIROZ SARDAR, merger and acquisition professional; b. Karachi, Pakistan, Feb. 27, 1950; s. Sardar Mohammad Shroff and Kulsum (Bano) Dhanji; m. Munira Firoz, Oct. 27, 1977; children: Khurram, Sara, Ally. Grad. high sch., Nairobi, Kenya. Apprentice, duty incharge Empire Investment Ltd., Nairobi, 1966-67; asst. mgr. to mgr. Trade Aids Inc., Karachi, 1967-69, asst. gen. mgr., 1969-72; gen. mgr. Canorient Overseas Distbrs. Ltd., London, 1972-74; dir., gen. mgr. Westland Securities Ltd., Nairobi, 1974-75; dep. mng. dir. Sasi Ltd., Karachi, 1975-78; dir. internat. expansion Sasi Group Cos., Karachi, 1978-80, mng. dir., 1984—; dir. operation Key Internat. S.A., London, 1980-84; participant Nat. Book Devel. Council, Singapore, 1980, Arthur D. Little Mgmt. Edn. Inst. and Pakistan Inst. Mgmt., 1986; trustee Sasi Found., Karachi, 1985; developer bus. info. and rsch. ctr.; advisor/cons. various corp. bodies on takeover acquisition of bus. in U.S., U.K. and the Pacific; involved in group discussions on internat. bus. opportunities, contacts in fin. circles. Recipient Cert. Recognition Asia-Pacific Real Estate Congress, 1987. Mem. Pakistan Pubs. and Booksellers Assn. (copyright com. 1975-80), Internat. Real Estate Fedn., Assn. Builders and Developers (convenor 1985), Internat. Real Estate Inst. (chpt. head 1986), Inst. Dirs., Pakistan C. of C. and Industry, United Coop. Credit Soc. (bd. dirs. 1977-79), Property Cons. Soc., Internat. Airline Passengers Assn. Clubs: Karachi Golf; Def. Lodge: Rotary. Avocations: reading, travel. Office: Sasi House G/2 Block 9, KDA Scheme No 5 Main Clifton Rd,

Khayaban-e-Iqbal Kehkashan Karachi 75600, Pakistan also: 12 Wynwood Dr Princeton Junction NJ 08550-2145

SHRONTZ, FRANK ANDERSON, airplane manufacturing executive; b. Boise, Idaho, Dec. 14, 1931; s. Thurlyn Howard and Florence Elizabeth (Anderson) S.; m. Harriet Ann Houghton, June 12, 1954; children: Craig Howard, Richard Whitaker, David Anderson. Student, George Washington U., 1953; LLB, U. Idaho, 1954; MBA, Harvard U., 1958; postgrad., Stanford U., 1969-70. Asst. contracts coordinator Boeing Co., Seattle, 1958-65, asst. dir. contract adminstrn., 1965-67, asst. to v.p. comml. airplane group, 1967-69, asst. dir. new airplane program, 1969-70, dir. comml. sales operations, 1970-73, v.p. planning and contracts, 1977-78; asst. sec. Dept. Air Force, Washington, 1973-76, Dept. Def., Washington, 1976-77; v.p., gen. mgr. 707/727/737 div. Boeing Comml. Airplane Co., Seattle, 1978-82, v.p. sales and mktg., 1982-84, pres., 1986—; pres., chief exec. officer The Boeing Co., Seattle, 1986—, chmn., chief exec. officer, 1988-96, chmn., 1996-97, chmn. emeritus, 1997—; bd. dirs. Citicorp, Boise Cascade Corp., 3M Co., Boeing, Chevron; mem. The Bus. Coun., 1987; vice chmn. New Am. Schs. Devel. Corp. Trustee Smithsonian Instn. 1st lt. AUS, 1954-56. Mem. Phi Alpha Delta, Beta Theta Pi. Clubs: Overlake Golf and Country, Columbia Tower. Office: Boeing Co 7755 E Marginal Way S Seattle WA 98108-4002

SHROPSHIRE, DONALD GRAY, hospital executive; b. Winston-Salem, N.C., Aug. 6, 1927; s. John Lee and Bess L. (Shouse) S.; m. Mary Ruth Bodenheimer, Aug. 19, 1950; children: Melanie Shropshire David, John Devin. B.S., U. N.C., 1950; Erickson fellow hosp. adminstrn., U. Chgo., 1958-59; LLD (hon.), U. Ariz., 1992; EdD (hon.), Tucson U., 1994. Personnel asst. Nat. Biscuit Co., Atlanta, 1950-52; asst. personnel mgr. Nat. Biscuit Co., Chgo., 1952-54; adminstr. Eastern State Hosp., Lexington, Ky., 1954-62; assoc. dir. U. Md. Hosp., Balt., 1962-67; adminstr. Tucson Med. Ctr., 1967-82, pres., 1982-92, pres. emeritus, 1992—, bd. dirs., 1995; pres. Tucson Hosps. Med. Edn. Program, 1970-71, sec., 1971-86; pres. So. Ariz. Hosp. Council, 1968-69; bd. dirs. Ariz. Blue Cross, 1967-76, chmn. provider standards com., 1972-76; chmn. Healthways Inc., 1985-92; bd. dirs. Tucson Med. Found., Tucson Electric Power Co.; adv. bd. Steele Meml. Pediatric Rsch. Ctr., U. Ariz. Coll. Medicine, 1996—; chmn. bd. La Posada at Park Centre, Inc., Green Valley, Ariz., 1996—. Bd. dirs. Health Planning Coun. Tucson, 1992, mem. exec. com., 1969-74; chmn. profl. divsn. United Way, Tucson, 1969-70, vice chmn. campaign, 1988, Ariz. Health Facilities Authority, bd. dirs., 1992—; chmn. dietary svcs. com., vice chmn., 1988, Md. Hosp. Coun., 1966-67; bd. dirs. Ky. Hosp. Assn., 1961-62, chmn. coun. profl. practice, 1960-61; past pres. Blue Grass Hosp. Coun.; trustee Assn. Western Hosps., 1974-81, pres., 1979-80; mem. accreditation Coun. for Continuing Med. Edn., 1982-87, chair, 1986; bd. govs. Pima C.C., 1970-76, sec., 1973-74, chmn., 1975-76, bd. dirs. Found., 1978-82, Ariz. Bd. Regents, 1982-90, sec., 1983-86, pres., 1987-88; mem. Tucson Airport Authority, 1987—, bd. dirs., 1990-95, pres., 1995; v.p. Tucson Econ. Devel. Corp., 1977-82; bd. dirs. Vol. Hosps. Am., 1977-88, treas., 1979-82; mem. Ariz. Adv. Health Coun. Dirs., 1976-78; bd. dirs. Tucson Tomorrow, 1983-87, Tucson Downtown Devel. Corp., 1988-95, Rincon Inst., 1992—, Sonoran Inst., 1992—; dir. Mus. No. Ariz., 1988—; nat. bd. advisors Coll. Bus. U. Ariz., 1992—, chmn. Dean's Bd. Fine Arts, 1992-96, pres. Ariz. Coun. Econ. Edn., 1993-95; vis. panel Sch. Health Adminstrn. and Policy Ariz. State U., 1990-92; bd. dirs. Tucson Cmty. Found., 1996—; mem. adv. bd. Steele Meml. Rsch. Ctr., U. Ariz. Coll. Medicine, 1996—. Named to Hon. Order Ky. Cols.; named Tucson Man of Yr. 1987; recipient Disting. Svc. award Anti-Defamation League B'nai B'rith, 1989. Mem. Am. Hosp. Assn. (nominating com. 1983-86, trustee 1975-78, ho. dels. 1972-78, chmn. coun. profl. svc. 1973-74, regional adv. bd. 1969-78, chmn. joint com. with NASW 1963-64, Disting. Svc. award 1989), Ariz. Hosp. Assn. (Salisbury award 1982, bd. dirs. 1967-72, pres. 1970-71), Ariz. C. of C. (bd. dirs. 1988-93), Assn. Am. Med. Colls. (mem. assembly 1974-77), Tucson C. of C. (bd. dirs. 1968-69), United Comml. Travelers, Nat. League for Nursing, Ariz. Town Hall (bd. dirs. 1982-92, chmn. 1990-92, treas. 1985), Pima County Acad. Decathlon Assn. (dir. 1983-85), The Rotary Ctr. of Tucson (pres. 1993-94). Baptist (ch. moderator, chmn. finance com., deacon, ch. sch. supt., trustee, bd. dirs. ch. found.). Home: 6734 N Chapultepec Circle Tucson AZ 85750 Office: Tucson Med Ctr 2195 E River Rd Ste 202 Tucson AZ 85718-6586 *It seems important to put something back into life - for all we take from it.*

SHROPSHIRE, WALTER, JR., biophysicist emeritus, pastor; b. Washington, Sept. 4, 1932; s. Walter and Mary Virginia (Anderson) S.; m. Audrey Marie McConkey, June 28, 1958; children—Janet Marie, Susan Lynn, Edward Allen. BS in Physics, George Washington U., 1954, MS in Botany, 1956, PhD in Plant Physiology, 1958; MDiv summa cum laude, Wesley Theol. Sem., 1990; postdoctoral fellow biophysics, Calif. Inst. Tech., 1957-59. Ordained to ministry United Meth. Ch., 1977. Physicist Smithsonian Instn., Washington, 1959-63; asst. dir. Smithsonian Environ. Rsch. Ctr., Washington, 1963-86; Gast prof. U. Freiburg, Germany, 1968-69; biophysicist, dir. Omega Lab., Cabin John, Md., 1986—; professorial lectr. botany George Washington U., 1960-85; Gast prof. U. Zurich, Switzerland, 1985-86; part-time adj. prof. Practice Min. & Mission Weslet Theol. Sem., 1990—. Editor: Phytochrome, 1972, Joys of Research, 1981, Photomorphogenesis, Vol 16A, 16B, 1983, Photobiology, 1984-85; Contbr. articles to profl. jours. Pastor, Foundry United Meth. Ch., Washington, 1991—. Recipient Smithsonian Outstanding Performance award, 1967, Smithsonian Research award, 1968, Merit award Soc. John Wesley, 1997; NSF grantee, 1960-66. Fellow Explorers Club. Office: Omega Lab PO Box 189 Cabin John MD 20818-0189 *The world is an incredible place, rich with unexplored and unexplained interconnections between the biological and physical domains. I am fortunate to have been born when science has begun to unravel some of the mysteries of these interconnections and especially fortunate to have had teachers who shared their enthusiasm for learning. I also have benefited from mystical religious experiences of others and my own that enable me to work at the interface between science and religion. My belief is that the pursuit of both subjective and objective knowledge of ourselves and the universe we live in is necessary to enable humanity to develop to its fullest potential. This is an exciting pursuit I hope to continue to participate in a long time.*

SHRUM, ALICIA ANN, elementary school educator, librarian; b. Miami, Okla., Sept. 8, 1946; d. Harold Richard Moye and Novella (Fields) Steen; m. Jimmie Ray Shrum, May 15, 1971. BS in Elem. Edn., Northeastern State U., Tahlequah, Okla., 1969, MS in Elem. Edn., 1978; student pubs. course, Inst. Children's Lit., 1990-91. Cert. elem. tchr., libr. media specialist, Okla. Tchr. 1st grade Justus Sch., Claremore, Okla., 1969-74, tchr. 3rd grade, 1974-81, tchr. remedial math., libr., 1981-83, libr./enrichment educator, 1983—; co-chair centennial com. Justis Sch., 1989; coach teams for 6th and 7th grades, 7th and 8th grades Acad. Bowl, 1993—. Justus Sch. rep. United Way, 1989-93. Mem. NEA, Okla. Edn. Assn. (grantee to establish new libr. 1984-87), Justus-Taiwah Edn. Assn. (sec./treas. 1988-90, pres. 1990-91, sec. 96-97). Democrat. Avocations: quilting, handicrafts, reading. Office: Justus Libr 3 Mile E Hwy # 20 Claremore OK 74018

SHTOHRYN, DMYTRO MICHAEL, librarian, educator; b. Zvyniach, Ukraine, Nov. 9, 1923; came to U.S., 1950; s. Mykhailo and Kateryna (Figol) S.; m. Eustachia Barwinska, Sept. 3, 1955; children: Bohdar O., Liudoslava V. Student, Ukrainian Free U., Munich, 1947-48, U. Minn., 1954; M.A. in Slavic Studies, U. Ottawa, Can., 1958, B.L.S., 1959, Ph.D. in Slavic Studies, 1970. Slavic cataloger U. Ottawa, 1959; cataloger NRC Can., Ottawa, 1959-60; Slavic cataloger, instr. library adminstrn. U. Ill., Urbana, 1960-64, head Slavic cataloging, asst. prof. library adminstrn., 1964-68, head Slavic cataloging, assoc. prof., 1968-75, head Slavic cataloging, prof., 1975-85, lectr. Ukrainian lit., 1975-91, assoc. Slavic librarian, prof., 1985-95, prof. Ukrainian lit., 1991—; lectr. Ukrainian lit. U. Ill., 1975-91; vis. prof. Ukrainian lit. U. Ottawa, 1974; assoc. prof. Ukrainian lit. Ukrainian Cath. U., Rome, 1978—; prof. Ukrainian lit. Ukrainian Free U., Munich, 1983—, Ukrainian lang. and lit., U. Ill., 1991—; chmn. Ukrainian Research Program U. Ill., 1984—. Editor: Catalog of Publications of Ukrainian Academy of Sciences, 1966, Ukrainians in North America: A Bibliographical Directory, 1975; author: Ukrainian Literature in the U.S.A.: Trends, Influences, Achievements, 1975, The Rise and Fall of Book Studies in Ukraine, 1986, Oleh Kandyba-Olzhych: Bibliography, 1992; editor: Bull. Ukrainian Libr. Assn. Am., 1982-88; mem. editl. bd. Ukrainian Historian, 1985—, Ethnic Forum, 1985-95, Crossroads, 1986—, Ukrainian Quar., 1993—. Counselor Boy Scouts Am., Champaign, Ill., 1967-85; bd. dirs. Ukrainian-Am. Found., Chgo., 1978-87. Recipient Grant Future Credit Union Toronto, 1956; recipient Grant U. Ill., 1977, 82, Silver medal Parliament of Can. Librarian, Ottawa, 1959, award Glorier Soc. Can., 1959. Fellow Shevchenko Sci. Soc. (exec. com.); mem. ALA (chmn. Slavic and East European sect. 1968-69), Ukrainian Libr. Assn. Am. (pres. 1970-74, 82-87), Ukrainian Acad. and Profl. Assn. (charter, sec. 1985-89, pres. 1989—), I. Franko Internat. Soc. (founding mem., pres. 1978-79, 81-82), Ukrainian-Am. Assn. Univ. Profs. (exec. com. 1981-96), Ukrainian Hist. Assn. (exec. com. 1983—), Ukrainian Acad. Arts and Scis. in U.S. (exec. com. 1993—), Ukrainian Congress Com. of Am. Scholarly Coun., Ukrainian Writers' Assn. Slovo, Libr. Congress Assocs. (charter mem.). Ukrainian Catholic. Home: 403 Park Lane Dr Champaign IL 61820-7729 Office: Dept Slavic Langs & Lits 3092 Fgn Langs Bldg 707 S Mathews Ave Urbana IL 61801-3625

SHU, CHI-WANG, mathematics educator, researcher; b. Beijing, People's Republic of China, Jan. 2, 1957; came to U.S., 1982, naturalized, 1993.; s. Kuang-Yao and Ding-Zhen (Shi) S.; m. Din-Sui Loh, May 1, 1984; 1 child, Hai-Shuo. BS, U. Sci. and Tech. of China, 1982; PhD, UCLA, 1986. Rsch. assoc. U. Minn., Mpls., 1986-87; asst. prof. applied math. Brown U., Providence, 1987-91, assoc. prof., 1992-96; prof., 1996—; cons. ICASE, NASA Langley Rsch. Ctr., Hampton, Va., 1988—. Mem. editorial bd. Mathematics of Computation, SIAM Jour. Numerical Analysis, Jour. Computational Math., 1993—, Comm. in Applied Analysis, 1996—; contbr. articles to profl. jours. Grantee NSF, NASA, Army Rsch. Office; recipient NASA Pub. Svc. Group Achievement award for pioneer work in computational fluid dynamics, 1992, First Feng Kang prize of Sci. Computing Chinese Acad. Sci., 1995. Mem. Am. Math. Soc., Soc. for Indsl. and Applied Math. Achievements include research in numerical solutions for discontinuous problems. Home: 135 Woodbury St Providence RI 02906-3511 Office: Brown U Div Applied Maths 182 George St Providence RI 02912-9056

SHU, WENLONG, environmental engineer, educator; b. Shanghai, China, Nov. 28, 1932; s. Junde and Yuying (Wang) S.; m. Manqing Chen, Mar. 10, 1957; children: Minmin, Hongmin. B in Engring., Qing Hua U., Beijing, China, 1953; MS in Environ. Engring., U. N.C., 1982. Cert. sr. engr. in water and wastewater engring. Bur. Staffs of Sci. and Tech., State Coun. China. Asst. tchr. Harbin (China) U. Tech., 1953-56; engr. Rsch. Inst. Bldg. and Constrn., Beijing, 1956-80; vis. scholar U. N.C., Chapel Hill, 1980, rsch. assoc., 1981-82; sr. engr. and vice chief engr. Rsch. Inst. Environ. Protection, Beijing, 1982-90, rsch. prof., 1990—; presenter in field; appraiser for proposals in environmental sciences of the Natl. Natural Science Found. of China, 1984—. Contbr. articles to profl. jours.; inventor in field. Recipient Lifelong Achievement award State Coun. China, Beijing, 1993—; Continuation Edn. grantee Ministry of Edn., Beijing, 1980-82; grantee UNEP Asia & Pacific Region Office, Bangkok, 1992. Mem. Am. Water Works Assn., Pacific Basin Consortium for Hazardous Waste Rsch., Chinese Soc. Water and Wastewater Engring. (com. 1985—), Rsch. Inst. Environ. Protection Metall. Industry (advisor to grads. 1984—). Avocations: traveling, writing, handiwork. Home: 33 Xitucheng Rd, Beijing 100088, China Office: Rsch Inst Environ Protect, 33 Xitucheng Rd, Beijing 100088, China

SHUART, JAMES MARTIN, academic administrator; b. College Point, N.Y., May 9, 1931; s. John and Barbara (Schmidt) S.; m. Marjorie Strunk, Apr. 5, 1953; children: James Raymond, William Arthur. BA, Hofstra U., 1953, MA, 1962; PhD, NYU, 1966. Group rep. Home Life Ins. Co., 1955-57; N.Y. Life Ins. Co., 1957-59; adminstr. Hofstra U., Hempstead, N.Y., 1959-70, asst. dir. admissions, asst. dean faculty, asst. pres., exec. dean student services, assoc. dean liberal arts scis., trustee, 1973-75; v.p. adminstrv. services Hofstra U., 1975-76, pres., 1976—; mem. higher edn. adv. com. N.Y. State Senate, 1979—; trustee Commn. on Ind. Colls. and Univs., N.Y. State, 1982-89, 92-95, chmn., 1988-89; mem. Am. Coun. on Edn.'s Labor/Higher Edn. Coun., 1983-88, Am. Coun. on Edns. Commn. on Leadership Devel., 1987-89, Peat Marwick Higher Edn. Pres.'s Adv. Com., 1988—; bd. dirs. Smith Barney Traveler's World Funds, European Am. Bank; chair Nassau County Property Tax Relief Commn., 1990-92; co-chair N.Y. State Temporary Commn. for L.I. Tax Relief. Trustee Molloy Coll., 1973-77; mem. adv. bd. Adelphi U. Sch. Social Work, 1973-84; dep. county exec. Nassau County, 1973-75, commr. social svcs., 1971-73, commr. L.I. Reg. Planning Bd., 1978-83, chmn., 1981-83; bd. dirs L.I. Assn., 1986-90; trustee Uniondale (N.Y.) Pub. Libr., 1966-68, L.I. Hosp. Planning Coun., 1971-75; pres., bd. dirs. Health Welfare Coun. Nassau County, 1971-80; chmn. Nassau Bd. Social Svcs., 1971-73; bd. dirs. Winthrop U. Hosp., 1979-86; mem. Nassau County Charter Revision Commn., 1993-96. Decorated officer Order of Orange Nassau (The Netherlands); recipient Founders Day award NYU, 1967, Alumnus of Yr. award Hofstra U., 1973, George M. estabrook Disting. svc. award Alumni Assn., 1974, Leadership in Govt. award C.W. Post coll., L.I. U., 1978, Man of Yr. award Hempstead C. of C., 1978, L.I. Pers. and Guidance Assn., award, 1977, Lincoln Day award Syosset-Woodbury Rep. Club, 1981, L.I. Bus. disting. Leadership award 1982, 96, Joseph Giacalone award 1986, Medal of Honor L.I.A., 1988, L.I. Achievement award Pub. Rels. Profls. of L.I., 1995, Award L.I. Bus. Devel. Coun., 1994; others; named to L.I. Hall of Fame, 1985. Home: 25 Cathedral Ave Garden City NY 11530-4412 Office: Hofstra U Office of Pres Hempstead NY 11550-1090

SHUB, HARVEY ALLEN, surgeon; b. Bklyn., Oct. 28, 1942; s. Irving and Sara (Levin) S.; m. Susan Jayne Smith, Dec. 26, 1970; children: Carolyn, Todd. Student, NYU, 1960-61, 1964-65; BS in Zoology, Physics, U. Miami, 1964; MD, U. Rome, Italy, 1971. Diplomate Am. Bd. Colon and Rectal Surgery. Intern, Beth Israel Med. Ctr., N.Y.C., 1971-72, resident in surgery, 1972-76; fellow in colon and rectal surgery, Muhlenberg Hosp., Plainfield, N.J., 1976-77; practice medicine specializing in colon and rectal surgery, Orlando, Fla., 1977—; chmn. dept. surgery Fla. Hosp., 1988-89; pres. Med. Staff Fla. Hosp., 1992-93; asst. consulting prof. dept. surgery Duke U., 1995; mem. staff Winter Park Meml. Hosp., Orlando Regional Med. Ctr., Columbia Park Hosp., South Seminole Community Hosp.; clin. asst. prof. dept. family medicine U. South Fla., Tampa, 1982—. Chmn. pub. edn. com. Am. Cancer Soc. Orange County 1982—. Served to capt. M.C., USAR, 1971-77. Recipient Physician's Recognition award, AMA, 1976, 79, 81, 83, 87, 91, 94, 96. Fellow ACS, Am. Soc. Colon and Rectal Surgeons, Internat. Coll. Surgeons, Southeastern Surg. Congress, Internat. Soc. Univ. Colon and Rectal Surgeons, Am. Soc. for Laser Medicine and Surgery; mem. AMA, So. Med. Assn., Fla. Med. Assn. (council splty. medicine), Orange County Med. Assn., Piedmont Soc. Colon and Rectal Surgeons (pres. elect 1997), Orange County Ostomy Assn. (med. adviser), Fla. Soc. Colon and Rectal Surgeons (sec.-treas. 1980-82, pres. 1983-84, sec.- treas. 1996—), Am. Soc. Gastrointestinal Endoscopy, Internat. Soc. Univ. Colon and Rectal Surgeons, Am. Soc. Laser Medicine and Surgery, Soc. Am. Gastrointestinal Endoscopic Surgeons. Consulting editor Jour. Fla. Med. Assn.; contbr. articles to profl. jours. Home: 1224 Roxboro Rd Longwood FL 32750-6815 Office: 308 Groveland St Orlando FL 32804-4019

SHUBART, DOROTHY LOUISE TEPFER, artist, educator; b. Ft. Collins, Colo., Mar. 1, 1923; d. Adam Christian and Rose Virginia (Ayers) Tepfer; m. Robert Franz Shubart, Apr. 22, 1950; children: Richard, Lorenne. *Dorothy Shubart's ancestors can be traced back to the days of Jefferson and Adams, with Christian Haufman (born January 1814). Her lineage also goes back to when humans came to America. Dorothy's great-grandfather, Ayers, gave up his knighthood in England and came to America to marry a Cherokee Indian princess. Her great-grandfather, Toepfer, a book binder, came to America in the 1870s from Altenstein, Germany. Many professions dot Dorothy's history, from a book binder to teacher, contractor, mid-wife to Dorothy's parents, who were homestead ranchers. Dorothy and her two sisters graduated from college as artists and art teachers. Several nieces and cousins are also musicians and artists.* Grad., Cleve. Inst. Art, 1944-46; AA, Colo. Women's Coll., 1944; grad., Cleve. Inst. Art, 1946; student, Western Res. U., 1947-48; BA, St. Thomas Aquinas Coll., 1974; MA, Coll. New Rochelle, 1978. Art tchr. Denver Mus., 1942-44, Cleve. Recreation Dept., 1944-50; ind. artist, portrait painter, ceramist-potter Colo., Cleve., N.Y., and N.Mex., 1944—; adult edn. art tchr. Nanuet (N.Y.) Pub. Schs., 1950-65, Pearl River (N.Y.) Adult Edn., 1950-51; rec. sec. Van Houten Fields Assn., West Nyack, N.Y., 1969-74. Exhbns. include Hopper House, Rockland Ctr. for Arts, CWC, Cleve. Inst. Art, Coll. New Rochelle, Rockland County Ann. Art Fair, Gonzalez Sr. Ctr., 1970-91. Leader 4-H Club, Nanuet, 1960-80, Girls Scouts U.S., Nanuet, 1961-68; mem. scholarship com., gen. com. PTA, Nanuet, 1964-68; rec. sec. Van Houten Fields assn., West Nyack, N.Y., 1969-74; com. mem. Eldorado (Santa Fe) Cmty. Improvement Assn.-Arterial Rd. Planning Com., 1992-94, Environ. Def. Fund, Union of Concerned Scientists, Nat. Com. to Preserve Social Security and Medicare; capt. Neighborhood Watch; local organizer Eldorado chpt.; mem. Eldorado Conservation Greenbelt Com., 1996-97; vol. Jim Baca Gov.'s campaign, 1994, Eric Serva's Campaign for Congress, 1996; mem. Eldorado Hist. Com., 1995-97; mem. El Dorado Arterial Road Planning Com., Habitat for Humanity. Gund scholar Cleve. Inst. Art, 1946. Mem. AAUW, NOW, Audubon Soc., Ams. for Dem. Action, Environ. Def. Fund, Union Concerned Scientists, Action on Smoking and Health, Wilderness Club, Delta Tau Kappa, Phi Delta Kappa. Democrat. Avocations: books, gardening, photography, bicycling, writing. Home: 8 Hidalgo Ct Santa Fe NM 87505-8898 *Spring is eternal, life is very fragile.*

SHUBB, WILLIAM BARNET, lawyer; b. Oakland, Calif., May 28, 1938; s. Ben and Nellie Bernice (Fruechtenicht) S.; m. Sandra Ann Talarico, July 29, 1962; children: Alisa Marie, Carissa Ann, Victoria Ann. AB, U. Calif., Berkeley, 1960, JD, 1963. Bar: Calif., 1964, U.S. Ct. Internat. Trade 1981, U.S. Customs Ct. 1980, U.S. Ct. Appeals (9th cir.) 1964, U.S. Supreme Ct. 1972. Law clk. U.S. Dist. Ct., Sacramento, 1963-65; asst. U.S. atty., Sacramento, 1965-71; chief asst. U.S. atty. (ea. dist.) Calif., 1971-74; assoc. Diepenbrock, Wulff, Plant & Hannegan, Sacramento, 1974-77, ptnr., 1977-80, 81-90; U.S. atty. Eastern Dist. Calif., 1980-81; judge U.S. Dist. Ct. (ea. dist.) Calif., 1990—; chmn. com. drafting of local criminal rules U.S. Dist. Ct. (ea. dist.) Calif., 1974, mem. speedy trial planning com., 1974-80; lawyer rep. 9th Cir. U.S. Jud. Conf., 1975-78; mem. faculty Fed. Practice Inst., 1978-80; instr. McGeorge Sch. Law, U. Pacific, 1964-66. Mem. ABA, Fed. Bar Assn. (pres. Sacramento chpt. 1977), Calif. Bar Assn., Assn. Def. Counsel, Am. Bd. Trial Advs., Sacramento County Bar Council. Office: US Courthouse 650 Capitol Mall Rm 2042 Sacramento CA 95814-4707*

SHUBERT, GABRIELLE S., museum executive director; b. Phila., Apr. 28, 1955; d. Albert H. and Florence (Reiff) S. B in Music, Oberlin Coll., 1977; M in Public Adminstrn., N.Y.U., 1989. Asst. to v.p./dir. of sales Columbia Artist Mgmt., N.Y.C., 1979-80; artist rep. Herbert Barrett Mgmt., N.Y.C., 1980-81; dir. sales Sheldon Soffer Mgmt., N.Y.C., 1981-87; dir. work study program The Parks Coun., N.Y.C., 1987-88; mgr. arts for transit Met. Transp. Authority, N.Y.C., 1988-91; exec. dir. N.Y. Transit Mus., N.Y.C., 1991—; guest lectr. N.Y.U., 1995, Yale U., New Haven, Conn., 1987; pub. art selection panel Dept. of Cultural Affairs, N.Y.C., 1992. Chmn. Concerned Citizens Upper Broadway, N.Y.C., 1983-85; fellow Coro Found. LEadership N.Y. program. Fellow Mus. Mgmt. Inst. Getty Mus., Berkeley, Calif., 1995, Mayor's Leadership Inst., N.Y.C., 1995. Fellow Mcpl. Art Soc. Office: NY Transit Museum 130 Livingston St Rm 9001 Brooklyn NY 11201-5106

SHUBERT, GUSTAVE HARRY, research executive, consultant, social scientist; b. Buffalo, Jan. 18, 1929; s. Gustave Henri and Ada Shubert (Smith) S.; m. Rhea Brickman, Mar. 29, 1952; children—Wendy J., David L. B.A., Yale U., 1948; M.A., NYU, 1951. Staff mem. Lincoln Lab., MIT, 1955-57; adminstr. systems engring. Hycon Eastern, Inc., Paris, 1957-59; with RAND Corp., Santa Monica, Calif., 1959—, corp. v.p. domestic programs, 1968-75, sr. v.p. domestic programs, 1975-78, sr. corp. v.p., 1978-89, trustee, 1973-89, sr. fellow, corp. advisor and adv. trustee, 1989—; founding dir. Inst. Civil Justice, 1979-87; dir. equities trust Neuberger & Berman, N.Y.C., 1989—; cons. Keene Corp., N.Y.C., 1990-92; pres. N.Y.C. Rand Inst., 1972-73, trustee, 1972-79; trustee Housing Allowance Offices Brown County, Wis. and South Bend, Ind., 1973-80; mem. adv. coun. Sch. Engring., Stanford U., 1976-79; mem. policy adv. com. clin. scholars program UCLA, 1975, 88; mem. adv. group evaluation and methodology divsn. GAO, 1986—; mem. adv. commn. on professionalism ABA, 1985-87; mem. Calif. jud. system com. Los Angeles County Bar Assn., 1984-85; mem. com. on evaluation of poverty rsch. NAS. Mem. history dept. adv. bd. Carnegie Mellon U., 1995—. With USAF, 1951-55. Decorated Air medal with 3 oak leaf clusters, Commendation medal. Mem. AAAS, Am. Judicature Soc. (bd. dirs. 1987-90), Inst. Strategic Studies (London) World Affairs Coun. (L.A. chpt.), Coun. of Fgn. Rels., Commonwealth Club of San Francisco, Town Hall Club Calif., Jonathan Club, Yale Club. Home: 13838 W Sunset Blvd Pacific Palisades CA 90272-4022 Office: RAND Corp 1700 Main St Santa Monica CA 90401-3208

SHUBERT, JOSEPH FRANCIS, librarian; b. Buffalo, Sept. 17, 1928; s. Joseph Francis and Lena M. (Kohn) S.; m. Dorothy Jean Whearty, Feb. 5, 1955 (div. Feb. 1980); children: Julia Ellen, Alan Joseph. BS, State U. Tchrs. Coll., Geneseo, N.Y., 1951; MA, U. Denver, 1957. Reference and extension librarian Nev. State Library, Carson City, 1951-57; library cons. Nev. State Library, 1957-59, state librarian, 1959-61; asst. dir. internat. relations office ALA, 1962-66; state librarian Ohio, 1966-77; state librarian, asst. commr. libraries N.Y. State Edn. Dept., 1977-96, state libr. emeritus, 1996—, sec., treas. chief officer state Library Agys., 1973-76, chmn., 1976-78; mem. adv. council to U.S. Pub. Printer, 1974-77; adv. com. White House Conf. Library and Info. Services, 1977-79; bd. dirs. Capital Dist. Regional Info. Svc. Network, State U. Albany; trustee Ohio Coll. Library Center, 1976-78; mem. adv. com. Center for the Book, Library of Congress, 1979-82, mem. network adv. coun., 1981-96; Disting. Alumnus lectr. U. Denver, 1979; mem. adv. coun. Sch. Library and Info. Sci., Pratt Inst., 1980—; bd. dirs. N.E. Document Conservation Center, 1980-82, treas. 1986-89, mem. 1989—; chmn. chief officers State Libraries in the NE, 1987-89; mem. design task force White House Conf. on Library and Info. Svcs., 1985. Editor: The Bookmark, 1987-96; contbr. to numerous periodicals. Mem. adv. com. U. Wis. Inst. on Edn., Federally Funded Literacy Program, 1992-94. Recipient Hall of Fame award Ohio Libr. Assn., 1991, Exceptional Achievement award ALA Assn. Specialized and Coop. Library Agy. Assn., 1985, Disting. Pub. Service award SUNY-Albany, Nelson A. Rockefeller Coll. of Pub. Affairs and Policy, 1987, Valma K. Moore award NY. State Assn. Libr. Bds., 1996; named Disting. Alumnus, SUNY-Geneseo, 1985. Mem. ALA (grass roots advocate 1996), Nat. Ctr. for Ednl. Stats., Nat. Commn. on Librs. and Info. Svcs., Task Force on Pub. Libr. Stats. (adv. com. 1990-96), chair advising com. on NCES Survey of State Libr. Agencies, 1993—, Assn . of Specialized and Coop. Lit. Agys. (pres. 1988-89), Nev. Libr. Assn. (pres.), North Collins Libr. Assn. (N.Y.), Meml. Libr. Assn., N.Y. Libr. Assn. (Outstanding Svc. awrad 1996), Chief Officers State Libr. Agys. (chmn. 1977-78), Nev. Congress Parents and Tchrs., Kappa Delta Pi. Roman Catholic. Home: 494 Madison Ave Albany NY 12208-3601 Office: NY State Libr State Edn Dept 33 Cultural Edn Ctr # 10A Albany NY 12230

SHUBIK, MARTIN, economics educator; b. N.Y.C., Mar. 24, 1926; s. Joseph Louis and Sara S.; m. Julia Kahn, Aug. 11, 1970; 1 child, Claire Louise. B.A., U. Toronto, 1947, M.A., 1949; Ph.D., Princeton U., 1953. Research asst. Princeton U., 1950-53, research asso., 1953-55; fellow Center for Advanced Study in Behavioral Scis., Palo Alto, Calif., 1955-56; cons. mgmt. consultation services Gen. Electric Co., 1956-60; adj. research prof. Pa. State U., 1957-59; vis. prof. econs. Yale U., New Haven, 1960-61; prof. econs. of orgn., dept. adminstrv. sci. Yale U., 1963-75, Seymour H. Knox prof. math. instl. econs., 1975—; bd. dirs. Equity Strategies, Third Ave. Fund; mem. staff T.J. Watson Rsch. Labs., IBM Corp., 1961-63; vis. prof. Escuela de Estudios Económicos U. Chile, Santiago, 1965, Inst. Advanced Studies, Vienna, Austria, 1968, 70, U. Melbourne, Australia, 1973; cons. Rand Corp., Santa Monica, Calif., 1963; dir. Cowles Found. for Rsch. In Econs., Yale U., 1973-76; mem. econs. bd. Santa Fe Inst., 1991—; cons. in field. Author or co-author: numerous books in field including The War Game, 1979, (with G. Brewer) The Aggressive Conservative Investor, 1979, (with M.J. Whitman) Market Structure and Behavior, 1980, (with R.E. Levitan) Game Theory in the Social Sciences, vol. 1, 1982, vol. 2, 1984; mem. editorial bd. Conflict Resolution; mem. editorial adv. bd. Internat. Studies Series; assoc. editor Mgmt. Sci, 1965-81; contbr. articles to profl. jours. Served to lt. Royal Can. Navy. Recipient Lanchester prize, 1983, Koopman prize mil. ops. rsch., 1996; named hon. prof. U. Vienna. Fellow Econometric Soc., World Acad. Arts and Scis.; mem. Social Systems Inc. (chmn. bd. dirs. 1978), Am. Acad. Arts and Scis., Conn. Acad. Arts and Scis. Home: 140 Edgehill Rd New Haven CT 06517-4011 Office: 30 Hillhouse Ave New Haven CT 06511-3704

SHUCK, ANNETTE ULSH, education educator; b. Harrisburg, Pa., Apr. 4, 1946; d. David Addison and Florence (Scholl) Ulsh; children: Ryan David Summers, Kirsten Annette Shuck. BS, Bloomsburg U., 1967; MS, W.Va. U., 1968, EdD, 1976; sch. psychology cert., Coll. Grad. Studies, 1983. Cert. elem., secondary, spl. edn. tchr., Pa., W.Va., sch. psychologist, W.Va. Elem. tchr. Pa. and W.Va. schs., 1968-70; instr. W.Va. U., Morgantown, 1972, grad. asst., 1972-75, instr. spl. edn. dept., 1976-77, asst. prof., 1977-83, assoc. prof., 1983-87; vis. assoc. prof. div. edn. U. V.I., Charlotte Amalie, St. Thomas, 1987-88, assoc. prof., 1988, prof. div. edn., 1989—; part-time instr. Lebanon Valley Coll. and Temple U., Harrisburg, Pa., 1970-72; cons. sch. psychology program Coll. Grad. Studies, Institute, W.Va., 1986; mem. Gov. of V.I. Spl. Edn. Task Force, 1988—. Author: International Parent Interventionist Booklet, 1976, 1988, rev. edit., 1997; contbr. chpt. to book and articles to profl. jours. Mem. com. St. Thomas Hist. Soc., 1988-95, Environ. Awareness and Action Com., St. Thomas, 1991—; hearing officer State Dept. Spl. Edn.; parent edn. interventionist, 1979—. NDEA fellow, 1967-68. Mem. Coun. for Exceptional Children, Am. Assn. Coll. Tchr. Edn., Phi Delta Kappa (v.p. 1975-76, pres. 1976-77). Avocations: research, writing, snorkeling, sailing, dancing. Office: U VI Tchr-Edn-208 Saint Thomas VI 00802

SHUCK, EDWIN HAYWOOD, III, surgeon; b. Chattanooga, Tenn., 1948. MD, Washington U., St. Louis, 1973. Diplomate Am. Bd. Surgery, Am. Bd. Colon and Rectal Surgery. Intern Tulane U. Hosps., New Orleans, 1973-74, resident, 1974-78; fellow in colon and rectal surgery Carle Clinic, Urbana, Ill., 1978-79; now with Meml. Hosp., Chattanooga, Tenn.; asst. prof. clin. surgery U. Tenn. Fellow ACS, Am. Soc. Colon and Rectal Surgery. Office: Colon & Rectal Surg Assoc Memorial Med Bldg W 721 Glenwood Dr Ste 473 Chattanooga TN 37404-1106

SHUCK, JERRY MARK, surgeon, educator; b. Bucyrus, Ohio, Apr. 23, 1934; s. James Edwin and Pearl (Mark) S.; m. Linda Wayne, May 28, 1974; children: Jay Steven, Gail Ellen, Kimberly Ann, Lynn Meredith, Steven James. BS in Pharmacy, U. Cin., 1955, MD, 1959, DSc, 1966. Intern Colo. Gen. Hosp., Denver, 1959-60; resident in surgery U. Cin. Integrated Program, 1960-66; mem. faculty dept. surgery U. N.Mex., Albuquerque, 1968-80; prof. U. N.Mex., 1974-80; founder burn and trauma unit; Oliver H. Payne prof. dept. surgery, chmn. dept. Case-Western Res. U., Cleve., 1980—; interim v.p. for med. affairs, 1993-95; dir. surgery Univ. Hosps. Cleve., 1980—; cons. FDA, 1972-77. Contbr. articles to profl. jours. Served to capt. U.S. Army, 1966-68. Mem. ACS, Am. Surg. Assn., Am. Bd. Surgery (bd. dirs., chmn. 1993-94), Soc. Univ. Surgeons, Am. Assn. Surgery Trauma, Am. Trauma Soc. (founding mem.), Univ. Assn. Emergency Medicine (founding mem.), Am. Burn Assn. (founding mem.), We. Surg. Assn., Ctrl. Surg. Assn. (pres. 1996—), Assn. Acad. Surgery, S.W. Surg. Assn., Cleve. Surg. Soc., Ohio Med. Assn., Acad. Medicine Cleve., Halsted Soc., Surg. Infection Soc. (founding mem.), B'nai B'rith, Jewish Cmty. Ctr. Club, The Temple Club. Democrat. Jewish. Office: Case Western Reserve U Dept Surgery 2074 Abington Rd Cleveland OH 44106-2602

SHUCK, LOLA MAE, retired elementary school educator; b. Eustis, Nebr., Mar. 22, 1929; d. Gust Adolf and Dora (Timm) Hueftle; m. Kenneth L. Shuck, Dec. 22, 1951 (div. Oct. 1969); children: David Lynn, Terri Kay, Lorie Jane Shuck Larson. BA, Nebr. Wesleyan U., 1951; MA, Ariz. State U., 1969. Elem. tchr. Springfield (Colo.) Pub. Sch., 1948-49; tchr. art David City (Nebr.) Pub. Schs., 1951-52, Alhambra Dist. 68 Pub. Schs., Phoenix, 1964-68, 69-92; ret., 1992. Vice pres. Women's Soc. Christian Svc., 1959-63; mem. ch. choir Meth. Ch., 1992—; committeewoman Phoenix Rep. Com., 1976-77. Named Ms. Personality, Ms. Nebr. Contest, 1949. Mem. Alpha Delta Kappa (pres. Xi chpt. 1981-82, chmn. bylaws 1991-93). Democrat. Avocations: china painting, acrylic, watercolor and oil painting. Home: 4766 W Palmaire Ave Glendale AZ 85301-2742

SHUCK, ROBERT F., financial executive; s. Robert F. II and Gertrude (Lehr) S.; m. Page Downe, May 30, 1969; children: Robert F. IV, Hollister A. BA in Acctg. with honors, S.E. Mo. Coll., 1959; MBA, Northwestern U., 1961. CPA, Ill.; cert. fin. planner. With Raymond James Fin., Inc., St. Petersburg, Fla., 1969—, vice chmn., 1991—; bd. dirs. RJ Comm., Inc. Bd. dirs. Southeast Mo. Univ. Found.; trustee All Children's Hosp.; mem. long range devel. com. Fla. Coun. Econ. Edn.; mem. policy bd. Tampa Bay Partnership for Regional Econ. Devel.; mem. devel. found. St. Petersburg Jr. Coll.; stewardship chmn. Our Savior Luth. Ch., St. Petersburg. Mem. Securities Industry Assn. (sales and mktg. com.), Internat. Assn. for Fin. Planning (past bd. dirs.), Nat. Endowment for Fin. Edn. (trustee, mem. exec. com.). Office: Raymond James Fin 880 Carillon Pky Saint Petersburg FL 33716-1102

SHUE, ELISABETH, actress; b. Wilmington, Del., Oct. 6, 1963; m. Davis Guggenheim. Student, Wellesley Coll.; grad., Harvard U.; studied with Sylvie Leigh, Showcase Theater. Appeared in Broadway plays including Some Americans Abroad, Birth and After Birth; appeared in films including The Karate Kid, 1984, Link, 1986, Adventures in Babysitting, 1987, Cocktail, 1988, Body Wars, 1989, Back to the Future Part II, 1989, Back to the Future Part III, 1990, Soapdish, 1991, The Marrying Man, 1991, Twenty Bucks, 1993, Heart and Souls, 1993, Radio Inside, 1994, Blind Justice, 1994, The Underneath, 1995, Leaving Las Vegas, 1995 (Oscar nominee for Best Actress), The Trigger Effect, 1996, The Saint, 1996, Palmetto, 1997, Deconstructing Harry, 1997, Cousin Bette, 1997; appeared in TV movies including Charles and Diana, Double Switch, 1987, Hale the Hero, 1992, Blind Justice; appeared in TV series Call to Glory, 1984. Office: Creative Arts Agy 9830 Wilshire Blvd Beverly Hills CA 90212-1804*

SHUER, LAWRENCE MENDEL, neurosurgery educator; b. Toledo, Apr. 12, 1954; s. Bernard Benjamin and Estelle Rose (Drukker) S.; m. Paula Ann Elliott, Sept. 4, 1976; children: Jenna, Tammy, Nichole. BA with high distinction, U. Mich., 1975, MD cum laude, 1978. Diplomate Am. Bd. Neurol. Surgery, Nat. Bd. Med. Examiners. Fellow in neurology Inst. Neurology, London, 1979; intern in surgery Stanford (Calif.) U. Sch. Medicine, 1978-79, resident in neuropathology, 1980, resident in neurosurgery, 1980-84, clin. asst. prof. surgery and neurosurgery, 1984-90, assoc. prof., 1990—, acting chmn. dept. neurosurgery, 1992-95, 96—, assoc. dean, 1996—, chief of staff Stanford Health Sys., 1996—; numerous presentations in field. Contbr. articles and abstracts to med. jours., chpts. to books. Recipient Kaiser tchr. award Stanford U., 1993; James B. Angell scholar. Mem. AMA, Am. Assn. Neurol. Surgeons, Congress Neurol. Surgeons, Western Neurosurg. Soc., Calif. Assn. Neurol. Surgeons (bd. dirs., treas. 1995—), Calif. Med. Assn., Am. Heart Assn. (fellow stroke coun.), Santa Clara County Med. Assn., San Francisco Neurol. Soc., Alpha Omega Alpha. Avocations: skiing, swimming, travel. Office: R155 Stanford U Med Ctr 300 Pasteur Dr Palo Alto CA 94304-2203

SHUEY, JOHN HENRY, diversified products company executive; b. Monroe, Mich., Mar. 14, 1946; s. John Henry and Bertha (Thomas) S.; children: Katherine, John Henry, John Joseph Satory. B.S. in Indsl. Engring., U. Mich., 1968, M.B.A., 1970. With Tex. Instruments Co., Dallas, 1970-74; asst. treas. The Trane Co., La Crosse, Wis., 1974-78, treas., 1978-81, v.p., treas., 1981-83, v.p. fin., chief fin. officer, 1983-86; also v.p., group exec. Am. Standard; sr. v.p. and chief fin. officer AM Internat. Inc., Chgo., 1986-91; exec. v.p. Amcast Indsl. Corp., Dayton, Ohio, 1991-93, pres., COO, 1993-95, pres., CEO, 1995—, also bd. dirs.; bd. dirs. Cooper Tire and Rubber Co., Findlay, Ohio. Bd. dirs., pres. Luth. Hosp. Found., 1983-87; bd. dirs. Wright State Univ. Found., 1996—; bd. trustees Dayton Ballet, 1996—, Ohio Found. of Ind. Colleges, 1994—. Mem. Fin. Execs. Inst., Manufacturers Alliance for Productivity & Innovation. Congregationalist. Office: Amcast Indsl Corp PO Box 98 Dayton OH 45401-0098 also: Elkhart Products Corp 1255 Oak St Elkhart IN 46514-2277

SHUFORD, HARLEY FERGUSON, JR., furniture manufacturing executive; b. Norfolk, Va., Oct. 7, 1937; s. Harley Ferguson Sr. and Nancy (Pope) S.; m. Helgi Kuuskraa; children: Linda, David. BA, U. N.C., 1959. Engr. Century Furniture Co., Hickory, N.C., 1959-60, mgr. data processing, 1960-63, v.p. mfg., 1964-67, pres., 1967-95; chmn. CV Industries (formerly Shuford Industries, Inc.), Hickory, 1994—; bd. dirs. 1st Union Bank N.C., Charlotte. Trustee Catawba Meml. Hosp., Hickory, 1971-77, chmn., 1977-81; bd. dirs. U. N.C. Sys., Chapel Hill, 1975-83; bd. dirs. N.C. Citizens Bus. and Industry, Raleigh, 1982-95; chmn. N.C. Arts Coun., Raleigh, 1985-93. Mem. Am. Furniture Mfrs. Assn. (bd. dirs. 1968-92, pres., chmn. 1980-82), Catawba County C. of C. (pres. 1976), Phi Beta Kappa. Republican. Mem. United Ch. of Christ. Office: CV Industries PO Box 608 Hickory NC 28603-0608

SHUGART, ALAN F., electronic computing equipment company executive; b. L.A., Sept. 27, 1930. BS in Engring. and Physics, U. Redlands, 1951. Dir. engring. IBM, San Jose, Calif., 1952-69; v.p. Memorex Corp., Sunnyvale, Calif., 1969-73; pres. Shugart Assocs., 1973-78; chmn., pres., chief exec. officer, coo Seagate Tech., Scotts Valley, Calif., 1978—, also bd. dirs. Office: Seagate Tech 920 Disc Dr Scotts Valley CA 95066-4544*

SHUGART, CECIL GLENN, retired physics educator; b. Ennis, Tex., Oct. 13, 1930; s. Clifford Clarence and Ethel Hazel (Venable) S.; m. Theresa Lively, Aug. 26, 1955 (div. July 1981); children: David Neal, Peter Gregory; m. Anita Brumbelow, Dec. 14, 1985. Student, Navarro Coll., Corsicana, Tex., 1954-55; BA, N. Tex. State U., 1957; MA, U. Tex., 1961, PhD, 1968. Rsch. scientist Def. Rsch. Lab., Austin, 1958-61; assoc. engr. IBM, San Jose, Calif., 1961-62; asst. prof., head dept. physics Hardin-Simmons U., Abilene, Tex., 1962-65; dir. Soc. Physics Students Am. Inst., N.Y.C., 1968-70; rsch. assoc. U. Tex.-Austin, 1967-68; prof. physics, chmn. Northeast La. U., Monroe, 1970-77; prof. chmn. physics U. Memphis, 1977-97; ret., 1997; cons. Tech. Legal Assocs., Memphis, 1978—. Author: (with Bedell and Genusa) Experiments for General Physics, 1975; co-author: (with Johnston) The Phenomena of Physics, 1982, Phenomenal Physics and Astronomy, 1991; editor: (with P. Barker) After Einstein, 1981, (with J. Payne) Scientists and Public Policy, 1982. Served with USAF, 1948-52. NSF fellow, 1966-67; NSF grantee, 1974-75, 79-80. Fellow AAAS; mem. Am. Assn. Physics Tchrs., Am. Phys. Soc. (vice chmn. southeastern sect. 1982-83, sect. chmn. 1983-84, sect. sec., 1991-95, sec. ea. region 1991-95), Sigma Pi Sigma (pres. 1972-76). Republican. Methodist. Home: 11483 Front Beach Rd TA0210 Panama City Beach FL 32907

SHUGART, HOWARD ALAN, physicist, educator; b. Orange, Calif., Sept. 21, 1931; s. Howard Ancil and Bertha Elizabeth (Henderson) S.; m. Elizabeth L. Hanson, Feb. 6, 1971. B.S., Calif. Inst. Tech., 1953; M.A., U. Calif.-Berkeley, 1955, Ph.D., 1957. Teaching asst. physics U. Calif.-Berkeley, 1953-56, assoc., 1957, lectr., 1957-58, acting asst. prof., 1958-59, asst. prof., 1959-63, assoc. prof., 1963-67, prof., 1967-93, prof. emeritus, 1993—, vice chmn., 1968-70, 79-87, 89—, acting chmn., summer 1979, 80, 81, 83, 84,87; atomic beam group leader Lawrence Berkeley Lab. Lawrence Berkeley Nat. Lab., 1965-79; cons. Convair divsn. Gen. Dynamics Corp., 1960-61; mem. com. nuclear constants NRC, 1960-63. Recipient Donald Sterling Noyce prize for excellence in undergrad. tchg. U. Calif., 1988, Berkeley citation, 1993. Fellow Am. Phys. Soc. (acting sec. Pacific Coast 1961-64, exec. com. div. electron and atomic physics 1972-74), Nat. Speleological Soc. (gov. 1954-56); mem. Sigma Xi. Office: U Calif Dept Physics Berkeley CA 94720-7300

SHUGART, JILL, school system administrator; b. Dallas, July 15, 1940; d. Claude Ernest and Allie Merle (Hamilton) S. BA, Baylor U., 1962; MA, Tex. Woman's U., 1972, PhD, 1980. Middle sch. English tchr. Garland (Tex.) Ind. Sch. Dist., 1962-63, high sch. social studies tchr., 1963-76, high sch. asst. prin., 1976-79, dir. communications, 1979-82, asst. supt., 1982-85, supt., 1985—; mem. legis. coun. U. Interscholastic League, Tex., 1989—; chmn. Dist. III music com., Tex., 1989-98; adj. prof. Tex. Women's U., Denton, 1983; chmn. Region X ESC Adv. Coun., rep. to commr.'s supt.'s com., 1993-95. Gen. chmn. Boy Scouts Am. Scouting Night, Dallas, 1988-89; chmn. City of Garland Comty. Rels. Coun., 1992; sec. Tex. Sch. Alliance, 1992-96; life mem. Tex. PTA; pres. Garland br. Am. Heart Assn., 1990-91; co-chmn. sustaining dr. Garland YMCA, 1995-96. Recipient Lamar award for excellence Masons, Award of Distinction, Tex. Ret. Tchrs. Assn.; named Top 100 Educators to Watch, Executive Educator mag., 1985, Finalist as Outstanding Tex. Sch. Supt., 1990, Woman of Distinction, Soroptimist Club; Paul Harris fellow. Mem. Am. Assn. Sch. Adminstrs. (suburban sch. com. 1990-93), Tex. Assn. Sch. Adminstrs., Tex. Assn. for Supr. Curriculum Devel., Garland Adminstr. Assn. (pres. 1978-79), Nat. Tex. PTA. Republican. Baptist. Avocations: snow skiing, tennis. Office: Garland Ind Sch Dist 720 Stadium Dr Garland TX 75040-4616

SHUGHART, DONALD LOUIS, lawyer; b. Kansas City, Mo., Aug. 12, 1926; s. Henry M. and Dora M. (O'Leary) S.; m. Mary I. Shughart, July 25, 1953; children: Susan C. Shughart Hogsett, Nancy J. Goede. AB, U. Mo., Columbia, 1949, JD, 1951. Bar: Mo. 1951, U.S. Dist. Ct. (we. dist.) Mo. 1951, U.S. Tax Ct. 1979. With Shughart, Thomson & Kilroy, P.C., Kansas City, Mo., 1951—; v.p. K.C. Mack Sales & Service Inc., R.D. Mann Carpet Co.; mem. Mo. Motor Carriers Assn. Pub. Service Com. Bd. dirs. Rockhurst Coll.; mem. adv. bd. St. Joseph Hosp. Served with AC, U.S. Army, 1944-47. Mem. Kansas City Bar Assn., Lawyers Assn. Kansas City, Mo. Bar Assn. (chmn. corp. com. 1980-81, 82-83), Kansas City Bar Assn. (chmn. bus. orgns. com. 1990-91), Am. Judicature Soc., Mo. Orgn. Def. Lawyers (pres. 1971-72), U. Mo. Law Soc., Homestead Country Club, Phi Delta Phi. Republican. Roman Catholic.

SHUHLER, PHYLLIS MARIE, physician; b. Sellersville, Pa., Sept. 25, 1947; d. Raymond Harold and Catherine Cecilia (Virus) S.; m. John Howard Schwarz, Sept. 17, 1983; 1 child, Luke Alexander. BS in Chemistry, Chestnut Hill Coll., 1971; MD, Mich. State U., 1976; diploma of Tropical Medicine and Hygiene, U. London, 1980. Diplomate Am. Bd. Family Medicine. With Soc. Cath. Med. Missionaries, Phila., 1966-82; ward clk., nursing asst. Holy Family Hosp., Atlanta, 1971-72; resident in family practice Somerset Family Med. Residency Program, Somerville, N.J., 1976-79; physician East Coast Migrant Health Project, Newton Grove, N.C., 1980; physician, missionary SCMM, Diocese of Sunyani, Berekum, Ghana, West Africa, 1980-81; emergency rm. physician Northeast Emergency Med. Assn., Quakertown, Pa., 1981-82; founder, physician Family Health Care Ctr., Inc., Pennsburg, Pa., 1982-90; physician Lifequest Med. Group, Pennsburg, 1990-93; pvt. practice Pennsburg, 1993—. Fellow Royal Soc. Tropical Medicine and Hygiene; mem. Am. Acad. Family Practice, Am. Bd. Family Practice, Am. Med. Women Assn. Pa. Acad. Family Practice, Lehigh Valley Women Med. Assn. Roman Catholic. Avocations: guitar, reading, bicycling, hiking. Office: 101 W 7th St Ste 2C Pennsburg PA 18073-1512

SHUKER, GREGORY BROWN, publishing and production company executive; b. Charleston, W.Va., Oct. 3, 1932; s. George and Florence (Brown) S.; m. Nancy Swift Frederick, June 9, 1956 (div. 1983); children: John Frederick, Allison Gregory, Frances Swift. B.S. in Journalism, Northwestern U., 1954. Corr. Life mag., 1959-60; producer Drew Assos., 1961-66, 73-78, Pub. Broadcast Lab., 1967-68; dir. programming CBS-EVR, 1969; program dir. Time-Life Video, RCA SelectaVision, 1970; exec. prod., v.p. Eden House Pub. Inc., N.Y.C., 1971—; exec. producer Playback Assos., Inc., 1972—, Communication for Edn. and Industry, 1981—; pres. GBS, Inc., media devel. group, 1991—; lectr. U. Mich. Sch. Comm., 1989-91; media devel., mgmt. cons. Am. Flywheel Sys., Inc., 1992; dir. corp. TV CEO Seminars, 1993, CD-ROM Devel. Series, 1994-95; exec. prodr. Brazil and Argentina Imax Documentary and Comms. Devel. Group, 1995—, Playback Holographic Data Storage, 1996; bd. dirs. The Loft Film and Theatre Ctr.; bd. dirs. The Environ. Bank, N.Y.C.; mng. dir. Tree-Free Print Out Devel. Group, 1995—; exec. prodr. dyslexia and speech disorders documentary film series, 1997; pres. mktg. devel. group; dir. Major Aviation and environ. groups, N.Y.C., 1997. Producer: documentary films TV Crisis: Behind a Presidential Committment, 1963 (summer of civil rights with John F. and Robert F. Kennedy),The Chair, 1963 (Grand Prix Cannes), Faces of November, 1964 (1st prize Venice), Letters from Vietnam (ABC-TV), 1964, Free at Last (Dr. Martin Luther king Jr.'s last days), . 1968 (1st prize Venice); exec. producer: documentary films TV What Do We Do Now? - The Need for Direction, 1976, Productivity Series, 1979-81, Corp. Media and HDTV Devel., 1984—; (David Susskind Prodns.) feature motion picture prodn., 1982—; producer, Aspira (AT&T), 1987, Lawrence of Arabia and Lowell Thomas, 1992, (TV series) Baltic Festival, 1994; line producer London-to-Peking, 1990; exec. prodr. (TV documentary) Peking-to-Paris Rally, 1997; author: Learning by Television (Ford Found.), 1966. Served to lt. (j.g.) USNR, 1955-58. Mem. Deru, Sigma Delta Chi, Alpha Tau Omega, Kappa Tau Alpha. Clubs: Bronxville Field, Little Forum. Home and Office: 12 Sunset Ave Bronxville NY 10708-2215 also: care NS Bienstock Inc 1740 Broadway New York NY 10019-4315 *God grant me the serenity to accept the things I cannot change, courage to change the things I can, and wisdom to know the difference.*

SHULA, DON FRANCIS, former professional football coach, team executive; b. Grand River, OH, Jan. 4, 1930; s. Dan and Mary (Miller) S.; children: David, Donna, Sharon, Anne, Michael; m. Mary Anne Shula. B.S., John Carroll U., Cleve., 1951, H.H.D. (hon.), 1972; M.A., Case Western Res. U., 1953; Sc.D. (hon.), Biscayne Coll., 1974. Profl. football player Cleve. Browns, 1951-52, Balt. Colts, 1953-56, Washington Redskins, 1957; asst. coach U. Va., 1958, U. Ky., 1959, Detroit Lions, 1960-62; head coach Baltimore Colts, 1963-69, Miami (Fla.) Dolphins, 1970-96; vice chmn. Miami Dolphins, 1996—. Author: The Winning Edge, 1972, (with Ken Blanchard) Everyone's A Coach, 1995. Fla. crusade chmn. Nat. Cancer Soc., 1975; co-chmn. Jerry Lewis March Against Dystrophy, 1975; nat. bd. dirs. Jesuit Program for Living and Learning, 1976; mem. nat. sports com. Multiple Schlerosis Soc., Muscular Dystrophy Assn.; bd. dirs. Heart Assn. Greater Miami; hon. chmn. Belen Jesuit Intercultural Fund Campaign To Build Schs.; established Don Shula Found., breast cancer rsch., 1991—; sponsor Don Shula Scholarship, 1978—. Coached 6 Superbowl teams, winning teams 1972, 73; recipient Coach of Yr. awards 1964, 66, 70, 71, 72, Coach of decade Profl. Football Hall of Fame, 1980, Pro Football's All-Time Winningest Coach, 1994, Brotherhood award Fla. region NCCJ, 1977, Light of Flames Leadership award Barry Coll., 1977, Concern award Cedars Med. Ctr., 1992, Solheim Lifetime Achievement award, 1992, Jim Thorpe award, 1993,Sportsman of Yr. Sports Illustrated, 1993, Horrigan award Pro Football Writers,1994, Horatio Alger award, 1995; named Balt. Colts Silver Anniversary Coach, 1977, elected to Pro Football Hall of Fame, 1997. Roman Catholic. Office: Miami Dolphins 7500 SW 30th St Davie FL 33314-1020 *Success is never final; defeat is never fatal.**

SHULA, ROBERT JOSEPH, lawyer; b. South Bend, Ind., Dec. 10, 1936; s. Joseph Edward and Bertha Mona (Buckner) S.; m. Gaye Ann Martin, Oct. 8, 1978; children: Deirdre Regina, Robert Joseph II, Elizabeth Martin. BS in Mktg., Ind. U., 1958, JD, 1961. Bar: Ind. 1961; Diplomate Ind. Def. Trial Counsel. Ptnr. Bingham Summers Welsh & Spilman, Indpls., 1965-82, sr. ptnr., 1982-89; ptnr. Price & Shula, Indpls., 1989-91, Lowe Gray Steele & Darko, Indpls., 1991—; mem. faculty Nat. Inst. Trial Advocacy; guest lectr. Brit. Medicine and Law Soc., 1979, Ind. U. Sch. Law; medico-legal lectr. Ind. U. Schs. Medicine, Dentistry, and Nursing. Bd. dirs. Arts Ind., Indpls., 1995—; pres. Oriental Arts Soc., Indpls., 1975-79, Meridian Women's Clinic, Inc., Indpls.; trustee Indpls. Mus. Art, 1975-78, life trustee, 1984—; bd. dirs. Ind. Repertory Theatre, Indpls., 1982-92, chmn. bd. dirs., pres., 1985-89; pres. Repertory Soc., 1993-96; v.p., bd. dirs. Flanner House of Indpls., Inc., 1977-88, chmn., 1988—; pres. Internat. Ctr. of Indpls., Inc., 1993-96. Maj. JAGC, USAFR, 1961-65. Fellow Internat. Soc. Barristers; mem. ABA, Fed. Bar Assn., Ind. State Bar Assn., Indpls. Bar Assn., Am. Bd. Trial Advs., Am. Law Inst., Ind. Def. Lawyers Assn., Am. Coll. Legal Medicine, Confrerie Chevaliers du Tastevin, Woodstock Country Club. Democrat. Episcopalian. Home: 4137 N Meridian St Indianapolis IN 46208-4014 Office: Lowe Gray Steele & Darko Bank One Ctr # 4600 111 Monument Cir Indianapolis IN 46204-5100

SHULDINER, ALAN RODNEY, physician, endocrinologist, educator; b. Irumagawa, Japan, Feb. 5, 1957; parents Am. citizens; s. Julius and Janet (Gursky) S.; m. Jill Francie Bresman, June 27, 1984; children: Seth David, Scott Ross. AB in Chemistry magna cum laude, Lafayette coll., 1979; MD with honors, Harvard U., 1984. Diplomate Am. Bd. Internal Medicine, Am. Bd. Endocrinology and Metabolism. Intern in medicine Columbia-Presbyn. Hosp., N.Y.C., 1984-85, resident in medicine, 1985-86; med. staff fellow Diabetes Br. Nat. Inst. Diabetes and Digestive and Kidney Diseases NIH, Bethesda, Md., 1986-88, sr. staff fellow, 1988-90; asst. prof. div. geriatric medicine and gerontology Sch. Medicine Johns Hopkins U., Balt., 1990-91, assoc. prof. div. geriatric medicine and gerontology; guest rschr. Nat. Insts. on Aging NIH, Balt., 1991-96, prof., head divsn. diabetes, obesity and nutrition U. Md. Sch. Medicine; lectr. Endocrine Soc. meetings, 1996, Japan Diabetes Soc. meeting, 1996, Am. Heart Assn. meeting, 1996, FASEB meeting, 1997, Am. Diabetes Assn. meeting, 1997. Co-author: Current Therapy in Endocrinology and Metabolism, 3d edit., 1988, 4th edit., 1991; contbr. articles to profl. jours. including Archives Biochem. Biophysics, Jour. Biol. Chemistry, New Eng. Jour. Medicine, Analytical Biochemistry, Endocrinology, Gene, Nucleic Acids Rsch., Procs. NAS, Biotechniques, Jour. Clin. Endocrinology Metabolism. Mem. AAAS, AMA, ACP, Am. Diabetes Assn. (Rsch. award 1996). Office: Univ of Maryland 725 W Lombard St Rm 5422 Baltimore MD 21201-1009

SHULER, ELLIE GIVAN, JR., retired military officer, military museum administrator; b. Raleigh, N.C., Dec. 6, 1936; s. Ellie Givan and Berta (Williams) S.; m. Annette Fontaine Maury, Mar. 22, 1961; children—Ellie Givan III, Franklin Maury, Gray Hays. B.S.C.E., The Citadel, 1959; M.S. in Mgmt., Rensselaer Poly. Inst., 1967; grad., Squadron Officer Sch., Maxwell AFB, Ala., 1964; postgrad., Naval War Coll.; grad. command and staff course, Nat. War Coll., 1976; grad. cen. flight instr. course, Castle AFB, Calif. Engr. in tng., S.C. Commd. 2d lt. U.S. Air Force, 1959, advanced through grades to lt. gen., 1988, various positions and locations, 1959-68; F-4C pilot, asst. flight comdr. 558th Tactical Fighter Squadron U.S. Air Force, Cam Ranh Bay AFB, Republic of Vietnam, 1968-69; indsl. engr., then asst. dep. chief Engring. Mgmt. Div., Hdqrs. 2d Air Force U.S. Air Force, Barksdale AFB, La., 1969-71; asst. exec. officer to comdr. in chief U.S. Air Force in Europe, Lindsey Air Sta., West Germany, 1972-73; base civil engr., comdr. 86th Civil Engring. Squadron U.S. Air Force in Europe, Ramstein Air Base, Fed. Republic Germany, 1973-75; dir. ops. 3902d Air Base Wing, comdr. 3902d Ops. Squadron Offutt AFB, Nebr., 1976; dir. programs Office Dep. Chief of Staff for Engring. and Services SAC, Offutt AFB, Nebr., 1976-77, exec. to comdr. in chief, 1977-79; vice comdr., then comdr. 19th Bombardment Wing Robins AFB, Ga., 1979-80; comdr. 42d Bombardment Wing Loring AFB, Maine, 1980-81; comdr. 4th Air Div. F.E. Warren AFB, Wyo., 1981-84; comdr. 3rd Air Div. SAC, Andersen AFB, Guam, 1984-86; asst. dep. then dep. chief of staff, ops. SAC Hqrs., Offutt AFB, Nebr., 1986-88; comdr. 8th Air Force SAC, Barksdale AFB, 1988-91; retired, 1991; chmn. bd., CEO 8th Air Force Heritage Ctr., 1993—. Bd. dirs. Longs Peak coun. Boy Scouts Am., 1983-84; trustee Falcon Found., USAF Acad. Decorated D.S.M. with oak leaf cluster, Legion of Merit with oak leaf cluster, D.F.C., Air medal with five oak leaf clusters, Air Force Commendation medal with oak leaf cluster. Mem. Soc. Am. Mil. Engrs. (chpt. pres. 1971), Am. Def. Preparedness Assn. (regional bd. dirs. 1981-84), Order of Dadaelians (hon. flight capt. 1981-85), Council on Am.'s Mil. Past, Mil. Order of World Wars, Tau Beta Pi. Republican. Episcopalian. Lodge: Kiwanis. Avocations: numismatics, golf, hunting, fishing, military history. Office: 675 Willow Way W Alexander City AL 35010-6253

SHULER, KURT EGON, chemist, educator; b. Nuremberg, Germany, July 10, 1922; came to U.S., 1937, naturalized, 1944; s. Louis and Donie (Wald) Schulherr; m. Beatrice Gwyn London, Nov. 11, 1944. B.S., Ga. Inst. Tech., 1942; Ph.D., Cath. U. Am., 1949; postdoctoral fellow, Johns Hopkins U., 1949-51. Sr. staff mem., asst. group supr., chem. physics group Applied Physics Lab., Johns Hopkins, 1951-55; supervisory phys. chemist Nat. Bur. Standards, 1955-58, cons. to dir., 1958-61, asst. dir., sr. research fellow, 1963-68; mem. research staff, sci. adviser to v.p. research Gen. Motors Corp., 1958; spl. asst. to dir. research Inst. Def. Analyses, 1961-63; vis. prof. chemistry U. Calif. at San Diego, La Jolla, 1966-67, prof. chemistry, 1968-91, prof. emeritus, 1991—, chmn. dept., 1968-70, 84-87; cons. to govt. and industry, 1956—; mem. Solvay Conf., 1962, 78; mem. adv. panel, chemistry div. NSF, 1973-75; assoc. Sotheby's, 1991—. Author, editor tech. books; assoc. editor: Jour. Math. Physics, 1963-66; bd. editors: Jour. Statis. Physics, 1968-80; mem. adv. bd.: Chem. Engring. News, 1967-70; contbr. articles to profl. jours. Served with U.S. Army, 1944-46. Recipient Distinguished Service award Nat. Bur. Standards, 1959, Gold medal award Dept. Commerce, 1968, Solvay Found. fellow, 1975. Fellow Am. Inst. Chemists, AAAS, Am. Phys. Soc., Washington Acad. Sci.; mem. Am. Chem. Soc., Washington Philos. Soc. Club: Rancho Santa Fe Golf. Home: PO Box 1504 Rancho Santa Fe CA 92067-1504 Office: Univ Calif at San Diego Dept Chemistry La Jolla CA 92093

SHULER, MICHAEL LOUIS, biochemical engineering educator, consultant; b. Joliet, Ill., Jan. 2, 1947; s. Louis Dean and Mary Clara (Boylan) S.; m. Karen Joyce Beck, June 24, 1972; children: Andrew, Kristin, Eric, Katherine. BSChemE, U. Notre Dame, 1969; PhDChemE, U. Minn., 1973. Asst. prof. biochem. engring. Cornell U., Ithaca, N.Y., 1974-79, assoc. prof., 1979-83, prof., 1984-91; Samuel B. Eckert prof. chem. engring. Cornell U., Ithaca, 1992—; dir. bioengring. program, 1994—; vis. scholar U. Wash., Seattle, 1980-81; vis. scientist U. Wis., Madison, 1988-89; guest prof. ETH, Zurich, Switzerland, 1995; bd. dirs. Phyton Inc., Ithaca. Editor 6 books;

contbr. numerous articles to profl. jours. and chpts. to books. Bd. dirs., treas., sec., v.p. Advs. for the Handicapped, Ithaca, 1978-88; sec., bd. dirs. Tompkins County Human Rights Commn., Ithaca, 1985-87; coach Spl. Olympics, 1994—; mem. adv. bd. Carnegie-Mellon Chem. Engring., Princeton U. Chem. Engring., Johns Hopkins U. Chem. Engring., Cambridge U. Press. Recipient Outstanding Paper award Am. Oil Chemist Soc., 1984, Coll. of Engring. Honor award U. Notre Dame, 1989, Amgen award Biochem. Engring., 1997. Fellow Am. Inst. Med. and Biol. Engrs. (founder, v.p. edn. com.); mem. NAE, AIChE (editor Biotech. Progress 1985-88, cons. editor jour. 1986—, mem. publ. com. 1988—, awards com. 1993—, chair Food Pharm. and Bioengring. divsn. 1994—, Food, Pharm., Engring. award 1989, Prof. Progress award 1991), Am. Acad. Arts and Scis., Am. Chem. Soc. (M.J. Johnson award 1986), Am. Soc. Microbiology, Am. Soc. Pharmacognosy, Biomed. Engring. Soc. Roman Catholic. Avocation: fishing. Office: Cornell U Dept Chem Engring 340 Olin Hall Ithaca NY 14853-5201

SHULER DONNER, LAUREN, film producer; b. Cleveland, OH. BS in Film and Broadcasting, Boston U. TV films include: Amateur Night at the Dixie Bar and Grill, 1979; films include: Thank God It's Friday, 1978 (assoc. prodr.), Mr. Mom, 1983, Ladyhawke, 1985, St. Elmo's Fire, 1985, Pretty in Pink, 1986, Three Fugitives, 1989, Radio Flyer, 1992, Dave, 1993, Free Willy, 1993, The Favor, 1994; (producer) Free Willy 2: The Adventure Home, 1995, Assassins, 1995, Free Willy 3, 1997, Volcano, 1997; (exec. prodr.). Office: Donner/Shuler-Donner Prodns Warner Bros 4000 Warner Blvd Burbank CA 91522-0001

SHULEVITZ, URI, author, illustrator; b. Warsaw, Poland, Feb. 27, 1935; came to U.S., 1959, naturalized, 1965; s. Abraham and Szandla (Hermanstat) S. Student, Tel-Aviv Art Inst., 1953-55; Tchrs. Cert., Tchrs. Coll. Israel, 1956; student, Bklyn. Museum Art Sch., 1959-61. Instr. illustrating and writing children's books The New Sch., 1970-86; dir. illustrating and writing children's books Hartwick Coll., 1974-92. Author, illustrator: The Moon In My Room, 1963, One Monday Morning, 1967, Rain Rain Rivers, 1969, Oh What a Noise, 1971, The Magician, 1973, Dawn, 1974, The Treasure, 1978, (Caldecott honor Book 1979), The Strange and Exciting Adventures of Jeremiah Hush, 1986, Toddlecreek Post Office, 1990, The Secret Room, 1993; author: Writing with Pictures: How to Write and Illustrate Children's Books, 1985; illustrator: The Fool of the World and the Flying Ship, 1968 (Caldecott medal 1969), The Twelve Dancing Princesses, 1966, SOldier and Tsar in the Forest, 1972, The Fools of Chelm, 1973, The Touchstone, 1976, Hanukah Money, 1978, The Lost Kingdom of Karnica, 1979, The Golem, 1982, Lilith's Cave: Jewish Tales of the Supernatural, 1988, The Diamond Tree, 1991, The Golden Goose, 1995. Served with Israeli Army, 1956-59. Mem Authors Guild. Office: care Farrar Straus & Giroux Inc 19 Union Sq W New York NY 10003-3307

SHULGASSER, BARBARA, writer; b. Manhasset, N.Y., Apr. 10, 1954; d. Lew and Luba (Golante) S. Student, Sarah Lawrence Coll., 1973-74; BA magna cum laude, CUNY, 1977; MS, Columbia U., 1978. Feature writer Waterbury (Conn.) Rep., 1978-81; reporter, feature writer Chgo. Sun Times, 1981-84; film critic San Francisco Examiner, 1984—; freelance book critic N.Y. Times Book Rev., N.Y.C., 1983—. Co-author: (screenplay, with Robert Altman) Ready to Wear, 1994; freelance video columnist N.Y. Times Sunday Arts & Leisure, 1989, features for Vanity Fair, Glamour and Mirabella mags. Office: San Francisco Examiner 110 5th St San Francisco CA 94103-2918

SHULKIN, JEROME, lawyer; b. Stanley, N.D., May 2, 1929; s. Max and Sophia (Harris) S.; m. Jane Pearl Israel, Dec. 30, 1956; 1 child, Shellie Jo. BA, U. Minn, 1951; LLB, U. Wash., 1956. Bar: Wash. 1956, Oreg. 1957, U.S. Dist. Ct. (we. dist.) Wash. 1956, U.S. Dist. Ct. (ea. dist.) Wash. 1959, U.S. Dist. Ct. Oreg. 1960, U.S. Ct. Appeals (9th cir.) 1958, U.S. Supreme Ct. 1963. Law clk. Wash. Supreme Ct., Olympia, 1956-57; assoc. Miracle, Treadwell & Pruzan, Seattle, 1957-61, ptnr., 1961-68; ptnr. Casey, Pruzan, Kovarik & Shulkin, Seattle, 1968-76; sr. ptnr. Shulkin, Hutton & Bucknell Inc., P.S., Seattle, 1976-93, Shulkin, Hutton Inc., PS, Seattle, 1993—. Contbr. to law rev. Col. JAG U.S. Army, 1952-54, USAR, 1954-81, ret. Fellow Am. Coll. Bankruptcy (bd. dirs.); mem. Am. Bankruptcy Inst. (bd. dirs.), Am. Bankruptcy Bd. of Certification (bd. dirs., v.p.), Wash. State Bar Assn. (lectr. 1975—), Oreg. State Bar Assn. Jewish. Avocation: classic automobiles. Office: Shulkin Hutton Inc PS 1201 3rd Ave Ste 1900 Seattle WA 98101-3083

SHULL, CLAIRE, documentary film producer, casting director; b. N.Y.C., Oct. 26, 1925; d. Barnet Joseph and Fannie (Florea) Klar; m. Leo Shull, Aug. 8, 1948; children: Lee Shull Pearlstein, David. Student, Am. Acad. Dramatic Arts, N.Y.C., 1943-44, NYU, 1973-74. Editor, assoc. pub. Show Bus. Publs., N.Y.C., 1957-85; owner, founder Claire/Casting, N.Y.C. and Miami, Fla., 1972—, Claire/Casting Film Prodns., N.Y.C. and Miami, 1978—; cons. dir., prodr., dir. film and TV, The Bass Mus., Miami Beach, Fla., 1992—. Actress in The Front Page, USO European tour, 1945-46, (on Broadway) Tenting Tonight, 1947; prodr., dir. HBO TV series How To Break into Show Business, 1980-81, Cable-TV series Join Us at the Bass, 1993-95. Recipient gold award and distinctive merit TV award Advt. Club. Hartford, Conn., 1984, Clio award, 1989. Mem. Ind. Casting Dirs. Assn. N.Y., Actors Equity Assn., Drama Desk.

SHULL, CLIFFORD G., physicist, educator; b. Pitts., Sept. 23, 1915; s. David H. and Daisy I. (Bistline) S.; m. Martha-Nuel Summer, June 19, 1941; children: John C., Robert D., William F. BS, Carnegie Inst. Tech., 1937; PhD, NYU, 1941. Research physicist Texas Co., 1941-46; chief physicist Oak Ridge Nat. Lab., 1946-55; prof. physics MIT, 1955-86, emeritus prof., 1986—; Chmn. vis. com. Brookhaven Nat. Lab., 1961-62; chmn. vis. com. Nat. Bur. Standard reactor, 1972-73; chmn. vis. com. solid state div. Oak Ridge Nat. Lab., 1974-75; chmn. policy com. Nat. Small-Angle-Scattering Center, 1978-81. Contbr. articles to sci. jours. Recipient award of merit Alumni Assn. of Carnegie Mellon U., 1968, Humboldt Sr. U.S. Scientist award, 1979, Disting. Scientist award Gov. of Tenn., 1986, Gregori Aminoff prize, 1993, Ilja Frank prize, 1993, Nobel Prize in Physics, 1994. Fellow Am. Phys. Soc. (Buckley prize 1956, chmn. solid state physics divsn. 1962-63), AAAS, Am. Acad. Arts and Scis., N.Y. Acad. Scis., Nat. Acad. Scis. (vice chmn. panel on neutron sci. 1977); mem. Am. Crystallographic Assn., Rsch. Soc. Am., Sigma Xi, Tau Beta Pi, Phi Kappa Phi, Phi Beta Kappa. Home: 4 Wingate Rd Lexington MA 02173-4516

SHULL, HARRISON, chemist, educator; b. Princeton, N.J., Aug. 17, 1923; s. George Harrison and Mary (Nicholl) S.; m. Jeanne Louise Johnson, 1948 (div. 1962); children: James Robert, Kathy, George Harrison, Holly; m. Wil Joyce Bentley Long, 1962; children: Warren Michael Long, Jeffery Mark Long, Stanley Martin, Sarah Ellen. A.B., Princeton U., 1943; Ph.D., U. Calif. at Berkeley, 1948. Assoc. chemist U.S. Naval Research Lab., 1943-45; asst. prof. Iowa State U., 1949-54; mem. faculty Ind. U., 1955-79, research prof., 1961-79, dean Grad. Sch., 1965-72, vice chancellor for research and devel., 1972-76, dir. Research Computing Center, 1959-63, acting chmn. chemistry dept., 1965-66, acting dean arts and scis., 1969-70, acting dean faculties, 1974; mem. faculty, provost, v.p. acad. affairs Rensselaer Poly. Inst., 1979-82; chancellor U. Colo., Boulder, 1982-85; prof. dept. chemistry U. Colo., 1982-88; provost Naval Postgrad. Sch., 1988-95; asst. dir. rsch., quantum chemistry group Uppsala (Sweden) U., 1958-59; vis. prof. Washington U., St. Louis, 1960, U. Colo., 1963; founder, supr. Quantum Chemistry Program Exchange, 1962-79; chmn. subcom. molecular structure and spectroscopy NRC, 1958-63; chmn. Fulbright selection com. chemistry, 1963-67; mem. adv. com. Office Sci. Personnel, 1957-60; chmn. First Gordon Research Conf. Theoretical Chemistry, 1962; mem. com. survey chemistry Nat. Acad. Sci., 1964-65; mem. adv. panel chemistry NSF, 1964-67; mem. adv. panel Office Computer Activities, 1967-70, cons. chem. information program, 1965-71, mem. adv. com. for research, 1974-76; mem. vis. com. chemistry Brookhaven Nat. Lab., 1967-70; mem. adv. com. Chem. Abstracts Service, 1971-74; dir. Storage Tech. Corp.; chief of Naval Ops. Exec. Panel, 1984-88. Assoc. editor: Jour. Chem. Physics, 1952-54; editorial adv. bd.: Spectrochimica Acta, 1957-63, Internat. Jour. Quantum Chemistry, 1967—, Proc. NAS, 1976-81; contbr. articles to profl. jours. Trustee Argonne U. Assn., 1970-75, Asso. Univs., Inc., 1973-76, U. Rsch. Assn., 1984-89, Inst. Defense Analysis, 1984-96. Served as ensign USNR, 1945. NRC postdoctoral fellow phys. scis. U. Chgo., 1948-49; Guggenheim fellow U. Uppsala, 1954-55; NSF sr. postdoctoral fellow, 1968-69; Sloan research fellow, 1956-58. Fellow Am. Acad. Arts and Scis. (v.p. 1976-83, chmn. Midwest Ctr. 1976-79), Am. Phys. Soc.; mem. AAAS, Nat. Acad. Scis. (com. on sci. and pub. policy 1969-72, coun., exec. com. 1971-74, chmn. U.S.-USSR sci. policy subgroup for fundamental rsch. 1973-81, naval studies bd. 1974-79, 96—, chmn. Commn. on Human Resources, 1977-81, nominating com. 1978), Am. Chem. Soc., Assn. Computing Machinery, Royal Swedish Acad. Scis. (fgn. mem.), Royal Acad. Arts and Scis. Uppsala (corr. mem.), Cosmos Club (Washington), Old Capital Club (Monterey), Phi Beta Kappa, Sigma Xi, Phi Lambda Upsilon. Office: Naval Postgrad Sch Code 09/hs Monterey CA 93940

SHULL, RICHARD BRUCE, actor; b. Evanston, Ill., Feb. 24, 1929; s. Ulysses Homer and Zana Marie (Brown) S.; m. Margaret Ann Haddy, July 14, 1951 (div. 1956); m. Peggy Joan Barringer, June 9, 1957 (div. 1967); m. Marilyn Sandra Swartz, July 6, 1969 (div. 1985, remarried July 7, 1989). BA in Drama, State U. Iowa, 1950; AA in Humanities, Kemper Mil. Sch., 1986. exec. asst. producer Gordon W. Pollock Prodns., 1953-56; stage mgr. Hyde Park Playhouse, 1954-55; prodn. mgr. Kaufman Auditorium, N.Y.C., 1956; gen. mgr. Music Circle Theatre, Detroit, 1957; prodn. supr. Ford Motor Co. Am. Road Show, 1959; prodn. mgr. (film) Dana Prodns. Inc., 1959-60; dir. Lake Luzerne Playhouse, 1962, 64, Showboat Dinner Theatre, 1968-69; art dir. (film) Tears are for Tomorrow, 1960. Freelance theatrical stage mgr. and dir., N.Y.C., 1950-70; appeared in plays, N.Y.C., including Each in His Own Way, 1950, Wake Up Darling, 1956, Minnie's Boys, 1970, Goodtime Charley (Tony nominee, Drama Desk nomination), 1975, Fools, 1981, Oh, Brother!, 1981, Desire Under the Elms, 1983, Fade the Game, 1984, The Marriage of Bette and Boo (Obie award), 1985, The Front Page, 1986, Opera Comique, 1987, Rough Crossing, 1990, One of the All-Time Greats, 1992, Ain't Broadway Grand, 1993, The Gig, 1994, Victor/Victoria, 1995-97; plays in L.A., including Mr. Ferris and The Model, 1967, The Tempest, 1979; film appearances include The Anderson Tapes and B.S., I Love You, 1970, Hail to the Chief and Such Good Friends, 1971, Slither and Ssssss, 1972, Cockfighter, 1974, The Fortune, The Black Bird and The Big Bus, 1975, The Pack, 1977, Lovesick, 1983, Spring Break, 1983, Unfaithfully Yours, 1984, Splash, 1984, Garbo Talks, 1984, My Blue Heaven, 1990, Tune in Tomorrow, 1990, Housesitter, 1992, For Love or Money, 1993, Trapped in Paradise, 1994, Café Society, 1995, Private Parts, 1996—; appearances on TV include Your Hit Parade, 1950, Robert Montgomery Presents, 1950, Diana, 1973, Ironsides, 1975, Goodtimes, 1975, Holmes and YoYo, 1976, The Rockford Files, 1978, Ziegfeld, A Man and His Women, 1978, Studs Lonigan, 1979, Hart to Hart, 1979, Lou Grant, 1980, The Ropers, 1980, Alice, 1980, Nurse, 1981, Will There Really Be a Morning?, 1982, The Boy Who Loved Trolls, 1984, Keeping the Faith, 1984, Seize the Day, 1985, The Conan O'Brien Show, 1993, As the World Turns, 1997; dir. Man Without a Shadow, 1958; author: motion picture story and screenplay Aroused, 1964, Pamela, Pamela You Are, 1967; program dir. Armed Forces Radio Sta. GYPSY; created AFKN Network program Concert in Jazz. Served with U.S. Army, 1951-53, Korea. Mem. AFTRA, Actors Equity Assn. (founding editl. bd., constl. rev. com. 1975), Screen Actors Guild, Acad. Motion Picture Arts and Scis., Episcopal Actors Guild (life), Actors Fund (life), SR, Soc. Colonial Wars, St. Nicholas Soc. (steward, bd. mgrs.), N.Y. Vet. Corps. Artillery (councillor), Gen. Soc. War of 1812 (pres. N.Y. State soc.), Colonial Order Acorn, Sons of Union Vets, Civil War (treas. Tilden Camp), First Families Ohio, Soc., Ind. Pioneers, Pioneer Assn. State Wash., Sons. Am. Colonists (gov. N.Y. chpt.), Hon. Order Ky. Cols., Lambs Club (life), Players Club, Friars Club, Dutch Treat Club, Univ. Club (N.Y.C.), Sloane Club (London), India House (N.Y.C.), Ends of the Earth, Pumpkin Papers Irregulars, Baker St. Irregulars. Democrat. Avocations: antique autos and railroading, animal protection. Office: Cheeriecrie Ltd 1501 Broadway Ste 1510 New York NY 10036-5601

SHULLICH, ROBERT HARLAN, systems analyst; b. Bklyn., Feb. 20, 1954; s. William and Vivian (Polowitz) S.; m. Phyllis Elaine Strickland, June 4, 1979 (dec. Oct. 1991). AS in Liberal Arts, Staten Island C.C., 1976; BS in Computer Sci., Coll. Staten Island, 1985, MS in Computer Sci., 1988; MBA in Mgmt., Baruch Coll., 1993. Cert. computer programmer, systems profl., data processor. Sr. systems analyst in ednl. adminstrv. systems Coll. of Staten Island, N.Y., 1981—. Mem. IEEE, Math. Assn. Am., Am. Mgmt. Assn., Assn. Computing Machinery, Data Processing Mgmt. Assn., Nat. Systems Programmer Assn., Tau Alpha Pi, Alpha Iota Delta. Roman Catholic. Avocations: bowling, concerts. Home: PO Box 021390 Brooklyn NY 11202-1390 Office: Coll Staten Island 2800 Victory Blvd Staten Island NY 10314-6609

SHULMAN, ARNOLD, judge, lawyer; b. Phila., Apr. 12, 1914; s. Edward Nathaniel and Anna (Leshner) S.; m. Mary Frances Johnson, Nov. 26, 1943; children: Diane Shulman Thompson, Warren Scott, Amy Lynn Shulman Haney. Student, Emory U., 1931; J.D., U. Ga., 1936. Bar: Ga. 1937. Mem. firm Shulman, Shulman, Bauer & Deitch (and predecessors), Atlanta, to 1977; judge Ga. Ct. Appeals, 1977-84, presiding judge, 1981-83, chief judge, 1983-84; of counsel Troutman, Sanders, Lockerman & Ashmore, Atlanta, 1984-87; appointed sr. appellate ct. judge, 1987—; chief judge settlement conf. div. Ct. Appeals Ga., 1989—; prof. Atlanta Law Sch., 1964-84; adj. prof. Ga. State U. Coll. Law, Atlanta. Author: (with Wiley H. Davis) Georgia Practice and Procedure, 1948, 3d edit., 1968, 4th edit., (with Warren S. Shulman), 1975; contbr. articles to legal jours. Chmn. DeKalb County (Ga.) Sch. Salary Commn., 1960-62, DeKalb County Sch. Study Commn., 1962-64; mem. Fulton County-Atlanta Ct. Study Commn., 1961-62. Served to capt. U.S. Army, 1941-46. Mem. ABA, Atlanta Bar Assn., Ga. State Bar, Lawyers Club (Atlanta). Home: 1527 September Chase Decatur GA 30033-1731 Office: 908 DeKalb County Courthouse Decatur GA 30030

SHULMAN, ARTHUR, communications executive; b. N.Y.C., Mar. 4, 1927; s. Jacob and Sarah (Hochman) S.; m. Jan. 30, 1958; children: James, Karen. BA, Syracuse U., 1950. Asst. to pub. TV Guide Mag., Radnor, Pa., 1958-72; pub. Seventeen Mag., N.Y.C., 1972-73; dir. regional ops. TV Guide, 1974-82; dir. comm. B'nai B'rith Internat., Washington, 1983-93. Author: How Sweet It Was, 1966, The Television Years, 1972. Dir. Penn Wynne (Pa.) Civic Assn., 1965-66. S/Sgt. US Army, 1945-46, Japan. Mem. Radio & TV Execs. Soc., Nat. Press Club, Overseas Press Club, Nat. Acad. TV Arts & Scis. Jewish. Address: 4017 Jardin Ln Sarasota FL 34238-4504

SHULMAN, CAROLE KAREN, professional society administrator; b. Mpls., Nov. 25, 1940; d. Allen Eldon and Beulah Ovidia (Blomsness) Banbury; m. David Arthur Shulman, Mar. 26, 1962; children: Michael, Krista, Tracy, Robbyn. Student, Colo. Coll., 1958-61; California Coast U., 1983-84. Profl. instr. Rochester (Minn.) Figure Skating Club, 1962-84, dir. skating, 1964-79, cons., 1979—; exec. dir. Profl. Skaters Assn., Rochester, 1984—; master rating examiner Profl. Skaters Guild, Rochester, 1971—, world profl. judge, 1976, 79, 87-88. Editor Professional Skater mag., 1984—; prodr. U.S. Open Profl. Figure Skating Championships, 1987, 89—. Pres. Rochester Arts Council, 1983. Named triple gold medalist U.S. Figure Skating Assn., Colorado Springs, Colo., 1959, 63, Master Rated Coach Profl. Skaters Assn., 1970, Sr. Rated Coach in Dance Profl. Skaters Assn., 1970. Mem. Am. Harp Soc. Mem. Covenant ch. Avocations: harp, skiing. Office: Profl Skaters Assn Internat 1821 2nd St SW Rochester MN 55902-0886

SHULMAN, DANIEL REES, lawyer; b. N.Y.C., Apr. 6, 1944; s. Max and Carol (Rees) S.; m. Margaret Phillips Marks, May 15, 1964; children: John, David, Amy, Ellen, Michael. BA, Harvard U., 1965, JD, 1970; MA, Yale U., 1967. Bar: Minn. 1970, U.S. Ct. Appeals (1st, 2d, 3d, 5th, 7th, 8th, 9th, 10th, 11th, fed. cirs.), U.S. Supreme Ct. With Gray, Plant, Mooty, Mooty & Bennett, Mpls., 1970-93; ptnr. Shulman Walcott & Shulman, Mpls., 1993—; gen. counsel Mpls. br. NAACP, 1972—, Mpls. Head Start, 1974—. Author: Winning Complex Litigation, 1984; contbr. articles on civil trial practice and antitrust law to profl. jours. Bd. dirs. Melpomene Inst., St. Paul, 1990-96. Recipient Disting. Svc. awards Mpls. br. NAACP, 1979, 88. Democrat. Avocations: literature, sports, music. Home: 2211 Kenwood Pky Minneapolis MN 55405-2329 Office: Shulman Walcott & Shulman 2999 Norwest Ctr 90 S 7th St Minneapolis MN 55402-3903

SHULMAN, GERALD I., clinical investigator; b. Detroit, Feb. 8, 1953; s. Herschel A. and Doris (Miller) S. BS with high honors and distinction, U. Mich., 1974; MD, PhD, Wayne State U., 1979. Intern Duke U., Durham, N.C., 1979-80, residency, 1980-81; fellowship in endocrinology and metabolism Mass. Gen. Hosp., Boston, 1981-84; asst. prof. medicine Harvard U., Boston, 1985-87; assoc. prof. Sch. Medicine Yale U., New Haven, 1989—; assoc. dir. Yale MD-PhD Program Sch. Medicine Yale U., New Haven, 1993—; prof. medicine, cellular and molecular psysiology; assoc. dir. Yale Diabetes Endocrine Rsch. Ctr. Contbr. articles to med. jours. Recipient of the Young Investigator award, Outstanding Investigator award. Fellow ACP; mem. Am. Soc. Clin. Investigation, Am. Diabetes Assn. (clin. rsch. grantee 1996), mem. Assn of Am. Physician, Endocrine Soc., Am. Physiol. Soc.,. Office: Yale Univ Sch Medicine Dept Internal Medicine 333 Cedar St Box 208020 New Haven CT 06520-8020

SHULMAN, LAWRENCE EDWARD, biomedical research administrator, rheumatologist; b. Boston, July 25, 1919; s. David Herman and Belle (Tishler) S.; m. Pauline K. Flint, July 19, 1946; 1 son, Lawrence E.; m. Reni Trudinger, Mar. 20, 1959; children: Kathryn Verena, Barbara Corina. AB, Harvard U., 1941, postgrad., 1941-42; PhD, Yale U., 1945, MD, 1949. Nat. Bd. Med. Examiners. Intern Johns Hopkins Hosp., 1949-50, resident and fellow in internal medicine, 1950-53; dir. connective tissue div. Johns Hopkins U., 1955-75, assoc. prof. medicine, 1964—; assoc. dir. div. arthritis, musculoskeletal and skin diseases NIH, Bethesda, Md., 1976-82, dir., 1982—; dir. Nat. Inst. Arthritis & Musculoskeletal & Skin Diseases NIH, 1986-94, dir. emeritus, 1994—, emissary for clin. rsch., 1995—; chmn. med. adminstrn. com. Arthritis Found., Atlanta, 1974-75, exec. com., 1972-77; dir. Lupus Found. Am.; med. adv. bd. United. Scleroderma Found., Watsonville, Calif., 1977-88; chair sci. group rheumatic diseases WHO, 1989. Discoverer: Eosinophilic Fasciitis, 1974, new med. sign friction rubs in scleroderma, 1961. Recipient Sr. Investigator award Arthritis Found., 1957-62, Disting. Svc. award, 1979, Heberden medal for rsch., London, 1975, Superior Svc. award USPHS, 1985, Spl. Recognition award Nat. Osteoporosis Found., 1991, Spl. award Am. Acad. Orthop. Surgeons, 1992, Presdl. citation for leadership Am. Acad. Dermatology, 1993, Leadership award Lupus Found. Am., 1994, Career Achievement award Am. Coll. Rheumatology, 1994, Outstanding Support Rsch. award Am. Soc. Bone Mineral Rsch., 1994, Gold medal Am. Coll. Rheumatology, 1995 Award of Merit, NASA; named W.R. Graham Meml. lectr., 1973, Cochrane Disting. lectr., 1993. Master ACP, Am. Rheumatism Assn. (pres. 1974-75); mem. Soc. Clin. Trials, Pan-Am. League Against Rheumatism (pres. 1982-86), Soc. Investigative Dermatology. Home: 6302 Swords Way Bethesda MD 20817-3350 Office: NIH Rm 4C-32 9000 Rockville Pike Bldg 31 Bethesda MD 20814-1436

SHULMAN, MAX REES, lawyer; b. Winston Salem, N.C., July 11, 1945. AB, Harvard U., 1967; JD, Columbia U., 1970. Bar: N.Y. 1972, U.S. Dist. Ct. (so. and ea. dists.) N.Y., 1974, U.S. Ct. Appeals (2nd cir.) 1982, U.S. Ct. Internat. Trade, 1982, U.S. Supreme Ct. 1987, U.S. Ct. Appeals (9th cir.) 1987, U.S. Ct. Appeals (fed. cir.) 1988, U.S. Ct. Appeals (5th cir.) 1989. Lawyer Cravath, Swaine & Moore, N.Y.C. Office: Cravath Swaine & Moore Worldwide Plz 825 8th Ave New York NY 10019-7416

SHULMAN, ROBERT GERSON, biophysics educator; b. N.Y.C., Mar. 3, 1924; s. Joshua S. and Freda (Lipshay) S.; m. Saralee Deutsch, Aug., 1952 (dec. Oct. 1983); children: Joel, Mark, James; m. Stephanie S. Spangler, May 11, 1986. AB, Columbia U., 1943, MA, 1947, PhD, 1949. Rsch. assoc. Columbia U. Radiation Lab., N.Y.C., 1949; AEC fellow in chemistry Calif. Inst. Tech., Pasadena, 1949-50; head semicondr. research sect. Hughes Aircraft Co., Culver City, Calif., 1950-53; mem. tech. staff Bell Labs., Murray Hill, N.J., 1953-66; head biophysics rsch. dept. Bell Labs., 1966-79; prof. molecular biophysics and biochemistry Yale U., 1979—, dir. divsn. biol. scis., 1981-87, Sterling prof. molecular biophysics and biochemistry, 1994—; Rask Oersted lectr. U. Copenhagen, 1959; vis. prof. Ecole Normale Superieur, Paris, 1962; Appleton lectr. Brown U., 1965; vis. prof. physics U. Tokyo, 1965; Reilly lectr. U. Notre Dame, Ind., 1969; vis. prof. biophysics Princeton U., 1971-72; Regents lectr. UCLA, 1978. Guggenheim fellow in lab. molecular biology MRC Cambridge (Eng.) U., 1961-62; recipient Havinga medal Leiden U., 1983, Gold medal Soc. Magnetic Resonance in Medicine, 1984,. Mem. Nat. Acad. Scis., Inst. Medicine. Achievements include research in spectroscopic techniques applied to physics, chemistry and biology. Office: Yale U MR Ctr Dept Molecular Bio PO Box 208043 New Haven CT 06520-8043

SHULMAN, ROBERT JAY, physician; b. Newark; s. Irving Jack and Shirley (Weinstock) S.; children: David Ian, Hannah Rachael. BA, Emory U., 1972; MD, Chgo. Med. Sch., 1976. Asst. prof. pediat. Baylor Coll. Medicine, Houston, 1982-89, assoc. prof., 1989-96, prof., 1996—; dir. nutritional support team Tex. Children's Hosp., Houston, 1982—. Author: Young Chef's Nutrition Guide and Cookbook, 1990, Keys to Child Nutrition, 1991, (with others) Principles and Practice of Pediatrics, 1994, Physiology of the Gastrointestinal Tract, 1994; mem. editl. bd. Jour. Pediat. Gastroenterology and Nutrition, 1994-96. Fellow Am. Acad. Pediat.; mem. Am. Gastroent. Soc., Am. Soc. Patenteral and Enteral Nutrition (pres. 1991-92), Am. Inst. Nutrition, N.Am. Soc. Pediat. Gastroenterology and Nutrition, Soc. Pediat. Rsch. Avocation: guitar. Office: Baylor Coll Medicine 1100 Bates Ave Houston TX 77030-2600

SHULMAN, STEPHEN NEAL, lawyer; b. New Haven, Apr. 6, 1933; s. Harry and Rea (Karrel) S.; m. Sandra Paula Still, Aug. 14, 1954; children—Harry, Dean, John. B.A., Harvard, 1954; LL.B. cum laude, Yale, 1958. Bar: Conn. 1958, D.C. 1960. Indsl. relations Bendix Aviation Corp., 1954-55; law clk. to Justice Harlan, U.S. Supreme Ct., 1958-59; vis. asst. pro. U. Mich. Law Sch., 1959; asso. firm Covington & Burling, Washington, 1959-60; asst. U.S. atty. Washington, 1960-61; exec. asst. to sec. labor, 1961-62, dept asst. sec. of def., 1962-65; gen. counsel U.S. Air Force, 1965-66; chmn. Equal Employment Opportunity Commn., 1966-67; mem. Kane, Shulman & Schlei, Washington, 1967-70; mem. firm Cadwalader, Wickersham & Taft, N.Y.C., also Washington, 1971-95, Freedman, Levy, Kroll & Simonds, Washington, 1995—; vis. prof. mgmt. U. Okla., 1965-66. Co-author: The Law of Equal Employment Opportunity, 1990; editor in chief Yale Law Jour., 1957-58. Mem. Book and Gavel, Order of Coif, Cum Laude Soc., Phi Alpha Delta. Home: 1332 Skipwith Rd Mc Lean VA 22101-1841 Office: Freedman Levy 1050 Connecticut Ave NW Washington DC 20036

SHULMAN, YECHIEL, engineering educator; b. Tel Aviv, Jan. 28, 1930; came to the U.S., 1950; s. David and Rachel (Chonowski) S.; m. Ruth Danzig, June 29, 1950; children: Elinor D., Ron E., Orna L. BS in Aero. Engring., MIT, 1954, BS in Bus. and Engring. Adminstrn., 1954, MS in Aero. Engring., 1954, DSc Aero. and Astro., 1959; MBA, U. Chgo., 1973. Assoc. prof. mech. engring. Northwestern U., Evanston, Ill., 1959-67; v.p. adv. engring. Anocut, Inc., Elk Grove Vill., Ill., 1967-72; v.p. corp. devel. Alden Press, Elk Grove Vill., Ill., 1973-84; pres. MMT Environ., Inc., Shoreview, Minn., 1984-87; cons. Shulman Assocs., Mpls., 1987-89; prof. mech. engring. dept. U. Minn., Mpls., 1989—, H. W. Sweatt chair in technol. leadership and dir. ctr. for devel. technol. leadership, 1989—, dir. grad. studies mgmt. of tech. program, 1990—. Mem. Am. Soc. Mech. Engrs., Inst. Indsl. Engrs. Office: U Minn 107 Lind Hall Minneapolis MN 55455

SHULTIS, ROBERT LYNN, finance educator, cost systems consultant, retired professional association executive; b. Kingston, N.Y., June 30, 1924; s. Albert H. and Dorothy Elizabeth (Jenkins) S.; m. Bernice Elizabeth Johnson, Jan. 20, 1946; 1 son, Robert Lee. BS, Columbia Univ. Sch. Bus., 1949, postgrad., 1949-51. Staff acct. Price Waterhouse, N.Y.C., 1949-52; credit mgr., controller Organon, Inc., West Orange, N.J., 1952-68; v.p., treas., chief fin. officer Arwood Corp., Rockleigh, N.J., 1968-72; v.p., controller Technicon, Tarrytown, N.Y., 1972-80; exec. dir. Inst. of Mgmt. Accts., Montvale, N.J., 1980-86; faculty, exec. dir. Ctr. for Exec. Devel. Coll. William & Mary, Williamsburg, Va., 1987-91; instr. Rutgers U., 1964-74, Fairleigh Dickinson U., 1967-68; mem. Fin. Acctg. Standards Adv. coun., 1981-86; cons. Acctg. and Cost Sys. design, 1990—; lectr., seminar leader, cons. on controllership, activity-based costing, cost mgmt., cost sys. design U. Calif, Berkeley, U. Minn., Michigan State U., So. Meth. U., Baldwin Wallace Coll., George Mason U., James Madison U., others, 1990—. Editor: Management Accountants' Handbook, and supplements, 1991-94. Mem. bd. advs. U. Fla. Sch. Accountancy, James Madison U. Sch. Accountancy; mem. fin. and budget com. Kingsmill Community Svcs. Assn. Served with USAF, 1943-45. Decorated Presdl. Unit Citation. Mem. AAUP, Fin. Execs. Inst., Assn. Systems Mgmt., Inst. of Mgmt. Accts., Am.

Acctg. Assn., Ross Inst. Acctg. Rsch., Kingsmill Club, Beta Alpha Psi (adv. forum).

SHULTS, ROBERT LEE, real estate executive, airline executive; b. Helena, Ark., Feb. 23, 1936; s. Albert and Mary S.; m. Belinda Housley, Aug. 21, 1965; children: Catherine Ann, Robert L. BS in Acctg. magna cum laude, U. Ark.-Fayetteville, 1961. CPA, Ark. Mgr., Arthur Andersen & Co., Memphis, 1961-70; exec. v.p. Allied Tel. Co., Little Rock, 1970-80; chmn. bd. Scheduled Skyways, Inc., Little Rock, 1980-88, chmn. bd., chief exec. officer, Fin. Ctr. Corp., Little Rock, 1980—, cons. Alltel Corp., Little Rock, 1980-90; chmn. bd., chief exec. Ranch Prop Inc., 1989—; chmn. bd. dir., chief exec. Fin. Ctr. Devel. Co., Air Midwest Inc.; past chmn. bd. Regional Airline Assn., Washington, 1984; chmn. bd. gov. advisory be. Telecom and Info Tech., 1996. Pres. bd. dirs. Ark. Children's Hosp., 1994—; bd. dirs., treas. Am. Cancer Soc., Ark., 1976-91, bd. dirs., Ark. Arts Ctr., 1996—, Inst. Pub. Utilities, Mich. State U., 1976-80; chmn. bd. trustees Trinity Cathedral, 1982-92, Fifty for Future Little Rock. With USMC, 1956-58. Recipient Pres.'s citation, U.S. Ind. Tel. Assn., 1978, 80. Mem. AICPA, Mo. Bd. Accts., Tenn. Bd. Accts., Met. Little Rock C. of C., Little Rock Club, The Capital Club, Summit Club, Little Rock Country Club, Rotary (bd. dirs. 1988-90). Episcopalian. Office: Fin Ctr Corp PO Box 56350 Little Rock AR 72215-6350

SHULTS, ROBERT LUTHER, JR., lawyer; b. Pine Bluff, Ark., Oct. 25, 1925; s. Robert Luther and Gay (Moseley) S.; m. Barbara Jo Taylor, Aug. 19, 1950; children—Steven Taylor, Elizabeth Gay. BSEE cum laude, La. State U., 1950; LLB cum laude, Harvard U., 1953; LLD (hon.), U. Ark., 1981. Bar: Ark. bar 1953. Assoc., ptnr. Wright, Lindsey, Jennings, Lester & Shults, Little Rock, 1953-65; ptnr. Lester and Shults, Little Rock, 1965-79, Shults, Ray & Kurrus, Little Rock, 1979—. Editor: Harvard Law Rev, 1952-53. Chmn. Little Rock Com. Fgn. Rels.; bd. dirs. Little Rock Ctrl. YMCA, Ark. chpt. Arthritis Found., Winrock Internat. Inst. for Agrl. Devel.; chmn. bd. Winthrop Rockefeller Found., Econ. Opportunity Agy. Pulaski County; trustee Winthrop Rockefeller Charitable Trust, Ark. Arts Ctr. 1st lt. AUS, 1943-46, ETO. Mem. ABA, Ark. Bar Assn. (chmn. legal edn. council 1963-66, chmn. exec. com. 1968-69), Am. Judicature Soc., Am. Inst. for Public Service (bd. of selectors), Nat. Audubon Soc. (dir. 1980-86), Sigma Chi, Tau Beta Pi, Omicron Delta Kappa. Democrat. Methodist. Clubs: Little Rock Country, Capital. Home: 11 Glenridge Rd Little Rock AR 72227-2208 Office: Shults Ray & Kurrus 200 W Capitol 1600 Boatmens Bank Bldg Little Rock AR 72201

SHULTS-DAVIS, LOIS BUNTON, lawyer; b. Elkton, Md., Sept. 29, 1957; d. Asa Grant Bunton and Carolyn Elizabeth Bunton Pate; m. David Reed Shults (Dec. 8, 1979 (div. Sept. 1990); children: Kenneth Grant, Joseph David, Lawrence Scott; m. Michael Howard Davis, June 14, 1992. BS, East Tenn. State U., 1977; JD, U. Tenn., 1980. Bar: Tenn. 1980, U.S. Dist. Ct. (ea. dist.) Tenn. 1985. Assoc. Jenkins & Jenkins, Knoxville, Tenn., 1980-82, R.O. Smith Law Offices, Erwin, Tenn., 1982-85; ptnr. Shults & Shults, Erwin, 1985—; gen. counsel Erwin Nat. Bank, 1985—. Bd. dirs. Unicoi County Heritage Mus., Erwin, 1986-87, Unicoi County Ambulance Authority, Erwin, 1990-91, YMCA, Erwin, 1991-94; pres. Unicoi Elem. PTO, 1994, Unicoi County Mid. Sch. PTA, 1997; mock trial coach Mock Trial Competition Young Lawyers, 1993, 95-96, 96-97. Recipient Contbn. to Edn. award Unicoi County Edn. Assn., 1994. Mem. Female Attys. of Mountain Empire, DAR (regent 1990-92), Internat. Platform Speakers Assn. Republican. Methodist. Avocations: snow skiing, reading, travel, gardening, home improvement. Home: RR 1 Box 258-b Unicoi TN 37692-9801 Office: Shults & Shults Law Offices 111 Gay St Erwin TN 37650-1227

SHULTZ, EMMET LAVEL, marketing executive; b. Blackfoot, Idaho, Apr. 23, 1934; s. Emmett Franklin and Alba Elizabeth (Larsen) S.; children: Joanne M. Shultz Greaney, Jeanette G. Shultz Yanez. Asst. to pres. Flying Diamond Corp., Salt Lake City, 1973-74; pres., also bd. dirs. Shuhart Industries, Inc., Salt Lake City, 1974-75; v.p. Hunstman Chem. and Oil Corp., Salt Lake City, 1975-76; exec. v.p. Huntsman Coal Corp., Salt Lake City, 1975-76; pres., chmn. bd. Gulf Energy Corp., Salt Lake City, 1976-90, Channel Energy Corp., 1983—, Kita Corp., 1985-90, Inst. for Adept Health Rsch., Inc., 1988-90; pres., chmn. bd. Ancestors, Inc., 1990—. Bd. Dirs. Ballet West, 1980-83, Utah Symphony, 1980-83. With USN, 1952-56. Republican. also: PO Box 3856 Ventura CA 93006 *Personal philosophy: Live life fully. Be kind and be generous with whatever you have. Your family is what you leave, not deeds.*

SHULTZ, GEORGE PRATT, former government executive, economics educator; b. N.Y.C., Dec. 13, 1920; s. Birl E. and Margaret Lennox (Pratt) S.; m. Helena M. O'Brien, Feb. 16, 1946; children: Margaret Ann Shultz Tilsworth, Kathleen Pratt Shultz Jorgensen, Peter Milton, Barbara Lennox Shultz White, Alexander George. BA in Econs., Princeton U., 1942; PhD in Indsl. Econs., MIT, 1949; Hon. degree, Yeshiva U., U. Tel Aviv, Technion-Israel Inst. Tech., Keio U., Tokyo. Mem. faculty M.I.T., 1949-57; assoc. prof. indsl. relations MIT, 1955-57; prof. indsl. relations Grad. Sch. Bus., U. Chgo., 1957-68, dean sch., 1962-68; fellow Ctr. for Advanced Study in Behavioral Scis., 1968-69; U.S. sec. labor, 1969-70; dir. Office Mgmt. and Budget, 1970-72; U.S. sec. treasury, also asst. to Pres., 1972-74; chmn. Council on Econ. Policy, East-West Trade Policy com.; exec. v.p. Bechtel Corp., San Francisco, 1974-75, pres., 1975-77; vice chmn. Bechtel Corp., 1977-81; also dir.; pres. Bechtel Group, Inc., 1981-82; prof. mgmt. and pub. policy Stanford U., 1974-82, prof. internat. econs., 1989-91, prof. emeritus, 1991—; chmn. Pres. Reagan's Econ. Policy Adv. Bd., 1981-82; U.S. sec. of state, 1982-89; disting. fellow Hoover Instn., Stanford, 1989—; bd. dirs. Bechtel Group, Inc., Gulfstream Aerospace Corp., AirTouch Comm.; mem. GM Corp. Adv. Coun.; mem. Gilead Scis. Bd.; chmn. J.P. Morgan Internat. Coun.; chmn. adv. coun. Inst. Internat. Studies, Calif. Gov.'s Econ. Policy Adv. Bd. Author: Pressures on Wage Decisions, 1951, (with Charles A. Myers) The Dynamics of a Labor Market, 1951, (with John R. Coleman) Labor Problems: Cases and Readings, 1953, (with T.L. Whisler) Management Organization and the Computer, 1960, (with Arnold R. Weber) Strategies for the Displaced Worker, 1966, (with Robert Z. Aliber) Guidelines, Informal Controls and the Market Place, 1966, (with Albert Rees) Workers and Wages in the Urban Labor Market, 1970, Leaders and Followers in an Age of Ambiguity, 1975, (with Kenneth W. Dam) Economic Policy Beyond the Headlines, 1977, Turmoil and Triumph: My Years as Secetary of State, 1993; also articles, chpts. in books, reports, and essays. Served to capt. USMCR, 1942-45. Mem. Am. Econ. Assn., Indsl. Relations Research Assn. (pres. 1968), Nat. Acad. Arbitrators. Office: Stanford U Hoover Instn Stanford CA 94305

SHULTZ, JOHN DAVID, lawyer; b. L.A., Oct. 9, 1939; s. Edward Patterson and Jane Elizabeth (Taylor) S.; m. Joanne Person, June 22, 1968; children: David Taylor, Steven Matthew. Student, Harvard Coll., 1960-61; BA, U. Ariz., 1964; JD, Boalt Hall, U. Calif., Berkeley, 1967. Bar: N.Y. 1968, Calif. 1978. Assoc. Cadwalader, Wickersham & Taft, N.Y.C., 1968-77; ptnr. Lawler, Felix & Hall, L.A., 1977-83, mem. exec. com., chmn. planning com., co-chmn. recruiting and hiring com.; ptnr. Morgan, Lewis & Bockius, L.A., 1983—, chmn. mgmt. com., mem. lateral entry com.; chmn. profl. evaluation com., chmn. bus. plan com., chmn. practice devel. com., chmn. recruiting com. Trustee St. Thomas Ch., N.Y.C., 1969-72, Shore Acres Point Corp., Mamaroneck, N.Y., 1975-77; mem. adv. bd. Internat. and Comparative Law Center, Southwestern Legal Found., 1981—; active Practicing Law Inst. Adv. Bd., Corp. and Securities Law, 1992—. Mem. ABA, Assn. Bar City N.Y., State Bar Calif., N.Y. State Bar Assn., Jonathan Club (L.A.), Phi Delta Phi, Sigma Chi. Episcopalian. Office: Morgan Lewis & Bockius 801 S Grand Ave Los Angeles CA 90017-4613

SHULTZ, LEILA MCREYNOLDS, botanist, educator; b. Bartlesville, Okla., Apr. 20, 1946; 1 child, Kirsten. BS, U. Tulsa, 1969; MA, U. Colo., 1975; PhD, Claremont Grad. Sch., 1983. Curator Intermountain Herbarium Utah State U., 1973-92; rschr. Harvard U., Cambridge, Mass., 1994—; rsch. assoc. prof. Utah St. U., 1994—. Co-author: Atlas of the Vascular Plants of Utah, 1988; taxon editor: Flora of North America (3 vols.), 1987. Mem. Am. Bot. Soc. (systematics rep. 1988-90), Am. Soc. Plant Taxonomists (coun. 1990-92). Office: Harvard U Herbaria 22 Divinity Ave Cambridge MA 02138-2020

SHULTZ, LINDA JOYCE, retired library director; b. South Bend, Ind., Aug. 25, 1931; d. Justin Russell and Gladys Ernstine (Miller) Nash; m. Dale Jay Shultz, Apr. 20, 1952; children: Donald Jay, Sally Janine, William Justin, Alan Joel, Kent Jon. AA, Stephens Coll., 1951; BS in Edn., Ind. U., Ft. Wayne, 1971, Cert. I in Libr. Edn., 1975. Sec. John R. Worthman, Inc., Ft. Wayne, 1951-54; farm wife, mother Noble County, Ind., 1954-68; libr. Noble County Pub. Libr., Albion, Ind., 1968-97; ret., 1997; mem. exec. bd. Tri-Alsa Libr. Svc. Authority, Ft. Wayne, 1988-90. Editor: Albion Memories, 1977. Mem. Albion Local Devel. Corp., 1989-92; sec. Cen. Noble Jr. Achievement, 1988-92. Named Albion Citizen of the Yr. Albion Rotary Club, 1977. Mem. DAR, Ind. Libr. Assn., Ind. Hist. Soc., Albion C. of C., Order Ea. Star, Rotary (pres. Albion club 1993-94), Toastmasters (pres. U.S. Six Shooters chpt. 1988-89), Gene Stratton Porter Meml. Soc., Ind. Soc. Mayflower Descendants, Geneal. Soc. (sec. 1985-95, pres. 1997—), Noble County Hist. Soc. Republican. Methodist. Avocation: genealogy.

SHULTZ, SILAS HAROLD, lawyer; b. Scribner, Nebr., Mar. 21, 1938; s. Harold Mohr and Arlene E. (Spath) S. BS, U. Pa., 1960; LLB, U. Ariz., 1966. Bar: Ariz. 1966, U.S. Supreme Ct. 1988, Colo. 1995; cert. specialist in personal injury and wrongful death, Ariz.; cert. civil trial specialist Nat. Bd. Trial Advocacy. Ptnr., dir. Fennemore, Craig, P.C., Phoenix, 1966-85; trial specialist Law Office of Richard Grand, Tucson, 1985-88; officer Shultz & Rollins, Ltd., Tucson, 1988—. 1st lt. U.S. Army Res., 1961-66. Mem. ATLA (Ariz. gov. 1994—), Am. Bd. Trial Advocates, Ariz. Trial Lawyers Assn. (bd. dirs. 1990—). Office: Shultz & Rollins Ltd 4280 N Campbell Ave Ste 214 Tucson AZ 85718-6585

SHUMACKER, HARRIS B., JR., surgeon, educator, author; b. Laurel, Miss., May 20, 1908; s. Harris B. and Corinne (Teller) S.; m. Myrtle E. Landau, Dec. 1, 1933; children—Peter D., James N. B.S., U. Tenn., Chattanooga, 1927; A.M., Vanderbilt U., 1928; M.D., Johns Hopkins U., 1932; D.Sc. (hon.), Ind. U., 1985. Diplomate Am. Bd. Surgery, Am. Bd. Thoracic Surgery. Asst. in surgery Johns Hopkins U., 1932-35, instr., 1938-41, asst. prof., 1941-46; asst. in surgery Yale U., 1936-37, instr., 1937-38, assoc. prof., 1946-48; prof. surgery Ind. U., 1948-70, chmn. dept., 1948-68, Disting. prof., 1970-78, Disting. prof. emeritus, 1978—; prof., sr. advisor Uniformed Svcs. U. of Health Scis., Bethesda, Md., 1981-87, Disting. prof. surgery, 1988—; pres. Uniformed Svcs U. Assocs., 1987-88; hon. mem. surg. faculties in Peoples Republic of China, 1979—; dir. sect. cardiovascular-thoracic surgery St. Vincent Hosp., 1973-78, sr. surg. cons., 1978-81. Served from capt. to lt. col. M.C., U.S. Army, 1942-46; cons. surgeon gen., 1949-60. Recipient Roswell Park award, 1968, Medal of Honor, Evansville U., 1970, Disting. Alumus award U. Chattanooga, Curtis medal, 1970, Spl. Alumnus award Johns Hopkins U., 1973, Disting. Svc. award Am. Soc. Abdominal Surgery, letter of commendation Surgeon-Gen. USN, 1987, Disting. Svc. medal Uniformed Svc. U. Health Scis., 1988, René Leriche prize Soc. Internat. de Chir., 1993. Fellow Royal Coll. Surgeons (hon.); mem. Am. Assn. Surgery of Trauma, Am. Surg. Assn. (1st v.p. 1961, sec. 1964-68), So. Surg. Assn., Central Surg. Assn., Pan-Pacific Surg. Assn. (trustee 1961-64, v.p., 1964-75, 78—, pres. 1975-78), AMA (chmn. sect. gen. surgery), Internat. Surg. Soc., Internat. Soc. Cardiovascular Surgeons (v.p. 1957-59, pres. N.Am. chpt. 1956-58), Soc. Clin. Surgery (pres. 1961-63), ACS (chmn. forum com. 1955-60, chmn. nat. TV com. 1964-68, Disting. Service award 1968), Soc. U. Surgeons (pres. 1951), Soc. for Vascular Surgery (pres. 1958-59), Am. Thoracic Surg. Assn., Soc. Thoracic Surgeons (hon.), Internat. Surg. Group (v.p. 1974-75, pres. 1975-76), Polish Surg. Assn. (hon.), Sociedad Cubana de Angiologia (hon.), Societa Italiana di Chirurgia (hon.), Internat. Surg. Group (hon.), Phi Beta Kappa, Sigma Xi, Alpha Omega Alpha.

SHUMAKER, JOHN WILLIAM, academic administrator; b. Pitts., Aug. 21, 1942; s. Thomas E. Shumaker and Sara Jane (Giffn) Cobun; children: Timothy, Brian. BA, U. Pitts., 1964; MA, U. Pa., 1966, PhD, 1969; LLD hon., Briarwood Coll., 1989; EdD (hon.), Kyung Hee U., 1992. Asst. assoc. prof. classics Ohio State U., Columbus, 1969-77, asst. dean Coll. Humanities, 1971-72, acting chmn. dept. classics, 1972-73, assoc. dean Coll. Humanities, 1973-77; dean Coll. Humanities and Fine Art SUNY, Albany, 1977-83, v.p. rsch. and ednl. devel., 1983-85, v.p. academic planning and devel., 1985-87; pres. Ctrl. Conn. State U., New Britain, 1987-95, U. Louisville, 1995—; exec. dir. Capital Dist. Humanities Program, Albany, 1978-83; trustee, chmn. Conn. Inst. for the ARts in Edn., New Britain, 1988-91; trustee Nat. Commn. for Coop. Edn., Boston, 1987—, exec. com. 1993—. Bd. dirs. New Britain Gen. Hosp., 1988—, Hartford chpt. ARC, 1988-91, A.W. Stanley Found., New Britain, 1988-93, Fleet Bank Adv. Bd., 1993—, World Affairs Coun., Hartford, Conn., 1994—, New Britain Found. for Pub. Giving, 1994—. Mem. Internat. Assn. Univ. Pres. (exec. com. 1987—, vice chmn. N.Am. coun. 1990—), Internat. Assembly Coop. Edn., Am. Assn. State Colls. and Univs. (com. on internat. programs 1987-88, com. state reps. 1988-89, com. diversity 1993—), New Eng. Bd. Higher Edn. (bd. govs. 1990—), New Britain C. of C. (bd. dirs. 1988-89), Phi Beta Kappa. Avocation: swimming. Office: University of Louisville Pres Office Louisville KY 40292*

SHUMAN, LARRY MYERS, soil chemist; b. Harrisburg, Pa., Apr. 3, 1944; s. Mark P. and Opal I. (Myers) Shuman; m. Catherine A. Yost, Mar. 21, 1970; children: Karen, Rebecca. BS, Pa. State U., 1966, MS, 1968, PhD, 1970. Asst. prof. soil chemistry U. Ga., Experiment, 1972-79, assoc. prof., 1979-91, prof., 1991—; USDA-OICD Exch. scientist to People's Republic of China, 1992. Co-editor, contbg. author Micronutrients in Agriculture, 1991; contbg. author: Zinc in Soils, 1979, Plant Environment Interactions, 1994, Methods of Soil Analysis, Part 3 - Chemical Methods, 1996; contbr. articles to profl. jours. Capt. M.S., U.S. Army, 1970-72. U.S. Aid grantee, 1980-81, USDA-CSRS grantee, 1992-94, Dept. Energy, 1995-96. Fellow Soil Sci Soc. Am. (soil chemistry divsn. chair 1994, assoc. editor jour. 1986-91); mem. Am. Soc. Agronomy, Coun. Agrl. Sci. and Tech., Soc. Environ. Geochemistry and Health. Home: 447 Trice Rd Milner GA 30257-3427 Office: U Ga Ga Experiment Sta Griffin GA 30223-1797

SHUMAN, MARK SAMUEL, environmental and electroanalytical chemistry educator; b. Yakima, Wash., July 29, 1936; s. Samuel and Ardella (Martin) S.; children—Kim, Donna, Bryce. B.S., Wash. State U., 1959; Ph.D., U. Wis., 1966. Chemist Atlantic Research Corp., Alexandria, Va., 1960-62; asst. prof. chemistry Tex. Christian U., Ft. Worth, 1966-69; vis. prof. Whitman Coll., Walla Walla, Wash., 1969-70; asst. prof. environ. chemistry U. N.C., Chapel Hill, 1970-75; assoc. prof. U. N.C., 1975-80, prof, 1980-92, prof. emeritus, 1992—. Contbr. articles to profl. jours., chpts. to books. Served to capt. U.S. Army, 1960-61. EPA fellow, 1970. Mem. Am. Chem. Soc. Office: 308 N 32nd Ave Yakima WA 98902-2216

SHUMAN, MICHAEL, think tank executive, attorney. AB in econs., internat. rels., Stanford U., 1979, JD, 1982. Bar: Calif., D.C. Founder Ctr. Innovative Diplomacy, 1982; co-dir., fellow Inst. Policy Studies, Washington. Author: Toward a Global Village, 1994; co-author: Citizen Diplomats: Pathfinders in Soviet-American Relations, 1986, Security Without War: A Post Cold War Foreign Policy, 1993; co-editor: (anthology) Conditions of Peace: An Inquiry, 1992, Technology for the Common Good, 1993; contbr. articles to profl. jours. Rsch. and Writing fellow John D. and Catherine T. MacArthur Found.; W.K. Kellogg Nat. Leadership fellow, 1987-90. Office: Inst Policy Studies Ste 1020 Washington DC 20005

SHUMAN, MICHAEL HARRISON, lawyer, policy analyst; b. N.Y.C., June 4, 1956; s. Jack Jacob and Bernadine Sydelle (Fine) S. AB, Stanford U., Palo Alto, Calif., 1979; JD, Stanford U., 1982. Bar: Calif. 1983, D.C. 1990. Intern NRDC, San Francisco, 1981-82; pres. Ctr. for Innovative Diplomacy, Irvine, Calif., 1982-91; fellow Inst. for Policy Studies, Washington, 1990—, dir., 1992—. Author: Citizen Diplomats, 1987, Conditions of Peace, 1991, Technology for the Common Good, 1993, Security Without War, 1993, Towards A Global Village, 1994, Home-Grown Prosperity, 1997. Kellogg Found. fellow, 1987-90. Avocations: roller skating, moose paraphernalia, film making, juggling. Office: Inst Policy Studies 733 H St NW Washington DC 20001-3733

SHUMAN, NICHOLAS ROMAN, journalist, educator; b. Chgo., June 30, 1921; s. Roman William and Pauline (Stasevich) S.; m. Marilyn Elaine Johnson, Feb. 23, 1952; children—Kristin Mary, Elizabeth Carol, Mark Nicholas. B.A., U. Ill., 1943. With Chgo. Jour. Commerce, 1938-46; mem. staff Herald-American, Chgo., 1946-51; asst. photo editor Herald-American, 1947-51; mem. staff Chgo. Daily News, 1951-78, fin. editor, 1961-65, asst. mng. editor, 1965-69, nat. and fgn. editor, 1969-77, chief editorial writer, 1977-78; editorial writer Chgo. Sun-Times, 1978-84; prof. journalism Columbia Coll., Chgo., 1984-91, cons., 1992—; columnist Chgo. Reporter, 1985-90; sr. editor World Book Ency., 1965-66; profl. instr. Medill Sch. Journalism, Northwestern U., 1954-61; freelance mag. writer, 1951—; TV commentator, 1958-61. Founding pres. Arlington Heights (Ill.) Human Relations Com., 1965. Served to 1st lt. AUS, 1943-46, ETO. Recipient awards Ill. AP, UPI, John Howard Assn., Inland Press Assn., Chgo. Newspaper Guild; nominated for Pulitzer prize 3 times. Mem. Alpha Kappa Lambda, Sigma Delta Chi. Home: 1001 W Clarendon Rd Arlington Heights IL 60004-4507

SHUMAN, R(OBERT) BAIRD, academic program director, writer, English language educator, educational consultant; b. Paterson, N.J., June 20, 1929; s. George William and Elizabeth (Evans) S. A.B. (Trustees scholar), Lehigh U., 1951; M.Ed., Temple U., 1953; Ph.D. (Univ. scholar), U. Pa., 1961; cert. in philology, U. Vienna, Austria, 1954. Tchr. Phila. Pub. Schs., 1953-55; asst. instr. English U. Pa., 1955-57; instr. humanities Drexel U., Phila., 1957-59; asst. prof. San José (Calif.) State U., 1959-62; asst. prof. English Duke U., 1962-63, asso. prof., 1963-66, prof. edn., 1966-77; prof. English, dir. English edn. U. Ill., Urbana-Champaign, 1977-85; dir. freshman rhetoric U. Ill., 1979-84, coord. Univ. Associates in Rhetoric Program, 1978-84, dir. devel., 1988-93, acting dir. Ctr. for Study of Writing, 1989-90, prof. emeritus, 1993—; vis. prof. Moore Inst. Art, 1958, Phila. Conservatory Music, 1958-59, Lynchburg Coll., 1965, King Faisal U., Saudi Arabia, 1978, 81, Bread Loaf Sch. English, Middlebury Coll., 1980, East Tenn. State U., Johnson City, 1980, Olivet Nazarene Coll., 1984, 86, 88, U. Tenn., Knoxville, 1987; cons. Ednl. Testing Svc., 1970—, Am. Coll. Testing Svc., 1975-82; cons. in lang. and lit. Coll. Engring., U. Ill., 1980—, Worldwide Youth in Sci. and Engring., 1995—; mem. William Inge Nat. Festival Com., 1989—. Author: Clifford Odets, 1962, Robert E. Sherwood, 1964, William Inge, 1965, rev. edit., 1989, Strategies in Teaching Reading: Secondary, 1978, (with Robert J. Krajewski) The Beginning Teacher: A Guide to Problem Solving, 1979, Elements of Early Reading Instruction, 1979, The First R: Strategies in Early Reading Instruction, 1987, rev. edit., 1989, Classroom Encounters: Problems, Case Studies, Solutions, 1989, (with Eric Hobson) Reading and Writing in High School, (with Denny T. Wolfe Jr.) Teaching English Through the Arts, 1990, Resources for Writers, 1992, American drama 1918-1960, 1992, Georgia O'Keeffe, 1993; editor: Nine Black Poets, 1968, An Eye for an Eye, 1969, A Galaxy of Black Writing, 1970, Creative Approaches to the Teaching of English: Secondary, 1974, Questions English Teachers Ask, 1977, Educational Drama for Today's Schools, 1978, Education in the 80's—English, 1980, The Clearing House: A Closer Look, 1984, 70th anniversary issue The Clearing House, 1995; exec. editor The Clearing House jour., 1976—; cons. editor Poet Lore, 1977-90, Cygnus, 1978—, Jour. Aesthetic Edn., 1978-82; contbg. editor Reading Horizons, 1975-85; editor quar. column Reading Horizons, 1975-85; editor Trends in English column Ednl. Leadership, 1989—. Active Nat. Trust Hist. Preservation. NEH researcher Trinity Coll., Dublin, Ireland, 1985. Mem. MLA, Nat. Coun. Tchrs. English (evaluator ERIC Clearing House, com. alt. careers for English profls.), Internat. Fedn. Tchrs. English, Internat. Coun. Edn. of tchrs., Nev. Coun. Tchrs. English, Conf. English Edn. (exec. com. 1976-79), Internat. Reading Assn. (coord. symposium on cultural literacy, Queensland, Australia 1988), Internat. Assn. Univ. Profs. English, Nat. Soc. Study Edn., Am. Fedn. Tchrs., Union Profl. Employees (editor newsletter 1988-92, exec. com. 1988-92). Democrat. Home: PO Box 27647 Las Vegas NV 89126-1647 Office: U Ill 208 English Bldg 608 S Wright St Urbana IL 61801-3613 *An education that does not produce people who are vibrantly alive, intoxicated with the wonder of existence, has fallen short. Joy of learning is the fulcrum upon which the human equation is balanced. I have always believed that emotion prevails over intellect and have led my life accordingly with the inevitable resultof being extraordinarily happy for most of my days.*

SHUMAN, SAMUEL IRVING, lawyer, law educator; b. Fall River, Mass., Aug. 7, 1925; s. Max and Fannie S.; m. Cynthia Webre, Mar. 25, 1990; children from previous marriage: Maxim Erric, Michael A. A.B., U. Pa., 1947, M.A., 1948, Ph.D., 1951; J.D., U. Mich., 1954; S.J.D., Harvard U., 1959. Bar: Mich. 1954, Tex. 1979. Research asst. Legis. Research Center, U. Mich., Ann Arbor, 1953-54; vis. prof. law Legis. Research Center, U. Mich., 1961; vis. prof. U. Rome, 1963-64; asst. prof. law Wayne State U., Detroit, 1954-55; assoc. prof. Wayne State U., 1955-56, prof., 1957-80; prof. dept. psychiatry Wayne State U. Med. Sch.; lectr. Internat. Faculty Comparative Law, Luxembourg, 1964; prof. forensic psychiatry, spl. counsel Lafayette Clinic, Mich. Dept. Mental Health; gen. counsel Mich. Psychiat. Assn., Epilepsy Center Mich. Author: Legal Positivism: Its Scope and Limitations, 1963, (with N.D. West) Introduction to American Law: Cases and Materials, 1971, Psychosurgery and the Medical Control of Violence: Autonomy and Deviance, 1977; editorial bd.: Am. Jour. Jurisprudence, 1969-79. Bd. dirs. Tex. Modern Art Found. Recipient Wayne State U. Bd. Govs. Faculty Recognition award, 1978; Probus Club award Disting. Acad. Achievement in Humanities, 1963; Fulbright fellow Italy, 1961; Rockefeller Found. grantee, 1959, 61; Fulbright travel grantee Germany, 1961; Wayne State U. research grantee, 1960-64; Internat. Research & Exchanges Bd. grantee, 1973. Mem. Am. Law Inst. (life).

SHUMAN, STANLEY S., investment banker; b. Cambridge, Mass., June 22, 1935; s. Saul A. and Sarah L. (Saxe) S.; m. Ruth H. Lande, 1967 (div. 1979); children: David Lande, Michael Adam; m. Sydney Roberts Gould, 1992. B.A., Harvard U., Boston, 1956, J.D., 1959, M.B.A., 1961. Bar: Mass. 1959, N.Y. 1991. Exec. v.p., mng. dir. Allen & Co., Inc., N.Y.C., 1961—; bd. dirs. Bayou Steel Corp., Global Asset Mgmt. (USA), Inc., Hudson Gen. Corp. Ltd., News Corp. Ltd., News Am. Holdings Inc., Sesac Inc.; mem. Pres.'s Fgn. Intelligence Adv. Bd., 1995—. Mem. Fin. Control Bd., N.Y.C., 1977-97; active Channel 13 WNET, 1990—, Carnegie Hall, 1990—, Mus. TV and Radio, 1996—, N.Y. Law Sch., 1990-96, The Markle Found., 1992—, Nat. Pub. Radio Found., 1992—; chmn. Nat. Econ. Devel. and Law Ctr., 1978-83; chmn. adv. bd. Inst. Policy Scis. and Pub. Affairs Duke U., 1992-96; bd. advisors DeWitt Wallace Ctr. Comm. and Journalism, 1994—, Bertlesmann Found. Media Workshop, 1994—; mem. exec. com. Harvard Campaign, 1995—; mem. adv. bd. Ctr. Health Comm. Harvard Sch. Pub. Health, 1996—; chmn. adv. coun. Ctr. for N.Y.C. Law, 1996—; trustee The Dalton Sch., 1977-84, hon. trustee, 1984—; active Devel. Bd. Phillips Acad., Andover, Mass., 1972-80; pres. Wiliwyck Sch., 1971-78; v.p. exec. com. Jewish Guild for the Blind, 1973-80; trustee Jewish Publ. Soc., 1986-90; mem. Coun. on Fgn. Rels., 1995—, sect. corp. banking and bus. law, 1974—. Clubs: Harvard (Boston), Harvard (N.Y.C.), Quaker Ridge Golf, East Hampton Tennis. Home: 25 Sutton Pl New York NY 10022 Office: Allen & Co Inc 711 5th Ave New York NY 10022-3108

SHUMATE, CHARLES ALBERT, retired dermatologist; b. San Francisco, Aug. 11, 1904; s. Thomas E. and Freda (Ortmann) S.; B.S., U. San Francisco, 1927, H.H.D., 1976; M.D., Creighton U., 1931. Pvt. practice dermatology, San Francisco, 1933-73, ret., 1973; asst. clin. prof. dermatology Stanford U., 1956-62; pres. E Clampus Vitus, Inc., 1963-64; hon. mem. staff St. Mary's Hosp. Mem. San Francisco Art Commn., 1964-67, Calif. Heritage Preservation Commn., 1963-67; regent Notre Dame Coll. at Belmont, 1965-78, trustee, 1977-93; pres. Conf. Calif. Hist. Socs., 1967; mem. San Francisco Landmarks Preservation Bd., 1967-78, pres., 1967-69; trustee St. Patrick's Coll. and Sem., 1970-86; dir. U.S. Catholic Hist. Soc., 1988—. Served as maj. USPHS, 1942-46. Decorated knight comdr. Order of Isabella (Spain); knight Order of the Holy Sepulchre, knight of St. Gregory, knight of Malta. Fellow Am. Acad. Dermatology; mem. U. San Francisco Alumni Assn. (pres. 1955), Calif. Book Club (pres. 1969-71), Calif. Hist. Soc. (trustee 1958-67, 68-78, pres. 1962-64), Soc. Calif. Pioneers (dir. 1979—), Drum Found. (v.p. 1986—). Clubs: Bohemian, Olympic, Roxburghe (pres. 1958-59) (San Francisco); Zamorano (Los Angeles). Author: Life of George Henry Goddard; The California of George Gordon, 1976, Jas. F. Curtis, Vigilante, 1988, Francisco Pacheco of Pacheco Pass, 1977; Life of Mariano Malarin, 1980; Boyhood Days: Y. Villegas Reminiscences of California 1850s, 1983, The Notorious I.C. Woods of the Adams Express, 1986, Rincon Hill and South Park, 1988, Captain A.A. Ritchie, Pioneer, 1991, Stormy Life of Major William Gouverneur Morris, 1993, Lord Sholto Douglas, Clamper, 1996. Mem. St. Andrew Soc. (hon. mem.). Home: 1901 Scott St San Francisco CA 94115-2613 Office: 490 Post St San Francisco CA 94102-1401

SHUMATE, JOHN PAGE, diplomat; b. El Paso, Tex., Sept. 18, 1934; s. John Page and Elizabeth (McWilliams) S.; m. Caroline Taylor, June 16, 1978. BA in Polit. Sci., UCLA, 1956; MAin Internat. Rels., U. So. Calif., 1970. Counsellor of Embassy, U.S. Embassy, Quito, Ecuador, 1970-72; dir. exec. tng. Fgn. Service Inst., Washington, 1972-75; dir. U.K. Affairs, Dept. State., 1975-78, exec. dir. Bur. Ednl. and Cultural Affairs, 1978-80, exec. dir. Bur. Adminstrn., Washington, 1981-84; staff dir. Sec. of State's Adv. Panel on Overseas Security, 1984-85; exec. v.p., chief exec. officer Am. Fgn. Service Protective Assn., 1986—, Assn. Fed. Health Orgns. (chmn. bd. dirs. 1992—); co-pres. U.S.-Mexico Cultural Commn. com., 1978-80; exec. dir. sr. living found. Am. Fgn. Svcs. Recipient Superior Honor award U.S. Dept. State., 1981; Phi Kappa Phi Cert. of Honor, 1970. Mem. Am. Fgn. Service Assn., Nat. Assn. Sr. Living Industries, Phi Kappa Phi. Clubs: Ft. Meyer Officers, Fgn. Service, Dacor Bacon House, Bethany West Tennis. Office: Am Fgn Svc Protective Assn 1716 N St NW Washington DC 20036-2907

SHUPACK, PAUL MARTIN, law educator; b. Bklyn., May 20, 1940; s. Ben and Florentina Marie (Leipniker) S.; m. Leslie Sloan, Dec. 23, 1989; stepchildren: Alexander Hoffert, Jason Hoffert. AB, Columbia U., 1961; postgrad., Harvard U., 1961-67; JD, U. Chgo., 1970. Bar: N.Y. 1971. Assoc. Cleary, Gottlieb, Steen & Hamilton, N.Y.C., 1970-77; asst. prof. Yeshiva U., N.Y.C., 1977-79, assoc. prof., 1980-84, prof., 1984—; vis. asst. prof. U. Chgo., 1979. Contbr. articles to profl. jours. Mem. Am. Law Inst., Assn. Bar City of N.Y. Home: 35 Sutton Pl Apt 7C New York NY 10022 Office: Yeshiva U 55 5th Ave New York NY 10003-4301

SHUR, MICHAEL, electrical engineer, educator, consultant; b. Kamensk-Yralski, Sverdlovsk, USSR, Nov. 13, 1942; came to U.S., 1976.; s. Saul and Anna (Katz) S.; m. Paulina Gimmelfarb, Sept. 25, 1966; children: Luba, Natasha. MS, Leningrad Elec. Tech. Inst., 1965; PhD, Ioffe Inst., Leningrad, 1967; DSc, Ioffe Inst., St. Petersburg, 1992; Hon. Doctorate, St. Petersburg State Tech. U., 1994. Scientist Ioffe Inst., 1965-75; asst. prof. Wayne State U., Detroit, 1976-77, Oakland U., Rochester, Mich., 1978; prof. U. Minn., Mpls., 1979-92; John Marshall Money prof. U. Va., Charlottesville, Va., 1989-96; Patricia W. and C. Sheldon Roberts prof. Rensselaer Poly. Inst., 1996—. Author 10 books; co-editor-in-chief Internat. Jour. High Speed Electronics and Systems; mem. hon. editl. bd. Solid State Electronics; contrbr. articles to profl. jours.; patentee in field. Fellow IEEE (assoc. editor IEEE Trans. 1990-93), Am. Phys. Soc.; mem. Eta Kappa Nu, Tau Beta Pi. *When we were penniless refugees, the United States adopted me and my family with compassion and friendship, gave us work and citizenship. Our debt of gratitude to the American people who accepted us as their own we will be never able to repay.*

SHURBAJI, M. SALAH, pathologist; b. Cairo, Apr. 18, 1957; came to U.S., 1984; s. Muhammad B. and Salma Shurbaji; m. Hilda Touma, 1984; 2 children. BS with distinction, Am. U. Beirut, 1979, MS, 1981, MD with distinction, 1984. Diplomate Am. Bd. Pathology; lic. physician Md., Tenn., Mich. Intern Am. U. Beirut Med. Ctr., 1983-84; resident pathology Johns Hopkins Hosp., Balt., 1984-87, resident dept. lab. medicine, 1987-89; clin. fellow dept. pathology Johns Hopkins U. Sch. Medicine, Balt., 1984-89, rsch. fellow dept. pathology, 1989-90; asst. prof. pathology East Tenn. State U., Johnson City, 1990-94, assoc. prof. pathology, 1994—; staff pathologist Univ. Physicians Practice Group, Johnson City, 1990—; staff pathologist Vets. Affairs Med. Ctr., Johnson City, 1990—, acting chief pathology and lab. medicine svc., 1993-94, chief pathology and lab. medicine svc., 1994—. Contbr. articles to profl. jours. Recipient John Abi Hashem Pediatric award Am. U. Beirut, 1982. Fellow Am. Soc. Clin. Pathologists, Coll. Am. Pathologists; mem. AAAS, A.P. Stout Soc. Surg. Pathologists, Am. Soc. Cytology, U.S. and Can. Acad. Pathology, Papanicolaou Soc. Cytopathology, Internat. Soc. Urologic Pathology, Sigma Xi, Alpha Omega Alpha. Achievements include contribution to understanding of certain factors that affect the prognosis of neoplasms especially prostate cancer. Office: E Tenn State U Coll Medicine Dept Pathology PO Box 70568 Johnson City TN 37614-0568

SHURE, MYRNA BETH, psychologist, educator; b. Chgo., Sept. 11, 1937; d. Sidney Natkin and Frances (Laufman) S.; student U. Colo., 1955; BS, U. Ill., 1959; MS, Cornell U., 1961, PhD, 1966. Asst. prof. U. R.I., head tchr. Nursery Sch., Kingston, 1961-62; asst. prof. Temple U., Phila., 1966-67, assoc. prof., 1967-68; instr. Hahneman Med. Coll., Phila., 1968-69, sr. instr. psychology, 1969-70, asst. prof., 1970-73, assoc. prof., 1973-80, prof., 1980—. NIMH research grantee, 1971-75, 77-79, 82-85, 87, 88-93. Recipient Lela Rowland Prevention award Nat. Mental Health Assn., 1982; . lic. psychologist, Pa. Fellow Am. Psychol. Assn. (Disting. Contbn. award div. community psychology 1984), Am. Psychol. Assn. (divsn. clin. psychology, child sect. 1994, Task Force on Prevention award 1987, Task Force on Model Programs award 1994, award U. Utah and Juvenile Justice Dept. of Delinquency Prevention, 1996); mem. Nat. Assn. Sch. Psychologists, Nat. Assn. Edn. Young Children, Soc. Research in Child Devel., Phila. Soc. Clin. Psychologists. Author: (with George Spivack) Social Adjustment of Young Children, 1974; (with George Spivack and Jerome Platt) The Problem Solving Approach to Adjustment, 1976; (with George Spivack) Problem Solving Techniques in Childrearing, 1978, (child curricula manual) I Can Problem Solve, 1992, (trade book) Raising a Thinking Child, 1994, (audiotape, workbook, paperback Parents' Choice award 1996), 1996; mem. editl. bd. Jour. Applied Developmental Psychology; spl. cons. to The Puzzle Place PBS Children's TV Show.

SHURICK, EDWARD PALMES, television executive, rancher; b. Duluth, Minn., Dec. 15, 1912; s. Edward P. and Vera (Wheaton) S.; m. F(lossie) Dolores Pipes, Aug. 1, 1933; children—Patricia Annette (Mrs. Robert Dube), Sandra Sue Shurick Dryden, Linda Jean (Mrs. James Elsea), Edward P. III. Student, U. Minn., 1932-33; B.A. in Econs, U. Mo., 1946. Gen. sales mgr. Intermountain Network, Salt Lake City, 1937-41; advt. mgr. sta. KMBC, Kansas City, Mo., 1941-47; research mgr. Free & Peters, N.Y.C., 1947-49; v.p. CBS TV, N.Y.C., 1949-57; exec. v.p. Blair TV, N.Y.C., 1957-62; chmn., treas. H-R TV, N.Y.C., 1962-76; dir. Seltel, Inc., N.Y.C.; v.p., owner Sta. KXXX-AM-FM, Colby, Kans., 1963-84; v.p. treas. H-R Rep. Cos., 1970-73; pres. S&S Enterprises, Charlottesville, Va., 1959-89, S & S Ranch Corp., Aspen, Colo., 1965-82; mem. bd. Chgo. Internat. Live Stock Expn., 1972-76. Author: First Quarter-Century of American Broadcasting, 1946. Pres. Shurick Rsch. Found., Bridgewater, 1959-72; v.p., originator Internat. Radio and TV Found., N.Y.C., 1964-73. Recipient Alumnus award U. Mo. at Kansas City, 1968; ordre du merit for contbns. to agr. Govt. France, 1970; Ordre du Charolais Francais, 1971. Mem. Internat. Radio and TV Soc. N.Y. (pres. 1967-69), Am. Internat. Charolais Assn. (pres. 1968-69), Colonial Charolais Breeders (dir. 1967-71), World Fedn. Charolais (pres. 1973-74), Broadcast Pioneers Assn., Am. Nat. Cattlemen's Assn. (tax com. 1968-76), Internat. Wine and Food Soc. (bd. dirs. 1985-88), Masons (32 degree), Shriners. Episcopalian (lay reader). Address: 1006 Fearrington Post Pittsboro NC 27312 *The opportunity to succeed as a self-made person still exists in the United States today. This may seem hackneyed and out-of-date, but it isn't. Honesty, dedication, long hours of hard work with an average amount of luck will build a fortune from a few cents to a million dollars.*

SHURKIN, LORNA GREENE, writer, publicist; b. N.Y.C., Mar. 5, 1944; d. Morris and Rita Rose (Cohen) Greene; m. Joel N. Shurkin, July 4, 1966 (div. Nov. 1981); children: Jonathan Greene, Michael Robert. BA, Bklyn. Coll., CUNY, 1964; postgrad., NYU, 1965-66; fundraising cert., U. Pa., 1997. English tchr. N.Y.C. Schs., 1963-64; asst. to articles editor Womans Day mag., N.Y.C., 1964-66; reporter, columnist News-Herald, Willoughby, Ohio, 1966-68; reporter, reviewer Phila. Inquirer, Reuters and others, 1974-76; pub. rels. rep., editor Thomas Jefferson U., Phila., 1976-79; account exec. Sommers/Rosen Pub. Relations, Phila., 1979-81; dir. pub. relations Swarthmore (Pa.) Coll., 1981-94; writer, publicist St. Davids, Pa., 1995—. Dem. cand. Radnor Twp. (Pa.) Sch. Bd., 1987, Radnor Dem. Com., 1988—; v.p. Footlighters Theater, Berwyn, Pa., 1985-88; ofcl. pronouncer Delaware County (Pa.) Spelling Bee, 1986—; mem. adv. bd. Ea. Pa. Theater Coun., 1986—; bd. dirs. Anti-Violence Partnership Phila., 1989—; twp. rep. Dem. County Coun., 1994, committeeperson, 1993—; bd. dirs. Friends of the Anthony Wayne Theatre, 1995—. Mem. Pub. Rels. Soc. Am., Del. County Press Club (bd. dirs. 1991—, program chmn. 1991-93), Nat. Writers Union, Phila. Pub. Rels. Assn. Jewish. Home: 435 E Lancaster Ave Apt 110 Saint Davids PA 19087-4221

SHURLEY, JAY TALMADGE, psychiatrist, medical educator, administrator, behavioral sciences researcher, polar explorer, author, genealogist; b. Sonora, Tex., Dec. 20, 1917; s. Ira L. and Jewell L. (Choate) S.; m. Erwina Bode Cornelison, Dec. 20, 1986. BA in Zoology, U. Tex.-Austin, 1940; MD, U. Tex. Med. Br., Galveston, 1942. Diplomate Am. Bd. Psychiatry and Neurology. Intern. Ind. U.-Indpls. Med. Ctr., 1943; Rockefeller fellow in neuropsychiatry dept. mental and nervous disease Inst. for Mental Hygiene Pa. Hosp., Phila., 1944-47; pvt. practice medicine specializing in psychiatry and psychoanalysis Phila., 1947-51, Austin, 1951-52; pvt. practice medicine specializing in psychiatry San Antonio, 1952-54, Chevy Chase, Md., 1955-57; pvt. practice medicine specializing in psychiatry, psychoanalysis and sleep disorders medicine Oklahoma City, 1978-90; acting chief lab. adult psychiat. investigation, clin. investigations NIMH, NIH, Bethesda, 1955-57; chief psychiatry service and mental hygiene clinic VA Hosp., Oklahoma City, 1957-62; sr. med. investigator in psychiatry, research service, dept. medicine and surgery VA, 1962-76; founder and dir. behavioral scis. labs VA Med. Ctr., Oklahoma City, 1962-78; sci. dir. Oklahoma Mental Health Research Inst., Oklahoma Dept. Mental Health, 1988-89; cons.-liaison in geropsychiatry O'Donoghue Rehab. Inst., Okla. Med. Ctr., 1990-91; med. dir. emeritus Willow View Mental Health Ctr., Oklahoma City, 1985-87; prof. psychiatry U. Okla., Oklahoma City, 1957-77, prof. psychiatry and behavioral scis. Coll. of Medicine and Grad. Coll., 1977-81; prof. emeritus psychiatry and behavioral scis. U. Okla. Coll. Medicine, Oklahoma City, 1981—; adj. prof. human ecology Coll. Health, U. Okla., 1967-81; mem. com. on polar rsch., chmn. panel on biology and medicine NAS/NRC, 1970-74; U.S. rep. Working Group on Biology XII Sci. Com. on Antarctic Rsch., Canberra and Melbourne, Australia, 1972; U.S. rep. Working Group on Human Biology and Medicine XIII Sci. Com. on Antarctic Rsch., Jackson Hole, Wyo., 1974; disting. vis. scientist Acad. Scis. USSR, Moscow and Leningrad, 1972; Centennial Yr. vis. prof. dept. psychol. medicine U. Otago, Dunedin, N.Z., 1975; mem. Health Rsch. Com., Okla. Ctr. for Sci. and Tech., 1986-91, Okla. Alzheimer Rsch. Adv. Coun., 1990-92. Editor: Relating Environment to Mental Health and Illness: The Eco-psychiatric Data Base, 1979, Symposium on Man on the South Polar Plateau, 1970; mem. editorial bd. Jour. Clin. Psychology, 1970-80; contbr. more than 100 articles to sci. publs. Served as capt. M.C. U.S. Army, 1952-54. Recipient Antarctic Svc. medal NSF/NAS, 1970, Disting. Profl. Svc. award Okla. Psychol. Assn., 1972, Sustained Superior Achievement cert. VA, 1974, Disting. Psychiatrist award Mid-Continent Psychiat. Assn., 1986, Okla. Psychiat. Assn., 1990, Sealy Inc. prize Assn. Profl. Sleep Socs., 1991; Shurley Ridge, Pensacola Mountains Antarctica named in his honor. Fellow Am. Psychiat. Assn. (life), Am. Coll. Psychiatrists (life); mem. AMA, Oklahoma County Med. Soc., Okla. State Med. Assn. (life), Okla. Psychiat. Assn. (pres. 1968, chair ethics com. 1989-91), Faculty House Club, Sigma Xi, Alpha Omega Alpha, Alpha Epsilon Delta. Democrat. Address: PO Box 1277 Bastrop TX 78602

SHURTLEFF, MALCOLM C., plant pathologist, consultant, educator, extension specialist; b. Fall River, Mass., June 24, 1922; s. Malcolm C. and Florence L. (Jewell) S.; m. Margaret E. Johnson, June 14, 1950; children: Robert Glen, Janet Lee, Mark Steven. BS in Biology, U. R.I., 1943; MS in Plant Pathology, U. Minn., 1950, PhD in Plant Pathology, 1953. Asst. plant pathologist Conn. Agrl. Expt. Sta., New Haven, 1942, R.I. Agrl. Expt. Sta., Kingston, 1943; asst. extension prof. U. R.I., Kingston, 1950-54; assoc. extension prof. Iowa State U., Ames, 1954-61; prof. plant pathology U. Ill., Champaign-Urbana, 1961-92, prof. emeritus, 1992—; cons., writer Urbana, 1992—. Author: How To Control Plant Diseases, 1962, 66 (award Am. Garden Guild 1961, 66), How To Control Lawn Diseases and Pests, 1973, How To Control Tree Diseases and Pests, 1975, Controlling Turfgrass Pests, 1987, 97, A Glossary of Plant Pathological Terms, 1997, The Plant Disease Clinic and Field Diagnosis of Abiotic Diseases, 1997; editor-in-chief Phytopathology News, 1966-69, Plant Disease, 1969-72; contbr. numerous articles to encys., profl. publs. and mags. Lt. (j.g.) USN, 1943-46, PTO. Recipient Disting. Svc. award U.S. Dept. Agriculture, Washington, 1986. Fellow Am. Phytopathological Soc. (councilor at large 1970-71, Excellence in Extension Plant Pathology award 1991); mem. Internat. Soc. Plant Pathology (chmn. extension com. 1975-80), Am. Phytopathological Soc. (mem. various coms.). Avocation: photography. Home: 2707 Holcomb Dr Urbana IL 61802-7724 Office: U Ill Dept Plant Pathology N-427 N Turner Hall Urbana IL 61801

SHURTLIFF, MARVIN KARL, lawyer; b. Idaho Falls, Idaho, Nov. 6, 1939; s. Noah Leon and Melba Dorothy (Hunting) S.; m. Peggy J. Griffin, Nov. 23, 1963; 1 dau., Jennifer Karyl. B.A., Idaho State Coll., 1962; J.D., U. Idaho, 1968. Bar: Idaho 1968. Tchr. pub. schs. Jefferson County, Idaho, 1964-65; atty. U.S. Dept. Justice, Washington, 1968-74; commr. Idaho Pub. Utilities Commn., 1974-75, pres., 1975-76; spl. asst., legal counsel Gov. of Idaho, Boise, 1977; U.S. atty. for Dist. of Idaho, Boise, 1977-81; practice law Boise, 1981—; mem. Idaho Ho. of Reps., 1962-64. Mem. Idaho State Bd. Edn., 1990-95. Mem. Idaho Bar Assn. Democrat. Home: 62 Horizon Dr Boise ID 83702-4419 Office: PO Box 1652 Boise ID 83701-1652

SHUSHKEWICH, KENNETH WAYNE, structural engineer; b. Winnipeg, Man., Sept. 22, 1952; m. Valdine Cuffe, Sept. 28, 1980. BSCE, U. Man., Winnipeg, 1974; MS in Structural Engring., U. Calif., Berkeley, 1975; PhD in Structural Engring., U. Alta., Edmonton, Can., 1985. Engr. Wardrop and Assocs., Winnipeg, 1974-78, Preconsult Can., Montreal, Que., 1978-80; prof. U. Alta., 1981-85, U. Man., 1985-87; engr. T.Y. Lin Internat., San Francisco, 1988-90, H.J. Degenkolb Assocs., San Francisco, 1990-92, Ben C. Gerwick, Inc., San Francisco, 1993-94, J. Muller Internat., Chgo., 1994-95, T.Y. Lin Internat., San Francisco, 1995—; mem. bridge design com., prestressed concrete com. ASCE-Am. Concrete Inst. Prin. works include design of prestressed concrete segmental bridges, seismic strengthening of San Francisco Ferry Building damaged in Loma Prieta earthquake, seismic retrofit of Presidio Viaduct in San Francisco; design mgr. for long-span west approach bridge of Northumberland Strait Crossing in Can.; contbr. articles to profl. jours. Recipient award for design of Vierendeel truss bridge, Man. Design Inst., 1977. Mem. ASCE, Am. Concrete Inst., Prestressed Concrete Inst., Internat. Assn. Bridge and Structural Engrs. Office: PO Box 2590 San Francisco CA 94126-2590

SHUSTER, ALVIN, journalist, newspaper editor; b. Washington, Jan. 25, 1930; s. Fred and Dora (Levy) S.; m. Miriam Schwartz, June 22, 1952; children: Fred, Jessica, Beth. AB, George Washington U., 1951. Reporter Washington Bur. N.Y. Times, 1952-61, asst. news editor, 1961-66, reporter London Bur., 1967-70; bur. chief Saigon, Vietnam, 1970-71, London, 1971-75, Rome, 1975-77; dep. editor editorial pages L.A. Times, 1977-83, fgn. editor, 1983-95, sr. consulting editor, 1995—; pres. Fgn. Corrs. Assn., London, 1973-74; trustee Monterey (Calif.) Inst. Internat. Studies, 1983—. Editor: The Witnesses, 1964, Washington: The New York Times Guide to the Nations' Capital, 1967, International Press Institute Report, 1995—. Nieman fellow Harvard U., 1966-67. Mem. Reform Club (London). Office: Los Angeles Times Times Mirror Sq Los Angeles CA 90053

SHUSTER, BUD, congressman; b. Glassport, Pa., Jan. 23, 1932; s. Prather and Grace (Greinert) S.; m. Patricia Rommell, Aug. 27, 1955; children: Peg, Bill, Debbie, Bobby, Gia. B.S., U. Pitts., 1954; M.B.A., Duquesne U., 1960; Ph.D. in Econs. and Mgmt., Am. U., 1967. Nat. account mgr. Univac div. Sperry Rand, 1956, Univac div. Remington Rand Co. (name now Sperry Rand), 1956-60; dist. mgr. Western Pa. RCA, 1960-62; mgr. ops. RCA, Washington, 1962-65; v.p. EPD div. RCA, 1965-68; pres. computer terminal co., 1968-72; mem. 93rd-105th Congresses from 9th Pa. dist., Washington, D.C., 1973—; pres. 93d Congress Rep. Freshman Class; chmn. Nat. Transp. Policy Study Commn., 1976, chmn. transp. and infrastructure com., 1995—. Author: Believing in America, 1983. Del. Rep. Nat. Conv., 1976, 80, 84, 88, 92, 96; co-chair Energy, Environment & Transp. Platform Subcom.; sr. transp. advisor Bush-Quayle Campaign; also mem. platform com.; chmn. Reagan-Bush Campaign in Western Pa.; sr. advisor to transition team for Dept. Transp., 1980-81; trustee J.F. Kennedy Ctr. for Performing Arts. Recipient Watchdog of Treasury award, Guardian of Small Bus. award, Golden Age Hall of Fame award. Mem. Pa. Soc., Chowder and Marching Soc., Phi Beta Kappa, Omicron Delta Kappa, Sigma Chi (Significant Sig award). Club: Capitol Hill. Office: US Ho of Reps 2188 Rayburn Bldg Ofc B Washington DC 20515-3809

SHUSTER, FREDERICK, internist; b. Newark, Sept. 12, 1933; s. Ralph and Anne (Weinstein) S.; m. Jane B. Block, June 11, 1958; children: Alan R., Robert G. BS, Rutgers U., 1955; MD, U. Chgo., 1959. Diplomate Am. Bd. Internal Medicine, Am. Bd. Gastroenterology. Intern U. Mich. Hosp., Ann Arbor, 1959-60, resident internal medicine, 1960-62; resident gastroenterology VA Hosp. U. Miami, Fla., 1962-63; pvt. practice N. Miami Beach, Fla., 1963—; from clin. instr. to assoc. prof. medicine U. Miami, Fla., 1963—; chmn. dept. medicine Parkway Regional Med. Ctr., N. Miami Beach, 1967, 70, chief of staff, 1974-75, chief divsn. gastroenterology, 1976-77, chmn. pharmacy and therapeutics com., 1978—. Chmn. med. advisory com. Crohn's and Colitis Found., S. Fla. chpt., Miami, 1979—. Major U.S. Army, 1967-69. Recipient Physician's Recognition award in Continung Edn., AMA, Chgo., 1970—. Fellow Am. Coll. Physicians, Am. Coll. Gastroenterology, Alpha Omega Alpha. Jewish. Avocations: bowling, ballroom dancing. Office: Drs Shuster & Reichbach PA 16800 NW 2nd Ave Ste 204 N Miami Beach FL 33169-5549

SHUSTER, JOHN A., civil engineer; b. Santa Fe, Jan. 18, 1939; s. William H. and Selma (Dingee) S.; m. Carol Habberley, July 1958 (div. Feb. 1960); m. Susan Handy, Aug. 20, 1962 (div. May 1992); children: David Brian, Karen. Student, U. N.Mex., 1961-63; BCE, U. Alaska, 1965; MCE, Stanford U., 1966. Registered profl. engr., Alaska, Calif., R.I., Mass., Va., Wash., Wis., Md., Del. Project engr. Woodward Clyde Assocs., Oakland, Calif., 1966-67, sr. project engr., 1969-72; resident project engr. Soil Cons. of S.E. Asia, Bangkok, Thailand, 1967-69; v.p. engring. Am. Drilling Co., Providence, 1972-74, also bd. dirs.; exec. v.p. Terrafreeze Corp., Lorton, Va., 1974-79, also bd. dirs.; pres. Geocentric Engring. Corp., Newington, Va., 1979-89; ind. profl. engr. Internat. Cons. Practice, Mason Neck, Va., 1989-91; pres. Geofreeze, Inc., Mason Neck, Va., 1991—; vis. lectr. on constrn. ground freezing and related techs., numerous univs. and profl. assns., 1975-88; bd. dirs. Geofreeze Corp., Lorton. Contbr. numerous tech. papers to internat. confs. Bd. dirs. Harbor View Civic Assn., Lorton, 1974-79; sect. dir. Operation Zap The Blackstone, Providence, 1972. Served with U.S. Army, 1957-61. Mem. ASCE, Internat. Soc. Soil Mechanics and Founds., Engring. Inst. Can., Am. Underground Space Assn. (charter), Deep Founds. Inst., Nat. Rsch. Coun. Transp. Rsch. Bd., Internat. Organizing Com. for Ground Freezing (internat. contractors rep.), Harbor View Recreation Club (bd. dirs. 1977-80). Democrat. Unitarian. Avocations: boating, fishing, skiing, motorcycling.

SHUSTER, ROBERT G., electronics company executive, consultant; b. N.Y.C., June 1, 1927; s. Robert Chandler and Therese G. (Giraud); m. Marianne B. Lynski, Apr. 20, 1970 (div. Jan. 1987); m. H. Elizabeth Young, May 20, 1989 (div. Dec. 1995). BSEE, CCNY, 1948; MSEE, Columbia U., 1955, postgrad., 1959-64. Test engr. Elec. Testing Labs., N.Y.C., 1948-50; project leader Sperry Gyroscope Co., Great Neck, N.Y., 1950-59; project mgr. RCA Advanced Communications Lab., N.Y.C., 1959-67; prin. scientist Tracor, Inc., Rockville, Md., 1967-75, v.p. electronics systems div., 1975-87; pres. Tracor Tech. Resources, Inc., Rockville, Md., 1984-90, RGS Assocs., McLean, Va., 1990—; v.p. C-Cubed Corp., Alexandria, Va., 1990-93; pres. C-Cubed Corp., 1993-95; sr. cons., 1996—. Mem. IEEE (sr.), AAAS, N.Y. Acad. Scis. Avocations: photography, hiking. Office: C-Cubed Corp 6800 Verser Ctr Springfield VA 22151-4177

SHUSTERMAN, NEAL DOUGLAS, author, screenwriter; b. N.Y.C., Nov. 12, 1962; s. Milton and Charlotte Ruth (Altman) S.; m. Elaine Gale Jones, Jan. 31, 1987; children: Brendan, Jarrod. BA in Psychology and Drama, U. Calif., Irvine, 1985. Author, screenwriter, 1987—. Author: Guy Talk, 1987, The Shadow Club, 1988 (Children's CHoice award Internat. Reading Assn. 1989), Dissidents, 1989, Speeding Bullet, 1991 (Best Book for Teens award N.Y. Pub. Libr., nominated Calif. Young Reader Medal 1995-96), Kid Heroes, 1991, What Daddy Did, 1991 (Best Book for Young Adults award ALA, Outstanding Work of Fiction award So. Calif. Coun. Lit. for Children and Young People, Children's Choice award and Young Adult Choice award Internat. Reading Assn., Pick of the List award ABA, Best Book for Teens award N.Y. Pub. Libr., Okla. Sequoyah award 1994), The Eyes of Kid Midas, 1992 (ALA Best Book for Reluctant Readers), Darkness Creeping, 1993, Piggyback Ninja, 1994, Scorpion Shards, 1995 (N.Y. Pub. Libr. Best Book for the Teenaged), Darkness Creeping II, 1995, Mindquakes, 1996 (ALA YALSA Quick Pick), Mindstorms, 1996, Mindtwisters, 1997, The Dark Side of Nowhere, 1997; screenwriter: Time Scavengers, 1990, Double Dragon, 1992, Evolver, 1993, The Eyes of Kid Midas, 1993; dir. Heart on a Chain, 1991 (Golden Eagle award CINE), What About the Sisters, 1993 (Golden Eagle award CINE), Games: How to Host a Teen Mystery, Hot Times at Hollywood High, 1994, How to Host a Murder: Roman Ruins, 1996, The Good, the Bad and the Guilty, 1997, Barbeque with the Vampire, 1997, (TV show) Goosebumps: The Werewolf of Fever Swamp, 1996, Goosebumps: Night of the Living Dummy III, 1997. Mem. PEN, Writers Guild Am. West, Soc. Children's Book Writers and Illustrators. Avocations: swimming, tennis, storytelling. Office: PO Box 18516 Irvine CA 92623-8516

SHUTE, MELODIE ANN, museum director; b. Ft. Worth, Apr. 17, 1947; d. James Roy and Annie Jo (Causseaux) S.; m. Robert Schmid, Aug. 31, 1968 (div. 1973). BA, Tex. Tech. U., 1969, postgrad. Art tchr. Lubbock (Tex.) H.S., 1969-73, Aspen (Colo.) Sch., 1973-77; educator Hillsborough County Schs., Tampa, Fla., 1978-81; sales rep. Jarvis Corp., Tampa, 1981-82; sales exec. Centel Bus. Sys., Tampa, 1982-86; account exec. Tel Plus, Tampa, 1986-88; supr. corp. comm. Siemens Info. Sys., Boca Raton, Fla., 1988-89; mgr. pub. rels. Siemens Pvt. Comm. Sys., Boca Raton, 1989-93; dir. comm. Boca Raton Mus. Art, 1993-95; dir. mktg. Morikami Mus. & Japanese Gardens, Delray Beach, Fla., 1995—. Mem. Greater Boca Raton C. of C., Palm Beach County Convention and Tourism Coun., Palm Beach County Cultural Coun., Palm Beach County Attractions Assn., Fla. Attractions Assn. Christian. Avocations: beach, biking, hiking, reading, pets. Office: Morikami Mus 4000 Morikami Park Rd Delray Beach FL 33446-2305

SHUTE, RICHARD EMIL, government official, engineer; b. Bklyn., May 1, 1938; s. William Leonard and Doris (Schlichting) S.; m. Linda Janan McElhiney, Mar. 7, 1960. B.S. in Mech. Engring., U. Miami, 1960; M.B.A., Fla. State U., 1970. Registered profl. engr., Fla. Engr. Pratt and Whitney Aircraft, West Palm Beach, Fla., 1960-62, Gen. Dynamics Corp., San Diego, 1962-64; aerospace engr. NASA/Kennedy Space Ctr., Fla., 1964-71; dir. planning and evaluation Fla. Dept. Health and Human Services, Tallahassee, 1971-76; dir. office program devel. Office Human Devel., HHS, Washington, 1976-87; dir. office of mgmt. and info. systems U.S. Dept. Commerce, Washington, 1987-90; pres. Richard E. Shute and Assocs. Mgmt. Cons., 1990—. Recipient Superior Achievement award NASA, 1966; recipient Spl. Achievement award HHS, 1977, Sr. Exec. award HHS, 1982. Mem. SAE, Nat. Assn. Security Dealers (bd. arbitrators).

SHUTER, DAVID HENRY, foreign language educator; b. Portsmouth, Ohio, Apr. 26, 1961; s. Paul H and Mary E. (Carr) S. BS in Edn., Ohio State U., 1982; MEd, U. Dayton, 1990; postgrad., Ohio U., 1991—. Cert. tchr., Ohio. Tchr. Amanda (Ohio) Clearcreek Local Sch. Dist., 1982-85, Vinton County Consol. Sch. Dist., McArthur, Ohio, 1986-91, 93—; instr. Ohio U., Athens, 1991-93; supr. Ohio U., Athens, 1992. Recipient Citizenship award, Lions Club, MInford, Ohio, 1979. Mem. ASCD, Inst. for Democracy in Edn., Ohio State U. Alumni Assn., Phi Delta Kappa. Avocations: farming, sports. Home: PO Box 116 Minford OH 45653-0116 Office: Vinton County High Sch 307 W High St Mc Arthur OH 45651-1093

SHUTIAK, JAMES, management consultant; b. Saskatoon, Sask., Can., July 1, 1932; s. Nicholas and Anna (Zabaczinski) S. MBA, Simon Fraser U., 1977. Chartered acct.; cert. mgmt. cons.; cert. fraud examiner. Ptnr. Winspear, Higgins, Stevenson & Co. (C.A.), 1951-61; comptroller, treas. Wainwright Producers & Refiners, Calgary, Alta., Can., 1961-63; sec., treas. Peace River Oil Pipeline Co., Ltd., Calgary, 1963-69; asst. to treas., asst. treas. Columbia Cellulose Co., Ltd., Vancouver, 1969-71; mgmt. cons. J. Shutiak (C.A.), Vancouver, 1971-73; asst. gen. mgr., dep. chmn. Man. Devel. Corp., Winnipeg, 1973-75; treas. Alta. Gas Trunk Line Co., Ltd., Calgary, 1975-79, also v.p. oil and gas subs., 1977-79; v.p. fin., CFO CDC Oil & Gas Ltd., Calgary, 1979-80; pres. IES Consulting, a divsn. of IES Resources Ltd., Calgary, 1980—; pvt. mgmt. cons., 1980—. Mem. Inst. Chartered Accts. Alta., Inst. Cert. Mgmt. Cons. Alta., Assn. Cert. Fraud Examiners, Fin. Execs. Inst., Simon Fraser U. Alumni Assn., Calgary Petroleum Club. Home: Box 1 Site 17 RR 1, De Winton, AB Canada T0L 0X0

SHUTLER, MARY ELIZABETH, academic administrator; b. Oakland, Calif., Nov. 14, 1929; d. Hal Wilfred and Elizabeth Frances (Gimbel) Hall; m. Richard Shutler Jr., Sept. 8, 1951 (div. 1975); children: Kathryn Allice, John Hall, Richard Burnett. BA, U. Calif., Berkeley, 1951; MA, U. Ariz., 1958, PhD, 1967. Asst., assoc., full prof. anthropology, chmn. dept. San Diego State U., 1967-75; prof. anthropology, dept. chmn. Wash. State U., Pullman, 1975-80; dean Coll. Arts and Scis., prof. anthropology U. Alaska, Fairbanks, 1980-84; vice chancellor, dean of faculty, prof. anthropology U. Wis. Parkside, Kenosha, 1984-88; provost, v.p. for acad. affairs, prof. anthropology Calif. State U., L.A., 1988-94; provost West Coast U., L.A., 1994—; mem. core staff Lahav Rsch. Project, Miss. State U., 1975—. Co-author: Ocean Prehistory, 1975, Deer Creek Cave, 1964, Archaeological Survey of Southern Nevada, 1963, Stuart Rockshelter, 1962; contbr. articles to jours. in field. Mem. coun. Gamble House. Fellow Am. Anthropol. Assn.; mem. Soc. for Am. Archaeology, Am. Schs. for Oriental Rsch., Am. Coun. Edn., Am. Assn. for Higher Edn., Am. Assn. State Colls. and Univs., Delta Zeta. Republican. Roman Catholic. Avocations: travel, gardening, cats. Office: West Coast U 440 Shatto Pl Los Angeles CA 90020-1704

SHUTRUMP, MARY JILL, writer, editor, photographer, educator; b. Youngstown, Ohio, Sept. 24, 1964; d. Albin George and Joanne Donna (Torello) S. BA in Journalism, Ohio State U., 1986; MFA in Creative Writing, Clayton U., 1990, PhD in Communications/English, 1991. Mgr. Riverwatch Tower, Columbus, Ohio, 1987-88; editor, writer UPS, Columbus, 1988-95; freelance writer Columbus, 1990-95, Folly Beach, S.C., 1995—; v.p. publicity Arc Entertainment, Columbus, 1992-94, copywriter, acct. mgmt. advt., 1993, asst. producer videos, 1994; publicist Pet Helpers Orgn., Folly Beach, S.C., 1995; writer The Connection Newspaper, Kiawah Island, S.C., 1995—; cons. Comms. and Advt., 1993-94; tech. writing cons. Mauswerks, Inc., Columbus, 1991; proofreader, Columbus, 1990-95; cons., commn./pub. rels. dir. FAN Engrng. (U.S.A.) Inc., 1993-95; owner, freelance cons. Profl. and Acad. Svcs., 1991; instr. dept. English Columbus State C. C., 1991-93; owner Au Natural internat. health and beauty products brokers, 1995-96; owner, publicist Moondog Cafè and Graphics Internat., 1995; comm. and speech instr. Trident Tech. Coll., Charleston, 1996—. Publicist and pub. rels. (rock band) Eurogression, 1991—; prodr. MD Entertainment, 1994, 96; model and actress in music field, Europe, 1992—; music editor/writer Atlantic Surfer mag., 1994; asst., publicist Innovative Resources LLC, 1995—; asst. publicist Coyote Enterprises, 1995—; publicity dir. Street Records, 1997—. Active Greenpeace, Washington, 1987—, Environ. Def. Fund, Washington, 1988—, World Wildlife Fund, PETA, 1987—. Mem. Humane Soc. of the U.S. Home: PO Box 1356 Folly Beach SC 29439-1356 Office: PO Box 1396 Folly Beach SC 29439-1396 also: 5742 Millcreek Blvd Youngstown OH 44512

SHUTT, FRANCES BARTON, special education educator; b. Pryor, Okla., Nov. 12, 1912; d. Edwin Harley and Bonnie (Heflin) Barton; m. John Paul Shutt, Dec. 24, 1932; children: Jon Edwin, Frances Paulette. BA, Northeastern Tchrs. U., 1941; MA, U. N.Mex., 1954, cert. in spl. edn., 1958. Classroom tchr. Pryor, Okla., 1932-40; classroom tchr. Albuquerque, 1941-55, homebound tchr. in spl. edn., 1955-72; substitute tchr. Las Cruces, N.Mex., 1973-75; ESL tchr. Las Cruces, 1974-97. Author: First Grade Guide, 1952. Mem. AAUW, 1962-68, Daus. of Nile, 1953; mission work in Japan, 1964, Samoa, 1972. Mem. N.Mex. Assn. Ednl. Retirees, Coun. for Exceptional Children (state pres. 1963-65), Ret. Tchrs. N.Mex. (sec. 1996), Order Eastern Star (worthy matron 1938), Pi Lambda Theta (pres. 1958-60), Alpha Delta Kappa (pres. 1968-70), Delta Kappa Gamma (pres. 1986-88), Kappa Kappa Iota (pres. 1990-93). Democrat. Baptist. Home: PO Box 697 Mesilla Park NM 88047-0697

SHUTT, RALPH P., research physicist. Rsch. scientist Brookhaven Nat. Lab., Upton, N.Y. Recipient W.K.H. Panofsky prize Am. Phys. Soc., 1993. Office: Brookhaven National Laboratory Upton NY 11973

SHUTTLEWORTH, ANNE MARGARET, psychiatrist; b. Detroit, Jan. 17, 1931; d. Cornelius Joseph and Alice Catherine (Rice) S.; A.B., Cornell U., 1953, M.D., 1956; m. Joel R. Siegel, Apr. 19, 1959; children: Erika, Peter. Intern, Lenox Hill Hosp., N.Y.C., 1956-57; resident Payne Whitney Clinic-N.Y. Hosp., 1957-60; practice medicine, specializing in psychiatry, Maplewood, N.J., 1960—; cons. Maplewood Sch. System, 1960-62; instr. psychiatry Cornell U. Med. Sch., 1960; mem. Com. to Organize New Sch. Psychology, 1970. Mem. AMA (Physicians Recognition award 1975, 78, 81, 84, 87, 90, 93, 96), Am. Psychiat. Assn., Am. Med. Women's Assn., N.Y. Acad. Scis., Acad. Medicine N.J., Phi Beta Kappa, Phi Kappa Phi. Home: 46 Farbrook Dr Short Hills NJ 07078-3007 Office: 2066 Millburn Ave Maplewood NJ 07040-3715

SHUTZ, BYRON CHRISTOPHER, real estate executive; b. Kansas City, Mo., Feb. 16, 1928; s. Byron Theodore and Maxine (Christopher) S.; m. Marilyn Ann Tweedie, Mar. 30, 1957; children: Eleanor S. Gaines, Byron Christopher, Collin Reid, Allison S. Moskow, Lindley Anne Baile. A.B. in Econs, U. Kans., 1949. Ptnr. Herbert V. Jones & Co., Kansas City, Mo., 1953-72; pres. Herbert V. Jones Mortgage Corp., Kansas City, 1967-72, The Byron Shutz Co., Kansas City, 1973—; dir. 1st Am. Financial Corp., Rothschild's, Inc. Chmn. bd. trustees U. Kansas City, 1979-81; trustee Pembroke-Country Day Sch., 1974-77, Midwest Rsch. Inst., 1980-89; chmn., bd. govs. Kansas City Art Inst., 1960-62; chmn. bd. dirs. Ctr. for Bus. Innovation, Inc., 1985-87; bd. dirs. Kansas City Crime Commn. 1st lt. USAF, 1951-53. Mem. Mortgage Bankers Assn. Am. (bd. govs. 1966-74), Am. Inst. Real Estate Appraisers. Clubs: Kansas City Country, University, Mercury (pres. 1978-79); Fla. Yacht (Jacksonville), Ocean Reef (Key Largo, Fla.). Home: 1001 W 58th Ter Kansas City MO 64113-1159 Office: 800 W 47th St Kansas City MO 64112-1251

SHYER, CHARLES RICHARD, screenwriter, film director; b. Los Angeles, Oct. 11, 1941; s. Melville Shyer and Lois Jones. Co-writer: (films) Goin' South, 1977, Housecalls, 1978; co-writer, prodr.: (film) Private Benjamin, 1980 (Acad. award nominee for screenplay 1980, Best Original Comedy award Writers Guild 1980); co-writer, dir.: (films) Irreconcilable Differences, 1984, Baby Boom, 1987, Father of the Bride, 1991, I Love Trouble, 1994, Father of the Bride, Part II, 1995. Mem. ASCAP, Acad. Motion Picture Arts and Scis., Writers Guild Am., Writers Guild Am. West, Dirs. Guild Am. *

SHYER, JOHN D., lawyer; b. Nashville, May 4, 1956; s. Michael and Hilda (Wertheim) S.; m. Marsha Anne Gisser, May 7, 1989; children: Allison Parcell, Michael Wertheim. AB, Princeton U., 1978; JD, Stanford U., 1981. Bar: N.Y. 1982, U.S. Ct. Appeals (2d cir.) 1983, U.S. Ct. Appeals (3d cir.) 1992. Assoc. Donovan, Leisure, Newton & Irvine, N.Y.C., 1981-85; assoc. Latham & Watkins, N.Y.C., 1985-89, ptnr., 1989—. Trustee Princeton (N.J.) Broadcasting Svc., 1985—. Mem. Assn. Bar City N.Y. Avocations: traveling, hiking, reading. Office: Latham & Watkins 885 3rd Ave Ste 1000 New York NY 10022-4834

SHYLLON, PRINCE E.N., lawyer, law educator; b. Freetown, Sierra Leone, Nov. 3, 1943; came to the U.S.; s. Henry W.O. and Lois (Johnson) S.; m. Millicent Boutchway, June 8, 1974; children: Nicky H., Selwyn A. BA in Economics, Shaw U., 1972; JD Sch. of Law, N.C. Ctrl. U., Durham, 1975. Bar: N.C. 1977, U.S. Dist. Ct. (ea. dist.), 1978, U.S. Ct. of Appeals (4th cir.), 1978. Ptnr. Shabica, Shyllon & Shyllon, Raleigh, N.C., 1977-79, Shyllon, Shyllon & Ratliff, Raleigh, N.C., 1979-85; prof. Bus. Law and Ins. Saint Augustines Coll., Raleigh, N.C., 1975-91; ptnr. Shyllon & Shyllon, Raleigh, N.C., 1986—; university counsel St. Augustines Coll., 1992—. Mem. ABA, N.C. Acad. of Trial Lawyers. Home: 1101 Athens Dr Raleigh NC 27606-2420 Office: Shyllon & Shyllon 4002 Barrett Dr Raleigh NC 27609-6604

SHYMANSKI, CATHERINE MARY, nursing education administrator; b. Omaha, Jan. 23, 1954; d. Leo Michael and Mildred Mary (Swank) Shymanski. AAS in Nursing, Iowa Western C.C., 1977; BSN, Pacific Western U., 1982; BFA, Drake U., 1980; MSN, Pacific Western U., 1992. Charge nurse Nebr. Psychiat. Inst., Omaha, 1977-78; staff nurse Menninger Found., Topeka, 1978-79; staff devel. instr., clin. coord. Stormont Vail Regional Med. Ctr., Topeka, 1979-80; charge nurse Allen County Hosp., Iola, Kans., 1980-81; asst. dir. nursing Arkhaven at Erie, Kans., 1980; dir. shift ops. Truman Med. Ctr., Kansas City, Mo., 1983; nursing supr. Osawatomie (Kans.) State Hosp., 1981-91; nursing orientation and insvc. coord. Topeka State Hosp., 1991-94, dir. nursing edn., 1993-94; coord. health occupation Kaw Area Tech. Sch., Topeka, Kans., 1994-95; supr. outpatient and partial hospitalization svcs. St. Catherine Hosp., Garden City, Kans., 1995; DON, Gardeeen Valley Retirement Village, Garden City, Kans., 1995-96; coord. quality assurance and edn. Beautiful Savior Home and Manor, Belton, Mo., 1996—. Mem. River City Players, Osawatomie, 1984-88. Mem. Bus. and Profl. Women (pres. Osawatomie chpt. 1985-86, 88-89, dist. dir. 1987-88, Young Career Woman award 1982, 84, Woman of Yr., 1982-83), Am. Psychiat. Nurses Assn., Kans. Nursing Assn. (pres. dist. 1985-86), Am. Cat Fanciers Assn., Topeka Cat Fanciers. Avocations: raise and show cats, gardening, reading. Office: Beautiful Savior Home and Manor 1003 S Cedar St Belton MO 64012

SHYY, WEI, aerospace, mechanical engineering researcher, educator; b. Tainan, Taiwan, China, July 19, 1955; came to U.S. 1979; s. Chiang-Chen and June-Hua (Chao) S.; m. Yuchen Shih; children: Albert, Alice, Andrew Chang, Kevin Chang. BS, Tsin-Hua U., Taiwan, 1977; MSE, U. Mich., 1981, PhD, 1982. Postdoctoral rsch. scholar U. Mich., Ann Arbor, 1982-83; rsch. scientist GE Corp. Rsch. and Devel. Ctr., Schenectady, N.Y., 1983-88; faculty mem. of aeronautics and astronautics Nat. Cheng-Kung U., Taiwan, 1987; assoc. prof. aerospace engrng., mechanics and engrng. sci. U. Fla., Gainesville, 1988-92, prof. aerospace engrng., mechanics and engrng. sci., 1992—, chmn. dept. aerospace engrng, mechs. and engrng. sci., 1996—; cons. numerous pvt., fed. agencies U.S., Taiwan; lectr. in field. Author: Computational Modeling for Fluid Flow and Interfacial Transport, 1994; co-author: Computational Fluid Dynamics with Moving Boundaries, 1996, Computational Technique for Complex Transport Phenemona, 1997; editor: Recent Advances in Comoputational Fluid Dynamics, 1989; mem. editl. adv. bd. Numerical Heat Transfer Jour.; reviewer U.S. govt., other govts., indsl. labs., profl. jours.; contbr. numerous articles to profl. jours. Recipient GE Rsch. and Devel. Ctr. 1986 Pubs. award, Chinese Soc. of Mech. Engrs. 1987 Rsch. Paper award, NASA/ASEE 1991 Cert. of Recognition. Fellow AIAA (assoc.); mem. ASME (Combustion and Fuel Com. 1984 Hon. Paper award), Minerals, Metals and Materials Soc., Am. Phys. Soc., Combustion Inst. Achievements include research in computational fluid dynamics, combustion and propulsion, gravity-induced thermofluid transport processes, materials processing and solidification, microgravity sciences and engrng. contributions to gas turbine, hydraulic turbine, high pressure lamp and electronic cooling. Office: U Fla Dept Aerospace Engrng 231 Aero Bldg Gainesville FL 32611

SIAS, JOHN B., multi-media company executive, newspaper publisher,publishing exec; b. 1927. A.B., Stanford U., 1949. Group v.p. Metromedia Inc., 1962-71; with Capital Cities Communications, 1971-93; pres. Fairchild Pubs. Inc., 1971-75, exec. v.p., pres. pub. div., 1975-85; pres. ABC-TV Network Group, N.Y.C., 1986-93; also former exec. v.p. Capital Cities/ABC Inc.(parent), N.Y.C.; pres., ceo Chronicle Pub. Co., San Francisco, 1993—. Served with AUS, 1945-46. Office: Chronicle Pub Co 901 Mission St San Francisco CA 94103-2905 also: Capital Cities/ABC Inc 24 E 51st St New York NY 10022-6801*

SIATRA, ELENI, English educator; b. Kozani, Greece, Oct. 22, 1961; came to U.S., 1985; d. Athanasios and Alexandra (Lanaras) S.; m. Todd Alan Reda, May 30, 1991. B of English, Aristotle U., 1983; MA in English, Miami U., 1990, PhD in English, 1996; MLS, Kent State U., 1986. Tchr. English as a 2d lang. Fgn. Langs. Inst., Kozani, Greece, 1983-85; asst. to dir. of ethnic studies ctr. Kent (Ohio) State U., 1986, student reference asst., 1985-86, instr., libr. adminstr., 1987; libr. readers' svcs. Bloomsburg (Pa.) U., 1987-88; grad. rsch. asst. Miami U., Oxford, Ohio, 1988-90, King Libr., Miami U., Oxford, Ohio, 1990-91; coord., portfolio rater Miami U., Oxford, Ohio, 1994-97, teaching assoc., 1991-94; vis. instr. Miami U., 1994—; mem. Coll. of Arts and Scis. Comparative Lit. Com., Miami U., 1995-96. Sinclair Meml. scholar, 1995-96. Fulbright scholar, 1985-86; recipient Gordon Wilson award, 1994. Fellow Phi Kappa Phi; mem. ALA, Am. Soc. 18th Century Studies, Nat. Coun. Tchrs. English, Modern Lang. Assn., Internat. Soc. Study of European Ideas (workshop chair, 1996. Greek Orthodox. Home: PO Box 416 West College Corner IN 47003-0416 Office: Miami U Dept English Oxford OH 45056

SIBBALD, JOHN RISTOW, management consultant; b. Lincoln, Nebr., June 20, 1936; s. Garth E.W. and Rachel (Wright) S.; BA, U. Nev., 1958; MA, U. Ill., 1964; m. Kathryn J. Costick ; children: Allison, John, Wright. Office mgr. Hewitt Assocs., Libertyville, Ill., 1964-66; coll. rels. mgr. Pfizer Inc., N.Y.C., 1966-69; pres., chief exec. officer Re-Con Systems, N.Y.C., 1969-70; v.p. Booz, Allen & Hamilton, N.Y.C., 1970-73, Chgo., 1973-75; pres., founder John Sibbald Assocs., Inc., Chgo., 1975; mem. Nat. Advisory Coun., Nat. Club Assn. Author: The Career Makers, 1990, 92, The New Career Makers, 1995; contbr. articles to profl. jours. Served to capt. AUS, 1958-64. Mem. Mid-Day Club Chgo., St. Louis Club. Episcopalian. Office: 7733 Forsyth Blvd Saint Louis MO 63105-1817

SIBLEY, CELESTINE (MRS. JOHN C. STRONG), columnist, reporter; b. Holly, Fla., May 23, 1917; d. W.R. and Evelyn (Barber) S.; m. James W. Little (dec. 1953); children: James W., Susan Little Bazemore, Mary Little Vance; m. John C. Strong (dec. 1988). Attended, U. Fla., Spring Hill Coll.; LHD (hon.), Spring Hill Coll. Columnist, reporter Atlanta Constitution, 1941—; twice juror Pulitzer Pirze newspaper awards. Author: The Malignant Heart, 1957, Peachtree Street, U.S.A.: An Affectionate Portrait of Atlanta, 1963, (stories) Christmas in Georgia, 1964, A Place Called Sweet Apple, 1967, Dear Store: An Affectionate Portrait of Rich's, 1967, Especially at Christmas, 1969, Mothers are Always Special, 1970, The Sweet Apple Gardening Book, 1972, Day by Day with Celestine Sibley, 1975, Small Blessings, 1977, Ah, Sweet Mystery: A Kate Mulcay Novel of Suspense, 1991, Straight As an Arrow: A Kate Mulcay Mystery, 1992, Dire Happenings at Scratch Ankle, 1993, A Plague of Kinfolks, 1995, others. Bd. vis. Grady Hosp.; mem. adv. bd. Neighborhood Justice Ctr.; mem. literary panel Ga. Coun. Arts; head fund appeal Atlanta Area Svcs. for Blind. Recipient Literary Achievement award Ga. Writers Assn., 1964, 2 Recognition awards Dixie Coun. Authors and Journalists, 2 AP awards, Radio and TV Big Story award Pall Mall, 2 awards Ga. Conf. Social Work, Nat. Christopher award, Wesley Woods award, Ralph McGill award Lifetime Achievement in Journalism by Soc. Profl. Journalists, numerous others; named Woman of Yr. in Arts, Atlanta, 1956. Democrat. Presbyterian. Office: Atlanta Constitution Metro Desk 72 Marietta St NW Atlanta GA 30303-2804

SIBLEY, CHARLES GALD, biologist, educator; b. Fresno, Calif., Aug. 7, 1917; s. Charles Corydon and Ida (Gald) S.; m. Frances Louise Kelly, Feb. 7, 1942; children: Barbara Susanne, Dorothy Ellen, Carol Nadine. A.B., U. Calif.—Berkeley, 1940, Ph.D., 1948; M.A. (hon.), Yale U., 1965. Biologist, USPHS, 1941-42; instr. zoology U. Kans., 1948-49; asst. prof. San Jose (Calif.) State Coll., 1949-53; assoc. prof. ornithology Cornell U., 1953-59, prof. zoology, 1959-65; prof. biology Yale U., 1965-86, prof. emeritus, 1986—, William Robertson Coe prof. ornithology, 1967-86, emeritus, 1986—; dir. div. vertebrate zoology, curator birds Peabody Mus., 1965-86, dir. mus., 1970-76; Dean's prof. sci., prof. biology San Francisco State U., 1986-92; cons. systematic biology, 1963-65; mem. adv. com. biol. medicine NSF, 1968—; exec. com. biol. agr. NRC, 1966-70. Co-author: (with Jon Ahlquist) Phylogeny and Classification of Birds, 1990, (with Burt Monroe) Distribution and Taxonomy of Birds of the World, 1990; mem. editorial bd. Jour. Molecular Evolution, 1983—, Molecular Biology and Evolution, 1986—. Served to lt. USNR, 1943-45. Guggenheim fellow, 1959-60. Fellow AAAS; mem. NAS (Daniel Giraud Elliot medal 1988), Soc. Study Evolution, Am. Soc. Naturalists, Soc. Systematic Biology, Am. Ornithologists' Union (pres. 1986-88, Brewster Meml. medal 1971), Royal Australian Ornithol. Union, Deutsche Ornithol. Gesellschaft, Internat. Ornithol. Congress (sec.-gen. 1962, pres. 20th congress 1986-90). Home: 433 Woodley Pl Santa Rosa CA 95409-6431

SIBLEY, HORACE HOLDEN, lawyer; b. Phila., Oct. 13, 1939; s. John Adams and Barbara (Thayer) S.; m. Beverly Bryan, Mar. 18, 1961; children: Clare, Holden, Eve. BA, Vanderbilt U., 1961; LLD, U. Ga., 1964; MBA, Ga. State U., 1971. Bar: Ga. 1964, U.S. Supreme Ct. 1975. Assoc. King and Spalding, Atlanta, 1968-72, ptnr., 1972—; chmn. Ga. Ctr. for Advance Telecom. Tech., So. Ctr. for Internat. Studies; bd. dirs. Atlanta Com. for Olympic Games; bd. advisors Carter Ctr. Trustee, mem. exec. com. Agnes Scott Coll., Atlanta, 1977; adv. trustee Henrietta Egleston Hosp. for Children, Atlanta, 1974-77, trustee, mem. exec. com., 1977—, chmn. bd. dirs., 1983-90; mem. exec. com. Atlanta Organizing Com. Summer Olympics, 1989—; chmn. bd. dirs. Butler St. YMCA, Atlanta, 1981; past bd. dirs. United Way, Nat. Assn. of Childrens' Hosp. and various other charitable orgns.; participant Leadership Ga., 1978, Leadership Atlanta, 1973, Soc. Internat. Bus. Fellows, 1982—; elder Trinity Presbyn. Ch., 1969-73. Capt. inf. U.S. Army, 1965-68, Germany. Mem. ABA, Ga. Bar Assn., Atlanta Bar Assn., World Trade Club Atlanta (bd. dirs. 1988-92), Japan-Am. Soc. (bd. dirs. 1981-87), Rotary, Blue Key Svc. Soc., Phi Kappa Phi, Omicron Delta Kappa. Democrat. Presbyterian. Avocations: tennis, running, fishing. Office: King & Spalding 191 Peachtree St NE Atlanta GA 30303-1740

SIBLEY, JAMES MALCOLM, retired lawyer; b. Atlanta, Aug. 5, 1919; s. John Adams and Nettie Whitaker (Cone) S.; m. Karen Norris, Apr. 6, 1942; children: Karen Mariea, James Malcolm Jr., Jack Norris, Elsa Alexandria Victoria, Quintus Whitaker. A.B., Princeton U., 1941; student, Woodrow Wilson Sch. Law, 1942, Harvard Law Sch., 1945-46. Bar: Ga. 1942. Assoc. King & Spalding, Atlanta, 1942-47, ptnr., 1947-91; bd. dirs. Summit Industries, Inc.; exec. com., mem. pub. affairs com. Coca-Cola Co., 1979-91; chmn. exec. com. John H. Harland Co., 1963-91; chmn. exec. com., mem. compensation com. Trust Co. of Ga., 1975-92; mem. exec. com., mem. compensation com. SunTrust Banks, Inc., 1985-92. Trustee Joseph B. Whitehead Found., Lettie Pate Evans Found., Emory U., A.G. Rhodes Home, Inc., Robert W. Woodruff Found., Inc. (formerly Trebor Found.), John H. and Wilhelmina D. Harland Charitable Found., Inc.; bd. dirs. emeritus Callaway Gardens Found. With USAF, 1942-45. Mem. ABA, Ga. Bar Assn., Atlanta Bar Assn., Am. Coll. Probate Counsel, Am. Bar Found., Am. Law Inst. Episcopalian. Clubs: Piedmont Driving, Commerce. Home: 63 Peachtree Circle Atlanta GA 30309-3556 also: King & Spalding 191 Peachtree St NE Atlanta GA 30303-1763

SIBLEY, WILLIAM ARTHUR, academic administrator, physics educator, consultant; b. Ft. Worth, Nov. 22, 1932; s. William Franklin and Sada (Rasor) S.; m. Joyce Elaine Gregory, Dec. 21, 1957; children: William Timothy, Lauren Shawn, Stephen Marshall. BS, U. Okla., 1956, MS, 1958, PhD, 1960. Tchg., rsch. asst. U. Okla., 1956-60; postdoctoral rsch. in defect solid state Kernforschungsanlage Julich and Tech. U. Aachen, Germany, 1960-61; rsch. solid state divsn. Oak Ridge Nat. Lab., 1961-70; prof., head physics Okla. State U., Stillwater, 1970-76; dir. Sch. Phys. and Earth Scis. Okla. State U., 1976-78, asst. v.p. rsch., 1978-88; program dir. NSF, Washington, 1988-89; acting divsn. dir. NSF Divsn. Materials Rsch., 1990; v.p. acad. affairs U. Ala.-Birmingham, 1990-96; program dir. NSF, Washington, 1996—; mem. solid state sci. com. NAS, 1977-83; bd. dirs. Oak Ridge Assoc. Univs., 1982-88, Coun. on Govt. Rels., 1987-93, Okla. Ctr. for Advancement Sci. and Tech., 1987-88; trustee, chmn. materials rsch. counsel Southeastern Univ. Rsch. Assn., 1992-95; cons. univ. edn. and rsch. Contbr. articles to profl. jours. Pres. Stillwater Indsl. Found., 1985-86. Served to lt. AUS, 1951-53. Maj. USAR, 1953-60. Fellow Am. Phys. Soc.; mem. Omicron Delta Kappa, Sigma Xi, Sigma Pi Sigma, Pi Mu Epsilon. Baptist. Home: 5901 Mount Eagle Dr Apt 814 Alexandria VA 22303-2508 Office: NSF Rm 815d Human Edn & Human Resources Dir Arlington VA 22230

SIBLEY, WILLIAM AUSTIN, neurologist, educator; b. Miami, Okla., Jan. 25, 1925; s. William Austin and Erna Johanna (Quickert) S.; m. Joanne Shaw, Sept. 4, 1954; children: John, Mary Jane, Peter, Andrew. B.S., Yale U., 1945, M.D., 1948. Intern Univ. Hosp., Cleve., 1948-50; asst. resident neurologist Neurol. Inst. Presbyn. Hosp., N.Y.C., 1953-55; chief resident neurologist Neurol. Inst. Presbyn. Hosp., 1955-56; asst. prof. neurology Western Res. U., Cleve., 1956-63; assoc. prof. Western Res. U., 1963-67; prof. U. Ariz. Coll. Medicine, Tucson, 1967—, head dept. neurology, 1967-82. Chmn. therapy com. Internat. Fedn. Multiple Sclerosis Socs., 1986-92, 96—. Served to capt. M.C. USAF, 1951-53. Recipient LaFayette B. Mendel prize in physiol. chemistry Yale U., 1945. Mem. Am. Neurol. Assn. (v.p. 1979-80), Am. Acad. Neurology (v.p. 1985-87), Central Soc. for Neurol. Research (pres. 1968). Helped establish effectiveness of beta-interferon therapy in multiple sclerosis. Home: 2150 E Hampton St Tucson AZ 85719-3810 Office: 1501 N Campbell Ave Tucson AZ 85724-0001

SIBLEY, WILLIAM RUCK, III (TREY SIBLEY), lawyer, oil and gas executive; b. Abilene, Tex., June 21, 1952; s. William R. Jr. and Sonoma (Rudman) S.; m. Sheila Herberger, Aug. 8, 1975; children: Heather Michelle, Jordan Matthew. BS, Tex. Tech U., 1975; JD, Miss. Coll., Jackson, 1978. Asst. v.p. oil and gas Southland Trust Co., Dallas, 1978-81; gen. counsel M.B. Rudman, Dallas, 1981-90, The Rudman Partnership, Dallas, 1990—. Coach, North Dallas Soccer Assn., Dallas, 1988, 90-92, Spring Valley Athletic Assn., Dallas, 1991, 92. Mem. State Bar Tex., Dallas Bar Assn., Am. Assn. Petroleum Landmen, Dallas Assn. Petroleum Landmen. Roman Catholic. Avocations: golf, hunting, fishing. Office: The Rudman Partnership 4700 First City Ctr 1700 Pacific Ave Ste 4700 Dallas TX 75201-7307

SIBLEY, WILLIS ELBRIDGE, anthropology educator, consultant; b. Nashville, Feb. 22, 1930; s. Elbridge and Elizabeth Reynolds (LaBarre) S.; m. Barbara Jean Grant, June 9, 1956; children: Sheila Katherine, Anthony Grant, Michael David. B.A., Reed Coll., 1951; M.A., U. Chgo., 1953, Ph.D., 1958. Instr. sociology and anthropology Miami (Ohio) U., 1956-58; asst. prof. anthropology U. Utah, 1958-60; from asst. prof. to prof. anthropology Wash. State U., 1960-71; prof. anthropology Cleve. State U., 1971—, chmn. dept., 1971-77, Cleve. (City) faculty fellow, 1987, interim chmn., 1989-90, prof. emeritus, 1990—; sr. program analyst EPA, Washington, 1977-78; Govtl. fellow Am. Coun. on Edn., 1978; Rockefeller Found. vis. prof. anthropology U. Philippines, Quezon City, 1968-69; postdoctoral fellow in society and tech. Carnegie-Mellon U., 1981-82. Fulbright grantee, 1954-55, 64; NIMH grantee, 1959-61; NSF grantee, 1964-71; Nat. Acad. Scis.-NRC travel grantee, 1966; Office Edn., HEW research grantee, 1967. Fellow AAAS, Am. Anthropol. Assn. (treas. 1989-91, alt. dir. Renewable Natural Resources Found.), Soc. Applied Anthropology (sec. 1977-80, pres. 1981-82); mem. AAUP (treas. Wash. State U. chpt. 1962-63, v.p. 1963-64, pres. 1965-66, pres. Cleve. State U. chpt. 1979-80, treas. 1980-81, interim pres. 1989-90), ACLU (pres. Pullman chpt. 1963, 66), Ctrl. States Anthropol. Soc. (past mem. exec. bd., treas. 1986-89), Wash. Assn. Profl. Anthropologists, Edgewater Yacht Club (Cleve., commodore 1991), Chesapeake Yacht Club (Shady Side, Md.). Home: 1190 Cedar Ave Shady Side MD 20764-9513 Office: Cleve State U Dept Anthropology Cleveland OH 44115

SIBOLSKI, ELIZABETH HAWLEY, academic administrator; b. Gt. Barrington, Mass., Aug. 18, 1950; d. William Snyder and Frances Harrington (Smith) Gallup; m. John Alfred Sibolski Jr., Aug. 15, 1970. BA, The Am. U., 1973, MPA, 1975, PhD, 1984. Acting dir. acad. adminstrn. The Am. U., Washington, 1974, planning analyst, 1974-79, asst. dir. budget and planning, 1980-83, dir. instl. rsch., 1984-85, dir. univ. planning and rsch., 1985—; trustee Mortar Bd. Nat. Found., 1989-95. Recipient Comencement award Am. U. Women's Club, 1973. Mem. ASPA, Assn. Instl. Rsch., Soc. Coll. and Univ. Planning (bd. dirs. 1995—), Am. Assn. for Higher Edn., Mortar Bd. (sect. coord. 1975-82), Pi Alpha Alpha, Phi Kappa Phi (chpt. officer 1986-92), Pi Sigma Alpha, Omicron Delta Kappa. Avocation: breed, raise and show Morgan horses. Home: 565 Wayward Dr Annapolis MD 21401-6747 Office: The Am Univ Office of Planning 4400 Massachusetts Ave NW Washington DC 20016-8001

SICES, DAVID, language educator, translator; b. N.Y.C., June 10, 1933; s. Harry and Henrietta (Finger) S.; m. Joan Picker, May 25, 1956 (div. 1961); children: Andrew M., Anne; m. Jacqueline Boulon, July 25, 1963; children: Laura, Harry J. AB, Dartmouth Coll., 1954, MA (hon.), 1971; PhD, Yale U., 1962. Instr. Dartmouth Coll., Hanover, N.H., 1957-62, asst. prof., 1962-67, assoc. prof., 1967-71, prof. French and Italian, 1971-75; prof. emeritus, 1995—; cons. NEH, Washington, 1986—, Can. Arts Council, Ottawa, 1979; mem. screening com. French Govt. Assistantships, N.Y.C., 1978-83. Author: Harmony of Contrasts, 1968, Theater of Solitude, 1974; co-author: French Idioms, 1996; co-author: 2001 French Idioms, 1982; co-editor, translator: Comedies of Machiavelli, 1985; translator: Comedies and Proverbs of Musset, 1994; co-editor, translator: Machiavelli and His Friends, 1996; translator: Historical Dramas of Musset, 1997. Fulbright-Hays fellow, Paris, 1956-57, Fulbright-Hays summer seminar, Rome, 1966; fellow Am. Council Learned Socs., 1969-70; humanities devel. grant Dartmouth Coll., Hanover, 1976. Mem. AAUP, Am. Literary Translators Assn., Am. Assn. Tchrs.

French, Am. Assn. Tchrs. Italian, Dante Soc. Am. Avocations: music, travel, photography.

SICHERMAN, MARVIN ALLEN, lawyer; b. Cleve., Dec. 27, 1934; s. Harry and Malvina (Friedman) S.; m. Sue Kovacs, Aug. 18, 1957; children: Heidi Joyce, Steven Eric. BA, Case Western Res. U., 1957, LLB, 1960, JD, 1968. Bar: Ohio 1960. Mng. prin. Dettelbach, Sicherman & Baumgart, Cleve., 1971—. Editorial bd.: Case-Western Res. Law Rev, 1958-60; Contbr. articles to legal jours. Mem. Beachwood (Ohio) Civic League, 1972—; mem. Beachwood Bd. Edn., 1978-86, pres., 1981, 85, v.p., 1984; trustee Beachwood Arts Council, 1977-84. Mem. ABA, Ohio Bar Assn. (lectr. truth in lending 1969, lectr. bankruptcy 1972, 81, 84; Meritorious Service awards 1971, 77, 78, 79, 83, 84, 85, 86, 87), Cleve. Bar Assn. (lectr. practice and procedure clinic 1960-80, 82-87, chmn. bankruptcy ct. com. 1971-73), Jewish Chautauqua Soc., Tau Epsilon Rho, Zeta Beta Tau. Jewish (trustee Temple brotherhood 1968-76, sec. 1971-73). Home: 24500 Albert Ln Cleveland OH 44122-2302 Office: Dettelbach Sicherman & Baumgart 1100 Ohio Savings Plz Cleveland OH 44114

SICILIANO, ELIZABETH MARIE, secondary education educator; b. Mansfield, Ohio, Apr. 22, 1934; d. Samuel Sevario and Lucy (Sferro) S. BS in Edn., Ohio State U., 1957; MA in Edn., Ea. Mich. U., 1971; MFA, Bowling Green U., 1975. Cert. tchr., Mich. Instr. adult edn. The Toledo (Ohio) Mus. Art, 1972-81; tchr. art Monroe (Mich.) Pub. Schs., 1975—; workshop facilitator; presenter in field; art tchr. computer graphics. Artist, working in oils, pastels and fabricating jewelry. Judge Monroe Bicentennial, Monroe Arts and Crafts League, other shows. Mem. NEA, Mich. Edn. Assn., Nat. Art Edn. Assn., Mich. Art Edn. Assn., Stratford Festival for the Arts, Toledo Craft Club, Toledo Fedn. Art Socs., Toledo Mus. Art. Avocations: swimming, skiing, classic cars, designing and creating jewelry, portraiture and landscape in oils. Home: 7179 Edinburgh Dr Lambertville MI 48144-9539 Office: Monroe High Sch 901 Herr Rd Monroe MI 48161-9702

SICILIANO, ROCCO CARMINE, institute executive; b. Salt Lake City, Mar. 4, 1922; s. Joseph Vincent and Mary (Arnone) S.; m. Marion Stiebel, Nov. 8, 1947; children: Loretta, A. Vincent, Fred R., John C., Maria. B.A. with honors, U. Utah, 1944; LL.B., Georgetown U., 1948; LHD, Hebrew Union Coll. Bar: D.C. bar 1949. Legal asst. to bd. mem. NLRB, Washington, 1948-50; asst. sec.-treas. Procon Inc., Des Plaines, Ill., 1950-53; asst. sec. labor charge employment and manpower Dept. Labor, Washington, 1953-57; spl. asst. to Eisenhower for personnel mgmt., 1957-59; ptnr. Wilkinson, Cragun & Barker, 1959-69; pres. Pacific Maritime Assn., San Francisco, 1965-69; undersec. of commerce Washington, 1969-71; pres., chmn. bd., chief exec. officer Ticor, Los Angeles, 1971-84; chmn., exec. com. Ticor, 1984-85; of counsel Jones, Day, Reavis & Pogue, 1984-87; chmn. bd., chief exec. officer Am. Health Properties, Inc., 1987-88; chmn. Dwight D. Eisenhower World Affairs Inst., Washington, 1991—; chmn. Ctr. for Govtl. Studies, 1992—; commr. Calif. Citizens Budget Commn.; bd. dirs. United TV, Inc.; mem. Fed. Pay Bd., 1971-73; trustee emeritus J. Paul Getty Trust. Bd. dirs. Eisenhower Inst., L.A. Philharm. Assn.; past chmn. Calif. Bus. Roundtable; trustee Com. for Econ. Devel.; co-chmn. Calif. Commn. on Campaign Financing; bd. govs. Cedars-Sinai Med. Ctr. 1st lt. AUS, 1943-46, MTO, ETO. Decorated Bronze Star; Order of Merit (Italy). Mem. Nat. Acad. Pub. Adminstrn., Met. Club (Washington), Calif. Club (L.A.). Home: 612 N Rodeo Dr Beverly Hills CA 90210-3208 Office: 918 16th St NW Ste 501 Washington DC 20006-2902 also: PO Box 2249 Beverly Hills CA 90213-2249

SICK, WILLIAM NORMAN, JR., investment company executive; b. Houston, Apr. 20, 1935; s. William Norman and Gladys Phylena (Armstrong) S.; m. Stephanie Anne Williams, Sept. 14, 1963; children: Jill Melanie, David Louis. BA, Rice U., 1957, BSEE, 1958. With Tex. Instruments Inc., various locations, 1958-87; exec. v.p. Tex. Instruments, Inc., Dallas, 1982-87; pres. semicondr. products group Tex. Instruments Inc., Dallas, 1982-86; bd. dirs. Tex. Instruments, Inc., 1985-87; CEO Am. Nat. Can Co., Chgo., 1988-89; also bd. dirs. Am. Nat. Can. Co., Chgo., 1988-89; mem. exec. com. Pechiney, Paris, 1989; bd. dirs. Pechiney Internat., 1989; vice, chmn., bd. dirs. Triangle Industries, N.Y.C., 1988; chmn., CEO, Bus. Resources Internat., Winnetka, Ill., 1989—; chmn. bd. dirs. Power Trends, Batavia, Ill.; bd. dirs. Metasolv, Dallas, Faroudja, Sunnyvale, Calif., McCabe Software, Columbia, Md., Hand Technologies, Austin, Tex.; guest lectr. Sophia U., Tokyo, 1973. Chmn. bd. trustees Shedd Aquarium, Chgo.; mem. bd. govs. Rice U., 1996—. Mem. Chgo. Com., Exec. Club Chgo., Glenview Club, Sigma Xi, Tau Beta Pi, Sigma Tau. Episcopalian. Office: Bus Resources Internat PO Box 500 Winnetka IL 60093-0500

SICKELS, ROBERT JUDD, political science educator; b. Nyack, N.Y., June 26, 1931; s. Robert and Dorothy (Judd) S.; m. Alice Esterer; children: Stephen Judd, Wendy. B.A., U. Chgo., 1950, M.A., 1954; Ph.D., Johns Hopkins U., 1960. Asst. staff dir. Pres.'s Commn. on Registration and Voting Participation, Washington, 1963-64; asso. dir. exec. insts. U.S. CSC, Washington, 1964-65; asso. prof. polit. sci. Purdue U., West Lafayette, Ind., 1965-68; assoc. prof. polit. sci. U. N.Mex., Albuquerque, 1968-73; prof. U. N.Mex., 1973-95; prof. emeritus U. N.Mex., Albuquerque, 1995—; chmn. dept. U. N.Mex., 1976-81. Author: Race, Marriage, and the Law, 1972, Presidential Transactions, 1974, The Presidency, 1980, John Paul Stevens and The Constitution: The Search for Balance, 1988; contbr. articles to profl. jours. Home: 1514 Harvard Ct NE Albuquerque NM 87106-3712

SICKELS, WILLIAM LOYD, secondary educator; b. Porterville, Calif., Mar. 26, 1936; s. Roy Ernest and Lula Mae (Weaver) S.; m. Donna Louise Eilers; 1 child, Alan Michael. AA, Porterville (Calif.) Coll., 1956; BA, San Jose (Calif.) State U., 1960, MA, 1965. Tchr. Redwood High Sch., Visalia, Calif., 1962-68; instr. Victor Valley Coll., Victorville, Calif., 1968-70; athletic dir., tchr. Tulare (Calif.) Western High Sch., 1970-96; retired, 1996. Pres. Sequoia Lake Conf. of YMCA's (pres. 1990-91, bd. dirs. 1982—). With U.S. Army, 1960-62. Named to Hall of Fame Visalia YMCA, 1990, Man of Yr., 1984. Fellow Y's Men Internat. (pres. 1985—), Calif. State Athletic Dirs. Assn. (v.p. 1984-94, Athletic Dir. of Yr. 1981, pres. 1995-96). Republican. Methodist. Avocations: back-packing, hiking. Home: 30312 Rd 152 Visalia CA 93292

SICURO, NATALE ANTHONY, academic and financial administrator, consultant; b. Warren, Ohio, July 19, 1934; s. Gaetano and Antonette (Montecalvo) S.; m. Linda Lou Rockman, Aug. 3, 1957; children: Michael, Christine, Paul. BS, Kent State U., 1957, PhD, 1964; MS in Pub. Health, U. N.C., Chapel Hill, 1958. Tchr., coach, recreation adminstr. schs. in N.E. Ohio, 1958-62; instr., grad. asst., teaching fellow Kent State U., 1962-64; asst. supt. Geauga (Ohio) County schs., 1964-65; dir. program planning, asst. dean regional campuses Kent State U., 1965-68, 70-72, dean continuing edn., assoc. provost med. affairs, 1972-78; sr. cons., mgr. Peat, Marwick, Mitchell, Washington and L.A., 1968-70; pres. So. Oreg. State Coll., Ashland, 1979-86, Portland State U., 1986-88, Roger Williams U., Bristol, R.I., 1989-93, Roger Williams U. Sch. Law, Bristol, 1992-93; Jones Disting. Univ. prof. Jones Inst. for Ednl. Excellence Tchrs. Coll., Emporia (Kans.) State U., 1993-94; pres. SICURO Ednl. Cons., 1994-96; investment mgmt. cons. Paine Webber Princeton Portfolio Mgmt. Group, Princeton, N.J., 1996—; pres. Ohio Council Continuing Edn., 1975-76; bd. dirs. So. Oreg. Coll. Found., 1979-86; state rep., chmn. fed. relations com. Am. Assn. State Colls. and Univs., 1979-86, bd. dirs. 1987-88, chmn.-elect, 1988; chmn. Govtl. Relations Commn., Am. Council on Edn., 1983-86; mem. council of presidents Nat. Assn. Intercollegiate Athletics; chmn. council of presidents Evergreen Conf.; co-chmn. council of presidents Columbia Football League; dir. Rogue Valley Physicians Service. Pres. United Way of Jackson County, Oreg., 1982; bd. dirs. Ashland YMCA, 1980-81, Ashland Indsl. Devel. Corp., 1982-85; mem. Jackson County Econ. Devel. Com., 1981-86, Am. Council on Edn., 1986-87. Mem. Nat. Challenges Commn. Higher Edn., Ashland Rotary, Bristol Rotary, Phi Delta Kappa, Phi Kappa Phi. Roman Catholic.

SIDAMON-ERISTOFF, ANNE PHIPPS, museum official; b. N.Y.C., Sept. 12, 1932; d. Howard and Harriet Dyer (Price) Phipps; m. Constantine Sidamon-Eristoff, June 29, 1957; children—Simon, Elizabeth, Andrew. BA, Bryn Mawr Coll., 1954. Chmn., bd. trustees Am. Mus. Natural History, N.Y.C.; dir.-at-large Black Rock Forest Consortium; trustee God Bless Am. Fund. Bd. dirs. Greenacre Found., Highland Falls (N.Y.) Pub. Libr., N.Y. Cmty. Trust, Storm King Art Ctr., Mountainville, N.Y., World Wildlife Fund.; former bd. dirs.Scenic Hudson, St. Bernard's Sch., N.Y.C., Mus. Modern Art, N.Y.C., Mus. Hudson Highlands. Home: 120 East End Ave New York NY 10028-7552

SIDAMON-ERISTOFF, CATHERINE BAXTER, securities broker; b. N.Y.C., Jan. 2, 1964; d. Comer Cash and Betty Nan (Carpenter) Baxter; m. Andrew Sidamon-Eristoff, Mar. 30, 1996. BA, Duke U., 1986, MBA, 1987. V.p. Morgan Stanley & Co., Inc., N.Y.C., 1987—; former alumni coun. mem. Fuqua Sch. Bus., Durham, N.C.; mem. alumnae bd. Hockaday Sch., Dallas. Chmn. bd. Burden Ctr. for Aging, N.Y.C., 1991—; bd. dirs. Jr. League, N.Y.C., 1982—; mem. jr. coun. Am. Mus. Natural History. Mem. NAFE, Am. Women's Econ. Devel. Assn. Republican. Presbyterian. Avocations: skiing, travel, reading. Office: Morgan Stanley & Co Inc 4th Flr 1221 Ave of the Americas New York NY 10020

SIDAMON-ERISTOFF, CONSTANTINE, lawyer; b. N.Y.C., June 28, 1930; s. Simon C. and Anne Huntington (Tracy) Sidamon-E.; m. Anne Phipps, June 29, 1957; children: Simon, Elizabeth, Andrew. B.S.E. in Geol. Engring, Princeton U., 1952; LL.B., Columbia U., 1957. Clk., then assoc. firm Kelley Drye Newhall Maginnes & Warren, N.Y.C., 1957-64; individual practice law N.Y.C., 1964-65, 74-77; exec. asst. to Congressman John V. Lindsay, 1964-65; city coordinator Lindsay Mayoral Campaign, N.Y.C., 1965; asst. to mayor City of N.Y., 1966, commr. hwys., 1967-68, transp. adminstr., 1968-73; ptnr. Sidamon-Eristoff, Morrison, Warren, & Ecker, N.Y.C., 1978-83; counsel Morrison & de Roos, 1984-88; pvt. practice N.Y.C., 1988-89; regional adminstr. Region II EPA, N.Y.C., 1989-93; of counsel Patterson, Belknap, Webb & Tyler, N.Y.C., 1993—; mem. N.Y. State Met. Transp. Authority Bd., 1974-89; commr. N.Y. State Jud. Commn. on Minorities, 1987-91; mem. Gov.'s Coun. on Hudson River Valley Greenway, 1989; trustee United Mut. Savs. Bank, N.Y.C., 1979-82; trustee Phipps Houses, N.Y.C., 1974—, chmn. 1986—. Trustee Allaverdy Found., N.Y.C., 1962—, Am. Farm Sch., Thessaloniki, Greece, 1973-79, Carnegie Hall, N.Y.C., 1967-92, Millbrook (N.Y.) Sch., 1971-89, hon. trustee, 1989—, Orange County (N.Y.) Citizens Found., 1974-81, Am. the Beautiful Fund (Washington), 1985—; bd. dirs. Caramoor Center for Music and Arts, Katonah, N.Y., 1961-80, Tolstoy Found., Inc., N.Y.C., 1975—, chmn., 1979-89, 94—, Boyce Thompson Inst. for Plant Rsch., Ithaca, N.Y., 1994—; bd. dirs., mem. exec. com. Mid-Hudson Pattern for Progress, Poughkeepsie, N.Y., 1975-89, chmn., 1981-85; bd. dirs. Coun. on Mcpl. Performance, N.Y.C., 1979-87, chmn., 1979-83, vice chmn., 1986, 87, N.Y. State Republican committeeman, 1980-89. Served to 1st lt. arty. AUS, 1952-54, Korea. Decorated Bronze Star; recipient Honor award Kings County chpt. N.Y. State Soc. Profl. Engrs., 1969, Honor award Greater N.Y. coun. Girl Scouts U.S., 1973, Board Leadership award Coun. Mcpl. Performance, 1984, Transp. Man of Yr. award Greater N.Y. March of Dimes, 1985, Award of Excellence Mid-Hudson Pattern for Progress, 1990, Honor award Nat. and N.Y. Parks and Conservation Assn., 1992, Bronze medal USEPA, 1993. Mem. ABA, N.Y. State Bar Assn., Assn. of Bar of City of N.Y., N.Y. County Lawyers Assn., Kent Moot Ct., AIME, Phi Delta Phi, Delta Psi. Eastern Orthodox. Clubs: Century Assn. (N.Y.C.), Knickerbocker (N.Y.C.), Racquet and Tennis (N.Y.C.). Office: Patterson Belknap Webb & Tyler LLP 1133 Avenue Of The Americas New York NY 10036-6710

SIDDALL, PATRICIA ANN, English language educator; b. North Adams, Mass., May 20, 1947; d. William W. and Shirley M. (Ogert) Hartman; m. Stephen B. Siddall, Apr. 18, 1970; 1 child, Michael William. BA in English, North Adams State Coll., 1969. Cert. secondary edn. tchr., English, Social Studies. English tchr. Bay Path Regional Vocat. Tech. High Sch., Charlton, Mass., 1977—, humanities cluster chmn., 1987-91. Del. Mass. Dem. State Conv., 1986, 87, 89, 90, 94. Mem. ASCD, NEA (bd. dirs. 1994—), Am. Vocat. Assn., Nat. Coun. Tchrs. English, Mass. Vocat. Assn. (sec. Ctrl. chpt. 1982-85), Mass. Tchrs. Assn. (exec. com. 1988-94, bd. dirs. 1984—). Roman Catholic. Avocations: photography, golf, environ. concerns, writing. Home: 5 Pinewood Dr Webster MA 01570-3122

SIDDAYAO, CORAZÓN MORALES, economist, educator, energy and environment consultant; b. Manila, July 26, 1932; came to U.S., 1968; d. Crispulo S. and Catalina T. (Morales) S. Cert. in elem. teaching, Philippine Normal Coll., 1951; BBA, U. East, Manila, 1962; MA in Econs., George Washington U., 1971, MPhil and PhD, 1975. Cert. Inst. de Francais, 1989. Tchr. pub. schs. Manila, 1951-53; exec. asst. multinational oil corps., 1953-68; asst. pensions officer IMF, Washington, 1968-71; cons. economist Washington, 1971-75; rsch. assoc. Policy Studies in Sci. and Tech. George Washington U., Washington, 1971-72, teaching fellow dept. econs., 1972-75; natural gas specialist U.S. Fed. Energy Adminstrn., Washington, 1974-75; sr. rsch. economist, assoc. prof. Inst. S.E.A. Studies, Singapore, 1975-78; sr. rsch. fellow energy/economist East-West Ctr., 1978-81, project dir. energy and industrialization, 1981-86; vis. fellow London Sch. Econ., 1984-85; sr. energy economist in charge energy program Econ. Devel. Inst., World Bank, Washington, 1986-94, ret., 1994; affiliate prof. econs. U. Hawaii, 1979—; vis. prof. econs. U. Philippines, intermittently, 1989—; co-dir. UPecon Inst. of Resource Studies, 1995—; vis. prof. econs. U. Montpelier, France, 1992, 1995-96; vis. prof. pub. policy Duke U., winter 1997; cons. internat. orgns. and govts., 1995—; spkr. at confs. and symposia. Author or co-author: Increasing the Supply of Medical Personnel, 1973, The Offshore Petroleum Resources of Southeast Asia: Some Potential Conflicts and Related Economic Factors, 1978, Round Table Discussion on Asian and Multinational Corporations, 1978, The Supply of Petroleum Resources in Southeast Asia: Economic Implications of Evolving Property Rights Arrangements, 1980, Critical Energy Issues in Asia and the Pacific: The Next Twenty Years, 1982, Criteria for Energy Pricing Policy, 1985, Energy Demand and Economic Growth, 1986; editor: Energy Policy and Planning series, 1990-92, Energy Investments and the Environment, 1993; co-editor: Investissements Energetiques et Environnement, 1993; co-editor: (series) Energy Projecy Analysis for the CIS Countries (Russian), 1993, Politique d'Efficacité de l'Énergie et Environnement, Expérience pratiques, 1994, Matérial Pedagogique sur la Politique d'Efficacité de l'Energie et Environnement, 1994; contbr. chpts. to books, articles to profl. jours. Grantee in field. Mem. Am. Econ. Assn., Internat. Assn. Energy Economists (charter), Alliance Francaise, Omicron Delta Epsilon. Roman Catholic. *Power and money never provided stimuli in my life. Rather, I have sought to do that which challenges, stimulates the spirit and the intellect, is useful - in the rather abstract global level or at the more concrete personal level - and which I am happy doing. As much as I would like to write about the past, I feel that there is so much to do in the present and for our future not to keep going. Also the less advantaged the individuals I deal with, the more help I feel they should get.*

SIDDERS, PATRICK MICHAEL, financial executive; b. Duluth, Minn., Oct. 19, 1940; s. Blaine L. and Elizabeth M. (Murphy) S.; m. Barbara E. Powers, Aug. 31, 1963; children: Patrick Michael, Kevin, Jennifer. BABA, St. Benedict's Coll., Atchison, Kans., 1963; postgrad., U. Minn. Grad. Sch. Bus. Adminstrn. Investment analyst Prudential Ins. Co., 1964-68; v.p. corp. fin. Dain Bosworth, Inc., Mpls., 1968-73; v.p. fin., treas. Modern Merchandising Inc., Minnetonka, Minn., 1973-79, exec. v.p., acting chief operating officer, 1979-81; pres. Modern Merchandising, Minnetonka, Minn., 1982-83; also dir. Modern Merchandising Inc., Minnetonka, Minn.; pres., chmn. and chief exec. officer Drag Spltys., Inc., Minnetonka, 1983-89, also dir.; CFO Salkin & Linoff, Mpls., 1989-90; sr. v.p., mng. dir. corp. fin. John G. Kinnard & Co., Mpls., 1990-94; exec. v.p. adminstrn., CFO, dir. Casino Magic Corp., Bay St. Louis, Miss., 1994-95; sr. v.p., mng. dir. corp. fin. R.J. Steichen & Co., Mpls., 1995—. Mem. Fin. Execs. Inst. Republican. Roman Catholic. Home: 2940 Pelican Point Ct Mound MN 55364-1941 Office: 1 Fin Plz 120000 6th St Minneapolis MN 55402

SIDDIQUI, DILNAWAZ AHMED, communications educator, international instructional communication planning advisor, consultant; b. Amroha, India, July 4, 1937; came to U.S., 1975; s. Aijaz Rosool and Safina (Begum) Khan; m. Narjis Bano Naqvi, May 18, 1963; children: Shajee Raza, Aamera. BEd, MA, Aligarh Muslim U. Aligarh, India, 1960; postgrad. London U., 1968, CAS, 1977; PhD, Syracuse U., 1980. Asst. prof. MSG Coll., Malegaon, India, 1961-63; edn. officer H.H. The Aga Khan & Ministry of Edn., Dar-es-salaam, Tanzania and Lusaka, Zambia, 1963-71; chmn. Evelyn Hone Coll., Can. Commn. Tech. Edn. and Vocat. Tng., CIDA, later under Ministry of Edn., Lusaka, 1971-75; rsch. asst. teaching asst. Syracuse U., N.Y., 1975-80; dir. Human Resources Planning and Devel. Action Programs Internat., Washington, 1980; prof. faculty communication Clarion U. Pa.; pres. Siddiqui Assocs., Shippenville, Pa; cons. Can. Commn. for Tech. Edn. and Vocational Tng., Lusaka, 1971-74; cons. IDD&E Syracuse U., N.Y., 1977-78; chief U.S. adviser human resources planning and devel. Cen. Planning Orgn., Prime Minister's Office, Yemen Arab Republic, Sana, 1980-82; adviser Mid-East/Africa API, Sheladia Assocs., 1983—; cons. Ariz. State U., 1983, chief of party U.S. evaluators' team to Hashemite Kingdom of Jordan Adminstrv. Tng. Project IV, 1992; human resource devel. master plan adviser to Govt. of Sudan, 1994-95. Active Internat. Congress for Univ. Adult Edn. Recipient contbn. to lit. for Edn. ERIC award 1977; rsch. and svc. East and Cen. Africa. Disting. contbn. to edn. adults award, ICAE award 1980; improtu lit. writing competition Gold Medal award 1958; named Academician honoris causa Russian Acad. Humanities, 1996. Advisor Interfaith Coun. Syracuse U., 1975-80; First Prize award Anjuman-e-Taraqqui-Urdu, Amroha, India, 1957; VC award for research in Africa, Syracuse U., 1978-79. Mem. Am. Assn. Tng. and Devel. (mem. editorial bd. jour.), Assn. Muslim Soc. Scis. (pres. 1993-95), Internat. Communication Assn. (mem. edit. bd. world -wide web jour. 1996—). Home: 510 Ridgewood Rd Marianne Est Shippenville PA 16254 Office: Clarion U Pa Dept Comm Clarion PA 16214

SIDDON, THOMAS EDWARD, Canadian government official, environmental consultant; b. Drumheller, Alta., Can., Nov. 9, 1941; s. Ronald Victor and Gertrude Violet (Humfrey) S.; m. Patricia Audrey Yackimetz, Sept. 1, 1962; children—Charles, David, Robert, Elizabeth, Katherine. BSME with distinction, U. Alta., 1963; MS in Aerospace Engring., U. Toronto, 1965, PhD in Aerodyn Noise, 1968. Assoc. prof. mech. engring. U. B.C., 1968-79; mem. House of Commons, Ottawa, Ont., Can., 1978-93; minister of state for sci. and tech. House of Commons, Ottawa, Ont., 1984-85, minister of fisheries and oceans, 1985-90, minister Indian Affairs and Northern Devel., 1990-93, min. nat. def., 1993; mem. Queen's Privy Coun., 1984—; founder acoustical engring. firm and audiometric testing bus.; acoustical cons., Can., U.S.; mem. priorities and planning com., 1988-93, environment, fed.-provincial rels. com., human rels. com., cultural affairs com.; lectr. environ. law Okanagan U. Coll.; pres. Bonaccord Consulting Group Environ. Solutions. Alderman Twp. of Richmond, B.C., 1975-77. Recipient Assn. Profl. Engrs. award, 1978. Fellow Acoustical Soc. Am. Anglican. Office: Box 118, Kaleden, BC Canada V0H 1K0

SIDDONS, SARAH MAE, chemist; b. Conway, S.C., July 20, 1939; d. Willie C. and Lelia (Parker) Crawford; m. John Lathan, June 26, 1958 (div.); m. Ronald Gladstone Siddons, June 26, 1965; 1 child, Ronald George. BA, Coll. New Rochelle, 1980; postgrad., Cornell U., 1975. Lab. technologist DC37-Local 144, Bronx, 1961-65, 65-82; jr. chemist DC37-Local 375, Bronx, 1982-85, assoc. chemist, 1985-90, assoc. chemist, supr., 1990—; del. DC37-Lcoal 144, 1962-84, DC37-Local 375, 1984—. Mem. Am. Assn. Clin. Chemistry, Dynamic Five Social Club (pres. 1988—, v.p. 1980-88). Home: 3924 Carpenter Ave Bronx NY 10466 Office: Lincoln Med Ctr 234 E 149th St Rm 432 Bronx NY 10451-5504

SIDEBOTTOM, WILLIAM GEORGE, communications executive; b. Greeley, Colo., July 21, 1948; s. William Carroll and Florence Elaine (Krusenstjerna) S.; m. Rosemary Russell, May 16, 1981; children: Faith Ann, William Jeremiah. BS in Mgmt. cum laude, U. West Fla., 1975; MA in Pub. Policy magna cum laude, Regent U., 1985. Mgr. Mgmt. Recruiters, Internat., Pensacola, Fla., 1976-79; div. mgr. Mgmt. Recruiters, Internat., Virginia Beach, Va., 1979-81; dir. communications Rock Ch., Virginia Beach, 1981-83; dir. devel., v.p. comm. Nat. Freedom Inst., Chesapeake, Va., 1983-86; pres. William G. Sidebottom & Assocs., 1986-96, InterAct Response Comms., 1997—. Author: Who Owns the Children, 1985; sr. editor: The Perspective Papers, 1985, Essential Lectures, 1985. Cons. Coral Ridge Ministries, 1990—, Am. Ctr. for Law and Justice, 1990—, Christian Advocates Serving Evangelism, 1995—, Cath. Alliance, 1997—. Capt. USMC, USN, 1970-76. Mem. Phi Kappa Phi, Pi Kappa Delta. Presbyterian. Office: PO Box 377 Lyndhurst VA 22952-0377

SIDER, HARVEY RAY, minister, church administrator; b. Cheapside, Ont., Can., June 20, 1930; s. Earl M. and Elsie (Sheffer) S.; m. Erma Jean Heise, July 20, 1957; children: Cheryl Sider Giles, Steven. BA, Western U., Ont., 1957; BD, Winona Lake Sch. Theology, Ind., 1962. Ordained to ministry Brethren in Christ Ch., 1953; cert. tchr., Ont. Pastor Brethren in Christ Ch., Toronto, Ont., 1957-61; missionary, adminstr. missions dept. Brethren in Christ Ch., Bihar, India, 1962-74; pastor Brethren in Christ Ch., Stayner, Ont., 1974-76; pres. Niagara Christian Coll., Ft. Erie, Ont., 1976-78; bishop Brethren in Christ Ch., Can., 1978-90; moderator Brethren in Christ Ch., N.Am., 1990—. Office: Brethren Christ Ch PO Box 290 Grantham PA 17027-0290

SIDER, RONALD J., theology educator, author; b. Stevensville, Ont., Can., Sept. 17, 1939; m. Arbutus Lichti Sider, Aug. 19, 1961; children: Theodore Ronald, Michael Jay, Sonya Maria. BA with honors, Waterloo Luth. U., 1962; MA in History, Yale U., 1963, BD, 1967, PhD in History, 1969. Lectr., asst. prof., then assoc. prof. Messiah Coll., 1968-78, acting dir., dean, 1971-75; assoc. prof. theology Ea. Bapt. Theol. Sem., Wynnewood, Pa., 1978-84, prof. theology, 1984—; coord., chair, convenor workshops in field; coord. Internat. Consultation on Simple Lifestyle, London, 1980; lectr. in field. Editor: Preaching on Peace, 1982, Lifestyle in the Eighties: An Evangelical Commitment to Simple Life-Style, 1982, Evangelicals and Development: Toward a Theology of Social Change, 1982, Living More Simply, 1980, Cry Justice: The Bible on Hunger and Poverty, 1988, 91; author: Christ and Violence, 1979, Karlstadt's Battle with Luther: Documents in a Liberal-Radical Debate, 1978, 82, Evangelism, 1985, Rich Christians in an Age of Hunger: A Biblical Study, 1977, rev. edit., 1984, 90, 96, German edit., 1979, Dutch edit., 1980, Portuguese edit., 1984, Japanese edit., 1989, Korean edit., 1995, Andreas Bodenstein Von Karlstadt, 1974, Genuine Christianity, 1996, (with Richard K. Taylor) Nuclear Holocaust and Christian Hope, 1982, English edit., 1984, (with Oliver O'Donovan) Peace and War: A Debate About Pacifism, 1985, (in chinese) Evangelical Faith and Social Ethics, 1986, Completely Pro-Life, 1987, (with Michael A. King) Preaching About Life in Threatening World, 1988, (with Kathleen Hayes), JustLife/88: A 1988 Election Study Guide for Justice, Life and Peace, 1988, Testing the Limits of Nonviolence, 1988, One-Sided Christianity? Uniting the Church to Heal a Lost and Broken World, 1993, Cup of Water, Bread of Life: Inspiring Stories About Overcoming Lopsided Christianity, 1994; editor, contbr.: The Chicago Declaration, 1974; contbr. numerous articles to profl. publs., chpts. to books. Head voter registration dr., New Haven, 1967; pres. Diamont St. Cmty. Ctr., 1986-91; exec. dir. Evangelicals for Social Action, 1987-92, pres., 1992—; exec. dir. Just Life, 1987-91, pres., 1991-94; bd. dirs. Bread for the World, 1978-84, Mennonite Ctrl. Com., 1978-80; co-chair Nat. Workshop on Race and Reconciliation, Atlanta, 1975. Malcolm Chase fellow, 1962-63, R.E. Darlin fellow, 1963-64, fellow Yale U., 1967-68, Inst. for Advanced Christian Studies, 1976. Mem. Nat. Assn. Evangelicals (mem. social action commn. 1975—). Mennonite. Home: 312 W Logan St Philadelphia PA 19144 Office: Ea Bapt Sem 6 E Lancaster Ave Wynnewood PA 19096-3430

SIDEROFF, BARRY, advertising executive; b. Mount Vernon, N.Y., Aug. 31, 1953; s. Milton and Beatrice (Plotkin) S.; m. Florence E. Flancbaum, July 25, 1979; children: Melissa Jane, Marc Adam. BA, SUNY, Binghamton, 1975; Mktg. and Advt. degree, NYU, 1982. Mgr. Comml. Investment Trust Fin. Corp., N.Y.C. and Livingston, N.J., 1980-83; asst. v.p. Mfrs. Hanover, N.Y.C., 1983-85; dir. mktg. Compu-U-Card Internat., Stamford, Conn., 1985-86; sr. v.p. D'Arcy, Masius, Benton & Bowles, Greenwich, Conn., 1986-93; sr. v.p./dir. mktg. Barry Blau & Ptnrs., Fairfield, Conn., 1993—; mem. Direct Mktg. Idea Exch., N.Y.C., 1983-86; guest lectr. in field. Mem. Direct Mktg. Assn. (moderator, spkr. nat. conv. 1992, Echo awards 1982, 84). Home: 18 Clover St Larchmont NY 10538 Office: Barry Blau & Ptnrs 241 Danbury Rd Wilton CT 06897-4046

SIDES, JACK DAVIS, JR., lawyer; b. Dallas, Sept. 18, 1939; s. Jack Davis Sr. and Edith Eugenia (Lowrie) S.; m. Nancy Pauline Cantwell, July 22, 1967 (div. Sept. 1976); children: Mary Katharine, Jack Davis III; m. Laura Gail Miller, Aug. 2, 1979; children: Susan Ashley, Stacy Anne. BBA, U. Tex., 1962, JD with honors, 1963. Bar: Tex. 1963. Assoc. Jackson, Walker, et al, Dallas, 1963-67, White, McElroy, White, Sides & Rector, Dallas, 1968-78; sole practice Dallas, 1978—. Editor: U. Tex. Law Review, 1963. With USAFNG, 1963-69. Fellow Dallas Bar Found., Tex. Bar Found. (life); mem.

ABA, Tex. Bar Assn. (grievance subcom. 1979-86), Dallas Bar Assn. (ethics com. 1973-77, jud. com. 1988—), Tex. Assn. Def. Counsel, Dallas Assn. Def. Counsel (sec. 1973-74). Republican. Methodist. Club: Brook Hollow Golf (Dallas). Avocations: reading, tennis, exercising. Office: 2301 Cedar Springs Rd Ste 350 Dallas TX 75201-7803

SIDES, LARRY EUGENE, advertising executive; b. Albany, Ga., Nov. 14, 1946; s. Robert N. and Florine (Stewart) S.; m. Kathy Ashworth, Aug. 13, 1950. BA in Radio and TV, U. Southwestern La., 1970, MS in Communications, 1975. News reporter Sta. KATC-TV, Lafayette, La., 1970-71; account exec. Herbert S. Benjamin Assocs., Lafayette, La., 1971-76; pres. Sides & Assocs., Lafayette, La., 1976—. Vice-chmn. Crimestoppers, Lafayette, 1985; bd. dirs. Episcopal Sch. Acadiana, Lafayette, 1987; pres. Gateway Found., 1990; active Leadership La., 1989, 90; mem. Coun. for a Better La., 1991—; bd. dirs. La. Coun. on Child Abuse, 1992—; active Leadership Lafayette, 1995. Named one of Outstanding Young Men of Am., Lafayette Jaycees, 1976; recipient Disting. Alumni award dept. comms. U. Southwestern La., 1995. Mem. Am. Assn. Advt. Agys. (pres. La. coun., 1989-90), Am. Soc. Hosp. Pub. Rels., Pub. Rels. Soc. Am., La. Assn. Advt. Agys., Pub. Rels. Assn. La., Acadiana Advt. Fedn., Lafayette C. of C. (pres. 1989, Entrepreneur of Yr. 1983), Sigma Nu (alumni pres. Lafayette chpt. 1977). Club: Beaver (pres. 1986, Outstanding Club Mem. award 1976). Home: 1015 W St Mary Blvd Lafayette LA 70506-3420 Office: 404 Eraste Landry Rd Lafayette LA 70506-2324

SIDEY, HUGH SWANSON, correspondent; b. Greenfield, Iowa, Sept. 3, 1927; s. Kenneth H. and Alice Margaret (Swanson) S.; m. Alice Anne Trowbridge, Dec. 5, 1953; children—Cynthia Anne, Sandra, Bettina, Edwin. B.S., Iowa State U., 1950. Reporter Adair County (Iowa) Free Press, 1950, The Nonpariel, Council Bluffs, Iowa, 1950-51, Omaha World-Herald, 1951-55, Life mag., 1955-58; corr. Time mag., 1958-96; columnist Time mag., Life mag. (The Presidency), 1966-96; chief Time mag. (Washington Bur.), 1969-78, Washington contbg. editor, 1978-96; contbr. Time mag., 1996—. Author: John F. Kennedy, President, 1963, A Very Personal Presidency, Lyndon Johnson in the White House, 1966, These United States, 1975, Portrait of a President, 1975, The Presidency, 1991; co-author: 1,000 Ideas for Better News Pictures, 1956, The Memories, 1961—JFK—1963, 1973; contbr.: The Kennedy Circle. Served with AUS, 1945-46. Office: 1050 Connecticut Ave NW Washington DC 20036

SIDMAN, RICHARD LEON, neuroscientist; b. Boston, Sept. 19, 1928; s. Manuel and Annabelle (Seltzer) S.; m. Ljiljana Lekic, 1974. A.B., Harvard U., 1949, M.D. (Jeffries Wyman scholar), 1953. Intern in medicine Boston City Hosp., 1953-54; asst. resident in neurology Mass. Gen. Hosp., Boston, 1955-56; staff scientist NIH, Bethesda, Md., 1956-58; instr. to prof. neuropathology Harvard U. Med. Sch., 1959—, Bullard prof., 1969—; chief div. neurogenetics New Eng. Regional Primate Rsch. Ctr. Harvard Med. Sch., 1991—; chief dept. neurosci. Children's Hosp., Boston, 1972-88; 1st Richard Stearns Meml. lectr. Albert Einstein Coll. Medicine, 1958; Bailey Meml. lectr. U. Sask., Can., 1978; Waisman Meml. lectr. U. Wis. Author: (with M. Sidman) Neuroanatomy - A Programmed Text, vol. 1, 1965, (with others) Catalog of the Neurological Mutants of the Mouse, 1965, (with R.D. Adams) Introduction to Neuropathology, 1968, (with others) Atlas of the Mouse Brain and Spinal Cord, 1971; contbr. numerous articles, book chpts., revs. on neuroembryology, pathology, and genetics to profl. publs. Mem. sci. adv. com. Retinitis Pigmentosa Found.; bd. sci. overseers Jackson Lab., Bar Harbor, Maine. Served with USPHS, 1956-58. Recipient Soma Weiss student research prizes Harvard U. Med. Sch., 1951-53, Boylston Soc. Essay prize, 1953; Harvard U. Mosley Travelling fellow, 1954-55; Neuroscis. Research Program fellow, 1971-79. Fellow Am. Acad. Arts and Scis., Nat. Acad. Sci.; mem. Am. Acad. Neurology, AAAS, Am. Assn. Anatomists, Am. Assn. Neuropathologists, Am. Soc. Cell Biology, Histochem. Soc., Internat. Brain Research Orgn., Soc. Devel. Biology, Internat. Soc. Devel. Neurobiology, Soc. Devel. Neurosci., Soc. Neurosci., Tissue Culture Assn. Office: New England Regional Primat Rsch Ctr Harvard Med Sch 1 Pine Hill Rd Southborough MA 01772-1312

SIDMAN, ROBERT JOHN, lawyer; b. Cleve., Aug. 4, 1943; s. Charles Frances and Louise (Eckert) S.; m. Mary Mato, July 29, 1967; children: Christa Mary, Alicia Mary. BA, Benedictine Coll., 1965; JD, U. Notre Dame, 1968. Bar: Ohio 1968, U.S. Dist. Ct. (so. dist.) Ohio 1970, U.S. Ct. Appeals (6th cir.) 1971, U.S. Supreme Ct. 1971. Law clk. U.S. Dist. Ct. (so. dist.) Ohio, Columbus, 1968-70; assoc. Mayer, Tingley & Hurd, Columbus, 1970-75; judge Bankruptcy Ct. U.S. Dist. Ct. (so. dists.) Ohio, Columbus, 1975-82; ptnr. Vorys, Sater, Seymour & Pease, Columbus, 1982—; prof. Ohio State U. Law Sch., Columbus, 1984, 85, 86. Mem. Nat. Conf. Bankruptcy Judges (bd. dirs. 1981-82), Assn. Former Bankruptcy Judges (bd. dirs. 1983-89, treas. 1986-87, pres. 1988-89). Office: Vorys Sater Seymour & Pease PO Box 1008 52 E Gay St Columbus OH 43215-3161

SIDNEY, SYLVIA (SOPHIA KOSSOW), actress; b. N.Y.C., Aug. 8, 1910; d. Victor and Rebecca (Saperstein) Kossow; m. Bennett Alfred Cerf, 1935 (div.); m. Luther Adler, 1938 (div.); 1 child, Jacob L.; m. Carlton Alsop, 1945 (div.). Attended, N.Y.C. pub. schs., Theater Guild Sch., 1925. Made stage debut starring as Prunella at the Garrick theater, 1926; subsequent stage appearances include The Challenge of Youth, Washington, 1926, The Squall, N.Y.C., 1927, Crime, 1927, Mirrors, 1928, The Breaks, 1928, The Gods of the Lightning, 1928, Nice Women, N.Y.C., 1929, Cross-Roads, 1929, Many a Slip, 1930, Bad Girl, 1930, To Quito and Back, N.Y.C., 1937, Pygmalion, 1938, The Gentle People, N.Y.C., 1939, Accent on Youth, 1941, Angel Street, 1942, 64, Pygmalion, 1943, Joan of Lorraine, 1947, Kind Lady, 1948, The Two Mrs. Carrolls, 1949, Pygmalion, 1949, O Mistress Mine, 1949, Goodbye My Fancy, 1950, Anne of the Thousand Days, 1950, Innocents, Black Chiffon, 1951, The Gypsies Wore High Hats, 1952, The Fourposter, 1952, A Very Special Baby, 1956, Auntie Mame, 1958, Enter Laughing, 1963, Silver Cord, 1964, Kind Lady, 1964, Come Blow Your Horn, 1968-69, Vieux Carré, Sabrina Fair, Morning's at 7, 1981, Shadow Box, 1981, Come Along with Me, 1981; appearances in Nat. Repertory Theatre plays include The Rivals, 1965-66, The Little Foxes, 1966, The Importance of Being Earnest, 1966, She Stoops to Conquer, 1968; film career began in 1930; movie appearances include Beetlejuice, Summer Wishes Winter Dreams (Acad. award nominee for best supporting actress), I Never Promised You A Rose Garden, Accent on Youth, 30 Day Princess, Behold My Wife, Sabotage, 1/3 of a Nation, Damien: Omen 2, Hammett, City Streets, An American Tragedy, Street Scene, Merrily We Go to Hell, Mary Burns, Fugitive, Madame Butterfly, Trail of the Lonesome Pine, Fury, You Only Live Once, Dead End, The Searching Wind, Love from a Stranger, Les Miserables, Used People, Mars Attacks; TV appearances include My Three Sons, Whiz Kids, Magnum PI, Trapper John, M.D.; TV movies include The Shadow Box, 1980, Raid on Entebbe, 1977, Snowbeast, 1977, Siege, 1978, A Small Killing, 1981, An Early Frost, André's Mother, 1990 (Golden Globe nominee); author: Sylvia Sidney's Needlepoint Book, 1968, The Sylvia Sidney Question and Answer Book on Needlepoint, 1975. Bd. dirs. Nat. Amyotrophic Lateral Sclerosis Found. Avocations: needlepoint, reading, watching TV. Office: care John Springer 130 E 67th St New York NY 10021-6136

SIDNEY, WILLIAM WRIGHT, retired aerospace company executive; b. Anaconda, Mont., Dec. 31, 1929; s. Paul and Lily Maud (Wright) S.; divorced; children: Kay Elise, Paul Daniel. Student U. Calif., Berkeley, 1953-56. Supr. prodn. Kaiser Aerospace, San Leandro, Calif., 1953-57, project engr., 1957-67, chief engr., 1967-69, gen. mgr., 1969-77; pres. Kaiser Aerotech, San Leandro, Calif., 1977-95, Kaiser Space Products, Pueblo, Colo., 1988-95, ret., 1995. With USN, 1948-52. Recipient NASA Pub. Svc. medal 1981. Home: 6025 Ridgemont Dr Oakland CA 94619-3721

SIDO, KEVIN RICHARD, lawyer; b. Alton, Ill., Nov. 22, 1951; s. Robert Frederick and Mary (Colligan) S.; m. Mary O'Neil, July 28, 1984. BA, U. Ill., 1972, JD, 1975. Bar: Ill. 1975, U.S. Dist. Ct. (no. dist.) Ill. 1975, U.S. Tax Ct. 1976, U.S. Ct. Appeals (7th cir.) 1977, U.S. Supreme Ct. 1979. Assoc. Hinshaw, Culbertson, Moelmann, Hoban & Fuller, Chgo., 1975-82, ptnr., 1982—, mem. exec. com., 1988—; lectr. Ill. Inst. CLE, 1977—; arbitrator Cir. Ct. of Cook County. Contbr. articles to profl. jours. Bd. dirs. Lake Barrington Shores (Ill.) Homeowners Assn., 1979. Mem. ABA, Ill Bar Assn., Chgo. Bar Assn., Def. Rsch. Inst. (lectr. 1983—, state chmn. No. Ill. 1988-94), Ill. Def. Counsel Assn. (bd. dirs. 1982-83, 87-94, editor 1984-87), Internat. Assn. Def. Counsel, Am. Arbitration Assn. (arbitrator), Phi Beta Kappa. Avocations: photography, antiques. Office: Hinshaw and Culbertson 222 N La Salle St Ste 300 Chicago IL 60601-1013

SIDON, CLAUDIA MARIE, psychiatric and mental health nursing educator; b. Bellaire, Ohio, Feb. 6, 1946; d. Paul and Nell (Bernas) DePaulis; m. Michael Sidon; children: Michael II, Babe. Diploma, Wheeling (W.Va.) Hosp. Sch., 1966; BS in Nursing summa cum laude, Ohio U., Athens, 1979; MS in Nursing, W.Va. U., Morgantown, 1982. Cert. social worker. Various staff positions Bellaire City Hosp., 1966-67, 72-77; adj. nursing faculty W.Va. No. Community Coll., Wheeling, 1977-82; nurse clinician, psychotherapist Valley Psychol. and Psychiat. Svcs., Moundsville, W.Va., 1984; psychotherapist, nurse clinician, case mgr. No. Panhandle Behavioral Health Ctr., Wheeling, 1984-88; assoc. prof. ADN program Belmont Tech. Coll., St. Clairsville, Ohio, 1988—; presenter in field. Mem. Tri-State Psychiat. Nursing Assn. (pres., v.p., program chmn.), Nat. League for Nursing (presenter), Phi Kappa Phi, Sigma Theta Tau. Home: 52295 Sidon Rd Dillonvale OH 43917-9538 Office: Belmont Tech Coll 120 Fox Shannon Pl Saint Clairsville OH 43950-8751

SIDRAN, MIRIAM, retired physics educator, researcher; b. Washington, May 25, 1920; d. Morris Samson and Theresa Rena (Gottlieb) S. BA, Bklyn. Coll., 1942; MA, Columbia U., N.Y.C., 1949; PhD, NYU, 1956. Rsch. assoc. dept. physics NYU, N.Y.C., 1950-55, postdoctoral fellow, 1955-57; asst. prof. Staten Island Community Coll., Richmond, N.Y., 1957-59; rsch. scientist Grumman Aerospace Corp., Bethpage, N.Y., 1959-67; prof. N.Y. Inst. Tech., N.Y.C., 1967-72; NSF rsch. fellow Nat. Marine Fisheries Svc., Miami, Fla., 1971-72; assoc. prof. then prof. physics Baruch Coll., N.Y.C., 1972-89, chmn. dept. natural scis., 1983-89, prof. emerita, 1990—; v.p. Baruch chpt. Profl. Staff Congress, 1983-89. Contbr. numerous articles to profl. and govtl. publs., chpts. to books. N.Y. State Regents scholar, 1937-41; NSF summer fellow, Miami, 1970. Mem. N.Y. Acad. Scis., Am. Assn. Physics Tchrs. Avocations: French and Hebrew languages, music, bicycling, poetry. Home: 210 W 19th St #5G New York NY 10011

SIDRANSKY, HERSCHEL, pathologist; b. Pensacola, Fla., Oct. 17, 1925; s. Ely and Touba (Bear) S.; m. Evelyn Lipsitz, Aug. 18, 1952; children: Ellen, David Ira. B.S., Tulane U., 1948, M.D., 1953, M.S., 1958. Diplomate: Am. Bd. Pathology. Intern Charity Hosp. La., New Orleans, 1953-54; vis. asst. pathologist Charity Hosp. La., 1954-58; practice medicine, specializing in pathology Washington, 1977—; pathologist Nat. Cancer Inst., NIH, Bethesda, Md., 1958-61; instr. pathology Tulane U., 1954-58; prof. pathology U. Pitts., 1961-72; prof., chmn. dept. pathology U. South Fla., Tampa, 1972-77, George Washington U., 1977—; cons. VA Hosp. and Children's Hosp., Washington. Mem. editl. bd. Jour. Nutrition, 1973-77, Cancer Rsch., 1974-77, Human Pathology, 1979-91, Am. Jour. Clin. Nutrition, 1979-82, Am. Jour. Pathology, 1980-85, Jour. Exptl. Pathology, 1982-92, Exptl. Molecular Pathology Jour., 1987—; contbr. articles to profl. jours. Served with AUS, 1944-46. Life Ins. Med. Research fellow, 1956-57; USPHS fellow, 1957-58, 67-68; NIH research grantee, 1961—. Mem. Am. Soc. for Investigative Pathology, Soc. Exptl. Biology and Medicine, Am. Assn. Cancer Rsch., Am. Inst. Nutrition, Am. Soc. Clin. Nutrition, U.S.-Can. Acad. Pathologists, Med. Mycology Soc. Ams., Reticuloendothelial Soc., N.Y. Acad. Scis., AAAS, Washington Acad. Medicine (pres. 1996—), Washington Soc. Pathologists, Assn. Pathology Chmn., Intersoc. Com. on Pathology Info., Sigma Xi. Home: 5144 Macomb St NW Washington DC 20016-2612 Office: 2300 I St NW Washington DC 20037-2336

SIEBEL, MATHIAS PAUL, mechanical engineer; b. Witten, Germany, Mar. 6, 1924; came to U.S., 1957, naturalized, 1962; s. Franz and Marie-Luise S.; m. Katherine Elizabeth Jente, May 27, 1960. B.S. in Mech. Engring, U. Bristol, Eng., 1949, Ph.D., 1952. From research and devel. engr. to asst. plant mgr. Tube Investments Ltd., Birmingham, Eng., 1952-57; research asso. Columbia U., N.Y.C., 1958-59; mgr. pressure equipment Pall Corp., Glen Cove, N.Y., 1959-64; v.p. ops. RDI Co., Westbury, N.Y., 1964-65; dir. mfg. engring. lab., then mem. sci. staff Marshall Space Flight Center, NASA, Huntsville, Ala., 1965-79; mgr. NASA Michoud Assembly Facility, New Orleans, 1979-87, cons., 1987—; assoc. dean Coll. Engring. U. New Orleans, 1989-92, adj. prof. mech. enring., 1993—. Author. Mem. Sigma Xi. Patentee in field. Home: 5204 Janice Ave Kenner LA 70065-3238

SIEBERT, CALVIN D., economist, educator; b. Hillsboro, Kans., Feb. 11, 1934; s. Ira and Margaret (Everett) S.; m. Valerie Dawn Nanninga, Feb. 18, 1960; children—Douglas Erik, Derek Christopher. BA, U. Kans., 1958, MA, 1960; PhD in Econs., U. Calif., Berkeley, 1966. Asst. prof. econs. U. Iowa, 1965-68, assoc. prof., 1968-75, prof., 1975—, chmn. dept., 1969-71, 75-79; Rockefeller Found. vis. asso. prof. U. Philippines, 1971-72. Contbr. articles to profl. jours. With U.S. Army, 1954-56. Ford Found. grantee, 1964-65. Mem. Am. Econ. Assn., Phi Beta Kappa. Home: 341 N 7th Ave Iowa City IA 52245-6003 Office: U Iowa Dept Econs W276 Pbab Iowa City IA 52242

SIEBERT, DIANE DOLORES, author, poet; b. Chgo., Mar. 18, 1948; m. Robert William Siebert, Sept. 21, 1969. RN. Author: Truck Song, 1984 (Notable Childrens Book award ALA 1984, Sch. Libr. Jour. one of Best Books 1984, Outstanding Childrens Book award N.Y. Times Book Rev. 1984, Reading Rainbow Selection book 1991), Mojave, 1988 (Childrens Editors Choice 1988, Internat. Reading Assn. Tchrs. Choice award 1989, others), Heartland, 1989 (award Nat. Coun. for Social Studies/Childrens Book Coun. 1989, on John Burroughs List Nature Book for Young Readers 1989, Ohio Farm Bur. Women award 1991), Train Song, 1990 (Notable Childrens Book award ALA, 1990, Redbook Mag. one of Top Ten Picture Books 1990, one of Best Books award Sch. Libr. Jour. 1990, others), Sierra, 1991 (Outstanding Sci. Trade Book for Children award NSTA 1991, Notable Childrens Trade Book in Field Social Studies award Nat. Coun. Social Studies 1991, Beatty award Calif. Libr. Assn. 1992), Plane Song, 1993 (Outstanding Sci. Trade Book for Children 1994, Platinum award Oppenheim Toy Portfolio, Tchrs. Choice award Internat. Reading Assn. 1994). Avocations: environmental affairs, running, classical guitar, motorcycle, animals. Home: 9676 SW Jordan Rd Culver OR 97734-9567

SIEBERT, KARL JOSEPH, food science educator; b. Harrisburg, Pa., Oct. 29, 1945; s. Christian Ludwig and Katharine (Springer) S.; m. Sui Ti Atienza, Mar. 14, 1970; children: Trina, Sabrina. BS in Biochemistry, Pa. State U., 1967, MS in Biochemistry, 1968, PhD in Biochemistry, 1970. Chemist Applied Sci. Labs., State College, Pa., 1968-70; rsch. assoc. Stroh Brewery Co., Detroit, 1971, head R & D sect., 1971-73, mgr. R & D lab., 1973-82, dir. rsch., 1982-90; v.p. Strohtech, Detroit, 1986-90; prof. Cornell U., Geneva, N.Y., 1990—, chmn. dept. food sci. and tech., 1990-95; also assoc. dir. Cornell Inst. Food Sci. Cornell U., Ithaca, 1990-95. Contbr. articles to profl. jours. Bd. visitors Oakland U. Biology Dept., Rochester, Mich., 1985-89; bd. dirs. Cornell Rsch. Found., 1990-96, Geneva Concerts Inc., 1991—. Capt. USAR, 1967-75. Recipient Presdl. award Master Brewers Assn., 1986, 90; named hon. prof. Moscow State Acad. Food Prodn., 1996. Fellow NSF; mem. Am. Chem. Soc. (divsn. agrl. and food chemistry, computers in chemistry divsn.), Master Brewer Assn. Ams., Am. Soc. Brewing Chemists (chmn. tech. com. 1986-88, mem. editl. bd. 1983-91, 96—), Inst. Food Technologists (divsn. fruit and vegetable tech., food chemistry, sensory analysis), Internat. Chemometrics Soc. (N.Am. chpt.). Avocations: computers, electronics. Home: 9 Parkway St Geneva NY 14456-9765 Office: NY State Agrl Expt Sta Cornell U Dept Food Sci Geneva NY 14456

SIEBERT, MURIEL, business executive, former state banking official; b. Cleve.; d. Irwin J. and Margaret Eunice (Roseman) Siebert; student Western Res. U., 1949-52; DCS (hon.), St. John's U., St. Bonaventure U., Molloy Coll., Adelphi U., St. Francis Coll., Mercy Coll., Coll. New Rochelle, St. Lawrence U., Manhattan Coll. Security analyst Bache & Co., 1954-57; analyst Utilities & Industries Mgmt. Corp., 1958, Shields & Co., 1959-60; partner Stearns & Co., 1961, Finkle & Co., 1962-65, Brimberg & Co., N.Y.C., 1965-67; individual mem. (first woman mem.) N.Y. Stock Exchange, 1967; chmn., pres. Muriel Siebert & Co., Inc., 1969-77; trustee Manhattan Savs. Bank, 1975-77; supt. banks, dept. banking State of N.Y., 1977-82; dir. Urban Devel. Corp., N.Y.C., 1977-82, Job Devel. Authority, N.Y.C., 1977-82, State of N.Y. Mortgage Agy., 1977-82; chmn., pres. Muriel Siebert & Co., Inc., 1983—; assoc. in mgmt. Simmons Coll.; mem. adv. com. Fin. Acctg. Standards Bd., 1981-84; guest lectr. numerous colls. Former mem. women's adv. com. Econ. Devel. Adminstrn., N.Y.C.; former trustee Manhattan Coll.; v.p., former mem. exec. com. Greater N.Y. Area council Boy Scouts Am.; mem. N.Y. State Econ. Devel. Bd., N.Y. Coun. Economy; bd. overseers NYU Sch. Bus., 1984-88; former bd. dirs. United Way of N.Y.C.; trustee Citizens Budget Commn., L.I. U.; mem. bus. com. Met. Mus., bus. com. of N.Y. State Bus. Coun.; active Women's Campaign Fund; bd. dirs. N.Y. Women's Agenda. Recipient Spirit of Achievement award Albert Einstein Coll. Medicine, 1977; Women's Equity Action League award, 1978; Outstanding Contbns. to Equal Opportunity for Women award Bus. Council of UN Decade for Women, 1979; Silver Beaver award Boy Scouts Am., 1981; Elizabeth Cutter Morrow award YWCA, 1983; Emily Roebling award Nat. Women's Hall of Fame, 1984; Entrepreneural Excellence award White House Conf. on Small Bus., 1986; NOW Legal Def. and Edn. Fund award, 1981, Brotherhood award Nat. Conf. of Christians and Jews, 1989, Women on the Move award Anti-Defamation League, 1990., award Borough of Manhattan, 1991, Benjamin Botwinick prize Columbia Bus. Sch.'s, 1992, Women in Bus. Making History award Women's Bus. Coun. N.Y. C. of C., 1993, Disting. Woman of the Yr. award Greater N.Y. Boy Scouts of Am., 1993, Woman of the Yr. award Fin. Women's Assn. N.Y., 1994, Medal of Honor award Ellis Island, 1994, Bus. Philanthropist of the Yr. award So. Calif. Conf. for Women Bus. Owner's., 1990, Corning Excellence award N.Y.S. Bus. Coun., 1993, Star award N.Y. Women's Agenda, Established Siebert Entrepreneurial Philanthropic Plan, N.Y. Urban Coalition's Achievement award, 1994, Women of Distinction award Crohn's and Colitis Found., Entrepreneurial Leadership award Nat. Found. Teaching Entrepreneurship, 1994; inductee Nat. Woman's Hall of Fame, Seneca Falls, N.Y., 1994, Internat. Women's Forum Hall of Fame, 1994. Mem. Women's Forum (founding mem., pres.), Com. 200, Fin. Women's Assn. (Community Svc. award 1993), River Club, Doubles Club, Westchester Country Club, West Palm Beach Polo and Country Club, Nat. Assn. Women Bus. Owners (Veuve Clicquot Bus. Women of Yr. award 1992, Lifetime Achievement award 1993), Econ. Club. Home: 435 E 52nd St New York NY 10022-6445 Office: Muriel Siebert & Co Inc 885 3rd Ave New York NY 10022-4834

SIEBERT, THOMAS L., ambassador; b. Cleve., May 2, 1946; m. Deborah Simpson; 4 children. BA, Georgetown U., JD. Intern Rep. Robert E. Sweeney, 1965-66; vol. Senator Robert F. Kennedy, 1966-68; aide Senator Carl Hayden, 1968-70; assoc. Pittman, Lovett, Ford & Hennessey, Washington, 1971-78; ptnr. Lovett, Ford, Hennessey, Stambler & Siebert, 1978-87; of counsel Besozzi & Gavin, 1987-93, Besozzi, Gavin & Craven, Washington, 1993; U.S. amb. to Sweden Dept. State, 1993—. Bd. Regents Cath. U.; bd. visitors St. John's Coll.; active U.S. Naval Acad. Midshipmen Program, Md. Hall for the Creative Arts. Mem. ABA, D.C. Bar, Fed. Comm. Bar Assn., Annapolis Assn. Office: Am Embassy, Strandvagen 101, S-115 89 Stockholm Sweden

SIEBERT, WILLIAM MCCONWAY, electrical engineering educator; b. Pitts., Nov. 19, 1925; s. Charles Theodore Jr. and Isabel (McConway) S.; m. Anne Decker, Sept. 10, 1949; children: Charles R. (dec.), Thomas McC., Peter W., Terry A., Theodore D. SB, MIT, 1943, ScD, 1952. Jr. engr. Westinghouse Rsch. Labs., 1946-47; group leader Lincoln Lab. MIT, Cambridge, Mass., 1953-55, mem. faculty, 1952-95, prof. elec. engring., 1963-95, sr. lectr., 1995—; cons. to govt. and industry, 1952—. With USNR, 1943-46. Fellow IEEE; mem. Acoustical Soc. Am., Sigma Xi, Tau Beta Pi, Eta Kappa Nu. Research in applications of communication theory to radar and biol. systems. Home: PO Box 505 17 Mountain View Rd Jackson NH 03846-0505 Office: MIT 77 Massachusetts Ave Cambridge MA 02139-4301

SIEDLE, ROBERT DOUGLAS, management consultant; b. Canton, Ohio, Aug. 8; m. Beverly Rose Scholl, Mar. 18, 1972 (div. Oct. 1983). BA in Econs., Hiram Coll., 1956; profl. cert. edn., Kent State/Western Res. Univs., 1963. Tchr., prin. Ohio secondary schs., 1957-65; salesman, area rep. visual products divsn. 3M Co., 1966-68; mgr. market devel. and tng. AV divsn. Bell & Howell, 1968-69; Chgo. br. mgr. info. systems divsn. Am. Std., 1969-72; mgr. edn. systems divsn. Audiotronics Corp., 1972-76; gen. mgr. Niles Entertainment/Wardway Films, 1977-80; pres. The Ultimate Image, Lakeland, Fla., 1985—. Producer: (films) New Dimensions in Learning II, 1969, District 65: The Exceptional Child, 1969, Career Exploration: Health, 1976, The Wide World of Work, 1976; author: Multisensory Learning: A Training Guide, 1973, Alphabet Zoo, 1973, City of Boston Young Adult Alternate Career Program, 1974, The Quick Job Hunt Guide, 1991; author, producer, dir.: (multimedia rd. show) "Rap" With Students, 1975; producer, editor: (film) Stampin' Ground, 1977; author poetry appearing in books and mags., 1983—; appeared on nat. radio and TV programs in U.S. and Can. Named Internat. Man of Yr., Internat. Biog. Ctr., Cambridge, Eng., 1992-93, recipient Internat. Order of Merit, 1993. Fellow Internat. Biog. Assn. (life), Am. Biog. Inst. (Man of Yr. and Most Admired Man of Decade 1993, Platinum Record award 1996, 500 Leadership Influence award 1996, Golden Record of Achievement 1996, Presdl. Seal of Honor 1996); mem. Internat. Biog. Ctr. (dep. dir. gen./life mem.), Am. Biog. Inst. Rsch. Assn. (dep. gov. life), U.S. Naval Aviation Mus. (life), U.S. Naval Inst. (life), Navy League of U.S. (life), World Future Soc., Internat. Platform Assn., Sun 'n Fun Air Mus. (life), Am. Air Mus. in Britain (founding mem.), Aircraft Owners and Pilots Assn., Aircraft Owners and Pilots Assn. Safety Found., Exptl. Aircraft Assn., Warbirds of Am., Soaring Soc. Am., Great Lakes Hist. Soc. (life), Air Force Assn., Nat. Space Soc. Baptist. Office: The Ultimate Image PO Box 91388 Lakeland FL 33804-1388

SIEDLECKI, NANCY THERESE, lawyer, funeral director; b. Chgo., May 30, 1954; d. LeRoy John and Dorothy Josephine (Wilczynski) Schielka; m. Jonathan Francis Siedlecki, June 18, 1977; children: Samantha Ann, Abigail Marie. Student Triton Jr. Coll., 1971-73; grad. funeral dir., Worsham Coll., 1974; student Loyola U., Chgo., 1974-76., U. Ill.-Chgo., 1976-77; JD with honors, Chgo.-Kent Coll. Law, 1980. Bar: Ill. 1980. Paralegal in real estate Rosenberg, Savner & Unikel, Chgo., 1974-77; pvt. practice law, Burr Ridge, Ill., 1980—; cons. probate and various small bus. corps., Chgo., 1980—. Mem. ABA, Ill. State Bar Assn., Chgo. Bar Assn. Roman Catholic. Office: 5300 Main St Downers Grove IL 60515-4846

SIEDLECKI, PETER ANTHONY, English language and literature educator; b. North Tonawanda, N.Y., May 19, 1938; s. Anthony Paul and Mary Barbara (Litwin) S.; m. Rose Mary Murphy, June 25, 1960 (div. 1978); children: Christopher, Gregory, Jeffrey, William; m. Lynnette Noreen Mende, Apr. 26, 1980; children: Peter Emmanuel Mende-Siedlecki. BA, Niagara (N.Y.) U., 1960, MA, 1966; PhD, SUNY, Buffalo, 1982. Tchr. English Lewiston-Porter Sr. High Sch., Youngstown, N.Y., 1960-64, Grand Island (N.Y.) Sr. High Sch., 1964-65; prof. English Rosary Hill Coll., Amherst, N.Y., 1965-74, Daemen Coll., Amherst, 1974—; prof. Am. Lit. Jagiellonian U., Krakow, Poland, 1982-84, Friedrich-Schiller U., Jena, 1988-89; commentator pub. radio, 1995-97. Author numerous poetry in jours. and revs.; contbr. articles to profl. jours. Fulbright Sr. lectr., Council for Internat. Exchange of Scholars, 1982-84, 88-89. Mem. MLA, Fulbright Alumni Assn. Democrat. Home: 249 Winspear Ave Buffalo NY 14215-1035 Office: Daemen College 4380 Main St Buffalo NY 14226-3544

SIEDLER, ARTHUR JAMES, nutrition and food science educator; b. Milw., Mar. 17, 1927; s. Arthur William and Margaret (Stadler) S.; m. Doris Jean Northrop, Feb. 23, 1976; children: William, Nancy Siedler Wilhite, Sandra Siedler Lowman, Roxanne Rose Butler, Randy Rose. BS, U. Wis., 1951; MS, U. Chgo., 1956, PhD, 1959. Chief div. biochemistry and nutrition Am. Meat Inst. Found., Chgo., 1959-64; group leader Norwich (N.Y.) Pharmacal Co., 1964-65, chief physiology sect., 1965-69, chief biochemistry sect., 1969-72; acting dir. div. nutritional scis. U. Ill., Urbana, 1978-81, head dept. food sci., 1972-89, prof. food sci., internal medicine and nutritional scis., 1972-94, prof. emeritus, 1994—. With USCG, 1945-46, PTO. NIH research grantee, 1960-63; Nat. Livestock and Meat Bd. grantee, 1959-64. Mem. Inst. Food Technologists, Am. Chem. Soc., Am. Inst. Nutrition, Coun. for Agrl. Sci. and Tech., Eagles, Moose, Rotary, Sigma Xi. Patentee in field. Home: 8 Stanford Pl Champaign IL 61820-7620 Office: 382M Ag Eng Sci 1304 W Pennsylvania Ave Urbana IL 61801-4726

SIEFER, STUART B., architect; b. Detroit, Nov. 28, 1942; s. Louis and Esther (Ressler) S.; m. Nancy Ann Feldman, Apr. 23, 1967; children: Eric S., Jeremy M., Ted B. BA, Wayne State U., 1965; postgrad., U. Detroit, 1965-68; BArch, Ariz. State U., 1971. Registered architect, Ariz. Designer, draftsman various firms, Detroit, 1966-68; rschr. Detroit Bd. Edn., 1967; archtl. designer Peace Corps, Tegucigalpa, Honduras, 1968-70; designer, job capt. various firms, Phoenix, 1970-73; prin. Siefer Assocs., Tempe, Ariz., 1973—. Bd. dirs. Downtown Tempe Community, Inc., 1993—; vol. bd. mem. Tempe Ctr. for Habilitation, 1993—; mem. Ariz. Town Hall, Phoenix, 1993—. Recipient 13 design awards Tempe Beautification Com., 1975—, merit & Crescordia award Valley Forward Assn. AIA Ariz., 1988, 93, Beautification award City of Mesa, Ariz., AIA Ariz. Archs. medal, 1996. Mem. AIA (pres. Rio Salado chpt.), Rio Salado Architecture Found. (exec. mem.), Tempe C. of C. (pres. 1992-93) Found. (founding bd. mem. 1995). Avocations: jogging, skiing, hiking, tennis.

SIEFERS, ROBERT GEORGE, banker; b. Pitts., Aug. 28, 1945; s. George Francis and Idella Alice (Eiler) S.; m. Janice Lynn Kirkpatrick, Mar. 25, 1970; children—Robert Scott, Jillian Stewart. B.A., Mt. Union Coll., 1967; M.B.A., Kent State U., 1971; J.D., Cleveland Marshall Law Sch., 1976. Security analyst Nat. City Bank, Cleve., 1971-76, v.p., investment rsch. dir., 1976-80, v.p. adminstrn. and rsch., 1980-82; sr. v.p. corp. planning Nat. City Corp., Cleve., 1982-85; sr. v.p. corp. banking Nat. City Bank, Cleve., 1985-86; pres., chief exec. officer Ohio Citizens Bank (affiliate Nat. City Corp.), Toledo, 1986-90; exec. v.p., chief fin. officer Nat. City Corp., Cleve., 1990—; bd. dirs. HCR Corp. Bd. trustees Mt. Union Coll. Republican. Presbyterian. Club: Chagrin Valley Country. Home: 10 Pebblebrook Ln Chagrin Falls OH 44022-2380 Office: Nat City Corp Nat City Ctr Cleveland OH 44022

SIEFERT-KAZANJIAN, DONNA, corporate librarian; b. N.Y.C.; d. Merrill Emil and Esther (Levins) S.; m. George John Kazanjian, June 15, 1974; 1 child, Merrill George. BA, NYU, 1969; MSLS, Columbia U., 1973; MBA, Fordham U., 1977. Asst. librarian Dun & Bradstreet, N.Y.C., 1969-73; research assoc. William E. Hill & Co., N.Y.C., 1973-76; sr. info. analyst Info. for Bus., N.Y.C., 1976-77; librarian Handy Assocs., N.Y.C., 1979-90; mgr. Infoserve Fuchs Cuthrell & Co., Inc., N.Y.C., 1991-94; libr. Heidrick & Struggles, Inc., N.Y.C., 1994—. Mem. Spl. Librs. Assn., Rsch. Roundtable, Am. Mensa Ltd. Roman Catholic. Office: Heidrick & Struggles Inc 245 Park Ave New York NY 10167-0002

SIEG, ALBERT LOUIS, photographic company executive; b. Chgo., Mar. 25, 1930; s. Albert Fredrick and Louise Augusta (Strege) S.; m. Irma Alice Spencer, Sept. 3, 1955; children—Karen, Diane, Susan. B.S. in Chemistry, U. Ill., 1951; Ph.D. in Organic Chemistry, U. Rochester, 1954; P.M.D., Harvard Bus. Sch., 1971. Supr. emulsion Eastman Kodak Co., Rochester, N.Y., 1970-72, corp. mgr. instant., 1972-76, mgr. paper mgt., 1976-81, v.p., dir., 1981-84; pres. Kodak Japan K.K., Tokyo, 1984-89; pres., rep. dir. Eastman Kodak Japan, Tokyo, 1989-91, also bd. dirs.; pres., rep. dir. Eastman Chems. Japan Ltd., Tokyo, 1989-91; v.p., dir. strategic resources, sec. imaging bd. Eastman Kodak Co., Rochester, 1991-92, ret., 1992; prin., cons. Albert L. Sieg Assocs., Rochester, 1992—; bd. dirs. Kodak Japan Industries, Ltd.; sr. lectr. U. Rochester, 1960-69. Co-author: 8th Here's How, 1972; co-author (with S. Bennett, Oliver Wight) Tokyo Chronicles, 1994; inventor in field. Bd. dirs., chmn. corp. gifts Rochester Philharm. Orch., 1982-84; chmn. corp. gifts Internat. Mus. Photography at George Eastman House, 1993, 94; pres. Reformation Luth. Ch., Rochester, 1978-83; bd. dirs. St. John's Home for the Aging, 1994—, vice chmn. bd. dirs., 1997—; bd. dirs. St. John's Nursing Home, 1994—, vice chmn. bd. dirs., 1997—. Served with Med. Svc. Corps, U.S. Army, 1955-57. Recipient George Eastman Medal Kodak Camera Clubs, 1980; Kiwanis Club Chgo. fellow, U. Ill., 1947-51; Am. Cyanamide fellow, 1953-54. Fellow Am. Inst. Chemists, Photog. Soc. Am. (v.p. 1969-84, Harold Lloyd award 1978, exec. v.p. 1995, progress medal 1995); mem. Am. Chem. Soc., Soc. Photog. Scientists and Engrs., AAAS, Rochester C. of C., Am. C. of C. in Japan (bd. govs. 1988-91, v.p. 1989-91), Internat. Stereoscopic Union (pres. 1993, 94). Republican. Club: American (Tokyo); Fgn. Correspondence. Avocations: skiing; photography; gardening. Home and Office: 159 Hillhurst Ln Rochester NY 14617-1938

SIEGAL, ALLAN MARSHALL, newspaper editor; b. N.Y.C., May 1, 1940; s. Irving and Sylvia Norma (Wrubel) S.; m. Gretchen M-P. Leefmans, May 31, 1977; children—Anna Marianita, Peter Bert. Grad., NYU, 1962. With New York Times, 1960—, editor Pentagon Papers, 1971, asst. fgn. editor, 1971-76, asst. to exec. editor, 1976-77, news editor, 1977-87, asst. mng. editor, 1987—, founding editor nat. edit., 1980; tchr. journalism NYU, 1966, Columbia U., 1967-69; juror Pulitzer Prize Nominating Com., 1987-89. Mem. Century Assn., Am. Soc. Newspaper Editors. Office: NY Times Co 229 W 43rd St New York NY 10036-3913

SIEGAL, BURTON LEE, product designer, consultant, inventor; b. Chgo., Sept. 27, 1931; s. Norman A. and Sylvia (Vitz) S.; m. Rita Goran, Apr. 11, 1954; children: Norman, Laurence Scott. BS in Mech. Engring., U. Ill., 1953. Torpedo designer U.S. Naval Ordnance, Forest Park, Ill., 1953-54; chief engr. Gen. Aluminum Corp., Chgo., 1954-55; product designer Chgo. Aerial Industries, Melrose Park, Ill., 1955-58; chief designer Emil J. Paidar Co., Chgo., 1958-59; founder, pres. Budd Engring. Corp., Chgo., 1959—; dir. Dur-A-Case Corp., Chgo.; design cons. to numerous corps. Holder more than 114 patents in more than 32 fields including multimemory for power seats and electrified office panel sys.; contbr. articles to tech. publs. Mem. math., sci. and English adv. bds. Niles Twp. High Schs., Skokie, Ill., 1975-79; electronic cons. Chgo. Police Dept., 1964. Winner, Internat. Extrusion Design Competition, 1975; nominated Presdl. Medal Technology Sen. Paul Simon and Rep. Dan Rostenkowski, 1986; named Inventor of Yr. Patent Law Assn. Chgo., 1986. Mem. ASME, Soc. Plastics Engrs., Soc. Mfg. Engrs., Inventor's Coun., Soc. Automotive Engrs., Pres.'s Assn. Ill. Office: 8707 Skokie Blvd Skokie IL 60077-2269 *A true professional can perform any time, any place, independent of his mood.*

SIEGAL, JACOB J., management and financial consultant; b. Phila., Apr. 4, 1929; s. Louis and Henrietta (Greenberg) S.; m. Dolores Berg, June 8, 1952; children: Marla, Karen, Leslie. B.S., Temple U., 1951, LL.B., 1954; postgrad., U. Chgo., 1973. Bar: Pa. 1955, Ill. 1973. With City of Phila., 1954-61, chief counselor, 1959-61, dep. city solicitor, 1958-61; pvt. practice law, partner firm Meltzer & Schiffrin, Phila., 1961-72; v.p., gen. counsel, dir. Bluebird Inc., Phila., 1972-74; exec. v.p. Bluebird Inc., 1974-78, pres., 1978-79, chmn., chief exec. officer, 1979; chmn. bd. Armen Cadillac-Osmobile, Inc. Mem. Am. Bar Assn., Am. Soc. Corp. Secs., Am. Meat Inst. (dir., conv. speaker 1978). Home: 101 Cheswold Ln Haverford PA 19041-1865 Office: PO Box 193 Plymouth Meeting PA 19462-0193

SIEGAL, KENNETH HARVEY, editor; b. Brookline, Mass., June 5, 1947; s. Samuel and Rose (Wolfson) S.; m. Jane Bolan, Mar. 29, 1970; children: Michele A., Joshua D. BS, Boston U., 1969. Reporter The Patriot Ledger, Quincy, Mass., 1969-75, copy editor, 1975-83; asst. mng. editor Boston Herald, 1983-88; mng. editor Digital News and Rev., 1988-93; dept. editor PC Week, 1993-95, mng. editor, 1995—. Officer Jaycees, Randolph, Mass., 1980-85. Home: 26 Katy Cir Randolph MA 02368-5414 Office: PC Week 10 Presidents Lndg Medford MA 02155-5148

SIEGAL, RITA GORAN, engineering company executive; b. Chgo., July 16, 1934; d. Leonard and Anabelle (Soloway) Goran; m. Burton L. Siegal, Apr. 11, 1954; children: Norman, Laurence Scott. Student, U. Ill., 1951-53; BA, DePaul U., 1956. Cert. elem. tchr., Ill. Tchr. Chgo. Public Schs., 1956-58; founder, chief exec. officer Budd Engring. Corp., Skokie, Ill., 1959—; founder, pres. Easy Living Products Co., Skokie, 1960—; pvt. practice in interior design, Chgo., 1968-73; dist. sales mgr. Super Girls, Skokie, 1976; lectr. Northwestern U., 1983; guest speaker nat. radio and TV, 1979—. Contbr. to profl. jours. Mem. adv. bd. Skokie High Schs., 1975-79; advisor Cub Scouts Skokie coun. Boy Scouts Am., 1975; bus. mgr. Nutrition for Optimal Health Assn., Winnetka, Ill., 1980-82, pres., 1982-84, v.p. med./profl., 1985-93; leader Great Books Found., 1972; founder Profit Plus Investment, 1970; bd. dirs. Noha, Internat. Recipient Cub Scout awards Boy Scouts Am., 1971-72, Nat. Charlotte Danstrom award Nat. Women of Achievement, 1988, Corp. Achievement award, 1988. Mem. North Shore Women in Mgmt. (pres. 1987-88), Presidents Assn. Ill. (bd. dirs 1990-94, membership com. 1991-93), Inventors Coun. Office: Budd Engring Corp 8707 Skokie Blvd Skokie IL 60077-2269 *Believe in yourself, if others can do it so can you. Prioritize so you are not overwhelmed by your responsibilities.*

SIEGAN, BERNARD HERBERT, lawyer, educator; b. Chgo., July 28, 1924; s. David and Jeannette (Seitz) S.; m. Sharon Goldberg, June 15, 1952 (dec. Feb. 1985); m. Shelley Zifferblatt, Nov. 19, 1995. AA, Herzl. Jr. Coll., Chgo., 1943, 46; Student, Roosevelt Coll., Chgo., 1946-47; J.D., U. Chgo., 1949. Bar: Ill. 1950. Practiced in Chgo.; partner firm Siegan & Karlin, 1952-73; pres., sec. various small corps. and gen. partner in partnerships engaged in real estate ownership and devel., 1955-70; weekly columnist Freedom newspaper chain, other papers, 1974-79; cons. law and econs. program U. Chgo. Law Sch., 1970-73; adj. prof. law U. San Diego Law Sch., 1973-74, prof., 1974-75, Disting. prof., 1975—, univ. prof., 1997—; adj. scholar Cato Inst., Washington, 1991—, Heritage Found., 1992—; cons. windfalls and wipeouts project HUD, 1973-74; cons. FTC, 1985-86, U.S. Justice Dept., dir. constl. bibliog. project, 1986-88; keynote speaker 5th Internat. Conf. on Urbanism, Porto Alegre, Brazil, 1989; nominated by Pres. Reagan to U.S. Ct. Appeals (9th cir.) Feb. 2, 1987, confirmation denied July 14, 1988 by party line vote Senate Judiciary Com. Author: Land Use Without Zoning, 1972, Spanish edit., 1995, Other People's Property, 1976, Economic Liberties and the Constitution, 1980, The Supreme Court's Constitution: An Inquiry Into Judicial Review and Its Impact on Society, 1987, Drafting a Constitution for a Nation or Republic Emerging into Freedom, 1992, 2d edit., 1994, Portuguese, Ukrainian, Polish and Spanish edits., 1993; editor: Planning without Prices, 1977, The Interaction of Economics and the Law, 1977, Regulation, Economics and the Law, 1979, Government, Regulation and the Economy, 1980. Mem. pres.-elect's Task Force on Housing, 1980-81; mem. Pres.'s Commn. on Housing, 1981-82; mem. Nat. Commn. on bicentannial of U.S. Constn., 1985-91; chmn. adv. com. Affordable Housing Conf., San Diego, 1985, Rights of Regulated Conf., Coronado, Calif., 1976; chmn. Conf. on the Taking Issue, 1976; mem. Houston Regional Urban Design Team, Study of Houston, 1990; mem. U.S. team Bulgarian Econ. Growth and Transition Project, 1990; mem. devel. bd. Mingei Internat. Mus. World Folk Art, 1981-84. Served with AUS, 1943-46. Research fellow law and econs. U. Chgo. Law Sch., 1968-69; Urban Land Inst. research fellow, 1976-86; recipient Leander J. Monks Meml. Fund award Inst. Humane Studies, 1972, George Washington medal Freedom Founds. at Valley Forge, 1981, Spl. award Liberal Inst. of Rio Grande do Sul, Porto Alegre, Brazil, 1989; named Chosen Univ. Prof., U. San Diego, 1997-98. Home: 6005 Camino De La Costa La Jolla CA 92037-6519

SIEGEL, ABRAHAM J., economics educator, academic administrator; b. N.Y.C., Nov. 6, 1922; s. Samuel J. and Dora (Drach) S.; m. Lillian Wakshull, Dec. 22, 1946; children: Emily Jean Siegel Stangle, Paul Howard, Barbara Ann Pugliese. B.A. summa cum laude, CCNY, 1943; M.A., Columbia U., 1949; Ph.D., U. Calif., Berkeley, 1961. Instr. dept. econs. CCNY, 1947-49; research economist Inst. Indsl. Relations, U. Calif., Berkeley, 1952-54; instr. dept. econs. M.I.T., Cambridge, 1954-56, asst. prof., 1956-59, assoc. prof., 1959-64, prof. dept. econs. Sloan Sch. Mgmt., 1964-93, assoc. dean Sloan Sch. Mgmt., 1967-80, dean, 1980-87, prof. emeritus, sr. lectr., 1993—; spl. lectr. Trade Union Program, Harvard U., 1961-64; vis. prof. Brandeis U., 1956-60; vis. prin. mem. div. Internat. Inst. Labour Studies, Internat. Labour Office, Geneva, 1964-65; asso. staff dir. Com. Econ. Devel., Study Group on Nat. Labor Policy, 1960-61; trustee, chmn. adminstrv. com. M.I.T. Retirement Plan for Staff Mems., 1970-91. Co-author: Industrial Relations in the Pacific Coast Longshore Industry, 1956, The Public Interest in National Labor Policy, 1961, The Impact of Computers on Collective Bargaining, 1969, Unfinished Business: An Agenda for Labor, Management and the Public, 1978. Bd. dirs. Whitehead Inst. Biomed. Rsch., Analysis Group, Inc., Internat. Data Group; mem. adv. group Internat. Inst. for Applied Systems Analysis, Laxenburg, Austria; mem. Framingham Sch. Com., South Middlesex Regional Dist. Vocat. Sch. Com., 1968-71. With USAF, 1943-46. Mem. Am. Econ. Assn., Indsl. Relations Research Assn., Nat. Acad. Arbitrators, Am. Arbitration Assn. (mem. various panels), Inst. Mgmt. Scis. Bus. Roundtable (exec. com.), Phi Beta Kappa. Clubs: Comml, St. Botolph's. Home: 112 Gardner Rd Brookline MA 02146-4537 Office: MIT Sloan Sch Mgmt 50 Memorial Dr Cambridge MA 02142-1347

SIEGEL, ALLEN GEORGE, lawyer; b. Chgo., May 19, 1934; s. David Harry and Jeanette (Morris) S.; m. Rochelle Robin, Mar. 12, 1961; children: Dina Robin, Jonathan Joseph. B.B.A., CCNY, 1957; LL.B. with distinction, Duke U., 1960. Bar: Fla. 1960, D.C. 1965. Pvt. practice law Jacksonville, Fla., 1960-62; field atty. NLRB, 1962-64; assoc. Arent, Fox, Kintner, Plotkin & Kahn, Washington, 1964-70, ptnr., 1970-80, sr. ptnr., 1980—; sr. lectr. in law Duke U., Durham, N.C., 1979—. Author: Confidential Supervisors Guide to Labor Relations, 1980, rev. edit., 1996, Confidential Supervisors Guide to Equal Employment, 1981, rev. edit., 1996; contbr. articles. Past pres. United Cerebral Palsy D.C., founder David H. Siegel Meml. Scholarship Duke U. Sch. Law, bd. dirs. pvt. adjudication ctr., 1986—; mem. bd. regents Cath. U. Am., 1990—; founder Rabbi Seymour Siegel Meml. Moot Ct. Competition Duke U. Law Sch.; founder Jeanette Siegel Meml. Scholarship, Phillip M. Siegel Meml. Scholarship; gen. counsel Jewish Social Svc. Agy. Washington, United Cerebral Palsy Assn. Washington and No. Va. Mordecai Soc. scholar; recipient Lehman-Piksen award Jewish Social Svc. Agy. Greater Washington, 1996. Mem. ABA, Fla. Bar Assn., D.C. Bar Assn., Am. Judicature Soc., Univ. Club Washington, Order of Coif. Republican. Jewish. Home: 7505 Connecticut Ave Chevy Chase MD 20815-4925 Office: Washington Square 1050 Connecticut Ave NW Washington DC 20036

SIEGEL, ARTHUR, corporate executive; b. N.Y.C., July 4, 1908; s. Louis and Helena (Kaufman) S.; m. Mirian Bierman, Sept. 3, 1939; children—Barbara Joan Siegel Frankfort, Louise Susan Siegel Riordan. B.S., N.Y. U., 1930. Vice pres. Congress Financial Corp., N.Y.C., 1963-68; v.p., dir. Commonwealth United Corp., Chgo., 1969—; pres., dir. Williams Electronics Inc., Chgo., 1969—; sr. v.p., dir. Seeburg Corp., Chgo., 1968—, Inland Credit Corp., N.Y.C., 1953-63; v.p., dir. Indsl. Equipment Credit Corp., N.Y., 1948-53. Home: 437 Golden Isles Dr Hallandale FL 33009 Office: 1500 N Dayton St Chicago IL 60622-2522

SIEGEL, ARTHUR HERBERT, accounting company executive; b. N.Y.C., Jan. 5, 1938; s. Joseph Kenneth and Gertrude Sylvia (Hecker) S.; m. Eleanor Novick, June 5, 1960; children: Joan Aileen, Linda Beth, Mark Eric. AB, Columbia, 1958, MBA, 1960. With Price Waterhouse, N.Y.C., 1960-61, mgr., L.I., 1961-72, ptnr., Boston, 1972—, nat. dir. acctg. svcs., N.Y.C., 1984-88, vice-chmn. bus. adv. and auditing svcs., 1988-95; mem. Fin. Acctg. Stds. Bd. Emerging Issues Task Force, 1985-88, Fin. Acctg. Stds. Adv. Coun., 1985-90; mem. adv. coun. Sch. Acctg. U. So. Calif., 1987-89; active World ABS Exec. Com., 1988-95, chmn., 1990-95, U.S. Mgmt. Com., 1988-95, World Mgmt. Coms., 1990-95. Past trustee, treas., 1st v.p. Temple Beth Avodah, Newton Centre, Mass.; bd. dirs. Nat. Multiple Sclerosis Soc., treas. exec. com., chmn. fin. com. Mem. AICPA (chmn. task force on risks and uncertainties 1987-98, chmn. SEC practice exec. com. 1994—), N.Y. Soc. CPAs (Silver Medal award), Mass. Soc. CPAs (pres.-elect 1983), Beta Gamma Sigma. Home: 179 E 70th St New York NY 10021-5154 Office: Price Waterhouse 300 Atlantic St Stamford CT 06901-3522

SIEGEL, BARRY ALAN, nuclear radiologist; b. Nashville, Dec. 30, 1944; s. Walter Gross Siegel and Lillian B. (Tumbarello) Ivener; m. Pamela M. Mandel, Aug. 18, 1968 (div. Mar. 1981); children: Peter A., William A.; m. Marilyn J. Siegel, Jan. 29, 1983. AB, Washington U., St. Louis, 1966, MD, 1969. Diplomate Am. Bd. Nuclear Medicine, Am. Bd. Radiology. Intern Barnes Hosp., St. Louis, 1969-70; resident in radiology and nuclear medicine fellow Mallinckrodt Inst. Radiology, Washington U., 1970-73, dir. div. nuclear medicine, 1973—, asst. prof., 1973-76, assoc. prof., 1976-79, prof. radiology, 1979—, assoc. prof. medicine, 1980-83, prof. medicine, 1983—; dir. Am. Bd. Nuc. Medicine, L.A., 1985-90, sec., 1990; chmn. adv. com. on med. uses of isotopes NRC, Washington, 1990-96; chmn. radiopharm. drugs adv. com. U.S. FDA, Rockville, Md., 1982-85, radiol. devices panel, 1992-95; mem. U.S. Pharmacopeia Adv. Panel on Radiopharms., 1975—, Armed Forces Radiobiol. Rsch. Inst., Bethesda. Author, editor 26 books; contbr. articles to profl. jours., chpts. to books. Maj. USAF, 1974-76. Recipient Commr.'s Spl. citation U.S. FDA, 1988, Honor citation U.S. Pharmacopeial Conv., 1995. Fellow ACP, Am. Coll. Radiology (vice chmn. commn. on nuclear medicine 1981—, editor in chief self evaluation program 1988—), Am. Coll. Nuclear Physicians; mem. AMA, Am. Roentgen Ray Soc., Assn. Univ. Radiologists, Radiol. Soc. N.Am., Soc. Nuclear Medicine (trustee 1981-85, 87-91). Office: Washington U Mallinckrodt Inst Radiology 510 S Kingshighway Blvd Saint Louis MO 63110-1016

SIEGEL, BERNARD, foundation administrator. Pres. The Harry and Jeanette Weinberg Found., Inc., Balt. Office: Harry and Jeanette Weinberg Found 7 Park Center Court Owings Mills MD 21117*

SIEGEL, BERNARD LOUIS, lawyer; b. Pitts., Sept. 15, 1938; s. Ralph Robert and Frieda Sara (Stein) S.; m. Marcia Margolis, Sept. 3, 1961 (div. Aug. 1982); children: Jonathan, Sharon. BA, Brandeis U., 1960; JD, Harvard U., 1963. Bar: Pa. 1964, U.S. Dist. Ct. (we. dist.) Pa. 1964, U.S. Dist. Ct. (ea. dist.) Pa. 1985, U.S. Ct. Appeals (3d cir.) 1985, U.S. Supreme Ct. 1985. Assoc. Silin, Eckert & Burke, Erie, Pa., 1963-66; ptnr. Silin, Eckert, Burke & Siegel, Erie, Pa., 1966-73; 1st asst. dist. atty. Erie County, 1972-76; dep. atty. gen. Pa. Dept. Justice, Phila., 1976-78; dep. dist. atty. Dist. Atty. of Phila., 1978-86; pvt. practice Phila., 1986—; adj. prof. La Salle U., Phila., 1986—; lectr. Fed. Law Enforcement Tng. Ctr., Glynco, Ga., 1986—, Mercyhurst Coll., Erie, 1974-76, Nat. Coll. Dist. Attys., Houston, 1978-85, Temple U. law sch., 1995—; mem. criminal rules com. Pa. Supreme Ct., Phila., 1976-85; commr. Pa. Crime Commn., Harrisburg, 1976-79. Author: (with others) Pennsylvania Grand Jury Practice, 1983, By No Extraordinary Means, 1986. Mem. ABA, Nat. Assn. Criminal Def. Lawyers, Pa. Assn. Criminal Def. Lawyers (bd. dirs. 1988—), Pa. Bar Assn. (chmn. criminal law sect. 1988-91), Phila. Bar Assn. (chmn. criminal justice sect. 1990-91). Democrat. Jewish. Avocations: bicycling, reading, hiking. Office: Packard Bldg 24th Fl 111 S 15th St Philadelphia PA 19102-2625

SIEGEL, BETTY LENTZ, college president; b. Cumberland, Ky., Jan. 24, 1931; d. Carl N. and Vera (Hogg) Lentz; m. Joel H. Siegel, June 6; children: David Jonathan, Michael Jeremy. B.A., Wake Forest Coll., 1952; M.Ed., U. N.C., 1953; Ph.D., Fla. State U., 1961; postgrad., Ind. U., 1964-66; hon. doctorate, Miami U., 1985, Cumberland Coll., 1985, Ea. Ky. U., 1992. Asst. prof. Lenoir Rhyne Coll., Hickory, N.C., 1956-59; assoc. prof., 1961-64; asst. prof. U. Fla., Gainesville, 1967-70; assoc. prof. U. Fla., 1970-72, prof., 1973-76, dean acad. affairs for continuing edn., 1972-76; dean Sch. Edn. and Psychology Western Carolina U., Cullowhee, N.C., 1976-81; pres. Kennesaw State Coll., Marietta, Ga., 1981—; bd. dirs. Atlanta Gas Light Co., Equifax Inc., Nat. Services Industries; cons. numerous sch. systems. Author: Problem Situations in Teaching, 1971; contbr. articles to profl. jours. Bd. dirs. United Way Atlanta, Woodruff Arts Ctr., Ga. Partnership for Excellence in Edn., Ga. Coun. Econ. Edn., Northside Hosp. Found., Atlanta Ballet. Recipient Outstanding Tchr. award U. Fla., 1969; Mortar Bd. Woman of Yr. award U. Fla., 1973, Mortar Bd. Educator of Yr., Ga. State U., 1983, CASE award, 1986, Alumna of Yr. award Wake Forest U., 1987, "Grad Made Good" award Fla. State U. Alumni Assn, Omicron Delta Kappa, 1991, Spirit of Life award City of Hope, 1992, Woman of Achievement award Cobb Chamber YWCA, 1992; named One of 100 Most Influential People in State of Ga., Ga. Trend Mag., Outstanding Alumni, Fla. State U. Coll. Edn. Alumni Assn., 1992, Cobb Citizen of the Yr. award, 1996. Mem. ASCD, Am. Psychol. Assn., Am. Assn. State Colls. and Univs. (bd. dirs., chmn. 1990), Am. Coun. Edn. (bd. dirs., bd. advisors), Am. Inst. Mng. Diversity (bd. dis.), Soc. Internat. Bus. Fellows, Internat. Alliance for Invitational Edn. (co-founder, co-dir.), Bus./Higher Edn. Forum, mem. exec. com.), Assn. Tchrs. Educators' Commn. on Leadership in Interprofl. Edn. (task force on techr. edn.), Cobb C. of C. (chair 1996), Kiwanis (Atlanta chpt.), Nat. Coun. for Accreditation of Tchr. Edn. (policy bd.), Phi Alpha Theta, Pi Kappa Delta, Alpha Psi Omega, Kappa Delta Pi, Pi Lambda Theta, Phi Delta Kappa, Delta Kappa Gamma. Baptist. Office: Kennesaw State Univ Office of the President 1000 Chastain Rd Kennesaw GA 30144-5588

SIEGEL, CAROLE ETHEL, mathematician; b. N.Y., Sept. 29, 1936; d. David and Helen (Mayer) Schore; m. Bertram Siegel, Aug. 18, 1957; children: Sharon, David. BA in Math., NYU, 1957, MS in Math., 1959, PhD in Math., 1963. With computer dept. Atomic Energy Commn., 1957-59; rsch. asst. Courant Inst. of Math. Sci., 1959-63; rsch. scientist dept. of engring. NYU, N.Y.C., 1963-64; rsch. math. Info. Scis. Div. Rockland Rsch. Inst., Orangeburg, N.Y., 1965-74; head Epidemiology and Health Svcs. Rsch. Lab Stat. Scis., Epidemiology Divsn./Nathan S. Kline Inst. Rsch., Orangeburg, N.Y., 1974—; rsch. prof. dept. psychiatry NYU, 1987—; dep. dir. WHO Collaborating Ctr., Nathan S. Kline Inst., 1987—; grant reviewer NIHM, 1988—; co-prin. investigator Ctr. for Study of Issues in Public Mental Health, NIMH, 1993-95, prin. investigator, dir., 1995—. Editor: (with S. Fischer) Psychiatric Records in Mental Health Care, 1981; contbr. articles to profl. jours. Recipient grants NIMH, 1993—, 88-91, Nat. Ctr. for Health Svcs. Rsch., 1979-82, Nat. Inst. Alcohol Abuse, 1978-82. Mem. Assn. for Health Svcs. Rsch., Am. Soc. Clin. Pharmacology and Therapeutics, Assn. Women in Math., Am. Statis. Assn. Avocations: pottery, gardening, cooking. Office: Nathan S Kline Inst Orangeburg NY 10962

SIEGEL, DAVID BURTON, lawyer; b. N.Y.C., Mar. 22, 1949; s. Henry and Ruth (Rosenzweig) S.; m. Barbara Joan Brown, Aug. 6, 1972; children: Jeffrey Spencer, Carolyn Rose, Laura Ellen. AB, Columbia Coll., 1971; JD, NYU, 1974. Assoc. atty. Kelley Drye & Warren, N.Y.C., 1974-77; corp. counsel W.R. Grace & Co., N.Y.C., 1977-87, asst. gen. counsel, 1987-91; assoc. gen. counsel W.R. Grace & Co., Boca Raton, Fla., 1991-93; v.p., dep. gen. counsel W.R. Grace & Co., Boca Raton, 1993—. Mem. Econ. Coun. Palm Beach County, Fla., 1993—; mem. bd. dirs. Edn. Partnership of Palm Beach County, 1994-96, treas., 1995-96. Home: 5896 NW 23rd Way Boca Raton FL 33496 Office: WR Grace & Co One Town Center Rd Boca Raton FL 33486

SIEGEL, DAVID DONALD, law educator; b. Bklyn., Oct. 18, 1931; s. Harry Wilbur and Ida Claire (Scharaga) S.; m. Rosemarie Ann Duffy, Dec. 21, 1969; children: Sheila Nell, Rachel Ann. B.A., CUNY, 1953; J.D., St. John's U., 1958; LL.M., NYU, 1964. Bar: N.Y. 1958. Law sec. to chief judge N.Y. Ct. Appeals, 1958-59; practiced law N.Y.C., 1960-62; asst. prof. law St. John's U., 1962-65, assoc. prof., 1965-67, prof., 1967-72, vis. prof., 1972-84, McNiece prof., 1984-90; prof. Albany Law Sch., 1972-84, disting. prof., 1990—; vis. prof. NYU, 1967-70, 84-85, 88-89, SUNY, Buffalo, 1971-72, Cornell U., 1978, Hofstra U., 1980, Albany Law Sch., 1984-90; adv., cons. on procedure Am. Arbitration Assn.; mem. N.Y. adv. com. on civil practice, 1979—, chmn., 1979-81. Author: New York Practice, 1978, 2d edit., 1991, Conflict of Laws in a Nutshell, 1982, 2d edit., 1994, Practising Law Inst. Monograph on Fed. Jurisdiction and Practice, ann. commentaries N.Y. civil practice McKinney's Consolidated Laws and fed. jurisdiction and practice U.S. Code Annotated and Federal Rules Decisions; editor: N.Y. State Law Digest, 1977—, Siegel's Practice Rev., 1993—; draftsman Appellate Division Handbook, 1979, Court of Appeals Handbook, 1981, 2d edit., 1991. Served with U.S. Army, 1953-55. Mem. Am. Law Inst., ABA, N.Y. State Bar Assn., Assn. Bar City N.Y. Jewish. Office: Albany Law Sch 80 New Scotland Ave Albany NY 12208-3434

SIEGEL, FREDERIC RICHARD, geology educator; b. Chelsea, Mass., Feb. 8, 1932; s. Louis and Eva (Minsky) S.; m. Felisa Matilde Puszkin, Mar. 3, 1962; children: Gabriela Davina, Galia Dinah. BA, Harvard U., 1954; MS, U. Kans., 1958, PhD, 1961. Prof. titular Universidad Nacional de Tucuman, Argentina, 1961-63; head geochemistry divsn. Kans. Geol. Survey, Lawrence, 1963-65; assoc. prof. geochemistry George Washington U., Washington, 1965-69, prof., 1969—, dir. geochemistry program, 1965—, chmn. dept. geology, 1976-86; tech. cons. UN Devel. program, Havana, Cuba, 1980. Author: Applied Geochemistry, 1974, Geoquimica Aplicada, 1992, Natural and Anthropogenic Hazards in Development Planning, 1996; editor: Review of Research on Modern Problems in Geochemistry, 1979. With U.S. Army, 1954-56; ETO. Recipient Erasmus Haworth award Dept. Geology, U. Kans., 1958; Fulbright prof., 1970, Best Paper award Energy Minerals divsn. Am. Assn. Petroleum Geologists, 1989. Mem. Assn. Exploration Geochemists (councillor 1988-95), Geochem. Soc., Internat. Assn. Geochemists and Cosmochemists, Soc. Environ. Geochemistry and Health. Jewish. Home: 4353 Yuma St NW Washington DC 20016-2027 Office: George Washington U 2029 G St NW Washington DC 20006-4211

SIEGEL, GEORGE HENRY, international business development consultant; b. Bklyn., Oct. 8, 1926; s. Samuel S. and Sara Siegel; m. Lenore D. Greenberg, Oct. 28, 1951; children: Arthur B., Ellen S. BEE, CCNY, 1948; M.S. in Indsl. Engring, NYU, 1951. Registered profl. engr., N.Y. From engr. to gen. mgr. Gen. Electric Corp., Syracuse, Utica and Binghamton, N.Y., 1951-74; v.p., gen. mgr. flight systems div. Bendix Corp., 1974-77, chief tech. officer, 1977-79, v.p., gen. mgr. diesel engine controls, 1979-82;

v.p., group exec. Bendix Automation Co., Cleve., 1983-84; v.p. tech. Allied-Signal Internat., Morristown, N.J., 1984-90; v.p. Volt Tech. Svcs. Co., N.Y.C., 1991-93; pres. Point North Assocs., Inc., Madison, N.J., 1990—; invited guest lectr. UCLA, 1960-63. Bd. visitors Oakland U., Rochester, Mich., 1977-83. Served with AUS, 1944-46. Mem. IEEE (sr., life, sect. chmn. 1965), Soc. Automotive Engrs. Office: Point North Assocs Inc PO Box 907 Madison NJ 07940-0907

SIEGEL, HERBERT BERNARD, certified professional management consultant; b. N.Y.C., Mar. 10, 1934; s. Jacob and Clara Dora (Goldgeier) S.; m. Joan Miriam Goodkin, Nov. 6, 1955; children—Jeffrey Roy, Lori Robin, Amy Hope, Jonathan Stuart. Degree, N.Y. U., 1959, postgrad. in bus., 1960-63; postgrad. in bus., Harvard U., 1975; PhD candidate, Columbia Pacific U., 1995. With William Iselin & Co., Inc., N.Y.C., 1957-67; treas. Bates Mfg. Co., Inc., N.Y.C., 1968; pres. Emle Industries, Inc., N.Y.C., 1968-72; fed. trustee Interstate Stores, Inc., N.Y.C., 1973-78; pres. Nat. Silver Co., N.Y.C., 1973-78, F.B. Rogers Silver Co., N.Y.C., 1979-82; pres., chief exec. officer Quaker City Steel Co., 1980-86, Seal-Kap Packaging Co., N.Y.C., 1980-90, J. Ramsey Reese, Inc., Tarrytown, N.Y., 1980-87; exec. v.p. Deerhill Devel. Corp., 1980-87, Columbia Profl. Baseball Club, Inc., 1980-87; pres., chief exec. officer J.R. Reese Enterprises, Ltd., 1989-90, New Swissco, Inc., 1991; pres. T.P.C.C.-Brandon, Inc., 1991—; prin. officer Whitestone Cons. Group, Ltd., 1991—; trustee Dime Savs. Bank of Williamsburg, N.Y.C.; thesis examiner Grad. Sch. Banking, Rutgers U., 1963-64; lectr. Grad. Sch. Mgmt. and Orgn., Yale U.; bd. dirs. N.Y. Pacific Exch. Ltd., Silvergull Industries Inc. Author: A Trustee's View of Chapter Ten, 1981, Tomorrow's America, Made Today in the U.S.A., 1993, The Masquerade of Cost Cutting, 1995, The Entropy of Government Deficits, 1995. Bd. dirs. United Cerebral Palsy, Nassau, N.Y. Served with AUS, 1955-57. Mem. Am. Mgmt. Assn., Am. Bankruptcy Inst., N.Y. Acad. Sci., NYU Alumni Club, Turnaround Mgmt. Assn., Prime Raters Fin. Club (pres.), Am. Mensa Soc., Am. Cons. League. Office: 1 E Broadway Long Beach NY 11561-4126

SIEGEL, HERBERT JAY, communications executive; b. Phila., May 7, 1928; s. Jacob and Fritzi (Stern) S.; m. Ann F. Levy, June 29, 1950; children: John C., William D. BA in Journalism, Lehigh U., 1950. Sec., dir. Official Films, Inc., N.Y.C., 1951-54; v.p., dir. Bev-Rich Products, Inc., Phila., 1955-56, Westley Industries, Inc., Cleve., 1955-58, Phila. Ice Hockey Club, Inc., 1955-60; chmn. bd. Fort Pitt Industries, Inc., Pitts., 1956-58, Seeburg Corp., 1958-60, Centlivre Brewing Corp., Ft. Wayne, Ind., 1959-61; dir. Baldwin Rubber Co., Pontiac, Mich., Mono-Sol Corp., Gary, Inc., 1959-62; chmn. bd. Baldwin-Montrose Chem. Co., 1960-67; pres. Gen. Artists Corp., 1960-64, chmn., 1960-62; chmn. bd., pres. Chris-Craft Industries, Inc., 1968—, BHC Comm. Inc., 1989—; bd. dirs. United TV, Inc., 1981—, chmn. bd., pres., 1982-95, CEO, 1983-90; bd. dirs. Warner Communications, Inc., 1984-89. Bd. dirs. Phoenix House, 1978-81; bd. advisors Vets. Bedside Network, 1980-90; v.p. Friars Nat. Assn. Found., 1980—, Chas. A. Dana Found., Inc., 1996—; trustee Lehigh U., 1989-92, Blair Acad., 1985-92. Club: Friars. Office: Chris-Craft Industries Inc 767 5th Ave Fl 46 New York NY 10153-0001

SIEGEL, HOWARD JEROME, lawyer; b. Chgo., July 29, 1942; s. Leonard and Idele (Lehrner) S.; m. Diane L. Gerber; children: Sari D., Allison J., James G. BS, U. Ill., 1963; JD, Northwestern U., 1966. Bar: Ill. 1966, U.S. dist. Ct. (no. dist.) Ill. 1967. Assoc., Ancel, Stonesifer & Glink, Chgo., 1966-70; ptnr. Goldstine & Siegel, Summit, Ill., 1970-75; sole practice, Chgo., 1975-77; pres. Wexler, Siegel & Shaw, Ltd., Chgo., 1978-82; ptnr. Keck, Mahin & Cate, Chgo., 1982-95, Neal Gerber & Eisenberg, Chgo., 1995—; dir. various corps. Mem. ABA, Chgo. Bar Assn., Ill. Bar Assn., Internat. Council Shopping Ctrs., Urban Land Inst., Chgo. Real.Estate Bd. Clubs: Standard (Chgo.); Ravisloe Country (Homewood, Ill.). Office: Neal Gerber & Eisenberg 2 N La Salle St Ste 2100 Chicago IL 60602-3801

SIEGEL, IRA T., publishing executive; b. N.Y.C., Sept. 23, 1944; s. David Aaron and Rose (Minsky) S.; m. Sharon Ruth Sacks, Sept. 5, 1965. BS, NYU, 1965; MBA, L.I. U., 1968. Bus. mgr. Buttenheim Pub. Co., N.Y.C., 1965-72; corp. v.p. rsch. Cahners Pub. Co. div. Reed Pub. USA, Boston, 1972-86; pres., COO R.R. Bowker Pub. Co. div. Reed Pub. USA, New Providence, N.J., 1986-91; pres. Martindale-Hubbell div. Reed Pub. USA, New Providence, N.J., 1990-91, Reed Reference Pub. (includes R.R. Bowker Co., Martindale-Hubbell, Nat. Register Pub. Co., The Salesman's Guide, Marquis Who's Who), New Providence, N.J., 1991-95; pres., CEO Lexis-Nexis, Dayton, Ohio, 1995—. Mem. Am. Mktg. Assn., Info. Industry Assn. Office: Lexis-Nexis PO Box 933 Dayton OH 45401

SIEGEL, JACK MORTON, retired biotechnology company executive; b. Sioux City, Iowa, June 11, 1922; s. Harry and Rose (Perlman) S.; m. Betty Virginia Collins, Feb. 22, 1946 (dec. Feb. 1986); children: Jennifer L. Mastricola, Marjorie G., Thomas A.; m. Dolores E. Williams Kinert, Dec. 20, 1991. BS in Chemistry, UCLA, 1944; PhD in Chemistry, Washington U., St. Louis, 1950. Chemist The Clinton Labs., Oak Ridge, Tenn., 1944-46; asst. prof. chemistry U. Ark. Sch. Medicine, Little Rock, 1950-55; chemist, v.p. P-L Biochems. Inc., Milw., 1955-82; v.p., gen. mgr. Pharmacia P-L Biochems. Inc., Milw., 1982-87, pres., 1987-89. Contbr. articles to profl. jours. Mem. AAAS, Am. Chem. Soc. Democrat. Jewish.

SIEGEL, JEFFREY NORTON, lawyer; b. N.Y.C., Nov. 27, 1942; s. George Siegel and Rose (Friedman) Gerber; m. Judith Sharon Chused, June 11, 1966; children: Daniel, Linda. AB, Brown U., 1964; LLB, Harvard U., 1967. Bar: N.Y. 1968. Assoc., ptnr. Golenbock & Barell, N.Y.C., 1967-89; ptnr. Whitman & Ransom, N.Y.C., 1990-93, Shack & Siegel, P.C., N.Y.C., 1993—. Mem. bus. com. The Jewish Mus. Mem. ABA, Assn. Bar City N.Y. (com. securities regulation 1987-90, com. profl. responsibility 1979-84), Phi Beta Kappa. Home: 975 Park Ave New York NY 10028 Office: Shack & Siegel PC 530 5th Ave New York NY 10036-5101

SIEGEL, JOEL STEVEN, television news correspondent; b. Los Angeles, July 7, 1943; s. Robert and Libby (Kantor) S.; m. Jane Kessler, Nov. 21, 1976 (dec. 1982); m. Melissa Nina De Mayo, Aug. 27, 1985 (div.); m. Ena Swansea, June 21, 1996. BA, UCLA, 1965, postgrad., 1966-67. Copywriter, producer Carson & Roberts Advt., Los Angeles, 1967-72; freelance writer Rolling Stone mag., Los Angeles Times, others, 1967-77; news anchorman Sta. KMET-FM, Los Angeles, 1972; corr. Sta. WCBS-TV, N.Y.C., 1972-76; corr., film critic Sta. WABC-TV, N.Y.C., 1976—, Good Morning America, N.Y.C., 1980—. Author: (Broadway mus.) The First, 1981 (Tony award nomination 1981). Dir. voter registration drive SCLC/Dr. Martin Luther King, Macon, Ga., 1965; joke writer Robert F. Kennedy, 1968. Served with USAR, 1967-73. Recipient 6 Emmy awards, numerous nominations Nat. Acad. TV Arts and Scis. (N.Y. chpt.), Freedom award B'nai Brith/Anti-Defamation League, 1976. Mem. AFTRA, Dramatists Guild, Drama Desk, Gilda's Club (founding pres.). Democrat. Jewish. Office: Good Morning Am 147 Columbus Ave New York NY 10023-5900

SIEGEL, LAURENCE GORDON, conductor; b. N.Y.C., July 23, 1931; s. Jacob and Esther (Gordon) S.; m. Luz M. Morales, Oct. 15, 1959; 1 child, Carla. BA, CCNY, 1953; MusM, New Eng. Conservatory Music, 1955. Worked with Boris Goldovsky and Leonard Bernstein Berkshire Music Ctr.; Dr. Fritz Stiedry; condr. Orquesta Sinfonica del Salvador; Symphony of the Air, N.Y.C.; condr. Orquesta Sinfonica de Las Palmas, Spain, Manila Met. Philharm. Orch. and Opera Assn., Teatro Sperimentale di Spoleto (Italy), Belgrade (Yugoslavia) Symphony, Filharmonica de Stat Oradea (Romania), Honolulu Orch., Shreveport (La.) Festival Orch., Alexandria (Va.) Symphony, Jacksonville (Fla.) Symphony and Opera Co., 1975-85, Conn. Grand Opera Co.; music dir., condr. Puccini Festival Orch., Italy, Italy, 1984; condr. Orch. of the Radio Assn. Italiana, Milan, 1985-96; music dir. North Miami Beach (Fla.) Symphony, 1976—; recorded with various record labels including Audio Team, Miller Internat., Intercord Klassiche Discothek, CTA Records Co. Ltd., Golden Master Series, Stradivari Records, Germany, Pilz Records, Germany, Madacy, Can., Delta, Germany; cons. Miami Internat. Music Competition; music dir., condr. Festival of Continents, Key West, Fla., 1990; chief condr. Osaka (Japan) Opera, 1990; music dir. Panam. Sinfonica, Miami, 1991—; guest condr. Kensington Symphony, Calif., Orch. Sinfonia de Sao Paulo, Orch. Sinfonia de Paraguay, Asuncion, R.I.A. Milano Orch., Italy, 1994, 95; music dir., condr. Hollywood (Fla.) Philharmonic, 1997. Condr. numerous operas including The Impressario, Cosi Fan Tutte, La Perchole, Don Pasquale, Faust, I Pagliacci, Samson and Dalila, Madame Butterfly, Tosca, La Boheme, Elisir D. Amore, Hansel and Gretl, La Traviata, Fledermaus, Otello, Rigoletto, Il Trovatore, Carmen, Ernani, Merry Widow, Lucia di Lammermoor, Grafin Mariza; condr. albums Tschaikovsky with the New Philharm. Orch. London, Mozart Symphony 41, recs. with London Philharm., London Festival Orch., Royal Philharm. Recipient numerous citations and medals Country of Italy; named hon. Dr. of Music, London, Paris, Knight of Templar Order of Germany.

SIEGEL, LAWRENCE IVER, real estate development company executive; b. Cleve., Aug. 19, 1925; s. Edward I. and Mary (Mentz) S.; BBA, Western Res. U., 1949, LLB, 1952; m. Joyce Reske, Nov. 4, 1950; children—Leslie, Diane, Frederick, Edward. Pres., Lawrence I. Siegel Co., Baton Rouge, 1980—; chmn. bd. Lisscorp. Inc. Bd. dirs. Tara High Sch. Backers, Baton Rouge, Community Concerts Assn., New Orleans; Cub Scout master, 1967-68. Served with inf. U.S. Army, 1943-46; ETO, PTO. Col. on Staff of gov. La. Decorated Combat Inf. Badge Bronze Star. Mem Internat. Council Shopping Centers, Mortgage Bankers Assn. Am., Am. Bankers Assn., U.S. C. of C., Baton Rouge C. of C. Club: Kiwanis. Home: 7844-A Jefferson Place Blvd Baton Rouge LA 70809 Office: 10455 Jefferson Hwy Baton Rouge LA 70809-2732

SIEGEL, LLOYD HARVEY, architect, real estate developer, consultant; b. N.Y.C., Nov. 27, 1928; s. Saul M. and Lillian (Bell) S.; m. Margot Kopsidas Phillips, Oct. 25, 1987. BArch., Princeton U., 1949; MArch., MIT, 1953. Registered architect, N.Y., N.J., Conn., Ohio, Ill., Mich. Designer Skidmore, Owings & Merrill, then I. M. Pei & Assocs., then Antonin Raymond, N.Y.C., 1955-60; assoc. Kelly & Gruzen, N.Y.C., 1960-66; dep. health services adminstr. City of N.Y., 1966-70; dep. exec. dir. health and hosps. governing commn. Cook County, Chgo., 1970-76; prin. L.H.S. Cons. in Health Planning, Facility Design & Mgmt., Washington, 1976—, Siegel & Schroeder, P.C., Chgo., 1983-87; dir. Office Architecture & Engring., VA, Washington, 1987-94; dir. Facilities Quality Office VA, Washington, 1994—; prin. Yacht Harbor Devel. Co., South Haven, Mich., 1983-88, Siegel & Schroeder Developers Inc., Chgo., 1984-88; mem. adv. coms. HEW; mem. pub. adv. panels GSA; mem. adv. com. Legislature State of Ill.; mem. fellowship evaluation com. AIA-Am. Hosp. Assn.; mem. tech. adv. com. to Northeastern Ill. Planning Commn.; chmn. Com. on Architecture for Health, 1984. Author: Hidden Asset? Interstitial Space, A Critical Evaluation, 1987; photography in permanent collections Met. Mus. Art, N.Y.C., Mus. Modern Art, N.Y.C., others; prin. works include N.Y. World's Fair Spanish Pavilion, N.Y.C. (N.Y. chpt. AIA award 1964), Williams Meml. Residence, Flushing, N.Y. (Queens C. of C. award 1964), Hebrew Home for Aged, Riverdale, N.Y. (Bronx C. of C. award 1966). Fulbright fellow Università di Roma, 1954, Politecnico di Milano, 1955. Fellow AIA; mem. Urban Land Inst., The Arts Club, Univ. Club. Avocations: micology, microphagy, oenology. Home: 3133 Connecticut Ave NW Washington DC 20008-5147 Office: VA 810 Vermont Ave NW Washington DC 20420-0001

SIEGEL, LOUIS PENDLETON, forest products executive; b. Richmond, Va., Nov. 6, 1942; s. John Boschen Jr. and Francis Beale (Tyler) S.; m. Nancy Dicks Blanton, Apr. 10, 1974 (dec. July 1976); m. Nancy Northon, June 26, 1982; children: Kathryn Tyler. AB in Econs., Dartmouth Coll., 1967. Asst. cashier, security researcher First Nat. Citibank, N.Y.C., 1967-71; v.p. security rsch. Drexel Burnham Lambert, N.Y.C., 1971-79; with Potlatch Corp., San Francisco, 1979—, sr. v.p. fin. and adminstrn., 1989, group v.p. wood products and corp. planning, 1989-92, group v.p. pulp and paperboard and corp. planning, 1992-93, exec. v.p. pulp-based ops. and corp. planning, 1993-94, pres., COO, 1994—; bd. dirs. San Francisco Fed. Corp., 1985-96. Pres., bd. dir. Bay Area Sci. Fair, San Francisco, 1989-90; bd. dirs. Bay Area Coun. With USCG, 1964-65. Republican. Episcopalian. Avocations: golf, tennis, fishing. Office: Potlatch Corp 1 Maritime Plz San Francisco CA 94111-3404

SIEGEL, LUCY BOSWELL, public relations executive; b. N.Y.C., July 5, 1950; d. Werner Leiser and Carol (Fleischer) Boswell; m. Henry Winter Siegel, Nov. 11, 1979 (div.); children: David Alan Siegel, Joshua Adam Siegel. BA, Conn. Coll., 1972. Assoc. editor Conn. Western, Litchfield, Conn., 1972-73; assoc. editor, editor United Bus. Publ., N.Y.C., 1974-78; mgr. external communications Equitable Life Assurance Soc., N.Y.C., 1978-86; mgr. internat. affairs Cosmo Pub. Relations Corp., Tokyo, Japan, 1986-87; dir. internat. affairs Cosmo Pub. Relations Corp., Tokyo, 1987-88; pres. Cosmo Pub. Rels. Corp., N.Y.C., 1988-90, Siegel Assocs. Internat., N.Y.C., 1990—; bd. dirs. Cosmo Pub. Rels. Corp., Tokyo, N.Y.C., 1987-91. Contbr. articles to jours. and mags. Bd. dirs., sec. Am. Jewish Com. (N.Y.C. chpt.) 1993—. Mem. Pub. Rels. Soc. Am., Women Execs. in Pub. Rels., Japan Soc. Democrat. Jewish. Home: 41 W 96th St Apt 12B New York NY 10025-6519 Office: Siegel Assocs Internat Ltd 38 E 29th St Fl 7 New York NY 10016-7911

SIEGEL, MARC MONROE, television and film producer, writer, director; b. N.Y.C., Dec. 8, 1916; s. Isaac and Annie N. (Natelson) S.; m. Anne Dorothy Fishman, Sept. 8, 1940; 1 son, Peter Kieve. B.A., Washington Sq. Coll., 1936; M.A., N.Y. U. Sch. Edn., 1938. Free-lance mag. writer, especially for: New Yorker mag, 1948-50; writer: Eternal Light radio series, NBC, N.Y.C., 1950-60; writer-dir-producer: Directions, ABC-TV, N.Y.C., 1961-78; exec. producer chief writer: Heritage: Civilization and the Jews, WNET, N.Y.C., 1978-84; author: feature screenplays A Child is Crying, 1961, The Young Adventurers, 1963; ABC News Bicentennial spls. Rendezvous With Freedom, 1973, The Right to Believe, 1975, The Will to Be Free, 1976; ABC News feature The Panama Canal, 1977 (Writers Guild award); (Recipient numerous awards, including: Edinburgh Film Festival award 1948, Venice Film Festival award 1962, Cannes Film Festival award 1964, Eternal Light award Jewish Theol. Sem. Am. 1969). Served with USAAF, 1943-45. Peabody award, 1979, 84; Gabriel award Nat. Assn. Catholic Broadcasters, 1979; Emmy award, 1984, Christopher award, 1984; also several awards Freedoms Found. Mem. Nat. Acad. TV Arts and Scis., Writers Guild Am. East (council 1972-73, 78-79, 84-88, awards 1959, 73, 78, 85, Jablow Meml. award 1988), Dirs. Guild Am. Democrat. Home: 75 Central Park W New York NY 10023-6011

SIEGEL, MARTIN JAY, lawyer, investment advisor; b. N.Y.C., Apr. 12, 1942; s. Barney and Ruth (Baer) S. BA in Econs., Mich. State U., 1963; JD, Bklyn. Law Sch., 1966; MBA in Fin., Fordham U., 1980. Served to col. U.S. Army, 1966—, commd. 2d lt., 1966; advanced through grades to col., 1991, ret., 1996; fin. advisor, pvt. practice law, N.Y.C., 1971—. Col. USAR, 1990—. Office: 150 Broadway Rm 1400 New York NY 10038-4401

SIEGEL, MARVIN, newspaper editor; b. N.Y.C., June 23, 1935; s. Murray and Belle (Diamond) S.; 1 child, Joshua Murray. BA, U. Mich., 1957. Reporter The Record, Hackensack, N.J., 1957-59; free-lance writer Western Europe, 1960-62; reporter Fairchild Publs., N.Y.C., 1962-63; editor The World Telegram, N.Y.C., 1963-66; copy editor The N.Y. Times, 1966-67, asst. met. editor, 1967-76, founding editor Weekend sect., 1976-82; founding editor World of N.Y., 1982-86; founding editor Edn. Life The N.Y. Times, 1986, dep. editor Week in Rev., 1987, culture news editor, 1988-92, dep. editor Book Rev., 1992-95; asst. to mng. editor, 1995—. Co-author: The World of New York, 1985, The New York Times: Great Lives of the 20th Century, 1988; editor: The Seven Deadly Sins, 1994, The Last Word: The New York Times Book of Obituaries and Farewells, 1997. Pfc. U.S. Army. Jewish. Office: NY Times Co 229 W 43d St New York NY 10036-3913

SIEGEL, MICHAEL ELLIOT, nuclear medicine physician, educator; b. N.Y.C., May 13, 1942; s. Benjamin and Rose (Gilbert) S.; m. Marsha Rose Snower, Mar. 20, 1966; children: Herrick Jove, Meridith Ann. AB, Cornell U., 1964; MD, Chgo. Med. Sch., 1968. Diplomate Nat. Bd. Med. Examiners. Intern Cedars-Sinai Med. Ctr., L.A., 1968-69; resident in radiology, 1969-70; NIH fellow in radiology Temple U. Med. Ctr., Phila., 1970-71; NIH fellow in nuclear medicine Johns Hopkins U. Sch. Medicine, Balt., 1971-73, asst. prof. radiology, 1972-76; assoc. prof. radiology, medicine U. So. Calif., L.A., 1976—; prof. radiology, 1989—, dir. divsn. nuclear medicine, 1982—; dir. Sch. Nuclear Medicine, L.A. County-U. So. Calif. Med. Ctr., 1976—; dir. divsn. nuclear medicine Kenneth Norris Cancer Hosp. and Rsch. Ctr., L.A., 1983—; dir. dept. nuclear medicine Orthopaedic Hosp., L.A., 1981—, Intercommunity Hosp., Covina, Calif., 1981—, U. So. Calif. Univ. Hosp., L.A., 1993—; cons. dept. nuclear medicine Rancho Los Amigos Hosp., Downey, Calif., 1976—. Author: Textbook of Nuclear Medicine, 1978, Vascular Surgery, 1983, 88, and numerous others textbooks; editor: Nuclear Cardiology, 1981, Vascular Disease: Nuclear Medicine, 1983. Mem. Maple Ctr., Beverly Hills. Served as maj. USAF, 1974-76. Recipient Outstanding Alumnus award Chgo. Med. Sch., 1991. Fellow Am. Coll. Nuclear Medicine (sci. investigator 1974, 76, nominations com. 1980, program com. 1983, bd. trustees 1993, disting. fellow, 1993, bd. reps., 1993—, bd. dirs. 1994—, treas. 1996—, ann. sci. program chmn. 1996—); mem. Soc. Nuclear Medicine (sci. exhbn. com. 1978-79, program com. 1979-80, Silver medal 1975), Calif. Med. Assn. (sci. adv. bd. 1987—), Radiol. Soc. N.Am., Soc. Nuclear Magnetic Resonance Imaging, Alpha Omega Alpha. Lodge: Friars So. Calif. Research on devel. of nuclear medicine techniques to: evaluate cardiovascular disease and diagnose and treat cancer, clinical utilization of video digital displays in nuclear medicine development; inventor pneumatic radiologic pressure system. Office: U So Calif Med Ctr PO Box 693 1200 N State St Los Angeles CA 90033

SIEGEL, NATHANIEL HAROLD, sociology educator; b. Bklyn., May 17, 1929; s. Victor and Yetta (Kogel) S.; m. Annabelle Replansky, Mar. 3, 1958; children—Anthony, Jennifer. A.B., Bklyn. Coll., 1950; A.M., N.Y.U., 1952, Ph.D., 1956. Asst. prof. sociology Columbia, 1956-59; sociologist Hillside Hosp., Queens, N.Y., 1958-63; assoc. dir. behavioral research N.Y.C. Dept. Health, 1963-64; chief social sci. tng. sect. NIMH, 1964-67, cons., 1970-79; prof. sociology Queens Coll., 1967-79, chmn. dept., 1967-70, v.p., dean faculty, 1970-74, provost, 1974-77, acting pres., 1977-78; sr. v.p. acad. affairs SUNY Purchase, 1979-94; prof. sociology SUNY, 1979—. Served with M.C. AUS, 1950-51. Home: 8 Birchfield Rd Larchmont NY 10538-1505 Office: SUNY Dept Sociology Purchase NY 10577

SIEGEL, NORMAN JOSEPH, pediatrician, educator; b. Houston, Mar. 8, 1943; m. Rise Joan Ross, Dec. 24, 1967; children: Andrew, Karen. BA, Tulane U., 1964; MA, U. Tex. Med. Br., Galveston, 1968, MD, 1968. Intern, then resident Yale-New Haven Hosp., 1968-70; fellow Sch. Medicine, Yale U., New Haven, 1970-72, asst. prof. pediatrics and medicine, 1972-76, assoc. prof., 1976-82, prof., 1982—, vice chmn. pediatrics, 1979—; acting chmn. pediats. Yale U., 1995-97; physician-in-chief Yale-New Haven Children's Hosp. Contbr. articles to profl. jours., chpts. to books. Grantee NIH, Am. Heart Assn., Hood Found. Mem. Am. Pediatric Soc. (sec.-treas. 1993—), Am. Soc. Pediatric Nephrology (pres. 1988-89), Nat. Kidney Found. (chmn. com. on pediatric nephrology and urology 1987-91, grantee, scientific adv. com. 1988-91), Soc. Pediatric Rsch. (membership sec. 1979-85), Nat. Bd. Med. Examiners (pediatric test com. 1993-95), Phi Beta Kappa, Mu Delta. Office: Yale U Sch Medicine Dept Pediatrics 333 Cedar St PO Box 208064 New Haven CT 06520-8064

SIEGEL, PATRICIA ANN, association management consultant; b. Louisville, Mar. 29, 1955; d. Roy John and Theresa (Preate) S. BS in Human Svcs., U. Scranton, 1977; M Psychosocial Sci., Pa. State U., 1982, cert. cmty. psychologist, 1982. Field rep. Am. Cancer Soc., Bethlehem, Pa., 1978-80; teen dir. YWCA, Harrisburg, Pa., 1980-82; mgr. membership devel. AAUW, Washington, 1982-85; mgr. membership Boat Owners Assn. U.S. (BOAT/US), Alexandria, Va., 1985-88; asst. v.p. leadership and membership devel. Nat. Assn. Home Builders, Washington, 1988-95; prin. Siegel & Assocs. Internat., San Francisco, 1995—; founder, exec. dir. Ctr. for Excellence in Assn. Leadership; cons. to membership-based assns., San Francisco, 1995—. Contbg. author: The National-Chapter Partnership, 1993; contbr. articles to profl. publs. Mem. Am. Soc. Assn. Execs. (cert., trainer, presenter confs. and meetings 1990-95, bd. dirs. 1993-95, edn. com. 1995, charter chmn. chpt. rels. sect. 1993-95, award of membership excellence in membership 1992, cert. assn. exec. 1990). Avocations: fitness walking, reading, travel. Office: 236 W Portal Ave # 136 San Francisco CA 94127-1423

SIEGEL, RICHARD DAVID, lawyer, former government official; b. Lewistown, Pa., Oct. 13, 1939; s. Robert and Pearl Eleanor (Nieman) S.; m. Marjorie Esther Greenwald, Mar. 13, 1966; children—Andrew, Jonathan, Michele. B.A., U. Pa., 1960; J.D., Harvard U., 1963. Bar: Pa., D.C., U.S. Supreme Ct. Staff writer Phila. Inquirer, 1964-66; spl. asst. U.S. Rep. Richard Schweiker, Washington, 1966-69; legis. counsel U.S. Senator Richard Schweiker, Washington, 1969-71; assoc. minority counsel Senate Com. on Labor and Human Resources, Washington, 1971-73; sole practice Washington, 1978-79, mem. various firms, 1973-78, 80-81; dep. asst. sec. for natural resources and environment USDA, Washington, 1981-87; pvt. practice, Washington, 1987—. Contbr. articles to profl. jours. Treas. Com. for Senator Schweiker, Washington, 1974; mem. nat. coun. Am. Israel Pub. Affairs Com., Washington, 1974-77; v.p. Tifereth Israel Congregation, Washington, 1980-82, 93—; sec.-treas. North Am.-Israel Hort. Found., 1987-95. With USCGR, 1963-64. Mem. ABA, FBA, Pa. Bar Assn., Assn. Former Senate Aides. Republican. Jewish. Home: 3141 Aberfoyle Pl NW Washington DC 20015-2325 Office: 1400 16th St NW Washington DC 20036-2217

SIEGEL, RICHARD LAWRENCE, allergist, immunologist, pediatrician; b. Miami, Fla., Jan. 22, 1949. MD, Washington U., St. Louis, 1977; also PhD. Diplomate Am. Bd. Allergy and Immunology, Am. Bd. Diagnostic Lab. Immunology, Am. Bd. Pediats. Resident in pediats. Children's Hosp. Med. Ctr., Boston, 1977-79, fellow in allergy and immunology, 1979-81; now with U. Comm. Hosp., Tampa, Fla. Fellow AIS; mem. Am. Acad. Pediats., Am. Acad. Allergy and Immunology, Am. Coll. Allergy and Immunology. Office: 3450 E Fletcher Ave Ste 210 Tampa FL 33613-4600

SIEGEL, ROBERT, heat transfer engineer; b. Cleve., July 10, 1927; s. Morris and Mollie (Binder) S.; m. Elaine Jane Jaffe, July 19, 1951; children: Stephen, Lawrence. BS, Case Inst. Tech., 1950, MS, 1951; ScD, MIT, 1953. Heat transfer engr. GE, Schenectady, N.Y., 1953-54; heat transfer analyst Knolls Atomic Power Lab., Schenectady, 1954-55; rsch. scientist NASA Lewis Rsch. Ctr., Cleve., 1955—; adj. prof. U. Toledo, 1981, 85, 95, adj. prof. mech. engring. U. Akron (Ohio), 1987, adj. prof. mech. engring. Cleve. State U., 1989, 91; mem. adv. coun. U. Akron, 1989—. Author: Thermal Radiation Heat Transfer, 1972, 3d edit., 1992; tech. editor ASME, 1973-83, AIAA, 1986—; author numerous sci. papers. With U.S. Army, 1945-47. Recipient Exceptional Sci. Achievement medal NASA, 1986, Space Act award, 1993, ASME-AIChE Max Jakob Meml. award, 1996. Fellow ASME (Heat Transfer Meml. award 1970), AIAA (Thermophysics award 1993); mem. Sigma Xi, Tau Beta Pi. Jewish. Avocations: ballroom dancing, piano. Home: 3052 Warrington Rd Cleveland OH 44120-2425 Office: NASA Lewis Rsch Ctr 21000 Brookpark Rd Cleveland OH 44135-3127

SIEGEL, ROBERT CHARLES, broadcast journalist; b. N.Y.C., June 26, 1947; s. Joseph and Edith Ruth (Joffe) S.; m. Jane Claudia Schwartz, June 17, 1973; children: Erica Anne, Leah Harriet. BA, Columbia U., 1968, postgrad. sch. journalism, 1969-70. Newscaster Sta. WGLI, Babylon, N.Y., 1968-69; reporter, news dir. Sta. WRVR-FM, N.Y.C., 1971-76; assoc. producer, editor Nat. Pub. Radio, Washington, 1976-78, sr. editor, 1976-79, dir. news and info., 1983-87, host All Things Considered, 1987—; sr. editor Nat. Pub. Radio, London, 1979-83; host Ea. Europe: Breaking with the Past, The Learning Channel, Washington, 1990, Earth Scope, Arlington, Va., 1990-91. Editor: The NPR Interviews. Recipient DuPont-Columbia award Columbia U., 1984. Jewish. Avocations: reading, golf, baseball. Home: 1340 19th Rd S Arlington VA 22202-1637 Office: Nat Pub Radio All Things Considered 635 Massachusetts Ave NW Washington DC 20001-3752

SIEGEL, ROBERT TED, physicist; b. Springfield, Mass., June 10, 1928; s. Charles V.D. and Ida B. Siegel; m. Rebecca Weisberg, June 14, 1951; children: Carol D., Naomi L., Joan E., Jonathan D., Richard M.; m. Wendy P. Kramer. BS, Carnegie-Mellon U., 1948, MS, 1950, DS, 1952. Research assoc. Carnegie Mellon U., 1952-57, asst. prof. physics, 1957-60, assoc. prof., 1960-63; prof. Coll. William and Mary, 1963—, W.F.C. Ferguson prof. physics, 1979—, dean grad. studies, 1965-67, dir. space radiation effects lab., 1967-79. Fellow Am. Phys. Soc.; mem. AAAS, AAUP. Jewish. Office: Coll William and Mary Physics Dept Williamsburg VA 23185

SIEGEL, SAMUEL, metals company executive; b. Elizabeth, N.J., Oct. 30, 1930; s. Morris and Anna (Fader) S.; m. Raenea Kershenbaum, Mar. 29, 1953; children: Daryl Lynn, Annie Roslyn. BBA, CUNY, 1952. CPA, N.Y. Cost accountant Seaporcel Metals, Inc., Long Island City, N.Y., 1955-56; asst. to controller Deltown Foods, Inc., Yonkers, N.Y., 1956-57; sr. accountant DeLoitte & Touche, N.Y.C., 1957-61; vice chmn., chief fin. officer, treas., sec., dir. Nucor Corp., Charlotte, N.C., 1961—. Mem. AICPA, Am. Soc. Corp. Secs., Fin. Execs. Inst. Home: 3421 Windbluff Dr Charlotte NC 28277-9850 Office: Nucor Corp 2100 Rexford Rd Charlotte NC 28211-3484

SIEGEL, SARAH ANN, lawyer; b. Providence, Aug. 29, 1956. BA in History cum laude, Brandeis U., 1978; JD, Washington U., St. Louis, 1981. Bar: Mo. 1982, U.S. Dist. Ct. (ea. dist.) Mo. 1983. Assoc. atty. St. Louis, 1982-83; staff atty. Land Clearance for Redevel. Authority, St. Louis, 1983-85, gen. counsel, 1985-88; gen. counsel Econ. Devel. Corp., St. Louis, 1988-90, St. Louis Devel. Corp., 1990-91; spl. counsel for devel. City of St. Louis, 1991-92; assoc. Suelthaus & Walsh, P.C., St. Louis, 1992-95, prin., 1995—. Pres. Central Reform Congregation, St. Louis, 1991-93, v.p., 1989-91, bd. dirs. 1987-89. Mem. ABA, Mo. Bar Assn. (vice chair com. on eminent domain 1990-91, steering com. 1987-89, 95-96), Women's Lawyer Assn. (bd. dirs. 1985-90, v.p. 1989-90). Avocations: hiking, swimming. Office: Suelthaus & Walsh PC 7733 Forsyth Blvd Fl 12 Saint Louis MO 63105-1817

SIEGEL, SHELDON C., physician; b. Mpls., Jan. 30, 1922; s. Carl S.; m. Priscilla Rikess, Mar. 3, 1946; children—Linda, Nancy. A.A., Va. Jr. Coll., 1940; B.A., B.S., U. Minn., 1942, M.D., 1945. Intern U. Minn. Hosp., 1946, resident in pediatrics, 1947-48; fellow in pediatric allergy Rochester, N.Y., 1949-50; practice medicine specializing in pediatric allergy and pediatrics St. Paul, 1950-52, San Antonio, 1952-54, Los Angeles, 1954—; clin. instr. pediatrics U. Rochester, 1949-50, U. Minn., 1950-51; asst. prof. pediatrics U. Tex., 1952-54; asst. clin. prof. U. Calif. at Los Angeles Med. Sch., 1955, clin. asso. prof., 1957-62, clin. prof., 1963—, co-chief pediatric allergy clinic, 1957—; mem. staff Harbor Gen. Hosp., Torrance, Calif., Daniel Freeman Hosp., Inglewood, Calif., Centinela Valley Community Hosp., Inglewood, Hawthorne (Calif.) Community Hosp. Editorial bd.: Jour. Allergy, 1973-75; contbr. articles to med. jours. Fellow Am. Acad. Allergy (pres. 1974), Am. Coll. Allergists, Am. Acad. Pediatrics; mem. AMA, Allergy Found. Am. (pres. 1976), Calif., Los Angeles County med. assns., Los Angeles Pediatric Soc., Calif., Los Angeles socs. allergy, Western Pediatric Research Soc., Am. Bd. Med. Specialists, Sigma Xi. Office: 11620 Wilshire Blvd Los Angeles CA 90025-1706

SIEGEL, SID, composer, lyricist; b. Chgo., Jan. 20, 1927; s. Michael and Rose (Wolfson) S.; m. Carrie Patricia Zeigler, May 18, 1952; children: David, Jodi, Mark. BMus in Composition, Roosevelt Coll., Chgo., 1950. Composer-lyricist for local TV shows, nightclub performers and popular songs, also commls. for radio and TV, nightclub shows; composer-lyricist, arranger, condr. for radio and TV commls., films, slide presentations, industry shows.; (Recipient numerous awards for music for commls. and films including Cindy Indsl. Film Producers Am. and Capa Chgo. Audio-Visual Producers Assn.). With USNR, 1945-46. Mem. ASCAP, Am. Fedn. Musicians. Address: 326 Satinwood Ct N Buffalo Grove IL 60089-6611

SIEGEL, STANLEY, lawyer, educator; b. N.Y.C., Mar. 2, 1941; s. David Aaron and Rose (Minsky) S.; m. Karina Haum, July 20, 1986. B.S. summa cum laude, NYU, 1960; J.D. magna cum laude, Harvard U., 1963. Bar: N.Y. 1963, D.C. 1964, Mich. 1970, Calif. 1976; CPA, Md. Atty. Office Sec. of Air Force, 1963-66; asst. prof. law U. Mich., Ann Arbor, 1966-69, assoc. prof., 1969-71, prof., 1971-74; ptnr. Honigman, Miller, Schwartz & Cohn, Detroit, 1974-76; prof. law UCLA, 1976-86; prof. law NYU, 1986—, assoc. dean, 1987-89; vis. prof. Stanford Law Sch., 1973, Ctrl. European U., Budapest, 1993—, U. Konstanz, Germany, 1996; fellow Max-Planck Inst., Hamburg, 1988; cons. reorgn. U.S. Postal Svc., 1969-71; exec. sec. Mich. Law Revision Commn., 1973; mem. bd. examiners AICPA, 1980-83; mem. editl. bd. Lexis Electronic Author's Press, 1996—. Author: (with Schulman and Moscow) Michigan Business Corporations, 1979, (with Conard and Knauss) Enterprise Organization, 4th edit., 1987, (with D. Siegel) Accounting and Financial Disclosure: A Guide to Basic Concepts, 1983, (with others) Swiss Company Law, 1996. Served to capt. USAF, 1963-66. Mem. ABA, D.C. Bar Assn., Calif. Bar Assn., Assn. of Bar of City of N.Y., Am. Law Inst., AICPA. Office: NYU Law Sch 40 Washington Sq S New York NY 10012-1005

SIEGEL, STEVEN DOUGLAS, oncologist; b. Mt. Vernon, N.Y., Oct. 26, 1950; s. Arthur Bernard and Edith Mildred (Kleinman) S.; m. Betsy Daniel, June 27, 1987; children: Zoe Elizabeth, Satchel Armond. BA, SUNY, Albany, 1972; MD, Loyola U., Maywood, Ill., 1983. Diplomate Am. Bd. Internal Medicine, Am. Bd. Med. Oncology. Physician North Fla. Hem. Onc. Assocs., Jacksonville, 1988—. Office: North Fla Hem Onc Assocs 1801 Barrs St Ste 800 Jacksonville FL 32204-4751

SIEGEL, SYLVIA, law librarian; b. Siberia, Russia, Mar. 8, 1946; came to U.S., 1950; d. Harry and Greta (Gersten) S. AA of Law Libr., Columbia U., 1968. Law libr. Weil Gotshal Manges, N.Y.C., 1963—. Mem. Am. Libr. Assn., N.Y. Libr. Assn., Law Libr. Assn. Greater N.Y. (chair pro bono com.), Spl. Librs. Assn. Jewish. Avocations: theatre, art shows, reading. Home: 238 6th Ave Brooklyn NY 11215-2149 Office: Weil Gotshal & Manges 767 5th Ave New York NY 10153-0001

SIEGEL, THOMAS LOUIS, lawyer; b. N.Y.C., Oct. 7, 1939; s. Jack M. and Helen S. (Simpson) S.; m. Ruth L. Rosenthal, June 23, 1963; children: Peter, Karen. B.A., Rutgers U., 1961; J.D., Cornell U., 1964. Bar: N.Y. 1964, D.C. 1967, Tex. 1982. Atty. advisor Office of Gen. Counsel, FHA, Washington, 1968; assoc. mem. firm Arent, Fox, Kintner, Plotkin & Kahn, Washington, 1968-70; gen. counsel Group Health Assn., Inc., 1970-74; ptnr. Diuguid, Siegel & Kennelly, Washington, 1974-80; gen. counsel, div. fed. law and regulation Am. Hosp. Assn., 1980—; pvt. practice Dallas, 1982—; legal counsel St. Paul Hosp., Dallas; legal cons. div. organizational devel. HEW, 1974-80. Pres. bd. trustees St. Luke's House, Bethesda, Md. Served with USAF, 1965-67. Mem. N.Y. State Bar Assn., Tex. Bar Assn., Bar Assn. D.C., Dallas Bar Assn., Nat. Health Lawyers Assn., Rutgers, Cornell U. alumni assns. Home: 3739 Waldorf Dr Dallas TX 75229-3937 Office: 4100 Mcewen Rd Ste 285 Dallas TX 75244-5184

SIEGELMAN, DON EUGENE, state official; b. Mobil, Ala., Feb. 24, 1946; m. Lori Allen; c. Dana, Joseph. B.A., U. Ala.; J.D., Georgetown U., 1972; postgrad., Oxford U., Eng., 1972-73. Bar: Ala. 1972. Sec. of state State of Ala., Montgomery, 1979-87, atty. gen., 1987-94; lt. gov. State of Ala., 1996—. Office: Office of Lt Gov 11 S Union St Montgomery AL 36104-3760

SIEGER, CHARLES, librarian; b. Fountain Hill, Pa., Dec. 9, 1944; s. Charles Franklin and Kathryn (Farny) S.; m. Deborah Day Malone, May 13, 1972; children: C. Alexander, Meredith Kathryn. BA History, Wesleyan U., 1969; student, Duke U., 1969-71; MS Libr. Sci., UNC, 1979. Reference, U.S. Documents libr. Fairleigh Dickinson U., Rutherford, N.J., 1980-83, asst. dir. tech. svcs., 1983-85, assoc. dir., 1985-92, dir., 1992-94; dir. Lyndhurst (N.J.) Free Pub. Libr., 1994—. Contbr. articles to World Book ency., legal jours; contbr. chpts. to books. Coach, v.p., then pres. Lyndhurst Youth Soccer Club; treas. Minolta Suburban Youth Soccer League; mem. parent adv. com. Lyndhurst H.S.; v.p. Lipton Youth Soccer. With U.S. Army, 1966-68, Vietnam. Mem. ALA, Govt. Documents Roundtable, Documents Assn. N.J., Inc. Avocation: soccer. Home: 216 Stuyvesant Ave Apt 12 Lyndhurst NJ 07071-1707 Office: Lyndhurst Free Pub Libr 355 Valley Brook Ave Lyndhurst NJ 07071-1810

SIEGERT, BARBARA (MARIE), health care administrator; b. Boston, May 22, 1935; d. Salvatore Mario and Mary Kathleen (Wagner) Tartaglia; m. Herbert C. Siegert (dec. Apr. 1974); children: Carolyn Marie, Herbert Christian Jr. Diploma, Newton-Wellesley (Mass.) Hosp. Sch. Nursing, 1956; MEd, Antioch U., 1980. Diplomate Am. Bd. Med. Psychotherapists. Supr. nursing Hogan Regional Ctr., Hathorne, Mass., 1974-78; community mental health nursing advisor Cape Ann area office Dept. Mental Health, Beverly, Mass., 1978-79; dir. case mgmt. Dept. Mental Health, Beverly, 1979-87, dir. case mgmt. north shore area office, 1988-91; dir. case mgmt. Dept. Mental Health-north shore area-Lynn (Mass.) site, Lynn, Mass., 1991-92; mem. interdisciplinary faculty, profl. cons. com., lecture staff clin. pastoral counseling program Danvers State Hosp./Hogan/Berry Regional Ctrs., Hathorne, Mass., 1982-86; nursing edn. adv. com. North Shore Community Coll., Beverly, 1983-91; tng. staff Balter Inst., Ipswich, Mass., 1987-88. Mem. Internat. Cultural Diploma Honor, 1989—. Recipient Spl. Recognition award Lexington (Mass.) Pub. Schs., 1973, Peter Torci award Lexington Friends of Children in Spl. Edn., 1974; named Internat. Biog. Roll. of Honor, 1989—. Fellow Am. Biog. Inst. (life, Woman of Yr. 1990); mem. World Inst. Achievement. Home: 63 Willow Rd # B Boxford MA 01921-1218

SIEGESMUND, KENNETH AUGUST, forensic anatomist, consultant, educator; b. Milw., Nov. 28, 1932; s. August Emil and Martha Laura (Schwarz) S.; m. Patricia Diane Dreyer, Apr. 15, 1959; children: Mark, Sandra, Carolyn, John. BS, U. Wis., 1954, PhD, 1960. Rsch. assoc. Marquette U., Milw., 1960-62; asst. prof. anatomy Med. Coll. Wis., Milw., 1962-69, assoc. prof., 1969—; cons. Milwaukee County Hosp., 1962-67, VA Hosp., Milw., 1963-78, Trinity Hosp., Milw., 1977-86, St. Lukes Hosp., Milw., 1982-85. Contbr. numerous articles to profl. jours.; patentee in field. NIH grantee, 1985, 86-88, 89. Mem. Electron Microscope Soc. Am., Midwest Microscope Soc. Am. (pres. 1970-71), Am. Assn. Anatomy, Am. Acad. Forensic Sci., Neuroelectric Soc. Am., Casal Club. Avocations: photography, bridge, skiing, astronomy, chess. Home: 17825 Primrose Ln Brookfield WI 53045-1231 Office: Med Coll Wis 8701 W Watertown Plank Rd Milwaukee WI 53226-3548

SIEGFRIED, DAVID CHARLES, lawyer; b. N.Y.C., Feb. 15, 1942; s. Charles Albert and Marjorie Claire (Young) S.; m. Meri Stephanie Smith; children: Karin Elisabeth, Christine Elise. AB summa cum laude, Princeton U., 1964; JD, Harvard U., 1967. Bar: N.Y. 1970. Assoc. Milbank, Tweed, Hadley & McCloy, N.Y.C., 1968-76, ptnr., 1977-79, 83-85, 88—; resident ptnr. Milbank, Tweed, Hadley & McCloy, Hong Kong and Singapore, 1979-83, 85-88; bd. dirs. PALS; speaker at confs. and seminars. Served to 1st lt. USAR, 1967-74. Mem. ABA, Am. Soc. Internat. Law, South African Profl. Devel. Program (steering com.), Internat. Bar Assn., N.Y. State Bar Assn., Assn. of Bar of City of N.Y., Millburn-Short Hills Hist. Soc. (v.p.). Congregationalist. Clubs: Princeton (New York), Short Hills (N.J.), Am. (Hong Kong/Singapore), Tanglin (Singapore), Cricket. Avocations: running, tennis, historic reading. Home: 30 Western Dr Short Hills NJ 07078-3230

SIEGFRIED, TOM, newspaper editor. Sci. editor Dallas Morning News. Office: The Dallas Morning News Communications Ctr 508 Young St PO Box 655237 Dallas TX 75265-5237*

SIEGLER, MARK, internist, educator; b. N.Y.C., June 20, 1941; s. Abraham J. and Florence (Sternlieb) S.; m. Anna Elizabeth Hollinger, June 4, 1967; children:Dillan, Alison, Richard, Jessica. AB with honors, Princeton U., 1963; MD, U. Chgo., 1967. Diplomate Am. Bd. Internal Medicine. Resident, chief resident internal medicine U. Chgo., 1967-71; hon. sr. registrar in medicine Royal Postgrad. Med. Sch., London, 1971-72; asst. prof. medicine U. Chgo., 1972-78, assoc. prof. medicine, 1979-85, acting dir. div. gen. internal medicine, 1983-85, dir. Ctr. Clin. Med. Ethics, 1984—, prof. medicine, Lindy Bergman prof., 1985—, dir. nat. leadership tng. program in clin. med. ethics, 1986—; vis. asst. prof. medicine U. Wis., Madison, 1977; vis. assoc. prof. medicine U. Va., Charlottesville, 1981-82. Co-author: Clinical Ethics, 1981, 2d edit., 1986, 3d edit., 1992, An Annotated Bibliography of Medical Ethics, 1988, Institutional Protocols for Decisions About Life-Sustaining Treatment, 1988; co-editor: Changing Values in Medicine, 1985, Medical Innovations and Bad Outcomes, 1987; editl. bd. Am. Jour. Medicine, 1979-94, Archives Internal Medicine, 1979-90, Bibliography of Bioethics, Jour. Med. Philosophy, 1978-89, Jour. Clin. Ethics; contbr. articles to profl. jours. Bd. govs. Josephson Inst. for Advancement of Ethics, L.A., 1986-92; mem. adv. bd. Bioethics Inst., Madrid. Grantee Andrew W. Mellon Found., Henry J. Kaiser Family Found., Pew Charitable Trusts, Field Found. Ill., Ira De Camp Found.; Phi Beta Kappa vis. scholar, 1991-92, Chrione prize Italian Nat. Acad. Medicine, 1996, others. Fellow ACP (human rights com., ethics com. 1985-90), Hastings Ctr.; mem. ACS (mem. ethics com. 1992—), Assn. Am. Physicians, Chgo. Clin. Ethics Program (pres. 1989-90). Office: Univ Chgo MC 6098 MacLean Ctr Clin Med Ethics 5841 S Maryland Ave Chicago IL 60637-1463

SIEGLER, THOMAS EDMUND, investment banking executive; b. Bklyn., Oct. 12, 1934; s. John G. and Edna (Trill) S.; m. Mary V., July 7, 1956; children—Christopher, John, Mary, Therese, Ellen, James. B.B.A., St. John's U., 1959; M.B.A., NYU, 1966. Fin. analyst Exxon Corp., N.Y.C., 1952-66; sr. v.p., sec. Donaldson, Lufkin & Jenrette, Inc., N.Y.C., 1966—; arbitrator Nat. Assn. of Securities Dealers, N.Y.C. Mem. Am. Soc. Corp. Secs., Nat. Assn. Securities Dealers. Republican. Roman Catholic. Lodge: K.C. Avocations: cabinetry; running. Home: 39 Wildwood Dr Huntington Station NY 11746-6040 Office: Donaldson Lufkin & Jenrette 277 Park Ave New York NY 10172

SIEGMAN, ANTHONY EDWARD, electrical engineer, educator; b. Detroit, Nov. 23, 1931; s. Orra Leslie and Helen Salome (Winnie) S.; (married). AB summa cum laude, Harvard U., 1952; MS, UCLA, 1954; PhD, Stanford U., 1957. Mem. faculty Stanford (Calif.) U., 1957—, assoc. prof. elec. engring., 1960-65, prof., 1965—; dir. Edward L. Ginzton Lab., 1978-83; cons. Lawrence Livermore Labs., Coherent Inc., GTE; mem. Air Force Sci. Adv. Bd.; vis. prof. Harvard U., 1965. Author: Microwave Solid State Masers, 1964, An Introduction to Lasers and Masers, 1970, Lasers, 1986; contbr. over 200 articles to profl. jours. Recipient Schawlow award Laser Inst. Am., 1991; Guggenheim fellow IBM Rsch. Lab., Zurich, 1969-70; Alexander von Humboldt Found. sr. scientist Max Planck Inst. Quantum Optics, Garching, Fed. Republic Germany, 1984-85. Fellow AAAS, IEEE (W.R.G. Baker award 1971, J.J. Ebers award 1977), Am. Phys. Soc., Laser Inst. Am., Optical Soc. Am. (R.W. Wood prize 1980), IEEE Laser Electro-Optics Soc. (Quantum Electronics award 1989), Am. Acad. Arts and Scis.; mem. NAS, NAE, AAUP, Phi Beta Kappa, Sigma Xi. Patentee microwave and optical devices and lasers, including the unstable optical resonator. Office: Stanford U Ginzton Lab Stanford CA 94305-4085

SIEGMAN, HENRY, association executive, foreign policy analyst; b. Germany, Dec. 12, 1930; came to U.S., 1942, naturalized, 1948; s. Mendel and Sara (Scharf) S.; m. Selma Goldberger, Nov. 8, 1953 (div.); children: Bonnie, Debra, Alan; m. Miriam Cantor, Aug. 11., 1981. B.A., New Sch. Social Research, 1961, postgrad., 1961-64. Nat. dir. community activities div. Union Orthodox Jewish Congregations Am., 1953-59; exec. sec. Am. Assn. Middle East Studies, 1959-64; dir. internat. affairs Nat. Community Relations Adv. Council, N.Y.C., 1964-65; exec. v.p. Synagogue Council Am., N.Y.C., 1965-78; exec. dir. Am. Jewish Congress, N.Y.C., 1978-94; sr. fellow Coun. on Fgn. Rels., 1994—; guest lectr. U. Ill., Columbia, Williams Coll.; an organizer White House Conf. Civil Rights, 1967; nat. vice chmn. Religion in Am. Life, 1966—; exec. com. Interreligious Com. on Peace, 1966—; chmn. Interreligious Com. Gen. Secs. (Nat. Council Chs.-U.S. Cath. Conf.-Synagogue Council Am.), 1973. Editor: Middle East Studies, 1959-64; Contbr. articles to profl. jours. Served to 1st lt., chaplain AUS, 1952-54. Decorated Bronze Star; designated Disting. Am. by Pres. U.S., 1970. Mem. AAUP, Council on Fgn. Relations. Office: Coun on Fgn Rels 58 E 68th St New York NY 10021-5939 Address: 541 Huntingridge Rd Stamford CT 06903

SIEGMAN, MARION JOYCE, physiology educator; b. Bklyn., Sept. 7, 1933; d. C. Joseph and Helen (Wasserman) S. BA, Tulane U., 1954; PhD, SUNY, Bklyn., 1966. Instr. physiology Med. Coll. Thomas Jefferson U., Phila., 1967-68, asst. prof., 1968-71, assoc. prof., 1971-77, prof., 1977—; mem. physiology study sect. NIH. Editor: Regulation and Contraction of Smooth Muscle, 1987. Recipient award for excellence in rsch. and teaching Burlington No. Found., 1986, award for excellence in teaching Lindback Found., 1987, Outstanding Alumna award, Newcomb Coll./Tulane U., 1990; grantee NIH, 1967—. Mem. Am. Physiol. Soc., Biophys. Soc., Soc. Gen. Physiologists, Physiol. Soc. Phila. (pres. 1972-73). Avocation: photography. Office: Jefferson Med Coll 1020 Locust St Philadelphia PA 19107-6731

SIEK, RAINER, broadcast executive. Pres. CBS Enterprises, N.Y.C. Office: CBS Enterprises 51 W 52nd St New York NY 10019-6119*

SIEKERT, ROBERT GEORGE, neurologist; b. Milw., July 23, 1924; s. Hugo Paul and Elisa (Kraus) S.; m. Mary Jane Evans, Feb. 17, 1951; children: Robert G. Jr., John E., Friedrich A.P. BS, Northwestern U., 1945, MS, 1947, MD, 1948. Cert. Am. Bd. Psychiatry and Neurology. Instr. anatomy U. Pa., Phila., 1948-49; fellow neurology Mayo Found., Rochester, Minn., 1950-54; cons. Mayo Clinic, Rochester, 1954-91, head neurology sect., 1966-76, bd. govs., 1973-80, prof. neurology med. sch., 1969—; chmn. Internat. Stroke Conf. Am. Heart Assn., 1976-80. Editor Mayo Clinic Procs., 1982-86; cons. editor Jour. Stroke, 1992—; contbr. articles to profl. jours.; described transient cerebral ischemic attacks. Trustee Mayo Found., Rochester, 1973-81. Served to lt. j.g. M.C., USNR, 1950-52. Recipient Disting. Achievement award Am. Heart Assn., 1984, Merit award, 1989, Robert G. Siekert Young Investigator award Am. Heart Assn., 1986. Fellow Am. Coll. Physicians; mem. Am. Neurol. Assn., Northwestern U. Med. Sch. Alumni Assn. (Service award 1983), Swiss Neurol. Soc. (corr.), Alpha Omega Alpha. Avocation: philately. Office: Mayo Clinic 200 1st St SW Rochester MN 55902-3008

SIEKMAN, THOMAS CLEMENT, lawyer; b. Somerville, Mass., Sept. 22, 1941; s. Aloysius C. and Estelle M. (Forte) S.; m. Claire Dorgan, Oct. 15, 1966; children: Michael T., James T., Amy K. BS in Engring., Merrimack Coll., 1963; JD, Villanova U., 1966. Bar: Mass. 1966, U.S. Dist. Ct. Mass. 1969. Patent atty. Bethlehem (Pa.) Steel, 1966-68, Mohawk Data Scis., Stoneham, Mass., 1968-72, Chittick, Thompson & Pfund, Boston, Mass., 1972-73; from patent atty. to v.p. and gen. counsel Digital Equipment Corp., Maynard, Mass., 1973—; bd. dirs. Associated Industries Mass., Boston, N.E. Legal Found., Boston; mem. legal quality coun. Conf. Bd. Trustees Mass. Trustee Mass. Taxpayers Found.; mem. New Eng. Legal Found. Mem. ABA, Internat. Bar Assn., Law Coun. Mfrs.' Alliance for Productivity & Innovation. Avocations: squash, skiing. Home: 73 Edgewater Dr Needham MA 02192-2745 Office: Digital Equipment Corp 111 Powder Mill Rd Maynard MA 01754-1482

SIEKMANN, DONALD CHARLES, accountant; b. St. Louis, July 2, 1938; s. Elmer Charles and Mabel Louise (Blue) S.; m. Linda Lee Knowles, Sept. 10, 1966; 1 child, Brian Charles. BS, Washington U., St. Louis, 1960. CPA, Ohio, Ga. Regional mng. ptnr. Arthur Andersen & Co., Cin., 1960—. Columnist Cin. Enquirer, 1983-86, Gannett News Services, 1983-86; editor "Tax Clinic" column Tax Advisor mag., 1974-75. Mem. bd. Cin. Zool. Soc., 1985-88; officer, bd. dirs. Cin. Found. for Pub. TV, 1984-88, Cin. Symphony Orch., 1973-85, Cin. Ballet Co., 1973-88, Cin. Theatrical Assn., Jewish Hosp., 1993—, Cin. Assn. for Performing Arts, 1992—, Cin. United Way, 1992—, Cin. Pk. Bd. Found., 1995—; pres. Sch. Creative and Performing Arts Greater Cin. Arts and Edn. Ctr. Mem. AICPA, Ohio Soc. CPAs, Cin. Country Club (trustee 1983-88), Optimists Club (pres. Queen City chpt. 1986). Lutheran. Club: Cin. Country (trustee 1983-88). Home: 5495 Waring Dr Cincinnati OH 45243-3933 Office: Arthur Andersen & Co 425 Walnut St Ste 1500 Cincinnati OH 45202

SIELICKI-KORCZAK, BORIS ZDZISLAW, political educator, investigative consultant; b. Wilno, Lithuania, Poland, Feb. 11, 1939; came to U.S., 1980; s. Wiltold and Antonina (Arciszewski) Sielicki-Korczak; m. Barbara Maria Kaniewski, May 29, 1971; children: Robert, Sandra. MSC, Warsaw U., 1964, Kunstindustriskole, Copenhagen, 1971; PhD, Basel (Switzerland) U., 1973. Pres. Impolex Ltd., Copenhagen, 1970-79; field operative Europe CIA, 1983-90; pres., educator Anti-Soviet Rsch. Ctr., McLean, Va., 1981-84; export dir. Worldwide Investment Ltd., Arlington, Va., 1985-87; pres. Amexim Internat. Co. Ltd., Arlington, 1986-89, BK & Assocs., Arlington, 1990—, Boris S. de Korczak, Inc., Fairfax Station, Va., 1986—; pres. R.R. Internat. Ltd., Copenhagen, 1983-89; mng. dir. Securitas Inc., Arlington, 1986-87; multiple appearance on U.S. and fgn. TV shows as expert on terrorism, USSR and Russian intelligence and its ops. Author: A Man From Atlantis, 1976; designer anti-drug poster. Dir. Nat. Lyric Opera Co., Washington, 1981-91; chief investigator Nat. Police Def. Found. Republican. Avocations: chess, classic music, travel, art, history. Office: PO Box 7153 Fairfax Station VA 22039-7153

SIEMENS, RICHARD ERNEST, retired metallurgy administrator, researcher; b. Coeur d'Alene, Idaho, July 7, 1938; s. John Charles and Ruth Eva (Schumaker) S.; m. Louise Irene Niehaus, June 21, 1959; children: Rhonda Kaye, Leann Marie. BS, Oreg. State U., 1960, postgrad., 1961-65, 70-71; postgrad., Linfield Coll., McMinnville, Oreg., 1960-61. Rsch. physicist Albany (Oreg.) Rsch. Ctr. U.S. Bur. Mines, 1961-77, metallurgist, 1977-80, group supr., 1980-84, rsch. supr., 1984-89; sr. tech. monitor, contract officers' rep. pilot plant U.S. Bur. Mines, Tucson, 1980-81; acting rsch. dir. Tuscaloosa (Ala.) Rsch. Ctr. U.S. Bur. Mines, 1988, rsch. dir. Reno Rsch. Ctr., 1989-94; ret., 1994; mem. adv. com. Profl. Coun. Fed. Scientists and Engrs., 1990-94, MacKay Sch. Mines, U. Nev., Reno, 1991-94; presenter numerous tech. mtgs. Contbr. over 50 articles to profl. jours. and internal publs. Pres. Fed. Metals Cen. Credit Union, Albany, 1976-89. Recipient Meritorious Svc. award U.S. Dept. Interior, 1981, Raiffeisen award Nat. Credit Union Assn., 1988; NDEA fellow Oreg. State U., 1960-63. Mem. AIME, Sigma Xi. Achievements include patents for Process for Recovery of Non-Ferrous Metal from Oxide Ores and Concentrates, for Reduction of Laterite Ores, for Recovery of Valuable Organic and Aqueous Phases from Metallurgical Solvent Extraction Emulsions, for Process for Recovering Ni(II), Cu(II), and Co(II) from Ammoniacal-Ammonium Sulfate Leach Liquor; research on phase relations of metal alloy systems, on phase relations and superconductivity in metal alloys and compounds, and on hydrometallurgical process development. Home: 39416 Highway 62 Chiloquin OR 97624-7752

SIEMER, DEANNE CLEMENCE, lawyer; b. Buffalo, Dec. 25, 1940; d. Edward D. and Dorothy J. (Helsdon) S.; m. Howard P. Willens; 1 child, Jason L. BA, George Washington U., 1962; LLB, Harvard U., 1968. Bar: N.Y. 1968, D.C. 1969, Md. 1972, Trust Ter. 1976. Economist Office of Mgmt. and Budget, Washington, 1964-67; assoc., then ptnr. Wilmer, Cutler & Pickering, Washington, 1968-90; ptnr. Pillsbury, Madison & Sutro, Washington, 1990-95; mng. dir. Wilsie Co., Saipan, M.P., 1995—; gen. counsel U.S. Dept. of Def., Washington, 1977-79; spl. asst. to sec. U.S. Dept. of Energy, Washington, 1979-80. Author: Tangible Evidence, 1984, 3d edit., 1996, Understanding Modern Ethical Standards, 1985, Manual on Litigation Support Databases, 1986, supplement, 1992. Mem. Lawyers Com. for Civil Rights, Washington, 1973—; mediator D.C. Superior Ct., Washington, 1986—, U.S. Ct. Appeals, Washington, 1988—; trustee Nat. Inst. Trial Advocacy, 1989—, Am. Law Inst., 1990—. Recipient Citation Air Force Assn., 1977, Dist. Pub. Service medal Sec. of Def., 1979, Commendation Pres. of U.S. 1981. Mem. ABA, ATLA, D.C. Bar Assn., No. Marianas Bar Assn., Womens Bar Assn. Episcopalian. Office: Wilsie Co Macaranas Bldg 1st Fl PO Box 909 Saipan MP 96950

SIEMER, FRED HAROLD, securities analyst; b. Mt. Vernon, N.Y., Apr. 3, 1937; s. Fred Henry and Doris Sophie (Peymann) S.; m. Barbara Jean Behrmann, May 20, 1960 (div. 1980); children: Carolyn Doris Baird, Charles Frederick, Janet Ann Bruno; m. Mary Brittain Brown, Aug. 20, 1981 (dec. Sept. 1992). BA in Chemistry, Colgate U., Hamilton, N.Y., 1958; MBA, Fairleigh Dickinson U., Rutherford, N.J., 1970. CFA. Mgr. rsch. planning Allied Chem. Corp., Morristown, N.J., 1962-69; mgr. econ. evaluation BASF Corp., Parsippany, N.J., 1969-72; chems. analyst Prudential Ins. Co., Newark, 1972-74; v.p. rsch. F. Eberstadt & Co., Inc., N.Y.C., 1974-80, Smith Barney Harris Upham, N.Y.C., 1980-85; pres. Siemer & Co., N.Y.C., 1985-93, F.H. Siemer & Co., Inc., N.Y.C., 1993—. Editor: Chemical Research For Wall St.; contbr. articles to profl. jours. With U.S. Army, 1959-62. Mem. Am. Chem. Soc., N.Y. Soc. Securities Analysts, Assn. for Investment Mgmt. and Rsch., Chem. Analysts of N.Y. and Chem. Specialists of N.Y., Chem. Mktg. Rsch. Assn., Chem. Mktg. Rsch. and Econs. Grp., Soc. de Chemie Indsl. Avocations: reading, walking, tennis, music. Office: F H Siemer & Co Inc 158 Bellevue Rd Highland NY 12528

SIEMER, PAUL JENNINGS, public relations executive; b. St. Louis, Jan. 24, 1946; s. Robert Vincent and Pauline Mary (Nece) S.; m. Susan MacDonald Arnott, Aug. 26, 1967. Student, U. Notre Dame, 1964-67. Reporter South Bend Tribune, Ind., 1967-69; reporter St. Louis Globe-Democrat, 1969-76; account exec. Fleishman-Hillard Inc., St. Louis, 1976-79, v.p., sr. ptnr., 1979-84, exec. v.p., sr. ptnr., 1984-95; ptnr. Stolberg & Siemer Inc., St. Louis, 1995—. Mem. Pub. Relations Soc. Am. Roman Catholic. Club: St. Louis Press. Home: 2961 Hatherly Dr Saint Louis MO 63121-4551 Office: Stolberg & Siemer Inc 1608 Menard St Saint Louis MO 63104-3702

SIEPI, CESARE, opera singer; b. Milan, Italy, Feb. 10, 1923. Operatic debut in Rigoletto, Schio, 1941, Il Nabucco, LaScala Opera, Milan, 1946, Don Carlo, Met. Opera, N.Y.C., 1950; soloist debut in, Carnegie Hall, N.Y.C., 1951; sang in Mozart and Verdi requiems, Edinburgh Festival, Albert Hall, London; leading bass at, Salzburg Festival, LaScala, Milan; appeared in: play Bravo Giovanni, 1962; appeared: play Vienna Staatsoper; made many opera recordings for, London Records. (Winner Nat. Singing Competition, Florence 1941, recipient Italy's Orfeo award 1956). Operatic debut, Rigoletto, Schio, at age of 18. Home: 12095 Brookfield Club Dr Roswell GA 30075-1261

SIEPMANN, JOERN ILJA, chemistry educator; b. Cologne, Germany, June 28, 1964; came to U.S., 1993; m. Silke Schmid, Mar. 22, 1990; 1 child, Tim Christoph. PhD, Cambridge (Eng.) U., 1992. Postdoctoral fellow IBM Zurich Rsch. Lab., Rüschlikon, Switzerland, 1991-92, Koninklijke/Shell Lab., Amsterdam, The Netherlands, 1992-93; rsch. assoc. U. Pa., Phila., 1993-94; asst. prof. chemistry U. Minn., Mpls., 1994—. Recipient Dreyfus New Faculty award Dreyfus Found., 1994. Mem. AIChE, Am. Chem. Soc. Achievements include research on configurational bias Monte Carlo of complex fluids. Office: U Minn Dept Chemistry 207 Pleasant St SE Minneapolis MN 55455-0431

SIEPSER, STUART LEWIS, cardiologist, internist; s. Jesse and Miriam (Spector) S.; m. Lynn Perkel, Mar. 15, 1969; children: Gabrielle, Craig, Amy. BA, Columbia Coll., 1964; MD, NYU, 1968. Diplomate Am. Bd. Internal Medicine, Am. Bd. Cardiology. Intern Bellevue Hosp., 1968-69, resident in medicine, 1969-70; fellow in cardiology NYU Med. Ctr., 1970-72; ptnr. Cardiology Assocs. North Jersey, PA, Wayne, N.J., 1974—; clin. asst. prof. N.J. Med. Sch. Coll. Medicine and Dentistry N.J., 1976—; pres. med. dental staff Chilton Meml. Hosp.; cardiology liaison Morristown (N.J.) Meml. Hosp., 1993—; mem. med. care appraisal com. Chilton Meml. Hosp., 1980—, hosp. pharmacy and therapeutics com., 1980-84, 93—, chmn. sect. cardiology, 1993—. Maj. U.S. Army, 1972-74. Fellow Am. Coll. Cardiology, Am. Coll. Physicians; mem. AMA, Soc. Internal Medicine, Passaic County Med. Soc., Alpha Omega Alpha. Avocations: skiing, running, mountain biking. Home: 44 Littlewood Ct Wayne NJ 07470-2453 Office: Cardiology Assocs North Jersey PA 1777 Hamburg Tpke Wayne NJ 07470-5243

SIERCK, ALEXANDER WENTWORTH, lawyer; b. N.Y.C., Dec. 15, 1940; s. Herbert Wentworth and Phebe Ann (Steers) S.; m. Susan Stephanie Arthur, Aug. 29, 1964; children: Carsten Wentworth, Alexander Arthur, Sarah Stephanie. BA, U. Va., 1962, JD, 1965. Bar: N.Y. 1965, D.C. 1968. Assoc. Wald Harkrader & Ross, Washington, 1968-74, ptnr., 1974-78; dir. trade policy Antitrust div. U.S. Dept. Justice, Washington, 1978-80; ptnr. Beveridge & Diamond, Washington, 1980-92, Cameron & Hornbostel, Washington, 1992—. Office: Cameron & Hornbostel 818 Connecticut Ave NW Ste 700 Washington DC 20006-2702

SIERLES, FREDERICK STEPHEN, psychiatrist, educator; b. Bklyn., Nov. 9, 1942; s. Samuel and Elizabeth (Meiselman) S.; m. Laurene Harriet Cohn, Oct. 25, 1970 (div. Aug. 1990); children: Hannah Beth, Joshua Caleb. AB, Columbia U., 1963; MD, Chgo. Med. Sch., 1967. Diplomate Am. Bd. Psychiatry and Neurology. Intern Cook County Hosp., Chgo., 1967-68; resident in psychiatry Mt. Sinai Hosp., N.Y.C., 1968-69, Chgo. Med. Sch., 1969-71, chief resident, 1970-71; staff psychiatrist U.S. Reynolds Army Hosp., Ft. Sill, Okla., 1971-73; assoc. attending psychiatrist Mt. Sinai Hosp., Chgo., 1973-74; instr. psychiatry Chgo. Med. Sch., North Chicago, 1973-74, dir. undergrad. edn. in psychiatry, 1974-94, asst. prof., 1974-78, assoc. prof., 1978-88, prof., Finch U. Health Scis, Chgo. Med. Sch., 1988—, vice chmn., 1990-94, acting chmn., 1994-95, chmn., 1995—, chmn. edni. affairs com., 1983-85, 86—, chmn. univ. tenure com. 1983-84, 88-94; cons. psychiatry Cook County Hosp., 1974-79, St. Mary of Nazareth Hosp., 1979-84, Great Lakes Naval Hosp., 1987-90, Jackson Park Hosp., 1987-89, Mt. Sinai Hosp., 1988—, Elgin Mental Health Ctr., 1997—; chief Mental Health Clinic, North Chicago VA Hosp., 1982-85, chief psychiatry svc., 1983-85. Author: (with others) General Hospital Psychiatry, 1985, Behavioral Science for the Boreds, 1987, rev. 2d edit., 1989, rev. 3rd edit., 1993; editor: Clinical Behavioral Science, 1982, Behavioral Science for Medical Students, 1992; contbr. articles to profl. jours. Coach Glenview (Ill.) Youth Baseball, 1987-89, mgr., 1990 (age 10-12 Glenview World Series winner 1990), Glenview Tennis Club, 1986-90 (3.5 Men's Doubles League winner 1989-90). Maj., M.C., U.S. Army, 1971-73. Recipient Ganser Meml. award Mt. Sinai Hosp., 1970, Nancy C. Roeske award, 1991, Lawrence R. Medoff award, 1993; named Prof. of Yr. Chgo. Med. Sch., 1977, 80, 83, Disting. Alumnus, 1993; N.Y. State Regents scholar, 1959-63; NIMH grantee, 1974-83, Chgo. Med. Sch. grantee, 1974-83. Fellow Am. Psychiat. Assn. (coun. edn. & career devel. 1993-95); mem. Am. Coll. Psychiatrists, Ill. Psychiat. Soc. (fellowship com. 1985—), Columbia Coll. Alumni Secondary Schs. Com., Assn. Dirs. Med. Student Edn. in Psychiatry (exec. council 1985—, chmn. program com. 1987-88, treas. 1989-91, pres. elect 1991-93, pres. 1993-95, immediate past pres. 1995—), Alliance for Clin. Edn., Assn. of Chmn. of Depts. of Psychiatry (Chgo. consortium for psychiatric rsch. 1994—, sec. 1996—, treas. 1997—), Sigma Xi, Alpha Omega Alpha, Phi Epsilon Pi. Office: Finch U Health Sci Chgo Med Sch 3333 Green Bay Rd North Chicago IL 60064-3037

SIERRA, ROBERTO, composer, music educator; b. Vega Baja, P.R., Oct. 9, 1953. Grad., P.R. Conservatory of Music, U. P.R., 1976; postgrad., Royal Coll. Music, London, U. London, 1976-78, Inst. Sonology, Utrecht, The Netherlands, 1978; studied with Gyorgy Ligeti, Hamberg (Germany) Hochschule for Music, 1979-82. Asst. dir. cultural activities dept. U. P.R., 1983-85, dir., 1985-86, dean of studies, 1986-87; chancellor P.R. Conservatory of Music, 1987—; prof. composition Cornell U., Ithaca, N.Y., 1992—; composer-in-residence Milw. Symphony Orch., 1989-92. Compositions include: (orchestral) Jubilo, 1985, Cuatro ensayos orquestales, 1986, Glosas for piano and orch., 1987, Descargo, 1988, Sasima, 1990; (chamber) Tiempo Muerto for string quartet, 1978, Salsa on the C String for cello and piano, 1981, Seis piezas fáciles for two violins, 1982, Bongo-O for percussion, 1982, Salsa for wind quintet, 1983, Cinco bocetos for clarinet, 1984, Concierto Nocturnal for harsichord, flute, clarinet, oboe, violin and cello, 1985, Memorias Tropicales for string quartet, 1985, El sueño de Antonia for clarinet and percussion, 1985, Toccata y Lamento for guitar, 1987, Essays for wind quintet, 1987, Mano a Mano for two percussionists, 1987, Introducción y Descarga for piano, brass quintet and percussion, 1988, Tributo for harp, flute, clarinet and string quartet, 1988; (piano) Descarga en sol, 1981; (stage) El Mensajero de Plata for chamber opera, 1984, El Comtemplado for ballet, 1987; (harpsichord) Tres Miniaturas, 1982, Con Salsa, 1984; (vocal) Cantos populares for chorus, 1983, Doña Rosita, 1985, Invocaciones, 1986, Glosa a la sombra, 1987; also, Entre terceras for 2 synthesizers and computer, 1988. Office: Subito Music Publ 91 Christopher St Montclair NJ 07042-4227 also: American Int'l Artists 315 E 62nd St 6th Flr New York NY 10021*

SIERRA, RUBEN ANGEL GARCIA, professional baseball player; b. Rio Piedras, P.R., Oct. 6, 1965. Grad. high sch., Rio Piedras, P.R. Baseball player Tex. Rangers, 1982-92, Oakland Athletics, 1992-95, N.Y. Yankees, 1995-96, Detroit Tigers, 1996, Cin. Reds, 1997, Toronto Blue Jays, 1997—. Named Am. League Player of Yr., Sporting News, 1989, recipient Silver Slugger award, 1989; named to All-Star team, 1989, 91-92, 94; Am. League RBI Leader, 1989. Office: Toronto Blue Jays, 1 Blue Jays Way Ste 3200, Toronto, ON Canada M5V 1J1*

SIESS, ALFRED ALBERT, JR., engineering executive, management consultant; b. Bklyn., Aug. 16, 1935; s. Alfred Albert and Matilda Helen (Suttmeier) S.; m. Gale Murray Scholes, Dec. 17, 1966; children: Matthew Alan, Daniel Adam. BCE, Ga. Inst. Tech., 1956; postgrad. in bus. Boston Coll., 1968; MBA, Lehigh U., 1972. With fabricated steel constrn. div. Bethlehem Steel Corp. (Pa.), 1958-76, project mgr., 1969-76, engr., projects and mining div., 1976-86; sr. cons. T.J. Trauner Assocs., Phila., 1986-87; assoc. S.T. Hudson Internat., Phila., 1987-90; dir. mktg. SWIN Resource Systems, Inc., Bloomsburg, Pa., 1989-90; mem. adj. faculty Drexel U., 1976—. Weekly columnist Economic and Environmental Issues, East Pa. edit. The Free Press, 1981-86; co-patentee suspension bridge erection equipment. Founder S.A.V.E. Inc., Coopersburg, Pa., 1969, pres., 1970, 75, 81, bd. dirs., 1970—. Served with C.E., USN, 1956-58. Recipient Environ. Action award S.A.V.E. Inc., 1975. Mem. ASCE (chmn. environ. tech. com. Lehigh Valley sect. 1971-83), Chi Epsilon. Republican. Mem. United Church of Christ. Lodge: Lions. Home: 6460 Blue Church Rd Coopersburg PA 18036-9371 Office: C E Resource Group PO Box 39 Coopersburg PA 18036-0039

SIESS, CHESTER PAUL, civil engineering educator; b. Alexandria, La., July 28, 1916; s. Leo C. and Adele (Liebreich) S.; m. Helen Kranson, Oct. 5, 1941; 1 dau., Judith Ann. B.S., La. State U., 1936; M.S., U. Ill., 1939, Ph.D., 1948. Party chief La. Hwy. Commn., 1936-37; research asst. U. Ill., 1937-39; soil engr. Chgo. Subway Project, 1939-41; engr., draftsman N.Y.C. R.R. Co., 1941; mem. faculty U. Ill., 1941—, prof. civil engring., 1955-78, emeritus, head dept. civil engring., 1973-78; mem. adv. com. on reactor safeguards Nuclear Regulatory Commn., 1968-92, chmn., 1972. Recipient award Concrete Reinforcing Steel Inst., 1956, Alumni Honor award for disting. service in engring. U. Ill., 1985, Disting. Service award NRC, 1987; named to Engring. Hall of Distinction, La. State U., 1979. Mem. ASCE (hon. mem., Rsch. prize 1956, Howard medal 1968, Reese award 1970), Nat. Acad. Engring., Am. Concrete Inst. (pres. 1974-75, Wason medal 1949, Turner medal 1964, hon. mem.), Reinforced Concrete Rsch. coun. (chmn. 1968-80, Boase award 1974), Internat. Assn. Bridge and Structural Engring., Sigma Xi, Tau Beta Pi, Phi Kappa Phi, Omicron Delta Kappa, Gamma Alpha, Chi Epsilon (chap. hon., nat. hon.). Research in reinforced and prestressed concrete structures and hwy. bridges. Home: 401 Burwash Dr Savoy IL 61874-9573 Office: Newmark Lab 205 N Mathews Ave Urbana IL 61801-2350

SIEVERS, ALBERT JOHN, III, physics educator; b. Oakland, Calif., June 28, 1933; s. Albert John and Martha (McDowell) S.; m. Betsy Floy Ross, Feb. 6, 1959; children: Karla Jean, John Charles, Martha Caroline, Sylvia Jane. B.A., U. Calif.-Berkeley, 1958, Ph.D., 1962. Machinist, Varian Assocs., Palo Alto, Calif., 1951-58; research assoc. Cornell U., 1962-64, asst. prof. physics, 1964-67, asso. prof., 1967-71, prof., 1971—; cons. Lockheed Rsch. Coun., 1969—, GM Corp., 1978—; lectr. NATO Summer Sch., Italy, 1966, Holland, 1968; E.L. Nichols chair Cornell U., 1992—. Mem. editorial bd.: Solar Energy Materials. Named Alexander von Humboldt sr. scientist, 1985; NSF sr. postdoctoral fellow, 1970-71, Erskine fellow U. Canterbury, New Zealand, 1976, 93. Fellow Optical Soc. Am., Am. Phys. Soc. (Frank Isakson prize 1988); mem. AAAS, N.Y. Acad. Scis., Sierra Club., Phi Beta Kappa, Sigma Xi. Research far infrared spectroscopy of solids. Home: 115 Winston Dr Ithaca NY 14850-1935

SIEVERTS, FRANK ARNE, association executive; b. Frankfurt, Fed. Republic Germany, June 19, 1933; s. Helmut J. and Cecile M. (Behrendt) S.; m. Jane Woodbridge, Dec. 31, 1957 (div.); children: Lisa, Michael; m. Sue Hubbell, Feb. 13, 1988; 1 stepchild, Brian. BA, Swarthmore Coll., 1955; M in Philosophy (Rhodes Scholar), Balliol Coll. Oxford U., 1957; postgrad., Nuffield Coll., 1957-59. News corr. Time mag., London and Washington, 1959-60; legis. asst. U.S. Senator Washington, 1960-62; with Dept. of State, Washington, 1962-86, spl. asst. to ambassador at large Averell Harriman, 1966-68, adviser on prisoner of war matters to U.S. delegation to Vietnam peace talks, spl. asst. to dep. sec. of state for prisoner of war matters, 1969-75, dep. asst. sec. for prisoner of war and missing in action matters, 1976—, dep. asst. sec. for refugee and migration affairs, 1978—; minister-counselor for humanitarian affairs U.S. Mission, Geneva, 1980-81; spl. asst. for refugee programs, 1982-86; spokesman for Com. on Fgn. Relations U.S. Senate, 1987-95; asst. to head of delegation for U.S., Can. Internat. Com. Red Cross, Washington, 1995—; mem. advance team for release Am. prisoners of war, Hanoi, 1973. Mem. U.S. delegation to 20th Internat. Conf. Red Cross, Vienna, 1965, 21st Conf., Istanbul, 1969, 22d Conf., Tehran, 1973; chmn. 23d Conf., Bucharest, 1977, 24th Conf., Manila, 1981, 25th Conf., Geneva, 1986; U.S. del. Diplomatic Conf. on Humanitarian Law in Armed Conflicts, Geneva, 1974-77, to exec. com. of UN High Commn. for Refugees, 1978, 79, 80; staff dir. Indochinese Refugee panel, 1986. Mem. Am. Assn. Rhodes Scholars (bd. dirs.). Office: Internat Com Red Cross 2100 Pennsylvania Ave NW Washington DC 20037-3202

SIFFERT, ROBERT SPENCER, orthopedic surgeon; b. N.Y.C., June 16, 1918; s. Oscar and Sadye (Rusoff) S.; m. Miriam Sand, June 29, 1941; children: Joan, John. AB in Biology with honors, NYU, 1939, MD, 1943. Diplomate Am. Bd. Orthop. Surgery, Nat. Bd. Med. Examiners. Intern Kings County Hosp., Bklyn., 1943; resident in orthop. surgery Mt. Sinai Hosp., N.Y.C., 1946-49, fellow in pathology, 1949-52, mem. staff, 1949—, dir. orthor. surgery, orthop. surgeon in chief, 1960-86, Lasker/Siffert Disting. Svc. prof., 1986—; pvt. practice N.Y.C., 1949—; dir. dept. orthops. City Hosp., Elmhurst, 1965-86; sr. orthop. cons. N.Y.C. Dept. Health, 1952-60; attending orthop. surgeon Blythedale Children's Hosp., Valhalla, N.Y., 1960-86, cons., 1986-90; prof., chmn. dept. orthops. Mt. Sinai Sch. Medicine, 1966-86, Dr. Robert K. Lippman prof., 1983-86, acting chmn., 1993-94. Author: See How They Grow, 1985; co-author: (with J.F. Katz) Management of Hip Disorders in Children, 1983; contbr. over 100 articles to profl. jours. Mem. adv. bd. CARE-MEDICO, 1972-83, bd. dirs., 1981-83, chmn., 1981-83; bd. dirs. CARE, 1983-90; adv. bd. Orthopaedics Overseas, 1981-93; bd. dirs., mem. profl. adv. com. Easter Seal Soc. for Crippled Children and Adults, 1st v.p., 1977-79. Capt. USAAF, 1944-46, CBI. Decorated 4 Battle Stars; recipient annual award medicine N.Y. Pub. Health Assn., 1958, annual award medicine N.Y. Philanthropic League, 1959, Richman award for humanism in medicine Mt. Sinai Sch. Medicine, 1989. Fellow ACS, APHA; mem. Am. Orthop. Assn., Am. Acad. Orthop. Surgery (chmn. com. on care of handicapped child), Assn. Bone and Joint Surgeons, Internat. Soc. Orthop. Surgery and Traumatology, Internat. Skeletal Soc., Orthop. Rsch. Soc., N.Y. Acad. Medicine (fellow orthop. sect. 1952, sec. 1962-63, chmn. 1963-64), N.Y. State Med. Soc. (chmn. orthop. sect. 1967-68), Century Assn. (N.Y.C.), Phi Beta Kappa, Alpha Omega Alpha. Office: 955 5th Ave New York NY 10021-1738

SIFNEOS, PETER EMANUEL, psychiatrist; b. Greece, Oct. 22, 1920; came to U.S., 1941, naturalized, 1944; s. Demitrios Z. and Mary E. (Lucas) S.; divorced; children: Ann L., Peter G., Jean C. B.Sc., Sorbonne, 1940; M.D., Harvard U., 1946. Diplomate: Am. Bd. Psychiatry. Intern Boston City Hosp., 1946-47; resident in psychiatry McLean Hosp., Belmont, Mass., 1950-52; chief resident Mass. Gen. Hosp., Boston, 1952-53; mem. staff, chief psychiat. clinic Mass. Gen. Hosp., 1954-68; fellow Harvard U. Sch. Public Health, 1953-54; mem. faculty Harvard U. Med. Sch., 1952—, prof. psychiatry, 1973-91, prof. emeritus, 1991—; staff, assoc. dir. psychiatry dept. Beth Israel Hosp., Boston, 1968-94. Author: Ascent from Chaos, 1964, Short-Term Psychotherapy and Emotional Crisis, 1972, Short-Term Dynamic P)sychotherapy Evaluation and Technique, 1979, 2d edit., 1987, Short-Term Anxiety Provking Psychotherapy, 1992; editor-in-chief Psychotherapy and Psychosomatics, 1974-91; contbr. 125 articles to profl. jours. Served with AUS, 1944-46, 47-50. Fellow Am. Psychiat. Assn. (life); mem. AMA, Internat. Fedn. Med. Psychotherapy (v.p. 1976-88, bd. dirs. 1988-94), Am. Psychosomatic Soc., Boston Psychoanalytic Soc. (life), Hellenic Psychosomatic Soc. (hon.), Italian Psychosomatic Soc. (hon.). Democrat. Home and Office: 59 Common St Belmont MA 02178-3022 *The principles which helped me most have been a belief in good education, a fierce sense of non-conformity, a strong sense of independence, an admiration of creativity and new ideas, a love of writing, teaching, reading, classic music, traveling to lecture and conduct workshops, seminars all over North and South America and Europe, swimming, and luck in being healthy.*

SIFONTES, JOSE E., pediatrics educator; b. Arecibo, P.R.; s. Jose E. and Josefa M. (Fontan) S.; m. Iris J. Sotomayor, Dec. 20, 1952; children: J. Jaime, Mariat, Iris, J. Roberto, Myrta, J. Ricardo, Beatriz. MD, Syracuse U., 1948. Diplomate Am. Bd. Pediatrics. Dir. USPHS TB Rsch., San Juan, Puerto Rico, 1958-66; dean U. Puerto Rico Sch. of Medicine, San Juan, 1966-71; chief of pediatrics U. Puerto Rico Sch. Medicine, San Juan, 1974-77, chief pediatric pulmonary program, 1960-66, prof. pediatrics, 1966—; pvt. practice specializing in pulmonary pediatrics, San Juan, 1982—; cons. to many nat. and internat. health orgns. including WHO, UN, PAHTO, 1954-82. Author: (Spanish textbook) Neumologia Pediatrica, 1974; contbr. over 100 articles to profl. jours. Vol. Am. Thoracic Soc. ATS, AZA, 1953—. Surgeon USPHS, 1957-59. Grantee: USPHS, NIH, 1954-82. Mem. Am. Acad. Pediatrics (fellow chest sect., nat. chmn. 1964-65), Am. Pediatric Soc. Roman Catholic.

SIFTON, CHARLES PROCTOR, federal judge; b. N.Y.C., Mar. 18, 1935; s. Paul F. and Claire G. S.; m. Susan Scott Rowland, May 20, 1986; children: Samuel, Tobias, John. A.B., Harvard U., 1957; LL.B., Columbia U., 1961. Bar: N.Y. 1961. Assoc. Cadwalader, Wickersham & Taft, 1961-62, 64-66; staff atty. U.S. Senate Fgn. Rels. Com., 1962-63; asst. U.S. atty. N.Y.C., 1966-69; ptnr. LeBoeuf, Lamb, Leiby and MacRae, N.Y.C., 1969-77; judge U.S. Dist. Ct. (ea. dist.) N.Y., Bklyn., 1977—, chief judge, 1995—. Mem. Bar Assn. City of N.Y. Office: US Dist Ct US Courthouse 225 Cadman Plz E Rm 244 Brooklyn NY 11201-1818*

SIFTON, DAVID WHITTIER, magazine editor; b. N.Y.C., Sept. 12, 1940; s. David William and Dorothy (Whittier) S. B.A., Trinity Coll., Hartford, Conn., 1962; M.A., Stanford U., 1967. Editor Inside Edn., N.Y. State Edn. Dept., 1968-70; adminstrv. editor Med. Econs., Oradell, N.J., 1970-72; editor Drug Topics, Oradell, 1972-75; editor in chief Current Prescribing, Oradell, 1975-78, RN mag., Oradell, 1978-83; dir. spl. editorial projects Med. Econs. Co., 1983-90; mgr. PDR Devel., Oradell, 1990—; founder Physicians' Desk Reference on CD-ROM, PDR's Drug Interactions and Side Effects Index, PDR's Indications Index, Pocket PDR (handheld electronic database), The PDR Family Guide to Prescription Drugs, The PDR Family Guide to Women's Health, The PDR Family Guide to Nutrition and Health, The PDR Family Guide to Lifelong Health, The PDR Family Guide Encyclopedia of Medical Care, The PDR Family Guide to Over-the-Counter Drugs. Served to 1st lt. USAF, 1963-66. Decorated Air Force Commendation medal; grantee Ford Found., 1967. Mem. Am. Bus. Press (chmn. editorial com. 1975-76). Republican. Episcopalian. Office: Med Econs Co Inc 5 Paragon Dr Montvale NJ 07645-1725

SIGAL, ISRAEL MICHAEL, scientist; b. Kiev, Ukraine, Aug. 31, 1945; came to U.S., 1978; s. Moshe I. and Eva (Guz) S.; m. Brenda Lynn Tipper; children: Alexander, Daniel. BA, Gorky (Russia) U., 1968; PhD, Tel-Aviv U., 1976. Postdoctoral fellow Swiss Inst. Tech., Zürich, Switzerland, 1976-78; asst. prof. Princeton (N.J.) U., 1978-81; R.H. Revson sr. scientist Weizmann Inst., Rehovot, Israel, 1981-85; prof. U. Calif., Irvine, 1984-90, U. Toronto, Ont., Can., 1985—; invited spkr. various confs. in field including invited talk at Internat. Conf. Mathematicians, Kyoto, 1990; Jeffrey-Williams Lectureship, Can. Math. Soc., 1992. Editor Revs. Math. Physics, 1991—, Internat. Rsch. Notices, 1991—; contbr. articles to profl. and sci. publs. I.W. Killam Rsch. fellow I.W. Killam Found., 1989-91; recipient John L. Synge Award Royal Soc. Can., 1993. Fellow Royal Soc. Can. Office: U Toronto Dept Math, 100 St George St, Toronto, ON Canada M5S 3G3

SIGAL, MICHAEL STEPHEN, lawyer; b. Chgo., July 9, 1942; s. Carl I. and Evelyn (Wallack) S.; m. Kass M. Flaherty, May 16, 1971; 1 child, Sarah Caroline. BS, U. Wis.-Madison, 1964; JD, U. Chgo., 1967. Bar: Ill. 1967, U.S. Dist. Ct. (no. dist.) Ill. 1967. Assoc. firm Sidley & Austin and predecessor firm, Chgo., 1967-73, ptnr., 1973—. Mem. U. Chgo. Law Rev., 1965. Bd. dirs. EMRE Diagnostic Services, Inc., affiliate Michael Reese Hosp., Chgo., 1982-91, The Mary Meyer Sch., Chgo., 1986-87. Mem. ABA, Chgo. Bar Assn., Law Club, Mid-Day Club (Chgo.), Mill Creek Hunt Club (bd. dirs. 1992—, Wadsworth, Ill.), Phi Beta Kappa, Phi Kappa Phi, Phi Eta Sigma. Jewish. Home: 2180 Wilmot Rd Deerfield IL 60015-1556 Office: Sidley & Austin 1 First Natl Plz Chicago IL 60603-2003

SIGALL, HAROLD FRED, psychology educator; b. N.Y.C., June 29, 1943; s. Walter and Regine (Goldenberg) S.; m. Brenda Ann Alpert, Aug. 8, 1965; children: Elana, Jennifer, Emily. BS, CUNY, 1964; PhD, U. Tex., 1968. Asst. prof. psychology U. Rochester, N.Y., 1968-72; assoc. prof. U. Md., College Park, 1972-78, prof., 1978—, dir. grad. program in social psychology; consulting editor Journal of Applied Social psychology, 1992—; cons. social research and decision making to numerous orgns., lectr. Smithsonian Inst., Washington, 1984, 85. Editor Personality and Social Psychology Bull., 1977-81; contbr. numerous articles to profl. jours. Bd. dirs. Columbia (Md.) Jewish Congregation, 1985-87, Howard County (Md.) Jewish Cmty. Sch., Columbia, 1986-87; mem. Human Rights Commn., Howard County, 1994—. NDEA fellow, 1967-68, Danforth Found. fellow, 1970-71. Fellow Am. Psychol. Assn., Am. Psychol. Soc.; mem. Soc. Exptl. Social Psychology. Home: 5060 Castlemoor Dr Columbia MD 21044-1454 Office: U of Md Dept Psychology College Park MD 20742

SIGBAND, NORMAN BRUCE, management communication educator; b. Chgo., June 27, 1920; s. Max and Bessie S.; m. Joan C. Lyons, Aug. 3, 1944; children: Robin, Shelley, Betsy. BA, U. Chgo., 1940, MA, 1941, PhD, 1954; LHD (hon.), DePaul U., 1986. Asst. prof. bus. communication De Paul U., 1946-50, assoc. prof., 1950-54, prof., 1954-65; prof. mgmt. communication U. So. Calif., 1965—, chmn. dept. mktg., 1970-72; assoc. dean U. So. Calif. (Sch. Bus.), 1975-80, Disting. prof. emeritus, 1989—; Disting. Centennial lectr. U. Tex., Austin, 1986; cons. to industry; speaker, condr. workshops, seminars in field; Scholar in Residence, Va. Commonwealth U., 1987, DePaul U., 1988; Disting. emeritus prof. U. So. Calif., 1989,. Author books including: Practical Communication for Everyday Use, 25th edit., 1954, Effective Report Writing for Business, Industry and Government, 1960, Communication for Management, 1970, Communicacion Para Directivos, 1972, Management Communication for Decision Making, 1972, Communication for Management and Business, 1976, Communication for Managers, 6th edit., 1994, Communicating in Business, 1987, 3d edit., 1989, Patient-Pharmacist Consultation: A Communication Skills Approach, 1993, Communication for Pharmacists and Other Health Professionals, 1995, 2d edit., 1996; movies include: Communication Barriers and Gateways, 2d edit., 1993, Listening: A Key to Problem Solving (award winnter), 2d edit., 1993, The Grapevine, The Power of a Minute, 1992; gen. editor books including: Harcourt Brace Jovanovich Bus. series; contbr. numerous articles to profl. jours., mags. Served to capt. AUS, 1942-46, ETO. Decorated Bronze Star; recipient Excellence in Teaching award U. So. Calif., 1975, Dean's award, 1972, Outstanding Educator award, 1973, Disting. Emeritus award, 1989. Fellow Am. Bus. Communication Assn. (pres. 1964-65); mem. Internat. Communication Assn., Acad. Mgmt., Anti-Defamation League, Hadassah Assocs., Blue Key, Phi Kappa Phi, Alpha Kappa Psi, Beta Gamma Sigma. Democrat. Jewish. Home: 3109 Dona Susana Dr Studio City CA 91604-4355 Office: U So Calif Health Sci Campus 1985 Zonal Ave Los Angeles CA 90033-1058

SIGEL, JAY, insurance company executive; b. Berwyn, Pa., Nov. 13, 1943; m. Elizabeth Sigel; children: Jennifer, Amy, Megan. Prin. owner Sigel Ins. Group, Berwyn, Pa.; profl. golfer Sr. PGA Tour. Bd. trustees Wake Forest Coll. Inducted into Collegiate Golf Coaches of Am. Hall of Fame; career victoris include 1994 GTE West Classic, 1996 Energizer Srs. Tour Championship, Bob Jones award, 1984, Ben Hogan award, 1984; won U.S. Amateur, 1982, 83, Brit. Amateur, 1979. Office: care Profl Golfers Assn Box 109601 100 Ave of Champions Palm Beach Gardens FL 33410-9961

SIGEL, MARSHALL ELLIOT, financial consultant; b. Hartford, Conn., Nov. 25, 1941; s. Paul and Bessie (Somer) S.; m. Sybil R. Miller, Nov. 23, 1995. BS in Econs., U. Pa., 1963; JD, U. Miami, 1982, LLM in Taxation, 1983. Exec. v.p. Advo-System div. KMS Industries, Inc., Hartford, 1963-69, pres., 1969-72; pres. Ad-Type Corp., Hartford, 1963-69, Ad-Lists, Inc., Hartford, 1963-69; fin. cons. Hartford, 1972-83, Boca Raton, Fla., 1987—; pvt. practice law, 1983-87. Bd. dirs. Wharton Sch. Club of South Fla. Mem. FOPA, World Pres.' Orgn., citizens bd. U. Miami, Boca Grove Club, 100 Club of So. Palm Beach County. Home and Office: PO Box 273408 Boca Raton FL 33427-3408

SIGETY, CHARLES BIRGE, investment company executive; b. N.Y.C., Sept. 30, 1952; s. Charles Edward and Katharine Kinne (Snell) S.; m. Elizabeth Ross Pennington, Nov. 27, 1976; children: Austin Douglas, Katharine Colyer, Alexander Birge. BA in English Lit., Bates Coll., 1975. Lic. nursing home adminstr. Adminstr. in tng. Florence Nightingale Nursing Home, N.Y.C., 1972, asst. dir. facility ops., 1975, dir. facility ops., 1975-78, assoc. adminstr., 1978-81, exec. dir., 1981-82; pres., CEO Profl. Med. Products, Inc., Greenwood, S.C., 1982-96; dir. Upper Savannah Internat. Trade Assn., Greenwood, S.C., 1993-94; pres. Upper Savannah Internat. Trade Assn., Greenwood, 1993; CEO Bison Investments, Inc., Tampa, Fla., 1996; adv. bd. Liberty Mutual Ins. Cos. S.C., 1986-96, County Bank, Greenwood, 1981, Nation's Banks S.C., 1984-96; bd. dirs. Profl. Med. Products, Inc.; vice chmn. Upper Savannah Bus. Group on Health Care, Greenwood, 1982-87; mem. S.C. Bus. Roundtable for the Initiative for Work

Force Excellence, Columbia, 1988-92; dir., mem. exec. com. OSTEO Am., Inc., 1993-96; bd. dirs. Help for Incontinent People, 1993-96. Bd. visitors Med. U. S.C., 1988; active Young Pres. Orgn., 1988. Mem. Am. Coll. Health Care Adminstrs., Health Industry Mfrs. Assn. (ofcl. rep. 1982-96), Upper Savannah Internat. Trade Assn. (pres. 1993), Young Pres.'s Orgn. Republican. Presbyterian. Avocations: hunting, sailing, woodworking. Office: Bison Investments Inc 3225 S Macdill Ave # 236 Tampa FL 33629-8171

SIGETY, CHARLES EDWARD, lawyer, family business consultant; b. N.Y.C., Oct. 10, 1922; s. Charles and Anna (Toth) S.; m. Katharine K. Snell, July 17, 1948; children: Charles, Katharine, Robert, Cornelius, Elizabeth. BS, Columbia U., 1944; MBA, Harvard U., 1947; LLB, Yale U., 1951; LHD (hon.), Cazenovia Coll., 1994. Bar: N.Y. 1952, D.C. 1958. With Bankers Trust Co., 1939-42; instr. adminstrv. engring. Pratt Inst., 1948; instr. econs. Yale U., 1948-50; vis. lectr. acctg. Sch. Gen. Studies Columbia U., N.Y.C., 1948-50, 52; rapporteur com. fed. taxation for U.S. coun. Internat. C. of C., 1952-53; asst. to com. fed. taxation Am. Inst. Accts., 1950-53; with Compton Advt. Agy., N.Y.C., 1954; vis. lectr. law Yale U., 1952; pvt. practice law N.Y.C., 1952-67; pres., dir. Video Vittles, Inc., N.Y.C., 1953-67; dep. commr. FHA, 1955-57; of counsel Javits and Javits, 1959-60; 1st asst. atty. gen. N.Y., 1958-59; dir., mem. exec. com. Gotham Bank, N.Y.C., 1961-63; dir. N.Y. State Housing Fin. Agy., 1962-63; chmn. Met. Ski Slopes, Inc., N.Y.C., 1962-65; pres., exec. adminstr. Florence Nightingale Health Ctr., N.Y.C., 1965-85; chmn. bd. Profl. Med. Products, Inc., Greenwood, S.C., 1982-96; dir. Schaerer AG, Wabern, Switzerland, 1982-88; professorial lectr. Sch. Architecture, Pratt Inst., N.Y.C., 1962-66; mem. Sigety Assocs., cons. in housing mortgage financing and urban renewal, 1957-67; ho. cons. Govt. of Peru, 1956; mem. missions to Hungary, Poland, Fed. Republic Germany, Malta, Czechoslovakia, Russia, Israel, Overseas Pvt. Investment Corp., 1990-92; owner, operator Peppermill Farms, Pipersville, Pa., 1956—. Bd. dirs., sec., v.p., treas. Nat. Coun. Health Ctrs., 1969-85; bd. dirs. Am.-Hungarian Found., 1974-76, Pritikin Rsch. Found., 1991—, Stratford Arms Condo Assn., 1992-93, Global Leadership Inst., 1993—; trustee Cazenovia (N.Y.) Coll., 1981-95; del. White House Conf. on Aging, 1971, White House Conf. on Mgmt. Tng. and Market Econs. Edn. in Ctrl. and Ea. Europe, 1991; bd. visitors Lander Coll., U. S.C., Greenwood, 1982-84; mem. fin. com. World Games, Santa Clara, 1981, London, 1985, Karlsruhe, 1989, The Hague, 1993, Confrerie des Chevaliers du Tastevin, Confrerie de la Chaine des Rotisseurs, Wine and Food Soc., Wednesday 10. Recipient President's medal Cazenovia Coll., 1990, George Washington laureate Am. Hungarian Found., 1996; Baker scholar Harvard U., 1947. Mem. Harvard Bus. Sch. Assn. (exec. coun. 1966-69, area chmn. 1967-69), Townsend Harris Alumni Assn. (bd. dirs. 1993—), Yale Club (N.Y.C.), Harvard Bus. Sch. Club (N.Y.C., pres. 1964-65, chmn. 1965-66, bd. dirs. 1964-70), Harvard Club (N.Y.C.), Met. Club (Washington), Alpha Kappa Psi, Phi Delta Phi. Presbyterian. Office: Peppermill Farms 7155 Old Easton Rd # 156 Pipersville PA 18947-9701

SIGETY, CORNELIUS EDWARD, office manager; b. N.Y.C., June 6, 1958; s. Charles Edward and Katharine (Snell) S.; m. Virginia White, Oct. 28, 1995. BA, U. Rochester, N.Y., 1980; MBA, Harvard U., Boston, 1985. Asst. adminstr. Florence Nightingale Health Ctr., N.Y., 1980-83; v.p. Profl. Med. Products, Greenwood, S.C., 1985-88; mng. dir. Kenbar Group, N.Y., 1988—; bd. dirs. Heritage Conservancy. Mem. Union Club, Doylestown Country Club, Mantoloking Yacht Club. Presbyn. Avocations: sailing, golf, skiing. Home: PO Box 369 Pipersville PA 18947 Office: Kenbar Group 1760 3rd Ave New York NY 10029-6810

SIGGINS, JACK ARTHUR, librarian; b. Arp, Tex., July 11, 1938; s. Wilbur McCulla and Dayle Marie (Hensley) S.; m. Maureen Ellen Sullivan, Sept. 1, 1984. B.A., Princeton U., 1960; postgrad. law, U. Va., 1961-62; M.A., Am. U., 1967, U. Chgo., 1969. Research analyst Library of Congress, Washington, 1965-66; Librarian Far Eastern Library, U. Chgo., 1968-70; head East Asia Coll. U. Md., College Park, 1970-75, asst. dir. libraries, 1975-77, assoc. dir. libraries, 1977-82; dep. univ. librarian Yale U., New Haven, 1982-92; pvt. practice orgnl. cons. New Haven, 1993-94; univ. libr. George Washington U., Washington, 1995—; cons. Boston Coll. 1994, U. Mo., 1994, Harvard U., 1994, Nat. Libr. of Australia, 1993, Ctrl. Mich. U., 1993, Tulane U., 1993; advisor Md. Dept. Edn., Balt., 1978-82; mem. adv. com. Sch. Libr. Sci. So. Conn. State U., New Haven, 1981-88; vis. com. Princeton U. Libr., 1987-96. Contbr. articles to profl. jours. Served with U.S. Army, 1961-64, Japan. Far Eastern Studies fellow Ford Found., 1966; Title II fellow U. Chgo., 1967-70; fellow Davenport Coll., Yale U., 1983-92. Mem. ALA (univ. libr. standards com. 1985-88), Beta Phi Mu. Club: Princeton (N.Y.C.). Office: George Washington U Gelman Libr Washington DC 20052

SIGINER, DENNIS AYDENIZ, mechanical engineering educator, researcher; b. Ankara, Turkey, July 10, 1943; came to U.S., 1976; s. Kazim Siginer and Emine Turkoz; m. Julya Yalcin, Nov. 25, 1994. BS, MS with honors, Tech. U. Istanbul, 1966, ScD, 1971; PhD, U. Minn., 1982. Rsch. assoc. U. Minn., Mpls., 1976-80; asst. prof. U. Ala., Tuscaloosa, 1981-83; assoc. prof. Auburn (Ala.) U., 1984-92, prof. mech. engring., 1992—; organizer, chmn. several internat. and nat. confs.; invited speaker to several countries, fgn. and nat. instns., internat. and nat. meetings; reviewer NSF, Internat. Sci. Found., Jour. Non-Newtonian Fluid Mechanics, Jour. Engring. Sci., Rheologica Acta, Jour. Fluids and Structures, Jour. Fluids Engring., Jour. Heat Transfer, Jour. Dynamic Systems Measurement and Ctrl., Jour. Applied Mechanics, book revs. for pubs. Editor procs. of 1st East-West Conf. on advances in structured and heterogeneous continua, Moscow, 1993; editor numerous books on devels. in non-Newtonian flows, electrorheol. fluids and fluid mechanics phenomena in microgravity; editor-in-chief: Advances in the Flow and Rheology on Non-Newtonian Fluids, 1997; assoc. editor Jour. of Applied Mechanics, 1997; author books in field; contbr. more than 100 articles to profl. jours. Recipient 3 univ.-wide teaching awards; Summer faculty fellow NASA, 1991, 92. Fellow ASME (organizer, editor procs. Symposia on Applications and Devels. Non- Newtonian Flows 1995, Symposia on Rheology and Fluid Mechanics Nonlinear Materi als 1996, 97, svc. award 1993, 95, 96), Sci. and Tech. Rsch. Coun. Turkey; mem. Am. Soc. Engring. Edn. (rsch. award 1992), Soc. Rheology, Am. Acad. Mechanics, Am. Inst. Physics, Soc. Engring. Sci., N.Y. Acad. Scis., Sigma Xi, Pi Tau Sigma (hon.). Home: 3809 Flintwood Ln Opelika AL 36804-7613 Office: Auburn U Dept Mech Engring Auburn AL 36849-5341

SIGLER, HOLLIS, artist, educator; b. Gary, Ind., Mar. 2, 1948. Studied in Florence, Italy, 1968-69; BFA, Moore Coll. Art, 1970, DFA (hon.), 1994; MFA, Sch. Art Inst. Chgo., 1973. Mem. faculty Columbia Coll., Chgo., 1978—, instr. painting and drawing, 1984—. One-woman shows include Akron (Ohio) Art Mus., 1986, S.W. Craft Ctr., San Antonio, 1989, Nat. Mus. Women Arts, Washington, 1991, 93, Printworks Gallery, Chgo., 1991, 93, Priebe Art Gallery, U. Wis., Oshkosh, 1992, Susan Cummins Gallery, Mill Valley, Calif., 1992, 94, Steven Scott Gallery, Balt., 1993, 94, Hartman Ctr. Gallery, Bradley U., Peoria, Ill., 1994, Mus. Contemporary Art, Chgo., 1994, Suburban Fine Arts Ctr., Highland Park, Ill., 1994, Lakeview Mus. Arts and Sci., Peoria, 1994, Decordova Mus. and Sculpture Park, Lincoln, Mass., 1994, Leedy-Voulkos Art Ctr. Gallery, Kansas City, Mo., 1995, Ark. Art Ctr., Little Rock, 1996, Elvehjem Mus. Art., U. Wis., Madison, 1997; exhibited in group shows Whitney Mus. Art, N.Y.C., 1981, Walker Art Mus., Mpls., 1982, Mus. Modern Art, N.Y.C., 1984, Corcoran Gallery Art, Washington, 1985, Chgo. Cultural Ctr., 1992, The Drawing Ctr., N.Y.C., 1993, The Contemporary Mus., Honolulu, 1994, Butler Inst. Am. Art, Youngstown, Ohio, 1995, Nat. Mus. Am. Art, Smithsonian, Washington, 1996; represented in permanent collections Mus. Contemporary Art, Chgo., Indpls. Mus. Art, Seattle Art Mus., Madison Art Ctr., High Mus. Art, Atlanta, Nat. Mus. Am. Art, Smithsonian, Nat. Mus. Women in the Arts, Washington; also others. Recipient cash award Southwestern Ctr. for Contemporary Art, Winston-Salem, N.C., 1987, Childe Hassam purchase award AAAL, 1988; grantee Ill. Arts Coun., 1986, Nat. Endowment for Arts, 1987. Office: Columbia Coll 600 S Michigan Ave Chicago IL 60605-1901

SIGLER, JAY ADRIAN, political scientist, educator; b. Paterson, N.J., June 21, 1933; s. Benjamin and Lucille (Pakula) S.; m. Janet Barndt, May 5, 1984; children: Niall, Ian. B.A. with honors, Rutgers U., 1954, J.D. (Law Alumni scholar), 1957, M.A. (fellow), 1960, Ph.D., 1962. Asst. prof. polit. sci. Kent (Ohio) State U., 1961-63, U. Vt., Burlington, 1963-64; instr. dept. polit. sci. Rutgers U., Camden, N.J., 1960-61; asso. prof. Rutgers U., 1965-70, prof., 1970-73, Disting. prof. polit. sci., chmn. dept., 1973—; dir. Grad. Program in Public Policy, 1979—; dir. Forum for Policy Rsch. and Pub. Svc. Rutgers U., Camden, N.J., 1995—; asso. dean Grad. Program in Public Policy, 1970-71. Author: An Introduction to the Legal System, 1968, Double Jeopardy, 1969, The Conservative Tradition in American Thought, 1969, Courts and Public Policy, 1970, El Pensamento Conservador en los Estados Unidos, 1971, Contemporary American Government, 1972, The Performance of American Government, 1972, American Rights Policies, 1975, The Legal Sources of Public Policy, 1977, Understanding Criminal Law, 1981, Minority Rights, 1983, International Handbook of Race and Race Relations, 1987, Interactive Compliance, 1988, Corporate Lawbreaking and Interactive Compliance, 1991; contbr. articles to profl. jours. Mcpl. chmn. Democratic Party, Haddonfield, N.J., 1968-70; mem. Camden County Dem. Com., 1968-71. Served with U.S. Army, 1957-58. Recipient Lindback award for disting. teaching, 1981; Rutgers Research fellow, 1973-74; Eagleton fellow, 1978-79; Am. Polit. Sci. Assn. Project 87 fellow, 1979; Nat. Endowment for Humanities summer fellow, 1979; Warren Sussman Disting. Teaching award, 1995. Mem. AAUP, Law and Soc. Assn., Policy Studies Orgn., Nat. Assn. Schs. Public Affairs and Adminstrn., Am. Polit. Sci. Assn. Club: Rutgers Faculty. Home: PO Box 1932 Edgartown MA 02539-1932 Office: Rutgers U Grad Program Pub Policy 311 N 5th St Camden NJ 08102-1205 *The contemplation of the limits of a life, of the mixture of luck and planning for more luck, is a source of balance and calm. Discovering that a few persons mean more than any things is the hard and painful part.*

SIGLER, LEROY WALTER, banker, lawyer, entrepreneur; b. Racine, Wis., Aug. 3, 1926; s. LeRoy I. and Ruth Ann (Wacynski) S.; m. Joanne I. Nash, June 20, 1947 (dec. Jan. 7, 1966); m. Sylvia L. Schmidt, Sept. 20, 1969; children: Suzanne Sigler Storer, Cynthia Sigler Whittaker, Lee Scott, Robb Nash, Paul Grant. B.B.A., U. Wis., 1952, J.D., 1952. Bar: Wis. 1952, Ohio 1967. Corp. counsel, asst. sec. J.W. Butler Paper Co., 1952-66, Butler Paper Co., 1952-66; asst. mgr. law dept. Nekoosa Edwards Paper Co., 1952-66; asst. sec., gen. counsel Seilon, Inc., 1966-68, v.p., sec., gen. counsel, 1968-70, pres., gen. counsel, dir., 1970-79; pres., gen. counsel, dir. Bancorp. Leasing, 1973-79, Thomson Internat. Co., Thomson Veracruz S.A., Thomson-Poole, Inc., Inmobilaria Elda S.A., 1971-79, Air-Way Sanitizor, Inc., 1972-79; various positions including pres., vice chmn., dir., sec., gen. counsel Nev. Nat. Bank, 1969-76; v.p., sec. gen., counsel, dir. Nev. Nat. Bancorp., 1969-76; sec., gen. counsel Lamb Enterprises, Inc., Lamb Communications, Inc., 1970-79; chmn., dir. Greenwood's Bancorp., Inc., 1976-81; pres., dir. Nekoosa Port Edwards Bancorp., Inc., 1979—, Nekoosa Port Edwards State Bank, 1980-95; chmn., CEO, dir. Nekoosa Port Edwards State Bank, 1995—; bd. dirs. Gross Common Carrier, Inc., Opollo, Lou-Ques Corp., Broadline Leasing, Freightline; pres., dir. NeKossa Port Edwards Investment, Inc., 1994—; sec., treas. Riverview Health Care Found., Inc., 1996, vice chmn., 1997—. Chmn. fund drive South Wood County United Fund, NeKoosa Pub. Libr., 1995-97; co-chmn. Community Planning Commn.; pres. Port Edwards Water Utility, Tri City Airways, Village of Port Edwards;pres., dir. Riverview Hosp., Riverview Manor; dir. Tri City Health Care, Inc., Advanced Med. Equipment, Inc.; chmn. South Wood County Airport Commn.; mem. parish council, fin. com., treas. Sacred Heart Ch., sec., bd. dirs. Sacred Heart Parish Found., Inc.; chmn. Nekoosa Bus. Council, 1981-82; chmn. Nekoosa Indsl. Devel., 1983-86. Served with AUS, 1945-47. Mem. Wisconsin Rapids C. of C. (dir. 1960-66, 81-83, Spl. Citizen award 1964), Tri-City Bar Assn. (pres.), 7th Circuit Bar Assn. (v.p.), Toastmasters Club (v.p.), Phi Delta Phi. Lodges: Elk (exalted ruler, trustee); Rotary. Home: PO Box 86 Nekoosa WI 54457-0086 Office: 405 Market St Nekoosa WI 54457-1125 *Play all games possible. Play by the rules. Play to win.*

SIGLER, LOIS OLIVER, retired educator; b. Piney Flats, Tenn., Sept. 8, 1923; d. Willie Campbell and Lillie (Brown) Oliver; m. William Virgil Sigler Jr., Aug. 25, 1962; 1 child, William Oliver. BS, East Tenn. State U., 1944; MS, U. Tenn., 1952; postgrad., Memphis State U., U. Tenn. Home econs. tchr. Buchanan (Va.) pub. schs., 1944-46; area supr. home econs. edn. and sch. lunch prog. State Dept. Edn., Commonwealth of Va., 1946-54; asst. nat. advisor Future Homemakers of Am./New Homemakers of Am., HEW, Washington, 1954-56; nat. advisor Future Homemakers of Am./New Homemakers of Am., HEW, 1956-63; family living coord. Ohio State Dept. and Columbus (Ohio) Pub. Schs., Columbus Met. Housing Authority, 1963; tchr. Millington (Tenn.) High Sch., 1966-92; ret., 1992. Mem. Pres. Kennedy's Food for Peace Coun., Pres. Eisenhower's Adv. Com. on Youth Fitness. Named Tenn. Home Econs. Tchr. of Yr., 1975, Woman of Yr., 1991, Twentieth Century award for achievement, 1991. Mem. NEA, Am. Home Econs. Assn., Tenn. Home Econs. Assn., Am. Voc. Assn., Tenn. Voc. Assn., Nat. Voc. Home Econs. Tchrs. Assn., Tenn. Voc. Home Econs. Tchrs. Assn. (hon. 1992, past sec.-treas., Outstanding Svc. award 1986), W. Tenn. Home Econs. Edn. Assn. (past pres.), Tenn. Edn. Assn. (bd. dirs. 1977-80), W. Tenn. Edn. Assn., Shelby County Edn. Assn. (past sch. rep.), Future Homemakers Am. (nat. hon. 1956, state hon. 1991, master advisor award 1988, advisor mentor 1991), Omicron Nu, Pi Lambda Theta. Home: 4785 Rolling Meadows Dr Memphis TN 38128-4868

SIGLER, PAUL BENJAMIN, molecular biology educator, protein crystallographer; b. Richmond, Va., Feb. 19, 1934; s. George and Florence (Kaminsky) S.; m. Althea Jo Martin, Oct. 2, 1958; children—Jennifer, Michele, Jonathan, Deborah, Rebecca. A.B. in Chemistry summa cum laude, Princeton U., 1955; M.D., Columbia U., 1959; Ph.D. in Biochemistry, Cambridge U., 1967. Intern and resident dept. medicine Columbia-Presbyn. Med. Ctr., N.Y.C., 1959-61; research assoc. NIAMD, 1961-63, staff Lab. Molecular Biology, 1963-64; vis. fellow MRC Lab. Molecular Biology, Cambridge, Eng., 1964-67; assoc. prof. biophysics U. Chgo., 1967-73, prof. biophysics and theoretical biology, 1973-84, prof. biochemistry and molecular biology, 1984-88; prof. molecular biophysics and biochemistry Yale U., New Haven, 1989—; investigator Howard Hughes Med. Inst., 1989—. Served with USPHS, 1961-64. Recipient Research Career Devel. award USPHS, 1971-75; Guggenheim fellow, 1974; Katzir fellow, 1975. Fellow Am. Acad. Arts and Scis.; mem. NAS, Am. Crystallographic Assn. Jewish. Avocations: painting; bicycling. Office: Yale U HHMI 154BCMM 260 Whitney Ave # G423 New Haven CT 06511-7208

SIGMON, DANIEL RAY, foundation administrator; b. Orangeburg, S.C., Sept. 15, 1949; s. Carment Ray and Freida Marion (Stoudenmire) S.; m. Cheryl Mahaffey, Dec. 31, 1976; children: Ashley W. Truluck, Elizabeth Wakefield, Caroline Christine. BE, U. S.C., 1971, MA, 1972. Tchr. Calhoun County Sch. Dist., St. Matthews, S.C., 1971-72; hist. sites supt. S.C. Dept. Parks, Recreation & Tourism, Columbia, S.C., 1972-73; staff historian S.C. Dept. Parks, Recreation & Tourism, 1973-85; exec. dir. Hist. Camden (S.C.), 1985-87; dir. Alexander Homesite & History Mus., Charlotte, N.C., 1987-88; exec. dir. Hist. Columbia Found., Columbia, 1988—. Author: Huntington Beach State Park; A Visitor's Guide, 1984, Hampton Plantation; Visitor's Guide, 1983; editor: A Guide to Historic Sites in Camden, S.C., 1985. Mem. Columbia Action Coun., 1989—, Cultural Coun. Richland and Lexington County, Columbia, 1989—; bd. dirs. Sunrise Found., 1992—; mem. county commn. Palmetto Project Discovery '92, 1991-92. Mem. Nat. Trust Hist. Preservation, Am. Assn. State and Local History, Am. Assn. Mus., S.C. Confedn. Local Hist. Socs. (exec. coun. 1991—), S.C. Fedn. Mus. (pres. 1994-96), Palmetto Trust Hist. Preservation (exec. com. 1991-96), Greater Columbia C. of C. Methodist. Avocations: gardening, backpacking, canoeing, camping, traveling. Office: Hist Columbia Found 1601 Richland St Columbia SC 29201-2633

SIGMON, JOYCE ELIZABETH, professional society administrator; b. Stanley, N.C., Oct. 4, 1935; d. Rome Alfred and Pearl Elizabeth (Beal) S. BS, U. N.C., 1971; MA, Loyola U., 1980. Cert. dental asst., assn. exec. Dental asst. Dr. Paul A. Stroup, Jr., Charlotte, N.C., 1953-63; instr. Wayne Tech. Inst., Goldsboro, N.C., 1963-65, Ctrl. Piedmont Community Coll., Charlotte, 1965-69; dir. Dental Assisting Edn. ADA, Chgo., 1971-85, asst. sec. Coun. Prosthetics Svcs., 1985-87, mgr. Office Quality Assurance, 1987-80, exec. dir. Aux., 1990-92; dir. adminstrv. activities Am. Acad. of Implant Dentistry, Chgo., 1993—; exec. sec. Am. Bd. of Oral Implantology/Implant Dentistry, 1993—. Deacon 4th Presbyn. Ch., 1973-75, elder 1975-77, 88-91, trustee, 1991-94; moderator Presbyn. Women in 4th Ch., 1987-91. Mem. Am. Soc. Assn. Execs., Chgo. Soc. Assn. Execs. (chair CAE com. 1991-92), Am. Dental Assts. Assn., N.C. Dental Assn. (pres. 1968-69), Charlotte Dental Assts. Soc. Presbyterian. Home: 260 E Chestnut St Chicago IL 60611-2401 Office: Am Acad Implant Dentistry 211 E Chicago Ave Chicago IL 60611

SIGMOND, CAROL ANN, lawyer; b. Phila., Jan. 9, 1951; d. Irwin and Mary Florence (Vollmer) S. BA, Grinnell Coll., 1972; JD, Cath. U., 1975. Bar: Va. 1975, D.C. 1980, Md. 1988, N.Y. 1990, U.S. Dist. Ct. (ea. dist.) Va. 1975, U.S. Dist. Ct. (so. and ea. dist.) N.Y. 1991, U.S. Ct. Appeals (4th cir.) 1976, U.S. Ct. Appeals (fed. cir.) 1987. Asst. gen. counsel Washington Met. Area Transit Authority, 1978-85; acting assoc. gen. counsel for appeals and gen. law, 1985-86; assoc. Patterson, Belknap, Webb & Tyler, Washington, 1986-89, Berman, Paley, Goldstein & Kannry, N.Y.C., 1991-93; prin. Law Offices of Carol A. Sigmond, N.Y.C., 1993—; Mem. Women's Nat. Dem. Club. Mem. ABA, D.C. Bar Assn., Arlington County Bar Assn., Va. State Bar Assn., Md. State Bar Assn. Democrat. Mem. LDS. Avocations: piano, bridge.

SIGMOND, RICHARD BRIAN, lawyer; b. Phila., Dec. 7, 1944; s. Joseph and Jean (Nissman) S.; children: Michael, Catherine, Alina; m. Susan Helen Peteraf, Dec. 24, 1984. BS, Phila. Coll. Textiles & Sci., 1966; JD, Temple U., 1969. Bar: Pa. 1969, U.S. Supreme Ct. 1973, U.S. Dist. Ct. (ea. dist.) Pa. 1975, U.S. Ct. Appeals (3d cir.) 1975, N.Y. 1982, D.C. 1995. Atty. Pub. Defender Assn., Phila., 1969-70; ptnr. Meranze, Katz, Spear & Wilderman, Phila., 1970-84; sr. ptnr. Spear, Wilderman, Sigmond, Borish & Endy, Phila., 1985-89, Sagot, Jennings & Sigmond, Phila., 1989—; chmn., bd. dirs. Gatehouse Phila., 1972-83; lectr. Pvt. Industry Coun., Phila., 1985—, labor studies div., Pa. State U., 1978-82, 85-86. Mem. ABA (labor law com., litigation com.), AFL-CIO (lawyers coordinating com.), Pa. Bar Assn. (labor law com.), Phila. Bar Assn. (labor com.), Phi Alpha Delta. Avocations: sailing, writing. Office: Penn Mutual Towers 16th Fl 510 Walnut St Fl 16 Philadelphia PA 19106-3619

SIGMOND, ROBERT M., medical economist; b. Seattle, June 18, 1920; s. Harry and Alice (Gottfeld) S.; m. Barbara, June 29, 1941; children: Alison, Laurence. B.A., Pa. State Coll., 1941, M.A., 1942. Research asso. Gov.'s Commn. on Hosp. Facilities, Standards and Orgn., Phila., 1945-46, Hosp. Council Phila., 1946-50; asst. to v.p. Albert Einstein Med. Center, Phila., 1950-55; exec. v.p. for planning Albert Einstein Med. Center, 1968-70, exec. v.p., 1971-75, recipient trustee medal, 1975; dir. fiscal studies Nat. Commn. Financing of Hosp. Care, Chgo., 1952-54; exec. dir. Hosp. Coun. Western Pa., Pitts., 1955-64, Hosp. Planning Assn., Allegheny County, Pitts., 1964-68; dir. Cmty. Programs for Affordable Health Care, Chgo., 1981-85; cons. Blue Cross Assn. and Blue Cross of Greater Phila., 1976-77; adviser on hosp. affairs Blue Cross Blue Shield Assn., Chgo., 1977-96; sr. cons. Health Alliance Pa., 1995—; scholar-in-residence Sch. Bus. Adminstrn. Temple U., 1985—; past adj. prof. Robert F. Wagner Grad. Sch. of Pub. Policy, chmn. nat. steering com. hosp. cmty. benefit stds. program NYU, 1988-94; past adv. panel on cost effectiveness Congl. Office of Tech. Assessment; past cons. com. cmty. health care coun. on med. svcs. AMA, Social Security Adminstrn., Pa. Gov.'s Hosp. Study Commns., USPHS, OEO, Pitts. Found., U. Mich. Study of Hosp. and Med. Econs., hosp. utilization project Calif. Dept. Health; expert Office Asst. Sec. of Health HEW. Author: Methods of Making Experimental Inferences 2d edit, 1945; (with Thomas Kinser) The Hospital-Blue Cross Plan Relationship, 1976; numerous monographs for profl. jours. Chmn. nat. adv. com. Johnson Found. Community Hosp. Med. Staff Group Practice Program; trustee Dorothy Rider Pool Health Care Trust, Allentown, Pa., Integrated Mental Health Inc., Rochester, N.Y. Recipient 1st C. Rufus Rorem award, 1986, Disting. Svc. award Ohio State U., 1995; Edwin L. Crosby fellow Nuffield Provincial Hosps. Trust, London, 1976. Fellow Am. Pub. Health Assn. (mem. editorial bd. jour.); mem. Am. Hosp. Assn. (hon.), Am. Coll. Healthcare Execs. (Dean Conley award 1969), Forum for Healthcare Planning (award of merit 1984), Soc. Hosp. Planning (Corning award 1981), Internat. Hosp. Fedn., Hosp. Assn. Pa.(Disting. Svc. award 1992), Boondocks Med. Soc. Home: 2912 Carlton House 1801 John F Kennedy Blvd Philadelphia PA 19103-1731

SIGMUND, DIANE WEISS, judge; b. N.Y.C., Mar. 1, 1943. BS, Pa. State U., 1963; JD magna cum laude, Temple U., 1977. Bar: Pa. 1977. Lawyer Blank, Rome, Cominsky & McCauley, Phila.; judge U.S. Bankruptcy Ct. (Pa. ea. dist.), 3rd circuit, Phila., 1993—; mem. steering com. Ea. Dist. Pa. Bankruptcy Conf., 1995—, 3d Cir. Task Force Equal Treatment in Cts., Gender Commn., 1995—; chmn. Endowment Edn. Nat. Conf. Bankruptcy Judges., 1996—. Office: US Courthouse 601 Market St Ste 203 Philadelphia PA 19106-1713

SIGMUND, PAUL EUGENE, political science educator; b. Phila., Jan. 14, 1929; s. Paul Eugene and Marie (Ramsey) S.; m. Barbara Rowena Boggs, Jan. 25, 1964 (dec. 1990); children—Paul Eugene, David, Stephen. AB, Georgetown U., 1950; AB Fulbright scholar, U. Durham, Eng., 1950-51; M.A., Harvard, 1954, Ph.D., 1959; postgrad., U. Paris, France, U. Heidelberg, U. Cologne, Germany, 1955-56. Teaching fellow Harvard, 1953-55, 58-59, instr., 1959-63; assoc. prof. politics Princeton, 1963-70, prof. politics, 1970—. Author: Nicholas of Cusa and Medieval Political Thought, 1963, (with Reinhold Niebuhr) The Democratic Experience, 1969, Natural Law in Political Thought, 1971, 81, The Overthrow of Allende and the Politics of Chile, 1977, Multinationals in Latin America: The Politics of Nationalization, 1980, Liberation Theology at the Crossroads: Democracy or Revolution?, 1990, paperback, 92, The United States and Democracy in Chile, 1993; editor: The Ideologies of the Developing Nations, 1963, 67, 72, Models of Political Change in Latin America, 1970, (with Pedro Aspe) The Political Economy of Income Distribution in Mexico, 1983, Poder, Sociedad y Estado en USA, 1985; assoc. editor: World Politics; translator: The Military and the State in Latin America (A. Rouquié), 1987, St. Thomas Aquinas, On Politics and Ethics, 1988, Nicholas of Cusa, The Catholic Concordance, 1991, 95. Served to 1st lt. USAF, 1956-57. Mem. Am. Polit. Sci. Assn., Latin Am. Studies Assn., Phi Beta Kappa. Home: 8 Evelyn Pl Princeton NJ 08540-3818

SIGNORILE, VINCENT ANTHONY, lawyer; b. Jersey City, Mar. 22, 1959; s. Ralph R. and Rita (DeRosa) S. BS, St. Peter's Coll., Jersey City, 1981; JD, Seton Hall U., 1985. Bar: N.J. 1985, Pa. 1985. Aide Jersey City Mcpl. Coun., 1980-81, Office of Mayor, City of Jersey City, 1981; law clk. Corp. Counsel Jersey City, 1981-85; law sec. Superior Ct. N.J. for Hudson County, Jersey City, 1985-86; assoc. atty. Jersey City, 1986-89; ptnr. Signorile & Saminski, Jersey City, 1989—; judge Jersey City Mcpl. Ct., 1996—. Mem. Hudson County Dem. Com., 1977-81, Jersey City Environ. Com., 1989-93, Jersey City Planning Bd. Com., 1991-93, Jersey City Ins. Fund Com., 1989-93; co-chmn. Hudson County Columbus Parade, 1984-85; elected to Mcpl. Coun. Jersey City, 1989-93. Mem. ABA, N.J. Bar Assn., Pa. Bar Assn., Hudson County Bar Assn. (treas. Young Lawyer's Assn. 1987-88, scholar 1984-85), Assn. Trial Lawyers Am. Roman Catholic. Home: 1691 John F Kennedy Blvd Jersey City NJ 07305-1841 Office: Signorile & Saminski 309 Baldwin Ave Jersey City NJ 07306-1711

SIGNOROVITCH, DENNIS JAMES, communications executive; b. Norristown, Pa., July 23, 1945; s. James and Regina S.; m. Susan E. McLaughlin, 1968; children: James Edward, Sarah Elizabeth. BS in Fgn. Svc., Georgetown U., 1967; MA, Old Dominion U., 1972; postgrad., U. Toledo., 1972. Instr. U. Toledo, 1972-77; writer/editor Doehler Jarvis div. NL Industries, Toledo, 1977-78; mgr. pub. rels. Eltra Corp., N.Y.C., 1979, mgr. planning, 1980; various assignments AlliedSignal Corp., Morristown, N.J., 1980-92; v.p. pub. affairs AlliedSignal Corp., Torrance, Calif., 1992—; mem. Exec. Comm. Forum. With U.S. Army, 1967-70. Decorated Bronze Star with oak leaf cluster. Mem. The Conf. Bd. (corp. comm. coun. 1991), Vol. Ctr. of South Bay (bd. dirs. 1994), L.A. Music Ctr. Unified Fund (aerospace com. mem. 1992, 93, 96, vice chmn. corp. campaign 1997), Arthur W. Page Soc., San Francisco Acad. (trustee). Office: Allied Signal Aerospace 2525 W 190th St Torrance CA 90504-6002

SIGUION-REYNA, LEONARDO, lawyer, business executive; b. Dagupan City, The Philippines, Apr. 18, 1921; s. Lamberto and Felisa (Tiongson) S.; m. Armida Ponce-Enrile, Nov. 24, 1952; children: Monica, Leonardo, Carlos. LLB, U. Santo Tomas, Manila, 1946-48. Bar: Philippines, 1948. Sr. ptnr. Siguion Reyna, Montecillo, and Ongsiako, Makati Metro Manila; chmn. bd. Phimco Industries, Inc., Manila, Sandvick Philippines, Inc., Electrolux Mktg. Corp., Autocorp Group, Inc.; pres. Electronic Tele. Systems Industries, Inc., Philippines, Inc., Manila Meml. Park Cemetary, Inc.,

Valmora Investment & Mgmt. Corp.; dir. ABB (Phils) Inc., BA Fin. Corp., Inc., Crismida Realty Corp., Dole Philippines, Inc., Electrolux Philippines, Inc., Filflex Indsl. & Mfg. Corp., Goodyear Philippines, Inc., Indsl. Realties, Inc., Investment & Capital Corp. of the Philippines, Proton Pilipinas, Inc., Rizal Comml. Banking Corp., Unilever (Phil) Inc. Mem. Philippine Bar Assn., Casino Español de Manila. Roman Catholic. CLubs: Manila Yacht, Manila Polo, Rotary. Home: 7 Tangile Rd/North Forbes, Makati Manila The Philippines

SIGULER, GEORGE WILLIAM, financial services executive; b. Cleve., Apr. 26, 1947; s. John Frederick and Helen Alice (Popp) S.; m. Pamela Ann Mallon, Oct. 31, 1981; children: George William Jr., Emily Ann, Charles Arthur, Mary Elizabeth. AB, Amherst Coll., 1970; MBA, Harvard U., 1972. Ptnr. Harvard Mgmt. Co., Boston, 1974-83; chief of staff HHS, Washington, 1983-84; exec. v.p. Monarch Capital Corp., Springfield, Mass., 1984-87; vice chmn. bd. Monarch Capital Corp., Springfield, 1987-91; pres. Associated Capital Investor, San Francisco, 1990-91; mng. dir. Mitchell Hutchins Instl. Investors, Inc., N.Y.C., 1991-95; founder Siguler Guff & Co., 1995—; assoc. treas. Harvard U., 1973-88; bd. dirs. Bus. Mortgage Investors, Venture Lending and Leasing, Inc., Russia Ptnrs., L.P., Allied Capital Corp., Washington, Nova Care, King of Prussia, Pa., Healthcare Capital, Inc., Great Neck, N.Y. Mem. vis. com. Harvard U. Med. Sch., Boston, 1986—; mem. nat. adv. com. on community health resources HHS, Washington, 1985-90; trustee Perkins Sch. for Blind, Watertown, Mass., 1976-83, New Eng. Aquarium, 1989-91. Recipient Disting. Svc. award HHS, 1984. Republican. Presbyterian. Office: Siguler Guff & Co 630 5th Ave New York NY 10111-0100

SIH, CHARLES JOHN, pharmaceutical chemistry educator; b. Shanghai, China, Sept. 11, 1933; s. Paul Kwang-Tsien and Teresa (Dong) S.; m. Catherine Elizabeth Hsu, July 11, 1959; children—Shirley, Gilbert, Ronald. A.B. in Biology, Caroll Coll., 1953; M.S. in Bacteriology, Mont. State Coll., 1955; Ph.D. in Bacteriology, U. Wis., 1958. Sr. research microbial biochemist Squibb Inst. for Med. Research, New Brunswick, N.J., 1958-60; mem. faculty U. Wis.-Madison, 1960—, Frederick B. Power prof. pharm. chemistry, 1978, Hilldare prof., 1987—. Recipient 1st Ernest Volwiler award, 1977; Roussel prize, 1980, Am. Pharm. Assoc. award 1987. Mem. Am. Chem. Soc., Soc. Am. Biol. Chemists, Acad. Pharm. Scis., Soc. Am. Microbiologists. Home: 6322 Landfall Dr Madison WI 53705-4309

SIHLER, WILLIAM WOODING, finance educator; b. Seattle, Nov. 17, 1937; s. William and Helen Alice (Wooding) S.; m. Mary Elizabeth Unwin, Aug. 21, 1963; children: Edward Wooding, Jennifer Mary. A.B. summa cum laude in Govt. (Sheldon traveling fellow), Harvard U., 1959, MBA with high distinction, 1962, DBA, 1965. Instr., asst. prof. Harvard U. Bus. Sch., 1964-67; asso. prof. Darden Grad. Bus. Sch., U. Va., Charlottesville, 1967-72; prof. Darden Grad. Bus. Sch., U. Va., 1972-76, A.J. Morris prof., 1976-84; R.E. Trzcinski prof., 1984—, dir. D.B.A. Program, 1971-73, assoc. dean acad. affairs, 1972-77; exec. dir. BAFT/Ctr. for Internat. Banking Studies, 1977-91; bd. dirs. Curtiss-Wright Corp.; pres. Southeastern Cons. Group, Ltd. Co-author: Financial Management: Text and Cases, 2d edit., 1991, The Troubled Money Business, 1992, Financial Service Organizations: Cases in Strategic Management, 1993, Cases in Applied Corporate Finance, 1994; editor: Classics in Commercial Bank Lending, vol. 1, 1981, vol. 2, 1985; contbr. articles to mgmt. publs. and anthologies of readings. Class sec. Harvard M.B.A. Class, 1962, Case Western Res. U., mem. vis. com. Sch. Mgmt., 1976-86, bd. overseers, 1980-86. Recipient DeL. K. Jay prize Harvard U., Disting. Prof. award U. Va. Alumni Assn., 1982; C.J. Bonaparte scholar Harvard U. Mem. Fin. Mgmt. Assn., Am. Econ. Assn., Am. Fin. Assn., Eastern Fin. Assn., Univ. Club (N.Y.C.), Harvard Club (N.Y.C.), Greencroft Club (Charlottesville), Phi Beta Kappa, Beta Gamma Sigma. Home: 202 Sturbridge Rd Charlottesville VA 22901-2116 Office: PO Box 6550 Charlottesville VA 22906-6550

SIIMESTÖ, ORVO KALERVO, financial executive; b. Helsinki, Finland, Aug. 3, 1943; s. Idor and Ilma (Hukka) S.; m. Marja-Liisa Vehviläinen, May 30, 1964; children: Satu Kristiina, Katja Maarit. MBA, Helsinki Sch. Bus. Adminstrn., 1969. Dir. fin. Kone Oy, Hyvinkää, Finland, 1975-83; v.p. fin. Oy Wilhelm Schauman AB, Helsinki, 1983-88, A. Ahlstrom Corp., Helsinki, 1988—. Avocations: sailing, cross-country skiing, volleyball. Office: A Ahlstrom Corp, Eteläesplanadi 14, 00130 Helsinki Finland

SIIROLA, JEFFREY JOHN, chemical engineer; b. Patuxent River, Md., July 17, 1945; s. Arthur Raymond and Nancy Ellen (Harris) S.; m. Sharon Ann Atwood, Apr. 24, 1971; childen: John Daniel, Jennifer Ann. BS in Chem. Engring., U. Utah, 1967; PhD, U. Wis., 1970. Rsch. fellow Eastman Chem. Co., Kingsport, Tenn., 1972—; trustee CACHE Corp., Austin, Tex., 1983—. Co-author: Process Synthesis, 1973. Active Kingsport C. of C. Recycling, 1988—, Appalachian tr. maintenance Eastman Hiking Club, Kingsport, 1973—. With U.S. Army, 1970-72. Mem. AIChE (A.E. Marshall award 1967, Computing Practice award 1991, CAST divsn. programming chair 1988—), Nat. Acad. Engring., Accreditation Bd. for Engring. and Tech., Am. Chem. Soc., Am. Soc. for Engring. Edn., Am. Assn. for Artificial Intelligence. Achievements include development of the AIDES chem. process flowsheet invention procedure. Home: 2517 Wildwood Dr Kingsport TN 37660-4748 Office: Eastman Chem Co PO Box 1972 Kingsport TN 37662-5150

SIKER, EPHRAIM S., anesthesiologist; b. Port Chester, N.Y., Mar. 24, 1926; s. Samuel S. and Adele (Weiser) S.; m m . Eileen Mary Bohnel, Aug. 5, 1951; children—Kathleen Ellen, Jeffrey Stephen, David Alan, Paul William, Richard Francis. Student, Duke U., 1943-45; M.D., N.Y.U., 1949. Diplomate: Am. Bd. Anesthesiology (dir. 1971—, sec.-treas. 1974-82, pres. 1982-83) Nat. Bd. Med. Examiners. Intern Grasslands Hosp., Valhalla, N.Y., 1949-50, resident in anesthesia, 1950; resident dept. anesthesiology Mercy Hosp., Pitts., 1952-53; assoc. dir. dept. Mercy Hosp., 1955-62, chmn., 1962-92; practice medicine, specializing in anesthesiology Pitts., 1954—; pres. Pitts. Anesthesia Assocs., Ltd., 1967-89; dir. anesthesia services Central Med. Ctr., Pitts., 1973-89; courtesy staff St. Clair Meml. Hosp., Pitts., 1954-89, St. Margaret Meml. Hosp., 1962—; clin. prof. dept. anesthesiology U. Pitts. Sch. Medicine, 1968—; mem. exec. com. Am. Bd. Med. Spltys., 1978-81; Exch. cons. Welsh Nat. Sch. Medicine, Cardiff, 1955-56; mem. Pa. Gov.'s Commn. on Profl. Liability Ins., 1968-70; mem. adv. panel U.S. Pharmacopeia, 1970-76; mem. Am. acupuncture anesthesia study group of Nat. Acad. Scis. to Peoples Republic China, 1974; mem. adv. com. on splty. and geog. distbn. of physicians Inst. Medicine, Nat. Acad. Scis., 1974-76; trustee Ednl. Coun. for Fgn. Med. Grads., 1980-82, Mercy Hosp. Found., 1983-95; bd. dirs., sec. Anesthesia Patient Safety Foun., 1985-89, mem. exec. com., 1985-92, exec. dir., 1992—. Author: (with F.F. Foldes) Narcotics and Narcotic Antagonists, 1964; sect. on narcotic: (with F.F. Foldes) numerous other publs. in med. lit. Ency. Brittanica. Served to lt. M.C. USNR, 1950-52. USPHS postdoctoral research fellow, 1954; hon. fellow faculty anaesthetists Royal Coll. Surgeons, Eng., 1974; hon. fellow faculty anesthetists Coll. Medicine South Africa, 1983; recipient Hippocratic award Mercy Hosp., 1982. Fellow Royal Coll. Surgeons Ireland, Faculty Anaesthetists (hon. 1988); mem. Am. Soc. Anesthesiologists (pres. 1973—, bd. dirs. Disting. Svc. award 1984), AMA (alt. del. 1962), Pa. Med. Soc., Allegheny County Med. Soc., Pa. Soc. Anesthesiologists (pres. 1965, Disting. Svc. award 1986), Royal Soc. Medicine (Eng.), Pitts. Acad. Medicine, Am. Coll. Anesthesiologists (bd. govs. 1969-7l), World Fedn. Anesthesiologists (chmn. exec. com. 1980-84, v.p. 1984-88), Assn. Anesthesia Program Dirs. (pres. 1987-89). Developed Siker Laryngoscope, 1956. Home: 185 Crestvue Manor Dr Pittsburgh PA 15228-1814 Office: 1400 Locust St Pittsburgh PA 15219-5114 *If you have to tell someone who you are, then you probably aren't. People are measured by more than their deeds, and such estimations are frequently made on the basis of their inter-personal relationships. While achievement and effort usually bear a linear relationship to each other, the impact that the achiever has on society depends upon the impact he makes on individuals.*

SIKES, ALFRED CALVIN, communications executive; b. Cape Girardeau, Mo., Dec. 16, 1939; s. William Kendall and Marcia (Weber) S.; m. Martha Pagenkopf, Aug. 19, 1961; chldren: Deborah Sue, Christine Louise, Marcia Cay. AB, Westminster Coll., 1961; LLB, U. Mo., 1964. Asst. atty. gen. Senator John Danforth, State of Mo., Jefferson City, 1970-72; campaign mgr. Bond. for Gov. Com., Jefferson City, 1972; dir., gov.-elect transition staff Bond for Gov. Com., Jefferson City, 1972; dir. dept. community and consumer affairs State of Mo., Jefferson City, 1973-76; exec. v.p. Mahaffey Enterprises, Springfield, Mo., 1977-78; pres., CEO Sikes & Assocs., Springfield, Mo., 1978-86; asst. sec. nat. telecom. and info. adminstrn. U.S. Dept. Commerce, Washington, 1986-89; chmn. FCC, Washington, 1989-93; v.p., group head new media and tech. The Hearst Corp., N.Y.C., 1993—; bd. dirs. Reflection Tech., Books That Work, Internet Profiles, Kidsoft, New Century Network. contbr. articles to profl. jours. Pres. Springfield Coun. Chs., 1984; chmn. bd. N.Y. Ctr. for Comm., Westminster Coll. Student Sponsorship/Partnership, Sch. Choice Found. Recipient Alumni Achievement award Westminster Coll., 1987. Mem. Orgn. Mo. Jaycees (pres. 1968-69), U.S. Jaycees (v.p. 1969-70), Orgn. Internat. Jaycees (legal counsel 1971-72). Republican. Methodist. Avocations: fishing, hunting, skiing, sailing. Home: 1140 5th Ave # 14B New York NY 10128-0806

SIKES, CYNTHIA LEE, actress, singer; b. Coffeyville, Kans., Jan. 2, 1954; d. Neil and Pat (Scott) S.; m. Alan Bud Yorkin, June 24, 1989. Student, Am. Conservatory Theater, San Francisco, 1977-79. Appeared in TV series St. Elsewhere, 1981-83, L.A. Law, 1989; TV movies include His Mistress, 1990; films include Man Who Loved Women, That's Life, Arthur On The Rocks, Love Hurts, 1988; producer, actress (television) Sins of Silence, 1996; also Broadway musical Into The Woods, 1988-89. Active Hollywood Women's Polit. Com. Recipient Gov.'s Medal of Merit, Kans., 1986. Democrat. Avocations: hiking, writing, reading.

SIKKEMA, KENNETH R., state legislator; b. Cadillac, Mich., Feb. 10, 1951; s. Peter John and Kathryn Mae (Laarman) S.; m. Carla Chase, Oct. 12, 1985; 1 child, Zachary Chase. BA in History cum laude, Harvard U., 1974; MBA with distinction, U. Mich., 1984. Legis. asst. Mich. Ho. of Reps., Lansing, 1974-75; adminstrv. asst. Mich. State Senate, Lansing, 1975-79; mktg. mgr. Herman Miller, Inc., Zeeland, Mich., 1984-86; exec. dir. West Mich. Environ. Action, Grand Rapids, 1979-82; state rep. State of Mich., Lansing, 1987—. Republican. Mem. Reformed Ch. in Am. Home: 3885 Omaha St SW Grandville MI 49418-1865 Office: Ho of Reps 515 Olds Plz Lansing MI 48913

SIKORA, BARBARA JEAN, library director; b. Passaic, N.J., Apr. 12, 1943; d. Stanley Francis and Jean (Sobczyk) S.; m. Richard Bendoritis, July 15, 1970 (div.). BA in Edn., English, William Paterson Coll., 1969, MEd in Learning Disabilities, 1978; MLS, Rutgers U., 1978; Cert. in Fundraising Mgmt., Fairleigh Dickinson U., 1990. Profl. libr. N.J. Tchr. Clifton (N.J.) Pub. Schs., 1969-73; office mgr. Singer/TRW, Fairfield, N.J., 1974-76; prin. libr. Passaic Pub. Libr., 1978-88; asst. libr. dir. Pub. Libr. Livingston, N.J., 1989-90; libr. dir. Pub. Libr. Livingston, 1991—; adj. faculty William Paterson Coll., 1977-90; trustee Wayne Pub. Libr., 1986-88; v.p. Livingston Coun. for the Arts, 1994; pres. Coun. for the Arts of the Livingston Area, 1993. Mem. Polish Heritage Festival Com., Holmdel, N.J., 1987—; trustee, bd. dirs. Livingston Area C. of C.; pres. Libr. Pub. Rels. Coun., 1997. Grantee U.S. Dept. Edn. libr. literacy program, 1987, N.J. State Libr. Leadership Inst., 1988. Mem. ALA (ethics com. 1995—), AAUW, LVW, NAFE, N.J. Libr. Assn., Rotary (pres. Livingston chpt. 1994—), Rutgers Grad. Alumni Assn. (pres. 1991-94), Beta Phi Mu. Avocations: writing, lecturing, personal development, psychology, developing leadership skills. Home: The Mill 300 Main St Apt 314 Little Falls NJ 07424-1359 Office: Pub Libr Livingston Robert Harp Dr Livingston NJ 07039

SIKORA, JAMES ROBERT, educational business consultant; b. Sacramento, July 8, 1945; s. George Robert and Marian Frances (Fears) S.; m. Marie Lynore Nyarady, June 22, 1968. BEE, U. Santa Clara, 1967; postgrad., U. Calif., Santa Cruz, 1979—. Electronic engr. GTE-Sylvania, Santa Cruz, 1967-69; sys. analyst GTE-Sylvania, 1969-71; sr. support analyst GTE-Sylvania, Mt. View, Calif., 1971-73; coord. bus. sys. Santa Clara County Office Edn., San Jose, Calif., 1973-76, dir. dist. payroll, pers. svcs., 1976-85, dir. dist. bus. svcs., 1985-95; self-employed sch. bus. cons. Omniserve, Ben Lomond, Calif., 1995—; cons. records mgmt. County Santa Clara, San Jose, 1982; vice-chmn. Edn. Mandated Cost Network Exec. Bd., 1991-95; mem. Schs. Fin. Svcs. subcom. 1987-94; dean's assoc. Maui Arts and Cultural Ctr. Ilima Club, U. Calif. San Francisco. Author, co-editor Howdy Rowdy Memorial, 1979. Affiliate San Jose/Cleveland Ballet; sponsor Dixieland Monterey; patrons cir. Monterey Bay Aquarium; dir. cir. San Jose Repertory Theater; fellow Cabrillo Music Festival; ptnr. Second Harvest Food Bank; vol. Mountain Pks. Found.; active Ctr. Photog. Arts, Napa Valley Wine Libr. Assn., Long Marine Lab., Chancellor's Cir., U. Calif. Santa Cruz; sustaining mem. Omni Found., Team Shakespeare, Shakespeare Santa Cruz; bd. dirs., treas. Mountain Parks Found., 1997—. Mem. Pub. Agy. Risk Mgmt. Assn., Am. Diabetes Assn., Calif. Assn. Sch. Bus. Ofcls. (subsect. pres. 1984-85, sect. bd. dirs. 1987-93, sect. pres. 1991-92, state bd. dirs. 1991-92, state legis. com. 1989—, state risk mgmt. com. 1985-87, 96—, state strategic planning com. 1994), Norwegian Elkhound Assn. (pres. 1977-79), Wine Investigation for Novices and Oenephiles, Amnesty Internat., Calif. Trout, Trout Unltd., Calif. State Parks Found., Point Lobos Natural History Assn., Santa Cruz Mus. Arts and History, Waddell Creek Assn., Monterey Hot Jazz Soc., Planned Parenthood, Americans for Hope, Growth and Opportunity, Kenna Club, Nature Conservancy, Friends of Santa Cruz Pub. Librs., Am. Assn. Ret. Perons, Beer Drinkers Am., Redwood Coast Brewers Assn., Am. Assn. Individual Investors, Am. Dog Owners Assn., Sierra Club (life). Libertarian. Roman Catholic. Avocations: photography, travel, gardening, fishing, snorkelling. Home and Office: 400 Coon Heights Rd Ben Lomond CA 95005-9711

SIKORA, STEPHEN THEODORE, publisher; b. Ukiah, Calif., Sept. 17, 1943; s. John Paul and Florence Anholm (Smith) S.; m. Kathleen Faye Hagemeyer, Aug. 5, 1967 (div. Aug. 1987); children: Benjamin, Anna. BA, U. Calif., Berkeley, 1966; MA, San Francisco State U., 1974. Tchr. Nevada County Sch. Dist., North San Juan, Calif., 1969-71; carpenter, contractor pvt. practice, Calif., 1974-82; publisher pvt. practice, Albany, Calif., 1982—. Editor/publisher (mag.) The Letter Exchange, 1982—. Sgt. U.S. Army, 1966-68. Mem. Phi Beta Kappa. Avocations: Homeric Greek studies, bicycling. Office: The Letter Exch PO Box 6218 Albany CA 94706

SIKOROVSKY, EUGENE FRANK, retired lawyer; b. Jackson, Mich., Nov. 27, 1927; s. Frank Joseph and Betty Dorothy (Malik) S.; m. Patricia O'Byrne, July 11, 1953; children: Paul, Charles, Catherine, Elizabeth, Emily. BSEE, U. Mich., 1948; LLB, Harvard U., 1951. Bar: N.Y. 1952, Va. 1970, Ill. 1978. Assoc. predecessor firms Cahill, Gordon & Reindel, 1954-63, ptnr., 1964-68; v.p., gen. counsel, dir. Reynolds Metals Co., Richmond, Va., 1969-76; gen. counsel Gould Inc., Rolling Meadows, Ill., 1977-79; v.p. Gould Inc., 1977-81; dep. gen. counsel Bell & Howell Co., Skokie, Ill., 1981-83; v.p. Bell & Howell Co., Chgo., 1983-88, gen. counsel, 1983-92, sec., 1984-92, sr. v.p., dir., 1988-92. Served to lt. USNR, 1951-54. Mem. Ill. State Bar Assn., Tau Beta Pi, Eta Kappa Nu, Phi Eta Sigma, Phi Delta Theta. Episcopalian. Home: 720 Grandview Ln Lake Forest IL 60045-3953

SIKORSKI, JAMES ALAN, research chemist; b. Stevens Point, Wis., Nov. 9, 1948; s. John Paul and Florence Lucille (Wierzba) S.; m. Jeanne Delaney, Apr. 15, 1968 (div. 1975); 1 child, Christine René; m. Georgina Weber, Nov. 19, 1977. BS, Northeast La. State Coll., 1970; MS, Purdue U., 1976, PhD, 1981. With Monsanto Agrl. Co., St. Louis, 1976-91, sci. fellow, 1987-91; sci. fellow Monsanto Corp. Rsch., St. Louis, 1991-93; sci. fellow med. chem. G.D. Searle R&D, St. Louis, 1994—; instr. organic chemistry St. Louis C.C., 1977-78; adj. prof. biochemistry Ctrl. Meth. Coll., 1995—; invited spkr. tech. presentations and seminars. Contbr. chpts. to books, rev. articles, symposia-in-print and articles to profl. jours.; patentee and co-patentee in field. Mem. AAAS, Am. Chem. Soc., Internat. Soc. Heterocyclic Chemistry, Sigma Xi. Avocations: hiking, canoeing, skiing, photography, snorkeling. Office: GD Searle R&D 700 Chesterfield Pky N Saint Louis MO 63198

SIKORSKY, ROBERT BELLARMINE, syndicated columnist; b. Pitts., July 1, 1936; s. Anthony Joseph and Frances Dorothy (Latsko) S.; m. Rogga Bowie, May 26, 1972; 1 child, Kyle Joseph. BA, U. Ariz., 1965. Writer Ariz. Daily Star, Tucson, 1984-86; syndicated columnist N.Y. Times Syndicate, N.Y.C., 1984—; automotive cons. to govt. and pvt. industry, Tucson, Ariz., 1965—; lectr., leader siminars on car care and safety driving; keynote spkr. nat. convs. including Automotive Svc. Assn., Hughes Aircraft Co., nat. new car dealer assns.; founder U.S. Dept. Energy Driver Energy Conservation Awareness Tng. Program, 1978-79. Author: How to Get More Miles Per Gallon, 1978, Drive It Forever, 1983, 3d rev. edit., 1997, Break It iN Right, 1984, revised edit., 1988, Rip-Off Tip-Offs: Winning the Auto Repair Game, 1990, Car Tips for Clean Air, 1991, From Bumper to Bumper, 1991, How to Get More Miles Per Gallon in the 90s, 1991; (booklets) Ease the Squeeze, Drive-Wise; (video) Avoid Repair Rip-offs: How to Find an Honest Mechanic, 1988; contbr. articles to Reader's Digest, Parade Mag., Family Circle, can. Reader's Digest, others; appeared on nat. and local radio and TV shows including the Tonight Show, Today, Hour Mag., Regis and Kathy Lee Show, CNBC's Smart Money, Steals and Deals and more. With USMC, 1957-58. Recipient 12 MOTO awards ann. Automotive Journalism Conf., Las Vegas, Nev., awards from journalism groups, State of Ariz., various cities. Mem. Soc. Automotive Engrs., Soc. Tribologists and Lubrication Engrs., Svc. Technicians Soc. Office: NY Times Syndicate 122 E 42nd St New York NY 10168-0002

SILAK, CATHY R., judge; b. Astoria, N.Y., May 25, 1950; d. Michael John and Rose Marie (Janor) S.; m. Nicholas G. Miller, Aug. 9, 1980; 3 children. BA, NYU, 1971; M in City Planning, Harvard U., 1973; JD, U. Calif., 1976. Bar: Calif. 1977, U.S. Dist. Ct. (no. dist.) Calif. 1977, D.C. 1979, U.S. Ct. Appeals (D.C. cir.) 1979, U.S. Dist. Ct. (so. dist.) N.Y. 1980, Idaho 1983, U.S. Dist. Ct. Idaho 1983, U.S. Ct. Appeals (2nd cir.) 1983, U.S. Ct. Appeals (9th cir.) 1985. Law clk. to Hon. William W. Schwarzer U.S. Dist. Ct. (no dist.), Calif., 1976-77; pvt. practice San Francisco, 1977-79, Washington, 1979-80; asst. U.S. atty. So. Dist. of N.Y., 1980-83; spl. asst. U.S. atty. Dist. of Idaho, 1983-84; pvt. practice Boise, Idaho, 1984-90; judge Idaho Ct. Appeals, 1990-93; justice Idaho Supreme Ct., Boise, 1993—; assoc. gen. counsel Morrison Knudsen Corp., 1989-90; mem. fairness com. Idaho Supreme Ct. and Gov.'s Task Force on Alternative Dispute Resolution; instr. and lectr. in field. Assoc. note and comment editor Calif. Law Rev., 1975-76. Land use planner Mass. Dept. Natural Resources, 1973; founder Idaho Coalition for Adult Literacy; bd. dirs. Literacy Lab., Inc. Recipient Jouce Stein award Boise YWCA, 1992, Women Helping Women award Soroptimist, Boise, 1993. Fellow Idaho Law Found (ann., lectr.); mem. ABA (nat. conf. state trial judges jud. adminstrn. divsn.), Nat. Assn. Women Judges, Idaho State Bar (corp./securities sect., instr.). Office: PO Box 83720 Boise ID 83720-3720

SILANO, ROBERT ANTHONY, editor, defense analyst, educator; b. Bklyn., Sept. 10, 1942; s. Ralph Henry and Charlotte Tecla (Borst) S. BA, Cathedral Coll., 1964; postgrad., New Sch., 1965-66, U. Louvain, 1971-72, U. Kent, Canterbury, 1972-74. Tchr. Bd. of Coop. Ednl. Svcs., Patchogue, N.Y., 1964-65; instr. U.S. Army Spl. Warfare Sch., Ft. Bragg, N.C., 1967-69; rsch. scientist Human Scis. Rsch., Inc., Saigon, Vietnam, 1969-71; plans officer Hdqrs. Dept. of the Army, Washington, 1975-77; R&D coord. Army Materiel Systems Analysis Agy., Aberdeen Proving Ground, Md., 1977-79; rsch. scientist Mission Rsch. Corp., Washington, 1979-80; staff mem. Office of the Sec. of Def., Washington, 1980-81; exec. dir. Coun. on Econs. and Nat. Security, Washington, 1982-85; faculty mem. Inst. of Higher Def. Studies Nat. Def. U., Washington, 1986-92; editor Joint Force Quar. Nat. Def. U., 1992—; lectr. U. Saigon, 1969-70, Georgetown U., Washington, 1985; cons. U.S. Synthetic Fuels Corp., Washington, 1982, Human Sci. Rsch., Inc., Saigon, 1972. Bd. dirs. The Thomas More Soc. of Am., Washington, 1984-88; dep. dir. of planning Commn. on the Bicentennial of the U.S. Constn., Washington, 1986; mem. ABA Working Group on Chem. Weapons, Washington, 1984. Capt. U.S. Army, 1966-69, 75-79, 80-81. Mem. Internat. Inst. for Strategic Studies (London). Republican. Roman Catholic. Avocations: collecting modern first editions and Indosinica. Office: Nat Def U Fort Lesley J NcNair Washington DC 20319-5066

SILAS, CECIL JESSE, retired petroleum company executive; b. Miami, Fla., Apr. 15, 1932; s. David Edward and Hilda Videll (Carver) S.; m. Theodosea Hejda, Nov. 27, 1965; children: Karla, Peter, Michael, James. BSChemE, Ga. Inst. Tech., Atlanta, 1953. With Phillips Petroleum Co., Bartlesville, Okla., 1953-94; pres. Europe-Africa, Brussels and London Phillips Petroleum Co., 1968-74; mng. dir. natural resource group Europe/Africa Phillips Petroleum Co., London, 1974-76; v.p. gas and gas liquids div. natural resources group Phillips Petroleum Co., Bartlesville, 1976-78, sr. v.p. natural resources group, 1978-80, exec. v.p. exploration and prodn., minerals, gas and gas liquids, 1980-82, pres., chief operating officer, 1982-85, chmn., CEO, 1985-94; bd. dirs. Milliken & Co., Ascent Entertainment. Bd. dirs. Reader's Digest Assocs., Inc., bd. dirs. of Halliburton Co. COMSAT Corp, Boys/Girls Clubs Am., Atlanta, parton councillor Atlantic Coun. of the U.S.; bd. dirs. Ethics Resource Ctr., Inc., Okla. Found. for Excellence; trustee Frank Phillips Found.; active Trilateral Commn. Served to 1st lt. Chem. Corps, AUS, 1954-56. Decorated comdr. Order St. Olaf (Norway); inducted into Ga. Inst. Tech. Athletic Hall of Fame, 1959, recipient Former Scholar-Athlete Total Person award, 1988; inducted into Okla. Bus. Hall of Fame, 1989; named CEO of Yr., Internat. TV Assn., 1987. Mem. Am. Petroleum Inst., U.S. C. of C. (past chmn. bd. dirs.), 25 Yr. Club, Phi Delta Theta. Avocations: fishing, golf, hunting. Office: 2400 Terrace Dr Bartlesville OK 74006-6237

SILBAJORIS, FRANK RIMVYDAS, Slavic languages educator; b. Kretinga, Lithuania, Jan. 6, 1926; came to U.S., 1949; s. Pranas and Elzbieta (Bagdonaviciute) S.; m. Milda Zamzickaite, Aug. 31, 1955; children: Victoria, Alex. BA, Antioch Coll., 1953; MA, Columbia U., 1955; PhD, Columbia U., 1962; D Philology (hon.), Latvian Acad. Scis., Riga, 1991. Instr. to asst. prof. Oberlin Coll., Ohio, 1957-63; assoc. prof. Ohio State U., Columbus, 1963-67, prof. Slavic langs., 1967-91, chmn. dept., 1986-89, prof. emeritus, 1992—; cons. NEH, 1978-79, exchange fellow, USSR, 1977-79; dir. NEH summer seminars, 1975, 77, 83, 84, 86, 88. Author: Russian Versification: The Theories of Trediakovskij, Lomonosov and Kantemir, 1968, Perfection of Exile: Fourteen Contemporary Lithuanian Writers, 1970, Tolstoy's Aesthetics and His Art, 1991, War and Peace. Tolstoy's Mirror of the World, 1995; editor: The Architecture of Reading, 1976, Mind Against the Wall, 1983; contbr. articles to profl. jours. Cons., lectr., organizer cultural events Lithuanian-Am. Community Orgn., 1949—. Antioch Coll. scholar, 1950-53; fellow John Hay Whitney Found., 1953-54, Ford Found., 1954-56, Woodrow Wilson Ctr., 1984, IREX, USSR, 1963-64. Mem. Inst. Lithuanian Studies (pres. 1977-82), Assn. Advancement Baltic Studies (pres. 1973-74), Am. Assn. Tchrs. Slavic and East European Langs., Am. Assn. Advancement Slavic Studies, Assn. Russian-Am. Scholars. Avocations: photography; bicycling; swimming; travel. Home: 4082 Ruxton Ln Columbus OH 43220-4046 Office: Ohio State U Dept Slavic Langs Columbus OH 43210

SILBAUGH, PRESTON NORWOOD, lawyer, consultant; b. Stockton, Calif., Jan. 15, 1918; s. Herbert A. and Della Mae (Masten) S.; m. Maria Sarah Arriola; children: Judith Ann Freed, Gloria Stypinski, Ximena Carey Braun, Carol Lee Morgan. A.B. in Philosophy, U. Wash., 1940; J.D., Stanford U., 1953. Bar: Calif. With Lockheed Aircraft Corp., 1941-44, Pan Am. World Airways, 1944, Office Civilian Personnel, War Dept., 1944-45; engaged in ins. and real estate in Calif., 1945-54; mem. faculty Stanford Law Sch., 1954-59, assoc. prof. law, 1956-59, assoc. dean, 1956-59; chief dep. savs. and loan commr. for Calif., 1959-61, bus. and commerce adminstr., dir. investment, savs. and loan commr., mem. gov.'s cabinet, 1961-63; dir. Chile-Calif. Aid Program, Sacramento and Santiago, 1963-65; chmn. bd. Beverly Hills Savs. & Loan Assn., Calif., 1965-84; bd. dirs. Wickes Cos., Inc.; chmn. bd., pres. Simon Bolivar Fund, San Diego, Calneva Land and Cattle Co., San Diego; of counsel firm Miller, Boyko & Bell, San Diego. Author: The Economics of Personal Insurance, 1958; also articles. Mem. pres.'s real estate adv. com. U. Calif., 1966—; mem. Beverly Hills Pub. Bldg. Adv. Com., 1970—. Served with USMCR, 1942-43. Mem. ABA, San Diego County Bar Assn., Soc. Internat. Devel., Inter-Am. Savs. and Loan Union, Internat. Union Building Socs., U. Wash., Stanford, Calif. Aggie alumni assns., Order of Coif, Phi Alpha Delta. Clubs: Commonwealth (San Francisco), Town Hall (Los Angeles). Home: Costanera Sur, Zapallar Chile also: 14500 Johnson Rd Red Bluff CA 96080-9281 also: 44135 Tahoe Cir Indian Wells CA 92210

SILBER, JOHN ROBERT, academic administrator; b. San Antonio, Aug. 15, 1926; s. Paul G. and Jewell (Joslin) S.; m. Kathryn Underwood, July 12, 1947; children: David Joslin, Mary Rachel, Judith Karen, Kathryn Alexandra, Martha Claire, Laura Ruth, Caroline Jocasta. B.A. summa cum laude, Trinity U., 1947; postgrad., Northwestern U., summer 1944, Yale Div. Sch., 1947-48, U. Tex. Sch. Law, 1948-49; M.A., Yale, 1952, Ph.D., 1956; L.H.D., Kalamazoo Coll., 1970; many others. Instr. dept. philosophy Yale

U., 1952-55; asst. prof. U. Tex., Austin, 1955-59, asso. prof., 1959-62, prof. philosophy, 1962-70, chmn. dept. philosophy, 1962-67, Univ. prof. arts and letters, 1967-70, chmn. (Comparative Studies Program), 1967, dean (Coll. Arts and Scis.), 1967-70; Univ. prof., prof. philosophy and law Boston U., 1971—, pres., 1971-96, prof. internat. rels., 1996—, chancellor, 1996—; vis. prof. Bonn U., 1960; fellow Kings Coll. U. London, 1963-64. Author: The Ethical Significance of Kant's Religion, 1960, Straight Shooting: What's Wrong With America and How to Fix It, 1989, Ist Amerika zu retten?, 1992; editor: Religion Within the Limits of Reason Alone, 1960, Works in Continental Philosophy, 1967—; assoc. editor: Kant-Studien, 1968-87; contbr. to profl. jours. Chmn. Tex. Soc. to Abolish Capital Punishment, 1960-69; mem. Nat. Commn. United Meth. Higher Edn., 1974-77; exec. bd. Nat. Humanities Inst., 1975-78; trustee Coll. St. Scholastica, 1973-85, U. Denver, 1985-89, WGBH Ednl. Found., 1971-96, Adelphi U., 1989-97; bd. visitors Air U., 1974-80; bd. dirs. Greater Boston coun. Boy Scouts Am., 1981-93, v.p. fin., 1981-93, Silver Beaver award, 1989; mem. Nat. Humanities Faculty, 1968-73, Nat. Captioning Inst., 1985-94; bd. advisors Matchette Found., 1971—; mem. Nat. Bipartisan Commn. on Ctrl. Am., 1983-84, Presdl. Adv. Bd. Radio Broadcasting to Cuba, 1985-92; adv. bd. Schurman Libr. of Am. Hist., Ruprecht-Karl U., Heidelberg, 1986—, Jamestown Found., 1989—; mem. def. policy bd. U.S. Dept. Def., 1987-90; mem. internat. coun.advisors Inst. for Humanities at Salado, 1988—; bd. dirs. New Eng. Holocaust Meml. Com., 1989—, Brit. Inst. of U.S., 1989—; Dem. gubernatorial candidate of Mass., 1990; vice chmn. U.S. Strategic Inst.; bd. dirs. Americans for Med. Progress, 1992—, chmn., 1994-95, mem. exec. com. 1995—; bd. dirs. U.S. Surg. Corp., 1994—, Mutual Am. Inst. Funds, Inc., 1996—, N.E. Savs. Bank, 1988-95; chmn. Mass. Bd. Edn., 1996—; bd. advisors Nat. Assn. Scholars. Recipient E. Harris Harbison award for disting. tchg. Danforth Found., 1966, Wilbur Lucius Cross medal Yale Grad. Sch., 1971, Outstanding Civilian Svc. medal U.S. Army, 1985, Disting. Pub. Svc. award Anti-Defamation League of B'nai B'rith, 1989, Horatio Alger award, 1992, Am.-Swiss Friendship award, 1991, Israel Peace medal, 1985, Ehrenmedaille U. Heidelberg, 1986, White House Small Bus. award for entrepreneurial excellence, 1986, Cross of Paideia, Greek Orthodox Archdiocese of North and South Am., 1988, Pro Bene Meritis award U. Tex., Austin, 1997; Fulbright rsch. fellow Germany, 1959-60; Guggenheim fellow Eng., 1963-64; decorated with Knight Comdr.'s Cross with Star of Order of Merit Fed. Republic of Germany, 1983; commandeur Nat. Order of Arts and Letters (France), 1985. Fellow Royal Soc. Arts; mem. Am. Philos. Assn., Am. Soc. Polit. and Legal Philosophy, Royal Inst. Philosophy, Am. Assn. Higher Edn., Nat. Assn. Ind. Colls. and Univs. (dir. 1976-81), Phi Beta Kappa. Office: Boston U 147 Bay State Rd Boston MA 02215-1708

SILBER, JUDY G., dermatologist; b. Newark, July 26, 1953. MD, SUNY, Bklyn., 1978. Intern Brookdale Med. Ctr., Bklyn., 1978-79; resident in dermatology Kings County Hosp., Bklyn., 1979-82; pvt. practice dermatology; affiliated with Meadowlands Med. Ctr., Secaucus, N.J. Fellow Am. Acad. Dermatology; mem. AMA, N.J. Med. Soc. Office: 992 Clifton Ave Clifton NJ 07013

SILBER, NORMAN JULES, lawyer; b. Tampa, Fla., Apr. 18, 1945; s. Abe and Mildred (Hirsch) S.; m. Linda Geraldine Hirsch, June 10, 1979; 1 child, Michael Hirsch. BA, Tulane U., 1967, JD, 1969; postgrad. in bus. adminstrn. NYU, 1970-72. Bar: Fla. 1970, U.S. Dist. Ct. (so. dist. Fla.) 1975, U.S. Tax Ct. 1975, U.S. Ct. Appeals (5th cir.) 1975, U.S. Ct. Appeals (11th cir.) 1981. With legal dept. Fiduciary Trust Co. N.Y., N.Y.C., 1969-72, asst. trust officer, 1971-72; exec. v.p. I.R.E. Fin. Corp., Miami, Fla., 1972-76; mng. atty. Norman J. Silber, P.A., Miami, 1973-85; ptnr. McDermott, Will & Emery, 1985—. Mem. ABA, Fla. Bar (chmn. 11th jud. cir. grievance com. I 1982-84). Republican. Jewish. Home: 1232 Palermo Ave Miami FL 33134-6327 Office: McDermott Will & Emery 201 S Biscayne Blvd Miami FL 33131-4332

SILBER, WILLIAM LEO, finance educator; b. Yonkers, N.Y., Nov. 26, 1942; s. Joseph F. and Pauline (Rothstein) S.; m. Lillian Frank, Jan. 26, 1964; children: Jonathan Mark, Daniel Jay, Tammy Beth. BA, Yeshiva Coll., 1963; MA, Princeton U., 1966, PhD, 1966. Sr. economist Pres.'s Coun. of Econ. Advisors, Washington, 1970-71; prof. NYU, 1966-90; sr. v.p. Lehman Bros., Kuhn, Loeb, N.Y.C., 1983-84; Gitlow prof. of fin. NYU, 1990—; mem. Commodity Exch., N.Y.C., 1984—, N.Y. Merc. Exch., 1986-90, N.Y. Cotton Exch., 1987—, N.Y. Stock Exch. Options Divsn., 1984-87; cons. Standard & Poors Corp., N.Y.C., 1986-95, Odyssey Ptnrs., N.Y.C., 1988-96, U.S. Senate Budget Com., Washington, 1975; advisor Fed. Res. Bank, N.Y.C., 1978-80, 90—. Author: Principles of Money, Banking and Finance, 1973, 9th rev. edit., 1996, Money, 1970, 4th rev. edit., 1977, Portfolio Behavior, 1970; editor: Financial Options, 1990; assoc. editor Rev. of Econ. and Stats. jour., 1973-94. Trustee Sch. of Bus., Yeshiva U., N.Y.C., 1987—; investment com. Social Sci. Rsch. Coun., N.Y.C., 1980-83; econ. adv. coun. Fed. Res. Bank N.Y., 1990. Mem. Am. Econ. Assn., Am. Fin. Assn. Avocation: collecting antique phonographs. Home: 1048 E 9th St Brooklyn NY 11230-4108 Office: NYU 44 W 4th St New York NY 10012-1106

SILBERBERG, DONALD H., neurologist; b. Washington, Mar. 2, 1934; s. William Aaron and Leslie Frances (Stone) S.; m. Marilyn Alice Damsky, June 7, 1959; children: Mark, Alan. MD, U. Mich., 1958; MA (hon.), U. Pa., 1971. Intern Mt. Sinai Hosp., N.Y.C., 1958-59; clin. assoc. in neurology NIH, Bethesda, Md., 1959-61; Fulbright scholar Nat. Hosp., London, 1961-62; NINDB spl. fellow in neuro-ophthalmology Washington U., St. Louis, 1962-63; assoc. neurology U. Pa., 1963-65, asst. prof., 1965-67, assoc. prof., 1967-71, prof., 1971-73, acting chmn. dept., 1973-74, prof., vice chmn. neurology, 1974-82, chmn., 1982-94, assoc. dean internat. programs, 1994—; active staff U. Pa. Med. Ctr., Phila.; cons. Children's Hosp., Phila.; pres., CEO Betasteron Found., Inc., 1994—. Contbr. articles to profl. jours., abstracts, chpts. in books. Recipient grants in study of multiple sclerosis. Mem. Am. Acad. Neurology, Am. Assn. Neuropathologists, Am. Neurol. Assn., Am. Soc. Neurochemistry, Assn. Rsch. in Nervous and Mental Diseases, Coll. Physicians Phila., Internat. Brain Rsch. Orgn., Internat. Soc. Devel. Neuroscis., Internat. Soc. Neurochemistry, John Morgan Soc. U. Pa. (pres. 1974-75), N.Y. Acad. Scis., Nat. Multiple Sclerosis Soc. (trustee 1997—, rsch. programs adv. bd.), Assn. Univ. Profs. Neurology (pres.-elect 1993), Phila. Neurol. Soc. (pres. 1978-79), Soc. Neurosci., World Fedn. Neurology (co-chair rsch. group on organziation & delivery of neurol. care, pres. rsch. group assn., Inc.), Alpha Omega Alpha. Office: U Pa Med Ctr Dept Neurology 3400 Spruce St Philadelphia PA 19104

SILBERBERG, INGA, dermatologist; b. Kassel, Germany, Sept. 16, 1934; came to U.S., 1938; d. Willi and Erna (Rosenbaum) S.; m. Herbert M. Sinakin, Feb. 16, 1969; 1 child, William Elias. BA, Hunter Coll., 1955; MD, SUNY, 1959; MS in Dermatology, NYU, 1965. Diplomate Am. Bd. Dermatologists, 1964. Instr., clin. dermatology NYU Med. Ctr., N.Y.C., 1963-65, clin. asst. prof., 1965-66, asst. prof. dermatology, 1966-71, clin. assoc. prof. dermatology, 1971-76; cons., dermatology Newcomb Hosp., Vineland, N.J., 1975—. Jonas Salk scholar, City of N.Y., 1955-59, Henry Silver award, Dermatologic Soc. Greater N.Y., 1962, 65, Dermatology Found. Discovery award, 1993. Fellow Am. Acad. Dermatology; mem. AMA.

SILBERBERG, MICHAEL COUSINS, lawyer; b. N.Y.C., July 26, 1940; s. Samuel and Sophie (Cousins) S.; m. Paula Baller, Aug. 17, 1965 (div. 1983); children: Dana, Sara. AB, Colgate U., 1962; JD, U. Chgo., 1965. Bar: N.Y. 1966, D.C. 1966, U.S. Ct. Appeals (2d cir.) 1972, U.S. Supreme Ct. 1975. Trial atty. civil rights div. U.S. Dept. Justice, Washington, 1966-68; asst. U.S. atty. U.S. Dist. Ct. (so. dist.) N.Y., N.Y.C., 1968-71; assoc. Golenbock & Barell, N.Y.C., 1971-75, ptnr., 1976-89; ptnr. Morvillo, Abramowitz, Grand, Iason & Silberberg, P.C., N.Y.C., 1989—. Author: Civil Practice in the Southern District of New York, 1995. 1st. lt. JAGC, U.S. Army, 1969-70. Home: 160 W 66th St New York NY 10023 Office: Morvillo Abramowitz et al Iason & Silberberg PC 565 5th Ave New York NY 10017-2413

SILBERBERG, RICHARD HOWARD, lawyer; b. N.Y.C., Feb. 20, 1951. BA, U. Wis., 1972; JD, NYU, 1975. Bar: N.Y. 1976, U.S. Dist. Ct. (so. and ea. dists.) N.Y., 1976, U.S. Ct. Appeals (2d cir.) 1982, U.S. Ct. Appeals (3d cir.) 1991, U.S. Ct. Internat. Trade 1983, U.S. Supreme Ct. 1994, U.S. Ct. Appeals (11th cir.) 1996. Assoc. Delson & Gordon, N.Y.C., 1975-83, ptnr., 1983-87; ptnr. Dorsey & Whitney, N.Y.C., 1988—, mng. ptnr., 1994—; mem. panel arbitrators U.S. Dist. Ct. for Ea. Dist. N.Y., 1987—; mem. panel mediators U.S. Dist. Ct. for So. Dist. N.Y., 1992—; trustee Lawyers Com. for Civil Rights Under Law, 1992—. Mng. editor NYU Jour. Internat. Law and Politics, 1974-75. Mem. Am. Arbitration Assn. (panel of arbitrators and mediators 1988—). Office: Dorsey & Whitney 250 Park Ave New York NY 10177-0001

SILBERFARB, PETER MICHAEL, psychiatrist, educator; b. Jersey City, Oct. 28, 1938; m. Anne Wagner, 1962; children: Benjamin, Leah S. BS, Bucknell U., 1960; postgrad., NYU, 1960-61; MD, Hahnemann Coll., 1965; MA (hon.), Dartmouth Coll., 1986. Diplomate Nat. Bd. Med. Examiners, Am. Bd. Psychiatry and Neurology (sr. examiner 1985-90, bd. dirs. 1991—). Intern Hahnemann Med. Coll. Hosp., Phila., 1965-66; resident in internal medicine Dartmouth Affiliated Hosps., Hanover, N.H., 1966-68, resident in internal medicine and psychiatry, 1968-69, psychiatry resident, 1971-72, chief resident in psychiatry, 1972-73; instr. in psychiatry Med. Sch., Dartmouth Coll., Hanover, 1972-73, asst. prof. of psychiatry, 1973-77, assoc. prof. clin. psychiatry, assoc. prof. clin. medicine, 1977-80, dir. grad. edn. and residency tng., 1978-86, assoc. prof. psychiatry, assoc. prof. medicine, 1980-82, prof. psychiatry, assoc. prof. medicine, 1982-85, dir. tng. and edn., 1984—, prof. psychiatry, prof. medicine, 1986—, chmn. dept. psychiatry, 1986—, Raymond Sobel prof. psychiatry, 1993; cons. psychiatrist Mary Hitchcock Meml. Hosp., Hanover, 1973—; dir. psychiat. in-patient svc. Dartmouth-Hitchcock Med. Ctr., 1973-75, dir. cancer psychiatry program Norris Cotton Cancer Ctr., 1975—, acting dir. psychiatry consultation svc., 1977-79, assoc. dir. cancer control Norris Ctr., 1981-86; sec. psychiatry com. Cancer and Leukemia Group B, 1976-79, vice chmn., 1979—; mem. grant rev. com. for cancer control Nat. Cancer Inst., 1979, 80, mem. spl. grant rev. com., 1981, 82, 85, cons. to bd. sci. counselors, 1982, mem. cancer control grant rev. com., 1986-90; vice chmn. adv. com. for psychosocial and behavioral rsch. Am. Cancer Soc., 1982-88, chmn., 1988-89; cons. collaborative ctr. for cancer pain relief WHO, Milan, 1985; mem. accreditation coun. for grad. med. edn. Appeals Bd. for Psychiatry, Chgo., 1983, specialist site visitor, 1985-90, mem. residency rev. com. for psychiatry, 1991—; prin. investigator in field. Author chpts. to books; mem. editl. bd. Jour. Psychosocial Oncology, 1983—, Internat. Jour. Psychiatry in Medicine, 1986-90, Contemporary Psychiatry, 1987-91, Psychooncology, 1991—; referee numerous manuscripts; contbr. articles to profl. jours. Surgeon USPHS, 1969-71. Fellow Am. Psychiat. Assn. (cons. to task force on treatment if psychiat. disorders 1989), Am. Coll. Psychiatrists; mem. AMA, Am. Soc. Psychiat. Oncology/AIDS, Am. Soc. Clin. Oncology, Am. Assn. Dirs. Psychiat. Residency Tng. (mem. curriculum com. 1979-88, mem. task force on med. students and residents, chmn. com. regional dirs. 1984-88, mem. exec. com. 1984-88), Am. Psychosomatic Soc., N.H. Psychiat. Soc. (chmn. membership com. 1974-76, chmn. continuing edn. com. 1977-79), N.H. Med. Soc., Assn. Rsch. in Nervous and Mental Disease, Assn. Acad. Psychiatry, Benjamin Rush Soc. Home: Bragg Hill Norwich VT 05055 Office: Dartmouth Coll Med Sch Dept Psychiatry Lebanon NH 03756-0001

SILBERG, JAY ELIOT, lawyer; b. N.Y.C., Apr. 5, 1941; s. Arnold and Lillian (Liberman) S.; m. Ruth Vogel, June 22, 1975; children: Eric, Karen, Joanne. BA cum laude, Amherst Coll., 1963; LLB, Harvard U., 1966. Bar: N.J. 1966, U.S. Dist. Ct. N.J. 1966, U.S. Ct. Appeals (D.C. cir.) 1970, U.S. Ct. Appeals (7th cir.) 1982, U.S. Supreme Ct. 1983, U.S. Ct. Appeals (6th cir.) 1986. Atty. Office Gen. Counsel AEC, Washington, 1966-69; assoc. Shaw, Pittman, Potts & Trowbridge, Washington, 1969-72, ptnr., 1973—. Mem. Assn. of Bar of City of N.Y. (chmn. nuclear tech. and law com. 1988-91). Republican. Jewish. Home: 6109 Neilwood Dr North Bethesda MD 20852-3706 Office: Shaw Pittman Potts & Trowbridge 2300 N St NW Washington DC 20037-1122

SILBERGELD, ARTHUR F., lawyer; b. St. Louis, June 1, 1942; s. David and Sabina (Silbergeld) S.; m. Carol Ann Schwartz, May 1, 1970; children: Diana Lauren, Julia Kay. BA, U. Mich., 1968; M City Planning, U. Pa., 1971; JD, Temple U., 1975. Bar: N.Y. 1976, Calif. 1978, D.C. 1983, U.S. Ct. Appeals (2d, 9th and D.C. cirs.). Assoc. Vladeck, Elias, Vladeck & Lewis, N.Y.C., 1975-77; field atty. NLRB, Los Angeles, 1977-78; ptnr., head employment law practice group McKenna, Conner & Cuneo, L.A., 1978-89; ptnr., head labor and employment law practice group Graham & James, L.A., 1990-96; labor ptnr. Sonnenschein Nath & Rosenthal, L.A., 1996—; instr. extension divsn. UCLA, 1981-89. Author: Doing Business in California: An Employment Law Handbook, 2d edit. 1996, Advising California Employers, 1990, 91, 93, 94, 95 supplements; contbr. numerous articles to profl. jours. Founding mem. L.A. Mus. Contemporary Art; mem. Mus. Modern Art, N.Y., Art Inst. Chgo.; bd. dirs. Bay Cities unit Am. Cancer Soc., Calif., 1981-85, Jewish Family Svc. L.A., 1981-85, So. Calif. Employment Round Table, 1990-96, Leadership Coun., So. Poverty Law Ctr. Mem. ABA (com. on devel. law under NLRA 1975—), L.A. County Bar Assn. (exec. bd. labor law sect. 1984—, sect. sec. 1996-97). Office: Sonnenschein Nath & Rosenthal 601 S Figueroa St Fl 15 Los Angeles CA 90017-5704

SILBERGELD, ELLEN KOVNER, environmental epidemiologist and toxicologist; b. Washington, July 29, 1945; d. Joseph and Mary (Gion) Kovner; m. Alan Mark Silbergeld, 1969; children: Sophia, Nicholas. AB, Vassar Coll., 1967; PhD, Johns Hopkins U., 1972. Kennedy fellow Johns Hopkins Med. Sch., Balt., 1974-75; scientist NIH, Bethesda, Md., 1975-81; chief toxics scientist Environ. Def. Fund, Washington, 1982-90; prof. epidemiology, toxicology and pharmacology U.Md., Balt., 1990—, affil. prof. environ. law, 1990—, dir. program in human health and environ., 1996—; adj. prof. Johns Hopkins Med. Insts., 1990—; guest scientist NIH, 1982-84; mem. sci. adv. bd. EPA, 1983-89, 94—, Dept. Energy, 1994-95; mem. bd. on environ. sci. and toxicology NAS-NRC, 1983-89; mem. com. geosci. environment and resources, 1994—; mem. bd. sci. counselors Nat. Inst. Environ. Health Scis., 1987-93; cons. Oil and CHem. Atomic Workers, 1970, NSF, 1974-75, OECD, 1987—. Mem. editl. bd. Neurotoxicology, 1981-86, Neurobehavioral Toxicology, 1979-87, Am. Jour. Indsl. Medicine, 1980—, Hazardous Waste, 1985—, Archives Environ. Health, 1986—; mem. editl. bd. Environ. Rsch., 1983—, editor-in-chief, 1994—; contbr. articles to profl. jours. Mem. Homewood Friends Meeting. Recipient Wolman award Md. Pub. Health Assn., 1991, Barsky award APHA, 1992, Md. Gov. Excellence citation, 1990, 93; Fulbright fellow, London, 1967, Woodrow Wilson and Danforth fellow, 1967; NAS exch. fellow, Yugoslavia, 1976; MacArthur Found. fellow, 1993; Baldwin scholar Coll. Notre Dame. Mem. AAAS, Am. Soc. Pharmacology and Exptl. Therapeutics, Soc. for Occupational and Environ. Health (sec.-treas. 1983-85, pres. 1987-89), Soc. Toxicology, Soc. for Neurosci., Am. Pub. Health Assn., Collegium Ramazzini, Phi Beta Kappa. Office: U Md Med Sch Dept Epid Prev Medicine HH 102 Baltimore MD 21201

SILBERGELD, JEROME LESLIE, art historian, educator; b. Highland, Ill., Apr. 25, 1944; s. David and Sabina Silbergeld; m. Michelle DeKlyen, June 27, 1970; children: David, Emily. BA in History, Stanford U., 1966, MA in History, 1967, PhD in Art History, 1974; MA in Art History, U. Oreg., 1972. Vis. asst. prof. art history U. Oreg., Eugene, 1974-75; from asst. prof. to prof. U. Wash., Seattle, 1975—, chmn. art history dept., 1988-92, dir. sch. art, 1992-96; vis. prof. dept. fine arts Harvard U., Cambridge, Mass., 1996. Author: Chinese Painting Style, 1982 (Soc. for Tech. Achievement award 1983), Mind Landscapes: The Painting of C.C. Wang, 1987, Contradictions: Artistic Life, the Socialist State, and the Chinese Painter Li Huasheng, 1993 (among N.Y. Times Notable Books of 1993); editor, translator: Chinese Painting Colors (Yu Fei'an) 1988; contbr. articles to profl. jours. Grantee Nat. Endowment for Humanities, 1981, 92, J. Paul Getty Trust, 1987. Mem. Assn. Asian Studies, Coll. Art Assn. Avocations: classical piano, long-distance running. Office: U Wash Dept Art History 353440 Seattle WA 98195

SILBERMAN, ALAN HARVEY, lawyer; b. Chgo., Oct. 22, 1940; s. Milton J. and Mollie E. (Hymanson) S.; m. Margaret Judith Auslander, Nov. 17, 1968; children: Elena, Mark. BA with distinction, Northwestern U., 1961; LLB, Yale U., 1964. Bar: Ill., 1964, U.S. Dist. Ct. (no. dist.) Ill., 1966, U.S. Ct. Appeals (7th cir.) 1970, (5th and 9th cir.) 1977, (D.C. cir.) 1979, (4th cir.) 1980, (11th cir.) 1981, (3rd cir.) 1982, (8th and 10th cirs.) 1993, U.S. Supreme Ct. 1978. Law clk. U.S. Dist. Ct., Chgo., 1964-66; assoc. Sonnenschein Nath & Rosenthal, Chgo., 1964-71, ptnr., 1972—; mem. antitrust adv. bd. Bur. Nat. Affairs, Washington, 1985—; mem. Ill. Atty. Gen. Franchise Adv. Bd., 1996—. Contbr. articles to profl. jours. bd. dirs., v.p., sec. Camp Ramah in Wisc., Inc., Chgo., 1966-86, pres., 1986-94; bd. dirs. Nat. Ramah Commn., Inc. of Jewish Theol. Sem. Am., N.Y.C., 1970—, v.p., 1986-94, pres., 1994—. Mem. Ill. State Bar Assn. (chmn. antitrust sect. 1975-76), ABA (chmn. antitrust sect. FTC com. 1981-83, chmn. nat. insts. 1983-85, mem. coun. antitrust sect. 1985-88, fin. officer, 1988-90, sect. del. ho. of dels. 1990-92, chair elect 1992-93, chair 1993-94), Northwestern U. 1851 Soc. (chair 1994-97). Home: 430 Oakdale Ave Glencoe IL 60022-2113 Office: Sonnenschein Nath 233 S Wacker Dr Ste 8000 Chicago IL 60606-6342

SILBERMAN, CHARLES ELIOT, magazine editor, author; b. Des Moines, Jan. 31, 1925; s. Seppy I. and Cel (Levy) S.; m. Arlene Propper, Sept. 12, 1948; children—David, Richard, Jeffrey, Steven. A.B., Columbia, 1946, postgrad. in econs, 1946-49; L.H.D. (hon.), Kenyon Coll., 1972. Tutor econs. Coll. City N.Y., 1946-48; instr. econs. Columbia, 1948-53, lectr. econs., 1955-66; asso. editor Fortune mag., 1953-60, mem. bd. editors, 1961-71; dir. Study Law and Justice, 1972-79, dir. The Study of Jewish Life, 1979-85; Mem. joint commn. on juvenile justice standards Am. Bar Assn.; dir. Carnegie Corp. Study Edn. Educators, 1966-69. Co-author: Markets of the Sixties, 1960; author: Crisis in Black and White, 1964, The Myths of Automation, 1966, Crisis in the Classroom, 1970, The Open Classroom Reader, 1973, Criminal Violence, Criminal Justice, 1978, A Certain People, 1985; contbr. to various publs. Bd. dirs. Found. for Informed Med. Decision Making, West End Synagogue; bd. govs. Reconstructionist Rabbinical Coll. Lt. (j.g.) USNR, 1943-46. Field Found. fellow, 1971-72. Fellow Nat. Assn. Bus. Economists. Home and Office: 1629 Pelican Cove Rd BA 134 Sarasota FL 34231

SILBERMAN, CURT C., lawyer; b. Wuerzburg, Fed. Republic Germany; came to U.S., 1938, naturalized, 1944; s. Adolf and Ida (Rosenbusch) S.; m. Else Kleemann, 1935. Student, U. Berlin, U. Munich; JD summa cum laude, Wuerzburg U., 1931, Rutgers U., 1947. Bar: N.J. 1948, U.S. Supreme Ct., 1957. Pvt. practice internat. pvt. law, Florham Park, N.J., 1948—; counsel to Arnold R. Kent, Florham Park; lectr. internat. pvt. law, 1954, 81, 82, 87, 91, 95; prin. guest lectr. at Univ.'s 400th anniversary U. Wuerzburg, 1982. Pres., Am. Fedn. Jews from Cen. Europe, N.Y., 1962-86, chmn. bd., 1986—; pres. Jewish Philanthropic Fund of 1933, Inc., N.Y., 1971-87, chmn. bd. 1987—; trustee Leo Baeck Inst., N.Y., 1962—, N.Y. Found. Nursing Homes, Inc.; hon. trustee Jewish Family Svc. of Metro-West, N.J.; co-chmn. Coun. Jews from Germany, 1974—; chmn. Rsch. Found. for Jewish Immigration Inc. N.Y.; bd. dir. Conf. on Jewish Material Claims Against Germany. Recipient Golden Doctoral Diploma U. Wuerzburg Law faculty, 1982, Festschrift dedicated to him by Am. Fedn. Jews from Cen. Europe in N.Y., 1969, recipient Pub. Svc. medal. Mem. N.J. Bar Assn. (chmn. com. comparative jurisprudence 1966-73, chmn. com. internat. trade 1974-78), Essex County Bar Assn., German-Am. Lawyers Assn., German-Am. C. of C., Am. Coun. on Germany, Internat. Biographical Dictionary of Cen. European Emigrés (adv. bd.) Contbr. articles to legal jours.; lectr. on polit. edn. and contemporary Jewish history.

SILBERMAN, ENRIQUE, physics researcher and administrator; b. Buenos Aires, Dec. 9, 1921; came to U.S., 1966; m. 1949; 2 children. PhD in Engring., U. Buenos Aires, 1945. Investigator physics Argentina Atomic Energy Commn., Buenos Aires, 1953-58; head dept. Arg AEC, 1958-63; prof. U. Buenos Aires, 1963-66; prof. physics Fisk U., Nashville, 1966—; dir. photonic materials and devices NASA Ctr., 1992—; guest prof. U. Notre Dame, 1963; cons. Arg Nat. Coun. Sci. Rsch., 1964; vis. prof. Vanderbilt U., 1967—. Mem. AAAS, Am. Assn. Physics Tchrs., Am. Phys. Soc., Arg Physics Assn. Office: Fisk U Dept Physics Nashville TN 37208-3051

SILBERMAN, H. LEE, public relations executive; b. Newark, Apr. 26, 1919; s. Louis and Anna (Horel) S.; m. Ruth Irene Rapp, June 5, 1948; children: Richard Lyle, Gregory Alan, Todd Walter. B.A., U. Wis., 1940. Radio continuity writer Radio Sta. WTAQ, Green Bay, Wis., 1940-41; reporter Bayonne (N.J.) Times, 1941-42; sales exec. War Assets Adminstrn., Chgo., 1946-47; copy editor Acme Newspictures, Chgo., 1947; reporter, editorial writer Wichita (Kans.) Eagle, 1948-55; reporter Wall St. Jour., N.Y.C., 1955-57; banking editor Wall St. Jour., 1957-68; 1st v.p., dir. corporate relations Shearson-Hamill & Co., N.Y.C., 1968-74; N.Y. corr. Economist of London, 1966-72; contbg. editor Finance mag., 1970-74, editor in chief, 1974-76; v.p., dir. Fin. Services Group, Carl Boyir & Assos., Inc., N.Y.C., 1976-78, sr. v.p., 1978-80, exec. v.p., 1981-86; sr. counselor Hill & Knowlton, Inc., N.Y.C., 1986-93, sr. v.p., 1993-96, sr. mng. dir., 1996; pres. LSA Media Cons., 1997—. Contbr. articles to profl. jours. Served to capt. C.E. AUS, 1942-46. Recipient Loeb Mag. award U. Conn., 1965; Loeb Achievement award for distinguished writing on fin. Gerald M. Loeb Found., 1968. Mem. Soc. Profl. Journalists, Soc. Silurians, N.Y. Fin. Writers Assn., Deadline Club N.Y., Overseas Press Club, Zeta Beta Tau. Republican. Home: 80 Miller Rd Morristown NJ 07960-5237

SILBERMAN, IRWIN ALAN, public health physician; b. Newport News, Va., Sept. 1, 1932; s. Henry and Toby (Weiss) S.; m. Lynne Sussman, Feb. 1954 (div. 1961); children: Denise, Donn; m. Mitsue Fukuyama, May 1964 (div. 1984); children: Daniel, Dean, Dana; m. Andrea Z. George, Nov. 1993. BA, U. Calif., Berkeley, 1953; MD, U. Calif., San Francisco, 1956; MS, U. No. Colo., 1980. Intern L.A. County Harbor Gen. Hosp., Torrance, Calif., 1956-57; resident ob-gyn. Harbor/UCLA Med. Ctr., Torrance, 1957-61; commd. USAF, 1961, advanced through grades to col., 1973; staff obstetrician-gynecologist Tachikawa (Japan) Air Base, 1963-65; chief ob-gyn. Mather Air Force Base, Sacramento, 1965-66; chief aeromed. services Yokota Air Base, Tokyo, 1966-68; dir. base med. services Itazuke Air Base, Fukuoka, Japan, 1968-70, Kirtland Air Force Base, Albuquerque, 1970-72; chief hosp. services USAF Hosp. Davis-Monthan, Tucson, 1972-81; ret. USAF, 1981; med. dir. CIGNA Healthplan of Fla., Tampa, 1981-83; chief women's clinic H.C. Hudson Comprehensive Health Ctr., L.A., 1983-85; dir. maternal health and family planning programs Los Angeles County Dept. Health Svcs., L.A., 1985-91, dir. family health programs, maternal and child health, 1991—; mil. cons. to surgeon-gen. USAF, 1980-81; bd. dirs. L.A. Regional Family Planning Coun.; clin. prof. ob-gyn. U. So. Calif., Sch. Medicine, 1992—; pres. Perinatal Adv. Coun. of L.A. Comtys., 1993-94, Calif. Conf. of Local Dirs. of Maternal, Child and Adolescent Health, 1997—. Chmn. health profls. adv. com. March of Dimes, Los Angeles, 1988; camp physician Boy Scouts Nat. Jamboree, Fort Hill, Va., 1985. Recipient Meritorious Service medal, USAF, 1972, 81, Air Force Commendation medal, 1980, Air medal, 1969. Fellow Am. Coll. Obstetricians and Gynecologists, Am. Coll. Physician Execs., Am. Coll. Preventive Medicine; mem. APHA, Am. Acad. Med. Dirs., So. Calif. Pub. Health Assn. Avocations: skiing, photography. Home: 3716 Beverly Ridge Dr Sherman Oaks CA 91423-4509 Office: LA County Dept Health Svcs 241 N Figueroa St Los Angeles CA 90012-2601

SILBERMAN, JAMES HENRY, editor, publisher; b. Boston, Mar. 21, 1927; s. Henry R. and Dorothy (Conrad) S.; m. Selma Shapiro, Aug. 26, 1986; children by previous marriage: Michael, Ellen. AB, Harvard U., 1950. Asst. to pub. Writer, Inc., 1950-51; asst. to advt. mgr. Little, Brown & Co., 1951-53; publicity dir. Dial Press, Inc., 1953-55, editor, 1954-55, exec. editor, 1955-59, v.p., editor-in-chief, 1959-63; editor The Dial, 1959-62; sr. editor Random House, Inc., N.Y.C., 1963-65, exec. editor, 1965-66, exec. editor, v.p., 1966-68, v.p., editor in chief, 1968-76, also pub., 1975-76; pres., editor-in-chief Summit Books div. Simon & Schuster, 1976-91; v.p., sr. editor Little Brown & Co., N.Y.C., 1991—; judge First Novel, Am. Book Awards, 1982; mem. adv. com. George Polk Meml. Awards, 1980—. Served as pfc. AUS, World War II. Mem. PEN, Assn. Am. Pubs. (Freedom to Read com. 1971-80, Freedom to Pub. com. 1982), Book Table, Pubs. Lunch Club, Corp. of Yaddo (bd. dirs. 1987—, exec. com. 1989—). Clubs: Harvard (N.Y.C.); Century Assn. Home: 315 E 70th St New York NY 10021-8657 Office: Little Brown & Co Inc 1271 Avenue Of The Americas New York NY 10020-1300

SILBERMAN, JOHN ALAN, lawyer; b. Balt., Sept. 20, 1951; s. Ronnie A. and Dovera (Gogel) S. BA, Northwestern U., 1973; JD, Harvard U., 1976. Bar: N.Y. 1977, U.S. Dist. Ct. (so. and ea. dists.) N.Y. 1977. Assoc. Paul, Weiss, Rifkind, Wharton & Garrison, N.Y.C., 1976-84, ptnr., 1985-96; prin. John Silberman Assocs., N.Y.C., 1996—. Bd. dirs. Coun. on Econ. Priorities, N.Y.C., 1986-90, Young Audiences, N.Y.C., 1988-90. Office: John Silberman Assocs PC 712 5th Ave Fl 23 New York NY 10019-4108

SILBERMAN, LAURENCE HIRSCH, federal judge; b. York, Pa., Oct. 12, 1935; s. William and Anna (Hirsch) S.; m. Rosalie G. Gaull, Apr. 28, 1957; children: Robert Stephen, Katherine DeBoer Balaban, Anne Gaull. AB, Dartmouth Coll., 1957; LLB, Harvard U., 1961. Bar: Hawaii 1962, D.C. 1973. Assoc. Moore, Torkildson & Rice and Quinn & Moore, Honolulu, 1961-64; ptnr. Moore, Silberman & Schulze, Honolulu, 1964-67; atty. appellate divsn. gen. counsel's office NLRB, Washington, 1967-69; solicitor of labor U.S. Dept. Labor, Washington, 1969-70, undersec. labor, 1970-73; ptnr. Steptoe & Johnson, Washington, 1973-74; dep. atty. gen. U.S. Washington, 1974-75; amb. to Yugoslavia, 1975-77; mng. ptnr. Morrison & Foerster, Washington, 1978-79, 83-85; exec. v.p. Crocker Nat. Bank, San Francisco, 1979-83; judge U.S. Ct. Appeals (D.C. cir.), Washington, 1985—; lectr. labor law and legis. U. Hawaii, 1962-63; adj. prof. adminstrv. law Georgetown U., Washington, 1987-94, 97—, NYU, 1995, 96; Pres.' spl. envoy on ILO affairs, 1976; mem. gen. adv. com. on Arms Control and Disarmament, 1981-85; mem. Def. Policy Bd., 1981-85; vice chmn. State Dept.'s Commn. on Security and Econ. Assistance, 1983-84. Bd. dirs. Com. on Present Danger, 1978-85, Inst. for Ednl. Affairs, 1981-85; vice chmn. adv. coun. on gen. govt. Rep. Nat. Com., 1977-80. With AUS, 1957-58. Am. Enterprise Inst. sr. fellow, 1977-78, vis. fellow 1978-85. Mem. U.S. Fgn. Intelligence Surveillance Act Ct. of Rev., Coun. on Fgn. Rels.

SILBERMAN, ROBERT A. S., lawyer; b. Lebanon, Pa., Mar. 4, 1945; s. Henry T. and Genevieve (Mensh) S.; m. Nancy D. Netzer, Nov. 10, 1974. BA, Yale U., 1967; JD, Harvard U., 1970. Bar: Mass. 1970, Pa. 1984. Assoc. Csaplar & Bok, Boston, 1970-78, ptnr., 1978-90; ptnr. Gaston & Snow, Boston, 1990-91, Edwards & Angell, Boston, 1991—. Mem. citizens rev. com. United Way Massachusetts Bay, Boston, 1981-89; dir. All Newton (Mass.) Music Sch., 1994-96, v.p., 1995-96. Mem. ABA (vice chmn. health law com. sect. bus. law 1992-95, chmn., 1995—), Internat. Bar Assn., Boston Bar Assn., Nat. Health Lawyers Assn., Phi Beta Kappa. Office: Edwards & Angell 101 Federal St Boston MA 02110-1817

SILBERSACK, MARK LOUIS, lawyer; b. Cin., Dec. 27, 1946; s. Joseph Leo and Rhoda Marie (Hinkler) S.; m. Ruth Ann Schwallie, Sept. 7, 1985. AB, Boston Coll., 1968; JD, U. Chgo., 1971. Bar: Ohio 1971, U.S. Dist. Ct. (so. dist.) Ohio 1973, U.S. Ct. Appeals (6th cir.) 1974, U.S. Supreme Ct. 1975. Atty. Dinsmore & Shohl, Cin., 1971—; lectr. Ohio CLE Inst., Columbus, 1981-91. Co-author: Managed Care: The PPO Experience, 1990, Information Sharing Among Health Care Providers, 1994. V.p. Cin. Cmty. Chest, 1985-89, Ohio United Way, Columbus, 1989-94, chmn. bd. dirs., 1994-96; pres. Hyde Park Neighborhood Coun., Cin., 1989-91, Hyde Park Ctr. for Older Adults, 1989-91; mem. Cin. Bd. Health, 1991-97, chmn., 1995-97. Mem. ABA, Ohio State Bar Assn., Cin. Bar Assn., Fed. Bar Assn., Bankers Club, Hyde Park Golf And County Club. Republican. Roman Catholic. Avocations: reading, travel, theater. Home: 3465 Forestoak Ct Cincinnati OH 45208-1842 Office: Dinsmore & Shohl 1900 Chemed Ctr 255 E 5th St Cincinnati OH 45202-4700

SILBERSTEIN, ALAN MARK, financial services executive; b. Munich, Dec. 22, 1947; came to U.S., 1949; s. Leon and Rose (Rosenblatt) S.; m. Carol Krongold, Aug. 30, 1970; children: Eric, Adam, Meredith. BS in Engring., Columbia U., 1969; MBA, Harvard U., 1972. Design engr. Ford Motor Co., Dearborn, Mich., 1969-70; budget analyst N.Y.C. Bur. of Budget, 1972-74; various positions Chem. Bank, N.Y.C., 1974-88, exec. v.p., head Consumer Banking Group, 1990-92; exec. v.p. and dir. of retail banking Midlantic Corp., Edison, N.J., 1992-95; CEO claims divsn. Travelers Property Casualty Corp., Hartford, Conn., 1995-96, exec. v.p., 1997—; bd. dirs. N.Y. Switch Corp., 1990-92, Cirrus System, Inc., 1991. Trustee Tenafly Bd. Edn., N.J., 1983-86, Yeshiva U. Sy Syms Sch. Bus., 1989—; mem. consumer adv. coun. Fed. Res. Bd., 1989-91; bd. dirs. N.Y. State Tree Consortium Inc., 1990-92; mem. exec. Bergen County N.J. Boy Scouts Am., 1992—, exec. v.p. fin., 1995. Mem. Am. Bankers Assn. (chmn. retail banking exec. com. 1992—), Harvard Bus. Sch. Club N.Y. (sec. 1981-85, bd. dirs. 1982-83, 85-88). Office: Travelers 388 Greenwoods St New York NY 10013

SILBERSTEIN, DIANE, publishing executive. Publisher The New Yorker, 1995—. Office: Advance Publ Inc 20 W 43rd St New York NY 10036-7400*

SILBERT, LINDA BRESS, educational counselor, therapist; b. New Rochelle, N.Y., Sept. 14, 1944; d. Abram H. and Ann (Dreizen) Bress; m. Alvin Jay Silbert, Aug. 14, 1966; children: Brian R., Cheryl J. BS, SUNY, New Paltz, 1966; MS, We. Conn. State U., Danbury, 1989; PhD in Ednl. Adminstrn., Walden U., Mpls., 1993. Cert. in sch. counseling and elem. edn., N.Y. Children's writer Phone Programs, N.Y.C., 1984-86; owner, pub. Silbert & Bress, Inc., Mahopac, N.Y., 1976—, children's author, 1976—; owner, dir. Silbert Tutoring and Guidance Svc., Mahopac, 1968—; part-time prin. Temple Beth Shalom Hebrew Sch., Mahopac, 1985—; leader parent workshops Silbert Tutoring and Guidance, 1985—, leader gifted program, 1989; cons. Mahopac Ctrl. Sch. Dist., 1983-84; cons., developer Author in Your Sch. program, 1983-87. Author: Creative Thinking Workbooks, 1976, Understanding People Storybooks, 1978 (lifeskills programs) Strong Kids Program, 1991, Stong Kids Early Childhood Programs, 1993, Passport to Emotionally and Socially Strong Kids, 1995, Teacher's Handbook Strong Study Skills Program, 1997. Membership chair Temple Beth Shalom, Mahopac, 1980-85. Recipient Gabriel Schonfeld award for educator excellence Bd. of Jewish Edn. of Greater N.Y., 1991. Mem. Am. Counseling Assn., Orton Dyslexia Soc., Am. Mental Health Counselors Assn., United Jewish Fedn. (award 1983). Avocations: dancing, painting. Office: Silbert & Bress Inc PO Box 68 Mahopac NY 10541-0068

SILBEY, JOEL HENRY, history educator; b. Bklyn., Aug. 16, 1933; s. Sidney and Estelle (Mintzer) S.; m. Rosemary Johnson, Aug. 13, 1959; children: Victoria, David. BA, Bklyn. Coll., 1955; MA, U. Iowa, 1956, PhD, 1963. Asst. prof. San Francisco State Coll., 1960-64, U. Md., College Park, 1965-66; asst. prof. Am. History Cornell U., Ithaca, N.Y., 1966-67, assoc. prof., 1967-68, prof., 1968-86, Pres. White prof. history, 1986—; vis. asst. prof. history U. Pitts., 1964-65. Author: The Shrine of Party, 1967, The Transformation of American Politics, 1968, A Respectable Minority: The Democratic Party in the Civil War Era, 1977, The Partisan Imperative: The Dynamics of American Politics before the Civil War, 1985, The American Political Nation, 1838-1893, 1991; editor: (with others) Voters, Parties and Elections, 1972, American Political Behavior, 1984, The History of American Electoral Behavior, 1978; editor-in-chief: Encyclopedia of the American legislative System, 1993; editorial cons. numerous publs.; contbr. numerous articles to profl. jours. Am. Philos. Soc. fellow, 1969-70; NSF fellow, 1970-74; NEH fellow, 1980-81; vis. fellow Ctr. for Advanced Study in the Behavioral Scis., 1985-86; vis. scholar Russell Sage Found., 1988-89; John Simon Guggenheim Meml. fellow, 1989-90. Mem. Am. Hist. Assn. (program com. 1977), Orgn. Am. Historians (chmn. program com. 1983), So. Hist. Assn., Social Sci. History Assn. (co-chmn. membership com., mem. exec. com). Home: 105 Judd Falls Rd Ithaca NY 14850-2715 Office: Cornell U 452 Mcgraw Hall Ithaca NY 14853-4601

SILBEY, ROBERT JAMES, chemistry educator, researcher, consultant; b. N.Y.C., Oct. 19, 1940; s. Sidney Richard and Estelle (Mintzer) S.; m. Susan Sorkin, June 24, 1962; children: Jessica, Anna. BS, CUNY Bklyn. Coll., 1961; PhD, U. Chgo., 1965. Asst. prof. MIT, Cambridge, 1966-76, prof., 1976—, chmn. dept. chemistry, 1990-95; vis. prof. U. Utrecht, The Netherlands, 1972-73, U. Grenoble, France, 1983; cons. Exxon Rsch., Clinton, N.J., 1984—. Author: Physical Chemistry, 1991, 2d edit., 1997; editor: Conjugated Polymers, 1991; contbr. articles to profl. jours. Recipient Alexander von Humboldt Found. Sr. Scientist award, 1989, Max Planck award, 1992; Alfred P. Sloan fellow, 1968, John S. Guggenheim fellow, 1972; Dreyfus Found. Tchr.-Scholar grantee, 1969. Fellow AAAS, Am. Acad. Arts and Scis., Am. Phys. Soc. Avocations: swimming, sailing. Office: MIT Dept Chemistry 77 Massachusetts Ave Cambridge MA 02139-4301

SILBIGER, MARTIN L., radiologist, medical educator, college dean; b. Ravenna, Ohio, Mar. 17, 1938; s. Alfred James and Evelyn Norma (Cheswick) S.; m. Ruth Hope Steele, June 4, 1957; children: Martin, Eve, Jonathan, Holly, Wendy. BA, U. Pa., 1958; MD, Western Reserve U., 1962; MBA, U. South Fla., 1989. Diplomate Am. Bd. Radiology, Am. Bd. Nuclear Medicine. Intern Univ. Hosps. Cleve., 1962-63; resident Johns Hopkins Hosp., 1963-66; with NIH, 1966-68; radiologist Tampa (Fla.) Gen. Hosp., 1968—; prof. U. South Fla., Tampa, 1982—; chief of staff Tampa Gen. Hosp., 1978-80; chmn. dept. radiology U. South Fla. Coll. Medicine, 1982-95; dean coll. medicine U. South Fla., 1995—, v.p. health scis., 1995—. Founder Hillsborough County Med. assn. Found., Tampa, 1992; treas. Cmty. Found. Tampa, 1993-95; bd. dirs. Moffitt Cancer Ctr., Tampa, 1985—, Moffitt Cancer Ctr. Found., 1994—. Avocations: reading, rollerblading, golf, tennis. Home: 1827 Bayshore Blvd Tampa FL 33606 Office: 3301 Alumni Dr Tampa FL 33612-9413 also: Univ South Fl Coll of Med Box 66 1209 Bruce B Downs Blvd Tampa FL 33612-4799

SILBY, DONALD WAYNE, investment executive, entrepreneur; b. Charles City, Iowa, July 20, 1948; s. Bernard and Rita (Grad) S.; m. Joana Johnston Silby, Nov. 11, 1988 (div. Mar. 1994); 1 child, Georgina. BSE, U. Pa., 1970; JD, Georgetown U., 1975. Chmn. Calvert Group Funds, Washington, 1976-85; pres. Calvert Social Investment Fund, Washington, 1982—; sr. ptnr. Calvert Social Venture Ptnrs., Bethesda, Md., 1989—; bd. dirs. Acacia Mut. Life Ins. Co., Washington. Bd. dirs. Calif. Sch. Profl. Psychology, 1986-92; mem. bd. Inst. East-West Studies, 1994-95. Recipient hon. award Interfaith Ctr. Corp. Responsibility, N.Y.C., 1990. Mem. Am. Assn. Higher Edn. (bd. dirs. 1986-=92), Bus. Execs. Nat. Security (bd. dirs. 1986-89), Social Venture Network (bd. dirs., co-founder 1987-90), Social Investment Forum. Buddhist. Home and Office: 1715 18th St NW Washington DC 20009-2507

SILCOX, FRANCES ELEANOR, museum and exhibits planning consultant; b. Orange, Calif., Sept. 26, 1956; d. William Henry and M. Eleanor (Saulpaugh) S.; m. David William Smith, June 21, 1986; children: Lena Celeste, Reid Whitney. BA in English, U. San Francisco, 1979; MA in Mus. Studies, George Washington U., 1984. Intern divsn. performing arts Smithsonian Instn., Washington, 1978; adminstrv. asst. exhibits dept. Calif. Acad. Scis., San Francisco, 1979-81; gallery coord. The George Washington U., Washington, 1981-83; intern art dept. aide Smithsonian Instn., Washington, 1983-84; asst. dir. Torpedo Factory Arts Ctr., Alexandria, Va., 1983-84; accreditation coord. Am. Assn. Mus., Washington, 1984-86; interpretive planner Design and Prodn. Inc., Lorton, Va., 1986-88; mus. planner West Office Exhbn. Design, San Francisco, 1988-91; ind. mus. and exhibits planner, owner Dallas, 1991—. Bd. mem. St. Gerard Circle, St. Rita Cath. Cmty., Dallas, 1995—; contbr. numerous natural and cultural resources orgns. Scholar Nat. Endowment for the Arts-Am. Law Inst.-ABA, Washington, 1982. Mem. Am. Assn. for State and Local History, Am. Assn. Mus., Archaeol. Inst. Am., Internat. Coun. Mus., Nat. Assn. for Mus. Exhibition, Tex. Assn. Mus. Democrat. Avocations: travel, correspondence, photography, reading, walking. Home and Office: 5816 Lindenshire Dallas TX 75230

SILEN, WILLIAM, physician, surgery educator; b. San Francisco, Sept. 13, 1927; s. Dave and Rose (Miller) S.; m. Ruth Heppner, July 13, 1947; children: Stephen, Deborah, Mark. BA, U. Calif., Berkeley, 1946; MD, U. Calif., San Francisco, 1949; MA (hon.), Harvard U., 1966. Diplomate Am. Bd. Surgery. Intern U. Calif., San Francisco, 1949-50, asst. resident gen. surgery, 1950-56, chief resident gen. surgery, 1956-57; asst. chief surgery Denver VA Hosp., 1957-59, chief surgery, 1959-60; asst. chief surgery San Francisco Gen. Hosp., 1960-61, chief surgery, 1961-66; surgeon-in-chief Beth Israel Hosp., Boston, 1966-94; instr. surgery, asst. prof. surgery U. Colo. Med. Sch., Denver, 1957-60; asst. prof. then assoc. prof. surgery U. Calif. Sch. Medicine, San Francisco, 1960-66; prof. surgery Harvard Med. Sch., Boston, 1966—, Johnson and Johnson prof. surgery, 1966-94, Johnson & Johnson disting. prof. surgery, 1994—, faculty dean faculty devel. & diversity, 1995—; dir. Harvard Digestive Diseases Ctr. NIH, Bethesda, Md., 1984-94. Author: Cope's Early Diagnosis of the Acute Abdomen, 1995, Conservative Management of Breast Cancer, 1983, Atlas of Techniques in Breast Surgery, 1995. With USAF, 1950-52. Mem. AMA, ACS, Soc. Univ. Surgeons, H.C. Naffziger Surg. Soc., Phi Beta Kappa. Avocation: bonsai cultivation. Office: Beth Israel Hosp 330 Brookline Ave Boston MA 02215-5400

SILER, EUGENE EDWARD, JR., federal judge; b. Williamsburg, Ky., Oct. 19, 1936; s. Eugene Edward and Lowell (Jones) S.; m. Christy Dyanne Minnich, Oct. 18, 1969; children—Eugene Edward, Adam Troy. B.A. cum laude, Vanderbilt U., 1958; LL.B., U. Va., 1963; LL.M., Georgetown U., 1964. Bar: Ky. 1963, Va. 1963, D.C. 1963. Individual practice law Williamsburg, 1964-65; atty. Whitley County, Ky., 1965-70; U.S. atty. Eastern Dist. Ky., Lexington, 1970-75; judge U.S. Dist. Ct., Eastern and Western Dists., Ky., 1975-91; chief judge Eastern Dist., Ky., 1984-91; judge U.S. Ct. Appeals (6th cir.), 1991—. Campaign co-chmn. Congressman Tim L. Carter, 1966, 5th Congl. Dist.; campaign co-chmn. U.S. Senator J.S. Cooper, 1966; trustee Cumberland Coll., Williamsburg, 1965-73, 80-88; 1st v.p. Ky. Bapt. Convention, 1986-87; bd. dirs. Bapt. Healthcare Systems Inc., 1990—. Served with USN, 1958-60, with Res. 1960-83. E. Barrett Prettyman fellow, 1963-64; recipient medal Freedom's Found., 1968. Mem. FBA, Ky. Bar Assn. (Judge of Yr. award 1992), D.C. Bar Assn., Va. State Bar. Republican. Baptist. Home: PO Box 129 Williamsburg KY 40769-0129 Office: US Ct Appeals 1380 W 5th St Ste 200 London KY 40741-1615

SILER, SUSAN REEDER, communications educator; b. Knoxville, Tenn., May 31, 1940; d. Claude S. Jr. and Mary Frances (Cook) Reeder; m. Theodore Paul Siler Jr., Sept. 3, 1960; children: Mary Siler Walker, Theodore Paul III. BS in Communications and Journalism, U. Tenn., Knoxville, 1988, MS in Mass Comms., 1994. 2d grade tchr. Lawton (Okla.) Pub. Schs., 1961-62, substitute tchr., 1963-64; with By Design, 1987-88; English tutor, 1991-95; adj. instr. comm. U. Tenn., 1994—, U. Tenn., Pellissippi State Tech. C.C., Knoxville, Tenn.; bd. dirs. Hlen Ross McNabb Mental Health Ctr., Knoxville. Tutor Episc. Ch. Ascension, Knoxville, 1990—; instr. United Meth. Ch., Knoxville, 1985-92; chmn. Dogwood Arts Festival, Knoxville, 1980-85; chmn. bd. Govs. of East Tenn. Presentation Soc., 1988-96, Dogwood Trails; chmn., sec. bd. dirs. YWCA, Knoxville, 1982-88, editor newsletter, membership chmn., placement adv., sec.; Knoxville Jr. League, 1979-95; bd. dirs. Knoxville Women's Ctr., 1993-94; spl. events chmn. St. Mary's Med. Ctr. Found., 1986-89; Pres. Knoxville area Literacy Assn., 1989-92, tutor Episcopal Ch. Literacy program, Knoxville, 1990-95. Mem. Internat. Mass Comm. Assn., Soc. Profl. Journalists, Am. Journalism Historians Assn., Assn. for Edn. in Journalism and Mass Comms., Kappa Tau Alpha, Golden Key. Home: 717 Kenesaw Ave Knoxville TN 37919-6662

SILER, WALTER ORLANDO, JR., retired business executive; b. Atascadero, Calif., May 21, 1920; s. Walter Orlando and Hylda Ruth Martyn (Jackson) S.; m. Carolyn Louise Townsend, 1978; children by previous marriage: Robert Eugene, Barbara Ellen, Susan Jane,Donald Walter, David Brian. B.S., U. So. Calif., 1941. C.P.A., Calif. Partner Arthur Andersen & Co. (C.P.A.'s), Phoenix, 1958-61; pres., treas., dir. Bargain City, U.S.A., Inc., Phila., 1962; treas., dir. Getty Oil Co., Los Angeles, 1963-67; v.p. Getty Oil Co., 1966-67, asst. controller, 1968-70; controller Fluor Corp., Los Angeles, 1970-72; gen. mgr. Saudi Arabian ops. Whittaker Corp., 1972-73; bus. mgr. Northrop Aircraft Div., Taif, Saudi Arabia, 1973-74; v.p. fin. Fluor Arabia Ltd., Dhahran, Saudi Arabia, 1974-77; mgr. accounting The Ralph M. Parsons Co., Pasadena, Calif., 1977-78; v.p., treas., sec. Parsons Constructors Inc., Pasadena, 1978-85; treas., dir. Mission Corp., 1963-68; treas. Mission Devel. Co., 1963-67; dir. Skelly Oil Co., 1963-68. Served to maj. USAAF, 1941-46. Mem. AICPA, Fin. Execs. Inst. (bd. dirs. L.A. chpt. 1990-93), Calif. Soc. CPAs, Univ. Club of Pasadena (bd. govs. 1990-91), Town Hall Calif. (L.A.), Sigma Nu, Phi Kappa Phi, Beta Gamma Sigma, Beta Alpha Psi. Republican. Home: 703 N Stoneman Ave Apt G Alhambra CA 91801-1410

SILER-KHODR, THERESA MARIE, biochemistry educator; b. Pomona, Calif., June 17, 1947; d. Joseph Horace and Anna Marie (Ary) Siler; m. Gabriel Shukri, Jan. 26, 1974; children: Tanya Ann Khodr, Christina Emilie Knodr, Zeina Gabriella Khodr. BA in Chemistry, Immaculate Heart Coll., L.A., 1968; Phd in Biochemistry, U. Hawaii, 1971. Cert. profl. chemist, Am. Chem. Soc. Nuclear medicine technician St. Vincent's Hosp., L.A., 1968; NIH predoctoral fellow dept biochemistry and biophysics U. Hawaii, Honolulu, 1968-70, predoctoral Ford Found. fellow, 1970, postdoctoral Ford Found. fellow anatomy/reproductive biology, 1971; chief adenohypophyseal hormone sect. InterSci. Inst., L.A., 1972; asst. rsch. biologist dept. reproductive medicine U. Calif., San Diego, 1972-74; asst. prof. dept. ob-gyn. Am. Univ. Beirut Hosp., 1974-76; with U. Tex. Health Sci. Ctr., San Antonio, 1976—, assoc. prof. dept. ob-gyn., 1979-86, prof., 1986—, dir. clin. endocrine infertility lab.; participant preceptor tng. programs including AID program for Internat. Edn. in Gynecology and Obstetrics, Dept. Ob-Gyn., Am. Univ. Beirut Hosp., 1974-76, Reproductive Endocrinology Fellowship Program, Health Sci. Ctr., U. Tex., 1987—; cons. rev. bd. for NIH Intramural Grants, S.W. Biomed. Rsch. Found., 1985-87; extramural reviewer Med. Rsch. Coun. Can., 1985, 86, 87, NICHD, 1985, NSF, 1981; presenter profl. confs. including XI World Congress of Gynecology and Obstetrics, West Berlin, 1985, 1stInternat. Meeting on Human Fetal Membranes, London, Ont., Can., 1986. Contbg. author: Radioimmunoassay Methods, 1971, Biorhythym in Human Reproduction, 1973, Advances in the Biosciences 15, 1975, Physiology and Pathophysiology of Reproduction, 1979, Clinics in Perinatology, 1983, Neonatal and Fetal Medicine, 1989, others; contbr. numerous articles to profl. publs.; mem. editorial bd. Jour. Endocrinological Investigation, 1978-83, Endocrinology, 1987—; ad hoc reviewer Obstetrics and Gynecology, 1982, Psychoneuroendocrinology, 1983, 84, 85, Neuroendocrinology, 1985,86, Placenta, 1987,88. Recipient Wyeth award The Pacific Coast Fertility Soc., 1972, 79, 80, Purdue Frederick Pres.'s award Congress for Am. Coll. Ob-Gyn., 1972, 1st prize Armed Forces Congress of Ob-Gyn., 1971; rsch. grantee Syntex Labs., U. Tex. Health Sci. Ctr., 1980-85, WHO, Am. U. Beirut Hosp., 1975-76, co-investigator, preceptor or cons. many other rsch. grants. Mem. AAAS, NIH (mem. reproductive endocrinology study sect. 1986-89, 90, 93-94, rsch. grantee 1976—), The Endocrine Soc., Soc. for Study of Reprodn., Soc. for Gynecologic Investigation, Am. Endocrine Soc., Assn. Profs. of Gynecology and Obstetrics, U. Tex. Health Sci. Ctr. Women's Faculty Assn., Sigma Xi. Office: Univ Tex Health Sci Ctr 7703 Floyd Curl Dr San Antonio TX 78284-6200

SILETS, HARVEY MARVIN, lawyer; b. Chgo., Aug. 25, 1931; s. Joseph Lazarus and Sylvia (Dubner) S.; m. Elaine L. Gordon, June 25, 1961; children: Hayden Leigh, Jonathan Lazarus (dec.), Alexandra Rose. BS cum laude, DePaul U., 1952; JD (Frederick Leicke scholar), U. Mich., 1955. Bar: Ill. 1955, U.S. Dist. Ct. (no. dist.) Ill. 1955, N.Y. 1956, U.S. Tax Ct. 1957, U.S. Ct. Mil. Appeals 1957, U.S. Ct. Appeals (7th cir.) 1958, U.S. Supreme Ct. 1959, U.S. Ct. Appeals (6th cir.) 1965, U.S. Ct. Appeals (2d cir.) 1971, U.S. Ct. Appeals (5th cir.) 1972, U.S. Ct. Appeals (11th cir.). Assoc. Paul, Weiss, Rifkind, Wharton & Garrison, N.Y.C., 1955-56; asst. atty. U.S. Dist. Ct. (no. dist.) Ill., 1958-60; chief tax atty. U.S. atty. No. Dist. Ill., Chgo., 1960-62; ptnr. Harris, Burman & Silets, Chgo., 1962-79, Silets & Martin, Ltd., Chgo., 1979-92; asst. advance tng. program IRS, U. Mich., 1952-53; law lectr. advance fed. taxation John Marshall Law Sch., 1962-66; adj. prof. taxation Chgo.-Kent Coll. Law, 1985—; gen. counsel Nat. Treasury Employees Union, 1968-92; mem. adv. com. tax litigation U.S. Dept. Justice, 1979-82; mem. Tax Reform Com., State of Ill., 1982-83; mem. Speedy Trial Act Planning Group U.S. Dist. Ct. (no. dist.) Ill., 1976-79; mem. civil justice reform act adv. com. U.S. Dist. Ct. (no. dist.) Ill., 1991-94; lectr. in field. Contbr. articles to profl. jours. Trustee Latin Sch., Chgo., 1970-76; active Chgo. Crime Commn., 1975-93, Govv.'s Commn. Reform Tax Laws, Ill., 1982-83. With AUS, 1956-58. Fellow Am. Coll. Trial Lawyers (chmn. com. on fed. rules of criminal procedure 1982-91, fed. rules of evidence com. 1988-93, mem. judiciary com., Upstate Ill. com. chmn. 1990-91), Am. Coll. Tax Counsel, Internat. Acad. Trial Lawyers; mem. ABA (active various coms.), Bar Assn. 7th Fed. Cir. (chmn. com. criminal law and procedure 1972-82, bd. govs. 1983-86, sec. 1986-88, v.p. 1989-90, pres. 1990-91), Fed. Bar Assn. (bd. dirs. 1971—, pres. 1977-78, v.p. 1976-77, sec. 1975-76, treas. 1974-75, active various coms.), Chgo. Bar Assn. (tax com. 1958-66, com. devel. law 1966-72, 78—, com. fed. taxation 1968—, com. evaluation candidates 1978-80, exec. com. tax sect. 1994—), Am. Bd. Criminal Def. Lawyers, Chgo. Soc. Trial Lawyers, Decalogue Soc. Lawyers, Bar Assn. N.Y. City, Nat. Assn. Criminal Def. Lawyers, Standard Club, Cliff Dwellers Club, Chgo. Club, Phi Alpha delta, Pi Gamma Mu. Office: Katten Muchin & Zavis 525 W Monroe St Ste 1600 Chicago IL 60661-3629

SILFVAST, WILLIAM T., laser physics educator, consultant; b. Salt Lake City, June 7, 1937; s. Andrew William and Dorothy Phyllis (Hobba) S.; m. Susan Carol Denton, Sept. 19, 1959; children: Scott William, Robert Denton, Stacey Marie. BS in Physics, BS in Math., U. Utah, 1961, PhD in Physics, 1965. Rsch. assoc. U. Utah, Salt Lake City, 1965-66; NATO postdoctoral fellow Oxford (Eng.) U., 1966-67; mem. tech. staff Bell Labs., Holmdel, N.J., 1967-82; Guggenheim fellow Stanford (Calif.) U., 1982-83; disting. mem. tech. staff AT&T Bell Labs., Holmdel, 1983-89; prof. physics and elec. engring. U. Cen. Fla., Orlando, 1990-94, chair dept. physics, 1994—. Contbr. numerous articles to sci. jours.; numerous patents relating to lasers. Trustee 1st Presbyn. Ch., Matawan, N.J., 1979-82, 88-89; chmn. bd. trustees Monmouth County Arts Coun., Red Bank, N.J., 1987-88. Fellow IEEE (assoc. editor IEEE Jour. Quantum Elecs. 1986-91), Optical Soc. Am. (chmn. tech. coun. 1988-89), Am. Phys. Soc. Avocations: writing, golf, tennis, skiing, automobile restoration. Office: U Cen Fla CREOL PO Box 162700 Orlando FL 32816-2700

SILHAVY, THOMAS JOSEPH, molecular biology educator; b. Wauseon, Ohio, Jan. 13, 1948; s. W.J. and Helen (Batdorf) S.; Daileen K. Stutzman, June 27, 1969; children—Marc Thomas, Ned Thomas. B.S. in Pharmacy, Ferris State Coll., 1971; A.M. in Biochemistry, Harvard U., 1974, Ph.D. in Biochemistry, 1975; D.S., Ferris State Coll, 1982. Instr. Harvard U. Med Sch., Boston, 1978-79; head genetics sect. Nat. Cancer Inst., Frederick, MD., 1979-81, dir. genetics, 1981-84; instr. Advanced Bacterial Genetics, Cold Spring Harbor, N.Y., 1981-85; prof. molecular biology Princeton U., 1984—. Co-author: Experiments with Gene Fusions, 1984, The Power of Bacterial Genetics: A Literature-based Course, 1992; contbr. over 100 articles to profl. jours. Patentee in field. Recipient Advanced Tech. Achievement award Litton, 1982, Wellcom vis. professorship in microbiol. scis., 1990, Pres.'s award for disting. teaching, 1993; Jane Coffin Childs fellow, 1975-77, Med. Rsch. Found. fellow, 1978-79. Fellow Am. Soc. Microbiology, Am. Acad. Microbiology; mem. AAAS, Am. Soc. Biol. Chemists, Am. Soc. Cell Biology. Home: 22 Van Doren Way Belle Mead NJ 08502-5508 Office: Princeton U Dept Molecular Biology Princeton NJ 08544

SILINS, INTS M., ambassador; b. Riga, Latvia, Mar. 25, 1942; m. Elizabeth Louise Adolphson, 1976; children: Kate, Matthew, Lucas, Nicholas. BA with honors in Philosophy, Princeton U., 1965; postgrad., U. Coll., London. With Washington Star; sr. advisor State Dept., Duc Thanh, Mekong Delta, Vietnam, 1970-71; exec. secretariat State Dept., Washington, 1975-76, Romania desk officer, 1976-78; amb. aide U.S. Embassy, Saigon, Vietnam, 1971-73; econ., comml. officer U.S. Embassy, Bucharest, Romania, 1973-75; polit. officer U.S. Embassy, Port au Prince, Haiti, 1978-80; polit. counselor U.S. Embassy, Stockholm, 1983-86; chargé d'affaires U.S. Embassy, Riga, Latvia, 1991-92, U.S. Amb., 1992-95; dep. prin. officer U.S. Consulate Gen., Leningrad, USSR, 1981-83; fellow Ctr. Internat. Affairs Harvard U., Cambridge, Mass., 1986-87; U.S. consul gen. Strasbourg, France, 1989-91. Recipient Valor award Dept. State, 1980, Meritorious Honor award Dept. State, 1985, Superior Honor award, 1988, 92, Three Stars Order, Rep. of Latvia, 1995. Office: U Chgo Harris Sch of Policy Studies 1155 E 60th St Chicago IL 60637-2745

SILIPIGNI, ALFREDO, opera conductor; b. Atlantic City, Apr. 9, 1931; s. Alfredo and Elisabeth (Calhoun) S.; m. Gloria Rose DiBenedetto, Apr. 11, 1953; children: Marisa, Elisabetta Luisa, Afredo Roberto. Student, Westminster Choir Coll., 1948, Juilliard Sch. Music, 1953; HHD (hon.), Kean Coll. N.J., 1978. Prin. condr., gen. dir., artistic dir. N.J. State Opera, Newark, 1965—, founder Young Artist Program, 1969—; guest lectr. Glassboro (N.J.) State Coll. Carnegie Hall debut with Symphony of the Air, 1956; condr. NBC Symphony, Boston, Bklyn. and Conn. operas, Newark Symphony; guest condr. Vienna State Opera, 1976, Grand Liceo di Barcelona, Spain, 1976, London, 1977, also numerous cos. Eng., Venezuela, France, Italy, Mex. and Can. with frequent appearances at L'Opera de Montreal; made recs. fo Zaza by Leoncavallo, "Adriana Lecouvrer" by Cilea; prin. guest condr. and advisor Bellas Artes, Mex., 1993-94. Recipient Centennial medal St. Peter's Coll., 1972, Disting. Svc. to Culture award City of San Remo, Columbia Found. award, Boys Town of Italy award, Music award N.J. Edn. Assn., 1988. Office: NJ State Opera 50 Park Pl Ste 10 Newark NJ 07102-4305

SILJAK, DRAGOSLAV D., engineering educator; b. Belgrade, Yugoslavia, Sept. 10, 1933; came to U.S. 1964, naturalized; s. Dobrilo T. and Ljubica Z. (Zivanovic) S.; m. Dragana T. Todorovic, Sept. 28, 1967; children—Ana, Matija. BSEE, U. Belgrade, 1958, MSEE, 1961, ScD, 1963. Docent prof.

U. Belgrade, 1963-64; assoc. prof. U. Santa Clara, Calif., 1964-70; prof. engring. U. Santa Clara, 1970-84, B. and M. Swig Univ. chair, 1984—. Author: Nonlinear Systems, 1969, Large Scale Systems, 1978, Decentralized Control of Complex Systems, 1991; mem. editl. bd. Jour. Difference Equations, Nonlinear World, Comm. in Applied Analysis, Nonlinear Studies, Dynamics of Cont., Disc. and Impulsive Systems, Math. Problems in Engring. Disting. prof. Fulbright Found., 1984. Fellow IEEE; mem. Serbian Acad. Scis. and Arts (hon.). Mem. Christian Orthodox Ch.

SILK, ALVIN JOHN, business educator; b. Winnipeg, Manitoba, Can., Dec. 31, 1935; came to U.S., 1959, naturalized, 1975; s. John Edward and Bertha Lena (Kirton) S.; m. Diane D. Wilson; children: Jonathan, Andrea, Stephanie. BA, U. Western Ont., 1959; MBA, Northwestern U., 1960, PhD, 1968. Asst. prof. mgmt. UCLA, 1963-66; asst. prof. U. Chgo., 1966-68; from assoc. prof. to prof. Sloan Sch. Mgmt., MIT, Cambridge, 1968-88; dep. dean MIT Sloan Sch. Mgmt., Cambridge, 1981-87; Lincoln Filene prof. Grad. Sch. Bus. Adminstrn. Harvard U., Boston, 1988—; vis. rsch. fellow Mktg. Sci. Inst., Cambridge, Mass., 1970-71, trustee, 1984-96; Ford Found. vis. prof. European Inst. for Advanced Studies in Mgmt., Brussels, 1975-76, Harvard Bus. Sch., 1987—; bd. dirs. Reed and Barton, Inc., Taunton, Mass., Boston 1784 Funds. Co-editor: Behavioral and Management Science in Marketing, 1978; assoc. editor: Management Science, 1969-77; mem. editorial bd.; Jour. Marketing Research, 1969-73, Jour. Marketing, 1978-81, Marketing Science, 1980-93; author, co-author numerous articles to profl. jours. Mem. Am. Mktg. Assn. (O'Dell award 1983), Am. Statis. Assn., Assn. for Consumer Rsch., Econometric Soc., Inst. for Mgmt. Scis. (Achievement award 1982, 83), Psychometric Soc., Beta Gamma Sigma, Zeta Psi. Home: 327 Commonwealth Ave Boston MA 02115-1900

SILK, ELEANA S., librarian; b. Detroit, Aug. 10, 1951; d. John and Helen (Kavenski) S. BS in Zoology, Mich. State U., 1972; BS in Geology, George Washington U., 1979; MDiv, St. Vladimir's Sem., 1986, MA in Religious Edn., 1988; MLS, Columbia U., 1989. Asst. libr. St. Vladimir's Sem., Crestwood, N.Y., 1985-90, libr., 1990—; mem. history and archives commn., bicentennial commn. Orthodox Ch. in Am., Syosset, N.Y., 1989—. Editor: The Legacy of St. Vladimir, 1989; contbr. articles to religious jours. Mem. ALA, N.Y. Area Theol. Libr. Assn., Oral History Assn., Fellowship Orthodox Stewards, Orthodox Theol. Soc. Am., Federated Russian Orthodox Clubs (chpt. pres. 1978-80, gov. 1981-82). Office: St Vladimir's Sem 575 Scarsdale Rd Tuckahoe NY 10707-1659

SILK, FREDERICK C.Z., financial consultant; b. Pretoria, Transvaal, South Africa, July 29, 1934; arrived in Canada, 1964; s. Frederick Charles and Edythe D'Olier (Ziervogel) S.; m. Margaret Colbourne, May 12, 1962; children: Michael, Alison, Jennifer. BS, Rhodes U., Grahamstown, Republic South Africa, 1954; cert. acctg. theory, U. Witwatersrand, Johannesburg, Republic South Africa, 1957. Acct., cons. Deloitte, Plender, Haskins & Sells, Johannesburg, London and N.Y.C., 1954-64; mgmt. cons. P.S. Ross & Ptnrs., Montreal, Que, Can., 1964-68; v.p. fin. and adminstrn. J&P Coats (Can.) Ltd., Montreal, 1968-74; treas. Standard Brands, Ltd., Montreal, 1974-75; asst. treas. Standard Brands, Inc., N.Y.C., 1975-78; treas. Harlequin Enterprises, Ltd., Toronto, Ont., Can., 1978-82; v.p., treas. Nabisco Brands, Ltd., Toronto, 1982-95; pvt. treas. cons. Toronto, 1995—. Fellow Inst. Chartered Accts. (Eng., Wales), Inst. Chartered Accts. (South Africa), Fin. Execs. Inst. Avocations: music, choral music, Gilbert and Sullivan operettas. Office: Ste 418, 80 Front St E, Toronto, ON Canada M5E 1T4

SILK, GEORGE, photographer; b. Levin, New Zealand, Nov. 17, 1916; s. Arthur and Constance (Naylor) S.; m. Margery G. Schieber, Nov. 28, 1947; children—Stuart, Georgiana B., Shelley G. Ed., New Zealand schs. With photographic store in New Zealand, 1935-39; ofcl. photographer Australian Inf. Forces in Middle East, 1940-42, New Guinea, 1942-43; photographer Life mag., 1943-73; corr. in Life mag., ETO, 1944-45, PTO, 1945, China, 1946, N.Y.C., 1947-73; free lance photographer, 1973—. Pictures in color sect. 1959 annual Ency. Brit.; photographs in Fine Arts exhibit, 1962, 63. Recipient gold medal Art Dirs. Club, 1961; Photographer of Year award Ency. Brit., 1960; Am. Soc. Mag. Photographers Meml. award, 1962; Photographer of Year awards Nat. Press Photographers Assn., U. Mo., World Book, 1960, 62, 63, 64; Brehm Meml. award Rochester Inst. Tech., 1966. Home: Owenoke Park Westport CT 06880-6851

SILKENAT, JAMES ROBERT, lawyer; b. Salina, Kans., Aug. 2, 1947; s. Ernest E. and Mildred R. (Iman) S.; children: David Andrew, Katherine Anne. BA, Drury Coll., 1969; JD, U. Chgo., 1972; LLM, NYU, 1978. Bar: N.Y. 1973, D.C. 1980. Assoc. Cravath, Swaine & Moore, N.Y.C., 1972-80; counsel Internat. Fin. Corp., Washington, 1980-86; ptnr. Morgan, Lewis & Bockius, N.Y.C., 1986-89, Morrison & Foerster, N.Y.C., 1989-92, Winthrop, Stimson, Putnam & Roberts, N.Y.C., 1992—; chmn. Council N.Y. Law Assocs., 1978-79, Lawyers Com. Internat. Human Rights, 1978-80. Editor ABA Guide to Fng. Law Firms, Moscow Conf. on Law Bilateral Econ. Rels., ABA Guide to Internat. Bus. Negotiations; contbr. over 70 articles on law and pub. policy to profl. jours. Served to capt. U.S. Army, 1972-73. Fellow NEH, 1977, U.S. Dept. State, 1981. Fellow Am. Bar Found.; mem. ABA (chmn. internat. law and practice sect. 1989-90, chmn. sect. officer's conf. 1990-92, mem. ho. of dels. 1989—, bd. govs. 1994—). Office: Winthrop Stimson Putnam & Roberts One Battery Park Plz New York NY 10004

SILKETT, ROBERT TILLSON, food business consultant; b. Columbia, Mo., Nov. 12, 1929; s. Ross Jacob and Marion Dorchester (Tillson) S.; m. Sally Forrest Lash, Dec. 23, 1954; children—Robert Tillson, Elizabeth L. B.A., Duke U., 1951; M.B.A. with distinction, Wharton Grad. Sch., U. Pa., 1956. With mktg. dept. Anderson Clayton Co., 1956-58; with Gen. Foods Corp., 1958-78, group exec. corp. mktg. and sales, 1976-78; chmn. bd., chief exec. officer Reckitt & Colman N.A., Rochester, N.Y., also R.T. French Co., 1978-86; exec. v.p., dir. Curtice-Burns Foods, Rochester, 1986-90; owner, pres. The RTS Group, Rochester, 1990—. Past bd. dirs. Rochester United Way, Rochester Mus.; mem. exec. bd. Wharton Grad. Sch., Rochester council Boy Scouts Am. Served to lt. USNR, 1951-54. Mem. Wharton Grad. Sch. Alumni Assn. (past chmn.), Beta Gamma Sigma. Republican. Episcopalian. Clubs: Rochester Country, Wilton Riding (past pres.); Wharton M.B.A. (N.Y.C.) (past dir.), Mid Ocean (Bermuda), Key Largo Anglers, Card Sound (Key Largo).

SILLARS, MALCOLM OSGOOD, communication educator; b. Union City, N.J., Feb. 12, 1928; s. Malcolm Osgood and Dorothy Edna (Browning) S.; m. Charlotte Jane Grimm, June 1, 1948; children—Paul Louis, Bruce Malcolm, Alan Leslie. B.A., U. Redlands, 1948, M.A., 1949; Ph.D., U. Iowa, 1955. Asst. prof. communication Iowa State U., Ames, 1949-53; asst. prof. Calif. State U., Los Angeles, 1954-56; prof., dean Calif. State U., Northridge, 1956-71; pres. Calif. State U., 1969-70; prof. U. Mass., Amherst, 1971-74; prof. communication U. Utah, Salt Lake City, 1974—; dean humanities U. Utah, 1974-81. Author: Speech: Content and Communications, 6th edit., 1991, Argumentation and Critical Decision Making, 4th edit., 1996, Messages, Meanings, and Culture, 1991; contbr. articles to profl. jours. Recipient Silver Beaver award Boy Scouts Am. Mem. Speech Communication Assn. (pres.), Western Speech Communication Assn. (pres.), AAUP, ACLU. Democrat. Home: 3508 Eastoaks Dr Salt Lake City UT 84124-3811 Office: U Utah Dept Communication Salt Lake City UT 84112

SILLECK, HARRY GARRISON, lawyer; b. Putnam Valley, N.Y., Mar. 19, 1921; s. Harry Garrison and Bertha May (Barrett) S.; m. June Baird, Mar. 4, 1977. B.A., Union Coll., 1940; LL.B., Columbia U., 1943. Bar: N.Y. 1944, U.S. Supreme Ct. 1966, U.S. Ct. Appeals (2d cir.) 1966 (6th cir.) 1976. Assoc. Dorr Hand Whittaker & Watson, N.Y.C., 1945-55, ptnr., 1955-63; ptnr. Mudge Rose Guthrie Alexander & Ferdon, N.Y.C., 1963-86, chmn., 1978-85. Served to 1st lt. AC, U.S. Army, 1943-45, ETO. Mem. Phi Beta Kappa. Home: 131 E 69th St New York NY 10021-5158

SILLIMAN, RICHARD GEORGE, retired lawyer, retired farm machinery company executive; b. Elgin, Ill., Aug. 11, 1922; s. Charles B. and Mabel Ellen (Winegar) S.; m. Mary L. Yost, June 12, 1945; children—Martha Jane, Charles R. B.A. in History, Cornell Coll., Mt. Vernon, Iowa, 1946; J.D., Northwestern U., 1949. Bar: Ill. 1949. Atty. various U.S. agys., Chgo., 1949-52; atty., asst. sec. Elgin Nat. Watch Co., Ill., 1952-59, sec., gen. atty., 1959-62; asst. gen. counsel Deere & Co., Moline, Ill., 1962-75, assoc. gen. counsel, 1975-82, sec., assoc. gen. counsel, 1982-87. Mem. editorial bd. Ill. Law Rev., 1948-49. Contbr. articles to profl. jours. Past pres., hon. dir. Quad-City Symphony Orch., Moline and Davenport, Iowa, 1968-87; bd. dirs., trustee Upper Rock Island County YMCA, Moline, 1965-87; bd. dirs. Police-Fire Commn., Elgin, 1957-61; bd. dirs., sec. Elgin YMCA, 1955. Served with USN, 1943-46. Mem. Ill. State Bar Assn. (past chmn. com. on corp. law dept.), Short Hills Country Club (Moline), Union League (Chgo.). Avocations: golf, music, sailing. Home: 4817 6th Street Ct East Moline IL 61244-4274

SILLIN, LELAN FLOR, JR., retired utility executive; b. Tampa, Fla., Apr. 19, 1918; s. Lelan Flor and Ruth (Berry) S.; m. Joan Outhwaite, Sept. 26, 1942; children: Lelan Flor, John Outhwaite, Andrew Borden, William Berry. AB with distinction, U. Mich., 1940, JD, 1942; LLD (hon.), Wesleyan U., 1969. Bar: N.Y. 1946. With Gould & Wilkie, N.Y.C., 1945-51; with Central Hudson Gas & Electric Corp., Poughkeepsie, N.Y., 1951-68, v.p., asst. gen. mgr., 1955-60, pres., 1960-68, chief exec. officer, 1964-67, also trustee; pres. Northeast Utilities, Hartford, Conn., 1968-70, chmn. bd., 1970-83, chief exec. officer, chmn. bd., 1968-83, also trustee; chmn. bd. Conn. Yankee Atomic Power Co., 1971-83, Northeast Energy, 1970-83; former chmn., dir. Fuel Cell User Group; bd. dirs. Waterbury Rep & Am.; past chmn. nat. power survey exec. adv. com. FPC, 1965-72; dir. Inst. Nuclear Power Ops., 1979-85, chmn., 1982-84; chmn. utility nuc. power oversight task com., 1986. Former mem. steering com. Nat. Urban Coalition; former mem. Pres.'s Adv. Com. Environ. Quality; former bd. dirs. Nat. Office Social Responsibility, New Eng. Council; trustee emeritus Edwin Gould Found. for Children, Woodrow Wilson Nat. Fellowship Found., New Eng. Natural Resources Ctr.; trustee emeritus Wesleyan U., former vice-chmn. bd. trustees; past mem. adv. com. White House Conf. on Balanced Nat. Growth and Econ. Devel.; past mem. Pub. Com. on Mental Health; former mem. Am. Arbitration Assn.; former bd. dirs. Conn. Bus. and Industry Assn.; trustee emeritus Vassar Bros. Hosp., Poughkeepsie. Maj. USMCR, 1942-45. Recipient Raymond E. Baldwin medal Wesleyan U., 1986, Oliver Townsend award Atomic Indsl. Forum, 1986. Former mem. Conf. Bd. (sr.). Clubs: Hartford; Dauntless (Essex, Conn.); Century Association, University (N.Y.C.). Office: NE Utilities Millstone Nuclear Power Sta Tng Ctr Box 128 Waterford CT 06385

SILLMAN, ARNOLD JOEL, physiologist, educator; b. N.Y.C., Oct. 10, 1940; s. Philip and Anne L. (Pearlman) S.; m. Jean Fletcher Van Keuren, Sept. 26, 1969; children—Andrea Jose, Diana Van Keuren. A.B., U. Calif.-Los Angeles, 1963, M.A., 1965, Ph.D., 1968. Asst. prof. U. Calif.-Los Angeles, 1969-73, Davis, 1975-78, assoc. prof., 1978-85, prof. 1985—; asst. prof. U. Pitts., 1973-75. Contbr. articles to profl. jours. USPHS trainee, UCLA, 1966-67; fellow NSF, 1967-68, Fight for Sight, Inc., 1968-69. Mem. Am. Physiol. Soc., Soc. Gen. Physiologists, Am. Soc. Zoologists, Assn. Research in Vision and Ophthalmology, AAAS, N.Y. Acad. Sci. Jewish. Home: 1140 Los Robles St Davis CA 95616-4927 Office: U Calif Sect Neurobiology Physiology & Behavior Divsn Biol Scis Davis CA 95616

SILLS, HILARY H., public relations executive; b. Chgo., Feb. 24, 1947. Cert. in EEC Studies, U. Brussels, 1968; BA in History, Hollins Coll., 1969. With staff of William Whitehurst U.S. Ho. Reps.; with The Daily Bond Buyer, GE; dir. energy and environment Govt. Rsch. Corp., 1975-87; v.p. Govt. Rsch. Group, 1988-89; sr. cons. Pub. Affairs Comm. Mgmt., 1987-88; v.p. Hill & Knowlton, 1989-91; sr. prin. Capitoline/MS&L, 1991—. former contbg. editor Economist Intelligence Unit. Mem. Women in Govt. Rels. Office: Capitoline/MS&L 1615 L St NW Ste 1150 Washington DC 20036-5624

SILLS, NANCY MINTZ, lawyer; b. N.Y.C., Nov. 3, 1941; d. Samuel and Selma (Kahn) Mintz; m. Stephen J. Sills, Apr. 17, 1966; children: Eric Howard, Ronnie Lynne Sills Lindberg. BA, U. Wis., 1962; JD cum laude, Union U., 1976. Bar: N.Y. 1977, U.S. Dist. Ct. (no. dist.) N.Y. 1977, U.S. Tax Ct. 1984. Asst. editor fin. news Newsweek mag., N.Y.C., 1962-65; staff writer, reporter Forbes mag., N.Y.C., 1965; rsch. assoc. pub. rels. Ea. Airlines, N.Y.C., 1965-67; asst. editor Harper & Row, N.Y.C., 1968-69; freelance writer, editor N.Y.C., Albany, 1967-70; confidential law sec. N.Y. State Supreme Ct., Albany, 1976-79; assoc. Whiteman, Osterman & Hanna, Albany, 1979-81, Martin, Noonan, Hislop, Troue & Shudt, Albany, 1981-83; ptnr. Martin, Shudt, Wallace & Sills, Albany, 1984; of counsel Krolick and DeGraff, Albany, 1984-89; ptnr. Hodgson, Russ, Andrews, Woods & Goodyear, Albany, 1990-91; pvt. practice Albany, 1991—; of counsel Lemery & Reid, Albany and Glens Falls, N.Y., 1993-94; asst. counsel N.Y. State Senate, 1983-88; cons. The Ayco Corp., 1975; jud. screening com. Third Jud. Dept., 1997—. Editor: Reforming American Education, 1969, Up From Poverty, 1968; rschr.: The Negro Revolution in America, 1963; contbr. articles to mags. Bd. dirs. Jewish Philanthropies Endowment, 1983-86, United Jewish Fedn. N.E. N.Y. Endowment Fund, 1992-96, Daus. Sarah Found., 1994—, Albany Jewish Cmty. Ctr., 1984-87; mem. Guilderland (N.Y.) Conservation Adv. Coun., 1993-96; mem. planned giving tech. adv. com. Albany Law Sch., Union U., 1991-95, chmn., 1992-95; mem. regional cabinet State of Israel Bonds Devel. Corp. for Israel, 1991-92. Mem. ABA, N.Y. State Bar Assn., Albany County Bar Assn., Warren County Bar Assn., N.Y. Criminal and Civil Cts. Bar Assn., Estate Planning Coun. Ea. N.Y., Aux. Albany County Med. Soc., Capital Dist. Trial Lawyers Assn., Capital Dist. Women's Bar Assn., Phi Beta Kappa, Sigma Epsilon Sigma. Republican. Home: 16 Hiawatha Dr Guilderland NY 12084-9526 Office: 126 State St Albany NY 12207-1637

SILLS, RICHARD REYNOLDS, scientist, educator; b. N.Y.C., Sept. 19, 1946; s. Leonard Harold and Carol (Rudin) S. BA, Boston U., 1968. Tchr. N.Y.C. Pub. Schs., 1968-70, 79-81; v.p. Plutronics, Inc., N.Y.C., 1981-85; pvt. practice N.Y.C., 1985—. Author: (children's book) Jonny the Jester, 1977; contbr. articles to profl. jours.; patentee method and apparatus for encoding and decoding signals, method and apparatus for modifying synthesized sound signals, analog processing system. Mem. Rep. Nat. Com., Washington, 1981—; rep. Presdl. Task Force, Washington, 1982—. Named Educator of Decade, Found. for Universal Brotherhood Inc., 1978. Mem. AAAS, Intellectual Property Owners, N.Y. Acad. Scis. Avocations: running, weight lifting.

SILVA, ERNEST R., visual arts educator, artist; b. Providence, R.I., Dec. 11, 1948. BFA, U. R.I., 1971; MFA, Tyler Sch. Art, 1974. Instr. U. R.I., Kingston, 1977-79; lectr. dept. visual arts U. Calif. San Diego, La Jolla, 1979-87, prof. dept. visual arts, 1987—; represented by Jan Baum Gallery, L.A., Lenore Gray Gallery, Providence, R.I.; bd. dirs. Installation Gallery, San Diego, mem. arts adv. bd., 1992—, exec. com., 1993—; lectr. Phila. Coll. Art, 1973, U. R.I., 1974, 84, 91, RISD, 1977, Tyler Sch. Art, Elkins Park, Pa., 1979, U. Calif. Irvine, 1981, Southwestern Coll., Chula Vista, 1982, San Diego State U., 1985, Nat. Soc. Arts and Letters, Washington, 1986, Friends of Jung, San Diego, 1991. One-person exhbns. include Inst. Contemporary Art, Boston, 1972, Artists Space, N.Y.C., 1975, Anyart Contemporary Art Ctr., Providence, R.I., 1976, Lenore Gray Gallery, Providence, 1978, 79, 92, Roy Boyd Gallery, L.A., 1982, 84, 87, Quint Gallery, San Diego, 1982, 83, 86, Jan Baum Gallery, L.A., 1989, 91, Tuttle Gallery, McDonogh, Md., 1990, Porter Randall Gallery, La Jolla, 1994, Mus. Contemporary Art, Roskilde, Denmark, 1995, many others; group exhbns. include Mus. Phila. Civic Ctr., 1973, Cheltenham (Pa.) Art Ctr., 1973, Pratt Graphic Ctr., N.Y.C., 1975, Corcoran Art Gallery, Washington, 1975, Ft. Worth Art Mus., 1976, Baker Gallery, La Jolla, 1980, Ind. Contemporary Exhbns., L.A., 1982, Navy Pier, Chgo., 1983, 84, 85, Roy Boyd Gallery, Chgo., 1983, 85, 86, Heckscher Mus. Art, Huntington, N.Y., 1984, Indpls. Mus. Art, 1984, Forum Internat. Kunstmesse, Zurich, Switzerland, 1984, Nat. History Mus., San Diego, 1985, Visual Arts Ctr. Alaska, Anchorage, 1985, San Francisco Airport Mus., 1985, Sonrisa Gallery, L.A., 1985, Alaska State Mus., Juneau, 1986, Foire Internat. De L'Art Contemporain, Nice, France, 1986, Lyceum Theatre, San Diego, 1987, Installation Gallery, San Diego, 1986, 87, 88, Chgo. Internat. Art Exposition, 1987,L.A. Convention Ctr., 1987, Cmty. Arts, San Francisco, 1989, 90, Annex Gallery, La Jolla, 1990, Bill Bace Gallery, N.Y.C., 1991, David Lewinson Gallery, Del Mar, Calif., 1991, Southwestern Coll. Art, Chula Vista, Calif., 1992, Boehm Gallery Palomar Coll, San Marcos, Calif., 1993, Porter Randall Gallery, La Jolla, 1992, numerous others; represented in permanent collections Fogg Art Mus. Harvard U., Cambridge, Mass., Grand Rapids (Mich.) Art Mus., La Jolla Mus. Contemporary Art, Laguna Mus. Art, De Saisset Mus. U. Santa Clara, Newport Harbor Art Mus., Newport Beach, Calif., Mus. Contemporary Art, San Diego, La Jolla, San Jose Mus. Art, San Diego Mus. Art; subject reviews, articles, 1974—. Office: U Calif San Diego Visual Arts 0327 9500 Gilman Dr La Jolla CA 92093-0327*

SILVA, EUGENE JOSEPH, lawyer; b. Gloucester, Mass., May 23, 1942; s. Edward Joseph and Rose (Lebre) S.; m. Nancy Blue-Pearson, Jan. 8, 1972; children: Eugene Joseph II, Michael Joseph. BS with honors, Maine Maritime Acad., 1964; JD, U. Notre Dame, 1972. Bar: Calif. 1972, U.S. Dist. Ct. (so. and cen. dists.) Calif. 1972, Tex. 1977, U.S. Dist. Ct. (so. and ea. dists.) Tex. 1978, U.S. Ct. Appeals (5th, 2d and 11th cirs.) 1978, U.S. Supreme Ct. 1981; lic. Master Mariner. Assoc. Luce, Forward, Hamilton & Scripps, San Diego, 1972-77; assoc. Vinson & Elkins, Houston, 1977-79, ptnr., 1980—. Bd. dirs. Cabrillo Festival Inc., San Diego, 1974-77, San Jose Clinic, Inc., 1990—, pres. 1993-95; bd. dirs. Portuguese Heritage Scholarship Found., 1995—, St. Joseph Hosp. Found., 1996—. Decorated Knight Comdr. Equestrian Order of Holy Sepulchre of Jerusalem; recipient Outstanding Alumni award Maine Maritime Acad., 1990. Mem. Houston Bar Assn., Calif. Bar Assn., Tex. Bar Assn., Internat. Bar Assn., Grays Inn U. Notre Dame Sch. Law (pres. 1970-72), Southeastern Admiralty Law Inst., Maritime Law Assn. U.S. (proctor in admiralty 1974—), Portuguese Union Calif. (bd. dirs. 1973-74), Portuguese Am. League San Diego (pres. 1974-75), Portuguese Am. Leadership Coun. U.S., Asia-Pacific Lawyers Assn., Notre Dame Club (pres. San Diego chpt. 1976-77), Houston Ctr. Club, The Naval Club (London). Roman Catholic. Home: 8 Smithdale Estates Dr Houston TX 77024-6600 Office: Vinson & Elkins 2500 First City Tower 1001 Fannin St Houston TX 77002-6706

SILVA, FELIPE, former tobacco company executive; b. Cienfuegos, Cuba, Feb. 27, 1919; came to U.S., 1960, naturalized, 1968; s. Felipe and Hortensia (Cardenas) S.; m. Dolores Alvarez, Feb. 3, 1945; children: Ana, Felipe Rafael, Maria Dolores, Lourdes. Student, U. Mich., 1936-38; D. Law, U. Havana, 1942, Public Acct., 1943. Pres. Tabacalera Cubana S.A., 1949-60; spl. sales rep. ACC div. Am. Tobacco Co., St. Petersburg, Fla., 1960-62; mgr. P.R. br. ACC div. Am. Tobacco Co., San Juan, 1963-67; export mgr. Am. Tobacco Co. div. Am. Brands, Inc., N.Y.C., 1968-78; pres. Am. Cigar div. Am. Brands, Inc., 1979-80, pres., chief exec. officer Am. Cigar div., 1981-83, chmn., chief exec. officer cigar div., 1983-84. Mem. U. Mich. Alumni Assn. Roman Catholic. Lodge: Rotary. Home: 600 Grapetree Dr Apt 7bs Miami FL 33149-2703

SILVA, JOANNA KONTAXIS, dietitian; b. Psari Trifilias, Greece, Nov. 19, 1940; came to U.S., 1967; d. George Demetrios and Sophia George (Naisopoulos) Kontaxis; m. Michael Andrew Silva, Oct. 4, 1969; children: Mark Alexander, Paul Richard. BA, Harokopios Coll., Kalithea, Athens, Greece; BS, U. Calif., Berkeley. Chief clin. dietitian A.H.E.P.A. Hosp., Salonika, Greece, 1961-67; clin. dietitian Providence Hosp., Oakland, Calif., 1967-92; renal dietitian B.M.A. Berkeley Dialysis Unit, 1990—; cons. dietitain Calif. Hosp., Oakland, 1976-81, C.D.C. Dialysis Unit, Vallejo, Claif., 1993—, C.A.P.D. Dietitien for Total Renal Care, Walnut Creek, Calif., 1992—. Mem. Am. Dietetic Assn. (registered), Bay Area Dietetic Assn. (hospitality chmn. 1979-87), Calif. Dietetic Assn., Daus. of Penelope (pres. 1990-92). Greek Orthodox. Avocations: swimming, Greek dancing, reading, gardening, traveling. Home: 4 Rita Way Orinda CA 94563-4132 Office: BMA Dialysis 3017 Telegraph Ave Berkeley CA 94705-2049

SILVA, JOHN PHILIP COSTA, newspaper editor; b. Providence, Jan. 19, 1951; s. Silvano Costa and Florence Josephine (Russo) S.; m. Deborah Helen Radovsky, May 8, 1977; children: Daniel David, Matthew Philip. BA in Journalism, U. R.I., 1973. Staff writer Providence Jour.-Bull., 1973-79; staff writer Miami (Fla.) News, 1979-81, asst. city editor, 1981-82; spl. corr. The Wall St. Jour., Miami, 1980-81; city editor Lexington (Ky.) Herald-Leader, 1982-84; night city editor L.A. Herald Examiner, 1984-85, assignment editor, 1985-87; asst. mng. editor Ariz. Daily Star, Tucson, 1987—. Recipient 1st place for spot news UPI Newspapers New Eng., 1977. Mem. Nat. Assn. Hispanic Journalists, Investigative Reporters and Editors Assn., Ariz. Assoc. Press Mng. Editors Assn. Avocations: writing historical research, computer technology. Home: 9433 N Albatross Dr Tucson AZ 85742 Office: Ariz Daily Star 4850 S Park Ave Tucson AZ 85714-1637

SILVA, JOSEPH DONALD, English language educator; b. Lowell, Mass., Jan. 19, 1935; s. Joseph Maria and Edna (Talbot) S.; m. Lucy Niles, June 22, 1957; children: Joseph Alden, Maria Margriet, Paul Frederic, Amanda Elizabeth. BA, U. N.H., 1957, MA, 1965. From instr. to assoc. prof. U. N.H., Durham, 1963-85, prof., 1985—; chmn. N.E. Regional Conf. on English, 1977-79. Author: A Bibliography on the Madeira Islands, 1987, World Bibiliographical Series Madeira Islands, 1997. Pastor New Castle (N.H.) Congl. Ch., 1967—; moderator Rockingham (N.H.) Assn. United Ch. of Christ, 1987-89. 1st lt. U.S. Army, 1958. Mem. AAUP (chmn. Durham chpt. 1983-84), Nat. Coun. Tchrs. English, Conf. Coll. Composition and Communication. Avocations: travel, photography, hiking, swimming, gardening. Home: 55 Main St New Castle NH 03854-0132

SILVA, OMEGA LOGAN, physician; b. Washington, Dec. 14, 1936; d. Louis Jasper and Ruth (Dickerson) Logan; m. C. Francis A. Silva, Oct. 25, 1958 (div. 1981); 1 child, Frances Cecile; m. Harold Bryant Webb, Nov. 28, 1982. Grad., Howard U., Washington, 1958, MD, 1967. Bio-chemist NIH, Bethesda, Md., 1958-63; asst. chief endocrinology Vets. Affairs Med. Ctr., Washington, 1967-96; physician Mitchell-Trotman Med. Group, P.C., 1996-97; assoc. prof. George Washington U., Washington, 1975-91, prof. 1991—; prof. Howard U., Washington, 1977-96. Author: (with others) Endocrinology, 1990; contbr. articles to profl. jours. Charter mem. Nat. Mus. of Women in the Arts, Washington, 1986; health cons. River Pk. Mutual Homes, Inc., Washington, 1987; vol. Career Day Chillum Elem. Sch., Career Week, George Washington U., Washington, 1988; trustee Howard U., 1991-97; gov. Region III, chmn. leadership com. Fellow ACP (Best Sci. Presentation award 1974); mem. Am. Chem. Soc., Am. Med. Women's Assn. (br. I v.p. 1986-87, pres. 1987-88, anti-smoking task force 1989-92, hair govtl. affairs nominations com. 1992), Howard U. Med. Alumni (pres. 1983-88), Alpha Omega Alpha. Avocations: dress and hat design, furniture design, home contruction.

SILVA-RUÍZ, SERGIO ANDRÉS, biochemist; b. San Juan, P.R., Jan. 12, 1944; s. Sergio A. and América (Ruíz) Silva-Izquierdo; m. Iris M. Piñero, Dec. 28, 1973; children: Maite Ira, Javier Juan, Siris Anya. BS in Chemistry, U. P.R., Rio Piedras, 1965, MS in Biochemistry, 1977, PhD, 1978. Scientist Schering-Plough, Manati, P.R., 1978-79, sr. scientist, 1979-82; mgr. R & D lab. Schering Corp., Manati, P.R., 1982-85; sr. scientist Schering Manati, Inc., Manati, P.R., 1986-91; mgr. fermentation plant Schering-Plough Products, Manati, P.R., 1991-93, plant mgr. antibiotics, 1993—; mem. adv. com. for biotech. Bachelors Degree, U. P.R., Rio Piedras, 1986-87; adv. bd. U. P.R. Minority Rsch. Ctr. for Excellence, Mayaquez, P.R., 1991-94; mem. adv. com. Lawrence Berkeley Lab., Jackson State U., Ana G. Méndez U. System Sci. Consortium, 1994-96; mem. program com. Am. Soc. Microbiology Biotech. Conf., 1991; mem. planning com. Am. Soc. Microbiology Conf. on Water Quality in Western Hemisphere, P.R., 1992-93. Pres. Sci. Rev. Com. Arecibo's Edn. Region, Dept. Edn., 1992-93. Recipient Dept. Def. fellowship, 1973-74, Merck Manual, U. P.R. Med Scis. Campus, 1978. Mem. AAAS (Caribbean Div. pres. 1992-93, coun, mem. 1993-94), Parenteral Drug Assn. (v.p. P.R. chpt. 1991-93), Sociedad Microbiólogos de P.R. (pres. 1982-83), Am. Soc. for Microbiology (mem. coun. 1983-85), N.Y. Acad. Sci., Sigma Xi. Office: Schering-Plough Products PO Box 486 Manati PR 00674-0486

SILVEIRA, AUGUSTINE, JR., chemistry educator; b. Mattapoisett, Mass., July 17, 1934; s. Augustine and Mildred (Lewis) S.; m. Beverly Ann Washburn, Aug. 20, 1960; children: Linda Ann, Karen Louise. BS, U. Mass., Dartmouth, 1957, ScD (hon.), 1975; PhD., U. Mass., Amherst, 1962. Research chemist Acushnet Process Co., Mass., 1957-58; instr. U. Mass., 1960-62; asst. prof. Rutgers U., 1962-63; assoc. prof SUNY, Oswego, 1963-64, prof., 1964-67, prof., chmn. dept. chemistry, 1967—, disting. teaching prof., 1976—; Am. Council on Edn. fellow U. Calif., Irvine, 1969-70, vis. prof., 1976-77, 83-84, 91; vis. prof. Calif. State U., Long Beach, 1976-77; cons. to edn. and industry; guest lectr.; evaluator SUNY Grad. Programs, 1968—, Patent Policy Bd., 1971; mem. commn. higher edn. Middle States

Assn., 1971—; mem. alumni adv. council U. Mass., 1971-75; mem. N.Y. State Bd. Optometry, 1981-91. Contbr. articles to profl. jours. Recipient N.Y. State/United Univ. Professions Excellence award, 1990; named to Fairhaven H.S. Hall of Fame Lifetime Achievement award; SUNY faculty exch. scholar, 1981—; SUNY rsch. grantee. Fellow Am. Inst. Chemists; mem. AAUP (v.p. 1965-66), Am. Chem. Soc. (dist. rep., Syracuse sect. award 1988), Sigma Xi (pres. 1972-73, 78-79), Delta Kappa Phi, Alpha Kappa Phi, Phi Kappa Phi. Home: 88 Co Rt 24 PO Box 98 Minetto NY 13115-0098 Office: SUNY Oswego Chemistry Dept Oswego NY 13126

SILVER, ALAN IRVING, lawyer; b. St. Paul, Sept. 17, 1949; s. Sherman J. Silver and Muriel (Bernstein) Brawerman; m. Janice Lynn Gleekel, July 8, 1973; children: Stephen, Amy. BA cum laude, U. Minn., 1971, JD cum laude, 1975. Bar: Minn. 1975, U.S. Dist. Ct. Minn. 1975, U.S. Dist. Ct. (ea. dist.) Wis. 1975, U.S. Ct. Appeals 8th and 10th cirs.) 1975. Assoc. Doherty, Rumble & Butler, P.A., Mpls., 1975-80; ptnr. Doherty, Rumble & Butler, P.A., St. Paul, 1980—; mem. 2d Jud. Dist. Ethics Com., St. Paul, 1985-88, 4th Jud. Dist. Ethics Com., Mpls., 1990-97. Author numerous continuing edn. seminar material. Vol. atty. Legal Assistance Ramsey County, St. Paul, 1975-82; mem. St. Louis Park (Minn.) Sch. Bd., 1993—, chair, 1995-97; mem. St. Louis Park Human Rights Commn., 1987-91; chmn. site mgmt. coun. Susan Lindgren Sch., St. Louis Park, 1986-93; bd. dirs. Jewish Cmty. Rels. Coun., Anti-Defamation League Minn. and Dakotas, 1987-93, treas., 1992-93. Mem. ABA, Minn. Bar Assn. (exec. bd. antitrust sect. 1984), Hennepin County Bar Assn. Avocations: running, guitar, reading. Home: 4320 W 25th St Minneapolis MN 55416-3841 Office: Doherty Rumble & Butler PA 150 S 5th St Minneapolis MN 55402-4200

SILVER, CASEY, broadcast executive. Screenwriter; from past v.p. prodn. to past sr. v.p. prodn. TriStar Pictures; past dir. devel. and prodn. Simpson-Bruckheimer; from exec. v.p. prodn. to chmn. Universal Pictures, 1987—. Asst. to dir. (film) Flashdance. Office: Universal Pictures 100 Universal City Plaza Universal City CA 91608*

SILVER, CHARLES MORTON, communications company executive; b. New Haven, Sept. 22, 1929; s. Sam and Rose (Fischman) S.; m. Rose Charek, Mar. 27, 1960; children—Ronni Ellen, Suzanne Paula, Steven Mitchell. B.S., U Conn., 1954. With Arthur Andersen & Co., N.Y.C., 1954-61, ITT, N.Y.C., 1961-88; ret. as v.p. and assoc. treas. ITT, 1988. Served with U.S. Army, 1947-48, 50-51. Mem. AICPA, Roxbury Swim and Tennis Club. Home: 51 Akbar Rd Stamford CT 06902-1401 also: PO Box 420275 Summerland Key FL 33042-0275

SILVER, DANIEL B., lawyer; b. Phila., Aug. 14, 1941; s. Samuel and Marjorie (Euster) S.; m. Sybil F. Michelson, Jan. 20, 1963; children—Abigail Ruth, Rachel Ann, Alexander Joseph. A.B., U. Calif., Berkeley, 1961; M.A., Harvard U., 1965, Ph.D., 1967, LL.B., 1968. Bar: D.C. 1968, U.S. Ct. Appeals (D.C. cir.) 1975, U.S. Supreme Ct. 1975. Assoc. Cleary, Gottlieb, Steen & Hamilton, Washington, 1968-70, 73-76, Brussels, Belgium, 1973-76, ptnr., Washington, 1976-78, 81-83, 85-96, Brussels, 1983-85, counsel, 1997—; gen. counsel NSA, Washington, 1978-79, CIA, Washington, 1979-81; adj. prof. Georgetown U. Law Ctr., 1981-83, 89-92, 94; disting. vis. from prac., 1993. Trustee The Textile Mus. Recipient Exceptional Civilian Service award NSA, 1979; Disting. Intelligence medal CIA, 1981. Mem. ABA (sects. antitrust law, pub. contract law, internat. law), Security Affairs Support Assn. (gen. counsel 1982-91), Coun. Fgn. Rels. Democrat. Jewish. Author: (with P. Fabrega) Illness and Shamanistic Curing in Zinacantan, 1975. Office: 1752 N St NW Washington DC 20036-2907

SILVER, DAVID, financial executive, lawyer; b. N.Y.C., Jan. 27, 1931; s. Sol and Fannie (Stein) S.; m. Meryl Young, Sept. 14, 1952 (dec.); children: Daniel, Matthew, Joshua; m. Ann Schwartz, June 4, 1993. B.A., CCNY, 1953; LL.B. cum laude, Harvard U., 1958. Bar: N.Y. 1958, D.C. 1979. Pvt. practice law N.Y.C., 1960-61; spl. counsel SEC, Washington, 1961-65; gen. counsel Investors Planning Corp., N.Y.C., 1965-66; asst. counsel Investment Co. Inst., Washington, 1966-69, gen. counsel, 1969-77, pres., 1977-91; cons. securities regulation Govt. of India, 1964; pres. ICI Mut. Ins. Co., 1987—; lectr. Law Sch., Boston U., 1995—. Served with U.S. Army, 1953-55. Mem. Fed. Bar Assn. (exec. council securities com., past chmn. investment co. com.). Home: 9410 Brooke Dr Bethesda MD 20817-2110 Office: ICI Mutual Insur 1401 H St NW Washington DC 20005-2110

SILVER, DAVID MAYER, former university official; b. West Pittston, Pa., July 16, 1915; s. Morris Jacob and Flora (Mayer) S.; m. Anita Rose Cohen, May 10, 1942; children: Gregory, Terence. AB magna cum laude, Butler U., 1937; AM, U. Ill., 1938, PhD, 1940; LittD (hon.), Butler U., 1990. Mem. faculty Butler U., 1940-85, prof. history, 1954-85, dean Coll. Liberal Arts and Scis., 1963-83, assoc. v.p. grad. studies and research, 1983-85; cons.-evaluator North Ctrl. Assn., 1974-85, mem. commn. higher edn., 1981-85. Author: Lincoln's Supreme Court, 1956, also articles. Pres. Indpls. Bd. Pub. Safety, 1956-63; mem. youth study com. Ohio Valley Council of Hebrew Congregations, 1963-65; Research dir. Ind. Democratic Central Com., 1944; Dem. nominee Ind. Legislature, 1944; Dem. candidate for Indpls. City Council, 1955; Bd. dirs. Indpls. Jewish Social Services, 1953-56. Recipient medal Butler U. Alumni Assn., 1987; U. Ill. scholar history, 1938, fellow, 1938-40; Butler U. faculty fellow, 1950-51. Mem. AAUP, Am. Hist. Assn., Orgn. Am. Historians, Supreme Ct. Hist. Soc., Ind. Hist. Soc., Ind. Conf. Acad. Deans (chmn. 1972), Ind. CLU, B'nai B'rith, Phi Beta Kappa, Phi Kappa Phi, Phi Eta Sigma, Sigma Alpha Mu. Jewish (bd. dirs., pres. Indpls. Hebrew congregation). Club: Broadmoor Country. Home: 8230 N Illinois St Indianapolis IN 46260-2943 *I have learned throughout my life that one succeeds the most when you respect those you deal with - just do the right thing, follow high moral and ethical standards, respect your fellow human beings, be optimistic, and success will come!.*

SILVER, DONALD, surgeon, educator; b. N.Y.C., Oct. 19, 1929; s. Herman and Cecilia (Meyer) S.; m. Helen Elizabeth Harnden, Aug. 9, 1958; children: Elizabeth Tyler, Donald Meyer, Stephanie Davies, William Paige. AB, Duke U., 1950, BS in Medicine, MD, 1955. Diplomate Am. Bd. Surgery, Am. Bd. Gen. Vascular Surgery, Am. Bd. Thoracic Surgery. Intern Duke Med. Ctr., 1955-56, asst. resident, 1958-63, resident, 1963-64; mem. faculty Duke Med. Sch., 1964-75, prof. surgery, 1972-75; cons. Watts Hosp., Durham, 1965-75, VA Hosp., Durham, 1970-75; chief surgery VA Hosp., 1968-70; prof. surgery, chmn. dept. U. Mo. VA Med. Ctr., Columbia, 1975—; cons. Harry S. Truman Hosp., Columbia, 1975—; mem. bd. sci. advisers Cancer Research Center, Columbia, 1975—; mem. surg. study sect. A NIH. Contbr. articles to med. jours., chpts. to books; editorial bds.; Jour. Vascular Surgery, Postgrad. Gen. Surgery, Vascular Surgery. Served with USAF, 1956-58. James IV Surg. traveler, 1977. Fellow ACS (gov. 1994—), Deryl Hart Soc.; mem. AMA, AAAS, Mo. Med. Assn., Boone County Med. Soc., Internat. Cardiovascular Soc., Soc. Univ. Surgeons, Am. Heart Assn. (Mo. affiliate rsch. com.), Soc. Surgery Alimenatry Tract, Assn. Acad. Surgery, So. Thoracic Surg. Assn., Internat. Soc. Surgery, Soc. Vascular Surgery, Am. Assn. Thoracic Surgery, Am. Surg. Assn., Ctrl. Surg. Assn. (pres.-elect 1990-91, pres. 1991-92), Western Surg. Assn., Midwestern Vascular Surg. Soc. (pres. 1984-85), Ctrl. Surg. Assn. Found. (treas. 1992-93, wd v.p. 1993-94, 1st v.p. 1994-95, pres. 1995-96). Home: 1050 Covered Bridge Rd Columbia MO 65203-9569 Office: U Mo Med Ctr Dept Surgery # M580 Columbia MO 65212

SILVER, GEORGE ALBERT, physician, educator; b. Phila., Dec. 23, 1913; s. Morris M. and Sara (Tutelman) S.; m. Mitzi Blieden, June 5, 1937; children—James David, Jane, Judith Ellen. B.A., U. Pa., Phila., 1934; M.D., Jefferson Med. Coll., Phila., 1938; M.P.H., Johns Hopkins U., Balt., 1948; M.A. (hon.), Yale U., New Haven, 1969. Diplomate Am. Bd. Preventive Medicine. Asst. demonstrator Jefferson Med. Coll., Phila., 1939-42; health officer Balt. City Health Dept., 1948-51; asst. prof. Johns Hopkins U., Balt., 1948-51; chief div. social medicine Montefiore Hosp., N.Y.C., 1951-65; assoc. prof. health adminstrn. Columbia U., N.Y.C., 1952-59; prof. social medicine Albert Einstein Coll. Medicine, N.Y.C., 1959-65; dep. asst. sec. health and sci. affairs HEW, Washington, 1965-68; health exec. Nat. Urban Coalition, Washington, 1968-71; prof. pub. health Yale U., New Haven, 1969-84, emeritus prof. pub. health, 1984—; chair com. on health policy Fedn. Am. Scientists. Author: Family Medical Care, 1963, Spy in the House of Medicine, 1974, Child Health: America's Future, 1978; contbg. editor Am. Jour. Pub. Health. Served to maj. M.C., U.S. Army, 1942-46. Recipient Superior Svc. award HEW, 1966; named to Soc. of Scholars, Johns Hopkins U., 1993; fellow Branford Coll., Yale U. Fellow APHA (assoc. editor jour. 1993—), Nat. Acad. Social Ins., N.Y. Acad. Medicine, Inst. Medicine; mem. NAS (sr.), Elizabethan Club, Sigma Xi. Democrat. Jewish. Home: 590 Ellsworth Ave New Haven CT 06511-1636 Office: Yale U 89 Trumbull St New Haven CT 06511-3723

SILVER, HARRY R., lawyer; b. Phila., Aug. 8, 1946; s. Jerome Benjamin Silver and Josephine Sandler (Steinberg) Furr; m. Jessica Dunsay, Nov. 23, 1972; children: Gregory, Alexander. BA, Temple U., 1968; JD, Columbia U., 1971. Bar: N.Y. 1972, D.C. 1973, U.S. Dist. Ct. D.C., U.S. Ct. Claims, U.S. Ct. Appeals (1st, 4th, 5th, 7th, 8th, 9th, 10th, fed. and D.C. cirs.), U.S. Supreme Ct. Law clk. to presiding justice U.S. Ct. Appeals (2d cir.), N.Y.C., 1971-72; assoc. Arent, Fox, Kintner, Plotkin & Kahn, Washington, 1972-74; atty. U.S. Dept. Justice, Washington, 1974-77, U.S. Dept. Energy, Washington, 1977-78; assoc. Akin, Gump, Strauss, Hauer & Feld, Washington, 1978-81, ptnr., 1981-88; ptnr. Oppenheimer, Wolff & Donelly, Washington, 1988-91, Davis Wright Tremaine, Washington, 1991-94, Ober, Kaler, Grimes & Shriver, Washington, 1994—. Mem. ABA, Fed. Bar Assn. Avocations: running, music, travel. Home: 6829 Wilson Ln Bethesda MD 20817-4948 Office: Ober Kaler Grimes & Shriver 1401 H St NW Ste 500 Washington DC 20005-2110

SILVER, HERBERT, physician; b. Bklyn., Feb. 18, 1932; s. Ben and Sylvia (Weinstock) S.; m. Judith Elaine Miller, Aug. 28, 1966; children: Rand Kenneth, David Jeffrey. BA, Adelphi U., 1953; MD, SUNY, Buffalo, 1957. Diplomate Am. Bd. Pathology. Intern Maimonides Med. Ctr., 1957-58; resident Nassau County Med. Ctr., 1958-60, Hosp. of U. of Pa., 1960-62; assoc. pathologist, dir. blood bank/hematology Jewish Hosp., St. Louis, 1964-70; dir. transfusion medicine Hartford (Conn.) Hosp., 1970—; assoc. prof. U. Conn. Med. Ctr., Farmington, 1970-90, U. Conn. Sch. of Allied Health, Storrs, 1977—; cons. Mt. Sinai Hosp., Hartford, Conn., 1978-92, Conn. Children's Med. Ctr., 1980—; med. dir. Hartford Med. Lab, 1985—. Author, editor: Probability of Inclusion in Paternity Testing, 1982, Problem Solving in Immunohematology, 1987; guest editor Transfusion Jour., 1992—; contbr. articles to profl. jours. Bd. dirs. Emanuel Synagogue, West Hartford, Conn. Capt. U.S. Army Med. Corps, 1962-64. Recipient Disting. Svc. award Am. Assn. Blood Banks, 1993. Mem. Am. Assn. Blood Banks (bd. dirs. 1987-92), Am. Soc. Clin. Pathology. Democrat. Jewish. Avocations: bicycling, clarinet. Home: 32 Beacon Hill Dr West Hartford CT 06117-1003 Office: Hartford Hospital 80 Seymour St Hartford CT 06102-5037

SILVER, JOEL, producer. Film producer: The Warriors, 1979, Xanadu, 1980, 48 Hours, 1982, Jekyll & Hyde...Together Again, 1982, Streets of Fire, 1984, Brewster's Millions, 1985, Weird Science, 1985, Commando, 1985, Jumpin' Jack Flash, 1986, Lethal Weapon, 1986, Predator, 1987, Action Jackson, 1988, Die Hard, 1988, Lethal Weapon 2, 1989, Roadhouse, 1989, Ford Fairlane, 1990, Die Hard 2, 1990, Predator 2, 1990, Hudson Hawk, 1991, Ricochet, 1991, The Last Boy Scout, 1991, Lethal Weapon 3, 1992, Demolition Man, 1993, Richie Rich, 1994, Demon Knight, 1994, Assassins, 1995, Fair Game, 1995, Executive Decision, 1996, Bordello of Blood, 1996. Office: Silver Pictures 4000 Warner Blvd Burbank CA 91522-0001

SILVER, JONATHAN MOSES, investment management executive; b. Cleve., Sept. 3, 1957; s. Daniel Jeremy and Adele Francis (Zeidman) S.; m. Melissa Moss, 1995. BA with honors, Harvard U., 1979; C.E.P., Inst. Polit. Studies, Paris, 1980; postgrad. Grad. Inst. Internat. Studies, U. Geneva, 1981-82. Asst. to exec. v.p. Manpower Demonstration Rsch. Corp., N.Y.C., 1980-81; asst. polit. dir. John Glenn Presdl. Campaign, Washington, 1983-84; assoc. Mckinsey and Co., N.Y.C., 1984-88; COO Tucker Comm., Inc., Cross River, N.Y., 1988-90; exec. v.p. John Blair Comm. Inc., N.Y.C., 1990-91; COO, mng. dir. Tiger Mgmt. Inc., N.Y.C., 1991-92; asst. dep. sec. U.S. Dept. Commerce, Washington, 1992-94, counselor to the sec. of the interior, 1994-95; gen. ptnr. Commonwealth Holdings, Inc., Washington, 1995—, Millennium Capital, 1996—; ptnr. HS Ptnrs., N.Y.C., 1993—; trustee Jonathan M. Silver Charitable Trust, N.Y.C., 1993—; vis. com. grad. faculty The New Sch. Bd.; chmn. bd. dirs. Am. Forests, Pub. Allies, Nat. Found. for Jewish Culture, Friends of Harvard Judaica (pres.). Harvard Coll. fellow, Cambridge, Mass., 1975-78, John Harvard fellow, 1979, Rotary grad. fellow, Paris, 1979, Fulbright grad. fellow, Swiss Univ. Exchange Grant, 1982. Jewish. Home: 3027 N St NW Washington DC 20007 Office: Commonwealth Holdings Inc 805 15th St NW Ste 500 Washington DC 20005-2207

SILVER, LAWRENCE ALAN, marketing executive; b. New Haven, Sept. 5, 1943; s. Herman B. and Marcia (Azersky) S.; m. Deena Rae Rosenberg, Feb. 26, 1967; children: Cheryl Ann, Elyse Stephanie, Marc Aaron. BJ, Boston U., 1965, MS, 1966. Reporter New Haven Register, 1958-66; dir. pub. rels. Spear & Staff, Inc., Babson Park, Mass., 1966-70; pres. Silver Assocs. Pub. Rels. & Advt., Holliston, Mass., 1971-82; pres. RJ Communication, Inc., St. Petersburg, Fla., 1982—; sr. v.p., dir. mktg. Raymond James & Assocs., Inc., St. Petersburg, 1982—; v.p. investor rels. Raymond James Fin., Inc., St. Petersburg, 1983—; chmn. Raymond James Fin. Mktg. Com., St. Petersburg, 1984—; coord. quality svcs. Raymond James Fin., St. Petersburg. 1989—; instr. journalism Framingham (Mass.) State Coll., 1974-80. Mem. Holliston Bylaw Study Com., 1978-82, U Tampa Ctr. Quality Steering Com., 1993-95, 96—; founding pres. Temple Beth Torah, Holliston, 1972-73; bd. dirs. Temple Ahavat Shalom Men's Club, Palm Harbor, 1983-84; trustee Temple Ahavat Shalom, 1985-86, Am. Stage Theatre, St. Petersburg, 1994-96; pres. Temple Ahavat Shalom Brotherhood, 1985-86; founding bd. dirs. Jewish Cmty. Ctr. Greater Framingham, 1969-72; mem. Fla. Edn. and Industry Coalition, 1988-95, St Petersburg Jr. Coll. Cmty. Outreach program, 1988-89; mem. Fla. Sch. Adv. Coun., 1990-93; mem. adv. coun. Clearwater Jr. League, 1993-94, sch. adv. coun. Tarpon Springs H.S., 1988-93. With U.S. Army, 1967-69. Mem. Securities Industry Assn. (Pub. Rels. Advt. Roundtable 1986-90, Mktg. Roundtable 1988—, sales and mktg. com. 1991—, editor Marketshare 1994-96), Boston U. Nat. Alumni Coun. Assoc. editor Venture Capital Jour., 1978-82. Home: 90 Greenhaven Cir Oldsmar FL 34677-4842 Office: Raymond James & Assocs 880 Carillon Pkwy Saint Petersburg FL 33716-1102

SILVER, LEONARD J., insurance and risk management company executive; b. Philadelphia, Sept. 19, 1927; s. Jacob and Mollie (Milgram) S.; m. Eva Penny Parris, Nov. 20, 1949; children: Jill Denise Silverstein, Brian B. CPCU, cert. risk mgmt. assoc. Pres. Ins. Offices of Leonard J. Silver, Inc., Phila., 1948-58, Am. Excess Co., Phila., 1953-58; pres. 1st Risk Mgmt. Co., Jenkintown, Pa., 1958—, San Juan, P.R., 1963-94; Pres. legal div. First Risk Mgmt., 1991—. With U.S. Army, 1947-48, Korea. Mem. Soc. Risk Mgmt. Cons. (bd. dirs. 1990-91), Ins. Cons. Soc. (founding mem., sec. 1969-70, v.p. 1970-71, pres. 1971-72, bd. dirs.), Ins. Inst. P.R., Am. Inst. Property and Liability Underwriters. Avocations: photography, sailing. Home: 213 Glenwood Rd Elkins Park PA 19027-3522 Office: 1st Risk Mgmt 636 Old York Rd Ste 220 Jenkintown PA 19046-2858

SILVER, MALCOLM DAVID, pathologist, educator; b. Adelaide, South Australia, Apr. 29, 1933; s. Eric Bertram and Stella Louisa (Riley) S.; m. Meredith May Galloway, Jan. 19, 1957; children: Stuart Faulkner, Claire Eleanor, Caryl Louise. M.D., U. Adelaide; Ph.D., McGill U. Diplomate: Am. Bd. Pathology. Resident med. officer Royal Adelaide Hosp., 1957-58; resident in pathology Royal Victoria Hosp.-Pathol. Inst., McGill U., Montreal, Que., Can., 1958-63; research fellow dept. exptl. pathology John Curtin Sch. Med. Research, Australian Nat. U., Canberra, 1963-65; asst. prof. pathology U. Toronto, 1965-68, assoc. prof., 1968-74, prof., 1974—, chmn. dept. pathology, 1985-95; staff pathologist Toronto Gen. Hosp., 1965-72, sr. staff pathologist, 1972-79; prof., chmn. dept. pathology U. Western Ont., London, Ont., Can., 1979-85; chief pathology Univ. Hosp., London, 1979-85; pathologist in chief Toronto Gen. Hosp., 1985-89; pathologist in chief The Toronto Hosp. (Toronto Gen. and Toronto Western Divs.), 1989-91, sr. staff pathologist, 1991—. Edtl. bd. Jour. Cardiovascular Pathology, Jour. Long-Term Effects of Med. Implants; contbr. articles to profl. jours. Fellow Royal Coll. Pathololgists of Australia, Royal Coll. Physicians and Surgeons Can.; mem. Can. Assn. Pathologists (chmn. membership com. 1975-77), Ont. Assn. Pathologists, Internat. Acad. Pathology, Can. Cardiovascular Soc., Am. Heart Assn., AAAS. Office: U Toronto Dept Pathology, 100 College St, Toronto, ON Canada M5G 1L5

SILVER, MARY WILCOX, oceanography educator; b. San Francisco, July 13, 1941; d. Philip E. and Mary C. (Kartes) Wilcox; children: Monica, Joel. BA in Zoology, U. Calif., Berkeley, 1963; PhD in Oceanography, U. Calif., La Jolla, 1971. Asst. prof. biology San Francisco State U., 1971-72; prof. marine sci. U. Calif., Santa Cruz, 1972—, chmn. dept., 1992-95. Contbr. numerous articles on biol. oceanography to profl. jours. Grantee NSF, 1979—; recipient Bigelow medal, 1992. Mem. AAAS, Am. Soc. Limnology and Oceanography, Am. Phycological Soc. Office: U Calif Dept Ocean Sci Santa Cruz CA 95064

SILVER, MICHAEL, school superintendent; b. Landsberg, Germany, Jan. 30, 1948; came to U.S., 1949; s. Norman and Esther Silver; m. Beverley Ann Moss, May 16, 1971; children: Sabina, Joseph. AB, Washington U., 1970, MEd, 1973, PhD, 1982. Cert. supt. Mo., Wash. Tchr. Normandy Sch. Dist., St. Louis, 1970-72; tchr. Parkway Sch. Dist., St. Louis, 1972-75, asst. prin., 1976-79, adminstrv. asst., 1979-83, asst. to supt., 1983-84, asst. supt., 1984-86; supt. South Ctrl. Sch. Dist., Seattle, 1986—; bd. dirs. Cities in Schs., Seattle; mem. adv. bd. Sta. KCTS, Seattle, 1990—; vis. exec. Seattle U. Sch. Edn., 1995. Author: Values Education, 1976, Facing Issues of Life and Death, 1976. Pres. SeaTac Task Force, Seattle, 1989; bd. dirs. Anti-Defamation League, Seattle, 1987—; mem. City of Tukwila (Wash.) 2000 Com., 1988-90. Recipient A Plus award Wash. Coun. Econ. Edn., 1992; named Exec. Educator, 100 Exec. Educator Mag., 1985, 1996 Associate for Inst. for Ednl. Inquiry Leadership Program; I/D/E/A fellow Charles F. Kettering Found., 1978, 88, Title VI fellow Washington U., 1971-73. Mem. ASCD, Am. Assn. Sch. Adminstrs., Wash. Assn. Sch. Adminstrs. (met. chpt., pres. 1989-90), King County Supts. (chmn. adv. com. 1989-90, 95-96), Southcenter Rotary Club (Paul Harris fellow 1994), Southwest King County C. of C., Phi Delta Kappa. Home: 14127 SE 50th St Bellevue WA 98006-3409 Office: South Central SD 406 4640 S 144th St Seattle WA 98168-4134

SILVER, MICHAEL JOEL, lawyer; b. Balt., Feb. 8, 1955; s. Edgar P. and Ann W. (Wolf) S.; m. Abbe Rebecca Levitt, May 14, 1983; children: Rachel, Lucy. AB, Harvard U., 1977; JD, U. Chgo., 1980. Bar: Md. 1980. Assoc. Piper & Marbury, Balt., 1980-87; ptnr. Piper & Marbury, Balt. & N.Y.C., 1987-92; now ptnr. Hogan & Hartson LLP, Balt. Office: Hogan & Hartson LLP 111 S Calvert St Fl 16 Baltimore MD 21202-6174

SILVER, MORRIS, economist, educator; b. N.Y.C., July 9, 1931; s. Julius and Lilly S.; m. Sondra P. Hartman, Jan. 26, 1958; children: Gerald David, Ronald Alan. B.A., CCNY, 1958; Ph.D. (Earhart Found. fellow, Ford Found. fellow), Columbia U., 1964. Mem. faculty City Coll. CUNY, 1964—, assoc. prof. econs., 1968—, prof., 1972—, chmn. dept., 1969-95; research asso. Nat. Bur. Econ. Research, 1967-71; cons crime deterrence and offender career Hudson Inst., 1974, Nat. Center for Health Services Research, 1970—. Author: (with R.D. Auster) The State as a Firm, 1979, Affluence, Altruism, and Atrophy: The Decline of Welfare States, 1980, Prophets and Markets: The Political Economy of Ancient Israel, 1983, Enterprise and the Scope of the Firm, 1984, Economic Structures of the Ancient Near East, 1985, Foundations of Economic Justice, 1989, Taking Ancient Mythology Economically, 1992, Economic Structures of Antiquity, 1995. Served with AUS, 1953-55. Mem. Am. Econ. Assn. Jewish. Office: Dept Econs City Coll 133 D St New York NY 10031

SILVER, NEIL MARVIN, manufacturing executive; b. Bklyn., June 2, 1928; s. Jack and Rose (Eisenberg) S.; m. Leah Rebecca Coffman Silver, Sept. 4, 1949; children: Pamela Sue, Carole Beth. Student, U. Mich., 1945-46, 48-49; BS, Ind. U., 1951. Asst. mgr. Wolverine Parking Co., Lansing, Mich., 1951-54; treas. Capitol Parking Co., Indpls., 1955-60; controller, asst. to pres. Eberhart Steel Products, Inc., Mishawaka Tool & Die, Inc., Ind., 1961-63; PRES. Allied Quality Products, Inc., Mishawaka, Ind., 1964-67; treas. Allied Screw Products, Inc., Mishawaka, Ind., 1968-88, chmn., sec., 1989—. Bd. dirs. Ind. State Anti-Defamation League, 1955-57; bd. dirs., treas., pres., chmn. Fin. Commn., Family and Children's Ctr., Inc., Mishawaka, Ind., 1957-77; bd. dirs., treas. Family Svc. Assn. St. Joseph County, Ind., 1955-57. With U.S. Army, 1946-48. Mem. AIAA, Soc. Mfg. Engrs., SAE Internat., Internat. Computing Soc., ASM Internat., B'nai B'rith. Avocations: photography, travel. Office: Allied Screw Products Inc PO Box 543 815 E Lowell Ave Mishawaka IN 46546-0543

SILVER, PAUL ROBERT, marketing executive, consultant; b. Balt., Mar. 15, 1931; s. Harry and Frieda (Rosengarten) S.; m. Natalie Nessa Nechamkin, May 17, 1957; children: Geri Ellen, Steven Marc, Lawrence Alan. BA, U. Md., 1949; BS, U. Balt., 1958; postgrad., Eckerd Coll., 1984. Pres., CEO Sterling Prodns. Inc., Balt., 1950-51; advt. mgr. Hecht Co., Washington, 1951-53; pres., CEO Artists & Models, Inc., Washington and Balt., 1974-76, The Charles Agy. Inc., Washington and Balt., 1955-80, The Golden Triangle Agy., Clearwater, Fla., 1980-82; COO Bridgman Assocs. Inc., Annapolis, Md., 1985-86; dir. promotions Internat. Beverage Expn., Washington, 1986; pres., CEO Prasco Inc., Tampa, Fla., 1982—; cons. Lewis and Ptnrs., Inc., San Francisco, Corp. Vision, Inc., L.A., Computer Response, Inc., Balt., Themes and Schemes, Inc., Dunedin, Fla., San Diego, 1984—, J&B Mgmt. Co., 1991, Alberee Products, Inc., 1992; v.p. Coupon Am., Bel Air, Md., 1987-88; dir. mktg. Miles Homes, Inc., Cheshire, Conn., 1993; CEO Universal Industries, Inc., 1994—; ptnr. Drakeford & Drakeford, PA, 1995-96; v.p. Chapman Security Inc., 1995—. Active in Radio Free Asia, 1972, Pinellas County Heart Savers, Clearwater, 1981; campaign mgr. for candidates for Balt. City Coun., U.S. Senate and U.S. Congress, 1968, 88, Fla. Commr. Agr., 1990. With U.S. Army, 1953-55, 72. Democrat. Jewish. Avocations: writing, art. Office: Prasco Inc PO Box 24461 Tampa FL 33623-4461

SILVER, R. PHILIP, metal products executive; b. 1942. Grad., U. Mo., 1967. With Amour & Co., Atlanta, 1967-68, Boise Cascade Corp., Idaho, 1968-75; exec. v.p. Fla. Gas Co., Orlando, Fla., 1975-80; pres. Continental Can, Norwalk, Conn., 1980-87; pres., treas. Silgan Corp., Stamford, Conn., 1987-93; chmn bd. dirs., co-chief exec. officer Silgan Corp, Stamford, Conn., 1993—. Office: Silgan Corp 4 Landmark Sq Stamford CT 06901-2502*

SILVER, RALPH DAVID, distilling company director; b. Chgo., Apr. 19, 1924; s. Morris J. and Amelia (Abrams) S.; m. Lois Reich, Feb. 4, 1951; children: Jay, Cappy. B.S., U. Chgo., 1943; postgrad., Northwestern U., 1946-48; J.D., DePaul U., 1952. Bar: Ill. bar 1952. Staff accountant David Himmelblau & Co. (C.P.A.'s), 1946-48; internal revenue agt. U.S. Dept. Treasury, 1948-51; practice in Chgo., 1952-55; atty. Lawrence J. West, 1952-55; fin. cons., bd. dirs. Barton Inc., Chgo., 1955-92; bd. dirs. Stone Fin. Corp., Stone Fin. II Corp., 1992-95; arbitrator N.Y. State Exch., Cir. Ct. of Cook County, Ill., Nat. Assn. Securities Dealers. Bd. dirs., pres. Ralph and Lois Silver Found. Lt. (j.g.) USNR, 1943-46. Mem. ABA, Chgo. Bar Assn., AICPA. Club: Green Acres Country. Home: 1124 Old Elm Ln Glencoe IL 60022-1235

SILVER, RICHARD TOBIAS, physician, educator; b. Jan. 18, 1929; m. Barbara Silver; 1 son, Adam Bennett. Diploma, A.B., Cornell U., 1950, M.D., 1953. Diplomate: Nat. Bd. Med. Examiners, Am. Bd. Internal Medicine, Am. Bd. Clin. Oncology. Intern N.Y. Hosp.-Cornell Med. Ctr., N.Y.C., 1953-54, asst. resident in medicine, 1956-57, resident in hematology, 1957-58; clin. assoc. gen. medicine br. Nat. Cancer Inst., NIH, Bethesda, Md., 1954-56; asst. in medicine Cornell U. Med. Coll., N.Y.C., 1956-58, instr. medicine, 1958-62, clin. asst. prof., 1962-67, clin. assoc. prof., 1967-73, clin. prof., 1973—; pres. N.Y. State Soc. Med. Oncologists and Hematologists, 1991—; asst. attending physician N.Y. Hosp., 1964-67, assoc. attending physician, 1967-73, attending physician, 1973—; asst. vis. physician 2d Cornell Med. div. Bellevue Hosp., N.Y.C., 1963-66; vis. Fulbright prof. U. Bahia Sch. Medicine, Brazil, 1958-59; vis. prof. Hershey Hosp.-Pa. State Hosp., 1976, Mayo Clinic, 1977, Upstate Med. Ctr., Binghamton, N.Y., 1977, Med. Coll. Va., 1979, Med. Sch. Colubia U., 1982, N.J. Coll. Medicine, New Brunswick, 1983, Meml. Med. Ctr. U. Ga., 1984, 86; invited lectr. Med. Coll. Shanghai and Chengchow, 1979, VIII Brazilian Hematology Congress, Salvador, 1981, 14th Internat. Congress Chemotherapy, Kyoto, Japan, 1985, XI Brazilian Congress of Cancerology, Florianopolis, Santa Catarina, 1987, 2d Internat. Conf. CML, Bologna, Italy, 1992, Internat. Symposium Myelo Proliferative Disorders, Mayo Clinic, Tochester Minn., 1994, 9th Internat. Symposium Molecular Biology Hematopolesis: Interferon in Myelo Proliferative Diseases, Genoa, Italy, 1995; vis. faculty curriculum Devel., Annenberg Ctr. Rancho Mirage, Calif., 1994—; mem. rev. bd. NIH,

Nat. Cancer Inst.; cons. Cancer Chemotherapy Investigative Rev. Bd., 1980, clin. trials com., 1979-81; mem. Cornell U. COuncil, 1987—. Author: Morphology of the Blood and Marrow in Clinical Practice, 1970; co-author: (with R.D. Lauper, C.I. Jarowski) A Synopsis of Cancer Chemotherapy, 1977, ed edit., 1987; editor, contbr.: Topics in Cancer, 1982; contbr. chpts. to books and articles to profl. jours., to nat. and internat. profl. confs., seminars and workshops in medicine. Fellow ACP; mem. N.Y. State Soc. Med. Hematologists and Oncologists (pres. 1991—), Cornell U. Med. Coll. Alumni Assn. (pres. 1973-76, sr. advisor 1976—), Am. Soc. Clin. Oncology, Internat. Soc. Hematology, Am. Soc. Hematology (chmn., guidelines com.), Chronic Myeloid leukemia, Sass Found Hematologic Rsch. (bd. advs.), N.Y. Soc. Study of Blood, N.Y. County Med. Soc., N.Y. State Med. Soc. Oncologists and Hematologists (pres. 1991-93), Harvey Soc., Am. Fedn. Clin. Rsch., Am. Assn. Cancer Rsch., Explorers Club (bd. dirs., chmn. sci. adv. com. 1987), Sigma Xi. Office: NY Hosp Cornell Med Ctr 525 E 68th St New York NY 10021-4873 also: 1440 York Ave New York NY 10021-2577

SILVER, SAMUEL MANUEL, rabbi, author; b. Wilmington, Del., June 7, 1912; s. Adolph David and Adela (Hacker) S.; m. Elaine Shapiro, Feb. 9, 1953; children: Lee, Joshua, Barry, Noah, Daniel. B.A., U. Del., 1933; M.H.L., Hebrew Union Coll., 1940, D.D., 1965. Ordained rabbi, 1940; dir. Hillel Found., U. Md., 1940-42; asst. rabbi in Cleve., 1946-52; rabbi Temple Sinai, Stamford, Conn., 1959-77, Jewish Community Center of Lee County, Cape Coral, Fla., 1977-79, Temple Sinai of South Palm Beach County, Fla., 1979-95; rabbi emeritus Temple Sinai, Delray Beach, Fla., 1995—; Sec. Temple of Understanding, Greenwich, Conn., 1969; v.p. Stamford-Darien Council of Chs. and Synagogues; exec. bd. Fellowship in Prayer, 1970—; pres. Rabbinical Assn. South Palm Beach County, 1980-82. Author: (with Rabbi M.M. Applebaum) Sermonettes for Young People, 1964, How To Enjoy This Moment, 1967, Explaining Judaism to Jews and Christians, 1971, When You Speak English You Often Speak Hebrew, 1973, Mixed Marriage Between Jew and Christian, 1977, Speak to the Children of Israel, 1977, What Happiness Is, 1995; editor: Am. Judaism, 1952-59, The Quotable Am. Rabbis, 1967; columnist Nat. Jewish Post, 1955—. Served as chaplain AUS, 1942-46. Mem. Central Conf. Am. Rabbis (nat. exec. bd. 1954-56), Jewish War Vets (chaplain 1966-70), Assn. Jewish Chaplains U.S. (pres. 1959-62), Stamford-Darien Ministers League (pres. 1961-62), Zionist Orgn. Am. (pres. Southeast region 1984—), Alpha Epsilon Pi. Home and Office: 2309 NW 66 Dr Boca Raton FL 33496-3602 *The greatest of all miracles is that we need not be tomorrow what we are today but that we can improve if we make use of the potential implanted within us by God.*

SILVER, SHEILA JANE, composer, music educator; b. Seattle, Oct. 3, 1946; d. Robert Eugene and Fannie (Horowitz) S.; m. John Feldman, Dec. 11, 1988. BA, U. Calif., Berkeley, 1968; postgrad., Hochschule fur Musik, Stuttgart, Fed. Republic Germany, 1969-71; MFA, Brandeis U., 1972, PhD, 1974. Assoc. prof. music SUNY, Stony Brook, 1979—; Barlow Found. Commn., 1996. Composer classical works for orch., string orch., opera, chamber orch., string quartet, various instruments, also vocal and choral compositions and feature film scores; Bellagio Residency/Rockefeller Found., 1995. Radcliffe Inst. fellow, 1977-78, Koussevitzky fellow, 1972, Nat. Endowment for the Arts Composer fellow, 1995; recipient Composer award Am. Inst. and Acad. Arts and Letters, 1986, Prix de Rome, Am. Acad. in Rome, 1978-79, CARY Trust Recording award, 1995; winner Nat. Composers' Competition, Internat. Soc. Contemporary Music, 1981-82, competition Indpls. Symphony Orch., 1977, IV Internat. Wettbewerb fur Komponistinnen, 1976. Mem. Am. Acad. in Rome, Am. Music Ctr., N.Y. Women Composers, Rockefeller Found. Jewish. Home and Office: 68-37 Dartmouth St Forest Hills NY 11375-5046

SILVER, SHELDON, state legislator, lawyer; b. N.Y.C., Feb. 13, 1944; s. Nathan and Frieda (Bearman) S.; m. Rosa Mandelkern, June 25, 1967; children: Edward, Janine, Michelle, Esther. BA, Yeshiva U., 1965; JD, Bklyn. Coll., 1968. Bar: N.Y. 1969, U.S. Dist. Ct. (so. and ea. dists.) N.Y. 1970. Assoc. Schechter & Schwartz, N.Y.C., 1968-71; law sec. to Judge Francis Pecora N.Y.C., 1971-76; ptnr. Agri, Bilder & Silver, N.Y.C., 1976-81; pvt. practice N.Y.C., 1981—; mem. N.Y. State Assembly, 1977—, chmn. ways and means com., 1992, speaker, 1994. Vice pres. Bialystoker Synagogue, Young Israel Synagogue. Named Man of Yr., Harry S. Truman Dem. Club, 1977, United Jewish Appeals, 1983, also others. Democrat. Office: 270 Broadway Ste 1800 New York NY 10007-2306

SILVER, SHELLY ANDREA, media artist; b. N.Y.C., July 16, 1957; d. Reuben and Anita (Kuriloff) S. BA, BFA, Cornell U., 1980. program fellow Japan/U.S. Friendship Commn. Artist Exch., 1994, Deutscher Akademischer Austauschdienst Berliner Kunstlerprogramm, 1992; vis. prof. Deutsche Film und Fernsehakadamie, 1992; vis. artist Art Inst. Chgo., 1991; adjunct prof. Tisch Sch. of the Arts, N.Y.C., 1996; freelance editor Sesame St., Frontline, Saturday Night Live, HBO, MTV, Showtime, others. Represented in exhbns. including The New Mus., N.Y.C., 1987, The Mus. of Modern Art, 1991, 95, 96, 97, The N.Y. Film Festival (video sect.), 1994, 96, The Mus. of Kyoto, Japan, 1994, The London Film Festival, 1991, Internat. Ctr. Photography, N.Y.C.,. Japan Found. Film & Video grantee, 1995, N.Y. State Coun. Arts Project grantee, 1987, 89, 95, Checkerboard Found. grantee, 1990, Media Bur. Finishing Funds grantee; fellow U.S./Japan Artists Exch., 1993, Nat. Endowment Arts, 1989, 91, N.Y. Found. Arts, 1986, 91. Home and Office: 22 Catherine St Apt 6 New York NY 10038

SILVER, STEPHEN HAL, stockbroker, financial planner; b. Indpls., Oct. 7, 1949; s. C. Hal and Betty (Jean) S.; m. Mary Starr Wilson, Oct. 22, 1977; children: Marisa, Scott, Stephanie. BA, Hanover (Ind.) Coll., 1972. Cert. fin. planner. Buyer men's sportswear Meier & Frank, Portland, Oreg., 1974-80, mdse. mgr., 1980-81; v.p. investments Dean Witter, Portland, 1981—. Deacon, St. Andrews Presbyn. Ch., Portland, 1984; leader Cub Scouts troop Boy Scouts Am., Tigard, Oreg., 1992; coach Tigard Little League, 1989. Recipient Pres.'s Merit award, 1983. Mem. Director's Club. Republican. Avocations: golf, skiing, collecting antique swords. Home: 9595 SW Ventura Ct Tigard OR 97223-9167 Office: Dean Witter 10260 SW Greenburg Rd Portland OR 97223-5500

SILVERBERG, DAVID S., financial consultant; b. Oelwein, Iowa, Mar. 3, 1936; s. Harold and Rose (Fishman) S.; m. Mary Ellen Silverberg, July 20, 1988; children: Laura, Sara, Stanley. Student, U. Minn., 1954-57; LUTC, Life Underwriter Coll., Sioux City, Iowa, 1976; CFP, Coll. Fin. Planning, Denver, 1979. Fin. cons. Smith Barney, Sioux City, 1978—; instr. Western Iowa Tech. Coll., Sioux City, 1980-87, Inst. of Banking, Sioux City, 1990. Pres. Sioux City Jewish Fedn., 1991-94; pres. Sioux City Jewish Cemetery Assn., 1990—; bd. dirs. Job Tng. Partnership Act, Sioux City, 1990—; bd. dirs. Sioux City Sumphony, 1991-94; bd. dirs. KWIT Pub. Radio Sta., 1997—. With U.S. Army, 1958-63. Recipient Young Leadership award Sioux City Jewish Fedn., 1984. mem. Internat. Assn. Fin. Planners, Landmark Lodge AF&AM, Scottish Rite (32nd degree), Shriners, Sioux City Country Club. Avocations: golf, fish. Home: 26 W 45th St Sioux City IA 51104-1002 Office: Smith Barney 600 4th St Sioux City IA 51101-1744

SILVERBERG, LEWIS HENRY, management consultant; b. L.A., Nov. 1, 1934; s. Milton Henry and Marjorie Vella (Coates) S.; m. Amelia Francis Backstrom, June 9, 1959 (div. 1979); children: Stephen, Richard, Donna; m. Alice Ellen Deakins, Mar. 9, 1979. BA, Pomona Coll., 1955; JD, UCLA, 1958. Bar: Calif. 1959, U.S. Supreme Ct. 1966. Pvt. practice San Diego, 1959-89; exec. v.p., dir. Liquor Barn, Inc., San Diego, 1989-93; bus. cons. San Diego, 1993—; referee Calif. inheritance tax and probate, 1972-88. Trustee San Diego Zool. Soc.; active various pub., charitable and ednl. orgns. Republican. Office: First Virtual Holding 11975 El Camino Real Ste 300 San Diego CA 92130-2543

SILVERBERG, MICHAEL JOEL, lawyer; b. Rochester, N.Y., Aug. 12, 1932; s. Goodman and Minnie (Krovetz) S.; m. Charlotte Goldman, June 19, 1955; children: Mark, Daniel. BA, U. Rochester, 1954; JD, Columbia U., 1957. Bar: N.Y. 1958, U.S. Dist. Ct. (so. dist.) N.Y. 1965, U.S. Dist. Ct. (ea. dist.) N.Y. 1990, U.S. Ct. Appeals (2d cir.) 1975, U.S. Supreme Ct. 1967. Instr. Columbia U. Law Sch., N.Y.C., 1957-58; assoc. Phillips, Nizer, Benjamin, Krim & Ballon, N.Y.C., 1960-67, ptnr., 1967—; pres. AMI/FAMI, N.Y., 1997—. Mem. exec. bd. N.Y. chpt. Am. Jewish Com. Fulbright scholar U. Strasbourg, France, 1958-59. Mem. ABA, N.Y. State Bar Assn. (com. on internat. litigation), Assn. Bar City N.Y. Home: 205 W End Ave New York NY 10023-4804 Office: Phillips Nizer Benjamin Krim & Ballon LLP 666 5th Ave New York NY 10103-0001

SILVERBERG, ROBERT, author; b. N.Y.C., 1935; s. Michael and Helen (Baim) S.; m. Barbara Brown, 1956; m. Karen Haber, 1987. B.A., Columbia U., 1956. Author: novels Thorns, 1967, The Masks of Time, 1968, Hawksbill Station, 1968, Nightwings, 1969, To Live Again, 1969, Tower of Glass, 1970, The World Inside, 1971, Son of Man, 1971, A Time of Changes, 1971, Dying Inside, 1972, The Book of Skulls, 1972, Born with the Dead, 1974, Shadrach in the Furnace, 1976, Lord Valentine's Castle, 1980, Majipoor Chronicles, 1982, Lord of Darkness, 1983, Valentine Pontifex, 1983, Gilgamesh the King, 1984, Tom O'Bedlam, 1985, Star of Gypsies, 1986, At Winter's End, 1988, To the Land of the Living, 1989, The New Springtime, 1990, (with Isaac Asimov) Nightfall, 1990, The Face of the Waters, 1991, (with Isaac Asimov) The Ugly Little Boy, 1992, Kingdoms of the Wall, 1993, (with Isaac Asimov) The Positronic Man, 1993, Hot Sky at Midnight, 1994, Mountains of Majipoor, 1995, Starborne, 1996, Sorcerers of Majipoor, 1997; non-fiction The Face of the Lost Cities and Vanished Civilizations, 1962, The Great Wall of China, 1965, The Old Ones: Indians of the American Southwest, 1965, Scientists and Scoundrels: A Book of Hoaxes, 1965, The Auk, the Dodo and the Oryx, 1966, The Morning of Mankind: Prehistoric Man in Europe, 1967, Mound Builders of Ancient America: The Archaeology of a Myth, 1968, If I Forget Thee, O Jerusalem: American Jews and the State of Israel, 1970, The Pueblo Revolt, 1970, The Realm of Prester John, 1971. Recipient Hugo award World Sci. Fiction Conv., 1956, 69, 87, 90; Nebula award Sci. Fiction Writers Am., 1970, 72, 75, 86. Mem. Sci. Fiction Writers Am. (pres. 1967-68). Address: PO Box 13160 Oakland CA 94661-0160

SILVERBERG, STEVEN MARK, lawyer; b. Bklyn., June 7, 1947; m. Arlene Leopold, July 4, 1971; 2 children. BA, Bklyn. Coll., 1969; JD, NYU, 1972. Bar: N.Y. 1973, U.S. Dist. Ct. (so. and ea. dists.) N.Y. 1974, U.S. Supreme Ct. 1976, U.S. Ct. Appeals (2nd cir.) 1978. Asst. dist. atty. Kings County Dist. Atty., Bklyn., 1972-75; dep. town. atty. Town of Greenburgh, N.Y., 1975-79; ptnr. Stowell, Kelly & Silverberg, White Plains, N.Y., 1979-83, Hoffman, Silverberg & Wachtell, Elmsford, N.Y., 1983-86, Hoffman, Silverberg, Wachtell & Koster, White Plains, N.Y., 1986-89; pvt. practice White Plains, 1989-92; ptnr. Kirkpatrick & Silverberg, White Plains, 1993—; adj. assoc. prof. N.Y. Law Sch., 1990-93. Co-author: Wetlands and Coastal Zone Regulations and Compliance, 1993; contbr. to profl. publs. Counsel Greenburgh Housing Authority, 1979-84, Town of Mamaroneck, N.Y., 1984-96; bd. dirs. Temple Beth Torah, Upper Nyack, N.Y., 1977-89, pres. 1984-86, N.J. West Hudson Valley Region Union of Am. Hebrew Congregations, 1986-88. Mem. ABA (urban, state and local govt. sect.), N.Y. State Bar Assn., Westchester County Bar Assn., Rockland County Bar Assn. Office: Kirkpatrick & Silverberg 81 Main St Ste 110 White Plains NY 10601-1711

SILVERBERG, STUART OWEN, obstetrician, gynecologist; b. Denver, Oct. 14, 1931; s. Edward M. and Sara (Morris) S.; BA, U. Colo., 1952, MD, 1955; m. Joan E. Snyderman, June 19, 1954 (div. Apr. 1970); children: Debra Sue Owen, Eric Owen, Alan Kent; m. 2d, Kay Ellen Conklin, Oct. 18, 1970 (div. Apr. 1982); 1 son, Cris S.; m. 3d, Sandra Kay Miller, Jan., 1983. Intern Women's Hosp. Phila., 1955-56; resident Kings County Hosp., Bklyn., 1958-62; practice medicine specializing in obstetrics and gynecology, Denver, 1962—; mem. staff Rose Med. Ctr., N. Suburban Med. Ctr., U. Hosp., St. Anthony Hosp.; med. exec. bd., chmn. dept. obstetrics and gynecology, 1976-77, 86-87, dir. Laser Ctr., 1994-95; clin. instr. U. Colo. Sch. Medicine, Denver, 1962-73, asst. clin. prof., 1972-88, assoc. clin. prof., 1989—, dir. gynecol. endoscopy and laser surgery, 1988-90; v.p. Productos Alimenticos, La Ponderosa, S.A.; dir., chmn. bd. Wicker Works Video Prodns., Inc., 1983-91; cons. Ft. Logan Mental Health Ctr., Denver, 1964-70; mem. Gov.'s Panel Mental Retardation, 1966; med. adv. bd. Colo. Planned Parenthood, 1966-68, Am. Med. Ctr., Spivak, Colo., 1967-70. Mem. Colo. Emergency Resources Bd., Denver, 1965—. Served to maj. AUS, 1956-58; Germany. Diplomate Am. Bd. Obstetrics and Gynecology, Am. Bd. Laser Surgery. Fellow Am. Coll. Obstetricians and Gynecologists, Am. Soc. Laser Medicine and Surgery, ACS; mem. Am. Internat. fertility socs., Colo. Gynecologists and Obstetricians Soc., Hellman Obstet. and Gynecol. Soc., Colo. Med. Soc. (bd. dirs. 1987-95, speaker of the house 1989-95), Clear Creek Valley Med. Soc. (trustee 1978, 80, 87, 93—, pres. 1995), Phi Sigma Delta, Flying Physicians Assn., Aircraft Owners and Pilots Assn., Nu Sigma Nu, Alpha Epsilon Delta. Jewish. Mem. editorial rev. bd. Colo. Women's Mag.; editor in chief First Image, Physicians Video Jour., 1984-86.

SILVERMAN, AL, editor; b. Lynn, Mass., Apr. 12, 1926; s. Henry and Minnie (Damsky) S.; m. Rosa Magaro, Sept. 9, 1951; children: Thomas, Brian, Matthew. B.S., Boston U., 1949, Litt.D., 1986. Assoc. editor Sport mag., 1951-52; sports editor True mag., 1952-54; asst. editor Argosy mag., 1954-55; free-lance mag. writer, contbr. Saturday Evening Post, Coronet, Pageant, This Week, Am. Weekly, Am. Heritage, Saturday Review, others, 1955-60; editor-in-chief Saga mag., Impact mag., Sport Library, Sport mag., 1960-72; exec. v.p., editorial dir. Book-of-the-Month Club, 1972—, pres., chief operating officer, 1981—, chmn., chief exec. office, 1985-88; v.p., contbg. editor Viking Penguin, 1989-92, sr. v.p., pub., editor in chief, 1992—; sr. v.p., editor-at-large Viking Penguin, N.Y.C., 1994—. Author: Warren Spahn, 1961, Best from Sport, 1961, (with Phil Rizzuto) The Miracle New York Yankees, 1962, The World of Sport, 1962, Mickey Mantle, Master Yankee, 1963, World Series Heroes, 1964, (with Paul Hornung) Football and the Single Man, 1965, The Specialist in Pro Football, 1966, Sports Titans of the 20th Century, 1968, (with Frank Robinson) My Life is Baseball, 1968, More Sport Titans of the 20th Century, 1969, Joe DiMaggio, The Golden Year, 1969, I Am Third, (with Gale Sayers), 1970, Foster and Laurie, 1974; editor: The Book of the Month, 1986; co-editor: The 20th Century Treasury of Sports, 1992. Mem. Authors Guild. Home: 15 Woods Way White Plains NY 10605-5446 Office: Penguin US 375 Hudson St New York NY 10014-3658

SILVERMAN, ALAN H., lawyer; b. N.Y.C., Feb. 18, 1954; s. Melvin H. and Florence (Green) S.; m. Gretchen E. Freeman, May 25, 1986; children: Willa C.F., Gordon H.F. BA summa cum laude, Hamilton Coll., 1976; MBA, U. Pa., 1980, JD, 1980. Bar: N.Y. 1981, U.S. Dist. Ct. (so. and ea. dist.) N.Y. 1981, U.S. Ct. Internat. Trade 1981, D.C. 1986, U.S. Supreme Ct. 1990. Assoc. Hughes, Hubbard & Reed, N.Y.C., 1980-84; asst. counsel Newsweek, Inc., N.Y.C., 1984-86; v.p., gen. counsel, sec., dir. adminstrn. Cable Onc, Inc., Phoenix, 1986—. Contbr. articles to profl. jours. Mem. prevention adv. com. Gov. Pa. Justice Commn., 1975-79; bd. dirs. Lawyers' Alliance for N.Y., 1982-85, N.Y. Lawyers Pub. Interest, 1983-85, Nat. Assn. JD-MBA Profls., 1983-85, Bus. Vols. for Arts, Inc., Phoenix, 1989-93, Ariz. Vol. Lawyers for the Arts, Inc., 1994-97; mem. Maricopa County Citizens Jud. Adv. Coun., 1990-93. Mem. ABA, Assn. of Bar of City of N.Y., D.C. Bar Assn., Phi Beta Kappa. Home: 5833 N 30th St Phoenix AZ 85016 Office: Cable One Inc 4742 N 24th St Ste 270 Phoenix AZ 85016-4860

SILVERMAN, ALBERT A., retired lawyer, manufacturing company executive; b. Copenhagen, Oct. 14, 1908; came to U.S., 1909, naturalized, 1921; s. Louis and Anna (Mendelsohn) S.; m. Gertrude Adelman, 1929 (div. 1934); 1 child, Violet (Mrs. Robert Blumenthal); m. Florence Cohen, Aug. 5, 1939 (dec. 1966); m. Francie Seifert, Oct. 1, 1975. Student, Northwestern U., 1929-34; AA, Cen. YMCA Coll., Chgo., 1936; JD, Loyola U., Chgo., 1940. Bar: Ill. 1940, Wis. 1959, U.S. Supreme Ct. 1960. With Cen. Republic Bank & Trust Co., Chgo., 1926-32; sec.-treas. Cen.-Ill. Co., 1932-42; corp. atty., sec. Republic Drill & Tool Co., 1942-44; asst. to treas. Hansen Glove Corp., Milw., 1944-45; v.p. Vilter Mfg. Corp., Milw., 1945-49, pres., 1949-88, 89-92, chmn., chief exec. officer, 1970-92, chmn. emeritus, 1992—; bd. dirs., pres. Vilter Found., Inc.; mem. coun. Marquette U. Engring. Sch., 1974-96, assoc., 1995—. Council, Med. Coll. Wis.; bd. dirs. Albert J. and Flora H. Ellinger Found., 1974-96. Named Man of Yr. Milw. chpt. Unico Nat., 1967; recipient Francis J. Rooney-St. Thomas More award Loyola U. Law Sch., Chgo., 1974, Community Relations award Milw. police chief, 1974, Antonio R. Rizzuto Gold Medal award Unico Nat., Community Svc. award, VFW, 1989, award Wis. Reg. Bd. NCCJ, 1989; honored by VFW for community svc., 1988. Mem. ABA, ASHRAE, Wis. Bar Assn., Milw. Bar Assn., Chgo. Bar Assn., Am. Zool Soc., Loyola U. Alumni Assn. (hon.), Milw. Athletic Club, Wis. Club, Univ. Club of Milw., Tripoli Country Club, Milw. Athletic Club, Milw. Press Club (Knight of Bohemia award 1979, Headliner award 1981, NCJJ award 1989), Masons (past master Milw. Harmony Lodge 1961, 32 deg.), Shriners, Beta Gamma Sigma (hon.). Jewish. Office: 2405 W Dean Rd River Hills WI 53217-2008 *As we go through life, we experience good and bad times, tragedies and happiness, successes and failures. Sometimes we are even handed lemons. Problems are opportunities, and with lemons one can make lemonade.*

SILVERMAN, ALBERT JACK, psychiatrist, educator; b. Montreal, Que., Can., Jan. 27, 1925; came to U.S., 1950, naturalized, 1955; s. Norman and Molly (Cohen) S.; m. Halina Weinthal, June 22, 1947; children: Barry Evan, Marcy Lynn. B.Sc., McGill U., 1947, M.D., C.M., 1949; grad., Washington Psychoanalytic Inst., 1964. Diplomate: Am. Bd. Psychiatry and Neurology. Intern Jewish Gen. Hosp., Montreal, 1949-50; resident psychiatry Colo. U. Med. Center, 1950-53, instr., 1953; from assoc. to assoc. prof. psychiatry Duke Med. Center, 1953-63; prof. psychiatry, chmn. dept. Rutgers U. Med. Sch., 1964-70; prof. psychiatry U. Mich. Med. Sch., Ann Arbor, 1970-90, prof. emeritus, 1990—; chmn. dept. U. Mich. Med. Sch., 1970-81; cons. Dept. of Def., 1974—; mem. biol. scis. tng. rev. com. NIMH, 1964-69, chmn., 1968-69, mem. rsch. scientist devel. award com., 1970-75, chmn., 1973-75, mem. merit rev. bd. in behavioral scis. VA, 1975-78, chmn., 1976-78, mem. small grants awards com., 1985-89; bd. mgrs. N.J. Neuropsychiat. Inst., 1965-69; trustee N.J. Fund Rsch. and Devel. Nervous and Mental Diseases, 1965-67; bd. dirs. N.J. Mental Health Assn., 1964-69; mem. behavioral sci. com. Nat. Bd. Med. Examiners, 1978-82, chmn., 1984-87, mem. comprehensive com., 1986-93, task force for nervous system, 1989-91; chmn. task force on Cons. Liaison Psychiat., 1991-92. Cons. editor: Psychophysiology, 1970-74, Psychosomatic Medicine, 1972-87; Contbr. articles in field. Served as capt. M.C. USAF, 1955-57. Fellow Am. Coll. Psychiatry (charter), Am. Psychiat. Assn. (chmn. coun. on med. edn. 1970-75, chair task force on DSM III ednl. materials 1979-81), Am. Acad. Psychoanalysis, Am. Coll. Neuropsychopharmacology; mem. Am. Psychosomatic Soc. (coun. 1964-68, 70-74, pres. 1976-77, vis. scholar com. 1992-96, co-chair program com. 1992-93), N.J. Psychoanalytic Soc. (trustee 1968-70), Assn. Rsch. Nervous and Mental Diseases, N.J. Neuropsychiat. Assn. (coun. 1966-69), Group Advancement Psychiatry (chmn. com. psychopathology 1968-74), Soc. Psychophys. Rsch., Soc. Biol. Psychiatry, Mich. Psychiat. Soc. (coun. 1975-77). Home: 19 Regent Dr Ann Arbor MI 48104-1738 Office: Mental Health Rsch Inst 205 Zina Pitcher Pl Ann Arbor MI 48109-0720

SILVERMAN, ALVIN MICHAELS, public relations consultant; b. Louisville, 1912; s. Alvin and May (Michaels) S.; m. Phyllis Israel, Nov. 22, 1936; children: Lora (Mrs. A. Gene Samburg), Jane (Mrs. Carl Culos). Student, Adelbert Coll., Western Res. U., 1930-32. With Cleve. Plain Dealer, 1930-65, beginning as sportswriter, successively schs. editor, city hall reporter, state house corr., Columbus, editorial columnist, day city editor, 1930-57, chief Washington bur., 1957-65; pres., chief exec. officer Pearl-Silverman Agy. (pub. relations consultants), Washington, 1965—; dir. Tiffin Amusement Co., Ellet Co., Bklyn. Devel. Corp. Author: The American Newspaper, 1965. Trustee Ctr. to Protect Workers' Rights. Mem. White House Corrs. Assn., Ohio Legis. Corrs. Assn., D.C. Friends of Ireland, Nat. Press Club, Woodmont Country Club, Gridiron Club, Fed. City Club, Sigma Delta Chi, Zeta Beta Tau. Home: 4100 Cathedral Ave NW Washington DC 20016-3584 Office: 1125 17th St NW Washington DC 20036-4707

SILVERMAN, ARNOLD, physician; b. N.Y.C., Feb. 15, 1933; s. Sol and Gertrude (Cohen) S.; m. Bonnie J. Fenson, Aug. 28, 1955; children: Jeffrey R., Paul A., David E. B.A., U. Colo., 1954, M.A., 1957, M.D., 1961. Diplomate: Am. Bd. Pediatrics. Intern Colo. Gen. Hosp., Denver, 1961-62; resident in pediatrics U. Minn. Hosp., Mpls., 1962-64; fellow in pediatric gastroenterology U. Colo. Med. Center, Denver, 1964-65; mem. faculty U. Colo. Med. Center, 1965—, assoc. prof. pediatrics, 1975-80; prof. U. Colo. Med. Ctr. (Health Sci. Ctr.), 1980-93, prof. emeritus, 1994—; dir. grad. edn. Denver Children's Hosp., 1967-75, chief gastroenterology svc., 1967-75; dir. pediat. svc. Denver Gen. Hosp., 1975-92; cons. Surgeon Gen. Fitzsimons Army Med. Hosp., 1976-95; mem. Nat. Commn. Digestive Diseases, 1979-80. Author: (with C.C. Roy and D. Alagille) Pediatric Clinic Gastroenterology, 4th edit., 1995. Mem. Am. Acad. Pediatrics, Am. Gastroenterology Assn., Am. Pediatric Soc., Am. Gastroenterology Assn., N.Am. Soc. Pediatric Gastroenterology, Am. Assn. Study Liver Disease, Denver Med. Soc., Alpha Omega Alpha. Jewish. Home: 3335 S Newport St Denver CO 80224-2823

SILVERMAN, ARNOLD BARRY, lawyer; b. Sept. 1, 1937; s. Frank and Lillian Lena (Linder) S.; m. Susan L. Levin, Aug. 7, 1960; children: Michael Eric, Lee Oren. B Engring. Sci., Johns Hopkins U., 1959; LLB cum laude, U. Pitts., 1962. Bar: U.S. Dist. Ct. (we. dist.) Pa. 1963, Pa. 1964, U.S. Patent and Trademark Office 1965, U.S. Supreme Ct. 1967, Can. Patent Office 1968, U.S. Ct. Claims 1975, U.S. Ct. Appeals (3d cir.) 1982, U.S. Ct. Appeals (fed. cir.) 1985. Patent atty. Alcoa, New Kensington, Pa., 1962-67, 68-74, sr. patent atty., 1972-76; ptnr. Price and Silverman, Pitts., 1967-68; v.p., gen. patent counsel Joy Mfg. Co., Pitts., 1976-80; ptnr. Murray Silverman & Keck, Pitts., 1980-81, Buell, Blenko, Ziesenheim & Beck, Pitts., 1984; ptnr. intellectual property sect. Eckert, Seamans, Cherin & Mellott, Pitts., 1984—, chmn., 1992—; spl. asst. atty. gen. State of W.Va., 1985—; spl. counsel patents U. Pitts., 1975—; spkr. on patents, trademarks, copyright, computer law; nat. panel of arbiters Am. Arbitration Assn., 1987—; chair Info. Tech. Practice Group, 1995—. Contbr. articles to profl. jours. Mem. Churchill CSC (Pa.), 1967-90, chmn., 1975-90; mem. Pitts. law com. Anti-Defamation League, 1981—, regional adv. bd., 1982—, ch-chmn. Pitts. region ann. dinner, 1983, mem. chmn. by-laws com., 1983; bd. govs. Slippery Rock U. Found., 1985-91; Pitts. steering com. MIT Enterprise Forum, 1986-87. With U.S. Army, 1963-64. Recipient Am. Spirit Honor medal, Ft. Knox, 1963,. Mem. ABA, ASME, Allegheny County Bar Assn. (chmn. pub. rels. com. 1978-80, vice-chmn. intellectual property sect. 1981-83), Pitts. Patent Law Assn. (chmn. pub. rels. com., 1968-69, chmn. patent laws com., 1970-72, chmn. nominating com., 1973, chmn. legis. action com., 1972-75, bd. mgrs. 1974-88, newsletter editor 1974-88, sec.-treas. 1976-84, v.p. 1984-85, pres. 1985-86, pub. rels. com. 1994-95, program com. 1995-96), Am. Intellectual Property Law Assn. (membership com. 1985-88, mem. pub. rels. com. 1994—), U.S. Trademark Assn. (chmn. task force on advt. agys. 1981, membership com. 1987-89), D.C. Bar Assn., Pa. Bar Assn., Nat. Assn. Coll. and Univ. Attys., Am. Chem. Soc. (chemistry and the law sect.), Licensing Execs. Soc. (co-chmn. Pitts. 1994-96 chemistry and law sect.), Brit. Inst. Chartered Patent Agts. (fgn. mem.), Johns Hopkins U. Alumni Assn. (chmn. publicity com. 1963-66, exec. com. 1966-87, v.p. 1969-70, pres. 1971-72, nat. alumni coun. 1989-92), U. Pitts. Gen. Alumni Assn., U. Pitts. Law Alumni Assn. (bd. dirs. 1992—), Robert Bruce Assn. Law Fellows (life), Golden Panthers, Stratford Cmty. Assn. (v.p. 1966-67, gov. 1966-70, pres. 1967-68), Mensa (fellow, lawyers in Mensa 1978—, nat. assoc. counsel patents and trademarks copyrights 1980-82, inventors' spl. interest group 1980-86), Intertel (treas. Pitts. Forum 1983—), Duquesne Club, Order of Coif, Tau Epsilon Rho, Psi Chi. Republican. Jewish. Home: 2019 High Point Dr Murrysville PA 15668-8515 Office: 600 Grant St Ste 42 Pittsburgh PA 15219-2703 *Welcome challenge and perform all tasks with enthusiasm, in a moral manner and to the very best of your ability.*

SILVERMAN, ARTHUR CHARLES, lawyer; b. Lewiston, Maine, June 13, 1938; s. Louis A. and Frances Edith (Brownstone) S.; BS in Elec. Engring., BS in Indsl. Mgmt., MIT, 1961; JD, Columbia U., 1964; m. Donna Linda Zolov, June 18, 1961; children: Leonard Stephen, Daniel Edward. Bar: N.Y. 1965, U.S. Supreme Ct. 1971. Engr., engring. asst. Gen. Electric Co., Pittsfield, Mass. and Phila., 1958-62; assoc. Baer & Marks, N.Y.C., 1965-68; assoc. Golenbock and Barell, N.Y.C., 1968-72, ptnr., 1972-89, Reid & Priest, N.Y.C., 1989—, dep. chair, 1997—. Treas., trustee Ramaz Sch., 1977-84, vice chmn., 1984-85, 86-88, chmn., 1988-92, hon. chmn., 1992—; bd. govs. MIT Hillel Found., 1979-84; mem. Bd. Jewish Edn. of City of N.Y., 1981-84; mem. exec. com. Nat. Jewish Ctr. for Learning and Leadership, 1984-90. Mem. IEEE, ABA, NSPE, N.Y. State Bar Assn., Fed. Bar Council, Assn. Bar City N.Y., N.Y. Soc. Architects, Internat. Bar Assn., Inter-Pacific Bar Assn., Constrn. Mgmt. Inst. Home: 200 E 74th St New York NY 10021 Office: Reid & Priest LLP 40 W 57th St New York NY 10019-4001

SILVERMAN, BRUCE GARY, advertising executive; b. N.Y.C., Feb. 16, 1945; s. Edward E. and Lillian (Brill) S.; children: Jennifer, Matthew; m. Nancy Cole, 1996. BA, Adelphi U., 1965; JD, Albany Law Sch., 1967. Sr.

v.p., exec. creative dir. Ogilvy & Mather Inc., N.Y.C., 1967-80; exec. v.p., exec. creative dir. Bozell & Jacobs Inc., Dallas, 1981-83, Batten, Barton, Durstine & Osborn Inc., L.A., 1984-85; exec. v.p., creative dir. Asher/Gould Advt. Inc., L.A., 1986-89, pres., chief creative officer, 1989-95, pres., COO, 1996-97; pres. Western Internat. Advocacy Group, L.A., 1997—. V.p., bd. dirs. Los Angeles Children's Mus., 1984-88; chmn. Resource Devel. com. Starbright Pavillion Found., 1993. Mem. Acad. TV Arts and Scis. Home: 3168 Dona Mema Pl Studio City CA 91604-4264 Office: Western Internat Advocacy Group 8544 Sunset Blvd Los Angeles CA 90069-2310

SILVERMAN, BURTON PHILIP, artist; b. Bklyn., June 11, 1928; s. Morris Daniel and Anne (Firstenberg) S.; m. Claire Guss, June 12, 1969; children: Robert Arthur, Karen Lila. BA, Columbia Coll., 1949. Freelance illustrator Life, Fortune, Esquire, Time, Newsweek, Sports Illus., New York, The New Yorkers mags., 1959—; instr. Sch. Visual Arts, N.Y.C., 1964-67. Co-author: Abel, 1968, A Portfolio of Drawings, 1968; author: Painting People, 1977, Breaking the Rules of Watercolor, 1983; contbr. articles and drawings to profl. jours.; one-man exhbns. include Davis Gallery, N.Y.C, 1956, 58, 62, Kenmore Galleries, Phila., 1963, 67, 70, FAR Gallery, N.Y.C., 1965, 70, 75, 77, Genesis Gallery, N.Y.C., 1979, Sindin Galleries, N.Y.C., 1983, Capricorn Galleries, Bethesda, Md., 1979, 91, Gallery 52, South Orange, N.J., 1967, 70, 77, Harbor Gallery, L.I., 1971, 74, U. Utah, 1967, Doll and Richards, Boston, 1980, Grand Central Galleries, N.Y.C., 1988, Cudahy's Gallery, N.Y.C., 1990, Joseph Keifer, Inc., N.Y.C., 1993, Gerold Wooderlich & Co., N.Y.C., 1996, Merrill Gallery, Denver, 1996; group exhbns. include Butler Inst. Am. Art, Youngstown, Ohio, 1954-71, 74, 76, 79, 88, 90, 93, NAD, N.Y.C., 1958-96, Am. Watercolor Soc., N.Y.C., 1978-82, 84-87, 89-91, 95-96, Pa. Acad. Fine Art, 1949, New Britain (Conn.) Mus. Am. Art, 1964, Wadsworth Atheneum, Hartford, Conn., 1961, Am. Acad. Arts and Letters, 1967, 74, 76, 79, N.Y. Hist. Soc., 1976, Pa. State Mus. Art, Portsmouth (Va.) Mus. Art, 1976, 79-80, 82 (Purchase prize, 1979, 82), Mexico City Mus. Art, 1990, Nat. Portrait Gallery, Washington, 1993, Hofstra Mus., N.Y.C., 1993, South Bend (Ind.) Mus. Art, 1994, Old Forge (N.Y.) Mus. and Gallery, 1994. With AUS, 1951-53. Named to Hall of Fame, Soc. of Illustrators, N.Y., 1990, Pastel Soc. Am., 1992. Mem. NAD (numerous awards and prizes including Joseph Isidor Gold medal 1992, Ranger Purchase prize 1962, 84, Benjamin Altman figure prize 1969), Am. Watercolor Soc. (numerous awards and prizes including Gold medal 1979, Silver medal 1984, 95, annuals). Home and Studio: 324 W 71st St New York NY 10023-3502 *In art I am wary of things too facile, or appealing. My painting is rooted in a realist tradition that is equally concerned with objective facts and subjective realities. It is a visual language that allows me to explore the tensions and ambiguities engendered by this dual aspect of human experience. Art is my life and my life is in my art.**

SILVERMAN, CHARLOTTE, federal agency administrator, medical epidemiologist; b. N.Y.C., May 21, 1913; d. Harry and Gussie (Goldman) S. BA, Bklyn. Coll., 1933; MD, Woman's Med. Coll. Pa., 1938; MPH, Johns Hopkins U., 1942, DrPH, 1948. Diplomate Am. Bd. Preventive Medicine. Intern Beekman Hosp., N.Y.C., 1939-40; resident Sea View Hosp., Staten Island, N.Y., 1940-41; asst. dir., dir. Bur. Tuberculosis Balt. City Health Dept., 1946-56; chief epidemiology, planning and rsch. Md. State Dept. Health, Balt., 1956-62; med. officer in various programs NIMH, Bethesda, Md., 1962-68; dep. dir. div. biol. effects and other positions Bur. Radiol. Health USPHS, Rockville, Md., 1968-83; assoc. dir. for human studies FDA, Rockville, 1983-92; mem. faculty dept. epidemiology Johns Hopkins U. Sch. Hygiene and Pub. Health, Balt., 1950—. Author: Epidemiology of Depression, 1968; contbr. articles to profl. jours. Sr. Surg. USPHS, 1944-45. Recipient Mary Pemberton Nourse Meml. award AAUW, 1941-42, Merit award FDA, 1974, Alumni Life Achievement award Bklyn. Coll., 1994. Fellow APHA, Am. Coll. Preventive Medicine, Am. Orthopsychiat. Assn., Am. Coll. Epidemiology; mem. Delta Omega. Home: 4977 Battery Ln Bethesda MD 20814-4927

SILVERMAN, DAVID ALAN, screenwriter, television story consultant; b. Whittier, Calif., Jan. 18, 1952; s. Sol Robert and Jeanne Delores (Weiser) S. Student, George Washington U., 1969; BA in Psychology with honors, Stanford U., 1974; MA in Cinema, U. So. Calif., 1978. Story cons. TV show Alice, 1982-85; contbg. writer TV shows Mork & Mindy, 1979, The Jeffersons, 1979-80, What's Happening Now, 1985, ALF, 1986; story editor TV show One Day At A Time, 1981-82; staff writer TV show New Love American Style, 1985-86; story cons. TV show 9 to 5, 1987; screenwriter De-Laurentis Entertainment Group, 1987—; story analyst Am. Internat. Pictures, Los Angeles, 1979, Babes TV shows, 1988-89. Writer: (TV pilots) Jr. Exec., 1984, For Better Or Worse, 1985, (screenplay) Stepping Out, 1987; exec. story cons. TV show The Jackie Thomas Show, 1990-91; exec. story editor TV show Tom, 1991-92; prodr.: (TV show) The Good Life, 1992-93, Wild Oats, 1992-94; supervising prodr.: (TV show) Cleghorne, 1994-95; co-creator, co-exec. prodr.: (TV show) Secret Service Guy, 1995-96. Mem. Writers Guild Am., ASCAP, U. So. Calif. Alumni Assn. (Cinema Circulus), Stanford Alumni Assn. Democrat. Home: 1230 Casa Del Rey Dr La Habra CA 90631-8330 Office: care Fox Broadcasting Co PO Box 900 Beverly Hills CA 90213-0900

SILVERMAN, FRANKLIN HAROLD, speech pathologist, educator; b. Providence, Aug. 16, 1933; s. Meyer and Reba (Sack) S.; m. Ellen-Marie Loebel, Feb., 1967 (div. Feb. 1981); 1 child, Catherine; m. Evelyn Ellen Chanda, Nov. 13, 1983. BS in Speech, Emerson Coll., 1960; MA, Northwestern U., 1961; PhD, U. Iowa, 1966. Lic. speech-lang. pathologist, Wis. Rsch. assoc. U. Iowa, Iowa City, 1965-67; asst. prof. U. Ill., Champaign, 1968-71; assoc. prof. Marquette U., Milw., 1971-77, prof., 1978—; clin. prof. Med. Coll. Wis., Wauwatosa, 1978—; mem. adv. bd. Wis. Telecomm. Relay Svcs., Madison, 1991—; cons. USAID Palestinian Speech Pathology Tng. Program, Gaza City, Gaza Strip, 1993—, Joint Centre for Rsch. Prosthetics and Orthotics and Rehab. Programmes, Riyadh, Saudi Arabia, 1995—. Author: Speech, Language, and Hearing Disorders, 1995, Communication for the Speechless, 3d edit., 1995, Stuttering and Other Fluency Disorders, 2d edit., 1996, Computer Applications for Augmenting the Management of Speech, Language and Hearing Disorders, 1997; contbr. numerous rsch. papers to profl. jours. Fellow Am. Speech-Lang.-Hearing Assn.; mem. Text and Acad. Authors Assn. (sec. 1993-94, pres.-elect 1996, pres. 1997). Jewish. Avocation: photography. Home: 5918 Currant Ln Greendale WI 53129 Office: Marquette U Dept Speech Pathology Milwaukee WI 53201-1881

SILVERMAN, FRED, television producer; b. N.Y.C., 1937. Student, Syracuse U.; M in TV and Theatre Arts, Ohio State U. With Sta. WGN-TV, Chgo.; then Sta. WPIX-TV, N.Y.C.; then dir. daytime programs CBS-TV, N.Y.C., v.p. programs, 1970-75; pres. ABC Entertainment, N.Y.C., 1975-78; pres., chief exec. officer NBC-TV, N.Y.C., 1978; now pres. Fred Silverman Co., L.A.; co-founder Pierce/Silverman TV Prodn. Co., 1989. Exec. producer TV series Perry Mason Movies, Matlock, In the Heat of the Night, Jake and the Fatman, Father Dowling Mysteries, Diagnosis Murder Starring Dick Van Dyck. Office: Fred Siverman Prod 12400 Wilshire Blvd Ste 920 Los Angeles CA 90025-1030*

SILVERMAN, FREDERIC NOAH, physician; b. Syracuse, N.Y., June 6, 1914; s. Max and Sophia S.; m. Carolyn R. Weber, Jan. 14, 1945. A.B., Syracuse U., 1935, M.D., 1939. Intern Yale U., 1939-40; resident in pediatrics Johns Hopkins U., Balt., 1940-41; fellow in pediatric pathology Columbia U., N.Y.C., 1941-42; in pediatric radiology Babies Hosp., N.Y.C., 1945-47; dir. dept. radiology Children's Hosp., Cin., 1947-75; asst. prof. to prof. radiology and pediatrics U. Cin., 1947-76; prof. clin. radiology and pediatrics Stanford (Calif.) U., 1976-79, emeritus, 1979—; ad hoc cons. HEW, NAS. Chief editor Caffey's Pediatric X-Ray Diagnosis, 1978—; mem. editorial bd. pediatric and radiol. jours.; contbr. articles to profl. jours. With AUS, 1942-46, South West Pacific area. Decorated Combat Med. Badge; recipient medal Centre Antoine Bèlère, Paris, 1981, Gold medal Assn. Univ. Radiologists, 1993. Mem. Am. Acad. Pediatrics, Am. Pediatric Soc., Soc. Pediatric Research (past v.p.), Soc. for Pediatric Radiology (past pres., Gold medal 1988); hon. mem. Am. Roentgen Ray Soc., European Soc. Pediatric Radiology, Spanish Radiology Soc., El Salvador Pediatrics Soc., Chilean Radiol. Soc., regional radiol. socs. Home: 850 Webster St Apt 735 Palo Alto CA 94301-2838 Office: Dept Radiology Stanford U Med Center Stanford CA 94305

SILVERMAN, GARY WILLIAM, financial planner; b. L.A., Nov. 30, 1957; s. Albert and Anna Marie (Robinson) S.; m. Joanne Marie Robinson, Aug. 29, 1976. BS summa cum laude Psychology/Counseling, Miami (Fla.) Christian Coll., 1987; MBA, U. Dallas, 1992. CFP. Tng. supr. Tex. Utilities, Glen Rose, Tex., 1982-92; registered rep. Waddell & Reed, Ft. Worth, 1990-94; tng. dir. Howmet Refurbishment, Wichita Falls, Tex., 1992-94; owner, fin. planner Personal Money Planning, Wichita Falls, 1993—. Grad. Leadership Wichita Falls, 1993; loaned exec. Wichita Falls United Way, 1993; instr. ARC, 1983—; Wichita Falls Gold Coast ambassador; mem. Job. Svc. Employer Com.; columnist Wichita Women mag. Mem. Inst. Cert. Fin. Planners, Registry Cert. Fin. Planners, Internat. Assn. Fin. Planning, S.W. Wichita Falls Rotary, Sigma Iota Epsilon. Office: Personal Money Planning 4245 Kemp Blvd Ste 818 Wichita Falls TX 76308-2829

SILVERMAN, GEORGE ALAN, broadcasting executive; b. Boston, Aug. 27, 1946; s. Sam and Ann S.; m. Sunnie Gozansky, Sept. 1, 1968; children—Rebecca, Marjorie, Jennifer. B.B.A. in Mktg, U. Miami, Fla., 1969. Gen. sales mgr. CBS, Sta. WEEI-FM, Boston, 1972-75; pres. Sunshine Group Broadcasting, Portland, Maine, 1977—; instr. mktg. Husson Coll., Bangor, Maine. Bd. dirs. Greater Portland Landmarks, Gulf of Marine Aquarium, 1979-80; mem. Greater Portland Arts Council; bd. dirs. Multiple Sclerosis Soc. Mem. Greater Portland Radio Broadcasters Assn. (past pres.), New Eng. Broadcast Assn., Maine Assn. Broadcasters. Home: 98 Carroll St Portland ME 04102-3526 Office: Sunshine Group Broadcasting 1555 Islington St Portsmouth NH 03801-4215

SILVERMAN, GERALD BERNARD, journalist; b. Mineola, N.Y., June 2, 1959; s. Martin and Esther S.; m. Robyn G. Silverman, Aug. 29, 1982; children: Rebecca, Joshua. BA in English, SUNY, New Paltz, 1981; Cert. in Labor Studies, Cornell U., 1987. Reporter Register-Star, Hudson, N.Y., 1981-83; N.Y. corrs. Bur. Nat. Affairs, Inc., Albany, 1982—; columnist The Saratogian, Saratoga Springs, N.Y., 1994—. Contbr. articles to profl. jours. Bd. dirs. Spring Hill Waldorf Sch., Saratoga Springs, N.Y., 1992-93. Mem. Soc. Profl. Journalists (pres. Empire State chpt. 1991—), The Newspaper Guild (shop steward 1992-95), Legis. Corrs. Assn. Avocations: cooking, jazz, camping, poetry. Home: 2 Frank St Ballston Lake NY 12019-2400

SILVERMAN, HAROLD IRVING, pharmaceutical executive; b. Lawrence, Mass., Apr. 27, 1928; s. Jack David and Norma (Illman) S.; m. Arlene Jacobowitz, Nov. 25, 1951; children: Robert L., Richard L. BSc, Phila. Coll. of Pharmacy, 1951, MSc, 1952, DSc, 1956. Instr. Phila. Coll. Pharmacy, 1952-56; prof. pharmaceutics L.I. U., Bklyn., 1956-64; sr. scientist Warner Lambert Rsch. Inst., Morris Plains, N.J., 1958-60; v.p. sci. dir. Knoll Pharm. Co., West Orange, N.J., 1964-68; prof., assoc. dean Mass. Coll. Pharmacy, Boston, 1968-85, prof. emeritus, 1985—; sr. v.p. Thompson Med. Co., N.Y.C., 1985-92; sr. v.p. for med. rsch. Bascomb Found. for Med. Rsch., Boston, 1992—; lectr. Boston U. Sch. Medicine, 1971-73, New Eng. Coll. of Optometry, Boston, 1971-80. Contbr. numerous articles to sci. jours. Mem. human subcom. Peter Bent Brigham, Boston, 1980-85, Boston U., 1983-85; cons. Mass. Bd. Optometry, Boston, 1974-80, WHO, Washington, 1985. Named Man of Yr., Boston Assn. Druggists, 1977; recipient Disting. Svc. award Am. Optometric Assn., 1974. Fellow Soc. Cosmetic Chemists; mem. AAAS, Am. Pharm. Assn. (Phytochemistry award 1956), Am. Chem. Soc., Am. Oil Chemists Soc., Am. Assn. Pharm. Scientists. Avocations: boating, painting. Home and Office: 45 Crest Rd Framingham MA 01702-5606

SILVERMAN, HENRY JACOB, history educator; b. New Haven, Feb. 22, 1934; s. Morris Samuel and Ethel (Ullman) S.; m. Ann Beryl Snyder, Apr. 12, 1957; children—Edwin Stodel, Emily Davies. B.A. (Univ. scholar), Yale U., 1955, M.A., 1956; M.A. (Ford Found. fellow); postgrad., Stanford U., 1959-60; Ph.D., U. Pa., 1963. Fgn. service officer Dept. States, 1961-63; bibliographer Am. history Library of Congress, Washington, 1963-64; asst. prof. Am. thought and lang. Mich. State U., East Lansing, 1964-68, assoc. prof., 1968-71, prof., 1971-89, prof. history, 1988—, chmn. dept. Am. thought and lang., 1977-87, sec. for acad. governance, 1989-95; chmn. dept. history Mich. State U., 1995—. Author: American Radical Thought, 1970. Fulbright scholar, Munich, 1956-57; Danforth Found. Assoc., 1969-73; Nat. Endowment for Humanities/U. Iowa grantee, 1979. Mem. AAUP (mem. exec. bd. Mich. State U. chpt. 1975-77), ACLU (mem. Laxing exec. bd., 1975-78, v.p. 1991-96, pres. 1996—, , Mich. exec. bd. 1993—), Am. Hist. Assn., Am. Studies Assn., Orgn. Am. Historians. Home: 1099 Woodwind Trl Haslett MI 48840-8978 Office: Mich State U Dept History East Lansing MI 48823

SILVERMAN, HENRY RICHARD, diversified business executive, lawyer; b. N.Y.C., Aug. 2, 1940; s. Herbert Robert and Roslyn (Moskowitz) S.; m. Susan H. Herson, June 13, 1965 (div. Jan. 1977); children: Robin Lynn, Deborah Leigh; m. Nancy Ann Kraner, Jan. 22, 1978; 1 child, Catherine Anne. Grad. cum laude, Hackley Sch., Tarrytown, N.Y., 1957; B.A. with honors, Williams Coll., 1961; LL.B., U. Pa., 1964; postgrad. in corp. fin. and taxation, NYU, 1965. Bar: N.Y. 1965, U.S. Tax Ct. 1965, U.S. Ct. Appeals (2d cir.) 1965. Practice law, 1965-66; with White, Weld & Co., beginning 1966; then gen. ptnr. Oppenheimer & Co., until 1970; pres., chief exec. officer ITI Corp., 1970-72; founder, pres. Trans-York Securities Corp., 1972; exec. v.p., chmn. exec. com. Ladenburg, Thalmann & Co., 1973; pres., chief exec. officer Vavasseur Am. Ltd., subs. U.K. mcht. bank, 1974-75; gen. ptnr. Brisbane Ptnrs., 1976-77; prin. various investment groups, 1977—, Silverman Energy Co., N.Y.C., 1977—, NBC Channel 20, Springfield, Ill., 1977-83, ABC Channel 9, Syracuse, N.Y., 1977-81; prin., dir. Delta Queen Steamboat Co., New Orleans, 1977-86; also prin. outdoor advt., music pub., motion picture prodn., radio broadcasting & hardware mfg. cos.; pres., chief exec. officer Reliance Capital Corp., subs. Reliance Group Holdings, Inc., N.Y.C., 1982—; sr. v.p. bus. devel. Reliance Group Holdings, Inc., N.Y.C., 1982-90; chmn., chief exec. officer Days Inns Am., Inc., Atlanta, 1984-89; also dir.; pres., chief exec. officer Telemundo Group, Inc., N.Y.C., 1986-90; gen. ptnr. Blackstone Group, N.Y.C., 1990-91; chmn., CEO HFS Inc., N.Y.C., 1990—. Bd. dirs. N.Y. Univ. Hosp., N.Y.C., 1987—. Served to lt. USNR, 1965-73. Republican. Jewish. Club: Harmonie (N.Y.C.). Avocation: tennis. Office: 712 5th Ave Fl 41 New York NY 10019-4108

SILVERMAN, HERBERT R., corporate financial executive; b. N.Y.C., June 10, 1914; s. Jacob and Minnie (Stein) S.; m. Roslyn Moskowitz, Dec. 17, 1933 (dec. Dec. 1965); children: Karen Silverman Mayers, Henry; m. Nadia Gray, Oct. 17, 1967 (dec. June 1994). BS, NYU, 1932; JD, St. Lawrence U., 1935. Bar: N.Y. bar 1935. Organizer, pres. Centaur Credit Corp. (merged with James Talcott, Inc. of N.Y.), 1945; v.p. James Talcott, Inc., 1944-46, exec. v.p., 1956-58, dir., 1956-75, pres., 1958-64, chmn. bd., chief exec. officer, 1961-73; chmn., chief exec. officer Talcott Nat. Corp., 1968-73, also chmn. exec. com., dir., 1968-75; pres. Nat. Comml. Fin. Conf., 1948-52, chmn., 1952-58; bd. dir. Baer-Am. Banking Corp., Partners Fund, Inc., Selected Sectors Fund, Inc.; sr. advisor Bank Julius Baer; adj. prof. fin. NYU Coll. Bus. and Pub. Adminstrn., 1973—; trustee med. ctr., vice chmn. bd. NYU. Named Man of Yr. banking and finance Phi Alpha Kappa; recipient Golden Medallion for humanitarian services B'nai B'rith, Albert Gallatin award NYU, 1978. Mem. ABA, N.Y. Bar Assn., N.Y. Univ. Alumni Fedn. (pres. 1958-60), Phi Alpha Kappa, Iota Theta. Clubs: Harmonie (N.Y.C.); Navesink Country (Middletown, N.J.); N.Y. Univ. (past pres.). Home: 150 Central Park S New York NY 10019-1566

SILVERMAN, HUGH J., philosophy educator; b. Boston, Aug. 17, 1945; s. Leslie and Eleanore (Riffin) S.; m. L. Theresa Watkins, June 22, 1968 (div. Apr. 1983); children: Claire Christine, H. Christopher; m. Gertrude Postl, Sept. 1, 1987. BA, Lehigh U., 1966, MA, 1967; postgrad., U. Paris, 1968, 71-72; PhD, Stanford U., 1973. Lectr. Stanford U., Calif., 1973-74; asst. prof. SUNY, Stony Brook, 1974-79, assoc. prof., 1979-83, prof. philosophy and comparative lit., 1983—; vis. sr. lectr. U. Warwick, Coventry, Eng., 1980, U. Nice, France, 1980, 81; vis. prof. Duquesne U., Pitts., 1978, NYU, 1978-80, 85-86, U. Leeds, Eng., 1988, U. Torino, Italy, 1989, U. Vienna, Austria, 1993, 94, U. Nice, France, 1994, 97, U. Helsinki, Finland, 1997; co-dir. Internat. Philos. Seminar, Alto Adige, Italy, 1991—. Author: Inscriptions: Between Phenomenology and Structuralism, 1987, Textualities: Between Hermeneutics and Deconstruction, 1994 (German translation 1997), Inscriptions: After Phenomenology and Structuralism, 1997; editor: Piaget, Philosophy and the Human Sciences, 1980, 97 (Spanish translation 1989), Philosophy and Non-Philosophy since Merleau-Ponty, 1988, 97, Derrida and Deconstruction, 1989, Postmodernism - Philosophy and the Arts, 1990 (Korean translation 1990), Gadamer and Hermeneutics, 1991, Writing the Politics of Difference, 1991, Questioning Foundations: Truth/Subjectivity/Culture, 1993, Cultural Semiosis: Training the Signifier, 1997; co-editor: Jean-Paul Sartre: Contemporary Approaches to His Philosophy, 1980, Continental Philosophy in America, 1983, Hermeneutics and Deconstruction, 1985, Descriptions, 1985, Critical and Dialectical Phenomenology, 1987, Horizons of Continental Philosophy, 1987, Postmodernism and Continental Philosophy, 1988, The Textual Sublime: Deconstruction and its Differences, 1990, Merleau-Ponty: Texts and Dialogues: On Philosophy, Politics and Culture, 1992, 96, Textualität der Philosophie-Philosophie und Literatur, 1994; series editor: Routledge Continental Philosophy series, 1986—; co-editor: Humanities Press Contemporary Studies in Philosophy and the Human Sciences series, 1989—, assoc. editor, 1979-89; Humanities Press Series in Philosophy and Literary Theory, 1989—, SUNY Press Contemporary Studies in Philosophy and Literature, 1988-96, Northwestern U. Press Series in Philosophy and Literature, 1996—; Bull. for Rsch. in Humanities, 1983-84; mem. editorial bd. Rsch. in Phenomenology, 1981—, Rev. of Existential Psychology and Psychiatry, 1979—; translator: Consciousness and the Acquisition of Language, 1973; contbr. numerous articles to profl. jours., and chpts. in books. Fulbright-French Govt. and Alliance Francaise fellow, Paris, 1971-72; faculty rsch. fellow SUNY-Stony Brook, 1977, 78, 81; rsch. fellow Am. Coun. Learned Socs., 1981-82; Experienced Faculty Travel fellowship, 1985, 88, 93; recipient MLA travel grant (Brazil), 1993, N.Y. Coun. for Humanities grant, 1976-77, SUNY Chancellor's award for excellence in teaching, 1977, medal U. Helsinki, 1997. Mem. Soc. Phenomenology and Existential Philosophy (exec. co-dir. 1980-86), Internat. Assn. Philosophy and Lit. (exec. com. 1976—, exec. sec. 1979-87, exec. dir. 1987—), Brit. Soc. Phenomenology (exec. com. 1980-95), Merleau-Ponty Circle (chmn. publs. com. 1978—), Heidegger Conf., Am. Soc. Aesthetics, Am. Philos. Assn. (program adv. com. 1986-89, lectures publs. and rsch. com. 1991-94). Home: 105 Bleeker St Port Jefferson NY 11777-1232 Office: SUNY Dept Philosophy Stony Brook NY 11794-3750

SILVERMAN, IRA NORTON, news producer; b. Bklyn., May 17, 1935; s. Joseph and Mildred (Axelrod) S.; m. Elizabeth Parsons Aspray, June 16, 1979; children by previous marriage: Gary, Bruce; stepchildren: Elizabeth, Aime, Alison. AB, Columbia U., 1957. Newspaper, mag. and book editor, 1957-67; producer, writer NBC News, 1967-79; sr. producer spl. projects NBC Nightly News, Washington, 1979-95; contbr., editl. cons. The New Yorker, N.Y.C., 1995—. Co-author: The Pleasant Avenue Connection, 1976. Recipient Nat. Headliner award, 1977, 78, 81, 87, Alfred I. DuPont-Columbia U. award, 1983-84, 85-86, Emmy award for news and documentary, 1985, 87, award Overseas Press Club Am., 1987, 90, George Polk award L.I. U., 1988, Excellence in TV award Channels mag., 1990, George Foster Peabody award U. Ga., 1991, Citation for Excellence Overseas Press Club, 1992. Avocation: climbing. Office: The New Yorker 20 W 43rd St New York NY 10036-7400

SILVERMAN, JEFFREY STUART, manufacturing executive; b. N.Y.C., Nov. 25, 1945; s. Harry T. and Roberta S.; m. Pamela Silverman (div.); children: Jason S., Amanda P.; m. Joy Silverman (div.); children: Evan M., Jessica Jaye; m. Lisa Tarnopol, Aug. 1995. BS in Fin., L.I. U., 1967. Mem. N.Y. Stock Exchange, 1968-72; pres. Basil Cable, N.Y.C., 1975-82, Silba Enterprises, N.Y.C., 1975-82; chmn. bd. dirs., CEO Ply-Gem Industries, N.Y.C., 1982—. Office: Ply-Gem Industries Inc 777 3rd Ave Fl 30 New York NY 10017-1401

SILVERMAN, JOSEPH, chemistry educator, scientist; b. N.Y.C., Nov. 5, 1922; s. Jakob and Mary (Chechick) S.; m. Joan Aline Jacks, Jan. 14, 1951; children: Joshua Henry, David Avrom. B.A., Bklyn. Coll., 1944; A.M., Columbia U., 1948, Ph.D., 1951. Head research dept. Walter Kidde (nuclear labs.), Garden City, N.Y., 1952-54; v.p., tech. dir. RAI Research Corp., L.I. City, N.Y., 1954-59; assoc. prof. chemistry State U. N.Y., Stony Brook, 1959-60; prof. dept. materials and nuclear engring. U. Md., College Park, 1960-92, prof. emeritus, 1992—; cons. Danish AEC, Indsl. Research Inst., Japan, Boris Kidric Inst., Yugoslavia, Bechtel Co., GPU Nuclear Corp., GE, IAEA, Vienna; disting. vis. prof. Tokyo U., 1974; gen. chmn. 2d Internat. Meeting on Radiation Processing, Miami, Fla., 1978, 3d Tokyo, 1980, hon. chmn. 6th, Ottawa, 1987; trustee Washington Inst. Values in Pub. Policy, 1981-87. Editor Internat. Jour. Applied Radiation and Isotopes, 1973-78, Trans. 1st Internat. Meetings on Radiation Processing, 1977, 3d edit., 1981; mem. editorial adv. bd. Radiation Physics and Chemistry, 1978-95. Served with AUS, 1944-46. Recipient Founders award 6th Internat. Mtg. on Radiation Processing, 1987, Centennial medal U. Md. Coll. Engring., 1994; Rsch. fellow Brookhaven Nat. Lab., 1949-51; Guggenheim fellow, 1966-67. Fellow Nordic Soc. Radiation Chemistry and Tech., Am. Phys. Soc., Am. Nuclear Soc. (Radiation Industry award 1975); mem. Am. Chem. Soc., Sigma Xi. Home: 320 Sisson St Silver Spring MD 20902-3156 Office: U Md Dept Materials and Nuclear College Park MD 20742-2115

SILVERMAN, JOSEPH HILLEL, mathematics educator; b. N.Y.C., Mar. 27, 1955; s. Harry and Shirley (Seiner) S.; m. Susan Leslie Greenhaus, June 13, 1976; children: Deborah, Daniel, Jonathan. ScB, Brown U., 1977; MA, Harvard U., 1979, PhD, 1982. Moore instr. MIT, Cambridge, 1982-86; assoc. prof. Boston U., 1986-88; assoc. prof. math. Brown U., Providence, 1988-91, prof., 1991—. Author: Arithmetic of Elliptic Curves, 1986; editor: Arithmetic Geometry, 1987, Rational Points on Elliptic Curves, 1992, Advanced Topics in Arithmetic of Elliptic Curves, 1995. Fellow NSF, 1983-86, Sloan fellow Sloan Found., 1987. Mem. Am. Math. Soc. Avocation: bridge. Office: Brown U Dept Math PO Box 1917 Providence RI 02912-9079

SILVERMAN, KENNETH EUGENE, English educator, writer; b. N.Y.C., Feb. 5, 1936; s. Gustave and Bessie (Goldberg) S.; children: Willa Zahava, Ethan Leigh. B.A., Columbia U., 1956, M.A., 1958, Ph.D., 1964. Instr. English U. Wyo., Laramie, 1958-59; preceptor in English Columbia U., N.Y.C., 1962-64; prof. English, co-dir. The Biography Seminar NYU, N.Y.C., 1964—; adv. council Inst. Early Am. History and Culture 1984-87. Author: Timothy Dwight, 1969, A Cultural History of the American Revolution, 1976, The Life and Times of Cotton Mather, 1984, Edgar A. Poe: Mournful and Never-ending Remembrance, 1991, Houdini!!! The Career of Ehrich Weiss, 1996; editor: anthology Colonial American Poetry, 1968; compiler: Selected Letters of Cotton Mather, 1976; mem. editorial bd.: Early Am Lit., 1969-72, 77-80, William and Mary Quar., 1984-87, Am. Lit. 1987-90. Recipient Bancroft prize in Am. history, 1985, Pulitzer Prize for biography, 1985, Edgar Allan Poe award Mystery Writers Am., 1992; grantee Bicentennial award NEH, 1972-74, Am. Philos. Soc., 1986, Am. Coun. Learned Socs., 1986; Guggenheim fellow, 1989-90. Mem. MLA (chmn. Early Am. lit. group 1975), Soc. Am. Historians, Am. Antiquarian Soc., PEN Am. Ctr., Authors Guild, Soc. Am. Magicians,. Jewish. Office: NYU Dept English 19 University Pl New York NY 10003-4556

SILVERMAN, LEONARD M., university dean, electrical engineering educator. B.S., Columbia U., 1962, M.S., 1963, Ph.D., 1966. Prof. elec. engring. U. So. Calif., Los Angeles, dean sch. engring. Mem. Nat. Acad. Engring. Office: U So Calif Sch Engring University Pk Los Angeles CA 90089-1450

SILVERMAN, MARCIA, public relations executive; b. Lexington, Ky., Dec. 4, 1943; d. Harry and Rebecca (Green) S.; m. Stephen Regenstreif, Mar. 13, 1977; 1 child, Jacob Anthony. AB in Polit. Sci., U. Pa., 1965, MA in Econs., 1966. Reporter Nat. Jour., Washington, 1969-72; pub. rels. exec. J. Walter Thompson, N.Y.C., 1979-80; pub. rels. exec. Ogilvy, Adams & Rinehart, Washington, 1981-95, pres., 1992-95. Bd. dirs. Washington Internat Sch., 1994-95, Mex. Am. Legal Def. & Edn. Fund, L.A., 1994-95, vice chair, 1997, Women's Campaign Fund, Washington, 1993-94. Recipient Pub. Rels. Star award Inside PR mag. Office: Ogilvy Adams & Rinehart 1901 L St NW Ste 300 Washington DC 20036-3515

SILVERMAN, MARTIN MORRIS BERNARD, secondary education educator; b. Boston, May 27, 1936; s. Joseph Lazarus and Sonya Lillian (Feldman) S.; m. Joseph Harvey. BS in Chemistry, U. Mass., 1960, MEd, 1962; MEd, Columbia U., 1974, EdD, 1985. Math./sci. tchr. Northampton (Mass.) Pub. Schs., 1960-62, U.S. Dept. of Def., Korea and Bermuda, 1963-66; tchr. math, sci. N.Y.C. Bd. Edn., 1966-91; rsch. scholar biophysics NYU,

1986—; biochemistry rsch. asst. Harvard U. Med. Sch., Boston, 1960; supr., dir. various sci. fairs and competitions; cons. in field. Writer, musician, composer and performer; photographer Explorers Jour., U. Mo. Archives collection, Jour. Violin Soc. Am. Recipient scholarship Internat. Ctr. Photography, N.Y.C., 1975. Mem. Violin Soc. Am., Jour. Violin Soc. Am., Nat. Assn. Watch Clock Collectors Assn., Musical Box Soc. Internat., Mensa, Explorers Club. Home: 25 Montgomery St New York NY 10002-6557

SILVERMAN, MARYLIN A., advertising agency executive; b. N.Y.C., Mar. 15, 1941; d. Morris George and Sophie (Betesh) Adler; m. Joseph Elias Silverman, May 30, 1965; children: Lisa, Jennifer. BA, Ind. U.-Bloomington, 1962; student Baruch Grad. Sch. Bus., CUNY, 1963-65. Research analyst Compton Advt., N.Y.C., 1962-63; account research supr. Foote, Cone & Belding, N.Y.C., 1963-68; self-employed market research cons., N.Y.C., 1968-78; research group head Ogilvy & Mather, Inc., N.Y.C., 1978-82; sr. v.p., assoc. research dir. Backer Spielvogel Bates, Inc., N.Y.C., 1982-88, exec. dir. strategic planning and internat. rsch., 1989-91, exec. v.p. strategic planning Bates Worldwide, 1991—; cons. Am. Assn. Advt. Agys., Boys Clubs Am., N.Y.C.; bd. dirs. Women at Risk. Co-author: Marketing Review, 1980, American Demographics, 1990, Marketing Review, 1997. Mem. exec. council Washington Sq. Park Council, 1969-74; mem. exec. bd. Friends Sem. PTA, N.Y.C., 1980-82, Advt. Rsch. Found., Children's Research Council Devel. Com. Mem. Am. Mktg. Assn. (chair Effie awards), Women in Communications, Am. Assn. Advt. Agys. (research com.), Grenwich Ho. Potters and Sculptors Assn. Office: Bates Worldwide 405 Lexington Ave New York NY 10174-0002

SILVERMAN, MELVIN, medical research administrator; b. Montreal, Que., Can., Jan. 4, 1940. BSc, McGill U., 1960, MD, CM, 1964. Rotating intern Montreal Gen. Hosp., 1964-65, resident, 1968-69; resident Bellevue Hosp., N.Y.C., 1965-66; assoc. rsch. scientist dept. medicine NYU, 1966-68; Med. Rsch. Coun. Centennial fellow McGill U. Med. Clinic Montreal Gen. Hosp., 1969-71; asst. prof. dept. medicine McGill U., 1970-71; asst. physician Montreal Gen. Hosp., 1970-71; staff physician nephrology Toronto Gen. Hosp., Ont., Can., 1971-84; asst. prof. to assoc. prof. medicine U. Toronto, 1971-84, assoc. prof. physics, 1975-81, prof. medicine and physics, 1981—; dir. trihosp. Nephrology Svc., Toronto Gen. Hosp., Mt. Sinai Hosp. and women's Coll. Hosp., 1984-90, sr. staff physician, 1990—; dir. MRC Group Membrane Biology, dept. medicine U. Toronto, 1987—, subspecialty tng. program, 1990-91, dir. Inst. Med. Sci., 1991—, dir. MD/PhD program, 1983—; mem. sci. coun. Kidney Found. Can., 1977-85, 94—, Med. Rsch. Coun. Can., 1984-89, 96—, Alta. Heritage Found. Med. Rsch., 1994—. Recipient J. Francis Meml. prize in medicine, 1964, Starr medal, 1974, William Goldie prize, 1975, Trillium award, 1990, Dept. Med. Rsch. award U. Toronto, 1993; numerous grants from various orgns., 1972—. Fellow Royal Coll. Physicians Can.; mem. Am. Soc. Clin. Investigator, Am. Physiol. Soc., Am. Soc. Nephrology, Am. Biophys. Soc., N.Y. Acad. Sci. Office: U Toronto Dept Medicine, Med Sci Bld Rm 7207, Toronto, ON Canada M5S 1A8

SILVERMAN, MERVYN F., health science association administrator, consultant. BS cum laude, Washington and Lee U., 1960; MD, Tulane U., 1964; MPH, Harvard U., 1969. Diplomate Am. Bd. Preventive Medicine. Physician Peace Corps, Thailand, 1965-67; regional med. dir. East Asia and the Pacific Peace Corps, Washington, 1967-68; spl. asst. to commr. FDA, Washington, 1969-70, dir. Office of Consumer Affairs, 1970-72; dir. health Wichita (Kans.)-Sedgwick County Dept. Cmty. Health, 1972-77; med. dir. Planned Parenthood Kans., Wichita, 1976-77; dir. health Dept. Health, San Francisco, 1977-85; health care cons. Mervyn F. Silverman & Assocs., Inc., 1985—; dir. AIDS health svcs. program Robert Wood Johnson Found., 1986-92; nat. spokesperson Am. Found. for AIDS Rsch., 1986-96, pres., also bd. dirs.; resident physician Sta. KPIX-TV, San Francisco, 1979-85; dir., prodr., host weekly health program Sta. KMPX Radio, 1980-82; sr. tech. advisor Acad. Ednl. Devel.-AIDSCOM, 1990-92; advisor to pres. Pan Am. AIDS Found., 1991-93, advisor to mayor of San Juan, Puerto Rico, 1991-93; former med. advisor to bd. dirs. Golden Gate chpt. ARC, San Francisco; past vice chmn. Adv. Health Coun., State of Calif.; former assoc. clin. prof. Wichita State U.; former assoc. clin. prof. U. Hawaii; former adj. assoc. prof. Sch. Pub. Health and Tropical Medicine Tulane U.; former adj. prof. Inst. Health Policy Studies, Sch. Medicine, U. Calif., San Francisco; former mem. nat. adv. coun. Harvard AIDS Inst.; spkr., presenter in field. Author: (with others) Humanistic Perspectives in Medical Ethics, 1972, What to Do About AIDS, 1986, AIDS and Patient Management: Legal, Ethical and Social Issues, 1986, AIDS: Facts and Issues, 1986, AIDS in Children, Adolescents and Heterosexual Adults: An Interdisciplinary Approach to Prevention, 1988, others; contbg. and consulting editor Modern Medicine Publs., Mpls., 1970-75; contbg. editor Healthline, 1983-85; contbr. articles to profl. jours. Bd. dirs., vice-chmn. U.S.-China Ednl. Inst. Recipient Award for Courageous Leadership, San Francisco Found., Award of Excellence, KAIROS Support for Care Givers, Civic Achievement award Bay Area Non-Partisan Alliance; Wear Found. fellow Wichita State U.; adj. scholar Kans. Newman Coll. Mem. APHA, AMA, Omicron Delta Kappa, Delta Omega. Address: 119 Frederick St San Francisco CA 94117-4046

SILVERMAN, MICHAEL, manufacturing company executive; b. Poland, May 9, 1913; arrived in U.S., 1920; m. Frances Setnor, Aug. 26, 1945; children: Leslie, Evan. Cutting rm. mgr. Rockland (Mass) Sportswear, 1938-58; owner Garmet Cutting Svc., Brockton, Mass., 1958-70; cons. Boston, 1970-73; cutting rm. mgr. Recent Mfg., Miami, 1973-85. Author: The New Breakthrough in Plaid Cutting, 1990, Marker Making Manual, 1955; inventor plaid matching device. Avocations: playing in poker tournament, gag writing (New Yorker, Jay Leno show).

SILVERMAN, MOSES, lawyer; b. Bklyn., Mar. 3, 1948; s. Bernard and Anne Silverman; m. Betty B. Robbins, Jan. 19, 1980; children: Benjamin, Rachel. AB, Colby Coll., 1969; JD, NYU, 1973. Bar: N.Y. 1974, U.S. Dist. Ct. (so. and ea. dists.) N.Y. 1974, U.S. Ct. Appeals (2d cir.) 1974, U.S. Ct. Appeals (D.C. cir.) 1977, U.S. Supreme Ct. 1977, D.C. 1982, U.S. Ct. Appeals (fed. cir.) 1985, U.S. Ct. Appeals (11th cir.), 1986 . Assoc. Paul, Weiss, Rifkind, Wharton & Garrison, N.Y.C., 1973-81, ptnr., 1981—. Vol. U.S. Peace Corps., Istanbul, Turkey, 1969-70. Mem. ABA, Assn. of Bar of City of N.Y. Home: 7 Gracie Square New York NY 10028 Office: Paul Weiss Rifkind Wharton & Garrison 1285 Avenue Of The Americas New York NY 10019-6028

SILVERMAN, NORMAN ALAN, cardiac surgeon; b. Boston, Dec. 19, 1946. BA, Dartmouth Coll., 1968; MD, Boston U., 1971. Prof. surgery U. Ill., Chgo., 1980-89; divsn. head Henry Ford Hosp., Detroit, 1989—; prof. surgery Case-Western Res. U., Cleve., 1992—. Contbr. 200 scientific articles to profl. jours. Lt. comdr. USPHS, 1973-75. Fellow Am. Coll. Surgeons, Am. coll. Cardiology, Am. Coll. Chest Physicians. Avocation: sailing. Office: Henry Ford Hosp 2799 W Grand Blvd Detroit MI 48202-2608

SILVERMAN, OZZIE, Canadian government official; b. Montreal, Que., Can., Jan. 30, 1939; s. Louis and Fanny (Black) S.; m. Sheela Marsha Zangwill, Aug. 22, 1962; children: Caroline, Marjorie. BSME, McGill U., Montreal, Que., 1963, diploma in mgmt., 1968, MBA, 1969. Cert. Que. Order of Engrs. Supr. quality control engring. United Aircraft, Montreal, 1964-68, sr. mktg. rschr., 1969-70; asst. chief internat. Dept. Industry, Trade and Commerce, Ottawa, Ont., Can., 1972-77; dir. industry projects Ministry of State for Sci. and Tech., Ottawa, 1978-85; dir. strategic techs. planning Industry, Sci. and Tech. Can., Ottawa, 1986-91; dir. gen. sci. strategy Industry Can., Ottawa, 1992—; chmn. com. for sci. and tech. policy Orgn. for Econ. Coop. and Devel., Paris, 1995—. Avocations: Inuit and Japanese graphic art. Home: 112 Pigeon Terr, Ottawa, ON Canada K1V 9H7 Office: Industry Can, 235 Queen St, Ottawa, ON Canada K1A 0H5

SILVERMAN, PAUL HYMAN, parasitologist, former university official; b. Mpls., Oct. 8, 1924; s. Adolph and Libbie (Idlekope) S.; m. Nancy Josephs, May 20, 1945; children: Daniel Joseph, Claire. Student, U. Minn., 1942-43, 46-47; BS, Roosevelt U., 1949; MS in Biology, Northwestern U., 1951; PhD in Parasitology, U. Liverpool, Eng., 1955, DSc, 1968. Rsch. fellow Malaria Rsch. Sta., Hebrew U., Israel, 1951-53; rsch. fellow dept. entomology and parasitology Sch. Tropical Medicine, U. Liverpool, 1953-56; sr. sci. officer dept. parasitology Moredun Inst., Edinburgh, Scotland, 1956-59; head dept. immunoparasitology Glaxo, Allen & Hanbury, Ltd., Ware, Eng., 1960-62; prof. zoology and vet. pathology and hygiene U. Ill., Urbana, 1963-72, chmn., head dept. zoology, 1963-68; prof., chmn. dept. biology, v.p. for rsch. U. N.Mex., 1972-77; provost, rsch. and grad. studies Ctrl. Adminstrn. SUNY, Albany, 1977-79, pres. Rsch. Found., 1979-80; pres. U. Maine, Orono, 1980-84; fellow biol. divsn. Lawrence Berkeley Lab. U. Calif., Berkeley, 1984-86; head biomed. divsn. Lawrence Berkeley Lab. Lawrence Berkeley Lab., Berkeley, 1986-87; adj. prof. med. parasitology Sch. Pub. Health U. Calif., Berkeley, 1986, assoc. lab. dir. for life scis., dir Donner Lab., 1987-90, dir. systemwide biotech. rsch. and edn. program, 1989-90; dir. Beckman's Scientific Affairs, Fullerton, Calif., 1990-93; assoc. chancellor Ctr. for Health Scis., adj. prof. medicine U. Calif., Irvine, 1993-96; exec. assoc. AAAS, Irvine, Calif., 1997—; dir. Western Ctr., Am. Acad. Arts and Scis., 1997—; cons., Commn. Colls. and Univs., North Central Assn. Colls. and Secondary Schs., 1964—; chmn. Commn. on Instns. Higher Edn., 1974-76; Fulbright prof. zoology Australian Nat. U., Canberra, 1969; adjoint prof. biology U. Colo., Boulder, 1970-72; mem. bd. Nat. Council on Postsecondary Accreditation, Washington, 1975-77; dir. research in malaria immunology and vaccination US AID, 1965-76; bd. dirs. Inhalation Toxicology Research Inst., Lovelace Biomed. and Environ. Research Inst., Albuquerque, 1977-84; mem. N.Y. State Gov.'s High Tech. Opportunities Task Force; chmn. research and rev. com. N.Y. State Sci. and Tech. Found.; mem. pres.'s council New Eng. Land Grant Univs.; bd. advs. Lovelace-Bataan Med. Center, Albuquerque, 1974-77; adv. com. U.S. Army Command and Gen. Staff Coll., Ft. Leavenworth, Kans., 1983-84. Contbr. articles to profl. jours. Chmn. rsch. rev. com. N.Y. State Sci. and Tech. Found. Fellow Meridian Internat. Inst., 1992; assoc. The Hastings Ctr., 1995—. Fellow Royal Soc. Tropical Medicine and Hygiene, N.Mex. Acad. Sci.; mem. AAAS, Am. Soc. Parasitologists, Am. Soc. Tropical Medicine and Hygiene, Am. Soc. Immunologists, Brit. Soc. Parasitology (coun.), Brit. Soc. Immunologists, Soc. Gen. Microbiology, Soc. Protozoologists, Am. Soc. Zoologists, Human Genome Orgn., Am. Inst. Biol. Scis., N.Y. Acad. Scis., N.Y. Soc. Tropical Medicine, World Acad. Art and Sci., B'nai B'rith, Sigma Xi, Phi Kappa Phi. Office: Am Acad Arts and Scis 3000 Berkeley Pl Irvine CA 92697-7425

SILVERMAN, PERRY RAYNARD, lawyer, consultant; b. N.Y.C., Nov. 5, 1950; s. Harry and Mary Sheila (Diamond) S.; m. Ruth Klarin, Oct. 7, 1979; children: Aaron, Rachel. BA, SUNY, Albany, 1971; JD, Boston U., 1974; MA, Ohio State U., 1981. Bar: N.Y. 1975, Ohio 1976, U.S. Dist. Ct. (so. dist.) Ohio 1977, U.S. Dist. Ct. (no. ist.) Ohio 1978, U.S. Ct. Claims 1977, U.S. Supreme Ct. 1978. Rsch. assoc. Polimetrics Lab. Ohio State U., Columbus, 1974-75, rsch. assoc. Behavioral Scis. Lab., 1974-76; asst. atty. gen. Ohio Atty. Gen.'s Office, Columbus, 1976-84; prin. Perry R. Silverman Co., LPA, Columbus, 1984—; spl. counsel Atty. Gen. of Ohio, 1984-95; adj. prof. Capital U., Columbus, 1978, 82; cons. Survey Rsch. Assocs., Columbus, 1975-77. Trustee, Congregatoin Beth Tikvah, Worthington, Ohio, 1992-94. Mem. ATLA, Ohio State Bar Assn., Columbus Bar Assn., Ohio Assn. Trial Lawyers, Nat. Assn. Retail Collection Agys. (v.p. 1995—). Office: Perry R Silverman Co LPA 8351 N High St Columbus OH 43235-1440

SILVERMAN, RICHARD BRUCE, chemist, biochemist, educator; b. Phila., May 12, 1946; s. Philip and S. Ruth (Simon) S.; m. Barbara Jean Kesner, Jan. 9, 1983; children: Matthew, Margaret, Philip. BS, Pa. State U., 1968; MA, Harvard U., 1972, PhD, 1974. Postdoctoral fellow Brandeis U., Waltham, Mass., 1974-76; asst. prof. Northwestern U., Evanston, Ill., 1976-82, assoc. prof., 1982-86, prof., 1986—, Arthur Andersen Tchg. and rsch. prof., 1996—, mem. Inst. for Neurosci., 1990—; cons. Procter and Gamble Co., Cin., 1984, Abbott Labs, North Chicago, 1987, Searle R&D, St. Louis, 1988-90, DuPont, 1991, Dow, 1991, Leytig, Voit & Mayer law offices, 1992—, DowElanco, 1993-95, G.D. Searle, 1995, Affymax, 1995; mem. adv. panel NIH, Bethesda, Md., 1981, 83, 85, 87-91; expert analyst CHEMTRACTS. Mem. editorial bd. Jour. Enzyme Inhibition, 1988—, Archivies Biochemistry and Biophysics, 1993—, Jour. Medicinal Chemistry, 1995—, Archiv der Pharmazie-Pharmaceutical and Medicinal Chemistry, 1995—; contbr. articles to profl. jours.; patentee in field. Served with U.S. Army, 1969-71. Mem. adv. bd. Ill. Math. and Sci. Acad., 1988. Recipient Career Devel. award USPHS, 1982-87; DuPont Young Faculty fellow, 1976, Alfred P. Sloan Found. fellow, 1981-85; grantee various govt. and pvt. insts., 1976—. Fellow AAAS, Am. Inst. Chemists; mem. Am. Chem. Soc. (nat. elected nominating com. div. biol. chemistry, treas. divsn. biol. chemistry 1993—), Am. Soc. Biochem. Molecular Biology. Avocations: tennis, family interactions. Office: Northwestern U Dept Chemistry 2145 Sheridan Rd Evanston IL 60208-0834

SILVERMAN, ROBERT JOSEPH, lawyer; b. Mpls., Apr. 4, 1942; s. Maurice and Toby (Goldstein) S.; 1 child, Adam Graham-Silverman; m. Suzanne M. Brown; 1 child, Thomas B. BA, U. Minn., 1964, JD, 1967. Bar: Minn. 1967. Assoc. Dorsey & Whitney, Mpls., 1967-72, ptnr., 1972—; lectr. William Mitchell Coll. Law, St. Paul, 1977-78, Hamline Law Sch., St. Paul, 1990—, Minn. Continuing Legal Edn., Mpls, 1985—. Bd. dirs. Courage Ctr., Golden Valley, Minn., 1978-84, 85-95, v.p., 1983-86, pres., 1988-89. With USAR, 1967-73. Mem. ABA, Minn. Bar Assn., Hennepin County Bar Assn. Jewish. Office: Dorsey & Whitney 220 S 6th St Minneapolis MN 55402-4502

SILVERMAN, SAMUEL JOSHUA, lawyer; b. Odessa, Russia, Sept. 25, 1908; came to U.S., 1913; s. Benjamin and Ida (Kagarlitzky) S.; m. Claire Gfroerer, Aug. 21, 1941. Student, NYU, 1925; A.B., Columbia U., 1928, LL.B., 1930. Bar: N.Y. With firm Gilman & Unger, 1930-32, Engelhard, Pollak, Pitcher, Stern & Clarke, 1932-35; asst. corp. counsel N.Y.C., 1938-40; partner firm Paul, Weiss, Rifkind, Wharton & Garrison, N.Y.C., 1946-62; of counsel Paul, Weiss, Rifkind, Wharton & Garrison, 1985—; assoc. justice N.Y. Supreme Ct., 1963-66, 71-75; surrogate N.Y. County, 1967-70; assoc. justice appellate div. N.Y. Supreme Ct., 1976-84, spl. master appellate div., 1st dept., 1985-90, mem., spl. counsel, disciplinary com. 1st judicial dept., 1986—, chmn. and chmn. emeritus adv. com. on judicial ethics, 1987—; lectr. Nat. Coll. State Trial Judges, Boulder, Colo., 1966. Bd. dirs. Univ. Settlement, N.Y.C., 1960-74. Fellow Am. Coll. Trial Lawyers; mem. ABA, Assn. Bar City N.Y., Am. Law Inst. Democrat. Home: 210 E 68th St New York NY 10021-6047 Office: 1285 Avenue Of The Americas New York NY 10019-6028

SILVERMAN, STANLEY WAYNE, chemical company executive; b. Phila., June 18, 1947; s. Sidney and Ruth (Epstein) S.; m. Ellen J. Seligsohn, June 10, 1970; children: Robert, Eric. BSChemE, Drexel U., 1969, MBA, 1974; AMP, Harvard U., 1989. Process engr. Atlantic Richfield Co., Phila., 1969-71, PQ Corp., Phila., 1971-74; mgr. oper. planning PQ Corp., Valley Forge, Pa., 1974-76, product mgr., 1976-80, mktg. mgr., 1980-82; nat. sales mgr. PQ Corp., Valley Forge, 1982-84; pres. Nat. Silicates Ltd. subs. PQ Corp., Toronto, Ont., Can., 1984-87; pres. ind. chem. group PQ Corp., Valley Forge, 1987-90, exec. v.p., chief oper. officer, 1990—. Mem. Drexel U. Coll. Engring. Adv. Coun. Avocations: sailing, jogging, polit. sci. Office: PQ Corp 1200 W Swedesford Rd Berwyn PA 19312-1078

SILVERMAN, STEPHEN MEREDITH, journalist, screenwriter, producer; b. L.A., Nov. 22, 1951; s. Raymond and Shirley (Garfein) S. BA, U. Calif., Irvine, 1973; MS, Columbia U., 1975. Editor-in-chief Coast Mag., L.A., 1975-77; chief entertainment writer N.Y. Post, 1977-88; film critic New Woman Mag., 1986-88; editor-in-chief Hollywood Mag., L.A., 1989-90; writer People Mag., 1996; editor People Daily Online, 1996—; adj. prof. Hunter Coll., N.Y.C., 1978, Marymount Manhattan, 1979, Columbia U., 1995—; juror Internat. film festivals, Berlin, Edinburgh, 1991. Author: Public Spectacles, 1981, The Fox That Got Away: The Last Days of the Zanuck Dynasty, 1988, David Lean, 1989, Where There's A Will: Who Inherited What and Why, 1991, Dancing on the Ceiling: Stanley Donen and His Movies, 1996, The Last Remaining Seats: The Movie Palaces of Tinsel Town, 1997; TV scriptwriter: Hot On the Trail: The Search for Love, Sex and Romance in the Old West and the New, TBS, 1993. Named Disting. Alumnus of Yr., U. Calif., Irvine, 1997. Avocation: global exploring. Office: People Mag 1271 Avenue Of The Americas New York NY 10020-1300

SILVERMAN, SYDEL FINFER, anthropologist; b. Chgo., May 20, 1933; d. Joseph and Elizabeth (Bassman) Finfer; m. Mel Silverman, Dec. 27, 1953 (wid. Sept. 1966); children: Eve Rachel, Julie Beth; m. Eric R. Wolf, Mar. 18, 1972. MA, U. Chgo., 1957; PhD, Columbia U., 1963. From lectr. to prof. anthropology Queens Coll., CUNY, Flushing, 1963-75; prof., exec. officer PhD program anthropology Grad. Sch. CUNY, N.Y.C., 1975-86, acting dean of Grad. Sch., 1982-83; pres. Wenner-Gren Found. for Anthropol. Rsch., N.Y.C., 1987—; bd. dirs. Social Sci. Rsch. Coun., N.Y.C., 1984-87. Author: Three Bells of Civilization, 1975; editor: Totems and Teachers, 1981, Inquiry and Debate in the Human Sciences, 1992, Preserving the Anthropological Record, 1995; contbr. articles to profl. jours. Recipient fellowship Am. Coun. Learned Socs., 1986, NEH, 1973-74, NIH, 1960-63, NSF, 1959; grantee Am. Phil. Soc., 1985. Jewish. Office: Wenner-Gren Found 220 5th Ave New York NY 10001-7708

SILVERMAN, WILLIAM A., public relations executive; b. Toledo, Mar. 27, 1930. BA in English, Ctr. Coll. Ky., 1953; cert. in Spanish Studies, U. Madrid, 1957. Reporter Cleve. News, 1948-58, United Press, Madrid, 1948-58; mgr. pub. rels. Reynolds Metals Co., 1958-61; dir. pub. rels. Fuller, Smith & Ross, 1961-65; v.p. Edward Howard & Co., 1965-68; pres. William Silverman & Co., 1968-73, 1980-93, chmn. bd. dirs.; chmn. Carter, Silverman & Assocs., 1973-80. Mem. Pub. Rels. Soc. Am., Cleve. City Club. Office: 1414 Statler Office Towers Cleveland OH 44115

SILVERMAN-DRESNER, TOBY ROSLYN, psychologist, educator; b. Bklyn., Feb. 24, 1941; d. Harry and Sylvia Silverman; B.A., Bklyn. Coll., 1961; M.A., Columbia U., 1962; Ph.D., N.Y.U., 1967; m. Israel Desner, Aug. 5, 1968; children: Avi, Tamar. Tchr.-in-tng., student tchr. Lexington Sch. Deaf, N.Y.C., 1960-64; tchr. slow learners Gilbert Sch., Bklyn., 1961; speech therapist Bklyn. Hebrew Home and Hosp. for Aged, 1963; biometrics researcher Columbia Psychiat. Inst.-Bklyn. State Hosp., 1963-64; research psychologist Lexington Sch. for Deaf, 1964-73; prin. investigator Deafness Research and Tng. Center, N.Y.U., 1972; assoc. prof. psychology William Paterson Coll., Wayne, N.J., 1975—; Mem. Am. Psychol. Assn., Am. Ednl. Research Assn., Council Exceptional Children, A.G. Bell Assn. for Deaf, Eastern Psychol. Assn., N.J. Psychol. Assn. Jewish. Author papers in field. Home: PO Box 1611 Hemlock Farms Hawley PA 18428 Office: William Patterson Coll 300 Pompton Rd Wayne NJ 07470-2103

SILVERN, LEONARD CHARLES, retired engineering executive; b. N.Y.C., May 20, 1919; s. Ralph and Augusta (Thaler) S.; m. Gloria Marantz, June 1948 (div. Jan. 1968); 1 child, Ronald; m. Elisabeth Beeny, Aug. 1969 (div. Oct. 1972); m. Gwen Taylor, Nov. 1985. BS in Physics, L.I. U., 1946; MA, Columbia U., 1948, EdD, 1952. Registered profl. consulting engr., Calif. Tng. supr. U.S. Dept. Navy, N.Y.C., 1939-49; tng. dir. exec. dept. N.Y. Div. Safety, Albany, 1949-55; resident engring. psychologist Lincoln Lab. MIT for Rand Corp., Lexington, 1955-56; engr., dir. edn., tng., rsch. labs. Hughes Aircraft Co., Culver City, Calif., 1956-62; dir. human performance engring. lab., cons. engring. psychologist to v.p. tech. Northrop Norair, Hawthorne, Calif., 1962-64; prin. sci., v.p., pres. Edn. and Tng. Cons. Co., L.A., 1964-96, Sedona, Ariz., 1980, pres. Systems Engring. Labs. div., 1980-96; cons. hdqrs. Air Tng. Command USAF, Randolph AFB, Tex., 1964-68, Electronic Industries Assn., Washington, 1963-69, Edn. R and D Ctr., U. Hawaii, 1970-74, Ctr. Vocat. and Tech. Edn., Ohio State U., 1972-73, Coun. for Exceptional Children, 1973-74, Canadore Coll. Applied Arts and Tech., Ont., Can., 1974-76, Centro Nacional de Productividad, Mexico City, 1973-75, N.S. Dept. Edn., Halifax, 1975-79, Aeronutronic Ford-Ford Motor Co., 1975-76, Nat. Tng. Systems Inc., 1976-81, Nfld. Pub. Svc. Commn., 1978, Legis. Affairs Office USDA, 1980, Rocky Point Techs., 1986; adj. prof. edn., pub. adminstrn. U. So. Calif. Grad. Sch., 1957-65; vis. prof. computer scis. U. Calif. Extension Div., L.A., 1963-72. Dist. ops. officer, disaster communications svc. L.A. County Sheriff's Dept., 1973-75, dist. communications officer, 1975-76; bd. dirs. SEARCH, 1976—; mem. adv. com. West Sedona Community Plan of Yavapai County, 1986-88; councilman City of Sedona, 1988-92; rep. COCOPAI, 1988-89; vol. earth team Soil Conservation Svc., U.S. Dept Agr., 1989-92; Verde Resource Assn., 1988-90, Group on Water Logistics, 1989-90; chair publs. com. Ariz. Rural Recycling Conf., 1990. With USN, 1944-46. Mem. IEEE (sr.), APA, Am. Radio Relay League (life), Nat. Solid Waste Mgmt. Symposium (chmn. publs. com. 1988-89), Ariz. Rural Recycling Conf. (chair publs. com. 1990), Friendship Vets. Fire Engine Co. (hon.), Soc. Wireless Pioneers (life), Quarter Century Wireless Assn. (life), Sierra Club (treas. Sedona-Verde Valley Group 1991-93), Assn. Bldg. Coms., Vox Pop (chmn. bd. dirs. Sedona, 1983-93, dir. 1993-95), Nat. Parks and Conservation Assn., Wilderness Soc., Ariz. Ctr. Law in Pub. Interest, Old Old Timers Club. Contbg. editor Ednl. Tech., 1968-73, 81-85; reviewer ACM Computing Revs., 1962-92, 96—. Contbr. numerous articles to profl. jours. Office: PO Box 2085 Sedona AZ 86339-2085

SILVERS, EILEEN S., lawyer; b. N.Y.C., Sept. 21, 1948; d. Sidney and Ethel Lynne (Starobin) Swertloff; m. Richard J. Bronstein; children: Steven Jay, Sharron Roth. BA magna cum laude, SUNY-Buffalo, 1970; JD, Columbia U., 1975. Bar: N.Y. 1977, U.S. Tax Ct. 1981, U.S. Ct. Claims 1983, D.C., 1984. Assoc., Paul, Weiss, Rifkind, Wharton & Garrison, N.Y.C., 1975-83, ptnr., 1983-94; v.p. taxes Bristol-Myers Squibb Co., N.Y.C., 1994—; mem. tax com. Nat. Fgn. Trade Coun. (steering com.); tax subcom. PhRMA; exec. com. PRUSA. Mem. ABA (tax sect.), N.Y. State Bar Assn. (chmn. persona l income com. tax sect. 1983-85 , exec. com. 1982-85, 1990-91), Internat. Fiscal Assn., Tax Execs. Inst. Home: 20 Mountain Peak Rd Chappaqua NY 10514-2110 Office: Bristol-Myers Squibb Co 345 Park Ave New York NY 10154-0004

SILVERS, GERALD THOMAS, publishing executive; b. Cin., Aug. 26, 1937; s. Steve Allen and Tina Mae (Roberts) S.; m. Ann Gregory Woodward, July 25, 1964. BA, U. Ky., 1960. Asst. research svcs. mgr. Cin. Enquirer, 1963-72, research svcs. dir., 1972-74, research dir., 1974-90, v.p. mktg. svcs., 1990-94, v.p. market devel., 1994—. Mem. Ky. Devel. Coun., Lexington, 1986—; trustee Neediest Kids of All, 1991—. 1st lt. U.S. Army, 1960-62. Recipient Thomas H. Copeland award of merit, 1991. Mem. U. Ky. Alumni Assn. Cin. Chpt. (pres. 1985), Newspaper Research Council (pres. 1985,86), Internat. Newspaper Market Assn., Am. Mktg. Assn. Presbyterian. Home: 229 Watch Hill Rd Fort Mitchell KY 41011-1822 Office: Cin Enquirer 312 Elm St Cincinnati OH 45202-2739

SILVERS, ROBERT BENJAMIN, editor; b. Mineola, N.Y., Dec. 31, 1929; s. James J. and Rose (Roden) S. A.B., U. Chgo., 1947; grad., Ecole des Sci. Politiques, Paris, France, 1956. Press sec. to Gov. Bowles of Conn., 1950; mem. editorial bd. Paris Rev., 1954—; assoc. editor Harper's mag., 1959-63; co-founder, co-editor N.Y. Rev. Books, 1963—. Editor: Writing in America, 1960, Hidden Histories of Science, 1995; co-editor: The First Anthology: 30 Years of The New York Review of Books 1963-93; translator: La Gangrene, 1961; mem. editorial com. Rivista dei Libri, Italy, 1991—. Bd. dirs. Am. Ditchley Found., 1993—. With AUS, 1952-53. Named Chevalier de l'Ordre Nat. du Merite, France, 1988—. Mem. Coun. Fgn. Rels., Am. Acad. Arts and Scis., Century Assn. Club (N.Y.C.), Coffee House Club (N.Y.C.). Office: NY Rev of Books 1755 Broadway Fl 5 New York NY 10019-3743

SILVERS, SALLY, choreographer, performing company executive; b. Greeneville, Tenn., June 19, 1952; d. Herbert Ralston and Sara Elizabeth (Buchanan) S.; life ptnr. Bruce Erroll Andrews. BA in Dance and Polit. Sci., Antioch Coll., 1975. Artistic dir. Sally Silvers & Dancers, N.Y.C., 1980—; mem. faculty Leicester Poly., 1986, 87, 89, summer choreography project Bennington Coll., 1988-92, Chisenhale Dance Space, London, 1989, 91, Am. Dance Festival, Durham, N.C., 1990, 92; guest tchr. European Dance Devel. Ctr., Arnhem, The Netherlands, 1992—. Choreographer: Politics of the Body Microscope of Conduct, 1980, Social Movement, 1981, Connective Tissue, 1981, Less Time You Know Praxis, 1981, Don't No Do And This, 1981, Lack of Entrepreneurial Thrift, 1982, Celluloid Sally and Mr. E, 1982, Mutate, 1982, Being Red Enough, 1982, Disgusting, 1982, Bedtime at the Reformatory, 1982, Eat the Rich, 1982, They Can't Get It in the Shopping Cart, 1982, Blazing Forceps, 1982, And Find Out Why, 1983, Tips for Totalizers, 1983, Choose Your Weapons, 1984, And Find Out Why, 1984, Extend the Wish for Entire, 1985, No Best Better Way, 1985, Every All Which is Not Us, 1986, Swaps Ego Say So, 1986, Be Careful Now, You Know Sugar Melts in Water, 1987, Fact Confected, 1987, Both, Both, 1987, Tizzy Boost, 1988, Moebius, 1988, Whatever Ever, 1989, Get Tough, Sports and Divertissement, 1989, Flap, 1989, Swan's Crayon, 1989, Fanfare Tripwire, 1990, Harry Meets Sally, 1990, Along the Skid Mark of Recorded History, 1990, Matinee Double-You, 1991, Grand Guignol, 1991, Dash Dash Slang Plural Plus, 1992, The Bubble Cut, 1992, Vigilant Corsage, 1992, Oops

Fact, 1992, Small Room, 1993, Exwhyzee, 1993, Elegy, 1993, Now That It Is Now, 1994, Give Em Enough Rope, 1994, Swoon Noir, 1994, Radio Rouge, 1995, Braceletizing, 1995, Hush Comet, 1995, Bite the Pillow, 1995, Pandora's Cake Stain, 1996, Secrets Of, 1997, and others; filmmaker: Little Lieutenant, 1993 (Silver award), N.Y. Dance on Camera Festival, Mechanics of the Brain, 1997; co-author: Resurgant New Writings By Women, 1992; contbr. articles to profl. jours. Grantee Nat. Endowment Arts, 1987, 89, 90, 91, Jerome Found., 1993, Meet the Composer N.Y. Found. for the Arts, 1995, 96; Guggenheim Found. fellow, 1988. Mem. Segue Found. (bd. dirs. Segue Performance Space 1992—). Avocations: reading, writing, art events, costume design. Home: 303 E 8th St Apt 4F New York NY 10009-5212

SILVERS, WILLYS KENT, geneticist; b. N.Y.C., Jan. 12, 1929; s. Lewis Julian and Miriam Elizabeth (Rosenzweig) S.; m. Abigail M. Adams, Sept. 29, 1956; children: Deborah Elizabeth, Willys Kent. BA, Johns Hopkins U., 1950; PhD, U. Chgo., 1954. Assoc. staff scientist Jackson Lab., Bar Harbor, Maine, 1956-57; assoc. mem. Wistar Inst., Phila., 1957-65; mem. faculty U. Pa. Med. Sch., 1965—, prof. genetics, 1967—; mem. allergy and immunology study sect. NIH, 1962-66, adv. bd. primate rsch. ctrs., 1968-71, com. cancer immunobiology Nat. Cancer Inst., 1974-78, bd. sci. overseers Jackson Lab., Bar Harbor, 1980-89. Author: The Immunobiology of Transplantation, 1971, The Coat Colors of Mice: A Model for Mammalian Gene Action and Interaction, 1979; mem. editorial bd. Transplantation, 1963-71, Jour. Exptl. Zoology, 1965-70, 81-86, Jour. Immunology, 1973-77, Jour. Reticuloendothelial Soc., 1974-77; contbr. articles to profl. jours. Mem. Am. Genetic Assn. (coun. 1980-83, pres. 1983). Home: 210 Millcreek Rd Ardmore PA 19003-1506 Office: U Pa Dept Genetics Sch Medicine Philadelphia PA 19104

SILVERSTEIN, ARTHUR MATTHEW, ophthalmic immunologist, educator, historian; b. N.Y.C., Aug. 6, 1928; s. Sol and Beatrice (Pearl) S.; m. Frances Swimmer, 1950; children—Alison, Mark, Judith. A.B., Ohio State U., 1948, M.Sc., 1951; Ph.D., Rensselaer Poly. Inst., 1954; D.Sc. (hon.), U. Granada, Spain, 1986. Research asst. Sloan Kettering Inst., N.Y.C., 1948-49; biochemist N.Y. Health Research Lab., N.Y.C., 1949-52; sr. biochemist N.Y. Health Research Lab., Albany, 1952-54; chief immunobiology Armed Forces Inst. Pathology, Washington, 1956-64; assoc. prof. Johns Hopkins Sch. Medicine, Balt., 1964-67; prof. Johns Hopkins Sch. Medicine, 1967-89, prof. emeritus, 1989—; cons. NIH, 1963-77. Author: Pure Politics and Impure Science: The Swine Flu Affair, 1981, A History of Immunology, 1989; mem. editorial bd. various sci. jours.; contbr. articles to profl. jours. Served to 1st lt. U.S. Army, 1954-56. Recipient Doyne Meml. medal Oxford Ophthal. Congress, Eng., 1974, Endowed Professorship Ind. Order Odd Fellows, 1964-89; Congl. Sci. fellow Fedn. Am. Socs. Exptl. Biology, 1975-76. Mem. AAAS, Am. Assn. Immunologists, Brit. Soc. Immunology, Assn. Research in Vision and Ophthalmology (trustee 1984-87, pres. 1988), Phi Beta Kappa, Sigma Xi. Home: 2011 Skyline Rd Baltimore MD 21204-6442 Office: Johns Hopkins Inst History Medicine 1900 E Monument St Baltimore MD 21205-2113

SILVERSTEIN, BARBARA ANN, conductor, artistic director; b. Phila., July 24, 1947; d. Charles and Selma (Brenner) S.; m. Bernard J. Taylor II, Aug. 19, 1978. Student Bennington Coll., 1965-67; B.Mus., Phila. Coll. Performing Arts, 1970. Assoc. music dir. Suburban Opera Co., Chester, Pa., 1967-75; asst. condr. Toledo Opera Assn., 1975-76; asst. condr., coach Curtis Inst. Music, Phila., 1973-77; asst. condr. Phila. Lyric Opera, 1971-74, Des Moines Opera Festival, Indianola, Iowa, 1974-78; music dir., condr. Savoy Co., Phila., 1977-80, Miss. Opera, Jackson, 1979-82; artistic dir., condr. Pa. Opera Theater, Phila., 1976-93; guest condr. Anchorage Opera, 1982, Opera Del., Wilmington, 1981, 83, Utah Festival Opera Co., 1993-96, Lyric Opera of Kansas City, 1995—. Recipient Alumni award U. of Arts, 1989, Wash. H.S., 1991, Greater Phila. Mem. Am. Fedn. Musicians, Music Fund Soc., Pa. Council on the Arts (adv. panel 1987-90) OPERA Am. (bd. dirs. 1987-93, exec. com. 1988-93) . Jewish. Avocations: scuba diving; reading.

SILVERSTEIN, JOSEPH HARRY, musician; b. Detroit, Mar. 21, 1932; s. Bernard and Ida (Katz) S.; m. Adrienne Shufro, Apr. 27; children—Bernice, Deborah, Marc. Student Curtis Inst. Music, 1945-50; hon. doctoral degrees Tufts U., 1971, Rhode Island U., 1980, Boston Coll., 1981, New Eng. Conservatory, 1986, Susquehanna. Violinist, Houston Symphony Orch., Phila. Orch.; concertmaster Denver Symphony Orch., Boston Symphony Orch.; formerly chmn. string dept. New Eng. Conservatory Music; also chmn. faculty Berkshire Music Sch.; mem. faculty Boston U. Sch. Music, Yale U. Sch. Music; music dir. Boston Symphony Chamber Players, Boston U. Symphony Orch., Chautauqua (N.Y.) Instn., 1987—; interim music dir. Toledo Symphony Orch.; prin. guest condr. Balt. Symphony Orch., 1981; condr. Utah Symphony, music dir., 1983—; mus. dir. Worcester Orch., Mass., until 1987. Recipient Silver medal Queen Elizabeth of Belgium Internat. contest, 1959, Naumberg found. award, 1960; named one of ten outstanding young men, Boston C. of C., 1962. Fellow Am. Acad. Arts and Scis. Office: care Utah Symphony Orch 123 W South Temple Salt Lake City UT 84101-1403*

SILVERSTEIN, LOUIS, art director, designer, editor; b. Bklyn., Oct. 10, 1919; s. Hyman and Yetta (Brodsky) S.; m. Helen Abby Becker, May 23, 1951; children: Jamie Richard (dec.), Anne Leith. B.F.A., Pratt Inst., Bkyln., 1940; M.A. credit, Inst. of Design, Chgo., 1948-50. Art. dir. Denhard & Stewart Advt., N.Y.C., 1942-43, 46-47; art. dir. Amerika (Russian lang. mag. distbn. USSR), Dept. State Publs., N.Y.C., 1947-48; promotion art dir. N.Y. Times, N.Y.C., 1952-67, corporate art dir., 1967-85, asst. mng. editor, 1969-85; cons. art director N.Y.C., 1985—; designer, cons. various newspapers, mags., U.S. and fgn. lectr. Am. Press Inst., Reston, Va., 1978-85; tchr. Sch. Visual Arts, N.Y.C., 1958-59; lectr. in field; bd. dirs. Am. Inst. Graphic Arts, N.Y.C., 1958-59, Soc. Publ. Designers, 1976-78; cons. Toronto Star, 1988—; founder Louis Silverstein Design Assn.; lectr. Ctr. Ind. Journalism, Prague, Czechoslovakia, 1991. Co-author: America's Taste, 1961; editor, art dir.: The Earth Times, 1993—, exec. editor, 1994—; exhibited in group shows and galleries, 1951—, Am. Fedn. Arts, 1963, USIA Exhbn., USSR, 1964; designer film strips Am. Fedn. Labor, 1950-52; one-man shows include Cooper Union, 1988, U. Montreal, 1988, Walker Art Ctr., Mpls.; author: Newspaper Design for the Times, 1989; design cons.: The Hill, 1994—, The American, 1996. Served with USAF, 1943-46. Recipient Spl. Gold award N.Y. Times Op-Ed Page, N.Y. Arts Dirs. Club, 1972, Hall of Fame, 1984, Gold Medal Lifetime Achievement award Soc. Publ. Designers, N.Y.C., 1984, Am. Inst. Graphic Arts Design Leadership award, Spl. medal for best design of Am. publs., 1989, Pulitzer prize nominee, 1984, 94, numerous awards Art Dir. Clubs, other profl. groups. Mem. Alliance Graphique Internationale, N.Y. Art Dirs. Club (bd. dirs. 1978-80, 82-84, 86—), Soc. Newspaper Design, Am. Abstract Artists. Jewish. Avocations: tennis; amateur poker. Home: 36 Highland Rd Southampton NY 11968-3612

SILVERSTEIN, MARTIN ELLIOT, surgeon, author, consultant; b. N.Y.C., Sept. 6, 1922; s. Louis and Ethel (Statman) S.; m. Mabelle A. Cremer, Dec. 10, 1962. AB cum laude, Columbia U., 1945; MD, N.Y. Med. Coll., 1948. Instr. bacteriology N.Y. Med. Coll., 1953-57, asst. to dean for clin. scis., 1953-58, instr. surgery, 1953-55, asst. dean, 1958; asst. vis. surgeon Bird S. Coler Hosp., N.Y.C., 1953-57, assoc. vis. surgeon, 1957-60; asst. vis. surgeon Met. Hosp., N.Y.C., 1953-57, assoc. vis. surgeon, 1957-60; asst. attending surgeon Flower and 5th Ave. Hosps., N.Y.C., 1953-57; asst. attending surgeon Monorah Med. Ctr. U. Kans. Sch. Medicine, N.Y.C., 1963-65; exec. dir. Monorah Med. Ctr. U. Kans. Sch. Medicine, Kansas City, 1963-65; exec. dir. Danciger Inst. for Health Scis. U. Kans. Sch. Medicine, Kansas City, Mo., 1963-66; chmn. dept. exptl. surgery Danciger Inst. for Health Scis. U. Kans. Sch. Medicine, Kansas City, 1963-66; chmn. dept. Surgery Menorah Med. Ctr. U. Kans. Sch. Medicine Affiliate, Kansas City, 1963-66; assoc. clin. prof. surgery U. Kans. Sch. Medicine, Kansas City, 1966-67; surgeon courtesy staff N.Y. Infirmary, 1969; surgeon Grand Canyon Med. Group and Hosp., 1979-70; chief sect. on surgery of trauma, dept. surgery U. Ariz. Coll. Med., Tucson, 1974-80, adj. assoc. prof. optical scis., 1979-83, assoc. prof. surgery, 1974-83, dir. quality assurance Univ. Hosp., 1983-84, rsch. prof. family and community medicine, internat. medicine, 1984-85, rsch. prof. surgical biology, 1984-85; sr. fellow in sci. and tch. Ctr. for Strategic and Internat. Studies Georgetown U., Washington, 1983-87; pres. Claude Gips Found. Inc., N.Y.C., 1967-93; disting. vis. prof. Uniformed Svcs. U. Health Scis., 1984, clin. prof. surgery F. Edward Hebert Sch. Medicine, 1984—; disting. vis. prof. Tulane U. Med. Sch., 1984; mem. internat. adv. bd. Univ. Microfilms Internat. Collections on Terrorism, 1987—; internat. cons. Disaster Mgmt. and Disaster Medicine, Australia, India, others, 1983—; gov. emeritus Internat. Coun. for Computer Comm., 1996—, exec. com., v.p., 1972-92. Author: Disaster: Your Right to Survive, 1991; mem. editorial bd. Terrorism, 1976—, Prehosp. and Disaster Medicine, 1989—; assoc. editor Jour. Prehosp. Care, 1984-85; contbr. articles to profl. jours. With U.S. Army, 1943-45; lt. (j.g.) USNR, 1946-53. Fgn. fellow NSF, 1974. Fellow ACS (chmn. Ariz. State com. on trauma 1979-84), Am. Assn. for Surgery of Trauma, Am. Coll. Emergency Physicians, Am. Coll. Gastroenterology, Am. Coll. Nuc. Medicine; mem. World Assn. for Emergency and Disaster Medicine (exec. com. 1987-92), Critical Care Soc. Republican.

SILVERSTEIN, MICHAEL ALAN, judge; b. Providence, Sept. 28, 1933; s. Barney and Pearl (Israel) S.; m. Phyllis J. Feer, Sept. 6, 1969; 1 child, Marc R. AB, Brown U., 1956; JD, Boston U., 1959. Bar: R.I., U.S. Dist. Ct. R.I., U.S. Ct. Appeals (1st cir.). Assoc. Higgins & Silverstein, Woonsocket, R.I., 1959-67, ptnr., 1967-89; mng. ptnr. Hinckley, Allen, Snyder & Comen, Providence, Boston, 1989-93; justice R.I. Superior Ct., Providence, 1994—. Bd. dirs., past chmn. Woonsocket Indsl. Devel. Corp., 1967—; trustee Roger Williams U., Bristol, R.I., 1982—. Mem. ABA (corp. banking and bus. law sect.), R.I. Bar Assn., Comml. Law League Am., Assn. Comml. Fin. Attys. Home: 28 Kennedy Blvd Lincoln RI 02865-3602 Office: Rhode Island Superior Ct Licht Judicial Ctr 250 Benefit St Providence RI 02903-2719

SILVERSTEIN, RICHARD, advertising agency executive. Grad., Parsons Sch. of Design. Prin., co-creative dir. Goodby, Silverstein & Ptnrs., San Francisco, 1983—. Office: Goodby Silverstein & Ptnrs 921 Front St San Francisco CA 94111-1426*

SILVERSTEIN, SAMUEL CHARLES, cellular biology and physiology educator, researcher; b. N.Y.C., Feb. 11, 1937; s. Paul Robert and Jeanette (Kamen) S.; m. Jo Ann Kleinman, Apr. 2, 1967; children: David Paul, Jennifer Kate. AB, Dartmouth Coll., 1958; MD, Albert Einstein Coll. Medicine, 1963. Intern in medicine U. Colo. Med. Center, 1963-64; postdoctoral fellow dept. cell biology Rockefeller U., 1964-67, asst. prof. cellular physiology and immunology, 1968-71, assoc. prof., physician, 1972—; John Dalton prof. physiology Columbia U. Coll. Physicians and Surgeons, N.Y.C., 1983—, chmn. dept., 1983—; asst. resident in medicine Mass. Gen. Hosp., Boston, 1967-68; established investigator Am. Heart Assn., 1972-77; mem. sci. adv. com. Cancer Rsch. Fund of Damon Runyon-Walter Winchell Found., 1975-79, bd. dirs., 1990—; mem. sci. adv. com. N.Y. Blood Ctr.; cons. Nat. Inst. Gen. Med. Scis., 1985-89, Am. Heart Assn., 1986-89; mem. coun. Am. Soc. Cell Biology, 1988-92; chmn. Gordon Conf. Lysosomes, 1982; founder, dir. Columbia U. Summer Rsch. Program for Sci. Tchrs.; bd. dirs. Rsch. Am.; cons. Nat. Inst. Allergy and Infectious Diseases, 1977-78, mem. adv. coun., dir., 1995—; mem. sci. adv. com. Keystone Symposia, 1993—, mgmt. com., 1996—. Editor: Transport of Macromolecules in Cellular Systems, 1979; chmn. editl. bd. Jour. Cell Biology, 1979-82, editor, 1978-89. Helen Hay Whitney fellow, 1964-67, John Simon Guggenheim fellow, 1997; recipient John Oliver LaGorce medal Nat. Geog. Soc., 1967, Marie Bonazinga Rsch. award Soc. Leukocyte Biology, 1984, Disting. Alumnus award Albert Einstein Coll. Medicine, 1987. Fellow AAAS chair-elect sect. Medicine), Am. Soc. Microbiology; mem. Am. Soc. Cell Biology, Am. Soc. Clin. Investigation, Am. Assn. Immunologists, Infectious Diseases Soc. Am., Am. Soc. Biol. Chemists, Am. Physiol. Soc., Assn. Am. Physicians, Practitioners Soc. N.Y., Fedn. Am. Socs. for Exptl. Biology (bd. dirs. 1991-96, v.p. 1993-94, pres. 1994-95, chmn. Pub. Affairs adv. coun. 1995-96), Inst. Medicine, Nat. Acad. Scis. Clubs: Am. Alpine (dir. 1963-64, 69-74), Explorers. Achievements include research and numerous publications in field of virology, cell biology, immunology, science policy and mountaineering. Home: 110 Riverside Dr New York NY 10024-3715 Office: Columbia U Coll Physicians & Surgeons 630 W 168th St New York NY 10032-3702

SILVERSTEIN, SHELBY (SHEL SILVERSTEIN), author, cartoonist, composer, folksinger; b. Chgo., 1932; 1 daughter. Former corr., cartoonist Stars and Stripes, Pacific area; now cartoonist, writer Playboy Mag., Chgo., 1956—. Author: (books) Now Here's My Plan, 1960, Lafcadio, the Lion Who Shot Back, 1963, Uncle Shelby's ABZ Book, 1961, Giraffe and a Half, The Giving Tree, 1964, A Playboy's Teevee Jeebies, 1963, More Playboy's Teevee Jeebies, 1965, L'Arbe Au Grand Coeur, 1973, Now Here's My Plan, 1976, Uncle Shelby's Zoo: Don't Bump the Glump, Where the Sidewalk Ends, 1974, The Missing Piece, 1976, The Missing Piece Meets the Big O, 1981, A Light in the Attic, 1981; co-author: Things Change, 1988, The Best American Short Plays 1992-1993: The Theatre Annual Since 1937, 1993; (drawings) Different Dances, 1979, Who Wants a Cheap Rhinoceros, 1964, Uncle Shelby's ABZ, 1985; plays: The Lady or the Tiger, 1981; composer: Comin' After Jinny, Boa Constrictor, A Boy Named Sue, One's On the Way, The Unicorn, So Good to So Bad, Yes, Mr. Rogers, Conch Train Robbery, Freakin' at the Freakers Ball, Where the Side Walk Ends; albums include: Dirty Feet, 1968, Ned Kelly, 1970, Freakin' at the Freakers' Ball, 1972, Sloppy Seconds, 1972, Dr. Hook, 1972, Bobby Bare Sings Lullabys, Legends and Lies, 1973, Drain My Brain, 1980; appeared in film: Who is Harry Kellerman and Why is He Saying Those Terrible Things About Me?, 1971. AUS Japan, Korea, 1950s. Office: Harper Collins Pubs Inc 10 E 53rd St New York NY 10022-5244*

SILVERSTONE, ALICIA, actress; b. Calif., Oct. 4, 1976. Stage debut in Carol's Eve at Met Theater, L.A.; starred in three Aerosmith videos, including Cryin'; appeared in feature films: The Crush, 1993, The Babysitter, 1995, True Crime, 1995, Le Nouveau Monde, 1995, Hideaway, 1995, Clueless, 1995; appeared in TV programs including Torch Song, 1993, Shattered Dreams, 1993, The Cool and the Crazy, 1994, The Wonder Years, Batman and Robin, 1997; appeared in, prodr. (film) Excess Baggage, 1997. Office: care Premiere Artists Agy 8899 Beverly Blvd Ste 102 Los Angeles CA 90048-2433 Office: First Kiss Prodns care Columbia Pictures Capra Bldg Ste 106 10202 W Washington Blvd Culver City CA 90232*

SILVERSTONE, DAVID, advertising executive; b. N.Y.C., Sept. 21, 1932; m. Caroline A. Hill, June 14, 1963; children: Eva Hilary, Joshua David. Grad., Queens Coll., 1954; postgrad., Columbia U., Baruch Sch., UCLA. Sr. research analyst McCann-Erickson Inc., N.Y.C., 1956-63, mgr. media research, 1963-68, v.p., dir. mktg., Dataplan, 1968, supr. mktg. devel., 1972-74, mgr. mktg. planning and research, 1974-77, dir. research, 1977-80, sr. v.p., dir. mktg. planning, 1981—; founder, dir. Media Info. Svcs., 1969-72; mem. Advt. Agy. Rsch. Dirs. Coun., 1977-82; mem. Queens Coll. Corp. Adv. Bd., 1986—, adj. prof., 1990—. Author: (with D.E. Sexton, Jr.) Understanding the Computer, Marketing Managers Handbook, 1973. Bd. dirs. United Way of Larchmont, 1974-77, Castle Gallery Coll. of New Rochelle, 1984-92; mem. adv. coun. Sch. Gen. Studies, Columbia U., 1991—. Developer of pioneer system for defining television marketing areas (1968), measuring consumer need states (1975), consumer language of product benefits (1978), global studies of business to business marketing (1981), consumer products (1988), and global brand tracking systems (1989-90). Home: 22 Glenn Rd Larchmont NY 10538-1543

SILVERSTONE, DAVID EDWARD, ophthalmologist; b. N.Y.C., Feb. 16, 1948; s. Sidney Milton and Estelle (Cohen) S.; m. Linda Carol Thalberg, June 19, 1969; 1 child, Scott. AB, Columbia Coll., 1969; MD, NY Med. Coll., 1973. Cert. Ophthalmology, Am. Bd. Ophthalmology, 1977. Acad. internat. eye fellow Albert Schweitzer Hosp., Deschapples, Haiti, 1976; instr. dept. ophthalmology and visual scis. Yale Sch. Medicine, New Haven, Conn., 1976-77; asst. clin. prof. Dept. Ophthalmology and Visual Scis. Yale Sch. Medicine, Newhaven, Conn., 1977-86, assoc. clin. prof. Dept. Ophthalmology and Visual Scis., 1986-91, clin. prof. Dept. Ophthalmology and Visual Scis., 1991—; chief ophthalmology VA Hosp., West Haven, Conn., 1977-85; attending physician Yale-New Haven Hosp., New Haven, Conn., 1976—, asst. chief ophthalmology, 1988—; dir. continuing edn. Am. Soc. Cataract and Refractive Surgery, Washington, 1991—; mem. Bd. Permanent Officers Yale Sch. Medicine, New Haven, 1991—. Author: Automated Visual Field Testing, 1986; contbr. articles to profl. jours. Recipient Med. Student Essay award Am. Sc. Pharmacology and Experimental therapeutics, 1971, Moshy Book award N.Y. Med. Coll., N.Y.C., 1973, Physician's regognition award AMA, Chgo., 1976, 79, 82, 85, 96, Honor award Am. Acad. Ophthalmology, San Francisco, 1990. Fellow Am. Acad. Ophthalmology; mem. New England Ophthalmological Soc., AMA, Conn. State Med. Soc., Conn. Soc. Eye Physicians, New Haven County Med. Assn., Yale Alumni Ophthalmology, Assn. for Rsch. in Vision and Ophthalmology. Avocation: computers. Office: Temple Eye Physicians 60 Temple St New Haven CT 06510-2716

SILVERSTONE, HARRIS J., chemistry educator; b. N.Y.C., Sept. 18, 1939; s. Sidney M. and Estelle Silverstone; m. Ruth C. Federman, 1960; children: Robert, Aron, Nancy, Murray. AB, Harvard U., 1960; PhD, Calif. Inst. Tech., 1964. Asst. prof. Johns Hopkins U., Balt., 1965-68, assoc. prof., 1968-71, prof., 1971—. Contbr. articles to profl. jours. NSF Postdoctoral fellow Yale U., 1964. Mem. Am. Phys. Soc., Am. Chem. Soc., Internat. Soc. Theoretical Chem. Physics. Office: Johns Hopkins U 3400 N Charles St Baltimore MD 21218-2608

SILVERSTONE, LEON MARTIN, dental research cariologist, neuroscientist, educator, researcher; b. London, May 21, 1939; came to U.S., 1976; s. Jack Stanley and Sadie (Osen) S.; m. Susan Petyan, Dec. 20, 1964; children; Samantha, Frances, Mark. Student, Queen Mary Coll., London, 1958-59; L.D.S., U. Leeds, U.K., 1963, B.Ch.D., 1964, D.D.Sc., 1971; L.D.S., Royal Coll. Surgeons, Eng., 1964; Ph.D., U. Bristol, Eng., 1967; postgrad., U. London, 1969-76. House surgeon Leeds Dental Hosp., Eng., 1963-64; research fellow Med. Research Council Unit, Bristol Dental Sch., 1964-67; lectr. in dental surgery U. Bristol, 1967-68; sr. lectr. child dental health Med. Coll., Royal London Hosp., 1969-75, reader in preventive and pediat. dentistry, 1975-76; cons. Royal London Hosp., 1973-76; vis. Lasby prof. Dental Sch. U. Minn., Mpls., 1974-75; prof., head div. cariology Dows Inst. Dental Research, Coll. Dentistry, U. Iowa, Iowa City, 1976-82; assoc. dean for research Dental Sch. U. Colo. Health Scis. Ctr., Denver, 1982-89; dir. Oral Scis. Research Inst. U. Colo. Health Scis. Ctr., 1986-89; biomed. cons., 1990; v.p. R & D The Synaptic Corp., La Jolla, Calif., 1990-95; dir. R&D BioSciences Systems, LaJolla, Calif., 1995—; vis. Nicholaysen prof. U. Oslo, 1972; cons. Pan Am. Health Orgn., 1973-85, dental rsch. Va, 1978-85; mem. study sect. and program adv. com. NIH-Nat. Inst. Dental Rsch., 1976-84, chmn. subcom. on dental caries, 1982-83, chmn. program adv. com., 1983-84. Mem. editorial bd. Caries Rsch., 1976-86; contbr. chpts. to books, articles in field to profl. publs. Recipient Nobel-Pharma A.B. Bofors prize in child dental health, 1971, ORCA-ROLEX rsch. prize, 1973, Disting. award in child dental health, 1981; NIH/Nat. Inst. Dental Rsch. grantee, 1976-89. Mem. European Orgn. Caries Research (mem. bd., sci. councillor 1971-83, pres. 1977-79), Internat. Assn. Dental Research (pres. cariology group 1982-83, Disting. Scientist award 1984), Am. Assn. Dental Research (pres. cariology group chpt. 1982-83, chmn. publs. com. 1985-86), Brit. Dental Assn., Internat. Assn. Dentistry for Children (exec. com. 1972-79, jour. editor 1971-79), AAAS, Soc. Exptl. Biology and Medicine, Space Medicine Com., AAUP, Am. Acad. Pedodontics, Omega Kappa Upsilon, Sigma Xi. Office: PO Box 3051 La Jolla CA 92038-3051

SILVERTHORNE, MICHAEL JAMES, classics educator; b. Bristol, Eng., Dec. 20, 1941; emigrated to Can., 1966; s. Frederick J. and Freda (Fox) S.; m. Ann Frances O'Malley, Aug. 6, 1966; children: Christopher, Stephen, Katherine. B.A., Oxford U., 1964, B.Litt., 1966, M.A., 1967, D.Phil., 1973. Lectr. McGill U., Montreal, 1966-68; asst. prof. McGill U., 1968-74, assoc. prof. dept. classics, 1974—, chmn. dept., 1981-86, 88-91, 94—. Can. Council fellow, 1969-73; Social Sci. and Humanities Research Council Can. grantee, 1980-83, 92-95. Mem. Classical Assn. Can. (sec. 1991-95), Conf. Social and Polit. Thought. Office: McGill U Classics Dept, 855 Sherbrooke St W, Montreal, PQ Canada H3A 2T7

SILVESTRI, ALAN ANTHONY, film composer; b. N.Y.C., Mar. 26, 1950; s. Louis and Elizabeth (Clarke) S.; m. Sandra Dee Shue; children: Alexandra, Joseph, James. PhD in Music (hon.), Berklee Coll. Music, Boston, 1995. Film scores include The Doberman Gang, 1972, The Amazing Dobermans, Las Vegas Lady, 1976, Romancing the Stone, 1984, Par ou t'es rentre? On t'as vu sortir, 1984, Fandango, 1984, Cat's Eye, 1984, Back to the Future, 1985 (Grammy award nominations best instrumental composition and best album of original score for a motion picutre, 1985), Summer Rental, 1985, Clan of the Cave Bear, 1986, The Delta Force, 1986, American Anthem, 1986, Flight of the Navigator, 1986, No Mercy, 1986, Critical Condition, 1987, Outrageous Fortune, 1987, Predator, 1987, Overboard, 1987, Who Framed Roger Rabbit?, 1988 (Grammy award nominations best instrumental composition and best album of original score for a motion picture, 1988), My Stepmother Is an Alien, 1988, Mac and Me, 1988, She's Out of Control, 1989, Downtown, 1989, The Abyss, 1989, Back to the Future II, 1989, Back to the Future III, 1990, Young Guns II, 1990, Predator II, 1990, Soapdish, 1991, Dutch, 1991, Ricohet, 1991, Shattered, 1991, Father of the Bride, 1991, Ferngully: The Last Rainforest, 1992, Death Becomes Her, 1992, Stop! Or My Mom Will Shoot, 1992, The Bodyguard, 1992, Cop and a Half, 1993, Sidekicks, 1993, Super Mario Bros., 1993, Judgment Night, 1993, Grumpy Old Men, 1993, Clean Slate, 1994, Blown Away, 1994, Forrest Gump, 1994 (Academy award nomination best original score 1994, Grammy award nomination best instrumental performance 1994, Golden Globe award nomination best original score 1994), Richie Rich, 1994, The Quick and the Dead, 1994, The Perez Family, 1995, Judge Dredd, 1995, Father of the Bride II, 1995, Sgt. Bilko, 1995, Grumpier Old Men, 1995, Eraser, 1996, Long Kiss Goodnight, 1996, Fools Rush In, 1996, Volcano, 1997, Contact, 1997; TV themes include CHiPs, 1978-83, Manimal, 1983. Recipient ACE award Nat. Acad. Cable Programming for Tales from the Crypt - All Through the House, 1990, Saturn award Acad. Arts and Sci. for fantasy and horror film, 1987. Mem. Nat. Acad. Recording Arts and Scis., Acad. Motion Picture Arts and Scis.

SILVESTRI, PHILIP SALVATORE, lawyer; b. San Francisco, Nov. 10, 1944; s. Philip and Olga (Difilipo) S.; m. Dianne Loveland, June 22, 1968; children: Lauren, Steven, Karin. BA, U. San Francisco, 1966, JD, 1969. Bar: Calif. 1969; cert. family law specialist State Bar Calif. Assoc. Goth, Dennis & Aaron, Redwood City, Calif., 1969-84; ptnr. Goth, Aaron & Silvestri, Redwood City, 1984-87, Goth & Silvestri, A.P.C., Redwood City, 1987—. With N.G., 1969-75. Republican. Avocations: weight training, running. Office: Goth & Silvestri APC 1000 Marshall St Ste B Redwood City CA 94063-2027

SILVESTRI, ROBERT, electric company executive; b. New Haven, Nov. 9, 1954; s. Danny and Helen (Turek) S.; m. Debra Ann Summa, Oct. 4, 1980; 1 child, Jason Dante. BS, Fairfield (Conn.) U., 1976; MS, U. New Haven, 1986. Cert. lab. dir. State of Conn. Dept. Health Svcs.; assoc. safety profl.; cert. hazardous materials mgr. Lectr., rschr. Yale U., New Haven, 1976; sr. chemist Mitchell-Bradford Internat., Milford, Conn., 1977-81; dir. C.A.L., Inc., Hamden, Conn., 1981-89; supr. environ. reporting and support svcs. United Illuminating, New Haven, 1989-90, mgr. environ. licensing and regulatory affairs, 1990-94, mgr. environ. ops. and safety, 1994—; chair Bus. Recycling Coun., New Haven, 1990-94; lectr. Middlesex C.C., Middletown, Conn., 1992-95; dir. Bus. Environ. Coun., Bristol, Conn., 1993-95; mem. adv. coms. Conn. Dept. Environ. Protection, 1989—. Co-author comty. planning report; contbg. author: Connecticut's Environment, 1995, 97. Mem. State of Conn. Environ. Permitting Task Force, Hartford, 1992-94; lobbyist United Illuminating, New Haven, 1991—; dir. Eli Whitney Mus., 1994—. Recipient Keynote Speaker award Conn. Forum of Regulated Environ. Profls., 1991, cert. of merit for bus. recycling Conn. Dept. Environ. Protection, 1991, Green Ribbon award Greater New Haven C. of C., 1991. Mem. Am. Electroplater's Soc. (cert. electroplater finisher), Am. Chem. Soc., Am. Indsl. Hygiene Assn., Air and Waste Mgmt. Assn. (dir. 1993—), Electric Coun. New Eng., Conn. Bus. and Industry Assn. (steering com. 1995—), Civitan (dir. New Eng. dist. 1992-95), Hamden Soccer Assn. (asst. coach 1996, coach 1997—, referee 1997—). Avocations: woodworking, music, antique automobiles. Home: 1140 Mount Carmel Ave Hamden CT 06518-1610 Office: United Illuminating 157 Church St New Haven CT 06510-2100

SILVESTRO, CLEMENT MARIO, museum director, historian; b. New Haven, Sept. 7, 1924; s. Joseph and Rose (Griego) S.; m. Betty C. Mack, June 26, 1950; 1 dau., Elizabeth J. Silvestro Casner. B.S., Central Conn. State Coll., 1949; M.S., U. Wis., 1951; Ph.D., 1959. Asst. to dir. Wis. Hist. Soc., 1956-57; dir. Am. Assn. State and Local History, 1957-64; editor History News, 1957-64; assoc. dir. Chgo. Hist. Soc., 1964-65, dir., 1965-74, sec., 1970-74; dir. Mus. of Our Nat. Heritage, Lexington, Mass., 1974-92;

Mem. exec. com. Am. Assn. Museums, 1965-71, v.p., 1966-71; vis. lectr. Northeastern U., 1983-85. Co-author: A Decade of Collecting: Maps, 1985. Mem. Chgo. Archtl. and Landmark Com., 1968-74; mem. Ill. Historic Sites Adv. Council, 1970-74, U.S. ICOM, Nat. Com., 1970-74; chmn. Pres.'s Adv. Council on Historic Preservation, 1974-77; mem. adv. bd. Eleutherian Mills-Hagley Found., 1973-76; U.S. rep. to UNESCO Internat. Adv. Com. to Safeguard City of Venice, 1975; trustee U.S. Capitol Hist. Soc.; trustee, pres. Fruitlands Mus., 1982-85. Served with USAAF, 1943-45. Decorated Air medal with oak leaf clusters. Mem. Am. Assn. Mus., Orgn. Am Historians (chmn. hist. sites com. 1973-78), Chgo. Hist. Soc., Colonial Soc. Mass., Bostonian Soc., Mass. Hist. Soc. (resident), Union Club Boston, Masons. Home: PO Box 119 West Shore Rd Hancock ME 04640

SILVEY, ANITA LYNNE, editor; b. Bridgeport, Conn., Sept. 3, 1947; d. John Oscar and Juanita Lucille (McKitrick) S.; m. Bill Clark, 1988. BS in Edn., Ind. U., 1965-69; MA in Comm. Arts, U. Wis., 1970. Editorial asst. children's book dept. Little Brown and Co., Boston, 1970-71; asst. editor Horn Book Mag., Boston, 1971-75; mng. editor, founder New Boston Rev., 1975-76; mktg. mgr. children's books, libr. svcs. mgr. trade divsn. Houghton Mifflin, Boston, 1976-84; editor-in-chief Horn Book Mag., Boston, 1985-95; v.p., pub. Children's Books Houghton Mifflin Co., Boston, 1995—. Editor: Children's Books and Their Creators, 1995, Help Wanted: Stories About Young People and Work, 1997; contbr. articles to profl. jours. Named one of 70 Women Who Have Made a Difference, Women's Nat. Book Assn., 1987. Mem. ALA (chmn. children's librs., Laura Ingalls Wilder award 1987-89), Internat. Reading Assn. (mem. IRA Book award com. 1985-87), Assn. Am. Pubs. (libr. com.), New England Round Table (chmn. 1978-79). Office: Houghton Mifflin 222 Berkeley St Boston MA 02116-3748

SILVEY, JAMES L., religious publisher. Exec. dir. Baptist Pub. House Baptist Missionary Assn. of Am., Texarkana, Tex. Office: Bapt Missionary Assoc Am Publications Dept 311 Main St Texarkana TX 75501-5604*

SILVIA, DAVID ALAN, insurance broker; b. Taunton, Mass., Mar. 5, 1953; s. Edward J. and Loretta (Sousa) S.; m. Janet E. McMahon, Apr. 16, 1988 (div. Jan. 1996); 1 child, David. BA, Roger Williams U., 1975. Sales rep. New England Brass, Taunton, Mass., 1976-81; ins. agt. Prudential Ins., Raynham, Mass., 1981-82; owner, ptnr. CS Assocs., North Attleboro, Mass., 1982-86; broker Fin. Mktg. Assocs., North Dighton, Mass., 1986—. Sec., treas. United Meth. Mens Club, Taunton, 1994, pres., 1995—. Independent. Office: Fin Mktg Assocs 495 Somerset Ave North Dighton MA 02764-1809

SILVIUS, DONALD JOE, educational consultant; b. Kingman, Kans., July 30, 1932; s. Henry Edgar and Gladys Mae (Beaty) S.; m. Jean Anne Able, Aug. 30, 1951; children: Laurie Dawn Silvius Gustin, Steven Craig, Jonathan Mark, Brian James. Student So. Calif. Coll., 1949-52; AA, Bakersfield Coll., 1962; BA, Fresno State Coll., 1963, MA, 1968. Radio/TV announcer, musician, music arranger and copyist, life ins. underwriter, other positions, 1953-62; jr. high sch. English tchr., elem. and jr. high counselor, child welfare, attendance and guidance supr., supr. pupil personnel svcs. Standard Sch. Dist., Oildale, Calif., 1963-92; ret. 1992; edn., guidance and computer cons., 1992—; tchr. counseling/guidance and spl. edn. various colls. Pres. North of the River Sanitation Dist. # 1. Recipient Standard PTA-Hon. Service award, Bakersfield "Up With People" Appreciation award, Golden Apple Service award Standard Sch. Dist. Tchrs. Assn., Innovations award Calif. Tchrs. Assn., Hon. Service award Kern chpt. Calif. Assn. Sch. Psychologists, Outstanding Ednl. Leader award West Kern chpt. Assn. Calif. Sch. Adminstrs., 1977-78, 7th Dist. PTA-Silver Service award, Continuing Service award Highland-Wingland PTA, Outstanding Community Service for Developmentally Disabled award. Mem. NEA, Calif. Tchrs. Assn., North of the River C. of C., Calif. Assn. Supervision of Child Welfare and Attendance, Assn. Calif. Sch. Adminstrs., Am. Assn. Curriculum Devel., Am. Assn. Counseling and Devel., ACES, ASCD, AMECD, ARVIC, Mental Health Assn. (Calif. exec. bd.), Assn. Kern County, Mensa, PTA, Calif. Assn. Counseling and Devel., Calif. Assn. for Counseling Edn. & Supervision, Calif. Assn. for Adult Devel. & Aging, Calif. Assn. for Measurement & Evaluation in Counseling, Calif. Assn. for Relig. Values & Issues in Counseling, v.p. Calif. Ret. Tchr. Assn., Oildale Lions Club, Phi Delta Kappa.

SILVOSO, JOSEPH ANTON, accounting educator; b. Benld, Ill., Sept. 15, 1917; s. Biagio and Camilla (Audo) S.; m. Wilda Lucille Miller, Nov. 16, 1942; children: Joseph A., Gerald R. EdB, Ill. State U., 1941; AM, U. Mo., 1947, PhD, 1951. CPA, Mo., Kans. Instr. U. Mo., 1947-48, 50-51; asst. U. Ill., 1948-49; staff acct/ Deloitte Touche (and predecessor, CPAs), Kansas City, Mo., 1951-55; ednl. dir. Deloitte Touche (and predecessor, CPAs), Detroit, 1956; assoc. prof. accountancy U. Mo., Columbia, 1955-58, prof., 1958-88, prof. emeritus, 1988—, sesquicentennial prof. accountancy, 1990—, KPMG Peat Marwick prof. profl. acctg., 1978-88, chmn. dept. accountancy, 1964-75; dir. Sch. Accountancy, 1975-79; cons. in field, 1956-94. Author: Auditing, 1965, Illustrative Auditing, 1965, Audit Case, 1966. Chmn. Joint Adv. Council Accounting, 1962-64. Served with USAAF, 1942-45. Recipient Shutz Teaching award U. Mo., 1985; Fedn. Sch. Accountancy Faculty Award of Merit renamed FSA Joseph A. Silvoso Faculty Award of Merit in his honor, 1989; established chairs in the sch. of accountancy, specifically the KPMG Peat Marwick/Joseph A. Silvoso Disting. prof., 1992, The Price Waterhouse/Joseph A. Silvoso Disting. prof., 1993, The Joseph A. Silvoso Disting. dir., 1993, The Arthur Andersen/Joseph A. Silvoso Disting. prof., 1994. Mem. Am. Acct. Assn. (chmn. membership com. Mo. 1956-58, nat. chmn. acctg. careers com. 1961-63, sec. treas. 1971-73, pres. 1980-81), AICPA (hon., contbg. editor jour. 1958-61, editorial bd. 1970-72, mem. coun. 1981-86, bd. dirs. 1983-86, Outstanding Acctg./ Educator award 1986, Disting. Svc. award 1986, nominations com. 1988-89), Mo. Soc. CPAs (chmn. acctg. careers com. 1966-67, dir., sec. ednl. found. 1968-70, bd. dirs. 1983-86, Max Myers Disting. Svc. award 1984), Ctrl. States Conf. CPAs (treas. 1975, sec. 1976, v.p. 1977, pres. 1978), Fedn. Schs. Accountancy (dir. 1977-78, v.p. 1981-82, pres. 1982-83), Nat. Assn. Accts., Inst. Internal Auditors, Fin. Exec. Inst., Midwest Econs. Assn., Delta Sigma Pi, Beta Gamma Sigma, Alpha Pi Zeta, Beta Alpha Psi (named Nat. Acad. Acct. of Yr. 1977). Methodist. Avocations: exercise, reading, gardening. Home: 827 Greenwood Ct Columbia MO 65203-2841 Office: U Mo 312 Sch Accountancy Columbia MO 65211

SIM, CRAIG STEPHEN, investment banker; b. Bklyn., Apr. 23, 1942; s. William Henry Craig and Lenore (Overton) S.; m. Susan Hart; children: Brandon Craig William, Stephanie Brooke. BA, Gettysburg Coll., 1965. Account exec. Francis I. duPont & Co., N.Y.C., 1969-72; v.p. E.F. Hutton & Co., N.Y.C., 1972-75; sr. v.p. Donaldson, Lufkin & Jenrette, N.Y.C., 1975-83; exec. v.p. Shearson Am. Express, N.Y.C., 1983-84; mng. dir. Donaldson, Lufkin & Jenrette, N.Y.C., 1984—. Trustee Gettysburg Coll. Served to capt. USMC, 1965-69. Mem. Bond Club N.Y. (gov. 19779-80, 84-85, 90-93), Lawrence Beach Club, The Leash, India House, St. Andrew's Soc. (N.Y.C.), L.I. Wyandanch Club, Seawanhaka Corinthian Yacht Club, Army and Navy Club (Washington). Office: Donaldson Lufkin & Jenrette Securities Corp 277 Park Ave New York NY 10172

SIM, ROBERT WILSON, accountant; b. Three Rivers, Quebec, Can., June 10, 1944; came to U.S., 1955; s. James Wilson and Winnifred May (Stephenson) S.; m. Maureen Ann McCune, Mar. 28, 1970; children: Patricia Marie, Catherine Ann, Jennifer May. BSBA, U. Fla., 1966. CPA, Fla., Mo. Staff acct. Arnold and Co., Sarasota, Fla., 1964-66; audit supr. Ernst and Ernst, Atlanta, 1968-74; audit mgr. Tornwall, Lang and Lee, St. Petersburg, Fla., 1974-76; ptnr. Grant Thornton, St. Petersburg, Fla., 1976-80, Kansas City, Mo., 1980-85, Miami/Ft. Lauderdale, Fla., 1985-90; owner, practitioner Robert W. Sim, CPA, Hollywood, Fla., 1990—. Treas. Mental Health Assn. Pinellas County, Inc., St. Petersburg, 1976-80; sec./treas. Suncoast Rotary Club St. Petersburg, 1976-80; organizer Chinese/Am. Soc. Kansas City, 1983-85. With U.S. Army, 1966-68. Recipient Cert. of Appreciation, St. Petersburg C. of C., 1975, Univ. Fla., 1992; plaque CPA Club Miami, 1990, Youth Orch. Fla., 1992. Mem. Fla. Inst. CPAs (chmn. com. on Univ. Fla. Acctg. Conf. 1993), Women in Distress of Broward County, Inc. (fund raising com. 1992, vol. cons. 1975-80), Miami Fin. Group. Republican. Presbyterian. Avocations: golf, travel/camping, weight lifting, car buff, spectator sports. Office: Robert W Sim CPA 6565 Taft St Ste 211 Hollywood FL 33024-4000

SIMAAN, MARWAN A., electrical engineering educator; b. July 23, 1946; m. Rita Simaan. MSEE, U. Pitts., 1970; PhD in Elec. Engring., U. Ill., 1972. Registered profl. engr., Pa. Rsch. engr. Shell Devel. Co., Houston, 1974-76; assoc. prof. elec. engring. U. Pitts., 1976-85, prof., 1985-89, Bell of Pa./Bell Atlantic prof., 1989—, chmn. dept. elec. engring., 1991—; cons. Gulf Rsch. and Tech., Pitts., 1979-85, ALCOA, Pitts., 1986-89. Editor: Vertical Seismic Profiles, 1984, Two-dimensional Transforms, 1985, Artificial Intelligence in Petroleum Exploration, 1989, Expert Systems in Exploration, 1991, (series) Advances in Geophysical Signal Processing; co-editor jour. Multidimensional Systems and Signal Processing; contbr. over 200 articles on signal processing and control to profl. jours. Grantee NSF, ONR, Ben Franklin, Gulf, ALCOA; recipient Outstanding ECE Alumnus U. Ill. Fellow IEEE (Best Paper award 1985); mem. Soc. Exploration Geophysics, Am. Assn. Artificial Intelligence, Eta Kappa Nu, Sigma Xi (Best Paper award ALCOA chpt. 1988). Achievements include patent in application of signal processing technology in aluminum manufacturing. Office: Univ Pitts Dept Elec Engring Pittsburgh PA 15261

SIMANDLE, JEROME B., federal judge; b. Binghamton, N.Y., Apr. 29, 1949; s. Paul R. Sr. and Mary F. Simandle; married; children: Roy C., Liza Jane. BSE magna cum laude, Princeton U., 1971; JD, U. Pa., 1976; diploma in Social Scis., U. Stockholm, 1974-75. Bar: Pa. 1977, N.J. 1978. Law clk. to Hon. John F. Gerry U.S. Dist. Ct., N.J., 1976-78; asst. U.S. atty. Dist. N.J., 1978-83; U.S. magistrate judge U.S. Dist. Ct., N.J., 1983-92, judge, 1992—; mem. lawyers adv. com. U.S. Dist. Ct. N.J., 1984-95; ct. adminstrn. case mgmt. com. Jud. Conf. U.S., 1991—. Internat. grad. fellow Rotary Found., 1974-75. Fellow Am. Bar Found.; mem. ABA, Fed. Judges Assn. (bd. dirs. 1997—), N.J. Bar Assn., Camden Inn of Ct. (master 1987—, program chmn. 1990-93, vice chmn. 1996—). Office: US Dist Ct US Courthouse One John F Gerry Plz Camden NJ 08101-0888

SIMARD, CYRIL, cultural organization administrator, architect; b. Baie-Saint-Paul, Que., Can., May 23, 1938; s. Lionel and Adrienne (Fortin) S.; m. Monique Gauthier, Aug. 27, 1966; children: Marie-Eve, Dominique, Marisol. BPhil, U. Laval, Que., 1959, PhD, 1986; BArch, U. Montreal, Que., 1965, MA in Design, 1976. Owner archtl. firm Montreal, 1965-72; prof. Sch. Architecture U. Montreal, 1967-72; mng. dir. Centrale d'Artisanat du Que., Montreal, 1972-77; visual arts dir. Que. Govt., 1977-83; dir. dept. planning Mus. Nat. Que., 1983-87; pres. Assn. Musées Nat. Que., 1983-87, Commn. des Biens Culturels Que., 1988—; UNESCO-ICOM prof., Brno, Czech Republic, 1992. Author: (dictionary) Artisanat Québécois, 1975-86 (Best Seller), Les Papiers Saint-Gilles, 1988 Economuséologie, 1986; editor: (ency.) Les Chemins de la Mémoire, 1991-97. Trustee Found. René-Richard, Montreal, 1991; pres. Papeterie Saint-Gilles, Charlevoix, 1984; founder, pres. Found. Internat. Économusées, Que., 1992. Recipient medal Lt. Gov. of Que., 1965, Nat. Innovation Tourist prize Govt. of Que., 1989, medal Gov. Gen. Ottawa, 1993, Lt. Gov. Que., 1994. Mem. Royal Soc. Can., Assn. Architects, Assn. Designers (hon.), Internat. Assn. Art Critics, Soc. Que. Ethnology, Icom Can. Unesco, Icomos Can. Unesco. Avocations: reading, music, travel. Office: Comn Biens Culturels Que, 12 Rue Sainte-Anne, Quebec, PQ Canada G1R 3X2

SIMATOS, NICHOLAS JERRY, aerospace company executive, consultant; b. Argostoli, Kefalonia, Greece, Aug. 21, 1948; came to U.S., 1955; s. Jerry Nicholas and Jenny (Kostantakis) S.; children: Alexander Nicholas, Diana Lindsay. AD, Hudson Valley Community Coll., Troy, N.Y., 1972; BS, Embry Riddle Aero. U., Daytona, Fla., 1974; MS, Embry Riddo Aero. U., Miami, Fla., 1978, M in Mgmt., 1978. Charter pilot Piedmont Aviation, Miami, 1977-78; instr. pilot Flight Safety Acad., Vero Beach, Fla., 1978-79; commd. 2d lt. U.S. Air Force, 1979, advanced through grades to capt.; space systems dir. 19th Surveillance SON, Diyarbakir, Turkey, 1983-84; astronaut, instr. NASA Johnson Space Ctr., Houston, 1984-87; resigned U.S. Air Force, 1987; aggressor pilot Flight Internat., Jacksonville Naval Air Sta., Fla., 1987-88; asst. prof. Embry-Riddle Aero. U., Daytona, 1989-96; pres. Apollo Aero. Internat. Inc., Daytona Beach, Fla., 1996—; mem. Life Support Systems for Space Exploration/Ops.; guest cosmonaut candidate, Star City, Russia; aerospace cons. Dept. Edn., State of Fla., 1989—; recert. dir. NASA, Houston, 1986-87. Author: Futuristic Spacecraft Systems, 1989, Space Transportation Systems, 1990, Space Flight Technologies, 1991. State advisor U.S. Congressional Adv. Bd., Washington, 1982; chmn. Hellenic Profl. Soc. Scholarship Program, Houston, 1986. Decorated Recognition award Turkish Air Force, award of excellence Dutch Air Force, Aerospace award Russian Space Forces, 1996. Mem. AIAA (sr.). Republican. Eastern Orthodox. Avocations: snow and water skiing, flying, swimming, jogging. Home: 120 Bittern Ct Daytona Beach FL 32119 Office: Apollo Aerospace Internat Inc PO Box 11461 Daytona Beach FL 32120

SIMCHES, SEYMOUR OLIVER, language educator; b. Boston, Sept. 22, 1919; s. Meyer and Rebecca (Nadell) S.; m. Marcia Harriet Goldberg, Sept. 13, 1953; children: Judith Ellen, Jonathan David. AB, Boston U., 1941; MA, Harvard U., 1942, PhD, 1950. Tchg. fellow Romance langs. Harvard U., 1947-50, resident tutor Adams Ho., 1947-53, mem. upper-commons rm. Adams Ho., 1995—, instr., 1950-53; asst. prof. Amherst Coll., 1953-54; mem. faculty Tufts U., 1954-90, chmn. dept. Romance langs., 1958-70, John Wade prof. modern langs., 1962-90, John Wade prof. emeritus, 1990—, co-founder, bd. dirs. Tufts Exptl. Coll., 1964-68; dir. Tufts Coll. Within, 1971-74, Ctr. for European Studies, 1978-83; founding dir. Tufts European Ctr., 1983—; mem. Mass. Adv. Com. on Fgn. Langs., 1961—; cons. U.S. Office Edn., 1964; dir. Fgn. Lang. Insts., NDEA, 1960-62, 65; mem. bd. examiners advanced placement Coll. Entrance Exam. Bd., 1968—; mem. Mass. Adv. Bd. on Non-Traditional Edn. Author: (with H.H. Golden) Modern French Literature and Language: A Bibliography of Homage Studies, 1956, Modern Iberian Literature and Language: A Bibliography of Homage Studies, 1958, Modern Italian Literature and Language: A Bibliography of Homage Studies, 1958, Le Romantisme et le Gout Esthetique du XVIIIième Siecle, 1964, The Theatre of Jacinto Grau, The Mythic Quest in Ionesco's Plays. Served with USAAF, 1942-46. Decorated Medaille Aero., chevalier officier and commandeur Palmes Academiques (France).; Sheldon traveling fellow Harvard, 1949. Mem. MLA, AAUP, Am. Assn. Tchrs. of French (pres. Boston chpt. 1958-60), Renaissance Soc. Am., New England MLA (chmn. Ea. Mass. chpt. 1955-56), N.E. Conf. Fgn. Lang. Tchrs. (vice chmn. 1964-65), Phi Beta Kappa, Phi Sigma Iota (hon.). Home: 5 Burbank Rd Medford MA 02155-2928

SIMCOX, CRAIG DENNIS, aeronautical engineer; b. Iowa Falls, Iowa, Sept. 18, 1939; s. Clair Mock and Alice Mae (Shane) S.; m. Molly A. H. Simcox, Aug. 4, 1961; 1 child, Vichi Rae Simcox Smokoff. BS in Aero. Engring., Iowa State U., 1962; MS in Aero. and Astro., Stanford U., 1965; PhD, Purdue U., 1969; postgrad., Columbia U., 1981. Research scientist Ames Research Ctr., NASA, Moffett Field, Calif., 1962-65; instr., cons. Purdue U., West Lafayette, Ind., 1965-68; research mgr. Boeing Comml. Airplanes Co., Renton, Wash., 1969-75; lab. mgr. Boeing Comml. Airplanes Co., Seattle, 1975-85; chief engr. Boeing Comml. Airplanes Co., Everett, Wash., 1985-90; dir. customer svcs. Boeing Comml. Airplanes Co., Seattle, 1990—; chmn. numerous nat. and internat. confs. Assoc. editor Tech. Periodic Jur. Aircraft, 1978-87; contbr. articles to profl. jours. V.p. Somerset Assn., Bellevue, Wash., 1978-80; v.p. civic affairs Boeing Mgmt. Assn., Seattle, 1986-88; pres. Eidelweiss Assn., Bellevue, Wash., 1991-92. Fellow AIAA (chmn. 1976-77, dep. dir. 1978-84, sec. aircraft design tech. com. 1988-91). Mem. Christian Ch. Avocations: skiing, golf, photography, music, boating. Home: 4640 132nd Ave SE Bellevue WA 98006-2131 Office: Boeing Comml Airplanes Co PO Box 3707 Seattle WA 98124-2207

SIME, DONALD RAE, retired business administration educator; b. Los Angeles, July 20, 1926; s. Chester I. and Gaynal (Ramage) S.; m. Patricia Evelyn Hawes, Sept. 4, 1949; children: Julia, Paul, Jill. B.A., Pepperdine Coll., 1949, MA, 1951; BD, Princeton Sem., 1954; PhD, U. Chgo., 1962. Prof. religion harding Grad. Sch. Harding Coll., 1954-66; prof. dept. religion and psychology Pepperdine Coll., 1966-68, chmn. dept. bus. adminstrn., 1968-69; dean Sch. Bus. and Mgmt. Pepperdine U., 1969-78, v.p., 1973-81, prof., 1978-96; cons. orgnl. devel., affirmative action programs Webco, Page Group, Los Angeles Cons. Group, Conceptual Consultants. Contbr. articles to bus. and religious publs. Served with USNR, 1944-46. Home: 20166 Village 20 Camarillo CA 93012-7506

SIMECKA, BETTY JEAN, marketing executive; b. Topeka, Apr. 15, 1935; d. William Bryan and Regina Marie (Rezac) S.; m. Alex Pappas, Jan. 15, 1956 (div. Apr. 1983); 1 child, Alex William. Student, Butler County Community Coll., 1983-85. Freelance writer and photographer L.A., also St. Marys, Kans., 1969-77; co-owner Creative Enterprises, El Dorado, Kans., 1977-83; coord. excursions into history Butler County Community Coll., El Dorado, 1983-84; dir. Hutchinson (Kans.) Conv. & Visitors Bur., 1984-85; dir. mktg. div. Exec. Mgmt., Inc., Wichita, 1985-87; exec. dir. Topeka Conv. and Visitors Bur., 1987-91, pres., CEO, 1991-96; pres. Internat. Connections, Inc., 1996—, Simecka and Assoc., 1996—; dir. promotion El Dorado Thunderboat Races, 1977-78. Contbr. articles to jours. and mags.; columnist St. Marys Star, 1973-79. Pres. El Dorado Art Assn., 1984; chmn. Santa Fe Trail Bike Assn., Kans., 1988-90; co-dir. St. Marys Summer Track Festival, 1973-81; chmn. spl. events Mulvane Art Mus., 1990, sec., 1991-92; membership chmn., 1993-94, bd. dirs., 1995-96; bd. dirs. Topeka Civic Theater, 1991-96, co-chmn. spl. events, 1992; Kans. chmn. Russian Festival Com., 1992-93; vice-chmn. Kans. Film Commn., 1993-94, chmn., 1994; bd. dirs. Kans. Expoctr. Adv. Bd., 1990-96; pres. Kans. Internat. Mus., 1994-96. Recipient Kans. Gov.'s Tourism award Kans. Broadcaster's Assn., 1993, Disting. Svc award City of Topeka, 1995, Hist. Ward Meade Disting. award Topeka Parks & Recreation Dept., 1995; named Kansan of Yr., Topeka Capitol-Jour., 1995, Sales and Mktg. Exec. of Yr., 1995, Internatn. Soroptimists, Topeka chpt., Woman of Distinction, 1996. Mem. Nat. Tour Assn., Sales and Mktg. execs. (bd. dirs. 1991-92), Internat. Assn. Conv. and Visitors Burs. (co-chmn. rural tourism com. 1994), Am. Soc. Assn. Execs., Travel Industry Assn. Kans. (membership chmn. 1988-89, sec. 1990, pres. 1991-92, Outstanding Merit award 1994), St. Marys C. of C. (pres. 1975), I-70 Assn. (v.p. 1989, pres. 1990), Optimists (social sec. Topeka chpt. 1988-89). Republican. Methodist. Avocations: writing, painting, photography, masters track. Holder Nat. AAU record for 100-yard dash, 1974.

SIMEONE, FREDERICK ANTHONY, neurosurgeon, researcher; b. Phila., June 8, 1936; s. Anthony and Emma Celeste (Grimaldi) S.; m. Catherine Eliz Walsh, Oct. 4, 1975 (div. 1989); 1 child, Christina. BA, Temple U., 1956; MD, Temple Med., 1960. Neurosurgical fellow Mayo Clinic, Rochester, Minn., 1961-63; neurosurgical resident U. Pa., Phila., 1963-65; asst. prof. Harvard Med., Boston, 1965-68; prof. U. Pa., Phila., 1968-94; prof., chmn. neurosurgery Jefferson Med. Coll., Phila., 1994—; chmn. Neurosurgery Pa. Hosp., 1969—, Jefferson Med. Coll., 1994, Wills Neurosurgery, 1994—. Author: The Spine, 1972—; contbr. articles to profl. jours. major U.S. Army, 1961-78. Mem. Am. Assoc. of Neurosurgeons, Am. Acad. Neurol. Surgeons, Congress of Neurosurgeons, Soc. Neurol. Surgeons. Republican. Roman Catholic. Avocations: sports car historical collection, automobile history writing. Home: 8700 Seminole St Philadelphia PA 19118 Office: Penn Hosp 800 Spruce St Philadelphia PA 19107-6130

SIMERAL, WILLIAM GOODRICH, retired chemical company executive; b. Portland, Oreg., May 22, 1926; s. Claire Cornelius and Geneva B. (Goodrich) S.; m. Elizabeth Louise Ross, June 25, 1949; children: Linda Simeral McGregor, Karen Simeral Schousen, William Goodrich Jr., John David. B.S. in Physics, Franklin and Marshall Coll., Lancaster, Pa., 1948; Ph.D. in Physics, U. Mich., 1953. With E.I. duPont de Nemours and Co., Inc., 1953-87; v.p., gen. mgr. plastics dept. E.I. duPont de Nemours and Co., Inc., Wilmington, Del., 1974-76; v.p., gen. mgr. plastic products and resins dept. E.I. duPont de Nemours and Co., Inc., 1976-77, sr. v.p., dir., mem. exec. com., 1977-81, exec. v.p., dir., mem. exec. com., 1981-87; vice chmn. bd., chief operating officer Conoco Inc., 1984-85. Trustee Franklin and Marshall Coll., 1977—, chmn. bd., 1991-94; trustee, bd. dirs. Wilmington Med. Ctr., 1978-93, chmn. bd., 1982-86; bd. dirs. YMCA Wilmington and New Castle County, 1978-81. Mem. Chem. Mfrs. Assn. (vice chmn. bd. 1980-81, chmn. exec. com. 1981-82, chmn. bd. 1982-83), Am. Phys. Soc., Phi Beta Kappa, Sigma Xi, Wilmington Country Club, Quail Creek Country Club, The Club Pelican Bay.

SIMEROTH, DEAN CONRAD, chemical engineer; b. Marysville, Calif., Mar. 21, 1946; s. Raphael Conrad and Mary Beatrice (Watson) S.; m. Phyllis Deborah Minakowski, Feb. 7, 1971 (div. Nov. 1994); 1 child, Brian Conrad. BS in Chem. Engring., U. Calif., Davis, 1968. From air pollution specialist to chief engr. evaluation br. Calif. Air Resources Bd., Sacramento, 1969-87; chief criteria pollutant br. Calif. Air Resources Bd., 1987—. Served in U.S. Army, 1969-71, Korea. Mem. AIChE, Air Waste Mgmt. Assn., Kiwanis (treas. Woodland, Calif. chpt. 1988-96). Democrat. Roman Catholic. Avocations: hunting, fishing, tennis, history. Office: Calif Air Resources Bd PO Box 2815 2020 L St Sacramento CA 95812

SIMES, DIMITRI KONSTANTIN, international affairs expert and educator; b. Moscow, Oct. 17, 1947; came to U.S., 1973; s. Konstantin M. and Dina (Kaminsky) S.; m. Anastasia Ryurikov, May 27, 1993. MA, Moscow State U., 1969. Sr. research fellow Ctr. for Strategic and Internat. Studies, Washington, 1973-76, dir. Soviet studies, 1976-80; prof. Soviet studies, exec. dir. Soviet and East European research program Sch. Advanced Internat. Studies, Johns Hopkins U., Washington, 1980-83, lectr., 1983-90; sr. assoc. Carnegie Endowment for Internat. Peace, Washington, 1983-94; pres. Nixon Ctr. for Peace and Freedom, Washington, 1994—; vis. prof. polit. sci. U. Calif., Berkeley, 1982; adj. prof. govt. Columbia U., N.Y.C., 1985, 92; cons. CBS News, N.Y.C., 1985-87, NBC News, 1987-94; commentators Voice of Am., 1990—. Author: Detente and Conflict: Soviet Succession: Leadership in Transition, 1978; columnist: Christian Sci. Monitor, Boston, 1983-87, L.A. Times Syndicate, 1987-89, Newsday, 1991—; contbr. articles to newspapers and jours. Vice chmn. Fund for Democracy and Devel. Mem. Coun. on Fgn. Rels. Office: Nixon Ctr Peace and Freedom 1620 I St NW Ste 900 Washington DC 20006-4005

SIMIC, CHARLES, English language educator, poet; b. Beograd, Yugoslavia, May 9, 1938; came to U.S., 1954, naturalized, 1971; s. George and Helen (Matijevich) S.; m. Helen Dubin, Oct. 1964; children: Anna, Philip. BA, NYU, 1967. Editl. asst. Aperture, Quar. of Photography, N.Y.C., 1966-69; prof. English Calif. State U., Hayward, 1970-73, U. N.H., Durham, 1973—; vis. tchr. Boston U., spring 1975, Columbia U., fall 1979. Author: poems What the Grass Says, 1967, Somewhere Among us a Stone is Taking Notes, 1969, Dismantling the Silence, 1971, White, 1972, Return to a Place Lit by a Glass of Milk, 1974, Biography and a Lament, 1976, Charon's Cosmology, 1977, Classic Ballroom Dances, 1980, Austerities, 1982, Weather Forecast for Utopia and Vicinity, 1983, Selected Poems, 1985, Unending Blues, 1986, The World Doesn't End, 1989 (Pulitzer Prize for poetry 1990), The Book of Gods and Devils, 1990, Hotel Insomnia, 1992, A Wedding in Hell, 1994, Walking the Black Cat, 1996; prose The Uncertain Certainty, 1985, Wonderful Words, Silent Truth, 1990, The Unemployed Fortune Teller; translator, editor: (with C.W. Truesdale) poems Fire Gardens, 1970, (with Mark Strand) Another Republic, 1976, (with others) Selected Poems of Tomaz Salamun, 1987, RollCall of Mirrors, 1987; translator: Four Modern Yugoslav Poets, 1970, (with P. Kastmiler) Atlantis, 1983; contbr. poems to mags. and anthologies. With U.S. Army, 1961-63. Recipient PEN Internat. award for translation, 1970, 80, Edgar Allan Poe award Am. Acad. Poets, 1975, Nat. Inst. Arts and Letters and AAAL award, 1976, Harriet Monroe poetry award U. Chgo., 1980, DiCastignola award Poetry Soc. Am., 1980, Pulitzer prize for poetry, 1990; Guggenheim fellow, 1972-73; Nat. Endowment for Arts fellow, 1974-75, 79-80; Fulbright Travelling fellow, 1982, Ingram Merrill fellow, 1983-84; Mac Arthur fellow, 1984-89. Mem. Am. Acad. Arts and Letters. Home: PO Box 192 Strafford NH 03884-0192 Office: U NH Dept English PO Box 192 Strafford NH 03884-0192

SIMINI, JOSEPH PETER, accountant, financial consultant, author, former educator; b. Buffalo, Feb. 15, 1921; s. Paul and Ida (Moro) S.; BS, St. Bonaventure U., 1940, BBA, 1949; MBA, U. Calif.-Berkeley, 1957; DBA, Western Colo. U., 1981; m. Marcelline McDermott, Oct. 4, 1968. Insp. naval material Bur. Ordnance, Buffalo and Rochester, N.Y., 1941-44; mgr. Paul Simini Bakery, Buffalo, 1946-48; internal auditor DiGiorgio (Fruit) Corp., San Francisco, 1950-51; tax accountant Price Waterhouse & Co., San Francisco, 1953; sr. accountant Richard L. Hanlin, C.P.A., San Francisco, 1953-54; prof. accounting U. San Francisco, 1954-79, emeritus prof., 1983—; mem. rev. bd. Calif. Bd. Accountancy, 1964-68. Mem. council com. Boy Scouts Am., Buffalo, San Francisco, 1942-65, Scouters Key, San Francisco council; bd. dirs. Nat. Italian Am. Found., Washington, 1979-85. Served to lt. jg. USNR, 1944-46. Recipient Bacon-McLaughlin medal St. Bonaventure U., 1940, Laurel Key, 1940; Outstanding Tchr. award Coll. Bus. Adminstrn.,

U. San Francisco, 1973; Disting. Tchr. award U. San Francisco, 1975, Joseph Peter Simini award, 1977. Crown Zellerbach Found. fellow, 1968-69; Gold Medal Associazione Piemontese nel Mondo, Turin, Italy, 1984; decorated Knight Order of Merit, Republic of Italy, 1982. CPA, Calif. Mem. Am. Inst. C.P.A.s, Calif. Soc. C.P.A.s (past chmn. ednl. standards, student relations com. San Francisco chpt.), Inst. of Mgmt. Accts. (past pres. San Francisco chpt.), Am. Acctg. Assn., Am. Mgmt. Assn. (lectr. 1968-78), Delta Sigma Pi (past pres. San Francisco alumni club), Beta Gamma Sigma. Roman Catholic. Clubs: Serra (past pres. Golden Gate chpt.), Il Cenacolo (past pres.), Toastmasters (past pres. Magic Word, treas. Dist. 4, 1996-97). Lodges: K.C., Rotary (past pres. Daly City). Author: Accounting Made Simple, 1967, 2d rev. edit., 1987, Cost Accounting Concepts for Nonfinancial Executives, 1976, Become Wealthy! Using Tax Savings and Real Estate Investments, 1982, Balance Sheet Basics for the Nonfinancial Managers, 1989, Petals of the Rose, 1990, How to Become Financially Independent, 1996. Tech. editor, Accounting Essentials, 1972. Patentee Dial-A-Trig and Verbum Est card game. Home: 977 Duncan St San Francisco CA 94131-1800 Office: PO Box 31420 San Francisco CA 94131-0420 *Personal philosophy: You can succeed! but you must program yourself for success and know what you want.*

SIMINOVITCH, LOUIS, biophysics educator, scientist; b. Montreal, Que., Can., May 1, 1920; s. Nathan and Goldie (Wachman) S.; m. Elinore Esther Faierman, July 2, 1944 (dec. 1995); children: Harriet Jane, Katherine Anne, Margo Ruth. B.Sc., McGill U., 1941, Ph.D., 1944; D honoris causa, Meml. U., 1978, McMaster U., 1978, U. Montreal, 1990, McGill U., 1990, U. Western Ont., 1990, U. Toronto, 1995. Mem. staff Nat. Research Council Can., 1944-47; Canadian Royal Soc. fellow Pasteur Inst., Paris, 1947-49; mem. staff Centre Nationale de la Recherche Scientifique, 1949-53; Nat. Cancer Inst. Can. fellow U. Toronto, Ont., Can., 1953-56; asst. prof. dept. med. biophysics U. Toronto, 1956-58, assoc. prof. med. biophysics, 1958-60, prof. med. biophysics, 1960-85, chmn. dept. med. cell biology, 1969-72, assoc. prof. pediatrics, 1972-78, prof. med. genetics, 1972-79, prof. Inst. Med. Sci., 1968-85, prof. dept. med. cell. biology, 1969-85, Univ. prof., 1976-85, univ. prof. emeritus, 1985—; dir. rsch. Samuel Lunenfeld Rsch. Inst., Mt. Sinai Hosp., Toronto, 1985-94; dir. emeritus Samuel Lunenfeld Rsch. Inst. Mt. Sinai Hosp., Toronto, 1994—; scientist divsn. biol. rsch. Ont. Cancer Inst., 1956-69. Editor Virology, 1960-80, Bacteriological Revs., 1969-72, Jour. Molecular and Cellular Biology, 1980-90; founding mem., pres. editl. bd. Sci. Forum, 1966-79; mem. editl. bd. Cell, 1973-81, Somatic Cell Genetics, 1974-84, Jour. Cytogenetics and Cell Genetics, 1974-80, Mutation Rsch., 1976-82, Jour. de Microscopie et de Biologie Cellulaire, 1976-86, Cancer Genetics and Cytogenetics, 1979-84, Jour. Cancer Surveys, 1980-89; corr. editor Proc. Royal Soc. B, 1989-93; contbr. numerous articles to sci. jours. Mem. adv. com. Can. Med. Discoveries Fund, 1994—. Decorated officer Order of Can.; recipient Queen Elizabeth II Silver-Jubilee award 1977, U. Toronto Alumni Assn. award, 1978, Izaak Walton Killam meml. price, 1981, Wightman award Gairdner Found., 1981, Medal of Achievement, Inst. de Recherches Cliniques de Montreal, 1985, Environ. Mutagen Soc. award, 1986, R.P. Taylor award Can. Cancer Soc., Nat. Cancer Inst., 1986, Disting. Rsch. award Can. Soc. Clin. Investigation, 1990, Toronto Biotech. Initiative Community Svc. award, 1991; named Companion of the Order of Can., 1989, The Gov. Gen. Commemorative medal for the 125th Anniversary of Can. Confederation, 1992. Fellow Royal Soc. Can. (mem. AIDS study steering com. 1987-88, mem. adv. com. on evaluation rsch. 1989-92, Centennial medal 1967, Flavelle medal 1978, Royal Soc. London; mem. AAAS. Home: 130 Carlton St # 805, Toronto, ON Canada M5A 4K3 Office: Samuel Lunenfeld Rsch Inst, Mt Sinai Hosp 600 University Ave, Toronto, ON Canada M5G 1X5

SIMIS, THEODORE LUCKEY, investment banker, information technology executive; b. N.Y.C., June 17, 1924; s. Theodore William Ernest and Helen (Luckey) S.; m. Laura Cushman Ingraham, Sept. 8, 1946; children—Nancy Simis Ricca, Theodore Steven, Karen Simis Woods, June Simis Sobocinski. B.S., NYU, 1950, M.B.A., 1952. With Bell System, 1941-79; various positions to officer level with N.Y. Telephone Co., N.J. Telephone Co., and AT&T; v.p. Warner Amex Cable Co., 1980-81; sr. v.p. E.F. Hutton, Sarasota, Fla., 1982-87; vice chmn., bd. dirs. XMX Corp., Burlington, Mass., 1986—; pres. Pvt. Transatlantic Telecommunication System Inc., McLean, Va., 1987-89; chmn. Value Added Network System, Inc., Sarasota, Fla., 1990-91; dir. Liebenzell Mission, Schooleys Mountain, N.J.; vis. Nieman fellow Harvard U., 1977. Mem. Republican Nat. Com., 1981—. 1st lt. U.S. Army, 1942-53, ETO. Mem. N.Y. Acad. Scis., U.S. C. of C., NYU Club. Lutheran. Home: 6025 Manasota Key Rd Englewood FL 34223-9245

SIMITIS, SPIROS, legal educator; b. Athens, Greece, Oct. 19, 1934; s. George and Fanny (Christopoulo) S.; m. Ilse Grubrich, Aug. 3, 1963. JD, U. Marburg, Fed. Republic Germany, 1956. Assoc. prof. U. Frankfurt, Fed. Republic Germany, 1963; prof. U. Frankfurt, 1969, U. Giessen, Fed. Republic Germany, 1964-69; vis. prof. London Sch. Econs., U. Calif. - Berkeley, 1976, U. Pa., 1980, U. Strasbourg, France, 1987-88, Paris, 1990—, Yale U., New Haven, Conn., 1981—; sec. gen. Internat. Civil Status Commn., 1966-80; chmn. Data Protection Experts Com. of the Coun. of Europe, Strasbourg, 1982-86, Hesse Data Protect commr., 1975-91; mem. rsch. coun. European Univ. Inst. Contbr. numerous articles to legal publs. Mem. German Lawyers Assn. (bd. dirs. 1970-82), German Coun. Pvt. Internat. Law. Office: Johann Wolfgang Goethe U, Senckenberganlage 31 Postfach, 111932 60054 Frankfurt Germany

SIMKHOVICH, SEMEN LASAREVICH, cryogenic engineer, researcher, educator; b. Cherven, Minsk, USSR, July 25, 1940; came to U.S., 1994; s. Lasar A. and Liliya S. (Rosengaus) S.; m. Marianna M. Fridman, Sept. 3, 1966; 1 child, Galina. MS in Hydromechanics, Novosibirsk State U., USSR, 1965; PhD in Hydromechanics, Inst. Physics and Optics, Moscow, 1974. Asst. prof. Poly. Inst., Omsk, USSR, 1965-67; asst. prof. Bauman's Tech. U., Moscow, 1967-76, prof., 1987-94; sr. rschr. Inst. Cryogenic Engring., Moscow, 1973-81, lead rschr., 1981-90; ind. cons. Bklyn., 1994-97; technical specialist Guardian Life Ins. Co. Am., N.Y.C., 1997—. Contbr. numerous articles to profl. jours. Recipient USSR Inventor award USSR State Com. Inventions & Discoveries, 1981. Achievements include over 30 patents in field of cryogenic engineering and space technology; research in fields of hydrodynamics and cryogenics; participation in Soviet Space Exploration program. Home: 1702 W 6th St Apt 1D Brooklyn NY 11223 Office: 201 Park Ave S New York NY 10003-1601

SIMKIN, PETER ANTHONY, physician, educator; b. Morgantown, W.Va., Nov. 22, 1935; s. William Edward and Ruth Helen (Commons) S.; m. Penelope Hart Payson, Aug. 9, 1958; children—Andrew, Caroline, Mary, Elizabeth. B.A., Swarthmore Coll., 1957; M.D., U. Pa., 1961. Intern N.C. Meml. Hosp., Chapel Hill, 1961-62; resident N.C. Meml. Hosp., 1962-63, Univ. Hosps. Cleve., 1965-66; fellow in medicine U. Wash., Seattle, 1966-69; asst. prof. U. Wash., 1969-74, assoc. prof., 1974-84, prof., 1984—. Mem. editorial bd.: Arthritis and Rheumatism, 1981-85, BIMR Rheumatology, 1980-84; contbr. articles to profl. jours. Bd. dirs. Wash. chpt. Arthritis Found., 1974-90, chmn. med. and sci. com., 1974-78. Served with U.S. Army, 1963-65. Fellow Am. Coll. Rheumatology; mem. Western Soc. Clin. Research, Am. Fedn. Clin. Investigation, Orthopaedic Research Soc. Quaker. Office: Rheumatology 356428 U Wash Seattle WA 98195-6420

SIMKO, JAN, English and foreign language literature educator; b. Zlaté Moravce, Slovakia, Oct. 30, 1920; came to U.S., 1967; s. Simon Simko and Terezia Simkova; m. Libusa Safarikova, Dec. 20, 1950 (div. 1970); children: Jan, Vladimir (dec.). Diploma in English, U. Bratislava, 1942, Diploma in German, 1943, PhD in English, 1944; MPhil in English, U. London, 1967. Tchr. English and German various bus. schs., 1942-45; asst. depts. English and German U. Bratislava, 1945-46; instr. English Econom U., 1946-47; mem. faculty U. Bratislava, 1950-68, from asst. prof. to assoc. prof. English, 1957-68; prof. English Rio Grande Coll., Ohio, 1968-75; instr. Shakespeare Georgetown U., 1982-84; vis. prof. English, scholar-in-residence W.Va. U., Parkersburg, 1989-90; instr. Slovak, Fgn. Svc. Inst., Washington, 1974, 96, fed. govt., 1989, 91-93, IMF & World Bank, 1994-95; external examiner critical langs. program Kent (Ohio) State U., 1974-91; feature writer Voice of Am., 1983-96; translator U.S. Dept. State, 1997—; numerous lectureships. Author: 3 English textbooks, 2 bilingual dictionaries, 1 linguistics monograph, numerous linguistics and literature articles, editor: Lectures in the Circle of Modern Philology, 2 vols., 1965-66; chief consulting editor: textbooks of Slovak and Czech, 1993-96; contbg. editor: The Review, 1995-96. With inf. Czecho-Slovak Army, 1946. Brit. Coun. grantee, 1947-49; Folger Shakespeare Libr./U.S. Dept. State, 1967-68; Internat. Rsch. and Exch. Bd. grantee, 1982, others. Mem. MLA (life), Slovak Studies Assn., Soc. for Scis. and Arts, Met. Opera Guild, Shakespeare Theater Guild, Nat. Symphony Orch. Assn. Roman Catholic. Avocations: classical music, opera, theatre, fine arts, hiking, swimming. Home: 1356 E Capitol St NE Washington DC 20003-1533

SIMMEL, MARIANNE LENORE, graphic designer; b. Jena, Germany; d. Hans E. and Else R. (Rapp) S. A.B., Smith Coll., 1943; A.M., Harvard U., 1945, Ph.D., 1949. Diplomate Am. Bd. Examiners Profl. Psychology. Intern psychology Worchester (Mass.) State Hosp., 1943; research asst. Neurol. Lab., Boston Dispensary, Tufts Coll. Med. Sch., Boston, 1943-45; instr. psychology Cambridge (Mass.) Jr. Coll., 1945-46; vol. asst. neurol. unit Childrens Hosp., Harvard Med. Sch., 1945-46; instr. psychology Hofstra Coll., 1946-48; vis. lectr. dept. psychology Wellesley Coll., 1948-49; from instr. to clin. assoc. prof. psychology dept. psychiatry Coll. Medicine, U. Ill., 1950-58; psychophysiologist, head psychol. lab. Ill. State Psychopathic Inst., Chgo., 1952-58; asst. dir. Ill. State Psychopathic Inst., 1952-55; vis. lectr. med. psychology Duke Med. Sch., 1958-59; spl. research fellow USPHS, NIMH, 1959-61, 69-70; asst. psychologist in neurosurgery Mass. Gen. Hosp., 1959-61, from 63; research assoc. dept. psychology Brandeis U., 1959-61, from assoc. prof. to prof., 1963-78, adj. prof., from 1978, prof. emeritus psychology, 1987—; research assoc. in neurology Mt. Sinai Hosp., N.Y.C., 1961-67; now graphic designer. Contbr. articles to profl. jours.; Editor: The Reach of Mind: Essays in Memory of Kurt Goldstein, 1968. Recipient Research award Am. Rehab. Counseling Assn., 1964. Fellow Am. Psychol. Assn.; mem. Eastern Psychol. Assn., Psychonomic Soc., AAUP, Am. Soc. Aesthetics, Phi Beta Kappa, Sigma Xi. Home: PO Box 562 North Eastham MA 02651-0562 *Methodology is the last refuge of a sterile mind.*

SIMMERMON, JAMES EVERETT, credit bureau executive; b. Arnold, Pa., Mar. 23, 1926; s. Joseph C. and Melba J. (McGeary) S.; m. Lois Bowden, Apr. 19, 1952; children: James, Thomas, John, Lisa, William. BS in Bus. Adminstrn, Ashland (Ohio) U., 1949. Chmn. Collection Service Ctr., New Kensington, Pa., 1955—; mem. adv. bd. Associated Credit Bus., Houston, 1965-73, bd. dirs., 1984—; bd. dirs. Consumer Credit Counseling Svc. of Western Pa., 1975—; vice chmn. Citizens Gen. Enterprises Inc., 1986—. Trustee Ashland (Ohio) U., 1986—; bd. dirs. Citizens Gen. Hosp., New Kensington, Pa., 1972—. With USNR, 1944-46. Mem. Rotary Club of Fox Chapel (past dist. gov. dist. 7300, 1982-83, Oakmont Country Club, Green Valley Country Club. Home: 302 Fox Chapel Rd Apt 316 Pittsburgh PA 15238-2337

SIMMONDS, RAE NICHOLS, musician, composer, educator; b. Lynn, Mass., Feb. 25, 1919; d. Raymond Edward and Abbie Iola (Spinney) Nichols; m. Carter Fillebrown, Jr., June 27, 1941 (div. May 15, 1971); children: Douglas C. (dec.), Richard A., Mary L., Donald E.; m. Ronald John Simmonds, Oct. 9, 1971 (dec. Nov. 1995). AA, Westbrook Coll., Portland, Maine, 1981; B in Music Performance summa cum laude, U. Maine, 1984; MS in Edn., U. So. Maine, 1989; PhD, Walden U., 1994. Founder, dir. Studio of Music/Children's Studio of Drama, Portsmouth, N.H., 1964-71, Studio of Music, Bromley, Eng., 1971-73, Bromley Children's Theatre, 1971-73, Oughterard Children's Theatre, County Galway, Ireland, 1973-74, Studio of Music, Portland, Maine, 1977-96; resident playwright Children's Theatre of Maine, Portland, 1979-81; organist/choir dir. Stevens Ave. Congl. Ch., Portland, 1987-95; field faculty advisor Norwich U., Montpelier, Vt., 1995; field advisor grad. program Vt. Coll., Norwich U., 1995; cons./educator mus. tng. for disabled vets. VA, Portsmouth, N.H., 1966-69; show pianist and organist, mainland U.S.A., 1939-59, Hawaii, 1959-62, Rae Nichols Trio, 1962—. Author/composer children's musical: Shamrock Road, 1980 (Blue Stocking award 1980), Glooscap, 1980; author/composer original scripts and music: Cinderella, If I Were a Princess, Beauty and the Beast, Baba Yaga - A Russian Folk Tale, The Journey - Musical Bible Story, The Perfect Gift - A Christmas Legend; original stories set to music include: Heidi, A Little Princess, Tom Sawyer, Jungle Book, Treasure Island; compositions include: London Jazz Suite, Bitter Suite, Jazz Suite for Trio, Sea Dream, Easter (chorale), others. Recipient Am. Theatre Wing Svc. award, 1944, Pease AFB Svc. Club award, 1967, Bumpus award Westbrook Coll., 1980; Nat. Endowment for Arts grantee, 1969-70; Women's Lit. scholar, 1980, Westbrook scholar, 1980-81, Nason scholar, 1983; Kelaniya U. (Colombo, Sri Lanka) rsch. fellow, 1985-86. Mem. ASCAP, Internat. Soc. Poets, Musicians Assn. of Hawaii, Internat. League Women Composers, Music Tchrs. of Maine, Am. Guild of Organists, Music Tchrs. Nat. Assn., Internat. Alliance for Women in Music, Doctorate Assn. N.Y. Educators, Inc., Delta Omicron, Phi Kappa Phi. Democrat. Episcopalian. Avocations: travel, philately. Home: RR 1 Box 950 West Baldwin ME 04091-9715

SIMMONS, ALAN JAY, electrical engineer, consultant; b. N.Y.C., Oct. 14, 1924; s. George and Cherry (Danzig) S.; m. Mary Marcella Bachhuber, April 12, 1947; children, G. David, Peter A., Michael A.; Philip E., Paul I. BS in Physics and Chemistry, Harvard U., 1945; MSEE, MIT, 1948; PhDEE, U. Md., 1957. Electronic scientist Naval Rsch. Lab., Washington, 1948-57; dir. rsch. TRG Inc., Boston, 1957-65; div. mgr. TRG div. Control Data Corp., Boston, 1965-71; group leader MIT Lincoln Lab., Lexington, 1971-87; cons. Winchester, Mass., 1987—. Contbr. articles to profl. jours.; patentee in field. Mem. Town Dem. Com., Winchester, Mass., 1963. Lt. (j.g.) USN, 1943-46. Fellow IEEE (life); mem. AAAS (life), Antennas and Propagation Soc. (pres. 1986). Avocations: gardening, hiking, tennis, travel. Home and Office: PO Box 207 Center Sandwich NH 03227-0207

SIMMONS, ALAN JOHN, philosophy educator; b. Dover, N.J., May 4, 1950; s. Alan Gleason and Jessie May (Ahrens) S.; m. Jean Claire Dreyfus, Mar. 26, 1969 (div. Aug. 1982); 1 child, Shawn Kathleen Simmons; m. Nancy Ellen Schauber, May 30, 1987. AB summa cum laude, Princeton U., 1972; MA, Cornell U., 1975, PhD, 1977. Asst. prof. philosophy U. Va., Charlottesville, 1976-81, assoc. prof. philosophy, 1981-89, prof. philosophy, 1989—, Commonwealth prof. philosophy, 1997—; vis. asst. prof. philosophy Johns Hopkins U., Balt., 1981; cons. FBI, Quantico, Va., 1982-88; vis. Prof. Philosophy U. Hawaii, Manoa, 1990. Author: Moral Principles and Political Obligations, 1979, The Lockean Theory of Rights, 1992, On the Edge of Anarchy, 1993; editor: International Ethics, 1985, Punishment, 1995; contbr. articles to profl. jours.; editor Philosophy and Pub. Affairs, 1982—. NEH fellow, 1987-88. Mem. Am. Soc. Polit. Legal Philosophy (v.p. 1997—), N. Am. Soc. Social Philosophy (exec. bd. 1983-84), Va. Philosophical Assn., Am. Philosophical Assn., Phi Beta Kappa, Ctr. Advanced Studies. Office: U Va Dept Philosophy 521 Cabell Hall Charlottesville VA 22903-3125

SIMMONS, ANNE L., federal official; b. Spencer, Iowa, Jan. 4, 1964; d. Donald Lewis and Lois Amber (Blass) S. B in Spl. Studies, Cornell Coll., 1986. Intern for Congressman Berkley Bedell Washington, 1986; field staff Iowans for Clayton Hodgson, Sioux City, Iowa, 1986; exec. sec. Atomic Indsl. Forum, Bethesda, Md., 1986-87; staff asst. House Armed Svcs. Com., Washington, 1987; legis. asst. to Congressman Tim Johnson Washington, 1988-93; staff dir. gen. farms commodities subcom. House Agriculture Com., Washington, 1993, staff dir. environ., credit and rural devel. subcom., 1994, minority resource conservation rsch. and forestry subcom., 1995-96. Profl. Staff Ho. Com. on Agrl., 1997—. Music scholar Cornell Coll., 1982-86. Mem. Delta Phi Alpha. Democrat. Office: House Agriculture Com 1301 Longworth Bldg Ofc Bldg Washington DC 20515-0004

SIMMONS, BILL, political editor; b. Little Rock, Ark., Sept. 23, 1941; s. William F. and Pauline (Hollenberger) S.; m. Jane, Dec. 27, 1962; children: Theodosia Jane, William Tobias. Newsman AP, Little Rock, Ark., 1962-90, chief of bur., 1990-96; polit. editor Ark. Dem.-Gazette, Little Rock, 1996—. Author (short stories) Hunter, Negro; also poems. Named Journalist of Yr., U. Ark., Little Rock, 1983. Home: 13803 Alexander Rd Alexander AR 72002-1509 Office: Ark Dem-Gazette 5th and Scott St Little Rock AR 72203

SIMMONS, CAROLINE THOMPSON, civic worker; b. Denver, Aug. 22, 1910; d. Huston and Caroline Margaret (Cordes) Thompson; m. John Farr Simmons, Nov. 11, 1936; children: John Farr (dec.), Huston T., Malcolm M. (dec.). AB, Bryn Mawr Coll., 1931; MA (hon.), Amherst Coll. Chmn. women's com. Corcoran Gallery Art, 1965-66; vice chmn. women's com. Smithsonian Assocs., 1969-71; pres. Decatur House Council, 1963-71; mem. bd. Nat. Theatre, 1979-80; trustee Washington Opera, 1955-65; bd. dirs. Fgn. Student Svc. Coun., 1956-79; mem. Washington Home Bd., 1955-60; bd. dirs. Smithsonian Friends of Music, 1977-79; commr. Nat. Mus. Am. Art, 1979-89; mem. Folger com. Folger Shakespeare Libr., 1979-86, trustee emeritus, 1986—; mem. Washington bd. Am. Mus. in Britain, 1970-93; bd. dirs. Found. Preservation of Historic Georgetown, 1975-89; trustee Marpat Found., 1987—, Amherst Coll., 1979-81, Dacor-Bacon House Found., Phillips Collection, 1990—, Georgetown Presbyn. Ch., 1989-91; v.p. internat. coun. Mus. Modern Art, N.Y.C., 1964-90, emeritus trustee; bd. dirs. Alliance Francaise. Recipient award for eminent svc. Folger Shakespeare Libr., 1986. Mem. Soc. Women Geographers, Sulgrave Club, Chevy Chase Club. Address: 1508 Dumbarton Rock Ct NW Washington DC 20007-3048

SIMMONS, CHARLES, author; b. N.Y.C., Aug. 17, 1924; s. Charles and Mary (Landrigan) S.; m. Helen Elizabeth Fitzgerald, Feb. 8, 1947 (div.); children: Deirdre, Maud; m. Nancy Nicholas, Sept. 17, 1977 (div.). A.B., Columbia U., 1948. Picture editor Unicorn Press, N.Y.C., 1948-51; mem. staff N.Y. Times, 1951-84, asst. book rev. editor, 1963-84; exec. editor Memories mag., 1988-90; editor-at-large Travel Holiday, 1991-93; contbg. editor Penthouse, 1991-92; author/editor Wordworks, 1993-96; vis. writer Am. Acad. in Rome, 1981; regents' lectr. U. Calif. at Santa Barbara, 1981; adj. prof. Sch. Arts, Columbia U., 1981. Author: Powdered Eggs, 1964 (William Faulkner award notable 1st novel), An Old Fashioned Darling, 1971, Wrinkles, 1978, The Belles Lettres Papers, 1987, also stories, articles, lit. criticism: editor (with Nona Balakian) The Creative Present: Notes on Contemporary American Fiction, 1963, (with Alexander Coleman) All There Is to Know: Readings from the Illustrious 11th Edition of Encyclopedia Britannica, 1994. Served with AUS, 1943-46. Home: 221 W 82nd St New York NY 10024-5406

SIMMONS, CLEATOUS J., lawyer; b. Panama City, Fla., Nov. 17, 1944. BS, USAF Acad., 1967; MS, U. Mich., 1970; JD, Vanderbilt U., 1977. Bar: Fla. 1977. Asst. prof. USAF Acad., Colo., 1970-73; mem. Lowndes, Drosdick, Doster, Kantor & Reed, Orlando, Fla. Mng. editor Vanderbilt Jour. Transactional Law, 1976-77. Capt. USAF, 1967-74, lt. col. Res. ret. Mem. Fla. Bar, Orange County Bar Assn. Office: Lowndes Drosdick Doster Kantor & Reed PO Box 2809 215 N Eola Dr Orlando FL 32801-2095

SIMMONS, CLYDE, professional football player; b. Lanes, S.C., Aug. 4, 1964. Student, Western Carolina. Former defensive end Phila. Eagles, 1986-94; with Ariz. Cardinals, 1994—. Named NFL All-Pro team defensive end, The Sporting News, 1991. Played in Pro Bowl, 1991, 92. Office: Ariz Cardinals PO Box 888 Phoenix AZ 85001-0888*

SIMMONS, DEIDRE WARNER, performing company executive; b. Easton, Pa., May 11, 1955; d. Francis Joseph and Irene Carol (Burd) Mooney; m. Robert D. Jacobson, June 27, 1981 (div. Mar. 1989); m. William Richard Simmons, Aug. 18, 1990; children: Caitlin Dawn, Abigail Patricia, Samantha Irene. BA in Music, Montclair State Coll., 1978. Music tchr. Warren Hills Regional Sch., Washington, N.J., 1978-80; devel. dir. N.J. Shakespeare Festival, Madison, 1981-83; dir. contbns. Parent Found., Lancaster, Pa., 1983-86; exec. dir. Fulton Opera House, Lancaster, 1986—, capital campaign counsel, 1990-95; mem. adv. bd. Mellon Bank. Vice chmn. bd. dirs. Ind. Eye, Lancaster, 1986-89; mem. adv. com. Lancaster Cultural Coun., 1988—. Mem. Theatre Communications Group, League Hist. Theatres. Avocations: piano, singing. Office: Fulton Opera House 12 N Prince St PO Box 1865 Lancaster PA 17608

SIMMONS, EDWIN HOWARD, marine corps officer, historian; b. Paulsboro, N.J., Aug. 25, 1921; s. Edwin Lonsdale and Nettie Emma (Vankirk) S.; m. Frances Bliss, Apr. 25, 1962; children: Edwin Howard, Clarke Vankirk, Bliss, Courtney. B.A., Lehigh U., 1942; M.A., Ohio State U., 1955; postgrad., Amphibious Warfare Sch., 1949-50, Nat. War Coll., 1966-67. Commd. 2d lt. USMC, 1942, advanced through grades to brig. gen., 1967; asst. prof. NROTC, Ohio State U., 1952-55; with Hdqrs. Marine Corps, 1955- 59; naval attache Dominican Republic, 1959-60; with Hdqrs. Marine Corps and Joint Staff, 1962-65, 3d Marine Div., 1965-66, 1st Marine Div., Vietnam, 1970-71; dep. fiscal dir. Marine Corps, 1967-70; dir. Marine Corps history and museums USMC Hdqrs., Arlington, Va., 1971-95, dir. emeritus, 1996—; pres. Am. Mil. Inst., 1979; v.p. U.S. Commn. Mil. History, 1979-83; exec. v.p. Marine Corps Hist. Found., 1979—; pres. Coun. Am. Mil. Past, 1991-95. Author: The United States Marines, 1974, Marines, 1987; Mng. editor: Marine Corps Gazette, 1946-49; sr. editor: Publs. Group, Marine Corps Schs., 1960-61; Contbr. to numerous books, encys., mags., jours. and annuals. Decorated D.S.M., Silver Star, Legion of Merit with two gold stars, Bronze Star with gold star, Meritorious Service medal, Navy Commendation medal, Purple Heart; knight Nat. Order of Vietnam, Vietnamese Cross of Gallantry with 2 palms and silver star; recipient Centennial Disting. Grad. medallion Ohio State U., 1970. Fellow Co. Mil. Historians; mem. Am. Soc. Mil. Comptrollers (nat. v.p. 1967-69, pres. 1969-70), Nat. War Coll. Alumni Assn. (v.p. 1969-70, 74-75), Phi Beta Kappa, Omicron Delta Kappa, Phi Sigma Kappa. Home: 9020 Charles Augustine Dr Alexandria VA 22308-2822 Office: USMC Mus MC Hist Ctr Navy Yard Bldg 160 Washington DC 20374-0580

SIMMONS, ELROY, JR., retired utility executive; b. Johnstown, Pa., Sept. 23, 1928; s. Elroy and Hazel Maria (Shomo) S. BS in Bus. Adminstrn., U. Pitts., 1951. With Pa. Electric Co., Johnstown, 1953, system treasury asst., 1969-71, system coordinator, treasury services, 1971-74, asst. treas., 1974-79, sec., treas., 1979-90; ret., 1990. Bd. dirs. Community Arts Ctr. of Cambria County, 1987-95. With CIC, U.S. Army, 1951-53. Mem. Pa. Electric Assn. (customer relations com. 1965-69), Nat. Corp. Cash Mgmt. Assn., Nat. Assn. Accts., Nat. Assn. Corp. Treas. Republican. Methodist. Home: 1023 Hillside Trl Johnstown PA 15905-1234

SIMMONS, EMORY G., mycologist; b. Ind., Apr. 12, 1920. AB, Wabash Coll., 1941; AM, DePauw U., 1946; PhD in Botany, U. Mich., 1950; DSc in Microbiology (hon.), Kasetsart U., Thailand, 1988. Instr. bacteriology & botany DePauw U., Greencastle, Ind., 1946-47; asst. prof. botany Dartmouth Coll., Hanover, N.H., 1950-53; mycologist U.S. Army Natick Labs., 1953-58, head mycology lab., 1958-74; prin. investor Devel. Ctr. Cult Collection of Fungi, 1974-77; prof. botany U. Mass., Amherst, 1974-77, prof. microbiology, 1977-87, ret., 1987; rsch. assoc. Wabash Coll., Crawfordsville, Ind., 1987—; chmn. adv. com. fungi Am. Type Cult Collection; U.S. rep. Expert Group on Fungus Taxonomy, Orgn. Econ. Coop. & Devel.; rsch. fellow Sec. Army, Thailand Indonesia, 1968-69; adj. prof. U. R.I., 1972-74; mem. exec. bd. U.S. Fedn. Cult Collections, 1974-76, pres., 1976-78; pres., chmn. bd. dirs. Second Internat. Mycology Congress Inc., 1975-78; mem. adv. com. cult collections UN Environ. Program/UNESCO/Internat. Cell Rsch. Orgn., 1977—. Mem AAAS, Mycological Soc. Am. (sec.- treas. 1963-65, v.p. 1966, pres. 1968, Disting. Mycologist award 1990), Brit. Mycological Soc., Internat. Assn. Plant Taxonomists. Achievements include research in taxonomic mycology, taxonomy of Fungi imperfecti, taxonomy and cultural characteristics of Ascomycetes. Office: 717 Thornwood Rd Crawfordsville IN 47933-2760

SIMMONS, GARY M., writer, small business owner; b. Chgo., Dec. 21, 1961; s. Larry Franklin S. and Carol T. Berry. Student, W. Ky. Tech., 1982-83. Respiratory therapist Loures Hosp., Paducah, Ky., 1982-96; owner Pets Plus, Sympsonia, Ky., 1990-91; retail mgr. Dippin' Dots Inc., Paducah, Ky., 1991-95; owner Pen, Inc., Paducah, 1995—; spkr. Kingsbury Enterprises, 1994, Bus. Events Internat., Escondido, Calif., 1995-96, Visionary Voices, Mission Viejo, Calif., 1997—; cons., websited designer Debco Software, Paducah, Ky. Author: Nature's Impressions, 1995, The Bahamian: Under Friendly Fire, 1997; assisted (video, cassette, book) BECOMING (Donna Loesh and Jack Canfield), Internetcolumnist, "Mr. Businessman Advice". Mem. Am. Rivers (Washington), Poets of the Western Rivers (Paducah, Ky.), Philosophy Round Table (Paducah, Ky.), Club Theatrical Arts (pres. 1981-82). Avocations: piano, swimming, weight lifting, fishing. Home: 2912 Fisher Rd West Paducah KY 42086-9736

SIMMONS, GENE, musician; b. Haifa, Israel, Aug. 25, 1949; came to U.S., 1958, naturalized, 1963; A.B.A., Sullivan Coll., SUNY, 1970; B.A., Richmond Coll., CUNY, 1972. Singer, songwriter, actor, 1970—; founder, 1973 thereafter mem. group Kiss. Albums include: Alive, 1975, Kiss-The

Originals, 1976, Destroyer, 1976, Rock & Roll Over, 1976, Love Gun, 1977, Alive II, 1977, Double Platinum, 1978, Gene Simmons, 1978, Dynasty, 1979, Unmasked, 1980, Music From the Elder, 1981, Creatures of the Night, 1982, Lick It Up, 1983, Animalize, 1984, Kiss, 1974, Hotter Than Hell, 1974, Dressed to Kill, 1975, Beth, 1976, I Was Made for Lovin' You, 1979, Asylum, 1985, Crazy Nights, 1987, Hot In The Shade, 1989, Smashes, Thrashes and Hits, 1989, Revenge, 1992, Alive!, 1993, Alive II, 1993, Alive III, 1993; film appearance in Kiss-Attack of the Phantom, 1978, Runaway, 1984-85. Winner 16 Gold Record Albums, 12 Platinum Record Albums, 2 Gold Single Records. Mem. Am. Fedn. Musicians, AFTRA, ASCAP. Inventor of Axe bass guitar, 1980. Office: care Polygram Records Inc Worldwide Pla 825 8th Ave New York NY 10019-7416 *Listen to everyone around you, but do only what you believe.**

SIMMONS, GEORGE FINLAY, mathematics educator; b. Austin, Tex., Mar. 3, 1925; s. George Finlay and Armede Victoria (Hatcher) S.; m. Hope Bridgeford, Sept. 11, 1954; 1 child, Nancy Bingham. BS, Caltech, 1946; MS, U. Chgo., 1948; PhD, Yale U., 1957. Instr. U. Chgo., 1947-50, U. Maine, Orono, 1950-52, Yale U., New Haven, 1952-56; asst. prof. U. R.I., Kingston, 1956-58, Williams College, Williamstown, Mass., 1958-62; assoc. prof. math. Colo. Coll., Colorado Springs, 1962-65, prof., 1965-90, prof. emeritus, 1990—. Author: Introduction Topology and Modern Analysis, 1962, Differential Equations, 1972, 2d edit., 1991, Precalculus Mathematics in a Nutshell, 1981, Calculus with Analytic Geometry, 1985, 2d edit., 1995, Calculus Gems: Brief Lives and Memorable Mathematics, 1992. Mem. Math. Assn. Am. Avocations: travel, cooking, trout fishing, billiards. Home: 1401 Wood Ave Colorado Springs CO 80907-7348 Office: Colorado College Dept Math Colorado Springs CO 80903

SIMMONS, HOWARD LEE, education educator; b. Mobile, Ala.. BS in Secondary Edn., Spring Hill Coll., 1960; MAT in Slavic langs. and Lit., Ind. U., 1965; PhD in Design and Mgmt. of Postsecondary Edn., Fla. State U., 1975; LHD (honoris causa), Sojourner-Douglass Coll., 1995. Assoc. dir. , asst. exec. sec. Commn. on Higher Edn. Middle States Assn. of Colls. & Schs., Phila., 1974-95, exec. dir., 1988-95; assoc. dean, prof., coord. edn. leadership in higher edn. Ariz. State U., Tempe, 1996—; vis. lectr. in Russian Lafayette Coll., Easton, Pa., 1970-71; part-time Russian/Spanish instr. Clayton (Mo.) High Sch., 1965-67; dean instructional svcs. Northampton Community Coll., Bethlehem, Pa., 1969-74; chmn. dept. fgn. lang. Forest Park Community Coll., Mo., 1964-69; sr. researcher Ariz. State U., nat. Ctr. for Postsecondary Governance and Fin., 1986-87; cons. in field; keynote speaker in field; researcher on accreditation and blacks in higher edn. Contbr. articles to profl. jours. NDEA grantee Spring Hill Coll., 1958-60, grantee Japan-U.S. Friendship Commn., 1993-94; NDEA fellow Ind. U., 1963-64, Edn. Professions Devel. Act fellow Fla. State U., 1973-75, fellow Am. Coun. Edn., 1972-73; USIA Acad. Specialist grantee, Quito, Ecuador, 1996. Mem. Am. Ednl. Rsch. assn., Am. Assn. for Community and Jr. Colls. (assoc.), Assn. for the Study of Higher Edn., Assn. of Tchrs. of Slavic and East European Langs., Assn. Caribbean Tertiary Instn., Internat. Accreditation Specialist, 1996—, Am. Assn. for Higher Edn. (exec. bd. black caucus, nat. cultural diversity award by caucuses 1992), Phi Delta Kappa, Kappa Delta Pi. Home: 2008 N Squire Ave Tempe AZ 85281-1330 Office: Ariz State U Coll Edn PO Box 872411 Tempe AZ 85287-2411

SIMMONS, JAMES CHARLES, lawyer; b. N.Y.C., June 5, 1935; s. James Knight and Helen (Bielefeld) S.; m. Carolyn Ann Edwards, June 12, 1957; children: James M., Shawn M. Dzielawa. BSMetE, Lehigh U., 1957; JD, Duquesne U., 1965. Bar: Pa. 1965, U.S. Dist. Ct. (we. dist.) Pa. 1965, U.S. Ct. Appeals (3rd cir.) 1965, U.S. Ct. Appeals (fed. cir.) 1977. Metall. engr. Crucible Steel Co. Am., Midland, Pa., 1957-66; contract adminstr. Nuclear Materials & Equipment Corp., Apollo, Pa., 1966-67; patent atty. Bausch & Lomb, Rochester, N.Y., 1967-69; asst. gen. patent counsel Air Products and Chem., Inc., Allentown, Pa., 1969-94; sr. atty. Ratner & Prestia, Valley Forge, Pa., 1994-97; ptnr. Ratner & Prestia, Valley Forge, 1997—. Mem. ABA, Am. Intellectual Property Law Assn. (sec. 1993-96), Pa. Bar Assn., Fed. Cir. Bar Assn., Phila. Intellectual Property Law Assn., Bar Assn. Lehigh County, Benjamin Franklin Am. Inn of Ct. Office: Ratner & Prestia Ste 301 One Westlakes PO Box 980 Valley Forge PA 19482

SIMMONS, J(AMES) GERALD, management consultant; b. Atlanta, Sept. 17, 1929; s. Joseph D. and Nell (Ray) S. BBA, U. Miami, 1956; student advanced mgmt. program, Harvard U., 1969. With IBM Corp., 1956-71; dir. mktg. Data Processing divsn. IBM, White Plains, N.Y., 1969-71; v.p., gen. mgr. dept. and splty. store divsn. Revlon Inc., N.Y.C., 1971-73; v.p. mktg. Wiltek Inc., Norwalk, Conn., 1973-76; pres. Handy HRM Corp., N.Y.C., 1976-96, vice chmn. emeritus, 1997—. With U.S. Army, 1951-54. Mem. Greenwich (Conn.) Country Club. Avocations: tennis, squash, golf. Office: Handy HRM Corp 250 Park Ave New York NY 10177-0001

SIMMONS, JEAN ELIZABETH MARGARET (MRS. GLEN R. SIMMONS), chemistry educator; b. Cleve., Jan. 20, 1914; d. Frank Charles and Sarah Anne (Johnston) Saurwein; m. Glen R. Simmons, Nov. 14, 1935; children: Sally Anne, (Frank) Charles, James Fraser. B.A., Western Reserve U., 1933; Ph.D. (Stieglitz fellow 1935-37), U. Chgo., 1938. Faculty Barat Coll., Lake Forest, Ill., 1938-58; prof., chmn. dept. chemistry Barat Coll., 1948-58; faculty Upsala Coll., East Orange, N.J., 1959—; prof. Upsala Coll., 1963-84, prof. emeritus, 1984—, chmn. dept. chemistry, 1965-71, 74, 76-81, chmn. sci. curriculum study, Luth. Ch. Am. grantee, 1965-68, chmn. div. natural scis. and maths., 1965-69, asst. to pres., 1968-73, 78-86; Coordinator basic scis. Evang. Hosp. Sch. Nursing, Chgo., 1943-46; lectr. sci. topics; participant various White House Confs. Contbr. articles to publs. in field. Troop leader Girl Scouts U.S.A., Wheaton, Ill., 1952-58, neighborhood chmn., 1956-57, dist. chmn., DuPage County, 1958; chmn. U. Chgo. Alumni Fund Dr., Wheaton, 1957, 58, Princeton, N.J., 1964, 65; mem. nursing adv. com. East Orange (N.J.) Gen. Hosp., 1963-73; pres. Virginia Gildersleeve Internat. Fund, 1975-81, bd. dirs., 1969-83, chmn. nominating com., 1985-87, oral history com., 1981, hon. mem., 1996. Recipient Lindback Found. award for disting. teaching, 1964; vis. fellow Princeton U., 1977. Fellow Am. Inst. Chemists, AAAS (council 1969-71); mem. Am. Chem. Soc., AAUW (br. treas. 1960-62, chmn. sci. topic 1963-65, state v.p. program 1964, nat. sci. topic implementation chmn. 1965, 66, state dir. 1967-68, 71-72, state pres. 1968-70, 50 Yr. Cert. 1989), Fedn. Orgns. Profl. Women (nat. pres. 1974-75), Internat. Fedn. Univ. Women (alt. del. for U.S. at conf. 1968, 77, 83, del. conf. 1974, ofcl. observer UN Conf. Vienna 1979, Nairobi 1981, convenor membership com. 1980-84, adv. bd. 1980—, oral history com. 1990), AAUP (charter, past chpt. pres.), Phi Beta Kappa (pres. North Jersey alumni assn. 1973-74), Sigma Xi, Sigma Delta Epsilon (nat. pres. 1970-71, dir. 1972-78, edn. liaison 1978-87, chmn. nom. 1986-87, hon., award sci. edn. 1989). Episcopalian. Home: 53 South St Jamaica Plain Boston MA 02130

SIMMONS, JOHN DEREK, investment banker; b. Essex, Eng., July 17, 1931; came to U.S., 1952; s. Simon Leonard and Eve (Smart) S.; m. Rosalind Wellish, Mar. 5, 1961; children: Peter Lawrence, Sharon Leslie. BS, Columbia, 1956; MBA, Rutgers U., 1959; postgrad. NYU, 1959-62.Chief cost acct. Airborne Accessories, Hillside, N.J., 1952-57; sr. cost analyst Curtiss-Wright Corp., Wood Ridge, N.J., 1957; sr. fin. analyst internat. group Ford Motor Co., Jersey City, N.J., 1958-60; rsch. assoc. Nat. Assn. Accts., N.Y.C., 1960-64; asst. to v.p. fin. Air Reduction Co., Inc., 1965-67; mgr. corp. planning Anaconda Wire & Cable Co., N.Y.C., 1968; ind. fin. cons., 1968-71; assoc. cons. Rogers, Slade and Hill, Inc., N.Y.C., 1969-71; v.p., security analyst, economist Moore & Schley, Cameron & Co. (name now changed to Fourteen Rsch. Corp.), 1972-81; v.p., security analyst Merrill Lynch Capital Markets, N.Y.C., 1981-88; security analyst Arnhold and S. Bleichroeder, Inc., N.Y.C., 1988-89; v.p., security analyst, corp. fin. specialist Smith Barney, Harris Upham & Co., Inc., N.Y.C., 1989-90; sr. cons. Carl Byoir & Assocs., N.Y.C., 1991-94; assoc. mng. dir. Commonwealth Assocs., N.Y.C., 1994-95; mng. dir. State St. Capital Markets Corp., N.Y.C., 1996; v.p. GKN Securities Corp., N.Y.C., 1996—; lectr. profl. socs. and confs.; lectr. econs., mgmt., polit. sci. Rutgers U., 1957-64. Contbr. articles on econs. of underdeveloped nations, polit. sci., mgmt., fin. to U.S. and fgn. publs. Served to 1st lt. Brit. Army, 1950-52. Granted personal coat of Arms By Queen Elizabeth II: manorial Lord of Ash., Suffolk, Eng. Mem. Am. Econ. Assn., N.Y. Soc. Security Analysts, Knight Templar Sovereign Mil. Order of Temple of Jerusalem. Home: 360 E 72nd St New York NY 10021-4753 Office: GKN Securities Corp 61 Broadway New York NY 10006-2701

SIMMONS, JOSEPH THOMAS, accountant, educator; b. Forest Lake, Minn., Jan. 23, 1936; s. Roland Thomas and Erma (Rabe) S.; m. Winola Ann Zwald, Aug. 18, 1962 (div.); children: Thomas E, Kevin M. BS in Bus. and Econs., Morningside Coll., 1964; MBA, U. S.D., 1965; PhD in Bus., U. Nebr., 1974. CPA, S.D. Prof. acctg. and fin. U. S.D., Vermillion, 1966-69, 75—, dir. Sch. Bus., 1975—; prof. U. Nebr., Lincoln, 1969-71, U. Man., Winnipeg, Can., 1971-75; prin. Simmons and Assocs. Mgmt. Cons., Rapid City, S.D., 1981—; pvt. practice acctg. Rapid City, 1982—; pres. Simmons Profl. Fin. Planning, Vermillion, 1983—; bd. dirs. Powerhouse Computers, Sioux Falls, N.D., v.p. fin., 1992-93; bd. dirs. MDU Resources Inc., Bismarck, N.D., RE/spec, Rapid City, Gro-Tech, Rapid City, Dairlean Inc., Sioux Falls; vis. prof. U. Warsaw, Poland, 1994. Served with U.S. Army, 1958-60. Mem. Fin. Mgmt. Assn. Republican. Methodist. Home and Office: Ponderosa Acres Lot 2 Burbank SD 57010-9731

SIMMONS, LAWRENCE WILLIAM, health care company executive; b. Omaha, May 7, 1947; s. Albin Pachola and Leella Clarice (Franklin) S.; m. Leanna Carol McGee, Nov. 3, 1968; children: Scott, Anthony. Assoc. Gen. Studies, U. Nebr., 1977, B Gen. Studies, 1978. Pharm. sales rep. 3M Pharms., Omaha, 1972-83; dist. sales mgr. 3M Pharms., Chgo., 1983-89; regional sales mgr. midwest region 3M Pharms., St. Paul, 1989-92; group bus. mgr. pharm. and personal care 3M Pharms., Mexico City, 1992-95; group bus. dir. 3M Mexico/Div. V Health Care, 1995—; cluster mem. Xavier U., New Orleans, 1987—; minority outreach rep. 3M, St. Paul, 1987—. With U.S. Army, 1968-71, Vietnam. Mem. Kappa Alpha Psi (polemarch 1981-83, best chpt. award 1983). Office: PO Box 60326 Aptdo # 345 Houston TX 77205

SIMMONS, LEE HOWARD, book publishing company executive; b. N.Y.C., Aug. 17, 1935; s. Lee H. and Frances (Goodell) S.; m. Barbara E. Beck, Sept. 6, 1961; children: Christopher, Elizabeth. A.B., Duke U., 1958; M.A., NYU, 1960. Sales mgr. The Orion Press, N.Y.C., 1959-60; advt. mgr. Doubleday & Co., N.Y.C., 1960-61; account exec. Franklin Spier, N.Y.C., 1961-68, v.p., 1968-78, pres., 1978-86; exec. v.p., assoc. pub. Arbor House Pub. Co., N.Y.C., 1986-88; pres. Lee Simmons Assocs. Inc., Port Washington, N.Y., 1988—; chmn. Oblivion Press, N.Y.C., 1977-82, N.Y. is Book Country, N.Y.C., 1986-87. Treas. Port Washington Estates Assn., 1975-78. Episcopalian. Home: 40 Richards Rd Port Washington NY 11050-3416 Office: Lee Simmons Assocs Inc 4 Boylston St Port Washington NY 11050

SIMMONS, LORNA WOMACK, elementary school educator; b. Enid, Okla., Dec. 25, 1954; d. Doyle Alex and Ruth Phyllis (Wiens) Nunneley; m. Daniel Bruce Womack, June 7, 1975 (widowed Jan. 1981); children: Zachary Womack, Travis Womack, Shawn Simmons, Shayla Simmons; m. H. Lynn Simmons, Feb. 14, 1982. BS cum laude, U. Tex., 1977. Spl. edn. tchr. Sand Springs (Okla.) I.S.D., 1977-78; pvt. therapist Alphabetic Phonics, Big Spring, Tex., 1981-87; dyslexia cons. Big Spring (Tex.) I.S.D., 1987-88; chpt. I tchr. Forsan I.S.D., Big Spring, Tex., 1988-91; cons. Classroom Phonics, Big Spring, Tex., 1991—. Author: Classroom Phonics, 1989, Classroom Phonics II, 1991, Classroom Phonics Spelling, 1991, Classroom Phonics Kid Cards, 1994, Classroom Phonics Comprehension Tests, 1994, Saxon Phonics K, 1996, Saxon Phonics 1, 1996, Saxon Phonics 2, 1996. Mem. Assn. Tex. Profl. Educators. Republican. Mem. Ch. of God. Home: 3200 Wasson Dr Big Spring TX 79720-7302

SIMMONS, LYNDA MERRILL MILLS, educational administrator; b. Salt Lake City, Aug. 31, 1940; d. Alanson Soper and Madeline Helene (Merrill) Mills; m. Mark Carl Simmons, Nov. 17, 1962; children: Lisa Lynn Simmons Morley, William Mark, Jennifer Louise, Robert Thomas. BS, U. Utah, 1961, MS, 1983. Cert. sch. adminstr., Utah. Tchr. Wasatch Jr. H.S./Granite Dist., Salt Lake City, 1961-64, Altamont (Utah) H.S./Duchesne Dist., 1964-66; tchr. spl. edn. Park City (Utah) H.S., 1971-73; resource tchr. Eisenhower Jr. H.S., Salt Lake City, 1979-88; tchr. specialist Granite Sch. Dist., Salt Lake City, 1985-90; asst. prin. Bennion Jr. H.S., Salt Lake City, 1990-93; prin. Hartvigsen Sch., Salt Lake City, 1993—; adj. prof. spl. edn. U. Utah, Salt Lake City, 1987—, Utah Prin. Acad., 1994-95, co-chair Utah Spl. Educators for Computer Tech., Salt Lake City, 1988-90; mem. adv. com. on handicapped Utah State Office Edn., 1990-93; presenter at confs. Author: Setting Up Effective Secondary Resource Program, 1985; contbr. articles to profl. publs. Dist. chmn. Heart Fund, Cancer Dr., Summit Park, Utah, 1970-82; cub pack leader Park City area Boy Scouts Am., 1976-80; bd. dirs. Jr. League Salt Lake City, 1977-80; cookie chmn. Park City area Girl Scouts U.S., 1981; dist. chmn. March of Dimes, 1982—. Recipient Amb. award Salt Lake Conv. and Vis. Bur., 1993; nominee Clubwoman of Yr., 1997. Mem. Nat. Assn. Secondary Sch. Prins., Park City Young Women's Mut. (pres. 1989-93, family history cons. 1993—), Women's Athanaeum (v.p. 1990-93, pres. 1994—), Gen. Fedn. Women's Clubs (v.p. Salt Lake dist., 1996—, comty.-improvement chairperson Utah 1996—) Coun. for Exceptional Children (pres. Salt Lake chpt. 1989-90, pres. Utah Fedn. 1991-93, Spl. Educator of Yr. 1995), Granite Assn. Sch. Adminstrs. (sec.-treas. 1992-94). Mem. LDS Ch. Avocations: reading, cooking, writing, sports, handiwork. Office: Hartrigsen Sch 350 E 3605 S Salt Lake City UT 84115

SIMMONS, MARVIN GENE, geophysics educator; b. Dallas, May 15, 1929; s. Burt H. and Mable (Marshall) S.; divorced; children—Jon Eric, Debra Lynn, Sandra Kay, Pamela Jean. B.S., Tex. Agrl. and Mech. Coll., 1949; M.S., So. Methodist U., 1958; Ph.D., Harvard U., 1962. Petroleum engr. Humble Oil Co., 1949-51; propr. gravel business, 1953-58; asst. prof. So. Meth. U., 1962-65; prof. geophysics MIT, 1965-89, prof. emeritus, 1989—; prin. Hager-Richter Geoscience Inc., 1989—; Cons. NASA, 1965-72; chief scientist NASA (Manned Spacecraft Center), Houston, 1969-71; cons. on siting of nuclear facilities; sec. Internat. Heat Flow Com., 1967-71; chmn. com. drilling for sci. purposes Nat. Acad. Scis., 1965; Mem. geophysics panel NSF. Served with USAF, 1951-53. NSF postdoctoral fellow, 1961-62. Fellow Geol. Soc. Am., Am. Geophys. Union; mem. ASTM (com. C-18 on dimension stone 1986—), Boston Geol. Soc. (pres. 1967-68), Soc. Exploration Geophysicists, Sigma Xi, Tau Beta Pi. Research on physical properties of materials, lunar exploration, marine geophysics, temperature of earth, regional geophysics, engineering geology and geophysics. Home: 180 N Policy St Salem NH 03079-1916 Office: 8 Industrial Way Unit D10 Salem NH 03079-2837

SIMMONS, MERLE EDWIN, foreign language educator; b. Kansas City, Kans., Sept. 27, 1918; s. Walter Earl and Mabel Sophronia (Shoemaker) S.; m. Concepcion Rojas, Sept. 8, 1948; children: Martha Irene, Mary Alice. AB, U. Kans., 1939, MA, 1941; teaching fellow, Harvard U., 1946-47; PhD, U. Mich., 1952. Mem. faculty Ind. U., Bloomington, 1942—; prof. Spanish Ind. U., 1962-83, prof. emeritus, 1983—, dir. grad. studies dept. Spanish and Portuguese, 1967-76, chmn. dept., 1976-81. Author: The Mexican Corrido, 1957, A Bibliography of the Romance and Related Forms in Spanish America, 1963, Folklore Bibliography for 1974, 1977, for 1975, 1979, for 1976, 1981, Santiago F. Puglia, An Early Philadelphia Propagandist for Spanish American Independence, 1977, U.S. Political Ideas in Spanish America Before 1830: A Bibliographical Study, 1977, Los escritos de Juan Pablo Viscardo y Guzmán, 1983, Obra completa de Juan Pablo Viscardo y Guzmán, 1988, La Revolución Norteamericana y la Independencia de Hispanoamérica, 1992, also articles. Decorated Gran Oficial of the Order of the Sun (Peru); grantee Am. Philos. Soc., 1955, 76; grantee Am. Coun. Learned Socs., 1962. Mem. AAUP, Am. Folklore Soc., Am. Assn. Tchrs. Spanish and Portuguese, Conf. Latin Am. History, MLA, Midwest MLA, Midwest Assn. Latin Am. Studies, Nat. Acad. History of Venezuela (corr.), Phi Beta Kappa, Phi Sigma Iota. Home: 4233 Saratoga Dr Bloomington IN 47408-3196 Office: Ind U Ballantine Hall # 857 Bloomington IN 47405

SIMMONS, MICHAEL ANTHONY, dean; m. Margaret Clare Martindale; children: Kristen Ann, Jeffrey Michael, Jennifer Clare Roe, Jason Davis. AB cum laude, Harvard Coll., 1963, MD, 1967. Diplomate Am. Bd. Pediatrics, Am. Bd. Neonatal-Perinatal Medicine. Intern Harriet Lane Svc., Johns Hopkins Hosp., Balt., 1967-68, asst. resident, 1968-69, sr. asst. resident, 1969; chief resident Dept. Pediatrics, U. Colo. Med. Ctr., Denver, 1971-72, rsch. fellow in perinatal medicine, 1972-74, clin. instr. in pediatrics, 1974-77, assoc. prof. pediatrics, 1977; assoc. prof. pediatrics and obstetrics Johns Hopkins U. Sch. Medicine, Balt., 1977-83; prof., chmn. dept. pediatrics U. Utah Sch. of Medicine, Salt Lake City, 1983-94; prof. pediatrics, dean U. N.C. at Chapel Hill Sch. Medicine, 1994—; adj. prof. dept. obstetrics and gynecology U. Utah Sch. of Medicine, Salt Lake City, 1984-94; co-dir. newborn svcs. U. Colo. Med. Ctr., Denver, 1974-77, Johns Hopkins Hosp., 1977-83; mem. staff Denver Gen. Hosp., 1976-77, Denver Children's Hosp., 1976-77; vice chmn. clin. affairs dept. pediatrics Johns Hopkins Hosp., 1981-83; chief of pediatrics U. Utah Med. Ctr., Salt Lake City, 1983-94; med. dir. Primary Children's Med. Ctr., 1983-94; bd. dirs. Triangle Univs. Licensing Consortium, U. N.C. Hosps. Contbr. numerous articles to profl. jours. Fellow Am. Acad. of Pediatrics (excellence in pediatric rsch. com. 1991—, coun. on govt. affairs 1992—); mem. Perinatal Rsch. Soc. (coun. 1982-84, pres.-elect 1985-87, pres. 1989), Western Soc. for Pediatric Rsch. (coun. 1985-86, pres.-elect 1987, pres. 1988), Soc. for Pediatric Rsch., Am. Bd. Pediatrics (sub-bd. of neonatal-perinatal medicine 1983-89, chmn. 1984-88). Office: U NC Sch of Medicine 509 Burnette-Womack/CB 7220 Chapel Hill NC 27599-7220*

SIMMONS, MIRIAM QUINN, state legislator; b. Jackson, Miss., Mar. 28, 1928; d. Charles Buford and Viola (Hamill) Quinn; m. Willie Wronal Simmons, July 10, 1952; children: Dick, Sue, Wronal. BS, Miss. U. for Women, 1949. Tchr. Columbia (Miss.) City Schs., 1949-51, 53-54, literacy coord., 1986-87; home demonstration agt. Coop. Extension Svc., Bay Springs, Miss., 1951-52; tchr. Marion County Schs., Columbia, 1952-53, 54-55, Columbia Tng. Sch., 1961-63, Columbia Acad., 1970-73; rep. Miss. Ho. of Reps., Jackson, 1988—; adv. bd. Magnolia Fed. Bank for Savs; trustee State Inst. Higher Learning, Jackson, 1972-84; dir. Miss. Authority for Ednl. TV, Jackson, 1976-88. Named Marion County Outstanding Citizen Columbia Jr. Aux., 1981. Mem. Miss. Fedn. Women's Clubs, Bus. and Profl. Women's Club, Hilltop Garden Club, Delta Kappa Gamma. Democrat. Methodist. Home: 45 Old Highway 98 E Columbia MS 39429-8172

SIMMONS, PETER, law and urban planning educator; b. N.Y.C., July 19, 1931; s. Michael L. and Mary A. S.; m. Ruth J. Tanfield, Jan. 28, 1951; children: Sam, Lizzard. A.B., U. Calif., Berkeley, 1953, LL.B., 1956; postgrad. (Alvord fellow), U. Wis., 1956-58. Prof. SUNY, Buffalo, 1963-67; mem. faculty Ohio State U., 1967-75, U. Ill., 1972, Case Western Res. U., 1974-75; prof. law and urban planning Rutgers U. Coll. Law, Newark, 1975—, dean, 1975-93; university prof. Rutgers U., 1993—. Contbr. articles to profl. jours. Mem. Ohio Housing Commn., 1972-74; commr. Ohio Reclamation Rev. Bd., 1974-75; chmn. N.J. Criminal Disposition Commn., 1983-84; mem. N.J. Law Revision Commn., 1987—. Mem. Am. Planning Assn., Urban Land Inst., Am. Law Inst., AAUP (nat. council 1973-75). Office: Rutgers U Law Sch 15 Washington St Newark NJ 07102-3105

SIMMONS, RALPH OLIVER, physics educator; b. Kensington, Kans., Feb. 19, 1928; s. Fred Charles and Cornelia (Douglass) S.; m. Janet Lee Lull, Aug. 31, 1952; children: Katherine Ann, Bradley Alan, Jill Christine, Joy Diane. B.A., U. Kans., 1950; B.A. (Rhodes scholar), Oxford U., 1953; Ph.D., U. Ill., 1957. Research assoc. U. Ill., Urbana, 1957-59, faculty physics, 1959—, assoc. prof., 1961-65, prof. physics, 1965—, head physics dept., 1970-86; vis. scientist Ctr. for Study Nuclear Energy, Mol, Belgium, 1965; mem. governing bd. Internat. Symposia on Thermal Expansion, 1970-88; cons. Argonne Nat. Lab., 1978-86, Los Alamos Nat. Lab., 1983-84, State U. Sys. Fla., 1989-91; chmn. Office of Phys. Scis., NRC, 1978-81; mem. Assembly of Math. and Phys. Scis., 1978-81, Geophysics Rsch. Bd., 1978-81; trustee Argonne Univs. Assn., 1979-83. Mem. internat. adv. bd.: Jour. Physics C (Solid State Physics), 1971-76; mem. editorial bd.: Physical Review B, 1978-81. Recipient Sr. U.S. Scientist Rsch. award Alexander von Humboldt Found., 1992; sr. postdoctoral fellow NSF, 1965. Fellow Am. Phys. Soc. (vice chmn., chmn. divsn. solid state physics 1975-77, coun. 1988), AAAS (chmn. sect. B Physics 1985-86); mem. Am. Crystallographic Assn., Am. Assn. Physics Tchrs., Phi Beta Kappa, Sigma Xi, Pi Mu Epsilon. Research on atomic defects in solids, neutron and x-ray scattering, quantum solids, molecular crystals, crystal dynamics, radiation damage. Home: 1005 Foothill Dr Champaign IL 61821-5622

SIMMONS, RAYMOND HEDELIUS, lawyer; b. Salinas, Calif., May 27, 1958; s. Raymond Hedelius and Antoinette (Lynch) S. BA magna cum laude, U. Calif., San Diego, 1979; JD magna cum laude, U. Calif., San Francisco, 1982. Bar: Calif. 1982, U.S. Dist. Ct. (no. dist.) Calif. 1982, Ga. 1987. Assoc. Farella, Braun & Martel, San Francisco, 1982-85; atty., v.p. Barnett-Range Corp., Atlanta, 1985-86; counsel Nationwide Capital Corp. subs. HomeFed. Bank, Atlanta, 1986, HomeFed. Bank, San Diego, 1987-90; gen. counsel, sr. v.p., sec. ITT Fed. Bank, San Francisco, 1990-95; also ITT Residential Capital Corp., ITT Residential Capital Servicing Corp., San Francisco; pvt. practice, Newport Beach, Calif., 1995—. Mem. ABA, Calif. Bar Assn., Ga. Bar Assn., Calif. Scholarship Fedn. (life), Order of Coif, Thurston Soc.

SIMMONS, RICHARD DE LACEY, mass media executive; b. Cambridge, Mass., Dec. 30, 1934; s. Ernest J. and Winifred (McNamara) S.; m. Mary DeWitt Bleecker, May 20, 1961; children: Christopher DeWitt, Robin Bleecker. Grad., 1951; AB, Harvard Coll., 1955; LLB, Columbia U., 1958. Bar: N.Y. 1959. V.p., gen. counsel Dun & Bradstreet Corp., N.Y.C., 1969-73, exec. v.p., 1976-79, vice chmn., 1979-81; pres. Moody's Investors Svc., N.Y.C., 1973-75, Dun & Bradstreet, Inc., N.Y.C., 1975; pres., chief oper. officer Washington Post Co., Washington, 1981-91; pres. Internat. Herald Tribune, Paris, 1989-96; bd. dirs. Washington Post Co., J.P. Morgan & Co., Inc., Morgan Guaranty Trust Co. N.Y., Union Pacific Corp., Yankee Pub., Inc.; mem. equity adv. bd., adv. bd. dirs. GE Investment Corp. Mem. coun. White Burkett Miller Ctr. Pub. Affairs, U. Va. Office: 105 N Washington St Ste 202 Alexandria VA 22314-3022

SIMMONS, RICHARD L., surgeon; b. Boston, Feb. 23, 1934; s. Nathanial J. and Anne Dorothy (Levenson) S.; widowed (Feb. 1993); children: Nicole, Janine. AB in Biochem. Scis. magna cum laude, Harvard U., 1955; MD summa cum laude, Boston U., 1959. Diplomate Am. Bd. Surgery. Intern, resident in surgery Columbia Presbyn. Med. Ctr., N.Y.C., 1959-66; clin. and rsch. fellow Mass. Gen. Hosp., Boston, 1965; rsch. fellow in surgery Harvard Med. Sch., Boston, 1965; instr. surgery Columbia U. Coll. P&S, N.Y.C., 1965-68; from asst. prof. to assoc. prof. surgery U. Minn., Mpls., 1968-72, prof. surgery and microbiology, 1972-87; George V. Foster prof. surgery, chair dept. surgery U. Pitts., 1987—, assoc. dean for clin. affairs Sch. Medicine, 1989—, prof. molecular genetics and biochemistry, 1992—; assoc. v.p. for clin. affairs U. Pitts. Med. Ctr., 1989—, med. dir., 1996; chief of surgery Presbyn.-Univ. Hosp., Pitts., 1987—; staff Children's Hosp. of Pitts.; cons. staff VA Med. Ctr. Author/co-author 11 books; contbr. more than 1200 articles to profl. jours. Recipient Disting. Svc. Prof. Surgery, 1994, other awards and grants. Mem. AMA, AAAS, ACS (pres. Southwestern Pa. chpt. 1992), NAS Inst. Medicine, Am. Soc. for Microbiology, Am. Soc. Transplant Physicians (pres. 1980-81), Am. Assn. Immunologists, Am. Assn. Pathologists, Am. Surg. Assn. (chmn. program com. 1990), Assn. for Acad. Surgery, Ctrl. Surg. Assn., Cell Transplant Soc., Halsted Soc., Infectious Diseases Soc. Am., Midwest Surg. Soc. (hon.), Reticuloendothelial Soc., Soc. for Leukocyte Biology, Soc. for Microbiology, Soc. Clin. Oncologists, Surg. Infection Soc. (pres. 1988), Soc. Surg. Chmn., Soc. Univ. Surgeons (exec. coun. 1973-81, pres. 1977-78), Allegheny County Med. Soc., Transplantation Soc. (councillor 1974-80), others. Office: U Pitts Sch Medicine Dept Surgery 3500 Terrace St Pittsburgh PA 15213-2500

SIMMONS, ROBERT RUHL, state legislator, educator; b. N.Y.C., Feb. 11, 1943; s. Charles Herbert Jr. and Roxane Page (Ruhl) S.; m. Edith Heidi Paffard, June 22, 1974; children: Jane Adams, Robert Waldo Ruhl. BA, Haverford Coll., 1965; MPA, Harvard U., 1979. Ops. officer CIA, Washington, 1969-79; legis. asst. U.S. Senator John H. Chafee, Washington, 1979-81; staff dir. intelligence com. U.S. Senate, Washington, 1981-85; vis. lectr. Yale U., New Haven, Conn., 1985—; mem. Conn. Gen. Assembly, Hartford, 1991—. Contbr. articles to profl. jours. Col. U.S. Army Res. Decorated Bronze Star with 1 oak leaf cluster, Army Commendation medal with 1 oak leaf cluster, Vietnam Svc. medal with four campaign stars, Nat. Def. medal, Army Res. Achievement medal. Episcopalian. Avocations: Chinese art, forestry. Home: 268 N Main St Stonington CT 06378-2910 Office: Legislative Office Bldg The Capital Ste 4200 Hartford CT 06106

SIMMONS, ROBERTA JOHNSON, public relations firm executive; b. St. Louis, June 28, 1947; d. Robert Andrew and Thelma Josephine (Bunch) J.; m. Clifford Michael Simmons, Aug. 10, 1968; children: Andrew Park, Matthew Clay, Jordan Michael. BA, Ind. U., South Bend, 1972. Lic. real estate broker, Ind.; accredited pub. rels. practitioner; mem. Inst. Residential

Mktg. Account exec., supr. Juhl Advt., Inc., Mishawaka, Ind., 1971-74, pub. rels. dir., 1974-79, v.p., 1979; v.p., pub. rels. dir. Juhl Advt., Inc., Mishawaka and Indpls., 1984-89; v.p. E.L. Yoder & Assocs., Inc., Granger, Ind., 1979-80; pres. Simmons Communications, Inc., Mishawaka, 1981-82; v.p., gen. mgr. Juhl Bldg. Communications, Inc., South Bend, 1983-84; sr. v.p. Wyse Advt., Inc., Indpls., 1989-90; v.p., pub. rels. dir. Caldwell VanRiper, Inc., Indpls., 1990-94; v.p. Pub. Rels. Network, Indpls., 1995—. Contbr. articles to profl. publs. Mem. pub. rels. com. Ind. Adult Literacy Coalition, Indpls., 1989; chairperson pub. rels. com. Crossroads of Am. coun. Boy Scouts Am., Indpls., 1990-91; dep. community info. com. Indpls. C. of C. Infrastructure Study, 1990-91. Mem. PRSA (accredited, mem. counsellors acad., Hoosier chpt. job bank com. 1993—, Nat. Assembly Del., 1996—, v.p. programs, 1997), Nat. Sales Mktg. Coun. (trustee 1991-92), Inst. Residential Mktg. Elder Christian Ch. (Disciples of Christ). Avocations: travel, reading. Office: Pub Rels Network 111 Monument Cir Ste 702 Indianapolis IN 46204

SIMMONS, ROY, JR., university athletic coach. Head coach lacrosse team Syracuse U. Orangemen, 1971—. Coached team to Divsn. IA Lacrosse Championship, 1983, 88-90, 93. Office: Syracuse Univ Manley Field House Syracuse NY 13244-5020*

SIMMONS, ROY WILLIAM, banker; b. Portland, Oreg., Jan. 24, 1916; s. Henry Clay and Ida (Mudd) S.; m. Elizabeth Ellison, Oct. 28, 1938; children—Julia Simmons Watkins, Matthew R., Laurence E., Elizabeth Jane Simmons Hoke, Harris H., David E. Asst. cashier First Nat. Bank Layton, Utah, 1944-49; Utah bank commr., 1949-51; exec. v.p. Bank of Utah, Ogden, 1951-53; pres. Lockhart Co., Salt Lake City, 1953-64, Zion's First Nat. Bank, Salt Lake City, 1964-81; chmn. bd. Zion's First Nat. Bank, 1965—; chmn., CEO Zion's Bancorp, 1965-91, chmn. bd., 1991—; chmn. bd. Zion's Savs. & Loan Assn., 1961-69; pres. Lockhart Co., 1964-87; bd. dirs. Beneficial Life Ins. Co., Ellison Ranching Co. Chmn. Utah Bus. Devel. Corp., 1969-80; Mem. Utah State Bd. Regents, 1969-81. Mem. Salt Lake City C. of C. (treas. 1964-65), Sigma Pi. Republican. Mem. Ch. of Jesus Christ of Latter Day Saints. Home: 817 E Crestwood Rd Kaysville UT 84037-1712 Office: Zions Bancorp 1000 Kennecott Bldg Salt Lake City UT 84133

SIMMONS, RUSSELL, recording industry executive; b. Hollis, N.Y., 1957; s. Daniel S. Attended, CCNY. Co-founder, owener Def Jam Records, N.Y.C., 1985—; owner Rush Artist Mgmt.; chmn. Rush Comms.; owner 6 record labels. Co-prodr. films Krush Groove, 1985, Tougher Than Leather, 1988; dir. music videos; HBO appearance Russell Simmons Def Comedy Jam; mgmt. co. represents Public Enemy, LL Cool J, others. Office: Def Jam Records 652 Broadway New York NY 10012-2316*

SIMMONS, RUTH J., academic administrator; b. Grapeland, Tex., July 3, 1945; 2 children. Student, Universidad Internacional, Saltillo, Mex., 1965, Wellesley Coll., 1965-66; BA, Dillard U., 1967; postgrad., Universite de Lyon, 1967-68, George Washington U., 1968-69; AM, Harvard U., 1970, PhD in Romance Langs., 1973; LLD (hon.), Amherst Coll., 1995; LHD (hon.), Howard U., 1996, Dillard U., 1996; LLD (hon.), Princeton U., 1996. Interpreter lang. svcs. divsn. U.S. Dept. State, Washington, 1968-69; instr. French George Washington U., 1968-69; admissions officer Radcliffe Coll., 1970-72; asst. prof. French U. New Orleans, 1973-75, asst. dean coll. liberal arts, asst. prof. French, 1975-76; adminstrv. coord. NEH liberal studies project Calif. State U., Northridge, 1977-78, acting dir. internat. programs, vis. assoc. prof. Pan-African studies, 1978-79; asst. dean grad. sch. U. So. Calif., 1979-82, assoc. dean grad. sch., 1982-83; dir. studies Butler Coll. Princeton (N.J.) U., 1983-85, acting. dir. Afro-Am. studies, 1985-87, asst. dean faculty, 1986-87, assoc. dean faculty, 1986-90, vice provost, 1992-95; provost Spelman Coll., 1990-91; pres. Smith Coll., Northampton, Mass., 1995—; peer reviewer higher edn. divsn. NEH, 1980-83, bd. cons., 1981; mem. grad. adv. bd. Calif. Student Aid Commn., 1981-83; chair com. to visit dept. African-Am. studies Harvard U., 1991—; mem. strategic planning task force N.J. Dept. Higher Edn., 1992-93; mem. nat. adv. commn. EQUITY 2000, Coll. Bd., 1992-95; mem. adv. bd. ctrl. N.J. NAACP Legal Def. Fund, 1992-95; mem. Mid. States Assn. Accreditation Team, Johns Hopkins U., 1993; chair rev. panel for model instns. planning grants NSF, 1993. Mem. editl. bd. World Edn. series Am. Assn. Collegiate Registrars and Admissions Officers, 1984-86; contbr. articles to profl. jours.; presenter, speaker and panelist in field. Mem. adv. bd. N.J. Master Faculty program Woodrow Wilson Nat. Fellowship Found.,m 1987-90, bd. trustees, 1991—. KYOK scholar, 1963; Worthing Found. scholar, 1963-67; Danforth fellow, 1967-73; Fulbright scholar U. de Lyon, 1967-68; Sr. Fulbright fellow, 1981; Rsch. grantee AACRAO, 1987-88; recipient Disting. Svc. award Assn. Black Princeton Alumni, 1989, Dillard U., 1992, Pres.'s Recognition award Bloomfield Coll., 1993, TWIN award Princeton Area YWCA, 1993, Women's Orgn. Tribute award Princeton U., 1994, Leadership award Third World Ctr. Princeton U., 1995, Tex. Excellence award Leap Program, 1995, Benjamin E. Mays award A Better Chance, 1995. Office: Smith College Office of the President Northampton MA 01063

SIMMONS, S. DALLAS, university president; b. Ahoskie, N.C., Jan. 28, 1940; s. Yvonne Martin; m. Mary A. Simmons, Feb. 10, 1963; children: S. Dallas Jr., Kristie Lynn. BS, N.C. Cen. U., 1962, MS, 1967; PhD, Duke U., 1977. Asst. prof. bus. adminstrn. N.C. Cen. U., Durham, 1967-71, asst. to chancellor, 1971-77, vice chancellor for univ. relations, 1977-81; pres. St. Paul's Coll., Lawrenceville, Va., 1981-85, Va. Union Univ., Richmond, 1985—; faculty cons. IBM, Research Triangle Park, N.C., 1968-71; cons. for edn. devel. officers Nat. Lab. for Higher Edn., Durham, 1972-73; staff asst. to Pres., White House Advance Office, Washington, 1975-76; univ. fed. liaison officer Moton Coll. Service Bur., Washington, 1972-80; mem. competency testing commn. N.C. Bd. Edn., 1977-81; bd. dirs., mem. loan com., mem. planning com. Pace Am. Bank, Lawrenceville, 1984-85. Bd. dirs. N.C. Mus. Life and Sci., Durham, 1972-75, Volunteer Services Bur, Inc., Durham, 1972-77, Va. Poly. Inst. and State U., 1982-83; mem. Durham Civic/Conv. Ctr. Commn., 1972-73, U.S./Zululand Ednl. Found., 1985; trustee, mem. exec. and pers. com. N.C. Cen. U., 1983-85; active various coms. United Negro Coll. Fund; mem. exec. bd. John B. McLendon Found., Inc., 1985. Named one of Outstanding Young Men Am., 1972, Citizen of Yr. Omega Psi Phi, 1983-84, Bus. Assoc. of Yr. Am. Bus. Women's Assn., 1984. Mem. Assn. Episc. Colls. (pres.-elect), Cen. Intercollegiate Athletic Assn. (exec. com. 1981—, bd. dirs. 1981—), Nat. Assn. for Equal Opportunity in Higher Edn. (bd. dirs., chmn. leadership awards com. 1984-85), Am. Mgmt. Assn., Data Processing Mgmt. Assn. (cen. Carolina chpt.), Am. Assn. Sch. Adminstrs., Am. Assn. Univ. Adminstrs., Kappa Alpha Psi (Kappa of Month Dec. 1981), Sigma Pi Phi (alpha beta boulé). African Methodist Episcopalian. Club: Downtown. Lodges: Masons (32 degree), Shriners, Kiwanis, Optimists. Home: 1200 W Graham Rd Richmond VA 23220-1409 Office: Va Union U 1500 N Lombardy St Richmond VA 23220-1711

SIMMONS, SHARON DIANNE, elementary education educator; b. Woodruff, S.C., Apr. 5, 1961; d. James Madison and Lucy Nell (Carlton) Crow; m. Wayne Roy Simmons, Mar. 29, 1986; children: Zachary, Luke. BA in Elem. Edn., U. S.C., 1983, M of Elem. Edn., 1987. Tchr. 3d grade M.S. Bailey Elem. Sch., Clinton, S.C., 1984-85, tchr. 4th grade, 1985-86; tchr. 5th grade Eastside Elem. Sch., Clinton, S.C., 1986-88, tchr. 4th & 5th grades, 1988-90, 91-92, tchr. 5th grade, 1990-91, tchr. 4th grade, 1993-95, tchr. 3rd grade, 1995-96; tchr. R.P. Dawkins Middle Sch., Moore, S.C., 1996—; pilot tchr. authentic assessment Eastside Elem. Sch., 1992-93, mem. sch. libr. com., 1993—96 tchr. chair 4th grade, 1993-94, tchr. grad. course authentic assessment, 1996. Pres. libr. coun. Spartanburg-Woodruff (S.C.) Br. Libr., 1993-95, v.p., 1995—. Recipient Ambassador award The Edn. Ctr., 1993-94. Mem. S.C. Math. Tchrs. Assn., Sch. Improvement Coun. Baptist. Avocations: piano, cross stitch, travel, sports, reading. Home: 651 Parsons Rd Woodruff SC 29388-8700 Office: RP Dawkins Middle Sch 1300 E Blackstock Rd Moore SC 29369-9656

SIMMONS, SHERWIN PALMER, lawyer; b. Bowling Green, Ky., Jan. 19, 1931; A.B., Columbia U., 1952, LL.B., 1954, J.D., 1969. Bar: Tenn. 1954, Fla. 1957. Assoc., Fowler, White, Collins, Gillen, Humkey & Trenam, Tampa, Fla., 1956-60, ptnr. 1960-70; ptnr. Trenam, Simmons, Kemker, Scharf & Barkin, Tampa, 1970-77; stockholder, pres. Trenam, Simmons, Kemker, Scharf, Barkin, Frye & O'Neill, P.A., Tampa, 1977-94; ptnr. chair tax dept. Steel Hector & Davis, Miami, 1994—; atty. adv. U.S. Tax Ct., Washington, 1954-56, mem. nominating commn., 1978-79; mem. adv. group Commr. of IRS, 1978-79, 1989-90, U.S. Dept. Justice, 1979-80; adj. prof. U. Miami, 1995—. Trustee, Hillsborough County Soc. Crippled Children & Adults, 1956-65, pres., 1960-61; treas., chmn. Hillsborough County Public Edn. Study Commn., 1965-66; mem. adv. bd. Salvation Army, 1959-62, 1964-66, sec., 1960-61; chmn., bd. dirs. The Fla. Orchestra, 1987-89; founding trustee, pres. Am. Tax Policy Inst., 1989—; trustee Tampa Bay Performing Arts Ctr., Inc., 1984-93, program adv. com. 1985-89, investment com. 1986-91. Fellow Am. Coll. Trust and Estate Counsel (bd. regents 1982-88), Am. Bar Found. (fellow 1969—, devel. com. 1992-94), Am. Coll. Tax Counsel (regent 1987-93, vice-chmn. 1989-91, chmn. 1991-93); mem. ABA (vice chmn. adminstrn. taxation sect. 1972-75, chmn. 1975-76, Ho. of Dels. 1985-90, bd. govs. 1990-93), Am. Bar Retirement Assn. (bd. dirs. 1984-90, v.p. 1987-88, pres. 1988-89), Am. Law Network (chmn. subcom. on continuing profl. edn. 1983—), Fed. Bar Assn., Fla. Bar Assn. (chmn. taxation sect. 1964-65), Am. Judicature Soc., So. Fed. Tax Inst. (trustee, pres. 1974, chmn. 1975), Internat. Acad. Estate and Trust Law, Internat. Fiscal Assn., Am. Law Inst. (mem. coun. 1986—, exec. com. 1994—). Author: Federal Taxation of Life Insurance, 1966; bd. of advisors mag. The Tax Times, 1986-87; contbr. articles to legal jours. Office: Steel Hector & Davis 200 S Biscayne Blvd Ste 4100 Miami FL 33131-2310

SIMMONS, SYLVIA JEANNE QUARLES (MRS. HERBERT G. SIMMONS, JR.), university administrator, educator; b. Boston, May 8, 1935; d. Lorenzo Christopher and Margaret Mary (Thomas) Quarles; B.A., Manhattanville Coll., 1957; M.Ed., Boston Coll., 1962, PhD, 1990, DHL (hon.) St. Joseph's Coll., 1994; m. Herbert G. Simmons, Jr., Oct. 26, 1957; children: Stephen, Alison, Lisa. Montessori tchr. Charles River Park Nursery Sch., Boston, 1970-76; registrar Boston Coll. Sch. Mgmt., Chestnut Hill, Mass., 1966-70; dir. fin. aid Radcliffe Coll., Cambridge, Mass., 1970-75, assoc. dean admissions and fin. aid, 1972-75, assoc. dean admissions, fin. aid and women's edn., 1975; assoc. dean admissions and fin. aid Harvard and Radcliffe, from 1975; assoc. v.p. for acad. affairs, central adminstrn. U. Mass., Boston, 1976-79, spl. asst. to chancellor, 1979; v.p. field services Am. Student Assistance, 1982-84, sr. v.p., 1984-93, exec. v.p. 1993-95; mem. faculty Harvard U., 1970-77; pres. faculty Harvard U., 1995-96; cons. Mass. Bd. Higher Edn., 1973-77; lectr. Boston U., 1991—. Bd. dirs. Rivers Country Day Sch., Weston, Mass., Simon's Rock Coll., Great Barrington, Mass., Wayland (Mass.) Fair Housing, Cambridge Mental Health Assn., Family Service Greater Boston, Concerts in Black and White, Mass. Higher Edn. Assistance Corp.; chmn. bd. dirs. North Shore Community Coll., 1986-88, mem. bd. dirs., 1985—; trustee and alumnae bd. dirs. Manhattanville Coll., 1986—. Mem. adv. com. Upward Bound, Chestnut Hill Boston Coll., 1972-74, Women in Politics Johm McCormack Inst., 1994—; Camp Chimney Corners, Becket, Mass., 1971-77; bd. dirs. Am. Cancer Soc., Mass., 1987-89, Boston Coll., 1990—, Merrimack Coll., 1992—, Mass. Found. for the Humanities, 1990-92, Mass. Bay United Way, 1990-94, Grimes King Found., 1992—, St. Elizabeta's Hosp., 1991, Anna Stearns Found., 1996—, Regis Coll., 1997—; overseer Mt. Ida Coll., 1990—. Recipient Educator of the Year award Boston and Vicinity Club, 1989; named One of Ten Outstanding Young Leaders, Boston Jr. C. of C., 1971, Sojourner's Daughters: 25 African women who have made a difference, 1991; recipient Bicentennial medal Boston Coll., 1976; Achievement award Greater Boston YMCA, 1977, Human Rights award Mass. Tchrs. Assn., 1988, Pres.' award Mass Ednl. Opportunity Assn., 1988. Mem. Women in Politics, Nat. (exec. council 1973-75), Eastern (1st v.p. 1973) assns. financial aid officers, Coll. Scholarship Service Council, Links, (pres. local chpt. 1967-69), Nat. Inst. Fin. Aid Adminstrs. (dir. 1975-77), Jack and Jill Am. (pres. Newton chpt. 1972-74, Delta Sigma Theta, Delta Kappa Gamma (pres. 1988-90). Club: Manhattanville (pres. Boston 1966-68). Home: 3 Dean Rd Wayland MA 01778-5007 Office: 330 Stuart St Boston MA 02116-5229

SIMMONS, TED CONRAD, writer; b. Seattle, Sept. 1, 1916; s. Conrad and Clara Evelyn (Beaudry) S.; m. Dorothy Pauline Maltese, June 1, 1942; children: lynn, Juliet. Student U. Wash., 1938-41, UCLA and Los Angeles State U., 1952-54, Oxford (Eng.) U., 1980. Drama critic Seattle Daily Times, 1942; indsl. writer, reporter-editor L.A. Daily News, 1948-51; contbr. Steel, Western Metals, Western Industry, 1951—; past poetry dir. Watts Writers Workshop; instr. Westside Poetry Center; asst. dir. Pacific Coast Writers Conf., Calif. State Coll. Los Angeles. Served with USAAF, 1942-46. Author: (poetry) Deadended, 1966; (novel) Middlearth, 1975; (drama) Greenhouse, 1977, Durable Chaucer, 1978, Rabelais and other plays, 1980, Dickeybird, 1981 (nominated TCG Plays-in-Progress award 1985), Alice and Eve, 1983, Deja Vu, Deja Vu, 1986, The Box, 1987, Ingrid Superstar, 1988, Three Quarks for Mr. Marks, 1989, Ingrid: Skier on the Slopes of Stromboli, 1990, A Midsummer's Hamlet, 1991, Hamlet Nintendo, After Hours, Dueling Banjoes, Viva el Presidente, Climate of the Sun, 1992, Nude Descending Jacob's Ladder, 1993, Almost an Opera, 1994, Landscape with Inverted Tree and Fred Astaire Dancing, 1995, O.J. Othello, Fast Track, Searching for Alice Liddell, Mr. Blue of Freaky Animals, Inc., 1997, Rosenstern & Guildencrantz II, 1997, Rosa/Rosa of the Centuries/Rosa of the Thorns, 1997, Joyce, 1997; writer short story, radio verse; book reviewer Los Angeles Times; contbr. poetry to The Am. Poet, Prairie Wings, Antioch Rev., Year Two Anthology; editor: Venice Poetry Company Presents, 1972. Grantee Art Commn. King County, 1993.

SIMMONS, VAUGHAN PIPPEN, medical consultant; b. Balt., Nov. 19, 1922; s. Harry S. and Sarah Jane (Pippen) S.; m. Marguerite Carolyn Massino, Dec. 27, 1947 (dec. 1990); children: Malynda Sarah, Jefferson Vaughan. Student, Ill. Inst. Tech., 1943-44; B.S., U. Chgo., 1947, M.D., 1949. Diplomate Am. Bd. Life Ins. Medicine. From instr. to asst. prof. Marquette U. Sch. Medicine, Milw., 1950-56; asst. med. dir. Northwestern Mut. Life Ins. Co., Milw., 1956-60; med. dir. Fidelity Mut. Life Ins. Co., Phila., 1961-73, v.p., 1968-73; v.p., med. dir. Colonial Penn Life Ins. Co., Phila., 1973-84; vis. lectr. ins. medicine Temple U. Sch. Medicine, Phila., 1966-84; asst. prof. anatomy Jefferson Med. Coll., Phila., 1977-88, hon. asst. prof. anatomy, 1988—. Patentee in field (3); contbr. articles to profl. jours. Mem. ofcl. bd. St. Luke United Methodist Ch., Bryn Mawr, Pa., 1963-83, chmn. commn. membership and evangelism, 1963-71, trustee, 1968-83. Served with M.C., U.S. Army, 1943-45, as lt. (j.g.) USNR, 1952-54; Korea. Fellow Coll. Physicians Phila. (chmn. pub. health sect. 1967-68, ins. medicine sect. 1970-72, planning com. 1981-82, adv. bd. Francis C. Wood Inst. History of Medicine 1984-88), Milw. Acad. Medicine, Am. Geriatrics Soc., N.Y. Acad. Medicine; mem. Am. Acad. Ins. Medicine (founding editor Ins. Medicine 1969-71, exec. coun. 1970-72, publs. com. 1967-75), Am. Life Ins. Assn. (sec. med. sect. 1974-77), Pa. Hist. Soc., Am. Assn. Automotive Medicine (dir. 1980-83), Am. Legion, Sigma Xi, Alpha Kappa Kappa. Clubs: Union League (bd. dirs. 1982-85, v.p. 1985-86), Sketch (Phila.). Avocations: photography, amateur radio, drawing, painting, med rsch. and writing. Home: 4665 S Landings Dr Fort Myers FL 33919-4683

SIMMONS, WILLIAM, physicist, aerospace research executive; b. Chgo., Apr. 24, 1932; s. Walter Garfield and Edna Dean (Winch) S.; m. Barbara Millet Haury, Oct. 4, 1954; children: Sheryl Lee, Cynthia Jane, Shelly Jean. BA in Physics, Carleton Coll., 1953; MS in Physics, U. Ill., 1955, PhD in Physics, 1960. Mem. tech. staff Space Tech. Labs., Redondo Beach, Calif., 1960-62; sr. rsch. scientist Gen. Tech., Torrance, Calif., 1962; sr. rsch. scientist TRW, Redondo Beach, 1962-71, dir. rsch., 1984-89, chief engr. spl. projects assigned to Lawrence Livermore (Calif.) Labs., 1989-92; engring. mgr. Lawrence Livermore Labs., 1972-84, rsch. reviewer, 1985-89; prof. engring. UCLA, 1968-72; tech. panel mem. U. Calif., Berkeley, 1985; tech. reviewer Dept. Energy, Washington, 1986—, mem. rev. com., 1987—. Editor, reviewer 2 books, 1982, 83; contbr. numerous articles to profl. jours. 10 patents in electro-optics devices. Named Disting. Engring. Prof. of Yr. UCLA, 1972, one of Top 100 Innovators in U.S.A, Sci. Digest, 1986; George F. Baker Found. scholar Carleton Coll., 1949-53. Mem. IEEE (sr. mem., gen. chmn. symposia 1988, 89, Simon Ramo Major medal 1987), Laser Inst. Am., Laser Engring. and Optical Soc., Am. Phys. Soc., Soc. of Photographic and Instrumentation Engrs., U.S. Chess Club, Phi Beta Kappa, Sigma Xi. Republican. Avocations: chess, table tennis, bridge. Office: Systems Solutions 1621 W 25th St Ste 231 San Pedro CA 90732-4300

SIMMS, AMY LANG, writer, educator; b. Bryn Mawr, Pa., Sept. 21, 1964; d. Eben Caldwell and Anna Mary L.; children: Harrison Lang, Maud Whittingon. BA in French and Sociology, Bucknell U., 1986; postgrad., Sch. Museum of Fine Arts, 1988, Cambridge Ctr. Adult Edn., 1988, Bryn Mawr Coll., 1988, Vassar Coll., 1993, U. Pa., 1995—. Assoc. dir. pub. rels. Haverford (Pa.) Coll., 1995-96; copywriter, media and prodn. asst. DBM Assocs., Cambridge, Mass., 1986-88; teaching asst. sociology dept. Bucknell U., Lewisburg, Pa., 1989; staff reporter Lewisburg Daily Jour., 1989-92, asst. editor, 1991; asst. editor Milton (Pa.) Standard, 1991; co-founder, co-editor Lewisburg Holiday Herald, 1990; co-founder Environ. Advisor Newsletter, Lewisburg, 1990-91. Assoc. editor: Main Line Life; contbr. articles to profl. jours. Media corr. Elem. Related Arts Com., Lewisburg, 1989; mem. adv. bd. Union County Children and Youth Svcs., Lewisburg, 1991-92; trustee Sarah Hull Hallock Meml. Libr., Milton, N.Y., 1993-95. Recipient Hon. Speakers award Lewisburg Lions Club, 1990. Mem. AAUW. Avocations: cats, books, food, travel, photography. Home and Office: 606 Trowill Ln Wayne PA 19087

SIMMS, ARTHUR BENJAMIN, management consultant, financier; b. Atlanta, Sept. 20, 1921; s. Arthur B. and Eva (Hurt) S.; m. Jane Laurice Griffin, Nov. 7, 1953; children: Arthur Benjamin IV, Jane Griffin, Anne Woodruff. Grad., Darlington Sch., 1938; student, Ga. Inst. Tech., 1939-40; B.S., U. Pa., 1942; M.B.A., Harvard, 1947. Bus. cons. Elec. Bond & Share Co., N.Y.C., 1947-50; pres. A. B. Simms & Assos. (mgmt. cons.), Atlanta, 1950—; prof. bus. adminstrn. Ga. State U., 1951-52; pres., chmn. bd. Peachtree House, Inc., 1957-65, S. & L. Corp., 1959-62, 1st Atlanta Investment Corp., 1960-65, Consol. Equities Corp., Atlanta, 1965-91; chmn. Realty Capital Corp., 1967-91, Growth Realty, Inc., 1961-65, Bayshore Towers, Inc., Tampa, Fla., 1961-65, Atlanta Towers, Inc., 1961-65; hon. bd. dirs. Atlanta and Edgewood St. Railway Co. Trustee Pop Warner Little Scholars, Inc.; bd. dirs. Lay Involvement for Evangelism, Atlanta, 1978—. Served from ensign to lt. USNR, 1942-46, ETO. Mem. Am. Mktg. Assn., Atlanta Apt. Assn. (dir. 1964-65), Nat. Assn. Small Bus. Investment Cos. (gov. 1963), So. Regional Assn. Small Bus. Investment Cos. (pres. 1963), Am. Mgmt. Assn., Atlanta C. of C., A.I.M. (mem. pres.'s council), Newcomen Soc. N.Am. (Ga. com.), Soc. Colonial Wars, Sigma Alpha Epsilon (past dir.). Presbyn. (deacon, elder). Clubs: Kiwanian. (Atlanta), Breakfast (Atlanta), Harvard Bus. Sch. (Atlanta) (past dir.), Piedmont Driving (Atlanta), Capital City (Atlanta); Harvard (N.Y.C.). Home: 2637 Peachtree Rd NE Atlanta GA 30305

SIMMS, CHARLES AVERILL, environmental management company executive; b. Hundred, W.Va., Apr. 12, 1937; s. Charles R. and Ada Faith (Devine) S.; m. Linda Magalis, June 24, 1961; children: Brian M., Eric C. BSBA, W.Va. U., 1959. Cert. internal auditor, Md. Jr. acct. Potomac Edison Co., Hagerstown, Md., 1960-61; internal auditor Potomac Edison Co., Hagerstown, 1961-66, supr. internal audits, 1966-69; constrn. audit mgr. Eastalco Aluminum Co., Frederick, Md., 1969-71, gen. acctg. mgr., 1971-73, exec. asst. to pres., 1973-74; contr. Teledyne Nat., Cockeysville, Md., 1974-77, dir. fin. and adminstrn., Northridge, Calif., 1977-79, v.p. ops., Timonium, Md., 1979-83; pres. Nat. Ecology, Inc., Timonium, 1983-89; pres., chief exec. officer Rescon Inc., Balt., 1989-93; dir. Md. Environ. Svc., Annapolis, 1993—; chmn. exec. com., bd. dirs. Am. Ecology Corp., Houston, 1984-94. 1st lt. U.S. Army, 1959-67. Mem. Solid Waste Assn. N.Am., Shriners (Cumberland, Md.). Republican. Home: 12231 Bare Bush Path Columbia MD 21044 Office: Md Environ Svc 10320 York Rd Cockeysville Hunt Valley MD 21030-3203

SIMMS, ELLENESE BROOKS, civic leader, retired school system administrator; b. New Orleans, Sept. 10, 1939; d. Annias and Ellen (Lyons) Brooks; m. Clarence Joseph Simms, June 16, 1960 (div. June 1967); 1 child, Stacy René; m. Melvin Simms, Apr. 27, 1968; 1 adopted child, Darrell Dean; 1 child, Christel Melvanesia. BA, Dillard U., 1962; MEd, Loyola U., New Orleans, 1976. Elem. tchr. New Orleans Pub. Schs., 1962-76, prin. Helen S. Edwards Elem. Sch., 1976-86, prin. Robert Russa Moton Elem. Sch., 1986-92, adminstr. for consol. programs, 1992-94; mem. ednl. task force La. Dept. Edn., 1975-76; pres. Golden Svcs. Inc., exec. dir., 1990—; pres. Profl. Assn. Creative Educators, ednl. cons., 1982-96; coord. Orleans Parish schs. area So. Assn. Colls. and Schs., 1982-93; designer, implementer year round sch. pilot project Orleans Parish Schs., 1989-92; mem. internat. curriculum devel. seminar in Cameroon, U. New Orleans, 1983. Mem. Brechtel Park Adv. Bd., 1984-94, Mayor's Algiers Task Force Com., 1984-85; chairperson Algiers Enterprise Cmty. Coun., Inc., 1996—; pres. Desire/Fla. Cmty. Coun., 1996—; mem. ednl. cmty. adv. bd. Fla./Desire, 1977-94; founder, v.p. Holly Park Civic Assn., pres., 1973-76; co-founder, past sec. Algiers-Gretna br. NAACP, 1990; co-chmn. Citizens Adv. Com. for minority Participation, 1989; commr. Regional Transit Authority, 1991-95, chmn. bd. commrs., 1991-94; founder Greater New Orleans Regional Transit Task Force, 1990, Transit Task Force for Civil Rights, 1993; bd. dirs. Health Edn. Authority of Wis., 1994-97, Total Cmty. Action, nc., 1997—. Recipient area chmn. citation New Orleans Sickle Cell Anemia Found., Inc., 1979, Leadership and Svc. award La. Assn. Sch. Execs., 1982, Outstanding Educator award Negro Bus. and Profl. Women's Club New Orleans, 1988, Outstanding Svc. award Prins. Assn. New Orleans Pub. Schs., 1992, New Orleans City Coun., 1992, Woman of Distinction award Austin Met. Bus. Resource Ctr., 1993, Gov.'s award State of La., 1994, cert. of appreciation Nat. Coun. Negro Women, 1994; also others. Mem. Am. Pub. Transit Assn. (v.p. human resources 1992-94, co-chmn. diversity coun. 1992-95; mem. transti 2000 comm. oversight com. 1992), Nat. Assn. for Yr. Round edn. (bd. dirs. 1991-94), Ind. Women's Orgn., La. PTA (hon. state life), Delta Sigma Theta (life, Vol. Svc. award New Orleans Alumnae chpt. 1977). Baptist. Avocations: cooking, crafts. Home: 3701 Mansfield Ave New Orleans LA 70131-5625

SIMMS, FRANCES BELL, elementary education educator; b. Salisbury, N.C., July 29, 1936; d. William Taft and Anne Elmira (Sink) Bell; m. Howard Homer Simms, June 24, 1966 (dec. Oct. 1993); 1 child, Shannon Lara. AB in English, U. N.C., 1958; MEd, U. Fla., 1962; postgrad., Boston U., 1963—, U. Va.; Queen's Coll., Cambridge, U.K. Playroom attendant dept. neurology Children's Hosp., Boston, 1958-60; reading clinician Mills Ctr., Inc., Ft. Lauderdale, Fla., 1960-61; reading/lang. arts tchr. Arlington (Va.) Pub. Schs., 1962—; adv. bd. mem. ad hoc com. Edn. Tech., Arlington, 1965-67; reading instr. Va. Poly. Inst. and State U., Arlington, 1974; prodr., dir. Barcroft Newsbag-CATV, Arlington, 1982—; chair self-study Elem. Sch., Arlington, 1987, 93; adv. bd. Reading is Fundamental of No. Va., Arlington, 1988—. Lay leader, choir mem. Cherrydale Meth. Ch., Arlington, 1976—; laborer Christmas in April, Arlington, 1990—; tutor, vol. instr. Henderson Hall Marine Corps, Arlington, 1990—; organizer, instr. Better Beginnings, Arlington, 1994—, The Reading Connection, P.R., 1994—. Recipient Literacy award, Margaret McNamara award Reading is Fundamental of No. Va., 1994-95. Mem. Va. State Reading Assn. (mem. conf. coms.), Arlington Edn. Assn. (contbg. editor newsletter 1967-69), Greater Washington Reading Coun. (com. chairperson 1962—, Tchr. of Yr. 1995-96), Delta Kappa Gamma (Alpha Omicron former news writer, v.p., program chairperson, news editor). Avocations: water color, singing in choir, writing poetry, journal keeping, traveling, producing children's musicals. Home: 6110 23rd St N Arlington VA 22205-3414

SIMMS, JOHN CARSON, logic, mathematics and computer science educator; b. Columbus, Ind., Oct. 24, 1952; s. Roberta Ann (Cooke) Burns; m. Florence Chizue Miyamoto, June 22, 1974; 1 child, Carson Chizumi. BA with highest distinction, Ind. U., 1972, MA, 1974; PhD, Rockefeller U., 1979. Assoc. instr. Ind. U., Bloomington, 1973-74; grad. fellow Rockefeller U., N.Y.C., 1974-78; vis. lectr. Tex. Tech U., Lubbock, 1978-80; v.p. Custom Computation, Inc., Lubbock, 1980-81; computer programmer and analyst Furr's Inc., Lubbock, 1981-82; contract computer programmer Lubbock, 1982-83; asst. prof. math. and computer sci. Marquette U., Milw., 1983-92, assoc. prof. math. and computer sci., 1992—. Assoc. editor Modern Logic, Modern Logic Books, 1990—; contbr. articles to profl. jours. Mem. AAAS, Assn. for Symbolic Logic, Kurt-Gödel-Gesellschaft (Collegium Logicum lectr. 1990), Am. Math. Soc., Interest Group in Pure and Applied Logic, Pi Mu Epsilon, Sigma Xi, Phi Beta Kappa. Achievements include research on new semantics for second-order logic, on a natural argument against the continuum hypothesis, on a natural argument against the axiom of choice, on applications of natural probabilistic notions to the foundations of mathematics. Home: 8969 N Pelham Pky Bayside WI 53217-1954 Office: Dept Math Stats Computer Sci Marquette Univ PO Box 1881 Milwaukee WI 53201-1881

SIMMS, LILLIAN MILLER, nursing educator; b. Detroit, Apr. 13, 1930; d. John Jacob and Mary Agnes (Knight) Miller; m. Richard James Simms, Feb. 2, 1952; children: Richard James Jr., Frederick William, Andrew

Michael. BSN, U. Mich., 1952, MSN, 1966, PhD in Ednl. Gerontology, 1977. Program dir., assoc. prof. nursing health svcs. adminstrn. U. Mich., Ann Arbor, 1977-82, interim assoc. dir. nursing, asst. dean clin. affairs, 1981-82, assoc. prof. nursing adminstrn. and health gerontology, 1982-90, assoc. prof. nursing, 1990—; prof. emeritus, 1995; spkr., presenter in field; mem. spl. study sect. NIH, 1986; mem. adv. com., panel of judges for inquiry and practice of nursing svc. adminstr. Intra and Interdisciplinary Invitational Conf., 1990; series editor Delmar Pubs., Inc., 1991-93; mem. med. delegation People to People Citizen Amb. Program, Australia and New Zealand, 1982, People's Republic of China, Hong Kong and Korea, 1989; dir. China project that developed acad. relationships with schs. of nursing in People's Republic of China, 1991-94. Developer nursing concept of work excitement; co-author: Administracion de Servicios de Enfermeria, 1986, A Guide to Redesigning Nursing Practice Patterns, 1992, The Professional Practice of Nursing Administration, 2d edit., 1994; contbr. numerous articles to profl. publs.; reviewer for various publs. in field. Bd. dirs. Domino House Sr. Ctr., Ann Arbor, 1990-95. Recipient Excellence in Nursing Edn. award Rho chpt. Sigma Theta Tau, 1995; grantee U. Mich., 1983-84, 84-87, 87-88, Presdl. Initiatives, 1990-92, W.K. Kellogg Found., 1991-93. Fellow Am. Acad. Nursing; mem. ANA, Am. Orgn. Nurse Execs., Midwest Nursing Rsch. Soc., Coun. on Grad. Edn. for Adminstrn. in Nursing (sec. 1986-88, chair publs. com. 1988-89), U. Mich. Nursing Alumni Assn., Sigma Theta Tau. Avocations: reading, gardening, international travel. Home: 1329 Wines Dr Ann Arbor MI 48103-2543 Office: U Mich Sch Nursing 400 N Ingalls St Rm 2174 Ann Arbor MI 48109-2003

SIMMS, LOIS AVERETTA, retired secondary education educator, musician; b. Charleston, S.C., May 27, 1919; d. Jasper Simeon and Anna Inez (Ferguson) S. BA, Johnson C. Smith U., 1941; MA, Howard U., 1954. Cert. English and social studies educator, S.C. Directive tchr. Avery Normal Inst., Charleston, 1941-42; tchr. English and French Laing H.S., Mt. Pleasant, S.C., 1942-44; tchr. English and math. Henry P. Archer Sch., Charleston, 1944-45; tchr. social studies and English Burke H.S., Charleston, 1945-52; tchr. English Avery H.S., Charleston, 1952-54, Burke H.S., Charleston, 1954-73; tchr. English and history Charleston H.S., 1973-76; ret., 1976; co-adviser Dramatic Club, Burke H.S., 1945-46, trainer section of chorus, 1945-47, chief advisor 1961 Bulldog Yearbook, 1960-61; advisor Crochet Club, Avery H.S., 1952-54, Charleston H.S., 1973-76. Author: Growing Up Presbyterian: Life in Presbyterian Colleges and Churches, 1991, Profiles of African American Females in Low Country of South Carolina, 1992, A Chalk and Chalkboard Career in Carolina, 1995, A History of Zion, Olivet, and Zion-Olivet Churches 1850-1985, 1989; editor The Scroll newsletter, 1984-94. Sec. exec. bd. YWCA of Greater Charleston, 1950s; mem. YWCA, S.C. Hist. Soc., S.C. ETV Endowment. Recipient plaque Zion-Olivet Presbyn. Ch., 1987, C.L. Campbell award Presbyn. Ch., 1988, plaque Staff of The Scroll, 1990. Mem. NAACP, Charleston County Ret. Educators Assn. Unit 2, Pres.'s Club (plaque 1991), Avery Inst. Afro-Am. History and Culture (editor The Bull. 1990-96, Cert.), S.C. Soc. Avocations: reading, playing music, playing Scrabble, planting flowers, writing prose. Home: 28 Jasper St Charleston SC 29403

SIMMS, LOWELLE, synod executive; b. Sterling, Colo., June 16, 1931; s. Griffin L. and Irene O. (Geer) S.; m. Lois A. Streeter, Aug. 8, 1959. BA, Park Coll., 1953; MDiv, Union Theol. Sem., 1956. Ordained min. Presbyn. Ch., 1956. Pastor East Trenton Presbyn. Ch., Trenton, N.J., 1957-61, Calvary Presbyn. Ch., Phila., 1961-66; min. of mission First, North, Westminster Chs., Kalamazoo, Mich., 1966-69; assoc. exec. Presbytery of Sccoto Valley, Columbus, Ohio, 1969-80; administr. interims Presbytery and Synods Presbyterian Ch., 1980-83; synod exec. Synod of the Covenant, Columbus. Avocation: photography. Office: Synod of the Covenant 6172 Busch Blvd Ste 3000 Columbus OH 43229-2515*

SIMMS, MARIA ESTER, health services administrator; b. Bahia Blanca, Argentina; came to U.S., 1963; d. Jose and Esther (Guays) Barberio Esandi; m. Michael Simms, July 15, 1973 (div. Aug. 1993); children: Michelle Bonnie Lee Carla, Michael London Valentine, Matthew Brandon. Degree medicine, Facultad del Centenario, Rosario, Argentina, 1962; Physician Asst. Cert. (hon.), U. So. Calif., 1977. Medical diplomate. Pres. Midtown Svcs. Inc., L.A., 1973—; dir. internat. affairs, speaker Gov. of Papua, New Guinea, 1996—; dir., CFO World Film Inst., 1996—; dir. internat. affairs, speaker on humanitarian, cultural and econ. matters Govt. of Papua New Guinea; advocate, internat. spkr. for women, children and animal rights. Chmn. bd. Am.'s Film Inst., Washington; chmn. bd. trustees World Film Inst, Dir. Intl. Affairs, speaker-Humanitarian, Economic and Cultural Consulate of Papua New Guinea, Los Angeles, Calif. Nominated chairwoman of bd. trustees World Film Inst. Fellow Am. Acad. Physicians' Assts.; mem. Bus. for Law Enforcement (northeast divsn.), Physicians for Social Responsibility, Mercy Crusade Inc., Internat. Found. for Survival Rsch., Noetic Scis. Soc., Inst. Noetic Scis., So. Calif. Alliance for Survival, Supreme Emblem Club of U.S., Order Eastern Star, Flying Samaritans, Shriners. Avocations: coin collecting, designing, writing, oil painting, flying.

SIMMS, MARIA KAY, publishing and computer services executive; b. Princeton, Ill., Nov. 18, 1940; d. Frank B. and Anna (Haurberg) S.; m. Neil F. Michelsen, Oct. 2, 1987 (dec. 1990); children: Shannon Sullivan Stillings, Molly A. Sullivan, Elizabeth Maria Jossick. BFA, Ill. Wesleyan U., 1962. Cert. cons. profl. astrologer; ordained min. L.A. Cmty. Ch. of Religious Sci. Elder priestess Covenant of the Goddess; art tchr. elem. and jr. high pub. schs., Dundee, Northbrook, Ill., 1962-65; high sch. art tchr. Danbury, Conn., 1975-76; self employed gallery painter various cities, 1962-77, free-lance comml. illustrator, 1972-74, 86-87; shop, gallery, café owner Conn., 1976-79; art dir. ACS Pubs., Inc., San Diego, Calif., 1987-90; pres. Astro Comm Svcs., Inc. (formerly ACS Pubs.), San Diego, 1990—; conf. lectr. United Astrology Congress, 1986, 89, 92, 95, Am. Fedn. Astrologers Internat. Conv., 1982, 84, 86, 88, 90, 92, 94, 96. Author: Twelve Wings of the Eagle, 1988, Dial Detective, 1989; co-author: Search for the Christmas Star, 1989, Circle of the Cosmic Muse, 1994, Your Magical Child, 1994, Future Signs, 1996, The Witch's Circle, 1996; contbr. numerous articles to mags. High priestee Cir. of the Cosmic Muse; elder priestess Covenant of the Goddess, 2d officer Calafia Local Coun., 1995-96, pub. info. officer, 1996-97. Recipient numerous art awards. Mem. Nat. Assn. Women Bus. Owners, Nat. Coun. Geocosmic Rsch. Inc. (dir., pubs. dir. 1981-92, editor jour. 1984-92), Am. Fedn. Astrologers, Internat. Soc. Astrol. Rsch., New Age Pubs. Assn. Office: Astro Comm Svcs Inc 5521 Ruffin Rd San Diego CA 92123-1314

SIMMS, THOMAS HASKELL, police chief; b. Yuma, Ariz., Sept. 3, 1945; s. Jessie Lee and Mary Elizabeth (Servos) S.; divorced; m. Ginny Lee David, Mar. 26, 1988; children: Thomas Haskell Jr., Julie Marie. BA, St. Mary's Coll., Moraga, Calif., 1981; MS, Calif. Poly., Pomona, 1991. Officer Mountain View (Calif.) Police Dept., 1972-76; police sgt. East Bay Parks, Oakland, Calif., 1976-79; police lt. Town of Moraga, Calif., 1979-84, chief police, 1984-87; chief police City of Piedmont, Calif., 1987-91; chief of police City of Roseville, Calif., 1991—; mem. U. Calif.-Davis Med. Ctr. Leadership Coun.; bd. dirs. Child Abuse Prevention Coun. of Placer County, Sierra Family Svcs. Bd. dirs. Piedmont coun. Boy Scouts Am., 1988-89. Maj. U.S. Army, 1967-71, Vietnam. Mem. Calif. Chiefs Police Assn. (bd. dirs.), Calif. Peace Officers Assn., Calif. Peace Officers Meml. Found. (bd. dirs.), Rotary, Kiwanis (pres. Moraga 1982-83, Kiwanian of Yr. award 1983). Presbyterian. Avocations: hiking, photography, travel, golf, fly fishing. Office: Roseville Police Dept 311 Vernon St Roseville CA 95678-2649

SIMNAD, MASSOUD T., engineering educator; b. Teheran, Iran, Mar. 11, 1920; came to U.S., 1948; s. Reza an Ferhunde (Magari) S.; m. Lenora Virginia Brown, May 28, 1954; childrne: Jeffrey, Virginia. BS, London U., 1942; PhD, U. Cambridge, Eng., 1946. Rsch. fellow U. Cambridge, 1945-48; postdoctoral fellow Carnegie-Mellow U., Pitts., 1949-50, mem. faculty, 1950-56; with Gen. Atomics, San Diego, 1956-81; adj. prof., cons. in engring. U. Calif., San Diego, 1981—; vis. prof. MIT, Cambridge, 1962-63; mem. tech. coms. U.S. Dept. Energy, 1970—; cons. in field. Author papers, monographs in field; patentee in field. Fellow Am. Nuc. Soc., Am. Soc. Metals, AAAs; mem. AIAA, NAE, Electrochem. Soc., Inst. Global Conflict and Cooperation, World Affairs Coun., UN Club, Sierra Club. Avocations: art, music, gardening, sports, travel. Home: 6120 La Flecha Rd PO Box 1806 Rancho Santa Fe CA 92093 Office: U Calif Mail Code R-011 La Jolla CA 92093

SIMOKAITIS, FRANK JOSEPH, air force officer, lawyer; b. St. Louis, Dec. 12, 1922; s. Frank and Constance (Ladish) S.; m. Mary Jane Feeny; children: Peggy, Mary. Student, Washington U., St. Louis, 1945-47; LL.B., St. Louis U., 1950, J.D., 1970. Bar: U.S. Supreme Ct. U.S 1950, Mo. 1950, also other fed. cts. 1950. Commd. 2d lt. USAAF, 1943; advanced through grades to maj. gen. USAF, 1973; plans and ops. officer Hdqrs. Pacific Air Force, 1960-63; staff officer Hdqrs. USAF, Washington, 1963-69; exec. asst. to sec. air force Hdqrs. USAF, 1969-73; comdt. Air Force Inst. Tech., 1973-78; dir. Dept. Def. affairs Hdqrs. NASA, Washington, 1978-83, cons., 1983—. Bd. dirs. Dayton chpt. ARC, Greater Miami chpt., arbitrator Better Bus. Bur. Decorated D.S.M. with oak leaf cluster, Legion of Merit, Air medal with 4 oak leaf clusters, Air Force Commendation medal. Mem. Miami Air Force Assn. (bd. dirs.), Navy League (v.p. U.S. Miami coun.), Ft. Myer Officers Club. Home: 3100 S Manchester St Falls Church VA 22044-2711

SIMON, ALBERT, physicist, engineer, educator; b. N.Y.C., Dec. 27, 1924; s. Emanuel D. and Sarah (Leitner) S.; m. Harriet E. Rubinstein, Aug. 17, 1947 (dec. June 1970); children: Richard, Janet, David; m. Rita Shiffman, June 11, 1972. BS, CCNY, 1947; PhD, U. Rochester, 1950. Registered profl. engr., N.Y. State. Physicist Oak Ridge Nat. Lab., 1950-54, assoc. dir. neutron physics divsn., 1954-61; head plasma physics divsn. Gen. Atomic Co., San Diego, 1961-66; prof. dept. mech. engring. U. Rochester, N.Y., 1966—; prof. physics U. Rochester, 1968—, chmn. dept. mech. engring., 1977-84; mem. Inst. for Advanced Study, Princeton, 1974-75; sr. vis. fellow U.K. Sci. Rsch. Coun., Oxford U., 1975. Author: An Introduction to Thermonuclear Research, 1959; contbr. to: Ency. Americana, 1964, 74; editor Advances in Plasma Physics, 1967—. With USN, 1944-46. Recipient Univ. Mentor award, 1988-89; John Simon Guggenheim fellow, 1964-65. Fellow Am. Phys. Soc. (chmn. plasma physics divsn. 1963-64); mem. ASME, ASEE (chmn. nuc. engring. divsn. 1985-86). Home: 263 Ashley Dr Rochester NY 14620-3327

SIMON, ARTHUR, pharmacologist, research laboratory executive; b. Bklyn., June 1, 1942; s. Harry and Ann S.; m. Sandra Goldberg, July 10, 1966; children—Brett David, Kira Denise. B.S. in Biology, Phila. Coll. Pharmacy and Sci., 1965; M.S. cum laude, Fairleigh Dickinson U., 1969; Ph.D. in Pharmacology (NIH fellow), U. Cin., 1972. Lab. technician La Wall and Harrisson Research Lab., Phila., 1962-63; research asst. toxicology dept. Wyeth Labs., Paoli, Pa., 1965-66; research assoc. pharmacology dept. Warner Lambert Research Inst., Morris Plains, N.J., 1966-69; research investigator Squibb Inst. for Med. Research, Princeton, N.J., 1972-74; sr. cardiovascular pharmacologist USV Pharm. Corp., Tuckahoe, N.Y., 1974-76; dir. cardiovascular clin. research Bristol Myers Co. Internat. Div., 1974-82; pres., chief exec. officer Research Testing Labs., Inc., Great Neck, N.Y., 1982—. Mem. Dermal Clin. Evaluation Soc., Drug Info. Assn., Assocs. Clin. Pharmacologist, Regulatory Affairs Profl. Soc., Internat. Assn. Dental Rsch., Am. Assn. Dental Rsch. Home: 52 Tamarack Ln Pomona NY 10970-2012 Office: Rsch Testing Labs Inc 255 Great Neck Rd Great Neck NY 11021-3301

SIMON, BARRY PHILIP, lawyer, airline executive; b. Paterson, N.J., Nov. 22, 1942; s. Alfred Louis and Rhoda (Tapper) S.; m. Hinda Bookstaber, Feb. 9, 1964; children: Alan, John, Eric. BA, Princeton U., 1964; LLB, Yale U., 1967. Bar: N.Y. 1965, Tex. 1986. Assoc. atty. Hughes Hubbard & Reed, N.Y.C., 1967-69, Sullivan & Cromwell, N.Y.C., 1969-72, Shea & Gould, N.Y.C., 1972-73; v.p., gen. counsel Teleprompter Corp., N.Y.C., 1973-82; v.p., sec., gen. counsel Continental Airlines, L.A. and Houston, 1982-86; v.p. in-charge internat. div. Continental Airlines, Houston, 1987-90; sr. v.p. legal affairs, gen. counsel, sec. Continental Airlines, 1990-92; sr. v.p. Tex. Air Corp., 1986-87; sr. v.p. legal affairs, gen. counsel, sec. Ea. Airlines, Miami, 1987-90; exec. v.p., gen. counsel GAF Corp., Wayne, N.J., 1993—; sr. v.p. for Europe, Continental Airlines, Houston; bd. dirs. Amadeus Reservations Sys. Mem. copyright com. Nat. Cable TV Assn., Washington, 1974-76, mem. utilities com., 1973-82; bd. dirs. Houston Grand Opera, Inprint, Alley Theatre. Recipient Class of 1888 Lit. prize Princeton U., 1961. Home: 2003 Dunstan Houston TX 77005

SIMON, BERNECE KERN, social work educator; b. Denver, Nov. 27, 1914; d. Maurice Meyer and Jennie (Bloch) Kern; m. Marvin L. Simon, Feb. 26, 1939; 1 dau., Anne Elizabeth. B.A., U. Chgo., 1936, M.A., 1942. Social worker Jewish Children's Bur. Chgo., 1938-40, U. Chgo. Hosps. and Clinics, 1940-44; mem. faculty U. Chgo., 1944-81, instr., 1944-48, asst. prof., 1948-60, prof. social casework, 1960—, Samuel Deutsch prof. Sch. Social Service Adminstrn., 1960-81, emeritus, 1981—. Mem. bd. editors 17th Edit. Ency. Social Work, 1975-77, Social Svc. Rev., 1975—; bd. editors: Social Work, 1978-82, book rev. editor, 1982-87; cons. editor Journal of Social Work Education, 1991-94; contbr. articles to profl. jours., book chpts., monographs. Mem. Council Social Work Edn. (mem. nat. bd., sec. 1972-74), Nat. Assn. Social Workers, Acad. Cert. Social Workers, Nat. Acads. Practice: Social Work. Office: U Chgo Sch of Social Svc Administrn 969 E 60th St Chicago IL 60637-2640

SIMON, CARLY, singer, composer, author; b. N.Y.C., June 25, 1945; d. Richard S.; m. James Taylor, 1972 (div. 1983); children: Sarah Maria, Benjamin Simon; m. James Hart, Dec. 23, 1987. Studied with Pete Seeger. Singer, composer, rec. artist, 1971—. Appeared in film No Nukes, 1980; albums include Carly Simon, 1971, Anticipation, 1972, No Secrets, 1973, Hotcakes, 1974, Playing Possum, 1975, The Best of Carly Simon, 1975, Another Passenger, 1976, Boys in the Trees, 1978, Spy, 1979, Come Upstairs, 1980, Torch, 1981, Hello Big Man, 1983, Spoiled Girl, 1985, Coming Around Again, 1987, Greatest Hits Live, 1988, My Romance, 1990, Have You Seen Me Lately?, 1990, Carly Simon, This Is My Life, 1992, Letters Never Sent, 1994; single records: Nobody Does It Better, 1977, Let the River Run, 1988 (Academy award best original song, 1989), (with Frank Sinatra) In the Wee Small Hours of the Morning, 1993, Clouds in My Coffee, 1995, (with others) Come Upstairs, 1996; recipient Grammy award as best new artist 1971; TV appearance: Carly in Concert: My Romance, 1990; created opera Romulus Hunt, 1993. Office: Warner Bros Records 75 Rockefeller Plz New York NY 10019*

SIMON, CATHY JENSEN, architect; b. L.A., Sept. 30, 1943; d. Bernard Everett and Bitten Hanne (Smith) S.; m. Michael Palmer, Nov. 23, 1972; 1 child, Sarah Marina. B.A. Wellesley Coll., 1965; M. Arch., Harvard U., 1969. Registered architect, Calif. 1974, N.Y. 1988, Mass. 1988, Colo. 1995, Ariz. 1996. Architect Cambridge 7 Assocs., Mass., 1968-69, Building Systems Devel., San Francisco, 1970-72, Mackinlay Winnacker McNeil, Oakland, Calif., 1973-74; prin. Marquis Assocs., San Francisco, 1974-85; prin. Simon Martin-Vegue Winkelstein Moris, 1985—; sr. lectr. architecture U. Calif., Berkeley, 1982-85, vis. lectr., 1973-82; teaching coordinator Women's Sch. Planning and Arch., Santa Cruz, Calif., 1976; speaker ALA Nat. Conv., 1992, Les Grandes Bibliotheques de L'Avenin, Paris, 1991. Prin. works include San Diego New Main Lib., Yerba Buena Gardens Retail and Entertainment Complex, San Francisco, Mus. N.Mex. Master Plan, Santa Fe, San Francisco Ballet Pavilion, Lick Wilmerding High Sch. Master Plan, San Francisco, Bothell Br. Campus, Bothell, Wash., San Francisco New Main Libr., Oceanside Water Pollution Control Project, San Francisco, Newport Beach (Calif.) Ctrl. Libr., Coll. 8 U. Calif., Santa Cruz, Olin Humanities Bldg. Bard Coll., N.Y., San Francisco Day Sch., Fremont (Calif.) Main Libr., Peter J. Shields Libr. U. Calif., Davis, Elena Baskin Visual Art Studios U. Calif., Santa Cruz, Primate Discovery Ctr., San Francisco Zoo, Braun Music Ctr., Stanford U. The Premier, La Jolla Colony, La Jolla, Calif. Mem. exec. com. San Francisco Mus. Modern Art; active Leadership Commn. Design Industry; mem. tech. assistance com., San Francisco Redevel. Agy., San Francisco, 1982—; mem. adv. panel Calif. Bd. Archtl. Examiners; bd. dirs. Golden Gate Nat. Park Assn. Recipient Calif. Preservation award Chambord Apartments, 1984, Adaptive Re-use award Engr. Offices, Am. Soc. Interior Designer, 1982, Commodore Sloat Sch. Honor award Nat. Sch. Bds. Assocs., 1980, Marcus Foster Mid. Sch. Honor award East Bay AIA, 1980; NEA grantee 1983. Mem. Orgn. Women Architects (founding 1972), San Francisco chpt. AIA, AIA (jury mem. nat. honor awards 1980, Los Angeles chpt. awards jury 1984). Home: 265 Jersey St San Francisco CA 94114-3822 Office: Simon Martin-Vegue Winkelstein Moris 501 2nd St Ste 701 San Francisco CA 94107-1431

SIMON, DAVID FREDERICK, lawyer; b. El Paso, Tex., Apr. 14, 1953; s. Maurice and Susan (Bendekovits) S.; m. Deborah Hart, Mar. 1, 1980; children: Alison Mallory, Joshua Alan, Rebecca Elizabeth, Nathaniel Cody. BS magna cum laude, U. Buffalo, 1974; JD cum laude, U. Pa., 1977. Bar: Pa. 1977, N.J. 1978. Law clk. to presiding judge Phila. Ct. Common Pleas, 1977-79; assoc. Wolf, Block, Schorr & Solis-Cohen, Phila., 1979-85, ptnr., 1985-90; sr. v.p. U.S. Healthcare Inc., Blue Bell, Pa., 1990-96; chief legal officer Aetna U.S. Healthcare, Inc., Blue Bell, 1996—; mem. adv. coun. Pa. Dept. Conservation and Natural Resources, 1996—; Pa. Judicial Nominating Commr., Montgomery County, 1995—. Mem. Phila. Bar Assn. (mem. exec. com. young lawyers sect. 1983-85, chmn. computer law com. 1984-85), Pa. Bar Assn. (chmn. in-house counsel com. 1993-94), Pa. Bar Inst. (bd. dirs. 1992-96). Avocations: photography, electronics. Home: PO Box 551 Gwynedd Valley PA 19437-0551 Office: Aetna US Healthcare PO Box 1180 Blue Bell PA 19422-0020

SIMON, DAVID HAROLD, retired public relations executive; b. Washington, Dec. 3, 1930; s. Isaac B. and Marjorie S. (Felstiner) S.; m. Ruth Lurie, Mar. 2, 1962; children: Rachel, Jessie. BEE, Cornell U., 1954. Mktg. engr. Sylvania Elec. Products, Inc., Boston, 1957-58; advt. mgr. Sylvania Elec. Products, Inc., Mountain View, Calif., 1958-60; regional sales engr. Sylvania Elec. Products, Inc., L.A., 1960-63; mgr. advt. and pub. rels. Electronic Splty. Co., L.A., 1963-66; corp. dir. advt. and pub. rels. Teledyne, Inc., L.A., 1966-67; pres. Simon/Pub. Rels., Inc., L.A., 1967-91. Contbr. articles on pub. rels. to various publs. Res. dep. sheriff L.A. Sheriff's Dept., 1973—, capt., 1996; mem. L.A. Olympic Citizens' Adv. Commn., 1980-84; commr. City of L.A. Cultural Affairs Commn., 1987-92, pres., 1990-92; trustee Calif. Chamber Symphony, 1981-84; mem., founder L.A. Philharmonic, 1984—; mem. Philharmonic Men's Com., 1986—; bd. dirs. L.A. Mozart Orch., Odyssey Theater, L.A., 1992—, pres., 1995—. With USN, 1954-57. Named Res. Dep. Sheriff of Yr., L.A. Sheriff's Dept., 1994. Fellow Pub. Rels. Soc. Am. (chair-elect coll. of fellows, bd. mem. L.A. chpt.); mem. Nat. Assn. Sci. Writers, Nat. Assn. Corp. Dirs. (founding pres. L.A. chpt.), Opera Buffs Inc. (bd. dirs. 1986-87, vice chair Madrid Theatre, 1997—), Mensa. Home: 13025 Weddington St Van Nuys CA 91401-6160

SIMON, DOLORES DALY, copy editor; b. San Francisco, Nov. 18, 1928; d. Francis Edward and Jeannette (Cooke) Daly; m. Sidney Blair Simon, Aug. 24, 1952 (div. Nov. 1955); children: John Roderick, Douglas Brian. BA in Journalism, Pa. State U., 1950. County editor Centre Daily Times, State College, Pa., 1950-51; soc. editor Bradford (Pa.) Era, 1951-52; copy editor Harper & Bros., Pubs., N.Y.C., 1955-60; copy chief Harper & Row, Pubs., N.Y.C., 1960-88; freelance editor, copy editor Warwick, N.Y., 1988—. Co-author: Recipes into Type, 1993 (Best Food Reference 1994). Mem. James Beard Found., Phi Mu. Democrat. Avocations: book collecting. Office: Editl Svcs 63 Blooms Corners Rd Warwick NY 10990-2403

SIMON, DONALD JOHN, financial planner, insurance and investment broker; b. Chgo., July 16, 1947; s. Nicholas J. and Alice R. (Vaughan) S.; 1 child, Joshua K. BSBA, Oglethorpe U., 1969. CFP, CLU. Sales rep. D. W. Shaw, Inc., Berlin, N.J., 1969-74; owner Simon Fin. Co., Silver Spring, Md., 1975—. Bd. dirs. Orphans Found. of Am., Washington, 1994—. Mem. Nat. Assn. Life Underwriters. Avocations: music, tennis. Home: 12600 Eastbourne Dr Silver Spring MD 20904-2041

SIMON, DORIS MARIE TYLER, nurse; b. Akron, Ohio, Jan. 24, 1932; d. Gabriel James and Nannie Eliza (Harris) Tyler; m. Matthew Hamilton Simon, Apr. 20, 1952; children: Matthew Derek, Denise Nanette, Gayle Machele, Doris Elizabeth. ADN, El Paso (Tex.) Coll. Media, 1969, El Paso Community Coll., 1976; BSPA in Health Care Adminstrn., St. Joseph's Coll., North Windham, Maine, 1991. RN, Tex. Med. asst. Dr. Melvin Farris, Akron, 1962-63, Dr. Samuel Watt, Akron, 1967-68, Drs. May, Fox and Buchwald, El Paso, 1972-76; head nurse, home dialysis and transplant and CAPD Hotel Dieu Med. Ctr., El Paso, 1977-87; nurse mgr., transplant coord. Providence Meml. Hosp., El Paso, 1987-95, nurse clinician nephrology, 1995; transplant coord. Sierra Med. Ctr., El Paso, 1995—; med. asst. instr. Bryman Sch. Med. Assts., El Paso, 1970-72. Youth choir dir. Ft. Sill, Okla., 1964-67; choir dir. Ft. Sill area and Ft. Bliss, Tex., 1964-74; instr. in piano and music theory, Ft. Sill, 1964-67; leader Ft. Sill coun. Girl Scouts U.S., 1965-67; instr. Sch. for Handicapped, Lawton, Okla., 1965-67; nephrology nurse del. to People's Republic China Citizen Amb. Program, People to People Internat., 1988, to Russia and the Baltics Citizen Amb. Group Project Asst. Healthcare, 1992. Recipient Molly Pitcher award U.S. Army, 1963-67, Martin Luther King Jr. Share a Dream Svc. award, 1993, Delta Sigma Theta Outstanding Profl. of 1993 award; named One of 12 Outstanding Personalities of El Paso El Paso Times, 1993. Mem. ANA, Am. Med. Assts. Assn., Am. Nephrology Nurses Assn., Les Charmantes (Akron) (pres./sec. 1950-52), Links Inc. (pres. El Paso chpt. 1992-96), Interclub Coun. (pres. 1992—), Donor Awareness Coalition, Trid-Transplant Recipients Internat. Orgn. Baptist. Avocations: piano, organ, singing, sewing, bowling. Home: 8909 Parkland Dr El Paso TX 79925-4012 Office: Transplant Dept Sierra Med Ctr 1625 Medical Center St El Paso TX 79902-5005

SIMON, ECKEHARD (PETER), foreign language educator; b. Schneidemühl, Germany, Jan. 5, 1939; came to U.S., 1955, naturalized, 1960; s. Herbert and Doris (Keiler) S.; m. Eileen Higginbottom, Dec. 19, 1959; children: Anders, Conrad (dec.), Matthew, Frederick. A.B., Columbia U., 1960; A.M., Harvard U., 1961, Ph.D., 1964. Instr., German Harvard U., Cambridge, Mass., 1964-65; asst. prof. Harvard U., 1965-69, assoc. prof., 1969-71, prof., 1971—, head tutor and lang. coordinator, 1965-76, chmn. dept. German, 1976-82, 85-86, chmn. com. on medieval studies, 1992-95. Author: Neidhart von Reuental: Geschichte der Forschung und Bibliographie, 1968, Neidhart von Reuental, 1975, The Türkenkalender (1454) Attributed to Gutenberg and the Strasbourg Lunation Tracts, 1988; editor: The Theatre of Medieval Europe, New Research in Early Drama, 1991; mem. editorial adv. bd.: Dictionary of the Middle Ages, 1982-89; contbr. articles to profl. jours. Woodrow Wilson fellow, 1960-61; NEH Younger Scholar fellow, 1968-69; research fellow, 1977-78; Guggenheim fellow, 1968-69; Fulbright fellow U. Cologne, 1983. Mem. MLA, Am. Assn. Tchrs. German, Medieval Acad. Am. (asst. editor Speculum 1981-94, book review editor 1994—). Home: 11 Hayes Ave Lexington MA 02173-3521 Office: Harvard U Barker Ctr 345 Cambridge MA 02138-6531

SIMON, ERIC JACOB, neurochemist, educator; b. Wiesbaden, Germany, June 2, 1924; came to U.S., 1938, naturalized, 1945; s. Joseph and Paula (Meyer) S.; m. Irene M. Ronis, Aug. 9, 1947; children: Martin A., Faye Ruth, Lawrence D. BS, Case Inst. Tech., Cleve., 1944; M.S., U. Chgo., 1947, Ph.D., 1951; hon. doctorate, U. René Descartes, Paris, 1982. Postdoctoral trainee in biochemistry Columbia U. Coll. Physicians and Surgeons, 1951-53; lectr. in chemistry CCNY, 1952-59; research assoc. Cornell U. Med. Coll., 1953-59; asst. prof. medicine NYU Med. Center, 1959-64, assoc. prof. exptl. medicine, 1964-72, prof. exptl. medicine, 1972-80, prof. psychiatry and pharmacology, 1980—; Harry Williams Meml. lectr. Dept. Pharmacology Emory U., Atlanta, 1986; mem. initial rev. com. Nat. Inst. Drug Abuse, 1976-80, chmn. 1979-80, mem. Nat. Adv. Coun. on Drug Abuse, 1989-92; Sterling-Winthrop lectr. Albany Med. Coll., 1977; vis. prof. Coll. de France, Paris, 1990. Trustee Teaneck (N.J.) Bd. Edn., 1975-79. Served with U.S. Army, 1944-46. Recipient Rsch. Pace Setter award Nat. Inst. Drug Abuse, 1977, Louis and Bert Freedman Found. award N.Y. Acad. Scis., 1980, Nathan B. Eddy Meml. award Com. on Problems of Drug Dependence, Lexington, Ky., 1983, Alumni Profl. Achievement award U. Chgo., 1986; Health Rsch. Coun. N.Y.C. career scientist, 1959-75. Fellow AAAS, N.Y. Acad. Scis. (trustee 1986-89); mem. Am. Soc. Biol. Chemists, Am. Soc. Neurochemistry, Am. Soc. Pharmacology, Internat. Soc. Neurochemistry, Am. Chem. Soc., Sigma Xi. Lodge: B'nai B'rith. Research, publs. on opiate receptors, endorphins, biochemistry of analgesic action, vitamin E metabolism, acyl-coenzyme A synthesis. Office: 550 1st Ave New York NY 10016-6481

SIMON, EVELYN, lawyer; b. N.Y.C., May 13, 1943; d. Joseph and Adele (Holzschlag) Berkman; m. Frederick Simon, Aug. 18, 1963; children: Amy Jocelyn, Marcie Ann. AB in Physics, Barnard Coll., 1963; MS in Physics, U. Pitts., 1964; JD, Wayne State U., 1978; LLB, Monash U., Melbourne, Australia, 1980. Bar: Mich. 1980, Victoria (Australia) 1981. Supr. engring. Chrysler Corp., Detroit, 1964-72; edn. and profl. mgr. Engring. Soc. Detroit,

1972-78; solicitor Arthur Robinson & Co., Melbourne, 1980-81; sr. atty. Ford Motor Co., Detroit, 1981-89; assoc. gen. counsel Sheller-Globe Corp., Detroit, 1989-90; v.p. planning, gen. counsel United Techs. Automotive Inc., Dearborn, Mich., 1991-94, v.p. bus. devel. and legal affairs, 1995-96, v.p. Asian bus. devel., 1997—. Mem. ABA, Mich. Bar Assn. Home: 1787 Alexander Dr Bloomfield Hills MI 48302-1204 Office: United Tecs Automotive Inc 5200 Auto Club Dr Dearborn MI 48126-4212

SIMON, GARY LEONARD, internist, educator; b. Bklyn., Dec. 18, 1946; s. Bernard and Dorothy (Ligeti) S.; m. Vicki Thiessen, Aug. 29, 1970; children: Jason, Jessica. BS, U. Md., 1968; PhD, U. Wis., 1972; MD, U. Md., 1975. Diplomate Am. Bd. Internal Medicine, Am. Bd. Infectious Diseases. Asst. prof. dept. medicine George Washington U., Washington, 1980-84, assoc. prof., 1984-89, assoc. chmn. medicine, 1984—, prof., 1989—, dir. divsn. infectious diseases, 1993—; cons. on AIDS Assn. Am. Med. Coll., Washington, 1990—. Contbr. articles to profl. jours. on AIDS and infectious diseases. Fellow Am. Coll. Physicians, Infectious Disease Soc. Am.; mem. Am. Soc. Microbiology, Assn. Program Dirs. in Internal Medicine. Office: George Washington U 2150 Pennsylvania Ave NW Washington DC 20037-3201

SIMON, HAROLD, radiologist; b. Trenton, N.J., May 13, 1930; s. John and Rae B. (Gilinsky) S.; m. Jane L. Ludwig, Feb. 25, 1956; children—Steven Gregg, John Gregory. M.D., Duke U., 1955. Diplomate Am. Bd. Radiology, Am. Bd. Nuclear Medicine. Intern U.S. Naval Hosp., Chelsea, Mass., 1955-56; med. officer U.S. Navy, Newport, R.I., 1956-58; resident in radiology Mass. Gen. Hosp., Boston, 1958-61, Oak Ridge Inst. Nuclear Medicine, 1959; instr. radiology Med. Sch., Tufts U., Boston, 1961-63; clin. asst. prof. radiology Med. Sch., Tufts U., 1965, assoc. clin. prof., 1971-77, clin. prof. radiology, 1977—; practice medicine specializing in radiology and nuclear medicine Newton Lower Falls, Mass., 1963—; mem. staff Newton Wellesley Hosp., Newton, Mass.; assoc. chief radiology Newton Wellesley Hosp., 1977—, radiologist-in-chief, 1987-95; dir. Sch. nuclear Med. Tech.; bd. dirs. Grove Bank for Savs.; bd. dirs., mem. CRC com., mem. audit. com. Grove Bank, chmn. audit com. 1995-96; bd. dirs., treas. Newell Physicians, Inc., 1986-93; bd. overseers Newell Health Corp.; cons. in radiology VA Hosp., Boston, 1996—, West Palm Beach, Fla., 1996—. Contbr. articles to med. jours. Served with USNR, 1955-58. Fellow Am. Coll. Radiology; mem. Radiol. Soc. N.Am., Am. Roentgen Ray Soc., New Eng. Roentgen Ray Soc., Mass. Med. Soc. (mem. ins. com.), Mass. Radiology Soc., Pinebrook Country Club (pres. 1982-85), Belmont Country Club, Presdl. Country Club, Phi Beta Kappa, Phi Eta Sigma. Home: 252 Atlantic Ave Palm Beach FL 33480

SIMON, HERBERT, professional basketball team executive; b. Bronx. Grad., CCNY. With Albert Frankel Co., Indpls., 1959; co-founder Melvin Simon and Assocs., Inc., Indpls., 1959—, pres., 1973—; owner Ind. Pacers (Nat. Basketball Assn.), Indpls., 1983—. Office: Ind Pacers Market Sq Arena 300 E Market St Indianapolis IN 46204-2603*

SIMON, HERBERT A(LEXANDER), social scientist; b. Milw., June 15, 1916; s. Arthur and Edna (Merkel) S.; m. Dorothea Pye, Dec. 25, 1937; children: Katherine S. Frank, Peter Arthur, Barbara. AB, U. Chgo., 1936, PhD, 1943, LLD (hon.), 1964; DSc (hon.), Case Inst. Tech., 1963, Yale U., 1963, Marquette U., 1981, Columbia U., 1983, Gustavus Adolphus U., 1984, Mich. Tech. U., 1988, Carnegie-Mellon U., 1990; Fil. Dr. (hon.), Lund U., Sweden, 1968; LLD (hon.), McGill U., 1970, U. Mich., 1978, U. Pitts., 1979, U. Paul Valery, France, 1984, Harvard U., 1990; Dr. Econ. Sci. (hon.), Erasmus U. Rotterdam, Netherlands, 1973, Duquesne U., 1988; DSc (hon.), LHD (hon.), Ill. Inst. Tech., 1988; D in Polit. Sci. (hon.), U. Pavia, Italy, 1988; D in Psychology (hon.), U. Rome, 1993. Rsch. asst. U. Chgo., 1936-38; staff mem. Internat. City Mgrs.' Assn.; also asst. editor Pub. Mgmt. and Municipal Year Book, 1938-39; dir. adminstrv. measurement studies Bur. Pub. Adminstrn., U. Calif., 1939-42; asst. prof. polit. sci. Ill. Inst. Tech., 1942-45, assoc. prof., 1945-47, prof., 1947-49; also chmn. dept. polit. and social sci., 1946-49; prof. adminstrn. and psychology Carnegie Mellon U., Pitts., 1949-65, Richard King Mellon univ. prof. computer scis. and psychology, 1965—; head dept. indsl. mgmt. Carnegie Mellon U., 1949-60; assoc. dean Grad. Sch. Indsl. Adminstrn., 1957-73, trustee, 1972-93; emeritus trustee, 1993—; cons. to Internat. City Mgrs. Assn., 1942-49, U.S. Bur. Budget, 1946-49, U.S. Census Bur., 1947, Cowles Found. for Research in Econs., 1947-60; cons. and acting dir. Mgmt. Engring. br. Econ. Cooperation Adminstrn., 1948; Ford Disting. lectr. NYU, 1959; Vanuxem lectr. Princeton, 1961; William James lectr. Harvard, 1963, Sigma Xi lectr., 1964, 76-78, 86; Harris lectr. Northwestern U., 1967; Karl Taylor Compton lectr. MIT, 1968; Wolfgang Koehler lectr. Dartmouth, 1975; Katz-Newcomb lectr. U. Mich., 1976; Carl Hovland lectr. Yale, 1976; Ueno lectr., Tokyo, 1977; Gaither lectr. U. Calif., Berkeley, 1980; Camp lectr. Stanford U., 1982; Gannon lectr. Fordham U., 1982; Oates vis. fellow Princeton U., 1982; Marschak lectr. UCLA, 1983; Auguste Comte lectr. London Sch. Econs., 1987; Lee Kuan Yew lectr. U. Singapore, 1989, Hitchcock lectr. U. Calif., Berkeley, 1990, lectr. U. Roma Sapienza, 1993, Mattioli lectr. Bocconi U., Milan, 1993; hon. prof. Tianjin (China) U., 1980, Beijing (China) U., 1986; hon. rsch. scientist Inst. Psychology, Chinese Acad. Scis., 1985; chmn. bd. dirs. Social Sci. Rsch. Coun., 1961-65; chmn. Pa. Gov.'s Milk Inquiry Com., 1964-65; chmn. div. behavioral scis. NRC, 1968-70; mem. President's Sci. Adv. Com., 1968-72; trustee Carnegie Inst., Pitts., 1987-93, hon. trustee, 1993—; cons. bus. and govtl. orgns. Author or co-author books relating to field, including Administrative Behavior, 1947, 4th edit., 1997, Public Administration, 1950, with new Introduction, 1992, Models of Man, 1956, rev. edit., 1991, Organizations, 1958, with new Introduction, 1993, New Science of Management Decision, 1960, rev. edit., 1977, The Shape of Automation, 1965, The Sciences of the Artificial, 1968, 2d edit., 1981, 3d edit., 1996, Human Problem Solving, 1972, Skew Distributions and Business Firm Sizes, 1976, Models of Discovery, 1977, Models of Thought, Vol. I, 1979, Vol. II, 1989, Models of Bounded Rationality, Vols. I and II, 1982, Vol. III, 1997, Reason in Human Affairs, 1983, Protocol Analysis, 1984, with new Introduction, 1993, Scientific Discovery, 1987, Models of My Life, 1991. Recipient Adminstrs. award Am. Coll. Hosp. Adminstrs., 1957, Alfred Nobel Mem. prize in econ. scis., 1978, Dow-Jones award, 1983, scholarly contbns. award Acad. Mgmt., 1983, Nat. Medal Sci., 1986, Pender award U. Pa., 1987, Fiorino d'Oro City of Florence, Italy, 1988, Am. Psychol. Found. Gold medal, 1988, award for excellence in the scis. Gov. of Pa., 1990, rsch. excellence award Internat. Joint Conf. Artificial Intelligence, 1995. Fellow AAAS, APA (disting. sci. contbn. award 1969, lifetime contbn. award 1993), Am. Acad. Arts and Scis., Am. Assn. Artificial Intelligence, Am. Econ. Assn. (disting., Ely lectr. 1977), Econometric Soc., Am. Psychol. Soc. (William James fellow), Am. Sociol. Soc., Inst. Mgmt. Scis. (life, v.p. 1954, Von Neumann theory award 1988), Brit. Psychol. Assn. (hon.); mem. IEEE (hon.), Jewish Acad. Arts and Scis., Am. Polit. Sci. Assn. (James Madison award 1984), Am. Soc. Pub. Adminstrn. (Frederick Mosher award 1974, Dwight Waldo award 1995), Assn. Computing Machinery (A.M. Turing award 1975), NAS (com. on sci. and pub. policy 1967-69, 82-90, chmn. com. air quality control 1974, chmn. com. behavioral scis. NSF 1975-76, coun., 1978-81, 83-86, chmn. com. scholarly com. with PRC, 1983-87, co-chmn. com. behavioral sci. in prevention of nuclear war 1986-90), Cognitive Sci. Soc., Soc. Exptl. Psychologists, Am. Philos. Soc., Royal Soc. Letters (Lund; fgn. mem.), Orgnl. Sci. Soc. (Japan, hon.), Yugoslav Acad. Scis. (fgn.), Chinese Acad. Sci. (fgn.), Indonesian Economists Assn. (hon.), Univ. Club Pitts., Phi Beta Kappa, Sigma Xi (Proctor prize 1980). Democrat. Unitarian. Office: Carnegie Mellon U Dept Psychology Schenley Park Pittsburgh PA 15213

SIMON, H(UEY) PAUL, lawyer; b. Lafayette, La., Oct. 19, 1923; s. Jules and Ida (Rogere) S.; m. Carolyn Perkins, Aug. 6, 1949; 1 child, John Clark. B.S., U. Southwestern La., 1943; J.D., Tulane U., 1947. Bar: La. 1947; CPA, La. 1947. Pvt. practice New Orleans, 1947—; asst. prof. advanced acctg. and taxation U. Southwestern La., 1944-45; staff acct. Haskins & Sells (now Deloitte & Touche), New Orleans, 1945-53, prin., 1953-57; ptnr. Deutsch, Kerrigan & Stiles, 1957-79; sr. founding ptnr. Simon, Peragine, Smith & Redfearn, 1979—; mem. bd. adv. editors Tulane Law Rev., 1992—; mem. New Orleans Bd. Trade. Author: Community Property and Liability for Funeral Expenses of Deceased Spouse, 1946, Income Tax Deductibility of Attorney's Fees in Action in Boundary, 1946, Fair Labor Standards Act and Employee's Waiver of Liquidated Damages, 1946, Louisiana Income Tax Law, 1956, Changes Effected by the Louisiana Trust Code, 1965, Gifts to Minors and the Parent's Obligation of Support, 1968; co-author: Deductions—Business or Hobby, 1975, Role of Attorney in IRS Tax Return Examination, 1978; assoc. editor: The Louisiana CPA, 1956-60; mem. bd. editors Tulane Law Rev., 1945-46, adv. bd. editors, 1992—; estates, gifts and trusts editor The Tax Times, 1986-87. Bd. dirs., mem. fin. com. World Trade Ctr., 1985-86; mem. New Orleans Met. Crime Commn., Coun. for a Better La., New Orleans Met. Area Com., Bur. Govtl. Rsch., Pub. Affairs Rsch. Coun.; co-chmn. NYU Tax Conf., New Orleans, 1976; mem. dean's coun. Tulane U. Law Sch. Fellow Am. Coll. Tax Counsel; mem. ABA (com. ct. procedure tax sect. 1958—), AICPA, La. Bar Assn. (com. on legis. and adminstrv. practice 1966-70), New Orleans Bar Assn., Internat. Bar Assn. (com. on securities issues and trading 1970-88), Am. Judicature Soc., Soc. La. CPAs, New Orleans Assn. Notaries, Tulane U. Alumni Assn., New Orleans C. of C. (coun. 1952-66), Tulane Tax Inst. (program com. 1960—), Internat. House (bd. dirs. 1976-79, 82-85), Internat. Platform Assn., City Energy Club, Press Club, New Orleans Country Club, Phi Delta Phi (past pres. New Orleans chpt.), Sigma Pi Alpha. Roman Catholic. Home: 6075 Canal Blvd New Orleans LA 70124-2936 Office: 30th Fl Energy Ctr New Orleans LA 70163 *Developing and maintaining consistency and constancy in feeling and showing genuine respect towards others nourish and stimulate an individual to become day by day a better person. Whether alone or in the presence of others, one who daily abides by the guidance and rules he would advocate to others invariably finds the greatest reward of all—true respect for one's self.*

SIMON, JACK AARON, geologist, former state official; b. Champaign, Ill., June 17, 1919; s. Abraham and Lenore (Levy) S. B.A., U. Ill., 1941, M.S., 1946; postgrad., Northwestern U., 1947-49, D.Sc. (hon.), 1981. Tech. and research asst. Ill. State Geol. Survey, Urbana, 1937-42; asst. to assoc. geologist Ill. State Geol. Survey, 1945-53, geologist, head, coal sect., 1953-67, prin. geologist, 1967-74, asst. chief, 1973-74, chief, 1974-81, prin. scientist, 1981-83; occasional cons.; asso. prof. dept. metallurgy and mining engring. U. Ill., 1967-74, prof., 1974-77, 80-85, adj. prof. dept. geology, 1979-86. Served with F.A. AUS, 1942-43, F.A., USAAF, 1943-45. Decorated Air Medal with 4 oak leaf clusters; recipient Disting. Svc. award So. Ill. U., Edwardsville, 1982, Coal Day award So. Ill. U., Carbondale, 1982, Alumni Achievement award U. Ill. dept. geology, 1994. Fellow AAAS (sect. E chmn. 1980), Geol. Soc. Am. (chmn. coal geology div. 1962-63, Gilbert H. Cady award 1975, mem. council and exec. com. 1979-81); mem. Am. Assn. Petroleum Geologists (ea. sect. Gordon M. Wood Jr. Meml. award 1991), AIME (chmn. Midwest coal sect. 1966, Percy W. Nicholls award 1981), Am. Inst. Profl. Geologists (v.p. 1973), Am. Mining Congress, Assn. Am. State Geologists (hon.), Ill. Mining Inst. (hon. life; exec. sec.-treas. 1963-68, v.p. 1980-81, pres. 1981-82), Ill. Soc. Coal Preparation Engrs. and Chemists, Ill. Geol. Soc., Ill. Acad. Sci., Soc. Econ. Geologists (councillor 1982-84), B'nai Brith, Sigma Xi. Club: Exchange (Urbana) (pres. 1969). Home: 101 W Windsor Rd # 4204 Urbana IL 61802-6697

SIMON, JACQUELINE ALBERT, political scientist, journalist; b. N.Y.C.; d. Louis and Rose (Axelroad) Albert; m. Pierre Simon; children: Lisette, Orville. BA cum laude, NYU, MA, 1972, PhD, 1977. Adj. assoc. prof. Southampton Coll., 1977-79; mng. editor Point of Contact, N.Y.C., 1975-76; assoc. editor, U.S. bur. chief Politique Internationale, Paris, 1979—; sr. resident scholar Inst. French Studies, NYU, 1980—, assoc. prof. govt., 1982-83; assoc. Inst. on the Media for War and Peace; frequent appearances French TV and radio. Contbg. editor Harper's, 1984-92; contbr. numerous articles to French mags., revs., books on internat. affairs. Bd. dirs. Fresh Air Fund, 1984—. Mem. Women's Fgn. Policy Group, Women in The Media, Overseas Press Club of Am. (v.p. 1996—), CWG (v.p.), Phi Beta Kappa. Home: 988 5th Ave New York NY 10021-0143

SIMON, JAMES LOWELL, lawyer; b. Princeton, Ill., Nov. 8, 1944; s. K. Lowell and Elizabeth Ann (Unholz) S.; children: Heather Lyn, Brandon James. Student, U. Ill., 1962-63, JD with honors, 1975; BSEE magna cum laude, Bradley U., 1967. Bar: Fla. 1975, U.S. Dist. Ct. (mid. dist.) Fla. 1976, U.S. Ct. Appeals (11th cir.) 1981, U.S. Patent Office 1983. Engr. Pan Am. World Airways, Cape Kennedy, Fla., 1967-68; assoc. Akerman, Senterfitt & Eidson, Orlando, Fla., 1975-80; ptnr. Bogin, Munns, Munns & Simon, Orlando, 1980-87, Holland & Knight, LLP, 1987—. With Seminole County Sch. Adv. Coun., Fla., 1981-88, chmn., 1982, 83; with Forest City Local Sch. Adv. Com., Altamonte Springs, Fla., 1981-84, Code Enforcement Bd., Altamonte Springs, 1983-84, Cen. Bus. Dist. Study com., Altamonte Springs, 1983-85, Rep. Coun. of '76, Seminole County, 1982-87; mem. Seminole County Libr. Adv. Bd., 1989-92, sec., 1990, pres., 1991, Seminole County Citizens for Quality Edn., 1990-92; mem. Seminole County Sch. Dist. Strategic Planning Com., 1991—, Class '91 Leadership Orlando; bd. dirs. Found. for Seminole County Pub. Schs., Inc., 1992-95, chmn., 1993-94; bd. dirs. Greater Seminole C. of C., 1993. Capt. USAF, 1968-72. Mem. ABA, Orange County Bar Assn. (jud. rels. com. 1982-83, fee arbitration com. 1983—), Greater Orlando C. of C., Seminole County Bar Assn. (sec. trial lawyers sect. 1993-94), Phi Kappa Phi, Tau Beta Pi, Sigma Tau, Eta Kappa Nu. Republican. Mormon. Home: 482 N Pin Oak Pl # 100 Longwood FL 32779-2632 Office: Holland & Knight LLP 200 S Orange Ave Ste 2600 PO Box 1526 Orlando FL 32802

SIMON, JEANNE HURLEY, federal commissioner; m. Paul Simon; 2 children. BA, Barat Coll.; JD, Northwestern U. Legis. analyst Nat. Adv. Coun. Women's Ednl. Programs; mem. Ill. Gen. Assembly; chair Nat. Commn. Librs. and Info. Sci., Washington, 1993—; adj. prof. libr. affairs So. Ill. U., Carbondale, 1997—; cons. women's initiative Am. Assn. Ret. Persons, Nat. Security Archive, Emeritus Found.; mem. adv. com. White Ho. Conf. Libr. and Info. Svcs., 1979. Mem. ALA, AAUW, LWV, Ill. Bar Assn., Women's Bar Assn., D.C. Bar Assn., Chgo. Bar Assn. Office: Nat Comm on Libraries 1110 Vermont Ave NW Ste 820 Washington DC 20005-3522

SIMON, JIMMY LOUIS, pediatrician, educator; b. San Francisco, Dec. 27, 1930; s. Sylvain L. and Hilda H. (Netter) S.; m. Marilyn S. Wachter, June 21, 1953; children: Kent, Nancy. A.B., U. Calif.-Berkeley, 1952; M.D., U. Calif.-Berkeley, San Francisco, 1955. Diplomate Am. Bd. Pediatrics. Intern U. Calif., San Francisco, 1955-56; resident Grace-New Haven Hosp., 1956-57; sr. asst. resident Boston Children's Hosp., 1957-58; instr., asst. prof. pediatrics U. Okla., Oklahoma City, 1960-64; asso. prof. U. Tex. Med. Br., Galveston, 1966-72; prof. pediatrics U. Tex. Med. Br., 1972-74; prof., chmn. pediatrics Bowman Gray Sch. Medicine, Wake Forest U., Winston-Salem, N.C., 1974-96; prof., chmn. emeritus pediatric Bowman Gray Sch. Medicine Wake Forest U., Winston-Salem, N.C., 1996—. Served with USAF, 1958-60. Mem. Am. Pediatric Soc., Am. Acad. Pediatrics, So. Soc. Pediatric Rsch., Am. Bd. Pediatrics, Ambulatory Pediatric Assn., Alpha Omega Alpha. Office: Bowman Gray Sch Med Dept Pediatrics Medical Center Blvd Winston Salem NC 27157

SIMON, JOHN BERN, lawyer; b. Cleve., Aug. 8, 1942; s. Seymour Frank and Roslyn (Schultz) S.; children: Lindsey Helaine, Douglas Banning. BS, U. Wis., 1964; JD, DePaul U., 1967. Bar: Ill. 1967. Asst. U.S. atty. U.S. Justice Dept., Chgo., 1967-70, dep. chief civil div., 1970-71, chief civil div., 1971-74; spl. counsel to dir. Ill. Dept. Pub. Aid, Chgo., 1974-75; legal cons. to Commn. on Rev. of Nat. Policy Toward Gambling, Chgo., 1975-76; ptnr. firm Friedman & Koven, 1975-85, mem. exec. com., 1983-85; ptnr. firm Jenner & Block, 1986—; spl. cons. to adminstr. DEA Dept. Justice, 1976-77; counsel to Gov.'s Revenue Study Commn. on Legalized Gambling, 1977-78; spl. counsel Ill. Racing Bd., 1979-80; lectr. tng. seminars and confs.; instr. U.S. Atty. Gen.'s Advocacy Inst., Washington, 1974; lectr. Nat. Conf. Organized Crime, Washington, 1975, Dade County Inst. Organized Crime, Ft. Lauderdale, Fla., 1976; faculty Cornell Inst. Organized Crime, Ithaca, N.Y., 1976, judge Miner Moot Ct. competition Northwestern U., 1971-73; mem. law coun. DePaul U., 1974-83, pres. law alumni bd., 1984-85, chmn., 1975-79; adj. prof. DePaul U. Coll. Law, 1977, 81; faculty Practising Law Inst., Chgo., 1984. Contbr. articles to profl. jours. Bd. dirs. Cmty. Film Workshop of Chgo., 1977-90; bd. dirs. Friends of Glencoe Parks, 1977-78, sec., 1978-79; mem. nominating com. Glencoe Sch. Bd., 1978-81, chmn. rules com., 1980-81; pres. Glencoe Hist. Soc., 1979-82; mem. Glencoe Zoning Bd. Appeals, Zoning Commn., Sign Bd. Appeals, 1981-86, chmn., 1984-86; mem. Ill. Inaugural Com., 1979, 83, 87, 95; bd. dirs., mem. exec. con. Chgo. World's Fair Authority, 1983-85; mem. Chancery divsn. task force Spl. Commn. on Adminstrn. of Justice in Cook County, 1985—; trustee De Paul U., 1990, chair phys. plant and property com., 1992-94, vice chair, 1995—; commr. Ill. Racing Bd., 1990—; gen. trustee Lincoln Acad. Ill., 1993—; mem. Ill. Supreme Ct. Planning and Oversight Com. for Jud. Performance Evaluation Program, 1997—. Recipient Bankcroft-Whitney Am. Jurisprudence award, 1965, 66, Judge Learned Hand Human Rels. award Am. Jewish Com., 1994. Mem. ABA (com. on liaison with the judiciary 1983-95), FBA (fed. civil procedure com. 1979—, chmn. 1985-86, bd. mgrs. 1987-89, chmn. house com. 1989-90, treas. 1990-91, 2d v.p. 1991-92, 1st v.p. 1992-93, pres. 1993-94), Ill. State Bar Assn., Women's Bar Assn., Ill. Police Assn., Ill. Sheriffs Assn., U.S. Treasury Agts. Assn., Chgo. Bar Assn., DePaul U. Alumni Assn. (pres. 1985-87, chmn. spl. gifts com. campaign, chmn. Simon Commn. 1989-91, nat. chair for ann. giving 1991-94), Std. Club. Office: Jenner & Block One IBM Plz Chicago IL 60611

SIMON, JOHN GERALD, law educator; b. N.Y.C., Sept. 19, 1928; s. Robert Alfred and Madeleine (Marshall) S.; m. Claire Aloise Bising, June 14, 1958; 1 son, John Kirby (dec.). Grad., Ethical Culture Schs., 1946; AB, Harvard U., 1950; LLB, Yale U., 1953; LLD (hon.), Ind. U., 1989. Bar: N.Y. 1953. Asst. to gen. counsel Office Sec. Army, 1956-58; with firm Paul, Weiss, Rifkind, Wharton & Garrison, N.Y.C., 1958-62; mem. faculty Yale Law Sch., 1962—, prof. law, 1967-76, Augustus Lines prof. law, 1976—, dep. dean, 1985-90, acting dean, 1991; dir., co-chmn. program on non-profit orgns. Yale U., 1977-88. Author: (with Powers and Gunnemann) The Ethical Investor, 1972. Pres. Taconic Found., 1967—; trustee, sec. Potomac Inst., 1961-93; mem. grad. bd. Harvard Crimson, 1950—; chmn. bd. dirs. Coop. Assistance Fund, 1970-76, vice chmn., 1977—; mem. governing coun. Rockefeller Archives Ctr., 1982-86; trustee The Found. Ctr., 1983-92, Open Soc. Inst., N.Y., 1996—. 1st lt. U.S. Army, 1953-56. Recipient Certificate of Achievement Dept. Army, 1956. Mem. Phi Beta Kappa. Office: Yale U Law Sch New Haven CT 06520

SIMON, JOHN IVAN, film and drama critic; b. Subotica, Yugoslavia, May 12, 1925; came to U.S., 1941; s. Joseph and Margaret (Reves) Simmon. AB, Harvard U., 1946, AM, 1948, PhD, 1959; LittD (hon.), Adelphi U., 1996. Teaching fellow Harvard U., Cambridge, Mass., 1950-53; instr. U. Wash., 1953-54, MIT, Cambridge, 1954-55; asst. prof. Bard Coll., Annandale-on-Hudson, N.Y., 1957-59; assoc. editor Mid-Century Book Soc., 1959-61; drama critic The Hudson Rev., 1960-80, Theatre Arts Mag., 1962, Sta. WNET-TV, 1963, Commonweal, 1967-68; drama and film critic The New Leader, 1962-73, 75-77, cultural critic, 1974—; drama critic New York mag., 1968-75, 77—, film critic, 1975-77; film critic Esquire mag., 1973-75, Nat. Rev., 1978—; lang. critic Esquire mag., 1977-79; guest prof. U. Pitts.; lectr. in field. Author: Acid Test, 1963, Private Screenings, 1967, Movies into Film, 1971, Ingmar Bergman Directs, 1972, Uneasy Stages, 1976, Singularities, 1976, Paradigms Lost: Reflections on Literacy and its Decline, 1980, Reverse Angle: A Decade of American Films, 1982, Something to Declare: Twelve Years of Films from Abroad, 1983, The Sheep from the Goats: Selected Literary Essays, 1989; editor: Film 67/68, (with Richard Schickel) Fourteen for Now, 1969. With USAF, 1944-45. Recipient George Polk Meml. award in film criticism, 1968, George Jean Nathan award for dramatic criticism, 1969-70, Lit. award AAAL, 1976; Fulbright fellow U. Paris, 1949-50. Mem. PEN, N.Y. Drama Critics Circle, N.Y. Film Critics Circle. Office: New York Mag 444 Madison Ave New York NY 10022-6903

SIMON, JOSEPH PATRICK, food services executive; b. Phila., Nov. 9, 1932; s. Joseph Patrick and Elizabeth Gertrude (McLaughlin) S.; m. Vera Cornelia Steiner, Sept. 15, 1956; children: Joseph Walter, Walter Joseph, Leslie Vera, Ernest William. B.S., Cornell U., 1955. With Slater Systems, 1955-59; with ARA Services, Inc., Phila., 1959-72; regional v.p. ARA Services, Inc., 1964-66, area v.p., 1966-68, group v.p. and sr. v.p., 1968-70, pres. community and school food service div., 1970-71, gen. mgr., pres. internat. ops., 1971-72; v.p., gen. mgr. airline services div. Dobbs Houses Inc., Memphis, 1972-73; group v.p. Service Systems Corp., Buffalo, 1973-79; pres. Service Systems Corp., 1980-85, also nat. dir.; group v.p. P.J. Schmitt subs. Loblaw Ltd., 1984, sr. v.p., 1985-88, also bd. dirs., 1986, 87. Dist. chmn. Detroit United Fund, 1966-67, Nat. Alliance of Businessmen, 1969; mem. adv. bd. McComb Jr. Coll.; mem. council Cornell U., 1980-83; chmn. bd. Sheehan Emergency Hosp., Buffalo, 1984-85; trustee D'Youville Coll.; bd. dirs. United Fund, Buffalo, 1981-82, CODE Inc., 1986-87. Served as 1st lt. U.S. Army, 1955-56. Mem. Assn. Food Svc. Mgmt. (dir.), Nat. Automatic Merchandising Assn. (dir.), Buffalo C. of C. (dir. 1982-84), Cornell Hotel Soc. Mich. (pres.), Memphis Athletic Club, Detroit Athletic Club, Buffalo Club, Park County Club, The Meadows Country Club, Zeta Psi. Episcopalian. Home: 4422 Whisperwood Sarasota FL 34235-6924

SIMON, KENNETH MARK, lawyer; b. Pitts., Apr. 25, 1952; s. Harvey and Jean (Busis) S.; m. Janet Hahn, June 24, 1979; children: Eliza, Jessica, Zachary. BA, U. Pitts., 1974; JD, Georgetown U., 1977. Bar: D.C. 1977. Assoc. Dickstein, Shapiro & Morin, Washington, 1977-85, ptnr., 1985—; mem. exec. com. Dickstein, Shapiro & Morin, Washington, 1992-96; sec. Ocean State Power, Burrillville, R.I., 1989-96. Gen. counsel Conservation Internat., Washington, 1988-93. Mem. Fed. Energy Bar (com. on cogeneration and ind. power, vice-chmn. 1989-90, chmn. 1990-91), D.C. Bar Assn. (sect. on environment, energy and natural resources energy com., chmn. energy com. 1988-90), Electric Generation Assn. (gen. counsel 1992-95). Democrat. Office: Dickstein Shapiro Morin 2101 L St NW Washington DC 20037-1526

SIMON, LEE WILL, astronomer; b. Evanston, Ill., Feb. 18, 1940; s. Clarence Turkle and Dorothy Elizabeth (Will) S.; m. Mary Jo Welsh, Feb. 19, 1966; children: John, Dan, Steve. B.A., Northwestern U., 1962, M.S., 1964, Ph.D. in Astronomy, 1972. Staff astronomer, program supr. Adler Planetarium, Chgo., 1969-77; dir. Morrison Planetarium, Calif. Acad. Scis., San Francisco, 1977-83, astronomer, 1983-84. Mem. Am. Astron. Soc., Sigma Xi. Roman Catholic. Home and Office: 245 San Marin Dr Novato CA 94945-1220

SIMON, LEONARD SAMUEL, banker; b. N.Y.C., Oct. 28, 1936; s. Nathaniel and Lena (Pasternack) S.; m. Marion Appel, Sept. 1, 1957; children: Andrew, Jonathan. B.S., MIT, 1958; M.S., Columbia U., 1959, Ph.D., 1963. Mem. faculty Grad. Sch. Mgmt., U. Rochester, 1962-79, prof., 1974-79; v.p. Community Savs. Bank, Rochester, N.Y., 1969-74; sr. v.p. Community Savs. Bank, 1974-77, exec. v.p., 1977-83; exec. v.p. Rochester Community Sav. Bank, 1983-84, chmn., chief exec. officer, 1984—; chmn., CEO, pres. RSCB Fin., Inc., 1995—; bd. dirs. Fed. Home Loan Bank N.Y., Cmty. Landing Corp.; chmn. Telephone Computing Svc. Corp., 1974-79; trustee Tchrs. Ins. Annuity Assn. Editor-in-chief, founding editor: Interfaces, 1970-76; Author books and articles in field. Past chmn. Rochester-Monroe County chpt. ARC, Rochester Area Ednl. TV Assn., Career Devel. Svcs. of Rochester; past trustee Ctr. for Govt. Rsch.; mem. Urban Policy Conf., Brookings Instn., 1972-73, 64th Am. Assembly. Ford Found. grantee, 1964; recipient MIT Corp. Leadership award, 1987. Mem. Cmty. Bankers Assn. N.Y. State (bd. dirs.), Am.'s Cmty. Bankers, Genesee Valley Club, Beta Gamma Sigma. Office: Rochester Community Savs Bank 235 Main St E Rochester NY 14604-2103

SIMON, LOTHAR, publishing company executive; b. Wuppertal, Germany, Sept. 17, 1938; came to U.S., 1961, naturalized, 1973; s. Fritz and Erna (Backhaus) S.; m. Jeannine Rechtman, Oct. 30, 1964; 1 child, Charles. Mgr. book dept. Franz Bader Book Shop and Globe Book Shop, Washington, 1961-66; sales mgr. Humanities Press Inc., N.Y.C., 1966-73; pres. Longman Inc., N.Y.C., 1973-81; pub. cons., 1981-82; pres., chief exec. officer Sheridan House, Inc., Dobbs Ferry, N.Y., 1982—. Mem. Assn. Am. Pubs. Democrat. Club: Town (Scarsdale, N.Y.). Office: Sheridan House Inc 145 Palisade St Dobbs Ferry NY 10522-1617

SIMON, MARILYN WEINTRAUB, art educator, sculptor; b. Chgo., Aug. 25, 1927; d. William and Caroline Mabel (Bergman) Weintraub; m. Walter E. Simon, Mar. 19, 1950 (div. Sept. 1990); children: Nina Fay Simon-Rosenthal, Jacob Aaron, Maurine Joy Simon Rubinstein, Linda Gay Simon Shapiro. PhB, U. Chgo., 1947; MEd, Temple U., 1969. Cert. tchr., Pa. Bd. sec. Delaware Valley Smelting Corp., Bristol, Pa., 1957-89; art tchr. Calumet Sch. Dist., Ill., 1951-53; art tchr., chmn. elem. art program Cheltenham (Pa.) Sch. Dist., 1969—; real estate agt., Tullytown, Pa.; speaker in field; devel. dir., exec. bd. Art Forms, Manayunk, Pa. One woman show Hahn Gallery, Phila., 1985; permanent exhibits Elkins Park (Pa.) Libr., Univ. Hosp., Cleve.; also represented in med. offices, private collections; author publs. on using art reproductions in edn. Chmn. Phila. chpt. U. Chgo. Alumni Fund Assn., 1978-84. Recipient numerous art awards including 1st prize Doylestown Art League, 1986-87, Best Sculpture award Mummers's Mus. Phila., 1987, Juror's award Cheltenham Art Ctr., 1987-88, 3d prize Abington Art Ctr., 1988, 1st prize for sculpture Art Assn. of Harrisburg, 1989. Mem. Nat. Art Edn. Assn., Pa. Art Educators Assn. (regional rep. 1988-89, Outstanding Art Educator of Yr. award 1987), Oil Pastel Assn. N.Y.C. (invited mem.). Democrat. Jewish. Office: PO Box 29722 Elkins Park PA 19027-0922

SIMON, MARK, architect; b. N.Y.C., Sept. 5, 1946; s. Sidney Simon and Joan (Lewisohn) Crowell; m. Penelope Bellamy, June 22, 1980; children: Jessica Rabe, Thomas Jefferson. BA, Brandeis U., 1968; MArch, Yale U., 1972. Registered architect, N.Y., N.J., Mass., Conn., R.I., Md., Va. Drafter Lewis Assocs., New Haven, 1972-73, Warren Platner Architects, New Haven, 1973-74; project mgr. Chas. W. Moore Assocs., Essex, Conn., 1974-75; project mgr. Moore Grover Harper, Essex, Conn., 1975-78, ptnr., 1978-84; ptnr. Centerbrook Architects, Essex, Conn., 1984—; vis. critic Carnegie Mellon U., Pitts., 1979, Yale U., New Haven, 1979-82, 85-87, N.C. State U., Raleigh, 1982-83, U. Md., 1989-90, Harvard U., 1990. Contbr. articles to profl. jours.; work included in Centerbrook Reinventing American Archiecture (Michael J. Crosbie), 1993, Centerbrook, Vol. 2 (Andrea Oppenheimer Dean), 1996. Recipient Record House award Archtl. Record, 1978, 79, 85, Am. Wood Coun. award, 1983, 86, 90, 93, Builder's Choice award Builder mag., 1985, 87,90, Product Design award Inst. Bus. Designers, 1993; 40 under 40 honoree Interiors Mag., 1986; named Emerging Voice, N.Y. Archtl. League, 1986, Top 100 List of U.S. Architects, Archtl. Digest, 1991. Fellow AIA (chmn. com. on design 1986, Jour. Drawing award 1982, Design award 1982, LIC/AIA chpt. gold award 1984, design award 1996 , AIA/VA design award 1994, New Eng. design awards 1980, 86, 90, 96, Brick in Architecture award 1995); mem. Conn. AIA (bd. dirs. 1985-86, Honor award, 1978, 82, 88, 89, 90, 95, 96, Unbuilt Projects Honor award 1990, 92). Office: Centerbrook Architects and Planners PO Box 955 Essex CT 06426

SIMON, MARTIN STANLEY, commodity marketing company executive, economist; b. St. Louis, Sept. 6, 1926; s. Elmer Ellis and Bessye Marion (Werner) S.; m. Rita Edith Scheinhorn, June 18, 1950; children: Deborah, Richard. B.B.A., CCNY, 1949; M.A., NYU, 1953. Econ. statistician Indsl. Commodity Corp, N.Y.C., 1949-52; agrl. econ. statistician Dept. Agr., Washington, 1952-58; commodity analyst Connell Rice & Sugar Co., Inc., Westfield, N.J., 1958-62, asst. to pres., 1962-67, v.p., 1967-74; sr. v.p. Connell Rice & Sugar Co., Inc. (now The Connell Co.), Westfield, N.J., 1974—; cons. AID, Jamaica, 1963; mem. Rice Insp. Industry Adv. Com., Washington, 1971-72; adv. U.S. Del. to UN FAO Intergovtl. Meetings on Rice, 1981. Served with U.S. Army, 1944-46, ETO. Recipient Class of 1920 award for merit in econ. stats. CCNY, 1949. Mem. Am. Econ. Assn., Rice Millers Assn. (chmn. legis. options working group 1984-86, govt. programs com. 1986-87, chmn. PL480 subcom. 1988-90), Nat. Economists Club. Office: The Connell Co 45 Cardinal Dr Westfield NJ 07090-1019

SIMON, MARVIN KENNETH, electrical engineer, consultant; b. N.Y.C., Sept. 10, 1939; s. Sidney and Belle (Cone) S.; m. Anita Joyce Sauerhof; children: Brette, Jeffrey. BEE, CCNY, 1960; MSEE, Princeton U., 1961; PhD, NYU, 1966. Mem. tech. staff Bell Telephone Labs., Holmdel, N.J., 1961-63, 66-68; sr. rsch. engr. Jet Propulsion Lab., Pasadena, Calif., 1968—; adj. prof. Calif. Inst. Tech., Pasadena, 1986-87, 88-90. Author: Telecommunications Systems Engineering, 1973, Phase-Locked Loops and Their Application, 1978, reprinted, 1991, Spread Spectrum Communications, Vols. I, II, III, 1984, Introduction to Trellis-Coded Modulation with Application, 1990, Digital Communication Techniques, Vol. I: Signal Design and Detection, 1994, Spread Spectrum Communications Handbook, 1994, Mobile Communications Handbook, 1995; also numerous articles; patentee in field. Recipient NASA Exptl. Svc. medal, 1979, NASA Exptl. Engring. Achievement medal, 1995. Fellow IEEE (Bicentennial medal 1984), Inst. for Advancement Engring. Avocation: computer games. Office: Jet Propulsion Lab Mail Stop 238-343 4800 Oak Grove Dr Pasadena CA 91109-8001

SIMON, MELVIN, real estate developer, professional basketball executive; b. Oct. 21, 1926; s. Max and Mae Simon; m. Bren Burns, Sept. 14, 1972; children: Deborah, Cynthia, Tamme, David, Max. Bs in Acctg., CCNY, 1949, M in Bus., Real Estate, 1983; PhD (hon.), Butler U., 1986, Ind. U., 1991. Leasing sgt. Albert Frankel Co., Indpls., 1955-60; pres. Melvin Simon & Assocs., Indpls., 1960-73, chmn. bd., 1973—; co-owner Ind. Pacers, Indpls., 1983—; mem. adv. bd. Wharton's Real Estate, Phila., 1986—. Mem. adv. bd. dean's council Ind. U., Bloomington; bd. dirs. United Cerebral Palsy, Indpls., Muscular Dystrophy Assn., Indpls., Jewish Welfare Found., Indpls.; trustee Urban Land Inst., Internat. Council Shopping Ctrs. Recipient Horatio Alger award Boy's Club Indpls., 1986; named Man of Yr., Jewish Welfare Found., 1980. Democrat. Jewish. *

SIMON, MICHAEL ALEXANDER, photographer, educator; b. Budapest, Hungary, June 20, 1936; came to U.S., 1957, naturalized, 1962; s. Miklos and Magda (Schreiber) Stern; m. Carol Susan Winters, Jan. 21, 1961; children: Amy Catherine, Nicholas Andrew. Student, Budapest Tech. U., 1954-56, Pa. State U., 1957-58; MFA in Photography, Rochester Inst. Tech., 1986. Propr. Michael Simon Studio, N.Y.C., 1966-68; mem. faculty Beloit (Wis.) Coll., 1968—, asst. prof. dept. art, 1971-76, chmn. dept. art and art history, 1984—, assoc. prof., 1976-85, prof., 1985—; curator photography Theodore Lyman Wright Art Center, 1980—. Free-lance photographer, 1958-66, artist-in-residence, Nat. Park Service, Mus. Div., Harpers Ferry, W.Va., 1971, vis. artist, U. Del., Newark, 1974, Sch. of Art Inst. Chgo., 1978; numerous one-man shows of photography, 1964—, latest being, Wright Art Center, Beloit, 1977, 78, Mpls. Inst. Arts, 1979, U. Rochester, 1985; group shows include, Gallery 38A, Beloit Coll., 1974, U. Iowa, Iowa City, 1975, Columbia Coll. Gallery, Chgo., 1975, Mpls. Inst. Arts, 1976, Evanston (Ill.) Art Center, 1978, Purdue U., Lafayette, Ind., 1978, Kohler Art Center, Sheboygan, Wis., 1979, Madison Art Ctr., (Wis.), 1983; represented in permanent collections, Mus. Modern Art, N.Y.C., U. Kans., Lawrence, Mpls. Inst. Arts, Sheldon Meml. Art Gallery, Lincoln, Nebr.; Author: (with Dennis Moore) First Lessons in Black and White Photography, 1978; contbr. numerous articles on Hungarian photography to profl. publs. Wis. Arts Bd. fellow, 1980; Nat. Endowment for Arts grantee, 1980; Mellon Fund. grantee, 1977. Mem. Soc. for Photog. Edn. (chmn. nat. bd. 1979-81, chmn. Midwest region 1973-76), Szechenyi Soc. of Hungary. Research on history of Hungarian photography, the photographic snapshot. Office: Beloit Coll Dept Art Beloit WI 53511

SIMON, MORDECAI, religious association administrator, clergyman; b. St. Louis, July 19, 1925; s. Abraham M. and Rose (Solomon) S.; m. Maxine R. Abrams, July 4, 1954; children: Ora, Eve, Avrom. BA, St. Louis U., 1947; MA, Washington U., St. Louis, 1952; MHL, Rabbi, Jewish Theol. Sem. Am., N.Y.C., 1952, DD (hon.), 1977. Ordained rabbi, 1952. Rabbi in Mpls., 1952-56, Waterloo, Iowa, 1956-63; exec. dir. Chgo. Bd. Rabbis, 1963-80, exec. v.p., 1980-95, exec. v.p. emeritus, 1995—; nat. chaplain Jewish War Vets., 1977-78. Host: (weekly program) What's Nu?, Sta. WGN-TV, 1973-92. Mem. Jewish Cmty. Rels. Coun., Jewish United Fund; mem. nat. coun. Joint Distbn. Com., Religious Leaders Com. With AUS, 1943-46. Recipient citation Jewish War Vets., 1967, Boy Scouts Am., 1966, 74, 88, Chgo. chpt. Am. Jewish Congress, 1973, Chgo. Conf. Jewish Women's Orgns., 1973, Chgo. Bd. Rabbis, 1973, Rabbinical Svc. award of Appreciation, Jewish Theol. Sem. Am., 1988, Raoul Wallenberg Humanitarian award, 1989, citation and commendation Ill. Ho. Reps., 1995, Order of Merit, The Equestrian Order of the Holy Sepulchre of Jerusalem, 1996; Rabbi Mordecai Simon Day proclaimed by Gov. James Edgar, State of Ill., 1995. Mem. Rabbinical Assembly, Coun. Religious Leaders Met. Chgo. Home: 621 County Line Rd Highland Park IL 60035-5220 Office: 1 S Franklin St Chicago IL 60606-4609

SIMON, NANCY RUTH, lawyer; b. Gary, Ind., Apr. 25, 1960; d. Norbert Fred and Elizabeth Anna (Laird) S. BSEE, Iowa State U., 1985; MBA, U. Dallas, 1988; JD, So. Meth. U., 1991. Bar: Tex. 1991, Calif. 1994; registered to practice before U.S. Patent and Trademark Office 1992; lic. real estate developer. Elec. engr. Tex. Instruments, Dallas, 1986-88; law clk. to pvt. law firms Dallas, 1989-91; law clk. U.S. Attys. Office, 1991; assoc. Felsman, Bradley, Gunter & Dillon, LLP, Ft. Worth, 1991-93; patent counsel Apple Computer, Inc., Cupertino, Calif., 1993—; realtor Coldwell Banker, Los Gatos, Calif. Co-author: Attorneys' Fees in IPL Cases; mem. So. Meth. U. Law Rev. Jour. of Air Law and Commerce, 1990-91. Mem. ABA, State Bar Tex., State Bar Calif., Nat. Assn. Realtors, Calif. Assn. Realtors, Peninsula West Valley Assn. Realtors, Mensa Iowa State U. Student Alumni Assn. (mem. career awareness com. 1984-85), Sigma Iota Epsilon, Zeta Tau Alpha (social chmn. 1982-83, house mgr. 1983-84, chmn. jud. bd. 1984-85), Phi Delta Phi. Avocations: reading, music. Office: Apple Computer Inc MS 38 PAT 1 Infinite Loop Cupertino CA 95014-2083 also: Coldwell Banker 497 N Santa Cruz Ave Los Gatos CA 95030

SIMON, NEIL, playwright, television writer; b. N.Y.C., July 4, 1927; s. Irving and Mamie Simon; m. Joan Baim, Sept. 30, 1953 (dec.); m. Marsha Mason, 1973 (div.); m. Diane Lander, 1987. Student, NYU, 1946; LLD (hon.), Hofstra U., 1981, Williams Coll., 1984. Author materials for Tamiment (Pa.) revues, 1952-53; author: (with brother Danny) sketches Catch a Star, 1955, (with brother Danny) for New Faces of '56; book for musicals Little Me, 1962, Sweet Charity, 1966 (Evening Standard Drama award 1967), Promises, Promises, 1968 (Tony award nomination 1969), They're Playing Our Song, 1979, Little Me (Tony award nomination 1963 version, rev. version), 1982, The Goodbye Girl, 1993Rewrites: A Memoir, 1996; plays include Come Blow Your Horn, 1961, Barefoot in the Park, 1963 (Tony award nomination 1963), The Odd Couple, 1965 (Tony award 1965), The Star-Spangled Girl, 1966, Plaza Suite, 1968 (Tony award nomination 1968), Last of the Red Hot Lovers, 1969 (Tony award nomination 1970), The Gingerbread Lady, 1970, The Prisoner of Second Avenue, 1971 (Tony award nomination 1972), The Sunshine Boys, 1972, The Good Doctor, 1973, God's Favorite, 1974, California Suite, 1976, Chapter Two, 1977, I Ought to be in Pictures, 1980, Fools, 1981, Brighton Beach Memoirs, 1983, Biloxi Blues, 1985 (Tony award for Best Playwright 1985, Best Play 1985), The Odd Couple (female version), 1985, Broadway Bound, 1986 (Tony award nomination 1987), Rumors, 1988, Lost in Yonkers, 1991 (Pulitzer Prize for drama 1991, Tony award Best Play 1991), Jake's Women, 1992, Laughter on the 23rd Floor, 1993, London Suite, 1995; wrote screenplays adapted from own plays: Barefoot in the Park, 1967, The Odd Couple, 1968, Plaza Suite, 1971, Last of the Red Hot Lovers, 1972, The Prisoner of Second Avenue, 1975, The Sunshine Boys, 1975, California Suite, 1978, Chapter Two, 1979, Only When I Laugh (adapted from play The Gingerbread Lady), 1981, I Ought to be in Pictures, 1982, Brighton Beach Memoirs, 1986, Biloxi Blues, 1988, Broadway Bound, 1992 (TV motion picture), Lost in Yonkers, 1993, (TV motion picture) Jake's Women, 1996; other screenplays include After the Fox, 1966, The Out-of-Towners, 1970, The Heartbreak Kid, 1973, Murder by Death, 1976, The Goodbye Girl, 1977, The Cheap Detective, 1978, Seems Like Old Times, 1980, Max Dugan Returns, 1983, The Lonely Guy (adaptation), 1984, The Sluggers Wife, 1984, The Marrying Man, 1991; other motion pictures based on his stage plays: Come Blow Your Horn, 1963, Sweet Charity, 1969, The Star-Spangled Girl, 1971; wrote for TV shows: The Phil Silvers Arrow Show, 1958, The Tallulah Bankhead Show, 1951, The Sid Caesar Show, 1956-57 (Emmy award 1956-57), Phil Silvers Show, 1958-59 (Emmy award 1958-59), Garry Moore Show, 1959-60; also NBC spl. The Trouble with People, 1972. Served to cpl. USAAF, 1945-46. Recipient Sam S. Shubert award 1968, Writers Guild screen awards, 1968, 70, 75, Writers Guild Laurel award, 1979. Mem. Dramatists Guild, Writers Guild Am. (Laurel award 1979, screen awards 1968, 70, 75). Address: care A DaSilva 502 Park Ave New York NY 10022-1108*

SIMON, NORMA PLAVNICK, psychologist; b. Washington, Sept. 20, 1930; d. Mark and Mary Plavnick; m. Robert G. Simon, Dec. 18, 1949; children: Mark Allan, Susan. BA, NYU, 1952, cert. in psychoanalysis, 1977; MA, Columbia U., 1953, EdD, 1968. Diplomate Am. Bd. Profl. Psychology, 1988. Psychologist Queens Coll. Counseling Ctr., Flushing, N.Y., 1968-70, asst. dir., 1970-76, dir., 1976; gen. practice psychology N.Y.C., 1976—; faculty, supr. New Hope Guild, Bklyn., 1976—, dir. child and adolescent tng. prog., 1988—; adj. prof. clin. psychology Columbia U., N.Y.C., 1986—; supr. NYU Postdoctoral Prog. in Psychoanalysis, 1988—. Author: (with Robert G. Simon): Choosing a College Major: Social Science, 1981; mem. editorial bd. The Counseling Psychologist jour., 1986-89, Profl. Practice and Rsch. in Psychology, 1994-97. Vice chairperson N.Y. State Bd. for Psychology State Edn. Dept., Albany, 1978-82, chairperson, 1982-88; bd. dirs. Pelham (N.Y.) Guidance Coun., 1980-83; pres.-elect Assn. State and Provincial Psychology Bds., 1990, pres., 1991. Recipient Karl Heiser award, 1993. Fellow APA (mem. bd. profl. affairs 1987-89, chair bd. profl. affairs 1989-90, policy and planning bd. 1991-93, mem. ethics com. 1995-98, vice chair ethics com. 1996-97, John Black award 1994), Nat. Acads. of Practice (elected disting. practitioner). Office: 500A E 87th St # 5A New York NY 10128-7626

SIMON, PAUL, former senator, educator, author; b. Eugene, Oreg., Nov. 29, 1928; s. Martin Paul and Ruth (Troemel) S.; m. Jeanne Hurley, Apr. 21, 1960; children: Sheila, Martin. Student, U. Oreg., 1945-46, Dana Coll., Blair, Nebr., 1946-48; 39 hon. doctorates. Pub. Troy (Ill.) Tribune and 14 other So. Ill. weeklies, 1948-66; mem. Ill. Ho. of Reps., 1955-63, Ill. Senate, 1963-69; lt. gov. Ill., 1969-73; fellow John F. Kennedy Sch. Govt., Harvard U., 1972-73; founded pub. affairs reporting program Sangamon State U., Springfield, Ill., 1972-73; mem. 94th-98th Congresses from 22d and 24th Dists. 94th-98th Congresses from 24th and 22d Dists. Ill., Ill., 1975-85; U.S. Senator from Ill., 1985-96; dir. pub. policy So. Ill. U., 1996—; U.S. presdl. candidate, 1987-88. Author: Lovejoy: Martyr to Freedom, 1964, Lincoln's Preparation for Greatness, 1965, A Hungry World, 1966, You Want to Change the World, So Change It, 1971, The Tongue-Tied American, 1980, The Once and Future Democrats, 1982, The Glass House, Politics and Morality in The Nation's Capitol, 1984, Beginnings, 1986, Let's Put America Back to Work, 1986, Winners and Losers, 1989; (with Jeanne Hurley Simon) Protestant-Catholic Marriages Can Succeed, 1967; (with Arthur Simon) The Politics of World Hunger, 1973, Advice and Consent, 1992, Freedom's Champion: Elijah Lovejoy, 1994. With CIC, AUS, 1951-53. Recipient Am. Polit. Sci. Assn. award, 1957; named Best Legislator by Ind. Voters of Ill., 7 times. Mem. Luth. Human Rels. Assn., Am. Legion, VFW, NAACP, Urban League. Democrat. Lutheran. Office: So Ill U Pub Policy Inst Carbondale IL 62901-4429*

SIMON, PETER E., publishing executive; b. Bklyn., June 29, 1953. BA in English, CCNY, 1971; MA in Libr. Sci., Columbia U., 1980. Database mgr. R.R. Bowker, N.Y.C., 1982-84; v.p. R.R. Bowker/Reed Reference Pubs., 1984-93; sr. v.p. Reed Reference Pub., New Providence, N.J., 1993-95, exec. v.p., 1995-97; v.p. bus. devel. Nat. Info. Svcs., Bethesda, Md., 1997—. Mem. ABA (assoc.), Info. Industry Assn. (bd. dirs.), Book Industry Study Group, Phi Beta Kappa. Office: Nat Info Svcs 45-20 East-West Hwy Bethesda MD 20814*

SIMON, RALPH E., electronics executive; b. Passaic, N.J., Oct. 20, 1930; s. Paul and Sophie (Epstein) S.; m. Elena Schiffman, June 22, 1952; children: Richard L., David P., Michael A. BA, Princeton U., 1952; PhD, Cornell U., 1959. Mem. tech. staff RCA Labs., Princeton, N.J., 1958-67, dir., 1967-69; mgr. RCA Electronic Components, Lancaster, Pa., 1969-75; v.p. RCA Solid State Div., Lancaster, Pa., 1975-80; v.p. optoelectronics div. Gen. Instrument Corp., Palo Alto, Calif., 1980-84; pres. Lytel Inc., Somerville, N.J., 1984-87; pres., CEO QT Optoelectronics, Sunnyvale, Calif., 1989—; dir. Xsirius Scientific, Inc., Marina Del Rey, Calif., 1988-91, Applied Electron Corp., Santa Clara, Calif., 1987—. pres., mem. Lawrence Twp. Bd. Edn., Lawrenceville, N.J., 1964-69, Community Action Orgn., 1967-69. Recipient UK Zworykin prize IEEE, 1973. Office: QT Optoelectronics 610 N Mary Ave Sunnyvale CA 94086-2906

SIMON, ROBERT G., lawyer; b. N.Y.C., Feb. 21, 1927; s. Monroe and Claire S. S.; m. Norma Plavnick, Dec. 18, 1949; children: Mark A., Susan. BA, Cornell U., 1947; LLB, JD, Georgetown U., 1950; LLM, NYU, 1961. Bar: D.C. 1950, N.Y. 1951, U.S. Supreme Ct. 1955. Assoc. firms in N.Y.C., 1950-52; legal sec. to judge U.S. Dist. Ct. So. Dist. N.Y., 1953-58; assoc. Jaffe & Wachtell, N.Y.C., 1958-61; legal adv. TV series The Verdict Is Yours, 1958-60; successively dir. bus. affairs, v.p., sr. v.p., mgr. bus. affairs dept. McCann-Erickson, Inc., N.Y.C., 1961-80; sr. broadcast atty. The Interpublic Group of Cos., N.Y.C., 1980-95; adj. faculty Manhattan Community Coll., 1967, Baruch Coll., 1968, CCNY, 1968, New Sch. Social Research, 1972-73; speaker in field. Author: (with Norma Simon) Choosing a College Major: The Social Sciences, 1981; contbr. articles to profl. jours. Dem.-Liberal candidate for county clk. Westchester County, N.Y., 1952; chmn. Narcotics Guidance Coun., Pelham, N.Y., 1973; mem. Nat. Media Coun. on Disability, 1986-90; bd. dirs., gen. counsel Nat. Challenge Com. on Disability, 1986-88; mem. adv. bd. The Caption Ctr. WGBH Found., 1987—. With USAAF, 1944-46. Mem. NATAS (chpt. gov. 1972-85, 96-97, treas. 1976-81, 1st v.p. 1981-83, pres. 1983-85, nat. trustee 1981-85, 96-97), N.Y. County Lawyers Assn. (com. on comms. and entertainment law 1990-94), Am. Assn. Advt. Agys. (com. on broadcast adminstrn. policy 1985-93). Home: 2 Garden Pl Pelham NY 10803-3207

SIMON, RONALD CHARLES, curator; b. Phila., Feb. 23, 1951; s. Samuel Charles and Emily (Luzenberg) S. BA, Dickinson Coll., 1973; postgrad., Brit. Film and TV Inst., Stirling, Scotland, 1973, Columbia U., 1973-75. Researcher NBC, N.Y.C., 1974-77; mgr. media prodn. 1st Boston Corp., N.Y.C., 1978-78; curator TV, Mus. TV and Radio, N.Y.C., 1979—; adj. prof. Hunter Coll., CUNY, 1987—, Columbia U., N.Y.C., 1991—; cons., lectr. to mus. and colls., including Smithsonian Instn., Whitney Mus. Am. Art, NYU, Cooper Hewitt Mus., 1985—. Exhbns. curated include: The Television of Dennis Potter, Witness to History, Jack Benny: The Radio and Television Work; contbg. author Encyclopedia of TV, 1997; creative cons., host CD-ROM Total TV, 1997. Mem. NATAS (panelist and juror for numerous awards 1985—, editorial bd. TV Quar. 1987—), Internat. Radio and TV Soc. Home: 141 E 17th St New York NY 10003-3402 Office: Television & Radio 25 W 52nd St New York NY 10019-6104

SIMON, SEYMOUR, lawyer, former state supreme court justice; b. Chgo., Aug. 10, 1915; s. Ben and Gertrude (Rusky) S.; m. Roslyn Schultz Biel, May 26, 1954; children: John B., Nancy Simon Cooper, Anthony Biel. B.S., Northwestern U., 1935, J.D., 1938; LL.D. (hon.), John Marshall Law Sch., 1982, North Park Coll., 1986, Northwestern U., 1987. Bar: Ill. 1938. Spl. atty. Dept. Justice, 1938-42; practice law Chgo., 1946-74; judge Ill. Appellate Ct., Chgo., 1974-80; presiding justice Ill. Appellate Ct. (1st Dist., 3d Div.), 1977, 79; justice Ill. Supreme Ct., 1980-88; ptnr. Rudnick & Wolfe, Chgo., 1988—; former chmn. Ill. Low-Level Radioactive Waste Disposal Facility Siting Commn.; former dir. Nat. Gen. Corp., Bantam Books, Grosset & Dunlap, Inc., Gt. Am. Ins. Corp. Mem. Cook County Bd. Commrs., 1961-66, pres., 1962-66; pres. Cook County Forest Preserve Dist., 1962-66; mem. Pub. Bldg. Commn., City Chgo., 1962-67; Alderman 40th ward, Chgo., 1955-61, 67-74; Democratic ward committeeman, 1960-74; bd. dirs. Schwab Rehab. Hosp., 1961-71, Swedish Covenant Hosp., 1969-75. Served with USNR, 1942-45. Decorated Legion of Merit; recipient 9th Ann. Pub. Svc. award Tau Epsilon Rho, 1963, Hubert L. Will award Am. Vets. Com., 1983, award of merit Decalogue Soc. Lawyers, 1986, Judge Learned Hand award Am. Jewish Com., 1994, Frances Feinberg Meml. Crown award Associated Talmud Torahs of Chgo., 1995; named to Sr. Citizen's Hall of Fame, City of Chgo., 1989, Hall of Fame Jewish Comty. Ctrs. Chgo., 1989. Mem. ABA, Ill. Bar Assn., Chgo. Bar Assn., Chgo. Hist. Soc., Decalogue Soc. Lawyers (Merit award 1986), Izaak Walton League, Chgo. Hort. Soc., Comml. Club Chgo., Standard Club, Variety Club, Order of Coif; Phi Beta Kappa, Phi Beta Kappa Assocs. Home: 1555 N Astor St Chicago IL 60610-1673 Office: Rudnick & Wolfe 203 N La Salle St Ste 1800 Chicago IL 60601-1225

SIMON, SHELDON WEISS, political science educator; b. St. Paul, Jan. 31, 1937; s. Blair S. and Jennie M. (Dim) S.; m. Charlann Lilwin Scheid, Apr. 27, 1962; 1 child, Alex Russell. BA summa cum laude, U. Minn., 1958, PhD, 1964; MPA, Princeton U., 1960; postgrad., U. Geneva, 1962-63. Asst. prof., then prof. U. Ky., 1966-75; prof. polit. sci. Ariz. State U., 1975—, chmn. dept., 1975-79, dir. Ctr. Asian Studies, 1980-88; vis. prof. George Washington U., 1965, U. B.C., Can., 1972-73, 79-80, Carleton U., 1976, Monterey Inst. Internat. Studies, 1991, 96, Am. Grad. Sch. Internat. Mgmt., 1991-92; cons. USIA Rsch. Analysis Corp., Am. Enterprise Inst. Pub. Policy Rsch., Hoover Instn., Orkand Corp., Nat. Bur. Asian Rsch. Author: Asian Neutralism and U.S. Policy, 1975, The ASEAN States and Regional Security, 1982, The Future of Asian-Pacific Security Collaboration, 1988; editor: The Military and Security in the Third World, 1978, East Asian Security in the Post-Cold War Era, 1993, Southeast Asian Security in the New Millenium, 1996; also others; contbr. articles to profl. jours., chpts. to books. Mem. Com. Fgn. Relations, Phoenix, 1976—; bd. dirs. Phoenix Little Theater, 1976-79. Grantee Am. Enterprise Inst., 1974, Earhart Found., 1979, 81, 92, 84, 88, U.S. Inst. Peace, 1994-96; Hoover Instn. fellow, 1980, 85. Mem. Am. Polit. Sci. Assn., Assn. Asian Studies, Internat. Studies Assn. (profl. ethics com. 1987-91, v.p. 1991-93), Asia Soc. (contemporary affairs com. 1987—), U.S. Coun. for Asia-Pacific Security, Phi Beta Kappa. Democrat. Jewish. Avocations: acting, singing, tennis. Home: 5630 S Rocky Point Rd Tempe AZ 85283-2134 Office: Ariz State U Polit Sci Dept Tempe AZ 85287

SIMON, THEODORE RONALD, physician, medical educator; b. Hartford, Conn., Feb. 2, 1949; s. Theologos Lingos and Lillian (Faix) S.; m. Marcia Anyzeski, Apr. 5, 1974; children: Jacob T., Theodore H., Mark G. BA cum laude, Trinity Coll., Hartford, 1970; MD, Yale U., 1975. Diplomate Am. Bd. Nuclear Medicine, Diplomate Nat. Bd. Med. Examiners; lic. Calif., Tex. Intern in surgery Strong Meml. Hosp., Rochester, N.Y., 1975-76; resident in diagnostic radiology U. Calif., San Francisco, 1976-78; resident in nuclear medicine Yale-New Haven Hosp., Conn., 1978-80, chief resident, 1979-80; asst. prof. nuclear medicine U. Tex. Southwestern Med. Ctr., Dallas, 1980-88, assoc. prof., 1990—; cons. nuclear medicine St. Paul's Hosp., Dallas, 1981-88; cons. internal medicine Presbyn. Hosp., Dallas, 1981-88, 90, Med. City Hosp., Dallas, 1989—; cons. nuclear medicine VA Med. Ctr., Dallas, 1981-82, chief nuclear medicine svc., 1982-88; nat. dep. dir. nuclear medicine VA, 1985-88; dep. chief nuclear medicine NIH, Bethesda, Md., 1988-90; mem. del. Taiwan Atomic Energy, U.S. State Dept., 1990. Mem. editorial bd. Jour. History of Med. and Allied Scis., 1974-75; contbr. articles to Internat. Jour. Radiol. Applications, Jour. Nuclear Medicine, Am. Jour. Cardiology, Clin. Nuclear Medicine, Circulation, Yale Jour. Biol. Medicine, Radiology, Surg. Radiology, and others. Pres. Christ Lutheran Ch., University Park, Tex. Mem. Soc. Nuclear Medicine (treas. correlative imaging coun. 1988-90, mem. exec. com 1988—). Achievements include patent for Complex Motion Device to Enhance Single Photon Emission Computed Tomography Uniformity; research in single photon emission computed tomography as it related to substance abuse, schizophrenia, depression, neurotoxicity and chronic fatigue syndrome. Home and Office: 4429 Southern Ave Dallas TX 75205-2622

SIMON, WILLIAM, biomathematician, educator; b. Pitts., May 27, 1929; m. Maxine Check, June 27, 1965; children: Robert, Steven, Alan. B.S. in Physics, Carnegie Inst. Tech., 1950; M.A. in Applied Physics, Harvard U., 1952, Ph.D., 1958. Staff physicist Comstock & Wescott, Inc. (cons. engrs.), Cambridge, Mass., 1951-53; head instruments sect. Spencer Kennedy Lab., Boston, 1953-57; sr. systems engr. Nat. Radio Co., Malden, Mass., 1957-59; chief physicist Image Instruments, Inc., Newton Lower Falls, Mass., 1959-60; mem. staff M.I.T. Lincoln Lab. and Center for Computer Tech. in Biomed. Scis., 1961-64; research asso. dept. physiology, dir. biomed. tech. cons. group Harvard U. Med. Sch., 1964-68; asso. prof., head div. biomath. U. Rochester Sch. Medicine and Dentistry, 1968-77, prof., head div. biomath., 1977-82, prof. biochemistry and biophysics, 1982—, prof. med. info., 1989; vis. assoc. prof. dept. elec. engring. MIT, 1974-75. Author: Mathematical Techniques for Physiology and Medicine, 1972, Mathematical Techniques for Biology and Medicine, 1977; contbr. articles to profl. jours. Office: U Rochester Box BPHYS Rochester NY 14642

SIMON, WILLIAM EDWARD, investment banker, former secretary of treasury; b. Paterson, N.J., Nov. 27, 1927; m. Carol Girard, Sept. 9, 1950; children: William Edward Jr., John Peter, Mary Beth Simon Streep, Carol Leigh Simon Porges, Aimee Simon Bloom, Julie Ann Simon Munro, Johanna Katrina. BA in Govt. and Law, Lafayette Coll., 1952, LLD (hon.), 1973; other hon. degrees include LLD, Pepperdine U., 1975, Manhattanville Coll., 1978, Washington U., 1980, Boston U., 1980, Washington Coll., 1984, Rider Coll., 1984, Seton Hall U., 1984, Fairleigh Dickinson U., 1984, Rutgers U., 1985, U. Rochester, 1985; D of Civil Law, Jacksonville U., 1976; Scriptural Degree, Israel Torah Rsch. Inst., Jerusalem, 1976; Doctor Philosophiae honoris causa, Tel Aviv U., 1976; DSc, New Eng. Coll., 1977; HHD, Springfield U., 1986; D of Econs., Hanyang U., Seoul, Republic of Korea, 1988. With Union Securities Co., N.Y.C., 1952-57, asst. v.p., mgr. mcpl. trading dept., 1955-57; v.p. Weeden & Co., N.Y.C., 1957-64; joined Salomon Bros. & Hutzler, N.Y.C., 1964; sr. ptnr., mem. exec. com. Salomon Bros., N.Y.C., 1964-73; dep. sec. Dept. Treasury, Washington, 1973-74; adminstr. Fed. Energy Office, Washington, 1973-74; sec. of the treasury, 1974-77; sr. cons. Booz Allen & Hamilton Inc., 1977-79; sr. advisor Blyth Eastman

Dillon & Co. Inc., 1977-80; dep. chmn. Olayan Investments Co. Establishment, 1980-82; chmn. Crescent Diversified Ltd., 1980-82, Wesray Corp., 1981-86, Wesray Capital Corp., 1984-86; chmn. emeritus Wesray Corp., Wesray Capital Corp., 1987; currently chmn., pres. William E. Simon & Sons, Morristown, N.J.; co-chmn. WSGP Internat. Inc., L.A.; chmn. William E. Simon Found., Inc.; bd. dirs. Pompano Pk. Realty, Inc., Castleton, Inc.; former cons. W.R. Grace & Co., Brazilinvest, Allstate Ins. Co., Calvin Bullock Ltd., Johnson & Johnson; mem. pub. rev. bd. Arthur Andersen & Co.; past chmn. World Trade Bancorp.; lectr. numerous schs. including Harvard Bus. Sch., U. Mich., Georgetown U., Boston U., U. Chgo., Columbia U., Lafayette Coll., U. Notre Dame, Oxford U., USAF Acad., U.S. Mil. Acad., L.I. U., Washington U., St. Louis, Princeton U., Erasmus U., Rotterdam, The Netherlands, U. Rochester, Susquehanna U., Fairleigh Dickerson U.; lectr. confs., round tables, panels, corps., mem. adv. bd. Classics of Liberty Libr., Corp. for Devel. and Commerce, The Papers of Albert Gallatin. Author: A Time for Truth, 1978, A Time For Action, 1980; mem. editorial adv. bd. Gryphon Editions Inc., The Washington Times. Pres. John M. Olin Found., Richard Nixon Presdl. Libr. and Birthplace Found.; chmn. investment com. USAF Acad., USAF Acad. Academic Devel. Fund; former pres. and treas. U.S. Olympic Com., now mem. bd. adminstrs., fin. com.; mem. budget and fin. com., trustee Heritage Found.; trustee The Animal Med. Ctr., Nat. Investors Hall of Fame, Boston U.; hon. trustee Adelphi U., Newark Boys Chorus Sch.; trustee emeritus Lafayette Coll.; trustee, mem. investment com., mem. exec. adv. coun., trustee Simon Sch., U. Rochester; chmn. bd. trustees U.S. Olympic Found.; bd. dirs. Sequoia Inst., World Cup '94 Organizing Com., Kissinger Assocs., Nat. Football Found. and Hall of Fame Inc., dir. emeritus, Cath. Big Bros., Citizens Against Govt. Waste, Space Studies Inst., Boys Harbor Inc., Internat. Found. for Edn. and Self Help, Citizens Network for Fgn. Affairs, Atlantic Coun. of U.S., Target; bd. dirs., co-chmn. endowment com. Covenant House; hon. dir. The Gerald R. Ford Found.; bd. advisors Cath. League for Religious and Civil Rights; mem. nat. coun. trustees Freedoms Found. at Valley Forge; mem. adv. bd. Jesse Owens Found., sec./treas.; mem. bd. overseers Hoover Instn. on War, Revolution and Peace, Stanford U., Exec. Coun. on Fgn. Diplomacy; mem. adv. bd. Am. rep. Pacific Security Rsch. Inst., Sydney, Australia, U. So. Calif. Sch. Bus. Adminstrn., Nat. Ethnic Coalition of Orgns.; trustee Newark Acad., mem. nominating com.; mem. adv. bd., life mem. S.A.I.L., Inc.-Am. Tall Ship Syndicate, Pvt. Sector Initiatives Found., Women's Sports Found., U.S. Assn. Blind Athletes, Caths. Committed to Support the Pope, The Acton Inst., Ctr. for Internat. Mgmt. Edn., U. Dallas, Ctr. for Christianity and the Common Good; mem. nat. adv. bd. Sudden Infant Death Syndrome Alliance; hon. bd. govs. Tel Aviv U.; bd. dirs. U. Limerick Found.; mem. bd. advisors William J. Casey chair geopolit. studies John M. Ashbrook Ctr. Pub. Affairs; mem. fed. adv. bd. Commn. for Preservation of Treasury Bldg.; mem. Inaugural adv. bd. Gene Autry Western Heritage Mus.; mem. adv. coun. Consumer Alert; mem. internat. adv. coun. Internat. Ctr. for the Disabled; mem. com. Cardinal's Com. of the Laity; bd. govs. Hugh O'Brian Youth Fedn.; bd. govs., mem. fin., investment coms., spl. com. on hosp. environ., mem. internat. adv. bd. N.Y. Hosp.; bd. govs. Ronald Reagan Presdl. Found.; mem. Amb. John D. J. Moore Scholarship Fund, Univ. Coll., Dublin, Ireland, Pres.'s Com. on Arts and Humanities; mem. com. for restoration John B. Kelly Jr. Meml. Boathouse; mem. vis. com. Marine Scis. Rsch. Ctr., SUNY, Stony Brook; mem. internat. councillors Ctr. for Strategic and Internat. Studies; mem. hon. com. Women's Econ. Round Table; mem. exec. com. The Bretton Woods Com.; mem. policy coun. The Tax Found.; mem. of coun. Templeton Coll.; prin. Coun. for Excellence in Govt.; mem. exec. coun. Daytop Village, Inc.; mem. nat. steering com. Jefferson Energy Found.; mem. internat. com. Miles Jesu Internat. Com. for Human Dignity; mem. nat. planning bd. Morality in Media Inc.; mem. chmn.'s coun. Nat. Coun. on Alcoholism and Drug Dependence Inc.; mem. diplomatic coun. People to People Sports Com. Inc.; hon. chmn. Inst. Ednl. Affairs; hon. chmn. fund raising campaign Morris Ctr. YMCA; hon. co-chmn. Liberty Pk. Found., Suffolk County Vietnam Vets. Meml. Commn., U.S. Fitness Acad. Campaign, Nat. Fitness Found.; mem. adv. coun. William J. Donovan Meml. Found. Inc. Served with inf. U.S. Army, 1946-48. Decorated Order of the Nile (Egypt); recipient Investment Bankers Assn. Am. award, 1970, Small Bus. Adminstrn. citation, 1971, 2d ann. Youth Services award Wall St. div. B'nai B'rith, 1971, Outstanding Service to His Country award Port Authority N.Y., 1973, Merit award Securities Industry Assn., 1973, Outstanding Citizen of N.J. award Advt. Club N.J., 1974, Financial World award, 1974, Good Scout award Boy Scouts Am., 1974, Exec. Govt. award OIC Govt. Relations Service, 1974, Outstanding Citizen of Yr. award, 1974, U.S. Indsl. Payroll Savs. award, 1974, Civic Leadership award Am. Jewish Com., 1975, Dean's citation Am. U., 1975, Trustees medal Fairleigh Dickenson U., 1975, Gold medal Nat. Inst. Social Scis., 1975, Am. Eagle award Nat. Invest in Am. Coun., 1975, Achievement award Newark Acad. Alumni Assn., 1975, Bicentennial award U.S. Citizen's Congress, 1975, Young Americans For Freedom citation, 1975, Am. Inst. for Pub. Service award, 1976, Bus. in Pub. Affairs award C. of C. of Md., 1976, Flame of Truth award Fund for Higher Edn. in Israel, 1976, Disting. Achievements award Money Marketers of NYU, 1976, Pa. Soc. medal, 1976, NYU Coll. Bus. and Pub. Adminstrn. medal, 1976, Govt. Service award Pub. Relations Soc. Am., 1976, Carnauba Palm award S.C. Johnson and Son Inc., 1976, proclamation Pub. Relations Soc. Am., 1976, Pres.'s award for outstanding achievement, 1976, Econ. Forum citation Chapman Coll., 1977, Alexander Hamilton award Dept. Treasury, 1977, Am. Legion award, 1977, Brotherhood award NCCJ, 1977, Outstanding Achievement award Freedoms Found. at Valley Forge, 1978, Order of Anthony Wayne citation Valley Forge Mil. Acad. and Jr. Coll., 1978, Disting. Patriot award SAR, 1979, George Washington Kidd award Lafayette Coll. Alumni Assn., 1979, George Washington Honor medal Valley Forge Freedom Found., 1979, Eastside Conservative Club, 1980, Service Above Self award, Easton Rotary Club, 1980, Charles Edison Meml. award, Leadership award Columbia Bus. Sch., 1982, Cath. Big Bros. of Yr. award Lotus Club, 1982, Hall of Fame award Tri-County Scholarship, 1983, Disting. Service award The Liberty Bowl, 1983, Jesse Owens Internat. Amateur Athletic award, 1984, Reed K. Swenson Leadership award Nat. Jr. Coll. Athletic Assn., 1984, Gov.'s Com. on Scholastic Achievement award, 1985, Golden Medallion award Internat. Swimming Hall of Fame, 1985, Internat. Exec. of Yr. award Am. Grad. Sch. Internat. Mgmt., 1985, Humanitarian award Am. Sportscaster Assn., 1985, Man of Yr. award Morristown Rotary Club, 1986, Disting. Citizen award Greater N.Y. council Boy Scouts Am., 1986, Sportsman of Yr. award All-Am. Collegiate Golf Found., 1986, Golden Plate award Am. Acad. Achievement, 1986, Societe d'Honneur award Lafayette Coll., 1986, Kriendler award Marine Corps Sch., 1986, Reunion Alumni Achievement award Newark Acad., 1986, Disting. Service award Cons. Engrs. Council N.J., 1987, Charles McCaffree award Coll. Swimming Coaches Assn. Am. Inc., 1987, Covenant House award, 1988, 1st Ann. award Mid-Atlantic Legal Found., 1988, Pres.'s medal Adelphi U., 1989, Entrepreneur of Yr. award Henry Bloch Sch. Bus. and Pub. Adminstrn., U. Mo., Kansas City, 1989, Jesse Owens Internat. award U.S. Olympic Com., 1990, Ellis Island Medal of Honor award, 1990, Club of Champions Gold medal Cath. Youth Orgn. of Archdiocese N.Y., 1991; named to l'Ordre Olympique by le Comité Internat. Olympique, 1987, U.S. Olympic Com. Hall of Fame, 1991. Mem. Coun. on Fgn. Rels., The Soc. of Friendly Sons of St. Patrick, Pilgrims of U.S., Nat. Fedn. State high Sch. Assns. (chmn. bd. emeritus), Mont Pelerin Soc., Asia Soc. (former trustee), Explorers Club (bd. dirs. 1994), Assn. N.J. Rifle and Pistol Club, Am. Assn. Master Knights of Sovereign Milit. Order of Malta (exec. com.), Villa Taverna Soc. Clubs: Alfalfa (Washington); Balboa Bay (Calif.); Maidstone Inc., Sheriff's Jury Inc., Links, Brook Forum, N.Y. Yacht, Bond of N.Y., Mcpl. Bond of N.Y., N.Y. Athletic (N.Y.C., Man of Yr. 1984); Commonwealth of Calif. (San Francisco); Lyford Cay (Nassau, Bahamas); Mendham Valley Gun (N.J.); Country Club of Colo. (Colorado Springs); Gulf Stream Golf (Fla.); Rolling Rock (Ligonier, Pa.); Waialae Country, Oahu Country (Honolulu); Maui Country; Morris County Golf (N.J.); Robert Trent Jones Internat. Golf (founding bd. dirs.). Numerous scholarships and endowments established. Office: William E Simon & Sons Inc PO Box 1913 Morristown NJ 07960-7301

SIMON, WILLIAM LEONARD, film and television writer and producer, author; b. Washington, Dec. 3, 1930; s. Isaac B. and Marjorie (Felsteiner) S.; m. Arynne Lucy Abeles, Sept. 18, 1966; 1 child, Victoria Marie; 1 stepson, Sheldon M. Bermont. BEE, Cornell U., 1954; MA in Ednl. Psychology, Golden State U., 1982, PhD in Comm., 1983. Writer features and TV movies, documentary and indsl. films, TV programs, 1958—; lectr. George Washington U., Washington, 1968-70; juror Coun. on Nontheatrical Events Film Festival, 1975-90, Cindy Festival Blue Ribbon Panel, 1985—; jury chmn., bd. dirs. CINE film festival, 1990—. Writer more than 600 produced works for motion pictures and TV, including (screenplays) Fair Woman Without Discretion, Majorca, Swindle, A Touch of Love, (teleplays and documentaries) From Information to Wisdom, Flight of Freedom II, Missing You, (home video) Star of India, Combat Vietnam series; writer, prodr.: The Star of India: Setting Sail; co-author: Profit from Experience-The Story of Transformation Management (best seller, nominee Global book awards), 1995, Lasting Changes, 1997; author: Beyond the Numbers, 1996. Pres. Foggy Bottom Citizens Assn., 1963-65, mem. exec. bd., 1965-69; v.p. Shakespeare Summer Festival, 1966-67, trustee, 1965-70; mem. interview com. Cornell U., 1987-88. Lt. USN, 1954-58. Recipient 12 Golden Eagle awards Cine Film Festival, gold medal N.Y. Internat. Festival, gold medal Freedoms Found., IFPA Gold Cindy; awards Berlin, Belgrade and Venice film Festivals, numerous others. Mem. Nat. Acad. TV Arts and Scis. (gov. D.C. chpt. 1970-73), Writers Guild Am., Am. Film Inst., Internat. Documentary Assn., Rotary (bd. dirs., program chmn.), Eta Kappa Nu (chpt. pres. 1953-54), Tau Beta Pi. Republican. Avocations: crew member square-rigged brig Pilgrim, San Diego Museum ship Star of India, tennis. Home: 6151 Paseo Delicias PO Box 2048 Rancho Santa Fe CA 92067-2048

SIMONDS, CHARLES FREDERICK, artist; b. N.Y.C., Nov. 14, 1945; s. Robert and Anita I. (Bell) S. BA, U. Calif., Berkeley, 1967; MFA, Rutgers U., 1969. One man shows include Ctr. nat. d'Art contemporain, Paris, 1975, Mus. Modern Art, N.Y.C., 1976, Westfälischer Kunstverein, Munster, 1978, Mus. Ludwig, Cologne, 1979, Mus. Contemporary Art, Chgo., 1981, Phoenix (Ariz.) Mus. Art, 1982, Brooks Meml. Art Gallery, Memphis, 1982, Solomon R. Guggenheim Mus., N.Y., 1983, Leo Castelli Gallery, N.Y., 1984, Architekturmuseum, Bâle, 1985, Corcoran Gallery Art, Washington, 1988, Fundació "la Caixa," Barcelona, 1994, Galerie nat. Jeu Paume, Paris, 1994; exhibited in group shows Whitney Mus. Am. Art, N.Y., 1975, 77, Mus. d'Art moderne Ville de Paris, 1975, Stedelijk Mus., Amsterdam, 1978, Mus. Modern Art, N.Y., 1979, Hayward Gallery, London, 1980, Tate Gallery, London, 1983, Solomon R. Guggenheim Mus., N.Y., 1985, 87, 89; works included in publs. including Artforum, 1980, Art/Cahier, 1977, Sprache im Technischen Zeitalter, 1978, Art in America, 1983, Images and Issues, 1982, ARTnews, 1978, Beaux Arts, 1986. Fellow Am. Acad. Rome. Home: 26 E 22nd St New York NY 10010-6107

SIMONDS, JOHN EDWARD, newspaper editor; b. Boston, July 4, 1935; s. Alvin E. and Ruth Angeline (Rankin) S.; m. Rose B. Muller, Nov. 16, 1968; children—Maximillian P., Malia G.; children by previous marriage—Rachel F., John B. B.A., Bowdoin Coll., 1957. Reporter Daily Tribune, Seymour, Ind., 1957-58, UPI, Columbus, Ohio, 1958-60; reporter, asst. city editor Providence Jour. Bull., 1960-65, Washington Evening Star, 1965-66; corr. Gannett News Svc., Washington, 1966-75; mng. editor Honolulu Star Bull., 1975-80, exec. editor, 1980-87, sr. editor, editorial page editor, 1987-93; exec. Hawaii Newspaper Agy., Honolulu, 1993—. Served with U.S. Army, 1958. Mem. Am. Soc. Newspaper Editors, AP Mng. Editors, Soc. Profl. Journalists, Nat. Conf. Editorial Writers. Home: 5316 Nehu Pl Honolulu HI 96821-1941 Office: Hawaii Newspaper Agy 605 Kapiolani Blvd Honolulu HI 96813-5129

SIMONDS, JOHN ORMSBEE, landscape architect; b. Jamestown, N.D., Mar. 11, 1913; s. Guy Wallace and Marguerite Lois (Ormsbee) S.; m. Marjorie C. Todd, May 1, 1943; children: Taye Anne, John Todd, Polly Jean, Leslie Brook. BS, Mich. State U., 1935, DSc hon.; MLandscape Architecture (Eugene Dodd medal), Harvard U., 1939. Landscape architect Mich. Dept. Parks, 1935-36; ptnr. Simonds and Simonds, Pitts., 1939-70, Collins, Simonds and Simonds, Washington, 1952-70; ptnr. The Environ. Planning and Design Partnership, Pitts., also Miami Lakes, 1970-82, emeritus, 1983—; cons. Dept. Pks., Collier County, Fla., 1986-90, Land and Nature Trust, Lexington, Ky., 1987-92, SW Fla. Water Mgmt. Dist., 1987-89; lectr., vis. critic urban and regional planning Carnegie-Mellon U., 1955-67; vis. critic Grad. Sch. Planning, also Sch. Architecture, Yale, 1961-62; Cons. Chgo. Cen. Area Com., 1962, Allegheny County Dept. Regional Pks., 1961-74; U.S. cons. community planning Inter-Am. Housing and Planning Ctr., Bogota, Colombia, 1960-61; mem. jury Am. Acad. Rome, 1963, 65, 66, 69; mem. Nat. Adv. Com. on Hwy. Beautification; chmn. panel on pks. and open space White House Conf. on Natural Beauty; mem. Interprofl. Commn. on Environ. Design, Joint Com. on Nat. Capital; mem. and report editor urban hwy. adv. bd. U.S. Bur. Pub. Rds., 1965-68; mem. landscape architecture adv. panel U.S. C.E., 1968-71, Pres.'s Task Force on Resources and Environ., 1968-70; mem. design adv. panel Operation Breakthrough, HUD, 1970-71; mem. Mid-Atlantic regional adv. bd. Nat. Park Svc., 1976-78; assoc. trustee U. Pa., 1962-66, mem. bd. fine arts, 1962-66; chmn. joint com. planning Carnegie-Mellon U. and U. Pitts., 1959-60; overseer's vis. com. Harvard Grad. Sch. Design, 1962-68, exec. coun. alumni assn., 1960-63; adv. com. Sch. Design, N.C. State U., 1965-67; mem. Fla. Gov.'s Task Force on Natural Resources, 1979-80, Chgo. Bot. Garden 25th Anniversary, 1991, keynote address, 1991, Internat. Fedn. Landscape Architects, Seoul, Korea, 1992; speaker keynote address Internat. Congress Urban Green, Geneva, 1986. Author: Landscape Architecture, the Shaping of Man's Natural Environment, 1961, 2d rev. edit., 1997, Earthscape, a Manual of Environmental Planning, 1978, revised edit. 1986, Garden Cities 21, Creating a Livable Urban Environment, 1994; editor: Virginia's Common Wealth, 1965, The Freeway in the City, 1968; contbr. sect. on urban design Ency. Architecture, 1990, sect. on landscape architecture Ency. Urban Planning, 1980. Maj. works include master plans for Chgo. Bot. Garden, (with others) Mellon Sq., Pitts., (with others) Miami Lakes New Town, Va. I-66 Corridor, Fairfax and Arlington counties, Va., Pelican Bay Community, Fla., Weston New Town, Fla. Bd. dirs. Hubbard Ednl. Trust, 1974—; bd. govs. Pitts. Plan for Arts. Recipient citation Top Men of Year Engring. News-Record, 1973; Charles L. Hutchinson medal Chgo. Hort. Soc., John R. Bracken medal Dept. Landscape Architecture, Pa. State U., 1985, Sigma Lambda Alpha award Coun. Educators in Landscape Architecture, 1979. Fellow Am. Soc. Landscape Architects (mem. exec. com. 1959-67, pres. 1963-65, pres. Found. 1966-68, recipient medal 1973), Royal Soc. Arts (Gt. Britain); mem. Nat. Acad. (US), Archtl. League N.Y., Royal Town Planning Inst. (hon. corr.); hon. assoc. Pa. chpt. AIA, Harvard-Yale-Princeton Club. Presbyterian (ruling elder). Home: 17 Penhurst Rd Pittsburgh PA 15202-1023 Office: The Loft 17 Penhurst Rd Pittsburgh PA 15202 *Perhaps the most important lesson in life is to learn to address oneself with intensity to each person, object and event. One may be with friends without awareness of either friend or friendship, live with family as an almost stranger, partake of food and drink without savor, pass burgeoning tree, splashing stream, or splendid view without appreciation . . . unless one learns to address all powers of perception-first consciously, and then by habit, to the subject at hand. Only thus may each experience be made rich and rewarding, and life, the sum of experience, be lived to the full.*

SIMONDS, MARSHALL, lawyer; b. Boston, Sept. 17, 1930; s. Sidney Lawrence and Evelyn (Peterson) S.; m. Katharine Blewett, May 9, 1969; children: Robert Bradley, Joshua Lawrence. BA, Princeton U., 1952; LLB, Harvard U., 1955. Bar: Mass. 1955. Since practiced in Boston; ptnr. Goodwin, Procter & Hoar, Boston, 1965—; counsel Mass. Crime Commn., 1963-65; spl. asst. atty. gen. Commonwealth of Mass., 1964-66; dir. Dynatech Corp., 1960-85, Data Packaging Corp., 1972-79; trustee Middlesex Instn. Savs., 1974-79. Moderator of Carlisle, Mass., 1967—; trustee Trustees for Reservations, 1972-78; bd. dirs. South Boston Neighborhood House, 1972-78. Served with USMCR, 1955. Fellow Am. Coll. Trial Lawyers, Am. Bar Found., Mass. Bar Found.; mem. ABA, Mass. Bar Assn., Boston Bar Assn. (coun. 1980-82), New Eng. Legal Found. (dir.), Franklin Flaschner Jud. Inst. (acad. com.), Am. Kennel Club (del.), Labrador Retriever Club (bd. dirs.), Harvard Club (Boston), Orthopedic Found. for Animals (bd. dirs.). Address: Bliss Hill Rd Morrisville VT 05661

SIMONDS, PEGGY MUÑOZ, writer, lecturer, retired literature educator; b. New Rochelle, N.Y., Feb. 29, 1928; d. Francisco Javier Muñoz and Julia Pinckney Dunham; m. Roger Tyrrell Simonds, Nov. 21, 1956; children: Robin Pinckney, Martha Muñoz. BA in English, U. Del., 1949; MA in Creative Writing/Latin Am. Studies, U. of the Americas, Mexico City, 1956; PhD in Lit. and History of Art, Am. U., 1975. Journalist, arts critic Mexico City, 1949-55; tchr. English U. of the Ams., Mexico City, 1953-55; lectr. Greek drama Norfolk (Conn.) Music Sch. of Yale U., summer 1958; tchr. English Montgomery (Md.) Coll., 1966-88, prof. emeritus, 1988—; ind. scholar, 1988—; lectr. and presenter in field. Author: Myth, Emblem, and Music in Shakespeare's "Cymbeline": An Iconographic Reconstruction, 1992, Iconographic Research in English Renaissance Literature: A Critical Guide, 1995; contbr. essays to books, numerous articles to profl. jours. Recipient U. Del. Press award, 1990; NEH fellow, 1982. Mem. MLA, Assn. Lit. Scholars and Critics, Shakespeare Assn. Am., Internat. Shakespeare Assn., Renaissance Soc. Am., Southeastern Renaissance Soc., South Ctrl. Renaissance Soc., Internat. Soc. for Classical Tradition, Internat. Soc. for Emblem Studies, Internat. Assn. for Neo-Latin Studies, Sixteenth-Century Studies Conf., Phi Kappa Phi. Home and Office: 5406 Beech Ave Bethesda MD 20814

SIMONDS, STEPHEN PAIGE, former state legislator; b. Franconia, N.H., Nov. 25, 1924; s. Stephen Moses and Gertrude Martha (Jesseman) S.; m. Judith Cole, Sept. 13, 1952; children: Scott, Mark, Laura, Jane. BA, U. N.H., 1948; MA in Social Svcs. Adminstrn., U. Chgo., 1953. Caseworker N.H. Dept. Pub. Welfare, Woodsville, 1950-51; dist. supr. N.H. Dept. Pub. Welfare, Conway and Woodsville, 1953-56; field supr. Conn. Dept. Welfare, Hartford, 1958-60; dir. social welfare Maine Dept. Health and Welfare, Augusta, 1960-67; commr. Assitance Payments Adminstrn. HEW, Washington, 1967-69; commr. Cmty. Svcs. Adminstrn. HEW, Washington, 1969-71; founder, dir. Human Svcs. Devel. Inst., U. So. Maine, Portland, 1971-86, dir. Office Internat. Programs, 1986-92; mem. Maine Ho. of Reps., Augusta, 1990-94, mem. human resources com., edn. com. Past pres. World Affairs Coun. of Maine, Cmty. Counseling Ctr. Recipient Disting. Svc. award World Affairs Coun. Maine, 1991; Fulbright scholar, Eng., 1957-58. Mem. Ptnrs. of Ams., Chinese and Am. Friendship Assn. (a founder). Democrat. Avocations: flying, boating, canoeing, gardening. Home: 18 Brentwood Rd Cape Elizabeth ME 04107

SIMONE, ALBERT JOSEPH, academic administrator; b. Boston, Dec. 16, 1935; s. Edward and Mary (DiGiovanni) S.; m. Carolie Roberta Menko, Nov. 7, 1959; children: Edward, Karen, Debra, Laura. BA, Tufts U., 1957; PhD, MIT, 1962. Lectr. Coll. Bus. Adminstrn., Northeastern U., Boston, 1958-59; instr. econs. MIT and Tufts U., Boston, 1959-60; asst. prof. Northeastern U., Tufts U., 1960-63; assoc. prof. Coll. Bus. Adminstrn. Boston Coll., 1963-66, prof., dir. quantitative mgmt. program Coll. Bus. Adminstrn., 1966-68; prof., head dept. quantitative analysis Coll. Bus. Adminstrn. U. Cin., 1968-72, dean Coll. Bus. Adminstrn., 1972-83; v.p. acad. affairs U. Hawaii, Honolulu, 1983-84, acting pres., 1984-85; pres. U. Hawaii System, Honolulu, 1985-92; chancellor U. Hawaii at Manoa, 1985-92; pres. Rochester (N.Y.) Inst. Tech., 1992—; served on, chaired numerous univ. coms.; program chmn. 1970 Nat. Conf. of Am. Prodn. and Inventory Control Soc.; mem. accreditation com. Am. Assembly Collegiate Schs. Bus., 1978-83, visits to U. Ky., Carnegie-Mellon U., 1982; session chmn. various profl. confs.; cons. statis. forecasting, prodn. scheduling and sample design models various cos. including Cin. Gas & Electric Co., Cin. Milacron, Kroger Co.; econ. and mgmt. cons. Atty. Gen.'s Office, State of Mass.; mem. council econ. advisors to Gov., Commonwealth of Mass. Author: Matematica Finita Con Aplicaciones A Las Ciencias Administrativas, 1969, Foundations of Contemporary Mathematics with Applications in the Social and Management Sciences, 1967, Probability: An Introduction with Applications, 1967; (with L. Kattsoff) Finite Mathematics with Applications in the Social and Management Sciences, 1965, (with R. Wessel and E. Willett) Statistics as Applied to Economics and Business, 1965; also articles. Bd. dirs. Greater Rochester Visitors Assn., Inc., Marine Midland Bank, N.A., Rochester/So. Region, United Way of Greater Rochester, Vis. Nurse Svc. of Rochester and Monroe County, Inc., High Tech. of Rochester, Greater Rochester Metro C. of C., chmn. bd. trustees; bd. dirs. Indsl. Mgmt. Coun.; chmn. United Way Vol. Resources Divsn. Steering Com.; trustee George Eastman House; corp. mem. Hillside Children's Ctr. Fellow of grad. sch. U. Cin.; named Prof. of Yr., Delta Sigma Pi, Alpha Theta chpt., U. Cin., 1972; recipient Tree of Life award Jewish Nat. Fund. Fellow Am. Inst. Decision Scis. (v.p. publs. 1969-70, v.p. and student liaison 1972, pres. 1974-75, founding editor and editor-in-chief jour. 1970-72, Disting. Svc. award 1972); mem. Acad. Mgmt., Am. Econ. Assn., Am. Inst. Indsl. Engrs., Am. Prodn. and Inventory Control Soc., Am. Statis. Assn., Assn. Computing Machinery, Univs. Rsch. Assn., Assn. of Ind. Tech. Univs., The Conf. Bd. RIT Rsch. Corp. (chmn., bd. dirs.), Nat. Commn. for Coop. Edn., N.Y. Commn. for Ind. Coll. and Univs., Rochester Area Coll. Consortium, Econometric Soc., Fin. Execs. Inst., Inst. Mgmt. Sci., Ops. Rsch. Soc. Am., Phi Beta Kappa, Phi Kappa Phi, Beta Gamma Sigma. Office: RIT George Eastman Bldg One Lomb Meml Dr Rochester NY 14623-5604

SIMONE, ANGELA PAOLINO, elementary education educator; b. New Haven, Jan. 27, 1953; d. John L. and Mary (Solli) Paolino; 1 child, Dennis. BS, So. Conn. U., 1974, MS in Reading, 1976; AS, S. Cen. Community Coll., New Haven, 1972. Substitute tchr. City of West Haven, Conn., 1976-77; elem. tchr. St. Brenden's Sch., New Haven, 1985; elem. tchr. St. Lawrence Sch., West Haven, 1985—, co-coord. Writing to Read Program, 1994—; primary sci. facilitator Rainbow Program for All God's Children, West Haven. Mem. We Are the World Com. of West Haven Pub. Schs. Mem. AAUW, ASCD, Nat. Cath. Edn. Assn., Internat. Reading Assn. Office: St Lawrence Sch 231 Main St New Haven CT 06516-4536

SIMONE, JOSEPH R., lawyer; b. N.Y.C., Jan. 7, 1949; m. Virginia E. Simone, May 29, 1971; children: Jacquelyn, Robert. BA cum laude, Queens Coll., 1971; LLM in Taxation, NYU, 1977; JD cum laude, Fordham U., 1974. Bar: N.Y. 1975, U.S. Dist. Ct. (so. dist.) N.Y. 1975, U.S. Ct. Appeals (2d cir.) 1975. Ptnr. Patterson, Belknap, Webb & Tyler, N.Y.C., 1982-88, Schulte, Roth & Zabel, N.Y.C., 1988—. Author: (textbooks) Pension Answer Book, 5th edit., 1990, Essential Facts: Pension and Profit-sharing Plans, 1996; editl. advisor Jour. of Pension Planning. Mem. Am. Arbitration Assn. (panel on multiemployer pension plans, employee benefits law adv. com, cochair symposium employee benefits), Phi Beta Kappa. Office: Schulte Roth & Zabel 900 3rd Ave New York NY 10022-4728

SIMONE, REGINA, family practice physician; b. Trenton, N.J., Mar. 20, 1961; d. Michael Simone and Amelia Ann Mastrogiovanni. BS in Microbiology, Gannon U., 1983, MS in Microbiology, 1986; DO, U. New Eng. Coll. Medicine, 1993. Diplomate Am. Bd. Family Practice; cert. BCLS Level C, ACLS. Instr. microbiology/asst. rschr. Gannon U., Erie, Pa., 1984-86; rschr. microbiology Temple U. Sch. Medicine, Phila., 1986-87; supr. quality control Wissahickon Spring Water Co., Phila., 1987-89; instr./asst. microbiology U. New Eng. Coll. Medicine, Biddeford, Maine, 1989-91; student physician U. New Eng. Coll. Medicine, 1989-93; resident in internal medicine St. Vincent's Hosp., Worcester, Mass., 1993-94; chief resident in family practice Garden City (Mich.) Hosp., 1994-96; pvt. practice Livonia, Mich., 1996—; mem. house staff tng. com. Garden City Hosp., 1995-96. Mem. AMA, Am. Med. Women's Assn., Am. Osteo. Assn., Am. Coll. Osteo. Physicians, Am. Coll. Gen. Practitioners. Roman Catholic. Avocations: golf, writing, opera.

SIMONELLI, MICHAEL TARQUIN, chemical engineer; b. Chgo., July 27, 1946; s. Michael Eugene and Caroline S.; m. Nancy Jo Garnaas (div.); 1 child, Kimberly; m. Tania Kalikin, Nov. 15, 1986; children: Nicole, John. BS in Chem. Engring., U. Ill., Chgo., 1968; BA, Elmhurst Coll., 1969. R & D mgr. plastic divsn. product devel. Masonite Corp., St. Charles, Ill., 1968-71; dist. sales mgr. DeGaynor and Co., Hillside, Ill., 1971-75; chem. salesman Dearborn Chem. Co., Arlington Hgts., Ill., 1975-77; waste water divsn. mgr. H-O-H Chemicals, Inc., Palatine, Ill., 1977-80; pres. N. Am. Waste Systems, Inc., Rolling Meadows, Ill., 1980-84; product reliability mgr. Modular Controls, Inc., Carol Stream, Ill., 1984-89; sr. vendor quality engr., R&D project engr. Blaw-Knox Constrn. Equipment Corp., Mattoon, Ill., 1989-94, sr. vendor quality engr., 1994—. Author: (book) Hydraulics Manual, 1991; inventor: waste mgmt. system, 1981, burner controls (patent pending), hydraulic controls (patent pending), cardinogenic fume extraction unit (patent in U.S. and Europe). Recipient flying honors, USCG Aux., Glenview Naval Air Sta., 1978, valor award, USCG Aux., Glenview Naval Air Sta., 1980. Mem. Am. Std. for Testing Methods, Nat. Asphalt Paving Assn., Aircraft Owners & Pilots Assn., Exptl. Aircraft Assn., Delta Tau Alpha (pres. 1965-67). Avocations: aircraft pilot, photography, computers. Home: 320 N 35th St Mattoon IL 61938-2147

SIMONET, JOHN THOMAS, banker; b. Stillwater, Minn., Aug. 11, 1926; s. Joseph S. and Helen (Martin) S.; m. Helen Kennedy, Sept. 8, 1951; children: William T., Joseph K., Mary, Michelle, Anne. B.B.A., U. Minn., 1948, LL.B., 1951. With First Nat. Bank, St. Paul, 1951-72; cashier First

Nat. Bank, 1958-60, v.p., 1960-71; exec. v.p. First Trust Co., St. Paul, 1972-74; pres. First Trust Co., 1974-85, chief adminstrv. officer, 1974-81, chief exec. officer, 1981-85, ret., 1985; asst. treas. Port Authority St. Paul, 1966-71; bd. dirs. First Trust, St. Paul, Carondelet Life Care Corp., Donovan Cos. Inc., Mairs and Power Funds, Inc. Mem. lay adv. bd. exec. com. St. Joseph's Hosp., St. Paul, 1965-70, trustee, 1971-82, chmn. bd. trustees, 1976-79; pres. adv. bd. Catholic Social Service St. Paul, 1968-70; chmn. Archbishop's Appeal Com., 1970; exec. bd. dirs. St. Paul Council Arts and Scis., 1967-69; trustee St. Paul Sem., 1969-92, Tozer Found., 1981—; bd. dirs. United Way, St. Paul, 1976-82, pres., 1980-81; mem. governing bd. St. Paul Found., 1979-85; bd. dirs. Mairs and Power Growth Fund, Mairs and Power Income Fund, 1992—. Served with USNR, 1944-46, 53-55.

SIMONETT, JOHN E., state supreme court justice; b. Mankato, Minn., July 12, 1924; m. Doris Bogut; 6 children. BA, St. John's U., 1948; LLB, U. Minn., 1951. Pvt. practice law Little Falls, Minn., 1951-80; assoc. justice Supreme Ct. of Minn., St. Paul, 1980-94; ret., 1994. Office: 1700 Metropolitan Ctr 333 S 7th St Minneapolis MN 55402-2414*

SIMON-GILLO, JEHANNE E., physicist; b. Liege, Belgium, Mar. 27, 1963; came to U.S., 1967; d. Nicolas Victor and Noelle Marie (Van Den Peereboom) Simon; m. Andrew James Gillo, June 9, 1990. BS, Juniata Coll., 1985; PhD, Tex. A&M U., 1991. Postdoctoral work Los Alamos (N.Mex.) Nat. Lab., 1991-94, staff mem., physicist, 1994—; project mgr. PHENIX Multiplicity Vertex Detector. Mem. Am. Chem. Soc., Am. Phys. Soc. Republican. Roman Catholic. Achievements include work on E814, NA44, PHENIX experiments; exptl. physicist studying relativistic heavy-ion collisions, specifically low PT phenomena and deuteron formation; subsystem mgr. and detector coun. mem. for PHENIX multiplicity vertex detector. Office: Los Alamos Nat Lab H846 LANL Los Alamos NM 87545

SIMONIAN, JOHN S., lawyer; s. Samuel and Mary Simonian. BA, U. R.I.; JD, Boston U. Bar: R.I., U.S. Dist. Ct. R.I. state rep. R.I. Ho. of Reps., Providence, 1991—, dep. majority leader, 1993—, chmn. commn. on criminal justice, 1993—, mem. house com. on fin., 1993—, joint com. on veteran's affairs, 1991—. Democrat. Apostolic. Home: 43 Eldridge St Cranston RI 02910

SIMONIAN, SIMON JOHN, surgeon, scientist, educator; b. Antioch, French Ter., Apr. 20, 1932; came to U.S., 1965, naturalized, 1976.; s. John Simon and Marie Cecile (Tomboulian) S.; m. Arpi Ani Yeghiayan, July 11, 1965; children: Leonard Armen, Charles Haig, Andrew Hovig. MD, U. London, 1957; BA in Animal Physiology, St. Edmund Hall, U. Oxford, Eng., 1964; MA in Animal Physiology, U. Oxford, Eng., 1969; MSc in nutrition, immunology & genetics, Harvard U., 1967, ScD in nutrition, immunology & genetics, 1969. Diplomate Am. Bd. Surgery. Rsch. asst. immunology unit Lister Inst. Preventive Medicine, Elstree, Essex, U.K., 1952; intern in medicine Univ. Coll. Hosp., London, 1957; intern in surgery Edinburgh (Scotland) Royal Infirmary, 1957-58, resident in surgery, 1961-62; clin. clk. Nat. Hosp. & Inst. of Neurology, 1958; resident Edinburgh Western Gen. Hosp., 1958-59, City Hosp., Edinburgh, Birmingham Accident and Burns Hosp., U. Birmingham, Eng., 1959-60; demonstrator dept. anatomy Edinburgh U., 1960-61; rsch. fellow in pathology Lab. Chem. Pathology Harvard U., Boston, 1965-68; trainee NIH Harvard U., 1967; instr. immunology Harvard Med. Sch., Boston, 1966-70; instr., assoc. in surgery Harvard Med. Sch., 1968-70, surg. dir. course on transplantation, biology and medicine, 1968-70; vis. prof. Harvard Med. Sch., Mass. Gen. Hosp., Brigham and Womens Hosp., New Eng. Deaconess Hosp., 1982; dir. transplantation immunology unit, asst. in surgery Brigham and Womens Hosp., Boston, 1968-70; resident in surgery Boston City Hosp., 1970-74; attending surgeon in transplantation and gen. surgery services U. Chgo. Med. Ctr., 1974-77; asst. prof. surgery, mem. com. immunology U. Chgo., 1974-77; head div. renal transplantation Hahnemann U. Sch. Medicine and Hosp., 1978-87, prof. surgery, 1978-88, chmn. Transplantation Com., 1983-88, chmn. quality assurance of surgery com., 1986-88; dept. surgery coord. with joint commn. for accreditation of hosps. Hahnemann U. Sch. Medicine, 1986; chief and chmn. dept. surgery St. John Hosp. and Med. Ctr., Detroit, 1988-89, chmn. credentials com. of surgery and oper. rm. com., 1988-89, assoc. v.p. for med. affairs, 1989-90; pres., CEO Vein Inst. of Met. Washington, Inc., 1990—; assoc. Fairfax Hosp., Falls Church, Va., 1990-92, active faculty, 1992—; guest lectr., 1994; clin. assoc. prof. surgery Georgetown U. Sch. Medicine, Washington, 1992-95, clin. prof. surgery, 1995—; lectr. in field; vis. prof. Vanderbilt U., 1968, Cedars-Sinai Med. Ctr. UCLA, 1977, Addenbroke's Hosp., Cambridge U., 1977, Karolinska Inst., 1977, Huddinge Hosp. U. Stockholm, 1977, Med. Coll. Pa. and Hosp., 1980, 81, 85, Grad. Hosp. U. Pa., 1981, 85, U. Athens, 1981, U. Coll. Hosp., U. London, 1981, VA Hosp., Tufts U., 1982, Nat. Acad. Scis., Yerevan, Republic Armenia, 1995; cons. Michael Reese Hosp., Chgo., 1976-77, cons. in gen. surgery City of Phila., 1986-88, cons. in vascular surgery Coll. Podiatry, Phila., 1986-88, chief med. team support for U.S. Presdl. visits to Detroit, 1988, 89; vis. surgeon Inst. Vein Disease, Mich., 1989-90; vis. scientist Argonne (Ill.) Nat. Lab., 1969, 74-77; guest lectr., panelist 8th Internat. Congress of Nephrology, Athens, Greece, 1981, 1st Congress Internat. Soc. Edn. and Rsch. in Vascular Disease, San Diego, bd. dirs. 1992, 4th Internat. Dialogue Transition to Global Soc., U. Md., College Park, 1995; chmn. session 5th Armenian Med. World Congress, Paris, 1992, 11th World Congress Internat. Union of Phlebology, Montreal, 1992, 22d World Congress Inernat. Soc. for Cardiovasc. Surgery, Kyoto, Japan, 1995, 6th Annual Congress N. Am. Soc. of Phlebology, Lake Buena Vista, Fla., 1993, sec., bd. dirs. Woodrock, Inc., 1992-93; eminent scholar, external assessor U. Zambia, Lusaka, 1994; chmn. panel, session chmn., panel co-chmn., guest lectr., panelist 17th World Congress Internat. Union Angiology, London, 1995; chmn. panel, adv. bd. 12th World Congress Union Internat. Phlebologie, London, 1995; chmn. panel 9th ann. congress N. Am. Soc. Phlebology Ann. Congress, San Diego, 1996; mem. internat. adv. bd. 13th World Congress Union Internat. Phlebologie, Sydney, Australia, 18th World Congress Internat. Union Angiology, Tokyo, 1996; mem. Internat. Faculty on Chronic Venous Disorders, Paris, 1997. Co-author: Manual of Vascular Access Procedures, 1987; cons. to editorial bd. dateline: Issues in Transplantation, 1985-87; mem. editorial bd. Phila. Medicine, 1988, Transplantation Proc., 1987-96, Jour. Transplantation Abstracts, 1968-70; reviewer Jour. Oncology and Dermatologic Surgery, 1993, Jour. Dermatologic Surgery, 1997; contbr. articles to profl. jours. and books; appeared in med. movie Giving. Co-founder Armenian Youth Soc., Eng., 1953, pres. 1953-54; Armenian Studies Program U. Chgo., 1975; bd. govs. Friends Sch., London, 1964-65; Mass. del., co-founder Armenian Assembly, Washington, 1970-74; fellow-trustee, co-founder Entry into Manhood of Armenian Youth at Age 13, 1981; co-founder Armenian Am. Health Assn. of Greater Washington, 1992, mem. pharms. com. 1992—, chmn. nominating com., 1993; mem. Am. Friends of St. Edmund Hall, U. Oxford, 1992—, U.S. Campaign for St. Edmund Hall, 1995—, Rep. Presdl. Task Force; mem. St. Mary's Armenian Apostolic Ch., Washington, guest preacher, 1994, 95, 96; mem. Am. Friends Am. U. Armenia, Yerevan, 1994, bd. dirs. mammography unit, 1997—; bd. dirs. Arlington (Va.) Symphony Orch., 1992, sci. com. Armenia-U.S.A., 1996—; mem. regional com. U.S. Campaign for Univ. Oxford, 1993; bd. dirs. First Western Found., Inc., 1994; active amphitheatre endowment fund Boston City Hosp., 1994; dist. benefactor, fundraiser Eurasia Found., 1996. Nairn scholar, 1949-52; Middlesex scholar, 1952-57; recipient Suckling prize, 1956, Brit. Med. Research Council award, 1962-64, Alt prize, 1973, Thompson award, 1974-77, Johnson award, 1975-77, Presdl. Medal of Merit, 1982, Kabakjian award Armenian Student Assn. Am., 1986, Dist. Alumni award U. Oxford, 1997; named outstanding new citizen of Citizenship Coun. of Met. Chgo. and Dept. Justice, Washington, 1976-77, Jonathan E. Rhoads ann. orator, 1984; co-endowed The John and Marie J. Simonian Award, St. Nerces Sem., 1981, John R. Pfeifer, MD, Rsch. Award, Providence Hosp., Southfield, Mich., 1992; endowed the Dennis Knight prize Royal Acad. Music, London, 1991; endowed The Marie J. Simonian Prize, Georgetown U. Med. Sch., 1991 (prize com. 1991—); established The John N.D. Kelly Prize in Med. Studies St. Edmund Hall, U. Oxford, 1992, The Simon J. and Arpi A. Simonian Prize for scholastic excellence for doctoral candidates, Harvard U., 1992; recognized for philanthropy to Hahnemann U. by placques in med. sch. and hosp. lobbies., Simon and Arpi Simonian plasma physics room Sch. of Humanities and Scis. U. Yerevan, Armenia, 1994, plaque in Cyrus Vesuna Auditorium and Conf. Ctr., Fairfax Hosp., Falls Church, Va., 1995; grantee U.S. Govt., industry cos., founds. Fellow Royal Coll. Surgeons Edinburgh, ACS (Phila., Mich. and Washington chpts.), Phila. Acad. Surgery (Jonathan E. Rhoads ann. orator 1984—, Samuel D. Gross prize com. 1988, councillor 1988); mem. AAAS, AMA, AAUP, Royal Coll. Surgeons of Eng., Royal Coll. Physicians of London Licentiates, Nat. Assn. Armenian Studies and Rsch. (rep. Midatlantic region 1994—), Armenian Gen. Benevolent Union (pres.' club 1990—), Knights of Vartan, Am. Armenian Med. Assn. (co-founder 1972, treas. 1972-74), Brit. Med. Assn., Immunology Club Boston, Cancer Rsch. Assn. Boston, Physicians for Social Responsibility, Am. Pub. Health Assn., Assn. for Study of Med. Edn., Armenian Med. and Dental Assn. Greater Phila. (co-founder 1983, pres. 1983-85, Outreach award 1986), Assn. Acad. Surgery, Transplantation Soc. (mem. membership com. 1980-82), Am. Fedn. Clin. Rsch., N.Y. Acad. Scis., Am. Soc. Transplant Surgeons (co-founding mem. 1974, chmn. immunosuppression study com. 1974-77, membership com. 1985-87), Am. Venous Forum, Assn. of Ill. Transplant Surgeons, Chgo. Assn. Immunologists, Chgo. Soc. Gastroenterology, Phila. Acad. Scis. (co-chmn. membership com. 1980-88, guest lectr. 1982), Greater Delaware Valley Soc. Transplant Surgeons (councillor 1978-80, 85-88, pres. elect 1980-82, pres. 1982-85), Phila. County Med. Soc. (rep. City Ctr. br. 1981-83, pres. 1984, bd. dirs. 1985-87, chmn. long range planning com. 1986-88), Pa. Med. Soc., Samuel Hahnemann Surg. Soc., Am. Technion Soc., Am. Soc. Artificial Internal Organs, European Soc. Organ Transplant, Oxford and Cambridge Soc. of Phila. and Washington, Internat. Cardiovascular Soc. (N.Am. chpt.), N. Am. Soc. Phlebology (curriculum devel. projects com. 1992—, faculty 1993-96, panelist 10th ann. congress 1996), End Stage Renal Disease Network 24 (mem. med. rev. bd. 1980-82, 86-87), Am. Coll. Physician Execs., Detroit Acad. Surgery, Detroit Surgical Assn., Transplantation Soc. Mich., Organ Procurement Agy. Mich. (adv. bd. 1988-89), Wayne County Med. Soc., Mich. State Med. Soc., Fairfax County Med. Soc., Med. Soc. Va., Met. Vascular Conf., Soc. Brigham Surg. Alumni, Greater Washington Telecomm. Assn. (pres.'s club 1994), Chesapeake Vascular Soc., Oxford Soc. Washington, Harvard Club (Phila. and Washington), Med. Club (Phila.), U. Chgo. Club (Washington), Langley Hill Friends Meeting (mem. peace com. 1996—), Sigma Xi. Mem. Soc. of Friends. Achievement includes bilateral lung reimplantation, reversal of renal allograft rejection, prevention and tretment of massive gastroduodenal hemrrhage from hemorrhagic gastritis, co-dicovery essential aminoacids phenylalanine and tryptophan are essential for antibody formation, assistance in the lyophization of the smallpox vaccine, co-discovery of immunogenetic control of antibody formation, rsch. advantages and disadvantages and prevention of splenectomy in renal transplant recipients. Office: 3301 Woodburn Rd Annandale VA 22003-1229

SIMONICH, SANDRA SUE, elementary education educator; b. Moline, Ill., Aug. 8, 1942; d. Kenneth Fred and Vurl Barbara (Nicely) Liedtke; children: Cassandra Ann Oliver Phillips; m. Joseph Donald Simonich, Mar. 11, 1983. BS, Augustana Coll., 1974; MS, Western Ill. U., 1984. With Bank of Silvis, Ill., 1960; with farm implement John Deere Harvester, East Moline; with parts depot John Deere, East Moline, 1960-68; tchr. Millikin Sch., Geneseo, Ill., 1974-76; elem. edn. tchr. S.W. Sch., Geneseo, 1976—; Program initiator Raindows-Counseling for Children with a Loss of Some Kind, 1990, Family Math Program, 1994—; officer IMPACT, elem. coord., 1990—. Mem. Ill. Reading Coun., Rock Island, Ill., 1980—, Jr. Women's Club-Geneseo, 1988; pres. PTA, 1992-94, life mem. Avocations: aerobics, tennis, boating, skiing. Home: 203 Longview Dr Geneseo IL 61254-9113

SIMONS, ALBERT, JR., retired lawyer; b. Charleston, S.C., Nov. 20, 1918; s. Albert and Harriet Porcher (Stoney) S.; m. Caroline Pinckney Mitchell, June 18, 1948; children: Albert III, Julian Mitchell, Cotesworth Pinckney, Caroline Pinckney. A.B., Princeton U., 1940; LL.B., Yale U., 1947. Bar: S.C. 1947, U.S. Dist Ct. (ea. and we. dists.) S.C. 1948, U.S. Ct. Appeals (4th cir.) 1948, U.S. Supreme Ct 1960. Sole practice Charleston, 1948; assoc. Sinkler & Gibbs, Charleston, 1948; ptnr. Sinkler Gibbs & Simons, Charleston, 1949-87, Sinkler & Boyd, Charleston, 1987-91. Mem. City Coun., Charleston, 1954-59; mem. Charleston County Bd. of Assessment Control, 1965-82; bd. dirs. S.C. Mcpl. Coun., Legal Aid Soc., Family Agy. Maj. AUS, 1941-46. Decorated Bronze Star medal. Fellow Am. Coll. Probate Counsel; mem. Am., S.C., Charleston County bar assns., St. Cecilia Soc., S.C. Soc., Soc. of Cin., Soc. Colonial Wars, St. Georges Soc., Carolina Art Assn. (former dir.), S.C. Hist. Soc. (past dir.), Charleston Library Soc. (trustee), Hibernian Soc., Princeton Alumni Assn. of S.C. (past pres.), Masons (Charleston), Rotary (Charleston), Carolina Yacht Club (Charleston), Charleston Club, St. John's Hunting Club at Pooshee Plantation (Berkley County), Alpha Tau Omega, Phi Delta Phi. Episcopalian. Home: Apt 207 1 King St Charleston SC 29401-2719 Office: 160 E Bay St Charleston SC 29401-2120

SIMONS, ALBERT, III, lawyer; b. Charleston, S.C., Nov. 22, 1950; s. Albert Jr. and Caroline Pinckney (Mitchell) S.; m. Theodora Bonnell Wilbur, Jan. 28, 1970; children: Albert IV, Charles A. BA, U. Va., 1972, JD, 1976. Bar: S.C. 1977, N.Y. 1978. Assoc. Brown, Wood, Ivey, Mitchell & Petty (now Brown & Wood), N.Y.C., 1977-84; ptnr. Orrick, Herrington & Sutcliffe, N.Y.C., 1984—. Mem. S.C. Bar Assn., N.Y. State Bar Assn. Office: Orrick Herrington & Sutcliffe 666 Fifth Ave New York NY 10103-0001

SIMONS, BARBARA M., lawyer; b. N.Y.C., Feb. 7, 1929; d. Samuel A. and Minnie (Mankes) Malitz; m. Morton L. Simons, Sept. 2, 1951; 1 child, Claudia. BA, U. Mich., 1950, JD, 1952. Bar: N.Y. 1953, U.S. Supreme Ct. 1963, U.S. Ct. Appeals (D.C. cir.) 1971, (5th cir.) 1992, (1st cir.) 1994. Ptnr. Simons & Simons, Washington, 1962—. Active Forest Hills Citizens Assn., Washington; past pres. D.C. chpt. U. Mich. Alumnae, Washington. Alumnae scholar U. Mich., 1946-50. Mem. Washington Coun. Lawyers, Women's Legal Def. Fund, Sierra Club, Phi Beta Kappa, Phi Kappa Phi, Alpha Lambda Delta. Office: Simons & Simons 5025 Linnean Ave NW Washington DC 20008-2042

SIMONS, BARRY THOMAS, lawyer; b. Lynn, Mass., Dec. 14, 1946; s. Emanuel Isador and Betty (Darish) S.; m. Laurie Jean Louder, May 5, 1985; children: Britton Eugene, Brett Jacob. BS in Govt., Am. Univ., 1968; JD, NYU, 1971. Bar: Calif. 1971, U.S. Dist. Ct. (ctrl. dist.) Calif. 1972, U.S. Ct. Appeals (9th cir.) 1972, U.S. Supreme Ct. 1978, U.S. Dist. Ct. (so. and no. dists.) Calif. 1979. Pvt. practice Laguna Beach, Calif., 1971—. Editor (law rev.) N.Y. Law Forum, 1971. Apptd. mem. gen. plan revision com. and local coastal task force City of Laguna Beach, 1980. Mem. Orange County Bar Assn. (bd. dirs. 1981), Newport/Harbor Bar Assn. (bd. dirs. 1979), South Orange County Bar Assn. (pres. 1986, bd. dirs. 1980-95), Calif. Attys. for Criminal Justice (chair misdemeanor com. 1995), Nat. Assn. Criminal Def. Attys., Nat. Coll. D.U.I. Def. (founding mem.). Office: 260 Saint Anns Dr Laguna Beach CA 92651-2737

SIMONS, CHARLES EARL, JR., federal judge; b. Johnston, S.C., Aug. 17, 1916; s. Charles Earl Sr. and Frances (Rhoden) S.; m. Jean Knapp, Oct. 18, 1941 (dec. 1991); children: Charles Earl III, Paul Knapp, Richard Brewster, Jean Brewster Smith. AB, U. S.C., 1937, LLB cum laude, 1939. Bar: S.C. 1939. Ptnr. Lybrand & Simons, Aiken, S.C., 1939-50, Thurmond, Lybrand and Simons, Aiken, 1950-54, Lybrand, Simons & Rich, Aiken, 1950-54, 1954-64; mem. S.C. Ho. of Reps., 1942, 47-48, 61-64; mem. ways and means com., 1947-48, 61-64; judge U.S. Dist. Ct. S.C., Aiken, 1964—, chief judge, 1980-86; sr. status U.S. Dist. Ct., 1987—; mem. S.C. Constl. Revision Com., 1948, Bd. Discipline and Grievance, S.C. Bar, 1958-61, Ethics Adv. Panel, 1981-87; jud. rep. 4th cir. Jud. Conf. U.S., 1973-79; chmn. subcom. on fed. jurisdiction of Com. on Ct. Adminstrn., 1986-87. Mem. Chief Met. Dist. Judges Conf., 1980-89, chmn., 1986-89; bd. dirs. S.C. Athletic Hall of Fame; mem. Jud. Conf. Commn. on Jud. Br., 1988-92. With USN, World War II. Recipient Algernon Sidney Sullivan award, 1937, 64. Mem ABA, S.C. Bar Assn. (com. mem.), Am. Law Inst., Am. Legion, U. S.C. Alumni Assn. (past pres. 1964), S.C. Golf Assn., Aiken Bus. Men's Club (past pres.), Palmetto Golf Club (pres. 1994-97), Rotary. Baptist. Home: PO Box 2185 Aiken SC 29802-2185 Office: US Dist Ct SC Charles E Simons Jr Fed Courthouse PO Box 2185 Aiken SC 29802-2185

SIMONS, DOLPH COLLINS, JR., newspaper publisher; b. Lawrence, Kans., Mar. 11, 1930; s. Dolph Collins and Marie (Nelson) S.; m. Pamela Counseller, Feb. 7, 1952; children: Pamela, Linda, Dolph Collins, Dan. A.B., U. Kans., 1951; LL.D. (hon.), Colby Coll., 1972. Reporter Lawrence Jour.-World, 1953, asso. pub., 1957, pub., 1962—, editor, 1978—, pres., 1969—; reporter The Times, London, 1956, Johannesburg (South Africa) Star, 1958; pres. World Co.; mgr. WorldWest; bd. dirs. Commerce Bancshares, Kansas City, Mo.; mem. Pulitzer Awards Jury, 1977, 78, 80, 81. Trustee, past pres. William Allen White Found.; trustee Midwest Rsch. Inst., Menninger Found., Nat. Parks and Conservation Assn., The Kans. Nature Conservancy; former mem. governing bd. Children's Mercy Hosp., Kansas City, Mo.; trustee, chmn. U. Kans. Endowment Assn.; past bd. dirs. Greater Kansas City Community Found.; former trustee The Freedom Forum. Served to capt. USMRC, 1951-53. Recipient Elijah Parish Lovejoy award, 1972; Fred Ellsworth award for significant service to U. Kans., 1976; Disting. Service citation, 1980. Mem. Newspaper Advt. Bur. (past dir.), Am. Soc. Newspaper Editors, Inland Daily Press Assn. (past dir.), Kans. Press Assn. (past pres., dir.), AP (past dir.), Am. Newspaper Pubs. Assn. (past dir., past nat. sec.), Lawrence C. of C. (past pres., dir.), U. Kans. Alumni Assn. (past pres., dir.), Sigma Delta Chi, Phi Delta Theta. Republican. Episcopalian. Clubs: Lawrence Country, Kansas City Country, Kansas City River. Lodges: Masons, Rotary. Home: 2425 Vermont St Lawrence KS 66046-4761 Office: 609 New Hampshire St Lawrence KS 66044-2243

SIMONS, DONA, artist; b. Bryn Athyn, Pa., Aug. 10, 1953; d. Keneth Alden and Reta Isabel (Evens) S.; m. John Louis Vigo, May 17, 1986. Student, Phila. Coll. Art, 1974, Moore Coll. Art, 1976, Pa. Acad. Fine Arts, 1977-79. One-woman shows include Frank Tanzer Gallery, Boston, 1975, The Curaçao Mus., Netherlands Antilles, 1991, The Curaçao Seaquarium, Netherlands Antilles, 1991, Sylvia Schmidt Gallery, New Orleans, 1992, Mobil Oil Co. bldg. lobbies, 1997; exhibited in group shows at Berg Gallery, Jenkintown, Pa., 1973, United Artisans Gallery, Chalfont, Pa., 1974, 75, Arthur Roger Gallery, New Orleans, La., 1980, Arts Coun. New Orleans Acad. Fine Arts, La., 1982, Am. Italian Renaissance Found., New Orleans, 1985, Found. Prince Pierre de Monaco, Monaco, 1985, The Rittenhouse Galleries, Phila., 1993, 94, Sylvia Schmidt Gallery, New Orleans, 1993, 94, 95, 96,; commn. portrait of Manuel Piar, Curaçao, Netherlands Antilles, 1990; represented in permanent collection Percent for Art Program, City of New Orleans, 1997. Office: Sylvia Schmidt Gallery 400 Julia St # A New Orleans LA 70130-3606

SIMONS, ELIZABETH R(EIMAN), biochemist, educator; b. Vienna, Austria, Sept. 1, 1929; came to U.S., 1941, naturalized, 1948; d. William and Erna Engle (Weisselberg) Reiman; B.Ch.E., Cooper Union, N.Y.C., 1950; M.S., Yale U., 1951, Ph.D., 1954; m. Harold Lee Simons, Aug. 12, 1951; children—Leslie Ann Mulert, Robert David. Research chemist Tech. Operations, Arlington, Mass., 1953-54; instr. chemistry Wellesley (Mass.) Coll., 1954-57; rsch. asst. children's Hosp. Med. Center and Cancer Rsch. Found., Boston, 1957-59, rsch. assoc. pathology, 1959-62; research assoc. Harvard Med. Sch., 1962-66, lectr. biol. chemistry, 1966-72; tutor biochemical scis. Harvard Coll., 1971-94 (ret.); assoc. prof. biochemistry Boston U., 1972-78, prof., 1978—. Contbr. articles to profl. jours. Grantee in field. Mem. AAAS, Am. Chem. Soc., Am. Heart Assn., Am. Soc. Biol. Chemists, Am. Soc. Cell Biology, Am. Soc. Hematology, Assn. Women in Sci., Biophys. Soc., Internat. Soc. Thrombosis and Hemostasis, N.Y. Acad. Sci., Sigma Xi. Office: Boston U Sch Medicine 80 E Concord St Roxbury MA 02118-2307

SIMONS, GALE GENE, nuclear and electrical engineer, educator; b. Kingman, Kans., Sept. 25, 1939; s. Robert Earl and Laura V. (Swartz) S.; m. Barbara Irene Rinkel, July 2, 1966; 1 child, Curtis Dean. BS, Kans. State U., 1962, MS, 1964, PhD, 1968. Engr. Argonne Nat. Lab., Idaho Falls, Idaho, 1968-77, mgr. fast source reactor, head exptl. support group, 1972-77; prof. nuclear engring. Kans. State U., Manhattan, 1977—, assoc. dean for rsch., dir. rsch. coun. Coll. Engring., 1988-97, bd. dirs. Rsch. Found., 1988-97, Presdl. lectr., 1983—, career counselor, 1984—; cons. to pvt. and fed. agys., 1983—; bd. dirs. Kans. Tech. Enterprise Corp., Topeka; com. mem. Kans. Gov.'s Energy Policy Com., Topeka, 1992-97; numerous presentations in field; reviewer proposals fed. agys. Contbr. over 100 articles to sci. jours.; patentee radiation dosimeter. Expert witness State of Kans., Topeka, 1986. Fellow AEC, 1964-67; numerous grants from fed. agys., 1979—. Mem. AAAS, IEEE, Am. Nuclear Soc., Health Physics Soc., Am. Soc. for Engring. Edn., Masons, Rotary, Phi Kappa Phi, Tau Beta Pi, Pi Mu Epsilon. Home: 2395 Grandview Ter Manhattan KS 66502-3729 Office: Kans State U Durland Hall Rm 261 Manhattan KS 66506-5103

SIMONS, HELEN, school psychologist, psychotherapist; b. Chgo., Feb. 13, 1930; d. Leo and Sarah (Shrayer) Pomper; m. Broudy Simons, May 20, 1956 (May 1972); children: Larry, Sheri. BA in Biol., Lake Forest Coll., 1951; MA in Clin. Psychology, Roosevelt U., 1972; D of Psychology, Ill. Sch. Profl. Psychology, 1980. Intern Cook County Hosp., Chgo., 1979-80; pvt. practice psychotherapist Chgo., 1980—; sch. psychologist Chgo. Bd. Edn., 1974-79, 80—. Contbr. articles on psychotherapy of A.D.D. and P.T.S.D. children to profl. jours. Mem. APA, Nat. Sch. Psychologists Assn., Midwestern Psychol. Assn., Mental Health Assn. Ill., Ill. Psychol. Assn., Ill. Sch. Psychologists Assn., Chgo. Psychol. Assn., Chgo. Sch. Psychol. Assn., Internat. Coun. Psychologists. Avocations: music, dancing, reading. Home: 6145 N Sheridan Rd Apt 29D Chicago IL 60660-2883 Office: Brennemann Sch 4251 N Clarendon Ave Chicago IL 60613-1523

SIMONS, LAWRENCE BROOK, lawyer; b. N.Y.C., Oct. 19, 1924; s. Harry A. and Marion B. (Brook) S.; m. Annalou Kadin, Aug. 24, 1947; children: Barbara Flexner, Kenneth. Student, Duke U., 1941-43, 46-47; JD, Columbia U., 1949. Bar: N.Y. 1949, D.C. 1984, U.S. Dist. Ct. (so. dist.) N.Y. 1949, U.S. Supreme Ct. 1987. Assoc. Spring & Eastman, N.Y.C., 1949-53; v.p., gen. mgr. Caribe Knitting Mills, San Juan, P.R., 1953-58; pres. LBS Constrn. Co. Inc., S.I., N.Y., 1958-77; asst. sec. housing FHA commn. HUD, Washington, 1977-81; ptnr. Powell, Goldstein, Frazier & Murphy, Washington, 1981—; mem. Task Force on Quality of Life, Dept. of Def., 1995. Trustee Bayley Seton Hosp., S.I., 1981-90, NHP Found., Inc., 1991—; chmn. bd. dirs. N.Y. State Urban Devel. Corp., 1975-77, Nat. Housing Conf., 1981—, Pa. Ave. Devel. Corp., 1981-87; mem. Nat. Housing Task Force, 1988, Nat. Housing Trust, 1990—; trustee Affordable Housing Found., 1990-92, Ctr. for Democracy, 1990-96; pres. Ctr. for Housing Policy, 1992-96, bd. dirs., 1996—. With U.S. Army, 1943-46, ETO. Named Man of Yr. Nat. Housing Conf., Washington, 1985. Mem. ABA, Nat. Assn. Home Builders, Richmond County C. of C., Army Navy C. of C., Sea Pines Country Club, Lambda Alpha. Democrat. Jewish. Avocation: golf. Home: 40 Plantation Dr Hilton Head SC 29928 Office: Powell Goldstein Frazier Murphy 1001 Pennsylvania Ave NW Washington DC 20004-2505

SIMONS, LEWIS MARTIN, journalist; b. Paterson, N.J., Jan. 9, 1939; s. Abram and Goldie (Fleisher) S.; m. Carol Lenore Seiderman, Feb. 7, 1965; children: Justine, Rebecca, Adam P.D. BA, NYU, 1962; MS, Columbia U., 1964. Corr. AP, Kuala Lumpur, Singapore, Saigon, Denver, 1965-70, Washington Post, Bangkok, New Delhi, 1971-82; bur. chief Knight-Ridder Newspapers, Tokyo, 1982-95; fgn. policy corr. Time mag., 1996-97. Author: Worth Dying For, 1987. With USMC, 1962-64. Recipient Grand prize and Investigative Reporting award Am. Newspaper Guild, 1981, Citation for Excellence, Overseas Press Club Am., 1983, Jessie Meriton White award Friends World Coll., 1986, Investigative Reporters and Editors award U. Mo., 1986, Award of Excellence, World Affairs Coun., 1984, 86, 89, 92, Pulitzer Prize, 1986, George Polk award, 1985, Malcolm S. Forbes award Overseas Press Club Am., 1986, 92, Gerald Loeb award UCLA, 1993; Edward R. Murrow fellow Coun. of Fgn. Rels., 1970-71. Mem. Fgn. Corrs. Club Japan (bd. dirs. 1991-92, pres., 1993-94).

SIMONS, LYNN OSBORN, state education official; b. Havre, Mont., June 1, 1934; d. Robert Blair and Dorothy (Briggs) Osborn; BA, U. Colo., 1956; postgrad. U. Wyo., 1958-60; m. John Powell Simons, Jan. 19, 1957; children: Clayton Osborn, William Blair. Tchr., Midvale (Utah) Jr. High Sch., 1956-57, Sweetwater County Sch. Dist. 1, Rock Springs, Wyo., 1957-58, U. Wyo., Laramie, 1959-61, Natrona County Sch. Dist. 1, Casper, Wyo., 1963-64; credit mgr. Gallery 323, Casper, 1972-77; Wyo. state supt. public instrn., Cheyenne, 1979-91; sec.'s regional rep. region VIII U.S. Dept. Edn., Denver, 1993—; mem. State Bds. Charities and Reform, Land Commrs., Farm Loan, 1979-91; mem. State Commns. Capitol Bldg., Liquor, 1979-91; Ex-officio mem. bd. trustees U. Wyo., 1979-91; ex-officio mem. Wyo. Community Coll. Commn., 1979-91; mem. steering com. Edn. Commn. of the States, 1988-90; mem. State Bd. Edn., 1971-77, chmn., 1976-77; advisor Nat. Trust for Hist. Preservation, 1980-86. Bd. dirs. Denver Fed. Exec. Bd., 1995—. Mem. LWV (pres. 1970-71). Democrat. Episcopalian. Office: US Dept Edn 1244 Speer Blvd Ste 310 Denver CO 80204-3582

SIMONS, RICHARD DUNCAN, lawyer; b. Niagara Falls, N.Y., Mar. 23, 1927; s. William Taylor and Sybil Irene (Swick) S.; m. Muriel (Penny) E.

Genung, June 9, 1951 (dec. 1992); m. Esther (Esi) Turkington Tremblay, May 21, 1994; children: Ross T., Scott R., Kathryn E., Linda A. AB, Colgate U., 1949; LLB, U. Mich., 1952; LLD (hon.), Albany Law Sch., 1983. Bar: N.Y. 1952. Pvt. practice Rome, N.Y., 1952-63; asst. corp. counsel City of Rome, 1955-58, corp. counsel, 1960-63; justice 5th jud. dist. N.Y. Supreme Ct., 1964-83, assoc. justice appellate divsn. 3d dept., 1971-72, assoc. justice appellate divsn. 4th dept., 1973-82; assoc. judge N.Y. Ct. Appeals, 1983-96, acting chief judge, 1992-93; counsel McMahon, Grow & Getty, Rome, Ky., 1997—; mem. Law Sch. Admission Svcs., Bar Passage Study Com. Editorial staff: N.Y. Pattern Jury Instructions, 1979-83. Chmn. Republican City Com., 1958-62; vice chmn. Oneida County Rep. Com., 1958-62; bd. mgrs. Rome Hosp. and Murphy Meml. Hosp., 1953. Served with USN, World War II. NEH fellow U. Va. Law Sch., 1979. Fellow Am. Bar Found., N.Y. State Bar Found. (chmn. 1997); mem. ABA, N.Y. State Bar Assn., Oneida County Bar Assn., Rome Bar Assn., Am. Law Inst., Inst. Jud. Adminstrn. Home: 6520 Pillmore Dr Rome NY 13440-2704 Office: McMahon Grow & Getty 301 N Washington St Rome NY 13440-5105

SIMONS, STEPHEN, mathematics educator, researcher; b. London, Aug. 11, 1938; came to U.S., 1965; s. Jack Isidore Simons and Ethel Esther (Littman) Harris; m. Jacqueline Mania Berchadsky, Aug. 13, 1963; 1 son, Mark. BA, Cambridge U., Eng., 1959, PhD, 1962. Instr. U. B.C., Vancouver, Can., 1962-63; asst. prof. U. BC., Vancouver, Can., 1964-65; asst. prof. U. Calif., Santa Barbara, 1965-67, assoc. prof., 1967-73, prof., 1973—, chmn. dept., 1975-77, 88-89; trustee Math. Scis. Rsch. Inst., Berkeley, Calif., 1988-94. Peterhouse rsch. fellow, Cambridge U., 1963-64. Mem. Am. Math. Soc., Inst. for Ops. Rsch. and Mgmt. Scis. Office: Univ Calif Dept Math Santa Barbara CA 93106

SIMONS, THOMAS W., JR., ambassador; b. Crosby, Minn., Sept. 4, 1938; married; 2 children. BA, Yale U., 1958; MA, Harvard U., 1959, PhD, 1963. Joined Fgn. Svc., Dept. State, 1964; sec. del., tech. sec. U.S. Del. to 6th round trade negotiation in GATT, 1967-68; consular officer Am. Embassy, Warsaw, Poland, 1969-71; polit. officer Dept. State, Washington, 1971-72; Coun. on Fgn. Rels. fellow Hoover Instn., Stanford, Calif., 1972-74; internat. rels. officer Bur. Politico-Mil. Affairs, 1974-75, mem. policy planning staff, 1975-77; chief external reporting unit, polit. sect. Am. Embassy, Moscow, 1977-79; dep. chief of mission Am. Embassy, Bucharest, Romania, 1979-81; counselor for polit. affairs Am. Embassy, London, 1981-85; dir. for Soviet Union affairs Dept. State, 1985-86; mem. Sr. Seminar in Fgn. Policy, 1986-89; dep. asst. sec. for European and Can. affairs Dept. State, 1989-90; diplomat-in-residence, vis. scholar, adj. prof. history Brown U., Providence, 1990—.

SIMONSON, BRUCE MILLER, geologist, educator; b. Washington, May 13, 1950; s. Roy Walter and Susan (Miller) S.; m. Sue Mareske, June 28, 1974; children: Joseph Walter, Sonja Anne, Maya Beth. BA with high honors, Wesleyan U., Middletown, Conn., 1972; PhD, Johns Hopkins U., 1982. Field mapper Nat. Geog. Inst., Honduras, 1973-74; instr. dept. geology Oberlin (Ohio) Coll., 1979-81, asst. prof., 1982-85, assoc. prof., 1986-88, prof., 1989—, chmn. dept. geology, 1986-89, 93-97; adj. faculty Case We. Res. U., Cleve., 1983—; vis. scientist Geol. Survey, We. Australia, summers, 1985-87, 89, 93; tchr. U.S. Geol. Survey, Reston, Va., 1985; vis. prof. U.S. Geol. Survey, Denver, Colo., 1992-93. Contbr. articles to profl. jours. Grantee Nat. Geog. Soc., 1986-89, 93-94, 96-97, NSF, 1977-79, 84, 91-94, Rsch. Corp., 1983, Petroleum Rsch. Fund, 1982-84. Mem. Geol. Soc. Am., Geol. Soc. Australia, No. Ohio Geol. Soc., Soc. for Sedimentary Geology (sec. Gt. Lakes sect. 1986-90), Sigma Xi. Office: Oberlin Coll Dept Geology Oberlin OH 44074-1044

SIMONSON, DAVID C., retired newspaper association executive; b. N.Y.C., May 9, 1927; s. Simon and Rebecca (Coolman) S.; m. Lois E. Sneider, Nov. 1, 1952; children: Peter, Eric, John Frederick. BA, Hamilton Coll., 1948; postgrad., U. Vt., 1949, Art Student League of N.Y., 1949. Copywriter Forwell & Mart Advt., N.Y.C., 1949-50; reporter, editor Croton-Cortlandt News, Croton, N.Y., 1950-52; gen. mgr. Colony Publs., N.Y.C., 1952-54; editor, mgr. County Press Newspapers, Croton, 1955-59; promotion dir. Amcrete Corp., Peekskill, N.Y., 1959-60; various positions in mgmt. Patent Trader, Mt. Kisco, N.Y., 1960-72, pub., 1972-77; pres./pub. Pioneer Press Newspapers, Wilmette, Ill., 1977-86; exec. v.p., chief exec. officer Nat. Newspaper Assn., Washington, 1987-92; retired, 1992; bd. dirs. Christian Herald Assn., Chappaqua, N.Y.; lectr. Medill Sch. Journalism, Meridian House, U.S.A., numerous state press assns.; media cons.; seminar leader Eastern Europe for World Press Freedom Com.; cons. to Slovenian publs. for U.S. Info. Agy., 1993-94, cons. to Slovakian publs. for USIA, 1995; cons. to African publs. for UNESCO, 1995; cons. to Bulgarian Publs. for USIA, 1997; seminar leader Voice of Am. for Bulgarian pubs., 1997; participant Freedom Forum Roundtables. Chmn. planning bd. Town of Croton-on-Hudson, N.Y., 1962-67, trustee, 1967, mayor, 1969. With USNR, 1945-46. Mem. Suburban Newspapers Am. (pres. 1984-85, bd. dirs. 1980-84), Ill. Press Assn (bd. dirs. 1980-84, 1st v.p. 1986), N.Y. Press Assn. (bd. dirs. 1966-76, 1st v.p. 1976), Nat. Newspaper Assn. (bd. dirs. 1985-86), Cook County Pubs. Assn. (pres. 1983-84). Avocations: painting, cartooning. Home: 1805 28th St S Arlington VA 22202-1536

SIMONSON, JOHN ALEXANDER, banking executive; b. Port Huron, Mich., July 22, 1945; s. Fred Alexander and Harriet (Woolfolk) S.; m. Juleen Marie Sheridan, June 18, 1971 (div. 1991); children: Laura E., Anne M. AB, U. Mich., 1967; MBA, Mich. State U., 1968. Exec. v.p., treas. Key Corp., Inc., Cleve., 1992—. Home: 225 Westwind Dr Apt 49 Avon Lake OH 44012-2420 Office: Key Bank NA Key Tower 127 Paul St Cleveland OH 44146-4602

SIMONSON, LEE STUART, broadcast company executive; b. Balt., July 3, 1948; s. Theodore and Sara (Silver) S.; m. Nancy Paula Levin, Mar. 25, 1973; children: Laura Todd, Michael Theodore. BA, U. Md., 1970. Acct. exec. WGMS-AM-FM (subs. RKO Gen.), Washington, 1971-73, retail sales mgr., 1973-76; sales mgr. WFYR-FM (subs. RKO Gen.), Chgo., 1976-80; v.p., gen. mgr. WRKS-FM (subs. RKO Gen.), N.Y.C., 1980-84, WOR-AM (subs. RKO Gen.), N.Y.C., 1984-88; vice chmn., COO, owner radio stas. Broadcasting Ptnrs., Inc., N.Y.C., 1988-95; chmn., CEO Broadcasting Ptnrs. Holdings, LP, N.Y.C., 1997—. Bd. dirs. N.Y.C. chpt. March of Dimes, 1982—, IRTS Found., 1995—; bd. dirs. Broadcast Pioneers Libr., Washington, 1995—. With USAR, 1970-76. Jewish. Office: 350 Park Ave Fl 20 New York NY 10022-6022

SIMONSON, SUSAN KAY, hospital administrator; b. La Porte, Ind., Dec. 5, 1946; d. George Randolph and Myrtle Lucille (Opfel) Menkes; m. Richard Bruce Simonson, Aug. 25, 1973. BA with honors, Ind. U., 1969; MA, Washington U., St. Louis, 1972. Perinatal social worker Yakima Valley Meml. Hosp., Yakima, Wash., 1979-81, dir. patient support and hospice program, 1981—, dir. social svc., 1982—; instr. Spanish, ethnic studies, sociology Yakima Valley Coll., Yakima, Wash., 1981—; pres. Yakima Child Abuse Council, 1983-85; developer nat. patient support program, 1981. Contbr. articles to profl. jours. Mem. Jr. League, Yakima; mem. adv. council Robert Wood Johnson Found. Rural Infant Health Care Project, Yakima, 1980, Pregnancy Loss and Compassionate Friends Support Groups, Yakima, 1982—, Teen Outreach Program, Yakima, 1984—. Recipient NSF award, 1967, discharge planning program of yr. regional award Nat. Glasrock Home Health Care Discharge Planning Program, 1987; research grantee Ind. U., 1968, Fulbright grantee U.S. Dept. State, 1969-70; Nat. Def. Edn. Act fellowship, 1970-73. Mem. AAUW, Soc. Med. Anthropology, Soc. Hosp. Social Work Dirs. of Am. Hosp. Assn. (regional award 1989), Nat. Assn. Social Workers, Phi Beta Kappa. Office: Yakima Valley Meml Hosp 2811 Tieton Dr Yakima WA 98902-3761

SIMONSON, TED, principal. Prin. Los Gatos (Calif.) High Sch. Recipient Blue Ribbon Sch. award, 1990-91. Office: Los Gatos High Sch 20 High School Ct Los Gatos CA 95032-6917*

SIMONT, MARC, artist; b. Paris, France, Nov. 23, 1915; came to U.S., 1927, naturalized, 1936; s. Josep and Dolors (Basté) S.; m. Sara Dalton, Apr. 7, 1945; 1 son, Marc Dalton. Attended, Académie Julian, Academie Ranson, André Lhote Sch., all Paris, 1932-35, NAD, N.Y.C., 1936. Asst. to Ezra Winter on Jefferson Wing mural Library of Congress, 1940; author, illustrator 9 children's books, 1939—; illustrator 80 books; author, illustrator: Opera Soufflé, 1950, Polly's Oats, 1951, The Lovely Summer, 1952, (with Red Smith) How to Get to First Base, 1952, Mimi, 1955, The Plumber Out of the Sea, 1955, The Contest at Paca, 1959, How Come Elephants?, 1965, Afternoon in Spain, 1965, A Childs' Eye View of the World, 1972; translator, illustrator The Lieutenant Colonel and The Gypsy, 1971; translator Ibrahim, 1989. Recipient Caldecott honor, 1950, Caldecott award, 1957, citation merit Soc. Illustrators, 1965; Tiffany Found. fellow, 1937. Mem. Am. Vets. Com., Authors Guild. Home: 336 Town St West Cornwall CT 06796-1304

SIMONTACCHI, CAROL NADINE, nutritionist, retail store executive; b. Bellingham, Wash., July 6, 1947; d. Ralph Eugene and Sylvia Arleta (Tyler) Walmer; m. Bob Simontacchi, Oct. 3, 1981; children: Caryl Anne, Bobbie Anne, Melissa Anne, Laurie Anne. BS in Health and Human Svcs., Columbia Pacific U., 1996, postgrad., 1996—. Cert. nutritionist, Wash. CEO The Health Haus, Inc., Vancouver, Wash., 1985—; host radio program Back to the Beginning, Vancouver, 1990—; CEO The Natural Physician Ctr., Beaverton, Oreg., 1995—, Enique Internat., 1995—; chair bd. dirs. Enique Internat., 1996—. Author: Your Fat is Not Your Fault, 1994, 97, The Sun Rise Book: Living Beyond Depression, 1996. Mem. Soc. Cert. Nutritionists (pres. bd. 1992-93), Nat. Nutritional Foods Assn. (chair edn. com. 1996—), Internat. Assn. Clin. Nutritionists, Am. Assn. Clin. Nutritionists. Republican. Christian Ch. Office: The Health Haus Inc 101 E 8th St Ste 250 Vancouver WA 98660-3294

SIMOPOULOS, ARTEMIS PANAGEOTIS, physician, educator; b. Kampos-Avias, Greece, Apr. 3, 1933; came to U.S. 1949, naturalized 1955; d. Panageotis L. and Nena P. (Konteas) S.; m. Alan Lee Pinkerson, Jan. 10, 1957; children: Daphne, Lee, Alexandra. B.A., Barnard Coll., 1952; M.D., Boston U., 1956. Diplomate Am. Bd. Pediatrics. Pediatric intern Kings County Hosp., Bklyn., 1956-57; resident Kings County Hosp., 1957-58; fellow in hematology Children's Hosp., Washington, 1960-61, asst. chief resident in pediatrics, 1961-62, mem. acad. staff, 1962-67, assoc. staff in pediatric nursery service, 1967-71; spl. lectr. pediatrics Ewha Woman's U. Sch. Medicine, Seoul, Korea, 1958-59; asst. prof. pediatrics George Washington U. Sch. Medicine, 1962-67, clin. asst. prof., 1967-71; dir. nurseries George Washington U. Hosp., 1965-67; staff pediatrician Nat. Heart and Lung Inst., NIH, 1968-71, cons. endocrinology br., 1971-78; with div. med. scis. Nat. Acad. Scis., NRC, Washington, 1971-74; exec. sec. Nat. Acad. Scis., NRC, 1974-76, exec. dir. bd. maternal, child and family health research, 1974-76; cons. to dir. Nat. Inst. Child Health and Human Devel., NIH, Bethesda, Md, 1976-77; chief devel. biology and nutrition br., ctrs. for research for mothers and children Nat. Inst. Child Health and Human Devel., NIH, 1977; vice chmn. and exec. sec. nutrition coordinating com. NIH, 1977-78; cons. nutrition and health to spl. asst. to the Pres. for Consumer Affairs The White House, Washington, 1978-81; chmn. nutrition coordinating com. office of the dir. NIH, 1978-86; dir. divsn. nutrtional sci. Internat. Life Sci. Inst. Rsch. Found., Washington, 1986-88; dir. Ctr. for Genetics, Nutrition and Health, Washington, 1989-90, pres., 1990—; co-chmn., exec. sec. joint subcom. Human Nutrition Rsch., Office Sci. and Tech. Policy, Exec. Office of the Pres., 1979-83; vis. prof. Harokopio U., Athens, 1994-95. Editor World Rev. Nutrition and Dietetics, 1989—; contbg. editor Nutrition Revs., 1979—; mem. editorial bd. Jour. Nutrition, Growth, and Cancer, 1982—, Internat. Jour. Vitamin and Nutrition Research, 1986—, n=3 News, 1986-90, Annals Nutrition and Metabolism, 1991—, Food Revs. Internat., 1994—; cons. editor Nutrition Research, 1983—, Annals Internal Medicine, 1984—, Jour. AMA, 1985—, Food Reviews Internat., 1994—; contbr. articles in endocrinology, genetics, nutrition and fitness, omega-3 fatty acids, and obesity to profl. jours. Recipient 1st Presdl. award for studies in field of obesity and weight control Columbia-Presbyn. Med. Ctr., 1993, Outstanding Achievement award promoting nutrition and fitness and positive health Greek Govt., 1992; NIH grantee, 1960-61. Fellow Am. Acad. Pediatrics, Am. Coll. Nutrition; mem. Soc. Pediatric Rsch., Endocrine Soc., Maternity Ctr. Assn. (rsch. adv. com.), Am. Pediatric Soc., Am. Inst. Nutrition, Am. Soc. Clin. Nutrition, Am. Assn. for World Health (v.p. 1981-90, asst. treas. 1981-90, nat. chmn. for World Health Day 1982—, vice chmn. bd. 1991-92, chmn. pgm. com. 1993—, bd. dirs. 1993—), D.C. Med. Soc., N.Am. Assn. for Study Obesity, Internat. Life Scis. Inst. (trustee 1982-88, exec. com. 1982-85, trustee Nutrition Found. 1985-87), Internat. Soc. Study of Fatty Acids and Lipids (sec., treas. 1991-94, 95—). Greek Orthodox. Home: 4330 Klingle St NW Washington DC 20016-3577 Office: Ctr Genetics Nutrition and Health 2001 S St NW Ste 530 Washington DC 20009-1125

SIMOS, EVANGELOS OTTO, economist, editor; b. Patras, Achia, Greece, May 18, 1947; came to U.S., 1972; s. Otto Evangelos and Demetra E. Dervenis; m. Louisa E., Apr. 18, 1972; children: Demetra E., Maria E. BS, Athens (Greece) Grad. Sch. Bus. and Econs., 1972; MA, No. Ill. U., 1975, PhD, 1977. V.p., economist D-Glass Co., Piraeus, Greece, 1969-72; instr. econs. No. Ill., Dekalb, 1976-77; prof. econs. U. N.H., Durham, 1977—, chmn. econs. program, 1987-90; v.p., chief Economist Infometrica, Inc., 1993—; sr. ptnr., founder Global Numis. Prognostications, 1987-94; v.p. econ. devel. World Trade Group N.H., 1989-91; editor, chief economist IBR, Inc., Dover, N.H., 1982-85. Chief editor Internat. Bus. Conditions Digest, 1983-85; editor for internat. affairs Jour. of Bus. Forecasting, 1987—, Quar. Domestic and Global Forecasts of Key Econ. Indicators, 1987—; editorial rev. bd. Rev. of Bus.; mem. bd. dirs. Internat. Assn. Bus. Forecasting, 1988-89; contbr. articles to profl. jours. Mem. Beta Gamma Sigma, Omicron Delta Epsilon. Home: 24 Tennyson Ave Dover NH 03820-4147 Office: Univ NH WSBE Durham NH 03824

SIMPICH, WILLIAM MORRIS, public affairs consultant; b. Washington, Sept. 24, 1924; s. Frederick and Margaret (Edwards) S.; m. Margaret Pearson Hunter, Sept. 9, 1950; children: William Morris, Margaret Edwards, John Hunter, Joseph Pearson. Student, George Washington U., 1942-43; BS, U.S. Naval Acad., 1946. Assoc. Ivy Lee & T.J. Ross (name later changed to T.J. Ross & Assocs., Inc.), N.Y.C., 1949-51, 54-63, v.p., 1964, sec., treas., 1965-84, sr. v.p., 1977-84, ret. as exec. v.p., 1984, also bd. dirs. With U.S. Navy, 1946-49, 51-53. Episcopalian. Home: 10450 Lottsford Rd # 4117 Mitchellville MD 20721

SIMPKIN, LAWRENCE JAMES, utilities executive; b. Sault Ste Marie, Mich., Jan. 1, 1933; s. Fred Bernard and Helen Clara (Goetz) S.; m. Agnes Diane L'Huillier, Sept. 3, 1960; children: Lawrence J., Lynn Marie, Dawn Catherine. B.S. in Elec. Engring, Mich. Technol. Inst., 1954; M.S., Wayne State U., 1965. Registered profl. engr., Mich. Engr. Detroit Edison Co., 1957-67, supr. engring. instrumentation, 1967-69, dir. elec. div., 1969-72, dir. engring. research, 1972-75, dir. tech. systems planning, 1975-76, gen. dir. div. services, 1976-82, dir. outage mgmt., 1982-84, dir. nuclear engring., 1985-87, gen. dir. generation engring., 1987—; lectr. Lawrence Inst. Tech., 1965-72; adj. prof. U. Mich., 1974. Contbr. articles to profl. jours. Served to capt. USAF, 1954-57. Mem. IEEE, Engring. Soc. Detroit, Sigma Xi. Home: 22016 Clover Ln Novi MI 48375-5112

SIMPKINS, HENRY, medical educator. BS in Chemistry, U. London, 1964, PhD in Biophys. and Molecular Biology, 1967; MD, U. Miami, 1975. Rsch. biologist U. Calif., San Diego, 1967-69; head lab. molecular biology and biophys. Lady Davis Inst. Med. Rsch. of Jewish Gen. Hosp., Montreal, Can., 1969-75; asst. prof. dept. biochemistry U. Montreal, 1970-73, assoc. prof., 1973-75; resident U. Colo. Med. Ctr., Denver, 1975-78, instr. dept. pathology, 1976-78, asst. prof. dept. pathology, 1976-77, assoc. prof. dept. pathology, 1977-78; assoc. prof. dept. pathology U. Calif., Irvine, 1978-81, prof. dept. pathology, 1981-85; prof. pathology SUNY, N.Y.C., 1985-91; prof., chmn. dept. pathology and lab. medicine Temple U. Med. Sch., Phila., 1991—; head divsns. chem. pathology and hematopathology U. Calif., Irvine, 1978-81, head divsn. hematopathology, 1981-83, head divsn. hematopathology.blood bank, 1983-85, acting chmn. dept. pathology, 1984; cons. hematopathology Long Beach VA Hosp., 1979-85; dir. dept. pathology and lab. medicine U. Hosp. S.I., N.Y., 1985-91; presenter in field. Contbr. articles to profl. jours. Postdoctoral fellow King's Coll., London, 1964-67, U. Calif., San Diego, 1967-69; Ministry Edn. State scholar, Gt. Britain, 1961-64, Sci. Rsch. Coun. scholar, Gt. Britain, 1964-67; Can. MEd. Rsch. Coun. scholar, 1970-75. Mem. Am. Soc. Clin. Pathologists, Am. Assn. Blood Banks, Am. Soc. Hematology, Coll. Am. Pathologists, Internat. Acad. Pathology, The Pluto Club. Office: Temple U Sch Medicine Dept Pathology and Lab Med Philadelphia PA 19140*

SIMPLICIO, JOSEPH S.C., education educator; b. Long Branch, N.J.; s. Philip L. and Angelina (Scott) S.; m. Mary Joan Carnera, July 16, 1972; 1 child, Angela Marie. BA, Seton Hall U., 1971; MA in Teaching, Montclair State U., 1976; PhD, NYU, 1989. Cert. social studies tchr., N.J. Prof. Caldwell (N.J.) Coll., 1992—; mem. curriculum com. King of Kings Pvt. Sch.; panelist N.J. ASCD Ednl. Forum, 1994, Leadership Inst., 1994, The Pres.'s Forum, 1994; presenter in field. Contbr. articles to profl. jours. Dir. exec. bd. Coalition Adoptive Parents; mem. fundraising & orgnl. planning coms. Monmouth County Adoptive Parents Orgn., pub. rels. com. St. Mary's Sch. Adv. Coun. Named Honoree, Ednl. Opportunity Fund, 1995; recipient Excellence in Edn. award West Essex C. of C., 1994. Roman Catholic. Home: PO Box 877 New Monmouth NJ 07748 Office: Caldwell Coll 9 Ryerson Ave Caldwell NJ 07006-6109

SIMPSON, A. W. B., law educator; b. 1931. Fellow Oxford U., Eng., 1955-72; prof. U. Kent, Canterbury, Eng., 1972-84, U. Chgo., 1984-87, U. Mich., Ann Arbor, 1987—. Office: U Mich Law Sch 625 S State St Ann Arbor MI 48109-1215

SIMPSON, ALAN KOOI, former senator; b. Cody, Wyo., Sept. 2, 1931; s. Milward Lee and Lorna (Kooi) S.; m. Ann Schroll, June 21, 1954; children—William Lloyd, Colin Mackenzie, Susan Lorna. BS, U. Wyo., 1954, JD, 1958; LLD (hon.), Calif. Western Sch. of Law, 1983, Colo. Coll., 1986, Notre Dame U., 1987; JD (hon.), Am. U., 1989. Bar: Wyo. 1958, U.S. Supreme Ct. 1964. Asst. atty. gen. State of Wyo., 1959; city atty. City of Cody, 1959-69; partner firm Simpson, Kepler, and Simpson, Cody, Wyo., 1959-78; mem. Wyo. Ho. of Reps., 1964-77, majority whip, 1973-75, majority floor leader, 1975-77, speaker pro tem, 1977; legis. participant Eagleton Inst. Politics, Rutgers U., 1971; mem. U.S. Senate from Wyo., 1978-96, asst. majority leader, 1985-87, asst. minority leader, 1987-95, chmn. vets. affairs com., chmn. fin. subcom. on Social Security and Family Policy, chmn. subcom. on immigration and refugee policy; mem. Sen. Rep. Policy Com. Spec. Com. on Aging; guest lectr. London exchange program Regent's Coll., London, 1987. Formerly v.p., trustee N.W. C.C., Powell, Wyo., 1968-76; trustee Buffalo Bill Hist. Ctr., Cody, Grand Teton Music Festival; del. Nat. Triennial Episcopal Ch. Conv., 1973, 76. With U.S. Army, 1954-56. Recipient Nat. Assn. Land Grant Colls. Centennial Alum award U. Wyo., 1987, Lifetime Svc. award Vietnam Vets. Am., 1993. Mem. Wyo. Bar Assn., Park County Bar Assn., Fifth Jud. Dist. Bar Assn., Am. Bar Assn., Assn. Trial Lawyers Am., U. Wyo. Alumni Assn. (pres. 1962, 63, Disting. Alumnus award 1985), VFW (life), Am. Legion, Amvets. (Silver Helmet award). Lodges: Eagles, Elks, Masons (33 deg.), Shriners, Rotary (pres. local club 1972-73). *

SIMPSON, ALLAN BOYD, real estate company executive; b. Lakeland, Fla., Nov. 24, 1948; s. Alfred Forsythe and Ruth Jeanette (Coker) S.; 1 child, Lauren Leigh. B in Indsl. Ingring., Ga. Inst. Tech., 1970; MBA, U. Pa., 1972. Cert. rev. appraiser; lic. realtor, Ga. Dir. mortgage banking Ackerman & Co., Atlanta, 1972-73; v.p. B.F. Saul & Co., Atlanta, 1973-79; pres. L.J. Hooker, Atlanta, 1979-88; also bd. dirs. Hooker/Barnes, Atlanta; bd. dirs. Hooker Holdings (USA), Inc., Century Ins. Co., Hooker Internat. Devels. Ltd., Hooker Internat. Fin. BV, Charter Credit Corp. Ltd., Simpson Spring, Inc., Strategic Land, Inc., Dunwoody Retail, Inc.; bd. dirs., treas. Midtown Bus. Assn., 1979-88; chmn., CEO The Simpson Orgn., Inc., Coker Capital Corp., 1989—. Bd. dirs. YES Atlanta, 1991—, Atlanta Coll. Art, Theatrical Outfit. Mem. Am. Inst. Indsl. Engrs., MBA Execs. Assn., Bldg. Owners and Mgrs. Assn., Nat. Assn. Realtors, U.S. C. of C., Atlanta C. of C., Internat. Coun. of Shopping Ctrs., Urban Land Inst., Nat. Assn. of Office and Indsl. Pks., Cherokee Town and Country Club, Big Canoe Club, Amelia Island Club. Democrat. Methodist. Home: 1847 Homestead Ave NE Atlanta GA 30306-3163 Office: 600 W Peachtree St NW Atlanta GA 30308-3607

SIMPSON, ALLYSON BILICH, lawyer; b. Pasadena, Calif., Feb. 5, 1951; d. John Joseph and Barbaran Rita (Bessolo) Bilich; m. Roland Gilbert Simpson, Aug. 11, 1979; children: Megan Elise, Erin Marie, Brian Patrick. BS, U. So. Calif., L.A., 1973, JD, 1976. Bar: Calif. 1976. Staff atty. Gen. Telephone Co., Thousand Oaks, Calif., 1978-79; group staff atty., dir. legis. compliance Pacific Mut. Life Ins. Co., Newport Beach, Calif., 1980-86; corp. counsel and sec. Amicare Ins. Co., Beverly Hills, Calif., 1986; assoc. Leboeuf, Lamb, Leiby & MacRae, L.A., 1986-87; from assoc. to ptnr. Musick, Peeler & Garrett, L.A., 1988-94; ptnr. Sonnenschein Nath & Rosenthal, L.A., 1994-95; sr. v.p., sec., gen. counsel Fremont Compensation Ins. Group, Glendale, Calif., 1995—; vis. pro. bus. law U. So. Calif., L.A., 1981. Trustee St. Anne's Maternity Home Found., L.A., 1991-97; bd. dirs. St. Anne's Maternity Home, L.A., 1993-97. Mem. Western Pension and Benefits Conf., Conf. Ins. Counsel, Am. Corp. Counsel Assn. Republican. Roman Catholic. Avocations: music, reading, family. Office: Fremont Compensation Ins Group 500 N Brand Blvd Glendale CA 91203-1923

SIMPSON, ANDREA LYNN, energy communications executive; b. Altadena, Calif., Feb. 10, 1948; d. Kenneth James and Barbara Faries Simpson; m. John R. Myrdal, Dec. 13, 1986; 1 child, Christopher Ryan Myrdal. BA, U. So. Calif., 1969, MS, 1983; postgrad. U. Colo., Boulder Sch. Bank Mktg., 1977. Asst. cashier United Calif. Bank, L.A., 1969-73; asst. v.p. mktg. 1st Hawaiian Bank, Honolulu, 1973-78; v.p. corp. comm. BHP Hawaii, Inc. (formerly Pacific Resources, Inc.), Honolulu, 1978—. Bd. dirs. Arts Coun. Hawaii, 1977-81, Hawaii Heart Assn., 1978-83, Coun. Pacific Girl Scouts U.S., 1982-85, Child and Family Svcs., 1984-86, Honolulu Symphony Soc., 1985-91, Sta. KHPR Hawaii Pub. Radio, 1988-92, Kapiolani Found., 1990-95, Hanahauoli Sch., 1991—; bd. dirs., 2nd. v.p. Girl Scout Coun. Hawaii, 1994-96, adv. bd., 1996—; trustee Hawaii Loa Coll., 1984-86, Kapiolani Women's and Children's Hosp., 1988—, Hawaii Sch. For Girls at LaPietra, 1989-91, Kapiolani Med. Ctr. at Pali Momi, 1994—; commr. Hawaii State Commn. on Status of Women, 1985-87, State Sesquecentennial of Pub. Schs. Commn., 1990-91; bd. dirs. Hawaii Strategic Devel. Corp., 1991—, Children's Discovery Ctr., 1994—, Pacific Asian Affairs Coun., 1994-96, adv. dir. Hawaii Kids at Work, 1991—, Hawaii Mothers Against Drunk Driving, 1992-96. Named Panhellenic Woman of Yr. Hawaii, 1979, Outstanding Woman in Bus. Hawaii YWCA, 1980, Hawaii Legis., 1980, Outstanding Young Woman of Hawaii Girl Scouts Coun. of the Pacific, 1985, 86. Mem. Internat. Pub. Rels. Assn. (Golden World award 1997), Am. Mktg. Assn., Pub. Rels. Soc. Am. (bd. dirs. Honolulu chpt. 1984-86, Silver Anvil award 1984, Pub. Rels. Profl. Yr. 1991, Silver Anvil award of excellence 1996), Utilities Communicators Internat. (Communicator of Yr. 1984), Honolulu Advt. Fedn. (Advt. Woman of Yr. 1984), U. So. Calif. Alumni Assn. (bd. dirs. Hawaii 1981-83), Outrigger Canoe Club, Pacific Club, Rotary (pub. rels. chmn. 1988-97, Honolulu chpt.), Alpha Phi (past pres., dir. Hawaii), Hawaii Jaycees (Outstanding Young Person of Hawaii 1978). Office: BHP Hawaii Inc 733 Bishop St Ste 2700 Honolulu HI 96813-4016

SIMPSON, BERYL BRINTNALL, botany educator; b. Dallas, Apr. 28, 1942; d. Edward Everett and Barbara Frances (Brintnall) S.; children: Jonathan, Meghan. AB, Radcliffe Coll., 1964; MA, Harvard U., 1968, PhD, 1968. Rsch. fellow Arnold Arboretum/Gray Herbarium, Cambridge, Mass., 1969-71; curator Smithsonian Instn., Washington, 1971-78; prof. U. Tex., Austin, 1978—; chmn. U.S. Com. to IUBS, 1985-88; co-pres. Internat. Congress Systematic and Evolutionary Biology, 1980-85. Author: Economic Botany, 1994; editor: Mesquite, 1977; contbr. over 100 articles and notes to profl. jours. Recipient Greenman award Mo. Bot. Garden, 1970. Fellow AAAS, Am. Acad. Arts and Sci.; mem. Soc. for Study Evolution (coun. 1975-80, pres. 1985-86), Bot. Soc. Am. (prs. 1990-91, Merit award 1992), Bot. Soc. Washington (v.p. 1975), Am. Soc. Plant Tazonomists (pres. 1994, Cooley award), Am. Inst. Biol. Scis. (bd. dirs. 1993-95), U.S.-Mex. Found. for Sci. (bd. govs.). Office: Dept Botany BIO 308 U Tex Austin TX 78713

SIMPSON, BOB G., retired quality assurance professional; b. DeWitt, Ark., Feb. 20, 1932; s. Fearmon Lambert Simpson and Myrtle Elsie (Lowrance) Simpson Palmer. BS in Physics., U. Ctrl. Ark., 1962. Quality/reliabilty engr. Motorola Inc., Phoenix, 1963-70; reliability engr. Motorola Inc., Mesa, Ariz., 1973-74; component engr. Control Data Corp., Tucson, 1971-73; mgr., supr. quality assurance Engineered Sys. Inc., Tempe, 1976-97, plant facilities mgr., 1996-97. Mem. Greater Phoenix Ch. of God; former chmn. coun. Phoenix Ch. of God Internat.With USN, 1951-55; with AEC Contractor, 1957-59.

SIMPSON, CAROLE ESTELLE, broadcast journalist; b. Chgo., Dec. 7, 1940; d. Lytle Ray and Doretha Viola (Wilbon) S.; m. James Edward Marshall, Sept. 3, 1966; children: Mallika Joy, Adam. BA in Journalism, U. Mich., 1962; postgrad., U. Iowa, 1964-65. News reporter WCFL Radio, Chgo., 1965-68; reporter/anchorwoman WBBM Radio, Chgo., 1968-70; TV news reporter WMAQ-TV, Chgo., 1970-74; NBC news network corr. Midwest Bur., transferred to Washington, from 1974; anchorwoman World News Saturday, Washington, 1988-93, World News Sunday, Washington, 1993—; instr. journalism Tuskegee Inst., Ala., 1962-64; faculty Medill Sch. Journalism, Northwestern U., 1972-74; moderator 1992 Town Mtg. Presdl. Debate. Recipient med. journalism award AMA, Emmy award, Dupont award, Milestone in Broadcasting award Nat. Commn. on Working Women, Disting. Journalist award U. Mo., Star award Am. Women in Radio and TV, Journalist of Yr. award Nat. Assn. Black Journalists, 1992; named Outstanding Woman in Comm., YWCA Met. Chgo., 1974; named to U. Iowa Comm. Hall of Fame; established several coll. scholarships for women and minorities in broadcast journalism. Mem. Internat. Women's Media Found. (bd. of RFK Journalism awards), NAS (mem. of bd. of children and families), Radio TV News Dirs. Found. (trustee), Radio-TV Corrs. Assn. Washington. Office: ABC News Washington Bureau 1717 Desales St NW Washington DC 20036-4401*

SIMPSON, CHARLES EDMOND, crop science educator; b. Winters, Tex., Aug. 19, 1940; s. Robert Charles and Rosalie Helen Simpson; m. Lynann Kruse, Aug. 29, 1964; children: Melissa E. Heatley, Shay L. BS in Agrl. Edn., Tex. A&M U., 1963, MS in Plant Breeding, 1966, PhD in Plant Breeding, 1967. From asst. prof. to assoc. prof. Tex. Agrl. Exptl. Sta., Tex. A&M U., Stephenville, 1967-84, prof., 1984—. Contbr. 8 chpts. to books, numerous articles to profl. jours. Fellow Am. Peanut Rsch. and Edn. Soc. (pres. 1991-92); mem. Am. Soc. Agronomy, Am. Phytopathol. Soc., Coun. on Agrl. Sci. & Tech. Diversity, Crop Sci. Soc. Am. (Frank N. Meyer medal 1993). Lutheran. Avocation: peanut germplasm preservation and collection. Office: Tex A&M U Tex Agrl Exptl Sta PO Box 292 Stephenville TX 76401

SIMPSON, CHARLES REAGAN, retired judge; b. Danville, Ill., June 16, 1921; s. Frank and Mamie (Moreland) S.; m. Ruth V. Thomason, June 5, 1948. B.A. with highest honors, U. Ill., 1944, J.D. with high honors, 1945; LL.M., Harvard U., 1950. Bar: Ill. 1945. Practiced in Champaign, Ill., 1946-49; atty. OPS, 1951-52; with legislation and regulations div. Office Chief Counsel, IRS, 1952-65, dir. office, 1964-65; judge U.S. Tax Ct., 1965-88, ret., 1988; Teaching fellow Harvard Law Sch., 1950-51. Chmn. Champaign County chpt. Nat. Found. Infantile Paralysis, 1947-49; Mem. Ill. Gen. Assembly from 24th Dist., 1947-50. Recipient Justice Tom C. Clark award Fed. Bar Assn., 1964. Mem. ABA, Am. Law Inst., Am. Judicature Soc., Phi Beta Kappa, Order of Coif, Phi Kappa Phi. Office: US Tax Ct 400 2nd St NW Washington DC 20217-0001

SIMPSON, CURTIS CHAPMAN, III, lawyer; b. Leonia, N.J., Apr. 19, 1952; s. Curtis Chapman Simpson Jr. and Marguerite (Johnson) Host; m. Joy D.; children: Ashley Blake, Curtis Chapman. BA, George Washington U., 1977; JD, Calif. Western U., 1980. Bar: Calif. 1981, U.S. Dist. Ct. (cen. dist.) Calif. 1983, U.S. Ct. Claims 1991. Pres. Curtis C. Simpson, III, P.C., Santa Barbara, Calif., 1981-84; assoc. Schurmer & Drane, Santa Barbara, 1984-90; prin. Curtis Simpson Law Firm, Santa Barbara, Oxnard, Calif., 1991—; ct.-appointed arbitrator superior cts. Santa Barbara County, Ventura County, San Luis Obispo County, all Calif., 1991—. Contbr. to profl. jours. Co-chmn. youth group leader Montecito YMCA, 1992; bd. dirs. Montecito Ednl. Found., 1993—; co-pres. Montecito Ednl. Found., 1994—. Mem. Assn. Trial Lawyers Am., Consumer Attys. Calif. (cert. recognition 1991—), State Bar Calif., Santa Barbara County Bar Assn., Ventura County Bar Assn., Hon. Order Ky. Cols., Coral Casino Beach and Cabana Club. Episcopalian. Office: Curtis Simpson Law Firm 120 E De La Guerra St Santa Barbara CA 93101-2226

SIMPSON, DANIEL H., ambassador; b. Wheeling, W.Va., July 9, 1939; married; 4 children. BA, Yale U., 1961; cert. in African studies, Northwestern U., 1973. Joined Fgn. Svc., U.S. Dept. State, Washington, 1966—, staff asst. Bur. Security and Consular Affairs, 1966-67, speech writer for asst. sec. state for African affairs, 1968, desk officer for Rhodesia, Botswana, Lesotho, and Swaziland, 1973-74; tng. officer USIA, Washington, 1967-68; polit., econ. and consular officer Am. Embassy, Bujumbura, Burundi, 1968-70; polit. officer Am. Embassy, Pretoria, Republic South Africa, 1970-72; dep. chief mission Am. Embassy, Beirut, until 1989; amb. to Cen. African Republic, Bangui, 1989-93; dep. comdr. Army War Coll., Carlisle, Pa., 1993-94; ambassador to Somalia Mogadishu, 1994-95; ambassador to Zaire Kinshasa, 1995—. Home and Office: Am Embassy Kinshasa Unit 31550 APO AE 09828-1550

SIMPSON, DANIEL REID, lawyer; b. Glen Alpine, N.C., Feb. 20, 1927; s. James R. and Margaret Ethel (Newton) S.; m. Mary Alice Leonard, Feb. 25, 1930; children: Mary Simpson Beyer, Ethel B. Simpson Todd, James R. II. BS, Wake Forest U., 1949, LLB, 1951. Bar: N.C. 1951, U.S. Dist. Ct. (we. dist.) N.C. 1951, U.S. Ct. Appeals (4th and 5th cirs.) 1980. Dir. First Union Nat. Bank, Morganton, N.C. Mem. N.C. Ho. of Reps., 1959-65; mem. N.C. Senate, 1984-96. Hon. mem. bd. dirs. N.C. Restaurant Assns.; del. Rep. Nat. Conv., 1968, 76, mem. N.C. Rep. Exec. Com. Served with AUS, 1943-45, PTO. Recipient Guardian Small Bus. award Order of Longlead Pine. Mem. N.C. Bar Assn., Burke County Bar Assn., Masons. Baptist. Home: Box 2358 Nebo NC 28761 Office: Simpson Aycock PA 204 E Mcdowell St Morganton NC 28655-3545 also: PO Box 1329 Morganton NC 28680-1329 *When you get off your knees, leave your troubles on the floor. No mistake was ever corrected by worrying about it.*

SIMPSON, DAVID WILLIAM, artist, educator; b. Pasadena, Calif., Jan. 20, 1928; s. Frederick and Mary Adeline (White) S.; m. Dolores D. Debus, July 30, 1954; 1 stepchild, Gregory C. Vose; 1 child, Lisa C. B.F.A., Calif. Sch. Fine Arts, 1956; M.A., San Francisco State Coll., 1958. Instr. art Am. River Jr. Coll., Sacramento, 1958-60, Contra Costa Jr. Coll., San Pablo, Calif., 1960-65; prof. art U. Calif., Berkeley, 1967-91, prof. emeritus, 1991—. Exhibited in one-man shows including Robert Elkon Gallery, N.Y.C., 1961, 63, 64, San Francisco Mus. Art, 1967, Henri Gallery, Washington, 1968, Oakland Mus., 1978, Modernism, San Francisco, 1980-81, 84, 86, Sheldon Meml. Art Gallery, Lincoln, Nebr., 1990, Mincher/Wilcox Gallery, San Francisco, 1991, 92, 93, Angles Gallery, Santa Monica, Calif., 1991, 92, 94, Bemis Found., Omaha, Nebr., 1991, Anthony Ralph Gallery, N.Y.C., 1992, John Berggruen Gallery, San Francisco, 1994, Charlotte Jackson Fine Art, Santa Fe, 1995, Laguna Art Mus., Laguna Beach, Calif., 1995; group shows include Mus. Modern Art, N.Y.C., 1963, Carnegie Internat., Pitts., 1961-62, 66-67, L.A. Mus. Art, 1964, U. Ill., 1969, Expo '70, Osaka, Japan, 1970, Josly Art Mus., Omaha, 1970, John Berggruen Gallery, San Francisco, 1979, Janus Gallery, L.A., 1980, Gallery Show, Tokyo, 1984, Koplin Gallery, L.A., 1987, Angles Gallery, Santa Monica, 1988, 90, John Good Gallery, N.Y., 1992, John Berggruen Gallery, San Francisco, 1993, Cheryl Haines Gallery, San Francisco, 1996, Museo di Arte Moderna e Contemporanea, Trent, Italy, 1996, Studio La Cittal, Verona, Italy, 1996; represented in permanent collections including Phila. Mus. Art, Nat. Collection Fine Arts, Washington, Seattle Art Mus., La Jolla (Calif.) Mus. Art, Mus. Modern Art, N.Y.C., San Francisco Mus. Art, Oakland (Calif.) Mus., Panza Collection, Italy, Laguna Art Mus., Laguna Beach, Calif., Univ. Art Mus., Berkeley, Calif., Museo Cantonale d'Arte Lugano, Switzerland. Home: 565 Vistamont St Berkeley CA 94708 Office: U Calif Art Dept Berkeley CA 94720

SIMPSON, DENNIS ARDEN, lighting contracting company executive; b. Monroe, N.C., July 10, 1944; s. Arden L. and Lola M. Simpson; children from previous marriage: Anthony Dennis, Legare Catherine; m. Peggy Lee Kay, Oct. 22, 1983; 1 child, Andrew Dennis. AB in Econs., U. N.C., 1967. Trainee Jordan Marsh, Miami, Fla., 1966-67; with planning dept. Burlington Industries, Reidsville, N.C., 1967-69; with scheduling dept. Burlington Industries, N.Y.C., 1969-71; ops. mgr. Unifi/Summerfield, Rocky Mt., N.C., 1971-75; pres., CEO East Industries, Rocky Mt., 1974-88, Dennis A. Simpson, Inc., Rocky Mt., 1988—. Mem. Illuminating Engring. Soc., Assn. Energy Engrs., Benvenue Country Club. Republican. Baptist. Avocations: tennis, boating. Office: 1114 Instrument Dr PO Box 8526 Rocky Mount NC 27804

SIMPSON, DENNIS DWAYNE, psychologist, educator; b. Lubbock, Tex., Nov. 9, 1943; s. Homer Arnold and Georgie Lee (Barrett) S.; m. Sherry Ann Johnson, Aug. 20, 1965; children: Jason Renn, Jeffrey Todd, Jennifer Lynn. BA, U. Tex., 1966; PhD, Tex. Christian U., 1970. Asst. prof. psychology Tex. Christian U., Ft. Worth, 1970-74, assoc. prof., 1974-79, prof., 1979-82, dir., prof., 1989—, S.B. Sells prof. psychology, 1992—; dir., prof. Tex. A&M U., College Station, 1982-89; sci. adv. bd. NIDA Rsch. Ctrs., Washington, 1992—; adv. bd. Nat. Drug Treatment Evaluation Studies, Washington, 1992—; expert advisor U.S. Acctg. Office, Health and Human Svcs., others; cons. WHO, fgn. govts. regarding drug rsch. Mem. editl. bd. Am. Jour of Drug and Alcohol Abuse, 1992, Internat. Jour. of the Addictions, 1995, Substance Use and Misuse; contbr. over 150 articles to profl. jours.; author 5 books. Recipient Disting. Rsch. Achievement award Tex. Commn. on Alcohol and Drug Abuse, 1987; recipient numerous grants. Mem. APA, Am. Psychol. Soc., Am. Evaluation Assn., Soc. of Psychologists in Addictive Behaviors, Southwestern Psychol. Assn., Sigma Xi. Achievements include research emphasis on the process of treatment service delivery in relation client attributes and how they related to retention rates, relapse, posttreatment outcomes; research on drug use in the workplace, other areas. Office: Tex Christian U Inst Behavioral Rsch PO Box 298740 Fort Worth TX 76129

SIMPSON, FREDERICK JAMES, retired research administrator; b. Regina, Sask., Can., June 8, 1922; s. Ralph James and Lillian Mary (Anderson) S.; m. Margaret Christine Simpson, May 28, 1947; children: Christine Louise, Steven James, Leslie Coleen, Ralph Edwin, David Glen. B.Sc., U. Alta., Can., 1944, M.Sc. in Agr., 1946; Ph.D. in Bacteriology, U. Wis., 1952. With Nat. Research Council Can., 1946-84; asst. dir. Atlantic Research Lab., Halifax, N.S., 1970-73; dir. Atlantic Research Lab., 1973-84; sci. cons., 1985-90; vis. scientist U. Ill., Urbana, 1955-56, vis. prof., 1964; mem. exec. council Atlantic Provinces Interuniv. Com. on Scis., 1976-79, chmn., 1981-84; pres. Fed. Inst. Mgmt., Halifax, 1981-82. Contbr. numerous articles to profl. jours. Decorated Queen's Silver Anniversary medal. Fellow Royal Soc. of Arts (London); mem. Can. Soc. Microbiologists (hon., sec.-treas. 1969-70, v.p. 1971-72, pres. 1972-73), Nova Scotian Inst. Sci. (v.p. 1975-76, pres. 1977-78), Internat. Phycological Soc., Aquaculture Assn. Can., Sigma Xi. Mem. United Ch. of Canada.

SIMPSON, GEORGE TRUE, surgeon, educator; b. Aurora, Colo., Apr. 29, 1943; s. George True and Meryle Flora (Moore) S.; m. Sharon Louise Mason, Mar. 9, 1944; children: Amber-Louise Elizabeth, George True III. BA in History, LaSierra U., 1969; MD, Loma Linda U., 1973, MPH, 1975. Diplomate Am. Bd. Otolaryngology, Am. Bd. Laser Surgery, Nat. Bd. Med. Examiners. Surgery resident U. Ala. Hosp. & Clinics, Birmingham, 1973-75; surgeon Kalabo Hosp., Zambia, 1975; otolaryngology resident UCLA Head/Neck Surgery, L.A., 1975-78; pediatric otolaryngology fellow Children's Hosp, Boston, 1978-79; assoc. prof., acting chair Boston (Mass.) U., 1979-90; dir. dept. otolaryngology Boston (Mass.) City Hosp., 1979-90; otolaryngologist-in-chief U. Hosp., Boston, 1984-90; chmn. dept. otolaryngology SUNY, Buffalo, 1991—, Sisters of Charity Hosp., Buffalo, 1991—; pres. U. Head/Neck Surgery, Buffalo, 1991—; cons. Ministry Pub. Health, State of Kuwait, 1976, MIT, Cambridge, 1979—, Gillette Corp., Boston, 1984-90; pres. Boston City Hosp. Med. Staff, 1983, 85; bd. dirs. Voice Found. Sci. Adv., Phila.; chmn. otolaryngology sect. 10 Internat. Congress on Lasers in medicine and Surgery, Taipei, Taiwan, 1989; examiner Am. Bd. Otolaryngology, Chgo., 1992, 93, 94. Author: Lasers in Otolaryngology, 1985; author, editor: Textbook of General Medicine, 1987; editor: Lasers in Otolaryngology: OTOL Clinics of N.Am., 1990; contbr. articles to profl. jours. With U.S. Army, 1964-66. Recipient Caring Physician award Mass. Nursing Assn., Mass. Med. Assn., 1989. Fellow ACS, Am. Acad. Otolaryngology-Head/Neck Surgery (Honor award 1987), Am. Acad. Pediatrics, Am. Soc. Head/Neck Surgery, Am. Bronchoesophagological, Am. Acad. Facial Plastic and Reconstructive Surgery, Am. Acad. Cosmetic Surgery, Royal Soc. Medicine, Am. Bd. Laser Surgery; mem. Am. Assn. Acad. Depts. Otolaryngology, Assn. for Rsch. in Otolaryngology, Soc. Univ. Otolaryngologist, Internat. Soc. for History Otolaryngology (sec./treas. 1984-87, v.p. 1987—), Buffalo Otolaryngology Soc., Buffalo Canoe Club, Buffalo Club, Orchard Park Country Club, Alpha Omega Alpha. Avocations: medical history, personal computing, music, running, boating. Office: SUNY Buffalo Dept Otolaryngology 2121 Main St Ste 205 Buffalo NY 14214-2693

SIMPSON, H. RICHARD (DICK SIMPSON), retailer; b. Akron, Ohio, Oct. 10, 1930; s. Bert M. and Violet K. (Mathias) S.; m. Joan Rose Marshall, Mar. 22, 1970; children: Carla Sue, Barry Nelson, Richard Drew, Catherine, Irene Elizabeth, Student, U. Akron, 1949-50; BS, U. Md., 1955. Mgr. Tex. Gen. Motors Corp., Detroit, 1959-62; pres. Friendly Pontiac, Friendly Toyota, Derrick Chrysler, Simpson Oil Corp., Corp. S., Dick Tiger Homes, Austin, 1962-85. Served to lt. col. USAF, 1953-75; Korea. Decorated D.F.C., Air Medal. Mem. Soc. Automotive Engrs., Res. Officers Assn. Methodist. Clubs: Horseshoe Bay Yacht, Horseshoe Bay Country. Lodges: Rotary, Masons. Office: PO Box 8186 Marble Falls TX 78657-8186

SIMPSON, JOANNE MALKUS, meteorologist; b. Boston, Mar. 23, 1923; d. Russell and Virginia (Vaughan) Gerould; m. Robert H. Simpson, Jan. 6, 1965; children by previous marriage: David Starr Malkus, Steven Willem Malkus, Karen Elizabeth Malkus. BS, U. Chgo., 1943, MS, 1945, PhD, 1949; DSc (hon.), SUNY, Albany, 1991. Instr. physics and meteorology Ill. Inst. Tech., 1946-49, asst. prof., 1949-51; meteorologist Woods Hole Oceanographic Instn., 1951-61; prof. meteorology UCLA, 1961-65; dir. exptl. meteorology lab. NOAA, Dept. Commerce, Washington, 1965-74; prof. environ. scis. U. Va., Charlottesville, 1974-76; W.W. Corcoran prof. environ. scis. U. Va., 1976-81; head Severe Storms br. Goddard Lab. Atmospheres, NASA, Greenbelt, Md., 1981-88, chief scientist for meteorology, 1988—; Goddard sr. fellow, earth scis. dir. Goddard Space Flight Ctr., NASA, 1988—; project scientist tropical rainfall measuring mission, 1986—; mem. Bd. on Atmospheric Scis. and Climate, NRC/NAS, 1990-93, Bd. on Geophys. and Environ. Data, 1993-96. Author: (with Herbert Riehl) Cloud Structure and Distributions Over the Tropical Pacific Ocean; assoc. editor: Revs. Geophysics and Space Physics, 1964-72, 75-77; contbr. articles to profl. jours. Mem. Fla. Gov.'s Environ. Coordinating Coun., 1971-74. Recipient Disting. Authorship award NOAA, 1969, Silver medal Dept. Commerce, 1967, Gold medal, 1972, Vincent J. Schaefer award Weather Modification Assn., 1979, Cmty. Headliner award Women in Comm., 1973, Profl. Achievement award U. Chgo. Alumni Assn., 1975, 92, Lifetime Achievement award Women in Sci. Engring., 1990, Exceptional Sci. Achievement award NASA, 1982, William Nordberg award NASA, 1994; named Woman of Yr. L.A. Times, 1963; Guggenheim fellow, 1954-55, Goddard Sr. fellow, 1988—. Fellow Am. Meterol. Soc. (hon., mem. coun. 1975-77, 79-81, mem. exec. com. 1977, 79-81, commr. sci. and tech. activities 1982-88, pres.-elect 1988, pres. 1989, publs. commr. 1992—, Meisinger award 1962, Rossby Rsch. medal 1983, Charles Franklin Brooks award 1992), Am. Geophys. Union; mem. Cosmos Club, Phi Beta Kappa, Sigma Xi. Home: 540 N St SW Washington DC 20024-4557 Office: NASA Goddard Space Flight Ctr Earth Scis Dir Greenbelt MD 20771

SIMPSON, JOE LEIGH, obstetrics and gynecology educator; b. Birmingham, Ala., Apr. 4, 1943; s. Robert S. and Winnie (Leigh) S.; m. Sandra A. Carson, May 6, 1978; children: Scott, Reid. MD, Duke U., 1968. Diplomate Am. Bd. Ob-Gyn, Am. Bd. Med. Genetics. Fellow in ob-gyn Cornell Med. Coll., N.Y.C., 1968-73; clin. assoc. N.Y. Blood Ctr., N.Y.C., 1969-73; asst. clin. prof. ob-gyn U. Tex., San Antonio, 1973-75; assoc. prof., head ob-gyn Northwestern U. Med. Sch., Chgo., 1975-79, prof. ob-gyn, 1979-86; Faculty prof. chmn. dept. ob-gyn U. Tenn., Memphis, 1986-94; Ernst W. Bertner chmn. and prof. dept. ob-gyn., prof. dept. molecular and human genetics Baylor Coll. of Medicine, Houston, 1994—; mem. genetics grant rev. and adv. bd. HHS, 1979-82; mem. clin. rsch. panel March of Dimes, 1986-94, chmn. adv. panel reproductive hazards, 1988-92; mem. accreditation coun. grad. med. edn. Residency Rev. Com. Med. Genetics, 1993—. Author: Disorders of Sexual Development, 1976; author: (with others) Genetics in Obstetrics and Gynecology, 1982, 2d edit., 1992, Obstetrics: Normal and Problem Pregnancies, 1986, 2d edit., 1991; co-editor: Genetic Diseases in Pregnancy, 1981, Material Serum Screening for Fetal Genetic Disorders, 1992, Essentials of Prenatal Diagnosis, 1993; contbr. numerous articles to profl. jours. and chpts. to books. Maj. U.S. Army, 1973-75. Recipient numerous awards Nat. Insts. Child Health and Devel., March of Dimes, Wyeth-Ayerest pub. recognition award Assn. Profs. Ob-Gyn, 1992. Fellow Am. Coll. Obstetricians and Gynecologists (chmn. genetics subcom. 1981-84); mem. Am. Gynecol. and Obstet. Soc., Am. Fertility Soc. (bd. dirs. 1984-87, pres. 1993-94), Soc. Gynecologic Investigation (mem. coun., Pres.'s Achievement award 1986), Soc. Advancement Contraception (bd. dirs. 1988—, treas. 1992—), Am. Soc. Human Genetics (mem. program com. 1988-91). Office: Baylor Coll of Medicine Dept Ob/Gyn 6550 Fannin St Ste 729A Houston TX 77030-2717*

SIMPSON, JOHN ALEXANDER, physicist; b. Portland, Oreg., Nov. 3, 1916; s. John A. and Janet (Br) S.; m. Elizabeth Alice Hilts, Nov. 30, 1946 (div. Sept. 1977); children: Mary Ann, John Alexander; m. Elizabeth Scott Johnson, Aug. 23, 1980. A.B., Reed Coll., 1940, D.Sc. (hon.), 1981; M.S., NYU, 1942, Ph.D., 1943. Research assoc. OSRD, 1941-42; sci. group leader Manhattan Project, 1943-46; instr. U. Chgo., 1945-47, asst. prof., 1947-49, assoc. prof., 1949-54, chmn. com. on biophysics, 1951; prof. physics, dept. physics and Fermi Inst. Nuclear Studies, 1954- 68, Edward L. Ryerson Disting. Service prof. physics, 1968-74, Arthur H. Compton Disting. Service prof. physics, 1974-87, Arthur H. Compton Disting. prof. emeritus, 1987—; also dir. Enrico Fermi Inst., 1973-78; Mem. Internat. Com. IGY; chmn. bd. Ednl. Found. Nuclear Sci.; mem. tech. panel cosmic rays NRC; mem. Internat. Commn. Cosmic Radiation, 1962—; mem. astronomy missions bd. NASA, 1968; vis. assoc. physics Calif. Inst. Tech.; vis. scholar U. Calif., Berkeley.; founder Lab. Astrophysics and Space Research in Enrico Fermi Inst., 1962, Space Sci. Working Group, Washington, 1982; lectr. Victor Hess Meml., 1997. Bd. overseers, vis. com. astronomy Harvard; mem. Pres. Ford's Sci. Adv. Group on Sci. Problems, 1975-76; life trustee Adler Planetarium, 1977—. Recipient medal for exceptional sci. achievement NASA, Quantrell award for excellence in teaching, Gagarin medal Nat. Soviet Socialists Rep. Acad. of Scis., Cospar award UN Com. on Space Rsch., 1990; fellow Ctr. Policy Study, U. Chgo., Guggenheim fellow, 1972, 84-85; Nora and Edward Ryerson lectr., 1986; A. H. Compton Centennial lectr., 1992. Fellow Am. Acad. Arts and Scis., Am. Geophys. Union (Parker lectr. 1992), Am. Phys. Soc. (chmn. cosmic physics div. 1970-71); mem. NAS (mem. space sci. bd., Henryk Arctowski medal and premium 1993), Am. Philosophical Soc. (elected 1996, First Norman MacLean Faculty award for educating young scientists 1997), Internat. Union Pure and Applied Physics (pres. cosmic ray commn. 1963-67), Atomic Scientists Chgo. (chmn. 1945-46, bd. bull. 1945—, pres. bull. bd. sponsors 1993—), Am. Astron. Soc. (Bruno Rossi prize 1991), Internat. Acad. Astronautics, Smithsonian Inst. (Martin Marietta chair in history of space sci. 1987-88, Glennan, Webb, Seamans Group 1986—), Phi Beta Kappa, Sigma Xi. Achievements include research in nuclear radiation and instrumentation inventions, also origin of cosmic radiation, solar physics, magnetospheric physics, high energy astrophys. problems, and acceleration and isotopic and elemental composition of charged particles in space; prin. investigator for 33 expts. in earth satellites and deep space probes, also 1st probes to Mercury, Mars, Jupiter and Saturn, fly by at Venus, 9 planetary encounters, comet dust expts. on the 2 Vega spacecraft to Halley's comet, 1986; Ulysses space craft experiments over poles of the sun, 1990—, Pioneer 10 space craft outside solar system to 68 astronomical units. Office: Fermi Inst 5630 S Ellis Ave Chicago IL 60637-1433

SIMPSON, JOHN AROL, retired government executive, physicist; b. Toronto, Ont., Can., Mar. 30, 1923; came to U.S., 1926; naturalized, 1938; s. Henry George and Verna Lavinia (Green) S.; m. Arlene Badel, Feb. 11, 1948; 1 child, George Badel. BS, Lehigh U., 1946, MS, 1948, PhD, 1951. Rsch. physicist Nat. Bur. Standards, Washington, 1948-62, supervisory physicist, 1962-69, dep. chief optical physics div., 1969-75, chief mechanics div., 1975-78; dir. Ctr. for Mfg. Engring. Nat. Bur. Standards, Gaithersburg, Md., 1978-91; dir. Mfg. Engring. Lab., Nat. Inst. Standards and Tech., Gaithersburg, 1991—; ret. Contbr. articles on electron optics to profl. jours. With U.S. Army, 1943-46. Recipient Silver medal Dept. Commerce, 1964, Gold medal, 1975; Allen V. Austin Measurement Sci. award, 1984; Disting. Exec. award Sr. Exec. Svc., 1985, Am. Machinist award, 1986. Fellow Am. Phys. Soc.; mem. NAE, Sigma Xi. Home: 312 Riley St Falls Church VA 22046-3310

SIMPSON, JOHN JOSEPH, physics educator, researcher; b. North Bay, Ont., Can., May 26, 1939; s. John William and Teresa (Hagarty) S.; m. Marianne Cornelia Van der Veen, July 5, 1968; children: J. James R., Sarah J. BSc, U. Toronto, Ont., 1961, MA, 1962; PhD, U. Oxford, U.K., 1966. Rsch. assoc. U. Oxford, U.K., 1965-66, Weizmann Inst., Rehovot, Israel, 1966-68, U. Toronto, Can., 1968-69; asst. prof. U. Guelph, Ont., 1969-73, assoc. prof., 1973-80, prof., 1980—; vis. rsch. fellow Max Planck Inst., Heidelberg, Fed. Republic Germany, 1973, Niels Bohr Inst., Copenhagen, 1975-76; sci. assoc. CERN, Geneva, Switzerland, 1982-83. Fellow Royal Soc. Can. (Rutherford Meml. medal 1985), Can. Assn. Physicists. Office: U Guelph, Dept Physics, Guelph, ON Canada N1G 2W1

SIMPSON, JOHN M., lawyer; b. Ponca City, Okla., Sept. 26, 1950. AB, Harvard U., 1972; JD, Columbia U., 1978. Bar: D.C. 1979, N.C. 1988. Mem. Fulbright & Jaworski L.L.P., Washington. Office: Fulbright & Jaworski LLP Market Square 801 Pennsylvania Ave NW Washington DC 20004-2604

SIMPSON, JOHN MATHES, newspaper editor; b. Madison, Wis., Jan. 7, 1948; s. Robert C. and Mary (Mathes) S.; m. Carol Flaker, July 2, 1977; children: Kate, Alexis. BA, SUNY, Binghamton, 1969. Reporter, editor Sun-Bulletin, Binghamton, 1970-76; mng. editor Ithaca (N.Y.) Jour., 1976-78; mng. editor, exec. editor Pacific Daily News, Agana, Guam, 1978-83; internat. mng. editor USA Today, Washington, 1984-86, 88-97, spl. projects mng. editor, 1986-87, dep. editor, 1997—; dir. corp. projects Gannett Internat., Washington, 1987-88. Dir. World Press Freedom Com. Mem. Am. Soc. Newspaper Editors, Inter Am. Press Assn. (bd. dirs.), World Editors Forum Adv. Com., Nat. Press Club. Office: USA Today Internat 1000 Wilson Blvd Arlington VA 22209-3901

SIMPSON, JOHN NOEL, healthcare administrator; b. Durham, N.C., Feb. 27, 1936; s. William Hays and Lucile (McNab) S.; A.B., Duke U., 1957; M.H.A., Med. Coll. Va., 1959; m. Virginia Marshall, June 27, 1959; children: John Noel, William M. Asst. adminstr. Riverside Health Sys., Newport News, Va., 1962-65, assoc. adminstr., 1965-70; assoc. adminstr. Richmond (Va.) Meml. Hosp., 1970-74, sr. v.p., adminstr., 1974-77, exec. v.p., 1977-80, pres., 1980-85; pres. Health Corp. Va., 1985-96; chmn. bd. Bon Secours-Richmond Health System, 1996—; preceptor Sch. Health Adminstrn., Duke U. and Med. Coll. Va., Washington U., St. Louis; bd. dirs. Sun Health, Inc./Sun Alliance, 1979-92, vice chmn., 1984, chmn., 1985-87; vice-chmn. Med./Bus. Coalition, 1981-83; participant Leadership Met. Richmond; bd. dirs. Ctrl. Va. Health Sys. Agy., 1980-84, Richmond chpt. ARC, 1980-83; mem. Va. Bd. Med. Assistance, 1980-84; mem. joint subcom. studying Va.'s med. malpractice laws divsn. legal svcs. Gen. Assembly of Comm. of Va., 1984; chmn. Va. Health Network, 1989-91; chmn. Hanover Bus. Coun., 1994-95; mem. Gov.'s Regional Econ. Devel. Adv. Coun., 1994-95. Served with Med. Service Corps, U.S. Army, 1959-62. Fellow Am. Coll. Healthcare Execs. (Council of Regents 1976-82, Edgar C. Hayhow award 1976, bd. govs. 1990-94, regents award sr. exec. level 1995); mem. Am. Hosp. Assn. (chmn. RPBIII 1994—, del. 1989-93, mem. bd. trustees 1994—, Va. Hosp. Assn. (dir. 1974—, chmn.-elect, chmn. 1984-85), Va. Ins. Reciprocal (chmn. 1977-79), Met. Richmond C. of C. (bd. dirs.). Republican. Presbyterian. Home: 9127 Carterham Rd Richmond VA 23229-7752 Office: Bon Secours-Richmond Health Sys 1300 Westwood Ave Richmond VA 23227-4612

SIMPSON, JOHN WISTAR, energy consultant, former manufacturing company executive; b. Glenn Springs, S.C., Sept. 25, 1914; s. Richard Caspar and Mary (Berkeley) S.; m. Esther Slattery, Jan. 17, 1948; children: John Wistar, Carter B., Patricia A., Barbara J. Student, Wofford Coll., 1932-33, DSc, 1972; BS, U.S. Naval Acad., 1937; MS, U. Pitts., 1941; DSc (hon.), Seton Hill Coll., 1970. With Westinghouse Electric Corp., 1937-77; mgr. Navy and Marine switchboard engring., switchgear div., on leave as mgr. nuclear engring. Daniels pile group, Oak Ridge Nat. Lab., successively as Westinghouse Electric Corp. (Bettis Atomic Power div.), 1949-58; v.p. Westinghouse Electric Corp.; gen. mgr. Westinghouse Electric Corp. (Bettis atomic power lab.), 1958-59, v.p., gen. mgr. atomic power divs., 1959-62, v.p. engring. and research, 1962-63, v.p. electric utility group, 1963-69, pres. power systems, corp. exec. v.p., dir., 1971-77; chmn. bd. Internat. Energy Assocs. Ltd., 1976-80; pres. Simpson Bus. Services, Inc., 1980-86; v.p. Sea

Pines Assocs., Hilton Head Island, S.C., 1989-91, also bd. dirs., 1987-91; bd. dirs. Sea Pines Real Estate Cos., Hilton Head Island, S.C., 1987-91; pvt. energy cons.; mem. adv. bd. Lawrence Livermore Nat. Lab. Fusion, 1975-88; mem. Naval Tech. Mission to Japan, 1945; del. 1st Internat. Conf. on Peaceful Uses Atomic Energy, Geneva, Switzerland, 1955, Conf. on Peaceful Uses Atomic Energy (2d Internat. Conf.), 1958; chmn. Atomic Indsl. Forum, 1974-75; mem. energy research adv. bd. Dept. Energy, 1981-83; chmn. com. on outlook for fusion hybrid and tritium breeding fusion reactors NRC; mem. sci. adv. bd. Notre Dame, 1974-86. Author: Nuclear Power from Underseas to Outer Space, 1994. Mem. governing bd. Nat. Coun. Chs., 1979-81; trustee Seton Hall Coll., 1969-76, Point Park Coll., 1973—, Wofford Coll., 1973-87. Recipient Navy cert. of merit for civilian svc. in World War II, 1947, Gold medal for advancement of rsch. Am. Soc. Metals, 1973, Disting. Alumnus award U. Pitts., 1975. Fellow IEEE (Edison medal 1971), ASME (hon. mem., George Westinghouse Gold medal 1975), Am. Nuclear Soc. (pres. 1973, Henry Dewolf Smyth Nuclear Statesman award 1997); mem. Nat. Acad. Engring., Franklin Inst. (Newcomen Gold medal), Rolling Rock Club (Ligonier, Pa.), Melrose Club, Bear Creek Golf Club, Sea Pines Club (Hilton Head, S.C.). Home and Office: 36 E Beach Lagoon Rd Hilton Head Island SC 29928-5714 *The guiding principles of my career have been to work in an area I considered to be of major importance, to have the most competent people working for me, to know enough technically that I could properly evaluate performance and, as far as possible, always make my position clear to all.*

SIMPSON, LISA ANN, government agency administrator, physician; b. Lagos, Nigeria, Feb. 9, 1958; (parents Am. citizens); d. Howard Russell and Mary Alice (Turner) S. MB, B of Surgery, Trinity Coll., Dublin, Ireland, 1981; MPH, U. Hawaii, 1986. Diplomate Am. Bd. Pediat. Resident in pediat. U. Hawaii, Honolulu, 1982-85; resident in preventive medicine U. N.C., Chapel Hill, 1987-88; dir. Maternal and Child Health Bur. State Dept. Health, Honolulu, 1988-90; policy advisor Office of Asst. Sec. for Health HHS, Washington, 1993-94; sr. advisor Agy. for Health Care Policy and Rsch. HHS, Rockville, Md., 1994-95, acting dep. adminstr. Agy. for Health Care Policy and Rsch., 1995-96, dep. adminstr. Agy. for Health Care Policy and Rsch., 1996—; mid-career fellow Inst. Health Policy Studies, San Francisco, 1991-93; adj. faculty dept. health policy and mgmt. Johns Hopkins U., Balt., 1995—. Contbr. articles to profl. jours. Recipient Preventive Medicine traineeship Pub. Health Svc., 1986. Fellow Am. Acad. Pediat.; mem. APHA (governing coun. 1994-96), Assn. for Health Svcs. Rsch. Avocations: hiking, cuisine. Home: 7419 Oak Ln Chevy Chase MD 20815 Office: Agy for Health Care Policy & Rsch 2101 E Jefferson Rockville MD 20852

SIMPSON, LOUIS A., insurance company executive; b. Chgo., Dec. 23, 1936; s. Irving and Lillian (Rubin) S.; m. Margaret Rowley, Dec. 16, 1959; children: Irving, Kenneth, Edward. Student, Northwestern U., 1954-55; BA, Ohio Wesleyan U., 1958; AM, Princeton U., 1960. Instr. econs. Princeton U., 1961-62; assoc., ptnr. Stein Roe & Farnham, Chgo., 1962-69; v.p. Shareholders Mgmt., Los Angeles, 1969-70; sr. v.p., exec. v.p., pres. Western Asset Mgmt., Los Angeles, 1970-79; vice chmn. bd. Geico Corp., Washington, 1979-93, pres., chief exec. officer capital ops., 1993—; bd. dirs. Potomac Capital Investment, Salomon, Inc., Potomac Electric Power, Pacific Am. Income Shares, Western Asset Trust, Thompson PBE, Cohr Inc. Mem. endowments com. Ohio Wesleyan U.; regent Loyola Marymount U., L.A.; trustee Woodrow Wilson Nat. Fellowship, Cate Sch. Woodrow Wilson fellow, 1958. Mem. San Diego Soc. Fin. Analysts, Calif. Club, L.A. Country Club, Arts Club Chgo., Chevy Chase Club, Met. Club. Episcopalian. Office: Geico Corp 1 Geico Plz Washington DC 20076

SIMPSON, LOUIS ASTON MARANTZ, English educator, author; b. Jamaica, W.I., Mar. 27, 1923; s. Aston and Rosalind (Marantz) S.; m. Jeanne Claire Rogers, 1949 (div. 1954); 1 child, Louis Matthew; m. Dorothy Mildred Roochvarg, 1955 (div. 1979); children: Anne Borovoi, Anthony Rolf; m. Miriam Butensky Bachner, 1985. Higher schs. certificate, Munro Coll., Jamaica, 1939; B.S., Columbia U., 1948, A.M., 1950, Ph.D., 1959; D.H.L., Eastern Mich. U., 1977; DLitt, Hampden Sydney Coll., 1990. Editor Bobbs-Merrill Pub. Co., N.Y.C., 1950-55; instr. Columbia U., 1955-59; prof. English U. Calif., Berkeley, 1959-67; prof. English SUNY, Stony Brook, 1967-91, Disting. prof., 1991—. Author: (poems) The Arrivistes, 1949, Good News of Death, 1955, A Dream of Governors, 1959, At the End of the Open Road, 1963 (Pulitzer prize for poetry 1964), Selected Poems, 1965, Adventures of the Letter I, 1971, Searching for the Ox, 1976, Caviare at the Funeral, 1980, The Best Hour of the Night, 1983, People Live Here: Selected Poems 1949-83, 1983, Collected Poems, 1988, In the Room We Share, 1990, Wei Wei and Other Friends, 1990, Jamaica Poems, 1993, There You Are, 1995, Nombres et poussière, 1996, (prose) Riverside Drive, 1962, James Hogg: A Critical Study, 1962, North of Jamaica, 1972, Three on the Tower: The Lives and Works of Ezra Pound, T.S. Eliot and William Carlos Williams, 1975, A Revolution in Taste: Studies of Dylan Thomas, Allen Ginsberg, Sylvia Plath and Robert Lowell, 1978, A Company of Poets, 1981, The Character of the Poet, 1986, Selected Prose, 1989, Ships Going into the Blue, 1994, The King My Father's Wreck, 1995; editor: The New Poets of England and America, 1957, An Introduction to Poetry, 1967. Served with AUS, 1943-45. Decorated Purple Heart, Bronze Star with oak leaf cluster; Hudson Rev. fellow, 1957, Guggenheim fellow, 1962, 70; Am. Coun. Learned Socs. grantee, 1963; recipient Prix de Rome, 1957, Millay award, 1960, Distinguished Alumnus award Columbia U., 1960, medal for excellence Columbia U., 1965; American Acad. of Arts and Letters award in literature, 1976; Centenary medal Inst. of Jamaica, 1980, Jewish Book Coun. award for poetry, 1981, Elmer Holmes Bobst award, 1987. Fellow Am. Acad. in Rome. Home: 186 Old Field Rd Setauket NY 11733-1636

SIMPSON, MADELINE LOUISA, psychologist; b. Norfolk, Va., June 22, 1923; d. David Edward and Zenobia Eleanor (Ross) S. BA, Fisk U., 1944; MS, Boston U., 1951; MA, The New Sch., 1967; PhD, U. Md., 1981; MPA, Va. Commonwealth U., 1985. Psychologist, N.Y. Practitioner Norfolk County Dept. Pub. Welfare, Portsmouth, Va., 1946-51, N.Y.C. Dept. Hosps. and the Hosp. for Joint Diseases, 1951-56; founder, dir. Centre d'Etudes Sociales, Port-au-Prince, Haiti, 1959-61; social work practitioner and supr. Child Welfare Agy., N.Y.C., 1961-68; asst. prof. pscychol. Del. State Coll., Dover, 1969-71; assoc. prof. psychol. Cheyney (Pa.) State Coll., 1972-75, 78; asst. prof. psychol. Longwood Coll., Farmville, Va., 1979-85; assoc prof. St. Paul's Coll., Lawrenceville, Va., 1985-90; psychologist Office Mental Retardation and Devel. Disability State of N.Y., 1990—. Mem. local human rights com. Va. Dept. Mental Health, Mental Retardation and Substance Abuse Svcs., Piedmont Geriatric Hosp., Burkeville, Va., 1983-89, recipient Cert. of Recognition, 1988. Mem. Gold Circle Club of Am. Psychol. Assn., Delta Sigma Theta (life).

SIMPSON, MARY MICHAEL, priest, psychotherapist; b. Evansville, Ind., Dec. 1; d. Link Wilson and Mary Garrett (Price) S. B.A., B.S., Tex. Women's U., 1946; grad. N.Y. Tng. Sch. for Deaconesses, 1949; grad., Westchester Inst. Tng. in Psychoanalysis and Psychotherapy, 1976; S.T.M., Gen. Theol. Sem., 1982. Missionary Holy Cross Mission, Bolahun, Liberia, 1950-52; mem. Order of St. Helena, 1952—; acad. head Margaret Hall Sch., Versailles, Ky., 1958-61; sister in charge Convent of St. Helena, Bolahan, 1962-67, novice dir., 1968-74; pastoral counselor on staff Cathedral St. John the Divine, N.Y.C., 1974-87, canon residentiary, canon counselor, 1977-87, hon. canon, 1988—; ordained priest Episcopal Ch., 1977; cons. psychotherapist Union Theol. Sem., 1980-83; dir. Cathedral Counseling Service, 1975-87; priest-in-charge St. John's Ch. Wilmot, New Rochelle, N.Y., 1987-88; pvt. practice psycholanalyst, 1974—; priest assoc. Ch. of the Good Shepherd, 1995—; Bd. dirs. Westchester Inst. Tng. in Psychoanalysis and Psychotherapy, 1982-84; trustee Council on Internat. and Pub. Affairs, 1983-87; interim pastor St. Michael's Ch., Manhattan, 1992-94; cons. Diocese of N.Y., 1992—. Mem. Nat. Assn. Advancement of Psychoanalysis, N.Y. State Assn. Practicing Psychotherapists, N.Y. Soc. Clin. Psychologists. Author: The Ordination of Women in the American Episcopal Church: the Present Situation, 1981; contbg. author: Yes to Women Priests, 1978. Home and Office: 151 E 31st St Apt 8H New York NY 10016-9502

SIMPSON, MICHAEL, metals service center executive; b. Albany, N.Y., Dec. 10, 1938; s. John McLaren Simpson and Constance (Hasler) Ames; B.A., U. Mich., 1965, M.B.A., 1966; m. Barbara Ann Bodtke, Jan. 5, 1963; children: Leslie Simpson Wikstrom, Elizabeth McLaren. Product mgr. Armour & Co., Chgo., 1966-68; with A. M. Castle & Co., Franklin Park, Ill., 1968—, pres. Hy-Alloy Steels Co. div., 1974-79, v.p. Midwestern region, 1977-79, chmn. bd., 1979—, dir., 1972—. Trustee, Rush-Presbyterian St. Luke's Med. Ctr., Chgo., 1978—, exec. com., 1980—, vice-chmn., 1991—; trustee Oldfields Sch., Glencoe, Md., 1982-87, 95—. Served in USMC, 1957-58. Mem. Steel Service Center Inst. (chmn. exec. com. 1982-84, bd. dirs. 1981—). Republican. Episcopalian. Clubs: Shore Acres; Onwentsia; Racquet of Chicago. Office: A M Castle & Co 3400 N Wolf Rd Franklin Park IL 60131-1319

SIMPSON, MICHAEL HOMER, dermatologist; b. Hamilton, Tex., Mar. 8, 1938; s. Edgar Randell and Lucille (Patterson) S.; m. Bertha Delia Meraz. BA, N. Tex. U., 1959; MD, U. Tex. S.W. Med. Sch., 1963. Diplomate Am. Bd. Dermatology. Intern Dallas VA Hosp., 1963-64; resident in dermatology U. Tex. Med. Br., Galveston, 1966-69; pvt. practice dermatology El Paso, Tex., 1970—. Capt. USAF., 1964-66. Office: 1501 Arizona Ave Ste 1A El Paso TX 79902-5007

SIMPSON, MICHAEL KEVIN, academic administrator, political science educator; b. Bellafonte, Pa., Apr. 22, 1949; s. Robert Paul and Helen Elisabeth (Popso) S.; m. Carol Anne Martin, June 27, 1970; children: Jennifer Lyn, Robert Manton. BA, Fordham Coll., 1970; MA, Tufts U., 1974, MA in Law and Diplomacy, 1976, PhD, 1976; MBA, Syracuse U., 1983. Instr. Newbury Jr. Coll., Boston, 1976-77; asst. prof. then prof. polit. sci. Utica (N.Y.) Coll. of Syracuse U., 1976—, v.p., 1987-88, pres., 1988—; Fulbright lectr. Univ. Nancy II, France, 1981-82; vis. prof. Syracuse U. Program in Strasbourg, 1981-82, 85-87; resident dir. Internat. Programs, Strasbourg, 1985-87; trustee Savs. Bank of Utica. Contbr. articles to profl. jours. Mem. exec. com. Land of Oneidas coun. Boy Scouts Am., 1991; bd. dirs. United Way of Greater Utica, 1987, mem. campaign cabinet, mem. exec. com.; mem. Leadership Coun., N.E./Midwest Inst., 1989; chmn. Health and Hosp. Coun., 1989-90; mem. joint hosp. bd. Mohawk Valley Network; dir. ministers and missionaries benefit bd. Am. Bapt. Chs., 1995. Decorated Def. Meritorious Svc. medal; recipient Grad. Alumni award Syracuse U. Sch. Mgmt., 1983, Disting. Teaching award Utica Coll., 1983, Silver Beaver award Boy Scouts Am.; Paul Harris fellow Rotary Internat. Mem. Internat. Studies Assn., Naval Res. Assn., Rotary (bd. dirs. Utica club 1988—, v.p. 1991-92, pres., 1992), Phi Beta Kappa. Democrat. Home: 22 Ironwood Rd New Hartford NY 13413-3904 Office: Syracuse U Utica Coll 1600 Burrstone Rd Utica NY 13502-4857

SIMPSON, MICHAEL MARCIAL, science specialist, consultant; b. Honolulu, Sept. 24, 1954; s. Marcial Tolentino and Beatrice (Martin) S. AB in Biol. Scis., U. Calif., Berkeley, 1976; MS in Biol. Scis., U. San Francisco, 1977; MS in Energy and Resources, U. Calif., Berkeley, 1979; PhD in Environ. Scis. and Engring., UCLA, 1986. Assoc. researcher NASA, Moffett Field, Calif., 1973; radio program host, producer Sta. KUSF-FM, San Francisco, 1976-78; rsch. asst. Lawrence Berkeley Lab., Berkeley, Calif., 1977-79; rsch. assoc. UCLA/U.S. Dept. Energy, 1979-81; congl. fellow, environ. health U.S. Congress, Washington, 1981-82; head, biomed. policy sect. and specialist in life scis. U.S. Congl. Rsch. Svc., Washington, 1982—; adv. bd. Banbury Ctr., Cold Spring Harbor, N.Y., 1985—; adj. faculty The Washington Ctr., 1992—. Contbr. articles to profl. jours. Values clarification educator, Alexandria, Va., 1985—. Fellow AAAS (Named Congl. Sci. fellow 1981-82); mem. Washington Acad. Sci., Library of Congress Profl. Assn., UCLA in Washington (exec. steering com. 1986-92). Avocations: photography, bicycle touring, short story writing, travel. Office: US Congl Rsch Svc CRS-SPR-LM413 Washington DC 20540-7490

SIMPSON, MURRAY, engineer, consultant; b. N.Y.C., July 27, 1921; s. George and Sonia (Vernov) S.; m. Ethel Gladstein, June 29, 1947; children: Anne Simpson Everett, David, Mindy, Jonathan. BEE, CCNY, 1942; MEE, Polytech. Inst. of N.Y., 1952. Engr. Internat. Tel.&Tel., N.Y.C., 1942-44; sr. engr. Raytheon Co., Waltham, Mass., 1946-48; sect. mgr. Fairchild Guided Missles div., Farmingdale, N.Y., 1948-50; v.p. Maxson Elec. Co., N.Y.C., 1950-62; pres. SEDCO Systems Inc. subs. Raytheon Co., Melville, N.Y., 1963-86; cons. M. Simpson Assocs., West Hempstead, N.Y., 1986—; former chmn. bd. dirs. Radyne Corp. Contbr. articles to profl. jours. former bd. dirs. United Way of L.I., N.Y., 1984-87. Served to lt. (j.g.) USNR, 1944-46, PTO. Fellow IEEE (chmn. L.I. sect. 1963-64); mem. Inverrary Country Club. Avocations: boating, skiing, golf, tennis. *Don't be afraid to take risk in the hope of great reward and satisfaction. The worst that could happen is that you may fail. A much greater loss is that you never tried and perhaps missed the great opportunity of your life.*

SIMPSON, O. J. (ORENTHAL JAMES SIMPSON), former professional football player, actor, sports commentator; b. San Francisco, July 9, 1947; s. Jimmie and Eunice (Durton) S.; m. Marguerite Whitley, June 24, 1967 (div.); children: Arnelle, Jason; m. Nicole Brown, 1985 (div. 1992); children: Sydney, Justin. Student, U. So. Calif.; grad., City Coll. San Francisco. Halfback Buffalo Bills, 1969-78, San Francisco 49'ers, 1978-79; sports commentator ABC Sports, 1979-86; analyst ABC Monday Night Football broadcasts, 1984-1985; co-host NBC Sports NFL Live. Motion picture appearances include The Towering Inferno, 1974, The Cassandra Crossing, 1977, Killer Force, 1976, Capricorn One, 1978, Firepower, 1979, Hambone & Hillie, 1984, The Naked Gun, 1988, The Naked Gun 2 1/2: The Smell of Fear, 1991, The Naked Gun 33 1/3: The Final Insult, 1994; TV films include A Killing Affair, 1977, Goldie and the Boxer, 1979, The Golden Moment: An Olympic Love Story, 1980, Student Exchange, Cocaine and Blue Eyes; co-host "NFL" Live on NBC, 1990—; author: I Want to Tell You, 1995. Recipient Heisman trophy N.Y. Downtown Athletic Club, 1968; voted Coll. Player of Decade ABC Sports, 1970; named to Am. Football League All-Star Team, 1970, ProBowl Team, 1972, 73, 74, 75, 76; named Nat. Football League Player of Decade Pro Football Monthly, 1979; inducted into Pro Football Hall of Fame, 1985; mem. world record 440 yard relay team (38.6 seconds), 1967; former record holder for most yards rushing gained in a season, most yards rushing gained in a game. *

SIMPSON, OCLERIS C., agricultural research administrator; b. Normangee, Tex., Sept. 10, 1939. BS, Prairie View A&M U., 1960; MS, Iowa State U., 1962; PhD in Animal Sci., U. Nebr., 1965. Assoc. prof. Ft. Valley State Coll., Ga., 1965-69; rsch. instr. Med. Coll. Ga., 1970-71; rsch. assoc. meharry Med. Coll., Nashville, 1972-74; rsch. coord. Ft. Valley State Coll., Ga., 1974-78; rsch. dir. Prairie View A&M U., 1978-83, asst. dir. planning and evaluation, 1983; dean rsch. and ext., rsch. dir. and ext. adminstr. Langston (Okla.) U., 1983—. Mem. U.S. Investigation Team China, Joint Coun. Food and Agr. Sci., 1890 Land-Grant Colls. and Univs., Internat. Sci. and Edn. Coun. (tech. assistance sub-com.). Office: Langston U Agrl Rsch & Extention PO Box 730 Langston OK 73050-0730 Office: Langston U PO Box 730 Langston OK 73050

SIMPSON, PAMELA HEMENWAY, art historian, educator; b. Omaha, Sept. 8, 1946; d. Myrle E. and Leone K. (Cook) Hemenway; m. Henry H. Simpson III, Apr. 4, 1970; 1 child, Peter Stuart Hay. BA, Gettysburg Coll., 1968; MA, U. Mo., 1970; PhD, U. Del., 1974. Instr. art history Pa. State Extension Campus, Media, 1973, Washington and Lee U., Lexington, Va., 1973-74; asst. prof. Washington and Lee U., Lexington, 1974-79, assoc. prof., 1979-85, prof. art history, 1985—, Ernest Williams prof., 1993, chair art dept., 1987—, assoc. dean of coll., 1981-86; chair co-edn. steering com. Washington and Lee Univ., Lexington, 1984-86; cons., head county survey Va. Hist. Landmarks Commn., Richmond, 1977-81. Author: Architecture of Historic Lexington, 1977 (Am. Assn. for State and Local History award 1977), The Sculptor's Clay: Charles Gafly, 1862-1929, 1996 (SECAC award); book reviewer Women's Art Jour., columnist, 1990—; contbr. articles to profl. jours. Officer Rockbridge Hist. Soc., Lexington, 1980—, Rockbridge Valley Nat. Orgn. for Women, Rockbridge County, Va., 1984—, Historic Lexington (Va.) Found., 1987—; founder, officer Rockbridge Area Coalition Against Sexual Assault, Lexington, 1990—. Recipient Outstanding Faculty award State Coun. of Higher Edn., State of Va., 1995; grantee Nat. Endowment for Arts, 1974, NEH, 1975, 77, Glenn, Washington and Lee U., 1980-81, 91; NEH Summer Inst. scholar, 1989; Hagley-Winterthur Mus. fellow, 1991, 96. Fellow Nat. Humanities Ctr.; mem. Southeastern Soc. Archtl. Historians (bd. dirs. 1990-94, v.p. 1993-94, pres. 1994-95), Soc. Archtl. Historians, Coll. Art Assn., Vernacular Architecture Forum (bd. dirs. 1982-84, 2d v.p. 1988-91, pres. 1997—), southeastern Coll. Art Conf. (pres. 1986-90, 2d v.p. 1994—, editor rev. 1979-82). Democrat. Episcopalian. Avocations: painting, reading mysteries. Office: Washington & Lee Univ Dupont Hall Lexington VA 24450

SIMPSON, RICHARD LEE, sociologist, educator; b. Washington, Feb. 2, 1929; s. Donald Dake and Lottie (Lee) S.; m. Ida Ann Harper, July 10, 1955; children: Robert Donald, Frank Daniel. A.B., U. N.C., 1950, Ph.D., 1956; M.A., Cornell U., 1952. Instr. Pa. State U., University Park, 1956-57; asst. prof. sociology Northwestern U., Evanston, Ill., 1957-58; asst. prof. U. N. C., Chapel Hill, 1958-61, assoc. prof. sociology, 1961-65; prof. U. N. C., Chapel Hill, 1965-80, Kenan prof. sociology, 1980—; acting dir. Inst. Research Social Sci., Chapel Hill, 1966-67. Author numerous research papers, articles and book chpts. in field; editor: Social Forces, 1969-72, 83—; co-editor Research in Sociology of Work, 1981-96. Mem. Am. Sociol. Assn., So. Sociol. Soc. (pres. 1971-72), Sociol. Research Assn. Methodist. Home: 604 Brookview Dr Chapel Hill NC 27514-1406 Office: Univ NC Dept Sociology Cb 3210 Hamilton Hall Chapel Hill NC 27599-3210

SIMPSON, ROBERT EDWARD, economist, consultant; b. Chgo., July 7, 1917; s. James Albert and Mabel Grace (Farrell) S.; m. Anna Margareta Nelson, May 22, 1954; children: Karen Anne, Heather Margot, John Frederick II. A.B., Amherst Coll., 1938; student, Nat. Inst. Pub. Affairs, 1939; M.A., George Washington U., 1964. Student U.S. Central Statis. Bd., 1938-39; economist U.S. Nat. Resources Com., 1939-40; personnel work Office Sec. of War, 1941; economist civilian supply div. WPB, 1941-42; econ., adminstrv. work Nat. Housing Adminstrn., 1946-47; asst. dir. European div., later dept. asst. dir. for econ. affairs Office Internat. Trade U.S. Dept. Commerce, 1947-53; dir. Office Econ. Affairs, Bur. Fgn. Commerce, 1953-61, Office Regional Econs., Bur. Internat. Commerce, 1961-70, Office Internat. Comml. Relations, 1970-73; counsellor for econ. and comml. affairs Am. Embassy, Canberra, Australia, 1973-77; dir. Office Country Affairs, U.S. Dept. Commerce, Washington, 1978-79; cons. economist, 1980—; mem. pub. adv. com. Met. Washington Council of Govts., 1987-88; assigned Nat. War Coll., Washington, 1961-62. Mem. U.S. dels. to various internat. confs., 1948-79; bd. examiners for U.S. Fgn. Svc.; mem. gov. bd. Common Cause, Md., 1985-88, v.p. 1987-88; v.p. Montgomery County Civic Fedn., 1985-96; mem. Montgomery County Econ. Adv. Coun., 1989—; treas. Montgomery County Citizens PAC, 1993—. Comdr. USNR, 1942-46, PTO, ETO. Decorated Bronze Star. Mem. Nat. Economists Club, Phi Beta Kappa, Delta Tau Delta, Kappa Theta. Office: PO Box 386 Glen Echo MD 20812-0386

SIMPSON, ROBERT GLENN, lawyer; b. Seattle, June 27, 1932; s. Harold Vernon and Anna Rondeau (McCabe) S.; m. Josephine Anne Heald, June 7, 1959; children: Jenifer Jane, Thomas Glenn, Mary Elizabeth. BS, U. Oreg., 1954; LLB, Willamette U., 1959. Bar: Oreg. 1959. Assoc. William B. Adams Law Office, Portland, Oreg., 1959-67; ptnr. Adams McLaughlin & Simpson, Portland, 1967-70, Schwabe Williamson & Wyatt, Portland, 1970—. Trustee, sec. Legacy Good Samaritan Hosp. & Med. Ctr., Portland, 1983-89, mem. cmty. bd., 1989—; trustee, chancellor Episcopal Diocese of Oreg., Portland, 1988—. Mem. Oreg. State Bar (exec. com. health law sect. 1987-90), Am. Acad. Hosp. Attys. (program com. 1987-88), Oreg. Acad. Hosp. Attys. (pres. 1977-78, legis. com. 1989), Multnomah Athletic Club, Univ. Club, City Club. Home: 13345 SW Iron Mountain Blvd Portland OR 97219-9306 Office: Schwabe Williamson & Wyatt 1211 SW 5th Ave Ste 1800 Portland OR 97204-3718

SIMPSON, R(OBERT) SMITH, author, retired diplomat; b. Arlington County, Va., Nov. 9, 1906; s. Hendree Paine and Edith Lydia (Smith) S.; m. Henriette S. Lanniée, Nov. 7, 1934; children: Margaret Lanniée Simpson Maurin-Stunkard, Zélia Tinsley. B.S., U. Va., 1927, M.S., 1928; LL.B., Cornell U., 1931; postgrad., Columbia U., 1931-32. Spl. labor adviser, exec. NRA, 1933-34; trade. assn. exec., adminstrv. agt. Asphalt, Shingle and Roofing Code Authority, 1934-35; instr., then asst. prof. bus. law U. Pa., 1935-44; spl. adviser Pa. Unemployment Relief and Assistance Commn., co-drafter Pa. Unemployment Compensation Act, 1936; adviser N.J. Civil Service Commn., 1939; adv. unemployment compensation and relief joint Pa. State Commn., 1939-42; asst. dir. fgn. div. recruitment and manning orgn. War Shipping Adminstrn., 1942-43; with Dept. State, 1943-62, 65-66; fgn. svc. officer, 1944-62; consul gen. Mozambique, 1954-57; adv. African affairs Dept. Labor, 1958-60, dir. office country programs, 1960-61; dep. examiner bd. fgn. service examiners Dept. State, 1961-62, cons., 1965-66; lectr. Georgetown U., 1973, research prof. diplomacy, 1974-77; del. and/or mem. numerous nat. and internat. meetings; founding mem., bd. dirs. Inst. Study Diplomacy, Georgetown U., Washington, 1978-94, emeritus founding mem., 1995—; co-drafter UN Charter and Food and Agrl. Orgn. (Rome) Constitution, 1944; co-organizer Divsn. Internat. Labor, Health and Social Affairs Dept. State, and Labor attache program of Fgn. Svc. Author: Anatomy of the State Department, 1967, The Crisis in American Diplomacy, 1980, Some Perspectives on the Study of Diplomacy, 1986, Education in Diplomacy, 1987; editor: Belgium in Transition, 1946, Resources and Needs of American Diplomacy, 1968; Instruction in Diplomacy: The Liberal Arts Approach, 1972. Annual diplomacy debate named in his honor Univ. Va. Mem. Am. Fgn. Svc. Assn., Consular Officers Assn., Assn. for Diplomatic Studies and Tng., Inst. for Study of Diplomacy (Georgetown U., founding mem., bd. dirs.), Jefferson Lit. and Debating Soc. (U. Va. assoc.), Raven Soc., Phi Beta Kappa, Phi Sigma Kappa. Presbyterian. Address: 250 Pantops Mountain Rd #41 Charlottesville VA 22911-8680 *I can remember standing on a slope of the Arlington National Cemetery as a teenager one Christmas Day, down apiece from the broken mast of the battleship Maine and, as I laid a wreath on the grave of an ancestor, vowing to do whatever I could the rest of my life for good will and peace among men. From that day, this has been my consuming objective. The broken mast of the Maine has been a kind of compass needle by which my private and diplomatic life has been guided.*

SIMPSON, RUSSELL GORDON, lawyer, mayor, counselor to not-for-profit organizations; b. Springfield, Mass., May 22, 1927; s. Archer Roberts and Maude Ethel (Gordon) S.; m. Bickley S. Flower, Sept. 11, 1954; children: Barbara G., Elisabeth Pires-Fernandes, Helen Blair. B.A., Yale U., 1951; J.D., Boston U., 1956; postgrad., Parker Sch. Internat. Law, 1962. Bar: Mass. 1956, U.S. Dist. Ct. (fed. dist.) Mass. 1957, U.S. Ct. Appeals (2d cir.) 1958, U.S. Supreme Ct. 1980. Advt. mgr. Burden Bryant Co., Springfield, 1951-53; assoc. Goodwin, Procter & Hoar, Boston, 1956-64, ptnr., 1965-87, of counsel, 1987—; sr. advisor to pres. World Learning, Inc., Brattleboro, Vt., 1988-89, exec. v.p., 1989-90, sr. v.p., 1990-91, trustee, 1991—, exec. com., 1994—; trustee, mem. exec. com. Save the Children Fedn., Westport, Conn., 1995—; mem. exec. group Internat. Save the Children Alliance, Geneva, Switzerland, 1996—; dir., mem. exec. com. Cmty. Found. Palm Beach and Martin Counties, West Palm Beach, Fla., 1994—; counselor to not-for-profit orgns., 1991—. Author: The Lawyer's Basic Corporate Practice Manual, 1971, rev. edit., 1978, 84, 87. Mayor Jupiter Island, Fla., 1993—; hon. consul New Eng. of Bolivia, 1958-82, mem. spl. com. to revise Mass. Corrupt Practices Act, 1961-62. Named Outstanding Young Man of Greater Boston, 1963. Fellow Am. Bar Found., Mass. Bar Found.; mem. Mass. Bar Assn. (chmn. banking and bus. law sect. 1980-83, bd. dels., exec. com. 1983-87, v.p. 1985-87), ABA (corp. banking and bus. law sect., com. on law firms, co-chmn. com. on law firm governance, panel on corp. law ednl. programs). Home: 101 Harbor Way Box 1106 Hobe Sound FL 33475

SIMPSON, SCOTT, professional golfer. Profl. golfer, 1979—; PGA tour victories include: Western Open, 1980, Westchester Classics, 1984, Greater Greensboro Open, 1987, U.S. Open, 1987. Office: care PGA 100 Avenue Of Champions Palm Beach Gardens FL 33418*

SIMPSON, STEVEN DREXELL, lawyer; b. Sturgis, Mich., Sept. 20, 1953; s. Drexell and Lorraine Simpson; m. Peggy Deibert, Apr. 28, 1979; children: Andrew Drexell, Christine Elizabeth, Marianne Tyner. BA, Hillsdale (Mich.) Coll., 1975; JD, Wake Forest U., 1978; LLM in Taxation, Georgetown U., 1981. Bar: Fla. 1978, D.C. 1980, N.C. 1984. Assoc. Bradford, Williams et al, Miami, Fla., 1978-80, Webster & Chamberlain, Washington, 1980-82, Fisher, Wayland et al, Washington, 1982-84, Maupin, Taylor & Ellis, P.A., Raleigh, N.C., 1984—. Author: Taxation of Broadcasters, 1984, Tax-Exempt Organizations: Organization, Operation and Reporting Requirements, 1995; contbr. articles to profl. jours. Mem. ABA (exemp orgns. com.). Republican. Methodist. Avocations: golf, running. Home: 3212

Anderson Dr Raleigh NC 27609-7854 Office: Maupin Taylor & Ellis PA PO Box 19764 Raleigh NC 27619-9764

SIMPSON, THOMAS WILLIAM, physician; b. Winston-Salem, N.C., Jan. 24, 1918; s. Thomas William Sr. and Sara Elizabeth (McGee) S.; m. Doris McElroy Cullings, June 2, 1941; children: Lucia Elisabeth Simpson Shen. BS with honors, Southwestern (Rhodes), 1940; MD, John Hopkins, 1943. Diplomate Am. Bd. Internal Medicine. Med. resident Vets. Adminstrn., Columbia, S.C., 1947-49; med. faculty Wake Forest Univ., Winston-Salem, N.C., 1949-66; med. officer Panama Canal Zone, Coco Solo, 1966-67; med. faculty U. Hawaii, Honolulu, 1967-70; med. faculty Johns Hopkins U., Balt., 1970-83, faculty emeritus, 1983—; health dir. Va. Health Dept.; chief med. cons. U. Hawaii, Okinawa, 1967-70; trop med. cons. DOD, 1967-70; resident coord. Johns Hopkins CMRT, Calcutta, India, 1970-72, acting dir., 1973-74. Author: (with others) Hunter's Tropical Medicine, 1984; contbr. articles to profl. jours. Oral fluid therapy cholera, Johns Hopkins U., 1971-72, health status migrant workers, Del Marva, 1983-85. Lt. USN, 1943-47. Recipient Commendation N.C. Health Dept., 1966, Va. Mental Hygiene Dept., 1988. Fellow ACP (coms.), Royal Soc. Tropical Medicine and Hygiene; mem. Am. Ornithologists Union, Am. Soc. Tropical Medicine and Hygiene (coms.). Democrat. Presbyterian. Achievements include incrimination of pigs as important amplifying host of Japanese encephalitis, restoration of Okinawan health care system after WW2, crucial early field trial of oral fluid therapy for cholera in West Bengal, improvement of health care for Haitian and Hispanic migrant farm workers. Office: Johns Hopkins Instn 615 N Wolfe St Baltimore MD 21205-2103

SIMPSON, VINSON RALEIGH, manufacturing company executive; b. Chgo., Aug. 9, 1928; s. Vinson Raleigh and Elsie (Passeger) S.; m. Elizabeth Caroline Matte, Sept. 9, 1950; children: Kathleen Simpson Jackson, Nancy Simpson Ignacio, James Morgan. S.B. in Chem. Engring, Mass. Inst. Tech., 1950; M.B.A., Ind. U., 1955. With Trane Co., LaCrosse, Wis., 1950-75, mgr. mktg. services, 1957-64, mgr. dealer devel., 1964-66; mng. dir. Trane Ltd., Edinburgh, Scotland, 1966; v.p. internat. Trane Co., LaCrosse, Wis., 1967, exec. v.p., 1968-70; exec. v.p., gen. mgr. comml. air conditioning div., 1970-73, pres., 1973-75; pres. Simpson and Co., La Crosse, 1975-76; pres., chief operating officer Marathon Electric Mfg. Corp., Wausau, Wis., 1976-80; chmn., pres., chief exec. officer Marion Body Works, Inc., Wis., 1980-93, chmn., 1993—; bd. dirs. Clintonville Area Found. Regional chmn. edn. coun. MIT; trustee Northland Coll., Fox Valley Tech. Coll.; bd. dirs., pres. Fox Valley Tech. Coll. Found.; past pres., bd. dirs. Wausau Area Jr. Achievement; mem. Marion Minutemen, Adv. Team, U. Wis. With USAF, 1951-53. Decorated Korean War Commendation ribbon. Mem. Fire Apparatus Mfrs., Nat. Truck Equipment Assn., Am. Legion, Kappa Kappa Sigma, Alpha Tau Omega, Beta Gamma Sigma (dirs. table). Congregationalist. Lodges: Masons, Shriners, Jesters, Rotary (past. pres. Marion club, Paul Harris fellow). Avocations: running, handball, snorkeling, water skiing, cross country skiing. Home: 171 Fairway Dr Clintonville WI 54929-1071 Office: Marion Body Works Inc 211 W Ramsdell PO Box 500 Marion WI 54950-9623

SIMPSON, W(ILBURN) DWAIN, physicist, corporate executive, computer systems, telecommunications, and advanced fueling systems consultant; b. Long Grove, Okla., Oct. 4, 1937; s. Joseph Charles and Wilma Ruby (Smith) S.; m. Ann Marie Coratello, Aug. 27, 1967; children: Ketah Marie, Rebecca Elizabeth. BS, U. Miss., 1959, MS, 1961, MA, Rice U., 1963, PhD, 1965. Research assoc. Rice U., Houston, 1965-67; asst. physicist Brookhaven Nat. Lab., Upton, N.Y., 1967-69; v.p., sec., founder Periphonics Corp., Bohemia, N.Y., 1969-80; dir. R&D Periphonics Corp., 1972-78; v.p., sec., founder, dir. R&D Alta Tech. Inc., Stamford, Conn., 1980-85; pres., founder W.D. Simpson Tech., Inc., Wilton, Conn., 1985-91; v.p., founder Saber Equipment Corp., Fairfield, Conn., 1989-97; pres., founder Synergetic Techs. Inc., Wilton, Conn., 1996—; cons. Ayentka Cons. Corp., Bay Shore, N.Y., 1980-81. Author: New Techniques in Software Project Management, 1987; patentee in computers and electronically controlled advanced fueling systems; over 15 patents issued. Fellow NSF, 1961; NASA, 1963. Mem. AAAS, IEEE, Am. Phys. Soc., N.Y. Acad. Scis., Data Processing Mgmt. Assn. Methodist. Avocations: robotics, computer controlled systems. Home: 124 Catalpa Rd Wilton CT 06897-2004 Office: Synergetic Techs Inc 124 Catalpa Rd Wilton CT 06897-2004

SIMPSON, WILLIAM KELLY, curator, Egyptologist, educator; b. N.Y.C., Jan. 3, 1928; s. Kenneth Farrand and Helen L.K. (Porter) S.; m. Marilyn E. Milton, June 19, 1953; children: Laura Knickerbacker Simpson Thorn, Abby Rockefeller Simpson Mydland. BA, Yale U., 1947, MA, 1948, PhD, 1954. Asst. in Egyptian art Met. Mus. Art, 1948-54; rsch. fellow Center Middle East Studies, Harvard U., 1957-58; mem. faculty Yale U., New Haven, 1958—; prof. Egyptology Yale U., 1965—, chmn. dept. Near Eastern langs., 1966-69; curator Egyptian and ancient Near Eastern art Mus. Fine Arts, Boston, 1970-86; ltd. partner Kin and Co., 1967-69; ltd. ptnr. Venrock, 1970—; dir. editor of papers Penn-Yale Archaeol. Expdn. to Egypt, 1960—; mem. adv. council fgn. currency program Smithsonian Instn., 1966-69. Author: Papyrus Reisner I-Records of a Building Project, 1963, Hekanefer and the Dynastic Material from Toshka, 1963, Papyrus Reisner II-Accounts of the Dockyard Workshop, 1965, Papyrus Reisner III: Records of a Building Project in the Early Twelfth Dynasty, 1969, The Terrace of the Great God at Abydos, 1974, The Mastabas of Qar and Idu, 1976, The Offering Chapel of Sekhem-ankh-ptah, 1976, The Offering Chapel of Kayemnofret in the Museum of Fine Arts Boston, 1992, The Inscribed Material from the Pennsylvania-Yale Excavations at Abydos, 1995, (with others) The Ancient Near East, A History, 1971, The Literature of Ancient Egypt, 1972, The Mastaba of Queen Mersyankh III, 1994. Trustee Am. Sch. Classical Studies, Athens, Am. U. in Cairo; mem. internat. council Mus. Modern Art, N.Y.C.; pres. Wrexham Found., 1965-67. Fulbright fellow Egypt, 1955-57; Guggenheim fellow, 1965. Mem. Am. Oriental Soc., Am. Philos. Soc., Archaeol. Inst. Am., Internat. Assn. Egyptologists, Egypt Exploration Soc., Soc. française d'egyptologie, German Archaeol. Inst., Foundation egyptologique Reine Elisabeth. Clubs: Century (N.Y.C.), Met. Opera (N.Y.C.), University (N.Y.C.), Union (N.Y.C.), River (N.Y.C.); Union Boat (Boston); Bedford (N.Y.); Golf and Tennis. Home: 129 Katonah Woods Rd Katonah NY 10536-9532

SIMPSON, WILLIAM STEWART, retired psychiatrist, sex therapist; b. Edmonton, Alta., Can., Apr. 11, 1924; came to U.S., 1950, naturalized, 1963; s. William Edward And Ethel Lillian (Stewart) S.; m. Eleanor Elizabeth Whitbread, June 17, 1950; children—David Kenneth, Ian Stewart, James William, Bert Edward. B.Sc., U. Alta., 1946, M.D., 1948. Diplomate Am. Bd. Psychiatry and Neurology, Am. Bd. Sexology. Rotating intern U. Alta. Hosp., 1948-49, resident in internal medicine, 1949-50; resident in psychiatry Topeka State Hosp., 1950-53, cons., 1967-68, asst. sect. chief, 1953-54, clin. dir., 1954-59, 68-72; fellow Menninger Sch. Psychiatry, Topeka, 1950-53; sect. chief C.F. Menninger Meml. Hosp., 1959-66, dir. edn., 1963-66; assoc. dir. Menninger Sch. Psychiatry, 1966-68; dir. field services Menninger Found., 1972-74, sr. staff psychiatrist adult outpatient dept., 1977-84, assoc. dir. adult outpatient dept., 1984-88; dir. Ctr. for Sexual Health, 1986-92; dir. Psychopharmacotherapy Clinic Menninger Clinic, 1989-90; chief psychiatry service, residency tng. program Topeka VA Hosp., 1974-77; dir. Midwest Impotence Ctr., Kansas City, Mo., 1988-91; mem. faculty Menninger Sch. Psychiatry, 1953-92, Ann. Seminar Inst. on Alcoholism, U. Wis., 1973-74; guest lectr. sex therapy Chinese Med. Assn., Rep. of China, 1985, Med. Sch. Tokai (Japan) U., 1985, dept. psychology U. Warsaw, Poland, 1987; cons. Osawatomie State Hosp., 1954-68, Colmery-O'Neill VA Hosp., 1983-92; mem. staff Stormont-Vail Hosp., Topeka, St. Francis Hosp., Topeka, Kans. Rehab. Hosp., Topeka, 1988-92; cons. in sex therapy Colmery-O'Neill VA Hosp., Topeka, 1983-92. Assoc. editor Bull. Menninger Clinic, 1963-70; cons. editor Jour. Med. Aspects of Human Sexuality, 1991-92. Bd. dirs. Topeka Civic Symphony Soc., 1953-55, Topeka People to People Council, 1963-66; ruling elder local Presbyn. ch., 1960—; mem. Kans. Citizens' Adv. Com. on Alcoholism, 1973-78; co-founder Topeka affiliate Nat. Council on Alcoholism, 1964, pres., 1964-65, bd. dirs., 1964, bd. dirs. N.Y.C., 1967, v.p., 1971-73, pres., 1973-75, mem. exec. com., 1967. Recipient Bronze Key award, Topeka affiliate Nat. Council on Alcoholism; 1972, Silver Key award, 1975, Outstanding Achievement award U. Alta. Med. Alumni Assn., 1975. Fellow Am. Psychiat. Assn. (life); mem. Topeka Inst. Psychoanalysis (cert.), Am. Assn. Sex Educators, Counselors and Therapists (cert. sex therapist, sex educator, supr.), Am. Psychoanalytic Assn. (cert.), AMA, Kans. Psychiat. Soc., Kans. Med. Soc., Shawnee County Med. Soc., Topeka Psychoanalytic Soc., Menninger Sch. Psychiatry Alumni Assn. (pres. 1979-80), Soc. for Sci. Study of Sex, Soc. for Sex Therapy and Research, Am. Assn. Sex Educators, Counselors and Therapists, Phi Delta Theta (Phi of Yr. award Kansas Beta chpt. 1964). Democrat. Presbyterian. Club: Saturday Night Literary (pres. 1990-91). Lodge: Rotary. Avocations: reading, classical music, photography, masters swimming. Home: 834 SW Buchanan St Topeka KS 66606-1428

SIMS, ALBERT MAURICE, marketing professional; b. N.Y.C., Jan. 22, 1930; s. Samuel Lee and Jennie (Rosenberg) S.; m. Estelle Deiner-Sims, Nov. 15, 1963 (div. June 1985). Diploma in Physics, Adelphi Coll., 1960; postgrad., Bklyn. Coll., 1968-72. Analytic engr. Stratos Divsn. Fairchild, Bayshore, N.Y., 1954-60; program mgr. EDO Corp., College Point, N.Y., 1960-76; mktg. mgr. Sperry, Great Neck, N.Y., 1976-85; dir. programs devel. PRC, McLean, Va., 1986-95; dir. bus. devel. Grumman Data Systems, Herndon, Va., 1986-95; v.p. programs Info. Tech. Solutions, Reston, Va., 1995—; v.p. mktg. EPI, Fairfax, Va., 1989-96; cons. Naval Studies Bd., D.C., 1982-83; adv. bd. SDS, Fairfax, 1990—; pres. Performance Engring., Fairfax, 1980—. Editor: Patron mag., 1956-50. Lobbyist PEI, Fairfax, 1980-95; campaigner fgn. aid issues, 1992-94; mem. U.S. Congl. adv. bd., D.C., 1982. Mem. Armed Forces Comms./Electronics Assn., Navy League, Nat. Def. Transp. Assn., Assn. of Old Crows. Avocations: music, swimming, skiing, photography, boating.

SIMS, BENNETT JONES, minister, educator; b. Greenfield, Mass., Aug. 9, 1920; s. Lewis Raymond and Sarah Cosette (Jones) S.; children: Laura (Mrs. John P. Boucher), Grayson, David. AB, Baker U., 1943, LHD (hon.), 1985; postgrad., Princeton Theol. Sem., 1946-47; B.D., Va. Theol. Sem., 1949, D.D., 1966; D.D., U. of South, 1972; Merrill fellow, Harvard U., 1964-65; postgrad., Cath. U., 1969-71. Ordained to ministry Episc. Ch. as deacon, 1949, priest, 1950. Rector Ch. of Redeemer, Balt., 1951-64; dir. continuing edn. Va. Theol. Sem., 1966-72; bishop of Atlanta, 1972-83; vis. prof. theology Emory U., Atlanta, 1980-88, pres. Inst. for Servant Leadership, 1988—; priest-in-charge St. Alban's Ch., Tokyo, 1962, 69. Author: Servanthood: Leadership for the Third Millennium, 1997. Trustee U. of South. With USNR, 1943-46. Named Young Man of Yr. Balt. C. of C., 1953; Disting. Alumnus of Yr., Baker U., 1972. Office: Inst Servant Leadership Hendersonville NC 28793

SIMS, DAVID BRYSON, JR., engineer; b. Memphis, Aug. 12, 1947; s. David Bryson and Ruth (Gnuse) S.; widowed; children: Jennifer Braddock, David Bryson III. BSChemE, U. Tenn., 1969; MS Mech. Engring., U. Memphis, 1972, MS Civil Engring., 1974. Registered profl. engr., Ga., Mi., Va., Kans., N.C., Tenn., S.C., La., Ohio, Ind., Fla., Md. Engr. DuPont, Memphis, 1969-73; cons. engr. Elles, Reaves, Fanning & Oakley, Memphis, 1973-75; engr. W.R. Grace, Memphis, 1975-79; engring. mgr. W.R. Grace, Wilmington, N.C., 1979-85; prin. David Sims & Assocs., Wilmington, 1985—; trustee Cape Fear Acad., Wilmington, 1987-92; part-time instr. Cape Fear C.C., Wilmington, 1981-86. Bd. dirs., pres. Bradley Creek Boatominium, Wilmington, 1990-97. Mem. NSPE, ASHRAE, AIChE (sec. 1972, pres. 1973), Nat. Fire Protection Assn. Republican. Presbyterian. Home: 2721 Shandy Ln Wilmington NC 28409-2042 Office: David Sims & Assocs 108 N Kerr Ave Ste K-1 Wilmington NC 28405-3406

SIMS, DEBBIE DEANN, psychotherapist; b. Ft. Wayne, Ind., Dec. 18, 1948; d. Richard and Helen (Becker) Brudi; m. Andrew J. Dodzik (div. 1983); children: Julie Kristine, Peter Allen, Stephanie Ann; m. Tom E. Sims, Oct. 5, 1985. RN, Parkview Sch. Nursing, Ft. Wayne, 1969; BA, Concordia Sr. Coll., 1976; MS, St. Francis Coll., 1979. Cert. clin. specialist in adult psychiat. and mental health nursing; cert. clin. social worker; cert. marriage and family therapist; lic. profl. clin. counselor; cert. nat. counselor. Staff nurse Parkview Meml. Hosp., Ft. Wayne, 1969-74, clin. supr., 1991-95; sr. psychotherapist, intake clinician Psychiat. Svcs., Inc., Ft. Wayne, 1974-91; therapist Parkview Sch. Nursing, Ft. Wayne, 1980-89; ptnr. Psychiat. Care Inc., Ft. Wayne, 1995—; cons., therapist Parkview Sch. Nursing, Ft. Wayne, 1980-89. Mem. Am. Mental Health Counselor Assn., Am. Assn. Counseling & Devel. Roman Catholic. Avocation: travel. Home: 4814 Golfview Dr Fort Wayne IN 46818-9338 Office: 415 E Cook Rd Ste 100 Fort Wayne IN 46825-3657

SIMS, DOUGLAS D., bank executive; b. 1946. Grad., U. Ill., Urbana, 1968. With St. Louis Bank for Cooperatives, St. Louis, 1969-74; v.p. Ctrl. Bank for Coops., 1974-78; pres. St. Louis Bank for Coops., 1978-84; exec. v.p. Farm Credit Banks of St. Louis, 1984-86, pres., 1986-88; pres. Nat. Bank for Cooperatives, Englewood, Colo., 1988-93; CEO CoBank, Englewood, 1994—. Office: CoBank 5500 S Quebec St Englewood CO 80111-1914

SIMS, EDWARD HOWELL, editor, publisher; b. Orangeburg, S.C., May 29, 1923; s. Hugo Sheridan and Jesse Lucile (Howell) S.; m. Frances Dell Hartt, Jan. 5, 1946; m. Martha Lurene Bass, July 18, 1960; children—Edward H., Robert; m. Bente Thorlund Christensen, Oct. 4, 1969; children—Edward Christian, Frederik. A.B., Wofford Coll., 1943; postgrad., Emory U., 1946-47. Mng. editor Orangeburg Times and Democrat, 1946, editor, 1952—; Washington corr., founder Washington bur. for number S.C. dailies, 1947; dir. Sims Pub. Co., Orangeburg. Columnist: Looking South From Washington, 1948—; Washington Bur. chief: Editor's Copy syndicate, 1950-52; editor-pub., 1952—; radio news analyst: The News of The Week In Washington, 1951—; Author: American Aces, 1958, Greatest Fighter Missions, 1962, The Fighter Pilots, 1967, Fighter Tactics 1914-70, 1972, Aces Over the Oceans, 1987; contbr. articles to publs. White House corr. covering Pres."s confs., 1948—; mem. Senate and House press galleries, 1947—; Am. consul Munich, Germany, 1963-65; cons. Exec. Office of White House, 1966-67; consul gen. Zurich, 1992; apptd. mem. Commn. to Preserve Am. Heritage Abroad, 1987. Served to 1st lt. USAF, World War II. Recipient Young Man of the Year award S.C. Jr. C. of C., 1959. Mem. White House Corrs. Assn., Am. Legion, V.F.W. Methodist. Clubs: Rotary, Nat. Press; Metropolitan (Washington); R.A.F. (London). Home: 3803 Pin Oaks St Sarasota FL 34232-1241 also: PO Box 400 Fairview NC 28730-0400 Office: PO Box 532 Orangeburg SC 29116-0532

SIMS, EVERETT MARTIN, publishing company executive; b. Morristown, N.J., June 27, 1920; s. Walter Leonard and Amy Ethel (Coleman) S. B.A., Drew U., Madison, N.J., 1941; M.A., Harvard U., 1947. Dir. project planning div. Prentice-Hall, Inc., Englewood Cliffs, N.J., 1950-60; asst. v.p. Prentice-Hall, Inc., 1956-60; with Harcourt Brace Jovanovich, Inc., N.Y.C., 1960-82; v.p. Harcourt Brace Jovanovich, Inc., 1970-80, sr. v.p., 1980-82; dir. coll. dept., 1970-82; pres. Media Systems Corp., 1974-77, chmn., 1977-81; pres. Telamon Enterprises, Inc., 1982—. Served with USAAF, 1942-45; Served with USAF, 1950-51, ETO. Decorated Air medal Croix de Guerre, (France). Home and Office: 180 Sebonac Rd Southampton NY 11968-2727

SIMS, EZRA, composer; b. Birmingham, Ala., Jan. 16, 1928; s. Ezra G. and Kathryn W. (Wallace) S. BA, Birmingham So. Coll., 1947; postgrad., Birmingham Conservatory Music, 1945-48; MusB in Composition, Yale U. Sch. Music, 1952; MA in Composition, Mills Coll., 1956. Librarian Harvard Music Library, Cambridge, Mass., 1958-62, 65-74; music dir. New Eng. Dinosaur Dance Theatre, Boston, 1968-78; instr. theory New Eng. Conservatory Music, Boston, 1976-78; instr. microtonal theory Mozarteum, Salzburg, 1992-93; freelance composer Cambridge, 1974—; dir. Dinosaur Annex Music Ensemble, Cambridge, pres. 1977-81; guest composer 23d Ann. Contemporary Music Festival, Ill. Wesleyan U., 1977; lectr. various colls. including Warwick U., Cleve. Inst. Music, Internat. Christian U., Westport Friends of Music, Schlumberger-Doll Rsch., Webster U., Mozarteum, Northwestern U., Hochschule für Musik, Hamburg. Composer over 100 works, predominantly microtonal music for various mediums including Chamber Cantata on Chinese Poems, 1954, Mass, 1955, Two Folk Songs, 1958, String Quartet, 1959, Sieben-Spencer Lieder, 1960, Sonate Concertanti, 1961, Third Quartet, 1962, Buchlein for Lyon, 1962, Cantata III, 1963, Octet for Strings, 1964, In Memoriam Alice Hawthorne, 1967, Antimatter: Three Dances for Toby, 1968, A Frank Overture: Four Dented Interludes and Coda, 1969, Pastorale, 1970, Clement Wenceslaus Lothaire Nepomucene, Prince Mettermich (1773-1859), In Memoriam, 1970, Real Toads, 1970, Interlope, 1971, Tango Variations, 1971, Museum Piece, 1972, Where the Wild Things Are, 1973, String Quartet #2 1962, 1974, After Lyle or Untitled, 1975, When the Angels Blow Their Trumpets, 1976, Celebration of Dead Ladies, 1976, Elegie-nach Rilke, 1976, Collage XIII, 1977, Aeneas on the Saxophone, 1977, Come Away, 1978, Midorigaoka, 1978, 5 Songs, 1979, -And, As I Was Saying..., 1979, Two for One, 1980, Sextet, 1981, All Done From Memory, 1980, Phenomena, 1981, Solo After Sextet, 1981, Quartet, 1982, Pictures for an Institution, 1983, Tune and Variations, 1983, Brief Elegies, 1983, String Quartet #4, 1984, The Conversions, 1985, Wedding Winds, 1986, Quintet, 1987, Chase, 1987, Solo in four movements, 1987, AEDM in memoriam, 1988, Flight, 1989, Night Piece: IN Girum Imus nocte et Consuminur Igni, 1989, Concert Piece, 1990, Duo, 1992, Invocation, 1992, Stanzas, 1995, If I Told Him, 1996, Duo, 1996; contbr. articles to profl. jours. Served as pvt. U.S. Army, 1952-54. Recipient Composers Forum award, 1959, Koussevitzky Found. commn., 1983, Am. Acad. Arts and Letters award, 1985; grantee Cambridge Arts Coun., 1975, 76, Martha Baird Rockefeller Found., 1977; fellow Guggenheim Found., 1962, Nat. Endowment for Arts, 1976, 78, Mass. Artists Found., 1979, Fulbright Sr. Scholar, 1992. Mem. Am. Composers Alliance, Broadcast Music, Inc. Home and Office: 1168 Massachusetts Ave Cambridge MA 02138-5205

SIMS, HENRY P., JR., management educator. Prof. mgmt. U. Md., College Park. Author: The Thinking Organization: Dynamics of Organizational Social Cognition, 1986, Super Leadership: Leading Others to Lead Themselves, 1989, The New Leadership Paradigm: Social Learning and Cognition in Organizations, 1992, Business Without Bosses: How Self-Managing Teams Are Building High-Performance Companies, 1993, Company of Heroes: Unleashing the Power of Self Leadership, 1996. Office: U Md Dept Mgmt College Park MD 20742-0001

SIMS, JAMES HYLBERT, English educator, former university administrator; b. Orlando, Fla., Oct. 29, 1924; s. James W. and Anna L. (Hylbert) S.; m. Ruth Elizabeth Gray, Jan. 3, 1944; children: James W., Timothy C., Suzannah C., C. Andrew, John M. BA in English, History and Psychology, U. Fla., 1949, MA in English, 1950, PhD in English Lit., 1959. Lic. comml. pilot FAA. Instr. English Tenn. Temple Coll., 1950-51; pres., instr. English Tri-State Bapt. Coll., Evansville, Ind., 1951-54; instr. English U. Fla., Gainesville, 1955-57, 58-59; prof. English, chmn. dept. Tift Coll., Forsyth, Ga., 1959-61, Austin Peay State U., Clarksville, Tenn., 1961-66; prof. U. Okla., Norman, 1966-76; prof. English and dean Coll. Liberal Arts U. So. Miss., Hattiesburg, 1976-82, v.p. acad. affairs, 1982-89, Disting. prof. English, v.p. emeritus for Acad. affairs, 1989-95, prof. emeritus, 1995—; Clyde Kilby lectr. Wheaton (Ill.) Coll., 1991-92, Charles G. Smith lectr. in English Baylor U., 1994. Author: Biblical Allusions in Shakespeare's Comedies, 1960, The Bible in Milton's Epics, 1962, Dramatic Uses of Biblical Allusions in Marlowe and Shakespeare, 1966, Milton and Scriptural Tradition: The Bible Into Poetry, 1984, A Comparative Literary Study of Daniel and Revelation: Shaping the End, 1995; contbr. chpts. to books; contbr. numerous articles on lit. criticism, comparative lit. and lit. history to scholarly jours.; assoc. editor: Seventeenth-Century News, 1968—. Bd. dirs. Baptist Faith Missions, Internat. Bd. Jewish Missions. Served with USN, 1943-46. Fellow Southeastern Inst. Medieval and Renaissance Studies, 1965-66, NEH, summer 1974, NEH-Huntington Libr., 1973, 78-79; recipient Regents' Superior Tchg. award U. Okla., 1968. Mem. MLA, John Donne Soc., Milton Soc. Am. (pres. 1976), South Atlantic MLA, South Ctrl. MLA, South Ctrl. Renaissance Conf. (pres. 1983), Conf. Christianity and Lit. (chmn. South Ctrl. 1981-82, 87-88, nat. pres. 1990-92), Rotary (Paul Harris fellow). Democrat. Baptist. Home: 3103 Delwood Dr Hattiesburg MS 39401-7214 Office: U So Miss English Dept Hattiesburg MS 39406

SIMS, JAMES LARRY, hospital administrator, healthcare consultant; b. Birmingham, Ala., Feb. 16, 1936; s. James Alexander and Elsie Lee (Coleman) S.; m. Sandra Anne Hanzel, July 25, 1981. AB, Birmingham Southern, 1958; cert., U. Ala., 1970. Diplomate Am. Acad. Med. Adminstrs. Sgt. USAF res. Fellow Am. Acad. Med. Adminstrs., Royal Soc. Health, Am. Coll. Healthcare Execs.; mem. Fla. Hosp. Personnel Dirs. Assn. (pres. 1964-65), South Fla. Hosp. Personnel Dirs. Assn. (pres. 1967-68), Fla. Hosp. Pub. Rels. Assn. (pres. 1970-71), South Fla. Pub. Rels. Coun. (pres. 1963-64). Democrat. Methodist. Home: Flying S Ranch PO Box 7825 Las Cruces NM 88006

SIMS, JANETTE ELIZABETH LOWMAN, educational director; b. Lincolnton, N.C., July 21, 1934; d. Lee Hobson and Myrtle Elizabeth (Travis) Lowman; m. Mickey Ray Sims, Feb. 2, 1951; children: Carol Lee Sims Walden, Rickey Ray. BS, Lenoir-Rhyne Coll., 1968; MAT, U. N.C., 1973; EdD, U. N.C., Greensboro, 1989. N.C. "G" tchg. cert; cert. devel. edn. specialist. Quality control supr. Kiser Roth Hosiery, Inc., Maiden, N.C., 1959-63; 9th grade phys. sci. and math. tchr. Cherryville (N.C.) Jr. H.S., 1968; phys. sci., chemistry and astronomy tchr. Maiden (N.C.) H.S., 1968-75; dir. studies lab. coord. Catawba Valley C.C., Hickory, N.C., 1975-79; physics, chemistry, math. and computer sci. instr. Catawba Valley C.C., Hickory, 1979-90, dir. developmental studies and learning assistance ctr., 1990—; trustee Catawba County Assn. for Spl. Edn., Conover, 1978-79, Catawba Valley Found., Hickory, 1993-96, chair, 1996; apprentice program instr. Meredith/Burda Corp., Newton, N.C., 1979-88. Coun. mem., choir mem., tchr. Faith Luth. Ch., Conover, 1980—. Mem. NEA, N.C. Assn. Educators (local unit pres.), Nat. Assn. Developmental Educators, N.C. Assn. Developmental Educators (regional chair 1990), Atlantic Assn. Physics Tchrs. (chair nominations com. 1992), N.C. Math. Assn. Two-Yr. Colls. (chairperson devel. math. com. 1991-93, sec. 1996—), Am. Legion Aux., Delta Kappa Gamma. Avocations: golfing, sewing, cooking. Home: 300 Parlier Ave Conover NC 28613-9312 Office: Catawba Valley CC 2550 Us Highway 70 SE Hickory NC 28602-8302

SIMS, JOE, lawyer; b. Phoenix, Sept. 29, 1944; s. Joe and Pauline Jane (Saunders) S.; m. Robin Ann Reed, Jan. 30, 1965; 1 child, Shannon Dane. BS in Fin., Ariz. State U., 1967, JD, 1970. Bar: Ariz. 1970, U.S. Supreme Ct. 1975, D.C 1978. Trial atty. antitrust div. Dept. Justice, Washington, 1970-73; spl. asst. to asst. atty. gen., 1973-75; dep. asst. atty. gen. for policy planning and legislation, 1975-77, dep. asst. atty. gen. for regulatory matters and fgn. commerce, 1977-78; mem. firm Jones, Day, Reavis & Pogue, Washington, 1978-79; ptnr. Jones, Day, Reavis & Pogue, 1979—; resident fellow Am. Enterprise Inst. for Pub. Policy Rsch., Washington, 1978-79, vis. fellow, 1979-81; prin. Coun. for Excellence in Govt. Contbr. various articles to prof. jours. Mem. ABA (chmn. antitrust law sect. one com. 1987-90, bus. law sect. antitrust law com. 1988-91, antitrust law civil practice and procedure com. 1990-91), Am. Law Inst., D.C. Bar Assn., City Club Washington, Tournament Players Club (Potomac, Md.), Firestone Country Club (Akron, Ohio), Collecton River Plantation (Hilton Head Island, S.C.). Republican. Home: 10100 New London Dr Potomac MD 20854-4849 Office: Jones Day Reavis & Pogue 1450 G St NW Ste 600 Washington DC 20005-2001

SIMS, JOHN ROGERS, JR., lawyer; b. Red Star, W.Va., Apr. 10, 1924; s. John Rogers and Myrtle (Hutchison) S.; m. Geraldine L. Bucklew, Oct. 8, 1966; children: John Rogers III, Joyce Rebecca. B.S. in Commerce, U. Va., 1950, LL.B., 1952. Assoc. firm Dow, Lohnes & Albertson, Washington, 1953-57; gen. counsel D.C. Transit System, Inc., Washington, 1957-65; individual practice law Washington, 1965-68; partner firm Wrape and Hernly, Arlington, Va., 1968-71, Sims, Walker & Steinfeld (and predecessor firm), Washington, 1972-95; pvt. practice Nellysford, Va., 1995—; Chmn. bd. dirs. John Sims Assocs., Inc., Purnell Bros. Transport, Ltd., 1981-91; co-founder, bd. dirs., gen. counsel A Presdl. Classroom for Young Ams., Inc., chmn. bd. dirs., 1979-83; dir., v.p., gen. counsel, sec. SunWorld Internat. Airways, Inc., 1984-88. Vice chmn. Falls Church (Va.) Planning Commn., 1958-64; pres. Falls Church Republican Party, 1961-62; bd. dirs. Heart Assn. No. Va., Inc., pres., 1963-64; bd. dirs., v.p., gen. counsel Commonwealth Doctors Hosp., Fairfax, Va., 1967-74. Served with Armed Forces, 1943-45. Mem. ABA, W.Va. Bar Assn., D.C. Bar Assn., Va. State Bar, Motor Carrier Lawyers Assn. (nat. pres. 1971-72), Assn. for Transp. Law, Logistics and Policy, Va. Trial Lawyers Assn., Rotary, Masons (Shriner), Washington Golf and Country Club, Farmington Country Club (Charlottesville, Va.). Presbyterian. Home: 31 Sawmill Creek Dr Nellysford VA 22958

SIMS, JOHN WILLIAM, lawyer; b. Vicksburg, Miss., Mar. 25, 1917; s. John Ernest and Helen Ross (Moore) S.; m. Marie Elise Hebert, Sept. 28, 1940; 1 dau., Helen Moore. B.A., Tulane U., 1937, LL.B., 1939. Bar: La. 1939. Of counsel Phelps Dunbar; mem. permanent adv. bd.-planning com. Admiralty Law Inst., Tulane U., New Orleans, 1966—, chmn., 1985-91, adj. prof. law, 1981-95. Assoc. editor Am. Maritime Cases, 1974-96; mem. editl. bd. Lloyd's Maritime and Comml. Law Quar., 1984-92; mem. bd. adv.

editors Tulane Law Rev., 1985-93, Maritime Advisor-Ct. Case Digest, 1985-96; contbr. articles to profl. jours. Trustee Gulf South Rsch. Inst., 1965-68, Children's Hosp., 1975-78; bd. dirs. Coun. for Better La., Bur. Govt. Rsch., 1973-84, USCG Found., 1986-91, La. World Expn., Inc., 1980-84, World Trade Ctr., 1985—; bd. dirs., v.p. New Orleans Opera Assn., 1974-93; mem. men's adv. bd. Christian Woman's Exch. Lt USCGR, 1942-45. Named Rex, King of Carnival Mardi Gras, New Orleans, 1981; recipient Disting. Pub. Service award Dept. Transp. U.S. Coast Guard, 1985. Fellow Am. Coll. Trial Lawyers; mem. Am., La. (past sec.-treas.), New Orleans Bar assns., Maritime Law Assn. U.S. (2d v.p. 1976-78, 1st v.p. 1978-80, pres. 1980-82, com. Supreme Ct. admiralty rules 1963-69, com. limitation of liability 1963-96, com. Comite Maritime Internat. 1965-80, com. uniformity admiralty law 1975-92, com. liquified natural gas transp. 1978-80, del. Comite Maritime Internat. conv. N.Y.C. 1965, Rio de Janeiro, 1977, Montreal, 1981, adv. cons. Hamburg 1974, titular mem. Comite Maritime Internat. 1979—, del. Comite Maritime Internat. Lisbon Conv., 1985), SAR, Soc. Colonial Wars, Order of Coif, Phi Beta Kappa, Omicron Delta Kappa, Phi Delta Theta, Phi Delta Phi. Clubs: Boston, Louisiana. Office: Texaco Ctr 400 Poydras St Fl 30 New Orleans LA 70130-3245

SIMS, KEITH, professional football player; b. Balt., June 17, 1967. BS in Indsl. Tech., Iowa State U. Guard Miami Dolphins, 1990—; player AFC Championship Game, 1992. Named to Pro Bowl Team, 1993. *

SIMS, KENT OTWAY, economist; b. Chickasha, Okla., Nov. 2, 1940; s. Jesse Otway and Mable Vela (Bear) S.; m. Jeanette McCollum, June 9, 1961; children: Marketa, Adam. B.A., U. Colo., 1963, Ph.D., 1966. registered investment advisor. Economist Urban Renewal Authority, Denver, 1965-66, U.S. Dept. State mission to Pakistan, 1966-69; economist Fed. Res. Bank of San Francisco, 1969-71, asst. v.p., 1971-72, v.p., dir. research, 1972-74, sr. v.p., 1974-82, exec. v.p., chief fin. officer, 1982-85; fin. advisor, investment mgr., mgmt. cons. Theodore R. Seton, 1985-86; ptnr. C&K Partnership, 1987-89; pres. Her Equal Share, Inc., 1986-89, San Francisco Econ. Devel. Corp., 1988-91; dir. econ. planning and devel. Mayor's Office, San Francisco, 1992-93, San Francisco Redevel. Agy., 1993-96; dir. spl. projects City Mgr.'s Office, Oakland, Calif., 1997. Bd. govs. Econ. Lit. Coun. Calif., Long Beach, 1983-88; trustee Strybing Arboretum Soc. Golden Gate Park, San Francisco, 1993-96; bd. dirs. Jewish Community Mus., San Francisco, 1986-93, Design Coun. San Francisco Bay Area, 1989-90, Career Resources Devel. Ctr., 1991-92; adv. bd. St. Lukes Hosp., San Francisco, 1988-96. Mem. Am. Econs. Assn., Nat. Audubon Soc. Am. Clubs: Sierra.

SIMS, KONSTANZE OLEVIA, social worker, case manager; b. Dallas, Dec. 20, 1944; d. Kenneth Winn and Odie Lee (Wells) S. Student, U. Dallas, 1963-64; BA, U. Tex., Arlington, 1968; MEd, U. North Tex., 1972. Sec. Stillman Coll. Regional Campaign Fund, Dallas, 1969; employment interviewer Zale Corp., Dallas, 1969-71; sch. counselor Bishop Dunne High Sch, Dallas, 1973-78; dir. guidance Notre Dame High Sch., Wichita Falls, Tex., 1978-81; taxpayer svc. rep. IRS, Dallas, 1981-83, acct. analyst, 1983-88; freelance Dallas, 1989-90; social worker Tex. Dept. Human Svcs., Dallas, 1991-96, Tex. Workforce Commn., 1996—. Reader, North Tex. Taping & Radio for the Blind, Dallas, 1991—; ; mem. Whale Adoption Project; mem. Union Chorale. Mem. AAUW, Am. Counseling Assn., Nat. Specialty Merchandising Assn., Am. Multicultural Counseling Assn., Am. Bible Tchrs. Assn., Tex. Counseling Assn., Tex. Multicultural Counseling Assn., Assn. Rsch. and Enlightenment, Inc., Assn. for Spiritual, Ethical, and Religious Values in Counseling, U. Tex Arlington Alumni Assn., U. North Tex. Alumni Assn. Avocations: reading, crossword puzzles, singing. Office: Tex Workforce Commn 2922 Martin Luther King Jr Blv Dallas TX 75215-2321

SIMS, LARRY KYLE, secondary school educator; b. Ft. Worth, Dec. 28, 1944; s. Kyle G. and Gladys (Holloway) S.; m. Stephenie Chandler, Aug. 30, 1968; children: Alan Dean (dec.), Roy B. BBA, Howard Payne, Brownwood, Tex., 1969; MEd, Colo. State U., 1975. Cert. tchr., Tex., Wyo.; lic. real estate broker, Tex., Wyo. Coord. Breckenridge (Tex.) High Sch., 1970-74; multi-occupations coord. Lander (Wyo.) Valley High Sch., 1974-76; diversified occupations coord. Riverton (Wyo.) Career Ctr., 1977-79; mktg. edn. coord. Stephenville (Tex.) High Sch., 1986—, tech prep coord., 1994—. Author: Little Spotted Moo, 1991. Mem. Am. Vocat. Assn., Nat. Mktg. Educators, Tex. Vocat. Assn. Consortium, Mktg. Educators Tex. (state pres. 1989-90). Baptist. Avocations: snow skiing, gold hunting, photography. Home: PO Box 1606 Stephenville TX 76401-7606 Office: 726 N Clinton St Stephenville TX 76401-3003

SIMS, MARCIE LYNNE, English language educator, writer; b. Monrovia, Calif., Feb. 22, 1963; d. Charles Eugene and Delores May (Wonert) S.; m. Douglas Todd Cole; 1 child, Marcus Anthony Cole. BA in English, Calif. State Poly., 1986; MA in English, San Diego State U., 1990. Page U.S. Senate, Washington, 1979; instr. Calif. Conservation Corps, San Diego, 1990; instr. in English Shoreline C.C., Seattle, 1990-94, Seattle Ctrl. C.C., 1990-94, Green River C.C., Auburn, Wash., 1994—; founder Wild Mind Women Writers Workshop, Seattle, 1992—. Author: Soul-Making: John Keats and the Stages of Death, 1990; contbg. author Moms on Line, 1996—; co-editor: The Great Tchrs. Almanac, 1988-90. Vol. cons. Camp Fire, Wash., 1994-96. Mem. Am. Fedn. Tchrs., The Keats-Shelley Orgn., Wash. Fed. Tchrs. (exec. bd. mem. 1993-94), Phi Kappa Phi, Sigma Tau Delta. Democrat. Avocations: cooking, tennis. Office: Green River CC 12401 SE 320th St Auburn WA 98092-3622

SIMS, PAUL KIBLER, geologist; b. Newton, Ill., Sept. 8, 1918; s. Dorris Lee and Vere (Kibler) S.; m. Dolores Carsell Thomas, Sept. 15, 1940; children: Thomas Courtney, Charlotte Ann. AB, U. Ill., 1940, MS, 1942; PhD, Princeton, 1950. Spl. asst. geologist Ill. Geol. Survey, 1942-43; geologist U.S. Geol. Survey, 1943-61; prof. geology, dir. Minn. Geol. survey U. Minn., 1961-73; research geologist U.S. Geol. Survey, 1973-95, rsch. geologist emeritus, 1995—; pres. Econ. Geology Pub. Co., 1979-96; Bd. dirs. North Star Research and Devel. Inst., Mpls., 1966-73. Co-editor: Geology of Minnesota, 1972, 75th anniversary vo.. Economic Geology, 1981. Adviser Minn. Outdoor Recreation Resources Commn., 1963-67. Served with USNR, 1943-46. Recipient Meritorious Service award U.S. Dept. Interior, 1984; Goldich medal Inst. on Lake Superior Geology, 1985, Disting. Svc. award U.S. Dept. Interior, 1991. Fellow Geol. Soc. Am., Soc. Econ. Geologists (hon.; councilor 1965-68, pres. 1975, Ralph W. Marsden award medal 1989); mem. Internat. Assn. on Genesis of Ore Deposits, Internat. Union Geol. Sci. (subcom. Precambrian stratigraphy, sec. 1976-84), Assn. Am. State Geologists (hon.), Colo. Sci. Soc. (hon.). Research geology metalliferous ore deposits Colo., Minn., Wis., N.J., Ariz., Wash., Wyo., also early evolution earth's crust in N. Am. Home: 1315 Overhill Rd Golden CO 80401-4238 *Hard work and diligence can cover for a lot of deficiencies.*

SIMS, REBECCA GIBBS, accountant, certified fraud examiner; b. Houston, Mar. 13, 1951; d. Shelton P. Gibbs and Elizabeth Gill Bisby; m. Morris Raymond Sims (div. 1977); children: Diana Elizabeth, Aaron Redding. BFA, U. Houston, 1977. Cert. fraud examiner. V.p. Lexley U.S.A., Inc., Houston and Mexico City, 1977-81; acct. self-employed, Houston, 1982-87, journalist/investigator, 1987—, fin. fraud investigator, 1991—; mng. ptnr. Boynton & Assocs., 1996—. Editor, rschr.: Mafia, CIA and George Bush, 1992; screenwriter; journalist Bilanz mag., Switzerland, 1989-91; author article. Childbirth instr. Houston Orgn. Parent Edn., Houston, 1974-77. Mem. Investigative Reporters and Editors, Nat. Writers Union, Assn. Cert. Fraud Examiners, Mensa. Democrat. Avocations: painting, gardening. Office: 440 Louisiana St Ste 1720 Houston TX 77002-1636

SIMS, RICHARD LEE, hospital administrator; b. Columbus, Ohio, Jan. 6, 1929; s. Dorwin Delos and Christine Anna (Hanstein) S.; m. Marilyn Lou Atkinson, June 2, 1951; children: John Christopher, Steven Paul. B.S., Ohio State U., 1951. Past pres. Doctors Hosp. Found., Columbus; preceptor faculty Ohio State U. Coll. Health Care Adminstrn.; past chmn. hosp. council Franklin County; ret., 1995; past chmn. Hosp. Shared Svc. Inc., Found. Osteo Health Svcs., 1989-93. Past pres. Franklin County chpt. ARC; past chmn. 1st Comty. Village Bd.; past chmn. governing bd. 1st Comty. Ch.; treas. Scioto Valley Health Systems Agy., 1986—; bd. dirs. Columbus Speech and Hearing Ctr.; past chair Columbus area chpt. ARC, emeritus bd. dirs. Recipient Distinguished Service award Columbus Jr. C. of C., 1960-63. Fellow Am. Coll. Healthcare Execs. (life), Am. Coll. Osteo. Healthcare Execs.; mem. Am. Osteo. Healthcare Assn. (chmn. 1988), Ohio Trade Assn. Execs. (past pres.), Ohio Hosp. Assn. (past chmn. bd.), Ohio Osteo. Hosp. Assn. (past pres.), Am. Legion (past post comdr.), Rotary (pres. 1978-79), Columbus Club, Sigma Chi. Home: 1180 Kenbrook Hills Dr Columbus OH 43220-4941

SIMS, ROBERT BARRY, lawyer; b. N.Y.C., Aug. 20, 1942; s. Irving Zach and Laura (Levine) S.; m. Roberta Jane Donner, Nov. 17, 1973; children: Alexandra Lauren, Andrew Michael, Amanda Morgan. AB, Franklin and Marshall Coll., 1964; JD, George Washington U., 1967; MBA, NYU, 1969. Bar: N.Y. 1968, D.C. 1969, Conn. 1980, Tex. 1995, U.S. Dist. Ct. D.C. 1969, U.S. Dist. Ct. (so. and ea. dists.) N.Y. 1970, U.S. Dist. Ct. Conn. 1978, U.S. Ct. Appeals (2d and D.C. cirs.) 1969, U.S. Ct. Claims 1977, U.S. Ct. Customs and Patent Appeals 1978, U.S. Supreme Ct. 1979, U.S. Ct. Internat. Trade 1981. Assoc. firm Cahill, Gordon & Reindel, N.Y.C., 1967-69, Whitman & Ransom, N.Y.C., 1969-72; asst. counsel Gen. Signal Corp., N.Y.C., Stamford, Conn., 1972-76; v.p., sec., gen. counsel Raymark Corp. (formerly Raybestos-Manhattan, Inc.), Trumbull, Conn., 1976-82; assoc. gen. counsel Lever Bros. Co., N.Y.C., 1983; asst. to pres., corp. counsel Math. Applications Group, Inc., Elmsford, N.Y., 1984; sr. v.p., sec., gen. counsel Summagraphics Corp., Austin, Tex., 1984-95; atty. at law, pres. Consulcor LLC, 1995—. Mem. ABA, N.Y. State Bar Assn., Assn. Bar City N.Y., D.C. Bar Assn., Conn. Bar Assn., Coporate Bar Assn., Tex. Bar Assn. Office: Summagraphics Corp 8500 Cameron Rd Austin TX 78754-3900

SIMS, ROBERT BELL, professional society administrator, public affairs official, newspaper publisher; b. Alamo, Tenn., Nov. 26, 1934; s. Robert Leslie and Lucille (Bell) S.; m. Patricia June Lytton, June 25, 1961; children—Jacqueline, James, Carolyn, William. B.A., Union U., Jackson, Tenn., 1956; postgrad., U. Sydney, Australia, 1957; M.A. in Polit. Sci., U. Wis., Madison, 1971, M.A. in Journalism, 1971; Grad., Nat. War Coll. Reporter Jackson Sun, Tenn., 1955-56; dir. pub. relations Union U., Jackson, 1958; commd. ensign USN, 1958, served to capt., 1984; spl. asst. to Pres., dir. pub. affairs NSC, Washington, 1982-83; spl. asst. to Pres., dep. press sec. for fgn. affairs The White House, Washington, 1983-85; asst. sec. def. pub. affairs Dept. of Def., Washington, 1985-87; v.p. communications Nat. Geographic Soc., Washington, 1987-89, sr. v.p., 1989—; owner, pub. The Crockett Times, Alamo, Tenn., 1974—. Author: Pentagon Reporters, 1983. Mem. bd. visitors U. Tenn. Coll. Arts and Scis., 1992—; bd. dirs. Mag. Pubs. Assn. Decorated Legion of Merit; Rotary Internat. Found. fellow, 1957; recipient Disting. Service award Union U., 1985. Mem. Sigma Delta Chi. Republican. Lodge: Masons. Home: 2701 O St NW Washington DC 20007 Office: Nat Geog Soc Washington DC 20036

SIMS, ROGER W., lawyer; b. Cleve., Aug. 3, 1950. BA with high honors, U. Fla., 1972, JD, 1974. Bar: Fla. 1975. Mem. Holland & Knight, Orlando, Fla. Mem. Moot Ct. U. Fla.; contbr. to profl mags and jours. Mem. ABA, Fla. Bar Assn. (chmn. environ., land use law sect. 1988-89), Phi Beta Kappa, Phi Kappa Phi, Omicron Delta Kappa, Phi Alpha Delta, Fla. Blue Key. Office: Holland & Knight PO Box 1526 200 S Orange Ave Ste 2600 Orlando FL 32801-3439

SIMS, WILLIAM RILEY, design and facility management educator, consultant; b. Gulfport, Miss., Dec. 17, 1938; s. William Riley and Hallie Pauline (Mills) S.; m. Jean Lee Booth, June 17, 1962; 1 child, Hallie Jean. B.Arch., U. N.Mex., 1963; M.Arch., M.C.P., U. Pa., 1965; Ph.D., MIT, 1973. Cert. facility mgr. Internat. Facility Mgmt. Assn., 1993. Planner, urban designer Phila. City Planning Commn., 1964; planner, urban designer Wallace McHarg Assocs., Phila., 1965; lectr. dep. city and regional planning U. Calif., Berkeley, 1966-68; asst. prof. dept. urban planning U. Wash., Seattle, 1970-73; assoc. prof. dept. city and regional planning Ohio State U., Columbus, 1973-80; prof., chmn. dept. design and environ. analysis Cornell U., Ithaca, N.Y., 1980—, co-dir. Internat. Facility Mgmt. program, 1989-93; co-dir. Workplace Studies Program, 1993—; cons. Columbus, Ohio, 1978-80; prin. Orbit-II Study, Ithaca, 1984—, Becker-Sims Assocs. (formerly Facility Rsch. Assocs.), Ithaca, 1984—. Author: Neighborhoods, 1975, Managing the Reinvented Workplace, 1996; (with others) Taos Adobes, 1965; editor (jour.) Design Guidelines from Post Occupancy Evaluation, 1980; U.S. editor Internat. Jour. Facilities Mgmt.; contbr. articles to profl. jours.; mem. publs. bd. Jour. Interior Design Edn. and Research, 1986-89. Trustee Columbus Landmarks Found., 1978-80; mem. bldgs. and properties com. Cornell U. Trustees. Fulbright scholar U.S. Inst. Internat. Edn., Norway, 1965-66; Mellon faculty fellow U. Wash., 1969, Ford faculty fellow Ohio State U., 1974. Mem. ASTM (chmn. assessing bldg. performance 1988-92), Internat. Facility Mgrs. Assn. (bd. dirs. 1984-87, cert. and accreditation task forces 1989—), Environ. Design Rsch. Assn., Assn. for Study of Man and Environ. Rels. (editl. bd. 1978-86), Am. Assn. Housing Educators (editl. bd. 1978-85). Home: 735 Ridge Rd Lansing NY 14882-8805 Office: Cornell U Dept Design & Environ Analysis Ithaca NY 14853-4401

SIMS, WILSON, lawyer; b. Nashville, Dec. 24, 1924; s. Cecil and Grace (Wilson) S.; m. Linda Bell, Aug. 12, 1948; children: Linda Rickman, Suzanne, Wilson. B.A., U. N.C., 1946; J.D., Vanderbilt U., 1948. Bar: Tenn. 1948. Since practiced in Nashville; ptnr. Bass, Berry & Sims, 1948—; gen. counsel, dir. Baird Ward Printing Co., Tenn., 1950-76, Southeastern Capital Corp., 1955-60, Martha White Foods, Synercon Corp., 1968-76, Forrest Life Ins. Co., 1970-75, Charter Co., 1983-84, The Bailey Co., Kenworth of Tenn., Inc. Chmn. Tenn. Commn. for Human Devel., 1970, Tenn. Commn. on Continuing Legal Edn., 1986-90; mem. Tenn. Gen. Assembly, 1959; bd. dirs. Nashville YMCA, United Cerebal Palsy, Kidney Found., Matthew 25, McKendree Village; trustee Meharry Med. Coll., Webb Sch., Bell Buckle, Tenn.; adv. bd. Jr. League; mem. bd. visitors U. N.C. 1st lt. USMCR, 1942-45, 50-52. Fellow Am. Bar Found. (life), Nashville Bar Found.; mem. ABA, Tenn. Bar Assn. (past speaker ho. of dels., past pres.), Nashville Bar Assn. (past pres., dir., Pub. Svc. award), Tenn. Bar Found. (past chmn.), Am. Judicature Soc., Am. Acad. Polit. Sci., Vanderbilt U. Law Alumni Assn. (past pres., Disting. Alumnus award), Nashville C. of C. (2 terms bd. govs.), Belle Meade Country (bd. dirs.), Wade Hampton Golf Club. Methodist. Home: 22 Foxhall Close Nashville TN 37215-1862 Office: Bass Berry & Sims 2700 First Am Ctr Nashville TN 37238

SIMSON, BEVLYN, artist; b. Columbus, Ohio, Sept. 9, 1917; d. Amon and Fannie Florence (Gilbert) Thall; m. Theodore Richard Simson, Mar. 25, 1938; children: Sherran Blair, Douglas A. BFA, Ohio State U., 1969, MFA, 1972. One woman shows include J.B. Speed Art Mus., Louisville, 1970, Huntington Gallery, Columbus, Ohio, 1970, 73, United Christian Ctr., Columbus, 1970, Bodley Gallery, N.Y., 1971, 74, Gilman Galleries, Chgo., 1971, Gallery 200, Columbus, 1972, Hopkins Hall Gallery, Ohio State U., Columbus, 1972, Meth. Theol. Sch., Delaware, Ohio, 1973, Columbus Pub. Libr., 1973, Garfinkels, Washington, 1973, City Hall, Mayor's Office, Columbus, 1974, 82, Capital U., Bexley, Ohio, 1977, Hillel Found., Ohio State U., 1978, Columbus Tech. Inst., 1979, Springfield (Ohio) Art Mus., 1980, Peace Luth. Ch., Gahanna, Ohio, 1981, Franklin U. Gallery, Columbus, 1981, Columbus Mus. Art, Collectors Gallery, 1983; exhibited in group shows at Columbus Mus. Art-Columbus Art League, 1968, 70, 71, 73, 74, 75, 77, 78, 79, 80, 86, Ohio Statehouse and State Office Tower, Columbus, 1968-78, Battelle Meml. Inst., Columbus, 1969-73, 75, 78, 81-82, Schumacher Gallery, Capital U., Columbus, 1969-85, 87, 88, Salles d'Exposition, Paris, 1969, Am. Cultural Ctr., Kyoto, Japan, 1970, Cin. Art Mus., 1970, J.B. Speed Art Mus. Collector's Gallery, Louisville, 1970-85, Studio San Guiseppe, Mt. St. Joseph Coll., Cin., 1971, Mansfield (Ohio) Art Ctr., 1971, Collector's Showroom, Chgo., 1971-82, Gov.'s Mansion State of Ohio, 1972, 74, Western Ill. U., 1972, Albatross Gallery, Rome, 1972, Palazzo Dell Exprizioni, Rome, 1972, Place-Allrich Gallery, San Francisco, 1973-75, Chautauqua Assn., N.Y., 1973, Butler Inst. Am. Art, Youngstown, Ohio, 1973, 76, Huntington Gallery, Columbus, 1973, 74, Gallery 200, Columbus, 1972-76, Columbus C. of C., 1974, 75, Zanesville (Ohio) Art Ctr., 1976, Columbus Inst. Contemporary Art, 1978, Nationwide Plaza Gallery, Columbus, 1980, Franklin U., Columbus, 1980, Columbus Art League, 1987, Jeffrey Mansion, Bexley, Ohio, 1996, 10th Ann. Women Artists Expo Seal of Ohio Girl Scout Coun., Inc. Columbus, 1996, Financial Group Gallery, Worthington, Ohio, 1997, Columbus (Ohio) Art League, 1997; represented in permanent collections Columbus Mus. Arts, J.B. Speed Art Mus., Louisville, Capital U., Bexley, Fordham U., N.Y.C., Kyoto City U. Fine Arts, Springfield Art Mus., Tyler (Tex.) Mus. Art, Wichita (Kans.) Mus. Art, Zanesville Art Ctr., Ohio State U., Columbus, Meth. Theol. Sch., Delaware, Ohio, Yerke Morgtgage Co., Columbus, Marcorp, N.Y., Kresge Co., Detroit, IBM, Columbus, Chase Manhattan Bank, N.Y.C., Chase Bank of Ohio, Am. Bancorp., Columbus, Ohio Nat. Bank Plaza, Columbus, Pan Western Life Ins. Co., Columbus, First Investment Co., Columbus, Redwood Bank, San Francisco, Children's Hosp., Phila., Franklin County Crippled Children's Ctr., Columbus, Zenith East, N.Y.C., First Cmty. Bank, Columbus, Ronald McDonald House, Columbus, Columbia Gas of Ohio, Columbus, Midland Title Security Co., Columbus, Huntington Nat. Bank Ctr., Columbus, Price Waterhouse Co., Columbus, Lehman Bros., N.Y.C., Columbus Sch. for Girls, Grand Prix Assocs., Inc., Columbus, Grant Hosp. Med. Ctr., Columbus; represented in pvt. collections. Mem. Nat. League Am. Pen Women, Nat. Artists Equity Assn., Bexley Art League, Columbus Mus. Art, Columbus Art League (bd. dirs. 1965-96, treas., sec., pres. 1977), Ohio State U. Alumni Assn., Winding Hollow Country Club, Phi Sigma Sigma. Avocations: golf, theater, symphony, travel. Studio: Bevlyn Simson Studio 4300 E Broad St 1st Cmty Bank Bldg Columbus OH 43213-1243

SIMSON, GARY JOSEPH, legal educator; b. Newark, Mar. 18, 1950; s. Marvin and Mildred (Silberg) S.; m. Rosalind Slivka, Aug. 15, 1971; children: Nathaniel, Jennie Anne. BA, Yale Coll., 1971; JD, Yale U., 1974. Bar: Conn. 1974, N.Y. 1980. Law clk. to judge U.S. Ct. Appeals 2d Cir., 1974-75; asst. prof. law, U. Tex., 1975-77, prof. law, 1977-80; vis. prof. law Cornell U., Ithaca, N.Y., 1979-80, prof. law, 1980-97, prof. law, assoc. dean, 1997—; vis. prof. law U. Calif., Berkeley, 1986; chair adv. bd. law casebook series Carolina Acad. Press; mem., atty adv. bd. Nat. Com. for Pub. Edn. and Religious Liberty. Author: Issues and Perspectives in Conflict of Laws, 1985, 3d edit., 1997. Mem. ABA, ACLU, Phi Beta Kappa. Contbr. articles to legal publs. Office: Cornell U Law Sch Myron Taylor Hall Ithaca NY 14853

SIMSON, JO ANNE, anatomy and cell biology educator; b. Chgo., Nov. 19, 1936; d. Kenneth Brown and Helen Marjorie (Pascoe) Valentine; m. Arnold Simson, June 1961 (div.); 1 child, Maria; m. Michael Smith, Nov. 10, 1971 (div.); children: Elizabeth Smith, Briana Smith. BA, Kalamazoo Coll., 1959; MS, U. Mich., 1961; PhD, SUNY, Syracuse, 1969. Postdoctoral fellow Temple U. Health Sci. Ctr., Phila., 1968-70; asst. prof. Med. U. S.C., Charleston, 1970-76, assoc. prof., 1976-83, prof. anatomy and cell biology, 1983-96; prof. emerita, 1997—; featured in Smithsonian exhibit, Sci. in Am. Life, 1994—. Contbr. articles to profl. jours.; author short stories and poems. Active adult edn. Unitarian Ch., Charleston, 1973-75, social action, 1990-92. Grantee NSF, 1959-60, NIH, 1966-67, 72-87, 91-95. Mem. Am. Assn. Anatomists, Am. Soc. Cell Biology, Histochem. Soc. (sec. 1979-82, exec. com. 1985-89), Fogarty Internat. Fellowship Bioctr. (Basel, Switzerland, 1987-88), Amnesty Internat. (newsletter editor Group 168 1982-86), Phi Beta Kappa. Home: 1760 Pittsford Cir Charleston SC 29412-4110 Office: Med U SC Anatomy 171 Ashley Ave Charleston SC 29425-0001 *In the end, it is only what a person has created and given to the rest of the world that endures.*

SIMUNICH, MARY ELIZABETH HEDRICK (MRS. WILLIAM A. SIMUNICH), public relations executive; b. Chgo.; d. Tubman Keene and Mary (McCamish) Hedrick; m. William A. Simunich, Dec. 6, 1941. Student Phoenix Coll., 1967-69, Met. Bus. Coll., 1938-40. Exec. sec. sales mgr. Sta. KPHO radio, 1950-53; exec. sec. mgr. Sta. KPHO-TV, 1953-54; account exec. Tom Rippey & Assos., 1955-56; pub. rels. dir. Phoenix Symphony, 1956-62; co-founder, v.p. Paul J. Hughes Pub. Rels., Inc., 1960-65; owner Mary Simunich Pub. Rels., Phoenix, 1966-77; pub. rels. dir. Walter O. Boswell Meml. Hosp., Sun City, Ariz., 1969-85; pub. rels. cons., 1985—; pres. DARCI PR, Phoenix, 1994—, Cityscape, Inc. (formerly Citynet, Inc.), 1994—; instr. pub. rels. Phoenix Coll. Evening Sch., 1973-78. Bd. dirs. Anytown, Ariz., 1969-72; founder, sec. Friends Am. Geriatrics, 1977-86. Named Phoenix Advt. Woman of Year, Phoenix Jr. Advt. Club, 1962; recipient award Blue Cross, 1963; 1st Pl. award Ariz. Press Women, 1966. Mem. NAFE, Women in Comm., Internat. Assn. Bus. Communicators (pres. Ariz. chpt. 1970-71, dir.), Pub. Rels. Soc. Am. (sec., dir. 1976-78), Am. Soc. Hosp. Pub. Rels. (dir. Ariz. chpt. 1976-78), Nat., Ariz. Press Women. Home: 4133 N 34th Pl Phoenix AZ 85018-4771 Office: DARCI Group 2425 E Camelback Rd Ste 450 Phoenix AZ 85016-4236

SINAI, ALLEN LEO, economist, educator; b. Detroit, Apr. 4, 1939; s. Joseph and Betty Paula (Feinberg) S.; m. Lee Davis Etsten, June 23, 1963; children: Lauren Beth, Todd Michael. AB, U. Mich., 1961; MA, Northwestern U., 1966, PhD, 1969. Asst. prof. to assoc. prof. econs. U. Ill.-Chgo., 1966-75; chmn. fin. info. group, chief fin. economist Data Resources, Lexington, Mass., 1971-83; chief economist, mng. dir. Lehman Bros. and Shearson Lehman Bros. Inc., N.Y.C., 1983-87; chief economist, exec. v.p. The Boston Co. Inc., 1988-93; pres., CEO The Boston Co. Econ. Advisors Inc., Boston and N.Y.C., 1988-93, Econ. Advisors, Inc., Boston, 1993-96; mng. dir., chief global economist dir. global econs. Lehman Bros., N.Y.C., 1993-96; pres., CEO, chief global economist Primark Decision Econs., Boston, 1996—; chief global economist, vice chmn. The WEFA Group, Boston, 1997—; cons. Laural Cons., Lexington and Evanston, Ill., 1966; vis. assoc. prof. econs. and fin. MIT, Cambridge, 1975-77; adj. prof. econs. Boston U., 1977-78, 81-83, NYU, 1984-88; adj. prof. econs. and fin. Lemberg Sch., Brandeis U., 1988—; vis. faculty Sloan Sch., MIT, 1989-91. Contbr. articles to profl. jours. and books. Mem. reducing the fed. budget deficit task force Roosevelt Ctr., Washington, 1984; bd. govs. Com. on Developing Am. Capitalism, 1984—, chmn., 1990-95; bd. economists Time Mag., 1991—. Recipient Alumnus Merit award Northwestern U., 1985. Mem. Am. Econ. Assn., Econometric Soc., Ea. Econs. Assn. (v.p. 1988-89, pres. 1990-91, Otto Eckstein prize 1988, fellow 1994), Western Econ. Assn. (exec. com.), Econometric Soc., Nat. Assn. Bus. Econs. Jewish. Avocations: tennis; skiing. Home: 16 Holmes Rd Lexington MA 02173-1917 Office: Primark Decision Econs 260 Franklin St Fl 15 Boston MA 02110-3112

SINATRA, FRANK (FRANCIS ALBERT SINATRA), singer, actor; b. Hoboken, N.J., Dec. 12, 1915; s. Anthony and Natalie (Garaventi) S.; m. Nancy Barbato, Feb. 4, 1939 (div.); children: Nancy, Frank Wayne, Christine; m. Ava Gardner (div.); m. Mia Farrow, 1966 (div.); m. Barbara Marx, 1976. Student, Demarest High Sch., Hoboken, Drake Inst.; hon. doctorate, Stevens Inst. Tech., Hoboken, 1985. Sang with sch. band and helped form sch. glee club; worked after sch. on news truck of Jersey Observer; copy boy on graduation with sports div. covering coll. sports events (won first prize on Maj. Bowes Amateur Hour, touring with co. for 3 months); sustaining programs on 4 radio stas. and in Rustic Cabin, N.J., toured with Harry James Band, then Tommy Dorsey's, solo night club and concert appearances; starred on radio program Lucky Strike Hit Parade; appeared in motion pictures From Here to Eternity (Acad. award as best supporting actor 1953), Las Vegas Nights, 1946, Ship Ahoy, 1942, Miracle of the Bells, 1948, Kissing Bandit, 1949, Take Me Out to the Ball Game, 1949, Higher and Higher, 1942, Step Lively, 1944, Anchors Aweigh, 1945, It Happened in Brooklyn, 1947, Guys and Dolls, 1956, Not as a Stranger, 1955, The Tender Trap, 1955, The Man With the Golden Arm, 1955, Johnny Concho, 1956, The Pride and the Passion, 1957, Pal Joey, 1957, Some Came Running, 1959, Never So Few, 1960, Can-Can, 1960, Oceans 11, 1960, Pepe, 1960, The Devil at 4 O'Clock, 1961, The Manchurian Candidate, 1962, Come Blow Your Horn, 1963, Robin and the Seven Hoods, 1963, None But the Brave, 1964, Assault on a Queen, 1965, Von Ryan's Express, 1966, Tony Rome, 1966, Lady in Cement, 1967, The Detective, 1968, Dirty Dingus McGee, 1970, Who Framed Roger Rabbit (voice), 1988, (TV film) Sinatra: 80 Years My Way, 1995, Listen Up: The Lives of Quincy Jones, 1991; actor, producer motion picture The First Deadly Sin, 1980, TV movie Contract on Cherry Street, 1977; hit songs include Night and Day, 1943, Nancy, 1945, Young at Heart, 1954, Love and Marriage, 1955, The Tender Trap, 1955, How Little We Know, 1956, Chicago, 1957, All the Way, 1957, High Hopes, 1959, It Was a Very Good Year, 1965, Strangers in the Night, 1966, My Way, 1969, (with Nancy Sinatra) Somethin Stupid, 1969; albums include Songs for Swingin' Lovers, 1956, Come Dance With Me, 1959, Come Fly With Me, 1962, September of My Years (Grammy award for best album), 1965, Moonlight 1966, Greatest Hits, 1968, My Way, 1969, Greatest Hits, Volume 2, 1970, L.A. is My Lady, 1984, The Very Good Years, 1991, Where Are You, 1992, The World We Knew, Duets, 1993, Duets II, 1994, You Make Me Feel So Young, 1995, Hello, Young Lovers, 1996; (with Bing Crosby) All the Best, 1995; (with Luciano Pavarotti) Live in Concert, 1995; (with Tommy Dorsey Orch.) There Are Such Things, 1996; author: A Man and His Art, 1990. Recipient Spl. Oscar award Acad. Motion Picture Arts and Scis., 1945, Sylvania TV award, 1959, Grammy awards for album of yr., 1959, 65, 66, best vocalist, 1959, 65, 66, rec. of yr., 1966, Peabody and

Emmy awards, 1965, Jean Hersholt award Acad. Motion Picture Arts and Scis., 1971, Golden Apple award as male star of yr. Hollywood Women's Press Club, 1977, Humanitarian award Variety Clubs Internat., 1980, Cross of Sci. and the Arts, Austria, 1984, Presdl. Medal of Freedom, 1985, Kennedy Ctr. honor, 1986, Life Achievement award NAACP, 1987, Grammy Lifetime Achievement award, 1994. Club: Friars (abbot). Office: care Thomas Cassidy Inc 366 Horseshoe Dr Basalt CO 81621-9104 also: care Sinatra Enterprises 9100 Wilshire Blvd # 455 Beverly Hills CA 90212-3415 also: care Sinatra Enterprises Goldwin Studios 1041 N. Formosa Los Angeles CA 90046*

SINAY, HERSHEL DAVID, publisher; b. Chgo., Mar. 15, 1938; s. Irving Paul and Gertrude (Drucker) S. BA, U. So. Calif., 1960. Telecom. and Cinema account exec. Wall St. Jour., L.A., 1961-63; account exec. R.J. Friedman Assocs., L.A., 1963-66; dir. sales Performing Arts Mag., L.A., 1966-72; pub. East, West Network, L.A., 1972-79, 85-87; pres., pub. Calif. Bus. Mag., L.A., 1979-85; pub., editor-in-chief Ranch & Coast Mag., DelMar, Calif., 1987-88; pub. Am. Film. Mag., L.A., 1988-91; pres. Project Mktg. Custom Publ. Specialists divsn. Sinai Comm., Inc., L.A., 1991—. Pub. Am. Cinema Editors Tribute Program, 1993—, Billboard Music Awards Tribute Book, 1993, 1st Ann. Thurgood Marshall Lifetime Achievement Award Tribute Book, NAACP Legal Def. and Ednl. Fund, 1993, 96. Recipient 32 Maggie awards Western Pub. Assn., 1979-93. Mem. Am. Film Inst., Western Pub. Assn. (bd. dirs.), L.A. Advt. Club. Avocations: yachting, jogging, gardening, photography. Office: 810 S Hauser Blvd Los Angeles CA 90036-4726

SINAY, JOSEPH, retail executive; b. Chgo., Dec. 5, 1920; s. Hyman and Ella S.; m. Ruth Milman, Mar. 7, 1961; 1 dau., Elise Sinay Spilker. Student, Herzl Jr. Coll., 1939. Gen. mgr. Fanchon & Marco Theatres, Los Angeles, 1943-54; v.p., founder Interstate United, Chgo., 1953-56; partner Josam Investment Co., Los Angeles, 1956—; chmn. bd., pres., chief exec. officer R B Industries Inc., L.A., 1956-89, now cons. Bd. dirs. Am. Acad. Dramatic Arts; pres. Variety Clubs Internat., 1985-87; gen. chmn. United Jewish Welfare L.A., 1976; pres. We. region Am. Friends Hebrew U., 1980; Calif. fin. chmn. Muskie for Pres., 1972; trustee Idyllwild Arts Found., 1968-73; bd. dirs. Constl. Rights Found., 1973-78. Mem. Nat. Home Furnishing Assn. Jewish. Office: Josam Investment Co 1801 Century Park E Los Angeles CA 90067-2302

SINBAD, actor, comedian; b. Benton Harbor, Mich.; m. Meredith; children: Paige, Royce. Student, U. Denver. Stand-up comedian various comedy clubs and concerts nationwide; regular on TV series A Different World, NBC, 1987—, other TV appearances include Starch Search (winner stand-up comedian competition 1984), The Cosby Show, Keep on Cruisin, The Redd Foxx Show; occasional co-host Showtime at the Apollo; toured with The Pointer Sisters, Anita Baker, Luther Vandross, Smokey Robinson. Office: Carsey-Werner Co CBS/MTM Bldg 3 4024 Radford Ave Studio City CA 91604-2101

SINCLAIR, ALASTAIR JAMES, geology educator; b. Hamilton, Ont., Can., Aug. 1, 1935; s. Burton Leslie and Grace (Isherwood) S.; m. Elizabeth Mary Sylvia Hill, June 13, 1964; children: Alison Trevena, Fiona Tamsin. BS, U. Toronto, 1957, MS, 1958; PhD, U. B.C., 1964. Asst. prof. U. Wash., Seattle, 1962-64; asst. prof. U. B.C., Vancouver, 1964-68, assoc. prof., 1968-74, prof., 1974—, head dept. geol. scis., 1985-90, dir. Geol. Engring., 1979-80, 81-82, 92—; pres. Sinclair Cons. Ltd., Vancouver, 1980—. Contbr. numerous articles to profl. jours. Killam Sr. fellow, 1990-91. Fellow Geol. Assn. Can. (treas. mineral deposits divsn. 1978-89), Soc. Econ. Geologists; mem. Assn. Profl. Engrs. B.C., Internat. Assn. Math. Geologists, Assn. Exploration Geochemists (councillor 1992-96), Can. Inst. Mining, Metallurgy and Petroleum (life, Robert Elver award 1991), Geol. Soc. Brazil (hon. mem. sci.-tech. comm. geochemistry 1982), Brazilian Geochem. Soc. (hon. 1987). Avocations: classical music, skiing. Home: 2972 W 44th Ave, Vancouver, BC Canada V6N 3K4 Office: U BC, Dept Geological Sciences, Vancouver, BC Canada V6T 1Z4

SINCLAIR, CAROLE, publisher, editor, author; b. Haddonfield, N.J., May 13, 1942; d. Earl Walter and Ruth (Sinclair) Dunham; 1 child, Wendy. Student, U. Florence, Italy, 1963; BA in Polit. Sci., Bucknell U, 1964. Advt. copywriter BBD&O Advertising, N.Y.C., 1966-67; sales promotion mgr. Macmillan Pub. Co., N.Y.C., 1967-71; mktg. mgr. Doubleday & Co., Inc., N.Y.C., 1972-74, promotion dir., 1974-76, advt. mgr., sales and promotion, chmn. mktg. com., 1976-80; v.p. mktg., editorial dir. Davis Pubs., N.Y.C., 1980-83; founder, pub., editorial dir., sr. v.p. Sylvia Porter's Personal Fin. Mag., N.Y.C., 1983-90; pres. The Sylvia Porter Orgn., Inc., N.Y.C., 1980-91; founder, pres. Sinclair Media Inc., N.Y.C., 1990—; mktg. dir. Denver Pub. Inst., summers 1975-78; lectr. Columbia U. Bus. Sch. and Sch. of Journalism, 1976; host nationally syndicated TV show, Sylvia Porter's Money Tips, syndicated daily radio show, Sylvia Porter's Personal Fin. Report, audio cassette series on fin. topics. Author: Keys for Women Starting and Owning a Business, 1991, Keys to Women's Basic Professional Needs, 1991, When Women Retire, 1992; contbg. editor Pushcart Prize, 1977; contbr. The Business of Publishing, 1980. Renaissance Art Program fellow, Florence, Italy, 1963; White House intern, 1962. Mem. Women's Forum, Intercorp. Communications Group, Mag. Pubs.' Assn., Advt. Women in N.Y., Spence Sch. Parent's League. Presbyterian. Club: Pubs. Lunch. Avocation: boating.

SINCLAIR, DAISY, advertising executive, casting director; b. Perth Amboy, N.J., Mar. 22, 1941; d. James Patrick and Margaret Mary (McAniff) Nieland; m. James Pratt Sinclair, May 25, 1978; children: Duncan, Gibbons. BA, Caldwell Coll., 1962. Jr. copywriter Young & Rubican, N.Y.C., 1962-64; various positions in casting dept. Ogilvy & Mather, N.Y.C., 1964-90, sr. v.p., dir. casting, 1990—. Mem. Am. Assn. Advt. (talent agt. com. 1972—), Drama League N.Y. (3d v.p. 1982—), The Knickerbocker Greys (v.p.), Edgartown Yacht Club, Chapaquoit Yacht Club, The Tuxedo Club. Republican. Episcopalian. Avocations: opera, theater, sailing, skiing. Home: 4 E 95th St New York NY 10128-0705 Office: Ogilvy & Mather Advt Worldwide Plz 309 W 49th St New York NY 10019-7316

SINCLAIR, GLENN BRUCE, mechanical engineering educator, researcher; b. Auckland, New Zealand, Mar. 7, 1946; came to U.S., 1969; s. Alan John and Piri (Vincent) S.; m. Della Jane Sutton, Dec. 23, 1972; children—Heidi Lee, Heather Ann, Hillary Colleen, Christopher Alan. B.Sc., U. Auckland, 1967, B.E., 1969; Ph.D., Calif. Inst. Tech., 1972. J. Willard Gibbs instr. mech. engring. Yale U., New Haven, 1972-74; lectr. U. Auckland, 1974-77; asst. prof. Carnegie-Mellon U., Pitts., 1977-80, assoc. prof., 1980-82, prof., 1982—, head, 1986-92; vis. prof. Cambridge U., Eng., 1981; research scientist Dept. Sci. and Indsl. Research, Wellington, New Zealand, 1968-69; summer prof. Pratt & Whitney, Hartford, Conn., 1978, Aircraft Corp., West Palm Beach, Fla., 1979; cons. in field. Contbr. articles to profl. jours. Fulbright scholar, 1969-72. Mem. Am. Acad. Mechanics. Office: Carnegie-Mellon Univ Dept Mech Engring 5000 Forbes Ave Pittsburgh PA 15213-3815

SINCLAIR, JAMES BURTON, plant pathology educator, consultant; b. Chgo., Dec. 21, 1927; s. James Lawrence Sinclair and Helen Marie (Thompson) Owens. BSc, Lawrence U., 1951; PhD, U. Wis., 1955. Grad. rsch. asst. U. Wis., Madison, 1951-55, grad. rsch. assoc., 1955-56; from asst. prof. to assoc. prof. La. State U., Baton Rouge, 1956-65, prof., 1965-68, adminstrv. asst. to chancellor, 1966-68; prof. U. Ill., Urbana, 1968—, dir. nat. soybean rsch. lab., 1992-96. Co-author: Basic Plant Pathology Methods, 1985, Principles of Seed Pathology, 1987, Anatomy and Physiology of Diseased Plants, 1991; contbr. articles to profl. jours. Sgt. U.S. Army, 1946-47. Recipient Soybean Rsch. Recognition award Am. Soybean Assn., 1983, Prodn. Rsch. award, 1989, Paul A. Funk award, 1984, Disting. Svc. award USDA, 1988, Disting. Svc. award Phytopathol. Soc. (north ctrl. divsn.), 1991, Rsch. award Land of Lincoln Soybean Assn., 1992. Fellow Am. Phytopathol. Soc., Nat. Acad. of Scis./India; mem. Ill. Crop Improvement Assn. (hon.), Am. Soc. Agronomy (hon.), Rotary (chmn. internat. com. Savoy chpt. 1990-91, v.p. 1991-93, pres. 1993-94). Home: 408 Arbours Dr Savoy IL 61874-9752 Office: U Ill Dept Plant Pathology 1102 S Goodwin Ave Urbana IL 61801-4730

SINCLAIR, JOSEPH SAMUELS, broadcasting company executive, retail merchant; b. Narragansett, R.I., June 14, 1922; s. James and Bertha (Samuels) S.; m. Betty Virginia Hintz, Feb. 16, 1946 (dec. 1968); children: Sherry Murr, Lani Patricia, Jodie Carol; m. Rosalyn K. Dwares, Oct. 24, 1969; children: Sara Ellen Sinclair, Steven Dwares. Student, Williams Coll., 1940-41; BS, U.S. Naval Acad., 1945; DBA (hon.), Johnson and Wales Coll., 1976. Asst. to program mgr. Sta. WJAR-TV, Providence, 1949-57, mgr., 1957-60; dir. Outlet Co., 1955-58, mem. exec. com., 1958-60, v.p., 1960, pres., 1960-68, chmn. bd. dirs., 1968-84; pres. Sinclair Communications, Sinclair Assn., Sinclair Ventures, Providence, 1984—. Mem. pres.'s coun. Providence Coll.; trustee R.I. Coun. Econ. Edn., U. R.I. Found.; mem. adv. bd. Salve Regina Coll.; mem. Wheeler Sch. bd., Providence; bd. visitors U.S. Naval Acad., 1960-64, chmn., 1962-64. Lt. (j.g.) 1945-47, lt. USNR, 1950-52. Decorated Italian Star Solidarity; recipient R.I. Advt. Silver medal, 1968. Mem. Navy League R.I., Naval War Coll. Found., Nat. Assn. Broadcasters (bd. dirs.), TV Pioneers, Internat. Radio and TV Soc., World Bus. Coun., Nat. Broadcasters Club, R.I. Assn. Broadcasters (v.p.), R.I. Commodores (adm.), R.I. 100 Club (pres.), Sports Car Am. Club, Point Judith Country Club, Dunes Club, Aurora Club, Palm Beach Polo and Country Club, Univ. Club, Maralago Club, Agawam Country Club. Home and Office: 170 Westminster St Providence RI 02903-2101

SINCLAIR, JULIE MOORES WILLIAMS, consulting law librarian; b. Montgomery, Ala., May 2, 1954; d. Benjamin Buford and Marilyn Moores (Simpson) Williams; m. Winfield James Sinclair, Dec. 16, 1978. BA, U. of South, 1976; MLS, U. Ala., Tuscaloosa, 1977; JD, Washington U., St. Louis, 1987. Bar: Ala. 1989, U.S. Dist. Ct. (no. dist.) Ala. 1989. Serials libr. Ala. Dept. Archives and History, Montgomery, 1977; cataloguing libr. Ala. Pub. Libr. Svc., Montgomery, 1978; league libr. Ala. League Municipalities, Montgomery, 1978-84; asst. libr. Mo. Ct. Appeals, St. Louis, 1984-86, law clk., 1987-88; cons. Law Libr. Cons., Birmingham, Ala., 1988—. Contbr. numerous articles to profl. jours. Mem. Ala. Bar Assn., Ala. Libr. Assn., Am. Assn. Law Librs., Law Libr. Assn. Ala. (charter, v.p. 1992-93, pres. 1993-94), Ala. Fedn. Bus. and Profl. Women (sec. 1993-94, 2d v.p. 1994-95, 1st v.p. 1995-96, pres. 1997—), Order of Gownsmen, Phi Alpha Theta. Episcopalian. Avocations: travel and sightseeing, reading, attending theatre, especially Shakespeare. Office: 3045 Independence Dr Birmingham AL 35209

SINCLAIR, KENT, law educator; b. San Diego, July 8, 1946; s. Kent and Ruth Melva (Wilson) S.; m. Kathryn Spining; children: K. Scott, Keith A. AB, U. Calif., 1968, JD, 1971. Bar: Calif. 1972, U.S. Dist. Ct. (so. dist.) N.Y. 1972, U.S. Ct. Appeals (2d cir.) 1972, N.Y. 1973, Va. 1986, U.S. Supreme Ct. 1990. Law clk. to judge James Browning U.S. Ct. Appeals 9th Cir., San Francisco, 1971-72; chief staff atty. U.S. Ct. Appeals 9th Cir., 1972; atty. Shearman & Sterling, N.Y.C., 1972-77; judge-magistrate U.S. Dist. Ct. So. Dist., N.Y.C., 1977-83; prof. law U. Va., Charlottesville, Va., 1983-89; prof. law, assoc. dean U. Va., 1989-93; spl. master U.S. Dist. Ct. SDN.Y., 1983-88; dep. spl. master Supreme Ct. U.S., 1989-94; reporter decisions Supreme Ct. Va., Richmond, 1985—; dir. Va. Judges Inst., Charlottesville, 1984-92. Author: Federal Civil Practice, 1992, Virginia Civil Procedure, 1993, Practice Before Federal Magistrates, 1984, Moore's Federal Practice, 1984, The Trial Handbook, 1989, Weinstein's Evidence Volume, 1996. Edn. dir. Va. State Bar, 1983-89, mem. Mem. Am. Law Inst., Va. Bar Assn. Avocation: computers. Office: U Va Sch Law 580 Massie Rd Charlottesville VA 22903-1738

SINCLAIR, MICHAEL GLENN, football player; b. Galveston, Tex., Jan. 31, 1968; m. Betty Sinclair; children: Michael, Michaela. Degree in phys. edn., Eastern N.Mex. U. Football player Seattle Seahawks, 1991—, Sacramento Surge (World League), 1992. Office: care Seattle Seahawks 11220 NE 53rd St Kirkland WA 98033*

SINCLAIR, ROLF MALCOLM, physicist; b. N.Y.C., Aug. 15, 1929; s. Nathan and Elizabeth (Stout) S.; m. Margaret Lee Andrews, June 13, 1959 (div. 1978); children: Elizabeth Ann, Andrew Caisley; m. Allyn J. Miner, July 29, 1991. B.S., Calif. Inst. Tech., 1949; M.A. (Reade scholar), Rice U., 1951, Ph.D. (Inst. fellow), 1954. Physicist, Westinghouse Research Labs., 1953-56; vis. scientist U. Hamburg, Germany, 1956-57, U. Paris, 1957-58, U.K. Atomic Energy Authority, Culham Lab., Eng., 1965-66; research physicist Princeton U., 1958-69; program dir. NSF, Washington, 1969—; mem. Solstice Project, 1978-91; NSF rep. U.S. Solar Eclipse Expdn. to India, 1980, Amundsen-Scott South Pole Sta., 1995, 96; Disting. vis. prof. N.Mex. State U., 1985; vis. prof. No. Ariz. U., 1986; vis. sci. Los Alamos Nat. Lab., 1988-89, guest scientist, 1989—; cons. to industry, 1960-69. Fellow Am. Phys. Soc. (panel pub. affairs 1976-77, nominating com. 1988-90), AAAS (sec. physics sect. 1972—, mem. coun. 1972-73, nominating com. 1982-83), Sigma Xi. Research and publs. on physics, archaeoastronomy, tech. and instrumentation. Home: 7508 Tarrytown Rd Chevy Chase MD 20815-6027 Office: Nat Sci Found Physics Divsn 4201 Wilson Blvd Arlington VA 22230-0001

SINCLAIR, SARA VORIS, health facility administrator, nurse; b. Kansas City, Mo., Apr. 13, 1942; d. Franklin Defenbaugh and Inez Estelle (Figenbaum) Voris; m. James W. Sinclair, June 13, 1964; children: Thomas James, Elizabeth Kathleen, Joan Sara. BSN, UCLA, 1965. RN, Utah; lic. health care facility adminstr.; cert. health care adminstr. Staff nurse UCLA Med. Ctr. Hosp., 1964-65; charge nurse Boulder (Colo.) Meml. Hosp., 1966, Boulder (Colo.) Manor Nursing Home, 1974-75, Four Seasons Nursing Home, Joliet, Ill., 1975-76; dir. nursing Home Health Agy of Olympia Fields, Joliet, Ill., 1977-79; dir. nursing Sunshine Terr. Found., Inc., Logan, Utah, 1980, asst. adminstr., 1980-81, adminstr., 1981-93; dir. divsn. health systems improvement Utah Dept. Health, Salt Lake City, 1993—; mem. long term care profl. and tech. adv. com. Joint Commn. on Accreditation Healthcare Orgns., Chgo., 1987-91, chmn., 1990-91; adj. lectr. Utah State u., 1991-93; mem. adj. clin. faculty Weber State U., Ogden, Utah; moderator radio program Healthwise Sta. KUSU-FM, 1985-93; spkr. Nat. Coun. Aging, 1993, Alzheimers Disease Assn. Ann. Conf., 1993; del. White House Conf. on Aging, 1995; chmn. Utah Dept. of Health's Ethics, Instnl. Rev. Bd. Com., 1995—, Utah Dept. Health Risk Mgmt. Com., 1995—; mem. Utah Long Term Care Coalition (exec. com. 1995, chmn. 1997), oversight com. and long term care tech. adv. group Utah Health Policy Commn., 1996—; Health Insight Utah State Coun, 1996—; presenter in field. Contbg. author: Associate Degree Nursing and The Nursing Home, 1988. Mem. dean's adv. coun. Coll. Bus. Utah State U., Logan, 1989-91, mem. presdl. search com., 1991-92; chmn., co-founder Cache Cmty. Health Coun., Logan, 1985; chmn. bd. Hospice of Cache Valley, Logan, 1986; mem. Utah State Adv. Coun. on Aging, 1986-93; apptd. chmn. Utah Health Facilities Com., 1989-91; chmn. Bear River Dist. Adv. Coun. on Aging, 1989-91; chmn. health and human svcs. subcom. Cache 2010, 1992-93; mem. long term care tech. adv. group, oversight com. Utah Health Policy Commn., 1997; dir. Health Insight, 1996. Recipient Disting. Svc. award Utah State U., 1989. Fellow Am. Coll. Health Care Adminstrs. (presenter 1992-93, 95, 1996 ann. convocations, v.p. Utah chpt. 1992-94, convocation and edn. coms. 1992-93, region IX vice gov. 1994-96, bylaws com. 1996—); mem. Am. Health Care Assn. (non-proprietary v.p. 1986-87, region v.p. 1987-89, presenter workshop conv. 1990-93, exec. com. 1993, presenter ann. convocation 1995), Utah Health Care Assn. (pres. 1983-85, treas. 1991-93, Disting. Svc. award 1991, Svc. award for long term care 1996), Utah Gerontol. Soc. (bd. dirs. 1992-93, 95—, chmn. nominating com. 1993-94, chmn. ann. conf. 1996, pres. 1997), Cache C. of C. (pres. 1991), Logan bus. and Profl. Women's Club (pres. 1989, Woman of Achievement award 1982, Woman of Yr. 1982), Rotary (Logan chpt., chair cmty. svc. com. 1989-90); hon. mem. Golden Key Nat. Honor Soc. Avocations: walking, reading. Office: Utah Dept Health Div Health Sys Improvement 288 N 1460 W Box 142851 Salt Lake City UT 84114-2851

SINCLAIR, VIRGIL LEE, JR., judge, writer; b. Canton, Ohio, Nov. 10, 1951; s. Virgil Lee and Thelma Irene (Dunlap) S.; children: Kelly, Shannon; m. Janet Brahler Sinclair. BA, Kent State U., 1973; JD, U. Akron, 1976; postgrad. Case Western Res. U., 1979. Adminstr. Stark County Prosecutor's Office, Canton, 1974-76; mem. faculty Walsh Coll., Canton, 1976-78; asst. pros. atty. Stark County, Canton, 1976-77; ptnr. Amerman Burt Jones Co. LPA, Canton, 1976-91, Buckingham, Doolittle and Burroughs Co., L.P.A., Canton, 1991-95; judge Stark County Common Pleas Ct., 1995—; legal adviser Mayor's Office, City of North Canton, Ohio, 1978-79; referee Stark County Family Ct., Canton, 1981, Canton Mcpl. Ct., 1991—; spl. referee Canton Mcpl. Ct., 1985-86. Author: Law Enforcement Officers' Guide to Juvenile Law, 1975, Lay Manual of Juvenile Law, 1976; editor U. Akron Law Rev.; contbr. to Ohio Family Law, 1983, also articles to profl. jours. Mem. North Canton Planning Comm., 1979-82; bd. mgrs. North Canton YMCA, 1976—, Camp Tippecanoe, Ohio, 1981—; profl. adviser Parents Without Partners, 1980—; spl. dep. Stark County Sheriff Dept., 1983—; trustee Palace Theatre Assn., Canton, 1982—. Recipient Disting. Service award U.S. Jaycees, 1984. Mem. ABA, Ohio Bar Assn., Stark County Bar Assn. (lectr. 1984), Ohio Trial Lawyers Assn., Assn. Trial Lawyers Am., Nat. Dist. Attys. Assn., Delta Theta Phi (bailiff 1976; nat. key winner 1975-76), Jaycees. Republican. Methodist. Lodge: Elks, Eagles, Masons.

SINCLAIR, WARREN KEITH, radiation biophysicist, organization executive, consultant; b. Dunedin, New Zealand, Mar. 9, 1924; came to U.S., 1954; naturalized, 1959; s. Ernest W. and Jessie E. (Craig) S.; m. Elizabeth J. Edwards, Mar. 19, 1948; children: Bruce W., Roslyn E. Munn. BSc, U. Otago, New Zealand, 1944, MSc, 1945; PhD, U. London, 1950. Cert. Am. Bd. Health Physics. Radiol. physicist U. Otago, 1945-47; radiol. physicist U. London Royal Marsden Hosp., 1947-54; chmn. dept. physics, prof. U. Tex. M.D. Anderson Hosp., 1954-60; sr. biophysicist Argonne (Ill.) Nat. Lab., 1960-85, div. dir., 1970-74, assoc. lab. dir., 1974-81; prof. radiation biology U. Chgo., 1964-85, prof. emeritus, 1985—; mem. Internat. Commn. on Radiation Units and Measurements, 1969-85, Internat. Commn. on Radiol. Protection, 1977—; alt. del. UN Sci. Com. on Effects of Atomic Radiation, 1979—; mem. Nat. Coun. on Radiation Protection and Measurements, 1967-91, pres., 1977-91, hon. mem., pres. emeritus, 1991—; L.S. Taylor lectr. Nat. Council on Radiation Protection and Measurements, 1993; H. M. Parker lectr. Battelle Found., 1992; mem. expert panel WHO; sec. gen. 5th internat. Congress Radiation Rsch., 1974; chmn. bd. on radiation effects NAS-NRC, 1992-96; cons. in field. Author: Radiation Research: Biomedical, Chemical and Physical Perspectives, 1975; Contbr. numerous articles to profl. jours., also chpts. to books. Served with N.Z. Army, 1942-43. Nat. New Zealand scholar, 1942-45. Fellow Inst. Physics; mem. Am. Assn. Physicists in Medicine (pres. 1961-62, Coolidge award 1986), Nat. Coun. on Radiation Protection and Measurements (pres. 1977-91, pres. emeritus 1991—), Radiation Rsch. Soc. (coun. 1964-67, pres. 1978-79, Failla award 1987), Brit. Inst. Radiology (coun. 1953-54), Internat. Assn. Radiation Rsch. (coun. 1966-70, 76-83), Radiol. Soc. N.Am., Biophys. Soc., Soc. Nuclear Medicine, Bioelectromagnetics Soc., Health Physics Soc., Soc. Risk Analysis, Hosp. Physicists Assn., Innominates Club (Chgo.), Cosmos Club (Washington). Home: 2900 Ascott Ln Olney MD 20832-2626 Office: 7910 Woodmont Ave Ste 800 Bethesda MD 20814-3015

SINCLAIR, WILLIAM DONALD, church official, fundraising consultant, political activist; b. L.A., Dec. 27, 1924; s. Arthur Livingston and Lillian May (Holt) S.; m. Barbara Jean Hughes, Aug. 9, 1952; children: Paul Scott, Victoria Sharon. BA cum laude, St. Martin's Coll., Olympia, Wash., 1975; postgrad. Emory U., 1978-79. Commd. 2d lt. USAAF, 1944, advanced through grades to col., USAF, 1970; served as pilot and navigator in Italy, Korea, Vietnam and Japan; ret., 1975; bus. adminstr. First United Methodist Ch., Colorado Springs, Colo., 1976-85; bus. adminstr. Village Seven Presbyn. Ch., 1985-87; bus. adminstr. Sunrise United Meth. Ch., 1987-89; vice-chmn. council fin. and adminstrn. Rocky Mountain conf. United Meth. Ch., U.S.A., 1979-83. Bd. dirs. Chins-Up Colorado Springs, 1983-86; chmn. bd. dirs. Pikes Peak Performing Arts Ctr., 1985-92; pres. Pioneers Mus. Found., 1985—; Rep. candidate for Colo. State Chmn., 1992-93, elected to Ho. of Reps., Colo. Legis., 1997—. Decorated Legion of Merit with oak leaf cluster, D.F.C., Air medal with 6 oak leaf cluster, Dept. Def. Meritorious Service medal, Vietnam Cross of Gallantry with Palms. Fellow Nat. Assn. Ch. Bus. Adminstrs. (nat. dir., regional v.p., v.p. 1983-85, pres. 1985-87, Ch. Bus. Adminstr. of Yr. award 1983, inducted hall of fame 1995), Colo. Assn. Ch. Bus. Adminstrs. (past pres.), United Meth., Assn. Ch. Bus. Admins. (nat. sec. 1978-81), Christian Ministries Mgmt. Assn. (dir. 1983-85), USAF Acad. Athletic Assn. Clubs: Colorado Springs Country, Garden of the Gods, Met. (Denver), Winter Night Club. Lodge: Rotary (pres. Downtown Colorado Springs club 1985-86), Order of Daedalians. Home: 3007 Chelton Dr Colorado Springs CO 80909-1008 *Ten words of two letters each, spoken by a black clergyman during the civil rights crusade of the 60s, are my guide to the future: "If it is to be, it is up to me." Only with this in mind can change occur.*

SINCOFF, JEROME J., architect. B in Architecture, Washington U., 1956. Advanced through ranks to pres. Hellmuth, Obata & Kassabaum, Inc., St. Louis, 1962—; bldg. rsch. bd. NRC/NAS; sch. architecture nat. coun. Washington U., 1993-96, mem.-at-large adv. bd., 1993-96, exec. com. alumni bd. govs., 1993-96, chmn., 1994-95. Bd. commrs. St. Louis Art Mus. Fellow AIA (co-founder large firm roundtable); mem. Constrn. Industry Pres.'s Forum. Office: Hellmuth Obata Kassabaum Inc 211 N Broadway Ste 600 Saint Louis MO 63102-2733

SINCOFF, MICHAEL Z., human resources and marketing professional; b. Washington, June 28, 1943; s. Murray P. and Anna F. (Jaffe) S. m. Kathleen M. Dunham, Oct. 9, 1983. BA, U. Md., 1964, MA, 1966; PhD, Purdue U., 1969. Instr. U. Tenn., Knoxville, 1968; asst. prof. Ohio U., Athens, 1969-74, dir. Ctr. for Comm. Studies, 1969-76, assoc. prof., 1974-76; vis. prof. U. Minn., St. Paul, 1974; dir. personnel devel. Hoechst-Celanese Corp. (formerly Celanese Corp.), N.Y., 1976-79; dir. employee comm. The Mead Corp., Dayton, Ohio, 1979-81, dir. edn., tng., 1981-83; assoc. dean Sch. of Bus. Adminstrn. Georgetown U., Washington, 1983-84; v.p. human resources ADVO, Inc. (formerly ADVO-Sys., Inc.), Hartford, Conn., 1984-87; v.p. human resources, corp. officer DIMAC Direct Inc., St. Louis, 1987-88; sr. v.p. human resources and adminstrn., sr. corp. officer DIMAC Mktg. Corp. (parent of DIMAC Direct Inc.), St. Louis, 1988-97, also sec., asst. treas., exec. com., 1988-97; sr. v.p. human resources, exec. corp. officer Brooks Fiber Properties, Inc., St. Louis, 1997—. Author, editor human resources sect. Am. Mgmt. Assn. Mgmt. Handbook, 3d edit., 1994; author approximately 50 books and articles; mem. edtl. adv. bd. Jour. Applied Comm. Rsch., 1991—. Life mem. Internat. Comm. Assn. (bus. mgr.-exec. sec. 1969-73, fin. com. 1982-85); mem. Am. Mgmt. Assn. (human resources coun. 1990—), Printing Industries of Am. (employer resources group 1989-97).

SINDEN, HARRY, professional hockey team executive; b. Collins Bay, Ont., Can., Sept. 14, 1932; m. Eleanor Sinden; children: Nancy, Carol, Donna, Julie. Player Hull-Ottawa Eastern Pro League hockey team; player-coach Kingston team, from 1961; coach numerous teams Central League, until 1967; coach Boston Bruins, Nat. Hockey League team, 1966-70, mng. dir., from 1972, now pres., gen. mgr., alt. gov.; TV hockey commentator, 1970-72; coach Team Can., 1973, Stanley Cup team, 1970. Office: Boston Bruins 1 Fleet Ctr Ste 250 Boston MA 02114-1303

SINDLINGER, VERNE E., bishop. Bishop Lincoln Trails Synod, Indpls. Office: Presbyterian Church USA 1100 W 42nd St Indianapolis IN 46208-3345*

SINEATH, TIMOTHY WAYNE, library educator, university dean; b. Jacksonville, Fla., May 21, 1940; s. Holcombe Asbury and Christine Marcel (Cook) S.; m. Patricia Ann Greenwood, June 8, 1962; children: Philip Greenwood, Paul Byron. B.A., Fla. State U., 1962, M.S., 1963; Ph.D. (Higher Edn. Act fellow), U. Ill., 1970. Reference librarian U. Ga., 1963-64, catalog librarian, 1964-66; acad. coordinator continuing edn. in library sci. U. Ill., 1966-68; asst. prof. library sci. Simmons Coll., 1970-74, coordinator doctoral program, 1974-77; prof., dean Coll. Libr. Sci. and Info. Sci. U. Ky., Lexington, 1977-87, prof., 1987—; cons. to libraries, schs., chs., industry; mem. Lexington (Ky.) Public Library Bd., 1978—. Author profl. reports; contbr. articles on library and info. sci., gen. info. mgmt., organizational and small group behavior to profl. jours. Mem. ALA, Am. Soc. Info. Sci., Assn. for Libr. and Info. Sci. Edn. (pres. 1993). Episcopalian. Home: 3418 Bay Leaf Dr Lexington KY 40502-3804 Office: U Ky MI King Bldg Lexington KY 40506-0039

SINEGAL, JAMES D., variety store wholesale business executive; b. 1936. With Fed-Mart Corp., 1954-77, exec. v.p.; v.p. Builders Emporium, 1977-78; exec. v.p. Price Co., 1978-79; with Sinegal/Chamberlin & Assocs., 1979-83; pres., chief oper. officer Costco Wholesale Corp., 1983—, chief exec. officer, 1988—, bd. dirs. Office: Costco Wholesale Corp 999 Lake Dr Issaquah WA 98027-5367*

SINFELT, JOHN HENRY, chemist; b. Munson, Pa., Feb. 18, 1931; s. Henry Gustave and June Lillian (McDonald) S.; m. Muriel Jean Vadersen, July 14, 1956; 1 son, Klaus Herbert. B.S., Pa. State U., 1951; Ph.D., U. Ill., 1954, D.Sc. (hon.), 1981. Research engr. Exxon Research Engring. Co., Linden, N.J., 1954-57; sr. research engr. Exxon Research Engring. Co., 1957-62, research assoc., 1962-68, sr. research assoc., 1968-72, sci. advisor, 1972-79, sr. sci. advisor, 1979-96, sr. sci. advisor emeritus, 1996—; vis. prof. chem. engring. U. Minn., 1969; Lacey lectr. Calif. Inst. Tech., 1973; Reilly lectr. U. Notre Dame, 1974; Frontiers in Chemistry lectr. Case Western Res. U., Cleve., 1978; Matthew Van Winkle lectr. U. Tex., 1979; Francois Gault lectr. catalysis Coun. Europe Rsch. Group Catalysis, 1980; Mobay lectr. in chemistry U. Pitts., 1980; disting. vis. lectr. in chemistry, U. Tex., 1981; Robert Welch Found. lectr. Confs. on Chem. Rsch., 1981; Camille and Henry Dreyfus lectr. UCLA, 1982; Edward Clark Lee Meml. lectr. U. Chgo., 1983; Dow disting. lectr. in chemistry Mich. State U., 1984; Arthur D. Little lectr. Northeastern U., 1985; Vollmer W. Fries lectr. Rensselaer Poly. Inst., 1986; disting. lectr. Ctr. Chem. Physics U. Fla., 1988; David M. Mason lectr. Stanford U., 1995, cons. prof. dept. chem. engring., 1996—. Contbr. articles to sci. jours. Recipient Dickson prize Carnegie-Mellon U., 1977, Internat. prize for new materials Am. Phys. Soc., 1978, Nat. medal of Sci., 1979, Perkin medal in chemistry Soc. Chem. Industry, 1984, Disting. Alumnus award Pa. State U., 1985; named to N.J. Inventors Hall of Fame, 1991. Fellow AIChE (Alpha Chi Sigma award 1971, Profl. Progress award 1975), Am. Acad. Arts and Scis., Am. Inst. Chemists (Chem. Pioneer award 1981, Gold medal 1984); mem. NAS (award for indsl. application of sci. 1996), NAE, Am. Chem. Soc. (Carothers lectr. Del. sect. 1982, Petroleum Chemistry award 1976, Murphree award 1986), Catalysis Soc. (Emmett award 1973), Am. Philos. Soc. Methodist. Achievements include introduction and development of concept of bimetallic clusters as catalysts; invention of polymetallic cluster catalysts used commercially in petroleum reforming. Office: Exxon Research Engineering Co Clinton Township Rte 22 E Annandale NJ 08801

SING, ROBERT FONG, physician; b. Camden, N.J., May 29, 1953; s. William Fong and Elizabeth (Maxwell) S.; m. Lauren McNamee, May 11, 1991. BS in Biology, Ursinus Coll., 1975; DO, Coll. Osteo. Medicine, Surgery, 1978. Intern, then resident Met. Hosp., Phila., 1978-80; dir. Emergency Dept. Springfield (Pa.) Hosp., 1984—; dir. sports medicine Sports Sci. Ctr., 1987—; med. dir. Emergency Ambulance Svcs., Inc., 1994-95; owner J. Enright Jewelers, Inc., Swarthmore, Pa., 1995—; owner, pres. Finish Line Sports, Inc., Phila., 1988-94; sch. and team physician Springfield Sch. Dist., 1989, Rose Tree-Media (Pa.) Sch. Dist., 1987; chief med. officer Kent Profl. Bicyling Tour of China, 1995, U.S. Olympic Cycling Trials, 1996. Author: Dynamics of the Javelin Throw, 1984. Med. dir. Springfield Ambulance Corp., 1988—. Named to Athletic Hall of Fame, 1985. Fellow Am. Coll. Emergency Physicians, Am. Coll. Sports Medicine, Am. Coll. Osteo. Emergency Physicians. Avocations: track and field, classical music, bicycling. Home: 1274 Gradyville Rd Glen Mills PA 19342-9614 Office: Sports Sci Ctr 700 S Chester Rd Swarthmore PA 19081-2224

SING, WILLIAM BENDER, lawyer; b. Houston, Oct. 16, 1947; s. William Bender Sr. and Alice Irene S.; m. Doris Anne Spradley, Sept. 1, 1967; children: Erin Elaine, Emily Elizabeth. BS cum laude, U. Houston, 1968, JD magna cum laude, 1971. Bar: Tex. 1971. Assoc. Fulbright & Jaworski, LLP, Houston, 1973-80, ptnr., 1980—. Elder, trustee St. Andrew's Presbyn. Ch., Houston; past pres., bd. dirs. St. Andrew's Presbyn. Sch., Houston; past pres. Houston C.C. Place Civic Assn. 1st lt. U.S. Army, 1971-73. Mem. ABA, Tex. Bar Assn., Houston Bar Assn., Order of the Barons Law Honor Soc., Phi Delta Phi, Phi Kappa Phi, Omicron Delta Epsilon. Presbyterian. Avocation: reading history and literature. Office: Fulbright & Jaworski LLP 1301 Mckinney St Houston TX 77010-3031

SINGER, ALLEN MORRIS, lawyer; b. Mpls., Dec. 30, 1923; s. William and Ida (Simenstein) S. JD, U. Chgo., 1948; LLM, Harvard U., 1958. Bar: Ill. 1948, Calif. 1949. Pvt. practice, 1950-55, 59—; v.p., sec., gen. counsel Am. Bldg. Maintenance Industries, San Francisco, 1969-85; assoc. prof. law U. Oreg., 1955-59; lectr. law Stanford (Calif.) U., 1960-62; of counsel Cooper, White & Cooper, San Francisco, 1970-97. Contbr. articles to profl. jours. Mem. U. Chgo. Nat. Alumni Cabinet, 1978-80. 2nd lt., USAAF, 1943-45. Mem. ABA, San Francisco Bar Assn., Calif. Bar Assn. Home and Office: 1070 Green St Apt 703 San Francisco CA 94133-3677 Office: Cooper White & Cooper 201 California St Fl 17 San Francisco CA 94111-5002

SINGER, ARMAND EDWARDS, foreign language educator; b. Detroit, Nov. 30, 1914; s. Elvin Satori Singer and Fredericka Elizabeth (Edwards) Singer Goetz; m. Mary Rebecca White, Aug. 8, 1940; 1 child, Fredericka Ann Hill. A.B., Amherst Coll., 1935; M.A., Duke U., 1939, Ph.D., 1944; diplôme, U. Paris, 1939; postgrad., Ind. U., summer 1964. Teaching fellow in sci. Amherst Coll., 1935-36; instr. French and Spanish, part-time Duke, 1938-40; teaching fellow Romance langs. W.Va. U., Morgantown, 1940-41, instr., 1941-47, asst. prof., 1947-55, assoc. prof., 1955-60, prof., 1960-80, prof. emeritus, 1980—, chmn. program for humanities, 1963-72, chmn. dept. integrated studies, 1963, acting chmn. dept. religion and program for humanities, 1973, dir. ann. colloquium on modern lit., 1976-80, 85-86, 96-97. Author: A Bibliography of the Don Juan Theme: Versions and Criticism, 1954, The Don Juan Theme, Versions and Criticism: An Annotated Bibliography, 1965, Paul Bourget, 1975, The Don Juan Theme: A Bibliography of Versions, Analogues, Uses, and Adaptations, 1993, The Armand E. Singer Tibet, 1809-1975, 1995, The Armand E. Singer Nepal, 1772-1961 and Beyond, 1997, (with J.F. Stasny) Anthology of Readings: Humanities I, 1966, Anthology of Readings: Humanities II, 1967; editor: (with Jürgen E. Schlunk) Martin Walser: International Perspectives, 1987; editor W.Va. U. Philol. Papers, 1948-50, 53-55, editor-in-chief, 1951-52, 55—, 1001 Horny Limericks by Ward Marden, 1996; editor, contbr. Essays on the Literature of Mountaineering, 1982; contbr. numerous articles to profl. and philatelic jours. Bd. dirs. Community Concert Assn., Morgantown, 1959-60, Humanities Found. W.Va., 1981-87. Recipient 4th Ann. Humanities award W.Va. Humanities Coun., 1990. Mem. MLA (internat. bibliography com. 1956-59, nat. del. assembly 1975-78), So. Atlantic MLA (exec. com. 1971-74), Am. Assn. Tchrs. Spanish and Portuguese, Am. Philatelic Soc., Nepal and Tibet Philatelic Study Circle, Nepal Philatelic Soc., Collectors Club of N.Y., Phi Beta Kappa. Republican. Home: 248 Grandview Ave Morgantown WV 26505-6925 *In an age of deteriorating standards, I want to be counted among those educators who stand against the tide. We ask too little of others, we ask too little of ourselves; others ask too little of us. When we constantly encounter shoddy construction, shoddy merchandise, shoddy performances, shoddy ethics, shoddy education, we may be tempted to forswear our standards. But through our hands pass tomorrow's leaders. As teachers we must help stop this erosion of our national pride. If we fail, make no mistake: it could well destroy us all.*

SINGER, ARTHUR LOUIS, JR., foundation executive; b. Scranton, Pa., Feb. 14, 1929; s. Arthur and Isabel S.; m. Joan Cristal, July 26, 1952; children—Arthur, Philip, Charles. A.B., Williams Coll., 1950; M.B.A., U. Mich., 1952. Adminstr. Mass. Inst. Tech., 1955-63; exec. asso. (Carnegie Corp.), N.Y.C., 1963-66; pres. Edn. Devel. Center, Newton, Mass., 1966-68; v.p. Alfred P. Sloan Found., N.Y.C., 1968-94, cons., 1994—. Served to lt. (j.g.) USNR, 1952-55. Home: 23 Owenoke Park Westport CT 06880-6834 Office: 630 5th Ave Ste 2550 New York NY 10111-0100

SINGER, BARBARA HELEN, photographer; b. N.Y.C., Jan. 29, 1927; d. Robert and Rose (Kaplowitz) S.; m. Nat Herz, Jan. 15, 1956 (dec. Nov. 1964); m. Melvin C. Zalkan, Sept. 7, 1983 (dec. Nov. 1993). BA in Biology, NYU, 1947; studied with Eli Siegel, 1944-76. Radiographer, 1951-90; instr. Meth. Hosp. Sch. Radiologic Tech., Bklyn., 1968-72; asst. to Benedict J. Fernandez & Lucien Clergue New Sch./Parsons, N.Y.C., N.Y., 1985-91; photographer N.Y.C., 1983—. Group exhbns. include Associated Artists Gallery, Winston-Salem, N.C., 1985, Donnell Libr., N.Y.C., 1986, Lincoln Sq. Gallery, N.Y.C., 1990, Konica Plz., Tokyo, 1990, Nikon House, N.Y.C., 1990, St. Margaret's House, N.Y.C., 1991, Duggal Downtown, N.Y.C., 1994, Salmagundi Club, N.Y.C., 1989, 90, 91, 92, 94, 95, 96, Coll. New Rochelle, N.Y., 1994, Artists Talk on Art, N.Y.C., 1994, Gallery Cedar Hollow, Malvern, Pa., 1995, Columbia U., N.Y.C., 1995, Erector Sq. Gallery, New Haven, Conn., 1995, Hudson Pk. Libr., N.Y.C., 1996, Learning Alliance, N.Y.C., 1996, 97, Lever House, N.Y.C., 1996, Severoceske Mus., 1996, Nat. Mus. Asian, African & Am. Cultures, Prague, Czech Republic, 1996, Time Life Bldg., N.Y.C., 1996, 97, Wildlife Conservation Soc., N.Y.C., 1996, The Wildlife Gallery at Central Park, N.Y.C., 1996, The Stone Gallery, Ft. Collins, Colo., 1997, Nassau C.C., Garden City, N.Y., 1997, Fulcrum Gallery, N.Y.C., 1997, Time Life Bldg., N.Y.C., 1997; CD-ROM Urbane Photography, 1996; photography published in Profl. Women Photographers Newsletter, 1985, 95, Light and Shade, 1985, Best of Photography Annual 1990, Women of Vision, 1990, Tear Sheet, 1995, Photonica 21, 1996, Fotophile, 1997. Photographers' Forum Finalist, 1990; recipient Photography award Beaux Arts Soc., 1994. Mem. Am. Soc. Picture Profls., Profl. Women Photographers, Pictorial Photographers Am., Artists Talk on Art, Am. Soc. Media Photographers. Avocation: ballroom dancing. Office: Madison Sq Sta PO Box 1150 New York NY 10159

SINGER, BURTON HERBERT, statistics educator; b. Chgo., June 12, 1938; married; 3 children. B.S., Case Inst. Tech., 1959, M.S., 1961; Ph.D. in Stats., Stanford U., 1967. From asst. to assoc. prof. stats. Columbia U., N.Y.C., 1967-77, prof. math. stats., 1977-85, chmn. dept. math. stats., 1985-89; then chmn. biostats., then chmn. and assoc. dean pub. health dept. epidemiology and pub. health Yale U., New Haven, 1989-91, chmn. epidemiology and pub. health, 1991-93, Ira Vaughan Hiscock prof. epidemiology and pub. health, 1991-94, prof. econs. and stats. dept. epidemiology and pub. health, 1991-94; prof. demography and pub. affairs Princeton (N.J.) U., 1994—; research assoc. statistician Princeton U., 1972-73. Mem. AAAS, Nat. Acad. Scis., Am. Statis. Assn., Psychometric Soc. Office: Princeton Univ Office Population Rsch 21 Prospect Ave Princeton NJ 08544

SINGER, CECILE DORIS, state legislator. BA, Queens Coll.; D (hon.), Pace U., 1997. Past rep. Spl. Svcs. for Children, N.Y.C.; past exec. dir. N.Y. State Assembly Social Svcs. and Judiciary Coms., Joint Legis. Com. on Corps., Authorities and Commns.; past pub. rep. Yonkers (N.Y.) Emergency Control Bd.; past coord. Westchester County Assembly Dels.; past chief of staff for dep. minority leader; mem. N.Y. State Assembly, Albany, 1988—, leadership sec. Rep. Conf., mem. assembly children & families com., mem. various other coms.; bd. dirs. Hudson Valley Bank; past rep. Temp. Commn. to Revise Social Svcs. Law; mem. Presdl. Commn. on Privacy Conf., N.Y. State Senate Transp. Conf.; mem. task force on substance abuse Am. Legis. Exch. Coun., task force on econ. devel., crime victims' rights, hosp. crisis, women's issues, com. on mass transit; sec. Rep. Conf. Nat. Adv. Panel Child Care Action Campaign; dir. Hudson Valley Bank; chmn. Westchester County Commn. on Pub. Financing of Campaigns; chmn. Lower Hudson Valley Adv. Com. N.Y. State Divsn. for Women. Mem. adv. bd. Legal Awareness for Women, Big Bros. and Big Sisters, Westchester C.C. Found., Westchester 2000 Rsch., Womens Adv. Bd. Westchester County; mem. task force on certiorari Westchester County Sch. Bds. Assn.; sch. and cmty. chmn. Yonkers PTA; bd. dirs. Yonkers Gen. Hosp., Yonkers chpt. United Jewish Appeal. Recipient Jenkins Meml. award, Nat. PTA award; inducted Women's Hall of Fame, 1996, Sr. Citizens Hall of Fame, 1996. Mem. Mental Health Assn. (bd. dirs., mem. nominating and pub. affairs coms. Westchester County chpt.), Rotary. Home: 117 Cliffside Dr Yonkers NY 10710-3144 Office: 21 Scarsdale Rd Yonkers NY 10707-3204

SINGER, CRAIG, broker, consultant, investor; b. N.Y.C., Aug. 13, 1947; s. Albert and Dorothy (Blackman) S.; m. Ellen Rappaport, Aug. 31, 1969; children: Chad Adam, Cara Danielle. BS, Cornell U., 1969; JD, Columbia U., 1972. Bar: N.Y. 1973. Exec. Continental Wingate Co., Inc., N.Y.C., 1972-74; exec. v.p. Integrated Resources, Inc., N.Y.C., 1974-87; chmn. bd. Integrated Resources Housing Corp., Integrated Funding, Inc., Resources Funding Corp., AIM Capital Mgmt. Corp., 1983-87; cons., investor, broker, Bedford Corners, N.Y., 1988—; pres. Westminster Fin. Group, Inc., 1989—. Former dir. Assn. Govt. Assisted Housing, Inc., 1976-84; former mem. exec. com. Coalition for Low and Moderate Income Housing; former mem. edn. adv. bd. Bur. Nat. Affairs Housing and Devel. Reporter. Home and Office: 148 Meeting House Rd RFD 4 Bedford Corners NY 10549

SINGER, DANIEL MORRIS, lawyer; b. Bklyn., Oct. 10, 1930; s. Samuel W. and Fannie G. (Sabloff) S.; m. Maxine Frank, June 15, 1952; children: Amy E., Ellen R., David B., Stephanie F. BA with honors, Swarthmore Coll., 1951; LLB, Yale U., 1954. Bar: N.Y. 1956, U.S. Dist. Ct. D.C. 1957, U.S. Ct. Appeals (D.C. cir.) 1957, U.S. Supreme Ct., 1959. Motions clk. U.S. Ct. Appeals D.C. Cir., 1956-57, law clk. to Judge George T. Washington, 1957-58; assoc. Fried, Frank, Harris, Shriver & Jacobson, Washington, 1958-64, ptnr., 1965-87, counsel, 1987—; arbitrator complex comml. case and constrn. nat. panels; mediator US Dist. Ct., Washington; vol. atty. Lawyers Com. for Civil Rights Under Law, 1965, 66; mem. exec. com. Washington Lawyers Com. for Civil Rights Under Law, 1973—; bd. mgrs. Swarthmore Coll., 1987-91. Bd. dirs., sec.-treas. Nat. Com. Tithing in Investment, 1964-65; dir. sec.-treas. Council for a Livable World, 1962-64; mem. gov. council, exec. com. Am. Jewish Congress, 1986—, v.p. 1988-92; dir. Am. Soc. for the Protection of Nature in Israel, 1986—. With Signal Corps, U.S. Army, 1954-56. Mem. ABA, D.C. Bar. Home: 5410 39th St NW Washington DC 20015-2902 Office: Fried Frank Harris Shriver 1001 Pennsylvania Ave NW Ste 800 Washington DC 20004-2505

SINGER, DAVID MICHAEL, marketing and public relations company executive; b. Bklyn., N.Y., Feb. 11, 1957; s. Seymour Allen and Ellen Sybil (Pavnick) S.; m. Pamela Rae Silton, July 20, 1986; 1 child, Max. BA in History, NYU, 1978; MA in Communications, Syracuse U., 1979; MA in Media, New Sch. Social Research, 1983; JD, Yeshiva U., 1981. Cons. pub. rels. Burson-Marsteller, N.Y.C., 1979-81, The Haas Group, N.Y.C., 1981-84, Braff & Co., N.Y.C., 1987-89; pub., editor-in-chief Lodestone Pub., N.Y.C., 1984-87; chief oper. officer Pentagon Ltd., N.Y.C., 1989-91; v.p. pub. rels. Braff & Co., N.Y.C., 1991-92; v.p. G.S. Schwartz & Co., N.Y.C., 1993—; lectr. evening div. NYU, 1982—; dir. media rels. Braff & Co. Contbr. articles and poems to profl. and consumer jours. and mags. Pres. Jewish Cultural Found., N.Y.C., 1976. Named Mem. of Yr., N.Y. State Kiwanis, 1976, Outstanding Young Man of Am., Jaycees, 1977; recipient Cert. Recognition Am. Film Inst., 1982, ANDY Design award Advt. Club N.Y., 1983, Proclamation Bklyn. Borough Pres., 1987. Mem. Alpha Epsilon Pi (Bro. of Yr. 1976). Avocations: baseball, politics, ping-pong, films, theater.

SINGER, DONALD IVAN, architect; b. Trenton, N.J., Feb. 20, 1938; s. Harold William and Beatrice (Lavine) S.; m. Elaine Ruth Segall, Aug. 23, 1959; children: Lauren Elizabeth, Susan Meredith. BArch, U. Fla., 1960; MS in Architecture, Columbia U., 1961. Registered architect, Fla. Draftsman Charles Reed, Jr. Architect, Hollywood, Fla., 1961-62; pvt. practice architecture Ft. Lauderdale, 1964—; mem. design adv. bd. Formica Corp., N.Y.C., 1977-82, design critique com. Dade County Aviation Authority, Miami, Fla., 1987-89. Prin. works include office bldg. R.J. Pavlik Corp. Hdqrs., 1980 (honor award Fla. Assn. AIA 1981), City Pk. Urban Pla. and Garage, Ft. Lauderdale, Fla., 1982 (honor award Fla. Assn. AIA 1983), office bldg. Fire Prevention Bur., 1987 (honor award Fla. Assn. AIA 1987), prototype sch. Forest Glen Middle Sch., 1989 (Fla. Concrete Assn. award 1990). Pres. Downtown Coun., Ft. Lauderdale, 1980-81; trustee Mus. Art, Ft. Lauderdale, 1980-85; vice chmn. Riverwalk Com., Ft. Lauderdale, 1989-91; chmn. Art-in-Pub. Places Com., Broward County, Fla., 1990-91; chmn. Design Broward, 1994-95. With USAF, 1961-62. Recipient Morretti award Broward Cultural Affairs Coun., 1983, Leadership award, 1995; Disting. Alumni award U. Fla. Sch. Architecture, 1991. Fellow AIA; mem. Fla. Assn. AIA (honor award for design 1984, chmn. conf. com. 1986-87, chmn. design awards com. 1988-89). Republican. Jewish. Avocation: photography. Office: 13 W Las Olas Blvd Fort Lauderdale FL 33301-1823 *We all wish for those moments during which our thoughts focus to a unity and we know something complete and of total simplicity. Architecture has the potential to afford those moments.*

SINGER, ELEANOR, sociologist, editor; b. Vienna, Austria, Mar. 4, 1930; came to U.S., 1938; d. Alfons and Anna (Troedl) Schwarzbart; m. Alan Gerard Singer, Sept. 8, 1949; children: Emily Ann, Lawrence Alexander. BA, Queens Coll., 1951; PhD, Columbia U., 1966. Asst. editor Am. Scholar, Williamsburg, Va., 1951-52; editor Tchrs. Coll. Press, N.Y.C., 1952-56, Dryden-Holt, N.Y.C., 1956-57; rsch. assoc., sr. rsch. assoc., sr. rsch. scholar Columbia U., N.Y.C., 1966-94; rsch. scientist Inst. for Social Rsch. U. Mich., Ann Arbor, 1994—; editor Pub. Opinion Quar., N.Y.C., 1975-86. Author: (with Carol Weiss) The Reporting of Social Science in the Mass Media, 1988, (with Phyllis Endreny) Reporting On Risk, 1993; editor: (with Herbert H. Hyman) Readings in Reference Group Theory and Research, 1968, (with Stanley Presser) Survey Research Methods: A Reader, 1989; contbr. articles to profl. jours. Mem. Am. Assn. Pub. Opinion Research (pres. N.Y.C. chpt. 1983-84, pres. 1987-88), Am. Sociol. Assn., Am. Statis. Assn. Office: U Mich Inst Social Rsch Box 1248 Ann Arbor MI 48106

SINGER, ERIC T., investment banker; b. N.Y.C., Apr. 11, 1952; s. Roger M. and Meredith Singer; m. Aet Paaro, Aug. 10, 1974; children: Brett A., Jamison P. BA, SUNY, Stony Brook, 1974; JD, Cornell U., 1977. Assoc. Barrett, Smith et al, N.Y.C., 1977-80; v.p. Smith Barney, N.Y.C., 1980-84; sr. v.p. PaineWebber, N.Y.C., 1984-88; exec. v.p. Metromedia Hotels, N.Y.C., 1988-90; exec. v.p., dir. corp. fin. Gerard Klauer Mattison, N.Y.C., 1990—. Mem. Cornell Law Rev. Mem. Heights Casino Club, Yale Club, Phi Beta Kappa. Republican. Avocation: squash. Home: 72 Hicks St Brooklyn NY 11201 Office: Gerard Klauer Mattison 529 5th Ave New York NY 10017-4608

SINGER, FREDERICK RAPHAEL, medical researcher, educator; b. St. Louis, June 27, 1939; s. Meyer and Lee (Minkle) S.; m. Sandra Joy Barnes, Aug. 16, 1964; children: Stefanie, Jeffrey. Student UCLA, 1956-59; BS, U. Calif.-Berkeley, 1960; MD, U. Calif.-San Francisco, 1963. Diplomate Am. Bd. Internal Medicine, Am. Bd. Endocrinology and Metabolism. Intern UCLA Affiliated Hosp., 1963-64; resident VA Hosp., Los Angeles, 1964-65, 68-69; instr. in medicine Harvard U., Boston, 1971-72; asst. prof. medicine UCLA, 1972-73; asst. prof. medicine U. So. Calif., L.A., 1973-74, assoc. prof., 1974-78, prof., 1978-89, prof. orthopaedic surgery, 1980-89; dir. Bone Ctr. Cedars-Sinai Med. Ctr., L.A., 1989-92; prof. medicine, UCLA, 1989-92, clin. prof. medicine, 1993—; dir. Osteoporosis/Metabolic Bone Disease program St. Johns Hosp. and Health Ctr., Santa Monica, 1992—; dir. Skeletal Biology Lab, John Wayne Cancer Inst., Santa Monica, 1992—; mem. endocrine and metabolic drug adv. com. FDA, USPHS, Bethesda, Md., 1983-87. Author: Paget's Disease of Bone, 1977. Contbr. numerous articles, revs. to profl. jours. Vice chmn. community adv. com. Univ. High Sch., L.A., 1984. Served as capt. USAF, 1965-67. Calif. State scholar, 1956-60; clin. investigator VA, 1971-73. Mem. Endocrine Soc., Am. Soc. Clin. Investigation, Am. Soc. Bone and Mineral Research (chmn. pub. affairs 1981-86, coun. 1987, pres.-elect 1989, pres. 1990), Paget's Disease Found. (chmn. bd. dirs. 1990—). Office: John Wayne Cancer Inst 2200 Santa Monica Blvd Santa Monica CA 90404-2302

SINGER, GERALD MICHAEL, lawyer, educator, author, arbitrator and mediator; b. Mpls., Sept. 9, 1920; s. Charles and Rachael Caroline (Feldman) S.; m. Lillian Kaplan, July 10, 1944; children: Barbara Ellen, Alan Mark. JD, Loyola U., L.A., 1968. Bar: Calif. 1969, U.S. Dist. Ct. Calif. (so dist.) 1969, U.S. Ct. Appeals (9th cir.) 1969, U.S. Supreme Ct. 1972. Pres. Bigg of Calif., Inc., 1948-69; pvt. practice, Encino, Calif., 1969—; adj. prof. law Loyola U., 1975-85, 92; judge pro tem Calif. Superior Ct., 1973—, arbitrator, 1976—; judge pro tem Calif. Mcpl. Ct., 1973—; arbitrator, mediator, 1988—; sr. panel mem. AAA Comml. Arbitrators, L.A., Internat. Arbitration World Ct., The Hague; lectr. to various law schs., bar assns. and legal groups, 1976—; freelance writer newspapers. Author: How To Go Directly Into Solo Law Practice (Without Missing a Meal), 1976, rev. edit. as How To Go Directly Into Your Own Computerized Solo Law Practice Without Missing a Meal (Or a Byte), 1986, updated, 1989, rev. edit. as How To Go Directly Into, and Manage, Your Own Solo Law Practice (Without Missing a Meal), 1993, 168-page supplement, 1996-97. Mem. Com. To Elect Ricard Nixon, Com. to Reelect Richard Nixon, Com. to Elect and Reelect Ronald Reagan, L.A. Staff sgt. Signal Corps, U.S. Army and USAAF, 1942-46. Mem. Am. Arbitration Assn. (arbitrator 1973—). Republican. Avocations: golf, sailing, horseback riding, photography, videography. Office: NPO 271 Box 555 38-180 Del Webb Blvd Palm Desert CA 92211

SINGER, HENRY A., behavioral scientist, institute director; b. Mt. Vernon, N.Y., Apr. 13, 1919; s. A.D. and Evelyn (Zierler) S.; m. Rosina Scimonelli, Jan. 7, 1944 (dec. Jan. 1991); children: Victoria, David Anthony. BS, Columbia U., 1942; MA, NYU, 1947, PhD (Rockefeller fellow 1947-48), 1950, PhD, 1973. Instr. Human Rels. Ctr. NYU, 1948-50; assoc. prof. SUNY, Fredonia, 1950-51; adviser U.S. Mission to Philippines, 1951-54; cons. Conn. Edn. Assn., 1954-56; dir. edn. Hilton Hotel Corp., 1956-58; cons. Conn. Assn. Mental Health, 1958-59; dir. edn. Remington Rand div. Sperry Rand, 1959-62; exec. dir. Soc. Advancement Mgmt., 1963-66; higher edn. officer CUNY, 1966-68; exec. dir. Human Resources Inst. Inc., Westport, Conn., 1969—; with Diebold Inst. Pub. Policy Studies, N.Y.C., 1981-87; exec. asst. Am. Nobel Com., N.Y.C., Conn., 1947-50, vice chmn., 1961-66, exec. officer, 1986-92, hon. chair, 1992—; vis. prof. Cornell U., 1949-83, U. Philippines, 1952-53, NYU, 1960-62, CUNY, 1962-63, Columbia U., 1963-64, Western Conn. U., 1964-70, U. Tehran, 1975, 77, Empire State Coll., SUNY, 1981; vis. prin. lectr. Hong Kong Poly., 1976-78, U. Hong Kong, 1992; sr. dir. Experience Compression Lab., Barnum Internat., 1960-93. Editor: Connecticut Teacher, 1954-56, Connecticut Mental Health News, 1958-59, Advanced Management, 1959-66; Contbr. articles to U.S. and internat. publs. vis. expert AID mission, Spain, 1962, Internat. Human Resources, Tehran, Iran, 1965, 75, 77; assoc. dir. engring. mgmt. workshops Columbia U., 1963-66; vis. lectr. Asian Inst. for Mgmt., 1977; bd. dirs. Conn. Assn. Mental Health, 1960-62, Mohonk Home for Boys, Westport, Conn., 1981—, NYU Alumni Coun., 1990—. Recipient award Council Internat. Progress in Mgmt., 1963; Rockefeller fellow, 1948-49. Fellow Am. Soc. Applied Anthropology, Hong Kong Psych. Soc., Internat. Acad. Counseling and Psychotherapy; Mem. APA (life). Clubs: Overseas Press (gov.), Columbia U., Princeton (N.Y.C.); Fgn. Corres. (Hong Kong). Office: 45 Southport Woods Dr Southport CT 06490-1117 Home: PO Box 20202 Sarasota FL 34276 *Perhaps life teaches us that relating successfully to others is the one sure road to survival in an increasingly crowded environment. One measurement of this successful human relationship is the degree to which one human being is able to inconvenience himself for another.*

SINGER, IRVING, philosophy educator; b. N.Y.C., Dec. 24, 1925; s. Isidore and Nettie (Stromer) S.; m. Josephine Fisk, June 10, 1949; children—Anne, Margaret, Emily, Benjamin. AB summa cum laude, Harvard U., 1948, MA, 1949, PhD, 1952. Instr. philosophy Cornell U., 1953-56; asst. prof. U. Mich., 1956-59; vis. lectr. Johns Hopkins U., 1957-58; mem. faculty M.I.T., 1958—, prof. philosophy, 1969—. Author: Santayana's Aesthetics, 1957, The Nature of Love: Plato to Luther, 1966, rev. edit., 1984, The Goals of Human Sexuality, 1973, Mozart and Beethoven, 1977, The Nature of Love: Courtly and Romantic, 1984, The Nature of Love: The Modern World, 1987, Meaning in Life: The Creation of Value, 1992, The Pursuit of Love, 1994, The Creation of Value, 1996, The Harmony of Nature and Spirit, 1996. Served with AUS, 1944-46. Fellow Guggenheim Found., 1965, Rockefeller Found., 1970, Bollingen Found., 1966; grantee Am. Council Learned Socs., 1966; Fulbright fellow, 1955. Mem. Am. Philos. Assn., Am. Soc. Aesthetics. Office: MIT Rm 20E210A Cambridge MA 02139

SINGER, JEFFREY MICHAEL, organic analytical chemist; b. N.Y.C., Feb. 2, 1949; s. Samuel and Theresa (Pohl) S.; m. Linda Arlene Prizer, Oct. 13, 1972; 1 child, Sarah. BA, CUNY, 1971; MS, Rensselaer Poly. Inst., 1976; MA, CUNY, 1979; PhD, Poly. U., Bklyn., 1987. Analytical chemist Equitable Environ. Health Inc., Woodbury, N.Y., 1979-80; group leader Chemtech Cons. Group, N.Y.C., 1980-81; sr. chemist/lab. supr. Revlon Health Care, Tuckahoe, N.Y., 1981-86; analytical devel. chemist Lederle Labs., Pearl River, N.Y., 1986-87; sr. chemist PepsiCo Inc., Valhalla, N.Y., 1987-89; lab. mgr. Pall Corp., Glen Cove, N.Y., 1989-90; mgr. analytical tech. support Du Pont Pharms., Garden City, N.Y., 1990-93; prin. scientist DuPont Pharms., Garden City, N.Y., 1993-94; mgr. analytical rsch. and devel. Clay-Park Labs., Bronx, N.Y., 1995-96; mgr. R&D contract product devel. Clay-Park Labs., Bronx, 1996—. Author: Analytical Profiles of Drug Substances, 1985. Charter mem. N.Y. Hall of Sci., Flushing, 1985; judge borough competition N.Y.C. Annual Sci. Fair, Flushing, 1987, 88, 90. Mem. AAAS, ASTM, Am. Chem. Soc., Assn. Official Analytical Chemists Internat. (program chairperson 1988-90, pres. N.Y.-N.J. sect. 1991-92), Parenteral Drug Assn., Am. Soc. Quality Control, N.Y. Acad. Scis., Sigma Xi. Achievements include research in chromatographic analytical methods development and validation of biologically and pharmacological active molecules; in pharmacognosy of novel natural products; in laboratory information management systems; in robotics, process optimization and technology transfer. Office: Clay Park Labs Inc 1700 Bathgate Ave Bronx NY 10457-7512

SINGER, JOEL DAVID, political science educator; b. Bklyn., Dec. 7, 1925; s. Morris L. and Anne (Newman) S.; m. C. Diane Macaulay, Apr., 1990; children: Kathryn Louise, Eleanor Anne. BA, Duke U., 1946; LLD (hon.), Northwestern U., 1983; PhD, NYU, 1956. Instr. NYU, 1954-55, Vassar Coll., 1955-57; vis. fellow social relations Harvard U., 1957-58; vis. asst. prof. U. Mich., Ann Arbor, 1958-60; sr. scientist Mental Health Research Inst. U. Mich., 1960-82, assoc. prof., 1964-65, prof. polit. sci., 1965—, coordinator World Politics Program, 1969-75, 81-90; vis. prof. U. Oslo and Inst. Social Research, 1963-64, 90, Carnegie Endowment Internat. Peace and Grd. Inst. Internat. Studies, Geneva, 1967-68, Zuma and U. Mannheim (W. Ger.), 1976, Grad. Inst. Internat. Studies, Geneva, 1983-84; cons. in field; U. Groningen, The Netherlands, 1991. Author: Financing International Organization: The United Nations Budget Process, 1961, Deterrence, Arms Control and Disarmament: Toward a Synthesis in National Security Policy, 1962, rev. 1984, (with Melvin Small) The Wages of War, 1816-1965: A Statistical Handbook, 1972, (with Susan Jones) Beyond Conjecture in International Politics: Abstracts of Data Based Research, 1972, (with Dorothy La Barr) The Study of International Politics: A Guide to Sources for the Student, Teacher and Researcher, 1976, Correlates of War I and II, 1979, 80, (with Melvin Small) Resort to Arms: International and Civil War, 1816-1980, 1982, Models, Methods, and Progress: A Peace Research Odyssey, 1990, (with Paul Diehl) Measuring the Correlates of War; monographs; contbr. articles to profl. jours.; mem. editorial bd. ABC: Polit. Sci. and Govt., 1968-84, Polit. Sci. Reviewer, 1971—, Conflict Mgmt. and Peace Sci., 1978—, Etudes Polemologiques, 1978—, Internat. Studies Quar., 1989—, Jour. Conflict Resolution, 1989—, Internat. Interactions, 1989—. With USNR, 1943-66. Ford fellow, 1956; Ford grantee, 1957-58; Phoenix Meml. Fund grantee, 1959,, 1981-82; Fulbright scholar, 1963-64; Carnegie Corp. research grantee, 1963-67; NSF grantee, 1967-76, 1986-89, 1992-94; Guggenheim grantee, 1978-79. Mem. Am. Polit. Sci. Assn. (Helen Dwight Reid award com. 1967, 95, chmn. Woodrow Wilson award com., chmn. nominating com. 1970), Internat. Polit. Sci. Assn. (chmn. conflict and peace rsch. com. 1974—), World Assn. Internat. Rels., Internat. Soc. Polit. Psychology, Internat. Soc. Rsch. on Aggression, Social Sci. History Assn., Peace Sci. Soc., Internat. Peace Rsch. Assn. (pres. 1972-73), Consortium on Peace Rsch., Edn. and Devel., AAAS, Fedn. Am. Scientists (nat. coun. 1991-95), Union Concerned Scientists, Arms Control Assn., Internat. Studies Assn. (pres. 1985-86), Com. Nat. Security, Am. Com. on East-West Accord, World Federalist Assn. Office: U Mich Dept Polit Sci Ann Arbor MI 48109 *As a researcher, teacher, consultant and activist, my goal has been to bring rigorous scientific methods to bear on the causes of war question, and to encourage the integration of ethical concern and hard evidence.*

SINGER, KURT DEUTSCH, news commentator, author, publisher; b. Vienna, Austria, Aug. 10, 1911; came to U.S., 1940, naturalized, 1951; s. Ignaz Deutsch and Irene (Singer) S.; m. Hilda Tradelius, Dec. 23, 1932 (div. 1954); children: Marian Alice Birgit, Kenneth Walt; m. Jane Sherrod, Apr. 9, 1955 (dec. Jan. 1985); m. Katherine Han, Apr. 8, 1989. Student, U. Zürich, Switzerland, 1930, Labor Coll., Stockholm, Sweden, 1936; Ph.D., Div. Coll. Metaphysics, Indpls., 1951. Escaped to Sweden, 1934; founder Ossietzky Com. (successful in release Ossietzky from concentration camp); corr. Swedish mag. Folket i Bild, 1935-40; founder Niemöller Com.; pub. biography Göring in Eng. (confiscated in Sweden), 1940; co-founder pro-Allied newspaper Trots Allt, 1939; corr. Swedish newspapers in, U.S., 1940; editor News Background, 1942; lectr. U. Minn., U. Kans., U. Wis., 1945-49; radio commentator WKAT, 1950; corr. N.Am. Newspaper Alliance, N.Y.C., 1953—; pres. Singer Media Corp., 1987—; dir. Oceanic Press Service, San Clemente, Calif. Author, editor: underground weekly Mitteilungsblätter, Berlin, Germany, 1933; author: The Coming War, 1934, (biog.) Carl von Ossietzky, 1936 (Nobel Peace prize), Germany's Secret Service in Central America, 1943, Spies and Saboteurs in Argentina, 1943, Duel for the Northland, 1943, White Book of the Church of Norway, 1944, Spies and Traitors of World War II, 1945, Who are the Communists in America, 1948, 3000 Years of Espionage, 1951, World's Greatest Women Spies, 1952, Kippie the Cow; juvenile, 1952, Gentlemen Spies, 1953, The Man in the Trojan Horse, 1954, World's Best Spy Stories, 1954, Charles Laughton Story; adapted TV, motion pictures, 1954, Spy Stories and Asia, 1955, More Spy Stories, 1955, My Greatest Crime Story, 1956, My Most Famous Case, 1957, The Danny Kaye Saga; My Strangest Case, 1958, Spy Omnibus, 1959, Spies for Democracy, 1960, Crime Omnibus Spies Who Changed History, 1961, Hemmingway-Life and Death of a Giant, 1961, True Adventures in Crime, Dr. Albert Schweitzer, Medical Missionary, 1962, Lyndon Baines Johnson-Man of Reason, 1964, Ho-i-man; juveniles, 1965; Kurt Singer's Ghost Omnibus, 1965; juvenile Kurt Singer's Horror Omnibus; The World's Greatest Stories of the Occult, The Unearthly, 1965, Mata Hari-Goddess of Sin, 1965, Lyndon Johnson-From Kennedy to Vietnam, 1966, Weird Tales Anthology, 1966, I Can't Sleep at Night, 1966, Weird Tales of Supernatural, 1967, Tales of Terror, 1967, Famous Short Stories, 1967, Folktales of the South Pacific, 1967, Tales of The Uncanny, 1968, Gothic Reader, 1968, Bloch and Bradbury, 1969, Folktales of Mexico, 1969, Tales of the Unknown, 1970, The House in the Valley, 1970, Hablan Los Artistas, 1970, Tales of the Macabre, 1971, Three Thousand Years of Espionage, 1971, El Mundo de Hoy, 1971, Cuentos Fantasticos del Mas, 1971, Aldous Huxley, El Camino al Infierno, 1971, Ghouls and Ghosts, 1972, The Unearthly, 1972, The Gothic Reader, 1972, Satanic Omnibus, 1973, The Plague of the Living Dead, 1973, Gothic Horror Omnibus, 1974, Dictionary of Household Hints and Help, 1974, Supernatural, 1974, They are Possessed, 1976, True Adventures into the Unknown, 1980, I Spied-And Survived, 1980, Great Adventures in Crime, 1982, The Oblong Box, 1982, Shriek, 1984, First Target Book of Horror, 1984, 2d, 1984, 3d, 1985, 4th, 1985, Solve A Crime, 1994, The Ultimate Quiz Book, 1994, The Complete Guide to Career Advancement, 1994, The Sex Quiz Book, 1994, The Marriage Quiz Book, The Psychology Quiz Book, The Teenage Quiz Book, Success Secrets, 1995, Conozcase Mejor y Triunfe, 1995, The Joy of Practical Parenting, 1995; editor: UN Calendar, 1959-58; contbr. articles to newspapers, popular mags., U.S., fgn. countries, all his books and papers in Boston U. Library-Spl. Collections, Awd Literatur Haus, Vienna, Austria. Mem. UN Speakers Research Com., UN Children's Emergency Fund, Menninger Found. Mem. Nat. Geog. Soc., Smithsonian Assos., Internat. Platform Assn. (v.p.), United Sch. Assemblies (pres.). Address: Singer Media Corp Seaview Business Pk 1030 Calle Cordillera # 106 San Clemente CA 92673-6234 *In the sunset years of my life, I feel stronger than ever that the most important contribution one makes in a lifetime is to plant as many seeds as possible with many people, and perhaps many countries. Who knows where the seeds of ideas survive and expand?.*

SINGER, MARCUS GEORGE, philosopher, educator; b. N.Y.C., Jan. 4, 1926; s. David Emanuel and Esther (Kobre) S.; m. Blanche Ladenson, Aug. 10, 1947; children: Karen Beth, Debra Ann. A.B., U. Ill., 1948; Ph.D. (Susan Linn Sage fellow), Cornell U., 1952. Asst. in philosophy Cornell U., Ithaca, N.Y., 1948-49; instr. philosophy Cornell U., 1951-52; instr. philosophy U. Wis.-Madison, 1952-55, asst. prof., 1955-59, assoc. prof., 1959-63, prof. philosophy, 1963-92, prof. emeritus, 1992—, chmn. dept. philosophy, 1963-68; chmn. philosophy dept. U. Wis. Center System, 1964-66; dir. pub. lectr. series Royal Inst. Philosophy, London, 1984-85; vis. fellow Birkbeck Coll., U. London, 1962-63; research assoc. U. Calif.-Berkeley, 1969; vis. Cowling prof. philosophy Carleton Coll., Northfield, Minn., 1972; vis. prof. humanities U. Fla., Gainesville, 1975; vis. fellow U. Warwick, 1977, 84-85; vis. Francis M. Bernardin disting. prof. humanities U. Mo., Kansas City, 1979; hon. research fellow Birkbeck Coll., U. London, 1984-85; acad. visitor London Sch. Econs., U. London, 1984-85. Author: Generalization in Ethics, 2d edit., 1971, Verallgemeinerung in der Ethik, 1975; editor: Morals and Values, 1977, American Philosophy, 1986, Reason, Reality, and Speculative Philosophy, 1996; contbr. Essays in Moral Philosophy, 1958, Ency. of Philosophy, 1967, Law and Philosophy, 1970, Skepticism and Moral Principles, 1973, Morals and Values, 1977, Acad. Am. Ency., 1982, 84, 89, World Book Ency., 1984, 86, Gewirth's Ethical Rationalism, 1984, Morality and Universality, 1985, American Philosophy, 1986, New Directions in Ethics, 1986, The Handbook of Western Philosophy, 1988, Applying Philosophy, 1988, Moral Philosophy: Historical and Contemporary Essays, 1989, Key Themes in Philosophy, 1990, Essays on Henry Sidgwick, 1992, Ency. of Ethics, 1992, A History of Western Ethics, 1992, Ethics, 1993, Cambridge Dictionary of Philosophy, 1995, Biographical Dictionary of Twentieth Century Philosophers, 1996, Pragmatism, Reason, and Norms, 1997; co-editor: Introductory Readings in Philosophy, 2d edit., 1974, Reason and the Common Good, 1963, Belief, Knowledge and Truth, 1970, Legislative Intent and other Essays on Law, Politics and Morality, 1993. Served with USAAF, 1944-45. Am. Philos. Assn. Western Div. fellow, 1956-57; Summer Research grant Social Sci. Research Council, 1958; Guggenheim fellow, 1962-63; Inst. for Research in Humanities fellow U. Wis., 1984. Mem. Am. Philos. Assn. (v.p. Western divsn. 1984-85, pres. Ctrl. divsn. 1985-86, bd. officers 1991-94), Royal Inst. Philosophy, AAUP, Aristotelian Soc., Mind Assn., Wis. Acad. Scis., Arts and Letters, Sidgwick Soc. (exec. dir.), Phi Beta Kappa, Phi Kappa Phi. Home: 5021 Regent St Madison WI 53705-4745

SINGER, MARKUS MORTON, retired trade association executive; b. N.Y.C., Dec. 20, 1917; s. Isadore and Nettie (Stromer) S.; m. Phyllis Berger, June 26, 1945; children—Fredric L., Robert B. B.C.S., NYU, 1939; postgrad., George Washington U., 1951-55. With Nat. Food Brokers Assn., Washington, 1946—, v.p., 1961-65, exec. v.p., 1965-71, pres., 1972-83, pres. emeritus, 1983—, acting pres., chief exec. officer, 1987-88; lifetime hon. trustee Nat. Food Brokers Assn. Edn. and Tng. Found. Served with AUS, 1942-45. Recipient Pres.'s award as Man of Yr. Can. Food Brokers Assn., 1976. Mem. European Food Brokers Assn. (hon. life), Frozen Food Industry Disting. Order of Zerocrats. Jewish.

SINGER, MAXINE FRANK, biochemist, think tank executive; b. N.Y.C., Feb. 15, 1931; d. Hyman S. and Henrietta (Perlowitz) Frank; m. Daniel Morris Singer, June 15, 1952; children: Amy Elizabeth, Ellen Ruth, David Byrd, Stephanie Frank. AB, Swarthmore Coll., 1952, DSc (hon.), 1978; PhD, Yale U., 1957; DSc (hon.), Wesleyan U., 1977, Swarthmore Coll., 1978, U. Md.-Baltimore County, 1985, Cedar Crest Coll., 1986, CUNY, 1988, Brandeis U., 1988, Radcliffe Coll., 1990, Williams Coll., 1990, Franklin and Marshall Coll., 1991, George Washington U., 1991, NYU, 1992, Lehigh U., 1992, Dartmouth Coll., 1993, Yale U., 1994, Harvard U., 1994; PhD honoris causa, Weizmann Inst. Sci., 1995. USPHS postdoctoral fellow NIH, Bethesda, Md., 1956-58; rsch. chemist biochemistry NIH, 1958-74; head sect. on nucleic acid enzymology Nat. Cancer Inst., 1974-79; chief Lab. of Biochemistry, Nat. Cancer Inst., 1979-87, rsch. chemist, 1987-88; pres. Carnegie Inst. Washington, 1988—; Regents vis. lectr. U. Calif., Berkeley, 1981; bd. dirs. Johnson & Johnson; mem. sci. coun. Internat. Inst. Genetics and Biophysics, Naples, Italy, 1982-86; mem. adv. bd. Chulabhorn Rsch. Inst., 1990—. Mem. editorial bd. Jour. Biol. Chemistry, 1968-74, Sci. mag., 1972-82; chmn. editorial bd. Procs. of NAS, 1985-88; author (with Paul Berg) 2 books on molecular biology; contbr. articles to scholarly jours. Trustee Wesleyan U., Middletown, Conn., 1972-75, Yale Corp., New Haven, 1975-90; bd. govs. Weizmann Inst. Sci., Rehovot, Israel, 1978—; bd. dirs. Whitehead Inst., 1985-94; chmn. Smithsonian Coun., 1992-93. Recipient award for achievement in biol. scis. Washington Acad. Scis., 1969, award for rsch. in biol. scis. Yale Sci. and Engring. Assn., 1974, Superior Svc. Honor award HEW, 1975, Dirs. award NIH, 1977, Disting. Svc. medal HHS, 1983, Presdl. Disting. Exec. Rank award, 1987, U.S. Disting. Exec. Rank award, 1987, Mory's Cup Bd. Govs. Mory's Assn., 1991, Wilbur Lucius Cross Medal for Honor Yale Grad. Sch. Assn., 1991, Nat. Medal Sci. NSF, 1992, Pub. Svc. award NIH Alumni Assn., 1995. Fellow Am. Acad. Arts and Scis.; mem. NAS (coun. 1982-85, com. sci., engring and pub. policy 1989-91), AAAS (Sci. Freedom and Responsibility award 1982), Am. Soc. Biol. Chemists, Am. Soc. Microbiologists, Am. Chem. Soc., Am. Philos. Soc., Inst. Medicine of NAS, Pontifical Acad. of Scis, Human Genome Orgn., N.Y. Acad. Scis. Home: 5410 39th St NW Washington DC 20015-2902 Office: Carnegie Inst Washington 1530 P St NW Washington DC 20005-1910

SINGER, NIKI, publishing executive, public relations executive; b. Rochester, N.Y., Sept. 10, 1937; d. Goodman A. and Evelyn (Simon) Sarachan; BA cum laude, U. Mich., 1959; m. Michael J. Sheets, 1973; children: Romaine Kitty, Nicholas Simon Feramorz. Mgr. advt. sales promotion Fairchild Publs., N.Y.C., 1959-67; account exec., account supr. Vernon Pope Co., N.Y.C., 1967-69, v.p., 1969-71; pres. Niki Singer, Inc., N.Y.C., 1971-93; sr. v.p. M. Shanken Comm., Cigar Aficionado, Wine Spectator Food, 1994—. Mem. Am. Inst. Wine and Food (bd. dirs.), Les Dames d'Escoffier. Home: 1035 5th Ave New York NY 10028-0135 Office: M Shanken Comm 387 Park Ave S New York NY 10016-8810

SINGER, NORMAN A., government official, former diplomat; b. Milw., Oct. 5, 1938; s. August S. and Lucille (Stachowski) S.; m. Dietlind Schmidt, May 15, 1964; children—Daniela, Dirk. B.A. in Polit. Sci., Sophia U., 1967, M.A. in Internat. Relations, 1970; M.A. in Mgmt., Syracuse U., 1976. Joined U.S. Fgn. Service, 1962; consul, chief consular services Am. Consulate Gen., Jerusalem, 1976-79; dir. Office of field support U.S. Dept. State, Washington, 1979-82; consul gen., prin. officer Am. Consulate Gen., Edinburgh, Scotland, 1982-86, sr. seminar, 1986-87, exec. dir. congl. commn. on migration and devel., 1987-88; the dean Consular Corps of Edinburgh-Leith, 1984-86; minster-counselor Mexico City, 1988-90, Bonn, Germany, 1990-94; consul-gen. Tijuana, Mex., 1994-96; dir. Am. C. of C., Scotland, 1997—. Served with U.S. Army, 1959-61. Recipient Meritorious Honor award U.S. Ambassador, Bonn, 1973; Superior Honor award Asst. Sec. for Near Eastern Affairs, 1979; Silver Cross of Orthodox Palestine Soc., Archimandrite of Jerusalem, 1979; Superior Honor award Asst. Sec. for European Affaris, 1984; John Jacob Rogers award, 1996. Mem. Edinburgh-Leith Petroleum Club. Roman Catholic. Clubs: New, Bruntsfield Links Golfing Soc. (Edinburgh). Avocations: golf, travel. Home: 3604 S 15th Pl Milwaukee WI 53221-1612 Office: 19 Scotland St, Edinburgh Scotland EH3 6PU

SINGER, NORMAN SOL, food products executive, inventor; b. Phila., Dec. 10, 1937; s. Herman and Thelma (Scheinberg) S.; m. Anne Goldstein, Aug. 23, 1959; children: Amy Debra, Judith Ellen. BS, Rutgers U., 1961. Sr. lab. technician Bur. Biological Rsch., New Brunswick, N.J., 1960-61; food scientist Thomas J. Lipton, Inc., Englewood Cliffs, N.J., 1961-68; rsch. dir. McCain Foods, Florenceville, Can., 1968-70; sr. scientist John Labatt Ltd., London, Ontario, Can., 1970-84; fellow/dir. exploration The NutraSweet Co., Deerfield, Ill., 1984-94; pres. Ideas Workshop Cons., Inc., Highland Park, Ill., 1994—; co-founder, CEO Sous Chef Culinary Supply, Inc., Highland Park, Ill., 1994—. Patentee in field. Recipient Outstanding Am. Inventor award Intellectual Property Owners Found., Washington, 1989. Mem. Inst. Food Technology, Product Devel. and Mgmt. Assn., Chgo. Horticultural Soc., Sigma Xi. Avocations: gourmet cooking, carving bone and antler, collecting amerind carvings, bicycling. Home: 40 Ridge Rd Highland Park IL 60035-4337 Office: Sous Chef Culinary Supply Highland Park IL 60035

SINGER, PAUL RICHARD, ophthalmologist; b. N.Y.C., Feb. 1, 1947; m. Katherine W. Singer, June 13, 1970; children: Amy E., Evan P. BA with honors, U. Rochester, N.Y., 1969, MD, 1973. Diplomate Am. Bd. Ophthalmology. Internal medicine intern U. N.C., Chapel Hill, 1973-74, resident in neurology, 1974-75; resident in ophthalmology Washington U. Sch. Medicine, St. Louis, 1975-78, Fight for Sight postdoctoral rsch. fellow dept ophthalmology, 1978-79; pres. Hartford (Conn.) Eye Physicians, 1980—; sr. staff dept. ophthalmology Hartford Hosp., 1980—. Chmn. bd. dirs. Prevent Blindness Conn., Middletown, 1990-92, Combined Health Appeal, Hartford, 1993-95. Recipient Cmty. Svc. award Hartford County Med. Assn., 1993, Robert Polk award for outstanding vol. svc. Prevent Blindness Conn., 1993. Office: Hartford Eye Physicians 55 Nye Rd Glastonbury CT 06033-1281

SINGER, PHILIP C., environmental engineer, educator; b. Bklyn., Sept. 6, 1942; married Ellen Becker, 1965; children: Naomi, Elizabeth, Robert, Jennifer. BCE, Cooper Union, 1963; MS, Northwestern U., 1965; SM, Harvard U., 1965, PhD, 1969. Diplomate Am. Acad. Environ. Engrs. Asst. prof. civil engring. U. Notre Dame, 1969-73; assoc. prof. environ. sci. and engring. U. N.C., Chapel Hill, 1973-78, prof., 1978—, dir. water resources engring. program, 1979—. Mem. ASCE, Nat. Acad. Engring., Am. Chem. Soc., Am. Water Works Assn., Water Environment Fedn., Assn. Environ. Engring. Profs., Internat. Ozone Assn. Office: Univ North Carolina Dept Environ Sci & Engring CB7400 Chapel Hill NC 27599

SINGER, ROBERT NORMAN, motor behavior educator; b. Bklyn., Sept. 27, 1936; s. Abraham and Ann (Norman) S.; m. Beverly; children: Richard, Bonni Jill. BS, Bklyn. Coll., 1961; MS, Pa. State U., 1962; PhD, Ohio State U., 1964. Instr. phys. edn. Ohio State U., Columbus, 1963-64, asst. prof., 1964-65; asst. prof. Ill. State U., Normal, 1965-67, dir. motor learning lab., 1965-69, assoc. prof., 1968-69, asst. dean Coll. Applied Sci. and Tech., 1967-69; asso. prof., dir. motor learning lab. Mich. State U., East Lansing, 1969-70; prof. Fla. State U., Tallahassee, 1970-87, dir. motor learning lab., 1970-72, dir. div. human performance, 1972-75, dir. Motor Behavior Ctr., 1975-87; chair dept. of exercise and sport scis. U. Fla., Gainesville, 1987—; lectr. in N.Am., S.Am., Africa, Australia, Asia and Europe; cons. in field. Author: Motor Learning and Human Performance, 1968, rev. edit., 1975, 80, Coaching, Athletics and Psychology, 1972, Physical Education, 1972, Teaching Physical Education, 1974, rev. edit., 1980, Laboratory and Field Experiments in Motor Learning, 1975, Myths and Truths in Sports Psychology, 1975, The Learning of Motor Skills, 1982, Sustaining Motivation in Sport, 1984, Peak Performance, 1986; editor: Readings in Motor Learning, 1972, The Psychomotor Domain, 1972, Foundations of Physical Education, 1976, Completed Research in Health, Physical Education and Recreation, 1968-74, Handbook of Research on Sport Psychology, 1993; mem. editl. bd. Rsch. Quar., 1968-81, Jour. Motor Behavior, 1968-81, Jour. Sport and Exercise Psychology, 1979-92, The Sport Psychologist, 1986-94, The Internat. Jour. Sport Psychology, 1977-88, Jour. Applied Sport Psychology, 1987-95; reviewer numerous jours.; contbr. articles to numerous anthologies and profl. jours. Served with U.S. Army, 1955-58. Recipient Disting. Alumnus award Bklyn. Coll., 1989. Mem. AAHPERD, APA (pres. divsn. of exercise and sport psychology 1995-97), Am. Acad. Kinesiology and Phys. Edn. (pres. 1995-96), Internat. Soc. Sport Psychology (prex. 1985-89, 90-93), Am. Ednl. Rsch. Assn., N.Am. Soc. Sport Psychology and Phys. Activity. Home: 6305 NW 56th Ln Gainesville FL 32653-3116 Office: U Fla 100 Florida Gym Gainesville FL 32653 *I have always enjoyed my activities and have looked forward to new challenges and horizons. Intrinsic motivational values have guided my involvement in various endeavors, and the outcomes have been extremely rewarding.*

SINGER, SAMUEL L(OEWENBERG), journalist; b. Phila., May 2, 1911; s. Benjamin and Hattie May (Loewenberg) S.; m. Betty Janet Levi, June 12, 1939; children—Ruth Babette, Samuel Lawrence, Robert Benjamin. B.S. in Journalism, Temple U., 1934. Mem. staff Phila. Inquirer, 1934-81, music editor, 1955-81, emeritus, 1981—, public service editor, 1973-81; tchr. undergrad. journalism course Temple U., 1946—, tchr. music criticism, 1965-70, adj. prof. journalism, 1973—; tchr. theatre and music reviewing Main Line Sch. Night, 1994—. Condr. radio program This Week's Music, 1961-72; author: Reviewing the Performing Arts, 1973. Organist Congregation Temple Judea, 1933-41, Phila. Ethical Soc., 1942-56, Main Line Reform Temple, 1951-55, Beth Israel, Phila., 1956-65, Coatesville, Pa., 1966-88, Zion Evang. Luth. Ch., 1956-82, St. Matthew's Evang. Luth. Ch., 1972-82, IHS Episcopal Ch., Drexel Hill, Pa, 1984—. Served with USNR, 1943-45. Named Outstanding 1934 Journalism Alumnus, Temple U., 1988. Mem. Am. Guild Organists (editor Phila. chpt. publ. Crescendo 1971-76), Newspaper Guild, Phila. Press Assn., Mus. Fund Soc. Phila., Music Critics Assn., Phila. Mus. Art, Phila. Orch. Assn., Sigma Delta Chi (life). Home: 1431 Greywall Ln Wynnewood PA 19096-3811 *Never do anything you can't tell your children.*

SINGER, SANDRA MARIA, forensic scientist; b. Wilkes-Barre, Pa., Sept. 9, 1964; d. Russell John and Anita Louise (Hovanec) S. BS in Chemistry, King's Coll., 1986; MS in Forensic Sci., George Washington U., 1989. Forensic analyst Collaborative Testing, Inc., Herndon, Va., 1988-89; forensic scientist Pa. State Police Crime Lab., Wyoming, 1990—. Mem. AAAS, Am. Acad. Forensic Sci., Am. Chem. Soc. Home: 203 Owen St Swoyersville PA 18704 Office: Pa State Police Wyoming Regional Crime Lab 479 Wyoming Ave Wyoming PA 18644-1823

SINGER, SARAH BETH, poet; b. N.Y.C., July 4, 1915; d. Samuel and Rose (Dunetz) White; m. Leon Eugene Singer, Nov. 23, 1938; children: Jack, Rachel. B.A., NYU, 1934; postgrad., New Sch. Social Research, 1961-63. Tchr. creative writing Hillside Hosp., Queens, N.Y., 1964-75, Samuel Field YMHA, Queens, 1980-82; mem. Pacific N.W. Writers Conf. Author: Magic Casements, 1957, After the Beginning, 1975, Of Love and Shoes, 1987, The Gathering, 1992, contbr. poetry to anthologies, poetry mags. and quars. including: Am. Women Poets, 1976, Yearbook Am. Poetry, 1981, The Best of 1980, 81, Filtered Images, 1992, the Croton Rev., The Lyric, Bitterroot, Judaism, Encore, The Jewish Frontier, Yankee, Hartford Courant, Poet Lore, N.Y.Times, Christian Sci. Monitor, Voices Internat., The Round Table, Orphic Lute, Brussels Sprout, Poetry and Medicine Column Jour. AMA, The Shakespeare Newsletter, Midstream (N.Y.C. Jewish Rev.), The Penwoman; cons. editor Poet Lore, 1975-81. Recipient Stephen Vincent Benet award Poet Lore, 1968, 71, Dellbrook award Shenandoah Valley Acad. Lit. and Dellbrook-Shenandoah Coll. Writers' Conf., 1978, 79, C.W. Post Poetry award, 1979-80, award for best poem Lyric quar., 1981, biennial award for achievement in poetry Seattle br. Nat. League Penwomen, 1988; award for traditional poetry Wash. Poets Assn., 1989, Wash. Poets Assn. 1995, cert. of merit Muse mag., 1990, Editor's Choice award for Haiku Brussels Sprout, 1992, poem chosen for Met. Bus. Poetry Project, Seattle, 1992, 96, Hon. Mention Wash. Poets Assn., 1997; poem Upon My Demise translated into Russian, recorded 1st prize Marj McAllister award Voices Internat., 1993. Mem. PEN, Poetry Soc. Am., Poets and Writers, Nat. League Am. Penwomen (poetry chmn. L.I. br. 1957-87, publicity chmn. 1990, sec. Seattle br. 1990, pres. 1992-94, v.p. 1994—, publicity chmn. State of Wash. 1992—, Marion Doyle Meml. award 1976, 1st prize nat. peotry contet 1976, Drama award 1977, Poetry award 1977, 1st prize modern rhymed poetry 1978, Lectr. award 1980, Sonnet award Alexandria br. 1980, 81, Catherine Cushman Leach award 1982; poetry award Phoenix br. 1983, Pasadena br. 1984, Alexandria br. 1985, 1st prize award Portland br. 1990, structured verse award Spokane br. 1992, Della Crowder Miller Meml. Petrarchan Sonnet award 1994, Honorable Mention Anita Marie Boggs Meml. award 1994, Owl award and Ann. award for achievement in poetry Seattle br. 1994, Poet's Choice award Portland br. 1995, 2d prize Internat. Poetry Contest, Palomar br., 1996, 3d prize in internat. poetry 1997), Poetry Soc. Am. (v.p. 1974-78, exec. dir. L.I., 1979-83, James Joyce award 1972, Consuelo Ford award 1973, Gustav Davidson award 1974, 1st prize award 1975, Celia Wagner award 1976). Address: 2360 43rd Ave E Apt 415 Seattle WA 98112-2703 *As a poet, I have sought never to compromise my standards as to what constitutes poetry, despite fads that come and go. My goal has been to achieve whatever perfection I can in my work, and to preserve enough humility to realize that the best is never good enough. My life has truly been enriched by vision and aspiration. As a poet, the important thing for me is to create something moving and beautiful. Publication is a welcome by-product, but in itself, is not the goal for which I strive.*

SINGER, SAUL, food industry execuvive, retired surgeon; b. N.Y.C, June 9, 1937; s. Jack and Renee (LeViloff) S.; m. Susan Green Hauff; children: Sharon Lynn, Sara Jean, Steven Mitchell. BA, Princeton U., 1959; MD, SUNY, Bklyn., 1963; grad., Culinary Inst. Am., Hyde Pk., N.Y., 1993. Diplomate Am. Bd. Surgery. Intern Presbyn. Hosp., N.Y.C., 1963-64, resident, 1964-69; surgeon in chief Humana Biscayne Hosp., North Miami, Fla., 1984-85; vice chief surgery Meml. Hosp., Hollywood, Fla., 1985-86, surgeon in chief, 1987—, ret., 1987; owner Singer Catering, Hollywood. Mem. schs. com. Princeton U., 1980-87; pres. Jewish Fedn. of South Broward, Hollywood, 1986-87, Am. Friends Hebrew U., Hollywood, 1987; nat. vice chmn. United Jewish Appeal, N.Y.C., 1987. Fellow ACS; mem. Alpha Omega Alpha. Home: 922 S South Lake Dr Hollywood FL 33019-1930

SINGER, S(IEGFRIED) FRED, geophysicist, educator; b. Vienna, Austria, Sept. 27, 1924; came to U.S., 1940, naturalized, 1944; s. Joseph B. and Anne (Kelman) S.; m. Candace Carolyn Crandall, 1990. B.E.E., Ohio State U., 1943, D.Sc. (hon.), 1970; A.M., Princeton, 1944, Ph.D. in Physics, 1948. Instr. physics Princeton, 1943-44; physicist, applied physics lab. Johns Hopkins, 1946-50; sci. liaison officer Office Naval Research, Am. embassy, London, 1950-53; asso. prof. physics U. Md., College Park, 1953-59; prof. U. Md., 1959-62; dir. Nat. Weather Satellite Center, Dept. Commerce, 1962-64; dean Sch. Environ. and Planetary Scis., U. Miami, 1964-67; dep. asst. sec. for water quality and research Dept. Interior, Washington, 1967-70; dep. asst. adminstr. EPA, Washington, 1970-71; prof. environ. scis. U. Va., Charlottesville, 1971-87; chief scientist U.S. Dept. Transp., Washington, 1987-89; pres. Sci. and Environ. Policy Project, 1989—; vis. prof. Jet Propulsion Lab., Calif. Inst. Tech., 1961-62; Fed. Exec. fellow Brookings Instn., 1971; vis. Sid Richardson prof. J.B. Johnson Sch., U. Tex., 1978; sr. fellow Heritage Found., 1982-83; vis. eminent scholar George Mason U., 1984-86, disting. rsch. prof., 1994—; head sci. evaluation group astronautics and space exploration com. U.S. Ho. of Reps., 1958; cons. U.S. Treasury Dept., GAO, Office Tech. Assessment, U.S. Congress; mem. bd. Nat. Com. on Am. Fgn.

Policy; mem. White House Panel on U.S.-Brazil Sci. and Tech. Exch., 1987; guest scholar Nat Air and Space Mus., Smithsonian Instn., 1991, Woodrow Wilson Internat. Ctr. for Scholars, 1991, Hoover Instn., 1992; disting. rsch. rpof. Inst. for Space Sci. and Tech., Gainesville, Fla., 1989—; bd. dirs. AMREP Corp., Patent Enforcement Fund, Inc. Author: Geophysical Research with Artificial Earth Satellites, 1956, Manned Laboratories in Space, 1970, Global Effects of Environmental Pollution, 1970, Is There an Optimum Level of Population, 1971, The Changing Global Environment, 1975, Arid Zone Development: Potentialities and Problems, 1977, The Economic Effects of Demographic Changes, 1977, Energy, 1979, Price of World Oil, 1983, Free Market Energy, 1984, Global Climate Change, 1990, Origins of The Universe, 1990, The Ocean in Human Affairs, 1990, The Greenhouse Debate Continued, 1992; sci. adv. com. Dept State 1981; vice chmn. Nat. Adv. Com. Oceans and Atmosphere, 1981-86; contbr. articles on space, energy, environment and population problems to profl. publs. Served with USNR, 1944-46. Recipient Presdl. commendation, 1958, gold medal for exceptional service Dept. Commerce, 1965; named Outstanding Young Man U.S. Jr. C. of C., 1959. Fellow AAAS (com. coun. affairs 1970), AIAA, Am. Geophys. Union, Am. Phys. Soc.; mem. Internat. Acad. Astronautics, European Acad. for Environ. Affairs, Pan Am. Med. Assn. (pres. sect. on environ. health scis. 1973—), Cosmos Club (Washington), Colonnade Club (Charlottesville). Office: 4084 University Dr Ste 101 Fairfax VA 22030-6803

SINGER, SUZANNE FRIED, editor; b. N.Y.C., July 9, 1935; d. Maurice Aaron and Augusta G. (Ginsberg) Fried; m. Max Singer, Feb. 12, 1959; children: Saul, Alexander (dec.), Daniel, Benjamin. BA with honors, Swarthmore Coll., 1956; MA, Columbia U., 1958. Program asst. NSF, Washington, 1958-60; assoc. editor Bibl. Archaeology Rev., Washington, 1979-84, mng. editor, 1984-96, exec. editor, 1996—; mng. editor Bibl. Rev., Washington, 1985-94, exec. editor, 1994—; mng. editor Moment, Washington, 1990—. Mem. Am. Schs. Oriental Rsch., Soc. Bibl. Lit. Jewish. Office: Bibl Archaeology Soc 4710 41st St NW Washington DC 20016-1700

SINGER, THOMAS ERIC, industrial company executive; b. Vienna, Austria, Mar. 6, 1926; came to U.S., 1938, naturalized, 1944; s. Henry and Berthe (dePokroi) S.; m. Ellen Colt, Dec. 20, 1952; children: Dominique, Mary F., Carlyle, Henry, Ellen. BA, George Washington U., 1950; MA, Harvard Coll., 1952. Fgn. affairs officer State Dept., 1952-55; export mgr. Polaroid Corp., Cambridge, Mass., 1955-58; with Gillette Co., 1958-79, exec. v.p., 1971-79; sr. v.p. Ingalls Assocs., Boston, 1979-81; chmn. Pontara Ltd., 1981-86; pres. Sontek Industries, 1983-84; prin. Thomas Singer and Daus., Boston, 1986—; bd. dirs. Galaxy Cheese Co. Trustee Faulkner Hosp., Boston; corporator Babson Coll., Wellesley, Mass., Childrens Mus., Boston; mem. Mayor's Com. for Cultural Affairs. With U.S. Army, 1944-46. Named hon. consul of Peru in Boston, 1969. Mem. Harvard Club (Boston, N.Y.C.), Essex County Club (Manchester, Mass.). Home: PO Box 362 Ipswich MA 01938-0362 Office: Thomas Singer and Daus 180 Beacon St Boston MA 02116-1401

SINGER, THOMAS KENYON, international business consultant, farmer; b. Wilson, N.Y., Jan. 30, 1932; s. Harold Thomas and Grace (Kenyon) S.; m. Jacqueline Germain Moulin, June 8, 1957; children: Marc Andre, Vivianne Grace Singer Scott, Claire Anne, Michelle Moulin Singer Ross, Gail Kenyon Singer Watson. BS in Econs., U. Pa., 1954. Dir. mktg. Europe Kaiser Aluminum & Chem. Corp., London, 1965-67; v.p. Kaiser LeNickel subs., Oakland, Calif., 1967-73, div. mgr., 1973-75; v.p. govt. relations Kaiser Aluminum & Chem. Corp., Washington, 1975-81; corp. v.p. Kaiser Aluminum & Chem. Corp., Oakland, Calif., 1977-86; pres. Kaiser Internat. Corp., Oakland, Calif., 1982-86, also dir.; dir., pres. IBA, Inc. Capt. USAF, 1955-57. Mem. French-Am. C. of C., Army and Navy Club (Washington), Niagara Falls Country Club. Republican. Episcopalian. Home: 6627 Hummingbird Ln Box 210 Appleton NY 14008 Office: 6730 Lake Rd Appleton NY 14008

SINGERMAN, MARTIN, newspaper publishing executive. Pub. N.Y. Post, N.Y.C. Office: NY Post 1211 6th Ave New York NY 10036*

SINGERMAN, PHILLIP A., federal agency administrator. BA, Oberlin Coll.; MA in Polit. Sci., Yale U., PhD in Polit. Sci. Past dir. mayor's office policy devel. City of Phila., past planning cons.; past exec. asst. to devel. adminstr. City of New Haven; pres., CEO Ben Franklin Tech. Ctr., Pa., 1983-95, also bd. dirs.; asst. sec. commerce econ. devel. Econ. Devel. Adminstrn., Washington, 1995—; past policy devel. dir. Conn. Conf. Municipalities; past instr. urban policy and regional devel. Bernard Coll., , U. Pa., Yale U.; past mem. gov.'s task force tech. transfer. Vol. Peace Corps, Columbia, S.Am., 1965-67; past bd. dirs. Phila.-Israel C. of C. W. Phila. Empowerment Zone Cmty. Trust. Office: Econ Devel Adminstrn 14th Constitution Ave NW Washington DC 20230*

SINGH, JYOTI SHANKAR, political organization director; b. Pathalgaon, India, Apr. 15, 1935; came to U.S., 1972; s. Brijnath Kumar and Tirthmani (Singh) S.; m. Maria Luz Molares, 1962; children: Anil, Rajeev, Ajit. BA, Banaras U., India, 1952, MA, 1954, LLB, 1955; MA, NYU, 1979; D (honoris causa), Internat. Inst. Integration, Bolivia, 1980. Assoc. sec. coordinating secretariat Leiden, The Netherlands, 1960-61, sec. gen. coordinating secretariat, 1961-64; programme cons. Internat. Youth Centre, New Delhi, 1965-66; sec. gen. World Assembly of Youth, Brussels, 1966-72; liaison officer Fund for Population Activities UN, N.Y.C., 1972-73, asst. exec. sec. World Population Yr., 1973-74, dep. chief info. and pub. affairs, 1975-80, chief info. and external rels., 1980-85, dir. info. and external rels., 1986-90; dir. tech. and evaluation div. UN Population Fund, N.Y.C., 1990-95; dep. exec. dir. UN Population Fund, 1995-96; spl. adviser to exec. dir. UNFPA, N.Y.C., 1996—; hon. prof. Cen. Am. U., Managua, Nicaragua, 1975; exec. coord. UN Internat. Conf. on Population, 1982-84; exec. coord. Internat. Conf. on Population and Devel., 1992-94; chmn. The Earth Times, 1996—. Author: A New International Economic Order, 1977; editor: World Population Policies, 1979; editor-in-chief Populi, 1980-90. Mem. Soc. for Internat. Devel., Asian Urban Info. Ctr. (mem. internat. adv. com./Kobe, Japan). Home: 10 Waterside Plz Apt 26D New York NY 10010-2606 Office: UNFPA 220 E 42nd St New York NY 10017-5806

SINGH, KRISHNA PAL, mechanical engineer; b. Patna, India, May 1, 1947; s. Balmiki Singh and Ram Rati Devi; m. Martha J. Trimble, May 18, 1974; children: Amy, Kris. BSME, BIT Sindri, India, 1967; MSME, U. Pa., 1969, PhD, 1972. Registered profl. engr., Pa., Mich. Prin. engr. Joseph Oat Corp., Camden, N.J., 1971-74, chief engr., 1974-79, v.p. engring., 1979-86; pres., CEO Holtec Internat., Cherry Hill, N.J., 1986—. Co-author: Mechanical Design of Heat Exchangers and Pressure Vessel Components, 1984; contbr. to profl. publs. Fellow ASME; mem. AICE, AM. Nuclear Soc., Thermal Exchangers Mfg. Assn. (vibration com.). Achievements include patents for heat exchanger for withstanding cycle changes in temperature and radioactive fuel cell storage rack. Office: Holtec Internat 555 Lincoln Dr W Marlton NJ 08053-3421*

SINGH, MANMOHAN, orthopedic surgeon, educator; b. Patiala, Punjab, India, Oct. 5, 1940; came to U.S., 1969; s. Ajmer and Kartar (Kaur) S.; m. Manjit Anand, Jan. 1, 1974; children: Kirpal, Gurmeet. MB, BS, Govt. Med. Coll., Patiala, 1964; MSurgery, Panjab U., Chandigarh, India, 1968. Diplomate Am. Bd. Orthopaedic Surgery. Rsch. fellow Inst. Internat. Edn., Chgo., 1969-74; resident in orthopedic surgery Michael Reese Hosp. and Med. Ctr., Chgo., 1974-78, mem. attending staff, dir. orthopedic rsch., 1979-94; fellow in orthopedic oncology Mayo Clinic and Mayo Found., Rochester, Minn., 1979; assoc. prof. U. Ill., Chgo., 1996—; pvt. practice, Chgo., 1979—; mem. vis. faculty Mayo Grad. Sch., Rochester, 1969. Developer x-ray method (Singh Index) and bone density method (Radius Index) for diagnosis of osteoporosis. Fulbright travel grantee, 1968. Fellow Am. Acad. Orthop. Surgeons, Am. Orthop. Foot and Ankle Soc.; mem. Orthop. Rsch. Soc., Am. Soc. for Bone and Mineral Rsch., Internat. Bone and Mineral Soc. Democrat. Sikh. Avocations: stamp collecting, photography, tennis. Office: 443 E 31st St Chicago IL 60616-4051

SINGH, RAJENDRA, mechanical engineering educator; b. Dhampur, India, Feb. 13, 1950; came to U.S., 1973; s. Raghubir and Ishwar (Kali) S.; m. Veena Ghungesh, June 24, 1979; children: Rohit, Arun. BS with honors, Birla Inst., 1971; MS, U. Roorkee, India, 1973; PhD, Purdue U., 1975. Grad. instr. Purdue U., West Layfayette, Ind., 1973-75; sr. engr. Carrier Corp., Syracuse, N.Y., 1975-79; asst. prof. Ohio State U., Columbus, 1979-83, assoc. prof., 1983-87, prof., 1987—; adj. lectr. Syracuse (N.Y.) U., 1977-79; bd. dirs. Nat. Conf. Fluid Power, Milw., Inst. of Noise Control Engring.; gen. chmn. Nat. Noise Conf., Columbus, 1985; leader of U.S. delegation to India-U.S.A. Symposium on Vibration and Noise Engring., 1996; vis. prof. U. Calif., Berkeley, 1987-88; cons., lectr. in field. Contbr. articles to profl. jours. Recipient Gold medal U. Roorkee, 1973, R. H. Kohr Rsch. award Purdue U., 1975, Excellence in Teaching award Inst. Noise Control Engring., 1989, George Westinghouse award Am. Soc. Engring. Edn., 1993, rsch. awards Ohio State U., 1983, 87, 91, 96. Fellow ASME, Acoustical Soc. Am.; mem. Soc. for Exptl. Mechanics, Inst. Noise Control Engring., Am. Soc. Engring. Edn. (George Westinghouse award 1993). Achievements include patent for rolling door; development of new analytical and experimental techniques in machine dynamics, acoustics, vibration and fluid control. Home: 4772 Belfield Ct Dublin OH 43017-2592 Office: Ohio State U 206 W 18th Ave Columbus OH 43210-1189

SINGH, VIJAY, professional golfer; b. Lautoka, Fiji, Feb. 22, 1963; m. Andrena Seth Singh; 1 child, Qass Seth. Winner Buick Classic, PGA European Tour Scandanavian Masters, 1994, Phoenix Open, 1995; mem. Pres. Cup Team, 1994; also won 10 other times worldwide. Set PGA Tour record for earnings in first two seasons. Office: care PGA Tour 112 Tpc Blvd Ponte Vedra Beach FL 32082-3046*

SINGHAL, AVINASH CHANDRA, engineering administrator, educator; b. Aligarh, India, Nov. 4, 1941; s. Shiam Sunder and Pushpa Lata (Jindal) S.; m. Uma Rani Sharma, Sept. 5, 1967; children: Ritu Chanchal, Anita, Neil Raj. BSc, Agra U., India, 1957; BSc in Engring., St. Andrews U., Dundee, Scotland, 1959, BSC in Engring. with honors, 1960; MS, MIT, 1961, CE, 1962, ScD, 1964. Registered profl. engr., N.Y., Que., Ariz. Rsch. engr. Kaman Aircraft, Burlington, Mass., 1964-65; prof. Laval U., Quebec, Can., 1965-69; asst. program mgr. TRW, Redondo Beach, Calif., 1969-71; mgr. GE, Phila., 1971-72; mgr. tech. svcs. Engrs. India Ltd., New Delhi, 1972-74; project engr. Weidlinger Assocs., N.Y.C., 1974-77; prof. Ariz. State U., Tempe, 1977—; dir. Cen. Bldg. Rsch. Inst., 1992-93; dir. Earthquake Rsch. Lab., Tempe, 1978-89; grad. coord. structural engring. Ariz. State U., Tempe, 1991-92, senator acad. senate, 1995—, chmn. governance grievance, 1995-96, faculty ombudsman, 1996-97, ASU com. on coms., 1997—, coord. Computer Aided Design and Modeling, 1997; cons. McDonnel Aircraft Corp., St. Louis, 1977-78, Sperry Corp., 1979-80, McDonnell Douglas Helicopter Co., 1990-91, Ariz. Nuclear Power Plant, 1991-92; reviewer of proposals NSF, Washington, 1980-91, 96-97, CSIR, India, 1990-93; U.S. del. U.S./China Workshop on Arch Dams, Beijing, 1987, Can. del. Shell Structures, USSR, 1964; session chmn. 5th Internat. Conf. on Soil Dynamics and Earthquake Engring., Karlsruhe, Fed. Republic of Germany, 1991; rsch. prof. Nat. Cen. U. Taiwan, Republic of China, 1990; vis. prof. U. Melbourne, Australia, 1983-84, U. Auckland, New Zealand, 1983-84; nodal dir. wood substitute rsch. program, India, 1992-93. Mem. editl. bd. Soil Dynamics and Earthquake Engring., 1991—, Advances in Earthquake Engring., 1995—; reviewer Jour. Psychol. Reports, Perceptual and Motor Skills; contbr. Nuclear Waste Storage, 1986, (proc. publ.) Earthquake Behavior of Buried Pipelines, 1989, Wood Substitute: A National Priority, 1992, System Flexibility and Reflected Pressures, 1993, Simulation of Blast Pressures on Flexible Panels, 1994; editor: Seismic Performance of Pipelines & Storage Tanks, 1985, Recent Advances in Lifeline Earthquake Engineering, 1987, Seismic Ground Motions Response, Repair and Instrumentation of Pipes and Bridges, 1992; contbr. articles to Jour. Performance of Constructed Facilities, ASCE, Jour. Computers and Structures, Jour. ASME, Jour. Aerospace Engring. ASCE; reviewer, bd. editors Jour. Earthquake Engring. and Structural Dynamics, Structural Engring. Papers Jour. ASCE. Mem., bd. dirs., pres. das Estadas Homeowner's Assn., Tempe, 1996-97; chmn. bd. dirs. India Assn. Greater Phoenix, 1985-86; pres. India Assn. Greater Boston, 1964-65, das Estadas, Tempe, Ariz., 1996—; v.p., treas. Dobson Ranch Homeowners Assn., Mesa, Ariz., 1988-91; founding mem. Asian Am. Assn. Ariz., Phoenix, 1987-89; founding mem., pres. Asian Am. Faculty Assn., Ariz. State U., Tempe, 1986-88; cons. UN Devel. Program New Delhi, 1991-92. McLintock fellow MIT, 1960, Carnegie fellow MIT, 1960-63, fellow Royal Astron. Soc., London, 1961-64, rsch. fellow Kobe U., Japan, 1990; Denninson scholar Instn. Civil Engrs., London, 1959; Henry Adams Rsch. medal Structural Engrs., London, 1972; grantee Can. Def. Rsch. Bd., 1966-69, NSF, 1978-82, Engring. Found., 1978-79, U.S. Army Corps Engrs., 1984-86, U.S. Dept. Interior, 1986-88, Office Naval Rsch., 1994; recipient 1st prize bridge bldg. Instn. Strucural Engrs., Merit award Inst. Engrs., India. Fellow ASCE, Ctrl. Bldg. Rsch. Inst. (chmn. mgmt. coun., chmn. APEX com.), Sigma Xi, Tau Beta Pi, Chi Epsilon. Achievements include research in computer engineering and computer modeling, blast effects on structures, in lifeline engineering, earthquake strengthening of deteriorated dams, steel and concrete buildings, bridges, building materials, non-linear finite element dynamics and engineering in mechanics. Home: 2258 W Monterey Ave Mesa AZ 85202-7330 Office: Ariz State U Dept Civil Engring 5306 Tempe AZ 85287-5306 *Service to mankind and love for the family and friends is the key to success and happiness.*

SINGHAL, KISHORE, engineering administrator; b. Allahabad, India, Dec. 28, 1944; came to U.S., 1966; s. Jagdish Chandra and Pushpa Lata (Mital) S.; m. Kumud Agrawal, Aug. 17, 1973; children: Monica, Nina. B Tech. with honors, Indian Inst. Tech., Kharagpur, 1966; MS, Columbia U., 1967, ScD in Engring., 1970. Postdoctoral fellow U. Waterloo, Ont., Can., 1970-71, lectr., 1972, asst. prof., 1973-77, assoc. prof., 1977-83, prof., 1983-88, adj. prof., 1988—, assoc. chmn. grad. studies in systems design, 1977-83; cons., then vis. mem. staff AT&T Bell Labs. (now Lucent Techs.), Murray Hill, N.J., 1984-85; supr. AT&T Bell Labs. (now Lucent Techs.), Allentown, Pa., 1985—; cons. Bell No., Ottawa, Ont., 1972-82. Author: Computer Aided Circuit Design, 1983 (transl. into Russian, Chinese and Pharsi), 2d edit., 1993; editor: Analog Circuit Design, 1987. Higgins fellow Columbia U., 1966, Boese fellow, 1967. Fellow IEEE. Avocations: reading, hiking. Office: Lucent Techs 1247 S Cedar Crest Blvd Allentown PA 18103-6201

SINGHVI, SURENDRA SINGH, finance and strategy consultant; b. Jodhpur, Rajasthan, India, Jan. 16, 1942; came to U.S., 1962, naturalized 1986; s. Rang Raj and Ugam Kanwar (Surana) S.; m. Sushila Bhandari, July 7, 1965; children: Seema, Sandeep. B in Commerce, Rajasthan U., 1961; MBA, Atlanta U., 1963; PhD, Columbia U., 1967. CPA, Cert. Mgmt. Acct. Asst. prof. fin. Miami U., Oxford, Ohio, 1967-69, assoc. prof., 1969-70; adj. prof. fin., 1970-95; fin. mgr. ARMCO Inc., Middletown, Ohio, 1970-79, asst. treas., 1979-83, gen. fin. mgr., 1983-86; v.p. and treas. Edison Bros. Stores, Inc., St. Louis, 1986-90; pres. Singhvi & Assocs., Inc., Dayton, Ohio, 1990—; bd. dirs. Columbia Indsl. Sales Corp., Hauer Music Co., Oasis Property Inc. Author: Planning for Capital Investment, 1980; co-editor: Frontiers of Financial Management, 4th edit., 1984, Global Finance 2000-A Handbook of Strategy and Organization (The Conference Board), 1996; contbr. over 90 articles to profl. jours. Recipient Chancellor's Gold medal Rajasthan U. Mem. Planning Forum, Inst. Mgmt. Accts. (Bayer Silver medal 1978), Fin. Execs. Inst., Asian Indian Am. Bus. Group in S.W. Ohio (pres. 1997—), Rotary (dir. internat. program Middletown chpt. 1973-86, Dayton chpt. 1995—), India Club (pres. Dayton chpt. 1980). Avocations: swimming, bridge, traveling, photography, writing. Home: 439 Ridge Line Ct Dayton OH 45458-9564 Office: Singhvi and Assocs Inc 515 Windsor Park Dr Dayton OH 45459-4112

SINGLE, RICHARD WAYNE, SR., lawyer; b. Balt., June 17, 1938; s. William and Lillian (Griffin) S.; m. Emily K. Kaffl, Nov. 4, 1962; children: Richard W. Jr., Stacey Lyn. AB, U. Md., 1959, JD, 1961. Bar: Md. 1961, U.S. Dist. Ct. Md. 1961, U.S. Supreme Ct. 1978. Staff atty. Legal Aid Bur. Balt., 1962-64; house counsel Gen. Automatic Prodns. Corp., Balt., 1964-67; resident counsel Nat. Industries, Inc., Odenton, Md., 1967-69; asst. counsel McCormick & Co., Inc., Hunt Valley, Md., 1969-72, asst. sec., asst. counsel, 1972-75, asst. sec., assoc. gen. counsel, 1975-82, div. gen. counsel, v.p., 1983-86, gen counsel, v.p., sec., 1986-96, v.p. govt. affairs, sec., 1996—, also bd. dirs.; bd. dirs. McCormick Can., Inc., London, Ont., Can., McCormick de Mexico, Mexico City, Helix Health System, Balt. Trustee Franklin Sq. Hosp., Balt., 1986—. Mem. ABA, Md. Bar Assn. Republican. Avocation: boating. Office: McCormick & Co Inc PO Box 6000 18 Loveton Cir Sparks MD 21152-6000

SINGLEHURST, DONA GEISENHEYNER, horse farm owner; b. Tacoma, June 19, 1928; d. Herbert Russell and Rose Evelyn (Rubish) Geisenheyner; m. Thomas G. Singlehurst, May 16, 1959 (dec.); 1 child, Suanna Singlehurst. BA in Psychology, Whitman Coll., 1950. With pub. rels. and advt. staff Lane Wells, L.A., 1950-52; staff mem. in charge new bus. Bishop Trust Co., Honolulu, 1953-58; mgr. Town & Country Stables, Honolulu, 1958-62; co-owner, v.p. pub. rels. Carol & Mary, Ltd., Honolulu, 1964-84; owner Stanhope Farms, Waialua, Hawaii, 1969—; internat. dressage judge, sport horse breeding judge Am. Horse Shows Assn.; sr. judge Can. Dressage Fedn. Chmn. ways and means com. The Outdoor Cir., Hawaii, 1958-64, life mem.; pres. emeritus Morris Animal Found., Englewood, Colo., 1988—, pres., 1984-88; bd. dirs., pres. Delta Soc., Renton, Wash., 1994—; mem. Jr. League of Honolulu. Recipient Best Friends award Honolulu Vet. Soc., 1986, Spl. Recognition award Am. Animal Hosp. Assn., 1988, Recognition award Am. Vet. Med. Assn. Mem. NAFE, Hawaii Horse Show Assn. (Harry Hutaff award 1985, past pres., bd. dirs.), Hawaii Combined Tng. Assn. (past pres. bd. dirs.), Calif. Dressage Soc., U.S. Dressage Fedn., U.S. Equestrian Team (area chmn. 1981-85), Hawaiian Humane Soc. (life), U.S. Pony Clubs (dist. commr. 1970-75, nat. examiner 1970-75), Pacific Club, Outrigger Canoe Club. Republican. Episcopalian. Avocations: music, travel. Home and Office: Stanhope Farms Waialua HI 96791

SINGLETARY, JAMES, JR., principal; b. Buffalo, Jan. 24, 1947; m. Carolyn Price, July 24, 1971; children: Arien, Craig, Brandon, Evan. Cert. sheet metal, Erie C.C., Buffalo, 1974; BS, SUNY, Buffalo, 1990; MS, Canisius Coll., 1993. Cert. tchr. permanent, 1988, sch. adminstr. and supr., 1993. Sheet metal worker Buffalo Sheets Metal, 1970-77; customer engr. IBM, Buffalo, 1977-83; sheet metal worker, drafting tchr. Buffalo Pub. Schs., 1983-93; acting asst. prin., asst. prin. Seneca Vocat. H.S., Buffalo, 1993—; 2d v.p. bd. dirs. Rev. Marvin W. Robinson Cmty. Ctr., Inc. Adv. coun. mem. SUNY and Buffalo Vocat. Tech. Edn. Coun., 1988-91. With USN, 1964-70. Mem. Am. Edn. Rsch. Assn., Am. Fedn. Sch. Adminstrs., N.Y. State Fedn. Suprs. and Adminstrs., Vocat. Tech. Guild Buffalo, Buffalo Coun. Suprs. and Adminstrs. (mem. grievance com.), Buffalo Secondary Asst. Prins. Assn. (v.p.), Buffalo State Coll. Alumni Assn., Canisius Coll. Alumni Assn., Jack and Jill of Am., Inc., Phi Delta Kappa. Avocations: bowling, tennis, roller skating. Home: 273 Humboldt Pky Buffalo NY 14208-1044 Office: Seneca Vocat HS 666 E Delavan Ave Buffalo NY 14215-3014

SINGLETARY, OTIS ARNOLD, JR., university president emeritus; b. Gulfport, Miss., Oct. 31, 1921; s. Otis Arnold and May Charlotte (Walker) S.; m. Gloria Walton, June 6, 1944; children: Bonnie, Scot, Kendall Ann. B.A., Millsaps Coll., 1947; M.A., La State U., 1949, Ph.D., 1954. Mem. faculty U. Tex., Austin, 1954-61, prof. history, 1960-61, assoc. dean Sch. Arts and Scis., 1956-59, asst. to pres., 1960-61; chancellor U. N.C., Greensboro, 1961-66; v.p. Am. Council on Edn., Washington, 1966-68; on leave as dir. Job Corps, OEO, Washington, 1964-65; exec. vice chancellor acad. affairs U. Tex. System, 1968-69; pres. U. Ky., Lexington, 1969-87, prof. emeritus, 1987—; bd. dirs. Howell Corp. Author: Negro Militia and the Reconstruction, 1957, The Mexican War, 1960; editor: American Universities and Colleges, 1968. Regional chmn. Woodrow Wilson Nat. Fellowship Found., 1959-61; chmn. N.C. Rhodes Scholarship Com., 1964-66; chmn. Ky. Rhodes Scholarship Com., 1970-71, 73-74, 77, 80-81, 84-86; mem. So. Regional Edn. Bd., 1969—; chmn. dept. Army history adv. com., 1972-80; bd. visitors Air U., Maxwell AFB, 1973-76. Served with USNR, 1943-46, 51-54. Recipient Scarborough Teaching Excellence award U. Tex., 1958, Students Assn. Teaching Excellence award, 1958, 59; Carnegie Corp. grantee, 1961. Mem. Am. Hist. Assn., So. Hist. Assn., Am. Mil. Inst. (Moncado Book Fund award 1954), Am. Assn. Higher Edn. (dir. 1969—), Phi Beta Kappa (senator 1977-94, v.p. 1985-88, pres. 1988-91), Phi Alpha Theta, Omicron Delta Kappa, Pi Kappa Alpha. Democrat. Methodist. Office: U of Ky 104 King Library N Lexington KY 40506

SINGLETERRY, GARY LEE, investment banker; b. Seattle, May 10, 1948; s. Richard W. and Anita J. (Fowler) S.; m. Mary Beth Burfeind, Nov. 29, 1969; children: Douglas, Laura. AB, Harvard U., 1970; MBA, Stanford U., 1974. Assoc. Morgan Stanley & Co., N.Y.C., 1974-79, Wm Sword & Co., Princeton, N.J., 1979-80; v.p. Thomson, McKinnon & Co., N.Y.C., 1981-82; mng. dir. Dean Witter Reynolds, N.Y.C., 1983-85, Prudential-Bache Securities, N.Y.C., 1985-91; pres. Singleterry & Co., Parsippany, N.J., 1991—. Mem. FNMA Nat. Adv. Coun., 1991. Republican. Office: Singleterry & Co 4 Campus Dr Parsippany NJ 07054-4401

SINGLETON, DONALD EDWARD, journalist; b. Morristown, N.J., Nov. 8, 1936; s. Edward Leslie and Charlotte (Angerbauer) S.; m. Maureen Ann McNiff, Aug. 8, 1959 (div. 1977); children: Nancy Ann, Mark Aram, Jill Susan. Student, Fairleigh Dickinson U., 1955-58. Reporter Dover (N.J.) Advance, 1959-61, Morristown Daily Record, 1961-63, Newark Eve. News, 1963-64; feature reporter-writer N.Y. Daily News, 1964—. Organizer Com. to Save Church Sq. Park, Hoboken, N.J.; vice chmn. Hoboken Environment Com.; mem. due process com. ACLU., Mem. bd. edn., City of Hoboken, 1974-77. Recipient Pub. Service award N.Y. Council Civic Affairs, 1967; President's Distinguished Service award N.Y.C. Council, 1969; Newspaper award merit Women's Press Club N.Y.C., 1970, 79; citation VFW, 1970; Heywood Broun Meml. award Am. Newspaper Guild, 1970; Silver medal for pub. service journalism N.Y. chpt. Pub. Relations Soc. Am., 1970; certificate merit Am. Bar Assn., 1971; Page One award Newspaper Guild N.Y., 1970; Feature award Newspaper Reporters Assn. N.Y., 1972; Consistent Excellence award Uniformed Firefighters Assn., 1991. Mem. Am. Newspaper Guild. Club: Press (N.Y.C.). Home: 366 Ogden Ave Jersey City NJ 07307-1115 Office: 220 E 42nd St New York NY 10017-5806 *In reporting, I try very hard to avoid gathering facts in such a way as to fulfill a preconception. I also attempt to force myself to review constantly my opinions about my subjects, and to keep my mind as open as possible. In writing, I try to ask myself the following questions regularly: "Is this what I really believe? Or am I simply writing this way because I believe that this is what some other person or group would like me to write?" Unless I can answer the first question in the affirmative, and the second in the negative, I am not satisfied with a particular story.*

SINGLETON, FRANCIS SETH, dean; b. Phila., July 13, 1940; s. William Francis and Anna A. (Setian) S.; m. Margaret Neff, June 14, 1962 (div. 1983); children: William, Andrew; m. Charlotte T. Kennedy, Jan. 16, 1988. AB, Harvard U., 1962; MA, Yale U., 1963, PhD, 1968. Budget examiner Bur. of Budget, Washington, 1964-65; dean Pearson Coll. Yale U., New Haven, 1966-69; lectr. U. Dares Salaam, Tanzania, 1969-70; asst. prof. U. Alta., Edmonton, Can., 1970-71; from assoc. prof. to prof., chair politics and govt. Ripon (Wis.) Coll., 1972-83; rsch. assoc. Russian Ctr., Harvard U., Cambridge, Mass., 1983-84; dean arts and scis. Pacific U., Forest Grove, Oreg., 1984-91, prof. govt., 1991—; academic dean Espiritu Santo U., Guayaquil, Ecuador, 1994—; ampart lectr. U.S.I.A., Africa, 1983, 90; bd. dirs. Oreg. Internat. Coun., Salem, 1986—; lectr. Ural U., Russia, 1991; cons. Russia Fedn. Govt., 1992. Author: Africa in Perspective, 1968; contbr. articles to profl. publs., chpts. to books. Bd. dirs. Com. Fgn. Rels., Portland, 1989—; mem. adv. com. Light Rail Tri-Met, Portland, Oreg., 1989—. Grantee Rockefeller Found., 1969-70, Nat. Coun. Soviet and E. Europe Rsch., 1983-84. Avocations: sailing, outdoor activities. Home: 3421 NW Thurman St Portland OR 97210 Office: Pacific U 2043 College Way Forest Grove OR 97116-1756

SINGLETON, HARRY MICHAEL, lawyer; b. Meadville, Pa., Apr. 10, 1949; s. Getdins T. and Rose Ann (Fucci) S.; children: Harry M. Jr., Leah Rose DiFucci. B.A., Johns Hopkins U., 1971; J.D., Yale U., 1974. Bar: D.C. 1975, U.S. Dist. Ct. D.C. 1975, U.S. Ct. Appeals (D.C. cir.) 1975, U.S. Ct. Mil. Appeals 1975, Pa. 1976. Assoc. Houston & Gardner, Washington, 1974-75, Covington & Burling, Washington, 1976-77; atty. FTC, Washington, 1975-76; dep. minority counsel Com. on D.C./U.S. Ho. of Reps., Washington, 1977-79, minority chief counsel, staff dir., 1979-81; dep. asst. sec. U.S. Dept. Commerce, Washington, 1981-82; asst. sec. U.S. Dept. Edn., Washington, 1982-86; pres. Harry M. Singleton & Assocs., Washington, 1986-91; pvt. practice law Washington, 1991—; legis. cons. Am. Enterprise Inst., Washington, 1975. Pres. bd. trustees Barney Neighborhood House, Washington, 1978-80; corp. bd. dirs. Children's Hosp. Nat. Med. Ctr., Washington, 1984-88; mem. crime com. Boys and Girls Clubs of Greater Washington, 1994—; mem. D.C. Rep. State Com., 1991—, Rep. Nat. Com., 1992—, R.N.C. exec. coun., 1993-95, resolutions com., 1997—. Mem. Rep.

Nat. Lawyers Assn. (bd. dirs. D.C. chpt. 1990-91), Coun. of 100 Black Reps. (bd. dirs. 1991-92), D.C. Black Rep. Coun. (chmn. 1992-93), Rep. Nat. African-Am. Coun. (nat. chmn. 1993—), D.C. Rep. Nat. African-Am. Coun. (chmn. 1993—), Rep. Nat. Hispanic Assembly Washington, Lions. Republican. Presbyterian. Office: 2300 M St NW Ste 800 Washington DC 20037-1434

SINGLETON, HENRY EARL, industrialist; b. Haslet, Tex., Nov. 27, 1916; s. John Bartholomew and Victoria (Flores) S.; m. Caroline A. Wood, Nov. 30, 1942; children: Christina, John, William, James, Diana. S.B., S.M., Mass. Inst. Tech., 1940, Sc.D., 1950. V.p. Litton Industries, Inc., Beverly Hills, Calif., 1954-60; CEO Teledyne Inc., Los Angeles, 1960-86; chmn. Teledyne Inc., 1960-91, Singleton Group, Beverly Hills, Calif., 1991-96; chmn. exec. com. Teledyne, Inc., L.A., 1991—. Office: 335 N Maple Dr Ste 177 Beverly Hills CA 90210-3858

SINGLETON, JAMES KEITH, federal judge; b. Oakland, Calif., Jan. 27, 1939; s. James K. and Irene Elisabeth (Lilly) S.; m. Sandra Claire Hoskins, Oct. 15, 1966; children: Matthew David, Michael Keith. Student, U. Santa Clara, 1957-58; AB in Polit. Sci., U. Calif., Berkeley, 1961, LLB, 1964. Bar: Calif. 1965, Alaska, 1965. Assoc. Delaney Wiles Moore and Hayes, Anchorage, 1963, 65-68, Law Offices Roger Cremo, Anchorage, 1968-70; judge Alaska Superior Ct., Anchorage, 1970-80, Alaska Ct. Appeals, Anchorage, 1980-90; judge U.S. Dist. Ct. for Alaska, Anchorage, 1990-95, chief judge, 1995—; chmn. Alaska Local Boundary Commn., Anchorage, 1966-69. Chmn. 3d Dist. Rep. Com., Anchorage, 1969-70. Mem. ABA, Alaska Bar Assn., Phi Delta Phi, Tau Kappa Epsilon. Office: US Dist Ct 222 W 7th Ave Unit 41 Anchorage AK 99513-7504

SINGLETON, JOHN, director, screenwriter; b. L.A., Jan. 6, 1968; s. Danny Singleton and Sheila Ward. BA, U. So. Calif., 1990. Writer, dir. Boyz N the Hood, 1991 (Acad. award nominee Best Dir. and Best Screenplay 1992); writer, dir., prodr. Poetic Justice, 1993, Higher Learning, 1995; dir., prodr., screenwriter Michael Jackson's Remember the Time video, 1992, Rosewood, 1997. First African-American and youngest person to be nominated for an Academy Award for Best Director. Office: United Talent Agy 9560 Wilshire Blvd 5th Fl Beverly Hills CA 90212-1804 also: New Deal Prodns 10202 Washington Blvd Culver City CA 90232-3119*

SINGLETON, JOHN VIRGIL, JR., retired federal judge, lawyer; b. Kaufman, Tex., Mar. 20, 1918; s. John Virgil Sr. and Jennie (Shelton) S.; m. Jane Guilford Tully, Apr. 18, 1953 (dec. Apr. 1991); m. Sylvia Gregg, May 13, 1991. BA, U. Tex., LLB, 1942. Bar: Tex. 1942. With U.S. Navy, 1942-46; lt. sr. grad. USS Demsey Gunnery Officer, 1942-45; exec. officer USS Green Wist, 1945-46; assoc., gen. counsel Houston Harris County Ship Channel Navigation Dist. Fulbright, Crooker, Freeman & Bates, 1946-54; ptnr. Bates, Riggs & Singleton, 1954-56, Bell & Singleton, 1957-61, Barrow, Bland, Rehmet & Singleton, 1962-66; judge U.S. Dist. Ct. (so. dist.) Tex., 1966-92, chief judge, 1979-88, sr. judge, 1988-92; pres. Houston Jr. Bar Assn., 1952-53; co-chmn. 5th cir. dist. judges divsn. Jud. Conf., 1969, chmn., 1970, rep. from 5th cir. Jud Conf. U.S., 1980-83, also chmn. legis. com.; mem. Fifth Cir. Jud. Coun., 1984—; bd. dirs. TransAmerican Waste Industries, Inc.; mem. Audit Com. Mem. Tex. Depository Bd., 1963-66; co-chmn. Harris County Lyndon B. Johnson for Pres. Com., 1960-61; del.-at-large Dem. Nat. Conv., 1956, 60, 64; regional coord. 7-state area Dem. Nat. Com., Lyndon B. Johnson-Hubert Humphrey Campaign for Pres., 1964; mem. exec. com., Tex. Dem. Com., 1962-65, chmn. fin. com. 1964-66; former bd. dirs. Houston Speech and Hearing Ctr.; trustee Houston Legal Found., Retina Rsch. Found.; mem. chancellor's coun. U. Tex.; mem. exec. com. Lombardi Awards Trophy; mem. tex. Longhorn Edn. Found.; sponsor Found. for Tex. Excellence; oversight com. renovation Meml. Park Golf Course, 1995. Named to Waxahachie High Sch. Hall of Fame. Mem. ABA (liaison rep. to spl. com. evaluation disciplinary enforcement, litigation sect. ad hoc com. on tng. for spl. masters, jury comprehension com.), Fed. Judges Assn. (bd. dirs. 1974—, mem. exec. com.), Houston Bar Assn. (v.p. 1956-57, editor Houston Lawyer 1954-55, chmn. unauthorized practice law com. 1961-62), Tex. Bar Found. (charter mem. fellows), Tex. Bar Assn. (dist. dir.), State Bar Tex. (adminstrn. justice com., chmn. unauthorized practice of law com., 1961-62, chmn. grievance com. 22d dist. 1965-66, bd. dirs. 1966, fed. jud. liaison to state bd. dirs. 1984-85, pres. state bar task force Thurgood Marshall Sch. Law, 1986—, charter mem. fellows Tex. Bar Found.), U. Tex. Ex-Students Assn. (life mem., pres. Houston chpt. 1961-62, mem. exec. com., chmn. scholarship com., at large mem. 1969-80, Pres's. Right Arm award 1978-79, Outstanding Com. chmn. 1978-79), Rotary, Cowboys (foreman, straw boss), Am. Judicature Soc., Order of Coif (Houston chpt. 1989—), Delta Tau Delta Gama Iota Chpt.(pres. 1940-41), Phi Alpha Delta, Lakeside Country Club (Houston, past sec., bd. dirs.). Episcopalian. Office: 314 N Post Oak Ln Houston TX 77024-5904

SINGLETON, MARVIN AYERS, otolaryngologist, senator; b. Baytown, Tex., Oct. 7, 1939; s. Henry Marvin and Mary Ruth (Mitchell) S.; B.A., U. of the South, 1962; M.D., U. Tenn., 1966. Intern, City of Memphis Hosps., 1966-67; resident in surgery Highland Alameda City Hosp., Oakland, Calif., 1967-68, resident in otolaryngology U. Tenn. Hosp., Memphis, 1968-71; Am. Acad. Otolaryngology and Ophthalmology fellow in otolaryngic pathology Armed Forces Inst. Pathology, Washington, 1971; fellow in otologic surgery U. Colo. at Gallup (N.Mex.) Indian Med. Center, 1972; practice medicine specializing in otolaryngology and allergies, Joplin, Mo., 1972—; founder, operator Home and Farm Investments, Joplin, 1975—, staff mem. Freeman Hosp., St. John's Hosp., Joplin, Oakhill Hosp.; cons. in otolaryngology Parsons (Kans.) State Hosp. and Tng. Center, Mo. Crippled Children's Service, Santa Fe R.R.; pres. Ozark Mfg. Co., Inc., Joplin. Mem. Internat. Arabian Racing Bd., 1983-88; mem. Mo. State Senate, 1990—, asst.minority leader; del. Rep. Nat. Conv., 1988, 92. Served with USNG, 1966-72. Diplomate Am. Bd. Otolaryngology. Fellow A.C.S., Am. Acad. Otolaryngologic Allergy, (past pres.), Am. Assn. Clin. Immunology and Allergy; mem. AMA (Mo. del.), Mo. State, So., Jasper County med. assns., Council of Otolaryngology, Mo. State Allergy Assn., Ear, Nose and Throat Soc. Mo. (past pres.), Joplin C. of C., Masons (32 degree), Sigma Alpha Epsilon, Phi Theta Kappa, Phi Chi. Methodist. Club: Elks. Contbr. articles to profl. jours. Home: 4476 Five Mile Rd Seneca MO 64865-8357 Office: 114 W 32nd St Joplin MO 64804-3701

SINGLETON, PHILIP ARTHUR, corporate executive; b. Detroit, May 2, 1914; m. Eleanor A. DeVilbiss, Aug. 16, 1941; children: Kimberley P., Janet D., John R.M., Tobias T. (dec.). BSME magna cum laude, U. Mich., 1935; cert., Harvard U. Bus. Sch., 1940; LL.B., Yale U., 1941, J.D., 1946. Bar: Conn. 1941, U.S. Supreme Ct 1946; enrolled Inns of Ct., London, Middle Temple, 1952-55; registered profl. engr. With Monsanto Chem. Co. (and asso. cos.), 1940-55; successively at Merrimac div., Everett, Mass.; asst. to pres. of Monsanto Co., Washington; exec. v.p. Nealco-Monsanto Co., Everett; asst. dir. fgn. dept. Monsanto Co., St. Louis, 1949-50; mng. dir. Monsanto Chems., Ltd., London, Eng., 1956; asst. to pres., sec. exec. com. Monsanto Chems. Co., St. Louis, 1956; dir., mem. exec. com. Forth Chems., Ltd., Scotland; dir. Monsanto Chems., India, Bombay, Monsanto Chem., Australia, Tororo Exploration Syndicate, Uganda, Monsanto Boussois S/A, Paris, Casco A/B, Stockholm, S.I.C.E., Milan, S.I.D.A.C. S/A, Brussels, 1951; exec. v.p. Prophy-lactic Brush Co., Florence, Mass., 1951-56; pres., dir. Prophy-lactic Brush Co., 1957-66; v.p. Vistron Corp.; pres. Pro Brush and Prolon Dinnerware divs., 1957-68; with Warner-Lambert Pharm. Co., Morris Plains, N.J., 1956-63, also sr. v.p. grand firm, 1960-63; with responsibility for indsl. divs. including Md. Glass Corp., Balt., Gulfport Glass Corp., Miss., Nepera Chem. Co.,, Harriman, N.Y.; chmn. chief exec. officer Singleton Assocs. Internat., Amherst, Mass., 1967-90; chmn. bd. Hoodfoam Industries, Inc., Marblehead, Mass., 1968-72; chmn. bd., dir. Mazzucchelli, Inc., N.Y.C., 1968-71; chmn., chief exec. officer Plastics Industry Adv. Services, Far East Trading and Tech.; pres. Environ. Research Services, High Arctic Tech. Services, 1986-94; ret., 1994; dir., mem. audit com., div. policy com. Mass. Mut. Life Ins. Co.; dir. Keuffel & Esser Co., Morristown, N.J., Davis Cos. Inc., Denver, Hood Enterprises Inc., Marblehead, Mass., Deerfield Plastics Co., South Deerfield, Mass., Barry Wright Corp., Watertown, Mass., Hardigg Industries Inc., South Deerfield, Mass., Howard Mfg. Co., Littleton, Colo., Amtel, Inc., Koehring Co., Compo Industries Inc., Davis Cos., Denver, Towle Mfg. Co., Courier Corp.; dir., mem. compensation com. and employee benefit com. Hershey Foods Corp., Pa.; chmn., dir., mem. audit com. Werner & Pfleiderer Corp.; mem. Park St. Investment Trust, Boston.; mem. regional appeals bd. War Manpower Commn., 1943-45; employer mem. U.S. delegation ILO, Geneva, Switzerland, 1953-54; pres. Plastics Industry Adv. Services, Amherst, Mass., 1968-83; chmn., chief exec. officer Polar Technology Services-High Arctic and Antarctica. Mem. nat. adv. council Hampshire Coll., Amherst; mem. corp. Northeastern U., Boston., Boston Mus. Sci.; mem. Park St. Ptnrs., 1982-97; founding bd. dirs. Plastics Edn. Found. Mem. NAM (dir. 1961-63), Am. Chem. Soc., Soc. Plastics Industry (dir.-at-large 1962-64, v.p. 1965-66, pres., dir. 1967-69), Pilgrims Soc., Soc. Chem. Industry London, U.S. C. of C. London (dir. 1953-56), Internat. C. of C. (overseas investment com., Paris 1953-55), Am. Brush Mfrs. Assn. (dir., pres.), Asso. Industries Mass. (v.p. 1963-65, dir. 1966-97), Explorers Club, Union Club (Boston), Royal Thames Yacht Club (London), Cruising Club Am., Edarmoc Club (Detroit), Rotary (Amherst club), Beta Gamma Sigma (hon.), Phi Kappa Psi, Tau Beta Pi (nat. officer, pres. Mich. chpt., editor Council Bull.), Phi Eta Sigma. Republican. Presbyterian. Clubs: Comml., Mchts., Union (Boston); Five Islands Yacht (Maine); Ends of the Earth, Philippics, Royal Cruising, Royal Thames Yacht (London); Intrepids, Travellers Century (Calif.); Beefeaters; Plastics Pioneers (N.Y.); Michigamua, Vulcans (Ann Arbor, Mich.). *Died Apr. 3, 1997.*

SINGLETON, SAMUEL WINSTON, physician, pharmaceutical company executive; b. Blackpool, Eng., Nov. 17, 1928; came to U.S., 1953, naturalized, 1955; s. Samuel Smith and Jessica Constance M. (Knights) S.; m. Sheila Yolande C. Kershaw, Aug. 23, 1953; 1 child, Diane Jane. M.B., Ch.B., U. Manchester, 1952. Diplomate: Am. Bd. Pediatrics. Intern Chester, Pa., 1953-54; pediatric resident Oakland, Calif., 1956-58; assoc. physician, dir. clin. investigation, med. dir., v.p. Burroughs Wellcome Co., Research Triangle Park, N.C., 1960-89; asst. clin. prof. pediatrics Duke U., Durham, N.C., 1972-90; past dir. B.W. Fund. Served with M.C. USNR, 1954-60. Home: 429 Tranquility Rd Moneta VA 24121

SINGLETON, STELLA WOOD, educator and habilitation assistant; b. Moore County, N.C., Nov. 3, 1948; d. Jay and Thelma A. Wood; m. Tommy Singleton, Dec. 21, 1968; children: Jennifer, Mike. Diploma, Hamlet Hosp. Sch. Nursing, Hamlet, N.C., 1975; postgrad., Appalachian State U., Boone, N.C., 1990—. RN, N.C. Dir. Hospice of Boone (N.C.) Area, 1982-83; Hospice dir. Hospice of Avery County, Newland, N.C., 1983-85; DON Toe River Health Dist., Newland, N.C., 1983-84; mental health nurse II New River Mental Health, Newland, N.C., 1977-82, 85-95; beauty cons. Mary Kay Cosmetics, 1986—; habilitation asst. Devl. Disabilities Svcs., Boone, N.C., 1995—; personal care supr. HomeCare Mgmt. Corp., Boone, N.C., 1996—; instr. Mayland C.C., Spruce Pine, N.C. Co-facilitator Avery County Alzheimer's Support Group, group facilitator Cancer Support Group Svc.; rehab. chmn. Am. Cancer Soc. Recipient Gov's. award for administrv. vol. Mem. N.C. Biofeedback Soc. Home: PO Box 483 Crossnore NC 28616-0483 Office: Devel Disabilities Svcs 404 Oak Summit Boone NC 28607 also: Mayland CC PO Box 547 Spruce Pine NC 28777

SINGLETON-WOOD, ALLAN JAMES, communications executive; b. Newport, Monmouthshire, Eng., Feb. 13, 1933; arrived in Can., 1968; s. Charles James and Violet Anne (Bond) S.-W.; m. Joan Davies, June 23, 1956; children: Ceri, Glendon. Student, London U., 1949-51. TV and radio musical dir., 1953-57, TV producer, 1957-61; freelance producer for BBC, 1962-64; indsl. advt. mgr. Western Mail, Cardiff, Wales, 1964; advt. dir. Voice of Brit. Industry Mags., London, 1966; mktg. svcs. exec. The Sun and The People, I.P.C. Newspapers, London, 1966-68; mktg. svcs. mgr. Fin. Post, Toronto, Ont., Can., 1969-71; rsch. mgr. Fin. Post, 1971-76, nat. sales mgr., 1976-77; pub. Fin. Post Mag., 1978-79, dir. advt. sales Fin. Post divsn., 1980-83; pub. Small Bus. Mag., 1983-87; v.p. pub. Bedford House Ltd., Toronto, 1987-88; pub. Small Bus. mag., v.p. CB Media Ltd., Toronto, 1988—; v.p. pub. Can. Bus. and Small Bus. mags., Who's Who in Can. Bus., Who's Who in Can. Fin., 1989—; corp. pub., gen. mgr. Sentry Comm., Willowdale, Ont., 1991-92; group pub. Bus. Publs. divsn. MacLean Hunter Ltd., Toronto, 1992-93; pres. Can. Productivity divsn. CB Media Ltd., Toronto, 1994-96; pres., CEO Singleton-Wood Comm. Inc., Toronto, 1996—; lectr. at various univs.; cons. in field; pres., founder Can. Info. Productivity Awards, 1994—. Composer: contemporary music including title theme of Swing High, BBC nat. network series, 1953-57. Mem. Anglican Ch. Achievements include development of first computer media evaluation program for Canadian advertising industry. Office: CIPA, CB Media Ltd, 777 Bay St, Toronto, ON Canada M5W 1A7

SINGLEY, GEORGE T., III, mechanical engineer, federal agency administrator; b. Wilmington, Del., Mar. 29, 1945; m. Maxine Verlander; 3 children. B in ME, U. Del., 1968; MBA, Coll. William and Mary, 1971; M in ME, Old Dominion, 1977. Aerospace engr. Aviation Applied Tech. Directorate, Ft. Eustis, Va., 1970-80; chief advanced concepts divsn., dep. project mgr. Army Aviation Sys. Command, St. Louis, 1980-85; asst. dir. Army Rsch. and Tech., Washington, 1985-87, dep. asst. sec.; program exec. officer Combat Support Aviation, 1987-88; prin. dep. to dir. Def. Rsch. and Engring., Washington, 1995—. With U.S. Army, 1968-70. Recipient Meritorious Exec. Presdl. Rank award, 1991, Engr. Alumnus of the Yr. award U. Del., 1991, Disting. Exec. Presdl. Rank award, 1993, Nat. Firepower award Am. Def. Preparedness Assn., 1993. Mem. Am. Helicopter Soc. (pres. 1996-97, Grover S. Bell award 1991). Office: Rsch and Engring 3030 Defense Pentagon Washington DC 20301-3030*

SINGLEY, JOHN EDWARD, JR., environmental scientist, consultant; b. Wildwood, N.J., July 31, 1924; s. John Edward Singley and Dorothy Mae (Pfrommer) S.; m. Virginia H. Ragsdale, Mar. 17, 1950; children: Gladys, Ann, Margaret, Patricia. BS, Ga. Inst. Tech, 1950; MS, Ga. Inst. Tech., 1952; PhD, U. Fla., 1966. Chemist Redstone Arsenal, Huntsville, Ala., 1950-51; dir. tech. svs. Tenn. Corp., College Park, Ga., 1951-64; lectr. chemistry Ga. State U., Atlanta, 1954-64, assoc. prof., 1964-67; prof. environ. engring. sci. U. Fla., Gainesville, 1967-90, prof. emeritus, 1990—; dir. TREEO Ctr., Gainesville, 1978-86; v.p. James M. Montgomery, Cons. Engrs., Inc., Gainesville, 1984-93, Montgomery Watson Cons. Engrs. Inc., Gainesville, 1993-96; sr. v.p. Environ. Scis. Engring. Inc., Gainesville, 1977-84; prin. Water and Air Rsch., Gainesville, 1970-77; v.p. Metcalf & Eddy, Gainesville, 1996—. Patentee in field of polymers. Mem. Fulton County Rep. Exec. Com., 1962-64; trustee Water for People, 1990-92. With USN, 1943-45. Recipient Donald R. Boyd award Met. Water Agys., 1992. Fellow Am. Inst. Chemists, Inst. Water and Environ. Mgmt.; mem. Am. Water Works Assn. (hon., life, bd. dirs. 1984-87, exec. com. 1986-87, 89-93, v.p. 1989-90, pres.-elect 1990-91, pres. 1991-92, Fuller award 1974, rsch. award 1983, Abel Wolman Excellence award 1995, Disting. Pub. Svc. award 1995), Fla. Water and Pollution Control Operators Assn. (Flanigan award 1979), Nat. Lime Assn. (Recognition award), Internat. Water Supply Assn., Nat. Assn. Corrosion Engrs., Internat. Ozone Assn. (bd. dirs. 1985-93). Presbyterian. Club: Gainesville, Civitan (pres. 1972, lt. gov. Fla. dist. 1973-76). Home: 1719 NW 23rd Blvd PHE Gainesville FL 32605-3082 Office: Metcalf & Eddy 3620 NW 43th St Ste C Gainesville FL 32606

SINGLEY, MARK ELDRIDGE, agricultural engineering educator; b. Delano, Pa., Jan. 25, 1921; s. Maurice and Clara (Rhodes) S.; m. Janet Twichell, Oct. 3, 1942; children: Donald Heath, Frances Marvin, Jeremy Mark, Paul Victor. BS, Pa. State U., 1942; MS, Rutgers U., 1949. Adminstrv. asst. UNRRA, 1946; prof. II biol. and agrl. engring. Rutgers U., New Brunswick, N.J., 1947-87; chmn. dept. Rutgers U., 1961-71; v.p. rsch. and devel. Bedminster Bioconversion Corp., Haddonfield, N.J., 1987-95; cons. New Holland N.Am., 1993—; bd. dirs. Agriplane. Chmn. Hillsborough Twp., Somerset County (N.J.) Planning Bd., 1956-73; pres. Hillsborough Twp. (N.J.) Democratic Club, 1979-80, Agrl. Mus. State of N.J., 1983—, pres. bd. trustee, 1984-89. With USNR, 1942-46. Named Prof. of Yr. Cook Coll., 1985. Fellow AAAS (sect. com. O), Am. Soc. Agrl. Engrs. (chmn. North Atlantic region 1966, bd. dir. 1973-75, Massey-Ferguson medal 1987); mem. Am. Forage and Grassland Council (bd. dir. 1966-69). Home and Office: 335 Amwell Rd Belle Mead NJ 08502-1203

SINGSTOCK, DAVID JOHN, military officer; b. Oshkosh, Wis., July 19, 1940; s. Arnold William and Viola Rufine (Gerdener) S.; children: Susan, Brian, Elissa, Timothy. BS with distinction, Maine Maritime Acad., 1964; student, U.S. Merchant Marine Acad., 1959-62; BSBA with distinction, George Washington U., 1973, MS, 1975. Lic. profl. marine engr. Commd. ensign USN, 1964, advanced through grades to comdr., 1984, various sea assignments including combat duty in Vietnam, 1964-69; engr. officer USS Harold J. Ellison USN, Norfolk, Va., 1969-71, ADP fin. mgr. Cinclantflt, 1971-73; planning and quality assurance officer supr. shipbuilding USN, Portsmouth, Va., 1973-76; prodn./repair officer supr. shipbuilding USN, Bath, Maine, 1976-79; ship maintenance mgr. chief naval ops. USN, Washington, 1980-83, dir. fleet modernization program space/naval warfare systems command, 1983-86, program mgr. USS Stark restoration naval sea systems command, 1986-88, tech. dir. dep. asst. sec. Navy for internat. programs, 1988-93; sr. tech. advisor Royal Saudi Naval Forces Ops. Desert Shield and Desert Storm, 1990-91; sr. naval tech. mem. to Sec. of Def. chartered delegation of sr. U.S. ofcls., Saudi Arabia, 1991; retired U.S. Navy, 1993. Asst. scoutmaster Boy Scouts Am., Dumfries, Va., 1985-90; coach Youth Soccer, Maine, Va., 1976-84; active local property owners civic orgns., Va., Maine, 1970—; instr. ARC, Seattle, 1967-68. Decorated Navy Commendation medal, Navy Achievement medal, Vietnamese Cross of Gallantry, Meritorious Svc. Medal, Joint Svc. Commendation medal, Bronze Star, Purple Heart; recipient Cert. of Appreciation and Gratitude, Comdr. of Saudi Arabian Armed Forces. Mem. Am. Soc. Naval Engrs. (dep. com. chmn., speaker 1988), Nat. Contract Mgmt. Assn. (cert. contracts mgr.), Ret. Officers Assn., Nat. Eagle Scout Assn., Mason (32 degree), Scottish Rite, Shriner. Presbyterian. Avocations: sailing, jogging, camping, golf, music. Home: 1125 Portner Rd Alexandria VA 22314-1314 Office: Vitro Corp Ste 100 Ml 2361 Jefferson Davis Hwy Arlington VA 22202-3876

SINHA, RAMESH CHANDRA, plant pathologist; b. Bareilly, India, Feb. 10, 1934; s. Bhawani Prasada and Ram Pyari; m. Indu Bala Sinha; children: Sanjeev, Sangita. BS, Bareilly Coll., 1953; MS, Lucknow (India) U., 1956; PhD, London U., 1960, DSc, 1975. Exptl. officer Rothamster Exptl. Sta., Harpenden, 1959-60; research assoc. U. Ill., Urbana, 1960-65; research scientist Agriculture Can., Ottawa, Ont., Can., 1965—, prin. research sci., 1965—. Contbr. articles in field. Fellow Royal Soc. Can.; mem. Can. Phytopathol. Soc., Indian Phytopathol. Soc. Avocations: badminton, golfing, bridge. Home: 21 Barran St, Nepean, ON Canada K2J 1G3 Office: Ea Cereal and Oil, Rsch Ctr, Ottawa, ON Canada K1A 0C6

SINICROPI, ANTHONY VINCENT, industrial relations and human resources educator; b. Olean, N.Y., Mar. 30, 1931; s. Anthony and Christina Maria (LaBella) S.; m. Margaret Frances Michienzi, June 16, 1956; children—Stephen, Christine, Angela, Anthony J., Annette, Joseph. B.A. in Econs. cum laude, St. Bonaventure Coll., 1956; M.I.L.R., Cornell U., 1958; Ph.D., U. Iowa, 1968. Instr. St. Bonaventure Coll., Olean, N.Y., 1958-60; asst. prof. Gannon Coll., Erie, Pa., 1960-63; John F. Murray prof dept. indsl. relations and human resources U. Iowa, Iowa City, 1963-93, John F. Murray prof. emeritus, 1993—, ombudsperson, 1985-89; labor arbitrator, Washington, 1963—. Co-author: Evidence in Arbitration, 1982, Remedies in Arbitration, 1983, Management Rights in Arbitration, 1986; contbr. numerous articles to profl. jours. Served with USAF, 1951-53. Mem. Indsl. Relations Research Assn., Soc. Profls. in Dispute Resolution (pres. 1979), Nat. Acad. Arbitrators (bd. govs. 1983—, v.p. 1983-91, pres. 1991-92). Avocation: music.

SININING, VICENTE C., education educator; b. Escalante, Philippines, May 15, 1968; s. Fortunato V. and Aida (Cabatania) S. BS in Chem. Engring., St. Augustine Coll., Philippines, 1988; BS in Computer Sci. with honors, Internat. U., Independence, Mo., 1991. Programmer/sys. analyst Portfolio Computer Sys., Philippines; faculty Internat. U., Philippines, 1991-92; tchr. Brownsville (Tex.) Ind. Sch. Dist., 1992, Mt. Bachelor Acad., Prineville, Oreg., 1993-94; vis. lectr. Mt. Carmel Coll., Escalante, Philippines, 1994—; founder, exec. dir. INFOSYS; tng. specialist ESL & computer literacy; founder Filipino Soc. Christian Svc.; mgmt. specialist; cons. Sada Internat. Co., Riyadh, Saudi Arabia; lectr./rschr. in field; cons./moderator The Carmelite Ember. Contbr. articles to profl. jours.; author: The Study of Human Behavior: An Integrated Approach, 1994; editor The Technoscope, The Eagle. Founder/dir. TRACEASKI Prodn. (non-profit orgn.). Avocations: reading, photography, painting, singing, making short films.

SINISE, GARY, actor, director; b. 1955. co-founder, artistic dir. Steppenwolf Theatre, Chgo. Appeared in (plays) The Indian Wants The Bronx, 1977, Getting Out, 1980 (Joseph Jefferson award), Of Mice And Men, 1980, Loose Ends, 1982, True West, 1983 (also dir., Obie award best dir. 1982-83), Balm in Gilead, 1984, Streamers, 1985, The Caretaker, 1986, Grapes of Wrath, 1990 (Tony award and Drama Desk), (TV films) The Final Days, 1989, My Name is Bill W., 1989, The Stand, 1994; (dir. theatrical films) Miles from Home, 1988, Of Mice and Men, 1991 (also actor); (actor) Jack The Bear, 1991, A Midnight Clear, 1991, Forrest Gump, 1994, The Quick and the Dead, 1995, Apollo 13, 1995; various TV appearances including Crime Story (also dir.), Hunter, True West, Grapes of Wrath; dir. (plays) Frank's Wild Years, Action, The Miss Firecracker Contest, Waiting for the Parade, Tracers, Orphans, Landscape of the Body, 1984, (TV tapes) thirtysomething, 1989, China Beach, 1991. Office: care CAA 9830 Wilshire Blvd Beverly Hills CA 90212-1804 Office: Licker & Ozurovich 2029 Century Park E Ste 500 Los Angeles CA 90067-2906

SINK, JOHN DAVIS, leadership consultant, scientist; b. Homer City, Pa., Dec. 19, 1934; s. Aaron Tinsman and Louella Bell (Davis) S.; m. Nancy Lee Hile, Nov. 9, 1956 (dec. Aug. 1961); 1 child, Lou Ann. (dec.); m. Claire Kaye Huschka, June 13, 1964 (div. Feb. 1987); children: Kara Joan, Karl John; m. Sharon Ferrando Padden, July 15, 1989; 1 child, Lisa Michelle Padden. BS in Animal/Vet. Sci., Pa. State U., 1956, MS in Biophysics/Animal Sci., 1960, PhD in Biochemistry/Animal Sci., 1962; EdD in Higher Edn., U. Pitts., 1986. Administrv. officer, exec. asst. to asst. agr. State of Pa., Harrisburg, 1962; prof., group leader dept. food, dairy and animal sci. Inst. Policy Rsch. and Evaluation, Pa. State U., University Park, 1962-79; pres. Collegian, Inc., 1971-72; joint planning and evaluation staff officer Sci. and Edn. Adminstrn., U.S. Dept. Agr., Washington, 1979-80; prof., chmn. intercoll. program food sci. and nutrition, interdivisional program agrl. biochemistry and div. animal and vet. scis. W.Va. U., Morgantown, 1980-85; pres., CEO Pa. State U.-Uniontown, 1985-92; pres. Sink, Padden & Assocs., Atlanta, 1992—, pastor, Sardis United Methodist Church, 1995—; dir. S.W. Inst., Uniontown, 1989-92; gen. mgr. Cavert Wire Co., Inc., Atlanta, 1993-97; exec. asst., naval rep. to gov. and adj. gen. State W.Va., Charleston, 1981-84; cons. Allied Mills, Inc., Am. Air Lines, Am. Home Foods, Inc., Apollo Analytical Labs., Armour Food Co., Atlas Chem. Industries, others. Mem. nat. adv. bd. Am. Security Council, 1981—; mem. nat. adv. council Nat. Commn. Higher Edn. Issues, 1980-82; bd. dirs. W.Va. Cattleman's Assn., 1981-83, W.Va. Poultry Assn., 1980-83, Pembroke Welsh Corgi Club Am., 1980-83, Penn State Stockmen's Club, 1969-71, Greater Uniontown Indsl. Fund, 1986-91, Fayette County Econ. Devel. Council, 1985-93, Westmoreland-Fayette coun. Boy Scouts Am., 1986-91, Westmoreland-Fayette Hist. Soc., 1986-91, Fayette County Soil Conservation Dist., 1990-93, Pa. Youth Found., 1989-93, Fayette County Coop. Extension Bd., 1992-93, Pa. Masonic Found., 1993. Capt. USNR, 1956-86, ret. Decorated Army commendation medal; recipient Nat. Merit Trophy award Nat. Block and Bridle Club, 1956; W.Va. Disting. Achievement medal; Disting. Leadership award Am. Security Council Found., 1983. Pa. Meat Packers Assn. scholar, 1958-62; hon. fellow in biochemistry U. Wis., 1965-65; NSF postdoctoral fellow, 1964-65; Darbaker prize Pa. Acad. Sci., 1967. Fellow AAAS, Am. Inst. Chemists, Inst. Food Technologists; mem. Am. Meat Sci. Assn. (pres. 1974-75), Pa. Air N.G. Armory (trustee 1968-80), Pa. Acad. Sci., U.S. Naval Inst., Naval Res. Assn., Navy League U.S., Res. Officers Assn., Armed Forces Communications and Electronics Assn., Acad. Polit. Sci. (world affairs coun. Pitts. chpt.), Am. Assn. Higher Edn., Am. Assn. Univ. Adminstrs., Am. Chem. Soc., Biophys. Soc., Am. Soc. Animal Sci., Inst. Food Technologists, Soc. Rsch. Adminstrs., Am. Cancer Soc. (bd. dirs. 1988-91), Greater Uniontown C. of C. (bd. dirs. 1989-93), Greater Connellsville C. of C. (pres., bd. dirs. 1989-91), North Fayette C. of C. (bd. dirs. 1986-89), Mon Valley Tri-State Network, Inc. (chmn. bd. dirs. 1989-92), Rotary (sec. State Coll. 1969-71, Paul Harris fellow 1991), Elks, Internat. Assn. of Turtles, Consistory, Shriners, Masons, Alpha Zeta, Omicron Delta Kappa, Gamma Sigma Delta, Sigma Xi, Phi Lambda Upsilon, Gamma Alpha, Phi Tau Sigma, Phi Sigma, Phi Delta Kappa, Pi Sigma Phi. Democrat. Author: The Control of Metabolism, 1974, Citizen Extraordinarire, 1993; contbr. numerous articles to profl. pubs. Home: 2726 Phillips Dr Marietta GA 30064-4224 Office: 3725 Powers Ferry Rd NW Atlanta GA 30342-4422

SINKFORD, JEANNE CRAIG, dentist, educator; b. Washington, Jan. 30, 1933; d. Richard E. and Geneva (Jefferson) Craig; m. Stanley M. Sinkford, Dec. 8, 1951; children: Dianne Sylvia, Janet Lynn, Stanley M. III. BS, Howard U., 1953, MS, 1962, DDS, 1958, PhD, 1963; DSc (hon.), Georgetown U., 1978, U. Med. and Dentistry of N.J., 1992, Detroit Mercy U., 1996. Instr. prosthodontics Sch. Dentistry Howard U., Washington, 1958-60, mem. faculty dentistry, 1964—, rsch. coord., co-chmn. dept. restorative dentistry, assoc. dean, 1968-75, dean, 1975-91, prof. Prosthodontics Grad. Sch., 1977-91; dean emeritus, prof. Sch. Dentistry Howard U.; spl. asst. Am. Assn. Dental Schs., 1991-93, dir. office women and minority affairs, 1993—; instr. rsch. and crown and bridge Northwestern U. Sch. Dentistry, 1963-64; cons. prosthodontics and rsch. VA Hosp., Washington, 1965—; resident Children's Hosp. Nat. Med. Ctr., 1974-75; cons. St. Elizabeth's Hosp.; mem. attending staff Freedman's Hosp., Washington, 1964—; adv. bd. D.C. Gen. Hosp., 1975—; mem. Nat. Adv. Dental Rsch. Coun., Nat. Bd. Dental Examiners; mem. ad hoc adv. panel Tuskegee Syphilis Study for HEW; sponsor D.C. Pub. Health Apprentice Program; mem. adv. coun. to dir. NIH; adv. com. NIH/NIDR/NIA Aging Rsch. Coun.; mem. dental devices classification panel FDA; mem. select panel for promotion child health, 1979-80; mem. spl. med. adv. group VA; bd. overseers U. Pa. Dental Sch., Boston U. Dental Sch.; bd. advs. U. Pitts. Dental Sch.; mem. anat. rev. bd. for D.C. NRC Gov. Bd.; cons. Food and Drug Adminstrn.; Nat. Adv. Rsch. Coun., 1993—; active Nat. Rsch. Coun. Governing Bd. Mem. editorial rev. bd. Jour. Am. Coll. Dentists, 1988—. Adv. bd. United Negro Coll. Fund, Robert Wood Johnson Health Policy Fellowships; mem. Mayor's Block Grant Adv. Com., 1982; mem. parents' coun. Sidwell Friends, 1983; mem. adv. bd. D.C., mem. Women's Health Task Force, NIH; bd. dirs. Girl Scouts U.S.A., 1993—. Louise C. Ball fellow grad. tng., 1960-63. Fellow Am. Coll. Dentists (sec.-treas. Wash. met. sect.), Internat. Coll. Dentists (award of merit); mem. ADA (chmn. appeal bd. coun. on dental edn. 1975-82), Am. Soc. for Geriatric Dentistry (bd. dirs.), Internat. Assn. Dental Research, Dist. Dental Soc., Am. Inst. Oral Biology, North Portal Civic League, Inst. Grad. Dentists (trustee), So. Conf. Dental Deans (chmn.), Wash. Coun. Adminstrv. Women, Assn. Am. Women Dentists, Am. Pedodontic Soc., Am. Prosthodontic Soc., Fed. Prosthodontic Orgn., Nat. Dental Assn., Inst. Medicine (coun.), Am. Soc. Dentistry for Children, N.Y. Acad. Scis., Smithsonian Assocs., Dean's Coun., Proctor and Gamble, Golden Key Honor Soc., Links Inc., Sigma Xi (pres.), Phi Beta Kappa, Omicron Kappa Upsilon, Psi Chi, Beta Kappa Chi. Address: 1765 Verbena St NW Washington DC 20012-1048

SINKIN, FAY MARIE, environmentalist; b. N.Y.C., Mar. 24, 1918; d. Joseph E. and Amelia (Kronish) Bloom; m. William R. Sinkin, May 31, 1942; children: Richard, Lanny. BA, Syracuse U., 1938. Pres. LWV, San Antonio, 1947-51; pres., organizer Vis. Nurse Assn., San Antonio, 1952-54; pres. Brandeis U. Women's Com., San Antonio, 1954-56; recruiter, cons. U.S. State Dept. (A.I.D.), Washington, 1963-67; pres. Aquifer Protection Assn., San Antonio, 1974-80, Portrait of Am. Women, San Antonio, 1976-82; chair Bexar County/Edwards Underground Water Dist., San Antonio, 1983-89; chairwoman Edwards Aquifer Preservation Trust, San Antonio, 1990. Editor (pamphlet) Is Applewhite Necessary?, 1978. Named Woman of Yr. Express New Publ., 1964, Sunday Woman San Antonio Light, 1965, Mother of Yr. Avance, 1988; recipient WICI award Women in Comm., 1989, Spirit of Giving award J.C. Penney, 1993; elected to Women's Hall of Fame, San Antonio, 1985. Mem. San Antonio 100, Tex. Internat. Woman's Forum. Democrat. Jewish. Avocations: folk art museum, needlepoint, swimming, reading. Home: 7887 Broadway St Apt 706 San Antonio TX 78209-2537

SINKIS, DEBORAH MARY, principal; b. Worcester, Mass., May 13, 1949; d. Peter Paul and Joanne Mary (Dumphy) Shemeth; m. Ben J. Sinkis, June 8, 1969; 1 child, Russell John. BS in Elem. Edn., Worcester State Coll., 1970, MEd, 1977, cert. in curriculum, 1981; cert. in interactive tech., Harvard U., 1989; EdD in Ednl. Adminstrn., U. Mass., 1993. Tchr. Worcester Pub. Schs., 1971-83, computer assisted instr., 1983-86, tchr. trainer for computers, 1986, citywide computer coord., 1986-89; prin. Millbury St. Sch., Worcester, 1989-90, F.J. McGrath Sch., Worcester, 1990—; adj. prof. edn. Worcester State Coll., 1996—; cons. computer edn. Author curriculum materials. Mem. computer coop. regional adv. coun. Mass. Commn. for Deaf and Hard of Hearing, 1989-90; bd. dirs. Montachusett coun. Girl Scouts U.S., 1996—. Named Woman of Distinction, Montachusett coun. Girl Scouts U.S., 1994. Mem. ASCD, NEA, Mass. Tchrs. Assn., Internat. Soc. Tech. in Edn., Internat. Cath. Deaf Assn., Harvard/Radcliffe Club, Quota Internat. (pres.-elect Worcester chpt. 1995, pres. 1996, Deaf Woman of Yr. 1991), Phi Delta Kappa (Adminstr. of Yr. 1994). Office: Worcester Pub Schs 20 Irving St Worcester MA 01609-2432

SINKLAR, ROBERT, insurance company executive. Chmn., pres., CEO Minn. Mutual Life Ins. Co., St. Paul. Office: Minn Mutual Life Ins Co 400 Robert St N Saint Paul MN 55101-2015*

SINKO, CHRISTOPHER MICHAEL, pharmaceutical scientist; b. Englewood, N.J., July 19, 1962; s. Patsy John and Patricia Lou (Anderson) S.; m. Angela Carole Small, Aug. 5, 1984. BS in Chem. Engring., Rutgers U., 1984; MS in Pharmaceutics, U. Mich., 1986, DPhil in Pharmaceutics, 1989. Scientist The Upjohn Co., Kalamazoo, 1989-91; rsch. scientist Pfizer, Inc., Groton, Conn., 1991-93, sr. rsch. scientist, 1993-95, sr. rsch. investigator, 1995—; lectr. U. Mich. Coll. Pharmacy, Ann Arbor, 1990. Contbr. articles to profl. jours. Pharmaceutical Mfrs. Assn. fellow, 1987; recipient North Jersey Sect. Rsch. award AICE, 1984. Mem. Am. Assn. Pharm. Scientists. Achievements include identification and definition of physical aging mechanisms in glassy polymers, flow testing technique which is now routinely used to characterize the flowability of pharmaceutical formulations during product development. Office: Pfizer Ctrl Rsch Eastern Point Rd Groton CT 06340

SINNETTE, JOHN TOWNSEND, JR., research scientist, consultant; b. Rome, Ga., Nov. 4, 1909; s. John T. Sinnette and Katherine Alice Lyon. BS, Calif. Inst. Tech., 1931, MS, 1933. Chemist Met. Water Dist., Banning, Calif., 1935-37, Boulder City, Nev., 1937-38; physicist U.S. Bur. Reclamation, Boulder City, 1938-41; rsch. scientist Nat. Adv. Com. for Aeronautics, Langley Field, Va., 1941-43, Cleve., 1943-51; cons. physicist U.S. Naval Ordnance Test Sta., Pasadena, Calif., 1951-58, Cleve. Pneumatic Industries, El Segundo, Calif., 1958-60; tech. dir. Hydrosystems Co., El Segundo, 1960-62; physicist Thrust Systems Corp., Costa Mesa, Calif., 1963-64; lectr. compressor design Case Inst. Tech., 1946-48; cons. many firms in aeronautical and related industries, 1950-79. Contbr. papers to sci. meetings and confs. Vol. Am. Cancer Soc., Costa Mesa, Calif., 1976-80, Cancer Control Soc., 1979-82; contbr. Action on Smoking and Health, Washington, 1985-96. Mem. AAAS, Am. Statis. Assn., Am. Math. Soc., Nat. Health Fed., N.Y. Acad. Sci., Common Cause, Sierra Club. Democrat. Achievements include patent dealing with a novel jet engine design (U.S., Britain); made first detailed measurement of silt flow (density currents) in Lake Mead and the deposition of the silt behind Boulder Dam, 1940; detailed rsch. on first government multi-stage axial-flow compressor suitable for jet engines; orginated and proved possibilities of extending useful operating range of axial-flow compressors by use of adjustable stator blades; used aerodynamic theory to design high-performance centrifugal compressors; development of statistical theory and demonstrated its usefulness in predicting the distribution of primes and factors of Fermat and related numbers. Home: 135 N B St Tustin CA 92780-3110

SINNING, MARK ALAN, thoracic and vascular surgeon; b. Holton, Kans., Apr. 24, 1953; s. Henry Harold andf Valere Madelene (Davey) S.; m. Kathy Diann Pugh, Sept. 25, 1982; children: Sarah, Emily, Mark, Rachel, Walter. BA, U. Kans., 1975; MD, U. Kans., Kansas City, 1978. Diplomate Am. Bd. Surgery, Am. Bd. Thoracic Surgery. Gen. surgery resident St. Luke's Hosp., Kansas City, Mo., 1978-83, thoracic surgery resident, 1983-85; pvt. practice Coastal Surg. Specialists, PA, New Bern, N.C., 1986—; attending staff Danbury (Conn.) Hosp., 1985-86, Craven Regional Med. Ctr., New Bern, 1986—; asst. clin. prof. East Carolina U., Greenville, 1992—. Fellow ACS, Am. Coll. Chest Physicians; mem. AMA, Soc. Thoracic Surgeons, So. Assn. Thoracic Surgery, N.C. Med. Soc., Phi Beta Kappa, Alpha Omega Alpha. Avocations: golf, snow skiing, music. Office: Coastal Surgical Specialists 800 Hospital Dr New Bern NC 28560-3452

SINNINGER, DWIGHT VIRGIL, engineer; b. Bourbon, Ind., Dec. 29, 1901; s. Norman E. and Myra (Huff) S.; student Armour Inst., 1928, U. Chgo., 1942, Northwestern U., 1943; m. Coyla Annetta Annis, Mar. 1, 1929; m. Charlotte M. Lenz, Jan. 21, 1983. Registered profl. engr., Ill. Electronics rsch. engr. Johnson Labs., Chgo., 1935-42; chief engr. Pathfinder Radio Corp., 1943-44, Rowe Engring. Corp., 1945-48, Hupp Electronics Co. div. Hupp Corp., 1948-61; dir. rsch. Pioneer Electric & Research Corp., Forest Park, Ill., 1961-65, Senn Custom, Inc., Forest Park and San Antonio, 1967—. Patentee in field. Mem. IEEE. Address: PO Box 982 Kerrville TX 78029-0982

SINNOTT, JOHN PATRICK, lawyer, educator; b. Bklyn., Aug. 17, 1931; s. John Patrick and Elizabeth Muriel (Zinkand) S.; m. Rose Marie Yuppa, May 30, 1959; children: James Alexander, Jessica Michelle. BS, U.S. Naval Acad., 1953; MS, U.S. Air Force Inst. Tech., 1956; JD, No. Ky. U., 1960. Bar: Ohio 1961, N.Y. 1963, U.S. Patent Office 1963, N.J. 1970, U.S. Supreme Ct. 1977. Assoc. Brumbaugh, Graves, Donohue & Raymond, N.Y.C., 1961-63; patent atty. Bell Tel. Labs., Murray Hill, N.J., 1963-64; patent atty. Schlumberger Ltd., N.Y.C., 1964-71; asst. chief patent counsel Babcock & Wilcox, N.Y.C., 1971-79; chief patent and trademark counsel Am. Standard Inc., N.Y.C., 1979-92; of counsel Morgan & Finnegan, N.Y.C., 1992—; adj. lectr. N.J. Inst. Tech., Newark, 1974-89; adj. prof. Seton Hall U. Sch. Law, Newark, 1989—. Author: World Patent Law and Practice, Vols. 2-20, 1993; A Practical Guide to Document Authentication, 6th edit. 1996, Counterfeit Goods Suppression, 1993; contbr. articles to profl. jours. Bd. dirs. New Providence Cmty. Swimming Pool (N.J.), 1970; mem. local Selective Svc. Bd., Plainfield, N.J., 1971. Capt. USAF, 1953-61, col. AUS (ret.), 1991. Decorated Legion of Merit. Mem. Am. Arbitration Assn. (arbitrator, WIPO Arbitration and Mediation Ctr.), N.Y. Patent Law Assn. (bd. dirs. 1974-82), N.J. Patent Law Assn. (com. chmn. 1981-82), Squadron A Club, Cosmos. Republican. Roman Catholic. Home: Two Blackburn Pl Summit NJ 07901 Office: Morgan & Finnegan LLP 345 Park Ave New York NY 10154-0004

SINNOTT, JOHN THOMAS, internist, educator; b. Reading, Pa., May 16, 1948; s. John Thomas and Josephine (Mallon) S.; m. Barbara Ballentine, May 30, 1970. BA, Columbus (Ga.) Coll., 1971; MA, U. South Fla., 1973; MD, U. South Ala., 1978. Diplomate Am. Bd. Internal Medicine, Am. Bd. Infectious Diseases. Internal medicine resident U. South Fla., Tampa, 1978-81, infectious disease resident, 1981-83, prof. and dir. infectious diseases Coll. medicine, 1991—, assoc. prof., 1987-92, asst. prof., 1983-87; vice chief of staff Tampa Gen. Healthcare, 1992-94, chief of staff, 1994-96, dir. epidemiology, 1985—; dir. S.W. Fla. Tissue Bank, 1987—. Editor jour. Infections in Medicine, 1994—. Fellow ACP, Infectious Disease Soc. Am. Avocation: fishing. Home: 9666 Oak St NE Saint Petersburg FL 33702 Office: Tampa Gen Hosp Infectious Disease Dept Tampa FL 33601-1289

SINOR, DENIS, Orientalist, educator; b. Kolozsvar, Hungary, Apr. 17, 1916; s. Miklos and Marguerite (Weitzenfeld) S.; m. Eugenia Trinajstic; children: Christophe (dec.), Sophie. BA, U. Budapest, 1938; MA, Cambridge (Eng.) U., 1948; doctorate (hon.), U. Szeged, Hungary, 1971. Attache Centre National de la Recherche Scientifique, Paris, 1939-48; univ. lectr. Altaic studies Cambridge U., 1948-62; prof. Uralic and Altaic studies and history Ind. U., Bloomington, 1962-81, disting. prof. Uralic and Altaic studies and history, 1975-86, disting. prof. emeritus Uralic and Altaic studies and history, 1986—, chmn. dept. Uralic and Altaic studies, 1963-1981, dir. Lang. and Area Ctr., 1963-88, dir. Asian studies program, 1965-67, dir. Asian Studies Rsch. Inst., 1967-79, dir. Rsch. Inst. for Inner Asian Studies, 1979-1981, 85-86; Sec. gen. Permanent Internat. Altaistic Conf., 1960—; rsch. project dir. U.S. Office Edn., 1969-70; sec. Internat. Union Orientalists, 1954-64; vis. prof. Institut Nat. des Langues et Civilizations Orientales, Paris, spring 1974; scholar-in-residence Rockefeller Found. Study Ctr., Bellagio, 1975; vice chmn. UNESCO Commn. for History Civilization Cen. Asia, 1981—, mem. consultative com. UNESCO Silk Rd. Project, 1990—; summer seminar dir. NEH, 1988. Author: Orientalism and History, 1954, History of Hungary, 1959, Introduction a l'étude de l'Eurasie Centrale, 1963, Aspects of Altaic Civilization, 1963, Inner Asia, 1968, Inner Asia and Its Contacts with Medieval Europe, 1977, Tanulmányok, 1982, Essays in Comparative Altaic Linguistics, 1990; editor, contbr.: Modern Hungary, 1977, Studies in Finno-Ugric Linguistics, 1977, Uralic Languages, 1988, Essays on Uzbek History, Culture and Languages, 1993, Cambridge History of Early Inner Asia, Hanbook of Uralic Studies, Jour. Asian History, Ind. U. Uralic and Altaic Series; mem. Am. editl. rev. bd. Britannica-Hungarica. Served with Forces Françaises de l'Intérieur, 1943-44; with French Army, 1944-45. NEH grantee, 1981, 87, 88; recipient Jubilee prize U. Budapest, 1938, Barczi Geza Meml. medal, 1981, Gold medal Permanent Internat. Altaistic Conf., 1982, 1996, Arminius Vambery Meml. medal, 1983, The Thomas Hart Benton Mural Medallion, Hungarian Order of Star, 1986; Am. Philos. Soc. Research grantee, 1963; Am. Council Learned Soc. research grantee, 1962; Guggenheim fellow, 1968-69, 1981-82. Fellow Körösi Csoma Soc. (hon.); mem. Royal Asiatic Soc. (hon. sec. 1954-64, Denis Sinor medal for Inner Asian Studies named in his honor 1992), Am. Oriental Soc. (pres. Midwest br. 1968-70, nat. pres. 1975-76), Assn. Asian Studies, Am. Hist. Soc., Soc. Asiatique (hon.), Tibet Soc. (pres. 1969-74), Mongolia Soc. (pres. 1987-94), Hungarian Acad. Scis. (hon.), Acad. Europaea (fgn.), Deutsche Morgenlandische Gesellschaft, Suomalais-Ugrilaisen Seura (hon. corr.), Soc. Uralo-Altaica (v.p. 1964-94, hon.), Internat. Union Oriental and Asian Studies (v.p. 1993—), Cosmos Club Washington, Explorers Club N.Y.C., United Oxford and Cambridge Club London, Correspondant de l'Académie des inscriptions et belles lettres (Paris). Home: 5581 E Lampkins Ridge Rd Bloomington IN 47401-8674 Office: Indiana U Dept Ctrl Eurasian Studies Goodbody Hall Bloomington IN 47405

SINOR, HOWARD EARL, JR., lawyer; b. New Orleans, Sept. 6, 1949; s. Howard E. and Beverly M. (Bourgeois) S.; m. Terran Ann Woodward, June 10, 1972; children: Sally, Vera Sue, Sarah, Sadie. BA with hons., U. New Orleans, 1971; JD cum laude, Harvard U., 1975. Bar: La. 1975, U.S. Supreme Ct. 1983, U.S. Ct. Appeals (5th and 11th cir.), U.S. Dist. Ct. (ea., middle, we.) Dist. La. Assoc. Jones, Walker, Waechter, Poitevent, Carrere & Denegre, New Orleans, 1975-80; sr. ptnr. Jones, Walker, Waechter, Poitevent, Carrere & Denegre, 1980—. Contbg. author: La. Appellate Practice Handbook, 1990, 93; editor: CLE Manual of Recent Developments, 1985, 2d edit., 1986; contbr. articles to profl. jours. Recipient Pres.'s award, La. State Bar Assn., 1987. Fellow La. Bar Found.; mem. ABA, Fed. Bar Assn., New Orleans Bar Assn., La. State Bar Assn. (chmn. antitrust sect. 1987-89). Avocations: golf, hiking, cross-country skiing. Office: Jones Walker Waechter Poitevent Carrere & Denegre 201 Saint Charles Ave New Orleans LA 70170-1000

SINSHEIMER, ROBERT LOUIS, retired university chancellor and educator; b. Washington, Feb. 5, 1920; s. Allen S. and Rose (Davidson) S.; m. Flora Joan Hirsch, Aug. 8, 1943 (div. 1972); children: Lois June (Mrs. Wickstrom), Kathy Jean (Mrs. Vandagriff), Roger Allen; m. Kathleen Mae Reynolds, Sept. 10, 1972 (div. 1980); m. Karen Current, Aug. 1, 1981. S.B., MIT, 1941, M.S., 1942, Ph.D., 1948. Staff mem. radiation lab. MIT, Cambridge, 1942-46; assoc. prof. biophysics, physics dept. Iowa State Coll., Ames, 1949-55; prof. Iowa State Coll., 1955-57; prof. biophysics Calif. Inst. Tech., Pasadena, 1957-77; chmn. div. biology Calif. Inst. Tech., 1968-77; chancellor U. Calif., Santa Cruz, 1977-87, chancellor emeritus, 1987—; prof. U. Calif., Santa Barbara, 1988-90, prof. emeritus, 1990—. Editor: Jour. Molecular Biology, 1959-67, Ann. Rev. Biochemistry, 1966-72. Named Calif. Scientist of Year, 1968; recipient N.W. Beijerinck-Virologie medal Netherlands Acad. Sci., 1969. Fellow Am. Acad. Arts and Scis.; mem. Am. Soc. Biol. Chemists, Biophys. soc. (pres. 1970), AAAS, Nat. Acad. Scis. (mem. council 1970-73, chmn. bd. editors Proc. 1972-80), Inst. Medicine. Achievements include discovery of single-stranded DNA, circular DNA; co-investigator in first in vitro replication of infective DNA. Office: Univ of Calif Dept Biol Sci Santa Barbara CA 93106

SINSHEIMER, WARREN JACK, lawyer; b. N.Y.C., May 22, 1927; s. Jerome William and Elizabeth (Berch) S.; m. Florence Dubin, Mar. 30, 1950; children: Linda Ruth, Ralph David, Alan Jay, Michael Neal. Student, Ind. U., 1943-47; JD cum laude, N.Y. Law Sch., 1950; LLM, NYU, 1957; MPhil, Columbia U., 1977. Bar: N.Y. bar 1950. Ptnr. Sinsheimer, Sinsheimer & Dubin, N.Y.C., 1950-78, Satterlee & Stephens, N.Y.C., 1978-86, Patterson, Belknap, Webb & Tyler, N.Y.C., 1986-91; counsel Patterson Belknap Webb & Tyler, N.Y.C., 1991-96; pres., bd. dirs. Neighborhood Bagel Corp., 1994—; pres. Plessey, Inc., N.Y.C., 1956-70, chmn., CEO, 1970-89; dir. oversees ops. and devel. The Plessey Co., Ltd., Illford, Essex, Eng., 1969-70, dep. chief exec., dir., 1976-89; dir. Plessey, Inc.; pres., chief exec. dir. The Neighborhood Bagel Corp.; trustee NYU Sch. Law, 1996—. Chmn. Com. of 68, 1964-67; Mem Westchester County Republican Com., 1956-73; chmn. Nat. Scranton for Pres. Com., 1964; mem. N.Y. State Assembly, 1965-66; Bd. visitors Wassaic State Sch., 1962-64; trustee Sch. Law, NYU, 1996—, bd. dirs. Shalom Hartman Inst., Jerusalem, 1991—, treas., 1996—. Served with USNR, 1944-45; with USAF, 1950-52. Mem. ABA, Assn. Bar City N.Y., Am. Digital Radio Soc. (pres. 1994), Torch and Scroll, Century Club (Purchase, N.Y., gov., treas. 1997—), Zeta Beta Tau. Jewish. Home: 22 Murray Hill Rd Scarsdale NY 10583-2828 Office: Westchester/Putnam Legal Svcs 4 Cromwell Pl White Plains NY 10601-5006

SINTROS, JAMES LEE, management consultant, arbitrator; b. Lowell, Mass., May 20, 1947; s. Constantine James and Martha Lou (Sawyer) S.; m. Effegenia Liakos, June 27, 1971 (div. Feb. 1993); 1 child, Sarah Gillian; m. Barbara Anne Kendall, Dec. 26, 1993; 1 child, Nathaniel David. BS, U. Mass., Lowell, 1970; JD, Suffolk U., 1974. Cert. registered arbitrator. Cons., Andover, Mass., 1974—; sr. cons. Cassidy & Assocs., Washington, 1985-95; clk. West of Ireland Edn. Fund, Inc., N.Y.C. and Galway, Ireland, 1990-96; dir. Mass. Ctr. for S.I.D.S., 1989—; clk., dir. S.I.D.S. Outreach Found., Inc., Mass., 1991—; exec. dir. Internat. Ednl. and Med. Alliance New Eng., Inc., Mass., 1989-96; exec. dir., treas. Joseph W. Stilwell Inst. Found., Ltd., Chongqing, China, 1989—; v.p., dir. G.T.N.Y. Found., Inc., N.Y.C., 1991-95; pres., treas., clk., bd. dirs. Global Brokers Internat. Ltd., Dublin, Ireland, 1993—; pres., treas., bd. dirs. Multinat. Bus. Devel. Coalition, Ltd., Hong Kong, 1990—; internat. cons. Suffolk U., Boston, 1992—; spl. asst. to pres. New Eng. Coll. Optometry, Boston, 1992-96; automobile racer in U.S. and abroad, 1965-82; dir. Phoenix Water Sys., Spokane, 1996—. Bd. dirs., vice chair Young Audiences of Mass., 1979-82; bd. dirs. Boston Classical Orch., 1985-89, Critical Langs. and Area Studies Consortium, 1990-93; corporator Merrimack Valley Cmty. Found., Inc.; treas. Am.-Ireland Ednl. Found., N.Y.C., Dublin, Ireland, 1995—. Mem. Am. Registry Arbitrators. Home: Brickend Farm 134 Boston Rd Chelmsford MA 01824-3965 Office: 93 Main St Andover MA 01810-3840

SINTZ, EDWARD FRANCIS, librarian; b. New Trenton, Ind., Feb. 6, 1924; s. John and Edith E. (Rudicil) S.; m. Donna Norris, Apr. 12, 1952; children—Ann Kristin, Lesley Elizabeth, Julie Melinda. B.A., U. Kans., 1950; M.A. in L.S, U. Denver, 1954; M.S. in Pub. Adminstrn, U. Mo., 1965. With Kansas City (Mo.) Pub. Library, 1954-66, asst. dir., 1964-66; asso. librarian St. Louis Pub. Library, 1966-68; dir. pub. libraries Miami, Fla., 1968-89, ret.; instr. Washington U., St. Louis, 1966-67; library surveys for Mo. State Library, 1967-68; library bldg. cons., 1965—. Editor: Mo. Library Assn. Quar, 1956-58. Served with USAAF, 1942-45. Mem. ALA, Fla. Library Assn. (pres. 1975-76), Southeastern Library Assn. Club: Kiwanian. Home: 7105 Lakeside Dr Charlotte NC 28215

SION, MAURICE, mathematics educator; b. Skopje, Yugoslavia, Oct. 17, 1928; came to Can., 1960; s. Max and Sarah (Alalouf) S.; m. Emilie Grace Chisholm, Sept. 15, 1957; children—Crispin, Sarah, Dirk. B.A., NYU, 1947, M.A., 1948; Ph.D., U. Calif.-Berkeley, 1951. Mathematician Nat. Bur. Standards, Washington, 1951-52; instr. U. Calif.-Berkeley, 1952-53; mem. Inst. for Advanced Study, Princeton, N.J., 1955-57, 62; asst. prof. U. Calif.-Berkeley, 1957-60; asst. prof. U. B.C., Vancouver, 1960, assoc. prof., 1961, prof., 1964-89, head math. dept., 1984-86; dir. Quadra Inst. Math., Vancouver, 1970-89, prof. emeritus, 1989—. Author: Introduction to Methods of Real Analysis, 1969; Theory Semi Group Valued Measures, 1973. Contbr. articles to profl. jours. Served with U.S. Army, 1953-55. Mem. Am. Math. Soc., Can. Math. Soc. (v.p. 1972-74). Office: U BC, Dept Math, Vancouver, BC Canada V6T 1Z2

SIOUI, RICHARD HENRY, chemical engineer; b. Bklyn., Sept. 25, 1937; s. Joseph Fernand and Ellen Annette (Johnson) S.; m. Mary Ann Kapinos, July 21, 1962; children: Kathleen, Thomas, Daniel, Rebecca, Linda, Michelle. BS, Northeastern U., 1964; PhD, U. Mass., 1968. Sr. rsch. engr. Norton Co., Superabrasives div., Worcester, Mass., 1968-71, rsch. supr., 1971-78, tech. mgr., 1978-83, rsch. dir., 1983-87, dir. of tech., 1987—. Com. chmn. Boy Scouts Am. Troop 178, Holden, Mass., 1981-86. With USAF, 1955-59. Recipient Outstanding Engring. Alumnus award U. Mass., 1995. Mem. AIChE, Am. Indian Sci. and Engring. Sci., Diamond Wheel Mfrs. Inst. (stds, safety and health com.). Achievements include patents relative to the manufacture and composition of abrasive products in which diamond or cubic boron nitride is the abrasive. Home: 22 Streeter Rd Hubbardston MA 01452-1433 Office: Norton Co 1 New Bond St Worcester MA 01606-2614

SIPER, CYNTHIA DAWN, special education educator; b. Bklyn., Apr. 16, 1965; d. Joel S. and Diana M. (Kessler) Rosenblatt; m. Alan Siper, Apr. 9, 1989; children: Rebecca Ruth, Daniel Louis. BS in Edn., SUNY, Plattsburgh, 1988; MEd, SUNY, New Paltz, 1992. Cert. K-12 spl. edn. tchr., N-6 elem. edn. tchr., N.Y. Tchr. spl. edn. Valley Cen. Sch. Dist., Montgomery, N.Y., 1988-90, Middletown (N.Y.) Enlarged City Sch. Dist., 1990—; spl. edn. tchr. rep. Coun. on Spl. Edn., Middletown, 1990—. Mem. Coun. for Exceptional Children, Middletown Tchrs. Assn., Kappa Delta Pi. Avocation: collecting Disneyana.

SIPES, JAMES LAMOYNE, landscape architect, educator; b. Elizabethtown, Ky., Jan. 28, 1957; s. William L. and Betty Jean (Miller) S.; m. Kimberly A. Blevins, Feb. 5, 1983; children: Matthew, Sara, Ally. BS in Landscape Architecture, U. Ky., 1982; M in Landscape Architecture, Iowa State U., 1984. Registered landscape architect, Tex. Teaching asst. U. Ky., Lexington, 1981-82; planning intern Lexington-Fayette Govt., 1982-83; teaching asst. Iowa State U., Ames, 1983-84; landscape architect Nat. Park Svc., Gunnison, Colo., 1984-85, Schrickel, Rollins Assocs., Arlington, Tex., 1985-88, U.S. Forest Svc., Dillon, Mont., 1989; computer graphic cons. Video Perspectives, Inc., Louisville, 1990; lectr. U. Idaho, Moscow, 1989-93; assoc. prof. landscape architecture Wash. State U., Pullman, 1988-94; dir. U. Okla., Norman, 1995—; cons. Computer Graphics and Simulations, Salt Lake City, 1993-94; mem. adv. bd. Cmty. Childcare Ctr., Pullman, 1992—. Computer editor Landscape Architecture Mag., Washington, 1994—; producer Animated World, PBS, 1994—; contbr. articles to profl. jours. Mem. Pullman Civic Trust, 1993-94. Recipient Cert. of Appreciation, Soil Conservation Svc., 1992, Cert. of Appreciation, U.S. Forest Svc., 1990. Mem. Am. Soc. Landscape Architects (Honor award 1984, 94, Tex. Design award 1992), Coun. Educators in Landscape Architecture, Nat. Computer Graphics Assn., Pacific N.W. Recreation Consortium, Gamma Sigma Delta, Phi Kappa Phi. Avocations: sports, art, reading, technology. Office: U Okla Landscape Architecture Dept Landscape Architecture Norman OK 73019

SIPES, KAREN KAY, newspaper editor; b. Higginsville, Mo., Jan. 8, 1947; d. Walter John and Katherine Marie (McLelland) Heins; m. Joel Rodney Sipes, Sept. 24, 1971; 1 child, Lesley Katherine. BS in Edn., Ctrl. Mo. State U., 1970. Reporter/news editor Newton Kansan, 1973-76; sports writer Capital-Jour., Topeka, 1976-83, spl. sects. editor, 1983-85, editl. page editor, 1985-92, mng. editor/features, 1992—. Co-chair Mayor's Commn. on Literacy, Topeka, 1995-96; mem. Act Against Violence Com., Topeka, 1995-96; mem. planning com. Leadership Greater Topeka, 1997. Mem. Ctrl. Mo. State U. Alumni Assn. (bd. dirs. 1996—). Avocations: music, gardening, art. Office: The Capital-Journal 616 SE Jefferson St Topeka KS 66607-1137

SIPFLE, DAVID ARTHUR, philosophy educator; b. Pekin, Ill., Aug. 29, 1932; s. Karl Edward and Louis Adele (Hinners) S.; m. Mary-Alice Slauson, Sept. 4, 1954; children: Ann Littlefield (dec.), Gail Elizabeth. BA in Math., Philosophy magna cum laude, Carleton Coll., 1953; MA, Yale U., 1955, PhD, 1958. Instr. philosophy Robert Coll., Istanbul, Turkey, 1957-58, Am. Coll. for Girls, Istanbul, 1957-60; asst. prof. Carleton Coll., Northfield, Minn., 1960-67, assoc. prof., 1967-70, chmn. dept., 1968-71, 89-92, prof., 1970-92, William H. Laird prof. philosophy and liberal arts, 1992—; vis. fellow Wolfson Coll., Cambridge U., 1975-76. Translator: (with Mary-Alice Sipfle) Emile Meyerson, The Relativistic Deduction: Epistemological Implications of the Theory of Relativity, 1985, Explanation in the Sciences, 1991; contbr. articles to profl. jours. NEH Younger Humanist fellow, Nice, France, 1971-72, NSF Sci. Faculty fellow, Cambridge, Eng., 1975-76; Carleton Coll. Faculty Devel. grantee, 1981-83, 86-87. Mem. Am. Philos. Assn., Metaphysical Soc. Am., Philosophy of Sci. Assn. Avocation: cross country skiing. Office: Carleton Coll 1 N College St Northfield MN 55057-4001

SIPIORA, LEONARD PAUL, retired museum director; b. Lawrence, Mass., Sept. 1, 1934; s. Walter and Agnes S.; m. Sandra Joyce Coon, 1962; children—Alexandra, Erika. A.B. cum laude, U. Mich., 1955, M.A., 1956. Dir. museums City of El Paso, Tex., 1967-90; ret.; co-founder, pres. El Paso Arts Council, 1969-71; sec.-treas. El Paso Council Internat. Visitors, 1968-71; trustee El Paso Mus. Art; bd. dirs. Tex. Com. Humanities, Assn. Southwestern Humanities Council; adv. bd. S.W. Arts Found. Bd. dirs. Community Concert Assn. El Paso, El Paso Symphony Orch., El Paso Hist. Soc. Mem. Assn. Mus. Dirs., Mountain Plains Mus. Assn. (pres. 1978-79), Tex. Assn. Museums (pres. 1977-79), Knights of Malfa (decorated Grand Cross), Prior of Tex., Kappa Pi. Republican. Lutheran. Home: 1012 Blanchard Ave El Paso TX 79902-2727

SIPPEL, WILLIAM LEROY, lawyer; b. Fond du Lac, Wis., Aug. 14, 1948; s. Alfonse Aloysious and Virginia Laura (Weber) S.; m. Barbara Jean Brost, Aug. 23, 1970; children: Katharine Jean, David William. BA, U. Wis., JD. Bar: Wis. 1974, U.S. Dist. Ct. (we. dist.) Wis. 1974, Minn. 1981, U.S. Dist. Ct. Minn. 1981, U.S. Ct. Appeals (10th cir.) 1984, U.S. Ct. Appeals (8th cir.) 1985. Research assoc. dept. agrl. econs. U. Wis., Madison, 1974-75; counsel monopolies and comml. law subcom. Ho. Judiciary Com., Washington, 1975-80; spl. asst. to asst. gen. antitrust div. U.S. Dept. of Justice, Washington, 1980-81; from assoc. to ptnr. Doherty, Rumble & Butler, Mpls. and St. Paul, Minn., 1981—; bd. dirs. World Trade Week. Co-author: The Antitrust Health Care Handbook, 1988. Mem. program com. Minn. World Trade Assn., Mpls., St. Paul, 1985-86, bd. dirs., 1986, Minn. With USAR, 1971-77. Mem. ABA (vice chmn. ins. industry com. 1990-91), Minn. Bar Assn. (co-chmn. antitrust sect. 1986-88, internat. law sect. coun. 1986-89, treas. 1989-90, sec. 1990-91, vice chmn. 1995-96, chmn. 1996-97), Minn. Med. Alley Assn. (co-chmn. internat. bus. com. 1990-95, Hennepin County Office Internat. Trade (bd. dirs. 1988-93), Phi Beta Kappa. Roman Catholic. Avocations: computers, reading. Home: 2151 Commonwealth Ave Saint Paul MN 55108 Office: Doherty Rumble & Butler PA 2800 Minnesota World Trade Ctr Saint Paul MN 55101

SIQUELAND, EINAR, psychology educator; b. Glasgow, Mont., Nov. 15, 1932; s. Harald and Anna Lydia (Kristensen) S.; m. Marian McGrail, Dec. 1960 (div. May 1970); children: Lynne Ruth, Beth Ann; m. Jillian E.A. Godfree, June 29, 1973. BA, Pacific Luth. U., 1954; MS, U. Wash., 1962, PhD, 1963. Rsch. assoc. pharmacology U. Wash., Seattle, 1958-59; clin. intern psychology VA Mental Hygiene Clinic, Seattle, 1960-61; asst. prof. dept. psychology Brown U., Providence, 1965-69, assoc. prof., 1969-88, prof., 1988—; rsch. scientist dept. Pediatrics Women's and Infants' Hosp., Providence, 1975—. Contbr. articles to profl. jours., chpts. to books. With U.S. Army, 1956-58, Korea. Predoctoral fellow USPHS, 1961-63, postdoctoral fellow, 1963-65. Mem. AAUP, APA, Am. Psychol. Soc., Soc. Rsch. in Child Devel., Sigma Xi. Office: Brown U Dept Psychology PO Box 1853 Providence RI 02912-1853

SIRI, WILLIAM E., physicist; b. Phila., Jan. 2, 1919; s. Emil Mark and Caroline (Schaedel) S.; m. Margaret Jean Brandenburg, Dec. 3, 1949; children: Margaret Lynn, Ann Kathryn. B.Sc., U. Chgo., 1942; postgrad. in physics, U. Calif.-Berkeley, 1947-50. Licensed profl. engr., Calif. Research engr. Baldwin-Lima-Hamilton Corp., 1943; physicist Manhattan Project Lawrence-Berkeley Lab., U. Calif., Berkeley, 1943-45, prin. investigator biophysics and research, 1945-74, mgr. energy analysis program, 1974-81, sr. scientist emeritus, 1981—; cons. energy and environment, 1982—; lectr. U. Calif. Summer Inst., 1962-72; vis. scientist Nat. Cancer Inst., 1970; exec. v.p. Am. Mt. Everest Expdn., Inc.; field leader U. Calif. Peruvian Expdns., 1950-52; leader Calif. Himalayan Expdn., 1954; field leader Internat. Physiol. Expdn. to Antarctica, 1957; dep. leader Am. Mt. Everest Expdn., 1963. Author: Nuclear Radiations and Isotopic Tracers, 1949, papers on energy systems analyses, biophys. research, conservation and mountaineering. Pres. Save San Francisco Bay Assn., 1968-88; bd. dirs. Sierra Club Found., 1964-78; gov. gen. Mountain Medicine Inst., 1988—; vice chmn. The Bay Inst., 1985—; bd. dirs. San Francisco Bay-Delta Preservation Assn., 1987-90. Lt. (j.g.) USNR, 1950-59. Co-recipient Hubbard medal Nat. Geog. Soc., 1963, Elsa Kent Kane medal Phila. Geog. Soc., 1963, Sol Feinstone Environ. award, 1977, Environ. award East Bay Regional Park Dist., 1984. Mem. Am. Phys. Soc., Biophys. Soc., Am. Assn. Physicists in Medicine, Sigma Xi. Democrat. Lutheran. Clubs: Sierra (dir. 1955-74, pres. 1964-66, William Colby award 1975, John Muir award 1994), American Alpine (v.p.), Explorers (certificate of merit 1964). Home: 1015 Leneve Pl El Cerrito CA 94530-2751

SIRICA, ALPHONSE EUGENE, pathology educator; b. Waterbury, Conn., Jan. 16, 1944; s. Alphonse Eugene and Elena Virginia (Mascolo) S.; m. Annette Marie Murray, June 9, 1984; children: Gabrielle Theresa, Nicholas Steven. MS, Fordham U., 1968; PhD in Biomed. Sci., U. Conn., 1977. Asst. prof. U. Wis., Madison, 1979-84; assoc. prof. Med. Coll. Va., Va. Commonwealth U., Richmond, 1984-90, prof. of pathology, 1990—, divsn. chair exptl. pathology, 1992—; regular mem. sci. adv. com. on carcinogenesis and nutrition Am. Cancer Soc., Atlanta, 1989-92, metabolic pathology study sect., NIH, Bethesda, 1991-95. Editor, author: The Pathobiology of Neoplasia, 1989, The Role of Cell Types in Hepatocarcinogenesis, 1992, Cellular and Molecular Pathogenesis, 1996; co-editor, author: Biliary and Pancreatic Ductal Epithelia: Pathobiology and Pathophysiology, 1997; mem. editl. bd. Pathobiology, 1990—, Hepatology, 1991-94; rev. bd. In Vitro Cellular and Devel. Biology, 1987—; contbr. rsch. papers to Am. Jour. Pathology, Cancer Rsch., others. Mem. AAAS, Am. Soc. Cell Biology, Am. Assn. Cancer Rsch. (chmn. Va. state legis. com. 1992-95), Soc. for In Vitro Biology, Assn.Clin. Scientist, Am. Soc. Investigative Pathology (chair program com. 1994-96), Am. Assn. Study Liver Diseases, N.Y. Acad. Scis., Soc. Exptl. Biology and Medicine, Hans Popper Hepatopathology Soc., Soc. Toxicology. Democrat. Roman Catholic. Achievements include development of collagen gel-nylon mesh system for culturing hepatocytes; first establishment and characterization of hyperplastic bile ductular epithelial cells in culture; research in hepato and biliary carcinogenesis, pathobiology of hepatocyte and biliary epithelial cells. Office: Med Coll Va Va Commonwealth U PO Box 980297 Richmond VA 23298-0297

SIRIGNANO, WILLIAM ALFONSO, aerospace and mechanical engineer, educator; b. Bronx, N.Y., Apr. 14, 1938; s. Anthony P. and Lucy (Caruso) S.; m. Lynn Haisfield, Nov. 26, 1977; children: Monica Ann, Jacqueline Hope, Justin Anthony. B.Aero.Engring., Rensselaer Poly. Inst., 1959; Ph.D., Princeton U., 1964. Mem. research staff Guggenheim Labs., aerospace, mech. scis. dept. Princeton U., 1964-67, asst. prof. aerospace and mech. scis., 1967-69, assoc. prof., 1969-73, prof., 1973-79, dept. dir. grad. studies, 1974-78; George Tallman Ladd prof., head dept. mech. engring. Carnegie-Mellon U., 1979-85; dean Sch. Engring., U. Calif.-Irvine, 1985-94, prof., 1994—; cons. indsutry and govt., 1966—; lectr. and cons. NATO adv. group on aero. rsch. and devel., 1967, 75, 80; chmn. nat. and internat. tech. congs.; chmn. acad. adv. coun. Indsl. Rsch. Inst., 1985-88; mem. space sci. applications adv. com. NASA, 1985-90, chmn. combustion sci. microgravity disciplinary working group, 1987-90; chmn. com. on microgravity rsch. space studies bd. NRC, 1991-94. Assoc. editor: Combustion Sci. and Tech., 1969-70; assoc. tech. editor Jour. Heat Transfer, 1986-92; contbr. articles to nat. and internat. profl. jours., also rsch. monographs. United Aircraft research fellow, 1973-74; Disting. Alumni Rsch. award U. Calif. Irvine, 1992. Fellow AIAA, ASME, AAAS, (Pendray Aerospace Lit. award 1991, Propellants and Combustion award 1992),(Freeman scholar 1992), Fellow Inst. Advancement Engring.; mem. IDERS (v.p. 1991-95, pres. 1995—, Oppenheim award 1993), Combustion Inst. (treas. internat. orgn., chmn. ea. sect., Alfred C. Egerton Gold medal 1996), Soc. Indsl. and Applied Math., Orange County Engring. Coun. (Excellence award 1994), Am. Electronics Assn. (recognition 1994). Office: U Calif Sch Engring S 3202 Engring Gateway Irvine CA 92717

SIRIS, ETHEL SILVERMAN, endocrinologist; b. Clifton, N.J., Aug. 21, 1945; s. Irving A. and Gertrude (Gollop) Silverman; m. Samuel G. Siris, June 2, 1971; children: Benjamin A., Sara A. AB in Biology magna cum laude, Radcliffe Coll. Harvard U., 1963-67; MD, Columbia U. Coll. Physicians and Surgeons, 1967-71. Nat. Bd. of Medical Examiners, Diplomate Am Bd. Internal Medicine, Diplomate Am. Bd. Internal Medicine, Certification in Endocrinology and Metabolism. Intern, asst. resident dept. medicine Presbyn. Hosp., N.Y.C., 1971-74, asst. attending physician, 1977-84, assoc. attending physician, 1984-91, attending physician, 1991—; NIH guest worker Reproduction Rsch. Br. Nat. Inst. Child Health and Human Devel., NIH, 1974-75, NIH rsch. fellow, 1975-76; fellow in Endocrinology Columbia U. Coll. of Physicians & Surgeons and Presbyn. Hosp., N.Y.C., 1976-77; bd. dirs. the Paget Found. for Paget's Disease of Bone and Related Disorders;; bd. trustees Nat. Osteoporosis Found.; dir. programs in osteoporosis Ctr. for Women's Health, 1993—; asst. prof. dept. medicine Columbia U., 1977-84, assoc. prof. clin. medicine, 1984-91, prof. clin. medicine, 1991-96, Madeline C. Stabile prof. clin. medicine, 1996—, dir. Toni Stabile Ctr. for Prevention and Treatment of Osteoporosis, 1996—, course dir. phys. diagnosis dept. medicine, 1985-96; mem. endocrinologic and metabolic drugs adv. com. FDA, 1992-95. Contbr. numerous articles to profl. jours. Upjohn award Columbia U. Coll. of Physicians and Surgeons, 1971, Mary Putnam Jacobi award for Clin. Rsch., 1979, Rsch. award The Paget's Disease Fdn., 1986, 87. Am. Soc. for Bone and Mineral Rsch., Endocrine Soc., Am. Assn. of Clin. Endocrinologists, Phi Beta Kappa, Alpha Omega Alpha. Home: 60 Prescott St Demarest NJ 07627-1420 Office: Dept Medicine Columbia U Coll Physicians & Surgeons 630 W 168th St New York NY 10032-3702

SIRKEN, MONROE GILBERT, statistician; b. N.Y.C., Jan. 11, 1921; s. Irving and Henrietta (Oram) S.; m. Blanche Skalak Horvitz (div. 1960); children: Robert, Philip. BA, UCLA, 1946, MA, 1947; PhD, U. Wash., 1950. Lectr. Med. Sch. U. Wash., Seattle, 1949; fellow Stats. Lab. U. Calif., Berkeley, 1950; statistician Census Bur., Suitland, Md., 1951-54, Pub. Health Svc., Washington, 1954-60, Nat. Ctr. Health Stats., Hyattsville, Md., 1961—; cons. NIH, 1980-85, Nat. Inst. Drug Addiction, 1976-80, NSF, 1986—, Health Care Fin. Adminstrn., 1989-90. Contbr. articles to Jour. Am. Statis. Assn., Biometrics, Demography, Jour. APHA, Pub. Health Reports, also others. Home: 3309 Claridge Ct Silver Spring MD 20902-2201

SIRKIN, JOEL H., lawyer; b. Pitts., Jan. 7, 1946; s. Sidney and Marion (Wolkin) S.; m. Karen Sargent, Aug. 7, 1977; children: Alex S., Jacob O. BA magna cum laude, Johns Hopkins U., 1967; JD cum laude, Harvard U., 1972. Bar: Mass. 1972. Prin. Cambridge (Mass.) Pilot Sch., 1970-71; staff atty. Cambridge-Somerville Legal Services, 1972-74; sr. ptnr. Hale & Dorr, Boston, 1974—. Author: Public School Law. Dir. Mass. Children's Lobby, Boston, 1980-84; mem. fin. com. Town of Wayland, Mass., 1993-96. Mem. Phi Beta Kappa. Avocations: gardening, tennis, golf. Home: 10 Wildwood Rd Wayland MA 01778-2122 Office: Hale & Dorr 60 State St Boston MA 02109-1800

SIRKIN, MICHAEL S., lawyer; b. Newark, Feb. 21, 1947. BSIE, Rutgers U., 1969; JD, Columbia U., 1972. Bar: N.Y. 1973. Mem. Proskauer Rose LLP, N.Y.C. Office: Proskauer Rose LLP 1585 Broadway New York NY 10036-8200

SIROIS, CHARLES, communications executive; b. Chicoutimi, Que., Can., May 22, 1954; children: Françoise-Charles, Marie-Hélène. Doctorate (hon.), U. Québec, Montréal, U. Ottawa (Can.). Founder Telesystem Ltd., Montreal, 1984—, Nat. Pagette Ltd., Montreal, 1986-88; chmn., CEO BCE Mobile Comms. Inc., Montreal, 1988-90, Teleglobe Inc., Teleglobe Can. Inc., Montreal, 1992—, Telesystem Ltd., Montreal, 1990—; chmn. Microcell Telecomms. Inc., Telesystem Internat. Wireless; bd. dirs. Hydro-Québec, Can. Imperial Bank Commerce, Radiomutuel, Inc., École nat. de l'humour, The Bus. Coun. on Nat. Issues; mem. adv. coun. Can. Info. Hwy.; mem. Global Info. Infrastructure Commn., Univ. du Québec á Montréal, chmn. fundraising campaign, 1994—. Co-author: The Medium and the Muse, 1995. Mem. Order of Can. (hon.). Office: Telesystem Ltd, 1000 de la Gauchetière St W 25th Fl, Montreal, PQ Canada H3B 4W5 also: Teleglobe Inc/Teleglobe Can Inc, 1000 de la Gauchetière St W 24th Fl, Montreal, PQ Canada H3B 4X5

SIROIS, GERARD, pharmacy educator; b. Andreville, Kamouraska, Que., Can., Dec. 5, 1934; s. Paul-Etienne and Marie-Anna (Caron) S.; children: Nathalie, Stephane. B.Pharm., U. Montreal, 1960; M.S., Purdue U., 1962, Ph.D., 1965. Lic. pharmacist, Que. Asst. prof. pharmacy U. Montreal, 1965-71, assoc. prof., 1971-76, prof., 1976—, pres. Ethic Com. for Health, 1984—. Grantee Med. Research Council Can., 1974-79; grantee Ministere d'Education du Que., 1972-74. Mem. Am. Pharm. Assn., Assn. Faculties of Pharmacy of Can., Am. Assn. Pharm. Scientists, Can. Soc. Hosp. Pharmacists, Sigma Xi. Roman Catholic. Home: 6352 Matte St, Montreal-Nord, PQ Canada H1G 2E8 Office: U Montreal Faculte Pharmacie, 2900 Blvd Edouard Montpetit, Montreal, PQ Canada H3C 3J7

SIROTKIN, PHILLIP LEONARD, educational administrator; b. Moline, Ill., Aug. 2, 1923; s. Alexander and Molly (Berghaus) S.; m. Cecille Sylvia Gussack, May 1, 1945; children—Steven Marc, Laurie Anne. B.A. (McGregor Found. scholar), Wayne State U., 1945; M.A., U. Chgo., 1947, Ph.D. (Walgreen Found. scholar, Carnegie fellow), 1951. Lectr. U. Chgo., 1949-50; instr. Wellesley Coll., 1950-52, asst. prof. polit. sci., 1953-57; asso. dir. Western Interstate Commn. Higher Edn., Boulder, Colo., 1957-60; exec. asst. to dir. Calif. Dept. Mental Hygiene, Sacramento, 1960-63; asst. dir. NIMH, 1964-66, asso. dir., 1967-71, cons., 1971-73; exec. v.p., acad. v.p. State U. N.Y. at Albany, 1971-76; exec. dir. Western Interstate Commn. Higher Edn., Boulder, Colo., 1976-90, sr. adviser, 1990—; sr. adviser Midwestern Legis. Higher Edn. Steering Com., Boulder, Colo., 1990-91; sr. cons. Midwestern Higher Edn. Commn., 1991—; bd. dirs. Boulder County Mental Health Ctr., 1992—; mem. ovesight commn. Hispanic Agenda, Larasa, 1992—; cons. Nebr. Post-Secondary Edn. Commn., 1994; mem. nat. adv. com. Soc. Coll. and Univ. Planning, 1976, adv. panel, rev. state system higher edn. in N.D., 1986, gov.'s com. on bi-state med. edn. plan for N.D. and S.D., 1988-90, Edn. Commn. States' Nat. Task Force for Minority Achievement in Higher Edn., 1989-91; cons. Bur. Health Manpower Edn., NIH, 1972-74, Nat. Ctr. Health Svcs. Rsch., 1975-85; spl. cons. AID, 1963-64; case writer Resources for the Future, 1954-55; mem. 1st U.S. Mission on Mental Health to USSR, 1967. Author: The Echo Park Dam Controversy and Upper Colorado River Development, 1959. Bd. dirs. Council Social Work Edn., 1959-60. Served to 1st lt. AUS, 1943-46. Recipient Superior Service award HEW, 1967; Wellesley Coll. Faculty Research award, 1956. Home: 299 Green Rock Dr Boulder CO 80302-4745 Office: PO Drawer P Boulder CO 80302

SIRPIS, ANDREW PAUL, insurance company executive; b. Portland, Maine, May 30, 1944; s. Alexander Fotis and Catherine (Nicholas) S.; m. Helene Victoria Scourby, June 18, 1967; children: Alexander Peter, Matthew Paul. BA, Lafayette Coll., Easton, Pa., 1967; MS, Rensselear Poly. Inst., 1981. CLU, ChFC, CMFC. Sales mgmt. trainee Procter & Gamble, Scarsdale, N.Y., 1967-68; ins. salesman Conn. Gen. Life, Washington, 1970-75; dir. pension mktg. Conn. Gen. Life, Hartford, 1975-77, dir. ins. products, 1978-80; dir. tng. CIGNA, Hartford, 1981-82, dir. fin. planning, 1982-84; sales mgr. CIGNA Individual Fin. Svcs., McLean, Va., 1984-91; asst. v.p. CIGNA Individual Fin. Svcs., Vienna, Va., 1992—. Capt. USAR, 1968-70. Mem. Nat. Assn. Life Underwriters, Gen. Agts. and Mgrs. Assn. (bd. dirs. Greater Washington chpt. 1989-90, sec.-treas. 1991-92, 2d v.p. 1992-93, v.p. 1993-94, pres. 1995-97, Career Devel. award 1995, 96, 97), Am. Soc. Pension Actuaries, No. Va. Soc. CLU's and ChFC's (bd. dirs. 1987-89), Internat. Assn. Fin. Planners. Greek Orthodox. Avocations: golf, fishing, woodworking. Home: 4908 Prestwick Dr Fairfax VA 22030 Office: CIGNA Fin Advisors Inc 2070 Chain Bridge Rd Ste 300 Vienna VA 22182-2536

SIS, PETER, illustrator, children's book author, artist, filmmaker; b. Brno, Czech Republic, May 11, 1949; came to U.S., 1982, naturalized, 1988; s. Vladimir and Alena (Petrvalska) S.; m. Terry Ann Lajtha, Oct. 23, 1990; children: Madeleine, Matej. BA, Acad. Fine Arts, Prague, Czech Republic, 1968, MA, 1974. Author, illustrator: Rainbow Rhino, 1987, Waving, 1988, Going Up, 1989, Beach Ball, 1990, Follow the Dream, 1991, An Ocean World, 1992, A Small, Tall Tale from the Far Far North, 1992, Komodo!, 1993, The Three Golden Keys, 1994, Starry Messenger, 1996; illustrator: Fairy Tales of the Brothers Grimm, 2 vols., 1976, 77, Hexe Lakritze and Buchstabenkonig, 1977, Zizkov Romances, 1978, Hexe Lakritze and Rhino Rhinoceros, 1979, Poetry, 1980, Baltic Fairy Tales, 1981, Little Singer, 1982, Bean Boy, 1983, Stories to solve, 1984, Whipping Boy, 1985 (Newberry medal 1987), Oaf, 1986, Three Yellow Dogs, 1986, Higgledy Piggledy, 1986, Jed and the Space Bandits, 1987, After Midnight, 1987, City Lights, 1987, Scarebird, 1988, Alphabet Soup, 1988, Halloween, 1989, The Ghost in the Noonday Sun, 1989, The Midnight Horse, 1990, More Stories to Solve, 1991, Rumpelstiltskin, 1993, The Dragons Are Singing Tonight, 1993, Still More Stories to Solve, 1994, The 13th Floor, 1995, Monday's Troll, 1996, Sleep Safe Little Whale, 1997; filmmaker: (TV series) Hexe Lakritze, 1982, (short films) Mimikry, 1975, Island for 6,000 Alarm Clocks, 1977, Heads, 1979 (Golden Bear award Berlin Film Festival 1980), Players, 1981 (Grand Prix Toronto Film Festival 1981), You Gotta Serve Somebody, 1983 (CINE Golden Eagle award 1983), Aesop's Fables, 1984, Twelve Months, 1985; artist one man shows include Gallery Martinska, Gallery Nerudova, Gallery Rubin, Prague, 1977-79, Gallery Klostermauer, St. Gallen, 1975, Gallery Ploem, Delft, 1977, Gallery Vista Nova, Zurich, 1980, Gallery Medici, London, 1981, Sch. Art U. Ohio, Athens, 1990. Recipient Best Illustrated Book award N.Y. Times, 1988, 90, 92, 93, 94, Gold medal Soc. Illustrators, 1993, Silver medal, 1994, Horn Book Honor Book award Boston Globe, 1993, 94, Caldecott honor, 1996. Home: 252 Lafayette St Apt 5E New York NY 10012-4064 Office: care Greenwillow Books 1350 Avenue Of The Americas New York NY 10019-4702

SIS, RAYMOND FRANCIS, veterinarian, educator; b. Munden, Kans., July 22, 1931; s. Frank J. and Edvie (Shimanek) S.; m. Janice L. Murphy, Aug. 31, 1953; children: Susan, Valerie, Mark, Michael, Amy. B.S., Kans. State U., 1953, D.V.M., 1957; M.S., Iowa State U., 1962, Ph.D., 1965. Clinician Blue Cross Animal Hosp., Albuquerque, 1957; asst. prof. small animal surgery Iowa State U., Ames, 1964-66; assoc. prof. anatomy Tex. A&M U., College Station, 1966-68, prof., 1968—, head dept. vet. anatomy, 1968-83. Served with USAF, 1957-61; mem. Res., 1961-91. Mem. Am. Vet. Med. Assn., Tex. Vet. Med. Assn. (dir. 1970-75), Tex. Assn. Lab Animal Sci. (pres. 1973), Am. Assn. Vet Anatomists (sec.-treas. 1973, pres. 1975), World Assn. Vet Anatomists, Am. Assn. Vet. Clinicians, Brazos Valley Vet. Med. Assn. (pres. 1971), Tex. Acad. Vet. Practice (v.p. 1973), Internat. Assn. for Aquatic Animal Medicine (bd. dirs. 1984-86, pres. 1991-92), World Aquaculture Soc., The Crustacean Soc., Tex. Aquaculture Assn., U.S. Aquaculture Soc., Serra Club (pres. 1985-86), Blue Key, Sigma Xi, Phi Zeta (exec. councilman 1969), Alpha Zeta, Phi Kappa Phi, Phi Sigma, Gamma Sigma Delta, Alpha Gamma Rho (adviser 1962-65, 77-85, pres. 1953, pres. alumni assn. 1976-83). Lodges: K.C. (trustee 1969, pres. 1968), Lions. Home: 2519 Willow Bend Dr Bryan TX 77802-2461 Office: Tex A&M U Dept Anatomy College Station TX 77843

SISCHY, INGRID BARBARA, magazine editor, art critic; b. Johannesburg, Republic of South Africa, Mar. 2, 1952; came to U.S., 1967; d. Benjamin and Claire S. BS, Sarah Lawrence Coll., 1973; PhD (hon.), Moore Coll. Art, 1987. Assoc. editor Print Collector's Newsletter, N.Y.C., 1974-77; dir. Printed Matter, N.Y.C., 1977-78; curatorial intern Mus. Modern Art, N.Y.C., 1978-79; editor ArtForum Mag., N.Y.C., 1979-88; editor-in-chief Interview, N.Y.C., 1989—. Office: Interview Magazine 575 Broadway Fl 5 New York NY 10012-3230*

SISCO, JOSEPH JOHN, management consultant, corporation director, educator, government official; b. Chgo., Oct. 31, 1919; m. Jean Churchill Head, Mar. 26, 1946; children: Carol Bolton, Jane Murdock. Student, Morton Jr. Coll., 1937-39; A.B. magna cum laude, Knox Coll., 1941; M.A., U. Chgo., 1947, Ph.D., 1950. Newspaper reporter, 1936-40; with City News Bur., Chgo., 1937; high sch. tchr., 1941, govt. service, 1950-51; staff Dept. State, 1951-76; successivley fgn. affairs officer, specialist internat. orgnl. affairs, officer-in charge Gen. Assembly, Security Council affairs, fgn. service officer, officer-in-charge UN polit. affairs, 1951-58; dep. dir. Office UN Polit. and Security Affairs, 1958-60, dir., 1960-63; dep. asst. sec. Bur. Internat. Orgn. Affairs, 1963-65, asst. sec. state internat. orgn. affairs, 1965-69; asst. sec. state Near East-South Asia, 1969-74; under sec. state for polit. affairs, 1974-76; pres. Am. U., Washington, 1976-80; chancellor Am. U., 1980-81; ptnr. Sisco Assocs. (mgmt. cons.), Washington, 1981—; bd. dirs. Raytheon Govt. Svcs., Inc., Newport News Shipbldg. InterPublic Group Inc., Braun Govt.; mem. U.S. delegation UN Collective Measures Com., 1952, U.S. delegations to UN Gen. Assembly, 1952-68; U.S. del. Spl. UN Gen. Assembly, session of Mid East, 1967; exec. officer, 1954=57; polit. adviser U.S. delegation Internat. Atomic Energy Agy., 1959; lectr. Fgn. Svc. Inst. Contbr. articles on internat. orgn., fgn. affairs to publs. Served as 1st lt., inf. AUS, 1941-45. Recipient Top Ten Career Service award Civil Service League, 1966, Rockefeller pub. service award, 1971; Silver Helmet Peace award Am. Vets. Com., 1973. Mem. Am. Acad. Diplomacy (bd. trustees), Coun. Fgn. Rels. (pvt. sector coun.). Clubs: Cosmos (Washington). Home: 2517 Massachusetts Ave NW Washington DC 20008-2823 Office: 1250 24th St NW Washington DC 20037-1124

SISISKY, NORMAN, congressman, soft drink bottler; b. Balt., June 9, 1927; m. Rhoda Brown, June 12, 1949; children: Mark B., Terry R., Richard L., Stuart J. BS in Bus. Adminstrn., Va. Commonwealth U., 1949; LLD (hon.), Va. State U. Pres., owner Pepsi-Cola Bottling Co. of Petersburg, Inc.; pres., dir. Lee Distbg. Co., Inc., Petersburg, Rhonor Corp., Petersburg; pres. Belfield Land, Inc., Petersburg; mem. Va. Gen. Assembly, Richmond, 1974-82, 98th-105th Congresses from 4th Va. dist., Washington, 1983—; mem. Ho. nat. security com., ranking mem. mil. readiness subcom., subcom. mil. procurement, panel on morale, welfare & recreation, Ho. small bus. com., subcom. procurement, exports & bus. opportunities; dir. Bank of Va., Richmond; vice-chair defense and security com. North Atlantic Assembly. Pres. Appomattox Indls. Devel. Corp.; bd. visitors Va. State U.; commr. Petersburg Hosp. Authority; trustee Va. State Coll. Found.; bd. dirs. Southside Va. Emergency Crew and Community Resource Devel. Bd. Served with USN 1945-46. Recipient Nat. Security Leadership award, Peace Through Stregnth Victory award, Douglas MacArthur award, Watchdog Treasury award, Thomas Jefferson award, 1994 Achievement award Va. Jaycees, Spirit of Enterprise U.S. C. of C., Small Bus. award Nat. Fedn. Ind. Bus. Mem. Nat. Soft Drink Assn. (chmn. bd. 1981-82), Petersburg C. of C. (v.p.). Democrat. Jewish. Club: Moose. Office: US Ho of Reps 2371 Rayburn Bldg Washington DC 20515-4604*

SISK, DANIEL ARTHUR, lawyer; b. Albuquerque, July 12, 1927; s. Arthur Henry and Myrl (Hope) S.; m. Katharine Banning, Nov. 27, 1954; children: John, Sarah, Thomas. B.A., Stanford U., 1950, J.D., 1954. Bar: N.Mex. 1955, Calif. 1954. Ptnr. firm Modrall, Sperling, Roehl, Harris & Sisk, Albuquerque, 1954-70, 71—; justice N.Mex. Supreme Ct., Santa Fe, 1970; chmn. bd. Sunwest Fin. Svcs., Inc., Albuquerque, 1975-90. Pres. Legal Aid Soc., Albuquerque, 1960-61; trustee Sandia Sch., 1968-72, Albuquerque Acad., 1971-73, A.T. & S.F. Meml. Hosps., Topeka, 1966-82; bd. dirs. N.Mex. Sch. Banking Found., 1981-85. Served with USNR, 1945-46, PTO; to capt. USMCR, 1951-52, Korea. Mem. N.Mex. Bar Assn., Albuquerque Bar Assn. (dir. 1962-63), ABA, State Bar Calif. Presbyn. (elder). Office: 500 4th St NW Albuquerque NM 87102-2183

SISK, MARK SEAN, priest, seminary dean, religious educator; b. Takoma Park, Md., Aug. 18, 1942; s. Robert James and Alma Irene (Davis) S.; m. Karen Lynn Womack, Aug. 31, 1963; children: Michael A., Heather K., Bronwyn E. BS, U. Md., 1964; MDiv, Gen. Theolog. Sem., 1967, DD, 1985. Asst. Christ Ch., New Brunswick, N.J., 1967-70; assoc. Christ Ch., Bronxville, N.Y., 1970-73; rector St. John's Ch., Kingston, N.Y., 1973-77; archdeacon Diocese of N.Y., N.Y.C., 1977-84; dean, pres. Seabury-Western Theol. Sem., Evanston, Ill., 1984—; sec. Coun. Episc. Sem. Deans, 1984-85; mem. task force for recruitment, tng. and deployment of black clergy, 1986-87. Pres. Anglican Theol. Review. Mem. Coun. for Devel. Ministry, 1988-93, exec. com., 1991-94; mem. Cornerstone Adv. Coun., 1996—. Named Hon. Canon Cathedral of St. John the Divine, N.Y.C., 1977. Mem. Soc. Bibl. Lit., Assn. Chgo. Theol. Schs. (pres. 1990-91), Soc. St. Francis (third order). Home: 625 Garrett Pl Evanston IL 60201-2903 Office: Seabury-Western Theol Sem 2122 Sheridan Rd Evanston IL 60201-2938

SISKE, ROGER CHARLES, lawyer; b. Starkville, Miss., Mar. 2, 1944; s. Lester L. and Helen (Cagan) S.; m. Regina Markunas, May 31, 1969; children: Kelly, Jennifer, Kimberly. BS in Fin. with honors, Ohio State U., 1966; JD magna cum laude, U. Mich., 1969. Bar: Ill. 1969. Assoc. Sonnenschein Nath & Rosenthal, Chgo., 1969-78, ptnr., 1978—, chmn. nat. employee benefits and exec. compensation dept. Past chmn., sec. coun. employee benefits Ill. State Bar Assn. Served to capt. U.S. Army, 1970-71. Decorated Bronze Star. Mem. ABA (past chmn. tax sect. employee benefits com., past chmn. joint com. on employee benefits and exec. compensation and bus. law sect., employee benefits and exec. compensation com.), Chgo. Bar Assn. (past chmn. employee benefits com., mem. exec. council of tax com.), Order of Coif (editor law review), Phi Alpha Kappa. Republican. Office: Sonnenschein Nath Rosenthal 233 S Wacker Dr Ste 8000 Chicago IL 60606-6342

SISKEL, GENE (EUGENE KAL SISKEL), film critic; b. Chgo., Jan. 26, 1946; s. Nathan W. and Ida (Kalis) S.; m. Marlene Iglitzen, 1980; children: Kate Adi, Callie Gray. BA, Yale U., 1967; postgrad., Dept. Def. Info. Sch., 1968; PhD of Letters (hon.), Ill. Coll., 1989. Fellow Coro Found., 1968; film critic Chgo. Tribune, 1969—, CBS This Morning, 1990—, WBBM-TV, Chgo., 1974—. Host. Nightwatch, Sta. WTTW-TV, 1979-80 (Emmy award 1979); co-host (with Roger Ebert) Sneak Previews, Sta. WTTW-TV and PBS Network, 1975-82 (Emmy award 1980), At the Movies, syndicated TV, 1982-86, Siskel & Ebert, syndicated TV, 1986—; author: (with Ebert) The Future of the Movies, 1991. Mem. Arts Club Chgo. *

SISKIN, EDWARD JOSEPH, engineering and construction company executive; b. Bklyn., Apr. 30, 1941; s. Haskell and Sylvia (Steckler) S.; m. Patricia Ann Moore, June 26, 1965 (div. Apr. 1990); children: Candice P. Howard, Cristin Jo; m. Jean Elizabeth Bowen, Dec. 17, 1994. BSEE, U. Pa., 1963; cert., Bettis Reactor Engring. Sch., West Mifflin, Pa., 1965; postgrad., George Washington U., 1963-67. Registered profl. engr., Pa., Mass., N.Y., N.J., Ill., Mich., Fla., W.Va., Ind., S.C., Tex., La., Nebr., Calif., Ala. Engr. U.S. AEC, Washington, 1963-67; field office mgr. U.S. AEC, Pitts., 1967-70, Groton, Conn., 1970-77; project mgr. Stone & Webster Engring. Corp., Boston, 1977-78, asst. engring. mgr., 1978-79; engring. mgr. Stone & Webster Engring. Corp., N.Y.C., 1979-83, v.p. & mgr., 1984-86; sr. v.p. & mgr. Stone & Webster Engring. Corp., Cherry Hill, N.J., 1987-88; exec. v.p. Stone & Webster Engring. Corp., Cherry Hill, 1988-90; dir. Stone & Webster Engring. Corp., Boston, 1985-90; gen. mgr. Superconducting Supercollider Lab., Dallas, 1990-94; pres. Enerjoin Svcs., Inc., 1994—; mem. adv. com. Inst. of Nuclear Power Ops., Atlanta, 1987-90, adv. bd. Ctr. for Chem. Plant Safety, N.Y.C., 1988-90. Bd. dirs. PenJerDel Coun., Phila., 1987-90. Lt. USN, 1963-69. Sr. mem. IEEE; mem. Am. Nuclear Soc., Am. Philatelic Soc. (State College, Pa.). Office: PO Box 17 Haddonfield NJ 08033-0016

SISKIND, ARTHUR, lawyer, director; b. N.Y., Oct. 11, 1938; s. William and Sylvia (Schuman) S.; m. Mary Ann Silverman, Nov. 10, 1962; children: Laura, Julie, Kenneth. BA in Liberal Arts, Cornell U., 1960, LLB with distinction, 1962. Ptnr. Squadron, Ellenoff, Plesent & Lehrer, N.Y., 1970-91; sr. exec. v.p., group gen. counsel, mem. exec. com., office chmn., dir. The News Corp. Ltd., N.Y., 1991—. Dir. Brit. Sky Broadcasting Group, PLC, Star TV Ltd. Active Cornell Law Sch. Adv. Coun. Capt. U.S. Army, 1963-65. Mem. ABA, City Bar Assn., Cornell Club. Office: The News Corp Ltd 1211 Avenue Of The Americas New York NY 10036-8701

SISKIND, DONALD HENRY, lawyer; b. Providence, Dec. 25, 1937; s. Samuel and Sadie (Wasserman) S.; m. Beth Mohel, July 15, 1962; children: Steven M., Edward M. BS, U. Pa., 1959; LLB, Columbia U., 1962. Bar: Mass. 1962, N.Y. 1963. Assoc. Marshall Bratter Greene Allison & Tucker, N.Y.C., 1962-69, ptnr., 1969-82; ptnr. Rosenman & Colin, N.Y.C., 1982—; bd. dirs. Chgo. Title Ins. Co.; chmn. various seminars Practicing Law Inst., 1974—; vis. lectr. Columbia U. Sch. Law, 1993—; mem. adv. bd. Wharton Real Estate Ctr. Mem. exec. com. of adv. bd. Real Estate Fin. Jour.; contbr. articles to profl. jours. Pres. Greenville Community Coun., 1974-76; pres. bd. edn. Union Free Sch. Dist., Scarsdale, N.Y., 1978-81. Mem. ABA, Am. Coll. Real Estate Lawyers (pres.), Anglo Am. Real Property Inst. (bd. govs.), N.Y. State Bar Assn., Assn. of Bar of City of N.Y., Phi Alpha Psi. Home: 876 Park Ave New York NY 10021-1832 Office: Rosenman & Colin 575 Madison Ave New York NY 10022-2511

SISKIND, RALPH WALTER, lawyer; b. Washington, May 29, 1949; m. Linda Paula Friedman. BS, Case Inst. Tech., 1971; MS, U. Pa., 1973; JD, Temple U., 1977. Bar: Pa. 1977, U.S. Dist. Ct. (ea. dist.) Pa. 1977. Engr. Westinghouse Electric Corp., Phila., 1971-74, Standard Pressed Steel, Jenkintown, Pa., 1974, U.S. Mint, Phila., 1975-78; atty. U.S. EPA, Phila., 1978-85; assoc. Blank, Rome, Comisky & McCauley, Phila., 1985-90; ptnr. Wolf, Block, Schorr & Solis-Cohen, Phila., 1990—. Co-author quar. articles Jour. Environ. Regulation, 1991-95; contbr. articles to profl. jours. Office: Wolf Block Schorr 12 Fl Packard Bldg SE Corner 15 & Chestnut Sts Philadelphia PA 19102-2678

SISLER, HARRY HALL, chemist, educator; b. Ironton, Ohio, Mar. 13, 1917; s. Harry C. and Minta A. (Hall) S.; m. Helen E. Shaver, June 29, 1940; children: Elizabeth A., David F., Raymond K., Susan C.; m. Hannelore L. Wass, Apr. 13, 1978. BSc, Ohio State U., 1936; MSc, U. Ill., 1937, PhD, 1939; Doctorate honoris causa, U. Poznan, Poland, 1977. Instr. Chgo. City Colls., 1939-41; from instr. to assoc. prof. chemistry U. Kans., Lawrence, 1941-46; from asst. prof. to prof. chemistry Ohio State U., Columbus, 1946-56; Arthur and Ruth Sloan vis. prof. chemistry Harvard, fall, 1962-63; prof., chmn. dept. chemistry U. Fla., Gainesville, 1956-68; dean Coll. Arts and Scis. U. Fla., 1968-70, exec. v.p., 1970-73, dean grad. sch., 1973-79, dir. divsn. sponsored rsch., 1976-79, Disting. Svc. prof. chemistry, 1979—; indsl. cons. W.R. Grace & Co., Martin Marietta Aerospace, Naval Ordnance Lab., TVA; chemistry adv. panel, also vis. scientists panel NSF, 1959-62; cons. USAF Acad., Battelle Meml. Inst., chmn. interinstl. com. nuclear research, Fla., 1958-64; mem. Fla. Nuclear Devel. Commn. Teaching Sci. and Math., 1958; chemistry adv. panel Oak Ridge Nat. Lab., 1965-69; dir. sponsored rsch. U. Fla., 1976-79. Author: Electronic Structure, Properties, and the Periodic Law, 2d edit, 1973, Starlight-A Book of Poems, 1976, Of Outer and Inner Space—A Book of Poems, 1981, Earth, Air, Fire and Water-A Book of Poems, 1989, (with others) Gen. Chemistry: A Systematic Approach, 2d edit, 1959, Coll. Chemistry: A Systematic Approach, 4th edit, 1980, Essentials of Chemistry, 2d edit, 1959, A Systematic Laboratory Course in Chemistry, 1950, Essentials of Experimental Chemistry, 2d edit, 1959, Semimicro Qualitative Analysis, 1958, rev. edit., 1965, Comprehensive Inorganic Chemistry, Vol. V, 1956, Chemistry in Non-Aqueous Solvents, 1961, The Chloramination Reaction, 1977, Dying-Facing the Facts, 1988, Inorganic Reactions and Methods, Vol. 7, 1988, Encyclopedia of Inorganic Chemistry, Vol. 5, Nitrogen: Inorganic Chemistry, 1994, Autumn Harvest-A Book of Poems, 1996; cons. editor: (with others) Dowden, Hutchinson & Ross, 1971-78; series editor: (with others) Phys. and Inorganic Textbook Series, Reinhold Pub. Corp, 1958-70; contbr. (with others) articles to profl. jours. Decorated Royal Order North Star(Sweden); Named Outstanding Chemist in South, Am. Chem. Soc., 1969, Outstanding Chemist in Southeast, Am. Chem. Soc., 1960, James Flack Norris award Am. Chem. Soc., 1979; recipient Outstanding Centennial Achievement award Ohio State U., 1970. Mem. Am. Chem. Soc. (nat. chmn. div. chem. edn. 1957-58, exec. com. 1957-60, bd. publ. Jour. Chem. Edn. 1956-58), Phi Beta Kappa, Sigma Xi, Phi Delta Kappa, Phi Lambda Upsilon, Phi Kappa Phi, Alpha Chi Sigma. Methodist. Patentee in field. Home: 6014 NW 54th Way Gainesville FL 32653-3265

SISLER, WILLIAM PHILIP, publishing executive; b. Yonkers, N.Y., May 4, 1947; s. William Andrew and Doris Elizabeth (Krasko) S.; m. Elaine Herg, Aug. 23, 1969; 1 child, Jonathan William. BA magna cum laude, Canisius Coll., 1969; PhD, Johns Hopkins U., 1977, M in Adminstrv. Sci., 1983. Asst. then assoc., sr. humanities editor Johns Hopkins U. Press, Balt., 1973-83; exec. editor Oxford U. Press, N.Y.C., 1983-86, v.p., exec. editor humanities and social scis., 1987-90; dir. Harvard U. Press, Cambridge, Mass., 1990—. Johns Hopkins U. fellow, 1969-73. Mem. Century Assn., Harvard Club of N.Y.C. Roman Catholic. Office: Harvard U Press 79 Garden St Cambridge MA 02138-1423

SISLEY, BECKY LYNN, physical education educator; b. Seattle, May 10, 1939; d. Leslie James and Blanche (Howe) S.; m. Jerry Newcomb, 1994. BA, U. Wash., 1961; MSPE, U. N.C., Greensboro, 1964; EdD, U. N.C., 1973. Tchr. Lake Washington High Sch., Kirkland, Wash., 1961-62; instr. U. Wis., Madison, 1963-65, U. Oreg., Eugene, 1965-68; prof. phys. edn. U. Oreg., 1968—, women's athletic dir., 1973-79, head undergrad. studies in phys. edn., 1985-92. Co-author: Softball for Girls, 1971; contbr. articles to profl. jours. Admitted to Hall of Fame, N.W. Women's Sports Found., Seattle, 1981, Honor award, N.W. Dist. Assn. for Health, Phys. Edn., Recreation and Dance, 1988, State of Oreg. Sports Hall of Fame, 1993; recipient Honor award Nat. Assn. for Girls and Women in Sports, 1995, Disting. Alumni award Sch. Health & Human Performance U. N.C., Greensboro; U.S. record holder Age 50-54 Triple Jump, Javelin, High Jump, Age 55-50 Javelin, Pole Vault; world record holder Age 55-59 Pole Vault. Mem. AAHPERD, Oreg. Alliance Health, Phys. Edn., Recreation and Dance (hon. life mem.), Western Soc. for Phys. Edn. of Coll. Women (exec. bd. 1982-85), Oreg. High Sch. Coaches Assn., N.W. Coll. Women's Sports Assn. (pres. 1977-78), Oreg. Women's Sports Leadership Network (dir. 1987—), Phi Epsilon Kappa, others. Office: University of Oregon Phys Activity & Recreation Svcs Eugene OR 97403

SISLEY, G. WILLIAM, lawyer; b. Morristown, N.J., Feb. 25, 1944; s. George William and Dorothy (Woods) S.; m. Doris Mortenson, Feb. 3, 1979; children: Amanda, Andrew. A.B., Princeton U., 1966; J.D., NYU, 1969. Bar: N.J. 1970, N.Y. 1970, Conn. 1983. Legal sec. Superior Ct. N.J., 1969-70; assoc. Pitney, Hardin & Kipp, Newark, 1970-74; corp. atty., counsel to bus. equipment group SCM Corp., N.Y.C., 1974-78; asst. gen. counsel The Continental Group Inc., Stamford, Conn., 1978-85, corp. sec., 1980-85; ptnr. Davidson, Dawson & Clark, New Canaan, Conn., 1986-89; of counsel Winthrop, Stimson, Putnam & Roberts, Stamford, Conn., 1989-91, ptnr., 1991—. Mem. Am. Soc. Corp. Secs., Corp. Bar Assn., Assn. of Bar of City of N.Y. Clubs: Princeton (N.Y.C.); Innis Arden Golf (Old Greenwich, Conn.). Home: 26 Keofferam Rd Old Greenwich CT 06870-2127 Office: Wintrop Stimson et al 695 E Main St Stamford CT 06904-6760

SISLEY, NINA MAE, physician, public health officer; b. Jacksonville, Fla., Aug. 19, 1924; d. Leonard Percy and Verna (Martin) S.; m. George W. Fischer, May 16, 1962 (dec. 1990). BA, Tex. State Coll. for Women, 1944; MD, U. Tex., Galveston, 1950; MPH, U. Mich., 1963. Intern City of Detroit Receiving Hosp., 1950-51; resident in gen. practice St. Mary's Infirmary, Galveston, Tex., 1951-52; sch. physician Galveston Ind. Sch. Dist., 1953-56; dir. med. svcs. San Antonio Health Dept., 1960-63, acting dir., 1963-64; resident in pub. health Tex. Dept. Pub. Health, San Antonio, 1963-65; dir. cmty. health svcs. Corpus Christi-Nueces County (Tex.) Health Dept., 1964-67; dir. Corpus Christi-Nueces County (Tex.) Dept. Pub. Health, 1987—; dir. Tb control region 5 Tex. Dept. Health, Corpus Christi, 1967-73; dir. pub. health region 11 Tex. Dept. Health, Rosenberg, 1978-87; chief chronic illness control City of Houston Health Dept., 1973-78; lectr. Incarnate Word Coll., San Antonio, 1963-64; adj. prof. U. Tex. Sch. Pub. Health, Houston, 1980—; guest lectr. Corpus Christi State U., 1987—; pvt. practice Galveston, Stockdale, Hereford and Borger, Tex., 1952-59; mem. adv. bd. N.W. Cmty. Adv. Coun., North Bay Longterm Health Adv. Coun. Bd. dirs. Coastal Bend chpt. ARC, Corpus Christi, 1990-94, pres., 1990-91; bd. dirs. United Way-Coastal Bend, Coastal Bend Coalition on AIDS, 1988-94, Coastal Bend chpt. Am. Diabetes Assn., 1990—; mem. Nueces County Child Fatality Rev. Com. Fellow Am. Coll. Preventive Medicine; mem. AMA, APHA, Tex. Med. Assn., Nueces County Med. Soc. (pres.-elect 1996, pres. 1997—), Tex. Assn. Pub. Health Physicians, Tex. Pub. Health Assn. (pres. 1991-92). Episcopalian. Avocations: fishing, crossword puzzles, raising African violets. Home: 62 Rock Creek Dr Corpus Christi TX 78412-4214 Office: Corpus Christi-Nueces County Dept Health 1702 Horne Rd Corpus Christi TX 78416-1902

SISMAN, ELAINE ROCHELLE, musicology educator; b. N.Y.C., Jan. 20, 1952; d. Irving and Margot (Weintraub) S.; m. Martin Fridson, June 14, 1981; children: Arielle, Daniel. AB, Cornell U., 1972; MFA, Princeton U., 1974, PhD, 1978. Instr. music history U. Mich., Ann Arbor, 1976-79, asst. prof., 1979-82; asst. prof. Columbia U., N.Y.C., 1982-90, assoc. prof., 1990-94, prof., 1995—; vis. prof. Harvard U., 1996. Author: Haydn and the Classical Variation, 1993, Mozart's "Jupiter" Symphony, 1993; assoc. editor: 19th Century Music, Beethoven Forum; also articles; co-editor; Beethoven Forum. Recipient Gt. Tchr. award Columbia U., 1992, Alexander Hamilton medal Columbia U., 1994; fellow NEH, 1981-82; travel grantee Am. Coun. Learned Socs. Mem. Am. Musicological Soc. (pres. Greater N.Y. chpt. 1982-84, bd. dirs. 1992-94, Einstein award 1983, mem. editl. Jour. of AMS), Am. Brahms Soc. (bd. dirs. 1993—), Soc. Fellows in Humanities Columbia U. (chmn. 1992-94). Office: Columbia U Dept Music 703 Dodge New York NY 10027

SISODIA, RAJENDRA SINGH, business educator, researcher, consultant; b. Ratlam, India, June 28, 1958; came to U.S., 1981; s. Narayan S. and Usha K. (Pawar) S.; m. Shailini Malhotra, Mar. 29, 1986; children: Alok, Priya, Maya. BE with honors, Birla Inst. Tech. and Sci., Pilani, India, 1979; M of Mgmt. Studies, Bajaj Inst. Mgmt., Bombay, 1981; MPhil, Columbia U., 1987, PhD, 1989. Asst. prof. Boston U., 1985-88; assoc. prof. George Mason U., Fairfax, Va., 1988—; cons. IBM, Washington, 1991, UN, N.Y.C., 1991, IRS, Washington, 1992, Sprint, 1993, 97, Price Waterhouse, 1994, Bell Core, 1993, Bell South, 1994, Ernst & Young, 1996, Motorola, 1997. Booz Allen fellow, 1982-84. Mem. Am. Mktg. Assn., Inst. Mgmt. Scis., Decision Scis. Inst., Acad. Mktg. Sci., Beta Gamma Sigma. Avocations: writing, jogging, tennis. Home: 10218 Eagle Landing Ct Burke VA 22015-2524 Office: George Mason U Sch Bus Adminstrn Fairfax VA 22030

SISSEL, GEORGE ALLEN, manufacturing executive; b. Chgo., July 30, 1936; s. William Worth and Hannah Ruth (Harlan) S.; m. Mary Ruth Runsvold, Oct. 5, 1968; children: Jenifer Ruth, Gregory Allen. B.S. in Elec. Engring., U. Colo., 1958; J.D. cum laude, U. Minn., 1966. Bar: Colo. 1966, Ind. 1973, U.S. Supreme Ct. 1981. Assoc. Sherman & Howard, Denver, 1966-70; with Ball Corp., Muncie, Ind., 1970—; assoc. gen. counsel Ball Corp., 1974-78, gen. counsel, 1978-95, corp. sec., 1980-95, v.p., 1981-87, sr. v.p., 1987-95; acting pres., CEO Ball Corp., Muncie, 1994-95, bd. dirs., pres., CEO, 1995—, chmn. bd., 1996—; bd. advisors First Chgo. Equity Capital, 1995—; bd. dirs. First Merchants Corp. Assoc. editor: U. Minn. Law Rev., 1965-66. Served with USN, 1958-63. Mem. ABA, Con. Mfrs. Inst. (bd. dirs., chmn.), Nat. Assn. Mfrs. (bd. dirs.), Am. Soc. Corp. Secs., Colo. Bar Assn., Ind. Bar Assn., Ind. C. of C. (bd. dirs.), Order of Coif, MIT Soc. Sr. Execs., (bd. govs. 1987-95), Sigma Chi, Sigma Tau, Eta Kappa Nu. Methodist. Lodge: Rotary. Home: 2600 W Berwyn Rd Muncie IN 47304-5115 Office: Ball Corp 345 S High St Muncie IN 47305-2326

SISSOM, LEIGHTON ESTEN, engineering educator, dean, consultant; b. Manchester, Tenn., Aug. 26, 1934; s. Willie Esten and Bertha Sarah (Davis) S.; m. Evelyn Janelle Lee, June 13, 1953; children: Terry Lee, Denny Leighton. B.S., Middle Tenn. State Coll., 1956; B.S. in Mech. Engring., Tenn. Technol. U., 1962; M.S. in Mech. Engring., Ga. Inst. Tech., 1964, Ph.D., 1965. Diplomate Nat. Acad. Forensic Engrs.; registered profl. engr., Tenn. Draftsman Westinghouse Electric Corp., Tullahoma, 1953-57; mech. designer ARO, Inc., Tullahoma, 1957-58; instr. mech. engring. Tenn. Technol. U., Cookeville, 1958-62, chmn. dept. mech. engring., 1965-79, dean engring., 1979-88, dean of engring. emeritus, 1988—; prin. cons. Sissom & Assocs., Cookeville, Tenn., 1962—; bd. dirs. Accreditation Bd. Engring. and Tech., N.Y.C., 1978-86, treas., 1982-86. Author: (with Donald R. Pitts) Elements of Transport Phenomena, 1972, Heat Transfer, 1977, 1,000 Solved Problems in Heat Transfer, 1991; contbr. An Attorney's Guide to Engineering, 1986; contbr. articles to various publs. Fellow ASME (sr. v.p. 1982-86, gov. 1986-88, Golden medallion), Am. Soc. Engring. Edn. (bd. dirs. 1984-87, pres. 1991-92), Accreditation Bd. Engring. and Tech.; mem. NSPE, Soc. Automotive Engrs., Nat. Engring. Deans Coun. (chmn. 1984-87), Order of the Engr. (chmn. bd. govs. 1994-96), Tau Beta Pi (v.p. 1986-89, councillor 1986-89). Home and Office: 1151 Shipley Church Rd Cookeville TN 38501-7730

SISSON, JEAN CRALLE, middle school educator; b. Village, Va., Nov. 16, 1941; d. Willard Andrew and Carolyn (Headley) Cralle; m. James B. Sisson, June 20, 1964 (div. Oct. 1994); 1 child, Kimberly Carol. BS in Elem. Edn., Longwood Coll., 1964; MA in Adminstrn. and Supervision, Va. Commonwealth U., 1979. Tchr. 2nd grade Tappahannock (Va.) Elem. Sch., 1964-67; tchr. 2nd and 4th grades Farnham (Va.) Elem. Sch., 1967-71; tchr. 6th grade Callao (Va.) Elem. Sch., 1971-81; tchr. 6th and 7th grades Northumberland Mid. Sch., Heathsville, Va., 1981—; sr. mem. Supt. Adv. Com., Heathsville, 1986-93. Author: My Survival, 1994; author of children's books, short stories and poetry. Lifetime mem. Gibeon Bapt. Ch., Village, Va., 1942—. Mem. NEA, ASCD, People for Ethical Treatment of Animals, Aerobics & Fitness Assn. Am., Va. Mid. Sch. Assn., Exercise Safety Assn., Nat. Coun. of English Tchrs., Nat. Wildlife Fedn., PETA. Republican. Avocations: aerobics, dance, music, art, travel. Home: RR 1 Box 39A Callao VA 22435-9706 Office: Northumberland Mid Sch PO Box 100 Heathsville VA 22473-0100

SISSON, RAY L., retired dean; b. Pueblo, Colo., Apr. 24, 1934; s. William Franklin and Lillie Mae (Hall) S.; m. Dixie Lee McConnell, Oct. 5, 1952; children: Mark Lynn, Bryan Keith, Tammy Sue Ann. BSEE, U. Colo., 1960; MSEE, Colo. State U., 1966; AA, Pueblo Coll., 1958; EdD, U. No. Colo., 1973. Electronic technician TV Svcs. Co., Pueblo, 1958, Sid's Appliance Ctr., Tucson; from instr. engring. to asst. prof. So. Colo. State Coll., Pueblo, 1960-63, assoc. prof., 1963-76, engring., electronics dept. head, 1968-70; dean Sch. Applied Sci. and Engring. Tech. U. So. Colo., Pueblo, 1973-84, prof., 1976—, interim dean Coll. Engring. and Sci., 1984-85, dean Coll. Applied Sci. and Engring. Tech., 1985-96, dean, prof. emeritus, 1996—; cons. Escuela Superior Politecnica del Litoral, Ecuador, 1979-82, SUNY, Alfred, Farmingdale, 1982, Moorhead U., 1985, N.Mex. Highlands U., 1985, 90, Kans. State U., Salina, 1994, Ministry Edn., Republic of Yemen, 1996. Bd. dirs. Colo. Transp. Inst., 1993—; exec. dir. So. Colo. Bus. and Tech. Ctr., 1994-96. With USN, 1952-56. Recipient James H. McGraw award Am. Soc. Engring. Edn., 1990; NSF grantee, 1964, 65, 67, 68, 80-83. Mem. IEEE, ABET (tech. accreditation commn. 1990-96, chmn. definition com. 1991, vice chmn. tech. accreditation commn., 1993-96), Am. Soc. Engring. Edn. (active, spectrum com. 1989-90, chmn. definition com. 1991, fellow 1993), Engring. Tech. Leadership Inst. (founding mem., bd. dirs. 1983-88, chmn. 1984-85), Profl. Engrs. Colo. (So. chpt., assoc. mem., chair young engrs. 1969, scholarship, edn. com. 1969, chair state scholarship com. 1968), Pueblo Pachyderm Club (pres.-elect 1997), Phi Delta Kappa, Eta Kappa Nu, Tau Alpha Pi. Home: 403 Starlite Dr Pueblo CO 81005-2685

SISSON, ROBERT F., photographer, writer, lecturer, educator; b. Glen Ridge, N.J., May 30, 1923; s. Horace R. and Frances A. S.; m. Patricia Matthews, Oct. 15, 1978; 1 son by previous marriage, Robert F.H.; 1 stepson, James A. Matthews. With Nat. Geographic Soc., Washington, 1942-88, chief nat. sci. photographer, 1981-88; free-lance photographer, 1988—; lectr. in field; mem. nature staff Sarasota Mag., 1989; owner Macro/Nature Workshops, Englewood, Fla. Photographer one-man shows, Nat. Geog. Soc., Washington, 1974, Washington Press Club, 1976, Berkshire (Mass.) Mus., 1976, Brooks Inst., Santa Barbara, Calif., 1980, U. Miami, 1993, Sea Ctr., Santa Barbara, Calif., 1993, Corcoran Gallery of Art's Spl. World Tour, 1988, permanent collections, Mus. Art, N.Y.C. Recipient 1st prize for color photograph White House News Photographers Assn., 1961; recipient Canadian Natural Sci. award, 1967, Louis Schmidt award, 1991. Aellow Biol. Photographers Assn.; mem. Biol. Photog. Assn. (awards for color prints 1967), Nat. Audubon Soc., Nat. Geog. Soc., Nat. Wildlife Fedn., Soc. Photog. Scientists and Engrs., N.Y. Acad. Scis., N.Am. Photography Assn. (bd. dirs. 1996), N.Am. Mature Photography Assn. (bd. dirs. 1996—), Sigma Delta Chi. Office: Macro/Nature Photography PO Box 1649 Englewood FL 34295-1649 *The true wonders of the natural world gave me inspiration and a challenge. My cameras and I are privileged to share images of this world with all people.*

SISSON, VIRGINIA BAKER, geology educator; b. Boston, Apr. 8, 1957; d. Thomas Kingsford and Edith Virginia (Arnold) S.; m. William Bronson Maze, Oct. 14, 1989. AB, Bryn Mawr Coll., 1979; MA, Princeton U., 1981, PhD, 1985. Rsch. assoc. Princeton (N.J.) U., 1985-86; rsch. assoc. Rice U., Houston, 1986-87, lectr., 1987-92, asst. prof. geology, 1992—; cons. U.S. Geol. Survey, Anchorage, 1984-95. Contbr. more than 30 articles to sci. publs. Rsch. grantee, NSF, Houston and Calif., 1984, 1988, Houston and Scotland, 1990, Alaska, 1990, Venezuela, 1990, Alaska, 1993. Mem. Assn. Women Geologists, Am. Women in Sci., Am. Geophys. Union, Geol. Soc. Am., Mineral Soc. of Am., Mineral Assn. Can. Avocations: pilot, cross-country skiing, soccer, recorder playing. Home: 4118 Lanark Ln Houston TX 77025-1115 Office: Rice U Dept Geology and Geophys 6100 Main St # 126 Houston TX 77005-1827

SISSONS, JOHN ROGER, educational administrator; b. Monroe, Wis., Aug. 10, 1938; s John F. and Pearl J. (Eichstadt) S.; m. Patricia M. Wiese, May 21, 1960; children: John A., Theresa M. Sissons, Kirstein. BA, U. Wis., Whitewater, 1971, MA, 1980. Cert. elem. tchr., Wis. Tchr. Postville Sch., Blanchardville, Wis., 1959-62; jr. high sch. tchr. Hollandale (Wis.) Sch., 1962-64; jr. high tchr., prin. DeSoto (Wis.) Sch. Dist., 1964-65; jr. high math. and sci. tchr. Walworth (Wis.) Grade Sch., 1965-68; math. sci. tchr. Reek Elem. Sch., Lake Geneva, Wis., 1968-81; dist. mgr. World Book, Inc., Chgo., 1981-92; goal tchr. Black Hawk Tech. Coll., Janesville, Wis., 1990-92; CEO, adminstr. Kid's Sta., Inc., Walworth, 1990—; computer cons. So. Lakes United Educators, Burlington, Wis., 1983-86. Mem. Am. Legion, K.C. Democrat. Roman Catholic. Avocations: RV camping, nature walks, classic cars. Office: Kid's Sta Inc PO Box 323 507 N Main St Walworth WI 53184-0323

SISTO, ELENA, artist, educator; b. Boston, Jan. 11, 1952; d. Fernando Jr. and Grace Sisto; m. John David Kirkpatrick. BA, Brown U., 1975; grad., N.Y. Studio Sch., 1977; postgrad., Yale U., Norfolk, Conn., 1975, Skowhegan (Maine) Sch., 1976. Gallery artist Vanderwoude Tanabaum, N.Y.C., 1983-89; gallery artist Damon Brandt Gallery, N.Y.C., 1989-91, Germans Van Eck, N.Y.C., 1991-94; tchr. R.I. Sch. Design, Providence, 1987—, N.Y. Studio Sch., N.Y.C., 1987—, SUNY-Purchase, 1988, Bard Coll., summer, 1990, Columbia U., N.Y.C., Yale U. Exhibited in one-man shows at David Beitzel Gallery, 1995, Greenville County Mus., S.C., Wurtz Gallerie, San Francisco; represented in various pub. and pvt. collections. Fellow Skowhegan Sch., 1970, Yale Norfolk, 1975, NEA, 1983, 89-90, Millary Colony, 1987, Fine Arts Work Ctr., Handhollow Found., Provincetown, Mass., 1995.

SISTO, FERNANDO, mechanical engineering educator; b. La Coruña, Spain, Aug. 2, 1924; s. Fernando Cartelle and Clara (Reiss) S.; m. Grace Jeanette Wexler, June 27, 1946; children: Jane Caroll, Ellen Gail, Todd Frederic. Student, NYU, 1940-43; BS, U.S. Naval Acad., 1946; ScD, MIT, 1952; M Engring. (hon.), Stevens Inst. Tech., 1962. Registered profl. engr., N.J. Commd. ensign USN, 1946, service in the Pacific, ret., 1949; propulsion div. chief Curtiss-Wright Research, Clifton, N.J., 1952-58; prof. mech. engring. Stevens Inst. Tech., Hoboken, N.J., 1959-96, chmn. dept., 1966-79, George Meade Bond prof., 1978-96; prof. emeritus Stevens Inst. Tech., Hoboken, 1996—; dean of the grad. sch. Stevens Inst. Tech., Hoboken, N.J., 1993-94; bd. dirs., trustee Am. Capital Mut. Funds, Houston, 1960—, chmn. bd., 1992-95; co-chmn. merged bd. Van Kampen Am. Capital, 1995—; bd. dirs. Dynalysis of Princeton; cons. UN Devel. Program at Nat. Aero. Lab., Bangalore, India, 1978. Co-author: (textbook) A Modern Course in Aeroelasticity, 1978, 3d edit., 1995. Lt. USN, 1943-49. R.C. DuPont fellow MIT, 1951-52. Fellow ASME; mem. Adirondack Mountain Club. Avocations: skiing, tennis, woodworking, sculling. Office: Stevens Inst Tech Dept Mech Engring Hoboken NJ 07030-5991

SITARZ, ANNELIESE LOTTE, pediatrics educator, physician; b. Medellin, Colombia, Aug. 31, 1928; came to U.S., 1935; d. Hans and Elisabeth (Noll) S. BA cum laude, Bryn Mawr (Pa.) Coll., 1950; MD, Columbia U., 1954. Diplomate Nat. Bd. Med. Examiners, Am. Bd. Pediatrics., Am. Bd. Pediatric Hematology and Oncology. With Columbia U., N.Y.C., 1957—, assoc. prof. clin. pediatrics, 1974-83, prof. clin. pediatrics, 1983—; cons. pediatrics, hematology and oncology Harlem Hosp., N.Y.C., 1967-72, Overlook Hosp., Summit, N.J., 1975—. Contbr. numerous articles to profl. jours. Pres. Mt. Prospect Assn., Summit, 1987—. Fellow Am. Acad. Pediatrics; mem. Am. Assn. Cancer Rsch., Am. Soc. Clin. Oncology, Am. Soc. Hematology, Internat. Soc. Hematology, Harvey Soc. Republican. Episcopalian. Avocations: gardening, sewing, skiing, hiking, stamp collecting. Office: Babies and Children's Hosp Harkness Pavilion 180 Fort Washington Ave New York NY 10032-3710

SITES, JAMES PHILIP, lawyer, consul; b. Detroit, Sept. 17, 1948; s. James Neil and Inger Marie (Krogh) S.; m. Barbara Teresa Mazurek, Apr. 9, 1978; children: Philip Erling, Teresa Elizabeth. Student, U. Oslo, Norway, 1968-69; BA, Haverford Coll., 1970; JD, Georgetown U., 1973, ML in Taxation, 1979. Bar: Md. 1973, D.C. 1974, U.S. Supreme Ct. 1978, Mont. 1984, U.S. Tax Ct. 1984, U.S. Dist. Ct. Mont. 1984, U.S. Ct. Appeals (9th cir.) 1988. Law clk. to judge James C. Morton, Jr. Ct. Spl. Appeals Md., Annapolis, 1974-75; law clk. to judge Orman W. Ketcham Superior Ct. D.C., Washington, 1975-76; gen. atty. U.S. Immigration & Naturalization Svc., Washington, 1976-77; trial atty. tax div. U.S. Dept. Justice, Washington, 1977-84; ptnr. Crowley, Haughey, Hanson, Toole & Dietrich, Billings, Mont., 1984—; consul for Govt. of Norway State of Mont., Billings,

1987—; instr. Norwegian Ea. Mont. Coll., 1987-88, Sons of Norway, 1989—; v.p. Scandinavian Studies Found., 1989—; bd. dirs. Billings Com. on Fgn. Rels., 1988—; mem. Mont. Coun. for Internat. Visitors, The Norsemen's Fedn. Chair local exec. bd. Mont. State U., Billings, 1993—. U. Oslo scholar, 1969; recipient Peace Rsch. award Haverford Coll., 1970. Mem. Md. State Bar Assn., Mont. State Bar (co-chmn. com. on income and property taxes 1987-91, chair tax and probate sect. 1991-92, chair tax litigation subcom. 1992—), D.C. Bar Assn., Am. Immigration Lawyers Assn., Norwegian-Am. C. of C., Hilands Golf Club, Kenwood Golf and Country Club, Billings Stamp Club, Elks, Masons. Avocations: philately, sports card collecting, hiking, Nordic skiing. Office: Crowley Haughey Hanson Toole & Dietrich Consulate for Norway 490 N 31st St Billings MT 59101-1256

SITOMER, SHEILA MARIE, television producer, director; b. Hartford, Conn., Aug. 25, 1951; d. George W. and Mary E. (Chaponis) Bowe; m. Daniel J. Sitomer, Aug. 25, 1985. BA, Smith Coll., 1973. Field producer, dir. Good Morning Am., ABC-TV, N.Y.C., 1981-86; field producer Evening Magazine, WWOR-TV, KDKA-TV, Secaucus, Pitts., N.J., Pa., 1978-79, 88; supervising producer The Reporters, Fox Broadcasting, N.Y.C., 1988; producer Inside Edition, King World Prodns., N.Y.C., 1988-95; co-exec. prodr. Inside Edition and Am. Jour., 1995—. Vol. Nathaniel Witherell Nursing Home, Greenwich, Conn., 1988—. Recipient 3 Emmies, New England chpt. TV Acad. Arts & Scis., 1975-78, 2 Emmys, N.Y. chpt. TV Acad. Arts & Scis., 1979, 89, recipient first prize Internat. Film & TV Festival N.Y., 1988, No. N.J. Press Club award, 1988. Mem. Dirs. Guild Am., Actors Equity Assn. Office: Inside Edition 402 E 76th St New York NY 10021-3104

SITRICK, JAMES BAKER, lawyer; b. Davenport, Iowa, Feb. 21, 1935; s. Philip and Miriam (Baker) S.; m. Anne H.M. Helmers, Aug. 21, 1971; children: James Baker Jr., Margaret A., Catherine Baker. BA, U. Wis., 1957; LLM, Yale U., 1960. Bar: N.Y. 1961. Spl. asst. to asst. sec. treasury for internat. taxation U.S. Treasury, Washington, 1965-67; ptnr. Courdert Bros., N.Y.C., 1975—; chmn. exec. com. Coudert Bros., N.Y.C., 1982-93, sr. ptnr., 1993—; lectr. numerous confs. and orgns. Contbr. articles to profl. jours. Mem. Coun. on Fgn. Rels.; chmn. Benjamin Franklin Found. for Bibliotuque Nat., Paris, English Chamber Orch. Soc. Am.; mem. bd. overseers faculty arts and scis. NYU; trustee French Inst. Alliance-Francais, Folger Shakespeare Libr. Washington, Pierpont Morgan Libr.; dep.-chmn. Coun. for U.S. and Italy; bd. dirs. Am. Friends Tate Gallery. 1st lt. U.S. Army, 1960-61. Frick Collection fellow. Mem. Robert Browning Soc. (bd. dirs.), Glyndebourne Opera Assn., Grolier Club, Century Assn., Knickerbocker Club, Racquet and Tennis Club, Meadow Club. Office: Coudert Bros 1114 Avenue Of The Americas New York NY 10036-7703

SITRICK, MICHAEL STEVEN, communications executive; b. Davenport, Iowa, June 8, 1947; s. J. Herman and Marcia B. (Bofman) S.; m. Nancy Elaine Eiseman, July 1, 1969; children: Julie, Sheri, Alison. BS in Bus. Adminstrn. and Journalism, U. Md., 1969. Coordinator press services Western Electric, Chgo., 1969-70; asst. dir. program services City of Chgo., 1970-72; asst. v.p. Selz, Seabolt & Assocs., Chgo., 1972-74; dir. communications and pub. affairs Nat. Can Corp., Chgo., 1974-81; dir. communications Wickes Cos., Inc., San Diego, 1981-82; v.p. communications Wickes Cos., Inc., Santa Monica, Calif., 1982-84, sr. v.p. communications, 1984-89; chmn., chief exec. officer Sitrick and Co., L.A. and N.Y.C., 1989—. Office: Sitrick and Co 2029 Century Park E Ste 1750 Los Angeles CA 90067-3003

SITTER, JOHN EDWARD, English literature educator; b. Cumberland, Md., Jan. 4, 1944; s. Vivian S. Snider; m. Deborah Ayer, June 19, 1971; children: Zachary, Amelia, Benjamin. AB, Harvard U., 1966; PhD, U. Minn., 1969. Asst. prof. English U. Mass., Amherst, 1969-75, assoc. prof. English, 1975-80; prof. English Emory U., Atlanta, 1980-85, Dobbs prof. English, 1985-93, Charles Howard Candler prof., 1993—, chmn. dept. English, 1982-85, 94-97; vis. lectr. U. Kent, Canterbury, Eng., 1974-75. Author: The Poetry of Pope's "Dunciad", 1971, Literary Loneliness, 1982 (Gottschalk prize 1982), Arguments of Augustan Wit, 1991; editor: The Eighteenth Century Poets, 2 Vols., 1990-91; contbr. articles to profl. jours. Nat. Def. Edn. Act fellow U. Minn., 1966-69, Nat. Humanities Ctr fellow, 1978-79. Mem. Am. Assn. Univ. Profs., Modern Language Assn., Am. Soc. 18th Century Studies. Office: Emory U Dept Of English Atlanta GA 30322

SITTON, CLAUDE FOX, newspaper editor; b. Emory, Ga., Dec. 4, 1925; s. Claude B. and Pauline (Fox) S.; m. Eva McLaurin Whetstone, June 5, 1953; children: Lea Sitton, Clinton, Suzanna Sitton Greene, McLaurin. A.B., Emory U., 1949, L.H.D., 1984. Reporter Internat. News Service, 1949-50; with U.P., 1950-55; writer-editor U.P., N.Y.C., 1952-55; information officer USIA, 1955-57; mem. staff N.Y. Times, 1957-68, nat. news dir., 1964-68; editorial dir. The News and Observer Pub. Co., Raleigh, N.C., 1968-90; dir. The News and Observer Pub. Co., 1969-90, v.p., 1970-90; editor News and Observer, 1970-90; sr. lectr. Emory U., Atlanta, 1991-94; active Pulitzer Prize Bd., 1985-94, chmn., 1992-93; bd. counselors Oxford Coll. Emory U., 1993—. Lay mem. Commn. on Evaluation of Disciplinary Enforcement, Ga. Supreme Ct., 1995-96; mem. Ga. First Amendment Found. Bd., 1994-97. With USNR, 1943-46, PTO. Recipient Pulitzer prize for commentary, 1983. Mem. Am. Soc. Newspaper Editors (dir. 1977-83). Home: PO Box 1326 Oxford GA 30267-1326

SIVASUBRAMANIAN, KOLINJAVADI NAGARAJAN, neonatologist, educator; b. Coimbatore, Madras, India, May 9, 1945; came to U.S., 1971; s. Kolinjavadi Ramaswamy and Sukanthi (Subramanian) Nagarajan; m. Kalyani Hariharier, Feb. 5, 1975; children: Ramya, Rajeev, Ranjan. BSc, Madras U., 1964, MD, 1969. Diplomate Am. Bd. Pediatrics and Neonatal-Perinatal Medicine. Intern in pediat. Jewish Hosp. and Med. Ctr., Bklyn., 1971-72; resident in pediat. U. Md. Hosp., Balt., 1972-74; fellow in neonatology Georgetown U. Hosp., Washington, 1974-76, attending neonatologist, 1976—, dir. nurseries, chief neonatology, 1981—, vice chair pediat., 1988—, prof. pediat. and ob-gyn. Editor: Trace Elements/Mineral Metabolism During Development, 1993; editor pub. SIDS Series, 1985; editor jour. Current Concepts in Neonatology, India, 1990—; internat. editor Indian Jour. Pediat., India, 1988—. Chmn. Siva Vishnu Temple, Lanham, Md., 1981-91; mem. Fetus and New Born Com., Washington, 1988; founder, bd. dirs. Coun. of Hindu Temples U.S.A.; founder, coord. United Hindu Temples of Met. Washington; 1st v.p. Interfaith Conf., Washington. Recipient "Preemies" cover article Newsweek, 1988; featured in "Washingtonian" jour., 1996. Fellow Am. Coll. Nutrition, Am. Acad. Pediat.; mem. AAAS, N.Y. Acad. Scis., Internat. Soc. for Trace Element Rsch. in Humans, Soc. for Bioethics Consultation, Am. Soc. Law, Medicine and Ethics. Hindu. Achievements include research in neonatology, trace elements kinetics, reduction in infant mortality, neonatal immunology, and bioethics. Office: Georgetown U Hosp 3 South Hospital 3800 Reservoir Rd NW Washington DC 20007-2113

SIVCO, DEBORAH LEE, research materials scientist; b. Somerville, N.J., Dec. 21, 1957. BA in chem. edn., Rutgers Univ., 1980; MS in material sci., Stevens Inst., 1988. III-V processing tech. Laser Diode Labs, New Brunswick, N.J., 1980-81; materials scientist Bell Labs. Lucent Technologies, Murray Hill, N.J., 1981—. Recipient Newcomb Cleveland prize AAAS, 1993-94, Electronics Letters premium Instn. Elec. Engrs. U.K., 1995. Office: Bell Labs Lucent Technologies 600 Mountain Ave New Providence NJ 07974-2008

SIVE, DAVID, lawyer; b. Bklyn., Sept. 22, 1922; s. Abraham Leon and Rebecca (Schwartz) S.; m. Mary Robinson, July 23, 1948; children: Rebecca, Helen, Alfred, Walter, Theodore. A.B., Bklyn. Coll., 1943; LL.B., Columbia U., 1948. Bar: N.Y. 1948, U.S. Supreme Ct. 1964. Partner Sive, Paget & Riesel, and predecessors, N.Y.C., 1957—; prof. Pace U. Law Sch., White Plains, N.Y., 1995—; adj. prof. law Columbia Law Sch. and other law schs., 1965—; short term sr. Fulbright scholar, 1994. Author: (with Reed Rowley) Rowley on Partnerships, 1959; contbr. articles to law revs. Dem. candidate for N.Y. State Supreme Ct., 1965; Dem. candidate for Congress, 1958; trustee Natural Resources Def. Coun., Inc., 1969-93. With U.S. Army, 1943-45. Decorated Purple Heart and oak leaf cluster. Mem. Am., N.Y. State (Root/Stimson award for pub. service 1977) bar assns., Assn. of Bar of City of N.Y. (mem. exec. com. 1972-76, chmn. environ. law com. 1971-75), Am. Law Inst., Sierra Club (chmn. Atlantic chpt. 1968-69, nat. dir. 1968-69). Home: Millbrook Rd Margaretville NY 12455 Office: Pace Univ Law Sch 78 N Broadway White Plains NY 10603-3710 also: care Sive Paget & Riesel 460 Park Ave New York NY 10022

SIVE, REBECCA ANNE, public affairs company executive; b. N.Y.C., Jan. 29, 1950; d. David and Mary (Robinson) S.; m. Clark Steven Tomashefsky, June 18, 1972. BA, Carleton Coll., 1972; MA in Am. History, U. Ill., Chgo., 1975. Asst. to chmn. of pres.' task force on vocations Carleton Coll., Northfield, Minn., 1972; asst. to acquisitions librarian Am. Hosp. Assn., Chgo., 1973; rsch. asst. Jane Addams Hull House, Chgo., 1974; instr. Loop Coll., Chgo., 1975, Columbia Coll., Chgo., 1975-76; cons. Am. Jewish Com., Chgo., 1975, Ctr. for Urban Affairs, Northwestern U., Evanston, Ill., 1977, Ill. Consultation on Ethnicity in Edn., 1976, MLA, 1977; dir. Ill. Women's History Project, 1975-76; founder, exec. dir. Midwest Women's Ctr., Chgo., 1977-81; exec. dir. Playboy Found., 1981-84; v.p. pub. affairs/pub. rels. Playboy Video Corp., 1985; v.p. pub. affairs Playboy Enterprises, Inc., Chgo., 1985-86; pres. The Sive Group, Inc., Chgo., 1986—; guest speaker various edni. orgns., 1972—; instr. Roosevelt U., Chgo., 1977-78; dir. spl. projects Inst. on Pluralism and Group Identity, Am. Jewish Com., Chgo., 1975-77; cons. Nat. Women's Polit. Caucus, 1978-80; bd. dirs. NOVA Health Systems, Woodlawn Community Devel. Corp.; trainer Midwest Acad.; mem. adv. bd. urban studies program Associated Colls. Midwest; proposal reviewer NEH. Contbr. articles to profl. jours. Commr. Chgo. Park Dist., 1986-88; mem. steering com. Ill. Commn. on Human Rels., 1976; mem. structure com. Nat. Women's Agenda Coalition, 1976-77; del.-at-large Nat. Women's conf., 1977; mem. Ill. Gov.'s Com. on Displaced Homemakers, 1979-81, Ill. Human Rights Com., 1980-87, Ill. coordinating com., Internat Womens Yr.; coord. Ill. Bicentennial Photog. Exhbn., 1977; mem. Ill. Employment and Tng. Coun.; mem. employment com. Ill. Com. on Status of Women; bd. dirs. Nat. Abortion Rights Action League and NARAL Found., Ill. div. ACLU, Midwest Women's Ctr. Recipient award for outstanding community leadership YWCA Met. Chgo., 1979, award for outstanding community leadership Chgo. Jaycees, 1988. Home: 3529 N Marshfield Ave Chicago IL 60657-1224 Office: The Sive Group 359 W Chicago Ave Ste 201 Chicago IL 60610-3025

SIVERD, ROBERT JOSEPH, lawyer; b. Newark, July 27, 1948; s. Clifford David and Elizabeth Ann (Klink) S.; m. Bonita Marie Shulock, Jan. 8, 1972; children: Robert J. Jr., Veronica Leigh. AB in French, Georgetown U., 1970; JD, 1973; postgrad. LaSorbonne, Paris, 1969. Bar: N.Y. 1974, U.S. Dist. Ct. (so. and ea. dists.) N.Y. 1974, U.S. Ct. Appeals (2nd cir.) 1974, U.S. Supreme Ct. 1980, U.S. Dist. Ct. (ea. dist.) Pa. 1984, U.S. Ct. Appeals (3rd cir.) 1984, (6th cir.) 1985, Ohio 1991, Ky. 1992. Assoc. Donovan Leisure Newton & Irvine, N.Y.C., 1973-83; staff v.p., litigation counsel Am. Fin. Group, Inc., Greenwich, Conn., 1983-86, v.p. litigation counsel, 1986-87, v.p. assoc. gen. counsel, Cin., 1987-92; sr. v.p., gen. counsel and sec. Gen. Cable Corp., 1992-94, exec. v.p., gen. counsel and sec., 1994—. Mem. ABA, Cin. Bar Assn., Assn. of Bar of City of N.Y., Ky. Bar Assn. Republican. Office: Gen Cable Corp 4 Tesseneer Dr Newport KY 41076-9753

SIVERSON, RANDOLPH MARTIN, political science educator; b. Los Angeles, July 29, 1940; s. Clifford Martin and Lorene (Sanders) S.; m. Mary Suzanne Strayer, Dec. 31, 1966; children: Andrew, Erica, Courtney. AB, San Francisco State U., 1962, MA, 1965; PhD, Stanford U., 1969. Lectr. polit. sci. Stanford U., Calif., 1967; asst. prof. U. Calif., Riverside, 1967-70; asst. prof. U. Calif., Davis, 1970-75, assoc. prof., 1975-81, prof., 1981—; Fulbright lectr. El Colegio de Mexico, Mexico City, 1974-75; vis. prof. Naval Postgrad. Sch., Monterey, Calif., 1980. Co-author: The Diffusion of War, 1991; editor: (with others) Change in the International System, 1980; editor Internat. Interactions, 1984-91; mem. editorial bd. Am. Polit. Sci. Rev., 1989-91. Mem. Internat. Studies Assn., Am. Polit. Sci. Assn., Western Polit. Sci. Assn. (pres. 1991), Midwest Polit. Sci. Assn. Roman Catholic. Office: U Calif Davis Dept Polit Sci Davis CA 95616

SIVIN, NATHAN, historian, educator; b. May 11, 1931; m. Carole Delmore. BS in Humanities and Sci., MIT, 1958; MA in History of Sci., Harvard U., 1960, PhD in History of Sci., 1966. Prof. Chinese history and history of sci., dept. history and sociology of sci. U. Pa., Phila., 1977—, acting chmn. dept., 1989; vis. lectr., Singapore U., 1962; vis. prof. Rsch. Inst. Humanistic Studies, Kyoto, Japan, 67-68, 71-72, 74, 79-80; vis. scientist Sinologisch Inst., Leiden, The Netherlands, Cambridge U., Eng., People's Republic China; vis. assoc., dir. Needham Rsch. Inst., Cambridge, 1987—; advisor Acad. Traditional Chinese Medicine, Beijing; numerous lectures and colloquia in Europe, Asia, N.Am. Author: (monograph) Chinese Alchemy: Preliminary Studies, 1968, Chinese trans. 1973, Cosmos and Computation in Early Chinese Mathematical Astronomy, 1969, Traditional Medicine in Contemporary China, 1987, Science in Ancient China: Researches and Reflections, 1995, Medicine, Philosophy and Religion in Ancient China: Researches and Reflections, 1995; author with others, editor or co-editor: Chinese Science, 1973, Science and Technology in East Asia, 1977, Astronomy in Contemporary China, 1979, Science and Civilisation in China, Vol.5, 1980, Science and Medicine in Twentieth-Century China, 1989, The Contemporary Atlas of China, 1989, Science in Ancient China, 1995, Medicine, Philosophy and Religion in Ancient China, 1995; also numerous articles for profl. jours., essays, prefaces to books, book revs.; editor, pub. Chinese Science, 1973-92; mem. editorial bd. U. Pa. Press, 1980-83, numerous jours.; gen. editor: (monograph series) Science, Medicine and Technology in East Asia, 3 Vol. MIT E. Asian Sci. Series, 6 vol.; adv. editor Tech. and Culture, 1973—. Mem. adminstrv. bd. Chinese Cultural and Community Ctr., Phila., 1983-84. Guggenheim fellow, 1971-72; Japan Soc. Promotion of Sci. rsch. fellow, 1979-80; grantee NSF, 1968-70, 79-81, Ford Found., 1970, Nat. Libr. Medicine NIH, 1976, IBM Corp., 1985, Nat. Program Advanced Study and Rsch. China, Com. Scholarly Communication with People's Republic China, 1986-87. Fellow Am. Acad. Arts and Scis.; mem. Am. Soc. for Study of Religion (exec. com. 1982-83, v.p. 1993—), Soc. for Studies Chinese Religion (bd. dirs., exec. coun. 1986-89), T'ang Studies Soc. (bd. dirs. 1986—), Internat. Soc. for History East Asian Sci., Tech. and Medicine (pres. 1990-93), Chinese Acad. Scis. (hon. prof. 1989—), Franklin Inn Club (pres. 1995), Acad. Internat. D'histoire des Scis. Home: 8125 Roanoke St Philadelphia PA 19118-3949 Office: U Pa Dept History & Sociology Sciences Philadelphia PA 19104-3325

SIX, FRED N., state supreme court justice; b. Independence, Mo., Apr. 20, 1929. AB, U. Kans., 1951, JD with honors, 1956; LLM in Judicial Process, U. Va., 1990. Bar: Kans. 1956. Asst. atty. gen. State of Kans., 1957-58; pvt. practice Lawrence, Kans., 1958-87; judge Kans. Ct. Appeals, 1987-88; justice Kans. Supreme Ct., Topeka, 1988—; editor-in-chief U. Kans. Law Review, 1955-56; lectr. on law Washburn U. Sch. Law, 1957-58, U. Kans., 1975-76. Maj. USMC, 1951-53; USMCR, 1957-62. Recipient Disting. Alumnus award U. Kans. Sch. Law, 1994. Fellow Am. Bar Found. (chmn. Kans. chpt. 1983-87); mem. ABA (jud. adminstrn. divsn.), Am. Judicature Soc., Kans. Bar Assn., Kans. Bar Found., Kans. Law Soc. (pres. 1970-72), Kans. Inn of Ct. (pres. 1993-94), Order of Coif, Phi Delta Phi. Office: Kans Supreme Ct 301 SW 10th Ave Topeka KS 66612-1502

SIZEMORE, BARBARA ANN, Black studies educator; b. Chgo., Dec. 17, 1927; d. Sylvester Walter Laffoon and Delila Mae (Alexander) Stewart; m. Furman E. Sizemore, June 28, 1947 (div. Oct. 1964); children: Kymara, Furman G.; m. Jake Milliones, Sept. 29, 1979 (div. Feb. 1992). BA, Northwestern U., 1947, MA, 1954; PhD, U. Chgo., 1979; LLD (hon.), Del. State Coll., 1974; LittD (hon.), Cen. State U., 1974; DHL (hon.), Bal. Coll. of Bible, 1975; D of Pedagogy (hon.), Niagara U., 1994. Tchr., prin., dir. Chgo. Pub. Schs., 1947-72; assoc. sec. Am. Assn. Sch. Adminstrs., Arlington, Va., 1972-73; supt. schs. D.C. Pub. Schs., Washington, 1973-75; edni. cons. Washington and Pitts., 1975—; prof. Black studies U. Pitts., 1977-92; dean Sch. of Edn. DePaul U., Chgo., 1992—. Author: The Ruptured Diamond, 1981; bd. mem. Jour. Negro Edn., 1974-83, Rev. Edn., 1977-85. Candidate city coun. Washington, 1977; mem. NAACP. Recipient Merit award Northwestern U. Alumni Assn., 1974, Excellence award Nat. Alliance Black Sch. Educators, 1984, Human Rights award UN Assn., 1985, Racial Justice award YMCA, 1995; named to U.S. Nat. Com., UNESCO, 1974-77. Mem. Nat. Coun. for Black Studies, African Heritage Studies Assn. (bd. mem. 1972—), Nat. Alliance Black Sch. Educators, Delta Sigma Theta. Democrat. Baptist. Avocations: reading, writing. Office: DePaul U Sch of Edn 2320 N Kenmore Ave Chicago IL 60614-3210

SIZEMORE, CAROLYN LEE, nuclear medicine technologist; b. Indpls., July 22, 1945; d. Alonzo Chester and Elsie Louise Marie (Osterman) Armstrong; m. Jessie S. Sizemore Sr., June 9, 1966; 1 child, Jessie S. Jr. AA in Nuclear Medicine, Prince George's Community Coll, Largo, Md., 1981; BA in Bus. Adminstrn., Trinity Coll., 1988. Registered technologist (nuclear medicine); cert. nuclear medicine technologist, Md.; lic. nuclear med. technologist. Nuclear med. technologist Washington Hosp. Ctr., 1981-88; chief technologist, mem. com. Capitol Hill Hosp., Washington, 1988-91; supr. diagnostic imaging, asst. radiation safety officer Nat. Hosp. Med. Ctr., Arlington, Va., 1991-97; mem. Am. Registry of Radiologic Technologists Nuclear Medicine Exam. Com., 1990-93. Contbr. articles to profl. jours. Mem. com. Medlantic Rsch. Found., Washington, 1989-93; sec. Crestview Area Citizens Assn., 1994-95. Mem. Va. Soc. Radiol. Technologists, Potomac Dist. Soc. Radiol. Technologists, Med. Soc. Radiol. Technologsts, Med. Soc. Nuclear Medicine Technologists, Soc. Nuclear Medicine (chmn. membership 1983-85, sec. 1985-87, 88-89, co-editor Isotopics 1991, editor Isotopics 1992-96, nominating com. 1995-96), Nuclear Medicine Adv. Bd., Am. Legion Aux. (exec. com. 1975-76), Internat. Platform Assn., Crestview Area Citizens Assn. (sec. 1994-95), Native Am. Resource Group. Republican. Lutheran. Avocations: various crafts, reading, aerobics, weight lifting, Native American earth astrology. Home: 6700 Danford Dr Clinton MD 20735-4019

SIZEMORE, HERMAN MASON, JR., newspaper executive; b. Halifax, Va., Apr. 15, 1941; s. Herman Mason and Hazel (Johnson) S.; m. Connie Catterton, June 22, 1963; children: Jill, Jennifer. AB in History, Coll. William and Mary, 1963; postgrad., U. Mo., 1965; MBA, U. Wash., 1985. Reporter Norfolk (Va.) Ledger-Star, summers 1961, 62, 63; copy editor Seattle Times, 1965-70, copy-desk chief, 1970-75, asst. mng. editor, 1975-77, mng. editor, 1977-81, prodn. dir., 1981-83, asst. gen. mgr., 1984, v.p., gen. mgr., 1985, pres., chief operating officer, 1985—; vis. instr. Sch. Comms. U. Wash., 1972-78; bd. dirs. Times Comms. Co., Walla Walla Union-Bull, Inc., Yakima Herald-Republic, Times Community Newspapers, Inc., Northwestern Mut. Life Ins. Co., 1993—, mem. policyowner examining com., 1985, chmn., 1986. Bd. dirs. Ctrl. Puget Sound Campfire Coun., 1985-91, pres., 1989-90; bd. dirs. Ptnrs. in Pub. Edn., 1987-88, United Way of King County, 1994—, Downtown Seattle Assn.; adv. coun. Puget Sound Blood Ctr. and Program; adv. bd. USO-Puget Sound Area. Named Seattle Newsmaker of Tomorrow, 1978. Mem. AP Mng. Editors, Soc. Profl. Journalists, Pacific N.W. Newspaper Assn., Allied Daily Newspapers Washington (bd. dirs.), Coll. William and Mary Alumni Assn. (bd. dirs.), Greater Seattle C. of C. (bd. dirs.), U. Wash. Exec. MBA Alumni Assn. (pres. 1988, bd. dirs.), Wash. Athletic Club (bd. dirs.), Rainier Club, Rotary. Methodist. Office: Seattle Times PO Box 70 Seattle WA 98111-0070

SIZEMORE, NICKY LEE, computer scientist; b. N.Y.C., Feb. 13, 1946; s. Ralph Lee and Edith Ann (Wangler) S.; m. Frauke Julika Hoffmann, Oct. 31, 1974; 1 child, Jennifer Lee Sizemore; 1 stepchild, Mark Anthony Miracle. BS in Computer Sci., SUNY, 1989. Sgt. first class U.S. Army, 1964-68, 70-86; computer operator UNIVAC, Washington, 1968-69, programmer, 1969-70; programmer/analyst Ultra Systems, Inc., Sierra Vista, Ariz., 1986-87; computer scientist Comarco, Inc., Sierra Vista, 1987-92, ARC, Profl. Svcs. Group, Sierra Vista, 1992-93, Computer Scis. Corp., Ft. Huachuca, Ariz., 1994; sr. cons. Inference Corp., 1995; subject matter expert Northrop Corp., Sierra Vista, Ariz., 1995—; sr. info. sys. engr. Harris Corp., Sierra Vista, Ariz., 1996—; speaker numerous confs., seminars, symposia. Mem. AIAA (mem. artificial intelligence standard com.), Computer Soc. IEEE, Am. Assn. for Artificial Intelligence (co-dir. workshop on verification, validation, and test of knowledge-based sys. 1988), Assn. for Computing Machinery, Armed Forces Comms.-Electronics Assn., Am. Def. Preparedness Assn. Avocations: chess, jogging/aerobics, karate. Home: 880 E Charles Dr Sierra Vista AZ 85635-1611 Office: Harris Tech Svcs Corp 101 E Wilcox Dr Sierra Vista AZ 85635-2540

SIZEMORE, TOM, actor; b. 1963. Appeared in films Lock Up, 1989, Flight of the Intruder, 1991, Guilty By Suspicion, 1991, Harley Davidson & The Marlboro Man, 1991, Passenger 57, 1992, Heart and Souls, 1993, Striking Distance, 1993, Wyatt Earp, 1994, Natural Born Killers, 1994, Devil in a Blue Dress, 1995, Strange Days, 1995, Heat, 1995, The Relic, 1997. Office: Creative Artists Agy 9830 Wilshire Blvd Beverly Hills CA 90212*

SIZEMORE, WILLIAM HOWARD, JR., newspaper editor; b. South Boston, Va., Dec. 8, 1948; s. W. Howard and Genevieve T. (Walton) S.; m. Mary K. Lamont, Jan. 29, 1972; children: Justin, Jennifer, Julie. BA in Philosophy, Coll. William and Mary, 1971. Editor The Clarksville (Va.) Times, 1972-75; reporter The Roanoke (Va.) Times, 1975-76, The Times-Herald, Newport News, Va., 1976-81; editor, pub. The York Town Crier, Yorktown, Va., 1981-88; copy editor The Ledger-Star, Norfolk, Va., 1982-89, news editor, 1989-95; writer, editor The Virginian-Pilot, Norfolk, Va., 1995—. Recipient various Excellence in Writing and Layout awards Va. Press Assn., 1972-96. Avocations: tennis, music, bicycling, camping. Home: 107 Azalea Dr Yorktown VA 23692-4645 Office: Virginian-Pilot/Ledger-Star 150 W Brambleton Ave Norfolk VA 23510-2018

SIZER, IRWIN WHITING, biochemistry educator; b. Bridgewater, Mass., Apr. 4, 1910; s. Ralph Waldo Emerson and Annie Jenkins (Scott) S.; m. Helen Whitcomb, June 23, 1935; 1 child, Meredith Ann (Mrs. Twomey). A.B., Brown U., 1931, Sc.D. (hon.), 1971; Ph.D., Rutgers U., 1935. Teaching fellow Rutgers U., 1931-35; dir. oyster pest control investigation for N.J. U.S. Bur. Fisheries, 1935; instr. MIT, Cambridge, 1935-39; asst. prof. MIT, 1939-42, assoc. prof. physiology, 1942-56, prof. biochemistry, 1956—, exec. officer biology, 1954-55, acting head biol. dept., 1955-56, head biol. dept., 1956-67, dean Grad. Sch., 1967-75, cons. resource devel., 1975-85; pres. Whitaker Health Sci. Fund, Inc., 1974-84; cons. in resource devel. MIT, 1992-95; bd. dirs. Boston Fed. Savs. Bank, Lexington, Mass.; cons. in biochemistry to pharm. industry Ford Found., 1990-95; dir. Biol. Scis. Curriculum Study. Contbr. sci. papers, enzymology, biochemistry to profl. jours.; mem. adv. bd. Tech. Rev. Trustee, bd. govs. Rutgers U.; trustee Boston Biomed. Research Inst.; corp. mem. Lesley Coll.; trustee Mus. of Sci., Theobold Smith Research Inst. Honored byIrwin Sizer award for acad. innovation, 1975—; named hon. mem. MIT Class of 1924, hon. mem. MIT Alumni Assn. Fellow Am. Acad. Arts and Sci., Am. Inst. Chemists; mem. Am. Physiol. Soc., Am. Soc. Zoologists, Am. Soc. Biol. Chemists, Am. Chem. Soc., Sigma Xi (pres. Mass. Inst. Tech. 1958-59), Phi Beta Kappa (hon. mem.), Delta Omega. Home: 52 Dartmouth Ct Bedford MA 01730-2908

SIZER, PHILLIP SPELMAN, consultant, retired oil field services executive; b. Whittier, Calif., Apr. 11, 1926; s. Frank Milton and Helen Louise (Saylor) S.; m. Evelyn Sue Jones, Aug. 16, 1952; children: Phillip Spelman, Ves Warner. BME, So. Meth. U., 1948. Registered profl. engr., Tex. With Otis Engring. Corp., Dallas, 1948-91; project engr. Otis Engring. Corp., 1958-62, chief devel. engr., 1962-70, v.p. R & D, 1970-73, v.p. engring. and rsch., 1973-76, sr. v.p., tech. dir., 1977-91, bd. dirs., 1975-91; pres. Sizer Engring. Inc., 1992—; prin. Crawford-Sizer Devel. Co., 1996—; bd. dirs. DHV Internat., Inc.; cons. in field; mem. exec. com. Offshore Tech. Conf., 1976-79. Patentee in field. Mem. U. Tex. Mech. Engring. Dept. Vis. Com., 1977-83. Named to Hall of Achievement Coll. Engring., U. Tex., Arlington, 1983. Fellow ASME (chmn. exec. com. petroleum divsn. 1974-75, SPEE-1 chmn. main com. 1981-88, Engr. of Yr. award North Tex. sect. 1971, centennial medal 1980, OILDROP award petroleum divsn. 1982, Dedicated Svc. award 1985, Silver Patent award 1990); mem. Soc. Petroleum Engrs., S.W. Rsch. Inst. (trustee 1982—), Petroleum Engrs. Club of Dallas, Rotary Internat., Kappa Sigma, Tau Beta Pi, Kappa Mu Epsilon. Home: 14127 Tanglewood Dr Dallas TX 75234-3851

SIZER, REBECCA RUDD, performing arts educator, arts coordinator; b. Melrose, Mass., July 28, 1958; d. David William and Harriet Fay (Sart) Rudd; m. Theodore Sizer II, June 21, 1980; children: Caroline Foster, Lydia Catherine Rachel, Theodore Rudd. AB, Mount Holyoke Coll., 1980; MFA, Rochester Inst. Tech., 1983; postgrad., Eastman and Westminster Choir Coll. Cert. tchr. music and art K-12, N.J. Dir. music Christian Bros. Acad., Lincroft, N.J., 1991-93, Peddie Sch., Hightstown, N.J., 1993-94; chair dept. fine and performing arts, arts curriculum coord. Ranney Sch., Tinton Falls, N.J., 1994—; dir. after sch. art program Upstairs Youth Agy., Rochester, N.Y., 1984-85; music dir. Peninsula Opera Rep. Co., Rumson, N.J., 1986-88, local music. theatre, Red Bank, N.J., 1986—; freelance artist, musician. Illustrator: (books) China: A Brief History, 1981, Making Decisions, 1983. Joseph A. Skinner fellow Mt. Holyoke Coll., 1981, Dodge fellow Geraldine R. Dodge Found., 1993. Mem. Music Educators Nat. Conf., Local 399 Musicians Union. Avocation: tennis. Home: 385 Branch Ave Little Silver NJ 07739-1102

SIZER, THEODORE R., educational director; b. New Haven, Conn., June 23, 1932; m. Nancy Faust; 4 children. BA in English Lit., Yale U., 1953; MAT in Social Studies, Harvard U., 1957, Phd in Edn. and Am. History, 1961; PedD (hon.), Lawrence U., 1969; LittD (hon.), Union Coll., 1972; LLD (hon.), Conn. Coll., 1984; LHD (hon.), Williams Coll., 1984; MA ad eundem, Brown U., 1985; LHD (hon.), U Mass., Lowell, 1985, Dartmouth Coll., 1985, Lafayette Coll., 1991, Webster U., 1992, Ind. U., 1993, Mt. Holyoke Coll., 1993, U. Maine, 1993, Iona Coll., 1995, L.I. U., 1996, Bridgewater State Coll., 1996. English and math. tchr. Roxbury Latin Sch., Boston, 1955-56; history and geography tchr. Melbourne (Australia) Grammar Sch., 1958; asst. prof. edn., dir. MA in tchrs. program Harvard U., Cambridge, Mass., 1961-64; dean grad. sch. edn. Harvard U., Cambridge, 1964-72; headmaster, instr. in history Phillips Acad., Andover, Mass., 1972-81; chmn. A Study of High Schs., 1981-84; prof. edn. Brown U., Providence, 1984-96, chmn. edn. dept., 1984-89, Walter H. Annenberg prof. edn., 1993-94, dir. Annenberg Inst. Sch. Reform, 1994-96, chmn. Coalition of Essential Schs., 1996—; vis. prof. U. Brisol, U.K., 1971, Brown U., Providence, spring 1983. Author: Secondary Schools at the Turn of the Century, 1964, The Age of the Academies, 1964, Religion and Public Education, 1967, (with Nancy F. Sizer) Moral Education: Five Lectures, 1970, Places for Learning, Places for Joy: Speculations on American School Reform, 1972, Horace's Compromise: The Dilemma of the American High School, 1984, rev. edit., 1985, Horace's School: Redesigning the American High School, 1992, Horace's Hope: What Works for the American High School, 1996. Active Nat. Adv. Coun., Scholastic, Inc., 1996. Capt. U.S. Army, 1953-55. Named Guggenheim fellow, 1971; recipient citations Am. Fedn. Tchrs., Nat. Assn. Secondary Sch. Prins., Phillips Exeter Acad., Boston C. of C., Andover C. of C., Lehigh U. Edn. Alumni, 1991, Nat. Assn. Coll. Admissions Counsellors, 1991, Anthony Wayne award Wayne State U., 1981, Gold medal for excellence in undergrad. teaching CASE, 1988, Tchrs. Coll. medal Tchrs. Coll., Columbia U., 1991, Harold W. McGraw prize in edn., 1991, James Bryant Conant award Edn. Commn. States, 1992, Disting. Svc. award Coun. Chief State Sch. Officers, 1992, Coun. Am. Private Edn., 1993, Nat. award of Distinction U. Pa., 1993, Alumni award Harvard Grad. Sch. Edn., 1994. Fellow Am. Acad. Arts and Scis., Am. Philos. Soc.; mem. Nat. Acad. Edn. Office: Brown Univ Coalition of Essential Schs PO Box 1969 Providence RI 02912-1969

SJOBLAD, STEVEN A., architectural firm executive. Chmn. Ellerbe Becket Co., Mpls. Office: Ellerbe Becket Co 800 Lasalle Ave Minneapolis MN 55402-2006

SJOERDSMA, ALBERT, research institute executive; b. Lansing, Ill., Aug. 31, 1924; s. Sam and Agnes S.; m. Fern E. MacAllister, Dec. 2, 1950; children—Leslie, Ann, Albert, Britt. Ph.B., U. Chgo., 1944, B.S., 1945, Ph.D., 1948, M.D., 1949. Research asst. U. Chgo., 1947-49, NIH postdoctoral research fellow, 1950; intern U. Mich. Hosp., Ann Arbor, 1949-50; resident physician Michael Reese Hosp., Chgo., 1951; resident in internal medicine USPHS Hosp., Balt., 1951-53; sr. investigator, chief exptl. therapeutics br. Nat. Heart and Lung Inst., Bethesda, Md., 1953-71; v.p. Merrell Internat. Co., Strasbourg, France, 1971-78; v.p. pharm. research and devel. Richardson-Merrell Inc., 1978-81; v.p. pharm. research Merrell Dow Pharms., Cin., 1981-83; pres. Merrell Dow Research Inst., Cin., 1983-89; pres. emeritus Merrell Dow Research Inst., Cin., 1989-94; med. scis. cons., 1994—; vis. spl. fellow Gen. Hosp., Malmo, Sweden, 1959-60; spl. lectr. George Washington U., 1959-71; Anton Julius Carlson lectr. U. Chgo., 1984; hon. chmn. 2d World Conf. on Clin. Pharmacology and Therapeutics, Washington, 1983; clin. prof. medicine U. Cin. Med. Ctr., 1986-91. Mem. AAAS (Theobold Smith award med. scis. 1958), Am. Soc. Pharm. and Exptl. Therapeutics (Harry Gold award in clin. pharmacology 1977, Exptl. Therapeutics award 1990), Am. Soc. Clin. Pharmacology and Therapeutics (Oscar B. Hunter Meml. award in therapeutics 1981), Internat. Soc. Hypertension, Coun. High Blood Pressure Rsch., Am. Heart Assn., Am. Fedn. Clin. Rsch., Am. Soc. Clin. Investigation, Am. Soc. Exptl. Biology and Medicine, Assn. Am. Physicians, Am. Coll. Neuropsychopharmacology. Home and Office: 263 N Dogwood Trail Kitty Hawk NC 27949

SJOGREN, ROBERT WILLIAM, internist; b. Ft. Collins, Colo., Aug. 4, 1919; s. John William and Flora Anne (Anderson) S.; m. Amenta Margaret Robeson, June 18, 1942; children: Robert Jr., Jane Durbin Fitch, Margaret Leigh. BS in Biology, Va. Poly. U., 1940; MD, U. Va., 1943. Diplomate Am. Bd. Internal Medicine. Home: HC 73 Box 856B Locust Grove VA 22508-9572

SJOLANDER, GARY WALFRED, physicist; b. Bagley, Minn., Dec. 5, 1942; s. Tage Walfred and Evelyn Mildred (Kaehn) S.; m. Joann Lorraine Tressler, June 18, 1966; 1 child, Toby Ryan. BS in Physics, U. Minn., 1970, MS in Physics, 1974, PhD in Physics, 1975. Rsch. assoc. U. Minn., Mpls., 1975-76; rsch. scientist Johns Hopkins U., Balt., 1977-78, sr. physicist, 1978-82; sr. engr. Westinghouse Electric Corp., Annapolis, Md., 1982-85; sr. staff engr. Lockheed Martin Astronautics, Denver, 1985-95; engring. scientist data techs. divsn. TRW, Aurora, Colo., 1996—; pres. Cypress Improvement Assn., Inc., Severna Park, Md., 1984-85; advisor Inroads/Denver, Inc., 1986-88. Author numerous articles in field. With USAF, 1960-64. Mem. AIAA, Internat. Soc. for Optical Engring., Am. Geophys. Union, The Planetary Soc. Lutheran. Avocations: tennis, motorcycling, wooden-ship models, piano, woodworking. Home: 811 W Kettle Ave Littleton CO 80120-4443

SJOSTRAND, FRITIOF STIG, biologist, educator; b. Stockholm, Sweden, Nov. 5, 1912; s. Nils Johan and Dagmar (Hansen) S.; m. Marta Bruhn-Fahraeus, Mar. 24, 1941 (dec. June 1954); 1 child, Rutger; m. Ebba Gyllenkrok, Mar. 28, 1955; 1 child, Johan; m. Birgitta Petterson, Jan. 23, 1969; 1 child, Peter. M.D., Karolinska Institutet, Stockholm, 1941, Ph.D., 1945; Ph.D. (hon.), U. Siena, 1974, North-East Hill U., Shillon, India, 1989. Asst. prof. anatomy Karolinska Institutet, 1945-48, assoc. prof., 1949-59, prof. histology, 1960-61; research assoc. MIT, 1947-48; vis. prof. UCLA, 1959, prof. zoology, 1960-82, prof. emeritus molecular biology, 1982—. Author: Über die Eigenfluoreszenz Tierischer Gewebe Mit Besonderer Berücksichtigung der Sägertierniere, 1944, Electron Microscopy of Cells and Tissues, Vol. I, 1967, Deducing Function from Structure, Vols. I and II, 1990; also numerous articles. Decorated North Star Orden Sweden; recipient Jubilee award Swedish Med. Soc., 1959, Anders Retzius gold medal, 1967; Paul Ehrlich-Ludwig Darmstaedter prize, 1971. Fellow Royal Micros. Soc. (hon., London), Am. Acad. Arts and Scis.; mem. Electron Microscopy Soc. Am. (hon., Disting. Scientist award 1992), Japan Electron Microscopy Soc. (hon.), Scandinavian Electron Microscopy Soc. (hon.). Achievements include development technique for high resolution electron microscopy of cells, fluorescence microspectrography; inventor ultramicrotome.

SKADDEN, DONALD HARVEY, professional society executive, accounting educator; b. Danville, Ill., Jan. 26, 1925; s. Harvey Frank and Lois Mary (Strawbridge) S.; m. Barbara Ann Meade, June 16, 1946 (dec.); children: John D., David H.; m. Karin Matson, Mar. 18, 1985. BS, U. Ill., 1948, MS, 1949, PhD, 1955. CPA, Ill. Asst. prof. acctg. U. Ill., Urbana, 1955-58, assoc. prof., 1958-61, prof., 1961-73, assoc. dean Coll. Commerce and Bus. Adminstrn., 1969-71; sr. acct. Haskins & Sells, 1957-58; Arthur Young prof. accounting U. Mich., Ann Arbor, 1973-87, chmn. acctg. faculty, 1976-79, assoc. dean for acad. affairs, 1979-87; v.p. taxation AICPA, 1987-92; exec. dir. Am. Tax Policy Inst., 1992—; dir. Paton Acctg. Ctr., 1976-79; mem. Fin. Acctg. Stds. Adv. Commn., 1980-84, ABA Commn. on Taxpayer Compliance, 1984-88; mem. commrs. adv. group IRS, 1990-91; active Nat. Conf. Lawyers and CPAs, 1993—. Author: Federal Income Tax: Student Workbook, 1965; Co-author: Principles of Federal Income Taxation; Editor: The Illinois CPA, 1964-66; editorial bd.: The Tax Adviser, 1969-74, The Accounting Review, 1973-75. Alderman, City of Urbana, 1961-69, mayor, 1969. With AUS, 1943-46, ETO. Decorated Combat Inf. badge. Mem. Am. Inst. CPA's (exec. com. of fed. tax div. 1979-82, council 1980-83), Ill. Soc. CPA's (bd. dirs. 1966-68, chair in accountancy 1968-73), Am. Acctg. Assn. (pres. 1979-80), Am. Taxation Assn. (pres. 1977-78), Urbana Assn. Commerce and Industry (bd. dirs. 1970-73), Beta Gamma Sigma, Phi Kappa Phi, Beta Alpha Psi. Methodist. Home: 3112 Chipping Wedge Ct Sanford NC 27330-8336

SKAFF, ANDREW JOSEPH, lawyer, public utilities, energy and transportation executive; b. Sioux Falls, S.D., Aug. 30, 1945; s. Andrew Joseph and Alice Maxine (Skaff) S.; m. Lois Carol Phillips, Oct. 4, 1971; children—Amy Phillips, Julie Phillips. B.S. in Bus. Adminstrn, Miami U., Oxford, Ohio, 1967; J.D., U. Toledo, 1970. Bar: Calif. 1971, U.S. Supreme Ct. 1974. Prin., sr. counsel Calif. Public Utilities Commn., 1977; gen. counsel Delta Calif. Industries, Oakland, 1977-82; sec. Delta Calif. Industries, 1978-82; mem. Silver Rosen, Fischer & Stecher, San Francisco, 1982-84; sr. ptnr. Skaff and Anderson, San Francisco, 1984-90; pvt. practice Law Office of Andrew J. Skaff, 1990-95; ptnr. Knox Ricksen LLP, Oakland, 1995—; officer Delta Calif. Industries and subs. Contbr. articles to legal jours.; contbg. mem. law rev. U. Toledo, 1970. Mem. Calif. Bar Assn., Conf. Calif. Pub. Utilities Counsel, Calif. Cogeneration Coun., Assn. Transp. Practitioners, Alameda County Bar Assn. Office: Lake Merritt Plz 1999 Harrison St Fl 17 Oakland CA 94612-3520

SKAFF, JOSEPH JOHN, state agency administrator, retired army officer; b. Charleston, W.Va., June 13, 1930; s. Michael Joseph and Zahia S.; m. Maree A. Fleming, Aug. 4, 1957; children: Joseph M., Lynn M. Johnson, Gregory M., Nancy E. Kochman. B.S., U.S. Mil Acad., 1955; M.S., George Washington U., 1968. Commd. 2d lt. U.S. Army, 1955; commanded 1/27 FA battalion, 1968-69; advanced through grades to maj. gen.; dep. dir. internat. negotiations U.S. Army Joint Chiefs of Staff, Washington, 1979-81; mem. staff and faculty U.S. Mil. Acad., 1972-76; also dep. commr. U.S. del. Standing Consultative Commn., Geneva, 1979-81; dep. dir. ops. readiness and moblzn. Hdqrs. Dept. Army, Washington, 1981-83; dep. comdr./chief staff U.S. Army in Japan, 1982-84; dep. commdg. gen., commdg. gen. 1st U.S. Army, Fort Devens, Mass., 1985-89, adj. gen. W.Va., 1989-95; cabinet sec. mil. affairs and pub. safety W.Va., 1989-97. Decorated D.S.M., Def. Superior Svc. medal, Legion of Merit, Bronze Star, Air medal, others. Mem. Assn. Grads. U.S. Mil. Acad., Assn. U.S. Army, Arty. Assn., Adj. Gens. Assn. U.S., Nat. Guard Assn. U.S., Officers Christian Fellowship, Fellowship Christian Athletes. Eastern Orthodox.

SKAGGS, ARLINE DOTSON, elementary school educator; b. Houston, Sept. 10, 1935; d. Gordon Alonzo and Fannie Mae (O'Kelley) Dotson; m. May 24, 1958 (div. Dec. 1969); children: Fred Mack, Ray Gordon. BS, U. Houston, 1957. Recreation leader VA Hosp., Houston, 1957-59; 4th and 5th grade tchr. Houston Ind. Sch. Dist., 1967-91; ret., 1991—; sponsor Number Sense, 1975-87, Sci. Fair, 1984-85. Auditor PTA, 1985, 87, 88; treas. Mt. Olive Luth. Sch. PTO, 1967-68; pres. Gulfgate Lioness Club, 1966-67; mem. Delphian Soc., 1965, Ch. of Houston Bread Distbn. program, 1990-91; treas. Houston Night Chpt. Women's Aglow, 1982; tchr. Children's Ch., 1972, 83, 84; prayer ptnr. Trinity Broadcasting Network, 1989-90, Christian Broadcasting Network, 1982-83; Braves scorekeeper Braes Bayou Little League, 1969-71; mem. United Way Funding Com., Salvation Army, Star of Hope & United Svcs. Orgn., 1974-76. Winning sponsor Citywide Math. Competition, Houston Ind. Sch. Dist., 1982, N.E. Area Math. Competition, 1976, 78, 79, 81, 82, 83, Lockhart Math. Contest, 1987. Mem. NEA (del. 1974), Houston Tchrs. Assn. (sch. rep. 1968-77, exec. bd. 1972-74, dir. N.E. area 1972-74, by-laws chmn. 1976), Tex. State Tchrs. Assn. (life, del. convs. 1968-75). Avocations: reading, grandparenting, travel. Home: 4437 Vivian St Bellaire TX 77401-5630

SKAGGS, BEBE REBECCA PATTEN, college dean, clergywoman; b. Berkeley, Calif., Jan. 30, 1950; d. Carl Thomas and Bebe (Harrison) P. BS in Bible, Patten Coll., 1969; BA in Philosophy, Holy Names Coll., 1970; MA in Bibl. Studies New Testament, Wheaton Coll., 1972; PhD in Bibl. Studies New Testament, Drew U., 1976; MA in Philosophy, Dominican Sch. Philosophy & Theology, 1990; postgrad., U. Calif., Berkeley, 1991-92. Ordained to ministry Christian Evang. Ch., 1963. Co-pastor Christian Cathedral, Christian Evang. Chs. Am., Inc., 1964—; assoc. prof. Patten Coll., Oakland, Calif., 1975-82, dean, 1977—, prof. N.T., 1982—; presenter in field. Author: Before the Times, 1980, The Word of the Early Church, 1990; contbg. author: Internat. Standard Bibl. Ency., rev. edit., 1983. Active Wheaton Coll. Symphony, 1971-72, Drew U. Ensemble, 1971-75, Young Artists Symphony, N.J., 1972-75, Somerset Hill Symphony, N.J., 1973-74, Peninsula Symphony, 1977, 80-81, Madison Chamber Trio, N.J., 1973-75. Named one of Outstanding Young Women of Am., 1976, 77, 80-81, 82; St. Olaf's Coll. fellow, 1990. Mem. AAUP, Am. Acad. Religion, Soc. Bibl. Lit., Internat. Biographical Assn., Christian Evang. Chs. of Am., Inc. (bd. dirs. 1964—), Christian Assn. for Student Affairs, Assn. for Christians in Student Devel., Inst. for Bibl. Rsch., Phi Delta Kappa.

SKAGGS, DAVID E., congressman; b. Cin., Feb. 22, 1943; s. Charles and Juanita Skaggs; m. Laura Locher, Jan. 3, 1987; 1 child, Matthew; stepchildren: Clare, Will. BA in Philosophy, Wesleyan U., 1964; student law, U. Va., 1964-65; LLB, Yale U., 1967. Bar: N.Y. 1968, Colo. 1971. Assoc. Newcomer & Douglass, Boulder, Colo., 1971-74, 77-78; chief of staff Congressman Tim Wirth, Washington, 1975-77; ptnr. Skaggs, Stone & Sheehy, Boulder, 1978-86; mem. 100th-105th Congresses from 2d Colo. dist., Washington, 1987—; mem. Appropriations com., subcoms. Commerce and Justice, Interior; mem. Ho. Permanent Select Com. on Intelligence; mem. Colo. Ho. of Reps., Denver, 1980-86; minority leader, 1982-85. Former bd. dirs. Rocky Mountain Planned Parenthood, Mental Health Assn. Colo., Boulder County United Way, Boulder Civic Opera. Served to capt. USMC, 1968-71, Vietnam; maj. USMCR, 1971-77. Mem. Colo. Bar Assn., Boulder County Bar Assn., Boulder C. of C. Democrat. Congregationalist. Office: US House of Reps 1124 Longworth Bldg Washington DC 20515-0602 also: 9101 Harlan St Unit 130 Westminster CO 80030-2925

SKAGGS, MERTON MELVIN, JR., environmental engineer; b. Kerrville, Tex., Nov. 16, 1953; s. Merton Melvin and Peggy LaNell (Dechert) S.; m. Susan Marie Frawley, Aug. 9, 1980; children: Alan, Marie, Bridget. B-SChemE, Tex. A&M U., 1976; MS in Biology, U. Houston, Clear Lake City, Tex., 1979. Registered profl. engr., Tex. Process engr. Diamond Shamrock Chems. Co., Pasadena, Tex., 1976-78, environ. engr., 1979-80, sr. environ. engr., 1981-84; ctrl. ops. mgr. Maxus Energy Corp., Dallas, 1985-91, gen. mgr. environ. affairs, 1991-96; pres. Chem. Land Holdings, Inc., Dallas, 1994—, Maxus Agrl. Chems., Inc., Dallas, 1994-96. Coach Odyssey of the Mind, Southlake, Tex., 1993-95. Mem. AIChE, Soc. Petroleum Engrs. (chmn. environ. study group 1993-96, sect. treas. 1996-97), Water Environ. Federation, Air and Waste Assn. Methodist. Achievements include management of projects to clean up and/or close five major hazardous waste disposal sites and five related publications. Home: 600 Llano Ct Southlake TX 76092-4817 Office: Chemical Land Holdings Inc 717 N Harwood St Dallas TX 75201-6538

SKAGGS, RICHARD WAYNE, agricultural engineering educator; b. Grayson, Ky., Aug. 20, 1942; s. Daniel M. and Gertrude (Adkins) S.; m. Judy Ann Kuhn, Aug. 25, 1962; children: Rebecca Diane Skaggs Ramsey, Steven Glen. BS in Agr. Engring., U. Ky., 1964, MS in Agr. Engring., 1966; PhD, Purdue U., 1970. Registered profl. engr., N.C. Grad. asst. U. Ky., Lexington, 1964-66; grad. instr. in rsch. Purdue U., West Lafayette, Ind., 1966-70; asst. prof. agrl. engring. N.C. State U., Raleigh, 1970-74, assoc. prof., 1974-79, prof., 1979-84, William Neal Reynolds prof., 1984—, disting. univ. prof., 1991—; cons. on drainage U.S. Aid, Egypt, 1989—; cons., lectr. on water mgmt., India, 1992, Malaysia, 1993, 95, New Zealand, 1993. Contbr. over 240 articles on water mgmt. and hydrology to profl. jours. Recipient Outstanding Young Scientist award N.C. State U. chpt. Sigma Xi, 1978; Alumni Rsch. award N.C. State U. Alumni Assn., 1983, Alumni Disting. Profl. award for grad. tchg., 1991, Alexander Q. Holladay Award for Excellence, N.C. State U., 1994, Superior Svc. award USDA, 1986, 90, O. Max Gardner award The U. of N.C. Sys., 1997; named to Drainage Hall of Fame, Ohio State U., 1984, Engring. Hall of Distinction, U. Ky., 1994; named Outstanding Alumnus Agrl. Engr., U. Ky., 1985, Disting. Engring. Alumnus, Purdue U., 1997. Fellow Am. Soc. Agrl. Engrs. (chmn. nat. drainage symposium com. 1976, mem. nominating com. 1979, 95-96, Hancor Soil and Water Engring. award 1986, bd. dirs. 1992-94, John Deere Gold medal 1993); mem. NRC (com. on wetland characterization), NAE. Avocations: basketball, golf, reading. Home: 2824 Sandia Dr Raleigh NC 27607-3150 Office: NC State U Dept Biol-Agrl Eng PO Box 7625 Raleigh NC 27695-7625

SKAGGS, RICKY, country musician; b. Ky., July 18, 1954; s. Hobert and Dorothy S.; m. Sharon White, 1981; 4 children. First profl. job, age 15, playing mandolin with Ralph Stanley group Clinch Mountain Boys; subsequently with Country Gentlemen, J.D. Crowe and New South; then formed own group Boone Creek; joined Emmylou Harris backup group Hot Band, 1977; played with The Whites; joined Grand Ole Opry, 1982; albums include Waitin' for the Sun to Shine, 1981, Highways and Heartaches, Don't Cheat in Our Hometown, Country Boy, 1984, Favorite Country Songs, Live in London, Love's Gonna Get Ya!, Comin' Home To Stay, 1988, Kentucky Thunder, 1989, My Father's Son, 1991, Super Hits, 1993, Solid Ground. Recipient Horizon award for best newcomer Country Music Assn., male vocalist of yr. award, 1982, best instrumental group award, 1983, 84, 85, 6 Country Music Assn. awards including Entertainer of Yr. award, 1985, Vocal Event of Yr. award, 1991, Grammy award for best country instrumental, 1984, 85, 86, Grammy award for best country vocal collaboration, 1992, 6 Acad. of Country Music awards, MusicDove award Gospel Music Assn., Playboy Reader's Poll Best Country Instrumental Performance, 1989, Eng.'s Country Music Round Up Most Popular Internat. Male, 1986-87, Edison award, 1987, 50th Anniversary award USO, 1989, various awards Music City News, Cash Box, Radio and Records; named Christian Country Artist of Yr. Gospel Voice Mag., 1993, Musician of Yr. award Christian Country Music Assn., 1994. Office: 54 Music Sq E Ste 301 Nashville TN 37203-4315*

SKAGGS, SANFORD MERLE, lawyer; b. Berkeley, Calif., Oct. 24, 1939; s. Sherman G. and Barbara Jewel (Stinson) S.; m. Sharon Ann Barnes, Sept. 3, 1976; children: Stephen, Paula Ferry, Barbara Gallagher, Darren Peterson. BA, U. Calif., Berkeley, 1961; JD, U. Calif., 1964. Bar: Calif. 1965. Atty. Pacific Gas and Electric Co., San Francisco, 1964-73; gen. counsel Pacific Gas Transmission Co., San Francisco, 1973-75; ptnr. Van Voorhis & Skaggs, Walnut Creek, Calif., 1975-85, McCutchen, Doyle, Brown & Enersen, San Francisco and Walnut Creek, 1985—; mem.Calif. Law Revision Commn., 1990—, chmn. 1993; dir. John Muir/Mt. Diablo Health Sys., 1996—. Councilman City of Walnut Creek, 1972-78, mayor 1974-75, 76-77; bd. dirs. East Bay Mcpl. Utility Dist., 1978-90, pres., 1982-90; dir. Calif. Symphony, 1992-96; trustee Contra Costa County Law Libr., 1978—. Mem. Calif. State Bar Assn., Contra Costa County Bar Assn., Urban Land Inst., Lambda Alpha, Alpha Delta Phi, Phi Delta Phi. Republican. Office: McCutchen Doyle Brown & Enersen PO Box V Ste 700 1331 N California Blvd Walnut Creek CA 94596

SKAGGS, WAYNE GERARD, financial services company executive, retired; b. Bonneterre, Mo., Dec. 12, 1929; s. Jasper Pinkney and Lattie May (Duren) S.; m. Hana Kaneko, June 1, 1952; children: Robert Kenneth, Melody Jane, Joy Elizabeth. Student, Mo. Inst. Acctg. and Law, 1947-48, U. Mo., Columbia, 1954-55. With Advantage Capital Corp. (formerly Am. Capital Corp.), Houston, 1955-96, ret., 1996; pres., COO Mktg. Group of Cos., Houston, 1976-80, corp. v.p., cons., 1972-90. Served with USAF, 1950-54, Korea. Mem. Nat. Assn. Securities Dealers (nat. vice chmn. 1977, dist. chmn. 1972), Nat. Bus. Conduct (gov., chmn. 1976), Investment Co. Inst. Republican. Presbyterian. Club: Optimists (pres. club 1966, life mem.). Home: PO Box 726 Wimberley TX 78676-0726

SKAL, DEBRA LYNN, lawyer; b. Dayton, Ohio, Oct. 2, 1958; d. Lawrence and Anne Bernice (Cunix) S. BS with high distinction, Ind. U., 1986; JD, Duke U., 1989. Bar: Ga. 1989. Assoc. Powell, Goldstein, Frazer & Murphy, Atlanta, 1989—. Exec. editor: Alaska Law Rev., 1987-89. Mem. Lupus Found. Am., Atlanta, 1992—; coun. mem. Yes!Atlanta, 1990—; mem. Sjogren's Found., Port Washington, N.Y., 1992—. Mem. State Bar Assn. Ga., mem. counsel, Atlanta, 1990—; mem. Southern Ooverty Law Ctr., Montgomery, Ala., mem. Lupus Found. of Am., Atlanta, 1992—, mem. Arthritis Found., mem. Sjogren's Found., Port Wash. N.Y., 1992—, mem. Am. Diabetes Assn., 1996—, Beta Gamma Sigma. Office: 2504 Northlake Ct NE Atlanta GA 30345-2228

SKALA, GARY DENNIS, electric and gas utilities executive management consultant; b. Bay Shore, N.Y, Oct. 15, 1946; s. Harry A. and Emily Skala. BS in Mgmt. Engring., Rensselaer Polytech. Inst., 1969; MA in Psychology, Hofstra U., 1972; postgrad., Chgo. Theol. Sem., 1996-97. Engr. L.I. Lighting Co., Hicksville, N.Y., 1969-71; labor rels. coord. L.I. Lighting Co., 1971-73; mgmt. cons. Gilbert/Commonwealth, N.Y.C., 1973-74; sr. mgmt. cons. Booz, Allen & Hamilton, San Francisco, 1974-78; mgr. utility cons. A.T. Kearney, Chgo., 1978-81; mng. cons. Cresap, div. Towers Perrin, Chgo., 1981-85; pres. Gary D. Skala & Assocs. Mgmt. Cons., Chgo., 1985—; lectr. on utility bus. issues Edison Electric Inst., Utility Exec. Mgmt. Com., Internat. Maintenance Conf., Assn. Rural Electric Coops., Inst. Indsl. Engrs.; subcontracting cons. Arthur D. Little Inc., Liberty Cons. Group, Ernst & Young, Cresap, A.T. Kearney, Towers Perrin, Michael Paris Assocs. Ltd., Planmetrics. Contbr. articles to profl. jours. Trustee, strategic planning com. Samaritan Inst. for Religious Studies; mem. bd. Ordained Ministry of Great Lakes Dist. of Universal Fellowship Met. Cmty. Chs.; vice moderator bd. dirs. Good Shepherd Parish Met. Cmty. Ch. of Chgo; vol. The Night Ministry of Chgo. Mem. Inst. Indsl. Engrs. (sr. mem. utility div. 1978—, charter), Am. Inst. Indsl. Engrs. (chmn. Midwest chpt. utility div. 1980-81). Avocations: managing the Jerry Lee Lewis Archives, Jason D. Williams Archives.

SKALAK, RICHARD, engineering mechanics educator, researcher; b. N.Y.C., Feb. 5, 1923; s. Rudolph and Anna (Tuma) S.; m. Anna Lesta Allison, Jan. 24, 1953; children: Steven Leslie, Thomas Cooper, Martha Jean, Barbara Anne. BS, Columbia U., 1943, CE, 1946, PhD, 1954; MD (hon.), Gothenburg U., Sweden, 1990. Instr. civil engring. Columbia U., N.Y.C., 1948-54, asst. prof., 1954-60, assoc. prof., 1960-64, prof., 1964-77, James Kip Finch prof. engring. mechanics, 1977-88, emeritus, 1988—, dir. Bioengring. Inst., 1978-88; prof. bioengring. U. Calif., San Diego, 1988—, dir. Inst. for Mechs. and Materials, 1992-96; Hunter lectr. Clemson U., 1994; mem. panel Gov.'s Conf. on Sci. and Engring., R&D, 1989-90. Contbr. articles to sci. jours. Bd. dirs. Biotech. Inst., Gothenburg, Sweden, 1978—; mem. adv. bd. Ctr. for Biomed. Engring., N.Y.C., 1994—. Recipient Great Tchr. award Columbia Coll. Soc. of Older Grads., 1972, Merit medal Czechoslovakian Acad. Scis., 1990. Fellow AAAS, ASME (Centennial medal 1980, Melville medal 1990, editor jour. 1984), Am. Acad. Mechanics, Soc. Engring. Sci., Am. Inst. Med. and Biol. Engring. (founding); mem. NAE, Soc. Rheology, Am. Heart Assn., Microcirculatory Soc., Internat. Soc. Biorheology (Poiseuille medal 1989), Biomed. Engring. Soc. (Alza medal 1983), Cardiovascular System Dynamics Soc., Am. Soc. for Engring. Edn., Tau Beta Pi, Sigma Xi. Democrat. Presbyterian. Home: 8916 Montrose Way San Diego CA 92122 Office: U Calif San Diego Dept Bioengring La Jolla CA 92093-0412

SKALE, LINDA DIANNE, elementary education educator; b. Lansing, Mich., May 24, 1947; d. Louis and Dolores Louise (Clum) Pascotto; m. Arthur Skale, Sept. 9, 1967; children: Michelle, John, David, Jennifer. BA, Mich. State U., 1969, MA, 1971. Tchr. 3rd grade Ionia (Mich.) pub. schs., 1971—; reading cons. Benton Harbor (Mich.) schs.; elem. tchr. 3rd-5th grades, curriculum chair lang. arts portfolio assessment Berrien Springs (Mich.) Sch., reading tchr., coord.; interim prin. Sylvester Elem. Sch., 1994-95. Named 1989 Outstanding Employee of the Yr., Berrien Springs Schs., 1988. Mem. ASCD, Internat. Reading Assn., Mich. Reading Assn. (lectr.), Tri County Reading Assn., Mich. Elem. and Mid. Sch. Prins. Assn. Home: 4384 Laurel Dr Saint Joseph MI 49085-9311

SKALKA, HAROLD WALTER, ophthalmologist, educator; b. N.Y.C., Aug. 22, 1941; s. Jack and Sylvia Skalka; m. Barbara Jean Herbert, Oct. 2, 1965; children: Jennifer, Gretchen, Kirsten. AB with distinction, Cornell U., 1962; MD, NYU, 1966. Intern Greenwich (Conn.) Hosp., 1966-67; resident in ophthalmology Bellevue Hosp., Univ. Hosp., Manhattan VA Hosp., 1967-70; fellow in retinal physiology and ultrasonography, 1970-71; cons. in ophthalmology St. Jude's Hosp., Montgomery, Ala., 1971-73; asst. prof. ophthalmology U. Ala., Birmingham, 1973-75, assoc. prof., 1975-80, prof., 1980-81, assoc. prof. dept. medicine, 1980—, chmn. combined program in ophthalmology, 1981—, Nathan E. Miles prof., 1986—; acting chmn. combined program ophthalmology U. Ala., 1974-76; ophthalmologist Lowndes

County Bd. Health Community Health Project, 1972. Contbr. articles to Am. Jour. Ophthalmology, Eye, Ear, Nose and Throat Monthly, Annals of Ophthalmology, Ophthalmic Surgery, Jour. Clin. Ultrasound, Jour. Pediatric Ophthalmology and Strabismus, The Lancet, AMA Archives of Ophthalmology, Jour. So. Med. Assn., Acta Ophthalmologica, Metabolic and Pediatric Ophthalmology, Applied Radiology, British Jour. Ophthalmology, Blood, Neuro-Ophthalmology; editorial bd.: Ala. Jour. Med. Sci. Major USAFMC, 1971-73. Mem. AAAS, AMA, ACS, SIDUO, Ala. Sight Conservation Assn., Ala. Conservancy, Ala. Wildlife Fedn., Eye Bank Bd., Am. Acad. Ophthalmology, Am. Inst. Ultrasound in Medicine, Internat. Soc. for Clin. Electrophysiology of Vision, Internat. Soc. on Metabolic Eye Disease, Assn. for Rsch. in Vision and Ophthalmology, AAUP, Am. Intraocular Implant Soc., Am. Assn. Ophthalmology, Pan Am. Assn. Ophthalmology, So. Med. Assn., Rsch. to Prevent Blindness, Ala. Acad. Ophthalmology, Ala. Med. Assn., Jefferson County Med. Soc., Contact Lens Assn. Ophthalmologists, Ala. Ultrasound Soc., Royal Soc. Medicine, N.Y. Acad. Scis., Am. Soc. Standardized Ophthalmic Echography (charter exec. bd. mem.), Am. Coll. Nutrition. Office: Eye Found Hosp U Ala 700 18th St S Ste 300 Birmingham AL 35233-1856

SKALKO, RICHARD GALLANT, anatomist, educator; b. Providence, Apr. 10, 1936; s. Francis Charles and Emilie Margaret (Gallant) S.; m. Louise Marie Luchetti (div. 1982); m. Priscilla Ann Brown, 1985; children—Patricia, Margaret, Christine. A.B., Providence Coll., 1957; M.S., St. John's U., 1959; Ph.D., U. Fla., 1963. Instr. anatomy Cornell U. Med. Coll., 1963-66, asst. prof., 1966-67; asst. prof. anatomy La. State U. Med. Ctr., New Orleans, 1967-69, assoc. prof., 1969-70; dir. Embryology Lab., Birth Defects Inst., N.Y. State Health Dept., Albany, 1970-77; assoc. prof. anatomy and toxicology Albany Med. Coll., 1970-76, prof., 1976-77; prof. anatomy and cell biology East Tenn. State U. Coll. Medicine, Johnson City, 1977—, chmn. dept., 1977—; mem. sci. adv. bd. NCTR, FDA, 1976-79; vis. prof. Institut fur Toxikologie und Embyronalpharmakologie, Freie U., Berlin, 1978; mem. human embryology and devel. study sect., NIH, 1990-94. Mem. Am. Assn. Anatomists, Teratology Soc., Soc. Devel. Biology, European Teratology Soc., Soc. Toxicology. Democrat. Roman Catholic. Author: Basic Concepts in Teratology, 1985; editor: Heredity and Society, 1973; Congenital Defects, 1974. Home: 3302 Pine Timbers Dr Johnson City TN 37604-1404 Office: East Tenn State U Coll Medicine Dept Anatomy and Cell Biology Johnson City TN 37614-0582

SKALLA, JOHN LIONELL, insurance agent; b. Marysville, Kans., July 25, 1933; s. Ernest John and Charlotte Violet (Ricker) S.; m. Allene Davison, Aug. 17, 1957; children: Camille, Johnette. BA, U. Nebr., 1957. CLU, ChFC. Agt. Conn. Mut. Life Ins. Co., Lincoln, Nebr., 1957-61; gen. agt. Conn. Mut. Life Ins. Co., Des Moines, 1961-69, Houston, 1969—; bd. dirs., mem. strategy and ops. com. Conn. Mut. Life Ins., Hartford, chmn. adv. com. Conn. Mut. Gen. Agts., 1989; nat. bd. dirs. Gen. Agts. and Mgrs. Conf., Washington; bd. dirs. Univ. of Houston Sch. of Ins. and Fin. Svcs. Contbr. articles to profl. jours. Trustee U. Nebr. Found. Bd., Lincoln; gen. chmn. Vice Lombardi Award Dinner, Houston, 1978; past pres. Whitehall Club, Houston; bd. dirs. Am. Cancer Soc., Houston; trustee Goodwill Industries, Houston; mem. Houston Bus. and Estate Planning Coun., Houston Estate and Fin. Forum. Recipient Mgr. of Yr. award Houston Gen. Agts. and Mgrs. Assn., 1995, Swgama Trail Boss award, 1996. Mem. Nat. Assn. Life Underwriters (Nat. Quality awards 1962-95), Million Dollar Round Table, Am. Soc. CLU and ChFc (Woody Woodson award 1993, Hall of Fame 1993), Tex. Assn. Life Underwriters, Houston Assn. Life Underwriters, Houston Estate and Fin. Forum, Rotary, Houston Bus. & Estate Planning Coun. Republican. Episcopalian. Avocations: travel, reading, writing, speaking. Office: John L Skalla & Assocs 4265 San Felipe St Fl 7 Houston TX 77027-2920

SKAMBIS, CHRISTOPHER CHARLES, JR., lawyer; b. Painesville, Ohio, Jan. 21, 1953; s. Christopher Charles and Anne (haritos) S.; m. Susan Elaine Adrianson, Dec. 18, 1976; children: Adrianne Elaine, Christopher Roy. Student, U. Pa., 1970-72; BA, U. Conn., 1972-74; JD, Ohio State U. Coll. Law, Columbus, 1975-78. Bar: Fla. 1978, Fla. Supreme Ct., 1978, U.S. Dist. Ct. (ctrl. dist.), 1979, U.S. Ct. Appeals (5th and 11th cir.) 1981, U.S. Supreme Ct. 1989. Assoc. VandenBerg, Gay & Burke, Orlando, Fla., 1978-81, ptnr., 1982; ptnr. VandenBurg, Gay, Burke, Wilson & Arkin, Orlando, Fla., 1982-85, Foley & Lardner, Orlando, Fla., 1985-96, Moran & Shams PA, Orlando, Fla., 1996—; mem. Orange County Bar Assn., Orlando, Fla., 1978, Fla. Bar 9D Grievance Commn., Orlando, Fla., 1989; arbitrator Fla. Bar 9th Cir. Fee Arbitration Commn., Orlando, Fla., 1987; co-chair Federal and State Trial Practice Co., Orlando, Fla., 1992—. Mem. Am. Judicature Soc., ABA. Avocations: amateur ham radio operator, little league, coalition for homeless. Office: Moran & Shams PA PO Box 472 111 N Orange Ave Ste 1200 Orlando FL 32801-0472

SKATES, RONALD LOUIS, computer manufacturing executive; b. Kansas City, Mo., Sept. 25, 1941; s. Raymond and Suzanne (Lispi) S.; m. Mary Austin; children: Melissa, Elizabeth. AB cum laude, Harvard U., 1963, MBA, 1965. Acct. Price Waterhouse, Boston, audit ptnr., 1976-86; sr. v.p. fin. and adminstrn. Data Gen. Corp., Westboro, Mass., 1986-88, dir., exec. v.p., chief oper. officer, 1988-89; pres., CEO Mass. Gen. Hosp., Boston, 1990—, overseer, 1992—. Overseer Mus. Fine Arts, 1989. Mem. AICPA, Mass. Soc. CPAs. Office: Data Gen Corp 3400 Computer Dr Westborough MA 01581-1771

SKAUEN, DONALD MATTHEW, retired pharmaceutical educator; b. Newton, Mass., May 14, 1916; s. Marcus and Mary A. (Duncan) S.; m. Rachel M. Burns, Oct. 25, 1942; children: Deborah Skauen Hinchcliffe, Bruce. BS, Mass. Coll. Pharmacy, 1938, MS, 1942; PhD, Purdue U., 1949. Dir. pharm. svc. Children's Hosp. Med. Ctr., Boston, 1940-46; teaching asst. Purdue U., West Lafayette, Ind., 1946-48; asst. prof. pharmaceutics U. Conn., Storrs, 1948-53, assoc. prof., 1953-59, prof., 1959-79, prof. emeritus, 1979—; mem. del. of med. scientists to discuss biol. and pharm. uses of ultrasound Nat. Coun. U.S.-China Trade, People's Republic China, 1979. Co-author: American Pharmacy, 4th edit., 1955, 5th edit., 1961, 6th edit., 1966, Husa's Pharmaceutical Dispensing, 1959, 2d edit., 1966, Radioecology, 1963; contbr. numerous articles to Sci., Nature, Jour. Am. Pharm. Assn. Mem. Am. Pharm. Assn., Am. Soc. Hosp. Pharmacists, Sigma Xi. Achievements include research on effects of ultrasound on pharmaceutical and biological systems; radioecology, including gross beta levels in oysters and other organisms in Thames River, Connecticut, and zinc-65 levels in oysters. Home: 16 Storrs Heights Rd Storrs Mansfield CT 06268-2322

SKED, MARIE JOSEPHINE, financial service owner, nurse; b. Stroudsburg, Pa., June 15, 1935; d. Newell Walter and Marjorie Frances (Keegan) Felton; m. Henry Daniel Kehr, Sept. 25, 1955 (div. Dec. 1972); children: Wendy Carol, John Francis, Newell Walter; m. Ogden Stanley Sked, Mar. 10, 1973. Student, Temple U., 1953-55; AAS in Nursing, Mercer County C.C., 1970; postgrad., Stockton State Coll., 1973-74. RN, Pa. LPN, emergency rm. and float nurse Zurbrugg Meml. Hosp., Riverside, N.J., 1964-67; LPN, staff nurse State of N.J. E.R. Johnstone Rsch. for Mentally Retarded, Bordentown, 1967-70, head nurse, 1970-71; asst. oper. rm. supr. Hamilton Hosp., Trenton, N.J., 1971-76; pvt. scrub nurse Dr. Ralph Ellis, Trenton, 1977-78; owner Income Tax Svc., Newfoundland, Pa., 1985—. Sec.-treas. Panther Lake Homeowner's Assn., 1984-94; mem. Pa. Hist. Mus. Commn. State of N.J. scholar, 1968. Mem. AARP (dist. coord. income tax vols. 1985—). Avocations: downhill skiing, bowling, reading, gardening, volunteer tax service. Home: Pine Grove Rd PO Box 216 Newfoundland PA 18445

SKEEN, JOSEPH RICHARD, congressman; b. Roswell, N.Mex., June 30, 1927; s. Thomas Dudley and Ilah (Adamson) S.; m. Mary Helen Jones, Nov. 17, 1945; children: Mary Elisa, Mikell Lee. B.S., Tex. A&M U., 1950. Soil and water engr. Ramah Navajo and Zuni Indians, 1951; rancher Lincoln County, N.Mex., 1952—; mem. N.Mex. Senate, 1960-70, 97th-103rd Congresses from 2nd N.Mex. dist., Washington, D.C., 1981—; mem. appropriations com., subcom. agr., chmn. appropriations com., subcom. def., mem. subcom. interior. Chmn. N.Mex. Republican Party, 1963-66. Served with USN, 1945-46; Served with USAFR, 1949-52. Mem. Nat. Woolgrowers Assn., Nat. Cattle Growers Assn., N.Mex. Woolgrowers Assn., N.Mex. Cattle Growers Assn., N.Mex. Farm and Livestock Bur. Republican. Club: Elks. Office: House of Representatives Washington DC 20515

SKEES, WILLIAM LEONARD, JR., lawyer; b. Indpls., Jan. 26, 1947; s. William Leonard and Marian Catherine (Fagan) S.; children: Kristina Suzanne, Elizabeth Ann; m. Dena Kay Wynalda, July 23, 1983; children: Catherine Fagan, William Leonard III (dec.), Samuel Jackson. BA, Ball State U., 1969; JD, Ind. U., 1971. Bar: Ind. 1971, Ky. 1981. Law clk. U.S. Dist. Ct. (no. dist.), Fort Wayne, Ind., 1971-72; assoc. Ice, Miller Donadio & Ryan, Indpls., 1972-80; mem. Brown, Todd & Heyburn, P.L.L.C, Louisville, 1981—. Contbr. articles to jours. in field. Mem. bd. visitors Ind. U. Sch. Law, 1975-91; bd. dirs., past pres. Louisville Housing Partnership, 1978—; bd. dirs. Stage One, Louisville Children's Theatre, pres., 1990-91; bd. dirs. Ky. chpt. Nat. SIDS Found.; mem. Leadership Ky., 1996. Recipient Disting. Citizen award Mayor of Louisville, 1983, Cert. Merit Bd. Aldermen, Louisville, 1984, Cert. Appreciation Fiscal Ct., Louisville, 1986. Mem. ABA, Ky. Bar Assn., Ind. Bar Assn., Louisville Bar Assn., Nat. Assn. Bond Lawyers. Office: Brown Todd & Heyburn 3200 Providian Center Louisville KY 40202-2873

SKEFF, KELLEY MICHAEL, health facility administrator; b. Center, Colo., 1944. MD, U. Chgo., 1970. Diplomate Am. Bd. Internal Medicine. Intern Harbor Gen. Hosp., Torrance, Calif., 1970-71; resident in internal medicine U. Colo. Med. Ctr., Denver, 1974-75; resident in internal medicine Stanford (Calif.) U. Hosps., 1975-76, fellow in internal medicine, 1976; program dir. Stanford U. Recipient Alpha Omega Alpha award Assocs. Am. Med. Coll., 1994. Office: Stanford U Dept Med 300 Pasteur Dr Palo Alto CA 94304-2203

SKELLY, THOMAS FRANCIS, manufacturing company executive; b. Boston, Jan. 19, 1934; s. Michael Gerard and Katherine Agnes (Kelly) S.; m. Patricia A. Limerick, Sept. 6, 1958; children—Thomas Francis, John M., Peter G., Matthew M. B.S., Northeastern U., 1956; M.B.A., Babson Coll., 1966. Mgr. Peat, Marwick, Mitchell & Co. (C.P.A.'s), Boston, 1957-67; with Gillette Co., Boston, 1967—; controller Gillette Co., 1973—, v.p., 1979-80, sr. v.p. fin., 1980—; mng. dir. Gillette Overseas Fin. Corp. N.V., Netherlands Antilles; dir. Neworld Bank, Boston. Bd. dirs. nat. coun. Northeastern U., bd. trustees; bd. dirs. Nat. Fgn. Trade Coun. Capt. AUS, 1957-59. Home: 54 Magnolia Dr Westwood MA 02090-3215 Office: Gillette Co Prudential Tower Bldg Boston MA 02199

SKELTON, BYRON GEORGE, federal judge; b. Florence, Tex., Sept. 1, 1905; s. Clarence Edgar and Avis (Bowmer) S.; m. Ruth Alice Thomas, Nov. 28, 1931; children: Sue, Sandra. Student, Baylor U., 1923-24; AB, U. Tex., 1927, MA, 1928, LLB, 1931. Bar: Tex. 1931, Circuit Ct. Appeals 1937, U.S. Supreme Ct. 1946, FCC 1950, Tax Ct. U.S 1952, U.S. Treasury Dept 1952, ICC 1953. Practice of law Temple, Tex., 1931-66; partner Saulsbury & Skelton, 1934-42, Saulsbury, Skelton, Everton, Bowmer & Courtney, 1944-55, Skelton, Bowmer & Courtney, 1955-66; judge U.S. Ct. Claims, Washington, 1966-77; sr. fed. judge U.S. Ct. Claims, 1977-82, U.S. Ct. Appeals (fed. cir.), Washington, 1982—; county atty., Bell County, Tex., 1934-38; spl. asst. U.S. amb. to Argentina, 1942-45; city atty., Temple, 1945-60; dir. First Nat. Bank of Temple. Dem. nat. committeeman for Tex., 1956-64; del. Dem. Nat. Conv., 1948, 56, 60, 64; del. Tex. Dem. Conv., 1946, 48, 50, 52, 54, 56, 58, 60, 62, 64, vice chmn., 1948, 58; chmn. Dem. Adv. Coun. of Tex., 1955-57; former pres. Temple YMCA; pres. Temple Indsl. Found., 1966. Appointed Ky. Col. and Adm. in Tex. Navy, 1959; recipient Legion of Honor DeMolay, 1980, Temple Outstanding Citizen award, 1984. Mem. ABA, State Bar Tex., Bell-Lampasas and Mills Counties Bar Assn. (past pres.), Am. Law Inst., Am. Judicature Soc., Temple C. of C. (past pres., dir.), Ex-Students' Assn. U. Tex. (past pres., mem. exec.coun.), Gen. Soc. Mayflower Descs., Masons (past worshipful master), Shriners, Kiwanis (past pres.), Phi Beta Kappa, Pi Sigma Alpha, Sigma Delta Pi, Delta Theta Phi. Democrat. Methodist. Home: 1101 Dakota Dr Temple TX 76504-4905 Office: US Ct Appeals 305 Fed Bldg Temple TX 76501

SKELTON, DIANN CLEVENGER, elementary education educator; b. Kennett, Mo., Nov. 26, 1956; d. Opie O'Neal and D. Charlenene (Duke) C.; m. Jason Skelton. BSEd in Early Childhood Edn., Ark. State U., 1978, MSEd in Spl. Edn., 1979, MSEd in Early Childhood Edn., 1989. Spl. edn. tchr. Blytheville (Ark.) Pub. Sch., 1978-82; tchr. early childhood edn. Hayti (Mo.) Pub. Schs., 1982-86, tchr. kindergarten, 1986-91, tchr. 2d grade, 1991—. Mem. Mo. State Tchrs. Assn., Assn. Supervision and Curriculum Devel., Beta Sigma Phi, Kappa Delta Pi, Delta Kappa Gamma. Republican. Baptist. Avocations: cross stitch, sporting events, Am. Kennel Club registered Dobermans. Office: Hayti Pub Schs 500 N 4th St Hayti MO 63851-1116

SKELTON, DON RICHARD, consulting actuary, retired insurance company executive; b. Des Moines, Dec. 9, 1931; s. Donald Harold and Wanda Mae (Johnson) S.; m. Barbara Joan Harris, Mar. 17, 1956 (dec. 1962); children: David, Janet; m. Alyce Mae Washington, May 15, 1964 (div. 1979); children: Laura, Lisa, James; m. Patricia Ann Matroni, July 10, 1981. BSBA, Drake U., 1953. Actuarial trainee Monarch Life Ins. Co., Springfield, Mass., 1953-57, mgr. group ins. dept., 1957-58, asst. actuary, 1958-64, group pensions actuary, 1964-67, asst. v.p., group actuary, 1967, v.p. R & D, 1967-83; v.p. Monarch Capital Corp., Springfield, Mass., 1980-91; sr. v.p. Monarch Life Ins. Co., Springfield, 1988-91; v.p. Monarch Fin. Svcs., Inc., 1989-91; pres., chief exec. officer First Variable Life Ins. Co., 1985-87, 91, also bd. dirs., ret., 1992; cons. actuary Longmeadow, Mass., 1992—. Mem. budget com. Pioneer Valley United Way, Springfield, 1964-69, chmn. 1969-70. Fellow Soc. Actuaries, Life Office Mgmt. Assn.; mem. Am. Acad. Actuaries, Coll. Life Underwriters. Republican. Clubs: Hartford (Conn.) Actuaries; Boston Actuaries. Avocations: golf, sailing, physical fitness. Home: 8 Althea Dr Longmeadow MA 01106-1707

SKELTON, DOROTHY GENEVA SIMMONS (MRS. JOHN WILLIAM SKELTON), art educator; b. Woodland, Calif.; d. Jack Elijah and Helen Anna (Siebe) Simmons; BA, U. Calif., 1940, MA, 1943; m. John William Skelton, July 16, 1941. Sr. rsch. analyst War Dept., Gen. Staff, M.I. Div. G-2, Pentagon, Washington, 1944-45; vol. rschr. monuments, fine arts and archives sect. Restitution Br., Office Mil. Govt. for Hesse, Wiesbaden, German, 1947-48; vol. art tchr. German children in Bad Nauheim, Germany, 1947-48; art educator, lectr. Dayton (Ohio) Art Inst., 1955; art educator Lincoln Sch., Dayton, 1956-60; instr. art and art edn. U. Va. Sch. Continuing Edn., Charlottesville, 1962-75; rschr. genealogy, exhibited in group shows, Calif., Colo., Ohio, Washington and Va.; represented in permanent collections Madison Hall, Charlottesville, Madison (Va.) Ctr. Recipient Hon. Black Belt Karate Sch. of Culpeper, Va., 1992. Vol. art cons.; bd. dirs. Va. Rappahannock-Rapidan Vol. Emergency Med. Svcs. Coun., 1978—. Mem. Nat. League Am. Pen Women, AAUW, Am. Assn. Museums, Coll. Art Assn. Am., Inst. for Study of Art in Edn., Dayton Soc. Painters and Sculptors, Nat. Soc. Arts and Letters (life), Va. Mus. Fine Arts, Cal. Alumni Assn., Air Force Officers Wives Club. Republican. Methodist. Club: Army Navy Country. Chief collaborator: John Skelton of Georgia, 1969; author: The Squire Simmons Family, 1746-1986, 1986. Address: Lotos Lakes Brightwood VA 22715

SKELTON, DOUGLAS H., architect; b. Cottage Grove, Oreg., Apr. 17, 1939; s. Harry Edward and Mary Jane (Caldwell) S.; m. Bonita L. Baker, June 17, 1961; children: Paul D., Cynthia J., Justin D. Student, Oreg. State U., 1957-59; degree in architecture, U. Oreg., 1963. Registered architect, Oreg. Draftsman Payne & Struble Architecture, Medford, Oreg., 1965-66; intern architect Wayne Struble Architect, Medford, Oreg., 1966-70, assoc., 1973-78; project architect William Seibert Architect, Medford, Oreg., 1970-73; ptnr. Struble & Skelton Architects, Medford, Oreg., 1978-83; owner Douglas Skelton Architect, Medford, Oreg., 1983-89; ptnr. Skelton, Straus & Seibert Architects, Medford, Oreg., 1989—; mem. law rev. com. State Bd. Architects, Oreg., 1991. Design bldg. renovation (911 Mag. award 1991, Excellence in Sch. Architecture AS&U mag. 1987). Bd. dirs. Rogue Valley Christian Ch., 1994. Recipient Outstanding Sch. Bldg. award Am. Sch. and Univ. mag., 1987. Mem. AIA (v.p. So. Oreg. chpt. 1972, pres. 1973), Architects Coun. Oreg. (del., treas. 1989), Rotary (v.p., bd. dirs. Jacksonville/Applegate chpt. 1994). Avocations: camping, fishing, boating, bicycling, cross-country skiing. Office: Skelton Straus & Seibert 26 Hawthorne St Medford OR 97504-7114

SKELTON, GORDON WILLIAM, data processing executive, educator; b. Vicksburg, Miss., Oct. 31, 1949; s. Alan Gordon and Martha Hope (Butcher) S.; m. Sandra Lea Champion, May 1974 (div. 1981); m. Janet Elaine Johnson, Feb. 14, 1986; 1 stepchild, Brian Quarles. BA, McMurry Coll., 1974; MA, U. So. Miss., 1975, postgrad., 1975-77, MS, 1987; postgrad., U. South Africa, 1994—. Cert. in data processing. Systems analyst Criminal Justice Planning Commn., Jackson, Miss., 1978-80; cord. Miss. Statis. Analysis Ctr., Jackson, 1980-83; data processing mgr. Dept. Adminstrn. Fed.-State Programs, Jackson, 1983-84; mgr. pub. tech. So. Ctr. Rsch. and Innovation, Hattiesburg, Miss., 1985-87; internal cons. Sec. of State, State of Miss., Jackson, 1987; system support mgr. CENTEC, Jackson, 1987-88; instr. dept. computer sci. Belhaven Coll., Jackson, 1988—; v.p. info. svcs. Miss. Valley Title Ins. Co., Jackson, 1988—. Author: (with others) Trends in Ergonomics/Human Factors, 1986. Treas. Singles and Doubles Sunday Sch. Class, Jackson, 1989, 91. With U.S. Army, 1970-73, Vietnam. Recipient Cert. of Appreciation, U.S. Dept. Justice/Bur. Justice Stats., 1982. Mem. IEEE Computer Soc., Data Processing Mgmt. Assn. (chpt. pres. 1991, 92, program chair 1990), Assn. Computing Machinery, Am. Soc. Quality Control. Presbyterian. Avocations: gardening, collecting baseball cards, collecting Civil War relics. Office: Miss Valley Title Ins Co 315 Tombigbee St Jackson MS 39201-4604

SKELTON, HOWARD CLIFTON, advertising and public relations executive; b. Birmingham, Ala., Mar. 6, 1932; s. Howard C. and Sarah Ethel (Holmes) S., Sr.; B.S., Auburn U., 1955; m. Winifred Harriet Karger, May 19, 1962; 1 dau., Susan Lynn. Copywriter, Rich's, Inc., Atlanta, 1955-59, Ga. Power Co., Atlanta, 1959-61; dir. advt. and sales promotion Callaway Mills, Inc. LaGrange, Ga., 1961-65; dir. advt. and sales promotion Thomasville (N.C.) Furniture Industries, 1965-66; v.p. in charge of fashion and textiles Gaynor & Ducas, N.Y.C., 1966-70; dir. comm. Collins & Aikman, N.Y.C., 1970-73; v.p. Marketplace, Inc., Atlanta, 1973-74; v.p. comm. and mktg. Internat. City Corp., Atlanta, 1974-75; chmn. Howard Skelton Assocs., Sarasota, 1976—. Served with Signal Corps, AUS, 1956-58. Recipient Danforth Found. award, 1950, United Cerebral Palsy Fundraiser award, Salvation Army Bell Ringer award, 200 Addy awards. Mem. N.Y. Advt. Fedn., Atlanta Advt. Fedn., Sarasota Advt. Fedn., Tampa Advt. Fedn., United Way (Sarasota chpt. past bd. dirs.), Salvation Army (past bd. advisors), Sarasota, Tampa C. of C., Centre Club (Tampa), Omicron Delta Kappa, Lambda Chi Alpha, Sigma Delta Chi. Home and Office: 4881 Tivoli Ave Sarasota FL 34235-3650

SKELTON, ISAAC NEWTON, IV (IKE SKELTON), congressman; b. Lexington, Mo., Dec. 20, 1931; s. Isaac Newton and Carolyn (Boone) S.; m. Susan B. Anding, July 22, 1961; children: Ike, Jim, Page. AB, U. Mo., 1953, LLB, 1956. Bar: Mo. 1956. Pvt. practice Lexington; pros. atty. Lafayette County, Mo., 1957-60; spl. asst. atty. gen. State of Mo., 1961-63; mem. Mo. Senate from 28th dist., 1971-76, 95th-105th Congresses from 4th Mo. Dist., 1977—; ranking minority mem. nat. security subcom. on mil. procurement 95th-104th Congresses from 4th Mo. Dist. Active Boy Scouts Am. Mem. Phi Beta Kappa, Sigma Chi. Democrat. Mem. Christian Ch. Clubs: Masons, Shriners, Elks. Home: 1814 Franklin St Lexington MO 64067-1708 Office: US Ho of Reps 2227 Rayburn House Bldg Washington DC 20515*

SKELTON, RED (RICHARD SKELTON), comedian, artist; b. Vincennes, Ind., July 18, 1913; s. Joseph and Ida (Mae) S.; m. Edna Marie Stillwell, June 1932 (div. 1940, dec.); m. 2d, Georgia Maureen Davis, Mar. 1945 (dec.); children: Valentina Maureen Alonso, Richard Freeman (dec.); m. 3d, Lothian Toland, Oct., 1973. HHD, Ball State U., 1986. Began acting career at age of 10 yrs.; successively with a tent show, a minstrel show, on a show boat, a clown in Hagenbeck & Wallace Circus, on burlesque in the Midwest, Walkathon contests (as master of ceremonies); appeared at Loew's Montreal Theatre in vaudeville (developed the doughnut dunking pantomime), 1936; made Broadway debut, June 1937; first motion picture appearance in Having a Wonderful Time, 1939; has since appeared in Flight Command, 1940, The People vs. Dr. Kildare, 1941, Dr. Kildare's Wedding Day, 1941, Lady Be Good, 1941, Whistling in the Dark, 1941, Whistling in Dixie, 1942, Maisie Gets Her Man, 1942, Panama Hattie, 1942, Ship Ahoy, 1942, I Dood It, 1943, Whistling in Brooklyn, 1943, DuBarry Was A Lady, 1943, Thousands Cheer, 1943, Bathing Beauty, 1944, Ziedfield Follies, 1946, The Show Off, 1946, Merton of the Movies, 1947, The Fuller Brush Man, 1948, A Southern Yankee, 1948, Neptune's Daughter, 1949, The Yellow Cab Man, 1950, Three Little Words, 1950, Watch the Birdie, 1950, The Fuller Brush Girl, 1950, Dutchess of Idaho, 1950, Excuse My Dust, 1950, Texas Carnival, 1951, Lovely to Look At, 1952, The Clown, 1952, Halfa Hero, 1953, The Great Diamond Robbery, 1953, Susan Slept Here, 1954, Around the World in 80 Days, 1956, Public Pigeon Number One, 1957, Ocean's Eleven, 1960, Those Magnificent Men in Their Flying Machines, 1965, Eighteen Again, 1988; had first own radio program, 1937, Red Skelton's Scrpabook of Satire, 1942; The Red Skelton Show on TV, 1951-71; nightclub performer, also writer and composer for radio, TV, movies; entertained service men World War II and Korea as pvt. in F.A.; artist original oil paintings and hand sketched linens. Bd. dirs. Red Skelton Needy Children's Fund. Recipient AMVETS Silver Helmet Americanism award, 1969, Freedom's Found. award, 1970, Nat. Comdrs. award Am. Legion, 1970; winner 3 Emmy awards, Golden Globe award, 1978, Ann. Achievement award SAG, 1987, Am. Comedy Hall of Fame award, 1993, Gourgas Gold medal Masonic Order, 1995. Address: PO Box 390190 Anza CA 92539-0190

SKELTON, WILLIAM DOUGLAS, physician. MD, EMory U., 1963. Sr. v.p. rsch. & health affairs Mercer U. Sch. Med., Macon, Ga., 1985—. Office: Mercer Univ Sch Medicine 1550 College St Macon GA 31201-1554

SKENE, G(EORGE) NEIL, publisher, lawyer; b. Jackson, Miss., Aug. 29, 1951; s. George Neil and Louise (Pate) S.; m. Madelyn Miller, Aug. 4, 1984; children: Christopher, Jennifer, Katherine. BA, Vanderbilt U., 1973; JD, Mercer U., 1977. Bar: Fla. 1978. Intern Macon (Ga.) Telegraph & News, 1968-70; reporter Tampa (Fla.) Times, 1973-74; reporter St. Petersburg (Fla.) Times, 1977-78, asst. city editor, 1978-80; capital bur. chief St. Petersburg (Fla.) Times, Tallahassee, 1980-84; editor Evening Ind., St. Petersburg, 1984-86; exec. editor Congl. Quar. Inc., Washington, 1986-89, pres., editor, pub., 1990-97; sr. v.p., editor-in-chief Individual, Inc., Burlington, Mass., 1997—. Mem. bd. visitors Law Sch. Mercer U., Macon, Ga., 1986-94; trustee Poynter Inst. for Media Studies, St. Petersburg, 1988—; mem. bd. advisors Grad. Sch. Journalism U. Calif., Berkeley, 1991-96. Mem. Fla. Bar Assn. Office: Individual Inc 8 New Eng Exec Park W Burlington MA 01803

SKENE, NEIL, publishing executive. Office: Congressional Quarterly Svc 1414 22nd St NW Washington DC 20037-1003

SKERRITT, TOM, actor; b. Detroit, Aug. 25, 1933. Student, Wayne State U. Films: War Hunt, 1962, One Man's Way, 1964, Those Calloways, 1964, M*A*S*H, 1970, WIld Rovers, 1972, Fuzz, 1972, Big Bad Mama, 1974, Thieves Like Us, 1974, The Devil's Rain, 1975, The Turning Point, 1977, Up In Smoke, 1978, Alien, 1979, Ice Castles, 1979, Silence of the North, 1981, A Dangerous Summer, 1981, Savage Harvest, 1981, Fighting Back, 1982, The Dead Zone, 1983, Top Gun, 1986, Space Camp, 1987, The Big Town, 1987, Wisdom, 1987, Opposing Force, 1987, Maid to Order, 1987, Poltergeist III, 1988, Steel Magnolias, 1989, Big Man On Campus, 1990, The Rookie, 1991, Blue Movie Blue, 1991, Poison Ivy, 1991, A River Runs Through It, 1992, Contact, 1997; TV shows: Ryan's Four, 1983, Contact, 1997, On The Edge, 1987, Cheers, 1987-88, Picket Fences, 1992-96 (Emmy award Outstanding Lead Actor in a Drama Series, 1993); TV movies: The Bird Man, The Last Day, Maneaters Are Loose!, Calendar Girl Murders, Miles to Go, True Believer, Parent Trap II, A Touch of Scandal, Poker Alice, Nightmare At Bitter Creek, Moving Target, The Heist, Red King White Knight, The China Lake Murders, Child of the Night, In Sickness and In Health, Getting Up and Going Home, Divided By Hate, 1997. Office: Guttman Assocs 118 S Beverly Dr Beverly Hills CA 90212-3003

SKERRY, PHILIP JOHN, English educator; b. Boston, May 6, 1944; s. Angelina (Creilson) S.; m. Amy Simon, June 15, 1968; children: Jessica Blythe, Ethan Amadeus. BA in English, U. Mass., 1966; MA in English, Case Western Res. U., 1968; PhD, Indiana U. of Pa., 1975. Instr. English Lakeland Community Coll., Mentor, Ohio, 1968-69, prof., 1973—, chmn. dept., 1991-93; assoc. prof. Tarrant County Jr. Coll., Hurst, Tex., 1971-73; project dir. Early English Composition Assessment Program Ohio Bd. Regents, Columbus, 1985-92, 96-97; participant Dir. Guild Am. summer sem., 1988, 92. Host TV talk show Western Res. Connection, 1980-86;

contbg. author: Superman at 50: The Persistence of a Legend, 1987, Beyond the Stars IV, 1993, Beyond the Stars V, 1996; contbr. articles to profl. jours. Chmn. Jump Rope for your Heart program Am. Heart Assn., Cleve., 1980-83, mem. adv. com., 1984; trustee, pres. Sussex Community Assn., Shaker Heights, Ohio, 1982; mem. adv. com. N.E. Ohio Assn. for Children with Learning Disabilities, 1975-76; bd. dirs. Shaker Heights Youth Ctr., 1991-92. Grantee NEH, 1983, Martha Holden Jennings Found., 1991-92; Humanities scholar Ohio Program for the Humanities, 1983—. Mem. NEA, Nat. Coun. Tchrs. English, Popular Culture Assn. Democrat. Avocations: collecting movies, coffee roasting. Home: 3655 Sutherland Rd Shaker Heights OH 44122-5134 Office: Lakeland Cmty Coll 7700 Clocktower Dr Kirtland OH 44094-5198

SKIDD, THOMAS PATRICK, JR., lawyer; b. Norwalk, Conn., July 2, 1936; s. Thomas Patrick and Anna (Sims) S.; m. Judith Chase Roberts, Sept. 10, 1960; children: Suanne C., Sherry E., Thomas Patrick III, Jody E. BA in Econs., Georgetown U., 1958; LLB, Yale U., 1961. Bar: Conn. 1961, U.S. Supreme Ct. 1963. Ptnr. Cummings & Lockwood, Stamford, Conn., 1961—; bd. dirs., mem. exec. com. Conn. Attys. Title Ins. Co., Rocky Hill, Conn. Mem. Conn. Bar Assn. (real estate sect. and land use sect.), Stamford-Norwalk Regional Bar Assn., Roton Point Club (Rowayton, Conn.). Roman Catholic. Avocation: phonograph record collector. Office: Cummings & Lockwood 107 Elm St Stamford CT 06902-3834

SKIDDELL, ELLIOT LEWIS, rabbi; b. Chelsea, Mass., Mar. 3, 1951; s. Jack and Evelyn (Starr) S.; m. Julie F. Goldberg, May 27, 1979; children: Sarit, Elanit. BA, U. Mass., 1974; MA, Temple U., 1979. Ordained rabbi, 1980. Rabbi Temple Beth El, Newark, Del., 1977-80; asst. rabbi Har Zion Temple, Penn Valley, Pa., 1980-82; rabbi Ramat Shalom Synogogue, Plantation, Fla., 1982—; placement dir. Reconstructionist Rabbinical Assn., Wyncote, Pa., 1985—; pres. Jewish Nat. Fund Broward and Palm Beach, 1987-89, North Broward Bd. Rabbis, Ft. Lauderdale, 1986-87, Reconstructionist Rabbinical Assn., 1980-82. Co-editor booklet: Mordecai Kaplan Centennial Resource Booklet, 1981. Bd. dirs. Jewish Fedn. Greater Ft. Lauderdale, 1986-89. Office: 11301 W Broward Blvd Fort Lauderdale FL 33325-2521 *I believe that the most important task facing us today is the creation of community and a sense of belonging to a community. For our own sake and for future generations, the sense of belonging to something larger than ourselves needs to be instilled.**

SKIDMORE, DONALD EARL, JR., government official; b. Tacoma, Apr. 27, 1944; s. Donald E. and Ingeborg (Johnsrud) S.; BSc, Evangel Coll., 1968. With Dept. Social and Health Svcs., State of Wash., Yakima, 1967-74; quality rev. specialist Social Security Adminstrn., Seattle, 1974-76, program analyst, Balt., 1976-79, Seattle, 1979-81, quality assurance officer, mgr. Satellite office, Spokane, Wash., 1981-84, program analyst, Seattle, 1984-90, mgmt. analyst, 1990—. Pres., bd. dirs. Compton Court Condo Assn., 1980-81; v.p., trustee Norwood Village, 1987-90; vice chair ops. subcom., mem. citizen's adv. com. METRO, 1987-89; mem. citizen's adv. com. land use planning, Bellevue, Wash., 1988-90. Grad. Bellevue Police Citizen's Acad., 1992. Office: Ste 510B 2201 6th Ave Seattle WA 98121-1832

SKIDMORE, HOWARD FRANKLYN, public relations counsel; b. Bklyn., Sept. 24, 1917; s. William F. and Mae (White) S.; m. Zaza Irina O'Hara, Dec. 4, 1943; children: Joel Michael, Susan Irina. Student, Coll. City N.Y., 1938-39. Editorial staff N.Y. Herald Tribune, 1937-42, 45-47; asst. to dir. pub. relations C. & O. Ry., N.Y.C., 1948; exec. asst. to v.p. passenger traffic, pub. relations, advt. C. & O. Ry., Cleve., 1949-53; dir. pub. relations C. & O. Ry., 1954-59, spl. asst. to chmn. bd., 1954-77, dir. pub. relations and passenger traffic, 1959-63; v.p. C. & O. Ry., also B. & O. Ry., 1963-77, Western Md. Ry., 1973-77, Chessie System, Inc., 1974-77; pres. Howard Skidmore Co., Inc., Cleve., 1977-83. Trustee Cleve. Music Sch. Settlement, 1958—. Served with USNR, 1942-45. Mem. Soc. Silurians, R.R. Pub. Relations Assn. (pres. 1958), Pub. Relations Soc. Am., Soc. Profl. Journalists. Clubs: Nat. Press (Washington); Carmel Valley Racquet; Canterbury Golf (Cleve.). Home: 26360 Monte Verde St Carmel CA 93923-9233

SKIDMORE, JAMES ALBERT, JR., management, computer technology and engineering services company executive; b. Newark, June 30, 1932; s. James A. and Frances W. (Barker) S.; m. Peggy Ann Young, July 10, 1954; children: Jacqueline Sue Skidmore, James Albert III. BA, Muhlenberg Coll., 1954. Customer sales rep. N.J. Bell Telephone Co., Newark, 1957-65, then dist. sales mgr., div. mktg. mgr.; asst. to pres. for pub. affairs Pepsi Co., Inc., N.Y.C., 1966-69; asst. to Pres. of U.S., 1968-69; v.p. Handy Assoc., N.Y.C., 1969-70, pres., 1971-72; pres., CEO Sci. Mgmt. Corp., Basking Ridge, N.J., 1972—, chmn. bd. dir. Newark Brush Co., 1974-79; bd. dirs. Franklin State Bank, Somerset, N.J., Franklin Bancorp, United Jersey Banks, United Jersey Bank Franklin State exec. com. UJB Fin., 1985-93, Blue Cross & Blue Shield N.J., Inc., Enterprise Holding Co., Inc.; trustee Blue Cross of N.J., 1983—; dir. Coca Cola, N.Y., 1980-85, Mariner Communications, 1983-85; mem., chmn. mktg. com. Seton Hall Commn., 1987; mem. dean's adv. coun. Rutgers U. Grad. Sch. Mgmt., 1989—; trustee Pub. Affairs Rsch. Inst. N.J., 1989—; lectr. U. Amsterdam (The Netherlands), 1967, U. Toronto (Ont., Can.), U. Helsinki (Finland), 1967, Tokyo U. Mem. Nat. Council on Crime and Delinquency, 1965-66; mem. Nat. Commn. on Youth Employment, 1966-67; state chmn. N.J. Nat. Found. March of Dimes, 1966-73; mem. exec. bd. Watchung Area council Boy Scouts Am., 1972-77, dir. NE region, 1983-90; mem. Citizen's Adv. Bd. on Youth Opportunity 1969-75; state chmn. United Citizens for Nixon-Agnew, N.J., 1968; bd. govs. Alpha Tau Omega Found., 1967-73; bd. dirs. Muhlenberg Coll., Allentown, Pa., 1980-92, N.E. region Boy Scouts Am., 1983—. Recipient Disting. Citizens award Boy Scouts Am., 1983, Private Sector Initiative award Pres. Reagan, 1985. Trustee Brick Twp. Hosp., Inc., Brick Town, N.J., 1976-80; bd. dirs. Am. Christmas Trains and Trucks, chmn., 1966; pres. Project Concern, San Diego,1966-78. Served to capt. USMC, 1954-57. Decorated Order of St. John (Eng.); recipient Internat. Understanding award, Brussels, 1966, Disting. Service award, St. Paul, 1966, Freedom Found. George Washington Medal of Honor award, 1965, Outstanding Achievement in Life award Muhlenberg Coll. Alumni, 1966, Ambassador award U.S. Jaycees, 1977, Trinidad and Tobago award Prime Minister of Ireland, 1970 Human Relations award Soc. Advancement of Mgmt., 1982; Statesman award N.J. Jaycees, 1983; Disting. Citizens award Boy Scouts Am., 1983; inducted into U.S. Jaycees Hall of Leadership, 1983. Mem. N.J. State C. of C. (bd. dirs.), Muhlenberg Coll. Alumni Assn., Alpha Tau Omega. Clubs: Sky N.Y.C., Baltusrol Golf, Longboat Key. Guest columnist Rotary Internat. mag., 1966-68, Kiwanis mag., 1966-68, Japan Times on Community Responsibility and Leadership, 1965-67. Home: 641 Ocean Ave Sea Girt NJ 08750 also: 1465 Gulf Of Mexico Dr Longboat Key FL 34228-3418 Office: Sci Mgmt Corp 721 Us Highway 202 Bridgewater NJ 08807-2510 also: 177 Sutton Dr Berkeley Heights NJ 07922-2512

SKIDMORE, JOYCE THORUM, public relations and communications executive; b. Murray, Utah, Dec. 30, 1926; d. Rolla Arden and Alice Luetta (Fox) Thorum; m. E. Douglas Jacobsen, Mar. 20, 1956 (dec.); 1 son, Kelly Douglas Jacobsen; m. Clarence E. Skidmore Jr., Aug. 9, 1969. B.S., U. Utah, 1950, postgrad., 1953-55; postgrad. U. So. Calif., 1964, U. Calif.-Irvine, 1973-74; student Cambridge U., Eng. Sales and promotion devel. JBL Internat., Los Angeles, 1959-69. Adminstrv. asst. world hdqrs. Toastmasters Internat., Santa Ana, Calif., 1973; adj. prof. communications Pepperdine U., 1974, developer human resources, Oran, Algeria, 1975; promotions coordinator Utah Bicentennial Project, Salt Lake City, 1976; editor Saga Weekly Post, and editor Children's Page, Stavanger and Bergen, Norway, 1976-78; press. sec. Utah Auditor's Office, Salt Lake City, 1979-81; pres., owner Joyce Skidmore Cons./Snowflake Prodns., pub. relations, communications and devel. in arts, bus., edn. and govt., Sandy, Utah, 1980—; Utah dir. Nat. Health Screening Coun. for Vol. Orgns., Bethesda, Md., 1982-83; adj. prof. Westminster Coll., 1978-79, 1992-93, Brigham Young U., 1978—; cons. pub. relations, health costs and tourism C. of C. of Salt Lake Area; adj. prof. mktg. and communication dept. and theatre/film dept. Colo. Mountain Coll., 1985-86; bus. cons., prof. mktg. and communications Mountainwest Coll. Bus. and Brigham Young U., Salt Lake City; cons. Hema U.S.A., Westline and Bunell Inc.; guest dir. Westminster Theatre, 1974; guest dir./ writer Cablevision, Newport Beach, Calif., 1975. Author: Happy Holidays, 1968; assoc. editor Utah Symphony newsletter; newsletter editor Nat. Auditor's Assn., 1979-81, State Auditor's Assn., 1979-81, Utah Health Fairs, 1982-83; journalist The Butler Banner; contbr. weekly columns to The Rifle Telegram; contbr. articles to Calif., Colo., Norwegian and Utah newspapers; author nat. bus. newsletters and family history newsletters; lectr. in field; writer pub. svc. announcements; initiated use of old copper from Utah Capitol dome as collector's item, 1980. Organizer Stavanger Theatre Guild and Workshops, 1977, Bookcliffs Arts and Humanities Council, 1984-86; originator, organizer Hurlburt Days, Grand Valley and Parachute, Colo.; initiator, dir. Reader's Theatre, Community Christmas Festival; dir. Storytelling Festival, Neil Simon Night; promoter Salt Lake Arts Festival, Am. Genealogical Lending Libr. World Hdqrs., appearance Japanese condr. in Salt Lake City; Sister-City exch. Salt Lake and Matsumoto, Japan; fundraiser Utah Symphony Guild; dir. theatre Art Barn, Salt Lake City; mem. steering com. for first nat. competition Utah Playwriting Conf., Sundance, 1979-80; mem. local econ. devel. council.; polit. dist. del., 1986. Initiated invitation from Bergen Internat. Festival to Utah Symphony, 1981; campaign mgr. Mayor Lake Valley City (Utah), 1982; cons. Cottonwood Heights (Utah) Council, 1982-83; cons. to Utah pres. Instrumentation Soc. Am.; co-chair advt. Utah Symphony Guild; winter and summer fundraisers Carousel Ball and Taste of the Town, 1988-89; guest dir. and Historian MMB Reading Arts Soc., 1988-89; promoter Utah Arts Orgns.; missionary leader Ch. of Jesus Christ of Latter-day Saints; v.p. Pub. Awareness RP Found. Fighting Blindness; dir. Internat. First Night Festival, Salt Lake City, 1993-94; bd. dirs. Utah Centennial Commn., The Found. Fighting Blindness, 1st Night Festival of Arts. Recipient Best Dir. statue, Colo., 2 Top Editor's awards Calif. Press Women, 1977, 4 writing awards 1977-78; Internat. Yr. of Child award Family Acad., San Francisco and Stavanger, 1979; Colo. Oscar award for Best Dir., 1986; Congl. Cup Utah Polo Club; nat. Zeta Phi Eta scholar, 1948; U. Utah fellow, 1953-55; So. Calif. Credit Assn. scholar, 1964. Mem. LWV (dist. pres. 1976), Pub. Relations Soc. Am. (student adv. 1980-82), Utah Press Women (6 writing awards 1979-81; 3d v.p. 1981-82), Instrument Soc. Am., Friendship Force Utah, MMB Reading Arts Soc. (v.p. devel.), Internat. Platform Assn., Daus. of Utah Pioneers, Utah Polo Club (bd. dirs.), Japan-Am. Soc. (bd. dirs.), Utah Storytelling Guild, UN Assn. Utah, Babcock Performing Readers (pres. 1996—). Avocations: historian, extensive genealogical research, global business and education research programs, screenwriting for film and TV. Home and Office: 2629 Oak Creek Dr Sandy UT 84093-6522

SKIDMORE, LINDA CAROL, science and engineering program administrator, consultant; b. Salisbury, Md., July 15, 1948; d. David Donaldson Skidmore Sr. and Mabel Frances Matthews Shockley; m. Charles Raymond Dix, Sept. 13, 1969 (div. Dec. 1991); 1 child, Larisa-Rose. BA, Loyola Coll., Balt., 1972; MEd, Salisbury (Md.) State Coll., 1982. Advanced profl. Md. State Dept. Edn. Tchr. secondary schs. Balt., 1972-73; tchr. James M. Bennett Sr. H.S., Salisbury, 1973-77, coord. English dept., 1978-81; adminstrv. asst. Commn. Human Resources Nat. Rsch. Coun., Washington, 1981-82; adminstrv. assoc. Office Sci. Engring. Pers. Nat. Rsch. Coun., Washington, 1982-84, adminstrv. officer, 1984-87, program officer, 1987-90, study dir., 1990-94, dir. com. on women in sci. and engring., 1994—; instr. English Salisbury State Coll., 1979; cons. leadership tng. program for women Md. State Tchrs. Assn., Balt., 1978-81, Anne Arundel County Pub. Schs., Annapolis, Md., 1982-90; prin. investigator Engring. Personnel Data Needs in the 1990's, Edn. and Employment Engrs., Minorities Sci. and Engring., Women Sci. and Engring.; staff officer Com. on the Internat. Exch. and Movement Engrs., Com. Engring. Labor-Market Adjustments, Com. on Scientists and Engrs. in Fed. Govt.; panel on gender differences in the career outcomes of PhD scientists and engrs.; presenter Computer Math. Sci. Fair, 1990—; lectr. in field. Editor: Women: Their Underrepresentation and Career Differentials in Science and Engineering, 1987, Minorities: Their Underrepresentation and Career Differentials in Science and Engineering, 1987, On Time to the Doctorate, 1989, (with Alan K. Campbell) Recruitment, Retention and Utilization of Federal Scientists and Engineers, 1990, (with Marsha Lakes Matyas) Science and Engineering Programs: On Target for Women?, 1992, Women Scientists and Engineers Employed in Industry: Why So Few?, 1994; author: Women and Minorities in Science and Engineering, 1989, Databook: Female Engineering Faculty, 1997; contbr. articles to profl. jours. Original appointee Wicomico County Commn. Women, 1977-81; Sunday sch. tchr. Severna Park, Md. United Meth. Ch., 1985-91; mem. Heartfriends, 1987—, co-chmn., 1989-90. Recipient cert. of Appreciation Wicomico County Bd. Edn., 1980; named Outstanding Young Woman Wicomico County Jaycees, 1977. Mem. AAAS, AAUW (chair women's issues Severna Park, Md. br. 1990-92, 1st v.p. 1992-95), Am. Assn. Higher Edn., Assn. for Women in Sci., Commn. on Profls. in Sci. and Tech., Fedn. Orgns. for Profl. Women, Nat. Coun. for Rsch. on Women, N.Y. Acad. Scis., Scho. Sci. and Math. Assn., Am. Ednl. Rsch. Assn. (spl. interest group on women and edn.), Nat. Coalition for Women and Girls in Edn., Women in Engring. Program Adv. Network, Women in Tech. Internat., Am. Legion Aux., Nat. Mus. Women Arts (charter), Md. State Tchrs. Assn. (chair women's caucus 1977-78, human rights com. 1979-81, meritorious svc. 1978, 80), Wicomico County Edn. Assn. (pres. 1978-79), Sigma Delta Epsilon. Democrat. Avocations: cross-stitching, writing poetry, reading historical novels, sailing. Home: 912 Winsap Ct Baltimore MD 21227 Office: NRC Office Sci and Engring Pers Rm Tj 2011 2101 Constitution Ave NW Washington DC 20418-0007

SKIDMORE, REX AUSTIN, social work educator; b. Salt Lake City, Dec. 31, 1914; s. Charles H. and Louise (Wangsgaard) S.; m. Knell Spencer, Aug. 31, 1939; children: Lee Spencer, Larry Rex. BA, U. Utah, 1938, MA, 1939; PhD, U. Pa., 1941; PhD (hon.), U. Utah, 1996, HHD (hon.), 1996. Instr. sociology U. Pa., 1940-41, Utah State Agrl. Coll., Logan, 1941-42; spl. agt. FBI, Miami, Fla., San Francisco, San Antonio, 1943-45; dir. bur. student counsel U. Utah, 1947-57, asso. prof., 1947-50, prof., 1950-85, dean Grad. Sch. Social Work, 1956-75. Author: Mormon Recreation: Theory and Practice, 1941, Building Your Marriage, 1951, 3d edit., 1964, Marriage Consulting, 1956, Introduction to Social Work, 1964, 7th edit., 1997, Introduction to Mental Health, 1979, Social Work Administration, 1983, 3d edit., 1995; contbr. articles to sociol. jours. Chmn. Western Mental Health Council, Western Interstate Commn. Higher Edn., 1964-65; mem. Nat. Adv. Council Nat. Manpower and Tng. Recipient Disting. Svc. award Cmty. Svc. Coun., NASW, 1975, Utah Conf. on Human Svcs., 1976, U. Utah Prof. Emeritus Svc. award, 1994. Mem. Coun. on Social Work Edn., Phi Kappa Phi, Pi Kappa Alpha, Pi Gamma Mu. Mem. Ch. of Jesus Christ Latter-Day Saints. Home: 1444 S 20th E Salt Lake City UT 84108 *A significant idea for successful living is knowing that: Loving is the central ingredient in human relationships; and the essence of loving is giving, not getting.*

SKIENS, WILLIAM EUGENE, electrical interconnect systems scientist, polymer engineer; b. Burns, Oreg., Feb. 21, 1928; s. William Poleman and Eugenia Glenn (Hibbard) S.; m. Vesta Lorraine Franz, Nov. 4, 1955; children: Rebecca, Beverly, Michael. Student, N.W. Nazarene Coll., 1946-48; BS in Chemistry, Oreg. State U., 1951; PhD in Phys. Chemistry, U. Wash., 1957. Chemist Dow Chem. Co., Pittsburg, Calif., 1951-53; research chemist Dow Chem. Co., Midland, Mich. and Walnut Creek, Calif., 1957-58, 1958-73, E.I DuPont de Nemours, Wilmington, Del., 1955; sr. research chemist Battelle Meml. Inst., Richland, Wash., 1973-84, also cons., 1984—; mgr. media system devel. Optical Data, Inc., Beaverton, Oreg., 1984-89; chief scientist Precision Interconnect, Portland, Oreg., 1989—; cons. WHO, Geneva, 1978-85, PI Med., Portland, 1991—. Contbr. chpts. to books, articles to profl. jours.; patentee in field. Com. chmn. Concord, Calif. council Boy Scouts Am., 1969-72; sec. Tri-Cities Nuclear Council, Richland, Wash., 1984. Named Alumni of Yr. N.W. Nazarene Coll., 1982. Mem. Am. Chem. Soc. (chmn. Richland sect. 1982), Sigma Xi. Republican. Mem. Ch. Nazarene. Avocations: skiing, photography, backpacking, golf. Home: 31179 SW Country View Ln Wilsonville OR 97070-7479 Office: Precision Interconnect 16640 SW 72nd Ave Portland OR 97224-7756

SKIGEN, PATRICIA SUE, lawyer; b. Springfield, Mass., June 16, 1942; d. David P. and Gertrude H. (Hirschhaut) S.; m. Irwin J. Sugarman, May 1973 (div. Nov. 1994); 1 child, Alexander David. BA with distinction, Cornell U., 1964; LLB, Yale U., 1968. Bar: N.Y. 1968, U.S. Dist. Ct. (so. dist.) N.Y. 1969. Law clk. Anderson, Mori & Rabinowitz, Tokyo, 1966-67; assoc. Rosenman Colin Kaye Petschek Freund & Emil, N.Y.C., 1968-70; assoc. Willkie Farr & Gallagher, N.Y.C., 1970-75, ptnr., 1977-95; v.p., corp. fin. group legal dept. Chase Manhattan Bank, N.Y.C., 1995—; dep. supt., gen. counsel N.Y. State Banking Dept., N.Y.C., 1975-77, 1st dep. supt. banks, 1977; adj. prof. Benjamin Cardozo Law Sch. Yeshiva U., 1979. Contbr. articles to profl. jours. Cornell U. Dean's scholar, 1960-64, Regent's scholar, 1960-64, Yale Law Sch. scholar, 1964-68. Mem. ABA (corp. banking and bus. law sect.), Assn. of Bar of City of N.Y. (chmn. com. banking 1991-94, long range planning com. 1994—, audit com. 1995—), Phi Beta Kappa, Phi Kappa Phi. Office: Chase Manhattan Bank 270 Park Ave New York NY 10017-2014

SKILBECK, CAROL LYNN MARIE, elementary educator and small business owner; b. Seymour, Ind., May 1, 1953; d. Harry Charles and Barbara Josephine (Knue) S.; div.; 1 child, Michael Charles. Postgrad., U. Cin., 1977, Wright State U., 1985-86, Northern Ky. U., 1995—. Cert. tchr., Ohio. Sec. Procter & Gamble, Cin., 1971-76; classified typist The Cin. Enquirer, Cin., 1976; tchr. St. Aloysius Sch., Cin., 1977-79, St. William Sch., Cin., 1979-82; legal sec. County Dept. Human Svcs., Cin., 1982-86; tchr. St. Jude Sch., Cin., 1986-91; educator, owner CLS Tutoring Svcs., Cin., 1991—; comm. edn. tchr. No. Ky. U., 1996; photographer Interstate Studio and Am. Sch. Pictures, 1994—; sales rep. Am. Sch. Pictures, 1997—; tchr. St. Martin Gifted Program, Cin., 1992-93, Oak Hills Schs. Cmty. Edn., Cin., 1990—, Super Saturday Gifted Program, Cin., 1990—; adult leader antidrug program Just Say No, Cin., 1989-92. Author: Study Skills Workshop, 1993; writer, dir. Christmas play, 1993; contbr. poetry to lit. publs. Vol. interior designer for homeless shelter St. Joseph's Carpenter Shop, Cin., 1990; mem. LaSalle PTA, 1993—; vol. Habitat for Humanity. Mem. Nat. Tchrs. Assn. Democrat. Roman Catholic. Avocations: writing, jazz/tap dance, community theatre, interior decorating, aerobics instructor. Home and Office: 3801 Dina Ter Cincinnati OH 45211-6527

SKILES, JAMES JEAN, electrical and computer engineering educator; b. St Louis, Oct. 16, 1928; s. Coy Emerson and Vernetta Beatrice (Maples) S.; m. Deloris Audrey McKenney, Sept. 4, 1948; children: Steven, Randall, Jeffrey. BSEE, Washington U., St. Louis, 1948; MS, U. Mo.-Rolla, 1951; PhD, U. Wis., 1954. Registered profl. engr., Wis. Engr. Union Electric Co., St. Louis, 1948-49; instr. U. Mo.-Rolla, 1949-51; prof. elec. engring. U. Wis., Madison, 1954-89, prof. emeritus, 1989—, chmn. Dept. Elec. Engring., 1967-72, dir. Univ. Industry Rsch. program, 1972-75, dir. Energy Rsch. Ctr., 1975-95; cons. in field. Contbr. articles to profl. jours. Mem. Monona Grove Dist. Schs. Bd., Wis., 1961-69; mem. adv. com. Wis. Energy Office, Madison, 1979-80, Wis. Pub. Service Commn., 1980-81. Recipient Wis. Electric Utilities Professorship in Energy Engring. U. Wis., 1975-89; recipient Benjamin Smith Reynolds Teaching award, 1980, Kiekhofer Teaching award, 1955, Acad of Elec. Engring. award U. Mo.-Rolla, 1982. Mem. IEEE (sr.), Am. Soc. Engring. Edn. Home: 8099 Coray Ln Verona WI 53593-9073 Office: Univ of Wisconsin Dept Elec & Computer Engring 1415 Engineering Dr Madison WI 53706-1607

SKILLERN, FRANK FLETCHER, law educator; b. Sept. 26, 1942; s. Will T. and Vera Catherine (Ryberg) S.; m. Susan Schlaefer, Sept. 3, 1966; children: Nathan Edward, Leah Catherine. AB, U. Chgo., 1964; JD, U. Denver, 1966; LLM, U. Mich., 1969. Bar: Colo. 1967, Tex. 1978. Pvt. practice law Denver, 1967; gen. atty. Maritime Adminstrn., Washington, 1967-68; asst. prof. law Ohio No. U., 1969-71; asst. prof. law Tex. Tech U., Lubbock, 1971-73, assoc. prof. law, 1973-75, prof. law, 1975—; vis. prof. U. Tex. Law Sch., summer 1979, U. Ark. Law Sch., 1979-80, U. Tulsa Coll. Law, 1981-82; cons. and speaker in field. Author: Environmental Protection: The Legal Framework, 1981, 2d edit. published as Environmental Protection Deskbook, 1995, Regulation of Water and Sewer Utilities, 1989, Texas Water Law, Vol. I, 1988, rev. edit., 1992, Vol. II, 1991; contbr. chpts. to Powell on Real Property, Zoning and Land Use Controls, others; author cong. procs. and numerous articles. Mem. ABA (mem. publs. com. Sect. Natural Resources Law 1984—, vice chair internat. environ. law com. Sect. Natural Resources Law 1987). Office: Tex Tech U Sch Law PO Box 40004 Lubbock TX 79409-0004

SKILLICORN, JUDY PETTIBONE, gifted and talented education coordinator; b. Cleve., June 16, 1943; d. C. Arthur and Dorothy Laura (Parratt) Pettibone; m. Robert Charles Skillicorn, Aug. 21, 1965; children: Jodie Lynn, Brian Jeffrey, Jennifer Laura. BS in Edn., Ohio State U., 1965; MEd, Cleve. State U., 1988. 6th grade tchr. Windermer Sch., Upper Arlington, Ohio, 1965-68; pvt. tutor, 1968-71; adminstr. Westshore Montessori Sch., Elyria, Lorain & Amherst, Ohio, 1981; ch. educator First Congl. Ch., Elyria, 1982-84, St. Peters United Ch. of Christ, Amherst, Ohio, 1984; tchr. gifted Clearview Local Schs., Lorain, 1985-90; coord. gifted Ednl. Svc. Ctr. Lorain County, Elyria, 1990—; planning dir. county-wide sch. creative & performing arts Lorain County Bd. Edn., Elyria; founder Arts Advocacy of Lorain County, 1994, pres. 1996; founder Arts Connected Tchg. pilot program in 4 sch. dists., 1995-96; mem. planning com. and curriculum com. Lorain County Alternative Sch. Author: Young Authors Handbook, 1991, 92, 93, 94, 95, 96, 97. Chairperson tickets Elyria 150th Bicentennial Celebration; pageant dir. Ch. Medieval Feast, Elyria, 1988-91; chmn. diaconate First Congl. Ch., Elyria, 1990-93; mem. com. Lorain County Beautiful, Seventh Generation, 1995-97. Recipient Partnership in Edn. for Young Authors Program grades K-6 Nat. Assn. Coll. Stores, Oberlin, 1993-97, for Writers conf. Program grades 7-9, 1993-97; Jennings scholar tchr. Martha Holden Jennings Found., 1990-91. Mem. Writing Tchrs. Network (publ. com. 1991-93), North Ctrl. Consortium for Gifted (treas., v.p. 1991-93), Lorain County Elem. Sch. Adminstrs. (sec.-treas. 1993, v.p. 1993-94, pres. 1994-95, nominating com. 1997), Consortium Ohio Coords. for Gifted, Ohio Assn. Gifted Children, Chautauqua Lit. Soc., Internat. Network for Visual and Performing Arts Schs., Phi Delta Kappa. Avocations: reading including children's literature, travel, attending plays, arts actvities and concerts, gardening. Office: Ednl Svc Ctr Lorain County 1885 Lake Ave Elyria OH 44035-2551

SKILLIN, EDWARD SIMEON, magazine publisher; b. N.Y.C., Jan. 23, 1904; s. Edward Simeon and Geraldine Madeleine (Fearons) S.; m. Jane Anne Edwards, Jan. 27, 1945; children: Edward John, Elizabeth Ann Skillin Flanagan, Arthur Paul, Susan Geraldine Skillin Thuvanuti, Mary Jane Skillin Davis. Grad., Phillips Acad., Andover, Mass., 1921; AB, Williams Coll., 1925; MA, Columbia U., 1933; LHD (hon.), St. Benedict's Coll., Atchison, Kans., 1954, Fordham U., 1974; LLD, St. Vincent's Coll., Latrobe, Pa., 1959, St. Francis Xavier U., Antigonish, N.S., Can., 1966, Stonehill Coll., 1979. With ednl. dept. Henry Holt & Co., N.Y.C., 1925-32; mem. staff Commonweal Found., N.Y.C., 1933-38, editor, 1938-67, pub., 1967—. Editor: The Commonweal Reader, 1949. Recipient Centennial citation St. John's U., Collegeville, Minn., 1957, St. Francis de Sales award Cath. Press Assn., 1987, Pax Christi award St. John's U., 1990. Mem. Cath. Commn. on Intellectual and Cultural Affairs, Phi Beta Kappa, Phi Gamma Delta. Office: Commonweal Found 15 Dutch St New York NY 10038-3719 *Grateful for many things: faith, family, the influence of 3 friends, good health, and 60 years with a socially-minded Christian journal of opinion.*

SKILLING, DAVID VAN DIEST, manufacturing executive; b. St. Louis, Sept. 16, 1933; s. David Miller Jr. and Eloise Margaret (van Diest) S.; m. Barbara Jo Chaney, Aug. 4, 1956; children: Kimberly Alice, Mark Chaney. BS, Colo. Coll., 1955; MBA, Pepperdine U., 1977. With TRW, Inc., Los Angeles, 1970-83, Cleve., 1983-93, Orange, Calif., 1993-96; exec. v.p., gen. mgr. infosystems and svcs. TRW, Inc., Los Angeles, 1989-96; chmn., CEO Experian Inc., Orange, Calif., 1996—; bd. dirs. Lamson & Sessions, Cleve. Bd. dirs. ISI, 1988—; trustee The Colo. Coll., 1994—. Mem. NAM (bd. dirs. 1988-93), Assn. for Corp. Growth, Calif. Bus. Roundtable (exec. com. 1994—), Orange County C. of C. (bd. dirs. 1993-96). Republican. Office: Experian Inc 505 City Pkwy W Orange CA 92868-2914

SKILLING, JOHN BOWER, structural and civil engineer; b. L.A., Oct. 8, 1921; s. Harold C. and Helen M. (Bower) S.; m. Mary Jane Stender, May 1, 1943; children: William, Susan, Ann. B.S., U. Wash., 1947. Design engr. W.H. Witt Co., Seattle, 1947-52; partner successor firm Worthington, Skilling, Helle and Jackson, Seattle, 1959-67, Skilling, Helle, Christiansen, Robertson, Seattle, 1967-82; chmn., CEO successor firm Skilling Ward Rogers Barkshire, Inc., Seattle, 1983-87; chmn. Skilling Ward Magnusson Barkshire, Inc. and successor firm, Seattle, 1987—; mem. Bldg. Research Adv. Bd. Mem. Seattle Found. Fellow ASCE; mem. NAE, Am. Concrete Inst., Internat. Assn. Shell Structures, Structural Engrs. Assn. Wash., AIA (hon.), Am. Inst. Steel Constrn., Wash. Athletic Club, Seattle Tennis Club, Broadmoor Golf Club, Lampda Alpha. Clubs: 101; Dean's, Pres.'s (Univ. Wash.). Home: 539 Mcgilvra Blvd E Seattle WA 98112-5047 Office: Skilling Ward Magnusson Barkshire Inc 1301 5th Ave Ste 3200 Seattle WA 98101-2603

SKILLING, THOMAS ETHELBERT, III, meteorologist, meteorology educator; b. Pitts., Feb. 20, 1952; s. Elizabeth Clarke. Student, U. Wis., 1970-74; Dr. Humanities (hon.), Lewis U., Romeoville, Ill., 1995. Meteorologist Sta. WKKD-AM-FM, Aurora, Ill., 1967-70, Sta. WLXT-TV, Aurora, 1969-70, Sta. WKOW-TV, Madison, Wis., 1970-74, Sta. WTSO, Madison, 1970-74, Sta. WTLV-TV, Jacksonville, Fla., 1974-75, Sta. WITI-TV, Milw., 1975-78, Sta. WAUK, Waukesha, Wis., 1976-77, Sta. WGN-TV, Chgo., 1978—; weather forecaster Wis. Farm Broadcast Network, Madison, 1970-74; weather cons. Piper, Jaffray & Hopwood, Madison, 1972-74; instr. meteorology Columbia Coll., Chgo., 1982-92, Adler Planetarium, Chgo., 1985-86. Vol. Chgo. chpt. Muscular Dystrophy Assn. Recipient Emmy award for "It Sounded Like a Freight Train," 1991, "The Cosmic Challenge, " 1994; Peter Lisagor awards for weather spls. aired on WGN, 1991, 93. Fellow Am. Meteorol. Soc. (v.p. Chgo. chpt. 1985-86, TV Seal of Approval, Outstanding Svc. award 1997), Nat. Weather Assn., Soc. Profl. Journalists, Chgo. Acad. TV Arts and Scis. Avocations: hiking, cross country skiing. Home: 6033 N Sheridan Rd Apt 31C Chicago IL 60660-3022 Office: Sta WGN-TV 2501 W Bradley Pl Chicago IL 60618-4701

SKILLINGSTAD, CONSTANCE YVONNE, social services administrator, educator; b. Portland, Oreg., Nov. 18, 1944; d. Irving Elmer and Beulah Ruby (Aleckson) Erickson; M. David W. Skillingstad, Jan. 12, 1968 (div. Mar. 1981); children: Michael, Brian. BA in Sociology, U. Minn., 1966; MBA, U. St. Thomas, St. Paul, 1982. Cert. vol. adminstr.; lic. social worker. Social worker Rock County Welfare Dept., Luverne, Minn., 1966-68; social worker Hennepin County Social Svcs., Mpls., 1968-70, vol. coord., 1970-78; vol. coord. St. Joseph's Home for Children, Mpls., 1978-89, mgr. community resources, 1989-94; exec. dir. Mpls. Crisis Nursery, 1994—; mem. community faculty Met. State U., St. Paul and Mpls., 1982—; faculty U. St. Thomas Ctr. for Non Profit Mgmt., 1990—; trainer, mem. adv. commn. Mpls. Vol. Ctr., 1978-90, cons., 1980—, chmn. Contbr. articles to Jour. Vol. Admintrn. Mem. adv. bd. Mothers Against Drunk Driving, Minn., 1986-88; vice chmn., chmn. adminstrv. coun., lay leader Hobart United Meth. Ch.; lay rep. to Minn. Ann. Conf. of Meth. Chs., 1989-92; mem. social concerns. commn. Park Ave United Meth. Ch., 1992—; bd. dirs. Ctr. for Grief, Loss and Transition. Named one of Outstanding Young Women Am., 1974, Woman of Distinction Mpls. St. Paul Mag./KARE-TV, 1995. Mem. Minn. Assn. Vol. Dirs. (pres. 1975, sec., ethics chmn. 1987—), Assn. for Vol. Adminstrn. (v.p. regional affairs 1985-87, mem. assessment panel 1986—, coord. nat. tng. team, cert. process for vol. adminstrs. 1988-92, profl. devel. chair 1990-92), Minn. Social Svcs. Assn. (pres. 1981, pres.-elect 1997-98. Disting. Svc. award 1987). Mem. Dem.-Farmer-Labor Party. Methodist. Avocations: bridge, volleyball, accordian, traveling, reading. Office: Mpls Crisis Nursery 4255 3rd Ave S Minneapolis MN 55409-2105

SKILLMAN, THOMAS GRANT, endocrinology consultant, former educator; b. Cin., Jan. 7, 1925; s. Harold Grant and Faustina (Jobes) S.; m. Elizabeth Louise McClellan, Sept. 6, 1947; children: Linda, Barbara. B.S., Baldwin-Wallace Coll., 1946; M.D., U. Cin., 1949. Intern Cin. Gen. Hosp., 1949-50, resident, 1952-54; instr. medicine U. Cin., 1952-57; asst. prof. medicine Ohio State U., Columbus, 1957-61; dir. endocrinology and metabolism Coll. Medicine Ohio State U., 1967-74, Ralph Kurtz prof. endocrinology, 1974-81, prof. emeritus, 1981—, cons. to v.p. med. affairs, 1981—; asso. prof. medicine Creighton U., Omaha, 1961-67. Editor: Case Studies in Endocrinology, 1971; Contbr. numerous articles to med. jours. Served with USNR, 1943-45; 1950-52, Korea. Recipient Golden Apple award Student Am. Med. Assn., 1966. Mem. Am. Diabetes Assn., Central Soc. Clin. Investigation, Am. Fedn. for Clin. Research, Alpha Omega Alpha. Club: Ohio State Golf (Columbus). Home: 4179 Stoneroot Dr Hilliard OH 43026-3023 Office: Ohio State U Hosps Meiling Hall # 200G Columbus OH 43210

SKILLMAN, WILLIAM ALFRED, consulting engineering executive; b. Lakehurst, N.J., Jan. 22, 1928; s. Wilbur Newton and Greta Alfreda (Ekman) S.; m. Anne Marie Cavender, Sept. 19, 1948; children—Thomas R., Gregory A., Karen L. B.S. in Engring. Physics, Lehigh U., 1952; M.S. in Physics, U. Rochester, 1954. Assoc. engr. Westinghouse Electric Corp., Balt., 1954-56, engr., 1956-58, sr. engr., 1958-61, supervisory engr., 1961-64, advisory engr., 1964-73, sr. adv. engr., 1973-85, cons. engr., 1986-93, cons. electronic systems group, 1993—. Author: Radar Calculations Using the TI-59 Programmable Calculator, 1983; author: (with others) Radar Handbook, 2d edit., 1990. Patentee in field. Served with USN, 1946-48. Fellow IEEE (life); mem. Aerospace and Electronic Sys. Soc. (Pioneer award 1995), Phi Beta Kappa. Republican. Methodist. Avocations: photography; canoeing; hiking; programming. Home and Office: 605 Forest View Rd Linthicum Heights MD 21090-2819

SKILLRUD, HAROLD CLAYTON, minister; b. St. Cloud, Minn., June 29, 1928; s. Harold and Amanda Skillrud; m. Lois Dickhart, June 8, 1951; children: David, Janet, John. BA magna cum laude, Gustavus Adolphus Coll., 1950; MDiv magna cum laude, Augustana Theol. Sem., Rock Island, Ill., 1954; STM, Luth. Sch. Theology, Chgo., 1969; DD (hon.), Augustana Coll., 1978, Newberry Coll., 1988. Ordained to ministry Evang. Luth. Ch. in Am., 1954. Supply pastor Saron Luth. Ch., Big Lake, Minn., 1950-51; mem. staff 1st Luth. Ch., Rock Island, Ill., 1951-52; intern, organizer new mission Faith Luth. Ch., Syosset, N.Y., 1952-53; sr. pastor St. John's Luth. Ch., Bloomington, Ill., 1954-79, Luth. Ch. of the Redeemer, Atlanta, 1979-87; bishop Southeastern Synod Evang. Luth. Ch. in Am., Atlanta, 1987-95, regional rep. bd. pensions, 1995—; del. to various convs. Luth. Ch. in Am., Luth. World Fedn. in Helsinki, 1963, mem. bd. publ., 1976-84, pastor-evangelist Evang. Outreach Emphasis program, 1977-79, mem. exec. bd. Ill. synod, 1977-79, pres. bd. publ., 1980-84, leader stewardship cluster Southeastern synod, 1983, mem. exec. bd. Southeastern synod, 1984-87; mem. exec. coun., Luth. Ch. in Am., 1984-87; mem. task force on new ch. design Commn. on New Luth. Ch., task force on ch. pub. house, 1985; del. constituting conv. Evang. Luth. Ch. in Am., 1987, del. assemblies Evang. Luth. Ch. in Am., 1989, 91, 93, 95; mem. commn. on clergy confidentiality Luth. Coun. in USA, 1987; co-chair USA Luth.- Roman Cath. Dialogue; mem. Task Force on Theol. Edn. Author: LSTC: Decade of Decision, 1969; co-editor Scripture and Tradition, Lutherans and Catholics in Dialogue, 1995; mem. edtl. bd. Partners mag., 1978-80; contbr. articles and sermons to religious jours. Former bd. dirs. Augustana Theol. Sem.; bd. dirs. Augustana Coll., 1969-77, chmn. bd., 1976-77; bd. dirs. Kessler Reformation Collection, Newberry Coll., Luth. World Relief, Augsburg Fortress; chmn. bd. dirs. Luth. Sch. Theology, Chgo., 1962-69; mem. Leadership Atlanta, 1980-81, United Way, Atlanta, 1980-81; mem. Bishop's Commn. on Econ. Justice, 1985-86; pres. bd. dirs. Atlanta Samaritan House, 1986-87. Recipient Alumni award Luth. Sch. Theology, Chgo., 1976, award Leadership Atlanta, 1981, The Rev. John Bachman award, Luth. Theol. Sem., Columbia, S.C., 1996. Mem. Luth. Sch. Theology Alumni Assn. (pres. 1975-77), Conf. of Bishops, Kiwanis (pres. Midtown chpt. 1984-85). Avocations: travel, photography. Home: 368 E Wesley Rd NE Atlanta GA 30305-3824

SKINGER, KENNETH ROBERT, communications executive, engineer, lawyer; b. New Britain, Conn., June 18, 1941; s. Dennis Leonard and Genevive (Backus) S.; m. Nancy Lee Christien, July 6, 1963 (div. 1984); children: Robin Lee, Todd Kristopher; m. Maryellen Kernen, Feb. 14, 1988; 1 child, Christopher D'Entremont. BS in Engring., U. Conn., 1963; JD cum laude, New Eng. Sch. Law, Boston, 1978. Bar: Mass. 1978, U.S. Dist. Ct. 1979, Mass. 1979, U.S. Ct. Appeals (1st cir.) 1979, U.S. Supreme Ct. 1982; profl. engr., Conn., Mass., N.Y., Tex., R.I., Fla. Sales engr. GE, N.Y.C., 1963-69; utility sales mgr. GE, Albany, N.Y., 1969-74; elec. engr. Stone & Webster Engring. Corp., Boston, 1974-78, mgr. mktg. svcs., 1978-85, mgr. engring. svcs., 1985-86, prin. elec. engr., 1986-88, project mgr., 1989-95, v.p. comm. svcs. group, 1995—; exec. com., bd. dirs. New Eng.-Can. Bus. Coun., Boston, 1993—, v.p., 1994-95. Contbr. articles to IEEE Transactions, FAA Tech. Forum, tech. mags. Mem. IEEE (sr. mem.). Avocations: sailing, cross country skiing. Office: Stone & Webster Engrg Corp 245 Summer St Boston MA 02210-1116

SKINNER, ALASTAIR, accountant; b. Hamilton, Ont., Can., Apr. 4, 1936; s. Allistair and Isabelle (Drysdale) S.; m. Patricia Skinner; children: Lisa, Iain, James, Graeme. CA, Queens U., Kingston, Ont., Can., 1959; MBA, Harvard U., 1963. Cert. mgmt. cons. Served to maj. Can. Army Res., 1954-71; nat. mng. ptnr. MacGillivray & Co. (name now Doane Raymond), 1977-83; ptnr.-in-charge Toronto (Ont.) Office, Spicer MacGillivray (name now Doane Raymond), 1984-86, 88-91; ptnr. Doane Raymond, Toronto, 1991—. Co-author: profl. manuals. Fellow Inst. Chartered Accts. of Ont. (pres. 1983-84), Soc. Mgmt. Accts. of Can. (bd. dirs.); mem. Inst. Mgmt. Cons. of Ont., Can. Tax Found. (bd. govs.), Pub. Accts. Coun. Ont. Club: Albany (Toronto), Devil's Glen Country Club. Avocations: skiing, bridge. Office: Doane Raymond Ste 1900, Royal Bank Plz Box 55, Toronto, ON Canada M5J 2P9

SKINNER, ANDREW CHARLES, history educator, religious writer; b. Durango, Colo., Apr. 25, 1951; s. Charles La Verne and Julia Magdalena (Schunk) S.; m. Janet Corbridge, Mar. 22, 1974; children: Cheryl Lyn, Charles Lon, Kelli Ann, Mark Andrew, Holly, Suzanne. BA with disting., U. Colo., 1975; MA with disting., Iliff Sch. of Theology, Denver, 1978; ThM, Harvard U., 1980; PhD, U. Denver, 1986. Group mgr. May Co. Dept. Store, Denver, 1980-83; assoc. studio dir. Talking Books Pub. Co., Denver, 1984-88; instr. history Metro. State Coll., Denver, 1984-88; prof. history Ricks Coll., Rexburg, Utah, 1988-92; prof. ancient scripture Brigham Young U., Provo, Utah, 1992—, chmn. ancient scripture, 1997—; vis. instr. ancient scripture Brigham Young U., Provo, Utah, 1987; vis. prof. Jerusalem Ctr. for Nr. Eastern Studies, Israel; cons. Univ. Without Walls, Loretto Heights Coll., Denver, 1985-88; mem. editorial staff Dead Sea Scrolls, publ. bd. Israel Antiquities Authority. Author chpts. numerous books and encyclopaedia articles; co-author: Jerusalem-The Eternal City. Bishop Mormon Ch., Denver, 1986-88, Utah, 1996—; varsity scout leader Teton Parks coun. Boy Scouts Am., Rexburg, 1988-89; host Internat. Scholars Conf. on Holocaust and the Chs., 1995. Mil. history fellow U.S. Mil. Acad., 1989. Mem. Am. Hist. Assn., Soc. Bibl. Lit., Mormon History Assn., Phi Theta Kappa, Phi Alpha Theta. Mem. LDS Ch. Office: Brigham Young U Dept Ancient Scripture JSB 270-M Provo UT 84602

SKINNER, BRIAN JOHN, geologist, educator; b. Wallaroo, South Australia, Dec. 15, 1928; came to U.S., 1958, naturalized, 1963; s. Joshua Henry and Joyce Barbara Lloyd (Prince) S.; m. Helen Catherine Wild, Oct. 9, 1954; children: Adrienne Wild, Stephanie Wild, Thalassa Wild. B.Sc., U. Adelaide, Australia, 1950; A.M., Harvard U., 1952, Ph.D., 1955. Lectr. U. Adelaide, 1955-58; research geologist U.S. Geol. Survey, 1958-62, chief br. exptl. geochemistry and mineralogy, 1962-66; prof. geology and geophysics, chmn. dept. Yale U., New Haven, 1966-73; Eugene Higgins prof. Yale U., 1972—; Hugh Exton McKinstry Meml. lectr. Harvard U., 1978; Alex L. du Toit lectr. Combined Socs. South Africa, 1979; Cecil H. and Ida Green lectr. U. B.C., 1983; Thayer Lindsley Meml. lectr. Soc. Econ. Geologists, 1983; Soc. Econ. Geologists Overseas lectr., 1985; Hoffman lectr. Harvard U., 1986, Joubin-James lectr. U. Toronto, 1987; mem. exec. com. divsn. earth scis. NRC, 1966-69; chmn. com. mineral resources and the environ. Nat. Acad. Scis.-NRC, 1973-75; mem. Lunar Sample Analysis Planning Team, 1968-70, Lunar Sci. Rev. Bd., 1971-72, U.S. Nat. Com. for Geochemistry, 1966-67, U.S. Nat. Com. for Geology, 1973-77, 85-93, chmn., 1987-93, chmn. bd. earth scis. NRC, 1987-88, earth scis. and resources, 1989-90; mem. bd. Internat. Geol. Correlation Program, UNESCO-IUGS, 1985-89, 90-96, chmn., 1986-89; cons. Office Sci. and Tech. Policy, 197-80, NSF, 1977-82; dir. Econ. Geology Pub. Co.; chmn. governing bd. Am. Jour. Sci., 1972—; pres. Econ. Geology Pub. Co., 1996—. Author: Earth Resources, 1969, 77, 86, Man and the Ocean, 1973, Physical Geology, 1974, 77, 87, Rocks and Rock Minerals, 1979, The New Iron Age Ahead, 1987, Resources and World Development, 1987, The Dynamic Earth, 1989, 92, 95, The Blue Planet, 1995, Environmental Geology, 1996; editor: Econ. Geology, 1969-96, Oxford Univ. Press Monographs in Geological Sciences, 1979—; editl. bd. Am. Scientist, 1974-90, chmn., 1987-90. Trustee Hopkins Grammar Sch., 1978-83. Recipient Disting. Contbns. award Assn. Earth Sci. Editors, 1979, Silver medal Soc. Econ. Geologists, 1981, Neil Miner award Nat. Assn. Geology Tchrs., 1995; Guggenheim fellow, 1970. Fellow Geol. Soc. Am. (councillor 1976-78, chmn. spl. publs. com. 1980-81, chmn. com. on coms. 1983, pres. 1985); mem. Geochem. Soc. (pres. 1972-73), Conn. Acad. Sci. and Engring. (div. chmn. 1978-80, council 1982-87), Soc. Econ. Geologists (pres. 1995). Home: PO Box 894 Woodbury CT 06798-0894

SKINNER, CHARLES SCOFIELD, technology management service executive, consultant, mechanical engineer; b. Cleve., Feb. 10, 1940; s. Harry Harrison and Margaret Charlotte (Scofield) S.; m. Nancy Lee Cleveland, Sept. 20, 1974; children: Jeffrey Charles, Melinda Lee. MME, Cornell U., 1969; MBA, Case Western Res. U., 1979; BSME, Cornell U., 1963; postgrad., MIT, 1972, Stanford U., 1977, Harvard U., 1982. Registered profl. engr., N.Y., Ohio. Mfg. engr. GM, Detroit, 1963-64; market researcher Exxon Corp., N.Y.C., 1964-65; sr. ptnr. Booz-Allen & Hamilton, Inc., N.Y.C., 1970-85; pres., CEO Strategic Technology Inc., Cleve., 1985—; cons. Booz-Allen & Hamilton, Inc., 1970-85, Strategic Tech., Inc., 1985—, also bd. dirs.; cons. First Pacific Networks, Inc., Sunnyvale, Calif., 1988-89. Author: CIM Implementation Planning Guide, 1988, (with others) The Management of Productivity, 1986; contbr. numerous articles to profl. jours. Fundraiser Culver (Ind.) Ednl. Found., 1969-92, Cornell U., Ithaca, N.Y., 1975—, Old Trail Sch., Akron, Ohio, 1988—, Univ. Sch., Shaker Hts., Ohio, 1991—. Capt. U.S. Army, 1965-68. Decorated Air medal with 23 oak leaf clusters, Vietnam Campaign medal with device, Aviator medal, Vietnam Service medal, Exxon Corp. grantee, 1968-69. Mem. Soc. Mfg. Engrs. (chmn. mfg. and planning divsn., tech. coun. 1982-83), Culver Legion (life), Cornell Club of N.Y., Mid-Day Club, Cornell Club of N.E. Ohio (treas. 1993), Sigma Chi (treas. 1962-63), SAR, We. Res. Soc., Scabbard and Blade (hon.), Phoebus (hon.), Masons, Shriners, Vietnam Vets. Am., VFW. Avocations: squash, golf, piloting. Office: Strategic Tech Inc 24200 Chagrin Blvd Cleveland OH 44122-5550

SKINNER, DAVID BERNT, surgeon, educator, administrator; b. Joliet, Ill., Apr. 28, 1935; s. James Madden and Bertha Elinor (Tapper) S.; m. May Elinor Tischer, Aug. 25, 1956; children: Linda Elinor, Kristin Anne, Carise Berntine, Margaret Leigh. BA with high honors, U. Rochester, N.Y., 1958, ScD (hon.), 1980; MD cum laude, Yale U., 1959; MD (hon.), U. Lund, 1994, Technishe U. Munich, 1995. Diplomate: Am. Bd. Surgery (dir. 1974-80), Am. Bd. Thoracic Surgery. Intern, then resident in surgery Mass. Gen. Hosp., Boston, 1959-65; sr. registrar in thoracic surgery Frenchay Hosp., Bristol, Eng., 1963-64; teaching fellow Harvard U. Med. Sch., 1965; from asst. prof. surgery to prof. Johns Hopkins U. Med. Sch., also surgeon Johns Hopkins Hosp., 1968-72; Dallas B. Phemister prof. surgery, chmn. dept. U. Chgo. Hosps. and Clinics, 1972-87; prof. surgery Cornell U., 1987—; pres., CEO N.Y. Hosp., 1987—, vice chair, CEO N.Y. & Presbyn. Hosps., 1996—; dir. Omnis Surg. Inc., 1984-85, Churchill Livingston, 1990-93, Lab. Corp. Am.; mem. Pres.' Biomed. Rsch. Panel, 1975-76. Author: Atlas of Esophageal Surgery, 1991; author: (with others) Gastroesophageal Reflux and Hiatal Hernia, 1972, Management of Esophageal Diseases, 1988; editor: Surgical Practice Illustrated, 1988-95; editor Current Topics in Surg. Rsch., 1969-71, Jour. Surg. Rsch., 1972-83; co-editor: Surg. Treatment of Digestive Disease, 1985, Esophageal Disorders, 1985, Reconstructive Surgery of the Gastrointestinal Tract, 1985, Primary Motility Disorders of the Esophagus, 1991; mem. editl. bd. Jour. Thoracic and Cardiovasc. Surgery, Annals of Surgery; contbr. profl. jours., chpts. in books. Elder Fourth Presbyn. Ch., Chgo., 1976-87, clk. of session, 1978-82, 84-87; bd. visitors Cornell U. Med. Coll., 1980-87. Served to maj. M.C. USAF, 1966-68. Decorated Chevalier Nat. Order of Merit (France); John and Mary Markle scholar acad. medicine, 1969-74. Fellow ACS; mem. AMA, Internat. Surg. Group (pres.-elect), Am., Western, So. Surg. Assns., Soc. Univ. Surgeons (pres. 1978-79), Am. Soc. Artificial Internal Organs (pres. 1977), Soc. Surg. Chmn. (pres. 1980-82), Am. Assn. Thoracic Surgery (pres. 1996-97), Soc. Vascular Surgery, Soc. Thoracic Surgery, Soc. Pelvic Surgeons, Soc. Surgery Alimentary Tract, Soc. Internat. de Chirurgie, Collegium Internat. de Chirurgie Digestivae, Am. Coll. Chest Physicians, Ctrl. Surg. Soc., Internat. Soc. Diseases Esophagus (pres. 1992-95), Assn. Acad. Surgery, Halsted Soc., Soc. Clin. Surgery (pres. 1986-88), Phi Beta Kappa, Alpha Omega Alpha. Clubs: Quadrangle (Chgo.); Cosmos (Washington); University (N.Y.C.); River (N.Y.C.). Home: 79 E 79th St New York NY 10021-0202 Office: New York Hosp Cornell Univ Office Pres 525 E 68th St New York NY 10021-4873

SKINNER, G(EORGE) WILLIAM, anthropologist, educator; b. Oakland, Calif., Feb. 14, 1925; s. John James and Eunice (Engle) S.; m. Carol Bagger, Mar. 25, 1951 (div. Jan. 1970); children: Geoffrey Crane, James Lauriston, Mark Williamson, Jeremy Burr; m. Susan Mann, Apr. 26, 1980; 1 dau., Alison Jane. Student, Deep Springs (Calif.) Coll., 1942-43; B.A. with distinction in Far Eastern Studies, Cornell U., Ithaca, N.Y., 1947, Ph.D. in Cultural Anthropology, 1954. Field dir. Cornell U. S.E. Asia program, also Cornell Research Center, Bangkok, Thailand, 1951-55; rsch. assoc. in Indonesia, 1956-58; asso. prof., then prof. anthropology Cornell U., Ithaca, N.Y., 1960-65; asst. prof. sociology Columbia, 1958-60; sr. specialist in residence East-West Ctr. Honolulu, 1965-66; prof. anthropology Stanford, 1966-89; Barbara Kimball Browning prof. humanities and scis., 1987-89; prof. anthropology U. Calif., Davis, 1990—; vis. prof. U. Pa., 1977, Duke U., spring, 1978, Keio U., Tokyo, spring 1985, fall 1988, U. Calif.-San Diego, fall 1986; field rsch. China, 1949-50, 77, S.E. Asia, 1950-51, Thailand, 1951-53, 54-55, Java and Borneo, 1956-58, Japan, 1985, 88, 95; mem. joint com. on contemporary China Social Sci. Research Coun.-Am. Acad. Learned Socs., 1961-65, 80-81, internat. com. on Chinese studies, 1963-64, mem. joint com. on Chinese studies, 1981-83; mem. subcom. rsch. Chinese Soc. Social Sci. Rsch. Coun., 1961-70, chmn., 1963-70; dir. program on East Asian Local Systems, 1969-71; dir. Chinese Soc. Bibliography Project, 1964-73; assoc. dir. Cornell China Program, 1961-63; dir. London-Cornell Project Social Rsch., 1962-65; mem. com. on scholarly communication with People's Republic of China, Nat. Acad. Scis., 1966-70, mem. social scis. and humanities panel, 1982-83; mem. adv. com. Ctr. for Chinese Rsch. Materials, Assn. Rsch. Libraries, 1967-70; mem. policy and planning com. China in Time and Space, 1993—. Author: Chinese Society in Thailand, 1957, Leadership and Power in the Chinese Community of Thailand, 1958; also articles; Editor: The Social Sciences and Thailand, 1956, Local, Ethnic and National Loyalties in Village Indonesia, 1959, Modern Chinese Society: An Analytical Bibliography, 3 vols, 1973, (with Mark Elvin) The Chinese City Between Two Worlds, 1974, (with A. Thomas Kirsch) Change and Persistence in Thai Society, 1975, The City in Late Imperial China, 1977, The Study of Chinese Society, 1979. Served to ensign USNR, 1943-46. Fellow Center for Advanced Study in Behavioral Scis., 1969-70; Guggenheim fellow, 1969; NIMH spl. fellow, 1970. Mem. NAS, AAAS, Am. Anthrop. Assn., Am. Sociol. Assn., Assn. Asian Studies (bd. dirs. 1962-65, chmn. nominating com. 1967-68, pres. 1983-84), Soc. for Cultural Anthropology, Internat. Union for Sci. Study of Population, Social Sci. History Assn., Am. Ethnol. Soc., Population Assn. Am., Siam Soc., Soc. Qing Studies, Soc. Econ. Anthropology, Phi Beta Kappa, Sigma Xi. Office: Dept Anthropology U Calif Davis CA 95616

SKINNER, HARRY BRYANT, orthopaedic surgery educator; b. Cleve., Oct. 13, 1943; s. Harry Bryant and Marion (Eastlick) S. BS, Alfred U., 1965; MS, PhD, U. Calif., Berkeley, 1970; MD, Med. U. S.C., 1975. Asst. prof. Youngstown (Ohio) State U., 1970-71; postdoctoral research assoc. Clemson (S.C.) U., 1971-72; lectr. Calif. State U., Sacramento, 1977-79; asst./assoc. prof. Tulane U., New Orleans, 1979-82; assoc. prof. orthopaedic surgery U. Calif., San Francisco, 1983-86, prof., 1986-94; prof. mech. engring. U. Calif., Berkeley, 1993—; chair grad. group U. Calif., Berkeley and San Francisco; prof., chmn. dept. orthopedic surgery U. Calif., Irvine, 1994—, prof. mech. and aerospace engring. Engring. Sch., 1995—; adj. asst./assoc. prof. Sch. Engring., Tulane U., New Orleans, 1979-82; dir. rehab. research and devel. VA Med. Ctr., San Francisco, 1983—. Mem. editorial bd. Orthopaedics jour., 1984-88, guest editor, 1985, Jour. Biomed. Materials Research, 1983—; contbr. articles to profl. jours. Grantee NIH, 1978-84, Nat. Inst. Dental Rsch., 1978-84, VA, 1978—, Schleider Found., 1980-82, Am. Fedn. Aging Rsch., 1986-89. Fellow ACS, Am. Acad. Orthopaedic Surgeons; mem. Orthopaedic Rsch. Soc., Soc. for Biomaterials (charter), Am. Orthopaedic Assn., The Hip Soc., Sigma Xi. Office: U Calif Dept Orthopaedic Surgery 29A 101 City Dr S Orange CA 92668

SKINNER, HELEN CATHERINE WILD, biomineralogist; b. Bklyn., Jan. 25, 1931; d. Edward Herman and Minnie (Bertsch) Wild; m. Brian John Skinner, Oct. 9, 1954; children: Adrienne, Stephanie, Thalassa. BA, Mt. Holyoke Coll., 1952; MA, Radcliffe/Harvard, 1954; PhD, Adelaide (Australia) U., 1959. Mineralogist sect. molecular structure Nat. Inst. Arthritis and Metabolic Diseases, NIH, 1961-65; with sect. crystal chemistry Lab. Histology and Pathology Nat. Inst. Dental Rsch., NIH, 1965-66; lectr. dept. geology and geophysics Yale U., 1967-69, rsch. assoc. dept. surgery, 1967-72, sr. rsch. assoc. dept. surgery, 1972-75; Alexander Agassiz vis. lectr. dept. biology Harvard U., 1976-77; lectr. dept. biology Yale U., 1977-83; assoc. prof. biochemistry in surgery Yale U., New Haven, 1978-84, lectr. dept. orthopedic surgery, 1972—, lectr., rsch. affiliate in geology and geophysics, 1967—; pres. Conn. Acad. Arts and Scis., 1986-94, publs. chair, 1994—; mineralogist AEC, summer 1953; master Jonathan Edwards Coll., Yale U., 1977-82; Alexander Agassiz vis. lectr. dept. biology Harvard U., 1976-77; vis. prof. sect. ecology and systematics dept. biology Cornell U., 1980-83; disting. prof. geology Adelaide U., 1990-91, U. Wyo., 1996; dental adv. com. Yale-New Haven Hosp., 1973-80; mem. faculty adv. com. Yale-New Haven Tchrs. Inst., 1983—; chmn. site visit team nat. Inst. Dental Rsch., 1974-75; mem. pubs. com. Am. Geolog. Inst., 1993-96. Author: (with others) Asbestos and Other Fibrous Materials: Mineralogy, Crystal Chemistry and Health Effects, 1988; co-editor: Biomineralization Processes of Iron and Manganese: Modern and Ancient Environments, 1992; contbr. over 50 articles to profl. jours.; tech. abstractor Geol. Soc. Am., 1961-65; sect. editor Am. Mineralogist, 1978-82. Mem. bd. edn. com. Conn. Fund for Environ., 1983-89, mem. sci. adv. com., 1989-92; founder, pres. Investor's Strategy Inst., New Haven, 1983-85; trustee Miss Porter's Sch., Farmington, Conn., mem. edn. com., 1986-88, mem. salaries and benefits com., 1988-91; treas. YWCA, New Haven, 1983-84. Fellow AAAS, Geol. Soc. Am., Mineral. Soc. Am. (mem. various coms., councilor 1979-81, Pub. Svc. award 1991); mem. Am. Soc. Bone and Mineral Rsch., Am. Assn. Crystal Growth, Am. Assn. Dental Rsch., Internat. Assn. Dental Rsch., Mineral Soc. Can. Home: PO Box 894 Woodbury CT 06798-0894 Office: Yale U Dept Geology Geophysics PO Box 208109 New Haven CT 06520-8109

SKINNER, JAMES LAURISTON, chemist, educator; b. Ithaca, N.Y., Aug. 17, 1953; s. G. William and Carol (Bagger) S.; m. Wendy Moore, May 31, 1986; children: Colin Andrew, Duncan Geoffrey. AB, U. Calif., Santa Cruz, 1975; PhD, Harvard U., 1979. Rsch. assoc. Stanford (Calif.) U., 1980-81; from asst. prof. to prof. chemistry Columbia U., N.Y.C., 1981-90; Hirschfelder prof. chemistry, dir. Theol. Chemistry Inst. U. Wis., Madison, 1990—; vis. scientist Inst. Theol. Physics U. Calif., Santa Barbara, 1987; vis. prof. physics U. Jos. Fourier, Grenoble, France, 1987, U. Bordeaux (France), 1995. Contbr. articles to profl. jours. Recipient Fresenius award Phi Lambda Upsilon, 1989, Camille and Henry Dreyfus Tchr.-Scholar award, 1984, NSF Presdl. Young Investigator award, 1984, Humboldt Sr. Scientist award, 1993; NSF grad fellow, 1975, NSF postdoctoral fellow, 1980, Alfred P. Sloan Found. fellow, 1984, Guggenheim fellow, 1993. Mem. AAAS, Am. Chem. Soc., Am. Phys. Soc. Achievements include fundamental research in condensed phase theoretical chemistry. Office: U Wis Dept Chemistry Theoretical Chem Inst 1101 University Ave Madison WI 53706-1322

SKINNER, JAMES LISTER, III, English language educator; b. Emory, Ga., Sept. 24, 1938; s. James Lister and Josephine Norvell (Fry) S.; m. Ramona Ann York Skinner, Apr. 2, 1961; 1 child, James Lister Skinner IV. AB in English, N. Ga. Coll., Dahlonega, 1960; MA in English, U. Ark., Fayetteville, 1962; PhD in English, 1965. Comdr. Headquarters and Headquarters Battery 28th Artillery Group, Selfridge AFB, Mich., 1964-65; assoc. prof. English Presbyterian Coll., Clinton, S.C., 1965-70; prof. English, 1970-92, Charles A. Dana prof. English, 1992—, chmn. The Russell Program, 1986—; co-chmn. English dept. Presbyn. Coll., 1996—; NDEA fellow U. Ark., Fayetteville, 1960-63; NEH summer fellow Yale U., New Haven, Conn., 1976; hon. vis. fellow Leicester (Eng.) U., 1983; sec. Presbyterian Coll. Faculty, Clinton, S.C., 1995—. Editor: The Autobiography of Henry Merrell: Industrial Missionary to the South, 1991; co-editor: The Death of a Confederate, 1996. 1st lt. U.S. Army, 1963-65. Recipient Commendation medal U.S. Army, 1965; named Presbyterian Prof. of Yr. Presbyterian Coll., Clinton, S.C., 1991, State Prof. of Yr. Coun. for Advancement and Support of Edn., 1991, Gov's. Prof. of Yr., Gov. of S.C., Columbia, 1991. Mem. Phi Beta Kappa, Omicron Delta Kappa, Alpha Psi Omega, Phi Alpha Theta. Democrat. Presbyterian. Home: 108 E Maple Clinton SC 29325 Office: Presbyterian Coll Broad St Clinton SC 29325

SKINNER, JAMES STANFORD, physiologist, educator; b. Lucedale, Miss., Sept. 22, 1936; married, 1963 (div. 1994); 2 children. BS, U. Ill., 1958, MS, 1960, PhD in Phys. Edn. and Physiology, 1963. Assoc. physiologist sch. medicine George Washington U., 1964, asst. prof. lectr., 1964-65; rsch. assoc. cardiologist sch. medicine U. Wash., Seattle, 1965-66; asst. prof. lab. human performance rsch. Pa. State U., University Park, 1966-70; rsch. assoc. med. clin. U. Freiburg, Germany, 1970-71; assoc. prof. phys. edn., rsch. assoc. inst. cardiology U. Montreal, 1971-77; prof. phys. edn. U. Western Ont., 1977-82, Ariz. State U., Tempe, 1982-95; prof. kinesiology Ind. U.,

Bloomington, 1996—; adj. prof. medicine Ind. U., Indpls., 1996—; dir. exercise and sport rsch. inst. Ariz. State U., 1983-95; chair sci. commn. Confederacion Panamericana de Medicina del Deporte, 1994—. Fellow Am. Coll. Sports Medicine (pres. 1979-80, Citation award 1986, treas. 1994-96), Am. Heart Assn., Am. Acad. Phys. Edn. (sec.-treas. 1990-92); mem. Can. Assn. Sports Sci. (sec. 1976-78), Am. Assn. Health, Phys. Edn. and Recreation, Internat. Coun. Sport Sci. and Phys. Edn. (v.p. 1994—, Philip Noel Baker rsch. award 1996). Achievements include research in physiology of exercise, especially pertaining to cardiovascular disorders, in exercise, training and genetics.

SKINNER, KNUTE RUMSEY, poet, English educator; b. St. Louis, Apr. 25, 1929; s. George Rumsey and Lidi (Skjoldvig) S.; m. Jeanne Pratt; 1953; divorced 1954; 1 child, Frank; m. Linda Kuhn, Mar. 30, 1961 (div. Sept. 1977); children: Dunstan, Morgan; m. Edna Kiel, Mar. 25, 1978. Student, Culver-Stockton Coll., 1947-49; B.A., U. No. Colo., 1951; M.A., Middlebury Coll., 1954; Ph.D., U. Iowa, 1958. Instr. English U. Iowa, Iowa City, 1955-56, 57-58, 60-61; asst. prof. English Okla. Coll. for Women, 1961-62; lectr. creative writing Western Wash. U., Bellingham, 1962-71; asso. prof. English Western Wash. U., 1971-73, prof. English, 1973-97; pres. Signpost Press Inc., nonprofit corp., 1983-95. Author: Stranger with a Watch, 1965, A Close Sky Over Killaspuglonane, 1968, 75, In Dinosaur Country, 1969, The Sorcerers: A Laotian Tale, 1972, Hearing of the Hard Times, 1981, The Flame Room, 1983, Selected Poems, 1985, Learning to Spell "Zucchini," 1988, The Bears and Other Poems, 1991, What Trudy Knows and Other Poems, 1994, The Cold Irish Earth: New and Selected Poems of Ireland, 1965-1995, 1996; editor: Bellingham Rev., 1977-83, 93-95; contbr. poetry, short stories to anthologies, textbooks, periodicals. Nat. Endowment for the Arts fellow, 1975. Mem. Am. Conf. Irish Studies, Wash. Poets Assn. Office: Western Wash U HU 323 Bellingham WA 98225-9055

SKINNER, NANCY JO, municipal recreation executive; b. Ogallala, Nebr., Nov. 5, 1956; d. Dale Warren Skinner and Beverly Jane (Fister) Berry. AA, Platte Community Coll., 1977; BS, U. Ariz., 1981; MBA, U. Phoenix, 1990; diploma, Nat. Exec. Devel. Sch., 1992. Cert. leisure profl. Sports specialist YWCA, Tucson, 1981, asst. dir. summer day camp, 1981, dir. health, phys. edn. and recreation, 1981-82; sr. recreation specialist Pima County Parks and Recreation Dept., Tucson, 1983, recreation program coord., 1983-90; recreation coord. III Phoenix Parks, Recreation and Libr. Dept., 1990-94, recreation supr., 1994—; labor mgmt. quality of work life rep. Pima County Govt., 1987; dist. coord. Atlantic Richfield Co. Jesse Owens Games, Tucson, 1986-89; adv. Pima County Health Dept. Better Health Through Self Awareness, 1982-83. Dir. tournament Sportsman Fund-Send a Kid to Camp, Tucson, 1984, 85, 86; mem. labor mgmt. quality of working life com. Pima County Govt., 1987; dist. coord. Nat. Health Screening Coun., Tucson, 1982-85; event coord. Tucson Women's Commn. Saguaro Classic, 1984; com. mem. United Way, Tucson, 1982-83; panelist Quality Conf. City of Phoenix, 1992. Musco/APRf Grad. scholar; recipient City of Phoenix Excellence award, 1994. Mem. Nat. Recreation and Parks Assn., Ariz. Parks and Recreation Assn. (cert., treas. dist. IV 1987, pres. 1988, 89, state treas. 1990, pub. rels. chair 1993, Tenderfoot award 1984, co-chair state conf. ednl. program com. 1995, nat. cert. bd. rep. Ariz. C.L.P. cert. program coord. 1997), Delta Psi Kappa. Democrat. Methodist. Avocations: music, reading, travel, tennis, golf. Office: Phoenix Pks Recreation & Libr Dept 3901 W Glendale Ave Phoenix AZ 85051-8132

SKINNER, PATRICIA MORAG, state legislator; b. Glasgow, Scotland, Dec. 3, 1932; d. John Stuart and Frances Charlotte (Swann) Robertson; m. Robert A. Skinner, Dec. 28, 1957; children: Robin Ann, Pamela. BA, NYU, 1953. Mdse. trainee Lord & Taylor, N.Y.C., 1955-59; adminstrv. asst. Atlantic Products, N.Y.C., 1954-59; newspaper corr. Salem Observer, N.H., 1964-84; mem. N.H. Ho. of Reps., 1973-94, chmn. labor, human resources and rehab. com., 1975-86, House Edn. Com., 1987, chmn., 1989-94, exec. com. Nat. Conf. State Legislatures, 1987-90; chmn. N.H. Adv. Council Unemployment Compensation, 1984-94. Bd. dirs. chmn. Castle Jr. Coll., 1975, chmn. bd., 1988-96; v.p. bd. Swift Water council Girl Scouts U.S., v.p. 1987-92; N.H. Voc-Tech. Coll., Nashua, 1978-83; trustee Nesmith Library, Windham, N.H., 1982—, chmn. bd. trustees, 1994-97. Mem. N.H. Fedn. Women's Clubs (parliamentarian, legis chmn. 1984-86, 1994-96), N.H. Fedn. Republican Women's Clubs (pres. 1979-82). Christian Scientist. Club: Windham Woman's (pres. 1981-83). Lodge: Order Eastern Star..

SKINNER, ROBERT EARLE, JR., civil engineer, engineering executive; b. Washington, Aug. 10, 1946; s. Robert Earle and Dorothy Inez (Ballance) S.; m. Dianne Lynette Sands; children: Martha, Jeffrey. BSCE, U. Va., 1969; MS in Civil Engring., MIT, 1971. Registered profl. engr., Va. Sr. assoc. PRC Voorhees, McLean, Va., 1971-79, v.p., 1979-83; sr. staff officer Transp. Rsch. Bd., Washington, 1983-86, dir. studies and info. svc., 1986-94, exec. dir., 1994—; adv. bd. Nat. Transit Inst., New Brunswick, N.J., 1994—; exec. com. Hwy. Innovative Tech. Evaluation Ctr., Washington, 1994—; adv. coun. MIT Ctr. for Transp. Studies, Cambridge, 1994—; adv. com. Ctr. for Transp. and the Environment, Raleigh, N.C., 1995—; mem. ITS Am. Coord. Coun., Washington, 1994—. Contbr. articles to profl. jours.; mem. editorial bd. Jour. Trans. and Stats., 1996. Mem. Md. Transp. Adv. Coun.; mem. adv. coun. U. Va., 1995—. With U.S. Army N.G., 1970-76. Mem. ASCE, Internat. Soc. Asphalt Pavements (ex-officio). Methodist. Avocations: woodworking, tennis. Office: Transportation Research Bd 2101 Constitution Ave NW Washington DC 20418-0007

SKINNER, SAMUEL BALLOU, III, physics educator, researcher; b. Russellville, S.C., Sept. 24, 1936; s. Samuel Ballou Jr. and Mary (Timmons) S.; m. Beverly Corinne Jones, Dec. 21, 1958; children: Teresa Lynn, Curtis Ballou, Mary Angela. BS, Clemson U., 1958; MA in Teaching, U. N.C., 1963, PhD, 1970. Sci. tchr. Franklin (Tenn.) High Sch., 1959-60, Irmo (S.C.) High Sch., 1960-62; asst. prof. physics St. Andrews Presbyn. Coll., Laurinburg, N.C., 1964-67; assoc. prof. physics Columbia (S.C.) Coll., 1970-72; prof. physics S.C. Coastal Carolina U., Conway, S.C., 1972—; dir. acad. affairs U. S.C. Coastal Carolina U., Conway, 1972-74; advisor Gov.'s Nuclear Adv. Coun., Columbia, 1977-80, S.C. Joint Legis. Com. on Energy, Columbia, 1980-85; U.S.A. rep. Internat. Symposium on Nuclear Waste, Vienna, Austria, 1980; researcher in current aerospace problems, nuclear radiation physics and crit. thinking devel.; project counselor Space Life Sci. Tng. Program, Kennedy Space Ctr., 1990. Author: Education and Psychology, 1973, Energy and Society, 1981; contbr. articles to profl. jours. Pres. Horry County Am. Cancer Soc., Conway, 1974-75, Horry County Literacy Coun., 1989-93; mem. Horry County Assessment Appeals Bd., 1981-91. Recipient fellowships NASA (6), 1987-93, Dept. Energy (5), 1972-86, USAF, 1985; grantee Dept. Energy, 1984; physics edn. del. to Vietnam, Citizen Amb. Program, 1993; participant Institut Teknologi MARA Mucia Program, Malaysia, 1993-94. Mem. Am. Assn. Physics Tchrs., Am. Assn. Higher Edn., S.C. Acad. Sci., U. S.C. Coastal Carolina Athletic Club (bd. dirs.), Lions (pres. Conway Club 1977-78). Presbyterian. Avocations: tennis, camping, sports spectator, travel. Home: 126 Citadel Dr Conway SC 29526-8870 Office: Coastal Carolina U Physics Dept Conway SC 29526

SKINNER, STANLEY THAYER, utility company executive, lawyer; b. Fort Smith, Ark., Aug. 18, 1937; s. John Willard and Irma Lee (Peters) S.; m. Margaret Olsen, Aug. 16, 1957; children—Steven Kent, Ronald Kevin. B.A. with honors, San Diego State U., 1960; M.A., U. Calif., Berkeley, 1961, J.D., 1964. Bar: Supreme Ct. Calif. bar 1965, U.S. Circuit Ct. Appeals for 9th Circuit bar 1965, 10th Circuit bar 1966. Atty. Pacific Gas and Electric Co., San Francisco, 1964-73; sr. counsel Pacific Gas and Electric Co., 1973, treas., 1974-76, v.p. fin., 1976, sr. v.p., 1977, exec. v.p., 1978-86, exec. v.p., chief fin. officer, 1982-85, vice chmn. bd., 1986-91, pres., chief oper. officer, 1991-94; pres., CEO Pacific Gas and Electric Co., San Francisco, 1994-95; chmn. bd. dirs., CEO Pacific Gas and Electric Co., 1995—; bd. dirs. Fed. Res. Bank of San Francisco, Pacific Gas Transmission Co. Bd. dirs. United Way of Bay Area, campaign chmn., 1992; trustee, former chmn. bd. dirs Golden Gate U.; bd. dirs. Bay Area chpt. ARC, Bay Area Coun., Bay Area Econ. Forum. Mem. Calif. State Bar Assn., Calif. State C. of C. (bd. dirs.), San Francisco C. of C. (bd. dirs.), Bus. Coun., Bay Area Coun., Bus. Roundtable, Moraga Country Club. Republican. Presbyterian. Office: Pacific Gas & Electric Co 77 Beale St San Francisco CA 94105-1814

SKINNER, THOMAS, broadcasting and film executive; b. Poughkeepsie, N.Y., Aug. 17, 1934; s. Clarence F. and Frances D. S.; m. Elizabeth Burroughs, June 22, 1957; children: Kristin Jon, Karin Anne, Erik Lloyd. BS, SUNY, Fredonia, 1956; MA, U. Mich., 1957, PhD, 1962. Instr. speech U. Mich., 1960; assoc. prof., exec. producer dept. broadcasting San Diego State U., 1961-66; asst. mgr. Sta. WITF-TV, Hershey, Pa., 1966-70; v.p. Sta. WQED-TV, Pitts., 1970-72; exec. v.p., COO QED Communications Inc. (WQED-TV, WQED-FM, Pittsburgh mag., WQEX-TV), 1972-93; founder, pres., exec. prodr. Windrush Assocs., 1993—; v.p. Programming Resolution Prodns., Burlington, Vt., 1996—. Exec. prodr. spls. and series including (for PBS) Nat. Geog. spls. Planet Earth, The Infinite Voyage, Conserving Am., (for TBS) Pirate Tales, (for A&E) Floating Palaces, Calif. and the Dream Seekers, The Story of Money (for Discovery) Battleship. Recipient award as exec. prodr. DuPont Columbia, 1979, Oscar award as dir. Acad. Motion Picture Arts and Scis., 1967, Emmy award as exec. prodr. Nat. Acad. TV Arts and Scis., 1979, 83-84, 86-87, Peabody award as exec. prodr., 1980, 86. Episcopalian. Address: PO Box 446 Suttons Bay MI 49682-0446

SKINNER, WALTER JAY, federal judge; b. Washington, Sept. 12, 1927; s. Frederick Snowden and Mary Waterman (Comstock) S.; m. Sylvia Henderson, Aug. 12, 1950; 4 children. A.B., Harvard, 1948; J.D., 1952. Bar: Mass. 1952, U.S. Dist. Ct. 1954. Assoc. firm Gaston, Snow, Rice & Boyd, Boston, 1952-57; pvt. practice law Scituate, Mass., 1957-63; asst. dist. atty. Plymouth County, 1957-63; town counsel Scituate, 1957-63; asst. atty. gen., chief Criminal Div., Commonwealth of Mass., 1963-65; mem. firm Wardwell, Allen, McLaughlin & Skinner, Boston, 1965-74; judge U.S. Dist. Ct. of Mass., 1974—; sr. status, 1992—. Bd. dirs. Douglas A. Thom Clinic, 1966-70. Mem. ABA, Mass. Bar Assn., Boston Bar Assn., Eight O'Clock Club (Newton, Mass.). Office: US Dist Ct US Courthouse 90 Devonshire St Rm 1503 Boston MA 02109-4501

SKINNER, WICKHAM, business administration educator; b. Cin., Feb. 20, 1924; s. Charles Wickham and Ruth (Hargrave) S.; m. Alice Sturges Blackmer, May 18, 1946; children: Polly Gay (Mrs. David Light), Charles Barry. B.Engring., Yale U., 1944; M.B.A., Harvard U., 1948, D.B.A., 1961. Chem. engr. Manhattan project at Los Alamos, 1946-48; with Honeywell Corp., 1948-58, asst. sec., 1957-58; mem. faculty Harvard Grad. Sch. Bus. Adminstrn., 1960-86, prof., 1967-74, James E. Robison prof. bus. adminstrn., 1974-86, asso. dean, 1974-77, dir. div. internat. activities, 1967-70; tchr. Pakistan, France, Vietnam, Australia, Singapore, Turkey, Tunisia, Ital; bd. dirs. Wilevco Corp., Helix Tech. Corp., Somerset Industries. Author: American Industry in Developing Economies, 1968, Manufacturing in Corporate Strategy, 1977, Manufacturing: The Formidable Competitive Weapon, 1985; also articles. Mem. spl. coms. Weston (Mass.) Sch. Com., 1962-64, 64-68; acad. adv. Bunting Inst., Work-in-Am. Inst.; mem. planning com., Wayzata, Minn., 1955-56; pres. Eastern Acad. Mgmt., 1968-69; Candidate for mayor, Wayzata, 1955; bd. dirs. Fla. Philharmonic Orch., 1956-58; bd. dirs. Nat. Resources Council Maine, 1986-93, pres. 1989-92; class agt. Yale Alumni Fund, 1944-69; trustee, treas. Urbana (Ohio) U., 1960-70; trustee Babson Coll., 1981-85, Mass. Audubon Soc., 1983-84, U. Maine System, 1995—; mem. Mfg. Studies Bd. NAS, 1979-84, chmn. 1987-89; bd. dirs. Farnsworth Mus., Rockland, Maine, 1990—, v.p., 1991-94, pres., 1994—. Served with AUS, 1944-46. Recipient McKinsey prize Harvard Bus. Rev., 1986. Fellow Acad. Mgmt.; mem. Ops Mgmt. Assn. (bd. dirs. 1987—). Mem. Swedenborgian Ch. Home: PO Box 282B Saint George ME 04857-9998 Office: Harvard U Bus Sch Soldiers Field Rd Boston MA 02163

SKIPP, TRACY JOHN, academic advisor, counselor; b. Bourne, Mass., Feb. 10, 1966; s. Herbert Bucklin and Nanette Marie (Fisher) S.; m. Karyn Shayann Brennan, Nov. 24, 1986; children: Tracy John Jr., Brennan Ross Anthony, Megan Shaylynn. Paralegal grad., Albuquerque Career Inst., 1989; B cum laude Univ. Studies, U. N.Mex., 1995. Med. asst. pvt. psychiat. practice, Albuquerque, 1987-89; owner Skipp's Legal Support Resources, Albuquerque, 1990-95; academic advisor, counselor U. N.Mex., Albuquerque, 1996—; cons. webmaster and internet. Co-author, illustrator: The Gift of the Apple, The Birth of a Star. Active Secular Franciscan Order, 1996—; rep. gen. honors coun., internat. affairs coun. Associated Stuents U. N.Mex., co-chmn. U. N.Mex. Vol. Svc. Coalition; med. missionary to Mex. St. Mark's United Meth. Ch. of El Paso; participant in 1996 Rolex Awards for Enterprise. Named Man of the Yr., Am. Biog. Inst., 1995; L.B. Reeder scholar, 1992-95, Fulbright scholar Dudley Wynn Honors Ctr., 1996. Fellow Internat. Bio. Assn.(Internat. Order of Merit Award, 1994); assoc. Am. Bio. Inst. (dep. gov., 1994—); mem. Internat. Platform Assn., Am. Freedom Coalition, Nat. Notary Assn., Legal Assts. N.Mex., Nat. Fedn. Paralegal Assn., N.Mex. Acad. Sci., Blue Key, Phi Beta Delta, Phi Delta Kappa. Roman Catholic. Avocations: reading, making art. Office: U New Mexico Bachelor Univ Studies Program Univ Coll Albuquerque NM 87123-1456

SKIPPER, NATHAN RICHARD, JR., lawyer; b. Wilmington, N.C., May 29, 1934; s. Nathan Richard and Mary Dell (Sidbury) S.; m. Barbara Lynn Renton, Sept. 5, 1959 (div. June 1978); children: Nathan Richard III, Valerie Lynne; m. Karen Marie Haughton, Sept. 26, 1987. AB, Duke U., 1956, JD, 1962; AAS, Oakland Community Coll., 1980. Bar: N.Y. 1963, U.S. Dist. Ct. (so. dist.) N.Y. 1964, Mich. 1971, U.S. Dist. Ct. (ea. dist.) Mich. 1979, N.C. 1991. Assoc. Cravath, Swaine & Moore, N.Y.C., 1962-70; counsel financings Ford Motor Co., Dearborn, Mich., 1970-78; gen. counsel, sec. Volkswagen Am., Inc., Troy, Mich., 1978-89, consulting counsel, 1989-91; assoc. Ward and Smith, P.A., New Bern, N.C., 1990-93, ptnr., 1994—. Served to capt. USAF, 1956-59, USAFR, 1962-75. Mem. ABA, SAR, N.C. Bar Assn., Ea. Carolina Yacht Club, Phi Delta Phi. Avocations: photography, boating, tennis. Home: 1108 Country Club Dr New Bern NC 28562-7102

SKIRNICK, ROBERT ANDREW, lawyer; b. Chgo., Apr. 23, 1938; s. Andrew and Stella (Sanders) S.; children: Rebecca, David; m. Maria Ann Castellano, Oct. 4, 1974; 1 child, Gabriella. BA, Roosevelt U., 1961; JD, U. Chgo., 1966. Bar: U.S. Dist. Ct. (no. dist.) Ill. 1966, U.S. Ct. Appeals (7th cir.) 1968, U.S. Supreme Ct. 1970, U.S. Ct. Appeals (5th and 9th cirs.) 1982, N.Y. 1982, U.S. Ct. Appeals (3rd cir.) 1983, U.S. Dist. Ct. (ea. dist.) Mich. 1988, (so. and ea. dists.) N.Y. 1989, U.S. Ct. Appeals (2nd cir.) 1990, U.S. Dist. Ct. (no. dist.) Calif. 1992, U.S. Ct. Appeals (11th Cir.) 1992, U.S. Dist. Ct. (so. dist.) Tex. 1992, U.S. Dist. Ct. Ariz. 1993. Atty. office gen. counsel honors program HEW, Washington, 1966-68; ptnr. Fortes, Eiger, Epstein & Skirnick, Chgo., 1975-77, Much, Shelist, Freed, Chgo., 1977-79, Wolf, Popper, Ross, Wolf & Jones, N.Y.C., 1979-87, Kaplan, Kilsheimer & Foley, N.Y.C., 1988-89, Wechsler, Skirnick, Harwood, Halebian & Feffer, N.Y.C., 1989-95, Lovell & Skirnick, LLP, N.Y.C., 1995—; instr. NYU, 1979-80; cons. Nat. Legal Aid and Def. Assn., Chgo., 1968-69; spl. asst. atty. gen. Ill. Atty Gen. Office, Chgo., 1972-73; spl. antitrust counsel State of Conn., 1976-77; mem. adv. bd. Small Bus. Legal Def. Commn., San Francisco, 1982—; lectr. Practicing Law Inst., N.Y.C., 1986-87; spl. master So. Dist. N.Y., 1988-91. Author: (with others) Federal Subject Matter Jurisdiction of U.S. District Courts, Federal Civil Practice, 1974, Antitrust Class Actions-Twenty Years Under Rule 23, 1986, The State Court Class Action-A Potpourri of Difference in the ABA Forum, Summer 1985; contbg. author: Multiparty Bargaining in Class Actions, Attorneys' Practice Guide to Negotiations, 2d edit., 1996; bd. editors Ill. Bar Antitrust Newsletter, 1969-73; topic and articles editor Jour. Forum Com. on Franchising, 1981-86. Atty. Office Gen. Counsel Honors Program, U.S. Dept. HEW, 1966-68; chmn. Ill. Legis. Com. Antitrust Section Ill. Bar., 1970-71; Topic and Articles Editor, Jour. Forum Com. on Franchising, 1981-86; mem., bd. dirs., Nat. Assn. for Pub. Interest Law fellowships, Washington, 1991—, v.p., 1994—. Mem. ABA (co-chair securities law subcom., litigation sect. 1987, mem. com. on futures regulation, mem. forum com. on franchising), ATLA, Fed. Bar Coun. (mem. com. on second cir cts. 1983-86), N.Y. State Bar Assn. (mem. class action com.), N.Y. State Trial Lawyers Assn., Ill. Bar Assn. (chmn. antitrust sect. Ill. legis. com. 1970-71), Nat. Assn. for Pub. Interest Law Fellowships (mem. exec. com., mem. selection com., mem. investment and fin. com., bd. dirs. 1991—, v.p. 1994—), Navy League of U.S. (N.Y. coun., mem. jour. com. 1995—), Carlton Club, Plandome Country Club. Office: Lovell & Skirnick 63 Wall St New York NY 10005-3001

SKLANSKY, JACK, electrical and computer engineering educator, researcher; b. N.Y.C., Nov. 15, 1928; s. Abraham and Clara S.; m. Gloria Joy Weiss, Dec. 24, 1957; children: David Alan, Mark Steven, Jeffrey Paul. BEE, CCNY, 1950; MSEE, Purdue U., 1952; D in Engring. Sci., Columbia U., 1955. Research engr. RCA Labs., Princeton, N.J., 1955-65; mgr. Nat. Cash Register Co., Dayton, Ohio, 1965-66; prof. elec. and computer engring. U. Calif., Irvine, 1966—; pres. Scanicon Corp., Irvine, 1980-89. Author: (with others) Pattern Classifiers and Trainable Machines, 1981; editor: Pattern Recognition, 1973, (with others) Biomedical Images and Computers, 1982; editor-in-chief: Machine Vision and Applications, 1987. Recipient best paper award Jour. Pattern Recognition, 1977; rsch. grantee NIH, 1971-84, Army Rsch. Office, 1984-91, NSF, 1992-96, Office of Naval Rsch., 1995—. Fellow IEEE, Internat. Assn. for Pattern Recognition; mem. ACM. Office: U Calif Dept Elec-Computer Engring Irvine CA 92697-2625

SKLAR, ALEXANDER, electric company executive, educator; b. N.Y.C., May 18, 1915; s. David and Bessie (Wolf) S.; student Cooper Union, N.Y.C., 1932-35; M.B.A., Fla. Atlantic U., 1976; m. Hilda Rae Gevarter, Oct. 27, 1940; 1 dau., Carolyn Mae (Mrs. Louis M. Taff). Chief engr. Aerovox Corp., New Bedford, Mass., 1933-39; mgr. mfg., engring. Indsl. Condenser Corp., Chgo., 1939-44; owner Capacitron, Inc., 1944-48; exec. v.p. Jefferson Electric Co., Bellwood, Ill., 1948-65; v.p., gen. mgr. electro-mech. div. Essex Internat., Detroit, 1965-67; adviser, dir. various corp., 1968—; vis. prof. mgmt. Fla. Atlantic U., Boca Raton, 1971-92; ret. 1993; lectr. profl. mgmt. U. Calif. at Los Angeles, Harvard Grad. Sch. Bus. Adminstrn., U. Ill. Mem. Acad. Internat. Bus., Soc. Automotive Engrs. Address: 4100 Galt Ocean Dr Fort Lauderdale FL 33308-6030

SKLAR, HOLLY L(YN), nonfiction writer; b. N.Y.C., May 6, 1955. BA, Oberlin Coll., 1977; MA in Polit. Sci., Columbia U., 1980. Rschr. UN Ctr. Transnat. Corps., N.Y., 1978; writer, rschr. N. Am. Congress Latin Am., N.Y., 1981-82; exec. dir. Inst. New Communications, N.Y., 1982-84; writer, lectr. N.Y., Boston; review panelist NEH, Washington, 1989; del. Soviet-Am. Women's Summit, N.Y., Washington, 1990. Author, co-author books, including: Trilateralism, 1980, Poverty in the American Dream: Women and Children First, 1983, Washington's War on Nicaragua, 1988, Streets of Hope: The Fall and Rise of an Urban Neighborhood, 1994, Chaos or Community? Seeking Solutions, Not Scapegoats for Bad Economics, 1995. Mem. adv. bd. Nationwide Women's Program, Am. Friends Svc. Com., The Progressive Media Project, Polit. Rsch. Assocs.; bd. dirs. United for a Fair Economy; nat. judge Project Censored; mem. steering com. Caribbean Basin Info. Project, 1982-85. Recipient Outstanding Book award Gustavus Myers Ctr. for Study Human Rights in U.S., 1988, Assocs. award Polit. Rsch. Assocs., Cambridge, 1991-97; fellow Columbia U. Grad. Sch. Arts and Scis., 1978-80. Mem. Nat. Writers Union, Acad. Polit. Sci. Office: 97 Sheridan St Boston MA 02130-1857

SKLAR, KATHRYN KISH, historian, educator; b. Columbus, Ohio, Dec. 26, 1939; d. William Edward and Elizabeth Sue (Rhodes) Kish; m. Robert A. Sklar, 1958 (div. 1978); children: Leonard Scott, Susan Rebecca Sklar Friedman; m. Thomas L. Dublin, Apr. 30, 1988. B.A. magna cum laude, Radcliffe Coll., 1965; Ph.D., U. Mich., 1969. Asst. prof., lectr. U. Mich., Ann Arbor, 1969-74; assoc. prof. history UCLA, 1974-81, prof., 1981-88, chmn. com. to administer program in women's studies Coll. Letters and Sci., 1974-81; Disting. Prof. history SUNY, Binghamton, 1988—; Pulitzer juror in history, 1976; fellow Newberry Libr. Family and Community History Seminar, 1973; active Calif. Coun. for Humanities, 1981-85, N.Y. Coun. for Humanities, 1992—. Author: Catharine Beecher: A Study in American Domesticity, 1973 (Berkshire prize 1974); editor: Catharine Beecher: A Treatise on Domestic Economy, 1977, Harriet Beecher Stowe: Uncle Tom's Cabin, or Life Among the Lowly: The Minister's Wooing, Oldtown Folks, 1981, Notes of Sixty Years: The Autobiography of Florence Kelley, 1849-1926, 1984, (with Thomas Dublin) Women and Power in American History: A Reader (2 vols.), 1991, (with Linda Kerber and Alice Kessler-Harris) U.S. History as Women's History: New Feminist Essays, 1995; co-editor: The Social Survey Movement in Historical Perspective, 1992, Florence Kelley and the Nation's Work: The Rise of Women's Political Culture, 1830-1900, 1995 (Berkshire prize 1996); mem. editl. bd. Jour. Women's History, 1987—, Women's History Rev., 1990—, Jour. Am. History, 1978-81; contbr. chpts. to books. Fellow Woodrow Wilson Found., 1965-67, Danforth Found., 1967-69, Radcliffe Inst., 1973-74, Nat. Humanities Inst., 1975-76, Rockefeller Found. Humanities, 1981-82, Woodrow Wilson Internat. Ctr. for Scholars, 1982, 1992-93, Guggenheim Found., 1984, Ctr. Advanced Study Behavioral and Social Scis., Stanford U., 1987-88, AAUW, 1990-91; Daniels fellow Am. Antiquarian Soc., 1976, NEH fellow Newberry Library, 1982-83; Ford Found. faculty rsch. grantee, 1973-74; grantee NEH, 1976-78, UCLA Coun. for Internat. and Comparative Studies, 1983. Mem. Am. Hist. Assn. (chmn. com. on women historians 1980-83, v.p. Pacific Coast br. 1986-87, pres. 1987-88), Orgn. Am. Historians (exec. bd. 1983-86, Merle Curti award com. 1978-79, lectr. 1982—), Am. Studies Assn. (coun. mem.-at-large 1978-80), Berkshire Conf. Women Historians, Am. Antiquarian Soc., Phi Beta Kappa. Avocation: photography. Office: SUNY Dept History Binghamton NY 13902

SKLAR, LOUISE MARGARET, service executive; b. L.A., Aug. 12, 1934; d. Samuel Baldwin Smith and Judith LeRoy (Boughton) Nelson; m. Edwynn Edgar Schroeder, Mar. 20, 1955 (div. July 1975); children: Neil Nelson, Leslie Louise Schroeder Grandclaudon, Samuel George; m. Martin Sklar, Oct. 17, 1983. Student, U. So. Calif., 1952-54, UCLA, 1977-79. Acct. Valentine Assocs., Northridge, Calif., 1976-78, programmer, 1978-79; contr. Western Monetary, Encino, Calif., 1979-81; pres. Automated Computer Composition, Chatsworth, Calif., 1984—. Mem. Am. Contract Bridge League (bd. govs. 1993—, mem. nat. charity com. 1982, mem. nat. goodwill com. 1994—), Assn. Los Angeles County Bridge Units (bd. dirs. 1990—, sec. 1984-86), DAR, Conn. Soc. Genealogists, Ky. Hist. Soc., So. Calif. Assistance League, Heart of Am. Geneal. Soc., Chatsworth C. of C., Greater L.A. Zoo Assn., Safari Club Internat., Zeta Tau Alpha. Republican. Avocations: tournament bridge, travel. Office: Automated Computer Composition Inc 21356 Nordhoff St Chatsworth CA 91311-6917

SKLAR, MORTY E., publisher, editor; b. Sunnyside, N.Y., Nov. 28, 1935; s. Jack and Selma (Ehrlich) S.; m. Shelley Joy Sterling, Aug. 17, 1981 (div. 1983); m. Marcela B. Bruno, June 7, 1993; children: Patricio Bruno, Marcos Bruno. BA in English, U. Iowa, 1972. Founding editor, pub. The Spirit That Moves Us Press, Jackson Heights, N.Y., 1974—. Author: The Night We Stood Up For Our Rights, 1977; editor: The Casting of Bells, 1983 (Jaroslav Seifert, Nobel prize 1984). Founder (with others) Phoenix House, N.Y.C., 1966; active Increase the Peace Vol. Corps., N.Y.C., 1992—. With U.S. Army, 1954-56. Mem. PEN, Acad. Am. Poets, Small Press Ctr. Democrat. Jewish. Avocations: photography, reading. Office: The Spirit That Moves Us Press PO Box 720820-WW Jackson Heights NY 11372

SKLAR, RICHARD LAWRENCE, political science educator; b. N.Y.C., Mar. 22, 1930; s. Kalman and Sophie (Laub) S.; m. Eva Molineux, July 14, 1962; children: Judith Anne, Katherine Elizabeth. A.B., U. Utah, 1952; M.A., Princeton U., 1957, Ph.D., 1961; UCLA. Mem. faculty Brandeis U., U. Ibadan, Nigeria, U. Zambia, SUNY-Stony Brook, UCLA; now prof. emeritus polit. sci. UCLA; mem. fgn. area fellowship program Africa Nat. Com., 1970-73; Simon vis. prof. U. Manchester, Eng., 1975, Fulbright vis. prof. U. Zimbabwe, 1984; Lester Martin fellow Harry S. Truman Rsch. Inst., Hebrew U. Jerusalem, 1979; fellow Africa Inst. of South Africa, 1994—. Author: Nigerian Political Parties: Power in an Emergent African Nation, 1963, Corporate Power in an African State, 1975; co-author: Postimperialism: International Capitalism and Development, 1987, African Politics and Problems in Development, 1991; contbr. articles to profl. jours. Served with U.S. Army, 1952-54. Rockefeller Found. grantee, 1967. Mem. Am. Polit. Sci. Assn., African Studies Assn. (dir. 1976-78, 80-83, v.p. 1980-81, pres. 1981-82), AAUP (pres. Calif. Conf. 1980-81). Home: 1951 Holmby Ave Los Angeles CA 90025-5905

SKLAR, WILLIAM PAUL, lawyer, educator; b. N.Y.C., Sept. 10, 1958; s. Morris and Helen (Meyers) S.; m. Lori Ann Hodges, Jan. 5, 1985. BBA magna cum laude, U. Miami, 1977, JD, 1980. Bar: Fla. 1980, N.Y. 1986, U.S. Dist. Ct. (so. dist.) Fla. 1981, U.S. Tax Ct. 1980, U.S. Ct. Appeals (5th cir.) 1980, U.S. Ct. Appeals (11th cir.) 1981. Assoc. Wood, Cobb, Murphy & Craig, West Palm Beach, Fla., 1980-85; ptnr. Wood, Cobb, Murphy & Craig, West Palm Beach, 1985-88; ptnr. Foley & Lardner, West Palm Beach, 1989—, ptnr.-in-charge, 1995—; chmn. Fla. Real Estate Dept., 1991—; adj. prof. law Sch. Law, U. Miami, Coral Gables, Fla., 1980—; dir. Inst. on

Condo. and Cluster Devels., Inst. on Real Property Law, 1986—. Co-author: Cases and Materials in Condominium and Cluster Developments, 1980; author, co-editor; Florida Real Estate Transactions, 1983; contbr. articles to profl. jours. Mem. atty. adv. bd. Morse Geriatric Ctr., West Palm Beach, 1984-88. Mem. ABA (chmn. subcom. on condominium and coop. housing sect. gen. practice 1983-88), Fla. Bar (com. condominium and planned devels. 1980—, bd. cert. real estate lawyer 1994), Palm Beach County Bar Assn., Phi Delta Phi, Pi Sigma Alpha. Republican. Avocations: travel, tennis. Home: 7238 Montrico Dr Boca Raton FL 33433-6930 Office: Foley & Lardner East Tower 777 S Flagler Dr Ste 202 West Palm Beach FL 33401-6161

SKLAREN, CARY STEWART, lawyer; b. Bklyn., Sept. 26, 1943; s. Jules Joseph and Florence (Somber) S.; m. Linda Genero, May 25, 1972; children: Robyn Alison, Adam William. BA, NYU, 1964; JD, Fordham U., 1967. Bar: N.Y. 1969, Mich. 1980. Assoc. product liability counsel Bristol-Myers Co., N.Y.C., 1969-79; sr. atty. Ford Mtr. Co., Dearborn, Mich., 1979-81; asst. gen. counsel Am. Mtrs. Corp., Southfield, Mich., 1981-84; ptnr. Herzfeld & Rubin, P.C., N.Y.C., 1984—. Contbr. articles to profl. jours.; author: (with others) Practical Products Liability, 1988, Products Liability, 1989. Capt. U.S. Army, 1967-69. Mem. ABA, Assn. Bar City of N.Y. Home: 851 President St Brooklyn NY 11215-1405 Office: Herzfeld & Rubin PC 40 Wall St New York NY 10005-2301

SKLAREW, ROBERT JAY, biomedical research educator, consultant; b. N.Y.C., Nov. 25, 1941; s. Arthur and Jeanette (Laven) S.; m. Toby Willner, July 15, 1970; children: David Michael, Gary Richard. BA in Zoology, Cornell U., 1963; MS, NYU, 1965, PhD in Biology, 1970. Assoc. rsch. scientist Sch. of Medicine NYU, N.Y.C., 1965-70, rsch. scientist Sch. of Medicine, 1971-73, sr. rsch. scientist Sch. of Medicine, 1973-79; rsch. asst. prof. pathology Sch. of Medicine Goldwater Meml. Hosp., N.Y.C., 1979-87, rsch. assoc. prof. pathology Sch. of Medicine, 1987-88, dir. cytokinetics and imaging lab. NYU Rsch. Svc., 1980-88; prof. cell biology, anatomy and medicine N.Y. Med. Coll., Valhalla, 1988—; rsch. assoc. dept. pathology Lenox Hill Hosp., N.Y.C., 1981-88; pres., CEO R.J. Sklarew Imaging Assoc., Inc., Larchmont, N.Y., 1990—; chmn. consensus panel for diagnostic cancer imaging Nat. Cancer Inst., 1994. Author: Microscopic Imaging of Steroid Receptors, 1990; sr. author: Cytometry, Jour. Histochem. Cytochem., Cancer, Exptl. Cell Rsch. Mem. Beth Emeth Synagogue, Larchmont, 1974—; group leader Boy Scouts Am., Larchmont, 1978-80. Grantee Am. Cancer Soc., Nat. Cancer Inst./NIH Conc. for Tobacco Rsch., R.J. Reynolds Industries Found., NYU; recipient Shannon award Nat. Cancer Inst., 1991. Mem. AAAS, Cell Kinetics Soc. (sec. 1983-85, 85-87, v.p. 1987-88, pres. 1988-89, chmn. nominations 1991, 93), N.Y. Acad. Sci., Soc. for Analytic Cytology, Soc. for Cell Biology, Tissue Culture Assn., Union Concerned Scientists, Kappa Delta Rho. Democrat. Achievements include development of methodology, algorithms and Receptogram analytic software for application of microscopic imaging in medical research and in pathodiagnosis of cancer, imaging methods for simultaneous densitometry and autoradiographic analysis; research in diagnostic imaging of steroid receptors, oncogenes and DNA ploidy in cancer, proliferative patterns and cell cycle kinetics of human solid tumors. Home: 8 Vine Rd Larchmont NY 10538-1247 Office: NY Med Coll Cancer Rsch Inst 100 Grasslands Rd Elmsford NY 10523-1110

SKLARIN, ANN H., artist; b. N.Y.C., May 21, 1933; d. Sidney and Revera (Myers) Hirsch; m. Burton S. Sklarin, June 29, 1960; children: Laurie Sklarin Ember, Richard, Peter. BA in Art History, Wellesley Coll., 1955; MA in Secondary Art Edn., Columbia U., 1956. Art tchr. jr. high sch. N.Y.C. Sch. System, 1956-61, chmn. art. dept. jr. high sch., 1957-61. One-woman shows include Long Beach (N.Y.) Libr., 1973, Silvermine Guild Ctr. Arts, New Canaan, Conn., 1986, Long Beach Mus. Art, 1986, Discovery Art Gallery, Glen Cove, N.Y., 1987—, Freport (N.Y.) Libr., 1997; exhibited in juried shows at Nassau C.C., Garden City, N.Y., 1970, Nassau County (N.Y.) John F. Kennedy Ctr. Performing Arts, 1970 (1st Pl. award 1970), Long Beach Art Assn., 1970 (1st Pl. award 1970), Gregory Mus., 1973-74, L.I. Arts 76, Hempstead, N.Y., 1976, 5 Towns Music and Art Found., Woodmere, N.Y., 1980 (1st Pl. award 1981, Honorable Mention award 1981), 83 (3d Pl. award 1983), 85, Long Beach Art Assn. and Long Beach Mus. Art, 1982 (1st Pl. award 1982), 84, 85 (3d Pl. award 1985), Silvermine Guild Arts, 1984 (Richardson-Vicks Inc. award 1985), 87 (Pepperidge Farm Inc. award 1987), Long Beach Mus. Art, 1985 (Best in Show-Grumbacher award 1985), Heckscher Mus., Huntington, N.Y., 1985, 87, Fine Arts Mus. L.I., Hempstead, 1985, 91, Long Beach Art League and Long Beach Mus. Art, 1986 (2d Pl. award 1986), Wunsch Arts Ctr., Glen Cove, 1986, 87, Smithtown Twp. Arts Coun., St. James, 1989 (Honorable Mention award 1989); exhibited in group shows at Hewlett-Woodmere Libr., 1969, B.J. Spoke Gallery, Port Washington, N.Y., 1985, Shirley Scott Gallery, Southampton, N.Y., 1986, Smithtown Twp. Arts Coun., St. James, N.Y., 1988, 90, N.Y. Inst. Tech., Old Westbury, N.Y., 1989, Dowling Coll., Oakdale, N.Y., 1990, Discovery Art Gallery, 1992, 93, 94, 95, Silvermine Guild Arts Ctr., 1992, Sound Shore Gallery, Stamford, Conn., 1993, Krasdale Foods Gallery, N.Y.C., 1993. Mem. exec. bd. 5 Towns Music & Art Found., 1960—, pres., 1971-74. Mem. Silvermine Guild Artists, Discovery Gallery (artist mem.). Avocations: tennis, jogging, hiking, traveling, reading. Studio: 501 Broadway Lawrence NY 11559-2501

SKLARIN, BURTON S., endocrinologist; b. N.Y.C., Feb. 28, 1932; s. Louis and Molla (Beiser) S.; m. Ann Hirsch, June 29, 1960; children: Laurie, Richard, Peter. A.B., NYU, 1953, M.D., 1957. Diplomate: Am. Bd. Internal Medicine, Am. Bd. Endocrinology and Metabolism. Intern Bellevue Hosp., N.Y.C., 1957-58, resident, 1958-61, asst. vis. clin. physician, 1961—; practice medicine specializing in endocrinology Lawrence, N.Y., 1961—; chief endocrinology St. John's Episcopal Hosp., 1961—, pres. med. staff, 1978-80, also chmn. med. exec. com.; asst. prof. clin. medicine NYU, 1961—, asst. in medicine Univ. Hosp., 1961; endocrinologist, staff physician L.I. Jewish Hosp.; cons. Franklin Gen Hosp. Contbr. articles on endocrinology to profl. pubis. Vice pres. bd. trustees Woodmere Acad. Fellow ACP, Am. Coll. Endocrinology, N.Y. Acad. Medicine, Soc. Nuclear Medicine; mem. Nassau County Med. Soc., N.Y. Diabetes Assn., Endocrine Soc., Rockaway Med. Soc. (past pres.), Am. Assn. Clin. Endocrinologists. Home and Office: 501 Broadway Lawrence NY 11559-2501

SKLARSKY, CHARLES B., lawyer; b. Chgo., June 13, 1946; s. Morris and Sadie (Brenner) S.; m. Elizabeth Ann Hardzinski, Dec. 28, 1973; children: Jacob Daniel, Katherine Gabrielle, Jessica Leah. AB, Harvard U., 1968; JD, U. Wis., 1973. Bar: Wis. 1973, Ill. 1973, U.S. Dist. Ct. (no. dist.) Ill. 1973, U.S. Ct. Appeals (7th cir.) 1978, U.S. Ct. Appeals (2nd cir.) 1986. Asst. states atty. Cook County, Chgo., 1973-78; asst. U.S. atty. U.S. Dist. Ct. (no. dist.) Ill., Chgo., 1978-86; ptnr. Jenner & Block, Chgo., 1986—. Mem. ABA, Am. Coll. Trial Lawyers, Chgo. Bar Assn. Office: Jenner & Block One IBM Plz Chicago IL 60611-3586

SKLENAR, HERBERT ANTHONY, industrial products manufacturing company executive; b. Omaha, June 7, 1931; s. Michael Joseph and Alice Madeline (Spicka) S.; m. Eleanor Lydia Vincenz, Sept. 15, 1956; children: Susan A., Patricia I. BSBA summa cum laude, U. Omaha, 1952; MBA, Harvard U., 1954; LLD (hon.), Birmingham-So. Coll., 1996. CPA, W.Va. V.p., comptr. Parkersburg-Aetna Corp., W.Va., 1956-63; v.p., dir. Marmac Corp, Parkersburg, 1963-66; mgr. fin. control Boise-Cascade Corp., Idaho, 1966-67; exec. v.p. fin. and adminstrn., sec. Cudahy Co., Phoenix, 1967-72; chmn. bd. dirs., CEO Vulcan Materials Co., Birmingham, Ala., 1972—; bd. dirs. Amsouth Bancorp., Birmingham, Protective Life Corp., Birmingham, Temple-Inland, Inc., Diboll, Tex. Author: (with others) The Automatic Factory: A Critical Examination, 1955. Trustee So. Rsch. Inst., Leadership Birmingham, Leadership Ala.; chmn. bd. trustees Birmingham-So. Coll. Recipient Alumni Achievement award U. Nebr.-Omaha, 1977, cert. merit W.Va. Soc. CPAs, Elizah Watts Sells award AICPA, 1965, Brotherhood award NCCJ, 1993. Mem. Shoal Creek Club, Birmingham Country Club, The Club, Univ. Club N.Y.C., Chgo. Club, Delta Sigma Pi (Leadership award 1952), Omicron Delta Kappa, Phi Kappa Phi, Phi Eta Sigma. Republican. Presbyterian. Home: 2809 Shook Hill Cir Birmingham AL 35223-2618 Office: Vulcan Materials Co 1 Metroplex Dr Birmingham AL 35209-6805

SKLOVSKY, ROBERT JOEL, naturopathic physician, pharmacist, educator; b. Bronx, N.Y., Nov. 19, 1952; s. Nathan and Esther (Steinberg) S. BS, Bklyn. Coll., 1975; MA in Sci. Edn., Columbia U., 1976; PharmD, U. of Pacific, 1977; D in Naturopathic Medicine, Nat. Coll. Naturopathic Medicine, 1983. Intern Tripler Army Med. Ctr., Honolulu, 1977; prof. pharmacology Nat. Coll. Naturopathic Medicine, Portland, Oreg., 1982-85; pvt. practice Milwaukie, Oreg., 1983—; cons. State Bd. Naturopathic Examiners, Oreg., Hawaii, Clackamas County Sheriff's Dept., Internat. Drug Info. Ctr., N.Y.C., 1983—, Albert Roy Davis Scientific Rsch. Lab, Orange Park, Fla. 1986. Recipient Bristol Labs. award, 1983. Mem. Am. Assn. Naturopathic Physicians, Oreg. Assn. Naturopathic Physicians, N.Y. Acad. Sci. Avocations: classical and jazz music, tap dance, art, botany, acting. Office: 6910 SE Lake Rd Portland OR 97267-2101

SKODON, EMIL MARK, diplomat; b. Chgo., Nov. 25, 1953; s. Emil John and Anne (Soltes) S.; m. Dorothea Shaffer, Mar. 6, 1982; children: Catherine Marie, Christine Louise. BA, U. Chgo., 1975, MBA, 1976. Consular officer U.S. Embassy, Bridgetown, Barbados, 1977-79; econ. officer U.S. Embassy, East Berlin, Germany, 1979-81, Office of So. African Affairs, Dept. State, Washington, 1982-84; econ. officer U.S. Embassy, Vienna, Austria, 1984-88, Kuwait City, Kuwait, 1989-91; dep. chief mission U.S. Embassy, Singapore, 1995—; consul gen. U.S. Consulate Gen., Perth, Australia, 1991-94. Mem. Nat. Trust for Hist. Preservation. Avocations: visiting historic sites, good food, spending time with family. Office: US Embassy, 27 Napier Rd, Singapore 258508, Singapore also: US Embassy Singapore Psc 470 # Dcm FPO AP 96534-0470

SKOGLUND, JOHN C., former professional football team executive. Former treas., chmn. bd., bd. dirs. Minn. Vikings Ventures, Inc.; chmn. Minn. Vikings Football Club; chmn. bd., pres. Skoglund Comms., Inc., Duluth, Minn. Office: Minn Vikings 9520 Viking Dr Eden Prairie MN 55344-3825*

SKOGMAN, DALE R., bishop. Bishop No. Great Lakes Synod, Marquette, Mich. Address: Evangelical Lutheran Church 1029 N 3rd St Marquette MI 49855-3509*

SKOL, MICHAEL, management consultant; b. Chgo., Oct. 15, 1942; s. Ted and Rebecca (Williams) S.; m. Claudia Serwer, Sept. 29, 1973. BA, Yale U., 1964. U.S. fgn. svc. officer Dept. State, 1965-95; polit. officer U.S. Embassy, Buenos Aires, 1966-67, Saigon, Viet Nam, 1968-70; desk officer Dept. State, Washington, 1970-72; comml. attache U.S. Embassy, Santo Domingo, Dominican Republic, 1972-75; econ. comml. officer U.S. Consulate Gen., Naples, Italy, 1975-76; comml. attache U.S. Embassy, Rome, 1976-78; polit. counselor U.S. Embassy, San Jose, Costa Rica, 1978-82; dep. dir. policy planning Inter-Am. Affairs Bur. Dept. State, Washington, 1982-85; dep. chief of mission U.S. Embassy, Bogota, Colombia, 1985-87; dir. Andean affairs Dept. State, Washington, 1987-88; dep. asst. sec. state for S. Am. U.S. Dept. of State, Washington, 1988-90; amb. U.S. Embassy, Caracas, Venezuela, 1990-93; prin. dep. asst. sec. for Latin Am./Caribbean Dept. State, Washington, 1993-95; sr. v.p. Diplomatic Resolutions, Inc., Washington, 1995—. Mem. Yale Club of Colombia, Yale Club of Venezuela, Yale Club of Washington, Yale Club of N.Y. Home: 3033 Cleveland Ave NW Washington DC 20008-3532 Office: 1420 16th St NW Washington DC 20036-2218

SKOLAN-LOGUE, AMANDA NICOLE, lawyer, consultant; b. Los Angeles, Feb. 19, 1954; d. Carl Charles and Estelle (Lubin) Skolan; m. James Edward Logue, Dec. 10, 1983. BS, U. Calif., Los Angeles, 1973; MBA, U. So. Calif., 1976; JD, Southwestern U., Los Angeles, 1982. Bar: Calif. 1982, U.S. Dist. Ct. (cen., no. and ea. dists.) Calif. 1982, N.Y. 1986. Sr. internal cons. Getty Oil Co., Los Angeles, 1976-80; atty. litigation ACLU of So. Calif., Los Angeles, 1982-83; corp. atty. Am. Can Co., Greenwich, Conn., 1983-86; assoc. Shereff, Friedman, Hoffman & Goodman, N.Y.C., 1986-88; region counsel Gen. Electric Capital Corp., Danbury, Conn., 1988—. Mem. ABA, N.Y. State Bar Assn. Republican. Home: 33 Musket Ridge Rd New Fairfield CT 06812-5101 Office: Gen Electric Capital Corp 44 Old Ridgebury Rd Danbury CT 06810-5107

SKOLER, LOUIS, architect, educator; b. Utica, N.Y., Apr. 5, 1920; s. Harry and Etta (Mitkoff) S.; m. Celia Rebecca Stern, 1952; children: Elisa Anne, Harry Jay. BArch, Cornell U., 1951. Maj. designer Sargent, Webster, Crenshaw & Folley, Syracuse, N.Y., 1951-59; design critic Cornell U., Ithaca, N.Y., 1956-57; pvt. practice architecture, Syracuse, 1956-69; faculty, Sch. Architecture Syracuse (N.Y.) U., 1959-92, prof. emeritus, 1990—; head of Masters in Architecture I Program, 1980-82, head undergrad. program, 1989-90, architecture programs abroad, London, 1977, Scandinavia, 1985, Japan, 1988; ptnr. Architects Partnership, Syracuse, 1969-71; pres. Skoler & Lee Architects, P.C., Syracuse, 1971-89; lectr. Nanjing Inst. Tech., China, 1986; arbitrator Am. Arbitration Assn., 1980—. Named Best in Residential Design, Design-in-Steel, 1968-69. Mem. AIA. Home: 213 Scottholm Ter Syracuse NY 13224-1737 *A guiding principle over many years of teaching and practice, is the interrelationship of theory and work-of idea and circumstance, of imagination and the forces generated by day to day life.*

SKOLFIELD, MELISSA T., government official; b. New Orleans, June 25, 1958; m. Frank W. Curtis. BA in Econ. and Behavioral Sci., Rice U., 1980; MA in Pub. Affairs, George Washington U., 1986. Account exec. McDaniel & Tate Pub. Rels., Houston, 1981-84; press sec. Rep. Michael Andrews of Tex., 1985-87; press. sec. Senator Dale Bumpers of Ark., 1987-93; dep. asst. sec. for pub. affairs for policy and strategy Dept. Health and Human Svcs., Washington, 1993-95, asst. sec. pub. affairs, 1995—. Press asst. Dem. Nat. Com., Dem. Nat. Conv., 1988, Clinton Pres. Campaign, Dem. Nat. Com., 1992. Mem. Senate Press Secs. Assn. (pres.), Assn. Dem. Press Assts., Pub. Rels. Soc. Am. Office: Dept Health & Human Svcs 200 Independence Ave SW Washington DC 20201-0004

SKOLNICK, JEROME H., legal educator; b. 1931. B.B.A., CCNY, 1952, M.A., 1953; Ph.D., Yale U., 1957. Research assoc. Yale U., New Haven, 1956-60, asst. prof., 1960-62; asst. prof. U. Calif.-Berkeley Law Sch., 1962-67, prof., 1970—, Claire Clements Deans prof. law emeritus Jurisprudence and Social Policy, 1970—; vis. assoc. prof. NYU, 1966; vis. prof. U. Denver, 1967; assoc. prof. U. Chgo., 1967-69; prof. U. Calif.-San Diego, 1969-70; dir. Ctr. Study of Law and Soc., 1972—; cons. Bd. dirs. Pres.'s Commn. on Causes and Prevention of Violence, 1968-69; disting. vis. prof. John Jay Coll. Criminal Justice, 1995-96; adj. prof., co-dir. Ctr. for Rsch. in Crime and Justice NYU Sch. Law, 1996-97. Carnegie fellow, 1956-66; Guggenheim fellow, 1980. Mem. Am. Criminol. Assn., ACLU, Am. Soc. Criminology (pres.), Law and Soc. Assn. (trustee). Author: (with D. Bayley) The New Blue Line, 1986, Justice Without Trial, 1966; House of Cards, 1978; (with R.D. Schwartz) Society and the Legal Order, 1970, (with J. Fyfe) Above the Law, (with J. Kaplan and M. Feeley) Criminal Justice. Office: NYU Sch Law 40 Washington Sq S New York NY 10012-1005

SKOLNICK, LAWRENCE, neonatologist, medical administrator; b. N.Y.C., July 29, 1947; s. Harry and Sylvia (Hausman) S.; m. Tamar Tumarkin, Apr. 7, 1970; children: Daniel, Michael, Rachel. BS, CUNY, 1968; MD, NYU, 1972; MPH, U. N.C., 1980. Dir. newborn medicine Hosp. of Albert Einstein Coll. Medicine, Bronx, N.Y., 1977-80; dir. neonatology Morristown (N.J.) Meml. Hosp., 1980—.

SKOLNICK, MALCOLM HARRIS, biophysics researcher, educator, patent lawyer, mediator; b. Salt Lake City, Aug. 11, 1935; s. Max Cantor and Charlotte Sylvia (Letman) S.; m. Lois Marlene Ray, Sept. 1, 1959; children: Michael, David, Sara, Jonathan. BS in Physics (with honors), U. Utah, 1956; MS in Physics, Cornell U., 1959, PhD in Theoretical Nuclear Physics, 1963; JD, U. Houston, 1986. chmn. health care tech. study sect. Nat. Ctr. Health Svcs. Rsch. HHS, 1975-79; editl. assocs. Cts., Health Sci. and Law, Washington, 1989-93; bd. dirs. Medquest Svcs., Inc., Biodyne, Inc. Staff scientist Elem. Sci. Study, Watertown, Mass., 1962-63; mem. Inst. for Advanced Study, Princeton, N.J., 1963-64; instr. Physics Dept. MIT, Cambridge, Mass., 1964-65; staff scientist dir. Edn. Devel. Ctr., Watertown, 1965-67; assoc. prof. physics Physics Dept. SUNY, Stony Brook, 1967-70; assoc. prof. dir. comm. Health Sci. Ctr. SUNY, Stony Brook, 1968-71; prof. biophysics grad. sch. biomed. sci. U. Tex. Health Scis. Ctr., Houston, 1971-94, prof. biomedical comm., 1971-83, prof. health svcs. rsch., 1988-95, dir. neurophysiology rsch. ctr., 1985-91; dir office tec. mgmt. U. Tex. Health Sci. Ctr., Houston, 1991-96; prof. tech. and health law U. Tex. Sch. Pub. Health, Houston, 1994—; chmn. health care tech. study sect. Nat. Ctr. Health Svcs. Rsch. HHS, 1975-79; editorial assoc. Cts., Health Sci. and Law, Washington, 1989-93; bd. dirs. Medquest, Inc., Biodyne, Inc., Cryogenic Solutions, Inc. Patentee in field; contbr. numerous articles to profl. jours. With USNR, 1953-61, hon. discharge. Recipient Silver Beaver award Boy Scouts Am., 1978; Ford Found scholar, U. Utah, 1952; rsch. grantee Nat. Inst. for Drug Abuse. Mem. ABA, IEEE, Soc. Neurosci., Licensing Exec. Soc., Am. Intellectual Property Law Assn., Tex. Tech. Transfer Assn. (bd. dirs.), Houston Intellectual Property Law Assn., Houston Soc. Engring. in Medicine and Biology (bd. dirs.), Am. Soc. Law and Medicine, S.W. Assn. Biotech. Cos. (bd. dirs.), Am. Bd. Forensic Examiners, Soc. Accident Reconstrn., Tex. Empowerment Network (pres., bd. dirs.), Assoc. Univ. Tech. Mgrs., Soc. Auto. Engrs., Am. Pub. Health Assn. Office: Sch of Pub Health Rm 342W PO Box 20186 Houston TX 77225-0186

SKOLNIK, BARNET DAVID, entrepreneur; b. N.Y.C., Feb. 8, 1941; s. Jack and Edythe (Savitz) S.; m. Patricia L. Krohn; children: Sarah, Deborah, Daniel, Joseph, Benjamin, Rebecca. AB in Am. Govt. cum laude, Harvard U., 1962, LLB, 1965. Bar: D.C. 1966, Md. 1984, Maine 1991. Atty. criminal div. U.S. Dept. Justice, Washington, 1966-68; asst. U.S. atty. for Dist. Md., Balt., 1968-78; chief public corruption unit U.S. Atty.'s Office, Balt., 1973-78; pvt. practice law Washington, 1978-83, 89-91, Balt., 1983-89, Portland, Maine, 1991-94; entrepreneur Maine, 1994—; tchr., lectr. on trial practice, white collar criminality, public corruption. Recipient Spl. Achievement award Dept. Justice, 1972, 74, Spl. Commendation for Outstanding Svc., Dept. Justice, 1978, Younger Fed. Lawyer award Fed. Bar Assn., 1974, Atty. Gen.'s Disting. Service award, 1974, Legal award Assn. Fed. Investigators, 1977. Home and Office: 4 Wilson St Topsham ME 04086

SKOLNIK, MERRILL I., electrical engineer; b. Balt., Nov. 6, 1927; s. Samuel and Mary (Baker) S.; m. Judith Magid, June 4, 1950; children: Nachama, Martin Allen, Julia Anne, Ellen Charlotte. BEng, Johns Hopkins U., 1947, MSEng, 1949, DEng, 1951. Research scientist Johns Hopkins U., Balt., 1947-54; vis. prof. Johns Hopkins U., 1973-74; engring. specialist Sylvania Electric, Boston, 1954; staff mem. MIT Lincoln Lab., Lexington, Mass., 1954-59; research mgr. Electronic Communications, Timonium, Md., 1959-64, Inst. Def. Analyses, Arlington, Va., 1964-65; supr. radar div. Naval Research Lab., Washington, 1965-96, radar sys. cons., 1996—; mem. bd. visitors Duke U. Engring. Sch., Durham, N.C., 1976-93; disting. vis. sci. Jet Propulsion Lab., 1990-92; mem. Md. Gov.'s Exec. Adv. Com., 1993-95. Author: Introduction to Radar Systems, 1962, 2d edit., 1980, Radar Handbook, 1970, 2d edit., 1990; editor: Radar Applications, 1988. Recipient Heinrich Hertz premium Instn. Electronic and Radio Engrs., London, 1964, Disting. Civilian Service award U.S. Navy, 1982; Meritorious Exec. award Sr. Exec. Service, 1986; Disting. Alumnus award Johns Hopkins U., 1979; named to Soc. of Scholars, Johns Hopkins U., 1975. Fellow IEEE (editor Proceedings 1986-89, Harry Diamond award 1983, Centennial medal 1984); mem. Nat. Acad. Engring. Home: 8123 McDonogh Rd Baltimore MD 21208-1005 Office: Naval Rsch Lab Washington DC 20375

SKOLNIK, MIRIAM, lawyer; b. Caracas, Venezuela, 1956; came to U.S., 1963; BA magna cum laude, Yeshiva U., 1976; JD, Columbia U., 1979. Bar: N.Y. 1980, U.S. Dist. Ct. (so. and ea. dists.) N.Y. 1980, U.S. Ct. Appeals (2nd cir.) 1982. Asst. corp. counsel City of N.Y., 1981-86; assoc. Herzfeld & Rubin, N.Y.C., 1986-95, ptnr., 1995—. Mem. N.Y. State Bar Assn. (com. on cts. of appellate practice 1994-96). Office: Herzfeld & Rubin PC 1143 E 12th St Brooklyn NY 11230-4811

SKOLNIKOFF, EUGENE B., political science educator; b. Phila., Aug. 29, 1928; s. Benjamin H. and Betty (Turoff) S.; m. Winifred S. Weinstein, Sept. 15, 1957; children: David, Matthew, Jessica. B.S., M.I.T., 1950, M.S., 1950, Ph.D., 1965; B.A., Oxford (Eng.) U., 1952, M.A., 1955. Registered profl. engr. Rsch. asst. in elec. engring. Uppsala U., Sweden, 1950; prof. polit. sci. M.I.T., 1965—, chmn. polit. sci. dept., 1970-74; dir. Center for Internat. Studies, 1972-87; vis. rsch. prof. Carnegie Endowment for Internat. Peace, Geneva, 1969-70; vis. fellow Balliol Coll., U. Oxford, 1989; systems analyst Inst. for Def. Analyses, Washington, 1957-58; mem. White House staff Office Spl. Asst. to Pres. for Sci. and Tech., Washington, 1958-63; adj. prof. Fletcher Sch. Law and Diplomacy, Tufts U., Medford, Mass., 1965-72; sr. cons. White House Office of Sci. and Tech. Policy, 1977-81, also vice chmn. adv. com. on sci., tech. and devel.; mem. policy rev. com. on nat. low-level nuclear waste mgmt., 1980-86; cons. Dept. State, Office of Tech. Assessment, AID, OECD, Resources for the Future, Am. Soc. Internat. Law, Ford Found., Inst. Def. Analyses; chmn., pres. Sci. and Public Policy Studies Group, 1967-73; mem. Internat. Council Sci. Policy Studies; Montague Burton vis. prof. U. Edinburgh, 1977. Author: Science, Technology and American Foreign Policy, 1967, International Imperatives of Technology, 1972, The Elusive Transformation: Science, Technology, and the Evolution of International Politics, 1993; co-editor: World Eco-Crisis, 1972, Visions of Apocalypse, End or Rebirth?, 1985; contbr. articles to publs.; chmn. editorial bd. Pub. Sci., 1971-75; mem. editorial bd. Tech. Rev., 1976-78, Social Studies of Sci., 1970-75, Internat. Orgn., 1974-80. Trustee German Marshall Fund, 1979-87, chmn., 1980-86; trustee UN Rsch. Inst. for Social Devel., 1979-85; bd. dirs. Saco Def., 1984-86; mem. Overseas Devel. Coun.; mem. U.S. del. UN Commn. for Social Devel., 1979; mem. State Dept. Adv. Com. on Sci. and Tech., 1987—. Served with U.S. Army Security Agy., 1955-57. Rhodes scholar, 1950-52; Rockefeller Found. fellow, 1963-65; decorated Comdr.'s Cross Fed. Republic Germany, Order of Rising Sun, Golden Rays, Neck Ribbon, Japan. Fellow Am. Acad. Arts and Scis. (councillor 1973-77), AAAS (sec. sect. K 1967-69, mem. com. on sci. and pub. policy 1973-74, com. on sci., engring. and pub. policy 1984-89); mem. UN Assn., Am. Coun. on Germany, Fedn. Am. Scientists (coun. 1981-85), Coun. Fgn. Rels., Am. Assn. Rhodes Scholars, Soc. for Internat. Devel., Soc. for Social Studies of Sci., Sigma Xi, Tau Beta Pi, Eta Kappa Nu. Patentee hybrid circuits. Home: 3 Chandler St Lexington MA 02173-3601 Office: MIT E51-263A 77 Massachusetts Ave # E51-263A Cambridge MA 02139-4301

SKOLOVSKY, ZADEL, concert pianist, educator; b. Vancouver, B.C., Can.; came to U.S., 1923, naturalized, 1929; s. Max and Kate (Jones) S.; m. Alice Maffett Glass, July 29, 1947 (div. 1953). Diploma, Curtis Inst. Music, 1937; studied piano with, Isabelle Vengerova and Leopold Godowsky; conducting with, Fritz Reiner and Pierre Monteux; violin with, Edwin Bachmann. Prof. music Ind. U., 1975-87, prof. emeritus, 1987—; juror NYU Internat. Tchaikovsky Piano Competition, 1978, 3d Latin Am. Teresa Carreno Piano Competition, Caracas, Venezuela, 1978, U. Md. Internat. Piano Competition, 1981, Joanna Hodges Internat. Piano Competition, Palm Desert, Calif., 1983; tchr. master classes; concert tour of U.S., S. Am. and Far East, 1989-90. Debut at Town Hall as winner of the Walter W. Naumburg award, 1939; appearances in recitals in Carnegie Hall, N.Y.C., 1939—, ann. concert tours U.S.A. and Can., 1939—, biennial tours Europe, Israel, S.Am., Far East, also condr. master classes, 1986—; soloist with N.Y. Philharmonic Symphony Orch.; soloist under condrs. Dimitri Mitropoulos, Charles Munch, Leonard Bernstein, Lorin Maazel, Erich Leinsdorf, Jan Kubelik, Paul Kletzki, Arthur Rodzinski, Paul Paray; appeared as a soloist Lewishohn Stadium, N.Y. and Robin Hood Dell, Phila., under condrs. Vladimir Golschmann, Pierre Monteux, Alexander Smallens; soloist with NBC Orch., Nat. Orch. Assn., Phila. Orch., Nat. Orch., Washington, San Francisco Symphony, Israel Philharmonic, Residentie Orch. at The Hague, L'Orchestre Nat. de Belgique, B.B.C. Scottish Orch., orchs. of Luxembourg, Lisbon, Portugal, Hilversum Radio, Holland, Paris, London, Ravinia, Chgo., N.Y.C.; also appeared on TV; first performance Second Piano Concerto by Prokofieff with N.Y. Philharmonic Orch. under Charles Munch, 1948; world premier Concerto No. 4 of Darius Milhaud with Boston Symphony, 1950; 1st extensive European tour, 1953; appeared with Residency Orch. of the Hague, 2d tour, appeared as soloist with Israel Philharmonic Orch. at opening concert World Festival Music, 1954, appeared in Mexico, 1965, European tour, Eng., Holland, Scandinavia, Belgium, 1965-66, 67, recital, Queen Elizabeth Hall, London, Eng., 1971, 73, recitals, B.C., 1975; concert tour of, S. Am., 1978, U.S., Can. and Europe, 1981-82, Can., 1991; 1st concert tour of Far East, 1983; mus. films for TV., recorded for Columbia Masterworks Records, Philips Records; transcontinental Can. tour, 1991, U.S.A, 1991; annual concert tours U.S.A., Can., Europe, 1992-93. Recipient prizes from Nat. Fedn. Music Clubs, 1943, Nat. Music League, 1940, Robin Hood Dell Young Am. Artists award 1943; recipient Walter W. Naumburg award, 1939. Democrat. Jewish. Club: Lotos (N.Y.C.). Avocations: tennis, chess, literature, theater.

SKOMAL, EDWARD NELSON, aerospace company executive, consultant; b. Kansas City, Mo., Apr. 15, 1926; s. Edward Albert and Ruth (Bangs) S.; m. Elizabeth Birkbeck, Mar. 4, 1951; children: Susan Beth, Catherine Anne, Margaret Elaine; m. Joan Kerner, Apr. 9, 1988. BA, Rice U., Houston, 1947, MA, 1949. Engr., Socony Rsch. Labs., Dallas, 1949-51; asst. sect. head Nat. Bur. Standards, Washington, 1951-56; project engr. Sylvania Research Lab., Palo Alto, Calif., 1956-59; mgr. applications engring., chief applications engr. Motorola Solid State Systems Div., Phoenix, 1959-63; dir. communications dept. Aerospace Corp., El Segundo, Calif., 1963-86, ret., 1986; mem. Presdl. Joint Tech. Adv. Com. on Electromagnetic Compatibility, Washington, 1965-70, 71-75. Author: Man Made Radio Noise, 1978, Automatic Vehicle Location Systems, 1980; Measuring the Radio Frequency Environment, 1985; contbr. articles to profl. jours. Patentee in field of radio systems, solid state devices, radar cross sect. reduction of ballistic rentry vehicles and solid state microwave components. Elder Presbyn. Ch., Redlands, Calif. Served with USN, 1944-6. Fellow IEEE (life, chmn. tech. adv. com. 1982-86, chmn. tech. com. electromagnetic environments 1976-82, standards com. 1980—, nat. com. standards coordinating com. on definitions 1986—, Richard A. Stoddart award 1980, cert. of Achievement 1971, Paper of Yr. award 1970); mem. IEEE Electromagnetic Soc. (life), Am. Phys. Soc., Internat. Union Radio Scientists, Sigma Xi. Republican. Presbyterian. Home: 1831 Valle Vista Dr Redlands CA 92373-7246

SKOMOROWSKY, PETER P., accounting company executive, lawyer; b. Leipzig, Germany, Nov. 14, 1932. BA, Columbia U.; MBA, CCNY; JD, NYU Law Sch. Home: 25 E 86th St New York NY 10028-0553 Office: care Grant Thornton 605 3rd Ave New York NY 10158

SKONEY, SOPHIE ESSA, educational administrator; b. Detroit, Jan. 29, 1929; d. George Essa and Helena (Dihmes) Cokalay; PhB, U. Detroit, 1951; MEd, Wayne State U., 1960, EdD, 1975; postgrad. Ednl. Inst. Harvard Grad. Sch. Edn., 1986-96; m. Daniel J. Skoney, Dec. 28, 1957; children: Joseph Anthony, James Francis, Carol Anne. Tchr. elem. sch. Detroit Bd. Edn., 1952-69, remedial reading specialist, 1969-70, curriculum coord., 1970-71, region 6 article 3 title I coord., 1971-83, area achievement specialist, 1984-88, adminstrv. asst. Office Grant Procurement and Compliance, 1988—; mem. dean's adv. coun. Coll. Edn. Wayne State U., 1995—; cons. in field. Recipient Disting. Alumni award Wayne State U., 1993. Editor newsletter Alliance to the Mich. Dental Assn., 1993—. Mem. Wayne State U. Edn. Alumni Assn. (pres. bd. govs. 1979-80, newsletter editor 1975-77, 80—), Macomb Dental Aux. (pres. 1969-70), Mich. Dental Aux. (pres. 1980-81), Am.-Assn. Sch. Adminstrs., Wayne State U. Alumni Assn. (dir., v.p. 1985-86), Internat. Reading Assn., Mich. Reading Assn., Mich. Assn. State and Fed. Program Specialists, Profl. Women's Network (newsletter editor 1981-83, pres. 1985-87, Anthony Wayne award for leadership 1981), Assn. for Supervision and Curriculum Devel., Delta Kappa Gamma, Beta Sigma Phi, Phi Delta Kappa (v.p. 1988-90, pres. 1990-91, Educator of Yr. 1985, 91, 96). Roman Catholic. Home: 20813 Lakeland St Saint Clair Shores MI 48081-2104 Office: Detroit Pub Schs 5057 Woodward Ave Detroit MI 48202-4050

SKOOG, DONALD PAUL, retired physician, educator; b. Sioux City, Iowa, Sept. 29, 1931; m. Mary Ann Bunn, 1955; children: Robert Eugene, David Alan (dec.), Kristin Marie. BA magna cum laude, Midland Lutheran Coll., Fremont, Nebr., 1953; MD cum laude, U. Nebr., 1958; DSci (hon.), Midland Luth. Coll., 1993. Diplomate Am. Bd. Pathology. Intern, then resident in pathology Bishop Clarkson Meml. Hosp., Omaha, 1958-62; resident in pathology Parkland Meml. Hosp., Dallas, 1962-63; fellow in pathology U. Tex. Southwestern Med. Sch., Dallas, 1962-63; practice medicine specializing in pathology Omaha, 1963-92; pathologist Bishop Clarkson Meml. Hosp., 1963-88, chmn. dept. pathology, 1978-80, dir. dept., 1986-87, chmn. med. edn. com., 1978-83, sec.-treas. med. staff, 1982-87; prof. pathology and microbiology U. Nebr. Med. Sch., 1977-93, mem. dean's faculty adv. coun., 1977-79, mem. grad. and continuing edn. com., 1980-85, mem. council for affiliated instns., 1981-83, mem. admissions com. 1986-91, sr. cons. pathology and microbiology, 1993—; assoc. med. dir. ARC Blood Svcs., Midwest region, Omaha, 1988, med. dir./dir. 1989-91, dir./prin. officer, 1991-92, mem. computer systems selection com., 1991; med. affairs com. ARC Blood Svcs., Washington, 1991-92; bd. dirs., exec. com. Health Planning Coun. of the Midlands, 1975-77; mem. exec. com., chmn. loan com. Nebr. Med. Edn. Fund, 1983-91, sec., treas., 1984-91. Mem. editorial bd. Lab. Medicine, 1979—; contbr. articles to med. jours. Councilman Luther Meml. Luth. Ch., Omaha, 1966-72, 87-91, vice chmn., 1969-72; trustee Midland Luth. Coll., 1968-87, chmn., 1973-75. Recipient Alumni Achievement award Midland Luth. Coll., 1972, Disting. Svc. award Sch. of Allied Health Program, U. Nebr. Med. Ctr., 1990. Fellow Am. Soc. Clin. Pathologists (hematology profl. self-assessment com. 1972, 75,78, adv. coun. 1972-78, chmn. coun. hematology 1978-81, editor Hematology Check Sample 1983-88, Disting. Svc. award Commn. on Continuing Edn. 1985, mem. bd. censors 1987-89, mem. nat. meeting activities com. 1989-92, chmn. 1990-92, Israel Davidsohn disting. svc. award 1993), Coll. Am. Pathologists (hematology resource com. 1981-86, vice chmn. 1982-85); mem. AMA, Am. Assn. Blood Banks, Nebr. Assn. Pathologists, Nebr. Med. Assn., Met. Omaha Med. Soc. (coun. on grievances and profl. ethics 1983-91), Midland Luth. Coll. Alumni Assn. (pres. 1969-70), Alpha Omega Alpha (pres. U. Nebr. chpt. 1976-77, counsellor 1984-90). Home: 706 S 96th St Omaha NE 68114-4918

SKOOG, FOLKE KARL, botany educator; b. Fjärås, Sweden, July 15, 1908; came to U.S., 1925, naturalized, 1935; s. Karl Gustav and Sigrid (Person) S.; m. Birgit Anna Lisa Bergner, Jan. 31, 1947; 1 dau., Karin. BS, Calif. Inst. Tech., 1932, PhD, 1936; PhD (hon.), U. Lund, Sweden, 1956; DSc (hon.), U. Ill., 1980; DAgr. Sci., U. Pisa, Italy, 1991, Swedish U. Agrl. Scis., Uppsala, 1991. Teaching asst., research fellow biology Calif. Inst. Tech., 1934-36; NRC fellow U. Calif., Berkeley, 1936-37, summer 1938; instr., tutor biology Harvard U., 1937-41, research assoc., 1941; assoc., assoc. prof. biology Johns Hopkins U., 1941-44; chemist Q.M.C.; also tech. rep. U.S. Army ETO, 1944-46; asso. prof. botany U. Wis.-Madison, 1947-49, prof., from 1949, C. Leonard Huskins prof. botany, now emeritus.; vis. physiologist Pineapple Research Inst., U. Hawaii, 1938-39; assoc. physiologist NIH, USPHS, 1943; vis. lectr. Washington U., 1946, Swedish U. Agrl. Scis., Ultuna, 1952; v.p. physiol. sect. Internat. Bot. Congress, Paris, 1954, Edinburgh, 1964, Leningrad, 1975. Editor: Plant Growth Substances, 1951, 80; contbr. articles to profl. jours. Track and field mem. Swedish Olympic Team, 1932. Recipient cert. of merit Bot. Soc. Am., 1956, Nat. Medal of Sci., U.S., 1991, Cosimo Ridolfi medal, 1991, John Ericsson medal, 1992. Mem. NAS, Bot. Soc. Am. (chmn. physiol. sect. 1954-55), Am. Soc. Plant Physiologists (v.p. 1952-53, pres. 1957-58, Stephen Hales award 1954, Reid Barnes life mem. award 1970), Soc. Devel. Biology (pres. 1971), Am. Soc. Gen. Physiologists (v.p. 1955-57, pres. 1957-58), Internat. Plant Growth Substances Assn. (hon. life mem., v.p. 1976-79, pres. 1979-82), Am. Soc. Biol. Chemists, Am. Acad. Arts and Scis., Deutsche Akademie der Naturforscher Leopoldina, Swedish Royal Acad. Scis., Tissue Culture Assn. (hon. life mem. 1991, Life Achievement award 1992), Russian Soc. Plant Physiologists (hon. life mem.). Achievements include patents in field. Home: 2820 Marshall Ct Madison WI 53705-2270 Office: U Wis Dept Botany Madison WI 53706

SKOOG, GERALD DUANE, science educator; b. Sioux City, Iowa, Feb. 27, 1936; s. Paul and Mary Ann Skoog; m. Elizabeth Ann Lee, Dec. 28, 1962; children: Jeffrey, John, Sarah. B.S., U. Nebr., 1958; M.A., U. No. Iowa, 1963; Ed.D., U. Nebr., 1969. Tchr. various schs., Nebr., Ill., 1958-69; instr. U. Nebr., Lincoln, summer 1969; asst. prof. curriculum and instrn. Tex. Tech U., Lubbock, 1969-72, assoc. prof., coordinator program, 1972-74, assoc. prof., chmn. secondary edn., 1976-80, prof., chmn. secondary edn., 1980-90, prof., chmn. curriculum and instrn., 1990—; pres. faculty senate Tex. Tech U., 1986-87; Helen DeVitt Jones prof., 1997—; vis. prof. Western Ill. U., summer 1972; lectr. in field; participant, facilitator numerous workshops; cons. Contbr. numerous articles to profl. jours., also reviewer articles and papers; co-author secondary sch. science textbooks. Bd. dirs. Gloria Dei Luth. Ch., Lubbock, 1971-74, 92-93; bd. dirs. Luth. Coun. Cmty. Action, 1970-71, Good Neighbor Ministry, 1982-84; leader Boy Scouts Am., 1978-79; foster parent Luth. Social Svcs. Tex.; bd. dirs. Triangle Coalition for Sci. and Tech., 1986-95. Recipient Pres.'s Faculty Achievement award Tex. Tech. U., 1986, Disting. Leadership award, 1996. Fellow AAAS; mem. Nat. Sci. Tchrs. Assn. (life, bd. dirs. 1977-79, pres. 1985-86, various coms., Disting. Svc. to Sci. Edn. award 1994), Nat. Assn. Rsch. Sci. Teaching, Assn. Edn. Tchrs. Sci., Assn. Supervision and Curriculum Devel., Nat. Sci. Suprs. Assn., Sci. Tchrs. Assn. Tex. (hon. mem., past pres.), Nat. Assn. Biology Tchrs., Tex. Assn. Tchr. Edn. (com. 1981-82), Soc. Study Edn., Phi Delta Kappa. Home: 3214 67th St Lubbock TX 79413-6206 Office: Tex Tech U Coll Edn Lubbock TX 79409

SKOOG, WILLIAM ARTHUR, former oncologist; b. Culver City, Calif., Apr. 10, 1925; s. John Lundeen and Allis Rose (Gatz) S.; m. Ann Douglas, Sept. 17, 1949; children: Karen, William Arthur, James Douglas, Allison. AA, UCLA, 1944; BA with gt. distinction, Stanford U., 1946, MD, 1949. Intern in medicine Stanford Hosp., San Francisco, 1948-49, asst. resident medicine, 1949-50; asst. resident medicine N.Y. Hosp., N.Y.C., 1950-51; sr. resident medicine Wadsworth VA Hosp., Los Angeles, 1951, attending specialist internal medicine, 1962-68; practice medicine specializing in internal medicine, Los Altos, Calif., 1959-61; pvt. practice hematology and oncology Calif. Oncologic and Surg. Med. Group, Inc., Santa Monica, Calif., 1971-72; pvt. practice med. oncology, San Bernardino, Calif., 1972-94; assoc. staff Palo Alto-Stanford (Calif.) Hosp. Center, 1959-61, U. Calif. Med. Center, San Francisco, 1959-61; assoc. attending physician U. Calif. at Los Angeles Hosp. and Clinics, 1961-78; vis. physician internal medicine Harbor Gen. Hosp., Torrance, Calif., 1962-65, attending physician, 1965-71; cons. chemistry Clin. Lab., UCLA Hosp., 1963-68; affiliate cons. staff St. John's Hosp., Santa Monica, Calif., 1967-71, courtesy staff, 1971-72; courtesy attending med. staff Santa Monica Hosp., 1967-72; staff physician St. Bernardine (Calif.) Hosp., 1972-94, hon. staff, 1994—; staff physician San Bernardino Cmty. Hosp., 1972-90, courtesy staff, 1990-94; chief sect. oncology San Bernardino County Hosp., 1972-76; cons. staff Redlands (Calif.) Cmty. Hosp., 1972-83, courtesy staff, 1983-94, hon. staff, 1994—; asst. in medicine Cornell Med. Coll., N.Y.C., 1950-51; jr. rsch. physician UCLA Atomic Energy Project, 1954-55; instr. medicine, asst. rsch. physician dept. medicine UCLA Med. Center, 1955-56, asst. prof. medicine, asst. rsch. physician, 1956-59; clin. asso. hematology VA Center, Los Angeles, 1956-59; co-dir. metabolic rsch. unit UCLA Center for Health Scis., 1955-59, 61-65; co-dir. Health Scis. Clin. Rsch. Ctr., 1965-68, dir., 1968-72; clin. instr. medicine Stanford, 1959-61; asst. clin. prof. medicine, assoc. rsch. physician U. Calif. Med. Center, San Francisco, 1959-61; lectr. medicine UCLA Sch. Medicine, 1961-62, assoc. prof. medicine, 1962-73, assoc. clin. prof. medicine, 1973—. Served with USNR, 1943-46, lt. M.C., 1951-53. Fellow ACP; mem. Am., Calif. med. assns., So. Calif. Acad. Clin. Oncology, Western Soc. Clin. Research, Am. Fedn. Clin. Research, Los Angeles Acad. Medicine, San Bernardino County Med. Soc., Am. Soc. Clin. Oncology, Am. Soc. Internal Medicine, Calif. Soc. Internal Medicine, Inland Soc. Internal Medicine, Phi Beta Kappa, Alpha Omega Alpha, Sigma Xi, Alpha Kappa Kappa. Episcopalian (vestryman 1965-70). Club: Redlands Country. Contbr. articles to profl. jours. Home: 1119 Kimberly Pl Redlands CA 92373-6786

SKOPIL, OTTO RICHARD, JR., federal judge; b. Portland, Oreg., June 3, 1919; s. Otto Richard and Freda Martha (Boetticher) S.; m. Janet Rae Lundy, July 27, 1956; children: Otto Richard III, Casey Robert, Shannon Ida, Molly Jo. BA in Econs., Willamette U., 1941, LLB, 1946, LLD (hon.), 1983. Bar: Oreg. 1946, IRS, U.S. Treasury Dept., U.S. Dist. Ct. Oreg., U.S. Ct. Appeals (9th cir.), U.S. Supreme Ct. 1946. Assoc. Skopil & Skopil, 1946-51; ptnr. Williams, Skopil, Miller & Beck (and predecessors), Salem, Oreg., 1951-72; judge U.S. Dist. Ct., Portland, 1972-79; chief judge U.S. Dist. Ct., 1976-79; judge U.S. Ct. Appeals (9th cir.), Portland, 1979—; chmn. com. adminstrn. of fed. magistrate sys. U.S. Jud. Conf., 1980-86; co-founder Oreg. chpt. Am. Leadership Forum; chmn. 9th cir. Jud. Coun. Magistrates Adv. Com., 1988-91; chmn. U.S. Jud. Conf. Long Range Planning Com., 1990-95. Hi-Y adviser Salem YMCA, 1951-52; appeal agt. SSS, Marion County (Oreg.) Draft Bd., 1953-66; master of ceremonies 1st Gov.'s Prayer Breakfast for State Oreg., 1959; mem. citizens adv. com., City of Salem, 1970-71; chmn. Gov.'s Com. on Staffing Mental Instns., 1969-70; pres., bd. dirs. Marion County Tb and Health Assn., 1958-61; bd. dirs. Willamette Valley Camp Fire Girls, 1946-56, Internat. Christian Leadership, 1959, Fed. Jud. Ctr., 1979; trustee Willamette U., 1969-71; elder Mt. Park Ch., 1979-81. Served to lt. USNR, 1942-46. Recipient Oreg. Legal Citizen of Yr. award, 1986, Disting. Alumni award Willamette U. Sch. Law, 1988. Mem. ABA, Oreg. Bar Assn. (bd. govs.), Marion County Bar Assn., Am. Judicature Soc., Oreg. Assn. Def. Counsel (dir.), Def. Research Inst., Assn. Ins. Attys. U.S. and Can. (Oreg. rep. 1970), Internat. Soc. Barristers, Prayer Breakfast Movement (fellowship council). Clubs: Salem, Exchange (pres. 1947), Illahe Hills Country (pres., dir. 1964-67). Office: US Ct Appeals 232 Pioneer Courthouse 555 SW Yamhill St Portland OR 97204-1336

SKORTON, DAVID JAN, university official, physician, educator, researcher; b. Milw., Nov. 22, 1949; s. Samuel and Pauline (Millstein) S.; 1 child, Joshua Samuel. BA, Northwestern U., 1970; MD, Northwestern U., Chgo., 1974. Diplomate Nat. Bd. Med. Examiners, Am. Bd. Internal Medicine, Am. Bd. Cardiovascular Disease. Resident UCLA, 1974-77, fellow in cardiology, 1977-80, chief resident in medicine, 1978-79, adj. asst. prof., 1978-80; instr. medicine U. Iowa, Iowa City, 1980-81, asst. prof., 1981-84, asst. prof. elec. and computer engring., 1982-84, assoc. prof. medicine and elec. and computer engring., 1984-88, prof., 1988—; acting dir., then dir. div. gen. internal medicine U. Iowa Coll. Medicine, 1985-89, assoc. chmn. for clinical programs, 1989-92, v.p. for rsch., 1992—; dir. echocardiology lab. VA Med. Ctr., Iowa City, 1980-89; mem. internat. and coop. projects study sect. NIH, 1988-92, chmn., 1990-92; lectr. in field numerous sci. sessions, nat. and internat. meetings; manuscript reviewer maj. jours. in field. Editor: Cardiac Imaging and Image Processing, 1986, Cardiac Imaging, 1990, 2d edit., 1996; mem. editl. bd. Am Jour. Cardiac Imaging, Am. Jour. Noninvasive Cardiology, Echocardiography, Circulation, 1986-88, Jour. Am. Coll. Cardiology, 1989-93, Jour. Am. Soc. Echocardiography, 1990-91, Internat. Jour. Cardiac Imaging, Ultrasonic Imaging, Cardiovascular Imaging (Italy), Clin. Cardiology, 1988-93; sect. editor Jour. Am. Soc. Echocardiography; contbr. numerous articles and sci. abstracts to profl. jours., chpts. to books. Regents' scholar UCLA, 1967-68; named Intern-of-Yr., UCLA, 1975; recipient Rsch. Assoc. Career Devel. award VA, Iowa City, 1981-84, Rsch. Career Devel. award Nat. Heart Lung & Blood Inst., Iowa City, 1984-89. Fellow ACP (governing coun. Iowa 1983-85), Am. Coll. Cardiology (chmn. computer applications com. 1984-90, gov. Iowa sect. 1987-90, trustee 1991-96), Am. Heart Assn., Am. Physiol. Soc.; mem. AAAS, Am. Soc. Echocardiography (bd. dirs. 1983-86), Am. Inst. Ultrasound in Medicine (bd. govs. 1986-89), Am. Fedn. for Clin. Rsch., Assn. Univ. Cardiologists, Internat. Soc. for Adult Congenital Cardiac Disease, Soc. Magnetic Resonance Imaging, Soc. Magnetic Resonance in Medicine. Jewish. Office: U Iowa VP for Rsch 201 Gilmore Hall Iowa City IA 52242-1320

SKORUPSKI, DIANE CHRISTINE, school library media specialist; b. Southbridge, Mass., Mar. 24, 1948; d. Axel Hector and Naomia Maxine (Willis) Johnson; m. Alfred Robert Skorupski, Oct. 9, 1971; children: Kurt (dec.), Gregory R., Kayle J. BS in Edn., North Adams State Coll., 1970; MLS, U. Ariz., 1988. Tchr., Ariz. Tchr. Town of Dudley, Mass., 1970-71, Sowest Supervisory Sch. Union, Bennington, Vt., 1971-73; sch. libr. media specialist Sunnyside Sch. Dist. # 12, Tucson, 1987—; bd. mem. Sch. Libr. Media Divsn., 1988-91, pres.-elect, 1992-93, pres. 1993-94. Contbr.: Information Literacy: Educating Children for the 21st Century, 1994. Brownie/Jr. Scout Leader Sahuaro Girl Scout Coun., Tucson, 1985-92. Grantee Tech. for Tchg. US West, Am. Assn. Sch. Adminstrs., Autodesk, AT&T, 1991-93, Murtle Island Project Nat. Indian Youth Leadership Project grantee, 1996-97. Mem. ALA, NEA, Am. Assn. Sch. Librs., Ariz. Libr. Assn., Ariz. Reading Assn., Tucson Area Reading Coun. (bd. dirs., v.p.-elect 1995-96). Avocations: reading, travel, camping, sewing, crafts. Home: 7810 N Rasmussen Ave Tucson AZ 85741-1448 Office: Liberty Elem School 5495 S Liberty Ave Tucson AZ 85706-3257

SKOTAK, ROBERT F., film production company executive; b. Dearborn, Mich.. Visual effects artist Hollywood, Calif., 1976—; co-founder, pres., visual effects dir. 4-Ward Prodns., Inc., L.A., 1989—. Visual effects artist, designer, supr. (films) Battle Beyond the Stars, Escape from New York, To Be or Not To Be, Strange Invaders, Forbidden World (Top Honor in visual effects French Film Festival 1982), Aliens (Am. and Brit. Acad. award 1986), The Abyss, 1989, (with 4-Ward Prodns.) Tremors, Darkman, 1989, Clifford, True Identity, Cast A Deadly Spell, Terminator 2, (Am. and British Acad. award, Saturn award Acad. of Sci. Fiction 1991), Batman Returns (Am. and British Academy award nominations), 1992, Honey, I Blew Up the Baby, 1992, Dracula, 1992, Heart and Souls, 1993, Fatal Instinct, 1993, No Escape, 1994, The Arrival, 1995, Terminator 2-3D, 1995, Mars Attacks, 1996, The Flood, 1997, Titanic, 1997; visual effects artist, designer, supr., co-prodn. designer (films) Galaxy of Terror, Creature (Acad. Sci. Fiction Best Visual Effects nomination 1984); author: Alien Worlds, 1978; universal filmscript series: This Island Earth, 1990; pub. Fantascene Mag., 1975-78. Mem. Writers Guild Am., Acad. Motion Picture Arts & Scis. Office: 4-Ward Prodns Inc 2801 Hyperion Ave # 104 Los Angeles CA 90027-2571

SKOTHEIM, ROBERT ALLEN, museum administrator; b. Seattle, Jan. 31, 1933; s. Sivert O. and Marjorie F. (Allen) S.; m. Nadine Vail, June 14, 1953; children—Marjorie, Kris, Julia. BA, U. Wash., 1955, MA, 1958, PhD, 1962; LLD (hon.), Hobart and William Smith Colls., Geneva, N.Y., 1975; LittD (hon.), Whitman Coll., 1988; LHD (hon.), Coll. Idaho, 1988, Occidental Coll., 1989, Ill. Wesleyan U., 1990; DFA (hon.), Willamette U., 1989. Prof. history U. Wash., 1962-63; prof. history Wayne State U., Detroit, 1963-66; prof. UCLA, 1966-67, U. Colo., Boulder, 1967-72; provost, dean faculty Hobart and William Smith Colls., 1972-75; pres. Whitman Coll., Walla Walla, Wash., 1975-88, Huntington Libr., Art Collections & Bot. Gardens, San Marino, Calif., 1988—. Author: American Intellectual Histories and Historians, 1966, Totalitarianism and American Social Thought, 1971; Editor: The Historian and the Climate of Opinion, 1969; co-editor: American Social Thought: Sources and Interpretations, 2 vols, 1972. Guggenheim fellow, 1967-68. Mem. Phi Beta Kappa (hon.). Office: Huntington Library Art Collections & Bot Gardens 1151 Oxford Rd San Marino CA 91108-1218

SKOV, ARLIE MASON, petroleum engineer, consultant; b. Perry, Okla., Sept. 21, 1928; s. Arnold and Mary (Mason) S.; m. Luella Luticia Sloan, July 31, 1951; children: Gregory Morgan, Jeffrey Markham, Tamara Kay. BS in Petroleum Engring., U. Okla., 1956; postgrad., U. Va., 1966. Engr. Sohio Petroleum Co., Pauls Valley, Okla., 1957-58; staff engr. Sohio Petroleum Co., Oklahoma City, 1958-65, mgr. spl. projects, 1966-75, asst. mgr. engring., 1975-76; mgr. prodn. planning BP Alaska Inc., San Francisco, 1977-80; project advisor Sohio Gas Pipeline Co., San Francisco, 1980-81; mgr. new tech. devel. Sohio Petroleum Co., San Francisco, 1981-83; dir. prodn. tech. Sohio Petroleum Co. and Standard Oil Prodn., Dallas, 1983-88; sr. cons. BP Exploration, Inc., Houston, 1989-92; owner Arlie M. Skov, Inc. Petroleum Consulting, Houston, 1993—. Recipient Disting. Svc. award Okla. Petroleum Coun. 1973. Mem. AIME (bd. dirs. 1977-79, trustee 1990-92, 95-97) Soc. Petroleum Engrs. (bd. dirs. 1972-74, exec. com. 1990-92, pres. 1991, Disting. mem.), Nat. Petroleum Coun. Avocations: reading, travel. Office: A M Skov Inc 1155 Dairy Ashford St Ste 216 Houston TX 77079-3011

SKOVE, THOMAS MALCOLM, retired manufacturing company financial executive; b. Cleve., June 27, 1925; s. Thomas Malcolm and Ethel C. (Rush) S.; m. Helen Busing, June 12, 1948; children: Margaret, Thomas, Richard, Marcie, Douglas. B.S., Bucknell U., 1949. Controller, treas. Cleve. Twist Drill Co., 1949-68; treas. Acme-Cleve. Corp., 1968-81, dep. treas., 1981-86, treas., 1986-88. Councilman, City of Aurora, Ohio, 1977-83; chmn. Aurora Meml. Library Trust, 1984-89. Served with USN, 1943-46. Mem. Sugar Mill Country Club (pres. 1993-94). Republican. Home: 209 Bromely Cir New Smyrna Beach FL 32168-2006

SKOWRONSKI, VINCENT PAUL, concert violinist, recording artist, executive producer, producer classical recordings; b. Kenosha, Wis., Jan. 22, 1944. MusB, Northwestern U., 1966, MusM, 1968. V.p. Eberley-Skowronski, Inc., Evanston, Ill., 1973-92; internat. dir. mktg. and pub. rels. Vincent Skowronski: Producer of Classical Recordings, Evanston, 1993—; internat. broker rare instruments Strings & Things, Evanston, 1973-92; owner Vincent Skowronski: Fine Violins, Evanston, 1993—; internat. dir. mktg. and pub. rels. EB-SKO Prodns., Evanston, 1978-92; dir. media comm. E-S Mgmt., Evanston, 1985-92; instr. violin Northwestern U., 1969-71; asst. prof. violin U. Wyo., 1971-72; pvt. violin tchr., chamber music coach, lectr., master classes. Solo violinist debut Chgo. Youth Orch., 1959; soloist Chgo. Civic Orch., 1968, guest solo artist Am. Artist Gala, Nat. Puerto Rican TV, 1960; solo guest artist Young Am. Musicians Sta. WKAR-TV Mich. State U., 1966, N.Am. premiere R. Nanes' Rhapsody Pathetique for violin and orch., Chgo. Cultural Ctr., 1994, Beijing, 1994, DePaul U. Ctr., Chgo., 1994, Skowronski in Recital: 20 Years Remembered, Northwestern U., Evanston, Ill., 1994, IV Internat. Tchaikovsky Competition Commemorative Recital-Moscow Remembered: 1970-95, Evanston, Ill., 1995, J.L. Kellogg Sch. Mgmt. Recital Northwestern Univ., Ill., 1996; featured solo artist Artist Showcase, Sta. WGN-TV Chgo., 1966-71; featured soloist Honors Concert-Northwestern U., 1966, guest solo artist A.M. Am., Sta. ABC-TV, 1977—; numerous concerts and recitals in Europe, Cen.Am., Mex. and U.S.; solo guest artist radio appearances include Continental Bank Concerts, Sta. WFMT-FM Chgo., 1983, 85-86, 88, 90, United Airlines Presents, Live!, Sta. WFMT-FM Chgo., Schumann, 1986, Szymanowski, 1987, Bloch, 1988, Saint-Saens, 1989, Grieg, 1991, Excursions in Music: The Artistry of Vincent P. Skowronski, Sta. KQED-FM San Francisco, 1979, Skowronski: Musical Giant, Interlake Profiles, Sta. WFMT-FM Chgo., 1980, Skowronski at 50: A Birthday Celebration Sta. WNIB-FM, Chgo., 1994; guest solo artist Chgo. Musicians Sta. WNIB-FM, 1996-97; guest solo artist, producer, annotator Separate but Equal, 1976, All Brahms, 1977; solo artist, exec. producer, annotator Gentleman Gypsy, 1978, Strauss and Szymanowski, 1979, Franck and Szymanowski, 1982, Skowronski Alone, 1996; producer, annotator Opera Lady I, 1978, Eberley Sings Strauss, 1980, American Girl, 1983, Opera Lady II, 1984; guest performances numerous TV stas. Guest dignitary papal audience, Vatican, Italy, 1995; bd. dirs. Chgo. Youth Orch., 1973-77, v.p., 1974-77; artistic cons. Classical and Protege Symphony Orchs., Chgo., 1994—; adjudicator ice skating shows and competitions Wilmette (Ill.) Park Dist., 1985-89; guest panelist classical performance-career forum Sch. of Music, Northwestern U., Evanston, 1992, 94; guest cons. career symposium Edwin G. Foreman High Sch., Chgo., 1989; mem. mayor's founding com. Evanston Arts Coun., 1974-75. Recipient Excellence in Performance award Northwestern Univ., 1959, Nat. H.S. Inst., 1958, 59, 60, Roy Harris award Inter-Am. U., San German, P.R., 1960, award Am. Fedn. Musicians, 1961, award Soc. Am. Musicians, 1961, McCormick Found. award Chgo. Tribune, 1965, Wade Fetzer award for excellence in performance Northwestern U., 1966, award Crescendo Musical Club, 1967; selected as one of 7 violinists chosen to represent U.S. in IV Internat. Tchaikovsky Competition, Moscow, 1970; guest dignitary Papal Audience, The Vatican, 1995. Mem. Sigma Nu, Internat. Platform Assn.

SKRAMSTAD, HAROLD KENNETH, JR., museum administrator, consultant; b. Washington, June 3, 1941; s. Harold K. and Sarah (Shroat) S.; m. Susan Chappelear, Dec. 28, 1963; children: Robert, Elizabeth. AB, George Washington U., 1963, PhD, 1971. Asst. dir. Am. studies program Smithsonian Instn., Washington, 1969-71, spl. asst. to dir. Nat. Mus. Am. History, 1971, chief spl. projects Nat. Mus. Am. History, chief exhibit programs Nat. Mus. Am. History, 1971-74; dir. Chgo. Hist. Soc., 1974-80; pres. Henry Ford Mus. and Greenfield Village, Dearborn, Mich., 1981—; mem. Nat. Coun. on Humanities, 1994; mem. mus. mgmt. adv. com. J. Paul Getty Trust, L.A., 1984-90. Chmn. bd. Met. Detroit Conv. and Visitors Bur., 1993, chmn., mem. exec. com., 1985—; trustee Coll. Art and Design, Detroit, 1981—; mem. Mich. Travel Commn., 1989—. Recipient Charles Frankel prize Nat. Endowment for the Humanities, 1992. Mem. Am. Assn. Mus. (v.p. 1984-88, accreditation commn. 1982, ethics commn. 1992-93), Smithsonian Instn. Nat. Air and Space Mus. (pub. programming adv. com. 1990—), Nat. Coun. on the Humanitites, 1994, Greater Detroit and Windsor Japan-Am. Soc. (bd. dirs. 1989—), Detroit Club, Cosmos Club (Washington). Home: Stone Mill 20900 Oakwood Blvd Dearborn MI 48124 Office: Henry Ford Mus Greenfield Village Dearborn MI 48124

SKRAMSTAD, ROBERT ALLEN, retired oceanographer; b. Montevideo, Minn., Apr. 3, 1937; s. Vernon Donald and Ann May (Tollefsen) S. Student, St. Olaf Coll., 1958-60; BS in Geol. Engring., S.D. Sch. Mines and Tech., 1965. Geologist Naval Oceanographic Office, Washington, 1965-70, oceanographer, 1970-75; oceanographer Naval Oceanographic Office, Bay St. Louis, Miss., 1975-82, phys. scientist, 1982-95; ret., 1995. With U.S. Army, 1957-60. Mem. Am. Soc. Photogrammetry and Remote Sensing, Nat. Geographic Soc. Republican. Avocations: photography, jogging, travel, mineral collecting. Home: 1308 Birch St Marshall MN 56258-0746

SKRATEK, SYLVIA PAULETTE, mediator, arbitrator, dispute systems designer; b. Detroit, Dec. 23, 1950; d. William Joseph and Helen (Meskauskas) S.; m. John Wayne Gullion, Dec. 21,1984. BS, Wayne State U., 1971; MLS, Western Mich. U., 1976; PhD, U. Mich., 1985. Media specialist Jackson (Mich.) Pub. Schs., 1971-79; contract specialist Jackson County Edn. Assn., 1976-79; field rep. Mich. Edn. Assn., E.Lansing, 1979-81; contract adminstr. Wash. Edn. Assn., Federal Way, 1981-85, regional coord., 1985-88, program adminstr., from 1988; dir. mediation svcs. Conflict Mgmt. Inst., Lake Oswego, Ore., 1986-87; exec. dir. N.W. Ctr. for Conciliation, 1987-88; served in Wash. State Senate, 1990-94; tng. cons. City of Seattle, 1986—; trustee Group Health Coop. of Puget Sound, Wash., 1984-87; sole proprietor Skratek & Assocs., 1980—; pres. Resolutions Internat., 1990-96; v.p. Mediation Rsch. and Edn. Project, Inc., 1990—. Contbr. articles to legal jours. Mem. Soc. for Profls. in Dispute Resolution, Indsl. Rels. Rsch. Assn. Avocations: swimming, piano, Asian cooking, cross country skiing.

SKREBNESKI, VICTOR, photographer; b. Chgo., Dec. 17, 1929; s. Joseph and Anna (Casper) S. Student, Art Inst. Chgo., 1945, Inst. Design, 1947. Propr. Skrebneski Studio, Chgo., 1956—. Author: Skrebneski, 1969, The Human Form, 1973, Skrebneski Portraits: A Matter of Record, 1978. Exhbns. include Charles Cowles Gallery, N.Y.C., 1992. Bd. dirs. Chgo. Internat. Film Festival. Recipient award Art Directors Soc., 1958-75. Mem. Dirs. Guild Am., Soc. Photographers in Communications. Club: Arts (Chgo.). Address: 1350 N La Salle Dr Chicago IL 60610-1911

SKRETNY, WILLIAM MARION, federal judge; b. Buffalo, Mar. 8, 1945; s. William S. and Rita E. (Wyroski) S.; m. Carol Ann Mergenhagen; children: Brian Alexander, Brooke Ann, Nina Clare. AB, Canisius Coll., 1966; JD, Howard U., 1969; LLM, Northwestern U., 1972. Bar: Ill. 1969, U.S. Dist. Ct. (no. dist) Ill. 1969, N.Y. 1972, U.S. Ct. Appeals (7th cir.) 1972, U.S. Dist. Ct. (we. dist.) N.Y. 1973, U.S. Ct. Appeals (2d cir.) 1976, U.S. Supreme Ct. 1980. Asst. U.S. atty. Office of U.S. Atty. No. Dist. Ill., Chgo., 1971-73; asst. U.S. atty. Office U.S. Atty. We. Dist. N.Y., Buffalo, 1973-81, 1st asst., 1975-81; gen. ptnr. Duke, Holzman, Yaeger & Radlin, Buffalo, 1981-83; 1st dep. dist. atty. Office Dist. Atty Erie County, Buffalo, 1983-88; assoc. Gross, Shuman, Brizdle and Gilfillan, PC, Buffalo, 1988; of counsel Cox, Barrell, Buffalo, 1989-90; judge U.S. Dist. Ct. (we. dist.) N.Y., Buffalo, 1990—; task force atty. tng. Office U.S. Atty Gen., 1978; spl. counsel U.S. Atty Gen.'s Advocacy Inst., 1979; staff atty. Office Spl. Prosecutor, Dept. Justice, Washington, 1980; faculty advisor Nat. Coll. D.A.s, Houston, 1987; lectr. Northwestern U., Chgo., 1980; jud. conf. com. on security, space and facilities, 1994. Contbr. articles to profl. jours. Bd. dirs. Sudden Infant Death Found. We. N.Y., 1979, Cerebral Palsy Foun. We. N.Y., 1985; co-v.p. PTA Harlem Rd. Sch., 1982; chmn. major corps. divsn. Studio Arena Theatre, Buffalo, 1982; chmn. Polish Culture, Canisius Coll., 1985, trustee, 1989; pres. Canisius Coll. Alumni Assn., 1989; regional chmn. Cath. Charities Appeal, 1986-87. Scholar Howard U., 1966; fellow Ford Found., 1969; named Citizen of Yr. Am Pol Eagle Newspaper, 1977, 90, Disting. Grad. Nat. Cath. Edn. Assn. Dept. Elem. Sch., 1991, Disting. Alumnus Canisius Coll., 1993. Mem. ABA, Fed. Bar Assn., Fed. Judges Assn., Western N.Y. Trial Lawyers Assn., Erie County Bar Assn., Chgo. Bar Assn., Thomas More Legal Soc. (pres. 1980), Advocates Soc. Western N.Y., Di Gamma, Phi Alpha Delta. Republican. Roman Catholic. Office: US District Court 68 Court St Rm 507 Buffalo NY 14202-3406

SKRIP, LINDA JEAN, nursing administrator; b. Neenah, Wis., Apr. 16, 1963; d. Donald Charles and Kathryn Amelia Patrikus; m. Stephen Michael, May 21, 1988. BSN, U. Wis., 1986. Staff nurse U. Hosp. Ill., Chgo., 1986-87; asst. clin. nurse mgr. Northwestern Meml. Hosp., Chgo., 1987-88; nursing coord. Pitt County Meml. Hosp., Greenville, N.C., 1988-91; nursing supr. Chesapeake (Va.) Gen. Hosp., 1991-92, case mgmt. coord., 1992—, cert. case mgr., 1993—. Roman Catholic. Avocations: tennis, travel. Home: 1253 Smokey Mountain Trl Chesapeake VA 23320-8187

SKROMME, LAWRENCE H., consulting agricultural engineer; b. Roland, Iowa, Aug. 26, 1913; s. Austin G. and Ingeborg B. (Holmedal) S.; m. Margaret Elizabeth Gleason, June 24, 1939; children: Cherlyn Sue Granrose, Inga Jean Hill, Karen Ann Sequino. B.S. with honors, Iowa State U., Ames, 1937. Registered profl. engr., Pa. Design and test engr. Goodyear Tire and Rubber Co., Akron, Ohio, 1937-41; project engr., asst. chief engr. Harry Ferguson Inc., Detroit, 1941-51; chief engr. Sperry New Holland div. Sperry Corp., New Holland, Pa., 1951-61, v.p. engring., 1961-78; cons. agrl. engr. Lancaster, Pa., 1978—; mem. adv. bd. U.S. Congress Com. on Sci. and Tech., 1989—; cons. AID, World Bank, others, 1978-85, Saudi Arabia, 1985-86. Patentee; contbr. articles to profl. jours. Rsch. adv. com. U.S. Dept. Agr., Washington, 1964-68; gov.'s com. agr. and land preservation Gov. of Pa., 1965-69; bd. dirs. awards com. Engrs. Joint Coun., N.Y.C., 1967-75; dir., v.p., pres. Farm and Home Found. Lancaster County, 1968—; Lancaster County Agrl. Land Preservation Bd., 1978—, sec.-treas. 1989—. Mem. Am. Soc. Agrl. Engrs. (gold medal 1974, v.p. 1952-55, pres. 1959-60, fellow 1965—), NAE (peer and membership com. 1978—), Nat. Soc. Profl. Engrs., Internat. Assn. Agrl. Engrs. (v.p. 1974-79, pres. farm machine div.), Am. Soc. Engring. Edn., Phi Kappa Phi, Alpha Zeta, Tau Beta Pi. Republican. Methodist. Avocations: collecting old tools and antiques, farm machinery history.

SKROWACZEWSKI, STANISLAW, conductor, composer; b. Lwow, Poland, Oct. 3, 1923; came to U.S., 1960; s. Pawel and Zofia (Karszniewicz) S.; m. Krystyna Jarosz, Sept. 6, 1956; children: Anna, Paul, Nicholas. Diploma faculty philosophy, U. Lwow, 1945; diploma faculties composition and conducting, Acad. Music Lwow, 1945, Conservatory at Krakow, Poland, 1946; L.H.D., Hamline U., 1963, Macalester Coll., 1972; L.H.D. hon. doctorate, U. Minn. Guest condr. in Europe, S.A., U.S., 1947—; Composer, 1931—, pianist, 1928—, violinist, 1934—, condr., 1939—; permanent condr., music dir. Wroclaw (Poland) Philharmonic, 1946-47, Katowice (Poland) Nat. Philharmonic, 1949-54, Krakow Philharmonic, 1955-56, Warsaw Nat. Philharmonic Orch., 1957-59, Minnesota Orch., 1960-79; prin. condr., mus. adviser Halle Orch., Manchester, Eng., 1984-91; musical advisor St. Paul Chamber Orchestra, 1986-87; first symphony and overture for orch. written at age 8, played by Lwow Philharm. Orch., 1931. Composer: 4 symphonies Prelude and Fugue for Orchestra (conducted first performance Paris), 1948, Overture, 1947 (2d prize Szymanowski Concours, Warsaw 1947); Cantiques des Cantiques, 1951, String Quartet, 1953 (2d Prize Internat. Concours Composers, Belgium 1953), Suite Symphonique, 1954 (first prize, gold medal Composers Competition Moscow 1957), Music at Night, 1954, Ricercari Notturni, 1978 (3d prize Kennedy Center Friedheim Competition, Washington), Concerti for Clarinet and Orch., 1980, Violin Concerto, 1985, Concerto for Orch., 1985, Fanfare for Orch., 1987, Sextett for Oboe, Violin, Viola, Orchestra, 1980, String Trio for Violin, Viola, 1990, Triple Concerto for Violin, Clarinet, Piano, Orchestra, 1992, Fantasie per Tre (Flute, Oboe, Cello), 1993, Chamber Concerto, 1993, Passacaglia Immaginaria for Orch., 1995; also music for theatre, motion pictures, songs and piano sonatas, English horn concerto; rec. by Mercury, Columbia, RCA Victor, Vox, EMI, Angel. Recipient nat. prize for artistic activity Poland, 1953; First prize Santa Cecilia Internat. Concours for Condrs., Rome, 1956. Mem. Union Polish Composers, Internat. Soc. Modern Music, Nat. Assn. Am. Composers-Condrs., Am. Music Center. Office: Orch Hall 1111 Nicollet Mall Minneapolis MN 55403-2406

SKUBE, MICHAEL, journalist, critic; b. Springfield, Ill.; 1 child, Noah. Degree in polit. sci., La. State U. Former tchr. math and sci. La.; formerly with U.S. Customs Svc., Miami, Fla.; book reviewer Miami Herald, from 1974; Raleigh (N.C.) bur. chief Winston-Salem (N.C.) Jour., 1978-82; editorial writer The News and Observer, Raleigh, 1982-86, became book editor, 1986; columnist, critic Atlanta Jour. and Constn., 1987—. Recipient Pulitzer Prize for criticism, 1989, Disting. Writing award for commentary and column writing Am. Soc. Newspaper Editors, 1989, 1st Pl. award for columns N.C. Press Assn. Office: Atlanta Jour and Constn 72 Marietta St NW Atlanta GA 30303-2804*

SKULINA, THOMAS RAYMOND, lawyer; b. Cleve., Sept. 14, 1933; s. John J. and Mary B. (Vesely) S. AB, John Carroll U., 1955; JD, Case Western Res. U., 1959, LLM, 1962. Bar: Ohio 1959, U.S. Supreme Ct. 1964, ICC 1965. Ptnr. Skulina & Stringer, Cleve., 1967-72, Riemer Oberdank & Skulina, Cleve., 1978-81, Skulina, Fillo, Walters & Negrelli, 1981-86, Skulina & McKeon, Cleve., 1986-90, Skulina & Hill, Cleve., 1990—; atty. Penn Cen. Transp. Co., Cleve., 1960-65, asst. gen. atty., 1965-78, trial counsel, 1965-76; with Consol. Rail Corp., 1976-78; tchr. comml. law Practicing Law Inst., N.Y.C., 1970; practicing arbitrator Am. Arbitration Assn., 1987—, Fed. Mediation and Conciliation Svc., 1990—; arbitrator Mcpl. Securities Rulemaking Bd., 1994—, N.Y. Stock Exch., 1995—, NASD, 1996—; mediator NASD, 1997—, AAA Comml., 1997—; mediator vol. panel EEOC, 1997—. Contbr. articles to legal jours. Income tax and fed. fund coord. City of Warrensville Heights, Ohio, 1970-77; spl. counsel City of North Olmstead, Ohio, 1971-75, spl. counsel to Ohio Atty. Gen., 1983-93, Cleve. Charter Rev. Commn., 1988; pres. Civil Svc. Commn., Cleve., 1977-86, referee, 1986—; fact-finder State Employees Rels. Bd., Ohio, 1986—. With U.S. Army, 1959. Mem. ABA (R.R. and motor carrier com. 1988-96, jr. chmn. 1989-96), Soc. Profls. in Dispute Resolution, Cleve. Bar Assn. (grievance com. 1987-93, chmn. 1989-90, trustee 1993-96), Ohio Bar Assn. (bd. govs. litigation sect. 1986-96, negligence law com. 1989-96, ethics and profl. responsibility com. 1990—, ADR com. 1996—), Fed. Bar Assn., Am. Arbitration Assn. (labor panel 1988—), Nat. Assn. R.R. Trial Counsel, Internat. Assn. Law and Sci., Pub. Sector Labor Rels. Assn., Indsl. Rels. Rsch. Assn. Democrat. Roman Catholic. Home: 3162 W 165th St Cleveland OH 44111-1016 Office: Skulina & Hill 24803 Detroit Rd Cleveland OH 44145-2547

SKUPINSKI, BOGDAN KAZIMIERZ, artist; b. Poland, July 16, 1942; came to U.S., 1971, naturalized, 1976; s. Kazimierz Stanislaw and Jrena Lucja (Kanar) S. BA, Acad. Fine Arts, Krakow, Poland, 1969, MA, 1971; cert., Ecole Nationale Superieure de Beaux Arts, Paris, 1971. Pres. Bogdan & Assoc., N.Y.C. Graphic artist: painting Proclamation, 1968, Escape, 1968, Return, 1969, Good Journey, (permanent collection N.J. State Mus., 1971, The Stable, (permanent collection Library of Congress), 1971, Nouvel Ordre, 1970 (annual prize Ministry of Cultural Affairs of France), Gare du Nord, 1970 (award Commn. Fine Arts. Paris), anti-war themes, 1969-76; life and work of John F. Kennedy and Albert Michelson, 1969-76. Recipient Grand Prix, Nat. Salon Young Artists, 1968, People's Choice award 2d Nat. Graphic Rev., Karkow, 1969, ann. Bartoczek and Babrowski award Polish Ministry Art and Culture, 1970, lst prize for prints and drawings Nat. Conn. Acad. Exhbn., Hartford, 1971, medal Internat. Exhbn. Graphic Art, Frechen, Fed. Republic Germany, 1976, Presdl. Medal of Merit, 1990; fellow Ecole Nat. Superieure Beaux Arts. Fellow Pratt Inst.; mem. NAD (Cannon prize for graphics 1971), Kosciuszko Found., Rep. Presdl. Task Force. Roman Catholic. Home: Cathedral Sta PO Box 849 215 W 104th St New York NY 10025-4230

SKUPSKY, STANLEY, laser fusion scientist. Group leader theory and computation lab. laser energetics U. Rochester, N.Y. Recipient award for Excellence in Plasma Physics Rsch. Am. Phys. Soc., 1993. Office: U Rochester Lab for Laser Energetics Rochester NY 14627

SKURDENIS, JULIANN VERONICA, librarian, educator, writer, editor; b. Bklyn., July 13, 1942; d. Julius J. and Anna M. (Zilys) S.; A.B. with honors, Coll. New Rochelle, 1964; M.S., Columbia U., 1966; M.A., Hunter Coll., 1974; m. Lawrence J. Smircich, Aug. 21, 1965 (div. July 1978); m. 2d, Paul J. Lalli, Oct. 1, 1978; 1 adopted dau., Kathryn Leila Skurdenis-Lalli. Young adult librarian Bklyn. Pub. Library, 1964-66; periodicals librarian, instr. Kingsborough Community Coll., Bklyn., 1966-67; acquisitions librarian Pratt Inst., Bklyn., 1967-68; acquisitions librarian, asst. prof. Bronx (N.Y.) Community Coll., 1968-75, head tech. services, assoc. prof., 1975—, acting dir. Libr. Resource Learning Ctr., 1994—. N.Y. State fellow, 1960-66, Columbia U. fellow, 1964-66, Pratt Inst. fellow, 1965. Mem. AAUP, Library Assn. CUNY (chairwoman numerous coms.), Archaeol. Inst. Am. Author: Walk Straight Through the Square, 1976, More Walk Straight Through the Square, 1977; contbg. editor Internat. Travel News, 1989—, Travel Your Way/New York Times, 1996—; travel editor Archaeology mag., 1986-89; contbr. over 250 travel, hist., and archaeol. pieces. Avocations: archaeology, travel, travel writing. Office: CUNY Bronx CC University Ave Bronx NY 10453-6994

SKURLA, LAURUS See LAURUS

SKUTNIK, BOLESH, optics scientist, lay worker, lawyer; b. Passaic, N.J., Aug. 19, 1941; s. Boleslaw Stanley and Helen Marie (Dzierzynska) S.; m. Phyllis Victoria Wojciechowski, Sept. 2, 1967 (div. July 1991); children: Pam, Janeen, Todd; m. Anita Marie Bacon, Aug. 2, 1997. BS, Seton Hall U., 1962; MS, Yale U., 1964, PhD, 1967; JD, U. Conn., 1995. Bar: N.Y. 1996, Conn. 1996. Chief scientist Ensign Bickford Coating Co., Simsbury, Conn., 1979-91; prin. B.J. Assocs., New Britain, Conn., 1991—; patent atty., chief Sci. Fiberoptic Fabrications, Inc., East Longmeadow, Mass., 1995-97, dir. rsch., dir. patents and licensing, 1997—; lector, mem. parish coun. St. Catherine of Siena, West Simsbury, Conn., 1980-85, St. Maurice, New Britain, Conn., 1985—; chmn., del. synod Archdioces of Hartford, Conn., 1990-96; chmn. parish Holy Family Retreat League, New Britain, 1989—; pres. Enbic Employees Credit Union, Simsbury, 1988-91; asst. prof. chemistry Fairfield U., Conn., 1973-79; rep. AYA, 1997—. Patentees in field; contbr. articles to profl. jours. Interviewer Yale Alumni Schs. Com., L.I. and Hartford, Conn., 1969—; mem. Yale Assn. of Yale Alumni Rep., New Britain Club, 1997—. Mem. ABA (subcom. chair 1993, 94, 96), Conn. Bar Assn., N.Y. State Bar Assn., Conn. Patent Lawyers Assn., Am. Intellectual Property Lawyers Assn., Nat. Coun. Intellectual Property Lawyers Assn., Soc. Photo-optical Engrs., Am. Ceramic Soc., (coord. symposium 1991), Materials Rsch. Soc. (chair symposium 1987-89), Am. Chem. Soc. (alt. coun. 1988-90. sect. chair 1994, vice chair 1993, bd. dirs. 1985—), Porsche Club Am. (various positions Conn. Valley region), Yale Club New Britain (dir. 1994—). Democrat. Roman Catholic. Home: PO Box 602 New Britain CT 06050 Office: Fiber Optic Fabrications Inc 515 Shaker Rd East Longmeadow MA 01028-3126 *The human spirit is stronger than anything that can happen to it.*

SKUTT, THOMAS JAMES, insurance company executive; b. Omaha, Nov. 1, 1930; s. Vestor Joseph and Angela (Anderson) S.; m. Jeanne Cecille Plunkett, Sept. 3, 1955; children: Mary Elizabeth Sutton, Kimberly Ann Davis, Thomas V.J. BA, Yale U., 1952; LLB, Creighton U., 1957; postgrad., Harvard U., 1979. Ptnr. Spire, Morrow & Skutt, Omaha, 1961-69; with Mut. of Omaha, 1969—, exec. v.p., sec., 1980-81, vice chmn. bd. dirs., 1981-84, 1st vice chmn. bd. dirs., chief exec. officer, 1984-86; chmn. bd. dirs., chief exec. officer Mutual of Omaha Ins. Co., 1986-96; chmn. bd. dirs., chief exec. officer United of Omaha subs. Mut. of Omaha, 1986-96; chmn. bd. dirs. United Mutual of Omaha Life Ins. Co., 1996—; chmn. bd., dir. United of Omaha Life Ins. Co., 1996—; bd. dirs. United of Omaha, Mut. Omaha Ins. Co., Companion Life Ins. Co., United World Life Ins. Co. Past pres., selected Citizen of Yr., Mid-Am. Coun. Boy Scouts Am., 1987, 89, 93.mem. exec. bd. 1980—; mem. consultation com. SAC, Omaha, 1984; bd. dirs. Omaha Zool. Soc., 1978—, pres., 1987-88, past. bd. dirs.; gen. chmn. campaign United Way of Midlands, 1979-80, bd. dirs., 1981—; bd. dirs. Creighton U., Omaha, 1983—. Recipient Humanitarian award Nat. Conf. Christians and Jews, 1992. Mem. Greater Omaha C. of C. (bd. dirs. 1979—, chmn. 1983, past chmn.), Mpls. Club, Yale Club N.Y.C., Knights of Ak-Sar-Ben (bd. govs. 1985, King XCVI 1992). Republican. Roman Catholic. Avocations: golf, tennis. Home: 400 N 62nd St Omaha NE 68132-1955 Office: Mut Omaha Ins Co 10250 Regency Cir Ste 175 Omaha NE 68114-3735*

SKVORECKY, JOSEF VACLAV, English literature educator, novelist; b. Nachod, Czechoslovakia, Sept. 27, 1924; arrived Can., 1969; s. Josef Karel and Anna (Kurazova) S.; m. Zdenka Josefa Salivarova, Mar. 30, 1958. Ph.D., Charles U., Czechoslovakia, 1951; LHD (hon.), SUNY, 1986; postgrad., Masaryk U., 1991, U. Calgary, 1992, U. Toronto, 1992. Vis. lectr. U. Toronto, Ont., Can., 1969-70; writer-in-residence U. Toronto, 1970-71, assoc. prof., 1971-75, prof. English, 1975-90; prof. emeritus, 1990—; lectr. on lit. topics Voice of Am., 1973—; adv. to Pres. Vaclav Havel, 1990. Editor: Sixty Eight Publ. Corp., Toronto, 1972—; author: The End of the Nylon Age, 1967, Republic of Whores, 1969, The Miracle Game, 1972, The End of Lieutenant Boruvka, 1975, The Swell Season, 1975, The Bass Saxophone, 1979, The Cowards, 1980, The Return of Lieutenant Boruvka, 1980, The Engineer of Human Souls, 1984, Miss Silver's Past, 1985, Dvorak in Love, 1986, The Bride from Texas, 1992, Headed for the Blues, 1996, The Two Murders in My Double Life, 1996; short story collections: The Menorah, 1964, The Life of High society, 1965, The Mournful Demeanor of Lieutenant Boruvka, 1966, A Babylonian Story, 1967, The Bitter World, 1969, Sins for Father Knox, 1973, Oh, My Papa! 1972, The Edenvale Stories, 1996; plays: The New Men and Women CBC Radio 1977, God in Your House, 1980 (1st prize Multicultural Theatre Festival Hamilton 1980); films: The Tank Battalion, 1991, The Swell Season, 1994; essays: Reading Detecive Stories, 1965, They-Which Is We, 1968, All the Bright Young Men and Women, 1972, Working Overtime, 1979, Talkin' Moscow Blues, 1989. Decorated Order of the White Lion; apptd. mem. Order of Can., 1992; Recipient Neustadt Internat. prize for lit., U. Okla., 1980, Gov. Gen. Can.'s award, 1985, lit. prize Echoing Green Found., 1990; Guggenheim fellow, 1980. Fellow Royal Soc. Can.; mem. Can. Writers' Union, Authors' League Am., Crime Writers Can., Mystery Writers Am., The Internat. PEN Club, Can. br. Czechosolovak Nat. Assn. Can. (mem. Presidium), Coun. Free Czechoslovakia (mem. Presidium), Order of Can. Progressive Conservative. Roman Catholic. Avocation: swing music. Home: 487 Sackville St, Toronto, ON Canada M4X 1T6

SKWIERSKY, PAUL, accountant; b. N.Y.C., Aug. 14, 1925; s. Abraham and Dora (Rainer) S.; m. Gloria Evelyn Lederman, Dec. 27, 1947; children: Janet S., Denise C. Skwiersky Cohen. BS, NYU, 1948. CPA, N.Y., N.J. Mng. ptnr. Benjamin Nadel & Co., N.Y.C., 1942-87, Skwiersky, Alpert & Bressler, N.Y.C., 1987—; bd. dirs. Philip & Janice Levin Found., North Plainfield, N.J., Darcy Found., Inc., N.Y.C., 1980-87, Levin Mgmt. Corp., North Plainfield, Allstate Constrn. Corp., North Plainfield; panelist, arbitrator Am. Arbitration Assn., N.Y.C. Dir. Birchwood Park Civic Assn., Syosset, N.Y., 1962. Sgt. U.S. Army, 1943-46. Mem. Fiber Producers Credit Assn., Textile Distbrs. Assn., Inc., N.Y. Credit & Fin. Mgmt. Assn., N.Y. State Soc. CPAs, Masons (master 1977-79), Fountains of Palm Beach Country Club. Avocations: reading, travel, golf. Office: Skwiersky Alpert Bressler 462 7th Ave New York NY 10018-7606

SKYLSTAD, WILLIAM S., bishop; b. Omak, Wash., Mar. 2, 1934; s. Stephen Martin and Reneldes Elizzbeth (Danzl) S. Student, Pontifical Coll., Josephinum, Worthington, Ohio; M.Ed., Gonzaga U. Ordained priest Roman Catholic Ch., 1960; asst. pastor Pullman, Wash., 1960-62; tchr. Mater Cleri Sem., 1961-68, rector, 1968-74; pastor Assumption Parish, Spokane, 1974-76; chancellor Diocese of Spokane, 1976-77; ordained bishop, 1977; bishop of Yakima, Wash., 1977-90, Spokane, Wash., 1990—. Office: Diocese of Spokane PO Box 1453 1023 W Riverside Ave Spokane WA 99210-1103 Home: 1025 W Cleveland Ave Spokane WA 99205-3320*

SKYLV, GRETHE KROGH, rheumatologist, anthropologist; b. Copenhagen, Denmark, May 31, 1938; d. Aage Krogh and Herdis Fischer (Lindeskov) Christoffersen; m. Axel Skylv, Jan. 12, 1962 (div. Feb. 1994); children: Lise, Kirsten, Mikael; m. Klaus Bruhn Jensen, Oct. 15, 1994. MD, U. Copenhagen, 1967, MA in Anthropology, 1990. Resident various hosps., Copenhagen, 1967-79; pvt. practice Hillerod, Denmark, 1979-84; dept. head Rehab. Ctr. for Torture Victims, Copenhagen, 1985-92; cons. Danish Red Cross, 1993—; rsch. scholar on cross-cultural interpersonal comm. Faculty of Humanities, U. Copenhagen, 1994—; cons. Orgn. for Manual Therapy, Denmark, 1985—, Internat. Rehab. Medicine Assn., 1991—, various Danish treatment ctrs. for torture victims & refugees, 1993—; com. mem. North-South issues Univ.-wide rsch., 1995-96; mem. interdisciplinary rsch. groups comm. med. contexts, 1994—; bd. dirs. Network for Interdisciplinary Qualitative Rsch., Denmark, 1989—. Guest editor: Danish Soc. for Anthropology Soc. Jour., 1988-89; contbr. articles to profl. jours. Recipient Honorary award Cranio-Facial Pain Ctr. 1990. Fellow European Assn. Social Anthropologists, Danish Med. Assn. (bd. for ethnic minorities 1996—), Danish Manual Therapy Orgn., Danish Assn. for Rheumatology, Danish Assn. Internal Medicine, Danish Soc. for Social Anthropology, Physicians for Human Rights. Avocation: black belt in jujitsu. Home: Mosesvinget 54, DK-2400 Copenhagen Denmark

SLAATTÈ, HOWARD ALEXANDER, minister, philosophy educator; b. Evanston, Ill., Oct. 18, 1919; s. Iver T. and Esther (Larsen) S.; m. Mildred Gegenheimer, June 20, 1951; children: Elaine Slaatte Tran, Mark, Paul. A.A., Kendall Coll., 1940; B.A. cum laude, U. N.D., 1942; B.D. cum laude, Drew U., 1945, Ph.D., 1956; Drew fellow, Mansfield Coll., Oxford (Eng.) U., 1949-50. Ordained to ministry Meth. Ch. as elder, 1943. Pastor Detroit Conf. United Meth. Ch., 1950-65; assoc. prof. systematic theology Temple U., 1956-60; vis. prof., prof. philosophy and religion McMurry Coll. (now named McMurry U.), 1960-65; prof. dept. philosophy Marshall U., Huntington, W.Va., 1965-89, prof. emeritus, 1989—, chmn. dept., 1966-81, mem. grad. council, 1970-73, mem. research bd., 1974-76, mem. acad. standards and policy com., 1975-77, research grantee, 1976, 77; mem. bd. Campus Christian Center, 1973-75; prof. ethics St. Leo (Fla.) Coll., 1993; lectr. Traverse City (Mich.) State Hosp., 1966-71, Am. Ontoanalytical Assn. internat. conf., Acapulco, Mex., 1970, World Congress Logotherapy, San Diego, 1980, other orgns.; mem. W.Va. Conf., United Meth. Ch., 1965-85. Author: Time and Its End, 1962, Fire in the Brand, 1963, The Pertinence of the Paradox, 1968, The Paradox of Existentialist Theology, 1971, Modern Science and the Human Condition, 1974, The Arminian Arm of Theology, 1977, The Dogma of Immaculate Perception, 1979, Discovering Your Real Self, 1980, The Seven Ecumenical Councils, 1980, The Creativity of Consciousness, 1983, Contemporary Philosophies of Religion, 1986, Time, Existence and Destiny, 1988, Critical Survey of Ethics, 1988; co-author: The Philosophy of Martin Heidegger, 1983, Religious Issues in Contemporary Philosophy, 1988, Our Cultural Cancer and Its Cure, 1995, A Re-Appraisal of Kierkegaard, 1995; contbr. Analecta Frankliana, 1981; gen. editor: (series) Contemporary Existentialism; contbr. to theol. and philos. jours. Mem. W.Va. Conf. United Meth. Ch., 1966—; bd. dirs. Inst. for Advanced Philos. Research, 1979-90; chmn. bd. dirs. Salvation Army of Huntington, W. Va. Recipient Outstanding Educators of Am. award, 1975, Profl. Excellence award Faculty Merit Found., State of W.Va., 1986; named to Honorable Order of Ky. Colonels, W.Va. Ambassador of Good Will; named Internat. Man of Yr., 1993; NSF fellow, 1965, Benedum Found. rsch. grantee, 1970, NSF rsch.-grantee, 1965, 71. Mem. W.Va. Philos. Assn. (pres., 1966-67, 83-84), Am. Philos. Assn., AAUP, Am. Acad. Religion. Home: 14123 Oak Knoll St Spring Hill FL 34609-3157 *Most knowledge is relative, a balanced existential position with empirical implications, except for the divine Absolute encountered by faith in existence. The revealed principles opened up thereby, especially the ultimacy of sacrifical love (Agape), give basis and motivation for vital morality and a healthy culture. True freedom springs from commitment to these principles.*

SLABY, LILLIAN FRANCES, home finance counselor, real estate professional; b. Cleve., June 9, 1931; d. Bismarck Otto and Marie Theresa (Emo) Newman; m. Jack Glenn Slaby, Sept. 22, 1951; children: Lonna, Jan, Jeffrey, James, Jack. Student, Dyke Coll., 1949-50. Lic. realtor, Ohio. Home fin. counselor, real estate assoc. HGM Hilltop, Rocky River, Ohio, 1978-88, Realty One, Westlake, Ohio, 1988-91; with Riveredge Realty, Rocky River, Ohio, 1993—. Mem. Internat. Graphoanalysis Soc. (cert.), World Assn. of Document Examiners. Roman Catholic. Avocations: landscaping design, fashion design, health sciences. Home: 5106 NW 16th Pl Gainesville FL 32605-3302 Office: Riveredge Realty Detroit Rd Rocky River OH 44116

SLACK, DONALD CARL, agricultural engineer, educator; b. Cody, Wyo., June 25, 1942; s. Clarence Raibon and Clara May (Beightol) S.; m. Marion Arline Kimball, Dec. 19, 1964; children: Jonel Marie, Jennifer Michelle. BS in Agrl. Engring., U. Wyo., 1965; MS in Agrl. Engring., U. Ky., 1968, PhD in Agrl. Engring., 1975. Registered profl. engr., Ky., Ariz. Asst. civil engr. City of Los Angeles, 1965; research specialist U. Ky., Lexington, 1966-70; agrl. engring. advisor U. Ky., Tha Phra, Thailand, 1970-73; research asst. U. Ky., Lexington, 1973-75; from asst. prof. to assoc. prof. agrl. engring. U. Minn., St. Paul, 1975-84; prof. U. Ariz., Tucson, 1984—, head dept. agrl. and biosystems engring., 1991—; tech. advisor Ariz. Dept. Water Resources, Phoenix, 1985—, Tucson active mgmt. area, 1996—; cons. Winrock Internat., Morrilton, Ark., 1984, Water Mgmt. Synthesis II, Logan, Utah, 1985, Desert Agrl. Tech. Systems, Tucson, 1985—, Portek Hermosillo, Mex., 1989—, World Bank, Washington, 1992—, Malawi Environ. Monitoring Project, 1996, Mex. Inst. for Water Tech., 1997; dep. program support mgr. Rsch. Irrigation Support Project for Asia and the Near East, Arlington, Va., 1987-94; mem. adv. team Cearan Found. for Meteorology and Hydrology, Fortaleza, Brazil, 1995—; mem. internat. adv. panel Matrou Resources Mgmt. Project, World Bank, Egypt, 1996—. Contbr. articles to profl. jours. Fellow ASCE (Outstanding Jour. Paper award 1988), Am. Soc. Agrl. Engrs. (Ariz. sect. Engr. of Yr. 1993); mem. Am. Geophys. Union, Am. Soc. Agronomy, Soil Sci. Soc. Am., Am. Soc. Engring. Edn., SAR, Brotherhood of Knights of the Vine (master knight), Sigma Xi, Tau Beta Pi, Alpha Epsilon, Gamma Sigma Delta. Democrat. Lutheran. Achievements include 3 patents pending; developer of infrared based irrigation scheduling device. Avocations: hunting, camping, hiking, model railroading. Home: 9230 E Visco Pl Tucson AZ 85710-3167 Office: U Ariz Agrl Biosystems Engring Tucson AZ 85721 *Personal philosophy: Don't take yourself too seriously and don't take anyone else too seriously either.*

SLACK, EDWARD DORSEY, III, financial systems professional, consultant; b. Fairmont, W.Va., June 2, 1942; s. Edward Dorsey Jr. and Margaret Elaine (Higgs) S.; m. Donna Jean Carter, Oct. 19, 1944; children: Ted, Robyn. BS in Indsl. Engring., W.Va. U., 1965, postgrad., 1965-66. Registered profl. engr., W.Va. Assoc. systems and procedures analyst Westinghouse Atomic Power divs., Pitts., 1966-69; systems and procedures analyst Westinghouse Nuclear Energy Systems, Pitts., 1969-72, sr. systems analyst, 1972-75, mgr. payroll and fin. systems, 1975-77; mgr. standard ledger conversion Westinghouse Energy Systems, Pitts., 1977, mgr. fin. systems and control, 1978-90, mgr. fin. systems and standard ledger, 1990-91, mgr. payroll, cost and fin. systems control, 1991-94; data processing analyst & decision support coord. Braddock (Pa.) Med. Ctr., 1995-96; systems analyst, decision support coord. U. Pitts. Med. Ctr., Braddock, Pa., 1996—. Developer computer programs; designer and installer computer modules, report writer. Mem. NSPE, W.Va. Soc. Profl. Engrs. Avocations: walking, jogging, basketball, spectator sports, sports cards. Home: 179 Autumn Dr Trafford PA 15085-1448 Office: Braddock Med Ctr 400 Holland Ave Braddock PA 15104-1599

SLACK, LEWIS, organization administrator; b. Phila., Apr. 15, 1924; s. Lewis and Martha (Fitzgerald) S.; m. Sarah Hunt Wyman, Dec. 29, 1948; children—Elizabeth Wyman, Susan Towne, Christopher Morgan. S.B., Harvard U., 1944; Ph.D., Washington U., St. Louis, 1950. Physicist U.S. Naval Research Lab., 1950-54; assoc. prof. physics George Washington U., Washington, 1954-57; prof. physics George Washington U., 1957-62, acting head physics dept., 1957-60; asst. exec. sec. div. phys. scis. Nat. Acad. Scis.-NRC, Washington, 1962-67; sec. com. nuclear sci. NRC, 1962-67, mem. commn. human resources, 1974-78; dir. ednl. programs Am. Inst. Physics, N.Y.C., 1967-87; cons. Gen. Atomics div. Gen. Dynamics Corp., La Jolla, Calif., summers, 1959, 60; chmn. phys. scis. Am. exhibit Internat. Conf. Peaceful Uses Atomic Energy, Geneva, Switzerland, 1958; mem. Sci. Manpower Commn., 1968-87, pres., 1974-75, treas., 1976; mem. U.S. nat. com. Internat. Union for Pure and Applied Physics, 1972-78, sec., 1974-78; Mem. adv. com. Physics Today, 1963-67, chmn., 1967. Mem. Bruce Mus., Greenwich, Conn. (collections com., edn. com., exhbns. com., 1988-95). With USNR, 1943-46. Fellow Washington Acad. Scis., AAAS (mem. council 1971-72, 76-78); mem. Am. Phys. Soc., Am. Assn. Physics Tchrs. Episcopalian. Research beta ray and gamma ray spectroscopy. Home: 2104 Tadley Dr Chapel Hill NC 27514-2109

SLADE, BERNARD, playwright; b. St. Catharines, Ont., Can., May 2, 1930; s. Frederick and Bessie (Walbourne) Newbound; m. Jill Florence Hancock, July 25, 1953; children: Laurel, Christopher. Ed., Caernarvon Grammar Sch. Eng. Actor: Garden Ctr. Theatre, Vineland, Ont., Crest Theatre, Toronto, CBC-TV, Citadel Theatre, Edmonton, Alta.; screenwriter of over 20 hour TV plays for CBC, CBS, ABC, NBC, 1957—; writer/creator (TV series) Love on a Rooftop, The Patridge Family, The Flying Nun, The Girl with Something Extra, Bridget Loves Bernie; story editor, writer 15 episodes of TV series Bewitched; writer/creator (plays) A Very Close Family, 1962, Same Time Next Year (Drama Desk award 1975, Tony award nomination 1975), Tribute, 1978, Romantic Comedy, 1979, Special Occasions, 1981, Fatal Attraction, 1984, Return Engagements, 1986, Sweet William, 1987, An Act of the Imagination, 1987, I Remember You, 1991, You Say Tomatoes, 1993, Everytime I See You, 1994, Same Time, Another Year; feature films: Same Time, Next Year, 1977, Tribute, 1978, Romantic Comedy, 1979. Recipient Acad. award nomination Motion Picture Arts and Scis., 1978. Mem. Dramatists Guild Am., Writers Guild Am. (award nomination), Acad. Motion Picture Arts and Scis. (Acad. award nomination 1978), Soc. Authors and Artists (France). Avocation: tennis. Office: care Jack Hutto Agy 405 W 23rd St New York NY 10011-1404 *I am a prisoner of a childhood dream: to write for the theatre. The fulfillment of that dream has lived up to all my expectations. I believe the theatre should be a celebration of the human condition and that the artist's job is to remind us of all that is good about ourselves. I feel privileged to be given a platform for my particular vision of life, and, whether my plays succeed or fail, I am always grateful for the use of the hall.*

SLADE, BERNARD NEWTON, electronics company executive; b. Sioux City, Iowa, Dec. 21, 1923; s. William Charles and Katherine Gertrude Slotsky; m. Margot Friedlein, Aug. 18, 1946; children: Steven P., Eric J. BSEE, U. Wis., 1948; MS, Stevens Inst. Tech., 1954. Devel. engr. tube div. RCA, Harrison, N.J., 1948-55; devel. engr. RCA Labs., Princeton, N.J., 1955-56; mgr. tech. program IBM, Poughkeepsie, N.Y., 1956-60; mgr. product ops. IBM, Hopewell Junction, N.Y., 1960-64; mgr. mfg. tech. IBM World Trade Corp., Armonk, N.Y., 1964-65; corp. dir. of mfg. tech. IBM Corp., Armonk, 1965-84; sr. cons. Arthur D. Little, Inc., Cambridge, Mass., 1984-86, Gemini Cons., Morristown, N.J., 1986-93; founder and v.p. Yieldup Internat. Corp., 1993-97, also bd. dirs.; bd. dirs. V3 Semicondr. Corp. Co-author: Winning the Productivity Race, 1985; author: Compressing the Product Development Cycle, 1992; contbr. numerous articles to tech. jours.; patentee in field; contbg. author: Transistors, 1956, Handbook of Semiconductor Electronics, 1962. 2d lt. AUS, 1943-46. Mem. IEEE (sr.), Sigma Xi. Home: 12 Merry Hill Rd Poughkeepsie NY 12603-3214

SLADE, GERALD JACK, publishing company executive; b. Utica, N.Y., May 24, 1919; s. John H. and Sada (Jacobson) S.; m. Dorothy Casler, Oct. 24, 1942; children—John, Carolyn, David. B.A. summa cum laude, Colgate U., 1941; M.B.A., Harvard, 1943. Chmn. bd., pres., chief exec. officer Western Pub. Co., Racine, Wis.; dir. Mattel, Inc., Wells-Gardner Electronics Corp., 1st Nat. Bank of Racine, Joseph Schlitz Brewing Co.; Past pres. Nat. Assn. Electronic Organ Mfrs. Mem. Phi Beta Kappa, Kappa Delta Rho. Home: 3352 SE Fairway W Stuart FL 34997-6030

SLADE, LLEWELLYN EUGENE, lawyer, engineer; b. Carroll, Iowa, May 1, 1911; s. Llewellyn and Mary (Veach) S.; m. Jane England Dickinson, June 8, 1945 (dec. Dec. 1992); 1 child, Yvonne Slade Tidd. B.S. in Elec. Engring., Iowa State U., 1938, M.S., 1942; J.D., Drake U., 1951. Registered profl. engr., Iowa. Rsch. engr. Iowa State U. Ext. Svc., 1938-40; With Iowa Power & Light Co., Des Moines, 1940-68; exec. v.p. ops., dir. Iowa Power & Light Co., 1964-68; cons. Nebr. Public Power Dist. nuclear project; pvt. practice as exec. counsellor, atty., profl. engr., 1968—; fed. ct. bankruptcy trustee, Solid Waste Com. City of Des Moines; past mgmt. adv. and dir. Wright Tree Service Cos.; mem. panel arbitrators U.S. Fed. Mediation and Conciliation Service, Iowa Pub. Employees Relations Bd.; active participant in major nuclear litigation. Former chmn., trustee Des Moines Metro Transit Authority. Mem. Fed., Am., Iowa, Polk County bar assns., Iowa Engring. Soc. (Anson Marston award for outstanding svc. 1957, Outstanding Svc. award 1987), Nat. Soc. Profl. Engrs., Engrs. Club Des Moines, Atomic Indsl. Forum, Greater Des Moines C. of C., Iowa Arboretum (bd. dirs.), Des Moines Club, Men's Garden Club of Am., Masons (32 deg.), Shriners, Rotary. Lutheran. Home: 5833 Pleasant Dr Des Moines IA 50312-1211

SLADE, LYNN HEYER, lawyer; b. Santa Fe, N.Mex., Jan. 29, 1948; m. Susan Zimmerman, 1 child, Benjamin, 1 child from a previous marriage, Jessica. BA in Econs., U. N.Mex., 1973, JD, 1976. Bar: N.Mex. 1976, U.S. Dist. Ct. N.Mex. 1976, U.S. Ct. Appeals (10th cir.) 1978, U.S. Ct. Appeals (D.C. cir.) 1984, U.S. Supreme Ct. 1984. Dir. Modrall, Sperling, Roehl, Harris & Sisk, PA, Albuquerque, 1976—; adj. prof. U. N.Mex. Sch. Law, Albuquerque, 1990. Editor N.Mex. Law Rev., 1975-76; contbr. articles to profl. jours. Fellow N.Mex. Bar Found.; mem. ABA (sect. of natural resources, energy and environ. law, chair com. on Native Am. natural resources 1991-94, coun. mem. 1995—), N.Mex. State Bar (bd. dirs. sect. of natural resources 1983-87, bd. dirs. Indian law sect. 1987-90). Home: 143 Olglin Rd Corrales NM 87048 Office: Modrall Sperling Roehl Harris & Sisk PA 500 4th St NW Ste 1000 Albuquerque NM 87102-2183

SLADE, ROY, artist, college president, museum director; b. Cardiff, U.K., July 14, 1933; came to U.S., 1967, naturalized, 1975; s. David Trevor and Millicent (Stone) S. N.D.D., Cardiff Coll. Art, 1954; A.T.D., U. Wales, 1954; D of Arts, Art Inst. So. Calif., 1994. Tchr. art and crafts Heolgam High Sch., Wales, 1956-60; lectr. art Clarendon Coll., Nottingham, Eng., 1960-64; sr. lectr. fine art Leeds Coll. Art, Eng., 1964-67; prof. painting Corcoran Sch. Art, Washington, 1967-68, assoc. dean, 1969-70, dean, 1970-77; dir. Corcoran Gallery of Art, Washington, 1972-77; pres., dir. Cranbrook Acad. Art, Bloomfield Hills, Mich., 1977-94; sr. lectr. Leeds Coll. Art, Eng. 1968-69; vis. Boston Mus. Fine Arts, 1970. Exhibited one-man shows Howard Roberts Gallery, Cardiff, Wales, 1958, New Art Ctr., London, 1960, U. Birmingham, 1964, 69, Herbert Art Gallery and Mus., Coventry, 1964, Va. State Art League, 1967, Mus. of Arts and Crafts, Columbus, Ga., 1968, Jefferson Place Gallery, Washington, 1968, 70, 72, 73, Park Sq. Gallery, Leeds, 1969, St. Mary's Coll., Md., 1971, Guelph U., Ont., Can., 1971, Hood Coll., 1974, Pyramid Gallery, Washington, 1976, Robert Kidd Gallery, 1981, 92, Herman Miller, Inc., Mich., 1985; group shows in U.K., Washington, Can.; represented in permanent collections Arts Council Gt. Brit., Contemporary Art Soc., Nuffield Found., Ministry of Works, Eng., Brit. Embassy, Washington, Brit. Overseas Airways Corp., U. Birmingham, Wakefield City Art Gallery, Clarendon Coll., Cadbury Bros., Ltd., Eng., Lord Ogmore, Local Edn. Authorities. Mem. D.C. Commn. on Arts.; bd. dirs. Artists for Environment Found., Nat. Assn. Schs. Art; chmn. Nat. Council Art Adminstrs., 1981. Served with Brit. Army, 1954-56. Decorated knight 1st class Order of White Rose (Finland), Royal Order of Polar Star (Sweden); recipient award Welsh Soc., Phila., 1974, Gov.'s Arts Orgn. award, 1988; Fulbright scholar, 1967-68. Mem. Nat. Soc. Lit. and Arts, AIA (hon. Detroit chpt.), Assn. Art Mus. Dirs. (hon.). Home: PO Box 48 Harsens Island MI 48028-0048

SLADE, THOMAS BOG, III, lawyer, investment banker; b. Balt., June 22, 1931; s. Thomas Bog Jr. and Blanche Evangeline (Hall) S.; m. Sunya Johanna Bowen, July 25, 1959 (div. 1976); children: Sunya Kirsten, DeWitt Bowen, Vivian Watson; m. Mary Stewart Bolton, Apr. 3, 1976. BA, U. Va., 1953, LLB, 1954. Bar: Fla. 1956, U.S. Supreme Ct. 1966. Assoc. Patterson, Freeman, Richardson & Watson, Jacksonville, Fla., 1956-61; ptnr. Freeman, Richardson, Watson, Slade, McCarthy & Kelly, Jacksonville, 1961-80; pvt. practice Jacksonville, 1980-81; ptnr. Foley & Lardner, Jacksonville, 1981-92; sr. v.p. Gardnyr Michael Capital, Inc., Jacksonville, 1992—. Served to 1st lt., U.S. Army, 1954-56. Mem. Fla. Bar (bd. govs. 1966-69, pres. young lawyers sect. 1967-68), Nat. Assn. Bond Lawyers, Jacksonville Bar Assn., Fla Yacht Club, Univ. Club of Jacksonville. Office: Gardnyr Michael Capital Inc 2764 Vernon Ter Apt B1 Jacksonville FL 32205-8823

SLADEK, LYLE VIRGIL, mathematician, educator; b. Pukwana, S.D., Oct. 13, 1923; s. Charles Frank and Emma Margaret (Swanson) S.; m. Patricia Knotts, Sept. 12, 1948; children: Susan, Ann, Laura, Karen. B.S., S.D. State U., 1948; M.A., U. S.D., 1949, Stanford U., 1963; Ph.D., UCLA, 1970. Tchr. high sch. Mitchell, S.D., 1950-56; asst. prof. math. Black Hills State Coll., S.D., 1957-62; prof. math. Calif. Luth. Univ., Thousand Oaks, 1963-94, prof. emeritus, 1994—; lectr. in field. Contbr. short stories, poems to mags. and newspapers. Pres. congregation Our Savior's Lutheran Ch., Spearfish, S.D., 1961. Served as officer U.S. Army, 1943-46, PTO, ETO. Shell Merit fellow, 1956; NSF fellow, 1956-57, 62-63; recipient Meritorious Achievement award edn. S.D. Mines and Tech., 1957; Fulbright-Hays lectr. Bahamas, 1980-81. Mem. Math. Assn. Am., Blue Key, Pi Kappa Delta, Phi Delta Kappa. Home: 3243 Pioneer St Thousand Oaks CA 91360-2730 *I learned from my parents during the dust bowl years that adversity often can be overcome through patience and determination, and that problems provide challenges that add spice to life. I have sought to return full measure to society for all the opportunities and joys of life that have come my way.*

SLADEK, RONALD JOHN, physics educator; b. Chgo., Sept. 19, 1926; s. James Joseph and Rose (Vachulka) S.; m. Jeanne T. McFadden, Sept. 19, 1953; children—Linda, James, Frances, Stephen, Rosemarie, Edward. Ph.B., U. Chgo., 1947, S.B., 1949, S.M., 1950, Ph.D. (AEC fellow), 1954. Research physicist Westinghouse Research Labs., Pitts., 1953-60, fellow scientist, 1960-61; assoc. prof. physics Purdue U., West Lafayette, Ind., 1961-66, prof., 1966-91, prof. physics emeritus, 1992—, acting head dept. physics, 1969-71, assoc. dean sci., 1974-87; vis. scientist Sci. Center, N.Am. Rockwell Corp., Thousand Oaks, Calif., summer 1967; sabbatical scientist Xerox Research Center, Palo Alto, Calif., 1976-77. Contbr. articles to profl. jours. With USNR, 1945-46. Fellow Am. Phys. Soc. Home: 963 Ridgeview Dr Reno NV 89511-8506

SLAGER, JOAN K., nurse midwife; b. Hastings, Mich., June 10, 1958; d. Richard E. and Pauline B. (First) Wolverton; m. Vernon R. Slager, Dec. 4, 1982; children: Michele E., Mark R., Meredith P. BS in Nursing cum laude, Nazareth Coll., 1980; cert in Nurse-midwifery, Frontier Sch. of Midwifery, Hyden, Ky., 1991; MS in Nursing, Case Western Reserve U., 1992. Staff nurse neonatal ICU Bronson Hosp., Kalamazoo, 1979-81; staff nurse Lehigh (Fla.) Acres Gen. Hosp., 1981; clinic nurse Kalamazoo County Health Dept., 1981-84; staff nurse birthing ctr. Borgess Med. Ctr., Kalamazoo, 1984-91; cert. nurse midwife Family Health Ctr. of Battle Creek, Mich., 1991-93; cert. nurse midwife Bronson Women's Svc., Kalamazoo, 1993—, dir. nurse-midwifery, 1995—; com. mem. Infant Mortality Rev. Com., Family Health Ctr., Battle Creek, 1992-93; guest speaker Sales Tng. Upjohn Co., Kalamazoo, 1992—; acad. faculty Frontier Sch. Midwifery and Family Nursing, 1997—. Mem. Am. Coll. of Nurse Midwives (cert. nurse midwife, sec. Region IV, chpt. XIII 1992-94, chpt. chair ACNM region IV chpt. XIII 1996-97). Avocations: vocal music, raising Labrador Retrievers. Home: 3681 S 26th St Kalamazoo MI 49001-9611 Office: Bronson Women's Svc 252 E Lovell St Kalamazoo MI 49007

SLAGLE, JACOB WINEBRENNER, JR., food products executive; b. Balt., Jan. 18, 1945; s. Jacob Winebrenner and Anna Dorothea (Vernon-Williams) S.; m. Sharon Carol Muth, Nov. 18, 1973 (div. 1982); children: Alexander, Dylan; m. Nina Kathleen Tou, May 20, 1994. Student, U. Ariz., 1963-65; BA in Sociology, U. Md., 1969; diploma, Broadcasting Inst. Md., Balt., 1975. Claims adjuster Govt. Employees Ins. Co., Towson, Md., 1969-71; exec. Slagle & Slagle, Inc., Balt., 1971-81, pres., 1981-92; pres. Denzer's Food Products, Balt., 1992—; bd. dirs. H.S.A., Inc., Marietta, Ga., 1992, 93; freelance writer for various nespapers and mags.; monthly columnist Jake About Town, Balt. Chronicle, 1989-93; mem. bd. advisors Broadcasting Inst. Md., 1990-93. Contbg. author: Baltimore: A Living Renaissance, 1981; contbg. writer Food Distbn. Mag., 1994-96. Bd. dirs. Hist. Balt. Soc., 1979-96, v.p., 1989-96; bd. dirs. Intervention with Pact, Balt., 1982-89; pres. Hanover House Condominium Assn., Balt., 1983—; arbitrator BBB Greater Md., Balt., 1983-91; mem. Greater Balt. Com. Leadership Group, 1996. Mem. Homebuilders Assn. Md. (bd. dirs. remodelers coun. 1989-93, Remodeling Assoc. of Yr. 1992), Md. Splty. Foods Assn. (bd. dirs. 1994—, sec. 1995, pres. 1996), Balt. Blues Soc. (bd. dirs. 1992—, sec. 1995—), Mid-Atlantic Specialty Foods Assn. (mng. dir. 1996—), Mid-Atlantic Food Dealers Assn. (bd. dirs., 1997—), Rotary (bd. dirs. Balt. 1992-94, 96—).

SLAGLE, JAMES ROBERT, computer science educator; b. Bklyn., 1934; married; 5 children. BS summa cum laude, St. John's U., 1955; MS in Math., MIT, 1957, PhD in Math., 1961. Staff mathematician Lincoln Lab. MIT, 1955-63; group leader Lawrence Livermore Radiation Lab. U. Calif., Livermore, 1963-67; chief heuristics lab. divsn. computer rsch. and tech. NIH, Bethesda, Md., 1967-74; chief computer sci. lab. comm. scis. divsn. Naval Rsch. Lab., Washington, 1974-81, spl. asst., 1981-84; Disting. prof. computer sci. U. Minn., Mpls., 1984—; mem. faculty dept. elec. engring. MIT, 1962-63; mem. faculty dept. computer sci. and elec. engring. U. Calif., Berkeley, 1964-67; mem. faculty dept. computer sci. Johns Hopkins U., 1967-74; cons. in field. Author: Artificial Intelligence: The Heuristic Programming Approach, 1971. Contbr. articles to profl. jours. Named one of Ten Outstanding Young Men of Am., U.S. Jaycees, 1969; recipient Outstanding Handicapped Fed. Employee of Yr. award, 1979; Mary P. Oenslager Career Achievement award, Recording for the Blind, 1982. Fellow AAAS, IEEE, Am. Assn. Artificial Intelligence; mem. Computer Soc. of IEEE. Office: U Minn Computer Sci Dept 4-192 EE/Csi Bldg 200 Union St SE Minneapolis MN 55455-0154

SLAGLE, LARRY B., human resources specialist; b. Templeton, Pa., Dec. 17, 1934; s. William Harry and Luella (Armstrong) S. AB, Wabash Coll., 1956; postgrad., Am. U., 1967-71. Dep. admistr. for mgmt. and budget USDA Animal & Plant Health Inspection Svc., Washington, 1978-88, assoc. adminstr., 1988-90; dir. pers. USDA, Washington, 1990-94; pvt. practice human resources and orgnl. cons., 1994—; bd. dirs. Fgn. Aid Through Edn. With U.S. Army, 1957-59, Korea. Named Meritorious Exec. President Reagan, 1985, President Bush, 1991. Avocation: cycling. Home and Office: 208 6th St SE Washington DC 20003-1134

SLAIBY, THEODORE GEORGE, aeronautical engineer, consultant; b. Washington, Conn., Apr. 12, 1929; s. George and Afifi (Buzaid) S.; m. Margaret Sullivan, June 29, 1957; children: Peter E., Jeffrey M., Barbara E. BS in Aero. Engring., Rensselaer Poly. Inst., 1950. Engr. tech. and rsch. group Pratt & Whitney Aircraft Engines, East Hartford, Conn., 1950-56, asst. project engr., tech. and rsch. group, 1956-60, devel. engr., advanced engines, 1960-67, mgr. new project devel. programs, 1967-76, dir. design & analytical engring., 1976-81, v.p. product integrity, 1981-83, v.p. engring., 1983-87, ret., 1987; engring. cons. United Techs. Corp., Hartford, Conn., 1987—; cons. to various engring. cos. Author or co-author numerous tech. papers, 1958-70; patentee in field. Avocations: farming, hunting, fishing, history, language study. Home: 251 Spring St Manchester CT 06040-6640

SLAIGHT, GARY, broadcasting executive; b. Edmonton, Alta., Can., 1951; married; 2 children. BA in English, U. Western Ont. Media estimator McLaren Advt., 1973; promotion mgr. Quality Records, 1974-75, WEA Records, 1975; account exec. Q107, 1977, program dir., 1978, v.p., gen. mgr., 1982; v.p., gen. mgr. MIX 99.9, 1987—; pres., CEO Std. Radio, Inc., Toronto, 1987—; gen. mgr. CFRB, Toronto, 1987—; creator Homegrown Contest. Spl. events chmn. United Way, 1986; mem. bd. Learning Partnership, Toronto Raptors. Recipient ann. music industry awards Gen. Mgr. of Yr., 1986, Program Dir. of Yr., 1987, Broadcast Exec. of Yr., 1992, 93, 96. Office: Standard Radio Inc, 2 St Clair Ave W, Toronto, ON Canada M4V 1L6

SLAIN, JOHN JOSEPH, legal educator; b. Jan. 21, 1927. A.B., Providence Coll., 1952; LL.B., NYU, 1955. Bar: N.Y. 1956. Assoc. Cravath, Swaine & Moore, 1955-60; v.p., gen. counsel AIM Cos., Inc., 1961-66, dir., 1964-71; assoc. prof. law Ind. U.-Indpls., 1965-70; prof. law Ohio State U., Columbus, 1970-77, NYU, N.Y.C., 1977—. Dir., treas. Indpls. Legal Services Orgn., 1966-71; dir. Ohio Catholic Charities, 1975-77. Republican. Episcopalian. Office: NYU Law Sch 40 Washington Sq S New York NY 10012-1005

SLAKEY, LINDA LOUISE, biochemistry educator; b. Oakland, Calif., Jan. 2, 1939; d. William Henry and Georgia Evelyn Slakey. BS, Siena Heights Coll., 1962; PhD, U. Mich., 1967; postgrad., U. Wis., 1970-73. Elem. sch. tchr. Saint Edmund's Sch., Oak Park, Ill., 1958-61; tchr. Resurrection H.S., Lansing, Mich., 1962-63; instr. in chemistry St. Dominic's Coll., St. Charles, Ill., 1967-69; rsch. assoc. Argonne (Ill.) Nat. Libr., 1969-70; project assoc., dept. physiol. chemistry U. Wis., Madison, 1970-73; asst. prof. dept. biochemistry U. Mass., Amherst, 1973-79, assoc. prof., 1979-87, prof., 1987—, head dept. biochemistry and molecular biology, 1986-91, dean Coll. Natural Scis. and Math., 1993—; adv. com. arteriosclerosis and hypertension Nat. Heart & Lung and Blood Inst., Washington, 1978-81, mem. rev. com. B, 1981-87; vis. scientist Clin. Rsch. Ctr, Harrow, Eng., 1984-85. Contbr. articles to profl. jours. NSF predoctoral fellow U. Mich., 1963-67, NIH spl. fellow, 1970-73. Fellow Am. Heart Assn. (established investigator 1977-82), Arteriosclerosis Soc. of Am. Heart Assn.; mem. Am. Soc. Cell Biology, Am. Soc. for Biochemistry and Molecular Biology, Sigma Xi, Sigma Delta Epsilon. Office: U Mass Coll Natural Sci & Math 722 Lederle Tower B Amherst MA 01003

SLANE, HENRY PINDELL, retired broadcasting executive; b. Peoria, Ill., Dec. 29, 1920; s. Carl P. and Frances (Pindell) S.; children by previous marriage: John, Elizabeth Jean, Henry Pindell, Barbara. A.B., Yale U., 1943. Became pub. Peoria Newspapers, Inc., Peoria Broadcasting Co.; pres. Peoria Jour. Star, Inc., now ret.; pres. PJS Publs., Inc. (Sew News, Shooting Times and Rotor & Wing, Profitable Crafts Merchandising and Crafts mags.), ret. Served with USNR, 1943-46. Mem. Am. Soc. Newspaper Editors, Peoria country Club, Mt. Hawley Country Club. Clubs: Peoria Country, Creve Coeur (Ill.) Country, Sturgeon Bay (Wis.). Home: PO Box 3535 Peoria IL 61614-3535

SLANSKY, JERRY WILLIAM, investment company executive; b. Chgo., Mar. 8, 1947; s. Elmer Edward and Florence Anna (Kosobud) S.; m. Marlene Jean Cannella, Jan. 29, 1950; children: Brett Matthew, Blake Adam. BA, Elmhurst Coll., 1969; MA, No. Ill. U., 1971. Mktg. rep. Bantam Book Co., Chgo., 1972-73, Charles Levy Circulating Co., Chgo., 1973-76; account exec. Merrill Lynch, Chgo., 1976-77; account exec. Oppenheimer & Co., Inc., Chgo., 1977—, asst. v.p., 1978, v.p., 1979, sr. v.p., 1981, mng. dir., 1986, ptnr., 1986—. Bd. dirs. Lake Geneva (Wis.) Beach Assn., 1987—, Glen Ellyn Youth Ctr., Glenbard West H.S. Mem. Nat. Assn. Securities Dealers (arbitrator 1988—), N.Y. Stock Exch., Chgo. Bd. Options, Am. Arbitration. Assn, Omaha C. of C. Presbyterian. Avocations: swimming, water skiing, golf. Office: Oppenheimer & Co Inc 311 S Wacker Dr Chicago IL 60606-6627

SLASH (SAUL HUDSON), guitarist; b. Stoke-on-Trent, Eng., July 23, 1965; s. Anthony and Ola Hudson; m. Renée Suran, Oct. 10, 1992. Guitarist Guns n' Roses, 1985—. Albums: (with Guns N' Roses) Live Like a Suicide, 1986, Appetite for Destruction, 1987, GN'R Lies, 1988, Use Your Illusion I, 1991, Use Your Illusion II, 1991, The Spaghetti Incident?, 1993, (with Slash's Snakepit) It's Five O'Clock Somewhere, 1995; worked as guitarist with Iggy Pop, Bob Dylan, Michael Jackson, Lenny Kravitz. Office: care Geffen Records 9130 W Sunset Blvd Los Angeles CA 90069-3110*

SLATE, FLOYD OWEN, chemist, materials scientist, civil engineer, educator, researcher; b. Carroll County, Ind., July 26, 1920; s. Ora George and Gladys Marie (Miller) S.; m. Margaret Mary Maggie, Oct. 14, 1939; children: Sally Lee Slate McEnteer, Sandra Kay Slate Miller, Rex Owen. B.S., Purdue U., 1941, M.S., 1942, Ph.D., 1944. Chemist Manhattan Project, N.Y.C., Oak Ridge and Decatur, Ill., 1944-46; asst. prof. civil engring. Purdue U., Lafayette, Ind., 1946-49; v.p., dir. Geotechnics & Resources Inc., White Plains, N.Y., 1959-63; prof. engring. materials Cornell U., Ithaca, N.Y., 1949-87; prof. emeritus, 1987; internat. lectr., cons. concrete, low-cost housing. Author books, research papers on concrete, low-cost housing, soil stabilization, 1944—. Recipient Excellence in Teaching award Cornell U., 1976, sr. fellow East-West Center, 1976, NSF research grantee, 1960-86. Fellow Am. Concrete Inst. (hon., Wason Research medal 1957, 65, 74, 86, Anderson award 1983), Am. Inst. Chemists; mem. ASCE, ASTM, Am. Chem. Soc. Research on internal structure of concrete vs. properties, chemistry applied to engring. problems, and low-cost housing for developing countries. Home: 255 The Esplanade N Apt 306 Venice FL 34285-1518 Office: Hollister Hall Cornell U Ithaca NY 14853 *Think positively and be optimistic. Be considerate of others, try to help others, and enjoy life.*

SLATE, JOE HUTSON, psychologist, educator; b. Hartselle, Ala., Sept. 21, 1930; s. Murphy Edmund and Marie (Hutson) S.; m. Rachel Holladay, July 1, 1950; children: Marc Allan, John David, James Daryl. B.S., Athens Coll., 1960; M.A., U. Ala., 1965, Ph.D., 1970. Mem. faculty Athens (Ala.) State Coll., 1965-92, prof. psychology, 1974-92, chmn. behavioral scis., 1974-92; pvt. practice psychology Athens, 1970-92, Hartselle, 1992—; v.p. Slate Security Systems, Hartselle, Ala., 1984—. Author: Psychic Phenomena, 1988, Self-Empowerment, 1991, Psychic Empowerment, 1995, Psychic Empowerment for Health and Fitness, 1996. Named hon. prof. Montevallo U., 1973, prof. emeritus Athens State, Coll., 1992. Mem. APA, Am. Soc. Clin. Hypnosis, Inst. Parapsychol. Rsch. (founder), Coun. for Nat. Register Health Svc. Providers in Psychology, NEA, Ala. Edn. Assn., Delta Tau Delta, Phi Delta Kappa, Kappa Delta Pi. Home and Office: 1807 Highway 31 NW Hartselle AL 35640-4442

SLATE, JOHN BUTLER, biomedical engineer; b. Schenectady, N.Y., Sept. 27, 1953; s. Herbert Butler and Violet (Perugi) S. BSEE, U. Wis., 1975, MEE, 1977, PhDEE, 1980. Spl. fellow of cardiovascular surgery U. Ala., Birmingham, 1980-81, dept. biomed. research engr., 1981-82; microbiology fellow, 1981-82; sr. research engr. IMED Corp., San Diego, 1982-83, sr. research scientist, 1983-86; sci. dir. Pacesetter Infusion Ltd. (dba MiniMed Technologies), Sylmar, Calif., 1986-87; v.p. tech. MiniMed Technologies, Sylmar, Calif., 1987-91; v.p. R & D Siemens Infusion Systems, Sylmar, Calif., 1991-93; v.p. tech. devel. Via Med., San Diego, 1993-94; pres. Slate Engring., San Diego, 1994—, Avant Drug Delivery Systems, Inc., San Diego, 1997—. Mem. IEEE (IEE Ayrton award), Biomed. Engring. Soc., Sigma Xi. Office: Slate Engring 3914 Kendall St San Diego CA 92109-6129

SLATE, MARTIN IRA, pension benefit executive. Grad., Harvard U., 1967; JD, Yale U., 1970; LLM in Taxation, Georgetown U., 1988. Dir. field svcs. EEOC, 1980-81; dir. ERISA program IRS, 1986-92; exec. dir. Pension Benefit Guaranty Corp., 1993—; adj. prof. in taxation Georgetown Law Ctr., 1988-92. Contbr. articles to profl. publs. Mem. Phi Beta Kappa. Office: Pension Benefit Guar Corp 1200 K St NW Washington DC 20005-4025

SLATER, BENJAMIN RICHARD, JR., lawyer; b. Riverside, La., Jan. 10, 1929; s. Benjamin Richard and Ila Celestine (Hyde) S.; m. Gloria S. Slater, Dec. 17, 1948; children: Benjamin R. III, Pamela M., Charlotte A., Elizabeth S. Borgen; m. Carol E. Vallette, Apr. 8, 1996. BS, Tulane U., 1949, JD, 1953. With Jones, Walker, Waechter, New Orleans, 1953-56, Martin & Slater, Pt. Sulphur, La., 1956-60, Monroe & Lemann, New Orleans, 1960-94, Slater Law Firm, New Orleans, 1994—. Fellow Am. Coll. Trial Lawyers; mem. FBA, La. Bar Assn., New Orleans Country Club. Office: Slater Law Firm 2600 Poydras Ctr 650 Poydras St New Orleans LA 70130-6101

SLATER, CATHRYN BUFORD, federal agency administrator; married; 5 children. BSE in English with honors, U. Ark., 1969, MA in English with high honors, 1972; postgrad., Duke U., 1990. Spl. asst., liaison natural & cultural resources State Ark., Little Rock, 1984-88; state hist. preservation officer, dir. Ark. Hist. Preservation Program, Little Rock, 1988—; lectr. English dept. U. Ark., Little Rock, 1975-84, 88—. Bd. dirs. Nat. Conf. State Hist. Preservation Officers, 1990-94, exec. com., 1992-94, chmn. critical issues com., 1992-94, sec., 1993-95; bd. dirs. Shelter Battered Women, Pulaski County, Ark., Ctrl. H.S. Parent Tchr. Student Assn., Little Rock, Pulaski Heights United Meth. Ch. Mem. Nat. Pks. & Conservation Assn., Nature Conservancy, Nat. Trust Hist. Preservation, Sierra Club, Wilderness Soc., Audubon Soc. Avocations: reading, hiking, canoeing, camping, backpacking. Address: 38 River Ridge Cir Little Rock AR 72207 Office: 1100 Pennsylvania Ave NW Washington DC 20004-2501*

SLATER, CHARLES JAMES, construction company executive; b. Munich, Feb. 16, 1949; s. Robert Marsh and Mary Elizabeth (James) S.; m. Pamela S. Senning, Sept. 17, 1974 (div. Apr. 1992); children: Mary Katherine, Robert Charles; m. Kristie J. Alexander, May 11, 1992. BA in Polit. Sci., U. Tenn., 1974. Safety mgr. Daniel Internat. Co., Kingsport, Tenn., 1981-83; safety and med. mgr. Daniel Internat. Co., Georgetown, S.C., 1983-84; risk mgmt. mgr. Yeargin Inc., Kingsport, 1985-88, Omaha, 1990; resident engr. Yeargin Inc., Frankfort, Ind., 1991, Florence, S.C., 1991; safety and risk mgmt. dir. Harbert-Yeargin Inc., Greenville, S.C., 1992-96; safety and health mgr. Fluor-Daniel Inc., Seaford, Del., 1996—; bd. advisors Assoc. Bldrs. and Contractors/Nat. Safety Coun., Washington, 1993—. Pres. Tenn. Vol. Firefighters Assn., Sullivan County, 1987-89, Kingsport Area Safety Coun., 1989. Mem. Am. Inst. Constructors (chpt. pres. 1993-94), Am. Soc. Safety Engrs., Nat. Safety Mgmt. Soc., Constrn. Industry Coop. Alliance (instr. 1992), Safety Dirs. League (charter), Constrn. Specifications Inst. Episcopalian. Avocations: golf, chess, reading, cinematography. Home: PO Box 361 Seaford DE 19973-0361 Office: Fluor-Daniel Inc 500 Woodland Rd Seaford DE 19973-4312

SLATER, DORIS ERNESTINE WILKE, business executive; b. Oakes, N.D.; d. Arthur Waldemar and Anna Mary (Dill) Wilke; m. Lawrence Bert Slater, June 4, 1930 (dec., 1960). Grad. high sch. Sec. to circulation mgr. Mpls. Daily Star, 1928-30; promotion activities Lions Internat. in U.S., Can., Cuba, 1930-48; exec. sec. parade and spl. events com. Inaugural Com., 1948-49; exec. sec. Nat. Capital Sesquicentennial Commn., 1949-50, Capitol Hill Assos., Inc., 1951, Pres.'s Cup Regatta, 1951; adminstrv. asst. Nat. Assn. Food Chains, 1951-60; v.p., sec.-treas. John A. Logan Assos., Inc., Washington, 1960—; v.p., sec.-treas. Logan, Seaman, Slater, Inc., 1962—; mng. dir. Western Hemisphere, Internat. Assn. Chain Stores, 1964—. With pub. relations div. Boston Met. chpt. ARC, 1941-42; mem. Nat. Cherry Blossom Festival Com., 1949—; mem. Inaugural Ball Com., 1953, 57, 65. Methodist. Lion. Home and Office: 2500 Wisconsin Ave NW Washington DC 20007-4504

SLATER, JAMES MUNRO, radiation oncologist; b. Salt Lake City, Jan. 7, 1929; s. Donald Munro and Leone Forestine (Fehr) S.; m. JoAnn Strout, Dec. 28, 1948; children: James, Julie, Jan, Jerry, Jon. B.S. in Physics, U. Utah, Utah State U., 1954; M.D., Loma Linda U., 1963; Dsc Honoris Causa, Andrews U., Berrien Springs, Mich., 1996. Diplomate: Am. Bd. Radiology. Intern Latter Day Saints Hosp., Salt Lake City, 1963-64; resident in radiology Latter Day Saints Hosp., 1964-65; resident in radiotherapy Loma Linda U. Med. Ctr., White Meml. Med. Center, Los Angeles; fellow in radiotherapy Loma Linda U. Med. Ctr., White Meml. Med. Center, 1967-68, U. Tex.-M.D. Anderson Hosp. and Tumor Inst., Houston, 1968-69; mem. faculty Loma Linda (Calif.) U., 1975—, prof. radiology, 1979—, chmn. radiation scis. dept., 1979-89, dir. nuclear medicine, 1970—, dir. radiation oncology, 1975-79, chmn. dept. radiation oncology, 1990—, dir. Cancer Inst., 1993—, exec. v.p. Med. Ctr., 1994-95; treas. Med. Ctr., 1995—; co-dir. cmty. radiology oncology program L.A. County-U. So. Calif. Comprehensive Cancer Ctr., 1978-83; mem. cancer adv. coun. State of Calif., 1980-85; clin. prof. U. So. Calif., 1982—; founding mem. Proton Therapy Coop. Group, 1985—, chmn. 1987-91; cons. charged particle therapy program Lawrence Berkeley Lab., 1986-94; cons. R&D monoclonal antibodies Hybritech Inc., 1985-94, bd. dirs., 1985-94; cons. Berkeley lab., 1986-94; mem. panel cons. Internat. Atomic Energy Agy. UNA 1994—; cons. Sci. Applications International. Corp., 1979, 89-91. Bd. dirs. Am. Cancer Soc., San Bernardino/Riverside, 1976—, exec. com., 1976—; pres. Inland Empire chpt., 1981-83. NIH fellow, 1968-69; recipient exhbn. awards Radiol. Soc. N.Am., 1973, exhbn. awards European Assn. Radiology, 1975, exhbn. awards Am. Soc. Therapeutic Radiologists, 1978, Alumnus of Yr. award, 1993, 94. Fellow Am. Coll. Radiology; mem. AMA, ACS (liaison mem. to commn. on cancer 1976-84), Am. Radium Soc., Am. Soc. Clin. Oncology, Am. Soc. Therapeutics Radiologists, Assn. Univ. Radiologists, Calif. Med. Assn., Calif. Radiol. Soc., Gilbert H. Fletcher Soc. (pres. 1981-82), Loma Linda U. Med. Sch. Alumni Assn., Radiol. Soc. N.Am., Bernardino County Med Soc., Soc. Chairmen Of Acad. Radiation Oncology Programs, Alpha Omega Alpha. Achievements include development of world's first proton accelerator system for treating patients with cancer and some benign diseases in a hospital enviroment; development of world's first computer assisted radiation treatment planning system utilizing patient's digitized anatomic images with overlying radiation distribution images. Home: 1210 W Highland Ave Redlands CA 92373-6659 Office: Loma Linda U Radiation Medicine Loma Linda CA 92354

SLATER, JILL SHERRY, lawyer; b. N.Y.C., Apr. 8, 1943. BA with distinction and honors, Cornell U., 1964; JD cum laude, Harvard U., 1968. Bar: Mass. 1968, Calif. 1971, U.S. Dist. Ct. (cen. dist.) Calif. 1971, U.S. Ct. Appeals (9th cir.) 1974, U.S. Dist. Ct. (so. dist.) Calif. 1977, U.S. Dist. Ct. (ea. dist.) Calif. 1984, U.S. Dist. Ct. (no. dist) Calif. 1985, U.S. Ct. Appeals (Fed. cir.) 1982, U.S. Supreme Ct. 1986, N.Y. 1988. Atty. Boston Redevel. Authority, 1968-70; from assoc. to ptnr. Latham & Watkins, N.Y.C., 1970—. Woodrow Wilson fellow, 1964. Mem. ABA., Phi Beta Kappa. Office: Latham & Watkins 885 3rd Ave Ste 1000 New York NY 10022-4834

SLATER, JOAN ELIZABETH, secondary education educator; b. Paterson, N.J., Aug. 27, 1947; d. Anthony Joseph and Emma (Liguori) Nicola; m. Francis Graham Slater, Nov. 16, 1974; children: David, Kristin, Kylie. BA in English, Montclair State Coll., 1968, MA in English, 1971. Cert. English, speech and theater arts tchr., N.J., Tex. Tchr. Anthony Wayne Jr. High Sch., Wayne, N.J., 1968-70, Wayne Valley High Sch., Wayne, N.J., 1970-74, Strack Intermediate Sch., Klein, Tex., 1987—; cons. Tex. Assessment Acad. Skills, Houston Post Newspaper, 1994—; adv. bd. Tex. Edn. Assn., winter 1993; sch. dist. rep. Southern Assn. Colls. and Schs., 1993; editor, advisor Pawprints Lit. Mag., 1989—. Co-author: Klein Curriculum for the Gifted and Talented, 1992-93. Com. chairperson Klein After-Prom Extravaganza, 1994-95; parent supporter Challenge Soccer Club, Klein, 1993—; mem. Klein H.S. Girls Soccer Team Bd., 1995-96. Mem. North Harris County Coun. Tchrs. English (sec. 1992-95), Klein Edn. Assn., Nat. Coun. Tchrs. English, Tex. Mid. Sch. Assn., Internat. Reading Assn., Greater Houston Area Reading Coun., Nat. Charity League. Avocations: aerobics, interior decorating, reading. Home: 6018 Spring Oak Holw Spring TX 77379-8833 Office: Strack Intermediate Sch 18027 Kuykendahl Rd Klein TX 77379-8116

SLATER, JOHN BLACKWELL, landscape architect; b. Kansas City, Mo., Mar. 20, 1943; s. Marcus Bedford and Helen (Butler) S.; m. Sue Stallings, June 22, 1968; 1 child, Alice Butler. B in Landscape Architecture, Syracuse U., 1965; student, SUNY, Syracuse U. Registered landscape architect, Md., N.Y., Va. Landscape architect A.E. Bye Assocs., Cos Cob, Conn., 1969-71, The Rouse Co., Columbia, Md., 1971-74, Slater Assocs., Columbia, 1974—; mem. Md. Bd. Examiners of Landscape Architects State of Md., 1991—. Prin. works include design Sully Plantation Hist. Park, Oakland Mills Courtyard, Benjamin Banneker Hist. Park, Port Deposit Hist. Restoration of Streetscape, Columbia Town Ctr. Park, S.I. Mall Expansion. Lt. USN, 1966-69. Fellow Am. Soc. Landscape Architects (trustee 1981-87, v.p. 1987-88, awards Md. chpt. 1979, 89, 90), Howard County Assn. Landscape Architects (pres. 1991), Rotary (past pres. Columbia Town Ctr. club). Avocations: sailing, gardening, photography, golf. Home: 4993 Dalton Dr Columbia MD 21045-1805 Office: Slater Assocs Inc 5560 Sterrett Pl Ste 302 Columbia MD 21044-2629

SLATER, JOHN GREENLEAF, financial consultant; b. Milw., Mar. 25, 1935; s. Thomas McIndoe and Margaret Mary (McAnarney) S.; m. Colleen Mary Conway, July 19, 1958; children: James C., John T., Ann E. Borngesser. BS in Econs, Marquette U., 1958, MA, 1960. With First Wis. Nat. Bank, Milw., 1960-69; with First Wis. Nat. Bank, Madison, 1969-79, exec. v.p., dir., 1973-79; sr. v.p. Fifth Third Bank, Cin., 1979-82; pres., chief exec. officer Slater Carley Group, Inc., Cin., 1982-85; exec. v.p., bd. dirs. E. W. Buschman Co., Cin., 1985-94; pres., CEO Diamond Machine Co., Inc., Cin., 1994-96; pvt. practice Cin., 1996—; bd. dirs. Bhat Industries, CinTech Inc. Mem. Madison Adv. Com. Drug Abuse, 1970-71; mem. long-range planning com. Edgewood High Sch., Madison, 1972-75; mem. long-range planning task force OKI Regional Planning Commn., 1980-81; bd. dirs. First Offenders Sch., 1975-79. Mem. Wis. Bus. Economists Assn. (pres. 1973), Nat. Assn. Bus. Economists, Cin. Inst. for Small Enterprise, Fin. Execs. Inst., Nat. Venture Capital Assn., Conveyer Equipment Mfrs. Assn., Cin. New Bus. Devel. Council (chair 1989), Phi Gamma Mu. Roman Catholic. Home and Office: 5666 Cedar Beach Ln Belgium WI 53004-9726

SLATER, JOSEPH ELLIOTT, educational institute administrator; b. Salt Lake City, Aug. 17, 1922; m. Annelore Kremser, Dec. 20, 1947; children: Bonnie Karen Hurst, Sandra Marian Slater. BA with honors, U. Calif., Berkeley, 1943, postgrad., 1943; LLB with honors, Colo. Coll.; PhD (hon.), U. Denver, U. N.H., Kung Hee, Korea. Teaching asst., reader U. Calif.-Berkeley, 1942-43; dep. U.S. sec. Allied Control Council, Berlin, Germany, 1945-48; UN planning staff Dept. State, Washington, 1949; sec.-gen. Allied High Commn. for Germany, Bonn, 1949-52; exec. sec., U.S. spl. rep. in Europe, U.S. sec. to U.S. del. to NATO and OEEC, Paris, France, 1952-53; chief economist Creole Petroleum Corp. (Standard Oil Co. N.J.), Caracas, Venezuela, 1954-57; mem. and dir. internat. affairs program Ford Found., 1957-68, study dir. spl. com. to establish policies and programs, 1961-62; asst. mng. dir. Devel. Loan Fund, Washington, 1960-61; dep. asst. sec. state for edn. and cultural affairs, 1961-62; pres. Salk Inst., LaJolla, Calif., 1967-72, hon. trustee, pres. emeritus; pres., CEO trustee Aspen Inst. for Humanistic Studies, 1969-86, pres. emeritus, trustee, sr. fellow, 1986—; chmn. John J. McCloy Internat. Ctr., 1986—; pres. Anderson Found., N.Y.C., 1969-72; adv. bd. Volvo Internat.; dir. Volvo N.Am. Sec. Pres.'s Com. on Fgn. Assistance (Draper Com.), 1959; del. Atlantic Conf., 1959; mem. devel. assistance panel Pres.'s Sci. Adv. Com., 1960-61; cons. Dept. State, 1961-68; founder, dir., bd. dirs. Creole Found., 1956-57; trustee Carnegie Hall Corp., 1960-86, Asia Soc., 1971-86, Am. Coun. on Germany, 1971—; mem. vis. com., dept. philosophy MIT, 1971-83; trustee Acad. for Ednl. Devel., Internat. Council Ednl. Devel., John J. McCloy Fund; bd. dirs. Eisenhower Exchange Fellowships, Internat. Inst. Environ. Devel., Ctr. for Pub. Resources. Served to lt. USNR, 1943-46; mil. govt. planning officer London, Paris, Berlin; trustee Lovelace Med. Found., 1993—. Decorated Order of Merit Fed. Republic Germany). Mem. NAS (mem. pres.'s cir.), Inst. Strategic Studies (London), Coun. Fgn. Rels., Ctr. for Inter-Am. Rels., Am. Acad. Arts & Scis., Am. Coun. for Jean Monnet Studies (dir.), Inst. for East-West Dynamics (dir.), N.Y. Acad. Scis., Phi Beta Kappa. Clubs: Century Assn. (N.Y.C.), Mid-Atlantic (N.Y.C.). Home: 870 United Nations Plz New York NY 10017 Summer address: 83 Halsey St Southampton NY 11968

SLATER, KRISTIE, construction company executive; b. Rock Springs, Wyo., Nov. 14, 1957; d. Fredrick Earl and Shirley Joan (McWilliams) Alexander; m. C. James Slater, May 11, 1992. A in Bus. Adminstrn., Salt Lake City Coll., 1978. EMT, Wyo. Cost engr., material coord. Project Constrn. Corp., LaBarge, Wyo., 1985; cost engr., scheduler Flour Daniel Constrn. Co., Salt Lake City, 1985-86, Bibby Edible Oils, Liverpool, Eng., 1986-87; cost engr., safety technician Sunvic, Inc./I.S.T.S., Inc., Augusta, Ga., 1987-88; cost engr. Brown & Root, Inc., Ashdown, Ark., 1988-89, Wickliffe, Ky., 1989; sr. cost engr. Brown & Root, Inc., Pasadena, Tex., 1989-90, LaPorte, Tex., 1990-91; project controls mgr. Yeargin Inc., Thousand Oaks, Calif., 1991-92; corp. controls mgr. Suitt Constrn. Co., Greenville, S.C., 1993-95; site scheduler, planner Fluor Daniel Constrn. Co., Seaford, Del., 1996—. Pres. 4-H State Coun., Laramie, Wyo., 1976; mem. com. Houston Livestock Show and Rodeo. Mem. LDS Ch. Avocations: horseback riding, reading, golf. Office: Fluor Daniel Inc Box 361 Seaford DE 19973

SLATER, MARILEE HEBERT, theatre administrator, producer, director, consultant; b. Laredo, Tex., Feb. 25, 1949; d. Minos Joseph and Eulalie (Fisher) Hebert; m. Stewart E. Slater, Dec. 3, 1972 (div. July 1978). BA, Baylor U., 1970, MA, 1972. Cert. secondary sch. tchr., Tex. Actress, dir., assoc. producer Everyman Players, Ky. and La., 1972-80; community rels. dir. Actors Theatre of Louisville, 1973-74, dir. children's theatre, lunchtime & cabaret theatre, 1974-76, dir., apprentice intern program, 1974-77, new play festivals coord., 1979-81, mgr. internat. touring, 1980—, assoc. dir., 1981—; guest dir. Louisville Children's Theatre, 1978; grants panelist Ky. Arts Coun., La. Arts Coun.; conf. lectr. Ky. Arts Coun., Va. Arts Commn., Southeastern Theatre Conf., S.W. Theatre Conf., So. Arts Fedn. Author: (play) Hey Diddle Diddle!, 1976. Pres. Ky. Citizens for Arts, 1985-86, 90-92; co-chmn. subcom. on arts Edn. Workforce, 1990-93; grad. Leadership Louisville, 1989, bd. dirs., 1992—; vice-chmn. Focus Louisville, 1994-96; chmn. Louisville Downtown Mgmt. Dist., 1996-97, Leadership Ptnrs., 1996—; chmn. Farm Works Coun., 1997—; mem. Downtown Devel. Implementation com., Louisville, 1991-93; Louisville Forum adv. coun., 1995-96; bd. dirs. Louisville Ctrl. Area, 1996--97; pres. Park IV Condo Assn., 1989-91, sec. Main St. Assn., 1992-96, v.p., 1997—; staging dir., cons. Walnut St. Bapt. Ch., 1980—. Bingham fellow, 1995-96; recipient Ky. Commonwealth award 1996, NACL Disting. Leadership award, 1997. Democrat. Baptist. Avocations: photography, travel, hiking, music. Office: Actors Theatre Louisville 316 W Main St Louisville KY 40202-2916

SLATER, RODNEY E., federal official; b. Tutwyler, Miss., Feb. 23, 1955; m. Cassandra Wilkins; 1 child. BS, Ea. Mich. U., 1977; JD, U. Ark., 1980. Asst. atty. gen. State of Ark., 1980-82; spl. asst. for community and minority affairs Gov. of Ark., 1983-85, exec. asst. for econ. and community programs, 1985-87; dir. intergovernmental rels. Ark. State U., 1987-93; adminstr. fed. hwy. adminstrn. U.S. Dept. Transp., Washington, 1993-97, sec., 1997—; mem. Ark. State Hwy. and Transp. Commn., 1987-93, chair, 1992-93; dep. campaign mgr., sr. traveling advisor Clinton for Pres. Campaign, 1992; dep. to chair Clinton/Gore Transition Team, 1992-93. Ark. liaison Martin Luther King, Jr. Fed. Holiday Commn., 1983-87; mem. Ark. Sesquicentennial Commn., 1986. Mem. Ark. Bar Assn. (sec.-treas. 1989-93), W. Harold Flowers Law Soc. (pres. 1985-92). Office: Office Sec Dept Transp 400 7th St SW Washington DC 20590-0001*

SLATER, SHELLEY, operations process manager; b. Ogden, Utah, June 26, 1959; d. Lynn Russell and Darlene (Allen) Slater; m. Dale Thomas Hansen, Jan. 26, 1977 (div. Feb. 1979); 1 child, Thomas Arthur; m. Eugene Allan DuVall, Mar. 8, 1981 (div. Dec. 1985); 1 child, Gregory Allan; m. Steven Blake Allender, June 9, 1990 (div. May 1993). BBA cum laude, Regis U., 1992, postgrad., 1992—. Installation, repair technician MT Bell, Clearfield, Utah, 1977-81; ctrl. office technician MT Bell, Salt Lake City, 1981-83, engring. specialist, 1983-86; engring. specialist U.S. West Comm., Englewood, Colo., 1986-93; network analyst, documentation and tng. mgr. Time Warner Comm., Englewood, Colo., 1993-97; ICG comm. process mgr. Time Warner Connect, Englewood, Colo., 1997—; bus. cons. Jr. Achievement, Denver, 1988-89. Day capt. AZTEC Denver Mus. of Natural History, 1992; loaned exec. Mile High United Way, 1993. Mem. Soc. Cable Telecomms. Engrs. (bd. dirs., pres. Rocky Mountain chpt.), Women in Cable and Telecomms. Democrat. Avocations: snow skiing, biking, softball, golf. Office: Time Warner Comm 160 Inverness Dr W Englewood CO 80112-5001

SLATER, THOMAS GLASCOCK, JR., lawyer; b. Washington, Mar. 15, 1944; s. Thomas G. and Hylton R. S.; m. Scott Newell Brent, Aug. 31, 1996; children: Thomas Glascock, Tacie Holden, Andrew Fletcher. B.A., Va. Mil. Inst., 1966; LL.B., U. Va., 1969. Bar: Va. 1969, U.S. Dist. Ct. (ea. dist.) Va. 1970, U.S. Dist Ct. (we. dist.) Va. 1979, U.S. Ct. Appeals (4th cir.) 1975, U.S. Ct. Appeals D.C. 1980, U.S. Supreme Ct. 1981. Assoc. Hunton & Williams, Richmond, Va., 1969-76, ptnr., 1976—; lectr. Pres. VMI Found. Fellow ABA, Va. Law Found.; mem. 4th Cir. Jud. Conf., Va. Bar Assn., Va. State Bar Coun. (exec. com.), D.C. Bar Assn., Richmond Bar Assn. (pres. 1989-90), Va. Mil. Inst. Alumni Assn. (past pres.). Office: Hunton & Williams Riverfrnt Plaza East Tower 951 E Byrd St Richmond VA 23219-4040

SLATER, WILLIAM ADCOCK, retired social services organization executive; b. Kiangsu, People's Republic China, July 26, 1933; (parents U.S. citizens); s. Paul Raymond and Daisy Roberta (Butcher) S.; m. Karen C. Crutchfield, Sept. 4, 1956; children: Kathleen Ann, Bryan Paul. BA in Sociology and History, Wichita State U., 1958; MSW, Denver U., 1960. Juvenile probation officer Hennepin County Dept. Ct. Svcs., Mpls., 1960-63, program dir., 1963-65, dir. social svcs., 1965-67; clin. dir. St. Cloud (Minn.) Children's Home, 1967-70; exec. dir. Gillis Ctr., Women's Christian Assn., Kansas City, Mo., 1970-88, mng. exec. dir., 1988-95; ret., 1995; team leader Coun. on Accreditation Svcs. for Families and Children, Washington, 1975—; presenter various child welfare confs., Okla., Kans., Mo., 1980-88; mem. Mo. Residential Treatment Task Force, Mo. Licensing Standards Task Fopce; mem. levels of care com. Kans. Dept. Social Svcs.; mem. EEO panels Fed. Exec. Bd., 1978, 79; mem. mental health tour People to People, People's Republic China, 1990. Contbr. articles to profl. jours. Mem. spkr.'s bur. United Way Kansas City, 1970—, chmn. agy. rels. com., agys. div., mem. homeless com.; mem. adv. bd. Bingham Jr. High Sch., Kansas City, 1984-86; mem. Kansas City-Xiao Sister City Com. With U.S. Army, 1953-55. Mem. NASW, Acad. Cert. Social Workers, Mo. Assn. Social Welfare, Mo. Child Care Assn. (bd. dirs. 1972-74, 84-88), Kans. Assn. Lic. Pvt. Child Care Agys., Children's Residential Treatment Assn. Kansas City (chmn.), Child Welfare League Am. (steering com. midwest region, nat. adv. coun. to exec. dir. 1976-80), U.S.-China Peoples Friendship Assn. (Kansas City chpt., bd. dirs. Midwest Region), Waldo Bus. Assn. (v.p.), Alpha Kappa Delta. Mem. Christian Ch. (Disciples of Christ). Avocations: history, photography. Home: 9328 Woodson Dr Shawnee Mission KS 66207-2437 Office: Women's Chrstian Assn 8150 Wornall Rd Kansas City MO 64114-5806

SLATKIN, LEONARD EDWARD, conductor, music director, pianist; b. L.A., Sept. 1, 1944; s. Felix Slatkin and Eleanor Aller; m. Linda Hohenfeld, Mar. 29, 1986. Began violin study, 1947; piano study with, Victor Aller and Selma Cramer, 1955; composition study with, Castelnuovo-Tedesco, 1958; viola study with, Sol Schoenbach, 1959; conducting study with, Felix Slatkin, Amerigo Marino and Ingolf Dahl; student, Ind. U., 1962, L.A. City Coll., 1963, Juilliard Sch.; student (Irving Berlin fellow in musical direction), beginning 1964; student of, Jean Morel and Walter Susskind. Founder, music dir., condr. St. Louis Symphony Youth Orch., 1969—, mus. advisor, 1979-80; mus. dir., condr. St. Louis Symphony Orch., 1979-96; mus. dir. Nat. Symphony Orch., Washington, 1996—; current mgmt. ICM Artist, Ltd., Harold Holt, Ltd., Konzertdirektion/Schmidt. Conducting debut as asst. condr., Youth Symphony of N.Y., Carnegie Hall, 1966; asst. condr., Juilliard Opera Theater and Dance Dept., 1967, St. Louis Symphony Orch., 1968-71, assoc. condr., 1971-74; guest conductor Concertgebouw, Royal Danish Orch., Tivoli, English Chamber Orch., BBC Manchester, London Philarmonic, London Synphony Orch., Philarmonia Orch., Nat. Orch. Paris, Stockholm, Oslo, Goetborg, Scottish Nat. Orch., NHK Tokyo, Israel, Berlin, Vienna State Opera, Lyric Opera Chgo., Stuttgart Opera and throughout the world; debut with Chgo. Symphony Orch., 1974, N.Y. Philharmonic, 1974, Phila. Orch., 1974, European debut with Royal Philharmonic Orch., 1974, debut with USSR orchs., 1976-77, Tokyo debut, 1986, Met. Opera debut, 1991; prin. guest condr. Minn. Orch., beginning 1974; summer artistic dir., 1979-89, music dir., New Orleans Philharmonic Symphony Orch., 1977-78, artistic dir. Great Woods, 1990; artistic adminstr. Blossom, 1991; composer: The Raven, Dialogue for Two Cellos and Orchestra, (string quartets) Extensions 1, 2, 3, 4; numerous recordings for RCA, Angel EMI, Vox. Telarc, Philips, Warner Bros. and others. Recipient 2 Grammy awards for Prokofiev Symphony No. 5 with St. Louis Symphony Orch. Nat. Acad. Rec. Arts and Scis., 1985, Declaration of Honor in Silver Austrian Govt., 1986, 5 Honorary Doctorates. Mem. Nat. Acad. Rec. Arts and Scis. (Chgo. chpt. bd. govs.). Office: National Symphony Orchestra John F Kennedy Ctr Washington DC 20566*

SLATKIN, MURRAY, paint sundry distribution executive; b. N.Y.C., June 6, 1905; s. Hyman Noah and Rose (Goldman) S.; m. Lillian Selsky, June 19, 1938; children—Joan, Robert. A.B., Johns Hopkins U., 1925; J.D., U. Md., 1929. Bar: Md. With Felmor Corp., Balt., 1925-38, pres., 1938-92; pres. Nat. Paint Distbrs., Des Plaines, Ill., 1966-68; Chmn. bd. dirs. Felmor Corp., Balt., 1992. Hon. v.p. Zionist Orgn. Am., 1980—. Recipient 1st Judge Sobeloff award, 1973. Mem. Screen Actors Guild, Am. Fedn., T.V. & Radio Artists. Democrat. Jewish. Lodge: B'nai B'rith (Man of Yr. award Menorah lodge 1969, hon. pres. 1982—). Office: Felmor Corp 2020 Hollins Ferry Rd Baltimore MD 21230-1607

SLATON, JOSEPH GUILFORD, social worker; b. N.Y.C., Sept. 29, 1951; s. Joseph Slachta and Hilda Elizabeth (Sims) S.; 1 child, Nicholas Michael. BS, E. Carolina U., 1974; MSW, U. N.C., 1977. Cert. pub. mgr. Cottage parent supr. N.C. Div. Youth Svcs., Rocky Mount, 1974-75; juvenile evaluation counselor N.C. Div. Youth Svcs., Rocky Mount and Butner, N.C., 1975-77; social worker Murdoch Ctr., N.C. Dept. Human Resources, Butner, 1977-78; facility survey cons., mental retardation profl. N.C. Div. Facility Svcs., Raleigh, 1978-81, facility survey cons. long-term care programs, 1981-83, program mgr. health care facilities br., 1983-87, human svcs. planner cert. of need program, 1987-94; sr. analyst, 1994—; asst. Scoutmaster BSA Troop 300, speaker in field. Author: Guide for the Newly Active Democrat, 1996. Mem. N.C. Rehab. Task Force, Raleigh, 1988-90; chmn. subcom. N.C. Mental Retardation Task Force, Raleigh, 1982-83; active N.C. Regional Strategic Planning Task Force, Raleigh, 1982-83; active N.C. Regional Strategic Planning Task Force on Mental Retardation, 1982; mem. allocations panel Wake County United Way, Raleigh, 1984-95; mem. planning com. Wake County Ptnrs. Program Sta. WRAL-TV, Raleigh, 1980, coord. Auction Day, 1981, mem. exec. planning com., 1982; campaign mgr., vol. coord., treas. rep. for N.C. Ho. Reps.; treas. Wake County Dem. Party, 1997—; charter pres. Cary Civitan Club, 1997—. Mem. NASW (legis. policy com.), Acad. Cert. Social Workers, Triangle Health Execs.' Forum, Am. Health Planning Assn. Episcopalian. Avocations: sailing, woodworking, golf. Office: NC Div Facility Svcs PO Box 29530 Raleigh NC 27626-0530

SLATTER, JOHN GREGORY, research scientist; b. Guelph, Ont., Can., Feb. 7, 1955; came to U.S., 1988; s. Wallace Osborne Conway and Nancy Dalzel (Hanna) S.; m. Vandana Khare, July 23, 1988. BSc in Biology and Chemistry with honors, Lakehead U., Thunder Bay, Ont., 1977; MSc in Pharm. Scis., U. B.C., Vancouver, Can., 1983, BSc in Pharm. Scis., 1988, PhD in Pharm. Scis., 1988. Lic. pharmacist, B.C. Postdoctoral fellow U. Wash., Seattle, 1988-90; rsch. scientist Upjohn Co., Kalamazoo, 1990-94, sr. scientist, 1994—. Contbr. articles to profl. jours. including Drug Metabolism and Disposition, Chem. Rsch. in Toxicology, Xenobiotica. U. B.C. grad. fellow, 1983. Mem. Am. Chem. Soc., Internat. Soc. for Study Xenobiotics, Kalamazoo Over-30 Hockey Assn. (2d v.p. 1992-94). Achievements include co-discovery of structure of transport form of methyl isocyanate in biological systems; research in toxic symptoms of survivors of the Bhopal Industrial Accident. Home: 3041 Hunters Hl Kalamazoo MI 49004-

9113 Office: Pharmacia & Upjohn Co Drug Metabolism Rsch Portage Rd Kalamazoo MI 49007

SLATTERY, CHARLES WILBUR, biochemistry educator; b. La Junta, Colo., Nov. 18, 1937; s. Robert Ernest Slattery and Virgie Belle (Chamberlain) Tobin; m. Arline Sylvia Reile, June 15, 1958; children: Scott Charles, Coleen Kay. BA, Union Coll., 1959; MS, U. Nebr., 1961, PhD, 1965. Instr. chemistry Union Coll., Lincoln, Nebr., 1961-63; asst. prof., assoc. prof. chemistry Atlantic Union Coll., South Lancaster, Mass., 1963-68; rsch. assoc. biophysics MIT, Cambridge, 1967-70; asst. prof., then prof. biochemistry Loma Linda U., Calif., 1970-80, prof. biochemistry-pediatrics, 1980—, chmn. dept., 1983—; vis. prof. U. So. Calif., L.A., 1978-79. Contbr. articles to profl. jours. NIH grantee, 1979-82, 86-89, Am. Heart Assn. (Calif.), 1981-83, 83-84. Mem. AAAS, Am. Chem. Soc. (biochemistry div.), Am. Dairy Sci. Assn., Am. Heart Assn. Thrombosis Coun., N.Y. Acad. Scis., The Protein Soc., Am. Soc. Biochemistry and Molecular Biology. Internat. Soc. for Rsch. on Human Milk and Lactation, Sigma Xi. Office: Loma Linda U Sch of Medicine Dept of Biochemistry Loma Linda CA 92350

SLATTERY, EDWARD J., bishop; b. Chgo., Aug. 11, 1940. Student, St. Mary of the Lake Sem., Mundelein, Ill., Loyola U., Chgo. Ordained priest Roman Cath. Ch., 1966. Ordained priest Chgo., 1966; v.p. Cath. Ch. Ext. Soc., 1971-76, pres., 1976-94; ordained bishop Diocese of Tulsa, 1994—. Office: Diocese of Tulsa Chancery Office PO Box 2009 Tulsa OK 74101-2009*

SLATTERY, JAMES JOSEPH (JOE SLATTERY), actor; b. Memphis, Feb. 7, 1922; s. James Joseph and Katie May (Carlin) S.; m. Mary Margaret Costello, May 23, 1944 (dec. Aug. 1987); children: James Joseph, John P., Ann, Mary, Nancy; m. Marilyn Daus, Sept. 16, 1989. A.B., Hendrix Coll., Conway, Ark., 1947. pres. Am. Fedn. TV and Radio Artists, 1976-79; dir. Bank No. Ill., Waukegan. Actor. Served with USAAF, 1942-46; to lt. col. USAF (ret.). Recipient Disting. Grad. award Hendrix Coll., 1986. Mem. Screen Actors Guild. Roman Catholic. Address: 5 The Court Of Bayview Northbrook IL 60062-3201

SLATTERY, WILLIAM JOSEPH, school psychologist; b. N.Y.C., May 11, 1955; s. William Joseph and Theresa Mary (Cummings) S. BA, Manhattan Coll., 1977; MS in Edn. with honors, Pace U., 1979; postgrad., U. Fla., 1988—. Cert. sch. psychologist, N.Y., Fla.; nat. cert. sch. psychologist. Team leader, therapy aide Bronx (N.Y.) Psychiat. Ctr., 1978-79; sch. psychologist Middletown (N.Y.) Pub. Schs., 1979-84, N.Y. State Div. for Youth, Middletown, 1983, Bd. Coop. Ednl. Svcs. Orange County, Goshen, N.Y., 1985-86; sch. psychologist, cons. group home div. Piux XII Youth and Family Svcs., Middletown, 1980-85, adminstrv. aide, psychologist foster care div., 1984-85; therapist IV, Univ. Hosp. Jacksonville, Fla., 1986-88; coord. dist. crisis team Duval County Pub. Schs., Jacksonville, 1988-90; sch. psychologist Sch. Bd. Alachua County, Gainesville, Fla., 1990-94; sch. psychologist, program mgr. multidisciplinary diagnostic and tng. program U. Fla., 1994—. Recipient Merit Edn. award Univ. Hosp. Jacksonville, 1988, Outstanding Svc. award Duval County Pub. Schs., 1990. Mem. NASP, Fla. Assn. Sch. Psychologists (rsch. com. 1990-92), Am. Assn. Suicidology, Sertoma (chater Gainesville chpt.), Phi Delta Kappa. Avocations: swimming, scuba diving. Home: 75 SW 75th St Apt B-8 Gainesville FL 32607 Office: U Fla Multidiscplinary Diagnostic & Tng Prog 1341 Norman Hall Gainesville FL 32611

SLAUGH, LYNN H., chemist. With Shell Devel. Co., Houston. Author 132 patents; inventor two indsl. processes; contbr. articles to profl. jours. Recipient Indsl. Chemistry award Am. Chem. Soc., 1995. Office: Shell Chem Comp PO Box 1380 Houston TX 77251-1380

SLAUGHTER, ALEXANDER HOKE, lawyer; b. Charlottesville, Va., Nov. 24, 1937; s. Edward Ratliff and Mary (Hoke) S.; m. Virginia Borah, 1964 (div.); 1 child, David A.; m. Mary Peeples, 1971. BA, Yale U., 1960; LLB, U. Va., 1963. Episcopalian. Home: 1410 Pump House Dr Richmond VA 23221-3915 Office: McGuire Woods Battle & Boothe LLP One James Ctr 901 E Cary St Richmond VA 23219-4057

SLAUGHTER, EDWARD RATLIFF, JR., lawyer; b. Raleigh, N.C., Sept. 15, 1931; s. Edward Ratliff and Mary McBee (Hoke) S.; m. Anne Limbosch, July 25, 1957; children: Anne-Marie, Hoke, Bryan. A.B., Princeton U., 1953; postgrad. (Rotary Found. fellow), U. Brussels, 1955-56; LL.B., U. Va., 1959. Bar: Va. 1959, D.C. 1981. Assoc. firm McGuire, Woods & Battle (now McGuire, Woods, Battle & Boothe) and predecessors, Charlottesville, Va., 1959-64; ptnr. McGuire, Woods & Battle and predecessors, 1964-79, head dept. litigation, 1964-79; spl. asst. for litigation to atty. gen. U.S., 1979-81; ptnr. firm Whitman & Ransom, Washington, 1981-84; prin. Slaughter & Redinger, P.C., Charlottesville, 1984-95, Slaughter, Izakowitz, Clarke & Nunley, P.C., 1995-96, Woods, Rogers & Hazlegrove, P.L.C., 1996—; vis. lectr. trial advocacy U. Va., 1970-77, Va. procedure, 1986-91; disting. lectr. U. Tunis, 1996. Chmn. Albemarle County (Va.) Dem. Com., 1969-73; pres. Charlottesville-Albemarle United Way, 1972; commr. accounts Albemarle County, 1986—; trustee Lime Kiln Arts, Inc., 1992—. Served with USNR, 1953-55. Fellow Am. Bar Found., Am. Coll. Trial Lawyers; mem. Am. Bar Assn., D.C. Bar, Charlottesville-Albemarle Bar Assn. (pres. 1976-77), Va. Bar Assn. (pres. 1978), Va. State Bar (bd. govs. internat. practice sect. 1992—), Va. Trial Lawyers Assn., Thomas Jefferson Inn Ct. (pres. 1995-96). Club: Boar's Head Sports, Farmington Country. Home: 111 Falcon Dr Charlottesville VA 22901-2035 Office: Woods Rogers & Hazlegrove PLC PO Box 2964 250 W Main St Ste 300 Charlottesville VA 22902-2964

SLAUGHTER, ENOS, retired baseball player; b. Roxboro, N.C., Apr. 27, 1916. Baseball player St. Louis Cardinals, 1938-42, 46-53, N.Y. Yankees, 1954-59, Kansas City Athletics, 1955-56, Milw. Braves, 1959. Named to Baseball Hall of Fame, 1985; selected All-Star Team, 1941-42, 46-53; mem. World Series Champions, 1942, 46, 58. Office: care Nat Baseball Hall Fame PO Box 590 Cooperstown NY 13326

SLAUGHTER, FRANK GILL, author, physician; b. Washington, Feb. 25, 1908; s. Stephen Lucius and Sallie Nicholson (Gill) S.; m. Jane Mundy, June 10, 1933; children: Frank G., Randolph M. A.B., Duke U., 1926; M.D., Johns Hopkins U., 1930; L.H.D., Jacksonville U., 1975. Diplomate Am. Bd. Surgery. Intern, asst. resident and resident surgeon Jefferson Hosp., Roanoke, Va., 1930-34; practice medicine specializing in surgery Jacksonville, Fla., 1934-42; ret., 1946; lectr. W. Colston Leigh, Inc., N.Y.C., 1947-49. Author: That None Should Die, 1941, Spencer Brade, M.D, 1942, Air Surgeon, 1942, Battle Surgeon, 1944, A Touch of Glory, 1945, In a Dark Garden, 1946, The New Science of Surgery, 1946, The Golden Isle, 1947, Sangaree, 1948, Medicine for Moderns, 1948, Divine Mistress, 1949, The Stubborn Heart, 1950, Immortal Magyar, 1950, Fort Everglades, 1951, The Road to Bithynia, 1951, East Side General, 1952, The Galileans, 1953, Storm Haven, 1953, The Song of Ruth, Apalachee Gold, 1954, The Healer, Flight from Natchez, 1955, The Scarlet Cord, 1956, The Warrior, 1956, Sword and Scalpel, 1957, The Mapmaker, 1957, Daybreak, 1958, The Thorn of Arimathea, 1958, The Crown and the Cross, 1959, Lorena, 1959, The Land and the Promise, 1960, Pilgrims in Paradise, 1960, Epidemic, 1961, The Curse of Jezebel, 1961, David: Warrior and King, 1962, Tomorrow's Miracle, 1962, Devil's Harvest, 1963, Upon This Rock, 1963, A Savage Place, 1964, The Purple Quest, 1965, Constantine: The Miracle of the Flaming Cross, 1965, Surgeon, U.S.A, 1966, God's Warrior, 1967, Doctor's Wives, 1967, The Sins of Herod, 1968, Surgeon's Choice, 1969, Countdown, 1970, Code Five, 1971, Convention M.D, 1972, Women in White, 1974, Stonewall Brigade, 1975, Plague Ship, 1976, Devil's Gamble, 1977, The Passionate Rebel, 1979, Gospel Fever, 1980, Doctor's Daughters, 1981, Doctors At Risk, 1983, No Greater Love, 1984, Transplant, 1987. Served from maj. to lt. col. M.C., U.S. Army, 1942-46. Fellow ACS. Presbyterian (elder). Home: PO Box 14 Jacksonville FL 32210-0014

SLAUGHTER, JAMES C., trading company executive; b. N.Y.C., Aug. 9, 1927; s. Joseph C. and Grace (Redell) S.; m. Lee Slaughter, June 14, 1956. BA, U. Va., 1949, LLB, 1951. Assoc. Otterbourg, Steindler, Houston & Rosen, N.Y.C., 1951-54, Hahn & Golin, N.Y.C., 1954-59; ptnr. Hahn & Golin, 1959-62; v.p. Reeves Bros. Inc., N.Y.C., 1962-69; ptnr. Hahn Hessen Margolis & Ryan, N.Y.C., 1969-73; chief exec. officer, chmn. bd. James Talcott Inc., N.Y.C., 1973-76; v.p. Assoc. Metals & Minerals, N.Y.C., 1976-85; chmn. bd. Assoc. Metals & Minerals, 1985—. Trustee Jerusalem Found., N.Y.C., 1988—, Am. Assn. of Royal Acad., 1990—; mng. dir. Horace Goldsmith Found., N.Y.C., 1980—; adv. dir. Met. Opera Assn., 1990—. With U.S. Army, 1944-46. Mem. Assn. of the Bar of City of N.Y., ABA, N.Y.C. Lawyers Assn., Harmonie Club, City Athletic Club, Turf & Field. Democrat. Jewish. Office: Associated Metals & Mineral 3 Corporate Park Dr White Plains NY 10604-3803

SLAUGHTER, JOHN BROOKS, university administrator; b. Topeka, Mar. 16, 1934; s. Reuben Brooks and Dora (Reeves) S.; m. Ida Bernice Johnson, Aug. 31, 1956; children: John Brooks, Jacqueline Michelle. Student, Washburn U., 1951-53; BSEE, Kans. State U., 1956, DSc (hon.), 1988; MS in Engring., UCLA, 1961; PhD in Engring. Scis, U. Calif., San Diego, 1971; D Engring. (hon.), Rensselaer Poly. Inst., 1981; DSc (hon.), U. So. Calif., 1981, Tuskegee Inst., 1981, U. Md., 1982, U. Notre Dame, 1982, U. Miami, 1983, U. Mass., 1983, Tex. So. U., 1984, U. Toledo, 1985, U. Ill., 1986, SUNY, 1986; LHD (hon.), Bowie State Coll., 1987; DSc (hon.), Morehouse Coll., 1988, Kans. State U., 1988; LLD (hon.), U. Pacific, 1989; DSc (hon.), Pomona Coll., 1989; LHD (hon.), Alfred U., 1991, Calif. Luth. U., 1991, Washburn U., 1992. Registered profl. engr., Wash. Electronics engr. Gen. Dynamics Convair, San Diego, 1956-60; with Naval Electronics Lab. Center, San Diego, 1960-75, div. head, 1965-71, dept. head, 1971-75; dir. applied physics lab. U. Wash., 1975-77; asst. dir. NSF, Washington, 1977-79; dir. NSF, 1980-82; acad. v.p., provost Wash. State U., 1979-80; chancellor U. Md., College Park, 1982-88; pres. Occidental Coll., Los Angeles, 1988—; bd. dirs., vice chmn. San Diego Transit Corp., 1968-75; mem. com. on minorities in engring. Nat. Rsch. Coun., 1976-79; mem. Commn. on Pre-Coll. Edn. in Math., Sci. and Tech. Nat. Sci. Bd., 1982-83; bd. dirs. Monsanto Co., ARCO, Avery Dennison Corp., IBM, Northrop Grumman Corp.; chmn. advancement com. Music Ctr. of L.A. County, 1989-93. Editor: Jour. Computers and Elec. Engring, 1972—. Bd. dirs. San Diego Urban League, 1962-66, pres., 1964-66; mem. Pres.'s Com. on Nat. Medal Sci., 1979-80; trustee Rensselaer Poly. Inst., 1982; chmn. Pres.'s Com. Nat. Collegiate Athletic Assn., 1986-88; bd. govs. Town Hall of Calif., 1990; bd. dirs. L.A. World Affairs Coun., 1990. Recipient Engring. Disting. Alumnus of Yr. award UCLA, 1978, UCLA medal, 1989, Roger Revelle award U. Calif.-San Diego, 1991, Disting. Svc. award NSF, 1979, Svc. in Engring. award Kans. State U., 1981, Disting. Alumnus of Yr. award U. Calif.-San Diego, 1982; Naval Electronics Lab. Ctr. fellow, 1969-70; elected to Topeka High Sch. Hall of Fame, 1983, Hall of Fame of Am. Soc. Engring. Edn., 1993; named Kansan of Yr. by Kans. Native Sons and Daus., 1994. Fellow IEEE (chmn. com. on minority affairs 1976-80), Am. Acad. Arts and Scis.; mem. NAE, Nat. Collegiate Athletic Assn. (chmn. pres. commn.), Am. Soc. for Engring. Edn. (inducted into Hall of Fame 1993), Phi Beta Kappa (hon.), Tau Beta Pi, Eta Kappa Nu. Office: Occidental Coll 1600 Campus Rd Los Angeles CA 90041-3314

SLAUGHTER, LOUISE MCINTOSH, congresswoman; b. Harlan County, Ky., Aug. 14, 1929; d. Oscar Lewis and Grace (Byers) McIntosh; m. Robert Slaughter, 1956; children: Megan Rae, Amy Louise, Emily Robin. BS, U. Ky., 1951, MS, 1953. Bacteriologist Ky. Dept. Health, Louisville, 1951-52, U. Ky., 1952-53; market researcher Procter & Gamble, Cin., 1953-56; mem. staff Office of the Lt. Gov. N.Y., Albany, 1978-82; state rep. N.Y. Gen. Assembly, Albany, 1983-86; mem. 100th-103rd Congresses from 30th (now 28th) N.Y. dist., Washington, D.C., 1987—; mem. Ho. Govt. Reform and Oversight com., Ho. Budget com. Del. Dem. Nat. Conv., 1972, 76, 80, 88, 92; mem. Monroe County Pure Water Adminstrn. Bd., Nat. Ctr. for Policy Alternatives Adv. Bd., League of Women Voters, Nat. Women's Polit. Caucus. Office: US Ho of Reps Office of House Mems 2347 Rayburn Bldg Washington DC 20515-3228

SLAUGHTER-DEFOE, DIANA TRESA, education educator; b. Chgo., Oct. 28, 1941; d. John Ison and Gwendolyn Malva (Armstead) S.; m. Michael Defoe (div.). BA, U. Chgo., 1962, MA, 1964, PhD, 1968. Instr. dept. psychiatry Howard U., Washington, 1967-68; rsch. asso., asst. prof. Yale U. Child Study Ctr., New Haven, 1968-70; asst. prof. dept. behavioral scis. and edn. U. Chgo., 1970-77; assoc. prof. edn. and African Am. studies and Ctr. for Urban Affairs and Policy Rsch. Northwestern U., Evanston, Ill., 1977-90, prof., 1990—; mem. nat. adv. bd. Fed. Ctr. for Child Abuse & Neglect, 1979-82, coord. Human Devel. and Social Policy Program, 1994—; mem. nat. adv. bd. Learning Rsch. and Devel. Ctr. U. Pitts., Ednl. Rsch. & Devel. Ctr., U. Tex., Austin; chmn., dir. public policy program com. Chgo. Black Child Devel. Inst., 1982-84; dir. Ill. Infant Mental Health Com., 1982-83; mem. res. adv. bd. Chgo. Urban League, 1986—. Fellow APA (mem. divsn. ethnic and minority affairs, com. on children, youth & families, bd. sci. affairs 1995—, mem. editl. bd. Child Devel., 1995—, Disting. Contbn. to Rsch. in Pub. Policy award 1993); mem. Soc. for Rsch. in Child Devel. (governing coun. 1981-87), Am. Ednl. Rsch. Assn., Assn. Black Psychologists, Nat. Head Start (mem. R & E adv. bd.), Nat. Acad. Scis. (com. on child devel. and publ. policy, 1987-93), Delta Sigma Theta. Contbr. articles to profl. jours. Home: 835 Ridge Ave Evanston IL 60202-1776 Office: 2115 N Campus Dr Evanston IL 60208-0002

SLAVENS, THOMAS PAUL, library science educator; b. Cincinnati, Iowa, Nov. 12, 1928; s. William Blaine and Rhoda (Bowen) S.; m. Cora Pearl Hart, July 9, 1950; 1 son, Mark Thomas. B.A., Phillips U., 1951; M.Div., Union Theol. Sem., 1954; M.A., U. Minn., 1962; Ph.D., U. Mich., 1965. Ordained to ministry Christian Ch., 1953. Pastor First Christian Ch., Sac City, Iowa, 1953-56, Sioux Falls, S.D., 1956-60; librarian Divinity Sch., Drake U., Des Moines, 1960-64; teaching fellow Sch. Info., U. Mich., Ann Arbor, 1964-65; instr. U. Mich., Ann Arbor, 1965-66, asst. prof., 1966-69, assoc. prof., 1969-77, prof., 1977—; vis. prof. U. Minn., 1967, U. Coll. of Wales, 1978, 80, 93; vis. scholar U. Oxford, Eng., 1980; adv. bd. Marcel Dekker Inc., N.Y.C., 1982—; cons. Nutrition Planning Abstracts-UN, N.Y.C., 1977-79. Author-editor: Library Problems in the Humanities, 1981, (with John F. Wilson) Research Guide to Religious Studies, 1982, (with W. Eugene Kleinbaur) Research Guide to History of Western Art, 1982, (with Terrence Tice) Research Guide to Philosophy, 1983, Theological Libraries at Oxford, 1984, (with James Pruett) Research Guide to Musicology, 1985, The Literary Adviser, 1985, A Great Library through Gifts, 1986, The Retrieval of Information, 1989, Number One in the U.S.A.: Records and Wins in Sports, Entertainment, Business, and Science, 1988, 2d edit., 1990, Doors to God, 1990, Sources of Information for Historical Research, 1994, Introduction to Systematic Theology, 1992, Reference Interviews Questions and Materials, 3d edit., 1994. Served with U.S. Army, 1946-48. Recipient Warner Rice Faculty award U. Mich., 1975; H.W. Wilson fellow, 1960; Lilly Endowment fellow Am. Theol. Library Assn., 1963. Mem. ALA (chmn. coms. 1964—), Assn. Libr. and Info. Sci. Edn. (pres. 1972), Beta Phi Mu. Home: 3745 Tremont Ln Ann Arbor MI 48105-3022 Office: University of Michigan School of Information 550 E University Ave Ann Arbor MI 48109-1092

SLAVICH, DENIS MICHAEL, engineering and construction company executive; b. San Francisco, June 1, 1940; s. Francis Luke and Betsy Florence (Carpenter) S.; m. Michele Christine Meyer, June 15, 1963 (div. July 1, 1979) 1 child: Samantha Nicole; m. Debbie Teh-Yan Chao, Nov. 22, 1980; children: David Francis, Destinie Florence. BSEE, U. Calif., Berkeley, 1964; MBA, U. Pitts., 1967; PhD, MIT, 1971. Elec. engr. Douglas Aircraft, Santa Monica, Calif., 1964-65, Hughes Aircraft, Culver City, Calif., 1965-66; prof. Boston U., 1969-71, Stanford U., Palo Alto, Calif., 1984; sr. v.p. Bechtel Group, Inc., San Francisco, 1971-91; v.p. Fluor Daniel, Inc., Irvine, Calif., 1991-95; exec. v.p., CFO Morrison Knudsen Corp., Boise, 1995—. Contbr. articles to profl. jours. Mem. Am. Fin. Assn., Nat. Assn. Bus. Econs., U. Calif. Engring. Alumni Soc., San Francisco C. of C. (bd. dirs. 1987-89), Olympic Club, Pacific Union Club, Beta Gamma Sigma. Avocations: golf; hiking. Office: Morrison Knudsen Corp PO Box 73 Boise ID 83729

SLAVICK, ANN LILLIAN, art educator, arts; b. Chgo., Sept. 29, 1933; d. Irving and Goldie (Bernstein) Friedman; m. Lester Irwin Slavick, Nov. 21, 1954 (div. Mar. 1987); children: Jack, Rachel. BFA, Sch. of Art Inst. of Chgo., 1973, MA in Art History, Theory, Criticism, 1991. Dir. art gallery South Shore Commn., Chgo., 1963-67; tchr. painting, drawing, crafts Halfway House, Chgo., 1972-73; tchr. studio art Conant H.S., Hoffman Estates, Ill., 1973-74; tchr. art history and studio arts New Trier H.S., Winnetka and Northfield, Ill., 1974-80; tchr. 20th century art history New Trier Adult Edn. Program, Winnetka, 1980-81; tchr. art adult edn. program H.S. Dist. 113, Highland Park, Ill., 1980-81; rschr., writer Art History Notes McDougall-Littel Pub., Evanston, Ill., 1984-85; tchr. art and art history Highland Park and Deerfield (Ill.) H.S., 1980—; tchr. art history Coll. of Lake County, Grayslake, Ill., 1986-88; faculty chair for visual arts Focus on the Arts, Highland Park H.S., 1981-85, faculty coord. Focus on the Arts, 1987—. One woman show Bernal Gallery, 1979, U. Ill., Chgo., 1983, Ann Brierly Gallery, Winnetka, 1984; exhibited paintings, drawings, prints and constrns. throughout Chgo. area; work represented by Art Rental and Sales Gallery, Art Inst. Chgo., 1960-87, Bernal Gallery, 1978-82; group shows at Bernal Gallery; work in pvt. collections in Ill., N.Y., Calif., Ariz., Ohio. Recipient Outstanding Svc. in Art Edn. award Ea. Ill. U., 1992, Mayors award for contbn. to the arts, Highland Park, 1995. Mem. Nat. Art Edn. Assn., Ill. Art Edn. Assn. Avocations: cooking, reading, theatre. Home: 5057 N Sheridan Rd Chicago IL 60640-3127 Office: Highland Park High Sch 433 Vine Ave Highland Park IL 60035-2044

SLAVIN, ARLENE, artist; b. N.Y.C., Oct. 26, 1942; d. Louis and Sally (Bryck) Eisenberg; m. Neal Slavin, May 24, 1964 (div. 1979); m. Eric Bregman, Sept. 21, 1980; 1 child, Ethan. BFA, Cooper Union for the Advancement of Sci. and Art, 1964; MFA, Pratt Inst., 1967. One woman exhbns. include Fischbach Gallery, N.Y., 1973,74, Brooke Alexander Gallery, N.Y., 1976, Alexander Milliken Gallery, N.Y.C., 1979, 80, 81, 83, U. Colo., 1981, Pratt Inst., N.Y.C., 1981, Am. Embassy, Belgrad, Yugoslavia, 1984, Heckscher Mus., Huntington, N.Y., 1987, Katherine Rich Perlow Gallery, 1988, Chauncey Gallery, Princeton, N.J., 1990, The Gallery Benjamin N. Cardoza Sch. Law, 1991, Norton Ctr. for Arts, Danville, Ky., 1992, Kavesh Gallery, Ketchum, Idaho, 1993; exhibited in group shows at Bass Mus. Art, Fla., Whitney Museum of Art, 1973, The Contempory Arts Center, Cinn., Oh., 1974, Indianapolis Museum of Art, 1974, Madison (Wis.) Art Ctr., Santa Barbara (Calif.) Mus., Winnipeg (Can.) Art Gallery, Gensler Assocs., San Francisco, 1986, Eliane Benson Gallery, Bridgehampton, N.Y., 1987, 89, 91, 93, City of N.Y. Parks and Recreation Central Park, N.Y.C. 1989, Benton Gallery, Southampton, N.Y., 1991, Parish Mus., Southampton, 1991, Michele Miller Fine Art, 1993 ; executed murals N.Y. Aquarium, Bklyn., 1982, Pub. Art Fund, N.Y.C., 1983, Albert Einstein Sch. of Medicine, Bronx, N.Y., 1983, Hudson River Mus., Yonkers, N.Y., 1983, Bellevue Hosp. Ctr., N.Y.C., 1986; represented in permanent collections at Met. Mus. of Art, N.Y.C, Bklyn. Mus., Fogg Art Mus., Cambridge, Mass., Hudson River Mus., Yonkers, N.Y., Heckscher Mus., Huntington, N.Y., Cin. Art Mus., Readers' Digest, Pleasantville, N.Y., Guild Hall, East Hampton, N.Y., Allen Meml. Art Mus., Oberlin, Ohio, Norton Mus., Palm Beach, Fla., Portland (Oreg.) Mus., Orlando (Fla.) Mus. Art, Neuburger Mus., Purchase, N.Y.; pub. commd. work iron gates Cathedral St. John the Divine, N.Y.C., 1988, 55' steel fence Henry St Settlement, N.Y., 1992, metal work stairway De Soto Sch., N.Y. Sch. Art, 1994-95, ornamental railings N.J. Transit, Newport, 1997, Liberty State Pk. Sta. 6 arts elements, 1997, 220' narrative fence Kissena Park, Queens, N.Y., 1997. Grantee Nat. Endowment for Arts, 1977-78, Threshold Found., 1991. Home and Studio: 119 E 18th St New York NY 10003-2107

SLAVIN, CRAIG STEVEN, management and franchising consultant; b. Tucson, Sept. 7, 1951; s. Sidney and Eileen (Gilbert) S.; m. Carol Lynn Haft, Aug. 30, 1982; children: Carly Blair, Samantha Illyna. Student, U. Ariz., 1969073, U. Balt., 1978. Dir. franchising and sales Evelyn Wood Reading Dynamics, Walnut Creek, Calif., 1974-75; dir. franchising Pasquale Food Co., Birmingham, Ala., 1975-77; exec. v.p. Franchise Concepts, Flossmoor, Ill., 1977-80; pres. Franchise Architects, Chgo., 1980-88; mng. dir. franchise practice Arthur Andersen & Co., Chgo., 1988-91; chmn. Franchise Architects, Riverwoods, Ill., 1991—; founder, bd. dirs. Franchise Broadcast Network, Riverwoods, 1991—; founder Franchise Success System, 1991, The Original Franchise Match, 1992. Author: Complete Guide to Self-Employment in Franchising, 1991, Franchising for the Growing Company, 1993, AMACON, The Franchising Handbook. Mem. ABA (faculty), Am. Arbitration Assn., Internat. Franchise Assn., Nat. Assn. Info. Suppliers, Water Quality Assn., Inst. Mgmt. Cons., Coun. Franchise Suppliers (adv. bd. dirs.), Nat. Restaurant Assn. Avocations: golf, chess, saltwater fish. Home and Office: The Franchise Architects 3 Metawa Ln Deerfield IL 60015-3551

SLAVIN, RAYMOND GRANAM, allergist, immunologist; b. Cleve., June 29, 1930; s. Philip and Dinah (Baskind) S.; m. Alberta Cohrt, June 10, 1953; children: Philip, Stuart, David, Linda. A.B., U. Mich., 1952; M.D., St. Louis U., 1956; M.S., Northwestern U., 1963. Diplomate: Am. Bd. Internal Medicine, Am. Bd. Allergy and Immunology (treas.). Intern U. Mich. Hosp., Ann Arbor, 1956-57; resident St. Louis U. Hosp., 1959-61; fellow in allergy and immunology Northwestern U. Med. Sch., 1961-64; asst. prof. internal medicine and microbiology St. Louis U., 1965-70, assoc., 1970-73, prof., 1973—, dir. div. allergy and immunology, 1965—; mem. NIH study sect., 1985-89; cons. U.S. Army M.C. Contbr. numerous articles to med. publs.; editorial bd.: Jour. Allergy and Clin. Immunology, 1975-81, Tice Practice Medicine, 1973-84, Jour. Club of Allergy, 1978-80. Chmn. bd. Asthma and Allergy Found. Am., 1985-88. With M.C., U.S. Army, 1957-59. Grantee NIH, 1967-70, 84—, Nat. Inst. Occpl. Safety and Health, 1974-80. Fellow ACP, Am. Acad. Allergy and Immunology (exec. bd., historian, pres. 1983-84); mem. Am. Assn. Immunologists, Central Soc. Clin. Research, AAAS. Democrat. Jewish. Home: 631 E Polo Dr Saint Louis MO 63105-2629 Office: 1402 S Grand Blvd Saint Louis MO 63104-1004

SLAVIN, ROBERT EDWARD, research scientist, educator; b. Bethesda, Md., Sept. 17, 1950; s. Joseph George and Miriam Helen (Crohn) S.; m. Nancy Abigail Madden, July 22, 1973; children: Jacob, Benjamin, Rebecca. BA, Reed Coll., 1972; PhD, Johns Hopkins U., 1975. Tchr. Beaverton (Oreg.) Pub. Schs., 1972-73; prin. rsch. scientist Johns Hopkins U., Balt., 1975—. Author: Educational Psychology, 5th edit., 1997, Preventing Early School Failure, 1994, Every Child Every School: Success for All, 1996. Recipient As They Grow award Parents Mag., 1994, Charles Dana award Charles Dana Found., 1994. Mem. Am. Ednl. Rsch. Assn. (chair publs. com. 1990-92, mem. at large 1996-99, Raymond Cattell award 1986, Palmer O. Johnson award 1988), Internat. Assn. for Study of Cooperation in Edn. (pres. 1988-90). Office: Ctr Social Orgn Schs 3505 N Charles St Baltimore MD 21218-2404

SLAVIN, SIMON, social administration educator; b. N.Y.C., Jan. 20, 1916; s. Isadore and Mary (Sushansky) S.; m. Jeannette Rose Littinsky, Jan. 16, 1938; children: Rayna (Mrs. Robert Epstein dec.), Vicky Jane, Johanna. B.S. in Social Sci, CCNY, 1937; M.A., Columbia U., 1938, Ed.D., 1953. Regional supr. United Service Orgn. Jewish Welfare Bd., Chgo., 1945-46; exec. dir. YM-YWHA, Mt. Vernon, N.Y., 1946-53; exec. sec. div. recreation and group work and sect. on services to handicapped Welfare and Health Council of N.Y.C., 1953-54; exec. dir. Ednl. Alliance, N.Y.C., 1954-60; asso. prof. social work Columbia U., 1960-63; prof., 1963-68, chmn. community orgn. area, 1960-66, chmn. advanced programs, 1966-67; Simon Sr. Research fellow U. Manchester, Eng., 1967-68; dean Sch. Social Adminstrn., Temple U., 1968-78, prof., 1978-80, prof., founding dean emeritus, 1983—; chmn. regional adv. com. Region III Dept. Pub. Welfare, Phila., 1972-74; instr. Adelphi Coll., 1955-58, N.Y. U., 1956-57, Chgo. U., 1958-59; cons. N.Y.C. Commr. of Drug Addiction Services. Author, co-editor: Leadership in Social Administration, 1980; editor: Social Administration: The Management of Social Services, 1978, Applying Computers in Social Service and Mental Health Agencies, 1983, An Introduction to Human Services Management, 1985, Managing Finances, Personnel and Information in Human Services, 1985; contbr. chpts. to Migration and Social Welfare, 1971, Evaluation of Social Intervention, 1972, A Design for Social Work Practice, 1974, Social Work Futures, 1983, Educating Managers of Nonprofit Organizations, 1988; editor in chief Adminstrn. in Social Work, 1977-92; book series editor Haworth Press, 1990—; also numerous articles to profl. jours. Mem. personnel adv. com. Nat. Urban League, 1964-66. Recipient Assn. for Community Orgn. and Social Adminstrn. Outstanding Life Achievement award, 1993. Home: Kimball Fams 235 Walker St Lenox MA 01240

SLAVITT, DAVID WALTON, retired lawyer; b. Chgo., Mar. 15, 1931; s. Isaac and Fay (Goldstein) S.; m. Roberta Chelnek, July 26, 1953; children: Steven, Denise, Howard. B.S., UCLA, 1952, J.D., 1955. Bar: Calif. 1956; C.P.A., Calif. Since practiced in Los Angeles; pres. Slavitt & Borofsky (P.C.), 1969-87; moderator continuing edn. programs. Author articles in field. Served with USNR, 1955. Mem. Am. Assn. Atty.-C.P.A.s (pres.

1964), ABA, State Bar Calif., Calif. Assn. Atty.-C.P.A.s (pres. 1963), Beverly Hills Bar Assn. (vice chmn. continuing edn. of bar 1970, asst. chmn. law practice mgmt. com. 1973).

SLAVITT, EARL BENTON, lawyer; b. Chgo., Sept. 12, 1939; s. Harold Hal and Rose (Hoffman) S.; m. Amy Lerner, July 12, 1987; 1 child, Gabriel Harrel; children from previous marriage: Andrew Miller, Lesley Deborah. BS in Econs., U. Pa., 1961, JD, 1964. Bar: Ill. 1964, U.S. Dist. Ct. (no. dist.) Ill. 1964, U.S. Supreme Ct. 1971. Assoc. Wisch, Crane & Kravets, Chgo., 1964-67, Ressman & Tishler, Chgo., 1967-69; assoc., then ptnr. Levy & Erens, Chgo., 1969-78; ptnr. Tash & Slavitt, Chgo., 1978-81, Katten Muchin & Zavis, Chgo., 1981—. Contbr. articles to profl. jours.; author poems and plays. Vol. Hospice of Ill. Masonic Med. Ctr., Chgo., 1987-89, Pro bono Advocates, 1989, Chgo. Ho., 1991 (recipient Outstanding Vol. award), Lawyers for the Creative Arts, Bus. Vols. for the Arts, 1992—; bd. dirs. Playwrights Ctr., Chgo., 1987, Jewish Reconstructionist Congregation, Chgo., 1978, 91, 92, Legal Clinic for the Disabled, 1993—, pres., 1995—, Sarah's Circle, 1994—. Mem. Ill. State Bar Assn. (mem. real estate com. 1976, recipient Pro Bono Cert. Accomplishment 1994), Chgo. Bar Assn. (mem. real estate com. 1976, real estate fin. com. 1982), Chgo. Coun. Lawyers (mem. jud. selection com. 1969), Lawyers in Mensa (bd. govs. 1983). Democrat. Jewish. Office: Katten Muchin & Zavis 1999 Ave Of Stars Ste 1400 Los Angeles CA 90067-6115

SLAVKIN, HAROLD CHARLES, biologist; b. Chgo., Mar. 20, 1938; m. Lois S. Slavkin; children: Mark D., Todd P. BA (hon.), U. So. Calif., 1961, DDS (hon.), 1965; Doctorate (hon.), Georgetown U., 1990, U. Paris, 1996, U. Md., 1997. Mem. faculty grad. program in cellular and molecular biology U. So. Calif., L.A., 1968—, mem. faculty gerontology inst., 1969, prof. sch. dentistry, 1974—, chmn. grad. program in craniofacial molecular biology, 1975-85; dir. Ctr. for Craniofacial Molecular Biology, L.A., 1989-95; George & Mary Lou Boone prof. craniofacial molecular biology U. So. Calif. Sch. Dentistry, L.A., 1989-95; dir. Nat. Inst. Dental Rsch., NIH, Bethesda, Md., 1995—; vis. prof. Israel Inst. Tech., Haifa, 1987-88; cons. U.S. News and World Report, 1985-95, L.A. Edn. Partnership, 1983-95, Torstar Books, Inc., 1985-95. Contbr. articles to profl. jours. Mem. sci. adv. bd. Calif. Mus. Sci. and Tech., 1985-95. Rsch. scholar U. Coll. London, 1980. Mem. AAAS, Am. Assn. Anatomists, Am. Inst. Biol. Scis., Am. Soc. for Cell Biology, Am. Assn. for Dental Rsch. (pres. 1993-94), N.Y. Acad. Scis., Inst. Medicine of NAS, Internat. Coll. Dentistry, Am. Coll. Dentistry, Los Angeles County Art Mus. Assocs. Office: Nat Inst Dental Rsch Bldg 31 Rm 2C39 31 Center Dr MSC 2290 Bethesda MD 20892-2290

SLAYDEN, JAMES BRAGDON, retired department store executive; b. Seattle, Sept. 28, 1924; s. Philip Lee and Ruth Alwin (Bragdon) S.; m. Barbara Marie McBride, May 7, 1955; children: Tracy Anne, James Bragdon. B.A., U. Wash., 1948; M.B.A., U. So. Calif., 1949. Buyer Frederick & Nelson (dept. store), Seattle, 1949-59; div. mdse. mgr. Frederick & Nelson (dept. store), 1959-65; gen. mgr. Bullocks Westwood, Los Angeles, 1965-69; exec. v.p., gen. mdse. mgr. May D&F Co. dept. store, Denver, 1969-72; pres., CEO J. W. Robinson dept. store, L.A., 1972-78; exec. v.p. ops. Marshall Field & Co., Chgo., 1978-80; lectr. mktg. U. So. Calif., 1985-93. Active United Crusade United Way, L.A., 1973-78, Chgo. Heart Assn., 1978-79; chmn. Pvt. Industry Coun., 1982-95; cons. Internat. Exec. Svc. Corps., 1987—; mem. planning commn. Palos Verdes Traffic Com., 1997. With U.S. Army, 1943-45. Mem. Phi Kappa Psi. Republican. Christian Scientist. Home: 37 Mela Ln Palos Verdes Peninsula CA 90275-5086

SLAYMAKER, GENE ARTHUR, public relations executive; b. Kenton, Ohio, Sept. 15, 1928; s. Edwin Paul and Anne Elizabeth (Grable) S.; divorced; children: Jill Brook, Scott Wood, Leslie Beth; m. Julie Ann Graff, Feb. 3, 1979; 1 adopted child, Peter Fredric Bannon II; stepchildren: Jennifer Elizabeth Nash, David Frank Nash. B.A. in Radio Journalism, Ohio State U. Announcer, reporter WLWC-TV, Columbus, Ohio, 1951-52; anchor, reporter WKBN-AM-FM-TV, Youngstown, Ohio, 1952-56, KYW-TV, Cleve., 1956-60; editor news Sta. WFBM-AM-FM-TV, Indpls., 1960-68; dir. news, sports, pub. affairs WTLC-FM and WTUX-AM, Indpls., 1976-92; community rels. liaison Marion County Pros. Atty. Office, Indpls., 1993; pres., founder Slaymaker and Assocs., Indpls., 1969—. Mambo dancer (movie) Going All the Way, 1996. Past bd. dirs. Park-Tudor Father's Assn.; mem. Meridian Kessler Neighborhood Assn., pres., 1968-69. Recipient Disting. Service award (2). Mem. Ind. AP Broadcasters Assn. (awards), UPI (awards), Nat. Fedn. Press Women, Soc. Profl. Journalists (awards Ind. chpt., bd. dirs., chpt. pres. 1991-92), Radio-TV News Dirs. Assn. (region bd. dirs. 1987-91), Indpls. Press Club, Woman's Press Club Ind., Players Club, Lambs Club. Democrat. Clubs: Nat. Headliners, Unity. Avocations: writing, painting, singing, gardening, tennis. Home: 5161 N Washington Blvd Indianapolis IN 46205-1071 Office: Slaymaker Assoc 5161 N Washington Blvd Indianapolis IN 46205-1071

SLAYMAKER, H. OLAV, geography educator; b. Swansea, Wales, Jan. 31, 1939; came to Can., 1968; s. Arthur J. and Astri H. (Breen) S.; m. Margaret A. Rapson, Apr. 8, 1967; children—Karen M., Paul O., Sarah J., Heidi R. BA, King's Coll., Cambridge, Eng., 1961; AM, Harvard U., 1963; PhD, Cambridge U., 1968. Asst. lectr. U. Coll. Wales, Aberystwyth, 1964-66; lectr. U. Coll. Wales, 1966-68; asst. prof. geography U.B.C., Vancouver, Can., 1968-70, assoc. prof., 1970-81, prof., 1981—, head dept., 1982-91, assoc. v.p. rsch., 1991-95; cons. water quality br. Inland Waters, Vancouver, 1976—. Editor: Mountain Geomorphology, 1972, Field Experiments, 1978, High Mountains, 1981, Extreme Landforming Events, 1983, Geomorphology and Land Managment, 1986, Erosion Budgets and Their Hydrologic Basis, 1986, Canada's Cold Environments, 1993, Steepland Geomorphology, 1995, Geomorphic Hazards, 1996. Senate mem. Vancouver Sch. Theology, 1973-75; bd. dirs. Regent Coll., Vancouver, 1975-78, U. B.C., 1984-87. Research grantee Natural Sci. and Engring. Research Council, Ottawa, Ont., Can., 1968—. Mem. Can. Assn. Geographers (pres. 1991-92), Am. Geophys. Union, Internat. Geog. Union (commn. chmn., sec., chmn. Can. nat. com. 1984-88), Internat. Assn. Geomorphologists (v.p. 1993—), Faculty Club (Vancouver). Anglican. Avocations: mountain hiking; philately. Office: Univ BC Dept Geography, 1984 West Mall, Vancouver, BC Canada V6T 1Z2

SLAYMAN, CLIFFORD LEROY, biophysicist, educator; b. Mt. Vernon, Ohio, July 7, 1936; s. Clifford Leroy and Ethel May (Stantz) S.; m. Carolyn Ruth Walch, Dec. 26, 1959; children: Andrew Lowell, Rachel Whitehouse. AB, Kenyon Coll., 1958; PhD, Rockefeller Inst., 1963; DSc (hon.), Kenyon Coll. 1991. NSF fellow Cambridge (Eng.) U., 1963-64; asst. prof. Western Res. U., Cleve., 1964-67; from asst. prof. to prof. physiology Yale U., New Haven, 1967—; mem panel on pre-doctoral fellowships NSF, Washington, 1969-71; DOE-DOA-NSF panel on Plant Sci. Ctrs., Washington, 1988. Editor: Electrogenic Ion Pumps, 1982; contbr. articles to profl. jours. and revs.; editorial bd. Bio Sci. Jour., 1985-88, Jour. Membrane Biology, 1982—. Mem. Hamden (Conn.) Neighborhood Preservation Com., 1980-82. Grantee NIH, 1964-91, NSF, 1979-82, DOE, 1985—. Mem. AAAS, Am. Physiol. Soc., Am. Soc. Plant Physiologists, N.Y. Acad. Scis., Soc. Gen. Physiologists, Conn. Acad. Arts and Scis. Avocations: antique house restoration, conservation, nature watching. Office: Yale Sch Medicine 333 Cedar St New Haven CT 06510-3206

SLAYTON, GUS, foundation administrator; b. Pocahontas, Ark., Jan. 20, 1937; s. Alvin M. and Eula Inis (Milam) S.; m. Ruth Virginia Furr, May 27, 1961 (dec. Nov. 1989). B.A., U. Md., College Park, 1973. Served as enlisted man U.S. Army, 1957-63, commd. 2d lt., 1963, advanced through grades to lt. col., 1978; various operational and research and devel. assignments, including The Pentagon, 1974-78, ret., 1980; exec. dir. Assn. of Old Crows, Alexandria, Va., 1980-92, AOC Ednl. Found., 1992—. Decorated Legion of Merit (2), Bronze Star (2). Republican. Avocation: real estate investment. Home: 25165 Elk Lick Rd Chantilly VA 22021-4267

SLAYTON, JOHN ARTHUR, electric motor manufacturing executive; b. St. Joseph, Mo., Aug. 12, 1918; s. Ernest Roy and Cora Belle (Hutchison) S.; m. Elizabeth Van Horn Duerr, Aug. 15, 1942; children: Richard, Elizabeth, Jane, James, Robert, Sarah, Mary. B.S., U. Mo., 1940. Salesman Burroughs Co., Chgo., 1940-42; acct. Standard Brands, Green Bay, Wis., 1945-48; exec. v.p. Marathon Electric, Wausau, Wis., 1948-88, pres., vice chmn., 1988—. Pres. C. of C. Found., Wausau, 1981-89, Woodson YMCA Found., 1977—; bd. dirs. Wausau Hosp. Ctr., 1976-82, North Ctrl. Mental Health Found., 1980-85, Wausau Area Vol. Exch., 1983-89, Wasau Health Found., 1975—; pres., bd. dirs. Grant Theatre Found., 1985—; bd. dirs., treas. Lehigh Yawkey Woodson Art Mus., 1985—, pres., 1996—; trstuee, elder 1st Presbyn. Ch., 1960-65. Served in USN, 1942-44. Recipient Citation of Merit U. Mo., Columbia, 1976,W ausau Disting. Community Service award, 1983, Wis. Gov.'s award, 1986; Paul Harris fellow, 1977. Mem. Wausau Area C. of C. (pres., dir. 1977-81). Republican. Clubs: Wausau Country (pres., dir. 1958-61), Wausau, YMCA (pres., dir. 1961-67). Lodge: Rotary (pres., dir. 1960-63). Home: 1804 Town Line Rd Wausau WI 54403-9119 Office: Marathon Electric 100 W Randolph St Wausau WI 54401-2569

SLAYTON, WILLIAM LAREW, planning consultant, former government official; b. Topeka, Dec. 2, 1916; s. Clarence Harvey and Mary (Larew) S.; m. Mary Prichard, Aug. 30, 1941; children: Mary Elizabeth Slayton Campbell, Barbara Slayton Shelton. Student, U. Omaha, 1937-39; A.B., U. Chgo., 1940, M.A., 1942; D.H.L. (hon.), Clarkson Coll. Tech., 1965. Polit. sec. Alderman Paul H. Douglas, Chgo., 1940-42; planning analyst Milw. Planning Commn., 1944-45, 46-47; municipal reference librarian Milw., 1947-48; asso. dir. Urban Redevel. Study, Chgo., 1948-50; field rep. div. slum clearance and urban redevel. HHFA, Washington, 1950; dir. redevel. Nat. Assn. Housing and Redevel. Ofcls., Washington, 1950-55; v.p. planning, redevel. Webb & Knapp, Inc., Washington, 1955-60; planning partner I.M. Pei & Partners, N.Y.C., 1956-61; commr. Urban Renewal Adminstrn., HHFA, HUD, Washington, 1961-66; dir. Urban Policy Center, Urban Am., Inc., Washington, 1966; exec. v.p. Urban Am., Inc., 1966-69, pres., 1969; exec. v.p. AIA, Washington, 1969-77, AIA Found., 1970-77; mem. bd. AIA Corp., 1970-77; vice chmn. AIA Research Corp., 1973-77; chmn. urban devel. advisory com. HUD, 1967-68; mem. U.S. del. Econ. Commn. for Europe, 1970; dep. asst. sec. of state for fgn. bldgs., 1978-83; cons. Nat. Assn. Housing and Redevel. Ofcls., 1983-87, Am. Planning Assn., 1987—. Bd. dirs. Met. Washington Ear, 1995—. With USNR, 1945-46. Recipient gold medal Royal Instn. Chartered Surveyors, Great Britain, 1965, Justin Herman award Nat. Assn. Housing and Redevel. Ofcls., 1994. Mem. Potomac Inst. (dir.), AIA (hon.), Am. Planning Assn., Am. Inst. Cert. Planners.

SLECHTA, ROBERT FRANK, biologist, educator; b. N.Y.C., June 4, 1928; s. Frank C. and Helen (Pospisil) S.; m. Betty S. Youngren, May 16, 1953; 1 son, Marc William. A.B., Clark U., 1949, M.A., 1951; postgrad., Columbia, 1951-52; Ph.D., Boston U., 1955. Research asst. Worcester Found., Shrewsbury, Mass., 1952-53; biologist U.S. Army Med. Nutrition Lab., Denver, 1953-55; instr., research asso. Tufts U., 1955-58; mem. faculty Boston U., 1958—, prof. biology, 1965-91, prof. emeritus, 1991—, assoc. dean Grad. Sch., 1967-78. Author: (with M. Hawthorne and E. Blaustein) Laboratory Manual for General Biology, 1965; also articles and book revs. Mem. Boston Zool. Soc. (dir. 1967-78, trustee 1978-79), Am. Inst. Biol. Scis., AAAS, Microcirculation Soc., Am. Soc. Zoologists, Soc. Study Reprodn., Sigma Xi. Research on limb regeneration in urodeles, starvation in prisoners of war, human factors in aircraft seating, effects on progestational compounds on reprodn. (early work on contraceptive pill), quantitative studies of blood flow in living microscopic vessels in mammals and amphibians. Home: 101 Wilson Rd Bedford MA 01730-1320 Office: Boston U Biology Dept 2 Cummington St Boston MA 02215-2425

SLEDGE, CLEMENT BLOUNT, orthopedic surgeon, educator; b. Ada, Okla., Nov. 1, 1930; s. John B. and Mollie D. (Blount) S.; m. Georgia Kurrus, Apr. 13, 1957; children—Margaret, John, Matthew, Claire. M.D., Yale U., 1955; M.A. (hon.), Harvard U., 1970; ScD (hon.), U. The South, 1987. Diplomate: Am. Bd. Orthopedic Surgery. Intern Barnes Hosp., St. Louis, 1955-56; resident in orthopedic surgery Harvard U., 1960-63; fellow in orthopedic pathology Armed Forces Inst. Pathology, 1963; vis. scientist Strangeways Research Lab., Cambridge (Eng.) U., 1963-66; asst. prof. orthopedic surgery Harvard U., 1963-67, assoc. prof., 1967-70, prof., 1970—; chmn. Brigham and Women's Physician Hosp. Orgn., 1995—; chmn. dept. orthopedic surgery Brigham and Women's Hosp., 1970-96. Editor: Textbook of Rheumatology, 1981, 85, 89, 93, 97; contbr. more than 100 articles to sci. jours. Active Arthritis Found.; chmn. Nat. Arthritis Adv. Bd., 1978-80. Served with M.C. USNR, 1956-58. Fellow Med. Found. Boston, 1963-66; Gebbie research fellow, 1968; NIH grantee, 1967—. Mem. Am. Acad. Orthopedic Surgeons (pres. 1985-86), Orthopedic Rsch. Soc. (pres. 1978-80), Am. Rheumatism Assn., Inst. of Medicine, Nat. Acad. Sci., Interurban Orthopedic Club, The Hip Soc. (pres. 1985). Episcopalian. Office: Brigham and Women's Hosp 75 Francis St Boston MA 02115-6110

SLEDGE, JAMES SCOTT, judge; b. Gadsden, Ala., July 20, 1947; s. L. Lee and Kathryn (Privott) S.; m. Joan Nichols, Dec. 27, 1969; children: Joanna Scott, Dorothy Privott. BA, Auburn U., 1969; JD, U. Ala., 1974, postgrad., 1989. Bar: Ala. 1974, U.S. Ct. Appeals (5th cir.) 1975, U.S. Ct. Appeals (11th cir.) 1981. Ptnr. Inzer, Suttle, Swann & Stivender, P.A., Gadsden, 1974-91; mcpl. judge, Gadsden, 1975-91; judge U.S. Bankruptcy Ct. No. Dist. Ala., 1991—; exec. com. Nat. Conf. Fed. Judges, 1996—; instr. U. Ala., Gadsden, 1975-77, Gadsen State Community Coll., 1989-90. Lay minister, vestryman Holy Comforter Episc. Ch., Gadsden, 1976—; mem. Ala. Coun. on the Arts, 1994—; incorporator Episc. Day Sch., Gadsden, 1976, Kyle Home for Devel. Disadvantaged, Gadsden, 1979; bd. dirs. Salvation Army, 1984-91, Etowah County Health Dept., 1975-91, Episc. Day Sch., 1992—, Gadsden Symphony, 1993—; mem. Ala. Dem. Exec. Com., 1990-91, Etowah County Dem. Exec. Com., 1984-91; founder Gadsden Cultural Arts Found., 1983, chmn., 1986-91. Capt. U.S. Army, 1969-71, Vietnam. Decorated Bronze Star, Legion of Honor (Vietnam); recipient Governor's award for art Ala. Coun. of the Arts, 1993. Mem. Gadsden-Etowah C. of C. (gen. counsel, v.p., bd. dirs. 1986-93), Phi Kappa Phi, Phi Eta Sigma. Lodge: Kiwanis (bd. dirs. 1981-84). Home: 435 Turrentine Ave Gadsden AL 35901-4059

SLEED, JOEL, columnist; b. N.Y.C., Jan. 29, 1929; m. MaryLou Kalwara, Nov. 15, 1983; children: Jodie, Jill, Jeffrey, Kristin Kalwara, Karen Hepler. Former travel editor The Star-Ledger, Newark, N.J.; travel columnist Epicurious Travel (Interactive Divsn. Conde Nast Publs.); columnist travel sect. Star-Ledger. Office: Newhouse Newspapers 140 E 45th St New York NY 10017-3144

SLEICHER, CHARLES ALBERT, chemical engineer; b. Albany, N.Y., Aug. 15, 1924; s. Charles Albert and Beatrice Eugena (Cole) S.; m. Janis Jorgensen, Sept. 5, 1953; children—Jeffrey Mark, Gretchen Gail. B.S., Brown U., 1946; M.S., M.I.T., 1949; Ph.D., U. Mich., 1955. Asst. dir. M.I.T. Sch. Chem. Engring.; Practice Bangor, Maine, 1949-51; research engr. Shell Devel. Co., Emeryville, Calif., 1955-59; assoc. prof. chem. engring. U. Wash., Seattle, 1960-66, prof., 1966-92, prof. emeritus, 1993—, dept. chmn., 1977-89; cons. Westinghouse-Hanford Co.; profl. photographer, 1994—. Contbr. articles on extraction, heat transfer, fluid mechanics, pesticide transport to profl. jours. Served with USN, 1943-47. NSF postdoctoral fellow, 1959-60; SEED grantee, 1973-74; research grantee NSF; research grantee Chevron Research Corp.; research grantee Am. Chem. Soc. Fellow AIChE (program awards coms.), AAAS; mem. Am. Chem. Soc., N.Am. Nature Photography Assn., Photographic Soc. Am., Sigma Xi. Chem. reactor design patentee. Home: 5002 Harold Pl NE Seattle WA 98105-2809 Office: U Wash Dept Chem Engring Box 351750 Seattle WA 98105

SLEIGH, SYLVIA, artist, educator; b. Llandudno, North Wales; came to U.S., 1961; d. John Harold and Katherine Amy (Miller) S.; m. Lawrence Alloway, June 28, 1954. Student, Sch. Art, Brighton, Sussex, Eng., 1932-36; diploma, U. London Extra-Mural Dept., 1947. Vis. asst. prof. SUNY-Stony Brook, 1978; instr. New Sch. Social Research, N.Y.C., 1974-77, 78-80; Edith Kreeger Wolf disting. prof. Northwestern U., Evanston, Ill., 1977; vis. artist Baldwin Seminar Oberlin Coll., Ohio, 1982, New Sch. Social Rsch., N.Y.C. One person shows include Bennington (Vt.) Coll., 1963, Soho 20 Art Gallery, N.Y.C., 1974, 76, 80, 82, A.I.R. Gallery, N.Y.C., 1974, 76, 78, Ohio State U., Columbus, 1976, Matrix, Wadsworth Atheneum, Hartford, Conn., 1976, Marianne Deson Gallery, Chgo., 1990, G.W. Einstein, Inc., N.Y.C., 1980, 83, 85, U. Mo., Saint Louis, 1981, Zaks Gallery, Chgo., 1985, 95, Milw. Art Mus., Butler Inst., Youngstown, Ohio, 1990, Stiebel Modern, N.Y.C., 1992, 94, Gallery 609, Denver, Canton (Ohio) Art Inst.; exhibited in group shows Newhouse Gallery, S.I., N.Y., Stamford (Conn.) Mus., 1985, Albany (N.Y.) Inst. Art, Cin. Art Mus., New Orleans Mus. Art, Denver Art Mus., Pa. Acad. Fine Arts, 1989, Calsten Art Gallery, Stevens Point, Wis., 1993, Rutgers U., New Brunswick, 1996, Stiebel Modern, N.Y.C., 1994, Soho 20, N.Y.C., 1993, 96, Katzen Brown Gallery, N.Y.C., 1989, Zaks Gallery, Chgo., 1986, Steinbaum Krauss Gallery, 1997, Deven Golden Fine Arts, Ltd., N.Y.C., 1997, Rutgers U., New Brunswick, N.J., 1984, RioArriba Gallery, Abiquiu, N.Mex., 1996, Milw. Art Mus., 1996. Panelist Creative Artists Pub. Service Program, N.Y.C., 1976. Nat. Endowment for Arts grantee, 1982, Pollock-Krasner Found. grantee, 1985. Home: 330 W 20th St New York NY 10011-3302

SLEIGHT, ARTHUR WILLIAM, chemist; b. Ballston Spa, N.Y., Apr. 1, 1939; s. Hollis Decker and Elizabeth (Smith) S.; AB, Hamilton Coll., 1960; PhD, U. Conn., 1963; m. Betty F. Hilberg, Apr. 19, 1963; children: Jeffrey William, Jeannette Anne, Jason Arthur. Faculty, U. Stockholm, Sweden, 1963-64; with E.I. du Pont de Nemours & Co., Inc., Wilmington, Del., 1965-89, rsch. mgr. solid state/catalytic chemistry, 1981-89; Harris Chair prof. materials sci. Oreg. State U., Corvallis, 1989—; adj. prof. U. Del., 1978-89. Mem. Presdl. Commn. Superconductivity, 1989. Recipient Phila. chpt. Am. Inst.. Chemists award, 1988, Gold Medal award Nat. Assn. Sci. Tech. and Soc., 1994. Mem. Am. Chem. Soc. (award Del. sect. 1978, Chemistry of Materials award 1997). Editor Materials Rsch. Bull., 1994—; editorial bd. Inorganic Chemistry Rev., 1979—, Jour. Catalysis, 1986—, Applied Catalysis, 1987—, Solid State Scis., 1987—, Chemistry of Materials, 1988—, Materials Chemistry and Physics, 1988—, Jour. of Solid State Chemistry, 1988—; patentee in field; contbr. articles to profl. jours. Home: PO Box 907 Philomath OR 97370-0907 Office: Oreg State U Dept Chemistry 153 Gilbert Hall Corvallis OR 97331-8546

SLEIK, THOMAS SCOTT, lawyer; b. La Crosse, Wis., Feb. 24, 1947; s. John Thomas and Marion Gladys (Johnson) S.; m. Judith Mattson, Aug. 24, 1968; children: Jennifer, Julia, Joanna. BS, Marquette U., 1969, JD, 1971. Bar: Wis. 1971, U.S. Dist. Ct. (we. dist.) Wis. 1971. Assoc. Hale Skemp Hanson Skemp & Sleik, La Crosse, 1971-74, ptnr., 1975—. State pres. Boy Scouts Am., 1981-83, bd. dirs. Gateway Area Coun., 1973—, pres., 1980-81; trustee La Crosse Pub. Libr., 1981—; v.p. La Crosse Pub. Edn. Found., 1997, bd. dirs. La Crosse Cmty. Theatre, 1979-83, Greater La Crosse Area United Way, 1985-92, campaign chmn., 1986, pres., 1987; mem. Sch. Dist. La Crosse Bd. Edn., 1973-77, v.p., 1977. Fellow Am. Acad. Matrimonial Lawyers; mem. ABA, ATLA, Wis. Acad. Trial Lawyers, State Bar Wis. (bd. govs. 1987-94, exec. com. 1990-93, pres. 1992-93, bd. dirs. family law sect. 1984-87, office mgmt. sect. 1990-91, chmn. conv. and entertainment com. 1989-91, bd. liaison lawyer referral and info. svc. 1989-91, speaker litigation sect. and family law seminars), La Crosse County Bar Assn. Roman Catholic. Home: 4082 Glenhaven Dr La Crosse WI 54601-7503 Office: HSHS&S 505 King St Ste 300 La Crosse WI 54601-4062

SLEMON, GORDON RICHARD, electrical engineering educator; b. Bowmanville, Ont., Can., Aug. 15, 1924; s. Milton Everitt and Selena (Johns) S.; m. Margaret Jean Matheson, July 9, 1949; children: Sally, Stephen, Mark, Jane. B.A.Sc., U. Toronto, 1946, M.A.Sc., 1948; D.I.C., Imperial Coll. Sci., London (Eng.) U., 1951, Ph.D., 1952; D of Engring. (hon.), Meml. U. Nfld., 1994. Asst. prof. elec. engring. N.S. Tech. Coll., Can., 1953-55; assoc. prof. U. Toronto, Ont., Can., 1955-63, prof., 1964-90, chmn. dept. elec. engring., 1966-76, dean of faculty of applied sci. and engring., 1979-86, prof. emeritus, 1990—; Colombo plan adviser, India, 1963-64; pres. Elec. Engring. Consociates, 1976-79; bd. dirs. Inverpower Controls Ltd., Innovations Found. Author: (with J.M. Ham) Scientific Basis of Electrical Engineering, Magnetoelectric Devices, (with A. Straughen) Electric Machinery; (with S.B. Dewan, A. Straughen) Power Semiconductor Drives, Electric Machines and Drives; contbr. articles to profl. jours. Chmn. Innovations Found., 1980-93, vice chmn., 1993—; chmn. Microelectronics Devel. Ctr., 1983-88. Recipient excellence in teaching award Western Electric, 1965, Can. Centennial medal, 1967, Ross medal, 1978, 83, Gold medal Jugoslav Union of Nikola Tesla Socs., Engring. Alumni medal, Educator of Yr. award Can. Engrs., 1992, Hall of Distinction award U. Toronto, 1992, Achievement award IEEE Magnetics Soc., 1997, Arbor award U. Toronto, 1997. Fellow Can. Acad. Engring., Engring. Inst. Can., Instn. Elec. Engrs. (hon. fellow 1995), Officer of Order of Can. 1995, IEEE (Centennial medal 1984, Nikola Tesla award); mem. Am. Soc. Engring. Edn., others. Patentee in field. Home: 40 Chatfield Dr, Don Mills, ON Canada M3B 1K5 Office: U Toronto, Faculty Applied Sci and Engring, Toronto, ON Canada

SLENKER, RICHARD DREYER, JR., broadcast executive; b. New Rochelle, N.Y., June 2, 1957; s. Richard D. and Ellen (Mullins) S.; m. Maria Pope, July 10, 1982; children: Scarlett Anne, Jessica Martha, Elizabeth Ellen, Martha Maria, Richard III. BA in Communications, Colgate U., 1979; MS in Tech. Mgmt., N.Y. Poly. U., 1986. Engr. WPIX, Inc., N.Y.C., 1979-82, engring. supr., 1982-86, dir. tech. ops., 1986-91; v.p. ops. and engring. Sta. WTTG-TV, Fox TV, Washington, 1991-96; v.p. engring. & ops. Fox TV Stas., Inc., 1995-96; exec. v.p., 1997—; sr. v.p., chief tech. officer Am. Sky Broadcasting, 1996—; cons. Archdiocese of N.Y., N.Y.C., 1987—. Sr. mem. CAP, Westchester, N.Y., 1989. Mem. NATAS, Soc. Motion Picture and TV Engrs., Aircraft Owners and Pilots Assn. Avocations: flying, piano playing, golf, scuba diving. Office: Fox TV Stas Inc 5151 Wisconsin Ave NW Washington DC 20016-4124

SLEPIAN, DAVID, mathematician, communications engineer; b. Pitts., June 30, 1923; s. Joseph and Rose Grace (Myerson) S.; m. Janice Dorothea Berek, Apr. 18, 1950; children: Steven Louis, Don Joseph, Anne Maria. Student, U. Mich., 1941-43; MA, Harvard U., 1947, PhD, 1949; postdoctoral studies, Cambridge U., Eng., 1949, Sorbonne, Paris, 1950. With AT&T Bell Labs., Murray Hill, N.J., 1950-82, head math. studies dept., 1970-82; prof. elec. engring. U. Hawaii, Honolulu, 1970-81; McKay prof. elec. engring. U. Calif., Berkeley, 1957-58, Regents lectr., 1977. Editor, author: Development of Information Theory, 1973; contbr. articles to profl. jours.; patentee in field. Served with U.S. Army, 1943-46, ETO. Von Neumann lectr. Soc. for Indsl. and Applied Math., 1982; Parker fellow in physics Harvard U., 1949-50. Fellow IEEE (editor Procs. 1969-70, Alexander Graham Bell award 1981), AAAS, Inst. Math. Stats.; mem. NAS, NAE, Am. Acad. Arts and Scis. Avocations: music, travel, languages. Home: 212 Summit Ave Summit NJ 07901-2966

SLEPIAN, PAUL, mathematician, educator; b. Boston, Mar. 26, 1923; s. Philip and Ida (Goldstein) S.; children—Laura, Jean. S.B., Mass. Inst. Tech., 1950; Ph.D., Brown U., 1956. Mathematician Hughes Aircraft Co., 1956-60; assoc. prof. math. U. Ariz., 1960-62; assoc. prof. Rensselaer Poly. Inst., Troy, N.Y., 1962-65; prof. math. Rensselaer Poly. Inst., 1965-69; prof., chmn. dept. math. Bucknell U., Lewisburg, Pa., 1969-70; prof. math. Howard U., Washington, 1970—; summer vis. staff mem. Los Alamos Sci. Lab., 1976, 78, 79. Mem. Am. Math. Soc., Soc. Indsl. and Applied Math., Math. Assn. Am. Home: 1331 W 40th St Baltimore MD 21211-1728

SLESNICK, WILLIAM ELLIS, mathematician, educator; b. Oklahoma City, Feb. 24, 1925; s. Isaac Ralph and Adele (Miller) S. B.S., U.S. Naval Acad., 1945; B.A., U. Okla., 1948; B.A. (Rhodes scholar), Oxford (Eng.) U., 1950, M.A., 1954; A.M., Harvard, 1952; A.M. (hon.), Dartmouth, 1972. Math. master St. Paul's Sch., Concord, N.H., 1952-62; vis. instr. Dartmouth Coll., 1958-59, mem. faculty, 1962-94, prof. math., 1971-94; prof. emeritus, 1994—; asst. dir. ednl. uses Kiewit Computation Center, 1966-69; mem. N.H. Rhodes Scholar Selection Com.; mem. advanced placement exam. com. math. Coll. Entrance Exam. Bd., 1967-71; mem. Nat. Humanities Faculty, 1972—. Co-author: 12 math. textbooks including (with R.H. Crowell) Calculus With Analytic Geometry, 1968. Active Boy Scouts Am., 1937—, attache world bur., 1955, 67, coun. exec. bd., 1964—, dist. chmn., 1974-76; mem. nat. com. Order of Arrow, 1965—, mem. internat. com., 1974-93; mem. Nat. Jewish Com. Scouting, 1973—, internat. ambassador, 1993—; mem. assembly of overseers Mary Hitchcock Meml. Hosp., Hanover; trustee Lawrence L. Lee Mus., Hanover-Norwich Youth Fund, New Hampton (N.H.) Sch., 1975-81; mem. selection com. Okla. Found. for Excellence, 1986-91. With USN, 1942-47. Recipient Vigil Honor, 1948, Nat. Disting. Svc. award Order of Arrow, 1967, Silver Beaver award Boy Scouts Am., 1967, Silver Antelope award, 1972, Disting. Svc. award Daniel Webster Coun., 1994, Wendell C. Badger award Dartmouth Coll., 1978, Disting. Eagle Scout award, 1979, Shofar award, 1980, Silver Buffalo award, 1990, Presidential medal Dartmouth Coll., 1991. Mem. Nat. Council Tchrs. Math., Math. Assn. Am., Assn. Tchrs. Math. in New Eng., Assn. Am.

Rhodes Scholars, Phi Beta Kappa (chpt. pres. 1974-77), Phi Eta Sigma, Pi Mu Epsilon, Alpha Phi Omega. Home: 306 Kendal at Hanover 80 Lyme Rd Hanover NH 03755-1225

SLETTEBAK, ARNE, astronomer, educator; b. Free City of Danzig, Aug. 8, 1925; came to U.S., 1927, naturalized, 1932; s. Nicolai and Valerie (Janczak) S.; m. Constance Pixler, Aug. 28, 1949; children: Marcia Diane, John Andrew. B.S. in Physics, U. Chgo., 1945, Ph.D. in Astronomy, 1949. Mem. faculty Ohio State U., Columbus, 1949—, prof. astronomy, 1959-94, chmn. dept. astronomy, 1962-78, prof. emeritus, 1994—; dir. Perkins Obs., Delaware, Ohio, 1959-78, mem. steering com. Earth Sci. Curriculum Project, 1963-68; mem. NRC Commn. on Astronomy adv. to Office Naval Research, 1963-65, chmn., 1965-66; mem. adv. panel for astronomy NSF, 1968-71; Fulbright lectr., vis. prof. U. Vienna, 1974-75, 81, 91; vis. prof. U. Louis Pasteur, Strasbourg, 1991; mem. nat. screening com. grad. study grants Fulbright Com., 1987-89. Fulbright rsch. fellow Hamburg, Fed. Republic Germany, 1955-56, Japan Soc. for Promotion Sci. fellow, 1988. Mem. Assn. Univs. for Research Astronomy (dir. 1961-79, chmn. sci. com. 1970-73), Am. Astron. Soc. (coun. 1964-67), Internat. Astron. Union (v.p. commn. 45, 1976-79, pres. 1979-82, chmn. working group on Be stars, 1982-85), Sigma Xi. Home: 601 Seabury Dr Worthington OH 43085-3557 Office: Ohio State U Dept Astronomy Columbus OH 43210

SLETTEN, JOHN ROBERT, construction company executive; b. Gt. Falls, Mont., Sept. 19, 1932; s. John and Hedvig Marie (Finstad) S.; m. Patricia Gail Thomas, Dec. 16, 1962; children: Leighanne, Kristen Gail, Erik John. BS in Archtl. Engring., Mont. State U., 1956. Estimator Sletten Constrn. Co., Gt. Falls, 1956-63; v.p., area mgr. Sletten Constrn. Co., Las Vegas, Nev., 1963-65; pres., chief exec. officer Sletten Constrn. Co., Gt. Falls, 1969—; bd. dirs. 1st Banks, Gt. Falls, Blue Cross-Blue Shield, Helena, Mont. Chmn. Gt. Falls Mil. Affairs Com., 1985; pres. President's Cir., Mont. State U., Bozeman, 1986; trustee Mont. Hist. Soc., Helena, 1987. with USMC, 1950-52. Mem. Mont. Contractors Assn. (bd. dirs. 1969-75, pres. 1974), Mont. C. of C. (chmn. 1984), Pachyderm Club, Rotary (bd. dirs. Gt. Falls), Elks. Republican. Lutheran. Avocations: skiing, fishing, hunting. Office: Sletten Inc 1000 25th St N PO Box 2467 Great Falls MT 59403-2467

SLEWITZKE, CONNIE LEE, retired army officer; b. Mosinee, Wis., Apr. 15, 1931; d. Leo Thomas and Amelia Marie (Hoffman) S. BSN, U. Md., Balt., 1971; MA in Counseling and Guidance, St. Mary's U., San Antonio, 1976. Commd. 1st lt. U.S. Army, 1957, advanced through grades to brig. gen., 1987; ret., 1987; chief dept. nursing Letterman Army Med. Ctr. U.S. Army, San Francisco, 1978-80; asst. chief nurse Army Nurse Corps U.S. Army, Washington, 1980-83; chief brigadier gen. U.S. Army, 1983-87; mem. Va. Adv. Com. on Women Vets. Contbr. articles to profl. jours. Decorated D.S.M., Legion of Merit, Bronze Star medal. Mem. ANA, Va. Nurses Assn., Alumni Assn. U.S. Army War Coll., Assn. U.S. Army, Women in Mil. Svc. for Am. Found. (v.p.), Am. Assn. for History of Nursing, Sigma Theta Tau. Avocations: photography; travel; music.

SLICHTER, CHARLES PENCE, physicist, educator; b. Ithaca, N.Y., Jan. 21, 1924; s. Sumner Huber and Ada (Pence) S.; m. Gertrude Thayer Almy, Aug. 23, 1952 (div. Sept. 1977); children: Sumner Pence, William Almy, Jacob Huber, Ann Thayer; m. Anne FitzGerald, June 7, 1980; children—Daniel Huber, David Pence. AB, Harvard U., 1946, MA, 1947, PhD, 1949; DSc (hon.), U. Waterloo, 1993; LLD (hon.), Harvard U., 1996. Research asst. Underwater Explosives Research Lab., Woods Hole, Mass., 1943-46; mem. faculty U. Ill., Urbana, 1949—, prof. physics, 1955—, prof. Ctr. for Advanced Study, 1968—, prof. chemistry, 1986—; Morris Loeb lectr. Harvard U., 1961; mem. Pres.'s Sci. Adv. Com., 1964-69, Com. on Nat. Medal Sci., 1969-74, Nat. Sci. Bd., 1975-84, Pres.'s Com. Sci. and Tech., 1976. Author: Principles of Magnetic Resonance, 1963, 3d edit., 1989; Contbr. articles to profl. jours. Former trustee, mem. corp. Woods Hole Oceanog. Instn.; mem. Harvard Corp., 1970-95. Recipient Langmuir award Am. Phys. Soc., 1969, Buckley prize, 1996; Alfred P. Sloan fellow, 1955-61. Fellow AAAS, Am. Physical Soc.; mem. NAS (Comstock prize 1993), Am. Acad. Arts and Scis., Am. Philos. Soc., Internat. Soc. Magnetic Resonance (pres. 1987-90, Trienniel prize 1986). Home: 61 Chestnut Ct Champaign IL 61821-7121

SLIDER, DORLA DEAN (FREEMAN), artist; b. Tampa, Fla., Sept. 9, 1929; d. Samuel Manning and Ida Caroline (Heller) Weeks; m. James Harold Slider, July 8, 1951; 1 child, Cindi Darnel Slider Dvornicky. Studied with Dr. Walter Emerson Baum, Allentown, Pa., 1940-48. Profl. advisor Pottstown (Pa.) Area Artists Guild, 1967-94; mem. jury of selection Nat. Soc. Painters in casein and acrylic, N.Y.C., 1992, 95; juror selection and awards Fla. Keys Watercolor Soc., Key West, 1987-90; nat. art judge and juror nat. and regional art shows. Exhibited in group shows at Am. Watercolor Soc., The Nat. Acad. of Design, Allied Artists, Audubon Artists, KnickerbockerArtists, Nat. Arts Club, Nat. Soc. Painters in Casein and Acrylic, N.Y.C., Pa. Acad. Fine Arts, Phila. Mus. Art, William Penn Mus., Pa., Butler Inst. Am. Art, Ohio, Watercolor U.S.A., Mainstreams Nat., Ohio, The Salt Palace, Utah, others; represented in permanent collections Brandywine River Mus., Chadds Ford, Pa., Berman Art Mus., Collegeville, Pa. Recipient Doris Kennedy Meml. award, Audubon Artists N.Y., 1979, C.L. Wolfe Art Club Gold medal, N.Y.C., 1970; Best of Show award Miami Water Color Soc., 1984, Arjomari/Arches/Rives award Nat. Soc. Painters Acrylic, 1991, award of excellence Nat. League Am. Pen Women, Washington, 1996, top awards Mainstream Internat., Allentown Art Mus., Internat. Soc. Artists, Salmagundie Club, Nat. Soc Painters in Caseim and Acrylic, Marion F. Gourville award Bianco Gallery, 1996, others. Mem. Am. Watercolor Soc. (Herb Olsen award 1972), Nat. Soc. Painters in Casein and Acrylic, Knickerbocker Artists (gold medal 1977), Audubon Artists (Savoir Faire award 1993, Yarka award 1995), Am. Artist Profl. League N.Y., Artists Equity, Phila. Watercolor Club (bd. dirs. 1996—, Dawson Meml. award 1994). Home: 268 Estate Rd Boyertown PA 19512-1922

SLIDER, MARGARET ELIZABETH, elementary education educator; b. Spanish Fork, Utah, Nov. 27, 1945; d. Ira Elmo and Aurelia May (Peterson) Johnson; m. Richard Keith Slider, Oct. 25, 1968; children: Thomas Richard, Christopher Alan. AA, Chaffey Coll., 1966; BA, Calif. State U., San Bernardino, 1968, MEd in English as Second Lang., 1993. Cert. elem. tchr., Calif. Tchr. Colton (Calif.) Unified Sch. Dist., 1968—; lead sci. tchr. McKinley Sch., 1994-96; mem. sci. steering com. Colton Joint Unified Sch. Dist., 1996—; mem. kindergarten assessment com. Colton Joint Unified Sch. Dist., Colton, 1988-90, dist. math. curriculum com., 1992-94; trainer Calif. State Dept. Edn. Early Intervention for Sch. Success, 1993—, demonstrator on-site classroom, 1994. Treas. McKinley Sch. PTA, Colton, 1989-91. Mem. NEA, ASCD, AAUW, Calif. Tchrs. Assn., Calif. Elem. Edn. Assn., Calif. Assn. of Tchrs. of English to Students of Other Langs., Calif. Mathematics Coun., Assn. Colton Educators, Pi Lambda Theta. Avocations: needlework, reading, bicycling. Home: 1628 Waterford Ave Redlands CA 92374-3967 Office: Colton Unified Sch Dist 1212 Valencia Dr Colton CA 92324-1731

SLIEPCEVICH, CEDOMIR M., engineering educator; b. Anaconda, Mont., Oct. 4, 1920; s. Maksim and Jovanka (Lubibratich) S.; m. Cleo L. Whorton, Oct. 21, 1955. BS, U. Mich., 1941, MS, 1942, PhD, 1948. Assoc. prof. dept. chem. and metall. engring. U. Mich., 1946-55; prof., chmn. Sch. Chem. Engring.; also assoc. dean Coll. Engring., U. Okla., 1955-62, George Lynn Cross Rsch. prof., 1963-91, Robert W. Hughes Centennial prof. engring., 1989-91, prof. emeritus, 1991—; pres. Univ. Engrs., Inc., 1965-78, Univ. Technologists, Inc., 1977—; cons. chem. engr. Author numerous tech. papers. Recipient Curtis W. McGraw Research award, 1958; Internat. Ipatieff award, 1959; George Westinghouse award, 1964; Sesquicentennial award U. Mich., 1967; Okla. Outstanding Scientist award, 1975; Disting. Service citation U. Okla., 1975; William H. Walker award, 1978; Gas Industry Research award 1986; named Okla. Profl. Engr. of Yr., 1973, Nat. Profl. Engr. of Year, 1974; inducted into Okla. Hall Fame, 1974. Fellow AAAS, AIChE; mem. Nat. Acad. Engrs., U. Okla. Coll. Engring. Disting. Grads. Soc. (1st hon. mem.). Home: RR 1 Box 41-b1 Washington OK 73093-9801

SLIFKA, ALFRED A., oil corporation executive; b. Boston, June 3, 1932; s. Abraham and Sonya S.; m. Gilda Koritz; children: Adam, Jennifer, Eric. Grad. high sch., Boston, 1949. Pres., dir., co-owner Global Petroleum Corp., Waltham, Mass., CEO; bd. dirs. New England Fuel Inst., 1974—, Better Home Heat Coun., Petroleum Inst. Rsch. Found., N.Y.C.; past bd. dirs. U.S. Trust Co., Boston. Contbr. articles to profl. jours. vice chmn. Hebrew Rehab. Ctr., Boston; trustee Combined Jewish Philanthropies, Boston; bd. dirs. Griffith Consumers Co., Cheverly, Md. With U.S. Army. Mem. N.Y. Merc. Exch., Pine Brook Country Club (past gov. 1985-89). Avocations: jogging, golf, tennis. Office: Global Petroleum Corp 800 South St Waltham MA 02154-1439*

SLIFKIN, LAWRENCE MYER, physics educator; b. Bluefield, W.Va., Sept. 29, 1925; s. Isaac L. and Eva (Baden) S.; m. Miriam Kresses, July 4, 1948; children: Anne, Rebecca, Merle, Naomi. BA, NYU, 1947; PhD, Princeton U., 1950. Rsch. assoc., rsch. asst. prof. U. Ill., Urbana, 1950-54; asst prof. U. Minn., Mpls., 1954-55; asst. prof., then prof. physics U. N.C., Chapel Hill, 1955-91, Bowman Gray prof., 1979-82, Alumni Disting. prof., 1983-91, prof. emeritus, 1991—; liaison sci. U.S. Office Naval Rsch., London, 1969-70; collaborateur étranger, CEN-Saclay, France, 1975-76. Editor: (with J. H. Crawford): Point Defects in Solids, vol. I, 1972, vol. II, 1975; contbr. more than 125 articles to profl. jours. and books. With U.S. Army, 1944-46, PTO. Fellow Am. Phys. Soc. (exec. com. div. condensed matter physics 1978-80, Jesse Beams award rsch. excellence S.E. Sect. 1977), Soc. Photographic Scientists and Engrs.; mem. Am. Assn. Physics Tchrs. Democrat. Jewish. Avocations: music, travel, reading, grandfathering. Home: 313 Burlage Cir Chapel Hill NC 27514-2703 Office: U NC-Chapel Hill Cb 3255 Phillips Hall Chapel Hill NC 27599

SLIFKIN, MALCOLM, clinical microbiologist, educator; b. Newark, Nov. 9, 1933; s. William and Raye (Nalebuff) S.; B.S., Furman U., 1955; M.S. in Pub. Health, U. N.C., 1956, M.S., 1959, Ph.D., Rutgers U., 1964; Diplomate Am. Bd. Med. Microbiology in Pub. Health and Med. Lab. Microbiology; m. Janet E. Saperstein, July 31, 1966; children—Joshua Michael, Robert Seth. Instr., Yale U. Sch. Medicine, New Haven, 1962-64; head. microbiology sect. Allegheny Gen. Hosp., Pitts., 1964—; adj. assoc. prof. microbiology Pa. State U., 1965—; clin. asst. pathology U. Pitts., 1955-71; cons. Coll. Am. Pathologists, Chgo. 1978-80; sr. scientist Allegheny Gen. Hosp., 1980—; prof. lab. medicine and pathology Allegheny U., 1990—, prof. microbiology and immunology, 1991—; assoc. editor Med. Microbiology Letters, 1991-97. Mem. Pitts. Savoyard Orch., 1965—, Pitts. Woodwind Quintet, 1964—. Am. Cancer Soc. grantee, 1969-70, NIH grantee, 1971-72. Fellow Am. Acad. Microbiology (com. on postdoctoral ednl. programs 1974-79); mem. Western Pa. Soc. Clin. Microbiologists (pres. 1971—), Am. Soc. Microbiology (ethical practices com.), AAAS, N.Y. Acad. Scis., Sigma Xi. Jewish. Contbr. numerous sci. articles to profl. publs. Home: 1230 Wightman St Pittsburgh PA 15217-1221 Office: Allegheny Gen Hosp 320 E North Ave Pittsburgh PA 15212-4756

SLIGER, HERBERT JACQUEMIN, JR., lawyer; b. Urbana, Ill., Nov. 21, 1948; s. Herbert Jacquemin and Marina (Mantia) S.; m. Sandra Ann Ratti, May 3, 1996; children: Lauren Christine, Matthew Ryan, Nicholas Adam, Claire Nicole, Adam Gregory. BS in Fin., U. Ill., 1970; JD, U. Ariz., 1974. Bar: Ariz. 1974, Ill. 1975, U.S. Supreme Ct. 1983, Okla. 1984, U.S. Ct. Appeals (7th cir.) 1980, U.S. Tax Ct. 1980; CPA, Okla. Lawyer Charles W. Phillips Law Offices, Harrisburg, Ill., 1974-75; trust counsel Magna Trust Co., F/K/A Millikin Nat. Bank, Decatur, Ill., 1976-80, First of America Trust Co., Springfield, Ill., 1980-83; mgr. employee benefits trust dept. First Interstate Bank of Okla., NA, Oklahoma City, 1983-89; v.p., pension counsel Star Bank, NA, Cin., Cin., 1989-90; asst. gen. counsel Bank One Ariz. Corp., Phoenix, 1990-95; asst. gen. counsel, nat. practice group head Banc One Corp., Columbus, Ohio, 1995—; state gen. counsel for Ariz. and Utah Banc One Corp., Phoenix, 1996-97; sec. of bd. and cashier Bank One, Ariz. NA, 1996—; sec. of bd. and statutory agt. Banc One Ariz. Corp., 1996-97; sec. bd. Bank One trust Co. N.A., Columbus, 1996—; co-chmn. Nat. Conf. Lawyers and Corp. Fiduciaries, 1992-94. Contbr. articles to profl. jours. Mem. ABA (sect. bus. law, banking law com., trust and investment svcs. subcom. 1991—, sect. real property, probate and trust law 1974—, fiduciary income taxation subcom. 1994—, fiduciary environ. problems com. 1993—, section of taxation, employee benefits com. 1991—), State Bar of Ariz., Okla. Bar Assn., Am. Bankers Assn. (chmn. trust counsel com. 1992-94, mem. and head of fiduciary law dept. Nat./Grad. Trust Sch. Bd. of Faculty Advisors 1994-95, faculty mem. teaching "fiduciary duties under ERISA" Nat. Employee Benefit Trust Sch. 1994-96, spokesman Environ. Risk Task Force 1994-95, mem. trust and investment divsn. exec. com. 1992-94, mini-adv. bd. chairperson trusts and estates 1995—). Roman Catholic. Avocations: phys. fitness, original print collecting. Home: 8011 N 7th St # 1069 Phoenix AZ 85020 Office: Bank One Corp 100 E Broad St 5th Fl Columbus OH 43271-0158 also: 201 N Central Ave 22nd Fl Phoenix AZ 85004

SLIKER, TODD RICHARD, accountant, lawyer; b. Rochester, N.Y., Feb. 9, 1936; s. Harold Garland and Marion Ethel (Caps) S.; BS with honors (Ford Found. scholar), U. Wis., 1955; PhD, Cornell U., 1962; MBA, Harvard, 1970; JD, U. Denver, 1982; m. Gretchen Paula Zeiter, Dec. 27, 1963; children: Cynthia Garland, Kathryn Clifton. Bar: Colo. 1983. With Clevite Corp., Cleve., 1962-68, head applied physics sect., 1965-68; asst. to pres. Granville-Phillips Co., Boulder, Colo., 1970; v.p., gen. mgr. McDowell Electronics, Inc., Metuchen, N.J., 1970-71; pres. C.A. Compton, Inc., mfrs. audio-visual equipment, Boulder, 1971-77; chief acct. C&S Inc., Englewood, Colo., 1977-80, v.p., 1980-82; sole practice law, Boulder, 1983-88; owner, mgr. real estate, 1972—. Del., Colo. Rep. Assembly, 1974, 76; Rep. dist. fin. coordinator, 1974-75; precinct committeeman, 1974-86, 92-94; chmn. Boulder County Rep. 1200 Club, 1975-79; mem. Colo. Rep. State Cen. Com., 1977-81, asst. treas., 1979-87; sect. corr. Harvard U., 1981—. Served to 1st lt. USAF, 1955-57. Recipient paper award vehicular communication group IEEE, 1966. Lic. real estate salesman, securities salesman; CPA, Colo. Mem. Colo. Soc. CPAs (govt. relations task force 1983-86), Colo. Bar Assn. (publs. com. 1982-84), Am. Phys. Soc., Optical Soc. Am. (referee Jour.), Colo. Harvard Bus. Sch. Club, Hist. Boulder Club, Rotary, Sigma Xi, Phi Kappa Phi, Theta Chi, Beta Alpha Psi. Contbr. articles to profl. jours. Patentee in field. Home: PO Box 715 12500 Oxford Rd Niwot CO 80544-0715 *Personal philosophy: The good will last.*

SLINGER, MICHAEL JEFFERY, law library director; b. Pitts., Apr. 12, 1956; s. Maurice and Mary Helen (Kengerski) S.; m. Cheryl Blaney, Apr. 19, 1980; children: Rebecca, Sarah. BA, U. Pitts., 1978; M Librianship, U. S.C., 1979; JD, Duquesne U., 1984. Reference libr. Duquesne U. Sch. Law, Pitts., 1983-84; rsch. libr. U. Notre Dame (Ind.) Sch. Law, 1984-85, head rsch. svcs., 1985-86, assoc. dir. pub. svcs., 1986-90; law libr. dir., assoc. prof. law Suffolk U. Sch. Law, Boston, 1990-93, law libr. dir., prof. law, 1994-95; law libr. dir., prof. law Cleve. State U., 1995—. Contbr. articles to profl. jours., chpt. to book. Mem. ABA, ALA, Am. Assn. Law Librs., Am. Assn. Law Schs. (exec. bd. sect. on law librs. 1993-94), New Eng. Law Libr. Consortium (treas. 1992-95), Ohio Regional Assn. Law Librs. (v.p. 1987-88, pres. 1988-89, Pres. award 1989). Avocations: reading, sports, family. Office: Cleveland-Marshall Coll Law Bartunek Law Libr 1801 Euclid Ave Cleveland OH 44115-2223

SLIVE, SEYMOUR, museum director, fine arts educator; b. Chgo., Sept. 15, 1920; s. Daniel and Sonia (Rapoport) S.; m. Zoya Gregorevna Sandomirsky, June 29, 1946; children: Katherine, Alexander, Sarah. AB, U. Chgo., 1943, PhD, 1952; MA (hon.), Harvard U., 1958, Oxford (Eng.) U., 1972. Instr. fine arts Oberlin (Ohio) Coll., 1950-51; chmn. art dept. Pomona (Calif.) Coll., 1952-54; mem. faculty Harvard U., Cambridge, Mass., 1954—, prof. fine arts, 1961—, Gleason prof. fine arts, 1973-91, Gleason prof. fine arts emeritus, 1991—, chmn. dept. fine arts, 1968-71, dir. Fogg Art Mus., 1975-82; Elizabeth and John Moors Cabot dir. emeritus Harvard art museums, 1982; exchange prof. Leningrad (USSR) U., 1961; Ryerson lectr. Yale U., 1962; Slade prof. Oxford (Eng.) U., 1972-73. Author: Rembrandt and His Critics, 1630-1730, 1953, The Rembrandt Bible, 1959, Catalogue of the Paintings of Frans Hals, 1962, Drawings of Rembrandt, 1965, (with Jakob Rosenberg and E.H. ter Kuile) Dutch Art and Architecture 1600-1800, 2nd edit., 1978, Rembrandt's Drawings, 1965, Frans Hals, 3 vols., 1970-74, Jacob van Ruisdael, 1981, Frans Hals, 1989, Dutch Painting: 1600-1800, 1995. Trustee Solomon R. Guggenheim Found., 1978—, Norton Simon Mus., 1989-91; bd. dirs. Burlington mag. Found., 1987—. Lt. (j.g.) USNR, 1943-46, PTO. Decorated officer Order Orange Nassau Netherlands, 1962; Fulbright fellow Netherlands, 1951-52; Guggenheim fellow, 1956-57, 78-79; Fulbright research scholar Utrecht (Netherlands) U., 1959-60. Fellow Am. Acad. Arts and Scis.; mem. Karel van Mander Soc. (hon.), Coll. Art Assn. (dir. 1958-62, 65-69), Renaissance Soc., Dutch Soc. Scis. (fgn. mem.), Brit. Acad. (corr. fellow). Office: Harvard U Sackler Art Museum Cambridge MA 02138

SLOAN, ALLAN HERBERT, journalist; b. Bklyn., Nov. 27, 1944; s. Samuel and Doris (Shanblott) S.; m. Nancy Nolan, June 29, 1969; children: Sharon R., Susan M., Dena A. BA, Bklyn. Coll., 1966; MS, Columbia U., 1967. Reporter Charlotte (N.C.) Observer, 1968-72, Detroit Free Press, 1972-79; assoc. editor, staff writer Forbes Mag., N.Y.C., 1979-81; staff writer Money Mag., N.Y.C., 1982-84; sr. editor Forbes Mag., N.Y.C., 1984-88; columnist N.Y. Newsday, N.Y.C., 1989-95; Wall St. editor Newsweek Mag., N.Y.C., 1995—. Author: Three Plus One Equals Billions: The Bendix-Martin Marietta War, 1982. Recipient Loeb award for fin. journalism Loeb Found., 1974, 84, 91, 93, Hancock award for fin. journalism Hancock Found., 1992. Office: Newsweek 251 W 57th St New York NY 10019-1802

SLOAN, DAVID EDWARD, retired corporate executive; b. Winnipeg, Man., Can., Mar. 29, 1922; s. David and Annie Maud (Gorvin) S.; m. Kathleen Lowry Craig, Dec. 26, 1947; children: Pamela Jane, John David, Kathleen Anne. B.Commerce, U. Man., 1942. With Monarch Life Assurance Co., Winnipeg, 1946-47; with Can. Pacific Ltd., 1947-88, treas., 1969-88; pres. and chief exec. officer Can. Pacific Securities Ltd., 1985-88; mem. adv. com. Can. Pension Plan, Can. Govt., 1967-76, chmn., 1974-76. Lt. Royal Can. Army Service Corps, 1942-45. Mem. Fin. Exec. Inst. Can. (past pres. Montreal chpt.), Toronto Soc. Fin. Analysts, Soc. Internat. Treas. (internat. chmn. 1985-86, mem. coun. advisors 1978-87), Assn. Investment Mgmt. and Rsch., U. Man. Alumni Assn., The Toronto Hunt Club. Mem. United Ch. Can. Home: 316 Rosemary Rd, Toronto, ON Canada M5P 3E3

SLOAN, DAVID W., lawyer; b. Rahway, N.J., June 23, 1941; s. Harper Allen and Margaret (Walker) S.; m. Margaret J. Neville, Oct. 23, 1965; children: Matthew A., John S. AB, Princeton U., 1963; MS, Stanford U., 1965; JD, Harvard U., 1970. Bar: Calif. 1971, Ohio 1974. Assoc. Brobeck, Phleger & Harrison, San Francisco, 1970-73; assoc. and ptnr. Burke, Haber & Berick, Cleve., 1973-83; ptnr. Jones, Day, Reavis & Pogue, Cleve., 1983—; adj. prof. law Case Western Reserve U., 1975. Vol. Peace Corps., Turkey, 1965-67; sr. warden St. Paul's Episcopal Ch., Cleveland Heights, 1993-96. Mem. ABA (former council mem. sect. on science and technology), Ohio Bar Assn., Cleve. Bar Assn., Computer Law Assn., Sigma Xi, Alzheimer's Assn. (former trustee and v.p.). Office: Jones Day Reavis & Pogue North Point 901 Lakeside Ave E Cleveland OH 44114-1116

SLOAN, EARLE DENDY, JR., chemical engineering educator; b. Seneca, S.C., Apr. 23, 1944; s. Earle Dendy and Sarah (Bellotte) S.; m. Marjorie Nilson, Sept. 7, 1968; children: Earle Dendy III, John Mark. BSChemE, Clemson U., 1965, MSChemE, 1972, PhD in Chem. Engring., 1974. Engr. Du Pont, Chattanooga, 1965-66, Seaford, Del., 1966-67; cons. Du Pont, Parkersburg, W.Va., 1967-68; sr. engr. Du Pont, Camden, S.C., 1968-70; postdoctoral fellow Rice U., 1975; prof. chem. engring. Colo. Sch. Mines, Golden, 1976—, dir. Ctr. for Rsch. on Hydrates and Other Solids, 1990—, Gaylord and Phyllis Weaver dist. prof. chem. engring., 1992—; pres. faculty senate Colo. Sch. Mines, 1989-90; Tokyo Electric Power Co. chair Keio U., Japan, 1996. Author: Clathrate Hydrates of Natural Gases, 1990, 2d edit., 1997; chmn. pub. bd. Chem. Engring. Edn., 1990—. Scoutmaster local Cub Scouts, 1978-81; elder Presbyn. Ch., Golden, Colo., 1977-79, 92-94. Fellow AIChE (chmn. area Ia thermodynamics and transport 1990-93); mem. Am. Soc. for Engring. Edn. (chmn. ednl. rsch. methods divsn. 1983-85, chmn. chem. engring. divsn.), Am. Chem. Soc., Soc. Petroleum Engrs. (Disting. Lectr. 1996—). Avocations: long distance running, piano, philosophy. Office: Colo Sch of Mines Ctr for Hydrate Rsch Golden CO 80401

SLOAN, FRANK ALLEN, economics educator; b. Greensboro, N.C., Aug. 15, 1942; s. Harry Benjamin and Edith (Vortrefflich) S.; m. Paula Jane Rackoff, June 22, 1969; children: Elyse Valerie, Richard Matthew. A.B., Oberlin Coll., 1964; Ph.D., Harvard U., 1969. Research economist Rand Corp., Santa Monica, Calif., 1968-71; asst. prof. econs. U. Fla., Gainesville, 1971-73, assoc. prof., 1973-76; prof. econs. Vanderbilt U., Nashville, 1976-84; Centennial prof. econs. Vanderbilt U., 1984-93, chmn. dept., 1986-89; J. Alexander McMahon Prof. econs. Duke University, Durham, NC, 1993—; dir. Health Policy Ctr. Vanderbilt U. Inst. Pub. Policy Studies, 1976-93; mem. Inst. Medicine, Washington, 1982—, mem. prospective payment rev. commns., 1996—; mem. Nat. Coun. Health Care Tech., Washington, 1979-81, Nat. Allergy and Infectious Disease Council, Washington, 1971-74; cons. adv. coun. Social Security, Washington, 1983. Co-author: Private Physicians and Public Programs, 1978, Hospital Labor Markets, 1980, Insurance, Regulation and Hospital Costs, 1980, Uncompensated Hospital Care: Rights and Responsibilities, 1986, Insuring Medical Malpractice, 1991. Mem. Am. Econ. Assn., So. Econ. Assn., Western Econ. Assn. Home: 109 Millbrae Ln Chapel Hill NC 27514 Office: Duke University Ctr for Health Policy PO Box 90253 Durham NC 27708

SLOAN, FRANK KEENAN, lawyer, writer; b. Johnson City, Tenn., Oct. 11, 1921; s. Z. Frank and Maria Pearl (Witten) S.; m. Helen Rhett Yobs, Feb. 23, 1946 (dec. 1978); children: Richard O., Lewis W., Christine McC., Frank Keenan; m. Alice E. Hamburger, June 22, 1979; children: Carl Francis, Alline Elizabeth. BA, U. S.C., 1943, LLB, JD, 1948. Bar: S.C. 1948. With firm Cooper & Gary, Columbia, S.C., 1948-62; dep. asst. sec. Dept. Def., Washington, 1962-65; S.E. regional dir. OEO, Atlanta, 1965-67; sole practice law Columbia, 1967-77, 87—; chief dep. atty. gen. State of S.C., Columbia, 1977-87; from instr. to assoc. prof. law U. S.C., 1954-62; syndicated columinst, Columbia, 1989-94. Author: (with J.F. Flanagan) S.C. Rules of Civil Procedure; contbr. articles to legal jours. Exec. dir., sec. S.C. Dem. Party, 1960-62, county atty., county exec., Richland County, S.C., 1970-72. Served with USN, 1943-46, 51-52; capt. Res. (ret.). Mem. Mil. Order of World Wars, Rotary (Columbia club), Forest Lake Club (Columbia), Phi Beta Kappa. Democrat. Lutheran. Home: 3320 Devereaux Rd Columbia SC 29205-1919

SLOAN, HAROLD DAVID, chemical engineering consultant; b. Olney, Tex., Jan. 4, 1949; s. James Robert Jr. and Laura Faye (Riddle) S.; m. Barbara Ellen Wilson, Dec. 17, 1970 (div. 1982); m. Maureen Ann Moriarity, Mar. 17, 1983; children: Christa Lauren, Elizabeth Michele. BSChemE, Tex. Tech U., 1972. Registered profl. engr., Tex. Field engr. Halliburton Svcs., Corpus Christi, Tex., 1972-73; mgr. tech. svc. Engelhard Corp., Houston, 1987-90; systems engr., process engr., then process mgr. M.W. Kellogg Co., Houston, 1973-87, sr. product tech. cons., 1990-94, refining product tech. mgr., 1994-95; product dir. Rose, 1995-97, product dir. resid upgrading, 1997—. Contbr. articles to tech. jours. and mags. Pres. Sagemeadow Civic Club, Houston, 1978; v.p. West Harris County Mcpl. Utility Dist. 10, Houston, 1985; Sunday sch. tchr. Met. Bapt. Ch., Houston, 1992—. Mem. AIChE, Tex. Soc. Profl. Engrs. (pres. Sam Houston chpt. 1980, Outstanding Young Engr. award 1978), NRA (life), Tex. State Rifle Assn., Nat. Petroleum Refiners Assn. (co. rep.), Am. Petroleum Inst. (co. rep.), Sigma Xi. Achievements include research on role of delayed coking in a clean fuels environment, economic options for heavy crude upgrading, processing heavier crude blends, process integration for optimizing distillate production, akylation: the ideal process for the reformulated gasoline era; resid upgrading optimization using the ROSE Process, advances in resid upgrading technology optimizing resid upgrading with ROSE and IGCC. Home: 16631 Avenfield Rd Tomball TX 77375-9034 Office: MW Kellogg Co 601 Jefferson St Houston TX 77002-7900

SLOAN, HERBERT ELIAS, physician, surgeon; b. Clarksburg, W.Va., Oct. 10, 1914; s. Herbert Elias and Luella (Dye) S.; m. Doris Edwards, May 3, 1943; children: Herbert, Ann, Elizabeth, John, Robert. A.B., Washington and Lee U., 1936; M.D., Johns Hopkins U., 1940. Diplomate Am. Bd. Surgery, Am. Bd. Thoracic Surgery (bd. dirs. 1966-86, v.p. 1971-73, sec.-treas. 1973-86). Resident in surgery Johns Hopkins Hosp., 1941-44; instr. dept. surgery Johns Hopkins U., 1943-44; resident in thoracic surgery U. Mich. Hosp., Ann Arbor, 1947-49, instr. thoracic surgery, 1949-50; asst. prof. U. Mich., Ann Arbor, 1950-53, assoc. prof., 1953-62, prof. surgery, 1962-87, head sect. thoracic surgery, 1970-85; chief clin. affairs U. Mich. Hosps., Ann Arbor, 1982-86, med. dir. operating room, 1986-87, prof. emeritus surgery, 1987—; med. dir. managed health care U. Mich., Ann Arbor, 1989-96; mem. staff VA Hosp., Ann Arbor, 1953—, cons., 1968—. Author:

(with Marvin M. Kirsh) Blunt Chest Trauma, General Principles of Management, 1977; editor Annals of Thoracic Surgery, 1969-85; contbr. (with Marvin M. Kirsh) chpts. to books, articles to profl. jours. Served to maj. M.C. U.S. Army, 1944-47. Recipient Bruce Douglas award in thoracic diseases, 1974, Med. Alumni Svc. award Johns Hopkins Sch. Medicine, 1973, Disting. Svc. award Johns Hopkins U. Sch. Medicine, 1983, Disting. Svc. award Mich. Med. Ctr. Alumni Soc., 1988. Mem. ACS, Am. Surg. Assn., Am. Heart Assn., Am. Assn. Thoracic Surgery (pres. 1979-80), Soc. Thoracic Surgeons (pres. 1974-75, Disting. Svc. award 1981), Central Surg. Assn., Soc. Univ. Surgeons, So. Thoracic Surgery Assn. (hon.), Thoracic Soc. Gt. Britain (hon.), John Alexander Soc., Western Thoracic Surg. Assn. (hon.), Cardiovascular Surgeons Club, Detroit Heart Club, Am. Trudeau Soc., Mich. Heart Assn., Mich. Trudeau Soc., Am. Acad. Pediatrics, Soc. Vascular Surgery, Frederick A. Coller Surg. Soc., U. Mich. Med. Alumni Soc. (Disting. Svc. award 1988), Rsch. Club, Phi Beta Kappa, Alpha Omega Alpha, Omicron Delta Kappa, Sigma Xi. Club: Ann Arbor Figure Skating (pres. 1965-66). Home: 471 Barton N Dr Ann Arbor MI 48105-1017

SLOAN, HUGH WALTER, JR., automotive industry executive; b. Princeton, N.J., Nov. 1, 1940; s. Hugh Walter and Elizabeth (Johnson) S.; m. Deborah Louise Murray, Feb. 20, 1971; children: Melissa, Peter, Jennifer, William. A.B. in History with honors, Princeton U., 1963. Staff asst. to Pres. U.S., White House, Washington, 1969-71; treas. Pres. Nixon's Re-election Campaign, Washington, 1971; spl. asst. to pres. Budd Co., Troy, Mich., 1973-74, exec. asst. internat., 1974-77, mgr. corp. mktg., 1977-79; pres., gen. mgr. Budd Can. Inc., Kitchener, Ont., 1979-85; pres. automotive The Woodbridge Group, Troy, Mich., 1985—; bd. dirs. Woodbridge Foam Corp., Mfrs. Life Ins. Co., Schneider Corp. Trustee Princeton U.; bd. dirs. The Cmty. House, Jr. Achievement of Can.; dir. Beaumont Found. Lt. USNR, 1963-65. Recipient Outstanding Bus. Leader award Wilfrid Laurier U., 1987. Mem. World Pres. Orgn., Automotive Parts Mfrs. Assn. (past chmn.), Am. Soc. Employers (bd. dirs.), Automotive Market Rsch. Coun. (past pres.), Bloomfield Hills (Mich.) Country Club. Republican. Office: Woodbridge Group 2500 Meijer Dr Troy MI 48084-7146

SLOAN, JEANETTE PASIN, artist; b. Chgo., Mar. 18, 1946; d. Antonio and Anna (Baggio) Pasin; children: Eugene Blakely, Anna Jeanette. BFA, Marymount Coll., Tarrytown, N.Y., 1967; MFA, U. Chgo., 1969. Exhibited in one-woman shows G.W. Einstein Gallery, N.Y.C., 1977-85, Landfall Press Gallery, Chgo., N.Y.C., 1978, 87, Roger Ransay Gallery, Chgo., 1987, 89, 92, Tatischeff Gallery, Santa Monica, Calif., 1989, Steven Scott Gallery, Balt., 1989, Butters Gallery, Portland, Oreg., 1989, 91, 94, 96, Tatischeff Gallery, N.Y.C., 1995, 97, Ouarter Editions, N.Y.C., 1995, Elliot Smith Gallery, St. Louis, 1994, Peltz Gallery, Milw., 1994-95, Gerhard Wurzer Gallery, Houston, 1997; represented in permanent collections Art Mus. Chgo., Cleve. Mus. Art, Ill. State Mus., Indpls. Mus. Art, Canton (Ohio) Art Inst., Ball State Bus., Mpls., Inst. Art, Fogg Mus. Harvard U., Yale U. Art Gallery, Snite Mus. U. Notre Dame, Met. Mus. Art, N.Y.C., Herbert F. Johnson Mus. Cornell U., Ithaca, N.Y.; exhibited in group shows. Studio: 535 Keystone Ave River Forest IL 60305-1611

SLOAN, JERRY (GERALD EUGENE SLOAN), professional basketball coach; b. Mar. 28, 1942; m. Bobbye; 3 children: Kathy, Brian, Holly. Student, Evansville Coll., Evansville, Ind. Professional basketball player, Baltimore, 1965-66, Chicago Bulls, NBA, 1966-76; head coach Chicago Bulls, 1979-82; scout Utah Jazz, NBA, Salt Lake City, 1983-84, asst. coach, 1984-88, head coach, 1988—; player 2 NBA All-Star games; named to NBA All-Defensive First Team, 1969, 72, 74, 75. Office: care Utah Jazz Delta Ctr 301 W South Temple Salt Lake City UT 84101-1216*

SLOAN, O. TEMPLE, JR., automotive equipment executive; b. Sanford, N.C., Feb. 21, 1939; s. Orris Temple and Thelma (Hamilton) S.; m. Carol Carson; children: C. Carson Henline, O. Temple Sloan III, Mark H. Sloan. BA in Bus. Adminstrn., Duke U., 1961. Founder, pres. Gen. Parts Inc., Raleigh, N.C., 1961—; now chmn. Gen. Parts Inc., Raleigh; chmn. bd. dirs. Highwoods Properties Inc., Raleigh; bd. dirs. So. Equipment Co., Raleigh, CARQUEST Corp., Denver, Al Smith Buick Inc., NationsBank Corp., Charlotte. Trustee Boys & Girls Homes N.C., Lake Waccamaw, 1973—, Glenaire Retirement Ctr., Raleigh, 1985—; adv. bd. Salvation Army, Raleigh, 1973-87, chmn., 1976-77; exec. bd., v.p., treas. Occoneechee council Boy Scouts Am., 1967—; bd. visitors Peace Coll., Raleigh, 1985-87, trustee, 1987—, vice chmn.; trustee St. Andrew's Presbyn. Coll., 1990—; bd. dirs. Rex Hosp. Found., 1989-90; elder Presbyn. Ch. Recipient Automotive Edn. Rep. award Boy Scouts Am., also Dist. award of merit Disting. Eagle awrd Boy Scouts Am.; Disting. Svc. citation Automotive Hall of Fame, 1997. Mem. Automotive Warehouse Distbrs. Assn. Inc. (dir. 1969—, chmn. 1976-77, scholarship award 1977, Automotive Man of Yr. award 1989), The Fifty Group (bd. dirs. 1983-88, pres. 1986-87), Greater Raleigh C. of C. (bd. dirs. 1989-91). Republican. Club: Carolina Country (Raleigh). Avocations: fishing, hunting, ranching. Home: 5528 Knightdale Eagle Rock Rd Knightdale NC 27545-8416 Office: Gen Parts Inc PO Box 26006 Raleigh NC 27611-6006

SLOAN, REBA FAYE, dietitian, consultant; b. South Bend, Ind., Feb. 5, 1955; d. Kenneth and Ruby Faye (Long) Lewis; m. Gilbert Kevin Sloan, May 22, 1976. BS, Harding U., 1976; MPH, Loma Linda U., 1989; Cert. Tng. in Child/Adolescent Obesity, U. Calif., San Francisco. Registered dietitian; lic. dietitian and nutritionist; cert. advanced clin. tng. adolescent obesity. Dietetic intern Vanderbilt U. Med. Ctr., Nashville, 1978, rsch. dietitian, 1979-80; therapeutic dietitian Bapt. Hosp., Nashville, 1981-85; staff dietitian Nautilus Total Fitness Ctrs., Nashville, 1983-86; cons. dietitian Nashville Met. Govt., 1986-95, Bapt. Hosp. Ctr. for Health Promotion, Nashville, 1987-91, Parkwest Eating Disorder Clinic, Nashville, 1989-91; nutrition therapist, pvt. practice Nashville, Tenn., 1992—; adj. prof. Vanderbilt U., 1995—; nutrition cons. The Nashville Striders, 1979-81; cons. nutritionist; mem. Vanderbilt U. Eating Disorder Com. Vol. Belmont Ch. Ministries, Nashville, 1981—; speaker Am. Heart Assn., Nashville, 1990—. Recipient cert. of appreciation Am. Heart Assn., 1990; Leaders fellow YMCA. Mem. Am. Dietetic Assn., Sports and Cardiovascular Nutritionists, Cons. Nutritionists, Am. Coll. Sports Medicine, Am. Running and Fitness Assn., Nashville Dist. Dietetic Assn. (contbr. diet manual 1984), Nat. Assn. for Chrisian Recovery, Alpha Chi. Avocations: travel, running, fitness, reading. Home: 1817 Shackleford Rd Nashville TN 37215-3525 Office: 121 21st Ave N Ste 208 Nashville TN 37203-5213

SLOAN, RICHARD, artist; b. Chgo., Dec. 11, 1935; s. Samuel Theodore and Lelia (Beach) S.; m. Arlene Florence Miller, Aug. 11, 1962 (dec. June 1994). Attended, Am. Acad. Art, 1951-53. Advt. illustrator; staff artist Lincoln Park Zoo., Chgo.; master wildlife artist Leigh Yawkey Woodson Art Mus., 1994. Exhbns. include Explorer's Hall Nat. Geographic Soc., Brit. Mus. Natural History, Royal Scottish Acad., Carnegie Mus., Calif. Acad. Scis., Boston Mus. Sci., Am. Mus. Natural History, Nat. Collection Fine Art Smithsonian Inst., Washington, 1979, Leigh Yawkey Woodson Art Mus. (13 exhbns., 1979—), Beijing Mus. Natural History, 1987; Roger Tory Peterson Inst. Natural History nat. mus. tour, 1993, James Ford Bell Mus. Nat. History, U. Minn., 1994; spl. guest artist 1st Vancouver Internat. Wildlife Art Show, 1994; permanent collections Smithsonsian Inst., Leigh Yawkey Woodson Art Mus., Ill. State Mus.; pvt. collections throughout world; contbr. Nat. Wildlife Stamp Program, World Wildlife Fund, international stamps; paintings featured Nat. and Internat. Wildlife Mag., U.S. Art, Wildlife Art News, Ariz. Wildlife Mag., numerous others; artist, illustrator Encyc. Brit., 1963, (book) Raptors of Arizona, 1994. Recipient Award of Excellence Cin. Mus. Nat. History, 1984, Award of Merit Anchorage Audubon Soc., 1985. Mem. Soc. Animal Artists (award of excellence 1990). Home: 1623 S W Pineland Way Palm City FL 34990

SLOANE, BEVERLY LEBOV, writer, consultant; b. N.Y.C., May 26, 1936; d. Benjamin S. and Anne (Weinberg) LeBov; m. Robert Malcolm Sloane, Sept. 27, 1959; 1 child, Alison Lori Sloane Gaylin. AB, Vassar Coll., 1958; MA, Claremont Grad. Sch., 1975, doctoral study, 1975-76; cert. in exec. mgmt., UCLA Grad. Sch. Mgmt., 1982, grad. exec. mgmt. program, UCLA 1982; grad. intensive bioethics course Kennedy Inst. Ethics, Georgetown U., 1987, advanced bioethics course, 1988; grad. sem. in Health Care Ethics, U. Wash. Sch. Medicine, Seattle, summer 1988-90, 94; grad. Summer Bioethics Inst. Loyola Marymount U., summer, 1990; grad. Annual Summer Inst. on Teaching or Writing, Columbia Tchrs. Coll., summer 1990; grad. Annual Summer Inst. on Advanced Teaching of Writing, summer, 1993, Annual Inst. Pub. Health and Human Rights, Harvard U. Sch. Pub. Health, 1994, grad. profl. pub. course Stanford U., 1982, grad. exec. refresher course profl. pub. Stanford U., 1994; cert. Exec. Mgmt. Inst. in Health Care, U. So. Calif., 1995, cert. advanced exec. program Grad. Sch. Mgmt. UCLA, 1995; cert. in ethics corps tng. program, Josephson Inst. of Ethics, 1991, cert.; ethics fellow Loma Linda U. Med. Ctr., 1989; cert. clin. intensive biomedical ethics, Loma Linda U. Med. Ctr., 1989. Circulation libr. Harvard Med. Libr., Boston, 1958-59; social worker Conn. State Welfare, New Haven, 1960-61; tchr. English, Hebrew Day Sch., New Haven, 1961-64; instr. creative writing and English lit. Monmouth Coll., West Long Branch, N.J., 1967-69; freelance writer, Arcadia, Calif., 1970—; v.p. council grad. students, Claremont Grad. sch., 1971-72, adj. dir. Writing Ctr. Speaker Series Claremont Grad. Sch., 1993—, spkr., 1996, 97; mem. adv. coun. tech. and profl. writing Dept. English, Calif. State U., Long Beach, 1980-82; mem. adv. bd. Calif. Health Rev., 1982-83; mem. Foothill Health Dist. Adv. Coun. L.A. County Dept. Health Svcs., 1987-93, pres., 1989-91, immediate past pres., 1991-92; vis. scholar Hastings Ctr., 1996; spkr. N.Y. Task Force, 1996. Ann. Key Mem. award, 1990. Author: From Vassar to Kitchen, 1967, A Guide to Health Facilities: Personnel and Management, 1971, 2nd edit. 1977, 3d edit., 1992. Mem. pub. relations bd. Monmouth County Mental Health Assn., 1968-69; chmn. creative writing group Calif. Inst. Tech. Woman's Club, 1975-79; mem. ethics com., human subjects protection com. Jewish Home for the Aging, Reseda, Calif., 1994-97; mem. task force edn. and cultural activities, City of Duarte, 1987-88; mem. strategic planning task force com., campaign com. for pre-eminence Claremont Grad. Sch., 1986-87, mem. alumni coun., 1993-96, bd. dirs., governing bd. alumni assn., 1993-96, mem. alumni coun., mem. steering com. annual alumni day 1994-96, mem. alumni awards com., 1994-96, mem. alumni events com., 1994-96, mem. vol. devel. com., 1994-96; Vassar Coll. Class rep. to Alumnae Assn. Fall Coun. Meeting, 1989,, class corr. Vassar Coll. Quarterly Alumnae Mag., 1993—; co-chmn. Vassar Christmas Showcase New Haven Vassar Club, 1965-66, rep. to Vassar Coll. Alumnae Assn. Fall Coun. Meeting, 1965-66; co-chmn. Vassar Club So. Calif. Annual Book Fair, 1970-71; chmn. creative writing group Yale U. Newcomers, 1965-66, dir. creative writing group Yale U. Women's Orgn., 1966-67; grad. AMA Ann. Health Reporting Conf., 1992, 93; mem. exec. program network UCLA Grad. Sch. Mgmt., 1987—; trustee Ctr. for Improvement of Child Caring, 1981-83; mem. League Crippled Children, 1982—, bd. dirs., 1988-91, treas. for gen. meetings, 1990-91, chair hostesses com., 1988-89, pub. rels. com., 1990-91; bd. dirs. L.A. Commn. on Assaults Against Women, 1983-84; chmn. 1st. ann. Rabbi Camillus Angel Interfaith Svc. Temple Beth David, 1978, v.p., 1983-86, spkr., 1997; mem. cmty. rels. com. Jewish Fedn. Council Greater L.A., 1985-87; del. Task Force on Minorities in Newspaper Bus., 1987-89; cmty. rep. County Health Ctrs. Network Tobacco Control Program, 1991; with N.Y. Citizens Com. Health Care Decisions. Recipient cert. of appreciation City of Duarte, 1988, County of L.A., 1988, Alumni Coun. Claremont Grad. Sch. 1996; Coro Found. fellow, 1979; named Calif. Communicator of Achievement, Woman of Yr. Calif. Press Women, 1992. Fellow Am. Med. Writers Assn. (pres. Pacific Southwest chpt. 1987-89, dir. 1980-93, Pacific S.W. del. to nat. bd. 1980-87, 89-91, chmn. various conv. coms., chmn. nat. book awards trade category 1982-83, chmn. Nat. Conv. Networking Luncheon 1983, 84, chmn. freelance and pub. relations coms. Nat. Midyr. Conf. 1983-84, workshop leader ann. conf. 1984-87, 90-92, 95—, nat. chmn. freelance sect. 1984-85, gen. chmn. 1985, Asilomar Western Regional Conf., gen. chmn. 1985, workshop leader 1985, program co-chmn. 1987, speaker 1985, 88-89, program co-chmn. 1989, nat. exec. bd. dirs. 1985-86, nat. adminstr. sects. 1985-86, pres.-elect Pacific S.W. chpt. 1985-87, pres. 1987-89, immediate past pres. 1989-91, bd. dirs., 1991-93, moderator gen. session nat. conf. 1987, chair gen. session nat. conf., 1986-87, chair Walter C. Alvarez Meml. Found. award 1986-87, Appreciation award for outstanding leadership 1989, named to Workshop Leaders Honor Roll 1991); mem. Women in Comm. (dir. 1980-82, 89-90, v.p. cmty. affairs 1981-82, N.E. area rep. 1980-81, chmn. awards banquet 1982, sem. leader, speaker ann. nat. profl. conf., 1985, program adv. com. L.A. chpt. 1987, v.p. activities 1989-90, chmn. L.A. chpt. 1st ann. Agnes Underwood Freedom of Info. Awards Banquet 1982, recognition award 1983, nominating com. 1982, 83, com. Women of the Press Awards luncheon 1988, Women in Comm. awards luncheon 1988), Am. Assn. for Higher Edn., AAUW (legis. chmn. Arcadia br. 1976-77, books and plays chmn. Arcadia br. 1973-74, creative writing chmn. 1969-70, 1st v.p. program dir. 1975-76, networking chmn. 1981-82, chmn. task force promoting individual liberties 1987-88, named Woman of Yr., Woman of Achievement award 1986, cert. of appreciation 1987), Coll. English Assn., APHA, Am. Soc. Law, Medicine and Ethics, Calif. Press Women (v.p. programs L.A. chpt. 1982-85, pres. 1985-87, state pres. 1987-89, past immediate past state pres. 1989-91, chmn. state speakers bur. 1989—, del nat. bd. 1989—, moderator ann. spring conv., 1990, 92, chmn. nominating com. 1990-91, Calif. lit. dir. 1990-92, dir. state lit. com. 1990-92, dir. family literacy day Calif., 1990, Cert. of Appreciation, 1991, named Calif. Communicator of Achievement 1992), AAUP, Internat. Comm. Assn., N.Y. Acad. Scis., Ind. Writers So. Calif. (bd. dirs. 1989-90, dir. Specialized Groups 1989-90, dir. at large 1989-90, bd. dirs. corp. 1988-89, dir. Speech Writing Group, 1991-92), Hastings Ctr. (vis. scholar 1996), AAAS, Nat. Fedn. Press Women, (bd. dirs. 1987-93, nat. co-chmn. task force recruitment of minorities 1987-89, del. 1987-89, nat. dir. of speakers bur. 1989-93, editor of speakers bur. directory 1991, cert. of appreciation, 1991, 93, Plenary of Past Pres. state 1989—, workshop leader-speaker ann. nat. conf. 1990, chair state women of achievement com. 1986-87, editor Speakers Bur. Addendum Directory, 1992, editor Speakers Bur. Directory 1991, 92, named 1st runner up Nat. Communicator of Achievement 1992), AAUW (chpt. Woman of Achievement award 1986, chmn. task force promoting individual liberties 1987-88, speaker 1987, Cert. of Appreciation 1987, Woman of Achievement-Woman of Yr. 1986), Internat. Assn. Bus. Communicators, Soc. for Tech. Comm. (workshop leader, 1985, 86), Kennedy Inst. Ethics, Soc. Health and Human Values, Assoc. Writing Programs, Authors Guild. Clubs: Women's City (Pasadena), Claremont Colls. Faculty House, Pasadena Athletic, Town Hall of Calif. (vice chair cmty. affairs sect. 1982-87, speaker 1986, faculty-instr. Exec. Breakfast Inst. 1985-86, mem. study sect. coun. 1986-88), Authors Guild. Lodge: Rotary (chair Duarte Rotary mag. 1988-89, mem. dist. friendship exch. com. 1988-89, mem. internat. svc. com. 1989-90, info. svc. com. 1989-90) Home and Office: 1301 N Santa Anita Ave Arcadia CA 91006-2419

SLOANE, CARL STUART, business educator, management consultant; b. N.Y.C., Feb. 9, 1937; s. George and Dorothy (Cohen) S.; m. Toby Tatlebaum, Dec. 27, 1958; children: Lisa Beth, Amy Rachel, Todd Cowan. BA, Harvard U., 1958, MBA, 1960. Asst. to pres. Revlon, Inc., N.Y.C., 1960-62; mgmt. cons. Harbridge House, Inc., Boston, 1962-69 ; exec. v.p., treas. Temple, Barker & Sloane, Inc., Lexington, Mass., 1970-78, pres., CEO, 1978-90, chmn., CEO, 1990-91; prof. bus. adminstrn. Harvard Grad. Sch. Bus. Adminstrn., 1991—; mem. policyholders' examining com. N.W. Mut. Life Ins. Co.; mem. bus. adv. com. Transp. Ctr., Northwestern U., 1984-91; mem. adv. com. Ctr. for Sci. and Internat. Affairs, Kennedy Sch. Govt., Harvard U., 1984—; bd. dirs. Am. Pres. Co.'s Ltd., Oakland, Calif., 1983-90, Moore McCormack Resources Inc., Stamford, Conn., 1976-88, Leaseway Transp., Inc., 1993-95, Ionics, Inc., 1995—, Sapient Corp., 1995—, Rayonier, Inc., 1997—. Bd. dirs. Harvard-Radcliffe Hillel, Cambridge, Mass., 1987—, chmn., 1994—; bd. dir., trustee Beth Israel Deaconess Med. Ctr., Boston, 1993—, vice chmn., 1996—; nat. fund chmn. Harvard U. Bus. Sch., 1987-89, also vis. com. Mem. Assn. Mgmt. Cons. Firms (chmn. 1984-86), Harvard U. Bus. Sch. Alumni Assn. (v.p. 1989, pres. 1989-91), Boston Yacht Club (Marblehead). Home: Sargent Rd Marblehead MA 01945-3744 Office: Harvard Bus Sch Soldiers Field Boston MA 02163

SLOANE, MARSHALL M., banker; b. Somerville, Mass., 1926; s. Jacob and Rose (Jacobson) S.; m. Barbara Gluck, Mar. 7, 1954; children—Barry Richard, Jonathan Gary, Linda Ruth. Chmn. bd., CEO, founder Century Bank and Trust Co., Somerville, Mass., 1969—; chmn. bd., pres. Century Bancorp Inc., Somerville, 1972—, Sloane Furniture Co., 1952-68. Chmn. bd. visitors Boston U.; bd. trustees Boston U.; exec. bd. Boy Scouts Am., trustee Nat. Mus. Boy Scouts Am.; trustee Catholic Found. of the Archdiocese of Boston, Boston Regional Office Cath. Charities; active Mass. Gen. Hosp. Coun., Corp. Ptnrs. Health Care Sys., Inc., Corp. Perkins Sch. for Blind. Served with USN. Recipient Good Scout award Greater Boston Council Boy Scouts Am., 1983, Shofar award Nat. Jewish Relationships Council Boy Scouts Am., 1984, Mortimer Schiff award Jewish Relationships Com. Boy Scouts Am., Commendation from Nat. Baptist Relationships Boy Scouts Am., 1985, Silver Beaver award Boy Scouts Am., 1979, Silver Antelope award, 1983, Silver Buffalo award, 1988, Allah-O-Akbar award Nat. Islamic Com. on Scouting, 1985, Theo. Storer award for svc. to Boston community, 1986, Israeli Peace medal, 1987, St. George medal Nat. Cath. Community, BSA, 1990, Bus. and Profl. award Religious Heritage, 1991, Sword of Hope award Am. Cancer Soc., 1992; named Baden Powell inductee World scout Found. Boy Scouts Am., 1989; decorated Knight of St. Gregory The Great by Pope John Paul II, 1994. Mem. Mass. Bankers Assn., Exec. Club, Algonquin Club, Pinebrook Club, Masons. Jewish. Office: Century Bancorp Inc 400 Mystic Ave Medford MA 02155-6316

SLOANE, NEIL JAMES ALEXANDER, mathematician, researcher; b. Beaumaris, Wales, Oct. 10, 1939; came to U.S., 1961; s. Charles Ronald and Jessie (Robinson) S.; m. Susanna Stevens Cuyler, Mar. 8, 1980. BA with honors, U. Melbourne, Australia, 1959, BEE, 1960; MS, Cornell U., 1964, PhD, 1967. Asst. prof. Cornell U., Ithaca, N.Y., 1967-69; mem. tech. staff ATT Bell Labs., Murray Hill, N.J., 1969-96; prin. mem. tech. staff AT&T Rsch. Labs, 1996—. Author: Handbook of Integer Sequences, 1973; co-author: (with F.J. MacWilliams) Theory of Error-Correcting Codes, 1977, (with J.H. Conway) Sphere-Packings, Lattices and Groups, 1988, 2d edit., 1993, (with A.D. Wyner) Claude Elwood Shannon: Collected Papers, 1993, (with S. Plouffe) Encyclopedia of Integer Sequences, 1995. Fellow IEEE (editor in chief Trans. Info. Theory jour. 1978-80); mem. Math. Assn. Am. (Chauvenet prize 1979, Earle Raymond Hedrick lectr. 1984), Am. Math. Soc. Avocation: rock climbing. Office: AT&T Labs Rsch PO Box 971 180 Park Ave Rm C233 Florham Park NJ 07932-0971

SLOANE, ROBERT MALCOLM, healthcare consultant; b. Boston, Feb. 11, 1933; s. Alvin and Florence (Goldberg) S.; m. Beverly LeBov, Sept. 27, 1959; 1 dau., Alison. A.B., Brown U., 1954; M.S., Columbia U., 1958. Adminstrv. resident Mt. Auburn Hosp., Cambridge, Mass., 1957-58; med. adminstr. AT&T, N.Y.C., 1959-60; asst. dir. Yale New Haven Hosp., 1961-67; assoc. adminstr. Monmouth Med. Center, Long Branch, N.J., 1967-69; adminstr. City of Hope Nat. Med. Center, Duarte, Calif., 1969-80; pres. Los Angeles Orthopedic Hosp., Los Angeles Orthopedic Found., 1980-86; pres., CEO Anaheim (Calif.) Meml. Hosp., 1986-94; pres. Vol. Hosp. Am. West, Inc., L.A., 1995; healthcare cons. Arcadia, Calif., 1996—; mem. faculty Columbia U. Sch. Medicine, 1958-59, Yale U. Sch. Medicine, 1963-67, Quinnipac Coll., 1963-67, Pasadena City Coll., 1972-73, Calif. Inst. Tech., 1973-85, U. So. Calif., 1976-79, clin. prof. 1987—, UCLA, 1985-87; chmn. bd. Health Data Net, 1971-73; bd. dirs. Intervalley Health Plan; pres. Anaheim Meml. Devel. Found., 1986-94, InTech Health Sys., Inc., 1996—; sr. cons. APM, Inc., 1996—. Author: (with B. L. Sloane) A Guide to Health Facilities: Personnel and Management, 1971, 2d edit., 1977, 3d edit., 1992; mem. editl. and adv. bd. Health Devices, 1972-90; contbr. articles to hosp. jours. Bd. dirs. Health Systems Agy. Los Angeles County, 1977-78, Vol. Hosps. of Am., 1986-95, chmn., 1993-94, pres., 1995; bd. dirs. Calif. Hosp. Polit. Action Com., 1979-87, vice chmn., 1980-83, chmn., 1983-85. Served to lt. (j.g.) USNR, 1954-56. Fellow Am. Coll. Hosp. Adminstrs. (regent 1989-93, nominations com. 1994—); mem. Am. Hosp. Assn., Hosp Coun. So. Calif. (bd. dirs. , sec. 1982, treas. 1983, chmn. elect 1984, chmn. 1985, past chmn. 1986, 89), Calif. Hosp. Assn. (bd. dirs. exec. com. 1984-86, 89), Anaheim C. of C. (bd. dirs. 1994). Home: 1301 N Santa Anita Ave Arcadia CA 91006-2419 Office: 150 N Santa Anita Ave Ste 300 Arcadia CA 91006-3113

SLOANE, THOMAS O., speech educator; b. West Frankfort, Ill., July 12, 1929; s. Thomas Orville and Blanche (Morris) S.; m. Barbara Lee Lewis, Nov. 1, 1952; children—Elizabeth Alison, David Lewis, Emily. B.A., So. Ill. U., 1951, M.A., 1952; Ph.D., Northwestern U., 1960. Instr. English, Washington and Lee U., 1958-60; asst. prof. speech U. Ill., 1960-65, assoc. prof., 1965-70, assoc. head dept., 1967-68, asst. dean liberal arts and scis., 1966-67; prof. rhetoric, chmn. rhetoric dept. U. Calif., Berkeley, 1970-92, pres.'s chair, 1987-90; dir. Nat. Endowment Humanities Summer Seminar for Coll. Tchrs., 1979. Editor: The Oral Study of Literature, 1966, The Passions of the Minde in Generall (Thomas Wright), 1971, (with Raymond B. Waddington) The Rhetoric of Renaissance Poetry, 1974, (with Joanna H. Maclay) Interpretation, 1972; Donne, Milton and the End of Humanist Rhetoric, 1985, On the Contrary, 1997; contbr. articles to profl. jours. Served to lt. USNR, 1952-55. Faculty research fellow, 1964; U. Ill. instructional devel. awardee, 1965; Henry H. Huntington Library research awardee, 1967; U. Calif. humanities research fellow, 1974; Guggenheim fellow, 1981-82. Mem. MLA, Renaissance Soc. Am., Speech Communications Assn. Office: U Calif Berkeley CA 94720

SLOCOMBE, DOUGLAS, cinematographer; b. London, Eng., Feb. 10, 1913. Cinematographer: (films) (with Wilkie Cooper) The Big Blockade, 1942, (with Ernest Palmer) For Those in Peril, 1944, The Girl on the Canal, 1947, The Loves of Joanna Godden, 1947, Another Shore, 1948, (with Jack Parker) The Captive Heart, 1948, It Always Rains on Sunday, 1949, Kind Hearts and Coronets, 1949, Saraband, 1949, Cage of Gold, 1950, Dance Hall, 1950, (with J. Saeholme) Hue and Cry, 1950, A Run for Your Money, 1950, The Lavender Hill Mob, 1951, Crash of Silence, 1952, His Excellency, 1952, The Man in the White Suit, 1952, The Titfield Thunderbolt, 1953, Lease of Life, 1954, The Love Lottery, 1954, The Light Touch, 1955, Decision Against Time, 1957, Panic in the Parlour, 1957, The Smallest Show on Earth, 1957, All at Sea, 1958, Davy, 1958, Tread Softly Stranger, 1959, The Boy Who Stole a Million, 1960, Circus of Horrors, 1960, The Mark, 1961, Scream of Fear, 1961, Freud, 1962, The L-Shaped Room, 1962, Wonderful to Be Young!, 1962, Guns at Batasi, 1964, The Servant, 1964 (British Academy award best cinematography 1964), The Third Secret, 1964, A High Wind in Jamaica, 1965, The Blue Max, 1966, Promise Her Anything, 1966, Fathom, 1967, The Fearless Vampire Killer; or, Pardon Me but Your Teeth Are in My Neck, 1967, Robbery, 1967, Boom!, 1968, The Lion in Winter, 1968, The Italian Job, 1969, The Buttercup Chain, 1971, Murphy's War, 1971, The Music Lovers, 1971, Travels with My Aunt, 1972 (Academy award nomination best cinematography 1972), Jesus Christ, Superstar, 1973, The Destructors, 1974, The Great Gatsby, 1974 (British Academy award best cinematography 1974), Hedda, 1975, The Maids, 1975, Rollerball, 1975, That Lucky Touch, 1975, The Bawdy Adventures of Tom Jones, 1976, Nasty Habits, 1976, The Sailor Who Fell from Grace with the Sea, 1976, Julia, 1977 (Academy award nomination best cinematography 1977, British Academy award best cinematography 1977), Close Encounters of the Third Kind, 1977, Caravans, 1978, Lost and Found, 1979, The Lady Vanishes, 1980, Nijinsky, 1980, (with Paul Beeson) Raiders of the Lost Ark, 1981 (Academy award nomination best cinematography 1981), Never Say Never Again, 1983, The Pirates of Penzance, 1983, Indiana Jones and the Temple of Doom, 1984, Water, 1985, Lady Jane, 1986, (with Beeson and Robert Stevens) Indiana Jones and the Last Crusade, 1989, (TV movie) The Corn Is Green, 1979; dir. photography: (films) Dead of the Night, 1945, Ludwig II, 1954, Heaven and Earth, 1956; photographer: (TV movie) Love Among the Ruins, 1975, (documentary) Lights Out in Europe. Address: 24 Hereford Sq, London SW7, England Office: London Mgt, 235/241 Regent St, London WI 2J7, England*

SLOCOMBE, WALTER BECKER, government official, lawyer; b. Albuquerque, Sept. 23, 1941; m. Ellen Seidman; children: Sarah Cody, Merrin Hayes, Benjamin William. B.A., Princeton U., 1963; postgrad., Balliol Coll., Oxford U., 1963-65; LL.B., Harvard U., 1968. Bar: D.C. 1970. Law clk. Justice Abe Fortas, U.S. Supreme Ct., 1968-69; mem. Nat. Security Council staff, 1969-70; rsch. assoc. Internat. Inst. Strategic Studies, London, 1970-71; mem. firm Caplin and Drysdale, Washington, 1971-76, 81-93; ptnr. Caplin and Drysdale, 1974-76, 81-93; dep. under-sec. for policy planning U.S. Dept. Def., Washington, 1979-81, prin. dep. under-sec., 1993-94, under-sec. of def. for policy, 1994—; prin. dep. asst. sec. for internat. security affairs, dir. Def. Dept. SALT Task Force, Dept. Def., Washington, 1977-79. Rhodes scholar, 1963-65. Mem. Council Fgn. Relations, Internat. Inst. Strategic Studies, Am. Bar Assn., ACLU. Democrat. Office: The Pentagon PDUSD(P) Rm 4E808 Washington DC 20301-2000*

SLOCUM, DONALD HILLMAN, product development executive; b. Flushing, N.Y., Jan. 6, 1930; s. John G. and Frances H. S.; m. June Manning, Sept. 22, 1952 (dec. 1976); children: Richard, Mark, Carol; m. Barbara M. Ruane, Nov. 1, 1985. BS, Davis and Elkins Coll., 1951; MS, U. Vt., 1956; PhD, Ohio State U., 1958; LLD, Fla. Tech. Inst., 1968; MBA, Rider Coll., 1971; ScD, Norton U., 1972; Dr. Profl. Studies, Pace U., 1974. Rsch. chem. Charles Pfizer, Inc., Bklyn., 1954; rsch. scientist Procter & Gamble,

Cin., 1958-68; mgr. product devel. E.I. DuPont de Nemours & Co., Wilmington, Del., 1960-68; dir. new ventures N.L. Industries, N.Y.C., 1968-71; dir. fin. planning Hoffmann LaRoche, Nutley, N.J., 1971-74; v.p. Curtiss-Wright Corp., Woodridge, N.J., 1974-78; sr. v.p. Masonite-USG/Internat. Paper, Chgo., 1978-85; pres. Doner-Viking Corp., Madison, N.J., 1985-87, Woodtec, Inc. subs. Masco, Taylor, Mich., 1987-96, Versitec Industries, 1996—. Author: New Venture Methodology, 1974; contbr. articles to tech. and bus. publs.; patentee in field. Lt. U.S. Army, 1951-54, Korea, Col. Res., ret. Home: 61 Chimney Ridge Dr Morristown NJ 07960-4722 Office: SRA 3400 Bee Ridge Rd Sarasota FL 34239-7223

SLOCUM, DONALD WARREN, chemist; m. Laurel Hopper, 1990; children from previous marriage: Warren, Matthew. BS in Chemistry, BA in English, U. Rochester; PhD in Chemistry, NYU, 1963. Postdoctoral rsch. assoc. Duke U., Durham, N.C., 1963-64; asst. prof. chemistry Carnegie Inst. Tech., Pitts., 1964-65; from asst. to assoc. prof. chemistry So. Ill. U., Carbondale, 1965-72; prof. So. Ill. U., 1972-81, adj. prof., 1981-84; program dir. chem. dynamics sect., chemistry div. NSF, Washington, 1984-85; program leader div. ednl. programs, sr. scientist chem. tech. div. Argonne (Ill.) Nat. Lab., 1985-90; head dept. chemistry Western Ky. U., Bowling Green, 1990-95, prof. chemistry, 1995—; sr. scientist Gulf Rsch. and Devel. Co., Pitts., 1980-82; vis. prof. U. Ill., 1970, U. Bristol, Eng., 1973, U. Cin., 1976; vis. fellow U. Bristol, 1972; vis. lectr. Carnegie-Mellon U., 1983-84, U. Pitts., 1983-84; organizer symposia on organometallic chemistry and catalysis; bd. dirs. Ctrl. States Univs., Inc., 1986-88, Arts at Argonne, 1988-90; cons. in field; mem. nat. organizing com. XVth Internat. Conf. on Organometallic Chemistry Wayne State U., Detroit, 1990; mem. internat. adv. bd. WVth Internat. Conf. on Organometallic Chemistry, Warsaw, 1992; mem. NSF/EPSCoR subcom., Ky., 1993-94; mem. coun. on undergrad. rsch. Instnl. Liaison Rep. to Western Ky. U., 1995—. Co-editor: Advances in Chemistry Series of Am. Chem. Soc., Vol. 230, 1992, Methane and Alkane Activation (Plenum), 1995; contbr. over 60 articles to profl. jours., chpts. to books. Recipient Rsch./Creativity award Ogden Coll. of Sci., Technology and Health, Western Ky. U., 1996. Mem. Am. Chem. Soc. (sec. gen. elect catalysis and surface sci. secretariat 1992, sec. gen. 1993, organic divsn. rep. to catalysis and surface sci. secretariat, 1993—, co-chmn. symposium, San Diego, 1994), Chem. Soc. Gt. Britain, Catalysis Soc., Sigma Xi. Avocations: music, literature, sports. Office: Western Ky U Dept Chemistry Bowling Green KY 42101

SLOCUM, GEORGE SIGMAN, energy company executive; b. East Orange, N.J., Sept. 9, 1940. B.A., Cornell U., 1962, M.B.A., 1967. Mgmt. trainee Richardson-Merrell, Inc., 1962; v.p. Citibank N.A., 1967-78; v.p. fin. Transco Energy Co., Houston, 1978-80, sr. v.p., 1980-81, exec. v.p., CFO, dir., 1981-84, pres., COO, dir., 1984-87, pres., CEO, dir., 1987-92; bd. dirs. Enron Global Power and Pipelines LLC, James River Coal Co., AnAerobics. Bd. dirs. Houston Hospice, Soc. for Performing Arts, Houston; trustee Boy Scouts Am., Cornell U.; mem. alumni adv. coun. Cornell U. Grad. Sch. Mgmt. Served with U.S. Army, 1963-65. Avocation: tennis. Home: 10776 Bridlewood St Houston TX 77024-5413 Office: Cayuga Lake Farm 3533 R and 90 Aurora NY 13026

SLOCUM, R.C., university athletic coach. Asst. football coach Tex. A&M U. Aggies, 1972-80, 82-89, U. So. Calif., 1981; head football coach Tex. A&M U. Aggies, 1989—. Office: Texas A&M Univ Athletics Dept College Station TX 77843-1228*

SLOCUM, ROSEMARIE R., physician management search consultant; b. Port Arthur, Tex., Dec. 19, 1948; d. Edly and Ella (McNeely) Raccard; m. James Rubenstein; 1 child, Blair Ashton Slocum. BS, La. State U., Baton Rouge, 1971. Cert. tchr., La. Edn. specialist La. Dept. Occupl. Stds., Baton Rouge, 1971-74; account exec. Uarco, Inc., Baton Rouge, 1974-77; owner, broker Rosemarie Slocum Real Estate, Baton Rouge, 1977-91; physician recruiter MSI, New Orleans, 1985-86; assoc. dir. physician recruitment Physician Search, Inc., Fairfax, Va., 1986-88; spl. cons. Caswell/Winters Physician Search Cons., Milw., 1988-89; v.p. U.S. Med. Search, Inc. subs. of Caswell/Winters, Milw., 1988-89; dir. physician recruitment/mktg. East Range Clinics, Ltd., Virginia, Minn., 1989-91; pres. RSI, Edina, Minn., 1991—. Avocations: healthcare research, antiques, historical preservation. Office: RSI 6400 Barrie Rd Apt 1000 Edina MN 55435-2316

SLOCUMB, HEATHCLIFF, professional baseball player; b. Jamaica, N.Y., June 7, 1966. Grad. H.S., Flushing, N.Y. With Chgo. Cubs, 1991-93, Cleve. Indians, 1993; pitcher Phila. Phillies, 1994-95, Boston Red Sox, 1996—. Selected to N.L. All-Star Team, 1995. Office: Boston Red Sox 4 Yawkey Way Boston MA 02215*

SLOGOFF, STEPHEN, anesthesiologist, educator; b. Phila., PA, July 7, 1942; s. Israel and Lillian (Rittenberg) S.; m. Barbara Anita Gershman, June 2, 1963; children: Michele, Deborah. AB in Biology, Franklin and Marshall Coll., 1964; MD, Jefferson Med. Coll., 1967. Diplomate Am. Bd. Med. Examiners, Am. Bd. Anesthesiology (jr. assoc. examiner 1977-80, sr. assoc. examiner 1980-81, bd. dirs. 1981-93, pres. 1989-90, joint coun. on in-tng. exams, vice chmn. 1983-86, chmn. 1986-92). Intern Harrisburg (Pa.) Hosp., 1967-68; resident in anesthesiology Jefferson Med. Coll. Hosp., 1968-71; chief anesthesia sect. U.S. Army, Brooke Army Med. Ctr., Fort Sam Houston, Tex., 1971-74; staff anesthesiologist Baylor Coll. Medicne, Houston, 1974-75; attending cardiovascular anesthesiologist U. Tex. Health Sci. Ctr., Houston, 1974-93, clin. asst. prof., 1977-81, clin. assoc. prof., 1981-85, clin. prof., 1985-93; prof., chmn. dept. anesthesiology Loyola U., Chgo., 1993—; chmn. rsch com., co-dir. rsch. labs Tex. Heart Inst., Houston, 1990-93. Contbr. articles to profl. jours. Mem. Am. Soc. Anesthesiologists, Alpha Omega Alpha. Avocations: tennis,jogging. Office: Loyola U Med Ctr Dept Anesthesia 2160 S 1st Ave Maywood IL 60153-3304

SLOMANSON, LLOYD HOWARD, architect, musician; b. N.Y.C., July 31, 1928; s. Albert Jerome and Dorothea (Jacobson) S.; m. Joan Barbara Kanel; children: Peter, Eric. BArch, Syracuse U., 1949. Registered architect, 18 states including N.Y. and N.J.; NCARB; registered profl. planner, N.J.; registered interior designer, Tex. Archtl. draftsman Rich & Conn Architects, Bklyn., 1949-50; project architect Fordyce & Hamby/Raymond Loewy, N.Y.C., 1951-53; project architect, assoc. ptnr. Serge P. Petroff, Architect, N.Y.C., 1953-58; project dir. Robert W. Hegardt, Architect, N.Y.C., 1959-60; project architect, ptnr. Fordyce & Hamby Assocs., N.Y.C., 1960-67; ptnr. Fordyce, Hamby & Kennerly, N.Y.C., 1967-69, Hamby, Kennerly & Slomanson, N.Y.C., 1969-72, Kennerly, Slomanson & Smith, N.Y.C., 1972-81; mng. ptnr. Slomanson, Smith & Barresi, N.Y.C., 1981—; arbitrator Am. Arbitration Assn., N.Y.C. Author articles. Served with U.S. Army, 1950-51. Recipient 1st prize for design S.I. C. of C., 1967, 84. Mem. AIA, N.Y. Soc. Architects (Store of Yr. award 1985, Design award 1993), N.Y. State Assn. Architects, Bldg. Ofcls. Conf. Am., Univ. Club, The Players. Avocations: playing music with a big band, photography. Office: Slomanson Smith & Barresi 65 Bleecker St New York NY 10012-2420

SLONAKER, NORMAN DALE, lawyer; b. Havre, Mont., Sept. 16, 1940; s. Frederick and Agnes (Monson) S.; m. Helen Bogumil, Aug. 29, 1964. BS, U. Wash., Seattle, 1962; LLM, Harvard U., 1965. Bar: N.Y. 1966. Assoc. Brown & Wood, LLP, N.Y.C., 1965-72, ptnr., 1973—. Office: Brown & Wood LLP 1 World Trade Ctr New York NY 10048-0202

SLONE, SANDI, artist; b. Boston, Oct. 1, 1939; d. Louis and Ida (Spind) Sudikoff; children: Erric Solomon, Jon Solomon. Student, Boston Mus. Fine Arts Sch., 1970-73; BA magna cum laude, Wellesley Coll., 1974. Sr., grad. painting faculty Boston Mus. Fine Arts Sch./Tufts U., 1975—; instr. grad. program Sch. Visual Art, N.Y.C., 1989-90; lectr. painting Harvard U., Cambridge, Mass., 1982; vis. artist Triangle Artists Workshop, N.Y., 1982, 87, 90; co-founder, dir. Art/Omi Internat. Artists Found., N.Y.C., 1992—. Solo shows including ICA, Boston, 1977, Harcus Krakow Gallery, Boston, 1978, 79, 80, 82, 84, 86, Acquavella Contemporary Art, N.Y., 1977, 79, 80, 82, 84, Contemporary Art, N.Y., 1977, 79, 80, 82, 84, Stephen Rosenberg Gallery, N.Y., 1988, Levinson Kane Gallery, Boston, 1989, Smith Jariwala Gallery, London, 1990, Jersey City Mus., 1996, J.J. Brookings Gallery, San Francisco, 1996; group shows include at Mus. Fine Arts, Boston, 1977, Corcoran Gallery of Art 35th Biennile, Washington, 1977, Edmonton Art Gallery, 1977, 85, Hayden Gallery MIT, Cambridge, Mass., 1978, New Generation Andre Emmerich Gallery, N.Y., 1980-81, Am. Ctr., Paris, 1980-81, Amerika Haus, Berlin, 1980-81, Carpenter Ctr., Harvard U., Ctr. de la Cultura Contemporanea, Barcelona, 1987, Federated Union of Black Artists, Johannesburg, South Africa, 1989, Jan Weiss Gallery, N.Y., 1990, Olympia Internat. Art Fairs, London, 1991, Gallery Korea, N.Y., 1992, Klarfeld Perry Gallery, N.Y., 1994, Out of the Blue Gallery, Edinburgh, Scotland, 1994, Gallery One, Toronto, 1996, fine Arts Ctr., U. R.I., Kingston, 1996, Crieger Dane Gallery, Boston, 1996, others; represented in permanent collections Mus. Modern Art, N.Y.C., Mus. Contemporary Art, Barcelona, Mus. Fine Arts, Boston, Hirshhorn Mus., Washington; artist-in-residence City Hall, Barcelona, 1987, 89, Artists Mus., Lodz, Poland, 1997. Mus. Fine Arts Boston fellow, 1977, 81; Ford Found. grantee, 1979. Studio: 13 Worth St New York NY 10013-2925

SLONECKER, CHARLES EDWARD, anatomist, medical educator, author; b. Gig Harbor, Wash., Nov. 30, 1938; s. William Mead and Helen Spencer (Henderson) S.; m. Jan Hunter, June 24, 1961; children—David Charles, Derron Scott, John Patrick. Student, Olympic Coll., 1957-58; student in Sci., U. Wash., 1958-60, DDS, 1965, PhD in Biol. Structure, 1967. Sci. asst. in pathology U. Bern, Switzerland, 1967-68; asst. prof. U. B.C., Vancouver, Canada, 1968-71, assoc. prof., 1971-76, prof., 1976, head of anatomy, 1981-92, dir. ceremonies and univ. rels., 1989—. Advisor Community Unit YMCA, Vancouver, 1981-92; group com. chmn. Boy Scouts, Can., 1976-82; mem. cabinet United Way Lower Mainland, 1997. Served with U.S. Army, 1956-61. Recipient Award of Merit Am. Acad. Dental Medicine, 1965; recipient Award of Merit Wash. State Dental Assn., 1965, Dennis P. Duskin Meml. award U. Wash., 1965, Master Tchr. award, Cert. of Merit U. B.C., 1975-76. Fellow Am. Coll. Dentists; mem. Am. Assn. Anatomists (Centennial Gold medal 1987, program sec. 1982-90, v.p. 1991-93, pres. 1994), Can. Assn. U. Tchrs., Sigma Xi (pres. U. B.C. 1981-82, 88-89), Omicron Kappa Upsilon (chpt. sec.), U. B.C. Faculty Club. Anglican. Home: 6007 Dunbar St, Vancouver, BC Canada V6N 1W8 Office: Univ BC, 6251 Cecil Green Park Rd, Vancouver, BC Canada V6T 1W5

SLORP, JOHN S., academic administrator; b. Hartford, Conn., Dec. 5, 1936. Student, Ocean Coll., Calif., 1956, Taft Coll., Calif., 1961; BFA Painting, Calif. Coll. Arts and Crafts, 1963, MFA Painting, 1965. Grad. tchr. U. N.D., Grand Forks, 1964; in house designer Nat. Canner's Assn., Berkeley, Calif., 1965; mem. faculty Md. Inst. Coll. Art, Balt., 1965-82; chair Found. Studies Md. Inst. Coll. Art, 1972-78; mem. faculty Emma Lake program U. Sask., Can., 1967-68, 70; selection, planning group for Polish Posters Smithsonian Instn., Md. Inst. Coll. Art, Warsaw, Poland, 1977; planner, initiator visual arts facility, curriculum Balt. High Sch. Arts, 1979-81; adjudicator Arts Recognition and Talent Search, Princeton, N.J., 1980-82; mem. Commn. Accredation Nat. Assn. Schs. Art and Design, 1985-88; pres. Memphis Coll. Art, 1982-90, Mpls. Coll Art and Design, 1990—; com. Advanced Placement Studio Art Ednl. Testing Svc., Princeton, N.J., 1975-82; chair Assn. Memphis Area Colls. and Univs., 1986-88. Prodr. film A Romance of Calligraphy; calligrapher various brochures, manuscripts, album covers, children's books. Mem. Hotel adv. com. City of Memphis and Shelby County Convention Hotel, 1982; adv. bd. Memphis Design Ctr.; bd. trustees Opera Memphis, 1985—, ART Today Memphis Brooks Mus., 1988—. Avocations: painting, calligraphy, computer graphics. Office: Mpls Coll Art Design Office of President 2501 Stevens Ave Minneapolis MN 55404-4347*

SLOSBERG, MIKE, advertising executive; b. Phila., Aug. 29, 1934; s. Sam. M. and Florence (Frank) S.; m. Joan Shidler, Aug. 29, 1957 (div. 1984); children: Sydney Ellen, Robert Morton; m. Janet Cohn, June 10, 1987. BSBA, U. Denver, 1960. Copy writer Young & Rubicam, Inc., N.Y.C., 1960-65, v.p. creative supr., 1965-69, sr. v.p., assoc. creative dir., 1971-78; v.p. creative dir. Young & Rubicam, Inc., Los Angeles, 1969-71; pres. Wunderman, Rocotta & Kline, N.Y.C., 1978-83; exec. v.p., exec. creative dir. Marsteller, Inc., N.Y.C., 1983-84; exec. v.p., exec. creative dir. Bozell Jacobs, Kenyon & Eckhardt, N.Y.C., 1984-86, pres. direct mktg. div., 1986-87; exec. creative dir. Bronner Slosberg Humphrey, Boston, 1987—. Author: The August Strangers, 1978. Mem. Direct Mktg. Assn., Boston Advt. Club, New Eng. Direct Mktg. Assn., The One Club, Direct Mktg. Idea Exchange, Friars Club, N.Y. Athletic Club. Avocations: writing novels, skiing. Office: Bronner Slosberg Humphrey Prudential Tower 800 Boylston St Boston MA 02199

SLOSSER, JEFFERY ERIC, research entomologist; b. Winslow, Az., Dec. 1, 1943; s. Ernest Clair and Geneva Lee (Hutchison) S.; m. Harolyn Christine, July 27, 1968; children: Tamara Joanne, Tracy Suzanne. BS, Arizona State U., 1966; MS, U. Arizona, 1968, PhD, 1971. Postdoctoral rsch. assoc. U. Ark., Fayetteville, 1972-75; asst. prof. Tex. Agrl. Expt. Sta., Vernon, 1975-79, assoc. prof., 1979-86, prof., 1986—; editor Southwestern Entomologist, Southwestern Entomologist Soc., College Station, Tex., 1986-90. Contbr. articles to profl. jours. Grantee boll weevil and bollworm rsch. Cotton Inc., 1977-82, 94-97, greenbug rsch. Tex. Wheat Prodrs. Bd., 1985-88, cotton aphid rsch. Nat. Cotton Coun., Cotton, Inc., 1992-97, boll weevil rsch. Plains Cotton Growers, 1989-95, (horse fly rsch. Waggoner Found., 1996-97); recipient award in excellence for rsch. Tex. A&M Univ. Sys., 1990. Mem. Entomol. Soc. Am. (CIBA Plant Protection award 1995), Southwestern Entomol. Soc. (pres.-elect 1992, pres. 1992), Sigma Xi. Republican. Baptist. Avocations: astronomy, astrophotography. Office: Tex Agrl Expt Sta PO Box 1658 Vernon TX 76385-1658

SLOTKIN, RICHARD SIDNEY, American studies educator, writer; b. Bklyn., Nov. 8, 1942; s. Herman and Roselyn B. (Seplowitz) S.; m. Iris F. Shupack, June 23, 1963; 1 child, Joel Elliot. B.A., Bklyn. Coll., 1963; Ph.D., Brown U., 1967; M.A. (hon.), Wesleyan U., Middletown, Conn., 1976. Mem. faculty Wesleyan U., 1966—, prof. English, 1976—, Olin prof., 1982—, chmn. dept. Am. studies, 1976—. Author: Regeneration Through Violence: The Mythology of the American Frontier, 1600-1860, 1973 (Albert Beveridge award Am. Hist. Assn.), (with J.K. Folsom) So Dreadfull a Judgement: Puritan Responses to King Philip's War, 1675-1677, 1978, The Crater: A Novel of the Civil War, 1980, The Fatal Environment: The Myth of the Frontier in the Age of Industrialization, 1800-1890, The Return of Henry Starr, 1988, Gunfighter Nation: The Myth of the Frontier in Twentieth Century America, 1992 (National Book award nominee, 1993); and articles. Fellow Center Humanities; fellow Wesleyan U., 1969-70, 74-75, 80—; fellow NEH, 1973-74, Rockefeller Found., 1976-77; recipient Don D. Walker prize AQ; lit. award Little Big Horn Assocs., 1986. Fellow Soc. Am. Historians; mem. MLA, AAUP, PEN, Am. Film Inst., Am. Studies Assn. (Mary Turpie prize for tchg. and program-bldg. 1995), Am. Hist. Assn., Orgn. Am. Historians, Western History Assn., Authors Guild, Western Writers Assn. Jewish. Office: Wesleyan Univ English Dept Middletown CT 06459

SLOTKIN, TODD JAMES, holding company executive, venture capitalist; b. Detroit, Mar. 19, 1953; s. Hugo Slotkin and Babette Walsey Okin; m. Judy Scavone, Jan. 30, 1988; children: Matthew Hugo, William Joseph, Thomas Samuel, Peter Benjamin. BS, Cornell U., 1974, MBA, 1975. With Citicorp, 1975-92, sr. credit officer, 1984-92, head divsn. corp. fin., 1988-90, sr. mng. dir., 1990-92; sr. exec. v.p. MacAndrews & Forbes Holdings, Inc., N.Y.C., 1992—. Mem. exec. com. United Jewish Appeal, N.Y.C., 1989—. Home: 876 Park Ave Apt 11 N New York NY 10021-1832 Office: MacAndrews & Forbes Holding 35 E 62nd St New York NY 10021-8016

SLOTNICK, MORTIMER H., artist; b. N.Y.C., Nov. 7, 1920; s. Max S. and Sarah B. S.; m. Phyllis June Gluckin, July 26, 1953; children: Debra Jan, Mark Stuart. B.S.S., CCNY, 1942; M.A., Tchrs. Coll., Columbia U., 1942. Tchr. visual arts, public schs. New Rochelle, N.Y., 1946-64; supr. arts and humanities City Sch. Dist., 1964-72; prin. Davis Elem. Sch., 1972-84; adj. prof. art CCNY, 1964-72; prof. art Coll. New Rochelle, N.Y., 1972-78; adj. prof. edn. Pace U., 1988-93. One-man shows include Ada Ahrtz Galleries, N.Y.C., 1959, Westport (Conn.) Art Gallery, 1986, New Rochelle Coun. on the Arts, 1989; exhibited in group shows Nat. Acad. N.Y., World Trade Ctr., N.Y.C., Lever House, N.Y.C., Am. Artists Profl. League, Nat. Arts Club, Salmagundi Club; represented in permanent collections Nat. Mus. Am. Art, Smithsonian Instn., New Britain Mus. Am. Art, Johnson Mus. Art Cornell U., Nat. Archives, Washington, Truman Home, Independence, Mo., F.D.R. Mus., Hyde Park, N.Y.; also pvt. and corp. collections; works published in Artists of Am. Calendar. Mem. City Art Commn. New Rochelle, 1977-80. Served with AUS, 1942-46, ETO, PTO. Mem. N.Y. Artists Equity Assn., Allied Artists Am., Am. Artists Profl. League, Coll. Art Assn., Nat. Assn. Humanities Edn., Art. Pub., Am. Artists Group, Bernard Picture Co., McLeery-Cumming Co., Donald Art. Co., Scafa-Tornabene Art Publ., A. B. Franklin Gallery, Internet, Masons. Club: Masons. Home: 43 Amherst Dr New Rochelle NY 10804-1814 *An artist must respect the totality of his art. His work must express his integrity, his honesty and his wish to communicate with the viewer. It must strive toward the sublime. Anything less is unworthy of being called art.*

SLOVES, MARVIN, advertising agency executive; b. N.Y.C., Apr. 22, 1933; s. John H. and Evelyn S. (Wishan) S. AB, Brandeis U, 1955; postgrad., Oriental Inst., U. Chgo., 1955-61. Staff researcher Leo Burnett Co., Chgo., 1962; dir. rsch. Earle Ludgin Co., Chgo., 1963-64; account exec. Ted Bates Co., N.Y.C., 1964; account supr., v.p. Papert, Koenig, Lois, N.Y.C., 1965-67; pres., chief exec. officer Scali, McCabe, Sloves, Inc., N.Y.C., 1967-81, chmn., chief exec. officer, 1981-93; vice chmn. The Lowe Group, 1993—. Bd. dirs. Burden Ctr. for Aged, N.Y.C., Chamber Music Soc. Lincoln Ctr., N.Y.C., Santa Fe Chamber Music Festival, Santa Fe Opera, N.Y. Coun. for Humanities, Hope House, Santa Fe, Nat. Cultural Alliance, Washington, D.C. NEA fellow. Mem. Am. Assn. Advt. Agys. Democrat. Jewish. Avocations: boxing; memorabilia collecting. Home: PO Box 50 Bogtown House North Salem NY 10560-0050

SLOVIK, SANDRA LEE, art educator; b. Elizabeth, N.J., Mar. 22, 1943; d. Edward Stanley and Frances (Garbus) S. BA, Newark State Coll., 1965, MA, 1970. Cert. art tchr. Art tchr. Holmdel (N.J.) Twp. Bd. Edn., 1965—; computer art in-sv. tng. Holmdel Bd. Edn., 1990; computer art workshop Madison (N.J.) Bd. Edn., 1991. Charter supporter, mem. Statue of Liberty/Ellis Island Found., 1976—; charter supporter Sheriffs' Assn. N.J., 1993—; mem. PTA, Holmdel, 1965—. Recipient Curriculum award N.J. ASCD, 1992; grantee Holmdel Bd. Edn., 1989, 90, N.J. Bus., Industry, Sci., Edn. Consortium, 1990. Mem. NEA, Nat. Art Edn., Assn., N.J. Art Educators Assn., N.J. Edn. Assn., Monmouth County Edn. Assn., Holmdel Twp. Edn. Assn. (sr. bldg. rep. 1977-79). Avocations: travel, sports. Office: Village Sch 67 Mccampbell Rd Holmdel NJ 07733-2231

SLOVIKOWSKI, GERALD JUDE, manufacturing company executive; b. N.Y.C., Feb. 9, 1949; s. Felix J. and Wilhelmina S. BS in Mech. Engring. with honors, Pratt Inst., Bklyn., 1970; MBA magna cum laude, Wagner Coll., N.Y.C., 1975. Registered profl. engr., N.J. Project engr. Mobil Oil Corp., N.Y.C., 1970-72; project mgr. Am. Home Products, N.Y.C., 1972-74; ops. mgr. Continental Oil Corp., Houston, 1974-75, bus. devel. mgr., 1975-77; v.p. and gen. mgr. Herman, Sommer & Assocs., Newark, 1977-80; exec. v.p. and gen. mgr. Engineered Products Co., Inc., Oldbridge, N.J., 1980—; v.p. Equity Investment Co., Clark, N.J.; bd. dirs. Urban Assocs., Holmdel, N.J., Engineered Products Co., Perth Amboy, N.J., GS Indsl. Co., N.J.; prof. bus. adminstrn. Middlesex Coll., Edison, N.J., 1981—. Cons. Woodbridge Twp. Econ. Devel. Council, Woodbridge, N.J., 1980. Recipient Cons. Engrs. award N.Y. Cons. Engring. Assn., 1970, Dow Jones Fin. award Dow Jones Wall Street Jour., 1975. Mem. ASME, Am. Nuclear Soc. (assoc.), Am. Inst. Chem. Engrs. (assoc.), Tau Beta Pi, Pi Tau Sigma, Delta Mu Delta, Pi Mu Epsilon. Home: 29 Buchannan Way Flemington NJ 08822-3205

SLOVITER, DOLORES KORMAN, federal judge; b. Phila., Sept. 5, 1932; d. David and Tillie Korman; m. Henry A. Sloviter, Apr. 3, 1969; 1 dau., Vikki Amanda. AB in Econs. with distinction, Temple U., 1953, LHD (hon.), 1986; LLB magna cum laude, U. Pa., 1956; LLD (hon.), The Dickinson Sch. Law, 1984, U. Richmond, 1992; LL.D. (hon.), Widener U., 1994. Bar: Pa. 1957. Assoc., then ptnr. Dilworth, Paxson, Kalish, Kohn & Levy, Phila., 1956-69; mem. firm Harold E. Kohn (P.A.), Phila., 1969-72; assoc. prof., then prof. law Temple U. Law Sch., Phila., 1972-79; judge U.S. Ct. Appeals (3d cir.), Phila., 1979—, chief judge, 1991—; mem. bd. overseers U. Pa. Law Sch. Mem. S.E. region Pa. Gov.'s Conf. on Aging, 1976-79, Com. of 70, 1976-79; trustee Jewish Publ. Soc. Am., 1983-89; Jud. Conf. U.S. com. Bicentennial Constn., 1987-90, com. on Rules of Practice and Procedure, 1990-93. Recipient Juliette Low medal Girl Scouts Greater Phila., Inc., 1990, Honor award Girls High Alumnae Assn., 1991, Jud. award Pa. Bar Assn., 1994, U. Pa. James Wilson award, 1996, Temple U. Cert. of Honor award, 1996; Disting. Fulbright scholar, Chile, 1990. Mem. ABA, Fed. Bar Assn., Fed. Judges Assn., Am. Law Inst., Nat. Assn. Women Judges, Am. Judicature Soc. (bd. dirs. 1990-95), Phila. Bar Assn. (gov. 1976-78), Order of Coif (pres. U. Pa. chpt. 1975-77), Phi Beta Kappa. Office: US Ct Appeals 18614 US Courthouse 601 Market St Philadelphia PA 19106-1713

SLOVITER, HENRY ALLAN, medical educator; b. Phila., June 16, 1914; s. Samuel and Rose (Seltzer) S.; m. Dolores Korman, Apr. 3, 1969. A.B., Temple U., 1935, A.M., 1936; Ph.D., U. Pa., 1942, M.D., 1949. Chemist, U.S. Naval Base, Phila., 1936-45; intern Hosp. U. Pa., 1949-50; research fellow U. Pa. Sch. Medicine, 1945-49, asst. prof., 1952-56, asso. prof., 1956-68, prof., 1968—; vis. scientist biochemistry dept. Tokyo U.; U.S. project officer USPHS Fogarty Internat. Center program Inst. for Biology, Belgrade, Yugoslavia, 1971, 74; vis. prof. Academia Sinica, China, 1983; rsch. scientist Tokyo Met. Inst. Med. Rsch., 1984; vis. lectr. King Edward Meml. Hosp., Bombay, 1990. Contbr. articles profl. jours. Am. Cancer Soc. fellow Nat. Int. Med. Rsch., London, 1950-52; Coll. de France endocrinology dept. rsch. fellow Paris, 1952; sr. internat. fellow USPHS Fogarty Internat. Ctr., St. Mary's Hosp. Med. Sch., London, 1978; recipient glycerine rsch. award, 1954; exch. scholar Tokyo U., 1963, USSR, 1965, 71, India, 1967; recipient alumni award Temple U., 1992. Fellow AAAS; mem. Internat. Soc. Neurochemistry, Am. Soc. Biol. Chemists, Internat. Soc. Blood Transfusion, Am. Physiol. Soc., Belgian Soc. for Anesthesia and Reanimation (hon.), Hungarian Soc. Hematology and Blood Transfusion. Home: 310 S Front St Philadelphia PA 19106-4310 Office: U Pa Sch Medicine Philadelphia PA 19104

SLOVUT, GORDON, reporter. Health and science reporter The Mpls. Star Tribune, Minn. Office: Mpls. Star Tribune 425 Portland Ave Minneapolis MN 55415-1511

SLOWIK, RICHARD ANDREW, air force officer; b. Detroit, Sept. 9, 1939; s. Louis Stanley and Mary Jean (Zaucha) S. BS, USAF Acad., 1963; BS in Bus. Adminstrn., No. Mich. U., 1967; LLB, LaSalle Extension U., 1969; MBA, Fla. Tech. U., 1972; MS in Adminstrn., Ga. Coll., 1979; MA, Georgetown U., 1983; postgrad. cert., Va. Polytech. Inst. and State U., 1986. Commd. 1st lt. U.S. Air Force, 1963, advanced through grades to lt. col.; pilot Craig AFB, Ala., 1963-64, Sawyer AFB, Mich., 1964-68; forward air contr. Pacific Air Forces, South Vietnam, 1968-69; pilot SAC, McCoy AFB, Fla., 1969-71; asst. prof. aerospace studies Va. Poly. Inst. and State U., Blacksburg, 1972-76; br. chief current ops. br. Robins AFB, Ga., 1976-80; asst. dep. chief ops. group Hdqrs. Air Force, Pentagon, Washington, 1980-82; Western Hemisphere and Pacific Area desk officer Nat. Mil. Command Center, Pentagon, Washington, 1982-83; mil. rep. Ops. Ctr., Dept. State, Washington, 1983-85; ops. officer 97th Bombardment Wing, Blytheville AFB, Ark., 1985-87, chief base ops. and trg. div., 97th Combat Support Group, Blythville AFB, 1987-88, chief airfield mgmt. div. Eaker AFB, Ark., 1988-91, free-lance writer, 1991—. Group ops. officer CAP, Marquette, Mich., 1967-68, Orlando, Fla., 1970-72, sr. programs officer, Blacksburg, 1972-76, Warner Robins, Ga., 1976-80, wing plans and programs officer, Washington, 1980—. Contbr. articles profl. jours. Decorated Defense Meritorious Service Medal, 10 Air medals, 3 Air Force Meritorious Service medals, 2 Commendation medals, Cross of Gallantry with Palm, Presdl. Legion of Merit, others; recipient Presdl. Legion of Merit, Presdl. Medal of Merit (3), Presdl. Achievement award (3). Mem. Acad. of Mgmt., Air Force Assn., Cato Inst., Heritage Found., Mil. Order World Wars, Am. Def. Preparedness Assn., Am. Security Council, Order of Daedalians. Roman Catholic. Home and Office: 1708 N Broadway St Blytheville AR 72315-1313

SLOYAN, GERARD STEPHEN, religious studies educator, priest; b. N.Y.C., Dec. 13, 1919; s. Jerome James and Marie (Kelley) S. A.B., Seton Hall U., 1940; S.T.L., Cath. U. Am., 1944, Ph.D., 1948; DLitt, Seton Hall U., 1984; HHD, St. Ambrose U., 1995. Ordained priest Roman Cath. Ch., 1944. Asst. pastor in Trenton, Maple Shade, N.J., 1947-50; mem. faculty Cath. U. Am., Washington, 1950-67, chmn. dept. religion, 1957-67; prof. N.T. studies Temple U., Phila., 1967-90, chmn. dept. religion, 1970-74, 84-86; vis. prof. Cath. U. Am., Washington, 1992—, Iowa State U., 1995.

English editor: N.T., The New American Bible, 1970; author: Jesus on Trial: Development of the Passion Narratives, 1973, Commentary on the New Lectionary, 1975, Is Christ the End of the Law?, 1978, Jesus in Focus, 1983, 2d edit., 1993, The Jesus Tradition, 1986, John: "Interpretation" Commentary, 1988, Jesus, Redeemer and Divine Word, 1989, What Are They Saying About John?, 1991, Walking in the Truth: 1, 2, and 3 John, 1995, The Crucifixion of Jesus, History, Myth, Faith, 1995. Recipient Pro Ecclesia et Pontifice medal, 1970, Johannes Quasten medal Cath U. Am., 1985, Michael Mathis award Notre Dame Ctr. Pastoral Liturgy, 1994. Mem. AAUP, Cath. Bibl. Assn., Soc. Bibl. Lit., Cath. Theol. Soc. Am. (John Courtney Murray award 1981, pres. 1993-94), Coll. Theology Soc. (pres. 1964-66), Liturg. Conf. (pres. 1962-64, v.p. 1970-71, 75-88, chmn. bd. dirs. 1980-88), N.Am. Acad. Liturgy (Berakah award 1986). Democrat.

SLOYAN, PATRICK JOSEPH, journalist; b. Stamford, Conn., Jan. 11, 1937; s. James Joseph and Annamae (O'Brien) S.; m. Phyllis Hampton, Nov. 19, 1960; children: Nora, Amy, Patrick, John. BS, U. Md., 1963. Reporter Albany (N.Y.) Times-Union, 1957-58, Balt. News Post, 1958-60, United Press Internat., Washington, 1960-69, Hearst News Svc., Washington, 1969-74; reporter Newsday, Washington, 1974-81, bur. chief, 1986-88, sr. corr., 1988—; bur. chief Newsday, London, 1981-86; chmn. Fund for Investigative Journalism, Washington, 1987—. With U.S. Army, 1955-57. Recipient Best Writing award Am. Soc. Newspaper Editors, 1982, War Reporting award George Polk Awards, 1992, Pulitzer Prize for internat. reporting, 1992. Mem. Gridiron Club. Roman Catholic. Avocations: swimming, tennis, gardening. Home: 17115 Simpson Circle Paeonian Springs VA 22129-9701 Office: Newsday 1730 Pennsylvania Ave NW Washington DC 20006

SLOYAN, SISTER STEPHANIE, mathematics educator; b. N.Y.C., Apr. 18, 1918; d. Jerome James and Marie Virginia (Kelley) S. BA, Georgian Ct. Coll., 1945; MA in Math., Cath. U. Am., 1950, PhD, 1952. Asst. prof. math. Georgian Ct. Coll., Lakewood, N.J., 1952-56, assoc. prof., 1956-59, prof., 1959—, coll. pres., 1968-74; lectr. Grad. Sch. Arts and Scis., Cath. U. Am., Washington, 1960-82. Mem. Math. Assn. Am. (bd. govs. 1988-91), Am. Math. Soc., Sigma Xi. Democrat. Roman Catholic. Office: Georgian Ct Coll Dept Math Lakewood NJ 08701-2697

SLUDIKOFF, STANLEY ROBERT, publisher, writer; b. Bronx, N.Y., July 17, 1935; s. Harry and Lillie (Elberger) S.; m. Ann Paula Blumberg, June 30, 1972; children: Lisa Beth, Jaime Dawn, Bonnie Joy. B.Arch., Pratt Inst., 1957; grad. student, U. So. Calif., 1960-62. Lic. architect, real estate broker. Project planner Robert E. Alexander, F.A.I.A. & Assos., Los Angeles, 1965-66, Daniel, Mann, Johnson & Mendenhall (City and Regional Planning Cons.), Los Angeles, 1967-70; pres., editor, pub. Gambling Times Inc., also Two Worlds Mgmt., Inc., Los Angeles, 1971—; v.p. Prima Quality Farms, Inc., P.R.; chmn. Creative Games, Inc., 1992—; pres. Las Vegas TV Weekly, also Postal West, Las Vegas, 1975-79; founder Stanley Roberts Sch. Winning Blackjack, 1976; instr. city and regional planning program U. So. Calif., 1960-63; founding mem. Mfrs. Direct, 1996. Author: (under pen name Stanley Roberts) Winning Blackjack, 1971, How to Win at Weekend Blackjack, 1973, Gambling Times Guide to Blackjack, 1983; author: The Beginner's Guide to Winning Blackjack, 1983, Begin to Win at Blackjack, 1997, Begin to Win at Video Poker, 1997, Begin to Win at Craps, 1997; also monthly column, 1977—; inventor Daily Digit lottery game; patentee in field. Mem. Destination 90 Forum, Citizens Planning Group, San Fernando Valley, Calif., 1966-67, Rebuild L.A. land use com., 1992—. Served to lt. col. U.S. Army, now Res. ret. Recipient commendation from mayor Los Angeles for work on model cities funding, 1968. Mem. AIA, Am. Planning Assn., Am. Inst. Cert. Planners, Internat. Casino Assn. (sec. 1980—), Res. Officers Assn. (life), Mensa (life). Home: 17147 Vintage St Northridge CA 91325-1653 Office: 16140 Valerio St # B Van Nuys CA 91406-2916 *The challenge of being alive lies in the development of one's maximum potential. To do less is to fly in the face of the gifts of creation, to shorten the aspect of one's life and to deny the fullness of existence. "The weakness of the flesh" prevents anyone's full development from reaching fruition but the personal and societal loss lies in giving up too soon, before we have fully tested our limits.*

SLUNG, HILTON B., surgeon; b. Louisville, May 10, 1950. MD, U. Louisville, 1976. Diplomate Am. Bd. Surgery, Am. Bd. Colon and Rectal Surgery. Intern Georgetown U. Hosp., Washington, 1976-77, resident in gen. surgery, 1977-79; resident in gen. surgery Marshall U. Hosp., Huntington, 1980-82; fellow in colon and rectal surgery Grant Hosp., Columbus, Ohio, 1983-84; mem. staff Jewish Hosp., Louisville, 1984—, Suburban Hosp., 1984—; mem. courtesy staff Bapt. East Hosp., 1984—, Audubon Hosp., 1984—; clin. instr. surgery U. Louisville. Fellow ACS; mem. Am. Soc. Colon and Rectal Surgery, So. Med. Assn., Jefferson County Med. Soc. Office: Doctors Office Bldg 250 E Liberty St Ste 610 Louisville KY 40202-1536

SLUSHER, KIMBERLY GOODE, researcher; b. Benham, Ky., Oct. 4, 1960; d. Herschel James and Nevelyn Faye (Hayes) Goode; m. Joe Allan Slusher, May 1, 1985; 1 child, Tarah Rene. BS in Agr., Ea. Ky. U., 1982; MS in Agr., U. Tenn., 1989. Rsch. asst. U. Tenn., Knoxville, 1983-89; info. analyst Oak Ridge (Tenn.) Nat. Lab., 1989—, tchr., cons. sci. honors program, 1993. Author: (army study) Drinking Water Contamination Study, 1995; contbr. chpt.: Teratogens: Chemicals Which Cause Birth Defects, 1993. Methodist. Avocations: gardening, piano. Office: Biomed & Environ Info Analysis Sect 1060 Commerce Park Dr Oak Ridge TN 37830-8026

SLUSSER, WILLIAM PETER, investment banker; b. Oakland, Calif., June 20, 1929; s. Eugene and Thelma (Donovan) S.; m. Joanne Eleanor Briggs, June 20, 1953; children: Kathleen E., Martin E., Wendelin M., Caroline E., Sarah A. BA cum laude, Stanford U., 1951; MBA, Harvard U., 1953. Mgr. spl. situations dept. Dean Witter & Co., N.Y.C., 1955-60; partner, sr. v.p. in charge corp. fin. dept., 1960-75, also dir.; mem. exec. com. Shields & Co.; co-mgr. investment banking div., sr. v.p. Paine Webber Inc., 1975-80; mng. dir., head merger and aquisitions dept. Paine Webber, Inc., N.Y.C., 1980-88; pres. Slusser Assocs., Inc., N.Y.C., 1988—; underwriter or fin. cons. Square D. Co., Times Mirror Co., Ashland Oil, Inc., Ga. Pacific, TRW, Inc., Avon Products, TransAm. Realty Investors, Atex, Inc. subs. Eastman Kodak Co., Perini Corp., Downey Savs. & Loan, Booth Newspapers, Inc., Holly Hill Lumber Co., Stanhome, Inc., Santee Portland Cement Co., Grow Group, Crown Cork & Seal Co., Dr. Pepper Co. of So. Calif., Sparton Corp., Cap Gemini Sogeti, Ltd., London, De La Rue, P.L.C., London, VNU Inc., Haarlem, Netherlands, Bertlesmann Pub. Co., Fed. Republic Germany, ADT Ltd., London, Bank of Guam, Houghton Mifflin Co., Orion Research, Inc., Pacific Holding Co., also vice chmn., 1969-73; bd. dirs. Ampex Corp., ADT Ltd.; founder original Stockholder Assoc. Mortgage Cos. Lectr. to profl. assns. Mem. Ends of the Earth; bd. fin. advisors Columbia U. Bus. Sch., Calif. Senate Commn. on Local Govt. Investments, mem. Calif. Senate commn. on corp. governance. Served to 1st lt. USAF, 1953-55. Mem. Investment Assn. N.Y., Soc. Calif. Pioneers, Alpha Delta Phi (exec. council 1956-62, treas. 1961). Clubs: Knickerbocker, Downtown, Stanford Assocs., Harvard (N.Y.C.); Lawrence Beach, Stanford of N.Y. Author numerous articles; contbr.; Handbook of Mergers, Acquisitions and Buyouts, The Mergers & Acquisitions Handbook. Home: 901 Lexington Ave New York NY 10021-5902 also: Slusser Ranch Windsor CA 95492 Office: Slusser Assocs Inc 1 Citicorp Ctr 153 E 53rd St Rm 5100 New York NY 10022-4611

SLUTSKY, KENNETH JOEL, lawyer; b. N.Y.C., Sept. 18, 1953; s. Clement and June (Gross) S.; m. Nancy Ellen Goldfarb, Jan. 15, 1978; children: Rachel, Jason, Jenna. BA, Columbia U., 1975; JD, Harvard U., 1978. Bar: N.J. 1978, U.S. Dist. Ct. N.J. 1978. Assoc. Lowenstein, Sandler, Brochin, Kohl, Fisher & Boylan, Roseland, N.J., 1978-83; mem. firm Lowenstein, Sandler, Kohl, Fisher & Boylan, P.A., Roseland, N.J., 1984—. Mem. met. N.J. chpt. Am. Jewish Com., Millburn, Jewish Family Svc. Metrowest N.J., Florham Park. Mem. ABA, N.J. Bar Assn. Home: 2 Hampton Ct N Caldwell NJ 07006-4701 Office: Lowenstein Sandler Kohl Fisher & Boylan PA 65 Livingston Ave Roseland NJ 07068-1725

SLUTSKY, LORIE ANN, foundation executive; b. N.Y.C., Jan. 5, 1953; d. Edward and Adele (Moskowitz) S. BA, Colgate U,, 1975; MA in Urban Policy and Analysis, New Sch. for Social Rsch., N.Y.C., 1977. Program officer N.Y. Cmty. Trust, N.Y.C., 1977-83, v.p., 1983-87, exec. v.p., 1987-89, pres., CEO, 1990—; former mem. and chmn. bd. Coun. on Founds., Inc., Washington, 1986-95. Trustee, chmn. budget com. Colgate U., Hamilton, N.Y., 1989—; vice chmn., bd. dirs. Found. Ctr., Inc., N.Y.C., United Way, N.Y.C.; bd. dirs. L.A. Wallace Fund for Metro. Mus. Art, N.Y.C., D. Wallace Fund for Meml. Sloan Kettering. Office: NY Community Trust 2 Park Ave New York NY 10016-5675

SLY, RIDGE MICHAEL, physician, educator; b. Seattle, Nov. 3, 1933; s. Ridge Joseph and Eva Jean (Ruddell) S.; m. Ann Turner Jennings, June 12, 1957; children: Teresa Ann Perper, Cynthia Marie Schattenfield. A.B., Kenyon Coll., 1956; M.D., Washington U., St. Louis, 1960. Diplomate Am. Bd. Pediatrics, Am. Sub-Bd. Pediatric Allergy, Am. Bd. Allergy and Immunology. Intern, resident in pediatrics St. Louis Children's Hosp, 1960-62; chief resident in pediatrics U. Ky. Med. Ctr., Lexington, 1962-63; fellow in allergy and immunology UCLA Med. Ctr., 1965-67; asst. prof., assoc. prof., prof. pediatrics La. State U. Med. Ctr., New Orleans, 1967-78; dir. allergy and immunology Children's Nat. Med. Ctr., Washington, 1978—; prof. pediatrics George Washington U., Washington, 1978—. Author: Textbook of Pediatric Allergy, 1985; mem. editl. bd. Annals of Allergy, Asthma, & Immunology, 1982—, Jour. Asthma, 1982-93, Clin. Revs. in Allergy, 1982—, Pediat. Asthma, Allergy, & Immunology, 1987—; assoc. editor Annals of Allergy, Asthma, & Immunology, 1989-90, editor, 1990—; contbr. articles to profl. jours. Served to capt. USAF, 1963-65. Recipient La. plaque Am. Lung Assn. of La., 1978. Fellow Am. Acad. Allergy, Asthma & Immunology (chmn. com. on drugs 1981-87), Am. Acad. Pediats. (sect. on allergy com. 1972-75), Am. Coll. Allergy, Asthma, and Immunology (Disting. Fellow award 1993); mem. Am. Thoracic Soc., Am. Assn. for Care of Asthma (pres. 1980-81, dir. postgrad. courses 1980—, Peshkin Meml. award 1983), Am. Med. Writer's Assn., Coun. Biology Editors, Phi Beta Kappa. Republican. Baptist. Avocations: music (organ, piano). Office: Children's Nat Med Ctr 111 Michigan Ave NW Washington DC 20010-2916

SLY, WILLIAM S., biochemist, educator; b. East St. Louis, Ill., Oct. 19, 1932. MD, St. Louis U., 1957. Intern, asst. resident Ward Med Barnes Hosp., St. Louis, 1957-59; clin. assoc. nat. heart inst. NIH, Bethesda, Md., 1959-63, rsch. biochemist, 1959-63; dir. divsn. med. genetics, dept. medicine and pediatrics, sch. medicine Washington U., 1964-84, from asst. prof. to prof. medicine, 1964-78, from asst. prof. to prof. pediatrics, 1967-78, prof. pediatrics, medicine and genetics, 1978-84; prof. biochemistry, chmn. E. A. Doisy dept. biochemistry, prof. pediatrics sch. med. St. Louis U., 1984—; vis. physician Nat. Heart Inst., 1961-63, pediatric genetics clinic U. Wis., Madison, 1963-64; Am. Cancer Soc. fellow lab. enzymol Nat. Ctr. Sci. Rsch., Gif-sur-Yvette, France, 1963, dept. biochemistry and genetics U. Wis., 1963-64; attending physician St. Louis County Hosp., Mo., 1964-84; asst. physician Barnes Hosp., St. Louis, 1964-84, St. Louis Children's Hosp., 1967-84; genetics cons. Homer G. Philips Hosp., St. Louis, 1969-81; mem. genetics study sect. divsn. rsch. grants NIH, 1971-75; mem. active staff Cardinal Glennon Children's Hosp., St. Louis, 1984—; mem. med. adv. bd. Howard Hughes Med. Inst., 1989-92. Recipient Merit award NIH, 1988; named Passano Found. laureate, 1991; Travelling fellow Royal Soc. Medicine, 1973. Mem. NAS, AMA, AAAS, Am. Soc. Human Genetics (mem. steering com. human cell biology program 1971-73, com. genetic counseling 1972-76), Am. Soc. Clin. Investigation, Am. Chem. Soc., Genetics Soc. Am., Am. Soc. Microbiology, Soc. Pediatric Rsch., Sigma Xi. Achievements include research in biochemical regulation, enveloped viruses as membrane probes in human diseases, lysosomal enzyme replacement in storage diseases, somatic cell genetics. Office: St Louis U Med Sch Dept Biochemistry 1402 S Grand Blvd Saint Louis MO 63104-1004*

SLYE, CARROLL JAMES, instructional supervisor; b. Harrisonburg, Va., July 23, 1953; s. Junior Lee and Phyllis Ann (Dovel) S.; 1 child, Kelsey Alexandra. BS, James Madison U., 1979, MEd, 1991. Collegiate profl. lic. Classroom tchr., coach Rockingham County Schs., Harrisonburg, Va., 1980-91; asst. prin. H.S. Rockingham County Schs., Harrisonburg, 1991-95, gen. supr., 1995—; mem. com. on tchr. edn. Ea. Mennonite U., Harrisonburg, 1995—. Named Educator of the Yr., Elkton (Va.) Lions Club, 1990, Elkton (Va.) Combined PTA, 1991. Mem. ASCD, Va. H.S. Coaches Assn., Phi Delta Kappa. Avocations: fishing, golfing, reading, snow skiing, hunting. Home: Rt 2 Box 739 McGaheysville VA 22840 Office: Rockingham County Schs 304 County Office Bldg Harrisonburg VA 22801

SLYE, LEONARD FRANKLIN See ROGERS, ROY

SMAGORINSKY, JOSEPH, meteorologist; b. N.Y.C., Jan. 29, 1924; s. Nathan and Dinah (Azaroff) S.; m. Margaret Knoepfel, May 29, 1948; children: Anne, Peter, Teresa, Julia, Frederick. BS, NYU, 1947, MS, 1948, PhD, 1953; ScD (hon.), U. Munich, 1972. Research asst., instr. meteorology N.Y. U., 1946-48; with U.S. Weather Bur., 1948-50, 53-65, chief gen. circulation research sect., 1955-63; meteorologist Inst. Advanced Study, Princeton, N.J., 1950-53; acting dir. Inst. Atmospheric Scis. Environ. Scis. Services Adminstrn., Washington, 1965-66; dir. Geophys. Fluid Dynamics Lab. Environ. Scis. Services Adminstrn.-NOAA, Washington and Princeton, 1964-83; cons., 1983—; vice chmn. U.S. Com. Global Atmospheric Research Program, Nat. Acad. Sci., 1967-73, 80-87, officer, 1974-77, mem. climate bd., 1978-87, chmn. com. on internat. climate programs, 1979, bd. internat. orgns. and programs, 1979-83, chmn. climate research com., 1981-87; chmn. joint organizing com. Global Atmospheric Research Program, Internat. Council Sci. Unions/World Meteorol. Orgn., 1976-80, officer, 1967-80; chmn. Joint Sci. Com. World Climate Research Program, 1980-81; chmn. climate coordinating forum Internat. Council Sci. Unions, 1980-84; vis. lectr. with rank of prof. Princeton U., 1968-83, vis. sr. fellow, 1983—; Sigmx Xi nat. lectr., 1983-85; Brittingham vis. prof. U. Wis., 1986. Contbr. to profl. publns. 1st lt. USAAF, 1943-46. Decorated Air medal; recipient Gold medal Dept. Commerce, 1966, award for sci. research and achievement Environ. Sci. Services Adminstrn., 1970, U.S. Presdl. award, 1980, Buys Ballot Gold medal Royal Netherlands Acad. Arts and Scis., 1973, IMO prize and Gold medal World Meteorol. Orgn., 1974. Fellow AAAS, Am. Meteorol. Soc. (hon. mem., councilor 1974-77, assoc. editor jour. 1965-74, Meisinger award 1967, Wexler Meml. lectr. 1969, Carl-Gustaf Rossby Research Gold medal 1972, Cleveland Abbe award for disting. service to atmospheric sci. 1980, pres. 1986, Charles Franklin Brooks award 1991); mem. Royal Meteorol. Soc. (hon., Symons Meml. lectr. 1963, Symons Meml. gold medal 1981). Home: 21 Duffield Pl Princeton NJ 08540-2605

SMAILI, AHMAD, mechanical engineering educator; b. Gaza, Lebanon, Nov. 4, 1955; came to U.S., 1976; s. Abdulkarim and Fatme (Mourad) S.; m. Maha Hazime, Aug. 10, 1989; children: Layla, Ali. BS, Tenn. Technol. U., 1979, MS, 1981, PhD, 1986. Asst. prof. Miss. State U., Starkville, 1987-91; asst. prof. Tenn. Technol. U., Cookeville, 1991-95, assoc. prof., 1995—; cons. Waste Policy Inst., Washington, 1992, U. Tenn. Space Inst., Tullahoma, 1993-94, Marine Gears, Greenville, Miss., 1990-91, Geka Thermal Sys., Atlanta, 1994—. Contbr. articles to profl. jours. Co-chmn. Cookeville Refugee Support Com., 1993—. Named Outstanding Faculty Mem., Student Assn. Miss. State U., 1989; recipient Kinslow Rsch. award Tenn. Technol. U., 1996. Mem. ASME (faculty advisor), Am. Soc. Engring. Edn., Pi Tau Sigma (Purple Shaft Trophy 1989, 90), N.Y. Acad. Scis., Tau Beta Pi. Muslim. Achievements include introduction for the first time the concept of "Robomechs" parallel-drive linkage arms for multi-function task applications. Avocations: Karate (2d degree black belt), travel, soccer. Home: 799 W Oak Dr Apt D-1 Cookeville TN 38501-3743 Office: Tenn Technol U W 10th St Box 5014 Cookeville TN 38505

SMALDONE, EDWARD MICHAEL, composer; b. Wantagh, N.Y., Nov. 19, 1956; m. Karen Ajamian, Aug. 5, 1979; children: Laura, Gregory, Julia. BA in Music, Queens Coll., 1978, MA in Music, 1980; PhD in Music, CUNY, 1986. Lectr. SUNY, Purchase, 1986-90; adj. asst. prof. Hofstra U., Hempstead, N.Y., 1988-90; vis. asst. prof. New Sch. for Social Rsch., N.Y.C., 1988; adminstrv. dir. Speculum Musicae, N.Y.C., 1988-89; artistic dir. Sounds for the Left Bank, Rego Park, N.Y., 1985-92; asst. prof. Copland Sch. of Music, CUNY, Flushing, 1990—; composer in residence N.Y.C. Pub. Schs., 1994, 95; Carlisle Project Choreographer and Composer Collaboration Commn., 1994. Composer: Two String Quartets, 1980, 86, Dialogue for orch., 1987, Double Duo (flute, clarinet, violin, cello), 1987, Transformational Etudes (solo piano), 1990, Rhapsody for piano and orch., 1992, Suite for violin and piano, 1993, Three Scenes from "The Heartland" for solo piano, 1994, Saxophone Quartet, 1995, Rituals: Sacred and Profane for flute, cello and piano, 1996, American Spiritual Fantasy for string orch., 1997. Recipient Standard award ASCAP, 1986—, Creative Incentive award CUNY Rsch. Found., 1992, 95, 97; residency fellow Yaddo Corp., 1986, 87, Composer's fellow Charles Ives Ctr. for Am. Music, 1990, residency fellow MacDowell Colony, 1994, Goddard Lieberson fellow Am. Acad. Arts and Letters, 1993; prize winner Percussive Arts Soc., 1994. Home: 228 Manhasset Ave Manhasset NY 11030-2220 Office: Copland Sch of Music Queens College Flushing NY 11030

SMALE, JOHN GRAY, diversified industry executive; b. Listowel, Ont., Can., Aug. 1, 1927; s. Peter John and Vera Gladys (Gray) S.; m. Phyllis Anne Weaver, Sept. 2, 1950; children: John Gray, Catherine Anne, Lisa Beth, Peter McKee. BS, Miami U., Oxford, Ohio, 1949, LLD (hon.), 1979; LLD (hon.), Kenyon Coll., Gambier, Ohio, 1974; DSc (hon.), DePauw U., 1983; DCL (hon.), St. Augustine's Coll., 1985; LLD (hon.), Xavier U., 1986. With Vick Chem. Co., 1949-50, Bio-Rsch., Inc., N.Y.C., 1950-52; pres. Procter & Gamble Co., 1974-86, chief exec., 1981-90, chmn. bd., 1986-90; dir. General Motors Corp., Detroit, 1992-95, chmn. of exec. com. of bd., 1996—; chmn. exec. com. Gen. Motors Corp., Detroit, 1996—; also bd. dirs. General Motors Corp., Detroit; bd. dirs. Gen. Motors Corp. Bd. govs. Nature Conservancy; emeritus trustee Kenyon Coll. With USNR, 1945-46. Mem. Bus. Coun., Comml. Club, Queen City Club, Cin. Country Club. Office: GM PO Box 599 Cincinnati OH 45201-0599

SMALES, FRED BENSON, corporate executive; b. Keokuk, Iowa, Oct. 7, 1914; s. Fred B. and Mary Alice (Warwick) S.; m. Constance Brennan, Dec. 11, 1965; children: Fred Benson III, Catherine (Mrs. Jonathan Christensen); children by previous marriage: Patricia (Mrs. Murray Pilkington), Nancy (Mrs. Bruce Clark). Student public schs., Los Angeles. With Champion Internat., Inc., 1933-68, successively San Francisco mgr., 1938-44, Los Angeles, Western div. mgr., 1944-55, v.p. Western sales div., 1955-65, v.p., regional dir., 1965-68; pres. Lewers & Cooke, Inc. div. Champion Internat., Inc., Honolulu, 1966-68; chmn. Securities of Am., Inc., 1968-70; chmn., dir. Hawaiian Cement Co., 1970-84; pres. Transpacific Cons., 1984-94, Plywood Hawaii, 1995—. Trustee Hawaii-Pacific U., Hawaii Maritime Ctr. Recipient Disting. Citizen award Nat. Govs. Assn., 1986. Mem. C. of C. Hawaii (past chmn.), So. Calif. Yachting Assn. (sr. staff commodore), Balboa Yacht Club (Newport Beach, Calif, sr. staff commodore), Transpacific Yacht (bd. dirs.), Waikiki Yacht (staff commodore), Pacific Club (past pres.), Royal Hawaiian Ocean Racing (vice commodore), Sequoia Yacht Club (Redwood City, Calif., sr. staff commodore). Home: 46-422 Hulupala Pl Kaneohe HI 96744-4243 Office: 1062 Kikowaena Pl Honolulu HI 96819-4413

SMALKIN, FREDERIC N., federal judge. BA, Johns Hopkins U., 1968; JD, U. Maryland, 1971. Atty. office of judge advocate gen. Dept. Army, 1972-74, asst. to gen. counsel, 1974-76; pvt. practice Monkton, Md., 1976; magistrate U.S. Dist. Ct. Md., Balt., 1976-86, judge, 1986—; lectr. comml. law U. Md., Balt., 1978—, SMH bar rev., Balt., 1985-86, 93-95, BRI/Modern Bar Rev. Course, Inc., Balt., 1980-81; panel spkr. on Utilization of Magistrates at the 1985 fourth cir., Jud. Conf. Capt. U.S. Army, 1968-76, lt. col. CAP (USAF Auxiliary). Mem. Fed. Bar Assn., Order of Coif, Phi Beta Kappa. Office: US Dist Ct 101 W Lombard St Baltimore MD 21201-2626

SMALL, ALDEN THOMAS, judge; b. Columbia, S.C., Oct. 4, 1943; s. Alden Killin and Shirley Edna (Eldridge) S.; m. Judy Jo Worley, June 25, 1966; children—Benjamin, Jane. AB, Duke U., 1965; JD, Wake Forest U., 1969. Bar: N.C. 1969. Asst. v.p. First Union Corp., Greensboro, N.C., 1969-72; assoc. dir., gen. counsel Community Enterprise Devel. Corp. Alaska, Anchorage, 1972-73, v.p., assoc. gen. counsel, First Union Corp., Raleigh, N.C., 1973-82; judge U.S. Bankruptcy Ct. (ea. dist.) N.C., 1982—, chief judge, 1992—; bd. govs. Nat. Conf. of Bankruptcy Judges, 1987-90; adj. prof. law Campbell U. Sch. Law, 1980-82; bd. dirs. Am. Bankruptcy Inst., 1989-95, Fed. Jud. Ctr., 1997—; chmn. Nat. Conf. Bankruptcy Judges Ednl. Endowment, 1993-94; mem. long range planning com. U.S. Judicial Conf., 1991-95, adv. com. bankruptcy rules, 1996—; mem. faculty Nat. Comml. Lending Sch., 1981-82; cons. Nat. Coalition for Bankruptcy Reform, 1981-82. Contributing editor Norton Bankruptcy Law and Practice. Mem. ABA, Am. Bankers Assn. (bankruptcy task force 1980-82), N.C. Bankers Assn. (bank counsel com. 1980-82), N.C. Bar Assn. (bankruptcy council), Kappa Sigma, Phi Alpha Delta. Republican. Office: US Bankruptcy Ct PO Box 2747 Raleigh NC 27602-2747

SMALL, BRUCE W., sales and marketing executive; b. Waltham, Mass., Oct. 3, 1950; s. W. Harold Jr. and Ruth M. (Lovejoy) S.; m. Ursula E. Briggs, Sept. 7, 1974. BA in English, BA in Psychology, Gettysburg Coll., 1972. Cert. hotel sales exec. Sales mgr. Boston (Mass.) Statler Hilton, 1972-75; dir. of sales Logan Airport Hilton, Boston, 1975-77, Dallas (Tex.) Hilton, 1977-80, Fontainebleau Hilton, Miami Beach, Fla., 1980-81; dir. of mktg. Fontainebleau Hilton, Miami Beach, 1981-84; dir. sales and mktg. Hyatt Regency Grand Cypress, Orlando, Fla., 1984-88; corp. dir. sales and mktg. pre-openings and acquisitions Hyatt Hotels Corp., Chgo., 1988-92, divisional dir. sales and mktg., 1992-96; dir. sales and mktg. nat. sales force Hyatt Hotels and Resorts, Chgo., 1996—. Mem. Profl. Conv. Mgmt. Assn. (assoc.), Am. Soc. Assn. Execs. (assoc.), Relig. Conv. Mgmt. Assn. (assoc.), Mtg. Planners Internat. (assoc.). Avocations: equestrian (show Engish Hunters), golf. Office: Hyatt Hotels & Resorts Nat Sales Force 200 W Madison St Chicago IL 60606-3414

SMALL, CLARENCE MERILTON, JR., lawyer; b. Birmingham, Ala., July 24, 1934; s. Clarence Merilton and Elva (Roberts) S.; m. Jean Russell, Nov. 18, 1935; children—William Stephen, Elizabeth Ann, Laura Carol. B.S., Auburn U., 1956; LL.B., U. Ala., 1961. Assoc., pres. Rives & Peterson, Birmingham, Ala., 1961—. Served to 1st lt. arty., AUS, to capt. JAGC. Fellow Am. Bar Found., Internat. Acad. Trial Lawyers, Am. Coll. Trial Lawyers; mem. Birmingham Bar Assn. (pres. 1979), Ala. Def. Lawyers Assn., ABA (ho. of dels. 1984-86), Ala. Bar Assn. (pres. 1992-93), Internat. Assn. Defense Counsel. Office: 1700 Financial Ctr Birmingham AL 35203

SMALL, DONALD MACFARLAND, biophysics educator, gastroenterologist; b. Newton, Mass., Sept. 15, 1931; s. Grace (MacFarland) S.; m. Elisabeth Chan, July 8, 1957 (div. 1979); children: Geoffrey, Philip; m. Kathryn Ross, July 26, 1986; 1 child, Samuel. BA, Occidental Coll., 1954; MA (hon.), Oxford (Eng.) U., 1964; MD, UCLA, 1960. Intern, asst. resident in medicine Mass. Meml. Hosps., Boston, 1960-62; sr. resident Boston City Hosp., 1962-63, vis. physician med. svcs., 1965—; asst. prof. medicine Boston U. Sch. Medicine, 1968-69, assoc. prof. medicine and biochemistry, 1969-73, prof., 1973—, prof. biophysics, chmn. dept., 1989—, dir. Biophysics Inst., 1972—; spl. tng. in phys. chemistry of lipids Inst. Pasteur, Paris, 1963-65; mem. adv. bd. Gladstone Found Labs., San Francisco, 1980—, Liver Ctr., U. Colo., Denver, 1985—; George Lyman Duff Meml. lectr. Coun. Arteriosclerosis, Am. Heart Assn., 1986; cons. Nat. Inst. Arthritis and Metabolic Diseases, NIH, 1968-72, mem. task force Nat. Heart, Lung and Blood Inst., 1990; also others. Author, editor: Physical Chemistry of Lipids, 1986; mem. editl. bd. Gastroenterology, 1967-74, Arteriosclerosis, 1980—, Jour. Biol. Chemistry, Current Opinions in Structural Biology, 1990; sub-editor: Jour. Lipid Rsch., 1974-78, editor, 1979-83; editor: (with R. Havel) Advances in Lipid Rsch., 1989—; mem. internat. bd. editors Jour. Nutritional Biochemistry, 1989—; contbr. articles and revs. to profl. jours.; author: (with A. Adams) The Healthy Meateaters Cookbook, 1991. Bd. dirs. Franconia (N.H.) Ski Racing Club, 1974-77. Recipient Eppinger prize IV Internat. Congress on Liver Disease, 1976, Disting. Achievment award Modern Medicine, 1978, UCLA Sch. Medicine Alumni Assn., 1988; Marshall scholar Magdalen Coll., Oxford, 1956-58, Aesculapian scholar UCLA, 1958-60, Markle scholar, 1966-70; also others. Mem. AAAS, Am. Heart Assn. (fellow coun. arteriosclerosis, chmn. program com. 1988-90, chmn. coun. 1992-94), Am. Assn. Physicians, Am. Soc. Biol. Chemists, Biophys. Soc., Am. Soc. Clin. Investigation, Am. Gastroent. Assn. (Ann. Disting. Achievement award 1972), Am. Oil Chemists Soc., Am. Fedn. Clin. Rsch., Am. Chem. Soc., Mass. Med. Soc., Suffolk Dist. Med. Soc., Phi Beta Kappa, Alpha Omega Alpha, Sigma Xi. Achievements include patent on method for making meat products having a reduced saturate fat and cholesterol content. Office: Boston U Sch Medicine Dept Biophysics 80 E Concord St Roxbury MA 02118-2307

SMALL, ELISABETH CHAN, psychiatrist, educator; b. Beijing, July 11, 1934; came to U.S., 1937; d. Stanley Hong and Lily Luella (Lum) Chan; m. Donald M. Small, July 8, 1957 (div. 1980); children Geoffrey Brooks, Philip Willard Stanley; m. H. Sidney Robinson, Jan. 12, 1991. Student, Immaculate Heart Coll., Los Angeles, 1951-52; BA in Polit. Sci., UCLA, 1955, MD, 1960. Intern Newton-Wellesley Hosp., Mass., 1960-61; asst. dir. for venereal diseases Mass. Dept. Pub. Health, 1961-63; resident in psychiatry Boston State Hosp., Mattapan, Mass., 1965-66; resident in psychiatry Tufts New Eng. Med. Ctr. Hosps., 1966-69, psychiat. cons. dept. gynecology, 1973-75; asst. clin. prof. psychiatry Sch. Medicine Tufts U., 1973-75, assoc. clin. prof., 1975-82, asst. clin. prof. ob-gyn, 1977-80, assoc. clin. prof. ob-gyn, 1980-82; assoc. prof. psychiatry, ob-gyn U. Nev. Sch. Med., Reno, 1982-85; practice psychiatry specializing in psychological effects of bodily changes on women, 1969—; clin. prof. psychiatry U. Nev. Sch. Medicine, Reno, 1985-86, prof. psychiatry, 1986-95, clin. assoc. prof. ob-gyn, 1985-88, emeritus prof. psychiatry and behavioral scis., 1995—; mem. staff Tufts New Eng. Med. Ctr. Hosps., 1977-82, St. Margaret's Hosps., Boston, 1977-82, Washoe Med. Ctr., Reno, Sparks (Nev.) Family Hosp., Truckee Meadows Hosp., Reno, St. Mary's Hosp., Reno; chief psychiatry svc. Reno VA Med. Ctr., 1989-94; lectr. various univs., 1961—; cons. in psychiatry; mem. psychiatry adv. panel Hosp. Satellite Network; mem. office external peer rev. NIMH, HEW; psychiat. cons. to Boston Redevelopment Authority on Relocation of Chinese Families of South Cove Area, 1968-70; mem. New Eng. Med. Ctr. Hosps. Cancer Ctr. Com., 1979-80, Pain Control Com., 1981-82, Tufts Univ. Sch. Medicine Reproductive System Curriculum Com., 1975-82. Mem. editorial bd. Psychiat. Update Am. (Psychiat. Assn. ann. rev.), 1983-85; reviewer Psychosomatics and Hosp. Community Psychiatry, New Eng. Jour. of Medicine, Am. Jour. of Psychiatry Psychosomatic Medicine; contbr. articles to profl. jours. Immaculate Heart Coll. scholar, 1951-52; Mira Hershey scholar UCLA, 1955; fellow Radcliffe Inst., 1967-70. Mem. AMA, Am. Psychiat. Assn. (rep. to sect. com. AAAS, chmn. ad hoc com. Asian-Am. Psychiatrists 1975, task force 1975-77, task force cost effectiveness in consultation 1984—, caucus chmn. 1981-82, sci. program com. 1982-88, courses subcom. chmn. sci. program com. 1986-88), Nev. Psychiat. Assn., Assn. for Acad. Psychiatry (fellowship com. 1982), Washoe County Med. Assn., Nev. Med. Soc., Am. Coll.Psychiatrists (sci. program com. 1989-98). Avocations: snow skiing, culinary arts. Home: 602 Alley Oop Reno NV 89509-3668 Office: 475 Hill St Reno NV 89501-1824

SMALL, ERWIN, veterinarian, educator; b. Boston, Nov. 28, 1924. Cert., Vt. State Sch. Agr., 1943; BS, U. Ill., 1955, DVM, 1957, MS, 1965. Diplomate: Am. Coll. Vet. Internal Medicine, Am. Coll. Vet. Dermatology. Intern Angell Meml. Animal Hosp., Boston, 1957-58; with U. Ill. Coll. Vet. Medicine, Urbana, 1958-92; prof. vet. clin. medicine U. Ill. Coll. Vet. Medicine, 1968-92, assoc. dean alumni and public affairs, chief of medicine, 1970-84, asst. dept. chmn., 1989-92; prof. emeritus, assoc. dean alumni and pub. affairs U. Ill. Coll. Vet. Medicine, Urbana, 1992—. Contbr. articles to profl. jours. Served with USMC, 1944-46, 50-51, PTO. Recipient Nat. Gamma award Ohio State U., 1971, Ill. State VMA Svc. award, 1973, Nat. Zeta award Auburn U., 1974, Bustad Companion Animal Veterinarian award, 1993, Disting. Svc. award U. Ill. Alumni Assn., 1995; named Outstanding Tchr., Nordens Labs., 1967, Outstanding Educator, 1973, Outstanding Faculty Mem., Dad's Assn. U. Ill., 1990, Veterinarian of Yr., Mass. Soc. for Prevention Cruelty to Animals, 1993. Fellow Am. Coll. Vet. Pharmacology and Therapeutics; mem. AVMA (chmn. coun. edn. 1981-82, chmn. program com. 1983-87, Pres.'s award 1992), Am. Animal Hosp. Assn. (award 1983, Midwest Region Svc. award 1989), Am. Coll. Vet. Dermatology (pres.), Internat. Vet. Symposia (pres.), Am. Assn. Vet. Clinics (pres., Faculty Achievement award 1992), Ill. Vet. Med. Polit. Action Com. (past chmn.), Chgo. Vet. Med. Assn. (lifetime achievement award 1997), Am. Coll. Vet. Internal Medicine (Robert W. Kirk award 1997), Am. Legion, VFW, Moose, Omega Tau Sigma (pres. 1971-79), Phi Zeta, Gamma Sigma Delta. Republican. Jewish. Home: 58 E Daniel St A-4 Champaign IL 61820-5921 Office: Vet Med Adminstrn U Ill Coll Vet Medicine Urbana IL 61801

SMALL, GEORGE LEROY, geographer, educator; b. Malden, Mass., Mar. 27, 1924; s. George Arthur and Alice Mildred (Weston) S.; m. Geraldine H. Koepke, July 4, 1970; 1 dau., Elizabeth Mary. B.A., Brown U., 1950; M.I.A., Columbia U., 1952, Ph.D., 1968. French tchr. pvt. schs. Ariz., 1955-62; instr. geography Hunter Coll., 1964-68; assoc. prof. geography Coll. S.I., CUNY, 1968—; cons. problems of whaling to environ. groups. Author: The Blue Whale, 1971. Served with U.S. Army, 1942-46. Recipient Nat. Book award, 1972; Rotary Found. fellow, 1952-53. Mem. Assn. Am. Geographers. Office: CUNY Coll Staten Is New York NY 10301

SMALL, HAMISH, chemist; b. Newtown Crommelin, North Ireland, Oct. 5, 1929; s. Johnston and Jean (Wilson) S.; m. Beryl Maureen Burley, Mar. 27, 1954; children: Deborah Jane, Claire Leslie. BS, Queens U., Belfast, Northern Ireland, 1949; MS, Queens U., Belfast, Northern Irelend, 1953. Chemist U.S. Atomic Energy Authority, Harwell, England, 1949-55; rsch. scientist Dow Chem. Co., Midland, Mich., 1955-83; chemist ind. rsch. and consulting, 1983—. Author: Ion Chromatography, 1990; patentee in field; contbr. 30 articles to profl. jours. Recipient Albert F. Sperry award Instrument Soc. Am., 1978, A.O. Beckman award, 1983, Herbert H. Dow Gold Medal Dow Chem. Co., 1983, Stephen Dal Nogare award, 1984, Am. Chem. Soc. award in Chromatography, 1991. Mem. Am. Chem. Soc. Avocations: painting, sketching, music, walking. Home: 4176 Oxford Dr Leland MI 49654-9716

SMALL, JENNIFER JEAN, writer, journalist; b. Chgo., Dec. 16, 1951; d. Len Howard and Jean Alice (Shaver) S. BA in Comparative Lit., Sarah Lawrence Coll., 1974. Wire filer, radio copy editor, features writers UPI, San Francisco, 1974-76; reporter statehouse bur. UPI, Montpelier, Vt., 1976-78; from Washington corr. to editorial dir. Small Newspaper Group, 1979-88, v.p., bd. dirs., 1979-89; freelance writer The Daily Jour., Kankakee, Ill., 1971-74, 78-79, The Aspen (Colo.) Times, summer 1973, The People's Almanac, 1974, UPI Paris bur., fall 1978, Small Newspaper Group, Paris, fall, 1978, The Illini Daily News, U. Ill., 1980; writer UPI articles for Atlanta Jour. and Констн., Boston Herald Am., Boston Globe, Cin. Post, Christian Sci. Monitor, Hartford Courant, L.A. Times, Miami Herald, NASA Current News, Pitts. Press, Providence Jour., Stars and Stripes, Star-Ledger (Newark), Washington Post; fiction contbr. Bread Loaf Writer's Conf. Middleberry Coll., 1989, 90. Bd. deacons Georgetown Presbyn. Ch., 1989-90, The Phillips Contemporaries Steering Com., The Phillips Collection, 1993-94; alumnae/alumni trustee Sarah Lawrence Coll., 1990-94; mem. arts and media com. Threshold Found., 1991, 92; bd. dirs. Organizing for Devel., an Internat. Inst., Washington, 1994-95. Recipient 1st pl. Investigative News award Nat. Newspaper Assn., 1987, citation for Best Consumer Journalism Nat. Press Club, 1986, 2d pl. Best Series award Calif./Nev. UPI Newspaper Contest, 1986, 2d pl. Investigative Reporting award Ill. UPI Newspaper Contest, 1986, 1st pl. award, 1985, Peter Lisagor award for Exemplary Journalism nominee, Chgo. Headline Club, 1986, Spl. Svc. award for Journalistic Excellence Ill. Valley Area C. of C., 1984, Livingston Awards for Young Journalists finalist, 1985. Mem. Washington Area Alumnae Assn. Sarah Lawrence Coll. (chair 1988-90). Avocations: the arts, progressive philanthropy, walking, swimming, enjoying nature. Office: 1155 Connecticut Ave NW Ste 500 Washington DC 20036-4306

SMALL, JONATHAN ANDREW, lawyer; b. N.Y.C., Dec. 26, 1942; s. Milton and Teresa Markell (Joseph) S.; m. Cornelia Mendenhall, June 8, 1969; children: Anne, Katherine. BA, Brown U., 1964; student, U. Paris, 1962-63; LLB, Harvard U., 1967; MA, Fletcher Sch. of Law and Diplomacy, 1968; LLM, NYU, 1974. Bar: N.Y. 1967. VISTA vol. Washington and Cambridge, Mass., 1968; law clk. to judge U.S. Ct. Appeals (2d cir.), 1968-69; assoc. Debevoise & Plimpton, N.Y.C., 1969-75, ptnr., 1976—; cons. Spl. Task Force on N.Y. State Taxation, 1976. Trustee Brearley Sch., 1985-95; bd. dirs. Nonprofit Coordinating Com. of N.Y., 1985—, Muscular Dystrophy Assn., 1986-88. Mem. ABA, N.Y. State Bar Assn. (chmn. tax sect. com. exempt orgns. 1980-82, co-chmn., 1995), Assn. Bar City N.Y., Nonprofit Forum, Phi Beta Kappa. Home: 60 E End Ave New York NY 10028 Office: Debevoise & Plimpton 875 3rd Ave New York NY 10022-6225

SMALL, JONATHAN ANDREW, lawyer; b. Balt., June 30, 1959; s. Marvin Myron and Suzanne (Bierstock) S. AA, Foothill Jr. Coll., 1980; BS in Math. with honors, Calif. Poly. State U., 1983; JD, U. Santa Clara, 1986. Bar: Calif. 1987, U.S. Dist. Ct. (no. and so. dists.) Calif. 1987, U.S. Patent Office 1987, U.S. Ct. Appeals (fed. cir.) 1987. Patent atty. Townsend & Townsend, San Francisco, 1986-89; counsel Xerox Corp., Palo Alto, Calif., 1989-92, 97—; assoc. Weil, Gotshal & Manges, Menlo Park, Calif., 1992-93; also gen. counsel Komag Inc., Milpitas, 1993-97. Editor-in-chief Santa Clara Computer and High-Tech. Law Jour., 1985-86; contbr. articles to legal jours. Mem. ABA, Am. Intellectual Proerty Law Assn. Avocations: bicycle touring, kayaking. Office: Xerox Palo Alto Rsch Ctr 3333 Coyote Hill Rd Palo Alto CA 94304-1314

SMALL, JOYCE GRAHAM, psychiatrist, educator; b. Edmonton, Alberta, Can., June 12, 1931; came to U.S., 1956; d. John Earl and Rachel C. (Redmond) Graham; m. Iver Francis Small, May 26, 1954; children: Michael, Jeffrey. BA, U. Saskatchewan, Can., 1951; MD, U. Manitoba, Can., 1956; MS, U. Mich., 1959. Diplomat Am. Bd. Psychiatry and Neurology, Am. Bd. Electroencephalography. Instr. in psychiatry Neuropsychiat. Inst. U. Mich., Ann Arbor, 1959-60; instr. in psychiatry med. sch. U. Oreg., Portland, 1960-61, asst. prof. in psychiatry med. sch., 1961-62; asst. prof. in psychiatry sch. of medicine Washington U., St. Louis, 1962-65; assoc. prof. in psychiatry sch. of medicine Ind. U., Indpls., 1965-69, prof. psychiatry sch. of medicine, 1969—; mem. initial rev. groups NIMH, Washington, 1972-76, 79-82, 87-91; assoc. mem. Inst. Psychiat. Rsch., Indpls., 1974—. Editorial bd.: Quar. Jour. of Convulsive Therayp, 1984, Clin. Electroencephalography, 1990, and more than 150 publs. in field; contbr. articles to profl. jours. Rsch. grantee NIMH, Portland, Oreg., 1961-62, St. Louis, 1962-64, Indpls., 1967—, Epilepsy Found., Dreyfus Found., Indpls., 1965; recipient Merit award NIMH, Indpls., 1990. Fellow Am. Psychiat. Assn., Am. Electroencephalographic Soc. (councillor 1972-75, 1982); mem. Soc. Biol. Psychiatry, Cen. Assn. Electroencephalographers (sec., treas. 1967-68, pres. 1970, councillor 1971-72), Sigma Xi. Office: Larue D Carter Meml Hosp 2601 Cold Spring Rd Indianapolis IN 46222-2202

SMALL, KENNETH ALAN, economics educator; b. Sodus, N.Y., Feb. 9, 1945; s. Cyril Galloway and Gertrude Estelle (Andrews) S.; m. Adair Bowman, June 8, 1968; 1 child, Gretchen Lenore. BA, BS, U. Rochester, 1968; MA, U. Calif., Berkeley, 1972, PhD, 1976. Asst. prof. Princeton (N.J.) U., 1976-83; rsch. assoc. Brookings Inst., Washington, 1978-79; assoc. prof. U. Calif., Irvine, 1983-86, prof. econs., 1986—, assoc. dean social sci., 1986-92, chmn. econs., 1992-95; vis. prof. Harvard U., Cambridge, Mass., 1991-92; cons. N.Y. State Legislature, Albany, 1982-83, Rand Corp., Santa Monica, Calif., 1985-86, ECO N.W., Eugene, Oreg., 1987—, World Bank, Washington, 1990—, Port Authority of N.Y. and N.J., 1994, Nat. Coop. Highway Rsch. Program, 1992-94; mem. study com. on urban transp. congestion pricing NRC, 1992-94, mem. highway cost allocation rev. com., 1995-96. Co-author: Futures for a Declining City, 1981, Urban Decline, 1982, Road Work, 1989; author: Urban Transportation Economics, 1992; co-editor: Urban Studies, Glasgow, Scotland, 1992-97, Kluwer Acad. Publs. book series, Dordrecht, The Netherlands, 1993—; assoc. editor Regional Sci. and Urban Econs., Amsterdam, The Netherlands, 1987—; editl. bd. mem. Jour. Urban Econs., San Diego, 1989—, Transportation, Dordrecht, 1993—, Jour. Transport Econs. and Policy, Bath, U.K., 1995—. Grantee NSF, 1977-87, Inst. Transp. Studies U. Calif., 1984-89, Haynes Found., 1987-88, U.S. and Calif. Depts. Transp., 1988-94, Nat. Coop. Highway Rsch. Program, 1995-96, ITF Intertraffic, 1996—. Mem. Am. Econ. Assn. (com. on status of women in econs. profession 1995-97), Econometric Soc., Transp. Rsch. Bd., Royal Econ. Soc., Regional Sci. Assn., Am. Real Estate and Urban Econs. Assn. Office: Dept Econs Univ Calif Irvine CA 92697-5100

SMALL, LAWRENCE FARNSWORTH, history educator; b. Bangor, Maine, Dec. 30, 1925; s. Irving Wheelock and Geneva May (Turner) S.; m. Elfie Joan Ames, Aug. 9, 1947; children: Kathleen Ann, Linda Jean, Lawrence Farnsworth, Daniel Irving (dec.). BD, Bangor Theol. Sem., 1948; BA, U. Maine, 1948, MA, 1951; PhD, Harvard U., 1955, LHD (hon.), 1991. Ordained to ministry Congregational Ch., 1950; minister Paramus (N.J.) Congl. Ch., 1955-59; asso. prof. history Rocky Mountain Coll., Billings, Mont., 1959-61; prof. Rocky Mountain Coll., 1975-90, dean of Coll., 1961-65, acting pres., 1965-66, pres., 1966-75; chmn. Mont. commn. Higher Edn. Facilities Act, 1965-75; exec. dir. Mont. Assn. Chs., 1984-90. Author: Montana Passage, A Century of Politics on the Yellowstone, Journey with the Law, The Life of Judge William J. Jameson; editor: Religion in Montana, Pathways to the Present, vols. I and II. Pres. Yellowstone County Council Chs., 1968-70; treas. Mont. Conf., United Ch. of Christ, 1970-73; chmn. bd. dirs. Western Independent Colls. Found.; bd. dirs. Community Concert Assn., Yellowstone County Mental Health Assn., Billings Citizens for Community Devel., Billings United Fund; trustee Billings Deaconess Hosp.; chmn. bd. dirs. Inst. for Peace Studies, Mont. Mem. Phi Beta Kappa, Phi Kappa Phi. Club: Kiwanis (pres. Billings, lt. gov.). Home: 7320 Sumatra Pl # 4 Billings MT 59106-2526 *One does not have to be great to embrace great ideas, but having done so, one's life will be changed for the better.*

SMALL, MARSHALL LEE, lawyer; b. Kansas City, Mo., Sept. 8, 1927; s. Phillip and Lillian (Mendelsohn) S.; m. Mary Rogell, June 27, 1954; children: Daniel, Elizabeth. B.A., Stanford U., 1949, J.D., 1951. Bar: Mo. 1951, Calif. 1955, N.Y. 1990. Law clk. to Justice William O. Douglas U.S. Supreme Ct., Washington, 1951-52; assoc. Morrison & Foerster, San Francisco, 1954-60, ptnr., 1961-92, sr. of counsel, 1993—; reporter corp. governance project Am. Law Inst., 1982-92. 1st lt. U.S. Army, 1952-54. Mem. ABA (com. corp. laws 1975-82), Phi Beta Kappa, Order of Coif. Office: Morrison & Foerster 425 Market St San Francisco CA 94105

SMALL, MELVIN, history educator; b. N.Y.C., Mar. 14, 1939; s. Herman Z. and Ann (Ashkinazy) S.; m. Sarajane Miller, Oct. 23, 1958; children: Michael, Mark. BA, Dartmouth Coll., 1960; MA, U. Mich., 1961, PhD, 1965. Asst. prof. history Wayne State U., Detroit, 1965-68, assoc. prof., 1968-76, prof., 1976—, chmn. dept. history, 1979-86; vis. prof. U. Mich., Ann Arbor, 1968, Marygrove Coll., Detroit, 1971, Aarhus (Denmark) U., 1972-74, 83, Windsor (Ont., Can.) U., 1977-78. Author: Was War Necessary, 1980, Johnson, Nixon and the Doves, 1988, Covering Dissent, 1994, Democracy and Diplomacy, 1996; co-author: Wages of War, 1972, Resort to Arms, 1982; editor: Public Opinion and Historians, 1970; co-editor: International War, 1986, Appeasing Fascism, 1991, Give Peace a Chance, 1992; mem. editl. bd. Internat. Interactions, 1987-91, Peace and Change, 1989—; restaurant critic Detroit Metro Times, 1982-95; history book reviewer Detroit Free Press, 1988-95. Mem. hon. bd. Swords into Plowshares Mus., 1992—. Recipient Disting. Faculty award Mich. Assn. Governing Bds., 1993; Am. Coun. Learned Socs. fellow, 1969; Stanford Ctr. for Advanced Study fellow, 1969-70; grantee Am. Coun. Learned Socs., 1983, Johnson Libr., 1982, 88, Can. Govt., 1987; NATO rsch. fellow, 1996. Mem. Coun. on Peace Rsch. in History (nat. coun. 1986-90, pres. 1990-92), Am. Hist. Assn., Atlantic Coun. (acad. assoc.), Orgn. Am. Historians, Soc. for Historians of Am. Fgn. Rels. (Warren Kuehl prize 1989). Home: 1815 Northwood Blvd Royal Oak MI 48073-3919 Office: Wayne State U Dept History 3119 Fab Detroit MI 48202

SMALL, MELVIN D., physician, educator; b. Somerville, Mass., May 22, 1925; s. Sidney J. and Ida (Gelbsman) S.; m. Judith Nogee, Dec. 23, 1962; children: Michael Dorian, Michele. AB, U. Wis., 1953; MD, Duke U., 1959; studied under Dr. Gregory Pincus, Worcester Found. Exptl. Biol. and Medicine, 1950-53; studied under Prof. Brian Abel-Smith, London Sch. Econs, 1986-90. Lic. physician, Fla., Md., D.C., Va. Intern Georgetown U. Med. Ctr., Washington, 1959-60, resident, 1960-61; chief gastrointestinal rsch. Georgetown U. Med. Ctr., 1961-64, instr. medicine, 1961-66, asst. prof. medicine, 1966-67, asst. clin. prof. medicine, 1967-81, 93—; chief gastroenterology sect. Georgetown divsn. D.C. Gen. Hosp., 1964-68; cons. Children's Hosp., Washington, 1962-66; active staff Fairfax (Va.) Hosp., 1961-73, Commonwealth Drs. Hosp., Fairfax, 1969-74, Arlington (Va.) Hosp., 1961-85, Circle Terr. Hosp., Alexandria, 1965-85, Mt. Vernon Hosp., Alexandria, 1976-85; hon. staff mem. Alexandria Hosp., 1985-89, 92—; attending physician D.C. Gen. Hosp., 1961-68, Georgetown U. Hosp., 1961-81, 93—, Mt. Sinai Hosp., Miami Beach, Fla., 1992—; chief animal experimentation Cancer rsch. under Dr. Sidney Farber Children's Med. Ctr., Boston, 1948-50; rsch. asst. Boston U. Sch. Medicine, 1956-57; chmn. dept. medicine Alexandria Hosp., 1964-85; founder, chmn., No. Va. Consortium for Continuing Med. Edn., 1974-86, chmn. emeritus, 1986; lectr. in field. Author publs. in field. Trustee Jefferson Meml. Hosp., 1965-74, mem. founding group, 1965, chmn. pharmacy com., 1965-76, co-chmn. tissue com., 1965-74; nominated candidate for Palm Beach (Fla.) Town Coun., 1995-96; chmn., chief med. officer Regi-Med. Corp. Rsch. fellow under Norman Zamcheck Mallory Inst. Pathology, Boston, 1953-59, Gastroenterology rsch. under Franz Ingelfinger, Evans Meml. Hosp., Boston, AEC, 1951-53. Mem. AMA, Am. Coll. Gastroenterology, ACP, Am. Gastroent. Assn., Am. Inst. Nutrition, Am. Physiol. Soc., Am. Soc. Gastrointestinal Endoscopy, D.C. Med. Soc., Med. Soc. Va. (chmn. commn. on continuing med. edn. 1978-81), Alexandria Med. Soc. (v.p. 1979-80), Royal Soc. Medicine, Fla. Med. Soc., Palm Beach County Med. Soc. Home: 47 Saint George Pl Palm Beach Gardens FL 33418

SMALL, MICHAEL, composer; b. 1939. Scores include (films) Out of It, 1969, Puzzle of a Downfall Child, 1970, Jenny, 1970, The Revoltionary, 1970, The Sporting Club, 1971, Klute, 1971, Child's Play, 1972, Dealing: Or the Berkeley-to-Boston Forty-Brick Lost-Bag Blues, 1972, Love and Pain and the Whole Damned Thing, 1973, The Parallax View, 1974, The Drowning Pool, 1975, The Stepford Wives, 1975, Night Moves, 1975, Marathon Man, 1976, Audrey Rose, 1977, Girlfriends, 1978, The Driver, 1978, Comes a Horseman, 1978, Going in Style, 1979, Those Lips, Those Eyes, 1980, The Postman Always Rings Twice, 1981, Continental Divide, 1981, Rollover, 1981, The Star Chamber, 1983, Kidco, 1984, Firstborn, 1984, Target, 1985, Dream Lover, 1986, Brighton Beach Memoirs, 1986, Black Widow, 1987, Orphans, 1987, Jaws the Revenge, 1987, 1969, 1988, See You in the Morning, 1989, Mountains of the Moon, 1990, Mobsters, 1991, Consenting Adults, 1992, Wagons East!, 1994, (documentaries) Pumping Iron, 1977, American Dream, 1989, (TV movies) The Boy Who Drank Too Much, 1980, The Lathe of Heaven, 1980, Chiefs, 1983, Nobody's Child, 1986, Queen, 1993. Office: Marks Mgt 20121 Ventura Blvd Ste 305 Woodland Hills CA 91364-2559

SMALL, NATALIE SETTIMELLI, pediatric mental health counselor; b. Quincy, Mass., June 2, 1933; d. Joseph Peter and Edmea Natalie (Bagnaschi) Settimelli; m. Parker Adams Small, Jr., Aug. 26, 1956; children: Parker Adams III, Peter McMichael, Carla Edmea. BA, Tufts U., 1955; MA, EdS, U. Fla., 1976; PhD, 1987. Cert. child life specialist. Pediatric counselor U. Fla. Coll. Medicine, Gainesville, 1976-80; pediatric counselor Shands Hosp.-U. Fla., Gainesville, 1980-87, supr. child life dept. patient and family resources, 1987—; adminstrv. liaison for self-dir. work teams, mem. faculty Ctr. for Coop. Learning for Health and Sci. Edn., Gainesville, 1988—, assoc. dir., 1996; cons. and lectr. in field. Author: Parents Know Best, 1991; co-author team packs series for teaching at risk adolescent health edn. and coop. learning. Bd. dirs. Ronald McDonald House, Gainesville, 1980—, mem. exec. com., 1991—; bd. dirs. Gainesville Assn. Creative Arts, 1994—; mem. health profl. adv. com. March of Dimes, Gainesville, 1986-96, HIV prevention planning partnership, 1995-96. Boston Stewart Club scholar, Florence, Italy, 1955; grantee Jessie Ball Du Pont Fund, 1978, Children's Miracle Network, 1990, 92, 93, 94, 95; recipient Caring and Sharing award Ronald McDonald House, 1995, Appreciation award March of Dimes, 1996. Mem. ACA, Nat. Bd. Cert. Counselors, Am. Assn. Mental Health Counselors, Assn. for the Care of Children's Health, Fla. Assn. Child Life Profls., Child Life Coun. Roman Catholic. Avocations: traveling, reading, swimming. Home: 3454 NW 12th Ave Gainesville FL 32605-4811 Office: Shands Hosp Patient and Family Resources PO Box 100306 Gainesville FL 32610

SMALL, PARKER ADAMS, JR., pediatrician, educator; b. Cin., July 5, 1932; s. Parker Adams and Grace (McMichael) S.; m. Natalie Settimelli, Aug. 26, 1956; children: Parker Adams, Peter McMichael, Carla Edmea. Student, Tufts U., 1950-53; MD, U. Cin., 1957. Med. intern Pa. Hosp., Phila., 1957-58; research assoc. Nat. Heart Inst. NIH, Washington, 1958-60; research fellow St. Mary's Hosp., London, Eng., 1960-61; sr. surgeon NIMH, Washington, 1961-66; prof. immunology and med. microbiology U. Fla., 1966-95, chmn. dept., 1966-75, prof. pediatrics, 1979—, prof. pathology, 1995—; dir. Ctr. for Coop. Learning for Health Sci. Edn., U. Fla., 1988—; vis. prof. U. Lausanne, Switzerland, 1972, U. Lagos, Nigeria, 1982, Al Hada Hosp., Saudi Arabia, 1983; vis. scholar Assn. Am. Med. Colls., Washington, 1973; assoc. life scis. panel Nat. Acad. Scis., 1981-88, co-chmn., 1982-83; bd. dirs. Biol. Sci. Curriculum Study, 1984-90, exec. bd., 1987-90; mem. edn. adv. com. Nat. Fund Med. Edn., 1984-87; mem. study com. Nat. Bd. Med. Examiners, 1983-85, mem. nat. vaccine adv. com., 1987-91, chmn. subcom. on new vaccines, 1987-91; cons. in field. Creator patient oriented problem solving system/POPS, for teaching immunology and coop. learning to med. students and Team Packs for teaching K-12 & college students health edn. and coop. learning; editor: The Secretory Immunologic System, 1971; mem. editorial bd. Infection and Immunity, 1974-76, Jour. Med. Edn., 1978-80; cons. editor Microbios, Cytobios; contbr. articles to profl. jours. Sec., treas. Oakmont, Md., 1964-65, mayor, 1965-66; chmn. Citizens for Pub. Schs. Gainesville, Fla., 1969-70. With USPHS, 1958-60, 61-66. Named Tchr. of Yr. U. Fla. Coll. Medicine, 1978-79, Disting. Lectr. AMA, 1986; recipient Presdl. medallion U. Fla., 1987, Nat. Basic Sci. Disting. Teaching award Alpha Omega Alpha, 1993, Jacob Ehrenzeller award, 1995, Pres.'s Faculty Humanitarian award U. Fla., 1996; NIH spl. fellow, 1960-61, rsch. grantee, 1966—, U. Fla. Tchr./Scholar and commencement spkr., 1987; invited lectr. Assn. Am. Med. Colls., 1992. Mem. AAAS, Am. Assn. Immunologists (edn. com. 1983-86), Physicians for Social Responsibility, Fla. Med. Assn., Phi Beta Kappa, Sigma Xi, Theta Delta Chi. Home: 3454 NW 12th Ave Gainesville FL 32605-4811 Office: U Fla Coll Med PO Box 100275 Gainesville FL 32610-0275

SMALL, RALPH MILTON, publisher, clergyman; b. Richland Center, Wis., Oct. 26, 1917; s. John Marion and Jessie Angeline (Rowe) S.; m. Patricia Courson Small, June 11, 1977; children—Gregory, Randall. B.A. cum laude, Cin. Bible Sem., 1939, postgrad, 1939-41; postgrad, U. Cin., 1941, Clarion State Tchrs. Coll., 1941, Lincoln Christian Coll., 1947; D.D., Pacific Christian Coll., 1971. Ordained to ministry Ch. of Christ, 1939. Minister Antioch Ch. of Christ, Hoopeston, Ill., 1939-63; Bible Sch. cons. Standard Publ. Co., Cin., 1963; weekly columnist The Lookout, 1964-69, dir. dept. ch. growth, 1964-70; editor Seek, 1970, exec. editor, 1970, v.p., publisher, 1971-86; sr. adults min. Clovernook Christian Ch., Cin., 1992—; cons. Standard Pub. Co. Moderator: The Living Word, WDAN-TV, 1954-59. Trustee Milligan Coll., chmn., 1990-91; nat. chmn. Milligan Coll. Capital Funds Campaign, 1989-91; dir. Nat. Christian Edn. Conv., 1965-86; bd. dirs. Fellowship, Inc., Muscular Dystrophy, Danville, Ill.; sec. bd. advisers Directory of Ministry, Christian Chs./Chs. of Christ, 1973-83; sec. bd. dirs. Christian Ch. Found. for the Handicapped, Knoxville, Tenn., 1981—. Chaplain AUS, 1945. Mem. Delta Aleph Tau. Home: 207 W Sequoya Trl Greensburg IN 47240-8302

SMALL, RICHARD DAVID, research scientist; b. Syracuse, N.Y., Jan. 6, 1945; s. Sydney Morton Small and Gertrude (Burman) Goldberg; m. Tsipora Meirson, Dec. 11, 1977; children: Eileen Lara, Carrie Ayala, Sharon Yael. BS, Rutgers U., 1967, MS, 1968, MPhil., 1969, PhD, 1971. Instr. Rutgers U., New Brunswick, N.J., 1970-71; sr. lectr. Technion, Haifa, Israel, 1971-78; rsch. scientist, dir. for thermal scis. Pacific-Sierra Rsch. Corp., L.A., 1979-94; pres. Eastwind Rsch. Corp., Belmont Shore, CA, 1994—; vis. asst. prof. U. Calif., L.A., 1977-79; vis. scholar U. Calif., 1979-81, San Francisco State U., 1994——; lectr. various univs. and confs.; adv. com. City Savs. and Loan Assn., 1985; mem. adv. and rev. coms. NAS, other sci. orgns. Author: Fires From Nuclear Weapon Fires, 1992; contbr. more than 100 tech. articles; reviewer profl. jours., confs. and symposia. With Israeli Army, 1977. Recipient Rothschild Fund. prize, 1974; NDEA fellow, 1967-70; N.J. Soc. Profl. Engrs. scholar, 1967. Mem. AAAS, AIAA, Sigma Xi. Jewish. Achievements include research in environmental consequences of conflict with determining analyses on impact of Kuwait oil fires and nuclear winter and development of a series of theoretical models of large fires. Office: Eastwind Rsch Corp PO Box 13081 Long Beach CA 90803-8081

SMALL, RICHARD DONALD, travel company executive; b. West Orange, N.J., May 24, 1929; s. Joseph George and Elizabeth (McGarry) S.; A.B. cum laude, U. Notre Dame, 1951; m. Arlene P. Small; children: Colleen P., Richard Donald, Joseph W., Mark G., Brian P. With Union-Camp Corp., N.Y.C., Chgo., 1952-62; pres. Alumni Holidays, Inc., 1962—, AHI Internat. Corp., 1962—, All Horizons, Inc., 1982—; chmn. AHI, Inc., 1982-89; bd. dirs. French Cruise Lines, Des Plaines, Ill., Russian Cruise Lines. Bd. dirs. Alumni Campus Abroad, 1994. Recipient Munich Ptnr. award, 1989. Mem. Univ. Club (Chgo.). Home: 190 N Sheridan Rd Lake Forest IL 60045-2429 also: 2202 Wailea Elua Wailea Maui HI 96753 Office: 1st National Bank Bldg 701 Lee St Des Plaines IL 60016-4329

SMALL, SALLY CHRISTINE (CHRIS), registered nurse; b. Science Hill, Ky., Feb. 10, 1951; d. William Roland Van Hoosier and Georgia (Mayfield)

Miller; m. Larry W. Small, May 24, 1968; children: Jeanette L., Larry W., Charlotte A., Daniel J. AS in Nursing, Seward County C.C., Liberal, Kans., 1983; BSN, Fort Hays State U., 1992. RN, Kans.; cert. BLS, Am. Heart Assn.; cert. ACLS, Am. Heart Assn., trauma nurse core course; cert. EMT, Kans.; cert. nurse aide. Nurse aide Satanta (Kans.) Dist. Hosp., 1981-82, LPN, 1982-83, RN, 1983—, infection control RN, 1984-93, labor and delivery supr. RN, 1985-93, asst. dir. RN, 1988-93; contract RN Bob Wilson Meml. Hosp., Ulysses, Kans., 1984, Stevens County Hosp., Hugoton, Kans., 1984-85, St. Catherine's Hosp., Garden City, Kans., 1986; child-birth class instr., Haskell County, 1985-93. EMT Satanta Emergency Med. Svc., 1984—, tech. tng. officer, 1986—; CPR instr. Haskell County schs. and bus., 1988—, ACLS instr.; dir. communicable disease prevention program Satanta H.S., 1991. Republican. Avocations: reading, camping. Home: PO Box 505 Satanta KS 67870-0505 Office: Satanta Dist Hosp Box 159 Satanta KS 67870

SMALL, WILLIAM ANDREW, mathematics educator; b. Cobleskill, N.Y., Oct. 16, 1914; s. James Arner and Lois (Patterson) S.; m. Bela Small; children: Lois (Mrs. Paul Gindling), James (dec.). B.S., U.S. Naval Acad., 1936; A.B., U. Rochester, 1950, M.A., 1952, Ph.D., 1958. Commd. ensign U.S. Navy, 1936, advanced through grades to lt. comdr., 1944; comdt. cadets, instr. DeVeaux Sch., Niagara Falls, N.Y., 1945-48; instr. U. Rochester, 1951-55; Alfred (N.Y.) U., 1955-56; asst. prof. math. Grinnell (Iowa) Coll., 1956-58, assoc. prof., chmn. dept., 1958-60; prof. math. Tenn. Tech. U., 1960-62, State Univ. Coll., Geneseo, N.Y., 1962-85; chmn. dept. math. State Univ. Coll., 1962-78; prof. emeritus, disting. service prof. SUNY, 1985—; Fulbright-Hays lectr. math. Aleppo U., Syrian Arab Republic, 1964-65. Contbr. articles to profl. jours. Mem. Math. Assn. Am., U.S. Naval Inst., Mil. Order World Wars, Ret. Officers Assn., Seneca Army Depot Officers Club, Am. Legion, Rotary (pres. Geneseo club 1990-91), Phi Beta Kappa. Episcopalian. Home: 28 Court St PO Box 367 Geneseo NY 14454-0367

SMALL, WILLIAM EDWIN, JR., association and recreation executive; b. Jackson, Mich., Jan. 18, 1937; s. William Edwin and Lena Louisa (Hunt) S.; m. Ruth Ann Toombs, Mar. 28, 1959; children: Suzanne Marie, William Edwin III, Bryan Anthony. AS, Jackson C.C., 1959; BS in Geology, Mich. State U., 1961, MA in Journalism, 1964. Reporter Sci. Svc., Washington, 1961-62; writer sci. U. Chgo., 1963-64; sci. info. officer Pa. State U., State College, 1964-66; corr. McGraw-Hill, Washington, 1966-69; staff com. pub. works U.S. Senate, 1969; founding editor Biomed. News, 1969-71; dir. pub. info. Nat. Bur. Standards, Washington, 1972-76; editor Am. Pharmacy Jour., 1979-82; dir. media and info. svcs. AMA, Washington, 1982-86; exec. dir. Nat. Found. Infectious Diseases, Washington, 1986-91, Assn. Biotech. Cos., 1991-93; CEO, Bioconfs. Internat., Bethesda, Md., 1993-95, WESmall & Assocs., Assn. Execs., Louisa, Va., 1976—; owner recreation resort Small Country, Louisa, 1976—; exec. dir. Va. Biotech. Assn., 1996—. Author: Third Pollution, 1971. With Security Agy., AUS, 1955-59. Recipient Superior Accomplishment award U.S. Dept. Commerce, 1974. Fellow AAAS; life mem. Nat. Assn. Sci. Writers. Office: PO Box 343 Louisa VA 23093-0343

SMALLEY, ARTHUR LOUIS, JR., engineering and construction company executive; b. Houston, Jan. 25, 1921; s. Arthur L. and Ebby (Curry) S.; m. Ruth Evelyn Britton, Mar. 18, 1946; children: Arthur Louis III, Tom Edward. BSChemE, U. Tex., Austin, 1942. Registered profl. engr., Tex. Dir. engring. Celanese Chem. Co., Houston, 1964-72; mktg. exec. Fish Engring. Co., Houston, 1972-74; pres. Matthew Hall & Co., Inc., Houston, 1974-87; cons. Davy McKee Corp., Houston, 1987-95; exec. v.p. Offshore Gas Devels. Ltd., San Marino, Calif., 1995—; dir. Walter Internat., 1991. Life mem. Houston Livestock and Rodeo; mem. Engring. Found. Adv. Coun. U. Tex. Recipient Silver Beaver award Boy Scouts Am., 1963; named Disting. Engring. Grad., U. Tex., 1987. Mem. Am. Inst. Chem. Engrs., Am. Petroleum Inst., Pres. Assn., Petroleum Club (Houston), Chemists Club of N.Y., Oriental Club (London), Houston Club, Traveler's Century Club, Rotary. Republican. Episcopalian. Mem. internat. adv. bd. Ency. Chem. Processing and Design. Home: 438 Hunterwood Dr Houston TX 77024-6936 Office: 7887 Katy Fwy Houston TX 77024-2012

SMALLEY, CHRISTOPHER JOSEPH, pharmaceutical company professional; b. Phila., June 26, 1953; s. Charles Wilfred and Verna May (Coulter) S.; m. Maria Visniskie, Aug. 9, 1974; children: Christa Maria, Mark Charles, Lora Loray. BS, Phila. Coll. Pharmacy and Sci., 1976; MBA, Temple U., 1982; PhD, LaSalle U., 1991. Ordained elder, Presbyn. ch. Mfg. pharmacist supr. McNeil Labs., Fort Washington, Pa., 1976-77; mfg. pharmacist group supr. McNeil Consumer Products Co., 1978-79, mfg. pharmacist mgr., 1980-85; tech. svcs. mgr. Janssen Pharmaceutica, 1985-88, plant mgr., 1988-94; quality assurance dir. Sanofi rsch. divsn. Sanofi Pharms., Inc., Malvern, Pa., 1994—. Mem. Rep. Nat. Com., 1979—. With USNR Med. Corps., 1986-95, with USAF, 1995—. Mem. Am. Pharm. Assn., Assn. Mil. Surgeons of U.S., Am. Assn. Pharm. Scientists, Internat. Soc. Pharm. Engrs., Aerospace Med. Assn., Am. Acad. Med. Adminstrs., Assn. Med. Svc. Corps Officers, Pa. Pharm. Assn., Inst. Environ. Scis., Eastern Assn. GMP Trainers, Parenteral Drug Assn. (chmn. tng. com.), Pharm. Mfrs. Assn. (prodn. sect.), Phila. Pharm. Forum, USN Inst., NRA, Kappa Psi. Presbyterian. Home: 421 Drayton Rd Oreland PA 19075-2010 Office: 9 Great Valley Pkwy Malvern PA 19355-1304

SMALLEY, DAVID VINCENT, lawyer; b. N.Y.C., Mar. 27, 1935; s. Vincent R. and Ethel A. (Sullivan) S.; m. Patricia Doyle Tolles, Nov. 28, 1964; children—Brian W., Gregory T. B.A., Hamilton Coll.; LL.B., Harvard U. Bar: N.Y. 1960. Assoc. Debevoise & Plimpton, N.Y.C., 1959-67, ptnr., 1968—. Mem. ABA, Assn. of Bar of City of N.Y. Home: 34 Pembroke Sq, London W8 6PD, England Office: Debevoise & Plimpton, 1 Creed Covat 5 Ludgate Hill, London EC4M 7AA, England

SMALLEY, EUGENE BYRON, plant pathology educator, forest pathologist, mycologist; b. L.A., July 11, 1926; s. Guy Byron and Lena Ernestina S.; m. Gladys Louise Doerksen, Feb. 5, 1954 (div. 1974): children: Daniel B., Lisa L., Sara C., Anthony B., Andrew J.; m. Joan Alice Potter, June 4, 1978. BS, UCLA, 1949; MS, U. Calif., Berkeley, 1953, PhD, 1957. Rsch. asst. plant pathology U. Calif., Berkeley, 1953-57; asst. prof. plant pathology U. Wis., Madison, 1957-64, assoc. prof., 1964-69, prof., 1969-94, prof. emeritus, 1994—, acting chair dept. plant pathology, 1988-89; mem. exec. com. Ctr. Environ. Toxicology, 1967—; rsch. advisor Elm Rsch. Inst., Harrisville, N.H., 1974—, Pitney Bowes Elms Across Europe, 1979—; U.S. advisor EEC Dutch Elm Disease Program, 1979; lectr. Gordon Rsch. Conf., 1967, 86. Contbr. articles to profl. jours.; patentee in field. Mem. com. NRC, 1982-83. With USN, 1944-46. Recipient numerous rsch. grants, B.Y. Morrison Meml. Lectr. award USDA/Agrl. Rsch. Svc., 1995. Mem. AAAS, Am. Phytopath. Soc., Wis. Arborists Assn. (hon.), Mycological Soc. Am., Sigma Xi, Gamma Sigma Delta. Democrat. Episcopalian. Home: 2831 Pleasant View Hts Cottage Grove WI 53527-9517 Office: U Wis Dept Plant Pathology 1630 Linden Dr Madison WI 53706-1520

SMALLEY, RICHARD ERRETT, chemistry and physics educator, researcher; b. Akron, Ohio, June 6, 1943; s. Frank Dudley and Virginia (Rhoads) S.; m. Judith Grace Sampierj, May 4, 1968; (div. July, 1979); 1 child, Chad; m. Mary Lynn Chapieski, July 10, 1980 (div. Nov. 1994); m. JoNell Marie Chauvin, Mar. 1, 1997. BS in Chemistry, U. Mich., 1965; MA in Chemistry, Princeton U., 1971, PhD in Chemistry, 1973; PhD (hon.), U. Liege, Belgium, 1991; DSc (hon.), U. Chgo., 1995. Assoc. The James Franck Inst., Chgo., 1973-76; from asst. prof. to prof. William Marsh Rice U., Houston, 1976-82, Gene & Norman Hackerman prof. chemistry, 1982—; prof. dept. physics Rice U., Houston, 1990—; chmn. Rice Quantum Inst., Houston, 1986-96; dir. Rice Ctr. for Nanoscale Sci. and Tech., 1996—. Contbr. numerous articles to profl. jours. Recipient Franklin medal, Franklin Inst., Phila., 1996, Nobel prize in chemistry, 1996. Fellow Am. Phys. Soc. (divsn. chem. physics, Irving Langmuir prize 1991, Internat. New Materials prize 1992); mem. AAAS, NAS, Am. Chem. Soc. (divsn. phys. chemistry, William H. Nichols medal 1993, S.W. regional award 1992, Harrison Howe award Rochester sect. 1994, Madison Marshall award North Ala. sect. 1995), Materials Rsch. Soc., Am. Acad. Arts and Scis., Sigma Xi. Office: Ctr for Nanoscale Sci & Tech Rice Univ 6100 Main MS 100 Houston TX 77005

SMALLEY, ROBERT MANNING, government official; b. Los Angeles, Nov. 14, 1925; s. William Denny and Helen (McConnell) S.; m. Lois Louisa Williamson, Nov. 28, 1948 (div.) m. Rosemary Sumner, Jan. 4, 1957; children—Leslie Estelle, David Christian. Student, UCLA, 1946-48. Radio news editor Mut. Radio Broadcasting System, Los Angeles, 1950-55; mgr. Agrl. Info. Inc., Sacramento, Calif., 1957-59; with Whitaker & Baxter, San Francisco, 1956-57, 59-61; sec. Mayor, San Francisco, 1961-63; asst. dir. pub. relations Republican Nat. Com., 1964; press sec. Republican vice presdl. candidate William E. Miller, 1964; dir. pub. relations Republican Nat. Com., 1965; v.p. Whitaker & Baxter, San Francisco, 1966-68; asst. press sec. Republican vice presdl. candidate Spiro Agnew, 1968; spl. asst. Sec. Commerce, Washington, 1969-72; adminstrv. asst. U.S. Senator Robert P. Griffin, Washington, 1972-73; dir. corp. affairs Potomac Electric Power Co., Washington, 1973-75; U.S. rep. devel. assistance com. O.E.C.D., Paris, France, 1975-77; spl. asst. U.S. Senator Robert P. Griffin, Washington, 1977-78; asst. to campaign mgr. Reagan for Pres. Com., Washington, 1979; sr. advisor mgmt. communications IBM, 1979-82; dep. asst. sec. of state pub. affairs Dept. of State, Washington, 1982-87, U.S. amb. to Kingdom of Lesotho, 1987-89; lectr. in pub. policy The Kendig Group, Columbia Artists Mgmt., Inc., N.Y.C., 1990—; sr. cons. Capitoline/MS & L, Washington. Served with USN, 1944-46, PTO. Episcopalian. Office: PO Box 823 Arlington VA 22216-0823

SMALLEY, WILLIAM EDWARD, bishop; b. New Brunswick, N.J., Apr. 8, 1940; s. August Harold and Emma May (Gleason) S.; m. Carole A. Kuhns, Sept. 12, 1964; children: Michelle Lynn, Jennifer Ann. BA in Sociology, Lehigh U., 1962; MDiv, Episcopal Theol. Sch., 1965; MEd, Temple U., 1970; D of Ministry, Wesley Theol. Sem., 1987. Ordained to ministry Episcopal Ch., 1965, bishop, 1989. Vicar St. Peter's Episcopal Ch., Plymouth, Pa., 1965-67, St. Martin-in-the-Fields Ch., Nuangola, Pa., 1965-67; rector All Saints' Episcopal Ch., Lehighton, Pa., 1967-75; fed. program adminstr. Lehighton Area Schs., 1970-72; rector Episcopal Ministry of Unity, Palmerton, Pa., 1975-80, Ch. of Ascension, Gaithersburg, Md., 1980-89; bishop Episcopal Diocese Kans., Topeka, 1989—. Pres. Gaithersburg (Md.) Pastoral Counseling Inc., 1986-89; bd. dirs. Washington Pastoral Counseling, 1988-89; chmn. Turner House Inc., Kansas City, Kans., 1989—, Episcopal Social Svcs., Wichita, Kans., 1989—; bd. dirs. Christ Ch. Hosp., Topeka, 1989—, St. Francis Acad., Atchison, Kans., 1989—; v.p. Province VII, The Episcopal Ch., 1993-95, pres. Province VII, 1995—; pres. Province VII Hosp of Bishops; mem. Ch. Deployment Bd., vice chair, 1997—; chair Presiding Bishop's Coun. Advice; mem. joint nominating com. for Presiding Bishop. Mem. Omicron Delta Kappa. Democrat. Avocations: gardening, swimming, cross-stitching, reading. Address: 833-35 Polk St Topeka KS 66612

SMALLMAN, BEVERLEY N., biology educator; b. Port Perry, Ont., Can., Dec. 11, 1913; s. Richard Benjamin and Ethel May (Doubt) S.; m. Hazel Mayne, Dec. 11, 1937 (dec. 1962); 1 child, Sylvia Gail; m. Florence Hazel Cook, July 27, 1965. B.A., Queens U., Kingston, Ont., 1936; M.Sc., Western U. Ont., Can., 1938; Ph.D., U. Edinburgh, Scotland, 1941; LL.D.(hon.), Trent U., Ont., 1982. Mem. staff Stored Grain Insect Investigations Bd. of Grain Commnrs., Winnipeg, 1941-45; officer-in-charge Stored Products Lab., Agrl. Can., Winnipeg, 1945-50; head entomol. sect. rsch. inst. Agrl. Can., London, 1950-57; chief entomol., rsch. dir. entomology, plant pathology Agrl. Can., Ottawa, 1957-63; prof., head dept. biology Queens U., Kingston, Ont., Can., 1963-73, prof. biology, 1973-78, prof. emeritus biology, 1979—; vis. scientist Nat. Inst. Med. Rsch., London, Eng., 1954-56, CSIRO Labs., Brisbane, Australia, 1970-71, 76; apiary insp. Province of Ont., 1981-91; cons., lectr. in field. Prin. author: Agricultural Science in Canada, 1970, Queen's Biology, 1992; co-author: Good Bye Bugs, 1983. Contbr. articles to profl. jours. Fellow Royal Soc. Can.; mem. Entomol. Soc. Can., Zool. Soc. Can., Entomol. Soc. Man. (founding pres. 1945), Entomol. Soc. Ont. Avocations: Mini-farming; beekeeping; writing popular science reviews. Home: RR 2, Yarker, ON Canada K0K 3N0

SMALLWOOD, FRANKLIN, political science educator; b. Ridgewood, N.J., June 24, 1927; s. J. William and Carolyn (Linkroum) S.; m. Ann Logie, Sept. 8, 1951; children: Susan, Sandra, David, Donald. A.B., Dartmouth Coll., 1951, A.M. (hon.), 1968; M.P.A., Harvard U., 1953, Ph.D., 1958. With AEC, 1953-57; asst. to pres. Dartmouth Coll., 1957-59, mem. faculty, 1959-92, prof. govt., 1967-92, Nelson A. Rockefeller prof. govt. emeritus, 1992—; U. Vt., Burlington, 1989—; chmn. city planning and urban studies program Dartmouth Coll., 1965-72, chmn. social sci. div., 1968-72, asso. dean faculty, 1968-72, acting dean, 1972, v.p. student affairs, 1975-77, chmn. policy studies program, 1977-83, dir. Nelson A. Rockefeller Center for Social Scis., 1983-86; chmn. Vt. Gov.'s Comm. Higher Edn., 1973-80, Vt. Adv. Commn. on Intergovtl. Relations, 1985-86, Vt. Legis Apportionment Bd., 1990—; fenceviewer Norwich, Vt., 1976-90. Author: Metro Toronto: A Decade Later, 1963, Greater London: The Politics of Metropolitan Reform, 1965, Free and Independent, 1976, The Politics of Policy Implementation, 1980, The Other Candidates, 1983, Thomas Chittenden, Virginia's First Governor, 1997. Mem. Vt. Senate, 1973-75; trustee Vt. State Colls., 1967-73, chmn., 1973. Served with AUS, 1945-46. Recipient Superior Achievement award AEC, 1957, Dartmouth Presdl. Leadership medal, 1991; fellow Inst. Pub. Adminstrn., 1960; Dartmouth Coll. Faculty fellow, 1962-63; Nuffield Coll. (Oxford U.), vis. fellow, 1981, 86-87. Mem. Am. Soc. Pub. Adminstrn., Phi Beta Kappa. Office: 38 Northshore Dr Burlington VT 05401-1259

SMALLWOOD, GLENN WALTER, JR., utility marketing management executive; b. Jeffersonville, Ind., Oct. 12, 1956; s. Glenn Walter and Darlene Ruth (Zeller) S. BSBA, S.E. Mo. State U., 1978; MA in Bus., Webster U., 1992, MBA, 1993. Cert. counselor. Customer svc. advisor Union Electric Co., Mexico, Mo., 1979-95, Cape Girardeau, Mo., 1995—; instr. Mexico Vo-Tech Sch., 1981; panelist on home design Mo. Extension Svc., 1984; co. advisor Mo. Bus. Week. Coord. local United Way, 1984; mem., chair Gt. Rivers coun. Boy Scouts Am.; panelist Mo. Freedmon Forum, 1990; charter mem. class Mo. Leadership; chmn. Leadership Mexico Program; coordinating advisor Jr. Achievement, Mexico H.S.; committeeman, chmn. Republican Party of Audrain County; bd. dirs. Mo. Rep. Grassroots Caucus. Named among Ten Outstanding Young Missourians, Mo. Jaycees, 1993; recipient Disting. Svc. award Mexico, Mo. Jaycees, 1993. Mem. Am. Mktg. Assn. (profl.), Nat. Eagle Scout Assn., Cooper Dome Soc., Boy Scouts Am. Alumni Family, Mexico Area C. of C. (bd. dirs.), Semo U. Alumni Assn., Inst. Cert. Profl. Mgrs. (cert. mgr.), Adminstrv. Mgmt. Soc., Optimists (youth appreciation award 1974), Kiwanis (cert. appreciation 1984), Mexico Noon (bd. dirs. 1990, treas. 1990-91, v.p. 1991-92, pres. 1993-94), Audrain County Pachyderm Club (bd. dirs., 2d v.p. 1990-92, pres. 1993), Southeast Mo. Pachyderm Club (founder, pres. 1997—), Sons of Confederate Vets., Honorable Order Ky. Cols. Republican. Avocations: music, spectator sports, baseball, basketball, tennis. Office: Union Electric Co PO Box 40 Cape Girardeau MO 63701-0040

SMALLY, DONALD JAY, consulting engineering executive; b. Cleve., 1922; s. Daniel James and Alice (Rohrheimer) S.; m. Ruth Janet Glasser, July 8, 1944; children: Alan Jon, Leonard Arthur. B.M.E., U. Cin., 1949. Prodn. engr. N. Ransohoff, Inc., Cin., 1949-50; chief engr. Mosby Engring. Assocs., Sarasota, Fla., 1952-55; prin. Smally, Wellford & Nalven, Inc., Sarasota, 1956-91; mem. tech. adv. com. Manatee Community Coll., Sarasota, 1965-90; mem. adv. com. Vocat.-Tech. High Sch., Sarasota, 1968-80. V.p. Sarasota YMCA, 1968-71, Sarasota Opera Assn., 1975-88, pres., 1988-89; chmn. Sarasota Vol. Talent Pool, 1973-76; sec.-treas. Civitan Found., 1965-79; bd. dirs. Suncoast Heart Assn., 1976; mem. Fla. Coordinating Coun. for Vocat. and Adult Edn., 1984-95, chmn., 1987-88; chmn. Sarasota Hist. Preservation Bd., 1988-91; pres. Sarasota County Rd. Improvement Task Force, 1990-93; mem. Sarasota County Pub. Sch. Found., 1990-95, chmn., 1990-91; v.p. Hist. Soc. Sarasota, 1990-91, Children's Haven and Adult Ctr. Bd., 1983—, pres., 1991-94; pres. John Ringling Ctr. Found., 1991—; mem. Plymouth Harbor Bd., 1994—. Recipient Good Citizenship award SAR, 1975, Disting. Alumni award U. Cin. Engring. Coll., 1985, Outstanding Svc. award Myakna Chpt. Fla. Engring. Soc., 1993; named Citizen of Yr. Sarasota Civitan Club, 1975, Engr. of Yr. Sarasota-Manatee Engrs. Soc., 1976. Fellow Am. Cons. Engrs. Council (treas. 1980-82), Fla. Engring. Soc. (pres. Sarasota-Manatee chpt. 1956-58); mem. Sarasota County C. of C. (past dir., v.p. 1983), Cons. Engrs. Council Fla. (pres. 1968), Fla. Soc. Profl. Land Surveyors (chpt. pres. 1973), Am. Water Works Resources Assn. (pres. Fla. Soc. 1981), Sarasota-Manatee Engring. Soc.

SMARANDACHE, FLORENTIN, mathematics researcher, writer; b. Balcesti-Vilcea, Romania, Dec. 10, 1954; came to U.S., 1990; s. Gheorghe and Maria (Mitroiescu) S.; m. Eleonora Niculescu; children: Mihai-Liviu, Silviu-Gabriel. MS, U. Craiova, 1979; postgrad., Ariz. State U., 1991. Mathematician I.U.G., Craiova, Romania, 1979-81; math. prof. Romanian Coll., 1981-82, 1984-86, 1988; math. tchr. Coop. Ministry, Morocco, 1982-84; French tutor pvt. practice, Turkey, 1988-90; software engr. Honeywell, Phoenix, 1990-95; prof. math. Pima C.C., Tucson, 1995—. Author: Nonpoems, 1990, Only Problems, Not Solutions, 1991, numerous other books; contbr. articles to profl. jours. Mem. U.S. Math. Assn., Romania Math. Assn., Zentralblatt fur Math. (reviewer). Achievements include development of Smarandache function, numbers, quotients, double factorials, consecutive sequence, reverse sequence, mirror sequence, destructive sequence, symmetric sequence, permutable sequence, consecutive sieve, prime base, cubic base, square base, class of paradoxes, multi-structure and multi-space, paradoxist geometry, anti-geometry, inconsistent systems of axioms. Home: 2456 S Rose Peak Dr Tucson AZ 85710-7413

SMARDON, RICHARD CLAY, landscape architecture and environmental studies educator; b. Burlington, Vt., May 13, 1948; s. Philip Albert and Louise Gertrude (Peters) S.; m. Anne Marie Graveline, Aug. 19, 1973; children: Regina Elizabeth, Andrea May. BS cum laude, U. Mass., 1970, MLA, 1973; PhD in Environ. Planning, U. Calif., Berkeley, 1982. Environ. planner, landscape architect Wallace, Floyd, Ellenzweig, Inc., Cambridge, Mass., 1972-73; assoc. planner Exec. Office Environ. Affairs, State of Mass., Boston, 1973-75; environ. impact assessment specialist USDA extension svc. Oreg. State U., Corvallis, 1975-76; landscape architect USDA Pacific S.W. Forest and Range Expt. Sta., Berkeley, 1977; rsch. landscape architect U. Calif., Berkeley, 1977-79; prof. landscape architecture, sr. rsch. assoc. SUNY Coll. Environ. Sci. and Forestry, Syracuse, 1979-86, prof. environ. studies, 1987—, dir. Inst. for Environ. Policy and Planning, 1987-95, chair faculty of environ. studies, 1996; co-dir. Gt. Lakes Rsch. Consortium, Syracuse, 1986-96; chair Randolf G. Pack Environ. Inst., 1996; guest lectr. numerous univs.; adj. asst. prof. U. Mass., Amherst, 1974-75, chair faculty Environment Studies, 1996, dir. R.G. Pack Environment Inst., 1996; Sea Grant trainee Inst. for Urban and Regional Devel., Berkeley, 1976; condr., presenter numerous seminars and workshops; cons. to numerous orgns.; mem. com. on environ. design and landscape Transp. Rsch. Bd.-NAS, 1985-95; mem. tech. adv. bd. Wetlands Rsch., Inc., Chgo., 1985; mem. adv. bd. Wetlands Fund, N.Y., 1985; v.p. Integrated Site Inc., Syracuse. Co-editor: Our National Landscape, 1979, spl. issue Coastal Zone Mgmt. Jour., 1982, The Future of Wetlands, 1983, Foundations for Visual Project Analysis, 1986, The Legal Landscape, 1993, Protecting Floodplain Resources, 1995; mem. editl. bd. Northeastern Environ. Sci. Jour., 1981, Landscape and Urban Planning, 1991; contbr. over 100 articles to profl. jours. Bd. dirs. Sackets Harbor Area Hist. Preservation Found., Watertown, N.Y., 1984-90; pres. Save the County, Inc., Fayetteville, N.Y., 1986-88; apptd. to Great Lakes (N.Y.) Adv. Commn., chmn., 1993. Recipient Beatrice Farrand award U. Calif., 1979, Am. Soc. Landscape Architects award, 1972, Pub. Svc. award in edn., 1990, Progressive Architecture mag. award 1992, Pres.'s Pub. Svc. award 1994. Mem. AAAS, Am. Land Resource Assn. (charter), Internat. Assn. for Impact Assessment, Coastal Soc., Alpha Zeta (life), Sigma Lambda Alpha. Avocations: folk guitar, hiking, skiing, travel. Office: SUNY Faculty Environ Studies Syracuse NY 13210 Office: Integrated Site Inc 886 E Brighton Ave Syracuse NY 13205-2538

SMARG, RICHARD MICHAEL, insurance and employee benefits specialist; b. Orange, N.J., July 25, 1952; s. Nicholas and Dorothy Smarg; m. Lynda E. Broms, Oct. 18, 1975; 1 child, Daniel. BS in Econs., U. N.H., 1974. CLU, ChFC. With New Eng. Mut. Life Ins. Co., Manchester, N.H., 1975-78; assoc. Baldwin & Clarke Cos., Bedford, N.H., 1978-88; founder Retirement & Ins. Assocs., Naples, Fla., 1988—; instr. Am. Coll., Bryn Mawr, Pa., 1985—; mem. M Fin. Group, Portland, Oreg., 1997—; speaker in field. Contbr. articles to profl. jours. Philanthropist; fundraising cons. Mem. Estate Planning Coun., Fla., Million Dollar Round Table (life, state coord. 1987-91), Rotary Internat. (Paul Harris fellow 1991), English-Speaking Union (v.p. Naples, Fla.). Republican. Episcopalian. Avocations: golf, running, photography, travel, sports cars. Office: Retirement & Ins Assocs 4001 Tamiami Trl N Ste 215 Naples FL 34103-3591

SMART, CHARLES RICH, retired surgeon; b. Ogden, Utah, Nov. 7, 1926; s. Junius Hatch and Avon (Rich) S.; m. Dorothea Jean Cannon Sharp, Dec. 23, 1952; children—Thomas, Edward, Christopher, Angela, Cynthia, David. B.S. with honors, U. Utah, 1945; M.D. with honors, Temple U., 1955. Intern Los Angeles County Hosp., 1955-56; resident Hosp. U. Pa., Phila., 1956-61; asst. prof. surgery in residence UCLA, 1963-66; assoc. prof. surgery Coll. Medicine, U. Utah, 1966-69, cancer coordinator, 1967-69, clin. assoc. prof. surgery, 1969-75, clin. prof. surgery, 1975-85; mem. staff, chief of surgery Latter-day Saints Hosp., 1974-84; chmn. SEER Group Nat. Cancer Inst., 1976-78, chief community oncology and rehab. br., 1985-86, chief early detection br., 1987-92; ret., 1992; dir. Rocky Mountain Coop. Tumor Registry, 1969-85; bd. dirs. Am. Cancer Soc., 1976-79. Contbr. research articles to med. jours. Fellow ACS; mem. Utah Med. Assn., AMA, Pan-Pacific Surg. Soc., Bay Surg. Soc., Los Angeles Surg Soc., Salt Lake Surg. Soc., Internat. Soc. Chemotherapists, Am. Assn. Cancer Edn., Am. Soc. Clin. Oncology, Soc. Head and Neck Surgeons, Am. Soc. Surg. Oncologists, Alpha Omega Alpha. Republican. Mormon. Home: 1262 Chandler Dr Salt Lake City UT 84103-4240

SMART, JACKSON WYMAN, JR., business executive; b. Chgo., Aug. 27, 1930; s. Jackson Wyman and Dorothy (Byrnes) S.; m. Suzanne Tobey, July 6, 1957; 1 son, Jackson W. III. B.B.A., U. Mich., 1952; M.B.A., Harvard, 1954. With First Nat. Bank Chgo., 1956-64; exec. v.p. comml. banking Bank of Commonwealth, Detroit, 1964-69; pres., dir. MSP Industries Corp. (subsidiary W.R. Grace & Co. 1972), Center Line, Mich., 1969-71, pres., CEO, 1971-75; chmn., pres., treas., dir. The Delos Internat. Group, Inc. (subs. Automatic Data Processing Inc. 1976), Princeton, N.J., 1975-77; chmn., pres., CEO, dir. Central Nat. Bank (merged with Exch. Nat. Bank, Chgo. 1982), Chgo., 1977-82; chmn. fin. com. Exch. Internat. Corp., Chgo., 1982-83; chmn. exec. com. Thomas Industries, Inc., Louisville, Ky., 1983-87; chmn., CEO, dir. MSP Communications, Inc., Chgo., 1988—; bd. dirs. Fed. Express Corp., Memphis, 1976—, chmn. fin. com., 1976-78; bd. dirs. Goldman Sachs Funds Group, N.Y.C.; chmn. Terminal Data Corp., Moorpark, Calif., 1992-94 (merger Banctec 1994); bd. dirs. 1st Commonwealth Inc., Chgo., 1988—, chmn. exec. com., 1996—; bd. dirs. Inroads Capital Ptnrs. Bd. dirs. Evanston (Ill.) Hosp., Hadley Sch. Blind, Winnetka, Ill., chmn. 1987-89. Mem. Chief Execs. Orgn., Birmingham Club (Mich.), Athletic Club, Comml. Club, Econ. Club, Univ. Club, Hundred Club of Cook County, Chgo. Club, Indian Hill Club, Ocean Club of Fla. (Ocean Ridge), Country Club of Fla. (Golf), Coral Beach and Tennis Club (Bermuda), Old Elm Club (Highland Park, Ill.). Office: 1 Northfield Plz Northfield IL 60093-1251

SMART, JACOB EDWARD, management consultant; b. Ridgeland, S.C., May 31, 1909; s. William Edward and Alma (Nettles) S.; m. Elizabeth Gohmert, Feb. 20, 1932 (div. 1946); children—Joan Elizabeth, Jacklyn Cabell, William Edward, Rosemary. Student, Marion Mil. Inst., 1926-27; B.S., U.S. Mil. Acad., 1931; student, Nat. War Coll., 1949-50. Commd. lt. USAF, 1931, advanced through grades to gen., 1963; served various posts U.S. and Europe, 1931-55; asst. vice chief of staff USAF, Washington, 1955-59; comdr. (12th Air Force), Waco, Texas, 1959-60; vice comdr. tactical air command Langley AFB, 1960-61; comdr. 5th Air Force and U.S. Forces in Japan, Japan, 1961-63, Cinc. Pacific Air Forces, 1963-64; dep. comdr. in chief (Hdqrs. U.S. European Command), 1964-66; ret., 1966; spl. asst. to adminstr. NASA, 1966-67, asst. adminstr. for policy, 1967-68; asst. adminstr. for Dept. Def. and inter-agy. affairs, 1968-73; v.p. Earth Satellite Corp., Washington, 1973-75; cons., 1975—. Decorated D.S.C., D.S.M. with 4 oak leaf clusters, Legion of Merit, D.F.C., Air medal with 3 oak leaf clusters, Purple Heart, Commendation Ribbon; hon. comdr. Order Brit. Empire; Order of Service Merit 1st class Korea; Medal of Cloud and Banner with Grand Cordon China; comdr. Legion of Honor France; Order of Sacred Treasures Japan). Mem. Assn. Grads. U.S. Mil. Acad., Air Force Assn. Home: PO Box 2440 Ridgeland SC 29936-0925

SMART, MARRIOTT WIECKHOFF, research librarian consultant; b. Memphis, Aug. 26, 1935; d. Gerhard Emil and Beatrice (Flanegan)

Wieckhoff; m. John A. Smart, May 9, 1959; children: Denise, Holly. BS in Geology, U. Tex.-Austin, 1957; MLS, U. Pitts., 1976. Geophysicist Mobil Corp., New Orleans, 1957-59; geologist Hanson Oil Co., Roswell, N.Mex., 1959-62; info. specialist Gulf Corp., Pitts., 1977-79, library mgr., Denver, 1979-84, library cons. team, Pitts., 1984; supr. Library-Info. Ctr., Amoco Minerals Co., Englewood, Colo., 1984; dir. Library-Info. Ctr., Cyprus Minerals Co., 1985-92; cons. Ask Marriott, Littleton, Colo., 1992—. Choir mem. Grace Presbyn. Ch., Littleton, 1979—. Mem. Spl. Libraries Assn. (bull. bus. mgr. 1982, treas. petroleum and energy divsn. 1984-86, chmn. petroleum and energy divsn. 1987-88, pres. Rocky Mountain chpt. 1991-92), Colo. Info. Profls. Network, Women in Mining, Alpha Chi Omega. Home: 3337 E Easter Pl Littleton CO 80122-1910

SMART, MARY-LEIGH CALL (MRS. J. SCOTT SMART), civic worker; b. Springfield, Ill., Feb. 27, 1917; d. S(amuel) Leigh and Mary (Bradish) Call; m. J. Scott Smart, Sept. 11, 1951 (dec. 1960). Diploma, Monticello Coll., 1934; student, Oxford U., 1935; B.A., Wellesley Coll., 1937; M.A., Columbia U., 1939, postgrad., 1940-41; postgrad., N.Y. U., 1940-41; painting student, with Bernard Karfiol, 1937-38. Dir. mgmt. Cen. Ill. Grain Farms, Logan County, 1939—; owner Lowtrek Kennel, Ogunquit, Maine, 1957-73, Cove Studio Art Gallery, Ogunquit, 1961-68; art collector, patron, publicist, 1954—, cons., 1970—. Editor: Hamilton Easter Field Art Found. Collection Catalog, 1966; originator, dir. show, compiler of catalog Art: Ogunquit, 1967; Peggy Bacon-A Celebration, Barn Gallery, Ogunquit, 1979. Program dir., sec. bd. Barn Gallery Assocs., Inc., 1958-69, pres., 1969-70, 82-87, asst. treas., 1987-92, hon. dir., 1970-78, adv. trustee, 1992-94, v.p., 1994—; curator Hamilton Easter Field Art Found. Collection, 1978-79, curator exhbns., 1979-86, chair exhbn. com., 1987-94; mem. acquisition com. DeCordova Mus., Lincoln, Mass., 1966-78; mem. chancellor's coun. U. Tex., 1972—; mem. pres.'s coun. U. N.H., 1978—; bd. dirs. Ogunquit C. of C., 1966, treas., 1966-67, hon. life mem., 1968—; bd. overseers Strawbery Banke, Inc., Portsmouth, N.H., 1972-75, 3d vice chmn., 1973, 2d vice chmn., 1974; bd. advisors U. Art Galleries, U. N.H., 1973-89, v.p., bd. overseers, 1974-81, pres., 1981-89; bd. dirs. Old York Hist. and Improvement Soc., York, Maine, 1979-81, v.p., 1981-82; adv. com. Bowdoin Coll. Mus. Art Invitational exhibit, 1975, '76 Maine Artists Invitational Exhbn., Maine State Mus., Maine Coast Artists, Rockport, 1975-78, All Maine Biennial '79, Bowdoin Coll. Mus. Art juried exhbn.; mem. jury for scholarship awards Maine com. Skowhegan Sch. Painting & Sculpture, 1982-84; nat. com. Wellesley Coll. Friends of Art, 1983—; adv. trustee Portland Mus. Art, 1983-85, fellow, 1985—; mem. mus. panel Maine State Commn. on Arts and Humanities, 1983-86; adv. com. Maine Biennial, Colby Coll. Mus. Art, 1983; coun. advisors Farnsworth Libr. & Art Mus., Rockland, Maine, 1986—; collections com. Payson Gallery, Westbrook Coll., Portland, 1987-91; dir. Greater Piscataqua Cmty. Found., N.H. Charitable Fund, 1991—; mem. corp. Ogunquit Mus. Am. Art, 1988-90, 95—; mem. Maine Women's Forum, 1993—; founder N.H. Charitable Fund, 1991-97. Lt. (j.g.) WAVES, 1942-45. Recipient Deborah Morton award Westbrook Coll., 1988, Friend of the Arts award Maine Art Dealers Assn., 1993. Mem. Springfield Art Assn., Jr. League Springfield, Western Maine Wellesley Club. Episcopalian. Address: 30 Surf Point Rd York ME 03909-5053

SMART, STEPHEN BRUCE, JR., business and government executive; b. N.Y.C., Feb. 7, 1923; s. Stephen Bruce and Beatrice (Cobb) S.; m. Edith Minturn Merrill, Sept. 10, 1949; children: Edith Minturn Smart Moore, William Candler, Charlotte Merrill Smart Rogan, Priscilla Smart Schwarzenbach. Student, Milton Acad.; AB cum laude, Harvard U., 1945; SM, MIT, 1947. Sales engr. Permutit Co., N.Y., 1947-51; various sales, gen. mgmt. positions Continental Group, Inc. (formerly Continental Can Co.), N.Y.C., 1953-85, v.p. Central metal divsn., 1962-65, v.p. marketing and corporate planning, 1965-67, v.p., asst. gen. mgr. paper ops., 1967-69, group v.p. paper ops., 1969-71, exec. v.p. paper ops., 1971-73, vice chmn. bd. dirs., 1973-75, pres., 1975-85, chmn., CEO, 1981-85; undersec. for internat. trade U.S. Dept. Commerce, Washington, 1985-88; cons. U.S. Dept. State, Washington, 1988-89; sr. fellow World Resources Inst., Washington, 1989-95, also bd. dirs. Editor: Beyond Compliance: A New Industry View of the Environment, 1992. Bd. dirs. League of Conservation Voters; chmn. bd. dirs. Notre Dame Acad., Middleburg, Va. Mem. Coun. Fgn. Rels., Bus. Coun., Pequot Yacht Club, Sigma Xi. Home and Office: 20561 Trappe Rd Upperville VA 20184-9708

SMARTSCHAN, GLENN FRED, educational administrator; b. Allentown, Pa., Dec. 11, 1946; s. Fred Gotfred and Joyce Isabel (Hensinger) S.; m. Linda Susan Bastinelli, Mar. 18. 1972; children: Erin Joy, Lauren Nicole. BS in Edn., Kutztown State Coll., 1968; MS in Edn., Temple U., 1972; EdD in Ednl. Adminstrn., Lehigh U., 1979. Cert. tchr. history and comprehensive social studies, secondary prin., supt., Pa. Tchr. 8th grade social studies South Mountain Jr. High Sch., Allentown Sch. Dist., 1968-76, adminstrv. asst. to prin. Raub Jr. High Sch., 1976-78, prin., 1978-80, dist. dir. curriculum, 1980-84, asst. to supt. for curriculum and community services, 1984-86; supt. of schs. Brandywine Heights Area Sch. Dist., Topton, Pa., 1986-90; supt. of sch. Mt. Lebanon Sch. Dist., Pitts., 1990—; adj. prof. Cedar Crest Coll., 1986-88; chief exec. officer Ednl. Dynamics Cons.; assoc. The Cambridge Group, 1993—; speaker, cons. on alternative edn., scope and sequence devel., criterion referenced testing, strategic planning; bd. dirs. Alternative House Inc., Bethlehem, Pa., 1976-81, chairperson program com., 1977-78, v.p., 1979, pres., 1980; mem. adv. com. Lehigh County (Pa.) Hist. Mus., 1980-86; bd. dirs. Girls' Club Allentown, 1983-86, v.p., 1985. Mem. Assn. Supervision and Curriculum Devel., Pa. Assn. Supervision and Curriculum Devel. (exec. com., registrar eastern regional meeting, v.p. Eastern region, pres. Eastern region 1988), Am. Assn. Sch. Adminstrs., Pa. Assn. Sch. Adminstrs. (pres. 1996), Pa. Sch. Bds. Assn., Alumni Coun. Lehigh U. (pres. 1986), Phi Delta Kappa, Fleetwood Club, Rotary (charter mem. Allentown club, exec. com. 1985). Roman Catholic. Home: One Spalding Cir Pittsburgh PA 15228 Office: Mt Lebanon Sch Dist 7 Horsman Dr Pittsburgh PA 15228-1128

SMATHERS, FRANK, JR., banker, horticulturist; b. Atlantic City, July 17, 1909; s. Frank and Lura (Jones) S.; m. Mary Belle Wall, Mar. 27, 1935; children: Lowry, Pamela Smathers MacCorquodale, Ann Smathers Prescott, Lura Smathers Bergh. Student, U. N.C., 1928-30; LLB, U. Miami, 1933; student, Grad. Sch. Banking, Rutgers U., 1939-42. Bar: Fla. 1933. Asst. state atty. State of Fla., 1934-35; asst. trust officer Miami Beach (Fla.) 1st Nat. Bank, 1936-39, v.p., trust officer, dir., 1936-56, asst. pres., trust officer, 1956-57, pres., 1957-67, chmn., 1966-74; chmn. bd. United Nat. Bank, Miami, 1964-74; chmn. Coral Gables 1st Nat. Bank, 1966-74, United Bancshares, 1966-73, Security Exch. Bank, West Palm Beach, Fla., 1970-73; vice chmn. United Nat. Bank, Dadeland, 1968-74; chmn. United Nat. Bank, Westland, Fla., 1972-74; pres., chief exec. officer United 1st Fla. Banks, Inc., 1973-74; chmn., chief exec. officer Flagship Banks Inc., 1974-75. Pres. Fedn. Econ. Concern, Dade County, Fla.; vice chmn. Assn. Governing Bds. Colls. and Univs.; trustee U. Miami, Rutgers U., Grad. Sch. Banking, St. Francis Hosp., Miami Beach., Fairchild Tropical Garden; bd. dirs. Fla. Coun. 100. With U.S. Army, 1928, 42-43; with Office Price Adminstrn., Washington, 1944-45. Mem. Iron Arrow Hon. Soc., SAR, Metropolitan Club (Washington), Indian Creek Country Club, Coral Reef Yacht Club, Yale Club (N.Y.C.), Royal and Ancient Golf Club, Pine Valley Golf Club, Delta Kappa Epsilon. Methodist. Home: 11511 SW 57th Ave Miami FL 33156-5002

SMATHERS, JAMES BURTON, medical physicist, educator; b. Prairie du Chien, Wis., Aug. 26, 1935; s. James Levi and Irma Marie (Stindt) S.; m. Sylvia Lee Rath, Apr. 20, 1957; children—Kristine Kay, Kathryn Ann, James Scott, Ernest Kent. B.Nuclear Enging., N.C. State Coll., 1957, M.S., 1959; Ph.D., U. Md., 1967. Diplomate Am. Bd. Radiology, Am. Bd. Health Physics, Am. Bd. Medical Physics; cert. in radiation oncology physics; registered profl. engr., D.C., Tex., Calif. Research engr. Atomics Internat., Canoga Park, Calif., 1959, Walter Reed Army Inst. Research, Washington, 1961-67; prof. nuclear enging. Tex. A. and M. U., College Station, 1967-80; prof., head bioengring. Tex. A. and M. U., 1976-80; prof., head med. physics, dept. radiation oncology UCLA, 1980—; cons. U.S. Army, Dept. Energy, also pvt.; industry. Served with U.S. Army, 1959-61. Recipient Excellence in Teaching award Gen. Dynamics, 1971; Excellence in Research award Tex. A. and M. U. Former Students Assn., 1976. Mem. Am. Nuclear Soc., Health Physics Soc., Am. Assn. Physcists in Medicine, Am. Soc. Enging. Edn. (Outstanding Tchr. award in nuclear enging. div. 1972), Radiation Research Soc., Nat. Soc. Profl. Engrs., Calif. Soc. Profl. Engrs., Sigma Xi, Sigma Pi Sigma, Phi Kappa Phi. Home: 18229 Minnehaha St Northridge CA 91326-3427 Office: UCLA Dept Radiation Oncology B265 200 UCLA Med Plz Los Angeles CA 90095-6951

SMEAD, BURTON ARMSTRONG, JR., lawyer, retired; b. Denver, July 29, 1913; s. Burton Armstrong and Lola (Lewis) S.; m. Josephine McKittrick, Mar. 27, 1943; children: Amanda Armstrong, Sydney Hall. BA, U. Denver, 1934, J.D., 1950; grad. Pacific Coast Banking Trust Sch., 1955. Bar: Colo., 1950. With Norwest Bank Denver (formerly Denver Nat. Bank), 1934-78, trust officer, 1955-70, v.p. and trust officer, 1970-78, sec. bd. dirs., 1976-78; pvt. practice law, Englewood, Colo., 1978—; of counsel Buchanan & Thomas, Lakewood, Colo., 1985—; bd. dirs., trust counsel, Resources Trust Co., Englewood, Colo. Author: History of the Twelfth Field Artillery Battalion in the European Theater of Operations, 1944-45, Captain Smead's Letters to Home, 1944-45; editor: Colorado Wills and Estates, 1965. Pres., trustee Stebbins Orphans Home Assn. Chmn. bd. dirs. Am. Cancer oc., N.Y.C., Colo. div., 1961-68. Maj. U.S. Army, 1941-45; ETO. Decorated Bronze Star, Croix de Guerre (France). Mem. ABA, Arapahoe Bar Assn., Colo. Bar Assn. (treas. 1970-88, chmn. probate and trust law sect. 1967-68, exec. coun., bd. govs. 1970-88, coun. bd. gov. 1970-88, hon. 1989—, award of merit 1979), Denver Estate Planning Coun. (co-founder, pres. 1971-72), Univ. Club (Denver). Republican. Episcopalian. Home and Office: 3130 Cherryridge Rd Englewood CO 80110-6057

SMEAL, CAROLYN A., community health nurse, educator; b. Guilford, N.Y., Jan. 30, 1930; d. Charles C. and Margaret C. (Wilson) Bloom; m. William C. Smeal, May 28, 1949; children: Dale, Sandra Smeal Barlow, Stacey (dec.), William M. Diploma, Millard Fillmore Hosp., Buffalo, 1950; BS, SUNY, Buffalo, 1967. Cert. community health nurse, sch. nurse-tchr. Staff nurse in oper. rm., emergency rm. Niagara Falls (N.Y.) Meml. Med. Ctr.; staff nurse Niagara Falls Air Base; sch. nurse tchr. Bd. Edn., Niagara Falls; community health nurse Niagara County Health Dept., Niagara Falls; retired, 1995. Bd. dirs. Ctr. for Young Parents, Cerebral Palsy Recreation Group. Mem. Assn. for Retarded Children (bd. dirs., past pres.). Home: 710 Chilton Ave Niagara Falls NY 14301-1008

SMEAL, JANIS LEA, operating room nurse, health facility administrator; b. Johnstown, Pa., Aug. 31, 1953; d. Charles Truman S. and Clara Belle (Smeal) Satterlee. RN, Mercy Hosp. Sch. Nursing, 1974; BS summa cum laude, U. Houston, 1996. ACLS, 1982; CNOR, 1988. Staff, relief chage nurse emergency room Mercy Hosp., Altoona, Pa., 1974-85; staff nurse operating room McAllen (Tex.) Med. Ctr., 1985-87, Rio Grande Regional Hosp., McAllen, Tex., 1987-88; co-owner Associated Hypnotherapy and Pain Mgmt. Svcs. Tex., Bellaire, 1991—; staff nurse operating room Meml. City Hosp., Houston, 1992—; co-owner, cons. J.L. Med. Svcs., McAllen, Tex., 1988-94. Recognition Golden Key Nat. Honor Soc., 1993, Phi Kappa Phi, 1994, Natural Sci. and Math. Scholars and Fellows, 1995. Mem. AORN, NOW, Golden Key, Phi Kappa Phi. Avocations: travel, dog training, interior design. Office: Assoc Hypnotherapy/Pain Svc 6300 West Loop S Ste 333 Bellaire TX 77401-2913

SMEAL, PAUL LESTER, retired horticulture educator; b. Clearfield, Pa., June 11, 1932; s. Walter Vernon and Agatha (Cowder) S.; m. Gladys Matilda Smeal, July 17, 1954; children: Lester Alan, Gwen Hope, Tracy Gay. BS, Pa. State U., 1954; MS, U. Md., 1958, PhD, 1961. Asst. prof. horticulture Va. Poly. Inst. and State U., Blacksburg, 1960-61, assoc. prof., 1961-67, prof., 1967-92, prof. emeritus, 1993—; pres. faculty senate Va. Poly. Inst. and State U., 1984-86. Advisor Alpha Zeta, 1984-86. Recipient Quill and Trowel Comm. award Garden Writers Assn. Am., 1986, 87, Disting. Svc. award Nat. Assn. Country Agrl. Agts., 1987, L.C. Chadwick Teaching award Am. Assn. Nurserymen, 1988, Nursery Ext. award Am. Assn. Nurserymen, 1990. Fellow Am. Soc. Hort. Sci. (mem. pub. affairs com. 1979-82, chmn. ad hoc com 1984-86, pres. so. region 1978-79, sec.-treas. 1989—, others, Carl S. Bittner Extension award 1984, Henry M. Covington Extension award 1991); mem. Internat. Plant Propagator's Soc. (chmn. rsch. com. ea. region 1987-90, bd. dirs. 1991, 2d v.p. 1991, v.p. 1992, pres. 1993), Va. Nurserymen's Assn. (hon.). Republican. Lutheran. Home: 1107 Kentwood Dr Blacksburg VA 24060-5656

SMEDINGHOFF, THOMAS J., lawyer; b. Chgo., July 15, 1951; s. John A. and Dorothy M.; m. Mary Beth Smedinghoff. BA in Math., Knox Coll., 1973; JD, U. Mich., 1978. Bar: Ill. 1978, U.S. Dist. Ct. (no. dist.) Ill. 1978. Assoc. McBride, Baker & Coles and predecessor McBride & Baker, Chgo., 1978-84, ptnr., 1985—; adj. prof. computer law John Marshall Law Sch., Chgo.; chair Ill. Commn. on Electronic Commerce and Crime, 1996—. Author Online Law, 1996. Mem. ABA (chair electronic commerce divsn. 1995—). Office: McBride Baker & Coles 500 W Madison St Fl 40 Chicago IL 60661-2511

SMEDLEY, ELIZABETH, researcher, codifier, consultant, historian, writer; b. Phila., Jan. 5, 1915; d. Elwood Quimby and Hazel deRemer (Ward) S. BA cum laude, Bryn Mawr Coll., 1936. Editor, rechr., writer Hist. Records Survey, Phila., 1939-43; rechr., writer U.S. Army Chief of Ordnance, Phila., 1943-45; local govt. specialist Bur. Mcpl. Affairs, Harrisburg, Pa., 1945-51; local govt. codifier, writer Penns Valley Pubs., State College, Pa., 1951-75; rschr., writer Pa. State Assn. Boroughs, Harrisburg, 1975-82; dir. codification, co-owner Century IV Codes, Inc., Hershey, Pa., 1982-95; owner, rechr. Century IV Codes, Inc., Hummelstown, Pa., 1995—; cons., writer Pa. State Assn. Boroughs, Harrisburg, 1962-65, Pa. Dept. Transp., Harrisburg, 1979-81. Author: Zion's Path of History, 1987, 1936: A 50 Year Perspective, 1986. Chmn. State College Govt. Study Commn., 1971-73. Mem. DAR, Daus. Am. Colonists. Republican. LDS. Avocations: collecting postcards and books, gardening, cooking, cats. Home and Office: 54 Ridgeview Rd Hummelstown PA 17036-9721

SMEDLEY, LAWRENCE THOMAS, retired organization executive; b. Lorain, Ohio, Sept. 2, 1929; s. Robert E. and Gerda Sofia (Johnson) S.; m. Carmen Nancy Suarez, June 29, 1962; children: Lorraine, Robert, Lawrence, Richard. BA, Bowling Green State U., 1952; MA, U. Mich., 1957; PhD, Am. U., 1972. Analyst Social Security dept. AFL-CIO, Washington, 1962-65, asst. dir. dept., 1965-73, assoc. dir. dept. occupation safety-health-social security, 1973-88; exec. dir. Nat. Coun. Sr. Citizens, Inc., Washington, 1988-96; former mem. numerous presdl. task forces and coms. on older Ams. and disabled; mem. planning and adv. coms. White House Conf. on Aging, 1971, 81; former mem. adv. coun. on employee welfare and pension plans Dept. Labor, also former mem. spl. task force examining policies relating to asset reversions from over-funded pension plans. Co-chmn. Leadership Coun. Aging Orgns., Washington, 1988-95; mem. exec. bd. Com. for Nat. Health Ins., WAshington, 1989—; mem. policy conv. White House Conf. on Aging, 1995. With M.I., U.S. Army, 1952-55, Korea. Recipient Disting. Svc. award Commn. on Accreditation of Facilities of Rehab., 1975, Dedicated Svc. award White House Conf. on Handicapped, 1977, award of honor Industry-Labor Coun., 1981, Outstanding Svc. award Pres.'s Com. on Employment of Handicapped, 1987. Democrat. Lutheran. Home: 1616 Winding Waye Ln Silver Spring MD 20902-1456 Office: Nat Council of Senior Citizens 1331 F St NW Washington DC 20004-1107

SMEDS, EDWARD WILLIAM, retired food company executive; b. Chgo., Feb. 15, 1936; s. Sigvard A. and Ida S.; m. Alice J. Lawler, Jan. 26, 1957; children—Ellen R., Brad W. BS, Carthage Coll., 1957; MS, U. Ill., 1959; grad. advanced mgmt. program, Harvard U., 1977. With Borg Warner Corp., 1958-61; with Kraft Foods div. Kraft Inc., 1961-75, v.p., dir. personnel, ops. group, 1976-78, v.p. human resources, 1978-79, sr. v.p. human resources, 1979-80, sr. v.p. fin. and adminstrn., 1980-84; pres. Kraft Asia Pacific, 1984-88; chmn. Kraft Foods Ltd., Australia, 1984-88; pres. Kraft Ltd. Can., 1988-89; sr. v.p. ops. and logistics Kraft Gen. Foods, Glenview, Ill., 1990-94; pres. customer svc. and ops. Kraft, Northfield, Ill., 1993—. Trustee Carthage Coll., Cornerstone Found. Mem. Global Bus. Mgmt. Coun., Econ. Club of Chgo., Chgo. Coun. on Fgn. Rels., Sunset Ridge Country Club, Club at Pelican Bay. Home: 10 Regentwood Rd Northfield IL 60093-2728 also: 6814 Pelican Bay Blvd Naples FL 34108-8218 Office: Kraft Gen Foods 3 Lakes Dr Northfield IL 60093

SMEETON, THOMAS ROONEY, governmental affairs consultant; b. Evanston, Ill., Sept. 26, 1934; s. Cecil Brooks, Jr. and Florence Mary (Rooney).; m. Susan Diane Tollefson, Feb. 23, 1963; children: Sean, Timothy, Shannon, Brendan, Colin. BS in History, Marquette U., 1958; postgrad., U. Notre Dame, 1958-59; grad., Armed Forces Staff Coll., 1972. Intellience officer U.S. CIA, Langley, Va., 1962-73; vp., gen. mgr. Nowicki Fla. Devel. Corp., Ft. Lauderdale, 1973-75; cons. spl. projects com. on fgn. affairs U.S. House Reps., Washington, 1975-86, minority counsel permanent select com. on intelligence, 1986-92, minority staff dir. Iran/Contra com., 1987-88, exec. dir. Rep. policy com., 1993-94; adminstr., chief investigator House Judiciary Com., Washington, D.C., 1995-96; govtl. affairs cons., 1996—. Contbg. author: (with Hyde) For Every Idle Silence, 1985. Bd. dirs. Sylvan Beach Found. With U.S. Army, 1959-62. Recipient Agy. Seal medallion CIA, 1993. Mem. Am. Legion, Notre Dame Club Washington (vice chmn. 1982-84), Amelia Island Club. Republican. Roman Catholic. Avocation: golf. Home and Office: 9414 Wallingford Dr Burke VA 22015-1733

SMEGAL, THOMAS FRANK, JR., lawyer; b. Eveleth, Minn., June 15, 1935; s. Thomas Frank and Genevieve (Andreachi) S.; m. Susan Jane Stanton, May 28, 1966; children: Thomas Frank, Elizabeth Jane. BS in Chem. Engring., Mich. Technol. U., 1957; JD, George Washington U., 1961. Bar: Va. 1961, D.C. 1961, Calif. 1964, U.S. Supreme Ct. 1976. Patent examiner U.S. Patent Office, Washington, 1957-61; staff patent atty. Shell Devel. Co., San Francisco, 1962-65; patent atty. Townsend and Townsend, San Francisco, 1965-91, mng. ptnr., 1974-89; sr. ptnr. Graham and James, San Francisco, 1992—; mem. U.S. del. to Paris Conv. for Protection of Indsl. Property. Pres. bd. dirs. Legal Aid Soc. San Francisco, 1982-84, Youth Law Ctr., 1973-84; bd. dirs. Nat. Ctr. for Youth Law, 1978-84, San Francisco Lawyers Com. for Urban Affairs, 1972—, Legal Svcs. for Children, 1980-88; presdl. nom., Legal Svcs. Corp., 1984-90, 93—. Capt. Chem. Corps, U.S. Army, 1961-62. Recipient St. Thomas More award, 1982. Mem. Ct. of Appeals for Federal Ct. (adv. com. 1992-96), ABA (chmn. PTC sect. 1990-91, ho. of dels. 1988—, mem. standing com. Legal Aid and Indigent Defendants, 1991-94, chair sect. officer conf., 1992-94, mem. bd. govs., 1994-97), Nat. Coun. Intellectual Property Law Assn. (chmn. 1989), Nat. Inventors Hall Fame (pres. 1988), Calif. Bar Assn. (v.p. bd. govs. 1986-87), Am. Patent Law Assn. (pres. 1986), Internat. Assn. Intellectual Property Lawyers (pres. 1995—), Bar Assn. San Francisco (pres. 1978), Patent Law Assn. San Francisco (pres. 1974). Republican. Roman Catholic. Clubs: World Trade, Olympic, Golden Gate Breakfast (San Francisco); Claremont (Berkeley). Contbr. articles to publs. in field. Office: Graham & James 1 Maritime Plz Ste 300 Alco San Francisco CA 94111-3404

SMELSER, NEIL JOSEPH, sociologist; b. Kahoka, Mo., July 22, 1930; s. Joseph Nelson and Susie Marie (Hess) S.; m. Helen Thelma Margolis, June 10, 1954 (div. 1965); children: Eric Jonathan, Tina Rachel; m. Sharin Fateley, Dec. 20, 1967; children: Joseph Neil, Sarah Joanne. B.A., Harvard U., 1952, Ph.D., 1958; B.A., Magdalen Coll., Oxford U., Eng., 1954; M.A., Magdalen Coll., Oxford U., 1959; grad., San Francisco Psychoanalytic Inst., 1971. Mem. faculty U. Calif., Berkeley, 1958-94, prof. sociology, 1962—, asst. chancellor ednl. devel., 1966-68; assoc. dir. Inst. of Internat. Studies, Berkeley, 1969-73, 80-89; Univ. prof. sociology U. Calif., Berkeley, 1972-94; prof. emeritus, 1994—; dir. edn. abroad program for U. Calif., Berkeley, 1977-79, spl. advisor Office of Pres., 1993-94, dir. Ctr. for Advanced Study in Behavioral Scis., 1994—; bd. dirs. Found. Fund for Rsch. in Psychiatry, 1967-70; bd. dirs. Social Sci. Rsch. Coun., 1968-71, chmn., 1971-73, mem. com. econ. growth, 1961-65; trustee Ctr. for Advanced Study in Behavioral Scis., 1980-86, 87-93, chmn., 1984-86; trustee Russell Sage Found., 1990—; mem. subcom. humanism Am. Bd. Internal Medicine, 1981-85, 89-90, mem. adv. com., 1992—, chmn. adv. com., 1995—; chmn. sociology panel Behavioral and Social Scis. survey NAS and Social Sci. Rsch. Coun., 1967-69; mem. com. on basic rsch. in behavioral and social scis. NRC, 1980-89, chmn., 1984-86, co-chmn., 1986-89. Author: (with T. Parsons) Economy and Society, 1956, Social Change in the Industrial Revolution, 1959, Theory of Collective Behavior, 1962, The Sociology of Economic Life, 1963, 2d edit., 1975, Essays in Sociological Explanation, 1968, Sociological Theory: A Contemporary View, 1971, Comparative Methods in the Social Sciences, 1976, (with Robin Content) The Changing Academic Market, 1980, Sociology, 1981, 2d edit., 1984, 3d edit., 1987, 4th edit., 1991, 5th edit., 1995, Social Paralysis and Social Change, 1991, Effective Committee Service, 1993, Sociology, 1994, Problematics of Sociology, 1997; editor: (with W.T. Smelser) Personality and Social Systems, 1963, 2d edit., 1971, (with S.M. Lipset) Social Structure and Mobility in Economic Development, 1966, Sociology, 1967, 2d edit., 1973, (with James Davis) Sociology: A Survey Report, 1969, Karl Marx on Society and Social Change, 1973, (with Gabriel Almond) Public Higher Education in California, 1974, (with Erik Erikson) Themes of Work and Love in Adulthood, 1980, (with Jeffrey Alexander et al) The Micro-Macro Lilnk, 1987, Handbook of Sociology, 1988, (with Hans Haferkamp) Social Change and Modernity, 1992, (with Richard Munch) Theory of Culture, 1992, (with Richard Swedberg) The Handbook of Economic Sociology, 1994; editor Am. Sociol. Rev., 1962-65, 89-90; adv. editor Am. Jour. Sociology, 1960-62. Rhodes scholar, 1952-54; jr. fellow Soc. Fellows, Harvard U., 1955-58; fellow Russell Sage Found., 1989-90. Mem. Am. Sociol. Assn. (coun. 1962-65, 67-70, exec. com. 1963-65, pres. elect 1995-96, pres. 1996-97), Pacific Sociol. Assn., Internat. Sociol. Assn. (exec. com. 1986-94, v.p. 1990-94), Am. Acad. Arts and Scis. (hon.), Am. Philos. Soc. (hon.), Nat. Acad. of Scis. (hon.). Home: 400 El Escarpado Stanford CA 94305

SMELT, RONALD, retired aircraft company executive; b. Houghtonle Spring, Durham, Eng., Dec. 4, 1913; came to U.S., 1948, naturalized, 1955; s. Henry Wilson and Florence (Bradburn) S.; m. Marie Anita Collings, Nov. 2, 1940 (dec. May 1964); 1 son, David; m. Jean Stuart, Jan. 15, 1965. B.A., King's Coll., Cambridge (Eng.) U., 1935, M.A., 1939; Ph.D., Stanford, 1961. With Royal Aircraft Establishment, 1935-48, chief high speed flight, 1940-45, chief guided weapons dept., 1945-48; dep. chief aeroballistic research dept. USN Ordnance Lab., 1948-50; chief gas dynamics facility ARO, Inc., Tullahoma, Tenn., 1950-57; dir. research and devel. Lockheed Aircraft Corp. (missile systems div.), Sunnyvale, Calif., 1958-59; mgr. Lockheed Aircraft Corp. (Discoverer Satellite system), 1959-60, chief scientist, 1960-62, v.p., gen. mgr. space programs div., 1962-63, v.p., chief scientist, 1963-78; Guggenheim lectr. Internat. Congress Aero. Sci., 1978; Mem. com. on space vehicle aerodynamics NASA, 1965-66, chmn. research adv. com. on space vehicles, 1966-73, chmn. research and tech. adv. council, 1973-77; chmn. tech. adv. bd. Dept. Transp., 1970-74; mem. engring. adv. com. Stanford U., 1988-89; adv. com. NASA-Stanford Ctr. for Turbulence Rsch. Fellow Cambridge Philos. Soc., Royal Aero. Soc. (London), Am. Astronautical Soc., AIAA (hon.; dir.-at-large 1966-68, pres. 1969, 70); mem. Nat. Acad. Engring.,. Home: 7250 Driver Valley Rd Oakland OR 97462-9679

SMERCINA, CHARLES JOSEPH, mayor, accountant; b. Cleve., Sept. 18, 1932; s. Edward Steven and Barbara Rose (Vincik) S.; m. Dorothy Rita Pazdernik, May 9, 1953; children: Cynthia Bomeli Smercina, David. ABA in Acctg., Fenn Coll.; ABA in Mgmt., BBA in Acctg., Cleve. State U.; postgrad., Kent State U., Case Western Res. U., Youngstown (Ohio) State U. CPA, Ohio. Chmn. CSC, Solon, 1956-66; councilman City of Solon, Ohio, 1966-68, vice mayor, 1966-67, income tax adminstr., 1968-73, mayor, 1974-75, 78-87; cons. taxation, mcpl. fin. various Ohio communities, 1970—; lectr. polit. sci., corp. fin. Case Western Res. U. Mem. Am. Soc. Pub. Adminstrs., Mayors Assn. Ohio, Cuyahoga County Mayors and City Mgrs. Assn., Mcpl. Fin. Officers Am., Nat. League of Cities, Nat. Soc. Pub. Accts., Ohio Assn. Pub. Safety Dirs., Ohio Assn. Tax Adminstrs. (past pres.), Ohio Mcpl. League, Water Pollution Control Fedn., Solon C. of C., VFW, Council on Human Relations, Ohio Nature Conservancy, Nat. Arbor Day Found. Democrat. Roman Catholic. Lodges: Rotary, KC. Home: 5075 Brainard Rd Cleveland OH 44139-1101

SMERDON, ERNEST THOMAS, academic administrator; b. Ritchey, Mo., Jan. 19, 1930; s. John Erle and Ada (Davidson) S.; m. Joanne Duck, June 9, 1951; children: Thomas, Katherine, Gary. BS in Engring., U. Mo., 1951, MS in Engring., 1956, PhD in Enging., 1959. Registered profl. engr., Ariz. Chmn. dept. agrl. engring. U. Fla., Gainesville, 1968-74, asst. dean for rsch., 1974-76; vice chancellor for acad. affairs U. Tex. System, Austin, 1976-82; dir. Ctr. for Rsch. in Water Resources U. Tex., 1982-88; dean Coll. Engring. and Mines U. Ariz., Tucson, 1988-92; vice provost, dean Enging U. Ariz., 1992—; mem. bd. sci. and tech. for internat. devel. NRC, 1990-94, mem. com. on planning and remediation for irrigation-induced water quality problems, 1990-96, chair com. Yucca Mountain peer rev., 1995, mem. com. study of rsch.-doctorate programs in U.S., 1991-95, other coms. Editor: Managing Water Related Conflicts: The Engineer's Role, 1989. Mem. Ariz.

Gov.'s Sci. and Tech. Coun., Tucson, 1989—; bd. dirs. Greater Tucson Econ. Coun., Tucson, 1990-95. Recipient Disting. Svc. in Engring. award U. Mo., 1982. Fellow AAAS, ASCE (hon. mem., Outstanding Svc. award irrigation and drainage divsn. 1988, Royce Tipton award 1989), NAE (peer com. 1986-90, acad. adv. bd. 1989-95, tech. policy options co. 1990-91, chair com. on career-long edn. for engrs.), Am. Soc. Agrl. Engrs., Am. Water Resources Assn. (Icko Iben award 1989), Am. Soc. Engring. Edn. (pres. elect, chmn., bd. dirs. engring. dean's coun.), Am. Geophys. Union, Univ. Coun. on Water Resources, Ariz. Soc. Profl. Engrs. (Engr. of Yr. award 1990), Sigma Xi, Phi Kappa Phi, Tau Beta Pi, Pi Mu Epsilon. Avocations: hiking, golf, scuba diving, painting. Office: University of Arizona Engineering Experiment Sta Tucson AZ 85721

SMERNOFF, RICHARD LOUIS, oil company executive; b. N.Y.C., July 26, 1941; s. George Stephen and Anna Theresa (Dutoit) S.; m. Agnes Elizabeth Neubauer, Sept. 27, 1969; children—Richard Louis Jr., Christopher Max. B.B.A., CCNY, 1966. CPA, N.Y. Asst. to controller F. Levy Levy & Co., N.Y.C., 1967-70; audit supr. Coopers & Lybrand, N.Y.C., 1970-74; dir. fin. controls Internat. Paper Co., N.Y.C., 1974-78; sr. v.p. Amerada Hess Corp., Woodbridge, N.J., 1978-91; pres. Am. Ultramar, Tarrytown, N.Y., 1991-92; fin. officer Datascope Corp., Montvale, N.J., 1992-94; fin. dir. Lasmo Plc, London, 1994—. Mem. AICPA. Republican. Roman Catholic. Avocations: golf, fishing. Home: 3 Trevor Sq Knightsbridge, London SW7 1DT, England Office: 100 Liverpool St, London EC2M 2BB, England

SMETHERAM, HERBERT EDWIN, government official; b. Seattle, Sept. 9, 1934; s. Francis Edwin and Grace Elizabeth (Warner) S.; m. Beverly Joan Heckert, Sept. 7, 1963; children: Alice, Helen, Charles. BA, U. Wash., 1956; diploma, Naval Intelligence Sch., 1962; MA, U. Md., 1971; diploma in Swedish, U.S. Fgn. Svc. Inst., 1978; MBA, Rollins Coll., 1991. Ensign USN, 1956, advanced through grades to capt., 1976; comdr. USS Lind (DD-703), 1971-73; attache to Sweden USN, Stockholm, 1978-81; comdr. Naval Adminstrn. Command, Orlando, Fla., 1981-84; ret. USN, 1984; strategic planner electronics, info. and missiles group Martin Marietta Corp., Orlando, 1985-93; exec. dir. re-use com. Naval Tng. Ctr., Orlando, 1993—, mem. retention com., 1991-93. Mem. ARC Ctrl. Fla.; mem. steering com. U.S. Congressman McCollum for Re-election; mem. U.S. Senator Hawkins Naval Acad. Nominating Com., Orlando, 1982-86, Fla. Gov.'s Def. Reinvestment Task Force, 1992-93; mem. Ctrl. Fla. coun. USO, Orlando, 1981-93, pres., 1991-93. Decorated Royal Order of North Star (Sweden). Mem. AIAA, SAR, Electronics Industry Assn. (requirements com. 1985-93), Nat. Assn. Installation Developers (southeast regional dir. 1996—, treas. 1996—), Ret. Officers Assn., Navy League, Fla. Tennis Assn., Army Navy Country Club, Orlando Tennis Ctr., Royal Tennis Club Stockholm, Delta Kappa Epsilon. Republican. Episcopalian. Avocation: tennis. Home: 3985 Lake Mira Dr Orlando FL 32817-1643

SMETHURST, E(DWARD) WILLIAM, JR., brokerage house executive; b. Newark, Apr. 15, 1930; s. Edward William and Helen Lea (Wiener) S.; m. Ludlow Bixby, June 30, 953; children: James, Andrew, Katherine. AB, Amherst Coll., 1952; MBA, Harvard U., 1958. Credit analyst Chase Manhattan Bank, N.Y.C., 1958-60; mgr. securities Irwin Mgmt. Co., Columbus, Ind., 1961-64; ptnr. Wertheim & Co., N.Y.C., 1965-79; sr. v.p. Cyrus J. Lawrence Inc., N.Y.C., 1980-87; mng. dir. Wertheim Schroder & Co. Inc., N.Y.C., 1988-95; pres., chief investment officer Schroder Wertheim Investment Svcs., N.Y.C., 1990-96; chmn., trustee Wertheim Series Trust, N.Y.C.; retired, 1996; chmn. Ctr. Redevel. Corp., South Hadley, Mass., 1988—. Trustee Mount Holyoke Coll., South Hadley, Mass., 1982—. Lt. USN, 1952-55. Episcopalian. Home: 861 Bingham Rd Ridgewood NJ 07450-2111 Office: Wertheim Schroder & Co Inc 787 7th Ave New York NY 10019-6018

SMETHURST, ROBERT GUY, retired lawyer; b. Calgary, Alta., Can., May 28, 1929; s. Herbert Guy and Muriel (Wilson) S.; m. Carol Ann Higgins; children from previous marriage: Linda Anne, David Guy. Student, U. B.C., 1946-47; LL.B., U. Man., 1952. Bar: Man. 1953, created Queen's counsel 1968. Practice in Winnipeg, 1954-87; partner firm D'Arcy and Deacon (formerly D'Arcy, Irving, Haig & Smethurst), 1965-87; exec. dir. B.C. br. Can. Bar Assn., 1987—; commr. Uniform Law Conf., 1964-86, pres., 1978-79; counsel Man. Pub. Utility Bd., 1968-69; Mem. Man. Law Reform Com., 1971-80; pres. Victorian Order Nurses Can., 1976-79. Mem. Can. Bar Assn. (pres. Man. br. 1971-73), Man. Bar Assn. (pres. 1969-70), Can. Bar Ins. Assn. (pres. 1983-85), Phi Delta Theta. Office: 845 Cambie St 10th flr, Vancouver, BC Canada V6B 5T3

SMIACH, DEBORAH, accountant, educator, consultant; b. Johnstown, Pa., Mar. 10, 1960; d. Frank Raymond and Pearl Lillian (Rudeck) S. BA in Acctg., U. Pitts., Johnstown, 1982; MBA, Katz Grad. Sch. Bus., Pitts., 1989, M of Info. Systems, 1991. CPA Pa., CGFM Va. Staff acct. C.E. Wessel & Co., Johnstown, Pa., 1982-84; sr. acct. Sickler, Reilly & Co., Altoona, Pa., 1984-86; assoc. prof. acctg. U. Pitts., Johnstown, 1986—, chmn. dept. bus., 1995—; cons. Cambria-Somerset Coun. for Health Profls., Johnstown, 1986—; internal inspector Walter Hopkins & Co., Clearfield, Pa., 1995, Wessel & Co., Johnstown, 1992—. Mem. bd. dirs. Bottleworks Ethnic Arts Ctr., Johnstown, Pa., 1993—, Am. Red Cross-Keystone chpt., 1995—; coun. mem. Our Lady of Mount Carmel, South Fork, Pa., 1993-95. Mem. AICPA, Pa. Inst. Cert. Pub. Accts., Pa. Bus. and Profl. Women (dist. 5 chair public relations com. 1993-95, chair woman of the yr. com. 1995-96, chair issues mgmt. 1996-97), Johnstown Bus. and Profl. Women (pres., pres-elect, v.p., treas.). Democrat. Roman Catholic. Avocations: exercising, baking, reading, crafts. Office: U Pitts Johnstown 104 Krebs Hall Johnstown PA 15904

SMIDDY, JOSEPH CHARLES, retired college chancellor; b. Jellico, Tenn., June 20, 1920; s. Joseph F. and Sara Nan (Tye) S.; m. Reba Graham, Sept. 6, 1985; children—Joseph F., Elizabeth Lee. BA, Lincoln Meml. U., 1948, LHD, 1970; MA, Peabody Coll., 1952; LLD, U. Richmond, 1975; LHD, Coll. William and Mary, 1986; DAm, Cumberland Coll., 1993. Tchr. Jonesville High Sch., 1948-51, prin., 1951-52; sec.-treas. Powell Valley Oil Co., Big Stone Gap, Va., 1952-53; prof. biology Clinch Valley Coll., U. Va., Wise, 1953-56; dean Clinch Valley Coll., U. Va., 1956-57, dir., 1957-68, chancellor, 1968-85, chancellor emeritus, 1985—; mem. Charter Day Award Emory and Henry Coll., 1980, Commonwealth Day awrd James Madison U., 1985. Folk music performer, collector and composer. Trustee Bapt. Sem. at Richmond, Va., William King Regional Arts Ctr. Served with AUS, 1942-45, PTO. Recipient Laurel Leaves award Appalachian Consortium, 1995, Kanto Ednl. award Wise County, 1995. Mem. Baptist Gen. Assn. Va. (pres. 1974—). Clubs: Masons, Shriners, Kiwanis. Home: Ridgefield Acres Wise VA 24293 Office: PO Box 3160 Wise VA 24293-3160

SMIETANA, WALTER, educational research director; b. New Bedford, Mass., Nov. 8, 1922; s. Stanislaw and Frances (Wojtal) S. AB in Edn., U. Mich., 1948; MS, Boston U., 1956, EdD, 1965; ScD (hon.), U. Mass., Dartmouth, 1975. Cert. tchr., Mich. Tchr. sci. and math. Somerset (Mass.) Pub. Schs., 1948-65; prof. edn. Elmhurst (Ill.) Coll., 1965-69; prof. edn. Alliance Coll., Cambridge Springs, Pa., 1969-87, chmn. divsn. social sci., pres., 1971-72; dir. rsch. SYLLAGENES, New Bedford, 1987—; liaison Study of Undergrad. Experience in Am., Carnegie Found. for Advancement of Teaching, Alliance Coll., 1984; participant Pa. Dept. Edn. ETS, Tchr. Cert. Test Devel., 1986-87; develop and accredite new tchr. edn. programs, state, regional and nat. levels, 1965-87; develop and evaluate year abroad and exch. programs Alliance Coll./Jagiellonian U., Cracow, Poland in coop. with U.S. Office Edn., 1969-85. Chmn. city com. Rep. Party, New Bedford, 1953-58; mem. citizens adv. com. Heritage State Park, New Bedford, 1989-93; chmn. bd. trustees Inst. Tech., New Bedford, 1963-64; chmn. adv. com. The Rsch. Found., New Bedford, 1962-64. Recipient Cert. of Merit for non-English Lang. Resources Rsch., Yeshiva U., 1981; U.S. Office Edn./ERIC grantee, 1969. Mem. World Future Soc., Inst. for Global Ethics, Nat. Space Soc., Inst. Noetic Scis., Libr. of Congress Assocs. (charter mem.). Republican. Roman Catholic. Avocations: astronomy, photography.

SMILES, RONALD, management educator; b. Sunderland, Eng., June 15, 1933; s. Andrew and Margaret (Turns) S.; m. Evelyn Lorraine Webster, Apr. 12, 1959 (div. June 1981); children: Tracy Lynn, Scott Webster, Wendy Louise; m. Linda Janet Miller, June 23, 1990. Assoc. in Bus. Adminstrn., U. Pa., 1968; BSBA, Phila. Coll. Textiles & Sci., 1969; PhD, Calif. Western U., 1977; MA, U. Tex., Arlington, 1985, PhD, 1987. V.p. Liquid Dynamics Corp., Southampton, Pa., 1968-71; pres., gen. mgr. Internat. Election Systems Corp., Burlington, N.J., 1971-76; plant mgr. Rack Engring. Co., Connellsville, Pa., 1977-80; v.p. Ft. Worth (Tex.) Houdaille, 1980-85; chmn. grad. sch. bus. Dallas Bapt. U., 1987-92, prof., 1987—, assoc. dean Coll. Bus., 1996—. Author: Impact on Legislation of Competition in the Voting Machine Industry, 1978, A Study of Japanese Targeting Practices and U.S. Machine Tool Industry Responses, 1985, Occupational Accident Statistics: An Evaluation of Injury and Illness Incidence Rates, 1987. Mem. Burlington County (N.J.) Selective Svc. Bd., 1974-76. Served with Royal Arty., 1951-53. Mem. Greater Connellsville C. of C. (v.p. 1979-80), Night Watch Honor Soc., Sigma Kappa Phi, Alpha Delta Epsilon (award 1968). Home: 2818 Timber Hill Dr Grapevine TX 76051-6432 Office: Dallas Bapt Univ Off Dean Coll Bus Dallas TX 75211

SMILEY, FREDERICK MELVIN, education educator, consultant; b. Yuba City, Calif., Apr. 13, 1943; s. Lester Boomer and Claire Leone (DeChesne) S. AA, Yuba Coll., 1963; BA, Chico State U., 1966; MA in Edn., Chapman Coll., 1973, MA in English, 1978, MA in Spl. Edn., 1982; PhD, U. Santa Barbara, 1982; EdD, Okla. State U., 1992. Tchr., coach, v.p. McDermitt (Nev.) High Sch., 1978-80; resource specialist Eagle Mt. (Calif.) High Sch., 1980-81; instr. spl. edn. Mary Stone Sch., San Mateo, Calif., 1981-86; dept. leader Quaezar Corp., Bridgeport, Conn., 1986-87; cons., researcher Multi-functional Resource Ctr., Stillwater and Norman, Okla., 1988-91; asst. prof. edn. Cameron U., Lawton, Okla., 1991—. Contbr. articles to profl. jours.; contbg. editor Think!, The Writing Teacher. Mary Aaron scholar Mary Aaron Trust, Marysville, Calif., Blue Key scholar Chico State U.. Mem. TESOL, Coun. for Exceptional Children, AAUP, Am. Assn. for Teaching and Curriculum, ASCD, Okla. Assn. Tchr. Educators, Soc. Educators and Scholars, Kappa Delta Pi, Phi Delta Kappa. Democrat. Lutheran. Avocations: reading, writing, racing, tennis, golf. Office: Cameron U 2800 W Gore Blvd Lawton OK 73505-6320

SMILEY, JANE GRAVES, author, educator; b. L.A., Sept. 26, 1949; d. James La Verne and Frances Nuelle (Graves) S.; m. John Whiston, Sept. 4, 1970 (div.); m. William Silag, May 1, 1978 (div.); children: Phoebe Silag, Lucy Silag; m. Stephen Mark Mortensen, July 25, 1987; 1 child, Axel James Mortensen. BA, Vassar Coll., 1971; MFA, U. Iowa, 1976, MA, 1978, PhD, 1978. Asst. prof. Iowa State U., Ames, 1981-84, assoc. prof., 1984-89, prof., 1989-90, Disting. prof., 1992—; vis. asst. prof. U. Iowa, Iowa City, 1981, 87. Author: (fiction) Barn Blind, 1980, At Paradise Gate, 1981 (Friends of American Writers prize 1981), Duplicate Keys, 1984, The Age of Grief, 1987 (Nat. Book Critics Cirle award nomination 1987), The Greenlanders, 1988, Ordinary Love and Goodwill, 1989, A Thousand Acres, 1991 (Pulitzer Prize for fiction 1992, Nat. Book Critics Cirle award 1992, Midland Authors award 1992, Amb. award 1992, Heartland prize 1992), Moo: A Novel, 1995; (non-fiction) Catskill Crafts: Artisans of the Catskill Mountains, 1987. Grantee Fulbright U.S. Govt., Iceland, 1976-77, NEA, 1978, 87; recipient O. Henry award, 1982, 85, 88. Mem. Author's Guild, Screenwriters Guild. Avocations: cooking, swimming, playing piano, quilting. Office: Iowa State U Dept English 201 Ross Ames IA 50011-1401*

SMILEY, LOGAN HENRY, journalist, public concern consultant; b. Atlanta, Feb. 1, 1926; s. Logan Smiley and Gladys (McCullum) Butcher. BA in Cinema, U. So. Calif., 1950; MS in Journalism, U. Calif., L.A., 1953. Pub. rels. dir. L.A. Open Golf Tournament, 1953-54; producer, dir., co-founder Bishop's Co., Westwood, Calif., 1953-55; producer ABC-TV, Hollywood, Calif., 1957-58; asst. producer Marlon Brando Prodns., Paramount Pictures, Hollywood, Calif., 1957-58, Paris, 1959-60; cons. L.A. C. of C., 1953-56, United Artists Corp., L.A., 1958-60, Russell Birdwell, Pub. Rels., N.Y.C. and London, 1960-64; pres. Pub. Concern Films, Ft. Lauderdale, Fla., 1990—, Nat. Comm. Assocs., Miami, also Jalapa, Mex., 1948—. Writer, columnist San Antonio Light, 1948-50; editor Art Direction Mag., 1968-70, Group Travel Mag., 1970-71; editor, assoc. pub. CLIO Mag., 1968-74, Musical Am. Mag., 1964-66; editor, designer New Spirit Mag. of Social Svc., 1978-80. Mem. Fla. press corps Jimmy Carter for Pres., Atlanta, 1976; chmn. So. Fla. Jerry Brown for Pres., Miami, 1992. With USNR, 1943-45. Recipient Barnett Peace prize Southwestern U., 1944, scholarship S.W. State Tchrs. Coll., 1943, 1st place award Tex. Secondary Sch. System, 1943. Democrat. Avocations: art and book collector, journal/diary writing. Home: 18301 NE 11th Ave Miami FL 33179-4606 Office: Nat Comms Assn PO Box 630715 Miami FL 33163

SMILEY, MARILYNN JEAN, musicologist; b. Columbia City, Ind., June 5, 1932; d. Orla Raymond and Mary Jane (Bailey) S. BS (State scholar), Ball State U., 1954; MusM, Northwestern U., 1958; cert., Ecoles d'Art Americaines, Fontainebleau, France, 1959; Ph.D. (Grad. scholar, Delta Kappa Gamma scholar), U. Ill., 1970. Public sch. music tchr. Logansport, Ind., 1954-61; faculty music dept. SUNY-Oswego, 1961—, Disting. Teaching prof., 1974—, chmn. dept., 1976-81; presenter papers at confs. Contbr. articles to profl. jours. Bd. dirs. Oswego Opera Theatre, 1978—, Oswego Orch. Soc., 1978—, Penfield Libr. Assocs., 1985—. Recipient Chancellor's award for Excellence in Tchg., 1973, SUNY Rsch. Found. fellow, summers 1971, 72, 74. Mem. AAUW (br. coun. rep. dist. III, N.Y. State div. 1986-88, br. coun. coord. N.Y. State div. 1988-90, pres. Oswego br. 1984-86, N.Y. divsn. area interest rep. cultural interests 1990-92, grantee 1984, N.Y. divsn. diversity dir. 1993-96), NEH (rsch. grantee 1990-91), Am. Musicological Soc. (chmn. N.Y. chpt. 1975-77, chpt. rep. to AMS Coun. 1993-96, bd. dirs. N.Y. State-St. Lawrence chpt. 1993-96), Medieval Acad. Am., Music Libr. Assn., Coll. Music Soc., Renaissance Soc. Am., Sonneck Soc. Am., Oswego County Hist. Soc., Heritage Found. of Oswego, Delta Kappa Gamma, Phi Delta Kappa, Delta Phi Alpha, Pi Kappa Lambda, Sigma Alpha Iota, Sigma Tau Delta, Kappa Delta Pi, Phi Kappa Phi. Methodist. Office: SUNY Dept Music Oswego NY 13126

SMILEY, RICHARD WAYNE, research center administrator, researcher; b. Paso Robles, Calif., Aug. 17, 1943; s. Cecil Wallace and Elenore Louise (Hamm) S.; m. Marilyn Lois Wenning, June 24, 1967; 1 child, Shawn Elizabeth. BSc in Soil Sci., Calif. State Poly. U., San Luis Obispo, 1965; MSc in Soils, Wash. State U., 1969, PhD in Plant Pathology, 1972. Asst. soil scientist Agrl. Rsch. Svc., USDA, Pullman, Wash., 1966-69; rsch. asst. dept. plant pathology Wash. State U., Pullman, 1969-72; soil microbiologist Commonwealth Sci. and Indsl. Rsch. Orgn., Adelaide, Australia, 1972-73; rsch. assoc. dept. plant pathology Cornell U., Ithaca, N.Y., 1973-74, asst. prof., 1975-80, assoc. prof., 1980-85; supt. Columbia Basin Agr. Rsch. Ctr., prof. Oreg. State U., Pendleton, 1985—; vis. scientist Plant Rsch. Inst., Victoria Dept. Agr., Melbourne, Australia, 1982-83. Author: Compendium of Turfgrass Diseases, 1983, 2d edit., 1992; contbr. more than 200 articles to profl. jours.; author slide set illustrating diseases of turfgrasses. Postdoctoral fellow NATO, 1972. Fellow Am. Phytopath. Soc. (sr. editor APS Press 1984-87, editor-in-chief 1987-91); mem. Am. Soc. Agronomy, Internat. Turfgrass Soc., Am. Sod Producers Assn. (hon. life), Coun. Agrl. Sci. and Tech., Rotary (pres. Pendleton chpt. 1991-92, Paul Harris fellow 1993). Achievements include discovery of the etiology of a serious disease of turfgrasses, which led to a redefinition of studies and disease processes in turfgrasses. Office: Oreg State U Columbia Basin Agr Rsch Ctr PO Box 370 Pendleton OR 97801-0370

SMILEY, ROBERT HERSCHEL, university dean; b. Scottsbluff, Nebr., Mar. 17, 1943; s. Eldridge Herschel and Lucile Agnes (Kolterman) S., m. Sandra P. Mason (div. 1975); children: Peter, Michael, Robin; m. JoAnn Charlene Cannon, June 3, 1978; 1 child, Matthew. BS, UCLA, 1966, MS, 1969; PhD, Stanford U., 1973. Sr. aerospace engr. Martin Marietta Co., Littleton, Colo., 1966-67; mem. tech. staff, engr. Hughes Aircraft Co., Culver City, Calif., 1967-69; prof. econs. and policy, assoc. dean Grad. Sch. Mgmt. Cornell U., Ithaca, N.Y., 1973-89; dean, prof. mgmt. Grad. Sch. Mgmt. U. Calif., Davis, 1989—; econ. cons. IBM, GM, Amex, SBA, Air Transport Assn., others; mem. rsch. adv. bd. NFIB, 1988—, policy adv. com. Ctr. for Coops., Davis, 1989—, adv. bd. Tech. Devel. Ctr., Davis, 1990—. Editor Sinergie, 1984—, Small Bus. Econs., 1988—; mem. editorial bd. Comstock's Mag., 1989—; contbr. articles to econs. and mgmt. jours. Bd. dirs. Sacramento Valley Forum, 1990—, Japan-Am. Conf., Sacramento, 1991—; chair sponsors com. Access '91, Sacramento, 1991; bd. govs. Capitol Club. SBA grantee, DOE grantee. Mem. Am. Econs. Assn., European Assn. for Rsch., Western Econs. Assn., Beta Gamma Sigma, Capitol Club. Avocations: skiing, tennis, swimming, biking. Office: U Calif-Davis AOB4 Dept Grad Sch Mgmt Davis CA 95616-8609

SMILEY, ROBERT WILLIAM, industrial engineer; b. Phila., Oct. 18, 1919; s. Albert James and Laura Emma (Hoiler) S.; children from previous marriage: Robert, James, Lauralee, Mary; m. Gloria Morais, June 30, 1990; stepchildren: Deborah, Sheila, Vicki, James, Sonja, Michelle. Certificate in Indsl. Engring, Gen. Motors Inst., 1942; student, U. Rochester, 1948; student mgmt. program for execs., U. Pitts. Grad. Sch. Bus., 1968; student, San Jose State Coll., 1969; BSBA, Coll. Notre Dame, Belmont, Calif., 1972, MBA, 1974. Registered profl. engr., Calif. With A.S. Hamilton (cons. engrs.), Rochester, N.Y., 1946-48; commd. lt. comdr. USN, 1952, advanced through grades to comdr., 1960; engaged in tech. contract mgmt. (Poseidon/Polaris and Terrier Missile Programs), 1952-64; officer in charge (Polaris Missile Facility Pacific), Bremerton, Wash., 1964-66; resigned, 1966; mgr. product assurance Missile Systems div. Lockheed Missiles and Space Co., Sunnyvale, Calif., 1966-72; mgr. materiel Missile Systems div. Lockheed Missiles and Space Co., 1972-77; mgr. product assurance McDonnell Douglas Astronautics, 1977-78; dir. product assurance Aerojet Tactical Systems, Sacramento, 1978-83; dir. quality assurance Aerojet Solid Propulsion Co., Sacramento, 1984-92, Tahoe Surg. Instruments, Inc., 1992—; frequent guest lectr. at colls. on quality control and reliability; chmn. Polaris/Minuteman/Pershing Missile Nondestruct Test Com., 1958-64; quality control cons. Dragon Missile Program, U.S. Army, 1971. Contbr. articles to sci. jours., chpt. to Reliability Handbook, 1966, Reliability Engineering and Management, 1988. Docent Calif. State Railroad and Mus., 1994—; chmn. sec. chpt. svc. Corps Retired Exec., 1992, dist. mgr., 1995. With USNR, 1942-46, 51-52; now capt. ret. Recipient letters of Commendation for work on Polaris/Poseidon Sec. of Navy, 1960, certificate of Honor Soc. for Nondestructive Testing, 1966. Fellow Am. Soc. Quality Control (chmn. San Francisco sect. 1969-70, exec. bd. 1966—, chmn. reliability divsn. 1971, 81, nat. v.p. 1984-85; mem. SCORE (chmn. Sacramento chpt. 1993-94, dist. mgr. 1996—), Aircraft Industries Assn. (chmn. quality assurance com.), Navy League, AAAS, Am. Mgmt. Assn. Home and Office: 9144 Green Ravine Ln Fair Oaks CA 95628-4110 *A man can consider himself successful only if he leaves the world better than he found it partly through his efforts.*

SMILEY, ROBERT WILLIAM, JR., investment banker; b. Lansing, Mich., Nov. 17, 1943; s. Robert William Sr. and Rebecca Lee (Flint) S. AB in Econs., Stanford U., 1970; postgrad., San Fernando Valley Coll. Law, 1973-75; MBA in Corp. Fin., City U. Los Angeles, 1979; LLB, LaSalle U., 1982. Bar: Calif. 1984. Sr. v.p. mktg. Actuarial Systems Inc., San Jose, Calif., 1972-73; founder, chmn. Benefit Systems Inc., L.A., and SE Nev., 1973-84, Brentwood Square Savs. and Loan, Los Angeles, 1982-84; chmn., CEO The Benefit Capital Cos. Inc., L.A. and S.E. Nev., 1984—; lectr. U. Calif. Extension, Los Angeles and Berkeley, 1977—; instr. Am. Coll. Life Underwriters. Editor, contbg. author: Employee Stock Ownership Plans: Business Planning, Implementation, Law and Taxation, 1989—; contbg. author: The Handbook of Employee Benefits, 1984, 4th edit., 1996; contbr. articles to profl. jours. Mem. nat. adv. coun., trustee Reason Found., L.A., 1983-91; bd. dirs. Nat. Ctr. for Employee Ownership, Oakland, Calif. With USN, 1961-64, Vietnam. Recipient Spl. Achievement award Pres.' Commn. on Pension Policy, 1984. Fellow Life Mgmt. Inst.; mem. Employee Stock Ownership Plan Assn. (founder, pres., bd. dirs., lifetime dir.), Assn. for Corp. Growth, Western and SW Pension Confs., Nat. Assn. Bus. Economists, ABA, Calif. Bar Assn. Office: The Benefit Capital Cos Inc PO Box 542 Logandale NV 89021-0542

SMILIE, JAMES WILLIAM, JR., editor; b. Columbus, Ohio, May 6, 1962; s. James William and Nancy Edgar (Wickert) S.; m. Rebecca Lynne Mathews, Nov. 19, 1988. BA in Journalism, U. Ala., 1984. Entertainment editor Town Talk, Alexandria, 1988—, special projects editor, 1994—. Appeared in (plays) Brighton Beach Memoires, 1988, Arsnic and Old Lace, 1989, The Front Page, 1990. Bd. dirs. United Way Ctrl. La., Alexandria, 1990-96. Mem. La. Press Women (v.p. 1987-89, pres. 1989-91), Lions (bd. dirs. Alexandria chpt. 1994—). Republican. Methodist. Avocations: animation cel collector, coin collector, volleyball, acting. Office: Alexandria Daily Town Talk 1201 3rd St Alexandria LA 71301-8246

SMILLIE, DOUGLAS JAMES, lawyer; b. Glen Ridge, N.J., Aug. 16, 1956; s. James and Nancy (Albright) S.; m. Nancy Marie McKenna, Jan. 27, 1990; children: Sara Grace, Jeffrey Douglas, Heather Patricia. BA in Polit. Sci. cum laude, Muhlenberg Coll., 1978; JD, Villanova U., 1982. Bar: Pa. 1982, U.S. Dist. Ct. (ea. dist.) Pa. 1982, U.S. Ct. Appeals (3d cir.) 1983, N.J. 1984, U.S. Dist. Ct. N.J. 1984, U.S. Dist. Ct. (mid. dist.) Pa. 1995. Assoc. Clark, Ladner, Fortenbaugh & Young, Phila., 1982-90, ptnr., 1991-96; shareholder, chair litigation sect. Fitzpatrick Lentz & Bubba, P.C., Center Valley, Pa., 1996—. Author: When Worlds Collide: The Impact of the Bankruptcy Stay on Environmental Clean-Up Litigation, 1989, The Absolute Priority Rule: Catch 22 for Reorganizing Closely-Held Businesses, 1992; editor (newsletter) Environ. Impact, 1985-96; contbr. articles to profl. jours. Mem. ABA, Nat. Bus. Inst. (seminar spkr. 1991), Am. Bankruptcy Inst. (seminar spkr. 1986), Comml. Law League Am. (bankruptcy and insolvency sect.), Assn. Comml. Fin. Attys., Robert Morris Assocs. (seminar spkr. 1995), N.J. Bar Assn. (bankruptcy sect., environ. law sect.), Phila. Bar Assn. (ea. dist. bankruptcy conf.). Avocation: Second City Troop Rugby Football Club. Office: Fitzpatrick Lentz & Bubba PO Box 219 Saucon Valley Rd at Rt 309 Center Valley PA 18034-0219

SMILLIE, THOMSON JOHN, opera producer; b. Glasgow, Scotland, Sept. 29, 1942; s. John Baird and Mary (Thomson) S.; m. Anne Ivy Pringle, July 14, 1965; children: Jane, Jonathan, Julia, David. MA, Glasgow U., 1963. Dir. pub. rels. Scottish Opera, 1966-78; artistic dir. Wexford Festival, Ireland, 1973-78; gen. mgr. Opera Co., Boston, 1978-80; gen. dir. Ky. Opera, Louisville, 1981—. Contbr. articles to various publs. Avocations: reading, collecting antiques. Home: 4701 Kitty Hawk Way Louisville KY 40207-1752*

SMIRNI, ALLAN DESMOND, lawyer; b. N.Y.C., Aug. 27, 1939; s. Donald W. and Ruby M. (King) S.; m. Barbara Smirni; 1 child, Amie Joy. BA, CUNY, 1960; JD, U. Calif., Berkeley, 1971. Bar: Calif. 1972, U.S. Dist. Ct. (no. dist.) Calif. 1972, U.S. Ct. Appeals (9th cir.) 1972. Assoc. Brobeck, Phleger & Harrison, San Francisco, 1971-74; asst. gen. counsel Envirotech Corp., Menlo Park, Calif., 1975-81; chief counsel sec. Televideo Systems, Inc., Sunnyvale, Calif., 1982-86; v.p., gen. counsel, sec. Memorex Corp., Santa Clara, Calif., 1987-89, Siemens Pyramid Info. Sys., Inc., San Jose, Calif., 1989—. Adv. bd. dirs. Social Advocates for Youth, Cupertino, Calif., 1985—. Capt. USAF, 1961-67. Mem. Am. Corp. Counsel Assn., Am. Soc. Corp. Secs., Charles Houston Bar Assn. Roman Catholic. Avocations: reading, walking, movies, theatre. Home: 1363 Lennox Way Sunnyvale CA 94087-3129 Office: Pyramid Tech Corp 3860 N 1st St San Jose CA 95134-1702

SMISKO, NICHOLAS RICHARD, bishop, educator; b. Perth Amboy, N.J., Feb. 23, 1936; s. Andrew and Anna (Totin) S. BTh, Christ the Saviour Sem., 1959; BA, U. Youngstown, 1961; Lic. in Theology, Halki (Greece) Sch. Theology, 1965. Ordained priest Carpatho-Russian Orthodox Greek Cath. Ch., 1959. Pastorate Sts. Peter and Paul Ch., Windber, Pa., 1959-62; prefect of discipline Christ the Saviour Sem., Johnstown, Pa., 1963-65; pastor Sts. Peter and Paul Ch., Homer City, Pa., 1965-71, St. Michael's Ch., Clymer, Pa., 1971-72; pastorate St. Nicholas Ch., N.Y.C., 1972-77; abbot Monastery of the Annunciation, Tuxedo Park, N.Y., 1978-83; bishop of Amissos Carpatho-Russian Orthodox Diocese, 1983—; mem. del. Ecumenical Patriarchate World Coun. Chs. 6th Gen. Assembly, Vancouver, B.C., Can.; mem. standing conf. Canonical Orthodox Bishops in Ams.; active Orthodox-Cath. Consultation of Hierarchs. Mem. Halki Alumni Assn. Am., Christ the Saviour Sem. Alumni Assn., Am. Soc. Constantinople. Home and Office: 312 Garfield St Johnstown PA 15906

SMISKO, RICHARD G. See NICHOLAS

SMIT, HANS, law educator, academic administrator, lawyer; b. Amsterdam, Netherlands, Aug. 13, 1927; came to U.S. 1952; s. Eylard Albertus and Trijntje (de Jong) S.; m. Beverly M. Gershgol, Aug. 1, 1954; children: Robert Hugh, Marion Tina. LLB with highest honors, U. Amsterdam, 1946, JD with highest honors, 1949; AM, Columbia U., 1953, LLB with highest honors, 1958; D. (hon.), U. Paris I, 1991. Bar: Supreme Ct. Netherlands 1946, N.Y. 1974. Ptnr. Bodenhausen, Blackstone, Rueb, Bloemsma & Smit, The Hague, 1952-58; assoc. Sullivan & Cromwell, N.Y.C., 1958-60; mem. faculty law Columbia U., N.Y.C., 1960—, assoc. prof., 1960-62, prof., 1962—, Stanley H. Fuld prof. law, 1978—; dir. Parker Sch. Fgn. and Comparative Law; vis. prof. U. Paris, Sorbonne-Pantheon, 1975-76, 89-90, 92-94; dir. Project on Internat. Proc., Columbia U.; reporter U.S. Com. on Internat. Rules Jud. Procedure, 1960-67; bd. dirs. Project on European Legal Inst., 1968, Leyden-Amsterdam-Columbia Summer Program in Am. Law; cons. internat. comml. transactions, internat. litig.; arbitrator ICC and AAA. Author: International Co-operation in Litigation, 1963, (with others) Elements of Civil Procedure, 5th edit., 1985, International Law, 3d edit., 1993, (with Pechota) World Arbitration Reporter, 1986, (with Herzog) The Law of the European Economic Community, 1978; editor-in-chief Am. Rev. of Internat. Arbitration. Mem. All-Dutch Waterpolo team 1946-48, All-Am. Waterpolo team, AAU, 1954. Knight Order of Netherlands Lion, 1987. Mem. ABA, Internat. Bar Assn., Am. Fgn. Law Assn., Assn. of Bar of City of N.Y., Am. Soc. Internat. Law, German-Am. Lawyers' Assn., Internat. Assn. Jurists of U.S.A.-Italy, Internat. Acad. Comparative Law, Royal Dutch Soc. Arts and Scis. (assoc.), Am. Arbitration Assn., Internat. C. of C. Home: 351 Riverside Dr New York NY 10025-2739 Office: Columbia U Sch Law 435 W 116th St New York NY 10027-7201

SMITH, A. ROBERT, editor, author; b. York, Pa., Feb. 13, 1925; s. Arthur R. and Inez (Dunnick) S.; m. Yvonne Franklin, 1945 (div. 1965); 1 child, Dana C.; m. Elizabeth McDowell Morgan, 1967 (div. 1988); children: Philip S. Morgan IV, Edward A. M. Morgan, Elizabeth A. Morgan; m. Jane Dreifus, 1993. BS, Juniata Coll., 1950; postgrad., George Washington U., 1950. Reporter Huntingdon (Pa.) Daily News, 1947, Evening Star, Washington, 1950; Washington corr. Eugene (Oreg.) Register-Guard, 1951-78, Portland Oregonian, 1952-72, King Broadcasting, 1976-78; assoc. editor Virginian-Pilot, Norfolk, 1978-83; editor Venture Inward, Assn. Rsch. and Enlightenment mag., Virginia Beach, Va., 1984—. Author: The Tiger in the Senate, 1962, Hugh Lynn Cayce: About My Father's Business, 1988; co-author: (with Eric Sevareid and Fred J. Maroon) Washington: Magnificent Capital, 1965, (with James V. Giles) An American Rape, 1975. With USNR, 1943-46, PTO. Office: ARE 67th And Atlantic Ave Virginia Beach VA 23451

SMITH, AARON, health researcher, clinical psychologist; b. Boston, Nov. 3, 1930; s. Harry and Anne (Gilgoff) S.; m. Sept. 7, 1952 (div.); children—Naomi E., Jeffrey O., David G., Andrew H.; m. D. Sharon Casey, Jan. 7, 1972. A.B., Brown U., 1952; Ph.D., U. Ill., 1958. Co-dir., Northeast Psychol. Clinic, Phila., 1959-75; dir. research Haverford State Hosp., Pa., 1962-73, asst. hosp. dir., 1973-75; assoc. rsch. prof. U. Nev., Reno, 1975—; dir. rsch VA Med. Ctr., Reno, 1975—; exec. dir. Sierra Biomedical Rsch. Corp., 1989—; chmn. Nev. Legislature Mental Health Task Force, Carson City, 1978; sci. adviser Gov.'s Com. on Radiation Effects, Carson City, 1979-82. Co-author: Anti-depressant Drug Studies 1956-66, 1969; Medications and Emotional Illness, 1976; co-editor: Goal Attainment Sealing: Application, Theory, and Measurement, 1994; contbr. chpts. to books and articles to profl. jours. Grantee Squibb Inst. Med. Research, 1965-69, NIMH, 1965-69, Smith Kline & French Labs., 1968-69, VA Health Services Research, 1976-93. Mem. Am. Psychol. Assn., Western Psychol. Assn., Gerontol. Soc. Am., Assn. Health Svcs. Rsch. Home: 12790 Roseview Ln Reno NV 89511-8671 Office: VA Med Ctr 1000 Locust St Reno NV 89520-0102

SMITH, ADA L., state legislator; b. Amherst County, Va.; d. Thomas and Lillian Smith. Grad., CUNY. Dep. clk. N.Y.C.; state senator N.Y. Legislature, Albany, 1988—; mem. various coms. N.Y. Legislature, ranking corp. commn. and authorities, 1994, minority whip; mem. Senate Dem. Task Force Women's Issues, Senate Dem. Task Force Financing Affordable Housing, Senate Dem. Task Force Child Care 2000, Sen. Dem. Task Force Affirmative Action and Econ. Devel., Senate Dem. Task Force Primary Health Care, Senate Minority Puerto Rican and Hispanic Task Force; chair Senate Minority Task Force on Privatization of Kennedy and Laguardia Airports. Trustee, life dir. Coll. Fund Baruch Coll. Recipient Outstanding Alumni award Baruch Coll. Mem. African Am. Clergy and Elected Ofcls., Inc. (treas.), N.Y. Assn. of State Black and Puerto Rican Legislators (vice chair), Baruch Coll. Alumni Assn. (pres., Disting. Svc. award, Outstanding Achievement award). Office: NY State Senate Rm 304 Legis Office Bldg Albany NY 12247 also: Queens Dist Office 116-43 Sutphin Blvd Jamaica NY 11434

SMITH, ADAM See **GOODMAN, GEORGE JEROME WALDO**

SMITH, ADRIAN DEVAUN, architect; b. Chgo., Aug. 19, 1944; s. Alfred D. and Hazel (Davis) S.; m. Nancy L. Smith, Aug. 17, 1968; children: Katherine, Jason. Student, Tex. A&M U., 1962-66; B.Arch., U. Ill., Chgo., 1969. Registered architect Ill., Ohio, N.J., N.Y., Mass., Iowa, Md., Conn., D.C., Fla., Ind., Mo., R.I., Tex. Design ptnr. Skidmore, Owings, & Merrill, Chgo., 1967—, ptnr., 1980—, CEO, 1994-96; vis. faculty Sch. Architecture, U. Ill., Chgo., 1984; chmn. Senator Richard A. Newhouse Bldg. Competition Jury, 1982, U. Ill. Sch. Archtl. Alumni Assn., AIA Jury on Inst. Honors; chmn. Skidmore Owings Merrill Found., 1990-95; pres., Chgo. Ctrl. Area; recipient U. Ill. Alumni Achievement award. cons. and lectr. in field. Designer numerous projects including Jin Mao Tower (World's Tallest Mixed-Use Project), Shanghai, China, Banco de Occidente, Guatemala City (CCAIA Interior Architecture award 1981, NAIA Honor award 1982), Three 1st Nat. Bank Chgo. (CCAIA Lighting Soc. award 1984), United Gulf Bank, Manama, Bahrain (Progressive Architecture award 1984, CCAIA Disting. Bldg. award 1988, NAIA Honor award 1988, CCAIA Disting. Detail Honor award 1989), 222 N. LaSalle, Chgo. (Disting Bldg. award CCAIA 1988), Art Inst. Chgo. 2d Fl. Galleries (CCAIA Disting. Bldg. award 1987), Rowes Wharf, Boston (Build Am. award 1988, Build Mass. award 1989, ULI award 1989, PCI Profl. Design award 1989, CCAIA Hon. award 1990, Nat. AIA Honor award 1994), AT&T Corp. Ctr., Chgo. (recipient Gold Metal Ill. Ind. Masonry award), NBC Tower (Chgo. Sun Times Bldg. of Yr. award 1989, CCAIA Disting. Bldg. award 1990, PCI Design award 1989), 75 State St., Boston (Archtl. Woodwork Inst. award 1989, Nat. Comml. Builder's Coun. Merit award 1990, Bldg. Stone Inst. Tucker Archtl. award 1990), Arthur Anderson Training Ctr. (Masonry award 1988), St. Charles, Ill., USG Hdqs., Chgo., Heller Internat. Tower, Chgo., State St Revovation designer numerous other fgn. projects including: Monterey Cultural Ctr., Mex., 1978; hdqrs. Banco de Occidente, Guatemala City, 1978 (AIA Nat. Honor award, Bus. Interior Design award Guatemala 1981, CCAIA Interior Architecture award 1982, NAIA Honor award), Canary Wharf Fin. Ctr., London, Eng., 1988, 10 Ludgate (CCAIA 1994 Honor award), 100 Ludgate, London, 1992, Aramco Hdqs. Dhahran Saudi Arabia ; contbr. articles to profl jours.; subject numerous publs. in architecture. Mem. com. Task Force for New City Plan, Chgo., Light Up Chgo., Cen. Area Com. Task Force, Chgo.; chmn. Senator Richard A. Newhouse Bldg. Competition Jury, 1982, Progressive Architecture Design Jury, 1985. Fellow AIA (mem. Young Architects Award Design Jury, 1987, Mich. Jury 1988, Disting. Bldg. award 1990), Royal Inst. Brit. Architects, Archtl. Registration Coun. U.K., Nat. Coun. Archtl. Registration Bds., Architecture Soc. of Art Inst. Chgo., Chgo. Arch. Found. (bd. dirs.), Chgo. Archtl. Club, Urban Land Inst. (bd. dirs.), University Club, Arts Club. Home: 1100 W Summerfield Dr Lake Forest IL 60045-1545 Office: Skidmore Owings & Merrill LLP 224 S Michigan Ave Ste 1000 Chicago IL 60604-2505

SMITH, ALAN JAY, computer science educator, consultant; b. N.Y.C., Apr. 10, 1949; s. Harry and Elsie Smith. SB, MIT, 1971; MS, Stanford (Calif.) U., 1973, PhD in Computer Sci., 1974. From asst. prof. to full prof. U. Calif., Berkeley, 1974—; assoc. editor ACM Trans. on Computers Systems, 1982-93; vice-chmn. elec. engring. & computer sci. dept. U. Calif., Berkeley, 1982-84; nat. lectr. ACM, 1985-86; mem. editorial bd. Jour. Microprocessors and Microsystems, 1988—; subject area editor Jour. Parallel and Distbn. Computing, 1989—; mem. IFIP working group 7.3. Fellow IEEE (disting. visitor 1986-87); mem. Assn. for Computing Machinery (chmn. spl. interest group on computer architecture 1991-93, chmn. spl. interest group on ops. systems 1983-87, bd. dirs. spl. interest group on performance evaluation 1985-89, bd. dirs. spl. interest group on computer architecture 1993—), Computer Measurement Group. Office: U Calif Dept of Computer Sci Berkeley CA 94720

SMITH, ALBERT ALOYSIUS, JR., electrical engineer, consultant; b. Yonkers, N.Y., Dec. 2, 1935; s. Albert Aloysius and Jean Mary (Misiewicz) S.; B.S.E.E., Milw. Sch. Engring., 1961; M.S.E.E., N.Y.U., 1964; m. Rosemarie Torricelli, Apr. 4, 1964 (dec. 1982); children—Denise, Matthew. Staff engr. Adler/Westrex, New Rochelle, N.Y., 1961-64; adv. engr. IBM, Kingston, N.Y., 1964-78, sr. engr., Poughkeepsie, N.Y., 1978-85, Kingston, N.Y., 1985-91; cons., 1991—. Com. chmn. Woodstock Boy Scout Troup 34, 1978-79; com. chmn. Woodstock Cub Pack 34, 1976-78. Served with USN, 1953-56. Recipient Outstanding Alumnus award Milw. Sch. Engring., 1981. Invention Achievement awards IBM, 1979, 90, Div. award, 1981. Fellow IEEE (tech. com. on electromagnetic environments, assoc. editor Trans. on EMC); mem. Am. Nat. Standards Com. Roman Catholic. Author: Coupling of External Electromagnetic Fields to Transmission Lines, 1977; Measuring the Radio Frequency Environment, 1985. Home: 11 Streamside Ter Woodstock NY 12498-1521

SMITH, ALBERT CHARLES, biologist, educator; b. Springfield, Mass., Apr. 5, 1906; s. Henry Joseph and Jeanette Rose (Machol) S.; m. Nina Grönstrand, June 15, 1935; children: Katherine (Mrs. L. J. Campbell), Michael Alexis; m. Emma van Ginneken, Aug. 1, 1966. AB, Columbia U., 1926, PhD, 1933. Asst. curator N.Y. Bot. Garden, 1928-31, asso. curator, 1931-40; curator herbarium Arnold Arboretum of Harvard U., 1940-48; curator div. phanerogams U.S. Nat. Mus., Smithsonian Instn., 1948-56; program dir. systematic biology NSF, 1956-58; dir. Mus. of Natural History, Smithsonian Instn., 1958-62, asst. sec., 1962-63; prof. botany, dir. research U. Hawaii, Honolulu, 1963-65; Gerrit Parmile Wilder prof. botany U. Hawaii, 1965-70, prof. emeritus, 1970—; Ray Ethan Torrey prof. botany U. Mass., Amherst, 1970-76; prof. emeritus U. Mass., 1976—; editorial cons. Nat. Tropical Bot. Garden, Hawaii, 1977-91; bot. expdns., Colombia, Peru, Brazil, Brit. Guiana, Fiji, West Indies, 1926-69; del. Internat. Bot. Congresses, Amsterdam, 1935, Stockholm, 1950; v.p. systematic sect., Montreal, 1959, Internat. Zool. Congress, London, 1958; pres. Am. Soc. Plant Taxonomists, 1955, Bot. Soc. Washington, 1962, Biol. Soc. Washington, 1962-64, Hawaiian Bot. Soc.. 1967. Author: Flora Vitiensis Nova: a New Flora of Fiji, Vol. I, 1979, Vol. II, 1981, Vol. III, 1985, Vol. IV, 1988, Vol. V, 1991, Comprehensive Indices, 1996; also tech. articles; Editor: Brittonia, 1935-40, Jour. Arnold Arboretum, 1941-48, Sargentia, 1942-48, Allertonia, 1977-88; editorial com.: International Code Botanical Nomenclature, 1954-64. Recipient Robert Allerton award for excellence in tropical botany, 1979, Asa Gray award Am. Soc. Plant Taxonomists, 1992, Charles Reed Bishop medal, 1995; Bishop Mus. fellow Yale U., 1933-34, Guggenheim fellow, 1946-47. Fellow Am. Acad. Arts and Scis.; mem. NAS, Bot. Soc. Am. (Merit award 1970), Assn. Tropical Biology (pres. 1967-68), Internat. Assn. Plant Taxonomy (v.p. 1959-64), Fiji Soc. (hon.), Washington Biologists' Field Club (pres. 1962-64). Home: 2474 Aha Aina Pl Honolulu HI 96821-1048

SMITH, ALDO RALSTON, JR., brokerage house executive; b. Yonkers, N.Y., Mar. 19, 1947; s. Aldo Ralston Sr. and Maggie (Allen) S.; m. Linda McKenney Davila, Oct. 15, 1983; children: Damian Allen, Caitlin Victoria McKenney. BA in Psychology summa cum laude, Talladega Coll., 1973; postgrad., CUNY, 1973-76. Account exec. trainee Advest Inc., N.Y.C., 1978-79; account exec. Merrill, Lynch, Pierce, Fenner & Smith, N.Y.C., 1979-80, Lehman Brothers Kuhn Loeb, N.Y.C., 1980-82; fin. cons. Shearson Am. Express, N.Y.C., 1982-84; v.p. instl. mcpl. bond sales A.L. Haven Securities, N.Y.C., 1984; v.p. Prescott Ball & Turben, Inc., N.Y.C., 1984-85; v.p. instl. sales Baird Patrick & Co Inc., N.Y.C., 1985-91, Lincoln Pvt. Bank, 1991—; account exec. North Fork Bank Corp., 1995. Bd. dirs. Hale House for Human Potential, N.Y.C., 1978-80; dist. leader Yonkers Rep. Party, 1985—; mem. Mayor's Citizens Adv. Budget Com., 1993; chmn. Yonkers Police Citizens Profl. Standards Adv. Com., 1992. With U.S. Army, 1967-70. Named Outstanding Young Men of Am. Nat. Jr. C. of C., 1981. Mem. Yonkers Lions Club (bd. dirs. 1985—, pres. 1991-92, zone chmn. 1992-93), Masons, Alpha Chi. Republican. Episcopalian. Avocations: scuba diving, photography, horticulture, cooking. Home: 96 Edgecliff Ter Yonkers NY 10705-1609

SMITH, ALEXANDER GOUDY, physics and astronomy educator; b. Clarksburg, W.Va., Aug. 12, 1919; s. Edgell Ohr and Helen (Reitz) S.; m. Mary Elizabeth Ellsworth, Apr. 19, 1942; children: Alexander G. III, Sally Jean. B.S., Mass. Inst. Tech., 1943; Ph.D., Duke U., 1949. Physicist Mass. Inst. Tech., Radiation Lab., Cambridge, 1943-46; research asst. Duke U., Durham, 1946-48; asst. prof. to prof. physics U. Fla., Gainesville, 1948-61; asst. dean grad. sch. U. Fla., 1961-69, acting dean grad. sch., 1971-73, chmn. dept. astronomy, 1962-71, prof. physics and astronomy, 1956—, Disting. prof., 1981—; dir. U. Fla. Radio Obs., 1956-85, Rosemary Hill Obs., 1989—. Author: (with others) Microwave Magnetrons, 1958, (with T.D. Carr) Radio Exploration of the Planetary System, 1964 (also Swedish, Spanish and Polish edits), Radio Exploration of the Sun, 1966; also numerous articles in field. Fellow AAAS, Optical Soc. Am., Am. Phys. Soc., Royal Micros. Soc.; mem. Am. Astron. Soc. (editor Photo-Bull. 1975-87), Astron. Soc. Pacific, Internat. Astron. Union, Internat. Sci. Radio Union, Fla. Acad. Scis. (treas. 1957-62, pres. 1963-64, medal 1965), Assn. Univs. for Rsch. in Astronomy (dir., cons.), S.E. Univs. Rsch. Assn. (trustee 1981-91), Soc. Photog. Scientists and Engrs., Athenaeum Club (past pres.), Db Racquet Club, Gainesville Country Club, Sigma Xi (nat. lectr. 1968, past pres. Fla. chpt.), Phi Kappa Phi, Sigma Pi Sigma. Republican. Christian Scientist. Home: 1417 NW 17th St Gainesville FL 32605-4014 Office: U Fla Dept Astronomy 211 Space Scis Bldg Gainesville FL 32611

SMITH, ALEXANDER JOHN COURT, insurance executive; b. Glasgow, Scotland, Apr. 13, 1934; s. John Court and Mary Walker (Anderson) S.; m. Margaret Gillespie, Oct. 15, 1968. Student, Scottish schs. Actuarial trainee Scottish Mut. Ins. Co., Glasgow, 1957; asst. actuary Zurich Life Ins. Co., Toronto, Can., 1958-61; from actuary to exec. v.p. William M. Mercer Ltd., Toronto, 1961-74; pres. William M. Mercer, Inc., Toronto, 1974-82; sr. v.p., dir. Marsh & McLennan, Inc., N.Y.C., 1974-78; group v.p. Marsh & McLennan Cos. Cons. and Fin. Svcs. Group, N.Y.C., 1982-84, pres., 1984-85; vice chmn. Marsh & McLennan Cos., N.Y.C., 1984-86, pres., 1986-92, chmn., CEO, 1992—. Trustee The Putnam Funds, 1986—, Cen. Park Conservancy, 1988—, Carnegie Hall Soc., 1992—. Fellow Faculty Actuaries Edinburgh, Can. Inst. Actuaries, Conf. Cons. Actuaries; mem. Soc. Actuaries (assoc.), Am. Acad. Actuaries, Internat. Congress Actuaries, Internat. Assn. Cons. Actuaries, Racquet and Tennis Club, Royal Can. Yacht Club, Apawamis Club, Caledonian Club, Blind Brook Club Inc. Home: 630 Park Ave New York NY 10021-6544 Office: Marsh & McLennan Cos Inc 1166 Avenue Of The Americas New York NY 10036-2708*

SMITH, ALEXANDER WYLY, JR., lawyer; b. Atlanta, June 9, 1923; s. Alexander Wyly and Laura (Payne) S.; m. Betty Rawson Haverty, Aug. 31, 1946; children—Elizabeth Smith Crew, Clarence Haverty, Laura Smith Brown, James Haverty, Edward Kendrick, Anthony Marion, William Rawson. Grad., Marist Sch., 1941; student, Holy Cross Coll., 1941-42; B.B.A., U. Ga., 1947, LL.B. cum laude, 1949. Bar: Ga. 1948. Practiced in Atlanta, 1948—; ptnr. Smith, Gambrell & Russell and predecessor, 1949-94; ret., 1994. Bd. dirs. Our Lady of Perpetual Help Free Cancer Home; bd. dirs., planning and devel. coun. Cath. Archdiocese Atlanta, Marist Sch., Atlanta, John and Mary Franklin Found. Served with USAAF, 1943-46. Mem. Ga. Bar Assn., Atlanta Bar Assn., Phi Delta Phi, Chi Phi, Piedmont Driving Club Atlanta, Peachtree Golf Club Atlanta (pres. 1989-91). Home: 158 W Wesley Rd NW Atlanta GA 30305-3523 Office: 300 Promenade II 1230 Peachtree St NE Atlanta GA 30309-3575

SMITH, ALEXIS, artist, educator; b. L.A., Aug. 24, 1949; d. Dayrel Driver and Lucille Lloyd (Doak) Smith; m. Scott Grieger, June 11, 1990. BA in Art, U. Calif., Irvine, 1970. Teaching position Calif. Inst. Arts, 1975, 96; teaching position U. Calif., Irvine, 1976, San Diego, 1977-78; teaching position UCLA, 1979-82, 85-88, Skowhegan (Maine) Sch. Painting and Sculpture, 1990, So. Meth. U., 1993; vis. artist and lectr. in field. One person exhbns. include Whitney Mus. Am. Art, N.Y.C., 1975, Nicholas Wilder Gallery, L.A., 1977, Holly Solomon Gallery, N.Y.C., 1977, 78, 79, 81, Walker Art Ctr., Mpls., 1986, Bklyn. Mus., 1987-88, Margo Leavin Gallery, L.A., 1982, 85, 88, 90, 93, 94, 95, Retrospective Whitney Mus. Am. Art, N.Y.C., 1991, MOCA, L.A., 1991-92, Gerald Peters Gallery, Dallas, 1995, Wexner Ctr. for the Arts, Columbus, Ohio, 1997; exhibited in group shows at Pasadena (Calif.) Art Mus., Mus. Modern Art, Whitney Mus. Am. Art, Musee d'art Moderne, Paris, Inst. Contemporary Art, Boston, Contemporary Arts Mus., Houston, Hirshhorn Mus. and Sculpture Garden, Washington, Mus. Contemporary Art, Chgo., Los Angeles County Mus. Art, UCLA, Getty Ctr for History of Art and Humanities, Santa Monica, Calif., others; numerous commns. including The Stuart Collection U. Calif., San Diego, slate and concrete pathway, La Jolla, Calif., terrazzo floor designs for L.A. Conv. Ctr. Expansion Project; subject of numerous articles. Mem. artist adv. coun. L.A. Mus. Contemporary Art, 1979-90; trustee Beyond Baroque Lit. Arts Ctr., 1990-95; bd. govs. Skowhegan Sch., 1990-93. Recipient New Talent award Los Angeles County Mus. Art, 1974; Nat. Endowment for the Arts grantee, 1976, 87. Office: Margo Leavin Gallery 812 N Robertson Blvd Los Angeles CA 90069-4929

SMITH, ALFRED GOUD, anthropologist, educator; b. The Hague, Netherlands, Aug. 20, 1921; s. William G. and Joan (Wraslouski) S.; m. Britta Helen Bonazzi, May 30, 1946. A.B. (Simon Mandlebaum scholar, Am. Council Learned Socs. fellow in Oriental Langs.), U. Mich., 1943; postgrad., Princeton U., Yale U., 1943; M.A., U. Wis., 1947, Ph.D., 1956. Far East analyst OSS and Dept. State, Washington, 1944-46; asst., instr. philosophy and anthropology U. Wis., 1946-50; supr. linguistics, Pacific area specialist Trust Ter. Pacific Islands and Dept. Interior, Micronesia and Washington, 1950-53; asst. prof. anthropology Antioch Coll., Yellow Springs, Ohio, 1953-56; asst. prof., asso. prof. anthropology Emory U., Atlanta, 1956-62; asso. prof., prof. anthropology, community service and pub. affairs. U. Oreg., Eugene, 1962-73; dir. Center for Communication Research, U. Tex., Austin, 1973-78; prof. anthropology Ctr. Communication Research Sch. Communication, U. Tex., 1973—; cons. Ga. Dept. Pub. Health, 1956-60, Peace Corps, 1965-69, Job Corps, 1968-70, USIA, 1972-79, 82; U.S. State Dept. specialist, Mex., 1978; cons. on problems of comm. and anthropology to state and fed. agys., industry, museums, instns. of higher learning; staff mem. AID Comm. Seminars, 1966-81; lectr. in field, Eng., Mex., Venezuela, Germany, and Can. Author: Communication and Culture, 1966, Cognitive Styles in Law Schools, 1979; mem. editl. bd. Communication and Info. Scis., Info. and Behavior, Progress in Communication Scis.; contbr. articles to profl. jours., chpts. to books; further reprintings and revs. Served to 1st lt. AUS, 1942-45. Fellow Am. Anthrop. Assn., AAAS; mem. Internat. Communication Assn. (pres. 1973-74, dir.), Sigma Xi, Alpha Kappa Delta, Phi Kappa Phi. Club: Town and Gown. Home: 1801 Lavaca St Austin TX 78701-1304 Office: U Tex Coll Communication Austin TX 78712

SMITH, ALLIE MAITLAND, university dean; b. Lumberton, N.C., June 9, 1934; s. Allie McCoy and Emma Hattie (Wright) S.; m. Sarah Louise Whitlock, June 16, 1957; children: Sara Leianne, Hollis Duval, Meredith Lorren. BME with honors, N.C. State U., Raleigh, 1956, MS, 1961, PhD, 1966. Assoc. engr. Martin Co., Balt., 1956-57; devel. engr. Western Electric Co., 1957-60; mem. tech. staff Bell Tel. Labs., Burlington, N.C., 1960-62; instr., then asst. prof. extension N.C. State U., 1958-62; rsch. project engr. Rsch. Triangle Inst., Durham, N.C., 1962-66; rsch. supr. Sverdrup/ARO, Inc., Arnold Air Force Sta., Tenn., 1966-79; adj. prof. U. Tenn., Tullahoma, 1967-79; prof. mech. engring., dean Sch. Engring. U. Miss., 1979—; bd. dirs., mem. scholarship bd. Miss. Mineral Resources Inst.; exec. chmn. 14th conf. Southeastern Conf. on Theoretical and Applied Mechanics, mem. exec. com. 13th through 16th confs., mem. ops. com. and policy com., 1990—, session chair, 1994; mem. organizing com., internat. sci. adv. bd., plenary session presiding officer Internat. Conf. on Hydrosci. and Engring., 1993, 95; mem. organizing com., plenary session chair Conf. on Mgmt. of Landscapes Disturbed by Channel Incision, 1997. Author: Fundamentals of Silicon Integrated Device Technology, Vol. I: Oxidation, Diffusion and Epitaxy, 1967, also articles, revs.; editor: Radiative Transfer and Thermal Control, 1976, Thermophysics of Spacecraft and Outer Planet Entry Probes, 1977, Fundamentals and Applications of Radiation Heat Transfer, 1987, Developments in Theoretical and Applied Mechanics, Vol. XIV, 1988, Radiation Heat Transfer: Fundamentals and Applications, 1990, Fundamentals of Radiation Heat Transfer, 1991, Radiative Heat Transfer: Theory and Applications, 1993, Solution Methods for Radiative Heat Transfer in Participating Media, 1996. Fellow ASME (mem. aerospace heat transfer com. 1975—), AIAA (chmn. thermophysics tech. com. 1975-77, chmn. terrestrial energy sys. tech. com. 1979-81, chmn. confs. 1975, 79, assoc. editor jour. 1975-77, 86—, mem. nat. publ. com. 1979-83, Nat. Thermophysics award 1978, Hermann Oberth award 1984-85, Space Shuttle Flag Challenger plaque 1984, supernumerary dir. Ala.-Miss. sect. 1994—); mem. AAUP, NSPE (pres. N.E. Miss. chpt. 1990-91), Am. Soc. Engring. Edn. (host Nat. Engring. Deans' Inst. 1991), N.Y. Acad. Scis., Rotary, Sigma Xi, Phi Kappa Phi, Tau Beta Pi, Pi Tau Sigma, Upsilon Pi Epsilon, Sigma Pi (scholar 1955), Order of the Engr., Rotary Club. Achievements include discovery of anomalous refraction maxima phenomenon. Home: PO Box 1857 University MS 38677-1857 Office: U Miss 101 Carrier Hall University MS 38677

SMITH, ALMA DAVIS, elementary education educator; b. Washin[...] June 27, 1951; d. Wyatt Deeble and Martha Elizabeth (Lingenfelter) [...] m. Perry James Smith, Jan. 1, 1979; children: Lauren, Hunter. BS[...] Madison U., 1973; MEd, U. Va., 1978. Cert. elem. tchr. and pri[...] Tchr. Robert E. Lee Elem. Sch., Spotsylvania, Va., 1973-79, C[...] Elem. Sch., Salem, Va., 1979, Hopkins Rd. Elem. Sch., Rich[...] 1980-87; tchr. Reams Rd. Elem. Sch., Richmond, Va., 1987-95[...] summer sch., 1990; tchr. Crestwood Elem. Sch., Richmond, [...] Bd. mem. PTA, 1994-95, life mem., 1995. Mem. NEA, Spo[...] Assn. (numerous chair positions), Chesterfield Edn. Assn.[...] Ellesmere Dr Midlothian VA 23113-3800

SMITH, ALMON R., labor union administrator. [...] Realtors, Chgo. Office: Nat Assn Realtors 430 N Mich[...] 60611-4002*

SMITH, ANDERS DOWNEY, financial services [...] Glen Ridge, N.J., July 5, 1964; s. Steven Lee a[...] strom) S. BA, U. Ill., 1986. CFP. Registered [...] Boston, 1986; telesvcs. rep. MFS, Boston, 198[...] regional mgr. Pacific Northwest Region, 19[...] Northwest Region MFS Fin. Svcs., Inc., Bost[...] mgr. MFS Fund Distbrs., Inc., Boston, 19[...] ternat. Assn. Fin. Planners. Republican. [...] raquetball, biking, scuba diving. Home: 2[...] 02116 Office: MFS Fin Svcs Inc 500 Boy[...]

SMITH, ANDERSON DODD, psyc[...] 1944; s. John Edward and Nancy (D[...] Lexington, Va., 1966; M.A., U. V[...] (Francis DuPont fellow), 1970; m[...] children: Nancy Taylor, Leigh-Ell[...] U. Va., 1966-70; mem. faculty [...] psychology, 1980-86, dir. psyc[...] 1995—; affiliate scientist Yerk[...] U. Assoc. editor: Aging in [...] Gerontology, 1980-86; cont[...] Neighborhood Planning U[...] dirs. Northside Shepard's [...] 1997—; vestryman St. A[...] Retirement, Inc. Recipi[...] Monie Ferst Sustaine[...] 1972—, NIMH, 197[...] and edn. coms., pre[...] mem. Psychonomi[...] lectrs. 1987—), P[...] Dr NW Atlant[...] Atlanta GA 3[...]

SMITH, AN[...] 3, 1947; s. [...] Howard [...] Architect[...] dinator [...] N.Y.C[...] Assn.[...] Assn.[...] Planning [...] Hallmark meda[...]

Nat. Assn. Housing and Redevel. Ofcls. (v.p. N.Y. Met. chpt. 1993-96, exec. v.p. 1996—), Urban Land Inst. (assoc.), Howard U. Alumni Assn. (regional rep. 1978-79, 82-86, pres. L.I. chpt. 1983-85), Sierra Club, Nat. Travel Club. Democrat. Avocations: scuba diving, horseback riding, travel photographing, fundraising, arts and crafts collecting. Home: 84-55 Daniels St Apt 6L Briarwood NY 11435-2014 Office: NYC Planning Commn 22 Reade St New York NY 10007-1216

SMITH, ANDREW JOSEF, historian, publishing executive, naturalist, writer; b. Suffern, N.Y., June 3, 1954; s. Andrew and Anna May (Gannon) S. BA in Integrated Social Scis., Empire State Coll., 1988, BS in Earth and Life Scis., 1995; MS in Environ. Sci., Columbia Pacific U., 1991, MA in History, 1994. Ordained to min. Universal Life Ch., 1979; lic. Nat. Assn. Underwater Instrs., 1980; lic. FCC technician class amateur radio. Sr. dist. forester Palisades Interstate Park Commn., Bear Mountain, N.Y., 1978-92; founder, dir. rsch., curator rsch. libr. Ctr. for Study Natural and Historical Anomalies, Tomkins Cove, N.Y., 1993—; curator of history and mycology Trailside Mus., Bear Mountain, 1992—; publisher Dutch-Way Publ. and Rustic Resources Newsletter, Stony Point, 1995—; pastoral counselor in pvt. practice, 1990—; instr. history and sci. North Rockland Sch. Dist., Thiells, N.Y., 1989—; adj. prof. history and sci. Rockland C.C., Suffern, 1990-91; adj. prof. environ. sci. The Nature Pl. Kennedy-Western U., 1992-93; adj. prof. sci. Empire State Coll., Nyack, N.Y., 1995—; conservation cons. Town of Stony Point, N.Y., 1990-92; vis. scientist North Rockland Sch. Dist., 1992—; vis. historian Rockland C.C., 1991; lectr., leader historic & natural sci. symposiums, hikes, horseback field excursions, 1996—. Author: The Way It Was Up Home, 1995, Exploring the Edible Landscape, 1997; editor: Safe on the Mountain, 1996; monthly column pub. in Beartracks newsletter Trailside Mus., Bear Mountain; sci. columnist Home and Store News, 1993-94; hist. columnist Rockland Rev., 1996—; contbr. articles to profl. jours. and newspapers; photographs exhibited at shows, 1987—; appeared as guest naturalist and historian CBS Today, C-Span, and local cable TV networks. Active preserving historic and natural landmarks, Rockland County, N.Y., 1989—, preserving landmarks in Hudson Valley and Highlands; founder, chmn. Bear Mountain Historic Preservation Alliance; co-founder N.Y. State Park Police underwater search and recovery unit, 1980-92; sci. and history home instructor Mahwah Sch. Dist., 1996—; mem. Orange County Directory of Environ. Educators, Pace Univ. Directory of Environ. Educators, N.Y. 20th Congl. Dist.'s Adv. Coun. on Sci. and Tech., N.Y. 20th Congl. Dist.'s Adv. Coun. on the Environment; founder, curator Mus. of the Hamlets, St. John's in the Wilderness Church, Stony Point, N.Y.; assoc. breeder Shetland Collies, Mary Dell Kennels, Pearl River, N.Y., 1973-74. Recipient Commn. award Palisades Interstate Park Commn., 1986, Cert. of Merit and Appreciation, County of Rockland and N.Y. State Dept. VA, 1996; named to Gallery of Disting. Alumni SUNY Empire State Coll., 1997. Mem. Mensa, Rural Culture Heritage Soc. (founder, dir. 1995—, curator Rsch. Libr. 1995—), Rockland County Hist. Soc., Masons, N.J. Assn. Rifle and Pistol Clubs, German Am. Soc., Rockland County Repeater Assn. Avocations: mycophagy, edible and medicinal plants, early Am. culture, hiking, target shooting. Home: PO Box 27 Tomkins Cove NY 10986 Office: Trailsides Mus Interstate Park Commn Bear Mountain NY 10911

SMITH, ANDREW VAUGHN, telephone company executive; b. Roseburg, Oreg., July 17, 1924; s. Andrew Britt and Ella Mae (Vaughn) S.; m. Dorothy LaVonne Crabtree, Apr. 25, 1943; children: Janet L., James A. B.S. in Elec. Engring, Oreg. State U., 1950. Registered profl. engr., Oreg. With Pacific N.W. Bell Tel. Co., 1951-89; asst. v.p. ops. Pacific N.W. Bell Tel. Co., Seattle, 1965, v.p. ops., 1970-78; v.p., gen. mgr. Pacific N.W. Bell Tel. Co., Portland, Oreg., 1965-70; v.p. ops. Pacific N.W. Bell Tel. Co., 1970-78; pres. Pacific N.W. Bell Tel. Co., Seattle, 1978-88; pres. ops. U.S. West Communications, 1988-89; exec. v.p. U.S. West Inc., 1989; pres. Telephone Pioneers of Am., 1989-90; ret. U.S. West Inc., 1989; bd. dirs. Bell Comms. Rsch., N.J., Horizon House, Seattle, Bellevue Prime Source, U.S. Bancorp. Hon. trustee Oreg. State U. Found.; trustee U. Wash. Grad. Sch. Bus., 1985, chmn. bd. trustees, 1984-85; gen. chmn. United Way of King County, 1980-81; mem. Wash. State Investment Com., Olympia, 1989-92; mem. bd. regents U. Wash., 1989-95; trustee Horizon House, Seattle. With USNR, 1943-46. Mem. Seattle C. of C. (chmn. 1985-86). Mem. Wash. Athletic Club (pres. 1982-83), Seattle Yacht Club, Rainier Club, Overlake Golf and Country Club, Multnomah Club (Portland), Columbia Tower Club (Seattle), Desert Island Country Club (Palm Desert, Calif.), The Palm Springs (Calif.) Club. Episcopalian. Office: 1600 Bell Plz Rm 1802 Seattle WA 98191

SMITH, ANN C., nursing educator; b. Weehawken, N.J., Aug. 11, 1937; d. John Aloysius Smith and Ruth Dorothea-Louise Wiese. Diploma, Bellevue Schs. of Nursing, N.Y.C., 1959; BS, MA, NYU, 1966, 68; MA, New Sch. for Social Rsch., N.Y.C., 1982; MSN, CUNY, 1988. Gerontol. nurse practitioner, N.Y. Prof. Bronx (N.Y.) Community College/CUNY. Capt. USAR Nurse Corp, 1959-63. Mem. ANA, Nat. League Nursing, N.Y. State Nurses Assn., N.Y. State Coalition Nurse Practitioners, Sigma Theta Tau.

SMITH, ANNA DEAVERE, actress, playwright; b. Balt., Sept. 18, 1950; d. Deavere Young and Anna (Young) S. BA, Beaver Coll., Pa., 1971, hon. doctorate; MFA, Am. Conservatory Theatre, 1976; hon. doctorate, U. N.C.; on. degree, Wheelock Coll., 1995, Colgate U., 1997, Sch. Visual Arts, 1997, Vesleyan U., 1997, Northwestern U., 1997, Coll. of the Holy Cross, 1997. nn O'Day Maples prof. arts and drama Stanford U. Playwright, performer e-woman shows On the Road: A Search for American Character, 1983, e, Aye, Aye, I'm Integrated, 1984, Piano, 1991 (Drama-Logue award), s in the Mirrors, 1992 (Obie award 1992, Drama Desk award 1992), ight: Los Angeles 1992 (Obie award, 2 Tony award nominations, Drama s Cir. spl. citation, Outer Critics Cir. award, Drama Desk award, co award, Beverly Hills, Hollywood NAACP theatre awards); writer o for Judith Jamison, performer Hymn, 1993; appeared in (films) Dave, Philadelphia, 1993, The American President, 1995. Named One of of Yr., Glamour mag., 1993; fellow Bunting Inst., Radcliffe Coll.; ellow The MacArthur Found., 1996. Office: 1460 4th St Ste 212 onica CA 90401-3414 also: Stanford Univ Dept of Drama Memorial nford CA 94305 Address: c/o Robert Bookman 9830 Wilshire Blvd Hills CA 90212

ANNA NICOLE, model; b. Mexia, Tex.; 1 child, Daniel; m. J. arshall II, Jun. 27, 1994 (dec.). Model for Guess? jeans. Ap- ms Naked Gun 33 1/3: The Final Insult, 1994, The Hudsucker cover model Playboy, 1992 (Playmate of the Yr. 1994). Office: s 121 Madison Ave New York NY 10016-7033*

NIE LEE NORTHERN, school system administrator; b. 27, 1932; d. Lee Fletcher and Christine (Johnson) Williams; er Williams; m. Louis Northern, Dec. 23, 1956 (dec. 1965); 1 2d Jules Smith, Jan 28, 1967. B.S., Tex. So. U., 1954, M.Ed., 1978, Tex. A & M U., 1988; CSD (hon.) Guadalupe Coll., 8; cert. mid-mgmt., 1959. Tchr. Stone Crest Nursery Sch., 7, Cypress Fairbanks Ind. Sch. Dist. (Tex.), 1957-59, Dist., 1959-75; instructional coordinator, 1975-77, prin., Houston Ind. Sch. Dist., 1990-94; ret. 1994. instr. Nat. ashville; speaker in field. Active Houston YWCA; re- youth coord., pulpit com., St. John Bapt. Ch., 1977—. g Performance award Houston Ind. Sch. Dist., 1974, ert. Appreciation City of Houston, 1986, State of Tex., award Spinal Health Edn., Outstanding Leadership vc. award H.A.S.A., 1994, Elrod Sch. Houston Ind. son Washington Family, 1994, Leadership award St. Dept., Houston, 1994, Women of Distinction award . Task Force, 1994, Black Togetherness award As- ess, 1995, Key to City award, City of Miami, Fla., vc. award H.H.C.R.T.A., 1996, others. Mem. NEA, . Coun. Negro Women, Nat. Coun. Black Edu- n., Houston Tchrs. Assn., Houston Prins. Assn., Tex. Elem. Sch. Tchrs. Assn., Nat. Women of —, reg. dir. 1991—, nat. pres. 1991-95, service 3, bd. dirs. 1995—), Am. Legion Aux., Mamie r, reporter, sec., Outstanding Leadership award (service award 1976-80, Outstanding Educator ard 1994, spl. recognition cert. 1995), Eta Phi Beta (achievement award 1993). Address: 2922 S Peach Hollow Cir Pearland TX 77584-2032

SMITH, APOLLO MILTON OLIN, retired aerodynamics engineer; b. Columbia Mo., July 2, 1911; s. Orsino Cecil and Blanche Alice (Whitaker) S.; m. Elisabeth Caroline Krost, Dec. 5, 1943; children: Tove Anne, Gerard Nicholas, Kathleen Roberta. BS in Mech. Engring., Calif. Inst. Tech., 1936, MS, 1937, MS in Aero. Engring., 1938; DSc (hon.), U. Colo., 1975. Asst. chief aerodynamicist Douglas Aircraft Co., El Segundo, Calif., 1938-42, 1944-48, supr. design rsch., 1948-54; supr. aerodynamic rsch. McDonnell Douglas Corp., Long Beach, Calif., 1954-69; chief engr. Aerojet Engring. Corp., Pasadena, Calif., 1942-44; chief aerodynamics engr. rsch. McDonnell Douglas Corp., Long Beach, 1969-75; adj. prof. UCLA, 1975-80; cons. aerodyn. engr., San Marino, Calif., 1975-86. Author: (with others) Analysis of Turbulent Boundary Layers, 1974, contbr. over 65 tech. papers. Recipient Robert H. Goddard award Am. Rocket Soc., 1954, Engring. Achievement award Douglas Aircraft Co., 1958, Casey Baldwin award Can. Aeros. and Space Inst., 1971, Fluids Engring. award ASME, 1985. Fellow AIAA (hon.); Wright Bros. lectr. 1974); mem. NAE. Home: 2245 Ashbourne Dr San Marino CA 91108-2304

SMITH, ARTHUR, radio and television producer, composer; b. Clinton, S.C., Apr. 1, 1921; s. Clayton Seymour and Viola (Fields) S.; m. Dorothy Byars, Apr. 12, 1941; children: Arthur Reginald, Constance (Mrs. Wiley Brown), Robert Clayton. Grad. high sch. Rec. artist RCA Victor, 1936-38; band leader, composer Sta. WSPA, Spartanburg, S.C., 1938-41, Sta. WBT, Charlotte, N.C., 1941-43; band leader, composer, producer CBS Radio, WBT, WBTV, Charlotte, 1945-70; producer WSOC-TV Cox Broadcasting Co., Charlotte, 1970—; dir. Hardware Mut. Ins. Co., Am. Bank & Trust Co., Meat Centers; pres. Clay Music Corp., Charlotte, 1960-76; owner Arthur Smith Studios, Charlotte, 1961—; v.p. CMH Records, L.A.; founder Arthur Smith King Mackerel Tournament, Myrtle Beach, S.C., 1976, Arthur Smith Kingfish, Dolphin, Wahoo Tournament of the Palm Beaches (Fla.), 1983, Queen City Records, 1997. Prin.: The Arthur Smith Show, 1971-76; composer: numerous compositions, including Guitar Boogie, 1946; also rec. artist: more than 100 albums for MGM, DOT, Monument and Starday, numerous compositions, including Dueling Banjos, 1973 (BMI Song of Year 1973); composer: (with Clay Smith) sound track of film Death Driver, 1975, Dark Sunday, 1976; musical score for Living Legend and Lady Grey-Superstar, 1979; co-host with Clay Smith of syndicated radio show "The Arthur Smith Sportsman Journal". Bd. dirs. Charlotte Sch. of Arts, Am. Heart Assn., Marine Sci. Coun.; trustee, dir. Gardner Webb Coll.; trustrr Boys Home N.C.; founder, chmn. Arthur Smith Bluefish Tournament of N.Y.; chmn. Alzheimer's Assn. Served with USN, 1943-45. Named Bapt. Layman of Yr. Southeastern Sem. Louisville, 1969; named to N.C. Broadcasters Hall of Fame, 1990; recipient Religion Emphasis award Am. Legion, 1971, S.C. Tourism award State of S.C., 1979, Cine Golden Eagle award for film The Hawk and John McNeely, 1980, Lung Assn. award, 1993. Mem. Am. Fedn. Musicians (dir. local 342, pres. local 342 1943-76), AFTRA, Salt Water Anglers Tournament Soc. (founder, chmn. bd.), U.S. Sportsfishing Assn. (chmn. 1985). Democrat. Clubs: Masons, Shriners, Kiwanis, Charlotte City, Red Fez. Home: 7224 Sardis Rd Charlotte NC 28270-6062 Office: Arthur Smith Studios 100 Smithfield Dr Charlotte NC 28270-6543 *To me, success is not a destination - it's a journey. Integrity is not a business principle - it's a matter of right or wrong. Whatever I shall achieve in this world I owe to complete trust in, and commitment to God through Christ, a loving and understanding wife and family and loyal associates.*

SMITH, ARTHUR B(EVERLY), JR., lawyer; b. Abilene, Tex., Sept. 11, 1944; s. Arthur B. and Florence B. (Baker) S.; children: Arthur C., Sarah R. BS, Cornell U., 1966; JD, U. Chgo., 1969. Bar: Ill. 1969, N.Y. 1976. Assoc. Vedder, Price, Kaufman & Kammholz, Chgo., 1969-74; asst. prof. labor law N.Y. State Sch. Indsl. and Labor Rls., Cornell U., 1975-77; ptnr. Vedder, Price, Kaufman & Kammholz, Chgo., 1977-86; founding mem. Murphy, Smith & Polk, Chgo., 1986—; guest. lectr. Northwestern U. Grad. Sch. Mgmt., 1979, Sch. Law, spring 1980; mem. hearing bd. Ill. Atty. Registration and Disciplinary Commn. Recipient award for highest degree of dedication and excellence in teaching N.Y. State Sch. Indsl. and Labor Relations, Cornell U., 1977. Mem. ABA (co-chmn. com. on devel. law under Nat. Labor Relations Act, Sect. Labor Rels. Law 1976-77), N.Y. State Bar Assn., Phi Eta Sigma, Phi Kappa Phi. Presbyterian. Clubs: Chgo. Athletic Assn., Monroe (Chgo.). Author: Employment Discrimination Law Cases and Materials, 4th edit., 1994; Construction Labor Relations, 1984, supplement, 1993; co-editor-in-chief: 1976 Annual Supplement to Morris, The Developing Labor Law, 1977; asst. editor: The Developing Labor Law, 3d edit., 1992; contbr. articles to profl. jours. Office: Murphy Smith & Polk 2 First National Plz Fl 25 Chicago IL 60603

SMITH, ARTHUR JOHN STEWART, physicist, educator; b. Victoria, B.C., Can., June 28, 1938; s. James Stewart and Lillian May (Geernaert) S.; m. Norma Ruth Askeland, May 20, 1966; children: Peter James, Ian Alexander. B.A., U. B.C., 1959, M.Sc., 1961; Ph.D., Princeton U., 1966. Postdoctoral fellow Deutsches Electronen-Synchrotron, Hamburg, W. Germany, 1966-67; mem. faculty dept. physics Princeton U., 1967—, prof., 1978—, Class of 1909 prof., 1992—, assoc. chmn. dept., 1979-83, chmn. dept. physics, 1990—; vis. scientist Brookhaven Nat. Lab., 1967—, Fermilab, 1974—, Superconducting Supercollider Lab., 1990-94. Assoc. editor Phys. Rev. Letters, 1986-89; contbr. articles to profl. jours. Fellow Am. Phys. Soc. (chmn. divsn. of particles and fields 1991). Achievements include research on experimental high-energy particle physics; kaon decays and quark structure of hadrons. Home: 4 Ober Rd Princeton NJ 08540-4918 Office: PO Box 708 Princeton NJ 08544-0708

SMITH, ARTHUR KITTREDGE, JR., academic administrator, political science educator; b. Derry, N.H., Aug. 15, 1937; s. Arthur Kittredge and Rena Belle (Roberts) S.; m. June Mary Dahar, Nov. 28, 1959; children: Arthur, Valerie, Meredith. BS, U.S. Naval Acad., 1959; MA, U. N.H., 1966; PhD, Cornell U., 1970. Vis. prof. El Colegio de Mexico, Mexico City, 1968-69; asst. prof. polit. sci. SUNY-Binghamton, 1970-74, assoc. prof., 1974-84, prof., 1984-88, provost for grad. studies and research, 1976-83, v.p. for adminstrn., 1982-88; prof. govt. and internat. studies U. S.C., Columbia, 1988-91, exec. v.p. for acad. affairs, provost, 1988-90, 91, interim pres., 1990-91; pres., prof. polit. sci. U. Utah, Salt Lake City, 1991-97; chancellor U. Houston Sys., 1997—, pres., prof. polit. sci., 1997—. Author: (with Claude E. Welch, Jr.) Military Role and Rule: Perspectives on Civil-Military Relations, 1975; contbr. articles to profl. jours. Active Am. Stores Co., First Security Corp. Served with USN, 1959-65. Lehman fellow, 1966-69, NDEA fellow, 1969-70. Mem. Am. Polit. Sci. Assn., L.Am. Studies Assn., Inter-Univ. Sem. on Armed Forces and Soc., Am. Coun. on Edn., World Affairs Coun. (pres. Binghamton chpt. 1976-76), Phi Beta Kappa, Pi Sigma Alpha, Omicron Delta Kappa, Phi Delta Kappa, Beta Gamma Sigma, Phi Kappa Phi. Home: 1505 S Boulevard Houston TX 77006 Office: U Houston Sys Office of the Chancellor 1600 Smith St Fl 34 Houston TX 77002-7362

SMITH, ARTHUR LEE, lawyer; b. Davenport, Iowa, Dec. 19, 1941; s. Harry Arthur Smith (dec.) and Ethel (Hoffman) Duerre; m. Georgia Mills, June 12, 1965 (dec. Jan. 1984); m. Jean Bowler, Aug. 4, 1984; children: Juliana, Christopher, Andrew. BA, Augustana Coll., Rock Island, Ill., 1964; MA, Am. U., 1968; JD, Washington U., St. Louis, 1971. Bar: Mo. 1971, D.C. 1983. Telegraph editor Davenport Morning Democrat, 1962-64; ptnr. Peper Martin Jensen Maichel & Hetlage, 1971-95, Husch & Eppenberger, St. Louis, 1995—; arbitrator Nat. Assn. Security Dealers, 1980—, Am. Arbitration Assn., 1980—; mem. Utility Com. Ctr. Pub. Resources. Columnist St. Louis Lawyer. Lt. USN, 1964-68. Mem. ABA, D.C. Bar Assn. (chmn. law practice mgmt. 1990-91), Fed. Energy Bar Assn., Mo. Bar Assn. (chair adminstrv. law com. 1995—, vice-chair ins. programs com. 1981-83, vice-chair antitrust com. 1981-83), P. Buckley Moss Soc. (dir. 1994—), Bar Assn. Met. St. Louis (chmn. law mgmt. com. 1993—, chair internet com. 1996-97, Pres.'s award for Exceptional Svc. 1995), Securities Industry Assn. (legal and compliance div.), Futures Industry Assn. (legal and compliance div.), Fed. Bar Assn., Order of Coif. Home: 1320 Chesterfield Estate Dr Chesterfield MO 63005-4400 Office: Husch & Eppenberger 100 N Broadway Ste 1300 Saint Louis MO 63102-2706

SMITH, BAKER ARMSTRONG, management executive, lawyer; b. Brunswick, Ga., Oct. 3, 1947; s. William Armstrong and Priscilla (Baker) S.; m. Deborah Elizabeth Ellis, Nov. 13, 1982; children: Ellis Armstrong, Elizabeth Anne, Everett Baker, Emery Manning. BS, U.S. Naval Acad., 1969; MBA, Northeastern U., 1975; JD cum laude, Suffolk U., 1977; LLM in Labor, Georgetown U., 1981. Bar: Ga. 1977, D.C. 1978, U.S. Supreme Ct. 1980; cert. turnaround profl., 1994. Commd. ensign U.S. Navy, 1969, advanced through grades to lt., 1974; exec. dir., founder The Center on Nat. Labor Policy, Inc., North Springfield, Va., 1977-81; asst. to sec., dir. labor relations U.S. Dept. HUD, Washington, 1981-83; exec. v.p. U.S. Bus. and Indsl. Council, Nashville, 1983-84; pres. Am. Quality Builders, Inc., Nashville, 1984-86; v.p. Hopeman Bros., Inc., Waynesboro, Va., 1986-88; ptnr. Morris, Anderson, Atlanta, 1988—; sec., founder U.S. Constitutional Rights Legal Def. Fund, Inc., Atlanta, 1983—; trustee Leadership Inst., Springfield, Va., 1978—; dir. Turnaround Mgmt. Assn., 1994—; v.p. Assn. Cert. Turnaround Profls., Boston, 1996—; mem. Coun. for Nat. Policy, Washington, 1981—, Civil Rights Reviewing Authority U.S. Dept. Edn., Washington, 1984-88; transition team leader Office of the Pres.-Elect of the U.S., NLRB, Occupational Safety and Health Review Commn., Fed. Mediation and Conciliation Service, Nat. Mediation Bd., Fed. Labor Relations Authority, Washington, 1980-81; instr. law, faculty sec. No. Va. Law Sch., Alexandria, Va., 1980-83; instr. law D.C. Law Sch., Washington, 1978-80. Contbg. author: Mandate for Leadership, 1981; contbr. articles to profl. jours. Served to lt. USN, 1969-74. Mem. St. George's House, Windsor Castle (assoc.), ABA (Nat. Law Day chmn. 1976-77, Silver Key award 1977), Phila. Soc., U.S. Supreme Ct. Hist. Soc., Federalist Soc., Joseph Story Soc., Beta Gamma Sigma, Phi Delta Phi (pres. 1989-91). Republican. Presbyterian. Club: Capitol Hill (Washington), Piedmont (Winston-Salem). Home: 3360 E Terrell Branch Ct Marietta GA 30067-5164

SMITH, BARBARA ANN, gifted education coordinator; b. Oak Park, Ill., Mar. 20, 1950; d. William J. and Mary T. (Barlow) S. BS in Edn., No. Ill. U., 1971, MS in Edn., 1974, cert. advanced study in edn., 1977, EdD, 1994; EdD, No. Ill. U., 1994. Cert. tchr., adminstr. gifted edn., verification, Ill.; lic. counselor, Ill. Coord. gifted edn. Dist. 45 Elem. Schs., Villa Park, Ill., 1986—, counselor to group on leadership devel., tchr. Author numerous articles on gifted edn., self-esteem enhancers, sch.-bus. partnerships. Mem. AACD, ASCD, NEA (chpt. sec., treas.), ACA, Ill. West Suburban Reading Coun., AAUW (coord. families facing change group), Delta Kappa Gamma (chpt. pres.), Phi Delta Kappa. Office: Sch Dist 45 255 W Vermont St Villa Park IL 60181-1943

SMITH, BARBARA ANNE, healthcare management company consultant; b. N.Y.C., Oct. 10, 1943; d. John Allen and Lelia Maria (De Silva) Santoro; m. Joseph Newton Smith, Feb. 5, 1963 (div. Sept. 1984); children: J. Michael, Robert Lawrence. Student, Oceanside/Carlsbad Coll. Real estate agt. Routh Robbins, Inc., Washington, 1973-75; gen. mgr. Mall Shops, Inc., Kansas City, Kans., 1975-80; regional mgr. FAO Schwarz, N.Y.C., 1980-84; clin. adminstr. North Denver Med. Ctr., Thornton, Colo., 1984-88; adminstrv. dir. Country Side Ambulatory Surgery Ctr., Leesburg, Va., 1989-91; pres. SCS Healthcare Mgmt. Inc., Washington, 1991—; bd. dirs. Franz Carl Weber Internat., Geneva, 1982-84. Pres. Am. Women Chile, 1968; v.p. Oak Park Assn., Kansas City, 1977-78, pres., 1978-79; vol. Visitor Info. and Assn. Reception Ctr. program Smithsonian Instn., Washington. Mem. NAFE, Network Colo., Profl. Bus. Women Assn., Med. Group Mgmt. Assn., Federated Ambulatory Surgery Assn.

SMITH, BARBARA BARNARD, music educator; b. Ventura, Calif., June 10, 1920; d. Fred W. and Grace (Hobson) S. B.A., Pomona Coll., 1942; Mus.M., U. Rochester, 1943, performer's cert., 1944. Mem. faculty piano and theory Eastman Sch. Music, U. Rochester, 1943-49; mem. faculty U. Hawaii, Honolulu, 1949—; assoc. prof. music U. Hawaii, 1953-62, prof., 1962-82, prof. emeritus, 1982—; sr. fellow East-West Center, 1973; lectr., recitals in Hawaiian and Asian music, U.S., Europe and Asia, 1956—; field researcher Asia, 1956, 60, 66, 71, 80, Micronesia, 1963, 70, 87, 88, 90, 91, Solomon Islands, 1976. Author publs. on ethnomusicology. Mem. Internat. Soc. Music Edn., Internat. Musicol. Soc., Am. Musicol. Soc., Soc. Ethnomusicology, Internat. Coun. for Traditional Music, Asia Soc., Am. Mus. Instrument Soc., Coll. Music Soc., Soc. for Asian Music, Music Educators Nat. Conf., Pacific Sci. Assn., Assn. for Chinese Music Rsch., Phi Beta Kappa, Mu Phi Epsilon. Home: 581 Kamoku St Apt 2004 Honolulu HI 96826-5210

SMITH, BARBARA JANE, assistant school superintendent; b. Lyons, N.Y., Aug. 23, 1941; d. George M. and Alice R. (Norris) S. BS in Elem. Edn., SUNY, Oswego, 1963, BS in Secondary English, 1974; MS in Curriculum, Instrn., Supervision, U. Albany, 1981. 5th grade tchr. Newark (N.Y.) Ctrl. Sch. Dist., 1963-68, jr. high English tchr., 1968-71, high sch. English tchr., 1971-84, instrnl. supr. English, 1974-84, staff developer-writing process, 1982-84; elem. prin. Marion (N.Y.) Ctrl. Sch. Dist., 1984-86; dir. instrnl. svcs. Jefferson-Lewis Bd. Coop. Svcs., Watertown, N.Y., 1986-93; asst. supt. for instrn. Oakfield (N.Y.)-Ala. Ctrl. Sch. Dist., 1993-95; dir. instrn. and learning Pioneer Ctrl. Sch. Dist., 1995-96; adj. instr. St. Bonaventure (N.Y.) U., 1996—; dir. secondary reading program North Rose (N.Y.) Ctrl. Sch., summer 1965; curriculum cons. N.Y. State Edn. Dept., Albany, 1968-91; sch. improvement cons. Jefferson-Lewis Bd. of Coop. Svcs., 1986-93, team bldg. cons., 1989—. Author (booklet) Teaching Science Fiction-Fantasy, 1971. Mem. adv. bd. Salvation Army, Watertown, N.Y., 1991-93, Ch. of the Nazarene, Watertown, 1992-93; co-chair edn. divsn. adv. bd. United Way, Botavia, N.Y., 1994—; mem. ch. bd. Nazarene Ch., Arcade, N.Y. Recipient Secondary Educators of Am. award Secondary Educators, 1975. Mem. ASCD, Delta Kappa Gamma (scholarship 1983), Phi Delta Kappa. Democrat. Avocations: travel, folk music, reading, golf. Home: 205 Park St Arcade NY 14009-1501 Office: Pioneer Ctrl Sch Box 579 County Line Rd Yorkshire NY 14173

SMITH, BARBARA JEAN, lawyer; b. Washington, Jan. 9, 1947; d. Harry Wallace and Jean (Fraser) S.; m. Philip R. Chall, July 13, 1991; children: Brian C.S. Brown, Craig F.S. Brown, Amy E. Chall, Carrie A. Chall. BA, Old Dominion Coll., 1968; MBA, Pepperdine U., 1974; JD, Case Western Res. U., 1977. Bar: Ohio 1977. Assoc. Squire, Sanders & Dempsey, Cleve., 1977-88, ptnr., 1988-93; shareholder McDonald, Hopkins, Burke & Haber Co., L.P.A., Cleve., 1993—. Bd. editors Health Law Jour. of Ohio, 1989-95; contbr. articles to health jours. and periodicals. Trustee Urban Community Sch., Cleve., 1984-86. Mem. Ohio Women's Bar Assn. (pres. 1994-95), Cleve. Bar Assn. (trustee 1992-95, chair health law sect. 1991-92, Appreciation award 1989, 91), Nat. Health Lawyers Assn., Am. Acad. Hosp. Attys., Ohio State Bar Assn. (health law com. 1991—), Soc. Ohio Hosp. Attys. Democrat. Mem. United Ch. of Christ. Avocations: reading, hiking. Home: 220 Grey Fox Run Chagrin Falls OH 44022-3398 Office: McDonald Hopkins Burke & Haber 2100 Bank One Ctr 600 Superior Ave E Cleveland OH 44114-2611

SMITH, BARBARA MARTIN, art educator; b. St. Louis, Feb. 3, 1945; d. Charles Landon and Mary Louise (Nolker) Martin; m. Timothy Van Gorder Smith, Nov. 27, 1976; children: Brian Eliot, Marjorie Van Gorder. BA, Lawrence U., 1967; MFA, So. Ill. U., 1975. Cert. tchr., Mo. Art instr. Horton Watkins High Sch., Ladue, Mo., 1968-76; leader Experiment in Internat. Living, Brattleboro, Vt., 1974; art tchr. Michigan City (Ind.) Ctr. for the Arts, 1979-80, Cleve. Mus. of Art, 1981-83; art instr. Villa Duchesne, St. Louis, 1986—; edn. dir. Dunes Art Found., Michigan City, 1979; co-chmn. Internat. Wives Group, Cleve. Coun. on World Affairs, 1982-84; bd. dirs. Webster Groves (Mo.) Sch. Found., 1992. Exhibited in shows at Art Inst. of Chgo., 1979, So. Ill. U. Alumnae Exhibit, 1982, Focus Fiber, Cleve. Mus. of Art, 1982, Nova, Wearable Art, Kuban Gallery, Cleve., 1983, Drawings & Prints, St. Louis Artist's Guild, 1986. Recipient Grad. Fellowship Ann. Grad. award So. Ill. U., 1975; named Artist in Residence/ Artist in Schs. Ind. Arts Commn./NEA, 1978-79; named to Honors Seminar for Advancement of Art Edn., R.I. Sch. of Design, 1988, Mem. Art Edn. Delegation to Japan, 1992. Mem. Nat. Art Edn. Assn., Internat. Soc. for Edn. through Art, St. Louis Art Mus., St. Louis Artist Guild. Home: 135 Jefferson Rd Webster Grv MO 63119-2934 Office: Villa Duchesne Oak Hill Sch 801 S Spoede Rd Des Peres MO 63131-2606

SMITH, BARNARD ELLIOT, management educator; b. Mpls., May 6, 1926; s. Sheldon Strong and Jessie (Gould) S.; m. Betty Lou Strohschein, Aug. 28, 1949; children: Carolyn Louise, Eileen Elizabeth. B.S. in Mech. Engring. with distinction, U. Minn., 1949, M.S., 1950; Ph.D., Stanford U.,

1961; M.A. (hon.), Dartmouth Coll., 1971. Asst. prof. mech. engring. U. N.D., 1950-51; mfg. specialist A.O. Smith Co., Milw., 1951-54; asst. prof. indsl. engring. Oreg. State Coll., 1954-58, Stanford U., 1958-61; asso. prof. mgmt. Sloan Sch. Mgmt., MIT, 1961-68; prof. mgmt. Indian Inst. Mgmt., Calcutta, 1965-68; prof. engring. Thayer Sch. Engring. Dartmouth Coll., 1968-71; dean Stuart Sch. Mgmt. and Finance, Ill. Inst. Tech., 1971-75, prof. mgmt., 1975-80; David M. French disting. prof. mgmt. U. Mich., Flint, 1980-89, emeritus, 1989; pres. Vineyards of the Acad., 1989, The Acad. of Wine of Oreg. Inc., 1993—; cons. in field. Served with USNR, 1944-46. Mem. Phi Tau Sigma, Beta Gamma Sigma. Home: 18200 Highway 238 Grants Pass OR 97527-8631

SMITH, BARRY DAVID, obstetrician-gynecologist, educator; b. Suffern, N.Y., July 3, 1938; s. Alexander N. and Beatrice (Morris) S.; m. Maryann Blair, Oct. 11, 1963; children: Gillian, Adam. AB, Dartmouth Coll., 1959; MD, Cornell U., 1962. Diplomate Am. Bd. Ob-Gyn. Resident in ob-gyn N.Y. Hosp. Cornell U. Med. Ctr., N.Y.C., 1963-67, chief resident, instr., 1967-68; staff obstetrician/gynecologist Mary Hitchcock Meml. Hosp., Hanover, N.H., 1970—; asst. prof. Dartmouth Coll., Hanover, 1970-78, assoc. prof., 1979—; chief sect. ob-gyn. Hitchcock Clinic, 1977-95, bd. govs., 1975-85, bd. dirs., 1980-86; chief sect. ob-gyn. Dartmouth Med. Ctr., 1977—, chmn. dept. ob-gyn., 1992-95, vice chair dept., 1995-97, chair dept., 1997—. Treas., pres. Norwich (Vt.) Recreation and Conservation Council, 1975-77. Served to comdr. USNR. Fellow Am. Coll. Ob-gyn. (v.p. N.H. sect. 1991-94, pres. 1994—, chair N.H. sect. 1994—), Am. Fertility Soc., Am. Soc. Colposcopy. Avocations: skiing, tennis, sailing. Office: Dartmouth Hitchcock Clinic 1 Medical Center Dr Lebanon NH 03756-0001

SMITH, BARRY MERTON, financial planner, consultant; b. Dunedin, Fla., Oct. 18, 1943; s. Ollie Morris and Leila Elizabeth (Crisman) S.; m. Susan Gay Stewart, Aug. 13, 1977; children: Jason, Justin, Joshua. Student, U. Fla., 1961-65, St. Petersburg Jr. Coll., 1963; BS in Agr., U. Fla., 1971; postgrad., U. Ctrl. Fla., 1980-83. CFP. Loan svc. rep. Columbia (S.C.) Bank for Coops., 1972; v.p. Apopka (Fla.) Growers Supply Inc., 1972-78, V-J Growers Supply Inc., Apopka, 1978-81, Estimation, Inc., Timonium, Md., 1981, Benbow Industries, Apopka, 1982; ptnr. Billy H. Wells and Assocs., Sanford, Fla., 1982-85; dist. mgr. The Equitable Life of N.Y., Orlando, Fla., 1982-85; v.p. CFS Securities Corp., Longwood, Fla., 1985-90, pres., CEO, 1991—. Capt. U.S. Army, 1966-70, Vietnam. Mem. Internat. Assn. for Fin. Planners (bd. dirs. ctrl. Fla. chpt. 1989-91), Inst. CFPs, Fla. Foliage Assn. (bd. dirs. 1978, treas. 1979-80, Sertoma Club (v.p. 1978-79). Avocations: jogging, baseball. Office: CFG Securities Corp 2180 State Road 434 W Ste 1150 Longwood FL 32779-5008

SMITH, BARRY SAMUEL, physiatrist; b. Windber, Pa., Jan. 15, 1947. MD, Thomas Jefferson U., 1969. Diplomate Am. Bd. Phys. Medicine and Rehab. Intern Reading (Pa.) Hosp., 1969-70; resident in phys. medicine and rehab. Inst. Phys. Med. Rehab., Louisville, 1970-73; now with Baylor U. Med. Ctr., Dallas, chief in phys. medicine and rehab. Mem. AMA, Am. Acad. Phys. Medicine and Rehab., Am. Congress Rehab. Medicine, Assn. Acad. Physiatrists, Am. Assn. Electrodiagnostic Medicine, Nat. Bd. Med. Examiners (diplomate). Office: Baylor U Med Ctr Dept Phys Medicine and Rehab 3500 Gaston Ave Dallas TX 75246-2017

SMITH, BENJAMIN ERIC, venture capitalist, executive; b. L.A., Mar. 22, 1915; s. Jesse Oliver and Clara Louise (Ferris) S.; m. Donelle Ray, Jan. 6, 1956 (div. 1971); children: Lee Fleming, Deidre Ray Folsom. BA, U. Redlands, 1937; postgrad., Yale U., 1938-39; MA, U. So. Calif., 1940. Mgr. Birch-Smith Storage Co., L.A., 1940-42; div. mgr. Bekins Van & Storage Co., L.A., 1946-50; nat. sales mgr. Meletron Corp., L.A., 1952-56; v.p. Leo G. MacLaughlin Co., Pasadena, Calif., 1956-57; sr. cons. Barry & Co., L.A., 1957-65; pres. Benjamin E. Smith & Assoc., L.A., 1965—, Lancer Pacific Inc., Carlsbad, Calif., 1973-79, Aries Group, San Diego, 1979—; mem., dir. Corp. Fin. Coun., San Diego, 1976—; faculty mem. Southwestern U., L.A., 1941-42, U. So. Calif., 1959-60; mem. San Diego in the Global Economy Com., San Diego, 1990-91. Author: Love, War, and Laughter, 1995, Two Paths, 1995; columnist West Coast Cmty. Newspapers, 1985-92; contbr. articles to profl. jours. Chmn. 57th Assembly Dist. Rep. Ctrl. Com., Hollywood, 1958-62; exec. dir. L.A. County Ctrl. Com., 1957; charter mem. Smithsonian Nat. Mus. of Am. Indian; mem. Libr. of Congress Assocs. Lt. col. U.S. Army, 1942-46, 50-52. Republican. Episcopalian. Avocations: writing, poetry, golf, swimming. Home: 3017 Azahar Ct Carlsbad CA 92009-8301 Office: Aries Group 5841 Mission Gorge Rd Ste B San Diego CA 92120-4015

SMITH, BENNETT WALKER, minister; b. Florence, Ala., Apr. 7, 1933; s. Pearline Smith; m. Marilyn J. Donelson, Dec. 29, 1985; children from previous marriage: Debra T., Bennett Jr., Lydia R., Matthew T. BS, Tenn. State U., 1958; DD (hon.), Cin. Bapt. Theol. Sem., 1967; LHD (hon.), Medaille Coll., 1979. Ordained to ministry Progressive Nat. Bapt. Conv., 1962. Pastor 1st Bapt. Ch., Cin., 1963-65, Lincoln Heights Bapt. Ch., Cin., 1965-72, St. John Bapt. Ch., Buffalo, 1972—; instr. Congress Christian Edn., 1968-80; first v.p. Progressive Bapts., 1988—. Author: Tithing Handbook, 1980; contbg. editor missionary handbook. Bd. dirs. People United to Serve Humanity, Buffalo, 1974—; pres. Va./Mich. Housing Co., 1982—. Recipient Outstanding Leadership award 1490 Entreprise, Inc., 1982, Community Leadership award Black Elected Officials, 1982, Outstanding Clergy award Black Religious Broadcasters, 1983. Mem. NAACP (life, Medgar Evers award 1982), Ptnrs. in Ecumenism, Operation PUSH (nat. bd. dirs., chaplain), Masons (32d degree), Kappa Alpha Psi. Democrat. Home: 292 Red Oak Dr Buffalo NY 14221-2219 Office: St John Bapt Ch 184 Goodell St Buffalo NY 14204-1251

SMITH, BERNALD STEPHEN, retired airline pilot, aviation consultant; b. Long Beach, Calif., Dec. 24, 1926; s. Donald Albert and Bernice Merrill (Stephens) S.; m. Marilyn Mae Spence, July 22, 1949; children: Lorraine Ann Smith Foute, Evelyn Donice Smith DeRoos, Mark Stephen, Diane April (dec.). Student, U. Calif., Berkeley, 1944-45, 50-51. Cert. airline transport pilot, flight engr., FAA. Capt. Transocean Air Lines, Oakland (Calif.) and Tokyo, 1951-53, Hartford, Conn., 1954-55; 1st officer United Air Lines, Seattle, 1955, San Francisco, 1956-68; tng. capt. United Air Lines, Denver and San Francisco, 1961-68; capt. United Air Lines, San Francisco, 1968-86, 2d officer, 1986-93, ret., 1993; founder, v.p. AviaAm., Palo Alto, Calif., 1970-72, AviaInternat., Palo Alto, 1972-74; cons. Caproni Vizzola, Milan, 1972-84; prin., cons. Internat. Aviation Cons. and Investments, Fremont, Calif., 1985—; instr. aviation Ohlone Coll., Fremont, 1976; founder Pacific Soaring Coun.; founder, trustee AirSailing, Inc., 1970—, Soaring Safety Found., 1985—. Author/editor: American Soaring Handbook, 1975, 80; contbr. articles to profl. jours. Trustee Nat. Soaring Mus., 1975—, pres. 1975-78; active RTCA, SSA del., 1992—, FAI del., 1996. Comdr. USNR. Fellow Internat. GPS Svc. for Geodynamics; mem. AIAA (pub. bd. 1977-94), Soaring Soc. Am. (pres. 1969-70, chmn. pub. bd. 1971-84, ins. com. 1975-93, bd. dirs. 1963—, Warren Eaton Meml. trophy, 1977, Exceptional Svc. award 1970, 75, 82, 88, 91, Exceptional Achievement award 1996, named to Hall of Fame 1984), Soc. Automotive Engrs., Nat. Aero. Assn., Exptl. Aircraft Assn., Aircraft Owners and Pilots Assn., Airline Pilots Assn., Seaplane Pilots Assn., Orgn. Scientifique et Technique Internat. du Vol a Voile (bd. dirs., U.S. del. 1981—), Fedn. Aeronatique Internat. (Paul Tissandier diploma 1992, Lilienthal medal 1993), Commn. de Vol A Voile (U.S. del. 1970-71, 78, 85-97, v.p. 1988-96), U. Calif. Alumni Assn. (life), Inst. Navigation, Civil GPS Svc. Interace Com. Democrat. Methodist. Office: Internat Aviation Cons Investments PO Box 3075 Fremont CA 94539-0307

SMITH, BERNARD JOSEPH CONNOLLY, civil engineer; b. Elizabeth, N.J., Mar. 11, 1930; s. Bernard Joseph and Julia Susan (Connolly) S.; BS, U. Notre Dame, 1951; BS in Civil Engring., Tex. A&M U., 1957; MBA in Fin., U. Calif.-Berkeley, 1976; m. Josephine Kerley, Dec. 20, 1971; children: Julia Susan Alice Birmingham, Teresa Mary Josephine, Anne Marie Kathleen. Asst. Bernard J. Smith, cons. engr. office, Dallas, 1947-57; hydraulic engr. C.E., U.S. Army, San Francisco, 1957-59, St. Paul dist., 1959-60, Kansas City (Mo.) dist., 1960-63, Sacramento dist., 1963-65; engr. Fed. Energy Regulatory Commn., San Francisco Regional Office, 1965—. Served with U.S. Army, 1952-54. Registered profl. engr., Calif., Mo.; lic. real estate broker, Calif. Mem. ASCE (sec. power div. San Francisco sect. 1969), Soc. Am. Mil. Engrs. (treas. Kansas City post 1962), Res. Officers Assn. (chpt. pres. 1973). Club: Commonwealth of Calif. Home: 247 28th Ave San Francisco CA 94121-1001 Office: Fed Energy Regulatory Commn 901 Market St San Francisco CA 94103-1729

SMITH, BETTY, writer, nonprofit foundation executive; b. Bonham, Tex., Sept. 16; d. Sim and Gertrude (Dearing) S. Student, Stephens Coll.; BJ, U. Tex. Women's editor Daily Texan; pres. Hope Assocs. Corp., N.Y.C., 1948-50; pres., owner Betty Smith Assocs., N.Y.C., 1950—. Author: A Matter of Heart, 1969. Pres. Melchior Heldentenor Found., N.Y.C., 1987-97, Gerda Lissner Found., 1994—; v.p. Herman Lissner Found., 1990—. Mem. Author's Guild. Home: 322 E 55th St New York NY 10022-4157 Office: care Lissner Found 135 E 55th St New York NY 10022-4049

SMITH, BETTY DENNY, county official, administrator, fashion executive; b. Centralia, Ill., Nov. 12, 1932; d. Otto and Ferne Elizabeth (Beier) Hasenfuss; m. Peter S. Smith, Dec. 5, 1964; children: Carla Kip, Bruce Kimball. Student, U. Ill., 1950-52; student, L.A. City Coll., 1953-57, UCLA, 1965, U. San Francisco, 1982-84. Freelance fashion coordinator L.A., N.Y.C., 1953-58; tchr. fashion Rita LeRoy Internat. Studios, 1959-60; mgr. Mo Nadler Fashion, L.A., 1961-64; showroom dir. Jean of Calif. Fashions, L.A., 1965—; freelance polit. book reviewer for community newspapers, 1961-62; staff writer Valley Citizen News, 1963. Bd. dirs. Pet Assistance Found., 1969-76; founder, pres., dir. Vol. Services to Animals L.A., 1972-76; mem. County Com. To Discuss Animals in Rsch., 1973-74; mem. blue ribbon com. on animal control L.A. County, 1973-74; dir. L.A. County Animal Care and Control, 1976-82; mem. Calif. Animal Health Technician Exam. Com., 1975-82, chmn., 1979; bd. dirs. L.A. Soc. for Prevention Cruelty to Animals, 1984-94, Calif. Coun. Companion Animal Advocates, 1993-97; dir. West Coast Regional Office, Am. Humane Assn., 1988-97; CFO Coalition for Pet Population Control, 1987-92; trustee Gladys W. Sargent Found., 1997; cons. Jungle Book II, Disney Studios, 1997; mem. Coalition to Protect Calif. Wildlife, 1996—; mem. Calif. Rep. Cen. Com., 1964-72, mem. exec. com., 1971-73; mem. L.A. County Rep. Cen. Com., 1964-70, mem. exec. com., 1966-70; chmn. 29th Congl. Cen. Com., 1969-70; sec. 28th Senatorial Cen. Com., 1967-68, 45th Assembly Dist. Cen. Com., 1965-68; mem. speakers bur. George Murphy for U.S. Senate, 1970; campaign mgr. Los Angeles County for Spencer Williams for Atty. Gen., 1966; mem. adv. com. Moorpark Coll., 1988—; mem. adv. bd. Wishbone Prodn., 1995—. Mem. Internat. Platform Assn., Mannequins Assn. (bd. dirs. 1967-68), Motion Picture and TV Industry Assn. (govt. rels. and pub. affairs com. 1992-97), Lawyer's Wives San Gabriel Valley (bd. dirs. 1971-74, pres. 1972-73), L.A. Athletic Club, Town Hall. Home: 1766 Bluffhill Dr Monterey Park CA 91754-4533

SMITH, BETTY ELAINE, geography educator; b. Paterson, N.J., Oct. 28, 1949; d. Robert Francis and Elaine Gertrude Clough; m. Harrison John Smith, Sept. 6, 1975. BA in Geography, U. Calif., Davis, 1971; MA in Geography, Calif. State U., Chico, 1987; PhD in Geography, SUNY, Buffalo, 1994. Asst. planner City of Sacramento, Calif., 1973-75; real estate broker Sun Realty, Redding, Calif., 1976-88, Medley Realty, Redding, 1976-88; rsch./tchg. asst. SUNY, Buffalo, 1991-94, instr., 1993-94; lectr. U. Wis., Oshkosh, 1994-95; asst. prof. Ea. Ill. U., Charleston, 1995—. Contbr. articles to profl. jours. Mem. Assn. Am. Geographers, Conf. Latinamericanist Geographers, Regional Sci. Assn. Internat., Sigma Xi (assoc.). Office: Ea Ill U Dept Geology and Geography Charleston IL 61920

SMITH, BEVERLY ANN EVANS, performance management consultant; b. Massillon, Ohio, Apr. 12, 1948; d. Louie Edward and Willa (Dumas) Evans; m. Stephen John Smith, Aug. 1971; children: Brian Stephen, Stacy Nicole. MEd, Kent State U., 1973; BS in Edn., Bowling Green State U., 1970; diploma exch. edn. program, Babson Coll., 1987. Tchr. Garfield High Sch., Akron, Ohio, 1971-72; fin. aids officer, Upward Bound dir. Kent (Ohio) State U., 1971-76; dean student affairs Ga. State U., Atlanta, 1971-76; varied mgmt. positions So. Bell, Atlanta, 1976-84; dist. mgr. AT&T, Atlanta, 1984-96; cons. in field. Bd. dirs., chmn. United Way, Cobb County, Ga., 1991; bd. dirs. Girls Inc., Cobb County, Women for a Meaningful Summit, Washington, 1988-90; appointee Ga. Clean and Beautiful Commn., Atlanta, 1984-88; mem. Leadership Cobb, 1988—, mem. governing bd., 1993—; cert. Stephen (lay) min. Episc. Ch., 1991—. Named Cobb County Ga. Woman of Yr. in Bus., Marietta (Ga.) Girls Club, 1984, Outstanding Young Profl., Washington, D.C. Bus. Exch., Outstanding Sr. Woman, Bowling Green State U., 1970, Outstanding Freshman Woman, 1967, recipient Disting. Svc. award, 1970; named one of Outstanding Young Women of Am., 1971, 80. Mem. Omicron Delta Kappa, Delta Sigma Theta (1st v.p. local chpt. 1986-88, nat. exec. dir. 1988-90). Avocation: classical piano. Home: 1152 Clarendon Dr Marietta GA 30068-2161

SMITH, BRADLEY YOULE, lawyer; b. N.Y.C., Feb. 11, 1948; s. Bradley and Christine (Brown) S.; m. Anne Barre, Dec. 31, 1986; children: Bradley McLaren, Andrew Robert, Lauren Barre, Timothy James, Lynden Eleanor, Christina McLaren. BA in History cum laude, Yale U., 1970; JD, NYU, 1974. Bar: N.Y. 1975, U.S. Dist. Ct. (so. dist.) N.Y. 1975, U.S. Ct. Appeals (2d cir.) 1975. With Davis Polk & Wardwell, N.Y.C., 1974—, ptnr., 1980—. Trustee Royal Coll. Surgeons Found., Inc. Mem. ABA (chmn. subcom. secured transactions 1983-87, moderator and panelist com. banking law and uniform comml. code), Am. Law Inst., N.Y. State Bar Assn. (mem. banking law com.). Office: Davis Polk & Wardwell 450 Lexington Ave New York NY 10017-3911

SMITH, BRENDA JOYCE, author, editor, social studies educator; b. Washington, Jan. 2, 1946; d. William Eugene and Marjorie (Williams) Young; m. Duane Milton Smith, Aug. 4, 1978. BA in History and Govt. cum laude, Ohio U., 1968, postgrad. in Am. and European History, 1972. Tchr. Jr. High Sch., Lancaster, Ohio, 1968-69, Reynoldsburg (Ohio) Mid. Sch. and High Sch., 1970-71; grad. teaching asst. Ohio U., Athens, 1969-70, 71-72; polit. speech writer Legis. Reference Bur., Columbus, Ohio, 1972-74; pub. rels. writer Josephinum Coll., Columbus, 1976-78; social studies editor Merrill Pub. Co., Columbus, 1979-91; freelance author/editor social studies Columbus, 1991—. Project editor: Human Heritage: A World History, 1985, 89, World History: The Human Experience, 1992; author: The Collapse of the Soviet Union, 1994, Egypt of the Pharaohs, 1995; writer-editor on African Am. history series, 5th grade; writer of 3 Am. history books; writer on state histories of N.Y. and Ind. Del. 1st U.S.-Russia Joint Conf. on Edn., 1994. Mem. Nat. Coun. Social Studies, Ohio Coun. Social Studies, Freelance Editl. Assn. Office: 3710 Harborough Dr Gahanna OH 43230-4037

SMITH, BRIAN DAVID, lawyer, educator; b. Fayetteville, Ark., Oct. 29, 1953; s. Samuel Charles and Janelle (McCaskill) S.; children: Garrett Walker, Brian Austin, Marshall David. JD, La. State U., 1977. Bar: La. 1978, U.S. Dist. Ct. (we. dist.) La. 1979, U.S. Tax Ct. 1980, U.S. Ct. Appeals (5th cir.) 1980, U.S. Supreme Ct. 1990, Tex. 1993. Law clk. to presiding justice 1st Jud. Cir. Ct. La., Shreveport, La., 1978-79; assoc. Nelson, Hammons & Johnson, Shreveport, 1979-84, Lunn, Irion, Johnson, Salley & Carlisle, Shreveport, 1984—; instr. legal asst. curriculum La. State U., Shreveport, 1984-87. Bd. dirs. YMCA of Shreveport-Bossier City, 1996—. Mem. La. Bar Assn., La. Assn. Def. Counsel, State Bar Tex., Mensa, Shreveport Country Club, Petroleum Club of Shreveport. Methodist. Avocations: golf, running, motorcycles. Home: 901 Monrovia St Shreveport LA 71106-1127 Office: Lunn Irion Johnson Salley & Carlisle PO Box 1534 Shreveport LA 71165-1534

SMITH, BRIAN WILLIAM, lawyer, former government official; b. N.Y.C., Feb. 3, 1947; s. William Francis and Dorothy Edwina (Vogel) S.; m. Donna Jean Holverson, Apr. 24, 1976; children: Mark Holverson, Lauren Elizabeth. BA, St. John's U., N.Y.C., 1968, JD, 1971; MS, Columbia U., 1981. Bar: N.Y. 1972, D.C. 1975, U.S. Dist. Ct. (ea. and so. dists.) N.Y. 1975, U.S. Supreme Ct. 1976, U.S. Dist. Ct. D.C. 1986. Atty. Am. Express Co., N.Y.C., 1970-73, CIT Fin. Corp., N.Y.C., 1973-74; assoc. counsel, mng. atty. Interbank Card Assn. (named changed to Master Card Internat., Inc.), N.Y.C., 1974-75, sr. v.p., corp. sec., gen. counsel, 1975-82; chief counsel Compt. of Currency, Washington, 1982-84; ptnr. Stroock & Stroock & Lavan, Washington, 1984-92, mng. ptnr., 1986-92; ptnr. Mayer, Brown & Platt, Washington and N.Y.C., 1992—; lectr. fin. industry. Editor: Bank Investment Products Deskbook, 1995. Capt., USAR, 1970-78. Mem. ABA, N.Y. State Bar Assn., D.C. Bar Assn., Assn. Bar City N.Y., Fed. Bar Assn., N.Y. Athletic Club, Met. Club N.Y. Home: 35 W Lenox St Chevy Chase MD 20815-4208 Office: Mayer Brown & Platt 2000 Pennsylvania Ave NW Washington DC 20006-1812

SMITH, BRUCE, professional football player; b. Norfolk, Va., June 18, 1963. Student, Va. Tech. U. With Buffalo Bills, 1985—; player Super Bowl XXV, 1990, XXVI, 1991, XXVII, 1992, XXVIII, 1993. Recipient Outland trophy, 1984; named to Pro-Bowl, 1987-90, 92, 93, 95, 96, Sporting News All-Pro team, 1987-88, 90, 92-95. Office: Buffalo Bills 1 Bills Dr Orchard Park NY 14127-2237*

SMITH, BRUCE DAVID, archaeologist; b. Iowa City, Iowa, Mar. 24, 1946; s. Goldwin Albert and Emily C. (Bateman) S.; m. Martha Mary Johnson, Sept. 22, 1973; children: David Vernon, Jonathan Oliver. B.A., U. Mich., 1968, M.A., 1971, Ph.D., 1973. Mem. faculty Loyola U., Chgo., 1973-74, U. Ga., Athens, 1974-77; curator N.Am. archaeology Nat. Mus. Natural History, Smithsonian Instn., Washington, 1977—, sr. scientist, dir. archaeobiology program, 1991—, spl. asst. to dir., 1983, asst. dir., 1986; mem. anthropology rev. panel NSF, 1982-83. Author: Mississippian Patterns of Animal Exploitation, 1975, Prehistoric Patterns of Human Behavior, 1978, Mississippian Settlement Patterns, 1978, Mississippian Emergence, 1990, Rivers of Change, 1992, Emergence of Agriculture, 1994, Mississippian Households and Communities, 1995. Horace H. Rackham prize fellow, 1971-73, Smithsonian Instn. Regents Pub. fellow, 1987; recipient James Henry Breasted prize Am. Hist. Assn., 1995. Mem. Soc. Am. Archaeology (sec. 1985-89, pres. 1993-95, Book award 1997), Southeastern Archaeol. Conf. (pres. 1982-84). Home: 2202 Whiteoaks Dr Alexandria VA 22306-2458 Office: Smithsonian Instn Nat Mus Natural History Dept Anthropology Washington DC 20560

SMITH, BRUCE R., English language educator; b. Jackson, Miss., Mar. 21, 1946. Student, U. Birmingham, England, 1966-67; BA magna cum laude in English with honors, Tulane U., 1968; MA, U. Rochester, 1971, PhD with distinction, 1973. From asst. prof. to assoc. prof. English Georgetown U., Washington, 1972-87, prof., 1987—; faculty Bread Loaf Sch. English, Middlebury Coll., 1994—. Author: Ancient Scripts and Modern Experience on the English Stage 1500-1700, 1988, Homosexual Desire in Shakespeare's England: A Cultural Poetics, 1991, Roasting the Swan of Avon: Shakespeare's Redoubtable Enemies and Dubious Friends, 1994; edit. bd. Shakespeare Quar., 1995—; contbr. chpts. to books, articles to profl. jours. Summer grantee Georgetown U. Acad. Rsch., 1976, 84, 87, 89, 91, 92; grantee Intercultural Curriculum Devel., 1982, Agecroft Assn., 1991; Mellon fellow Huntington Libr., 1996; jr. fellow Folger Inst., 1979-85, fellow, 1990, 96; ACLS fellow, 1979-80; NEH fellow, 1987-88; Va. Found. Humanites fellow, 1989. Mem. Shakespeare Assn. Am. (pres. 1994-95). Office: Georgetown U Dept English Washington DC 20057

SMITH, BRUCE WILLIAM, safety engineer; b. Louisville, Ky., July 23, 1932; s. Roy Sylvester and Anna Lois (Levine) S.; m. Barbara Ruth Lischin, Oct. 13, 1951; children: Carl Wayne, Joyce Leslie, Nancy Florence. Student, U. Cin., 1953-58, Miami U., Oxford, Ohio, 1950-52. Registered profl. engr., Ohio. Materials testing spec. Gen. Electric AE, Cin., 1952-56, systems engr., 1956-79, facitities engr., 1979-83, safety engr., 1983-91; ret. Gen. Electric AE, 1991; consulting engr. Exec. Resource Assocs., Inc., Cape Coral, Fla., 1991—. Paramedic, Community Medic Res., No. Hamilton County, 1975-84; asst. fire chief Springdale (Ohio) Vol. Fire Dept., 1956-84; councilman, Springdale, 1960-62; mem. Springdale Charter Comm., 1962. Recipient physics scholarship, Ohio Acad. Sci., 1950. Mem. Am. Soc. Safety Engrs., Nat. Fire Protection Assn. Avocations: sailing, photography. Home: 919 SE 26th Ter Cape Coral FL 33904-2919

SMITH, BYRON OWEN, retired lawyer; b. Mitchell, S.D., July 28, 1916; s. Frank B. and Elizabeth (Klostermann) S.; m. Jean Knox Harris, Dec. 20, 1938; children: Sheryl S. (Mrs. Kenneth P. King), Laird W. (dec.), Ryland R., Ford R. A.B., Stanford, 1937, J.D., 1940. Bar: Calif. 1940. Assoc. Stephens, Jones, Inch & LaFever, L.A., 1940-41; ptnr. Stephens, Jones, LaFever & Smith, L.A., 1945-77; ptnr. Adams, Duque & Hazeltine, L.A., 1977-95, of counsel, 1995-96; ret., 1996. Served to comdr. USNR, 1942-45, 51. Fellow Am. Coll. Trust and Estate Counsel; mem. Calif. State Club Assn. (dir., pres. 1974), So. Calif. Golf Assn. (Dir. 1966-71), Eldorado Country Club (sec., dir. 1970-72), Calif. Club, Phi Delta Phi, Alpha Delta Phi. Home: 75-701 Camino De Plata Indian Wells CA 92210

SMITH, C. KENNETH, business executive; b. Brackenridge, Pa., Feb. 1, 1918; s. Clarence H. and Mary (Ferguson) S.; m. AnnaBell Amlin. Degree in bus., U. Pitts., 1942. Mng. ptnr. Ernst & Young, CPAs, Columbus, Ohio, 1964-78; fin. dir., mem. mayor's cabinet City of Columbus, 1983; mng. dir. Fairoaks Internat., 1978—; profl. outside dir. various corps.; guest lectr. Ohio State U. Mem. exec. com. Nat. Football Found. and Hall Fame, Columbus Sports Arena Task Force; co-founder, past chmn. Greater Columbus Arts Coun.; advisor Columbus Found.; bd. govs. Westerville Fund, chmn., 1984-87; mem. Forward Columbus Com.; bd. dirs. Devel. Com. Greater Columbus, Quality Edn. Com., Columbus Zool Park, Columbus Jr. Achievement, Nat. Jr. Achievement; mem. Otterbein Coll. Theatre Adv. Bd.; trustee Columbus Symphony Orch., gen. chmn. symphony grand ball, 1975; trustee Franklin U., 1970—, chmn. bd.; adv. bd. Kenyon Rev., Kenyon Coll.; co-founder, trustee Columbus Leadership Program. Named One of 10 Top Men in Columbus, Columbus Citizen Jour., 1971; named in Columbus Dispatch Blue Chip Profile, 1977; named to Hon. Order Ky. Cols. Mem. AICPA, Am. Acad. Arts and Scis., Am. Mgmt. Assn. (pres.'s coun.), Am. Acctg. Assn., Columbus Soc. Fin. Analysts, Nat. Assn. Corp. Dirs., Columbus Assn. Performing Arts (pres., chmn. bd. 1970-72, chmn. profl. theatre com.), Columbus Mus. Art, Columbus Civic Ballet, Nat. Audubon Soc., Am. Forestry Assn., Am. Tree Farm Sys., Nature Conservancy, Ohio Hist. Soc., Columbus Area C. of C. (chmn. bd. 1968-70, Man of Yr. award 1979), Ohio C. of C. (dir. 1974). Conglist. Clubs: Mason (32 deg., Shriner), Rotarian (dir. 1976—, pres. 1978-79), Columbus (dir. 1968-74), Columbus Country, Royal Commonwealth (London), Torch (pres. 1979-80), Athletic (Columbus); Zanesfield Rod and Gun, Maennerchor, U. Pitts. Alumni Assn., Ohio State U. Alumni Assn. (life); Faculty (Ohio State U.), Presidents (Ohio State U.); Press of Ohio, Ohio Commodore. Home and Office: Fairoaks Farm Westerville OH 43081-9580 *To live life to the fullest, to love and be loved, to pursue knowledge and wisdom, to achieve goals, then set new ones, to be blessed with good health, to be at peace with God and man. This be my prayer.*

SMITH, C. LEMOYNE, publishing company executive; b. Atkins, Ark., Sept. 15, 1934; s. Cecil Garland and Salena Bell (Wilson) S.; m. Selma Jean Tucker, May 23, 1964; 1 child, Jennifer Lee. B.S., Ark. Tech. U., 1956; M.Ed., U. Ark., 1958. Tchr. pub. schs., Little Rock, 1956-58; instr. bus. adminstrn. Ark. Tech. U., Russellville, 1958-60; sales rep. South-Western Pub. Co., Cin., 1960-67, editorial staff, 1967-82, pres., chief exec. officer, 1982-90, chmn., 1990-91, ret., 1991. Bd. dirs. Cin. Council on World Affairs, 1983-95. Mem. Am. Vocat. Assn., Nat. Bus. Edn. Assn., Delta Pi Epsilon. Republican. Methodist. Avocations: bridge; travel. Office: South-Western Pub Co 5101 Madison Rd Cincinnati OH 45227-1427

SMITH, CAREY DANIEL, acoustician, undersea warfare technologist; b. Kenedy, Tex., July 10, 1932; s. Ernest Edwin and Nancy Margaret (Willoughby) S.; m. Fannie Belle Walker, Sept. 18, 1954; children: Daniel Carey, Bryan Owen, Ernest Price, Sara Elizabeth Babyak. BS in Math. and Physics, U. Tex., 1959. Rsch. physicist Def. Rsch. Lab./U. Tex., Austin, 1958-64; electro-acoustic engr. Bur. Ships, Washington, 1964-66; dir. sonar tech. office Naval Sea Sys. Command, Washington, 1966-79, dir. Undersea Warfare Tech. Office, 1979-86; sr. cons. U.S. Navy/Sec. of Def., Washington, 1987—; fgn. liaison specialist in undersea warfare as collatoral duty USN, 1966-86; chmn. sonar tech. panel Tech. Coop. Program of multiple allied nations, 1972-86; tech. advisor undersea warfare div. Am. Def. Preparedness Assn., 1976-86. Chair deacons McLean (Va.) Bapt. Ch., 1988-89, 96-97; chair Band Parents, McLean H.S., 1979-80, chair Sports Boosters, 1977-78. With USN, 1951-56. Decorated Legion of Honor (France); recipient Disting. Civilian Svc. award Sec. Navy, 1979, also Brit., Can., French, Japanese, and New Zealand navies commendations, 1985-86. Fellow Acoustical Soc. Am. Achievements include development of numerous advanced, innovative techniques incorporated in fleet sonar, torpedo, mine, countermeasure, acoustic communications, underwater combat control/ocean environmental acoustic systems; color display for high resolution sonars. Home and Office: 1638 Dinneen Dr Mc Lean VA 22101-4646

SMITH, CARL BERNARD, education educator, writer; b. Dayton, Ohio, Feb. 29, 1932; s. Carl R. and Elizabeth Ann (Lefeld) S.; m. Virginia Lee Cope, Aug. 30, 1958; children—Madonna, Anthony, Regina, Marla. B.A., U. Dayton, 1954; M.A., Miami U., Oxford, Ohio, 1961; Ph.D., Case Western Res. U., 1967. Tchr., Cathedral Latin High Sch., Cleve., 1954-57; customer corr. E.F. MacDonald Co., Dayton, 1958-59; tchr. Kettering (Ohio) High Sch., 1959-61; editor Reardon Baer Pub. Co., Cleve., 1961-62; tchr./researcher Case Western Res. U., Cleve., 1962-65, Cleve. Pub. Schs., 1966-67; asst. prof. edn. Ind. U., Bloomington, 1967-69, assoc. prof., 1970-72, prof., 1973—; dir. ERIC Ctr., 1988—, Family Literacy Ctr., 1990—; pres. Grayson Bernard Pub. Co., 1988—, Am. Family Learning Corp., 1996—. Pres. Bd. Edn., St. Charles Sch., Bloomington, 1976-80. Recipient Sch. Bell award NEA, 1967, Literacy award Ind. State Reading Assn., 1997. Mem. Internat. Reading Assn., Nat. Council Tchrs. of English, Assn. Supervision and Curriculum Devel., Am. Ednl. Research Assn., Phi Delta Kappa. Republican. Roman Catholic. Author: Reading Instruction through Diagnostic Teaching, (Pi Lambda Theta Best Book in Edn. award, 1972; Getting People To Read, 1978; sr. author: Series r, 1983, New View, 1993; Teaching Reading and Writing Together, 1984, Connect! Getting Your Kids to Talk to You, 1994, Word History A Resource Book, 1995, (videotape) Make a Difference, 1996. Home: 401 Serena Ln Bloomington IN 47401-9226 Office: ERIC Clearinghouse Smith Rsch Ctr Bloomington IN 47405

SMITH, CARL DEAN, JR., counselor, child advocate, business broker; b. Denver, Sept. 12, 1949; m. Patricia Ann O'Donnell, Aug. 18, 1973; children: Amanda Paige, Grant Carlton. BA, Springfield Coll., 1972; postgrad., Goethe Inst., Munich, 1972-73, Gordon Conwell Theol. Sem., Hamilton, Mass., 1986-88; MEd, Cambridge Coll., 1993. Bus. analyst Dun & Bradstreet, Inc., Boston, 1974-77; Western U.S. credit mgr. Salomon/N.Am., Inc., Peabody, Mass., 1977-81; regional credit mgr. Stride Rite Corp., Cambridge, Mass., 1981-82; sales mgr., franchisee V.R. Bus. Brokers of Chestnut Hill, Mass., 1982-85; pres. C.D. Smith Assocs., Wakefield, Mass., 1985-90; ind. cons. Swampscott, 1990-94; crisis clinician Ctr. for Mental Health, Lexington, Mass., 1994—; counselor HRI Counseling, Woburn, Mass., 1994—. Pres. coun. Gordon Conwell Theol. Sem., 1988—; Boston coord. Fellowship of Cos. for Christ, 1988—; leadership gifts solicitor United Way, 1987, 88, 89—; class agt. Brewster Acad., 1968—; basketball coach Shore Country Day, Beverly, 1993, Shady Hill Sch., Cambridge, 1996—; Stephens minister First Ch. Cong. of Swampscott, Mass., 1997—. Mem. Am. Assn. Christian Counselors (N.E. mem.). Avocation: basketball coaching. Home and Office: 314 Forest Ave Swampscott MA 01907-2109

SMITH, CARL RICHARD, association executive, former air force officer; b. New Holland, Pa., Dec. 20, 1933; s. Lemmon Lloyd and Martha Marie (Grabill) S.; m. Mariana Roth, June 15, 1956; children: Timothy Carl, Jeffry Francis, Desi Marie. B.S. in Econs., Franklin and Marshall Coll., Lancaster, Pa., 1955; M.S. in Bus. Adminstrn., George Washington U., 1966. Commd. 2d lt. U.S. Air Force, 1955, advanced through grades to lt. gen., 1986; served in Vietnam and Belgium; assigned Hdqrs. USAF, Washington, 1966-70, 76-78, 86-91; mil. asst. to sec. def., 1978-83; assigned comdr. Lackland AFB, Tex., 1983-86; asst. vice chief of staff Hdqrs. USAF, 1986-91, ret., 1991; exec. v.p. Armed Forces Benefit Assn., Alexandria, Va., 1991—. Decorated Def. D.S.M. with oak leaf cluster, Air Force D.S.M., Legion of Merit with oak leaf cluster, D.F.C., Bronze Star, Meritorious Service medal, Air medal with 2 oak leaf clusters, Air Force Commendation medal. Mem. Air Force Assn., Lambda Chi Alpha. Methodist. Home: 2345 S Queen St Arlington VA 22202-1550 Office: Armed Forces Benefit Assn 909 N Washington St Alexandria VA 22314-1555

SMITH, CARLTON MYLES, military officer; b. Sacramento, Sept. 21, 1920; s. Carl Walter and Minnie Clamina (Friberg) S.; m. Phyllis Lee Routzahn, Nov. 2, 1947; children: Fredrick Benjamin Brown, Brian Webb Smith, Randal Lee Smith, Dennis Stuart Smith. BA, U. Calif., Berkeley, 1946. Joined USAF, 1942, advanced through ranks to lt. col.; various intelligence assignments to chief Advanced Intelligence Courses Br./Def. Intelligency Agy., retired, 1972. Co-author: Stonyford Pedigree, 1988; compiler Genealogist's Historiograph, 1986, (computer program) Genealogist's Historiograph, 1988. Decorated Air medal, WWII, Bronze Star, Meritorious Svc. medal. Mem. Calif. State Geneal. Soc. (Merit award 1985), 303d Bomb Group Assn. (membership chmn. 1991-97). Avocations: geneal. and hist. rsch., travel, writing. Home: 12700 Red Maple Cir Sonora CA 95370-5269 *Success in life comes to some in the form of fame, an ego trip. True success and complete self-satisfaction comes to all whose fame stems from service to others, an excursion for the improvement of mankind.*

SMITH, CAROLE DIANNE, legal editor, writer, product developer; b. Seattle, June 12, 1945; d. Glaude Francis and Elaine Claire (Finkenstein) S.; m. Stephen Bruce Presser, June 18, 1968 (div. June 1987); children: David Carter, Elisabeth Catherine. AB cum laude, Harvard U., Radcliffe Coll., 1968; JD, Georgetown U., 1974. Bar: Pa. 1974. Law clk. Hon. Judith Jamison, Phila., 1974-75; assoc. Gratz, Tate, Spiegel, Ervin & Ruthrouff, Phila., 1975-76; freelance editor, writer Evanston, Ill., 1983-87; editor Ill. Inst. Tech., Chgo., 1987-88; mng. editor LawLetters, Inc., Chgo., 1988-89; editor ABA, Chgo., 1989-95; product devel. dir. Gt. Lakes divsn. Lawyers Coop. Pub., Deerfield, Ill., 1995-97; product devel. mgr. Midwest Market Ctr., Thomson Legal Pub. (formerly Lawyers Coop. Pub.), Deerfield, Ill., 1996-97; product devel. mgr. Midwest Mkt. Ctr.-West Group, Thomson Legal Pub., Deerfield, Ill., 1997—. Author Jour. of Legal Medicine, 1975, Selling and the Law: Advertising and Promotion, 1987; (under pseudonym Sarah Toast) 65 children's books, 1994-97; editor The Brief, 1990-95, Criminal Justice, 1989-90, 92-95 (Gen. Excellence award Soc. Nat. Assn. Pubs. 1990, Feature Article award-bronze Soc. Nat. Assn. Pubs. 1994), Franchise Law Jour., 1995; mem. editl. bd. The Brief, ABA Tort and Ins. Practice Sect., 1995—. Dir. Radcliffe Club of Chgo., 1990-93; mem. parents council Latin Sch. Chgo., 1995-96. Mem. ABA. Office: West Group 155 Pfingsten Rd Deerfield IL 60015

SMITH, CARTER BLAKEMORE, broadcaster; b. San Francisco, Jan. 1, 1937; s. Donald V. and Charlotte M. (Nichols) S.; children: Carter Blakemore, Clayton M. AA, City Coll. San Francisco, 1958; BA, San Francisco State U., 1960; postgrad. N.Y. Inst. Finance, 1969-70; Assoc. in Fin. PLanning, Coll. for Fin. Planning, 1984. Announcer, Sta. KBLF, Red Bluff, Calif., 1954-56; personality Sta. KRE-KRE FM, Berkeley, Calif., 1958-63, Sta. KSFO, San Francisco, 1963-72, Sta. KNBR, San Francisco, 1972-83, Sta. KSFO, San Francisco, 1983-86, Sta. KFRC, San Francisco, 1986-91, 93-94, Sta. KABL, San Francisco, 1996—; mem. faculty radio-TV dept. San Francisco State U., 1960-61. Mem. adv. bd. Little Jim Club Children's Hosp., 1968-71; bd. dirs. Marin County Humane Soc., 1968-73, San Francisco Zool. Soc., 1980-90; trustee Family Svc. Agy. Marin, 1976-85; mem. alumni bd. Lowell High Sch. Recipient award San Francisco Press Club, 1965; named one of Outstanding Young Men in Am. U.S. Jaycees, 1972. Mem. Amateur Radio Relay League (life), Quarter Century Wireless Assn., Alpha Epsilon Rho.

SMITH, CARY CHRISTOPHER, artist; b. Ponce, P.R., Oct. 1, 1955; s. Roger William and Headley Hall (Mills) S.; m. Virginia Vernon Knowles, Nov. 26, 1977; children: Emily Hall, Hayley Knowles. Student, Sir John Cass Art Sch., London, Eng., 1976; BFA, Syracuse U., 1977. One-man shows include Port Washington (N.Y.) Pub. Libr., 1980, Julian Pretto Gallery, N.Y.C., 1987, Koury Wingate Gallery, N.Y.C., 1988, 90, Galerie Six Friedrich, Munich, Germany, 1989, Lawrence Oliver Gallery, Phila., 1989, Ezra and Cecil Zilkha Gallery, Wesleyan U., Middletown, Conn., 1989, Linda Cathcart Gallery, Santa Monica, Calif., 1991, Rubin Spangle Gallery, N.Y.C., 1992, Roger Ramsay Gallery, Chgo., 1993, Salvatore Ala Gallery, N.Y.C., 1994, Galerie Jorg Paal, Munich, 1995, 97; exhibited in group shows at Stux Gallery, Boston, 1987, White Columns, N.Y.C., 1987, Mission West, N.Y.C., 1987, A.L.G.O. Gallery, N.Y.C., 1987, Postmasters Gallery, N.Y.C., 1988, Jacob Javits Ctr., N.Y.C., 1988, Koury Wingate Gallery, N.Y.C., 1988, 89, 90, Wolff Gallery, N.Y.C., 1988, Whitney Mus. Am. Art, N.Y.C., 1989, 91, 93, Rastovski Gallery, N.Y.C., 1989, Marc Richards Gallery, Santa Monica, 1990, Vrej Baghoomian Gallery, N.Y.C., 1990, Marilyn Pearl Gallery, N.Y.C., 1991, Fay Gold Gallery, Atlanta, 1991, Wadsworth Atheneum, Hartford, Conn., 1992, 96, Rubin Spangle Gallery, N.Y.C., 1992, Salvatore Ala Gallery, N.Y.C., 1993, 94, Pamela Archincloss Gallery, N.Y.C., 1995, Galerie Jorg Paal, Munich, 1996, Lawrence Markey Gallery, N.Y.C., 1996; represented in permanent collections Whitney Mus. Am. Art, N.Y.C., Bklyn. (N.Y.) Mus., Osaka (Japan) Mus., Wadsworth Ateneum, Hartford, New Britain (Conn.) Mus. Am. Art; illustrator: Cover Mag.; featured in Art News mag., ArtForum mag., Art in Am., N.Y. Times. Recipient Conn. Commn. on the Arts grant for painting, 1983, 86, Art in Pub. Spaces award Conn. Commn. on the Arts, 1985, Nat. Endowment for the Arts Fellowship in Painting, 1991-92, Pollock Krasner grant for painting, 1993. Address: PO Box 924 Farmington CT 06034

SMITH, CECE, venture capitalist; b. Washington, Nov. 16, 1944; d. Linn Charles and Grace Inez (Walker) S.; m. John Ford Lacy, Apr. 22, 1978. B.B.A., U. Mich., 1966; M.L.A., So. Meth. U., 1974. C.P.A., Tex. Staff accountant Arthur Young & Co. (C.P.A.s), Boston, 1966-68; staff accountant, then asst. to controller Wyly Corp., Dallas, 1969-72; controller, treas. sub. Univ. Computing Co., Dallas, 1972-74; controller Steak and Ale Restaurants Am., Inc., Dallas, 1974-76; v.p. fin. Steak and Ale Restaurants Am., Inc., 1976-80, exec. v.p., 1980-81; exec. v.p. Pearle Health Services, Inc.,, 1981-84, pres. Primacare div., 1984-86; gen. ptnr. Phillips-Smith Specialty Retail Group, 1986—; pres. Le Sportsac Dallas, Inc., 1981-87; bd. dirs. Henry Silverman Jewelers, Inc., Lil Things, Inc., Hot Topic, Inc.; chmn. Fed. Res. Bank of Dallas, 1994-96. Former co-chmn. pres.'s rsch. coun. U. Tex. S.W. Med. Ctr. Dallas; former mem. vis. com. U. Mich. Grad. Sch. Bus.; former exec. bd. So. Meth. U. Cox Sch. Bus.; former v.p., bd. dirs. Jr. Achievement Dallas, past pres. Charter 100; past treas. Dallas Assembly; former bd. dirs. Taco Villa, Inc., BizMart, Inc., A Pea in the Pod, Inc. Mem. Tex. Soc. CPAs (former dir.). Home: 3710 Shenandoah St Dallas TX 75205-2121 Office: 5080 Spectrum Dr Ste 700 W Dallas TX 75248-4658

SMITH, CHARLES CARTER, JR., publishing executive; b. Mobile, Ala., Jan. 14, 1930; s. Charles Carter Sr. and Sidney Taylor (Adair) S.; m. Elizabeth Covington, July 4, 1959; children: Adair, Carter, Adam. BA with high honors, U. South, 1951; postgrad., Northwestern U., 1954-55. Asst. to nat. housewares sales mgr. Sears-Roebuck & Co., Chgo., 1954-57; acct. supr. McAnn-Erickson Advt., Chgo., 1957-60; dir. mktg. Ency. Britannica Press, Chgo., 1960-63; pub. Systems for Edn., Inc., Chgo., 1963-67; asst. pub. Time-Life Books, N.Y.C., 1967-70; pres. Media Projects, Inc., N.Y.C., 1970—; adj. lectr. NYU, 1992-93; bd. dirs. Sharon (Conn.) Hist. Dist. Com., Sharon Hist. Soc., Sickness Prevention Achieved Through Regional Coordination Found.; mem. Madison coun. Libr. Congress, Washington, 1994-95. Author: Mobile: 1864, 3 vols., 1964, Images of Healing, 1980, Country Antiques and Collectibles, 1981, Decorating with Americana, 1985, A Day in the Life of a Medical Detective, 1985, Turning Points in American History: The Korean War, 1990, A Day in the Life of an FBI Agent in Training, 1991, Turning Points in American History: The Jamestown Colony, 1991; editor: American Heritage Illustrated History of the U.S., 18 vols., 1988, Images on File: The Faces of America, 1988, Images on File: Key Issues in Constitutional History, 1988, Images on File: The Civil War, 1989, Images on File: Colonial and Revolutionary America, 1990, Images on File: The Faces of America 2, 1990, American Albums from the Library of Congress: Colonial America, 6 vols., 1991, American Albums from the Library of Congress: The American West, 6 vols., 1991, American Albums from the Library of Congress: The Civil War, 6 vols., 1992, American Albums from the Library of Congress: The U.S. Presidency, 6 vols., 1993, Journeys Into the Past: Daily Life in Colonial America, 1993; contbr. articles to Saturday Rev., So. Accents. Trustee Day Sch., N.Y.C., 1980-82. Decorated Army Commendation medal, 1993; recipient VISTA Achievement cert. U.S. Office Econ. Opportunity, 1969. Mem. Am. Book Prodrs. Assn. (founder, pres. 1980-82), Century Assn., Sharon Country Club. Episcopalian. Avocations: tennis, gardening, collecting hist. Am. prints. Office: Media Projects Inc 305 2nd Ave New York NY 10003-2739

SMITH, CHARLES CONARD, refractory company executive; b. Mexico, Mo., Feb. 10, 1936; s. Charles Adelbert and Waldine (Barnes) S.; m. Constance Nagel, Oct. 6, 1962; children: Stewart Ashley, Graham Prior. BS in Ceramic Engring., Iowa State U., 1958; MBA, Stanford U., 1962. Process engr. Kaiser Refractory divsn. Kaiser Aluminum, Moss Landing, Calif., 1962-65; materials mgr. Kaiser Refractory divsn. Kaiser Aluminum, Mexico, Mo., 1965-67; divsn. planning Kaiser Refractory divsn. Kaiser Aluminum, Oakland, Calif., 1967-69; v.p., gen. mgr. Kaiser Refractories Argentina, Buenos Aires, 1969-74; with divsn. planning Kaiser Refractories divsn. Kaiser Aluminum, Oakland, 1974-77, mktg. mgr., 1977-80, gen. mgr. mfg., 1980-82, v.p., gen. mgr. refractories divsn., 1982-85; chmn., pres., CEO Nat. Refractories and Mineral Corp., Livermore, Calif., 1985—. Patentee in refractory field. Lt. USNR, 1958-60. Mem. Refractories Inst. (past chmn., exec. com.). Republican. Avocations: fishing, biking, kite flying, photography, music.

SMITH, CHARLES E., protective services official; b. Memphis; married; 3 children. B of Personnel Adminstrn. Firefighter Memphis Fire Dept., 1975-79, lt., 1979-84, capt., 1984-87, dist. chief fire fighting, 1987-91, divsn. chief tng., 1991-92, dir. fire svcs., 1992—; apptd. commr. Tenn. Commn. Fire Fighting Personnel Stds. & Edn. Bd. dirs. Cath. Charities, Inc., Fire Mus. Memphis. Mem. Nat. Inst. Urban Search & Rescue, NAt. Fire Protection Assn., Tenn. Fire Chiefs (bd. dirs.), Alliance for Fire and Emergency Mgmt. (stds. cabinet). Roman Catholic. Office: Office of Dir Fire Svcs 65 S Front St Memphis TN 38103-2411

SMITH, CHARLES EDWARD, state agency administrator; b. White County, Tenn., May 19, 1939; s. Cecil Edward and Christine (Newsome) S.; m. Shawna Lea Hickerson, Dec. 15, 1962; children: Chip, Tandy. B.S. in Journalism, U. Tenn., 1961; M.A. in English, George Peabody Coll., Nashville, 1966, Ph.D. in Higher Edn., 1976. Editor Sparta Expositor, Tenn., 1961-63; mng. editor Putnam County Herald-Cookeville Citizen, Cookeville, Tenn., 1963-64; asst. news editor Nashville Tennessean, 1964-67; news bur. dir. U. Tenn., Knoxville, 1967-68, pub. relations dir., 1968-70, exec. asst. to chancellor, 1971-73; exec. asst. to pres. U. Tenn. System, Knoxville, 1973-75; chancellor U. Tenn., Nashville, 1975-79; v.p. pub. service U. Tenn. System; editor Nashville Banner, 1979-80; chancellor U.Tenn.-Martin, 1980-85; v.p. adminstrn. state-wide system U. Tenn.-Knoxville, 1985-87; commr. edn. State of Tenn., Nashville, 1987-93; chancellor Tenn. Bd. Regents, Nashville, 1994—; trustee Am. Coll. Testing Bd., Iowa City, 1987-93; mem. So. Regional Edn. Bd., 1989-95, exec. com., 1991-95, vice chmn., 1994-95. Contbr. articles to profl. jours. Mem. Peabody Coll. Alumni Bd., 1994—. Recipient Single Best Editorial award Tenn. Press Assn., 1962, Peabody Coll. Disting. Alumnus award, 1993; named Fulbright fellow, 1980, One of Nation's Top 100 Coll. Educators, Bowling Green State U., 1986. Mem. Phi Kappa Phi. Democrat. Mem. Ch. of Christ. Home: 6340 Chickering Cir Nashville TN 37215-5301 Office: Tenn Bd Regents 1415 Murfreesboro Pike Ste 350 Nashville TN 37217-2829

SMITH, CHARLES EDWIN, computer science educator, consultant; b. Columbia, Mo., Apr. 15, 1950; s. William Walter and Nelletha Pearl (Lavendar) S.; m. Mary L. Davis, July 27, 1991. AA, Edison C.C., Ft. Myers, Fla., 1971; BS, Troy State U., 1979; MA, Webster U., St. Louis, 1989. Cert. computing profl. Enlisted USAF, Tyndall AFB, Fla., 1975; advanced through grades to maj. USAF; commd. 2d lt. USAF, Scott AFB, Ill., 1979; maj. USAFR, 1989-96, ret., 1996; adj. instr. Manatee C.C., Venice, Fla., 1989-90, Edison C.C., Punta Gorda, Fla., 1989-92; prof. computer sci. Edison C.C., 1992—; cons. Charles E. Smith Consulting, North Port, Fla., 1989-91. Assoc. mem. Charlotte County Econs. Devel. Coun., Port Charlotte, Fla., 1992—. Mem. Fla. Assn. C.C.s, Bass Anglers Sportsman's Soc. Republican. Avocations: reading, fishing, boating, astronomy. Office: Edison C C 26300 Airport Rd Punta Gorda FL 33950-5748

SMITH, CHARLES HADDON, geoscientist, consultant; b. Dartmouth, N.S., Can., Sept. 3, 1926; s. Albion Benson and Dora Pauline (McGill) S.; m. Mary Gertrude Saint, Sept. 5, 1949; children: Charles Douglas, Richard David, Alan Michael, Timothy McGill. B.Sc. and Diploma in Engring, Dalhousie U., Can., 1946, M.Sc. in Geology, 1948; M.S., Yale U., 1951, Ph.D. in Econ. Geology, 1952. Instr. Dalhousie U., Halifax, N.S., 1946-48; geologist Cerro de Pasco Copper Corp., Morococha, Peru, 1949, Geol. Survey of Can., Ottawa, Ont., 1952-64; chief petrological scis. div. Geol. Survey of Can., 1964-67, chief crustal geology div., 1967-68; sci. adviser Sci. Council Can., Ottawa, 1968-70; dir. planning Dept. Energy Mines and Resources, Ottawa, 1970-71; asst. dep. minister sci. and tech. Dept. Energy Mines and Resources, 1971-75, sr. asst. dep. minister, 1975-81; pres. Charles H. Smith Cons., 1982-94; mem. adv. coun. dept. geology and geophysics Princeton U., 1967-76; sci. advisor Can. Commn. for UNESCO, 1983-89; exec. dir. Can. Nat. Com./World Energy Conf., 1983-90; bd. govs. Can. Inst. Radiation Safety, 1983-86; hon. mem. Energy Coun. Can., 1991—; coord. 150th anniversary Geol. Survey Can., 1990-93. Mem. editl. bd. Am. Jour. Sci., 1967-72, Mineralium Deposita, 1968-83, Jour. Petrology, 1966-70, Econ. Geology, 1966-70; contbr. articles to profl. jours. Fellow Royal Soc. Can. (fgn. sec. 1986-90), Mineral. Soc. Am., Soc. Econ. Geologists (v.p. N.Am. 1968-70); mem. Can. Inst. Mining and Metallurgy (life mem., v.p. 1982-84), Assn. Profl. Engrs. Ont., Geol. Assn. Can., Can. Geosci. Coun. (pres. 1984), Rotary.

SMITH, CHARLES HENRY, JR., industrial executive; b. Cleve., July 28, 1920; s. Charles H. and Florence (Reno) S.; m. Rhea Day, Sept. 18, 1943 (dec. Jan. 1990); children: Charles Henry, Deborah Rhea Smith Potantus, Hudson Day; m. Florence M. Johnson, Mar. 9, 1991. B.S., Mass. Inst. Tech., 1942. Pres., dir. Steel Improvement & Forge Co. (name changed to Sifco Industries, Inc.), Cleve., 1943-70; chmn., chief exec. officer Steel Improvement & Forge Co. (name changed to Sifco Industries, Inc.), 1970-83, chmn., 1970—; pres. Can. Steel Improvement, Etobicoke, Ont., 1951-54; chmn. bd. Sifco Custom Machining Inc., Mpls., Sifco Selective Plating Inc., Cleve., Sifco Bearing Inc., Avon, Ohio, 1970-88; chmn., consultative coun. Sifco do Brazil, Sao Paulo, 1959-81; chmn. Sifco Turbine Component Svcs., Tampa, Fla.; dir. Sifco Turbine Components Ltd., Cork, Ireland; adv. com. bd. dirs. New Eng. Mut. Life Ins. Co., 1973-77; dir. Bharat Forge Co. Ltd., Poona, India, Aikoh Sifco Co. Ltd., Tokyo, 1970-83, Industrias Kaiser Argentina, 1958-63; mem. Com. on Manpower Resources for Nat. Security, 1953-54; U.S. employer del. Internat. Labor Conf., Geneva, 1956, 75-92, Buenos Aires, 1961; mem. adv. coun. U.S.-Japanese econ. rels. U.S. State Dept., 1970-75; dir., mem. com. experts study relationship between multinat. corps. and social policy ILO, mem. governing body, 1975-78; dir. U.S.-USSR Econ. and Trade Coun., 1975; chmn. U.S. sect. Brazil-U.S. Bus. Coun., 1976-77. Trustee Cleve. YMCA; chmn. bd. mgrs. Addison br., chmn. internat. adv. com. Center Internat. Mgmt. Studies, chmn., 1982-88; bd. dirs. YMCA of the U.S.A., 1983-88, chmn. internat. com.; vice chmn. No. Ohio Rep. Fin. Com.; chmn. No. Ohio Rep. Small Bus. Com., 1956, Partners of Alliance for Ohio, 1969-72; trustee Defiance Coll., 1958-74, St. Alexis Hosp., 1960-70, Booth Meml. Hosp., 1964-74, Judson Park; trustee Ednl. Research Council Am., 1976-86, chmn., 1978-86; pres. bd. trustees Forging Industry Edn. and Research Found., 1961-65; bd. dirs. Nat. Endowment for Democracy, 1983-91; adv. bd. Salvation Army. Named One of Ten Outstanding Young Men Am., 1955. Mem. Forging Industry Assn. (dir. 1954-55, pres. 1956-58), Young Pres.'s Orgn. (chmn. Cleve. chpt. 1956-57), U.S. C. of C. (dir. 1967-81, v.p. 1970-73, treas. 1973-74, chmn. bd. 1974-75, chmn. exec. com. 1975-76), The Ocean Club Fla. (Ocean Ridge), Union Club (Cleve.), Shaker Heights Country Club (dir.), Pine Lake Trout Club, Burning Tree Club (Bethesda, Md.), Va. Hot Springs Golf and Tennis Club, Pepper Pike Club, La Mirador (Mt. Pelerin, Switzerland), Delray Dunes Golf and Tennis Club (Boynton Beach, Fla.), Masons (33 degree). Home: 4565 S Lake Dr Boynton Beach FL 33436-5904 also: 3885 Lander Rd Chagrin Falls OH 44022-1368 also: North Ridge Hot Springs VA 24445

SMITH, CHARLES ISAAC, geology educator; b. Hearne, Tex., Feb. 9, 1931; s. Walter Lee and Nellie Lucille (Clearwater) S.; m. Anita Lou Howell, Aug. 22, 1961; children: Lanita Maylene, James Emmett, Timothy Stephen, Sheila Nell. B.S., Baylor U., 1952; M.A., La. State U., 1955; Ph.D., U. Mich., 1966. Geologist Shell Devel. Co., Houston, 1955-60, 62-65; prof. geology U. Mich., Ann Arbor, 1965-77, chmn. dept., 1970-77; prof. geology U. Tex., Arlington, 1977-93, prof. emeritus, 1994—, chmn. dept., 1977-89, cons. geologist, 1993—. Author research papers. Home: PO Box 2170r Dr Ruidoso NM 88345 Office: Univ Tex Dept Geology Arlington TX 76019

SMITH, CHARLES OLIVER, engineer; b. Clinton, Mass., May 28, 1920; s. Oliver E. and Flora (Small) S.; m. Mary J. Boyle, Feb. 9, 1946; children: Mary J., Charles M., John P., Susan M., Peter G., Robert A., Katherine M. BS in Mech. Engring., Worcester Poly. Inst., 1941; SM, MIT, 1947, ScD in Metallurgy, 1951. Instr. mech. engring. Worcester Poly. Inst., 1941-43; instr., then asst. prof. Mass. Inst. Tech., 1946-51; research engr. Alcoa Research Lab., 1951-55, Oak Ridge Nat. Lab. 1955-65; prof. engring. U. Detroit, 1965-76, U. Nebr., 1976-81, Rose-Hulman Inst. Tech., 1981-86. Author: Product Liability: Are You Vulnerable?, Nuclear Reactor Materials, Science of Engineering Materials, Introduction to Reliability in Design; also numerous papers on materials, design, product liability, engring. edn. Served with USNR, 1943-46. Recipient St. George award Boy Scouts Am. Fellow ASME (Triodyne Safety award 1992, Machine Design award, 1993), Am. Soc. Engring. Edn. (Fred Merryfield award 1981); mem. AIME, Am. Soc. Metals, Sigma Xi, Tau Beta Pi, Pi Tau Sigma, Phi Kappa Theta. Home: 1717 Homewood Blvd Apt 156 Delray Beach FL 33445

SMITH, CHARLES PAUL, newspaper publisher; b. Hartford, Conn., Nov. 1, 1926; s. Thomas S. and Kathryn (Klingler) S.; m. Carolyn Calkins, Feb. 12, 1966; children: Charles, Timothy. BS, U.S. Naval Acad., 1947. Commd. ensign USN, 1947, advanced through grades to lt., line officer, 1947-58, resigned; mgr. Container Corp. Am., Phila., 1958-66, Chattanooga, 1966-68; pub. Daily Intelligencer, Doylestown, Pa., 1968—. Roman Catholic. Office: Calkins Newspapers Inc 333 N Broad St Doylestown PA 18901-3407

SMITH, CHARLES THOMAS, retired dentist, educator; b. San Diego, Mar. 22, 1914; s. Sydney Alexander and Lydia Ellen (Hoff) S.; m. Ruth Anita Anderson, May 20, 1935 (dec. Jan. 1979); children: Charlyn Ruth, Charles Thomas; m. Mary Lou Sessums, July 21, 1979. A.B., Pacific Union Coll., 1935; D.D.S., Coll. Phys. and Surg., 1940; LL.H., Loma Linda U. Sch. of Dentistry, 1971. Tchr. Glendale Union Acad., 1935-36; pvt. practice dentistry San Diego, 1940-53; dean-elect Sch. Dentistry, Loma Linda U., 1959-60, dean, 1960-71, dean emeritus, 1971; prof. emeritus Loma Linda U., 1973—; program coordinator div. Physicians and Health Profession Edn., NIH, 1971-73; prof. dept. community dentistry U. Tex. at San Antonio, 1973-83, acting dean student affairs Dental Sch., 1975-76, assoc. dean for acad. affairs, 1976-77, acting chmn. dept. community dentistry, 1977-83; Cons. dental facilities rev. com. USPHS, 1964-69; mem. grants and allocations com. Am. Found. for Dental Health, 1973-80. Dir. Paradise Valley Sanitarium and Hosp., 1947-59, San Diego Union Acad., 1947-53; founder San Diego Children's Dental Health Center; exhibit chmn. Pacific Coast Dental Conf., 1957; pres. Am. Cancer Soc., 1950; trustee Loma Linda U., 1976-90. Served as maj. AUS Dental Corps, 1953-55. Fellow Am. Coll. Dentists (vice chmn. So. Calif. chpt. 1967-68, chmn. 1968-69), Internat. Coll. Dentists; mem. So. Calif. Dental Assn. (chmn. council on dental edn. 1963-68, treas. 1967-71), San Diego County Dental Soc. (pres. 1949), Am. Acad. Dental Practice Adminstrn., Western Dental Deans Assn. (chmn. 1960-67), Western Deans and Dental Examiners (v.p. 1969—, pres. 1970), Am. Assn. Dental Schs. (mem. exec. com., v.p. council deans 1971), Acad. Dentistry Internat. (v.p. 1985-89, treas. 1985-89, chmn. awards com. 1989-90, assoc. chmn., 1986—), Nat. Assn. Seventh Day Adventists, Am. Acad. Periodontology, Acad. Dentistry Internationale, Delta Sigma Delta, Tau Kappa Omega, Omicron Kappa Upsilon. Home: 34-895 Surrey Way Thousand Palms CA 92276-4121

SMITH, CHARLES WILLIAM, engineering educator; b. Christiansburg, Va., Jan. 1, 1926; s. Robert Floyd and Ollie (Surface) S.; m. Doris Graham Burton, Sept. 9, 1950; children: Terry Jane Kelley, David Bryan. BSCE, Va. Poly. Inst., 1947, MS in Applied Mechanics, 1949. Registered profl. engr., Va. Isntr. Va. Poly. Inst. and State U., Blacksburg, 1947-48, asst. prof., 1949-52, assoc. prof., 1953-57, prof. engring., 1958-81, alumni disting. prof., 1982-92, alumni disting. prof. emeritus, 1992—; advanced grad. engring. tng. program GE Co., Lynchburg, Va., 1962; grad. tng. program Western Elec.-Bell Labs., Winston-Salem, N.C., 1963, 64; bd. dirs. Local Water Authority, Blacksburg, 1975—. Author: (with others) Experimental Techniques in Fracture Mechanics, Vol. 2, 1973, Inelastic Behavior of Composite Materials, 1975, Mechanics of Fracture, Vol. 6, 1981, Handbook of Experimental Stress Analysis, 1986, Experimental Techniques in Fracture, Vol. 3, 1993; editor: Fracture Mechanics, Vol. 11, co-editor, Vol. 17; regional editor: Jour. of Theoretical and Applied Fracture Mechanics, 1984—; guest editor: (jour.) Optics and Lasers in Engineering, 1991; contbr. articles to profl. jours. Recipient Scientific Achievement award NASA Langley Rsch. Ctr., 1986,

Dan H. Pletta award for engring. educator of yr. Va. Consortium Engring. Schs., 1991. Fellow ASME, Soc. Exptl. Mechanics (numerous coms., M.M. Frocht award for outstanding educator in exptl. mechanics 1983, William M. Murray medal for contbns. to exptl. mechanics 1993, B.J. Lazan award for rsch. in exptl. mechanics 1995, Frank G. Tatnall award 1997), Am. Acad. Mechanics; mem. ASTM, NSPE (many coms. 1950-70), Am. Soc. Engring. Edn. (chmn. nominating com. 1971), Soc. Engring. Sci. (organizing com. 1977-81, ann. meetings co-chmn. 1984), Internat. Assn. Structural Mechanics in Reactor Tech. Methodist. Achievements include development of refined merger of optical methods to measure stress intensity factor distributions in three dimensional cracked bodies in nuclear, missile and aircraft industries. Office: Va Poly Inst and State Univ ESM-VPISU-0219 Blacksburg VA 24061

SMITH, CHARLES WILLIAM, social sciences educator, sociologist; b. Providence; s. Joseph and Clara (Loitman) S.; m. Rita Cope, Sept. 3, 1963; children: Abigail Cope, Jonathan Cope. AB, Wesleyan U., 1960; MA, Brandeis U., 1966, PhD in Sociology, 1966. Instr. sociology Simmons Coll., Boston, 1964-65; from lectr. to assoc. prof. Queens Coll., Flushing, N.Y., 1965-71, from assoc. to prof. sociology, 1979—; grad. faculty Grad. Ctr. CUNY, 1986—; vis. scholar Nuffield Coll., Oxford, Eng., 1979-80, Wesleyan U., Middletown, Conn., 1987-88; chair dept. sociology Queens Coll., Flushing, 1988-91, acting dean of faculty social sci., 1991-92, dean faculty social sci., 1992-97; cons. auctions, 1986—. Author: The Mind of the Market: A Study of Stock Market Philosophies, Their Uses and Implications, 1981, Critique of Sociological Reasoning: An Essay in Philosophic Sociology, 1982, Auctions: The Social Construction of Values, 1989; editor Jour. for Theory of Social Behavior, 1983—. Bd. dirs., pres. Cmty. Action Program of White Plains, N.Y., 1974-79; bd. trustees, v.p. Temple Israel Ctr. of White Plains, 1975-94; class agt., alumni activities Wesleyan U., Middletown, Conn., 1960—. Recipient FIPSE award Dept. Edn., 1993-96, Ford Found. Diversity grant, 1990-93, 96-98. Office: Queens Coll CUNY 65-30 Kissena Blvd Flushing NY 11367-1575

SMITH, CHARLES WILSON, JR., university dean; b. Ft. Lauderdale, Fla., Apr. 15, 1949; m. Constance Killen; children: Thaddeus, Cameron, Amber, Isaac, Jordan, Rachael. MD, U. N.C., 1974, BS, 1979. Diplomate Am. Bd. Family Practice (bd. dirs., com. mem., treas., pres. 1991-92). Resident in psychiatry U. N.C. Meml. Hosp., 1974-75, resident in family practice, 1975-78; pvt. practice, Muscatine, Ia., 1978-79; asst. prof. Wright State U., 1979-83, assoc. prof., 1983-86; chief of family medicine sch. of primary med. care U. Ala., Huntsville, 1986-87, assoc. dean clin. affairs, 1986-87, acting dean, 1986; assoc. dean U. Ala. Sch. of Medicine, Huntsville, 1986-89; exec. assoc. dean for clin. affairs U. Ark. for Med. Scis., Little Rock, 1989—, prof. family and community medicine, 1989—, exec. dir. faculty practice plan, 1991—; dir. family practice residency program Miami Valley Hosp., Dayton, Ohio, 1979-86. Co-author: Family Practice Desk Reference, 2d edit., 1995; editor Primary Care Currents, 1985—; dep. editor Am. Family Physician, 1987—; contbr. numerous articles to profl. jours. Bd. dirs. Nicholas J. Pisacano Found., 1990—. Mem. AMA, Am. Acad. Family Physicians (editor mag.), Ark. Acad. Family Physicians, Ark. Med. Assn., Pulaski County Med. Soc. Home: 4 Chelsea Rd Little Rock AR 72212-3723 Office: U Ark for Med Scis 4301 W Markham St # 719 Little Rock AR 72205-7101

SMITH, CHARLES Z., state supreme court justice; b. Lakeland, Fla., Feb. 23, 1927; s. John R. and Eva (Love) S.; m. Eleanor Jane Martinez, Aug. 20, 1955; children: Carlos M., Michael O., Stephen P., Felica L. BS, Temple U., 1952; JD, U. Wash., 1955. Bar: Wash. 1955. Law clk. Wash. Supreme Ct., Olympia, 1955-56; dep. pros. atty., asst. chief criminal div. King County, Seattle, 1956-60; ptnr. Bianchi, Smith & Tobin, Seattle, 1960-61; spl. asst. to atty. gen. criminal div. U.S. Dept. Justice, Washington, 1961-64; judge criminal dept. Seattle Mcpl. Ct., 1965-66; judge Superior Ct. King County, 1966-73; former assoc. dean, prof. law U. Wash., 1973; now justice Wash. Supreme Ct., Olympia. Mem. adv. bd. NAACP, Seattle Urban League, Wash. State Literacy Coun., Boys Club, Wash. Citizens for Migrant Affairs, Medina Children's Svc., Children's Home Soc. Wash., Seattle Better Bus. Bur., Seattle Foundation, Seattle Symphony Orch., Seattle Opera Assn., Community Svc. Ctr. for Deaf and Hard of Hearing, Seattle U., Seattle Sexual Assault Ctr., Seattle Psychoanalytic Inst., The Little Sch., Linfield Coll., Japanese Am. Citizens League, Kawabe Meml. Hous, Puget Counseling Ctr, Am. Cancer Soc., Hutchinson Cancer Rsch. Ctr., Robert Chinn Found.; pres. Am. Bapt. Chs. U.S.A., 1976-77, lt. col. ret. USMCR. Mem. ABA, Am. Judicature Soc., Washington Bar Assn., Seattle-King County Bar Assn., Order of Coif., Phi Alpha Delta, Alpha Phi Alpha. Office: Wash Supreme Ct Temple of Justice PO Box 40929 Olympia WA 98504

SMITH, CHARLOTTE REED, retired music educator; b. Eubank, Ky., Sept. 15, 1921; d. Joseph Lumpkin and Cornelia Elizabeth (Spenser) Reed; m. Walter Lindsay Smith, Aug. 24, 1949; children—Walter Lindsay IV, Elizabeth Reed. B.A. in Music, Tift Coll., 1941; M.A. in Mus. Theory, Eastman Sch. of Music, 1946; postgrad. Juilliard Sch., 1949. Asst. prof. theory Okla. Bapt. U., 1944-45, Washburn U., 1946-48; prof. music Furman U., Greenville, S.C., 1948-92; chmn. dept. music, 1987-92. Editor: Seven Penitential Psalms with Two Laudate Psalms, 1983; author: Manual of Sixteenth-Century Contrapuntal Style, 1989. Mem. Internat. Musicological Soc., Am. Musicological Soc., Soc. for Music Theory, AAUP (sec.-treas. Furman chpt. 1984-85), Nat. Fedn. Music Clubs, Pi Kappa Lambda. Republican. Baptist.

SMITH, CHESTER, broadcasting executive; b. Wade, Okla., Mar. 29, 1930; s. Louis L. and Effie (Brown) S.; m. Naomi L. Crenshaw, July 19, 1959; children: Lauri, Lorna, Roxanne. Country western performer on Capitol records, TV and radio, 1947-61; owner, mgr. Sta. KLOC, Ceres-Modesto, Calif., 1963-81, Sta. KCBA-TV, Salinas-Monterey, Calif.?; owner, gen. ptnr. Sta. KCSO-TV, Modesto-Stockton-Sacramento, 1966-97, Sta. KCVU-TV, Paradise-Chico-Redding, Calif., 1986—, Sta.; owner Sta. KBVU-TV, Eureka, Calif., 1990—, Sta. KNSO-TV, KCSO-TV, 1966-97 Merced-Fresno, KZVU-TV, Chico, Calif., K22EJ, Redding, Calif., KES-TV, Sacramento, 1996-97, KFWU-TV, 1996-97, Fort Bragg, Calif., 1996-97, KRVU-TV, Redding, 1997—. Mem. Calif. Broadcasters Assn. Republican. Mem. Christian Ch. original rec. Wait A Little Longer Please Jesus; rec. in Country Music Hall of Fame, Nashville, 1955, inductee Western Swing Hall of Fame, Sacramento, 1988.

SMITH, CHRISTINE, author, lecturer, former pharmaceutical executive; b. Bronx, N.Y., Oct. 28, 1958; d. Frank and Virginia (Milone) Michalchuk. AA, Suffolk County C.C., Farmingville, N.Y., 1978; AS, Suffolk County C.C., Farmingvale, N.Y., 1979; BA, SUNY, Stony Brook, 1980. Cert. dental asst., N.Y. Purchasing agt. Ctrl. Dental Supply Co., Hempstead, N.Y., 1981-82; sales mgr. Capital Credit Corp., Hempstead, N.Y., 1982-83; pharm. rep. Bristol Myers, Evansville, Ind., 1983-91, Syntex Labs., Palo Alto, Calif., 1991-93, Abbott Labs., Abbott Park, Ill., 1993-96; ptnr., author, lectr. Post-Divorce Reconstruction Publs., Huntington, N.Y., 1996—; pres., ptnr. The Image Consultants, Huntington, 1989-91. Mem. Tai-Zen Acad. Self-Def., U.S. Karate Studios. Roman Catholic. Avocations: creative writing, consulting to persons experiencing post-"break-up"-trauma.

SMITH, CHRISTOPHER ALLEN, technology company executive, marketing professional; b. Rockford, Ill., Nov. 16, 1961; s. Robert Lee and Martha Ann (Moody) S.; m. Mary G. Meany, Apr. 13, 1991. BA, Ind. U., 1983, postgrad., 1983; postgrad., Golden Gate U., 1986-87. Rates analyst North American Van Lines, Ft. Wayne, Ind., 1984-85; mgr., investor rels. BRAE Corp., San Francisco, 1985-87; fin. analyst CIS Corp., San Francisco, 1987-89; dir., corp. devel. Affiliated Computer Systems, Inc., San Francisco, 1989-96; bus. practice leader, outsourcing svcs. Sci. Applications Internat. Corp., San Francisco, 1996—. Contbr. articles to profl. jours. Vol. Rep. Party, Foster City, Calif., 1988; apptd. dir. Pvt. Industry Coun. Contra Costa County. With USMCR, 1982-83. Mem. Equipment Leasing Assn. Am. (Jour. award 1991), Ind. U. Alumni Assn. Republican. Roman Catholic. Avocations: freelance writing, photography, gardening. Office: Sci Applications Internat Corp 2000 Powell St Ste 1090 Emeryville CA 94608-1855

SMITH, CHRISTOPHER HENRY, congressman; b. Rahway, N.J., Mar. 4, 1953; s. Bernard Henry and Katherine Joan (Hall) S.; m. Marie Hahn, July 2, 1977; children: Melissa, Christopher, Michael Jonathan, Elyse. Student, Worcester Coll., Eng., 1973-74; B.A. in Bus. Adminstrn., Trenton State Coll., 1975. Exec. dir. N.J. Right to Life Com., 1976-77; dir. instl. sales Leisure Unltd. Inc., Woodbridge, N.J., 1978-80; mem. 97th-105th Congresses from 4th N.J. dist., Washington, D.C., 1981—; chmn. internat. rels. subcom. on internat. ops. and human rights 97th-105th Congresses from 4th N.J. dist., vice-chmn. vets. affairs com., co-chmn. Helsinki com., 1995—; U.S. rep. to UN internat. conf. immunizing world's children. Active human rights movements Romania, China, former Soviet Union, Vietnam; co-chmn. House Pro-Life Caucus. Named Legislator of Yr. VFW, Legislator of Yr. Internat. Assn. Chiropractors, Legislator of Yr. KC, 1989, Legislator of Yr. JWV of Am., 1996; recipient Leader for Peace award Peace Corps. Mem. Nat. Fedn. Ind. Bus. Republican. Roman Catholic. Office: 2370 Rayburn Ho Office Bldg Washington DC 20515

SMITH, CLARA JEAN, retired nursing home administrator; b. Berwick, Pa., Aug. 31, 1932; d. Barton Fredrick and Evelyn Miriam (Bomboy) Hough; RN, Williamsport (Pa.) Hosp., 1953; B.S. in Nursing Edn., Wilkes Coll., Wilkes-Barre, Pa., 1960; M.S. in Edn., Temple U., Phila., 1969; m. Robert W. Smith, June 7, 1958. From staff nurse to dir. nursing Retreat State Hosp., Hunlock Creek, Pa., 1953-80; dir. long term care facility Danville (Pa.) State Hosp., 1980-82; ret., 1982; dir. accrediatation coordination and quality assurance Nursing Home Adminstrs., 1980—; speaker, instr. in field. Author tng. and ednl. programs. Mem. Pa. State Employees Retirement Assn. (pres. Luzerne/Columbia County chpt., regional v.p. northeastern Pa.), Williamsport Hosp. Sch. Nursing Alumni, Sunshine Club, Town Hill Hobby Group, Town Hill Over 50 Group. Methodist. Home: PO Box 999 Berwick PA 18603-0699

SMITH, CLIFFORD NEAL, business educator, writer; b. Wakita, Okla., May 30, 1923; s. Jesse Newton and Inez Lane (Jones) S.; m. Anna Piszczan-Czaja, Sept. 3, 1951; children: Helen Inez Smith Barrette. BS, Okla. State U., 1943; AM, U. Chgo., 1948; postgrad. Columbia U., 1960. Selector, U.S. Displaced Persons Commn., Washington and Munich, Germany, 1948-51; auditor Phillips Petroleum Co., Caracas, Venezuela, 1951-58; planning analyst Mobil Internat. Oil Co., N.Y.C., 1960, 65-66, Mobil Oil A.G., Deutschland, Hamburg, Germany, 1961-63; asst. to v.p. for Germany, Mobil Inner Europe, Inc., Geneva, 1963-65; asst. prof. No. Ill. U. Sch. Bus., DeKalb, 1966-69, part-time prof. internat. bus., 1970—; owner Westland Publs.; lectr. in field. Author: Federal Land Series, vol. 1, 1972, vol. 2, 1973, vol. 3, 1980, vol. 4, part 1, 1982, vol. 4, part 2, 1986, Encyclopedia of German-American Genealogical Research, American Genealogical Resources in German Archives, 1977, numerous monographs in German-Am., Brit.-Am., French-Am. geneal. research series, German and Central European Emigration Series, Selections from the American State Papers; contbg. editor Nat. Geog. Soc. Quar., Geneal. jour. (Utah); contbr. articles to profl. jours. Mem. at large exec. com. Friends Com. on Nat. Legis., 1968-75; mem. regional exec. com. Am. Friends Service Com., 1969-76; v.p. Riverside Dem., N.Y.C., 1959-61; precinct committeeman, 1984—; mem. Ariz. State Central Com. of Dem. Party, 1984—; sec. Dem. Cen. Com. of Cochise County; mem. com. to Re-Elect Clinton for Pres. Recipient Distinguished Service medal Ill. Geneal. Soc., 1973, award for outstanding service to sci. genealogy Am. Soc. Genealogists, 1973; court appointed arbitrator for civil cases, 1992. Fellow Geneal. Soc. of Utah; mem. S.R., SAR, Soc. Descs. Colonial Clergy, Soc. Advancement Mgmt., Ill. Genealogic Soc. (dir. 1968-69), Phi Eta Sigma, Beta Alpha Psi, Sigma Iota Epsilon. Mem. Soc. of Friends. Club: American of Hamburg (v.p. 1962-63); contbr. articles to profl. jours. Address: PO Box 117 Mc Neal AZ 85617-0117

SMITH, CLODUS RAY, academic administrator; b. Blanchard, Okla., May 15, 1928; s. William Thomas and Rachel (Hale) S.; m. Pauline R. Chaat; children: Martha Lynn, William Paul, Paula Diane. Assoc. degree, Cameron State Coll., 1948; BS in Agrl. Edn., Okla. A & M Coll., 1950; MS in Vocat. Edn., Okla. State U., 1955; EdD in Vocat. Edn., Cornell U., 1960. Grad. asst. Cornell U., 1957-59; asst. prof. U. Md., 1959-62, assoc. prof., 1962-63, dir. Summer Sch., 1963-72, adminstrv. dean, 1972-73; spl. asst. to pres. Cleve. State U., 1973-74, v.p. for univ. rels., 1974-83; pres. Rio Grande Coll. and Rio Grande Community Coll., Ohio, 1983-86, Lake Erie Coll., Painesville, Ohio, 1986-92, Okla. Ind. Coll. Found., Oklahoma City, 1993—, Okla. Assn. Ind. Colls. and Univs., 1993—; cons. NEA, Naval Weapons Lab., Dehlgren, Va.; researcher Personal and Profl. Satisfactions; contract investigator Nat. Endowment for Humanities; dir. Human Resources and Community Devel., Prince George's County, Md. Author: Planning and Paying for College, 1958, Rural Recreation for Profit, 1971, A Strategy for University Relations, 1975, State Relations for the 1980 Decade, 1982. Amb. Natural Resources, Ohio, 1984, chmn. dept.; founder N.Am. Assn. of Summer Schs., 1979. Recipient Rsch. award Nat. Project in Agrl. Communications, 1959, Edn. award Prince George's C. of C., 1971. Mem. Am. Assn. U. Adminstrs., Am. Assn. for Higher Edn., Nat. Soc. for Study Edn., Coun. for Support and Advancement Edn., Am. Alumni Coun., Al Koran Hunter's Club, Shriners. Methodist. Avocations: hunting, fishing. Home: 6617 115th St Oklahoma City OK 73162 Office: Okla Ind Coll Found 114 E Sheridan Ave Ste 101 Oklahoma City OK 73104-2411

SMITH, CLYDE CURRY, historian, educator; b. Hamilton, Ohio, Dec. 16, 1929; s. Charles Clyde and Mabel Ethel Ola (Curry) S.; m. Ellen Marie Gormsen, June 13, 1953; children: Harald Clyde, Karen Margaret Evans. BA in Physics cum laude and MS, Miami U., Oxford, Ohio, 1951; BDiv, U. Chgo., 1954, MA, 1961, PhD, 1968. Ordained to ministry Christian Ch. (Disciples of Christ), 1954. Exec. asst. to dean Disciples Div. House, Chgo., 1956-57; lectr. in O.T., Univ. Coll. U. Chgo., 1957; asst. prof. St. John's Coll. U. Manitoba, Winnipeg, Can., 1958-63; instr. Brandeis U., Waltham, Mass., 1963-65; prof. ancient history and religious U. Wis., River Falls, 1965-90, prof. emeritus, 1990—; vis. prof. religious studies Culver-Stockton Coll., Canton, Mo., 1990, U. Newcastle-upon-Tyne, Eng., 1992-94; vis. lectr. div., Edge Hill Coll. of Edn., Ormskirk, Eng., 1970-71; postdoctoral fellow Johns Hopkins U., Balt., 1977; NEH fellow-in-residence U. Calif., Santa Barbara, 1978-79; vis. rsch. fellow, lectr. religious studies U. Aberdeen, Scotland, 1980, 85-86. Contbr. articles to profl. publs. Mem. Pierce County Hist. Assn., River Falls, 1965—, Wis. Dems., 1965—, Dem. Nat. Com., 1983—; charter mem. Sci. Mus. of Minn., St. Paul, 1973—, Libr. Congress, 1994—; charter assoc. Libr. of Congress, 1994—; founding mem. River Falls Cmty. Arts Base, 1996—, Kinnickinnic River Land Trust, 1996—. Recipient Gov.'s Spl. award State of Wis., 1990, several grants. Mem. Internat. Soc. Anglo-Saxonists, Assn. Ancient Historians, Can. Soc. Ch. History (founder, treas. 1960-63), N.Am. Patristic Soc., Can. Soc. for Mesopotamian Studies, Soc. Old Testament Study (Gt. Britain), Soc. for Promotion Roman Studies of London, Hellenic Soc. London, Brit. Sch. Archaeology in Iraq, Brit. Inst. Archaeology in Ankara, Internat. Soc. Anglo-Saxonists, Oriental Inst. U. Chgo., Phi Beta Kappa. Democrat. Avocations: outerspace, battleships, dinosaurs. Home: 939 W Maple St River Falls WI 54022-2055 *We can begin thought with the assumption that there is a world which knows neither origin nor end but which includes us; we can conclude with the affirmations that there was a "when" whatever is was not, and that whatever is will with time cease to be. Our concern then can be to enhance value and empower others, especially those who follow.*

SMITH, CLYDE R., counselor educator; b. Donaldson, Ark., June 15, 1933; s. Clyde Raymond Smith and Annie Pearl (Burnett) Cypert; m. Jannis Lowery, July 31, 1952; 1 child, Renee Lowery. BS, Ark. State U., 1957; MEd, U. Mo., 1958; EdD, U. Tenn., Knoxville, 1969. Employment placement counselor Mo. Bur. for the Blind, Kansas City, Mo., 1958-60; counselor Presbyn. Guidance Ctr., Rhodes U., Memphis, 1960-67; assoc. prof. edn. Bradley U., Peoria, Ill., 1969-97, prof. emeritus, 1997—; vocat. cons. Social Security Adminstrn. Bur. Hearings and Appeals, Memphis, 1963-69, Peoria, 1969-78. Contbr. articles to profl. jours. Bd dirs. Peoria Heights Sch. Dist. 325, 1974-76, Children's Home Assn. Ill., Peoria, 1978-80. Recipient Jefferson award Am. Inst. for Pub. Svc., 1978, Tom Connor award C. of C., Peoria, 1978, Others award Salvation Army, 1984. Mem. ACA (life), Nat. Career Devel. Assn., Peoria Lions (life, pres. 1975-76, bd. dirs. 1978-81, 85-91, dep. dist. gov. 1982-83, zone chmn. 1983-84, Melvin Jones fellow). Republican. Presbyterian. Avocations: reading, music, hiking, collecting old movies. Home: 1511 W Callender Ave Peoria IL 61606-1615 Office: Bradley U 306 Westlake Hall Peoria IL 61625

SMITH, CONSTANCE LEWIS, secondary school educator; b. Macon, Ga., May 29, 1936; d. Isiah and Anna (Duncan) Lewis; m. Willie S. Smith, Dec. 2, 1956; children: Glenda Smith Hubbard, Kristen Y. MA, Ft. Valley (Ga.) State Coll., 1981. Cert. early childhood edn. tchr., Ga. Tchr. pub. schs., Macon, 1971—. Mem. NEA, Ga. Assn. Educators, Bibb County Assn. Educators, Delta Sigma Theta. Roman Catholic. Avocations: reading, travel, music, ceramics, interior decorating. Home: 3703 Greenbriar Rd Macon GA 31204-4255

SMITH, CORLIES MORGAN, publishing executive; b. Phila., Mar. 31, 1929; s. Charles Ross and Mary Howard (Stewart) S.; m. Sheila de Peyster Carey, June 17, 1950; children: Mark, Nicholas, Peter, Baylies, Timothy. BA, Yale U., 1951. Assoc. editor J.B. Lippincott Co., Phila., 1955-62; sr. editor The Viking Press, N.Y.C., 1962-83; editorial dir. Ticknor & Fields, N.Y.C., 1984-89; editor in chief Harcourt Brace & Co., N.Y.C., 1990-94, editorial con., 1995—. Home and Office: 1435 Lexington Ave New York NY 10128-1625

SMITH, CORNELIA MARSCHALL, retired biology educator; b. Llano, Tex., Oct. 15, 1895; d. Ernst and Lucie (Meusebach) Marschall; m. Charles G. Smith, Sept. 9, 1926 (wid. Aug. 1967). BA in Pre-Med/Biology, Baylor U., 1918; MA in Biology, U. Chgo., 1925; PhD in Biology, Johns Hopkins, 1928. Prof. biology Waco (Tex.) High Sch., 1918-25; prof. botany Baylor U., Waco, 1928-30, asst. prof. biology, 1930-35, chmn. biology dept., 1940-67, dir. Strecker Mus., 1940-67; chmn. biology dept. John B. Stetson U., DeLand, Fla., 1935-40; sec. treas. Tex. Bd. Examiners of Basic Scis., 1960-67; v.p. Tex. Acad. Sci., 1954, treas. 1944-46. Editor: Spencer's Proverb Lore, 1970; author: Browning's Proverb Lore, 1989, A Monograph: The Artist Pen Browning, 1993, A Monograph: The Physical Browning, 1981. Recipient Herbert H. Reynolds award Baylor U., Waco, 1991; Cornelia M. Smith Professorship in Biology initiated 1980, Cornelia Marschall Smith Day of Celebration, 1992; named Minnie Piper Prof. of Yr., 1965. Mem. Mortar Bd. (hon.), Baylor Round Table, Beta Beta Beta, Omicron Delta Kappa (hon.), Sigma Xi. Democrat. Baptist. Avocations: attending symphony performances, hosting social parties, going to work daily. Home: 801 James Ave Waco TX 76706-1472 Office: Armstrong Browning Libr PO Box 97152 Waco TX 76798

SMITH, CRAIG RICHARDS, manufacturing executive; b. Los Angeles, June 2, 1940; s. Max Boley and Dorcas (Richards) S.; m. Diann Kuhni, June 2, 1960; children: Bradley, Hally, Sharee, Tracy, Cindy, Kristen, Michelle. BS in Physics, Brigham Young U., 1962, MBA, 1965. V.p. ops. WER Indsl. div. Emerson Electric, Grand Island, N.Y., 1972-76; v.p., gen. mgr. Carborundum Bonded Abrasives Div., Buffalo, 1976-70; v.p., div. mgr. Raymark Corp., Trumbull, Conn., 1980-85, now bd. dirs.; pres., chief exec. officer Raytech Corp., Shelton, 1985—, also bd. dirs. Republican. Mormon. Avocations: running, golf, tennis, basketball. Office: Raytech Corp 1 Corporate Dr Ste 512 Shelton CT 06484-6210

SMITH, CRAIG RICHEY, machinery executive; b. Cleve., May 30, 1925; s. Wilbur Thomas and Helen (Stearns) S.; m. Mary Wood Glover, Dec. 17, 1945; children: Timothy VanGorder, Craig Richey, Patricia Sodon, Marcia Colby. B.S. in M.E, Case Inst. Tech., 1945; postgrad., Harvard Bus. Sch., 1974. Mem. Warner & Swasey Co. (merger Bendix Corp. 1980, Allied Corp. 1983), 1946-84; gen. mgr. Wiedemann div. Warner & Swasey Co., King of Prussia, Pa.; v.p. Turning Machine Div. Warner & Swasey Co., Cleve., 1969-73, group v.p. machine tools, 1973-77, pres., chief operating officer, 1977-79, chmn., chief exec., 1979-80, pres. indsl. group, 1980-82, chmn. indsl. group, 1982-84; chmn. Prodn. Pub. Co., 1985-86; chmn., chief exec. officer Ransburg Corp., 1988-89, bd. dirs., 1979-89; chmn., chief exec. officer Ameritrust Corp., 1990-92, bd. dirs., 1980-92; bd. dirs. Lincoln Elec. Co., Cleve. Machine Controls Co. Campaign leader United Way Svcs., 1977-83; trustee Judson Park, 1977-84, Greater Cleve. Growth Assn., 1979-84, Case Western Res. U., 1979-95; trustee Vocat. Guidance & Rehab. Svcs., 1972-79, 1st v.p. 1976-79. Served with USN, 1943-46, 52-53. Mem. Soc. Mfg. Engrs. (hon.), Machine Tool Builders Assn., (dir. 1971-74, 79-84, chmn. 1980-81), Machinery and Allied Products Inst. (mem. exec. coun. 1979-84). Clubs: Union, Chagrin Valley Hunt, Cleve. skating. Home: 13754 County Line Rd Chagrin Falls OH 44022-4008

SMITH, CULLEN, lawyer; b. Waco, Tex., May 31, 1925; s. Curtis Cullen and Elizabeth (Brient) S.; m. Laura Risher Dossett, Mar. 6, 1948; children: Sallie Chesnutt Smith Wright, Alethea Risher Smith Gilbert, Elizabeth Brient Smith. Student, Emory U., 1943-44, Duke U., 1944; B.B.A., Baylor U., 1948, J.D., 1950. Bar: Tex. 1950. Ptnr. firm Smith, McIlheran & Smith, Weslaco, Tex., 1950-53, Naman, Howell, Smith & Lee (P.C.), Waco, 1953—; lectr. law Baylor U. Sch. Law, 1964-72. Contbr. articles to legal publs. Mem. standing com. Episcopal Diocese of Tex., 1960-63, 74-75; trustee Episcopal Theol. Sem. of S.W., 1962-67; mem. Waco City Coun., 1983-86; chmn. bd. Vanguard Sch., 1975; bd. dirs. G.H. Pape Found., 1993-94; bd. dirs., vice chmn. Tex. Ctr. for Legal Ethics and Professionalism, 1994—. 1st lt. USMCR, 1943-46. Named One of 5 Outstanding Young Texans Tex. Jr. C. of C., 1957, Baylor Lawyer of Yr., 1980. Fellow Am. Bar Found., Tex. Bar Found. (chmn. bd. 1973-74), fellow Coll. of Law Practice Mgmt.; mem. ABA (chmn. standing com. econs. law practice 1965-69, chmn. spl. com. on law book pub. practices 1970-72, chmn. gen. practice sect. 1973-74, mem. ho. of dels. 1974-81), Am. Law Firm Assn. (chmn. 1989-90), Waco-McLennan County Bar Assn. (pres. 1956-57), Mont. Bar Assn. (hon.), State Bar Tex. (pres. jr. bar 1957-58, chmn. profl. econs. com. 1959-61, chmn. spl. com. on revision Tex. Canons Ethics 1969-71, dir. 1971-74, pres. 1978-79), Baylor U. Law Alumni Assn. (pres. 1962-63), Order of Coif, Delta Sigma Phi, Phi Delta Phi. Clubs: Ridgewood Country (pres. 1965), Hedonia (pres. 1957). Lodge: Rotary. Avocation: photography. Home: Oak Grove Farm 447 Meandering Way China Spring TX 76633-2905 Office: Naman Howell Smith & Lee PC Tex Ctr PO Box 1470 Waco TX 76703-1470

SMITH, CURTIS JOHNSTON, government executive; b. Honolulu, Jan. 7, 1947; s. Robert Johnston and Sara Adelaide (Marshall) S.; m. Susan Helen Manell, June 17, 1967; 1 dau., Morgan Lynn. BA, Calif. Luth. Coll., Thousand Oaks, 1969; MA, Ohio State U., 1972, PhD, 1975. Legis. asst. Office of Pers. Mgmt., Washington, 1977-80, spl. asst. to assoc. dir. for compensation, 1980-82, dep. asst. dir. for pay and benefits policy, 1982-84, sr. examiner office mgmt. and budget, 1984-85, policy advisor to dir., 1985-86, assoc. dir. for career entry and employee devel., 1986-89, assoc. dir. ret., ins., 1989-94; dir. Office Exec. Resources and dir. Fed. Exec. Inst., Charlottesville, Va., 1994—; mem. Nat. Accountancy Pub. Adminstrs. panel on pub. svc. Assn. Va. Health Policy Ctr. Mem. Am. Soc. Pub. Adminstrn., Internat. Personnel Mgmt. Assn., Trout Unlimited. Avocations: fishing, golf, bicycling. Office: Fed Exec Inst Office Exec Resources 1301 Emmet St N Charlottesville VA 22903-4872

SMITH, D. ADAM, congressman; b. Washington, June 15, 1965; m. Sara Bickle-Eldridge, 1993. BA, Fordham U., 1987; JD, U. Wash., 1990. Driver United Parcel Svc., 1985-87; mem. Wash. State Senate, 1990-96; atty. Cromwell Mendoza Belur, 1992-93; asst. prosecuting atty. City of Seattle, 1993-96; mem. 105th Congress from 9th dist. Wash., 1997—. Democrat. Office: 1505 Longworth Washington DC 20515

SMITH, DALLAS R., federal official; b. Bolton, N.C., Oct. 1, 1942; s. John William and Bonnie Arlene (Jacobs) S.; m. Shirley Ann Turner, Apr. 10, 1966; 2 children. BS, N.C. Agrl. and Tech. U., 1965; postgrad., U. Md., 1968-69. Agrl. ext. agent N.C. ext. svc. tobacco and peanuts divsn. agrl. stabilization and conservation svc. USDA, Washington, 1965-68, cotton mktg. specialist, 1969-75, chief peanut br., 1976-77, dep. dir., 1977-85, dir., 1985-93, dep. under sec. internat. affairs and commodity programs office of sec., 1993—, now acting under sec. farm and fgn. agrl. svcs. Active Patuxent River 4-H Ctr. Sgt. U.S. Army, res. Nat. 4-H fellow. Presbyterian. Avocations: woodworking, tennis. Office: USDA Farm & Foreign Agrl Srvs Rm 205E 14th & Independence Ave SW Washington DC 20250-0002

SMITH, DANI ALLRED, sociologist, educator; b. Natchez, Miss., Dec. 12, 1955; d. Paul Hollis and Mary Frances (Byrd) Allred; m. Ronald Bassel Smith, Aug. 9, 1980. BS in Social Sci., Lee Coll., 1977; MA in Sociology, U. Miss., 1980; postgrad., U. Tenn., 1989—. Staff writer Natchez Dem., 1977; secondary tchr. Natchez Pub. Schs., 1977-78; instr. sociology U. Miss., 1980-81, 82, rsch. assoc., instr. mgmt. info. systems, 1982-87; secondary tchr.

Coffeeville (Miss.) Schs., 1981-82; asst. prof. sociology Lee Coll., Cleveland, Tenn., 1988-96; instr. sociology Fisk U., Nashville, 1996—; workshop speaker Ch. of God Prison Conf., Cleveland, 1993, 94, 95; speaker Bradley County Law Enforcement Tng. Assn., Cleveland, 1992; advisor Lee Collegian, 1988-93. Contbr. articles to profl. jours. and newspapers. Advisor Sociology Club, 1988-96, Alpha Kappa Delta, 1992-96, Soc. for Law and Justice, 1995-96. Mellon Appalachian fellow, 1993-94; named one of Outstanding Young Women Am., 1981. Mem. Am. Sociol. Assn., So. Sociol. Assn., Christian Sociol. Assn., Am. Soc. Criminology, Am. Mus. Natural History, Gt. Smoky Mountains Natural History Assn., Am. Hiking Soc., Smithsonian Assocs., Libr. of Congress Assocs., Phi Kappa Phi, Alpha Chi, Alpha Kappa Delta. Avocations: reading, hiking, camping, plate collecting, cross-stitching. Home: 430 20th St NE Cleveland TN 37311-3949 Office: Fisk Univ Dept Sociology Dept Sociology 1000 17th Ave N Nashville TN 37208-3045

SMITH, DANIEL CLIFFORD, lawyer; b. Cin., Aug. 9, 1936; s. Clifford John and Vivian Aileen (Stone) S.; m. Carroll Cunningham; children—Edward, Andrew, Scott. B.S., Ariz. State U., 1960; postgrad. George Washington U., 1961-62; J.D., Am. U., 1965. Bar: D.C. 1965, U.S. Ct. Appeals (D.C. cir.) 1966, U.S. Ct. Appeals (Fed. cir), U.S. Dist. Ct. D.C. 1966, Va. 1967, U.S. Supreme Ct. 1969, U.S. Ct. Appeals (4th cir., 5th cir., 7th cir., 9th cir., 11th cir.), U.S. Ct. Claims, U.S. Ct. Customs and Patent Appeals, U.S. Tax Ct. Assoc. Alpern & Feissner, Washington, 1963-66; atty. FTC, Washington, 1966-70; ptnr. Arent, Fox, Kintner, Plotkin & Kahn, Washington, 1970-93, Canfield & Smith, Washington, 1993—. Pres., dir. Country Pl. Citizens Assn., Inc., 1974-77; bd. dirs. Sea Watch Condominium, Ocean City, Md., 1978—, treas., 1982-86, pres. 1986—; active Supreme Ct. Hist. Soc., Smithsonian Inst. Assocs., Ariz. State Soc. Served with USMC. Mem. D.C. Bar Assn. (dir. 1974-76, chmn. consumer protection com. 1972-74, chmn. D.C. affairs sect. 1975-76), Va. State Bar Assn., ABA, Fed. Bar Assn., Assn. Trial Lawyers Am., Nat. Field Selling Assn. (gen. counsel), Ariz. State U. Alumni Assn., Delta Theta Phi. Clubs: Rotary (pres. 1987-88, 96-97), Optimist (pres. 1972-73), Country Glen, Internat. Town and Country (dir. 1969-73), Masons. Contbr. articles to legal jours. Office: Canfield & Smith Fed Bar Bldg 1815 H St NW Ste 1001 Washington DC 20006-3604

SMITH, DATUS CLIFFORD, JR., former foundation executive, publisher; b. Jackson, Mich., May 3, 1907; s. Datus Clifford and Marion (Houston) S.; m. Dorothy Hunt, Aug. 29, 1931 (dec. 1973); children: Sandra, Karen. B.S., Princeton U., 1929, M.A. (hon.), 1958. Grad. mgr. student employment Princeton U., 1929-30; editor Princeton Alumni Weekly, 1931-40; editor Princeton U. Press, 1941-53, dir. sec., 1942-53; assoc. prof. Princeton U., 1943-47, prof., 1947-53; pres. Franklin Book Programs, 1052-67; v.p. JDR 3d Fund, 1967-73; asso. John D. Rockefeller 3d, 1967-73; coordinator Japan philanthropy project Council on Founds., 1974-75; cons. Asia Soc., Nat. Endowment for Humanities, Hazen Found., Am. Council Learned Socs., Assn. Am. Pubs., Indo-U.S. Subcom. Edn. and Culture; past chmn. Found. Internat. Group; Bowker lectr. N.Y. Pub. Library, 1958; adv. council Ctr. for Book, Library of Congress; past pres. Assn. Am. Univ. Presses; dir. Am. Book Pub. Council.; Past chmn. editorial com. Pub. Opinion Quar.; vis. com. Harvard Press; Nat. Book Com.; trustee Center Applied Linguistics, Japan Center Internat. Exchange, Mason Early Edn. Found.; hon. life trustee Asia Soc., 1983—; trustee JDR 3d Fund, Haskins Labs.; pres. U.S. Bd. on Books for Young People, 1981-84. Author: Land and People of Indonesia, 1961, 83, Guide to Book Publishing, 1966, 68, 94, Economics of Book Publishing in Developing Countries, 1976; contbr. to Fgn. Affairs, Atlantic Monthly, Scholarly Pub., Internat. Ency. Book Pub., Ency. Asian History; project dir., Publishers Weekly; mng. editor Meadow Lark. Trustee, pres. U.S. Com. for UNICEF, 1977-79, vice chmn., 1979-81; past mem. U.S. nat. commn. UNESCO; sec. Meadow Lakes Forum; mem. Dem. County com., Mercer County. Decorated Order of Homayoun Iran; recipient Disting. Svc. award Assn. Am. Univ. Presses, 1975, Princeton in Asia award 1989, Helenka Pantaleoni award UNICEF, 1989, Asalaksen Internat. Publ. award, 1991; named to Pub. Hall of Fame, 1985. Mem. PEN, Am. Ctr. Home: 708 Meadow Lks Hightstown NJ 08520 Office: US Com for UNICEF 331 E 38th St New York NY 10016-2772

SMITH, DAVID BROOKS, federal judge; b. 1951. BA, Franklin and Marshall Coll., 1973; JD, Dickinson Sch. Law, 1976. Pvt. practice Jubelirer, Carothers, Krier, Halpern & Smith, Altoona, Pa., 1976-84; judge Ct. Common Pleas of Blair County, Pa., 1984-88, U.S. Dist. Ct. (we. dist.) Pa., Johnstown, 1988—; asst. dist. atty. Blair County, part-time, 1981-83, dist. atty. part-time, 1983-84; instr. Pa. State U., Altoona campus, 1977-87, St. Francis Coll., 1986—; adv. com. on criminal rules U.S. Jud. Conf., 1993—. Trustee St. Francis Coll. Mem. Pa. Bar Assn., Am. Judicature Soc., Pa. Soc., Amen Corner, Blair County Game, Fish and Forestry Assn., Fed. Judges Assn. (bd. dirs. 1993—), Inns of Ct., Allegheny County Bar Assn., Pi Gamma Mu. Office: US Courthouse 319 Washington St Ste 104 Johnstown PA 15901-1624

SMITH, DAVID BRUCE, lawyer; b. Moline, Ill., May 9, 1948; s. Neal Schriever and Barbara Jean (Harris) S.; m. Yvonne Bess Smith, May 27, 1972; children: Neal, Stephanie. BSME, U. Iowa, 1970; JD, U. Tex., 1973. Bar: Tex. 1973, Wis. 1975. Patent examiner U.S. Patent and Trademark Office, Washington, 1973-74; atty. Nilles & Kirby S.C., Milw., 1974-76, Globe-Union, Inc., Milw., 1976-77, Michael Best & Friedrich, Milw., 1978—. Pres. Milw. County coun. Boy Scouts Am., Milw., 1994-95. Mem. ABA, State Bar Wis., Wis. Intellectual Property Law Assn., Ozaukee Country Club, Milw. Club. Office: Michael Best & Friedrich 100 E Wisconsin Ave Milwaukee WI 53202-4107

SMITH, DAVID CLARK, research scientist; b. Owensboro, Ky., Feb. 8, 1937; s. Robert Emmitt and Mary Margaret (Flaherty) S.; m. Kathleen Sue Kohne, June 27, 1964; children: Christine, Jennifer, Paula. BSME, U. Dayton, 1959; MS, Northwestern U., 1961, PhD, 1964; postgrad. 1964. Rsch. scientist United Technologies Research Ctr., East Hartford, Conn., 1965-67, sr. rsch. scientist, 1967-68, prin. scientist, 1968-80, mgr. exptl. optics, 1980-82, mgr. optical physics, 1982-91, cons. DCS Assoc., 1992—, Conn. Tech. Assocs., 1992—. Author: (with G. Bekefi) Principles of Laser Plasmas, 1976. Contbr. articles to profl. jours. Patentee in field. Chmn. Youth and Family Resource Ctr. Commn., 1979-84; bd. dirs. Glastonbury A Better Chance, Conn., 1970-78; mem. Glastonbury Energy Com., 1979-83; tutor YMCA Read to Succeed Literacy; vol. Habitat for Humanity. Named Man of Yr., Friends of Glastonbury Youth, 1984; recipient Outstanding Svc. award, 1985, Glastonbury, Conn., United Technologies Outstanding Svc. award., 1987. Mem. IEEE, AAAS, AIAA, Am. Phys. Soc., Sigma Xi. Democrat. Roman Catholic. Avocations: tennis; sailing. Home: 44 Candlelight Dr Glastonbury CT 06033-2537 Office: DCS Assoc PO Box 167 East Glastonbury CT 06025-0157

SMITH, DAVID DOYLE, international management consultant, consulting engineer; b. Newport, Tenn., Aug. 17, 1956; s. Doyle E. and Lena Maude (Clemmons) S.; m. Judith Ann Craig, Nov. 1, 1991; children: Adam, Christine, James. BSEE, U. Tenn., 1981. Registered profl. engr., Tenn., Ga. Engring. apprentice E.I. DuPont, Brevard, N.C., 1976; field engr. IBM Corp., Knoxville, Tenn., 1977-79; rsch. asst. Office of Naval Rsch. U. Tenn., Knoxville, 1980-81; systems test engr. Tex. Instruments, Inc., Johnson City, Tenn., 1981-82, product engr., 1982-83, product mgr., 1983-87; missile design engr., supr. Tex. Instruments, Inc., Lewisville, Tex., 1987-89; sr. systems engr. U.S. Data Corp., Richardson, Tex., 1989-90; lead cons. Keane, Inc., Atlanta, 1991-94; mgr., admstr. cons. Ernst & Young LLP, Atlanta, 1994—; lectr. Tech. Inst., 1983-86; developer RTU Sys. for oil and gas, water, and electric utilities, 1990-92. Co-author profl. papers. Mem. IEEE, NSPE, Am. Prodn. and Inventory Control Socs. Avocations: archaeology, writing. Home: 1080 Allenbrook Ln Roswell GA 30075-2983 Office: Ernst & Young LLP 600 Peachtree St Atlanta GA 30308-2215

SMITH, DAVID ELVIN, physician; b. Bakersfield, Calif., Feb. 7, 1939; s. Elvin W. and Dorothy (McGinnis) S.; m. Millicent Buxton; children: Julia, Suzanne, Christopher Buxton-Smith, Sabree Hill. Intern San Francisco Gen. Hosp., 1965; fellow pharmacology and toxicology U. Calif., San Francisco, 1965-67, assoc. clin. prof. occupational medicine, clin. toxicology, 1967—, dir. psychopharmacology study group, 1966-70; practice specializing in toxicology/addiction medicine San Francisco, 1965—; physician Presbyn. Alcoholic Clinic, 1965-67, Contra Cost Alcoholic Clinic, 1965-67; dir. alcohol and drug abuse screening unit San Francisco Gen. Hosp., 1967-68; co-dir. Calif. drug abuse info. project U. Calif. Med. Ctr., 1967-72; founder, med. dir. Haight-Ashbury Free Med. Clinic, San Francisco, 1967—; rsch. dir. Merritt Peralta Chem. Dependency Hosp., Oakland, Calif., 1984—; chmn. Nat. Drug Abuse Conf., 1977; mem. Calif. Gov.'s Commn. on Narcotics and Drug Abuse, 1977—; nat. health adviser to former U.S. Pres. Jimmy Carter; mem. Pres. Clinton's Health Care Task Force on Addiction and Nat. Health Reform, 1993; with Office Drug Abuse Policy, White House Task Force Physicians for Drug Abuse Prevention; dir. Benzodiazepine Rsch. and Tng. Project, Substance Abuse and Sexual Concerns Project, PCP Rsch. and Tng. Project; cons. numerous fed. drug abuse agys. Author: Love Needs Care, 1970, The New Social Drug: Cultural, Medical and Legal Perspectives on Marijuana, 1971, The Free Clnic: Community Approaches to Health Care and Drug Abuse, 1971, Treating the Cocaine Abuser, 1985, The Benzodiazepines: Current Standard Medical Practice, 1986, Physicians' Guide to Drug Abuse, 1987; co-author: It's So Good, Don't Even Try it Once: Heroin in Perspective, 1972, Uppers and Downers, 1973, Drugs in the Classroom, 1973, Barbiturate Use and Abuse, 1977, A Multicultural View of Drug Abuse, 1978, Amphetamine Use, Misuse and Abuse, 1979, PCP: Problems and Prevention, 1981, Sexological Aspects of Substance Use and Abuse, Treatment of the Cocaine Abuser, 1985, The Haight Ashbury Free Medical Clinic: Still Free After All These Years, Drug Free: Alternatives to Drug Abuse, 1987, Treatment of Opiate Dependence, Designer Drugs, 1988, Treatment of Cocaine Dependence, 1988, Treatment of Opiate Dependence, 1988, The New Drugs, 1989, Crack and Ice in the Era of Smokeable Drugs, 1992, others; also drug edn. films; founder, editor Jour. Psychedelic Drugs (now Jour. Psychoactive Drugs), 1967—; contbr. over 300 articles to profl. jours. Mem. Physicians for Prevention White House Office Drug Abuse Policy, 1995; pres. Youth Projects, Inc.; founder, chmn. bd., pres. Nat. Free Clin. Coun., 1968-72. Recipient Rsch. award Borden Found., 1964, AMA Rsch. award, 1977, Cmty. Svc. award U. Calif.-San Francisco, 1974, Calif. State Drug Abuse Treatment award, 1984, Vernelle Fox Drug Abuse Treatment award, 1985, UCLA Sidney Cohen Addiction Medicine award, 1989, U. Calif. San Francisco medal of honor, 1995; named one of Best Doctors in U.S., 1995. Mem. AMA (alt. del.), CMA (alt. del.), Am. Soc. on Addiction Medicine (bd. dirs. pres. 1995), San Francisco Med. Soc., Am. Pub. Health Assn., Calif. Soc. on Addiction Medicine (pres., bd. dirs.), Am. Soc. Addiction Medicine, Sigma Xi, Phi Beta Kappa. Methodist. Home: 289 Frederick St San Francisco CA 94117-4051 Office: Haight Ashbury Free Clinics 612 Clayton St San Francisco CA 94117-2958

SMITH, DAVID ENGLISH, physician, educator; b. San Francisco, June 9, 1920; s. David English and Myrtle (Goodin) S.; m. Margaret Elizabeth Bronson, June 9, 1948; children: Ann English Smith Elbert, David Bronson, Mary Margaret. A.B., Central Coll. Mo., 1941; M.D. cum laude, Washington U., St. Louis, 1944. Intern, resident pathology Barnes Hosp., St. Louis, 1944-46; instr. pathology Washington U. Med. Sch., 1948-51, asst. prof., 1951-54, asst. head dept., 1953-54, assoc. prof., 1954-55; prof. pathology U. Va. Sch. Medicine, 1955-73, chmn. dept., 1958-73; dir. div. U. Va. Sch. Medicine (Cancer Studies), 1972-73; prof. pathology Northwestern U. Sch. Medicine, 1974-75, U. Pa. Sch. Medicine, 1976-80; prof. pathology Tulane U. Sch. Medicine, 1980-85, assoc. dean, 1980-85; prof. pathology U. Tex. Med. Br., 1986—; assoc. dir. Am. Bd. Med. Spltys., 1974-75; v.p., sec., dir. undergrad. evaluation Nat. Bd. Med. Examiners, 1975-80; trustee Am. Bd. Pathology, 1966-73, v.p., 1973; mem. Nat. Bd. Med. Examiners, chmn. pathology test com., 1966-72; chmn. test com. Ednl. Commn. for Fgn. Med. Grads., 1979-91; eligibility & due process com. Nat. Commn. Cert. Physician Assts., 1990—. Editor: Survey of Pathology in Medicine and Surgery, 1966-70; contbr. articles to profl. publs. Pres. Va. div. Am. Cancer Soc., 1967-69. Served from 1st lt. to capt. M.C. AUS, 1946-48. Paul Brindley Disting. scholar U. Tex. Med. Br., 1997. Mem. Va. Soc. Pathology (pres. 1960), Am. Assn. Pathologists, Internat. Acad. Pathology (council 1956-59, pres. 1964-65), Am. Soc. Clin. Pathologists (co-dir. self assessment program 1970-75), AMA, Am. Assn. Neuropathologists, AAAS, Sigma Xi, Alpha Omega Alpha, Phi Beta Pi, Alpha Epsilon Delta. Home: 59 Colony Park Cir Galveston TX 77551-1737

SMITH, DAVID EUGENE, business administration educator; b. Boise, Idaho, Dec. 14, 1941; s. Roy Arthur and Anna Margaret (Fries) S.; m. Patricia Stroy, Aug. 4, 1973; 1 child, Zachary Adam. BS in Applied Stats., San Francisco State Coll., 1964, MS in Mgmt. Sci., 1966; MBA, PhD in Bus. Adminstrn., U. Santa Clara, 1969. Asst. to dir. mgmt ctr. Grad. Sch. Bus., U. Santa Clara, Calif., 1966-69, lectr. mktg., 1968; asst. prof. bus. adminstrn. Mktg./Quantitative Studies Dept., San Jose State U., Calif., 1969-71, assoc. prof. bus. adminstrn., 1971-76, prof. bus. adminstrn., 1976—, chmn. dept., 1986-89. Author: Quantitative Business Analysis, 1977, Internat. Edit., 1979, 1982; contbr. articles to profl. jours. Mem. INFORMS, Phi Kappa Phi, Beta Gamma Sigma. Republican. Avocations: tennis, fishing, skiing. Home: 22448 Tim Tam Ct Los Gatos CA 95030-8521 Office: San Jose State U Mktg/MIS/Decision Scis One Washington Sq San Jose CA 95192

SMITH, DAVID GILBERT, political science educator; b. Norman, Okla., Oct. 10, 1926; s. Gilbert Harmer and Virginia (Haizlip) S.; m. Carlota Shipman (div. 1967); m. 2d, Eleanor Cowan; children: Alison Claire, Joel Anthony; stepchildren: Laura Gergen, Stan Gergen. BA, U. Okla., 1948, MA, 1950; PhD, Johns Hopkins U., 1953. Instr. polit. sci. Swarthmore (Pa.) Coll., 1953-55, asst. prof. polit. sci., 1957, prof., 1967—, Centennial prof., 1977-87, Richter prof. polit. sci., 1987-92, chmn., 1970-87, prof. emeritus, 1992—; asst. prof. polit. sci. Stanford U., Palo Alto, Calif., 1956-57; cons. HEW, NAS, NRC, Ford Found. Author: (with J. Roland Pennock) Political Science: An Introduction, 1965, The Convention and the Constitution, 1965, 2d edit., 1987, Paying for Medicare, 1992; also articles. Chmn. ACLU, Delaware County, Pa., 1965-70, Health and Welfare Coun., Delaware County, 1970-73; v.p. Delaware Valley HMO, Concordville, Pa., 1978-81; pres. Media (Pa.) Child Guidance, 1980-82; bd. dirs. Friends Life Care at Home, 1992—. Sgt. U.S. Army, 1945-46. Mem. Am. Soc. for Polit. and Legal Philosophy, Phi Beta Kappa. Democrat. Presbyterian. Home: 448 S Jackson St Media PA 19063-3716

SMITH, DAVID JEDDIE, American literature educator; b. Portsmouth, Va., Dec. 19, 1942; s. Ralph Geargld and Catherine Mary (Cornwell) S.; m. Deloras Mae Weaver, Mar. 31, 1966; children: David Jeddie, Lael Cornwell, Mary Catherine. BA, U. Va., 1965; MA, So. Ill. U., 1969; PhD, Ohio U., 1976. Staff creative writing Bennington (Vt.) Coll. summer prog., 1980-87; instr. English We. Mich. U., Kalamazoo, 1973-74; asst. prof. English Cottey Coll., Nevada, Mo., 1974-75; assoc. prof. English U. Utah, Salt Lake City, 1976-80; vis. prof. English SUNY, Binghamton, 1980-81; assoc. prof. English U. Fla., Gainesville, 1981-82; prof. Am. it. Va. Commonwealth U., Richmond, 1982-89; prof. Am. Lit. La. State U., 1990—; lectr. in field; cons. in field. Author: Local Assays, 1985, The Roundhouse Voices: Selected and new Poems, 1985, The Morrow Anthology of Younger American Poets, 1985, Gray Soldiers, 1984, Southern Delights, 1984, In the House of the Judge, 1983, The Pure Clear Word: Essays on the Poetry of James Wright, 1982, Onliness, 1981, Homage to Edgar Allan Poe, 1981, Cuba Night, 1990, Night Pleasures: New and Selected Poems, 1992, Fate's Kite: Poems 1991-1995, 1996, Floating on Solitude: Three Books of Poems, 1996, others; editor New Va. Rev., 1987, The Back Doors: A Poetry Mag., Southern Rev., 1990; contbr. articles to profl. jours. Recipient Va. Prize in Poetry, 1988, Prairie Schooner poetry prize, 1980, Portland Rev. poetry prize, 1979, Sou'wester poetry prize, 1973, others; Guggenheim fellow, 1981, Lyndhurst fellow, 1987, 88, 89, others. Mem. MLA, Poetry Soc. Am., Poetry Soc. Va., PEN, Nat. Book Critics Cir., Assoc. Writing Progs., So. MLA, Acad. Am. Poets, Fellowship of So. Writers. Office: La State U So Rev 43 Allen Hall Baton Rouge LA 70803

SMITH, DAVID JOHN, physicist, educator; b. Melbourne, Australia, Oct. 10, 1948; arrived in U.S., 1984; s. Arthur and Agnes Frances S.; m. Gwenneth Paula Bland, Sept. 18, 1971 (div. 1992); children: Heather F., Marion J. BSc with honors, U. Melbourne, Australia, 1970, PhD, 1978, DSc, 1988. Post-doctoral rsch. asst. Cavendish Lab. U. Cambridge, Eng., 1976-78, sr. rsch. assoc., 1979-84; assoc. prof. Ariz. State U., Tempe, 1984-87, prof., 1987—; dir. Cambridge U. High Resolution Electron Microscope, 1979-84, NSF Ctr. for High Resolution Electron Microscopy, Tempe, 1991-96. Author 7 chpts. in books; editor 13 confr. procs.; contbr. over 270 articles to profl. jours. Recipient Faculty Achievement award Burlington Resources Found., 1990. Fellow Inst. Physics (U.K., Charles Vernon Boys prize 1985); mem. Royal Micros. Soc. (U.K.), Am. Phys. Soc., Material Rsch. Soc., Microscopy Soc. Am. Office: Ariz State U Ctr Solid State Sci Tempe AZ 85287

SMITH, DAVID JOHN, JR., plastic surgeon; b. Indpls., Feb. 20, 1947; s. David John and Carolyn (Culp) S.; m. Nancy Loonsten, June 7, 1975; children: Matthew, Peter, Hadley. BA, Wesleyan U., 1969; MD, Ind. U., 1973. Diplomate Am. Bd. Plastic Surgery. Resident Emory U.-Grady Hosp., Atlanta, 1973-78; resident Ind. U. Med. Ctr., Indpls., 1978-80; Christine Kleinert fellow in hand surgery, 1979; asst. prof. surgery Ind. U. Sch. Medicine, 1980-84; assoc. prof. of surgery Wayne State U. Sch. Medicine, 1984-87; assoc. prof. plastic surgery, surgery sect. head U. Mich. Med. Ctr., Ann Arbor, 1987-92, prof. surgery sect. head, 1992—, assoc. chmn. surgery, 1995—; mem. Residency Rev. Com. for Plastic Surgery, 1992, vice chmn., 1994, chmn. 1996—. Mem. editl. bd. Jour. of Surg. Rsch., 1989-95, Annals of Plastic Surgery, 1992—, assoc. editor, 1994, Yearbook of Hand Surgery, 1989—; guest reviewer Surgery, 1988—, Plastic and Reconstructive Surgery, 1988—; contbr. articles to profl. jours. Recipient numerous grants. Fellow ACS (many coms.), Soc. Univ. Surgeons, Am. Assn. Plastic Surgeons, Am. Surg. Assn. (chmn. oral exam. 1995—), Am. Bd. Plastic Surgeons, Assn. for Acad. Surgery, Western Surg. Assn., Ctrl. Surg. Assn., Am. Soc. for Surgery of the Hand, Am. Soc. Plastic and Reconstructive Surgeons, Plastic Surgery Ednl. Found. (bd. dirs. 1988—, treas. 1994, v.p., pres.-elec., pres., other coms.), Plastic Surgery Rsch. Coun., Am. Burn Assn., Am. Burn Life Support Nat. Faculty, Am. Assn. for Hand Surgeons (pres. 1994). Home: 769 Heatherway St Ann Arbor MI 48104-2731 Office: U Mich Med Ctr 2130 Taubman Health Ctr 1500 E Medical Center Dr Ann Arbor MI 48109-0005

SMITH, DAVID JULIAN, educational consultant; b. Boston, Apr. 24, 1944; s. Julian John and Anita Regina (Goldman) S.; m. Suzanne Marilla Shaw, June 18, 1966. AB, Harvard U., 1966; MAT, Reed Coll., 1967. Cert. elem. tchr., Mass., Hawaii, Oreg. 10th grade tchr. Punahou Sch., Honolulu, 1967-69; 7th, 9th grades tchr. U. Hawaii Lab. Sch., Honolulu, 1969-70; 7th grade head tchr. Shady Hill Sch., Cambridge, Mass., 1970-92; pvt. practice ednl. cons. Cambridge, 1992—. Author: Mapping the World By Heart, 1992, Abigail's Atlas, 1992, Making Maps from Memory, 1989; contbr. articles to profl. jours. Bd. dirs. Cambridge Mental Health Assn., 1991—, Cambridge Ctr. for Adult Edn., 1988—; active Cambridge Civic Assn. Recipient Breaking the Mold award U.S. Dept. Edn., 1992. Mem. Nat. Coun. for Social Studies, Nat. Coun. for Geog. Edn., Assn. Am. Geographers (chair cartographic specialty group 1997—), Inst. British Geographers. Office: Mapping the World by Heart 4 Blanchard Rd Cambridge MA 02138-1009

SMITH, DAVID KINGMAN, retired oil company executive, consultant; b. Malone, N.Y., June 5, 1928; s. Ernest DeAlton and Louisa Kingman (Bolster) S.; m. Lois Louise Wing, June 13, 1959; children: Mara Louise, David Andrew. BS in Engring., Princeton U., 1952. Registered profl. engr., Tex. Civil engr., supt. Raymont Internat. Inc., N.Y.C., 1952-55, asst. v.p., 1970-71, v.p., 1971-74; group v.p. Raymont Internat. Inc., Houston, 1974-80; mgr. Raymond-Brown and Root, Maracaibo, Venezuela, 1955-70; sr. engring. assoc. Exxon Prodn. Rsch. Co., Houston, 1980-81, supr., 1982-95; cons. project mgmt., 1995—. Pres. Yorkshire Civic Assn., Houston, 1979-80, trustee, 1985-97. With U.S. Army, 1946-48, PTO. Mem. ASCE, NSPE, Soc. Petroleum Engrs. (continuing edn. com. Gulf Coast chmn. 1989-93, treas. 1987-88, nat. continuing edn. com. 1991-93, dir. Gulf Coast sect. 1994-95), Tex. Soc. Profl. Engrs., Men's Garden Club Houston, Am. Legion, Princeton Alumni Assn. (dir. Houston sect.), Cen Ners In Square Dance Club (pres. 1996-97). Republican. Methodist. Avocations: photography, gardening, tennis, golf, square dancing. Home: 611 W Forest Dr Houston TX 77079-6915

SMITH, DAVID LEE, newspaper editor; b. Shelby, Ohio, Apr. 4, 1939; s. Ferris Francis and Rita Ann (Metzger) S.; m. Betty Stewart Walker, Sept. 10, 1960; children: Stacie Lynn, Stefanie Linn, David Lee, II (dec.). Student, Pontifical Coll. Josephinum, Worthington, Ohio, 1953-56, Ohio State U., Mansfield, 1961. Sports writer Mansfield News-Jour., 1960-61; sports editor Ashland (Ohio) Times-Gazette, 1961-63, Miami (Fla.) News, 1963-67, Ft. Lauderdale (Fla.) News, 1967-70, Boston Globe, 1970-78, Washington Star, 1978-81; dep. mng. editor, exec. sports editor Dallas Morning News, 1981—; condr. seminars. Bd. dirs. Doak Walker Nat. Running Back Award, The Dallas Athletic Club, GTE-SMU Athletic Forum. Served with USMC, 1957-60. Mem. AP Sports Editors Assn. (1st pres. 1974-75), Baseball Writers Assn. (Red Smith award for major contbns. to sports journalism 1990), Football Writers Assn., Golf Writers Assn., Dallas Athletic Club (pres.), Dallas All Sports Assn. (bd. dirs.). Roman Catholic. Home: 5723 Berkshire Ln Dallas TX 75209-2401 Office: Dallas Morning News Communications Center Dallas TX 75265

SMITH, DAVID MARTYN, forestry educator; b. Bryan, Tex., Mar. 10, 1921; s. John Blackmer and Doris (Clark) S.; m. Catherine Van Aken, June 16, 1951; children: Ellen, Nancy. BS, U. R.I., 1941; postgrad., NYU, 1942; MF, Yale U., 1946, PhD, 1950; DSc (hon.), Bates Coll., 1986, U. R.I., 1993. From instr. to prof. Sch. Forestry and Environ. Studies, Yale U., 1946-90, asst. dean, 1953-58; Morris K. Jesup prof. silviculture Yale U., 1967-90, Morris K. Jesup prof. emeritus, 1990—; cons. Baskahegan Co.; vis. prof. U. Munich, 1981; mem. Conn. Forestry Practices Bd., 1991—; pres., bd. dirs. Connwood Foresters, Inc. Author: Practice of Silviculture, 1954, 86, 97. Capt. Weather Svc., USAAF, 1942-45. Fellow Soc. Am. Foresters (Disting. Svc. New Eng. sect. award 1969, 93); mem. Am. Forests (Disting. Svc. award 1990), Nat. Acad. Forest Scis. Mex. (corr.), Ecol. Soc. Am., Conn. Forest and Park Assn. (dir.), Sigma Xi, Phi Kappa Phi. Mem. United Ch. of Christ. Home: 55 Woodlawn St Hamden CT 06517-1338 Office: 360 Prospect St New Haven CT 06511-2104

SMITH, DAVID RYAN, museum director; b. Ft. Worth, Apr. 23, 1952; s. David Earnest and Helen Virginia (Armstrong) S.; m. Peggy Lou Bennett, Mar. 9, 1974; children: Jennifer Renee, Kenneth Ryan. BS in Am. Studies, Harding U., 1974; MA in History, U. Tex., 1979. Dir. Star of the Republic Mus., Washington, Tex., 1977-87, Panhandle-Plains Hist. Mus., Canyon, Tex., 1987-91; exec. dir. Tex. Energy Mus., Beaumont, Tex., 1992—; field reviewer Inst. Mus. Svcs., Wash., 1985—. Chmn. Tex. Antiquities Com., 1990-92; mem. Summerlee Commn. on Tex. History, 1989-92. Bd. dirs. Edison Pla. Mus., Beaumont, Beaumont Conv. and Visitors Bur.; mem. cmty. adv. coun. Mobil Refinery; chmn. Beaumont History Conf. Named Outstanding Alumnus Harding U., 1987. Mem. Am. Assn. Mus. (surveyor mus. assessment program), Tex. State Hist. Assn., Tex. Assn. Mus. (coun. 1979-81, 84-86), Cen. Tex. Mus. Assn. (chmn. 1979-81, 84-86), S.E. Tex. Mus. Assn. (treas. 1995—), Rotary. Mem. Ch. of Christ. Avocations: backpacking, canoeing, tennis, running. Home: 9265 Meadowbend Dr Beaumont TX 77706-3829 Office: Tex Energy Mus 600 Main St Beaumont TX 77701-3305

SMITH, DAVID SHIVERICK, lawyer, former ambassador; b. Omaha, Jan. 25, 1918; s. Floyd Monroe and Anna (Shiverick) S.; m. June Noble, Dec. 8, 1945 (div. 1968); children:Noble, David Shiverick, Jeremy T., Bradford D.; m. Mary Edson, Feb. 14, 1972. Degre Superieur, Sorbonne, Paris, 1938; B.A. magna cum laude, Dartmouth Coll., 1939; J.D., Columbia U., 1942. Bar: N.Y. 1942, Conn. 1950, D.C. 1954. Asso. Breed, Abbott & Morgan, N.Y.C., 1946-48; legal dept. ABC, N.Y.C., 1948-50; partner Chapman, Bryson, Walsh & O'Connell, N.Y.C. and Washington, 1950-54; spl. asst. to undersec. Dept. State, Washington, 1954; asst. sec. Air Force, 1954-59; dir. internat. fellows program Columbia U., 1959-75, coordinator internat. studies, 1960-75, asso. dean sch. internat. affairs, 1960-74; cons. AEC, 1959-60; partner Baker & McKenzie (and predecessor), N.Y.C. and Washington, 1960-75, Martin & Smith (and predecessors), Washington, 1975-76, 77-88; ambassador to Sweden, 1976-77; dir. United Svcs. Life Ins. Corp., Internat. Bank, USLICO Corp., Liberian Svcs., Inc.; mem. Coun. Fgn. Rels.; dir. Fgn. Policy Assn.; mem. adv. coun. Sch. Advanced Intenat. Studies, Johns Hopkins U., 1962—; pres., dir. Ctr. for Inter-Am. Rels., N.Y.C., 1969-74. Adv. and contbg. editor: Jour. Internat. Affairs, 1960-74; editor: The Next Asia, 1969, Prospects for Latin America, 1970, Concerns in World Affairs, 1973, From War to Peace, 1974. Chmn. bd. George Olmsted Found., 1977—; active in past various charitable orgns. Lt. USNR, 1942-54; PTO; col. USAFR, 1955-75. Decorated Purple Heart. Mem. ABA, Am. Soc. Internat. Law, Am. Fgn. Law Assn., N.Y. State Bar Assn., Conn. Bar Assn.,

Fed. Bar Assn. (v.p. for N.Y., N.J. and Conn.), Pilgrims of U.S., France-Am. Soc., English Speaking Union, Asia Soc., Coun. on Foreign Rels., Hudson Inst., Washington Inst. Fgn. Affairs, Coun. Fgn. Rels., Coun. Am. Ambs. (bd. dirs., sec.), Soc. Mayflower Descs., Brook Club (N.Y.C.), Met. Club (Washington), Chevy Chase Club, Bathing Corp. of Southampton (N.Y.), Meadow Club (Southampton), Bath and Tennis Club, Everglades Club (Palm Beach), The Crocodiles, Old Guard Soc. Palm Beach Golfers, Phi Beta Kappa. Home: 525 S Flagler Dr Apt 20-c West Palm Beach FL 33401-5922

SMITH, DAVID STUART, anesthesiology educator, physician; b. Detroit, May 29, 1946; s. Philip and Eleanor (Bishop) S.; m. Suzanne Wanda Zeleznik, Aug. 17, 1969; children: Katherine Michele, Lisa Anne. BA, Oakland U.; MD, Med. Coll. Wis., 1975, PhD, 1975. Intern Dept. of Medicine, Med. Coll. Wis., Milw., 1975-76; resident Dept. Anesthesia, U. Pa., Phila., 1976-78, fellow, 1978-80; dir., div. of neuroanesthesia Hosp. U. Pa., Phila., 1982—, attending anesthesiologist, 1980—; asst. prof. U. Pa., Phila., 1980-89, assoc. prof., 1989—; editorial bd. Jour. Neurosurgical Anesthesia, N.Y.C., 1987—. Co-editor: Anesthesia and Neurosurgery, 3d edit., 1994; author and co-author of numerous sci. papers, revs., and book chpts. Sr. fellow, Nat. Rsch. Svc. award, Phila., 1985-87. Fellow Coll. Physicians Phila.; mem. Am. Soc. Anesthesiologists, Soc. Neurosurg. Anesthesia and Critical Care (sec., treas. 1987-89, v.p. 1989-90, pres. elect 1990-91, pres. 1991-92), Assn. U. Anesthesiologists, Internat. Soc. Cerebral Blood Flow and Metabolism, Internat. Soc. Neurochemistry. Jewish. Office: Hosp U Pa Dept Anesthesia 3400 Spruce St Philadelphia PA 19104

SMITH, DAVID THORNTON, lawyer, educator; b. Pawtucket, R.I., Dec. 11, 1935; s. Herbert Jeffers and Harriet Amelia (Thornton) S.; m. Sandra June Gustavson, Dec. 20, 1958; children—David T., Douglas A., Daniel H. B.A., Yale U., 1957; J.D. cum laude, Boston U., 1960. Bar: Mass. 1961, U.S. Supreme Ct. 1964. Instr. law Ind. U., Bloomington, 1960-62; asst. prof. law Duquesne U., Pitts., 1962-63, Case Western Res. U., Cleve., 1963-65; asso. prof. Case Western Res. U., 1965-68; asso. prof. law U. Fla., Gainesville, 1968-69; prof. U. Fla., 1969—; lectr. Fla. Bankers Assn., Fla. Trust Sch., 1973—. Author: (with M. Sussman and J. Cates) The Family and Inheritance, 1970, Florida Probate Code Manual, 1975. Mem. Am. Bar Assn., Mass. Bar Assn., Am. Law Inst., Am. Judicature Soc., AAUP (past pres. U. Fla. chpt.), Fla. Blue Key, Selden Soc., Omicron Delta Kappa, Phi Alpha Delta. Lutheran. Home: 6405 NW 18th Ave Gainesville FL 32605-3209 Office: Univ Fla Coll Of Law Gainesville FL 32611

SMITH, DAVID TODD, publishing company executive; b. Stamford, Conn., Nov. 19, 1953; arrived in Can., 1956; m. Margaret Beryl Starke, Dec. 30, 1978; children: Erik Joseph, Maximilian Peter Starke. BBA in Fin. and Econs., Wilfrid Laurier U., Waterloo, Ont., Can., 1976; MBA in Fin., McMaster U., Hamilton, Ont., 1978. Cert. gen. acct., Ont. Fin. analyst Economical Mut. Ins. Co., Kitchener, Ont., 1976-78; portfolio mgr. Mcht. Trust Co., Toronto, Ont., 1978-80; treasury officer Harlequin Enterprises Ltd., Toronto, 1980-82, asst. treas., 1982-89; treas. Torstar Corp., Toronto, 1989—. Office: Torstar Corp, 1 Yonge St, Toronto, ON Canada M5E 1P9

SMITH, DAVID WALDO EDWARD, pathology and gerontology educator, physician; b. Fargo, N.D., Apr. 3, 1934; s. Waldo Edward and Martha (Althaus) S.; m. Diane Leigh Walker, June 18, 1960. BA, Swarthmore Coll., 1956; MD, Yale U., 1960. Intern, asst. resident, research fellow pathology Yale U. Med. Sch., 1960-62; research assoc. lab. molecular biology Nat. Inst. Arthritis and Metabolic Diseases, 1962-64, investigator lab. exptl. pathology, 1964-67; assoc. prof. pathology and microbiology Ind. U. Med. Sch., 1967-69; prof. pathology Northwestern U. Med. Sch., 1969—, dir. Ctr. on Aging, 1988—; Guest investigator Internat. Lab. Genetics and Biophysics, Naples, Italy, 1969; mem. ad hoc biochemistry study sect. NIH, 1974-75, mem. pathobiol. chemistry study sect., 1975-79, cons., 1982; sabbatical leave NIH, 1986-87; chmn. NIH Conf. on Gender and Longevity: Why Do Women Live Longer Than Men?, 1987. Author: Human Longevity, 1993, also research papers, chpts. in books.; editorial bd. Yale Jour. Biology and Medicine, 1957-60. Sr. surgeon USPHS, 1958-67. Recipient Career Devel. award NIH, 1968-69. Mem. AAAS, Am. Soc.for Investigative Pathology, Am. Soc. for Biochem. and Molecular Biology, Gerontol. Soc. Am., Sigma Xi, Alpha Omega Alpha. Home: 1212 N Lake Shore Dr Apt 33 Chicago IL 60610 Office: Northwestern U Med Sch Dept Pathology 303 E Chicago Ave Chicago IL 60611-3008

SMITH, DAVID WAYNE, psychologist, educator; b. Ind., Apr. 16, 1927; s. Lowell Wayne and Ruth Elizabeth (Westphal) S.; m. Marcene B. Leever, Oct. 20, 1948; children: David Wayne, Laurreen Lea. B.S., Purdue U., 1949; M.S., Ind. U., 1953, Ph.D., 1955. Prof. rehab., dir. Rehab. Center; assoc. dean, later asst. v.p. acad. affairs Ariz. Health Scis. Center, U. Ariz., Tucson, 1955-80; research prof. rehab., adj. prof. medicine, cons. in research S.W. Arthritis Center, Coll. Medicine, 1980-87; prof. rehab. and rheumatology, dept. medicine U. Ariz., 1987—, also dir. disability assessment program; pres. allied health professions sect. Nat. Arthritis Found.; bd. dirs. Nat. Arthritis Found. (S.W. chpt.); nat. vice chmn. bd. dirs.; mem. NIH Nat. Arthritis Adv. Bd., 1977-84; also chmn. subcom. community programs and rehab.; mem. staff Ariz. Legislature Health Welfare, 1972-73; Mem. Gov.'s Council Dept. Econ. Security, 1978-85; pres., bd. dirs. Tucson Assn. for Blind, 1974-86; chmn. Gov.'s Council on Blind and Visually Impaired, 1987—; active Gov.'s Coun. on Arthritis and Musculoskeletal Disease, 1987—. Author: Worksamples; contbr. chpts. to books and articles to profl. jours. Recipient Gov.'s awards for leadership in rehab., 1966, 69, 72, 73; awards for sci. and vol. services Nat. Arthritis Found., 1973, 75; 1st nat. Addie Thomas award Nat. Arthritis Found., 1983, Benson award, 1989, Govt. Affairs award, 1989; Arthritis Found. fellow, 1983. Mem. Am. Psychol. Assn. (div. 17 counseling psychology), Assn. Schs. Allied Health Professions, Nat. Rehab. Assn., Ariz. Psychol. Assn. Home: 5765 N Camino Real Tucson AZ 85718-4213 Office: U Ariz Arizona Health Scis Ctr Tucson AZ 85724

SMITH, DAVID YARNELL, financial consultant; b. Chattanooga, Apr. 9, 1963; s. Eugene Scott and Johnathan (Yarnell) S.; m. Donna Kathryn Swisher, July 1, 1989. BS in Bus. Adminstrn. with honors, U. Tenn., 1985; MBA, Ga. State U., 1989. CPA; cert. valuation analyst. Comml. banking officer, comml. bus. devel. coord., then asst. v.p. and asst. mgr. Trust Co. Bank, Atlanta, 1985-89; asst. v.p. Bank of Am., Nat. Trust & Savings Assn., Atlanta, 1989-91; fin. cons., mgr. Petty & Landis, CPAs, Chattanooga, 1991—. Mem. Am. Inst. of CPA's, Tenn. Soc. of CPA's, Nat. Assn. of CVA's. Avocations: golf, hunting. Office: Petty & Landis Krystal Bldg Ste 700 Chattanooga TN 37402

SMITH, DEAN, communications advisor, arbitrator; b. N.Y.C., Aug. 10, 1925; s. Franklin Grant and Anna Lucille (Kranebell) S.; m. Andree Marie Praileur, Aug. 9, 1947; children—David F., Christopher P. Student, NYU, 1945-46, Columbia U., 1946-47, N.Y. Sch. Printing, 1946-47. Editor ShowBill Mag., N.Y.C., 1945-47; news editor Boulder City (Nev.) Daily News, 1947-49; owner, pub., editor Tucson Sun-News, N.Y.C., 1949-51; dir. radio and TV news Sta. WBEN/WBEN-TV, Buffalo, 1951-53; dir. pub. svc. and promotion Indpls. Times, Buffalo, 1953-56; v.p., gen. mgr Kendall Assocs., Inc., N.Y.C., 1956-60; dir. Office Publs. and Info., Commerce Dept., Washington, 1961-70, dir. publs. div., 1970; asst. dir. Nat. Tech. Info. Svc., Springfield, Va., 1971-81, dir. office of market devel., 1982-83; assoc. dir. NTIS, Springfield, Va., 1984-85, self-employed communications advisor, 1986—. Chmn. for fed. mail list policy Vice Pres.'s Com. on Right of Privacy; chmn. presdl. domestic policy rev. work group on fed. acquisition of fgn. tech., 1979; bd. dirs. Commerce Fed. Credit Union. Served with AUS, 1943-45. Decorated Silver Star with oak leaf cluster, Bronze Star, Purple Heart with oak leaf cluster; recipient award Ariz. Newspaper Assn., 1950, Ind. Photo Journalism award, 1954. Mem. Am. Arbitration Assn. (panelist), Soc. Mayflower Descendants, Sons of Revolution (treas.), Flagon and Trencher, Soc. for the Descendants of the Colonial Clergy. Democrat. Home and Office: 2325 49th St NW Washington DC 20007-1002

SMITH, DEAN EDWARDS, university basketball coach; b. Emporia, Kans., Feb. 28, 1931; s. Alfred Dillon and Vesta Marie (Edwards) S.; m. Linnea Weblemoe, May 21, 1976; children: Sharon, Sandy, Scott, Kristen, Kelly. B.S. in Math. and Phys. Edn., U. Kans., 1953. Asst. basketball coach U.S. Air Force Acad., 1955-58; asst. basketball coach U. N.C., 1958-61, head basketball coach, 1961—; mem. U.S. and Canadian Basketball Rules Com., 1967-73; U.S. basketball coach Olympics, Montreal, Que., Can., 1976; lectr. basketball clinics, Germany, Italy. Served with USAF, 1954-58. Named Coach of Year Atlantic Coast Conf., 1967, 1968, 1971, 1976, 1977, 79, Nat. Basketball Coach of Year, 1977, Nat. Coach of Yr. U.S. Basketball Writers, 1979, Naismith Basketball Hall of Fame, 1982. Mem. Nat. Assn. Basketball Coaches (Nat. Basketball Coach of Year 1976, dir. 1972—, pres. 1981-82), Fellowship Christian Athletes (dir. 1965-70). Baptist. Office: U NC Office Basketball Coach PO Box 2126 Chapel Hill NC 27515-2126

SMITH, DEAN GORDON, economist, educator; b. Flint, Mich., Feb. 23, 1959; s. David Wade and Janet Pearl (Hendrickson) S. AB, U. Mich., 1981; PhD, Tex. A&M U., 1985. Economist RRC, Inc., Bryan, Tex., 1984-85, Parke-Davis, Ann Arbor, 1995-96; from rsch. investigator to asst. prof. U. Mich., Ann Arbor, 1985-94, assoc. prof., 1994—; faculty fellow Lincoln Nat. Life Ins. Co., Ft. Wayne, Ind., 1990. Contbr. articles to profl. jours. Economist, Mich. Med. Liability Rsch. Program, Lansing, 1990, Gov.'s Healthcare Cost Mgmt. Team, Lansing, 1989; bd. dirs. Care Am. Mich., Inc. Grantee Mercy Consortium for Rsch., 1990, Robert Wood Johnson Found., 1992-95. Mem. APHA, Am. Coll. Healthcare Execs., Am. Econ. Assn., Am. Fin. Assn., Assn. Univ. Programs in Health Adminstrn. (chair fin. faculty com. 1992-93), Care Am. Mich. (bd. dirs. 1996—). Avocations: bicycling, tennis. Office: Dept HSMP U Mich Dept HSMP 109 Observatory St Ann Arbor MI 48109-2029

SMITH, DENNIS A., insurance company executive; married; 3 children. Degrees in Polit. Sci. and Civil Engring., N.C. State U., 1972; postgrad., Harvard U., Ga. State U., U. Va. Casualty adjuster Crawford & Co., Greensboro, N.C., 1972-80, v.p., midwest regional mgr., 1980-86, sr. v.p., 1986-91; pres. internat. divsn. Graham Miller Crawford & Co., London, 1991-92; pres., COO claims svcs. bus. unit Crawford & Co., Atlanta, 1992-94, pres., COO, chmn. internat. ops., 1994-95, chmn., CEO, 1995—. Office: Crawford & Co 5620 Glenridge Dr NE Atlanta GA 30342-1334

SMITH, DENNIS (EDWARD), publisher, author; b. N.Y.C., Sept. 9, 1940; s. John and Mary (Hogan) S.; m. Patricia Ann Kearney, Aug. 24, 1963 (div. May 1988); children: Brendan, Dennis, Sean, Deirdre and Aislinn (twins). BA, NYU, 1970, MA, 1972. Adj. asst. prof. Coll. New Rochelle, 1973-74; fireman City of N.Y., 1963-80; founder, pub., editor in chief Firehouse Mag., N.Y.C., 1976-89. Author: Report from Engine Co. 82, 1972, Final Fire, 1975, Firehouse, 1977, Dennis Smith's History of American Firefighting, 1978, Glitter and Ash, 1980, The Aran Islands—A Personal Journey, 1980, Steely Blue, 1985, Firefighters, Their lives in Their Own Words, 1988, The Little Fire Engine That Saved the City, 1990. Mem. bd. advisors Boys and Girls Clubs Am., N.Y.C., N.Y.C. Cultural Affairs; bd. dirs. The New York Fire Safety Found.; bd. dirs., chmn. Kips Bay Boys and Girls Club, N.Y.C., N.Y. Acad. Art; bd. dirs., pres. Found. for Health and Safety Am. Firefighters; bd. dirs. Ireland House at NYU. With USAF, 1957-60. Recipient Christopher award for non-fiction, 1973. Mem. Union League Club, Irish Georgian Soc. (bd. dirs.). Democrat. Roman Catholic. Home and Office: 50 Hidden Cove Ct Southampton NY 11968-1520

SMITH, DENTYE M., library media specialist; b. Atlanta, July 21, 1936; d. William Harry and Gladys Magdalene (Bruce) S. AB, Spelman Coll., 1958; MLM, Ga. State U., 1975. Cert. Libr., media specialist. Tchr. English Atlanta Pub. Schs., 1961-82, supr. tchr., 1968-69, tchr. journalism, 1975-80, libr. media specialist, 1982-94; media specialist West Fulton High Sch., 1982-92, West Fulton Mid. Sch., 1992, Booker T. Washington Comprehensive High Sch., Atlanta, 1992-94; leader jur. gt. books Archer and West Fulton high schs.; coord. Atlanta Pub. Schs. reading cert., program West Fulton H.S.; vol. liaison Atlanta-Fulton Pub. Libr., 1987-94, local arrangements com. Atlanta Libr. Assn., 1990-91; seminar presenter in field; coord. study skills seminars Morris Brown Coll.'s Summer Upward Bound Program, 1993, 94, 95; mem. High Mus. of Art, Atlanta, Atlanta Hist. Soc., Ga. Pub. TV. Contbr. articles to profl. jours. Named to Acad. Hall of Fame, Atlanta Pub. Schs., 1990; recipient Tchr. of Yr. award West Fulton H.S., Atlanta, 1974, acad. achievement incentive program award in media APS, 1990. Mem. ALA, NEA, Nat. Ret. Tchrs. Assn., Nat. Coun. Tchrs. English, Am. Assn. Sch. Librs., Soc. Sch. Librs. Internat., Ga. Assn. Educators, Atlanta Assn. Educators, Ga. Libr. Assn., Ga. Libr. Media Assn., Nat. Alumnae Assn. Apelman Coll., Ga. State U. Alumni Assn., Nat. Trust Hist. Preservation, Ga. Trust Hist. Preservation, Atlanta Ret. Tchrs. Assn., Atlanta Hist. Assn., Ga. Ret. Tchrs. Assn., the Smithsonian Assocs., Libr. of Congress Assocs.

SMITH, DEREK ARMAND, publishing company executive; b. Hamilton, Ont., Can., Sept. 2, 1953; came to U.S., 1981; s. Alastair A.G. and Jessie Mead (Maben) S.; m. Rebecca Oldfield, Oct. 10, 1981; 1 child, Alastair Maben Oldfield. BCom., U. Toronto, 1976. Chartered acct.; CPA, Mass. Staff acct. Office of Auditor Gen., Ottawa, 1976-78; chartered acct. Peat Marwick Thorne, Ottawa, 1978-79; v.p. fin. adminstrn. Can. Dry Bottling Ltd., Kingston, Ont., 1979-81; supervising sr. Peat Marwick, Boston, 1981-82; mgr. corp. reporting Warren, Gorham & Lamont, Inc., Boston, 1981-82; asst. contr. Warren, Gorham & Lamont, Inc., N.Y.C., 1982-84, sr. v.p., CFO, 1988-90; sr. v.p., CFO Penguin Books USA Inc., N.Y.C., 1990-96; exec. v.p., 1995-96; exec. v.p., CFO Addison Wesley Longman Inc., Reading, Mass., 1996—; pres. Trinity Coll. Sch. Fund, Darien, Conn., 1992; gov. Trinity Coll. Sch., Port Hope, Ont., 1992. Trustee John Hart Hunter Ednl. Found., N.Y.C., 1992. Mem. Assn. of Chartered Accts. in the U.S. Ltd. (treas. 1990-93, dir. 1989-94, hon. dir. 1994—), Kappa Alpha Soc. (exec. coun., v.p. 1991-93, pres. 1993-95, past pres. 1995—). Episcopalian. Avocations: skiing, sailing, tennis, paddle tennis, golf. Office: Addison Wesley Longman Inc One Jacob Way Reading MA 01867-3999

SMITH, DERRIN RAY, information systems company executive; b. Columbus, Ohio, Feb. 19, 1955; s. Ray Stanley Smith and Clara (Diddle) Craver; m. Catherine Marie Massey, Aug. 18, 1979; children: Shannon Cathleen, Allison Collette, Micayla Colleen, Nicole Catherine. BS, Regis U., 1981; MBA, U. Phoenix, 1984; PhD, U. Denver, 1991. Test lab. mgr. Ball Aerospace Systems, Ball Corp., Boulder, 1975-84; sr. systems engr. Martin Marietta Info. Systems, Denver, 1984-87; tech. cons. MITRE Fed. R & D Ctr., Colorado Springs, 1988-92; pres. DRS Scis., Inc., Denver, 1992—; nat. program mgr. cable/telephone/full svc. network The Nat. Program Mgr. Time Warner, 1995—; tech. cons. U.S. Space Command—RAPIER, Colorado Springs, 1989-91, Unisys Corp., Greenwood Village, Colo., 1992; adj. prof. CIS dept. Univ. Coll., U. Denver, 1992; secretariat Corp. Planner's Roundtable, St. Louis, 1982-84; speaker in field. Author: Evolving the Mountain; Defense Acquisition Management of Strategic Command and Control System Procurements, 1991; contbr. articles to profl. jours. Res. police officer Federal Heights (Colo.) Police Dept., 1979-82. With USMC, 1978-84. Recipient Outstanding Achievement award Rocky Mountain News, 1981, Reservist of Yr. award Navy League U.S., 1981. Mem. Assn. Former Intelligence Officers (pres. Rocky Mountain chpt.). Roman Catholic. Avocations: martial arts, skiing, sailing, creative writing, mountaineering. Home: 3746 E Easter Cir S Littleton CO 80122-2033 Office: DRS Sciences Inc PO 2091 Littleton CO 80161-2091

SMITH, DICK MARTIN, oil field service company executive, owner; b. Alamosa, Colo., Nov. 20, 1946; s. Jack and Mary (Turnbull) S.; m. Janyce Wood Smith, Jan. 5, 1971 (div. May 1975); 1 child, DAnna Marie; m. Patricia Ann Connors, June 5, 1987; stepchildren: Shawna Parker, Scott Parker. Student, U. Md., 1969-72, U. York, Harrogate, Eng., 1969-72, U. N.Mex., 1975-79. With spl. ops. Nat. Security Agy., U.S. Govt., Ft. Meade, Md., 1969-74; with engring. rsch. U. N.Mex., Albuquerque, 1974-78; engr. fluids Internat. Mineral and Chem. Co., Houston, 1978-82; owner, pres., CEO Corrosions Monitoring Svcs. Inc., Casper, Wyo., 1981—; bd. dirs. Trenching Svcs., Casper, CMS Farms, Alamosa, Colo. With USN, 1964-68. Decorated Navy Unit Citation. Mem. Soc. Petroleum Engrs., Casper Wildcatters, Aircraft Owners Pilots Assn., DAV. Republican. Avocations: golf, flying, gardening, music. Home: 4471 E 12th St Casper WY 82609-0826 Office: CMS Inc PO Box 9826 Casper WY 82609-0826

SMITH, DOLORES MAXINE PLUNK, retired dancer, educator; b. Webster City, Iowa, Dec. 22, 1926; d. Herschel Swanson and Kathryn (Wilke) Hassig; m. Del O. Furrey, Aug. 26, 1945 (div. Feb. 1960); children: Bob H. Furrey, Jon B. Furrey, Kathryn E. Furrey Simmons; m. Dewey Pechota, 1962 (div. 1963); m. Leon Plunk, 1965 (div. 1967); m. Harold Burdick, 1974 (div. 1977); m. Floyd E. Smith, July 13, 1985. BS in Edn., Black Hills Tchrs. Coll., 1962; MA, Tex. Woman's U., 1964, PhD, 1974. Owner, operator pvt. dance studios, S.D., 1953-62; tchr. rural schs. Rosebud Reservation, S.D., 1945-49; tchr. Mellette County Pub. Schs., White River, S.D., 1958-60, St. Francis Indian Day Sch., 1960-61, Converse County (Wyo.) High Sch., 1961-62; grad. asst. Tex. Woman's U., Denton, 1962-64, 71; asst. prof. dance Sam Houston U., Huntsville, Tex., 1964-65; prof. Ctrl. Mo. State U., Warrensburg, 1965—; judge dance contest Kansas City Dance Theatre Co., 1987, 88, World Dance Assn., 1988, Mo. State Fair, 1989; judge Miss Am. Co-ed Pageants, 1991-93; dir. Dance Partisans Assn., Ctrl. Mo. State U., 1982-86, cmty. children's gymnastics program, 1982-87, tchr. cmty. dance program, 1985-87, dir. show dance team, 1991-97; dance coord. Internat. Coun. Health, Phys. Edn., Recreation, Sport and Dance, 1991—, mem. editl. bd., S.D., 1997; presenter Japanese Asia Dance Events, Malaysia, 1994, Dance Edn. Conf., Mich. State U., 1994. Contbr. articles to profl. jours. Bd. dirs. Kansas City Dance Theatre Co.; dir. Commn. on Dance, 1991-96, co-dir., 1994-96. Recipient Dance Scholar award ICHPER, 1993, Coun. for Health, Phys. Edn., Recreation, Sport and Dance scholar, 1995. Mem. Dance Masters Am. (sec. 1985-87, chmn. Mr. and Miss Dance Contest 1985, scholarships com. 1988-90), AAHPERD (honors award cen. dist. chpt., cen. dist. presentor 1991-92, dance chair, coll. chair, dance performance chair 1989-90, v.p. dance edn. 1991-93), Mo. Assn. Health, Phys. Edn., Recreation and Dance (pres. 1972, svc. award, 1996 Mahperd Dance scholar), Nat. Dance Assn. (future directions com. 1997, v.p. dance edn. 1991-93, chmn. Heritage luncheon 1968, 78, 87, Heritage award com. 1988-89, mem. ad hoc spl. svcs. com. 1989-91, pub. Spotlight 1989-90), Mid-Am. Dance Network (on-site coord. choreographers/dancers workshop 1992, bd. dirs., sec. 1992-94), Mo. Art Coun. Basic Arts Edn. (basic arts edn. task force higher edn.), Dance and Child Internat. (ctrl. dist. rep., USA Chpt., display chair, presider 1991), Asian Pacific Conf. Arts Edn. (presenter 1989), Assn. Supervision and Curriculum Devel., Internat. Congress Health, Phys. Edn. and Recreation Presenters (congress dels. representing dance, presenter 1991, 93), Internat. Phys. Edn. and Sports for Girls and Women, Phys. Edn. and Recreation, Mo. Alliance for Arts Edn. Avocations: raising and showing Belgium and Shire draft horses, draft ponies, jacks & jennies, mules, stained glass, cake decorating. Home: 130 SW 400th Rd Warrensburg MO 64093-8109

SMITH, DONALD ARTHUR, mechanical engineer, researcher; b. Hartford, Conn., Apr. 9, 1945; s. Winfred Arthur and Marguerite Elisabeth (Johnson) S.; m. Marianne Carol Taverna, June 17, 1967; 1 child, Adam James. BSME, U. Hartford, 1968. Rsch. engr. Combustion Engring. Inc., Windsor, Conn., 1968-71; supr. fluid rsch. Combustion Engring. Inc., Windsor, 1971-77, mgr. combustion rsch., 1977-84; dir. R&D Hartford Steam Boiler Inspection & Ins. Co., 1984—; co. rep. Indsl. Rsch. Inst., Washington, 1989—; treas. Am. Flame Rsch. Com., 1983—. Tech. editor: HSB Locomotive, 1990-91. Haddam (Conn.) Planning and Zoning Commn., 1991-95; pres. Sherwood Camp Assn., Haddam, 1971-81. Named Engr. Yr. ASME (Hartford sect.), 1989. Mem. Lions. Republican. Roman Catholic. Achievements include patents in spray atomizers, burners, ignitors and flame scanning systems for indsl. application. Established Combustion Engring.'s fluid mechanics and combustion rsch. facilities, Hartford Steam Boiler's corp. R&D program. Home: PO Box 95-42 Smith Hill Rd Haddam CT 06438 Office: Hartford Steam Boiler One State St Hartford CT 06102

SMITH, DONALD CAMERON, physician, educator; b. Peterborough, Ont., Can., Feb. 2, 1922; came to U.S., 1952, naturalized, 1960; s. James Cameron and Clarice (Leighton) S.; m. Jean Ida Morningstar, Sept. 11, 1946; children: Douglas Frazer, Scot Earle, Donald Ian. MD, Queen's U., 1945; MSc in Medicine, U. Toronto, 1948, DPH, 1949. Diplomate Am. Bd. Preventive Medicine (ofcl. examiner 1966-76), Am. Bd. Pediatrics. Intern Victoria Hosp., London, Ont., 1945-46; fellow in physiology U. Toronto, 1947-48; asst. med. officer health East York-Leaside (Ont.) Health Unit, 1949-50; lectr. pub. health adminstrn. U. Toronto, 1949-50; med. officer health Kent County (Ont.) Health Unit, 1950-51; Commonwealth Fund fellow in pediatrics U. Mich. Hosp., 1952-55; asst. prof. maternal and child health, clin. instr. pediatrics U. Mich., Ann Arbor, 1956-57; asso. prof. maternal and child health, research asso. pediatrics U. Mich., 1957-61; prof. maternal and child health U. Mich. (Sch. Pub. Health); prof. pediatrics U. Mich. (Med. Sch.), 1961-79, chmn. dept. health and human devel., 1961-79; prof. psychiatry and behavioral scis. Northwestern U. Med. Sch., Chgo., 1979-85; pres. Barton Hills Corp., 1970-72, 90—; mem. adv. coun. on health protection and disease prevention Dept. Health, Edn. and Welfare, 1969-72, chmn. med. assistance adv. coun., 1969-72; prin. advisor on health and med. affairs to gov. Mich., 1972-78; dir. Mich. Dept. Mental Health, 1974-78; chmn. health care policy bd. Mich. Dept. Corrections, 1986-91; chmn. State Pub. Health Adv. Coun., 1982-90; chmn. Expert Com. on AIDS, 1985-88; sr. v.p. Joint Commn. on Accreditation Hosps., Chgo., 1979-81; sr. med. adviser Sisters of Mercy Health Corp., 1978-86; dir. Office Behavioral Medicine, Cmty. Hosp. Authority Mich., 1986-91; pres. Mental Health Assn. Mich., 1992—; spl. cons. on maternal and child health and family planning programs South Korean Ministry Social Affairs, 1969; chmn., cross-nat. study of health care svcs. HEW, 1971; vis. prof. maternal and child health Harvard U., 1969-72; med. dir. Physician's Rev. Orgn. Mich., 1992—. Author: Contbr. to: Manual on Standards of Child Health Care, 1971, Barnett's Pediatrics, 1971, Pediatric Clinics of North America; also articles in med. and pub. health jours. Med. dir. Mich. Crippled Children Commn., 1962-64, Mich. United Fund, 1964-67. Served to Surgeon lt. Royal Canadian Navy, 1946-47. Fellow Am. Pub. Health Assn. (chmn. com. pub. med. care for children 1967-70, chmn. sect. maternal and child health 1968-70), Am. Acad. Pediatrics (chmn. com. on legis. 1966-73, chmn. council pediatric practice 1966-73), Royal Coll. of Physician and Surgeons of Canada; mem. AMA, Internat. Epidemiol. Assn., Delta Omega (pres. 1967-68). Home: 1000 Country Club Rd Ann Arbor MI 48105-1039

SMITH, DONALD E., broadcast engineer, manager; b. Salt Lake City, Sept. 10, 1930; s. Thurman A. and Louise (Cardall) S.; B.A. Columbia Coll., Chgo., 1955; B.S.; U. Utah, 1970; postgrad. U. So. Calif., U. Utah, PhD (hon.) Columbia Coll., 1985; m. Helen B. Lacy, 1978. Engr., Iowa State U., (WOI-TV), 1955-56; asst. chief engr. KLRJ-TV, Las Vegas, 1956-60; studio field engr. ABC, Hollywood, Cal., 1960; chief engr. Teletape, Inc., Salt Lake City, 1961; engring. supr. KUER, U. Utah, Salt Lake City, 1962-74, gen. mgr., 1975-85. Freelance cinematographer, 1950—; cons. radio TV (mgmt. engr. and prodn.), 1965—. Mem. Soc. Motion Pictures and TV Engrs., Lambda Chi Alpha. Home: 963 Hollywood Ave Salt Lake City UT 84105-3347

SMITH, DONALD E., banker; b. Terre Haute, Ind., Nov. 4, 1926; s. Henry P. and Ruth I. (Bius) S.; m. Mary F. Ryan, June 25, 1947; children: Virginia Lee, Sarah Jane. Student, Ind. U., 1945-47, Ind. State U., 1947-48. Chmn. Deep Vein Coal Co., Terre Haute, Ind., 1947—; with R.J. Oil Co., Inc., 1948—; chmn. Princeton Mining Co., Terre Haute, 1947—; pres. Terre Haute Oil Corp., 1947—; chmn. of bd. Terre Haute 1st Nat. Bank, 1969—; pres., CEO 1st Fin. Corp., Terre Haute, 1969—; bd. dirs. So. Ind. Gas and Electric Co. Trustee Ind. State U.; bd. mgrs. Rose-Hulman Inst. Tech., 1978—; pres. Alliance for Growth and Progress, 1987—; treas. Terre Haute Econ. Devel. Commn., 1981—; mem. Ind. Econ. Devel. Coun. Mem. Terre Haute C. of C. (bd. dirs. 1982—). Club: Country of Terre Haute. Lodge: Elks. Home: 94 Allendale Terre Haute IN 47802-4751 Office: Terre Haute First Nat Bank One First Financial Pla PO Box 540 Terre Haute IN 47807

SMITH, DONALD EUGENE, healthcare facility management administrator owner; b. Mishawaka, Ind., Oct. 15, 1936; s. Ernest Hartmann and Lucile Emma (Krumanaker) S.; m. Nancy Mae Jaffke, Sept. 2, 1961; children: Adam, Reid, Lynn. AB, Wabash Coll., 1959; MBA, U. Chgo., 1963. Adminstrv. resident Ind. U. Med. Ctr., 1960-61; assoc. dir. Ind. U. Hosps., 1966-72; pres. Henderson & Smith Corp., Indpls., 1978—; lectr. in health adminstrn. Ind. U., 1965-66, adj. asst. prof. in health adminstrn., 1966-78; ptnr. Covington (Ind.) Manor Health Care Ctr., Carmel (Ind.) Care Ctr., Countryside Manor, Anderson, Ind., Dearborn Enterprises, Lawrenceburg, Ind., Manor House at Riverview, Noblesville, Ind., Rawlins House, Pendleton, Ind., Manor House of Carmel, Ind., Northridge, Crawfordsville, Ind., Power Purchasing, Inc., Greenwood, Ind.; chmn. Ind. State Bd. Registration and Edn. Health Facility Adminstrs., 1969-82. Bd. dirs. Ind. U. Med. Ctr. Fed. Credit Union, 1965-68, Ind. Blue Cross, 1966-71; med. ctr. chmn. United Fund Drive, 1962-65; sec. Carmel (Ind.) Classic, 1979, v.p., 1981, pres., 1982-83; bd. trustees Wabash Coll., 1986—, mem. exec. com., 1986—, chmn. capital campaign drive, 1987-91, mem. long range planning com.,

1985; active Hamilton County Rep. Fin. Com., 1990—. Fellow ACHS; mem. Am. Health Care Assn., Ind. Health Care Assn., Wabash Coll. Alumni Assn., U. Chgo. Hosp. Adminstrn. Alumni Assn., Woodland Country Club, Skyline Club. Office: Henderson & Smith Corp 10333 N Meridian St Ste 250 Indianapolis IN 46290-1081

SMITH, DONALD EVANS, library consultant; b. Shanendoah, Iowa, Dec. 2, 1915; s. William Wesley and Bess Alice (Evans) S.; student Ricks Coll., 1939-40; BA, Hastings Coll., 1946; MLS, U. Wash., 1964. Tchr. English, librarian Tenino (Wash.) High Sch., 1950-51, Rochester (Wash.) High Sch., 1954-59; librarian North Thurston High Sch., Lacey, Wash., 1959-67; head librarian, coord. instructional materials Lakes High Sch., Lakewood Ctr., Wash., 1967-80; library cons., 1980—. Mem. awards com. Wash. Library Commn., 1964-66. With Signal Corps, AUS, 1942-45; to 1st lt., M.I., U.S. Army, 1951-54; to col. Wash. State Guard, 1971-80, now ret. Mem. Wash. Assn. Sch. Librarians (com. chmn.), Clover Park Edn. Assn. (com. chmn. 1970-71), Am. Legion, Phi Delta Kappa (del. nat. confs.). Home and Office: 4530 26th Loop SE Lacey WA 98503-3264

SMITH, DONALD L., social sciences educator; b. Richland, Wash., Feb. 1, 1949; s. Marcelle H. and Nettie B. (Lacher) S.; m. Sally Jane Carr, Aug. 15, 1971; children: Shannon, Stephanie. AA, Mesa Coll., 1969; BS in Edn., Southwest Mo. State U., 1971, MS in Edn., 1976. Cert. tchr., Mo. Tchr., chair dept. social scis. Ozark (Mo.) H. S., 1971-96; retired, 1996; rsch. technician Ctr. Archaeol. Rsch., S.W. Mo. State U., Springfield, 1978, rsch. assoc., 1979; adj. prof. Drury Coll., Springfield, 1983—; cons. mandatory statewide competency testing in social studies Mo. Dept. Elem. and Secondary Edn., Columbia, 1986. Special corr. Springfield Newspapers, Inc., 1996-97. V.p. Frisco Railroad Mus., Springfield, Mo., 1996-97. Nat. Endowment for Humanities scholar, 1985, Fulbright scholar U.S. Dept. Edn., Zimbabwe, Botswana, Malawi, 1991. Mem. Nat. Coun. Social Studies, Greater Ozarks Coun. Social Studies, Mo. State Tchrs. Assn. (pres. dept. social studies 1982-83, newsletter editor 1983-88), Archaeol. Inst. Am., Bibl. Archaeol. Soc. Avocations: travel, military history, aviation, computers, model railroading. Home: 1801 W Cherokee St Springfield MO 65807-2205

SMITH, DONALD NORBERT, engineering executive; b. Ft. Wayne, Ind., June 12, 1931. BS in Indsl. Mgmt., Ind. U., 1953; Diploma Grad. Sch. Bus., U. N.C., 1960. Asst. mgr. Ann Arbor (Mich.) Rsch. Labs/Burroughs Corp., 1961-64; dir. Indsl. Devel. Divsn. U. Mich., Ann Arbor, 1964-93; assoc. dir.-mfg. systems rsch. Office for Study Auto Transp. U. Mich. Transp. Rsch. Inst., Ann Arbor, 1993—. Co-author: Management Standards for Computers and Numerical Controls, 1977; contbr. articles to profl. jours. Recipient Peace award, Israel, 1967, Mfg. Tech. award ASTME, 1968, Engring. Merit award, San Fernando Valley Engrs. Coun., 1971, Man of Yr. award Great Lakes Chpt. Numerical Control Soc., 1975, Archimedes Engring. award Calif. Soc. Profl. Engrs., Disting. CAD/CAM Achievements award L.A. Coun. Engrs., 1982, Achievement award for promoting Swedish/Am. trade, Kingdom of Sweden, 1983, Tech. Transfer award NASA/Rockwell Internat., 1984. Fellow Soc. Mfg. Engrs. (Indsl. Tech. Mgmt. award 1978, internat. awards com. 1986, 88, 89, Joseph A. Siegel Internat. Svc. award 1988, Pres.'s award Robotics Internat. 1985). Roman Catholic. Avocation: boating. Office: Office Study Automotive Transp 2901 Baxter Rd Ann Arbor MI 48109-2150

SMITH, DORIS CORINNE KEMP, retired nurse; b. Bogalusa, La., Nov. 22, 1919; d. Milton Jones and Maude Maria (Fortenberry) Kemp; m. Joseph William Smith, Oct. 13, 1940 (dec.). BS in Nursing, U. Colo., 1957, MS in Nursing Adminstrn., 1958. RN, Colo. Head nurse Chgo. Bridge & Iron Co., Morgan City, La., 1941-45, Shannon Hosp., San Angelo, Tex., 1945-50; dir. nursing Yoakum County Hosp., Denver City, Tex., 1951-52; hosp. supr. Med. Arts Hosp., Odessa, Tex., 1952-55; dir. insvc. edn. St. Anthony Hosp., Denver, 1961-66; coord. Sch. Vocat. Nursing, Kiamichi Area Vocat.-Tech. Nursing Sch., Wilburton, Okla., 1969-77; supr. non-ambulatory unit Lubbock (Tex.) State Sch., 1978-85, ret., 1985; mem. steering com. Western Interstate Commn. on Higher Edn. for Nurses, Denver, 1963-65; mem. curriculum and materials com. Okla. Bd. Vocat.-Tech. Edn., Stillwater, 1971-76; mem. Invitational Conf. To Plan Nursing for Future, Oklahoma City, 1976-77; mem. survey team to appraise Sch. of Vocat.-Tech. Edn. Schs. for Okla. Dept. Vocat.-Tech. Edn., 1975-76. Author, editor: Survey of Functions Expected of the General Duty Nurse, State of Colorado, 1958; co-editor: Curriculum Guides; contbr. numerous articles to profl. jours. Recipient citation of merit Okla. State U., 1976. Mem. AAAS, ANA, AAUW (life), Nat. League for Nursing, Tex. League for Nursing, Tex. Nurses Assn., Dist. 18 Nurses Assn., Tex. Employees Assn. (v.p. 1984-85), U. Colo. Alumni Assn., Am. Bus. Women's Assn. (pres. Lubbock chpt. 1986-87, rec. sec. 1989-90, edn. chair 1994-95, hospitality chair 1995-96), Am. Bus. Women's Assn. (program co-chair 1996-97, Woman of Yr. Sunrise chpt. 1994-95), Bus. and Profl. Women's Assn. (sec. 1992-95), Chancellor's Club U. Colo., Pi Lambda Theta (sec. local chpt. 1957-58). Republican. Avocations: gardening, swimming, walking, travel, fishing. Home: 2103 55th St Lubbock TX 79412-2612

SMITH, DORIS VICTORIA, educational agency administrator; b. N.Y.C., July 5, 1937; d. Albin and Victoria (Anderson) Olson; m. Howard R. Smith, Aug. 21, 1960; children: Kurt, Steven, Andrea. BS in Edn., Wagner Coll., 1959; MA in Edn., Kean Coll., 1963, cert., 1980; EdD, Nova Southeastern U., 1995. Cert. adminstr., tchr. elem. edn., N.J. Thorough and efficient coord. East Hanover (N.J.) Twp. Sch. Dist., 1977-79; ednl. specialist N.J. State Dept. Edn., Morristown, 1979—, ednl. planner, 1982-87, ednl. mgr., 1987—; pres. N.E. Coalition Ednl. Leaders, Inc.; founding mem. Morris County Curriculum Network. Author: Affirmative Action—Rules and Regulations, 1982, Supervising Early Childhood Programs, 1984. Past pres. bd. trustees Florham Park Libr.; founding mem. Morris Area Tech. Alliance; founding mem., pres. Calvary Nursery Sch.; bd. of trust office N.J. Coun. Edn.; pres. bd. trustees Madison/Chatham Adult Sch.; trustee Morris County Children's Svcs. Tchr. insvc. grantee; recipient Disting. Svc. award N.E. Coalition Ednl. Leaders, 1991, Disting. Svc. award Morris County Prins. and Suprs. Assn., Outstanding Educator award N.J. ASCD, 1995. Mem. N.J. Coun. Edn., N.J. Schoolmasters Assn., Phi Delta Kappa.

SMITH, DOROTHY OTTINGER, jewelry designer, civic leader; b. Indpls.; d. Albert Ellsworth and Leona Aurelia (Waller) Ottinger; student Herron Art Sch. of Purdue U. and Ind. U., 1941-42; m. James Emory Smith, June 25, 1943 (div. 1984); children: Michael Ottinger, Sarah Anne, Theodore Arnold, Lisa Marie. Comml. artist William H. Block Co., Indpls., 1942-43, H.P. Wasson Co., 1943-44; dir. Riverside (Calif.) Art Center, 1963-64; jewelry designer, Riverside, 1970—; numerous design commns. Adviser Riverside chpt. Freedom's Found. of Valley Forge; co-chmn. fund raising com. Riverside Art Ctr. and Mus., 1966-67, bd. dirs. Art Alliance, 1980-81, Art Mus.; mem. Riverside City Hall sculpture selection panel Nat. Endowment for Arts, 1974-75; chmn. fund raising benefit Riverside Art Ctr. and Mus., 1973-74, trustee, 1980-84, chmn. permanent collection, 1981-84, co-chmn. fund drive, 1982-84; chmn. Riverside Mcpl. Arts Commn., 1974-76, Silver Anniversary Gala, 1992; juror Riverside Civic Ctr. Purchase Prize Art Show, 1975; mem. pub. bldgs. and grounds subcom., gen. plan citizens com. City of Riverside, 1965-66; mem. Mayor's Commn. on Civic Beauty, Mayor's Commn. on Sister City Sendai, 1965-66; bd. dirs., chmn. spl. events Children's League of Riverside Community Hosp., 1952-53; bd. dirs. Crippled Children's Soc. of Riverside, spl. events chmn., 1952-53; bd. dirs. Jr. League of Riverside, rec. sec., 1960-61; bd. dirs. Nat. Charity League, pres. Riverside chpt., 1965-66; mem. exec. com. of bd. trustees Riverside Arts Found., 1977-91, fund drive chmn., 1978-79, project rev. chmn., 1978-79; juror Gemco Charitable and Scholarship Found., 1977-85; mem. bd. women deacons Calvary Presbyn. Ch., 1978-80, elder, 1989-92; mem. incorporating bd. Inland Empire United Fund for Arts, 1980-81; bd. dirs. Hospice Orgn. Riverside County, 1982-84; Art Awareness chmn. Riverside Arts Found.; mem. Calif. Coun. Humanities, 1982-86. Recipient cert. Riverside City Coun., 1977, plaque Mayor of Riverside, 1977. Mem. Riverside Art Assn. (pres. 1961-63, 1st v.p. 1964-65, 67-68, trustee 1959-70, 80-84, 87-92), Art Alliance of Riverside Art Ctr. and Museum (founder 1964, pres. 1969-70). Recipient Spl. Recognition Riverside Cultural Arts Coun., 1981, Disting. Service plaque Riverside Art Ctr. and Mus., Jr. League Silver Raincross Community Svc. award, 1989, Cert. Appreciation Outstanding Svc. to the Arts Community Riverside Arts Found., 1990. Address: 3979 Chapman Pl Riverside CA 92506-1150

SMITH, DUDLEY RENWICK, retired insurance company executive; b. N.Y.C., June 10, 1937; s. Crosby Tuttle and Vernon (Siems) S.; m. Juliana Buros, Nov. 17, 1962; children: Clayton Tuttle, Bradley Renwick, Gregory Dudley. AB, Dartmouth Coll., 1960. V.p. Fed. Ins. Co., Warren, N.J.; sr. v.p. Chubb & Son Inc., Warren, 1961-96; trustee Chubb Found. Home: 60 Fairway Dr PO Box 1335 Grantham NH 03753-1335

SMITH, DWIGHT CHICHESTER, III, lawyer; b. Ft. Meade, Md., June 24, 1955; s. Dwight Chichester Jr. and Rachel (Stryker) S.; m. Mindy L. Kotler, Aug. 18, 1985; children: Dwight C. IV, Cornelia R. BA, Yale U., 1977, JD, 1981. Bar: D.C. 1982, N.Y. 1982. Para-legal House Ethics Com., Washington, 1977-78; law clk. to Hon. Hugh Bownes U.S. Ct. Appeals (1st cir.), Concord, N.H., 1981-82; assoc. Kaye, Scholer, Fierman, Hays & Handler, Washington, 1982-84, Covington & Burling, Washington, 1984-90; dep. chief counsel Office of Thrift Supervision, Dept. of Treas., Washington, 1990-94, dep. chief counsel for bus. transactions, 1995—. Article and book rev. editor Yale Law jour., 1980-81; contbr. articles to profl. jours. Mem. Potomac Boat club, City Tavern Club. Presbyterian. Avocation: rowing. Home: 3422 Q St NW Washington DC 20007-2718 Office: Dept Treas Office Thrift Supervision 1700 G St NW Washington DC 20006-4710

SMITH, DWIGHT MORRELL, chemistry educator; b. Hudson, N.Y., Oct. 10, 1931; s. Elliott Monroe and Edith Helen (Hall) S.; m. Alice Beverly Bond, Aug. 27, 1955 (dec. 1990); children—Karen Elizabeth, Susan Allison, Jonathan Aaron; m. Elfi Nelson, Dec. 28, 1991. B.A., Central Coll., Pella, Iowa, 1953; Ph.D., Pa. State U., 1957; ScD (hon.), Cen. Coll., 1986; LittD (hon.), U. Denver, 1990. Postdoctoral fellow, instr. Calif. Inst. Tech., 1957-59; sr. chemist Texaco Rsch. Ctr., Beacon, N.Y., 1959-61; asst. prof. chemistry Wesleyan U., Middletown, Conn., 1961-66; assoc. prof. Hope Coll., Holland, Mich., 1966-69, prof., 1969-72; prof. chemistry U. Denver, 1972—, chmn. dept., 1972-83, vice chancellor for acad. affairs, 1983-84, chancellor, 1984-89; pres., bd. trustees Hawaii Loa Coll., Kaneohe, 1990-92; bd. dirs. Aina Inst., Hawaii; mem. Registry for Interim Coll. and Univ. Pres.; mem. adv. bd. Solar Energy Rsch. Inst., 1989-91, Denver Rsch. Inst.; mem. vis. com. Zettlemoyer Ctr. for Surface Studies Lehigh U., 1990—; scientific adv. bd. Denver Rsch. Inst. Editor Revs. on Petroleum Chemistry, 1975-78; contbr. articles to profl. jours.; patentee selective hydrogenation. Chmn. Chs. United for Social Action, Holland, 1968-69; mem. adv. com. Holland Sch. Bd., 1969-70; bd. commrs. Colo. Adv. Tech. Inst., 1984-88, Univ. Senate, United Meth. Ch., Nashville, 1987-88, 91-93; mem. adv. bd. United Way, Inst. Internat. Edn., Japan Am. Soc. Colo., Denver Winter Games Olympics Com.; mem. ch. bds. or consistories Ref. Ch. Am., N.Y., Conn., Mich., United Meth. Ch., Colo. DuPont fellow, 1956-57, NSF fellow Scripps Inst., 1971-72; recipient grants Research Corp., Petroleum Research Fund, NSF, Solar Energy Research Inst. Mem. AAAS, Am. Chem. Soc. (chmn. Colo. 1976, sec. western Mich. 1970-71, award Colo. sect. 1986), Catalysis Soc., Soc. Applied Spectroscopy, Mile High Club, Pinehurst Country Club, Sigma Xi. Home: 1931 W Sanibel Ct Littleton CO 80120 Office: U Denver Dept Chem Univ Park Denver CO 80208

SMITH, DWIGHT RAYMOND, ecology and wildlife educator, writer; b. Sanders, Idaho, July 28, 1921; s. Andrew Leonard and Effie Elizabeth (Simons) S.; m. Carol Elizabeth Breclaw (dec. 1983); children Alan Dwight (dec.), Sharon Lee Smith Dequine, Gary Robert, Mark Jonathan (dec.). BS in Forestry, U. Idaho, 1949, MS in Wildlife Mgmt., 1951; PhD in Ecology, Utah State U., 1971. Rsch. biologist Idaho Fish and Game Dept., Salmon, 1950-52, area game mgr., 1953-56; range scientist U.S. Forest Svc., Ft. Collins, Colo., 1957-61, wildlife rsch. biologist, 1962-65; asst. prof. Colo. State U., Ft. Collins, 1965-70, assoc. prof., 1971-75, prof., 1975-83, prof. emeritus, 1983—; nature photographer Alan Landsburg Prodns., Hollywood, Calif., 1971; energy cons. CF&I Steel, Pueblo, Colo., 1981. Author: Above Timberline: A Wildlife Biologist's Rocky Mountain Journal, 1981; writer/photographer (film) Research in the Rockies: A Scientist Explores the Alpine, 1973; contbr. articles to profl. jours. Served to 2d lt. (via battlefield comm.) inf. U.S. Army, 1942-45, PTO, ETO. Decorated Bronze Star; rsch. grantee, fellow U.S. Fish and Wildlife Svc., 1949-50, Wildlife Mgmt. Inst., 1950, Nat. Wildlife Fedn., 1954-55. Fellow Explorers Club; mem. Toastmasters (ednl. v.p. local chpt. 1960-62, pres. 1963), Xi Sigma Pi, Sigma Xi, Gamma Sigma Delta, Phi Kappa Phi. Democrat. Roman Catholic. Avocations: photography, bicycling, skiing, square dancing. Home: 1916 Harmony Dr Fort Collins CO 80525-3442 Office: Desert House of Prayer Box 570 Cortaro AZ 85652 *Do not be afraid of enthusiasm. You can do nothing effectively without it.*

SMITH, DWYANE, university administrator; b. St. Louis, Feb. 16, 1961; s. Magnolia Smith. BS in Psychology, N.E. Mo. State U., 1983, MA in Edn. Adminstrn., 1991; postgrad., U. Mo., Columbia, Harvard U., 1995. Intern IRS, St. Louis, 1983; minority counselor N.E. Mo. State U., Kirksville, 1983-88, dir. minority svcs., 1988-91, asst. dir. admissions, asst. dean multicultural affairs, 1991—, assoc. dean multicultural affairs. Mem. Alpha Phi Alpha (chair statewide conv. 1990, Mo. Man of Yr. 1985), Alpha Phi Omega, Phi Kappa Phi, Habitat for Humanity. Avocations: reading, writing. Home: 1601 S Franklin St Kirksville MO 63501-4401

SMITH, EDGAR BENTON, physician; b. Houston, June 2, 1932; s. Burt Benton and Lela Elizabeth (Grant) S.; m. Francis Elaine Newton, Aug. 1, 1953; children—Sheri Elaine Smith Dinehart, Robin Marie Smith Fredrickson. Student, Rice U., 1950-53; BA, U. Houston, 1956; MD, Baylor U., 1957; diploma clin. medicine of the tropics, U. London, 1967. Intern Walter Reed Gen. Hosp., Washington, 1957-58; resident Brooke Gen. Hosp., Ft. Sam Houston, Tex., 1960-63; asst. prof. dermatology U. Miami Sch. Medicine, 1967-68, Baylor Coll. Medicine, Houston, 1968-71; asso. prof. medicine (dermatology) U. N.Mex. Sch. Medicine, Albuquerque, 1971-75; prof. U. N.Mex. Sch. Medicine, 1975-78; prof., chmn. dept. dermatology U. Tex. Med. Br., Galveston, 1978—. Contbr. articles in field to profl. jours. Served with U.S. Army, 1956-66. Recipient Khatali award U. N.Mex. Sch. Medicine, 1976; Fulbright scholar London Sch. Hygiene and Tropical Medicine, 1966-67; Alfred Stengel travelling scholar ACP, 1967. Mem. AMA, Am. Acad. Dermatology (bd. dirs. 1978-82, pres.-elect 1988, pres. 1989, Sulzberger internat. lectr. 1992), Assn. Profs. Dermatology (sec.-treas. 1979-82), Am. Dermatol. Assn. (bd. dirs. 1994—), Southwestern Dermatol. Soc. (sec. 1974-77, pres. 1978), South Ctrl. Dermatol. Congress (sec.-gen. 1973-76, pres. 1976-81), Tex. Dermatol. Soc. (trustee 1986), So. Med. Assn. (chmn. dermatology sect. 1988), Galveston Arty. Club, Yacht Club, Baker Street Irregulars, Alpha Omega Alpha. Democrat. Methodist. Home: 3017 Ave O Galveston TX 77550 Office: U Tex Med Br Dept Dermatology Galveston TX 77555-0783

SMITH, EDGAR EUGENE, biochemist, university administrator; b. Hollandale, Miss., Aug. 6, 1934; s. Sam and Augusta Lillie (McCoy) S.; m. Inez Oree Wiley, May 27, 1955; children—E. Donald, Anthony R., Stephen S., Gregory S. B.S., Tougaloo Coll., 1955; M.S., Purdue U., 1957, Ph.D., 1960. Rsch. fellow in surgery (biochemistry) Harvard Med. Sch., Boston, 1959-61; rsch. assoc. Harvard Med. Sch., 1961-68; assoc. in surg. rsch. Beth Israel Hosp., Boston, 1959-68; asst. prof. surgery (chemistry) Boston U. Sch. Medicine, 1968-70, assoc. prof. biochemistry, 1970-74; assoc. prof. biochemistry U. Mass. Med. Sch., Worcester, 1974-80, prof. emeritus biochemistry and molecular biology, 1991—; assoc. dean acad. affairs U. Mass. Med. Sch., 1974-77, provost, 1975-83; asst. dean minority affairs, prin. investigator Bur. Health Manpower Spl. Project grant Boston U. Sch. Medicine, 1972-74; v.p. acad. affairs U. Mass. System, 1983-91; v.p. Nellie Mae, 1990-93; acting pres. Tougaloo Coll., 1995, edn. cons., 1996—; mem. governing bd. Robert Wood Johnson Health Policy Fellowship Program, Inst. Medicine, NAS, 1978-85. Contbr. writings to sci. publs. Chmn. bd. overseers Sch. Medicine Morehouse Coll.; trustee Tougaloo Coll., Metco Scholarship Fund, Lexington, Mass.; bd. dirs. Dimock Community Health Center, Boston, New Urban League of Greater Boston, So. Edn. Found., 1976-79; chmn. Boston Com. for Nat. Med. Fellowships, Inc. Recipient research career devel. award Nat. Cancer Inst., 1969-74, award for outstanding achievement in biochemistry Nat. Consortium for Black Profl. Devel., 1976, human relations award Mass. Teachers Assn., 1977, health award NAACP, 1977; Robert Wood Johnson Health Policy fellow Inst. Medicine, Nat. Acad. Scis., 1977-78; named Alumnus of Yr. Tougaloo Coll., 1969, Disting. Alumnus Nat. Assn. for Equal Opportunities in Higher Edn., 1979, 92, Old Master Purdue U., 1978. Fellow Am. Inst. Chemists; mem. Am. Soc. Biol. Chemists, Am. Chem. Soc. (div. biol. chemists), AAAS, N.Y. Acad. Scis., Am. Assn. for Cancer Research, Boston Cancer Research Assn., Am. Polit. Sci. Assn., Am. Soc. Biol. Chemists (com. on minorities 1980-83), Josiah Macy, Jr. Found. Scholarship Com. Marine Biol. Lab., Woods Hole, Mass., Sigma Xi, Phi Lambda Upsilon, Alpha Phi Alpha. Home: 81 Hill St Lexington MA 02173-6532

SMITH, EDWARD HERBERT, radiologist, educator; b. N.Y.C., Feb. 18, 1936; s. Nathan Leon and Rebecca Ada (Brodsky) S.; m. Anne Chantler Oliphant, June 27, 1971; children: Peter Chantler, Jeffrey Martin. A.B., Columbia Coll., 1956; M.D., SUNY, 1960. Intern U. Calif. Hosp., San Francisco, 1960-61; resident in internal medicine Montefiore Hosp., N.Y.C., 1961-62; resident in radiology Kings County Hosp. Ctr., Bklyn., 1964-67, radiologist, 1967-69; instr. SUNY-Bklyn., 1967-69; radiologist Children's Hosp. Med. Ctr., Boston, 1969-70, Peter Bent Brigham Hosp., Boston, 1969-80; dir. div. radiology Charles A. Dana Cancer Research Ctr., Boston, 1974-80; instr. Harvard Med. Sch., Boston, 1969-70, asst. prof., 1970-75, assoc. prof., 1975-80, lectr. radiology, 1980—; radiologist U. Mass. Med. Ctr., Worcester, 1980—, prof., chmmn. dept. radiology, 1980—; prof. U. Mass. Med. Sch., Worcester, 1980—; prof. dept. surgery in urology U. Mass. Med. Sch., 1983—; vis. radiologist Rambam Govt. Hosp., Haifa, Israel, 1972; vis. prof. dept. ultrasound U. Copenhagen, Herlev, Denmark, 1977-78, Shanghai Med. Ctr., Peoples Republic China, 1987; cons. Tng. Program in Diagnostic Ultrasound for Physicians and Technologists, Va., 1974-75; reviewer profl. jours. Author: (with others) Abdominal Ultrasound: Static and Dynamic Scanning, 1980; contbr. articles to profl. jours. Fogarty sr. internat. fellow John E. Fogarty Internat. Ctr. for Advanced Study in Health Scis., NIH, Copenhagen, 1977-78. Fellow Am. Coll. Radiology, Soc. Radiologists in Ultrasound (charter); mem. Assn. Univ. Radiologists, Am. Inst. Ultrasound in Medicine, Am. Roentgen Ray Soc., Radiol. Soc. N.Am., New Eng. Soc. Ultrasound in Medicine (charter, pres. 1978-79), New Eng. Roentgen Ray Soc. (pres. 1989-90), Mass. Radiologic Soc. (exec. coun.). Office: U Mass Med Ctr Dept Radiology 55 Lake Ave N Worcester MA 01655-0002 *I have enjoyed a rewarding career in academic medicine but I am extremely concerned with the momentum shifting toward for profit "managed care", medicine will become a business with primary concern with the bottom line and we will lose the "care" in medical care and the American public will be the big loser.*

SMITH, EDWARD JUDE, biologist; b. Serabu, Sierra Leone, Oct. 31, 1961; s. Karimu and Yemah (Brewah) S.; m. Gilceria Estandien Pimentel, Oct. 9, 1991; children: Dehmeh, Ngeindaloh. BSc, U. Sierra Leone, 1984; MSc, Oreg. State U., 1989, PhD, 1991. Rsch. asst. Oreg. State U., Corvallis, Oreg., 1987-91; postdoctoral rsch. assoc. Iowa State U., Ames, 1991-92; asst. prof. Tuskegee (Ala.) U., 1992—. Contbr. articles to profl. jours. Sec. Pace, Auburn, Ala., 1994. Mem. Am. Soc. Genetics, USDA (sec. 1994, pres. 1995). Roman Catholic. Achievements include rsch. on discriminant analysis of selected lines; rsch. on candidate markers for tibial dyschondroplasia; rsch. on an animal model to study the molecular basis for heterosis. Home: 827 Cahaba Dr Auburn AL 36830-3201 Office: Tuskegee U 109 Milbank Hall Tuskegee AL 36088

SMITH, EDWARD K., economist, consultant; b. Buffalo, Apr. 12, 1922; s. Clifford Kershaw and Helen (Baro) S.; m. Mary Alice Pendergast, Dec. 20, 1948; children: Benjamin, Christopher, Loretta Christopher, Katherine Smith Fuscoe, Alice Ryan, Margarita Treuth, James, Daniel. B.A., Hobart Coll., 1946; M.A., U. Buffalo, 1950, Harvard U., 1955; Ph.D., Harvard U., 1960. From asst. to assoc. prof. econs. Boston Coll., 1956-64; dep. asst. sec. U.S. Dept. Commerce, Washington, 1965-68; prof., chmn. dept. econs. Colo. State U., Ft. Collins, 1968-70; v.p. Nat. Bur. Econ. Research, N.Y.C., 1970-77; sr. econ. cons. Brimmer & Co. Inc., Washington, 1977-83; dir. Internat. Banking Ctr., Fla. Internat. U., Miami, 1982, Bur. Ind. Econs., U.S. Dept. Commerce, Washington, 1983; assoc. dir. Bur. Econ. Analysis, 1984-88; cons. economist, 1988—; vis. prof. econs. U. Colo., 1965, Yale U., New Haven, 1971, Fla. Internat. U., Miami, 1982. Author: The Economic State of New England, 1954. Fiscal advisor Lt. Gov. Mass., Boston, 1955; mem. Pres.'s Task Force on Environ., 1966, Pres.'s Task Force on Housing, 1968, Gov. Carey's Task Force on Unemployment, N.Y.C., 1974; trustee St. Mary's Coll., Newburgh, N.Y., 1972-77. Served with U.S. Army, 1943-46. Mem. Am. Econs. Assn., Nat. Assn. Bus. Economists, So. Regional Sci. Assn., Nat. Economists Club (v.p. 1984, bd. dirs. 1985-86). Democrat. Episcopalian.

SMITH, EDWARD PAUL, JR., lawyer; b. Westbury, N.Y., Jan. 13, 1939; s. Edward Paul Sr. and Margaret (Eisenhauer) S.; m. Mary Elizabeth Neagle, Mar. 29, 1980; children: Nora, Edward, Brian, Thomas, Brendan. BA, Coll. of the Holy Cross, 1960; LLB, Columbia U., 1963. Bar: N.Y. 1964, Fla. 1966. Assoc. Chadbourne & Parke, N.Y.C., 1964-75, prin., 1975—; corp. sec. Am. Bur. Metal Statis., N.Y.C., 1978—. Author: Regulation of Employee Benefit Plans, Under Erisa, 1990. Capt. USAF, 1964-67. Mem. N.Y. State Bar Assn., Fla. Bar Assn. Roman Catholic. Home: 36 Avon Rd Bronxville NY 10708-1614 Office: Chadbourne & Parke 30 Rockefeller Plz New York NY 10112

SMITH, EDWARD REAUGH, retired lawyer, cemetery and funeral home consultant; b. Flora, Ill., Sept. 23, 1932; m. Jo Anne Myers, Sept. 10, 1954; children: Mark and Michael (twins), Jillian. BS, Midwestern U., 1953; LLB, So. Meth. U., 1957. Bar: Tex. 1957, U.S. Dist. Ct. (so. dist.) Tex. 1957, U.S. Dist. Ct. (no. dist.) Tex. 1961, U.S. Tax Ct. 1961, U.S. Ct. Appeals (5th cir.) 1971, U.S. Ct. Claims 1971, U.S. Supreme Ct. 1982; CPA, Tex. Atty. Vinson, Elkins, Weems & Searls, Houston, 1957-59, Nelson, McCleskey & Harringer, Lubbock, Tex., 1959-61; pvt. practice Lubbock, 1961-62; ptnr. Smith, Baker, Field & Clifford Inc. (formerly Smith & Baker Inc.), Lubbock, 1962-84; CPA Tex., 1955-92; chmn., CEO Resthaven Funeral Home and Cemetery, Lubbock, 1979-93; cons. Svc. Corp. Internat., Lubbock, 1993—; bd. dirs. Briercroft Savs. Assn., 1962-84, Tex. Cemetery Assn., 1986-87, 90-91; pres., bd. chmn. Resthaven Funeral Home, 1965-69, Resthaven of Lubbock, Inc., 1979-93, Lakeview Meml. Gardens, 1978-86; lectr. profl. meetings on taxes and estate planning; bd. visitors So. Meth. U. Law Sch., 1968-71; chmn. estate planning seminar for women Tex. Tech. Found., 1971; pres. South Plains Trust and Estate Coun., 1963-64, others. Contbr. articles to profl. jours. Mem. Lubbock Planning and Zoning Commn., 1964-65, chmn., 1966, budget divsn. United Fund; co-chmn. profl. divsn. United Way, 1981; tchr., bd. dirs. First Meth. Ch., Lubbock, 1963-88; pres. Haynes Elem. Sch. PTA, 1968-69; past mem. pres.'s adv. bd. Lubbock Christian Coll.; bd. dirs. Tex. Tech. U. Found., 1968-89, sec., 1969-76, vice-chmn., 1976-78, chmn., 1978-81, chmn. fund raising com., 1979-81; bd. dirs. Tex. Tech. U. Med. Sch. Found., 1970-78, vice-chmn., 1972-73, chmn., 1973-74; mem. pres.'s coun. Tex. Tech. U., 1978—; spkr. ann. banquet Flora Acad. Found., Flora H.S., 1991; bd. dirs. Lubbock Symphony Orch., 1996—. Mem. Am. Anthroposophical Soc., Tex. Cemeteries Assn. (hon. life), Alpha Chi. Avocations: mountain trails, research, writing.

SMITH, EDWARD SAMUEL, federal judge; b. Birmingham, Ala., Mar. 27, 1919; s. Joseph Daniel and Sarah Jane (Tatum) S.; m. Innes Adams Comer, May 5, 1942; children: Edward Samuel, Innes Smith Cameron Richards. Student, Ala. Poly. Inst., 1936-38; B.A., U. Va., 1941, J.D., 1947. Bar: Va. 1947, D.C. 1948, Md. 1953. Assoc., then ptnr. firm Blair, Korner, Doyle & Appel, Washington, 1947-54; ptnr. firm Blair, Korner, Doyle & Worth, 1954-61; gen. counsel Nat. Cath. Edn. Assn., 1958-61; chief trial sect., tax. div. Dept. Justice, 1961, asst. for civil trials, dep. asst. atty. gen., 1961-63; ptnr. firm, head tax dept. Piper & Marbury, Balt., 1963-78; mng. ptnr. Piper & Marbury, 1971-74; assoc. judge U.S. Ct. Claims, Washington, 1978-82; judge U.S. Ct. Appeals (Fed. Cir.), Washington, 1982—, sr. circuit judge, 1989—; liaison atty. gen. to Lawyers Com. Civil Rights Under Law, 1963; adj. faculty Cumberland Sch. Law, Samford U., 1992—. Bd. dirs. Roland Park Civic League, Inc., Balt., 1977-78; pres., St. Andrew's Soc. Washington, 1956-58. Served to lt. USNR, 1941-46; to comdr. USNR, Ret. 1968. Mem. ABA (chmn. com. on tax litigation 1977-78), Fed. Bar Assn., Md. State Bar Assn. (chmn. sect. of taxation 1971-72), D.C. Bar Assn., Va. State Bar, Met. Club, Chevy Chase Club, Lawyers Club of Washington, Summit Club (Birmingham), Lambda Chi Alpha. Democrat. Episcopalian. Office: Hugo Black US Courthouse 1729 5th Ave N Birmingham AL 35203-2000 also: US Ct Appeals Fed Crct Nat Cts Bldg 717 Madison Pl NW Washington DC 20439-0001 *The second most important rule of life is that we should never become disillusioned with the Golden Rule when others do not follow it.**

SMITH, EDWIN ERIC, lawyer; b. Louisville, Sept. 29, 1946; s. Lester Henry and Nancy Joy (Heyman) S.; m. Katharine Case Thomson, Aug. 16, 1969; children: Benjamin Clark, George Lewis, Andrew Laurence. BA, Yale U., 1968; JD, Harvard Law Sch., 1974. Bar: Mass. 1974, U.S. Dist. Ct. Mass. 1974. Assoc. Bingham, Dana & Gould, Boston, 1974-81, ptnr., 1981—; lectr. in field; Mass. commr. on uniform state laws; mem. uniform comml. code articles 5 and 9 drafting com.; U.S. del. to UN Commn. on Internat. Trade Law. Lt. USNR, 1969-74. Recipient Achievement Medal USN, 1971. Mem. ABA (chmn. uniform comml. code com. bus. law sect.), Am. Law Inst. (Uniform Comml. Code article 9 study com.), Am. Coll. Comml. Fin. Lawyers (bd. regents), Assn. Comml. Fin. Attys. Home: 4 Chiltern Rd Weston MA 02193-2714 Office: Bingham Dana & Gould 150 Federal St Boston MA 02110

SMITH, EDWIN IDE, medical educator; b. Norfolk, Va., May 13, 1924; s. Charles Carroll and Lila (Ide) S.; m. Matilda Janet Snelling, Mar. 31, 1951; children: Sarah Pinckney Smith Crotty, Susan Ide Smith Thurmond, Charles Carroll III. Student, Harvard Coll., 1942-44, Georgetown U., 1944-46; MD, Johns Hopkins U., 1948. Diplomate Am. Bd. Surgery. Intern Johns Hopkins Hosp., Balt., 1948-49; Halsted fellow in surgery Johns Hopkins Sch. Medicine, Balt., 1949-50; resident Boston Children's Hosp., 1950, 52-53, 55-56, Vanderbilt U. Hosp., Nashville, 1953-55; pvt. practice pediatric surgery Norfolk, Va., 1956-63; assoc. prof. surgery U. Mo. Coll. Medicine, Kansas City, 1963-68, U. Okla. Coll. Medicine, Oklahoma City, 1968-71; prof. surgery U. Okla. Coll. Medicine, 1971-89; prof. surgery U. Tex. S.W. Med. Ctr., Dallas, 1989-94, emeritus prof., 1994—; medical educator emeritus, 1994—; surgeon-in-chief Children's Mercy Hosp., Kansas City, Kans., 1963-68; chief pediatric surgery Children's Hosp. Oklahoma City, 1968-87, U. Tex. S.W. Med. Ctr., Dallas, 1989-92. Contbr. articles to profl. jours., chpts. to books. Mem. hosp. care commn. Am. Acad. Pediatrics, 1973-79, chmn. surg. sect., 1996-97; mem. select com. med. tech. Okla. Health Planning Commn., 1981-85; trustee Ctrl. Okla. Ambulance Trust, Oklahoma City, 1976-80. Mem. Am. Burn Assn., ACS, Am. Pediatric Surgery Assn., Am. Surg. Assn., Soc. Surg. Oncology, So. Surg. Assn. Republican. Episcopalian. Avocations: tennis, travel. Office: U Tex SW Med Ctr 5323 Harry Hines Blvd Dallas TX 75235-7208

SMITH, ELAINE DIANA, foreign service officer; b. Glencoe, Ill., Sept. 15, 1924; d. John Raymond and Elsie (Gelbard) S. BA, Grinnell Coll., 1946; MA, Johns Hopkins U., 1947; PhD, Am. U., 1959. Commd. fgn. service officer U.S. Dept. State, 1947; assigned to Brussels, 1947-50, Tehran, Iran, 1951-53, Wellington, N.Z., 1954-56; assigned to Dept. State, Washington, 1956-60, Ankara, Turkey, 1960-69, Istanbul, Turkey, 1969-72; assigned to Dept. Commerce Exchange, 1972-73; dep. examiner Fgn. Service Bd. Examiners, 1974-75; Turkish desk officer (Dept. State), Washington, 1975-78; consul gen., Izmir, Turkey, 1978—. Author: Origins of the Kemalist Movement, 1919-1923, 1959. Recipient Alumni award Grinnell Coll., 1957. Mem. U.S. Fgn. Svc. Assn., Phi Beta Kappa. Home: The Plaza 800 25th St NW Apt 306 Washington DC 20037-2207

SMITH, ELDON, dean. MD, Dalhousie U. From asst. prof. to assoc. prof. medicine and physiology Dalhousie U., Calgary, Alta., Can., 1973-80; prof. medicine and physiology and biophysics U. Calgary, 1980—, chief divsn. cardiology, 1980-86, chair dept. medicine, 1985-90, assoc. dean, clin., 1990-92, dead faculty of medicine, 1992—. Fellow Royal Coll. Physicians and Surgeons Can.; mem. Am. Coll. Cardiology. Office: U Calgary Faculty of Medicine, 3300 Hosp Dr, Calgary, AB Canada T2N 4N1

SMITH, ELDRED GEE, church leader; b. Lehi, Utah, Jan. 9, 1907; s. Hyrum Gibbs and Martha E. (Gee) S.; m. Jeanne A. Ness, Aug. 17, 1932 (dec. June 1977); children: Miriam Smith Skeen, Eldred Gary, Audrey Gay Smith Vance, Gordon Raynor, Sylvia Dawn Smith Isom; m. Hortense H. Child, May 18, 1978; stepchildren: Carol Jane Child Burdette (dec.), Thomas Robert Child. Employed with sales div. Bennett Glass & Paint Co., Salt Lake City, 6 years; mech. design engr. Remington Arms Co., 2 years; design engr., prodn. equipment design Tenn. Eastman Corp., Oak Ridge, Tenn., 3 years; now presiding patriarch Ch. Jesus Christ of Latter-day Saints. Home: 2942 Devonshire Cir Salt Lake City UT 84108-2526 Office: 47 E South Temple Salt Lake City UT 84150-1005

SMITH, ELDRED REID, library educator; b. Payette, Idaho, June 30, 1931; s. Lawrence E. and Jennie (Reid) S.; m. Judith Ausubel, June 25, 1953; children: Steven, Janet. B.A., U. Calif.-Berkeley, 1956, M.A., 1962; M.L.S., U. So. Calif., 1957. Aquisition reference librarian Long Beach State Coll. Library, 1957-59; reference librarian San Francisco State Coll. Library, 1959-60; bibliographer U. Calif.-Berkeley Library, 1960-65, head search div. acquisition dept., 1966-69, head loan dept., 1969-70, asso. univ. librarian, 1970-72, acting univ. librarian, 1971-72; dir. libraries, also prof. SUNY, Buffalo, 1973-76; univ. librarian U. Minn., 1976-87, prof., 1976-96; lectr. Sch. Library Sci., U. Wash., 1972; bd. dirs. Center for Research Libraries, 1975-77. Author: The Librarian, The Scholar, and the Future of the Research Library, 1990; contbr. articles to libr. jours. Council on Library Resources fellow, 1970. Mem. ALA, Assn. Research Libraries (dir. 1979-85, pres. 1983-84), Assn. Coll. and Research Libraries (pres. 1977-78, dir. 1976-79, com. on academic status 1969-74, chmn. univ. libraries sect. 1974-75). Home: 847 Gelston Pl El Cerrito CA 94530-3046

SMITH, ELEANOR JANE, university chancellor; b. Circleville, Ohio, Jan. 10, 1933; d. John Allen and Eleanor Jane (Dade) Lewis; m. James L. Banner, Aug. 10, 1957 (div. 1972); 1 child, Teresa M. Banner Watters; m. Paul M. Smith Jr. BS, Capital U., 1955; PhD, The Union Inst., Cin., 1972. Tchr. Columbus (Ohio) Pub. Schs., 1956-64, Worthington (Ohio) Pub. Schs., 1964-72; from faculty to administrator U. Cin., 1972-88; dean Smith Coll., Northampton, Mass., 1988-90; v.p. acad. affairs, provost William Paterson Coll., Wayne, N.J., 1990-94; chancellor U. Wis.-Parkside, Kenosha, 1994—; dir. Afrikan Am. Inst., Cin., 1977-84; adv. bd. Edwina Bookwalter Gantz Undergrad. Studies Ctr., Cin. Spl. Arts Night Com., Northampton, 1988-89. Named career woman of achievement YWCA, Cin., 1983. Mem. Nat. Assn. Women in Higher Edn., Am. Assn. for Higher Edn., Leadership Am. (bd. dirs., treas. 1993-95), Nat. Assn. Black Women Historians (co-founder, co-dir. 1979-82), Am. Coun. on Edn. (mem. com. on internat. edn. 1994—, bd. dirs. 1995—), Am. Assn. State Colls. and Univs. (mem. com. on policies and purposes 1994—). Avocations: music, travel, reading. Home: 40 Harborview Dr Racine WI 53403-1098 Office: U Wis Parkside 900 Wood Rd Kenosha WI 53144-1133

SMITH, ELISE FIBER, international non-profit development agency administrator; b. Detroit, June 14, 1932; d. Guy and Mildred Geneva (Johnson) Fiber; m. James Frederick Smith, Aug. 11, 1956 (div. 1983); children: Gregory Douglas, Guy Charles. BA, U. Mich., 1954; postgrad., U. Strasbourg, France, 1954-55; MA, Case Western Res. U., 1956. Tchr. U.S. Binat. Ctr., Caracas, Venezuela, 1964-66; instr. English Am. U., 1966-68; prof. lang. faculty Catholic U., Lima, Peru, 1968-70; coord. English lang. and culture program, lang. faculty El Rosario U., Bogota, Colombia, 1971-73; lang. specialist, mem. faculty Am. U., English Lang. Inst., 1975-78; exec. dir. OEF Internat. (name formerly Overseas Edn. Fund), Washington, 1978-89, bd. dirs.; dir. Leadership Program, Winrock Internat. Inst. for Agrl. Devel., 1989—; v.p., bd. dirs. Pvt. Agys. Collaborating Together, N.Y.C., 1983-89; trustee Internat. Devel. Conf., Washington, 1983—, mem. exec. com., 1985-90; mem. hon. com. for Global Crossroads Nat. Assembly, Global Perspectives in Edn., Inc., N.Y.C., 1984, Washington, 1984-92, mem. gen. assembly, 1992; mem. nat. com. Focus on Hunger '84, L.A.; sec. bd. dirs. U.S. Binat. Sch., Bogota, Colombia, 1971-73; ofcl. observer UN Conf. on Status Women, 1980, UN 3rd World Conf. on Women, 1985, del. NGO Forum, UN 4th World Conf. on Women, del. NGO Forum, 1995; mem. mental health adv. com. Dept. State, 1974-76; U.S. del. planning seminar integration women in devel. OAS, 1978; participant Women, Law and Devel. Forum; mem. exec. com., co-chair commn. advancement women Interaction (Am. Coun. for Vol. Internat. Action), 1994—; bd. dirs. Sudan-Am. Found.; mem. adv. bd. Global Links Devel. Edn., Washington, 1985-86; adv. coun. Global Fund for Women, 1988-93. Co-editor: Toward Internationalism: Readings in Cross-cultural Communication, 1979, 2d edit. 1986. Bd. dirs. Internat. Ctr. Rsch. on Women, 1992—; mem. adv. com. on vol. fgn. aid U.S. AID, 1994—. Rotary Internat. fellow Strasbourg, France, 1954-55; grantee Dept. State, 1975. Mem. Soc. Internat. Devel., Assn. Women in Devel., Soc. Intercultural Edn. Tng. and Rsch., Coalition Women in Internat. Devel. (co-founder 1979, chair 1993—), Pvt. Agys. in Internat. Devel. (co-chmn. 1980-82, pres. 1982-85), Nat. Assn. Fgn. Student Affairs (grantee 1975), U. Mich. Alumni Assn., Women's Fgn. Policy Group, Rotary Internat. (mem. global com. Women in Future Soc. 1996). Unitarian. Home: 4701 Connecticut Ave NW Apt 304 Washington DC 20008-5617 Office: Winrock Inst 1611 N Kent St Ste 600 Arlington VA 22209-2111

SMITH, ELIZABETH HEGEMAN, mental health therapist, hypnotherapist; b. Mineola, N.Y., Oct. 5, 1942; d. Andrew Burt and Ruth Eliza (Velsor) Hegeman; m. Lloyd W. Smith, June 11, 1966; children: Warren Willits, Lisa Velsor. BA, Adelphi U., 1964; MEd, Temple U., 1969. Cert. tchr., Pa.; registered hypnotherapist. Tchr. health, phys. edn. Friends Acad., Locust Valley, N.Y., 1964-66, Darby (Pa.)-Colwyn Schs., 1966-70; pvt. practice mental health therapy Wallingford, Pa., 1980-85, Charlotte, N.C., 1985—; cons. Dynamic Health Systems, Charlotte, 1989—. Mem. LWV, Wallingford, 1976-85; pres., editor Taxpayers for Quality Edn., Wallingford, 1976-85; chmn. Raintree Archtl. Rev. Com., Charlotte, 1989-91, com. mem., 1987-88; treas. Raintree Homeowners Assn. Mem. Am. Guild Hypnotherapists, Raintree Homeowners Assn. (treas. 1993-95, pres. 1995-96); Village of Raintree and the Southeast Coalition of Neighborhoods (pres. 1996—). Mem. Soc. of Friends. Avocations: horseback riding, tennis, skiing, photography, gardening. Home and Office: 3609 Windbluff Dr Charlotte NC 28277-9897

SMITH, ELIZABETH PATIENCE, oil industry executive, lawyer; b. N.Y.C., June 21, 1949; d. Harry Martin and Frances (Blauvelt) S.; m. Kwan-Lan Mao, Apr. 1, 1989. BA cum laude, Bucknell U., 1971; JD, Georgetown U., 1976. Atty. Texaco Inc., White Plains, N.Y., 1976-84, dir. investor rels., 1984-89, v.p. corp. communications div., investor rels., 1989-92, v.p. investor rels. and shareholder svcs., 1992—. Mem. bd. trustees Marymount Coll., Tarrytown, N.Y.; bd. dirs. Westchester Edn. Coalition, Texaco Found. Mem. Petroleum Investor Rels. Assn., Nat. Investor Rels. Inst., Investor Rels. Assn. (pres.), N.Y. Bar Assn. Office: Texaco Inc 2000 Westchester Ave White Plains NY 10650-0001

SMITH, ELIZABETH SHELTON, art educator; b. Washington, Feb. 12, 1924; d. Benjamin Warren and Sarah Priscilla (Harrell) Shelton; m. John Edwin Smith, Aug. 16, 1947 (dec. July 1992); children: Shelley Hobson, Dale Henslee, John Edwin Jr.; m. Headley Morris Cox Jr., Dec. 30, 1994. BA in Art, Meredith Coll., 1946; MEd in Supervision and Adminstrn., Clemson U., 1974. Youth dir. St. John's Bapt. Ch., Charlotte, N.C., 1946-47; art tchr. Raleigh (N.C.) Pub. Schs., 1947-49, East Mecklenberg H.S., Charlotte, 1968-69, D. W. Daniel H.S., Central, S.C., 1970-86; art instr. U. S.C., Columbia, 1966-68; adj. prof. Clemson (S.C.) U., 1991-93; artist-in-residence edn. program S.C. Arts Commn., Columbia, 1991—. Exhibited in numerous one and two person shows and in group exhibits, 1946—. Vol. worker, editor newsletter Pickens County Habitat for Humanity, Clemson, 1981—; vol. art tchr. St. Andrew's Elem. Sch., Columbia, 1962-68. Recipient Clemson Sertoma Club Svc. to Mankind award, 1997; named S.C. Tchr. of Yr., S.C. Dept. Edn. and Ency. Britannica, 1976, Citizen of Yr., Clemson Rotary Club, 1979. Mem. S.C. Art Edn. Assn. (pres. 1978, Lifetime Svc. award 1990, Lifetime Achievement in Art Edn. award 1995), Nat. Art Edn. Assn. (ret. art educator affiliate, pres. 1994—, Disting. Svc. award 1995), S.C. Watercolor Soc., Upstate Visual Artists (Best in Show award). Baptist. Avocations: travel, reading, writing, music. Home: 1604 Six Mile Hwy Central SC 29630-9483

SMITH, ELMER W., retired federal government administrator; b. Trenton, N.J., June 10, 1928; s. Elmer Watson and Violet Mae (Thatcher) S.; m. Caroline Jo Elliott Crea, June 23, 1956; children: Caroline Elinore, Elliott Pearson, David Grant, Eric Graham. BA, Drew U., 1951; MPA, Syracuse U., 1952. Budget analyst Dept. HEW, Washington, 1956-64; exec. officer Welfare Adminstrn., Washington, 1964-67; dep. regional commr. Social and Rehab. Svc., Charlottesville, Va., 1968-70; regional commr. Social and Rehab. Svc., N.Y.C., 1970-76; assoc. commr. for policy and planning Social Security Adminstrn., Balt., 1976-79; dir. office of eligibility policy Health Care Financing Adminstrn., Balt., 1979-90, sr. program advisor Medicaid Bur., 1990-93, dir. Medicaid Spec. program initiatives staff, 1993-95, tech. dir. Office of Long Term Care Svc. Medicaid Bur., 1995-96; ret., 1996; pres., bd. dirs. Wm. H. Masson & Co., Balt., 1992—. Vestry mem. Christ the King Ch., Woodlawn, Md., 1977-88. Mem. Am. Soc. for Pub. Adminstrn. Episcopalian. Avocations: coin collecting, gardening, hiking.

SMITH, ELSKE VAN PANHUYS, retired university administrator; b. Monte Carlo, Monaco, Nov. 9, 1929; came to U.S., 1943; d. Johan Abraham AE and Vera (Craven) van Panhuys; m. Henry J. Smith, Sept. 10, 1950 (dec. July 1983); children: Ralph A., Kenneth A. BA, Radcliffe U., 1950, MS, 1951, PhD, 1956. Rsch. assoc. Sacramento Peak Observatory, Sunspot, N.Mex., 1955-62; rsch. fellow Joint Inst. for Lab. Astrophysics, Boulder, Colo., 1962-63; assoc. to prof. U. Md., College Park, 1963-80, asst. provost, 1973-78, asst. vice chancellor, 1978-80; dean, coll. humanities and scis. Va. Commonwealth U., Richmond, 1980-92, interim dir. environ. studies, 1992-95; ret., 1995; cons. NASA, Greenbelt, Md., 1964-76, reviewer, Washington, 1970's, NSF, Washington, 1970's, 86; vis. com. Assn. of Univ.'s for Rsch. in Astronomy, Tucson, 1975-78. Author: (with others) Solar Flares, 1963, Introductory Astronomy and Astrophysics, 1973, 3d edit., 1992; also numerous articles. Mem. various environ. orgns. Rsch. grantee Rsch. Corp., 1956-57, NSF, 1966-69, 90, NIH, 1981-90, NASA, 1974-78; program grantee Va. Found. for Humanities, 1985, NEH, 1987, Assn. Am. Colls., 1987, EPA, 1994. Fellow AAAS; mem. Am. Astron. Soc. (counselor 1977-80, vis. prof. 1975-78), Internat. Astron. Union (chief U.S. del. 1979, U.S. Nat. com.), Coun. Colls. of Arts and Scis. (bd. dirs. 1989), Phi Beta Kappa. Democrat. Avocations: hiking, travel, environmental issues. Home: 68 Old Stockbridge Rd Lenox MA 01240

SMITH, ELVIE LAWRENCE, corporate director; b. Eatonia, Sask., Can., Jan. 8, 1926; s. Harry Burton and Laura Mae (Fullerton) S.; m. Jacqueline Moy Colleary, Dec. 15, 1956; children: Ronald, Paul, David, Marguerite. BS with great distinction, U. Sask., 1947; MSME, Purdue U., 1949; LLD (hon.), Concordia U., 1983; D in Engring., Carleton U., 1984, Purdue U., 1987; DS (hon.), U. Saskatchewan. Exptl. engr. Nat. Research Council, Ottawa, Ont., Can., 1949-56; with Pratt & Whitney Can. Inc., 1957—, exec. v.p. ops., 1978-80, pres., CEO, 1980-84, chmn., 1984-94, dir., 1970-96. Decorated Order of Can., 1992; recipient Sawyer award ASME, 1986, Gold Medal Polish People's Republic, 1985, Aerospace Leadership award SAE, 1994; named to Can. Aviation Hall of Fame, 1993. Fellow Can. Aeronautics and Space Inst. (McCurty award 1976, C.D. Howe award 1983); mem. Aerospace Industries Assn. Can. (life, chmn. 1982-83), Gatineau Gliding Club. Office: Pratt & Whitney Can Inc, 1000 Marie Victorin, Longueuil, PQ Canada J4G 1A1

SMITH, ELWIN EARL, mining and oil company executive; b. Ellicottville, N.Y., Sept. 30, 1922; s. Henry B. and Beatrice M. (Spellman) S.; m. Mary Ellen Kirchmaier, Nov. 4, 1944; children: Peter E., Michael E., Timothy E. Student, U. Ala., 1941-43, NYU, 1954, Internat. Program, Harvard Bus. Sch., 1962. Sales engr. Cities Service Oil Co., N.Y.C., 1949-55; gen. sales mgr. Climax Molybdenum Co., N.Y.C., 1955-64; Exec. v.p., dir. Lithium Corp. Am., Gastonia, N.C., 1964-69; pres., chief exec. officer Lithium Corp. Am., 1969-77; v.p., dir. Gulf Resources & Chem. Co., Houston, 1970-77; pres., dir. Asia Lithium Corp., Osaka, Japan, 1970-77; pres. Amax Iron Ore, Greenwich, Conn., 1977-80; corp. v.p., group exec. for indsl. minerals and resources group Amax Iron Ore, 1978-80; exec. v.p. Amax Inc., Greenwich, 1981-82, sr. exec. v.p., 1982-85; prin. Elwin Smith Internat. Sales Engrs., Darien, Conn., 1986—; dir. Essex Chem. Corp., 1983-88, Freeport Mac Mo Ran Copper Co., 1988—, Am. Metal & Coal Co., Greenwich, Ct., Ethanol Corp., Sydney, Australia, First Dynasty Mines, Denver; chmn. Seven Seas Cinema, Stamford, Conn., 1985-95. Served to 1st lt. U.S. Army Paratroopers, 1943-48. Decorated Combat Inf. badge, Bronze Star, sr. parachute badge. Mem. AIME, Am. Petroleum Inst., Am. Chem. Soc., Am. Australian Assn., Japan Soc., Asia Soc., Mining and Petroleum Club of Sydney (Australia), Copper Club N.Y., Weeburn Country Club, Masons. Republican. Home and Office: 7 Tokeneke Trl Darien CT 06820-6126

SMITH, EMIL L., biochemist, consultant; b. N.Y.C., July 5, 1911; s. Abraham and Esther (Lubart) S.; m. Esther Press, Mar. 29, 1934; children—Joseph Donald, Jeffrey Bernard. B.S., Columbia U., 1931, Ph.D., 1936. Instr. biophysics Columbia U., N.Y.C., 1936-38; John Simon Guggenheim fellow Cambridge U., Eng., 1938-39, Yale U., New Haven, 1939-40; fellow Rockefeller Inst., N.Y.C., 1940-42; biophysicist, biochemist E. R. Squibb & Sons, New Brunswick, N.J., 1942-46; assoc. prof. to prof. biochemistry U. Utah, Salt Lake City, 1946-63; prof. biol. chemistry Sch. Medicine UCLA, 1963-79, prof. emeritus, 1979—; cons. NIH, Am. Cancer Soc., Office Naval Research. Author: (with others) Principles of Biochemistry, 7th edit., 1983; also numerous articles. Recipient Stein-Moore award Protein Soc., 1987. Mem. NAS, Am. Acad. Arts and Scis., Am. Philos. Soc., Am. Soc. Biol. Chemists, Am. Chem. Soc., Protein Soc., Acad. Scis. USSR (fgn.). Office: UCLA Sch Medicine Los Angeles CA 90095-1737

SMITH, EMMITT J., III, professional football player; b. Pensacola, Fla., May 15, 1969; s. Emmitt Jr. and Mary Smith. Student, U. Fla. With Dallas Cowboys, 1990—; player Pro-Bowl, 1990-92, NFC Championship game, 1992, 93, Super Bowl XXVII, 1992, Super Bowl XXVIII, 1993; owner Emmitt Inc. Recipient MVP award for season, 1993, MVP award for Super Bowl, 1993; named Running Back, Sporting News Coll. All-Am. team, 1989, Offensive Rookie of Yr., 1990, Running Back, Sporting News NFL All-Pro team, 1992, 93, NFL Player of Yr., Sporting News, 1993; named to Pro-Bowl, 1993, 95. Led NFL in rushing, 1991-93, 95; Led NFL running backs in scoring, 1992, 95. Office: Dallas Cowboys One Cowboys Pky Irving TX 75063*

SMITH, EPHRAIM PHILIP, university dean, educator; b. Fall River, Mass., Sept. 19, 1942; s. Jacob Max and Bertha (Horvitz) S.; m. Linda Sue Katz, Sept. 3, 1967; children—Benjamin, Rachel, Leah. B.S., Providence Coll., 1964; M.S., U. Mass., 1965; Ph.D., U. Ill., 1968. Chmn. dept. acctg. U. R.I., Kingston, 1972-73; dean Sch. Bus. Shippensburg State Coll., Pa., 1973-75; dean Coll. Bus. Adminstrn. Cleve. State U., 1975-90; dean Sch. Bus. Adminstrn. and Econ. Calif. State U., Fullerton, 1990—. co-author: Principles of Supervision: FIrst and Second Level Management, 1984, Federal Taxation-Advanced Topics, 1995, Federal Taxation-Basic Principles, 1997, Federal Taxation Comprehensive Topics, 1997; contbr. articles to profl. jours. Mem. Am. Acctg. Assn., Am. Taxation Assn., Am. Inst. for Decision Scis., Fin. Execs. Inst., Beta Gamma Sigma, Beta Alpha Psi. Office: Calif State U Sch Bus Adminstrn and Econ 800 N State College Blvd Fullerton CA 92831-3547

SMITH, ERIC MORGAN, virology educator; b. Lafayette, Ind., Feb. 13, 1953; s. James E. and Betty Carolyn (Hanlin) S.; m. Janice Marie Kelly, May 26, 1979; children: David Kendall, Ben Pham. BS cum laude, Syracuse U., 1975; PhD, Baylor Coll. of Medicine, 1980. Postdoctoral fellow Dept. Microbiology, U. Tex. Med. Br., Galveston, Tex., 1979-81, asst. prof., 1982-85, assoc. prof., 1985-90, prof., 1990—; editl. bd. Progress in Neuro-Endocrin Immunology, Washington, 1988-92, Behavior and Immunity, 1993—, Cellular and Molecular Neurobiology, 1994—; mem. mental health AIDS and immunity rev. com. NIMH, 1992-96. Founding co-editor Advances in Neuroimmunology, 1991; contbr. over 100 articles to profl. jours. Mem. Galveston Hist. Found., 1980—. Mem. AAAS, Am. Soc. for Microbiology, Am. Assn. Immunologists, Internat. Soc. Immunopharmacology, Internat. Working Group on Neuroimmunomodulation, Assn. Immuno-Neurobiologists (co-founding pres.), Galveston Yacht Club, Syracuse Scuba Soc. (v.p. 1975). Avocations: racing sailboats., photography, scuba diving. Office: U Tex Med Br Dept Psychiatry Galveston TX 77550

SMITH, ERIC PARKMAN, retired railroad executive; b. Cambridge, Mass., Mar. 23, 1910; s. B. Farnham and Helen T. (Blanchard) S.; AB, Harvard U., 1932, MBA, 1934. Staff fed. coordinator transp., Washington, 1934; with traffic and operating depts. N.Y. New Haven & Hartford R.R., Boston and New Haven, Conn., 1934-53; with Maine Central R.R., Portland, 1953-82, sec. adv. bd. retirement trust plan, 1958-82, asst. treas., dir. cost analysis, 1970-82, bd. dirs., 1981-82. Trustee parish donations 1st Parish in Concord, Unitarian-Universalist Ch., 1960-96, trustee emeritus, 1996—. Mem. New Eng. R.R. Club (hon., pres. 1973-74), Louisa May Alcott Meml. Assn. (dir. 1984—, treas. 1987—), The Thoreau Soc. (dir. 1987-95, treas. 1987-95). Author: Verses on an Icelandic Vacation, 1965, The Church in Concord and its Ministers, 1971, In All That Dwell Below the Skies, 1972; contbr. The Meeting House on the Green, 1985. Home and Office: 35 Academy Ln Concord MA 01742-2431

SMITH, ERNEST KETCHAM, electrical engineer; b. Peking, China, May 31, 1922; (parents Am. citizens); s. Ernest Ketcham and Grace (Goodrich) S.; m. Mary Louise Standish, June 23, 1950; children: Priscilla Varland, Nancy Smith, Cynthia Jackson. BA in Physics, Swarthmore Coll., 1944; MSEE, Cornell U., 1951, Ph.D., 1956. Chief plans and allocations engr. Mut. Broadcasting System, 1946-49; with Nat. Bur. Stds. Ctrl. Radio Propagation Lab., 1951-65; chief ionosphere research sect. Nat. Bur. Standards, Boulder, Colo., 1957-60; div. chief Nat. Bur. Standards, 1960-65; dir. aeronomy lab. Environ. Sci. Services Adminstrn., Boulder, 1965-67; dir. Inst. Telecommunication Scis., 1968, dir. univ. relations, 1968-70; assoc. dir. Inst. Telecommunications Scis. Office of Telecommunications, Boulder, 1970-72, cons., 1972-76; mem. tech. staff Jet Propulsion Lab. Calif. Inst. Tech., Pasadena, 1976-87; adj. prof. dept. Elec. and Computer Engring. U. Colo., Boulder, 1987—; vis. fellow Coop. Inst. Rsch. on Environ. Scis., 1968; assoc. Harvard Coll. Obs., 1965-75; adj. Prof. U. Colo.m 1969-78, 87—; internat. vice-chmn. study group 6, Internat. Radio Consultative Com., 1958-70, chmn. U.S. study group, 1970-76; mem. U.S. nat. com. Internat. Sci. Radio Union, mem.-at-large U.S. nat. com., 1985-88; convenor Boulder Gatekeepers to the Future, 1990—. Author: Worldwide Occurrence of Sporadic E, 1957; (with S. Matsushita) Ionospheric Sporadic E, 1962. Contbr. numerous articles to profl. jours. Editor: Electromagnetic Probing of the Upper Atmosphere, 1969; assoc. editor for propagation IEEE Antennas and Propagation Mag., 1989—. Mem. 1st Congl. Ch., moderator, 1995-97. Recipient Diplôme d'honneur, Internat. Radio Consultative Com., Internat. Telecom. Union, 1978. Fellow IEEE (fellow com. 1993, 94, 95), AAAS; mem. Am. Geophys. Union, Electromagnetics Acad., Svc. Club, Kiwanis, Univ. Club, Athenaeum Club (Pasadena), Boulder Country Club, Sigma Xi (pres. U. Colo. chpt. 1994-95, v.p. 95-97). Home: 5159 Idylwild Trl Boulder CO 80301-3667 Office: U Colo Dept Elec and Computer Engring Campus Box 425 Boulder CO 80309 *A weakness of many large organizations is that it is difficult for senior administrators to step down after peaking in their 40s. I'm grateful for a crisis at age 50 which resulted in my taking early retirement at age 54 and then accepting a more modest job until age 65.*

SMITH, ESTHER THOMAS, editor; b. Jesup, Ga., Mar. 13, 1939; d. Joseph H. and Leslie (McCarthy) Thomas; m. James D. Smith, June 2, 1962; children: Leslie, Amy, James Thomas. BA, Agnes Scott Coll., 1962. Staff writer, Sunday women's editor Atlanta Jour.-Constn., 1961-62; mng. editor Bull. of U. Miami Sch. Medicine, 1965-66; corr. Atlanta Jour.-Constn. and Fla. Times-Union, 1964, 67-68; founding editor Bus. Rev. of Washington, 1978-81; founding editor, gen. mgr. Washington Bus. Jour., 1982; pres., bd. dirs. Tech News, Inc., 1986-96, ceo, 1995-96; founder, editor-at-large Washington Tech., 1986—, Tech. Transfer Bus. Mag., 1992-95; bd. dirs. MIT Enterprise Forum of Washington/Balt., 1981-82, TechNews, Inc., 1986-96; mem. Greater Washington Board of Trade, Internat. Task Force, Women's Forum, Washington, 1981—; mem. No. Va. Bus. Round Table (exec. com. 1993—); mem. adv. bd. Va. Math Coalition, 1991-94; bd. trustees Ctr. for Excellence in Edn., 1993-96; bd. dirs. INOVA Health Svcs. Capital Region Technology Investors Conf., bd. trustees; bd. advs. George Washington U., Va., 1996—. Mem. Assn. Tech. Bus. Couns. (chmn. bd. advisors 1989-94), Pres.'s Forum, Mid-Atlantic Venture Assn., No. Va. Tech. Coun. (mem. exec. com., bd. dir. 1994—), Suburban Maryland High Tech. Coun. Office: 8500 Leesburg Pike Ste 7500 Vienna VA 22182-2409

SMITH, EUGENE WILSON, retired university president and educator; b. Forrest City, Ark., June 10, 1930; s. Milton Saumel and Frank Leslie (Wilson) S.; m. Rebecca Ann Slaughter, May 27, 1956; children: Lucinda Anne, Bradley Eugene. B.A., Ark. State U., 1952; M.Ed., U. Miss., 1955, Ed.D., 1958. Mem. faculty Ark. State U., State University, 1958-92, prof. edn., 1971-92, v.p. adminstrn., 1968-71, dean Grad. Sch., 1971-84, interim pres., 1980, sr. v.p., 1980-84, pres., 1984-92, 94-95; pres. emeritus Ark. State U., State University, 1992—, interim pres., 1994-95; pres. Jonesboro Indsl. Devel. Corp., 1983-94; mem. exec. com. Conf. So. Grad. Schs., 1973-74, Ark. State Coun. on Econ. Edn., 1987-90; pres. Am. South Athletic Conf., 1987-89; dir. Mercantile Bank of Jonesboro, Union Planters Bank of Northeast

Ark. Alderman, City of Jonesboro, 1982-84. Served to 1st lt. AUS, 1952-54, Korea. W.K. Kellogg Found. rsch. fellow, 1954-58. Mem. Ark. Adv. Council Elem. and Secondary Edn., Jonesboro C. of C. (dir. 1967-69, 80-85, v.p. 1981-82, pres. 1982-83), Phi Kappa Phi, Phi Delta Kappa, Kappa Delta Pi. Club: Rotary (pres. 1974-75). Home: 407 Lynne Ct Jonesboro AR 72401-8807

SMITH, FERN M., judge; b. San Francisco, Nov. 7, 1933. AA, Foothill Coll., 1970; BA, Stanford U., 1972, JD, 1975. Bar: Calif. 1975. children: Susan Morgan, Julie. Assoc. firm Bronson, Bronson & McKinnon, San Francisco, 1975-81, ptnr., 1982-86; judge San Francisco County Superior Ct., 1986-88, U.S. Dist. Ct. for Northern Dist. Calif., 1988—; mem. U.S. Jud. Conf., Adv. Com. Rules of Evidence, 1993-96, chair, 1996—; mem. hiring, mgmt. and pers. coms., active recruiting various law schs. Contbr. articles to legal publ. Apptd. by Chief Justice Malcolm Lucas to the Calif. Jud. Coun.'s Adv. Task Force on Gender Bias in the Cts., 1987-89; bd. visitors Law Sch. Stanford U. Mem. ABA, Queen's Bench, Nat. Assn. Women Judges, Calif. Women Lawyers, Bar Assn. of San Francisco, Fed. Judges Assn., 9th Cir. Dist. Judges Assn., Am. Judicature Soc., Calif. State Fed. Judicial Coun., Phi Beta Kappa.*

SMITH, FLOYD LESLIE, insurance company executive; b. Silver Creek, N.Y., Nov. 12, 1931; s. Harry Lee and Fanny Diem (Arnold) S.; m. Jane Kathryn Elters, Feb. 18, 1956; children: Keith Arnold, Bruce Erik. A.B., Oberlin Coll., (Ohio), 1953; M.B.A., NYU, 1962. Investment trainee Mut. of N.Y., N.Y.C., 1953-64, dir. investments, 1964-66; asst. v.p. securities investment Mut. of N.Y., N.Y.C., 1966-69; 2d v.p. securities investment Mut. of N.Y., N.Y.C., 1969-74, v.p. securities investment, 1974-78, sr. v.p., 1978-81, chief investment officer, 1981-83, exec. v.p., chief investment officer, 1983-89; vice chmn., chief investment officer Mut. of N.Y., 1989-91; trustee The Mut. Life Ins. Co. of N.Y., 1988-91; dir. MONY Series Fund, 1983—, Empire Fidelity Investments Life Ins. Co., 1994—; trustee MONY Real Estate Investors, N.Y.C., 1981-90; bd. dirs., chmn. exec. com. Ins. Systems Am., Atlanta, 1974-82. Trustee Friends Sem., N.Y.C., 1975-84, Village of Saltaire, 1984-87; dir. St. Maarten Condo. Assn., Naples, Fla., 1993—; mem. Saltaire (N.Y.) Zoning Bd. Appeals, 1982-84. With Signal Corps, U.S. Army, 1954-56. Mem. Ft. Worth Boat Club, Edgewater Club.

SMITH, FLOYD RODENBACK, retired utilities executive; b. San Francisco, June 25, 1913; s. Floyd M. and Elizabeth (Rodenback) S.; m. Marion LaFrae Blythe, Oct. 5, 1935; children: Marion Katherine Smith White, Virginia Helene. Student, Long Beach (Calif.) Jr. Coll., 1931-33; B.S., N.Mex. State U., 1935; postgrad., Harvard Bus. School, 1962. Registered profl. engr., Tex. With Gulf States Utilities Co., Beaumont, Tex., 1935-78; dir. Gulf States Utilities Co., 1965-78, v.p. Baton Rouge div., 1965-67, v.p. div. ops., 1967-69, exec. v.p., 1969, pres., 1970-73, prin. exec. officer, 1970-78, chmn. bd., prin. exec. officer, 1973-78; pres. S.W. Atomic Energy Assocs., 1971-77; mgmt. cons., 1978-85. Bd. dirs., past chmn. Beaumont chpt. ARC; bd. dirs. Central City Devel. Corp., 1971-81, YMCA, 1980-83; trustee United Appeals, pres., 1975; pres. Tex. Atomic Energy Research Found., 1976-78. Named Disting. Alumnus Engring. Sch., N.Mex. State U., 1977. Mem. Tex. Atomic Energy Rsch. Found. (bd. dirs. 1970-78, pres. 1976-78), Southeastern Elec. Exch. (pres. 1975-76, bd. dirs. 1970-78), Tex. Rsch. League (bd. dirs. 1970-78), Assn. Electric Cos. of Tex. (chmn. 1978-79), Utility Shareholders Assn. of Tex. (chmn. 1986-93), Beaumont C. of C. (bd. dirs. 1970-76). Presbyterian. Clubs: Beaumont Country, Beaumont (bd. dirs. 1974-76), Tower Club. Home: 21 Cheska Hollow Beaumont TX 77706-2750

SMITH, FRANCIS XAVIER, accountant; b. Jenkintown, Pa., Oct. 11, 1960; s. William Joseph and Patricia Josephine (Leaper) S. BBA, U. Pa., 1986. CPA, Pa. Pvt. practice Jenkintown, 1990—. Mem. AICPA, Pa. Inst. of CPAs, Wharton Club of Phila., Faculty Club of U. of Pa. Republican. Roman Catholic. Office: 1653 The Fairway Ste 203 Jenkintown PA 19046-1420

SMITH, FRANK EARL, retired association executive; b. Fremont Center, N.Y., Feb. 4, 1931; s. Earl A. and Hazel (Knack) S.; m. Caroline R. Gillin, Aug. 14, 1954; children—Stephen F., David S., Daniel E. B.S., Syracuse U., 1952. With Mellor Advt. Agy., Elmira, N.Y., 1954-55; asst. mgr. Assn. of Commerce, Elmira, N.Y., 1955-56, C. of C., Binghamton, N.Y.; mgr. Better Bus. Bur., Broome County, N.Y., 1956-60; exec. v.p. C. of C., Chemung County, Elmira, 1960-65, Schenectady County (N.Y.) C. of C., 1965-69, Greater Cin. C. of C., 1969-78; pres. Greater Detroit C. of C., 1978-95. Dir. Presbyn. Devel. Corp. Detroit. Served to 1st lt. USAF, 1952-54. Named Young Man of Yr. Jr. C. of C. Elmira, 1964. Mem. C. of C. Execs. Mich., Am. C. of C. Execs. (past chmn.), N.Y. State C. of C. Execs. (past pres.), Ohio C. of C. Execs. (past pres.), C. of C. of U.S. (past bd. dirs., past chmn. nat. bd. regents, Inst. for Orgn. Mgmt.), Lochmoor Golf Club. Presbyterian. Home: 59 Greenbriar St Grosse Pointe Shores MI 48236-1507

SMITH, FRANK FORSYTHE, JR., lawyer; b. Crystal City, Tex., June 2, 1942; s. Frank F. and Allyne Y. (Allen) S.; m. Martha S. Strack, Aug. 7, 1965; children: Martha Lee, Amanda L. BA, U. Tex., 1964, JD, 1968; MA, U. Mich., 1965. Bar: Tex. 1968. Assoc., ptnr. Vinson & Elkins, Houston, 1968—. Contbr. articles to profl. jours. Mem. Am. Land Title Assn. Lender's Coun., State Bar of Tex., Am. Coll. Real Estate Lawyers. Office: Vinson & Elkins 3536 First City Tower 1001 Fannin St Houston TX 77002-6706

SMITH, FRANKLIN SUMNER, JR., retired insurance executive; b. Athens, Ga., Jan. 11, 1924; s. Franklin Sumner and Florence (Davis) S.; m. Eleanor Deanne Milligan, Feb. 22, 1947 (dec. Dec. 1982); children: Franklin Sumner III, Katharine Ruth; m. Jane Martin, Apr. 6, 1986. Student, Davidson Coll., 1940-41, Furman U., 1941-42. V.p., sec. Frank S. Smith Co., Inc., Columbia, S.C., 1946-60; resident mgr. Dick & Merle-Smith, N.Y.C., 1961-66; with Colonial Life & Accident Ins. Co., Columbia, 1966-93, vice chmn. bd., 1987-92, pres., CEO, 1992-93; vice chmn. bd. Colonial Cos., Inc., Columbia, 1989-92, pres., CEO, 1992-93, bd. dirs., 1989-94. Mem. Richland County Coun., Columbia, 1965-70, chmn. 1967-69; chmn. bd. trustees Richland Meml. Hosp., 1971-80, 93—; mem. United Way of Midlands, S.C., gen. campaign chmn., 1977, pres., 1979; pres. Greater Columbia C. of C., 1974-75, S.C. C. of C., 1987-88, U.S. Ednl. Found., 1992—. Recipient Vol. of Yr. award United Way of S.C., 1977, Humanitarian of Yr. award United Way of Midlands, 1989, Amb. of Yr. award Greater Columbia C. of C., 1991, Humanitarian award Richland Meml. Hosp. Found., 1993, Outstanding Philanthropist award Assn. Fund-raising Execs. (Ctrl. S.C. chpt.), 1994. Mem. Assn. of S.C. Life Ins. Cos. (pres. 1973, 82), S.C. Mcpl. Assn. (pres. 1964-65), Assn. of U.S. Army (pres. Palmetto chpt. 1978-82, Civilian of Yr. award 1983), Pine Tree Hunt Club (pres. 1954-56), The Palmetto Club (pres. 1976-89, chmn. 1990—). Presbyterian. Home: 4720 Wrenwood Ln Columbia SC 29206-4650 Mailing Address: PO Box 61047 Columbia SC 29260

SMITH, FRED DOYLE, nurse; b. Ferris, Tex., Mar. 12, 1930; s. Luther Lee and Willie Lane (Coats) S.; children: Ronald, Patricia, Donald, Stacy, Rhonda. Student, Southwestern Bus. U., Houston, 1950-51; diploma blood gasses analyst, East Tenn. Children's Hosp., Knoxville, 1985; LPN, Tenn. LPN Program, 1983. LPN, Tenn. Respiratory therapy asst. Claiborne County Hosp., Tazewell, Tenn., 1984-87; nurse Clairborne County Nursing Home, Tazewell, 1987, Brakebill Nursing Home, Knoxville, Tenn., 1987-89; nurse med.-surg. wing East Tenn. Bapt. Hosp., Knoxville, 1988-89; nurse Hancock County Health Dept., Sneedville, Tenn.; respiratory therapy asst. Wariota Health Care Ctr. (formerly Meadowbrook Manor), Maynardville, Tenn., 1987-88, nurse, 1989—. Parent Foster Parent Assn., Tazewell. With USN, 1951-59. Mem. Highlander Club, Hutt River Command. Democrat. Baptist. Avocations: singing, cooking. Home: RR 2 Box 97 Thorn Hill TN 37881-9422 Office: Wariota Health Care Ctr 215 Richardson Way Maynardville TN 37807-3803

SMITH, FREDDYE L(EE), financial planner; b. Oklahoma City, Oct. 16, 1938; d. Frederick Douglass and Leeoshia M. (Harris) Moon; divorced; children: Karyn Smith Cole, Stanford Brandon. BA, Fisk U., 1959; MA, U. Chgo., 1964. CFP, 1984. Tchr. of French Chgo. Bd. Edn., 1961-69, guidance counselor, 1969-80; fin. planner Waddell & Reed, Chgo., 1980—. Contbr. articles to profl. jours. Adv. bd. Cmty. Mental Health Coun., Chgo., 1994—. Named Fin. Planner of Yr., Eta Phi Beta, 1996; honoree Alpha Gamma Pi Sorority. Mem. Internat. Assn. for Cert. Fin. Planners, Internat. Bd. Stds. and Practices for CFP, Zonta Internat., Alpha Gamma Pi, Alpha Kappa Alpha. Mem. Trinity United Ch. Christ. Avocation: interior design. Office: Waddell & Reed 1525 E 53rd St Ste 803 Chicago IL 60615-4530

SMITH, FREDERICK COE, manufacturing executive; b. Ridgewood, N.J., June 3, 1916; s. Frederick Coe and Mary (Steffee) S.; m. Ruth Pfeiffer, Oct. 5, 1940; children: Frederick Coe, Geoffrey, Roger, William, Bart. B.S., Cornell U., 1938; M.B.A., Harvard U., 1940. With Armstrong Cork Co., Lancaster, Pa., 1940-41; with Huffy Corp., Dayton, Ohio, 1946-86; pres., chief exec. officer Huffy Corp., 1961-72, chmn., chief exec. officer, 1972-76, chmn., 1976-78, chmn. exec. com., 1979-86. Chmn. Sinclair C.C. Found.; past chmn. nat. bd. dirs. Planned Parenthood Fedn.; former dir. Internat. Parenthood Fedn.; past chmn. Dayton Found.; trustee emeritus Alan Gutmacher Inst., Ohio United Way; chmn. employment and tng. com. Gov.'s Human Investment Coun. Lt. col. USAAF, 1941-46. Decorated Legion of Merit.

SMITH, F(REDERICK) DOW(SWELL), physicist, retired college president; b. Winnipeg, Man., Can., Jan. 2, 1921; came to U.S., 1948, naturalized, 1955; s. Edgar Nelson and Clara Branum (Dowswell) S.; m. Margaret Lavinia Watson, July 2, 1949; children: Eric, Douglas, Linda, Murray. B.A. with honors, Queen's U., 1947, M.A., 1948; Ph.D., U. Rochester, 1951. Research asst. Nat. Research Council of Can., 1947-48, Bausch & Lomb Optical Co., Rochester, N.Y., 1949-51; instr. dept. physics Boston U., 1951-52, asst. prof., 1952-54, asso. prof., 1955-58, chmn. dept. physics, 1953-58; dir. Boston U. Phys. Research Lab.), 1955-58; dir. research Itek Corp., Boston, 1958-63; mgr. optics div. Itek Corp., 1963-67, v.p., 1967-74; pres. New Eng. Coll. Optometry, Boston, 1979-85; v.p., treas. Internat. Commn. Optics, 1975-81. Fellow Optical Soc. Am. (pres. 1974, treas. 1979-91, recipient dist. svc. award, 1994), AAAS, Assn. Schs. and Colls. Optometry (sec.-treas. 1983-85); mem. Sigma Xi. Home: River Rd Groton RR 2 Box 505 Rumney NH 03266

SMITH, FREDERICK ROBERT, JR., social studies educator; b. Lynn, Mass., Sept. 19, 1929; s. Frederick Robert and Margaret Theresa (Donovan) S. m. Mary Patricia Barry, Aug. 28, 1954; children: Brian Patrick, Barry Frederick, Brendan Edmund. A.B., Duke U., 1951; M.Ed., Boston U., 1954; Ph.D., U. Mich., 1960. Tchr. social studies public Jackson, Mich., 1954-58; instr. Eastern Mich. U., 1959, U. Mich., 1959-60; mem. faculty Sch. Edn., Ind. U., Bloomington, 1960-94; prof. Sch. Edn., Ind. U., 1969-94, chmn. social studies edn., 1965-69, chmn. secondary edn. dept., 1969-72, chmn. dept. curriculum and instrn., 1983-84, assoc. dean adminstrn. and devel., 1975-78, dir. external rels., 1991-94; dir. devel. Bloomington campus and annual giving Ind. U. Found., 1984-90; prof. emeritus retired, 1994; vis. prof. U. Wis., summer 1967, U. Hawaii, summer 1972. Co-author: New Strategies and Curriculum in Social Studies, 1969, Secondary Schools in a Changing Society, 1976; co-editor 2 books. Bd. overseers St. Meinrad Coll. and Sem., 1991—, trustee, 1995—. With USAF, 1951-53. Recipient Booklist award Phi Lambda Theta, 1965, 69. Mem. Ind. Coun. Social Studies (pres. 1968-69), Phi Delta Kappa, Kappa Sigma, Phi Kappa Phi. Roman Catholic. Home: 2306 E Edgehill Ct Bloomington IN 47401-6839 Office: Indiana Univ Sch of Edu Rm 3032 Bloomington IN 47405

SMITH, FREDERICK WALLACE, transportation company executive; b. Marks, Miss., Aug. 11, 1944; s. Frederick Smith; m. Diane Avis. Grad., Yale U., 1966. Cert. comml. pilot. Owner Ark Aviation, 1969-71; founder, pres. Fed. Express Corp., Memphis, 1971—, chmn. bd., pres, CEO, 1975—. Served with USMC, 1966-70. Office: Fed Express Corp 2005 Corporate Ave PO Box 727 Memphis TN 38132

SMITH, FREDRIC CHARLES, electronic technician, consultant; b. Chgo., May 30, 1947; s. Fredric Louis and Beverly Jean (Bito) S.; m. Marylou Yanowsky, Feb. 5, 1965 (div. Sept. 1978); m. Kim Nio Song, Aug. 5, 1985; children: Tracy Lynn, Fredrick Dylan, David Sean. AAS in Electronic Engring., Middlesex County C.C., 1991. Indsl. electrician Bristol-Meyers Squibb, New Brunswick, N.J., 1985—; electronic technician Bristol-Meyers Squibb, Lawrenceville, N.J., 1990-91; mgr. cons., David & Smith Engring., Princeton Junction, N.J., 1993—. With U.S. Army, 1966-68. Mem. IEEE, Internat. Soc. Electronic Technicians. Avocations: programming-amateur radio, poetry, creative writing. Home: 3 Marsh Ct Lawrenceville NJ 08648-2622 Office: Bristol-Meyers Squibb PO Box 191 New Brunswick NJ 08903

SMITH, FREDRICA EMRICH, rheumatologist, internist; b. Princeton, N.J., Apr. 28, 1945; d. Raymond Jay and Carolyn Sarah (Schleicher) Emrich; m. Paul David Smith, June 10, 1967. AB, Bryn Mawr Coll., 1967; MD, Duke U., 1971. Intern, resident U. N.Mex. Affiliated Hosps., 1971-73; fellow U. Va. Hosp., Charlottesville, 1974-75; pvt. practice, Los Alamos, N.Mex., 1975—; chmn. credentials com. Los Alamos Med. Ctr., 1983—, chief staff, 1990; bd. dirs. N.Mex. Physicians Mut. Liability Ins. Co., Albuquerque. Contbr. articles to med. jours. Mem. bass sect. Los Alamos Symphony, 1975—; mem. Los Alamos County Parks and Recreation Bd., 1984-88, 92-96, Los Alamos County Med. Indigent Health Care Task Force, 1989—; mem. ops. subcom. Aquatic Ctr., Los Alamos County, 1988—. Fellow ACP, Am. Coll. Rheumatology; mem. N.Mex. Soc. Internal Medicine (pres. 1993-96), Friends of Bandelier. Democrat. Avocations: swimming, music, reading, hiking. Office: Los Alamos Med Ctr 3917 West Rd Los Alamos NM 87544-2222

SMITH, G. E. KIDDER, architect, author; b. Birmingham, Ala., Oct. 1, 1913; s. F. Hopkinson and Annie (Kidder) S.; m. Dorothea Fales Wilder, Aug. 22, 1942; children: G.E. Kidder, Hopkinson Kidder. A.B., Princeton U., 1935, M.F.A., 1938; student, Ecole Americaine, Fontainbleau, France, 1935. Registered architect, N.Y., Ala., N.C. Architect Princeton Expdn. to, Antioch, Syria, 1938; designer, site planner, camoufleur with Caribbean Architect-Engr. on Army bases, Caribbean, 1940-42; own archtl. practice, 1946—; lectr. numerous European archtl. socs., also many Am. univs. and museums; archtl. critic Yale U., 1948-49; vis. prof. MIT, 1955-56; guest arch. Archtl. Inst. Japan, 1988. Author: (with P.L. Goodwin) Brazil Builds, 1943, Switzerland Builds, 1950, Italy Builds, 1955, Sweden Builds, 1950, rev. edit., 1957, The New Architecture of Europe, 1961, The New Churches of Europe, 1963, A Pictorial History of Architecture in America, 1976, The Architecture of the United States, 3 vols, 1981, The Beacon Guide to New England Churches, 1989, Looking at Architecture, 1990, Source Book of American Architecture, 1995; also contbr. articles to encys.; exhibits, Stockholm Builds, 1940, Brazil Builds, 1943; installed: Power in the Pacific, USN, 1945 (all at Museum Modern Art, N.Y.C); New Churches of Germany, Goethe House, N.Y.C., and Am. Fedn. Arts, 1957-58, Masterpieces of European Posters (donated), Va. State Mus., Richmond, 1958; Work of Alvar Aalto, Smithsonian Instn., 1965-82, Am.'s Archtl. Heritage for, Smithsonian Instn., 1976, Smithsonian, 1976, photographs in collection, Mus. Modern Art, Met. Mus., N.Y.C. Served to lt. USNR, 1942-46. Recipient Butler prize Princeton, 1938; fellow Am. Scandinavian Found., 1939-40; Guggenheim Found. fellow, 1946-47; President's fellow Brown U., 1949-50; research Fulbright fellow Italy, 1950-51; research Fulbright fellow India, 1965-66; Samuel H. Kress grantee India, 1967; Brunner scholar, 1959-60; Graham Found. for Advanced Study in Arts-Nat. Endowment on Arts joint fellowship, 1967-69; Nat. Endowment Arts fellow, 1974-75; Ford Found. grantee, 1970-71, 75-76; decorated Order So. Cross Brazil; Premio ENIT gold medal Italy; recipient gold medal (archtl. photography) AIA, 1964; E.M. Conover award, 1965; subject of public TV spl., 1976. Fellow AIA, Internat. Inst. Arts and Letters (life; Switzerland); mem. Soc. Archtl. Historians, Assn. Collegiate Schs. of Architecture, Municipal Art Soc. N.Y.C., Coll. Art Assn. Episcopalian. Clubs: Century Assn. (N.Y.C.); Cooperstown Country. Address: 163 E 81st St New York NY 10028-1806

SMITH, G. ELAINE, religious organization executive. Pres. ABC Bd. of Nat. Ministries, Valley Forge, Pa. Office: ABC Board of National Ministries PO Box 851 Valley Forge PA 19482-0851

SMITH, GARDNER WATKINS, physician; b. Boston, July 2, 1931; s. George Van Siclen and Olive (Watkins) S.; m. Susan Elizabeth Whiteford, Sept. 6, 1958; children—Elizabeth Whiteford, Rebecca Tremain, George Van Siclen II. Grad., Phillips Acad., 1949; M.D., Harvard, 1956; A.B., Princeton, 1969. Diplomate: Am. Bd. Surgery, Am. Bd. Thoracic Surgery. Intern Johns Hopkins Hosp., Balt., 1956-57; asst. resident Johns Hopkins Hosp., 1958-59, fellow, 1957-58, asst. in surgery, 1957-59, prof. surgery, 1970-96, emeritus prof. surgery, 1996—, dep. dir. dept. surgery, 1978-85; asst. resident U. Va., Charlottesville, 1959-61, resident, 1961-62, asst. in surgery, 1959-63, cardiovascular resident, 1962-63, instr., 1963-65, asst. prof., 1965-68, assoc. prof., 1968-70, surgeon, 1963-70; chief surgery Balt. City Hosp., 1970-79, vis. surgeon, 1979-85; chmn. sect. surg. scis. Johns Hopkins Bayview Med. Ctr., 1985-96, active staff, 1996—; cons. Greater Balt. Med. Ctr., 1970-91, Lock Haven VA Hosp., Balt., 1971-92, Walter Reed Army Med. Ctr., 1976-90, Nat. Naval Med. Ctr., 1984-90. Contbr. articles to med. jours. Mem. Soc. U. Surgeons, Am., So. surg. assns., A.C.S., Am. Gastroenterol. Assn., Assn. for Acad. Surgery, Balt. City Med. Soc., Halsted Soc., Med. and Chirurgical Faculty of Md., Soc. Surgery Alimentary Tract, Soc. Vascular Surgery, Internat. Cardiovascular Soc., So. Soc. Clin. Surgeons, Southeastern Surg Congress, So. Assn. Vasular Surgery, Va. Surg. Assn., Cum Laude Soc., Alpha Omega Alpha, Nu Sigma Nu. Home: 1503 Old Orchard Ln Baltimore MD 21204-3654 Office: Johns Hopkins Bayview Med Ctr 4940 Eastern Ave Baltimore MD 21224-2735

SMITH, GEOFFREY ADAMS, special purpose mobile unit manufacturing executive; b. Bay Shore, N.Y., Mar. 17, 1947; s. Ian Morrison and Dorothy Brumbach (Adams) S.; m. Linda Ann Lehmann, July 15, 1972; 1 child, Chad William. BS in Managerial Sci., Lehigh U., 1969. Supr. Roadway Express, South Kearny, N.J., 1969-72; v.p. mktg. Med. Coaches, Inc., Oneonta, N.Y., 1972-76, pres., CEO, 1976—, chmn. bd., 1976; dir. Wilber Nat. Bank, Oneonta, 1996—, Preferred Mut. Ins., New Berlin, N.Y., 1979—; bd. dirs. and v.p. Wilderness Properties Ltd., Oneonta, 1986—; bd. dirs. Moex, Inc., Jefferson, Oreg. Bd. dirs., v.p. Thomas A. Dooley Found., 1984—; trustee A.O. Fox Meml. Hosp. Found., 1984—; adv. com. Oneonta Ctr. for Econ. and Community Devel; advocacy com. Nat. Soccer Hall Fame; mem. Hartwick Coll. Adv. Coun.; coun. mem. citizens bd. Hartwick Coll.; bd. dirs. Future of Oneonta Found., MSRT, Indpls.; mem. N.Y. State Govs. Bus. Adv. Coun. Served with Army N.G., 1969-76. Mem. Greater Oneonta C. of C. (pres., bd. dirs. 1976-82), Am. Legion, Oneonta Country Club (bd. dirs.), Rotary (pres., bd. dirs. Oneonta club 1975-82), Elks, Sigma Beta Delta (hon.). Republican. Methodist. Avocations: racquetball, softball, photography, travelling, golf. Home: Hcr # 862 West Oneonta NY 13861 Office: Medical Coaches Inc PO Box 129 Hemlock Rd Oneonta NY 13820

SMITH, GEORGE CURTIS, judge; b. Columbus, Ohio, Aug. 8, 1935; s. George B. and Dorothy R. S.; m. Barbara Jean Wood, July 10, 1963; children: Curtis, Geoffrey, Elizabeth Ann. BA, Ohio State U., 1957, JD, 1959. Bar: Ohio 1959, U.S. Dist. Ct. (so. dist.) Ohio 1987. Asst. city atty. City of Columbus, 1959-62; exec. asst. to Mayor of Columbus, 1962-63; asst. atty. gen. State of Ohio, 1964; chief counsel to pros. atty. Franklin County, Ohio, 1965-70, pros. atty., 1971-80; judge Franklin County Mcpl. Ct., Columbus, 1980-85; judge Franklin County Common Pleas Ct., 1985-87; judge U.S. Dist. Ct. (so. dist.) Ohio, 1987—; mem. Ohio Supreme Ct. Coun. on Victims Rights, 1988-94; judge in residence Law Sch. U. Cin., 1993; faculty Ohio Jud. Coll., Litigation Practice Inst.; chmn. 1994, Fed. Bench-Bar Conf., 1995; lectr. ABA Anti-Trust Sec., 1995; alumni spkr. law graduation Ohio State U., 1995; pres. Young Rep. Club, 1963, Perry Group, 1996; exec. com. Franklin County Rep. Party, 1971-80; Elder Presbyn. Ch. Recipient Superior Jud. Service award Supreme Ct. Ohio; Resolution of Honor, Columbus Bldg. and Constrn. Trades Coun. Mem. Ohio Pros. Attys. Assn. (pres., Ohio Prosecutor of Yr, Award of Honor, Leadership award), Columbus Bar Assn., Assn. Trial Lawyers Am., Columbus Bar Found., Fed. Bar Assn., Ohio Mcpl. Judges Assn. (v.p. 1983), Columbus Athletic Club (pres., dir.), Lawyers Club of Columbus (pres. 1975), Masons (33d degree), Aladdin Shrine. Presbyterian. Office: 85 Marconi Blvd Columbus OH 43215-2823

SMITH, GEORGE DRURY, publisher, editor, collagist, writer; b. Dayton, Ohio, Mar. 10, 1927; s. Martin Jefferson and Viola (Haas) S.; m. Anne Liard Jennings, Apr. 1967 (div. 1975). A.B. cum laude, Marietta Coll., 1953; Diplome de Phonetique, U. Grenoble, 1950; student, U. Madrid, 1950-51, Heidelberg U., 1951-52, U. Minn., 1953-55, U. Calif.-Berkeley, 1965, UCLA, 1968. CFO Argonaut newspaper, 1972-96; dir. Lambda Point Cons. and Pentacle Group, 1984—. Editor: Beyond Baroque, 1968-80, NewLetters, 1969-75, (book series) NewBooks, 1976-78. Founder, bd. dirs. Beyond Baroque Found., Venice, Calif., 1968-80; mem. Mcpl. Arts Adv. Bd., L.A., 1980-82; chmn. Save Westminster Auditorium Com., Venice, 1977-80; advisor Venice Cultural Ctr. Com., 1981-83. With U.S. Army, 1945-47. Grantee Nat. Endowment for Arts, 1973-80, Calif. Arts Coun., 1977-80, Mcpl. Arts Commn., 1977-80, Coordinating Coun. Lit. Mags., 1974-80. Mem. Rosicrucians. Democrat. *I believe that if we have faith we can live without fear; that the universe is benevolent if we can love unconditionally; that we can live righteously and prosper if we are honest and seek divine guidance; and that our mission is to enjoy life and strive for beauty.*

SMITH, GEORGE FOSTER, retired aerospace company executive; b. Franklin, Ind., May 9, 1922; s. John Earl and Ruth (Foster) S.; m. Jean Arthur Farnsworth, June 3, 1950; children—David Foster, Craig Farnsworth, Sharon Windsor. B.S. in Physics, Calif. Inst. Tech., 1944, M.S., 1948, Ph.D. magna cum laude (Standard Oil fellow 1949-50), 1952. Founding staff mem. Engring. Research Assos., St. Paul, 1946-48; teaching fellow, resident asso. Calif. Inst. Tech., 1948-52; mem. staff Hughes Research Labs., Malibu, Calif., 1952-87; asso. dir. Hughes Research Labs., 1962-69, dir., 1969-87; v.p. Hughes Aircraft Co., 1965-81, sr. v.p., 1981-87, mem. policy bd., 1966-87; adj. asso. prof. elec. engring. U. So. Calif., 1959-62; cons. Army Sci. Adv. Panel, 1975-78. Contbr. numerous articles to profl. jours. Adv. local Explorer post Boy Scouts Am., 1965-70; bd. mgrs. Westchester YMCA, 1974—, chmn., 1979-81; chmn. trustees Pacific Presbyn. Ch., Los Angeles, 1959-62. Served to lt. (j.g.) USNR, 1944-46. Recipient Disting. Alumnus award Calif. Inst. Tech., 1991. Fellow IEEE (pres. Sorenson fellows 1972-73, Frederick Philips award 1988), Am. Phys. Soc.; mem. AAAS, Caltech Assocs. (bd. dirs. 1990—, pres. 1993-94), Sierra Club, Sigma Xi (chpt. pres. 1957-58), Tau Beta Pi. Achievements include 6 patents in field; directed leading industrial research in electronics, lasers, and electro-optics; conducted first laser range finder experiments. Office: Hughes Elecronics Corp Rsch Labs 3011 Malibu Canyon Rd Malibu CA 90265-4737

SMITH, GEORGE LEONARD, industrial engineering educator; b. State College, Pa., Sept. 6, 1935; s. George Leonard and Frieda Regina (Droege) S.; m. Patricia Gallagher, Dec. 29, 1962; children: Stephanie Ann, Seana Maureen. BS in Indsl. Engring., Pa. State U., 1957; MS in Indsl. Engring., Lehigh U., 1958, MS in Psychology, 1967; PhD in Indsl. Engring., Okla. State U., 1969. Registered profl. engr., Pa. Asst. prof. Ohio State U., Columbus, 1968-72, assoc. prof., 1972-77, prof. indsl. engring., 1977-95, prof. emeritus, 1995, chmn. dept. indsl. and systems engring., 1982-94, assoc. dean for acad. affairs, 1991-93; v.p. Breakthrough Performance, Inc., Lexpert; arbitrator Fed. Mediation and Conciliation Service, 1970—; vis. Disting. Prof. New U. of Lisbon, Portugal, 1990—. Editor: Human Factors, 1980-83; author: Work Measurement: A Systems Approach, 1978. Pub. mem. Ohio Power Siting Commn., 1970-75. Recipient Disting Teaching award Coll. Engring., Ohio State U., 1982. Fellow Inst. Indsl. Engrs. (Human Factors Soc., div. dir. 1979-81, v.p. edn. rsch. 1988-91, Spl. citation ergonomics divsn.), Soc. for Engring. and Mgmt. Systems (pres. 1996), World Acad. of Productivity Sci., Human Factors and Ergonomics Soc.; mem. Am. Soc. Engring. Edn. Democrat. Roman Catholic. Home: 858 Katherines Ridge Ln Columbus OH 43235-3462 Office: 858 Katherines Ridge Ln Columbus OH 43235-3462

SMITH, GEORGE LESTER, lawyer; b. Ft. Meade, Md., July 14, 1951; s. Dale Ellison and Jane (Sheppard) S.; m. Patricia P. Smith, July 25, 1981; 1 child, Bradford D. BA, Claremont McKenna Coll., 1973; JD, U. Calif., Davis, 1976; LLM, U. Fla., 1987. Bar: Wash. 1980, Calif. 1976; CPA, Calif., Wash. Acct. Touche Ross & Co., San Francisco, 1976-78; assoc. Graham & Dunn, Seattle, 1982-87; ptnr. Foster Pepper & Shefelman, Seattle, 1987-96; founder, prin. Smith & Zuccarini, P.S., Bellevue, 1996—. Capt. JAGC, U.S. Army, 1978-82. Office: 777 108th Ave NE Ste 2250 Bellevue WA 98004-5118

SMITH, GEORGE PATRICK, II, lawyer, educator; b. Wabash, Ind., Sept. 1, 1939; s. George Patrick and Marie Louise (Barrett) S. BS, Ind. U., 1961,

JD, 1964; certificate, Hague Acad. Internat. Law, 1965; LLM, Columbia U., 1975. Bar: Ind. 1964, U.S. Supreme Ct. 1968. Kannert teaching fellow Ind. U. Sch. Law, 1964-65; instr. law U. Mich. Sch. Law, 1965-66; practiced in Ind. and Washington, 1965—; legal adviser Fgn. Claims Settlement Commn., Dept. State, Washington, 1966; asst. prof., asst. dean State U. N.Y. at Buffalo Law Sch., 1967-69; vis. asst. prof. law George Washington U., Nat. Law Center, summer 1968; assoc. prof. law U. Ark., 1969-71; spl. counsel EPA, Washington, 1971-74; adj. prof. law Cath. U. Law Sch., Washington, 1973-74, prof., 1977—; adj. prof. law Georgetown U. Law Ctr., 1971-75; assoc. prof. law U. Pitts. Sch. Law, 1975-78; Commonwealth fellow in law, sci. and medicine Yale U., New Haven, 1976-77; vis. prof. law U. Conn., 1977; disting. vis. scholar Kennedy Bioethics Inst., Georgetown U., 1977-81; vis. scholar Cambridge (Eng.) U., summer 1975, spring 1978-79, Hoover Inst. on War, Revolution and Peace Stanford (Calif.) U., summer 1983, Inst. Soc., Ethics and Life Scis., Hastings Ctr., N.Y., 1981, Lilly Rare Books Libr., Ind. U., July 1981, The Kinsey Inst. for Rsch. in Sex, Gender and Reproduction, U. Ind., July 1981, Am. Bar Found., Chgo., 1986, 87, Vatican Libr., Rome, July, 1989; Rockefeller Found. resdl. scholar, Bellagio, Italy, 1980; lectr. Sch. Medicine, Uniformed Svcs. U. Health Scis., Bethesda, Md., 1979-87; cons. environ. legislation Govt. of Greece, 1977; spl. counsel to Gov. Ark. for environ. affairs, 1969-71; cons. Ark. Planning Commn., 1970-71; mem. Ark. Waterway Commn., 1970-71; chmn. Ark. Com. on Environ. Control, 1970-71; mem. com. on hwy. rsch. NRC, NAS, 1971-81; life mem. Ind. U. Found.; univ. fellow Columbia U. Law Sch., 1974-75; fellow Max Planck Inst., Heidelberg, Fed. Republic of Germany, summer 1983; mem. Pres. Reagan's Pvt. Sector Survey on Cost Control, 1982; vis. fellow Clare Hall Cambridge U., 1983-84, summer 87, law, sci. and medicine Hughes Hall, Cambridge (Eng.) U., 1989, also vis. mem. law faculty, Apr.-Aug., 1989; Fulbright vis. prof. U. New South Wales, Syndey, Australia, 1984, vis. prof., vis. fellow Ctr. for Law and Tech., 1987; vis. fellow Inst. Advanced Study, Ind. U., 1985; vis. prof. law U. Notre Dame, 1986; vis. scholar Am. Bar Found., Chgo., 1986, 87; sr. vis. fellow U. Singapore, 1987; vis. fellow McGill U. Ctr. for Medicine, Ethics and Law, Montreal, 1988, Ctr. for Biomed. Ethics U. Va. Health Scis. Ctr., Charlottesville, 1990, Ctr. for Bioethics Monash U., Melbourne, Australia, 1990, Working Ctr. Studies in German and Internat. Med. Malpractice Law Free U. Berlin, 1992; vis. rsch. fellow Ctr. for Advanced Study of Ethics Georgetown U., Washington, 1990-91; rsch. fellow Divinity Sch. Yale U., New Haven, 1991; assoc. Med. Inst. for Law Faculty, Cleve. Clinic Ctr. Creative Thinking in Medicine Cleve. State U., 1991; vis. prof. rsch. U. Auckland Law Faculty, 1991, U. Sydney Law Faculty, 1991, U. Victoria Law Faculty, B.C., Can., 1992, Trinity Coll., 1992, Dublin U., Ireland, 1992, Wolfson Coll. Cambridge U., 1992, Ind. U. Sch. Public and Environ. Affairs, 1992, Queensland U. Faculty Law, Australia, 1993; vis. scholar Ctr. Biomed. Ethics U. Minn. Med. Sch., Mpls., 1991, Ctr. for Socio-Legal Studies Oxford U., July 1992, Princeton (N.J.) Theol. Sem., 1993, Ctr. Med. Ethics Pritzker Sch. Medicine U. Chgo., 1993; vis. fellow Ctr. for Internat. Malpractice Law Free U. Berlin, Jan. 1992, King's Coll. Ctr. for Med. Law and Ethics U. London, June 1992; vis. sr. fellow Ctr. for Study Aging and Human Devel. Duke U. Med. Ctr., 1994; vis. prof. Rsch. U. Otiago, 1994; faculty of law, vis. fellow U. Bioethics Rsch. Ctr., Dunedin, New Zealand, 1994; vis. scholar Poynter Ctr. for Study of Ethics Am. Instns., Ind. U., Bloomington, 1994, law, medicine and ethics Schs. Medicine and Pub. Health Boston U., 1995, Ctr. Law and Health Ind. U., Indpls., 1995; vis. fellow U. Pa. Sch. Medicine, Phila., 1996, Inst. Study Applied & Profl. Ethics, Dartmouth Coll., Hanover, N.H., 1996, Cambridge (Eng.) U. Rsch. Ctr. Internat. Law, 1996; vis. scholar Vanderbilt U. Divinity Sch., Nashville, 1996, Northwestern U. Med. Sch., Med. Ethics & Humanities Program, Chgo., 1997, Hoover Instn., Stanford U., Palo Alto, Calif., 1997, Ind. U. Sch. Medicine Program Med. Ethics, Indpls., 1997; vis. prof. legal rsch. Ind. U. Law Sch., Bloomington, 1997. Author: Restricting the Concept of Free Seas, 1980, Legal, Ethical and Social Issues of the Brave New World, 1980, Genetics, Ethics and the Law, 1981, Medical-Legal Aspects of Cryonics, 1983, The New Biology, 1989, Final Choices: Autonomy in Health Care Decisions, 1989, Bioethics and the Law, 1993, Legal and Healthcare Ethics for the Elderly, 1996; contbr. articles to profl. jours. U. Ark. del. Pacem In Maribus Conf., Malta, 1970. Recipient Disting. Alumni award Ind. U. Bd. Trustees, 1985, citation for Path-Breaking Work; establishment of George P. Smith II Disting. Research Professorship, Ind. U., Bloomington, 1986. Mem. ABA (rep. UN Conf. on Human Environ., Stockholm 1972, rep. Law of Sea Conf., UN, N.Y.C. 1976, Switzerland 1979, cons. UNESCO Declaration on the Production of the Protection of the Human Genome, Paris 1995), Am. Assn. Bioethics, Am. Law Inst., Soc. Ind. Pioneers, Am. Friends of Cambridge U., Order of St. John Hospitaller, Alpha Kappa Psi, Phi Alpha Delta, Sigma Alpha Epsilon, Order of Omega. Republican. Club: Cosmos (Washington). *Think big, work hard and, above all, have a dream: these are the simple guideposts for a fulfilling life.*

SMITH, GEORGE S., JR., communications financial executive; b. Newark, Dec. 8, 1948; m. Pamela Smith. BS in Acctg., Hiram Scott Coll., Scott's Bluff, Nebr., 1971. Cash mgr. Diamondhead Corp., N.Y.C., 1971-75, Texasgulf Inc., N.Y.C., 1975-77; dir. fin. svcs. Viacom Internat. Inc., N.Y.C., 1977-79, dir. fin. planning, 1979-81, controller radio div., 1981-83, v.p. fin. and adminstrn. broadcast group, 1983-85, v.p., controller, 1985-87, sr. v.p., chief fin. officer Viacom Inc., 1987—. Mem. Broadcast Cable Fin. Mgmt. Assn., Fin. Execs. Inst. Office: Viacom Inc 1515 Broadway New York NY 10036

SMITH, GEORGE THORNEWELL, retired state supreme court justice; b. Camilla, Ga., Oct. 15, 1916; s. George C. and Rosa (Gray) S.; m. Eloise Taylor, Sept. 1, 1943 (dec.). Grad., Abraham Baldwin Agrl. Coll., 1940; LLB, U. Ga., 1948. Bar: Ga. 1947. Assoc. Cain & Smith, Cairo, Ga., 1947-71; city atty. Cairo, 1949-58; atty. Grady County, 1950-59; solicitor Cairo City Ct., 1951-59; mem. Ga. Ho. of Reps., 1959-67, speaker of the house, 1963-67; lt. gov. State of Ga., 1967-71; city atty. East Point, Ga., 1973-76; judge Ga. Ct. Appeals, 1976-81; justice Ga. Supreme Ct., Atlanta, 1981-91, presiding justice, 1990-91; of counsel Barnes, Browning Tanksley and Casurella, Marietta, Ga., 1992—; past mem. exec. com. Nat. Conf. Appellate Judges; vice chmn. Nat. Conf. Lt. Govs. Trustee Nat. Arthritis Found. Lt. comdr. USN, 1940-45. Only person in the state's history to serve in an elective capacity in all 3 brs. of govt. Mem. State Bar Ga., Cobb County Bar Assn., Lawyers Club Atlanta, Am. Legion, VFW, Moose, Kiwanis. Avocations: hunting, bowling, golf. Office: Barnes Browning Tanksley and Casurella 166 Anderson St Ste 225 Marietta GA 30060-1984

SMITH, GEORGE WOLFRAM, physicist, educator; b. Des Plaines, Ill., Sept. 19, 1932; s. Murray Sawyer and Alice Lucile (Wolfram) S.; m. Mary Lee Sackett, Sept. 7, 1956; children—Dean, Grant. B.A., Knox Coll., 1954; M.A., Rice U., 1956, Ph.D., 1958. Welch Found. fellow Rice U., 1958-59; sr. rsch. physicist GM, Warren, Mich., 1959-76; dept. rsch. scientist GM, 1976-81, sr. staff rsch. scientist, 1981-87, prin. rsch. scientist, 1987—; lectr. physics and astronomy Cranbrook Inst. Sci., Bloomfield Hills, Mich., 1963-87, mem. sci. adv. com., 1989—; instr. Lawrence Inst. Tech., 1963-65; vice chmn. Gordon Rsch. Conf. on Orientational Disorder in Crystals, 1976, chmn., 1978; co-chmn. Internat. Symposium on Particulate Carbon, 1980; mem. rev. com. Liquid Crystal Inst., Kent (Ohio) State U., 1984-85; mem. adv. com. Conf. on Electrorheological Fluids, 1991, 93; mem. adv. bd. NSF Sci. and Tech. Ctr. for Advanced Liquid Crystalline Optical Materials, 1996—. Co-editor: Particulate Carbon: Formation During Combustion, 1981; editl. cons. Ency. Applied Physics, 1988—; contbr. Handbook of Chemistry and Physics; contbr. articles to sci. and tech. jours.; patentee on temperature measuring device, liquid crystal device tech., dielectric heating, graphite fiber growth, polymer-dispersed liquid crystals. Mem. Mich. Regtl. Civil War Roundtable, 1965—, pres., 1971-72. Recipient Knox Coll. Achievement award 1977, John M. Campbell Research award, 1980, Charles L. McCuen Achievement award, Gen. Motors, 1985. Fellow Am. Phys. Soc. (com. on applications of physics 1988-91, chmn. 1991, chmn. com. on tutorials 1991, mem. Pake Prize Com. 1993-94); mem. Soc. Info. Display (program com. 1990-93), Phi Beta Kappa, Sigma Xi (chpt. pres. 1980-81), Phi Delta Theta, Alpha Delta. Home: 1882 Melbourne St Birmingham MI 48009-1163 Office: GM Rsch and Devel Ctr Physics and Phys Chem Dept Warren MI 48090-9055

SMITH, GERARD PETER, neuroscientist; b. Phila., Mar. 24, 1935; s. Stanley Alward and Agnes Marie (McLarney) S.; m. Barbara McInnis, May 12, 1962; children: Christopher, Mark, Hilary, Maura. BS, St. Joseph's U., Phila., 1956; MD, U. Pa., 1960. Intern, resident N.Y. Hosp., 1960-62; asst. prof. physiology U. Pa. Sch. Medicine, Phila., 1964-68; from asst. to assoc. prof. Cornell U., N.Y.C., 1968—, prof. psychiatry (behavioral neurosci.), 1973—; vis. prof. MIT, 1973-74, Rockefeller U., 1979-80; adj. prof., 1982-86; cons. NIH; Curt Richter lectr. Johns Hopkins U., 1976; Leon lectr. U. Pa., 1990, Stellar lectr. U. Pa., 1993; Rushton lectr. Fla. State U., 1992, Merck, Sharpe, and Dohm prof. neurosci. U. Flinder, Australia, 1992; Loucks lectr. U. Wash., 1995; dir. Eating Disorders Inst., N.Y. Hosp.-Cornell Med. Ctr., 1984-88. Recipient Rsch. Scientist USPHS, 1982; NIH grantee. Mem. AAAS, Am. Physiol. Soc., Soc. for Neurosci., Am. Assn. for Rsch. in Nervous and Mental Disease, Endocrine Soc., Soc. for Study Ingestive Behavior (pres.), Internat. Behavioral Neurosci. Soc. (pres.), Alpha Omega Alpha, Alpha Sigma Nu. Office: NY Hosp Cornell Med Ctr EW Bourne Behavioral Rsch Lab 21 Bloomingdale Rd White Plains NY 10605-1504

SMITH, GERI GARRETT, nurse educator; b. Brownsville, Tenn., Nov. 21, 1948; d. F.G. and Willie Mae (Morris) Garrett; m. Lu Smith, Dec. 20, 1967 (dec.); children: Taylor, Alexandra, Amber; m. Tom Jeanes, July 16, 1984; children: Zachary, Garrett. BSN, U. Tenn., Memphis, 1987; MSN, U. Memphis, 1989; MS, Memphis State U., 1978; BS, U. Tenn., Martin, 1970. RN, Tenn.; NCAST instr.; cert. tchr., Fla., Tenn., Tex. Tchr. Aldine Schs., Houston, 1972-74, 1972-74; tchr. Shelby County Schs., Memphis, 1977-85; sch. nurse Memphis Shelby County Health Dept., Memphis, 1987-89, nurse supr. new mothers program, 1989-94; asst. prof. Sch. Nursing Union U., 1993—. Mem. NAACOG, ICEA, Tenn. Nurses Assn., Tenn. Pub. Health Assn., Sigma Theta Tau. Home: 70 Grassland Dr Jackson TN 38305-3808

SMITH, GLEE SIDNEY, JR., lawyer; b. Rozel, Kans., Apr. 29, 1921; s. Glee S. and Bernice M. (Augustine) S.; m. Geraldine B. Buhler, Dec. 14, 1943; children: Glee S., Stephen B., Susan K. AB, U. Kans., 1943, JD, 1947. Bar: Kans. 1947, U.S. Dist. Ct. 1951, U.S. Supreme Ct. 1973, U.S. Ct. Mil. Appeals 1988. Ptnr. Smith, Burnett & Larson, Larned, Kans., 1947—; of counsel Barber, Emerson et. al., Lawrence, Kans., 1992—, Kans. state senator, 1957-73, pres. Senate, 1965-73; mem. Kans. Bd. Regents, 1975-83, pres., 1976; bd. govs. Kans. U. Law Soc., 1967—; mem. Kans. Jud. Coun., 1963-65; county atty. Pawnee County, 1949-53; mem. bd. edn. Larned, 1951-63; Kans. commr. Nat. Conf. Commn. on Uniform State Laws, 1963—. Bd. dirs. Nat. Legal Svcs. Corp., 1975-79. Served to 1st lt. U.S. Army, 1943-45. Recipient Disting. Svc. award, U. Kans. Law Sch., 1976; Disting. Svc. citation U. Kans., 1984. Fellow Am. Coll. Probate Counsel, Am. Bar Found.; mem. ABA (bd. of govs. 1987-90, chmn. ops. com. 1989-90, exec. com. 1989-90, chmn. task force on solo and small firm practitioner 1990-91, chmn. com. on solo and small firm practitioners 1992-94, chmn. task force on applying fed. legis. to congress 1994-96), Kans. Bar Assn. (del. to ABA ho. of dels. 1982-92, bd. govs. 1982-92, leadership award 1973, medal of Distinction 1993), Southwest Kans. Bar Assn., Am. Judicature Soc. Republican. Presbyterian. Clubs: Kiwanis, Masons, Rotary. Home: 115 E 9th St Apt 5 Larned KS 67550-2647 Home: 4313 Quail Pointe Rd Lawrence KS 66047-1966

SMITH, GLENN A., lawyer; b. Oakland, Calif., July 11, 1946. BA, Pomona Coll., 1968; JD, U. Calif., Berkeley, 1971; LLM in Taxation, NYU, 1973. Bar: Calif. 1972, D.C. 1975. Law clerk to Hon. William M. Drennen U.S. Tax Ct., 1973-75; mem. Heller, Ehrman, White & McAuliffe, Palo Alto, San Francisco, Calif. Office: Heller Ehrman White & McAuliffe 525 University Ave Ste 1100 Palo Alto CA 94301-1908

SMITH, GLENN STANLEY, electrical engineering educator; b. Salem, Mass., June 1, 1945; s. Stanley Ernest and Florence Estelle (Chaney) S.; m. Linda Lee Holmquist, Aug. 4, 1968; children: Geoffrey Douglas, Eleanor Leigh. BS, Tufts U., 1967; MS, Harvard U., 1968, PhD, 1972. Postdoctoral rsch. fellow Harvard U., Cambridge, Mass., 1972-75; rsch. assoc., lectr. Northeastern U., Boston, 1973-75; asst. prof. elec. engring. Ga. Inst. Tech., Atlanta, 1975-79, assoc. prof., 1979-84, prof., 1984-89, Regents' prof., 1989—. Co-author: Antennas in Matter, 1981; assoc. editor Radio Sci., 1983-87. Fellow IEEE (editorial bd. IEEE Press 1988-91); mem. Internat. Union Radio Sci. Home: 2518 Hazelwood Dr NE Atlanta GA 30345-2145 Office: Sch Elec Engring Ga Inst Tech Atlanta GA 30332

SMITH, G(ODFREY) T(AYLOR), academic administrator; b. Newton, Miss., Nov. 12, 1935; s. Taylor and Edna (Blanton) S.; m. Joni Eaton, Sept. 1, 1956; children: Paul Brian, Sherry Lynn. BA, Coll. of Wooster, 1956; MPA with distinction, Cornell U., 1960; LLD (hon.), Bethany Coll., 1979. From assoc. dir. devel. to v.p. Cornell U., 1960-67; pres. Chapman U., Orange, Calif., 1977-88, pres. emeritus, 1988—; lectr. in field. Contbr. numerous articles on coll. mgmt. to profl. publs. Bd. dirs. Wayne County (Ohio) Indsl. Devel. Corp., 1966-72, World Affairs Coun. Orange Coun., Calif., 1978-89, Orange County chpt. NCCJ, 1979-86, Orange County coun. Boy Scouts Am., 1980-85, Coun. Ind. Colls., 1985-87; bd. dirs. div. higher edn. Christian Ch. (Disciples of Christ), 1980-86, chmn., 1984-86; bd. dirs., mem. exec. com. Ind. Colls. So. Calif., 1979-88, pres., 1981-82; mem. exec. com. Assn. Ind. Calif. Colls. and Univs., 1980-88, treas., 1982-87. Recipient Steuben Apple award for tchg. excellence Coun. for Advancement and Support Edn., 1984, Disting. Alumnus award Coll. of Wooster, 1991, Faith and Reason award Christian Ch. (Disciples of Christ), 1993, Laureate award Inst. for Charitable Giving, 1997; Smith Hall dedicated at Chapman U., 1988; Alfred P. Sloan fellow Cornell U., 1960. Presbyterian. Home: 2200 Lupine Dr Ashland OR 97520-3642 *If we treat people as they are, they will stay as they are. But if we treat them for what they might be and might become, they will become those better selves.*

SMITH, GOFF, industrial equipment manufacturing executive; b. Jackson, Tenn., Oct. 7, 1916; s. Fred Thomas and Mabel (Goff) S.; m. Nancy Dall, Nov. 28, 1942 (dec. 1972); children: Goff Thomas, Susan Knight; m. Harriet Schneider Oliver, June 23, 1973. BSE, U. Mich., 1938, MBA, 1939; MS, MIT, 1953. Trainee Bucyrus Erie, South Milwaukee, Wis., 1939-40; mem. sales staff Amsted Industries, Chgo. and N.Y.C., 1946-55; subsidiary pres. Amsted Industries, Chgo., 1955-60, v.p., 1960-69, pres., dir., 1969-74, pres., CEO, dir., 1974-80, chmn., 1980-82. Pres. Village of Winnetka, Ill., 1967-69; pres., bd. dirs. United Way Chgo., 1976-85; bd. dirs. Rehab. Inst., Chgo., Chgo. Theol. Sem., Presbyn. Home, Evanston, Ill.; trustee Sigma Chi Found. Maj. U.S. Army, 1940-46. Sloan Fellow MIT, 1952-53. Republican. Avocations: hunting, fishing, golf.

SMITH, GORDON E., religious organization executive. Exec. dir. ABC Ministers & Miss. Benefit Bd., Valley Forge, Pa., pres. Office: ABC Ministers & Miss Benefit Bd PO Box 851 Valley Forge PA 19482-0851*

SMITH, GORDON H., civil engineer; b. N.Y.C., Mar. 17, 1936; s. Henry and Theodora (Augenstern) S.; m. Norma Kaplan, Feb. 28, 1960; children: Randy Smith Aberg, Robin Smith Kolstad. B in Engring., Yale U., 1957. Registered profl. engr., Mich., N.Y. V.p., chief engr. Albro Metal Products Corp., N.Y.C., 1957-69, pres., 1969-75; pres. Gordon H. Smith Corp., N.Y.C., 1975—. Contbr. articles to Archtl. Record, Progressive Arch., ASTM, Chgo. High Rise Com. Mem. NSPE, ASTM, ASCE, AIA (Inst. Honors 1994), Nat. Assn. Archtl. Metal Mfrs. (v.p., prs., bd. dirs.), Archtl. Aluminum Mfrs. Assn. (v.p., bd. dirs.), Nat. Assn. Miscellaneous, Ornamental and Archtl. Metal Mfrs. (bd. dirs.), Constrn. Specifications Inst. Office: Gordon H Smith Corp 200 Madison Ave New York NY 10016-3903

SMITH, GORDON HAROLD, senator; b. Pendleton, Oreg., May 25, 1952; s. Milan Dale and Jessica (Udall) S.; m. Sharon Lankford; children: Brittany, Garrett, Morgan. BA in History, Brigham Young U., 1976; JD, Southwestern U., 1979. Law clk. to Justice H. Vern Payne N.Mex. Supreme Ct.; pvt. practice Ariz.; owner Smith Frozen Foods; mem. Oreg. State Senate, 1992-95, pres., 1995-96; U.S. senator from Oreg., 1997—; mem. Budget com. U.S. Senate; vice chair subcom. water and power, subcom. forests and pub. land mgmt., subcom. energy rsch., devel., prodn. and regulation Energy and Natural Resource com.; chair subcom. European affairs, subcom. Near Eastern and South Asian affairs, subcom. internat. ops. Fgn. Rels. com. Office: B40-2 Dirksen Senate Office Bldg Washington DC 20510-3701*

SMITH, GORDON HOWELL, lawyer; b. Syracuse, N.Y., Oct. 26, 1915; s. Lewis P. and Maud (Mixer) S.; m. Eunice Hale, June 28,1947; children: Lewis Peter, Susan S. Rizk, Catherine S. Maxson, Maud S. Daudon. B.A., Princeton U., 1932-36; LL.B., Yale U., 1939. Bar: N.Y. 1939, Ill. 1946. Asso. Lord, Day & Lord, N.Y.C., 1939-41, Gardner, Carton & Douglas, Chgo., 1946-51; partner Mackenzie, Smith & Michell, Syracuse, 1951-53; partner Gardner, Carton & Douglas, 1954-57, 60-85, of counsel, 1986—; sec., dir. Smith-Corona, Inc., 1951-54, v.p., Syracuse, 1957-60. Bd. dirs. Rehab. Inst. Chgo., chmn., 1974-78, 83-86; bd. dirs. United Way Met. Chgo., 1962-85. Served to lt. comdr. USNR, 1941-46. Mem. Am. Soc. Corporate Secs., Am., Ill., Chgo. bar assns. Clubs: Comml., Law, Econ., Legal, Chgo., Old Elm (Chgo.). Home: 1302 N Green Bay Rd Lake Forest IL 60045-1108 Office: 321 N Clark St Ste 3400 Chicago IL 60610-4717

SMITH, GORDON PAUL, management consulting company executive; b. Salem, Mass., Dec. 25, 1916; s. Gordon and May (Vaughan) S.; m. Daphne Miller, Nov. 23, 1943 (div. 1968); m. Ramona Chamberlain, Sept. 27, 1969; children: Randall B., Roderick F. B.S. in Econs, U. Mass., 1947; M.S. in Govt. Mgmt, U. Denver (Sloan fellow), 1948; postgrad. in polit. sci. NYU, 1948-50; DHL (hon.), Monterey Inst. Internat. Studies, 1994. Economist Tax Found., Inc., N.Y.C., 1948-50; with Booz, Allen & Hamilton, 1951-70; partner Booz, Allen & Hamilton, San Francisco, 1959-62, v.p., 1962-67, mng. pntr. Western U.S., 1968-70; partner Harrod, Williams and Smith (real estate devel.), San Francisco, 1962-69; state dir. fin. State of Calif., 1967-68; pres. Gordon Paul Smith & Co., Mgmt. Cons., 1968—; pres., chief exec. officer Golconda Corp., 1972-74, chmn. bd., 1974-85; pres. Cermetek Corp., 1978-80; bd. dirs., exec. com. First Calif. Co., 1970-72, Groman Corp., 1976-85; bd. dirs. Madison Venture Capital Corp.; adviser task force def. procurement and contracting Hoover Commn., 1954-55; spl. asst. to pres. Republic Aviation Corp., 1954-55; cons., Hawaii, 1960-61, Alaska, 1963; cons. Wash. Hwy. Adminstrn., 1964, also 10 states and fed. agys., 1951-70, Am. Baseball League and Calif. Angels, 1960-62; bd. dirs. Monterey Coll. Law; chmn. Ft. Ord Econ. Devel. Adv. Group, 1991; chmn. Coalition on Rsch. and Edn., 1993—; bd. dirs. Monterey Bay Futures Project; counsel Ctr. for Non-Proliferated Studies, 1995—; over 750 TV, radio and speaking appearances on econs., mgmt. and public issues. Author articles on govt., econs. and edn. Mem. 24 bds. and commns. State of Calif., 1967-72; mem. Calif. Select Com. on Master Plan for Edn., 1971-73; mem. alumni council U. Mass., 1950-54, bd. dirs. alumni assn., 1964-70; bd. dirs. Alumni Assn. Mt. Hermon Prep. Sch., 1963; bd. dirs. Stanford Med. Ctr., 1960-62, pres., chmn., 1962-66; chmn. West Coast Cancer Found., 1976-87, Coalition Rsch. and Edn., 1993—, Jim Tunney Youth Fund, 1994—; trustee, chmn. Monterey Inst. Internat. Studies, 1978-92, trustee emeritus, 1995—; trustee Northfield Mt. Hermon Sch., 1983-93, Robert Louis Stevenson Sch., 1993—; mem. devel. council Community Hosp. of Monterey Peninsula, 1983—; bd. dirs. Friends of the Performing Arts, 1985—; bd. dirs. Monterey County Symphony Orch., 1991—, Monterey Bay Futures Project, 1992—. Recipient spl. commendation Hoover Commn., 1955, Alumni of Yr. award U. Mass., 1963, Trustee of Yr. award Monterey-Peninsula, 1991, Monterey-Peninsula Outstanding Citizen of Yr. award, 1992, Laura Bride Powers Heritage award, 1991, U.S. Congl. award, 1992, Calif. Senate and Assembly Outstanding Citizen award, 1992, Wisdom award of honor Wisdom Soc., 1992; permanent Gordon Paul Smith Disting. Chair for Internat. Studies established at Monterey Inst. Internat. Studies; Gordon Paul Smith Scholarship Fund named in his honor Northfield Mt. Hermon Sch.; named to Honorable Order of Ky. Cols. Mem. Monterey History and Art Assn. (bd. dirs. 1987-92, pres. 1985-87, chmn. 1987-92, hon. lifetime dir. 1992—), The Stanton Ctr. Heritage Ctr. (chmn. 1987-92, chmn. emeritus 1992—), Salvation Army (bd. dirs., chmn. hon. cabinet), Monterey Peninsula Mus. Art, Carmel Valley (Calif.) Country Club, Monterey Peninsula Country Club, Old Capitol Club. Home: 253 Del Mesa Carmel CA 93923 *If the quest for personal success is only for an accumulation of prestige, power or wealth, then personal failure will be assured. Genuine personal success can surely be found, however, through a significant and lasting contribution toward helping the progress of others and raising the human worth. This is the true mark of leadership.*

SMITH, GRANT WARREN, II, university administrator, physical sciences educator; b. Kansas City, Mo., Jan. 21, 1941; m. Constance M. Krambeer, 1962; 1 child, Grant Warren III. BA, Grinnell Coll., 1962; PhD, Cornell U., 1966, postgrad., 1967. Asst. prof. chemistry Cornell U., Ithaca, N.Y., 1966-68, vis. prof., Am. Council on Edn. fellow, 1973-74; assoc. prof. U. Alaska, Fairbanks, 1968-77, prof., 1977-78, head dept. chemistry and chem. engring., 1968-73, acting head dept. gen. sci., 1972-73; pres. univ. assembly U. Alaska System, 1976-77; prof. phys. scis., dean Sch. Scis. and Techs. U. Houston, Clear Lake, 1979-84; prof. chemistry Southeastern La. U., Hammond, 1984-95, honors prof. arts and scis., 1995-97, v.p. for acad. affairs, 1984-86, pres., 1986-97; pres. Slippery Rock U., 1997—. Bd. dirs. Houston Area Research Ctr., 1982-83; violinist, pres. exec. bd. Clear Lake Symphony, 1980-84. NIH fellow, 1963-66, DuPont fellow, 1967. Fellow Royal Soc. Chemistry (London, chartered chemist), Explorers Club; mem. Am. Assn. Higher Edn., Am. Assn. Univ. Adminstrs. (bd. dirs. 1982-85, 86-88, v.p. 1988-90), AAAS, Am. Chem. Soc., Internat. Assn. Univ. Pres., Soc. Econ. Botany, Am. Soc. Pharmacognosy, Ethnopharmacology Soc., Soc. of Ethnobiology, Nat. Speleological Soc., Am. Spelean History Assn., Arctic Inst. N.Am., Hammond C. of C. (bd. dirs. 1988-90), Rotary, Sigma Xi, Phi Kappa Phi, Beta Gamma Sigma, Phi Eta Sigma. Office: Slippery Rock U Office of Pres Slippery Rock PA 16057-1326

SMITH, GREGORY ALLGIRE, academic director; b. Washington, Mar. 31, 1951; s. Donald Eugene and Mary Elizabeth (Reichert) S.; m. Susan Elizabeth Watts, Oct. 31, 1980; 1 child, David Joseph Smith-Watts. BA, The Johns Hopkins U., 1972; MA, Williams Coll., Williamstown, Mass., 1974. Adminstrv. asst. Washington Project for the Arts, 1975; intern Walker Art Ctr., Mpls., 1975-76; asst. devel. officer The Sci. Mus. of Minn., St. Paul, 1977; asst. dir. Akron (Ohio) Art Inst., 1977-80; asst. to dir. Toledo Mus. Art, 1980-82, asst. dir. adminstrn., 1982-86; exec. v.p. Internat. Exhbns. Found., Washington, 1986-87; dir. The Telfair Mus. Art, Savannah, Ga., 1987-94, Art Acad. of Cin., 1994—. Trustee Greater Cin. Consortium of Colls. and Univs., Assn. Ind. Colls. of Art and Design. Mem. Am. Assn. Mus. (surveyor mus. assessment program 1988—), Assn. Art Mus. Adminstrs. (founder 1984-85), Ohio Found. on the Arts (v.p. 1981-83, trustee 1981-84), Coll. Art Assn., Univ. Club, Rotary. Avocations: collecting arts & crafts movement objects, repairing old houses, landscape design. Home: 2533 Erie Ave Cincinnati OH 45208-2015 Office: Art Acad of Cin 1125 Saint Gregory St Cincinnati OH 45202-1734

SMITH, GREGORY SCOTT, medical researcher, educator; b. Troy, N.Y., Mar. 22, 1955; s. Oney Percy and Gloria Ann (Tetrault) S. BS in Biology, LeMoyne Coll., 1977; MS in Physiology, U. Tex. Houston, 1989, PhD in Physiology, 1993. From rsch. asst. to rsch. assoc. Surgery U. Tex. Med. Sch., Houston, 1979-90, postdoctoral fellow Pathology, 1993-94, asst. prof. surgery and pathology, 1994-95; assoc. prof. surgery and anatomy St. Louis U. Sch. Medicine, 1996—. Contbr. chpts. in books and articles to profl. jours. Head usher Braeburn Presbyn. Ch., Houston, 1987-95; judge Houston Sci. and Engring. Fair, 1993-95. Mem. Am. Physiol. Soc., Gastroenterology Rsch. Group, Am. Gastroenterology Assn., Shock Soc., Am. Assn. Lab. Animal Sci., Am. Assn. Anatomy. Republican. Avocations: woodworking, fishing, cooking.

SMITH, GREGORY WHITE, writer; b. Ithaca, N.Y., Oct. 4, 1951; s. William R. and Kathryn (White) S. BA, Colby Coll., 1973; JD, Harvard U., 1977, MEd, 1980. Bar: Mass., 1980. Fellow Thomas J. Watson, 1973-74; pres. Woodward/White, Inc.; overseer Colby Coll.; mem. bd. trustees Columbus Acad. Author: (with Steven Naifeh) Moving Up in Style, 1980, Gene Davis, 1981, How to Make Love to a Woman, 1982, What Every Client Needs to Know About Using a Lawyer, 1982, The Bargain Hunter's Guide to Art Collecting, 1982, Why Can't Men Open Up?: Overcoming Men's Fear of Intimacy, 1984, The Mormon Murders: A True Story of Greed, Forgery, Deceit, and Death, 1988, Jackson Pollock: An American Saga, 1989 (Nat. Book award nomination for nonfiction 1990, Pulitzer Prize for biography 1991), Final Justice: The True Story of the Richest Man Ever Tried for Murder, 1993, A Stranger in the Family: A True Story of Murder, Madness, and Unconditional Love, 1995; editor: (with Naifeh) The Best Lawyers in America, The Best Doctors in America. Office: Woodward/White 129 1st Ave Aiken SC 29801-4862*

SMITH, GRIFFIN, JR., editor; b. Fayetteville, Ark., June 29, 1941; s. Griffin and Mildred (Cross) S.; m. Mary Elizabeth Routh, Sept. 1, 1979. BA in History, Rice U., 1963; MA in Polit. Sci., Columbia U., 1965; postgrad. in philosophy, Oxford U., 1966; JD, U. Tex., 1969. Bar: Tex. 1969, U.S. Dist. Ct. (ea., we., no. and so. dists.) Tex. 1969, Ark. 1981, U.S. Dist. Ct. (ea. and we. dists.) Ark.1981. Spl. asst. to Senator Fulbright U.S. Senate, Washington, 1968-69; atty. estate and gift tax div. IRS, Houston, 1970; rsch. dir. Tex. gubernatorial campaign Paul Eggers, 1970; chief counsel constl. amendments com. Tex. Senate, 1971, chief counsel drug law reform com., 1971-73; editor natural areas survey Lyndon B. Johnson Sch. Pub. Affairs U. Tex., Austin, 1973-77; speech writer Pres. of U.S., 1977-78; ptnr. Smith & Nixon (formerly Smith, Smith, Nixon & Duke), Little Rock, 1984-92. Author: A Consumer Viewpoint on State Taxation, 1971, Marijuana in Texas, 1972, The Best of Texas Monthly, 1978, Texas Monthly's Political Reader, 1978, 80, Journey into China, 1982, Forgotten Texas: A Wilderness Portfolio, 1983, The Great State of Texas, 1985; sr. editor Tex. Monthly mag., 1973-77; exec. editor Ark. Dem. Gazette Newspaper, 1992—; contbr. articles to Nat. Geog., Saturday Rev., Atlantic Monthly, and others. Woodrow Wilson fellow, 1964. Mem. State Bar Tex., Tex. Inst. Letters (award for best work of journalism in Tex. 1974, 76). Episcopalian. Office: Ark Dem Gazdette 121 E Capitol Ave Little Rock AR 72201-3819

SMITH, GROVER CLEVELAND, English language educator; b. Atlanta, Sept. 6, 1923; s. Grover C. and Lillian Julia (McDaniel) S.; m. Phyllis Jean Snyder, June 19, 1948 (div. 1965); children: Alice Elizabeth, Charles Grover; m. Dulcie Barbara Soper, Dec. 29, 1965; children: Stephen Kenneth, Julia Margaret. BA with honors, Columbia U., 1944, MA, 1945, Ph.D. (Alexander M. Proudfit fellow), 1950. Instr. English Rutgers U., 1946-48, Yale U., 1948-52; instr. English Duke U., 1952-55, asst. prof., 1955-61, asso. prof., 1961-66, prof., 1966-93; prof. emeritus, 1993—; mem. summer faculty CUNY, 1946, 47, 48, Columbia U., 1963, 64, NYU, 1963, Wake Forest U., 1966, vis. lectr., 1963, 64. Author: T.S. Eliot's Poetry and Plays: A Study in Sources and Meaning, 1956 (Poetry Chapbook award) rev. 1974, Archibald MacLeish, 1971, Ford Madox Ford, 1972, The Waste Land, 1983, T.S. Eliot and the Use of Memory, 1996; editor: Josiah Royce's Seminar, 1913-1914: As Recorded in the Notebooks of Harry T. Costello, 1963, Letters of Aldous Huxley, 1969. Mem. Christian Gauss Award com., 1973-75. With U.S. Army, 1943. Guggenheim fellow, 1958; Am. Philos. Soc. grantee, 1965; Am. Learned Socs. grantee, 1965; Nat. Endowment Humanities grantee, 1979; fellow, 1980. Mem. T.S. Eliot Soc. (bd. dirs. 1986-94, 96—, v.p. 1986-88, editor News and Notes, 1987-88, 90-91, pres. 1989-91, sec. 1996—), Am. Lit. Assn. (rep. to coun. of Am. Author Socs. 1990-91), Nat. Assn. Scholars. Office: Duke U Dept English PO Box 90015 Durham NC 27708-0015

SMITH, GUY LINCOLN, IV, strategic and crisis communications company executive; b. New Orleans, Mar. 16, 1949; s. Guy Lincoln III and Laura Louise (Orr) S.; m. Marjorie Russell, June 19, 1971; children: Abigail, Guy Lincoln V, Laura. Student, Bowling Green State U., 1967-68, U. Tenn., 1968-70, Am. U., 1971, U.S. Dept. Agrl. Grad. Sch., Washington, 1971. Reporter, asst. city editor The Knoxville Jour., 1967-70; dir. info. Appalachian Regional Commn., Washington, 1970-72; dir. info., press sec. to mayor City of Knoxville, 1972-76; mgr. corp. affairs Miller Brewing Co., Milw., 1976-79; v.p. corp. affairs The Seven-Up Co., St. Louis, 1979-84, Philip Morris U.S.A., N.Y.C., 1984-88; v.p. corp. affairs Philip Morris Cos. Inc., N.Y.C., 1989-91, pub. Philip Morris Mag., 1986-91; COO Hill and Knowlton, Inc., N.Y.C., 1991-93; chmn. Smith Worldwide, Inc., N.Y.C., 1993—; mem. pvt. sect. com. on pub. rels. USIA. Bd. dirs. Barrier Island Trust, Tallahassee, Fla., 1991—, AmeriCares, Inc., Ptnrs. for Devel., Washington. Recipient Excellence in News Writing award William Randolph Hearst Found., 1969, Achievement award Puerto Rican Family Inst., 1988; named confrere Sovereign Military Order of St. John of Jerusalem, of Rhodes, and of Malta, 1986, Outstanding Pub. Rels.-Pub. Affairs Exec. of Yr. Gallagher Report, 1988. Mem. Nat. Press Club, Kappa Alpha. Roman Catholic. Office: Smith Worldwide Inc #204 171 Madison Ave New York NY 10016-5110

SMITH, HARMON LEE, JR., clergyman, moral theology educator; b. Ellisville, Miss., Aug. 23, 1930; s. Harmon Lee Sr. and Mary (O'Donnell) S.; children: Pamela Lee, Amy Joanna, Harmon Lee III. AB, Millsaps Coll., 1952; BD, Duke U., 1955, PhD, 1962. Ordain to priest Episcopal Ch., 1972. Asst. dean Duke U. Divinity Sch., Durham, N.C., 1959-65, asst. prof. Christian ethics, 1962-68, assoc. prof. moral theology, 1968-73, prof. moral theology, 1973—, prof. community and family medicine, 1974—; cons. med. ethics; vis. prof. U. N.C., 1964, 70, 72, U. Edinburgh, Scotland, 1969, U. Windsor, Ont., 1974. Author books on Christian theology, ethics and med. ethics; sr. editor Social Science and Medicine, 1973-89; contbr. articles on Christian ethics to various publs. Lilly Found. fellow, 1960; Gurney Harris Kearns Found. fellow, 1961; Nat. Humanities Ctr. fellow, 1982-83. Mem. Am. Assn. Theol. Schs., Am. Soc. Christian Ethics, Am. Acad. Religion, Soc. for Religion in Higher Edn., Soc. Health and Human Values. Home: 3510 Randolph Rd Durham NC 27705-5347 Office: Duke U The Divinity Sch Durham NC 27706

SMITH, HAROLD B., manufacturing executive; b. Chgo., Apr. 7, 1933; s. Harold Byron and Pauline (Hart) S. Grad., Choate Sch., 1951; B.S., Princeton U., 1955; M.B.A., Northwestern U., 1957. With Ill. Tool Works, Inc., Chgo., 1954—; exec. v.p. Ill. Tool Works, Inc., 1968-72, pres., 1972-81, vice chmn., 1981, chmn. exec. com., 1982—, also bd. dirs.; bd. dirs. W.W. Grainger, Inc., No. Trust Corp.; trustee Northwestern Mut. Life Ins. Co. Mem. Rep. Nat. Com., 1976—; chmn. Ill. Rep. Com., 1993—; del. Rep. Nat. Conv., 1964, 76, 88, 92, 96; bd. dirs. Adler Planetarium, Boys and Girls Clubs Am., Northwestern U., Rush-Presbyn.-St. Luke's Med. Ctr., Newberry Libr. Clubs: Chicago, Commercial, Commonwealth, Economic, Northwestern, Princeton (Chgo.). Office: Ill Tool Works Inc 3600 W Lake Ave Glenview IL 60025-1215

SMITH, HAROLD CHARLES, private pension fund executive; b. N.Y.C., Jan. 11, 1934; s. Harold Elmore and Hedwig Agnes (Gronke) S. BA cum laude with honors, Ursinus Coll., 1955, DD (hon.), 1993; MBA, NYU, 1958; M in Div., Union Theol. Sem., N.Y.C., 1958. DD Ursinus Coll., 1993. CFA; ordanined minister United Ch. of Christ, 1959. Vice pres. YMCA Retirement Fund, Inc., N.Y.C., 1958-69, portfolio mgr., 1960—, assoc. sec., 1969-77, v.p., 1977-80, exec. v.p., 1980-82, pres. elect, 1982-83, pres., 1983—; pastor 1st E&R Ch., Bridgeport, Conn., 1958-88, Unity Hill United Ch. of Christ, 1988—; assoc. prof. bus. and fin. L.I. U., 1969-71; trustee Bank Mart, Bridgeport, Conn., 1983-91; bd. dirs. Y Mut. Ins. Co., treas. 1988—, United Ch. Residencies, 1962-65. Trustee YWCA Greater Bridgeport, 1975-79, Pension Funds United Ch. of Christ, 1968—, Springfield Coll. (Mass.), 1983—, Mut. Ins. Co., 1989; pres. Cousing Investment, 1996; bd. dirs. YMCA Greater N.Y., 1983—, Bridgeport Area Found., 1989—, Ursinus Coll., Pa., 1994—, Coun. of Chs. of Greater Bridgeport, 1995-96; trustee United Ch. Found., 1968-95, vice chmn., 1995—. Mem. N.Y. Soc. Security Analysts, Am. Econs. Assn., Fin. Analysts Fedn., World and Trade Club, Mcht's Club, Masons, Marco Polo Club, Order Eastern Star. Author: Getting it All Together for Retirement, 1977. Office: YMCA Retirement 225 Broadway New York NY 10007-3001 *It is a great privilege to serve and to be a part of organizations dedicated to making life and this world better.*

SMITH, H(AROLD) LAWRENCE, lawyer; b. Evergreen Park, Ill., June 27, 1932; s. Harold Lawrence and Lorna Catherine (White) S.; m. Madonna Jeanne Koehl, June 9, 1956 (div. 1968); children: Lawrence Kirby, Sandra Michele, Madonna Clare Galloway; m. Nancy Leigh Baum, May 2, 1970 (dec.); m. Louise Fredericka Jeffrey, Nov. 2, 1984 (div. 1994); m. Marianne Lorraine Laug, Apr. 19, 1997. BS, U.S. Naval Acad., 1956; JD, John Marshall Law Sch., 1965. Bar: Ill. 1965, Mich. 1986,U.S. Dist. Ct. (no. dist.) Ill. 1965, U.S. Ct. Appeals (7th cir.) 1967, U.S. Ct. of Customs and Patent Appeals, 1976, U.S. Ct. Appeals (fed. cir.) 1982, U.S. Patent and Trademark Office 1968. Tech. asst. Langner, Parry, Card & Langner, Chgo., 1961-65, assoc., 1965-69; patent atty. Borg-Warner Corp., Chgo., 1970-74; sr. patent atty. Continental Can Co., Inc., Chgo. and Oak Brook, Ill., 1974-82, asst. gen. counsel, Stamford, Conn., 1982-86; ptnr. Varnum, Riddering, Schmidt & Howlett, Grand Rapids, Mich., 1986-96, counsel, 1996—; adj. prof. patent law Cooley Law Sch., 1991—. Served to lt. USN, 1956-61. Mem. Intellectual Property Law Assn. Chgo., Chartered Inst. Patent Agts. (London), World Affairs Coun. of Western Mich. (dir. 1996—). Club: Peninsular. Office: Varnum Riddering Schmidt & Howlett Bridgewater Pl PO Box 352 Grand Rapids MI 49501-0352

SMITH, HARRY DELANO, educational administrator; b. Florence, Ala., June 10, 1954; s. Cornelius Everett and Nadine (Olive) S.; m. Wanda Joy Skipworth, Nov. 23, 1978; children: Benjamin Delano, Rebekah Joy. BS, U. North Ala., 1975, MA, 1977, EdS, 1983; EdD, U. Ala., Tuscaloosa, 1989. Cert. class AA supr.-prin., Ala. Exec. dir. Christian Student Ctr., Florence, 1980-83; head dept. math. Mars Hill Bible Sch., Florence, 1983-87; tchr. math. and physics Muscle Shoals (Ala.) High Sch., 1975-80, asst. prin., 1987-88, prin., 1989—; farmer, Killen, Ala., 1974-80; tchr. summer sch. Sheffield (Ala.) High Sch., 1977-78; dir. scholars program Muscle Shoals Schs., 1987-88; asst. prin. Avalon Mid. Sch., Muscle Shoals, 1987-88, prin., 1988-89; math. cons. Cartersville (Ga.) City Schs., 1991-92; curriculum cons. Eufaula (Ala.) High Sch., 1991-92; co-chmn. Ala. Learner Outcomes Com., Montgomery, 1991-92; dist. judge All-State Acad. Team, Athens, Ala., 1991-92; coach Ala. Mathcounts team NSPE, Birmingham, 1985. Dir. music and edn. Shoals Ch. of Christ, 1992. Named Outstanding Young Educator, No. Dist. Ala. Jaycees, 1987; Beeson fellow Samford U., 1987. Mem. ASCD, Nat. Assn. Secondary Sch. Prins., Am. Assn. Sch. Adminstrs., Ala. Coun. Sch. Adminstrs. and Suprs., Ala. Assn. Secondary Sch. Prins., Kappa Delta Pi, Phi Kappa Phi. Avocations: travel, stamp collecting, reading, bowling. Home: 2201 E Jennifer St Muscle Shoals AL 35661-2637 Office: Muscle Shoals High Sch 100 E Trojan Dr Muscle Shoals AL 35661-3173*

SMITH, HARVEY ALVIN, mathematics educator, consultant; b. Easton, Pa., Jan. 30, 1932; s. William Augustus and Ruth Carolyn (Krauth) S.; m. Ruth Wismer Kolb, Aug. 27, 1955; children: Deirdre Lynn, Kirsten Nadine, Brinton Averill. B.S., Lehigh U., 1952; M.S., U. Pa., 1955, A.M., 1958, Ph.D., 1964. Asst. prof. math Drexel U., 1960-65; mem. tech. staff Inst. Def. Analyses, Arlington, Va., 1965-66; assoc. prof. math Oakland U., 1966-68; ops. research scientist Exec. Office of Pres., Washington, 1968-70; prof. math. Oakland U., 1970-77; prof. Ariz. State U., Tempe, 1977—; cons. Inst. Def. Analyses, 1967-69, Exec. Office Pres., 1967-73, U.S. Arms Control and Disarmament Agy, 1973-79, Los Alamos Nat. Lab., 1980-93. Author: Mathematical Foundation of Systems Analysis, 1969. NSF fellow, 1964-65; recipient Meritorious Service award Exec. Office of Pres., 1970. Mem. Soc. Indsl. and Applied Math., Am. Math. Soc., AAAS, Sigma Xi. Home: 18 E Concorda Dr Tempe AZ 85282-3517 Office: Ariz State U Dept Math Tempe AZ 85287-1804

SMITH, HEDRICK LAURENCE, journalist, television comentator, author, lecturer; b. Kilmacolm, Scotland, July 9, 1933; s. Sterling L. and Phebe (Hedrick) S.; m. Ann Bickford, June 29, 1957 (div. Dec. 1985); children: Laurel Ann, Jennifer Laurence, Sterling Scott, Lesley Roberts; m. Susan Zox, Mar. 7, 1987. Grad., Choate Sch., 1951; BA, Williams Coll., 1955, LittD (hon.), 1975; postgrad. (Fulbright scholar), Balliol Coll., Oxford, Eng., 1955-56; LittD (hon.), Wittenburg U., 1985, N.H. Coll., 1991; LHD (hon.), Columbia Coll., 1992; LittD (hon.), Amherst Coll., 1992; LHD (hon.), U. S.C., 1992; LittD (hon.), Furman U., 1996. With U.P.I., Memphis, Nashville, Atlanta, 1959-62; with N.Y. Times, 1962-88, Washington and S.E., 1962-63; with Vietnam, 1963-64; Middle East corr. N.Y. Times, Cairo, U.A.R., 1964-66; diplomatic news corr. N.Y. Times, Washington, 1962-64, 66-71; Moscow Bur. chief N.Y. Times, 1971-74, dep. nat. editor, 1975-76, Washington Bur. chief, 1976-79, chief Washington corr., 1980-85; Washington correspondent N.Y. Times mag., 1987-88; vis. journalist Am. Enterprise Inst., 1985-87; fellow Fgn. Policy Inst., Johns Hopkins U. Sch Advanced Internat. Studies, 1989—; panelist Washington Week in Rev., PBS, 1969-95. Author: The Russians, 1975 (Overseas Press Club award 1976), The Power Game: How Washington Works, 1988, The New Russians, 1990 (Overseas Press Club citation 1991), Rethinking America, 1995; co-author: The Pentagon Papers, 1972, Reagan the Man, the President, 1981, Beyond Reagan: The Politics of Upheaval, 1986, Seven Days That Shook the World, 1991; TV documentaries Star Wars, 1985, Moscow Jews, 1986, Space Bridge, Chernobyl: Three Mile Island, 1987, 4-part Power Game series, PBS, 1989, Countdown to White House: The Bush Transition, 1989, 4-part series Inside Gorbachev's USSR, 1990 (George Polk award Gold Baton award Columbia-Du Pont), Guns, Tanks and Gorbachev, 1991, Soviets, 1991 (George Peabody award), 4-part series PBS, Challenge to America, 1994, Across the River pub. TV program (Hillman award), 1995, The People and the Power Game, 1996. Trustee Williams Coll., 1982-97. With USAF, 1956-59. Recipient Pulitzer prize for pub. svc. Pentagon Papers Series, 1972, for internat. reporting from Soviet Union and Ea. Europe, 1974, William Allen White award U. Kans., 1996; Nieman fellow Harvard U., 1969-70. Mem. Gridiron Club, Phi Beta Kappa.

SMITH, HELEN ELIZABETH, retired military officer; b. San Rafael, Calif., Aug. 11, 1946; d. Jack Dillard and Marian Elizabeth (Miller) S. BA in Geography, Calif. State U., Northridge, 1968; MA in Internat. Rels., Salve Regina, Newport, R.I., 1983; MS in Tech. Comm., Rensselaer Poly. Inst., 1988; postgrad., Naval War Coll., 1982-83. Commd. ensign USN, 1968, advanced through grades to capt., 1989; adminstrv. asst. USN Fighter Squadron 101, Key West, Fla., 1969-70; adminstrv. officer Fleet Operational Tng. Group, Mountain View, Calif., 1970-72; leader human resource team Human Resource Ctr., Rota, Spain, 1977-79; adminstrv. officer Pearl Harbor (Hawaii) Naval Sta., 1979-80; dir. Family Svc. Ctr., Pearl Harbor, 1980-82; officer-in-charge R&D lab. Naval Ocean Systems Ctr., Kaneohe, Hawaii, 1983-85; exec. officer Naval ROTC, assoc. prof. Rensselaer Poly. Inst., Troy, N.Y., 1985-88; comdg. officer Navy Alcohol Rehab. Ctr., Norfolk, Va., 1988-90; faculty mem., commanding officer Naval Adminstrv. Command, dean adminstrv. support, comptr. Armed Forces Staff Coll., Norfolk, Va., 1990-93; ret., 1993; exec. dir. Calif. for Drug-Free Youth, 1995-96. Author: (walking tour) Albany's Historic Pastures, 1987; composer (cantata) Night of Wonder, 1983. Chair Hawaii State Childcare Com., Honolulu, 1981-82; coun. mem. Hist. Pastures Neighborhood Assn., Albany, N.Y., 1985-88; mem. working group Mayors Task Force on Drugs, Norfolk, 1989-90; chair, bd. dirs. Va. Coun. on Alcoholism, 1989-92, Calif. for Drug Free Youth, 1995-96; singer North County Baroque Ensemble. Mem. AAUW, Waves (nat. unit 126), Kiwanis. Republican. Presbyterian. Avocation: writing. Home: 32 Via Santa Barbara Paso Robles CA 93446

SMITH, HENRY CHARLES, III, symphony orchestra conductor; b. Phila., Jan. 31, 1931; s. Henry Charles Jr. and Gertrude Ruth (Downs) S.; m. Mary Jane Dressner, Sept. 3, 1955; children—Katherine Anne, Pamela Jane, Henry Charles IV. BA, U. Pa., 1952; artist diploma, Curtis Inst. Music, Phila., 1955. Solo trombonist Phila. Orch., 1955-67; condr. Rochester (Minn.) Symphony Orch., 1967-68; assoc. prof. music Ind. U., Bloomington, 1968-71; resident condr., ednl. dir. Minn. Orch., Mpls., 1971-88; prof. music U. Tex., Austin, 1988-89, Frank C. Erwin Centennial Prof. of Opera, 1988-89; music dir. S.D. Symphony, Sioux Falls, 1989—; prof. Ariz. State U., Tempe, 1989-93, prof. emeritus, 1993—; vis. prof. U. Tex., Austin, 1987-88; founding mem. Phila. Brass Ensemble, 1956—; music dir. World Youth Symphony Orch., Interlochen, Mich., 1981-96. Composer 5 books of solos for trombone including Solos for the Trombone Player, 1963, Hear Us As We Pray, 1963, First Solos for the Trombone Player, 1972, Easy Duets for Winds, 1972; editor 14 books 20th century symphonies lit. Served to 1st lt. AUS, 1952-54. Recipient 3 Grammy nominations, 1967, 76, 1 Grammy award for best chamber music rec. with Phila. Brass Ensemble, 1969. Mem. Internat. Trombone Assn. (dir.), Am. Symphony Orch. League, Music Educators Nat. Conf., Am. Guild Organists, Am. Fedn. Musicians, Tubist Universal Brotherhood Assn., Acacia Fraternity. Republican. Congregationalist. Home: 8032 Pennsylvania Rd Bloomington MN 55438

SMITH, HENRY CLAY, retired psychology educator; b. Catonsville, Md., May 9, 1913; s. Harry C. and Lovell (Figgins) S.; m. Nancy Woollcott, Aug. 27, 1938; children—David Barton, Woollcott Keston, Barbara Sunderland. A.B. magna cum laude, St. John's Coll., Annapolis, Md., 1934; Ph.D., Johns Hopkins U., 1939. Instr. psychology U. Vt., Burlington, 1940-43; dir. tng. and research Western Electric Co., Balt., 1943-45; asso. prof. Knox Coll., Galesburg, Ill., 1945-46; asso. prof. psychology, chmn. dept. Hamilton Coll., Clinton, N.Y., 1946-49; prof. psychology Mich. State U., East Lansing, from 1949; ret., 1983; Fulbright research fellow, Italy, 1955-56; cons. prof. Waseda U., Tokyo, 1960. Author: Sensitivity Training, 2d edit, 1973, Personality Development, 2d edit, 1974; co-author: Social Perception, 1968, Psychology of Industrial Behavior, 3d edit, 1972, Ten Keys to Understanding People, 1987. Fellow APA; mem. Phi Beta Kappa. Home: PO Box 3086 West Tisbury MA 02575-3086

SMITH, HILARY CRANWELL BOWEN, investment banker; b. Balt., Nov. 1, 1937; s. Henry Bowen and Clayton (Cranwell) S.; m. Janet Simmons, June 9, 1962. BA, Colgate U., 1960; MBA, U. Va., 1967. V.p. Goldman, Sachs & Co., N.Y.C., 1969-74, E. F. Hutton & Co., N.Y.C., 1974-77; sr. v.p. Blyth Eastman Dillon, N.Y.C., 1977-79; mng. dir. Salomon Bros., N.Y.C., 1979-90, Dillon, Read & Co., Inc., N.Y.C., 1990—. Lt. USN, 1960-63. Office: Dillon Read & Co Inc 535 Madison Ave Fl 15 New York NY 10022-4212

SMITH, HOKE LAFOLLETTE, university president; b. Galesburg, Ill., May 7, 1931; s. Claude Hoke and Bernice (LaFollette) S.; m. Barbara E. Walvoord, June 30, 1979; children by previous marriage: Kevin, Kerry, Amy, Glen. B.A. (Harold fellow), Knox Coll., 1953; M.A., U. Va., 1954; Ph.D. (fellow 1958), Emory U., 1958; hon. degree, Sung Kyun Kwan U., Korea, 1993, Knox Coll., 1995. Asst. prof. polit. sci. Hiram Coll., Ohio, 1958-64; assoc. prof. polit. sci. Hiram Coll., 1964-67; asst. to pres., prof. polit. sci. Drake U., Des Moines, Iowa, Md., 1967-70; chmn. interim governing com. Drake U., 1971-72, v.p. acad. adminstrn., 1970-79; pres. Towson (Md.) State U., 1979—; mem. univ. adv. council Life Ins. Council Am., 1969-71. Chmn. exec. com. Coun. Econ. Edn., Md., Towson, 1979—; bd. dirs. Balt. Coun. on Fgn. Rels.; chmn. Very Spl. Arts of Md. With U.S. Army, 1954-56. Recipient Eileen Tosney award Am. Assn. Univ Administrs., 1991; Congl. fellow Am. Polit. Sci. Assn., 1964-65. Mem. Am. Assn. State Colls. and Univs. (bd. dirs. 1984-88, bd. dirs. found., 1985-87, chmn. elect. 1985-86, chmn. 1986-87), Am. Coun. Edn. (bd. dirs., exec. com. 1988-94, chmn. elect 1991-92, chmn. 1992-93, past chmn. 1993-94), Am. Assn. Higher Edn., Soc. for Coll. and Univ. Planning (bd. dirs. 1986-88), Balt. C. of C. (adv. coun.), Renaissance Group (exec. com.), Met. and Urban Colls. and Univs. (co-chair 1996—), St. Petersburg Internat. Consortium of Colls. and Univs. (co-chair 1997), Phi Beta Kappa, Phi Kappa Phi, Omicron Delta Kappa, Delta Sigma Rho, Gamma Gamma, Pi Sigma Alpha. Office: Towson State U Office Pres Baltimore MD 21204

SMITH, HOWARD, film editor. Editor: (films) Live a Little, Steal a Lot, 1975, Mackintosh & T.J., 1975, Tex, 1982, Twilight Zone-The Movie ("Terror at 20,000 Feet"), 1983, (with David Garfield and Suzanne Petit) Sylvester, 1985, (with David Bretherton) Baby-Secret of the Lost Legend, 1985, At Close Range, 1986, Near Dark, 1987, (with Sonya Sones Tramer) River's Edge, 1987, The Abyss, 1989, Big Man on Campus, 1989, (with Joel Goodman and Conrad Buff) After Dark, My Sweet, 1990, Point Break, 1991, Glengarry Glen Ross, 1992, The Saint of Fort Washington, 1993, Two Bits, 1994, (TV movies) Flying Blind, 1990. Office: care Lawrence Mirisch The Mirisch Agency 10100 Santa Monica Blvd Ste 700 Los Angeles CA 90067-4011*

SMITH, H(OWARD) DUANE, zoology educator; b. Fillmore, Utah, June 25, 1941; s. Howard Martell and Mary Ellen (Mitchell) S.; m.. Dahnelle Bower, Dec. 18, 1961; children: Cory, Neichol. BS, Brigham Young U., 1963, MS, 1966; PhD, U. Ill., 1969. From asst. prof. to prof. Brigham Young U., Provo, Utah, 1969—; pvt. practice Orem, Utah, 1973—; dir. Life Sci. Mus. Co-author: Special Publications-Mammalogy, 1994; contbr. articles to profl. jours. Mem. Am. Soc. Mammalogists (sec.-treas. 1987—), Wildlife Soc., Ecol. Soc. Am., Rocky Mountain Elk Found., Sigma Xi (pres. 1996-97). Republican. Mormon. Avocations: hunting, fishing. Office: Brigham Young Univ 290 MLBM Provo UT 84602-1049

SMITH, HOWARD MCQUEEN, librarian; b. Charlotte, N.C., July 25, 1919; s. Daniel Holt and Pearl Elizabeth (Truitt) S.; m. Elaine Betty Wiefel, June 27, 1949; children: Leslie, Steven Holt. B.A., U. Va., 1941; A.B. in L.S, U. Mich., 1946, M. Pub. Adminstrn., 1947. Reference asst. Enoch Pratt Free Library, Balt., 1947-49; coordinator library activities Richmond (Va.) Area Univ. Center, 1949-50; exec. asst. to dir. Enoch Pratt Free Library, 1950-53, head films dept., 1953-55; personnel officer Free Library Phila., 1955-59; city librarian Richmond Pub. Library, 1959-84. Served to lt. (s.g.) USNR, 1942-46. Mem. ALA.

SMITH, HOWARD RUSSELL, manufacturing company executive; b. Clark County, Ohio, Aug. 15, 1914; s. Lewis Hoskins and Eula (Elder) S.; m. Jeanne Rogers, June 27, 1942; children: Stewart Russell, Douglas Howard, Jeanne Ellen Smith James. A.B., Pomona Coll., 1936. Security analyst Kidder, Peabody & Co., N.Y.C., 1936-37; economist ILO, Geneva, 1937-40; asst. to pres. Blue Diamond Corp., Los Angeles, 1940-46; v.p., gen. mgr., dir. Avery Dennison Corp., Pasadena, Calif., 1946-75, chmn. bd., 1975-84, chmn. exec. com., 1984-95; dir. emeritus, 1995—; chmn. bd. Kinsmith Fin. Corp., San Marino, Calif., 1979—. Bd. dirs., past pres., chmn. Los Angeles Philharm. Assn.; chmn. emeritus, bd. trustees Pomona Coll., Claremont, Calif.; past chmn. bd. Children's Hosp. Los Angeles, Community TV of So. Calif. (Sta. KCET), Los Angeles. Lt. USNR, 1943-46. Home: 1458 Hillcrest Ave Pasadena CA 91106-4503 Office: Avery Dennison Corp 150 N Orange Grove Blvd Pasadena CA 91103-3534

SMITH, HOWARD THOMPSON, business executive; b. Camden, Ark., Apr. 30, 1937; s. Howard Thompson and Pauline Virginia (Rogers) S.; m. Ann Monroe; children: Paul R., Elizabeth M. BS, Tulane U., 1960; postgrad. studies, La. State U., 1961-63; EPBA, Columbia U., 1978. Dir. planning Ethyl Corp., Baton Rouge, La., 1970-76; exec. v.p., gen. mgr. William Bonnell Co. subs. Ethyl Corp., Newman, Ga., 1976-81; pres. Steelcraft, Cin., 1981-84; v.p., group exec. Am. Standard, Cin., 1984-89; sr. v.p. Am. Standard, N.Y.C., 1989-94, also bd. dirs., 1989—; pres., CEO The Trane Co., N.Y.C., 1989-94; mng. ptrn. Septa Assocs., 1994—; pres. Thompson Smith Found., 1993—; chmn. bd. dirs. Trinity Mother Francis Health Sys., 1996—, Adobe Air. Bd. dirs. Salvation Army, 1988—, Tex. Rsch. League, Austin, 1989, U. Tex., Tyler, 1990—, Mother Francis Hosp. Found., 1991—; chmn. bd. dirs. East Tex. Communities Found., 1993—; elder, trustee 1st Presbyn. Ch.; trustee U. Tex., Tyler, East Tex. Pres. Found., Union Theol. Sem., 1994—. Mem. Tex. Assn. Taxpayers (dir.), Smith County C. of C. (bd. dirs. 1988-91), Tyler Petroleum Club, Hollytree Country Club, Willowbrook Country Club, Sawgrass Country Club. Republican. Presbyterian. Avocations: golf, tennis. Home: 6110 Covey Ln Tyler TX 75703-4507 Office: The Trane Co PO Box 9010 Tyler TX 75711-9010 also: 819 Spinnakors Reach Ponte Verda FL

SMITH, HOWARD WELLINGTON, education educator, dean; b. Granby, Mo., Jan. 19, 1929; s. Howard W. and Margaret L. (Sanderson) S.; m. Margaret E. Bell, Mar. 1, 1953; 1 child, Christopher Alan. BS, S.W. Mo. State U., 1954; MEd, U. Mo., 1955, EdD, 1959. Tchr. Newton County (Mo.) Pub. Schs., 1948-51; instr. U. Mo., Columbia, 1955-59; asst. prof. So. Meth. U., Dallas, 1959-61; from asst. to full prof. U. North Tex., Denton, 1961-95; assoc. dean Coll. Edn. U. North Tex., 1972-76, assoc. v.p. acad. affairs, 1976-79, v.p. acad. affairs, 1979-82, interim dean, 1994—; interim chancellor U. North Tex. Coll. Osteo. Medicine, Denton and Ft. Worth, 1981; sr. cons. Am. Assn. State Colls. and Univs., Washington, 1982; cons. Srinakharinwirot U., Thailand, 1986, Tex. Internat. Edn. Consortium, Austin, 1992, sr. author Operation Manual Al Akhawayn U., 1993; vis. prof. Shanxi Ednl. Coll. Taiyuan, China, 1993. Contbr. articles to ednl. jours. Prin. investigator Micro Tchg. Lab., 1967-69. With USAF, 1951-53. Democrat. Presbyterian. Avocations: travel, reading. Office: U North Tex Coll Edn Po Box 13857 UNT Denton TX 76203

SMITH, IAN CORMACK PALMER, biophysicist; b. Winnipeg, Man., Can., Sept. 23, 1939; s. Cormack and Grace Mary S.; m. Eva Gunilla Landvik, Mar. 27, 1965; children: Brittmarie, Cormack, Duncan, Roderick. BS, U. Man., 1961, MS, 1962; PhD, Cambridge U., England, 1965; Filosophie Doktor (hon.), U. Stockholm, 1986; DSc (hon.), U. Winnipeg, 1990; Diploma Tech. (hon.), Red River Coll., 1996. Fellow Stanford U., 1965-66; mem. rsch. staff Bell Tel. Labs., Murray Hill, N.J., 1966-67; rsch. officer divsn. biol. scis. NRC, Ottawa, 1967-87, dir. gen., 1987-91; dir.-gen. Inst. Biodiagnostics, Winnipeg, 1992—; adj. prof. chemistry and biochemistry Carleton U., 1973-90, U. Ottawa, 1976-92; adj. prof. chemistry, physics and anatomy U. Man., 1992—; adj. prof. biophysics U. Ill., Chgo., 1974-80; allied scientist Ottawa Civic Hosp., 1985—, Ottawa Gen. Hosp., 1989—, Ont. Cancer Found., 1989-91, St. Boniface Hosp., 1992—, Health Scis. Ctr., 1993—, Econ. Tech. Innovation Coun., Man., 1994—, exec. com., 1995—, Man. Health Rsch. Coun., 1995—, exec. com. 1996—. Contbr. chps. to books, articles in field to profl. jours. Recipient Barringer award Can. Spectroscopy Soc., 1979, Herzberg award, 1986, Organon Teknika award Can. Soc. Clin. Chemists, 1987, Sr. Scientist award Sigma Xi, 1995. Fellow Chem. Inst. Can. (Merck award 1978, Labatt award 1984), Royal Soc. Can. (Flavelle medal 1996), Soc. Magnetic Resonance Medicine (exec. com. 1989-94); mem. Internat. Coun. Sci. Unions (gen. com. 1993—), Am.

Chem. Soc., Biophys. Soc., Can. Biochem. Soc. (Ayerst award 1978), Biophys. Soc. Can. (pres. 1992-94), Internat. Union Pure and Applied Biophysics (coun. 1993—, v.p. 1996—), U. Man. Alumni Assn. (bd. dirs. 1993—). Office: Inst Biodiagnostics, Winnipeg, MB Canada R3B 1Y6

SMITH, ILEENE A., book editor; b. N.Y.C., Jan. 21, 1953; d. Norman and Jeanne (Jaffe) S.; m. Howard A. Sobel, June 3, 1979; children: Nathaniel Jacob, Rebecca Julia. BA, Brandeis U., Waltham, Mass., 1975; MA, Columbia U., 1978. Editorial asst. Atheneum Publishers, N.Y.C., 1979-82; sr. editor Summit Books, N.Y.C., 1982-91, lit. editor, 1991-92; edit. cons. The Elie Wiesel Found. for Humanity, 1993—; editl. cons. Marsalis on Music; cons. editor Paris Rev., N.Y., 1987—. Author introductory scripts for Met. Opera Telecasts, 1987-93. Jerusalem fellow, 1987; recipient Tony Godwin Meml. award, 1982, PEN/Roger Klein award for editl. excellence, 1988, Contbg. to Prodn. of Aida cert. NATAS, 1990.

SMITH, IVAN HURON, architect; b. Danville, Ind., Jan. 25, 1907; s. Calvin Wesley and Irma (Huron) S.; m. Sara Butler, Aug. 18, 1972; 1 child by previous marriage, Norma Smith Benton. Student, Ga. Inst. Tech., 1926; B.Arch., U. Fla., 1929. With Ivan H. Smith (architect), 1936-41; partner Reynolds, Smith & Hills (architects and engrs.), Jacksonville, Fla., 1941-70; chmn. bd. emeritus Reynolds, Smith & Hills (Architects, Engrs., Planners, Inc.), Jacksonville, Tampa, Orlando, Merritt Island and Ft. Lauderdale, Fla., 1971-77; sec. Jacksonville Bldg. Code Adv. Bd., 1951-68; mem. Duval County Govt. Study Commn., 1966-67; chmn. Jacksonville Constrn. Trades Qualification Bd., 1971. Important works include City Hall, Jacksonville, Duval County Ct. House, Jacksonville, Baptist Hosp, Jacksonville, Engring. Bldg, Nuclear Sci. Bldg, Fla. Field Stadium at, U. Fla.; dormitories Council Bldg, Jacksonville U.; fed. bldgs., Jacksonville, Gainesville, Fla., So. Bell Telephone bldgs; Internat. Airport, Tampa, Fla.; (with Edward Durell Stone) Fla. State Capitol Center. Mem. council Jacksonville U., 1958-76; pres. Jacksonville Humane Soc., 1956-59; bd. dirs. Jacksonville-Duval Safety Council. Served with USNR, 1943-45. Recipient U. Fla. Disting. Alumnus award, 1981, Jacksonville U. Order of the Dolphin, 1985; Paul Harris fellow, 1980. Fellow AIA (Outstanding Service award Fla. region 1965, chpt. pres. 1942, 56); mem. Fla. Assn. Architects (dir. 1957, Gold medal 1981), Jacksonville C. of C. (dir. 1957-59), Beta Theta Pi, Phi Kappa Phi, Sigma Tau. Clubs: Gargoyle (U. Fla.); River (Jacksonville), Univ. (Jacksonville), San Jose Country (Jacksonville), Epping Forest Yacht (Jacksonville), Rotary (Jacksonville, Paul Harris fellow 1980). Home: 6000 San Jose Blvd # 201 Jacksonville FL 32217-2381 Office: 4651 Salisbury Rd Jacksonville FL 32256-6107

SMITH, J. KELLUM, JR., foundation executive, lawyer; b. N.Y.C., June 18, 1927; s. James Kellum and Elizabeth Dexter (Walker) S.; m. Sarah Tod Lohmann, July 22, 1950 (div. 1993); children: Alison Andrews, Timothy Kellum, Jennifer Harlow, Christopher Lohmann; m. Angela Marina Brown, Feb. 3, 1995. Grad., Phillips Exeter Acad., 1945; A.B. magna cum laude, Amherst Coll., 1950; LL.B., Harvard, 1953. Bar: N.Y. 1955. Assoc. Lord, Day & Lord, N.Y.C., 1953-59; asst. sec. John Simon Guggenheim Meml. Found., 1960-62; mem. staff Rockefeller Found., 1962-74, asst. sec., 1963-64, sec., 1964-74; v.p., sec. Andrew W. Mellon Found., N.Y.C., 1974-89, sr. fellow, 1989-92; sr. advisor, 1992—. Trustee Nat. Sculpture Soc., 1955-71, Nat. Ins. Archtl. Edn., 1961-69, St. Bernard's Sch., N.Y.C., 1968-78, Found. for Child Devel., 1968-74; trustee Brearley Sch., N.Y.C., 1964-80, pres., 1973-78; trustee Am. Acad. in Rome, 1964-95, treas., 1965-66, 2d v.p., 1968-72, 84-88, sec., 1973-84, 89-95. With USAAF, 1945-46. Mem. Phi Beta Kappa. Club: Century Association (N.Y.C.). Home: 550 Number 37 Rd Saranac NY 12981-2956 Office: Mellon Found 140 E 62nd St New York NY 10021-8142

SMITH, J. ROY, education educator; b. Washington, Ga., Sept. 13, 1936; s. James Roy and Nellie Irene (Mansfield) S. BA, Mercer U., 1956; postgrad., Brown U., 1957; cert., Oxford U., Eng., 1963. Tchr. City of Cranston, R.I., 1957-59; with Charleston County, Charleston, S.C., 1962-64, 76-79; tchr. Fulton County, Fairburn, Ga., 1965-76, Berkeley County, Moncks Corner, S.C., 1979-94. Lt. (j.g.) USN, 1959-62. Charleston Area Writing Project fellow; recipient English Speaking Union scholarship Oxford U., 1963; Newspaper Fund of the Wall Street Jour. fellow. Mem. SAR (sec./treas. S.C. Soc. 1977-78), Soc. Second War with Great Britain, Sons and Daus. of Pilgrims (gov. Ga. br. 1976, hon. gov. 1976—), S.C. Hist. Soc., Ga. Hist. Soc., Kappa Phi Kappa (registered tour guide, lectr.). Home and Office: 110 Coming St Charleston SC 29403-6103

SMITH, JACK, food service executive. Prtn. Smith Realty, Grundy, Va., 1955—; chmn. K-VA-T Food Stores, Grundy, Va. Office: K-VA-T Food Stores 329 N Main St Grundy VA 24614*

SMITH, JACK CARL, foreign trade consultant; b. Cleve., Sept. 11, 1928; s. John Carl and Florence Agnes (O'Rourke) S.; m. Nannette June Boyd, Dec. 1, 1962; 1 dau., Colleen Wentworth. Student, Baldwin Wallace Coll., 1948-51, postgrad., 1958; B.A., Ohio U., 1954. Rep. Flying Tiger Line, Inc., Los Angeles, 1958-61; prin. Pub. Rep. bus., Cleve., 1961-64; pub. Penton Pub., Cleve., 1964-90; sr. fellow Am. Fgn. Policy Coun., Washington, 1990—; dir. Central Cleve. Corp., Nat. Distbn. Terminals; graduated Air Tng. Command Intelligence Officer Sch., served from 1958-62 AFR. Trustee Presdl. task force, Rep. Senatorial Inner Circle, Coun. of Logistics Mgmt., U.S. Bus. and Indsl. Coun. With USAF, 1954-58. Mem. Am. Mgmt. Assn., Material Handling Inst., Am. Trucking Assn., Nat. Council Phys. Distbn. Mgmt., Family Motor Coach Assn., Recreation Vehicle Industry Assn., Am. Bus. Press, Mag. Pubs. Assn., Sci. Research Soc., Internat. Platform Assn., Sigma Xi, Sigma Chi. Club: Wings (N.Y.C.). Home: 457 Devonshire Ct Bay Village OH 44140-3009 Office: Am Fgn Policy Coun 621 Pennsylvania Ave SE Washington DC 20003-4327 *Do your best and God will forgive you the rest.*

SMITH, JACK LEE, bank executive; b. Yale, Okla., Feb. 2, 1948; s. George W. and Alta E. (Tilley) S.; m. Rose Mary Cantrell, Feb. 3, 1968 (div. Feb. 1980); children: Anissa Kay, Melany Elaine; m. Janice A. Houston, Aug. 2, 1981). BS, Okla. State U., 1972. Asst. v.p. Production Credit Assn., 1972-76; v.p., office mgr. Mountain Plains Prodn. Credit Assn., Ft. Collins, 1976-81; dist. mgr. Ralston Purina, St. Louis, 1981-83; 2d v.p. Omaha Nat. Bank, 1983-85; v.p., office mgr. FirsTier Bank, N.A., Omaha, Ft. Collins, 1985-93; mgr. western area agrl. lending FirsTier Bank, N.A., Omaha, Omaha, 1993-96; sr. v.p. agribus. fin. group Farm Credit Svcs., Greeley, Colo., 1996—; bd. dirs. Colo. Cattle Feeders Assn.; chmn. Allied Industry Coun. for Agr. Mem. Am. Bankers Assn., Colo. Bankers Assn., Nat. Cattlemen's Assn., Kans. Livestock Assn., Colo. Cattlemen's Assn., Elks. Republican. Avocations: photography, hiking, fishing, camping. Home: 2613 Jewelstone Ct Fort Collins CO 80525 Office: AgriBusiness Finance Group Farm Credit Svcs 2308 29th St Greeley CO 80631-8514

SMITH, JACK PRESCOTT, journalist; b. Paris, Apr. 25, 1945; s. Howard Kingsbury and Benedicte (Traberg) S.; divorced; 1 child, Alexander Kingsbury. BA in History, Carnegie-Mellon U., 1971, Oxford (Eng.) U., 1974. Writer-producer Sta. WIIC-TV News, Pitts., 1969-70; producer-reporter Sta. WLS-TV News, Chgo., 1974-76; fgn. corr. ABC-TV News, Paris, 1976-80; corr. ABC-TV News, Washington, 1980—. Served with inf. U.S. Army, 1964-67. Decorated Purple Heart, bronze star, Army Commendation medal; recipient citation for best mag. reporting in fgn. affairs Overseas Press Club, 1967. Office: ABC News 1717 Desales St NW Washington DC 20036-4401

SMITH, JACKIE, former professional football player. Student, Northwestern Louisiana State U. With St. Louis Cardinals, 1963-77, Dallas Cowboys, 1978. NFL Hall of Fame, 1994. Retired as the leading receiver among tightends. Office: care Pro Football Hall of Fame 2121 George Halas Dr NW Canton OH 44708-2630*

SMITH, JAMES A., lawyer; b. Akron, Ohio, June 11, 1930; s. Barton H. and Myrna S. (Young) S.; m. Melda I. Perry, Jan. 17, 1959; children: Hugh, Sarah Louise. AB, Western Res. U., 1952; postgrad., Columbia U., 1954-56, LLB, 1961; postgrad., Yale U., 1956-58. Bar: Ohio 1961, U.S. Dist. Ct. (no. dist.) Ohio 1963, U.S. Ct. Appeals (6th cir.) 1973, U.S. Supreme Ct. 1974, U.S. Ct. Appeals (11th cir.) 1983, U.S. Ct. Appeals (D.C. cir.) 1984. Assoc. Squire, Sanders and Dempsey, Cleve., 1961-70, ptnr., 1970-91, counsel, 1991-96; mem. spl. adv. com. Nat. Conf. Commrs. on Uniform State Laws, 1972-74. Trustee Chagrin Falls Community Park, 1968-78, Greater Cleve. Neighborhood Ctrs. Assn., 1973-78, Legal Aid Soc. Cleve., 1977-80, Cleve. Inst. Music, 1994—; mem. Charter Rev. Commn., Chagrin Falls, 1966. Lt. (j.g.) USNR, 1952-54. Fellow Am. Coll. Trial Lawyers; mem. ABA, Ohio Bar Assn., Cleve. Bar Assn. (trustee 1988-92), U.S. Ct. Appeals for 6th Cir. Jud. Conf. (life), Ohio Ct. Appeals for 8th Jud. Dist. Conf. (life), Am. Inns of Ct. (master of bench), Ct. of Nisi Prius (clk. 1975-76, judge 1994-95), Phi Beta Kappa, Omicron Delta Kappa, Delta Sigma Rho. Democrat.

SMITH, JAMES ALBERT, lawyer; b. Jackson, Mich., May 12, 1942; s. J. William and Mary Barbara (Browning) S.; m. Lucia S. Santini, Aug. 14, 1965; children: Matthew Browning, Aaron Michael, Rachel Elizabeth. BA, U. Mich., 1964, JD, 1967. Bar: Mich. 1968, U.S. Dist. Ct. (ea. dist.) Mich., U.S. Ct. Appeals (6th and D.C. cirs.), U.S. Supreme Ct. Assoc. Bodman, Longley & Dahling, Detroit, 1967-75, ptnr., 1975—; mem. panel Atty. Discipline Bd., Wayne County, Mich., 1987—; arbitrator Am. Arbitration Assn., 1975—; mem. Banking Commrs. com. on Contested Case Adminstrn., 1978. Mem. pro bono referral group Call For Action, Detroit, 1982—. Mem. ABA, State Bar Mich., Detroit Bar Assn., Detroit Athletic Club, Grosse Pointe Sail Club. Roman Catholic. Avocations: sailing, travel. Office: Bodman Longley & Dahling 100 Renaissance Ctr Ste 34 Detroit MI 48243-1003

SMITH, JAMES ALMER, JR., psychiatrist; b. Montclair, N.J., May 30, 1923; s. James Almer and Carrie Elizabeth (Moten) S.; m. Elsie Mae Brooks; children: James III, Roger, Margo, Melanie. BS, Howard U., 1947, MD, 1948. Diplomate Am. Bd. Psychiatry and Neurology. Staff psychiatrist Hartley Salmon Child Guidance Ctr., Hartford, Conn., 1955-60; assoc. psychiatrist Child Guidance Clinic Springfield (Mass.), 1960-83; cons. psychiatrist Gandara Mental Health Ctr., Springfield, 1984—; med. dir. Kolburne Sch., New Marlborough, Mass., 1969—; bd. dirs. Hampden Mental Health Dist., Springfield, 1968—; cons. psychiatrist Childrens' Services Hartford, 1956-60, Childrens' Study Ctr., Springfield, 1960—, W.W. Johnson Ctr., Springfield, 1979—. Bd. dirs. Springfield Commn. on Human Relations, 1961-62, Negro Cath. Scholarship Fund of Springfield, 1976—. Served to capt. M.C., U.S. Army, 1953-55. Recipient Dr. Anthony Brown award W. W. Johnson Ctr., 1987. Fellow Am. Orthopsychiat. Assn., Am. Assn. Psychoanalytic Physicians (pres. 1979-81), Soc. Psychoanalytic Physicians; mem. Am. Psychiat. Assn., Am. Soc. Psychoanalytic Physicians, Sigma Pi Phi. Baptist. Club: Squires of Springfield (pres. 1980-81). Home and Office: 96 Dartmouth St Springfield MA 01109-3909

SMITH, JAMES BARRY, lawyer; b. N.Y.C., Feb. 28, 1947; s. Irving and Vera (Donaghy) S.; m. Kathleen O'Connor, May 28, 1977; childen: Jennifer, Kelly. BA in Econs., Colgate U., 1968; JD, Boston U., 1974. Assoc. McDermott, Will & Emery, Chgo., 1974-78; assoc. Ungaretti & Harris, Chgo., 1978-80, ptnr., 1980O, head real estate dept., 1988O. Lt. U.S. Navy, 1968-70. Mem. Chgo. Bar Assn., Chgo. Mortgage Atty. Assn. Avocations: sports, reading, travel. Office: Ungaretti & Harris 3500 Three First Nat Pla Chicago IL 60602

SMITH, JAMES BROWN, JR., secondary school educator; b. Greenville, N.C., Apr. 6, 1943; s. James Brown Sr. and Clara Lucille (Avery) S.; m. Donna Drake, Aug. 12, 1967; children: Caryn Frances, James Brown III, Sarah Elizabeth. BS, East Carolina U., 1966; MEd, Va. State U., 1976. Cert. tchr., postgrad. prof., Va. Tchr. Great Bridge Jr. High Sch., Chesapeake, Va., 1966-68, Queen's Lake Sch., York County, Va., 1968-76, Bruton High Sch., York County, 1976—; cons. Acad. Tech, Hampton, Va., 1992-93; tchr. intern Va. Peninsula C. of C., Hampton, 1992. Mem. York County Edn. Assn., Va. Edn. Assn., NEA, Va. Vocat. Assn., Am. Vocat. Assn., Kiwanis (bd. dirs. 1984-92). Methodist. Avocations: photography, gardening, auto repair, fishing. Home: 135 John Pott Dr Williamsburg VA 23188-6328 Office: Bruton High Sch 185 Rochambeau Dr Williamsburg VA 23188-2121

SMITH, JAMES EARLIE, JR., accountant; b. Petersburg, Va., Nov. 25, 1945; s. Dorothy Mae (Brown) Crews; m. Sandra Kim Oh, Mar. 23, 1967 (div. 1981); children: Ricky Young Smith; m. Joanne Hamlin, May 17, 1986. BS in Acctg., BS in Fin., Kans. State U., 1985. Enlisted U.S. Army, 1964, advanced through grades to Master Sgt., 1983, retired, 1984; asst. bank examiner Fed. Deposit Ins. Corp., San Francisco, 1986-92; regional rep. Grant Thornton CPA Inc., San Antonio, 1992; loan acctg. officer Broadway Nat. Bank, San Antonio, 1992-93; staff acct. USAA Fed. Savs. Bank, San Antonio, 1993; chief internal control and analysis Def. Acctg. Office, Ft. Polk, La., 1993; rsch. acct. Grant Thornton CPA Inc., San Antonio, 1993-94; pres., CEO Smith Fin. Instn. Svcs., Universal City, Tex., 1995—. Author: Finance Procedures Handbook for Military Leaders, 1983. Mem. San Antonio Choral Soc., 1993—. Decorated Army Meritorious Svc. medal with 1st oak leaf cluster. Mem. Inst. Mgmt. Accts., San Antonio Area Bankers Compliance Assn., Greater San Antonio C. of C., Black Profl. Leadership Network, San Antonio Choral Soc. (bd. dirs. 1995—), Phi Beta Sigma. United Methodist. Avocations: weightlifting, traveling, theater, opera, music. Home and Office: 13438 Forum Rd Universal City TX 78148-2801

SMITH, JAMES EDWARD, newspaper company executive; b. N.Y.C., June 26, 1945; s. James Edward and Loretta Anne (Johnston) S.; m. Beverly Lynn Jermyn, Feb. 23, 1980; children: Allison Bridget, Cori Patricia. BA, State U. N.Y., 1969; MA, Cornell U., 1973, PhD, 1976. Asst. prof. Sociology, U. Miami, Coral Gables, Fla., 1973-80; research mgr. News & Sun-Sentinel Co., Ft. Lauderdale, Fla., 1980—; v.p. mktg., v.p./dir. mktg. and promotion Ft. Lauderdale Sun Sentinel, 1991—; bd. dirs. Newspaper Research Council Des Moines. Contbr. articles to profl. jours. Mem. Syndicated Research Task Force, N.Y.C., 1987--, Future Advt. Task Force on Mktg. Data, N.Y.C., 1986-87; pres. Econ. Forum Broward, 1982-85; research chmn. Broward Tourist Devel. Council, 1984-; research cons. Discovery Ctr., Ft. Lauderdale, 1988. Recipient Gavel award Am. Bar Assn., 1981. Mem. Leadership Broward (Best Group 1986), Leadership Broward Alumni. Home: 9321 NW 10th Ct Fort Lauderdale FL 33322-4929 Office: News & Sun-Sentinel Co 200 E Las Olas Blvd Fort Lauderdale FL 33301-2248*

SMITH, J(AMES) E(VERETT) KEITH, psychologist, educator; b. Royal, Iowa, Apr. 30, 1928; s. James H. and Naomi Dorothy (James) S.; m. Greta Standish, Sept. 10, 1949. B.S. in Math, Iowa State U., 1949; A.M. in Psychology, U. Mich., 1952, Ph.D., 1954. Staff psychologist Mass. Inst. Tech., Lincoln Lab., Cambridge, Mass., 1954-64; research psychologist Mental Health Research Inst., Ann Arbor, Mich., 1964-67; prof. psychology U. Mich., Ann Arbor, 1964-96; prof. statistics U. Mich., 1977-96, chmn. dept. psychology, 1971-76, prof. emeritus, 1996—; lectr. Brandeis U., 1960. Cons. editor Psychol. Bull., 1967-70; editor Jour. Math. Psychology, 1971-74. Mem. Commn. on Human Factors, NRC, 1980-82. hon. Research fellow Univ. Coll., London, 1972; mem. rev. panels NSF, 1972-74, Nat. Inst. Gen. Med. Sci., 1967-71; vis. scholar Beijing U., 1985; chmn. spl. study sect. NIH, 1985. Fellow Am. Psychol. Assn.; mem. Am. Statis. Assn., Psychometric Soc., Inst. Math. Statis., Sigma Xi, Phi Kappa Phi, Pi Mu Epsilon, Delta Upsilon. Home: 1160 Heatherway St Ann Arbor MI 48104-2838

SMITH, JAMES FREDERICK, securities executive; b. N.Y.C., Jan. 6, 1944; s. James Arthur and Agnes Rose (Kollenz) S.; m. Joan Ann Kelly, June 18, 1966; children: James Patrick, John Michael. BBA in Accountancy Practice, Pace U., 1970. CPA, N.Y.; registered fin. & operational prin., registered rep. Mgmt. trainee Chase Manhattan Bank, N.Y.C., 1965-67; internal auditor MW Kellogg & Co., N.Y.C., 1967-69; sr. acct. Price Waterhouse, N.Y.C., 1969-72; asst. treas. and contr. Henderson Bros. Inc., N.Y.C., 1972-80; pvt. practice Clearwater, Fla., 1980-82; sr. audit mgr. Price Waterhouse, N.Y.C., 1982-84; v.p. & contr. Integrated Resources, N.Y.C., 1984-86; pres., CFO, Freeman Securities, Jersey City, 1986—; pres., dir. First Summit Capital Mgmt., 1994—; dir. Summit High Yield Bond Fund. With USN, 1961-65. Mem. AICPA, Internat. Soc. CEBS (charter mem.), N.Y. State Soc. CPA, Securities Industry Assn., Pub. Securities Assn., Wall St. Tax Assn. Avocation: carpentry. Home: 3 Greenfield Ter Congers NY 10920-2606 Office: Freeman Securities 30 Montgomery St Jersey City NJ 07302-3821 also: 1st Summit Capital Mgmt 8044 Montgomery Rd Cincinnati OH 45236-2919

SMITH, JAMES GILBERT, electrical engineer; b. Benton, Ill., May 1, 1930; s. Jesse and Ruby Frances S.; m. Barbara Ann Smothers, July 29, 1955; 1 child, Julie. B.S. in Elec. Engring, U. Mo., Rolla, 1957, M.S., 1959, Ph.D., 1967. Instr., then asst. prof. U. Mo., Rolla, 1958-66; mem. faculty So. Ill. U., Carbondale, 1966-93, prof. elec. engring., 1972-93, chmn. dept. elec. scis. and systems engring., 1971-80, prof. emeritus, 1993—. Served with AUS, 1951-53, Korea. Decorated Bronze Star. Faculty fellow NSF, 1961. Mem. Rotary (Paul Harris fellow 1988). Office: So Ill U Coll Engring Carbondale IL 62901-6603

SMITH, JAMES JOHN, physiologist; b. St. Paul, Jan. 28, 1914; s. James W. and Catherine (Welsch) S.; m. Mariellen Schumacher, Mar. 17, 1945 (dec.); children: Philip W., Lucy S. Shaker, Paul R., Gregory K. M.D., St. Louis U., 1937; Ph.D., Northwestern U., 1946. Intern St. Paul-Ramsey Med. Ctr., 1937-38; fellow in pathology Cook County Hosp., Chgo., 1938-39; Koesler research fellow in physiology Northwestern U., Chgo., 1939-41; dean Stritch Sch. Med., Loyola U., 1946-50, assoc. prof. physiology, 1946-50; chief edn. div., dept. medicine and surgery VA, 1950-52; prof., dir. dept. physiology Med. Coll. Wis., Milw., 1952-79; prof. physiology and medicine Med. Coll. Wis., 1979—; dir. human performance lab. and dep. dir. Cardiopulmonary Rehab. Ctr. VA Med. Ctr., Milw., 1978-90; assoc. clin. prof. George Washington U. 1950-52 Fulbright research prof. U. Heidelberg, Physiology Inst., Germany, 1959-60; medico-legal cons. on retirement policy for high stress professions. Author textbooks on circulatory physiology, numerous articles in field. Decorated Legion of Merit; recipient Disting. Service award Med. Coll. Wis., 1982. Mem. Soc. Exptl. Biology, Am. Physiol. Soc., Am. Gerontol. Assn., Sigma Xi. Roman Catholic. Researcher in aviation medicine, U.S. Air Force, 1941-46. Home: 11050 W Maple Ln Milwaukee WI 53225-4428 Office: 8701 W Watertown Plank Rd Milwaukee WI 53226-3548

SMITH, JAMES LAWRENCE, research physicist; b. Detroit, Sept. 3, 1943; s. William Leo and Marjorie Marie (Underwood) S.; m. Carol Ann Adam, Mar. 27, 1965; children: David Adam, William Leo. BS, Wayne State U., 1965; PhD, Brown U., 1974. Mem. staff Los Alamos (N.Mex.) Nat. Lab., 1973-82, fellow, 1982-86, dir. ctr. materials sci., 1986-87, fellow, 1987—; chief scientist Superconductivity Tech. Ctr., 1988—; co-editor N.Am. Philos. Mag., 1990-95; editor Philos. Mag. B, 1995—. Contbr. articles to profl. jours. Recipient E.O. Lawrence award, 1986, Disting. Alumni award Wayne State U., 1993. Fellow Am. Phys. Soc. (internat. prize for new materials 1990); mem. AAAS, Materials Rsch. Soc., Minerals Metals Materials Soc., Am. Crystallographic Assn. Achievements include patents for design of magnetic field and high-strength conductors. Office: Los Alamos Nat Lab Superconductivity Tech Ctr Mail Stop K763 Los Alamos NM 87545

SMITH, JAMES LOUIS, III, lawyer; b. Fort Worth, Tex., Mar. 21, 1943; s. James Louis Jr. and Ellen Vickers (Smedley) S.; m. Jane Benton, Mar. 25, 1965 (div. Oct. 1982); children: Rebecca, Sarah; m. Sandra Howell, Dec. 29, 1984; stepchildren: Kristen, Mason. BA cum laude with distinction, Dartmouth Coll., 1965; JD, Duke U., 1968. Bar: Ga. Assoc. Sutherland, Asbill & Brennan, Atlanta, 1968-74, ptnr., 1974-82; shareholder Trotter Smith & Jacobs, Atlanta, 1983-92; ptnr. Troutman Sanders, Atlanta, 1992—. Contbr. articles profl. jours.; mng. editor Duke Law Jour. Chmn. legal divsn. United Way, 1989, fundraiser, mem. allocation com. homeless and hungry, 1991, 92; co-chmn. pledge fulfillment com. YES! Atlanta Coun., 1991-92; mem. adv. com. Atlanta Vols. Lawyers Found.; mem. Assn. Corp. Growth, Northwest Presbyn. Ch. Mem. ABA (fed. securities law com. 1933 act registration statements subcom., ptnrships and unicorp. bus. orgns. com. bus. law sect.), State Bar Ga. (chmn. corp. and banking law sect. 1979, chmn. gen. ptnrship and limited ptnrship law revision coms. corp. sect. 1982-91, chmn. subcom. Ga. bus. corp. code rev. com. 1987-89, exec. com. corp. and banking law sect. 1982-91, lectr. ann. corp. and banking law inst. 1983, 87-88, 90-91, 93), Atlanta Bar (lectr. ann. corp. bus. seminar 1983, 88, advanced securities seminar 1989, 94), Practicing Law Inst. (lectr. securities filings 1994-95), Order of Coif. Presbyterian. Avocations: canoeing, hiking, tennis, jogging, travel. Office: Troutman Sanders 600 Peachtree St NE Atlanta GA 30308-2214

SMITH, JAMES MORTON, museum administrator, historian; b. Bernie, Mo., May 28, 1919; BEd, So. Ill. U., 1941; MA, U. Okla., 1946; PhD, Cornell U., 1951; DHL (hon.), Widener U., 1984; m. Kathryn Hegler, Jan. 5, 1945; children: Melisa Jane, James Morton. Editor, Inst. Early Am. History and Culture, Williamsburg, Va., 1955-66; prof. history Cornell U., Ithaca, N.Y., 1966-70, U. Del., Newark, 1976-90; dir. State Hist. Soc. Wis., Madison, 1970-76, Henry Francis DuPont Winterthur (Del.) Mus., 1976-84. Lt. USCGR, 1943-45. Mem. Assn. Art Mus. Dirs., Am. Assn. Museums, Am. Hist. Assn., Orgn. Am. Historians, Am. Assn. State and Local History, Soc. Historians of Early Am. Republic. Author: Freedom's Fetters, 1956, Liberty and Justice, 1958, Seventeenth-Century America, 1959, George Washington: A Profile, 1969, The Constitution, 1971, Politics and Society in American History, 1973, The Republic of Letters, 1995. Home: 120 Sharpless Dr Elkton MD 21921-2073

SMITH, JAMES OSCAR (JIMMY SMITH), jazz organist; b. Norristown, Pa., Dec. 8, 1928; s. James and Grace Elizabeth (Weldon) S.; m. Edna Joy Goins, Mar. 31, 1957; children: James Oscar, Jia Charlene. Student, Ornstein Sch. Music, Phila., 1946-49. Jazz organist, 1951—; owner, dir. Edmy Music Pub. Co., 1962—, Trieste Builders Co., 1962—, Jay Cec Corp., 1962—; appeared at Antibes (Frances) Jazz Festival, 1962, Complain-de-Tour Jazz Festival, Belgium, 1963. composer, performer background music film Where the Spies Are, 1965; composer music film La Metamorphose de Clopertes, 1965; performed with Art Blakey, Stanley Turrentine, Jackie McLean, Hank Mobley, others; composer numerous organ pieces; compiler organ books; numerous recordings including The Sermon, A Walk on the Wild Side, Got My Mojo Working, Slaughter On Tenth Avenue, Bluesette, House Party, 1985, Plays the Blues, 1988, Midnight Special, 1989, Best Of, 1991, Fourmost, 1991, Sum Serious Blues, 1993. Recipient downbeat Mag's. Reader and Critics award, 1962, 63, 64; also downbeat Mag's. Reader's Poll, 1989. Mem. Broadcast Music Inc., AFTRA, NAACP, Nat. Acad. Recording Arts and Scis. Lodge: Masons. Office: care Fantasy Inc 10th & Parker Berkeley CA 94710 Office: care CEMA 1750 Vine St Los Angeles CA 90028-5209*

SMITH, JAMES PATRICK, economist; b. Bklyn., Aug. 3, 1943; s. James P. and Winefred (Harrison) S.; m. Sandra Berry, Oct. 25, 1983; children: Gillian Clare, Lauren Teresa. B.S., Fordham U., 1965; Ph.D., U. Chgo., 1972. Rsch. assoc. Nat. Bur. Econ. Rsch., N.Y.C., 1972-74; sr. economist Rand Corp., Santa Monica, Calif., 1974—, dir. of research labor and population, 1977-93 . bd. mem. Occupl. Safety and Health Standards State Calif. Editor: Female Labor Supply, 1980; bd. editors Am. Econ. Rev., 1980-83; author articles in field. Recipient Merit award NIH, 1995—. Mem. NIA (steering com., health and retirement survey); chair NAS panel on immigration. Mem. Am. Econ. Assn., Phi Beta Kappa. Office: RAND PO Box 2138 Santa Monica CA 90407-2138

SMITH, JAMES ROLAND, state legislator; b. Aiken, S.C., Feb. 26, 1933; s. Walter Daniel and Maebell Smith; m. Peggy Cato, Mar. 3, 1953; children: Garry R., Todd D., Caroline M. Student, Oral Roberts Univ., U. S.C., So. Meth. U.; DDiv, Universal Bible Inst., 1975. Rural postal carrier U.S. Postal Svc., Warrenville, S.C., 1969-88; min. Aiken, S.C., 1965—; legislator S.C. Ho. of Reps., Columbia, 1989—; mem. Ho. Ways & Means Com., Edn. Subcom. Commr. Beech Island (S.C.) Rural Water Dist., 1973-83; bd. dirs. Aiken County Bd. Edn., 1983-88. Mem. Am. Legion (post 153), Midland Valley C. of C., Midland Valley Lions Club, Graniteville (S.C.) Exch. Club, Beech Island Agriculture Club, Jackson Agriculture Club. Republican. Avocation: family. Home: 183 Edgar St Warrenville SC 29851 Office: SC Ho of Reps 416 Blatt Bldg Columbia SC 29210-4620

SMITH, JAMES STEPHEN, hockey player; b. Glasgow, Scotland, Apr. 30, 1963. Hockey player Edmonton Oilers Nat. Hockey League, 1985-91, hockey player Chgo. Blackhawks, 1991—; played in All-Star Game, 1991;

mem. Stanley Cup Championship team 1987, 88, 90. Office: Chgo Blackhawks 1901 W Madison St Chicago IL 60612-2459

SMITH, JAMES TODD See LL COOL J

SMITH, JAMES W., JR., judge; b. Louisville, Miss., Oct. 28, 1943. BS, U. So. Miss., 1965; JD, Jackson Sch. Law, 1972; MEd with honors, Miss. Coll., 1973. Bar: Miss. 1972, U.S. Dist. Ct. (no. and so. dists.) Miss. 1973, U.S. Ct. Appeals (5th cir.) 1974. Pvt. practice Pearl, 1972-78, Brandon, 1979-80; prosecuting atty. City of Pearl, 1973-80; dist. atty. 20th Jud. Dist., 1977-82; judge Rankin County, 1982-92; Supreme Ct. justice Cen. Dist., 1993—; instr. courtroom procedure and testifying Miss. Law Enforcement Tng. Acad., 1980-91. With U.S. Army, 1966-69. Named Wildlife Conservationist of Yr. Rankin County, 1988; recipient Outstanding Positive Role Model for Today's Youth award, 1991, Child Forever award Miss. Voices of Children and Youth, 1992, You've Made a Difference award, 1995, Alumnus of Yr. award Hinds C.C., 1996. Mem. VFW, Miss. State Bar Assn., Rankin County Bar Assn., Nat. Wildlife Fedn., Nat. Wild Turkey Fedn., Jackson Downtown Rotary Club. Office: Carroll Gartin Justice Bldg PO Box 117 Jackson MS 39201

SMITH, JAMES WALKER, lawyer; b. S.I., N.Y., May 11, 1957; s. James Patrick and Ann Catherine (Sullivan) S.; m. Erin Patricia Murphy, Aug. 15, 1982; children: Patrick James, Daniel Timothy, Meghan Kathleen, James John. BA magna cum laude, Fordham U., 1979, JD, 1982; LLM, NYU, 1988. BAr: N.Y. 1983, N.J. 1984, Pa. 1993, U.S. Supreme Ct. 1994. Assoc. Mendes & Mount, N.Y.C., 1982, Costello Shea & Gaffney, N.Y.C., 1982-86; ptnr. Anderson Kill Olick & Oshinsky P.C., N.Y.C., 1986-96, Smith Abbot, LLP, N.Y.C., 1996—; arbitrator N.Y.C. (N.Y.) Civil Ct., 1987-89; faculty chairperson hosp. law Fordham Law Sch., N.Y.C., 1989-93; mediator U.S. Dist. Ct. (so. dist.) N.Y., N.Y.C., 1992—. Author: Hospital Liability, 1985—; editor-in-chief: New York Practice Guide, 1993—; contbg. editor: Medical Malpractice Law and Strategy, 1993—; bd. editors Fordham Urban Law Jour., 1981-82. Mem. N.Y. County Lawyer's Assn. (com. on tort law 1993-95), Assn. of the Bar of the City of N.Y. (com. on tort law 1990-92, com. on state cts. 1994—). Roman Catholic. Avocations: golf, coaching youth basketball. Home: 28 Rokeby Pl Staten Island NY 10310 Office: Smith Abbot LLP Oshinsky 100 Maiden Ln New York NY 10038-4818

SMITH, JAMES WARREN, pathologist, microbiologist, parasitologist; b. Logan, Utah, July 5, 1934; s. Kenneth Warren and Nina Lou (Sykes) S.; m. Nancy Chesterman, July 19, 1958; children: Warren, Scott. BS, U. Iowa, 1956, MD, 1959. Diplomate Am. Bd. Pathology. Intern, Colo. Gen. Hosp., Denver, 1959-60; resident U. Iowa Hosps., Iowa City, 1960-65; asst. prof. pathology U. Vt., Burlington, 1967-70; prof. pathology Ind. U., Indpls., 1970—, chmn. dept. pathology and lab. med., 1992—. Contbr. articles to profl. jours. Served to lt. comdr. USN, 1965-67. Recipient Oustanding Contbrn. to Clin. Microbiology award South Central Assn. Clin. Microbiology, 1977. Fellow Coll. Am. Pathologists (chmn. microbiology resource com. 1981-85), Infectious Disease Soc. Am., Am. Soc. Investigative Pathology, Royal Soc. Tropical Medicine and Hygiene, AMA, Am. Soc. Clin. Pathology, Am. Soc. Microbiology, Am. Soc. Tropical Medicine and Hygiene, U.S.-Can. Acad. Pathology, Assn. Pathology Chairs, Binford Dammin Soc. Infectious Disease Pathologists. Soc. Protozoologists Office: Ind Univ Med Ctr 635 Barnhill Dr Rm 128A Indianapolis IN 46202-5126

SMITH, JANE FARWELL, civic worker; b. Chgo.; d. John Charles and Jessie Greene (Delaware) Farwell; m. Wakelee R. Smith, Feb. 7, 1929; children—Diana Jane Smith Gauss, Carol Louise Smith, Anderson. Student, U. Chgo., 1925-28. Pres. Infant Soc. Chgo., Beverly Hills (Ill.) Center, 1949; chmn. Am. heritage com. DAR, Ill., 1963-65; Am. heritage com. nat. vice chmn. DAR, 1965-68, Insignia chmn., Ill., 1966, Ill. treas., 1966-68, mem. nat. Americanism and manual for citizenship com., 1968, Ill. regent, 1969-71; mem. U.S.A. Bicentennial Commn., DAR, 1971-74; nat. corr. sec. gen. DAR, 1971-74, 1st. v.p. gen., 1974-75, pres. gen., 1975-77, hon. life pres. gen., 1977-81, mem. long range planning commn., 1988-93; trustee U.S. Capitol Hist. Soc., 1976-82; pres. 4th Div. Ex-Regents Club, 1981-82. Mem. Kate Duncan Sch. Bd., Grant, Ala., 1975-86, Tamassee Sch. Bd., Tamassee, S.C., 1975-77. Recipient Gold medal of appreciation Ill. chpt. S.A.R., 1970, resolution of congratulation Senate of 80th Assembly of State of Ill., 1977. Mem. Nat. Gavel Soc. (life), DAR (pres. exec. club 1983-85, pres. nat. officers' club 1986-88), DAR Museum (life), Daus. Colonial Wars, Nat. Soc. New Eng. Women, Alden Kindred Am., Colonial Dames Am., Daus. Am. Colonists, Daus. Founders and Patriots, Nat. Soc. Women Desc. Ancient and Hon. Arty. Co., Am. Nat. Soc. Old Plymouth Colony Descs., Soc. Mayflower Descs., Colonial Daus. 17th Century, Hereditary Order of First Families of Mass., Colonial Wars Nat. Soc., New. Eng. Women. Episcopalian. Home: 851 W Heather Ln Milwaukee WI 53217-2107

SMITH, JANE WARDELL, historian, philanthropist, entrepreneur; b. Detroit, Aug. 9, 1943; d. John Slater and Lucille Maude (Hoskins) Beck; m. marshall Smith, Oct. 31, 1964 (div. 1972); children: Aaron Wardell, Gerald Allen. Student, Detroit Bus. Coll., Cass Sch. Tech. Exec. sec. Wayne County Cir. Ct. 7th Dist., 1968-72, Wayne County Friend of Ct., Detroit, 1968-72; with exec. mgmt. City Detroit Pers. Dept., 1972-79; fin. analyst City of Detroit, 1979-82, Merlite Industries, N.Y.C., 1994—; salesperson Mason Shoe Co., Chippewa Falls, 1968-72; fin. analyst A. J. Valenci, Salem, W.Va., 1968-72; examiner Mich. State Dept., Detroit, 1972-79. Critic various consumer groups. Vol. Richard Austin polit. campaign, Grand River, Mich., 1975, John Conters polit. campaign, Livernois, Mich., 1980; with Mayor's Com. for Human Resources, Detroit, 1979; active local drama and theater clubs, Detroit, 1980—, local Bapt. Ch., 1984—. Recipient numerous awards, honors and achievements. Democrat. Avocations: swimming, bicycling, tennis, dance, roller skating.

SMITH, JANET MARIE, professional sports team executive; b. Jackson, Miss., Dec. 13, 1957; d. Thomas Henry and Nellie Brown (Smith) S. BArch, Miss. State U., 1981; MA in Urban Planning, CCNY, 1984. Draftsman Thomas H. Smith and Assocs. Architects, Jackson, 1979; mktg. coord. The Eggers Group, P.C. Architects and Planners, N.Y.C., 1980; program assoc. Ptnrs. for Livable Places, Washington, 1980-82; coord. asst. Lance Jay Brown, Architect and Urban Planner, N.Y.C., 1983-84; coord. architecture and design Battery Park City Authority, N.Y.C., 1982-84; pres., chief exec. officer Pershing Sq. Mgmt. Assn., L.A., 1985-89; v.p. stadium planning and devel. Balt. Orioles Oriole Park at Camden Yard, 1989-94; v.p. sports facilities Turner Properties, Atlanta, 1994-97; v.p. planning and devel. Atlanta Braves, Braves, 1994—; pres. TBS Sports Devel., Inc., 1997—; bd. dirs. Assn. Collegiate Schs. Architecture, Washington, 1979-82, Assn. Student Chpts. AIA, Washington, 1979-82. Guest editor: Urban Design Internat., 1985; assoc. editor: Crit, 1979-82; contbr. articles to profl. jours. Named Disting. Grad., Nat. Assn. State Univs. and Land Grant Colls., 1988, One of Outstanding Young Women of Am., 1982; recipient Spirit of Miss. award, Sta. WLBT, Jackson, 1987. Mem. AIA (assoc.), Urban Land Inst. Democrat. Episcopalian. Office: Turner Sports Devel Inc 1 Cnn Ctr NW Ste 275 Atlanta GA 30303-2705

SMITH, JEAN KENNEDY, ambassador; b. Brookline, Mass., Feb. 20, 1928; d. Joseph P. and Rose Kennedy; m. Stephen E. Smith (dec.); 4 children. BA, Manhattanville Coll. Founder, dir., chair Very Spl. Arts, 1974—; amb. to Ireland Dublin, 1993—. Author: (with George Plimpton) Chronicles of Courage, 1993; contbr. articles on the disabled to profl. jours. Trustee Joseph P. Kennedy, Jr. Found., 1964—, John F. Kennedy Ctr. Performing Arts. Recipient Sec.'s award Dept. Vets. Affairs, Vol. of Yr. award People-to-People Com. Handicapped, Margaret Mead Humanitarian award Coun. Cerebral Palsy Auxs., Jefferson award Am. Inst. Pub. Svc., Spirit of Achievement award Yeshiva U., Humanitarian award Capital Children's Mus. Address: Am Embassy, 42 Elgin Rd, Ballsbridge Dublin Ireland*

SMITH, JEAN WEBB (MRS. WILLIAM FRENCH SMITH), civic worker; b. L.A.; d. James Ellwood and Violet (Hughes) Webb; B.A. summa cum laude, Stanford U., 1940; m. George William Vaughan, Mar. 14, 1942 (dec. Sept. 1963); children: George William, Merry; m. William French Smith, Nov. 6, 1964. Mem. Nat. Vol. Svc. Adv. Coun. (ACTION), 1973-76, vice chmn., 1974-76; dir. Beneficial Standard Corp., 1976-85. bd. dirs. Cmty. TV So. Calif., 1979-93; mem. Calif. Arts Commn., 1971-74, vice chmn., 1973-74; bd. dirs. The Founders, Music Ctr., L.A., 1971-74; bd. dirs. costume coun. L.A. County Mus. Art, 1971-73; bd. dirs. United Way, Inc., 1973-80, Hosp. Good Samaritan, 1973-80, L.A. chpt. NCCJ, 1977-80, Nat. Symphony Orch., 1980-85, L.A. World Affairs Coun., 1990, L.A. chpt. ARC, 1994-95; bd. fellows Claremont Univ. Ctr. and Grad. Sch., 1987—; bd. dirs. Hosp. Good Samaritan, 1973-80; mem. exec. com., 1975-80; mem. nat. bd. dirs. Boys' Clubs Am., 1977-80; mem. adv. bd. Salvation Army, 1979—; bd. overseers The Hoover Instn. on War, Revolution and Peace, 1989-94; mem. President's Commn. on White House Fellowships, 1980-90, Nat. Coun. on the Humanities, 1987-90; bd. govs. Calif. Cmty. Found., 1990—; bd. regents Children's Hosp. L.A., 1993—. Named Woman of Yr. for cmty. svc. L.A. Times, 1958; recipient Citizens of Yr. award Boys Clubs Greater L.A., 1982, Life Achievement award Boy Scouts Am., L.A. coun., 1985. Mem. Jr. League of L.A. (pres. 1954-55, Spirit of Volunteerism award 1996), Assn. Jr. Leagues of Am. (dir. Region XII, 1956-58, pres. 1958-60), Phi Beta Kappa, Kappa Kappa Gamma. Home: 11718 Wetherby Ln Los Angeles CA 90077-1348

SMITH, JEFFREY E., historian, educator; b. Columbus, Ohio, July 5, 1956; s. George Edward and Anna Marie (Fisher) S.; m. Kristine Runberg, Aug. 15, 1987; 1 child, Lucy Kathryn. BA, Mount Union Coll., Alliance, Ohio, 1978; MFA, Syracuse U., 1981; PhD, U. Akron, 1991. Dir. Summit County Hist. Soc., Akron, Ohio, 1981-90; exec. dir. St. Louis Merc. Libr., St. Louis, 1990-94; instr. Washington U., St. Louis, 1992—; pres. Janus Applied History Group, St. Louis, 1994—; assoc. prof. history Lindenwood Coll., St Charles, Mo, 1996—; adj. prof. U. Akron, 1984-86. Contbr. articles to profl. jours. Mem. Am. Assn. for State and Local History (Award of Merit 1987), Ohio Assn. Hist. Socs. and Mus. (various award 1984-90), Orgn. Am. Historians, Ohio Mus. Assn. (sec., trustee), Hower House Mus. (bd. dirs.). Office: Janus Applied History Group 3920 Cleveland Ave Saint Louis MO 63110-4032

SMITH, JEFFREY EARL, management consulting executive; b. Dunkirk, N.Y., June 15, 1958; s. Earl Redmond and Ruth Aliene (Crawford) S.; m. Ellen Lori Pichney, Feb. 9, 1992; children: Daniel Edward, Benjamin Michael. BS in Civil Engring., Worcester (Mass.) Poly. Inst., 1981; BA in Physics, Coll. of the Holy Cross, 1981; MBA, U. Md., 1995. From ops. engr. to info. ctr. mgr. Dresser Atlas, Houston, 1981-83; group (multidivsnl.) info. sys. v.p. Dresser Industries, 1983-86; solution team mgr. AT&T Info. Sys., Houston, 1986; sr. mgmt. cons., nat. dir. Gemini Cons. Co., Morristown, N.J., 1986-89; prin., regional dir. Gen. Elec. Cons. Svcs., Phila., 1990-91; pres., mng. dir. Knowledge Cons. Co., Rockville, 1989-95; exec. cons. IBM Global Distbn. Svcs., Chgo., 1995—. Home: Knowledge Consulting Co 7440 Damascus Rd Laytonsville MD 20882 Office: IBM Cons Group 1 IBM Plz 6th Fl Dept PJE Chicago IL 60611

SMITH, JEFFREY GREENWOOD, industry executive, retired army officer; b. Ft. Sam Houston, Tex., Oct. 14, 1921; s. Henry Joseph Moody and Gladys Adrienne (Haile) S.; m. Dorothy Jane Holland, June 2, 1948; children: Meredith B. Exnicios, Jennifer H. Meyer, Jeffrey Greenwood, Tracy E. McDonald, Melissa A. Deutsch, Ashley A. Pollock. B.S. in Civil Engring, Va. Mil. Inst., 1943; M.S. in Mech. Engring, Johns Hopkins U., 1949; M.A. in Internat. Affairs, George Washington U., 1964. Commd. 2d lt. U.S. Army, 1944, advanced through grades to lt. gen., 1975; service in CBI, Korea, Germany and Vietnam; comdr. 2d Inf. Div., Korea, 1971-73; dep. chief staff ops. Hdqrs. Army Forces Command, Ft. McPherson, Ga., 1973-74; chief staff Hdqrs. Army Forces Command, 1974-75; comdr. 1st U.S. Army, Ft. Meade, Md., 1975-79; ret., 1979; dir. govt. rels. Ethyl Corp., Washington, 1980—, v.p. govt. rels., 1992—, ret., 1994. Decorated D.S.M., Silver Star, Legion of Merit with 3 oak leaf clusters, D.F.C., Bronze Star with V device and 2 oak leaf clusters, Air medal with 12 oak leaf clusters, Army Commendation medal with oak leaf cluster, Purple Heart with oak leaf cluster, Combat Inf. badge (2); breast Order Yun Hui Republic China; Order Security Merit Korea; Gallantry Cross with silver and gold stars (Vietnam) Army Distinguished Service Order. Mem. Assn. U.S. Army, Mil. Order Carabao, Kappa Alpha. Clubs: Army and Navy. Home: 3000 Sevor Ln Alexandria VA 22309-2221

SMITH, JEFFREY KOESTLIN, publishing executive; b. Cleve., June 25, 1948; s. James D. and Inez (Hobson) S.; m. Mary Frances Fitch, Dec. 29, 1971; children: Gwynneth F., Colin J., Douglas F. Student, U. Edinburgh, Scotland, 1968-69; BA, Duke U., 1970; MA, U. Wis., 1971. Editor Fed. Register, Washington, 1971-73; sales rep. Harper and Row, Cleve., 1974-76; acquisitions editor Harper and Row, N.Y.C., 1976-77; acquisitions editor Kluwer Acad. Pubs., The Hague, The Netherlands, 1977-81; acquisitions editor Kluwer Acad. Pubs., Boston, 1981-83, v.p., 1983—; pres. Kluwer Acad. Pubs., 1996—; also bd. dirs. Kluwer Acad. Pubs., Boston. Office: Kluwer Acad Pubs 101 Philip Dr Norwell MA 02061-1615

SMITH, JEFFREY L. (THE FRUGAL GOURMET), cook, writer; b. Seattle, Jan. 22, 1939; s. Emely S.; m. Patricia M. Dailey, 1964; children: Jason, Channing. BA, U. Puget Sound, 1962, DHL (hon.), 1987; MDiv, Drew U., 1965, DDiv (hon.), 1993. Ordained to ministry United Meth. Ch., 1965. Served Meth. chs. Hartsdale, N.Y., rural, Wash.; chaplain, asst. prof. religion U. Puget Sound, Tacoma, Wash., 1966-72; founder The Chaplain's Pantry, Tacoma, 1972-83; host Seattle Today TV program The Frugal Gourmet (formerly Cooking Fish Creatively), 1973-77; host PBS program The Frugal Gourmet, 1983—. Author: The Frugal Gourmet, 1984, The Frugal Gourmet Cooks with Wine, 1986, The Frugal Gourmet Cooks American, 1987, The Frugal Gourmet Cooks Three Ancient Cuisines: China, Greece and Rome, 1989, The Frugal Gourmet on Our Immigrant Ancestors: Recipes You Should Have Gotten From Your Grandmother, 1990, The Frugal Gourmet's Culinary Handbook, 1991, The Frugal Gourmet Celebrates Christmas, 1991, The Frugal Gourmet Whole Family Cookbook, 1992, The Frugal Gourmet Cooks Italian: Recipes from the New and Old World Simplified for the American Kitchen, 1993, The Frugal Gourmet Keeps the Feast: Past, Present and Future, 1995. Recipient Daytime Emmy nominations (5), Best of the West Edn. TV award Western Ednl. Network, 1986. Office: The Frugal Gourmet Inc 88 Virginia St Unit 2 Seattle WA 98101-1047

SMITH, JEFFREY MICHAEL, lawyer; b. Mpls., July 9, 1947; s. Philip and Gertrude E. (Miller) S.; 1 son, Brandon Michael. BA summa cum laude, U. Minn., 1970; student U. Malaya, 1967-68; JD magna cum laude, U. Minn., 1973. Bar: Ga. 1973. Assoc. Powell, Goldstein, Frazier & Murphy, 1973-76; ptnr. Rogers & Hardin, 1976-79; ptnr. Bondurant, Stephenson & Smith, 1979-85, Arnall, Golden & Gregory, 1985-92, Katz, Smith & Cohen, 1992—; vis. lectr. Duke U., 1976-77, 79-80, 89-93; adj. prof. Emory U., 1976-79, 81-82; lectr. Vanderbilt U., 1977-82. Co-author: Preventing Legal Malpractice, 1996, Legal Malpractice, 1996. Bd. visitors U. Minn. Law Sch., 1976-82. Mem. ABA (vice chmn. com. profl. officers and dirs. liability law, 1979-83, chmn. 1983-84, vice chmn. com. profl. liability 1980-82, mem. standing com. lawyer's profl. liability 1981-85, chmn. 1985-87, standing com. lawyer competency 1993-95), State Bar of Ga. (chmn. profl. liability and ins. com. 1978-89, trustee Inst. of Continuing Legal Edn. in Ga. 1979-80), Order of Coif, Phi Beta Kappa. Home: 145 15th St NE Apt 811 Atlanta GA 30309-3559 Office: Katz Smith & Cohen Ivy Place 2d Fl 3423 Piedmont Rd NE Atlanta GA 30305-1754

SMITH, JEFFREY P., supermarket chain executive; b. 1950. Student, Utah State U., 1968-70. With Smith's Food and Drug Ctrs., Salt Lake City, 1970—, pres., COO, 1984-88, chmn., CEO, 1988—, also bd. dirs. Office: Smith's Food & Drug Ctrs Inc 1550 S Redwood Rd Salt Lake City UT 84104-5105*

SMITH, JEFFRY ALAN, health administrator, physician, consultant; b. L.A., Dec. 8, 1943; s. Stanley W. and Marjorie E. S.; m. Jo Anne Hague. BA in Philosophy, UCLA, 1967, MPH, 1972; BA in Biology, Calif. State U., Northridge, 1971; MD, UACJ, 1977. Diplomate Am. Bd. Family Practice. Resident in family practice WAH, Takoma Park, Md., NIH, Bethesda, Md., Walter Reed Army Hosp., Washington, Children's Hosp. Nat. Med. Ctr., Washington, 1977-80; occupational physician Nev. Test Site, U.S. Dept. Energy, Las Vegas, 1981-82; dir. occupational medicine and environ. health Pacific Missile Test Ctr., Point Mugu, Calif., 1982-84; dist. health officer State Hawaii Dept. Health, Kauai, 1984-86; asst. dir. health County of Riverside (Calif.) Dept. Health, 1986-87; regional med. dir. Calif. Forensic Med. Group, Monterey, Calif., 1987-94; med. dir. Cmty. Human Svcs., Monterey, Calif., 1987-94, Colstrip (Mont.) Med. Ctr., 1994-97; cons. San Bernadino County, Calif., 1997—. Fellow Am. Acad. Family Physicians; mem. AMA, Am. Occupational Medicine Assn., Flying Physicians, Am. Pub. Health Assn. Avocations: pvt. pilot. Home: 1517 14th St W # 250 Billings MT 59102-3105 Office: 5225 Canyon Crest Dr Ste 71-448 Riverside CA 92507

SMITH, JEROME HAZEN, pathologist; b. Omaha, Oct. 9, 1936; s. Hazen Dow and Helen Kellogg (Hewitt) S.; m. Marilyn Kay Stauber, 1961; children: Nathaniel, Kathryn Hewitt, Andrew Kellogg. B.S. in Medicine, U. Nebr., 1960, M.D., 1963, M.S. in Anatomy, 1962; M.Sc. Hygiene in Tropical Pub. Health, Harvard U., 1969. Diplomate: Am. Bd. Pathology. Rotating intern Mpls.-Hennepin County Gen. Hosp., 1963-64; from jr. asst. resident in pathology to chief resident in clin. pathology Peter Bent Brigham Hosp., Boston, 1964-72, assoc. pathologist, 1973; from rsch. fellow in pathology to instr. Harvard U. Med. Sch., Boston, 1964-73; pathologist, head dept. Inst. Med. Evangelique, Kimpese, Congo, 1968; chief autopsy svcs. Inst.Tropical Medicine, Hosp. Mama Yemo, Fomeco, Kinshasa, Zaire, 1973-74; med. dir. anatomic pathology Inst. Tropical Medicine, Hosp. Mama Yemo, Fomeco, Kinshasa, Zaire, 1974; asst. prof. anatomic pathology U. Ariz. Med. Sch., Tucson; dir. anatomic pathology and microbiology Tucson VA Hosp., 1975-76; mem. faculty U. Tex. Med. Br., Galveston, 1976-84, 90—, prof. pathology, 1979-84, 90—, dir. autopsy service, 1977-84, dir. clin. parasitology lab., 1977-81, 90-94, dir. pathology edn., 1993-95, prof. grad. sch., 1980-84, 90—, adj. prof. pathology, 1989-90; cons. Shriners Burn Inst., Galveston, 1980-84, 90-91; prof pathology and lab. medicine Tex. A&M U. Coll. Medicine, College Station, 1984-88; pres. Birch Tree, Inc., 1995—. Contbr. numerous articles to med. jours. Comdr. M.C. USNR, 1969-71. Recipient Avalon tuition award, 1961; NSF fellow, 1959; Poynter fellow, 1960; USPHS trainee, 1961, 68-69. Mem. NRA (life), Am. Soc. Clin. Pathologists, U.S.-Can. Acad. Pathologists, Am. Soc. Parasitologists, N.Y. Acad. Scis., Tex. Med. Assn., Tex. Soc. Pathologists, Tex. Soc. Infectious Diseases, Galveston County Med. Soc., Am. Soc. Tropical Medicine and Hygiene, Houston Soc. Clin. Pathologists (Harlan Spjut award 1995), Houston Safari Club (bd. dirs. 1994-96), Sigma Xi. Republican. Home: 2706 Wilmington Dr Dickinson TX 77539-4664 Office: U Tex Med Br Dept Pathology Galveston TX 77550 *Your only lasting investment is in your fellow men. Your only certain investment is in God.*

SMITH, JERRY EDWIN, federal judge; b. Del Rio, Tex., Nov. 7, 1946; s. Lemuel Edwin and Ruth Irene (Henderson) S.; m. Mary Jane Blackburn, June 4, 1977; children: Clark, Ruth Ann, J.J. BA, Yale U., 1969, JD, 1972. Bar: Tex. 1972. Law clk. to judge U.S. Dist. Ct. (no. dist.) Tex., Lubbock, 1972-73; assoc. then ptnr. Fulbright & Jaworski, Houston, 1973-84; city atty. City of Houston, 1984-88; cir. judge U.S. Ct. Appeals (5th cir.), Houston, 1988—. Chmn. Harris County Rep. Party, Houston, 1977-78; committeeman State Rep. Exec. Com., Tex., 1976-88. Mem. State Bar Tex., Houston Bar Assn. Methodist. Home: PO Box 130608 Houston TX 77219-0608 Office: US Ct Appeals 12621 US Courthouse 515 Rusk St Houston TX 77002-2600*

SMITH, JESSE GRAHAM, JR., dermatologist, educator; b. Winston-Salem, N.C., Nov. 22, 1928; s. Jesse Graham and Pauline Field (Griffith) S.; m. Dorothy Jean Butler, Dec. 28, 1950; children: Jesse Graham, Cynthia Lynn, Grant Butler. B.S., Duke U., 1962, M.D., 1951. Diplomate: Am. Bd. Dermatology (dir. 1974-83, pres. 1980-81). Intern VA Hosp., Chamblee, Ga., 1951-52; resident in dermatology Duke U., 1954-56, assoc. prof. dermatology, 1960-62, prof., 1962-67; resident U. Miami, 1956-57, asst. prof., 1957-60; prof. dermatology Med. Coll. Ga., 1967-91, chmn. dept. dermatology, 1967-91, acting chmn. dept. pathology, 1973-75, acting v.p. devel., 1984-85; chief staff Talmadge Meml. Hosp., Augusta, Ga., 1970-72; prof. dermatology, chief div. of dermatology U. South Ala., Mobile, 1991—; mem. advisory council Nat. Inst. Arthritis, 1975-79. Editorial bd. Archives of Dermatology, 1963-72, Jour. Investigative Dermatology, 1966-67, Jour. AMA, 1974-80; editorial bd. So. Med. Jour., 1976—, assoc. editor, 1991-92, editor, 1992—; editor Jour. Am. Acad. Dermatology, 1978-88; contbr. chpts. to books, articles to profl. jours. Served with USPHS, 1952-54. Recipient Disting. Alumnus award Duke U. 1981. Fellow ACP, Royal Soc. Medicine; mem. Am. Acad. Dermatology (hon., dir. 1971-74, 78-88, pres.-elect 1988-89, pres. 1989-90), Can. Dermatol. Assn. (hon.), Am. Dermatol. Assn. (hon. sec. 1976-81, pres. 1981-82), Soc. Investigative Dermatology (dir. 1964-69, pres. 1979-80), S.E. Dermatol. Assn. (sec. 1970-71, pres. 1975-76), Ga. Soc. Dermatology (pres. 1979-80), So. Med. Assn. (chmn. sect. dermatology 1981-84), Assn. Profs. Dermatology (dir. 1976-77, 80-82, pres. 1984-86), Med. Rsch. Found. Ga. (bd. dirs. 1967-91, pres. 1974-75), Alpha Omega Alpha. Home: 4272 Bitand Spur # 4 Mobile AL 36608 Office: USAMC 3401 Medical Park Dr Ste 103 Mobile AL 36693-3318

SMITH, JO ANNE, writer, retired educator; b. Mpls., Mar. 18, 1930; d. Robert Bradburn and Virginia Mae S. BA, U. Minn., 1951, MA, 1957. Wire and sports editor Rhinelander (Wis.) Daily News, 1951-52; staff corr., night mgr. UPI, Mpls., 1952-56; interim instr. U. N.C., Chapel Hill, 1957-58; instr. U. Fla., Gainesville, 1959-65; asst. prof. journalism, communications U. Fla., 1965-68, assoc. prof., 1968-76, prof., 1976-88, disting. lectr., 1977. Author: JM409 Casebook and Study Guide, 1976, Mass Communications Law Casebook, 1979, 3d edit., 1985. Active, Friends of Libr., Alachua County Humane Soc. Recipient outstanding Prof. award Fla. Blue Key, 1976; Danforth assoc., 1976-85. Mem. Women in Communications, Assn. Edn. in Journalism, Phi Beta Kappa, Kappa Tau Alpha. Democrat. Unitarian. Home: 208 NW 21st Ter Gainesville FL 32603-1732

SMITH, JOAN H., women's health nurse, educator; b. Akron, Ohio; d. Joseph A. and Troynette M. (Lower) McDonald; m. William G. Smith; children: Sue Ann, Priscilla, Timothy. Diploma, Akron City Hosp., 1948; BSN in Edn., U. Akron, 1972, MA in Family Devel., 1980. Cert. in inpatient obstetric nursing. Mem. faculty Akron Gen. Med. Ctr. Sch. Nursing, 1964; former dir. obstet. spl. procedures Speakers Bur., Women's Health Ctrs. Akron Gen. Med. Ctr., 1988;, 1990; cons., speaker women's health care. Mem. Assn. Women's Health, Obstet. and Neonatal Nursing (charter, past sec.-treas., past vice chmn. Ohio sect., chmn. program various confs.). Home: 873 Kirkwall Dr Copley OH 44321-1751

SMITH, JOAN LOWELL, writer, public relations consultant; b. Orange, N.J., June 20, 1933; d. William Jr. and Katherine Margaret (Macpherson) Lowell; m. John A. Nave, Dec. 14, 1957 (div. May 1961); children: Deborah Lowell, Nancy Lowell; m. Warren W. Smith, July 19, 1969. Student, Lasell Coll., 1951-52, Drake Bus. Sch., N.Y.C., 1952-53. Exec. sec. Amb. Ernest A. Gross, N.Y.C., 1954-57; adminstrv. asst./v.p. J.B. Williams Co. (Geritol), Clark, N.J., 1966-74; pub. rels. dir. N.J. State Opera, Newark, 1974-78; talk show host-radio WJDM (AM) WFME (AM-FM), Elizabeth and West Orange, N.J., 1974-82; exec. dir. Chamber of Commerce, Westfield, N.J., 1976-79; legis. aide Assemblyman C. Hardwick, N.J., 1980-82; exec. dir. Alzheimer's Disease Fund, Westfield, N.J., 1986-87; pub. rels. dir. Children's Specialized Hosp., Mountainside, N.J., 1993-94; pres./owner Media Mgmt., Westfield, 1974—; weekly columnist on animals The Star Ledger, Newark, N.J., 1996—. Recipient 13 awards N.J. Press Woman, 1991—, 2d place award Nat. Fedn. Press Women, 2d place award Nat. Fedn. Press Women, 1997. Mem. DAR (regent 1987-89), Assn. Children with Learning Disabilities (chmn. bd. dirs. 1980-82), Westfield Day Care Ctr. (bd. dirs.), Geneal. Soc. of West Fields (bd. dirs. 1984-88), Daus. of Cin. Republican. Presbyterian. Avocations: Bible studies, tennis, duplicate bridge, snorkeling, geneology. Office: Media Mgmt 1739 Boulevard Westfield NJ 07090-2857

SMITH, JOAN PETERSEN, nursing administrator, educator; b. Aurora, Nebr., Apr. 4, 1943; d. Ardean Leroy and Leone Eleanor (Ketterer) Petersen; m. Tyrone Wilson Smith, Aug. 15, 1979; 1 child, Steven. BSN, Boston U., 1967; MPA, Roosevelt U., 1977. Dir. ambulatory nursing Michael Reese Hosp., Chgo., 1978-80; v.p. patient care svcs. Marin Gen. Hosp., Greenbrae, Calif., 1980-84, Alta Bates Hosp., Berkeley, Calif., 1984-86; assoc. dir. health and hosp. sys., dir. nursing Santa Clara Valley Med. Ctr., San Jose, Calif., 1986—; clin. prof. U. Calif. Sch. Nursing, San Francisco, 1985—. Recipient Tribute to Women in Industry award YWCA Santa Clara Valley, 1995; mgmt. fellow Nat. Assn. Pub. Hosps., 1991. Mem. Am. Orgn. Nurse Execs., Calif. Orgn. Nurse Execs., Sigma Theta Tau. Home: 1944 Melvin Rd

Oakland CA 94602-2027 Office: Santa Clara Valley Med Ctr 751 S Bascom Ave San Jose CA 95128-2604

SMITH, JOE DORSEY, JR., retired newspaper executive; b. Selma, La., Apr. 6, 1922; s. Joe Dorsey and Louise (Lindsay) S.; 1 child, Lawrence Dorsey. B.A., La. Coll. Pineville, 1939-43. Gen. mgr. Alexandria Daily Town Talk, La., 1958—; pub. Alexandria Daily Town Talk, 1965—; pres. McCormick & Co., Inc., 1968—, chmn., 1990-96. Served with USAF, 1942-45. Mem. Alexandria Golf and Country Club, Boston Club, New Orleans Club. Democrat. Episcopalian. Home: 2734 Georges Ln Alexandria LA 71301-4721 Office: Ste 1003 Hibernia Bldg 934 3rd St Alexandria LA 71301-8383

SMITH, JOEY SPAULS, mental health nurse, biofeedback therapist, bodyworker, hypnotist; b. Washington, Oct. 9, 1944; d. Walter Jr. and Marian (Och) Spauls; children: Kelly, Sean. BSN, Med. Coll. Va., 1966; MA in Edn., U. Nebr., Lincoln, 1975. RNC, ANA; cert. psychiat. and mental health nurse; cert. zero balancer, cert. hypnotist, cert. biofeedback therapist, cons. Staff nurse Booth Meml. Hosp., Omaha, 1969-71; asst. house supr. Nebr. Meth. Hosp., Omaha, 1971-72; head nurse, clin. instr. U. Calif., Davis, 1976-78; staff nurse Atascadero State Hosp., Calif. Dept. Mental Health, 1978-79; nurse instr. psychiat. technician Atascadero State Hosp., 1979-84, insvc. tng. coord., 1984-86; nursing coord. chem. dependency recovery program French Hosp. Med. Ctr., San Luis Obispo, Calif., 1986-87; relief house supr. San Luis Obispo County Gen. Hosp., 1982-88; regional program assoc. statewide nursing program Consortium Calif. Sate U., 1986-88; nurse instr., health svcs. staff devel. coord. Calif. Men's Colony, Dept. Corrections, San Luis Obispo, 1987-92; pvt. practice San Luis Obispo, Calif., 1990—; clin. instr. nursing divsn. Cuesta Coll., 1988—; relief house supr. San Luis Obispo County Gen. Hosp., 1982-88, regional program assoc. statewide nursing program Consortium Calif. State U., 1986-88. 1st lt. U.S. Army Nurse Corps., 1965-67. Mem. Assn. Applied Psychophysiology and Biofeedback, Central Coast Nurses Coop. Coun., Consol. Assn. Nurses in Substance Abuse (cert. chem. dependency nurse), Biofeedback Cert. Inst. Am. (cert. biofeedback therapist, stress mgmt. edn., cert. zero balancer), Alpha Sigma Chi, Phi Delta Kappa. Home: 1321 Cavalier Ln San Luis Obispo CA 93405-4905 Office: PO Box 4823 San Luis Obispo CA 93403-4823

SMITH, JOHN BREWSTER, teaching program administrator; b. Bryan, Tex., June 26, 1937; s. Elmer Gillam and Sara Roland (Lull) S.; m. Ida Hawa, Dec. 28, 1963; children: Susan Helen, Rona Esther. B.A., Tex. A & M U., 1960; M.S., Columbia U., 1963, cert. advanced librarianship, 1984, DLS, 1991. Asst. law librarian Columbia U., N.Y.C., 1963-66; asst. library dir. for pub. services Tex. A & M U., College Station, 1966-69, dir. libraries, 1969-74; dir. libraries, dean library scis. SUNY, Stony Brook, 1974-96, dir. library and info. sci. tchg. program, 1996-97; chief libr. Bronx Cmty. Coll., CUNY, 1997—. Named Librarian of Year Tex. Library Assn., 1972. Mem. ALA, N.Y. Libr. Assn. Home: 121 Gnarled Hollow Rd East Setauket NY 11733-1959 Office: Bronx Cmty Coll Univ Ave and West 181 St New York NY 10453

SMITH, JOHN EDWIN, philosophy educator; b. Bklyn., May 27, 1921; s. Joseph Robert and Florence Grace (Dunn) S.; m. Marilyn Blanche Schulhof, Aug. 25, 1951; children: Robin Dunn, Diana Edwards. AB, Columbia U., 1942, PhD, 1948; BD, Union Theol. Sem., N.Y.C., 1945; MA, Yale U., 1959; LL.D., U. Notre Dame, 1964. Instr. religion and philosophy Vassar Coll., 1945-46; instr., then asst. prof. Barnard Coll., 1946-52; mem. faculty Yale U., 1952—, prof. philosophy, 1959—, chmn. dept., 1961—, Clark prof. philosophy, 1972-91, Clark prof. philosophy emeritus, 1991—; vis. prof. Union Theol. Sem., 1959, U. Mich., 1958; guest prof. U. Heidelberg, Germany, 1955-56; Fagothey chair of philosophy U. Santa Clara, 1984, vis. prof. Boston Coll., 1992; Dudleian lectr. Harvard, 1960; lectr. Am. Week, U. Munich, Germany, 1961; Suarez lectr. Fordham U., 1963; pub. lectr. King's College, Univ. London, 1965; Aquinas lectr. Marquette U., 1967; Warfield lectr. Princeton Theol. Sem., 1970; Fulbright lectr. Kyoto U., Japan, 1971; Sprunt lectr. Union Theol. Sem., Va., 1973; Mead-Swing lectr. Oberlin Coll., 1975; H. Richard Niebuhr lectr. Elmhurst Coll., Ill., 1977; Merrick lectr. Ohio Wesleyan U., 1977; Roy Wood Sellars lectr. Bucknell U., 1978; O'Hara lectr. U. Notre Dame, 1984; Hooker disting. vis. prof. Mc Master U., 1985; mem. adv. com. Nat. Humanities Inst., New Haven, 1974, dir., 1977-80. Author: Royce's Social Infinite, 1950, Value Convictions and Higher Education, 1958, Reason and God, 1961, The Spirit of American Philosophy, 1963, The Philosophy of Religion, 1965, Religion and Empiricism, 1967, Experience and God, 1968, Themes in American Philosophy, 1970, Contemporary American Philosophy, 1970, The Analogy of Experience, 1973, Purpose and Thought: The Meaning of Pragmatism, 1978, America's Philosophical Vision, 1992, Jonathan Edwards, Puritan, Preacher, Philosopher, 1992, Quasi-Religions: Humanism, Marxism, Nationalism, 1994; translator: (R. Kroner): Kant's Weltanschauung, 1956; editor: (Jonathan Edwards): Religious Affections, Vol. 2, 1959; gen. editor, Yale edit.: Works of Jonathan Edwards; Editorial bd.: Monist, 1962—, Jour. Religious Studies, Philosophy East and West, Jour. Chinese Philosophy, The Personalist Forum, Jour. Faith and Philosophy, Jour. Speculative Philosophy. Named Hon. Alumnus, Harvard Div. Sch., 1960; recipient Herbert W. Schneider award Soc. for Advancement of Am. Philosophy, 1990, Founder's medal Metaphys. Soc. Am., 1996; Am. Coun. Learned Socs. fellow, 1964-65. Mem. Culinary Inst. Am. (dir. New Haven affiliate), Am. Philos. Assn. (v.p. 1980, pres. 1981), Am. Theol. Soc. (pres. 1967-68), Metaphys. Soc. Am. (pres. 1970-71, founder's medal, 1996), Hegel Soc. Am. (pres. 1971), Charles S. Peirce Soc. (pres. 1992). Home: 300 Ridgewood Ave Hamden CT 06517-1428 Office: PO Box 201562 New Haven CT 06520-1562

SMITH, JOHN FRANCIS, materials science educator; b. Kansas City, Kans., May 9, 1923; s. Peter Francis and Johanna Teresa (Spandle) S.; m. Evelyn Ann Ross, Sept. 1, 1947; children—Mark Francis, Letitia Ann Smith Harder. BA with distinction, U. Mo.-Kansas City, 1948; PhD, Iowa State U., 1953. Grad. asst. Iowa State U., Ames, 1948-53; faculty and research scientist Iowa State U., Ames, 1953-88; dept. chmn., div. chief Ames Lab. Iowa State U., Ames, 1966-70; cons. Tex. Instruments, Inc., Dallas and Attleboro, Mass., 1958-63, Argonne Nat. Lab., Ill., 1964-70, Iowa Hwy. Commn., Ames, Los Alamos Nat. Lab., N.Mex., 1984-88, bur. standards Nat. Inst. Standards and Tech., Gaithersburg, Md., 1988-91, Sandia Nat. Lab., Albuquerque, N.M., 1991-92, ASM Internat., Cleve., 1992—. Patentee ultrasonic determination of texture in metal sheet and plate, lead-free soldier; author: Phase Diagrams of Binary Vanadium Alloys; Hellcats Over the Philippine Deep; co-author: Thorium: Preparation and Properties, 1975; editor: Calculation of Phase Diagrams and Thermochemistry of Alloy Phases, 1978; editor Jour. Phase Equilibria; contbr. articles to profl. publs. Mem. former comdr. Ames-Boone Squadron CAP, 1970-75. With USN, 1942-46, PTO, comdr. USNR, 1946-64. Decorated Air medal with star; Disting. Svc. award Civil Air Patrol, Maxwell AFB, Ala., 1979; Faculty Citation Iowa State Alumni Assn., Ames, 1977. Fellow Am. Inst. Chemists, ASM (chmn. Des Moines chpt. 1966); mem. AIME, Materials Research Soc., Alpha Sigma Mu (trustee 1984-86). Roman Catholic. Clubs: Silent Knights, Inc. (trustee 1980—), Exptl. Aircraft Assn. Avocation: flying. Home: 2919 S Riverside RR 5 Box 343 Ames IA 50010-9520 Office: Iowa State U Ames Lab 104 Metallurgy Ames IA 50010

SMITH, JOHN FRANCIS, JR., automobile company executive; b. Worcester, Mass., Apr. 6, 1938; s. John Francis and Eleanor C. (Sullivan) S.; children: Brian, Kevin; m. Lydia G. Sigrist, Aug. 27, 1988; 1 stepchild, Nicola. B.B.A., U. Mass., 1960; M.B.A., Boston U., 1965. Fisher Body div. mgr. Gen. Motors Corp., Framingham, Mass., 1961-73; asst. treas Gen. Motors Corp., N.Y.C., 1973-80; comptroller Gen. Motors Corp., Detroit, 1980-81, dir. worldwide product planning, 1981-84; pres., gen. mgr. Gen. Motors Can., Oshawa, Ont., Can., 1984-85; exec. v.p. Gen. Motors Europe, Glattbrugg, Switzerland, 1986-87, pres., 1987-88; exec. v.p. internat. ops. Gen. Motors Corp., Detroit, 1988-90; vice chmn. internat. ops. Gen. Motors Corp., 1990, bd. dirs., mem. fin. com., 1990—, pres., COO, 1992—; CEO, pres., 1992-95; chmn. bd. Gen. Motors Corp., Detroit, 1996—; pres.'s coun. Global Strategy Bd.; bd. dirs. EDS, Hughes Electronics Corp., Gen. Motors Acceptance Corp.; mem. Bus. Roundtable Policy Com.; mem. U.S. Japan Bus. Coun., Am. Soc. Corp. Execs.; mem. Bd. of Detroit Renaissance; bus. coun. Meml. Sloan-Kettering Cancer Ctr.; bd. dirs. Procter & Gamble Co. Mem. chancellor's exec. com. U. Mass., dir.; trustee United Way S.E. Mich., New Am. Revolution, Boston U. Mem. Am. Soc. Corp. Execs., Am. Auto Mfrs. Assn. (bd. dirs.), Econ. Club Detroit (bd. dirs.), Beta Gamma Sigma (pres.), Dirs. Table. Roman Catholic. Office: GM 3044 W Grand Blvd Detroit MI 48202-3037 also: Globe Hqtrs at Renesonce Ctr PO Box 431301 100 Renesonce Ctr Detroit MI 48243-7301*

SMITH, JOHN GELSTON, lawyer; b. Chgo., Aug. 10, 1923; s. Fred G. and Ferne (Keiser) S.; m. JoAnn Stanton, Aug. 17, 1944; children: Carey S., JoAnne G. B.S., U. Notre Dame, 1949, LL.B., 1950. Bar: Ill. 1950. Assoc. Lord, Bissell & Brook, Chgo., 1950-54, 57, ptnr., 1958-90, of counsel, 1990—; asst. atty. gen. State of Ill., Springfield, 1954-56; bd. dirs. Lloyd's of London Press, Inc.; lectr. ins. law Northwestern U., Evanston, 1952, 56-57; chmn. 1st Non-Profit Ins. Co., 1991-93. Chmn. Gov.'s Transition Task Force, Ill. Dept. Ins., Springfield, 1969; chmn. Gov.'s Adv. Bd. Ill. Dept. Ins., 1969-73; atty.-in-fact Underwriters at Lloyd's, London, 1974-88; adv. com. William J. Campbell Library of U.S. Cts., Chgo., 1963-87; trustee Lake Bluff (Ill.) Village Bd., 1965-69. Served to 1st lt. USAAF, 1942-45. Home: 382 Ravine Park Dr Lake Forest IL 60045-1341 Office: Lord Bissell & Brook 115 S La Salle St Chicago IL 60603-3801

SMITH, JOHN JOSEPH, lawyer; b. Pitts., Nov. 14, 1911; s. John J. and Alta Ethel (McGrady) S.; m. Ruth Lee Snavely, July 11, 1942; children: John Joseph Jr., Robert William. AB, Birmingham So. Coll., 1931; AM, U. Va., 1932, postgrad. in Econs., 1932-34; JD, U. Ala., 1937. Bar: Ala. 1937, U.S. Dist. Ct. (no. dist.) Ala. 1940, U.S. Supreme Ct. 1945, U.S. Ct. Appeals (5th cir.) 1950. Assoc. Murphy, Hanna & Woodall, Birmingham, Ala., 1937; asst. prof. U. Va., Charlottesville, 1937-39; office solicitor U.S. Dept. Labor, Washington, 1939-42; enforcement atty. Office of Price Adminstrn., Atlanta, 1942-43; legal counsel Bechtel-McCone Corp., Birmingham, 1943-46; pvt. practice Birmingham, 1946—. Author: Selected Principles of the Law of Contracts, Sales and Negotiable Instruments, 1938. Founder, commr. Homewood (Ala.) Joy Open Baseball League, 1958-72, dir., 1972-90; gov's staff Ala., 1963-71; chmn. Homewood Citizens Action Com. Against Annexation; life mem. Ala. Sheriffs' Boys and Girls Ranches Builders Club; organizer, dir. Birmingham dist. Young Adult Fellowship Classes, Meth. Ch., hon. mem. adminstrv. bd. Recipient Youth Service award Pop Warner Conf., Phila., 1961, Clifford Crow Meml. Community Service award, Shades Valley Civitan Club, Homewood, 1981, Adminstrv. Bd. award for faithful svc. Meth. Ch., 1992. Mem. ABA, Ala. Bar Assn., Birmingham Bar Assn. (ethics com., unlawful practice of law com., fee arbitration com., econs. of law com., acct.'s liaison com., meml. com.), Order of Coif (founder Farrah Order of Jurisprudence, pres. 1937, alumni organizer U. Ala. Sch. Law chpt., pres. 1969-73, life historian), Tau Kappa Alpha, Pi Gamma Mu. Methodist. Clubs: The Club (Homewood); City Salesmen's (Birmingham) (Man of Yr. award 1986). Lodges: Masons (life mem., master 1956-57, chmn. legal adv. com. for grand lodge), KT (life), Shriners (life), Royal Order Scotland, Scottish Rite (So. jurisdiction). Home: 1506 Primrose Pl Birmingham AL 35209-5426 Office: Smith & Smith Marathon Bldg 618 38th St S Birmingham AL 35222-2414

SMITH, JOHN JOSEPH, JR., textile company executive, educator; b. Fall River, Mass., Feb. 11, 1913; s. John J. and Mabel E. (Reid) S.; m. Mary C. Moson, Aug. 8, 1936; children—Nancy S. (Mrs. John Lee Lesher, Jr.), Robert J. B.S. in Chem. Engring., Tufts U., 1935. With Johnson & Johnson subsidiary Chicopee Mfg. Corp., New Brunswick, N.J., 1935—; pres. Chicopee Mfg. Corp., 1959—, chmn., 1971-74; with Chicopee Mills, Inc., N.Y.C., 1959—; pres. Chicopee Mills, Inc., 1960—, chmn., 1971-75; dir. Johnson & Johnson, New Brunswick, 1961-74, mem. exec. com., 1966-74; chmn. Chicopee Cuyk Holland, Devro Moodiesburn Scotland; adj. prof. Fla. Atlantic U., Boca Raton, 1976-82. Mem. Am. Assn. Tech. Colorists and Chemists, Am. Chem. Soc., Gulf Stream Golf Club, The Little Club, Delray Beach (Fla.) Club, The Misquamicut Club, Watch Hill (R.I.) Yacht Club. Home: 1225 S Ocean Blvd Delray Beach FL 33483 Summer home: 7 Everett Ave Watch Hill RI 02891

SMITH, JOHN KERWIN, lawyer; b. Oakland, Calif., Oct. 18, 1926; 1 dau., Cynthia. BA, Stanford U.; LLB, Hastings Coll. Law, San Francisco. Ptnr., Haley, Purchio, Sakai & Smith, Hayward, Calif; bd. dirs. Berkeley Asphalt, Mission Valley Ready-Mix; gen. ptnr. Oak Hill Apts., City Ctr. Commercial, Creekwood I and Creekwood II Apts. Road Parks Commn., 1957, mem. city coun., 1959-66, mayor, 1966-70; chmn. Alameda County Mayors Conf., 1968; chmn. revenue taxation com. League Calif. Cities, 1968; vice-chmn. Oakland-Alameda County Coliseum Bd. Dirs.; bd. dirs. Coliseum Found., Mission Valley Rock, Rowell Ranch Rodeo; former pres. Hastings 1066 Found. (Vol. Svc. award 1990), Martin Kauffman 100 Club. Recipient Alumnus of Yr. award Hastings Coll. Law, 1989. Mem. ABA, Calif. Bar Assn., Alameda County Bar Assn., Am. Judicature Soc., Rotary. Office: 22320 Foothill Blvd Ste 620 Hayward CA 94541-2719

SMITH, JOHN LEE, JR., minister, former association administrator; b. Fairfax, Ala., Dec. 11, 1920; s. John Lee and Mae Celia (Smith) S.; m. Vivian Herrington, Aug. 15, 1942; children—Vicky Smith Davis, Joan Smith Wimberly, Jennifer Lee Smith Ruscilli. A.B., Samford U., 1950; student, New Orleans Bapt. Theol. Sem., 1950-51, 53; D.D., Ohio Christian Coll., 1967, Birmingham Bapt. Bible Coll., 1979; postgrad., Auburn U., 1956, Baylor U., 1972-73; LL.D., Nat. Christian U., 1974. Owner Smith's Grocery Co., Montgomery, Ala., 1945-47; ordained minister Bapt. Ch., 1947; pastor Dolomite Bapt. Ch., Birmingham, Ala., 1947-50, Elim Bapt. Ch., Brewton, Ala., 1950-51; pastor 1st Bapt. Ch., Tallapoosa, Ga., 1951-52, Villa Rica, Ga., 1952-54, Fairfax, Ala., 1954-57; pastor West End Bapt. Ch., Birmingham, 1957-59, 88-94, Dalraida Bapt. Ch., Montgomery, 1959-66, 83-86, 1st Bapt. Ch., Demopolis, Ala., 1966-69; assoc. exec. dir. Ala. Council Alcohol Problems, Birmingham, 1969-70, exec. dir., 1970-78; exec. dir. Am. Council Alcohol Problems, Washington, 1972-74, sec., 1974-79, v.p., 1979-87; pastor Benton (Ala.) Bapt. Ch., 1987-88, Vinesville (Ala.) Bapt. Ch., 1994—; tchr., dir. Bessemer Bapt. Inst., 1978-83; exec. dir. missions Bessemer Bapt. Assn., 1978-83; tchr. Mercer U. extension, Carrollton, Ga., 1953-54; tchr. Extension div. Samford U., Fairfax, Ala., 1955-57, South Ala. area dir., 1986-87; mem. bd. ministerial edn. Bapt. Ch., 1958-59, Christian Life Commn., 1959-60; pres. Bessemer Ministers Alliance, 1979-81. Contbr. profl. jours. Chmn. Marengo County Cancer Soc., 1967-68, Good News Ala., Jefferson County, 1977-79, Gov.'s Commn. on Pornography, 1970-78, Nat. Temperance and Prohibition Council, 1973-80, Nat. Coordinating Council on Drug Edn., 1972-78, Alcohol Drug Problems Assn. Am., 1972-78; exec. dir. Temperance Edn., Inc., Washington, 1972-74; trustee Internat. Reform Fedn., 1973-74; adv. bd. JCCEO, 1975-82; bd. dirs. Bessemer Rescue Mission, 1978-83, 89-94, Bessemer YMCA, 1978-83; mem. adv. bd. Bessemer Salvation Army, 1978-83. Served to capt. USAAF, 1942-45, ETO. Mem. C of C., Trident, Phi Kappa Phi. Club: Mason. Home: PO Box 535 Helena AL 35080-0535

SMITH, J(OHN) MALCOLM, political science educator; b. Vancouver, B.C., Can., Jan. 24, 1921; (parents Am. citizens); s. George John and Henrietta E. (Smith) S.; m. Connie Grace Shaw, June 2, 1943; children: Sheila C., Nancy L., Patricia L. BA, U. Wash., 1946; MA, Stanford U., 1948, PhD, 1951. Instr. polit. sci. Stanford (Calif.) U., 1947-50; instr. pub. law and govt. Columbia U., N.Y.C., 1950-52; organizer World Affairs Coun., L.A., 1952-54; asst. prof. polit. sci. U. Calif., Riverside, 1954-57; prof. polit. sci. Calif. State U., Hayward, 1965—; cons. Office of Sec. USAF, Washington, 1957-58, Commn. on Civil Rights, Washington, 1958-59; spl. asst. minority whip U.S. Senate, Washington, 1959-61; vis. prof. U. S.D., 1961-62, Ariz. State U., 1962-63; Merrill prof. Utah State U., 1976. Co-author: Powers of the President During Crisis, 1961, President and National Security, 1972; contbr. articles to profl. jours. Midshipman USN, 1940-43; 1st lt. infantry U.S. Army, 1943-45. Grantee Ford Found., 1955-56, John S. Sheppard, 1951-52. Mem. Acad. Polit. Sci., The Supreme Ct. Hist. Soc., Ctr. for Study of Presidency. Home: 2289 East Ave Hayward CA 94541-5631 Office: Calif State U Dept Polit Sci Hayward CA 94542

SMITH, JOHN MATTHEW, insurance company executive; b. Bklyn., Mar. 21, 1936; s. John Bernard and Mary (Lukas) S.; m. Kathryn Ellen Hurley, May 30, 1959; children—Mary Ellen, Kathryn Ann Jacques, Sarah Jane. B.A., Bklyn. Coll., 1959. With Met. Life Ins. Co., N.Y.C., 1959-68; with Guardian Life Ins. Co., N.Y.C., 1968—, sr. v.p., 1983-94, exec. v.p., 1995—; adj. prof. Coll. Ins., N.Y.C., 1975—; pres. Guardian Investor Svcs. Corp., N.Y.C., 1977—, Baillie Gifford Internat. Fund, N.Y.C., 1990—; exec. v.p. Guardian Ins. & Annuity Co., N.Y.C., 1981—. Served with U.S. Army, 1956-58. Mem. Nat. Assn. Securities Dealers (registered prin.). Democrat. Roman Catholic. Avocations: woodworking; electronics. Office: Guardian Life Ins Co 201 Park Ave S New York NY 10003-1601

SMITH, JOHN MCNEILL, JR., lawyer; b. Rowland, N.C., Apr. 9, 1918; s. John McNeill and Roberta (Andrew) S.; m. Louise Jordan; children: Louise Smith Nichols, Anne Smith Cole, John McNeill III, Eleanor. AB, U. N.C., 1938; LLB, Columbia U., 1941. Bar: N.C. 1941, N.Y. 1942. Assoc. Root Clark Buckner & Ballantine, N.Y.C., 1941, Smith Wharton & Jordan, Greensboro, N.C., 1945-48; ptnr. Smith Wharton Sapp & Moore and successor firm: Smith Helms Mulliss & Moore, Greensboro, 1948—; vis. prof. U. N.C. Law Sch., Chapel Hill, 1964-65; faculty Nat. Inst. Trial Advocacy. Author, editor: Equal Protection of the Laws in North Carolina, 1963; contbr. articles to jours in field. Mem. N.C. Ho. of Reps., 1970, N.C. Senate, 1971-78; bd. dirs. Alt. Energy Corp. N.C., 1980-88, N.C. Ctr. for Pub. Policy Rsch., 1980-92; chmn. N.C. State Bd. Ethics, 1980-84; pres. N.C. Vol. Lawyers for the Arts, 1984-89. Served to lt. comdr. USNR, 1941-48. Recipient award NCCJ, 1990; named one of 100 Most Influential Lawyers, Nat. Bar Jour., 1985, 88, 91. Mem. ABA (chmn. ind. rights and responsibilities 1972, mem. ho. dels. 1974, chmn. commn. on mentally disabled 1979, Ctrl. and Ea. European law initiate liaison to Estonia 1992-93), Internat. Bar Assn., N.C. Bar Assn. (chairperson constl. rights and responsibilities 1994—, Liberty Bell award 1990), Greensboro Bar Assn., N.C. Acad. Trial Lawyers, N.C. Assn. Def. Attys., Nat. Acad. Elder Law Attys., Am. Bus. Club (pres. 1968-70). Avocations: concert band, photography, bicycling, tennis. Home: 2501 W Market St Greensboro NC 27403-1519 Office: Smith Helms Mulliss & Moore PO Box 21927 300 N Greene St Ste 1400 Greensboro NC 27401-2167

SMITH, JOHN MICHAEL, lawyer; b. Summit, N.J., Sept. 23, 1959; s. Paul Harry and Mary (Konieczny) S. BA in Polit. Sci., Ursinus Coll., Collegeville, Pa., 1981; JD, Del. Law Sch., Wilmington, 1985; LLM in Environ. Law, George Washington U., Washington, 1995. Bar: Pa. 1985, U.S. Ct. Military Appeals 1986. Asst. staff judge adv. 4th Combat Support Group, Seymour Johnson AFB, N.C., 1986-87, 343d Combat Support Group, Eielson AFB, AK, 1987-88; area def. counsel USAF Judiciary, Eielson AFB, AK, 1988-90; asst. staff judge adv. Headquarters 7th Air Force, Osan AFB, Rep. of Korea, 1990-91; dep. staff judge adv. 438th Airlift Wing, McGuire AFB, N.J., 1991-94, Air Force Environ. Law & Litigation Divsn., Arlington, Va., 1995—; Mem. Pa. Bar Assn., 1985-88. Recipient Air Force Commendation medal USAF, 1987, 90, 91, Air Force Achievement medal USAF, 1992, Air Force Meritorious Svc. medal, 1995. Roman Catholic. Avocations: racquetball, computers, bicycling. Home: 5913 Parkridge Ln Alexandria VA 22310 Office: AFL/JACE 1501 Wilson Blvd Ste 629 Arlington VA 22209-2403

SMITH, JOHN N., film director; b. Montreal, Quebec, Canada, 1943. Dir. films A Gift for Kate, 1985, The Rebellion of Young David, 1985, First Stop China, 1985, Sitting in Limbo, 1985, Train of Dreams, 1986, The Boys of St. VIncent, 1993, Dieppe, 1984, Dangerous Minds, 1995, Sugartime, 1995; co-dir. The Masculine Mystique, 1983. Office: Internat Creative Mgmt 8942 Wilshire Blvd Beverly Hills CA 90211*

SMITH, JOHN ROBERT, physicist; b. Salt Lake City, Oct. 1, 1940; married; 2 children. BS, Toledo U., 1962; PhD in Physics, Ohio State U., 1968. Aerospace engr. surface physics Lewis Rsch. Ctr. NASA, 1965-68; sr. rsch. physicist, head surface and interface physics group Gen. Motors, Warren, Mich., 1972-80, sr. staff scientist, head solid state physics group, 1980-86, prin. rsch. scientist rsch. lab., 1986—, head engineered surfaces program, 1995—; adj. prof. dept. physics U. Mich., 1983—. Air Force Office Sci. Rsch., Nat. Rsch. Coun. fellow U. Calif., 1970-72. Fellow Am. Phys. Soc. (David Adler Lectureship award in field of materials sci. 1991); mem. Am. Vacuum Soc., Sigma Xi. Achievements include research in the theory and experiment of solid surfaces, electronic properties, magnetic properties and chemisorption, adhesion, metal contact electronic structure, defects and universal features of bonding in solids, as well as the application of thermal spray coatings in automobile engines. Office: General Motors Research Lab Physics Dept 30500 Mound Rd Warren MI 48092-2031

SMITH, JOHN STEPHEN, retired educational administrator, consultant; b. Wheeling, W.Va., Aug. 16, 1938; s. Carl Edward and Martha Ellen (Van Meter) S.; m. Bernice E. Eichenlaub, Sept. 7, 1963; children: Karl Bartholomew, Ann Kathryn, Suzanne Lee. BS, Wheeling Jesuit Coll., 1960; MS, Duquesne U., 1965; PhD, U. Pitts., 1971. Instr. biochemistry U. Pitts., 1962-69, mgr. budget systems, 1969-72; asst. dean, asst. to chancellor La. State U. Med. Ctr., New Orleans, 1972-74; asst. to v.p. health affairs U. Ala. Birmingham Med. Ctr., 1974-78, asst. v.p. health affairs, 1978-88, assoc. v.p. health affairs, 1988-96, ret., 1996; dep. dir. internat. program U. Ala. Birmingham, 1980-90; cons. in field. Contbr. articles to acad. jours. Active Boy Scouts Am., 1978—; chmn. spl. events Vulcan dist., Birmingham, 1986-90, chmn. comm. com. Birmingham Area coun., 1991-95; bd. dirs. Red Mountain Mus. Soc. Birmingham, 1982. Mem. Assn. Am. Med. Colls. (chmn. so. region planning 1979-80, nat. chmn. instnl. planning 1980-81), Assn. Instnl. Rsch., Soc. Coll. and Univ. Planning, Com. Fgn. Rels., Phi Beta Delta. Avocations: hiking, golf, reading. Office: U Ala Birmingham 604 Webb Bldg Birmingham AL 35294-3361

SMITH, JOHN STUART, lawyer; b. Rochester, N.Y., Sept. 4, 1943; s. Cecil Y. and Helen M. (Van Patten) S.; m. Nancy Schauman, Aug. 28, 1965; children—Kristan, Debra Barton. A.B. magna cum laude, Harvard U., 1965, LL.B. cum laude, 1968. Bar: N.Y. 1968, D.C. 1968, U.S. dist. ct. (we. dist.) N.Y. 1969, U.S. dist. ct. (so. dist.) N.Y. 1973, U.S. dist. ct. (no. dist.) N.Y. 1977, U.S. dist. ct. (no. dist.) Tex. 1980, U.S. Ct. Apls. (5th cir.) 1971, (2d cir.) 1972, (9th cir.) 1980, U.S. Sup. Ct. 1978. Assoc. Nixon, Hargrave, Devans & Doyle, Rochester, N.Y., 1968-74, mem., 1975—. Bd. dirs. Rochester Chamber Orch., 1970-75, Geva Theater, 1988. Mem. ABA, N.Y. State Bar Assn. (past chmn. criminal procedure subcom. antitrust sect.), Monroe County Bar Assn. Office: PO Box 1051 1 Clinton Sq Rochester NY 14603 also: 1 Thomas Cir NW Washington DC 20005-5802 also: # 702 1026 16th St NW Apt 702 Washington DC 20036-5712

SMITH, JOHN WEBSTER, retired energy industry executive; b. Atlanta, Del., May 3, 1921; s. Frank Louis and Dorothy (Andrew) S.; m. Patricia Catherine Metzner, Jan. 9, 1943 (div. 1958); 1 child, Edward Marc; m. Beverly Brabner, Aug. 21, 1958 (div. July 1983); 1 child, David Andrew; m. Sandra Seefeld, Jan. 5, 1985. BA, Washington Coll., Chestertown, Md., 1942; MS, George Washington U., 1973. Served to rear admiral USN, 1942-73, served in ETO, Korea, Vietnam, Pacific, other locations, 1942-73, ret., 1973; supt., prof. Tex. Maritime Coll./Tex. A&M U., Galveston, 1973-78; v.p. Sealcraft Ops., Inc., Galveston, 1978-83; dir. tng. Tidewater Marine Svcs. Assn., New Orleans, 1983-84; pres. various cos. Houston, 1984-86; mng. dir. Grand Hotel, Houston, 1986-87; exec. asst. to CEO Taylor Energy Co., New Orleans, 1988-97; exec. dir. Patrick F. Taylor Found, New Orleans, 1988-97; cons. Soc. Marine Cons., New Orleans, 1986-88; chmn. Galveston County Pvt. Industry Coun., 1980-82; chmn. bd. dirs. Gulf Coast Coun. Fgn. Affairs, Galveston, 1979-82; asst. in devel. of world's 1st nuclear radiation course after Bikini Atom Bomb test at Navy Dept.; trustee Patrick F. Taylor Found., 1997—. Contbr. articles, papers to profl. publs. Decorated 2 Legion of Merit medals, Bronze Star medal. Mem. Navy League of U.S. (bd. dirs. New Orleans coun.), Coun. Am. Master Mariners, La. Sheriffs Assn., Ret. Officers Assn., Pelican Club Galveston, Rotary (pres. Galveston chpt. 1983), Lambda Chi Alpha. Republican. Methodist. Avocations: reading, maps and charts, travel. Home: 113 Rue Holiday Slidell LA 70461-5312 Office: Patrick F Taylor Found 234 Loyola Ave New Orleans LA 70112-2001

SMITH, JOHN WILSON, III, newspaper editor, columnist, statistician; b. Pottsville, Pa., June 2, 1935; s. John Wilson II and Hannah (Morris) S.; m. Jean Ann Longenecker, Nov. 21, 1973; children: Jeffrey W., Jennifer L., Jodi A. BA in History magna cum laude, Franklin & Marshall Coll., 1957; MA in Journalism, Syracuse U., 1959. Sports writer Reading (Pa.) Eagle, 1958-81, sports editor, 1981-82; news editor, columnist Reading Eagle/Times, 1983-87, religion editor, columnist, 1988—; copy chief Reading Eagle, 1987—; statistician Ea. Pa. Football Conf., Hazleton, 1981—, Dist. 11, Allentown, Pa., 1984—; moderator Reading Bapt. Assn., 1966-68. Pres. Western Berks Jr. Baseball League, West Lawn, Pa., 1993—; sports ofcl. Pa. Interscholastic Athletic Assn., Mechanicsburg, 1955-95. Named to Pa. Am. Legion Sports Hall of Fame, 1972, St. Clair, Pa. Oldtimers Sports Hall of Fame, 1993. Mem. Religion Newswriters Assn., Phi Beta Kappa, Sigma Delta Chi. Am. Bapt. Avocation: youth baseball administrator and coach. Home: 1121 Whitfield Blvd West Lawn PA 19609 Office: Reading Eagle Times PO Box 582 Reading PA 19603

SMITH, JONATHAN DAVID, medical educator; b. Cleve., Jan. 10, 1955. BS, U. Calif., Santa Cruz, 1978; PhD, Harvard U., 1984. Postdoctoral Lab. Biochem. Genetics and Metabolism The Rockefeller U., N.Y.C., 1984-89, asst. prof., 1989-96, assoc. prof., 1996—. Contbr. articles to profl. jours. Recipient Nat. Rsch. Svc. award NIH, 1985-87, Program Project award, 1995—. Mem. AAAS, Am. Heart Assn. (Investigatorship award N.Y.C. affiliate 1989-92, Grant-in-Aid 1989-92, 92-95, Established Investigator 1994—). Achievements include identification of genes that regulate atherosclerosis; development of animal models useful for testing therapies to proevent atherosclerosis; characterization of novel functions of apolipoprotein E which are relevant to Alzheimer's disease, cardiovascular disease and longevity.

SMITH, JOSEF RILEY, internist; b. Council Bluffs, Iowa, Oct. 1, 1926; s. George William Smith and Margaret (Wood) Hill; divorced; children: Sarah L. Kratz, David L., Mary E. Loeb, John R., Ruthann P. Sherrier, Mark A.; m. Susan Frances Irwin, Feb. 9, 1973; 1 child, Christopher I. Student, Tulane U., 1944-46; BM, Northwestern U., 1950, MD, 1951; MSEE, Marquette U., 1964. Diplomate Am. Bd. Internal Medicine. Instr. internal medicine U. Miss. Med. Sch., Jackson, 1956-59; asst. prof. Marquette U. Med. Sch., Milw., 1959-63; from assoc. prof. to full prof. U. Mich. Med. Sch., Ann Arbor, 1963-72; physician Youngstown (Ohio) Hosp., 1972-79, Group Health Med. Assn., Tucson, 1979-84, Assocs. in Internal Medicine, Tucson, 1985-87; pvt. practice Tucson, 1987—. Co-author: Clinical Cardiopulmonary Physiology, 1960, Textbook of Pulmonary Disease, 1965, 2d rev. edit., 1974; contbr. articles to profl. jours. Controller Mahoning County TB Clinic, Youngstown, 1973-79. Served to lt. USNR, 1952-54. Fellow ACP, Sigma Xi; mem. Ariz. Med. Assn., Pima County Med. Assn., Am. Thoracic Soc., Ariz. Thoracic Soc., Bioengring. Med. Soc. (founder). Avocations: photography, computer programming. Office: 2224 N Craycroft Rd Ste 109 Tucson AZ 85712-2811

SMITH, JOSEPH A., urologic surgeon; b. Memphis, July 13, 1949; s. Joseph A. Smith and Virginia E. (Redd) Mulroy; m. Barbara Bradford, June 14, 1974; children: Carolyn, Bradford J., Christiane. BS, U. Tenn., Knoxville, 1971; MD, U. Tenn., Memphis, 1974. Diplomate Am. Bd. Urology. Prof. U. Utah, Salt Lake City, 1981-90; prof., chmn. dept. urol. surgery Vanderbilt U., Nashville, 1990—; vice chair Residency Rev. Com., Chgo., 1996—. Author: Lasers in Urologic Surgery, 1994. Fellow Am. Coll. Surgeons; mem. Am. Urol. Assn., Am. Soc. Clin. Oncology, Am. Assn. Genitourology Surgeons, Soc. Urol. Oncology (sec. 1995—). Office: Vanderbilt U A-1302 Med Ctr N Nashville TN 37232

SMITH, JOSEPH NEWTON, III, retired architect, educator; b. Jacksonville, Fla., July 4, 1925; s. Joseph Newton, Jr. and Oneal (Kemp) S.; m. Gloria Bevis, Aug. 24, 1946; 1 child, Gordon Kemp. B.S., Ga. Inst. Tech., 1948, B.Arch., 1949. Designer and/or architect archtl. firms in Miami, Fla., 1949-56; propr. Joseph N. Smith, Architect, Miami, 1956-63; partner firm Smith, Polychrone and Wolfcale, Atlanta, 1966-69; gen. cons. architecture, 1969-73; mem. faculty Sch. Architecture, Ga. Inst. Tech., 1963-82, prof. architecture, asst. dir. sch., 1971-77, asst. dean, 1977-82; v.p. interior design Thompson, Ventulett, Steinback and Assocs., Architects and Interior Designers, Atlanta, 1982-88; ptnr. TVS & Assocs.; adj. faculty, Atlanta Coll. Art, 1994—. One-man shows: Archtl. Book Show Atlanta, 1987, Connell Gallery, Atlanta, 1992. Served to lt. (j.g.) USNR, 1943-46. Recipient Birch Burdette Long Meml. award Archtl. League N.Y., 1956; award merit S. Atlantic region AIA for Key Biscayne (Fla.) Presbyn. Ch., 1964, for Friendship Center, low income housing Atlanta, 1970; named Honored Artist of Year, Young Women of Arts, 1974. Fellow AIA (chpt. pres., state pres., state Bronze medal, nat. continuing edn. com., nat. design jury, various state archtl. design juries, landscape architecture Nat. design jury, consulting engrs. coun.). Presbyterian. Home: 2466 Ridgewood Rd NW Atlanta GA 30318-1316

SMITH, JOSEPH PHELAN, film company executive; b. N.Y.C.; s. John William and Margaret Mary (Phelan) S.; m. Madelyn Eleanor Davis, Jan. 17, 1942; children: Kevin, Karen, Margaret, Lisa. BS, Columbia U. Former salesman Van Alstyne Noel & Co., N.Y.C.; former salesman RKO Radio Pictures, Inc., Boston, Omaha, div. mgr., Los Angeles, Portland, Oreg., San Francisco, 1938-47; former exec. v.p. Lippert Prodns., Hollywood, Calif.; former v.p., gen. mgr. sales Telepictures, N.Y.C.; founding pres. Cinema Vue Corp.; now chmn. Pathe News Inc., N.Y.C.; now pres. Pathe Pictures Inc., N.Y.C. Served with U.S. Army. Mem. Motion Picture Pioneers, Am. Film Inst., Elks. Republican. Office: Pathe News Inc 630 9th Ave Ste 305 New York NY 10036-3708

SMITH, JOSEPH PHILIP, lawyer; b. Jackson, Tenn., June 14, 1944; s. William Benjamin and Virginia Marie (Carey) S.; m. Deborah J. Smith, Dec. 22, 1972; 1 child, Virginia Louise. BA, U. Miss., 1967, JD, 1975; MEd, U. So. Miss., 1977; EdD, U. Memphis, 1997. Bar: Miss. 1975, Tex. 1979, N. Mex. 1991, Colo. 1991, Tenn. 1995, U.S. Dist. Ct. (no. dist.) Miss. 1975, U.S. Dist. Ct. (no. dist.) Tex. 1982, U.S. Dist. Ct. N.Mex. 1993, U.S. Dist. Ct. Colo. 1993, U.S. Ct. Appeals (10th cir.) 1993. Tchr. math. Marks (Miss.) Jr. H.S., 1971-73; tchr., then asst. prin. Biloxi (Miss.) City Schs., 1975-78; oil and gas landman Modling & Assocs., 1978-79; assoc., then ptnr. Byrnes, Myers, Adair, Campbell & Sinex, Houston, 1979-85; farmer Quitman County, Miss., 1988-90; pvt. practice Marks, Miss., Memphis, Raton, N.Mex., 1985—. Mem. Archdiocese of Santa Fe Sch. Bd., 1991-92. Capt. USAF, 1967-71. Mem. ABA, Colo. Bar Assn., Miss. Pub. Defender Assn. (treas. 1988-90), Rotary (pres., sec. Marks club 1985-90, mem. Raton club 1990-91). Republican. Roman Catholic. Home: 674 Saint Augustine Sq Memphis TN 38104-5054

SMITH, JOSEPH SETON, electronics company executive, consultant; b. N.Y.C., July 16, 1925; s. William Thomas and Loretto Agnes (Gorman) S.; m. Marion Susan McManus, June 14, 1952; children: Marion R., Loretto A., Joseph S., John J., Eleanor M., William T., Vincent C., Regina M. BSEE, Iowa State U., 1946; MEE, NYU, 1950, DSc, 1955. Rsch. assoc. prof. NYU, N.Y.C., 1947-55; asst. chief engr. Burroughs Corp., Bklyn., 1955-59; div. mgr. Sperry Rand Corp., Gt. Neck, N.Y., 1959-66; v.p. Litton Industries, Beverly Hills, Calif., 1966-72; sr. v.p. Figgie Internat. Corp., Cleve., 1972-79; pres. J.S. Smith Corp., Cleve., 1979-87; exec. dir. Ctr. for Venture Devel., Cleve., 1983-87; v.p., gen. mgr. CSD Telephonics Corp., Farmingdale, N.Y., 1987-93; v.p. Technology Telephonics Corp., 1993—; bd. dirs. Waterlox Corp., Cleve.; trustee Enterprise Devel. Inc. subs. Case Western Res. U., Cleve.; cons. on creation and growth tech. cos. Contbr. articles on radar, systems integration, instrumentation, and entrepreneurship to profl. jours. Organizer, keynote speaker Cleve. Entrepreneurship Confs., 1984, 85; music dir. Ch. St. Gregory the Great, Cleve. Lt. (j.g.) USN, 1943-46. Fellow IEEE (chmn. N.Y. sect. 1957-58); mem. Hermit Club (Cleve.), Mayfield Country Club (Cleve.), Sigma Xi, Eta Kappa Nu, Pi Mu Epsilon. Home: 4912 Countryside Rd Lyndhurst OH 44124-2515 Office: Telephonics Corp Command Systems Div 815 Broadhollow Rd Farmingdale NY 11735-3904

SMITH, JULIA LADD, medical oncologist, hospice physician; b. Rochester, N.Y., July 26, 1951; d. John Herbert and Isabel (Walcott) Ladd; m. Stephen Slade Smith; 1 child. BA, Smith Coll., 1973; MD, N.Y. Med. Coll., 1976. Diplomate Am. Bd. Internal Medicine, Am. Bd. Med. Oncology. Intern in medicine N.Y. Med. Coll., N.Y.C., 1976-77; resident in medicine Rochester Gen. Hosp., 1977-79; internist Genesee Valley Group Health, Rochester, 1979-80; oncology fellow U. Rochester, 1980-82, asst. prof. oncology in medicine sch. medicine & dentistry, 1986—; oncologist Med. Ctr. Clinic, Ltd., Pitts., 1982-83; oncologist, internist Rutgers Community Health Plan, New Brunswick, N.J., 1983-86; med. dir. Genesee Region Home Care Assn./Hospice, Rochester, 1988—. Bd. dirs. Am. Cancer Soc., Monroe County, 1988-92. Nat. Cancer Inst. rsch. grantee, 1993-95. Mem. ACP, Am. Soc. Clin. Oncology, Acad. Hospice Physicians. Unitarian-Universalist. Avocations: sailing, reading, movies, bridge. Address: Genesee Hosp 224 Alexander St Rochester NY 14607

SMITH, JULIAN CLEVELAND, JR., chemical engineering educator; b. Westmount, Que., Can., Mar. 10, 1919; s. Julian Cleveland and Bertha (Alexander) S.; m. Joan Elsen, June 1, 1946; children: Robert Elsen, Diane Louise Smith Brook, Brian Richard. B.Chemistry, Cornell U., 1941, Chem. Engr., 1942. Chem. engr. E. I. duPont de Nemours and Co., Inc., 1942-46; mem. faculty Cornell U., 1946—, prof. chem. engring., 1953-86, prof. emeritus, 1986—, dir. continuing engring. edn., 1965-71; assoc. dir. Cornell U. (Sch. Chem. Engring.), 1973-75, dir., 1975-83; vis. lectr. U. Edinburgh, 1971-72; cons. to govt. and industry, 1947—; UNESCO cons. Universidad de Oriente, Venezuela, 1975. Author: (with W. L. McCabe and P. Harriott) Unit Operations of Chemical Engineering, 1956, 5th edit., 1993, also articles; sect. editor: Perry's Chemical Engineers Handbook, 1963. Fellow Am. Inst. Chem. Engrs.; mem. Am. Chem. Soc., Sigma Xi, Tau Beta Pi, Phi Kappa Phi, Alpha Delta Phi. Clubs: Ithaca Country, Statler (Ithaca). Home: 711 The Parkway Ithaca NY 14850-1546

SMITH, JULIAN PAYNE, gynecological oncologist, educator; b. Portsmouth, Ohio, Mar. 23, 1930; s. Emory Farl and Lola Blanche (Payne) S.; m. Eleanore G. Stankunas, June 5, 1954; children: Susan Sharon, Charles Douglas, Geraldine Gigi, David James. Student, U. Mich., 1947-48; BA, Ohio Wesleyan U., 1951; MD, Columbia U., 1955. Diplomate Am. Bd. Ob-Gyn. Intern Univ. Hosps., Cleve., 1955-56; resident in ob/gyn Cornell N.Y. Hosp., 1956-57; resident in ob-gyn Columbia Presbyn. Med. Ctr., N.Y.C., 1957-59; fellow in gynecology-oncology U. Tex., Houston, 1963-66; pvt. practice Portsmouth, 1961-63; prof. U. Tex. System Cancer Center, M.D. Anderson Hosp. and Tumor Inst., Houston, 1973-77; prof. ob-gyn, dir. gynecologic oncology Wayne State U. Med. Sch., Detroit, 1977-83; pvt. practice medicine specializing in gynecologic oncology Southfield, Mich., 1983-86; prof. of ob-gyn Loyola U., Chgo., 1986-88; prof., dir. gynecology oncology Loyola U. Med. Ctr., Maywood, Ill., 1986-88; prof. ob-gyn, dir. gynecologic oncology U. Md. Sch. Medicine, Balt., 1988—. Editor: (with Gravlee) Endometrium, 1977, A Review of the World Literature, 1977, (with Delgado) Management of Complications in Gynecologic Oncology, 1982, (with Hafez) Carcinoma of the Cervix, 1982; contbr. articles to profl. jours. Bd. dirs. Am. Cancer Soc., Wayne County, Mich., 1980-81. Capt. M.C., USAR, 1959-61. Mem. Am. Coll. Ob-Gyn., Am. Radium Soc., Am. Assn. Ob-Gyn., Felix Rutledge Soc. (pres. 1968-70), Am. Gynecol. Soc., Am. Gynecol. and Obstet. Soc., Soc. Gynecol. Oncologists (pres. 1984-85), Soc. Pelvic Surgeons (pres. 1994-95), Mid. Atlantic Gynecol. Oncology Soc. (pres. 1991-92), Med. Ch. Soc. Md. Republican. Methodist. Home: 22 Treadwell Ct Lutherville Timonium MD 21093-3764 Office: U Md Sch Medicine Dept Ob-Gyn 22 S Greene St Baltimore MD 21201-1544

SMITH, JUNE ANN, counseling educator; b. Hanover, Jamaica, Sept. 8, 1952; d. Eddie E. and Roselyn V. (Hue) DeRoux; m. Alanzo H. Smith, June 19, 1977. MA, Andrews U., 1982, PhD, 1987; MSW, CSW, Yeshiva U., 1990. Cert. social worker, N.Y. Tchr. sci. and math. West Jamaica Conf., Montego Bay, Jamaica, 1976-81; counselor Andrews U., Berrien Springs, Mich., 1984-87; programs dir. Grand St. Settlement, N.Y.C., 1987-97; asst. prof. counseling Hofstra U., Hempstead, N.Y., 1990—. Author: Meaning of Marriage to Voluntarily Childless Couple, 1987. Mem. AACD, Assn. Counselor Edn. and Supervision, Am. Sch. Counselor, Am. Mental Health Counselors Assn., Phi Delta Kappa. Seventh-day Adventist. Avocations: computers, cooking, traveling, photography, piano. Office: Hofstra U 1000 Fulton Ave Hempstead NY 11550-1030

SMITH, JUNE BURLINGAME, English educator; b. Barrington, N.J., June 1, 1935; d. Leslie Grant and Esther (Bellini) Burlingame; m. Gregory Lloyd Smith, July 6, 1963; children: Gilia Cobb Burlingame Smith, Cyrus Comstock. BA, Reed Coll., 1956; MS, Ind. U., 1959; MA, Calif. State U., Dominquez Hills, 1986. Sec. to dean Reed Coll., 1956-57; residence hall supr. Ind. U., 1957-59; buyer Macy's Calif., 1959-63; residence hall supr. U. Wash., 1963, interviewer Tchr. Placement Bur., 1964; music tchr. Chinook Jr. High Sch., Bellevue, Wash., 1964-68; pvt. practice music tchr., 1971-83; gifted grant coord. South Shores/CSUDH Magnet Sch., 1981; tchr. cons. L.A. Unified Sch. Dist., 1981-82; assoc. prof. English L.A. Community Colls., Harbor Coll., Wilmington, Calif., 1989—; sexual harrassment officer Harbor Coll., Wilmington, Calif., 1991-92; pres. acad. senate Harbor Coll., 1997—. Chair Sex Equity Commn., L.A. Unified Sch. Dist., 1988-91; bd. dirs. Harbor Inter Faith Shelter, 1994—. Mem. AAUW (pres. San Pedro, Calif. br. 1989-90, mem. task force Initiative for Equity in Edn. 1991-95), Am. Acad. Poets, Phi Kappa Phi, Delta Kappa. Democrat. Home: 3915 S Carolina St San Pedro CA 90731-7115 Office: LA Community Coll Harbor 1111 Figueroa Pl Wilmington CA 90744-2311

SMITH, KAREN ANN, artist, graphic designer, educator; b. Trenton, N.J., May 25, 1964; d. James Roy and Clara Patricia (Walton) S. A in Comml. Art, Art Inst. Phila., 1984; BFA in Graphic Design and Art Therapy, U. Arts, Phila., 1989; grad. in graphic design, Basel Sch. for Design, 1991; MA in Expressive Therapies, Lesley Coll., 1993. Graphic designer Mercer County C.C., Trenton, 1984-86; mural painter, supr. Anti-Graffiti Network, Phila., 1988; tchr. drawing and set design Chestnut Hill (Mass.) Sch., 1995, 96; freelance graphic designer Swiss Fed. Rys., Bern, 1993-95; tchr. drawing Wentworth Inst. Tech., Boston, 1996, 97; tchr. design Northeastern U., Boston, 1997. One-woman show Contempo Galerie, Bern, Switzerland, 1994, Boston Archtl. Ctr. Atelier, 1997; exhibited in group shows including Howard Yezerski Gallery, Boston, 1994, Kingston Gallery, Boston, 1995. Scholar Women in Graphic Arts, 1987-89; grantee Mystic Studios Trust, 1994-97. Mem. Coll. Art Assn., Am. Coun. for the Arts. Studio: 549 Penn St Newtown PA 18940

SMITH, KATHLEEN ANN, mathematics educator; b. New Orleans, Sept. 8, 1948; d. Robert King and Catherine Rose (Peter) S. BA in Math., U. Dallas, 1970; MS in Math., U. Ctrl. Ark., 1975. Cert. secondary prin., elem. prin. and tchr., secondary math., phys. sci. tchr., Ark. Math., sci. tchr. Sacred Heart High Sch., Morrilton, Ark., 1970-73, West Jr. High Sch., West Memphis, Ark., 1973, Mount St. Mary Acad., Little Rock, 1974-76; math., sci. tchr. St. Joseph Sch., Conway, Ark., 1976-90, asst. prin., 1981-84, prin., 1986-90; math. instr. U. Ctrl. Ark., Conway, 1990—; adj. prof. math. Hendrix Coll., Conway, 1990-93. Named Tchr. of Yr., St. Joseph Sch., 1979. Mem. Math. Assn. of Am., Nat. Coun. Tchrs. Math. Roman Catholic. Avocations: needlework, camping.

SMITH, KATHLEEN TENER, bank executive; b. Pitts., Oct. 19, 1943; d. Edward Harrison Jr. and Barbara Elizabeth (McCormick) Tener; m. Roger Davis Smith, May 30, 1970 (dec.); children: Silas Wheelock, Jocelyn Tener, Luke Ewing Taft. BA summa cum laude, Vassar Coll., 1965; MA in Econs., Harvard U., 1968. Rsch. assoc. Harvard U. Grad. Sch. Bus., Cambridge, Mass., 1967-69; assoc. economist Chase Manhattan Bank, N.Y.C., 1969-70, asst. treas., 1971, 2d v.p., 1972, v.p., 1973—, sec. asset liability mgmt. com., 1985-90, treas. Global Bank, 1990-91, divsn. exec. structured investment products, 1991-93, global mktg. and comms. exec. Global Risk Mgmt. Sect., 1993-94, global mktg. and comms. product devel. exec., 1994-96, global asset mgmt. and pvt. bank mktg., 1996—. Editor: Commodity Derivatives and Finance, 1996. Trustee Vassar Coll., Poughkeepsie, N.Y., 1979-91, mem. exec. com., 1987-91; mem. subcom. on edn. Chase Manhattan Found., N.Y.C., 1985-90. NSF fellow, 1965-67. Mem. Am. Fin. Assn., Am. Econ. Assn., Fin. Mgmt. Assn., Yale Club, Phi Beta Kappa. Republican. Episcopalian. Home: 454 State Route 32 N New Paltz NY 12561-3040 Office: Chase Manhattan Bank 1211 Avenue Of The Americas New York NY 10036-8701

SMITH, KATHRYN ANN, advertising executive; b. Harvey, Ill., Mar. 30, 1955; d. Kenneth Charles and Barbara Joan (Wise) Smith; m. Christopher A. Erwin, July 16, 1994; stepchildren: Brian, Courtney, Misty. Student Art Inst. Chgo., 1973. Adv. salesperson Calumet Index, Inc., Riverdale, Ill., 1974-77, Towne & Country Ind., Hammond, 1977-78; owner, sales person Ad-Com, Merrillville, Ind., 1978-92, pres., Crown Point, Ind., 1978-92, corp. pres., chief exec. officer, 1993; pres. Smith-Halcomb Advt., Chgo., 1993; pres., owner Smith-Leonard & Assocs. Advt., Des Plaines, Ill., 1993—. Dir., producer cable TV comml., 1982; dir., producer TV comml., 1987-88. Recipient Silver Microphone award, 1987, 90; named Am. On Line Spl. Interest Forum Leader, 1991. Mem. Advt. Agy. Owners Assn. (chair 1985-88), Merrillville C. of C. Avocations: painting, fishing, antiques, computers, travel.

SMITH, KEITH, protective services official. Now fire chief City of Indpls. Office: Fire Dept 50 N Alabama St Ste 208E Indianapolis IN 46204-5308*

SMITH, KEN, landscape architect. BS in landscape architecture, Iowa State U., 1976; M in landscape architecture, Harvard U., 1986. Landscape architect N.Y., Calif., Mass., Iowa. Landscape architect State Conservation Commn. State Iowa, 1979-84, The Office of Peter Walker and Martha Schwartz, Inc., N.Y.C., San Francisco, 1986-89; cons. Dept. Environ. Mgmt. Commonwealth Mass., 1984-86; prin. Martha Schwartz Ken Smith David Meyer, Inc., San Francisco, 1990-92, Ken Smith Landscape Architect, N.Y.C., 1992—; adj. prof. CCNY Sch. Architecture Urban Landscape Program, 1992—; vis. design critic Harvard U. Grad. Sch. Design, 1995-96; vis. critic U. Pa. Sch. Fine Arts, 1997; vis. lectr. U. Va. Sch. Architecture, 1996. Contbr. articles to profl. jours. Ctr. Pub. Architecture fellow Randalls Island Project, N.Y.C., 1994; honorable mention Am. City Design Comp., Architecture Soc. Atlanta, 1994, San Diego Housing Commn., 1992; 1st place award limited design comp. Cumberland Park, Toronto, Ont., 1991, Bridging the Gaps Design Comp. Columbia U. Grad. Sch. Architecture Planning/Preservation and N.Y. Bldg. Arts Forum, 1990; spl. mention Boston Visions Comp. Boston Soc. Archs., 1988. Office: City Coll NY Urban Landscape Arch Program Convent Ave & 138th St New York NY 10031 Office: 108 Franklin St Apt 2W New York NY 10013-2952

SMITH, KEN A., physicist. BA, Rice U., 1970, MA, 1973, PhD, 1976. Exec. dir. Quantum Inst. Rice U. Office: Rice U Quantum Inst PO Box 1892 Houston TX 77005

SMITH, KENNETH ALAN, chemical engineer, educator; b. Winthrop, Mass., Nov. 28, 1936; s. James Edward and Alice Gertrude (Walters) S.; m. Ambia Marie Olsson, Oct. 14, 1961; children: Kirsten Heather, Edward Eric, Andrew Ian Beaumont, Thurston Garrett. S.B., MIT, 1958, S.M., 1959, Sc.D., 1962; postgrad., Cambridge (Eng.) U., 1964-65. Asst. prof. chem. engring. MIT, 1961-67, assoc. prof., 1967-71, prof., 1971—, Edwin R. Gilliland prof. chem. engring., 1989—, acting head dept., 1976-77, assoc. provost, 1980-81, assoc. provost, v.p. rsch., 1981-91, dir. Whitaker Coll. Health Sci. and Tech., 1989-91; cons. chem. and oil cos. NSF fellow, 1964-65, Overseas fellow, Churchill Coll., (Eng.), 1993. Mem. Am. Inst. Chem. Engrs., Nat. Acad. Engring., Am. Chem. Soc., AAAS, Sigma Xi, Phi Lambda Upsilon, Tau Beta Pi. Episcopalian. Home: 32 School St Manchester MA 01944-1336 Office: MIT Bldg 66-540 Cambridge MA 02139

SMITH, KENNETH BLOSE, former financial executive; b. Monmouth, Ill., Jan. 29, 1926; s. Elmer Edwin and Florence (Logan) S.; m. Julia M. Stupp, June 17, 1950; children: Donald E., Paul C., Marilyn D. B.S., U. Iowa, 1947. Internal auditor Deere & Co, Moline, Ill., 1947-52; treas. John Deere Chem. Co., Pryor, Okla., 1952-65; fin. mgr. Deere & Co, Moline, Ill., 1965-71, asst. treas., 1971-81, treas., 1981-85. Republican. Lutheran.

SMITH, KENNETH BRYANT, seminary administrator; b. Montclair, N.J., Feb. 19, 1931; m. Gladys Moran; children: Kenneth Bryant Jr., Kourtney Beth, Kristen Bernard. BA, Va. Union U., 1953; postgrad., Drew U., 1953-54; BD, Bethany Theol. Sem., 1960; DD (hon.), Elmhurst Coll., 1971, Shaw U., 1987; D Ps (hon.), Nat. Lewis U., 1981; LittD (hon.), Chgo. State U., 1990; STD, Olivet Coll., 1992; LhD, Roosevelt U., 1997. Ordained to ministry United Ch. of Christ, 1960. Assoc. min. Park Manor Congl. Ch., Chgo., 1957-61; min. Trinity United Ch. of Christ, Chgo., 1961-66; min. urban affairs The Community Renewal Soc., 1966-68; sr. min. Ch. of Good Shepherd, Chgo., 1968-84; pres. Chgo. Theol. Sem., U. Chgo., 1984—. Mem. Met. Chgo. YMCA, 1986—, Community Renewal Soc., 1966-68. Office: Chgo Theol Sem 5757 S University Ave Chicago IL 60637-1507

SMITH, KENNETH DAVID, performance technologist, musician; b. Newark, Mar. 25, 1963; s. David Morgan and Mary (Peperato) S. BA in Music, Psychology, Rutgers U., 1985; MA in Indsl./Orgnl. Psychology, Montclair State U., 1992. Tng. specialist KPMG Peat Marwick, Montvale, N.J., 1990-92, sr. instrnl. designer, 1992—. Recipient Windows World Open award Microsoft and Computer World, 1995, Outstanding Instructional Product award Internat. Soc. Performance Improvement, 1996. Mem. ASTD, Nat. Soc. for Performance and Instrn. (co-presenter 1995), Phi Beta Kappa. Avocations: photography, gardening. Office: KPMG Peat Marwick 3 Chestnut Ridge Rd Montvale NJ 07645-1842

SMITH, KENNETH JUDSON, JR., chemist, theoretician, educator; b. Raleigh, N.C., Sept. 4, 1930; s. Kenneth Judson and Irene (Strickland) S.; m. Dorothy Margaret Ratcliffe, Mar. 6, 1953; children: Patricia Lynne Smith Pittman, Pamela Jean. A.B., East Carolina U., 1957; M.A., Duke U., 1959, Ph.D., 1961. Research chemist Chemstrand Research Center, Durham, N.C., 1961-65; sr. research chemist Chemstrand Research Center, 1965-68; asst. prof. polymer research SUNY Coll. Environ. Sci. and Forestry, Syracuse, 1968-70; assoc. prof. SUNY Coll. Environ. Sci. and Forestry, 1970-73, prof., 1973-95, emeritus prof., 1995—, asst. dir. Polymer Research Center, 1971-79, acting dir., 1979-83, dir. Organic Materials Sci. Program, 1971-75, chmn. dept. chemistry, 1972-84; vis. prof. Instituto di Chimica Industriale, U. Genoa, Italy, 1979; cons. U.S. Army Materials and Mechanics Rsch. Ctr., Watertown, Mass., 1973-75, cert. of appreciation 1973, NRC, Washington, 1980-87; mem. adv. coun. Syracuse Met. Transp. Coun., 1975-84; mem. adv. bd. confs. in polymer sci. and tech. SUNY, New Paltz, 1977-85; mem. rsch. found. joint com. on procedures SUNY, Albany, 1974-81; cons. Hong Kong Rsch. Coun., 1995—. Contbr. articles to profl. jours. Served with USMC, 1951-54. Recipient cert. Appreciation U.S. Army Materials and Mechanics Rsch. Ctr., 1973. Mem. AAAS, Am. Chem. Soc. (dir. Syracuse sect. 1977-79, chmn. 1978, councilor 1979-82), Am. Phys. Soc. (com. on internat. freedom of scientists, small coms.), Am. Inst. Chemists, Soc. Plastics Engrs., Math. Assn. Am., N.Y. Acad. Scis., Sigma Xi, Phi Lambda Upsilon, Kappa Delta Pi. Achievements include research on statistical mechanics, mechanical properties and theoretical studies of polymers; rubber elasticity and thermoelasticity; crystallization of networks; structure-property relationships; ultimate properties of fibers. Home: 108 Scottholm Blvd Syracuse NY 13224-1728 Office: Coll Environ Sci and Forestry Suny Syracuse NY 13210

SMITH, KENT ASHTON, scientific and technical information executive; b. Boston, Sept. 3, 1938; s. Kent Wooliscroft and Dorothy Patten Smith; m. Mary Margaret Gaffney; children: Holly L. Smith Volz, Kent W. BA, Hobart Coll., 1960; MBA, Cornell U., 1962; postgrad., Am. U., 1978-79. Mgmt. analyst Office of Sec., HEW, Washington, 1962-65; adminstrv. officer divsn. rsch. facilities and resources NIH, Bethesda, Md., 1965-67, asst. exec. officer divsn. rsch. facilities and resources, 1967-68, exec. officer divsn. rsch. resources, 1968-71, asst. dir. adminstrn. Nat. Libr. Medicine, 1971-78, dep. dir., 1978—; mem. exec. bd. Internat. Coun. Sci. and Tech. Info., Paris, 1983-98, treas., 1986-88, pres.-elect, 1989, pres., 1990-94; treas. Nat. Fed. Abstracting and Info. Sci., Phila., 1986-88, exec. bd., 1985—, pres. elect, 1989, pres., 1990; v.p. U.S. Nat. Com. of UNESCO-PGI, Washington, 1983-85; mem. exec. adv. bd. Fed. Libr. and Info. Ctr. Com., Washington, 1984-89; exec. com. CENDI-Info. Consortia, Washington, 1985—. Contbr. articles to profl. jours., chpt. to book: Management of Federally Sponsored Libraries, 1995. Mem. Citizens Com. for Pub. Libr. Montgomery County, Bethesda, 1981-82; fin. dir. Christ Ch., Rockville, Md., 1990-91. Recipient Asst. Sec. for Health Exceptional Achievement award USPHS, 1978, Sr. Exec. Svc. award, 1996. Mem. ASPA (vice chmn. 1971-72), Am. Mgmt. Assn., Am. Soc. Info. Svcs., Med. Libr. Assn. (Pres. award 1997), Assn. Rsch. Librs., Assn. Advanced Sci., Cosmos Club, Washington. Episcopalian. Avocations: theater, golf, baseball, bird watching, genealogy. Home: Internat Coun Sci & Tech 17903 Gainford Pl Olney MD 20832 Office: Nat Libr Medicine 8600 Rockville Pike Bethesda MD 20894-0001

SMITH, K(ERMIT) WAYNE, computer company executive; b. Newton, N.C., Sept. 15, 1938; s. Harold Robert and Hazel K. (Smith) S.; m. Audrey M. Kennedy, Dec. 19, 1958; 1 son, Stuart W. BA, Wake Forest U., 1960; MA, Princeton U., 1962, PhD, 1964; postgrad., U. So. Calif., 1965; LLD (hon.), Ohio U., 1992. Instr. Princeton U., 1963; asst. prof. econs. and polit. sci. U.S. Mil. Acad., 1963-66; spl. asst. to asst. sec. def. for sys. analysis

Washington, 1966-69; program mgr. def. studies RAND Corp., Santa Monica, Calif., 1969-70; dir. program analysis NSC, Washington, 1970-72; group v.p. planning Dart Industries, L.A., 1972-73; group pres. resort devel. group Dart Industries, 1973-76; exec. v.p. Washington Group, Inc., 1976-77; mng. ptnr. Coopers & Lybrand, Washington, 1977-80, group mng. ptnr., 1980-83; chmn., CEO World Book, Inc., 1983-86; prof. Wake Forest U., 1986-88; CEO OCLC Online Computer Libr. Ctr., Inc., Dublin, Ohio, 1989—, also bd. dirs.; sr. cons. Dept. Def., Dept. State, NSC, NASA, Dept. Energy, OMB, GAO; bd. dirs. Excelco Corp., Nat. City Bank, Columbus, Info. Dimensions, Inc.; con. prof. (hon.) Tsinghua U., Beijing, 1996. Author: How Much is Enough? Shaping the Defense Program, 1961-69, 1971; contbr. articles to profl. jours. Mem. vis. com. Brookings Instn., Washington, 1971-79; mem. bd. visitors Wake Forest U., 1974-78, 82-90, chmn. bd. visitors, 1976-78, trustee, 1991-95, 96—; mem. bd. visitors Def. Sys. Mgmt. Coll., 1982-85, Lenoir Rhyne Coll., 1988-94, Mershon Ctr. Ohio State U., 1990-92, Columbus Assn. for Performing Arts, 1991-95, U. Pitts. Sch. Libr. and Info. Sci., 1992-95; mem. bd. visitors Bowman Gray Bapt. Hosp. Med. Ctr., 1992-95, chmn. bd. visitors, 1993-95. Danforth fellow, Woodrow Wilson fellow Princeton U., 1962. Mem. ALA, Coun. Fgn. Rels., Internat. Inst. Strategic Studies, Inst. Internat. Edn., Coun. Higher Edn., Am. Assn. Higher Edn., Am. Soc. Info. Sci., Washington Golf and Country Club, Chgo. Club, Lakes Golf and Country Club, Capital Club, PhiBeta Kappa, Omicron Delta Kappa, Kappa Sigma. Methodist. Home: 8530 Preston Mill Ct Dublin OH 43017-9648 Office: Online Computer Libr Ctr Inc 6565 Frantz Rd Dublin OH 43017-5308

SMITH, KERRY CLARK, lawyer; b. Phoenix, July 12, 1935; s. Clark and Fay (Jackson) S.; m. Michael Waterman, 1958; children: Kevin, Ian. AB, Stanford U., 1957, JD, 1962. Bar: Calif. 1963, U.S. Supreme Ct. 1980. Assoc. Chickering & Gregory, San Francisco, 1962-70, ptnr., 1970-81; ptnr. Pettit & Martin, San Francisco, 1981-95, Hovis, Smith, Stewart, Lipscomb & Cross, San Francisco, 1995—. Mem. editl. bd. Stanford Law Rev., 1961-62. Lt. USN, 1957-60. Mem. ABA (bus. law sect., mem. banking and savs. and loan coms.), Calif. Bar Assn. (bus. law sect.), San Francisco Bar Assn., Orinda Country Club, La Quinta Resort Golf Club, San Francisco World Travel Club. Office: Hovis Smith Stewart et al 21st Fl 100 Pine St Fl 21 San Francisco CA 94111-5102

SMITH, KEVIN, film director, writer. Dir. films Clerks, 1994, Mall Rats, 1996, Chasing Amy, 1997. Office: Endeavor Agy 9701 Wilshire Blvd 10th Fl Beverly Hills CA 90212*

SMITH, LAMAR SEELIGSON, congressman; b. San Antonio, Nov. 19, 1947; s. Campbell and Eloise Keith (Seeligson) S.; m. Elizabeth Schaefer, Mar. 20, 1992; children: Nell Seligson, Tobin Wells. BA, Yale U., 1969; JD, So. Meth. U., 1975. Mgmt. intern SBA, Washington, 1969-70; bus. writer The Christian Sci. Monitor, Boston, 1970-72; assoc. Maebius & Duncan, Inc., San Antonio, 1975-76; chmn. Rep. Party of Bexar County, San Antonio, 1978-81; state rep. Dist. 57-F, San Antonio, 1981-82; county commr. Precinct 3 Bexar County, 1982-85; mem. 100th-105th Congresses from 21st Tex. dist., 1987—; mem. budget com., jud. com., subcom. crime and criminal justice; ptnr. Lamar Seeligson Ranch, Premont, Tex., 1975—. Christian Scientist. Office: US Ho of Reps 2231 Rayburn Bldg Washington DC 20515-0005*

SMITH, LANE JEFFREY, automotive journalist, technical consultant; b. Honolulu, May 17, 1954; s. Gerald Hague and JoEllen (Lane) S.; m. Susan Elizabeth Gumm, May 24, 1980 (div. 1997); children: Amber Elizabeth, Graham Hague. BS in Journalism, Iowa State U., 1978. Feature editor Car Craft mag. Peterson Pub., L.A., 1979—, tech. editor, sr. editor, editor Hot Rod Mag., 1987-93, exec. editor, 1993—; speaker in field. Avocations: military history, aviation, building and racing high performance automobiles. Home: 18320 Citronia St Northridge CA 91325-1717 Office: Hot Rod Mag 6420 Wilshire Blvd Los Angeles CA 90048-5502

SMITH, LANTY L(LOYD), lawyer, business executive; b. Sherrodsville, Ohio, Dec. 11, 1942; s. Lloyd H. and Ellen Ruth (Newell) S.; m. Margaret Hays Chandler, June 11, 1966; children: Abigail Lamoreaux Presson, Margaret Ellen, Amanda Prescott. BS in Math. with honors, Wittenberg U., Springfield, Ohio, 1964; LLB with honors, Duke U., 1967. Bar: Ohio 1967. Assoc. Jones, Day, Cockley & Reavis, Cleve., 1967-73; ptnr. Jones, Day, Reavis & Pogue, Cleve., 1974-77; exec. v.p., sr. gen. counsel Burlington Industries, Inc., Greensboro, N.C., 1977-86, pres., 1986-88; chmn., CEO Precision Fabrics Group Inc., Greensboro, 1988—; chmn. The Greenwood Group, Inc., Raleigh, N.C., 1992—; chmn. bd. visitors Duke Univ. Sch. Law; bd. dirs., mem. exec. com. First Union Corp., PC Press, Inc., Wikoff Color; bd. trustees Duke U. Vice-chmn., bd. govs. Ctr. for Creative Leadership; chmn. Moses Cone Hosp.; mem. exec. com. Greensboro Devel. Corp.; trustee Kathleen Price Bryan Family Fund; bd. visitors N.C. Agrl. & Tech. State U. Mem. ABA, N.C. Inst. Medicine, N.C. Textile Found. Episcopalian. Home: 1401 Westridge Rd Greensboro NC 27410-2912 Office: 301 N Elm St Fl 6 Greensboro NC 27401-2149

SMITH, LARRY DENNIS, paper mill stores executive; b. Altoona, Pa., Dec. 12, 1954; s. Bernard Robert and Dollie Edith (Nofsker) S. BS in Art Edn., Ind. U. Pa., 1977. Audio artist, 1974—; artist Mail Art Network, 1980—; organizer, curator Manifesto Shnn Archives, East Freedom, Pa., 1982-86; established Patriots of the Am. Revolution Heraldic Register, 1993. Author: Manifesto Shnnalchemy, 1981, In the Wake of the Disaster Machine, 1981; editor: Artcomnet, 1981-87; artist The Labours of Grimnlaek, 1984; one-man shows in Rome, Stockholm, Zurich, Brusque and Helsinki; group show Seoul Internat. Bienale, 1984; editor 150th Anniversary History of Blair County, 1993-96. Mem. SAR. Republican. Avocations: genealogical research, rare book collector, gardening. Home: RR1 Box 704-A East Freedom PA 16637-9770 Office: Appleton Papers Inc 100 Paper Mill Rd Roaring Spring PA 16673-1480

SMITH, LARRY GLENN, retired state judge; b. Montgomery, Ala., Aug. 6, 1924; s. Alonzo Nathan and Louise (Norman) S.; m. Mary Emmalyn Murphree, Feb. 28, 1948; children: Cynthia Lynn Smith, Larry Glenn Jr., Celia Dell Smith Rudolph. Student, U. Ala., Tuscaloosa, 1942-43, 46-48; LLB, U. Fla., 1949. Bar: Fla. 1949. Pvt. practice, Panama City, Fla., 1949-53; assoc. Mathis & Mathis, Panama City, 1953-57; asst. state's atty. Office State's Atty. for 14th Cir., Panama City, 1953-57; rsch. asst. Fla. Supreme Ct., Tallahassee, 1958-60; ptnr. Baker, Baker & Smith, Orlando, Fla., 1960-64, Isler, Welch, Smith, Higby & Brown, Panama City, 1964-72; judge cir. ct. Fla. 14th Jud. Cir., Panama City, 1973-79; judge Fla. 1st Dist. Ct. Appeal, Tallahassee, 1979-94; ret., 1994; chief judge Fla. 1st Dist. Ct. Appeal, Tallahassee, 1987-89; ret., 1994; sr. judge State of Fla.; Mem. Fla. Bd. Bar Examiners, Tallahassee, 1967-72, Fla. Ct. Edn. Coun., Tallahassee, 1979-81, 86-91, Fla. Bench and Bar Commn., Tallahassee, 1990-91; pres. Fla. Conf. of Dist. Ct. Appeals Judges, Tallahassee, 1986-87. Mem. Panama City Airport Authority, 1952-55; past pres. Bay County Libr. Assn., Panama City. Lt. (j.g.) USNR, 1943-45. Mem. ABA, Fla. Bar, Tallahassee Bar Assn., Am. Judicature Soc. Avocations: hiking, biking, skiing, photography, reading. Home: 4115 W 17th St Panama City FL 32401-1122

SMITH, LAUREN ASHLEY, lawyer, journalist, clergyman, physicist; b. Clinton, Iowa, Nov. 30, 1924; s. William Thomas Roy and Ethel (Cook) S.; m. Barbara Ann Mills, Aug. 22, 1947; children: Christopher A., Laura Nan Smith Pringle, William Thomas Roy II. BS, U. Minn., 1946, JD, 1949; postgrad., U. Chgo., 1943-49; MDiv, McCormick Theol. Sem., 1950; postgrad., U. Iowa, 1992. Bar: Colo. 1957, Iowa 1959, Ill. 1963, Minn. 1983, U.S. Supreme Ct. 1967; ordained to ministry Presbyn. Ch., 1950. Pastor Presbyn. Ch., Fredonia, Kans., 1950-52, Lamar, Colo., 1952-57; pastor Congl. Ch., Clinton, 1975-80; editor The Comml., Pine Bluff, Ark., 1957-58; pvt. practice Clinton, 1959—; CEO LASCO Pub. Group, Clinton, 1995—; internat. conferee Stanley Found., Warrenton, Va., 1963-72; legal observer USSR, 1978; co-sponsor All India Renewable Energy Conf., Bangalore, 1981; law sch. conferee U. Minn., China, 1983; sr. assoc. Molecular Nanotech. Foresight Inst., Palo Alto, Calif. Author: (jurisprudence treatise) Forma Dat Esse Rel, 1975, (monograph) First Strike Option, 1983; coauthor: India On to New Horizons, 1989; columnist Crow Call, 1968—; coeditor Press and News of India, 1978-82; pub. Crow Call; pseudonym Christopher Crow, 1981—; editor Asian Econ. Cmty. Jour.; contbr. articles to religious publs. Minister-at-large Presbyn. Ch. U.S.A., Iowa, 1987—, mem. nat. New Spiritual Formation Network; bd. dirs. Iowa divsn. UN Assn. U.S.A., Iowa City, 1970-85; sr. assoc. Molecular Nanotechnology Foresight Inst., Palo Alto, Calif.; Franciscans United Nations Non Govt. Orgn.; assoc. Westar Inst. (The Jesus Seminar), Santa Rosa, Calif., 1997. Mem. Iowa Bar Assn., Ill. Bar Assn., St. Andrews Soc., Clinton County Bar Assn. (pres. 1968, Best in Iowa citation), Clinton Ministerial Assn., Samaritan Health Systems Chaplain Corps., Quaker Internat. Yokefellow, Nat. Network for New Spiritual Formation Presbyn. Ch. USA, Molecular Nanotechnology Foresight Inst. (sr. assoc.), Franciscans Internat., City Club of Quad Cities (bd. dirs.).

SMITH, LAWRENCE J., bishop. Pres., regionary bishop The Liberal Cath. Ch.-Province of the U.S.A., Evergreen Park, Ill. Office: Liberal Cath Ch 9740 S Avers Ave Evergreen Park IL 60805-2946*

SMITH, LAWRENCE LEIGHTON, conductor; b. Portland, Oreg., Apr. 8, 1936; s. Lawrence Keller and Bonita Evelyn (Wood) S.; children by previous marriage: Kevin, Laura, Gregory; stepchildren: Kristine, John. B.S. cum laude, Portland State Coll., 1956; grad. magna cum laude, Mannes Coll. Music, N.Y.C., 1959; Ph D (Hon.), Ind. U, 1992; D (hon.), U. Louisville, Ind. State U. Mem. faculty Mannes Coll. Music, 1959-62; prof. piano Boston U., 1963-64; asst. condr. Met. Opera, 1964-67; mem. faculty Curtis Inst., Phila., 1968-69, Calif. Inst. Arts, 1970-72, U. Tex., 1962-63; prin. guest condr. Phoenix Symphony, 1970-73; music dir., condr. Austin (Tex.) Symphony, 1971-72, Oreg. Symphony, Portland, 1973-80; pres., music dir. San Antonio Symphony, 1980-85; music dir., condr. Louisville Orch., 1983-95, condr. laureate, 1995-97; prin. guest condr. N.J. Symphony Orch., 1997—; faculty mem. Yale U., 1994—; guest condr. N.Y. Philharm., L.A. Philharm., Tulsa Philharm., Winnipeg (Man., Can.) Orch., Minn. Orch., Cin. Symphony, St. Louis Symphony, Moscow Philharm., Tokyo Philharm. Recipient 1st prize Met. Internat. Condrs. competition, 1964, Ditson Condrs. award Columbia U., 1988. Mem. Am. Fedn. Musicians, Mensa. Buddhist.

SMITH, LAWRENCE R., lawyer; b. Oak Park, Ill., Jan. 27, 1948. AB cum laude, Coll. of Holy Cross, 1970; JD, U. Mich., 1973. Bar: Ill. 1973. Ptnr. Querrey & Harrow Ltd., Chgo.; panel Am. Arbitration Assn. Mem. ABA, Am. Law Firm Assn. (bd. dirs.), Ill. State Bar Assn., Chgo. Bar Assn., Ill. Assn. Def. Trial Counsel (pres. 1988-89), Def. Rsch. Inst. Address: 180 N Stetson Ave Ste 3500 Chicago IL 60601-6714

SMITH, LEE ARTHUR, professional baseball player; b. Jamestown, La., Dec. 4, 1957. Student, Northwestern State U., La. Pitcher Chgo. Cubs, 1975-87, Boston Red Sox, 1987-90, St. Louis Cardinals, 1990-93, N.Y. Yankees, 1993-94; with Balt. Orioles, 1994, Calif. Angels, 1994-96, Cin. Reds, 1996, Montreal Expos, 1997—. Named Nat. League Fireman of Yr., Sporting News, 1991, 94; holder maj. league record for most consecutive errorless games by pitcher, Nat. League single-season record for most saves; Nat. League Saves Leader, 1983, 91-92; mem. Nat. League All-Star team, 1983, 87, 91-94; named Nat League Co-Fireman of Yr., Sporting News, 1983, 92. Office: Montreal Expos, 4549 Pierre-de-Coubertin Ave, Montreal, PQ Canada*

SMITH, LEE ELTON, surgery educator, retired military officer; b. Ventura, Calif., July 19, 1937; s. Raymond Elroy and Edith Irene (Jordan) S.; m. Carole Sue Smith; children: Justine Diane, Alexander Loren. BS, U. Calif., Berkeley, 1959; MD, U. Calif., San Francisco, 1962. Diplomate Am. Bd. Surgery, Am. Bd. Colon and Rectal Surgery (pres. 1992-93). Commd. ens. USN, 1960, advanced through grades to capt., 1977; intern U. Utah, Salt Lake City, 1962-63; resident USN, San Diego, Calif., 1966-70; staff surgeon USN, Bremerton, Wash., 1970-72; resident colorectal surgery U. Minn., Mpls., 1972-73; dir. colorectal surgery Nat. Naval Med. Ctr. USN, Bethesda, Md., 1973-82; ret. USN, 1983, Seattle, 1982; clin. prof. surgery Uniformed Svcs. U., Bethesda, 1976—; prof. surgery George Washington U., Washington, 1983-96, clin. prof. surgery, 1996—; dir. sect. of colon and rectal surgery Washington Hosp. Ctr., 1996—; pres. Am. Bd. Colon and Rectal Surgery, 1993-94. Editor: Practical Guide to Anorectal Physiology, 1990, 2d edit., 1995; assoc. editor Diseases of the Colon & Rectum, 1984-96, Perspectives in Colon and Rectal Surgery, 1989—. Mem. ACS (pres. Met. Washington chpt. 1993-94), Soc. Am. Gastrointestinal Endoscopic Surgeons (pres. 1989-90), Am. Cancer Soc. (v.p. D.C. chpt. 1985—). Home: 1200 N Nash St Apt 518 Arlington VA 22209-3614 Office: Washington Hosp Ctr 110 Irving St NW Washington DC 20010-2931

SMITH, LEE HERMAN, business executive; b. Ector, Tex., Jan. 7, 1935; s. Lee Herman and Willie Mae (Morrison) S.; m. Eva Landers, Feb. 18, 1960; 1 dau., Diette. B.S. in Math., Tex. A&M U., 1957, Ph.D. in Stats., 1964; M.S. in Engring. Adminstrn., So. Methodist U., 1961. Various engring. positions, 1957-65; asst. prof. Sch. Bus., U. Tex., Arlington, 1965-66, assoc. dean, assoc. prof., 1967-68; exec. planning adviser N.Am. Aviation Co., Los Angeles, summer 1966; prof., chmn. dept. quantitative mgmt. sci. U. Houston, 1969-71; dean faculties, prof. mgmt. sci. U. Tex., Dallas, 1971-72, v.p. acad. affairs, prof. mgmt. sci., 1972-74; pres. S.W. Tex. State U., San Marcos, 1974-81, TRAVELHOST, Inc., 1981-87, 89-93; chief exec. officer Neuro Systems Inc., 1984-85; pres. J & P Petroleum Products, Inc., 1986-87, Standard Life Ins. Co. of Miss., Jackson, 1987-89, Intercontinental Life Ins. Co. of N.J., 1987-89; exec. search cons. Sandhurst Assocs., 1993-94, 96—; pres. Voyager Expanded Learning Inc., 1995-96; cons. in field; mem. sci. adv. com. Callier Hearing and Speech Center, Dallas; mem. Am. Assn. State Colls. and Univs. trip to People's Republic of China, 1975, Republic of China, 1976; chmn. bd. Central Tex. Higher Edn. Authority, 1977-78; mem. Gov.'s Higher Edn. Mgmt. Effectiveness Council, 1980-81. Author books, articles, revs. in field. Tex. A & M Coll. Opportunity scholar, 1953-57; Iowa State U. Research Found. fellow, 1961; Gen. Electric Co. fellow, 1962; Ling-Temco-Vought fellow, 1963-64; U. Tex. travel grantee, 1967. Mem. Am. Statis. Assn. (pres. N.Tex. chpt. 1967-68), Ops. Research Soc. Am., Inst. Mgmt. Scis. (program chmn. meetings), Am. Inst. Decision Scis. (v.p. planning and devel. 1970-71, council 1971-72), S. Tex. C. of C., Delta Sigma Pi, Phi Kappa Phi. Home: 2300 Grayson Dr Apt 212 Grapevine TX 76051-7001

SMITH, LEE L., hotel executive; b. Long Beach, Calif., Oct. 15, 1936; s. Lowell Llake and Violet Margaret (Chrissman) S.; m. Sharon M.C. Lanahan, (div. 1977). AA, Long Beach City Coll., 1958; BA in Music, Chapman Coll., 1965; postgrad., Calif. State U., Long Beach, 1966-67, U. Calif., Santa Barbara, 1974. Cert. tchr. Calif.; lic. ins. agt., Calif. Owner, mgr. Lee's Land Cattle Ranch, Cuyama Valley, Calif., 1960—; tchr. Cuyama Valley Schs., New Cuyama, Calif., 1967-79; owner, mgr. Cuyama Buckhorn Restaurant & Motel, New Cuyama, 1979-83; owner Allstate Ins. Agy., Desert Hot Springs, Calif., 1987-91; owner, mgr. Caravan Resort Spa, Desert Hot Springs, 1983-91; owner S & S Printing, 1990—, Lee's Land Bed & Breakfast, 1992—. Violinist Bakersfield (Calif.) Symphony, 1967—, Brook String Quartet, Palm Springs, Calif., 1984-91; dir. Planning Commn., Desert Hot Springs, 1985-87; chmn. Environ. Rev., Desert Hot Springs, 1986-88; mem. Redevel. Com., Desert Hot Springs, 1983-88; mem. exec. bd. growth and devel. Boys and Girls Club; bd. dirs. Food Now Program, 1988-91. Mem. Am. Fedn. Musicians, Desert Hot Springs C. of C. (Bus. Person Yr. 1987), Taft C. of C. (pres. 1997), Breakfast Rotary (pres. 1987-88), Taft Rotary, Elks. Republican. Avocations: hiking, flying. Home: HC 1 Box 185B Maricopa CA 93252-9629 Office: S & S Printing 606 Center St Taft CA 93268-3125

SMITH, LEIGHTON WARREN, JR., naval officer; b. Mobile, Ala., Aug. 20, 1939; s. Leighton W. Sr. and Sara Wallace (Griffith) S.; m. Dorothy Dunn McDowell, June 23, 1962; children: Leighton W. III, Susan Page, Dorothy McDowell. BS, U.S. Naval Acad., 1962; postgrad., Air Command and Staff Coll., Montgomery, Ala., 1973-74; MS in Psychology, Troy State U., 1974. Commd. ensign USN, 1962, advanced through grades to 4 star adm., 1991; comdr. Attack Squadron 86 USN, Cecil Field, Fla., 1974-76; comdr. Light Attack Wing One USN, Cecil Field, 1980-81; comdr. Carrier Air Wing 15 USN, San Diego, 1976-78; head comdr. assignments Naval Mil. Pers. Command USN, Arlington, Va., 1978-80; comdg. officer USS Kalamazoo (AOR6) USN, Norfolk, Va., 1982-83; asst. chief staff readiness, Naval Air Force, U.S. Atlantic Fleet USN, Norfolk, Va., 1983-84, comdg. officer USS America, 1984-85; strategic studies group CNO fellow Naval War Coll. USN, Newport, R.I., 1985-86; dir. tactical readiness div. OPNAV Chief of NavalOps. USN, Washington, 1986-88; comdr. Carrier Group 6 USN, Mayport, Fla., 1988-89; dir. ops. U.S. European Command J-3 USN, Stuttgart, Fed. Republic Germany, 1989-91; dep. chief of naval ops. for plans, policy and ops. USN, 1991-94; comdr. in chief USN Forces Europe and NATO Allied Forces Southern Europe, 1994-96, comdr. joint task force provide promise, 1994-96; comdr. NATO Peace Implementation Force, Bosnia, 1995-96. Decorated D.S.M. Legion of Merit with two gold stars, DFC with one gold star, Meritorious Service medal with one gold star, 29 Air medals; received Order of Merit from Pres. of Hungary; hon. knight of the Brit. Empire by Her Majesty the Queen. Mem. Meninac Rotary (Jacksonville, Fla.), Rotary. Episcopalian. Avocations: golf, squash, racquet ball, fishing.

SMITH, LEO EMMET, lawyer; b. Chgo., Jan 6, 1927; s. Albert J. and Cecilia G. (Dwyer) S.; m. Rita Gleason, Apr. 14, 1956; children: Mary Cecilia, Gerianne, Kathleen, Leo A., Maureen. JD, DePaul U., 1950. Admitted to Ill. bar, 1950; assoc. with law firm also engaged in pvt. industry, 1950-54; asst. states atty. Cook County, Ill., 1954-57; asst. counsel Traffic Inst., Northwestern U., Evanston, Ill., 1957-60; asst. exec. sec. Comml. Law League Am., Chgo., 1960-61, exec. dir., 1961-83, editor Comml. Law Jour., 1961-89, editor emeritus, 1989—; assoc. Howe & Hutton, Ltd., Chgo., 1985—. Fellow Chgo. Bar Found. (life); mem. Chgo. Bar Assn. (chmn. libr. com. 1983, sec. sr. lawyers com. 1994-95), Am. Acad. Matrimonial Lawyers (exec. dir. 1982-84), World Assn. Lawyers (founding mem. 1975), Am. Soc. Assn. Execs., Chgo. Soc. Assn. Execs., Assn. Econs. Coun., Friends of Northwestern Sta. (spokesperson 1984). Contbr. articles to legal jours. Home: 1104 S Knight Ave Park Ridge IL 60068-4447 Office: Howe & Hutton Ltd 20 N Wacker Dr Ste 4200 Chicago IL 60606-3103

SMITH, LEO GILBERT, hospital administrator; b. Oroville, Calif., July 29, 1929; s. Leo Paul and Laura Mae (Hoffschulte) S.; m. Marcia Elise Ernest, Jan. 26, 1952; children: Matthew Paul, Mara Lee, Bridget Mari, Leo Ernest. B.S.C., U. Santa Clara, 1951; M.P.H., U. Calif., 1958. Adminstrv. resident San Diego County Gen. Hosp., 1958-59; asst. hosp. adminstr. Santa Clara Valley Med. Center, 1959-67, adminstr., 1967-76, dir. planning, 1976-77; health care cons., 1977-80; adminstr. Puget Sound Hosp., 1980-82; mgr. Tacoma Family Medicine dept Multicare Med. Ctr., Tacoma, Wash., 1982-86, dir. clinic services, 1986-91; clinic mgr. Providence Factoria Family Healthcare div. Providence Med. Ctr., Seattle, 1992; ret. Bd. dirs. Children's Home Soc. of Calif., chmn. dist. bd., 1969-70; chmn. br. bd. Children's Home Soc. of Wash., 1986—. Served in mil. 1952-54. Mem. Cen. Coast Hosp. Conf. (pres. 1970), Hosp. Coun. No. Calif. (dir. 1970-73), Am. Coll. Hosp. Adminstrs., Med. Group Mgrs. Assn., Tacoma Sunrise Rotary (pres. 1982-83, Dist. 5020 Youth Exch. officer 1991-96). Home: 7122 Turquoise Dr SW Tacoma WA 98498-6431

SMITH, LEONARD, JR., medical/surgical and oncology nurse; b. Ft. Lauderdale, Fla., Aug. 17, 1955; s. Leonard and Ruthe Mae (Taylor) S.; m. Koreen Andrea Smith, Dec. 31, 1989; children: Jessica, Sara Marie, Marcus Alan. BS in Biology and Chemistry, Jacksonville U., 1977; postgrad., Fla. Atlantic U., 1978-82, U. fla., 1984-87; AS in Nursing, Broward Community Coll., Ft. Lauderdale, 1990; cert. in theol. studies, Knox Theol. Sem., 1994. RN, Fla., BLS. Physician asst. trained East Broward Med. Ctr., Pompano, Fla., 1987-88; mental health technician, counselor CPR-Ft. Lauderdale, 1988-90; nurse med.-surg. and oncology units Broward Gen. Med. Ctr., Ft. Lauderdale, 1990—; nurse mgr. Ft. Lauderdale (Fla.) Hosp., 1992—; cmty. health nurse Staff Builders Profl. Nursing, Ft. Lauderdale, 1991-94; RN Broward County Hospice, North Lauderdale, Fla., 1994—; community health nurse Staff Builders Profl. Nursing, Ft. Lauderdale, 1991—. Mem. AANC (cert. med.-surg. nursing). Democrat. Presbyterian. Avocations: chess, movies, keyboard musician.

SMITH, LEONARD BINGLEY, musician; b. Poughkeepsie, N.Y., Sept. 5, 1915; s. Frank Roderick and Ethel (Schubert) S.; m. Helen Gladys Rowe, Apr. 20, 1940 (dec. 1993); 1 dau., Sandra Victoria. Student, N.Y. Mil. Acad., 1930-33, Ernest Williams Sch. Music, 1933-36, NYU, 1936-37, Curtis Inst. Music, 1943-45; H.H.D., Detroit Inst. Tech., 1965. Pres. Accompaniments Unltd., Inc., 1952—. Cornet soloist, Ernest Williams Band, 1933-36, The Goldman Band, summers 1936-42; 1st trumpet, Barrere Little Symphony, 1935-37, Detroit Symphony Orch., 1937-42, Ford Sunday Evening Hour, 1937-42; condr., The Leonard Smith Concert Band, 1945—, Detroit Concert Band, 1945—, U. Detroit Bands, 1949-50, Moslem AAONMS Band, 1945-57, Scandinavian Symphony Orch. of Detroit, 1959-61, guest condr., Indpls. Symphony Orch., 1967; guest condr., soloist, clinician numerous concerts, U.S., Can.; mus. dir. John Philip Sousa documentary for BBC, 1970; Sousa Am. Bicentennial Recorded Collection; record series Gems concert band, Blossom Festival Band; condr. Blossom Festival Concert Band, 1972—; The Indomitable Teddy Roosevelt; producer: Our Am. Heritage in Music, 1970; pres., Bandland, Inc., 1951-61; Author: Treasury of Scales; over 350 pub. compositions; mem. bd. advisors Instrumentalist mag. Chmn. music com. Mich. Civil War Centennial Commn., 1961-64; gov. bd. Mac Award. With USNR, 1942-45. Recipient spl. medal Mich. Polish Legion Am. Vets., Distinguished Service medal Kappa Kappa Psi; Mich. Minuteman Gov.'s award, 1973; Freedom Found. award, 1975; Gen. William Booth award, 1976, Embassy Mich. Tourism award, 1979; named Alumnus of Distinction N.Y. Mil. Acad., 1976. Mem. ASCAP, Philippine Bandsmen's Assn. (hon.), Am. Fedn. Musicians, Internat. Platform Assn., Assn. Concert Bands (pres. 1982-83). Clubs: Masons (33 deg.), Shriners, K.T, Jesters. Office: care Detroit Concert Band Inc 7443 E Butherus Dr Ste 100 Scottsdale AZ 85260-2423

SMITH, LEONARD WARE, lawyer; b. Lancaster, Ky., Jan. 1, 1938; s. William F. and Willie (Ware) S.; m. Carole Irene Binkley, Mar. 18, 1978; 1 stepchild, Gina Harper; children: Rebecca Ann, Andrew Ware. Student, Centre Coll., 1956-57; BA, Eastern Ky. U., 1961; JD, U. Ky., 1968. Bar: Ky. 1969, Tenn. 1988. Pvt. practice law Lancaster, 1969-70; atty. TVA, Knoxville, Tenn., 1970-86; sr. atty. TVA, Knoxville, 1986-92, ret., 1992; city atty. City of Lancaster, 1969-70; bd. dirs., chmn. TVA Employees Credit Union, 1980-84. Bd. govs. Shrine Hosp., Greenville, S.C. Capt., U.S. Army, 1961-66. Mem. Ky. Bar Assn., Masons (32 deg. Knight Comdr. Ct. of Honor), Scottish Rite, Shriners (Potentate Kerbela Shrine Temple 1989, mem. Imperial Shrine jurisprudence & laws com., imperial rep., 1988—, v.p. South Atlantic Shrine Assn. 1992—). Home and Office: 416 Kendall Rd Knoxville TN 37919-6803

SMITH, LEONORE RAE, artist; b. Chgo.; d. Leon and Rose (Hershfield) Goodman; m. Paul Carl Smith, Apr. 17, 1945; children: Jill Henderson, Laurie Christman. Student, Chgo. Art Inst., 1935-40, U. Chgo., 1939—. performer in many Broadway shows, with Met. Opera Quartet, Carnegie Hall, nat. concerts; portrait landscape painter; signature artist Oil Painters of Am., Chgo., 1992-96; ofcl. artist U.S. Coast Guard, Washington, 1989-95; cert. artist Am. Portrait Soc., Huntington Harbor, Calif., 1985; nat. adv. bd. The Portrait Club, N.Y.C., 1983. Pres. Pacific Palisades Rep. Women, Calif. Recipient Best of Show awards Salamagundi U.S. Coast Guard, N.Y.C., 1989, Pacific Palisades Art Assn., 1987, 1st prize in oils Greater L.A. Art Competition, Santa Monica, Calif., 1995, prize The Artist's Mag., 1995, Internat. Soc. Artists, 1977, 1st Pl. The Artists Mag. Internat. Dream Studies Competition, 1996. Mem. Salmagundi Club, Pacific Palisades Art Assn. (past pres.), Calif. Art Club, Oil Painters of Am., Am. Portrait Soc. Avocations: singing, acting.

SMITH, LEROY HARRINGTON, JR., mechanical engineer, aerodynamics consultant; b. Balt., Nov. 3, 1928; s. Leroy Harrington and Edna (Marsh) S.; m. Barbara Ann Williams, July 7, 1951; children: Glenn Harrington, Bruce Lyttleton, Cynthia Ann. BS in Engring., Johns Hopkins U., 1949, MS, 1951, Dr. Engring., 1954. Compressor aerodynamicist Gen. Electric Co., Cin., 1954-61, mgr. turbomachinery devel., 1961-68, mgr. compressor & fan design tech., 1968-75, mgr. turbomachinery aerodynamics tech., 1975-92; cons. technologist Turbomachinery Aerodynamics Gen. Electric Co., 1992—. Contbr. articles to ASME Trans.; holder 12 patents. Recipient Perry T. Egbert Jr. awards, 1969, 83, Charles P. Steinmetz award, 1987 Gen. Electric Co. Fellow ASME (Gas Turbine award 1981, 87, R. Tom Sawyer award 1987, Aircraft Engine Tech. award 1993); mem. NAE, Ohio River Launch Club. Office: GE Aircraft Eng Mail Drop A411 1 Neumann Way # A411 Cincinnati OH 45215-1915

SMITH, LESLIE ROPER, hospital and healthcare administrator; b. Stockton, Calif., June 20, 1928; s. Austin J. and Helen (Roper) S.; m. Edith Sue Fincher, June 22, 1952; children: Melinda Sue, Leslie Erin, Timothy Brian. A.B., U. Pacific, 1951; M.S. in Pub. Adminstrn, U. So. Calif., 1956. Adminstrv. asst. Ranchos Los Amigos Hosp., Downey, Calif., 1953-57; asst. adminstr. Harbor Gen. Hosp., Torrance, Calif., 1957-65; adminstr. Harbor Gen. Hosp., 1966-71; acting regional dir. Los Angeles County Coastal Health Services Region, 1973; pres. San Pedro Peninsula Hosp., San Pedro, Cal., 1974-86; exec. dir. Los Angeles County/U. So. Calif. Med. Center, 1971-73; adminstr. Long Beach (Calif.) Hosp., 1965-66; asso. clin. prof. community medicine and pub. health, also emergency medicine U. So. Calif., 1968-78; instr. U. So. Calif. (Sch. Pub. Adminstrn.), 1968; preceptor hosp. adminstrn. UCLA Sch. Pub. Health, 1964—; chief exec. officer French Hosp. Med. Ctr. and Health Plan, 1986-87; dir. health care services McCormack & Farrow, 1987—; lectr. in field, 1963—; cons. emergency health services HEW, 1970-73; chmn. com. diaster preparedness Hosp. Council So. Calif., 1966-72, sec., 1971—, pres., 1973; mem. Calif. Assembly Com. on Emergency Med. Services, 1970, Calif. Emergency Med. Adv. Com., 1972-75, Los Angeles County Commn. on Emergency Med. Services, 1975-83, Los Angeles Health Planning and Devel. Agy. Commn., 1980-83; bd. dirs. Blue Cross of So. Calif.; mem. hosp. relations com. Blue Cross of Calif.; mem. adv. com. on emergency health services Calif. Dept. Health, 1974-75; bd. dirs., mem. exec. com. Truck Ins. Exchange of Farmers Ins. Group, 1977-82; bd. dirs. Hosp. Council of So. Calif., 1966-76, 81-86, Health Resources Inst., 1985-86; chmn. Preferred Health Network, 1983-86. Mem. goals com., Torrance, 1968—; pres. Silver Spur Little League, Palos Verdes, 1969-70. Served with AUS, 1946-48. Recipient Silver Knight and Gold Knight award Nat. Mgmt. Assn., 1970, 85, Walker Fellowship award, 1976. Fellow Am. Coll. Health Care Execs. (life); mem. Am., Nat. mgmt. assns., Am. Hosp. Assn. (chmn. com. on community emergency health services 1973), Calif. Hosp. Assn. (chmn. com. emergency services 1965-70, trustee 1973-76, bd. dirs. Calif. Ins. Service Group 1980-82), County Suprs. Assn. Calif. (chmn. joint subcom. on emergency care 1970). Presbyn. (elder, trustee). Home: 27 Marseille Laguna Niguel CA 92677-5400

SMITH, LESTER MARTIN, broadcasting executive; b. N.Y.C., Oct. 20, 1919; s. Alexander and Sadie S.; m. Bernice Reitz, Sept. 28, 1962; 1 child, Alexander. B.S. in Bus. Adminstrn, NYU, 1940. Chief exec. officer Alexander Broadcasting Co., radio stas. in, 1954—; gen. partner 700 Investment Co.; past dir. Seattle C. of C.; past chmn. dir. Radio Advt. Bur. Served to maj. U.S. Army, 1942-46. Decorated Bronze Star. Mem. Nat. Assn. Broadcasters (past dir.), Oreg. Assn. Broadcasters (past pres.), Broadcast Pioneers. Clubs: Rotary (Seattle), Rainer (Seattle), Wash. Athletic (Seattle). Address: 700 112th Ave NE Bellevue WA 98004-5106

SMITH, LEVIE DAVID, JR., real estate appraiser, consultant; b. Lakeland, Fla., Oct. 19, 1924; s. Levie David and Grace (Ross) S.; m. Annie Laurie Hogan, Aug. 29, 1948; children: Nancy, L. David, Judy. Student, U. Miami, 1943; Columbia U., USNR Midshipmen's Sch.; BS, Fla. So. Coll., 1947. Salesman Smith & Smith, Realtors, Lakeland, 1947-50; staff appraiser Smith & Son, Appraisers, Lakeland, 1952-72; pres. Levie D. Smith & Assoc., Inc., Lakeland, 1973-95, cons., 1996—; chmn. bd. dirs. First Fed. of Fla., Lakeland, acting pres., 1992-95, dir. emeritus, 1996—; pres. Fla. Assn. Realtors, Orlando, 1970; chmn. Fla. Real Estate Commn., Orlando, 1979. Past trustee Polk Theatre, Inc., pres. 1989, chmn. adv. bd., 1994-95; mem. adv. bd. Imperial Symphony Orch., 1993—; mem. exec. bd. Gulf Ridge Coun. Boy Scouts Am., dist. chmn. 1995—; mem. real estate adv. bd. U. Fla.; bd. dirs. Fla. Presbyn. Homes, Inc., 1997—. Lt. USN, 1943-46, 50-52. Recipient Silver Beaver award Gulf Ridge Coun., Boy Scouts Am., 1984. Mem. Am. Inst. Real Estate Appraisers (govt. coun. 1976-83, v.p. 1982-83, SE Meritorious award 1987), Lakeland Rotary Club (pres. 1976-77, Paul Harris fellow, 4 way test award), Pi Kappa Alpha. Presbyterian. Avocations: gardening, camping, fishing. Home: 515 Laurel Ln Lakeland FL 33813-1650 Office: Levie D Smith & Assocs Inc 101 Doris Dr Lakeland FL 33813-1004

SMITH, LEWIS DENNIS, academic administrator; b. Muncie, Ind., Jan. 18, 1938; s. Thurman Lewis and Dorothy Ann (Dennis) S.; m. Suzanne F. Metcalfe; children: Lauren Kay, Raymond Bradley. AB, Ind. U., 1959, PhD, 1963. Asst. biologist Argonne (Ill.) Nat. Lab., 1964-67, assoc. biologist, 1967-69; assoc. prof. Purdue U., West Lafayette, Ind., 1969-73; prof. biology Purdue U., West Lafayette, 1973-87, assoc. head dept. biol. scis., 1979-80, head dept., 1980-87; prof. dept. devel. and cell. U. Calif., Irvine, 1987-94, dean Sch. Biol. Scis., 1987-90, exec. vice chancellor, 1990-94; pres. U. of Nebr., 1994—; instr. embryology Woods Hole (Mass.) Marine Biology Lab., summers 1972, 73, 74, 88, 89; mem. Space Sci. Bd., Washington, 1986-91; chmn. Space Biology and Medicine, Space Sci. Bd., 1986-91; mem. cell biology study sect. NIH, Bethesda, Md., 1971-75; chmn., 1977-79, bd. sci. counselors Nat. Inst. Child Health and Human Devel., 1990-95, chmn. 1992-95; mem. space biology peer rev. bd. AIBS, 1980-85. Guggenheim fellow, 1987. Mem. Am. Soc. Biochemistry and Molecular Biology, AAAS, Internat. Soc. for Devel. Biology, Soc. for Devel. Biology, Am. Soc. Cell Biology. Home: 9125 Pioneers Ct Lincoln NE 68520-9305 Office: Varner Hall 3835 Holdrege St Lincoln NE 68503-1435*

SMITH, LEWIS MOTTER, JR., advertising and direct marketing executive; b. Kansas City, Mo., Nov. 4, 1932; s. Lewis Motter and Virginia (Smith) S.; m. Alice Allen, June 28, 1975; children: Katherine Allen, Patience Allen. Student, Kenyon Coll., 1951-53, Columbia U., 1956-58. Copywriter mail order div. Grolier Soc., Inc., N.Y.C., 1957-59; free lance copywriter Santa Fe, N.M., 1960-61; v.p. creative services Grolier Enterprises Inc., N.Y.C., 1962-67; v.p., creative planning dir. Wunderman, Ricotta & Kline, Inc., N.Y.C., 1968-72; exec. v.p., creative dir., 1972-79; exec. v.p. Young & Rubicam Direct Mktg. Group, 1980; sr. v.p., dir. mktg. Book-of-the-Month Club, Inc., 1980-84, dir., 1981-84; exec. v.p., creative dir. SSC&B: Vos Direct Inc., N.Y.C., 1985-87; pres., dir. creative services Lintas: Direct Inc. (formerly SSC&B: Vos Direct Inc.), N.Y.C., 1987-89; pres. Lew Smith & Assocs., Inc., 1989—. Bd. dirs. Young Concert Artists, Inc., N.Y.C., 1966-67, Harlem Sch. Arts, 1967-68. Served with U.S. Army, 1953-56. Mem. Delta Phi. Episcopalian. Home and Office: 45 Knollwood Rd Rhinebeck NY 12572-2313

SMITH, LINDA A., congresswoman, former state legislator; m. Vern Smith; children: Sheri, Robi. Office mgr.; former mem. Wash. State Ho. of Reps.; mem. Wash. State Senate; congresswoman, Wash. 3rd Dist. U.S. House Reps., Washington, D.C., 1995—; mem. resources com., small bus. com.; mem. nat. parks & pub. lands, water & power, small bus. coms. Republican. Home: 10009 NW Ridgecrest Ave Vancouver WA 98685-5159 Office: 1317 Longworth Bldg Washington DC 20515-4703*

SMITH, LINDA LOU, city official; b. Fullerton, Ky., Jan. 26, 1943; d. James Oliver and Ethel Lucille (Stewart) Newman; m. Richard Glenn Smith, Aug. 28, 1959; children: Richard Jr., Janet Smith Sparks, Robert Orin. Student, Wayne County C.C., 1979, Detroit Bus. Inst., 1985; cert. mcpl. clk. with advanced edn., Mich. State U., 1992. Sec. Brownstown (Mich.) Twp., 1976-85, apptd. dep. clk., 1988, elected clk., 1988—, 1992-96, 96—. Bd. dirs. Downriver Comty. Conf., Southgate, Mich., 1988-92; sec., vice-chair Downriver Comty. Alliance, Southgate, 1992-95; mem. Wayne County Election Scheduling Bd., Detroit, 1988—; mem. dist 16 Mich. Dem. Party, Wayne, 1988-93; elected Brownstown Precinct Del., 1992—. Recipient Spl. Svc. award Downriver Human Svc. Ctr., 1984. Mem. LWV (dir. 1988—), Internat. Inst. Mcpl. Clks. (cert. mcpl. clk., advanced acad. edn.), Mich. Mcpl. Clks. Assn., Wayne County Clks. Assn. (sec.), South Wayne County C. of C., Jaycees (v.p. 1974, 77, pres. 1975, 78, Key Woman), Kiwanis. Avocations: golf, reading. Home: 24781 Pamela St Flat Rock MI 48134-9202 Office: Charter Twp Brownstown 21313 Telegraph Rd Trenton MI 48183-1314

SMITH, LIZ (MARY ELIZABETH SMITH), newspaper columnist, broadcast journalist; b. Ft. Worth, Feb. 2, 1923; d. Sloan and Sarah Elizabeth (McCall) S. BJ., U. Tex., 1948. Editor Dell Publns., N.Y.C., 1950-53; assoc. producer CBS Radio, 1953-55, NBC-TV, 1955-59; assoc. Cholly Knickerbocker newspaper column, N.Y.C., 1959-64; film critic Cosmopolitan mag., 1966; columnist Chgo. Tribune-N.Y. Daily News Syndicate (now Tribune Media Services), 1976-91; TV commentator WNBC-TV, N.Y.C., 1978-91; commentator Fox-TV, N.Y.C., 1991—; columnist Newsday, L.A. Times Syndicate, 1991—, Family Circle mag., 1993—; freelance mag. writer, also staff writer Sports Illus. mag.; commentator Gossip Show E! Entertainment, 1993—; columnist N.Y. Post, N.Y.C., 1995—, 1995—. Author: The Mother Book, 1978. Office: N Y Newsday 2 Park Ave New York NY 10016-5675 *A career in Journalism? Any career at all? I say learn to type. Read a lot. Keep on keeping on. Work is its own reward and success is loving your work. And remember, never give up. After the Middle Ages comes the Renaissance.*

SMITH, LLOYD, musician; b. Cleve., Dec. 1, 1941; s. Thomas George Russell and Anita May (Speer) S.; m. Rheta R. Naylor, Mar. 30, 1967 (div. Nov. 1994); 1 child, Peter Eldon; m. Nancy R. Bean, June 6, 1995. Mus.B., Curtis Inst. Music, 1965. Tchr. Settlement Music Sch., 1970-72, 92—. Cellist Pitts. Symphony, 1965-67, Phila. Orch., 1967—, asst. prin. cello, 1988—; soloist Indpls. Symphony, 1958, 68, Garden State Philharmonic, 1964, Lansdowne Symphony, 1965, West Jersey Chamber Orch., 1991, Haverford-Bryn Mawr Symphony, 1992; mem. Huntingdon Trio, 1974-93, Wister quartet, 1988—. Alumni rep. Curtis Inst. Music Bd. Trustees, chmn. Parents' Com., 1989-90; bd. dirs. Phila. Youth Orch., 1987-91, Community Out Reach Partnership, 1988-90. Mem. Am. Soc. Ancient Instruments (asst. artistic dir. 1975-77, music dir. 1977-80), Curtis Inst. Music Nat. Alumni Assn. (treas., bd. dirs. 1989-90), 1807 & Friends (bd. dirs. 1994—). Home: 5639 E Wister St Philadelphia PA 19144-1522 Office: 5639 E Wister St Philadelphia PA 19144-1522

SMITH, LLOYD HOLLINGSWORTH, physician; b. Easley, S.C., Mar. 27, 1924; s. Lloyd H. and Phyllis (Page) S.; m. Margaret Constance Avery, Feb. 27, 1954; children—Virginia Constance, Christopher Avery, Rebecca Anne, Charlotte Page, Elizabeth Hollingsworth, Jeffrey Hollingsworth. A.B., Washington and Lee U., 1944, D.Sc., 1969; M.D., Harvard, 1948. Intern, then resident Mass. Gen. Hosp., Boston, 1948-50; chief resident physician Mass. Gen. Hosp., 1955-56; mem. Harvard Soc. Fellows, 1952-54; asst. prof. Harvard Soc. Fellows (Med. Sch.), 1956-63; vis. investigator Karolinska Inst., Stockholm, 1954-55, Oxford (Eng.) U., 1963-64; prof. medicine, chmn. dept. U. Calif. Med. Sch., San Francisco, 1964-85, assoc dean, 1985—; Mem. Pres.'s Sci. Adv. Com., 1970-73. Bd. overseers Harvard, 1974-80. Served to capt., M.C. AUS, 1950-52. Mem. Am. Acad. Arts and Scis., Am. Soc. Clin. Investigation (pres. 1969-70), Western Soc. Clin. Rsch. (pres. 1969-70), Assn. Am. Physicians (pres. 1974-75), Am. Fedn. Clin. Rsch. Spl. research genetic and metabolic diseases. Home: 309 Evergreen Dr Kentfield CA 94904-2709 Office: U Calif San Francisco Med Ctr San Francisco CA 94143

SMITH, LOIS ANN, real estate executive; b. Chgo., Jan. 1, 1941; d. Alburn M. and Ruth A. (Beaver) Beaudoin; m. Dickson K. Smith, Mar. 24, 1962 (div. May 1982); children: Michelle D., Jeffrey D. BA, U. Utah, 1962; MBA, Marquette U., 1972. Asst. mgr. prodn. Northwestern Mut. Life Ins. Co., Milw., 1979-83, asst. mgr., asset mgr., 1983-88; assoc. dir., asset mgmt. Asset Mgmt., 1988-89; dir. asset mgmt. Northwestern Mut. Life Ins. Co., Milw., 1990-95, dir. real estate equities, 1995—. Cons. Girl Scouts Am., Milw., 1986, YWCA, Milw., 1986, bd. dirs. YWCA, 1981-87; bd. dirs. Wis. Rep. Orgn., 1985-87. Mem. Internat. Council Shopping Ctrs., Profl. Dimensions, Beta Gamma Sigma. Unitarian. Home: N21 W 24090 Cir E Pewaukee WI 53072 Office: Northwestern Mut Life Ins Co 720 E Wisconsin Ave Milwaukee WI 53202-4703

SMITH, LOIS ARLENE, actress, writer; b. Topeka, Nov. 3, 1930; d. William Oren and Carrie D. (Gottshalk) Humbert; m. Wesley Dale Smith, Nov. 5, 1948 (div. 1973); 1 child, Moon Elizabeth. Student, U. Wash., 1948-50; studied with Lee Strasberg, Actor's Studio, N.Y.C., 1955—. guest dir. Juilliard Sch., 1987; Clarence Ross fellow Am. Theater Wing at Eugene O'Neill Theater Ctr., 1983; mem. adv. panel program fund Pub. Broadcasting Service, 1981-82; hon. founder Harold Clurman Theatre Artists Fund, Ctr. for Arts, SUNY-Purchase, 1981. Author: play All There Is, 1982; debut in Time Out for Ginger, 1952; actress Broadway and off-Broadway prodns., 1952—; stage appearances include Theater of the Living Arts, Mark Taper Forum, Long Wharf Theater and Steppenwolf Theater Co.; appears on network and pub. TV programs; stage appearances include, The Young and the Beautiful, 1955, The Glass Menagerie, 1956, Blues for Mr. Charlie, 1964, Orpheus Descending, 1957, Miss Julie, 1966, Uncle Vanya, 1965, 69, The Iceman Cometh, 1973, Harry Outside, 1975, Hillbilly Women, 1979, 81, the Vienna Notes, 1985, The Stick Wife, April Snow, 1987, The Grapes of Wrath, 1988-89, 90, Measure for Measure, Beside Herself, 1989, Escape from Happiness, 1993, Buried Child, 1995-96; films include East of Eden, 1955, Five Easy Pieces, 1970, Next Stop Greenwich Village, 1975, Resurrection, 1980, Green Card, 1990, Fried Green Tomatoes, 1991, Falling Down, 1993, How to Make an American Quilt, 1995, Dead Man Walking, 1995, Larger than Life, 1996, Twister, 1996. Named Best Supporting Actress for Five Easy Pieces, Nat. Soc. Film Critics, 1971; recipient Tony nominations for Grapes of Wrath, 1990, Buried Child, 1996; named to Filmdom's Famous Fives for East of Eden, Failm Daily mag., 1955. Mem. SAG, AFTRA, Actors Equity Assn., Dramatists Guild, Actors Studio, Ensemble Studio Theater, Steppenwolf Theatre Co. Ensemble, Acad. Motion Picture Arts and Scis.

SMITH, LONNIE MAX, diversified industries executive; b. Twin Falls, Idaho, July 28, 1944; s. Lonnie E. and Christie (Stuart) S.; m. Cheryl Diane Smith, June 10, 1968; children: Kristen, Maryam, Rebecca, Michael, Catherine. BSEE, Utah State U., 1967; MBA, Harvard U., 1974. Engr., mgr. field services, mgr. tech. services to asst. to v.p. plans and control IBM Corp., San Francisco, Palo Alto, Calif., and White Plains, N.Y., 1967-74; mgr., corp. strategy, then cons. Boston Cons. Group, 1974-76; exec. v.p. Am. Tourister, Inc., Warren, R.I., 1978-81; sr. v.p. corp. planning Hillenbrand Industries, Inc., Batesville, Ind., 1977-78, sr. exec. v.p., 1982—, also bd. dirs.; pres., chmn. bd. Hillenbrand Internat. Sales Corp.; v.p., bd. dirs. Forecorp, Inc., Batesville; bd. dirs. Hillenbrand Investment Adv. Corp., Batesville Casket Co., Batesville Internat. Corp., Hill-rom Co., The Forethought Group, Inc., Hilico Life Inst. Co., Medeco Security Locks, Inc., Salem, Va. Served to 1st lt. U.S. Army, 1969-72. Republican. Mormon. Avocations: tennis, skiing. Office: Hillenbrand Industries Inc 700 State Route 46 E Batesville IN 47006-8928

SMITH, LOREN ALLAN, federal judge; b. Chgo., Ill., Dec. 22, 1944; m. Catherine Yore; children: Loren Jr., Adam. BA in Polit. Sci., Northwestern U., 1966, JD, 1969; LLD (hon.), John Marshall Law Sch., 1995, Capital U. Law Sch., 1996, Campbell U., 1997. Bar: Ill. 1970, D.C., U.S. Ct. Mil. Appeals 1973, U.S. Ct. Appeals (D.C. cir.) 1974, U.S. Supreme Ct. 1974, U.S. Ct. Claims, 1985, U.S. Ct. Appeals (fed. cir.) 1986. Gen. atty. FCC, 1973; asst. to spl. counsel to the pres. White House, Washington, 1973-74; spl. asst. U.S. atty. D.C., 1974-75; counsel Reagan for Pres. campaigns, 1976, 80; prof. Del. Law Sch., 1976-84; dep. dir. Office Exec. Br. Mgmt. Presdl. Transition, 1980-81; chmn. Adminstrv. Conf. U.S., 1981-85; appointed judge U.S. Claims Ct., 1985, designated chief judge, 1986—; adj. prof. Internat. Law Sch., 1973-74, Georgetown U. Law Ctr., 1992—, Am. U. Sch. Law, 1994—, Columbus Sch. Law Cath. U. Am., 1996—; past mem. Pres.'s Cabinet Coun. on Legal Policy, Pres.' Cabinet Coun. on Mgmt. and Adminstrn.; chmn. Coun. Ind. Regulatory Atys.; Allen chair U. Richmond Sch. Law, 1996. Contbr. articles to profl. jours. Recipient Presdl. medal Cath. U. Am. Law Sch., 1993, Romanian medal of justice Romanian Min. of Justice, 1995. Republican. Jewish.

SMITH, LORETTA MAE, contracting officer; b. Washington Twp., Pa., May 25, 1939; d. Irvin Calvin and Viola Mary (Deibler) Shambaugh; 1 child, Miriam Estella Smith. B in Humanities, Pa. State U., 1984. Bookkeeper Harrisburg (Pa.) Nat. Bank, 1957-62; contract specialist USN, Mechanicsburg, Pa., 1987—; founder Telecare, Harrisburg, Pa., 1972-82. Active ARC, instr. CPR, 1982—; active Girl Scouts U.S., trainer, 1972—. Recipient Hemlock award Hemlock coun. Girl Scouts U.S., Harrisburg, 1981; Merit scholar Hall Found., 1982. Mem. Nat. Contract Mgmt. Assn., Mensa. Avocations: walking in woods, birding, swimming, making music.

SMITH, LOUIS, sports association administrator; m. Sharon Smith; 4 children. BSEE, U. Mo., Rolla; MBA, Rockhurst Coll.; postgrad., U. Kans. Assoc. engr. to asst. gen. mgr. AlliedSignal Inc., Kansas City, Mo., 1966-86; v.p. prodn. ops. Bendix Aerospace Sector AlliedSignal Inc., Arlington, Va., 1986-88; v.p. mfg. AlliedSignal Aerospace Co., Torrance, Calif., 1988-89; asst. gen. mgr., adminstrn. AlliedSignal Inc., Kansas City, 1989-90, pres., 1990-95; pres., COO, bd. dirs. Ewing Marion Kauffman Found., Kansas City, 1995—; bd. dirs. Western Resources, Commerce Bank Kansas City. Bd. dirs. Kansas City Royals, Greater Kansas City C. of C., Midwest Rsch. Inst., Civic Coun. Greater Kansas City, The Learning Exch.; mem. exec. com. Kansas City Area Devel. Coun., Rockhurst Coll. Bd. Trustees; mem. numerous coms. U. Mo.-Rolla, U. Kans.; ;past chmn. corp. devel. coun., mem. Acad. Elec. Engring. U. Mo.-Rolla; adv. bd. U. Kans. Sch. Engring. Office: Kansas City Royals Kauffman Stadium PO Box 419969 Kansas City MO 64141-6969

SMITH, LUCIUS SKINNER, III, educational foundation administrator; b. Boulder, Colo., July 11, 1919; s. Lucius Skinner Jr. and Georgie Elizabeth (Hoxie) S.; m. Josephine Lamb Butler, 1942 (div. 1963); children: Lucius S. IV (dec.), Suzy Smith Hunt, Alexander Gavin Butler, Alan Bret, Anthony Butler Mason; m. Emilie Jensen, 1964 (div. 1974); m. Maria Katalin Feher, Sept. 27, 1974. BA in Modern European History, U. Calif., Berkeley, 1941. Cons., lobbyist Am. Bar Ctr. and Keogh Act for the Self-Employed, 1955-60; journalist Hearst Corp., Boston, 1970-75; pub. rels. and exec. search Washington and St. Louis, 1976-86; cons. Am. Freedom Train for Am.'s Bicentennial, 1975; adj. gen. Nat. Assn. Atomic Vets., Independence, Mo., 1985-90; pres. Atomic Libr. and Tech. Found., Washington, 1988—. Supported enactment of Radiation-Exposed Vets. Compensation Act, 1988. Naval aviator USMC, 1941-45, PTO, Lt. col. ret. USMC Res. Decorated DFC, Bronze star, Air medal with gold star, Presl. unit citation. Office: 218 N Washington St Du Quoin IL 62832-1769

SMITH, DAME MAGGIE, actress; b. Ilford, Eng., Dec. 28, 1934; d. Nathaniel and Margaret (Hutton) S.; m. Robert Stephens, 1967 (div. 1974); m. Beverley Cross, 1974. Grad., Oxford High Sch. Girls; D.Litt. (hon.), St. Andrews, 1971; DLitt (hon.), Oxford U., 1994. dir. United British Artists, 1982—. Stage and film actress, 1952—; stage appearances include: New Faces, debut N.Y.C., 1956, Share My Lettuce, 1957, The Stepmother, 1958, Rhinoceros, 1960, Strip the Willow, 1960, The Rehearsal, 1961, The Private Ear and the Public Eye, 1962, Mary, Mary, 1961; appearances at Old Vic, 1959-60, Nat. Theatre, London, 1963—; productions at Nat. Theatre include Private Lives, 1972, Othello, Hay Fever, Master Builder, Hedda Gabbler, Much Ado About Nothing, Miss Julie, Black Comedy, Stratford Festival, Ont., Can., 1976, 77, 78, 80, Antony and Cleopatra, Macbeth, Three Sisters, Richard III, Night and Day, London and N.Y.C., 1979-80, Virginia, London, 1981, Way of the World, Chichester Festival, London, 1984-85, Interpreters, London, 1985-86, Lettice and Lovage, 1988, also in N.Y., 1990, The Importance of Being Earnest, 1993, Three Tall Women, 1994, 95, Talking Heads, 1996; films include Othello, 1966, The Honey Pot, 1967, Oh What a Lovely War, 1968, Hot Millions, 1968, The Prime of Miss Jean Brodie, 1968 (Acad. award for best actress), Love and Pain and the Whole Damn Thing, 1971, Travels with My Aunt, 1972, Murder by Death, 1976, Death on the Nile, 1977, California Suite, 1978 (Acad. award for best supporting actress), Quartet, 1978, Clash of the Titans, 1981, Evil under the Sun, 1981, The Missionary, 1982, A Private Function, 1984 (Brit. Acad. of Film & TV Arts best actress award 1985), Lily in Love, 1985, A Room with a View, 1985, The Lonely Passion of Judith Hearn, 1987 (Brit. Acad. of Film & TV Arts award 1989), Paris by Night, 1988, Hook, 1991, Sister Act, 1992, The Secret Garden, 1993, Richard III, 1995, The First Wives Club, 1996; TV films include Memento Mori, 1992, Suddenly Last Summer, 1993 (Lead Actress-Miniseries Emmy nominee 1993); BBC-TV appearance Bed Among the Lentils, 1988. Recipient Best Actress award Eve. Std., 1962, 70, 82, 85, 94, Best Film Actress award Soc. Film and TV Arts U.K., 1968, Film Critics Guild, 1968, Taomina Gold award, 1985, Antoinette Perry award (Tony), 1990, Hanbury Shakespeare prize, 1991; decorated Dame Brit. Empire, 1989; named Actress of Yr., Variety Club, 1963, 72, Brit. Acad. Best Screen Actress, 1985; Brit. Film Inst. fellow, 1992, Theater Hall of Fame, 1994. Fellow BAFTA. Office: Write on Cue, 29 Whitcomb St, London WC2H7EP, England

SMITH, M(AHLON) BREWSTER, psychologist, educator; b. Syracuse, N.Y., June 26, 1919; s. Mahlon Ellwood and Blanche Alice (Hinman) S.; m. Jean Dresden Schwartz, June 1942 (div. 1945); m. Deborah Anderson, June, 1947; children: Joshua H., T. Daniel, Rebecca M., J. Torquil. Student, Reed Coll., Portland, Oreg., 1935-38; A.B., Stanford U., 1939, A.M., 1940; Ph.D., Harvard U., 1947. Rantoul scholar Harvard U., 1940-41; jr. analyst Office Coordinator of Information, U.S. Govt., 1941; Social Sci. Research Council fellow Harvard U., 1946-47; asst. prof. social psychology Harvard U. (Dept. Social Relations), 1947-49; prof. psychology, chmn. dept. Vassar Coll., 1949-52; staff Social Sci. Research Council, 1952-56; prof. psychology NYU, 1956-59; prof. psychology U. Calif. at Berkeley, 1959-68, dir. Inst. Human Devel., 1965-68; prof., chmn. dept. psychology U. Chgo., 1968-70; prof. psychology U. Calif. at Santa Cruz, 1970-88, prof. emeritus, 1988—, vice chancellor social scis., 1970-75; fellow Center Advanced Studies Behavioral Scis., 1964-65; Vice pres. Joint Commn. Mental Illness and Health, 1955-61. Author: Social Psychology and Human Values, 1969, Humanizing Social Psychology, 1974, Values, Self and Society, 1991; co-author: The American Soldier, 1949, Opinions and Personality, 1956; editor: Jour. Social Issues, 1951-55, Jour. Abnormal Soc. Psychology, 1956-61; contbr. articles to profl. jours. Served from pvt. to maj. Adj. Gen. Div. AUS, 1942-46; research officer Information and Edn. div. War Dept., 1943-46; research asso. spl. com. on soldier attitudes Social Sci. Research Council 1946. Decorated Bronze Star medal.; NIMH fellow, 1964-65, NEH fellow, 1975-76; Belding scholar Found. for Child Devel., 1982-83; Gold medal award lifetime contbn. to psychology in pub. interest Am. Psychol. Found., 1992. Fellow AAAS, APA (pres. 1978, Disting. Contbn. to Pub. Interest award 1988, Henry A. Murray award in personality psychology 1993); mem. Soc. Psychol. Study Social Issues (pres. 1959, Kurt Lewin Meml. award 1986), Western Psychol. Assn. (pres. 1986, Lifetime Contbn. award 1996), Psychologists for Social Responsibility (pres. 1987-90), Internat. Soc. Polit. Psychology (Harold Lasswell award 1993), Internat. Assn. Applied Psychology (pres. divsn. polit. psychology 1994—), Cosmos Club (Washington), Phi Beta Kappa, Sigma Xi. Democrat. Home: 316 Escalona Dr Santa Cruz CA 95060-2607

SMITH, MALCOLM BARRY ESTES, philosophy educator, lawyer; b. Houston, Oct. 24, 1939; s. Fairleigh Estes and Norna Barry (McNab) S.; m. Patricia Sweetser; children: Malcolm, Eric. BA, Va. Mil. Inst., 1961; PhD, Cornell U., 1969; JD, U. Calif., Berkeley, 1984. BarL Mass. 1985, U.S. Supreme Ct. 1992. Instr. philosophy Smith Coll., Northampton, Mass., 1967-69, asst. prof. philosophy, 1969-74, assoc. prof., 1974-79, prof., 1979—. Served to capt. USAR, 1964-66. Mem. ABA, Mass. Bar Assn., Am. Philos. Assn. Home: 9 Park St Northampton MA 01060-1236 Office: Smith Coll Dept Philosophy PO Box 839 Northampton MA 01061-0839

SMITH, MALCOLM BERNARD, investment company executive; b. Lynn, Mass., May 27, 1923; s. Philip and Ida (Zenis) S.; m. Betty Booth, June 20, 1948; children: Eric, Daniel. B.A. summa cum laude, Dartmouth Coll., 1944; M.A. in Econs., Harvard U., 1948; hon. degree, New Sch. for Social Rsch., 1995. Sec. Gen. Am. Investors Co., N.Y.C., 1956-57, treas., 1957-59, v.p., 1958-61, pres., 1961-89, vice chmn., 1989-97; sr. cons., 1997—. Chmn. fin. com. N.Y. Found., 1973-82, treas., 1979-82, trustee, 1973-89, 91—, chmn. 1982-85; chmn. New Sch. for Social Rsch., N.Y.C., 1985-95, trustee, 1982—, treas., 1982-84, chmn. ednl. policy com., 1984-85, chmn. exec. com., 1985-95; trustee John Simon Guggenheim Meml. Found., 1982-95, chmn. fin. com., 1985-95, Human Rights Watch, 1993—; mng. trustee Permanent Fund of MLA, 1987—; mem. investment com. Fedn. Jewish Philantrophies, N.Y., 1975-96, Phi Beta Kappa Found., 1987-96; bd. dirs. Learning Smith, Inc., 1992-93; Cybersmith, Inc., 1994—. With U.S. Army, 1943-46. Mem. AAAS (chmn. investment and fin. com. 1975—), Investment Co. Inst. (bd. govs. 1987-95), Assn. Publicly Traded Investment Funds (bd. dirs. 1970-87, chmn. 1971-79, Coun. on Fgn. Rels., N.Y. Soc. Security Analysts, Phi Beta Kappa Assocs. (adv. com. 1984-93, bd. dirs. 1993—), Phi Beta Kappa. Club: Harvard (bd. mgrs. 1984-86), Century Assn. (N.Y.C.). Home: PO Box 358 Pound Ridge NY 10576-0358 Office: 1150 Park Ave New York NY 10128-1244

SMITH, MALCOLM NORMAN, manufacturing company executive; b. Milw., Feb. 25, 1921; s. Samuel H. and Dorothea (Werner) S.; m. Muriel J. Foreman, Feb. 14, 1943; 1 dau., Louise K. BS in Econs, U. Pa., 1942. With Ekco Products Co., Chgo., 1946-50, 56-63; v.p. Ekco Products Co., 1956-63; dir. Platers & Stampers Ltd. (Brit. div. Ekco), London, 1950-56; pres., chief exec. officer, dir. Argus, Inc., Chgo., 1963-68; pres. Malcolm N. Smith & Co., Chgo., 1968-70; adminstrv. v.p., cashier Am. Nat. Bank and Trust Co., Chgo., 1970-75; pres. Macromatic div. Macromatic Inc., 1975-88; pres. Macromatic Divsn. of Milw. Electronics Corp., Chgo., 1988-93, Newmac, Inc., 1994—; profl. lectr. U. Chgo. Grad Sch. Bus., 1968-82; bd. dirs. Acorn Internat. Fund. Bd. dirs. The Acorn Fund, 1976-97. 1st lt. USMCR, 1942-46. Decorated Silver Star. Mem. Friends of Franklin, Inc. (dir. 1990—, pres. 1992-96), Lake Shore Country Club, The Casino, Royal Tennis Ct., Hampton Ct. Palace, Am. Ceramic Circle (dir. 1997—), Percival David Found. (London), Oriental Ceramic Soc. (London). Home: 309 Maple Ave Highland Park IL 60035-2056

SMITH, MALCOLM SOMMERVILLE, bass; b. Rockville Centre, N.Y., June 22, 1933; s. Carlton Newell and Margaret (Sommerville) S.; m. Margaret Yauger, Oct. 4, 1975. B.Music Edn., Oberlin Coll., 1957, B.Mus., 1960; M.A. in Ednl. Adminstrn, Columbia Tchrs. Coll., 1958; student, Ind. U. Sch. Music, 1960-62. Dir. choral music, Ramapo Regional High Sch., Wyckoff, N.J., 1958-60; basso, Lyric Opera, Chgo., 1961, 63; bass soloist Russian tour, Robert Shaw Choral, 1962; leading bass, N.Y.C. Opera, 1965-70, Deutsche Oper Am Rhein, Dusseldorf, Germany, 1971—, Vienna State Opera, 1973-74, 86 Met. Opera, Japan Tour, spring 1975, Met. Opera, N.Y.C., 1975-77, Paris Opera, 1978, Barcelona Opera, 1978, Sao Paulo, Brazil, 1978, Mexico City, 1979, 80, Berlin Opera, 1979, 80, Montreal Symphony, 1979, 80, 81, 82, Hamburg Opera, 1981, Köln Opera, 1980, Stuttgart Opera, 1980, Frankfurt Opera, 1980, Rome Opera, 1980, Trieste (Italy) Opera, 1981, Berlin Staatsoper, 1982, 85, Lyric Opera Phila, 1982, Los Angeles Philharm. at Hollywood Bowl, 1984, Mannheim Opera, Fed. Republic Germany, 1986, Turin Opera, Italy, 1986, 88, Bordeaux, France, 1987, Dresden Opera, German Dem. Republic, 1987, Hannover Opera, Fed. Republic Germany, 1987, Staats Oper Berlin Japan Tour, 1987, Polish TV, 1989, Oslo Opera, 1987, Paris Radio, 1988-89, Orange Festival, France, 1988, Penderecki Festival, Krakow, Poland, 1988; maj. soloist Schleswig Holstein Festival, Fed. Republic Germany, 1989, Krakow Philharmonic, Poland, 1988, Maggio Musicale, Florence, Italy,1988, Boston Symphony, Minn., Cin., Houston, Utah, Seattle, Chgo., Phila., Balt. Symphony, 1993, Mexico Nat. Symphony, 1993, Nat. symphonies, also, Cin. Summer Opera, Central City (Colo.) Summer Opera, Festival of two Worlds, Spoleto, Italy., Saratoga Festival, 1985, debut, La Scala, Milan, Italy, 1982, Salzburg Festival, 1986, Athens Festival, 1987, Bordeaux (France) Opera, 1987, Ft. Worth Opera, 1988, Orange Festival, France, 1988, Staatsoper Munich, 1990, Bastille Opera, Paris, 1991, Heidelberg Summer festival, 1991, 92,, Brussels Opera, 1992, 93, 94, 97, Opera Nice, France, 1992, Opera Montpelier, France, 1992, Cin. Opera, 1994, Düsseldorf Opera, 1994, tour Japan, 1994, Bregenz (Austria) Festival, 1996, Honolulu Opera, 1996, Baltimore Opera, 1996, Prague Autumn Festival, 1997; recorded War and Peace, 1986, Penderecki Requiem, 1990. Served with AUS, 1954-56. Recipient Kämmersanger title Dusseldorf (Germany) Opera, 1996. Congregationalist. Office: care Thea Dispeker Artists Rep 59 E 54th St New York NY 10022-4211 *Hard work and a sense of humor.*

SMITH, MARGARET TAYLOR, volunteer; b. Roanoke Rapids, N.C., May 31, 1925; d. George Napoleon and Sarah Luella (Waller) T.; m. Sidney William Smith Jr., Aug. 15, 1947; children: Sarah Smith, Sidney William Smith III, Susan Smith, Amy Smith. BA in Sociology, Duke U., 1947. Chair. bd. trustees Kresge Found., Troy, MI, 1985—; chmn. Nat. Coun. for Women's Studies Duke U., N.C., 1986—, chmn. Trinity Bd. Visitors, 1988—; bd. vis. Wayne State U. Med. Sch., 1993; bd. dirs., mem. exec. com. Detroit Med. Ctr. Recipient the Merrill-Palmer award Wayne State U., Detroit, 1987, disting. alumna award Duke U. Mem. The Village Club, Internat. Women's Forum, Pi Beta Phi, Phi Beta Kappa. Methodist.

SMITH, MARGHERITA, writer, editor; b. Chgo., May 24, 1922; d. Henry Christian and Alicia (Koke) Steinhoff; m. Rufus Zartman Smith, June 26, 1943; children: Matthew Benjamin, Timothy Rufus. AB, Ill. Coll., 1943. Proofreader Editorial Experts, Inc., Alexandria, Va., 1974; mgr. proofreading div. Editorial Experts, Inc., Alexandria, 1978-79, mgr. publs. div., 1979-81, asst. to pres., 1980-81; freelance editor, cons. Annandale, Va., 1981—; instr. proofreading and copy editing, George Washington U., Washington, 1978-82; presenter workshops on proofreading for various profl. orgns., 1981—. Author: (as Peggy Smith) Simplified Proofreading, 1980, Proofreading Manual and Reference Guide, 1981, Proofreading Workbook, 1981, The Proof Is In the Reading: A Comprehensive Guide to Staffing and Management of Typographic Proofreading, 1986, Mark My Words: Instructions and Practice in Proofreading, 1987, rev. edit., 1993, Letter Perfect: A Guide to Practical Proofreading, 1995; contbr. articles to revs. to various publs. Recipient Best Instrnl. Reporting award Newsletter Assn. Am., 1980, Disting. Achievement award for excellence in ednl. journalism Ednl. Press Assn. Am., 1981, Disting. Citizen award Ill. Coll., 1992. Avocation: writing verse. Home and Office: 9120 Belvoir Woods Pky # 110 Fort Belvoir VA 22060-2722

SMITH, MARION PAFFORD, avionics company executive; b. Waycross, Ga., Dec. 12, 1925; s. Rossa Elbert and Lillian Solee (Pafford) S.; m. Esther Pat Davis, Nov. 23, 1952; children: Bryan P., Danton D., Patricia Anne. Student, Okla. State U., 1944, Yale U., 1945; BS in EE, La. State U., 1949; postgrad., U. So. Fla., 1966-70. Engr. Bell Telephone Co., Baton Rouge, 1949-51; mgr. engring. Vitro Labs., Silver Spring, Md., 1952-57; design engring. mgr. dept. design and constrn. flight hand contrs. Space Shuttle and Space Sta. Honeywell Avionics Div., Clearwater, Fla., 1957—; vice chmn., bd. dirs. First Union, Largo, Fla., 1985-93; cons. U.S. Army Mgmt. Engring. Tng. Agy., 1975-79; U.S. Del. Internat. Elec. Tech. Commn., 1965-85, chmn. chief U.S. tech. adviser com. on reliability and maintainability, 1975-85, v.p., exec. com. U.S. nat. com., 1975-84; U.S. del. NATO Quality Conf., 1973; mem. White House Summit Conf. on Inflation, 1975; del. White House Conf. on Handicapped, 1977; mem. nat. adv. coun. on devel. disabilities HEW, 1974-78, Fla. Adv. Coun. on Devel. Ctr. for Persons with Disabilities, 1974-78, Fla. Advocacy, 1983—; mem. devel. coun. Morton Plant Hosp., Clearwater, 1971-74. 1st lt. Signal Corps, AUS, 1944-45, 51-52. Served to 1st lt. Signal Corps AUS, 1944-45, 51-52. Recipient McDonald award Fla. Rehab. Assn., 1968; Bilgore award Citizen of Year Clearwater, Fla., 1969; Outstanding Service award Am. Soc. Quality Control, 1968-69; United Comml. Travelers award Most Outstanding Service Retarded Fla., 1970; named Engr. of Year Fla. W. Coast, 1970; Service to Mankind award Sertoma Clubs, 1977. Fellow IEEE (dir., Nat. Reliability award 1979); mem. Assn. Retarded Citizens USA (pres. 1973-75, nat. govt. affairs chmn. 1975-83), Am. Assn. Mental Deficiency, Nat. Symposium Reliability Quality Control (gen. chmn.), Sigma Chi. Presbyterian elder. Club: Kiwanis (Marion P. Smith award established in his honor). Home: 1884 Oakdale Ln N Clearwater FL 34624-6441 Office: 13350 Us Highway 19 N Clearwater FL 33764-7226 *True turning points in life are sometimes difficult to recognize, but for those who have become parents of a handicapped child, particularly a mentally retarded child, then that turning point is easy to recognize. After the difficult period of adjustment, one becomes aware of a realization that all persons have human dignity and worth and can make a contribution to humanity and to society.*

SMITH, MARJORIE AILEEN MATTHEWS, museum director; b. Richmond, Va., Aug. 19, 1918; d. Harry Anderson and Adelia Charlotte (Howland) Matthews; m. Robert Woodrow Smith, July 23, 1945 (dec. Mar. 1992). Pilot lic., Taneytown (Md.) Aviation Svc., 1944, cert. ground sch. instr., 1945. Founder, editor, pub. Spinning Wheel, Taneytown, 1945-63; v.p. Antiques Publs., Inc., Taneytown, 1960-68; pres. Prism Inc., Taneytown, 1968-78; mus. dir. Trapshooting Hall of Fame, Vandalia, Ohio, 1976—, sec., 1993—. Co-author: Handbook of Tomorrow's Antiques, 1954; contbr. articles to profl. publs. Sec. Balt. area coun. Girl Scouts USA, 1950. Named to All-Am. Trapshooting team Sports Afield mag., 1960, 61. Mem. Nat. League Am. Pen Women, Amateur Trapshooting Assn. (life), Am. Contract Bridge League, Internat. Assn. Sports Mus. and Halls of Fame (bd. dirs. 1993-94). Lutheran. Avocations: duplicate bridge, trapshooting, antiques collecting. Office: Trapshooting Hall of Fame 601 W National Rd Vandalia OH 45377-1036

SMITH, MARK EUGENE, architectural engineering service company executive; b. Wareham, Mass., Apr. 1, 1951; s. Mark Alvin and Evelyn Marie (Somers) S.; m. Brigid Ann Murray, Oct. 17, 1979; children: Hugh Talmidge, Patrick Morgan. Student, Ea. Carolina U., 1970-71; AS, New England Inst. Tech., 1981; student, Boston U., 1982. Owner Marks Motor Co., Wareham, 1965-69; chief designer HF Scientific Instrument, Ft. Myers, Fla., 1981-83; chief designer HVE Keltron Corp., Waltham, Mass., 1984-85; chief exec. officer Home Svcs., Ft. Myers, 1985-90; cons. Underwood & Assocs., Cape Coral, Fla., 1981-89, Shaban Mfg. Co., Ft. Myers, 1982-83; chief designer Keltron Corp., Waltham, 1984-85. Co-author: The Art of Custom Painting, 1978. With USMC, 1969-72. Named Advanced Designer, Metalflake Design Group, Springfield, Mass., 1977. Mem. Soc. Mech. Engrs., Soc. Automotive Engrs., Am. Inst. for Design and Drafting (nat. drafting award 1981). Republican. Avocations: numismatics, antiquarian. Office: Gen Capitol PO Box 2044 Fremont NC 27830-1244

SMITH, MARK HALLARD, architect; b. Detroit, June 28, 1955; s. John Hallard and Barbara Ruth (Hinkle) S.; m. Janee Lynne Batey, July 18, 1981; children: Elizabeth Anne, Jacquelyne Ruth. BS, Ga. Inst. Tech., 1977, MArch, 1979. Registered architect, Fla.; cert. Nat. Coun. Archtl. Registration Bds. Draftsman Kirkland/Ogram Architects, Atlanta, 1979-80; project mgr. Bailey Vrooman Allegret, Atlanta, 1980-81, Rabun Hatch and Dendy, Atlanta, 1981; project architect C. Randolph Wedding & Assocs., St. Petersburg, Fla., 1981-83, Stearman Architects, St. Petersburg, 1983-90, Carl Abbott Arch. FAIA PA, Sarasota, Fla., 1990-94; prin. Smith Architects, Sarasota, 1994—; panelist Ringling Mus. Art, Sarasota, 1991. Asst. editor Centerline, 1990. Chmn. Sarasota Design Conf., 1994, 96; mem. steering com. John Ringling Ctr. Found., Sarasota, 1995; pres. Men's Club, St. Michael The Archangel Ch., 1993-96. Mem. AIA (archtl. juror Palm Beach chpt. 1993, pres. Fla. Gulf Coast chpt. 1994-95, Fla. award of excellence 1993, Fla. bd. dirs. 1995—, Fla. Pres. award 1994), Nat. Trust for Hist. Preservation, Tiger Bay Club. Republican. Roman Catholic. Avocation: tennis. Home: 5562 Cape Aqua Dr Sarasota FL 34242-1804 Office: Smith Architects Sarasota FL 34242

SMITH, MARK LEE, architect; b. L.A., Nov. 16, 1957; s. Selma (Moidel) Smith. BA in History of Architecture, UCLA, 1978, MA in Architecture, 1980. Registered architect Calif., Nev., Oreg., Wash., Tenn., Colo., N.Y., Ohio. Designer, drafter John B. Ferguson and Assocs., L.A., 1976-83, architect, 1983; pvt. practice architecture L.A., 1984—; mem. Los Angeles County Archtl. Evaluation Bd., 1990—. Contbr. articles to profl. jours. Bd. govs. UCLA John Wooden Ctr., 1978-80. Regents scholar, U. Calif., Berkeley, UCLA, 1975-78; UCLA Grad. Sch. Architecture Rsch. fellow, 1979-80. Mem. AIA (treas. San Fernando Valley chpt. 1986, bd. dirs. 1986—, v.p. 1987, pres. 1988, Design award 1988, 89, 90, 91, chmn. Design awards 1994, bd. dirs. Calif. coun. 1989-94, v.p. 1991-94, chmn. continuing edn. 1991-93, chmn. 1992 conf.), Phi Beta Kappa. Office: 18340 Ventura Blvd Ste 225 Tarzana CA 91356-4234

SMITH, MARKWICK KERN, JR., management consultant; b. N.Y.C., Feb. 14, 1928; s. Markwick Kern and Elizabeth (Morning) S.; m. Martia Reed, Mar. 2, 1951; children—Karen, Rebecca, Mark David, Jennifer. B.S., Mass. Inst. Tech., 1951, Ph.D., 1954; M.F.A., Vt. Coll., 1988. Vice pres., then exec. v.p. Geophys. Service Inc., Dallas, 1962-67, pres., 1967-69; v.p. Tex. Instruments, Dallas, 1967-73; mgmt. cons., author Norwich, Vt., 1973—. Served with USNR, 1946-48. Mem. NAE. Congregationalist. Address: PO Box 189 Main St Norwich VT 05055

SMITH, MARSHA H., state agency administrator, lawyer; b. Boise, Idaho, Mar. 24, 1950; d. Eugene F. and Joyce (Ross) Hatch; m. Terrell F. Smith, Aug. 29, 1970; 2 children. BS in Biology/Edn., Idaho State U., 1973; MLS, Brigham Young U., 1975; JD, U. Wash., 1980. Bar: Idaho, U.S. Dist. Ct. Idaho, U.S. Ct. Appeals (9th cir.), U.S. Ct. Appeals (D.C. cir.). Dep. atty. gen. Bus./Consumer Protection Divsn., Boise, 1980-81; dep. atty. gen. Idaho Pub. Utilities Commn., Boise, 1981-89, dir. policy and external rels., 1989-91, commr., 1991—, pres., 1991-95; mem. Harvard Electricity Policy Group, Nat. Coun. on Competition and The Electric Industry. Legis. dist. chair Ada County Democrats, Idaho, 1986-89. Mem. Nat. Assn. Regulatory Utility Commrs. (chair electric strategic issues subcom.), Idaho State Bar, Western Conf. Pub. Svc. Commrs. Office: Idaho Pub Utilities Commn PO Box 83720 Boise ID 83720-0074

SMITH, MARSHALL SAVIDGE, government official, academic dean, educator; b. East Orange, N.J., Sept. 16, 1937; s. Marshall Parsons and Ann Eileen (Zulauf) S.; m. Carol Goodspeed, June 25, 1960 (div. Aug. 1962); m. Louise Nixon Claiborn, Aug. 1964; children: Adam, Jennifer, Matthew, Megan. AB, Harvard U., 1960, EdM, 1963, EdD, 1970. Computer analyst and programmer Raytheon Corp., Andover, Mass., 1959-62; instr., assoc. prof. Harvard U., Cambridge, Mass., 1966-76; asst., assoc. dir. Nat. Inst. Edn., Washington, 1973-76; asst. commr. edn. HEW, Washington, 1976-79, chief of staff to U.S. Dept. Edn. sec., 1980; prof. U. Wis., Madison, 1980-86; prof., dean Sch. Edn. Stanford (Calif.) U., 1986-93; under-sec. edn. U.S. Dept. Edn., 1993—, acting dep. sec. edn., 1996—; task force, chmn. Clinton Presdl. Transition Team, 1992-93; chmn. PEW Forum on Ednl. Reform; chmn. bd. internat. com. studies in edn. NAS, 1992-93. Author: The General Inquirer, 1967, Inequality, 1972; contbr. several articles to profl. jours, chpts. to books. Pres. Madison West Hockey Assn., 1982-84. Mem. Am. Ednl. Rsch. Assn. (chmn. orgn. instl. affiliates 1985-86), Cleve. Conf., Nat. Acad. Edn., Cosmos Club. Democrat. Avocation: environmental issues, coaching youth soccer. Home: 900 N Stafford St Apt 1817 Arlington VA 22203-1848 Office: US Dept Edn Under Sec Edn 600 Independence Ave SW Washington DC 20202-0004 Also: Stanford U Edu Dept Stanford CA 94305

SMITH, MARTHA VIRGINIA BARNES, elementary school educator; b. Camden, Ark., Oct. 12, 1940; d. William Victor and Lillian Louise (Givens) Barnes; m. Basil Loren Smith, Oct. 11, 1975; children: Jennifer Frost, Sean Barnes. BS in Edn., Ouachita Bapt. U., 1963; postgrad., Auburn U., 1974, Henderson State U., 1975. Cert. tchr., Mo. 2d and 1st grade tchr. Brevard County Schs., Titusville and Cocoa, Fla., 1963-65, 69-70; 1st grade tchr. Lakeside Sch. Dist., Hot Springs, Ark., 1965-66, Harmony Grove Sch., Camden, 1972-76; 1st and 5th grade tchr. Cumberland County Schs., Fayetteville, N.C., 1966-69; kindergarten tchr. Pulaski County Schs., Ft. Leonard Wood, Mo., 1970-72; 3d grade tchr. Mountain Grove (Mo.) Schs., 1976—; chmn. career ladder com. Mountain Grove Dist., 1991-96. Children's pastor 1st Bapt. Ch., Vanzant, Mo., 1984-88. Mem. NEA (pres.-elect Mountain Grove chpt. 1995—), Kappa Kappa Iota. Avocation: antique and classic cars. Office: Mountain Grove Elem Sch 320 E 9th St Mountain Grove MO 65711-1119

SMITH, MARTIN BERNHARD, journalist; b. San Francisco, Apr. 20, 1930; s. John Edgar and Anna Sophie (Thorsen) S.; m. Joan Lovat Muller, Apr. 25, 1953; children: Catherine Joan, Karen Anne. AB, U. Calif., Berkeley, 1952, M Journalism, 1968. Reporter, city editor Modesto (Calif.) Bee, 1957-64; reporter, mng. editor Sacramento Bee, 1964-75; polit. editor, columnist McClatchy Newspapers, Sacramento, 1975-92; ret., 1992. Episcopalian.

SMITH, MARTIN CRUZ, author; b. Reading, Pa., Nov. 3, 1942; s. John and Louisa (Lopez) S.; m. Emily Stanton Arnold, June 15, 1968; children: Ellen, Luisa, Samuel. BA, U. Pa., 1964. Author: Gorky Park, 1981, Stallion Gate, 1986, Polar Star, 1989, Red Square, 1992, Rose, 1996.

SMITH, MARTIN HENRY, pediatrician; b. Gainesville, Ga., Nov. 3, 1921; s. Charles E. and Mamie Mae (Emmett) S.; m. Mary Gillis, Feb. 25, 1950; children: Susan, Margaret, Mary. MD, Emory U., 1945. Diplomate Am. Bd. Pediatrics. Intern City Hosp. System, Winston-Salem, N.C., 1945-46; fellow in infectious diseases Grady Meml. Hosp., Atlanta, 1948-49; resident Henrietta Egleston Hosp., Atlanta, 1949-50, Children's Hosp., Washington, 1950-51; practice medicine, specializing in pediatrics Gainesville, Ga.; ret., 1988; clin. asst. prof. Emory U. Hosp., Atlanta; chief of staff Hall County Hosp., Gainesville, 1965-66; mem. Nat. Vaccine Adv. Commn., 1990—, chmn., 1991. Contbr. articles to profl. jours. Chmn. Nat. Vaccine Adv. Com., 1991—. Capt. M.C., U.S. Army, 1946-48. Fellow Am. Acad. Pediatrics (chpt. chmn. 1966-69, dist. chmn. 1977-83, pres.-elect 1984-85, pres. 1985-86); mem. Hall County Med. Soc. (pres. 1960), Ga. Pediatric Soc. (pres. 1965-66), Med. Assn. Ga., AMA, Alpha Omega Alpha. Episcopalian. Clubs: Chattahoochee Country (Gainesville); Piedmont Driving (Atlanta).

SMITH, MARTIN JAY, advertising and marketing executive; b. N.Y.C., Feb. 1, 1942; s. Nathan and Helen (Schwartz) S.; m. Ellen Susan Chadakoff, Dec. 20, 1964; children: Hilary, Nancy. BA, U. Pitts., 1963. With sta. clearance dept. ABC Radio Network, N.Y.C., 1965-66; asst. account exec. Norman Craig & Kummel, N.Y.C., 1966-67, account exec., 1967-68; account exec. Gotham, Inc., N.Y.C., 1968-72, account supr., 1972-74, v.p., 1974-78, sr. v.p., 1978-80, exec. v.p., 1980-84, vice chmn., 1984—. Sgt. USAR, 1963-69. Mem. Am. Advt. Assn. Am. (mem. mgmt. com. 1987). Avocations: flying, tennis, golf. Home: 920 Park Ave New York NY 10028-0208 Office: Gotham Inc 260 Madison Ave New York NY 10016-2401

SMITH, MARTIN LANE, biomedical researcher; b. Seattle, Mar. 15, 1959; s. Melvin Dale and Rosemary (Nations) S. BA, Austin Coll., 1981; PhD, Emory U., 1990. Assoc. U. Pitts. Sch. Medicine, 1990-93, NIH, Bethesda, Md., 1993—; instr. biology Emory U., Altanta, 1985-89. Contbr. articles to profl. jours. NIH grantee, 1991-93; recipient Am. Cancer Soc. award, 1992. Mem. AAAS, Am. Assn. Cancer Rsch., Sigma Xi. Avocations: coin collecting, hiking, travel.

SMITH, MARVIN FREDERICK, JR., chemical engineer, consultant; b. Newark, N.J., Oct. 22, 1932; s. Marvin F. and Helen (Marsh) S.; m. Jacqueline Pettit, June 20, 1959; 1 child, Scott C. BSChE, Newark (N.J.) Coll. Engring., 1954. Field engr. E.I. DuPont, Newark, Del., 1954-55, Newport, Del., 1957-59; dir. mfg. and rsch. Bon Ami Co., N.Y.C., 1959-63; sr. rsch. engr. Exxon Rsch. & Engring. Co., Linden, N.J., 1964-68; project head, engring. assoc. Exxon Chem. Co., Linden, N.J., 1968-89; engring. assoc. Exxon Rsch. & Engring. Co., Linden, 1989-92; cons., expert witness Paul, Weiss, Rifkind, Wharton & Garrison, N.Y.C., 1992—. Presenter tech. papers Transactions of Soc. Automotive Engrs. ASTM, Nat. Petroleum Refiners Assn. Mgr. baseball team Aberdeen Little League, 1978-83; team mgr., dir. basketball league Aberdeen Recreation League, 1978; chmn. tennis com. Strathmore Bath and Tennis Club, Aberdeen, 1980-82. With U.S. Army, 1955-57. Fellow ASTM (chmn. high temperature rheology 1978-91, Appreciation award 1988, Excellence in Symposium Mgmt. award 1990, Merit award 1993); mem. Soc. Automotive Engrs. Achievements include patents for Petroleum Additives and a Shear-Stability Test Device; key innovations in high temperature and low temperature viscometers used by petroleum industry; concept and devel. of novel multigrade motor oils for autos and trucks. Avocation: senior singles competition in national and regional tennis tournaments. Home and Office: 81 Avondale Ln Aberdeen NJ 07747-1239

SMITH, MARY LEVI, academic administrator; b. Jan. 30, 1936. Pres. Ky. State U., Frankfort. Office: Kentucky State U Office of President Frankfort KY 40601

SMITH, MARY LOUISE, politics and public affairs consultant; b. Eddyville, Iowa, Oct. 6, 1914; d. Frank and Louise Anna (Jager) Epperson; BA, U. Iowa, 1935; LHD (hon.), Drake U., 1980; LLD (hon.), Grinnell Coll., 1984; m. Elmer Milton Smith, Oct. 7, 1934; children: Robert C., Margaret L., James E. Mem. Eagle Grove (Iowa) Bd. Edn., 1955-60; Republican precinct committeewoman, Eagle Grove, 1960-62, vice-chairwoman, Wright County, Iowa, 1962-63; mem. Rep. Nat. Com., 1964-84, mem. exec. com., 1969-84, mem. conv. reforms com., 1966, vice-chairwoman Steiger com. on conv. reform, 1973, co-chmn. nat. com., 1974, chmn. Com., 1974-77; vice-chairwoman U.S. Commn. on Civil Rights, 1982-83; vice-chairwoman Midwest region Rep. Conf., 1969-71; del. Rep. Nat. Conv., 1968, 72, 76, 80, 84, alt. del., 1964, hon officer, 1988, 92, organized and called to order, 1976; vice-chairwoman Iowa Presdl. campaign, 1964; nat. co-chmn. Physicians Com. for Presdl. Campaign, 1972; co-chairwoman Iowa Com. to Reelect the Pres., 1972; mem. Nat. Commn. on Observance Internat. Women's Year, 1975-77, del. Internat. Women's Yr. Conf., Houston, 1977; vis. fellow Woodrow Wilson Fellowship Found., 1979. Mem. U.S. del. to Extraordinary Session of UNESCO Gen. Conf., Paris, 1973; mem. U.S. del. 15th session population commn. UN Econ. and Social Council, Geneva, 1969; mem. Pres.'s Commn. for Observance of 25th Anniversary of UN, 1970-71; mem. Iowa Commn. for Blind, 1961-63, chairwoman, 1963; mem. Iowa Gov.'s Commn. on Aging, 1962; trustee Robert A. Taft Inst. Govt., 1974-84, Herbert Hoover Presdl. Libr. Assn., Inc., 1979-91. Pres. Eagle Grove Cmty. Chest; bd. dirs. Mental Health Center North Iowa, 1962-63, YWCA of Greater Des Moines, 1983-87, Orchard Place Resdl. Facility for Emotionally Disturbed Children, 1983-88, Learning Channel, cable TV, 1984-87, Iowa Peace Inst., 1985-90, Planned Parenthood of Greater Iowa, 1986-92, U. Iowa Found., 1987—; trustee Drake U., 1990—; bd. dirs. U.S. Inst. Peace, 1990—, Chrysalis Womens Found., 1994—; bd. dirs., nat. co-chair Rep. Mainstream Com.; bd. dirs. Alliance for Arts and Understanding, 1993-96, The Interfaith Alliance of Iowa, 1996—; mem. adv. coun. U. Iowa Hawkeye Fund Women's Program, 1982-87, co-founder Iowa Women's Archives, 1991; chairperson UN Day for Iowa, 1987; polit. communication ctr. conf. U. Okla., 1987; disting. vis. exec. Coll. Bus. Adminstrn. U. Iowa, 1988; co-chmn. select com. on drug abuse City of Des Moines, 1989-90; mem. bipartisan legislative com. on govt. ethics and procedures, 1992; mem. Gov.'s Blue Ribbon Task Force on Campaign Fin. Disclosure Law, 1989; mem. Des Moines Human Rights Commn., 1995—; hon. chmn. Iowa Student/Parent Mock Election, 1995-96. Named hon. col., mil. staff Gov. Iowa, 1973; Iowa Women's Hall of Fame, 1977; named to Iowa City H.S. Hall of Fame, 1995; recipient Disting. Alumni award U. Iowa, 1984, Hancher Medallion award, 1991; Cristine Wilson medal for equality and justice Iowa Commn. on Status of Women, 1984, Elinor Robson award Coun. for Internat. Understanding, 1992, Pres. award Midwest Archives Conf., 1994; Mary Louise Smith award named in her honor, YWCA, 1988; Mary Louise Smith endowed chair in Women and Politics, Iowa State U., 1995; Brotherhood/Sisterhood award Iowa region NCCJ, 1996. Mem. Women's Aux. AMA, UN Assn., Nat. Conf. Christians and Jews, Nat. Women's Polit. Caucus (adv. bd. 1978—), PEO, Kappa Alpha Theta. Address: 654 59th St Des Moines IA 50312-1250 *The concept of "giving back" to the community in return for the benefits you have received establishes a sound basis for public service. I also believe that a woman who has achieved any degree of success in any field has an obligation to help other women in their efforts to succeed.*

SMITH, MARYA JEAN, writer; b. Youngstown, Ohio, Nov. 12, 1945; d. Cameron Reynolds and Jean Rose (Sause) Argetsinger; m. Arthur Beverly Smith Jr., Dec. 30, 1968 (div. 1996); children: Arthur Cameron, Sarah Reynolds. BA, Cornell U., 1967. Editorial asst. Seventeen Mag., N.Y.C., 1967-68; promotion writer U. Chgo. Press, 1968-70; asst. account exec. Drucilla Handy Co., Chgo., 1970-72; feature writer various mags. Chgo., 1972-74; freelance writer Cornell U., Ithaca, N.Y., 1975-76, lectr., 1976-77; playwright Playwrights' Ctr. Prodn., Chgo., 1978; humor columnist various jours. Chgo., 1979-81, freelance writer, 1982—. Author: Across the Creek, 1989, Winter-Broken, 1990, Danish edit., 1991; (play) Hire Power, 1997; contbr. poetry Primavera, Ariel VI and VIII, 1974, 87, 89; contbr. articles and essays to mags. and papers, 1984—. Vol. reading tutor Literacy Vols. Western Cook County, Oak Park, Ill., 1988-89, Oak Park Pub. Libr. Reading Program, 1990-94. Recipient 1st Pl. for News Writing Associated Ch. Press, 1986, Poetry award Poets and Patrons, 1986, Triton Coll. Salute to Arts, 1987, 89. Mem. Nat. Writers Union, Soc. Children's Book Writers, Author's Guild, Soc. Midland Authors, Children's Reading Round Table. Roman Catholic.

SMITH, MAURICE EDWARD, lawyer, business consultant; b. Denver, Mar. 30, 1919; s. Edward Daniel and Junie Ardella (Fox) S.; m. Gloria Tanner, June 17, 1944; children: Christine, Kathryn, Carol (dec.), Daniel. Student, Brigham Young U., 1938-40; BS in Commerce, U. Denver, 1942; LLB, Stanford U., 1948. Mem. staff Ralph B. Mayo & Co., Denver, 1949-50; v.p. fin., gen. counsel Husky Oil Co., Cody, Wyo., 1950-61; exec. v.p. Cen. Nat. Ins. Group, Omaha, 1961-65; treas., legal counsel Sunnen Products Co., St. Louis, 1965-69; v.p., treas. Global Marine, Inc., Los Angeles, 1969-78; pvt. bus. cons., 1978—. Mem. Cody City Council, 1955-57. Served with USNR, 1942-45. Mem. Calif. Bar Assn., Kiwanis Club of Provo. Mem. Ch. Jesus Christ of Latter-day Saints. Home: PO Box 327 Provo UT 84603-0327

SMITH, MAURY DRANE, lawyer; b. Samson, Ala., Feb. 2, 1927; s. Abb Jackson and Rose Drane (Sellers) S.; m. Lucile West Martin, Aug. 15, 1953; children: Martha Smith Vandervoort, Sally Smith Legg, Maury D. Smith, Jr. BS, U. Ala., 1950, LLB, JD, 1952. Bar: Ala., 1952; U.S. Dist. Ct. (mid., no. and so. dists.) Ala. 1953; U.S. Ct. Appeals, 1957, U.S. Supreme Ct., 1957. Asst. atty. gen. State of Ala., Montgomery, 1952-55; asst. dist. atty. Montgomery County, 1955-63; ptnr. Balch & Bingham LLP, Montgomery, 1955—; chmn. lawyers adv. com. Mid. Dist. Ala., Montgomery, 1990—; mem. U.S. Ct. of Appeals 11th cir. adv. com. on rules, Montgomery, 1990—, U.S. Dist. Ct. Mid. Dist. civil justice reform act adv. com., Montgomery, 1991—. Pres. Montgomery Area United Way, Ala., 1987; mem. Leadership Montgomery, 1994. Fellow Am. Coll. Trial Lawyers, Am. Bar Found.; mem. Univ. Ala. System (bd. trustees 1991-97, trustee emeritus 1997—), Ala. Law Inst. (mem. coun.), ABA (mem. litigation sect.), Montgomery County Bar Assn. (pres. 1976), Montgomery Area C. of C. (pres. 1984), Ala. State Bar (chmn. jud. bldg. task force 1987-94). Avocations: farming, tennis. Home: 2426 Midfield Dr Montgomery AL 36111-1529 Office: Balch & Bingham LLP 2 Dexter Ave PO Box 78 Montgomery AL 36101

SMITH, MERLIN GALE, engineering executive, researcher; b. Germantown, Ky., May 12, 1928; s. Allen Edward and Gladys Myrtle (Kaiser) S.; m. Elinore Klein, Dec. 23, 1955; children: Laurence Robin, Derek Randall, April Rena. B.E.E., U. Cin., 1950; M.E.E., Columbia U., 1957. With IBM, N.Y.C. and Yorktown Heights, N.Y., 1952-92; engring. mgr. large scale integration IBM, Yorktown Heights, 1964-70; research staff mem. IBM, 1970-92; pvt. practice cons., 1992—; bd. govs. Computer Soc., 1970-80, 87-88, sec., 1972-73, v.p., 1975-76, 87-88, pres. 1977-78; bd. dirs. Nat. Computer Conf., 1973-77, chmn., 1975, conf. chmn., 1978. Contbr. articles to profl. jours. Served with Signal Corps AUS, 1951-52. Fellow IEEE (mem. tech. activities bd. 1977-78, 83-84, bd. dirs. 1983-86, exec. v.p. 1985, v.p. tech. activities 1986); mem. Am. Fedn. Info. Processing Socs. (dir. 1977-79, exec. com. 1978-79). Patentee in field. Home and Office: Farnham Point Rd PO Box 215 East Boothbay ME 04544-0215

SMITH, MERRITT ROE, history educator; b. Waverly, N.Y., Nov. 14, 1940; s. Wilson Niles and Mary Eleanor (Fitzgerald) S.; m. Bronwyn M. Mellquist, Aug. 24, 1974. AB, Georgetown U., 1963; MA, Pa. State U., 1965, PhD, 1971; LHD (hon.), Rensselaer Poly. Inst., 1997. Asst. prof. history Ohio State U., Columbus, 1970-74, assoc. prof., 1974-78; vis. prof. history and sociology of sci. U. Pa., Phila., 1976; prof. history tech. program in sci., tech. and society M.I.T., Cambridge, 1978—, Metcalfe prof. engring. and liberal arts, 1989-92, dir. progam in sci., tech. and society, 1992-96, Leverett and William King Cutten prof., 1993—. Author: Harpers Ferry Armory and the New Technology, 1977, Military Enterprise and Technological Change, 1985, Science, Technology and the Military, 2 vols., 1988, Does Technology Drive History?, 1994; mem. editorial bd. Tech. and Culture, 1973-91, Bus. History Rev., 1978-85, MIT Press, 1986-91, Archimedes, 1995—. Mem. Mass. Hist. Soc.; trustee Hagley Mus. and Libr., Mus. Am. Textile History, Charles Babbage Inst.; bd. advisors MIT Mus.; mem. Anne S.K. Brown mil. collection com. Brown U. Recipient Cert. of Commendation Am. Assn. State and Local History, 1978, Disting. Tchg. award Ohio State U., 1978; grantee Ohio State U., 1972, Am. Philos. Soc., 1974, Harvard Bus. Sch., 1974-75, Eleutherian Mills-Hagley Found., 1978-79, Alfred P. Sloan Found., 1994—; Guggenheim fellow, 1983-84, Regents fellow Smithsonian Instn., 1984-85. Mem. AAAS, Am. Acad. Arts and Scis., Soc. History Tech. (mem. exec. council, Dexter Prize com., Da Vinci medal 1994, mus. com., v.p., pres. 1989-91), Orgn. Am. Historians (Frederick Jackson Turner award 1977), Bus. History Conf., Am. Antiquarian Soc., Newcomen Soc. N. Am., Soc. Indsl. Archeology, History Sci. Soc. (Pfizer award 1978), Phi Kappa Phi, Phi Alpha Theta. Home: 17 Longfellow Rd Newton MA 02162-1505 Office: MIT Rm E51-110 Cambridge MA 02139

SMITH, MICHAEL, biochemistry educator; b. Blackpool, Eng., Apr. 26, 1932. BSc, U. Manchester, Eng., 1953, PhD, 1956. Fellow B.C. Rsch. Coun., 1956-60; rsch. assoc. Inst. Enzyme Rsch., U. Wis., 1960-61; head chem. sect. Vancouver Lab. Fisheries Rsch. Bd. Can., 1961-66; med. rsch. assoc. Med. Rsch. Coun. Can., 1966-71, career investigator, 1971—; assoc. prof. biochem. U. B.C., Vancouver, 1966-70, prof., 1970—, Peter Wall disting. prof. biotech., 1994—. Recipient Gairdner Found. Internat. award, 1986, Nobel Prize in Chemistry, 1993. Fellow Chem Inst. Can., Royal Soc. (London), Royal Soc. Can., Royal Soc. Chemistry; mem. Sigma Xi, Order of British Columbia, Companion of the Order of Can. Achievements include research in nucleic acid and nucleotide chemistry and biochemistry using in-vitro mutagenesis gene expression. Office: U BC Biotech Lab, 6174 University Blvd, Vancouver, BC Canada V6T 1Z3

SMITH, MICHAEL ALEXIS, petroleum geologist; b. Boston, Nov. 8, 1944; s. Albert Charles and Nina (Gronstrand) S.; m. Nancy Laura Wilson, Dec. 19, 1971; 1 child, Christine Lara. B.S., U. Mich., 1966; M.S., U. Kans., 1969; Ph.D., U. Tex., 1975. Marine geologist U.S. Geol. Survey, Washington, 1966-68, petroleum geologist, 1975-81, geochemist, 1976-81; rsch. geochemist Getty Oil Co., Houston, 1981-83, supr. basin evaluation and structural geology, 1983-84; rsch. assoc. Texaco Inc., Houston, 1984-92; chief geologist Geo-Strat, Inc., Houston, 1992—; adj. prof. geology Emory U., Atlanta, 1988-89; reg. deepwater geologist Minerals Mgmt. Svc., New Orleans, 1994—. Contbr. articles to profl. jours. and books. Fellow Geol. Soc. Am.; mem. Am. Assn. Petroleum Geologists, Am. Geophys. Union, Houston Geol. Soc., Am. Assn. of Stratigraphic Palynologists , Soc. Organic Petrology (founding mem.). Avocations: music, running. Research interest: geol. and depositional facies controls on petroleum occurrence; regional source-rock geochemistry and organic petrology; biostratigraphy, paleogeography, and paleoecology. Home: 1123 Shillington Dr Katy TX 77450-4204 Office: Geo-Strat Inc 1718 Triway Ln Houston TX 77043-3346

SMITH, MICHAEL CHARLES, personnel director, human resources specialist; b. DuQuoin, Ill., Apr. 1, 1947; s. Michael Paul and Audrey Elizabeth (Bigham) S.; m. Janelle Ann Hutchings, Apr. 10, 1971; 1 child, Rachel Elizabeth. BS, Murray State U., 1974. Dist. sales mgr. Protective Life Ins. Cos., Murray, Ky., 1973—; employee rels. rep. G.D. Freeman United Coal Co., DuQuoin, 1975-79; dir. personnel and safety Tuck Tape Inc., Carbondale, Ill., 1979-80; supr. personnel GTE Elec. Components and Materials Div., Muncy, Pa., 1980-82; human resources mgr. GTE Elec. Components Div., Williamsport, Pa., 1982-85, Muncy, Pa., 1985-88; human resources mgr. GTE Lighting Spl. Projects, Waldoboro, Maine, 1988-89, GTE Ctrl. Devices, Stanoish, Maine, 1989-92, Keebler Co., Macon, Ga., 1992—; chmn. and organizer State Employment Office for Employer Adv. Council Ill., Carbondale, 1979-80, chairperson Ill. Job Service Adv. Council, 1975; adult edn. instr. Rend Lake Community Coll., Pinckneyville, Ill., 1977-78. Charter pres. Murray State Jaycees, 1972. Served to sgt. USAF, 1967-71. Recipient P. Daniel Coyne Meml. award Maine Safety Coun., 1993; named to Hon. Order Ky. Cols. Mem. Cen. Pa. Safety Assn. Republican. Presbyterian. Lodge: Masons. Avocations: golf, fishing, tennis, reading, family activities. Home: 108 Saddle Run Ct N Macon GA 31210-8612 Office: Keebler Co 2475 Meade Rd Macon GA 31206

SMITH, MICHAEL CORDON, lawyer; b. Boise, July 30, 1954; s. Jay Myrven Jr. and Jena Vee (Cordon) S.; m. Candace Louise Langley, Dec. 10, 1977; children: Angela K., Nicole E., Jeremy L., Melanie D. BS with high honors, Brigham Young U., 1977; JD, UCLA, 1980. Assoc. Johnson & Poulson, L.A., 1980-87, ptnr., 1987-91; pvt. practice Torrance, Calif., 1992—; judge pro tem L.A. Mcpl. Ct., 1986-94, L.A. Superior Ct., 1991-95, ct. apptd. arbitrator, 1986-91. Mem. ATLA, Nat. Employment Lawyers Assn., Calif. Employment Lawyers Assn., L.A. County Bar Assn. (vice chair law office mgmt. sect. 1992-94, exec. com. 1985-95, state bar conv. del. 1995), Consumer Attys. Assn. L.A. Republican. Mem. LDS Ch. Avocations: genealogy, computers, audio-visual electronics. Office: 23133 Hawthorne Blvd Ste 300 Torrance CA 90505-3724

SMITH, MICHAEL JAMES, industrial engineering educator; b. Madison, Wis., May 12, 1945; s. James William and Ruth Gladys (Murphy) S.; m. Patricia Ann Bentley, June 22, 1968; children: Megan Colleen, Melissa Maureen. BA, U. Wis., 1968, MA, 1970, PhD, 1973. Rsch. analyst Wis. Dept. Industry Labor, Madison, 1971-74; rsch. psychologist Nat. Inst. for Occupational Safety and Health, USPHS, Cin., 1974-84; prof. U. Wis., Madison, 1984—; owner, prin. M.J. Smith Assocs. Inc., Madison, 1991—. Contbr. articles to profl. jours. Mem. APA, Inst. Indsl. Engrs. (sr.), Human Factors Soc., Assn. Computer Machinery, Am. Soc. Testing and Measurement. Avocation: tennis. Home: 6719 Shamrock Glen Cir Middleton WI 53562-1144 Office: U Wis Dept Indsl Engring Human Factors Rsch Lab 1513 University Ave Madison WI 53706-1539

SMITH, MICHAEL JOSEPH, composer, pianist, lecturer; b. Tiline, Ky., Aug. 13, 1938; s. Marvin Gilford and Bobbie Bell (Vinson) S.; m. Kerstin Alli-Maria Andersson, May 1973; children: Tanja Michaelsdotter, Kassandra Michaelsdotter; m. Wei Wei, 1994; children: Symington Wei, Remington Wei. Student, New Eng. Conservatory Music, Julliard Sch. Pres., bd. dirs. World Music (U.S.A.), Inc., Atlanta, 1993—; composer-in-residence, Ga., 1980, 88-90; lectr., performer Agnes Scott Coll., Atlanta, Bowdoin Coll., Maine, Royal Opera, Stockholm, Ctrl. Conservatory Music, Beijing and Xian, China; rschr. IBM Corp. Scandinavia and Roland Synthesizer Corp., 1986—. Performed 1st European concert tour, 1970; on concert tours of jazz and contemporary ensembles in Western Europe and U.S., from 1972; composer 10 major ballet works, scores for major films and TV projects, 560 works for various ensembles; commns. include Moscow Philharm., Tbilisi Chamber Orch., various European ensembles, ballet cos.; performances include Atlanta Olympics, 1996, Bolshoi Theatre, Moscow, Leningrad U., Royal Swedish Opera, Stockholm, Lincoln Ctr., N.Y.C., Carnegie Hall, N.Y.C., Philharm. Hall, Berlin, stadiums in Shanghai, Guanshou, Yunan, Beijing, and Hong Kong; numerous recs., from 1970. With USN, 1955-59. Mem. Swedish Composers Soc., Internat. Soc. Contemporary Music. Home and Office: PO Box 81107 Conyers GA 30208-9107

SMITH, MICHAEL LAWRENCE, computer company executive, consultant; b. Sheboygan, Wis., Aug. 29, 1958; s. Lawrence Eugene Patrick and Velma Mary (Baltus) S. BS in Computer Sci., U. Wis., 1980; MS in Computer Sci., U. So. Calif., 1988. Lab. asst. McArdle Lab. for Cancer Rsch., Madison, Wis., 1978-80; systems programmer/analyst Controls and Data Systems, Belvidere, Ill., 1980-82; sr. systems software engr. Ex-Cell-O Mfg. Systems Co., Rockford, Ill., 1982-85; artificial intelligence cons. McDonnell-Douglas Artificial Intelligence Ctr., Cypress, Calif., 1985-88; sr. artificial intelligence engr. Eaton Corp., Milw., 1988-92; sr. knowledge engr. Inference Corp., L.A., 1992-93, sr. cons., 1993-94; sr. cons. Compuware Corp., 1994—. Author: (chpt.) Cooperating Artificial Neural and Knowledge-Based Systems in a Truck Fleet Brake-Balance Application, 1991; contbr. articles to profl. jours. Founder, chmn. Computer Profls. for Social Responsibility, Milw., 1989-90. Mem. AAAS, Am. Assn. for Artificial Intelligence, N.Am. Fuzzy Info. Processing Soc., Internat. Neural Network Soc. Achievements include patents for fuzzy logic controlled washing machine; for fuzzy logic controlled automobile engine coolant valve; for knowledge-based ion-beam deposition semi-conductor mfg. system; for blackboard-based intelligent agts.; research in ability to train practical, real world artificial neural systems using scarce data and back propagation algorithm and cooperating knowledge bases, research in globally developed and deployed case-based reasoning systems; development and deployment of a systems engineering practice; development and deployment of intranet/extranet/World Wide Web applications. Home: 111 Marquette Ave Apt 1212 Minneapolis MN 55401-2029 Office: Compuware Corp 608 2nd Ave S Minneapolis MN 55402-1916

SMITH, MICHAEL PETER, social science educator, researcher; b. Dunkirk, N.Y., Aug. 2, 1942; s. Peter Joseph and Rosalie Barbara (Lipka) S.; m. Patricia Anne Lendway, Aug. 21, 1965. BA magna cum laude, St. Michael's Coll., 1964; MA in Polit. Sci., U. Mass., 1966, PhD in Polit. Sci., 1971. Instr., asst. prof. dept. govt. Dartmouth Coll., Hanover, N.H., 1968-71; asst. prof. dept. polit. sci. Boston U., 1971-74; assoc. prof., prof. dept. polit. sci. Tulane U., New Orleans, 1974-86; prof. community studies U. Calif., Davis, 1986—, chmn. dept. applied behavioral scis., 1986-91; vis. prof. pub. policy U. Calif., Berkeley, 1981, city planning U. N.C., Chapel Hill, 1982, city planning U. Calif., Berkeley, 1985; vis. scholar in govt. U. Essex, Eng., 1979; vis. scholar polit. and social sci. U. Cambridge, Eng., 1982; vis. scholar Inst. Urban and Regional Devel., U. Calif., Berkeley, 1990. Author: The City & Social Theory, 1979, City, State and Market, 1988; co-author: Restructuring the City, 1983, California's Changing Faces, 1993; editor: Cities in Transformation, 1984, Breaking Chains, 1991, After Modernism, 1992, Marginal Spaces, 1995, Comparative Urban & Community Research, 1986—; co-editor: The Capitalist City, 1987—, The Bubbling Cauldron, 1995; mem. editl. bd. U. Press Am., 1976—. Mem. Internat. Polit. Sci. Assn., Am. Polit. Sci. Assn., Internat. Sociol. Assn. Research Coms. on Urban & Regional Devel. and Comparative Community Research. Office: Dept Human & Cmty Devel Univ Calif Davis CA 95616

SMITH, MICHAEL TOWNSEND, author, editor, stage director; b. Kansas City, Mo., Oct. 5, 1935; s. Lewis Motter and Dorothy (Pew) S.; m. Michele M. Hawley, 1974; children: Julian Bach, Alfred St. John; m. Carol E. Storke, 1992. Student, Yale U., 1953-55. Theatre critic Village Voice, N.Y.C., 1959-68, 1971-74, assoc. editor, 1962-65; curator, judge Obie awards for theatre, 1962-68, 1971-74; playwright mem. Open Theatre, N.Y.C., 1962-66; mgr. Sundance Festival, Upper Black Eddy, Pa., 1966-68; dir. Theatre Genesis, N.Y.C., 1971-74; arts editor Taos (N.Mex.) News, 1977-78; music critic New London (Conn.) Day, 1982-86; instrument maker, adminstr. Zuckermann Harpsichords Inc., 1974-77, 79-85; dir. Boston Early Music Festival and Exhbn., 1983-85; asst. press sec., speechwriter Mayor Edward I. Koch, N.Y.C., 1986-89; mgr. 14th St. Stage Lighting, N.Y.C., 1989-90; lighting dir. The Living Theatre, N.Y.C., 1990-93; music critic Santa Barbara (Calif.) News-Press, 1992; arts editor Santa Barbara Ind., 1992-94; editor Santa Barbara Mag., 1995—. Author: (fiction) Getting Across, 1962; Near the End, 1965, Automatic Vaudeville, 1970, High Points of Youth, 1986; (poetry) American Baby, 1975, A Sojourn in Paris, 1985; (plays) I Like It, 1961; The Next Thing, 1963, A Dog's Love, 1965, Captain Jack's Revenge, 1970, Country Music, 1971, Double Solitaire, 1973, Prussian Suite, 1973, The Dinner Show, 1974, A Wedding Party, 1974, Cowgirl Ecstasy, 1976, Heavy Pockets, 1981, One Hundred Thousand Songs, 1982, Turnip Family Secrets, 1983, Half Life, 1984, Trouble (as Vernon Oreille), 1987, (with Alfred Brooks) Sameness, 1990, Life Before Death, 1992, Entertaining Vancouver, 1993, Come in Here, 1994; (memoir) Wild Dogs, 1991; translations Life Is Dream, 1978, (with Pascale Cheminee) Agatha, 1985; critical jour. Theatre Jour., 1968, Theatre Trip, 1969; also articles; editor: anthologies Eight Plays from Off-Off-Broadway, 1966, The Best of Off-Off-Broadway, 1969, More Plays from Off-Off-Broadway, 1971. Dir. Lobero Found., The Arts Fund of Santa Barbara. Recipient creative arts citation in theatre Brandeis U., 1965; Obie award, 1971; Rockefeller Found. award, 1976. Address: care Santa Barbara Mag 2064 Alameda Padre Serra Santa Barbara CA 93103-1704

SMITH, MICHAEL VINCENT, surgeon; b. Athens, Ga., Mar. 30, 1957; s. Thomas Allen and Lucile Vivian (Jackson) S.; m. Jeralyn Demetria Scott, July 28, 1979; 1 child, Demetria Joy. BS in Agr., U. Ga., 1979; MD, Med. Coll. of Ga., 1983. Diplomate Nat. Bd. Med. Examiners, Diplomate Am. Bd. Surgery, Am. Bd. Thoracic Surgery. Intern in surgery U. Ky. Med. Ctr., Lexington, 1983-84, resident in surgery, 1984-89, chief resident in gen. surgery, 1988-89; clin. asst. prof. surgery Sch. Medicine Morehouse Coll., Atlanta, 1989-90; assoc. vascular surgeon Midtown Vascular Surgery, Atlanta, 1989-90; attending surgeon Ga. Bapt. Med. Ctr., Atlanta, 1989-90, 96, Crawford Long Hosp. of Emory U., Atlanta, 1989-90, 96, Northlake Regional Med. Ctr./S.W. Cmty. Hosp. and Med., Atlanta, 1989-90, 96; assoc. cardiothoracic surgeon Atlanta Cardiac and Thoracic Surgery Assocs., 1995—; fellow in cardiothoracic surgery Coll. of Medicine Mt. Sinai Med. Ctr., N.Y.C., 1990-91; fellow cardiovascular rsch. U. Mass. Med. Ctr., Worcester, 1991-92, resident cardiothoracic, 1992-95; attending surgeon St. Joseph Hosp., Atlanta, 1996, cardiothoracic surgery chief resident, 1994-95; attending surgeon Piedmont Hosp., Atlanta, 1996, Dunwoody Med. Ctr., Atlanta, 1996, South Fulton Med. Ctr., Atlanta, 1989-90, 96, Southern Regional Med. Ctr., Riverdale, 1996; mem. ICU S.W. Community Hosp., Atlanta, 1989-90; mem. clin. pathway coms. St. Joseph Hosp., 1996, Ga. Bapt. Med. Ctr., 1996. Sunday sch. tchr. 1st African Meth. Episcopal Ch., Athens, Ga., 1975-79, Bethel African Meth. Episcopal Ch., Augusta, Ga., 1980-83, St. Paul African Meth. Episcopal Ch., Lexington, Ky., 1985-89. Sunday sch. tchr. First A.M.E. Ch., Athens, Ga., 1975-79, Bethel African Meth. Episcopal Ch., Augusta, Ga., 1980-83, St. Paul A.M.E. Ch., Lexington, Ky., 1985-89, St. Philip A.M.E. Ch., 1996. Nat. Achievement scholar, 1974; named one of Outstanding Young Men of the Yr., Jaycees, 1983. Mem. ACS (mem. candidate group), AMA, Atlanta Med. Assn., Southeastern Surg. Congres (assoc.), Assn. Acad. Surgery, Soc. Black Acad. Surgeons, Nat. Med. Assn., Mass. Med. Soc., Am. Heart Assn. (affiliate in tng.), Am. Coll. Cardiology, NAACP (Worchester chpt.), Alpha Phi Alpha. Avocations: computers, photography, music, reading. Office: St Joseph Med Ctr Ste 350 5671 Peachtree Dunwoody Rd NE Atlanta GA 30342-5003

SMITH, MICHAEL W., popular musician. Albums include The Big Picture, 1993, The First Decade 1983-1993, 1993, Go West Young Man, 1993, Christmas, 1993, (with Amy Grant) Change Your World, 1993, I'll Lead You Home, 1995. Recipient Best Pop/Contemporary Gospel album Grammy award, 1996. Office: Reunion Records 2908 Poston Ave Nashville TN 37203-1312*

SMITH, MICHAEL WILLIAM, biomedical engineer, consultant; b. Hancock, Mich., Mar. 14, 1957; s. Jackson B. and Vivian Elizabeth (Pier) S. AAS in Biomed. Engring., Western Wis. Tech. Coll., 1977; B of Biomed. Engring. Tech., Milw. Sch. Engring., 1983; MBA, No. Ill. U., 1997. Registered profl. engr., Wis. Quality engr. GE Med. Sys., Waukesha, Wis., 1984-85, supr., 1985-87, project leader, 1987-91; dir. engring. Miller Med. Sys., Indpls., 1991-93; med. sys. engr. Comdisco Med. Exch., Wood Dale, Ill., 1993—. Pres. Madison Home Owners Assn., Waukesha, 1989-91. Mem. IEEE, NSPE. Office: Comdisco Med Exch 1421 N Wood Dale Rd Wood Dale IL 60191-1078

SMITH, MICHELE, lawyer; b. Ogden, Utah, Feb. 12, 1955; d. Max S. and Grace B. (Gerstman) Smith; m. Philip A. Turner, Aug. 25, 1985. BA, SUNY, Buffalo, 1976; JD, U. Chgo., 1979. Law clk. U.S. Ct. Appeals (7th cir.), Chgo., 1979-81; asst. atty. no. dist. U.S. Atty's Office, Chgo., 1981-89; assoc. gen. counsel Navistar Internat. Transportation Corp., Chgo., 1989—. Mem. Am. Corp. Counsel Assn., Phi Beta Kappa. Office: Navistar Internat Transp Corp 455 N Cityfront Plaza Dr Chicago IL 60611-5503

SMITH, MIKEL DWAINE, physician, educator, researcher; b. Eugene, Oreg., Jan. 3, 1952; s. Charles G. and Helen Jean (Giles) S.; m. Barbara Anne Phillips, June 27, 1980 (div. April 1993); children: Ellen Anne, Benjamin Hatfield; m. Annette Louise Cater, Nov. 19, 1993. BS, Murray (Ky.) State U., 1973; MD Coll. Medicine, U. Ky., Lexington, 1977. Diplomate Nat. Bd. Med. Examiners, Am. Bd. Internal Medicine. Intern in internal medicine Med. Coll. Va., Richmond, 1977-78, resident in internal medicine, 1978-80, fellow in cardiology, 1980-82; instr. in medicine Coll. Medicine U. Ky., Lexington, 1982-83, asst. prof. medicine/cardiology, 1983-87, assoc. prof. medicine/cardiology, 1987-92, prof. medicine/cardiology, 1992—; dir. cardiovascular fellow Coll. Medicine U. Ky., Lexington, 1987—, dir. adult echocardiography, 1989—. Contbg. author 11 books in field; contbr. numerous articles to sci. jours. Recipient Outstanding Tchr. award Am. Coll. Physicians, U. Ky., 1996. Fellow Am. Coll. Cardiology, Am. Heart Assn. (com. on echo 1992-94); mem. Am. Soc. Echocardiography (bd. dirs. 1994—, com. on tng. 1993-95). Methodist. Avocations: basketball, tennis, golf. Office: U Ky Coll Medicine L-548 Kentucky Clinic Lexington KY 40536

SMITH, MILTON RAY, computer company executive, lawyer; b. Idaho, 1935. AA, Long Beach (Calif.) City Coll., 1958; BS, Portland State U., 1962; MS, Oreg. State U., 1969; JD, Lewis and Clark Coll., 1970. Bar: Oreg. 1970, U.S. Dist. Ct. Oreg. 1970, U.S. Ct. Appeals (9th cir.) 1971, U.S. Supreme Ct. 1973. Tech. writer Northrop Corp., Hawthorne, Calif., 1957-58; engring. writer Tektronix Inc., Beaverton, Oreg., 1958-60, design engr., 1960-63, project engr., 1963-65, program mgr., 1966-70; asst. engring. mgr. Eldorado Electronics, Concord, Calif., 1965-66; ptnr. Acker, Underwood & Smith, Portland, Oreg., 1970-86; chmn., chief exec. officer Floating Point Systems Inc., Beaverton, 1986-88, pres., chief exec. officer, 1991-92, also vice chmn. bd. dirs.; pres., chief exec. officer Thrustmaster Inc., Tigard, Oreg., 1992-94; pres., CEO Zeelan Tech., Inc., Beaverton, Oreg., 1994-95; mgmt. cons., 1995—; CEO, Test Sys. Strategies, Inc., Beaverton, 1992-93; bd. dirs. ThrustMaster, Inc., Beaverton, Distbn. Scis. Corp., Hillsboro, Oreg. Bd. dirs. Oreg. Bus. Council, Portland, 1986-88; mem. bd. visitors Northwestern Sch. Law, Portland, 1986—. With USN, 1953-56. Mem. Am. Electronics Assn. (exec. com. Oreg. coun. 1987-93, vice chmn. 1994-95, chmn. 1995-96), Oreg. State Bar, Founders Club Portland. Republican. Office: 6717 NE 126th St Vancouver WA 98686-3485

SMITH, MORTON EDWARD, ophthalmology educator, dean; b. Balt., Oct. 17, 1934. BS, U. Md., 1956, MD, 1960. Bd. cert. Ophthalmology Bd.; lic. physician Mo., Md., Wis. Rotating intern Denver Gen. Hosp., 1960-61; resident, nat. inst. of neurol. diseases and blindness fellow in opthalmology Washington U. Sch. Medicine-Barnes Hosp., 1961-63; NIH spl. fellow in ophthalmic pathology Armed Forces Inst. of Pathology, Washington, 1964; chief resident, instr. ophthalmology Washington U. Sch. Medicine, St. Louis, 1965-66, instr. ophthalmology, 1966-67, asst. prof. ophthalmology and pathology, 1967-69, assoc. prof. ophthalmology and pathology, 1969-75, prof. ophthalmology and pathology, 1975—, asst. dean, 1978-91, assoc. dean, 1991-96, prof. emeritus, assoc. dean emeritus, 1996—; prof. ophthalmology U. Wis., Madison, 1995—; vis. scholar Eye Inst., Columbia Presbyn. Med. Ctr., N.Y.C., 1966; prof./lectr. Montefiore Hosp., Pitts., 1969, U. Ark., 1970, 77, 80, 82, 84, 86, 88, U. Fla., 1972, 81, U. Tex. and Lackland AFB, San Antonio, 1973, U. Colo., 1974, 82, U. Mo., 1974, 79, 80, 88, So. Ill. U., Springfield, 1974, U. Md., 1975, Montreal (Can.) Gen. Hosp., 1975, U. Wis., 1976, 87, 93, U. Pitts., 1977, 83, 87, U. Iowa, 1977, 87, Cleve. Clinic, 1978, Colo. Ophthalmol. Soc., 1978, Brooke Army Hosp., San Antonio, 1979, Wills Eye Hosp., Phila., 1980, USPHS Hosp., San Francisco, 1981, U. Calif., Davis, 1981, Sinai Hosp., Balt., 1985, 89, 94, U. Calif., San Diego, 1985, Tufts U., Boston, 1985, Cornell U., N.Y.C., 1988, U. Wash., Seattle, 1990, Brown U., Providence, 1990, Vanderbilt U., Nashville, 1991, Duke U., Durham, N.C., 1992; Chandler lectr. Harvard U., 1988; The Lois A. Young-Thomas Meml. lectr. U. Md., 1991; Braley lectr. U. Iowa, 1993; Havener Meml. lectr. Ohio State, 1994. Editor pathology sect.: Perspectives in Ophthalmology, 1977; mem. editl. bd. Ophthalmic Plastic & Reconstructive Surgery, 1986-90; contbr. articles to profl. jours. With USAR M.C., 1958-66. Scholar U. Md., 1958, 59. Fellow Am. Acad. Ophthalmology (ophthalmic pathology com. 1977-83, chmn. ophthalmic com. 1979-83, Honor award for svc. 1981, Sr. Honor award 1992); mem. AMA, Am. Bd. Ophthalmology (diplomate, bd. dirs. 1992—), Assn. for Rsch. in Vision and Ophthalmology (chmn. sect. pathology ann. meeting 1971), Am. Assn. Ophthalmic Pathologists (pres. 1977-80), Assn. Am. Med. Colls. (group med. edn. 1985—), Mo. Med. Assn., Mo. Ophthalmol. Soc., Verhoeff Soc., Theobald Soc., St. Louis Med. Soc., St. Louis Ophthalmol. Soc., Soc. Med. Coll. Dirs. for Continuing Med. Edn., Alpha Omega Alpha (sec.-treas. Wash. U. chpt. 1993—). Office: U Wis Dept Ophthalmology F4/336 CSC 600 Highland Ave Madison WI 53792-0001

SMITH, MORTON HOWISON, religious organization administrator, educator; b. Roanoke, Va., Dec. 11, 1923; s. James Brookes and Margaret Morton (Howison) S.; m. Lois Virginia Knopf, July 7, 1925; children: Samuel Warfield, Susanne Rochet Margaret. BA, U. Mich., 1947; BD, Columbia Theol. Sem., 1953; ThM, ThD, Free U., Amsterdam, The Netherlands, 1962. Ordained to ministry Presbyn. Ch., 1954. Pastor Springfield-Roller Presbyn. Chs., Carroll County, Md., 1954; prof. bible Belhaven Coll., Jackson, Miss., 1954-63; guest lectr. Westminster Theol. Sem., Phila., 1963-64; prof. Reformed Theol. Sem., Jackson, 1964-79; stated clk. gen. assembly Presbyn. Ch. in Am., Decatur, Ga., 1973-88; prof. systematic theology, dean faculty Greenville Presbyn. Theol. Sem., 1987—; advisor to bd. dirs. Greenville (S.C.) Presbyn. Theol. Sem., 1986—; mem. bd. dirs. Presbyn. Jour., Asheville, N.C., 1965-87; lectr. on theology Republic of So. Africa , June-July, 1988, Riga, Latvia, 1992, Budapest, Hungary, 1994, Prague, Czech Republic, 1994, 95, Trinidad and Tobago, 1995, on mission, Republic of Korea, June-July, 1989. Author: Studies in Southern Presbyterian Theology, 1962, 2d edit. 1987, How Is the Gold Become Dim, 1973, (pamphlet) Reformed Evangelism, 1970, Testimony, 1986, Commentary on the Book of Church Order, 1990, Harmony of the Westminster Confession and Catechisms, 1990, Systematic Theology, 1994; contbr. articles to Reformed Theology in Am., 1985. Trustee Covenant Coll., Lookout Mountain, Tenn., 1982-90. 1st lt. USAAF, 1942-45. Fulbright fellow U.S. Govt., 1958. Mem. N.Am. Presbyn. and Reformed Coun. of Chs. (sec. 1977-92). Avocations: flying, traveling, genealogy. Office: Greenville Presbyn Theol Sem PO Box 9279 Greenville SC 29604-9279

SMITH, MURRAY THOMAS, transportation company executive; b. Hudson, S.D., 1939; s. Rex D. and Frances M. Smith; m. Diane R. Cramer, Dec. 4, 1959 (div. June 1994); children: Lisa B., Thomas M., Amy R.; m. Donna Thomas Kjonaas, Jan. 1995. V.p. Overland Express Inc., Indpls., 1978-82; v.p. ops. R.T.C. Transp. Inc., Forest Pk., Ga., 1982-83; with Midwest Coast Transport L.P., Sioux Falls, S.D., 1983—, sr. v.p., 1983-84;

pres. Midwest Coast Transport L.P., Sioux Falls, S.D., 1984-89, prin., pres., chief exec. officer, 1989—, also bd. dirs.; bd. dirs. Interstate Carrier Conf., Nat. Perishable Logistics Assn. Bd. dirs. Sioux Valley Hosp., 1991—, United Way, Sioux Falls, 1991—. Office: Midwest Coast Transport LP 1600 E Benson Rd Sioux Falls SD 57104-0871

SMITH, MYRON JOHN, JR., librarian, author; b. Toledo, May 3, 1944; s. Myron John and Marion Oliva (Herbert) S.; 1 son, Myron John III. Student, Coll. Steubenville, 1962; AB, Ashland Coll., 1966; MLS, Western Mich. U., 1967; MA, Shippensburg U., 1969; postgrad., U. Wis., Purdue U.; LittD, Cardinal Newman Coll., 1982. Rsch. librarian G.W. Blunt White Libr., Mystic Seaport, Conn., 1967-68; asst. librarian Western Md. Coll., Westminster, 1969-72; libr. dir. Huntington (Ind.) Pub. Libr., 1972-76; prof. history and libr. sci., dir. librs. Benedum Libr. Salem-Teikyo U.; dir., then assoc. dir. aviation program Salem (W.Va.) Coll., 1976-90; prof. history and libr. sci., libr. dir. Tusculum Coll., Greeneville, Tenn., 1990—; mem. Am. Com. on History 2d World War, Assn. for Bibliography of History. Author: American Naval Bibliography Series, 1972-74, Huntington Centennial Handbook, 1973, The Sophisticated Lady: The Battleship Indiana in World War II, 1973, World War II at Sea: A Bibliography of Sources in English, 1976, (with Robert Webber) Sea Fiction Guide, 1976, The Cloak and Dagger Bibliography, 1976, World War I in the Air, 1977, Air War Chronology 1939-45, 1977, Air War Bibliography Series, 1977—, The Mountain State Battleship: USS West Virginia, 1979, Air War Southeast Asia, 1979, The Soviet Navy, 1941-1978, 1979, The Secret Wars Series, 1980-81, The Soviet Air and Strategic Rocket Forces, 1941-1980, 1981, The Soviet Army, 1941-1980, 1981, Equestrian Studies: The Salem College Guide, 1981, The Cloak and Dagger Fiction Guide: An Annotated Guide to Spy Thrillers, 1981, (with Terry White) 3d edit., 1994, The Mountaineer Battlewagon: USS West Virginia, 1982, The Keystone Battlewagon: USS Pennsylvania, 1983, The Golden State Battlewagon: USS California, 1983, Watergate: A Bibliography, 1983 World War II: Mediterranean and European Theaters, 1984, The United States Navy and Coast Guard, 1946-1983: A Bibliography of English Language Works and 16mm Films, 1984, U.S. Television Network News: A Guide to Sources in English, 1984, Battleships and Battlecruisers, 1884-1984: A Bibliography and Chronology, 1985, Baseball: A Comprehensive Bibliography, 1986, 99th Infantry Division Bibliography, 1986, The Airline Bibliography: The Salem College Guide to Sources on Commercial Aviation, Vol. I, The United States, 1986, Vol. II, Airliners and Foreign Carriers, 1987, Passenger Airliners of the United States, 1926-86: A Pictorial Guide, 1987, rev. edit. through 1991, 1991, 3d rev. edit. through 1995, 1995, Brooklyn/Los Angeles Dodgers: A Bibliography, 1987, American Warplane Bibliography, 1989, Volunteer Battlewagon: The U.S.S. Tennessee (BB-43), 1989; editor: Sports Teams and Players Bibliography Series, 1987, Battle and Leaders Bibliography Series, 1988, 100 Years of Opportunity: A Pictorial History of Salem College, 1888-1988, 1988, Pro Football Bio-Bibliography, 1920-1988, 1989, Pearl Harbor, December 7, 1941: An Annotated Bibliography, 1991, Battles of the Coral Sea and Midway, 1942: A Bibliography, 1991, World War II at Sea, 1974-1989: A Bibliography, 1990, Professional Football: The Official Pro Football Hall of Fame Bibliography, 1993, Baseball: A Comprehensive Bibliography-1st Supplement: 1985-1991, 93, The College Football Bibliography, 1994, Glimpses of Tusculum College: A Pictorial History, 1794-1994, 1994, Airlines of the World, 1908-94, 97; contbr. articles to various jours. Recipient Nelson Ross award Profl. Football Rsch. Assn., 1993; 1st Am. recipient Richard Franck Gold medal Bibliothek für Zeitgeschichte, Stuttgart, Fed. Rep. Germany, 1981. Mem. ALA, U.S. Naval Inst., U.S. Mil. Inst., U.S. Air Force Found., Assn. Bibliog. of History (pres. 1981-82), Alliance of Librs. in Northeast Tenn. (pres. 1997—), Beta Phi Mu, Phi Alpha Theta. Club: Optimist. Office: Tusculum Coll PO Box 5005 Greeneville TN 37743-0001

SMITH, NANCY HOHENDORF, sales and marketing executive; b. Detroit, Jan. 30, 1943; d. Donald Gerald and Lucille Marie (Kopp) Hohendorf; m. Richard Harold Smith, Aug. 21, 1978 (div. Jan. 1984). BA, U. Detroit, 1965; MA, Wayne State U., 1969. Customer rep. Xerox Corp., Detroit, 1965-67; mktg. rep. Univ. Microfilms subs. Xerox Corp., Ann Arbor, Mich., 1967-73, mktg. coord., 1973-74, mgr. dir. mktg., 1975-76; mgr. mktg. Xerox Corp., Can., 1976-77; major account mktg. exec. Xerox Corp., Hartford, Conn., 1978-79, New Haven, Conn., 1979-80; account exec. State of N.Y. Xerox Corp., N.Y.C., 1981; N.Y. region mgr. customer support Xerox Corp., Greenwich, Conn., 1982, N.Y. region sales ops. mgr., 1982; State of Ohio account exec. Xerox Corp., Columbus, 1983; new bus. sales mgr. Xerox Corp., Dayton, Ohio, 1983, major accounts sales mgr., 1984; info. systems sales and support mgr., quality specialist Xerox Corp., Detroit, 1985-87, new product launch mgr., ops. quality mgr., 1988, dist. mktg. mgr., 1989-91, major accounts sales mgr., 1992—. Named to Outstanding Young Women of Am., 1968, Outstanding Bus. Woman, Dayton C. of C., 1984, Women's Inner Circle of Achievement, 1990. Mem. NAFE, Am. Mgmt. Assn., Women's Econ. Club Detroit, Detroit Inst. Arts Founders' Soc., Detroit Hist. Soc., Greater Detroit C. of C., Detroit Hist. Soc. Republican. Roman Catholic. Avocations: interior decorating, reading, music, art. Home: 23308 Reynard Dr Southfield MI 48034-6924 Office: Xerox Corp 300 Galleria Officentre Southfield MI 48034-4700

SMITH, NANCY LYNNE, journalist, real estate agent, public relations consultant; b. San Antonio, July 31, 1947; d. Tillman Louis and Enid Maxine (Woolverton) Brown; m. Allan Roy Jones, Nov. 28, 1969 (div. 1975); 1 dau., Christina Elizabeth Woolverton Jones. BA, So. Meth. U., 1968; postgrad. So. Meth. U., 1969-70, Vanderbilt U., 1964, Ecole Nouvelle de la Suisse Romande, Lausanne, Switzerland, 1962. Tchr. spl. edn. Hot Springs Sch. Dist. (Ark.), 1970-72; reporter, soc. editor Dallas Morning News, 1974-82; soc./celebrity columnist Dallas Times Herald, 1982—; owner, pub. High Soc., Soc. Fax; realtor, Ebby Halliday Realtors; stringer Washington Post, 1978; contbg. editor Ultra mag., Houston, 1981-82, Tex. Woman mag., Dallas, 1979-80, Profl. Woman mag., Dallas, 1979-80; mem. bd. advisors Ultra Mag., 1985—; owner Nancy Smith Pub. Rels. Appeared on TV series Jocelyn's Weekend, Sta. KDFI-TV, 1985. Bd. dirs. TACA arts support orgn., Dallas, 1980—, asst. chmn. custom auction, 1978-83; judge Miss Tex. USA Contest, 1984; bd. dirs. Am. Parkinson Disease Assn. (Dallas chpt.), mem. adv. bd. Cattle Baron's Ball Com., Dallas Symphony Debutante presentations; hon. mem. Dallas Opera Women's Bd., Northwood Inst. Women's Bd., Dallas Symphony League; mem. Friends of Winston Churchill Meml. and Library, Dallas Theatre Ctr. Women's Guild, Childrens' Med. Ctr. Auxiliary; mem. women's com. Dallas Theatre Ctr.; hon. mem. Crystal Charity Ball Com.; mem. Community Council Greater Dallas Community Awareness Goals Com. Impact '88, 1985—; co-chmn. Multiple Sclerosis San Simeon Gala, 1988; celebrity co-chmn. Greer Garson Gala of Hope 1990-91; gala chmn. Greer Garson Gala of Hope for Am. Parkinson's Disease Assn., 1991-93; chmn. gala benefit Northwood U., 1994; co-chmn. star studded stomp Mar. Dimes, 1994; mem. Femmes du Monde spl. activities com., com. Dallas Coun. World Affairs. Mem. Soc. Profl. Journalists (v.p. communications 1978-79), Nat. Press Club, Dallas Press Club, DAR, Daus. of Republic of Tex. (registrar 1972), Dallas So. Memorial Assn., Dallas County Heritage Soc., Dallas Mus. Art League, Dallas Opera Guild. Club: Argyle (sec. 1983-84), The 500 (Dallas). Home: 6324D Bandera Ave Dallas TX 75225-3614 Office: 8333 Douglas Ave Ste 100 Dallas TX 75225-5811

SMITH, NATHAN MCKAY, library and information sciences educator; b. Wendell, Idaho, Apr. 22, 1935; s. M. Blair and Vaunda H. (Hawkes) S.; m. Joyce A. Carman, July 5, 1953; children: Nathan M., Jeffrey M., Pamela J., Russell A., Kristen E. BS in Secondary Edn., Eastern Oreg. Coll., 1961; MS in Gen. Sci., Oreg. State U., 1965; MLS, Brigham Young U., 1969, PhD in Zoology, 1972. Tchr. sci. Dalles Jr. High Sch., The Dalles, Oreg., 1961-64; asst. sci. libr. Brigham Young U., Provo, Utah, 1968, life sci. libr., 1970-73, prof. Sch. Libr. and Info. Sci., 1973-82, dir. Sch. Libr. and Info. Sci., 1982-93, life sci. libr. Sch. Libr. and Info. Sci., 1993-97; cons. Weber County Library, Ogden, Utah, 1980—; back issues sec. Herpetologists League, 1976-81. Served to sgt. USAF, 1953-57. Yr. scholar NSF Acad., 1964; fellow NDEA Title IV, 1969; recipient research award Assn. Library and Info. Sci. Edn., 1983. Mem. ALA (councilor legis. council), Assn. Library Info. Sci. Edn., Mountain Plains Library Assn., Utah Library Assn. (exec. bd., pres.), N. Am. Soc. Adlerian Psychology, Phi Kappa Phi, Sigma Xi, Beta Phi Mu. Mem. LDS Ch. Home: 1606 Locust Ln Provo UT 84604-2806

SMITH, NEIL, professional football player; b. New Orleans, Apr. 10, 1966. Student, U. Nebr. Defensive end Kansas City Chiefs, 1988-96, Denver Broncos, 1997—. Played in Pro Bowl, 1991-93; named defensive lineman The Sporting News All-America team, 1987. Office: Denver Broncos 13655 Broncos Pky Englewood CO 80112*

SMITH, NEIL, professional sports team executive; b. Toronto, Ont., Can., Jan. 9, 1954; m. Katia Smith. Student, We. Mich. U. Selected NHL amateur draft N.Y. Islanders, with scouting dept., 1980-81; from dir. profl. scouting to dir. farm system Detroit Red Wings, 1982; dir. scouting, player procurement, gen. mgr./gov. Adirondack Red Wings (Am. Hockey League); gen. mgr. N.Y. Rangers, N.Y.C., 1989—, pres., 1992—. Bd. dirs. Nat. Child Abuse Prevention Ctr. Named All-Am. Defenseman We. Mich. U., to Hall of Fame, 1991, NHL Exec. Yr. Sporting News. Avocations: raquetball, movies. Office: NY Rangers 4 Pennsylvania Plz New York NY 10001*

SMITH, NEVILLE VINCENT, physicist; b. Leeds, Eng., Apr. 21, 1942; came to U.S., 1966; s. Horace J.H. and Ethel S.; m. Elizabeth Jane Poulson, 1970; children: Katherine, Elizabeth. BA, Cambridge (Eng.) U., 1963, MA, 1967, PhD, 1967. Rsch. assoc. Stanford (Calif.) U., 1966-68; mem. staff AT&T Bell Labs., Murray Hill, N.J., 1969-94, head condensed state physics rsch. dept., 1978-81; scientific program head Advanced Light Source Lawrence Berkeley Nat. Lab., Berkeley, Calif., 1994—. Contbr. articles to jours. in field. Fellow Am. Phys. Soc. (Davisson-Germer prize 1991). Office: Lawrence Berkeley Nat Lab 1 Cyclotron Rd Berkeley CA 94720

SMITH, NICK, congressman, farmer; b. Addison, Mich., Nov. 5, 1934; s. LeGrand John and Blanche (Nichols) S.; m. Bonnalyn Belle Atwood, Jan. 1, 1960; children: Julianna, Bradley, Elizabeth, Stacia. BA, Mich. State U., 1957; MS, U. Del., 1959. Radio & TV farm editor Sta. WDEL, Wilmington, Del., 1957-59; radio editor Sta. KSWD, Wichita Falls, Tex., 1959-60; capt. intelligence USAF, Tex., 1959-61; mem. twp. bd. Somerset Twp., Addison, 1962-68; asst. dep. adminstr. USDA, Washington, 1972-74; state rep. Mich. Ho. of Reps., Lansing, 1978-82; state senator Mich. State Senate, Lansing, 1982-92; mem. 104th-105th Congresses from 7th Mich. dist., 1993—; chmn. Senate Agrl. Com., 1982-92, Senate Corrections Appropriation Com., 1984-90, Senate Mil. Affairs Com., 1984-90, Senate Fin. Com., 1990-92; mem. agriculturecom., budget com. Leader's Task Force on Economy, 1993—. Del. Am. Assembly on World Population & Hunger, Washington, 1973; nat. del. on U.S.-Soviet Cooperation and Trade, 1991; former trustee Somerset Congl. Ch. Capt. USAF, 1959-61. Fellow Kellogg Found., 1965; named Hon. FFA State Star Farmer, 1987, SCF Conservator of Yr. Hillsdale County, 1988. Mem. Mich. Farm Bur. (bd. dirs.), Jackson C. of C., Mich. State U. Alumni Club, Masons. Republican. Office: US House of Reps 360 Longworth Hob Washington DC 20515-2207*

SMITH, NOEL WILSON, psychology educator; b. Marion, Ind., Nov. 2, 1933; s. Anthony and Mary Louise (Wilson) S.; m. Marilyn C. Coleman, June 17, 1954; children: Thor and Lance (twins). AB, Ind. U., 1955, PhD, 1962; MA, U. Colo., 1958; 1971-95. Asst. prof. psychology Wis. State U., Platteville, 1962-63; asst. prof. psychology SUNY, Plattsburgh, 1963-66, assoc. prof., 1966-71, prof., 1971-95, prof. emeritus, 1995—; courtesy prof. U. Fla., 1997—; courtesy prof. U. Fla., 1997—. Author: Greek and Interbehavioral Psychology, 1990, rev. edit., 1993, An Analysis of Ice Age Art: Its Psychology and Belief, 1992; co-author: The Science of Psychology: Interbehavioral Survey, 1975; sr. editor: Reassessment in Psychology, 1983; editor: Interbehavioral Psychology newsletter, 1970-77; contbr. articles to profl. jours. Fellow APA; mem. AAUP (pres. SUNY coun. 1980-82), Am. Psychol. Soc., Cheiron Internat. Soc. History of Behavior Sci., Sigma Xi. Home: 7 W Court St Plattsburgh NY 12901-2301 Office: SUNY Dept Psychology Beaumont Hall Plattsburgh NY 12901

SMITH, NONA COATES, academic administrator; b. West Grove, Pa., Apr. 1, 1942; d. John Truman and Elizabeth Zane (Trumbo) Coates; m. David Smith, Oct. 12, 1968 (div. May 1986); children: Kirth Ayrl, Del Kerry, Michael Sargent, Sherri Lee. BA, West Chester (Pa.) U., 1988; postgrad., Temple U., 1989—. Legal sec. Gawthrop & Greenwood, West Chester, 1968-73, MacElree, Gallagher, O'Donnell, West Chester, 1981-84; social sec. Mrs. John B. Hannum, Unionville, Pa., 1975-81; rsch. asst. West Chester U., 1984-88, cons., 1988; dir. faculty grants Bryn Mawr (Pa.) Coll., 1989—, chair rsch./tchg. evaluation, 1993-95. Treas. Kennett Vol. Fire Co., Kennett Square, Pa., 1984-86. recipient Scholastic All-Am. award U.S. Achievement Acad., 1988, Rsch. award Truman Libr., 1992, Goldsmith Rsch. award Harvard U., 1993; fellow Truman Dissertation, 1997—. Fellow Phi Alpha Theta; mem. AAUW, Am. Hist. Assn., Soc. Historians of Am. Fgn. Rels., Nat. Coun. Univ. Rsch. Adminstrs. (mem. nat. conf. com. 1995-96). Republican. Presbyterian. Avocations: reading, gardening, travel, cultural events. Home: Box 239 Unionville PA 19375 Office: Bryn Mawr Coll 101 N Merion Ave Bryn Mawr PA 19010-2859

SMITH, NORMA JANE, elementary education educator; b. N.Y.C., Aug. 19, 1933; d. Raymond and Thelma (Kavares) Schneider; m. Thomas Edward Smith; children: Robyn, Sharon, Ilene. BA, CUNY, 1955; cert. in art, N.Y. Inst. Tech., 1986; postgrad., L.I. U., 1990. Cert. tchr., N.Y. Tchr. grade 1 Plainedge (N.Y.) Pub. Schs., 1956-59; tchr., reading specialist Half Hollow Hills Schs., Dix Hills, N.Y., 1969-70, tchr. grade 4, 1970-95, tng. and supervision of student tchrs., 1972-93, drama dir., 1982-95, social studies coord., 1982, 83, sci. coord., 1988, 89; instr. in-svc. tchr. edn. courses Half Hollow Hills, 1989, 90, 91; advisor Math Olympiads, Chestnut Hills, 1994-95. Author: The Queen's Mirrors, 1973, Pot Pourri, 1984, Spelling Pizazz, 1992, A Fish Named Willie Blue, 1992, Who Turned Off the Sun?, Who Turned On the Moon?. Bd. dirs. San Remo (N.Y.) Civic Assn., Half Hollow Hills Active Ret. Tchrs. Assn. Recipient award for 20 yrs. of dedicated svc. to children of Chestnut Hill, Chestnut Hill PTA, 1990. Mem. ASCD, Half Hollow Hills Tchrs. Assn. (rep. 1974-79, newsletter publ. 1996—), Soc. of Children's Book Writers and Illustrators. Avocations: writing, piano, art, theater arts. Home: 17 Acacia Rd Kings Park NY 11754

SMITH, NORMAN CLARK, fund raising consultant; b. Hartford, Conn., Jan. 2, 1917; s. Raymond W. and Elinor (Smith) S. A.B., Middlebury Coll., 1939; postgrad., Hartford Coll. Law, Trinity Coll. Tchr. Loomis Sch., 1945-50, adminstr., tchr., 1952-53, asst. bus. mgr., 1953-55, bus. mgr., 1955-58, controller, 1958-63; treas. Vassar Coll., 1963-64; v.p. devel., planning Emory U., Atlanta, 1964-76; v.p. univ. devel. U. Del., 1976-79. Bd. dirs., past chmn. bd. Nat. Soc. Fund Raising Execs.; past trustee LoomisInst., Watkinson Sch.; past chmn. Ga. Conservancy; past pres. Mashantucket Land Trust of Southeastern Conn.; trustee emeritus, pas pres. Conn. River Mus., Essex; mem. Conn. State Coun. on Environ. Quality, Naval War Coll. Found.; mem. citizens adv. coun. Project Oceanology; trustee Conn. Antiquarian and Landmarks Soc.; former mem. Nat. Exec. Svc. Corps.; pres. Groton Edn. Found. Capt. USNR, 1941-45, 50-52; commanding officer Conn. State Naval Militia, 1946-50. Decorated Navy Cross. Mem. Chi Psi, Omicron Delta Kappa. Club: Rotary. Home and Office: 161 Pequot Ave Mystic CT 06355-1728

SMITH, NORMAN CUTLER, geologist, business executive, educator; b. Paterson, N.J., Mar. 18, 1915; s. Archibald Nicholas and Ruth (Cutler) S.; m. Dorothy Phyllis Barnes, June 12, 1942; children: Roxanne Lorraine, Lee Cutler. Student, Pennington Prep. Sch., 1930-33, Drew U., 1933-34; AB in Geology and Biology cum laude, Washington and Lee U., 1937; postgrad., Harvard U., 1940-42, U. Okla., 1947. Field geologist Standard Oil Co. Venezuela, 1938-40; teaching fellow Harvard Grad. Sch. Geology, 1941-42; geologist Humble Oil & Refining Co., 1946-49; cons. geologist and photogeol. specialist, 1949-62; exec. dir. Am. Assn. Petroleum Geologists, 1963-72; pres. Resource Devel. Internat., Inc., Atlanta, 1973-88; chmn. bd. and faculty N.C. Center for Creative Retirement U. N.C., Asheville, 1988-93, dir. Sr. Acad. for Intergenerational Learning; bd. dirs. Oil Mining Corp., Boulder, Colo., 1990—; founder, 1st pres. Coun. Sci. Socs., Dallas-Ft. Worth area, 1958, chmn bd., 1960; mem. standing com. Nat. Com. on Geology, 1962-72. Author articles, chpts. in books in field. Bd. dirs. Tulsa Sci. Found., 1967; trustee Tulsa Sci. Ctr., 1967-72; mem. Buncombe County Reorgn. Comm., 1992-93; bd. dirs. Colburn Gem. and Mineral Mus. Served to lt. (s.g.) USNR, 1942-46, PTO. Fellow AAAS, Geol. Soc. Am.; mem. Tulsa Soc. Assn. Execs. (pres. 1968; hon.), Dallas Geol. Soc. (prs. 1958-59, exec. com. 1956-60; hon.), Am. Assn. Petroleum Geologists, Soc. Petroleum Engrs., Soc. Exploration Geophysicists, Coun. Engrng. and Sci. Soc. Secs. Home: 105 Windward Dr Asheville NC 28803-9555

SMITH, NORMAN OBED, physical chemist, educator; b. Winnipeg, Man., Can., Jan. 23, 1914; came to U.S., 1950, naturalized, 1958; s. Ernest and Ruth (Kilpatrick) S.; m. Anna Marie O'Connor, July 1, 1944; children: Richard Obed, Graham Michael, Stephen Housley. B.Sc., U. Man., 1935, M.Sc., 1936; Ph.D., NYU, 1939. Teaching fellow NYU, 1936-39; mem. faculty dept. chemistry U. Man., Winnipeg, 1939-50; asst. prof. U. Man., 1946-49, assoc. prof., 1949-50; assoc. prof. Fordham U., N.Y.C., 1950-65; prof. chemistry Fordham U., 1965-84, prof. emeritus, 1984—, chmn. dept., 1974-78; sr. phys. chemist Arthur D. Little, Inc., Cambridge, Mass., 1957; indsl. cons. Author: (with others) The Phase Rule and Its Applications, 1951, Chemical Thermodynamics, A Problems Approach, 1967, Elementary Statistical Thermodynamics, A Problems Approach, 1982; contbr. to: Ency. Brit, 1974. Fellow Chem. Inst. Can.; mem. Am. Chem. Soc., Asso. Can. Coll. Organists, Am. Guild Organists (dir. chpt. 1964-66, 79-82, 91-92), Sigma Xi, Phi Lambda Upsilon. Home: 59 Monrovia Blvd Tuckahoe NY 10707-1023 Office: Fordham U Dept Chemistry New York NY 10458-5198

SMITH, NORMAN RAYMOND, college president; b. Toronto, Ont., Can., Oct. 24, 1946; s. William Raymond and Jeanne (Malin) S.; m. Susan Robinson, Dec. 26, 1981; 1 child, Caroline Robinson. BS, Drexel U., 1969, MBA, 1971; EdD, Harvard U., 1984. Assoc. dean students Drexel U., Phila., 1971-73; dean of students, professor Phila. Coll. Textiles and Sci., 1973-78; asst. dean Harvard Grad. Sch. Edn., Cambridge, Mass., 1978-80, John F. Kennedy Sch. Govt., Harvard U., Cambridge, 1980-84; exec. v.p. Moore Coll. Art, Phila., 1984-87; pres. Wagner Coll., S.I., N.Y., 1988—; dir. Dime Bancorp; assoc. Harvard U. Philosophy of Edn. Rsch. Ctr., Cambridge, 1987—. Author: How to Make The Right Decisions About College, 1993. Chair mayor's cabinet transition search City of Boston, 1983-84; trustee N.Y. Coun. of Ind. Colls. and Univs., 1994—. Lt. U.S. Army, 1969-73. Recipient U. medal Drexel U., 1993, Pres.'s medal NYU, 1994. Mem. Ind. Coll. Fund N.Y. (sec.-treas.), Harvard Club of N.Y.C., Richmond County Country Club. Home: 79 Howard Ave Staten Island NY 10301-4404 Office: Wagner College Office of Pres 631 Howard Ave Staten Island NY 10301-4428

SMITH, NORMAN T., lawyer; b. Akron, Ohio, Nov. 23, 1935; s. Norman and Margaret (Stall) S.; m. Marilyn Deanna Richards, Oct. 1, 1960; children: Brian T., Valerie E. Goettler, Gregory D. BS, Ohio State U., 1957; MBA, Case Western Res. U., 1959; JD, U. Mich., 1963. Bar: Ohio 1963. Of counsel Porter, Wright, Morris & Arthur (and predecessor firms), Columbus, Ohio, 1963—; past. exec. dir. Ohio Title Ins. Rating Bur., Columbus, 1972-89; instr. Capital U. Legal Assistant Program, Columbus, 1985—. Sr. warden St. Marks Episcopal Ch., Upper Arlington, Ohio, 1970-73, 85; pres. 412 Sycamore, Inc., Cin., 1983—; mem. bd. edn. Upper Arlington, 1980-83, Bd Zoning Adjustment, Columbus, 1977-85. Recipient Merit award Ohio Legal Ctr. Inst. Fellow Ohio State Bar Found., Columbus Bar Found.; mem. ABA, Ohio State Bar Assn. (coun. dels. 1985-95, chmn. real property bd. govs. 1980-82), Am. Coll. Real Estate Lawyers, Ohio Land Title Assn. (pres. 1976), Columbus Bar Assn., Nat. Conf. Bar Examiners (real property drafting com. multistate bar exam 1988-95), Columbus Athletic Club, Leatherlips Yacht Club (gov. 1970-71). Republican. Episcopalian. Office: Porter Wright Morris & Arthur 41 S High St Columbus OH 43215-6101

SMITH, NUMA LAMAR, JR., lawyer; b. Rock Hill, S.C., Nov. 22, 1915; s. Numa Lamar and Grace (Hanes) S.; m. Mary Catherine Gray, Mar. 24, 1941; children: Patricia Gray, Elizabeth Hanes, Lamar Douglas. A.B., Furman U., 1938; LL.B. with distinction, Duke U., 1941. Bar: N.Y. 1942, D.C. 1946. Assoc. firm White & Case, N.Y.C., 1941-42, Miller & Chevalier, Washington, 1946-49; partner Miller & Chevalier, 1949-83, counsel, 1983—; bd. visitors, 1973-83; sr. fellow Duke U. Law Sch., 1979-80. Assoc. editor: Duke Law Jour, 1940-41. Served with U.S. Army, 1942-46; with Judge Adv. Gen. Corps 1944-46. Recipient Gen. Excellence award Furman U., 1938. Fellow Am. Bar Found.; mem. ABA, D.C. Bar Assn., Am. Law Inst., Duke Law Alumni Assn. (pres. 1967-69), Order of Coif, Met. Club (Washington), Burning Tree Club (Bethesda, Md.), Washington Golf Club (Arlington, Va.), Sigma Alpha Epsilon. Baptist. Home: 7515 Pelican Bay Blvd Naples FL 34108-6518

SMITH, ORA EVERETT, corporate executive, lawyer; b. Kennett, Mo., Dec. 24, 1947; s. Everett and Thelma May (Johnson) S.; m. Sue Ellen Caldwell, Sept. 3, 1972; children: Everett Eugene, Nathan Thomas. BME and MME, MIT, 1970; JD, Harvard U., 1976. Bar: Mass. 1977, D.C. 1977, U.S. Dist. Ct. Mass. 1977, Calif. 1983, U.S. Dist. Ct. (cen. dist.) Calif. 1983, U.S. Ct. Appeals (9th cir.) 1983. Mgr. engring. U.S. EPA, Cin., 1970-73; atty. New Eng. Telephone, Boston, 1976-77; mng. dir. Gordian Assocs. Inc., Washington, 1977-79; dir. structural materials integrity Rockwell Internat., Thousand Oaks, Calif., 1979-81, dir. physics and chem., 1981-85, dir. external tech. devel., 1985-89; v.p. mktg. Conductors, Inc., Sunnyvale, Calif., 1989-90; pres., CEO Ill. Superconductors Corp., Mt. Prospect, 1990—; cons. Exec. Office of Pres. of U.S., Washington, 1985—. Patentee impact sensor and coding apparatus; contbr. articles to profl. jours. Served with USPHS, 1970-72. Mem. AEA Midwest Coun., Ill. Mfrs. Assn. (dir.). Republican. Home: 921 Fisher Ln Winnetka IL 60093 Office: Ill Superconductor Corp 451 Kingston Ct Mount Prospect IL 60056-6068

SMITH, ORIN ROBERT, chemical company executive; b. Newark, Aug. 13, 1935; s. Sydney R. and Gladys Emmett (DeGroff) S.; m. Stephanie M. Bennett-Smith; children: Lindsay, Robin; 1 stepchild, Brendan. BA in Econometrics, Brown U., 1957; MBA in Mgmt., Seton Hall U., 1964; PhD in Econs. (hon.), Centenary Coll., 1991; LLD (hon.), Monmouth Coll., 1994. Various sales and mktg. mgmt. positions Allied Chem. Corp., Morristown, N.J., 1959-69; dir. sales and mktg. Richardson-Merrell Co., Phillipsburg, N.J., 1969-72; with M&T Chems., Greenwich, Conn., 1972-77, pres., 1975-77; with Engelhard Minerals & Chems. Corp., Menlo Park, Edison, N.J., 1977-81, corp. sr. v.p., 1978-81, pres. div. minerals and chems., 1978-81, also bd. dirs., 1979-81, pres., dir. various U.S. subs., 1979-81; exec. v.p., pres. div. minerals and chems. Engelhard Corp., Menlo Park, Edison, 1981-84, bd. dirs., 1981—; pres., CEO, Engelhard Corp., Iselin, N.J., 1984-95, chmn., CEO, 1995—; also bd. dirs.; bd. dirs. Summit Bank Co., The Summit Bancorp, Vulcan Materials Co., La. Land and Exploration Co., Perkin-Elmer Corp., Ingersoll-Rand Corp., Minorco, Engelhard Corp., Mfrs. Alliance. Trustee N.J. State C. of C., Inst. for Tech. Advancement, Henry R. Kessler Found., Inc.; mem. bd. overseers N.J. Inst. Tech.; trustee Plimoth Plantation; 1st vice chmn. bd. trustees Centenary Coll.; past chmn. Ind. Coll. Fund N.J.; past dir.-at-large U. Maine Pulp and Paper Found. Lt. (j.g.) USN, 1957-59. Mem. Chem. Mfrs. Assn. (past bd. dirs.), Am. Mgmt. Assn. (gen. mgmt. coun.), Econ. Club (N.Y.C.), Union League Club (N.Y.C.), Duxbury Yacht Club, New Bedford Yacht Club, N.Y. Yacht Club. Office: Engelhard Corp 101 Wood Ave S Iselin NJ 08830-2703

SMITH, (TUBBY) ORLANDO HENRY, college basketball coach; b. Scotland, Md., June 30, 1951; m. Donna Smith; children: Orlando, Shannon, Saul, Brian. BS in Phys. Edn., High Point Coll., 1973. Head basketball coach Gt. Mills (Md.) H.S., 1973-77, Hoke County H.S., Raeford, N.C., 1977-79; asst. basketball coach Va. Commonwealth, 1979-86; asst. coach U. S.C., 1986-89, Ky. U., 1989-91; head coach U. Tulsa, 1991-95, U. Ga., Athens, 1995—. Winner 3 Sun Belt Conf. Championships; appeared in 5 NCAA Tournaments. Office: U Ga PO Box 1472 Athens GA 30603

SMITH, ORVILLE AUVERNE, physiology educator; b. Nogales, Ariz., June 16, 1927; s. Orville Auverne and Bess (Gill) S.; m. Clara Jean Smith; children—Nanette, Marcella. B.A. in Psychology, U. Ariz., 1949; M.A., Mich. State U., 1950, Ph.D., 1953. Instr. psychology Mich. State U., East Lansing, 1953-54; fellow U. Pa., Phila., 1954-56; trainee dept. physiology and biophysics U. Wash., Seattle, 1956-58, instr. physiology and biophysics, 1958-59, asst. prof., 1959-61, 62-63; asst. dir. Regional Primate Research Ctr., 1962-69, assoc. prof., 1963-67, prof., 1967—; assoc. dir. Regional Primate Research Center, 1969-71, dir., 1971-88. Contbr. articles to profl. jours. Mem. Am. Physiol. Soc., Am. Soc. Primatologists (pres. 1977-79), Internat. Congress Physiol. Scis., Am. Assn. Anatomists, AAAS, Pavlovian Soc. N.Am. (pres. 1977-78), Internat. Primatological Soc., AAUP, Neurosci. Soc. Home: 7521 30th Ave NE Seattle WA 98115-4719 Office: U Wash Regional Primate Research Ctr SJ-50 Seattle WA 98195

SMITH, OZZIE (OSBORNE EARL SMITH), professional baseball player; b. Mobile, Ala., Dec. 26, 1954; m. Denise Jackson, Nov. 1, 1980; children:

Osborne Earl Jr., Dustin Cameron. Grad., Calif. State Poly. U., San Luis Obispo. Shortstop San Diego Padres Baseball Club, Nat. League, 1977-82, St. Louis Cardinals Baseball Club, Nat. League, 1982-96; baseball analyst St. Louis Cardinals Sta. KPLR, St. Louis, 1997—. Player Nat. League All-Star Team, 1981-92, 94, All-Star Team Sporting News, 1982, 84-87, World Series Championship Team, 1982; recipient Most Valuable Player award Nat. League Championship Series, 1985, Gold Glove award, 1980-92, Silver Slugger award, 1987. Avocations: jazz, word puzzles, backgammon. Office: Sta KPLR 4935 Lindell Blvd Saint Louis MO 63108*

SMITH, PAT EVERETT, chemical company executive; b. San Diego, July 17, 1930; s. Jack and Eva (Coffman) S.; m. Sept. 16, 1961. BS in Chemistry, UCLA, 1954. Chemist Lever Bros., Los Angeles, 1959-64; dir. rsch. and devel. Cee Bee Chem. Co., Los Angeles, 1964-69; material and process engr. Gary Aircraft Corp., San Antonio, 1969-71; v.p., owner Eldorado Chem. Co., San Antonio, 1969—. Inventor U.S. Patent Process for Biochemical Reactions, 1975. Election judge City of Hill Country Village, Tex. 1983. With U.S. Army, 1955-59. Recipient Smalley award Am. Oil Chemists' Soc. 1961. Mem. Nat. Assn. Corrosion Engrs., Am. Soc. Test Methods, Soc. Automotive Engrs., Soc. for the Advancement of Material and Process Engrs., Aircraft Owners and Pilots Assn., Tech. Assn. of Pulp and Paper Engrs., Harp & Shamrock Soc. Avocations: natural science, painting, archaeology, languages, cooking. Office: Eldorado Chem Co PO Box 34837 San Antonio TX 78265-4837

SMITH, PATRICIA ANNE, special education educator; b. West Chester, Pa., Aug. 19, 1967; d. William Richard and Carol Anne (Benn) S. BS in Spl. Edn. cum laude, West Chester U., 1989; postgrad., Immaculata Coll., 1993—. Cert. mentally and physically handicapped tchr., Pa. Learning support tchr. Chester County Intermediate Unit, Downington, Pa., 1989-90, early intervention tchr., 1990-92; autistic support tchr. Coatesville (Pa.) Area Sch. Dist., 1992—, event coord. WOYC workshops, 1993—; presenter ann. conf. Pa. Assn. of Resources for People with Mental Retardation, Hershey, 1994; co-presenter ARC, 1996, Paoli Meml. Hosp., 1997; presenter info. sessions ann. conf. Del. Valley Assn. for Edn. of Young Children, Phila., 1994, Lions, Downingtown, Pa., 1992, early childhood conf. Capital Area Assn. for Edn. of Young Children, Harrisburg, Pa., 1995, vols. Caln Athletic Assn. Challenger League, 1995-96; mentor West Chester U., 1995—. Mem. recreation adv. bd. dirs. Assn. for Retarded Citizens, Exton, Pa., 1993—, Daisy Girl Scout Leader, 1995-96; vol. tutor Chester County Libr. Adult Literacy Program, 1995—; mem. Chester County Mental Health Mental Retardation Consultation and Edn. Bd., 1997—. Recipient Outstanding Svc. award Coatesville Area Parent Coun., 1994, 96, Vol. award Friendship PTA, 1993, 96, Pa. Early Childhood Edn. Assn. Workshop presenter award, 1993; grantee Pa.Dept. Edn., 1993, Coatesville Area Sch. Dist., 1990. Mem. ASCD, Nat. Assn. for the Edn. of Young Children, Autism Soc. Am., Kappa Delta Pi. Republican. Roman Catholic. Home: 501 Clover Mill Rd Exton PA 19341-2505 Office: Friendship Elem Sch 296 Reeceville Rd Coatesville PA 19320-1520

SMITH, PATRICIA GRACE, government official; b. Tuskegee, Ala., Nov. 10, 1947; d. Douglas and Wilhelmina (Griffin) Jones; m. J. Clay Smith, Jr., June 25, 1983; children—Eugene Douglas, Stager Clay, Michelle L., Michael L. B.A. in English, Tuskegee Inst., 1968; postgrad. Auburn U., 1969-71, Harvard U., 1974, George Washington U., 1983; cert. sr. exec. service 1987; exec. mgmt. tng. devel. assignments Dept. Def., 1986, U.S. Senate Commerce Com., 1987. Instr. Tuskegee Institute, Ala., 1969-71; program mgr. Curber Assocs., Washington, 1971-73; dir. placement Nat. Assn. Broadcasters, Washington, 1973-74, dir. pub. affairs, 1974-77; assoc. producer Group W Broadcasting, Balt., 1977, producer, 1977-78; dir. affiliate relations and programming Sheridan Broadcasting Network, Crystal City, Va., 1978-80; dep. dir. policy, assoc. mng. dir. pub. info. and reference svcs., FCC, Washington, 1992-94, acting assoc. mng. dir., pub. info. and reference svcs., 1994; dep. dir. Office Pub. Affairs, 1994—; chief of staff office assoc. adminstr. for comml. space transp., FAA, U.S. Dept. Transp., 1994-96, dep. assoc. adminstr. office assoc. adminstr. for comml. space transp., 1996-97, acting assoc. adminstr., 1997. vice chmn. Nat. Conf. Black Lawyers Task Force on Communications, Washington, 1975-87. Mem. D.C. Donor Project, Nat. Kidney Found., Washington, 1984—; trustee, mem. exec. com., nominating com., youth adv. com. Nat. Urban League, 1976-81; mem. communications com. Cancer Coordinating Council, 1977-84; mem. Braintrust Subcom. on Children's Programming, Congl. Black Caucus, 1976—; mem. adv. bd. Black Arts Celebration, 1978-83; mem. NAACP; mem. journalism and communications adv. council Auburn U., 1976-78; mem. Washington Urban League, 1985—; bd. dirs. Black Film Rev., 1989-91; mem D.C. Commn. on Human Rights, 1986-88, chmn. 1988-91; mem. adv. coun. Nat. Insts. Health, 1992-96; mem. bd. advisors The Salvation Army, 1993—. Named Outstanding Young Woman of Yr., Washington, 1975, 78; recipient Sustained Superior Performance award FCC, Washington, 1982-95, Disting. Alumnus award Tuskegee U., 1996. Mem. Women in Communications, Inc. (mem. nat. adv. com.), Lambda Iota Tau. Club: Broadcasters (bd. dirs. 1976-77). Democrat. Baptist. Avocations: writing, swimming. Home: 4010 16th St NW Washington DC 20011-7002 Office: DOT/OCST 400 7th St SW Rm 5415 Washington DC 20590-0001

SMITH, PATRICK JOHN, editor, writer; b. N.Y.C., Dec. 11, 1932; s. H. Ben and Geraldine (Wilson) S.; m. Elisabeth Munro, Nov. 27, 1964; children: Douglass Munro, Matthew Wilson. Student, Phillips Exeter, 1951; AB, Princeton U., 1955. Freelance writer and critic, 1958-70; editor, pub. The Mus. Newsletter, N.Y.C., 1970-77; pres. Music Critics Assn., Washington, 1977-81; dir. opera mus. theater program NEA, Washington, 1985-89; editor Opera News, N.Y.C., 1989—. Author: The Tenth Muse: A History of the Opera Libretto, 1970, A Year at the Met, 1983. Office: Opera News 70 Lincoln Center Plz New York NY 10023-6548

SMITH, PAUL EDMUND, JR., philosophy and religion educator; b. Northampton, Mass., Feb. 6, 1927; s. Paul Edmund and Mary Jane (Murphy) S.; B.A., U. Mass., 1948; postgrad. Harvard U., 1948-49; M.A., Boston U., 1957; B.D., Columbia Theol. Sem., 1957, M.Div., 1971; postgrad. U. N.C., 1967-68. Instr. Latin and French, Chester (Vt.) High Sch., 1949-53, Loris (S.C.) High Sch., 1953-54; lectr. history U. Ga., Albany, 1957-59; instr. Latin, Rocky Mount (Va.) High Sch., 1959-61; minister Henderson Presbyn. Ch., Albany, 1957-59, Rocky Mount (Va.) Presbyn. Ch., 1959-64; asst. prof. religion Ferrum (Va.) Coll., 1961-68; vis. lectr. history John Tyler C.C., Chester, Va., 1968-69; instr. philosophy and religion Richard Bland Coll., Petersburg, Va., 1968-71, asst. prof., 1971-76, asso. prof., 1976—, chmn. dept., 1971—. Mem. Am. Hist. Assn., Presbytery of the Peaks. Democrat. Presbyterian. Office: Richard Bland Coll Commerce Hall Petersburg VA 23805

SMITH, PAUL FREDERICK, plant physiologist, consultant; b. Copeland, Kans., Dec. 17, 1916; s. Frederick Eugene and Susie Irene (Wikoff) S.; m. Marjorie Haselwood, July 6, 1940; children: Gary Lynn, Carol Jeanne. BS, U. Okla., 1938, MS, 1940; PhD, U. Calif., 1944. Asst. plant physiologist USDA, Salinas, Calif., 1943-45, Orlando, Fla., 1946-50; assoc. physiologist USDA, 1950-55, plant physiologist, 1956-61, prin. physiologist, 1962-71, head physiologist, 1971-75, hort. cons., 1975—. Contbr. chpts. to books and articles to profl. publs. With USN, 1945-46. Fellow Am. Soc. Hort. Sci.; mem. Fla. Hort. Soc. (hon. life, Presdl. Gold medal 1970). Achievements include research in streamlining fertilization practices on citrus thereby avoiding deficiencies and excesses. Home and Office: 2695 Ashville St Orlando FL 32818-9018

SMITH, PAUL J., museum administrator; b. Buffalo; student Art Inst. Buffalo, Sch. Am. Craftsmen, Rochester, N.Y.; DFA (hon.) New Sch. Social Research, 1987. Staff mem. Am. Craft Coun., N.Y.C., 1957—, dir. Am. Craft Mus., 1963-87, dir. emeritus, 1987—; juror numerous exhibitions; lectr. and cons. in field of contemporary crafts and design. Trustee Louis Comfort Tiffany Found., Penland Sch. Crafts; adv. trustee Haystack Mountain Sch. Crafts, Deer Isle, Maine; nat. coun. Atlantic Ctr. for Arts, Inc. Office: PO Box 6735 Yorkville Station New York NY 10128

SMITH, PAUL LETTON, JR., geophysicist; b. Columbia, Mo., Dec. 16, 1932; s. Paul Letton and Helen Marie (Doersam) S.; m. Mary Barbara Noel; children: Patrick, Melody, Timothy, Christopher, Anne. BS in Physics, Carnegie Inst. Tech., 1955, MSEE, 1957, PhD in Elec. Engring., 1960. From instr. to asst. prof. Carnegie Inst. Tech., Pitts., 1955-63; sr. engr. Midwest Rsch. Inst., Kansas City, Mo., 1963-66; from rsch. engr. to sr. scientist and group head Inst. Atmospheric Scis., S.D. Sch. Mines and Tech., Rapid City, 1966-81; vis. prof. McGill U., Montreal, Que., Can., 1969-70; chief scientist Air Weather Svc. USAF, Scott AFB, Ill., 1974-75; dir. Inst. Atmospheric Scis., S.D. Sch. Mines and Tech., Rapid City, 1981-96, prof. emeritus, 1996—; lectr. Tech. Svc. Corp., Silver Spring, Md., 1972-91; vis. scientist Alberta Rsch. Coun., Edmonton, Can., 1984-85; dir. S.D. Space Grant Consortium, Rapid City, 1991-96; Fulbright lectr. U. Helsinki, 1986. Contbr. over 50 articles to profl. jours. Fellow Am. Meteorol. Soc. (Editor's award 1992); mem. IEEE (sr.), Weather Modification Assn. (Thunderbird award 1995), Sigma Xi. Home: 2107 9th St Rapid City SD 57701-5315

SMITH, PAUL THOMAS, financial services company executive; b. Garden City, N.Y., May 17, 1938; s. Leo Joseph and Martha Duncan (Perine) S.; m. Carole A. Dlugolenski, Sept. 1, 1962; children—Laura Jane, Paul Thomas, Elizabeth Ann, Kathryn Celinda. B.B.A., U. Notre Dame, 1960; M.B.A., Harvard U., 1964. C.P.A., N.Y. chartered fin. analyst. In charge accountant Deloitte & Touche, N.Y.C., 1964-67; from investment analyst to 2d v.p. N.Y. Life Ins. Co., N.Y.C., 1967-78, v.p. investments, 1978-83, v.p., chief equity investment officer, 1983-88, sr. v.p. corp. planning and devel., 1988-91, sr. v.p. venture capital, chief equity investment officer, 1991-96. Served to lt. USN, 1960-62. Mem. Inst. Chartered Fin. Analysts, N.Y. Soc. Security Analysts. Club: Cherry Valley. Office: 70 Brook St Garden City NY 11530-6313

SMITH, PAUL TRAYLOR, mayor, former business executive, former army officer; b. Burkesville, Ky., June 22, 1923; s. Samuel Joseph and Bonnie (Ferguson) S.; m. Elizabeth C. Nolte, July 2, 1942; m. Phyllis Jean Corbin, Oct. 11, 1975; children: Gregory L., Douglas B., Paula J. Smith Richardson, Mary K. B.A., U. Md., 1960, M.B.A., 1962. Enlisted in U.S. Army, 1940, advanced through grades to maj. gen., 1975; service in Japan, Ger., Korea, Vietnam; adj. gen. Continental Army Command, 1968-70, comdg. gen. U.S. Army Computer Systems Command, 1973-75; adj. gen. U.S. Army, 1975-77; exec. v.p. Taylorcraft Devel. Corp., Inc., Burkesville, Ky., 1977-82; mayor City of Burkesville, Burkesville, Ky., 1982. Bd. dirs. Lake Cumberland Area Devel. Dist. Inc., Lake Cumberland Housing Agy., Inc.; bd. dirs., mem. exec. com., legis. policy com. Ky. League of Cities, also trustee investemnt pool bd., 1st v.p.; chmn. Lake Area Inspection Svc. Inc.; chmn. bd. dirs. Lake Cumberland Area Devel. Dist., Revolving Loan Fund Com., Lake Cumberland Housing Agy., Burkesville Manor Corp.; trustee Ky. Mcpl. Risk Mgmt. Agy. Decorated D.S.M., Legion of Merit with 2 oak leaf clusters, Bronze Star. Mem. Assn. U.S. Army, Ret. Officers Assn. Address: PO Box 607 Burkesville KY 42717-0607 *Make sure the goals and standards you set for yourself are higher than others might set for you. You are the key to your own success or failure.*

SMITH, PAUL VERGON, JR., corporate executive, retired oil company executive; b. Lima, Ohio, Apr. 25, 1921; s. Paul Vergon and Aleta Rose (Bowers) S.; m. Alta Fern Chipps, Mar. 2, 1945; children: Douglas, Marsha, Jeffrey, Alison. AB, Miami U., Oxford, Ohio, 1942; MS, U. Ill., 1943, PhD, 1945. With Exxon Research & Engring. Co., 1946-66, 72-86, mgr. pub. affairs, 1972-80, mgr. ednl. and profl. soc. relations, Florham Park, N.J., 1981-86; asst. dir. chem. research Esso Petroleum Co., Abingdon, Eng., 1966-67; dir. chem. research Esso Research S.A., Brussels, 1967-71; mem. adv. bd. Cache, Inc., Austin, Tex., 1979-86; pres. APS Assocs., Westfield, N.J., 1986-90; bd. dirs., treas. Jets, Inc., Alexandria, Va.; dir. CENTCOM, Ltd.; mem. exec. bd. N.J. Bus./Industry/Sci. Edn. Consortium. Patentee in field; contbr. numerous articles to profl. jours., chpts. to books. Bd. dirs. United Way of Union County, N.J., 1980-86; chmn. research adv. council Miami U., 1980-84. Recipient Pres.'s award Am. Assn. Petroleum Geologists, 1955; Spl. award N.J. Sci. Tchrs. Assn., 1985. Mem. AAAS, Am. Chem. Soc. (dir. 1978-86, chmn. bd. 1984-86; Belden award 1984), Am. Soc. Engring. Edn. (dir. 1980-86, v.p. 1980-86), Country Club Naples, Phi Beta Kappa, Sigma Xi, Omicron Delta Kappa, Phi Eta Sigma, Alpha Chi Sigma, Pi Mu Epsilon, Sigma Pi Sigma, Phi Lambda Upsilon. Republican. Methodist.

SMITH, PAULA MARION, urology and medical/surgical nurse; b. Provincetown, Mass., Apr. 2, 1930; d. Manuel V. and Marion V. (Cabral) Raymond; m. George A. Smith, July 2, 1952; children: Steven, Michael, Elizabeth. Diploma in nursing, Quincy (Mass.) City Hosp., 1951; student, Boston Coll., U. S.C. RN, Tex., Kans., Mass. Operating room nurse Richland County Hosp., El Paso, Tex., 1958-62, Hotel Dieu, El Paso, 1962-64, U.S. Army Hosp., Ft. Riley, Kans., 1967-68; splty. head nurse urology unit Cape Cod Hosp., Hyannis, Mass., 1972-1994, Health Ctrl., Orlando, Fla., 1995—; cons. Urologic Nursing Jour. Past editor Uro-Gram. Recipient H. Harrison Hartwell award. Mem. ANA, Assn. Operating Rm. Nurses, Internat. Acad. Nurse Editors, Am. Urologic Assn. Allied (editor Uro-Gram, award New Eng. chpt. 1988).

SMITH, PETER, chemist, educator, consultant; b. Sale, Cheshire, Eng., Sept. 7, 1924; came to U.S., 1951; s. Peter and Winifred Emma (Jenkins) S.; m. Hilary Joan Hewitt Roe, 1951; children: Helen Andrews Winifred, Eric Peter, Richard Harry, Gillian Carol. B.A. Queens' Coll., Cambridge U., 1946, M.A., 1949, Ph.D., 1953. Jr. sci. officer Royal Aircraft Establishment, Farnborough, Hampshire, Eng., 1943-46; demonstrator chemistry dept. Leeds U., Yorkshire, England, 1950-51; postdoctoral research fellow in chemistry Harvard U., Cambridge, Mass., 1951-54; asst. prof. chemistry Purdue U., West Lafayette, Ind., 1954-59; asst. prof. chemistry Duke U., Durham, N.C., 1959-61, assoc. prof., 1961-70, prof., 1970-95, prof. emeritus chemistry, 1995—. Contbg. author: chem. research jours. Fulbright postdoctoral scholar Fulbright Commn., Harvard U., 1951-53. Mem. Am. Chem. Soc., Royal Soc. Chemistry, Am. Phys. Soc., Sigma Xi, Phi Lambda Upsilon, Alpha Chi Sigma. Home: 2711 Circle Dr Durham NC 27705-5726 Office: Dept Chemistry Paul M Gross Chem Lab PO Box 90346 Durham NC 27708-0346

SMITH, PETER JOHN, geographer, educator; b. Rakaia, New Zealand, Sept. 18, 1931; s. Sidney Charles and Ethel May (Pettit) S.; m. Sheana Mary Lee, May 30, 1959; children: Katrina, Hugh. BA, U. New Zealand, 1953, MA, 1954; diploma of town and regional planning (Central Mortgage and Housing Corp. planning fellow), U. Toronto, 1959; Ph.D., U. Edinburgh, Scotland, 1964. Tchr. schs. New Zealand and Gt. Britain, 1951-55; research planner Calgary City Planning Dept., 1956-59; mem. faculty dept. geography U. Alta., Edmonton, Can., 1959-94, prof., 1969-94, chmn. dept., 1967-75, prof. emeritus, 1994—; Planning cons., 1958—. Author: Population and Production: An Introduction to Some Problems in Economic Geography, rev. edit, 1971, The Edmonton-Calgary Corridor, 1978; editor: The Prairie Provinces, 1972, Edmonton: The Emerging Metropolitan Pattern, 1978, Environment and Economy: Essays on the Human Geography of Alberta, 1984, A World of Real Places: Essays in Honor of William C. Wonders, 1990. Recipient certificate of distinction Town Planning Inst. Can., 1959; Social Scis. and Humanities Research Council grantee, 1977, 84; Leave fellow Can. Council, 1970. Mem. Canadian Assn. Geographers (newsletter editor 1969-77, councillor 1966-70, v.p. 1972-73, pres. 1973-74, editor Can. Geographer 1978-84, award for svc. to the profession), Canadian Inst. Planners, Am. Assn. Geographers, Internat. Planning Hist. Soc. (councillor 1993—), Am. Soc. City and Regional Planning History. Home: 64 Marlboro Rd, Edmonton, AB Canada T6J 2C6

SMITH, PETER LANSDOWN, art director. Art dir.: (films) Chapter Two, 1979, Seems Like Old Times, 1980, The Last Married Couple in America, 1980, Paternity, 1981, Night Shift, 1982, Fandango, 1985, Jagged Edge, 1985, Big Trouble, 1986, Star Trek IV: The Voyage Home, 1986, Nadine, 1987, Blind Date, 1987, Tequila Sunrise, 1988, Fat Man and Little Boy, 1989, Groundhog Day, 1993; prodn. designer: (films) Going Berserk, 1983, The New Kids, 1985. Office: Society of Motion Pic & TV Dir 11365 Ventura Blvd Ste 315 Studio City CA 91604-3148*

SMITH, PETER WALKER, finance executive; b. Syracuse, N.Y., May 19, 1923; s. Stanley Sherwood and Elizabeth Wilkins (Young) S.; m. Lucile Elizabeth Edson, June 22, 1946; children: Andrew E., Laurie (Mrs. Samuel J. Falzone), Pamela C. (Mrs. Denison W. Schweppe, Jr.), Stanley E. B.Chem. Engring., Rensselaer Poly. Inst., 1947; M.B.A., Harvard U., 1948; LL.B., Cleve. Marshall Law Sch., 1955. Bar: Ohio 1955; Registered profl. engr., Ohio. Div. controller Raytheon Co., Lexington, Mass., 1958-66; v.p. finance, indsl. systems and equipment group Litton Industries Inc., Stamford, Conn., 1966-70; v.p. finance, treas. Copeland Corp., Sidney, Ohio, 1970-74; v.p. fin., treas., dir. Instrumentation Lab. Inc., Lexington, Mass., 1974-78; chief fin. officer, treas. Ionics, Inc., Watertown, Mass., 1978-80; v.p. fin., treas. Data Printer Corp., Malden, Mass., 1980-84, Orion Research Inc., Boston, 1984-87; pvt. practice cons. Concord, Mass., 1987—. Mem. fin. adv. bd., Northeastern U., Boston. Lt. AUS, 1943-46, 50-52. Mem. Fin. Execs. Inst., Am. Prodn. and Inventory Control Soc. (founding), Rensselaer Soc. Engrs., Sigma Xi, Tau Beta Pi. Home and Office: 155 Monument St Concord MA 01742-1808

SMITH, PETER WILLIAM EBBLEWHITE, electrical engineering educator, scientist; b. London, Nov. 3, 1937; m. Jacqueline Marie Mankiewicz, June 18, 1966; children: Christal, Dawn N. BSc, McGill U., Montreal, Que., Can., 1958, MSc, 1961, PhD, 1964. Mem. of staff Can. Marconi Co., Mont., 1958-59; mem. tech. staff Bell Labs., Holmdel, N.J., 1963-83; dist. mgr. Bellcore, Red Bank, N.J., 1984-87, div. mgr., 1989-92; prof. elec. and computer engring. U. Toronto, 1992—; exec. dir. Ont. Laser and Lightwave Rsch. Ctr., 1992-95. Editor-in-chief IEEE Press Progress in Lasers and Electro-Optics Series, 1987-92; editor Optics Letters, 1989-95; contbr. over 200 articles to profl. jours., books and refereed conf. proc. Board dirs. Monmouth Arts Found., Red Bank, 1965-82. Recipient Sr. Scientist award NATO, 1979. Fellow IEEE (Quantum Electronics award 1986), Optical Soc. Am. (bd. dirs., chmn. bd. editors); mem. IEEE Lasers and Electro-Optics Soc. (pres. 1984), Am. Phys. Soc., Can. Assn. Physicists. Achievements include first demonstration of waveguide gas laser, non-linear optical interface; development of hybrid bistable optical devices; 32 patents in field. Office: U Toronto, Dept Elec & Computer Engrin, Toronto, ON Canada M5S 1A4

SMITH, PETER WILSON, symphony orchestra administrator; b. Utica, N.Y., Mar. 15, 1938; s. Stanley W. and Frances (Brown) S.; m. Kay Gardner, 1960 (div. 1972); children: Juliana, Jennifer; m. Lynn Perrott, 1976. B.Mus., U. Mich., 1965. Asst. mgr. Indpls. Symphony, 1966-67; asst. mgr. St. Louis Symphony, 1967-68; exec. dir. Norfolk Symphony, Va., 1968-72; ops. mgr. Buffalo Philharmonic, 1972-74; ops. adminstr. Carnegie Hall Corp., N.Y.C., 1974-76; mng. dir. Ft. Wayne (Ind.) Philharmonic, 1976-85; exec. dir. Grand Rapids (Mich.) Symphony, 1985-95, pres., 1995—. Served to airman 1st class USAF, 1961-64. Mem. Met. Orch. Mgrs. Assn. (pres. 1979-81), Regional Orch. Mgrs. Assn. (v.p. 1987-89), Am. Symphony Orch. League (bd. dirs. 1989-91), Mgrs. Am. Orch. (vice-chmn. 1989-91). Office: Grand Rapids Symphony Ste 1 169 Louis Campau Promenade NW Grand Rapids MI 49503-2629

SMITH, PHILIP DANIEL, academic administrator, education educator; b. Dayton, Ohio, Dec. 25, 1933; s. Hubert Edgar and Edith (Parker) S.; m. Marilyn Brown, Nov. 25, 1953; children: Carolyn Smith Valentine, Norman Daniel, Stanley Nathan. BS cum laude, Bob Jones U., 1955; MEd, Miami U., Oxford, Ohio, 1956; EdD, Pa. State U., 1964. Dean coll. arts and sci. Bob Jones U., Greenville, S.C., 1961-65, registrar, 1965-81, prof. edn., 1956—, provost, 1981—; mem. edn. adv. bd. One Touch Systems, Inc., 1995—. cons. for books Beginnings for Christian Schools, English Skills for Christian Schools. Pres. Bob Jones U. Alumni Assn., Greenville, 1970-71; mem. coll. parallel adv. com. Tri-County Tech. Coll., Pendleton, S.C., 1973-86. Mem. Assn. Ednl. Communications and Tech. (life mem.; membership coordinator for profl. assns. 1969-72, vice chair nat. membership com. 1972-73, chair nat. membership com. 1973-75, council del. S.C. chpt. 1972-73, audiovisual instrn. editorial adv. com. 1974-75, del. to Lake Okoboji ednl. media leadership conf. 1972, 74), Assn. Ednl. Communications and Tech. of S.C. (bd. dirs. 1970-75, pres. 1972-73, award for outstanding contbns. and service 1971), Am. Assn. Collegiate Registrars and Admissions Officers, Phi Delta Kappa. Republican. Baptist. Office: Bob Jones U Off of Provost Greenville SC 29614

SMITH, PHILIP EDWARD LAKE, anthropology educator; b. Fortune, Nfld., Can., Aug. 12, 1927; s. George Frederick and Alice Maggie (Lake) S.; m. Fumiko Ikawa, 1959; 1 son, Douglas Philip Edward. B.A., Acadia U., 1948; M.A., Harvard U., 1957, Ph.D., 1962; postgrad., Universite de Bordeaux, 1958-59; D. Litt. (hon.), Meml. U. Nfld., 1976. Lectr. anthropology U. Toronto, Ont., Can., 1961-63; asst. prof. U. Toronto, 1963-65, asso. prof., 1965-66; asso. prof. archaeology Universite de Montreal, 1966-69, prof., 1969—; v.p. Ednl. Found. for Anthropology and the Public, 1981-84. Author: Le Solutreen en France, 1966, Food Production and Its Consequences, 1976, Japanese edit., 1986, Palaeolithic Archaeology in Iran, 1986; co-editor: The Hilly Flanks and Beyond, 1983; fgn. corr. L'Anthropologie (Paris); contbr. articles to profl. jours.; mem. internat. adv. com. Anthropologie et Societes (Que.). Can. Council Research grantee, 1969, 71, 74, 77; Leave grantee, 1970; research grantee, 1983; NRC research grantee, 1967; Soc. Sci. and Humanities Research Council Can. leave grantee, 1981; exchange research visitor to China, 1984. Fellow Royal Soc. Can., Am. Anthrop. Assn.; mem. Internat. Union Prehistoric and Protohistoric Scis. (permanent coun.), Current Anthropology (assoc.), Can. Soc. for Archaeology Abroad (past pres.), Internat. Union Anthrop. and Ethnol. Scis. (interim chmn. Can. del. to permanent coun. 1979-84, dept. chmn. 1981-84), Can. Inst. Baghdad. Archaeol. expdn. dir., Egypt, 1962-63, Iran, 1965, 67, 69, 71, 74, 77; other field work in Mex., U.S.A., France, Iraq, French W. Indies, India, 1954-82. Home: 3955 Ramezay Ave, Montreal, PQ Canada H3Y 3K3 Office: Univ de Montreal, Dept Anthropologie, Montreal, PQ Canada H3C 3J7

SMITH, PHILIP JOHN, industrial and systems engineering educator; b. Bradenton, Fla., July 11, 1953; s. John Fredrick and Valerie Eline (Polk) S. BA in Psychology, U. Mich., 1975, MS in Indsl. and Ops. Engring., 1976, PhD in Psychology and Indsl. Engring., 1979. Lectr. dept. indsl. engring. U. Mich., Ann Arbor, 1979-80, rsch. scientist Ctr. for Ergonomics, 1979-80; asst. prof. dept. indsl. engring. Ohio State U., Columbus, 1980-86, assoc. prof., 1986-92, prof. indsl. and sys. engring., 1992—; cons. Ford, Dearborn, Mich., 1986—, Travellers Ins. Co., Hartford, Conn., 1991—. Co-editor: Challenges in Indexing Electronic Text and Images, 1994; contbr. articles, paper to profl. publs. Mem. IEEE Sys., Man and Cybernetics, Am. Soc. for Info. Sci., Assn. Computing Machinery (spl. interest group for info. retrieval 1992-93), Human Factors Soc. Avocation: dressage. Home: 7197 Calhoun Rd Ostrander OH 43061-9420 Office: Ohio State U Engring Dept 1971 Neil Ave Columbus OH 43210-1210

SMITH, PHILIP JONES, lawyer; b. York, Pa., May 14, 1941; s. Clark S. and Margaret Ann (Jones) S.; m. Ann F. Johnson, Apr. 21, 1973; 1 child, James M. BA cum laude, Williams Coll., 1963; LLB, U. Va., 1966. Bar: Mass. 1967. Assoc. Ropes & Gray, Boston, 1967-76, ptnr., 1976—; lectr. Boston U. Sch. of Law, Boston, 1985—. Contbr. chpts. to books, articles to profl. jours. Bd. dirs., pres. Greater Boston Youth Symphony Orch., Boston, 1978—; bd. dirs., v.p. The Keewaydin Found., Salisbury, Vt., 1980—; bd. dirs., past treas. Project STEP, Boston, 1987-95; overseer, chair facilities com. New Eng. Conservatory, Boston, 1989-95. Fulbright scholar U. Madrid, 1966-67. Mem. ABA, Eastern Yacht Club (sec. 1977-83), N.Y. Yacht Club, Essex County Club, Order of Coif. Home: 35 Harbor Ave Marblehead MA 01945-3636 Office: Ropes & Gray One Internat Pl Boston MA 02110-2624

SMITH, PHILIP LUTHER, patent information scientist; b. Milan, Ind., Dec. 23, 1956; s. Donald Walter and Evelyn Emma (Vornheder) S.; m. Mary Ann Radike, Feb. 9, 1985; children: Martha Jesse, Philip Benjamin. BS, Purdue U., 1980. Rsch. asst. U. Cin. Coll. of Medicine, Cin., 1981-84; sr. phys. biochemist Med. Coll. of Ohio, Toledo, 1985-89; sr. rsch. molecular geneticist Marion Merrell Dow Rsch. Inst., Cin., 1990-95; patent info. scientist Hoechst Marion Roussel, Inc., Cin., 1996—. Contbr. articles to profl. jours. Mem. AAAS, Am. Radio Amateur Satellite Corp., Am. Chem. Soc., The Prot. Soc., Patent Info. Users Group, Am. Radio Relay League, Purdue U. Alumni Assn. (life). Roman Catholic. Achievements include rsch. in synthesis, purification and characterization of DNA/RNA oligonucleotides, peptides, proteins and synthetic compounds with a pharmaceutical significance; rsch. in protein chemistry with an emphasis on protein structure and function; rsch. info. sci. Avocations: amateur radio, electronics, volunteer teaching, FCC/ARRL accredited volunteer examiner and ofcl. observer.

SMITH, PHILIP MEEK, science policy consultant, writer; b. Springfield, Ohio, May 18, 1932; s. Clarenc Mitchell S. and Lois Ellen (Meek) Dudley. B.S., Ohio State U., 1954, M.A., 1955; DSc (hon.), N.C. State U., 1986. Mem. staff U.S. Nat. Com. for Internat. Geophys. Yr., Nat. Acad. Scis., 1957-58; program dir. NSF, 1958-63, dir. ops. U.S. Antarctic Research program, 1964-69, dep. head div. polar programs, 1970-73; chief gen. sci. br. Office Mgmt. and Budget Exec. Office of Pres., 1973-74; exec. asst. to dir. and sci. advisor to pres. NSF, 1974-76; assoc. dir. Office Sci. and Tech. Policy, Exec. Office of Pres., 1976-81; exec. officer NRC-Nat. Acad. Scis., Washington, 1981-94; ptnr. McGeary and Smith, Washington, 1995—; chmn. external adv. com. Nat. Computational Sci. Alliance, 1997—; bd. Aurora Flight Scis. Corp.; mem. adv. consulting bd. Geophys. Inst., U. Ala., 1994—; chmn. sci. adv. bd. Devel. Rsch. and Programs, Inc., 1997—; adviser Com. for Econ. Devel., 1997. Author: (with others) Defrosting Antarctic Secrets, 1962; The Frozen Future, a Prophetic Report from Antarctica, 1973; contbr. numerous articles to profl. jours. Bd. dirs. Washington Project for Arts, 1983-84, Washington Sculptors Group, 1983-84. 1st lt. U.S. Army, 1955-57. Mem. AAAS, Antarctican Soc., Cosmos Club (Washington), Am. Alpine Club (Golden, Colo.), Coun. Excellence Govt. (prin.). Office: McGeary and Smith 464 M St SW Washington DC 20024-2603

SMITH, PHILIP WAYNE, writer, communications company executive; b. Fayetteville, Tenn., Sept. 2, 1945; s. Clyde Wilson and Chastain (Finch) S.; m. Susan Jones, June 22, 1968; 1 child, Alan Wayne. Student, U. So. Miss., 1963-64, Athens Coll., 1964-65, 69-70. Reporter The Huntsville (Ala.) Times, 1964-66, The Elk Valley Times, Fayetteville, 1969-70; edn. reporter The Huntsville Times, 1970-71; Washington corr. The Huntsville Times, Washington, 1971-76; White House corr. Newhouse News Svc., Washington, 1977-80, Pentagon corr., 1981-84; writer Huntsville, 1984—; pres. P.S. Comms., Huntsville, 1994—; pub. rels. cons. Teledyne Brown Engring., Huntsville, 1984—; safety film producer VECO, Inc., Prudhoe Bay, Alaska, 1991. Co-author: Protecting the President, 1985 (Lit. Guild alt. selection 1986); screenwriter Our Land Too, 1987, Chemicals in War, 1989, Security: Everyone's Job, 1990, Face to Face Prospecting, 1992, Investigating Child Abuse, 1992, Lead Generation, 1993, Telephone Prospecting, 1993, Delayed Enlistment Program Management, 1993, Recruiter Sales Presentation, 1994, Duties and Responsibilities of Recruiting Station Commanders, 1994, Training Future Leaders, 1994, Rehabilitative Training Instructor Program, 1994, U.S. Army Program Executive Office for Tactical Missiles, 1995, Training: The Army Advantage, 1995, National Environmental Policy Act Compliance, 1996, Operations of the M21 Remote Sensing Chemical Agent Alarm, 1996, Buying Green: Purchasing Environmentally Friendly Products, 1997, Introduction to Terrorism, 1997, Terrorist Operations, 1997, Individual Protective Measures, 1997, Hostage Survival, 1997, Detecting Terrorist Surveillance, 1997, Buying Green: Using Environmentally Friendly Products, 1997. Sgt. USMC, 1966-69, Vietnam. Decorated Navy Achievement medal with combat V; named for Reporting Without Deadline, Ala. Press Assn., 1972, News Feature Writing, Ala. AP, 1975. Mem. Tenn. Screenwriting Assn., VFW. Democrat. Episcopalian. Avocations: tennis, swimming. Home and Office: 8007 Hickory Hill Ln SE Huntsville AL 35802-3252

SMITH, PHILLIP HARTLEY, steel company executive; b. Sydney, Australia, Jan. 26, 1927; came to U.S., 1950, naturalized, 1960; s. Norman Edward and Elizabeth (Williams) S.; m. Martha Frances Dittrich, June 4, 1955; children: Elizabeth, Thomas, Johanna, Alice, Margaret, Sarah. B.Engring. with 1st class honors in Mining and Metallurgy, U. Sydney, 1950; Metall. Engr., MIT, 1952; diploma indsl. rels., U. Chgo., 1958; LLD, Grove City Coll., 1975. Successively trainee, metallurgist, foreman Indiana Harbor, Ind., Inland Steel Co., 1952-55; successively trainee, metallurgist, dir. purchasing and planning La Salle Steel Co., Hammond, Ind., 1956-64; with Copperweld Corp., Pitts., 1964-77; pres. Copperweld Corp., 1967-77, chmn., 1973-77; pres., chief exec. officer Bekaert Steel Wire Corp., Pitts., 1978-82; mng. ptnr. Hartley Smith & Ptnrs., 1982-84; chmn. Smith, Yuill & Co. Inc., 1984—; bd. dirs. Mitech Labs. Inc., Jennmar Aust. Pty. Ltd.; adj. prof. bus. Grove City Coll.; vis. dean sr. exec. program Dalian U. Tech., Peoples Republic of China. Patentee in field; editor: Mechanical Working of Steel, 1961; author: Essays in Management, A Guide to Young Managers on the Way Up. Trustee Berea (Ky.) Coll., Wheeling Jesuit U., 1978-85; dir. Nat. Tech. Transfer Ctr.; chmn. Inroads Inc.; chair Sydney U. Found. Cadet officer Australian Mcht. Marine, 1942-43, Royal Australian Fleet Aux., 1943. Recipient Nat. Steelmaking award, 1955, Outstanding Chief Exec. Officer in Steel Industry award Fin. World, 1975; Nuffield scholar, 1949; Fulbright fellow, 1950. Mem. Univ. Club of Chgo., Duquesne Club of Pitts., Fox Chapel Golf Club, Rolling Rock Club (Ligonier, Pa.), Sigma Xi. Home: 102 Haverford Rd Pittsburgh PA 15238-1620

SMITH, PHILLIPS GUY, banker; b. Orange, N.J., Sept. 15, 1946; s. Phillips Upham and Helen Ottilie (Voderberg) S.; m. Ann Dixon Schickhaus, Dec. 29, 1973; children: Guy Dixon, William Schickhaus, Louisa Upham. B in Engring., Stevens Inst. Tech., Hoboken, N.J.; MBA, U. Pa., 1975. Comml. banking rep. The Bank of N.Y., N.Y.C., 1976-78, asst. treas., 1978-79, asst. v.p., 1979-80, v.p., 1980-85, sr. v.p., 1985-93; mng. dir. N.Am. Internat. Strategy Svcs., Inc., N.Y.C., 1993—. Vestryman Ch. of The Heavenly Rest, N.Y.C., 1983-88, treas., 1985-87; trustee Tabor Acad., Marion, Mass., 1987—, treas., 1991—. Lt. USN, 1970-74, Vietnam. Mem. Racquet and Tennis Club, Down Town Assn., Rockaway Hunting Club, Nantucket Yacht Club. Episcopalian. Home: 6 E 94th St New York NY 10128-1911 Office: Internat Strategy Svcs Inc 2 Wall St New York NY 10005-2001

SMITH, R. GORDON, lawyer; b. Roanoke, Va., May 28, 1938. BA with highest honors, U. Va., 1960; LLB magna cum laude, Harvard Law Sch., 1964. Bar: Va. 1964. Law clk. to judge U.S. Ct. Appeals (5th cir.), 1964-65; ptnr. McGuire, Woods, Battle & Boothe, Richmond, Va.; exec., legislation editor Harvard Law Rev., 1963-64. Fellow Am. Bar Found.; mem. Va. Bar Assn. (pres. 1987-88), Am. Law Inst., Phi Beta Kappa, Omicron Delta Kappa. Office: McGuire Woods Ste 800 One James River Plz Richmond VA 23219-3229

SMITH, RALPH ALEXANDER, cultural and educational policy educator; b. Ellwood City, Pa., June 12, 1929; s. J.V. and B. V. S.; m. Christiana M. Kolbe, Nov. 16, 1955. A.B., Columbia Coll., 1954; M.A., Teachers Coll., Columbia U., 1959, Ed.D., 1962. Faculty, art history and arts edn. Kent (Ohio) State U., 1959-61, Wis. State U., Oshkosh, 1961-63, SUNY, New Paltz, 1963-64; faculty edn. and art edn. U. Ill., Urbana-Champaign, 1964—, also prof. cultural and ednl. policy & aesthetic edn., prof. emeritus, 1996—; first Italo DeFrancesca Meml. lectr. Kutztown State U., 1974, Leon Jackman Meml. lectr., Perth, Australia, 1985, Dean's lectr. Coll. Fine Arts and Comm., Brigham Young U., 1985, Dunbar lectr. Millsaps Coll., 1993; disting. vis. prof. Ohio State U., 1987; sr. scholar Coll. Edn. U. Ill., 1991. Author: (with Albert William Levi) Art Education: A Critical Necessity, 1991; founder, editor Jour. Aesthetic Edn., 1966—; editor: Aesthetics and Criticism in Art Education, 1966, Aesthetic Concepts and Education, 1970, Aesthetics and Problems of Education, 1971, Regaining Educational Leadership, 1975, Cultural Literacy and Arts Education, 1991; co-author: Research in the Arts and Aesthetic Education: A Directory of Investigators and Their Fields of Inquiry, 1978, Excellence in Art Education: Ideas and Initiatives, 1987; editor: Discipline-Based Art Education, 1989, The Sense of Art: A Study in Aesthetic Education, 1989, (with Alan Simpson) Aesthetics and Arts Education, 1991, (with Bennett Reimer) The Arts, Education and Aesthetic Knowing, 1992, (with Ronald Berman) Public Policy and the Aesthetic Interest, 1992, General Knowledge and Arts Education, 1994, Excellence II: The Continuing Quest Art Education, 1995. Bd. govs. Inst. Study of Art in Edn.; trustee Nat. Ctr. Study of Art in Edn. With Med. Svc., U.S. Army, 1954-57. Recipient spl. merit recognition Coll. Edn., U. Ill., 1975, Disting. lectr. Studies in Art Edn. award, 1991. Fellow Nat. Art Edn. Assn. (Disting., Manuel Barkan Meml. award 1973); mem. Coun. Policy Studies in Art Edn. (first exec. sec. 1978-82), Ill. Art Edn. Assn. (Disting.). Home: 2909 Heathwood Ct Champaign IL 61821-7659 Office: U Ill 361 Education 1310 S 6th St Champaign IL 61820-6925

SMITH, RALPH LEE, author, musician; b. Phila., Nov. 6, 1927; s. Hugh Harold and Barbara (Schatkin) S.; m. Betty H. Smith, Sept. 1954 (div. Jan. 1963); children: David Bruce, Robert Hugh; m. Mary Louise Hollowell, 1971 (div. 1977); m. Shizuko Maruyama, 1977; 1 child, Lisa Koyuki. BA, Swarthmore Coll., 1951; MEd, U. Va., 1987. Folk musician on Appalachian dulcimer; recs. include Dulcimer: Old Time and Traditional Music, 1973, Tunes of the Blue Ridge and Great Smoky Mountains, 1983; author: The Story of the Dulcimer, 1986, American Dulcimer Traditions, 1997. Home: 1662 Chimney House Rd Reston VA 20190-4302 Office: 400 Prince Georges Blvd Upper Marlboro MD 20774-8731

SMITH, RALPH WESLEY, JR., federal judge; b. Ghent, N.Y., July 16, 1936; s. Ralph Wesley and Kathleen S. (Callahan) S.; m. Nancy Ann Fetzer, Dec. 30, 1961 (div. 1981); children: Mark Owen, Tara Denise, Todd Kendall; m. Barbara Anne Milian, Nov. 8, 1982; stepchildren: Kim Highter, Jeffrey Highter, Eric Highter. Student, Sorbonne, U. Paris, Paris, 1954-55; BA, Yale U., 1956; LLB, Albany Law Sch., 1966. Bar: N.Y. 1966, U.S. Dist. Ct. (no. dist.) N.Y. 1966. Assoc. Hinman, Straub Law Firm, Albany, N.Y., 1966-69; chief asst. dist. atty. Albany County, N.Y., 1969-73, dist. atty., 1974; regional dir. state nursing home investigation Asst. Atty. Gen., Albany, 1975-77; dir. State Organized Crime Task Force, 1978-82; U.S. magistrate judge U.S. Dist. Ct. (no. dist.) N.Y., Albany, 1982—; judge moot ct. Albany Law Sch., 1983—; lectr. N.Y. State Bar Assn., 1985—. Capt. USNR, 1957-82. Mem. Fed. Magistrate Judges Assn., Columbia County Bar Assn., Columbia County Magistrates Assn. Republican. Roman Catholic. Avocations: fishing, bicycling, skiing, sailing, camping. Home: 2375 Route 66 Chatham NY 12037-9717 Office: US Dist Ct 445 Broadway Ste 314 Albany NY 12207-2925

SMITH, RANDALL NORMAN, orthopedist; b. Hicksville, N.Y., Mar. 1, 1948; s. Lester I. and Meta (Moskowitz) S.; m. Marcia Hope Bluestein, Jan. 23, 1949; children: Todd Adam, Taryn Leigh. BS, Ohio U., 1969; MD, Temple U., 1973. Diplomate Am. Bd. Orthopedics. Intern Einstein Med. Ctr., Phila., 1973-74, orthopedic resident, 1974-78, chief resident, 1976-78, staff physician, 1978—; pvt. practice Phila., 1978—; dir. emergency rm. JFK Hosp., Phila., 1975-79; spkr. in field. Contbr. articles to profl. jours. Bd. dirs. Plymouth Soccer League, Plymouth Twp.hi , Pa., 1986-90; coach Plymouth Baseball and Basketball League, Plymouth Twp., 1982-89; referee Whitemarsh Soccer and Basketball, Lafayette Hill, Pa., 1985-91; mem. golf com. Meadowlands Country Club, Blue Bell, Pa., 1986-93. Recipient Pharmacy Family of Yr., Nat. Assn. Retail Druggists, 1972. Fellow Am. Acad. Orthopedics; mem. Am. Coll. Sports Medicine, Am. Coll. Occupl. Medicine, Ea. Orthopedic Assn., Am. Running and Fitness Assn., Brotherhood of Ami. Jewish. Avocations: golf, health club activities, children's sports, reading, chess. Office: Palmaccio Smith Assoc 12000 Bustleton Ave Philadelphia PA 19116-2151

SMITH, RANKIN M., JR., professional football team executive; b. Hot Springs, AR, Aug. 24, 1947; m. Rebecca Robinson; children: Caroline, Kathryn, Rankin M. III. BBA, U. Ga., 1971. Pres. Atlanta Falcons, 1977—. Mem. Ducks Unltd. Office: Atlanta Falcons Atlanta Falcons Complex One Falcon Place Suwanee GA 30174-2127*

SMITH, RAYMOND LEIGH, plastic surgeon; b. Norristown, Pa., Sept. 27, 1940; s. Walter Joseph and Pauline C. (Wolfskill) S.; m. Coralynn Elder, Jan. 8, 1966; children: Susan, Elizabeth, Christine. BS, Ursinus Coll., 1962; MD, Temple U., 1966. Diplomate Nat. Bd. Med. Examiners, Am. Bd. Plastic Surgery. Active staff Reading Hosp., Pa., 1976—, chief sect. of plastic surgery, 1994—, St. Joseph Hosp., Reading, 1976—, Cmty. Gen. Hosp., Reading, 1976—. Mem. ACS, Republican Majority Found., Washington Legal Found. Mem. Am. Soc. Plastic and Reconstructive Surgery, Robert H. Ivy Soc., Am. Assn. Hand Surgery, Northeastern Soc. Plastic Surgeons, Pa. Med. Soc., Lipoplasty Soc. N.Am., Berks County Med. Soc. Lutheran. Office: 926 Penn Ave Wyomissing PA 19610-3017

SMITH, RAYMOND LLOYD, former university president, consultant; b. Vanceboro, Maine, Jan. 25, 1917; s. Ivan and Genevieve (Gatcomb) S.; m. Beatrice Bennett, Dec. 4, 1943; children: Bennett Charles, Martin Lloyd. B.S. cum laude, U. Alaska, 1943; M.S. in Metall. Engring, U. Pa., 1951, Ph.D. in Metall. Engring, 1953; D.Sc. (hon.), Western Mich. U.; LL.D., No. Mich. U., D.Eng. (hon.), Mich. Technol. U., S.D. Sch. Mines and Tech. Instr. math. U. Alaska, 1946-47, asst. prof. metallurgy, 1948-49; rsch. assoc. dept. metallurgy U. Pa., 1949-53; sr. rsch. metallurgist Franklin Inst. Labs., Phila., 1953; sect. chief metallurgy Franklin Inst. Labs., 1954-56, assoc. dir., 1957, tech. dir., 1958-59; prof., head metall. dept. Mich. Technol. U., Houghton, 1959-64, coord. rsch., 1960-64, pres., 1965-79; pres. Am. Soc. Metals, 1979-80, Houghton (Mich.) Daily Mining Gazette, 1979-81, R. L. Smith, Inc.; Am. Soc. Metals/The Metallurgical Soc. joint disting. lectr. in materials, 1983; mem. indsl. adv. bd. mining engring. dept. Mich. Tech. U.; bd. dirs. Lake Superior & Ishpeming R.R.; lectr. in field. Contbr. numerous articles to metall. sci. jours.; patentee in field. Bd. dirs. Community Water Co., Green Valley. With AUS, 1943-46. Recipient Distinguished Alumnus award U. Alaska, Clair M. Donovan award Mich. Tech. U., D. Robert Yarnall award U. Pa. Engring. Sch.; Outstanding Service award Air Force ROTC; Rotary Paul Harris fellow. Fellow Metall. Soc., AIME (Henry Krumb meml. lectr. 1981), Am. Soc. for Metals (hon.); mem. Internat. Exec. Svc. Corps., Scabbard and Blade, Blue Key, Tau Beta Pi, Alpha Sigma Mu (hon. lectr. 1982), Alpha Phi Omega, Phi Kappa Phi, Theta Tau. Home: PO Box 726 Green Valley AZ 85622-0726 *A sense of humor is one of the important building blocks for that firm sense of balance so necessary to meet the challenges of life. It's like the seasoning of a chef's masterpiece.*

SMITH, RAYMOND THOMAS, anthropology educator; b. Oldham, Lancashire, Eng., Jan. 12, 1925; s. Harry and Margaret (Mulchrone) S.; m. Flora Alexandrina Tong, June 30, 1954; children: Fenela, Colin, Anthony. B.A., Cambridge (Eng.) U., 1950, M.A., 1951, Ph.D., 1954. Sociol. research officer govt. Brit. Guiana, 1951-54; research fellow U. W.I., 1954-59; prof. sociology U. Ghana, 1959-62; sr. lectr. sociology, prof. anthropology U. West Indies, 1962-66; prof. anthropology U. Chgo., 1966-95, prof. emeritus, 1995—, chmn. dept. anthropology, 1975-81, 84-85, 94-95; vis. prof. U. Calif. - Berkeley, 1957-58, McGill U., Montreal, 1964-65; mem. com. on child devel. research and public policy NRC, 1977-80; dir. Caribbean Consortium Grad. Sch., 1985-86. Author: The Negro Family in British Guiana, 1956, British Guiana, 1962, 2d edit., 1980, Kinship and Class In The West Indies, 1988, The Matrifocal Family, 1996; co-author: Class Differences in American Kinship, 1978; editor: Kinship Ideology and Practice in Latin America, 1984; contbr. articles to profl. jours. Co-investigator urban family life project U. Chgo., 1986-90. Served with RAF, 1943-48. Guggenheim fellow, 1983-84. Fellow Am. Anthrop. Assn.; mem. Assn. Social Anthropologists. Office: Univ Chicago Dept Anthropology 1126 E 59th St Chicago IL 60637-1539

SMITH, RAYMOND W., telecommunications company executive; b. Pitts., 1937. B.S., Carnegie-Mellon U., 1959; M.B.A., U. Pitts., 1967. Dir. budget planning and analysis comptroller dept. AT&T, 1976-77; with Bell of Pa., Phila., 1959-75, 77-85, div. ops. mgr. Western area, 1971-74; asst. v.p. pub. relations Bell of Pa. and Diamond State Telephone, Phila., 1974-75; v.p., gen. mgr. Eastern region Bell of Pa. and Diamond State Tel., Phila., 1977-81, v.p.-regulatory, 1981-83, pres., chief exec. officer, 1983-85; vice chmn., chief fin. officer, dir. parent co. Bell Atlantic Corp., Phila., 1985-88; pres., chief oper. officer Bell Atlantic Corp., 1988; chmn., chief exec. officer Bell Atlantic Corp., Phila., 1989—; bd. dirs. USAir Group, Core States Fin. Corp., Westinghouse Electric Corp.; mem. Bus. Roundtable, 1990—; mem. nat. adv. bd. Pvt. Sector Coun., 1990—; mem. James Madison nat. coun. Libr. of Congress, 1990—. Pub. playwright. Vice chmn. Phila. blood donor campaign ARC; mem. bd. advisors Arden Theatre Co., 1991—. With Signal Corps, U.S. Army, 1959-60. Office: Bell Atlantic Corp 1717 Arch St Philadelphia PA 19103-2713*

SMITH, REBECCA BEACH, federal judge; b. 1949. BA, Coll. William and Mary, 1971; postgrad., U. Va., 1971-73; JD, Coll. William and Mary, 1979. Assoc. Wilcox & Savage, 1980-85; U.S. magistrate Ea. Dist. Va., 1985-89; dist. judge U.S. Dist. Ct. (ea. dist.) Va., Norfolk, 1989—; exec. editor Law Review, 1978-79. Active Chrysler Mus. Norfolk, Jean Outland Chrysler Libr. Assocs., Va. Opera Assn., Friends of the Zoo, Friends of Norfolk Pub. Libr., Ch. of the Good Shepherd. John Marshall Soc. fellow; recipient Acad. Achievement and Leadership award St. George Tucker Soc.; named one of Outstanding Women of Am., 1979. Mem. ABA, Va. State Bar Assn., Fed. Bar Assn. Supreme Ct. Hist. Soc., Fourth Cir. Judicial Conf., The Harbor Club, Order of Coif., Phi Beta Kappa. Office: US Dist Ct US Courthouse 600 Granby St Ste 358 Norfolk VA 23510-1915*

SMITH, REBECCA MCCULLOCH, human relations educator; b. Greensboro, N.C., Feb. 29, 1928; d. David Martin and Virginia Pearl (Woodburn) McCulloch; m. George Clarence Smith Jr., Mar. 30, 1945; 1 child, John Randolph. BS, Woman's Coll., U. N.C., 1947, MS, 1952; PhD, U. N.C., Greensboro, 1967; postgrad., Harvard U., 1989. Tchr. pub. schs., N.C. and S.C., 1947-57; instr. U. N.C., Greensboro, 1958-66, asst. prof. to prof. emeritus human devel. and family studies, 1967-91, adj. prof. emeritus, 1991-94, dir. grad. program, 1975-82; adj. prof. ednl. cons. depts. edn. N.C., S.C., Ind., Ont., Man.; vis. prof. N.W. La. State U., 1965, 67, U. Wash., 1970, Hood Coll., 1976, 86. Named Outstanding Alumna Sch. Home Econs., 1976; recipient Sperry award for service to families N.C. Family Life Coun., 1979. Mem. Nat. Coun. Family Rels. (exec. com. 1974-76, treas. 1987-89, Osborne award 1973), U. N.C. at Greensboro Alumni Assn. (chair membership recruitment com. 1994-96). Author: Teaching About Family Relationships, 1975, Klemer's Marriage and Family Relationships, 2d edit., 1975, Resources for Teaching About Family Life Education, 1976, Family Matters: Concepts in Marriage and Personal Relationships, 1982; co-author: History of the School of Human Environmental Sciences: 1892-1992, 1992, assoc. editor Family Relations (Jour. Applied Family and Child Studies), 1980-90; ednl. cons. Current Life Studies, 1977-84. Home: 1212 E Ritters Lake Rd Greensboro NC 27406-7816 Office: U NC Dept Human Devel Sch Human Environ Scis Greensboro NC 27412

SMITH, REGINALD BRIAN FURNESS, anesthesiologist, educator; b. Warrington, Eng., Feb. 7, 1931; s. Reginald and Betty (Bell) S.; m. Margarete Groppe, July 18, 1963; children: Corinne, Malcolm. MB, BS, U. London, 1955; DTM and H, Liverpool Sch. Tropical Medicine, 1959. Intern Poole Gen. Hosp., Dorset, Eng., 1955-56, Wilson Meml. Hosp., Johnson City, N.Y., 1962-63; resident in anesthesiology Med. Coll. Va., Richmond, 1963-64; resident in anesthesiology U. Pitts., 1964-65, clin. instr., 1965-66; asst. prof., 1969-71, asso. clin. prof., 1971-74, prof., 1974-78, acting chmn. dept. anesthesiology, 1977-78; prof., chmn. dept. U. Tex. Health Sci. Center, San Antonio, 1978—; anesthesiologist in chief hosps. U. Tex. Health Sci. Ctr., 1978—, med. dir. hyperbaric medicine unit Univ. Hosp., 1993—; dir. anesthesiology Eye and Ear Hosp., Pitts., 1971-76; Univ. Hosp.; anesthesiologist in chief Presbyn. Univ. Hosp., Pitts., 1976-78. Contbg. editor: Internat. Ophthalmology Clinics, 1973, Internat. Anesthesiology Clinics, 1983; contbr. articles to profl. jours. Served to capt. Brit. Army, 1957-59. Fellow ACP, Am. Coll. Anesthesiologists, Am. Coll. Chest Physicians, Am. Coll. Hyperbaric Physicians; mem. AMA, Internat. Anesthesia Rsch. Soc., Am. Soc. Anesthesiologists (pres. Western Pa. 1974-75), Tex. Soc. Anesthesiologists, San Antonio Soc. Anesthesiologists (pres. 1990), Tex. Med. Assn., Bexar County Med. Soc. Home: 213 Canada Verde St San Antonio TX 78232-1104 Office: 7703 Floyd Curl Dr San Antonio TX 78284-6200

SMITH, REX WILLIAM, journalist; b. Danville, Ill., Oct. 19, 1952; s. Ralph William and Lillian Grace (Hart) S.; m. Marion Roach, July 15, 1989. BA cum laude, Trinity U., San Antonio, 1974; MS with highest honors, Columbia U., N.Y.C., 1980. Mng. editor Rensselaer (Ind.) Republican newspaper, 1974-75; legis. asst. U.S. Rep. Floyd J. Fithian, Washington, 1975-79; reporter, spl. writer Newsday, L.I., N.Y., 1980-87, chief Albany (N.Y.) bur., 1987-91; editor The Record, Troy, N.Y., 1991-95; mng. editor Times Union, Albany, N.Y., 1995—. Contbr. numerous articles to newspapers and mags. Recipient Community Svc. award Rensselaer C. of C., 1975, Media award World Hunger Fund, 1983, Disting. Svc. medal Soc. Profl. Journalists, 1987, Editorial award Common Cause, 1992, award for disting. community svc. N.Y. State Pubs. Assn., 1994; Rotary fellow, 1979, Pulitzer Travel fellow Columbia U., 1982. Presbyterian. Home: Fox Hollow Lodge Dill Brook Rd Petersburg NY 12138 Office: Times Union Box 15000 Albany NY 12212

SMITH, RICHARD ALAN, publishing and speciality retailing executive; b. Boston, 1924; married. BS, Harvard U., 1946; LLD (hon.), Boston Coll., 1988. With Smith Mgmt. Co., 1947-61; chmn. bd., CEO, Gen. Cinema Corp. (name changed to Harcourt Gen., Inc. 1993), Chestnut Hill, Mass., 1961-91, 96—, Neiman Marcus Group, Chestnut Hill, Mass., 1987—; chmn., CEO Harcourt Gen., Inc., Chestnut Hill, 1993—; chmn., CEO, pres. GC Cos., Inc., Chestnut Hill, 1993-95, chmn., 1995—. Office: Harcourt Gen Inc 27 Boylston St Chestnut Hill MA 02167-1719

SMITH, RICHARD ANTHONY, investment banker; b. St. Louis, July 17, 1939; s. Jack and Ruth Smith; children: Richard Adam, Jonathan. Student, Yale U., 1961. With Salomon Bros., N.Y.C., 1969-75, Morgan Stanley & Co., N.Y.C., 1975-92; mng. dir. Morgan Stanley, N.Y.C., 1983, mem. mgmt. com., 1988-92; bd. dirs. Chateau D'Eau, Paris, CMT Med. Tech., Haifa, Israel, 4 F Inv. Br., Paris. Bd. dirs. Rabbi Marc H. Tanenbaum Found. Mem. Bd. Am. Jewish World Svc., Shelter Island Yacht Club.

SMITH, RICHARD BOWEN, retired national park superintendent; b. Grandville, Mich., Mar. 8, 1938; s. William Jr. and Mary Elizabeth (Bowen) S.; m. Katherine Theresa Short, Sept. 21, 1980. BA in History, Albion Coll., 1960; MA in English, Mich. State U., 1967. Tchr. Grand Rapids (Mich.) Jr. H.S., 1960-66; vol. Peace Corps, Asuncion, Paraguay, 1968-70; ranger Nat. Pk. Svc., Yosemite, Calif., 1971-76; ranger. instr. Nat. Pk. Svc., Grand Canyon, Ariz., 1976-78; ranger, legis. specialist Nat. Pk. Svc., Washington, 1978-80; asst. supt. Nat. Pk. Svc., Everglades, Fla., 1980-83; assoc. regional dir. ops. Nat. Pk. Svc., Phila., 1984-86; supt. Nat. Pk. Svc., Carlsbad Caverns, N.Mex., 1986-88; assoc. regional dir. ops. Nat. Pk. Svc., Santa Fe, 1988-89; assoc. regional dir. resources mgmt. Nat. Park Service, Santa Fe, 1990-94; cons. on protected area mgmt. in L.Am., 1994—; temp. supt. Yellowstone Nat. Pk., 1994—; owner R & K Internat., 1994—; pres. Assn. Nat. Pk. Rangers, 1977-78; coord. Congress of the Internat. Ranger Fedn., San José, Costa Rica, 1997. Bd. dirs. Yellowstone Assn., 1995—. Recipient Meritorious Svc. award Dept. of Interior, 1992. Home: 2 Roadrunner Trl Placitas NM 87043-9424

SMITH, RICHARD CONRAD, JR., telecommunications company executive; b. Gadsden, Ala., Feb. 10, 1942; s. Richard Conrad and Anne Ruth (McFarlin) S.; m. Mary Elizabeth Dale, Mar. 18, 1967; children: Corinne Craig, Andrea Dale, Jason McFarlin. B Engring., Vanderbilt U., 1964; MS, MPhil, Yale U., 1966, PhD, 1970. Salesman Ins. Sys. Am., Atlanta, 1970-73, adminstr., 1973-76, sr. v.p., 1976-80; pres., CEO, ISACOMM, Inc., Atlanta, 1980-83; pres. U.S. Telecom-Corp. Network Svcs., Atlanta, 1983-86; pres. nat. accounts div. U.S. Sprint, Atlanta, 1986-89; pres. nat. markets div. U.S. Sprint, Kansas City, Kans., 1989-91; sr. v.p. quality devel. and pub. rels. Sprint Corp., Kansas City, Mo., 1991—. Bd. advisors Ctr. for Entrepreneurial Leadership, Kansas City, Mo., 1992; bd. dirs. Pvt. Industry Coun., Kansas City, Mo., 1992, Kansas City Crime Commn., 1992, St. Lukes Hosp., 1995; trustee U. Kansas City, 1993; mem. commn. on ministry Episcopal Diocese We. Mo., 1993. Mem. Kansas City (Mo.) C. of C. (bd. dirs.), Carriage Club, Mission Hills Country Club, Sigma Xi, Tau Beta Pi. Episcopalian. Avocation: photography. Office: Sprint Corp PO Box 11315 Kansas City MO 64112

SMITH, RICHARD ERNEST, retired insurance company executive; b. Adrian, Mich., Oct. 29, 1935; s. Albert Forrest and Thelma (Brock) S.; m. Joanne Piplow, Oct. 11, 1955; children: Kathryn, Albert, Sharon, Richard, Heidi. Student, Spring Arbor Coll., 1955. CLU. Mgr. White Hardware, Adrian, 1950-59; dist. mgr. Met. Life, Adrian and Lafayette, Ind., 1959-75; dir. regional Ohio Nat. Life, Cin., 1975-78; agy. v.p. Provident Life, Bismarck, N.D., 1978-86, pres., 1986-90; bd. dirs. Provident Life Ins. Co. Commr. City of Adrian, 1966-71; trustee Medctr. One, Bismarck, 1986—, Bismarck State Coll. Found., 1987-91; bd. dirs. Macinac Straits Hosp., St. Ignace, Mich., 1995—, Bismarck Devel. Assn., 1987-91, Greater Adrian Devel. Assn., 1966-70. Republican. Club: Apple Creek Country (Bismarck). Lodge: Elks. Avocation: travel. Home: N 5072 Epoufette Bay Naubinway MI 49762-9722

SMITH, RICHARD GRANT, retired telecommunications executive, electrical engineer; b. Flint, Mich., Jan. 19, 1937; s. Grand Ladd and Pauline Lorain (Lott) S.; m. Carol Ann Treanor, Apr. 18, 1965; children: Scott, Holly, Heather. BSEE, Stanford U., 1958, MSEE, 1959, PhDEE, 1963. Mem. tech. staff Bell Labs., Murray Hill, N.J., 1963-68, supr., 1968-82, dept. head, 1982-87; dir. AT&T Bell Labs., Breinigsville, 1987-93; ret., 1993; ind. cons., 1993—; chmn. CLEOS, 1980. Contbr. chpts. in books. Vice chmn.

Bernards Twp. Parks and Recreation, 1976-78. Fellow IEEE (Centennial award 1984), OSA; mem. Phi Beta Kappa, Tau Beta Pi, Theta Delta Chi.

SMITH, RICHARD HOWARD, banker; b. Tulare, Calif., Aug. 27, 1927; s. Howard Charles and Sue Elizabeth (Cheyne) S.; B.A., Principia Coll. 1958; LL.B., LaSalle U., 1975; postgrad. Sch. Banking U. Wash., 1970-72; m. Patricia Ann Howery, Mar. 12, 1950; children—Jeffrey Howard, Holly Lee, Gregory Scott, Deborah Elaine. Prin., Aurora Elementary Sch., Tulare, 1951-53; prin. Desert Sun Sch., Idyllwild, Calif., 1953-55; trust adminstr. trainee Bank of Am., San Diego, 1955-58, asst. trust officer, Ventura, Redlands, Riverside and L.A., 1958-65; asst. trust officer Security Pacific Bank, Fresno, Calif., 1965-68; trust officer, 1968-72, v.p., mgr., 1972-88, Pasadena, 1988-94; v.p. Bank of Am., L.A., 1994-95; ret., 1995; pres. Fiduciary Svcs., Fresno, 1995—; instr. San Bernardino Valley Coll., 1962—, Fresno City Coll., 1977—. With USN, 1945-46. Mem. Fresno Bar Assn. Home: 3222 W Dovewood Ln Fresno CA 93711-2125

SMITH, RICHARD JACKSON, elementary education educator; b. Mt. Airy, N.C., Feb. 17, 1947; s. Robert Wayne and Ruth (Jackson) S.; m. Sue Monday, Sept. 10, 1971 (dec. Nov. 21, 1981); 1 child, Richard Jackson Jr. BA, U. N.C., 1972; MA, Appalachian State U., 1975; EdD, U. N.C., 1994. Elem. tchr. Surry County Schs., Dobson, N.C., 1987-96, parent coord., 1992-96, K-5 instnl. facilitator, 1996—; part-time instr. grad. equivalency diploma/adult basic edn. and effective tchr. tng. classes Surry C.C., Dobson, 1988-92; cons. Eckerd Family Youth Alternatives, Inc., 1994—. Local and dist. chmn., state treas. N.C. Polit. Action Com. for Edn., Raleigh, 1976-81; state exec. com. N.C. Dem. Party, Raleigh, 1981-83; trustee, deacon First Bapt. Ch. of Pilot Mountain, 1988—, sec. bd. dirs., 1990, Sunday sch. dir., 1991—, vice chmn., 1996—. Mem. ASCD, NEA (congressional lobbying 1976-80), Internat. Reading Assn. (local unit chair 1986—), N.C. Assn. Educators (local, dist. pres. 1979-81, local, dist., state chmn. legis. commn. 1980-81), Pilot Mountain Jaycees (life, charter mem., pres. 1979-80, Officer of Yr. 1978, 79), Geneal. Soc. Rockingham & Stokes Counties, Stokes County Hist. Soc., Sons Confederate Vets. (Stokes County camp 1994—), Masons (32 degree, Scottish Rite, edn. chmn. 1986—, scholarship chmn. 1986—, Winston-Salem consisitory ambassador 1988, ambassador 1990—, lodge master 1990, Cert. of Meritorious Svc. 1988). Home: PO Box 127 517 E Main St Pilot Mountain NC 27041 Office: Surry County Schs PO Box 364 Dobson NC 27017

SMITH, RICHARD JOSEPH, history educator; b. Sacramento, Oct. 30, 1944; s. Joseph Benjamin and Margaret Elaine (Stoddard) S.; m. Alice Ellen Weisenberger, July 1, 1967; 1 child, Tyler Stoddard. BA, U. Calif., Davis, 1966, MA, 1968, PhD, 1972. Lectr. Chinese U. Hong Kong, 1972-73, U. Calif., 1972-73; asst. prof. history Rice U., Houston, 1973-78, assoc. prof., 1978-83, prof., 1983—, Minnie Stevens Piper prof., 1987, Sarofim Disting. Teaching prof., 1993-95; adj. prof. U. Tex., Austin, 1983—; cons. FBI, CIA, Washington, 1985—, NEH, Washington, 1983—, various mus., Houston, Boston, N.Y.C., 1987—. Author: Mercenaries and Mandarins, 1978, Traditional Chinese Culture, 1978, China's Cultural Heritage, 1983, 2d edit., 1994, Entering China's Service, 1986, Fortune-Tellers and Philosophers, 1991, Robert Hart and China's Early Modernization, 1991, Chinese Almanacs, 1993, Cosmology, Ontology and Human Efficacy, 1993, H.B. Morse: Customs Commissioner and Historian of China, 1995, Chinese Maps, 1996. adj. mem. Houston Mus. Fine Arts, 1986—; guest curator Children's Mus., Houston, 1987-89, 91—; pres. Tex. Found. for China Studies, Houston, 1988-93. Mem. Assn. for Asian Studies (pres. S.W. conf. 1990-91), Asia Soc. (bd. dirs. Houston Ctr. 1976—), Nat. Com. on U.S.-China Rels., Houston-Taipei Soc. (bd. dirs. 1990—), Phi Kappa Phi. Democrat. Avocations: sports, travel, music. Home: 2403 Goldsmith St Houston TX 77030-1813 Office: Rice U Dept History MS-42 6100 Main St Houston TX 77005-1827

SMITH, RICHARD MELVYN, government official; b. Lebanon, Tenn., May 2, 1940; s. Roy D. and V. Ruth (Draper) S.; m. Patti Hawkins, Feb. 29, 1964; 1 child, Douglas. B.S.E.E., Tenn. Technol. U., 1963. Asst. Engr.-in-charge FCC, Phila., 1972, Balt., 1971-72; chief investigations br. FCC, Washington, 1974-77, asst. chief enforcement div., 1977-80, dep. chief Field Ops. Bur., 1981-94, chief Office Engring. and Tech., 1994—. Recipient sr. exec. service award FCC, 1983, 84, 85, 86, 87, 88. Avocations: instrument-rated pvt. pilot. Office: FCC 2000 M St NW Ste 480 Washington DC 20036-3307

SMITH, RICHARD MILLS, editor in chief, magazine executive; b. Detroit, Jan. 12, 1946; s. William Steele Smith and Janet (Mills) Morrison; m. Lee Ann Vanderstoep (div.); children: Scott William, Anna Mills; m. Soon-Young Yoon, Oct. 20, 1978; 1 child, Song-Mee. BA summa cum laude, Albion Coll., 1968; postgrad., Columbia U., 1968-69, MS, 1970; LLD (hon.), Albion Coll., 1993. Reporter Associated Press, N.Y., 1969; assoc. editor foreign dept. Newsweek, N.Y., 1970-73, gen. editor nat. affairs dept., 1973-74; editor Asian region, bur. chief Hong Kong Newsweek, Asia, Hong Kong, 1974-77; mng. editor Newsweek Internat., N.Y., 1977-81; asst. mng. editor Newsweek, N.Y.C., 1982, exec. editor, 1983, editor in chief, 1984-91, editor in chief, pres., 1991—. Trustee Albion Coll.; bd. dirs. Cooper-Hewitt Nat. Design Mus., Smithsonian Institution. Recipient Disting. Alumni award Albion Coll., 1974. Mem. Am. Soc. Mag. Editors (mem. exec. com. 1985-88), Mag. Pubs. Assn. (chmn.), Coun. on Fgn. Rels., Century Assn., Phi Beta Kappa. Office: Newsweek Inc 251 W 57th St New York NY 10019-1802*

SMITH, RICHARD MULDROW, lawyer; b. Jefferson City, Mo., Sept. 2, 1939; s. Elmer Clyde and Mary (Muldrow) S.; children—Stephen, Michael. J.D., U. Ark., 1963; postgrad. U. Ill., 1963-64. Bar: Ark. 1963, D.C. 1980, U.S. Ct. Appeals (D.C. cir.) 1980, U.S. Supreme Ct. 1980. Asst. prof. U. N.C., Chapel Hill, 1964-67, assoc. prof., 1967-73, prof. 1973-79; spl. counsel FPC, Washington, 1976-77; mem. White House Energy Policy Staff, Washington, 1978-79; dir., Office of Policy Coordination, Dept. of Energy, Washington, 1978-79; ptnr. Mayer, Brown & Platt, Washington, 1979-91; pres. Little Creek Marina Inc., Norfolk, Va., 1992—. Author (with others) North Carolina Uniform Commercial Code Forms Annotated, 2 vols., 1967. Mem. ABA (pub. utility law sect., council mem. 1985-88, chmn. gas com. 1988-89, chmn. publ. com. 1989-91). Home: 4941 Adelia Dr Virginia Beach VA 23455-2227 Office: 4801 Pretty Lake Ave Norfolk VA 23518-2005

SMITH, RICHARD THOMAS, electrical engineer; b. Allentown, Pa., June 15, 1925; s. Raymond Willard and Mary (Rau) S.; m. Naomi Elsie Anthony, May 26, 1956; children: Cynthia Louise, Carol Ann. B.S. with high honors, Lehigh U., 1946, M.S., 1947; Ph.D., Ill. Inst. Tech., 1955. Registered profl. engr., Mass., Okla., Tex., Gt. Britain. Instr., Lehigh U., Bethlehem, Pa., 1947-50; analytical and design engr. Gen. Electric Co., Schenectady, 1952-58; asso. prof. U. Tex., Austin, 1958-61; George Westinghouse prof. elec. engring. Va. Poly. Inst., Blacksburg, 1961-62; project dir. Tracor, Inc., Austin, 1962-64; sr. engr., asst. dir., dir., v.p. Southwest Research Inst., San Antonio, 1964-66; Okla. Gas and Electric prof. elec. engring. U. Okla., Norman, 1966-68; prof. elec. machinery Rensselaer Poly. Inst., Troy, N.Y., 1968-70; NSF fellow U. Colo., 1970; Alcoa&UMR Disting. prof. elec. engring. U. Mo., Rolla, 1970-73; inst. engr., dir. Nondestructive Testing Info. Analysis Center, Southwest Research Inst., San Antonio, 1973-83; cons., 1983—; adj. prof. U. Tex., 1974-83, prof., 1983-87; cons., reviewer numerous cos. Author: Analysis of Electrical Machines, 1982. Recipient Excellence Fund U. Tex., 1959, DuPont Meml. prize Lehigh U., 1946. Fellow AIAA (assoc.), Instn. Elec. Engrs. (Eng.); mem. Am. Soc. Engring. Edn., I.E.E.E. (1st paper prize 1960, 63, sr.), N.Y. Acad. Scis., I.E.E.E. (numerous coms.), Internat. Electrotech. Commn. (adv. group 1971-74), Sigma Xi, Tau Beta Pi, Pi Mu Epsilon, Phi Eta Sigma, Eta Kappa Nu, Phi Kappa Phi. Office: 402 Yosemite Dr San Antonio TX 78232-1251

SMITH, RICHEY, chemical company executive; b. Akron, Ohio, Nov. 11, 1933; s. Thomas William and Martha (Richey) S.; m. Sandra Cosgrave Roe, Nov. 25, 1961; children: Mason Roe, Parker Richey. BS, U. Va., 1956. Asst. to pres. Sun Products Corp., Barberton, Ohio, 1960-64, v.p., 1964-67, gen. mgr., dir., 1967-69; chmn., CEO Sun Products Corp., 1969-76; prin. A.T. Kearney Co., Cleve., 1977-87; chmn., CEO Richey Industries, Inc., Medina, Ohio, 1987—; dir. Jaite Packaging, Inc. Mem. exec. com. Great Trail coun. Boy Scouts Am., 1973-75; chmn. capital funds dr. Summit County Planned Parenthood, 1970-71; trustee Old Trail Sch., Barberton Citizens Hosp., Medina County Arts Coun.; treas. Friends of Metro Park; vestryman St. Paul's Episcopal Ch.; corp. bd. Cleve. Mus. of Art. Mem. Bluecoats, Navy League (pres. Akron coun. 1972-73), Young Pres. Orgn., Portage Country Club (bd. dirs.), Mayflower Club, Sawgrass Club (Fla.) Farmington Club (Charlottesville, Va.), Rotary (trustee Akron Club 1974-75), Chi Psi. Home: 721 Delaware Ave Akron OH 44303-1303 Office: PO Box 928 910 Lake Rd Medina OH 44256-2453

SMITH, RITA SUE, administrator; b. Winter Haven, Fla., Apr. 19, 1954; d. Vernon Harris and Sarah Olive (Williams) S. AA, Polk C.C., 1974; BS in Psychology, Mich. State U., 1976. Childcare worker Wallace Village for Children, Broomfield, Colo., 1980-81; counselor, program supr. Alternatives to Family Violence, Commerce City, Colo., 1981-84; counselor Ending Violence Effectivly, Denver, 1984-86; dir. Women in Crisis, Arvada, Colo., 1986-88; freelance television and film prodn. Ctrl. Fla., 1989-92; dir. Nat. Coalition Against Domestic Violence, Denver, 1992—. Co-author: (manual) Family Violence: The LEgal Response, 1987. Vol. Peace River Legal Spouse Abuse Shelter, Lakeland, Fla., 1989-91, Refuge House, Tallahassee, 1991-92, Adams County (Colo.) Rape Task Force, 1982. Democrat. Avocations: reading, biking, racquetball. Office: Nat Coalition Against Domestic Violence PO Box 18749 Denver CO 80218

SMITH, ROBERT BOULWARE, III, vascular surgeon, educator; b. Atlanta, June 15, 1933; s. Robert Boulware Jr. Smith and Mary Eva (Black) Fanning; m. Florence Chance Limehouse, Aug. 22, 1953; children: Victoria Joanne Smith Harkins, Robert Boulware IV, Brian Scott. MD, Emory U., 1957. Diplomate Am. Bd. Surgery, Am. Bd. Vascular Surgery. Intern in surgery Columbia Presbyn. Hosp., N.Y.C., 1957-58, resident in surgery, 1960-65; asst. prof. surgery Emory U. Sch. Medicine, Atlanta, 1966-69, assoc. prof., 1969-77, prof., 1977—, head gen. vascular surgery, 1984—; chief surg. svc. VA Med. Ctr., Atlanta, 1969-88; assoc. med. dir. Emory U. Hosp., 1993-95, med. dir., 1995—. Contbr. numerous articles, book chpts. to profl. publs.; co-editor: Trauma to the Thorax and Abdomen, 1969, Medical Management of the Surgical Patient, 1982, 3d edit., 1995. Capt. M.C., U.S. Army, 1958-60. Mem. ACS, Am. Surg. Assn., So. Assn. Vascular Surgery (sec. 1986-91, pres. 1992-93), Soc. Vascular Surgery, Assn. VA Surgeons (pres. 1983-84, Disting. Svc. award 1988), Ga. Surg. Soc. (pres. 1992-93), Atlanta Vascular Soc. (pres. 1986-88), Internat. Soc. for Cardiovasc. Surg., 1996-97. Phi Beta Kappa, Alpha Omega Alpha. Republican. United Methodist. Avocation: music, travel. Home: 2701 Coldwater Canyon Dr Tucker GA 30084-2358 Office: The Emory Clinic 1365 Clifton Rd NE Atlanta GA 30322-1013

SMITH, ROBERT BRUCE, college administrator; b. Phila., July 8, 1937; s. Graeme Conlee and Margaret Edith (Moote) S.; m. Eileen Adele Petznick, Aug. 21, 1959; children: Monica, Sara, Douglas. BS, Wheaton (Ill.) Coll., 1958; PhD, U. Calif., Berkeley, 1962. Asst. prof. chemistry U. Nev., Las Vegas, 1961-66, assoc. prof., chmn. dept., 1966-68, prof., dean Coll. Sci., Engring. and Math., 1968-81; v.p. acad. affairs Weber State U., Ogden, Utah, 1981-93, provost, 1993-96, asst. to pres., 1996—; mem. Nev. Bd. Examiners Basic Scis., 1970-75, Nev. Bd. Pharmacy, 1972-77; mem. Commn. on Colls., N.W. Assn. Schs. and Colls., 1985-94, chmn. Commn. on Colls., 1989-94; dir. Am. Assn. State Colls. and Univs. Acad. Leadership Inst., 1986-96. NSF fellow, 1959-61. Mem. AAAS, Am. Assn. Higher Edn., Sigma Xi, Phi Kappa Phi. Home: 2732 Polk Ave Ogden UT 84403-0431 Office: Weber State Univ Office of the Pres 1001 University Cir Ogden UT 84408-1001

SMITH, ROBERT BRUCE, former security consultant, retired army officer; b. De Quincy, La., Apr. 22, 1920; s. Malcolm Monard and Jewell (Perkins) S.; m. Gladys Opal Borel, Feb. 22, 1941; children: Susan, Richard, Bruce. B.J., La. State U., 1941; grad., Command and Gen. Staff Coll., 1951-52, Army War Coll., 1958-59. Commd. 2d lt. U.S. Army, 1941, advanced through grades to maj. gen., 1969; plans and ops. officer 83d Div. Arty., Europe, 1943-45; personnel officer Philippine-Ryukyus Command, Manila, 1947-49; prof. mil. sci. and tactics ROTC, Lanier High Sch., Macon, Ga., 1949-51; chief res. officers sect., procurement br. Dept. Army, 1952-55; chief troop info. Office Chief Info., Dept. Army, 1962-63, dep. chief info., 1968-69; comdg. officer 8th F.A. Bn., 25th Inf. Div., Hawaii, 1955-56; G-1 25th Inf. Div. and U.S. Army Hawaii, Hawaii, 1956-58; mem. staff, faculty Command and Gen. Staff Coll., Fort Leavenworth, Kans., 1959-62; chief Alt. Nat. Mil. Command Center, Fort Ritchie, Md., 1963-64; dep. dir. ops. Office Joint Chiefs of Staff, 1964-65; asst. div. comdr. 7th Inf. Div., Korea, 1965-66; dep. comdt. Army War Coll., Carlisle, Pa., 1966-68; comdg. gen. Ryukyus Islands, 1969-72, 6th U.S. Army, Presidio of San Francisco, 1972-73; ret. active duty, 1973; reporter, news editor Lake Charles (La.), 1946-47; region adminstrv. mgr. Burns Security Service, Oakland, Calif., 1974-76; ptnr. constrn. co. Napa, Calif., 1976-77, Burns Security Service, 1978-81; now ret.; dir. 1st Am. Title Co., Napa, Calif., 1988-92. Trustee Queen of Valley Hosp. Found., 1987-89; mem. Nat. coun. Boy Scouts Am., 1969-70; pres. Silverado Property Owners Assn., Inc., 1990-92. Decorated D.S.M. with oak leaf cluster, Legion of Merit with 2 oak leaf clusters, Bronze Star with oak leaf cluster; inducted into La. State U.'s Manship Sch. of Mass Communication Hall of Fame, 1996. Club: Silverado Country (Napa, Calif.). Home: 350 St Andrews Dr Napa CA 94558-1544

SMITH, ROBERT CLINTON, senator; b. Trenton, N.J., Mar. 30, 1941; s. Donald and Margaret (Eldridge) S.; m. Mary Jo Hutchinson, July 2, 1966; children: Jennifer L., Robert Clinton, Jason H. A.A., Trenton Jr. Coll., 1963; B.A., Lafayette Coll., 1965; postgrad., Long Beach State U., 1968-69. Tchr., realtor Wolfeboro, N.H., 1975-85; chmn. Gov. Wentworth Dist. Sch. Bd., 1978-84; mem. 99th-101st Congresses from 1st N.H. dist., 1985-90; U.S. Senator from New Hampshire, 1990—; mem. armed svcs., environ. and pub. works, govt. affairs, ethic com. With USN, 1965-67, Vietnam; with USNR, 1962-65, 67-69. Decorated campaign medal (Republic of Vietnam). Mem. VFW, Am. Legion, NRA, Theta Xi. Republican. Roman Catholic. Office: US Senate 303 Dirksen Senate Ofc Washington DC 20510*

SMITH, ROBERT EARL, space scientist; b. Indpls., Sept. 13, 1923; s. Harold Bennett and Bernice (McCaslin) S.; m. Elizabeth Lee Usak, Jan. 3, 1947 (dec. 1984); children: Stephanie Lee, Robert Michael, Cynthia Ann, Kelly Andrew; m. Lyla Lee Lewellen, July 1, 1988. B.S., Fla. State U., 1959, M.S., 1960; M.S., U. Mich., 1969, Ph.D., 1974. Enlisted U.S. Army Air Force, 1943-44; advanced through grades to maj. U.S. Air Force, 1955; airway traffic controller Berlin, Germany, 1945; staff weather reconnaissance officer 9th Air Force, 1956; ret., 1963; project scientist Atmospheric Cloud Physics Lab.; dep. chief atmospheric scis. div. NASA/Marshall Space Flight Ctr., Ala., 1963-86; sr. scientific cons. Univs. Space Rsch. Assn., Huntsville, Ala., 1986-87; sr. computer cons. Computer Scis. Corp., Huntsville, 1987-89; chief space sci. and applications div. FWG Assocs., Inc., Huntsville, 1989-92; NASA program mgr. Physitron, Inc., Huntsville, 1992-96; sr. computer scientist Computer Scis. Corp., Huntsville, 1996—. Mem. AIAA, Pi Mu Epsilon, Sigma Phi Epsilon. Home: 125 Westbury Dr SW Huntsville AL 35802-1619 Office: NASA/MSFC Huntsville AL 35812

SMITH, ROBERT EVERETT, lawyer; b. N.Y.C., Mar. 15, 1936; s. Arthur L. and Augusta (Cohen) S.; m. Emily Lucille Lehman, July 17, 1960; children: Amy, Karen, Victoria. BA, Dartmouth Coll., 1957; LLB, Harvard U., 1960. Bar: N.Y. 1960, U.S. Dist. Ct. (so. dist.) N.Y. 1962, U.S. Ct. Appeals (2d cir.) 1963, U.S. Supreme Ct. 1967, U.S. Dist. Ct. (ea. dist.) N.Y. 1969, U.S. Ct. Appeals (3d cir.) 1982, U.S. Ct. Appeals (9th cir.) 1988. Assoc. Paul, Weiss, Rifkind, Wharton & Garrison, N.Y.C., 1960-65; from assoc. to ptnr. Baar, Bennett & Fullen, N.Y.C., 1965-74; ptnr. Guggenheimer & Untermyer, N.Y.C., 1974-85; ptnr. Rosenman & Colin LLP, N.Y.C., 1985—, chmn., 1994—. With U.S. Army, 1961-64. Mem. ABA, N.Y. State Bar Assn., Assn. of Bar of City of N.Y., Fed. Bar Coun., N.Y. County Lawyers Assn., Am. Arbitration Assn. (nat. panel arbitrators), The Am. Law Inst. Office: Rosenman & Colin 575 Madison Ave New York NY 10022-2511

SMITH, ROBERT F. (BOB SMITH), rancher, congressman; b. Portland, Oreg., June 16, 1931; m. Kaye Tomlinson; children: Christopher, Matthew, Tiffany. BA in Bus. Adminstrn. and Econs., Willamette U., 1953. Mem. Oreg. Ho. of Reps., 1960-73, spkr., 1969-73; mem. Oreg. State Senate, 1973-82, leader republican caucus, 1977-83; mem. 98th-105th Congresses from 2d dist. Oreg., 1983-94; pres. Smith West Co., Portland, 1995-96; dir. First State Bank Oreg., Key Bank; dir. exch. bd. Farmers Ins.; dir. bd. trustee Willamette U. Named one of Harry County, Oreg.'s Leading Citizens, 1957, one of Oreg.'s Outstanding Young Men, 1961. Republican. Office: 843 E Main St Ste 400 Medford OR 97504-7137

SMITH, ROBERT F., JR., civil engineer; b. Oneida, N.Y., Apr. 17, 1949; s. Robert F. and Lucy (Rice) S.; m. Lane K. McDonald, Nov. 21, 1984 (div. 1989); children: Sean Michael, Kevin Robert. BCE, Clarkson U., 1971. Registered profl. engr., N.Y., Ky. Asst. city engr. City of Oneida, 1971-78; chief stormwater mgmt. engr. Met. Sewer Dist., Louisville, 1978—. V.p. United Way, Oneida, 1976-77. Named Ky. Col., 1982. Mem. Nat. Soc. Profl. Engrs. (southeast region v.p. 1996—, chmn. profl. engrs. in govt., 1993-94), Ky. Soc. Profl. Engrs. (v.p. 1989-91, D.V. Terrell award 1990, Disting. Engr. 1983, 88), ASCE (chpt. pres. 1984, Zone II Govt. Civil Engr. of Yr. 1989), Am. Pub. Works Assn. Democrat. Roman Catholic. Achievements include development of stormwater utility for city of Louisville and Jefferson County, Kentucky. Office: Met Sewer Dist 700 W Liberty St Louisville KY 40203-1911

SMITH, ROBERT FRANCIS, psychologist, consultant, investment advisor; b. Independence, Mo., May 4, 1943; s. Ernest L. and Grace Evelyn (Buck) S.; m. Susan Marie Quanty, Sept. 3, 1976; children: Justin Quanty, Natalie Christine. BA, U. Mo., Kans. City, 1973, MA, 1976; PhD, U. Kans., 1984. Registered investment advisor. Assoc. field svc. engr. Diamond Power Speciality Corp., Lancaster, Ohio, 1968-71; rsch. assoc. Kans. U. Med. Ctr. Otolaryn. Dept., Kansas City, Kans., 1973-78; rsch. psychologist VA Behavioral Radiology Labs., Kans. City, Mo., 1978-95; chmn. subcom. working group on biorhythms for C95-1-IV, Am. Nat. Stds. Inst., Washington, 1983-91; cons. Midwest Rsch. Inst., Kansas City, Mo., 1982—, West Assocs. Energy Task Force, Rosemead, Calif., 1984-86; guest speaker NAS Workshop, Washington, 1985. Contbr. articles to profl. jours. Served in USN, 1962-68. Mem. Psi Chi. Avocation: tennis. Home: 9351 E 60th Ter Raytown MO 64133-3803

SMITH, ROBERT FREEMAN, history educator; b. Little Rock, May 13, 1930; s. Robert Freeman and Emma Martha Gottlieb (Buerkle) S.; m. Alberta Vester, Feb. 1, 1950 (dec. 1985); children: Robin Ann, Robert Freeman III; m. Charlotte Ann Coleman, Sept. 9, 1985. BA, U. Ark., 1951, MA, 1952; PhD, U. Wis., Madison, 1958. Instr. U. Ark., Fayetteville, 1953; asst. prof. Tex. Luth. Coll., Seguin, 1958-62; assoc. prof. U. R.I., Kingston, 1962-66, U. Conn., Storrs, 1966-69; prof. history U. Toledo, 1969-86, disting. univ. prof., 1986—; vis. prof. U. Wis., Madison, 1966-67. Author: The United States and Cuba: Business and Diplomacy 1917-1960, 1961 (Tex. Writers' Roundup award 1961), What Happened in Cuba: A Documentary History of U.S.-Cuban Relations, 1963, The United States and Revolutionary Nationalism in Mexico, 1916-1932, 1973 (Ohio Acad. History award 1973), The Era of Caribbean Intervention, 1890-1930, 1981, The Era of Good Neighbors, Cold Warriors, and Hairshirts, 1930-82, 1983, The Caribbean World and the United States: Mixing Rum & Coca-Cola, 1994; contbr. to numerous publs. Col. 7th Hist. Detachment, Ohio Mil. Res. 1st lt. U.S. Army, 1953-55. Knapp fellow in history U. Wis., 1957; Tom L. Evans rsch. fellow Harry S. Truman Libr., Independence, Mo., 1976-77, Mexican Ministry Fgn. Rels. fellow, 1991-92. Mem. Soc. Historians of Am. Fgn. Rels., Soc. Mil. History, U.S. Naval Inst., Ohio Acad. History, So. Hist. Assn., Orgn. Am. Historians, Assn. U.S. Army, State Guard Assn. of U.S., Am. Legion, Masons, Scottish Rite, Shriners, Phi Beta Kappa, Phi Alpha Theta. Episcopalian. Avocation: photography. Home: 4110 Dunkirk Rd Toledo OH 43606-2217 Office: U Toledo Dept History Toledo OH 43606

SMITH, ROBERT G. (BOB SMITH), lawyer, assemblyman, educator; b. Scranton, Pa., Mar. 25, 1947; s. Philip and Ruth (Delmar) S.; m. Ellen Theresa Foster, 1968; children: Karen Elizabeth, Lisa. BA in History, U. Scranton, 1969, MS in Chemistry, 1970; MS in Environ. Sci., Rutgers U., 1973; JD, Seton Hall U., 1981. Bar: N.J. 1981. Sci. tchr. Lourdesmont High Sch., Clark Summit, Pa., 1968-70; environ. health sci. curriculum coordinator Middlesex County Coll., Edison, N.J., 1972-73, adminstrv. asst. to dean sci., 1974-77, instr., 1970-74, asst. prof., 1974-76, assoc. prof., 1976-79, prof. chemistry and environmental sci., 1979-86; law clk. N.J. Dept. Environ. Protection, Trenton, 1980; prin., pvt. practice law Bob Smith and Assocs., Piscataway, N.J., 1981—; zoning bd. atty. City of New Brunswick, N.J., 1993—. Mayor of Piscataway Twp., 1981-86; N.J. assemblyman N.J. 17th Legis. Dist., 1986—, mem. appropriations com. and environ. quality com., assembly select com. on ocean pollution, 1988, assembly energy and hazardous waste com. policy and rules, 1994; parliamentarian Assembly Dem. caucus, 1988-90, chmn. task force on environment, 1987; chmn. Piscataway Dem. Orgn., 1981-90; counsel N.J. State Dem. Platform Com., 1987, 89; chmn. Middlesex County Dem. Orgn., 1991-92; Assembly Dem. Dep. Minority Leader, 1993-95; councilman-at-large Piscataway Twp., 1977-80, pres. council, 1979, v.p., 1978; mem. Middlesex County Transp. Coordinating Com., 1980-86; chmn. Piscataway Environ. Commn., 1971-75; mem. Piscataway Planning Bd., 1981-86, sec., 1975, chmn., 1976; bd. dirs. N.J. Conf. Mayors, 1984-86; mem. tech. adv. com. air pollution Middlesex County Planning Bd., 1973-74; mem. Greenbrook Basin com. Area 208 Mgmt. Planning Program, 1975-76; mem. commr.'s adv. com. N.J. Dept. Environ. Protection, 1972-86; mem. Joyce Kilmer dist. Thomas A. Edison council Boy Scouts Am., 1983-86. Recipient Disting. Citizen award Piscataway Jewish Congregation B'nai Shalom, 1982; named Legis. of Yr. Eden Inst., 1990, Environ Legislator of Yr., N.J. Environ. Fedn.; U. Scranton Presdl. scholar, 1965-69. Mem. Middlesex County Bar Assn. Roman Catholic. Contbg. author Jour. of Air Pollution Control Assn., 1976; contbg. author; Environmental Health Science, 1975; co-editor: New Jersey State Wastewater Treatment Operations Manual, 1979. Office: 216 Stelton Rd Piscataway NJ 08854-3284 also: 44 Stelton Rd Piscataway NJ 08854-2600

SMITH, ROBERT G., lawyer; b. Washington, Oct. 4, 1943. BA, Johns Hopkins U., 1965; LLB, Harvard U., 1968. Bar: Md. 1969. Ptnr. Venable, Baetjer and Howard, Balt. Mem. ABA, Md. Bar Assn., Bar Assn. Balt. City. Office: Venable Baetjer and Howard 1800 Merc Bank & Trust Bldg 2 Hopkins Plz Baltimore MD 21201-2930

SMITH, ROBERT G., JR., public official, retired hotel executive; b. Harrisburg, Pa., July 22, 1932; s. Robert Grant Sr. and Helen C. (Reitz) S.; m. Pamela Ann Pasquariello-Epstein, June 8, 1978 (dec. 1985); stepchildren: Rosalind Ann Giest, Tara Helene Epstein. Attended, U.S. Army Officer's Candidate Sch., 1950-53. Owner Bob Smith Luncheonette, Harrisburg, Pa., 1953-54; pres., chmn. Hook's Diner, Inc., Allentown, Pa., 1954-67, Top of the Mall, Inc., Whitehall, Pa., 1967-71, Sheraton Inn, Inc., Allentown, 1971-83. Chmn. Allentown Housing Rev. Bd., 1964-78, Pa. Ho. of Reps. Workman Compensation Com., 1995—, Allentown Housing Authority; v.p. Allentown City Coun., 1976-77; treas. City of Allentown, 1978-81, Rep. nominee for mayor, 1981; commr., chmn. Allentown Housing Authority, 1994—; active Mayor's Advancement Team, Allentown, 1993—; Rep. nominee for Pa. Senate, 1994. Mem. Pa. Soc., Rotary Club od Allentown, West Bethlehem Club, Sertoma Club, Zembo Temple, Harrisburg Consistory, Robert Burns Lodge, Tall Cedars of Lebanon, No. Rep. Club, Bethlehem Club, Northend Rep. Club, Ye Host's Square Club. Lutheran. Home: 230 N St George St Allentown PA 18104-5615

SMITH, ROBERT HOUSTON, archeologist, humanities and religious studies educator; b. McAlester, Okla., Feb. 13, 1931; s. Vaughn Hubert and Bobbie Louise (Nelson) S.; m. Geraldine Warshaw, Jan. 26, 1969; 1 child, Vanessa Eleanor. BA, U. Tulsa, 1952; BD, Yale U., 1955, PhD, 1960. Instr. Coll. Wooster, Ohio, 1960-62, asst. prof., 1962-65, assoc. prof., 1965-70, prof., 1970-72, Fox prof. religious studies, 1979-93, chmn. dept., 1981-93, chmn. archaeology program, 1979-93; Grosvenor lectr. Nat. Geographic Soc., Washington, 1985; dir. Coll. Wooster Archeol. Expdn. to Pella, Jordan, 1966-85; cons. on devel. bus. and profl. codes of ethics. Author: Excavations at Khirbet Kufin, 1962, Pella of the Decapolis, vol. 1, 1973, vol. 2, 1989, Patches of Godlight: The Pattern of Thought of C.S. Lewis, 1986, The Passmores in America: A Quaker Family Through Six Generations, 1992; co-author: Pella in Jordan 1, 1982, Pella in Jordan 2, 1992; lectr. Digging Up the Past, NBC-TV Edn. Exchange series, 1968; contbr. articles to profl. jours. Trustee Am. Ctr. Oriental Research, Amman, Jordan, 1979-85. NEH grantee, 1979-81, Nat. Geographic Soc. grantee, 1979-85; Yale U. fellow Am. Sch. Oriental Research, 1958-59. Mem. Am. Schs. Oriental Research, Soc. Profl. Archaeologists, Soc. Biblical Lit., Archaeological Inst. Am. Democrat. Presbyterian. Avocation: landscape painting. Home: 2900 Tice Creek Dr Walnut Creek CA 94595-3214

SMITH, ROBERT HUGH, engineering construction company executive; b. Wichita, Kans., Dec. 29, 1936; s. Richard Lyon and E. Eileen (O'Neal) S.; m. Melinda Louise Fitch, Sept. 26, 1959 (div. Dec. 1969); children: Robert Blake, Thomas Hugh; m. Margaret Anne Moseley, Dec. 11, 1977; 1 child, Steven Richard. BS, Kans. State U., 1959; MS, U. Kansas, 1964, PhD, 1970. Sr. process engr. FMC Corp., Lawrence, Kans., 1959-64; rsch. engr. Phillips Petroleum Co., Bartleville, Okla., 1964-66; group leader Standard Oil of Ohio, Warrenville Heights, Ohio, 1966-67; sr. rsch. assoc., group leader Atlantic Richfield, Plano, Tex., 1970-80; regional mgr., sr. mgr., sales mgr. Fluor Daniel, Houston and Marlton, N.J., 1980-90; v.p., gen. mgr. Badger Design & Construction, Tampa, Fla., 1990-93; exec. v.p., COO The Pritchard Corp., Overland Park, Kans., 1993—. Patentee in the field; contbr. to profl. jours. Adv. bd. dept. chem. engring U. Kans., Lawrence, 1993—. Mem. AIChE (chmn., vice chmn., sec. 1962—, Engr. of Yr. award Dallas 1980, exec. bd. Engr. and Cons. Contracting divsn.), Phi Lambda Upsilon, Sigma Xi. Avocations: tennis, sailing, skiing, reading.

SMITH, ROBERT JOHN, anthropology educator; b. Essex, Mo., June 27, 1927; s. Will Dan and Fern (Jones) S.; m. Kazuko Sasaki, Aug. 22, 1955. B.A. summa cum laude, U. Minn., 1949; M.A., Cornell U., 1951, Ph.D., 1953. Engaged in cultural anthrop. field research N.S., Can., 1950, Japan, 1951-52, 55, 57-58, Brazil, 1966-67; mem. faculty Cornell U., 1953—, prof. anthropology, 1963-74, Goldwin Smith prof. anthropology, 1974-97, prof. emeritus, 1997—, chmn. dept. Asian studies, 1961-66, chmn. dept. antropology, 1967-71, 76-82, prof. emeritus, 1997—; vis. prof. anthropology U. Ariz., 1971, U. Hawaii, 1978, Nat. Mus. Ethnology, Osaka, Japan, 1982. Author: (with Cornell) Two Japanese Villages, 1956, (with Cornell, Saito and Maeyama) Japanese and Their Descendants in Brazil, 1967; editor: (with Beardsley) Japanese Culture: Its Development and Characteristics, 1962, Social Organization and the Applications of Anthropology, 1974, Ancestor Worship in Contemporary Japan, 1974, Kurusu: The Price of Progress in a Japanese Village, 1951-75, 1978, (with Wiswell) Women of Suye Mura, 1982, Japanese Society: Tradition, Self and the Social Order, 1983, (with K. Smith) Diary of a Japanese Innkeeper's Daughter, 1984. Served with AUS, 1944-46. Tng. grantee Social Sci. Rsch. Coun., Japan, 1951-52; recipient Individual Exch. award to Japan Inst. Internat. Edn., 1957-58; Fulbright lectr. Tokyo Met. U., 1962-63; NSF rsch. grantee, 1965-67; Japan Found. grantee, 1979; awarded Order of the Rising Sun, Govt. of Japan, 1993. Fellow Am. Anthrop. Assn., Assn. for Asian Studies (v.p. 1987-88, pres. 1988-89), Soc. Applied Anthropology (editor jour. Human Orgn. 1961-66). Home: 107 Northview Rd Ithaca NY 14850-6039 Office: Cornell U Dept Anthropology Ithaca NY 14853

SMITH, ROBERT JOHN, JR., real estate executive; b. Rochester, N.Y., June 1, 1951; s. Robert and Irene (Frisbie) S.; m. Sherry L. Silberman, July 5, 1981; 1 child, Jordan. Student, Ohio U., 1969-73. CPA, Ohio. Gen. mgr. Televac, Inc., Athens, 1975—; CFO Practice Mgmt., Inc. (PMI), Cleve., 1988—. Bd. dirs. Cleve. Sports Stars Found., 1992—. Mem. AICPA. Office: Televac Inc PO Box 10 Athens OH 45701-0010

SMITH, ROBERT KEITH, exchange program associate; b. Ashland, Ky., Dec. 30, 1955; s. Robert French and Neva Lee (Stapleton) S.; m. Rebecca Slone, July 30, 1994; children: Jonathan Wesley, Robert Charles. BS in Police Adminstrn., Ea. Ky. U., 1977; MS in Sys. Mgmt., U. So. Calif., 1983. Commd. 2d lt., 1977; advanced through grades to lt. col. U.S. Army, 1989; internat. def. cons. TRW Sys. Overseas, Inc., Saudi Arabia, 1993-95; project mgr. Columbia Gas. Transmission, Inc., Charleston, W.Va., 1995—. With U.S. Army Res., 1993—. Mem. Am. Mgmt. Assn., Soc. Logistics Engrs., Inst. Indsl. Engrs., Project Mgmt. Inst. Republican. Baptist. Avocations: music, hunting, computing. Home: 13615 Bent Tree Cir Apt 102 Centreville VA 20121 Office: Columbia Gas Transmission PO Box 10146 Fairfax VA 20230

SMITH, ROBERT KIMMEL, author; b. Bklyn., July 31, 1930; s. Theodore and Sally (Kimmel) S.; m. Claire Medney, Sept. 4, 1954; children: Heidi Medney, Roger Kimmel. Student, CUNY Bklyn. Coll., 1947-48. Copywriter Doyle, Dane, Bernbach Advt., N.Y.C., 1957-61; copy chief Grey Advt., N.Y.C., 1961-63; group head, creative dir. West, Weir, Bartel Advt., N.Y.C., 1964-67; co-owner, creative dir. Boyce, Smith & Toback Advt., N.Y.C., 1967-69; author, playwright Bklyn., 1970—. Author: (novels) Ransom, 1971, Sadie Shapiro's Knitting Book, 1973, Sadie Shapiro in Miami, 1977, Sadie Shapiro, Matchmaker, 1980, Jane's House, 1982; (juveniles) Chocolate Fever, 1972, Jelly Belly, 1981, The War With Grandpa, 1984, Mostly Michael, 1987, Bobby Baseball, 1989, The Squeaky Wheel, 1990; (plays) A Little Singing, A Little Dancing, 1971, A Little Dancing, 1974. Bd. dirs. Prospect Pk. South Assn., Bklyn., 1976-86, pres., 1984-86. With U.S. Army, 1951-53. Recipient Best Book award ALA, 1983, Nene prize Hawaii Libr. Assn., 1984, Children's Book award S.C. Libr., 1984, 86, Tenn. Libr. Assn., 1988, Ga. Libr. Assn., 1989, Ala. Libr. Assn., 1989, Dorothy Canfield Fisher award Vt. Libr. Assn., 1986, Mark Twain award Mo. Libr. Assn., 1987, Golden Sower award Nebr. Libr. Assn., 1987, William Allen White Young Reader's Choice award Kans. Libr. Assn., 1987, Pacific N.W. Libr. Assn., 1987, Young Readers' medal Calif. Libr. Assn., 1990, Knickerbocker award N.Y. State Libr. Assn., 1995. Mem. Authors Guild, Writers Guild, Soc. Children's Book Writers, Eugene O'Neill Theater. Avocations: gardening, reading, cooking, tennis. Address: care Harold Ober Assocs 425 Madison Ave New York NY 10017-1110

SMITH, ROBERT L., principal. Prin. Thomson (Ga.) High Sch. Recipient Blue Ribbon award U.S. Dept. Edn., 1990-91. Office: Thomson High Sch PO Box 1077 Thomson GA 30824-1077

SMITH, ROBERT L., medical research administrator; b. N.Y.C., Mar. 29, 1941; m. Carolee Smith, 1968; children: Jana, Shayna, Marni. BEE, CCNY, 1962; MSEE, NYU, 1966; PhD in Neurosci., Syracuse U., 1973. Devel. engr. Wheeler Lab., Great Neck, N.Y., 1962-64; lectr. elec. engring. CCNY, 1964-66; instr. elec. engring. Syracuse U., 1970-74, from asst. prof. to assoc. prof. sensory rsch., 1974-85, prof. neurosci., 1985—, dir. Inst. Sensory Rsch., 1993—. Assoc. editor Jour. Acoustical Soc. Am., 1986-89. NIH fellow, 1979-84. Fellow Acoustical Soc. Am.; mem. Assn. Rsch. Otolaryngology, Soc. Neurosci., Sigma Xi. Achievements include research in neurophysiology and neural coding in the auditory nervous system; single unit recording from the cochiea, auditory nerve and cochlear nucleus; mathematical modeling of the results and systems analysis of the auditory system; biological engineering. Office: Syracuse U Inst for Sensory Rsch MerrillLn Syracuse NY 13244-5290*

SMITH, ROBERT LEE, agriculturalist; b. Ottawa, Ill., Apr. 2, 1921; s. Charles Emanuel and Helen Beatrice (Cray) S.; m. Lillian Pearl Francisco, 1947 (div. 1969); children: Charles, Jerome (dec.), Rodger, Lawrence, Eileen, Arlene. PhD in Humane Sci. (hon.), Cleo U., 1990. Elder, tchr. Meth. Ch., El Paso, Ill., 1955-67; dir. rsch. Ill. Farmers Union, Springfield, 1963-68; radio officer, pilot search and rescue unit Civil Air Patrol, Woodford County, 1964-69; lectr. U. Ill., Champaign, 1989-90. Contbr. articles to profl. jours. Dir. Ill. Youth Corps, No. Ill., 1965-68; Dem. candidate for state rep. Capt. USAF, 1944-46; with USAFR, 1955-68. Mem. Mensa (life, pres. cen. Ill. chpt. 1980-85, editor 1981-84), Moose. Avocations: writing, bridge, dancing, hiking, reading. Home: 1120 Northwood Dr N Champaign IL 61821-2116

SMITH, ROBERT LONDON, commissioner, retired air force officer, political scientist, educator; b. Alexandria, La., Oct. 13, 1919; s. Daniel Charleston and Lillie (Roberts) S.; m. Jewel Busch, Feb. 5, 1949; children: Jewel Diane, Robert London, Karl Busch. B.A., Coll. St. Joseph, 1954; M.A., U. Okla., 1955; Ph.D., Am. U., 1964. Commd. 2d lt. USAAF, 1941; advanced through grades to lt. col. USAF, 1961; various assignments in aircraft engring., command and logistics, 1941-60; rsch. logistics Hdqs. Office Aerospace Rsch., 1960-63; project sci., adminstr. postdoctoral rsch. program, asst. dir. NAS, Hdqs. Office Sci. Rsch., 1963-65; ret., 1965; asso. prof. polit. sci., head dept. eve. classes and corr. study U. Alaska, College, 1966-68, dean Coll. Bus., Econs. and Govt., 1968-70, prof., head dept. polit. sci., 1966-84, prof. emeritus, 1984—; commr. Alaska Dept. Health and Social Services, 1983—; mem. govt. panels and planning groups; dir. Arctic 1st Fed. Savs. & Loan Assn.; corporator Mt. McKinley Mut. Savs. Bank. Author: (with others) Squadron Adminstration, 1951; also publs. on nat. security and nat. def.; Contbr. to: (with others) The United Nations Peace University, 1965. Committeeman Western region Boy Scouts Am., 1968-73; mem. exec. bd. Midnight Sun council, 1973-74, committeeman-at-large nat. council, 1968—; mem. Alaska Gov.'s Employment Commn.; pres. United Service Orgn. Council, Fairbanks, Alaska; mem. active corps execs. SBA. Recipient Silver Beaver award Boy Scouts Am.; named Outstanding Prof. U. Alaska, 1975. Mem. Nat. Acad. Econs. and Polit. Sci., AAAS, Air Force Hist. Found., Nat. Inst. Social and Behavioral Scis., Nat. Inst. U.S. in World Affairs, Am. Polit. Sci. Assn., Assn. U.S. Army (bd. dirs. Polar Bear chpt.), Alaska C. of C. (edn. com.), Pi Gamma Mu, Pi Sigma Alpha. Roman Catholic. Club: Rotary. Home: Smithhaven 100 Goldizen Ave Fairbanks AK 99709-3634 also: Smithawaii Nani Kai Hale 73 N Kihei Rd Apt 607 Kihei HI 96753-8827 also: Costa Vida Unit #920-921, KM 4 456 Carr Apdo Postal 186, Puerto Vallarta Jalisco, Mexico

SMITH, ROBERT LOUIS, construction company executive; b. Parkersburg, W.Va., Apr. 19, 1922; s. Everett Clerc and Janet (Morrison) S.; m. June Irene Odbert, Oct. 25, 1948; children: Peter Clerc, Morrison James, Edna Louise. B.S. in Civil Engring., Lehigh U., 1944. Design engr. Chrysler Corp., 1944-46; engr. Harrison Constrn. Co., Charleston, W.Va., 1946-47; sr. engr. Creole Petroleum Co., Las Piedras, Venezuela, 1947-55; v.p. Rea Constrn. Co., Charlotte, N.C., 1955-64; exec. v.p. Warren Bros. Co., Cambridge, Mass., 1964-68; pres. Warren Bros. Co., 1968-79; also dir.; sr. v.p. Ashland Oil, Inc., Ky., 1974-79; pres. Robert L. Smith & Assos., Lexington, 1979—; pres., dir. Tree Farm Devel. Corp., Cambridge, 1979—; dir. Panastalto (S.A.), Wilder Constrn. Co., Inc., J.H. Shears Sons, Inc. Fellow ASCE; mem. Nat. Asphalt Pavement Assn. (dir.), Phi Beta Kappa, Tau Beta Pi, Sigma Chi. Republican. Unitarian. Home and Office: 1010 Waltham St Apt A 412 Lexington MA 02173-8044

SMITH, ROBERT LUTHER, management educator; b. Kutztown, Pa., Feb. 18, 1927; s. Paul Luther and Esther Florence (Schwoyer) S.; m. Canda Eure Banks, Aug. 18, 1951; children: Kimberley Smith Kidd, Valerie Smith Eudy, Alexandra. BS, U.S. Naval Acad., 1949; MSA, George Washington U., 1975, DBA, 1984. Commd. USN, 1949-72, advanced through grades to comdr.; commanding officer USS Grouper, 1962-65; engr. and repair officer U.S. Submarine Base, Groton, Conn., 1965-67; supt. of test Portsmouth Naval Shipyard, Portsmouth, N.H., 1967-70; asst. project mgr. Naval Systems Submarine Acquisition, Washington, 1970-72; project mgr. EG&G, Washington Analytical, Rockville, Md., 1972-80; pres. Interface Resources Ltd., Alexandria, Va., 1980—; lectr. George Mason U., Fairfax, Va., 1981-84; assoc prof. Coll. of Notre Dame of Md., Balt., 1984—; seminar leader various pvt. cos., 1980-85; faculty Dealer Mgmt. Inst., Columbus, Ohio, 1981-83; cons. in field. Contbr. articles to bus. publs. Sr. warden St. Paul's Episcopal Ch., Alexandria, 1980-81; mem. Alexandria Health Svcs., 1983—. Mem. ASTD, Assn. Quality and Participation, Acad. Mgmt., Ea. Acad. Mgmt., Organl. Behavior Tchg. Soc., Kiwanis Alexandria (pres. 1985-86, del. to internat. 1985), Masons, Beta Gamma Sigma. Republican. Home: 1102 Bayliss Dr Alexandria VA 22302-3506 Office: Coll Notre Dame Md 4701 N Charles St Baltimore MD 21210-2404

SMITH, ROBERT MASON, university dean; b. Fort Sill, Okla., May 5, 1945; s. Arnold Mason and Lillyan (Scott) S.; m. Ramona Lynne Stukey, June 15, 1968; children: David, Angela. BA, Wichita State U., 1967; MA, Ohio U., 1968; PhD, Temple U., 1976. Debate coach Princeton U. (N.J.), 1971-73, Wichita (Kans.) State U., 1973-87, assoc. dean Coll. Liberal Arts and Scis., 1977-87; dean coll. arts and scis. U. Tenn., Martin, 1987—, dir. Gov. Sch. for Humanities, 1996spl. asst. U.S. Dept. HHS, Washington, 1980-81; cons. in field; chmn. corp. communication bd. Ea. Airlines, Miami, Fla., 1984-86. Mem. State Behavorial Sci. Regulatory Bd., Topeka, 1985-87; trustee Leadership Kans., Topeka, 1986-87; founder, bd. dirs. WestStar Regional Tenn. Leadership Program, 1989—. Recipient Excellence in Tchg. award Coun. for Advancement and Support of Edn., 1984, Crystal Apple award for outstanding tchg., 1995, Nat. Assn. for Cmty. Leadership award for disting. leadership, 1995, HHS fellow, 1980. Mem. Kans. Speech Communication Assn. (Outstanding Coll. Speech Tchr. award 1977, pres. 1978), Assn. for Communication Adminstrn. (pres. 1988), Tenn. Coun. Colls. Arts & Scis. (pres. 1989-90), Tenn. Speech Comm. Assn. (pres. 1993-94), Phi Kappa Phi, Phi Eta Sigma, Beta Theta Pi, Phi Theta Kappa, Rotary. Baptist. Home: 168 Weldon Dr Martin TN 38237-1322 Office: U Tenn Coll Arts & Scis Martin TN 38238

SMITH, ROBERT MCNEIL, university dean; b. Balt., Jan. 14, 1932; s. Walter H. and Clara (Goodwin) S.; m. Bette A. Smith, June 15, 1961; children: David, Andrew, Michele, Denise, Jonathan, Kristen. B.S., U. Md., 1957; M.Ed., U. Ill., 1958, Ed.D., 1962. Asso. prof., research asso. cleft palate research center Sch. Dentistry, U. Pitts., 1963-66; asso. prof. U. Del., 1966-67; prof. spl. edn. Pa. State U., 1967-78, asst. provost, 1974-78; dean Coll. Edn., Va. Poly. Inst. and State U., Blacksburg, 1978-92; cons. in field. Author books, monographs, articles in field, also chpts. in books. Served with AUS, 1953-55. Fellow Am. Council Edn., 1973, U.S. Office Edn., 1961; resident fellow U. Md., 1958. Fellow Am. Assn. Mental Deficiency; mem. Coun. Exceptional Children, Am. Cleft Palate Assn., AAAS, Nat. Assn. Accts., Am. Coll. Sports Medicine, Phi Delta Kappa, Kappa Delta Pi, Iota Lambda Sigma Psi. Home: 3336 Mcever Rd Blacksburg VA 24060-8710 Office: Va Tech 300 War Memorial Hall Blacksburg VA 24061

SMITH, ROBERT MICHAEL, lawyer; b. Boston, Nov. 4, 1940; s. Sydney and Minnie (Appel) S.; m. Catherine Kersey, Apr. 14, 1981 (dec. 1983). AB cum laude, Harvard Coll., 1962; diploma, Centro de Estudos de Espanol, Barcelona, 1963; MA in Internat. Affairs, Columbia U., 1964, MS in Journalism with high honors, 1965; JD, Yale U., 1975. Bar: Calif., N.Y., D.C., U.S. Supreme Ct. Intern in econ. devel. UN, Geneva, 1964; corres. Time Mag., N.Y.C., 1965-66, The N.Y. Times, Washington, 1968-72, 75-76; atty. Heller, Ehrman, White & McAuliffe, San Francisco, 1976-78; spl. asst. Office of Atty. Gen. of U.S., Washington, 1979-80; dir. Office Pub. Affairs U.S. Dept. Justice, Washington, 1979-80; mem. U.S. delegation Internat. Ct. of Justice, The Hague, 1980; asst. U.S. atty. No. Dist. Calif., San Francisco, 1981-82; counsel, sr. counsel to sr. litigation counsel Bank of Am. NT & SA, San Francisco, 1982-86; pvt. practice law San Francisco, 1988—; lectr. FBI Acad., Quantico, Va., 1980, Internat. Bankers Assn. Calif., 1994, Cmty. Bankers No. Calif., 1994, 95; judge Golden Medallion Broadcast Media awards State Bar of Calif., 1985; judge pro tem Mcpl. Ct. City and County of San Francisco, 1989—. Author: Alternative Dispute Resolution for Financial Institutions, 1995; bd. editors Yale Law Jour., 1974-75; editor Litigation, jour. ABA litigation sect., 1978-81; mem. editl. adv. bd. Bancroft-Whitney, 1991-94; contbr. articles to profl. jours. Bd. dirs. Neighborhood Legal Assistance Found., San Francisco, 1985-87, Nob Hill Assn., San Francisco, 1985-93; bd. dirs., fin. com. St. Francis Found., San Francisco, 1993-94. 1st lt. inf., USAR, 1965-71. Recipient UPI Award for Newswriting, 1958; Harvard Coll. scholar, 1958-62, Fulbright scholar, 1962-63; Columbia U. Internat. fellow, 1964-65. Mem. ABA (corp. counsel com. 1986-96, alternative dispute resolution sect. 1994-96), Assn. Atty. Mediators (v.p. No. Calif. chpt. 1995), State Bar of Calif. (pub. affairs com. 1982-85, litigation sect. 1990-96), Bar Assn. of San Francisco (bench-bar media com. 1985-96, alternative dispute resolution com. 1994-96), Assn. Bus. Trial Lawyers No. Calif., Assn. of Former U.S. Attys. No. Dist. Calif., Am. Arbitration Assn. (mem. comml. arbitration panel, No. Calif. adv. coun., mediator Am. Arbitration Ctr. for Mediation), Profl. Atty. Mediators, Cmty. Bds. of San Francisco (conciliator), German-Am. C. of C. West U.S., Harvard Club of San Francisco (bd. dirs. 1986-94, pres. 1992-94), Yale Club of San Francisco (bd. dirs. 1989-94), Soc. Profls. in Dispute Resolution (assoc. mem.), Columbia U. Alumni Club of No. Calif. (exec. com. 1978-92). Home: 1250 Washington St San Francisco CA 94108

SMITH, ROBERT MOORS, anesthesiologist; b. Winchester, Mass., Dec. 10, 1912; s. Francis E. and Elsie C. (Davis) S.; m. Margaret Louise Nash, Aug. 7, 1937; children: Jonathan E., Marcia A., Karen E. A.B., Dartmouth Coll., 1934; M.D., Harvard U., 1938. Diplomate: Am. Bd. Anesthesiology. Rotating intern Faulkner Hosp., Jamaica Plain, Mass., 1938-39; asst. in pathology Faulkner Hosp., 1939; intern in surgery Boston City Hosp., 1939-41; gen. practice medicine Cohasset, Mass., 1941-42; anesthesiologist Children's Hosp. Med. Center, Boston, 1946-81; dir. anesthesiology Children's Hosp. Med. Center, 1946-80, pres. staff, 1966-68; assoc. anesthesiologist Peter Bent Brigham Hosp., Boston, 1958-61; asso. anesthesiologist Boston Lying-In Hosp., 1964-70; instr. anesthesia Harvard Med. Sch., Boston, 1948-63; assoc. in anesthesia Harvard Med. Sch., 1955, asst. clin. prof. anesthesia, 1963-66, assoc. clin. prof., 1966-81, clin. prof. anesthesia, 1976-81, clin. prof. emeritus, 1981—; chief anesthesiology Kennedy Meml. Children's Hosp., 1981-88; anesthesiologist Franciscan Children's Hosp., 1988-94. Bd. dirs. Minuteman council Boy Scouts Am. Served to maj. U.S. Army, 1941-46. Recipient Disting. Svc. award Am. Soc. Anesthesiologists, 1988. Fellow Am. Coll. Anesthesiologists (gov. 1952-58); mem. AMA, Mass. Med. Soc., New Eng. Soc. Anethesiologists (pres. 1966), Mass. Soc. Anesthesiologists (pres. 1955, dir. 1965-68), New Eng. Pediatric Soc., Assn. Univ. Anesthesiologists, Am. Acad. Pediatrics (chmn. com. pediatric anesthesiology 1963-64, 76-77), Royal Acad. Surgeons (Ireland) (hon.), Pan Am. Med. Soc. Home: 4 Leslie Rd Winchester MA 01890-3123

SMITH, ROBERT NELSON, former government official, anesthesiologist; b. Toledo, Apr. 2, 1920; s. Robert Frederick and Amy Laura (Nelson) S.; children: Sandralyn, Sharon, Robert Nelson, Marilyn Anne, Marcia, Elizabeth. Student, U. Mich., 1938-39; BS, U.S. Mil. Acad., 1943; MS, MIT, 1945; MD, U. Nebr., 1952. Diplomate Am. Bd. Anesthesiologists. Commd. capt. USAAF, 1943, resigned, 1948; intern Toledo Hosp., Ohio, 1952-53; resident Toledo Hosp., 1954-57; anesthesiologist KFC Med. Corp., Toledo, 1954-76; asst. sec. def. for health affairs Washington, 1976-78; bd. dirs. Ohio Med. Indemnity Corp., Columbus., 1968-78; mem. anesthetic and life support drugs adv. com. FDA, Dept. HHS, 1986-90; mem. disability adv. coun. SSA, Dept. HHS, 1986-89; mem. Ohio Pub. Health Coun., 1976—. Chmn. State Health Planning Council, 1974-76; mem. Statewide Health Coordinating Council, until 1976; gov. apptd. mem. Ohio Pub. Health Council, 1997-2002. Recipient Sec. Def. medal for outstanding pub. service, 1977. Mem. AMA (Ho. of Dels. Resolution of Commendation), Ohio Med. Assn. (pres. 1970, commendation 1977), Am. Soc. Anesthesiology, Inverness Club, Rotary. Club: Inverness (Toledo). Home: 3424 Gallatin Rd Toledo OH 43606-2442

SMITH, ROBERT POWELL, former ambassador, former foundation executive; b. Joplin, Mo., Mar. 5, 1929; s. Powell Augusta and Estella (Farris) S.; m. Alice Irene Rountree, Aug. 22, 1953; children: Michael Bryan, Steven Powell, Karen Louise, David Robert. B.A., Tex. Christian U., 1954, M.A., 1955. Fgn. svc. officer Dept. State, 1955-81; press officer Washington, 1955; vice-consul Lahore, West Pakistan, 1956-58; 2d sec. Beirut, Lebanon, 1959-61; consul and prin. officer Enugu, Nigeria, 1962-65; officer-in-charge Ghanaian Affairs, 1966; officer-in-charge Nigerian Affairs, dep. dir. Office West African Affairs, 1967-69; dep. chief of mission, counselor of embassy Pretoria, South Africa, 1970-74; ambassador to Malta, 1974-76, Ghana, 1976-79, Liberia, 1979-81. Pres. Africa Wildlife Leadership Found., 1981-85. Served with USMCR, 1946-49, 50-52. Decorated Air medal.; recipient Meritorious Honor award State Dept., 1967. Mem. Am. Fgn. Service Assn. Baptist.

SMITH, ROBERT RUTHERFORD, university dean, communication educator; b. Buffalo, Nov. 18, 1933; s. Thomas Newlands and Mary Jane (Rutherford) S.; m. Suzanne Louise Stines, June 7, 1958; children: Eric Anthony, Gwendolyn Anne. B.A. cum laude, U. Buffalo, 1955; M.A., Ohio State U., 1956, Ph.D., 1963. Prof. communication, chmn. div. broadcasting and film Sch. Pub. Communication, Boston U., 1961-78; prof., dean. Sch. Communication and Theater Temple U., Phila., 1978-95; cons. Nat. Endowment for Arts, others. Author: poems Participations, 1972; criticism Beyond the Wasteland, 1980; editorTV Quar., 1971, Feedback, 1973-76; contbr. articles to profl. jours. Mem. communication com. Mass. Council Chs., 1971-76. Served with AUS, 1959-61. Mem. Broadcast Edn. Assn. (pres. 1984-85), Speech Communication Assn., Broadcase Pioneers (pres. Phila. 1985-86), Soc. Profl. Journalists (pres. 1983-85), Appalachian Mountain Club (Boston), Delmont Club (pres. 1992-94). Home: 6 Trout Farm Ln Plympton MA 02367-1617 Office: Temple U Sch Communication Philadelphia PA 19122

SMITH, ROBERT SAMUEL, banker, former agricultural finance educator; b. Laconia, N.H., June 16, 1920; s. Samuel W. and Winnifred (Page) S.; m. Mary Morgan, June 20, 1942; children: Patricia, Peggy, Morgan Scott, Sharon, Starlee. BS, Cornell U., 1942, MS, 1950, PhD, 1952. County agrl. agt. Livingston County, Mt. Morris, N.Y., 1942-44, Lewis County, Lowville, N.Y., 1944, Belknap County, Laconia, 1947-49; assoc. prof. edn. Cornell U., Ithaca, N.Y., 1952-54, assoc. prof. farm mgmt., 1954-58, prof. agrl. fin., 1958-77, W.T. Myers prof. agrl. fin., 1977-81; chmn. Tompkins County Trust Co., Ithaca, 1978-92, chmn. emeritus, 1992—; trustee Mut. of N.Y./MONY Fin. Svcs., N.Y.C., 1981-93, emeritus, 1993—; bd. dirs. Challenge Industries, Ithaca, N.Y.; advisor Ministry of Agr., Israel, 1960-61, Agrl. Devel. Bank of Iran, 1968. Contbr. numerous articles to profl. jours. Elder First Presbyn. Ch., Ithaca, 1970; bd. dirs. Am. Agriculturist Found., Ithaca, 1980, East Lawn Cemetery Assn., Ithaca, 1987, Hospicare Found., Ithaca. 1st lt. U.S. Army, 1944-47, ETO. Recipient Tax Edn. award IRS, Buffalo, 1973, Disting. Svc. citation N.Y. State Agrl. Soc., 1982. Mem. Country Club of Ithaca, City Club Ithaca, Phi Kappa Phi, Epsilon Sigma Phi. Republican. Avocations: golf, bridge. Home: 60 Wedgewood Dr Ithaca NY 14850-1063 Office: Tompkins County Trust Co The Commons Ithaca NY 14850

SMITH, ROBERT SELLERS, lawyer; b. Samson, Ala., July 31, 1931; s. Abb Jackson and Rose (Sellers) S.; m. June Claire West, Feb. 2, 1963; children-Robert Sellers, David West, Rosemary True, Adam Douglas. BS, U. Va., 1953, LLB, 1958, LLM, 1990. Bar: Ala. 1959. Asst. counsel spl. com. to investigate campaign expenditures U.S. Ho. of Reps., 1960; counsel U.S. Senate Labor and Pub. Welfare Com., 1961-63; ptnr. firm Smith, Huckaby & Graves (P.A.), Huntsville, 1963-85, Bradley, Arant, Rose & White, Huntsville, 1985-95; ptnr. Foley, Smith & Mahmood, Huntsville, 1995—; instr. econs., Am. econ. history U. Ala., 1963-64; Mem. industry adv. com., select com. small bus. U.S. Senate. Author: West's Tax Law Dictionary and 11 other books; mem. bd. editors Ala. Lawyer, 1994—. Pres. Madison County (Ala.) Legal Aid Soc., 1971-75; pres. North Ala. Estate Planning Council, 1974. Served with U.S. Navy, 1953-57. Mem. ABA, Am. Immigration Lawyers Assn., Internat. Bar Assn., Ala. Bar Assn., Huntsville-Madison County Bar Assn. (pres. 1988). Episcopalian. Home: 6004 Macon Ct SE Huntsville AL 35802-1932 Office: Foley Smith & Mahmood 200 W Court Sq Huntsville AL 35801

SMITH, ROBERT VICTOR, university administrator; b. Glendale, N.Y., Feb. 16, 1942; s. Robert Arthur and Marie Marlene (Florence) S. BS in Pharm. Sci., St. John's U., Jamaica, N.Y., 1963; MS in Pharm. Chemistry, U. Mich., 1964, PhD in Pharm. Chemistry, 1968. Asst. prof., then assoc. prof. U. Iowa, Iowa City, 1968-74; assoc. prof., asst. dir. U. Tex., Austin, 1974-77, area coordinator basic pharmaceutics, 1975-76, assoc. dir. Drug Dynamics Inst., 1977-78, dir. Drug Dynamics Inst., Coll. Pharmacy, 1979-85, James E. Bauerle Centennial prof. Coll. Pharmacy, 1983-85; prof., dean Coll. Pharmacy Wash. State U., Pullman, 1985-86, vice provost for research, dean Grad. Sch., 1987—; cons. E. R. Squibb, New Brunswick, N.J., 1979-82, Upjohn Co., Kalamazoo, Mich., 1982-85; external examiner U. Malaysia, Penang, 1981-82; mem. sci. adv. bd. Biodecision Labs., Pitts., 1985-86; Wash. Biotech. Found., 1989-90; mem. noms. com. Coun. Grad. Schs., Washington, 1990-91; accreditation evaluator Northwest Assn. Schs. and Colls., Seattle, 1991—; mem. exec. com. grad. deans African-Am. Inst., N.Y., 1992—. Author: Textbook of Biopharmaceutic Analysis, 1981, Graduate Research: A Guide for Students in the Sciences, 1990, Development and Management of University Research Groups, 1986. Bd. dirs. Wash. Tech. Ctr., 1990-92. Grantee NIH, 1974-83; fellow Acad. Pharm. Scis., 1981, Am. Assn. Pharm. Scientists, 1987; recipient Disting. Alumnus award Coll. Pharmacy U. Mich., 1990, Outstanding Svc. award Wash. State U., Grad. and Profl. Student Assn., 1993. Mem. Am. Assn. Colls. Pharmacy (chmn. research and grad. affairs com. 1983-84), U.S. Pharmacopeia (revision com. 1985-90), Acad. Pharm. Scis. (chmn., vice chmn. 1983-85, 90, Presdl. citation 1985), Wash. Rsch. Found. (bd. dirs. 1989—). Unitarian. Home: 862 Indian Hills Dr Moscow ID 83843 Office: Wash State Univ Grad Sch Pullman WA 99164

SMITH, ROBERT WALTER, food company executive; b. Chgo., Nov. 11, 1937; s. Ernest Gilmer and Anna (Reptik) S.; m. Audrey Mavis Segar, Apr. 20, 1962; children: Melissa Ann, Kathleen Diane, Michael Robert. BS, U. Ariz., 1963. Mgmt. trainee Fleming Cos. Inc., Houston, 1963-64, mgr. store planning, 1964-65; mgr. store planning Fleming Cos. Inc., Austin, 1965-66, Phila., 1966-72; dir. site selection Fleming Cos. Inc., Topeka, 1972-75, dir. store devel., 1975-83; v.p. store devel. Fleming Cos. Inc., Oklahoma City, 1983—, sr. v.p. retail devel., 1993—. Mem. Nat. Assn. Corp. Real Estate

Execs., Internat. Coun. Shopping Ctrs. Republican. Lutheran. Office: Fleming Cos Inc Box 26647 6301 Waterford Blvd Oklahoma City OK 73126

SMITH, ROBERT WILLIAM, former insurance company executive, lawyer; b. Catskill, N.Y., Apr. 2, 1923; s. Victor and Leda Leone (Cline) S.; m. Inez R. Iuzzolino, Jan. 31, 1976; children: Jeffrey, Timothy, Kathy. BS cum laude, Syracuse U., 1948; JD cum laude, Seton Hall U. Coll. of Law, 1987. Bar: N.J. 1987; accredited pers. exec.; CLU. With Prudential Ins. Co. Am., Newark, 1948-84; sr. v.p. Prudential Ins. Co. Am., 1973-84; mem. adv. council on mgmt. and personnel research (Conf. Bd.), 1975-83, chmn., 1977-78; now ret.; chmn. LOMA Personnel Council, 1971-72; bus. adminstr., City of Newark, 1970. Trustee Coll. of Ins., 1974-83; trustee State Theater of N.J., 1983-92, chmn., 1984-87; cons. Nat. Exec. Svc. Corps, 1988—. Served to 1st lt. USAAF, 1942-45. Decorated Air medal with 5 oak leaf clusters. Mem. Beta Gamma Sigma, Alpha Kappa Psi, Sigma Phi Epsilon. Home: 41 Woodbine Rd Florham Park NJ 07932-2647

SMITH, ROBERTA HAWKING, plant physiologist; b. Tulare, Calif., May 3, 1945; d. William Brevard and Freda Lois (Kessler) Hawkins; m. James Willie Smith Jr., Sept. 17, 1968; children: James Willie III, Cristine Lois. BS, U. Calif., Riverside, 1967, MS, 1968, PhD, 1970. Postdoctoral fellow dept. plant sci. Tex. A&M U., College Station, 1972-73, asst. prof. dept. plant sci., 1974-79, assoc. prof. dept. plant sci., 1979-85, prof. dept. soil and crop sci., 1985-89; Eugene Butler prof., 1989—; asst. prof. Sam Houston State U., Huntsville, Tex., 1973-74. Editl. bd. In Vitro Cellular and Dev. Biology, 1991-96, Jour. Plant Physiology, 1994—; assoc. editor Jour. Crop Sci., 1995—. Mem. Crop Sci. Soc. Am. (chmn. C-7 divsn. 1990-91), Internat. Crops Rsch. Inst. Semi-Arid Tropics (bd. govs. 1989-95), Faculty of Plant Physiology (chmn. 1987-89), Soc. In Vitro Biology (chmn. plant divsn. 1983-86, pres. 1994-96). Republican. Methodist. Avocations: Western horseback riding, gardening, reading. Home: RR 1 Box 701 Hearne TX 77859-9734 Office: Tex A&M Univ Dept Soil And Sci College Station TX 77843

SMITH, ROBIN DOYLE, judge; b. Oklahoma City, Jan. 23, 1957; s. Travis Ray and Juanita May (Stephens) S. BS, Okla. State U., 1979; JD, Tex. Tech. U., 1981. Bar: Tex. 1982. Asst. city atty. City of Midland, Tex., 1982-83, presiding judge, 1984—; sole practice Midland, 1983-84; bd. dirs. Tex. Mcpl. Cts. Assn., 2 v.p., 1989-90, pres.-elect, 1990-91, pres., 1991-92, bd. tng. ctr., Austin. Contbg. author Tex. Mcpl. Court Procedures Manual, 1988, Tex. Mcpl. Ct. Tng. Ctr. Newsletter, 1987; pub. Tex. Mcpl. Ct. Justice Ct. News, 1987—. Grad. Leadership Midland, 1987. Named one of five outstanding young Texans Tex. Jr. C. of C., 1994. Mem. ABA (del. to conf. of spl. ct. judges 1988, 89, 90, 91, 92, 93, 94, 95, exec. com. 1990—, vice chair 1994-95, chair 1996-97), State Bar Tex. (chmn. mcpl. judges sect. 1988-89, state bar coll. 1986—). Republican. Avocations: water sports, scuba diving, sailing, outdoor activities. Home: PO Box 585 Midland TX 79702-0585 Office: City of Midland Tex PO Box 1152 Midland TX 79702-1152

SMITH, RODGER FIELD, financial executive; b. Milw., Jan. 23, 1941; s. Millard Beale and Alice Catherine (Field) S.; m. Sarah Godfrey, June 19, 1964; children: Rodger F. Jr., Scott G., Reid W. BSChemE, U. Wis., 1964, MBA in Fin. with distinction, 1965. V.p. Allis Chalmers, Milw., 1966-76; ptnr. Greenwich (Conn.) Assocs., 1976—; trustee Harbor Funds, Toledo, 1987—; bd. dirs. Arlington Capital, London. Author articles and spkr. on investing pension funds. Fund raiser United Way, Milw., 1966-76. Mem. U. Wis. Alumni Assn. (nat. bd. dirs. 1994—), Wee Burn Country Club, Bascom Hill Soc., Tau Beta Pi (chmn. trust adv. com. 1986—), Beta Gamma Sigma. Avocations: travel, golf, tennis, coin collecting. Office: Greenwich Assocs Office Park Eight Greenwich CT 06830

SMITH, ROGER DEAN, pathologist; b. N.Y.C., Oct. 6, 1932; s. Joseph Leslie and Matilda (Feigelson) S.; m. Margaret Helen Smith, Apr. 24, 1957; children—Wade Russell, Craig Andrew, Douglas Dean, Roger Len. A.B., Cornell U., 1954; M.D., N.Y. Med. Coll., 1958. Diplomate Am. Bd. Pathology, Nat. Bd. Med. Examiners (flex test com. 1982-94, chmn. 1983-90, U.S. med. licensing exam. step 3 devel. com. 1992-94, med. licensing exam. step 3 com. 1994—). Asst. prof. dept. pathology U. Ill. Coll. Medicine, Chgo., 1966; cons. renal pathology Presbyn. St. Lukes Hosp., W. Side VA Hosp., Chgo., 1969; assoc. prof. dept. pathology U. Ill. Coll. Medicine, Chgo., 1970, dir. ind. study program, asst. dean, 1971-72; Mary M. Emery prof. U. Cin., 1972—, dir. dept. pathology, 1972-90, dir. autopsy svc., 1991—; dir. lab. services U. Cin. Hosp.; mem. test coms. Nat. Bd. Med. Examiners, 1976—. Contbr. research papers to profl. jours. Capt. M.C. U.S. Army, 1959-61. Recipient Hoektoen award Chgo. Pathology Soc.; USPHS pathology research fellow, 1962-66; Am. Cancer Soc. grantee, 1965-68; NIH grantee, 1968-72, 75-79. Mem. Am. Assn. Pathologists (chmn. 1972, pres. 1985-88), Coll. Am. Pathologists (chmn. edn. com. and manpower task force 1983-90), Internat. Acad. Pathology, Am. Assn. Clin. Pathologists, Armed Forces Inst. Pathology (sci. adv. bd. 1989-94). Home: 1319 Dillon Ave Cincinnati OH 45208-4208 Office: U Cin Coll Medicine Dept Pathology Cincinnati OH 45267-0529

SMITH, ROGER KEITH, insurance agent; b. Hazard, Ky., Mar. 31, 1962; s. Homer and Ruth (Hampton) S.; m. Carla Slone, June 5, 1982. AA in Bus. Mgmt., U. Ky., Hazard, 1981. CLU; ChFC; LUTCF; lic. life, health, property, casualty, Ky. Heavy equipment operator Golden Oak Mining Co., Isom, Ky., 1981-84; debit agt. Commonwealth Life Ins. Co., Louisville, 1984-90, spl. agent, then account rep., 1990-96; agt. Blair Ins. Agy., Whitesburg, Ky., 1997—; guest speaker Southeast C.C., Whitesburg, Ky., 1990-92. Mem. exec. com. Letcher County Dems., 1996—. Recipient Guest Speaker award Big Sandy Assn. Life Underwriters, Prestonburg, Ky., 1992. Fellow Life Underwriters Tng. Coun.; mem. Nat. Assn. Life Underwriters (Nat. Quality award 1989-92, Nat. Sales Achievement award 1992), Big Sandy Assn. Life Underwriters (chmn. comty. svc. 1994-96, bd. dirs. 1994—, sec., treas. 1996-97), U.S. Jr. C. of C. (mgmt. devel. c.p. 1992-93, Key Man award, Most Outstanding Mgmt. Devel. v.p. 1992-93), Am. Soc. CLUs and ChFCs, Jaycees (pres. Letcher area 1993-94, regional dir. Ky. 1994-95), Letcher County C. of C. (v.p., chmn. tourism com., pres. 1995-96, past pres. 1996-97), Alpha Beta Gamma. Avocations: golf, bowling, fishing, walking, dog training. Home: HC 71 Box 800 Jeremiah KY 41826-9722 Office: Blair Ins Agy Inc 115 E Main St Whitesburg KY 41858-1133

SMITH, ROGER WINSTON, political theorist, educator; b. Birmingham, Ala., July 9, 1936; s. Buford Houston and Sarah Louise (Trucks) S.; m. Martha Christin Daniels, Jan. 16, 1960; children—Louisa, David. A.B. magna cum laude, Harvard U., 1958, postgrad. in law, 1958-59; M.A. in Polit. Sci., U. Calif.-Berkeley, 1963, Ph.D. in Polit. Sci., 1971. Teaching assoc. U. Calif.-Berkeley, 1965-66; asst. prof. govt. Coll. William and Mary, Williamsburg, Va., 1967-72, assoc. prof., 1972-80, prof, 1980—; sr. lectr. politics Glasgow (Scotland) U., 1977-78; lectr. N.E.H., 1988; cons. Nelson-Hall Pubs., Chgo.; mem. coun. Inst. Internat. Conf. on the Holocaust and Genocide, Jerusalem; co-founder, v.p. Assn. Genocide Scholars; film cons. Armenian Heritage Project. Co-author, editor: Guilt: Man and Society, 1971; co-author: Genocide and the Modern Age, 1986, Genocide, vol. 2, 1991, Bearing Witness to the Holocaust, 1939-89; contbg. editor Internet on the Holocaust and Genocide; contbr. articles to profl. jours. Served to 1st lt. U.S. Army, 1960-62, Japan. Fellow NSF, 1966, College of William and Mary, 1977. Mem. Am. Polit. Sci. Assn., Human Rights Watch, Cultural Survival. Democrat. Baptist. Avocations: gardening; walking. Home: 102 Lake Dr Williamsburg VA 23185-3113 Office: Coll William and Mary Dept Govt Williamsburg VA 23187

SMITH, RONALD EARL, aircraft design engineer; b. St. Louis, May 22, 1947; s. Lawrence Abner and Judith Evelyn (Roberson) S.; m. Sheila M. Smith; children: Kimberly A., Russell E. BSME, U. Mo., 1970, MS in Mech. and Aerospace Engring., 1971; PDD in Engring. Mgmt., U. Mo., Rolla, 1986; postgrad., Def. Sys. Mgmt. Coll., Ft. Belvoir, Va., 1990. Student coop. engr. McDonnell Douglas, St. Louis, 1966-70, design engr., 1971-90, head design dept., 1990-91; program mgr. MD-12 wing McDonnell Douglas, Long Beach, Calif., 1992; chief sys. engr. McDonnell Douglas, St. Louis, 1992-93, chief engr. F/A-18, 1993—. Editor newsletter Gateway News, 1992; contbr. articles to profl. jours. Team mgr. Creve Coeur Athletic Assn., St. Louis, 1987, team coach, 1986. Fellow AIAA (assoc., com. mem. 1976-86, treas. 1982-83, vice chmn. 1993-94, chmn. 1994-95, Sect. Svc. award 1996); mem. Tau Beta Pi. Avocation: skiing. Home: 14062 Forest Crest Dr Chesterfield MO 63017-3242

SMITH, RONALD EHLBERT, lawyer, referral-based distributor, public speaker, writer and motivator; b. Atlanta, Apr. 30, 1947; s. Frank Marion and Frances Jane (Canida) S.; m. Annemarie Krumholz, Dec. 26, 1969; children: Michele, Erika, Damian. BME, Stetson U., 1970; postgrad., Hochschule Fuer Musik, Frankfurt, Fed. Republic Germany, 1971-74; Masters in German Lit., Germany & Middlebury Coll., 1975; JD, Nova U., 1981. Bar: Fla. 1982, U.S. Dist. Ct. (mid. dist.) Fla. 1983, U.S. Ct. Appeals (11th cir.) 1990, Ga. 1994, U.S. Dist. Ct. (no. dist.) Ga. 1994. Asst. state atty. 10th Jud. Cir. Ct., Bartow, Fla., 1982-85; pvt. practice Lakeland, Fla., 1985-94, Atlanta, 1994—; rsch. asst. 10th Jud. Cir. Ct., Bartow, 1981-82; instr. Broward County C.C., Ft. Lauderdale, Fla., 1976-79, 91-94, pub. and pvt. schs., Broward County, Offenbach, Fed. Republic Germany, 1971-78; instr. Polk C.C. and Police Acad., Winter Haven, Fla., 1981-94; adj. prof. English, Ga. State U., 1996—; reader ETS GMAT, 1997—; part time police instr. Police Acad., Forsyth Ga., 1996—. Tchr., drama dir. Disciples I and II, United Meth. Ch., Lakeland, 1980-94, Glenn Meml. United Meth. Ch., Atlanta, 1994—; Billy Graham counseling supr., 1994—; active Atlanta Men for Christ, 1995—; promoter Promise Keepers, 1995—; spkr., promoter ProNet, 1996—. Freedom Bridge fellow German Acad. Exch. Svc., Mainz, 1974-75. Mem. ABA, Christian Legal Soc., Ga. Trial Lawyers Assn., Lakeland Bar Assn., Atlanta Bar Assn., Nat. Orgn. Soc. Sect. Claimant Rep., Ga. Assn. Criminal Def. Lawyers, Kiwanis. Democrat.

SMITH, RONALD EMORY, telecommunications executive; b. Shelburne, N.S., Can., May 26, 1950; s. Edgar Earle and Ida Mae (Porter) S.; children: Stephen, Sarah, Susan. BBA, Acadia U., Wolfville, N.S., 1971. Chartered acct., N.S. Staff acct., mgr. Clarkson Gordon (now Ernst & Young), Halifax, N.S., 1971-78, Toronto, Ont., Can., 1978-80; prin., ptnr. Woods Gordon (now Ernst & Young), Toronto, 1980-87; v.p. fin. and corp. svcs. Maritime Tel. & Tel., Halifax, 1987—; dir. Maritime Med. Care Inc., Dartmouth, N.S., 1995—; bd. dirs. The Island Telephone Co. Ltd., Charlottetown, P.E.I., Can., MT&T Leasing Inc., Halifax, MT&T Mobility Inc., Halifax. Dir. Coun. for Can. Unity, 1994—; bd. govs. Acadia U., 1994—; chmn. bd. trustees IWK/Grace Hosp., 1989—; trustee Atlantic Provinces Econ. Coun., Halifax, 1993-95, Acadia Sch. Bus. Adv. Bd., 1996—, L'Inst. Roeher Inst., 1997—; pres. Can. Assn. for Cmty. Living, 1989-93, chmn. Min.'s Task Force on Physician Policy Devel., N.S., 1991-93; mem. coun. fin. execs. Conf. Bd. Mem. Fin. Execs. Inst., Can. Inst. Chartered Accts., Inst. Chartered Accts. N.S., Ashburn Golf Club. Roman Catholic. Avocations: golf, hiking, travel. Office: Maritime Tel & Tel Co Ltd, 1505 Barrington St PO Box 880, Halifax, NS Canada B3J 2W3

SMITH, RONALD LYNN, health system executive; b. Algona, Iowa, Sept. 22, 1940; s. Russell Malcom and Helen Lucille (Gridley) S.; m. Jacqueline Sue Yarger, Dec. 23, 1962 (div. Aug. 1981); children: Sheri Rene, Gregory Mark, Brenton Alan; m. Sylvia Jo Grotjan, Dec. 31, 1982; 1 child, Russell Lynn. B.S., Iowa State U., 1962; postgrad., U. S.D., 1963; M.A., U. Iowa, 1965. With Harris Hosp.-Methodist, Ft. Worth, 1967-82, assoc. dir., 1974-76, exec. dir., 1977-82; pres. Harris Meth. Health System, Ft. Worth, 1982—; trustee Am. Healthcare Systems, Nat. Com. for Quality Health Care; mem. adv. coun. Hill-Rom Co., 1991; mem. healthcare exec. adv. coun. IBM, 1991; mem. bd. Tex. Commerce Bank. Trustee Tarrant County United Way, 1977-79, campaign chmn., 1992, chmn. bd. trustees 1993, chmn. bd. dirs., 1994, area-wide svcs. chair, 1988—, self-sufficiency task force; bd. mem. Tex. Rsch. League, 1990—, nat. bd. visitors Tex. Christian U., 1990—; bd. visitors Tex. Wesleyan U., 1995—. Fellow Am. Coll. Hosp. Execs.; mem. Tex. Hosp. Assn. (trustee 1983-87, chmn. 1986-87), Dallas-Ft. Worth Hosp. Coun. (pres. 1981), Ft. Worth C. of C. (bd. dirs. 1992), Rotary. Methodist.

SMITH, R(ONALD) SCOTT, lawyer; b. Washington, June 30, 1947; s. Joseph Peter Smith and Roberta Ann (Bailey) George; m. Cheryle Rae Coffman, Nov. 15, 1974 (div. July 1977); m. Gloria Jean Haralson, Nov. 30, 1985. BJ, U. Mo., 1970, JD, 1973. Bar: Mo. 1973, U.S. Dist. Ct. (we. dist.) Mo. 1973, U.S. Ct. Appeals (10th cir.) 1990, U.S. Ct. Appeals (8th cir.) 1992, U.S. Dist. Ct. (ea. dist.) Mo. 1996. Field dir. The Mo. Bar, Jefferson City, 1973-75; law clk. to judge Mo. Ct. Appeals (we. dist.), 1975-76; ptnr. Shirkey, Norton & Smith, Kansas City, 1976-77, Jackson & Sherman, P.C. and predecessors, Kansas City, 1977-84, Birmingham & Furry, Kansas City, 1984, Birmingham, Furry & Smith, 1985-92, Birmingham, Furry, Smith & Stubbs, 1992-95, Furry & Smith, Kansas City, 1996—. Author: (with others) Automobile Accident Handbook, 1984, rev., 1986, Vexatious Refusal and Bad Faith, 1990, Insurance Claims, 1993; editor: The Rights & Responsibilies of Citizenship in a Free Society, 1974, Due Process of Law, 1974, News Headnotes, 1976-84, Young Lawyer, 1977-80; mem. editorial bd. Mo. Bar Jour., 1978-81; (TV series) legal script advisor Lex Singularis, 1973-75; (multimedia) producer, author Freedoms Lost, 1976; producer, playwright (musical-comedy play) Silly ib Philly, 1987. Mem. ABA (mem. varius coms.), Mo. Bar Assn. (dist. 12 chmn. 1979—, mem. varius coms., Disting. Svc. award young lawyers sect. 1978, 79, 80), West Mo. Def. Lawyers Assn., Kansas City Met. Bar Assn. (pres. young lawyers sect. 1981-82, mem. various coms., Disting. Svc. award young lawyers sect. 1982, Leadership award st. sect. 1985, Dirst Ann. Pres. award sr. sect. 1987), Kansas City Claim Assn., Phi Delta Phi. Democrat. Roman Catholic. Home: 3411 Shady Bend Dr Independence MO 64052-2816 Office: 1600 Bryant Bldg 1102 Grand Blvd Kansas City MO 64106-2316

SMITH, ROWLAND JAMES, educational administrator; b. Johannesburg, S. Africa, Aug. 19, 1938; s. John James and Gladys Spencer (Coldrey) S.; m. Catherine Anne Lane, Sept. 22, 1962; children: Russell Claude, Belinda Claire. B.A., U. Natal, 1959, Ph.D., 1967; M.A., Oxford U., Eng., 1967. Lectr. English U. Witwatersrand, Johannesburg, S. Africa, 1963-67; asst. prof. Dalhousie U., Halifax, N.S., Can., 1967-70, assoc. prof. English, 1970-77, prof., 1977-88, McCulloch prof., 1988-94, chmn. English dept., 1977-83, 85-86, dir. Centre for African Studies, 1976-77, asst. dean arts and scis., 1972-74, dean arts and social scis., 1988-93, provost Coll. Arts and Scis., 1988-89, 90-91, 92-93; vis. prof., rsch. assoc. Multidisciplinary Ctr. Can. Studies, U. Rouen, 1994; prof. Wilfrid Laurier U., Waterloo, Ontario, 1994—, v.p. acad., 1994—. Author: Lyric and Polemic: The Literary Personality of Roy Campbell, 1972; editor: Exile and Tradition: Studies in African and Caribbean Literature, 1976, Critical Essays on Nadine Gordimer, 1990. Bd. govs. Halifax Grammar Sch., 1972-74, Neptune Theatre Found., 1977-78; mem. selection com. IODE Meml. Scholarships for N.S., 1969-71, Rhodes Scholarships N.S., 1972-74; mem. edn. com. Victoria Gen. Hosp., 1986-90; dir. publicity and promotion N.S. Rugby Football Union, 1987-89; chair liaison com. edn. dept. N.S. U., 1990-93; mem. book prize jury, Can. Fedn. for Humanities, 1990, regional judge (Can. and the Caribbean) Commonwealth Writers Prize, 1991; chair com. on employment and ednl. equity Coun. Ont. Univs., 1996—. Recipient Transvaal Rhodes scholar, 1960; vis. fellow Dalhousie U., 1965-66, vis. scholar Ctr. Canadian Studies U. Western Sydney, Macarthur, New South Wales; Can. Council leave fellow, 1974-75, research grantee, 1977; grantee Social Scis. and Humanities Research Council of Can., 1978, internat. grantee, 1985, grantee Cultural Personalities Exchange program Assn. Canadian Studies in Australia and New Zealand, 1996. Mem. Assn. Can. Univ. Tchrs. English (sec.-treas. 1968-70, profl. concern com. 1979-81), Can. Assn. for Commonwealth Lit. and Lang. Studies (exec. mem. 1989-92, pres. 1995—), Can. Assn. Chmn. English (v.p. 1981-82, pres. 1982-83, exec. mem.-at-large 1985-86), Can. Fedn. Humanities (aid to scholarly publs. com. 1979-85, bd. dirs. 1992-94), MLA (div. chmn. 1984). Office: Wilfrid Laurier U, Office of VP Acad, Waterloo, ON Canada N2L 3C5

SMITH, ROY FORGE, art director, production designer. Art dir.: (films) Far from the Madding Crowd, 1967, The Assassination Bureau, 1969, The Amazing Mr. Blunden, 1972, Yesterday, 1980, The Last Chase, 1981, Mrs. Soffel, 1984; prodn. designer: (films) Monty Python and the Holy Grail, 1974, The House By the Lake, 1976, Jabberwocky, 1977, The Hound of the Baskervilles, 1979, Running, 1979, Funeral Home, 1981, Melanie, 1983, Curtains, 1983, The Believers, 1987, Burnin' Love, 1987, The Kiss, 1988, Bill & Ted's Excellent Adventure, 1989, Teenage Mutant Ninja Turtles, 1990, Teenage Mutant Ninja Turtles II: The Secret of the Ooze, 1991, Warlock, 1991, Teenage Mutant Ninja Turtles III, 1993, Robin Hood: Men in Tights, 1993, The Page Master, 1994, (TV movies) Clown White, 1980, A Deadly Business, 1986, Haunted By Her Past, 1987, The Lost Capone, 1990, (TV series) SCTV, 1983. Office: Sandra Marsh Mgt 9150 Wilshire Blvd Ste 220 Beverly Hills CA 90212-3429*

SMITH, ROY JORDAN, religious organization administrator; b. Franklin, N.C., July 7, 1929; s. Sanford Jordan and Pearl Elizabeth (Kinsland) S.; m. Doris Elizabeth Pearce, Dec. 20, 1950; children: Ginger Smith Graves, Roy J. Jr., Tracy M. BA, Wake Forest U., 1952, DD (hon.), 1995; MDiv, Southeastern Bapt. Theol. Sem., Wake Forest, N.C., 1956; DD (hon.), Campbell U., 1981. Ordained to ministry Bapt. State Conv., 1954. Pastor Union Hope Bapt. Ch., Zebulon, N.C., 1954-57, Jersey Bapt. Ch., Lexington, N.C., 1957-62; regional missionary Bapt. State Conv., Sylva, N.C., 1962-67; dir. town and country missions Bapt. State Conv., Raleigh, N.C., 1967-78, assoc. exec. dir., 1978-84, exec. dir., 1984—; cons. on sem. extension, Nashville, 1962-77; cons. on leisure ministry Bapt. Home Mission Bd., Atlanta, 1962-77. Contbr. articles to religious publs. Chaplain Lions Club, Linwood, N.C., 1959-62, Sylva Fire Dept., 1964-67. Mem. Assn. State Exec. Dirs. (pres. 1994-95). Avocations: camping, gardening, fishing, travel. Home: 4746 Wildwood St Raleigh NC 27612 Office: Bapt State Conv PO Box 1107 Cary NC 27512-1107

SMITH, ROY PHILIP, judge; b. S.I., N.Y., Dec. 29, 1933; s. Philip Aloysius and Virginia (Collins) S.; m. Elizabeth Helen Wink, Jan. 23, 1965; children: Matthew P., Jean E. BA, St. Joseph's Coll., Yonkers, N.Y., 1956; JD, Fordham U., 1965. Bar: N.Y. Asst. reg. counsel FAA, N.Y.C., 1966-79; adminstrv. law judge U.S. Dept. Labor, Washington, 1979-83; adminstrv. appeals judge Benefits Rev. Bd., Washington, 1983—, chmn., chief adminstrv. appeals judge, 1988-90; adj. prof. aviation law Dowling Coll., Oakdale, N.Y., 1972-79; adj. prof. transp. law Adelphi U., Garden City, N.Y., 1975-79; vis. prof. Georgetown U. Law Sch., 1989—. With U.S. Army, 1957-59. Mem. Assn. of Bar of City of N.Y. (sec.-treas. aeronautics com. 1978-79), Fed. Adminstrv. Law Judges Conf. (treas. 1983-84, mem. exec. com. 1982-83), Internat. Platform Assn., Friendly Sons of St. Patrick, Edgemoor Club. Avocation: tennis. Home: 6700 Pawtucket Rd Bethesda MD 20817-4836 Office: Benefits Rev Bd 200 Constitution Ave NW Washington DC 20210-0001

SMITH, RUBY LUCILLE, librarian; b. Nobob, Ky., Sept. 19, 1917; d. James Ira and Myrtie Olive (Crabtree) Jones; AB, Western Ky. State Tchrs. Coll., 1943, MA, 1966; m. Kenneth Cornelius Smith, Dec. 25, 1946; children: Kenneth Cornelius, Corma Ann. Tchr. rural schs., Barren County, Ky., 1941-42; tchr. secondary sch. English, libr. Temple Hill Consol. Sch., Glasgow, Ky., 1943-47, 49-51, 53-56, sch. libr., 1956-83. Sec. Barren County Cancer Soc., 1968-70, Barren County Fair Bd., 1969-70; leader 4-H Club, 1957-72, mem. council Barren County; coord. AARP tax-aide program, 1985-88, dist. dir., 1988—. Trustee Mary Wood Weldon Meml. Libr., 1964—; trustee Barren County Pub. Libr., 1969—, sec., 1969—; instr. 55 Alive Mature Driving AARP, 1993—. Mem. NEA (life), Ky. Edn. Assn., Ky. Sch. Media Assn. (sec. 1970-71), 3d Dist. Libr. Assn. (pres. 1944, 66), Barren County Edn. Assn. (pres. 1960-62, treas. 1979-80), 3d Dist. Ret. Tchrs. Assn. (pres. 1991-92), Ky. Ret. Tchrs Assn. (v.p. 1992-93, pres.-elect 1993, pres. 1994-95), Ky. Audio Visual Assn., Glasgow-Barren County Ret. Tchrs. Assn. (pres. 1984-86, 96-97, sec. 1989, treas. 1990), Ky. Libr. Trustee Assn. (bd. dirs. 1985—, pres. 1986-88, 93-94, dir. Barren River region 1985—), Barren County Rep. Women's Club, Monroe Assn. Woman's Missionary Union (dir. 1968-72, 79-83, sec. 1985—), Monroe Assn. Bapts. (libr. dir. 1972-88, sec. 1985—), Ky. Libr. Assn., Delta Kappa Gamma (pres. Delta chpt. 1996—). Home: 54 E Nobob Rd Summer Shade KY 42166-8405

SMITH, RUSSELL FRANCIS, transportation executive; b. Washington, Mar. 26, 1944; s. Raymond Francis and Elma Gloria (Daugherty) S. Student East Carolina U., 1964, N.C. State U., 1964-65; BS with honors, U. Md.-Coll. Park, 1969, MBA, 1975. Exec. asst. mgr. Hotel Corp. Am. Internat. Inn and Mayflower Hotel, Washington, 1966-68; sr. venture capital cons. Initiative Investing Corp., Washington, 1968-69; pres., gen. mgr. Associated Trades Corp., Washington, 1970-74; cons. in fin., Greenbelt, Md., 1974-76; mng. cons. Bradford Nat. Corp., Washington, 1976-79; v.p. OAO Corp., Washington, 1979-81; ptnr. for fin. evaluation and ops. analysis Blake, Brunell, Lehmann & Co., Washington, 1981-86; v.p. mgmt. services adminstrn. United Airlines Svcs. Corp., Lakewood, Colo., 1986-91, cons. Venture Fund of Washington, 1991—. Chmn. com. on wildlife Prince George Humane Soc., Hyattsville, Md., 1968-71, Soc. for Prevention Cruelty to Animals, Hyattsville. 1971-75. Served with U.S. Army, 1963-66. Decorated Silver Star medal, Bronze Star medal with V device, Purple Heart. Mem. Am. Fin. Assn., Ops. Research Soc. Am., Am. Acctg. Assn., N.Am. Soc. Corp. Planners, Internat. Assn. Math. Modeling, Assn. MBA Execs. (registered investment advisor), Beta Gamma Sigma, Beta Alpha Psi. Libertarian.

SMITH, RUSSELL JACK, former intelligence official; b. Jackson, Mich., July 4, 1913; s. Lee C. and Georgia L. (Weed) S.; m. Rosemary Thomson, Sept. 5, 1938; children: Stephen M., Scott T., Christopher G. AB, Miami U., Oxford, Ohio, 1937; PhD, Cornell U., 1941. Asst. instr. English Cornell U., 1937-41; instr. English Williams Coll., 1941-45; with OSS, 1945; asst. prof. English Wells Coll., 1946-47; with CIA, 1947-74, mem. bd. nat. estimates, 1957-62, dir. current intelligence, 1962-66, dep. dir. for intelligence, 1966-71; spl. asst. U.S. Embassy, New Delhi, 1971-74; rsch. cons., 1975—; assigned Nat. War Coll., 1951-52, U.S. rep. Brit. Joint Intelligence Com., Far East, Singapore, 1954-56. Author: John Dryden, A Study in Controversy, 1941, The Unknown CIA: My Three Decades with the Agency, 1989, (novels) The Secret War, 1986, The Singapore Chance, 1991, Lodestone, 1993, Whirligig, 1994. Recipient Nat. Civil Svc. League award, 1971, Disting. Intelligence medal CIA, 1974. Mem. Phi Beta Kappa, Phi Delta Theta, Omicron Delta Kappa. Home: 1138 Bellview Rd Mc Lean VA 22102-1104

SMITH, RUTH LILLIAN SCHLUCHTER, librarian; b. Detroit, Oct. 18, 1917; d. Clayton John and Gertrude Katherine (Kastler) Schluchter; m. Thomas Guilford Smith, Sept. 28, 1946; 1 son, Pemberton, III. AB, Wayne State U., Detroit, 1939; AB in Libr. Sci., U. Mich., Ann Arbor, 1942. Libr. Detroit Pub. Libr., 1942-43; rsch. asst. Moore Sch. Elec. Engring. U. Pa., Phila., 1946-47; libr. Bethesda (Md.) Meth. Ch. Libr., 1955-61; reference libr., chief reader svcs. Inst. Def. Analyses, Arlington, Va., 1961-65, chief unclassified libr. sect., 1965-67, head libr., 1967-75, mgr. tech. info. svcs., 1975-81; dir. office customer svcs. Nat. Tech. Info. Svc., 1981-88, cons., 1988—; leader ch. libr. workshops, 1960—; speaker profl. meetings; founder, chmn. Com. Info. Hang-ups, 1969-86; mem. Depository Libr. Coun. to Pub. Printer, 1975-78, Def. Tech. Info. Ctr. Resource Sharing Adv. Group, 1980-82; chmn. edn. working group Fed. Libr. and Info. Ctr. Com., 1984-88, cons., 1988—. Author: Publicity for a Church Library, 1966, Workshop Planning, 1972, (with Claudia Hannaford) Promotion Planning, 1975, Getting the Books off the Shelves, 1975, rev. edit., 1985, 2nd rev. edit., 1991, Cataloging Made Easy, 1978, rev. edit., 1986, 2d rev. edit., 1997, Setting up a Library: How to Begin or Begin Again, 1979, rev. edit., 1987, 2nd rev. edit., 1994, Running a Library, 1982; contbr. articles to library and religious jours. Mem. ALA, Am. Soc. Info. Sci., Ch. and Synagogue Library Assn. (founding mem., life mem., pres. 1967-68), Fedn. Info. Users (v.p. interactive affairs 1973-75), Spl. Libraries Assn. (chmn. aerospace div. 1975-76, chmn. library mgmt. div. 1978-79, chmn. div. cabinet 1980-81, John Cotton Dana award 1979, SLA Fellow award 1987, Hall of Fame award 1988). Republican. Methodist. Home: 5304 Glenwood Rd Bethesda MD 20814-1406

SMITH, SALLY ELAINE BECKLEY, veterinary technician; b. Oneonta, N.Y., July 28, 1959; d. Clyde Allen Beckley and Doris Robinson; m. David Michael Smith, Apr. 17, 1983. AS, SUNY, Delhi, 1979. Lic. vet. technician; cert. kennel operator. Vet. technician Am. Animal Hosp., Mt. Freedom, N.J., 1979-81, hosp. adminstrs., 1981-87; dir. Golub Animal Hosp./Animal Inn, Ledgewood, N.J., 1987—; pres., cons. Companion Pet Enterprises, Blairstown, N.J., 1994—; bd. dirs. Airborne Animals, Inc., Ledgewood; spkr. and cons. in field. Mem. Am. Boarding Kennels Assn. (regional dir. 1995—, chair edn. com. 1989—, Nat. Appreciation award 1989, Golden Scoop 1994, pres.-elect 1997), N.J. Vet. Technicians (sec. 1985-88), Ind. Pet & Animal Transp. Assn. (sec. 1994—). Republican. Avocations: hiking, reading, cooking, gardening. Office: Animal Inn PO Box 425 Ledgewood NJ 07852

SMITH, SALLYE WRYE, librarian; b. Birmingham, Ala., Nov. 11, 1923; d. William Florin and Margaret (Howard) Wrye; m. Stuart Werner Smith,

Sept. 20, 1947 (dec. June 1981); children: Carol Ann, Susan Patricia, Michael Christopher, Julie Lynn, Lori Kathleen. BA, U. Ala., 1945; MA, U. Denver, 1969. Psychometrician U.S. Army, Deshon Gen. Hosp., Butler, Pa., 1945-46, U.S. Vet. Adminstrn. Vocat. Guidance, U. Ala., Tuscaloosa, 1946; clin. psychologist U.S. Army, Walter Reed Gen. Hosp., Washington, 1946-47, U.S. Army, Fitzsimons Gen. Hosp., Denver, 1948, U.S. Vets. Adminstrn., Ft. Logan, Colo., 1948-50; head sci.-engring. libr. U. Denver, Colo., 1969-72; instr., reference libr. Penrose Libr., U. Denver, 1972-80, asst. prof., reference libr., 1980-90, interim dir., 1990-92, asst. prof. emerita, 1992—; vis. prof. U. Denver Grad. Sch. Libr. Info. Mgmt., 1975-77, 83; info. broker Colo. Rschrs., Denver, 1979—; cons., presenter The Indsl. Info. Workshop Inst. de Investigaciones Tecnologicas, Bogota, Colombia, 1979, LIPI-DRI-PDIN workshop on R&D mgmt., Jakarta, Indonesia, 1982; mem. BRS User Adv. Bd., Latham, N.Y., 1983-86. Indexer: Statistical Abstract of Colorado 1976-77, 1977. Recipient Cert. of Recognition, Sigma Xi, U. Denver chpt., 1983. Mem. ALA, Spl. Libr. Assn., Colo. Libr. Assn., Phi Beta Kappa, Beta Phi Mu.

SMITH, SAM CORRY, retired foundation executive, consultant; b. Enid, Okla., July 3, 1922; s. Chester Hubbert and Nelle Kate (Corry) S.; m. Dorothy Jean Bank, Sept. 21, 1945; children: Linda Jean, Nancy Kay, Susan Diane. Student, Phillips U., 1940-43; BS in Chemistry, U. Okla., 1947, MS in Chemistry, 1948; PhD in Biochemistry, U. Wis., 1951. Asst. and assoc. prof. U. Okla., Oklahoma City, 1951-55; assoc. dir. grants Research Corp., N.Y.C., 1957-65, dir., 1965-68, v.p. grants, 1968-75; exec. dir. M.J. Murdock Charitable Trust, Vancouver, Wash., 1975-88; foundation cons., 1988—; pres. Pacific Northwest Grantmakers Forum, 1983-84. Contbr. sci. articles to profl. jours. Trustee Nutrition Found., Washington, 1976-84, Internat. Life Scis. Inst., Washington, 1984-86; bd. councilors U. So. Calif. Med. Sch., L.A., 1977-82; mem. adv. com. Coll. Natural Scis. Colo. State U., 1977-80; pres. Cardiopulmonary Rehab. Programs Oreg., 1990-91; bd. dirs. Clark Coll. Found., 1993—. Named Boss of Yr., Am. Bus. Women's Assn., 1982, Bus. Assoc. of Yr., 1983. Fellow AAAS; mem. Am. Chem. Soc. Avocations: tennis, photography, gardening. Home: 5204 DuBois Dr Vancouver WA 98661-6617 *Personal philosophy: "There is no limit to what a man can do or where he can go if he doesn't mind who gets the credit." Author unknown.*

SMITH, SAM PRITZKER, columnist, author; b. Bklyn., Jan. 24, 1948; s. Leon and Betty (Pritzker) S.; m. Kathleen Ellen Rood, Jan. 24, 1976; 1 child, Connor. BBA in Acctg., Pace U., N.Y.C., 1970; MA in Journalism, Ball State U., Muncie, Ind., 1974. Acct. Arthur Young & Co., N.Y.C., 1970-72; reporter Ft. Wayne (Ind.) News Sentinal, Ft. Wayne, 1973-76, States News Svc., Washington, 1976-79; press sec. U.S. Senator Lowell Weicker Jr., 1979; writer/reporter Chgo. Tribune, 1979-90, columnist, 1991—. Author: The Jordan Rules, 1991; Second Coming, 1995; contbr. articles to mags. including Inside Sports, Sport, Basketball Digest. With USAR, 1970-76. Recipient Journalism awards AP, UPI, Sigma Delta Chi; named Ball State U. Journalism Alumnus of Yr. Office: Chicago Tribune 435 N Michigan Ave Chicago IL 60611

SMITH, SAMUEL BOYD, history educator; b. Adams, Tenn., Oct. 23, 1929; s. Carl S. and Annie (Tolleson) S.; m. Martha Sue Fitzsimmons, Dec. 23, 1956; children—David Fitzsimmons, Mark Tolleson, Stephen Boyd. Student, Milligan Coll., 1947-48, U. Tenn., 1948-49, Syracuse U., 1951-52; B.S., Peabody Coll., 1956; M.A., Vanderbilt U., 1960, Ph.D., 1962. Asst. prof. history U. South Fla., 1961-64; state librarian and archivist, chmn. Tenn. Hist. Commn., 1964-69; lectr. history Peabody Coll., 1965-66; assoc. prof. history U. Tenn., 1969-71, prof., editor Andrew Jackson Presdl. Papers, 1972-79; prof. Tenn. State U., Nashville, 1979-97. Co-author: This is Tennessee, 1973; Editor and compiler: Tennessee History: A Bibliography, 1974; co-editor: The Papers of Andrew Jackson, vol. I, 1980. Served with USAF, 1951-54. Mem. Orgn. Am. Historians, Am. Hist. Assn., Tenn. Hist. Assn., Shakespeare Club, Univ. Club, Rotary. Democrat. Methodist. Home: 1135 Sewanee Rd Nashville TN 37220-1017 Office: Tenn State Univ History Dept Downtown Campus Nashville TN 37203

SMITH, SAMUEL DAVID, artist, educator; b. Thorndale, Tex., Feb. 11, 1918; s. Otto Frank and Jeanette (Joyce) S.; m. Elizabeth Marie Smith; children: Cezanne, Rembrandt, Michelangelo. Ed. pub. schs. Prof. art U. N.Mex., 1956-84, prof. art emeritus, 1984—. Illustrator: Roots in Adobe, 1967, Cowboy's Christmas Tree, 1956; also: Coronet mag; one man exhbns. include, Corcoran Gallery Art, Washington, 1949, Santa Fe Mus. Art, 1947, Roswell (N.Mex.) Mus. Fine Art, 1953, 64, Goodwell (Okla.) Hist. Mus., 1964, Panhandle Plains Mus., Canyon City, Tex., 1964, Biltomore Galleries, Los Angeles, 1946, First Nat. Bank, Los Alamos, 1968, group exhbns. include, Baker Galleries, Lubbock, Tex., 1964-73, Met. Mus., N.Y.C., 1944, Blue Door Gallery, Taos, N.Mex., 1946-53, Galeria del Sol, Albuquerque, 1968-73, Brandywine Galleries, 1972-73, Watercolor Workshop, Teluride, Colo., 1964; one-man show includes Retrospective Exhbn. U. of N.Mex., Albuquerque, 1986, World War II War Art Exibit, Nat. Bldg. Mus., 1995. Served as combat artist AUS, 1942-45. Hon. life mem. N.Mex. Art League. Mem. Artist Equity Assn. (pres. N.Mex. chpt. 1957-58, 66-67, 70-71), Elks. Gallery: PO Box 2006 Telluride CO 81435-2006

SMITH, SAMUEL HOWARD, academic administrator, plant pathologist; b. Salinas, Calif., Feb. 4, 1940; s. Adrian Reed and Elsa (Jacop) S.; m. Patricia Ann Walter, July 8, 1960; children: Samuel Howard, Linda Marie. BS in Plant Pathology, U. Calif., Berkeley, 1961, PhD, 1964; D (hon.), Nihon U., Tokyo, 1989. NATO fellow Glasshouse Crops Research Inst., Sussex, Eng., 1964-65; asst. prof. plant pathology U. Calif., Berkeley, 1965-69; assoc. prof. Pa. State U., Arendtsville, 1969-71; assoc. prof. Pa. State U., University Park, 1971-74, prof., 1974-85, head dept. plant pathology, 1976-81, dean Coll. Agr., dir. Pa. Agrl. Expt. Sta. and Coop. Extension Service, 1981-85; pres. Wash. State U., 1985—; bd. dirs. Assoc. Western Univs.; adv. com. Wash. Sch. Employees Credit Union, 1993-95; mem. adv. com. Battelle Pacific N.W. Lab., 1993—; chair Pacific-10 Conf. CEOs, 1993-94; bd. dirs. All-Nations Alliance for Minority Participation; mem. pres.' commn. NCAA, 1994—, divsn. I chair, 1995-96; chair Pres.'s Commn., 1996—. Bd. dirs. Forward Wash., 1986-95, The Technology Alliance, 1996—, China Rels. Coun.; mem. Wash. Coun. Internat. Trade, Western Insterstate Commn. Higher Edn.; bd. dirs. Assn. Western Univs., 1993—. Mem. AAAS, Am. Phytopath. Soc., Nat. Assn. State Univs. and Land-Grand Colls. (bd. dirs. 1994—, chair commn. info. tech. 1994-96), Gamma Sigma Delta, Alpha Zeta, Epsilon Sigma Phi, Sigma Xi, Omicron Delta Kappa, Golden Key, Pi Kappa Alpha (hon.). Home: 755 NE Campus St Pullman WA 99163-4223 Office: Wash State U French Adminstrn Bldg Pullman WA 99164-1048

SMITH, SAMUEL STUART, lawyer; b. Harrisburg, Pa., Nov. 18, 1936; s. Joseph and Fannie (Latt) S.; m. Susan Ruth Egert, Dec. 10, 1960; children: Jeffrey Alan, Gary Michael, Lauren Paige. BBA, U. Miami, 1958, JD, 1960. Bar: Fla. 1960, U.S. Dist. Ct. (so. dist.) Fla. 1960, U.S. Supreme Ct. 1960. Ptnr. Smith & Mandler, P.A., Miami Beach, Fla., 1960-87, Ruden, McClosky, Smith Schuster & Russell, Miami, Fla., 1987—. Bd. dirs. WPBT-TV, Miami, Jewish Family Svc., Miami, Guardianship Program Dade County, Comprehensive Personal Care Inc. Capt. U.S. Army, 1960-61. Fellow Am. Bar Found., Am. Coll. Trust and Estate Counsel (regent 1996—), Fla. Bar Found. (pres. 1989-90); mem. ABA (chmn. law econs. sect. 1979-80, gov. 1985-87, sec.-elect 1992-93, sec. 1993-96), The Fla. Bar (pres. 1980-81), Miami Beach Bar Assn. (pres. 1972-73), Dean's Nat. Adv. Coun. (chair 1992-93). Democrat. Avocations: tennis. Office: Ruden McClosky Smith Schuster & Russell 701 Brickell Ave Ste 1900 Miami FL 33131-2834

SMITH, SCOTT CLYBOURN, media company executive; b. Evanston, Ill., Sept. 13, 1950; s. E. Sawyer and Jerolanne (Jones) S.; m. Martha Reilly, June 22, 1974; children—Carolyn Baldwin, Thomas Clybourn. B.A., Yale U., 1973; M.Mgmt., Northwestern U., 1976. Comml. banking officer No. Trust Co., Chgo., 1973-77; fin. planning mgr. Tribune Co., Chgo., 1977-79, asst. treas., 1979-81, treas., 1981-82, v.p., treas., 1982-84, v.p. fin., 1984-89, sr. v.p., chief fin. officer, 1989-91, sr. v.p. for devel., 1991-93; pres., CEO, pub. Sun Sentinel Co., Ft. Lauderdale, Fla., 1993-97; pres., pub. Chgo. Tribune Co., 1997—. Episcopalian. Clubs: Glen View (Golf, Ill.), Lauderdale Yacht Club, Fort Lauderdale Country Club. Office: Chgo Tribune Co 435 N Michigan Ave Chicago IL 60611

SMITH, SELMA MOIDEL, lawyer, composer; b. Warren, Ohio, Apr. 3, 1919; d. Louis and Mary (Oyer) Moidel; 1 child, Mark Lee. Student U. Calif., 1936-39, U. So. Calif., 1939-41; JD, Pacific Coast U., 1942. Bar: Calif. 1943, U.S. Dist. Ct. 1943, U.S. Supreme Ct. 1958. Gen. practice law; mem. firm Moidel, Moidel, Moidel & Smith. Field dir. civilian adv. com. WAC, 1943; mem. nat. bd. Med. Coll. Pa. (formerly Woman's Med. Coll. Pa.), 1953—, exec. bd., 1976-80, pres., 1980-82, chmn. past pres. com., 1990-92. Decorated La Orden del Merito Juan Pablo Duarte (Dominican Republic). Mem. ABA, State Bar Calif. (servicemen's legal aid com., conf. com. on unauthorized practice of medicine, 1964, Disting. Svc. award 1993), L.A. Bar Assn. (psychopathic ct. com., Outstanding Svc. award 1993), L.A. Lawyers Club (pub. defenders com.), Nat. Assn. Women Lawyers (chmn. com. unauthorized practice of law, social commn. UN, regional dir. western states, Hawaii 1949-51, mem. jud. adminstrn. com. 1960, nat. chmn. world peace through law com. 1966-67, liaison to ABA sr. lawyers divsn. 1996—), League of Ams. (dir.), Inter-Am. Bar Assn., So. Calif. Women Lawyers Assn. (pres. 1947, 48), Women Lawyers Assn. L.A. (chmn. Law Day com. 1966, subject of oral hist. project, 1986), Coun. Bar Assns. L.A. County (charter sec. 1950), Calif. Bus. Women's Coun. (dir. 1951), L.A. Bus. Women's Coun. (pres. 1952), Calif. Pres.'s Coun. (1st v.p.), Nat. Assn. Composers U.S.A. (dir. 1974-79, ann. luncheon chmn. 1975), Nat. Fedn. Music Clubs (nat. vice chmn. for Western region, 1973-78), Calif. Fedn. Music Clubs (state chmn. Am. Music 1971-75, state conv. chmn. 1972), Docents of L.A. Philharm. (v.p. 1973-83, chmn. Latin Am. community rels. 1972-75, press and pub. rels. 1972-75, cons. coord. 1973-75), Assn. Learning in Retirement Orgns. in West (pres. 1993-94, exec. com. 1994-95, Disting. Svc. award 1995), Euterpe Opera Club (v.p. 1974-75, chmn. auditions 1972, chmn. awards 1973-75), ASCAP, Iota Tau Tau (dean L.A., supreme treas.), Plato Soc. of UCLA (Toga editor, 1990-93, sec. 1991-92, chmn. colloquium com. 1992-93, discussion leader UCLA Constitution Bicentennial Project, 1985-87, moderator UCLA extension lecture series 1990, Exceptional Leadership award 1994). Composer of numerous works including Espressivo-Four Piano Pieces (orchestral premiere 1987, performance Nat. Mus. Women in the Arts 1989). Home: 5272 Lindley Ave Encino CA 91316-3518

SMITH, SEYMOUR MASLIN, financial advisor, investment banker; b. Hartford, Conn., Sept. 19, 1941; s. Seymour Ewing and Margaret Ruth (Maslin) S.; m. Anita P. Streeter, Nov. 12, 1966. A.B., Hamilton Coll., 1963; M.B.A., Columbia U., 1970. With Conn. Bank and Trust Co., Hartford, 1970-85, sr. v.p., 1976-80, exec. v.p., treas., 1980-85; pres. Am. Cruise Lines Inc., 1986-87; exec. v.p., chief fin. officer New Eng. Savs. Bank, New London, 1989-93; fin. advisor, investment banker pvt. practice, Essex, Conn., 1993-94; v.p., CFO Patient Edn. Media, Inc. (an affiliate of Time Life, Inc.), 1995-97. Trustee Conn. Public Expenditure Council, Conn. State U., 1973-83. Served to lt. USN, 1963-68, Vietnam. Republican. Episcopalian.

SMITH, SHARMAN BRIDGES, state librarian; b. Lambert, Miss., Sept. 2, 1951; d. Gilbert Asa and Vivian Pearl Bridges; m. Gary Walter Smith, Oct. 3, 1975; children: Heather Elisabeth, Millicent Helen. BS, Miss. U. for Women, Columbus, 1972; MLS, George Peabody Coll., Nashville, 1975. Head libr. Clinton (Miss.) Pub. Libr., 1972-74; asst. dir. Lincoln-Lawrence-Franklin Regional Libr., Brookhaven, Miss., 1975-77, dir., 1977-78; info. svcs. mgr. Miss. Libr. Commn., Jackson, 1978-87, asst. dir. libr. ops., 1987-89, dir. libr. svcs. div., 1989-92; state librarian State Libr. of Iowa, Des Moines, 1992—; bd. trustees Bibliog. Ctr. for Rsch., Denver. Office: State Libr Iowa E 12th St Grand Des Moines IA 50319

SMITH, SHARON PATRICIA, university dean; b. Jersey City, Nov. 6, 1948; d. Vincent C. and Dorothy (Linehan) S. AB, Rutgers U., 1970, MA, 1972, PhD, 1974. Rsch. assoc. Princeton (N.J.) U., 1974-76, vis. sr. rsch. economist, 1988-90; economist Fed. Res. Bank, N.Y.C., 1976-81, sr. economist, 1981-82; dist. mgr. AT&T, N.Y.C. and Piscataway, N.J., 1982-90; prof. mgmt. systems, dean Coll. of Bus. Adminstrn. Fordham U., Bronx, 1990—; vis. assoc. prof. N.Y. State Sch. Indsl. and Labor Rels., Ithaca, N.Y., 1981; adj. assoc. Drew U., Madison, N.J., 1984. Author: Equal Pay in the Public Sector: Fact or Fantasy, 1977, (with Albert Rees) Faculty Retirement in the Arts and Sciences, 1991; contbr. articles to profl. jours. Adv. bd. Archbishop Hughes Inst. on Religion and Culture. NDEA fellow, 1970-73. Mem. Am. Econ. Assn., N.J. Human Resource Planners Assn., Indsl. Rels. Rsch. Assn., Security Traders Assn. (bd. govs., adv. com.), Am. Assn. for Higher Edn., Princeton Club N.Y. Democrat. Roman Catholic. Home: 45 Wellington Ave Short Hills NJ 07078-3307 Office: Fordham U Coll of Bus Adminstrn Faber Hall Rm 351 Bronx NY 10458

SMITH, SHARRON WILLIAMS, chemistry educator; b. Ashland, Ky., Apr. 3, 1941; d. James Archie and May (Waggoner) Williams; m. William Owen Smith, Jr., Aug. 16, 1964; children: Leslie Dyan, Kevin Andrew. BA, Transylvania U., 1963; PhD, U. Ky., 1975. Chemist, Procter & Gamble, Cin., 1963-64; tchr. sci. Lexington pub. schs., Ky., 1964-67; chemist NIH, Bethesda, Md., 1974-75; asst. prof. chemistry Hood Coll., Frederick, Md., 1975-81, assoc. prof., 1981-87, prof. 1987—, chair dept. chemistry, physics and astronomy, 1982-86, 95—, acting dean grad. sch. 1989-91, Whitaker prof. Chemistry, 1993—. NDEA fellow, 1967-70, Dissertation Yr. fellow U. Ky., Lexington, 1970-71; grantee Hood Coll. Bd. Assocs., 1981, 85, 91, Beneficial-Hodson faculty fellow Hood Coll., 1984, 92; grantee NSF, 1986. Mem. AAAS, Am. Chem. Soc., Middle Atlantic Assn. Liberal Arts Chemistry Tchrs. (pres. 1984-85). Democrat. Office: Hood Coll Dept Chemistry Frederick MD 21701

SMITH, SHEILA DIANE, medical transcriptionist; b. Caribou, Maine, Aug. 20, 1965; d. Melvin and Flora Jane (Michaud) Kennard; m. John Philip Smith, Aug. 25, 1984; children: Daniel Craig, Janelle Marie. Cert. legal asst., Hillcrest Inst., Portland, Maine, 1993; cert med. transcriptionist, At-Home Professions, Ft. Collins, Colo., 1993; cert. in fin. statement analysis, payroll I & collections, Am. Inst. Profl. Bookkeepers, 1995. Lic. occupl. sec., Fla. Sec., data entry processor Aroostook County Courthouse, Caribou, Maine, 1983; typist, adminstrv. asst. Continental Contracting Co., Mascoutah, Ill., Houston, 1986-87; sales assoc. AAFES Main Exch., Torrejon AB, Spain, 1990-91; family daycare provider MWR (USAF), Torrejon AB, Spain, 1991; med. clk., adminstrv. asst. 401st Hosp. (USAF), Torrejon AB, Spain, 1991-92; med. transcriptionist, sec. Bridgeway Ctr., Inc., Ft. Walton Beach, Fla., 1993-94; owner, med. transcriptionist, billing specialist Smith's Bus. Svcs., Eglin AFB, Fla., 1994—. Vol. Girl Scouts Am., Eglin AFB, 1994-95; mem. nat. steering com. Clinton/Gore '96 Campaign, Washington, 1995-96. Mem. AAUW, NAFE, Am. Inst. Profl. Bookkeepers, Smithsonian Inst. (assoc.). Roman Catholic. Avocations: snorkeling, travel, reading, cooking. Office: Smith's Bus Svcs 102 Fir St Eglin AFB FL 32542-1216

SMITH, SHERWOOD DRAUGHON, retired hospital administrator; b. Durham, N.C., Feb. 12, 1925; s. Cody Hood and Eula (Draughon) S.; m. Patricia Ann Collins, Jan. 27, 1952; children—David Cody, Kenneth Heber, Sherwood Allan, Steven Collins, Sarah Amy. B.A., Duke, 1950, M.S., 1952. Asst. adminstr. Hubbard Hosp., Nashville, 1952-54; adminstr. Hubbard Hosp., 1954-56; exec. dir. Lakeland (Fla.) Gen. Hosp., 1956-88, ret., 1988. Bd. dirs., exec. com. Suncoast Health Council; bd. dirs. Blue Cross Fla.; past pres., bd. dirs. Southeastern Hosp. Conf., del., 1968-80; pres. Central Fla. Hosp. Council, 1961-62; mem. Fla. Health Planning Council, 1971—; Mem. Adv. Com. Employment, Lakeland; mem. Polk County Planning Council, 1970—; bishop Ch. of Jesus Christ of Latter-day Saints. Served with AUS, 1942-46. Fellow Am. Coll. Hosps. Adminstrs. (regent dist. III 1970-73); mem. Fla. Hosp. Assn. (pres. 1966, bd. dirs.), Am. Hosp. Assn. (Fla. del. 1967-73, trustee 1974-80, chmn. regional adv. bd.). Club: Rotarian. Home: 1515 Leighton Ave Lakeland FL 33803-2518

SMITH, SHERWOOD HUBBARD, JR., utilities executive; b. Jacksonville, Fla., Sept. 1, 1934; s. Sherwood Hubbard and Catherine Gertrude (Milliken) S.; m. Eva Hackney Hargrave, July 20, 1957; children: Marlin Hamilton, Cameron Hargrave, Eva Hackney. AB, U. N.C., 1956, JD, 1960; D civil laws, St. Augustine's Coll., 1988; LDD, Campbell U., 1990; HHD, Francis Marion Coll., 1990. Bar: N.C. 1960. Assoc. Lassiter, Moore & Van Allen, Charlotte, 1960-62; ptnr. Joyner & Howison, Raleigh, 1963-65; assoc. gen. counsel Carolina Power & Light Co., Raleigh, 1965-70, sr. v.p., gen. counsel, 1971-74, exec. v.p., 1974-76, pres., 1976-92; CEO Carolina Power & Light Co., Raleigh, N.C., 1979-96; chmn. bd. Carolina Power & Light Co., Raleigh, 1980—; bd. dirs. Global TransPark Found., Inc., No. Telecom Ltd., Northwestern Mut. Life Inst. Co., Springs Industries, Wachovia Corp.; dir. Nuclear Energy Inst., 1994—; pres., dir. Global TransPark Authority; chmn. Am. Nuclear Energy Coun., 1980-83, Edison Electric Inst., 1985-86, Southeastern Elec. Reliability Coun., 1988-90, Nuclear Power Oversight Com., 1990-94. Mem. N.C. Coun. Mgmt. and Devel.; trustee Z Smith Reynolds Found., 1978-96, Nat. Humanities Ctr.; bd. dirs. N.C. Citizens for Bus. and Industry, chmn., 1985-86; bd. dirs. Rsch. Triangle Found. of N.C.; mem. Tirangle Univs. Ctr. Advanced Studies, 1986—; bd. dirs. Microelectronics Ctr. of N.C., 1980—; mem. Kenan Inst. Pvt. Enterprise; trustee Com. Econ. Devel.; mem. Bus. Coun., 1991—, Bus. Roundtable; former bd. trustees, chmn. Rex Hosp. Recipient Nat. Humanitarian award Am. Lung Assn., 1993, Outstanding Leadership award in Mgmt. scis. Am. Soc. Mech. Engrs., 1983, A.E. Finley Disting. Svc. award Greater Raleigh C. of C., 1985, Disting. Citizenship award N.C. Citizens Bus. and Industry, 1997. Mem. Elec. Power Rsch. Inst. (bd. dirs. 1984-89), Greater Raleigh C. of C. (pres. 1979), Am. Nuclear Soc., U.S. C. of C. (energy com.), Assn. Edison Illuminating Cos. (pres. 1990-91), Phi Beta Kappa. Home: 408 Drummond Dr Raleigh NC 27609-7006 Office: Carolina Power & Light Co PO Box 1551 411 Fayetteville Street Mall Raleigh NC 27602-1551

SMITH, SHERYL VELTING, elementary school executive director; b. Grand Rapids, Mich., Apr. 5, 1946; d. Louis and Martha (Kamminga) Velting; children: Laura, Paul. BA in Elem. Edn., Western Mich. U., Kalamazoo, 1968; MA in Adminstrn. and Supr./Edn., Akron U., 1980. Cert. edn. adminstr. and supr. Elem. tchr. Northview Pub. Schs., Grand Rapids, Mich., 1968-69, Ft. Knox (Ky.) Dependent Schs., 1969-70, Dept. of Def., Okinawa, 1970-71, Jefferson County Schs., Louisville, 1971-76, Hudson (Ohio) Local Schs., 1976-80; dir., preschool tchr. The Treehouse Preschool, 1981-83; exec. dir. High Meadows Sch., Roswell, Ga., 1993—; regional conf. bd. Assn. Gifted Children, Akron, Ohio, 1979; chairwomen bd. dirs. Friends of High Meadows, Roswell, Ga., 1990-94; mem. adv. bd. Mt. Pisgah Christian Schs., Alpharetta, Ga., 1991-92; mem. North Fulton Cmty. Found. Bd., 1996—. Avocations: sports, gardening, travel, reading. Office: High Meadows Sch 1055 Willeo Rd Roswell GA 30075-4131

SMITH, SHIRLEY, artist; b. Wichita, Kans., Apr. 17, 1929; d. Harold Marvin and Blanche Carrie (Alexander) S. BFA, Kans. State U., 1951; postgrad., Provincetown (Mass.) Workshop, 1962-66. One woman exhbns. 55 Mercer St. Gallery, N.Y.C., 1973, Wichita Art Mus, 1978, Stamford Mus. and Nature Ctr., Conn., 1987, Aaron Gallery, Washington, 1987, 88, Joan Hodgell Gallery, Sarasota, Fla., 1987; group exhbns. include Chrysler Mus., Provincetown, 1964, The Va. Mus., Richmond, 1970, Whitney Mus. Am. Art, 1971, Colo. Springs Fine Art Ctr., 1972, Everson Mus., Syracuse, N.Y., 1976-80, Nat. Acad. Design, N.Y.C., 1986, One Penn Pla., N.Y.C., 1987, 88, Am. Acad., Inst. Arts and Letters, N.Y.C., 1990, 91; permanent collections Whitney Mus. Am. Art, N.Y.C., U. Calif. Art Mus., Berkeley, Phoenix Art Mus., The Aldrich Mus. Contemporary Art, Ridgefield, Conn., Ulrich Mus., Wichita, Everson Mus., Syracuse, South County Bank collection, St. Louis, Prudential Life Ins., Newark, N.J., King Features Syndicate, N.Y.C., Chase Manhattan Bank Collection, N.Y.C., Senator Nancy Kassabaum Russel Senate Bldg., Washington. Recipient Grumbacher Cash award for mixed media New Eng. Exhibition, Silvermine, Conn., 1967, Acad. Inst. award Am. Acad. Arts and Letters, N.Y.C., 1991. Mem. Artist Equity. Democrat. Presbyterian. Avocation: bike riding. Home: 141 Wooster St New York NY 10012-3163

SMITH, SIBLEY JUDSON, JR., historic site administrator; b. Alexandria, La., June 26, 1955; s. Sibley Judson and Eunice Lee (Raulins) S.; m. Alice Laurie Casey, Nov. 28, 1980; children: Jacob Lee, Casey Raulins. Student, N.E. La. U., 1973-76; BA in History magna cum laude, Christopher Newport Coll., 1985; MA in Am. Studies, Coll. of William and Mary, 1992. Mus. interpreter Colonial Williamsburg (Va.) Found., 1979-87; coord. of interpretation Historic Hudson Valley, Inc., Tarrytown, N.Y., 1987-88; historic site mgr. Philipse Manor Hall State Historic Site, Yonkers, N.Y., 1988-91; exec. dir. Historic Allaire (N.J.) Village, Inc., 1991—. Mem. Alpha Chi, Alpha Psi Omega. Avocations: gardening, theater, movies, mus. Office: Allaire Village Inc PO Box 220 Farmingdale NJ 07727-0220

SMITH, SIDNEY OSLIN, JR., lawyer; b. Gainesville, Ga., Dec. 30, 1923; s. Sidney Oslin and Isabelle Price (Charters) S.; m. Patricia Irwin Horkan, Aug. 4, 1944; children—Charters Smith Wilson, Ellen Smith Andersen, Sidney Oslin III. A.B. cum laude, Harvard Coll., 1947; LL.B. summa cum laude, U. Ga., 1949. Bar: Ga. 1948. Ptnr. Telford, Wayne & Smith, Gainesville, Ga., 1949-62; asst. solicitor Superior Cts., Northeastern Jud. Cir. Ga., 1951-61, judge, 1962-65; judge U.S. Dist. Ct. (no. dist.) Ga., 1965-68, chief judge, 1968-74; ptnr. Alston, Miller & Gaines, Atlanta, 1974-82; ptnr. Alston & Bird, Atlanta, 1982-94, of counsel, 1994—. Chmn. Gainesville Bd. Edn., 1959-62; trustee Brenau Coll., Gainesville, 1974—, chmn., 1976-84; mem. state bd. regents Univ. System of Ga., 1980-87, chmn., 1984-85. Served to capt. U.S. Army, 1943-46, ETO. Fellow ABA, Am. Coll. Trial Lawyers; mem. Am. Law Inst., Am. Judicature Soc., Commerce Club, Chattahoochee Club, Phi Beta Kappa, Phi Kappa Phi, Phi Delta Phi, Phi Delta Theta. Democrat. Episcopalian. Home: 2541 Club Dr Gainesville GA 30506-1769 Office: Alston & Bird 1 Atlantic Ctr 1201 W Peachtree St NW Atlanta GA 30309-3400

SMITH, SIDNEY RUFUS, JR., linguist, educator; b. Greensboro, N.C., Sept. 18, 1931; s. Sidney Rufus and Page (Johnston) S.; m. Vera Pautzsch, Apr. 19, 1969 (div. 1975); children: Stephanie Alice, Eric Brian. B.A., Duke U., 1953; Ph.D., U. N.C., 1965. Asst. prof. U. Conn., Storrs, 1965-66; asst. prof. U. N.C., Chapel Hill, 1966-71, assoc. prof., 1971-79, prof., 1979—, chmn. Germanic langs., 1979-89, 94—, chmn. linguistics, 1981-84. Author numerous articles for profl. publs. Local troop leader Girl Scouts U.S.A. Served to sgt. AUS, 1953-56. Recipient Northeast Conf. Teaching Langs. Stephen Freeman award, 1969. Mem. Linguistic Soc. Am., MLA, Soc. Advancement Scandinavian Study, Am. Assn. Tchrs. German, S. Atlantic MLA, Internat. Brotherhood Magicians. Democrat. Office: U NC Dept Germanic Langs Chapel Hill NC 27599

SMITH, SINJIN, beach volleyball player; b. L.A., May 7, 1957. Former pres. Assn. Volleyball Profls.; pres. Internat. Volleyball Fedn., World Beach Coun. Bd. dirs. Big Bros., U.S. Volleyball Assn. Named Most Successful Player in History, 1996 Olympian. Office: 1156 Embury St Pacific Palisades CA 90272-2503

SMITH, SPENCER BAILEY, engineering and business educator; b. Ottawa, Ont., Can., Jan. 31, 1927; s. Sidney B. and Etta (Bailey) S.; m. Mildred E. Spidell, Dec. 31, 1954. B.Eng., McGill U., 1949; M.S., Columbia U., 1950, Eng.Sc.D., 1958. Adminstrv. engr. Mergenthaler Linotype Co., N.Y.C., 1953-58; ops. research mgr. Raytheon Co., Newton, Mass., 1958-61; ops research mgr. Montgomery Ward & Co., Chgo., 1961-66; assoc. prof., then prof. Ill. Inst. Tech., 1966-96, prof. emeritus, 1996—, chmn. dept. indsl. and systems engring., 1971-77, dir. Stuart Sch. Office of Research, 1977-82; tchr. TV courses Nat. Tech. U. Author: Computer-Based Production and Inventory Control, 1989; contbr. articles to profl. jours.; patentee on order quantity calculator, 1964. Vol. cons. on sch. redistricting Elem. Sch. Dist., Evanston, Ill., 1972-74. Research grantee Harris Trust and Savs. Bank, 1968-70, Ill. Law Enforcement Commn., 1972-74, U.S. Army C.E., 1981, Am. Prodn. and Inventory Control Soc., 1980. Mem. Ops. Rsch. Soc. Am., Inst. Mgmt. Sci., Inst. Indsl. Engrs., Am. Statis. Assn., ASME, Am. Prodn. and Inventory Control Soc., Soc. Mfg. Engrs. Presbyterian. Club: University (Chgo.). Home: 2530 Lawndale Ave Evanston IL 60201-1158

SMITH, STAN VLADIMIR, economist, financial service company executive; b. Rhinelander, Wis., Nov. 16, 1946; s. Valy Zdenek and Sylvia S.; children: Cara, David. BS in Ops. Research, Cornell U., 1968; MBA, U. Chgo., 1972, postgrad., 1973. Lectr. U. Chgo., 1973; economist bd. govs. Fed. Res. System, Washington, 1973-74; staff economist First Nat. Bank of Chgo., 1974; assoc. December Group, Chgo., 1974-77; founding pres. Seaquest Internat., Chgo., 1977-85; mgr., ptnr. Ibbotson Assocs., Chgo., 1981-85; pres. Corp. Fin. Group, Ltd., Chgo., 1981-85; expert econ. witness in field; adj. prof. Coll. Law DePaul U., Chgo. Author: Economic/Hedonic Damages, 1990; founding editor Stocks, Bonds, Bills and Inflation yearbook, 1983; bd. editors Jour. Forensic Economics, 1991—; also contbr. articles in field. Founder, exec. dir. Ctr. for Value of Life, 1996. Fellow Allied Chem.,

1967, John McMullen Trust, 1969; grantee Ford Found., 1972, U.S. Fed. Res., 1973. Mem. Am. Econ. Assn., Am. Fin. Assn., Nat. Assn. Forensic Econs., Nat. Acad. Econ. Arbitrators (founder 1989—), Am. Arbitration Assn. (arbitrator 1994-96), Nat. Future Assn. (arbitrator), Am. Bd. Forensic Examiners, Alpha Delta Phi. Office: Corp Fin Group 1165 N Clark St Ste 650 Chicago IL 60610-7861

SMITH, STANFORD SIDNEY, state treasurer; b. Denver, Oct. 20, 1923; s. Frank Jay and Lelah (Beamer) S.; m. Harriet Holdrege, Feb. 7, 1947; children: Monta Smith Ramirez, Franklin Stanley. Student, Calif. Inst. Tech., 1941-42, Stanford U., 1942-43; BS, U.S. Naval Acad., 1946. Pres. Vebar Livestock Co., Thermopolis, Wyo., 1961—; mem. Wyo. Senate, 1974-76; pres. Wyo. Wool GrowersAssn., 1976-78; mem. Wyo. Ho. of Reps., Cheyenne, 1978-82; treas. State Wyo., Cheyenne, 1983—; dir. Coun. of State Govts., 1990-92; v.p. Wyo. Wool Growers, dir., 1976-82. County commr. Hot Springs County, Wyo, 1966-74. Lt. USN, 1943-54. Decorated Bronze Star. Mem. Nat. Assn. State Treas. (pres. 1990-91). Republican. Methodist. Office: State of Wyoming State Capital Cheyenne WY 82002

SMITH, STANLEY BERTRAM, clinical pathologist, allergist, immunologist, anatomic pathologist; b. Phila., 1929. MD, Washington U., St. Louis, 1956. Diplomate Am. Bd. Clin. Pathology, Am. Bd. Allergy and Immunology, Am. Bd. Anatomic Pathology. Intern Barnes Hosp., St. Louis, 1956-57; resident in pathology Jackson Meml. Hosp., 1957-62; fellow in immunology Sch. Medicine Yale U., New Haven, 1963-65; chief of Pathology Lab Miami (Fla.) Children's Hosp. Mem. AAAS, ACP, AMA, Am. Acad. Allergy and Immunology, N.Y. Acad. Sci., Internat. Acad. Pathology, Internat. Soc. Analytic Cytology. Office: Miami Children's Hosp 3100 SW 62nd Ave Miami FL 33155-3009

SMITH, STANLEY KENT, economics and demographics educator; b. Peoria, Ill., Oct. 11, 1945; s. Tilman R. and Louella M. (Schertz) S.; m. Rita J. Kandel, Aug. 12, 1967; children: Ian, Rachel. BA with high honors, Goshen Coll., 1967; postgrad., Mich. State U., 1971-72; PhD, U. Mich., 1976. Asst. dir. Mennonite Cen. Com., Cochabamba, Bolivia, 1968-70; teaching fellow Mich. State U., East Lansing, 1971-72; econ. demography trainee U. Mich., Ann Arbor, 1972-76; asst. prof. econs. and demographics U. Fla., Gainesville, 1976-81, assoc. prof., 1981-90, prof., dir. bur. econ. and bus. rsch., 1990—; cons. numerous orgns. including GM, Petroleum Inst. Am., N.Y. Times, 1977—; Fla. rep. Fed.-State Coop. Program for Population Estimates and Projections, 1976—. Contbr. articles to profl. publs. Treas. Alachua County Boys Choir, Gainesville, 1984-86; coach Youth Soccer, Inc., Gainesville, 1985; moderator United Ch., Gainesville, 1988-89. Mem. Am. Econ. Assn., Population Assn. Am., So. Demographic Assn. Avocations: sports, music, travel. Office: Univ Fla Bur Economic & Business Rsch 221 Matherly Hall Gainesville FL 32611-2017

SMITH, STANTON KINNIE, JR., utility executive, lawyer; b. Rockford, Ill., Feb. 14, 1931; s. Stanton Kinnie and Elizabeth (Brown) S.; m. Mary Beth Sanders, July 11, 1953; children: Stanton E., Kathryn A., Dana. BA, Yale U., 1953; JD, U. Wis., 1956. Bar: Ill. 1956, Mich. 1976. Ptnr. Sidley & Austin, Chgo., 1964-84; vice-chmn., gen. counsel Am. Natural Resources Co., Detroit, 1984-87; sr. v.p. Costal Corp., Houston, 1985-87, also dir.; vice chmn., gen. counsel CMS Energy Corp., 1987-88, pres. 1988-92, vice chmn., 1992-96, also bd. dirs.; sr. counsel Skadden, Arps, Slate, Meagher & Flom; bd. dirs. Clarcor Corp. Trustee Founders Soc., Detroit Inst. Arts, Rockford Coll., Devel. Bd. Yale U., Mich. Opera Theater; bd. advisors U. Wis. Law Sch., Mich. State U., Pub. Utility Inst. Office: Skadden Arps Slate Meagher & Flom 919 3rd Ave New York NY 10022

SMITH, STEPHANIE MARIE, lawyer; b. Manhattan, Kans., May 15, 1955; d. William C. and Joyce A. (Davis) S. BS in Fgn. Studies (Economics), Georgetown U., 1977; JD, U. Mich., 1980. Bar: Colo. 1980, U.S. Dist. Ct. Colo. 1980, U.S. Ct. Appeals (10th cir.) 1980, (9th cir.) 1995, Ariz. 1985, Nev. 1985, U.S. Dist. Ct. Nev. 1985. Assoc. Fishman & Geman, Denver, 1980-81, Hart & Trinen, Denver, 1982-85; ptnr. Jolley, Urga, Wirth & Woodbury, Las Vegas, Nev., 1985—; lawyer rep. 9th Cir. Jud. Conf., 1994—, chmn. Nev. delegation, 1995. Mem. ABA, Nev. Bar Assn., Am. Bankruptcy Inst., So. Nev. Bankruptcy Lawyers' Assn. Office: Jolley Urga Wirth & Woodbury 300 S 4th St Ste 800 Las Vegas NV 89101-6018

SMITH, STEPHEN ALEXANDER, retail and wholesale food distribution company executive; b. Toronto, Ont., Can., Mar. 1, 1957; s. Alexander and Norma Eileen (McEwan) S.; m. Mary E. Cavasin, June 14, 1980; children: Lauren, Carolyn. B Commerce, U. Toronto, 1979. Chartered acctg., Ont. Acct. Price Waterhouse, Toronto, 1979-84, mgr., 1984-85; mgr. systems and internal control Loblaw Cos. Ltd., Toronto, 1985-86, asst. contr., 1986-87, contr., 1987—, v.p., 1989—, sr. v.p., 1994—. Office: Loblaw Cos Ltd, 22 St Clair Ave E Ste 1500, Toronto, ON Canada M4T 2S8

SMITH, STEPHEN DALE, safety engineer; b. Hamilton, Ohio, Dec. 2, 1951; s. Dale H. and Katherine M. (Schmidt) S.; m. Sabrina Gara Smith, May 29, 1982; 1 child, Corita K. BS, Miami U., Oxford, Ohio, 1975; MS, Ctrl. Mo. State U., Warrensburg, 1979. Driver edn. tchr. Switzerland County Schs., Vevay, Ind., 1975-78; grad. asst. Ctrl. Mo. State U., 1978-79; hwy. safety technician Nat. Hwy. Transp. Safety Adminstrn., U.S. Dept. Transp., Kansas City, Mo., 1979-80; safety advisor GCC Beverages, Boston, 1980-83; safety mgr. GCC Beverages/Pepsi-Cola, Miami, Fla., 1983-84; safety specialist Fed. Express, Parsippany, N.J., 1984-87; sr. safety specialist Fed. Express, Cin., 1987-96; sr. loss prevention cons. Acordia/Rauh, Cin., 1996—. Active Eagle Scout, Boy Scouts Am., Parsippany, also Fairfield, Ohio, 1983—. Mem. Am. Soc. Safety Engrs. (sec. S.W. Ohio chpt. 1994-95, v.p. 1995-96, pres. 1996-97). Home: 5100 W Scioto Dr Fairfield OH 45014-1563 Office: Acordia/Rauh 1014 Vine St Ste 1100 Cincinnati OH 45202-1119

SMITH, STEPHEN EDWARD, lawyer; b. Boston, Aug. 5, 1950; s. Sydney and Minnie (Appel) S.; m. Eileen Beth O'Farrell, June 15, 1986; children: Nora, Bennett, Liliana. AB in Polit. Sci., Boston U., 1972; JD, Washington U., St. Louis, 1976. Bar: Ill. 1976, Mass. 1985, U.S. Dist. Ct. (no. dist.) Ill. 1977, U.S. Dist. Ct. (no. dist.) Ind. 1986, U.S. Dist. Ct. Mass. 1987, U.S. Dist. Ct. (so. dist.) Wis. 1987, U.S. Ct. Appeals (7th cir.) 1981. Assoc., ptnr. Brown & Blumberg, Chgo., 1976-80; founding ptnr. Cantwell, Smith & Van Daele, Chgo., 1980-84; ptnr. Gottlieb & Schwartz, Chgo., 1984-85; of cousnel Siemon, Larsen & Prudy, Chgo., 1985-90; solo pracittioner Chgo., 1990-94; assoc. prof. clin. practice Ill. Inst. Tech. Chgo.-Kent Coll. law, Chgo., 1994-95; of counsel Field Golan & Swiger, Chgo., 1995—; mediator Ctr. for Conflict Resolution, Chgo., 1992—; cmty. adv. coun. WBEZ, Chgo., 1985—; arbitrator NASD, Chgo., 1994—; mediator, arbitrator Duke U. Pvt. Adjudication Ctr. Author: ADR for Financial Institutions, 1995. Past. bd. dirs., past pres. Jane Addams Ctr., Hull House Assn., Chgo. Mem. Am. Arbitration Assn. (comml. and internat. panels), Univ. Club of Chgo. Office: Field Golan & Swiger 21st Floor Three First Nat Plz Chicago IL 60602

SMITH, STEPHEN GRANT, journalist; b. N.Y.C., Mar. 6, 1949; s. John J. and Nora O.S.; m. Sarah Rowbotham Bedell, May 22, 1982; children: R. Kirk Bedell, Elisabeth DeCou Bedell, David Branson Smith. Student, Deerfield Acad.; BA, U. Pa., 1971. City Hall reporter Daily Hampshire Gazette, Northampton, Mass., 1971-73; spl. assignment reporter Albany Times-Union, 1973-74; dep. regional editor Phila. Inquirer, 1974-76; asst. met. editor Boston Globe, 1976-78; sr. editor Horizon Mag., 1978; staff writer Time Mag., 1978-80, sr. editor, 1980-82, Nation editor, 1982-85, acting asst. mng. editor, 1985-86; exec. editor Newsweek Mag., 1986-91; Washington news editor Knight-Ridder newspapers, 1991-94; founding editor Civilization Mag., Washington, 1994-96; editor Nat. Jour., 1996—; chmn. publs. com. U. Pa. Chmn. publs. com. U. Pa. Mem. Am. Soc. Mag. Editors, Coun. of Fgn. Rels., World Affairs Coun. Washington, U. Pa. Gen. Alumni Soc. (exec. com.), Fourth Estate Golf Soc. Clubs: St. Anthony Hall, Nat. Press, Brook, Century, Met., Beefsteak, White's. Home (summer): PO Box 183 Little Compton RI 02837-0183 Office: Nat Jour 1501 M St NW Washington DC 20005

SMITH, STEPHEN KENDALL, lawyer; b. Burlington, Vt., May 31, 1941; s. Lester Hurlin and Elizabeth Helen (Mitchell) S.; m. Margaret Anne Weir, Sept. 2, 1967; children: Andrew Kendall, Edward Anthony, Charles Franklin, Charlotte Catherine. AB with distinction, Ind. U., 1964; BA, Oxford U., 1966, MA, 1971; JD, Columbia U., 1972. Bar: Ind. 1972, U.S. Dist. Ct. (so. dist.) Ind. 1972, U.S. Dist. Ct. (no. dist.) Ind. 1978, U.S. Ct. Appeals (7th cir.). Assoc. Barnes, Hickam, Pantzer & Boyd and predecessors, Indpls., 1972-79, ptnr., 1980-81; ptnr. Barnes & Thornburg and predecessors, Indpls., 1981—, co-chair litigatin mgmt. and econs. com., 1991-94, co-chair equal opportunity in the law com., 1994—. Contbr. articles to legal jours. Sec. Indpls. Com. on Fgn. Rels., 1978-87, chmn., 1987-96. Capt. U.S. Army, 1966-69. Rhodes scholar, 1964. Mem. ABA (litigation sect., jury instrn. project 1983—), Fed. Bar Assn., Ind. Bar Assn., Indpls. Bar Assn., 7th Cir. Bar Assn., SAR (chancellor Ind. Soc. 1985—). Democrat. Presbyterian. Home: 4414 N Meridian St Indianapolis IN 46208-3534 Office: Barnes & Thornburg 11 S Meridian St Ste 1313 Indianapolis IN 46204-3506

SMITH, STEPHEN RANDOLPH, aerospace executive; b. Des Moines, Apr. 17, 1928; s. Norvin Ellis and Helen (Heberling) S.; m. Margaret Anne Graves, Dec. 20, 1950; children: Stephen Randolph Jr., Susan Canning, Sara Kutler, Anne Barrette, Julia Carroll. BSME, Stanford U., 1951, MSME, 1952; MBA Advanced Mgmt. Program, Harvard U., 1974. Registered profl. engr., Calif. Sr. analyst, preliminary design engr. Northrop & Garrett Corps., L.A. and Hawthorne, Calif., 1952-55; propulsion lead design engr. Northrop Corp., Hawthorne, 1955-59; engring. rep. ea. dist. Northrop Corp., Washington, 1959-60; T-38/F-5/F-20 program mgr. Northrop Corp., Hawthorne, 1960-75; v.p. Iran ops. Northrop Corp., Tehran, 1975-78; v.p. advanced stealth projects Northrop Corp., Hawthorne, 1978-83, v.p. engring. and advanced devel., 1983-86, v.p., program mgr. F-20/YF-23A, 1986-88, corp. v.p., gen. mgr. aircraft divsn., 1988-92; cons. tech. mgmt. Palos Verdes, Calif., 1992—; bd. mem. Quarterdeck Ptnrs., Inc., L.A. and Washington, 1992—, NASA Advanced Aeronautics Com., 1984-86; invited lectr. aircraft design USAF Acad., 1983. Author, designer, patentee in field. Bd. dirs. Boy Scouts Am., L.A. coun., 1986—, charter comm. chmn., 1996; pres. Penn Srs., Palos Verdes, Calif., 1996. Sgt. U.S. Army, 1946-48. Recipient Disting. Civilian Svc. medal for Tacit Blue, U.S. Dept. Def., Washington, 1983. Fellow AIAA (chmn. L.A. sect. 1985-86, adv. bd. 1988—, Spl. Citation 1994), Inst. Advancement Engring.; mem. Soc. Automotive Engrs. (chmn. aerotech. 1986-87, honors 1987), Sierra Club, Trailfinders Conservation Coun. (life, coun. chief 1940). Republican. Episcopalian. Avocations: competitive sailing, tennis, backpacking, skiing, running. Home and Office: 2249 Via Guadalana Palos Verdes Estates CA 90274

SMITH, STEVEN ALBERT, philosophy educator; b. What Cheer, Iowa, May 12, 1939; s. Irving James and Mary (Emmons) S.; m. Daryl Goldgraben, Aug. 2, 1970 (div. Mar. 1987); 1 child, David Irving; m. Patricia Adkisson, Aug. 11, 1991. BA, Earlham Coll., 1961; MA, Harvard U., 1963, PhD, 1972. Instr. Claremont (Calif.) McKenna Coll., 1968-72, asst. prof., 1972-75, assoc. prof., 1975-90, full prof. philosophy, 1990—. Author: Satisfaction of Interest and the Concept of Morality, 1974; editor: Ways of Wisdowm, 1983, Everyday Zen, 1989, Nothing Special, 1993, Now Zen, 1995; contbr. articles to profl. jours. Elected bd. mem. Mt. Baldy (Calif.) I&W Assn., 1973-75. Grantee Nat. Endowment for Humanities, 1972. Mem. Am. Philos. Assn., Am. Assn. Philosophy Tchrs., N.Am. Soc. Social Philosophy. Democrat. Quaker. Home: PO Box 16 Mt Baldy CA 91759 Office: Claremont McKenna Coll 890 Columbia Ave Claremont CA 91711-3901

SMITH, STEVEN COLE, engineering process consultant; b. Idaho Falls, Idaho, Oct. 3, 1952; s. Merrell Cordon and Myrtle Jean (McArthur) S.; m. Gay Lynn Pendleton, May 2, 1975; children: Jennifer, Melinda, Gregory, Aimilee. BS, Brigham Young U., 1977; MS, West Coast U., 1992. Engr. Gen. Dynamics, San Diego, 1978-81, Hughes Aircraft, L.A., 1981-82; cons. CAD/CAM Splty., L.A., 1982-83; system mgr. Solar Turbines, San Diego, 1983-87; mktg. support Evans and Sutherland, Costa Mesa, Calif., 1987-88; mktg. mgr. Computervision, San Diego, 1988—; instr. Southwestern C.C., San Diego, 1986-87. Mem. AIAA. Mormon. Office: Computervision 9805 Scranton Rd Ste 160 San Diego CA 92121-1765

SMITH, STEVEN DELANO, professional basketball player; b. Highland Park, Mich., Mar. 31, 1969. Student, Mich. State U. Guard Miami Heat, 1991-94; with Atlanta Hawks, 1994—. Named Sporting News All-Am. First Team, 1990, 91, NBA All-Rookie Team, 1992, Dream Team II, 1994. Office: Atlanta Hawks South Tower One CNN Ctr Ste 405 Atlanta GA 30303*

SMITH, STEVEN RAY, law educator; b. Spirit Lake, Iowa, July 8, 1946; s. Byrnard L. and Dorothy V. (Fischbeck) S.; m. Lera Baker, June 15, 1975. BA, Buena Vista Coll., 1968; JD, U. Iowa, 1971, MA, 1971. Bar: Iowa 1971, Ky. 1987, Ohio 1992. From asst. to assoc. dean Sch. Law U. Louisville, 1974-81, acting dean, 1974-75, 76, prof. law, 1971-88, assoc. in medicine Med. Sch., 1983-88; dep. dir/ Assn. Am. Law Schs., 1987-88; dean, prof. law Cleve. State U., 1988-96; pres., dean and prof. Calif. Western Sch. of Law, 1996—. Author: Law, Behavior and Mental Health: Policy and Practice, 1987; contbr. chpts. to books, articles to profl. jours. Trustee U. Louisville, 1980-82, SCRIBES, 1993—; chmn. faculty adv. com. Ky. Coun. Higher Edn., 1981-82; pres. Ky. Congress of Senate Faculty Leaders, 1982-84; bd. trustees Am. Bd. Profl. Psychology, 1994—. Recipient Grawemeyer award Innovative Teaching. Metroversity Consortium, 1983, Pres. award Cleve.-Marshall Law Alumni Assn., 1995. Fellow Ohio State Bar Found.; mem. ABA (stds. rev. com. 1991-95, govt. rels. com. 1993-95, joint commn. ABA/Assn. Am. Law Schs. financing of legal edn. 1993-94), APA (pub. mem. ethics com.), Am. Econs. Assn., Assn. Am. Law Schs. (chmn. librs. com., dep. dir. 1987-88, mem. accreditation com. 1993-96, chair accreditation com. 1994-96), Ohio State Bar Assn. (coun. of dels. 1992-96), Order of Coif, City Club of Cleve. (pres. 1994-95). Office: Calif Western Sch of Law Office of the Pres 225 Cedar St San Diego CA 92101-3046

SMITH, STEVEN SIDNEY, molecular biologist; b. Idaho Falls, Idaho, Feb. 11, 1946; s. Sidney Ervin and Hermie Phyllis (Robertson) S.; m. Nancy Louise Turner, Dec. 20, 1974. BS, U. Idaho, 1968; PhD, UCLA, 1974. Asst. research scientist Beckman Research Inst. City of Hope Nat. Med. Ctr., Duarte, Calif., 1982-84, staff Cancer Ctr., 1983—, asst. research scientist depts. Thoracic Surgery and Molecular Biology, 1985-87, assoc. research scientist, 1987-95; rsch. scientist City of Hope Nat. Med. Ctr., Duarte, 1995—; dir. dept. cell and tumor biology Beckman Research Inst. City of Hope Nat. Med. Ctr., Duarte, Calif., 1990—; Wellcome vis. prof. in basic med. scis. Okla. State U., 1995-96; cons. Molecular Biosystems Inc., San Diego, 1981-84, Am. Inst. Biol. Scis., Washington, 1994. Contbr. articles to profl. jours. Grantee NIH, 1983-93, Coun. for Tobacco Rsch., 1983-92, March of Dimes, 1988-91, Smokeless Tobacco Rsch. Coun., 1992—, Office of Naval Rsch., 1994—; Swiss Nat. Sci. Found. fellow U. Bern, 1974-77, Scripps Clinic and Rsch. Found., La. Jolla, Calif., 1978-82, NIH fellow Scripps Clinic, 1979-81. Mem. Am. Soc. Cell Biology, Am. Assn. Cancer Rsch., Am. Crystallographic Assn., Am. Chem. Soc., Am. Weightlifting Assn., Phi Beta Kappa. Avocation: backpacking. Office: City of Hope Nat Med Ctr 1500 Duarte Rd Duarte CA 91010-3012

SMITH, STEWART EDWARD, physical chemist; b. Balt., Oct. 5, 1937; s. Ambrose Jefferson and Gladys Ruth (Stewart) S.; children: Nicole Catherine, Stewart Bradford; m. Loretta Inez Moody, Mar. 9, 1994. BS, Howard U., 1960; PhD, Ohio State U., 1969. Chemist Du Pont, Gibbstown, N.J., 1963-64; rsch. chemist Du Pont, Wilmington, Del., 1972-74; tech. svc. rep. Du Pont, Wilmington, 1974-78; rsch. chemist Sun Oil, Marcus Hook, Pa., 1969-71; coal chemist Exxon Rsch. and Engring., Baytown, Tex., 1976-81, group head, 1981-82; relocation coord. Exxon Rsch. and Engring., Clinton, N.J., 1982-84; sr. staff chemist Exxon Rsch. and Engring., Baytown, 1984-86; adv. engr. Westinghouse-Bettis, West Mifflin, Pa., 1986—. Contbr. articles to profl. jours. Mem. jr. high sch. adv. bd., Wilmington, 1975; coach Little League Baseball, Clear Lake City, Tex., 1979. Lt. U.S. Army, 1961-63. Recipient Pres.'s award Howard U. Alumni, Wilmington, 1976. Mem. AAAS, Am. Chem. Soc., Am. Statis. Assn., Sigma Xi, Kappa Alpha Psi. Avocations: physical fitness, jogging, gourmet cooking. Home: 125 Amberwood Ct Bethel Park PA 15102-2252 Office: Westinghouse Elec Corp PO Box 79 West Mifflin PA 15122-0079

SMITH, S(TEWART) GREGORY, ophthalmologist, inventor, product developer, consultant, author; b. Wyandotte, Mich., Jan. 24, 1953; s. Stewart Gene and Veronica (Latta) S. BA in Econs. with distinction, U. Mich., 1974; MD, Wayne State U., 1978. Diplomate Am. Bd. Ophthalmology, Nat. Bd. Med. Examiners. Intern, Sacred Heart Med. Ctr., Spokane, Wash.,1978; resident in ophthalmology U. Minn., Mpls., 1979-82, fellow cornea and anterior segment surgery, 1982-83; practice medicine specializing in cornea and anterior segment surgery, and ophthalmology Wilmington, Del., 1983—; clin. prof. ophthalmology U. Pa., Hershey Med. Ctr., 1984—; clin. asst. prof. Thomas Jefferson U.; attending surgeon Wills Eye Hosp., Phila., 1995—; mem. sr. faculty 3M Vision Care Dept., Mpls., 1984-90, rsch. cons., 1984, lectr., 1983—, cons. Am. Cyanamid Opthalmic Divsn., 1990-94, Am. Home Product, 1995—; lectr. in field, Korea, Hong Kong, Thailand, Malaysia, Phillipines, France, Spain, Ireland, Portugal, Holland, Denmark, England, Sweden; cons. Am. Home Products, 1995—. Author: Complications ofIntraocular Lenses and Their Management, 1988, Can You Really See Perfectly Again Without Glasses?, 1996; co-author: Vision Without Glasses, 1990, Sight for Life, 1990; contbr. articles to Fly Fisherman Mag. and other profl. publs. Patentee investigational devices and pharmaceutical, tilt control for automotive vehicles. Recipient award for Best Sci. Poster, Contact Lens Assn. of Ophthalmologists, 1980; Best Film award Internat. Congress of Cataract Surgeons, 1985; Grand Prize Am. Soc. Cataract and Refractive Surgeons Film Festival, 1986. Fellow Am. Intraocular Implant Soc., Castroviejo Soc. (Best Paper award 1984), AMA, Eye Bank Assn. Am., Am. Soc. Cataract and Refractive Surgery Internat. Soc. Refractive Surgery, Am. Acad. Ophthalmology (Honor award 1996), Assn. for Rsch. and Vision in Ophthalmology, Internat. Intraocular Implant Club, Wills Eye Hosp. Alumni Soc., European Soc. Cataract & Refracture Soc. Avocations: fly fishing, hunting, saxophone, tennis, skiing. Home: Nine Gates Rd Yorklyn DE 19736 Office: 1100 N Grant Ave Wilmington DE 19805-2670

SMITH, STUART A., lawyer; b. N.Y.C., Mar. 16, 1941; s. Sydney S. and Gertrude (Blinder) S.; m. Helaine Levi, Mar. 14, 1982. AB, Columbia Coll., N.Y.C., 1961; LLB, Harvard U., 1964. Bar: N.Y. 1964, U.S. Tax Ct. 1965, U.S. Supreme Ct. 1967, D.C. 1970. Law clk. to chief judge U.S. Tax Ct., Washington, 1964-66; atty. U.S. Dept. Justice Tax Div., Washington, 1966-70; pvt. practice Washington, 1970-73; tax asst. to solicitor gen. U.S. Dept. Justice, Washington, 1973-83; pvt. practice N.Y.C., 1983-91; ptnr. Piper & Marbury LLP, N.Y.C., 1991—. Author: How You Can Get the Most from the New Tax Law, 1982; contbr. articles to law revs. Mem. ABA (chmn. tax sect. subcom.), Assn. of Bar of City of N.Y (fed. taxation com.), Am. Law Inst. (tax adv. group), Univ. Club (N.Y.C., Washington), RAC Club (London). Office: Piper & Marbury LLP 1251 Ave of Ams New York NY 10020-1104

SMITH, STUART LYON, psychiatrist, corporate executive; b. Montreal, Que., Can., May 7, 1938; s. Moe Samuel and Nettie (Krainer) S.; m. Patricia Ann Springate, Jan. 2, 1964; children: Tanya, Craig. BSc, McGill U., 1958, MD, CM, 1962, diploma in psychiatry, 1967; LLD (hon.), Mt. Allison U., 1992. Intern. Montreal Gen. Hosp., 1962-63, resident in psychiatry, 1963-67; from asst. prof. to assoc. prof. medicine McMaster U., Hamilton, Ont., Can., 1967-75; mem. Ont. Legislature, 1975-82, leader Ont. Liberal Party, 1976-82, leader of the opposition, 1977-82; chmn. Sci. Coun. Can., Ottawa, 1982-87; pres. RockCliffe Rsch. and Tech., Inc., 1987—, Philip Utilities Mgmt. Corp., Toronto, Ont., 1994—; sr. v.p. Philip Environment Inc., Toronto, 1994—; bd. dirs. Capital Alliance Ventures, Inc., Can. Trade Group Inc.; chmn. Ensyn Techs., Inc., 1990—; vis. prof. psychiatry McMaster U., 1982-93; adj. prof. U. Ottawa, 1986-94; chmn. com. on inquiry on Can. Univ. Edn., 1989-91; chmn. bd. trustees Ottawa Gen. Hosp., 1991-94; chmn. Nat. Roundtable on Environ. and Economy, Ottawa, 1995—. Mem. bd. govs. U. Ottawa, 1989-94. Decorated knight Nat. Order of Merit, France, 1988; McLaughlin travelling fellow, 1964-65. Fellow Royal Coll. Physicians and Surgeons of Can. Jewish. Office: 100 King St West, 22nd Flr, PO Box 2440 LED # 1, Hamilton, ON Canada

SMITH, STUART SEABORNE, writer, government official, union official; b. N.Y.C., Jan. 27, 1930; s. Purcell Leonard and Elizabeth (Wright) S.; m. Birte Moeller Jacobsen, Apr. 27, 1956 (div. 1972); children: Stuart Seaborne, Bjarne Moeller; m. Editha Maria Fuchs, Jan. 3, 1973; children: Cornelia Gerda, Melanie Carla. Grad., Lawrenceville (N.J.) Sch., 1948; student, Princeton U., 1948-51, U. Heidelberg, Germany, 1953-54, U. Madrid, Spain, 1954-55, U. Copenhagen, Denmark, 1955-56. Reporter Balt. Sun, 1957-65, fgn. corr. chief Bonn (Germany) bur., 1965-69, corr. Washington Bur., 1969-70; with ABA, 1970-71, Dept. Justice, Washington, 1971—; exec. dir. Capitol Employees Organizing Group, 1979—; pub. Balt. Banner, 1965. Served with AUS, 1951-53. Recipient Spl. award for meritorious svc. Washington-Balt. Newspaper Guild, 1965, meritorious award Dept. Justice, 1985, 87, Sustained Superior Performance award Dept. Justice, 1992, 93. Mem. Am. Fedn. State, County and Mcpl. Employees (pres. coun. 26 1977-80, 87-95, chief steward Local 2830 1975-80, 81-82, pres. 1982—, Meritorious Svc. award Local 2830, 1980). Home: 10522 Tyler Ter Potomac MD 20854-4059 Office: Office of Justice Programs Washington DC 20531 *I believe in honor and democracy and social justice. I further believe that for the most part we are the ignorant slaves of political and philosophical superstitions, but in the end the truth shall set us free.*

SMITH, SUE FRANCES, newspaper editor; b. Lockhart, Tex., July 4, 1940; d. Monroe John Baylor and Myrtle (Krause) Mueck; m. Michael Vogtel Smith, Apr. 20, 1963 (div. July 1977); 1 child, Jordan Meredith. B. Journalism, U. Tex., 1962. Feature writer, photographer Corpus Christi Caller Times, 1962-64; feature writer, editor Chgo. Tribune, 1964-76; features editor Dallas Times Herald, 1976-82; sales assoc. Bumpas Assocs., Dallas, 1982-83; asst. mng. editor for features Denver Post, 1983-84, assoc. editor, 1984-91; asst. mng. editor in charge of Sunday paper Dallas Morning News, 1991-94, asst. mng. editor Lifestyles, 1994-96, dep. mng. editor Lifestyles, 1996—; active Coun. Pres., 1993. Mem. Am. Assn. Sunday and Feature Editors (pres. 1993), Newspaper Features Coun. (bd. dirs., sec., treas.), Tex. Associated Press Mng. Editors (bd. dirs.), Delta Gamma. Home: 6060 Jereme Trl Dallas TX 75252-5130 Office: 508 Young St Dallas TX 75202-4808

SMITH, SUE PARKER, media administrator; b. Pendleton, N.C., June 19, 1946; d. Edward Eldridge and Mildred (Conner) Parker; m. Jay Wilson Smith Jr., Nov. 24, 1967; 1 child, Susan Leigh. BEd, East Carolina U., Greenville, N.C., 1967, MEd in LS, 1983. Cert. tchr., media coord., N.C. Librarian Fike High Sch., Wilson (N.C.) City Schs., 1968-72; media coord. Nash-Rocky Mount Sch. System, Elm City, N.C., 1978—. Contbr. articles to profl. jours. Deacon, Nashville (N.C.) Bapt. Ch., 1989—. Mem. N.C. Assn. Educators, N.C. Assn. Sch. Librarians, Order Ea. Star (worthy matron 1989-90). Democrat. Avocations: reading, gardening, walking. Home: PO Box 505 112 E Lucille St Nashville NC 27856-1340 Office: Coopers Elem Sch 6833 S NC58 Elm City NC 27822-9433

SMITH, SUSAN ELIZABETH, guidance director; b. Phila., Mar. 24, 1950; d. E. Burke Hogue and Janet Coffin Hogue Ebert; m. J. Russell Smith, June 17, 1972 (div. June 1989); 1 child, Drew Russell. BS in Elem. Edn., E. Stroudsburg Coll., 1972; MEd in Counseling, U. Okla., 1974, postgrad., 1976-77; postgrad., Trenton State Coll., 1989-90; EdM in Devel. Disabilities, Rutgers U., 1992, postgrad., 1994—. Cert. elem. tchr., N.C.; cert. elem. tchr., early childhood edn. tchr., guidance and counseling, Okla.; cert. elem. tchr., guidance and counseling, tchr. of handicapped, psychology tchr., supr. instrn., dir. student pers. svcs., N.J. Elem. tchr. Morton Elem. Sch. Onslow County Schs., Jacksonville, N.C., 1971-72; instr. U. Isfahan, Iran, 1974-76; guidance counselor Moore (Okla.) Pub. Schs., 1976-77; counselor Johnstone Tng. Ctr. N.J. Divsn. Devel. Disabilities, Bordentown, 1988-90; spl. edn. tchr. Willingboro (N.J.) Schs., 1990-91; guidance counselor Haledon (N.J.) Pub. Schs., 1991-92; spl. edn. adj. tchr. Gateway Sch., Carteret, N.J., 1991-93; guidance counselor Bloomfield (N.J.) Pub. Schs., 1992-94; dir. guidance Somerville (N.J.) Pub. Schs., 1994-95; adj. prof. in spl. edn. Essex County (N.J.) Coll., 1994; guidance Ft. Lee (N.J.) Schs., 1995—; cons., seminar and workshop presenter on behavior mgmt., parenting skills, and behavior modification techniques; cons. N.J. Fragile X Assn. Author: Motivational Awards for ESL Students, 1993, Parent Contracts to Improve School Behaviors, 1996; contbr. articles to profl. jours. Leader Boy Scouts Am., Oklahoma City, 1983-87, com. chmn., Redmond, Wash., 1987-88. Recipient Rsch. award ERIC/CAPS, 1992, Svc. award N.J. Fragile X Assn., 1993. Mem. ACA, Am. Sch. Counselor Assn. (grantee 1992), N.J. Counseling Assn., N.J. Sch. Counseling Assn., Assn. for Multicultural Counseling and Devel., AAUW, Assn. for Counselor Edn. and Supervision, N.J. Assn. for

Counselor Edn. and Supervision, N.J. Prins. and Suprs. Assn., Nat. Assn. Coll. Admissions Counselors (grantee 1995), Alpha Omicron Pi. Episcopalian. Home: 13 Yale St Nutley NJ 07110-3386

SMITH, TAD RANDOLPH, lawyer; b. El Paso, Tex., July 20, 1928; s. Eugene Rufus and Dorothy (Derrick) S.; m. JoAnn Wilson, Aug. 24, 1949; children: Laura Borsch, Derrick, Cameron Ann Compton. BBA, U. Tex. 1952, LLB, 1951. Bar: Tex. 1951; assoc. firm Kemp, Smith, Duncan & Hammond, P.C., El Paso, 1951, ptnr., 1952-81, CEO, 1975-95, shareholder, 1981—; bd. dirs. El Paso Indsl. Devel. Corp. Active United Way of El Paso; chmn. El Paso County Reps., 1958-61, Tex. Rep. State Exec. Com., 1961-62; alt. del. Rep. Nat. Conv., 1952, 62, del., 1964; dir. El Paso Electric Co., 1961-90, State Nat. Bank of El Paso, 1969-90, The Leavell Co., 1970-94; trustee Robert E. and Evelyn McKee Found. 1970-90, Property Trust of America, 1971-91; mem. devel. bd. U. Tex. El Paso, 1973-81, v.p., 1975, chmn. 1976; dinner treas. Nat. Jewish Hosp. and Research Ctr., 1977, chmn. 1978, presenter of honoree, 1985; bd. dirs. Southwestern Children's Home, El Paso, 1959-78, NCCJ, 1965-76, chmn. 1968-69; trustee Hervey Found., 1990—, Lydia Patterson Inst., 1994—. Named Outstanding Young Man El Paso, El Paso Jaycees, 1961; recipient Humanitarian award El Paso chpt. NCCJ, 1983. Fellow Tex. Bar Found.; mem. ABA, Tex. Bar Assn., El Paso Bar Assn. (pres. 1971-72), El Paso C. of C. (dir. 1979-82), Sigma Chi. Republican. Methodist. Home: 5716 Mira Grande Dr El Paso TX 79912-2006 Office: Kemp Smith Duncan & Hammond 2000 Norwest Plz 221 N Kansas St El Paso TX 79901-1443

SMITH, TAL, sports association administrator; b. Framingham, Mass., Sept. 27, 1933; m. Jonnie Smith; children: Valerie, Randy. Student, Culver (Ind.) Mil. Acad.; BA in Bus. Adminstrn., Duke U., 1955. Staff, farm dept. Cin. Reds, 1958-60; asst. to gen. mgr. Houston Astros, 1960-61, farm dir. Colt .45s, 1961-63; asst. to pres. Houston Sports Assn., 1963-65, v.p., dir. player personnel, 1965-72; v.p., dir. ops. Astrodome-Astrohall Stadium Corp., Houston, 1972-73; exec. v.p. N.Y. Yankees, N.Y.C., 1973-75; gen. mgr. Houston Astros, 1975-76, pres., 1976-81; owner, operator Tal Smith Enterprises, Houston, 1981-94; pres. Houston Astros, 1994—. Officer, USAF, 2 yrs. Named Major League Exec. of Yr., Sporting News, 1980. Office: Houston Astros PO Box 288 Houston TX 77001-0288

SMITH, TAYLOR, professional football team executive; b. Atlanta, GA, May 3, 1953; m. Louise; children: Ryan, Brooks, Rebecca. BBA, U. Ga., 1976. With Atlanta Falcons, Ga., former mem. front office staff, former corp. sec., former exec. v.p.; now pres. Atlanta Falcons, Atlanta, GA. Bd. dirs. Gwinnett Found.; active Falcons Youth Found. Mem. Rotary. Office: Atlanta Falcons 1 Falcon Pl Suwanee GA 30174*

SMITH, TED JAY, III, mass communications educator; b. Dobbs Ferry, N.Y., Sept. 14, 1945; s. Ted Jay Jr. and Marie Glencora (Hershey) S.; m. Rosemary Tibbe, June 12, 1971. Student, U. Pitts., 1963-64; Student, U. So. Miss., 1968-69; BA with high honors, Mich. State U., 1971, MA, 1972, PhD, 1978. Commd. 2nd lt. USAF, 1971, advanced through grades to 1st lt., 1973, from electronics technician to electronics instr., 1965-70; airman edn. & commissioning program student USAF, E. Lansing, Mich., 1970-71; info officer USAF, 1971-74, resigned, 1974; grad. teaching/rsch. asst. Mich. State U., E. Lansing, 1974-77; asst. prof. SUNY, Albany, 1977-79; lectr. I, Warrnambool Inst. Advanced Edn., Warrnambool, Australia, 1979-82; asst. prof. U. Va., Charlottesville, 1982-87, dir. grad. studies, 1984-87; assoc. prof. Va. Commonwealth U., Richmond, 1987—, dir. grad. studies, 1990-94; sr. rsch. fellow Ctr. for Media & Pub. Affairs, 1996—; Bradley resident scholar Heritage Found., Washington, 1992-93; pres. Applied Anaytics, Inc., Richmond, Va., 1986—; sr. analyst Rowan & Blewitt, Inc., Washington, 1986-90; co-founder, sr. rsch. fellow Ctr. for Comm. Rsch., Warrnambool, 1982—; mem. policy adv. coun. VA Inst. for Pub. Policy, 1996—; mem. nat. adv. bd. Comm. Rsch. Corp., Washington, 1986-95, nat. adv. coun. The Media Inst., Washington, 1987—; faculty adviser FBI Nat. Acad., Quantico, Va., 1983-87; bd. dirs. Nat. Assn. Scholars, 1990—; mem. Main St. Commn., Rockford Inst., 1992—; educators adv. bd. Inst. for Pub. Rels. Rsch. & Edn., 1992—; co-founder Statis. Assessment Svc., 1993. Author: The Vanishing Economy, 1988, Moscow Meets Main Street, 1988; co-author: What Do the People Want From the Press?, 1997; editor: Propaganda: A Pluralistic Perspective, 1989, Communication in Australia, 1983; co-editor: Communication and Government, 1986; co-editor human communication book series SUNY Press, Albany, 1987—; contbr. articles to profl. jours. Mem. The Nature Conservancy, Albany, 1977-79, Charlottesville, 1982—, Accuracy in Media, Washington, 1982—; contbg. mem. Va. Mus. Fine Arts, Richmond, 1987—. Grantee FBI, U. Va., Warrnambool Inst., Bradley Found., Raldolph Found., Scaife Found., Earhart Found. Mem. Am. Assn. for Pub. Opinion Rsch., Assn. for Edn. in Journalism and Mass Communication, Australian Communication Assn. (founding), Internat. Communication Assn., Anglican Guild of Scholars, Nat. Assn. Scholars (bd. dirs. 1990—), Pub. Rels. Soc. Am., Phila. Soc., Va. Assn. Scholars (founding bd. dirs., pres. 1990—), So. Speech Communication Assn., St. George Tucker Soc., Southern League, Va. Speech Communication Assn. (chair theory divsn. 1986-91, 1st v.p. 1991-94), Phi Kappa Phi, Kappa Tau Alpha. Republican. Anglican Catholic. Avocations: nature study, fine arts and crafts, classical music. Home: 4010 Sherbrook Rd Richmond VA 23235-1643 Office: Va Commonwealth U Sch Mass Communications 901 W Main St Richmond VA 23284-9014

SMITH, TEFFT WELDON, lawyer; b. Evanston, Ill., Nov. 18, 1946; s. Edward W. and Margery T. (Weldon) S.; m. Nancy Jo Smith, Feb. 25, 1967; children: Lara Andrea, Tefft Weldon II. BA, Brown U., 1968; JD, U. Chgo., 1971. Bar: Ill. 1971, U.S. Supreme Ct. 1977. Ptnr. Kirkland & Ellis, Chgo., 1971—. Mem. ABA (litigation sect., antitrust law sect.), Econ. Club., Univ. Club, Mid-Am. Club, Sea Pines Country Club (Hilton Head, S.C.). Avocations: squash, Ferraris, sculpture. Office: Kirkland & Ellis 200 E Randolph St Chicago IL 60601-6436 also: 655 15th St SW Washington DC 20005

SMITH, THELMA TINA HARRIETTE, gallery owner, artist; b. Folkston, Ga., May 5, 1938; d. Harry Charles and Malinda Estelle (Kennison) Causey; m. Billy Wayne Smith, July 23, 1955; children: Sherry Yvonne, Susan Marie, Dennis Wayne, Chris Michael. Student, U. Tex., Arlington, 1968-70; studies with various art instrs. Gen. office worker Superior Ins. Corp., Dallas, 1956-57, Zanes-Ewalt Warehouse, Dallas, 1957-67; bookkeeper Atlas Match Co., Arlington, 1967-68; sr. acct. Automated Refrigerated Air Conditioner Mfg. Corp., Arlington, 1968-70; acct. Conn. Gen. Life Ins. Corp., Dallas, 1972-74; freelance artist Denton, Tex., 1974—; gallery owner, custom framer Tina Smith Studio-Gallery, Mabank, Tex., 1983—. Painting in pub. and pvt. collections in numerous states including N.Y., Fla., Ga. and N.D.; editor Cedar Creek Art Soc. Yearbook, 1983—. Treas. Cedar Creek Art Soc., 1987-88, 89—; mem. com. to establish state endorsed Arts Coun. for Cedar Creek Lake Area, Gun Barrel City, Tex. Recipient numerous watercolor and pastel awards Henderson County Art League, Cedar Creek Art Soc., Cmty. Svc. award Mayor Wilson Tippit, Gun Barrel City, Tex., 1986. Mem. Southwestern Watercolor Soc. (Dallas), Soc. Outdoor Painters, Pastel Soc. of the S.W. (Dallas), Cedar Creek Art Soc. (Gun Barrel City)(v.p. 1983-86, treas.), Profl. Picture Framers Assn. Baptist. Avocations: water activities, gardening. Office: Tina Smith Studio-Gallery 139 W Main St Gun Barrel Cy TX 75147-9479

SMITH, THOMAS CLAIR, manufacturing company executive; b. Indiana, Pa., Mar. 14, 1925; s. William Bryan and Edna Louise (Thomas) S.; m. Marilyn Louise Globisch, May 29, 1948; children: Claudia Lynn Smith Holtry, Craig Randall. BSME, Pa. State U., 1946; A, Alexander Hamilton Bus. Inst., 1949. Registered profl. engr., Pa. Structural test engr. Chance Vought Aircraft Co., Bridgeport, Conn., 1946-48; test engr. Fed. Mogul Bearings Co., Lancaster, Pa., 1949-51; fuse engr. to mgr. materials Hamilton Watch Co. (name now Hamilton Tech.), Lancaster, Pa., 1952-70; plant mgr. Woodstream Corp., Lititz, Pa., 1970-79, v.p. mktg., 1980-96; faculty, coach Lacrosse Franklin and Marshall Coll., Lancaster, 1950-53. Pub. Smith, Bryan, Allison & Morris Geneal. Chart, 1989; author and pub. of 1600 person geneal. chart in Libr. of Congress, 1989; patentee electric watch, 1957, swivel snap, 1975; author Penna Law 110 of 1992 and Pa. Law 22 of 1994/saving ancestral cemetaries. Pres., bd. dirs. Lancaster County Mental Health Assn., 1952-60, Lancaster County Cmty. Svc. Ctr., 1968-78, Am. Cancer Soc., 1970-72; bd. dirs. Hearing Conservation Assn., Lancaster, 1955-60, ARC, Lancaster, 1967-86, United Way, Lancaster, 1968-72, Ephrata (Pa.) Area Rehab. Ctr., 1986—, Grave Concern, Inc., 1994—; mem. All-Am. Lacrosse Team, 1945, Heritage Ctr. Lancaster, 1980—, Ind. County Hist. Soc., 1984—, Greene County Hist. Soc., Waynesburg, Pa., 1985—, Selective Svc. Bd., 1992—; trustee Lancaster Hist. Soc., 1992—, mem., 1983—; judge elections, Lancaster County, 1994—. Recipient Outstanding Svc. award Mental Health Assn., Lancaster, 1961, Edward D. Eshelman award as Humanitarian of Yr., Am. Cancer Soc., Lancaster, 1991; named Boss of Yr. Am. Bus. Womens Assn., 1978, Man of Yr. Am. Cancer Soc., 1984, Tennis Family of Yr., Pa., N.J., Del., 1970, Am. Cancer Bldg. Lancaster, Pa. dedicated to Thomas C. Smith, 1996. Mem. Order of Crown of Charlemagne in U.S.A. (life), Pa. State U. Alumni Club (life), Pa. Sons of Revolution (bd. dirs., sec. 1990—), Phi Delta Theta (pres. Pa. State U. chpt. 1945), Wheatland Tennis Club (v.p. 1990-94, pres. 1995-96). Republican. Presbyterian. Club: Lancaster Country (chmn. tennis com. 1960-75). Avocations: genealogy, tennis, skiing. Home: 1420 Quarry Ln Lancaster PA 17603-2426 Office: Woodstream Corp 69 N Locust St Lititz PA 17543-1714 *You only go through this life on earth once. Don't waste that time. Put it to use in helping to make the earth a better place.*

SMITH, THOMAS EUGENE, investment company executive, financial consultant; b. Brown's Summit, N.C., Aug. 23, 1930; s. Howard Cleveland and Annie May (Warren) S.; m. Joan Cretcher Hopkins, Sept. 22, 1948; 1 dau., Vicki Joan. Student, George Washington U., 1948-50, Am. U., 1950-55 (intermittently). Pres., dir. T. Eugene Smith, Inc. investment co. and real estate and fin. cons. co., Falls Church, Va., 1950—; pres. The Potomac Corp., Falls Church, Va., 1960-74; pres., dir. Nat. Bank of Fairfax, Va., 1975-81, dir.; exec. v.p. First & Mchts. Nat. Bank, Richmond, Va., 1981-83; chmn., dir. Decisions and Designs, Inc., McLean, Va., 1983-86; ptnr. Braddock-Ravensworth Ltd. Partnership, 1964—; sec., dir. Port Royal, Inc., 1965—; ptnr. Lee Graham Shopping Ctr., 1969—; chmn., pres., dir. Am. Mobile Home Towns, Inc., holding co., 1969-85; dir., pres. Topsail, Inc., 1983-89; ptnr. Potomac Greens Assn., 1986—; bd. dirs. Growth Fund of Washington, Am. Funds Tax Exempt Series I, Washington Mut. Investors, M.G. Thalheimer Realty Advisors, Inc.; chmn., bd. dirs. River Capital Corp., Alexandria, Va., 1986-89, J. Webb, Inc., 1986—; acting dir., mem. mgmt. com. Alexandria 20/20, 1988-91, acting dir., 1988-89; pres., dir. Pender Marina Holdings, Inc., 1988—, Pender Land Holdings, Inc., 1990—; mem. CSX Realty Adv. Bd., 1992—. Bd. dirs. Wolftrap Found., Washington, 1974-84; trustee Sta. WETA-TV, 1978-86; mem. Nat. Capital Planning Commn., Washington, 1980-83, vice chmn., 1981-83; mem. Va. Hwys. and Transp. Commn., Richmond, 1982-86; trustee Ch. Schs., Diocese of Va., 1983-88; mem. Va. Gov.'s Coun. Econ. Advisors, 1985-94, Met. Washington Airports Authority, 1986-94; chmn. Fairfax County Transp. Commn. for the Future, 1988-89; dir. Air and Space Heritage Coun., 1987-90. Mem. Nat. Assn. Small Bus. Investment Cos. (treas. and bd. dirs. 1962-66), Commonwealth Club (Richmond), Met. Club (Washington). Democrat. Episcopalian. Home: 666 Tintagel Ln Mc Lean VA 22101-1835

SMITH, THOMAS HUNTER, ophthalmologist, ophthalmic plastic and orbital surgeon; b. Silver Creek, Miss., Aug. 10, 1939; s. Hunter and Wincil (Barr) S.; m. Michele Ann Campbell, Feb. 27, 1982; 1 child, Thomas Hunter IV. BA, U. So. Miss., 1961; MD, Tulane U., 1967; BA in Latin Am. Studies, Tex. Christian U., 1987, MA in Latin Am. History, 1995. Diplomate Am. Bd. Ophthalmology. Intern Charity Hosp., New Orleans, 1967-68; resident in ophthalmology Tulane U., New Orleans, 1968-71; dir., sec. bd. dirs. Ophthalmology Assocs., Ft. Worth, 1971—; clin. prof. Tex. Tech. U. Med. Sch., Lubbock, 1979—; bd. examiners Am. Bd. Ophthalmology, 1983-90; guest lectr., invited speaker numerous schs., confs., symposia throughout N.Am., Ctrl. Am., South Am., Europe and India; hon. mem. ophthalmology dept. Santa Casa de São Paulo Med. Sch. Contbr. articles to profl. jours. Cons. ophthalmologist Helen Keller Internat.; deacon South Hills Christian Ch.; mem. Rocky Mountain Coun. Latin Am. Studies. Recipient Tex. Chpt. award Am. Assn. Workers for the Blind, 1978, Recognition award Lions Club Sight & Tissue Found., Cen. Am., 1977-79; named to Alumni Hall of Fame U. So. Miss., 1989. Fellow ACS, Am. Acad. Ophthalmology (bd. counsellors 1995—), Am. Acad. Facial Plastic and Reconstructive Surgery; mem. Tex. Med. Assn. (com. socio-econs.), Pan-Am. Assn. Ophthalmology (adminstr. 1988-93, bd. dirs. 1993—), Internat. Cos. Cryosurgery, Royal Soc. Medicine (affiliate), Tex. Soc. Ophthalmology and Otolaryngology, Peruvian Ophthalmol. Soc. (hon.), Santa Casa De São Paulo (hon. assoc.), Tex. Ophthalmol. Assn. (past mem. exec. coun., treas.), Tex. Med. Assn., Tarrant County Med. Soc., Byron Smith Ex Fellows Assn., Tarrant County Multiple Sclerosis Soc. (past pres.), Tarrant County Assn. for Blind, Tulane Med. Alumni Assn. (bd. dirs.), S.Am. Explorers Club, Colonial Country Club, Petroleum Club Ft. Worth, Sigma Xi, Omicron Delta Kappa. Mem. Disciples of Christ. Avocations: hunting, fishing, flying, world travel. Office: Ophthalmology Assocs 1201 Summit Ave Fort Worth TX 76102-4413

SMITH, THOMAS J., surgeon, educator. BA cum laude, Amherst Coll., 1967; MD, Tufts U. Sch. Medicine, 1971. Diplomate Am. Bd. Surgery, Nat. Bd. Med. Examiners. Intern, resident in surgery Tufts New England Med. Ctr., Boston, 1971-73, chief resident in surgery, 1975-78; clin. assoc. surgery br. Nat. Cancer Inst., Bethesda, Md., 1978-80; from asst. prof. to assoc. prof. surgery Tufts U. Sch. Medicine, 1980-94; assoc. prof. U. South Fla., 1994; asst. prof. clin. surgery Columbia U., N.Y.C., 1995—; clin. prof. surgery UMDNJ Med. Sch., 1997—. Editl. bd. Internat. Jour. Cancer Rsch. & Treatment, Oncology; contbr. articles, abstracts to profl. jours. Mem. Am. Coll. Physician Execs., Soc. Study of Breast Disease, Soc. Surg. Oncology (edn. com. 1988—), Am. Cancer Soc. (sword of hope award com.). Office: Morristown Meml Hosp PO Box 1956 Morristown NJ 07962-1956

SMITH, THOMAS KENT, radiologist; b. Bowling Green, Ohio, Aug. 21, 1934; s. Robert O. and Roslyn Smith; m. Jaleh Saidi, Feb. 1, 1974; children: Jeffrey, Todd, Mark, Blake, Tyler. BS with high honors, U. Cin., 1957; MD, Case Western Res. U., 1961. Intern Nat. Naval Med. Ctr., Bethesda, Md., 1961-62; resident in radiology VA Med. Ctr., Long Beach, Calif., 1965-69; dir. radiology Harriman Jones Med. Group, Long Beach, 1969-88; fellow in MRI/CT U. Calif., San Francisco, 1988-89; dir. MRI Orange County MRI, Fountain Valley, Calif., 1989-90; chmn. dept. diagnostic imaging Kaiser Permanente Med. Ctr., Honolulu, 1990—; fellow in radiologic pathology Armed Forces Inst. of Pathology, Washington, 1968; mem. adv. bd. Hawaii Permanente Med. Group, Honolulu, 1990—; bd. dirs. Harriman Jones Med. Group, Harriman Jones Assocs.; assoc. clin. prof. radiology U. Hawaii, Honolulu, 1990—; asst. clin. prof. U. Calif., Irvine, 1970-88; clin. instr. U. Calif., San Francisco, 1988-89, asst. clin. prof., 1989—; cons. in radiologic devel. Kaiser Permanente Internat., 1996—. Lt. USN, 1961-65. Fellow Am. Coll. Radiology; mem. Hawaii Radiol. Soc. (pres. 1992-93), Radiol. Soc. N.Am., Internat. Soc. Magnetic Resonance in Medicine, Margulis Soc., Alpha Omega Alpha. Avocations: fishing, travel, viticulture. Home: 46-434 Haiku Plantation Dr Kaneohe HI 96744-4207 Office: Kaiser Permanente Med Ctr 3288 Moanalua Rd Honolulu HI 96819-1469

SMITH, THOMAS RAYMOND, III, software engineer; b. Phila., Dec. 6, 1946; s. Thomas Raymond and Naomi (Hart) S.; m. Marguerite Anne LeMoyne De Martigny, Sept. 6, 1969; children: Michelle Renée, Heather Anne, Thomas Raymond IV. Student, MIT, 1964-68. Sr. analyst Dabcovich and Co., Lexington, Mass., 1969-71; sr. analyst, prin. Multi-Logic Corp., Burlington, Mass., 1970-73; consulting software engr. Digital Equip. Corp., Maynard, Mass., 1974—. Co-editor: IEEE Dictionary, 1993; author, co-editor numerous stds. books for Internat. Electrotech. Commn. and IEEE, 1984-93. Mem. IEEE (chmn. various stds. coms., 1980—). Home: 36 Toppans Ln Newburyport MA 01950-3843 Office: Digital Equipment Corp ZK01-3/H42 110 Spit Brook Rd # 3 442 Nashua NH 03062-2711

SMITH, THOMAS SHORE, lawyer; b. Rock Springs, Wyo., Dec. 7, 1924; s. Thomas and Anne E. (McTee) S.; m. Jacqueline Emily Krueger, May 25, 1952; children: Carolyn Jane, Karl Thomas, David Shore. BSBA, U. Wyo., 1950, JD, 1959. Bar: U.S. Dist. Ct. Wyo. 1960, U.S. Ct. Appeals (10th cir.) 1960, U.S. Tax Ct. 1969, U.S. Supreme Ct. 1971. Of counsel Smith, Stanfield & Scott, LLC, Laramie, Wyo., 1963—; atty. City of Laramie, 1963-86; instr. mcpl. law U. Wyo., 1987, mem. dean's adv. com. Law Sch.; dir. budget and fin. Govt. of Am. Samoa, 1954-56. Bd. dirs. Bur. Land Mgmt., Rawlins, Wyo., 1984-89, chmn. bd. dirs., 1989; pres. Ivinson Hosp. Found., 1994-95; bd. dirs. U. Wyo. Found., 1991—, pres., 1996-97. Francis Warren scholar, 1958. Mem Wyo. Bar Assn. (pres. 1984-85), Albany County Bar Assn., Western States Bar Conf. (pres. 1985-86), Elks. Republican. Episcopalian. Avocation: golf. Office: Smith Stanfield & Scott LLC PO Box 971 515 E Ivinson Ave Laramie WY 82070-3157

SMITH, THOMAS WINSTON, cotton marketing executive; b. Crosbyton, Tex., Mar. 16, 1935; s. Lance L. and Willie Mae (Little) S.; m. Patricia Mae Zachary, Dec. 13, 1958; children—Janna Olean, Thomas Mark. B.S., Tex. A&M U., 1957; P.M.D., Harvard U., 1964. Various positions Calcot Ltd., Bakersfield, Calif., 1957-77, exec. v.p., pres., 1977—; v.p. Amcot, Inc., Amcot Internat., Inc., Bakersfield, 1977—, also bd. dirs.; bd. mgrs. N.Y. Cotton Exchange, N.Y.C., v.p., Memphis. Bd. dir. Greater Bakersfield Meml. Hosp.; mem. pres.'s adv. commn. Calif. State Coll., Bakersfield; v.p. Nat. Cotton Coun., Memphis. Mem. Rotary.

SMITH, THOMAS WOODWARD, cardiologist, educator; b. Akron, Ohio, Mar. 29, 1936; s. Luther David and Beatrice Pearl (Woodward) S.; m. Sherley Louise Goodwin, Sept. 13, 1958; children: Julia Goodwin, Geoffrey Woodward, Allison Lloyd. A.B., Harvard U., 1958, M.D., 1965. Diplomate: Am. Bd. Internal Medicine; Am. Bd. Cardiovascular Diseases. Intern in medicine Mass. Gen. Hosp., Boston, 1965-66, asst. resident in medicine, 1966-67, clin. and research fellow in cardiology, 1967-69, Nat. Heart and Lung Inst. spl. fellow, 1969-71, asst. in medicine, 1969-72, assoc. program dir. myocardial infarction research unit, 1972-74, asst. physician, 1972-77, cons. in medicine, 1977—; asst. prof. medicine Harvard U. Med. Sch., 1971-73, assoc. prof., 1973-79, prof., 1979—; physician Peter Bent Brigham Hosp. (now Brigham and Women's Hosp.), Boston, chief cardiovascular div.; cons. in cardiology Children's Hosp. Med. Ctr. and Sidney Farber Cancer Inst. (now Dana-Farber Cancer Inst.); prof. medicine MIT div. Health Scis. and Tech.; Hall vis. prof., Sydney, Australia, 1977; Sir Henry Hallett Dale vis. prof. Johns Hopkins U. Med. Sch., 1979; Nahum lectr. Yale U. Sch. Medicine, 1979. Reviewer med. jours.; contbr. articles to profl. publs. Mem. Am. Heart Assn. (council clin. cardiology, council basic sci., council on circulation, established investigator 1971-76 Rosenthal award), Am. Fedn. Clin. Research, Paul Dudley White Soc., AAAS, Am. Soc. Pharmacology and Exptl. Therapeutics, Am. Soc. Clin. Investigation, Am. Coll. Cardiology, ACP, Assn. Univ. Cardiologists, Am. Physiol. Soc., Assn. Am. Physicians, Soc. Gen. Physiologists, Alpha Omega Alpha. Home: 128 Wellesley St Weston MA 02193-1555 Office: Brigham and Women's Hosp 75 Francis St Boston MA 02115-6110

SMITH, TODD LAWRENCE, computer scientist; b. July 11, 1956; m. Dawn M. Simpson, Oct. 24, 1992. BS in Computer Sci. and Physics, Loyola Coll., 1978; MS in Ops. Rsch. & Mgmt. Sci., George Mason U., 1993. Comm. programmer Computer Data Systems, 1978-82; tech. staff TRW, Inc., Fairfax, Va., 1982-94; sr. engr. Washington Cons. Group, 1994-95; sr. software engr. Mitech, Inc., Rockville, Md., 1995-97; software engr. Sci. Applications Internat. Corp., McLean, Va., 1997—; sound technician, adminstrv. bd. mem. Manassas St. Thomas U.M.C., 1995—. Foreman, fed. jury duty Fed. Justice Ct., Alexandria, Va., 1991. Recipient Spl. Achievement plaque TRW Systems Integration Group, 1989. Mem. IEEE Computer Soc. Avocations: boating, hiking, model railroads, chess, piano. Home: 11050 Camfield Ct # 101 Manassas VA 20109-7507

SMITH, TODD MALCOLM, political consultant; b. Hallettsville, Tex., Aug. 7, 1961; s. Jerome Malcolm and Mary Eugenia (Devall) S. BS in Criminal Justice, S.W. Tex. State U., 1983; postgrad. in Criminal Justice Adminstrn., Sam Houston State U., 1988—; cert., Fed. Law Enforce. Tng. Acad., 1987. Chief juvenile probation officer 25th Jud. Dist. Tex., 1983-84; field coord. Mac Sweeney for Congress, Victoria, Tex., 1984; dist. coord. U.S. Congress-14th Congl. Dist. Tex., 1984-85; chief dep. sheriff Lavaca County Sheriff's Dept. Tex., 1985-88; dir. ops. Clayton Williams for Gov. Com., Austin, Tex., 1988-90; pres. Property Valuation Advisors, San Marcos, Tex., 1991-93; gen. ptnr. Wm. A. Tryon and Todd M. Smith Polit. Cons. Group, Austin, 1991-93; prin. Smith & Assocs. Polit. Cons. Group, Austin, 1993—; coord. Lavaca County Crime Stoppers, Hallettsville, 1985-88; apptd. by Tex. Gov. to Tex. Crime Stoppers Commn. Regulatory Agy., 1986-90; mem., appointee Golden Crescent Regional Planning Commn., Victoria, 1986-88; investigator U.S. Customs Svcs., Op. Blue Lightning Narcotics Task Force, Tex. 1988-89. Mem. Young Reps. Tex., Austin, 1989—, candidate selection com. Assoc. Reps. Tex., Austin, 1991—, rep. senatorial dist. 18 State Rep. Exec. Com., 1992-94; pres. Tex. Citizens United; chmn. Taxpayers Def. Fund. 2d lt. Tex. State N.G., 1990-92. Recipient Outstanding Svc. award Tex. Crime Stoppers Adv. Coun., 1990, Outstanding Coord. award Lavaca County Crime Stoppers, 1988, Outstanding ROTC Cadet award Daus. of Founders and Patriots, 1982. Mem. Am. Assn. Polit. Cons., Masons. Republican. Episcopalian. Avocation: politics. Home: 2204 Hazeltine Ln Austin TX 78747 Office: 807 Brazos St Ste 408 Austin TX 78701-2508

SMITH, V. KERRY, economics educator; b. Jersey City, Mar. 11, 1945; s. Vincent C. and Dorothy E. (Linehan) S.; m. Pauline Anne Taylor, May 10, 1969; children: Timothy, Shelley. AB, Rutgers U., 1966, PhD, 1970. Asst. prof., then assoc. prof. Bowling Green State U., Ohio, 1969-72; rsch. assoc. Resources for Future, Washington, 1971-73; assoc. prof. SUNY, Binghamton, 1973-75, prof., 1975-78; sr. fellow Resources for Future, Washington, 1976-79; prof. U. N.C., Chapel Hill, 1979-83; Centennial prof. Vanderbilt U., Nashville, 1983-87; Univ. Disting. prof. N.C. State U., 1987-94; Arts and Scis. prof. environ. econs. Duke U., 1994—; adviser energy div. Oak Ridge Nat. Lab., 1978-80, U. N.C. Inst. Environ. Studies, 1980-83; mem. panel NSF, 1981-83, sci. adv. bd. EPA. Author: Monte Carlo Methods, 1973, Technical Change, Relative Prices and Environmental Resource Evaluation, 1974, The costs of Congestion: An Econometric Analysis of Wilderness Recreation, 1976, Structure and Properties of a Wilderness Travel Simulator: An Application to the Spanish Peaks Area, 1976, The Economic Consequences of Air Pollution, 1976, Scarcity and Growth Reconsidered, 1979, (with others) Explorations in Natural Resource Economics, 1982, (with others) Environmental Policy Under Reagan's Executive Order, 1984, (with W.H. Desvousges) Measuring Water Quality Benefits, 1986, (with others) Environmental Resources and Applied Welfare Economics, 1988, (with R.J. Kopp) Valuing Natural Assets: The Economics of Natural Resource Damage Assessment, Resources for the Future, 1993, Estimating Economic Values for Nature, 1996; editor Advances in Applied Micro Econs. series; contbr. numerous articles to profl. jours. Guggenheim fellow, 1976; grantee Resources for Future, 1970, 73, 74, 86, Fed. Energy Adminstrn. 1975, N.Y. Sea Grant Inst., 1975, Ford Found., 1976, NSF, 1977, 79, 83, Electric Power Rsch. Inst., 1978, Nat. Oceanic and Atmospheric Adminstrn., 1980, Sloan Found., 1981, 86, EPA, 1983-88, N.C. Sea Grant Program, 1987-93. Russell Sage Found., 1989-91; recipient Frederick V. Waugh medal Am. Agrl. Econ. Assn., 1992. Mem. Am. Econ. Assn., Am. Statis. Assn., Econometric Soc., So. Econ. Assn. (exec. com. 1981-83, 1st v.p. 1987, pres. elect 1988, pres. 1989), Assn. Environ. and Resource Economists (bd. dirs. 1975-79, v.p. 1979-80, chmn. com. 1982-83, pres. 1985-86, Disting. Svc. award 1989).

SMITH, V. ROY, neurosurgeon; b. N.Y.C., Feb. 12, 1943; s. Leslie Ewart and Vera (Dhlosh) S.; m. Elizabeth Kay Bartlett, June 12, 1971; children: Rebecca L., Adam L., Andrew R. BA, Ohio State U., 1964, MD, 1967. Diplomate Am. Bd. Neurol. Surgeons. Ptnr. Fresno Neurol. Med. Group, Calif., 1975—; pres. med. staff St. Agnes Hosp., Fresno, Calif., 1987-89, chief of surgery, 1983-85, chmn. div. neurosurgery, 1993-95. Lt. U.S. Navy, 1969-71, Vietnam. Fellow Am. Coll. Surgeons; mem. AMA, Am. Coll. Surgeons, Am. Assn. Neurol. Surgeons. Home: 2627 E Birch Ave Clovis CA 93611-9167 Office: Fresno Neurosurg Med Group 6137 N Thesta St # 103 Fresno CA 93710-5266

SMITH, VALERIE GAY, school counselor; b. Austin, Tex., Oct. 31, 1947; d. James Griffin and Ida Mae (Routon) Black; m. James David Smith, July 20, 1993. BA in English, McMurry Coll., 1969; MEd in Counseling, U. North Tex., 1974. Lic. profl. counselor, Tex.; cert. sch. counselor, Tex. Tchr. Nimitz H.S., Irving, Tex., 1969-71; tchr. MacArthur H.S., Irving, Tex., 1971-74, counselor, 1974-89; counselor Ditto Elem. Sch., Arlington, Tex., 1989-94, Withers Elem. Sch., Dallas, 1994—. Mem. ACA, Am. Sch. Counselor Assn., Tex. Sch. Counselor Assn. (elem. v.p. 1990-92, senator 1988-90, sec. 1986-88, Rhosine Fleming Outstanding Counselor award 1987, pres.-elect 1992-93, pres. 1993-94), Tex. PTA (life), Tex. Counseling Assn. (region

4 dir. 1990-93, pres.-elect 1995-96, pres. 1996-97), Phi Delta Kappa. Home: 2120 Nob Hill Carrollton TX 75006 Office: Withers Elem Sch 3959 Northaven Rd Dallas TX 75229-2758

SMITH, VAN P., airplane engine company executive; b. Oneida, N.Y., Sept. 8, 1928; m. Margaret Ann Kennedy, Nov. 19, 1960; children: Lynn Ann Smith Walters, Mark Charles, Paul Gregory, Susan Colleen, Victor Patrick. AB in Pub. Adminstrn. and Econs., Colgate U., 1950; JD, Georgetown U., 1955; LLD (hon.), Ball State U., 1980; D of Bus. (hon.), Vincennes U., 1985; LLD (hon.), Ind. State U., 1986. Bar: D.C., Ind. Assoc. Warner, Clark & Warner, Muncie, Ind., 1955-56; co-founder, dir. Ontario Corp. of Muncie, 1956-63, sec. then v.p. sales, 1956-63, pres., chief exec. officer, 1963—, also chmn. bd., 1978—; chmn. bd. Ontario Forge Corp., Pyromet Industries Inc., Sherry Labs, Inc., Ontario Devel. Corp., Ontario Systems Corp., W.W. Rich Found., all in Muncie, Ontario Corp. Ltd., U.K., Pyromet Inc., Calif., Ontario Techs., Calif., CDS Engring., Calif., Dulond Toll and Engring. Inc, Fla., and other subs. Ontario Corp.; bd. dirs. N.G. Gilbert Corp., Muncie, Hoosier Motor Club, Indpls., Ind. Bell Telephone Co, Inc., Indpls., Indsl. Trust & Savs. Bank, Muncie, Lilly Indsl. Coatings, Inc., Indpls., Maxon Corp, Muncie, Pub. Service Ind., and other subs. Ontario Corp.; ptnr. Del. Aviation, Smittie's Men's Store, Village Developers, all in Muncie. Rep. mem. Ind. Ho. of Reps., 1960-62; del. Ind. and Nat. Rep. Conv.; pres. Muncie Police & Fire Commn., 1963-66; mem. parochial sch. bd. St. Mary's Sch., Muncie, 1968-70; mem. Ind. Employment Security Bd., 1969-71, Ind. Commn. Higher Edn., 1971—, Nat. Adv. Council SBA, 1982—, Gov.'s Fiscal Policy Adv. Council, 1982—, Ind. Labor & Mgmt. Council, 1983—, Ind. Econ. Devel. Council, 1985—, Presdl. Observation Team Phillipine Nat. election, 1986, Presdl. Trade Mission to several Far Eastern countries, 1984; bd. dirs. Bus.-Industry Polit. Action Com., 1984—; trustee Colgate U., 1985—, La Lumiere Sch., 1983—, Acad. for Community Leadership, 1975—; bd. dirs. Muncie Symphony Assn., 1980-88, pres. 1986-87; pres. Del. County United Way, 1969-70; bd. dirs. Newman Found. Ind., 1969—, Religious Heritage Am. 1986-88; active St. Mary's Cath. Parish, Muncie; mem. Diocese of Lafayette Bishop's Com. 100, 1969-80, pres. 1969-70; bd. regents Cath. U. Am., Washington, 1986-90, trustee 1990—; trustee Interlochen (Mich.) Ctr. for Arts, 1991—. Served 1st lt. USAF, 1951-53. Named one of Outstanding Young Men of Am., Jaycees, 1960; recipient Bus. and Layman award, Religious Heritage Am., 1984, Ind. Cath. Layman award, Faith, Family & Football of Ind., Inc. 1985, Civic Service award, Ind. Assn. Cities and Towns, 1985; invested Knight of Equestrian Order of Holy Sepulchre of Jerusalem, 1986. Mem. ABA, Ind. Bar Assn., Ind. Mfrs. Assn. (chmn. 1978-80, bd. dirs. 1978—), Forging Industry Assn. (pres. 1976-77), Alliance of Metalworking Industries (chmn. 1978-80), U.S. C. of C. (chmn. numerous coms., active panels and councils 1977—), Ind. State C. of C. (exec. com. 1982—), Rotary (past pres.), Meridian Hills Country Club, Theta Chi (pres. Iota chpt. 1950), Delta Theta Phi, Beta Gamma Sigma (hon.), Delta Sigma Pi (hon.). Clubs: Columbia, Skyline (Indpls.); Ind. Soc. of Chgo. Lodges: Rotary (local past pres.), Elks, KC. Home: 762 Bounty Dr Foster City CA 94404-4114 Office: 123 E Adams St Muncie IN 47305-2402

SMITH, VERNA MAE EDOM, sociology educator, freelance writer, photographer; b. Marshfield, Wis., June 19, 1929; d. Clifton Cedric and Vilia Clarissa (Patefield) Edom; children: Teri Freas, Anthony Thomas. AB in Sociology, U. Mo., 1951; MA in Sociology, George Washington, 1965; PhD in Human Devel., U. Md., 1981. Tchr. Alcohol Safety Action Program Fairfax County, Va., 1973-75; instr. sociology No. Va. C.C., Manassas, 1975-77, asst. prof., 1977-81, assoc. prof., 1981-84, prof., 1984-94, prof. emerita, 1995; coord. coop. edn. No. Va. Community Coll., Manassas, 1983-89; Chancellor's Commonwealth prof. Manassas, 1991-93; freelance writer, editor and photographer, 1965—; co-dir. Clifton C. Edom Truth With a Camera (photography seminars); asst. producer history of photography program Sta. WETA-TV, Washington, 1965; rsch. and prodn. asst., photographer, publs. editor No. Va. Ednl. TV, Sta. WNVT, 1970-71; cons. migrant div. Md. Dept. Edn., Balt., summer 1977; researcher, photographer Roundabout presch. high sch. series on Am. Values Sta. WNVT, 1970-71. Author, photographer: Middleburg and Nearby, 1986; co-author: Small Town America, 1993; contbr. photography to various works including Visual Impact in Print (Hurley and McDougall), 1971, Looking Forward to a Career in Education (Moses), 1976, Child Growth and Development (Terry, Sorrentino and Flatter), 1979, Photojournalism (Edom), 1976, 80, Migrant Child Welfare, 1977, (Cavenaugh), Caring for Children, 1973 (5 publs. by L.B. Murphy), Dept. Health, Edn. and Welfare, Nat. Geog., 1961, Head Start Newsletter, 1973-74. Mem. ednl. adv. com. Head Start, Warrenton, Va. Recipient Emmy Ohio State Children's Programming award; Fulbright-Hays Rsch. grantee, 1993. Mem. Va. Assn. Coop. Edn. (com. mem.). Democrat.

SMITH, VERNON G., education educator, state representative; b. Gary, Ind.. BS, Ind. U., 1966, MS, 1969, EdD, 1978; postgrad., Ind.U.-Purdue U., 1986-90. Tchr. Gary Pub. Schs. Systems, 1966-71, resource tchr., 1971-72; asst. prin. Ivanhoe Sch., Gary, 1972-78; prin. Nobel Sch., Gary, 1978-85, Williams Sch., Gary, 1985-92; part-time counselor edn. div. Ind. U. N.W., Gary, 1967-69, adj. lectr., 1987-92, asst. prof., 1992—; mem. Ind. Ho. of Reps., Indpls., 1990—; columnist Gary Crusader, 1969-71; speaker Devel. Tng. Inst., 1986—. Author: (with D. McClam) Building Bridges Instead of Walls—History of I.U. Dons, Inc., 1979; also articles. Mem. Gary City Coun., 1972-90; precinct committeeman Gary Dem. Com., 1972-92; founder, chmn. Gary City-wide Festival Com.; bd. dirs. N.W. Ind. Urban League; founder, pres. I.U. Dons, Inc.; past pres. Gary Cmty. Mental Health Bd.; v.p. Gary Common Coun., 1982, 85-87, pres., 1976, 83-84, 88; past mem. bd. dirs. Little League World series; founder, past sponsor Youth Ensuring Solidarity, Young Citizens' League; chmn. Ind. Commn. on Status of Black Males, 1992—; mem. Gov.'s Commn. for Drug-Free Ind., 1990—. Recipient citation in edn. Gary NAACP, 1970, Good Govt. award Gary Jaycees, 1977, Outstanding Svc. award Gary Young Dems., 1979, Businessman of Yr. award Gary Downtown Mchts., 1979, Bd. Dirs. Svcs. award Gary Cmty. Health Ctr., 1982, G.O.I.C. Dr. Leon H. Sullivan award, 1982, Gary Jaycees Youth award, 1983, Info Newspaper Outstanding Citizen of N.W. Ind. and Info. Newspaper's Outstanding Educator award, 1984, Post Tribune Blaine Marz Tap award, 1984, Gary Cmty. Sch. Corp. Speech Dept. Recognition award, 1984, Gary Cmty. Mental Health Ctr.'s 10th Yr. Svc. award, 1985, Roosevelt H.S. Exemplary Svc. award, 1985, Gary Crusader 25th Anniversary award, 1986, Purdue U. Ednl. Opportunity Programs Black History Svc. award, 1986, Educator Par Excellence awa4rd Williams Sch., 1987, Black Woman Hall of Fame Found. Success award, 1987, Black Women Hall of Fame Bethune-Tubman-Truth award, 1987, Our Lady of Perpetual Help Ch. Hon. Mem. award, 1987, Gary Educator of Christ Adminstr. Leadership award, 1988, NBC-LEO Appreciation award, 1988, Omega Psi Phi Citizen of Yr., 1989, Omicron Rho chpt. Appreciation award, 1991, Gary Cmty. Schs. Presenters award, 1991, Mr. G.'s Svc. award, 1991, Appreciation award Ind. Assn. Chiefs Police, 1992, Meth. Hosp., 1992, Bros. Keeper, 1992, Svc. award Ind. Assn. Elem. and Mid. Sch. Prins., 1992, I.U. N.W. Alumni Assn. Divsn. of Edn. Disting. Educator award, 1992, N.W. Ind. Black Expo's Sen. Carolyn Mosby Above and Beyond award, 1995. Mem. NAACP (life), Ind. Assn. Sch. Prins., No. Ind. Assn. Black School Educators (founder), Ind. U. N.W. Alumni Assn. (life, Disting. Educator award 1992), Phi Delta Kappa, Omega Psi Phi (life, Omega Man of Yr. award 1974, Citizen of Yr. award 10th dist. 1989, appreciation award Omicrono Rho chpt. 1991). Baptist. Home: PO Box M622 Gary IN 46401-0622 Office: Ind U NW 3400 Broadway Hawthorn #339 Gary IN 46408

SMITH, VERNON LOMAX, economist, researcher; b. Wichita, Kans., Jan. 1, 1927; s. Vernon Chessman and Lula Belle (Lomax) S.; m. Joyce Harkleroad, June 6, 1950 (div. Aug. 1975); m. Carol Breckner, Jan. 1, 1980. BSEE, Calif. Inst. Tech., 1949; MA in Econs., U. Kans., 1952; PhD in Econs., Harvard U., 1955; D of Mgmt. (hon.), Purdue U., 1990. Asst. prof. econs. Purdue U., West Lafayette, Ind., 1955-58, assoc. prof., 1958-61, prof., 1961-65, Krannert prof., 1965-67; prof. Brown U., Providence, 1967-68, U. Mass., Amherst, 1968-75; prof. U. Ariz., Tucson, 1975—, Regents' prof.; Contbr. articles to profl. jours. Fellow Ctr. for Advanced Study in Behavioral Scis., Stanford, Calif., 1972-73; Sherman Fairchild Disting. Scholar Calif. Inst. Tech., Pasadena, 1973-74; adj. scholar CATO Inst., Washington, 1983—. Fellow AAAS, Am. Acad. Arts and Scis., Econometric Soc., Am. Econ. Assn. (Disting. fellow); me. Pvt. Enterprise Edn. Assn. (Adam Smith award), Nat. Acad. Sci. Home: 6020 N Pontatoc Rd Tucson AZ 85719 Office: U Ariz Econ Sci Lab Tucson AZ 85718

SMITH, VERONICA LATTA, real estate corporation officer; b. Wyandotte, Mich., Jan. 13, 1925; d. Jan August and Helena (Hulak) Latta; m. Stewart Gene Smith, Apr. 12, 1952; children: Stewart Gregory, Patrick Allen, Paul Donald, Alison Veronica, Alisa Margaret Lyons, Glenn Laurence. BA in Sociology, U. Mich., 1948, postgrad., 1948. Tchr. Coral Gables (Fla.) Pub. Sch. System, 1949-50; COO Latta Ins. Agy, Wyandotte, 1950-62; treas. L & S Devel. Co., Grosse Ile, Mich., 1963-84; v.p. Regency Devel., Riverview, Mich., 1984—. Active U. Mich. Bd. Regents, 1985-92, regent emeritus, 1993—; mem. Martha Cook Bd. Govs., U. Mich., 1972-78, pres., 1976-78; del. Rep. County Conv., Grand Rapids, Mich., 1985, 87, 89, 91, 92, 94, 96, Lansing, Mich., 1996, Detroit, 1986, 88, 90, 92, 97; mem. pres. adv. com. Campaign for Mich., 1992—, mem. campaign steering com., 1992—. Mem. Mich. Lawyers Aux. (treas. 1975, chmn. 1976, 77, 78, 79), Nat. Assn. Ins. Women (cert.), Faculty Women's Club U. Mich. (hon.), Radrick Farms Golf Club (Ann Arbor), Pres.'s Club U. Mich., Investment Club (pres. 1976, sec. 1974-75, treas. 1975-76), Alpha Kappa Delta. Home: 22225 Balmoral Dr Grosse Ile MI 48138-1403

SMITH, VINCENT DACOSTA, artist; b. Bklyn., Dec. 12, 1929; s. Beresford Leopold and Louise S.; m. Cynthia I. Linton, July 15, 1972. Student, Art Students League, N.Y.C., 1953, Bklyn. Mus. Sch., 1955-56; B. Profl. Services, Empire State Coll., 1980. Instr. painting and graphics Whitney Mus. Art, N.Y.C., 1967-76; instr. painting Ceda Project, 1978-80; artist in residence Smithsonian Conf. Center, Elkridge, Md., 1967, Cite des Arts Internat., Paris, 1978; participant 2d World Black and African Festival Arts and Culture, Lagos, Nigeria, 1977; commns. include Impressions: Our World Portfolio of Prints, 1974, mural at Boys and Girls High Sch., Bklyn., 1976, mural for Tremont/Crotona Social Svc. Ctr. Human Resources Adminstrn. and CETA Project, N.Y.C., 1980, mural for Oberia D. Dempsey Multi-Svc. Ctr. for Cen. Harlem, Dept. Cultural Affairs, N.Y.C., 1988, 2 murals for 116 St. Sta., N.Y.C. Met. Transit Authority; film tapes and videos include Bernie Casey: Black Dimensions in Contemporary Am. Art, Carnation Co., Los Angeles, 1971, Tee Collins, Barbara Cobb: The First Water, Theatre Eleven, 1977, Robert Fassbinder: The Creative Pulse of Afro-Am. Culture, WTVG, N.J., 1978, Bearden Plays Bearden, Third World Cinema, 1980, Works on Paper, Storefront Mus./Paul Robeson Theatre, Jamaica, N.Y., 1981; host biweekly program, discussions with 45 activists WBAI-FM Radio. Illustrator: Folklore Stories from Africa, 1974; exhbns. include Hall of Springs Mus., Saratoga, N.Y., 1970, Contemporary Black Am. Artists, Whitney Mus. Am. Art, N.Y.C., 1971, Two Generations, Newark Mus., 1971, Mus. of Sci. and Industry, Chgo., 1975, Bronx Mus. Art, 1977, Bklyn. Mus., 1979; one-man exhbns. include Lacarda Gallery, N.Y.C., 1967, 68, 70, 73, 75, 77, Paa Ya Paa Gallery, Nairobi, Kenya, 1973, Chemchemi Creative Arts Center, Arusha, Tanzania, 1973, Kibo Art Gallery, Mt. Kilimanjaro, Tanzania, 1973, Portland (Maine) Art Mus., 1974, Reading (Pa.) Public Mus., 1974, Erie (Pa.) Art Center, 1977, Gallery 7, Detroit, 1977; represented in permanent collections, Mus. Modern Art, N.Y.C., Newark Mus., Bklyn. Mus., U. Va. Art Mus.; also subject of TV film; host Vincent Smith Dialogues with Contemporary Artists, Radio Sta. WPAI-FM, 1986-88. Served with U.S. Army, 1948-49. Recipient Thomas B. Clark prize N.A.D., 1974; Winslow and Newton prize Nat. Soc. Painters in Casein and Acrylic, 1978; John Hay Whitney fellow, 1959; Nat. Endowment Arts grantee, 1973; Nat. Inst. Arts and Letters grantee, 1968; Cultural Council Found. grantee, 1971. Mem. Nat. Conf. Artists. Home: 264 E Broadway New York NY 10002-5670 *I have tried to develop three things which I feel are necessary to achieving some success in one's chosen field: a philosophy in which one keeps physically fit, mentally aware and consistent in one's work. Through a belief in the importance of the work one can constantly strive to grow and reach new heights.*

SMITH, VINCENT MILTON, lawyer, designer, consultant; b. Barbourville, Ky., Nov. 21, 1940; s. Virgil Milton and Louis (McGalliard) S.; 1 child, Jessica Todd. BA, Harvard U., 1962; LLB, Yale U., 1965. Bar: N.Y. 1966. Assoc. Breed, Abbott & Morgan, N.Y.C., 1965-70; assoc. Debevoise & Plimpton, N.Y.C., 1970-75, ptnr., 1975-95; CEO Lang, Winslow & Smith Co., Chatham, N.J., 1995—; mem. adv. bd. Chgo. Title Ins. Co., N.Y.C., 1979—. Trustee Chatham Players, N.J., 1967-77, 87-91, Summit Friends Meeting, Chatham, 1973—, N.J. Shakespeare Festival, Madison, 1975-80, Playwrights Theatre N.J., 1989-91. Mem. ABA, N.Y. State Bar Assn., Assn. of Bar of City of N.Y., Am. Land Title Assn., Urban Land Inst. Mem. Soc. of Friends. Clubs: Harvard, N.Y. Athletic. Office: Debevoise & Plimpton 875 3rd Ave New York NY 10022-6225

SMITH, VIRGINIA A., marketing communications professional; b. Washington, Oct. 23, 1962; d. Kenneth Ross and Patricia Marcella (Maher) S. BBA, Va. Commonwealth U., 1986; postgrad., George Washington U., 1994—. Pub. rels. coord. Richmond Comedy Club, Va., 1987-90; media coord. Medalist Sports, Richmond, Va., 1991; event coord. ProServ, Washington, 1992; paralegal Law Resources, Washington, 1993-94; cons. internat. mktg. MCI, McLean, Va., 1994-96; mktg. comm. mgr. global alliance products MCI, 1996—; cons., media rels. Va. Internat. Gold Cup, Middleburg, Va., 1993-94, Project Life Animal Rescue, Washington, 1994, media chairperson; cons., media rels. The President's Golf Cup, Washington, 1994, 96. Editor: Tour DuPont Mag., 1991. Vol. Octagon Club, Winchester, Va., 1980-81, Senatorial Campaigns, Richmond, 1988, Washington, 1994. Mem. Smithsonian, Nat. Assn. Female Execs. Republican. Roman Catholic. Avocations: writing, golfing, reading. Home: 116 Stonewall Dr Winchester VA 22602

SMITH, VIRGINIA WARREN, artist, writer, educator; b. Atlanta, Mar. 7, 1947; d. Ralph Henry and Dorothy Jane (Kubler) S. AB in Philosophy, Ga. State U., 1976, M Visual Art in Art and Photography, 1978. dir. The Upstairs Artspace, Tryon, N.C., 1984-86; mng. editor Art Papers, Atlanta, 1986-88; art critic Atlanta (Ga.) Jour./Constn., Atlanta, 1987-92; adj. faculty Atlanta (Ga.) Coll. Art, 1991—, Ga. State U., Atlanta, 1991—. Author, photographer: Scoring in Heaven: Gravestones and Cemetery Art in the American Sunbelt States, 1991, Alaska: Trail Tails and Eccentric Detours, 1992; exhbns. include High Mus. Art, Atlanta, 1972, 78, 80, 81, 82, 84, 88, 89, Nexus Contemporary Art Ctr., Atlanta, 1986, 87, 91, Sandler Hudson Gallery, Atlanta, 1987, 89, 92, Jackson Fine Art, Atlanta, 1988, 91, 93, Aperture Found., N.Y.C., 1989, MS Found., N.Y.C., 1991, Albany (Ga.) Mus. Art, 1991, Montgomery (Ala.) Mus. Art, 1992, Bernice Steinbaum Gallery, N.Y.C., 1992, Wyndy MoreLead Gallery, New Orleans, 1991, 92, U.S. Info. Agy., Washington, 1994, Chatahouchee Valley Art Mus., Lagrange, Ga., 1994, others; works in permanent collections including Mus. Modern Art, N.Y.C., Mus. Fine Arts, Boston, High Mus. of Art, Atlanta, New Orleans Mus. Art, Harvard U., Rochester Inst. Tech., N.Y., U. N.Mex., Ctr. for Study of So. Culture U. Miss., Oxford, Miss., Columbia (S.C.) Mus. Art and Sci., Ringling Sch. Art, Sarasota, Fla., City of Atlanta, Franklin Furnace, N.Y.C. Bd. mem. Art Papers, Atlanta, 1983-88; adv. bd. memd. Arts Festival Atlanta, Ga., 1990-93. Mem. Coll. Art Assn., Soc. for Photog. Edn., Photography Forum of the High Mus. Art (v.p. 1994-95). Democrat. Avocation: collecting snowdomes. Home and Office: PO Box 1110 Columbus NC 28722

SMITH, W. JAMES, health facility administrator; b. Shenandoah, Iowa, Mar. 26, 1942; s. Willis C. and Lois M. (Hurst) S.; m. Sharon E. Hogue, May 4, 1940; children: Sharon Wendy, W. James II, Stacey E. BA in Psychology, Nat. Coll. Kansas City, 1960; MA in Psychology, Gerontology, John F. Kennedy U., 1969. Lic. nursing home adminstr., Fla., Iowa, Nebr., Calif. Pres. Retirement Svcs., Oakland, Calif., 1966-77; adminstr. Good Samaritan Soc., Sioux Falls, S.D., 1977-80; pres. Good Shepherd Ctrs., Palm Harbor, Fla., 1980-84; program coord. Hospice of Fla. Suncoast, Inc., Largo, Fla., 1984-91; pres., CEO Alzheimer's Ctrs., Inc., 1991—. Home: 491 Willow Ln Palm Harbor FL 34683-5828

SMITH, W. STUART, strategic planning director; b. Binghamton, N.Y., May 2, 1943; married. B, Washington & Lee U., 1965; M, Mich. State U., 1967, Va. Commonwealth U., 1974. Adminstrv. resident MUSC Med. Ctr., Charleston, 1973-74, asst. dir., 1974-79, assoc. dir., 1979-83, dir. ops., 1983-87, dir. mktg., 1987-92, exec. dir., 1993-94; dir. strategic planning, 1994—. Mem. S.C. Hosp. Assn. (bd. dirs.). Home: 516 Island Walk W Mount Pleasant SC 29464 Office: MUSC Med Ctr Med U SC 171 Ashley Ave Charleston SC 29425-0001

SMITH, WALDO GREGORIUS, former government official; b. Bklyn., July 29, 1911; s. John Henry and Margaret (Gregorius) S.; m. Mildred Pearl Prescott, July 30, 1935 (dec. Jan. 1992); 1 dau., Carole Elizabeth Smith Levin. Student CCNY, N.Y., 1928-29; BS in Forestry, Cornell U., 1933. Registered prof. engr., Colo. Forester Forest Svc., U.S. Dept. Agr., Atlanta, 1933-41, Ala. Div. Forestry, Brewton, 1941-42; engr., civil engring. technician Geol. Survey, U.S. Dept. Interior, 1942-71, cartographic technician, 1972-75; chmn. Public Transp. Council, 1975-89; legislator aide to individuals Colo. State Legis. Internship Program, 1987-95. Recipient 40 Yr. Civil Service award pin and scroll; 42 Yr. Govt. Service award plaque. Fellow Am. Congress Surveying and Mapping (life, sec.-treas. Colo. chpt. 1961, program chmn. 1962, reporter 1969, mem. nat. membership devel. com. 1973-74, rep. to Colo. Engring. Council 1976-77); mem. AAAS (emeritus), Denver Fed. Center Profl. Engrs. Group (U.S. Geol. Survey rep. 1973-76, Engr. of Yr. award 1975), Nat. Soc. Profl. Engrs. (pre-coll. guidance com. 1986-91, life 92—), Profl. Engrs. Colo. (chpt. scholarship chmn. 1979—, advt. corr., service award 1983), Cornell U. Alumni Assn. (alumni secondary schs. com. Quadrangle Club), Common Cause, Colo. Engring. Council (chmn. library com. 1970—, spl. rep. Regional Transp. Dist., 1974-75; mem. sci. fair com. 1970-71; rep. ex officio Denver Pub. Library Found. Bd. Trustees 1975-80, mem. historic agreement with Denver Pub. Libr. 1993, Pres.'s Outstanding Service award 1987), Environ. Concerns (chmn. com. 1988—, treas. 1989-91, mem. site specific adv. bd., restoration adv. bd. Rocky Mountain arsenal cleanup 1994—), Fedn. Am. Scientists, Am. Soc. Engring. Edn., People for Am. Way. Contbr. articles to profl. jours. Home: 3821 W 25th Ave Denver CO 80211-4417 *Personal philosophy: A new acronym: T'n'T=Truth and Trust; give posterity a decent break.*

SMITH, WALLACE BUNNELL, physician, church official; b. Independence, Mo., July 29, 1929; s. William Wallace and Rosamond (Bunnell) S.; m. Anne M. McCullough, June 26, 1956; children—Carolyn, Julia, Laura. A.A., Graceland Coll., Lamoni, Iowa, 1948; B.A., U. Kans., 1950, M.D., 1954. Diplomate: Am. Bd. Ophthalmology. Intern Charity Hosp. of La., 1955; resident in medicine U. Kans. Med. Center, 1958, resident in ophthalmology, 1959-62; pvt. practice medicine specializing in ophthalmology, 1962-76; ordained to ministry Reorganized Ch. of Jesus Christ of Latter Day Saints, 1945; also. pastor Walnut Park Congregation, Independence, Mo., 1966-70, Pleasant Heights Congregation, Independence, 1975-76; president-designate Reorganized Ch. of Jesus Christ of Latter Day Saints, 1976-78, pres., 1978-96, pres. emeritus, 1996—; clin. assoc. U. Kans. Med. Center, 1962-76; dir. Pacific Land Devel. Assn. Bd. dirs. Am. Lung Assn. West Mo., Truman Heartland Comm. Found. Lt. M.C., USNR, 1955-58. Fellow ACS, Am. Acad. Ophthalamology; mem. AMA, Jackson County Med. Soc., Independence C. of C., Rotary, Phi Beta Pi. Home: 337 E Partridge St Independence MO 64055-1452 Office: Auditorium PO Box 1059 Independence MO 64051-0559

SMITH, WALTER DOUGLAS, retired college president; b. Harriman, Tenn., Nov. 17, 1918; s. Walter Blaine and Jeanetta Mae (Scarborough) S.; m. Rhondda Verle Miller, Apr. 5, 1947; children: Ian Douglas Miller, Walter Henry. B.A., Lincoln Meml. U., Harrogate, Tenn., 1943; M.A., U. Mich., 1947, Ph.D., 1950. Faculty psychology Fla. State U., 1950-59; dean coll., prof. psychology Winthrop Coll., Rock Hill, S.C., 1959-66; v.p. acad. affairs, dean of faculty Winthrop Coll., 1966-68; pres. Salisbury (Md.) State Coll., 1968-70, Francis Marion Coll., Florence, S.C., 1970-83. Served with USNR, 1943-46. Mem. Am. Psychol. Assn. Presbyterian. Home: 609 S Graham St Florence SC 29501-5142

SMITH, WALTER S., JR., federal judge; b. Marlin, Tex., Oct. 26, 1940; s. Walter S. and Mary Elizabeth Smith; children—Debra Elizabeth, Susan Kay. BA, Baylor U., 1964, JD, 1966. Bar: Tex. Assoc. Dunnam & Dunnam, Waco, Tex., 1966-69; ptnr. Wallace & Smith, Waco, 1969-78, Haley & Fulbright, Waco, 1978-80; judge Tex. Dist. Ct., 1980-83; U.S. magistrate U.S. Dist. Ct. (we. dist.) Tex., 1983-84; judge U.S. Dist. Ct. (we. dist.) Tex., Waco, 1984—. Named Outstanding Young Lawyer of Yr., Waco-McLennan County Bar Assn., 1976. Office: US Dist Ct PO Box 1908 Waco TX 76703-1908*

SMITH, WALTER SAGE, environmental engineer, consultant; b. Hammond, Ind., Nov. 12, 1938; s. Reading Barlow and Lois Cora (Riddle) S.; m. Doris Jean Bryson, Oct. 23, 1961 (div. Sept. 1976); children: Cami Stryker Davis, Adam Smith, Kelly A. Stryker, Alex Smith; m. Jacqueline P. Stryker, June 4, 1977. BSChemE, Bucknell U., 1961. Registered profl. engr., N.C., N.J. Engr. Pub. Health Svc. Commn. Corp., Cin., 1961-72; co-owner, pres. Entropy Environmentalists, Inc., Research Triangle Park, N.C., 1972-92, pres., cons., 1974-76; owner, pres. Walter Smith & Assocs., Inc., Cary, N.C., 1993—; v.p. Nutech Corp., Raleigh, N.C., 1974-76, Housing Corp. of the South, Raleigh, 1977-78, Umstead Devel. Corp., Raleigh, 1977-80. Editor (newsletter) Stack Sampling News, Entropy Quarterly. Vice pres. Black Horse Run Homeowners Assn., Raleigh, 1984. Fellow Air and Waste Mgmt. Assn.; mem. Am. Acad. Environ. Engrs. (diplomate 1985), Carolinas Air Pollution Control Assn., Source Evaluation Soc. (founder 1984). Episcopalian. Avocations: swimming, sailing, reading. Home: 6225 Splitrock Trl Apex NC 27502-9778 Office: Walter Smith & Assocs Inc P O Box 117 Cary NC 27511-0117

SMITH, WALTON NAPIER, lawyer; b. Macon, Ga., Feb. 26, 1942; s. Robert Monroe and Marion Rose (Napier) S.; m. Susan Rush Baum, Oct. 10, 1970; children—Rush Hendley, Berkeley Bosman. A.B. cum laude, Dartmouth Coll., 1964; J.D., Harvard U., 1967. Bar: Ga. 1966, D.C. 1972, Ill. 1978, U.S. Supreme Ct. 1971. Counsel, Nat. R.R. Passenger Corp., Washington, 1971-75; assoc. Lord, Bissell & Brook, Washington and Chgo., 1975-79, ptnr., Chgo. and Atlanta, 1980—. Mem. bd. Upper Chattahoochee Riverkeeper Fund. Served to capt. JAGC, U.S. Army, 1964-71. Decorated Bronze Star, Army Commendation medal. Mem. ABA, Ill. Bar Assn., State Bar Ga., Nat. Assn. R.R. Trial Counsel. Democrat. Episcopalian. Clubs: Union League (Chgo.); Commerce Club. Office: Lord Bissell & Brook 1201 W Peachtree St NW Atlanta GA 30309-3400

SMITH, WARREN ALLEN, editor; b. Minburn, Iowa, Oct. 27, 1921; s. Harry Clark and Ruth Marion (Miles) S.; BA, U. No. Iowa, 1948; MA, Columbia U., 1949. Chmn. dept. Eng., Bentley Sch., N.Y.C., 1949-54, New Canaan (Conn.) High Sch., 1954-86; founder, pres., chmn. bd. Variety Sound Corp., N.Y.C., 1961-90; pres. Afro-Carib Records, 1971-90, Talent Mgmt., 1982-90, pres. AAA Rec. Studio, 1985-90; founder, pres. Variety Rec. Studio, 1961-96; instr. Columbia U., 1961-62. Pres., Taursa Fund, 1971-73; bd. dirs. 31 Jane Street Corp. Author: Humanists on Humanism: A Directory of Non-Believers or, Who's Who in Hell; book rev. editor The Humanist, 1953-58; editor (jour.) Taking Stock, 1967-93, Pique, 1990-93, Van Rijn's Pad, 1991; contbr. book revs. Libr. Jour.; editl. assoc. Free Inquiry, 1992—; contbg. editor GALHA, Eng., 1996—; syndicated columnist Manhattan Scene in W.I. newspapers; columnist, Humanist Potpourri in Free Inquiry, 1994—; drama critic Brontë Newsletter, 1995—. Treas. Secular Humanist Soc. N.Y., 1988-93; sec. Jane St. Corp., 1995-97. With ACT UP, Hume Soc.; founder Voltaire Soc. Am. With AUS, 1942-46. Recipient Leavey award Freedoms Found. at Valley Forge, 1985. Mem. ASCAP, Coun. Secular Humanism, Mensa, N.Y. Skeptics Soc. (bd. dirs. 1990-94), Internat. Press Inst., Am. Unitarian Assn., Rationalist Press Assn., Conn. Edn. Assn., Asociación Iberoamericana Ético Humanista (hon.), Brit. Humanist Assn., Humanist Book Club (pres. 1957-62), Bertrand Russell Soc. (v.p. 1977-80, bd. dirs. 1973—), Omaha Beach Veterans Assn., Stonewall Veterans Assn., Mensa Investment Club (chmn. 1967, 73—). Signer Humanist Manifesto II, 1973. Avocation: teratology. Home and Office: 31 Jane St Apt 10D New York NY 10014-1980

SMITH, WARREN JAMES, optical scientist, consultant, lecturer; b. Rochester, N.Y., Aug. 17, 1922; s. Warren Abrams and Jessica Madelyn (Forshay) S.; m. Mary Helen Geddes, May 18, 1944; children: David Whitney, Barbara Jamie. BS, U. Rochester, 1944; postgrad., U. Calif., Santa Barbara, 1960. Physicist Clinton Engr. Works, Tenn. Eastman Co., Oak Ridge, 1944-46; chief optical engr. Simpson Optical Mfg. Co., Chgo., 1946-59; mgr. optical sect. Raytheon Corp., Santa Barbara, 1959-62; v.p. R & D, Infrared Industries, Santa Barbara, 1962-87; chief scientist Kaiser Electro-Optics, Inc., Carlsbad, Calif., 1987—; lectr. U. Wis., Madison, 1972—, U. Rochester, 1988—, Genesee Computer Ctr., Rochester, 1982-93, Sinclair Optics, 1994—; cons. in field; expert witness. Author: Modern Optical

Engineering, 1966, 2d edit., 1990, Modern Lens Design, 1992, Practical Optical System Layout, 1997; editor McGraw-Hill series Optical and Electro-Optical Engineering; also articles. Fellow Optical Soc. Am. (pres. 1980, organizer, chmn. tech. confs.), Soc. Photo-Optical Instrumentation Engrs. (life), Internat. Soc. Optical Engring. (pres. 1983, organizer, chmn. tech. confs., Gold medal 1985, Dirs. award 1992), Sigma Chi. Avocations: tennis, sailing. Home: 1165 Countrywood Ln Vista CA 92083-5334 Office: Kaiser Electro-Optics Inc 2752 Loker Ave W Carlsbad CA 92008-6603

SMITH, WAYNE CALVIN, chemical engineer; b. Beaver, Okla., Mar. 19, 1935; s. Dean C. and Loraine S.; m. Suellyn Joyce Canon, Aug. 18, 1984. BS, Okla. U., 1958, MSChemE, 1964; PhDChemE, Colo. U., 1974. Registered profl. engr., Tex., Okla., Colo.; cert. emergency response specialist. Process engr. Shell Oil Co., Deer Park, Tex., 1958-59; sr. devel. engr. Monsanto, Pensacola, Fla., 1965-66; project leader Phillips Petroleum Co., Bartlesville, Okla., 1967-69; acting chief process control EPA Nat. Enforcement Investigations Ctr., Denver, 1971-78; firm wide mgr. pollution control Dames & Moore, Golden, Colo., 1978-81; regional mgr. Hittman Assocs., Englewood, Colo., 1981-82; pres. Encon Environs Control Svcs., Golden, Colo., 1982-83; chief hazardous waste mgmt. Woodward-Clyde Cons., Englewood, 1983-84; exec. cons. Kellogg Corp., Littleton, Colo., 1984-86; program mgr. Radian Corp., Austin, Tex., 1986-93; prin. engr., office mgr. Tetra Tech, Inc., Oklahoma City, 1993—. Contbr. over 30 articles to profl. jours. Capt. USMC, 1959-62. Scholar Magnolia Petroleum Co., 1956-58; fellow Phillips Petroleum Co., 1962-64, Marathon Oil Co., 1966-67, Gulf Oil Co., 1969-71. Mem. AICE, Am. Arbitration Assn., Water Pollution Control Fedn., Soc. Plastics Engrs., The Greens Country Club, Sigma Xi. Baptist. Avocations: golf, woodworking. Office: Tetra Tech Inc 806 W Curtis Dr Ste I Midwest City OK 73110-3041

SMITH, WAYNE H., forest resources and conservation educator. BS in Agronomy with high honors, U. Fla., 1960; MS in Soils-Forestry, Miss. State U., 1962, PhD in Forest Soils, 1965. Rsch. aide So. Sta. U.S. Forest Svc., Marianna, Fla., 1957-60; asst. prof. Sch. Forest Resources and Conservation U. Fla., Gainesville, 1964-70, assoc. prof., 1970-76, prof., 1976—, asst. dir. Sch. Forest Resources and Conservation, 1971-78, dir. Ctr. Environ. and Natural Resources Programs, 1978-84, dir. ctr. Biomass Programs, 1980—, dir. Fla. Energy Ext. Svc. Inst. Food and Agrl. Scis., 1990-95, dir. Inst. Food and Agrl. Svcs., 1995—; cons. on internat. bioenergy projects U.S. AID, 1980-83, agroforestry, Haiti, 1987, U.S. Dept. Energy resource assessment, Peru, 1978, UN, FAO, UNDP, Sch. Energy Studies, Punjab U., India, 1990, NRC, NAS, Biogas Program, Thailand, 1990; forest biologist Coop. State Rsch. Svc., Washington, 1973-74; prin. investigator Biomass and Chems. from Woody Plants in Fla., 1968-80; co-mgr. Intensive Practices Assessment Ctr., USDA Forest Svc. and forest industry, 1978-79; co-coord. Coop. Rsch. in Forest Fertilization Program, a Univ./Forestry Industry Coop. Rsch. Program, 1968-75; dir. Fed. Agy. Rels., 1985-86; Fla. coord. Solid Waste Mgmt. Iniative, 1988-95. Contbr. articles to profl. jours.; editor 5 books; N.Am. editor Biomass, 1984-90, Biomass and Bioenergy, 1990—. Recipient Hi Kellogg award Composting Coun., Disting. Svc. award USDA, Nat. award U.S. Dept. Energy. Mem. FORA (bd. dirs.). Office: U Fla Ctr Biomass Program 118 Newins-Ziegler PO Box 110410 Gainesville FL 32611-0410

SMITH, WAYNE RICHARD, lawyer; b. Petoskey, Mich., Apr. 30, 1934; s. Wayne Anson and Frances Lynetta (Cooper) S.; m. Carrie J. Swanson, June 18, 1959; children: Stephen, Douglas (dec.), Rebecca. AB, U. Mich., 1956, JD, 1959. Bar: Mich. 1959. Asst. atty. gen. State of Mich., 1960-62; pros. atty. Emmet County (Mich.), 1963-68; dist. judge 90th Jud. Dist. Mich., 1969-72; sr. ptnr. Smith & Powers, Petoskey; city atty. City of Petoskey, 1976—; lectr. real estate law U. Mich. Trustee North Central Mich. Coll., 1981—, chmn., 1992-97; mem. No. Mich. Cmty. Mental Health Bd., 1972-92, chmn. 1979-81. Mem. ABA, Am. Judicature Soc., Emmet-Charlevoix Bar Assn. (pres. 1967), State Bar Mich., Mich. State Bar Found. Presbyterian. Home: 201 Sunset Petoskey MI 49770-0111 Address: PO Box 636 2 Pennsylvania Plz Petoskey MI 49770-0636

SMITH, WENDELL MURRAY, graphic arts control and equipment manufacturing executive; b. Bklyn., May 15, 1935; s. J. Henry and Roberta (Foard) S.; m. Margaret McGregor, Aug. 24, 1957; children: Karen, Wendy, Kimberley, Kathryn, Jennifer. AB, Dartmouth Coll., 1957, MS in Engring., 1958. Devel. engr. Sikorsky Aircraft Co., Stratford, Conn., 1958-60; sales engr., mgr. Barnes Engring. Corp., Stamford, Conn., 1960-65; v.p. mktg. Baldwin-Gegenheimer Corp., Stamford, 1966-70, pres., chief exec. officer, 1971-79; founder, pres. Polestar Ltd., Bermuda, 1980—; pres., chmn. bd., chief exec. officer Baldwin Tech. Co., Inc., Rowayton, Conn., 1984-95, chmn., 1995—; bd. dirs. Globe Ticket and Label Co., Bowne & Co.; trustee Bermuda Biol. Sta. for Rsch. Recipient John L. Kronenberg Industry Leadership award, 1991. Mem. Rsch. and Engring. Coun. (bd. dirs.), Graphic Comms. Assn. (bd. dirs., vice chmn.), Soderstrom Soc. of Nat. Assn. Printers and Lithographers, Stamford Ctr. for the Arts (bd. dirs.), Stamford Yacht Club, N.Y. Yacht Club, Royal Bermuda Yacht Club, Mid-Ocean Club. Republican. Methodist. Home: 10 Manor House, Smith's FL07 Bermuda Office: Polestar Ltd, PO Box 551, Flatts FLBX, Bermuda

SMITH, WENDY HAIMES, federal agency administrator; b. Amarillo, Tex.; d. Ernest A. and Fannie Haimes; m. Jay L. Smith, 1983. BA in Econs., U. Mich.; postgrad., Ohio State U., Am. U., Washington Studio Sch. Cert. real estate agt. Office mgr. Haimes Travel Agy., Ohio, 1972-73; mgmt. intern U.S. Dept. Commerce, 1973-75, country specialist for Korea, 1973, spl. asst. to dep. asst. sec. for internat. commerce, 1973-74, project officer, maj. projects divsn., 1974-75, project mgr. indsl. sys., maj. projects divsn., 1975-77, country specialist for Brazil, 1978, project mgr. hydrocarbons and chem. process plants, maj. export projects divsn., 1977-79, exec. asst. to dep. asst. sec. of commerce for export devel. and staff dir. Pres. Export Coun., 1979-81, dir. Pres. Export Coun., 1981-92, acting dir. Office Planning and Coordination, 1988-89, dir. adv. coms. and pvt. sector programs Internat. Trade Adminstrn., 1992—; dir. Trade Info. Sys. Ctr., 1997—. Author, editor: U.S. Trade in Transition: Maintaining the Gains, 1988; co-author, editor: The Export Imperative, 1980, Coping with the Dynamics of World Trade in the 1980s, 1984, Artist exihibit, Courtyard Gallery, Brian Logan Artspace, Washington. Active Smithsonian Instn., Washington Studio Sch., Washington Opera Guild. Mem. Alpha Epsilon Phi (pres. Pi chpt. 1971). Office: Dept of Commerce Rm H2015B 14th and Constitution Ave NW Washington DC 20230

SMITH, WENDY L., foundation executive; b. Chgo., Sept. 12, 1950; d. John Arthur and Dolores Mae (Webb) Rothenberger; m. Alan Richard Smith; children: Angela Fuhs, Erica Smith. Ed., Oakton C.C., Des Plaines, Ill., 1986, Mundelein Coll., 1990. Purchasing clk. AIT Industries, Skokie, Ill., 1975-76; purchasing agt. MCC Powers, Skokie, 1976-78; office mgr. Spartan Engring., Skokie, 1978-80, Brunswick Corp., Skokie, 1980—; successively sr. sec., coord. indsl. rels., dir. Brunswick Found., Lake Forest, Ill., 1982-89; pres. Brunswick Found., Lake Forest, 1989—; asst. sec. Brunswick Pub. Charitable Found., Lake Forest, 1989—; mem. adv. com. Found. for Ind. Higher Edn., Stamford, Conn., 1989—, Coun. Better Bus. Burs., Arlington, Va., 1988-90; bd. dirs. Associated Colls. of Ill., 1991—; bd. dirs., mem. trustees com., mem. compensation and benefits com. Donors Forum of Chgo., 1988-93. Bd. dirs. INROADS/Chgo., Inc., 1994—; mem. steering com. Dist. 57 Edn. Found., Mt. Prospect, Ill., 1996—. Recipient Pvt. Sector Initiative Commendation, U.S. Pres., 1987-89. Mem. Donors Forum Chgo. (treas. 1988-91, bd. dirs., mem. exec. com., chairperson audit and fin. com., mem. trustees com. 1992—), Coun. on Founds., Ind. Sector Suburban Contbns. Network (chairperson 1987-89), Women in Philanthropy Corp. Founds. (mem. cmty. rels. com. 1985-87), Chgo. Women in Philanthropy. Avocations: antique restoration, pleasure reading, bowling, golf. Office: Brunswick Found 1 N Field Ct Lake Forest IL 60045-4810

SMITH, WHITNEY BOUSMAN, music and drama critic; b. Cin., May 31, 1956; s. Lawrance Spencer and Ruby Virginia (Bousman) S. BA in Journalism, Ind. U., 1978. Reporter South Bend (Ind.) Tribune, 1977, The Repository, Canton, Ohio, 1978-82; reporter Comml. Appeal, Memphis, 1982—, on spl. assignment in Italy, 1992. Office: Comml Appeal 495 Union Ave Memphis TN 38103-3242

SMITH, WILBUR LAZEAR, radiologist, educator; b. Warwick, N.Y., Oct. 11, 1943; s. Wilbur and Betty (Norris) S.; m. Rebecca Rowlands, June 19, 1965; children: Jason, Daniel, Joanna, Noah, Ethan, Jacob. BA, SUNY, Buffalo, 1965, MD, 1969. Diplomate Am. Bd. Radiology, Am. Bd. Pediatrics. Intern, then resident Buffalo Children's Hosp., 1969-71; resident in pediatric radiology Cin. Gen. and Children Hosp., 1971-74; asst. prof. pediatrics and radiology Ind. U., Indpls., 1975-78, assoc. prof., 1978-80, acting dir. pediatric radiology, 1979-80; assoc. prof. U. Iowa, Iowa City, 1980-82, prof., 1982—, dir. med. edn. radiology, 1980-86, vice chmn. dept. radiology, 1986-94, interim head, 1994-96, dir. pediatric radiology, 1980-92. Contbr. articles to profl. jours. Served with USAR, 1969-77. Assoc. editor Gastrointestinal Imaging in Pediatrics, Acad. Radiology, 1992—. Soccer coach Iowa City Kickers, 1980—; mem. equity adv. com. Iowa City Sch. Bd., 1983-87. Recipient Merke Prize Medicine award SUNY, 1968, Wurlitzer Prize Medicine SUNY, 1968. Fellow Am. Acad. Pediatrics, Am. Coll. Radiology; mem. AMA, Iowa Radiol. Soc. (pres. 1987-88), Assn. Univ. Radiologists (pres. 1995-96), Soc. Pediat. Radiology (treas. 1995—, rep. coun. of Academia Socs. of AAMC, 1996—). Mem. Soc. Friends. Avocation: photography. Home: 2271 Cae Dr Iowa City IA 52246-4515 Office: U Iowa Dept Radiology Iowa City IA 52242

SMITH, WILBURN JACKSON, JR., retired bank executive; b. Charlotte, N.C., June 13, 1921; s. Wilburn Jackson and Banna (Oswalt) S.; B.S. in Acctg., U. N.C., 1943; postgrad. in comml. banking Rutgers U. Sch. Banking, 1953, postgrad. in investment banking, 1956; m. Terry Mosteller, Jan. 4, 1944; children: Kenneth M., M. Scott (dec.), Wilburn Jackson III, Curtis Todd. With First Union Nat. Bank, Charlotte, 1946-74, exec. v.p., 1960-67, 1st exec. v.p., 1967-74; pres., mng. trustee Cameron-Brown Investment Group, Raleigh, N.C., 1974-78; chmn. loan policy com. N.C. Nat. Bank, Charlotte, 1979-88; bd. dirs. Burroughs & Chapin Co. Inc., Myrtle Beach, S.C.; cons. in field. Served with USN, 1943-46. Recipient Citizenship award Charlotte Civitan, 1972. Mem. Robert Morris Assocs. Baptist. Club: Myers Park Country (Charlotte).

SMITH, WILFRED IRVIN, former Canadian government official; b. Port La Tour, Can., May 20, 1919; s. Claude Albert and Deborah (Inglis) S.; m. Joan Eileen Capstick, Nov. 27, 1946; children: Gordon, Heather, Gail. B.A., Acadia U., Wolfville, N.S., Can., 1943, M.A., 1946, D.C.L., 1975; Ph.D., U. Minn., 1968. Lectr. U. Minn., 1948, U. Sask., 1948-50, Carleton U., 1955-60; mem. staff Pub. Archives Can., 1950-84, dir. hist. br., 1964-65, asst., then acting dominion archivist, 1965-70, dominion archivist, 1970-84; mem. Canadian Nat. Library Adv. Bd., Canadian Permanent Com. Geog. Names, Historic Sites and Monuments Bd. Can, Indian Hist. Manuscripts Commn.; former mem. internat. adv. com. documentation, libraries and archives UNESCO. Author: Code Word Canloan, 1992; contbr. articles to profl. jours. Served to maj. Canadian and Brit. armies, 1943-45. Decorated officer Order Can.; recipient Can. decoration, 1958, Centennial medal, 1967, Jubilee medal, 1978, Royal Soc. Can. medal, 1980, Outstanding Achievement award Can. Govt., 1983. Fellow Soc. Am. Archivists (past pres.); hon. life mem. Internat. Council Archives (sec. gen.), Canadian Hist. Assn. (past editor hist. booklets), Assn. Canadian Archivists, Order St. John; mem. Soc. Archivists, Am. Antiquarian Assn., Canadian Heraldry Soc. (hon. v.p.), United Empire Loyalists Assn. (hon. v.p.), Guards Assn., Friends of Can. War Mus., Canloan Assn. (pres.). Home: 201-71 Somerset St W, Ottawa, ON Canada K2P 2G2

SMITH, WILL, actor, rapper; b. Phila., Sept. 25, 1968; m. Sheree Smith; 1 child, Willard Smith III. Albums (as The Fresh Prince with DJ Jazzy Jeff): And in this Corner..., 1989, Homebase, 1991, Rock the House, 1991 reissue, He's the DJ, I'm the Rapper, 1988; TV series: The Fresh Prince of Bel-Air, 1990—; Movies: Where the Day Takes You, 1992, Made in America, 1993, Six Degrees of Separation, 1993, Bad Boys, 1995, Independence Day, 1996, Men In Black, 1997. Office: CAA 9830 Wilshire Blvd Beverly Hills CA 90212-1804*

SMITH, WILLIAM BARNEY, allergist; b. Memphis, Aug. 23, 1959; m. Carol Nix, 1985; children: Lauren Ashley, William Braden. BS magna cum laude, Memphis State U., 1980; MD, U. Tenn., 1985. Diplomate Am. Bd. Internal Medicine, Am. Bd. Allergy and Immunology; cert. Advanced Cardiac Life Support. Intern dept. internal medicine U. Tenn., Memphis, 1985-86, resident dept. internal medicine, 1986-88; fellow dept. allergy and immunology Vanderbilt U., Nashville, 1988-90, asst. clin. prof. dept. medicine, 1992—; pvt. practice Allergy and Asthma Assocs. of Mid. Tenn., Nashville, 1990—. Fellow Am. Coll. Allergy and Immunology; mem. ACP, Tenn. Med. Assn., Nashville Acad. Medicine, Alpha Epsilon Delta. Office: 300 20th Ave N Ste 100 Nashville TN 37203-2132 also: Ste 127-B 353 New Shackle Island Rd Hendersonville TN 37075

SMITH, WILLIAM BRIDGES, diversified company executive; b. Washington, Feb. 13, 1944; s. Harry Leroy and Laura Sloo (Johnson) S.; m. Marjorie Lee Donaghy, Dec. 11, 1965; children: Laura Lee, William Bridges. B.S.E.E., U. Md., 1962; M.S.E.E., Princeton U., 1963; Ph.D in Computer Info. Sci., U. Pa., 1968. Mem. tech. staff BTL, Holmdel, N.J., 1962-66; supr. BTL, Naperville, Ill., 1967-70; dept. head BTL, Holmdel, 1970-74; dir. BTL, Columbus, Ohio, 1974-78; exec. dir. BTL, Naperville, 1978-82; v.p. ITT, 1982-86; gen. tech. dir. for Europe ITT Europe Inc., Brussels, 1982-86; exec. dir. AT&T Bell Labs, 1986-91; SVP, chief info. and tech. officer US West, Inc., 1991-95; COO, pres. Telco Sys., Inc., 1995-96, pres., CEO, 1996—; grad. instr. Ill. Inst. Tech., Chgo., 1968-70; gen. chmn. COMPSAC '79, Chgo., 1979; dir. ITT-U.K., London, 1982—83, Standard Telecommunications Labs., Harlow, Eng., 1982—. Patentee in data signaling error control field, 1971; contbr. articles to profl. jours., 1971. Md. state treas. Children of the Revolution, 1959; mem. vestry Trinity Ch., Wheaton, Ill., 1981-82, Christ Ch., Shrewsbury, N.J., 1990-91; mem. Ill. Inst. Tech. bd. overseers, Armour Coll. Engring., 1981-82, Coll. Engring. Dept., U. Colo., 1994-95. Mem. IEEE (sr. chmn. computer group 1969-70). Republican. Episcopalian. Office: Telco Systems 63 Nahatan St Norwood MA 02062-5732

SMITH, WILLIAM BURTON, chemist, educator; b. Muncie, Ind., Dec. 13, 1927; s. Merrill Mark and Felice Hoy (Richardson) S.; m. Marian Louise Roseborough, Aug. 9, 1954; children: Mark W., Frederick D., Mary F. BA, Kalamazoo Coll., 1949; PhD, Brown U., 1954. Research asso. Fla. State U., 1953-54, U. Chgo., 1954-55; asst. prof., then asso. prof. Ohio U., 1955-61; R.A. Welch vis. prof. chemistry Tex. Christian U., 1960-61, prof. chemistry, chmn. dept., 1961-81; Research participant Oak Ridge Inst. Nuclear Studies, 1956—. Author: A Modern Introduction to Organic Chemistry, 1961, Molecular Orbital Methods in Organic Chemistry, 1974, Introduction to Theoretical Organic Chemistry and Molecular Modelling, 1996; also rsch. articles. Recipient Chancellor's award, 1989. Fellow Royal Soc. of Chemistry; mem. Am. Chem. Soc. (Doherty award 1990), Sigma Xi. Home: 3604 Wedghill Way Fort Worth TX 76133-2156

SMITH, WILLIAM CHARLES, lawyer; b. Batavia, N.Y., June 9, 1930; s. William F. and Verna B. (Busmire) S.; m. Lucia P. Pierce, July 10, 1954; children: William Charles, Leonard P., Victoria J. B.A., U. Buffalo, 1952; LL.B., Harvard U., 1955. Bar: Maine 1955, D.C. 1962, Fla. 1995, U.S. Dist. Ct. Maine, 1956, U.S. Tax Ct. 1960, U.S. Ct. Appeals (1st cir.) 1977, U.S. Ct. Claims 1985, U.S. Supreme Ct. 1960. Assoc. Portland, Maine, 1955-57; ptnr. Hutchinson, Pierce, Atwood & Allen, Portland, 1957-59; counsel Office Tax Legis. Counsel, U.S. Treasury Dept., Washington, 1959-61; ptnr. Pierce, Atwood, Scribner, Allen, Smith and Lancaster, Portland, 1961-96, of counsel, 1996—; exec. com. Fed. Tax Inst., New Eng. Vice chmn. budget com. United Community Services, 1966-68, chmn., 1968-70, nat. budget and consultation com., 1969-71; bd. dirs. Portland Goodwill, Inc., 1967-69, United Way, Inc., 1968-74, 75-80, Portland Widow's Wood Soc., 1962—; trustee Portland Regional Opportunity Program, 1967-68, Freyburg Acad., 1976-96 , Found. Blood Research, 1979-85. Mem. ABA, Maine Bar Assn., D.C. Bar, Fla. Bar, Cumberland County Bar Assn., Am. Law Inst., Am. Coll. Trust and Estate Counsel, Am. Coll. Tax Counsel. Republican. Unitarian. Clubs: Portland Country, Mid-Ocean (Bermuda); Naples Country (Maine); Meadows Country (Fla.). Home: 392 Spring St Portland ME 04102-3642 Office: Pierce Atwood Scribner Allen Smith & Lancaster One Monument Sq Portland ME 04101-1110

SMITH, WILLIAM HENRY PRESTON, writer, editor, former corporate executive; b. Pleasanton, Tex., Sept. 8, 1924; s. Sidney Newton and Willie Gertrude (Cloyd) S.; m. Frances Dixon, July 1, 1950; children: Juliet, Dixon, David. B.J., U. Tex., 1949. Reporter Dallas Morning News, 1949-52; advt. asst. Dallas Power & Light Co., 1952-55; dir. pub. relations Greater Boston C. of C., 1955-58; with New Eng. Telephone and Telegraph Co., Boston, 1958-86, asst. v.p., 1966-75, corp. sec., 1975-83, dir. pub. relations, 1983-86; free-lance writer Dover, Mass., 1986—. Editor: Bus. Ethics Resource Newsletter. Bd. dirs., v.p. Mass. Soc. for Prevention Cruelty to Children; bd. dirs. Bus. Ethics Found., Urban Dynamics Adv. Coun.; mem. support policies com. United Way Mass; bd. advisors to pres. Andover Newton Theol. Sch. With paratroopers U.S. Army, 1943-46. Decorated Purple Heart. Mem. Am. Soc. Corp. Secs., Friars, Dedham Country and Polo Club, Down Town Club, Wellesley Coll. Club, Sigma Delta Chi, Delta Kappa Epsilon. Republican. Home and Office: 10 Turtle Ln Dover MA 02030-2053

SMITH, WILLIAM HULSE, forestry and environmental studies educator; b. Trenton, N.J., May 9, 1939; s. Philip Andrews and Marion (Hulse) S.; m. Judith Chapin Pease, July 6, 1963 (div. 1982); children—Scott William, Philip Chapin; m. Deborah Banks Coit, June 17, 1983; 1 child, Tyler Banks. B.S., Rutgers U., 1961, Ph.D., 1965; M.F., Yale U., 1963. Asst. prof. forestry Rutgers U., 1965-66; asst. prof. Yale U., 1966-72, assoc. prof., 1972-75, prof., 1975—, dean, 1981-83, Clifton R. Musser prof. forest biology, 1985—; mem. sci. adv. bd. U.S. EPA, 1990—. Author: Tree Pathology, 1970, Air Pollution and Forest Ecosystems, 1981, 2d edit., 1990. Mem. Conn. Siting Council, 1985. NSF grantee, U.S. Dept. Agr. Forest Service grantee. Mem. Soc. Am. Foresters, Am. Phytopath. Soc., Ecol. Soc. Am. Home: 1 Northwinds Dr Ivoryton CT 06442-1261 Office: Sch Forestry and Environ Studies Yale U 370 Prospect St New Haven CT 06511-2104

SMITH, WILLIAM JAY, author; b. Winnfield, La., Apr. 22, 1918; s. Jay and Georgia (Campster) S.; m. Barbara Howes, Oct. 1, 1947 (div. June 1965); children: David Emerson, Gregory Jay; m. Sonja Haussmann, Sept. 3, 1966. Student, Institut de Touraine, Tours, France, 1938; B.A., Washington U., St. Louis, 1939, M.A., 1941; postgrad., Columbia U., 1946-47; postgrad. Rhodes scholar, Oxford U., 1947-48; postgrad., U. Florence, Italy, 1948-50; Litt.D., New Eng. Coll., 1973. Asst. in French Washington U., 1939-41; instr. English and French Columbia U., 1946-47; lectr. English Williams Coll., 1951, poet in residence, lectr. English, 1959-64, 66-67; Ford Found. fellow Arena Stage, Washington, 1964-65; writer in residence Hollins Coll., 1965-66, prof. English, 1967, 70-80, prof. emeritus, 1980; poet laureate Libr. of Congress, Washington, 1968-70, hon. cons. in Am. letters, 1970-76; vis. prof., acting chmn., writing divsn. Sch. Arts, Columbia U., 1973, 74-75; mem. staff Salzburg (Austria) Seminar, 1975; mem. jury Nat. Book award, 1962, 70, 75, Neustadt Internat. prize for lit., 1978, Com. of Pegasus Prize for Lit., 1979—; poet in residence Cathedral St. John the Divine, N.Y., 1985-88. Author: Poems, 1947, Celebration at Dark, 1950, Laughing Time, 1955, Poems, 1947-57, Boy Blue's Book of Beasts, 1957, Puptents and Pebbles: A Nonsense ABC, 1959, Typewriter Town, 1960, The Spectra Hoax, 1961, What Did I See, 1962, Ho for a Hat, 1964, (with Louise Bogan) The Golden Journey; Poems for Young People, 1965, The Tin Can and Other Poems, 1966, Poems from France, 1967, If I Had a Boat, 1967, Mr. Smith and Other Nonsense, 1968, New and Selected Poems, 1970, The Streaks of the Tulip, selected criticism, 1972, Poems from Italy, 1973, Venice in the Fog, 1975, The Telephone, 1977, Laughing Time, 1980, The Traveler's Tree, New and Selected Poems, 1980, Army Brat, a Memoir, 1980, A Green Place: Modern Poems, 1982, Plain Talk: Epigrams, Epitaphs, Satires, Nonsense, Occasional Concrete and Quotidian Poems, 1988, Ho for a Hat (rev.), 1989, Collected Poems 1939-1989, 1990, Laughing Time: Collected Nonsense, 1990, Birds and Beasts, 1990, Big and LIttle, 1992 (with Carol Ra) Behind the King's Kitchen: A Roster of Rhyming Riddles, 1992, The Cyclist, 1995 (with Carol Ra) The Sun is Up: A Child's Year of Poems, 1996; translator: (with Emanuel Brasil) Brazilian Poetry 1950-80, 1984, (with Ingvar Schousboe) The Pact: My Friendship with Isak Dinesen by Thorkild Bjørnvig, 1983, (with J.S. Holmes) Dutch Interior: Post-War Poetry of the Netherlands and Flanders, 1984, Scirocco by Romualdo Romano, 1951; Poems of a Multimillionaire by Valery Larbaud, 1955, Selected Writings of Jules Laforgue, 1956, Children of the Forest by Elsa Beskow, 1969, Two Plays by Charles Bertin: Christopher Columbus and Don Juan, 1970, The Pirate Book by Lennart Hellsing, 1972, (with Leif Sjöberg) Agadir by Artur Lundkvist, 1979, Moral Tales of Jules Laforgue, 1985, Collected Translations: Italian, French, Spanish, Portuguese, 1985, (with Dana Gioia) Poems from Italy, 1985, (with Leif Sjöberg) Wild Bouquet: Nature Poems by Harry Martinson, 1985, (with Sonja Haussmann Smith) The Madman and the Medusa by Tchicaya U Tam'Si, 1989, Songs of Childhood by Federico Garcia Lorca, 1994, Berlin: The City and the Court, 1995, (with Heif Sjoberg) The Forest of Childhood: Poems from Sweden; editor: Herrick, 1962, Light Verse and Satires by Witter Bynner, 1978, (with F.D. Reeve) An Arrow in the Wall: Selected Poetry and Prose by Andrei Voznesensky, 1986 (one of 16 Best Books of 1986, N.Y. Times), Life Sentence: Selected Poems of Nina Cassian, 1990. Mem. Vt. Ho. of Reps., 1960-62. Served to lt. USNR, 1941-45. Recipient Alumni citation Washington U., 1963; prize Poetry mag., 1945, 64; Henry Bellamann Major award, 1970; Russell Liones award Nat. Inst. Arts and Letters, 1972; Gold medal Labor Hungary 1978; Golden Rose award New Eng. Poetry Club, 1979, médaille de vermeil French Acad., 1991, Pro Cultura Hungarica medal, Hungary, 1993; Nat. Endowment for Arts fellow, 1972, 95; NEH fellow, 1975, 89; Ingram Merrill fellow, 1982; Camargo Found. fellow, 1986. Mem. Am. Acad. Arts and Letters (v.p. for literature 1986-89), Am. Assn. Rhodes Scholars, Acad. Am. Poets, Authors Guild (council), P.E.N. Club: Century. Home: 63 Luther Shaw Rd Cummington MA 01026-9787 also: 52-56 rue d'Alleray, 75015 Paris France

SMITH, WILLIAM K., real estate developer; b. 1944. BA, U. Redlands, 1966; JD, UCLA, 1969. With Mission Viejo (Calif.) Co., 1969—, officer, 1974—, now sr. v.p., gen. counsel. Office: Mission Viejo Co 26137 La Paz Rd Mission Viejo CA 92691-5309

SMITH, WILLIAM LEWIS, hotel executive; b. Cleve., Nov. 7, 1925; s. Floyd Holland and Florence (Goebelbecker) S.; m. Dorothy Losch, Aug. 2, 1945; children: Diane, William, Bradley, Tracey. Student, John Carroll U., Kent State U., Darden Sch., U. Va. Cert. hotel adminstr., cert. engring. ops. exec. With Halle Bros. Co., Cleve., 1946-58; with Hilton Hotel Corp., various locations, 1958-89, Statler Hilton, Cleve., 1958-61, Hilton Inn, Tarrytown, N.Y., 1961-63, N.Y. Hilton, N.Y.C., 1963-68, Conrad Hilton Hotel, Chgo., 1968-78, Fontainebleau Hilton, Miami Beach, Fla., 1978-80, Washington Hilton, 1980-84, Chgo. Hilton and Towers, 1984-89; asst. sec. Hilton Hotels Corp., 1971-89; with Bus. Cons. Internat., Barrington, Ill., 1989—; vis. lect. U. Wis.-Stout, 1974, U. Notre Dame, 1975, 76, U. Houston, 1980, Cornell U., Ithaca, N.Y., 1987. Bd. dirs. Mich. Blvd. Assn., 1968-78, Good Shepherd Manor, Momence, Ill., 1973-89, Maur Hill Prep. Sch., Atchison, Kans., 1973-79, Met. Fair and Expn. Authority Chgo., 1975-78, Chgo. Conv. and Vis. Bur., Chgo. Conv. and Tourism Bur., 1975-78, 84-89, Miami Beach Visitor and Conv. Authority, 1978-80, Burnham Park Planning Bd., 1984-86; mem. Nat. 4-H Service Com., 1969-76, mem. adv. com., 1977-78; mem. adv. bd. Mercy Hosp. and Med. Ctr., Chgo., 1973-78, 84—, Echols Internat. Hotel Schs., Inc., 1984-89; mem. D.C. Bldg. Code Adv. Com., 1981-84, Near South Task Force Chgo. Cen. Area Com., 1984-89; mem. exec. com. Washington Conv. and Visitors Assn., 1981-84; mem. hotel/motel mgmt. adv. bd. Howard U., 1983-84; mem. bus. adv. council Coll. Bus. Adminstrn., U. Ill., Chgo., 1984-86; mem. steering com. South Side Planning Bd., 1984-89. Served with USNR, 1943-45. Recipient Partner-in-4-H award, 1971; Good Scout award Boy Scouts Am., 1974; Ignatian award, 1975. Mem. Am. Hotel and Motel Assn. (life, exec. engr. com. 1983-89), Washington Hotel Assn. (bd. dirs. 1980-84), Ill. Restaurant Assn. (bd. dirs. 1984-89, chmn. 1989), Hotel-Motel Assn. Ill. (bd. dirs. 1986-89, life). Address: 16 Champlain Rd Barrington IL 60010-9312

SMITH, WILLIAM RANDOLPH, lawyer; b. Houston, July 30, 1928; s. Angie Frank and Bess Patience (Crutchfield) S.; m. Margaret Ann Pickett, Nov. 25, 1950; children: Sherren Bess (dec.), William Randolph Jr., Margaret Moody, David Christian. B.A., So. Meth. U., 1948; LL.B., U. Tex., 1951. Assoc. Vinson & Elkins, Houston, 1951-64, ptnr., 1965-91; dir. Weatherford Internat., Houston, 1979-95, several pvt. corps. Bd. dirs. Meth. Hosp. System, Houston, 1970—; trustee M.D. Anderson Hosp., 1975-92, So. Meth. U., Dallas, 1975-88, Briarwood Sch./Brookwood Community, Houston, 1970—. 1st lt. USAF, 1952-53. Mem. Houston Country Club, Ramada

Club (sec. 1978-94). Home: 58 E Broad Oaks Dr Houston TX 77056-1202 Office: Vinson & Elkins 3311 First City Tower 1001 Fannin St Houston TX 77002-6706

SMITH, WILLIAM RANDOLPH (RANDY SMITH), health care management association executive; b. Spartanburg, S.C., July 23, 1948; s. Jesse Edward and Helen (Knox) S.; m. Donna Marie HAwthorne, July 18, 1970; children: Kirstin Leigh, Andrea Marie. BA, Furman U., 1970; MHA, Duke U., 1972. Exec. dir. Riverside Hosp., Wilmington, Del., 1974-79; assoc. exec. dir. Brookwood Med. Ctr., Brimingham, Ala., 1979-81, exec. dir., 1983-85; v.p. ops. Am. Med. Internat., Atlanta, 1981-89; interim chief fin. officer Am. Med. Internat., Beverly Hills, Calif., 1989-90; chief adminstrv. officer Am. Med. Internat., Dallas, 1990, exec. v.p. ops., 1990-95; exec. v.p. Tenet Health Corp, Dallas, 1995—; bd. dirs. EPIC Healthcare Group, Dallas, 1989-92. Bd. dirs. Ala. Symphony Assn., Birmingham, 1985, State of Ala. Ballet, Birmingham, 1983-85. Lt. U.S. Army, 1972-74. Mem. Fedn. Am. Health Systems (bd. dirs. 1989—, pres. 1993, chmn. 1994). Episcopalian. Avocations: skiing, tennis, automobiles. Office: Tenet Healthcare Inc 14001 Dallas Pkwy Ste 200 Dallas TX 75240-4300

SMITH, WILLIAM RAY, retired biophysicist, engineer; b. Lyman, Okla., June 26, 1925; s. Harry Wait and Daisy Belle (Hull) S. BA, Bethany Nazarene Coll., 1948; MA, Wichita State U., 1950; PhD, UCLA, 1967. Engr., Beech Aircraft Corp., Wichita, Kans., 1951-53; sr. group engr. McDonnell Aircraft Corp., St. Louis, 1953-60; sr. engr. Lockheed Aircraft Corp., Burbank, Calif., 1961-63; sr. engr. scientist McDonnell Douglas Corp., Long Beach, Calif., 1966-71; mem. tech. staff Rockwell Internat., L.A., 1973-86, CDI Corp.-West, Costa Mesa, Calif., 1986-88, McDonnell Douglas Aircraft Corp., Long Beach, 1988-93; ret., 1993. tchr. math. Pasadena Nazarene Coll. (now Point Loma Nazarene Coll., San Diego), 1960-62, Glendale Coll., Calif., 1972; asst. prof. math. Mt. St. Mary's Coll., L.A., 1972-73; math. cons. L.A. Union Rescue Mission Bank of Am. Learning Ctr., 1995—; docent Will Rogers State Park Nature Mus., 1995—; deacon Presbyn. Ch. Recipient Recognition certificate NASA, 1982. Mem. Town Hall Calif., Yosemite Assocs., L.A. World Affairs Coun., UCLA Faculty Club, Sigma Xi, Pi Mu Epsilon. Republican. Avocations: sailing, photography, teaching Sunday sch. first grade. Home: 2405 Roscomare Rd Los Angeles CA 90077-1839

SMITH, WILLIAM RAYMOND, history educator, philosophy educator; b. Bowling Green, Ky., June 5, 1932; s. William Raymond and Rose Velta (Biggerstaff) S.; m. Robin Sommers, July 12, 1954 (div. Sept. 1977); children: Dana Leslie Henning, Lauren Reneé Imgrund; m. Lee Ann McClathchey, Dec. 31, 1994. BA in Liberal Arts, U. Chgo., 1953, MA in English, 1959, PhD in History of Culture, 1961. Lic. thorobred trainer. Asst. prof. English Pa. State U., Univ. Park, 1961-63, Haverford (Pa.) Coll., 1963-66; asst. prof. English Scripps Coll., Claremont, Calif., 1966-67, exec. officer literature divsn., 1966-67; chmn. integrative studies Shimer Coll., Mt. Carroll, Ill., 1967-70; asst. prof. humanities Reed Coll., Portland, 1970-71; prof. history and philosophy U. Pitts., Johnstown, Pa., 1971—, acad. dean, 1971-72; Fulbright prof. Am. studies U. Utrecht, Netherlands, 1969-70. Author: History as Argument, 1966, The Rhetoric of American Politics, 1969; contbr. chpts. to books The Colonial Legacy, 1971, Nineteenth Century Literary Criticism, 1986. Cpl. U.S. Army, 1955-57. Recipient fellow Union for Rsch. in Higher Edn., Kennebunkport, Maine, 1968. Avocations: fox hunting rider, steeplechase rider. Home: RD 2 Box 144 New Paris PA 15554 Office: U Pitts Johnstown 233 Biddle Hall 450 Schoolhouse Rd Johnstown PA 15904-2912

SMITH, WILLIAM ROBERT, utility company executive; b. Mount Clemens, Mich., Nov. 11, 1916; s. Robert L. and Elsie (Chamberlain) S.; BS, Detroit Inst. Tech., 1947; postgrad. Detroit Coll. Law, U. Mich. Grad. Sch. Bus. Adminstrn.; children: William R., Laura A. (dec.). Indsl. engr. Detroit Edison Co., 1934-60; mgr. econ. devel. East Ohio Gas Co., Cleve., 1960-80; mgr. nat. accounts Consol. Natural Gas Co., Cleve., 1980-85; dir. mktg. Edison Polymer Innovation Corp. 1985-88; exec. dir. Western Res. Econ. Devel. Coun., 1988—; pres. T.S.T. Corp. Bd. dirs. Animal Protective League and Humane Soc. Served with USAAF, 1942-45. Registered profl. engr., Mich., Ohio. Fellow Am. Indsl. Devel. Council; Indsl. Devel. Rsch. Coun., Assn. Ohio Commodores, Shaker Heights (Ohio) Country Club, Delta Theta Tau. Presbyterian. Home: 27750 Fairmount Blvd Cleveland OH 44124-4612 Office: Kent State Univ Coll Bus Adminstrn Goodyear Exec Office Kent OH 44242

SMITH, WILLIE TESREAU, JR., retired judge, lawyer; b. Sumter, S.C., Jan. 17, 1920; s. Willie T. and Mary (Moore) S. ; student Benedict Coll., 1937-40; AB, Johnson C. Smith U., 1947; LLB, S.C. State Coll., 1954, JD, 1976; m. Anna Marie Clark, June 9, 1955; 1 son, Willie Tesreau, III. Admitted to S.C. bar, 1954; began gen. practice, Greenville, 1954; past exec. dir. Legal Svcs. Agy. Greenville County, Inc.; state family ct. judge 13th Jud. Circuit S.C., 1977-91; ret. 1991. Mem. adv. bd. Greenville Tech. Edn. Ctr. Adult Edn. Program and Para-Legal Program, Greenville Tech. Coll. Found. Bd.; bd. visitors Presbyn. Coll., Clinton, S.C.; past bd. dirs. Greenville Urban League; past trustee Greenville County Sch. Dist. Served with AUS, 1942-45, USAF, 1949-52. Mem. Am., Nat. (jud. coun.), S.C., Greenville County bar assns., Southeastern Lawyers Assn., Nat. Coun. Juvenile and Family Ct. Judges, Am. Legion, Greater Greenville C. of C. (past dir.), Peace Ctr. for The Performing Arts (v.p.), Phillis Wheatley Assn. (dir.), NAACP, Omega Psi Phi, Delta Beta Boule, Sigma Pi Phi. Presbyterian (past chmn. bd. trustees Fairfield-McClelland Presbytery, past moderator Foothills Presbytery). Clubs: Masons, Shriners, Rotary. Home: 601 Jacobs Rd Greenville SC 29605-3318

SMITH, YVONNE SMART, advertising agency executive; b. Asheville, N.C., June 25, 1947; d. Gardner Ford and Yvonne (Boyd) Smart. BFA, Auburn U., 1969. Asst. art dir. Mademoiselle mag., N.Y.C.; art dir. Cargill, Wilson & Acree Advt. div. Doyle Dane Bernbach, Charlotte, N.C.; art dir., creative supr. Tracy-Locke Advt., Dallas; v.p., assoc. creative dir., exec. art dir. Chiat/Day Advt., L.A., sr. v.p., assoc. creative dir., Venice, Calif.; prin. Yvonne Smith, Inc.; sr. v.p., assoc. creative dir. Chiat/Day Advt., Venice, N.Y.C., London, Toronto; mng. ptnr., creative dir. TBWA Chiat/Day Advt., Venice, 1997—; guest lectr. UCLA, Art Ctr. Coll. Design, L.A., 1982; judge advt. awards. Subject of profl. articles. Recipient One Show award N.Y. Art Dirs. Club, Belding awards Los Angeles Advt. Club, 1976-83, Andy awards N.Y. Arts Dirs. Club, Art Dirs. Club award, Steven Kelly awards, Clio awards, CA awards. Mem. Communicating Arts (sec.), Los Angeles Creative Club. Club: N.Y. Jr. League (N.Y.C.). Office: TBWA Chiat/Day Advt 340 Main St Venice CA 90291

SMITH, ZACHARY TAYLOR, II, retired tobacco company executive; b. Mt. Airy, N.C., June 15, 1923; s. Eugene Gray and Leonita (Yates) S. AB in Econs., U. N.C., 1947; LLD (hon.), Wake Forest U., 1989. With R.J. Reynolds Tobacco Co., 1947-85, treas., dir., 1970-85. Trustee, past pres. Z. Smith Reynolds Found.; life trustee Wake Forest U.; bd. dirs. Mary Reynolds Babcock Found., past pres.; bd. dirs. Arts and Scis. Found., U. N.C.; mem. nat. devel. coun. U. N.C.; past bd. dirs. Med. Found. N.C.; past bd. dirs. Leadership Winston-Salem; past mem. adv. coun. The Carolina Challenge; past chmn. bd. visitors U. N.C. Chapel Hill; past mem. Reynolds Scholarship Com., past mem. bd. visitors Wake Forest U.; mem. adv. coun. to hosp., past mem. bd. visitors inst. policy studies and pub. affairs Duke U.; past bd. dirs., N.C. Sch. Arts Found., Devotion Found., N.C. Outward Bound Sch., Small Bus. Devel. Com., Winston-Salem Symphony, Citizens Planning Coun.; past trustee Forsyth Hosp. Authority; past pres., dir. Child Guidance Clinic Forsyth County, YMCA, Red Shield Boy's Clubs; past chmn. indsl. divsn. Arts Coun. fund drive; past v.p., dir. Arts Coun.; past v.p., dir. Amos Cottage; past bd. visitors Meredith Coll.; past trustee St. Augustine Coll.; past bd. dirs. alumni assn. U. N.C.; vice chmn., dir. Friends of U. N.C.-Greensboro Libr.; co-founder Club Med. Sch., U. N.C., Chapel Hill. Mem. Old Town Club, Rotary. Democrat. Episcopalian. Home: 2548 Forest Dr Winston Salem NC 27104

SMITHBURG, WILLIAM DEAN, food manufacturing company executive; b. Chgo., July 9, 1938; s. Pearl L. and Margaret L. (Savage) S.; children: Susan, Thomas. BS, DePaul U., 1960; MBA, Northwestern U., 1962. With Leo Burnett Co., Chgo., 1961-63, McCann-Erickson, Inc., Chgo., 1963-66; various positions Quaker Oats Co., Chgo., 1966-71, gen. mgr. cereals and mixes divsn., 1971-75, pres. food divsn., 1975-76, exec. v.p. U.S. grocery products, 1976-79, pres., 1979-83, chief exec. officer, 1979—, chmn., 1983—, also bd. dirs. Served with USAR, 1959-60. Roman Catholic. Office: Quaker Oats Co PO Box 049001 321 N Clark St Chicago IL 60610-4715*

SMITHEE, JOHN TRUE, lawyer, state legislator; b. Amarillo, Tex., Sept. 7, 1951; s. John J. and Mildred B. (True) S.; m. Becky Collins, Aug. 18, 1979; children: Jennifer, Rebecca, John True. BBA, West Tex. State U., Canyon, 1973; JD, Tex. Tech U., 1976. Bar: Tex. 1976, U.S. Supreme Ct., 1983. Atty. Templeton, Smithee, Hayes & Fields, Amarillo, Tex., 1976—; mem. Tex. Ho. of Reps., Austin, 1985—, chmn. ins. com., 1993—. Mem. State Bar Tex., Amarillo Bar Assn. Republican. Home: 2808 Parker St Amarillo TX 79109-3546 Office: Templeton Smithee Hayes & Fields 600 S Tyler St Ste 12075 Amarillo TX 79101-2351

SMITHER, HOWARD ELBERT, musicologist; b. Pittsburg, Kans., Nov. 15, 1925; s. Elbert S. and Ethel (Schwab) S.; m. Doris J. Arvin (div. 1976); children: Thomas A., Jesse N. Woodsmith; m. Ann M. Woodward. AB magna cum laude, spl. honors in music, Hamline U., 1950; MA in musicology, Cornell U., 1952; postgrad., U. Munich, 1953-54; PhD in musicology, Cornell U., 1960. Instr. Oberlin Coll. and Conservatory of Music, Oberlin, Ohio, 1955-57, asst. prof., 1957-60; asst. prof. U. Kans., Lawrence, 1960-63; assoc. prof. Tulane U., New Orleans, 1963-68; assoc. prof. U. N.C., Chapel Hill, 1968-71, prof., 1971-79, dir. grad. studies in music, 1977-79, 83-84, 86-88, James Gordon Hanes prof. humanities in music, 1979-92, James Gordon Hanes prof. emeritus humanities in music, 1992—; John Bird prof. of music U. Wales, Cardiff, 1993-95; Lectr., chmn. panels regional, nat. and internat. meetings, confs., symposiums, 1964-90. Author: A History of the Oratorio, Vol. 1, The Oratorio in the Baroque Era: Italy, Vienna, Paris, 1977 (transl. Italian), Vol. 2, The Oratorio in the Baroque Era: Protestant Germany and England, 1977 (Deems Taylor award ASCAP 1978), The Oratorio in the Classical Era, 1987; editor The Italian Oratorio 1650-1800, Vols. 1-3, 6, 8, 11, 12, 13, 16, 18, 19, 20, 24, 25, 27, 1986-87; editor, translator poems in Alfred Einstein's The Italian Madrigal, 1971; author publs. in periodicals, dictionaries, encys., congress reports, record-jacket notes, abstracts, revs.; music rev. editor Notes, 1967-69; mem. editorial bd. Detroit Monographs in Musicology, 1971-87; chmn. editorial bd. Early Musical Masterworks: Editions and Commentaries, 1978-83; mem. editorial bd. Videodisc Music Series, NEH, 1982-86; editor Oratorios of the Italian Baroque, 1983—. Fellow Cornell U., 1953-54, NEH, Italy, 1972-73, England, 1979-80, Guggenheim, 1984-85; Fulbright sr. rsch. grant in Italy, 1965-66, sr. Fulbright lectr. Moscow State Conservatory, 1990. Mem. Am. Mus. Soc. (chmn. S.E. chpt. 1969-71, mem. coun. 1969-71, 75-77, bd. dirs. 1977-79, pres. 1980-82, del. to Am. Coun. Learned Socs. 1984-88, to Internat. Congress Strasbourg 1982), Music Libr. Assn. (bd. dirs. 1968-70), Sonneck Soc. Avocations: hiking, photography.

SMITHEY, DONALD LEON, airport authority director; b. St. Louis, Aug. 31, 1940; children: Kelly, Jill. Student, St. Ambrose Coll., 1962; BS in Bus. Mgmt., So. Ill. U., 1966; postgrad., U. Mo., St. Louis, 1973-74. Asst. ops. dispatcher Ozark Airlines, 1971-72; transp. analyst Olin Corp., 1972-78, cost acct., 1978-80; commr. St. Louis Regional Airport Authority, 1971-80, chmn., 1974-80, airport dir., 1980-83; asst. dir. Cedar Rapids Mcpl. Airport, 1983-85; dir. adminstrn. Omaha Airport Authority, 1985-87, dep. exec. dir., 1987-89, exec. dir., 1989—. With USN Air Res. 1963-66, USN, 1966-68. Mem. Am. Assn. Airport Execs. (Great Lakes chpt.), Airports Coun. Internat., Iowa Airport Exec. Assn. (past pres.), Ill. Pub. Airports Assn. (past v.p.), Exptl. Aircraft Assn., Omaha Rotary Club, Masonic Lodge (Bethalto, Ill.), Tangier Shrine (Omaha), Quiet Birdmen Assn., Silver Wings Fraternity. Office: Omaha Airport Authority 4501 Abbott Dr Omaha NE 68110-2627

SMITHIES, OLIVER, geneticist, educator; b. Halifax, Eng., June 23, 1925; naturalized citizen; PhD in Biochemistry, Oxford U., Eng., 1951. Postdoctoral fellow phys. chemistry U. Wis., Madison, 1951-53, from asst. prof. to prof. genetics and med. genetics, 1960-63, Leon J. Cole prof., 1971-80, Hilldale prof., 1980-88; rsch. asst., assoc. Connaught Med. Rsch. Lab., Toronto, Can., 1953-60; Excellence prof. pathology U. N.C., Chapel Hill, 1988—; mem. nat. adv. med. sci. coun. NIH, 1985. Contbr. articles to profl. jours. Recipient William Allen Meml. award Am. Soc. Human Genetics, 1964, Karl Landsteiner Meml. award Am. Assn. Blood Banks, 1984, Internat. award Gairdner Found., 1990, 93, State of N.C. award, 1994, Alfred P. Sloan Jr. prize, 1994; Markle scholar, 1961. Fellow AAAS; mem. NAS, Am. Acad. Arts & Sci., Genetics Soc. Am. (v.p. 1974, pres. 1975). Achievements include research on targetted modification of specific genes in living animals. Office: Univ of N C Dept Pathology Chapel Hill NC 27599-7525

SMITHKEY, JOHN, III, public health nurse, consultant; b. Akron, Ohio, Nov. 14, 1953; s. John C. and Catherine V. (Ennis) S. BS in Edn., U. Akron, 1977, BS in Nursing, 1988; Med. Lab. Specialist, U.S. Acad. Health Scis., Ft. Sam Houston, Tex., 1983. RN, Ohio; cert. ARC nurse, advanced cardiac life support; cert. instr. , trainerCPR, HIV/AIDS, sch. nurse. Med. asst. instr. So. Ohio Coll., Mogadore, 1984-86; EMT Plain Twp. Fire Dept., 1985-88; commd. 2d lt. USAF, 1988, advanced through grades to 1st lt., 1990; staff nurse USAF, Goldsboro, N.C., 1988-91; pub. health nurse Summit County Health Dept., 1991-96, Physicians Indsl. and Instnl. Svcs., 1996—, Universal Nursing Svcs., Akron, 1997—. Author: Prevention is the Cure for Hearing Loss Caused by Noise in the Lab, 1991, The Use of Narcotics in Controlling Patient Pain, 1993; contbr. articles to profl. jours. Home: 1271 Overland Ave North Canton OH 44720 Office: 402 E Market St Akron OH 44304-1541

SMITH-LEINS, TERRI L., mathematics educator; b. Salina, Kans., Sept. 19, 1950; d. John W. and Myldred M. (Hays) Smith; m. Larry L. Leins, May 26, 1984. BS, Ft. Hays (Kans.) U., 1973, MS, 1976; AA, Stephen Coll., Columbia, Mo., 1970. Math tchr. Scott City (Kans.) Jr. H.S., Howard (Kans.) Schs.; instr. math. Westark C.C., Ft. Smith, Ark. Contbr. articles to profl. jours., chpts. to books. Mem. AADE, ASCD, Nat. Assn. Devel. Edn. (state sec. 1986-88, computer access com. 1980-85), Phi Delta Kappa (Kappan of Yr. 1985), Delta Kappa Gamma (state chairperson women in art 1993-95). Home: PO Box 3446 Fort Smith AR 72913-3446

SMITH-PIERCE, PATRICIA A., speech professional; b. Washington, May 24, 1939; d. Edward Milton and Mary Louise Anderson; m. Wayne D. Pierce, Mar. 25, 1978. BA, Ohio State U., 1961; MA, U. Utah, 1970; PhD, Wash. State U., 1977. Stewardess Am. Airlines, Chgo., 1962-63; selling supr. The Emporium, San Francisco, 1963-65; buyer Cain-Sloan Co., Nashville, 1967-68; speech coach William Rainey Harper Coll., Palatine, Ill., 1970-76, prof., 1970-95, chmn. speech dept., 1985-92, dir. corp. svcs., 1990-91; prof. emeritus, 1996—; owner, pres. Power Speaking Cons., 1991—; cons. Inst. Mgmt. Devel., Palatine, 1983—; bd. dirs. Ill. Women's Agenda, 1981-87, v.p., 1982-83, pres., 1983-85; bd. dirs. Women in Charge, Chgo., 1987-90; cons. various corp. and govtl. agys.; mem. com. Ill. Commn. on Status of Women, 1983-85; trainer Mex. Am. Legal Def. and Edn. Fund, Leadership Program Chgo., 1986-95. Mem. Ill. Minority and Female Bus. Enterprise Coun., 1984-94; mem. USAF Civic Leaders Tour, 1996. Mem. AAUW (1st v.p. state orgn. 1985-87, bd. dirs. 1981-87, nat. trainer 1987-95), Human Resources Mgmt. Assn. Chgo., Execs. Club Chgo. Avocations: reading, golf. Office: Power Speaking Consultants 112 Lynnfield Ln Schaumburg IL 60193-1030

SMITHSON, LOWELL LEE, lawyer; b. Kansas City, Mo., Apr. 29, 1930; s. Spurgeon Lee and Lena Louise (Ruddy) S.; m. Rosemary Carol Leitz, Jan. 30, 1960 (div. Sept. 1985); m. Phyllis Galley Westover, June 8, 1986; children: Carol Maria Louise, Katherine Frances Lee. AB in Polit. Sci., U. Mo., 1952, JD, 1954. Bar: Mo. 1954, U.S. Dist. Ct. (we. dist.) Mo. 1955, U.S. Supreme Ct. 1986. Ptnr. Smithson & Smithson, Kansas City, 1956-59; assoc. Spencer, Fane, Britt & Browne, Kansas City, 1959-64, ptnr., 1964—; adj. prof. law U. Mo., Kansas City, 1982. Pres. Kansas City Mental Health Assn., 1963-65; mem. bd. pres. All Souls Unitarian Ch. Kansas City, 1965-67; chmn. com. select dean for law sch. U. Mo., 1983. 1st lt. U.S. Army, 1954-56, Korea. Mem. Kansas City Bar Assn., Lawyers Assn. Kansas City, Assn. Trial Lawyers Am., Western Mo. Def. Lawyers Assn., Fed. Energy Bar Assn., Phi Beta Kappa, Phi Delta Phi. Democrat. Unitarian Ch. Avocations: skiing, reading, tennis, swimming, canoeing. Home: 1215 W 65th St Kansas City MO 64113-1803 Office: Spencer Fane Britt & Browne 1000 Walnut 1400 Commerce Bank Bldg Kansas City MO 64106

SMITH-THOMPSON, PATRICIA ANN, public relations consultant, educator; b. Chgo., June 7, 1933; d. Clarence Richard and Ruth Margaret (Jacobson) Nowack; m. Tyler Thompson, Aug. 1, 1992. Student Cornell U., 1951-52; BA, Centenary Coll., Hackettstown, N.J., 1983. Prodn. asst. Your Hit Parade Batten, Barton, Durstine & Osborne, 1953-54; pvt. practice polit. cons., 1954-66; legal sec., asst. Atty. John C. Cushman, 1966-68; field dep. L.A. County Assessor, 1968-69, pub. info. officer L.A. County Probation Dept., 1969-73; dir. consumer rels. Fireman's Fund, San Francisco, 1973-76; pvt. practice pub. rels. cons., 1976-77; spl. projects officer L.A. County Transp. Commn., 1977-78; tchr. Calif. State U.-Dominguez Hills, 1979-86; editor, writer Jet Propulsion Lab., 1979-80; pub. info. dir. L.A. Bd. Pub. Works, 1980-82; pub. info. cons. City of Pasadena, (Calif.), 1982-84; pub. rels. cons., 1983-90, community rels./Worldport L.A., 1990-92. Contbr. articles to profl. jours. Mem. First United Methodist Ch. Commn. on Missions and Social Concerns, 1983-89; bd. dirs. Depot, 1983-87; mem. devel. com. Pasadena Guidance Clinics, 1984-85. Recipient Pro award L.A. Publicity Club, 1978, Outstanding Achievement award Soc. Consumer Affairs Profls. in Bus., 1976, Disting. Alumni award Centenary Coll., 1992. Mem. Pub. Relations Soc. Am. (accredited mem.; award for consumer program 1977, 2 awards 1984, Joseph Roos Community Service award 1985), Nat. Press Women (pub. relations award 1986), Calif. Press Women (awards 1974, 78, 83, 84, 85, community relations 1stplace winner 1986, 87, 88, 89), Nat. Assn. Mental Health Info. Offices (3 regional awards 1986). Republican. Home and Office: Box 4300-41 24145 Jacaranda Tehachapi CA 93561

SMITS, EDWARD JOHN, museum consultant; b. Freeport, N.Y., Dec. 11, 1933; s. Karl M. and Jennie (Spring) S.; m. Ruth K. Hall; children: E. John, Robert K., Theodore R. BA, Hofstra U., 1955; MA, NYU, 1959. Curator Nassau County Hist. Mus., East Meadow, N.Y., 1956-70; dir. mus. svcs. Div. Mus. Svcs. Nassau County, Syosset, N.Y., 1971-92; Nassau County historian, 1985—; planning coord. Mus. at Mitchel Ctr., 1994—. Author: Long Island Landmarks, 1970, Creation of Nassau County, 1959, Nassau, Suburbia U.S.A., 1974. Trustee Friends for L.I.'s Heritage, Nassau County Hist. Soc.; trustee, past pres. Levittown Libr. Bd. 1st lt. U.S. Army, 1955-56. Fulbright grantee, 1965; recipient Nassau County disting. svc. award, 1970, alumni disting. svc. award Hofstra U., 1970, H. Sherwood Historic Preservation on L.I. award Soc. for the Preservation of L.I. Antiquities, 1975. Mem. Am. Assn. Mus. Avocations: book collecting, antique toys, golf. Home: 14 Wavy Ln Wantagh NY 11793-1202

SMITS, HELEN LIDA, physician, administrator, educator; b. Long Beach, Calif., Dec. 3, 1936; d. Theodore Richard Smits and Anna Mary Wells; m. Roger LeCompte, Aug. 28, 1976; 1 child, Theodore. BA with honors, Swarthmore Coll., 1958; MA, Yale U., 1961, MD cum laude, 1967. Intern, asst. resident Hosp. U. Pa., 1967-68; fellow Beth Israel Hosp., Boston, 1969-70; chief resident Hosp. U. Pa., 1970-71; chief med. clinic U. Pa., 1971-75; assoc. adminstr. for patient care svcs. U. Pa. Hosp., 1975-77; v.p. med. affairs Community Health Plan Georgetown U., Washington, 1977; dir. health standards and quality bur. Health Care Financing Adminstrn., HHS, Washington, 1977-80; sr. rsch. assoc. The Urban Inst., Washington, 1980-81; assoc. prof. Yale U. Med. Sch., New Haven, 1981-85; assoc. v.p. for health affairs U. Conn. Health Ctr., Farmington, 1985-87; prof. community medicine U. Conn. Sch. Medicine, Farmington, 1985-93; hosp. dir. John Dempsey Hosp., Farmington, 1987-93; dep. administr. Health Care Financing Adminstrn., Washington, 1993-96; pres., med. dir. Health Right, Inc., Meriden, Conn., 1996—; commr. Joint Com. on Accreditation Hosps., Chgo., 1989-93, chair, 1991-92. Contbr. numerous articles to profl. jours. Bd. dirs. The Ivoryton Playhouse Fedn., Inc., 1990-92, The Connecticut River Mus., 1990-93, Hartford Stage, 1990-93; mem. Dem. Town Com., Essex, Conn., 1982-89. Recipient Superior Svc. award HHS, Washington, 1982; Royal Soc. Medicine Found. fellow, London, 1973; Fulbright scholar, 1959-60. Mem. ACP (master, regent 1984-90), Phi Beta Kappa, Alpha Omega Alpha. Episcopalian. Avocations: sailing, cooking, gardening. Home: 81 Main St Ivoryton CT 06442-1032 Office: Health Right Inc 134 State St Meriden CT 06450-3293

SMITS, JIMMY, actor; b. N.Y.C., July 9, 1955; two children. Master's degree, Cornell Univ., 1982. Appearances include Off-Broadway prodns., tours with regional theatres; (TV series) Miami Vice, 1984, L.A. Law, 1986-91 (Outstanding Actor in Dramatics Series Emmy award 1990), NYPD Blue, 1994—; (TV movies) Rockabye, 1986, The Highwayman, 1987, Glitz, 1988, The Broken Cord, 1991, Stephen King's The Tommyknockers, 1992; (films) Running Scared, 1986, The Believers, 1987, Old Gringo, 1988, Vital Signs, 1989, Fires Within, 1989, Switch, 1990, Gross Misconduct, 1992, The Cisco Kid, 1993, Solomon & Sheba, 1994, My Family, 1994, Marshal Law, 1995, Murder in Mind, 1996, Lesser Prophets, 1997. Avocations: football, basketball, softball, reading. Office: care Sherman Mgmt 1516 S Beverly Dr Apt 304 Los Angeles CA 90035-3059

SMITTLE, NELSON DEAN, electronics executive; b. Peebles, Ohio, Sept. 19, 1934; s. Nelson John and Alma Katherine (Green) S.; m. Claire Wiggins, May 5, 1973. BS, BFA, U. Cin., 1962, MA, 1971. Commd. 2d lt. U.S. Army, 1962; staff officer U.S. Army Photo Agy. Pentagon, Washington, 1966; detachment comdr. tactical comms. Republic South Vietnam, 1967-68; comdr. 907th communications squadron Rickenbacker AFB, Ohio, 1972; dir. ops. fixed communications Air Combat Command Langley AFB, Va., 1982; dir. info. systems AWACS Saudi Arabia, 1984-85; dep. chief of staff standard systems Air Material Command Wright-Patterson AFB, Ohio, 1985; comdr. engring. installation divsn. Tinker AFB, Okla., 1988; commn. transferred to USAF, 1970, commd. col., 1988; ret. USAF, Cin., 1991; pres. Falcon Techs., Cin., 1991—; tchr. Princeton City Sch. Dist., Cin., 1992-94; cons. Air War Coll., Air Univ., Maxwell AFB, Ala., 1987—, Defense Systems Mgmt. Coll., Ft. Belvior, Va., 1988—. Author: (books) Army Visual Presentation, 1966 (medal 1966), Famous Moments in Aviation History, 1997. Mem. Batavia (Ohio) City Coun., 1972; pres. Ohio Buckeye Wing Assn., Columbus, 1973; mem. Air Force Policy Coun., Washington, 1978; congl. campaign mgr., 1993; bd. dirs. Cin. Art Club, 1995-96. Decorated Commendation medal; recipient Meritorious Svc. medal Dept. Def., 1986, 91. Mem. DAV, Air Force Assn., Res. Officers Assn., Am. Soc. Aviation Artists, The ZR-1 Registry. Avocations: freelance writer, exhibiting artist, walking, science fiction. Home and Office: Falcon Techs 198 Palisades Pointe Cincinnati OH 45238-5653

SMOCK, DONALD JOE, governmental liaison, political consultant; b. Ponca City, Okla., Sept. 24, 1964; s. Joe Clellan and Ruth Esther Smock. BA in Polit. Sci., U. Ctrl. Okla., 1991, MA in Urban Affairs, 1993. Founder Smock Polit. Systems, Edmond, Okla., 1990—; rschr. The Nigh Inst. State Govt., Edmond, 1993-94; U. Ctrl. Okla. del. to Ctr. Study of Pres. Symposium, Washington, 1993; govt. liaison Elizey Electric Motor Co., 1994-96; govt. affairs dir. Oklahoma City Met. Assn. Realtors, 1996—. Charter founder Ronald Reagan Rep. Ctr., 1989; del. State of Okla. Rep. Presdl. Task Force, 1996; mem. Rep. Presdl. Trust, 1996. Recipient Okla. Rep. Blue Key award, 1984, Presdl. Commn., 1992, Merit cert. Rep. Nat. Com., 1990; named to Ronald Reagon Rep. Ctr. Presdl. Commemorative Honor Roll, 1991; by order of President George Bush flag dedicated in name Rotunda of U.S. Capitol, 1990. Mem. Tau Kappa Epsilon (Delta Nu colony inductee, chpt. advisor 1990-92, Fraternity for Life iniductee, David Crain Leadership award 1986, Ed Howell Leadership award 1988-89, Red Carnation Ball dedicated in name 1989-90, 94, Top Alumnus 1990-91), Pi Sigma Alpha. Republican. Mem. Ch. of Christ. Home: PO Box 6323 Edmond OK 73083-6323

SMOCK, RAYMOND WILLIAM, historian; b. Jeffersonville, Ind., Feb. 8, 1941; s. Richard and Lottie (Paciorek) S.; m. Phyllis Lee Chadwick, Feb. 12, 1961. B.A., Roosevelt U., Chgo., 1966; Ph.D., U. Md., College Park, 1974. Rsch. asst. Md. Constl. Conv., Annapolis, 1967-68; lectr. in history U. Md., College Park, 1968-72; co-editor The Booker T. Washington Papers, 14 vols., 1972-83; pres. Instructional Resources Corp., Lanham, Md., 1976-83; pres. Rsch. Materials Corp., College Park, 1982-83, dir., 1982-85; historian, dir. Office for Bicentennial, U.S. Ho. of Reps., Washington, 1983-89, Office of Historian, U.S. Ho. of Reps., Washington, 1989-95; mem. adv. bd., editorial advisers Md. Historian, College Park, 1971—. Author: A Talent for Detail:

The Photographs of Miss Frances Benjamin Johnston 1889-1910, 1974; co-editor: A Guide to Manuscripts in the Presidential Libraries, 1985; editor-:Booker T. Washington in Perspective: The Essays of Louis R. Harlan, 1988. Ford Found. fellow, 1970; recipient Philip M. Hamer award Soc. Am. Archivists, 1979. Mem. Nat. Coun. Pub. History, Assn. for Documentary Editing (pres. 1983-84), Orgn. Am. Historians, So. Hist. Assn., Soc. History in Fed. Govt. Avocations: photography; astronomy.

SMOCK, TIMOTHY ROBERT, lawyer; b. Richmond, Ind., June 24, 1951; s. Robert Martin and Thelma Elizabeth (Cozad) S.; m. Martha Carolene Middleton, Apr. 4, 1992; children: Andrew Zoller, Alison Pierce. BA, Wittenberg U., 1973; JD cum laude, Ind. U., 1977. Bar: Ind. 1977, Ariz. 1979, U.S. Dist. Ct. (so. dist.) Ind. 1977, U.S. Dist. Ct. Ariz. 1979, U.S. Ct. Appeals (7th cir.) 1977, U.S. Ct. Appeals (9th cir.) 1979. Jud. clk. Ct. of Appeals of Ind., Indpls., 1977-79; assoc. Lewis and Roca, Phoenix, 1979-82; assoc./shareholder Gallagher & Kennedy, Phoenix, 1982-89; ptnr. Scult, French, Zwillinger & Smock, Phoenix, 1989-94, Smock and Weinberger, Phoenix, 1994—; judge, pro tempore Maricopa County Superior Ct., Phoenix, 1989—; faculty, State Bar Course on Professionalism, Ariz. Supreme Ct./State Bar, Phoenix, 1992—; speaker, Continuing Legal Edn., Maricopa County and Ariz. State Bar, 1988—. Mem. ABA, Ariz. Bar Assn., Maricopa Bar Assn., Def. Rsch. Inst. Office: Smock and Weinberger 2700 N Central Ave Ste 1125 Phoenix AZ 85004-1149

SMOLANSKY, OLES M., humanities educator; b. Ukraine, USSR, May 2, 1930; came to U.S. 1950; s. Mykola S. and Irene (Plinto) S.; m. Bettie Moretz, Dec. 29, 1966; chidlren: Alexandra, Nicholas. BA, NYU, 1953; MA, Columbia U., 1955, PhD, 1959. Instr. UCLA, 1960-62; asst. prof. Lehigh U., Bethlehem, Pa., 1963-66, assoc. prof., 1966-70, prof., 1970-85, univ. prof., 1985—. Author: The Soviet Union and the Arab East Under Khrushchev, 1974, The USSR and Iraq: The Soviet Quest for Influence, 1991; co-editor: Russia and America: From Rivalry to Reconciliation, 1993, Regional Power Rivalries in the New Eurasia: Russia, Turkey, and Iran, 1995; contbr. articles to profl. jours. Recipient joint fellowship, Rockefeller Found. and Ford Found., N.Y.C., 1962-63, sr. research joint fellowship, Research Inst. on Communist Affairs and Middle East Inst., Columbia U., N.Y.C., 1972-73, research fellowship, Ford Found., N.Y.C., 1980-81. Mem. Internat. Studies Assn., Am. Assn. for Advancement of Slavic Studies (Marshall Shulman award 1992), Middle East Studies Assn., Mid. East Inst. Democrat. Greek-Orthodox. Avocations: music, sports. Home: 3665 Walt Whitman Ln Bethlehem PA 18017-1553 Office: Lehigh U Dept Internat Rels Bethlehem PA 18015

SMOLENSKY, EUGENE, economics educator; b. Bklyn., Mar. 4, 1932; s. Abraham and Jennie (Miller) S.; m. Natalie Joan Rabinowitz, Aug. 16, 1952; children: Paul, Beth. B.A., Bklyn. Coll., 1952; M.A., Am. U., 1956; Ph.D., U. Pa., 1961. Prof. econs. U. Wis., Madison, 1968-88, chmn. dept., 1978-80, 86-88; dir. Inst. for Research on Poverty, U. Wis., 1980-83; dean Grad. Sch. Pub. Policy U. Calif., Berkeley, 1988—. Author: Public Expenditures, Taxation and the Distribution of Income: The U.S., 1950, 61, 70, 77. Mem. Nat. Acad. Pub. Adminstrn., 1994; mem. com. on child devel. rsch. and pub. policy NAS, Washington, 1982-87, mem. com. on status of women in labor market, 1985-87. With USN, 1952-56. Mem. Am. Econs. Assn. Democrat. Jewish. Avocation: collecting old master etchings and lithographs. Home: 669 Woodmont Ave Berkeley CA 94708-1233 Office: U Calif Dept Pub Policy 2607 Hearst Ave Berkeley CA 94709-1005

SMOLEV, TERENCE ELLIOT, lawyer, educator; b. Bklyn., Oct. 5, 1944; s. Lawrence and Shirley (Lebowitz) S.; m. Sherry Gale Rosen, Nov. 24, 1968 (div.); children: Cindy, Scott; m. Phyllis C. Rudko, Oct. 8, 1995. BBA, Hofstra U., 1966; JD, American U., 1969; LLM, NYU, 1974. Bar: N.Y. 1970. Acct. Peat Marwick & Mitchell, N.Y.C., 1969-70; dir. deferred giving Hofstra U., Hempstead, N.Y., 1971-74; editor Panel Publishers, Greenvale, N.Y., 1970-71; ptnr. Naidich & Smolev, P.C., Bellmore, N.Y., 1972-92; mem. bd. trustees Hofstra U., 1992—; adj. prof. Hofstra U., Hempstead, N.Y., 1971—; dist. counsel North Merrick (N.Y.) UFSD, 1975—. Author of book chpt. Mem. Nassau County, N.Y. Dem. Com., 1972-80, mem. judicial screening com., 1992—; mem. IRS Small Bus. Adv. Com., Washington D.C., 1975-77; bd. dirs. Arthritis Found. L.I., 1995—. Recipient George M. Estabrook award Hofstra U., 1991, Alumni Achievement award Hofstra U., 1993; named Senator of Yr., Hofstra U., 1985, Alumnus of Yr., 1996. Mem. ABA, N.Y. State Bar Assn., Nassau County Bar Assn., N.Y. State Assn. Sch. Attys. (pres. 1984), Hofstra U. Alumni Senate (pres. 1987-89), Hofstra U. Club (bd. dirs. 1981-95). Avocations: photography, golf. Office: One Old Country Rd Carle Place NY 11514

SMOLINSKI, EDWARD ALBERT, holding company executive, lawyer, accountant, deacon; b. N.Y.C., Jan. 6, 1928; s. Albert John and Adele (Weber) S.; m. Joan E. Winslow, Nov. 12, 1955; children: Albert, Edward, Linda, Donna. B.S. in Acctg., L.I. U., 1948; M.B.A., NYU, 1950, J.D., 1956. Bar: N.Y. 1957; C.P.A., N.Y.; ordained deacon Roman Cath. Ch., 1977. Acct. various cert. pub. acctg. firms. N.Y.C., 1948-53; acctg. supr. Curtiss Wright Co., Woodridge, N.J., 1953-60; mem. treasury staff Sperry-Rand Corp., Great Neck, N.Y., 1960-62; contr. PRD electronics Harris Corp., Hicksville, NY, 1962-68; corp. controller Fairchild Camera and Instrument Co., Syosset, N.Y., 1968-69; v.p., treas., chief fin. officer Grow Group, Inc., N.Y.C., 1969-89; asst. treas./sec. United Indsl. Corp., N.Y.C., 1989—; adj. asst. prof. Hunter Coll., 1989. Bd. dirs. Long Island U.-Bus. Game, N.Y.C., 1977-83, NYU Mgmt. Decision Lab., 1983-88; deacon Diocese of Bklyn., Roman Cath. Ch., 1977—. Mem. AICPA (com. on nat. def. 1963), N.Y. Bar, Fin. Execs. Inst. Roman Catholic. Lodge: Elks. Home: 70-19 Juno St Forest Hills NY 11375-5839 Office: United Indsl Corp 18 E 48th St New York NY 10017-1014

SMOLKER, GARY STEVEN, lawyer; b. L.A., Nov. 5, 1945; s. Paul and Shayndy Charolette (Sirott) S.; m. Alice Graham; children: Terra, Judy, Leah. BS, U. Calif.-Berkeley, 1967; MS, Cornell U., 1968; JD cum laude, Loyola U., L.A., 1973. Bar: Calif. 1973, U.S. Dist. Ct. (cen. dist.) Calif. 1973, U.S. Tax Ct. 1973, U.S. Ct. Appeals (9th cir.) 1973, U.S. Supreme Ct. 1978, U.S. Dist. Ct. (so., ea. and no. dists.) Calif. 1981. Guest researcher Lawrence Radiation Lab., U. Calif., 1967; teaching fellow Sch. Chem. Engring., Cornell U.; mem. tech. staff Hughes Aircraft Co., Culver City, Calif., 1968-70; in advanced mktg. and tech. TRW, Redondo Beach, Calif., 1970-72; sole practice, Beverly Hills, Calif., 1973-89, L.A., 1989—; guest lectr. UCLA Extension, 1973-74, Loyola U. Law Sch., 1979; speaker, panelist in field; adv. Loyola U. Law Sch., 1973—. Contbr. articles to profl. jours.; inventor self-destruct aluminum tungstic oxide films, electrolytic anticompromise process. Mem. Nat. Assn. Real Estate Editors, Calif. State Bar Assn., L.A. County Bar Assn., Beverly Hills Bar Assn. (sr. editor jour. 1978-79, contbg. editor jour. 1980-82, 86-90, editor-in-chief 1984-86, pub. Smolker Letter 1985—). Jewish. Lodge: B'nai B'rith (anti-defamation league). Office: 4720 Lincoln Blvd Ste 280 Marina Del Rey CA 90292

SMOLLA, RODNEY ALAN, lawyer, educator; b. Pueblo, Colo., Mar. 13, 1953; s. Richard Paul and Harriet (Waskowiak) S.; m. Linda A. Malone, Apr. 13, 1979. BA, Yale U., 1975; JD, Duke U., 1978. Bar: Ill. 1979, U.S. Supreme Ct. 1987. Law clk. to presiding judge U.S. Ct. Appeals, Jackson, Miss., 1978-79; assoc. Mayer, Brown & Pratt, Chgo., 1979-80; asst. prof. De Paul U. Sch. Law, Chgo., 1980-81, U. Ill. Coll. Law, 1981-83; prof. U. Ark. Sch. Law, 1983-87; vis. prof. U. Denver Coll. Law, 1987-88; Arthur B. Hanson prof. constl. law Coll. of William and Mary, Williamsburg, Va., 1988—, dir. Inst. Bill of Rights Law, 1988—. Author: Suing the Press: Libel, The Media & Power, 1986 (cert. of merit ABA 1987), Law of Defamation, 1986, Jerry Falwell V. Larry Flynt: The First Amendment on Trial, 1988; (with Banks and Braveman) Constitutional Law: Structure and Rights in Our Federal System, 1991, 3rd edit., 1996, Free Speech in an Open Society, 1992 (William O. Douglas award 1993), Smolla and Nimmer on Freedom of Speech, 1994, 3rd edit., 1996, Federal Civil Rights Acts, 1994; editor: A Year in the Life of the Supreme Court, 1995 (ABA Silver Gavel award). Fellow, cons. Annenberg Washington Program in Communications, 1987—; project dir. Annenberg Libel Reform Task Force, 1988-89; reporter Bill of Rights Adv. Com. to the Commn. on the Bicentennial of U.S. Constitution, 1989—. Recipient Disting. Prof. of Yr. award U. Ark., 1986. Mem. ABA, Ill. Bar Assn., AAUP (mem. litigation com. 1988—). Home: 119 Richneck Rd Williamsburg VA 23185-3245 Office: William and Mary Sch Law Inst Bill Of Law Williamsburg VA 23187

SMOLTZ, JOHN ANDREW, professional baseball player; b. Warren, Mich., May 15, 1967. With Detroit Tigers, 1985-87; pitcher Atlanta Braves, 1987—; player Nat. League All-Star Game, 1989, 92, 93, 96. Recipient Cy Young award Baseball Writers' Assn. Am., 1996; named Sporting News Nat. League Pitcher of the Yr., 1996. Leader in strikeouts in Nat. League, 1992. Office: Atlanta Braves PO Box 4064 Atlanta GA 30302*

SMOOK, MALCOLM ANDREW, chemist, chemical company executive; b. Seattle, Aug. 22, 1924; s. Joseph Murray and Bonnie (Hanson) S.; m. Mary Louise Nominee, Dec. 19, 1945; children—Frances Lynn, Valerie Dale. B.S., U. Calif., Berkeley, 1945; Ph.D. in Organic Chemistry, Ohio State U., 1949. With E. I. duPont de Nemours & Co., Wilmington, Del., 1949—; research supr. E. I. duPont de Nemours & Co., 1952-53, div. head, 1953-57, asst. lab. dir., 1957-60, lab. dir., 1960-63, asst. research dir., 1963-75, gen. lab. dir., 1975-80, mgr. patents and regulatory affairs, 1980-84; cons. Malcolm A. Smook, Inc.,, 1985—; mem. adv. com. NASA, 1971-76. Contbr. articles to profl. jours. Served to lt. (j.g.) USN, 1943-46. Socony Vacuum fellow, 1948-49. Mem. Am. Chem. Soc., Sigma Xi. Patentee in field (6). Home and Office: 59 Rockford Rd Wilmington DE 19806-1003

SMOOT, GEORGE FITZGERALD, III, astrophysicist; b. Yukon, Fla., Feb. 20, 1945. BS in math., BS in physics, MIT, 1966, Ph.D. in physics, 1970. Rsch. physicist MIT, 1970; rsch. physicist Univ. Calif., Berkeley, Calif., 1971—, prof. physics, 1993—; rsch. physicist Lawrence Berkeley Lab., 1974—; team leader, differential microwave radiometer experiment, COBE (Cosmic Background Explorer) satellite. Author: (with Keay Davidson) Wrinkles in Time, 1993. Recipient Space/Missiles Laurels award Aviation Week & Space Technology, 1992, Lawrence award US Dept of Energy, 1994. Mem. Internat. Astron. Union, Am. Phys. Soc., Am. Astron. Soc., Sigma Xi. Office: Bldg 50-205 LBNL Berkeley CA 94720

SMOOT, HAZEL LAMPKIN, retired piano teacher, poet; b. Kamiah, Idaho, Oct. 17, 1916; d. Albert Chuning and Cora Benson (Buckland) Weaver; m. Daniel Joseph Smoot, Feb. 18, 1939 (div. 1960); children: Daniel Jerome, David Reed. AA, Sacramento City Coll., 1937; student, Linfield Coll., 1938. Contbr. poetry to anthologies published by World of Poetry, also to Vantage Press and The Golden Treasury of Great Poems, Great American Poetry Anthology. Scholar Linfield Coll.; recipient Golden Poetry awards World of Poetry, 1987, 88, 89, 96, Best Poems of 1996 award Nat. Libr. of Poetry, 1996, A Sea of Treasures award Nat. Libr. of Poetry, 1996. Avocations: poetry, walking, reading, music, singing.

SMOOT, JOSEPH GRADY, university administrator; b. Winter Haven, Fla., May 7, 1932; s. Robert Malcolm and Vera (Eaton) S.; m. Florence Rozell, May 30, 1955 (dec.); m. Irma Jean Kopitzke, June 4, 1959; 1 child, Andrew Christopher. BA, So. Coll., 1955; MA, U. Ky., 1958, PhD, 1964. Tchr., Ky. Secondary Schs., 1955-57; from instr. to assoc. prof. history Columbia Union Coll., Takoma Park, Md., 1960-68, acad. dean, 1965-68; prof. history Andrews U., Berrien Springs, Mich., 1968-84, dean Sch. Grad. Studies, 1968-69, v.p. acad. adminstrn., 1969-76, pres., 1976-84; v.p. for devel. Pittsburg State U., Kans., 1984—; exec. dir. Pitts. State U. Found., 1985—; bd. dirs. 1st State Bank and Trust Co., Pitts., 1994—; founder Pitts. State U. Radio Sta.-KRPS-FM, 1988; commr. North Cen. Assn., 1987-91, cons., evaluator, 1978—; cons. internat. edn; trustee Loma Linda U., 1976-84, U. Ea. Africa, Baraton, Kenya, 1979-84, Hindsdale Hosp., Ill., 1973-84; chmn., bd. trustees Andrews Broadcasting Corp., 1976-84; bd. dirs. Internat. U. Thailand Found., 1987-95, trustee, 1994-95. Contbr. articles to profl. jours; editor: Spottiswoode Soc. Record, 1990—. Active Pitts. Area Festival Assn., 1984-86, bd. dirs. Pitts. United Way, 1987-92, Pitts. C. of C. Found., 1990-93; bd. advisors Pitts. Salvation Army, 1987-92, vice-chmn., 1990-91, chmn., 1991-92; bd. trustees Mt. Carmel Med. Ctr. Found., 1991-95; bd. dirs. S.E. Kans. Symphony Orch., 1995—, bd. trustees, 1996—. Recipient Disting. Pres. award Mich. Coll. Found., 1984. Mem. Inst. Early Am. History and Culture (assoc.), Am. Hist. Assn., So. Hist. Assn., Orgn. Am. Historians, Soc. for Historians of Early Am. Rep., Soc. History of Authorship, Reading & Pub., Phi Alpha Theta. Club: Crestwood Country. Lodge: Rotary (dist. chmn. scholarship com. 1986-88, Paul Harris Fellow) Home: 1809 Heritage Rd Pittsburg KS 66762-3556 Office: Office of V.P. for Development Pittsburg State U Pittsburg KS 66762

SMOOT, LEON DOUGLAS, chemical engineering educator, research director, former university dean; b. Provo, Utah, July 26, 1934; s. Douglas Parley and Jennie (Hallam) S.; m. Marian Bird, Sept. 7, 1953; children: Analee, LaCinda, Michelle, Melinda Lee. BS, Brigham Young U., 1956, B in Engring. Sci., 1957; MS, U. Wash., 1958, PhD, 1960. Registered profl. engr., Utah. Engr. Boeing Corp., Seattle, 1956; teaching and research asst. Brigham Young U., 1954-57; engr. Phillips Petroleum Corp., Arco, Idaho, 1957; engr., cons. Hercules Powder Co., Bacchus, Utah, 1961-63; asst. prof. Brigham Young U., 1960-63; engr. Lockheed Propulsion, Redlands, Calif., 1963-67; vis. asst. prof. Calif. Inst. Tech., 1966-67; assoc. prof. to prof. Brigham Young U., 1967—, chmn. dept. chem. engring., 1970-77, dean Coll. Engring. and Tech., 1977-94, dean emeritus, 1994—; dir. Advanced Combustion Engring. Rsch. Ctr., 1986—; expert witness on combustion and explosions; dir. Advanced Combustion Engring. Research Ctr. (NSF), 1986—; cons. Hercules, Thiokol, Lockheed, Teledyne, Atlantic Research Corp., Raytheon, Redd and Redd, Billings Energy, Ford, Bacon & Davis, Jaycor, Intel Com Radiation Tech., Phys. Dynamics, Nat. Soc. Propellants and Explosives, France, DFVLR, West Germany, Martin Marietta, Honeywell, Phillips Petroleum Co., Exxon, Nat. Bur. Standards, Eyring Research Inst., Systems, Sci. and Software., Los Alamos Nat. Lab., others. Author 5 books on coal combustion; contbr. over 200 articles and tech. jours. Former. Mem. AIChE, Am. Soc. Engring. Edn., Combustion Inst., Rsch. Soc. Am., Sigma Xi, Tau Beta Pi, Phi Lambda Epsilon. Republican. Mem. LDS Ch. Office: Brigham Young U Advanced Combustion Engring Rsch Ctr 45 Crabtree Tech Bldg Provo UT 84602

SMOOT, OLIVER REED, JR., lawyer, trade association executive; b. San Antonio, Aug. 24, 1940; s. Oliver Reed and Angie Frances (Watters) S.; m. Sandra Lee Curry, July 25, 1964; children: Stephen Reed, Sheryl Anne. BS, MIT, 1962; JD, Georgetown U., 1966. Bar: D.C. 1966, Va. 1967. Computer systems mgr. Inst. for Def. Analyses, Arlington, Va., 1962-69; program mgr., v.p., then exec. v.p. and treas. Info. Tech. Industry Coun., Washington, 1969—. Author: (with others) Computers and the Law, 3d edit., 1981; chpt. editor: Toward a Law of Global Communications Networks, 1986. Bd. dirs. exec. com. Am. Nat. Stds. Inst.; chmn. Info. Infrastructures Stds. Panel, 1994—. Mem. ABA (chmn. sci. and tech. sect. 1989-90), Computer Law Assn. (pres. 1990-91), Assn. for Computing Machinery. Methodist. Avocations: alpine skiing, gardening. Office: Info Tech Industry Coun 1250 I St NW Ste 200 Washington DC 20005-3922

SMOOT, WENDELL MCMEANS, JR., investment counselor; b. Salt Lake City, Jan. 15, 1921; s. Wendell M. and Rebecca (Clawson) S.; m. Barbara Davis, June 24, 1942; children: Wendell M. III, Margaret, David, John, Mary. B.A., U. Utah, 1942. Gen. ptnr. J.A. Hogle & Co., Salt Lake City, 1945-63, Goodbody & Co., N.Y.C., 1963-70; chmn. Smoot, Miller, Cheney & Co., Salt Lake City, 1971—. Pres. Great Salt Lake council Boy Scouts Am., 1968-70; chmn. Utah State Pioneer Meml. Theatre, 1978-79; pres. Mormon Tabernacle Choir. Served to capt., U.S. Army, 1942-45; ETO. Mem. Fin. Analysts Soc. Republican. Mem. Ch. of Jesus Christ of Latter Day Saints. Club: The Country. Lodge: Rotary.

SMORAL, VINCENT J., electrical engineer; b. Syracuse, N.Y., May 13, 1946; s. Anthony Vincent and Stephanie (Koutin) S.; m. Theresa W. Gut, Aug. 5, 1967; children: Jennifer, Laura, Anne. BSEE, Syracuse U., 1967. Jr. engr. Fed. Systems Div. IBM, Owego, N.Y., 1967-68; adv. engr. logic design IBM, Owego, 1968-80, sr. engr./systems, 1980-90, sr. engr./program mgr., 1990-93; sr. engr. Lockheed Martin Fed. Systems Co., Owego, 1994—. Designer 688 Class Sonar, An/UYS-1 Signal Processor, AWACS Computer, 3838 Array Processor, 1968-80; mgr. AN/UYK-43 Computer, AWACS Computer, Rugged Processor, F117 Processor, 1980-93; patentee in field. Fellow AIAA (assoc.; mem. nat. computer systems tech. com. 1990-95); mem. IEEE. Democrat. Roman Catholic. Avocations: swimming, sailing, fishing, skiing. Home: 812 Skylane Terr Endwell NY 13760 Office: Lockheed Martin-Fed Systems 1801 State Route 17C Owego NY 13827-3900

SMOTHERMON, PEGGI STERLING, middle school educator; b. Dallas, Nov. 11, 1948; d. Kiel Sterling and Ann C. (Wolfe) Sterling; m. William C. Smothermon Jr., June 20, 1981; children: Kirsten, Melinda, William III. BA, So. Meth. U., Dallas, 1973; MLA, So. Meth. U., 1978. Tchr. Richardson (Tex.) Ind. Sch. Dist., 1973-90; tchr. Coppell (Tex.) Ind. Sch. Dist., 1990-96, ret., 1996. J.J. Pearce scholar. Mem. Nat. Coun. Tchrs. Math., NSTA, NEA (faculty rep., membership chmn., sec.), Tex. Tchrs. Assn., Assn. Coppell Educators, Tex. Computer Edn. Assn., Tex. Coun. Tchrs. Math., Kappa Delta Pi. Home: 408 Greenridge Dr Coppell TX 75019-5714

SMOTHERS, DICK, actor, singer; b. Nov. 20, 1939; s. Thomas B. and Ruth Smothers; children: Susan, Dick, Steven, Andrew, Sara, Remick; m. Denby Franklin, Jan. 4, 1997. Student, San Jose State Coll. Night club appearances in Reno, Lake Tahoe, Las Vegas and various venues in U.S.; co-star half-hour situation comedy TV Series Smothers Bros. Show, 1965-66, TV show Smothers Bros. Comedy Hour, 1967-69, 70, weekly variety hour The Smothers Bros. Show, NBC-TV, 1975; appeared on Broadway in I Love My Wife, 1978; appeared in TV movie Terror at Alcatraz, 1982, feature film Casino, 1995; starred in Smothers Bros. Spl. and Series, 1988-89. Office: Knave Prodns Ste 107B 6442 Coldwater Canyon Ave North Hollywood CA 91606-1137

SMOTHERS, TOM, actor, singer; b. Feb. 2, 1937; s. Thomas B. and Ruth Smothers; children: Tom, Bo, Riley Rose; m. Marcy Carriker, Sept. 9, 1990. Student, San Jose State Coll. owner winery, Kenwood, Calif. Night-club appearances in Reno, Lake Tahoe, Las Vegas, Nev., and various venues in the U.S.; co-star TV situation comedy Smothers Brothers Show, 1965-66, Smothers Brothers Comedy Hour, CBS-TV, 1967-69, 70, weekly variety show The Smothers Brothers Show, NBC-TV, 1975; starred in films The Silver Bears, Get To Know Your Rabbit, A Pleasure Doing Business, Serial, There Goes the Bride, Pandemonium, Speed Zone; starred on Broadway in I Love My Wife, 1978-79; appeared in TV movie Terror at Alcatraz, 1982; starred in Smothers Brothers Spl. and Series, 1988-89. Office: Knave Prodns Ste 107B 6442 Coldwater Canyon Ave North Hollywood CA 91606-1137

SMOTHERS, WILLIAM EDGAR, JR., geophysical exploration company executive; b. Shawnee, Okla., July 9, 1928; s. William Edgar and Lena Rivers (Randolph) S.; m. Marilyn Myrtle Cales, Sept. 6, 1952; children: Bill, Susan. BS in Commerce, Okla. State U., 1950. Staff acct. Amoco Prodn. Co., Tulsa, 1953-56; chief internal auditor Seismography Svc. Corp., Tulsa, 1956-63, mgr. tax and auditing, 1964-77, v.p., treas., 1978—. Vice chmn. Tulsa United Way Drive, 1976, chmn., 1977. Capt. U.S. Army, 1951-53. Mem. Am. Mgmt. Assn., Tax Execs. Inst., Nat. Assn. Accts., Systems Mgmt. Assn., Petroleum Club, Tulsa Country Club. Democrat. Presbyterian. Home: 9103 E 38th Pl Tulsa OK 74145-3437 Office: Seismograph Svc Corp PO Box 1590 Tulsa OK 74102

SMOTRICH, DAVID ISADORE, architect; b. Norwich, Conn., Oct. 6, 1933; s. Max Z. and Ida (Babinsky) S.; m. Bernice D. Strachman, Mar. 25, 1956; children—Ross Lawrence, Maura Faye, Hannah. AB, Harvard U., 1955, MArch, 1960. Mem. master planning team Town of Arad, State of Israel, 1961-62; assoc. Platt Assocs. (architects), N.Y.C., 1963-65; gen. partner Smotrich & Platt (architects), N.Y.C., 1965-74, Smotrich Platt & Buttrick, 1975-76, Smotrich & Platt, 1976-85, David Smotrich & Ptnrs., 1985—; Cons. to Jerusalem Master Plan Office, Israel Ministry of Housing, 1967. Mem. planning bd. Town of New Castle, N.Y., 1974-81; mem. exec. bd. Road Rev. League, Bedford, N.Y., 1966-70. Served with AUS, 1955-57. Recipient Bard award, 1969, 85; Archtl. Record award, 1971, 73, 74, 75, 78; Design award HUD, 1980. Mem. AIA (Nat. Honor award 1969, N.Y. State Honor awards 1984, 94, Cmty. Design awards 1991, 93, AIA Coll. of Fellows 1993), Assn. Engrs. and Archs. in Israel, Phi Beta Kappa, Harvard Club (N.Y.C.). Home: 7 Mayberry Close Chappaqua NY 10514-1113 Office: David Smotrich & Ptnrs 443 Park Ave S New York NY 10016-7322

SMOUSE, H(ERVEY) RUSSELL, lawyer; b. Oakland, Md., Aug. 13, 1932; s. Hervey Reed and Vernie (Rush) S.; m. Creta M. Staley, June 15, 1955; children: Kristin Anne, Randall Forsyth, Gregory Russell. AB, Princeton U., 1955; LLB, U. Md., 1958. Bar: Md. 1958, U.S. Tax Ct. 1979, U.S. Ct. Appeals (4th cir.) 1960, U.S. Supreme Ct. 1974. Atty., Atty. Gen.'s Honors Program, Dept. Justice, Washington, 1958-60, asst. U.S. atty. Dist. Md., 1960-62; assoc. Pierson and Pierson, Balt., 1962-64; atty. B.&O. R.R., Balt., 1964-66; mem. Pierson and Pierson, 1966-69; mem. Clapp, Somerville, Black & Honemann, Balt., 1969-74; Law Offices H. Russell Smouse, 1974-81; mem. Melnicove, Kaufman, Weiner & Smouse, P.A., Balt., 1981-89, Whiteford, Taylor & Preston, Balt., 1989-93, chair, litigation dept., 1989-93; head gen. litigation Law Offices Peter G. Angelos, 1993—; spl. legal counsel Balt. Orioles, 1993—; v.p. Legal Aid Bur. Balt. City, 1972-73; bd. dirs. Md. Legal Svcs. Corp., 1987—. Fellow Am. Coll. Trial Lawyers; mem. ABA, Md. State Bar Assn. (gov. 1981-83), Bar Assn. Balt. City (chmn. grievance com. 1969-70, chmn. judiciary com. and nominating com. 1980, mem. exec. com. 1969-70, 80, chmn. exec. com. lawyers' com. for ind. judiciary 1989—), Nat. Assn. R.R. Trial Counsel (exec. com., v.p. ea. region 1986-92). Republican. Presbyterian. Office: 210 W Pennsylvania Ave Ste 515 Baltimore MD 21204-4592

SMUCKER, BARBARA CLAASSEN, former librarian, writer; b. Newton, Kans., Sept. 1, 1915; dual citizen U.S. and Can.; d. Cornelius Walter and Addie (Lander) Claassen; m. Donovan Ebersole Smucker, Jan. 21, 1939; children: Timothy, Thomas, Rebecca. BS, Kans. State U., 1936; postgrad., Rosary Coll., 1963-65; LittD (hon.), U. Waterloo, 1986; DHL (hon.), Bluffton Coll., 1989. English tchr. Harper (Kans.) High Sch., 1937-38; reporter Evening Kansan Republican, Newton, 1939-41; tchr. Ferry Hall Sch., Lake Forest, Ill., 1960-63; children's librarian Kitchener (Ont.) Public Library, 1969-77; reference librarian, head librarian Renison Coll., U. Waterloo, Ont., 1977-82, sr. fellow Renison Coll., 1982—; writer Am. Educator Ency., Lake Bluff, Ill., 1960-63; convocation speaker U. Waterloo, Ont., 1986. Author: Henry's Red Sea, 1955, Cherokee Run, 1957, Wigwam in the City, Susan, 1970, Underground to Canada, 1977, Runaway to Freedom, 1977, Under Jorden Til Canada, 1977, Les Chemins Secrets de la Liberte, 1978, Folge dem Nordstern, 1979, Days of Terror, 1980, June Lilly, 1981, Amish Adventure, 1983, Huida al Canada, 1983, Nubes Negras, 1984, Dagen Van Angst, 1985, White Mist, 1985, Jacob's Little Giant, 1987 (selected as gift to Prince Harry by govt. Ont.), Incredible Jumbo, 1990 (Ind. Order Dau. Empire award 1991), Race to Freedom, 1994, Selina and The Bear Paw Quilt, 1995, The Abiding Place, 1984, Garth and the Mermaid, 1992, Salina and the Shoe-Fly Pie, 1997; (interpretation) Oxford Companion to Canadian Literature, 1985, Michelle Landsberg's Guide to Children's Books, 1986; illustrator (autobiography) Something About the Author, 1991. Recipient prizes Can. Council, 1980, Ruth Schwartz Found., 1980, Disting. Service award Kans. State U., 1980, Brotherhood award NCCJ, 1980; $2000 Vicki Metcalf prize for outstanding contbn. to Can. children's lit. Can. Authors Assn., 1988, Kitchener award, 1990. Mem. AAUW, Canadian Assn. Univ. Women, Canadian Soc. Children's Authors, Illustrators and Performers, Children's Reading Round Table, Chgo. Home: 20 Pinebrook Dr Bluffton OH 45817-1145

SMUCKLER, HARVEY GLASGOW, financial consultant; b. Sturgeon Bay, Wis., Aug. 4, 1924; s. Joseph Max and Ruth Mary (Glasgow) S.; m. Harriet Carol Victor, June 28, 1949; children: Alan Lee, David Todd, Joel Jay. BBA, U. Wis., 1949; cert., The Am. Coll., Bryn Mawr, Pa., 1969, The Am. Coll., Bryn Mawr, Pa., 1984. CLU, ChFC; registered investment advisor, SEC and Calif. Asst. mgr. Mut. of N.Y., Chgo., 1955-59; gen. agt. Continental Assurance Co., Milw., 1959-64; pres. Mayflower Life of Wis., Milw., 1964-67; agy. v.p. Bankers Security Life Ins. Soc., Washington, 1967-70, sr. v.p., 1970-74; exec. v.p. Occidental Life Ins. N.C., Raleigh, 1974, pres., 1975-79; CEO Lincoln Am. Life Ins. Co., Memphis, 1979-80; pres., CEO Smuckler Fin., Tarzana, Calif., 1981—; registered rep. Titan Value Equities Group, Tustin, Calif., 1983—; chmn. SS Telecom Inc., Encino, Calif., 1991—. Avocations: golf, numismatist. Home: 4623 El Caballero Dr Tarzana CA 91356-4812 Office: Smuckler Fin 18801 Ventura Blvd Ste 304 Tarzana CA 91356-3362

SMUCKLER, RALPH HERBERT, university dean, political science educator; b. Milw., Apr. 10, 1926; s. Robert H. and Celia (Berliand) S.; m. Lillian Zembrosky, July 6, 1946; children: Gary, Sandra, Harold. BA, U.

Wis., 1948, MA, 1949, PhD, 1952. Mem. faculty Mich. State U., East Lansing, 1951-93, prof. polit. sci., 1963-93, dean internat. studies and programs, 1968-90, asst. to pres., 1987-91, emeritus prof., dean, 1993—; chief advisor tech. assistance team in Saigon, Mich. State U., 1955-56, 58-59; v.p. Edn. and World Affairs, N.Y.C., 1963-64; rep. Ford Found., Pakistan, 1967-69; dir. U.S. Internat. Sci. and Tech. Coop. Planning Office, Washington, 1978-79; mem. rsch. adv. com. AID, 1972-82, chmn., 1973-82, dep. asst. adminstr., 1991-92. Author: (with Leroy Ferguson) Politics in the Press, 1953, (with George Belknap) Leadership and Participation in Urban Political Affairs, 1956, (with R. Berg) New Challenges New Opportunities: U.S. Cooperation for International Growth and Development in the 1990s, 1988; contbr. articles to profl. jours. Bd. dirs. Midwest Univs. Consortium Internat. Activities, 1965-67, 69-90; trustee Inst. Internat. Edn., 1974-91; mem. adv. com. Kellogg Found. Nat. Fellowship Program, 1980-84; mem. bd. sci. and tech. for internat. devel. Nat. Acad. Sci., 1982-88, chmn., 1984-88; v.p. Mich. UN Assn., 1972-76; State of Mich. chmn. UN Day, 1960. With Inf. AUS, 1944-46. Decorated Bronze Star medal; recipient Disting. Citizen award Steuben Jr. High Sch., Milw., 1965, John Gilbert Winant Humanitarian award Marine City, Mich., 1976; Phi Beta Delta internat. scholar, Outstanding Faculty award, 1990. Mem. Am. Polit. Sci. Assn., Soc. Internat. Devel., Internat. Studies Assn., Assn. Internat. Edn. Adminstrs. (pres. 1986-87), Nat. Assn. State Univs. and Land-Grant Colls. (chmn. internat. acad. affairs com. 1986-90), Nat. Assn. Fgn. Student Affairs (governing bd. 1986, M. Houlihan award 1990), Mich. State Univ. Club, Phi Kappa Phi (named Disting. Mem. 1990). Jewish. Home: 4201 Cathedral Ave NW Apt 814W Washington DC 20016-4965

SMUIN, MICHAEL, choreographer, director, dancer; b. Missoula, Mont., Oct. 13, 1938; m. Paula Tracy; 1 child, Shane. Studied with Christensen Bros.; studied, San Francisco Ballet Sch.; DFA, U. Mont., 1984. Dancer U. Utah Ballet, Salt Lake City, 1955-57; dancer, choreographer, dir. San Francisco Ballet, 1957-62, 73-85; dancer Am. Ballet Theatre, N.Y. State Theatre, N.Y.C., 1967; prin. dancer, choreographer Am. Ballet Theatre, 1969-73; resident choreographer Am. Ballet Theatre, N.Y.C., 1992—; founder, dir. Smuin Ballets/SF, 1994—; worked as free-lance dancer with wife Paula Tracy, ind. choreographer; co-chmn. dance adv. panel Nat. Endowment for the Arts, Washington; mem. U.S. dance study team, People's Republic of China, 1983. Dir., musical stager, choreographer: (with Donald McKayle) Sophisticated Ladies, 1981 (Tony award nomination best direction of musical 1981, Outer Critics Circle award 1981); dir., choreographer: Chaplin, 1983, Shogun, 1990; choreographer: Anything Goes, 1987 (Tony award best choreography 1988, Drama Desk award best choreography 1988), Pulcinella Variations, Private Lives, 1991; staged dance works for Leslie Caron, Mikhail Baryshnikov, Rudolf Nureyev with Am. Ballet Theatre/Paris Opera Ballet, 1986; prodr. for San Francisco Ballet: Cinderella, Romeo and Juliet, The Tempest, A Song for Dead Warriors; dir.: Faustus in Hell, Peter and the Wolf; choreographer: (films) Rumble Fish, 1983, The Cotton Club, 1984, Fletch Lives, 1989, Bram Stoker's Dracula, 1992, So I Married an Axe Murderer, 1993, Angie, 1994, The Fantasticks, 1995; tech. adviser: (film) The Golden Child, 1986; choreographer: (TV) The Tempest, 1981 (Emmy award nomination outstanding achievement in choreography, 1981), A Song for Dead Warriors, 1984 (Emmy award outstanding achievement in choreography 1984), Cinderella, 1985, Romeo and Juliet; dir.: (TV spls.) Jinx, 1985, Voice/Dance: Bobby McFerrin and the Tandy Beal Dance Company, 1987; choreographer: (TV episode) Corridos! Tales of Passion and Revolution, 1987; creator: (TV show) The Omo, 1987; dir., choreographer: (TV spl.) Linda Ronstadt's Canciones de Mi Padre, 1989, Aid and Comfort. Recipient Dance Magazine award, 1983. Office: Smuin Ballets/SF 1314 34th Ave San Francisco CA 94122-1309*

SMUTNY, JOAN FRANKLIN, academic director, educator; b. Chgo.; d. Eugene and Mabel (Lind) Franklin; m. Herbert Paul Smutny; 1 child, Cheryl Anne. BS, Northwestern U., MA. Tchr., New Trier High Sch., Winnetka, Ill.; mem. faculty, founder, dir. Nat. High Sch. Inst., Northwestern U. Sch. Edn., Chgo.; mem. faculty, founder dir. high sch. workshop in critical thinking and edn., chmn. dept. communications Nat. Coll. Edn., Evanston, Ill., exec. dir. high sch. workshops, 1970-75, founder, dir. Woman Power Through Edn. Seminar, 1969-74, dir. Right to Read seminar in critical reading, 1973-74, seminar gifted high sch. students, 1973, dir. of Gifted Programs for 6, 7 and 8th graders pub. schs., Evanston, 1978-79, 1st-8th graders, Glenview (both Ill.) 1979—; dir. gifted programs Nat.-Louis U., Evanston, 1980-82, dir. Center for Gifted, 1982—; dir. Bright and Talented and Project 1986—, North Shore Country Day Sch., Winnetka, 1982—; dir. Job Creation Project, 1980-82; dir. New Dimensions for Women, 1973, dir. Thinking for Action in Career Edn. project, 1974-77 , dir. Individualized Career Edn. Program, 1976-79, dir. TACE, dir. Humanities Program for Verbally Precocious Youth, 1978-79; co-dir., instr. seminars in critical thinking Ill. Family Svc., 1972-75 . Writer ednl. filmstrips in Lang. arts and Lit. Soc. for Visual Edn., 1970-74 ; mem. speakers bur. Counc. Fgn. Rels., 1968-69 ; mem. adv. com. edn. professions devel. act U.S. Office Edn., 1969—; mem. state team for gifted, Ill. Office Edn., Office of Gifted, Springfield, Ill., 1977; writer, cons. Radiant Ednl. Corp., 1969-71 ; cons. ALA, 1969-71, workshop leader and speaker in area of gifted edn., 1971—; coord. of career edn. Nat. Coll. Edn., 1976-78, dir. Project 1987—, dir. Summer Wonders, 1986—, Creative Children's Acad., bd. dirs., Worlds of Wisdom and Wonder, 1978—; dir. Future Tchrs. Am. Seminar in Coll. and Career, 1970-72; cons. for research and devel. Ill. Dept. Vocat. Edn., 1973—; cons. in career edn. U.S. Office Edn., 1976—; evaluation cons. DAVTE, IOE, Springfield, Ill., 1977, mem. Leadership Tng. Inst. for Gifted, U.S. Office Edn., 1973-74; dir. workshops for high sch. students; cons., speaker in field; dir. Gifted Young Writer's and Young Writer's confs., 1978, 79; dir. Project '92 The White House Conf. on Children and Youth; mem. adv. bd. Educating Able Learners, 1991—; chmn. bd. dirs. Barbereux Sch., Evanston, 1992—; asst. editor, mem. editl. bd. Understanding Our Gifted, 1994—. Mem. AAUP, Nat. Assn. for Gifted Child (nat. membership chmn. 1991—, co-chmn. schs. and programs, co-editor newsletter early childhood divsn.), Nat. Soc. Arts and Letters (nat. bd., 1st and 3d v.p. Evanston chpt., dir. 1983-92, pres. Evanston chpt. 1990-92), Mortar Bd., Outstanding Educators of Am. 1974, Pi Lambda Theta, Phi Delta Kappa (v.p. Evanston chpt., rsch. chmn. 1990-92). Author: (with others) Job Creation: Creative Materials, Activities and Strategies for the classroom, 1982, A Thoughtful Overview of Gifted Education, 1990, Your Gifted Child - How to Recognize and Develop the Special Talents in Your Child from Birth to Age Seven, 1989, paperback, 1991, Education of the Gifted: Programs and Perspectives, 1990, The Young Gifted Child: An Anthology, 1997, Potential and Promise: The Gifted Young Chinld in the Regular Classroom, 1997; contbg. editor Roepper Review, 1994—; asst. editor Understanding Our Gifted, 1995—; editor, contbr. Maturity in Teaching; writer ednl. filmstrips The Brother's Grimm, How the West Was Won, Mutiny on the Bounty, Dr. Zhivago, Space Odessey 2001, Christmas Around the World; editor Jour. for Gifted, Ill., 1984—, Ill. Coun. Gifted Jour., 1985-93; contbg. editor Roeper Review, 1994—; editor IAGC Jour. for Gifted, 1994—; adv. bd. Gifted Education Press Quarterly, 1995—; contbg. editor numerous books in field; contbr. articles to profl. jours. including Chgo. Parent Mag. Reviewer of Programs for Gifted and Talented, U.S. Office of Edn., 1976-78. Home: 633 Forest Ave Wilmette IL 60091-1713 *Commitment to education is defined as contribution. We who are privileged to work in education know that the focus is the educant-the learner. Gifted education is particularly vital in that it discerns the needs of bright, talented children who have an immense amount to contribute to our country and our world. Gifted children are our country's most neglected resource--and most needed. It is my privilege to work in this area, to work with children, parents and teachers. The community of mankind is needed to support the talent and growth of the gifted. Then we are really contributing to the educant.*

SMYNTEK, JOHN EUGENE, JR., newspaper editor; b. Buffalo, Aug. 24, 1950; s. John Eugene and Leona (Kluczynski) S. BA, U. Detroit, 1972. Asst. instr. Mich. State U., East Lansing, 1981; features editor Free Press, 1985-92; dir. online svcs. and dir. libr. Free Press Plus, Detroit, 1992-95, spl. features and syndicate editor, 1995—; vis. fellow in journalism Duke U., 1988; profl. student publs. advisor U. Detroit Mercy, 1992-94. Recipient Fine Arts Reporting award Detroit Press Club, 1985. Roman Catholic. Office: Detroit Free Press 321 W Lafayette Blvd Detroit MI 48226

SMYRL, WILLIAM HIRAM, chemical engineering educator; b. Brownfield, Tex., Dec. 12, 1938; s. Garvin H. and Opal Faye (Coor) S.; m. Donna Kay Clayton, Nov. 29, 1964; children: Eliot K., Clifford G. BS in Chemistry, Tex. Tech U., 1961; PhD in Chemistry, U. Calif., Berkeley, 1966. Asst. prof. U. Calif., San Francisco, 1966-68; mem. tech. staff Boeing Sci. Rsch. Lab., Seattle, 1968-72, Sandia Nat. Lab., Albuquerque, 1972-84; prof., dir. corrosion rsch. ctr. U. Minn, Mpls., 1984-96. Contbr. over 100 articles to refereed jours. Mem. AAAS, AIChE, Am. Chem. Soc., Electrochem. Soc. (chair corrosion divsn. 1990-92, H.H. Uhlig award 1995), Sigma Xi (Am. editor Corrosion Sci.). Democrat. Baptist. Office: U Minn Corrosion Rsch Ctr 221 Church St SE Minneapolis MN 55455-0152

SMYSER, ADAM ALBERT, newspaper editor; b. York, Pa., Dec. 18, 1920; s. Adam Milton and Miriam (Stein) S.; m. Elizabeth Harrison Avery, Dec. 25, 1943 (dec. 1983); children: Heidi, Avery; m. Doris H. Prather, Apr. 24, 1984. B.A., Pa. State U., 1941. Rewrite man Pitts. Press, 1941-42; with Honolulu Star-Bull., 1946—, city editor, 1953-60, mng. editor, 1960-65, editor, 1966-75, editor editorial page, 1975-83, contbg. editor, 1983—; mem. Pulitzer Journalism Awards Jury, 1970. Author: Hawaii's Future in the Pacific: Disaster, Backwater or Future State?, 1988, Hawaii as an East-West Bridge, 1990; past freelance writer McGraw-Hill mags. Chmn. temp. commn. on statewide environ. planning, 1973; bd. dirs. Corp. for Community TV; chmn. steering com. Gov.'s Congress on Hawaii's Internat. Role, 1988; mem. community adv. bd. Tokai U. Pacific Ctr.; Lt. USNR, 1942-46, PTO. Recipient Disting. Alumnus award Pa. State U., 1976, Hawaii's Outstanding Journalist award, 1989, Award for Disting. Contbn. to Hawaii Journalism Honolulu Cmty.-Medic Coun., 1994, award for promotion of U.S.-Asia/Pacific rels. Pacific and Asian Affairs Coun., 1994. Mem. Hawaii Econ. Assn., Honolulu Social Sci. Assn., Honolulu Acad. Arts, Am. Soc. Newspaper Editors, Japan-Am. Soc. Hawaii, Honolulu Cmty.-Media Coun., Honolulu Press Club (named to Hall of Fame 1987), Honolulu Rotary. Home: 1052 Iiwi St Honolulu HI 96816-5111 Office: Honolulu Star-Bull 605 Kapiolani Blvd Honolulu HI 96813-5129

SMYTH, CRAIG HUGH, fine arts educator; b. N.Y.C., July 28, 1915; s. George Hugh and Lucy Salome (Humeston) S.; m. Barbara Linforth, June 24, 1941; children: Alexandra, Edward Linforth (Ned). BA, Princeton U., 1938, MFA, 1941, PhD, 1956; MA (hon.), Harvard U., 1975. Rsch. asst. Nat. Gallery Art, Washington, 1941-42; officer-in-charge, dir. Cen. Art Collecting Point, Munich, 1945-46; lectr. Frick Collection, N.Y.C., 1946-50; asst. prof. Inst. Fine Arts NYU, 1950-53, assoc. prof. Inst. Fine Arts, 1953-57, prof. Inst. Fine Arts, 1957-73, acting dir. Inst. Fine Arts, acting head dept. fine arts Grad. Sch. Arts and Scis., 1951-53, dir. inst., head dept. fine arts Grad. Sch., 1953-73; prof. fine arts Harvard U., 1973-85, prof. emeritus, 1985—; Samuel Kress prof. Ctr. for Advanced Study in Visual Arts Nat. Gallery Art, Washington, 1987-88; dir. Villa I Tatti Harvard U. Ctr. Italian Renaissance Studies, Florence, 1973-85; art historian in residence Am. Acad. in Rome, 1959-60; mem. U.S. Nat. Com. History Art, 1955-85; alt. U.S. mem. Comité Internat. d'Histoire de l'Art, 1970-83, U.S. mem., 1983-85; chmn. adv. com. J. Paul Getty Rsch. Inst. History of Art and Humanities, 1982—; mem. architect selection com. J. Paul Getty Trust, 1983-84; mem. organizing com., keynote speaker 400th Anniversary of Uffizi Gallery, 1981-82; vis. scholar Inst. Advanced Study, Princeton, N.J., 1971, mem., 1978, visitor, 1983, 85-86; vis. scholar Bibliotheca Hertziana, Max Planck Soc., Rome, 1972, 73; mem. vis. com. dept. art and archaeology Princeton U., 1956-73, 85-89; mem. adv. com. Villa I Tatti, 1985-92; trustee Hyde Collection, Glens Falls, N.Y., 1985-87, The Burlington mag., 1987—; mem. commn. Ednl. & Cultural Exch. between Italy and U.S., 1979-83. Author: Mannerism and Maniera, 1963, rev. edit. with introduction by E. Cropper, 1992, Bronzino as Draughtsman, 1971, Michelangelo Architetto (with H.M. Millon), 1988, English edit., 1988, Repatriation of Art from the Collecting Point in Munich After World War II, 1988; editor: Michelangelo Drawings (Nat. Gallery of Art), 1992; editor (with Peter M. Lukehart), contbr.: The Early Years of Art History in the United States, 1994; contbr.: (with H.M. Millon) articles on Michelangelo and St. Peter's to profl. jours. Hon. trustee Met. Mus. Art, N.Y.C., 1968—; trustee Inst. Fine Arts, NYU, 1973—; mem. mayor's com. Piazza Della Signoria, Florence, 1975-78. Lt. USNR, 1942-46. Decorated Chevalier Legion of Honor France, U.S. Army Commendation medal; sr. Fulbright Rsch. fellow, 1949-50. Mem. Am. Acad. Arts and Scis., Am. Philos. Soc., Coll. Art Assn. Am. (bd. dirs. 1953-57, sec. 1956), Accademia Fiorentina delle Arti del Disegno (academician, assoc.), Accademia di San Luca, Harvard Club (N.Y.C.), Century Assn. (N.Y.C.). Address: PO Box 39 Cresskill NJ 07626-0039

SMYTH, DAVID SHANNON, real estate investor, commercial and retail builder and developer; b. Denver, May 13, 1943; s. William James and Constance Ruth (Sherman) S.; student Regis Coll., 1967-69, USAF Acad., 1961-65, U. No. Colo., 1965-67; m. Sharon Kaye Swiderski, Jan. 3, 1980; children: Julia Caitlin, Alexander Jeremiah, Matthew Davis; 1 son by previous marriage, Shannon David. Accountant, Colo. Nat. Bank, 1966-69; bus. analyst Dun & Bradstreet, 1969-70; pres., dir. Georgetown Valley Water & Sanitation Dist., 1973-74, Realists, Inc., 1973-74, Silver Queen Constrn. Co., 1973-74; v.p., sec., dir. Georgetown Assocs., Inc. (Colo.), 1970-74; pres., chief ops. officer Lincoln Cos., Denver, 1975-76; project mgr., sales mgr., prin. Brooks-Morris Homes, Fox Ridge, Colo., 1976-77; project mgr. U.S. West Homes, Denver, 1977-78; pres., dir. Denver Venture Capital, 1978-81; prin., dir., exec. v.p. Shelter Equities, Inc., 1982-87; prin., dir., exec. v.p. Comml. Constrn. Mgmt. Services, Inc., 1987-88, Shelter Equities, Inc., 1984-87; owner, dir., exec. v.p. Maple Leaf Realty Corp.; v.p., dir. Gibraltar Devel. Corp., Dominion Properties Ltd., 1978-82; investment dir. Van Schaack & Co., 1987-91; prin. investor, head devel. The Farkas Group, 1991-92; sr. residential loan officer, Freedom Mortgage Co., 1992-93; sr. loan officer, dir. builder mktg. NVR Mortgage Co., Englewood, Colo., 1994-96; sr. loan officer Market St. Mortgage, 1996-97; dist. builder account mgr. N.Am. Mortgage Co., Denver, 1997—. Served with USAF, 1961-65. Lic. real estate broker. Home: 8680 S Aberdeen Cir Highlands Ranch CO 80126 Office: NAm Mortgage Co 4949 S Syracuse St Ste 500 Denver CO 80237-2747

SMYTH, DONALD MORGAN, chemical educator, researcher; b. Bangor, Maine, Mar. 20, 1930; s. John Robert and Selma (Eubanks) S.; m. Elisabeth Luce, Aug. 1, 1951; children: Carolyn, Joanne. BS in Chemistry, U. Maine, 1951; PhD in Inorganic Chemistry, MIT, 1954. Sr. chemist Sprague Electric Co., North Adams, Mass., 1954-58, sect. head, 1958-61, dept. head, 1961-71; assoc. prof. Lehigh U., Bethlehem, Pa., 1971-73, prof., 1973-95, dir. Materials Rsch. Ctr., 1971-92, Paul B. Reinhold prof. materials sci., engring. and chemistry, 1988-95; emeritus, 1995—; mem. various coms. Lehigh U., 1973-95; mem. materials rsch. adv. com. NSF, 1984-88, chmn., 1985-86, co-chair ad-hoc com. to brief dir., 1986; mem. coun. materials sci. Dept. Energy, 1986-90; presenter in field. Contbr. articles to profl. jours. Recipient Libsch Rsch. award Lehigh U., 1990, Buessem award Dielectrics Rsch. Ctr., Pa. State U., 1991; grantee in field. Fellow Am. Inst. Chemists, Am. Ceramic Soc. (com. edn. electronics divsn. 1974-78, chmn. Lehigh Valley sect. 1978-79, counselor 1982—, assoc. editor jour. 1988-92, best paper award 1987, 95, Kraner award Lehigh Valley sect. 1990, Sosman lectr. 1996); mem. Am. Chem. Soc., Nat. Acad. Engring., Materials Rsch. Soc., Electrochem. Soc. (various coms., sec. dielectrics and insulation divsn. 1967-69, vice chmn. 1969-70, chmn. 1970-71, rsch. award battery divsn. 1960). Achievements include patents (with others) for Solid-State Battery Cell with Complex Organic Electrolyte Material, Capacitor with Dielectric Film Having Phosphorous-Containing Component Therein, Solid Barrier Electrolyte Incorporating Additive, others; research in defect chemistry and electrical properties of complex oxides. Home: 3429 Mountainview Cir Bethlehem PA 18017-1807 Office: Lehigh U Materials Rsch Ctr 5 E Packer Ave Bethlehem PA 18015-3102

SMYTH, GLEN MILLER, management consultant; b. Abingdon, Va., July 26, 1929; s. Glen Miller and Kathleen (Dunn) S.; m. Cynthia Olson, Aug. 25, 1954 (div. 1967); children: Catherine Ellen, Glen Miller, III, Cynthia Allison; m. Lilian Castel Edgar, Oct. 31, 1968; children: Stephanie Castel, Kimberley Forsyth, Lindsay Dunn. BA, Yale U., 1951; MS in Psychology, Rutgers U., 1958. Mktg. rep. Wheeling Stamping Co., N.Y.C., 1953-56; personnel dir. Celanese Internat., N.Y.C., 1958-71; mgr. orgn. and Manpower Internat. and Can. group Gen. Electric Co., N.Y.C., 1971-73; sr. v.p. human resources Northwest Bancorp., Mpls., 1973-82; sr. v.p. Calif. Fed. Savs., L.A., 1983-85; v.p. Career Transition Group, L.A., 1985-87; pres. Fuchs, Cuthrell & Co., Inc., L.A., 1987-93, Fuchs & Co., L.A., 1993-94; pres., CEO Smyth, Fuchs & Co., Inc., L.A., 1995—; leader seminars. Co-author: International Career Pathing, 1971; Contbr. articles to profl. jours. Served with AUS, 1951-53. Mem. Am. Psychol. Assn., Nat. Fgn. Trade Coun. (founder, past chmn. human resources, orgn. com. 1966—), Human Resources Planning Soc., Employment Mgmt. Assn., Jonathan Club, Yale Club of N.Y., North Ranch Country Club, Phi Gamma Delta. Home: 1115 Westcreek Ln Westlake Vlg CA 91362-5467

SMYTH, JOEL DOUGLAS, newspaper executive; b. Renovo, Pa., Nov. 8, 1941; s. Bernard John and Eva Mae (Stone) S.; m. Madonna Robertson, Nov. 29, 1959; children: Deborah Sue, Susan Kelly, Michael Robertson, Patricia Ann, Rebecca Lee, Jennifer Neilia. Student, Lycoming Coll., 1959. Reporter Del. State News, Dover, 1960-62, news editor, 1962-65, mng. editor, 1965-70, editor, pres., 1970-78; editor Del. Sunday News, 1964-65; pres. Ind. Newspapers, Inc., Dover, 1970-89, chmn., CEO, 1989—. Founding pres. Valley Citizen's League, 1987-90. Recipient writing awards. Mem. AP Mng. Editors Assn. (dir.), Am. Soc. Newspaper Editors, Young Pres.'s Orgn., Sigma Delta Chi. Winter home: 33811 N 70th Way Scottsdale AZ 85262-7009 Summer home: 260 Forest Highlands Flagstaff AZ 86001-8422 Office: Independent Newspaper Inc PO Box 70001 Dover DE 19903

SMYTH, JOSEPH PATRICK, retired naval officer, physician; b. Norwalk, Conn., Mar. 2, 1933; s. Patrick and Helen (Heffernan) S.; m. Ursula Marie (Kirwin), Dec. 28, 1960; children: Donna, Jennifer, Joseph. BA, Fairfield U., 1960; MD, Creighton U., 1964. Diplomate Am. Bd. Med. Examiners. Commd. ensign USN, 1963, advanced through grades to rear adm., 1988; intern Phila. Naval Hosp., 1964-65, internal medicine resident, 1965-68, staff physician, 1968-69; internist, chief of medicine U.S. Naval Hosp., DaNang, Vietnam, 1969-70, Orlando, Fla., 1970-76; chief of medicine, exec. officer U.S. Naval Hosp., Yokosuka, Japan, 1976-80; exec. officer U.S. Naval Hosp., Oakland, Calif., 1980-82, comdg. officer, 1984-86; comdg. officer U.S. Naval Hosp., Okinawa, Japan, 1982-84, Naval Med. Command European Region, London, 1986-90; dep. dir. for med. readiness The Joint Staff, Pentagon, Washington, 1990-92; retired US Navy, 1992; med. dir. Volusia County (Fla.) Dept. of Corrections, 1994—; instr. medicine Jefferson Med. Coll., 1966-69; preceptor USN Physician Asst. Program, Orlando, 1971-76; inst. mgmt. course Navy Med. Dept., Washington, 1986; Joint Staff coord. for entire mil. med. build-up for Operation Desert Shield/Storm, Saudi Arabia, 1990-91. Physician Orange County, Fla. Alcohol Ctr., Orlando, 1974-76. Decorated Def. Superior Svc. medal, Legion of Merit, Meritorious Svc. medals with 2 oak leaf clusters, Navy Commendation medal. Mem. AMA, Assn. Mil. Surgeons of U.S., Am. Acad. Med. Adminstrs. (Levandowski award 1991), Fla. Med. Assn., Am. Acad. Physician Execs., Orange County Med. Soc. Republican. Roman Catholic. Home: 400 Sweetwater Blvd S Longwood FL 32779-3422

SMYTH, JOSEPH PHILIP, travel industry executive; b. N.Y.C., Aug. 16, 1939; s. Joseph P. and Virginia S. (Gibbs) S.; m. Janet Hughes; 1 child, Philip. BA, Hamilton U., 1961; MBA, Harvard U., 1967; student, Naval Intelligence Sch., 1961-62. Dir. planning N.E. Airlines, Boston, 1967-70; acct. supr. Wells, Rich, Greene, N.Y.C., 1970-72; sr. v.p. mktg. Inter-Continental, N.Y.C., 1972-86, Hilton Hotels, Beverly Hills, Calif., 1986-88; head of ops. Cunard, N.Y.C., 1988-94; sr. v.p. fleet ops. Holland Am., Seattle, 1994; chmn Gibbs Bros., Huntsville, Tx., 1995—. Bd. mem. First Nat. Bank Huntsville, Tex. Lt. USN, 1961-65, ETO. Mem. Univ. Club, Harvard Club. Avocation: running. Home: 1088 Park Ave New York NY 10128-1132 Office: Gibbs Bros PO Box 711 Huntsville TX 77342-0711

SMYTH, JOSEPH VINCENT, manufacturing company executive; b. Belfast, Ireland, July 18, 1919; s. Joseph Leo and Margaret M. (Murray) S.; m. Marie E. Cripe, Mar. 22, 1941; children: Kevin W., Brian J., Ellen M., Vincent P. B.S. cum laude, U. Notre Dame, 1941. With Arnolt Corp., Warsaw, Ind., 1946-63; exec. v.p., gen. mgr. Arnolt Corp., until 1963; pres., gen. mgr. Hills-McCanna Co., Carpentersville, Ill., 1963-72; pres. Lunkenheimer Co., Cin., 1972-79; v.p. Condec Flow Control Group, Chgo., 1979-82; cons., 1982—. Club: Pinecrest Golf and Country (N.C.). Lodge: K.C. Home: 740 Saint Andrews Ln Apt 34 Crystal Lake IL 60014-7043 also: 299 Peppard Dr Fort Myers Beach FL 33931-3136

SMYTH, NICHOLAS PATRICK D., surgeon; b. Dublin, Ireland, Apr. 1, 1924; came to U.S., 1951; s. Patrick Joseph and Nano Elizabeth (Dillon) S.; m. Elizabeth Stavely Long; children: Sheila, Brian, Nicholas, Augustine, Patrick. BSc, Univ. Coll. Dublin, 1946, MSc, 1948, MB BCh, 1949; MS, U. Mich., 1954. Diplomate Am. Bd. Surgery, Am. Bd. Thoracic Surgery. Intern Mater Misericordiae Hosp., Dublin, 1949-50, Norfolk and Norwich Hosp., Eng., 1950-51; resident in gen. surgery Henry Ford Hosp., Detroit, 1951-52, 53-55; resident in thoracic surgery George Washington U. Hosp., Washington, 1957-59; pvt. practice, Washington, 1959-86; clin. prof. surgery emeritus George Washington U. Sch. Medicine, Washington; mem. staff, Washington Hosp. Ctr., George Washington U. Med. Ctr.; consulting surgeon, VA Hosp., Washington, NIH, Bethesda, Md., Walter Reed Army Med. Ctr., Washington; pres. Potomac Fund Cardiovascular Rsch. Contbr. numerous articles to profl. jours.; patentee in field. Capt. M.C., U.S. Army, 1955-57. Fellow ACS, Am. Coll. Chest Physicians, Am. Coll. Cardiology; mem. D.C. Thoracic Soc., Washington Heart Assn., Am. Heart Assn., AMA, Med. Soc. D.C., Am. Assn. Thoracic Surgery, Washington Acad. Surgery, Am. Fedn. Clin. Rsch., Pan Am. Med. Assn., World Med. Assn., Soc. Thoracic Surgery, So. Thoracic Surg. Assn., So. Med. Assn., AAAS, Assn. Advancement Med. Instrumentation, Soc. Vascular Surgery, Internat. Cardiovascular Soc., N.Am. Soc. Pacing and Electrophysiology, Royal Soc. Medicine. Republican. Roman Catholic. Avocation: writing. Office: 3612 Winfield Ln NW Washington DC 20007-2385

SMYTH, PAUL BURTON, lawyer; b. Phila., Aug. 15, 1949; s. Benjamin Burton and Florence Elizabeth (Tomlinson) S.; m. Denise Elaine Freeland, May 31, 1975. BA, Trinity Coll, Hartford, Conn., 1971; JD, Boston Coll., 1974. Bar: Conn. 1974, D.C. 1975, U.S. Dist. Ct. D.C., 1980, U.S. Supreme Ct., 1985. With Dept. Interior, 1974—, atty. Office of Hearings and Appeals, Arlington, Va., 1974-76, atty. Office of Solicitor, Washington, 1976-82, asst. solicitor for land use and realty, Washington, 1982-87; deputy assoc. solicitor for energy and resources, Washington, 1987-93, acting dir. Office of Hearings and Appeals, Arlington, 1993-94, dep. assoc. solicitor. for energy and resources, Washington, 1994-95, for land and water resources, 1995—. Editor: Federal Reclamation and Related Laws Annotated, Reclamation Reform Act Compilation, 1982-88; contbr. articles to legal publs. Mem. ABA (coun. 1991-94, budget officer 1994—, sect. natural resources, energy and environ. law). Office: Office of Solicitor Dept Interior 18th and C Streets NW Washington DC 20240

SMYTH, PETER HAYES, radio executive; b. Apr. 25, 1952; s. Arthur and Irene (McNamara) S; m. Catherine Comerford Smyth, Aug. 8, 1976; children: Nancy, Colin, Kathleen. BA, Holy Cross Coll., Worcester, Mass., 1975; postgrad., Fordham U., 1975-76. Retail sales man Sta. WROR Radio, Boston, 1975-76, gen. sales mgr., 1976-83; gen. sales mgr. Sta. WOR Radio, N.Y.C., 1983-86; v.p. greater media radio sales, v.p. gen. mgr. Greater Boston Radio Stas., 1986—; cons. Greater Media Cable, North Oxford, Mass., 1988-89. Bd. dirs. Holy Cross Coll., Worcester, Univ. Club, Boston, United Way of Mass., 1993, 94. Mem. New England Broadcast Assn. (bd. dirs. 1987, v.p., pres. 1992—). Republican. Roman Catholic. Avocations: golfing, swimming, skiing. Office: Greater Boston Radio Stas 330 Stuart St Boston MA 02116-5229

SMYTH, REGINALD (REGGIE SMYTHE), cartoonist; b. Hartlepool, Eng., Oct. 7, 1917; s. Richard Oliver and Florence (Ritson) S.; m. Vera Toyne, Aug. 13, 1949. Student, Galleys Field Sch., 1922-31. With Brit. Civil Service, 1945-54; cartoonist, 1955—. Creator: Andy Capp daily comic strip, 1956. Served with Brit. Army, 1936-45. Recipient Best Brit. Cartoon award, 1961-65; Premio Cartoon award Lucca, 1969; Best Cartoonist award Genoa, 1973; Best Strip Cartoonist award Am. Cartoonists Soc., 1974. Mem. Nat. Cartoonists Soc. Mem. Ch. of Eng. Address: Whitegates 96 Caledonian Rd, Hartlepool England

SMYTH, RICHARD HENRY, foreign service officer; b. Oakland, Calif., June 12, 1951; s. Ronald Henry and Alyce Miriam (Swensson) S.; m. Janice Eileen Sullivan, Mar. 10, 1979; children: Caitlin, Alison. BA, U. Wash., 1973; grad. cert., U. Ala., Tuscaloosa, 1977; MS, Nat. War Coll., 1997. Cmty. planner Tuscaloosa, 1975-78; 3rd sec. U.S. Embassy, Kabul, Afghanistan, 1979-80; 2nd sec. U.S. Embassy, New Delhi, 1980-81, Jakarta, Indonesia, 1985-87; 1st sec. U.S. Embassy, Copenhagen, 1987-90; 2nd sec. Belgian Embassy, Baghdad, Iraq, 1981-84; with U.S. Dept. of State, Washington, 1990-92; consul gen. U.S. Consulate, Peshawar, Pakistan, 1992-96; dep. chief mission U.S. Embassy, Colombo, Sri Lanka, 1996—. Vol. U.S. Peace Corps, Kabul, Afghanistan, 1973-75. Mem. Assn. Am. Geographers, Am. Fgn. Svc. Assn. Avocations: Oriental studies, angling. Home and Office: 210 Galle Rd, Colombo 3, Sri Lanka

SMYTHE, CHEVES MCCORD, dean, medical educator; b. May 25, 1924. Student, Yale Coll., 1942-43; MD cum laude, Harvard, 1947. Diplomate Am. Bd. Internal Medicine, Am. Bd. Geriatrics. Intern, asst. resident Harvard Med. Svc., Boston City Hosp., 1947-49, chief resident, 1954-55; resident chest svc. Bellevue, 1949-50; rsch. fellow Presbyn. Hosp., N.Y.C., 1950-52; assoc. medicine Med. Coll. S.C. Sch. Medicine, 1956-58, asst. prof. medicine, 1958-60, assoc. prof. medicine, 1960-66, dean, 1963-65; attending physician Wesley Meml., Cook County North Side VA Hosps., Chgo., 1967-70; with Aga Khan U. Hosp., Karachi, Pakistan, 1990-91; dean faculty health scis., prof. medicine Aga Khan U., Karachi, Pakistan, 1982-85, prof., chmn. dept. medicine, 1990-91; chief Med. Svcs. at LBJ Hosp., Houston, 1991-95; prof. divsn. gen. medicine dept. internal medicine U. Tex. Med. Sch., Houston, 1970—, dean, 1970-75, dean pro tem, 1995-96; assoc. med. dir. Hermann Hosp., 1996—. Bd. dirs. Assn. Am. Assoc. Med. Colls.. Office: Univ Tex Med Sch 6431 Fannin MSB1.126 Houston TX 77030

SMYTHE, WILLIAM RODMAN, physicist, educator; b. Los Angeles, Jan. 6, 1930; s. William Ralph and Helen (Keith) S.; m. Carol Richardson, Nov. 27, 1954 (dec. Dec. 1987); children: Stephanie, Deborah, William Richardson, Reed Terry; m. Judith Brean Travers, Jan. 1, 1989. B.S., Calif. Inst. Tech., 1951, M.S., 1952, Ph.D., 1957. Engr. Gen. Electric Microwave Lab., Palo Alto, Calif., 1956-57; asst. prof. U. Colo., 1958-63, assoc. prof., 1963-67, prof., 1967—, chmn. nuclear physics lab., 1967-69, 81-83, 90-92. Group leader Rocky Mountain Rescue Group, 1967-68. Mem. Am. Phys. Soc. Club: Colorado Mountain (Boulder). Achievements include inventing negative ion cyclotron, fractional turn cyclotron. Home: 2106 Knollwood Dr Boulder CO 80302-4706

SMYTHE-HAITH, MABEL MURPHY, consultant on African economic development, speaker, writer; b. Montgomery, Ala., Apr. 3, 1918; m. Hugh H. Smythe, June 22, 1939 (dec. 1977); 1 child, Karen Pamela; m. Robert Haith, Jr., Oct. 18, 1985. Student, Spelman Coll., 1933-36, LLD (hon.), 1980; BA, Mt. Holyoke Coll., 1937, LHD (hon.), 1977; MA, Northwestern U., 1940; PhD, U. Wis., 1942, LLD (hon.), 1991; LHD (hon.), U. Mass., 1979. Asst. prof. Lincoln U., Mo., 1942-45; prof. Tenn. A. and I. U., 1945-46, Bklyn. Coll., 1946-47; vis. prof. Shiga U., Japan, 1951-53; dep. dir. rsch. for sch. segregation cases NAACP Legal Def. and Edn. Fund, 1953; tchr., prin. New Lincoln High Sch., N.Y.C., 1954-69; with Phelps-Stokes Fund, 1970-77, dir. research and publs., 1970-72, v.p., 1972-77; U.S. amb. to United Republic of Cameroon, Yaounde, 1977-80; U.S. amb. to Equatorial Guinea, 1979-80; dep. asst. sec. for African affairs Dept. State, 1980-81; Melville J. Herskovits prof. African studies Northwestern U., Evanston, Ill., 1981-83, disting. prof., 1983-85, prof. emeritus, 1985—, co-dir. internat. internship program, 1983-85; co-dir. African seminar Northwestern U., 1985; mem. Adv. Com. on Ednl. Exchange U.S. Dept. State, 1961-62, Adv. Commn. on Internat. Ednl. and Cultural Affairs, 1962-65; mem. Dept. State adv. coun. on African Affairs, 1962-65; U.S. del. 13th gen. conf. UNESCO, 1964; trustee Conn. Coll., 1964-65, 69-77, Mt. Holyoke Coll., 1971-76, vice chmn., 1975-76, trustee fellow, 1988—, Spelman Coll., 1980-89, life trustee, 1991—, Hampshire Coll., 1971-77, 85-88, vice chair, 1975-76; mem. U.S. Nat. Com. for UNESCO, 1965-70, Nat. Adv. rev. Bd., 1974-77; co-dir. African seminar for pres. black colls., 1971; bd. dirs. Nat. Corp. for Housing Partnerships, 1972-77; scholar-in-residence U.S. Commn. on Civil Rights, 1973-74; U.S. del. Internat. Conf. for Assistance to Refugees in Africa, Geneva, 1981, So. African Devel. Coordination Conf. II, 1980; guest scholar Woodrow Wilson Internat. Ctr. for Scholars, Smithsonian Instn., Washington, 1982; mem. Aspen Inst. Humanistic Studies Exec. Seminar, 1983; mem. study mission to Japan with Assn. Black Am. Ambassadors, 1984, 85; mem. com. on policy for racial justice Joint Ctr. for Polit. and Econ. Studies, 1983-92; co-leader: Md. Consortium to Togo, Sierra Leone, Senegal, Liberia and Cameroon from 1970; co-dir. Mission to Malawi Women's Commn. on Refugee Women and Children, Malawi, 1989; adv. commn. Howard Univ. Patricia Roberts Harris Public Affairs Program, 1989—; adv. bd. Lincoln Univ. (Pa.) Ctr. for Public Policy and Diplomacy, 1991—; bd. dirs. Ralph Bunche Inst. on UN, CUNY, 1986-94; co-chair African-Am. Inst. Del. to observe presdl. elections, Madagascar, Feb., 1993. Author introduction: A Slaver's Log Book or 20 Years Residence in Africa, 1976; co-author: The New Nigerian Elite, 3d edit, 1971, Intensive English Conversation, Vol. I, 1953, Vol. II, 1954; editor: The Black American Reference Book, 1976; co-editor: Curriculum for Understanding, 1965; contbr. chpts. to coop. books, articles to profl. jours. Bd. dirs. Refugee Policy Group, 1983-89, adv. coun., 1989—; cons. African Devel. Found., 1986—; mem. Friends Inst. for Democracy in South Africa (formerly Inst. for a Democratic Alternative in South Africa), 1990—. Decorated grand officer Order of Valor (Cameroon); Grand Dama D'Inore, Order of Royal Crown of Crete (Malta); recipient Top Hat award Pitts. Courier, 1979, Mary McLeod Bethune award, 1981, Decade of Service award Phelps-Stokes Fund, 1982, Ella T. Grasso award Mt. Holyoke Coll., 1982, Northwestern U. Alumna of Year award, 1983, Disting. Service award Nat. Coalition of 100 Black Women, 1984, Disting. Service award USIA, 1986, Am. Bicentennial Presdl. Inaugural award, 1989, Black History Makers award Associated Black Charities, 1990. Mem. Coun. Fgn. Rels., Nat. Coun. Women U.S., Coun. Am. Ambassadors, Assn. Black Am. Ambassadors (exec. com.). Hugh H. and Mabel M. Smythe Internat. Service citation awarded annually by InterFuture, Inc. Address: Watergate South Ste 317 700 New Hampshire Ave NW Washington DC 20037-2406 *Living in challenging times brings, along with its problems, opportunities for discovering new and better solutions to our difficulties, for making creative contributions to a world which so sorely needs positive input, for learning to enjoy the beauty and hope which are within our grasp.*

SMYTHE ZÄJC, M. CATHERINE, library administrator, development officer; b. Washington, Jan. 5, 1956; d. William Sterling Jr. and Anna Rosamund (Johnson) S.; m. John M. Zajc, Jr., May 27, 1995. BA in History, Westminster Coll., 1976; MLS, Syracuse U., 1982. Rsch. libr. White House Libr., Washington, 1982-86; dep. dir., rsch. libr. Time, Inc. Sports Libr., N.Y.C., 1986-89; dir. libr. svcs. Nat. Sports Daily, N.Y.C., 1989-90; rsch. assoc. Jury Verdict Rsch., Solon, Ohio, 1990-91; cons., owner Sports Source, Inc., Painesville, Ohio, 1990-92; dir. of prospect rsch. Baldwin-Wallace Coll., Berea, Ohio, 1992—; cons. Bowman Gray Sch. Medicine/Bapt. Hosp. Med. Ctr., Wake Forest U. N.C., Winston-Salem, 1990-93. Author: Geothesaurus, 1982. Mem. bd. Global Issues Resource Ctr.; mem. Adoption Network Cleve. Mem. Assn. of Profl. Rschrs. for Advancement, Coun. for Advancement and Support of Edn., Ohio Prospect Rschrs. Network, Ind. Coll. Advancement Assocs., Soc. for Am. Baseball Rsch., Ch. St. Ministries (fund raising adv. bd.), Cleve. Sight Ctr., Radio Reading Svc. Presbyterian. Avocations: reading, collecting Shelley china and Poole pottery, physical fitness, music, crossword puzzles. Home: 2672 W 14th St # 2 Cleveland OH 44113-5216

SNADER, JACK ROSS, publishing company executive; b. Athens, Ohio, Feb. 25, 1938; s. Daniel Webster and Mae Estella (Miller) S.; m. Sharon Perschnick, Apr. 4, 1959; children: Susan Mae, Brian Ross. BS, U. Ill., 1959. Cert. mgmt. cons. With mktg. Richardson-Merrell, Cin., 1959-65, Xerox Corp., N.Y.C., 1965-67, Sieber & McIntyre, Chgo., 1967-69; pres. Systema Corp., Northbrook, Ill., 1969—; bd. dirs. 1st Fed. Bank, Waukegan, Ill., Instrnl. Systems Assn. Author Systematic Selling, 1987, The Sales Relationship, 1981. Mem. ASTD, Inst. of Mgmt. Cons., Am. Mgmt. Assn. Office: Systema Corporation 60 Revere Dr Ste 600 Northbrook IL 60062-1578

SNAPP, ELIZABETH, librarian, educator; b. Lubbock, Tex., Mar. 31, 1937; d. William James and Louise (Lanham) Mitchell; BA magna cum laude, North Tex. State U., Denton, 1968, MLS, 1969, MA, 1977; m. Harry Franklin Snapp, June 1, 1956. Asst. to archivist Archive of New Orleans Jazz, Tulane U., 1960-63; catalog librarian Tex. Woman's U., Denton, 1969-71, head acquisitions dept., 1971-74, coord. readers svcs., 1974-77, asst. to dean Grad. Sch., 1977-79, instr. libr. sci., 1977-88, acting Univ. libr., 1979-82, dir. librs., 1982—, univ. historian, 1995—; chair-elect Tex. Coun. State U. Librs., 1988-90, chmn., 1990-92; mem. adv. com. on libr. formula Coordinating Bd. Tex. Coll. and Univ. System, 1981-92; del. OCLC Nat. Users Council, 1985-87, mem. by-laws com., 1985-86, com. on less-than-full-svcs. networks, 1986-87; trustee AMIGOS Bibliographic Coun., Inc., 1994—, sec. bd. trustees, 1996—; project dir. NEH consultancy grant on devel. core curriculum for women's studies, 1981-82; chmn. Blue Ribbon com. 1986 Gov.'s Commn. for Women to select 150 outstanding women in Tex. history; project dir. math./sci. anthology project Tex. Found. Women's Resources. Co-sponsor Irish Lecture Series, Denton, 1968, 70, 73, 78. Sec. Denton County Dem. Caucus, 1970. Recipient Ann. Pioneer award Tex. Women's U., 1986. Mem. AAUP, ALA (standards com. 1983-85), Tex. Libr. Assn. (program com. 1978, Dist. VII chmn. 1985-86, archives and oral history com. 1990-92, co-chair program com. Tex. Libr Assn. Ann. Conf. 1994, mem. Tall Texan selection com. 1995-96, treas. exec. bd. 1996—), Tex. Hist. Commn. (judge for Farenbach History prize 1990-93), Women's Collecting Group (chmn. ad hoc com. 1984-86), AAUW (legis. br. chmn. 1973-74, br. v.p. 1975-76, br. pres. 1979-80, state historian 1986-88), AAUW Ednl. Found. (rsch. and awards panel 1990-94), So. Conf. Brit. Studies, Tex. Assn. Coll. Tchrs. (pres. Tex. Woman's U. chpt. 1976-77), Alliance Higher Edn. (chair coun. libr. dirs. 1993-95), Woman's Shakespeare Club (pres. 1967-69), Beta Phi Mu (pres. chpt. 1976-78; sec. nat. adv. assembly 1978-79, pres. 1979-80, nat. dir. 1981-83), Alpha Chi, Alpha Lambda Sigma (pres. 1970-71), Pi Delta Phi. Methodist. Club: Soroptimist Internat. (Denton) (pres. 1986-88). Asst. editor Tex. Academe, 1973-76; co-editor: Read All About Her! Texas Women's History: A Working Bibliography, 1995; contbg. author: Women in Special Collections, 1984, Special Collections, 1986; book reviewer Library Resources and Tech. Services, 1973—. Contbr. articles to profl. jours. Home: 1904 N Lake Trl Denton TX 76201-0602 Office: TWU Sta PO Box 424093 Denton TX 76204-4093 *The idealistic dreams of youth can be translated into making a difference in the work place and in your personal life if you develop a big picture that includes the ideas of individuals of diversity and if you give life your full attention, enthusiasm, and courage and give a few your steadfast friendship.*

SNAPP, HARRY FRANKLIN, historian; b. Bryan, Tex., Oct. 15, 1930; s. H.F. and Ethel (Manning) S.; BA, Baylor U., 1952, MA, 1953; PhD, Tulane U., 1963; m. Elizabeth Mitchell, June 1, 1956. Instr., U. Coll. Tulane U., 1960-62; asst. prof. history Wofford Coll., 1963-64; asst. prof. history U. North Tex. (formerly North Tex. State U.), Denton, 1964-69, assoc. prof., 1969-94; dir. Tex. Rsch. Ctr. Biog. Study of Women, Denton, 1995—; pres., dir. Read All About Her Tex. Women's Biographic Ctr., Inc., 1995—. Editor Brit. Studies Mercury, 1970-84, Tex. Academy, 1973-76; co-editor: Read All About Her! Texas Women's History: A Working Bibliography, 1995; author: (with others) West Texas Historical Association Year Book, 1994, West Texas Historical Association Year Book, 1996; contbr. articles to profl. jours. Mem. Friends of Winchester Cathedral, Am. Com. Irish Studies; mem. adv. com. on acad. freedom and tenure policy, coordinating bd. Tex. Coll. and Univ. System. Recipient North Tex. State U. Faculty Rsch. award, 1966, 67. Mem. AAUP (pres. North Tex. chpt. 1968-69, pres. Southwestern regional conf. 1971-72, pres. Tex. conf. 1974-76, nat. coun. 1976-86), So. Conf. Brit. Studies (sec.-treas. 1969-84), Am. Hist. Assn., Tex. State Hist. Assn., Hist. Assn. (London), Libr. Rsch. Round Table, Libr. History Round Table, Northamptonshire Record Soc., Butler Soc. (Ireland), Econ. History Soc., Ch. Hist. Soc., Tulane U. Alumni Assn., Alpha Chi, Lambda Chi Alpha. Methodist. Home: 1904 N Lake Trl Denton TX 76201-0602 Office: Read All About Her Tex Women's Biographic Ctr Inc PO Box 424053 TWU Sta Denton TX 76204-4053

SNAPP, ROY BAKER, lawyer; b. Strang, Okla., May 9, 1916; s. Harry Moore and Verda Mildred (Austin) S.; m. Dorothy Faye Loftis, Jan. 27, 1942; children: Deborah, Bryan Austin, Martha Lynn, Barbara, James. Lawyer. B.S. in Pub. Adminstrn, U. Mo., 1936; LL.B., Georgetown U., 1941, LL.M., 1942. With U.S. State Dept., 1941; spl. adviser comdg. gen. (Manhattan (Atomic Bomb) Project), 1946; dir. internat. affairs U.S. AEC, 1947, 1st sec., 1948-54, asst. to chmn., 1954-55, sr. staff mem. nat. security coun., 1953-55; v.p. atomic div. (Am. Machine & Foundry), 1957; v.p. Am. Machine & Foundry Co., Washington office, 1961; bd. dirs. Electro-Nucleonics, Inc.; ptnr. Bechhoefer, Snapp and Trippe, 1966. Commd. ensign USNR 1942; assigned secretariat of U.S. Joint Chiefs of Staff and Combined (U.S.-Brit), Chiefs of Staff; naval mem. 1945; Intelligence Staff of Joint Cheifs Staff and Combined Chiefs Staff promoted to lt. comdr. 1945. Recipient D.S.M. AEC, 1955. Mem. SVC, Nat. Assn. Mgrs. (chmn. atomic energy com. 1963-64, dir. 1964-65), Phi Gamma Mu, Delta Theta Phi. Baptist. Clubs: Univ. (Washington), Columbia Country (Washington). Home: 11446 Savannah Dr Fredericksburg VA 22407-9108

SNAPPER, ERNST, mathematics educator; b. The Netherlands, Dec. 2, 1913; came to U.S., 1938, naturalized, 1942; s. Isidore and Henrietta (Van Buuren) S.; m. Ethel Lillian Klein, June 1941; children—John William, James Robert. MA, Princeton U., 1939, PhD, 1941; MA (hon.), Dartmouth Coll., 1964. Instr. Princeton, 1941-45, vis. asso. prof., 1949-50, vis. prof., 1954-55; asst. prof. U. So. Calif., 1945-48, asso. prof., 1948-53, prof., 1953-55; NSF post-doctoral fellow Harvard, 1953-54; Andrew Jackson Buckingham prof. math. Miami U., Oxford, Ohio, 1955-58; prof. math. Ind. U., 1958-63; prof. math. Dartmouth, 1963—, Benjamin Pierce Cheney prof. math., 1971—. Mem. Am. Math. Soc., Math. Assn. Am. (pres. Ind. sect. 1962-63, Carl B. Allendoerfer award 1980), Assn. Princeton Grad. Alumni (governing bd.), Soc. for Preservation Bridges of Konigsburg, Phi Beta Kappa (hon.), Pi Mu Epsilon (hon.). Home: PO Box 67 Norwich VT 05055-0067

SNAVELY, WILLIAM PENNINGTON, economics educator; b. Charlottesville, Va., Jan. 25, 1920; s. Tipton Ray and Nell (Aldred) S.; m. Alice Watts Pritchett, June 4, 1942; children: Nell Lee, William Pennington, Elizabeth Tipton. Student, Hampden-Sydney Coll., 1936-37; BA with honors, U. Va., 1940, MA, 1941, PhD, 1950; postgrad. (Bennett Wood Green fellow), Harvard U., 1946-47. Mem. faculty U. Conn., 1947-73, prof. econs., 1961-73, chmn. dept., 1966-72, economist econ. edn. workshop, summers 1954, 55, 56; prof. econs. George Mason U., 1973-86, chmn. dept., 1973-81; acting dean CAS, summer 1981, 85-86, assoc. dean, 1982-85; prof. econs. Liberty U., 1986-93; cons. Ford Found., Jordan Devel. Bd., Amman, 1961-62, Ministry of Planning, Beirut, Lebanon, 1964-65, Saudi Arabian Cen. Planning Orgn., Riyadh, 1964-65, Am. U. Beirut, 1969-70, Bahrain Ministry Fin. and Nat. Economy, 1974, 75, 76, UN, Jordan Nat. Planning Coun., Amman, 1972; mem. Danforth Workshop, summer 1966; mem. adv. com. Willimantic Trust Co., Conn., 1968-73; v.p. Champion Econs. & Bus. Assn., 1988—. Author: (with W.H. Carter) Intermediate Economic Analysis, 1961, Theory of Economic Systems, 1969, (with M.T. Sadik) Bahrain, Qatar and the United Arab Emirates, 1972; contbr. articles to jours.; articles Ency. Americana. Bd. regents Liberty U. Capt. AUS, 1942-46. Fellow Fund Advancement Edn. Harvard, 1951-52; faculty-bus. exchange fellow Chase Nat. Bank, N.Y.C., summer 1952; fellow Merrill Center Econs., summer 1957; Fulbright research fellow Rome, 1958-59. Mem. Am. Econ. Assn., So. Econ. Assn., Assn. Christian Economists, Assn. Comparative Econs., Va. Assn. Economists (pres. 1979-80), Phi Beta Kappa, Phi Kappa Phi. Home: 1551 Dairy Rd Charlottesville VA 22903-1303

SNEAD, DAVID L., superintendent; b. Detroit, Oct. 15, 1943; s. Herman Jr. and Edythe (Burrell) S.; children by previous marriage: Deborah, David, Brandon; m. Sharon McPhail, May 1995. BS in Edn. and Kinesiology, Tuskegee Inst., 1968; MA in Urban Edn. and Kinesiology, U. Mich., 1970, PhD in Ednl. Adminstrn., 1984. Cert. tchr., Mich. Tchr., coach Detroit Pub. Schs., 1968-74; dept. chair health, athletics and phys. edn. Ctrl. H.S., Detroit, 1974-85, supr. health, tchr. phys. edn., 1985; asst. prin. Osborn H.S., Detroit, 1985-87; prin. Redford H.S., Detroit, 1987-89, Cass Tech. H.S., Detroit, 1989-93; asst. supt. for parent and adult edn. Detroit Bd. Edn., 1993, gen. supt., 1993—. Contbr. articles to profl. jours. Vol. ARC, 1970—; mem. youth adv. bd. St. Matthews-St. Joseph Episc. Ch. With AUS, 1961-64. Mem. U. Mich. Accreditation Adv. Com., Oreg. Sch. Adminstrs. and Suprs., Contract Negotiating Team. Office: 5057 Woodward Ave Detroit MI 48202-4050

SNEAD, ELEANOR LEROY MARKS, secondary school educator; b. Florence, S.C., Oct. 21, 1943; d. Franklin Leroy and Hazel Eleanor (Wallace) Marks; m. Samuel Everette Snead, Aug. 14, 1965; children: Robin Lynne, Ashley Eleanor. BA, Meredith Coll., 1965; MA, U. N.C., Greensboro, 1985. Cert. secondary bus. and marketing tchr., N.C. Tchr. Selma (N.C.) High Sch., 1965, Laurinburg (N.C.) High Sch. (now Scotland High Sch.), 1965-76, 84—, Hoke County High Sch., Raeford, N.C., 1980-84; curriculum writer N.C. Dept. Pub. Instrn., Raleigh, 1985, 90; presenter workshops Mktg. Edn. divsn. Vocat. Edn., N.C. Dept. Pub. Instrn. Recipient N.C. DECA Profl. Divsn. award, 1997; named Scotland County Outstanding Young Educator. Mem. NEA, N.C. Assn. Educators, Mktg. Educator's Assn., N.C. Mktg. Educator's Assn. (treas. 1991—, Solid Gold Tchr. 1989, Gold Link Tchr. 1990, Outstanding Mem. of N.C. 1994), Am. Vocat. Assn., N.C. Vocat. Assn., Scotland County Area C. of C., Delta Kappa Gamma (treas. Delta Omicron chpt.), Delta Pi Epsilon. Methodist. Avocations: flower and shrub gardening, needlework, sewing. Office: Scotland High Sch 1000 W Church St Laurinburg NC 28352-3565

SNEAD, GEORGE MURRELL, JR., army officer, scientist, consultant; b. San Diego, Nov. 6, 1922; s. George Murrell and Helen (Olsen) S.; m. Kathleen Hill Dawson, Apr. 26, 1947; children: George Murrell III, James M., William M., John P., Edward W. B.S., Va. Mil. Inst., 1943; M.S., U. Ill., 1948; Ph.D., U. Va., 1953. Commd. 2d lt. U.S. Army, 1943, advanced through grades to brig. gen., 1969; with Central Germany campaign 805th Signal Co., Europe, 1945-46; Aleutian sector comdr. Alaska Communication System, 1948-50; sta. at Electronic Warfare Center Ft. Monmouth, N.J. and Ft. Huachuca, Ariz., 1953-56; student U.S. Army Command and Gen. Staff Coll., 1956-57; signal adviser MAAG Vietnam, 1957-58; signal officer Dept. Army, 1958-60; acting dir. research ballistic missile def. Advanced Research Projects Agy., 1960; with U.S. Army Satellite Communications Agy. Ft. Monmouth, 1960-63; student Nat. War Coll., 1963-64, div. signal officer 24th Inf. Div., 1964-65, comdg. officer 7th Signal Group, 1965; dir. Communication /ADP Lab. Ft. Monmouth, 1966-68; exec. asst. chief of staff Communications Electronics, Dept. Army, 1968; dir. army research Dept. Army Washington, 1968-71; dep. comdr. Army Strategic Communications Command, 1971-73; prin. scientist Gen. Research Corp. McLean, Va., 1973-82; pres. Nat. Sci. Ctr. Found., Burke, Va., 1982-84; chmn. bd. Am. Fed. Savs. & Loan Assn., Lynchburg, Va., 1985-86; sci./bus. cons., 1986—. Active Boy Scouts Am., 1958-68; bd. dirs. Ctrl. Youth Summer Activities, Ft. Monmouth, 1960-63, Arthritis Found., Washington, 1981-84, Lynchburg Symphony, 1990-95; pres. Acad. Music Theatre, Lynchburg, 1985-95; trustee Sci. Mus. Va., 1995—; elder Presbyn. Ch., 1986—. Decorated D.S.M., Legion of Merit with oak leaf cluster, Bronze Star, Air medal, Army Commendation medal with 4 oak leaf clusters. Mem. Assn. U.S. Army, Armed Forces Communications and Electronics Assn. (sec. Washington chpt. 1968-69), Sigma Xi, Kappa Alpha. Home: 957 Rothowood Rd Lynchburg VA 24503-1113 Office: PO Box 3306 Lynchburg VA 24503-0306

SNEAD, JAMES ARRINGTON, architect; b. Richmond, Va., June 24, 1950; s. John Elwood and Anna Ruth (Reiche) S. BA, U. N.C., 1972; MArch, Va. Tech. U., 1978. Designer Hord Coplan & Macht, Balt., 1978-80; assoc. CS&D Architects, Balt., 1980-84; v.p., pres. Ziger Hoopes & Snead, Balt., 1984-93; pres. Ziger/Snead Architects, Balt., 1994—. Trustee Gilman Sch., Balt., 1990—; mem. adv. bd. Md. Inst. Sch. Continuing Studies, Balt., 1991—. Mem. AIA. Democrat. Presbyterian. Avocations: golf, travel, sailing. Office: Ziger &Snead Architects 1006 Morton St Baltimore MD 21201-5411*

SNEAD, RICHARD THOMAS, restaurant company executive; b. Washington, Apr. 19, 1951; s. Walter Thomas and Ruth Claire (Reeves) S.; m. Marilyn Wolke; children: Richard Adam, Eric Thomas. BS in Engring., U. Tenn., 1973. Project mgr. First Fla. Bldg. Corp., Miami, 1974-78; constrn. mgr. Burger King Corp., San Francisco, 1978-79; nat. constrn. dir. Miami, 1979-81; dir. devel. Boston, 1981-84; regional v.p. Detroit, 1984-86; sr. v.p. devel. Miami, 1986-87, exec. v.p. devel., eastern div. mgr. (including responsibility for minority affairs), 1987-88; pres. Burger King Internat. Div., 1988-89; mng. dir. Burger King U.K., 1989-92, Lenscrafters div. of U.S. Shoe, U.K., 1992-93; sr. v.p. Lenscrafters U.S.A., Cin., 1993-94, pres. Sight & Save div. and new bus. devel. Internat. div., 1994-96; sr. v.p. ops. and retail devel. Casual Corner Group, Inc., Enfield, Conn., 1996-97; exec. v.p. internat. Friday's Hospitality Worldwide, Dallas, 1997—. Republican. Avocations: running, golf, snow skiing, motorcycling. Office: Friday's Hospitality Worldwide 7450 Lyndon B Johnson Fwy Dallas TX 75251-1413

SNEAD, SAMUEL JACKSON, former professional golfer; b. Hot Springs, Va., May 27, 1912; m. Audrey; children: Samuel Jackson, Terrance. Profl. golfer, from 1935. Author: How To Hit a Golf Ball, 1940, How To Play Golf, 1946, (with Al Stump) Education of a Golfer, 1962, The Driver, 1974, Golf Begins at Forty, 1978. Served with USNR, 1942-45. Recipient Vardon trophy Profl. Golfers' Assn., 1938, 49, 50, 55, Player of Year award, 1949, elected to Hall of Fame, 1963. Winner Profl. Golfers' Assn. Championship, 1942, 49, 51, Brit. Open, 1946, Masters Golf Tournament, 1949, 52, 54, Legends of Golf Championship, 1982. Office: care PGA of Am 100 Avenue Of Champions Palm Beach Gardens FL 33418*

SNEDAKER, CATHERINE RAUPAGH (KIT SNEDAKER), editor; b. Fargo, N.D., Apr. 2; d. Paul and Charity (Primmer) Raupagh; B.A., Duke U.; m. William Brooks; children—Eleanor, Peter William; m. 2d, Weldon Snedaker. Promotion mgr. sta. WINR-TV and WNBF-TV, Binghamton, N.Y.; TV editor, feature writer Binghamton Sun, 1960-68; mem. staff Los Angeles Herald Examiner, food editor, restaurant critic, 1978-80, food and travel editor; editor The Food Package. Author: The Great Convertibles; contbr. numerous articles on food and travel to nat. mags. and newspapers; guest editor Mademoiselle mag., 1942; contbg. writer Robb Report. Recipient 3 awards Los Angeles Press Club, VISTA award, 1979. Mem. Soc. Am. Travel Writers. Democrat. Home: 140 San Vicente Blvd Apt A Santa Monica CA 90402-1533

SNEDDEN, JAMES DOUGLAS, retired health service management consultant; b. Toronto, Ont., Can., Mar. 4, 1925; s. David Morrison and Sarah Hayton (Monteith) S.; m. Elizabeth Ann McCauley, Dec. 20, 1953. B.Comm., U. Toronto, 1948; C.A., Inst. Chartered Accts. Ont., 1951. With Hosp. for Sick Children, Toronto, 1952-86, asst. dir., 1961-67, adminstr., 1967-70, chief exec. officer, 1970-86; nat. dir. health and social service cons. Peat, Marwick & Ptnrs., 1986-87; pres. J. Douglas Snedden and Assocs., 1987-97; bd. dirs. Mallinckrodt Can., Cyberfluor Can. Hon. dir. Woodgreen Community Centre, Toronto, 1963-65, v.p., 1965-67, pres., 1967-69, hon. mem. bd. dirs., 1973—; past bd. dirs. Hosp. Coun. Met. Toronto; mem. Bd. Trade Met. Toronto, 1965—; bd. dirs. United Way Met. Toronto, 1986-89; bd. dirs. Wedgewood at Bonita Bay, Bonita Springs, 1990-94, pres., 1992-94. Served with RCAF, 1943-45. Decorated Can. Centennial medal. Fellow Can. Coll. Health Svc. Execs. (founding mem. 1970, bd. dirs. 1972-83, treas. 1978-81, chmn. 1981-82, past chmn. 1982-83), Inst. Chartered Accts. Ont. (life), Acad. of Medicine, Toronto; mem. Am. Coll. Healthcare Execs. Presbyterian. Clubs: University, Bd. of Trade. Home: 26550 Clarkston Dr Bonita Springs FL 34135

SNEDEKER, JOHN HAGGNER, university president; b. Plainfield, N.J., May 30, 1925; s. Alfred H. and Anna Marie (Ward) S.; m. Noreen I. Davey, Dec. 30, 1950; children—John D., Philip A., Patrick W. B.S. cum laude, N.Y. U., 1951, M.A., 1951; Ed.D., Ind. U., 1959. Dir. lab. human devel. U. Mont., 1952-56; cons. psychologist research Purdue U., 1955; assoc. prof., dir. bur. research Ball State U., 1956-61; prof. higher edn., research asso. Ind. U., 1958; prof., dean Western Wash. State U., Bellingham, 1961-62; pres. Western N.Mex. U., Silver City, 1962—; mem. exec. bd. Internat. Coun. Spl. Edn., 1952-56; Rocky Mountain regional rep. APA, 1953-56; mem. Gov. Wash. Com. Licensing Tchr. Edn., 1961, Wash. State Legislature Rsch. Tech. Com., 1961. Author or co-author rating scales, attitude and opinion measurement devices; contbr. jours. Bd. dirs. Nat. Sci. Fair; trustee N.Mex. Health Found. Served with U.S. Army, 1943-48. Fellow AAAS; mem. Midwest Psychol. Assn., Inter-Am. Soc. Psychology, Am. Ednl. Research Assn., Holland Soc. N.Y. Address: 2117 Pinon St Silver City NM 88061-7734

SNEED, ELLOUISE BRUCE, nursing educator; b. Monroe, La., June 21, 1945; d. Wesley Newton Bruce and Oza Celeste Parker; m. Gary Arnold, Aug. 10, 1978. RN, Mather Sch. Nursing, New Orleans, 1966; BS in Nursing, William Carey Coll., Hattiesburg, Miss., 1975; MS in Nursing, Med. Coll. Ga., Augusta, 1978; EdD, U. So. Miss., Hattiesburg, 1981. Instr. community-psychiat. nursing Charity Hosp. Sch. Nursing, New Orleans, 1975-77; family nurse cons. Drs. R. Gregory and G. Keller, Mandeville, La., 1978-83; assoc. prof. Sch. Nursing William Carey Coll., New Orleans, 1980-

88; employee well health and health fair cons. St. Tammany Parish Hosp., Covington, La., 1987-88; prof., Holder Coughlin Sanders chair nursing La. Coll., Pineville, 1988-95; retired, 1995; ednl. program cons., 1984-85; speaker-presenter for profl. orgns. and instns. throughout La. Contbg. author: Crisis Intervention Theory and Practice: A Clinical Handbook, 1980, Mosby's 1988, 92 Secured Assess Test: A Practice Test Exam for RN Licensure, 1988, 92. Active Am. Heart Assn. Named A Great One Hundred Nurse, New Orleans Dist. Nurses Assn., 1987. Mem. ANA (cert. cmty. nursing), ARC, Nat. League Nursing, La. Assn. Mental Health, La. Coun. Adminstrs. Nursing Edn., La. State Nurses Assn., Alexandria Dist. Nurses Assn., Sigma Theta Tau (officer). Home: 4703 Warwick Blvd Alexandria LA 71303-2610

SNEED, JOSEPH DONALD, philosophy educator, author; b. Durant, Okla., Sept. 23, 1938; s. Dabney Whitfield and Sallybelle (Atkinson) S. B.S., Rice U., 1960; M.S., U Ill., 1962; Ph.D., Stanford U., 1964. Prof. Stanford U., Palo Alto, Calif., 1966-73; policy analyst SRI Internat., Menlo Park, Calif., 1973-74; prof. U. Munich, 1974-75, U. Eindhoven, Holland, 1976-77, SUNY, Albany, 1977-79; prof. philosophy Colo. Sch. Mines, Golden, 1980—. Author: The Logical Structure of Mathematical Physics, 1971, (with W. Balzer and C. Moulines) An Architectonic for Science, 1987; editor: (with S. Waldhorn) Restructuring the Federal System, 1974. Mem. Am. Philos. Assn. Office: Colo Sch Mines Golden CO 80401

SNEED, JOSEPH TYREE, III, federal judge; b. Calvert, Tex., July 21, 1920; s. Harold Marvin and Cara (Weber) S.; m. Madelon Juergens, Mar. 15, 1944; children—Clara Hall, Cara Carleton, Joseph Tyree IV. B.B.A., Southwestern U., 1941; LL.B., U. Tex., Austin, 1947; S.J.D., Harvard, 1958. Bar: Tex. bar 1948. Instr. bus. law U. Tex., Austin, 1947; asst. prof. law U. Tex., 1947-51, asso. prof., 1951-54, prof., 1954-57, asst. dean, 1949-50; counsel Graves, Dougherty & Greenhill, Austin, 1954-56; prof. law Cornell U., 1957-62, Stanford Law Sch., 1962-71; dean Duke Law Sch., 1971-73; dep. atty. gen. U.S. justice dept., 1973; judge U.S. Ct. Appeals (9th cir.), San Francisco, 1973—, now sr. judge; Cons. estate and gift tax project Am. Law Inst., 1960-69. Author: The Configurations of Gross Income, 1967; Contbr. articles to profl. jours. Served with USAAF, 1942-46. Mem. ABA, State Bar Tex., Am. Law Inst., Order of Coif. Office: US Ct Appeals 121 Spear St San Francisco CA 94105-1558*

SNEED, MICHAEL (MICHELE), columnist; b. Mandan, N.D., Nov. 16, 1943; d. Richard Edward and June Marie (Ritchey) S.; m. William J. Griffin, Sept. 16, 1978; 1 child, Patrick. B.S., Wayne State U., 1965. Tchr. Barrington High Sch., Ill., 1965-66; legis. asst. Congressman Ray Clevenger, 1966-67; reporter City News Bur., Chgo., 1967-69; reporter Chgo. Tribune, 1969-86, columnist, 1981-86; pres. sec. Mayor Jane Byrne, Chgo., 1979; gossip columnist Chgo. Sun-Times, 1986—. Co-editor Chgo. Journalism Rev., 1971-72. Vice pres. No. Mich. U. chpt. Young Democrats, 1962. Roman Catholic. Club: Women's Athletic. Avocation: gardening. Office: Chgo Sun-Times Inc 401 N Wabash Ave Chicago IL 60611-5642*

SNEED, RAPHAEL CORCORAN, physiatrist, pediatrician; b. Selma, Ala., 1942. MD, U. Ala., 1968. Diplomate Am. Bd. Pediat., Am. Bd. Phys. Medicine and Rehab. Intern U. Ala. Hosp. Clinic, Birmingham, 1968-69, resident in pediat., 1969-71, resident in phys. medicine and rehab., 1981-83, fellow in phys. medicine and rehab., 1983-84; with Children's Rehab. Ctr. Miss. Med. Ctr., Jackson. Mem. Am. Acad. Pediat., Am. Acad. Phys. Medicine and Rehab. Office: U Miss Med Ctr Children's Rehab Ctr 2500 N State St Jackson MS 39216-4500

SNEED, RONALD ERNEST, engineering educator emeritus; b. Oxford, N.C., Nov. 23, 1936; s. Henry Ernest and Jewel Leigh (Hughes) S.; m. Shelba Jean Walters, June 8, 1958; children: Kathy Geneva Grosvenor, Jennie Leigh Berrier. BS in Agrl. Engring., N.C. State U., 1959, PhD in Biol. and Agrl. Engring., 1971. Registered profl. engr., N.C.; cert. irrigation designer. Sales trainee John Deere Co., 1959-60; ext. specialist N.C. State U., 1960-62, ext. instr., 1962-69, 70, ext. asst. prof., 1971-75, ext. assoc. prof., 1971-80, prof., 1980-92, prof. emeritus, 1993—; project engr. Agri-Waste Tech., Inc., 1993—, Irrigation Consulting and Engring., Inc., 1995; cons. Lexington (N.C.) Swine Breeders, 1973, 1st Colony Farms, Creswell, N.C., 1977-78, Greek Tobacco Co. Uruguay, 1973-84, Internat. Potato Ctr., Lima, Peru, 1981-85, Philip Morris Tobacco Co., Richmond, Va., 1992-94, Stowe's Nursery, Inc., Belmont, N.C., 1993-94, Floyd Harrell Farms, Inc., Conetoe, N.C., 1994, Gilliam & Mason, Inc., Harrellsville, N.C., 1994, Craven County Com. of 100, Ltd., 1995. Active Civitan, Raleigh, 1994—. Maj. Gen. retired, U.S. Army, 1960-95. Recipient Outstanding Paper award So. region Am. Soc. Horticultural Sci., 1986, 91; Ronald E. Sneed Irrigation Soc., Inc. scholarship established in his honor, 1991. Fellow Am. Soc. Agrl. Engrs. (ednl. aids competition Blue Ribbon 1963-64, 68, 78-79, 85, 89, 91-92, Gunlogson Countryside Engring. award 1992, Outstanding Paper award 1984), The Irrigation Assn. (life tech. mem., Man of Yr. 1981), N.C. Irrigation Soc., Inc. (Oustanding Contbn. to Irrigation award 1973, former tech. advisor), Soil and Water Conservation Soc., N.C. Land Improvement Contractors Assn. (former tech. advisor), Carolinas Irrigation Assn. (hon.), Res. Officers Assn. (life). Democrat. Baptist. Office: 3405 Malibu Dr Raleigh NC 27607-6505

SNEED, WILLIAM R., III, lawyer; b. Iowa City, 1949. BA cum laude, Yale U., 1972; JD, NYU, 1975. Bar: Pa. 1976. Mng. dir. A252 Digital Projects, Inc., Washington. Contbr. articles to profl. jours. Office: A252 Digital Projects Inc 1500 K St NW Ste 625 Washington DC 20005

SNEIRSON, MARILYN, lawyer; b. Yonkers, N.Y., July 23, 1946. BA, Brandeis U., 1968; JD, Rutgers U., 1981. Bar: N.J. 1981, N.Y. 1989, U.S. Ct. Appeals (3d cir.) 1988, U.S. Supreme Ct. 1989. Law clerk Hon. Sylvia Pressler Superior Ct. N.J. Appellate, Hackensack, N.J., 1981-82; assoc. Pitney, Hardin, Kipp & Szuch, Morristown, N.J., 1982-84, Cole, Schotz et als, Hackensack, 1984-89; ptnr. Beattie, Padovano, Montvale, N.J., 1989-94; ptnr., prin. Price, Sneirson, Shulman & Meese, Woodcliff Lake, N.J., 1994—; commentator Court TV. contbr. articles to profl. jours. Committeewoman Dem. County Com., Ridgewood, N.J., 1980—. Mem. N.J. Bar Assn., Justice Pashman Am. Inns Court (master), Bergen County Bar Assn. Avocation: art. Office: Price Sneirson Shulman & Meese 50 Tice Blvd Woodcliff Lk NJ 07675-7654

SNELL, BRUCE M., JR., state supreme court justice; b. Ida Grove, Iowa, Aug. 18, 1929; s. Bruce M. and Donna (Potter) S.; m. Anne Snell, Feb. 4, 1956; children: Rebecca, Brad. AB, Grinnell Coll., 1951; JD, U. Iowa, 1956. Bar: Iowa 1956, N.Y. 1958. Law clk. to presiding judge U.S. Dist. Ct. (no. dist.) Iowa, 1956-57; asst. atty. gen., 1961-65; judge Iowa Ct. Appeals, 1976-87; justice Iowa Supreme Ct., 1987—. Comments editor Iowa Law Rev. Mem. ABA, Iowa State Bar Assn., Am. Judicature Soc., Order of Coif. Methodist. Home: PO Box 192 Ida Grove IA 51445-0192 Office: Iowa Supreme Ct St Capitol Bldg Des Moines IA 50319

SNELL, ESMOND EMERSON, biochemist; b. Salt Lake City, Sept. 22, 1914; s. Heber Cyrus and Hedwig Emma (Ludwig) S.; m. Mary Caroline Terrill, Mar. 15, 1941; children: Esmond Emerson (dec.), Richard T., Allan G., Margaret Ann. B.A., Brigham Young U., 1935; M.A., U. Wis., 1936, Ph.D., 1938, D.Sc. (hon.), 1982. Rsch. assoc. chemistry U. Tex., 1939-41, asst. prof. chemistry, 1941-43, assoc. prof., 1943-45, prof. chemistry, 1951-56; assoc. prof. biochemistry U. Wis., 1945-47, prof., 1947-53, on leave 1951-53; prof. biochemistry U. Calif., 1956-76, chmn. dept., 1956-62; prof. microbiology and chemistry U. Tex., Austin, 1976-90, Ashbel Smith prof., 1981-90, prof. emeritus, 1990—, chmn. dept. microbiology, 1976-80; Guggenheim Meml. Found. fellow U. Cambridge, 1954-55, Max-Planck Institut für Zellchemie, München, 1962-63, U. Wash., Seattle, Rockefeller U., N.Y.C., Hebrew U., Jerusalem, 1969; Walker-Ames prof. biochemistry U. Wash., Seattle, spring 1953. Author numerous research articles in sci. jours.; Editor: Volume III Biochemical Preparations, 1963-64, Chemical and Biological Aspects of Pyridoxal Catalysis, 1963, Pyridoxal Catalysis, Enzymes and Model Systems, 1968; Mem. editorial bd. Jour. Am. Chem. Soc, 1948-58, Jour. Biol. Chemistry, 1949-59, Biochemistry, 1961-70, Biochem. and Biophys. Research Communication, 1970-85, Biofactors, 1988-91; editor: Ann. Rev. Biochemistry, 1969-83. Recipient U.S. Sr. Scientist award Alexander von Humboldt Found., 1977. Fellow AAAS, Am. Inst. Nutrition (Meade-Johnson B-Complex award 1946, Osborne-Mendel award 1951); mem. Nat. Acad. Scis., Am. Acad. Arts and Scis., Japanese Biochem. Soc. (hon.), Am. Chem. Soc. (chmn. div. biol. chemistry 1954, Kenneth A. Spencer award 1974, Nebr. Lectureship award 1983), Am. Soc. Biol. Chemists (pres. 1961-62, William Rose award 1985), Soc. Am. Bacteriologists (Eli Lilly award in bacteriology and immunology 1945), Am. Acad. Microbiology. Home: 5001 Greystone Dr Austin TX 78731-1118

SNELL, JACK EASTLAKE, federal agency administrator; b. Evanston, Ill., Nov. 29, 1935; s. Clarence Eastlake and Ruth (Meloy) S.; m. Elizabeth Kercher, Oct. 15, 1966; children: Jeffrey Eastlake, Julie Elizabeth. B.S.E. with honors in Aero. Engring, Princeton U., 1957; M.S. in Indsl. Engring, Northwestern U., 1965, Ph.D. in Civil Engring; Ph.D. (Walter P. Murphy scholar, Transp. Center fellow), 1966; grad., Fed. Exec. Inst., 1979. Aircraft maintenance engr. Pan Am. World Airways, N.Y.C., 1960; asst. prof. transp. engring., and dir. Transp. and Urban Systems Lab., Princeton U., 1966-71; chief bldg. service systems sect. Nat. Bur. Standards, Washington, 1971-73; asst. chief bldg. environ. div. Nat. Bur. Standards, 1973-74; chief Office Energy Conservation, 1974-76; dir. Office Energy Programs, 1976-81; dir. Ctr. Fire Research Nat. Engring. Lab., 1981-91, deputy dir. bldg. and fire rsch. lab., 1991—; mem. various fed. interagy. energy task forces, 1973-79; steering com. Intersoc. Energy Conversion Engring. Conf.; mem. Md. Gov.'s Sci. Adv. Council, 1976—; chmn. U.S.-Japan Panel on Fire Research and Safety. Contbr. articles to profl. jours. Served to 1st lt. USAF, 1953-60. Recipient Silver medal Dept. Commerce, 1975, Gold medal Dept. Commerce, 1987. Fellow ASME (chmn. advanced energy systems divsn. 1981), Nat. Fire Protection Assn. (bd. dirs. 1991-96, chmn. toxicity adv. com.). Presbyterian. Office: Natl Inst Standards & Technology Gaithersburg MD 20899

SNELL, JAMES LAURIE, mathematician, educator; b. Wheaton, Ill., Jan. 15, 1925; s. Roy Judson and Lucille (Ziegler) S.; m. Joan Perry, Dec. 30, 1952; children: John, Mary Paige. BA, U. Ill., 1947, MA, 1948, PhD, 1951. Instr. math. Princeton U., 1951-54; mem. faculty Dartmouth Coll., Hanover, N.H., 1954—, prof. math., 1962-95, prof. emeritus, 1995—. Author: (with J.G. Kemeny and G.L. Thompson) Introduction to Finite Mathematics, 1959, (with J.G. Kemeny) Finite Markov Chains, 1960, (with J.G. Kemeny and A.W. Knapp) Denumerable Markov Chains, 1966; Introduction to Probability, 1988. With USNR, 1944-46. Mem. Am. Math. Soc., Math. Soc. Am. Home: 34 E Wheelock St Hanover NH 03755-1514 Office: Dartmouth Coll Dept of Math Hanover NH 03755

SNELL, JOHN RAYMOND, civil engineer; b. Soochow, China, Dec. 9, 1912; (parents Am. citizens); s. John A. and Grace (Birkett) S.; m. Florence Moffett, Dec. 8, 1939; children: Dorothea Snell Fenska, Karen Snell Dailey, Martha E. Snell Rood, John Raymond, David Moffett. BE, Vanderbilt U., 1934; MS, U. Ill., 1936; DSc, Harvard U., 1939. Registered profl. engr., Mass., Mich., Ohio, Ill., Ind., La. Wis., N.Y., Tex. Fla., Idaho, Oreg., Ont., Can.; cert. san. engr.; diplomate Am. Acad. Environ. Engrs. Instr. civil engring. Hangchow U., 1934-35; with Water Supply Fed. Pub. Works Dept., Venezuela, 1939-40; design engr. Metcalf & Eddy, also Fay Spofford and Thorndyke, Stone & Webster, Boston, 1941-42; san. engr., head water and sewage sect. 1st Svc. Command, Boston, 1946; assigned UNRA restoration water, sewage, solid wastes 5 no. provinces China San. Engring. Services Inc., 1945-46; project engr. Burns & Kenerson, Boston, 1947; pres., chief engr. Engring. Svcs. Inc., Boston, 1948-51; lectr. MIT, 1949-51; prof., head dept. civil and san. engring. Mich. State U., 1951-55; owner John R. Snell & Assocs., 1956; sr. prin. Mich. Assocs., cons. engrs., 1956-60; pres. John R. Snell Engrs. Inc., 1960-75; pres. Snell Environ. Group, 1975-80, hon. chmn. bd., spl. cons., 1980-88; joint venturer Snell-Republic Assocs. Ltd., Lahore, West Pakistan, 1961-80; with Assoc. Architects & Engrs., Dacca, Bangladesh, 1965-80; pres. Caribbean Devel. Corp. and subs. Gen. Shrimp Ltd., Belize, 1984-92; sr. adj. scientist Mich. Biotech. Inst., 1990—; 1994 guest of China-Suzhou Hosp. 110 Aniv.; solid waste cons. Xiaogan Recycling Treatment Utilization of Organics, Peoples Republic of China, 1995; founder Trans Mich. Waterway Inc., S.W. Waterway (Ont.) Ltd., N.Y.; spl. cons. on ast high rate compost plant to Govt. of Japan, 1955-56; cons. in Orient, WHO, 1956; chmn. bd. Bootstrap Internat. Inc., 1972; expert witness on over 50 ct. cases. Author 12 sects. Environment Engineering Handbook; coauthor: Municipal Solid Waste Disposal; contbr. articles to profl. jours.; patentee in composting field. Maj. USPHS, 1945-47. Recipient Prescott Eddy award, 1944. Mem. Nat., Mich. (life) socs. profl. engrs., Am. Water Works Assn., Hwy. Rsch. Bd., ASTM, ASCE, Am. Pub. Works Assn., Water Pollution Control Fedn. (life), Mich. Engring. Soc. (life), Cons. Engrs. Coun. (past dir.), Cons. Engrs. Assn. Mich. (past pres.), Inter-Am. Assn. San. Engrs., World Aquaculture Soc., Composters Inc. (pres. Worldwide Techs. Inc. East Lansing 1980—), Rotary, Tau Beta Pi, Chi Epsilon. Home and Office: 918 Rosewood Ave East Lansing MI 48823-3127

SNELL, NED COLWELL, financial planner; b. Cowley, Wyo., May 16, 1944; s. Jay Hatton and Freda Hope (Colwell) S.; m. Barbara Anne Frandsen, Apr. 24, 1969; children: Taylor Anthony, Trevor Cameron. BA, U. Utah, 1969; CLU, Am. Coll., 1983, ChFC, 1985. English tchr. Granite Sch. Dist., Salt Lake City, 1969-71; ins. agt. Prudential Ins. Co., Salt Lake City, 1971-76; pres. Snell Fin. Corp., Salt Lake City, 1976—. Bd. dirs. Utah chpt. Arthritis Found., Salt Lake City, 1980-82, pres. 1982-83; missionary Mormon Ch. 1963-66; chmn. voting dist. 2604 Rep. Nominating Convs., 1986, 90. Recipient Golden Key Soc. Devel. award, 1990. Mem. NALU (Nat. Sales Achievement award 1971-89, Nat. Quality award), Am. Soc. CLU and ChFC (bd. dirs. Utah chpt. 1990-93, treas. 1993-94, v.p. 1994-96, pres. 1996-97), Million Dollar Round Table (knight 1988—), Salt Lake Assn. Life Underwriters (bd. dirs. 1974-76, 80-82). Republican. Avocations: creative writing, fly tying, fishing, basketball, tennis. Home: 1101 S 2000 E Salt Lake City UT 84108-1971 Office: 1800 S West Temple Ste 416 Salt Lake City UT 84115-1851

SNELL, PATRICIA POLDERVAART, librarian, consultant; b. Santa Fe, Apr. 11, 1943; d. Arie and Edna Beryl (Kerchmar) Poldervaart; m. Charles Eliot Snell, June 7, 1966. BA in Edn., U. N.M., 1965; MSLS, U. So. Calif., 1966. Asst. edn. libr. U. So. Calif., L.A., 1966-68; med. libr. Bedford (Mass.) VA Hosp., 1968-69; asst. law libr. U. Miami, Coral Gables, Fla., 1970-71; acquistions libr. U. N.Mex. Law Sch. Libr., Albuquerque, 1971-72; order libr. Los Angeles County Law Libr., 1972-76, cataloger, 1976-90; libr. Parks Coll., Albuquerque, 1990-92; records technician Technadyne Engring. Cons. to Sandia Nat. Labs., 1992-93; libr. Tireman Learning Materials Ctr. U. N.Mex., Albuquerque, 1993-96, instr. libr. sci. program Coll. Edn., 1991—; rsch. technician City of Albuquerque, 1996—. Ch. libr.. Beverly Hills Presbyn. Ch., 1974-90, ch. choir libr., 1976-90. Southwestern Library Assn. scholar 1965. Mem. ALA, N.Mex. Libr. Assn., Pi Lambda Theta. Avocations: travel, reading. Office: U N Mex Coll Edn EM/LS Program Ed Admin B 29 Albuquerque NM 87131

SNELL, RICHARD, holding company executive; b. Phoenix, Nov. 26, 1930; s. Frank L. and Elizabeth (Berlin) S.; m. Alice Cosette Wiley, Aug. 1, 1954. BA, Stanford U., 1952, JD, 1954. Bar: Ariz. Ptnr. firm Snell & Wilmer, Phoenix, 1956-81; pres., chmn., chief exec. officer Ramada Inc., Phoenix, 1981-89; chmn., chief exec. officer Aztar Corp., 1989-90, chmn., bd. dirs., 1990-92; chmn., chief exec. officer, pres. Pinnacle West Capital Corp., Phoenix, 1990—, bd. dirs.; bd.. dirs. Bank One Ariz. Corp., Bank One Ariz. NA, Aztar Corp.; bd. dirs., chmn. Ariz. Pub. Svc. Co. Trustee Am. Grad. Sch. Internat. Mgmt., Phoenix; past pres. YMCA Met. Phoenix and Valley of Sun. With U.S. Army, 1954-56. Mem. ABA, Ariz. Bar Assn., Paradise Valley Country Club, Phoenix Country Club. Republican. Lutheran. Office: Pinnacle West Capital Corp 400 E Van Buren St Phoenix AZ 85004 also: Arizona Public Service Co PO Box 53999 # 9960 Phoenix AZ 85072-3999*

SNELL, RICHARD SAXON, anatomist; b. Richmond, Surrey, Eng., May 3, 1925; came to U.S., 1963; s. Claude Saxon and Daisy Lilian S.; m. Maureen Cashin, June 4, 1949; children: Georgina Sara, Nicola Ann, Melanie Jane, Richard Robin, Charles Edward. MB, BS, Kings Coll., U. London, 1949, PhD, 1955, MD, 1961. House surgeon Sir Cecil P.G. Wakeley, Kings Coll. Hosp. and Belgrave Hosp. for Children, London, 1948-49; lectr. anatomy Kings Coll., U. London, 1949-59, U. Durham, Eng., 1959-63; asst. prof. anatomy and medicine Yale U., 1963-65, assoc. prof., 1965-67, vis. prof. anatomy, 1969; prof., chmn. dept. anatomy N.J. Coll. Medicine and Dentistry, Jersey City, 1967-69; vis. prof. anatomy Harvard U., 1970, 71, 80, 86; prof. anatomy Coll. Medicine, U. Ariz., Tucson, 1970; prof., chmn. dept. anatomy George Washington U. Med. Ctr., Washington, 1972-88, prof. emeritus, 1988—. Author: Clinical Embryology for Medical Students, 1972, 3d edit., 1983, Clinical Anatomy for Medical Students, 1973, 5th edit., 1995, Atlas of Normal Radiographic Anatomy, 1976, Atlas of Clinical Anatomy, 1978, Gross Anatomy Dissector, 1978, Clinical Neuroanatomy for Medical Students, 1980, 4th edit., 1997, Student's Aid to Gross Anatomy, 1986, Clinical Anatomy for Anesthesiologists, 1988, Clinical Anatomy of the Eye, 1989, 2d edit., 1997, Gross Anatomy: A Review with Questions and Explanations, 1990, Neuroanatomy: A Review with questions and Explanations, 1992, Clinical Anatomy for Emergency Medicine, 1993, Clinical Anatomy: An Illustrated Review with Questions and Explanations, 2d edit., 1996, Clinical Neuroanatomy: An Illustrated Review with Questions and Explanations, 2d edit., 1997; contbr. articles to med. jours. Med. Research Council grantee, 1959; NIH grantee, 1963-65. Mem. Anat. Soc. Gt. Britain, Am. Soc. Anatomists, Alpha Omega Alpha. Home: 518 Boston Post Rd Madison CT 06443-2930

SNELL, ROBERT, retail executive; b. 1949. CEO United Supermarkets, Lubbock, Tex., 1970—. Office: PO Box 6840 Lubbock TX 79493-6840*

SNELLING, GEORGE ARTHUR, banker; b. St. Petersburg, Fla., June 27, 1929; s. William Henry and Eula Hall S.; m. Carolyn Shiver, Mar. 3, 1963; children—George, John S. B.S.B.A., U. Fla., 1951. Partner Smoak, Davis, Nixon & Snelling, C.P.A.s, Jacksonville, Orlando, Fla., 1956-66; v.p. planning Barnett Banks of Fla., Jacksonville, 1966-76; exec. v.p. 1st Bancshares of Fla., Boca Raton, 1976-78; exec. v.p. Fla. Nat. Banks of Fla., Jacksonville, 1978-80; exec. v.p. corp. devel., chief fin. officer Sun Banks of Fla., Orlando, 1981-85; exec. v.p. corp. devel. SunTrust Banks, Inc., Atlanta, 1986-90; pres. Unicoy, Inc., Atlanta, 1991—. Trustee Fla. So. U. Served with USAF, 1951-55. Mem. AICPA. Democrat. Methodist. Home: 2682 Varner Dr NE Atlanta GA 30345-1559 Office: Unicoy Inc PO Box 996 Burnsville NC 28714-0996

SNELLING, NORMA JUNE, retired music educator, English educator; b. Brooten, Minn., June 1, 1928; d. Harold Melvin and Mabel Olga (Markuson) Hellickson; m. Douglas Howard Snelling, June 27, 1953; children: Julie Marie, Mary Merced, Steven Douglas. BA, Concordia Coll., Moorhead, Minn., 1949. Cert. tchr., Minn. Tchr. Wolverton (Minn.) Sch. Dist., 1949-51, Kimball (Minn.) Sch. Dist., 1951-52, Benson (Minn.) Sch. Dist., 1952-53, Belgrade (Minn.) Sch. Dist., 1953-57, Hutchinson (Minn.) Sch. Dist., 1964-66, Litchfield (Minn.) Sch. Dist., 1966-92; mem. staff edn. liaison 2d Congl. Dist. Minn., Litchfield, 1992—. Assoc. chairperson county level, del. Dem. Farmer Labor Party, Minn., 1992—, chair 1994; del. to Dem. Nat. Conv., 1984; co-chairperson Concert Series, Litchfield, 1962, Cancer Dr., Litchfield, 1960; dir. Choralaires, Eden Valley, Minn., 1976—; dir. music Zion Luth. Ch., Litchfield, 1962-85, poet ch. pubs., dedications, etc., also Big Grove Luth. Ch.; speech coach Litchfield Jr. H.S., 1972-77; mem. VFW Aux., Am. Legion Aux. 94m. NEA (life, congl. contact person 1985-90), Minn. Edn. Assn. (govtl. rels. uniserve chairperson, Leadership award medal 1986), Ret. Educators Minn. (legis. chairperson 1993—), Internat. Platform, Sons of Norway (musician, pres. Vannland Lodge 1993-94, Bronze medal 1993-94), Gen. Fedn. Women's Study Clubs, Halling Laget, Delta Kappa Gamma. Avocations: reading, bowling, flower arranging, painting, golf. Home: 621 W Crescent Ln Litchfield MN 55355-1830

SNELLING, ROBERT ORREN, SR., franchising and employment executive; b. Phila., Aug. 16, 1932; s. Louis Raymond and Gwendolyn Anne (Preble) S.; m. Joan E., 1951 (dec. 1979); children—Robert, Krista; m. Anne Morris, June 30, 1979; children—Rick Spragins, Leigh Crews, Linda Paulk. Student, Pa. State U., 1951-52; Dr. Lit. (hon.), Albright Coll., 1968. Profl. employment counsellor, Snelling & Snelling, Phila., 1952-53, gen. mgr., 1954-67, pres., 1962-68, chmn. bd., 1969—; speaker, lectr. in field. Author: The Opportunity Explosion, 1969, Jobs-What They Are-Where They Are-What They Pay, 1985, rev. edit., 1992, The Right Job, 1987, rev. edit., 1992; contbr. articles to profl. jours. Mem. long-range planning Sarasota 2000, 1976; mem. pvt. sector employment svcs. com. Dept. Labor, 1982; mem. Com. on Skilled Employment Brokering Svcs., 1984; mem. White Ho. Com. on Small Bus., 1986; mem. adv. com to U.S. Sec. William Brock, 1986; mem. Gov.'s Select Com. on Workforce 2000, 1988-89, chmn. govtl. regulations and benefits subcom., 1989; apptd. to Nat. Commn. for Employment Policy, 1994—. With U.S. Army, 1953-54. Recipient Golden Plate award, 1964; W.O. Blanchet award Pa. Assn. Personnel Service, 1976; Outstanding Citizen award Assn. Personnel N.Y., 1977; award for excellence Am. Acad. Achievement, 1964; Harold B. Nelson award, 1985. Mem. Internat. Franchise Assn., Nat. Assn. Personnel Cons., Nat. Assn. Temp. Svcs., U.S. C. of C. Republican. Avocations: reading, photography.

SNELSON, KENNETH DUANE, sculptor; b. Pendleton, Oreg., June 29, 1927; s. John Tavner and Mildred F. (Unger) S.; m. Katherine Eve Kaufmann, May 2, 1972; 1 child, Andrea Nicole. Numerous. Student, U. Oreg., 1946-47, Black Mountain Coll., 1948-49, Chgo. Inst. Design, 1950-51, Academie Montmartre, Paris, 1951-52; D of Arts and Humane Letters (honoris causa), Rensselaer Poly. Inst., 1985. Subject of articles in art publs.; one-man shows U.S. and Germany, Holland, including Portrait of an Atom, Balt., 1979-80, De Cordova and Dana Mus. and Park, Lincoln, Mass., 1984, Zabriskie Gallery, 1984, Yoh Art Gallery, Osaka, Japan, 1991, Contemporary Sculpture Ctr., Tokyo, 1995, Maxwell Davidson Gallery, N.Y.C., 1994; major retrospective, Hirshhorn Mus. and Sculpture Garden of Smithsonian Instn., 1981, Albright-Knox Art Gallery, Buffalo, 1981, N.Y. Acad. Scis., 1989; group shows include Mus. Modern Art, N.Y.C., 1967, Whitney Mus., N.Y.C., 1966, 69, 70, Albright Knox Gallery, 1968, Prospect '68, Dusseldorf, Germany, 1968, Salon International de Galeries Pilotes, Lausanne, Switzerland, 1970, Sammlun Etzold, Kolnischer Kunstverein, Cologne, Germany, 1970, Expo '70, Osaka, Japan, 1970, Fondation Maeght, St. Paul de Vence, France, 1970, Art Inst. Chgo., 1972; represented in permanent collections including, Mus. Modern Art, Whitney Mus. Am. Art, cities of Hannover and Hamburg, Germany, Rijksmuseum Kroller Muller, Otterlo, Holland, Rijksmuseum, Amsterdam, Holland, Japan Iron, Steel Fedn., Osaka, City of Balt., Hirshhorn Mus., Milw. Art Center, City of Buffalo, Mus. Modern Art, Shiga, Japan; author: Full Circle: Panoramas of Paris, Venice, Rome, Siena and Kyoto, 1990. Served with USNR, 1945-46. DAAD fellow Berlin Kunstlerprogram, 1976; recipient AIA Artist's medal, 1981, Art award Am. Inst. Arts and Letters, 1987, Prix Ars Electronica Siemens AG for Computer Graphics, Linz, Austria, 1989. Mem. Am. Acad. Arts and Letters. Patentee discontinuous compression structures, model for atomic forms. *My art is concerned with nature in its most fundamental aspect, the patterns of physical forces in space.*

SNETSINGER, DAVID CLARENCE, retired animal feed company executive; b. Barrington, Ill., Apr. 22, 1930; s. Clarence J. and Helen (Mills) S.; m. Phoebe Burnett; children: Penny, Tom, Carol, Susan. BS, U. Ill., 1952, MS, 1957, PhD, 1959. Registered profl. animal scientist. Asst. prof. U. Minn., 1959-62, assoc. prof., 1962-67; poultry area mgr. Purina Mills Inc., St. Louis, 1967-69, dir. poultry group, 1970-87, v.p. rsch., 1987-91; ret., 1991. Patentee in field of poultry feeding programs and equipment; author 116 sci. and popular trade articles on poultry nutrition. 1st lt. U.S. Army, 1952-54. Fellow Poultry Sci. Assn. (pres. 1988-89); mem. World's Poultry Sci. (v.p. 1989-92), Fedn. Food Animal Scis. (sec.-treas. 1989-92), Animal Sci. Assn., Am. Inst. Nutrition, Dairy Sci. Assn., Internat. Brotherhood Magicians (pres. 1982-83, 93-94), Soc. Am. Magicians (v.p. St. Louis chpt. 1980-81), Sigma Xi.

SNIBBE, RICHARD W., architect; b. Balt., Oct. 31, 1916; s. George W. and Mildred (Robinson) S.; m. Miriam Bergman, Jan. 3, 1942 (dec.); children: John Robinson, Paul Clor; m. Patricia Lois Miscall, Sept. 8, 1962. B.A., St. Johns Coll., 1939; postgrad., Harvard Grad. Sch. Design, 1939-41. Registered profl. architect, lic. architect N.Y. Asso. Edward D. Stone (architect), N.Y.C., 1951-56; partner Ballard, Todd & Snibbe, N.Y.C., 1957-61; individual practice architecture N.Y.C., 1962; partner Myller, Snibbe, Tafel, N.Y.C., 1962-67, Snibbe, Tafel, Lindholm, 1967-73, Wilson & Snibbe (architects, planners, engrs.), N.Y.C., from 1970; formed Snibbes Inc. (producers archtl. films), 1981; instr. Cooper Union, N.Y.C., 1949; vis. critic Columbia, N.Y.C., 1956, Pratt Inst., N.Y.C., 1962; founder Archtl. Film Library, 1982. Author: Small Commercial Buildings, 1956, Snibbe, Selected Works and Essays, 1983; important works include U.S. embassy, New Delhi,

India (as assoc.), 1955, Tennis Pavilion, Princeton, 1960 (AIA honor award 1962), grad. dormitories Princeton U., 1961, comprehensive campus plan and bldgs. State U. Coll, Geneseo, N.Y., 1962-72, Handloser Project, Future Town, 1973, entry to Paris Opera Competition, 1983; pub. L'Arca, 1990; exhibited in Mus. Modern Art, N.Y.C., Transformations in Modern Architecture, 1979; producer: (film) Maison La Roche-Jeanneret by Le Corbusier, 1983, (TV film) Great Modern Architecture of the Last 25 Years, 1994. Chmn. aesthetics com., bd. dirs. Gramercy Neighborhood Assn. Inc.; founder Archs. Com. N.Y., 1992, Bill Clinton for Pres., 1992. Brunner scholar N.Y. chpt. AIA, 1957. Fellow AIA (founder, chmn. nat. com. on aesthetics 1963, mem. emeritus 1990—); mem. Harvard Grad. Sch. Design Assn., Am. Arbitration Assn., Players Club. Patentee for suspended structure, Landspan. Address: 139 E 18th St New York NY 10003-2470

SNIDER, BARRY B., organic chemist; b. Chgo., Jan. 13, 1950; s. Gordon L. and Ruth C. (Tobias) S.; m. Katalin Boros, July 12, 1975; 1 child, Emily L. BS in Chemistry, U. Mich., 1970; PhD, Harvard U., 1973. Postdoctoral fellow Columbia U., N.Y.C., 1973-75; asst. prof. Princeton (N.J.) U., 1975-81; assoc. prof. Brandeis U., Waltham, Mass., 1981-85, prof., 1985—, chmn. dept. chemistry, 1992-95. Recipient scholar award Dreyfus Found., 1982; Sloan Found. fellow, 1979. Mem. Am. Chem. Soc. (Arthur C. Cope scholar 1995), Royal Soc. Chemistry. Office: Brandeis U Dept Chemistry Waltham MA 02254

SNIDER, EDWARD MALCOLM, professional hockey club executive; b. Washington, Jan. 6, 1933; s. Sol C. and Lillian (Bonas) S.; m. Martha McGeary, March 4, 1984; children: Craig Alan, Jay Thomas, Lindy Lou, Tina Suzanne, Sarena Lynn, Samuel Everett. B.S., U. Md., 1955. CPA, Md. Maj. stockholder, exec. v.p. Edge Ltd., Washington, 1957-63; v.p. Phila. Eagles Football Club, 1964-67; owner Phila. Flyers Hockey Club, 1967—; chmn. bd. Spectrum Arena, Phila., 1967—; bd. govs. NHL, 1967—; established spectator, sports, entertainment and comm. firm adv. bd. Sol C. Snider Entrepreneurial Ctr. U Pa.; bd. overseers Wharton Sch. U. Pa.; bd. dirs. Inst. for Cancer and Blood Diseases Hahnemann U., Simon Weisenthal Ctr.; bd. trustees Inst. for Objectivist Studies. Office: Phila Flyers CoreStates Ctr 3601 N Broad St Philadelphia PA 19140-4107*

SNIDER, EDWIN D., retired baseball player; b. L.A., Sept. 19, 1926. Baseball player Bklyn. Dodgers, 1947-57, N.Y. Mets, 1963, San Francisco Giants, 1964; scout L.A. Dodgers, 1965, 67-68; minor league mgr., 1965-68; batting instr., broadcaster San Diego Padres, 1969-71; broadcaster Montreal Expos, 1973. Named to Baseball Hall of Fame, 1980; selected to All-Star Team, 1950, 52-56, 63; mem. World Series Champions, 1954. Office: c/o Nat Baseball Hall Fame PO Box 590 Cooperstown NY 13326-0590

SNIDER, ELIOT I., lumber company executive; b. Cambridge, Mass., Apr. 10, 1921; s. Harry and Lena (Korelitz) S.; m. Ruth Freund, 1945; children: Andrew, Paul, Nancy. BA, Harvard U., 1941, MBA, 1943. Pres. Mass. Lumber Co., Cambridge, 1953-95; chmn., dir. George McQuesten Co., Inc., Eastern Terminals, Inc.; dir. Kravis Ctr.; dir. corps. Chmn. Beth Israel Hosp., Boston, 1982-86, trustee 1976—; overseer Mus. Fine Arts; mem. dean's coun. Harvard U. Sch. Pub. Health. Pres. Snider Charitable Trust; co-chair bd. overseers Beth Israel Deaconess Med. Ctr., 1996—; dir. Cmty. Found. for Palm Beach and Martin Counties, 1996—. Served to lt. USN, 1943-45. Mem. Chief Execs. Orgn., World Bus. Coun. Republican. Clubs: Longwood, Harvard, N.Y. Yacht, Rotary. Office: Mass Lumber Co 929 Massachusetts Ave Cambridge MA 02139-3143

SNIDER, GORDON B., retired medical educator; b. Columbus, Ohio, Dec. 19, 1928; s. James M. and Rose G. (Joyce) S.; m. Mary Louise Graham, July 19, 1952; children: Mary Katherine, Cynthia L., John M., James G., Martha R. BA in Bacteriology, Ohio State U., 1950, MD, 1954. Diplomate Am. Bd. Internal Medicine. Intern Mt. Carmel Hosp., Columbus, 1954-55, resident, 1955-57; Henry Ford Hosp., Detroit, 1957-58; pvt. practice Lancaster, Ohio, 1960-94; dir. med. edn. Fairfield Med. Ctr., Lancaster, 1994-97; clin. assoc. prof. medicine Ohio State U. Coll. Med., Columbus, 1981—; bd. dirs. Fairfield Med. Ctr., Lancaster, 1990-96. Founder, dir. paramedic program Lancaster fire Dept., 1985. Capt., M.C., U.S. Army, 1958-60. Fellow ACP, Lancaster Rotary (past pres.); mem. Fairfield Med. Soc. (past pres.), Ohio State Med. Assn., Ohio Soc. Internal Medicine (past pres.). Roman Catholic. Avocation: golf. Office: Fairfield Med Ctr 401 N Ewing St Lancaster OH 43130-3372

SNIDER, GORDON LLOYD, physician; b. Toronto, Apr. 11, 1922; came to U.S., 1946, naturalized, 1956; s. Isadore Leonard and Rebecca (Freeman) S.; m. Ruth Charlotte Tobias, May 18, 1945; children: Barry Bernard, Martin David, Rebecca Eve. MD, U. Toronto, 1944. Intern Toronto Gen. Hosp., 1944-45; resident in medicine Bronx Hosp., N.Y.C., 1946-47; resident in pathology Mass. Meml. Hosps., Boston, 1947-48; fellow in medicine Lahey Clinic, Boston, 1948-49; fellow in pulmonary medicine Trudeau San., Trudeau, N.Y., 1949-50; asst. dir. chest dept. Michael Reese Hosp., Chgo., 1950-61; attending physician Winfield (Ill.) Hosp., 1950-61; cons. physician, dir. pulmonary function lab. Mcpl. Tb San., Chgo., 1954-68; chief div. thoracic medicine Mt. Sinai Hosp., Chgo., 1961-66; acting chmn. depts. medicine Chgo. Med. Sch. and Mt. Sinai Hosp., 1965-66; chief pulmonary disease sect. Wood VA Hosp.; attending physician Milwaukee County Gen. Hosp., Wood, Wis., 1966-68; asst. prof. Chgo. Med. Sch., 1958-61, assoc. prof., 1961-64, prof., 1964-66; prof. Marquette U. Sch. Medicine, 1966-68; prof. medicine, head pulmonary medicine sect. Boston U. Sch. Medicine, 1968-87; chief pulmonary medicine sect., Boston VA Med. Ctr., 1968-88, chief med. svc., 1986—; pulmonary sect. mem. Evans Dept. Clin. Rsch., Univ. Hosp., Boston, 1968—; Maurice B. Strauss prof. medicine, Boston U. and Tufts U. Schs. Medicine, 1986-93, Boston U. Sch. Medicine, 1993—; Presdl. lectr. Soc. European Pulmonologists, 4th Ann. Congress, Stressa-Milan, Italy, 1986, Blankenhorn lectr. Cin. Soc. Ind. Medicine, 1989; Parker B. Francis lectr. 6th Thomas L. Petty Aspen Lung Conf., 1991, Theodore Badger Meml. lectr. Mass. Thoracic Soc., 1995; vis. prof. U. Cin. Sch. Medicine, 1989; Frank T. Fulton vis. physician-in-chief pro tempore R.I. Hosp. and Brown U., Providence, 1988; med. adv. bd. Puritan-Bennett Corp.; chmn. sci. adv. com. Norman B. Salvesen Emphysema Trust, U. Edinburgh, 1981-93; Theodore Badger Meml. lecture Mass. Thoracic Soc., 1995, Irving Kass lectr. U. Nebr., 1992. Served to capt. M.C. Royal Can. Army, 1945-46. Co-recipient Alton Ochsner award relating smoking and health, 1990; NIH grantee, 1962-91; Francis S. North travel fellow, 1978; 6th Robert K. Match Disting. scholar L.I. Jewish Hosp., 1991. Fellow Am. Coll. Chest Physicians (Simon Rodbard lectr. 1985), ACP; mem. Am. Fedn. Clin. Research, Am. Thoracic Soc. (pres. 1986, Amberson lectr. 1992), Central Soc. Clin. Research, Sigma Xi, Alpha Omega Alpha. Jewish. Home: 24 Holly Rd Newton MA 02168-1449 Office: VA Med Center 150 S Huntington Ave Jamaica Plain MA 02130-4817

SNIDER, HARLAN TANNER, former manufacturing company executive; b. Owensboro, Ky., July 20, 1926; s. George William and Lydia (Tanner) S.; m. Helen Boswell, Mar. 7, 1953; children—William Jeffrey, Katherine Snider. B.A., Transylvania U., 1949. Territory salesman Sunray DX Corp., Owensboro, 1950-57; dist. sales mgr. Sunray DX Corp., Ind., 1958-63; div. mgr. Sunray DX Corp., Iowa, 1963-65; dir. mktg. services Sunray DX Corp., Tulsa, 1955-67; pres. Red Bar Chems., Tulsa, 1967-69; dir. petrochems. Sun Oil Co., Phila., 1969-71; v.p. mktg. Sun Oil Co., 1973-75; pres. Sunmark Industries, Phila., 1975-79; sr. v.p., external affairs Sun Co., Inc., Radnor, Pa., 1980-84; sr. v.p. planning pub. affairs Sun Co., Inc., 1984-88; ret., 1988. Served with USAF, 1944-46. Mem. Am. Petroleum Industry, 25 Yr. Club Petroleum Industry. Club: Union League (Phila.), Aronimink Golf (Newtown Square, Pa.), Mariner Sands Golf Club (Stuart, Fla.). Home (winter): 1124 Saint Andrews Rd Bryn Mawr PA 19010-1936

SNIDER, HAROLD WAYNE, risk and insurance educator; b. Puyallup, Wash., Apr. 16, 1923; s. P. Marion and Grace Stevenson (Short) S.; m. Isobel Milne Dice, Jan. 20, 1961. BA, U. Wash., 1946, MA, 1950; PhD, U. Pa., 1955. Instr. bus. U. Wash., 1952-54; assoc. prof. Ill. Wesleyan U., 1954-57; asst. prof. U. Pa., 1957-64; prof. risk mgmt. and ins. Temple U., Phila., 1964-91, prof. emeritus, 1991—; dir. Planned Protection Ins. Co. Author: Life Insurance Investment in Commercial Real Estate, 1956, Risk Management, 1963, (with Denenberg and others) Risk and Insurance, 1964, The Automobile Accident Problem: Saskatchewan Approach, 1973, Employee Benefit Administration, 1981; contbg. author: The Job of Risk Management, 1962. Bd. dirs. Planned Parenthood Fedn. Am., 1980-83. Served with AUS, 1943-46. S.S. Huebner Found. fellow, 1950-52. Mem. Risk and Ins. Mgmt. Soc., Am. Mgmt. Assn., Am. Risk and Ins. Soc., Phi Beta Kappa, Beta Gamma Sigma. Home: Unit 2A The Meadows 501 N Bethlehem Pike Apt 2A Ambler PA 19002-2516 Office: Sch Bus Adminstrn Temple U Philadelphia PA 19122 *If one has not failed, one's aspiration levels have been too low.*

SNIDER, JAMES RHODES, radiologist; b. Pawnee, Okla., May 16, 1931; s. John Henry and Gladys Opal (Rhodes) S.; B.S., U. Okla., 1953, M.D., 1956; m. Lynadell Vivion, Dec. 27, 1954; children—Jon, Jan. Intern, Edward Meyer Meml. Hosp., Buffalo, 1956-57; resident radiology U. Okla. Med. Center, 1959-62; radiologist Holt-Krock Clinic and Sparks Regional Med. Center, Ft. Smith, Ark., 1962-66, dir. Fairfield Community Land Co., Little Rock, 1968-87, Fairfield Communities, Inc., 1968-87. Mem. Ark. Bd. Pub. Welfare, 1969-71. Bd. dirs. U. Okla. Assn., 1967-70, U. Okla. Alumni Devel. Fund, 1970-74; bd. visitors U. Okla. Served to lt. comdr. USNR, 1957-62. Mem. Am. Coll. Radiology, Radiol. Soc. N.Am., Am. Roentgen Ray Soc., AMA, Phi Beta Kappa, Beta Theta Pi, Alpha Epsilon Delta. Asso. editor Computerized Tomography, 1976-88. Home: 5814 S Cliff Dr Fort Smith AR 72903-3845 Office: 1500 Dodson Ave Fort Smith AR 72901-5128

SNIDER, JOHN JOSEPH, lawyer; b. Seminole, Okla., July 25, 1928; s. George Nathan and Katherine (Harris) S.; m. Harriet Jean Edmonds, June 14, 1952; children—John Joseph, Dorothy Susan (Mrs. Mark E. Blohm), William Arnold. A.B., U. Okla., 1950, LL.B., 1955. Bar: Okla. bar 1955. Since practiced in Oklahoma City; atty. Fellers, Snider, Blankenship, Bailey & Tippens, 1964-93, counsel to, 1993—; mem. Okla. adv. council Nat. Legal Services Corp., 1976-77. Pres. Okla. Soc. to Prevent Blindness, 1965-71; bd. dirs. Hosp. Hospitality House, Okla., 1978-86; bd. dirs. Nat. Soc. Prevention Blindness, 1971-75; vice chmn. Oklahoma City Crime Prevention Council, 1976-77. Served to 1st lt. USAF, 1950-53. Fellow Am. Bar Found. (Okla. chmn. 1986-88); mem. Oklahoma City C. of C., Okla. Bar Assn., Okla. County Bar Assn., Am. Judicature Soc., Phi Delta Phi, Phi Kappa Psi. Methodist. Home: 2018 Redbud Pl Edmond OK 73013-7733 Office: First Nat Bldg Oklahoma City OK 73102

SNIDER, L. BRITT, government executive; b. Rocky Mount, N.C., Jan. 12, 1945; s. Arnold Holmes and Kate Mills (Suiter) S.; m. Virginia Lansford, Aug. 24, 1974; 1 child, Britt Arnold. BA, Davidson (N.C.) Coll., 1966; JD, U. Va., 1969. Counsel judiciary subcom. on constl. rights U.S. Senate, Washington, 1971-75, counsel select com. on intelligence, 1975-76; ptnr. Ketner & Snider, Salisbury, N.C., 1976-77; counsel govt. ops. subcom. on govt. info. U.S. Ho. Reps., Washington, 1977; asst. dep. undersec. counter-intelligence and security Dept. Def., Washington, 1977-87; minority counsel U.S. Senate Intelligence Com., Washington, 1987-89, gen. counsel, 1989-95, staff dir. commn. on roles and capabilities of U.S. Intelligence Cmty., 1995-96; sr. fellow Ctr. for Study of Intelligence, 1996—; staff dir. Commn. to Rev. Security Practices and Procedures Dept. Def., Washington, 1985. Served to capt. U.S. Army, 1969-71, Vietnam. Mem. Va. Bar Assn., D.C. Bar Assn. Democrat. Episcopalian. Avocations: tennis, jogging, reading.

SNIDER, LAWRENCE K., lawyer; b. Detroit, Dec. 28, 1938; s. Ben and Ida (Hertz) S.; m. Maxine Bobman, Aug. 12, 1962; children: Stephanie, Suzanne. BA, U. Mich., 1960, JD, 1963. Bar: Mich. 1964, Ill. 1991. Ptnr. Jaffe, Snider, Raitt & Heuer, Detroit, 1968-91, Mayer, Brown & Platt, Chgo., 1991—; mem. Nat. Bankruptcy Conf., Am. Coll. Bankruptcy, 1991—. Contbr. articles to profl. jours. Mem. Mich. Coun. for the Arts, 1990-91. Avocations: photography, collections. Office: Mayer Brown & Platt 190 S La Salle St Chicago IL 60603-3410

SNIDER, ROBERT F., chemistry educator, researcher; b. Calgary, Alta., Can., Nov. 22, 1931; s. Edward C. and Agnes S. (Klaeson) S.; children: Wendy A., Timothy J., Terry E., Geoffrey Y, Eric A. M. Burrough. B.S., U. Alta., 1953; Ph.D., U. Wis., 1958. Postdoctoral fellow Nat. Research Council Can., Ottawa, 1958; instr. II U. B.C., Vancouver, 1958-60, asst. prof., 1960-65, assoc. prof., 1965-69, prof., 1969-96, prof. emeritus, 1997—; vis. research prof. U. Leiden, Netherlands, 1973-74. Recipient gov. gen. gold medal U. Alta., 1953; U. Wis. WARF unassigned fellow, 1953-55; Izaac Walton Killam Meml. fellowship, 1985-86. Fellow Chem. Inst. Can., Royal Soc. Can.; mem. Am. Phys. Soc., Can. Assn. Physicists. Home: 3952 W 29th St, Vancouver, BC Canada V6S 1T9 Office: U BC, 2036 Main Mall, Vancouver, BC Canada V6T 1Z1

SNIDER, ROBERT LARRY, management consultant; b. Muskogee, Okla., Aug. 10, 1932; s. George Robert and Kathryn (Smiser) S.; m. Gerlene Rose Tipton, Nov. 26, 1953; children: Melody Kathryn Porter, Rebecca Lee. BS in Indsl. Engring., U. Houston, 1955, postgrad., 1956; postgrad., Pomona Coll., 1960. Cert. mgmt. cons. Instr. U. Houston Coll. Engring., 1955-56; sr. indsl. engr. Sheffield Steel Corp., Houston, 1955-59, Kaiser Steel Co., Fontana, Calif., 1959-60; cons. Arthur Young & Co., L.A., 1960-61; mgmt. analyst Iranian Oil Exploration & Producing Co., Masjidi-Suliman, Iran, 1961-62; cons., 1962-65; v.p. operating methods divsn. Booz, Allen & Hamilton, Inc., Dallas, 1965-67; mngr., ptnr. RLS Profl. Svcs., LiLic, Houston, Tex., 1995—; prin., gen. cons. practice Peat Marwick Mitchell, CPAs, Houston, 1969-71; exec. v.p. mfg. Sterling Electronics Corp., Houston, 1971-72, COO, pres., 1972-77; CEO, pres. Rapoca Energy Corp., Cin., 1977-79; mng. ptnr., cons. Coopers & Lybrand, Southwest, Houston, 1979-81; mng. dir. S.W. region Korn Ferry Internat., Houston, 1981-86; ptnr.-in-charge Houston Mgmt. Cons. Practice, 1986-91; ptnr. cons. Southwest Enterprise Coopers & Lybrand, Houston, 1991-92; ptnr. S.W. Mfg. Cons. Process Improvement Group Coopers & Lybrand, Houston, Pakistan/Mid. Asia, 1992-93; internat. cons. ptnr. Coopers & Lybrand, Houston, 1993-95; mng. ptnr. RLS Profl. Svcs. LLC, 1995—. Past mem. bd. dirs., exec. com. Houston Jr. Achievement; pastchmn. bd. mem. found. bd.and adminstrv. bd. Chapel Wood Meth. Ch.; ret. exec. com., bd. dirs. Houston Grand Opera. With C.E. AUS, 1956. Recipient Outstandng Mil. Engr. award Soc. Mil Engrs., 1955; named Disting. Alumni, Cullen Coll. Engring., U. Houston, 1991. Mem. Soc. Mining Engrs., U. Houston Alumni Assn. (past bd. dirs., exec. com., past pres., chmn.), Houston club, Houstonian Club, Phi Theta Kappa, Phi Kappa Phi. Home: 11643 Greenbay St Houston TX 77024-6430 Office: RLS Profl Svcs 681 Teel Rd Montgomery TX 77356-3387

SNIDER, RUTH ATKINSON, retired counselor; b. Louisville, Jan. 7, 1930; d. Ellis Orrell and Fanola Blanche (Miller) Atkinson; m. Arnold Wills Snider, Feb. 17, 1950; children: Yvonne Marie, Ray Wills, Mark Alan. Student, Centre Coll., 1947-48; BS, Spalding U., 1965, MEd, 1970; rank I, Western Ky. U., 1981. Cert. sch. psychometrist, sch. prin., supr. of instrn. Tchr. Shelby County (Ky.) Bd. Edn., 1949-50, Louisville Pub. Schs., 1956-57; tchr. Jefferson County Pub. Schs., Louisville, 1965-67, counselor, 1967-92; vol. co-chairperson for mentor program Spalding U., Louisville, 1991. Vol. Ky. Ctr. for Arts, 1989, 90, 91, Actors Theatre of Louisville, 193-94, 95, 96, Klondike Elem. Sch. Libr., 1994-95; pub. chair World Day of Prayer, 1996; sec. adv. com. Beechwood Bapt. Ch. Mem. ACA (del.), Am. Sch. Counselors Assn. (del. nat. conf.), Ky. Assn. Counseling and Devel., Ky. Sch. Counselors Assn. (conf. chairperson), Spalding Soc. (pres. 1995-97), Spalding Alumni Assn. (sec. 1994-96, Caritas award), Jefferson County Ret. Tchrs. Assn., Christian Women's Club. Avocations: sewing, travel. Home: 2428 Chattesworth Ln Louisville KY 40242-2849

SNIDER, STEPHEN WILLIAM, art director, graphic designer; b. Boston, July 21, 1943; s. Louis Oscar and Etta Zelda (Rosenberg) S.; m. Marlene Sandra Shuman, Sept. 2, 1973; children: Emily Allison, Jill Tracy. Grad., Sch. Mus. Fine Arts, Boston, 1961-65. Asst. art dir. Arthur D. Little, Inc., Cambridge, Mass., 1965-70; creative dir. Snider Design, Boston, 1970-78; art dir. The Atlantic Monthly, Boston, 1978-81; design dir. Arnold & Co. Advt., Boston, 1981-85; creative dir. Snider Design, Wellesley, Mass., 1985-87; art dir. Little, Brown & Co., Boston, 1987-96; creative dir. St. Martin's Press, N.Y.C., 1996—. Recipient 1st place and Silver medal New Eng. Hatch awards, Boston, 1974, Gold medal N.Y. Art Dirs. Club, 1984, Best of Category Design, New Eng. Book Show, Boston, 1994. Mem. Boston Athaneum. Avocations: tennis, theatre, film, photography, antique collecting. Home: 99 Brook St Wellesley MA 02181-6644 Office: St Martin's Press 175 5th Ave New York NY 10010-7703 also: 226 E 25th St New York NY 10010

SNIERSON, LYNNE WENDY, communications executive; b. Laconia, N.H., Feb. 28, 1952; d. Bernard Irwin and Muriel Stella (Goldberg) S. BA, Duke U., 1975. Reporter, prodr. WMUR-TV, Manchester, N.H., 1981-83; sportswriter Boston Herald, 1983-87, Miami (Fla.) News, 1987-89, St. Louis Sun, 1989-90; contbg. reporter KMOX Radio, St. Louis, 1990-93; sportswriter The Racing Times, N.Y.C., 1991-92; dir. comm. Arlington Internat. Racecourse, Arlington Heights, Ill., 1992-95; dir. comm. and mktg. Rockingham Park, Salem, N.H., 1995—. Reporter (tv show) Arlington Weekend, 1993-94; contbr. articles to publs. Recipient Best Sports Story award New Eng. Womens Press Assn., 1986, award of excellence New Eng. Womens Press Assn., 1986; named one of 10 most powerful women in NFL, Coll. and Pro Football Weekly, 1988. Mem. Profl. Football Writers Am., Nat. Turf Writers Assn., New Eng. Turf Writers Assn. (sec.-treas. 1995-96, v.p. 1996—), Fla. Turf Writers Assn., Turf Publicists Am., (v.p. 1997—, Assn. for Women in Sports Media, NOW, Nat. Abortion Rights Action League, N.H. Women's Lobby. Democrat. Avocations: reading, traveling, fitness training, gardening. Office: Rockingham Park Rockingham Park Blvd Salem NH 03079

SNIFFEN, MICHAEL JOSEPH, hospital administrator; b. Ossining, N.Y., June 16, 1949; s. John Francis and Mary Agnes (Madden) S.; m. Anne Marie Gillick; children: Kevin, Kristina. BS, Fordham U., 1971; MBA in Hosp. Adminstrn., Baruch Coll., 1977. Dir. of fin. planning Westchester div. N.Y. Hosp., White Plains, N.Y., 1971-74; assoc. dir. N.Y. Hosp., N.Y.C., 1974-80, sr. assoc. dir., assoc. dean Cornell Med. Ctr., 1980-87; pres., COO Overlook Hosp., Summit, N.J., 1987—; exec. v.p., chief exec. officer Atlantic Health Sys., Florham Park, N.J., 1996—; exec. dir. Cornell Health Policy Program, N.Y.C., 1984-87; adminstr. program Commonwealth Fund, N.Y.C., 1978-81; adv. bd. Robert Wood Johnson Found.-Teaching Nursing Home Program, Princeton, N.J., 1980-86. Vol. March of Dimes, Tarrytown, N.Y., 1984-88; bd. dirs. St. Columbans Sch., Peekskill, N.Y., 1981-84; mem. various Father's Clubs, Westchester County, N.Y., 1976-91. Mem. Am. Coll. Healthcare Execs., Hosp. Fin. Mgmt. Assn. (advanced mem.), Echo Lake Country Club (Westfield, N.J.), Beacon Hill Country Club, Baltusrol Country Club (Springfield, N.J.)., Rotary. Roman Catholic. Avocations: golf, college basketball. Home: 49 Drum Hill Rd Summit NJ 07901-3141 Office: Atlantic Health Sys 325 Columbia Tpke Florham Park NJ 07932-1212

SNIFFIN, JOHN HARRISON, retail executive; b. N.Y.C., Feb. 25, 1942; s. Harrison Webb and Elizabeth (Wood) S.; m. Beverly Ann Bailey, Sept. 24, 1966; children: Christine, John, Ned, Ellen. BBA, Ga. State U., 1967, MBA, 1969. Internal audit mgr. Sears, Roebuck and Co., Atlanta, 1961-69; asst. controller Heilig-Meyers Co., Richmond, Va., 1969-72, asst. treas., 1972-84, treas., 1984-86, v.p., treas., sec., 1986, v.p. mdse., 1986-89, sr. v.p. merchandising, 1989-92; sr. v.p. govt. rels., 1992—. Mem. retail exec. adv. com. Ctr. for Retailing, James Madison U. Mem. Fin. Execs. Inst., So. Home Furnishings Assn. (pres., exec. com.), Va. Retail Mchts. Assn. (bd. dirs., exec. com., vice chmn.), N.C. Retail Mchts. Assn. (bd. dirs.), Ky. Retail Fedn. (bd. dirs.), Pa. Retailers Assn. (bd. dirs.), Fla. Retail Fedn. (bd. dirs.), Tenn. Coun. of Retail Merchants (chmn.), Ga. Retail Assn. Republican. Roman Catholic. Avocations: music, golf. Office: Heilig-Meyers Co 2235 Staples Mill Rd Richmond VA 23230-2942

SNIPES, WESLEY, actor. Grad., SUNY, Purchase, 1980. Appeared in Broadway plays Boys of Winter, Execution of Justice, Death and King's Horsemen; films include Streets of Gold, 1986, Vietnam War Story (ACE award for best actor 1989), Mo'Better Blues, 1989, Major League, 1989, New Jack City, 1991, Jungle Fever, 1991, The Waterdance, 1992, White Can't Jump, 1992, Passenger 57, 1992, Rising Sun, 1993, Demolition Man, 1993, Boiling Point, 1993, Sugar Hill, 1994, Drop Zone, 1994, To Wong Foo, Thanks for Everything, Julie Newmar, 1995, The Money Train, 1995, The Fan, 1996, America's Dream, 1996, U.S. Marshals, 1997, One Night, 1997, Murder at 1600, 1997, Blade, The Vampire Slayer, 1997. Address: Starr & Co 350 Park Ave 9th Fl New York NY 10022*

SNITOW, CHARLES, lawyer; b. N.Y.C., Feb. 7, 1907; m. Virginia Levitt, Nov. 2, 1935; children: Ann Barr, Alan Mark. AB, Cornell U., 1928, JD, 1930. Ptnr. Pomerance & Snitow, N.Y.C., 1931—; pres. Nat. Hardward Show Inc., N.Y.C., 1945-70, World Hobby Exposition, Chgo., Phila., 1948-53, Charles Snitow Orgn., N.Y.C., 1950-79, Internat. Auto Show, N.Y.C., 1952-80, Nat. Fancy Food Conf. Show, N.Y.C., 1955-70, U.S. World Trade Fair Inc., N.Y.C., San Francisco, 1957-66, Internat. Photography & Travel Show Inc., N.Y.C., 1960-72, Consumer Electronics Show, N.Y.C., 1967-77, Snitow Show Consultants, Inc., N.Y.C., 1975—; cons. Soviet Expn. Sci. and Tech., N.Y.C., 1959, N.C. Internat. Fair, Charlotte, 1959, Brit. Expn., N.Y.C., 1960, Cahners Expn. Group divsn. Reed Exhbn. Cos., N.Y.C., 1970-87, Brazil Expo, N.Y., Chgo., L.A., Dallas, Atlanta, Miami, Fla., 1981, Greater N.Y. Internat. Auto Show, 1982—, East/Cen. Europe Trade Expo, N.Y., 1994. Contbr. articles to Cornell Law Quar. Bd. dirs. Bill of Rights Found., N.Y.C., 1980; mem. Met. Opera Chorus, Schola Cantorum, Collegiate Chorale. Recipient cert. of honor March of Dimes, Gold Key-Medal of Honor, City of N.Y., 1960-62, Gran Prix Am., France, 1965, Garcia Moreno medal Equador, 1966; named Knight, Order of Merit, Republic of Italy, 1963; named to Order Hon. Ky. Cols., La. Cols. Mem. Nat. Assn. Expn. Mgrs. (hon., Kings Glove award for excellence 1991), Latin Am. C. of C., Cornell Club, Savage Club, Phi Beta Kappa, Alpha Kappa Delta. Avocation: singing. Home: 81 Walworth Ave Scarsdale NY 10583-1140 Office: Snitow Show Cons Inc 4 Sniffen Ct New York NY 10016-3505

SNITZER, ELIAS, physicist; b. Lynn, Mass., Feb. 27, 1925; s. Isaac and Jenny (Sussman) S.; m. Shirley Ann Wood, Nov. 22, 1950; children: Sandra, Barbara, Peter, Helen, Louis. B.S.E.E., Tufts U., 1946; M.S. in Physics, U. Chgo., 1950, Ph.D., 1953. Research physicist Honeywell Corp., Phila., 1954-56; assoc. prof. Lowell Technol. Inst., Mass., 1956-58; dir. research Am. Optical Co., Southbridge, Mass., 1959-76; mgr. applied physics United Technologies Research, East Hartford, Conn., 1977-84; mgr. fiber optics Polaroid, Cambridge, Mass., 1984-88; prof. Rutgers U., 1989-97, prof. emeritus, 1997—. Contbr. articles to profl. jours. Inventor glass laser. Served with USN, 1943-46. Fellow Optical Soc. Am. (John Tyndall award 1994), Ceramic Soc.; mem. NAE, IEEE (George Morey award 1971, Quantum Electronics award 1979, Charles Townes award 1991), Am. Phys. Soc. Democrat. Jewish. Home: 8 Smoke Tree Close Piscataway NJ 08854-5109 Office: Rutgers U Fiber Optics Materials Rsch Program PO Box 909 Piscataway NJ 08855-0909

SNIVELY, STEPHEN WAYNE, lawyer; b. Danville, Ill., Apr. 27, 1949; s. Roberts Eyster and Margaret Louise Snively; m. Heather Lea Patten, Mar. 19, 1988; children: Toby, Ben, Madeline, Taylor. BA, U. Ill., 1971, JD, 1975. Bar: Ill. 1975, Fla. 1980. Assoc. Kavanagh, Scully, Sudow, White & Frederick, Peoria, Ill., 1975-80, Maguire, Voorhis & Wells, P.A., Orlando, Fla., 1980—; seminar speaker, 1987. Contbr. articles to profl. jours. Bd. dirs. Found. for Orange County Pub. Schs., Orlando, 1987-96, officer, 1987-96, pres., 1993-94, chmn., 1994-96; bd. dirs. Found. for Hospice of Ctrl. Fla., Inc., 1995-96; treas., bd. dirs. HCF Found., Inc., 1996—. Mem. Fla. Bar (liaison to land surveyor com. 1982—), Orange County Ba Assn., Internat. Coun. Shopping Ctrs., Fla. C. of C. (Leadership Fla. 1991-92), Fla. Zool. Soc. (sec., bd. dirs. 1991-96), Univ. Club, Citrus Club, Tiger Bay Club, Econs. Club Orlando, Phi Beta Kappa. Republican. Presbyterian. Avocations: running, computers, photography. Office: Maguire Voorhis & Wells PA Two S Orange Ave Orlando FL 32801

SNODDON, LARRY ERLE, public relations executive; b. Grosse Pointe, Mich., June 10, 1945; s. Firman and Evelyn Marie (McDonnell) S.; m. Kathleen McGreevy, Mar. 2, 1985; children: Elizabeth, Sarah, Emily. B.A., U. Mich.; M.A., U. Wis.-Madison. Corp. pub. relations rep. Gen. Motors Corp., Detroit, 1968-70; corp. pub. relations mgr. Am. Express Co., N.Y.C., 1970-72; pres. for Ams. Burson-Marsteller, N.Y.C., 1972-87; pres. for Europe Burson-Marsteller, London, 1987-91; pres., CEO Burson-Marsteller, N.Y.C., 1992-95; vice chmn. Young & Rubicam, Inc., N.Y.C., 1995—; bd. dirs. Young & Rubicam, Inc. Bd. dirs. Am. II Syndicate for 1987 Am.'s Cup, U.S.-China Arts Exchange; mem. coun. Bus. in the Community, London. Fellow Royal Soc. London, Prince of Wales Bus. Leaders Forum; mem. Univ. Club, N.Y. Yacht Club, Greenwich Country Club, Riverside Yacht Club, Royal Automobile Club. Avocation: sailing. *

SNODDY, CHRIS RAYMOND, athletic trainer; b. Nashville, Nov. 19, 1959; s. Raymond Thomas and Farris (Duke) S. BS, David Lipscomb Coll., 1981; MA, Appalachian State U., 1987. Lic. athletic trainer. Real estate salesperson McKinney & Co., Nashville, 1980-89; head athletic trainer David Lipscomb U., Nashville, 1981-91; sr. athletic trainer Ctr. Sports Medicine, Bapt. Hosp., Nashville, 1993—; coord. sports medicine Bapt. Hosp., Nashville, 1997—; dir. sports medicine Pinnacle Rehab., Nashville, 1991-92; cons. sports medicine David Lipscomb H.S., Nashville, 1982-91; adj. faculty Free Will Bapt. Bible Coll., Nashville; cons. Lipscomb U. Sports Medicine. Editor: Where to Go Camping Guide, 1980; contbr. articles to Flying Eagle mag. Recipient Mayor's medallion City of Nashville, 1986, Silver Beaver award Boy Scouts Am., 1995, named Eagle Scout, 1976, Clin. Athletic Trainer of Yr., 1992. Mem. Nat. Athletic Trainers Assn., Tenn. Athletic Trainers Assn. Republican. Mem. Ch. of Christ. Lodges: Civitan (bd. dirs. Nashville 1986-87, pres. 1990), Wa-Hi-Nasa (lodge advisor 1995—), Order of Arrow (assoc. advisor Tenn. and Ky. chpts. 1984-87, Founder's award 1976). Avocation: skiing. Home: 315 Bowwood Dr Nashville TN 37217-2301

SNODDY, JAMES ERNEST, education educator; b. Perrysville, Ind., Oct. 6, 1932; s. James Elmer and Edna May (Hayworth) S.; m. Alice Joanne Crowder, Aug. 15, 1954; children: Ryan Anthony, Elise Suzanne. BS, Ind. State U., 1954; MEd, U. Ill., 1961, EdD, 1967. Tchr. Danville (Ill.) Pub. Schs., 1954-57, prin., 1961-64; instr. U. Ill., Champaign, 1965-67; prof. edn. Mich. State U., East Lansing, 1967-72, 78-96, chmn. dept. elem. and spl. edn., 1972-78, ret., 1996; dir. Program CORK, 1978-82. With U.S. Army, 1955-57. Mem. Am. Assn. for Adult and Continuing Edn., Commn. of Profs. of Adult and Continuing Edn. Methodist. Home: 2194 Lagoon Dr Okemos MI 48864-2711 Office: Mich State U 419 Erickson Hall East Lansing MI 48824-1034

SNODGRASS, ROBERT EUGENE, psychiatrist; b. Indpls., Feb. 27, 1930; s. William Howard and Della Gladys (Satterly) S.; m. Constance Fusco, Mar. 1, 1958; 1 child, Robert Brent. AB in Anatomy and Physiology, Ind. U., 1952, MD, 1955. Diplomate Am. Bd. Psychiatry and Neurology. Intern Marion County Gen. Hosp., Indpls., 1955-56; resident in psychiatry Ind. U. Med. Ctr., Indpls., 1964-67; pvt. gen. practice Greenwood, Ind., 1958-64; pvt. practice Indpls., 1967-90; staff psychiatrist Madison (Ind.) State Hosp., 1991—. Author: Beloved Madison, 1990; contbr. articles to profl. jours. Mem. Hist. Dist. Bd. Rev., Madison, 1991—. Capt. U.S. Army, 1956-58. Decorated Meritorious Svc. Commendation medal. Fellow Am. Psychiatric Assn.; mem. AMA, Ind. Psychiatric Soc. (past pres.), Jefferson County Hist. Soc. (bd. dirs. 1989—), Elks. Avocation: foreign languages. Home: 707 E Main St Madison IN 47250-3650 Office: Madison State Hosp 711 Green Rd Madison IN 47250-2143

SNODGRASS, W. D., writer, educator; b. Wilkinsburg, Pa., Jan. 5, 1926; s. Bruce DeWitt and Jesse Helen (Murchie) S.; m. Lila Jean Hank, June 6, 1946 (div. 1953); 1 child, Cynthia Jean; m. Janice Marie Ferguson Wilson, Mar. 19, 1954 (div. Aug. 1966); children—Kathy Ann Wilson (stepdau.), Russell Bruce; m. Camille Rykowski, Sept. 13, 1967 (div. 1977); m. Kathleen Brown, June 20, 1985. Student, Geneva Coll., 1943-44, 46-47; B.A., State U. Iowa, 1949, M.A., 1951, M.F.A., 1953; hon. doctorate, Allegheny Coll., 1991. Faculty English dept. Cornell U., Ithaca, N.Y., 1955-57; faculty English dept. U. Rochester, N.Y., 1957-58; prof. English Wayne State U., Detroit, until 1968; prof. English and speech Syracuse U., N.Y., 1968-76; Disting. prof. of creative writing and contemp. poetry U. Del., Newark, 1979-94, retired, 1994; faculty Morehead Writers' Conf., Ky., summer 1955, Antioch Writers' Conf., Yellow Springs, Ohio, summer 1958, 59; disting. vis. prof. Old Dominion U., Norfolk, Va.; instr. Narrative Poetry Workshop SUNY, Binghamton, 1977, Cranbrook Writers' Conf., Birmingham, Mich., 1981. Author: (poems) Heart's Needle (Pultizer prize 1960), 1959, After Experience, 1968, Remains (under pseudonym S.S. Gardons) 1970, The Fuhrer Bunker, 1977, If Birds Build With Your Hair, 1979, The Boy Made of Meat, 1982, Magda Goebbels (poems from The Fuhrer Bunker, 1983), Heinrich Himmler (poems from The Fuehrer Bunker) 1983, D.D. Byrde Calling Jennie Wrenne, 1984, A Colored Poem, 1986, The House the Poet Built, 1986, 1987, Selected Poems, 1957-87, W.D.'s Midnight Carnival: Poems by W.D. Snodgrass and Paintings by DeLoss McGraw, 1988, The Death of Cock Robin: Poems by W.D. Snodgrass and Paintings by DeLoss McGraw, 1989, Autumn Variations, 1990; translator: (with Lore Segal) Gallows' Songs of Christian Morgenstern, Six Troubadour Songs, 1977, Traditional Hungarian Songs, 1978, Six Minnesinger Songs, 1983, The Four Seasons (translations of Vivaldi's Sonnets) 1984, (essays) In Radical Pursuit, 1975, Star and Other Poems, 1990, Five Romanian Ballads, 1991, Snow Songs, 1992, Each in His Season, 1993, The Fuehrer Bunker: The Complete Cycle, 1995; contbr. essays, poems, translations to lit. mags. Recipient Ingram-Merrill award, 1958, Longview lit. award, 1959, spl. citation Poetry Soc. Am., 1960, Pulitzer prize for poetry, 1960, Guinness Poetry award, 1961, Miles Modern Poetry award, 1966; Hudson Rev. fellow in poetry, 1958-59; fellow Guggenheim Found., 1972-73, Acad. Am. Poets, 1973, Bi-Centennial Medal William and Mary Coll., 1976, Centennial Medal Govt. Romania, 1977; Ingram-Merrill fellow 1979; sabbatical grantee Nat. Council on Arts, 1966-67, Ctr. for Advanced Study U. Del. grantee, 1983-84. Mem. PEN, Nat. Inst. Arts and Letters (grantee 1960), Poetry Soc. Am. Home: RD 1 Box 51 Erieville NY 13061-9801

SNORTLAND, HOWARD JEROME, educational financial consultant; b. Sharon, N.D., June 22, 1912; s. Thomas and Aline (Vig) S.; m. Anna Adeline Anderson, Sept. 1, 1940; children—Jan Signe, Kristi Jo, Howard Jay. B.A., U. N.D., 1937, M.S., 1958. Cashier N.D. Workmen's Compensation Bur., 1937-42, N.D. State Treas.'s Office, 1945-48; with N.D. Dept. Pub. Instrn., Bismarck, 1948-81; supt. pub. instrn. N.D. Dept. Pub. Instrn., 1977-81; ednl. fin. cons., 1981—; pres. State Econ. Council, 1978; nat. pres. Com. Ednl. Data Systems, 1965-67. Chmn. Burleigh ARC, 1963-67, bd. dirs., 1946—, vice chmn., 1964—; bd. dirs. Burleigh County Tb Assn., 1950—; stated clk. United Presbyterian Ch., 1942—; pres. N.D. United Christian Campus Fellowship, 1964-67, N.D. Westminster Found., 1963-70; mem. N.D. Synod Council, 1970—; chmn. United Way Fund, 1983. Served with USAAF, 1942-45. Recipient Summit Conf. award for outstanding pub. service, 1976. Mem. NEA, N.D. Edn. Assn., N.D. Sch. Bus. Ofcls., N.D. Assn. Adminstrs., Nat. Assn. Adminstrs., N.D. Assn. Ret. Employees (pres. 1987—), Am. Assn. Ret. Persons (vice chmn. N.D. legis. com. 1992-94, chmn. 1994—), Kiwanis, Phi Beta Kappa, Phi Delta Kappa.

SNOUFFER, NANCY KENDALL, English and reading educator; b. Long Branch, N.J., Aug. 22, 1941; d. Percival Wallace and Ruby Mae (Braswell) Kendall; m. Eugene Joseph Snouffer, Aug. 27, 1966; 1 child, Kendall Ann. BA in English, Gettysburg (Pa.) Coll., 1962; MA in English and Journalism, U. N.C., 1964; MS in Edn. and Reading, Western Ill. U., 1974; postgrad., U. Mo., 1976-78. Instr. English U. N.C., Wilmington, 1963-65, Shaw U., Raleigh, N.C., 1965-66; from instr. to asst. prof. English Wright Coll. and Chgo. City Colls., 1967-74; from instr. to asst. prof. reading Western Ill. U., Macomb, 1974-81; prof. ESL and reading Del Mar Coll., Corpus Christi, Tex., 1982—; mem. adv. bd. Tex. A&M U., Corpus Chrisit, 1993—; cons. in field. Author: College Reading Power, 5th edit., 1976-82; assoc. editor jour. Epistle, 1980-83, mem. editoral bd., 1983-85; contbr. articles to profl. jours. Master Tchr. Del Mar, 1986. Grantee Western Ill. U., 1974-81, Del Mar Coll., 1982—, NISSOD Teaching Excellence award, 1993. Mem. Tex. Assn. Developmental Educators, Tex. Coll. Reading Learning Assn. (chair So. membership 1994—, state sec. 1995-97, pres. elect 1997—), Nat. Assn. Developmental Educators (co-chair nat. com., profl. liaison), Internat. Reading Assn., Corpus Christi Literacy Coun. (bd. dirs., sec. 1988-93, vice-chair 1991-92), Harbor Playhouse (bd. dirs. 1988, 91-93), Alliance Francaise. Republican. Episcopalian. Avocations: tennis, travel, reading. Home: 4206 Acushnet Dr Corpus Christi TX 78413-2004 Office: Del Mar Coll 101 Baldwin Blvd Corpus Christi TX 78404-3805

SNOW, ALAN ALBERT, publisher; b. Van Nuys, Calif., July 20, 1946; s. Perry William and Virginia (Show) S. BA, Pepperdine U., L.A., 1969; MA, Sch. of Theology, Claremont, Calif., 1974; Magister Operae Onerosae (hon.), Inst. Antiquity-Christianity, Claremont, 1972; ThD, Andersonville Bapt. Sem., 1994. Dir., min. Ch. of the Ams., Balboa Island, Calif.; pres. Alan Alber Snow Ins. Agy. Farmers Ins. Group of Cos., Fountain Valley, Calif.; bd. dirs. Inst. for Study of Judeo-Christian Origins Calif. State U., Long Beach; mem. Jesus seminar Westar Inst. Contbg. author to anthologies: The Book Your Church Does Not Want You to Read, 3d edit., 1997, Sydney Omarr's Astrol. Guides for Your, 1994, 95, 96, 97, (poetry) The Long and Winding Road, 1997. Mem. Am. Assn. Christian Counselors, Assn. Ind. Clergy, Nat. Notary Assn. (ethics com., Cert. Accomplishment), Am. Soc. Notaries, Dead Sea Scroll Rsch. Coun., Bibl. Archaeology Soc. Democrat. Home: 518 S Bay Front Newport Beach CA 92662

SNOW, CUBBEDGE, JR., lawyer; b. Macon, Ga., May 20, 1929. AB, Emory U., 1951; JD magna cum laude, Mercer U., 1952. Bar: Ga. 1952. Ptnr. Martin, Snow, Grant, Napier, Macon. Col. JAGC, USAFR, 1952-89. Fellow Am. Coll. Trial Lawyers, Am. Bar Found. (state chmn. 1988-92), Fedn. Ins. and Corp. Counsel, Ga. Def. Lawyers Assn., Am. Prepaid Legal Svcs. Inst. (bd. dirs. 1983-89); mem. ABA (ho. of dels. 1984—, chmn. prepaid legal svcs. com. 1986-88, bd. govs. 1993-96), Macon Bar Assn. (pres. 1967), State Bar Ga. (pres. 1974-75), Am. Judicature Soc. (bd. dirs. 1978-82, Herbert Harley award 1986), Phi Beta Kappa, Phi Alpha Delta, Omicron Delta Kappa. Office: Martin Snow 240 3rd St PO Box 1606 Macon GA 31202

SNOW, DAVID FORREST, judge; b. Boston, Mar. 15, 1932; s. Albert Grindle and Hope (Farrington) S.; m. Rosemary Allsman, Oct. 7, 1957 (div. Jan. 1982); children: Nicholas David, Sarah Alison, Catherine Ann; m. Joyce Neiditz, Mar. 15, 1985. BA, Dartmouth Coll., 1954; JD, Harvard U., 1960. Bar: Ohio 1961, U.S. Dist. Ct. Ohio 1965. Ptnr. Jones, Day, Reavis & Pogue, Cleve., 1960-88; assoc. prof. law U. Iowa, Iowa City, 1967-68; bankruptcy judge U.S. Dist. Ct., Cleve., 1988—. Mem. ABA, Cleve. Bar Assn. Home: 2330 Ardleigh Dr Cleveland OH 44106-3128 Office: US Bankruptcy Ct 127 Public Sq 3101 Key Tower Cleveland OH 44114-1309

SNOW, DEAN RICHARD, anthropology educator, archaeologist; b. Sleepy Eye, Minn., Oct. 18, 1940; s. Roger Pershing and Gloria Jane Snow; m. Janet Charlene Keller, Dec. 21, 1963; children: Katherine, Barbara, Joshua. BA, U. Minn., 1962; PhD, U. Oreg., 1966. Asst. prof. anthropology U. Maine, Orono, 1966-69; asst. prof. SUNY, Albany, 1969-74, assoc. prof., chmn., 1974-80, prof., assoc. dean, 1980-83, prof., 1983-89, prof., dept. chmn., 1989-91, prof., 1991-95; prof., head Penn State, 1995—. Author: The Archaeology of North America, 1976, Archaeology of New England, 1980, Archaeology of North American Indians, 1989; editor: Foundations of Northeast Archaeology; co-author: (with Michael Coe and Elizabeth Benson) Atlas of Ancient America. Pres. N.Y. Archaeol. Coun., 1987-89; active N.Y. State Bd. for Hist. Preservation, vice chair, 1985-95. Grantee Nat. Geog. Soc., 1983, 85, NEH, 1984-85, 85-86, 87-89, 91-93, NSF, 1991-92. Fellow AAAS, Am. Anthrop. Assn., N.Y. State Archaeol. Assn.; mem. Am. Soc. Ethnohistory (pres. 1978-79), N.E. Anthrop. Assn. (pres. 1984-86). Office: 409 Carpenter University Park PA 16802

SNOW, GEORGE ABRAHAM, physicist; b. N.Y.C., Aug. 24, 1926; s. Joseph and Anna (Snow) Ginsberg; m. Lila Alpert, June 20, 1948; children: Zachary, Andrew, Sara Ellen. B.S., CCNY, 1945; M.A., Princeton U., 1947, Ph.D., 1949. Jr. physicist Brookhaven Nat. Lab., Upton, N.Y., 1948-51; assoc. physicist Brookhaven Nat. Lab., 1951-55; physicist Naval Research Lab., Washington, 1955-58; vis. prof. dept. physics and astronomy U. Md., College Park, 1957-58, assoc. prof., 1958-61, prof., 1961-92, prof. emeritus, sr. rsch. scientist, 1992—; mem. Inst. for Advanced Study, Princeton, 1952-53; vis. lectr. U. Wis., Madison, 1955-56; vis. prof. U. Rome, 1965-66, U. Paris (France), Oxford, 1972-73, Tohoku U., Sendai, Japan, 1979; vis. scientist CERN, 1980, U. Bologna, 1986; mem. high energy physics adv. panel AEC, 1970-72; mem. high energy physics vis. com. Argonne Nat. Lab., 1969-71, Princeton-Pa. Accelerator, 1969-70, Lawrence Radiation Lab., Berkeley, Calif., 1980-83; mem. high energy physics adv. com. Brookhaven Nat. Lab., 1967-69; cons. to physics editor Prentice Hall, Inc., 1971-76. Cameraman, editor cable TV program: The Art Scene with Lila Snow, 1995—. Trustee URA, 1973-78, vice chmn., 1974, chmn. sci. com., 1975-77. Recipient Disting. Scholar-Tchr. award U. Md., 1988-89; NSF sr. postdoctoral fellow, 1961-62, John S. Guggenheim sr. fellow, Fulbright scholar, 1965-66; cited by Washington Acad. Scis., 1963. Fellow AAAS, Am. Phys. Soc. (mem. exec. coun. div. particles and fields 1968-70, vice chmn. div. particles and fields 1975, chmn. 1976, editor Phys. Rev. D 1981-83); mem. Fedn. Am. Scientists, European Phys. Soc., Phi Beta Kappa. Home: 4816 Essex Ave Bethesda MD 20815-5548 Office: U Md Dept Physics College Park MD 20742

SNOW, JAMES BYRON, JR., physician, research administrator; b. Oklahoma City, Mar. 12, 1932; s. James B. and Charlotte Louise (Andersen) S.; m. Sallie Lee Ricker, July 16, 1954; children: James B., John Andrew, Sallie Lee Louise. BS, U. Okla., 1953; MD cum laude, Harvard U., 1956; MA (hon.), U. Pa., 1973. Diplomate: Am. Bd. Otolaryngology (dir. 1972-90). Intern Johns Hopkins Hosp., Balt., 1956-57; resident Mass. Eye and Ear Infirmary, Boston, 1957-60; prof., head dept. otorhinolaryngology Sch. Medicine U. Okla., Oklahoma City, 1962-72; prof., chmn. dept. otorhinolaryngology and human communication U. Pa. at Phila., 1972-90; dir. Nat. Inst. on Deafness and Other Comm. Disorders/NIH, Bethesda, Md., 1990—; mem. nat. adv. coun. neurol. and communicative disorders and stroke NIH, 1972-76, 82-86; chmn. Nat. Com. Rsch. Neurol. and Communicative Disorders, 1979-80. Editor: Am. Jour. Otolaryngology, 1979-83; Contbr. articles to sci. and profl. jours. Served with M.C. AUS, 1960-62. Recipient Regents award for superior tchg. U. Okla., 1970, Golden award Internat. Fedn. Otorhinolaryngological Socs., 1989, Disting. Achievement award Deafness Rsch. Found., 1993, Presdl. Meritorious Exec. Rank award, 1994; named to Soc. Scholars Johns Hopkins U., 1991. Fellow Japan Broncho-Esophagological Soc. (hon.), Am. Laryngological Assn. (hon.); mem. ACS (regent 1982-90), AMA (coun. on sci. affairs 1975-86), Soc. Univ. Otolaryngologists (pres. 1975), Am. Acad. Otolaryngology-Head and Neck Surgery, Assn. Acad. Depts. Otolaryngology (pres. 1981-82), Am. Laryngol., Rhinol. and Otol. Soc., Am. Otol. Soc., Am. Laryngol. Assn. (editor 1983-89, pres. 1990-91), Am. Broncho-Esophagol. Assn. (editor trans. 1973-77, pres. 1979), Collegium Otorhinolaryngologicum, Phi Beta Kappa, Alpha Omega Alpha. Home: 119 Driscoll Way Gaithersburg MD 20878-5210 Office: Nat Inst Deafness & Other Comm Disorders 9000 Rockville Pike Bldg 31 Bethesda MD 20814-1436

SNOW, JEFFREY SCOTT, fuels engineer; b. Princeton, Ind., Feb. 27, 1959; s. Wilford Lee and Lois Jean (Spaw) S.; m. Debra Rose Stout, Mar. 27, 1982; children: Bryan Robert, Scott Harrison. AS in Mining Engring. Tech., U. So. Ind., Evansville, 1980, BS in Mining Engring. Tech., 1981; BS in Mgmt. of Human Res., Oakland City (Ind.) Coll., 1990; MS in Mgmt., Oakland City U., 1996. Engring. coop. Old Ben Coal Co., Oakland City, 1978-80; engring. asst. PSI, Plainfield, 1982-83; sr. engring. asst. Pub. Svc. Ind. Energy, Plainfield, 1983, sta. engring. technologist, 1983-85, site and fueling engr., 1985-96, analyst power ops., 1996—. Co-author: From Management to Leadership for the 21st Century, 1996. Mem. Soc. Mining Engrs. of AIME (assoc. 1983—), ASTM (mem. DO5 com. 1988—, E31 com. 1988—), Nat. Conf. on Weights and Measures, Omicron Psi. Lutheran. Achievements include coal handling system automation - Gibson Generating Station; avocations: golf, coin collecting. Office: PSI Energy Inc Gibson Generating Sta RR 1 Box 300 Owensville IN 47665

SNOW, JOEL ALAN, research director; b. Brockton, Mass., Apr. 1, 1937; s. George H. and Mary W. (Sproul) S.; m. Laetitia Harrer, June 29, 1957 (div. 1983); children: Jonathan, Nicholas; m. Barbara Kashian, Feb. 7, 1992; stepchildren: James, Alexander. BS in Physics, U. N.C., 1958; MA in Physics, Washington U., St. Louis, 1963, PhD in Physics, 1967. Fellow Ctr. Advanced Study U. Ill., Champaign, 1967-68; program dir. for theoretical physics NSF, Washington, 1968-70, head office of interdisciplinary rsch., 1970-71, dep. asst. dir. for sci. and tech., rsch. applications, 1971-74, dir. office of planning and resources mgmt., 1974-76, dir. div. of policy rsch. and analysis, 1976; sr. policy analyst, office of sci. and tech. policy Exec. Office of the Pres., Washington, 1976-77; assoc. dir. for rsch. policy U.S. Dept. Energy, Washington, 1977-81, dir. sci. and tech. affairs, 1981-88; assoc. v.p. for rsch. and Argonne, U. Chgo., 1988-92; dir. Inst. for Phys. Rsch. and Tech. Iowa State U., Ames, 1993—, prof. elec. and computer engring., 1993—; rsch. assoc. dept. physics U. Ill., Urbana, 1967-68; instr. physics and electronics U.S. Navy Nulcear Power Shc., New London, Conn., 1958-61; sci. organizer Pres.'s Conf. on Superconductivity, 1987, NSF program rsch. applied to nat. needs, 1971, NSF program interdisciplinary rsch. relevant to problems of society, 1969. Contbr. over 130 articles to mags. and profl. jours. Lt. (j.g.) USN, 1958-61. Recipient Meritorious Svc. award NSF, 1972, Meritorious award William A. Jump Found., 1973, Arthur S. Fleming award Downtown Jaycees, 1974; NSF postdoctoral fellow Ctr. for Advanced Study U. Ill., 1967-68; NSF fellow, 1963-65. Fellow AAAS, Am. Phys. Soc.; mem. Am. Chem. Soc., Am. Nuc. Soc., World Future Soc., Sigma Xi, Phi Beta Kappa. Achievements include pioneering development of federal programs in solar and geothermal energy and energy conservation and federal programs in technology transfer to industry. Office: IPRT/Iowa State U 112 Office Lab Bldg Ames IA 50011

SNOW, JOHN WILLIAM, railroad executive; b. Toledo, Aug. 2, 1939; s. William Dean and Catharine (Howard) S.; m. Fredrica Wheeler, June 11, 1964 (div. 1973); children: Bradley, Ian; m. Carolyn Kalk, Aug. 31, 1973; 1 child, Christopher. BA, Kenyon Coll./U. Toledo, 1962; PhD, U. Va., 1965; LLB, George Washington U., 1967. Asst. prof. econs. U. Md., College Park, 1965-67; assoc. Wheeler & Wheeler, Washington, 1967-72; asst. gen. counsel Dept. Transp., Washington, 1972-73, dep. asst. sec. for policy, plans and internat. affairs, 1973-74, asst. sec. for govtl. affairs, 1974-75, dep. under sec., 1975-76; adminstr. Nat. Hwy. Traffic Safety Adminstrn., Washington, 1976-77; v.p. govt. affairs Chessie System Inc., Washington, 1977-80; sr. v.p. corp. services CSX Corp., Richmond, Va., 1980-84, exec. v.p., 1984-85; pres., chief exec. officer Chessie System R.R.s, Balt., 1985-86, CSX Rail Transport, Jacksonville, Fla., 1986-87, CSX Transp., Jacksonville, Va., 1987-88; pres., chief operating officer CSX Corp., Richmond, Va., 1988-89, pres., chief exec. officer, 1989-91, chmn., pres., chief exec. officer, 1991—, also bd. dirs.; adj. prof. law George Washington U., 1972-75; vis. prof. econs. U. Va., Charlottesville, spring 1977; vis. fellow Am. Enterprises Inst., Washington, spring 1977; bd. dirs. NationsBank Corp., USX Corp., Textron Inc., Circuit City Stores, Inc. Bd. trustees Johns Hopkins U. Mem. Va. State Bar. Episcopalian. Clubs: Chevy Chase, Metropolitan (Washington); Commonwealth, Country of Va. (Richmond).

SNOW, KARL NELSON, JR., public management educator, university administrator, former state senator; b. St. George, Utah, July 1, 1930; s. Karl Nelson and Wanda (McGregor) S.; m. Donna Jean Dain, Jan. 29, 1960; children: Karl Nelson, III, Melissa, Daniel D., Jeanmarie, Elisabeth, Howard H. B.S., Brigham Young U., Provo, Utah, 1956; M.A. (State of Minn. Adminstrv. fellow 1956-57), U. Minn., 1958; M.P.A. (univ. fellow 1959-61), U. So. Calif., 1965, D.P.A., 1972. Budget examiner Minn. Dept. Adminstrn., 1956-59; staff asst., instr. Sch. Pub. Adminstrn. U. So. Calif., 1959-62; mem. faculty Brigham Young U., Provo, Utah, 1962—, dir. Inst. Govt., 1969-79, prof. public mgmt., 1979—, asst. exec. v.p., 1987-91; state legis. fiscal analyst, 1966-70; mem. Utah Senate from 16th Dist., 1972-85, majority leader, 1981-85; chmn. Utah State House Fellowship Commn., 1973-79, Utah Constl. Revision Commn., 1977-89; bd. dirs. Legis. Leaders Found., 1981-85; chmn. bd. trustees Utah Tech. Fin. Corp., 1983-94; pres., trustee Utah Tech. Equity Found., 1994-96; chmn. Conf. of State Sponsored Seed and Venture Funds, 1993-96. Bd. editors Public Adminstrn. Rev, 1969-70, State and Local Govt. Rev, 1977-83; contbr. articles to profl. jours. Missionary Mormon Ch., 1950-52, mem. stake high council, 1975-85, 91—, bishop, 1985-90; mem. Warren Burger Prison Task Force, 1983-87; bd. dirs. Utah Innovation Found., 1984-88. Mem. Am. Soc. Pub. Adminstrn. (chpt. pres. 1968-69), dir. nat. council (1969-72), Sons Utah Pioneers. Home: 1847 Oak Ln Provo UT 84604-2140

SNOW, MARINA SEXTON, author; b. Boston, Apr. 9, 1937; d. Charles Ernest Snow and Katherine Alice Townsend; m. Richard DeVere Horton, Aug. 30, 1958 (div. 1968); children: Heather Kertchem, James Horton; m. Charles A. Washburn, Jan. 7, 1978 (div. 1979). BA, U. Iowa, 1958; MA in Speech Pathology, N.Mex. State U., 1967; MA in Librarianship, San Jose State U., 1976; MA in Theatre Arts, Calif. State U., Sacramento, 1979. Cert. clin. competence Am. Speech and Hearing Assn. Tchr. ESL Inst. Colombo-Americano, Cali, Colombia, 1958-59; tchr. Las Cruces (N.Mex.) Pub. Schs., 1964-66; speech therapist Sutter County Schs., Yuba City, Calif., 1967-72; reference libr. Calif. State U. Libr., Sacramento, 1976-95. Contbr. articles to profl. jours.; author 2 plays: Apricot Coffee, Alkali Flat. Pres. Alkali Flat Neighborhood Assn., Sacramento, 1987-94. Mem. Sacramento Old City Assn. Avocations: theatre arts, historic preservation, gardening.

SNOW, MARLON O., trucking executive, state agency administrator; m. Ann; children. Gen. mgr. spl. commadities Milne Truck Lines, Phoenix, L.A., 1970-81; gen. mgr. spl. commodities, sales Motor Cargo, Salt Lake City, Utah, 1981-82; owner MST Trucking, Inc., Salt Lake City, Utah, 1982—. Mem. Utah Valley State Coll. Found. (bd. dirs. 1991—), Alpine Sch. Dist. Found. (bd. dirs. 1990—). Office: 1247 E 430 N Orem UT 84097-5400

SNOW, ROBERT ANTHONY, journalist; b. Berea, Ky., June 1, 1955; s. James Allen and Betty Jo (Threlkeld) S.; m. Jill Ellen Walker, Sept. 26, 1987; children: Kendall Elizabeth, Robert Walker, Kristin Anna. BA, Davidson Coll., 1977; postgrad. in Philosophy and Econs., U. Chgo., 1978-79. Editl. writer The Greensboro (N.C.) Record, 1979-81, The Virginian Pilot, Norfolk, 1981-82; editl. page editor The Daily Press, Newport News, Va., 1982-84; dep. editl. page editor The Detroit News, 1984-87, columnist, 1993—; editl. page editor The Washington Times, 1987-91; dep. asst. to pres. comm., dir. speechwriting The White House, Washington, 1991-92, dep. asst. for media affairs to Pres., 1992-93; columnist USA Today, Arlington, 1993—; syndicated columnist Creators Syndicate, 1993—; substitute host Rush Limbaugh Radio Program, 1994—; polit. analyst Good Morning America, 1995; host Fox News Sunday, 1996—. Active Leadership Washington. Mem. Coun. Fgn. Rels., Nat. Conf. Edtl. Writers. Avocations: sports, music, traveling, writing. Office: Fox News Sunday 400 N Capitol St NW Ste 550 Washington DC 20001-1511

SNOW, THEODORE PECK, astrophysics educator; b. Seattle, Jan. 30, 1947; s. Theodore P. and Louise (Wertz) S.; s. Constance M. Snow, Aug. 23, 1969; children: McGregor A., Tyler M., Reilly A. BA, Yale U., 1969; MS, U. Wash., 1970, PhD, 1973. Mem. rsch. staff Princeton (N.J.) U., 1973-77; prof. U. Colo., Boulder, 1977—, dir. Ctr. for Astrophysics and Space Astronomy, 1986-96. Author: (textbook) The Dynamic Universe, 1983, 4th edit., 1991, Essentials of the Dynamic Universe 4th edit., 1993 (textbook excellence award Text and Academic Authors Assn. 1994), Physics, 1986, Universe: Origins and Evolution, 1997; contbr. over 200 articles to profl. jours. Fellow Royal Astron. Soc.; mem. Am. Astron. Soc., Astron. Soc. Pacific, Sigma Xi. Achievements include discovery, through observations in ultraviolet visible, and infrared wavelengths, of several important processes involving interstellar gas and dust, and their roles in star formation and late stages of stellar evolution. Office: U Colo Ctr Astrophysics Space Astronomy Campus Box 389 Boulder CO 80309

SNOW, TOWER CHARLES, JR., lawyer; b. Boston, Oct. 28, 1947; s. Tower Charles and Margaret (Harper) S.; m. Belinda L. Snow. AB cum laude English, Dartmouth Coll., 1969; JD, U. Calif., Berkeley, 1973. Bar: Calif. 1973, U.S. Dist. Ct. (no. dist.) Calif. 1973, U.S. Ct. Appeals (9th cir.) 1973, U.S. Supreme Ct. 1976, U.S. Dist. Ct. (ea. dist.) Calif. 1979, U.S. Ct. Appeals (fed. cir.) 1980, U.S. Ct. Claims 1980, U.S. Ct. Appeals (2d cir.) 1987, N.Y. 1988, U.S. Dist. Ct. (ea. and so. dists.) N.Y. 1988, U.S. Dist. Ct. (ctrl. dist.) Calif. 1989, U.S. Dist. Ct. (no. dist.) Tex. 1995, U.S. Dist. Ct. (so. dist.) Calif. 1996, U.S. Dist. Ct. Ariz. 1996. Ptnr., chmn. litigation dept. Orrick, Herrington & Sutcliffe, San Francisco, 1973-89; ptnr. Shearman & Sterling, San Francisco, 1989-94; ptnr., chmn. securities litigation group, mem. policy com. Brobeck, Phleger & Harrison, San Francisco, 1995—; arbitrator Nat. Assn. Securities Dealers, Am. Stock Exch., N.Y. Stock Exch., Pacific Coast Stock Exch., Superior Ct. City and County San Francisco, Am. Arbitration Assn.; lectr. in field. Author numerous law handbooks and articles to prof. jours. Mem. San Francisco Mus. Soc., San Francisco Symphony, San Francisco Ballet, San Francisco Opera, Am. Conservatory Theatre. Mem. ABA (chmn. subcom. pub. offering litig. 1984-88, co-chair task force on securities arbitration 1988-89, vice chair securities litig. com. 1986-88), Continuing Edn. Bar (bus. law inst. planning com. 1986), Securities Industry Assn., Nat. Inst. Trial Advocacy, San Francisco Bar Assn. (pres. securities litig. sect. 1995). Democrat. Avocations: internat. travel, skiing, running, scuba diving, photography. Home: 177 Ridge Dr Napa CA 94558-9777 Office: Brobeck Phleger & Harrison Spear St Tower One Market St San Francisco CA 94105

SNOW, W. STERLING, secondary education educator, retired sports coach; b. Devils Lake, N.D., Feb. 14, 1947; s. Morgan Williams and Josephine Elizabeth Ann (Erickstad) S.; m. Barbara Kay Jolley, Aug. 29, 1976; 1 child, Michelle Rene. AB, U. Calif., Santa Cruz, 1970; postgrad., U. Calif., Santa Barbara, 1970-71; MA, Chapman Coll., 1976. Cert. secondary sch. tchr., Calif., Alaska, Ariz.; cert. in adminstrn., Calif., Ariz. Tchr., coach Monterey (Calif.) Peninsula Unified Sch. Dist., 1972-76; tchr., coach Anchorage (Alaska) Sch. Dist., 1976-96, athletic dir., 1987-92, tchr., 1992-96; sabbatical, 1996—; conf. asst. U. Calif., Santa Cruz, 1971-78. Bd. dirs. Dimond Alumni Found., Anchorage, 1987-92. Recipient Merit award for outstanding athletic program Alaska Dept. Edn., 1990, Appreciation award Dimond Alumni Found., 1990, Hall of Fame award, 1995. Mem. AAAS, ASCD, NSTA, Am. Chem. Soc., Nat. Assn. Biology Tchrs. (life), Nat. Interscholastic Athletic Adminstrs. Assn. (life), Alaska Sci. Tchrs. Assn., Alaska Athletic Adminstrs. Interscholastic Assn. (Athletic Dir. of Yr. 1990), N.Y. Acad. Scis., Kappa Delta Pi. Lutheran.

SNOWBARGER, VINCENT KEITH, congressman; b. Kankakee, Ill., Sept. 16, 1949; s. Willis Edward and Wahnona Ruth (Horger) S.; m. Carolyn Ruth McMahon, Mar. 25, 1972; children: Jeffrey Edward, Matthew David. BA in History, So. Nazarene U., 1971; MA in Polit. Sci., U. Ill., 1974; JD, U. Kans., 1977. Bar: Kans. 1977, U.S. Dist. Ct. Kans. 1977, Mo. 1987. Instr. Mid-Am. Nazarene Coll., Olathe, Kans., 1973-76; ptnr. Haskin, Hinkle, Slater & Snowbarger, Olathe, 1977-84, Dietrich, Davis, Dicus et al, Olathe, 1984-88, Armstrong, Teasdale, Schafly & Davis, Overland Park, Kans., 1989-92; Holbrook, Heaven & Fay, P.C., Merriam, Kans., 1992-94; ptnr. Snowbarger & Veatch LLP, Olathe, Kans., 1994-96; mem. 105th Congress from 3rd Kans. dist., 1997—. Mem. Kans. Legislature, Topeka, 1985-96; majority leader Ho. of Reps., 1993-96; mem. Olathe Planning Commn., 1982-84, Leadership Olalthe; divsn. chmn. United Way, Olathe, 1985-88, chmn. citizen rev. com., 1991-95. Mem. Kans. Bar Assn., Kans. Assn. Hosp. Attys., Johnson County Bar Assn., Olathe Area C. of C. (bd. dirs. 1984), Overland Park C. of C. Republican. Nazarene. Avocation: politics. Home: 1451 E Orleans Dr Olathe KS 66062-5728 Office: 509 Cannon House Off Bldg Washington DC 20515-1603

SNOWDEN, FRANK MARTIN, JR., classics educator; b. York County, Va., July 17, 1911; s. Frank Martin and Alice (Phillips) S.; m. Elaine Hill, June 8, 1935; children: Jane Alice, Frank Martin III. Grad., Boston Latin Sch., 1928; AB, Harvard U., 1932, AM, 1933, PhD, 1944; postgrad., Am. Acad. in Rome, summer 1938; Fulbright research scholar, Italy, 1949-50; LLD (hon.), Bard Coll., 1957; DLitt (hon.), Union Coll., 1979; LHD (hon.), Georgetown U., 1985, Howard U., 1985; LHD, U. Md., 1993. Instr. classics Va. State Coll., 1933-36, Spelman Coll., 1936-40; instr. classics Howard U., 1942-44, chmn. dept., 1942-77, asso. prof., 1944-45, prof., 1945-90, prof. emeritus, 1991—; dir. Howard U. (Summer Sch.), 1942-54, Howard U. (Evening Sch. and Adult Edn.), 1942-48; chmn. Howard U. (Humanities Program), 1950-51; dean Howard U. (Coll. Liberal Arts), 1956-68; specialist lectr. Internat. Information Adminstrn., Dept. State, French West Africa, Gold Coast, Nigeria, Libya, Italy, Greece, Austria, 1953; cultural attaché Am. Embassy, Rome, Italy, 1954-56; vis. lectr. Fgn. Service Inst., 1956-62, 66-68; U.S. specialist in, India, lectr., Bombay, New Delhi, Lucknow, Calcutta, Madras areas, 1957, lectr. as U.S. specialist, Brazil, summer 1960, studied higher edn., Soviet Union, 1958; participant internat. seminar University Today, Dubrovnik, Yugoslavia, 1958; mem. U.S. del. UNESCO, Paris, 1958, 60, U.S. nat. commn. for, 1958-61; mem. Nat. Humanities Faculty, 1969-70, mem. bd., 1970-73; ann. lectr. Archaeol. Inst. Am., 1970-71, 74-76; vis. scholar U. Center Va., 1971-72; mem. com. Internat. Exchange Persons, 1970-73; mem. jury to select fellows in classics Am. Acad. Rome, 1971-73; mem. com. Folger Fellowship Program, 1972-75; Am. Council Learned Socs. rep. Council on Internat. Exchange of Scholars, 1973-77; mem. D.C. com. on Fulbright scholarships, 1951-54, 68-74; fellow Woodrow Wilson Internat. Center for Scholars, 1977; scholar-in-residence Rockefeller Found., Bellagio, Italy, fall 1977; adj. prof. classics Georgetown U., 1991-92, Blegen vis. disting. rsch prof. Vassar Coll., 1992-93. Author: Blacks in Antiquity: Ethiopians in the Greco-Roman Experience, 1970; co-author: The Image of the Black in Western Art I: From the Pharaohs to the Fall of the Roman Empire (also pub. in French), 1976, Before Color Prejudice: The Ancient View of Blacks, 1983; contbr. chpts. to books, articles to classical and ednl. jours. Mem. D.C. Mayor's Commn. Arts and Humanities, 1972-74; vis. com. bd. overseers dept. classics Harvard Coll., 1977-83. Decorated Medaglia d'Oro for outstanding work in Italian culture and edn. Italy, 1958; Am. Council Learned Socs. fellow, 1962-63; NEH grantee, summer 1970. Mem. Am. Conf. Acad. Deans (sec., editor 1959-62, chmn. 1963-64), Am. Council on Edn., Vergilian Soc. Am. (trustee 1956-60), Am. Philol. Assn. (Charles J. Goodwin award of merit 1973, bd. dirs. 1976-79, 2d v.p. 1983-84), Archeol. Inst. Am. (pres. Washington soc. 1971), Classical Soc. Am. Acad. in Rome, Washington Classical Soc. (v.p. 1949-50, pres. 1974-75), Washington Fedn. Chs. (v.p. 1951-53). Clubs: Cosmos, Harvard. Home: 4200 Massachusetts Ave NW Washington DC 20016-4744

SNOWDEN, LAWRENCE FONTAINE, retired aircraft company executive, retired marine corps general officer; b. Charlottesville, Va., Apr. 14, 1921; s. Lawrence Fontaine Snoddy and Beatrice M. (Huffman) S.; m. Martha Roselyn Ham, Nov. 17, 1942; children: John Stephen, Brian Fontaine. Student, Stetson U., 1938-39; BS, U. Va., 1942; MA, Northwestern U., 1950; advanced mgmt. program, Harvard U., 1968; grad., Indsl. Coll. Armed Forces, 1967. Commd. 2d lt. USMC, 1942, advanced through grades to lt. gen., 1975; comdr. 7th Marine Regt., Vietnam, 1966; ops. officer III Marine Amphibious Force, Vietnam, 1967; asst. dir. personnel Hdqrs. Marine Corps, Washington, 1968-69; dir. systems support group Hdqrs. Marine Corps, 1969-70; dir. Marine Corps Devel. Ctr., Quantico, Va., 1970-72; chief of staff U.S. Forces, Japan, 1972-75; U.S. chmn. UN Bd., Japan, 1973-75; chief of staff Hdqrs. U.S. Marine Corps, 1977-79; ret., 1979; v.p. Far East Internat. Service Co. Hughes Aircraft Co., 1979-86; group v.p. Internat. Ground Systems Group Hughes Aircraft Co., Fullerton, Calif., 1986-88; pres. Snowden Internat. Assocs., Tallahassee, Fla., 1988—. Recipient Disting. Eagle Scout award, Silver Beaver award Boy Scouts Am.; decorated Legion of Merit (5), Army Commendation medal, Navy Commendation medal, D.S.M. (2), Purple Heart (2), Cross of Gallantry (3) Vietnam, Second Order of Sacred Treasure Japan). Mem. Marine Corps League, U.S. Navy League, Am. C. of C. in Japan , Am.-Japan Soc., Marine Corps Assn., Sigma Nu. Clubs: Tokyo, Killearn Country.

SNOWDEN, RUTH O'DELL GILLESPIE, artist; b. Gary, W.Va., Apr. 16, 1926; d. Haynes Thornton and Blanche Beaula (Boling) Gillespie; m. Eugene Louis Snowden, Dec. 21, 1946; children: Wanda Snowden Ballard, Eugene III, Ronald, Marian Snowden Warren, Jeffry. RN, Natharith Coll., 1946; postgrad., Transylvania U., 1983-84, U. Ky., 1985-89. RN. Painter, publicity chmn. Artists's Attic Inc., Lexington, Ky., 1988-89. Exhibited in group shows at U. Ky. Art Mus., Lexington, 1988, 5th Internat. Juried Exhibition Pastels, Nyack, N.Y., 1988, Small Paintings Nat., Ky. Highlands Mus., Ashland, 1988, The Appalachian Cen., U. Ky., 1988, Ft. Wayne (Ind.) Mus. Art, 1986, John Howard Sanden Nat. Artists Seminar, Washington, Nat. Artists' Seminar, Chgo., Huntington (W.Va.) Galleries, Nat. Nursing Art Exhibit, Meth. Med. Cen., Peoria, Ill., Chautauqua Art Assn. Galleries, N.Y., 1990, Central Bank gallery, Chatauqua, 1990, Pastel & Chisel Acad. Fine Arts, 1990, Opera House Gallery, 1990, Sacramento Fine Arts Ctr., 1990, Ariel Gallery, Soho, N.Y., 1990, 91, Sumi-e Soc. Am., Inc., 1993, Watercolor Soc. Ala., 1994; represented in the Director of American Portrait Artists, Am. Portrait Soc., Huntington Harbour, Calif.; numerous local and nat. shows; in pvt. collections. Recipient Assn. Alliance award Am. Frame Co., 1993, also various watercolor and oil painting awards. Mem. Oil Pastel Assn., Nyack, N.Y., Winchester Art Guild, Lexington Art League, Ky. Watercolor Assn. (Bluegrass regional dir. 1988, 89, 90, 91, 92), Ky. Guild Artists and Craftsmen, Inc., Berea, Northwest Pastel Soc., Seattle, Degas Pastel Soc., New Orleans. Avocations: golfing, bowling. Home: 2800 Old Boonesboro Rd Winchester KY 40391-8805 Office: Artists Attic Inc Victorian Square 401 W Main St Lexington KY 40507-1640

SNOWDON, JANE LOUISE, industrial engineer; b. Ann Arbor, Mich., July 17, 1959; d. John Colin and Anne Joy (Vickery) S. BS in Indsl. Engring., Pa. State U., 1981; MS in Indsl. Engring., U. Mich., 1982; PhD in Indsl. Engring., Ga. Inst. Tech., 1994. Semiconductor cost engring. coordinator IBM Corp., Hopewell Junction, N.Y., 1982-85; engagement mgr. IBM Corp., Boca Raton, Fla., 1990-96; mem. rsch. staff T.J. Watson Rsch. Ctr. IBM Corp., Yorktown Heights, N.Y., 1996—. Contbr. articles to profl. jours. Mem. Inst. Indsl. Engrs. (sr., Mid-Hudson chpt. devel. officer 1984-85, sec. 1983-84, N.Y.-Pa. Inst. Indsl. Engrs. scholar 1980, v.p. West Palm Beach chpt. 1991-93), Inst. Ops. Rsch. and Mgmt. Scis., Soc. Women Engrs., (Union Carbide scholar 1978), English Speaking Union, Pi Mu Epsilon, Alpha Pi Mu, Alpha Lambda Delta, Tau Beta Pi, Phi Mu (Mary King Shepardson scholar 1981, Lowe scholar, 1986, 88), Sigma Xi. Republican. Episcopalian. Avocations: travel, tennis, swimming, aerobic dancing, golf. Home: 44 Northfield St Greenwich CT 06830-4618

SNOWE, OLYMPIA J., senator; b. Augusta, Maine, Feb. 21, 1947; d. George John and Georgia G. Bouchles; m. John McKernan. BA, U. Maine, 1969; LLD (hon.), U. Maine, Machias, 1982, Husson Coll., 1981, Bowdoin Coll., 1985, Suffolk U., 1994, Colby Coll., 1996. Businesswoman; mem. Maine Ho. of Reps., 1973-76, Maine Senate, 1976-78; mem. 96th-103d Congresses from 2d Maine Dist., 1979-94, mem. budget com., foreign affairs com., com. on aging, 1979-94; co-chair Congl. Caucus for Women's Issues, 1983-94; dep. Republican whip, U.S. senator from Maine, 1995—; mem. commerce, sci. and transp. com., chmn. subcom. Oceans and Fisheries; mem. armed svcs. com., budget com., small bus. com., counsel to asst. senate majority leader; corporator Mechanics Savs. Bank. Republican. Greek Orthodox. Club: Philoptochos Soc. Office: US Senate 250 Russell Senate Bldg Washington DC 20510-1903

SNOWISS, ALVIN L., lawyer; b. Lock Haven, Pa., June 16, 1930; s. Benjamin and Lillian (Kalin) S.; m. Jean Yarnell, Mar. 16, 1973. BA, U. Pa., Phila., 1952, JD, 1955. Bar: Pa. 1956, U.S. Dist. Ct. (mid. dist.) Pa. 1958, U.S. Supreme Ct. 1972. Pvt. practice Lock Haven, 1955-61; ptnr. Lugg & Snowiss, Lock Haven, 1961-74, Lugg, Snowiss, Steinberg & Faulkner, Lock Haven, 1974-86, Snowiss, Steinberg & Faulkner, LLP, Lock Haven, 1987—; solicitor Clinton County, Lock Haven, 1964-72; dir. Mellon Bank, ctrl. region, State College, Pa. Chmn. bd. Lock Haven Hosp. Found., 1986-92; pres. Lock Haven Hosp., 1982-86; bd. govs. Clinton County Cmty. Found., Lock Haven, 1970-97; chmn. adv. bd. Palmer Mus. Art, State College; mem. Bucknell U. Ctr. Gallery, Lewisburg, Pa.; mem. nat. devel. coun. Pa. State U., State College, 1990-96; v.p. bd. trustees Ross Libr., Lock Haven, 1963-86; mem. exec. com. Pa. Rep. Com., Harrisburg, 1974-80; state committeeman Clinton County Rep. Com., Lock Haven, 1967-80. Fellow Am. Coll. Trust and Estate Counsel, Am. Bar Found., Pa. Bar Found. (founding, bd. dirs. 1984-95); mem. Pa. Bar Assn. (zone del. 1976-82, zone gov. 1983-86, treas. 1987-90), Clinton County Bar Assn. (pres. 1975-76), Kiwanis (pres. Lock Haven 1966-67). Republican. Avocations: art history, golf, historical research. Home: 414 W Main St Lock Haven PA 17745-1107 Office: 333 N Vesper St Lock Haven PA 17745-1342

SNYDER, ALAN CARHART, insurance company executive; b. N.Y.C., May 25, 1946; s. John I. and Elfrida (Bendix) S.; m. Mary Burgoyne, Feb. 9, 1974. BS, BA, Georgetown U., 1968; MBA, Harvard U., 1973. Cons. Reynolds Securities, N.Y.C., 1972-73; exec. v.p. Dean Witter Reynolds, N.Y.C., 1975-85; sole proprietor Shinnecock Ptnrs., N.Y.C., 1985-89, mng. ptnr., 1989—; pres., chief oper. officer, bd. dirs. First Exec. Corp., L.A., 1990-91; COO, Exec. Life Ins. Co., L.A., 1991-93; CEO, Aurora Nat. Life Assurance Co., LA, 1993-94; cons. Aurora Nat. Life Assurance Co., L.A., 1994-95; mng. ptnr. Shinnecock Group L.L.C., L.A., 1994—. Baker scholar Harvard Bus. Sch., 1973.

SNYDER, ALLEGRA FULLER, dance educator; b. Chgo., Aug. 28, 1927; d. R. Buckminster and Anne (Hewlett) Fuller; m. Robert Snyder, June 30, 1951 (div. Apr. 1975, remarried Sept. 1980); children: Alexandra, Jaime. BA in Dance, Bennington Coll., 1951; MA in Dance, UCLA, 1967. Asst. to curator, dance archives Mus. Modern Art, N.Y.C., 1945-47; dancer Ballet Soc. of N.Y.C. Ballet Co., 1945-47; mem. office and prodn. staff Internat. Film Found., N.Y.C., 1950-52; editor, dance films Film News mag., N.Y.C., 1966-72; lectr. dance and film adv., dept. dance UCLA, 1967-73, chmn. dept. dance, 1974-80, 90-91, acting chair, spring 1985, chair of faculty Sch. of the Arts, 1989-91, prof. dance and dance ethnology, 1973-91, prof. emeritus, 1991—; pres. Buckminster Fuller Inst., Santa Barbara, Calif.; chairwoman bd. dirs. Buckminster Fuller Inst.; vis. lectr. Calif. Inst. Arts, Valencia, 1972; co-dir. dance and TV workshop Am. Dance Festival, Conn. Coll., New London, 1973; dir. NEH summer seminar for coll. tchrs. Asian Performing Arts, 1978, 81; coord. Ethnic Arts Intercoll. Interdisciplinary Program, 1974-73, acting chmn., 1986; vis. prof. performance studies NYU, 1982-83; hon. vis. prof. U. Surrey, Guildford, Eng., 1983-84; cons. Thyodia Found., Salt Lake City, 1973-74; mem. dance adv. panel Nat. Endowment Arts, 1968-72, Calif. Arts Commn., 1974-91; mem. adv. screening com. Coun. Internat. Exch. of Scholars, 1979-82; mem. various panels NEH, 1979-85; core cons. for Dancing, Sta. WNET-TV, 1988—. Dir. film Baroque Dance 1625-1725, in 1977; co-dir. film Gods of Bali, 1952; dir. and wrote film Bayanihan, 1962 (named Best Folkloric Documentary at Bilboa Film Festival, winner Golden Eagle award); asst. dir. and asst. editor film The Bennington Story, 1952; created films Gestures of Sand, 1968, Reflections on Choreography, 1973, When the Fire Dances Between Two Poles, 1982; created film, video loop and text Celebration: A World of Art and Ritual, 1982-83; supr. post-prodn. film Erick Hawkins, 1964, in 1973. Also contbr. articles to profl. jours. and mags. Adv. com. Pacific Asia Mus., 1980-84, Festival of the Mask, Craft and Folk Art Mus., 1979-84; adv. panel Los Angeles Dance Currents II, Mus. Ctr. Dance Assn., 1974-75; bd. dirs. Council Grove Sch. III, Compton, Calif., 1976-81; apptd. mem. Adv. Dance Com., Pasadena (Calif.) Art Mus., 1970-71, Los Angeles Festival of Performing Arts com., Studio Watts, 1970; mem. Technology and Cultural Transformation com., UNESCO, 1977. Fulbright research fellow, 1983-84; grantee Nat. Endowment Arts, 1981, Nat. Endowment Humanities, 1977, 79, 81, UCLA, 1968, 77, 80, 82, 85; recipient Amer. Dance Guild Award for Outstanding Achievement in Dance, 1992. Mem. Am. Dance Therapy Assn., Congress on Rsch. in Dance (bd. dirs. 1970-76, chmn. 1975-77, nat. conf. chmn. 1972), Coun. Dance Adminstrs., Am. Dance Guild (chmn. com. awards 1972), Soc. for Ethnomusicology, Am. Anthrop. Assn., Am. Folklore Soc., Soc. Anthropology of Visual Comm., Soc. Humanistic Anthropology, Calif. Dance Educators Assn. (conf. chmn. 1972), L.A. Area Dance Alliance (adv. bd. 1978-84, selection com. Dance Kaleidoscope project 1979-81), Fulbright Alumni Assn. Home: 15313 Whitfield Ave Pacific Palisades CA 90272-2548 Office: Buckminster Fuller Inst 2040 Alameda Padre Serra Santa Barbara CA 93103-1760*

SNYDER, ARTHUR, publishing company executive; b. Valley Stream, N.Y., Feb. 6, 1925; s. Arthur and Kathryn (Staubitzer) S.; m. Betty Lain Harper, July 8, 1950; children: Susan, Arthur, Betsy, Jack, Heidi, Bonnie. B in Metall. Engring., Cornell U., 1950, MBA, 1952. Mfg. engr. Norton Co., Worcester, Mass., 1952-56; chief accountant Norton Co., 1956-58, asst. controller, 1958-59, mgr. data processing, 1959-61, controller, 1961-65; exec. v.p. A.M. Best Co., Oldwick, N.J., 1965-67; pres. A.M. Best Co., 1968—, chmn., 1971—. Author: Principles of Inventory Control and Managing Capital Expenditures. 1st lt. 95th Inf. div. AUS, 1942-45. Decorated Bronze Star with oak leaf cluster, Purple Heart. Mem. Fin. Execs. Inst., Cornell Soc. Engrs., Roxiticus Golf Club (Mendham, N.J.), Baltusrol Golf Club (Springfield, N.J.), U.S. Srs. Golf Assn., Lyford Cay Club (Nassau, Bahamas), Loch Lomond Golf Club (Scotland). Presbyterian. Home: Lloyd Rd Bernardsville NJ 07924-1710 Office: A M Best Company Inc Ambest Rd Oldwick NJ 08858

SNYDER, CAROLYN ANN, university dean, librarian; b. Elgin, Nebr., Nov. 5, 1942; d. Ralph and Florence Wagner; m. Barry Snyder, Apr. 24, 1969. Student, Nebr. Wesleyan U., 1960-61; BS cum laude, Kearney State Coll., 1964; MS in Librarianship, U. Denver, 1965. Asst. libr. sci. and tech. U. Nebr., Lincoln, 1965-67, asst. pub. svc. libr., 1967-68, 70-73; pers. libr. Ind. U. Librs., Bloomington, 1973-76, acting dean of univ. librs., 1980, 88-89, assoc. dean for pub. svcs., 1977-88, 89-91, interim devel. officer, 1989-91; adminstrv. army libr. Spl. Svcs. Agy., Europe, 1968-70; dean libr. affairs So. Ill. U., Carbondale, 1991—; team leader Midwest Univs. Consortium for Internat. Activities-World Bank IX project to develop libr. system and implement automation U. Indonesia, Jakarta, 1984-86; libr. devel. cons. Inst. Tech. MARA/Midwest Univs. Consortium for Internat. Activities Program in Malaysia, 1985; ofcl. rep. EDUCOM, 1996—. Contbr. chpt. to book and articles to profl. jours. Mem. Humane Assn. Jackson County, 1991—, Carbondale Pub. Libr. Friends, 1991—. Recipient Cooperative Rsch. grant Coun. on Libr. Resources, Washington, 1984. Mem. ALA (councilor 1985-89, Bogle Internat. Travel award 1988, H.W. Wilson Libr. Staff devel. grantee 1981), Libr. Adminstrn./Mgmt. Assn. (pres. 1981-82), Com. on Instnl. Coop./Resource Sharing (chair 1987-91), Coalition for Networked Info. (So. Ill. U. at Carbondale rep. 1991—), Coun. Dirs. State Univ. Librs. in Ill. (chair 1992-93), Ill. Assn. Coll. and Rsch. Librs. (chair Ill. Bd. Higher Edn. liaison com. 1993-94), Ill. Network (bd. dirs.), Ind. Libr. Assn. (chair coll./univ. divsn. 1982-83), U.S. Grant Assn. (bd. dirs. 1992—), Ill. Libr. Computer Sys. Orgn. (policy coun. 1992-95, 96—), Nat. Assn. State Univs. and Land-Grant Colls. (commn. on info. tech. and its distance learning bd. and libr. bds. 1994-96), NetIllinois (bd. dirs. 1994-96), OCLC Users Coun. (elected rep. 1995—). Avocations: antiques, theater, movies. Office: So Ill U Morris Libr Carbondale IL 62901-6632

SNYDER, CHARLES AUBREY, lawyer; b. Bastrop, La., June 19, 1941; s. David and Shirley Blossom (Haas) S.; m. Sharon Rae Veta, Aug. 29, 1963; children: David Veta, Shelby Haas, Claire Frances. B.B.A., Tulane U., 1963; J.D., La. State U., 1966. Bar: La. 1966. Assoc. firm. Milling, Benson, Woodward, Hillyer, Pierson & Miller, and predecessors, New Orleans, 1966-69, ptnr., 1969—; bd. dirs. Delta Petroleum Co., La. Motel and Investment Corp., Jerre aux Boeufs Corp. Trustee Kathyn O'Brien Found., 1970; bd. dirs. New Orleans Speech and Hearing Ctr., pres., 1978-80; bd. dirs. City Pk. Commn., 1991—, pres., 1995; fellow La. Coll. Securities Counsel. Mem. ABA, La. Bar Assn. (chmn. sect. on corp. and bus. law 1982-83), New Orleans Bar Assn., La. Law Inst. (coms. on mineral code and revision of partnership law and community property law), Beta Gamma Sigma. Clubs: Metairie Country, City Energy, Plimsoll. Home: 74724 River Rd Covington LA 70435 Office: Milling Benson Woodward Hillyer Pierson & Mill 909 Poydras St Ste 2300 New Orleans LA 70112-4024

SNYDER, CHARLES ROYCE, sociologist, educator; b. Haverford, Pa., Dec. 28, 1924; s. Edward D. and Edith (Royce) S.; m. Patricia Hanson, June 30, 1951; children—Stephen Hoyt, Christiana Marie, Constance Patricia, Daniel Edward. BA, Yale U., 1945, M.A., 1949, Ph.D., 1954. Mem. staff Ctr. Alcohol Studies Yale U., 1950-60, asst. prof. sociology, 1956-60; prof. sociology So. Ill. U., Carbondale, 1960-85; chmn. dept. So. Ill. U., 1964-75, 81-85, prof. emeritus, 1985—; vis. prof. human genetics Sackler Sch. Medicine, Tel Aviv U., 1980; cons. behavioral scis. tng. com. Nat. Inst. Gen. Med. Scis., NIH, 1962-64; mem. planning com., chmn. program 28th Internat. Congress Alcohol and Alcoholism, 1964. Author: Alcohol and the Jews, 1958; editor: (with D.J. Pittman) Society, Culture and Drinking Patterns, 1962; editorial bd. Quar. Jour. Studies on Alcohol, 1957-83; assoc. editor Sociol. Quar., 1960-63. Mem. theol. commn. United Ch. of Christ, 1964-71; bd. dirs. Ill. Stewardship Alliance, 1990-95. With USNR, WWII. Fellow Am. Sociol. Assn.; mem. Soc. Study Social Problems (v.p. 1963-64, rep. to council Am. Sociol. Assn. 1964-66), Midwest Sociol. Soc. (bd. dirs. 1970-71), AAUP. Home: 1223 Race St Apt 501 Denver CO 80206

SNYDER, CHARLES THEODORE, geologist; b. Powell, Wyo., July 19, 1912; s. Lee G. and Eda Belle (Hansen) S.; m. Marion Ruth Harris, Dec. 22, 1945 (dec. 1973); children: Anita Maria, Kristin Eileen; m. Alberta Irene Dangel, Oct. 15, 1973 (dec. 1994). BS, U. Ariz., 1948. Registered profl. geologist, Calif. Hydrologist U.S. Geol. Survey, Menlo Park, Calif., 1948-75; dir. Scotts Valley (Calif.) Water Dist., 1980-84; vis. scientist Carter County Mus., Ekalaka, Mont., 1983-84; researcher Resurgent Lakes in Western U.S. Author: Effect of Off-Road Vehicles, 1976. Disaster chmn. ARC, 1982-83. Mem. AAAS, Arctic Inst. N.Am., Soc. Vertebrate Paleontologists. Democrat. Presbyterian. Home: 552 Bean Creek Rd Scotts Valley CA 95066-3327

SNYDER, CLAIR ALLISON, banker; b. Reading, Pa., June 12, 1921; s. Augustus M. and Estella G. (Bright) S.; m. Jean Doris George, June 27, 1948 (dec. Feb. 1997); children: Joan Marie Snyder Ferguson, Jerry George. Student, W.Va. U., 1943-44, U. Mich., 1944-45. With Meridian Bancorp, Inc. and Meridian Bank, Reading, 1938-43, 46-88; exec. v.p., gen. banking Meridian Bancorp, Inc. and Meridian Bank, 1973-78, exec. v.p., chmn. credit policy com., 1978-86; pvt. practice fin. cons. Snyder Svcs. Co., Reading, 1987—; bd. dirs. Terre Hill (Pa.) Concrete Corp., Am. Beton Systems, Terre Hill; asst. sec. Bi-Products, Inc., Fairfax, Va. Bd. dirs. Pa. divsn. Am. Cancer Soc., 1965-87, chmn. bd. dirs., 1975-77; chmn. Hope Lodge Com.; chmn. Property Mgmt. Com. With U.S. Army, 1943-46. Recipient Luther Halsey Gulick award Camp Fire Girls, 1966; div. Bronze medal Am. Cancer Soc., also Sword of Hope award. Mem. Internat. Soc. for Philosophic Inquiry, Am. Bankers Assn. (cert.), Pa. Bankers Assn. (group chmn. 1972-73), Robert Morris Assocs. (pres. 1972-73), Am. Legion (post comdr. 1948-49), Old Point Golf and Country Club, Moselem Springs Golf Club, Belvedere Plantation Golf and Country Club. Republican. Mem. United Chs. of Christ. Home: Flying Hills 92 Medinah Dr Reading PA 19607-3313 also: 616 Sawgrass Rd Olde Point Hampstead NC 28443 *My life has been dedicated to personal achievement, but always with the knowledge that mankind's progress can only occur if each of us is willing to commit some of our efforts and resources to the future.*

SNYDER, DAVID L., film production designer; b. Buffalo, Sept. 22, 1944; s. Albert R. and Louise M. (Passero) S.; m. Terry Finn, Aug. 1, 1990; children: David Michael, Amy Lynne. Grad. high sch., Niagara Falls, N.Y. Ind. film prodn. designer Hollywood, Calif.; pres. Snyder Bros. Prodns., Inc., Hollywood; guest speaker Tokyo Internat. Film Festival, 1985. Art dir.: (films) In God We Trust, 1980, The Idolmaker, 1980, Blade Runner, 1982 (Academy award nomination best art direction 1982), Brainstorm, 1983; prodn. designer: (films) Strange Brew, 1983, Racing With the Moon, 1984, The Woman In Red, 1984, My Science Project, 1985, Armed and Dangerous, 1986, Back to School, 1986, Summer School, 1987, Moving, 1988, She's Out of Control, 1989, Bill & Ted's Bogus Journey, 1991, Class Act, 1992, Super Mario Brothers, 1993, Demolition Man, 1993, Terminal Velocity, 1994, Rainbow, 1995, Vegas Vacation, 1997, An Alan Smithee Film, 1997; assoc. prodr.: (film) Cold Dog Soup, 1990; exec. prodr. (film) Rainbow, 1995. Mem. NATAS, Soc. Motion Picture and TV Art Dirs., Acad. Motion Picture Arts and Scis., Dirs. Guild Am. Democrat. Avocation: researching history of the film industry in America. Office: Internat Creative Mgmt (ICM) c/o Paul Hook Talent Agy 8942 Wilshire Blvd Beverly Hills CA 90211

SNYDER, DAVID RICHARD, lawyer; b. Kalamazoo, Mich., Oct. 9, 1949; s. Richard E. and Margaret L. (Vanderplough) S.; m. Phyllis Alford, Aug. 14, 1971; children: Jason Richard, Carrie Lynn. BA with high honors, Mich. State U., 1971; JD with distinction, Cornell U., 1974. Bar: Calif. 1974. Assoc. Jenkins & Perry, San Diego, 1974-77, ptnr., 1978-83; ptnr. Aylward, Kintz & Stiska, San Diego, 1983-86, Luce, Forward, Hamilton & Scripps, San Diego, 1986-93, Pillsbury Madison & Sutro LLP, San Diego, 1993—; v.p., dir. San Diego Venture Group, 1989-91; adj. prof. Calif. Western Sch. Law, San Diego, 1982-84; lectr. Calif. Continuing Edn. of Bar, 1983—. Co-author: Drafting Legal Instruments, 1982; editor Cornell Law Rev., 1973-74. Bd. dirs. Boys Club Chula Vista, Calif., 1979-83; pres. Corpus Christi Parish Coun., Bonita, Calif., 1988-90; mem. Children's Hosp. Found., San Diego, 1988—, chmn., 1990-92. Mem. ABA (fed. securities law com. 1987—, vice chmn. subcom. on ann. rev. fed. securities regulation), State Bar Calif., San Diego County Bar Assn., Am. Electronics Assn. (bd. dirs., mem. exec. com. San Diego chpt. 1991-93), Order of Coif, Phi Beta Kappa. Republican. Roman Catholic. Office: Pillsbury Madison & Sutro 101 W Broadway Ste 1800 San Diego CA 92101-8219

SNYDER, DONALD EDWARD, corporate executive; b. Rochester, N.Y., Nov. 10, 1928; s. Benjamin Orman and Arlien Henrietta (Wing) S.; m. Dorothy Edna Stanke, Oct. 16, 1954; children—Donald Edward, Anne Arlien Snyder Marone, Barbara Lynn Snyder Mitchell, Richard John Snyder. A.B., Cornell U., 1950, J.D., 1952; postgrad., Ind. U., 1962. Bar: N.Y. 1953. Pvt. practice law, 1953-56; with Eastman Savs. and Loan Assn., 1956-68, pres., 1970-75, chmn. bd., 1979-88; asst. to treas. Eastman Kodak Co., Rochester, 1968-70; gen. credit mgr. Eastman Kodak Co., 1975-77, with Comptroller's div., 1977-78, asst. treas., 1978-79, treas., 1979-88; chmn. Eastman Kodak Credit Corp., 1985-88; chief exec. officer, chmn. bd., pres. Corp. Officers and Dirs. Assurance Ltd., Hamilton, Bermuda, 1990-93. Bd. dirs. Greater Rochester chpt. Epilepsy Found. Am., 1979-85, Allendale Mut. Ins. Co., 1983-92; bd. dirs. Luth. Ch.-Mo. Synod, 1983-95; vice chmn. bd., chmn. fin. com., mem., chmn. audit com., 1989-95; bd. dirs., mem. exec. com. ACE Ltd., 1985-90, EXEL Ltd., 1985-90, CODA Ltd., 1986-93; mem. investment rev. com. United Way of Greater Rochester, 1979—; trustee

Seneca Zool. Soc., 1983-90. With USNR, 1946-48. Mem. N.Y. State Bar Assn., Monroe County Bar Assn., Rochester C. of C. (trustee 1980-86), Cornell Club (Rochester), Phi Kappa Tau (nat. fin. advisor, mem. nat. coun. 1988-95, treas., mem. exec. com. Phi Kappa Tau Found. 1991—). Home and Office: 48 Church Hill Rd Henrietta NY 14467-9711

SNYDER, FRANKLIN FARISON, hydrologic engineering consultant; b. Holgate, Ohio, Nov. 11, 1910; s. Samuel Lewis and Nettie May (Farison) S.; m. Mary Elizabeth Bruton, Oct. 1, 1938; children: Marilyn Kay Snyder Lutz, Carol Lamb Snyder Garnett, Gregory Lewis(dec.). Student, U. Toledo, 1928-30; B.C.E., Ohio State U., 1932, C.E., 1942; postgrad., Dept. Agr. Grad. Sch., 1940-42, 62. Registered profl. engr., Ohio. Hydraulic engr. U.S. Geol. Survey, Washington, 1934-35; hydraulic engr. TVA, Knoxville, 1936-37, Pa. Dept. Forests and Waters, Harrisburg, 1938-39, U.S. Weather Bur., Pitts. and Washington, 1940-42, Office Chief Engrs., Washington, 1942-66; ptnr. Nunn, Snyder & Assocs., Fairfax, Va., 1972-78; hydrologic engring. cons., McLean, Va., Can., Mex., Sudan, Greece, Bangladesh, Pakistan, Colombia, Jamaica, 1954-90; mem. Internat. St. Lawrence River Bd. Control., 1961-74, U.S. Nat. Com. for Internat. Hydrol. Decade, 1964-67, mem. commn. for Hydrology, World Meteorol. Orgn., 1960-72. Contbr. articles to profl. publs. Supr. Citizens Assn. Security Patrol, Chesterbrook Woods, McLean, 1978-94. Recipient exceptional civilian service award War Dept., 1946, Outstanding Civil Engring. Alumnus award Ohio State U. Civil Engring. Alumni Assn., 1989, Disting. Alumnus award Ohio State U., 1990; named to Gallery of Disting. Civilian Employees, C.E., 1983. Fellow ASCE (Cross medal); mem. Am. Geophys. Union, Am. Meteorol. Soc., Nat. Acad. Engring., Cosmos Club Washington, Officers Club Ft. Myer, Va., Sigma Xi, Tau Beta Pi. Republican. Presbyterian. Avocations: genealogy; golf; travel. Address: 1516 Laburnum St Mc Lean VA 22101-2527

SNYDER, GARY SHERMAN, poet; b. San Francisco, May 8, 1930; s. Harold Alton and Lois (Wilkie) S.; m. Masa Uehara, Aug. 6, 1967 (div.); children: Kai, Gen; m. Carole Koda, Apr. 28, 1991. B.A., Reed Coll., 1951; postgrad., Ind. U., 1951-52, U. Calif.-Berkeley, 1953-56. Gen. Lookout Mount Baker Forest, 1952-53; research in Japan, 1956-57, 59-64; lectr. U. Calif., Berkeley, 1964-65; prof. U. Calif., Davis, 1985—. Author: poems Riprap, 1959, Myths and Texts, 1960, Six Sections, 1965, The Back Country, 1968, Regarding Wave, 1970, Turtle Island, 1974, Axe Handles, 1983, Left Out in the Rain, 1986, No Nature, 1992, Mountains and Rivers Without End, 1996; prose Earth House Hold, 1969, The Old Ways, 1977, He Who Hunted Birds in His Father's Village, 1979, The Real Work, 1980, Passage Through India, 1984, The Practice of the Wild, 1990, A Place in Space, 1995. Bollingen fellow, 1966-67, Guggenheim fellow, 1968-69; recipient Pulitzer prize for poetry, 1975, Bollingen prize for poetry, 1997. Mem. Am. Acad. Arts and Letters, Am. Acad. Arts and Scis. *My work as artist and citizen has been driven by the insight that all is connected and interdependent—nature, societies, rocks, stars. If I seem to set myself "against the times" it is in the name of a larger process; of clarity and of sanity.*

SNYDER, GEORGE EDWARD, lawyer; b. Battle Creek, Mich., Feb. 7, 1934; s. Leon R. and Edith (Dullabahn) S.; m. Mary Jane Belt, July 27, 1957 (div. Sept. 23, 1982); children: Sara Lynn, Elizabeth Jane; m. Claudia Gage Brooks, Feb. 25, 1984. B.S., Mich. State U., 1957; J.D., U. Mich., 1960. Bar: Mich. 1961, U.S. Dist. Ct. (we. and ea. dists.) Mich. 1961. With Gen. Electric Co., 1957-58; asso. firm Miller, Johnson, Snell & Commisky, Grand Rapids, 1960-62, Goodenough & Buesser, Detroit, 1962-66; partner firm Buesser, Buesser, Snyder & Blank, Detroit and Bloomfield Hills, 1966-85, Meyer, Kirk, Snyder & Safford, Bloomfield Hills, 1985—; dir. Bill Knapps Mich., Inc. Chmn. E. Mich. Environ. Action Council, 1974-78; pub. mem. inland lakes and streams rev. com. Mich. Dept. Natural Resources, 1975-76. Served as 2d lt. AUS, 1957. Fellow Am. Acad. Matrimonial Lawyers (pres. Mich. chpt. 1991-92), Am. Coll. Family Trial Lawyers, Am. Bar Found., Internat. Acad. Matrimonial Lawyers, Mich. Bar Found; mem. ABA, Am. Judicature Soc., Am. Arbitration Assn. (panel arbitrators), State Bar Mich. (chmn. family law com. 1968-72, mem. rep. assembly 1972-78, chmn. rules and calendar com. 1977-78, mem. family law sect. coun. 1973-76, environ. law sect. coun. 1980-85, prepaid legal svcs. com. 1973-82, com. on judicial selection 1974, com. on specialization 1976-82), Detroit Bar Assn. (chmn. family law com. 1966-68), Oakland County Bar Assn., Delta Upsilon (chmn. trustees, alumni chpt. dep. 1965-70), Tau Beta Pi, Pi Tau Sigma, Phi Eta Sigma. Episcopalian. Clubs: Detroit Athletic, Birmingham (Mich.) Athletic. Home: 32965 Outland Trl Bingham Farms MI 48025-2555 Office: Meyer Kirk Snyder & Safford Ste 100 100 W Long Lake Rd Bloomfield Hills MI 48304-2773

SNYDER, HARRY COOPER, retired state senator; b. July 10, 1928. Student, Wilmington Coll., Ohio U. Mem. Ohio State Senate, Columbus, 1979-96; ret., 1996; chmn. edn. and retirement com. Ohio State Senate, Columbus. Former mem. exec. com. Ohio Sch. Bds. Assn.; commr. Ohio High Speed Rail Devel. Authority; mem. Edn. Commn. of the States; chmn. Ohio Retirement Study Commn.; chmn. Legis. Office on Edn. Oversight; ad hoc mem. State Bd. Edn., Ohio Bd. Regents; mem. Jobs for Ohio Grads.; founder Clinton County Family Y; mem. Clinton County Bd. Edn. Recipient Outstanding Legis. Svc. award Citizens United for Responsible Edn., Ohio Ret. Tchrs. Assn., Ohio Coalition for Edn. of Handicapped Children, Ohio Assn. Civil Trial Attys., Guardian of Small Bus. award Nat. Fedn. Ind. Bus., Outstanding Contbr. to Edn. in Ohio award Ohio Confedn. Tchr. Edn. Orgn., Disting. Govtl. Svc. award Ohio Coun. Pvt. Colls. and Schs., Legis. of Yr. Ohio Sch. and Transit Assn. Mem. Am. Legis. Exch. Coun. (edn. com., Outstanding State Legis.-Jefferson award), Nat. Conf. State Legislatures (state/fed. assembly, edn. and job tng. com., assembly of legislature, edn. com.), Rotary Club (pres.), Great Oaks Task Force. Republican. Methodist. Avocations: reading, gardening, sailing. Home: 6508 Spring Hill Dr Hillsboro OH 45133-9209

SNYDER, HENRY LEONARD, history educator, bibliographer; b. Hayward, Calif., Nov. 3, 1929; s. Henry Runyon and Mary (Rosenberg) S.; m. Janette Marie Hannus, July 21, 1961; children: Michael Jesse, Christopher Henry, David Lyle. BA, U. Calif., Berkeley, 1951, MA, 1960, PhD, 1963. Sr. buyer Dohrmann Comml. Co., San Francisco, 1951-59; instr. to prof. U. Kans., Lawrence, 1963-78; assoc. dean to dean research adminstrn. U. Kans., 1967-78; prof. history, dean arts and scis. La. State U., Baton Rouge, 1979-86; prof. history U. Calif., Riverside, 1986—; dir. Ctr. for Bibliog. Studies, 1989—; dean humanities and social scis. U. Calif., Riverside, 1986; vis. lectr. Bedford Coll., U. London, 1965-66; Fulbright lectr., research scholar U. Hamburg, Fed. Republic Germany, 1974; dir. English Short Title Catalogue for N.Am., 1978—. Editor: The Marlborough Godolphin Correspondence, 1975; co-editor: The Scottish Heritage, 1981. Pres. Baton Rouge Opera, 1981-83, Riverside Opera, 1987-90; pres. United Way, Lawrence, 1977; bd. dirs. Arts and Humanities Com., Baton Rouge, 1981-85; Sigmund, Martin, Heller Traveling fellow U. Calif.-Berkeley, 1962-63. Am. Council Learned Soc. sr. fellow, 1969-70. Fellow Royal Hist. Soc. Gt. Brit. Bibliog. Soc. London; mem. Am. Soc. 18th Century Studies (pres. 1980-81), Conf. Brit. Studies (exec. com. 1978-83), Am. Hist. Assn., Internat. Fed. Librs. (chair rarebooks and ms. sect. 1995—). Republican. Congregationalist. Home: 220 Trinity Ave Kensington CA 94708-1139 Office: U Calif- Riverside Ctr for Bibliog Studies Riverside CA 92521-0154

SNYDER, JACK L., social sciences administrator. Past dir. Columbia U. Inst. War & Peace Studies; chmn. Columbia U. Dept. Polit. Scis., 1997—. Office: Columbia Univ Dept of Polit Scis 420 W 118th New York NY 10027*

SNYDER, JACK RALPH, lawyer; b. Gary, Ind., June 24, 1940; s. Jack T. and Margaret (Considine) S.; m. Barbara C. Goins, June 23, 1962 (div. Sept. 1985); children: John, Hilary, Alison, Alfred; m. Mary L. Brzezinski Forster, Oct. 1987. AB, Brown U., 1962; LLB, U. Mich., 1964. Bar: Ind. 1965, U.S. Dist. Ct. (so. dist.) 1965, U.S. Ct. Appeals (7th cir.) 1965, (D.C. cir.) 1980. Assoc. ICE Miller Donadio & Ryan, Indpls., 1965-71, ptnr., 1972—, mng. ptnr., 1990-93; bd. dirs. Indpls. Motor Speedway Corp. Counsel Midwestern Collegiate Conf.; trustee Marian Coll.; v.p. Ind. Sports Corp., 1989—. Recipient Louis A. Dawson Outstanding Vol. award Tabernacle Presbyn. Ch., 1980, Monsignor Albert Basalt Outstanding Vol. award Indsl. Cath. Youth Orgn., 1982, Knight of Svc. award Marian Coll., 1995. Fellow Ind. Bar Assn.; mem. ABA, Indpls. Bar Assn., Skyline Club (Indpls.), Ind. Conv. and Visitors Assn. (bd. dirs.), Phi Delta Phi, Delta Kappa Epsilon. Avocations: running, photography, sports, travel. Office: Ice Miller Donadio & Ryan 1 American Sq Indianapolis IN 46282-0001

SNYDER, JAN LOUISE, administrative aide, retired; b. Warrington Twp., Pa., Sept. 15, 1935; d. Wilbert Adam and Alice (Myers) March; divorced; children: Steven Michael Krone, David Sylvan Snyder. Grad. high sch., Dover, Pa. With McCrory Stores Divsn. McCrory Corp., York, 1966-97, receptionist exec. buying divsn.; retired, 1997. Active Northwestern region York Hosp. Aux., 1979—, York Symphony Assn., 1990—, membership com., 1992—; active York chpt. Am. Cancer Soc. Am., 1990—, York Chorus, 1988-90; mem. Ch. of the Open Door of Shiloh, 1956—, Dover Twp. Fire Co. Aux. for Women, 1975—, Harrisburg Jr. League Lectr. Series, 1980-95, York Jr. League Lectr. series, 1989-96. Mem. Am. Bus. Women's Assn. (pres. Colonial York charter chpt. 1980, mem. adv. bd. 1980-89, May queen 1950), nat. Trust for Historic Preservation. Democrat. Avocations: traveling, music, educational lecturing series, church activities, flower and vegetable gardening. Home: 2823 Grandview Ave York PA 17404-3905

SNYDER, JEAN MACLEAN, lawyer; b. Chgo., Jan. 26, 1942; d. Norman Fitzroy and Jessie (Burns) Maclean; m. Joel Martin Snyder, Sept. 4, 1964; children: Jacob Samuel, Noah Scot. BA, U. Chgo., 1963, JD, 1979. Bar: Ill. 1979, U.S. Dist. Ct. (no. dist.) Ill. 1979, U.S. Ct. Appeals (7th cir.) 1981. Ptnr. D'Ancona & Pflaum, Chgo., 1979-92; prin. Law Office of Jean Maclean Snyder, Chgo., 1993-97; trial counsel The MacArthur Justice Ctr. U. Chgo. Law Sch., 1997—. Contbr. articles to profl. publs. Mem. ABA (mem. coun. on litigation sect. 1989-92, editor-in-chief Litigation mag. 1987-88, co-chair First Amendment and media litigation com. 1995-96, co-chair the woman advicate com. 1996—, standing com. on strategic communications, 1996—), Am. Civil Liberities Union of Ill. (mem., bd. dirs. 1996—), Lawyers for the Creative Arts (mem., bd. dirs. 1995—). Office: The MacARthur Justic Ctr Univ of Chgo Law Sch 1111 E 60th St Chicago IL 60637

SNYDER, JOHN GORVERS, lawyer; b. Boston, June 20, 1960; s. Philip Francis and Sylvia (Gorvers) S.; m. Hinda Mala Simon, July 8, 1984; children: Monica Paige, Kimberly Blaine. BA, Johns Hopkins U., 1982; JD, Cornell U., 1987. Bar: Mass. 1988, U.S. Dist. Ct. Mass. 1989. Ptnr. banking law, bus. law and corp. law dept. Craig & Macauley P.C., Boston, 1995—, assoc. banking law, bus. law and corp. law dept., 1987-94; lectr. New England Banking Inst., 1994—. Active Combined Jewish Philanthropies, Boston, 1991—, Anti-Defamation League, Boston, 1993-94. Mem. Mass. Bar Assn., Boston Bar Assn., Phillips Exeter Acad. Alumni Assn., Phi Alpha Delta Internat., Omicron Delta Kappa (Johns Hopkins U. chpt., pres. 1981-82), Delta Upsilon (Johns Hopkins U. chpt.). Avocations: golf, tennis. Home: 7 Laurus Ln Newton Center MA 02159-3138 Office: Craig & Macauley PC Fed Res Plz 600 Atlantic Ave Boston MA 02210-2211

SNYDER, JOHN HENRY, computer science educator, consultant; b. Wichita, Kans., Mar. 16, 1947; s. Melvin Henry and Cathleen Ann (Collins) S.; m. Patricia Reilly, Mar. 11, 1984; children: Matthew Melvin George, Mark John Joseph. BA, U. Kans., 1970; MS, Nova U., Ft. Lauderdale, Fla., 1984. Cert. tchr. Nev., N.D. Computer sci. tchr. Hyde Park Jr. High Sch., Las Vegas, Nev., 1981-86, Chapparal High sch., Las Vegas, 1986-91, Cimarron Meml. High Sch., Las Vegas, 1991-94; chair dept. sci. & tech. Advanced Tech. Acad., Las Vegas, 1994—; copywriter pub. info. office CCSD, Las Vegas, 1982-84; chmn. gifted children spl. interest group, Am. Mensa, 1984; mem. tech. com. Nev. 2000 Task Force, 1994—, Nev. State Network Internet Com., 1994—; mem. sch. dist. tech. coord. task force, 1994—; cons. Office Supt. Clark County Sch. dist., Las Vegas, 1984, 85, IBM Corp., Atlanta, 1991—; systems analyst Homes & Narver, 1988 (summer); adminstrv. aide EG&G Energy Measurements, Las Vegas, 1989 (summer); adj. instr. computer sci. Nova U., 1984-93, U. Nev. Las Vegas, 1990—, The Meadows Sch., 1991-96; bd. dirs. Ctr. for Teaching Resources, The Mazer Corp., N.Y., Akron, Ohio, 1990—. Newsletter editor Nat. State Tchrs. of Yr., 1991—; contbr. articles to profl. jours. Co-chmn. Ednl. Exposition, Las Vegas, 1984; tech. cons. Harry Reid for U.S. Senate, 1986, 92; mem. Nevada 2000 Tech. Subcom., 1994—, Nev. State Network Internet Com., 1993—. Named Tchr. of Yr., State of Nev., 1989-90, U. Nev., Las Vegas, Southland Tchr. of Yr., 1990, Tandy Tech. Scholar, 1991, Nev. Educator of Yr., Milliken Family Found., 1992, Nev. Tchr. of the Yr. Microsoft Corp./Technology & Learning Mag., 1995; recipient Innovative Teaching award Bus. Week Mag., 1990, Mc Caulufffe fellowship, 1994l Impact Innovator grantee, 1996. Mem. NEA (Instrn. and Profl. Devel. chmn. 1979-80), ASCD, KC (sec., v.p., pres., past pres., local lodge newsletter editor), Am. Legion, Phi Delta Kappa (newsletter editor Overall Excellence award 1990). Democrat. Roman Catholic. Avocations: programming, guitar, classical music, website construction, virtual reality. Office: Advanced Tech Acad 2501 Vegas Dr Las Vegas NV 89106-1643

SNYDER, JOHN MILLARD, recreation resources executive, educator; b. Chelsea, Mass., Apr. 3, 1946; s. John Henry and Grace (Eby) S.; m. Barbara Ripple, Nov. 8, 1969 (div. 1979); 1 child, Logan; m. Glenda Allene Snyder, Sept. 10, 1983; children: Erika, Kimberly. BA, Franklin & Marshall Coll., 1968; MS, Colo. State U., 1974, PhD, 1982; cert., Harvard Sch. Design, 1987. Econ. rsch. asso. Coll. Natural Resources, Ft. Collins, Colo., 1972-76; econ devel. City Devel. Dept., Kansas City, Mo., 1976-77; v.p. Oblinger Smith Corp., Denver, 1977-79; sr. resource analyst Abt Assocs., Denver, 1979-80; dr. devel. analysis URS Engrs., Denver, 1980-83; pres. Strategic Studies, Inc., Littleton, Colo., 1983—; pres. Glacier Bay Outfitters, 1990—; co-founder Ecotourism Internat., 1994—; facculty environ. policy and mgmt. U. Denver, 1990—, dir. environ. policy and mgmt., 1997—; econ. faculty Regis U., 1984—. Author: (poems) A Far Off Place, 1995, Best Poems of 1995, 1995; contbr. articles to profl. jours. Econ. advisor Treas. and Gov. Colo., Denver, 1979-84; officer YMCA Guides Program, LIttleton, 1984-85; sr. advisor Spl. Family Recreation, Denver, 1985-90; benefactor Le Bal de Ballet, Denver, 1989—. 1st lt. U.S. Army military intelligence, 1968-72. Fellow nat. The Explorers Club, N.Y. Mem. Ctr. for Whale Studies, Stanford Libr. (assoc.), Denver Zoological Found., Nat. Parks and Conservation Assn., several environ. orgns., Phi Kappa Phi, Xi Sigma Pi. Office: Strategic Studies Inc PO Box 3460 Littleton CO 80161-3460

SNYDER, JOSEPH JOHN, editor, author, lecturer, historian, consultant; b. Washington, Aug. 27, 1946; s. Joseph John and Amy Josephine (Hamilton) S.; m. Sally Hale Walker, July 4, 1973; children: Lauren Elizabeth, Brian Joseph Seth. BA in Anthropology, George Washington U., 1968; MA in Anthropology, U. N.Mex., 1973. With U.S. CSC, Washington, 1974-77; editor, writer U.S. Nat. Park Svc., Harpers Ferry, W.Va., 1977-81; cons. editor Early Man mag., Evanston, Ill., 1978-83; cons. editor Sea Power Mag., 1987—; freelance writer, 1981—; pres. Sta. at Shepherdstown Inc., 1992—; pres., chmn. bd. dirs., Atlantic & Pacific High Speed Railway, Inc., 1993—; lectr. Maya archaeology Norwegian-Caribbean Lines, Miami, Fla., 1982; cons. mus. design. Chmn. parks com. Neighborhood Planning Adv. Group, Croydon Park, Rockville, Md., 1980-81; bd. dirs. Agrl. R & D Orgn, 1985—; v.p., bd. dirs., Hagerstown (Md.) Roundhouse Mus., 1989-91; v.p. bd. dirs. Hagerstown-Washington County Conv. and Visitors. Bur., 1993—, sec., 1993-96. With U.S. Army, 1970-71, Vietnam. Decorated Bronze Star. Mem. Coun. Md. Archaeology, Hakluyt Soc., Am. Com. to Advance Study of Petroglyphs and Pictographs (editor), Nat. Geog. Soc. (cons. 1987—), Nat. Ry. Hist. Soc. Cons. editor jour. Archaeoastronomy, 1987—; contbr. articles to popular mags. Democrat. Home: 2008 Ashley Dr Shepherdstown WV 25443

SNYDER, LESTER M., sports association executive; b. Red Lion, Pa.; m. Audrene Snyder; children: Kim, Ky. Degree, Millersville State U.; doctorate, U. Mich. Past v.p., treas., presdl. appointee to exec. com., Pacific region v.p., sect. del., pres. southwest sect., chmn. and mem. various coms. U.S. Tennis Assn., Tempe, Ariz., now pres., chmn. bd. dirs.; prof. counseling psychology Ariz. State U., Tempe, 1967—; founding dir. Rio Salado Bank; pres. The Heuristic Syss., Inc.; past mem. com. mgmt. Internat. Tennis Fedn., Davis Cup and budget coms., del.; bd. dirs., exec. com. Internat. Tennis Hall of Fame; past Grand Slam com. rep. to Women's Tennis Fedn. Office: 1324 E Whalers Way Tempe AZ 85283*

SNYDER, LEWIS EMIL, astrophysicist; b. Ft. Wayne, Ind., Nov. 26, 1939; s. Herman Lewis and Bernice (McKee) S.; m. Doris Jean Selma Lautner, June 16, 1962; children: Herman Emil, Catherine Jean. BS, Ind. State U., 1961; MA, So. Ill. U., 1964; PhD, Mich. State U., 1967. Research assoc. Nat. Radio Astronomy Obs., Charlottesville., Va., 1967-69; prof. astronomy dept. U. Va., Charlottesville, 1969-73, 74-75; vis. fellow Joint Inst. for Lab. Astrophysics, U. Colo., Boulder, 1973-74; prof. astronomy dept. U. Ill., Urbana, 1975—. Co-editor: Molecules in the Galactic Environment, 1973; contbr. articles to sci. jours. NASA-Am. Soc. Engring. Edn. summer fellow, 1972, 73; Alexander von Humboldt Found. sr. U.S. scientist award, 1983-84. Mem. AAAS, Astron. Soc. Pacific, Am. Phys. Soc., Am. Astron. Soc., Internat. Astron. Union, Union Radio Scientifique Internationale. Lutheran. Office: U Ill 1002 W Green St Urbana IL 61801-3074

SNYDER, LINDA ANN, marketing specialist; b. Pitts., Feb. 24, 1957; d. Arthur Anthony and Patricia Ann (Balzer) Krysinski; m. Christopher Lee Snyder, June 1, 1996. BFA, Carnegie Mellon U., 1979. Systems adminstr. Duncan, Lagnese & Assocs. (now known as Killam Assocs.), Pitts., 1979-86; editorial office supr. Materials Rsch. Soc., Pitts., 1986-94; monographs editor Air & Waste Mgmt. Assn., Pitts., 1994-95; mktg. specialist Killam Assocs., Warrendale, Pa., 1995-96; devel. editor Soc. of Automotive Engrs., Warrendale, Pa., 1996—; freelance corr. Pitts. Post-Gazette, 1990-93. Named Jaycee of Quar., North Hills Jaycees, 1990. Republican. Roman Catholic. Avocations: photography, gardening, hiking, writing. Home: 121 Hillcrest Dr Pittsburgh PA 15237-2424 Office: Soc of Automotive Engrs 400 Commonwealth Dr Warrendale PA 15086-7511

SNYDER, MARION GENE, lawyer, former congressman; b. Louisville, Jan. 26, 1928; s. M. G. and Lois (Berg) S.; 1 son, Mark; m. Patricia C. Robertson, Apr. 10, 1973; 3 step-children. LLB cum laude, Jefferson Sch. Law, Louisville, 1950; JD, U. Louisville, 1969. Bar: Ky. bar 1950, D.C. bar 1970. Practiced law Louisville, 1950-76; ret., farmer, 1957-80; city atty. Jeffersontown, 1953-57; magistrate 1st dist. Jefferson County, 1957-61; real estate broker, 1949—; mem. 88th Congress from 3d Ky. Dist., 1963-65; mem. 90th-99th congresses from 4th Ky. Dist., 1967-87, ret., 1987; sole practice, 1987-91; v.p. Ky. Magistrates and Commrs., 1958. Vice pres. Jeffersontown Civic Center, 1953-54; pres. Lincoln Republican Club Ky., 1960-61, 1st Magisterial Dist. Rep. Club, 1955-57. Mem. Ky. Bar Assn., Ky. Farm Bur., Ky. Real Estate Brokers, Lions, Optimists (prs. Jeffersontown club 1957-58), Jesters, Shriners, Masons. Home (winter): 383 Juli Fe Dr Naples FL 34110-1123

SNYDER, MARK IRWIN, marketing and public relations executive; b. Boston, June 11, 1954; s. Daniel Leonard and Maxine May (Goldman) S.; m. Pamela Diane Dana, May 14, 1989. BA, Curry Coll., 1976; MA, Marquette U., 1976-77. Cert. pub. rels. specialist. Asst. dir. pub. rels. Curry Coll., Milton, Mass., 1972-76; syndicated columnist Boston, 1979-88; talk show host Sta. WMRE, Boston, 1983-86, Stas. WTTP, WATD, WMSX, WMLN-FM, WJCC, Boston, 1983—; pub. Singles Lifeline mag., Randolph, Mass., 1983-90; CEO Profl. Mktg. & Promotions Co., Stoughton, Mass., 1986—; v.p. mktg. Tech. Mgmt. Advisors Corp., Norwood, Mass., 1989-92; owner PMP Media Group/PMP Modeling Promotions; event planning cons. Cystic Fibrosis Found., Brookline, Mass., 1985; host radio talk show Taylor Subscription Talk Network, 1996; internet talk show host Digital City Boston/Am. Online, 1996—. Author: Sex in Poetry, 1976, Feelings, 1977 (Mass. Book of Yr. award Boston Writers Coalition 1977), Rock and Roll Covers, 1984, What Am I Doing Here, 1986. Press sec. for candidate for state rep., 1984; mem. Randolph Town Meeting, 1987-90, Stoughton Town Meeting, 1992—; pub. rels. cons., mem. South Shore exec. bd. Am. Cancer Soc., 1988-92; mem. Stoughton Taxation and Fin. Com., 1992—. Named To Hall of Fame, Tandy Corp., 1979; recipient Sales Exec. of Yr., Lechmere Corp., 1980-83. Mem. South Shore Advt. Club, New Eng. Creative Writers League (pres. 1983-88), Neponset Valley C. of C. (chmn. bd.), Metro South C. of C. Office: PMP Media Group 24 Hollytree Rd Stoughton MA 02072-3019

SNYDER, MARVIN, neuropsychologist; b. Bklyn., Oct. 14, 1940; s. Samuel and Sarah (Seidman) S.; m. Arlyne S. Naphtali, June 23, 1963; 1 dau., Sian Leslie. BA (N.Y. State Regents scholar 1958-62, Meml. award psychology 1962), Bklyn. Coll., 1962; PhD (NDEA fellow 1962-65, USPHS fellow 1965-66, trainee 1966-67), Duke U., 1967. Research psychologist NIMH, 1967-71; Nat. Eye Inst., 1971-72; program dir., neuroscis. Nat. Inst. Drug Abuse, 1974-79, dir. div. research, 1979-90, dir. Office of Sci. Policy, Edn. and Legislation, 1990-94; acting dep. dir. Nat. Inst. on Drug Abuse, 1992-93; pres. Snyder Assocs., 1995; dir. life scis. rsch. office Fedn. of Am. Socs. for Exptl. Biology, 1995—; mem. sr. exec. svc. USPHS exec. com. AIDS, 1983-85; mem. Dept. Health and Human Svcs. Orphan Products Bd., 1982-88; mem. The White House Task Force on Drug Abuse Health Issues; co-chmn. Interagy. Com. on Smoking and Health, Interagy. Com. on New Therapies for Pain and Discomfort; exec. sec. Interagy. com. on Pain and Analgesia, chmn. subcom. on edn. and tng., 1985—; cons. to WHO on drug abuse policy issues, 1985-87; testifier on drug abuse sci. and policy issues to U.S. Congress; mem. Fed. Coordinating Com. for Sci., Engring. and Technology, Com. on Brain and Behavior, 1990-91, Devel. Guidelines for Protection Human Subjects in Drug Abuse Studies, 1991. Author papers and reports on comparative neurology, drug abuse, nutrition, and health policy. Recipient Michael Morrison award for excellence in sci. adminstrn. Com. on Problems of Drug Dependence, 1988, Presdl. Meritorious Rank award 1990. Office: Fedn Am Socs Exptl Biology Life Scis. Rsch Office 9650 Rockville Pike Bethesda MD 20814-3998

SNYDER, NATHAN, entrepreneur; b. Hartford, Conn., Oct. 7, 1934; s. Saul and Betsy (Wand) S.; m. Geraldine Wolff, Dec. 27, 1964; children: Hannah Abigail, Alexander Lowell Wolff. AB, Harvard U., 1956; LLB, Columbia U., 1963; postgrad. in bus., NYU, 1967-68. Bar: N.Y. 1963. Assoc. Paul, Weiss, Rifkind, Wharton & Garrison, N.Y.C., 1963-66; v.p., sec. Randolph Computer Corp., Greenwich, Conn., 1966-69, exec. v.p., gen. counsel, bd. dirs., 1969-73; exec. v.p., chief operating officer BanCal Tri-State Corp. (holding co. Bank of Calif.), San Francisco, 1974-76; v.p. acquisitions CBS Inc., N.Y.C., 1976-87; pres. VS & A Communications Ptnrs., N.Y.C., 1987-89, The Snyder Co., New Canaan, Conn., 1989—; lectr. of mgmt. Golden Gate U., San Francisco, 1974-76, Annenberg Sch. Comms., Phila., 1982-87; bd. dirs. Sogen Funds, N.Y.C. Editor: Columbia Law Rev., 1962-63. Vol. legal services Office Econ. Opportunity, 1963. Served to lt. USNR, 1956-60. Harlan Fiske Stone scholar, 1964-65. Mem. ABA, Econ. Club N.Y., Harvard Club (N.Y.C.), Harvard Club (v.p. Fairfield County). Office: The Snyder Co 163 Parish Rd New Canaan CT 06840-4427

SNYDER, PATRICIA DI BENEDETTO, theater director and administrator. BA in English and Speech Edn., SUNY, Albany, 1967; MA in Theater Arts, Syracuse U., 1967; PhD in Arts and Humanities, NYU, 1991. Tchr. English, speech and drama West Genesee Sr. High Sch., Camillus, N.Y., 1962-64; tchr. English and drama, chair humanities teaching team Chestnut Hill Mid. Sch., Liverpool, N.Y., 1964-66; grad. asst. Syracuse (N.Y.) U., 1966-67; instr. dept. theatre SUNY, Albany, 1967-74, spl. asst. to chancellor, adj. assoc. prof. dept. theatre, 1974-75, founder, producing dir. Empire State Youth Theatre Inst., 1975-92; exec. dir. Gov. Nelson A. Rockefeller Empire State Plz. Performing Arts Ctr. Corp., 1982-89; producing dir., CEO N.Y. State Theatre Inst. Corp., 1992—; cons. Spanish and Portuguese Mins., Madrid and Lisbon, 1968, U.S. Office Edn. 1979, Spanish Min. Culture, 1982, Time Warner, Inc., 1991; mem. edn. bd. Saratoga Performing Arts Ctr., 1973; apptd. arts and humanities planning com. N.Y. State Edn. Dept., 1975; mem. arts task force on arts in edn. NEH, 1977; apptd. N.Y. State Edn. Commr.'s Adv. Coun., 1978; panelist U.S. Children;s Lit. Assn., 1978; del. UNESCO Conf., Sibenek, Yugoslavia, 1979; lectr. Syracuse U., 1988; mem. acad. coun. Richard Porter Leach Fund for Arts, 1989; adj. prof. theatre Russell Sage Coll., 1992.; lectr. and presenter in field. Prodr. (stage prodns.) The Wizard of Oz, 1977, Lancashire Lad, 1980, Sleeping Beauty, 1981, 83, 90, Handy Dandy, 1985, Rag Dolly, 1986, Aladdin, 1987, Hizzoner!, 1988, 89, Beauty and the Beast, 1991, Slow Dance on the Killing Ground, 1993 (Best dir. theatre N.E. Metroland for '94); exec. prodr. (CD) Atlantic Theatre, A Tale of Cinderella, 1995; stage and video dir. A Tale of Cinderella, 1995; contbr. articles to profl. jours. Guest fellow Hungairan Theatre Inst., 1970, USSR Min. Culture, 1970, 84; recipient Mayor's medal City of Milan, Italy, 1977, Spl. Recognition award John F. Kennedy Ctr. for Performing Arts, 1978, 81, Recognition award NATAS, 1986, Albany League Arts award, 1986, Spl. Recognition award N.Y. State Theatre Edn Assn., 1993, silver award Worldfest, 1996, cert. merit Chgo. Internat. Film Festival, 1996. Mem. Am. Theatre Assn. (commn. on theatre devel. 1976, Spl. Recognition citation 1973, 74, Jennie Heiden award 1985), Children's Theatre Assn. Am. (Zeta Phi Eta award 1972), League Am. Theatres and

Prodrs., Soc. State Dirs. and Choreographers, Assn. Internat. du Theatre pour l'Enfants et al Jeunesse (del. 1968, 70, 74, 78, 79 congresses, exec. com. 1969, fundraiser 1972 conf., editor ofcl. report 1973, chair U.S. ctr. 1977), N.Y. Women in Film and TV, N.Y. League Profl. Theatre Women, U. Albany Alumni Assn. (Disting. Alumni award 1987), Cosmopolitan Club, Phi Delta Kappa. Home: 722 N Broadway Saratoga Springs NY 12866-1621 Office: NY State Theatre Inst PO Box 28 Troy NY 12181-0028

SNYDER, PETER LARSEN, public relations executive; b. Phila., Apr. 28, 1952; s. Philip Lerch and Adrienne Louise (Larsen) S.; m. Karen Suzanne Stachiw, June 1, 1973; children: P. Evan, Erik D. BS, Cornell U., 1975. Account exec. Gibbs & Soell Pub. Rels., N.Y.C., 1975-78; account assoc. Ruder & Finn Pub. Rels., N.Y.C., 1978-80; exec. v.p., mng. ptnr. Dorf & Stanton Communications, St. Louis, 1980—, COO, 1992—, pres., 1995—; mng. dir. Shandwick U.S.A. (merger with Dorf & Stanton), 1996—; pres. Miller/Shandwick Techs., St. Louis, 1997—. Cons. Harbor Festival '78, N.Y.C., 1978, St. Louis Pub. Sch. Partnership program, 1985-87, St. Louis area ARC, 1987-88, Muscular Dystrophy Assn. St. Louis, 1988; bd. dirs., capital chmn. Rohan-Woods Sch., Warson Woods, Mo., 1986-88; bd. dirs. Kirkwood/Webster YMCA, Webster Groves, Mo., 1984-87, The New Theater, St. Louis, 1994-96, Riverway Sch., 1994-95, Downtown St. Louis, 1995—, Emmanuel Ch. Found., 1989-92; co-founder, asst. scoutmaster Troop 39, Boy Scouts Am.; chmn. Downtown Parks Bus. Dist., 1990—; co-chair security com. Downtown St. Louis Inc., 1991—; comms. com. Diocese Mo. Episcopal Ch., 1993—; trustee world affairs coun. St. Louis, 1993, v.p. 1994-96; commr. downtown pks. taxing dist., 1994—. Mem. Nat. Agri-Mktg. Assn. (named Best of 1983), Cornell Club St. Louis (bd. dirs. 1988—), Media Club, The Newcomen Soc. Episcopalian. Avocations: sailing, scuba diving, skiing. Office: Miller/Shandwick Techs 515 Olive St Ste 1900 Saint Louis MO 63101-1804

SNYDER, PETER M., medical educator, medical researcher. BA in Biology summa cum laude, Luther Coll., 1984; MD, U. Iowa, 1989. Diplomate Am. Bd. Internal Medicine. Resident in internal medicine U. Tex., Dallas, 1989-92; fellow in cardiovascular diseases Dept. Internal Medicine U. Iowa Hosp. & Clinics, Iowa City, 1992-96, asst. prof. Dept. Internal Medicine, 1996—. Contbr. articles to profl. jours. Student Rsch. fellow U. Iowa, 1985; Student fellow Am. Heart Assn., 1987-88, recipient Clinician Scientist award, 1996. Mem. ACP, Alpha Omega Alpha. Achievements include research in sodium channel structure and function. Office: U Iowa Coll of Medicine Dept Internal Medicine 200 Hawkins Dr Iowa City IA 52242-1009

SNYDER, RICHARD ELLIOT, publishing company executive; b. N.Y.C., Apr. 6, 1933; s. Jack and Molly (Rothman) S.; children: Jacqueline, Matthew, Elliott; m. Laura Yorke, Jan.17, 1992. B.A., Tufts U., 1955. Asst. mktg. dir. Doubleday & Co., N.Y.C., 1958-60, sales mgr., 1960-64; dir. sales Simon & Schuster, N.Y.C., 1964-66, dir. mktg., 1967-68, pub., exec. v.p., 1969-75, pres., 1975—, chief exec. officer, 1979, chief exec. officer, chmn. bd., 1981-94; cons., 1994-95; chmn., CEO Golden Books Family Entertainment, Inc., N.Y.C., 1996—; bd. dirs. Reliance Group Holdings, Children's Blood Found., HSN, Inc. Contbr. articles to profl. jours. Chmn. N.Y. area com. PEN, 1988; co-chmn. benefit com., 1992, chmn. pubs. com. for 48th Internat. PEN Congress; founding mem. Nat. Book Found., Nat. Book Awards, Inc.; mem. bus. com. N.Y. Zool. Soc., Coun. on Foreign Rels., Soc. Fellows, libr. com. Am. Mus. Natural History; mem. bd. overseers Univ. Librs., Tufts U.; vice chmn. benefit Literacy Vols., N.Y.C., 1991. Mem. Assn. Am. Pubs. (bd. dirs. 1976-79, 82-85), Econ. Club of N.Y.C. Office: Golden Books Family Entertainment Inc 850 3rd Ave New York NY 10022-6222

SNYDER, ROBERT LYMAN, materials scientist, educator; b. Plattsburgh, N.Y., June 5, 1941; s. George Michael and Dorothy (Lyman) M.; m. Sheila Nolan, Sept. 1, 1963; children: Robert N., Kristina M. BA, Marist Coll., 1963; PhD, Fordham U., 1968. Postdoctoral fellow NIH U. Pitts., 1968; NRC fellow NASA Elec. Rsch. Ctr., Cambridge, Mass., 1969; asst. prof. ceramic sci. Alfred (N.Y.) U., 1970-77, assoc. prof., 1977-83, prof., 1983-96, dir. Inst. Ceramic Superconductivity, 1987-96; prof., chmn. dept. materials sci. and engring. Ohio State U., Columbus, 1996—; vis. prof. Lawrence Livermore (Calif.) Lab., 1977, 78, U.S. Nat. Bur. Stds., Gaithersburg, Md., 1980, 81, Siemens AG Ctrl. Rsch. Labs., Munich, 1983, 91; invited prof. U. Rennes, France, 1995. Author: Introduction to X-Ray Powder Diffractometry, 1996; author, editor 6 books; contbr. chpts. to books and 200 articles to profl. jours. Deputy mayor Village of Alfred, 1973-77; pres. Alfred Vol. Fire Co., 1979-88. Recipient Chancellor's award SUNY, 1980, numerous research grants; named Faculty Exch. scholar SUNY, 1978-96. Fellow Am. Ceramic Soc.; mem. NAS (U.S. nat. com. on crystallography 1991-95), Nat. Inst. Ceramic Engrs., Am. Crystallography Assn. (chmn. applied crystallography div. 1988-92), Materials Rsch. Soc., Ceramic Ednl. Coun., Internat. Ctr. Diffraction Data (bd. dirs. 1986-92, chmn. bd. dirs. 1996-94, elected chmn. bd. dirs. 1996—), Edward Orton Jr. Ceramic Found. (bd. dirs. 1996—), Alfred and Allegany County Fire Assn., Sigma Xi, Phi Kappa Phi. Democrat. Achievements include numerous patents for practical superconductors. Home: 8500 Stoneshot Loop Dublin OH 43017 Office: Ohio State U Dept Materials Sci and Engring 2041 College Ave Columbus OH 43209-2885

SNYDER, ROBERT M., communication company executive; b. Boston, Aug. 22, 1963; s. Richard J. Snyder and Joyce (Marshall) Serwitz; m. Michele Dannin, Nov. 5, 1988; children: Jennifer, Brett. BA, Am. U., Washington, 1985. Account exec. WMZO Country Radio 95.7FM, Washington, 1985-88; sports mktg. dir. WMAL News/Talk Radio 630AM, Washington, 1988-91; gen. sales mgr. WTEM Sports Radio 570AM, Washington, 1992-95, v.p., gen. mgr., 1995—; radio sales cons. Rick Scott & Assocs., Seattle, 1995—. Office: WTEM Sports Radio 570AM 1 Central Plaza Rockville MD 20852

SNYDER, ROBERT MARTIN, agriculture consultant, retired government official; b. Lahmansville, W.Va., Sept. 6, 1912; s. Noah W. and Maggie M. (Varner) S.; m. Gail M. Hiser, Nov. 25, 1937; children: Rebecca J. Snyder Peters, Margaret A. Snyder Bensenhaver, Shirley L. Snyder Williams, Robert Martin Jr. B.S. in Agr, W.Va. U., 1937. Engaged in farming, 1929-90; agrl. extension agt. Nicholas County, W.Va., 1937-41; adminstrn. commodity loans crop ins. and program performance AAA, Morgantown, W.Va., 1941-42; adminstrn. grain and oilseed program E central region, AAA USDA, 1942-47, asst. coordinator, CCC, 1947-50, coordinator dairy, poultry, fruit and vegetable programs, CCC, 1950-52; chief agriculturist U.S. mission to Karachi, Pakistan FOA, 1952-54; dir. U.S. Mission and counselor U.S. Embassy Afghanistan, Kabul, 1954-59; rep. ICA to, Brit. East Africa, Kenya, Uganda, Tanganyika, Zanzibar, 1959-60; food and agr. officer West African countries of Ivory Coast, Upper Volta, Niger, Dahomey, 1961-62; acting dir. U.S. AID Mission, Ivory Coast, 1961-63; agr. adviser, area office rep. AID mission to, Rhodesia and Nyasaland, 1964; attache, AID affairs officer Malawi, Africa, 1964-68; cons. World Bank, IBRD, 1967; detail officer fgn. direct investments Dept. Commerce, 1968; AID affairs officers Washington, 1968-69; food and agr. officer U.S. AID, Amman, Jordan, 1969-70; planning adviser Ministry Natural Resources, Nigeria, 1970-72; cons., 1972—; Mem. del. Gen. Mem. Agreements Tariffs and Trade Conf., Torquay, Eng., 1951; mem. Mus. Commn., Library Commn. Served to lt. USNR, 1944-46, PTO. Recipient nat. 4-H award Nat. 4-H Congress, Chgo., 1982, Disting. Alumnus award W.Va. Coll. Agriculture and Forestry, 1987; named to W.Va. Agrl. and Forestry Hall of Fame, 1991. Mem. Fgn. Service Assn., Am. Legion, W.Va. U. Alumni Assn., Am. Acad. Polit. and Social Sci., Soc. Internat. Devel., Internat. Platform Assn., U.S. Nat. Trust for Historic Preservation, Nature Conservancy, Commn. on Aging, Alpha Zeta. Clubs: Masons, Kiwanis, Explorers. Home: Noah Snyder Farm HC 84 Box 32 Lahmansville WV 26731-9702 *I feel that any success which I have achieved in life is in direct relationship to my interest in others and my ability to contribute to a better world situation in which each person can develop and achieve a better life for himself or herself and family.*

SNYDER, SCOTT WILLIAM, geology educator; b. Canton, Ohio, Apr. 8, 1946; s. Russell William and Merrie Elizabeth (Landis) S.; m. Lorna Jean Richmond, Sept. 3, 1966; 1 child, Kimberly Ann. BA in Geology, Coll. of Wooster, 1968; MS in Geology, Tulane U., 1970, PhD in Paleontology, 1974. Lic. geologist, N.C. Asst. prof. East Carolina U., Greenville, N.C., 1972-76, assoc. prof., 1976-83, prof., 1983—, chmn. geology dept., 1988—; acting assoc. dean Coll. Arts and Scis., 1990-91; scientist aboard R/V Glomar Challenger (sponsored by NSF), 1981, R/V Joides Resolution, 1993; mem. adv. com. N.C. State Geol. Map, Raleigh, 1983-85. Assoc. editor Jour. Foraminiferal Rsch., 1986-94, editor, 1995-97, Spl. Pub. #25 Cushman Found., 1988; co-editor: Ocean Drilling Program Scientific Results, Vol. 150X, 1997; contbr. articles to profl. jours. Mem. Nat. Wildlife Fedn., 1988—; bd. dirs. Cushman Found., 1991—. Grantee NOAA, 1982, 84, 91, 93, NSF, 1982, 86, Petroleum Rsch. Fund, Am. Chem. Soc., 1988. Fellow Cushman Found. for Foraminiferal Rsch.; mem. Geol. Soc. Am., Paleontol. Soc., Paleontol. Rsch. Inst., Am. Geophys. Union, N.Am. Micropaleontol. Soc., Nat. Assn. Geology Tchrs., Sigma Xi. Democrat. Avocations: jogging, woodworking. Office: East Carolina U Dept Geology Greenville NC 27858

SNYDER, SOLOMON HALBERT, psychiatrist, pharmacologist; b. Washington, Dec. 26, 1938; s. Samuel Simon and Patricia (Yakerson) S.; m. Elaine Borko, June 10, 1962; children: Judith Rhea, Deborah Lynn. M.D. cum laude, Georgetown U., 1962, D.Sc. (hon.), 1986; D.Sc. (hon.), Northwestern U., 1981; PhD (hon.), Ben Gurion U., 1990. Intern Kaiser Found. Hosp., San Francisco, 1962-63; rsch. assoc. NIMH, Bethesda, Md., 1963-65; resident psychiatry Johns Hopkins Hosp., Balt., 1965-68; assoc. prof. psychiatry and pharmacology Johns Hopkins Med. Sch., 1968-70, prof., 1970-77, disting. svc. prof. psychiatry and pharmacology, 1977-80, disting. svc. prof. neurosci., psychiatry, and pharmacology, 1980—, dir. dept. neurosci., 1980—; NIH lectr., 1979. Author: Uses of Marijuana, 1971, Madness and the Brain, 1973, Opiate Receptor Mechanisms, 1975, The Troubled Mind, 1976, Biologic Aspects of Mental Disorder, 1980, Drugs and the Brain, 1986, Brainstorming, 1989; editor Perspectives in Neuropharmacology, 1971, Frontiers in Catecholamine Research, 1973, Handbook of Psychopharmacology, 1974; contbr. articles to profl. jours. Served with USPHS, 1963-65. Recipient Outstanding Scientist award Md. Acad. Scis., 1969, John Jacob Abel award Am. Pharmacology Soc., 1970, A.E. Bennett award Soc. Biol. Psychiatry, 1970; Gaddum award Brit. Pharm. Soc., 1974, F.O. Schmitt award in neuroscis. MIT, 1974, Nicholas Giarman lecture award Yale U., 1975, Rennebohm award U. Uis., 1976, Salmon award 1977, Stanley Dean award Am. Coll. Psychiatrists, 1978, Harvey Lecture. award, 1978, Lasker award, 1978, Wolf prize, 1983, Dickson prize, 1983, Sci. Achievement award AMA, 1985, Ciba-Gaigy-Drew award, 1985, Strecker prize, 1986, Edward Sachar Meml. award Columbia U., 1986, Paul K. Smith Meml. lecture award George Washington U., 1986; Sense of Smell award Fragrance Rsch. Found., 1987, Julius Axelrod lecture award CUNY. 1988, John Flynn Meml. lecture award, Yale U., 1988, V. Erspamer lecture award Georgetown U., 1990, J. Allyn Taylor prize, 1990, Pasarow Found. award, 1991; Bower award Achievement Sci. Franklin Inst., 1991, Chauncey Leake Lecture award, 1992; William Veatch lecture award Harvard Med. Sch., 1992, Joseph Priestley prize Dickinson Coll., 1992, Konrad Bloch lecture award Harvard U., 1992, Basic Neurochem. lecture award Am. Soc. Neurochem., 1993, Nanine Duke lecture award Duke U., 1993, Salvador Luria lecture award MIT, 1993, Rudin lecture award Columbia U., 1995, Christian Herter lecture award NYU, 1995, Maclean lecture award, Baylor Med. Coll., 1995, Baxter award Am. Assn. Med. Colls., 1995, Bristol-Myers-Squibb Neurosci. prize, 1996. Fellow Am. Coll. Neuropsychopharmacology (Daniel Efron award 1974), Am. Psychiat. Assn. (Hofheimer award 1972, Disting. Svc. award 1989), Am. Acad. Arts and Scis., Am. Philosophical Soc.; mem. Nat. Acad. Scis., Soc. for Neuroscis. (pres. 1979-80), Am. Soc. Biol. Chemists, Am. Pharmacology Soc., Inst. Medicine. Home: 3801 Canterbury Rd Apt 1001 Baltimore MD 21218-2315 Office: Johns Hopkins U Med Sch Dept Neurosciences 725 N Wolfe St Baltimore MD 21205-2105

SNYDER, STEPHEN EDWARD, lawyer, mediator; b. Albuquerque, Sept. 14, 1942; s. John Royden and Elaine Stella (Draper) S.; m. Judith Anne Swall, Oct. 27, 1967; children: Sara, Katherine. BBA, U. N.Mex., 1965, MBA, 1967; JD, U. Tex., 1972. Bar: Colo. 1973, N.Mex. 1984. Ptnr. Holme Roberts & Owen, Denver, 1973-96. Author: Commercial Bankruptcy Litigation, 1989. Chmn. bd. trustees Mile High Transplant Bank, Denver, 1995; trustee The Transplant Found., 1992-96, Allosource, 1994-96. Lt. (j.g.) USN, 1967-70.

SNYDER, SUSAN BROOKE, retired English literature educator; b. Yonkers, N.Y., July 12, 1934; d. John Warren and Virginia Grace (Hartung) S. BA, Hunter Coll., CUNY, 1955; MA, Columbia U., 1958, PhD, 1963. Lectr. Queens Coll., CUNY, N.Y.C., 1961-63; instr. Swarthmore Coll., Pa., 1963-66, asst. prof. English lit., 1966-70, assoc. prof., 1970-75, prof., 1975-93, Eugene M. Lang research prof., 1982-86, Gil and Frank Mustin prof., 1990-93; ret.; prof. emeritus Swarthmore Coll., 1993—; scholar-in-residence Folger Shakespeare Libr., 1997—. Author: The Comic Matrix of Shakespeare's Tragedies, 1979; editor: Divine Weeks and Works of Guillaume de Saluste, Sieur du Bartas, 1979, Othello: Critical Essays, 1988, All's Well that Ends Well, 1993, Pastoral Process, 1998; mem. editl. bd. Shakespeare Quar., 1972—. Folger Library sr. fellow, 1972-73; Nat. Endowment for Humanities fellow, 1967-68; Guggenheim Found. fellow, 1980-81; Huntington Library summer grantee, 1966, 71; Folger Library grantee, 1969; Nat. Endowment for Humanities grantee, 1970; Nat. Endowment for Humanities summer grantee, 1976. Mem. Renaissance Soc. Am. (coun. 1979-81), Shakespeare Assn. Am. (trustee 1980-83).

SNYDER, SUSAN LEACH, science educator; b. Columbus, Ohio, Nov. 25, 1946; d. Russell and Helen Marie (Sharpe) Leach; m. James Floyd Snyder, June 18, 1988. BS in comprehensive sci. edn., Miami U., 1968; MS in entomology, U. Hawaii, 1970. Gen. and health sci. tchr. Columbus Pub. Schs., 1971-73; life, earth & physical sci. tchr. Upper Arlington (Ohio) Schs., 1975—; ednl. cons. Innovation Alliance, Columbus, 1990—. Author: The Ocean Environment, 1992, 96; co-author: Focus on Earth Science, 1987, 89, Merrill Earth Science, 1993, 95. Glencoe Earth Science, 1997; mem. author team: Science Interactions, 1993, 95; contbr. articles to profl. jours. Trustee N.Am. Astrophys. Obs., Delaware, Ohio, 1983—; pres. Consortium of Aquatic and Marine Educators Ohio, 1983-84; sec. Ohio chpt. Nat. Tchrs. of Yr., 1993-95. Named Outstanding Earth Sci. Tchr. of State of Ohio and East Cen Sect. Nat. Assn. Geology Tchrs., 1983, Ohio Tchr. of Yr. Ohio State Dept. Edn., 1986, Finalist Nat. Tchr. of Yr. Coun. of Chief State Sch. Officers, 1986; Pres. award for Excellence in Sci. and Math Teaching Nat. Sci. Tchrs. Assn., 1992, Outstanding Tchr. award Geological Soc. Am., 1992. Mem. Nat. Sci. Tchrs. Assn. (Exemplary Earth Sci. Teaching Team 1983, 84, 85, conf. workshop presenter 1985), Nat. Marine Educators Assn. (Nat. Outstanding Marine Sci. Tchr. 1984, bd. mem., conf. workshop presenter 1984), Sci. Edn. Coun. Ohio, NEA, Great Lakes Educators of Aquatic and Marine Educators. Avocation: photography. Home: 1361 Marlyn Dr Columbus OH 43220-3973 Office: Jones Middle Sch 2100 Arlington Ave Upper Arlngtn OH 43221-4314

SNYDER, THOMAS DANIEL, retired electronics engineer, consultant; b. Phila., Aug. 30, 1925; s. Thomas Daniel and Edith May (Lees) S.; Asso. in Applied Sci. in Radio and TV Tech., Milw. Sch. Engring., 1951; m. Mary Ann Wilson, Aug. 28, 1954; children: Thomas Daniel, Ellen Mary, John W. Foreman Prime Mfg. Co., Milw., 1951; with engring. dept. No. Light Co., Milw., 1951-52; communications clk. fgn. service U.S. Dept. State, 1952-55; electronics engr. U.S. Dept. Def., Warrenton, Va., 1955-85; staff cons. Am. Elect. Labs. Cons. accoustics and magnetics govt. agys., 1964—; lectr. metric conversion; participant Solid States Application Conf., Fla. Atlanta U., 1971; participant profl. seminars Mass. Inst. Tech., 1962, 64, 66, Columbia, 1963, Pa. State U., 1967, U. Wis., 1969. Pres., PTA, Fairfax, Va., 1971, county rep., 1972. Served with USNR, 1943-46; PTO. Recipient Meritorious award for outstanding design in electronics equipment, U.S. Govt., 1969. Mem. AAAS, IEEE, Optical Soc. Am., Metric Assn., Am. Nat. Metric Coun., Am. Legion, Cath. War Vets. (adj. 1964-67). Roman Catholic. Contbr. articles to profl. jours. Patentee in field. Home: 4246 Worcester Dr Fairfax VA 22032-1140

SNYDER, VIC, physician, congressman; b. Medford, Oreg., Sept. 27, 1947. BA in Chemistry, Willamette U., 1975; MD, U. Oreg., 1979; JD, U. Ark., 1977. Resident family practice U. Ark. Med. Scis., 1979-82; physician family practice Ark., 1982-96; mem. Ark. State Senate, 1991-96, U.S. Ho. Reps. from 2d Ark. dist., 1996—. Med. missions to Cambodian regufee camps, Thailand, El Salvadoran regufee camps, Honduras, mission hosp., Sierra Leone, Africa, Ethiopian refugee camp, Sudan. With USMC, 1967-69. Democrat. Office: 1319 Longworth House Office Bldg Washington DC 20515 also: 1527 Fed Bldg 700 W Capitol Ave Little Rock AR 72201

SNYDER, WILLARD BREIDENTHAL, lawyer; b. Kansas City, Kans., Dec. 18, 1940; s. N.E. and Ruth (Breidenthal) S.; m. Lieselotte Dieringer, Nov. 10, 1970 (dec. Nov. 1975); 1 child, Rolf; m. T.J. Sewall, May 17, 1996. BA, U. Kans., 1962, JD, 1965; postgrad., Hague Acad. Internat. Law, The Netherlands, 1965-66, U. Dijon, France, 1966; grad., Command and Gen. Staff Coll., Ft. Leavenworth, Kans., 1977. Bar: Kans. 1965, Mo. 1986, U.S. Tax Ct. 1977, U.S. Ct. Mil. Appeals 1981, U.S. Dist. Ct. Kans. 1965, U.S. Supreme Ct. 1977. Atty. Kansas City, 1970-80, 85—; trust officer, corp. trust officer Security Nat. Bank., Kansas City, 1980-83, corp. sec., 1983-85; pres. Real Estate Corp. Inc., Leawood, Kans., 1984—; dir., mem. trust and investment com. Blue Ridge Bank; German Consul (H) for Kans., Western Mo., 1972—. Mem. Platte Woods (Mo.) City Coun., 1983-84; mem. exec. bd. dirs. regional coun. Boy Scouts Am.; bd. govs. Liberty Meml. Assn.; bd. dirs., v.p. MacJannett Found., Talloires, France; pres. Breidenthal-Snyder Found.; bd. dirs., mem. exec. com. CORO Found.; trustee Hoover Pres. Libr. Col. Kans. Army N.G., ret.; col. USAR ret. Decorated Bundesverdienst Kreuz, 1982, BVK 1KL (Germany), 1992, Bundeswehr Kreuz (silver), 1987, Ge. Abn., Legion of Merit, Meritorious Svc. medal, Army commendation medal; KARNG medal of excellence; named to Hon. Order Ky. Cols., 1988; recipient Golden Honour badge German Vet. Orgn., Bavaria, 1988, Mil. Order of WW award, OCS Hall of Fame. Mem. Mo. Bar Assn., Kansas City Bar Assn., Kansas City Hosp. Attys., Kansas City Bd. Trade, Mil. Order of World Wars (chpt. comdr. 1983-84, regional comdr. 1987-91, Patrick Henry award), Nat. Eagle Scout Assn., Blue Ridge Bankshares (dir.). Avocations: scuba, hunting, Notgeld collections, cartridge collection. Office: 8014 State Line Rd Ste 203 Leawood KS 66208-3712

SNYDER, WILLIAM BURTON, insurance executive; b. Clarksburg, W.Va., July 9, 1929; s. William Burton and Mary Catherine (Cornwell) S.; m. Georgie Gaye, Oct. 27, 1951; children: William Burton, Melissa Ann. B.B.A. in Acctg. cum laude, Tex. Tech. U., 1955. With Travelers Ins. Co., 1955-77, v.p., 1970-77; with Govt. Employees Ins. Co., Washington, 1977-93; chmn., pres., CEO GEICO Corp., 1985-93; chmn. and mem. bd. So. Heritage Ins. Co./Merastar Ins. Co., 1991—; chmn., pres., CEO So. Heritage Holdings, Inc., Merastar Corp., Washington, 1993—; adv. bd. mem. Riggs Nat. Bank, Washington Mut. Investors Fund.; bd. mem. CACI, Inc., Phillips Publishing, Inc. Past chmn., mem. econ. adv. coun. Montgomery County; bd. dirs. Capital Area coun. Boy Scouts Am.; past chmn., mem. Nat. Assn. Ind. Insurers. Capt. USAF, 1950-53. Decorated Air medal. Mem. Kenwood Country Club (Bethesda, Md.). Republican. Baptist.

SNYDER, WILLIAM D., photojournalist; b. Henderson, KY, July 1, 1959; s. Charles Gordon and Mary Odette (Galloway) S.; m. Amy Barbara Lewy, Sept. 1, 1985; children: Cameron Reid Gray, Scott Ethan. BS with highest honors, Rochester Inst. Tech., 1981. Photographer/intern Henderson Gleaner, 1974-76; photographer Evansville (Ind.) Press, 1977-79; photo intern Ariz. Rep., Phoenix, 1980; photographer Miami News, Fla., 1981-83, Dallas Morning News, 1983—. Recipient Pro Football Photographer of Yr. award Pro Football Hall of Fame, 1986, Picture of Yr. award -1st pl. newspaper sports action U. Mo., 1986, 1st pl. news pictorial, 1986, Pulitzer prize for explanatory journalism, 1989, Pulitzer Prize for feature photography, 1991, Robert F. Kennedy journalism citation, 1991, Pulitzer Prize for spot news photography, 1993. Mem. Nat. Press Photographers Assn. Democrat. Episcopalian. Avocations: cinema, music. Office: Dallas Morning News PO Box 655237 Dallas TX 75265

SNYDER, WILLIAM HARRY, financial advisor; b. Newport, Pa., May 11, 1934; s. William Harry and Mary (Barner) S.; m. Irvil Kear, June, 1956 (div. 1961); 1 child, Geoffrey W.; m. Sandra Elizabeth Wolff, June 25, 1966; 1 child, Tara Elizabeth. BS in Indsl. Engring., Lehigh U., 1956; MS in Applied Stats., Rutgers U., 1961. Cert. fin. planner. Research engr. Johns-Manville Corp., Manville, N.J., 1956-61; indsl. engr., mgr. services and quality control Johns-Manville Corp., Nashua, N.H., 1961-69; mgr. phys. distbn. Johns-Manville Corp., N.Y.C., 1969-72; mgr. div. and corp. planning. Johns-Manville Corp., Denver, 1972-82; dir. corp. devel. Manville Corp. (formerly Johns-Manville Corp.), Denver, 1982-85; prin. Snyder Fin. Services, Littleton, Colo., 1985—; bd. dirs. Manville Employees Fed. Credit Union, Denver, 1985-88; rep. Fin. Network Investment Corp., 1988—; sec., founding mem. Manville Retirees Assn., 1992—; assoc. Fin. Network Adv. Corp., 1993—. Patentee process for making chalkboard; author: (with others) Standard Handbook of Plant Engineering, 1983. Vol. AARP Tax Coun. Program for the Elderly, 1987—; vol. ARC Disaster Action Team, 1994—. Served as 2d lt. U.S. Army, 1957-58. Mem. Colo. Soc. of Cert. Fin. Planners, Inst. of Cert. Fin. Planners, Pi Kappa Alpha (pres. 1954-55), Tau Beta Pi, Alpha Pi Mu. Republican. Methodist. Lodge: Mason. Avocations: backpacking, skiing, sailing, cycling. Home and Office: Snyder Fin Svcs 1952 W Ridge Rd Littleton CO 80120-3139

SNYDER, WILLIAM PENN, III, manufacturing company executive; b. Pitts., Mar. 11, 1918; s. William Penn and Marie Elise (Whitney) S.; m. Jean Evans Rose, Sept. 30, 1939; children: Marie Elise, J. Brandon. Student, U. Pitts. With The Wilpen Group Inc., now pres.; dir. H.J. Heinz Co., all Pitts., Whitney Nat. Bank, New Orleans. Bd. dirs. Pa. Economy League; chmn. bd. Allegheny Health, Edn. and Rsch. Found., Pitts.; v.p. bd. mgrs. Allegheny Cemetery; trustee Carnegie-Mellon U., Pitts., Carnegie Inst., Carnegie Hero Fund Commn., Western Res. Hist. Soc. Served as lt. (s.g.) USNR, 1942-45. Republican. Episcopalian. Clubs: Duquesne (Pitts.); Rolling Rock (Ligonier, Pa.); Allegheny Country (Sewickley, Pa.); Gulf Stream Golf (Delray Beach, Fla.). Home: Blackburn Rd Sewickley PA 15143-1416

SNYDERMAN, RALPH, medical educator, physician; b. Bklyn., Mar. 13, 1940; m. Judith Ann Krebs, Nov. 18, 1967; 1 child, Theodore Benjamin. BS, Washington Coll., Chestertown, Md., 1961; MD, SUNY, Bklyn., 1965, DSc (hon.) Health Sci. Ctr., 1996. Diplomate Am. Bd. Internal Medicine, Am. Bd. Allergy and Immunology. Med. intern Duke U. Hosp., Durham, N.C., 1965-66, med. resident, 1966-67, asst. prof. medicine and immunology, 1972-74, assoc. prof., 1974-77, chief divsn. rheumatology and immunology, 1975-87, prof. medicine and immunology, 1980-87, Frederic M. Hanes prof. medicine, prof. immunology, 1984-87, adj. prof. medicine, 1987-89; surgeon USPHS, NIH, Bethesda, Md., 1967-69; sr. staff fellow Nat. Inst. Dental Rsch., NIH, Bethesda, Md., 1969-70, sr. investigator immunology sect. lab. microbiology and immunology, 1970-72; chief divsn. rheumatology Durham VA Hosp., Bethesda, Md., 1972-75; v.p. med. R & D Genentech, Inc., South San Francisco, Calif., 1987-88, sr. v.p. med. R & D, 1988-89; chancellor for health affairs, dean Sch. Medicine Duke U., Durham, 1989—, James E. Duke prof. medicine, 1989—; CEO Duke U. Health Sys.; adj. asst. prof. oral biology U. N.C. Sch. Dental Medicine, Chapel Hill, 1974-75; Howard Hughes med. investigator, Durham, 1972-77; dir. Lab Immune Effector Function, Howard Hughes Med. Inst., Durham, 1977-87; adj. prof. medicine U. Calif., San Francisco, 1987-89. Editor: Contemporary Topics in Immunobiology, 1979, Inflammation: Basic Concepts and Clinical Correlates, 1988, 2nd edit., 1992, Medical Clinics of North America, 1997; contbr. articles to profl. jours. Recipient McLaughlin award for inflammation rsch., 1978, Alexander von Humboldt award Fed. Republic Germany, 1985, award for lifetime achievements in inflammation rsch. Ciba-Geigy Morris Ziff, 1991, Bonnizinga award for excellence in leukocyte biology rsch., 1993, Disting. Alumni Achievement award SUNY Bklyn., 1995, Disting. Alumni citation Washington Coll., 1996, others. Mem. NAS, Inst. Medicine, Assn. Am. Physicians, Am. Assn. Immunologists, Am. Soc. Clin. Investigation, Am. Acad. Allergy, Am. Assn. Cancer Rsch., Soc. for Leukocyte Biology, Am. Fedn. Clin. Rsch., Am. Assn. Pathologists, Am. Soc. for Biochemistry and Molecular Biology, Assn. Acad. Health Ctrs., Am. Coll. Rheumatology, Am. Assn. for Med. Colls., Soc. for Med. Adminstrs., Sigma Xi. Office: Duke U Sch Medicine PO Box 3701 Durham NC 27710

SNYDERMAN, SELMA ELEANORE, pediatrician, educator; b. Phila., July 22, 1916; d. Harry Samuel and Rose (Koss) S.; m. Joseph Schein, Aug. 4, 1939; children: Roland M. H., Oliver Douglas. AB, U. Pa., 1937, MD, 1940. Diplomate Am. Bd. Pediatrics, Am. Bd. Clin. Nutrition. Intern Einstein Med. Ctr., Phila., 1940-42; resident Bellevue Hosp., N.Y.C., 1944-45; fellow NYU Med. Ctr., N.Y.C., 1945-46; instr. pediat. NYU Sch.

Medicine, N.Y.C., 1946-50, assoc. prof., 1950-57, 1957-67, prof., 1967-95; assoc. prof. U. Tex. Med. Br., Galveston, 1952-53; attending physician Bellevue Hosp., 1947—; dir. Pediatric Metabolic Disease Ctr. Bellevue Med. Ctr., 1965-95; attending physician Tisch Hosp., N.Y.C., 1947-95; prof. human genetics and pediat., attending physician Mt. Sinai Med. Ctr., N.Y.C., 1995—, dir. Metabolic Disease Ctr., 1995—; mem. nutrition study sect. NIH, Bethesda, Md., 1973-77. Contbr. numerous med. articles to profl. jours. Named career scientist Health Rsch. Coun., 1961-75. Fellow Am. Acad. Pediatrics (Borden award 1975); mem. Am. Inst. Nutrition, Am. Pediatric Soc., Soc. for Pediatric Rsch., Am. Soc. Clin. Nutrition, Soc. Inherited Metabolic Disorders (v.p. 1978, pres. 1979, bd. dirs. 1980-83), Soc. Parenteral and Enteral Nutrition, Soc. for Study of Inborn Errors of Metabolism, Phi Beta Kappa. Jewish. Avocations: gardening, orchid growing, reading. Office: Mount Sinai Med Ctr Dept Human Genetics Fifth Ave & 100th St New York NY 10029

SNYDERS, DIRK JOHAN, electrophysiologist, biophysicist, educator; b. Wilrijk, Antwerpen, Belgium, July 18, 1955; came to U.S., 1984; s. Godlief Stefaan and Mariette L. (Dieu) S. BS in Med. Sci., U. Antwerp, Belgium, 1976; MD with great honor, U. Antwerp, 1980. Lic. physician, cert. cardiologist, Belgium. Resident then fellow in internal medicine and cardiology Univ. Hosp. Antwerp, 1980-84; postdoctoral fellow U. Calif., San Francisco, 1984-85; instr. medicine Vanderbilt U., Nashville, 1986-87, asst. prof., 1987-95, assoc. prof. medicine and pharmacology, 1995—. Co-author: The Heart and the Cardiovascular System, 1991; mem. editorial bd. Circulation Rsch.; reviewer Jour. Gen. Physiology, Cardiovascular Rsch., Jour. Molecular and Cellular Cardiology, Molecular Pharmacology, European Jour. Pharmacology, Biophys. Jour., Jour. Biol. Chemistry; contbr. articles to profl. jours. Lt. Med. Svc., Belgian Army, 1987-88, Germany. Recipient Specia award Specia NV., Belgium, 1980; hon. fellow Belgian Am. Ednl. Found., NATO rsch. fellow, 1984, med. rsch. fellow Alta. Heritage Found., 1984; rsch. grantee NIH, Am. Heart Assn. Mem. AAAS, Biophys. Soc., Soc. Gen. Physiologists, Am. Heart Assn. (Basic Sci. Coun.). Achievements include research on mechanism of action of "specific bradycardiac agents", use-dependent unblocking and voltage clamp validation of modulated receptor theory (cardiac sodium channels and antiarrhythmic agents), electrophysiology and pharmacology of cloned cardiac potassium channels (including human), ion channel structure-function relationships. Office: Vanderbilt U Med Ctr 554 MRB 2 Nashville TN 37232-6602

SNYDMAN, DAVID RICHARD, infectious diseases specialist, educator; b. Phila., Sept. 23, 1946; s. Leonard and Marie (Perrin) S.; m. Diane Canter, June 26, 1971; children: Laura Kate, Alexander Julian. BA, Williams Coll., 1968; MD, U. Pa., 1972. Diplomate Am Bd. Infectious Disease. Intern New Eng. Med. Ctr., Boston, 1972-73, resident in medicine, 1973-74; asst. prof. Sch. Medicine Tufts U., Boston, 1979-84, assoc. prof., 1984-90, prof. medicine and pathology, 1990—; hosp. epidemiologist New Eng. Med. Ctr., Boston, 1979-89, dir. clin. microbiology, 1987—; Epidemic Intelligence Svc. officer CDC, Atlanta, 1974-76. Assoc. editor: Yearbook of Infectious Diseases, 1986—; contbr. over 140 articles to New Eng. Jour. Medicine, Jour. Infectious Diseases, others. Lt. comdr. USPHS, 1974-76. Grantee NIH, 1982-93. Fellow Infectious Disease Soc. (Bristol fellow 1978-79); mem. ACP (Tchng. and Rsch. scholar 1979-82), Soc. Hosp. Epidemiologists, Am. Soc. Transplant Physicians. Achievements include first description of Lyme arthritis; rsch. in hosp. infections, intravenous catheter-associated infections, transplant-related infectious diseases, antibiotic resistance, sepsis, cytomegalovirus prevention; developer of cytomegalovirus immune globulin. Office: New Eng Med Ctr 750 Washington St Boston MA 02111-1526

SOARES, CARL LIONEL, metrologist, quality control engineer; b. New Bedford, Mass., Sept. 14, 1944; s. Lionel Francis and Sarah Vincent (Flor) S.; m. Jean Rosalee Bettencourt, Nov. 11, 1965 (div. Oct. 1974); children: Kevin Carl, Keith Christopher, Kenneth Craig. Student in Indsl. Tech., Fitchburg State Coll., 1980—. Quality assurance specialist Cornell-Dubilier Electronics, Inc., New Bedford, Mass., 1965-66; computer controlled test equipment technician Raytheon Co., Waltham, Quincy, North Dighton, Mass., 1966-79; quality control supt. Raytheon Co., Waltham, 1982-85, metrologist, dept. quality dir., 1979-96; pres., treas., mgr. S.&O. Cleaning Corp. d/b/a The MAIDS, New Bedford, 1995—. Choir mem. St. James Ch. With USN, 1963-65. Mem. Am. Soc. for Quality Control, Buttonwood Park Zool. Soc. (bd. dirs., membership chmn., newsletter editor, events chmn.), Friends of Dartmouth Librs., New Bedford C. of C., Am. Legion. Roman Catholic. Avocations: gardening, bicycling, records and CDs, home computing, music. Home: 205 Maple St New Bedford MA 02740-3513

SOAVE, ROSEMARY, internist; b. N.Y.C., Jan. 23, 1949. BS, Fordham U., 1970; MD, Cornell Med. Coll., 1976. Diplomate Am. Bd. Internal Medicine, Subspecialty Bd. in Infectious Diseases. Intern, resident N.Y. Hosp., N.Y.C., 1976-79; chief med. resident Meml.-Sloan Kettering Cancer Ctr., N.Y.C., 1979-80; fellow infectious diseases N.Y. Hosp., N.Y.C., 1980-82, asst. prof. medicine, 1982-89, assoc. prof. medicine and pub. health, 1989—; spkr. in field; mem. Nat. Insts. Allergy and Infectious Diseases-AIDS and Related Diseases Study Sect. Contbr. numerous articles to profl. jours., chpts. to books, reviews and abstracts to profl. jours. Recipient Mary Putnam Jacobi fellowship for rsch., 1981-82, Leopold Schepp Rsch. fellowship, 1983-84, Nat. Found. for Infectious Diseases Young Investigator Matching Grant award, 1984-85; NIH grantee, 1986-89, 83-86, 87-90. Fellow Am. Coll. Physicians, Infectious Diseases Soc. Am.; mem. AAAS, Am. Fedn. Med. Rsch., N.Y. Acad. Scis., Infectious Diseases Soc. Am., Am. Soc. for Microbiology, Harvey Soc., Sigma Xi. Office: NY Hosp Cornell Med Ctr 1300 York Ave New York NY 10021-4805

SOBCZAK, DARLENE MARIE, police officer; b. Chgo., Nov. 17, 1956; d. Richard and Marilyn (Fuesting) Dvorak; children: Christopher B., Gina K. A of Criminal Justice, Morton Coll., 1991; B in Criminal Justice, U. Ill., Chgo., 1993. Police officer Town of Cicero, Ill., 1984—; field tng. officer Cicero Police Dept., 1989—, detective, 1992-95, sgt., 1995—; Pres. Cicero Police Pension Bd. Active PTA, Cicero, 1984—. Named Police Officer of Yr., 1995. Fellow Ill. Police Assn., Fraternal Order Police; mem. Cicero Police Benevolent Assn. (pres. 1985—), Cicero Police Pension Bd. (bd. dirs. 1992—).

SOBCZAK, JUDY MARIE, clinical psychologist; b. Detroit, Dec. 28, 1949; d. Thaddeus Joseph and Bernice Agnes (Sowinski) Gorski; m. John Nicholas Sobczak, Aug. 17, 1974. BE cum laude, U. Toledo, 1971; postgrad., Ea. Mich. U., 1980-82; PhD, U. Toledo, 1987. Lic. psychologist. Tchr. Ottawa (Ohio)-Glandorf Schs., 1971-73; prin., tchr. St. Mary Sch., Assumption, Ohio, 1973-77; tchr. Our Lady of Perpetual Help Sch., Toledo, 1978-79; staff psychologist Outer Dr. Hosp., Lincoln Park, Mich., 1987-90; psychologist Adult/Youth Devel. Svcs., Farmington, Mich., 1991-95, Davis Counseling Ctr., Farmington Hills, Mich., 1996—; with Northwestern Cmty. Svcs., Livonia, Mich., 1996—, Orchard Hills Psychiat. Ctr., Plymouth, Mich., 1996—; adj. asst. prof. Madonna U., Livonia, Mich., 1987-94. Eucharistic minister St. Anthony Cath. Ch., Belleville, Mich., 1991—, parish coun. 1993-96; Cath. Svc. Appeal co-chmn., 1993—; sec. bd. dirs. Children Are Precious Respite Care Ctr., 1995. Fellow Mich. Women Psychologists (charter; newsletter editor 1987-92, treas 1989-93, Plaque of Appreciation 1992-96, sec. 1993—, pres.- elect 1997-98); mem. Mich. Psychol. Assn., Phi Kappa Phi. Home: 41498 Mckinley St Belleville MI 48111-3439 Office: Davis Counseling Ctr 37923 W 12 Mile Rd Farmington Hills MI 48331

SOBEL, ALAN, electrical engineer, physicist; b. N.Y.C., Feb. 23, 1928; s. Edward P. and Rose (Naftalison) S.; m. Marjorie Loebel, June 15, 1952; children: Leslie Ann, Edward Robert. BSEE, Columbia U., 1947, MSEE, 1949; PhD in Physics, Poly. Inst. Bklyn., 1964. Lic. Profl. Engr., N.Y. and Ill. Asst. chief engr. The Electronic Workshop, N.Y.C., 1950-51; head, functional engr. Fairchild Controls Corp., 1951-56; project engr. Skiatron Electronics and TV Corp., 1956-57; sr. rsch. engr. Zenith Radio Corp., Glenview, Ill., 1964-78; v.p. Lucitron inc., Northbrook, Ill., 1978-87, pres., 1987; pvt. practice cons. Evanston, Ill., 1988—; asst., instr. Poly. Inst. Bklyn.,1957-64; mem. program coms. SID Internat. Symposium, Internat. Display Rsch. Conf., 1970—. Inventor: 14 patents on various display and electron devices; author 50 papers on electronics, physics, electronic displays, etc.; editor Jour. Soc. Info. DIsplay, 1991—; contbg. editor Info. Display; assoc. editor: IEEE Trans. on Electron Devices, N.Y., 1970-77. Mem. Democratic Party of Evanston and Ward Orgn., various neighborhood orgns. NSF fellow, 1959, 60. Fellow Soc. Info. Display; mem. IEEE (sr., life), Am. Phys. Soc., Internat. Soc. for Optical Engring., SPIE, Sigma Xi. Democrat. Home and Office: 633 Michigan Ave Evanston IL 60202-2552

SOBEL, BURTON ELIAS, physician, educator; b. N.Y.C., Oct. 21, 1937; s. Lawrence J. and Ruth (Schoen) S.; m. Susan Konheim, June 19, 1958; children: Jonathan, Elizabeth. A.B., Cornell U., 1958; M.D. magna cum laude, Harvard U., 1962. Intern Peter Bent Brigham Hosp., Boston, 1962-63; resident Peter Bent Brigham Hosp., 1963-64, 66-67; clin. asso., cardiology br. NIH, Bethesda, Md., 1964-66, 67-68; asst. prof. medicine U. Calif. at San Diego, La Jolla, 1968-71; asso. prof. medicine, dir. myocardial infarction research unit, dir. coronary care, 1971-73; asso. prof. medicine Barnes Hosp.-Washington U., St. Louis, 1973-75; adj. prof. chemistry Washington U., St. Louis, 1979-94; prof. medicine Barnes Hosp.-Washington U., 1975—, dir. cardiovascular div., 1973—, program dir. specialized ctr. rsch. ischemic heart disease, 1975-89, program dir. specialized ctr. rsch. in coronary and vascular diseases, 1990-94, program dir. principles in cardiovascular rsch., 1975-94; chmn. and prof. medicine, prof. biochemistry U. Vt., Burlington, 1994—; physician-in-chief Med. Ctr. Hosp. Vt., Burlington, 1994—; physician-in-chief Fletcher Allen Health Care, Burlington, 1995—; program dir. Collaborative Clin. Trial Therapy to Protect Ischemic Myocardium, Washington U., 1977; chmn. cardio renal drugs U.S. Pharmacopeial Conv., 1990—; bd. dir. Scios Corp. Assoc. med. editor The Heart Bull, 1971-72; editor Clin. Cardiology, 1971-74, Clin. Guides to Med. Mgmt., 1996—; mem. circulation bd., 1971—; editor Circulation, 1983-88; mem. editorial bd. Circulation Research, 1974—, Annals of Internal Medicine, 1976—, Am. Jour. Cardiology, 1976—, Cardiology Digest, 1976-77, Jour. Continuing Edn. in Cardiology, 1978—, Cardiology in the Elderly, 1991—; mem. editorial bd., assoc. editor Jour. Clin. Investigation, 1977—; assoc. editor, Am. Jour. Physiology: Heart and Circulatory Physiology, 1978—; Churchill Livingstone editorial advisory bd. Internat. Seminars in Cardiovascular Medicine, 1978—, Cardiology in Review, 1992—; mem. editorial bd. Current Med. Lit., Current Opinion in Cardiology, editor, 1989—, Arteriosclerosis, Thrombosis, and Vascular Biology, 1996—, Clin. Therapeutics, 1996, Internat. Jour. Cardiology, Fibrinolysis, 1986, assoc. editor, 1990—; cons. editor Circulation, 1988—; editor Coronary Artery Disease, 1989—; mem. editorial bd. Can. Jour. Cardiology, 1995—. Served to lt. comdr. USPHS, 1964-68. Recipient Career Rsch. Devel. award USPHS, 1972, internat. recognition award Heart Rsch. Found., 1981, Disting. Achievement award Am. Heart Assn. Sci. Couns., 1984, award Robert J. and Claire Posatow Found., 1988, award Va. Heart Ctr., 1991, Drake award Maine Heart Assn., 1992. Fellow ACP, Molecular Medicine Soc.; mem. AAAS (councilor 1997—), Royal Soc. Medicine, Am. Fedn. Clin. Rsch. (councilor), Am. Heart Assn. (James B. Herrick award 1992), Am. Coll. Cardiology (Disting. Scientist award 1987), Assn. Univ. Cardiologists, Am. Soc. Clin. Investigation (councilor), Assn. Am. Physicians, Am. Physiol. Soc., Cardiac Muscle Soc., Western Soc. Clin. Rsch., Internat. Soc. Fibrinolysis and Thrombolysic (councilor), Assn. Profs. Cardiology (pres.-elect 1992), Internat. Soc. Applied Cardiovasc. Biology, Alpha Omega Alpha. Home: 2 Lost Cove Rd Colchester VT 05446-1840 Office: Fletcher Allen-MCHV Campus Fletcher 311 Burlington VT 05401

SOBEL, HOWARD BERNARD, osteopath; b. N.Y.C., May 15, 1929; s. Martin and Ella (Sternberg) S.; m. Ann Louise Silverbush, June 16, 1957 (dec. May 1978); children—Nancy Sobel Schumer, Janet Sobel Medow, Robert; m. Irene S. Miller, June 8, 1980; stepchildren—Avner Saferstein, Daniel Saferstein, Naomi Saferstein. A.B., Syracuse U., 1951; D.O., Kansas City Coll. Osteopathy and Surgery, 1955. Intern Zieger Osteo. Hosp., Detroit, 1955-56; gen. practice osteo. medicine Redford Twp., Mich., 1956-74, Livonia, Mich., 1974—; chief of staff Botsford Gen. Hosp., Farmington, Mich., 1978; mem. faculty Mich. State U. Coll. Osteo. Medicine, 1969—; clin. assoc. prof. family practice, 1973—; mem. exec. and med. adv. coms. United Health Orgn. Mich.; mem. Venereal Disease Action Com., Mich.; apptd. to asst. impaired osteo. physicians Mich., 1983. Mem. Am. Osteo. Assn. (ho. of dels. 1981—), Mich. Assn. Osteo. Physicians and Surgeons (ho. of dels.), Am. Coll. Osteo. Rheumatologists, Coll. Am. Osteo. Gen. Practitioners, Osteo. Gen. Practice Mich., Wayne County Osteo. Assn. (pres.). Jewish. Home: 6222 Northfield Dr West Bloomfield MI 48322-2431 Office: 28275 5 Mile Rd Livonia MI 48154-3944

SOBEL, KENNETH MARK, electrical engineer, educator; b. Bklyn., Oct. 3, 1954; s. Seymour Phillip and Marilyn (Nanus) S. BSEE, CCNY, 1976; MEngring, Rensselaer Poly. Inst., 1978, PhD, 1980. Sr. rsch. specialist Lockheed Calif. Co., Burbank, 1980-87; assoc. prof. dept. elec. engring. CCNY, 1987-93, prof., 1993—; mem. proposal rev. panel Nsf, 1991-93, PSC-CUNY, 1993-95; adj. lectr. Calif. State U., Northridge, 1981; adj. asst. prof. U. So. Calif., L.A., 1982-87; prin. investigator USAF, 1989, 91, mem. summer faculty fellowships, 1987, 88, 90; exec. com. PhD programs in engring. CUNY, 1989—, mem. exec. com. dept. elec. engring., CCNY, 1994—, mem. faculty senate, 1992-93, 95—, mem. disciplinary com., 1995-96. Co-author: Direct Adaptive Control Algorithms Theory and Applications, 1994; contbg. author: The Control Handbook, 1995; assoc. editor Jour. Guidance Control and Dynamics, 1993-95; contbr. over 80 articles to profl. jours. and confs., chpts. to books. Program vice-chmn. 1986 Am. Control Conf., Seattle. Recipient Prof. of Yr. award Beta Pi chpt. Eta Kappa Nu, 1991-92; Profl. Staff Congress-CUNY rsch. grantee, 1988-90. Fellow AIAA (assoc.); mem. IEEE (sr. exhibits chmn. 23rd conf. on decision and control 1988, tech. assoc. editor Control Sys. mag., 1986-94, program chmn. 1993 regional conf. on control sys. NJIT, control sys. soc. liaison to IEEE Press, 1993), Am. Radio Relay League (life) Control Sys. Soc. (bd. govs. 1990), Sigma Xi, Alpha Phi Omega. Office: CCNY Dept Elec Engring New York NY 10031

SOBELL, NINA R., artist; b. Patchogue, N.Y., May 4, 1947; d. Jack and Helen Ruth (Rosenberg) S.; m. Christopher Rogers Shearer, Sept. 8, 1982 (div. Mar. 1987); 1 child, Jacqueline Corianne. BFA, Temple U., 1969; MFA, Cornell U., 1971. Cert. educator N.Y. Vis. artist Calif. Inst. of the Arts, Valencia, 1975, Sch. of Architecture, London, 1976; vis. lectr. dept. art Reading (Eng.) U., 1976-77; vis. lectr. dept. design & sculpture UCLA, 1979, assoc. prof. electronic imagery, 1984-85; artist-in-residence interactive telecomm. program NYU, N.Y.C., 1991-92, artist-in-residence Ctr. Digital Multimedia, 1994—; instr. video prodn. Sch. Visual Arts, N.Y.C., 1992-93; dir. tech. integration Aux. Svc. High Schs., N.Y.C. Bd. Edn., 1994—; artist-lectr. Documenta VII, Kassel, Germany, 1977; juror U.S. Film and Video Festival, L.A., 1984; juror media arts divsn. N.Y. State Coun. on the Arts, N.Y.C., 1994; artist-presenter Siggraph, New Orleans, 1996. Prin. works include installation Interactive Brainwave Drawings, 1974—, interactive installation Videophone Relay, 1977-79; artist/dir. HIV-INFO Interactive Call-In TV Show, Manhattan Pub.-Access Cable, 1992, ParkBench Pub-Access Web Kiosks, 1994—; curriculum designer Online Art Network for At-Risk Youth, N.Y.C. Bd. Edn., 1996; represented in permanent collection Mus. Modern Art, N.Y.C., Whitney Mus. Art Whitney Web Site. Installation/Lecture grantee Found. Art Resources, 1981; Installation grantee N.Y. State Coun. Arts, 1981. Mem. Art and Sci. Collaborations, Inc., Coll. Art Assn., Assn. Ind. Video and Filmmakers, United Fedn. of Tchrs. Democrat. Jewish. Avocations: swimming, cooking, biking, birdwatching, skating. Home: 190 Eldridge St # 3S New York NY 10002-2911 Office: NYU Ctr Digital Multimedia 719 Broadway Fl 12 New York NY 10003-6802

SOBELLE, RICHARD E., lawyer; b. Cleve., Mar. 18, 1935. BA, Stanford U., 1956, JD, 1960; LLM, U. So. Calif., 1967. Bar: Calif. 1961, U.S. Supreme Ct. 1969. Exec. Tracinda Corp., Las Vegas. Mem. ABA (mem. corp., banking and bus. law sect. 1969—), State Bar Calif. (del. to conf. state bar dels. 1965-77, mem. exec. com. bus. law sect. 1977-78), L.A. County Bar Assn. (mem. exec. coun., jr. barristers 1965-68, mem. exec. com. bus. and corps. sect. 1973-75). Office: Tracinda Corp 4835 Koval Ln Las Vegas NV 89109-7308

SOBEN, ROBERT SIDNEY, computer scientist; b. Corpus Christi, Tex., Feb. 7, 1947; s. Sydney Robert and Rose Mary (Bailey) S.; 1 child, Dena Dianne. BS in Electrical Engring., La. Tech. U., 1973; MA in Communication, U. Okla., 1982; MS in Mgmt. Scis., Troy (Ala.) State U., 1988; PhD in Engring. Mgmt. Sci., LaSalle U., 1990. Digital computer sci. USAF Air Training Command, Keesler AFB, Miss., 1966-71; command pilot USAF, worldwide, 1971-82; NATO instr. pilot 80th Fighter Training Wing, Sheppard AFB, Tex., 1978-82; electro-optics br. chief Electronics Systems Test Div., Eglin AFB, Fla., 1982-84; mission ops. officer Deputate for Testing Engring., Eglin AFB, Fla., 1984-85, test support div. chief, 1985-93; sr. TQ analyst 46TW/OG-1 TQM in 46 OG, 1994-95; CEO ORCOM, Eglin AFB, 1985—; adj. asst. prof. Troy State U., Ft. Walton Beach, Fla., 1987—, St. Leo's Coll., Eglin AFB, 1988—. Author: Digital Computer Basics, 1970, Application of Expert Systems to Scientific and Technical Information Command, Control and Communication Management, 1990; author USAF tech. report Video Augmentation, 1984, tng. manual and system test engring., 1988, POGI for Quality Results, a mil. pub., 1995. Avocations: sailing, scuba diving, writing, racing cars. Home: 214 Stebbins Ter SE Pt Charlotte FL 33952-9145

SOBER, SIDNEY, retired diplomat, education educator; b. N.Y.C., Nov. 12, 1919; s. Isaac and Mary (Krug) S.; m. Elizabeth Holmes Sober, Apr. 2, 1948; children: Stephen, Elizabeth (dec.). BA magna cum laude, CCNY, 1939; MA, George Washington U., 1964. Fgn. svc. officer Dept. of State, Tananarive, Prague, Reykjavik, Ankara, Bombay, 1947-63; dir. regional affairs Bur. Near Ea. and So. Asian Affairs, Dept. of State, Washington, 1964-68; min. counselor Am. Embassy, Islamabad, Pakistan, 1969-73; dep. asst. sec. of state, 1974-78, chargé d áffaires, 1972-73; chair South Asia Seminar Fgn. Svc. Inst., Dept. of State, Washington, 1982-96; vis. prof., adj. prof. Am. U., Washington, 1978-87; cons. Sisco Assocs., Washington, 1984-93; declassification specialist Dept. of State, Washington, 1991—. Lt. (j.g.) USN, 1944-46. Mem. Am. Fgn. Svc. Assn., Diplomatic and Consular Officers Ret., Asia Soc., Phi Beta Kappa. Home: 4928 Sentinel Dr # 106 Bethesda MD 20816

SOBEY, DAVID FRANK, food company executive; b. Stellarton, N.S., Can., Mar. 22, 1931; s. Frank Hoyse and Irene (MacDonald) S.; m. Faye B. Naugle, June 2, 1953; children: Paul David, Janis Irene Hames. D of Commerce (hon.), St. Mary's U., 1991. With Sobeys Inc., Stellarton, 1949—, store mgr., dir. merchandising and advt., v.p., exec. v.p., pres., dep. chmn., chief exec. officer, dir., 1981-85, chmn., dir., 1985—; bd. dirs. Empire Co. Ltd., Sobey Leased Properties Ltd., Atlantic Shopping Ctrs. Ltd., Sobeys Land Holdings Ltd., Clover Group, Ea. Sign Print Ltd., Lumsden Bros. Ltd., Dominion Textile Inc., Evangeline Fin. Svcs. Corp., T.R.A. Foods Ltd., Hannaford Bros. Co., CHC Helicopter Corp.; chmn. The Sobey Found., Frank H. Sobey Fund for Excellence in Bus. Studies. Bd. dirs. Retail Coun. Can., Internat. Assn. Chain Stores, C.I.E.S., Food Mktg. Inst., Tim Horton Children's Found., The Sobey Art Found., Boy Scouts Can., Atlantic Salmon Fedn.; bd. govs. St. Mary's U., chmn. fin. campaign; mem. Halifax Bd. Trade. Mem. Order of Can., 1996. Clubs: Royal N.S. Yacht Squadron; Halifax; City (New Glasgow), Abercrombie Country. Office: Sobeys Inc, 115 King St, Stellarton, NS Canada B0K 1S0

SOBEY, DONALD CREIGHTON RAE, real estate developer; b. New Glasgow, N.S., Can.; s. Frank Hoyse and Irene (MacDonald) S.; m. Elizabeth H. Purvis; children: Robert George Creighton, Irene Elizabeth, Kent Richard. B of Commerce, Queen's U.; LLD (hon.), Dalhousie U., 1989. Vice chmn. Halifax Devels. Ltd., 1989—; pres. Empire Cos. Ltd., 1969; chmn. Empire Co. Ltd., 1985—; also bd. dirs.; bd. dirs. Paribas Participations Limitee PPL, Merchant Pvt. Ltd., Atlantic Shopping Ctrs. Ltd., Jannock Ltd., Tibbetts Paints Ltd., Toronto-Dominion Bank, Wajax Ltd., Sobeys Inc., Maritime Telegraph and Telephone Co. Ltd. Gov. Olympic Trust Can.; patron 1986 World Congress on Edn. and Tech.; bd. govs. Dalhousie U.; mem. task force Future of Port Halifax; mem. Conf. Bd. Can.; found. chmn. Camp Hill Med. Ctr.; mem. Club de Rels. d'Affaires Can.-France; chmn. Friends of the Nova Scotia Mus. Industry Soc.; co-chair fin. com. Gov. Gen.'s Can. Study Conf.; bd. dirs. Nat. Gallery Can. Mem. Internat. Assn. for Students Econs. and Commerce, Lloyd's of London (underwriting). Avocations: skiing, tennis, music, art, travel. Office: Empire Co Ltd, 115 King ST, Stellarton, NS Canada B0K 1S0

SOBEY, EDWIN J. C., museum director, oceanographer, consultant; b. Phila., Apr. 7, 1948; s. Edwin J. and Helen (Chapin) S.; m. Barbara Lee, May 9, 1970; children: Ted Woodall, Andrew Chapin. BS, U. Richmond (Va.), 1969; MS, Oreg. State U., 1974, PhD, 1977. Rsch. scientist Sci. Applications, Inc., Boulder, Colo., 1977-79, div. mgr., 1979-81; exec. dir. Sci. Mus., West Palm Beach, Fla., 1981-88, Mus. Sci. and History, Jacksonville, Fla., 1988, Nat. Invention Ctr., Akron, Ohio, 1989-92, Fresno (Calif.) Met. Mus., 1993-95; ednl. cons., 1995—; exec. prodr. (t.v. show) Idea Factory, KFSN-30, Fresno, 1995—. Alumni v.p. Leadership Palm Beach County; expdn. leader Expdn. Tng. Inst., S.E. Alaska, 1980; mem. U.S. Antarctic Research Program, 1974. Author: Complete Circuit Training Guide, 1980; Strength Training Book, 1981; (with others) Aerobic Weight Training Book, 1982, Increasing Your Audience, 1989, Inventing Stuff, 1995, Wrapper Rockets and Trombone Straws-Science at Every Meal, 1996, Car Smarts, 1997; mem. editorial adv. bd. Invent Mag., 1989-92. Founder, bd. dirs. Visually Impaired Sports Program, Boulder, 1978-81; fitness instr. YMCA Boulder, 1977-81; convener 1st Nat. Conf. Sports for the Blind, 1979; bd. dirs. Leadership Palm Beach; vice chmn. County Com. on Artificial Reefs; treas. Leaderdeship Akron Alumni Assn., 1990-91, class pres. Leadership Akron; v.p. Ohio Mus. Assn., 1991-92, pres., 1992-93; co-host Blow the Roof Off Ednl TV show, 1992; bd. dirs. Fla. Mus. Assn., 1988-89; mem. adv. bd. Marine Sci. Inst., 1990—. Lt. USN, 1970-73. Fellow Explorers Club; mem. Marine Tech. Soc. (sect. chmn. 1982-84), Coral Reef Soc. (chpt. pres. 1982-87), Nat. Inventive Thinking Assn. (bd. dirs. 1989—). Home: 8806 N 5th St Fresno CA 93720-1724

SOBH, TAREK MAHMOUD, computer science educator, researcher; b. Giza, Egypt, Feb. 16, 1967; came to U.S., 1988; s. Mahmoud Abd-El-Hakeem Sobh and Nagwa Abd-el-Meguid Reda; m. Nihal Samy Kandil, Sept. 16, 1992; 1 child, Omar Tarek. BSc in Engring. with honors, Alexandria (Egypt) U., 1988; MS in Engring., U. Pa., 1989, PhD in Computer and Info. Sci., 1991. Registered profl. engr., Utah. Postdoctoral rsch. fellow dept. computer and info. sci. Gen. Robotics and Active Sensory Perception Lab. U. Pa., Phila., 1991-92; rsch. asst. prof. dept. computer sci. Coll. Engring., U. Utah, Salt Lake City, 1992-95; assoc. prof., dir. robotics, intelligence sensing and contol lab, dept. computer sci. and engring. U. Bridgeport, Conn., 1995—; organizer session discrete event and hybrid sys. internat. conf. Intelligent Robots and Sys., 1994. Author chpts. to books; editor Jour. Robotics and Autonomous Sys., 1994; reviewer for books, jours.; contbr. articles to profl. jours. Grantee NSF, 1993, 94, Def. Advanced Rsch. Projects Agy./Office Navy Rsch., 1993—, Def. Advanced Rsch. Projects Agy., 1993—. Mem. IEEE (chair session on object recognition 1993 2nd CAD-Based Vision Workshop 1994, session chair internat. conf. robotics and automation 1994), IEEE Computer Soc. (mem. tech. com. on pattern analysis and machine intelligence), IEEE Robotics and Automation Soc. (co-chairperson discrete event dynamic sys. tech. com. 1992—), Internat. Soc. Optical Engring., Assn. Computing Machinery, Soc. Indsl. Computing, Tau Beta Pi (advisor Utah chpt.), Phi Beta Delta, Sigma Xi. Avocations: reading, squash, soccer, scuba diving, photography. Office: U Bridgeport Dept Computer Sci & Engring 169 University Ave Bridgeport CT 06604-5763

SOBIESKI, JAROSLAW, aerospace engineer; b. Wilno, Poland, Mar. 11, 1934; came to U.S., 1966; naturalized, 1971.; s. Stanislaw and Sabina Sobieszczanski; m. Wanda Dlugosz, Dec. 31, 1958; children: Margaret Ann, Ian Patrick. BS aeros., Tech. U. Warsaw, 1955, MS aeros., 1957, DEng, 1964. Cons. Polish Aircraft Industries, Warsaw, Poland, 1957-64; asst. and adj. prof. Tech. U. Warsaw, Warsaw, Poland, 1955-64; rsch. assoc. Tech. U. Norway, Trondheim, 1964-66; assoc. prof. St. Louis U., 1966-71; aerospace engr. NASA Langley Rsch. Ctr., Hampton, Va., 1971-89, head rsch. office, 1979-93, chief scientist, 1993-94, multidisciplinary rsch. coord., 1994—, mgr. computational AeroScis. team, 1996—; mem. faculty George Washington U., 1972-92, U. Va., 1992—; pres. and cons. engr. Tech. Analysis Optimization, Inc. Hampton, Va., 1982—. Co-editor: Structural Optimization jour., 1989—; contbr. articles to profl. jours. Recipient medal for exceptional achievement in engring. NASA, 1988. Fellow AIAA (mem. tech. com., Nat. Multidisciplinary Design Optimization award 1996). Home: 518 Elizabeth Lake Dr Hampton VA 23669-1724 Office: NASA Langley Rsch Ctr Hampton VA 23681-0001

SOBIN, JULIAN MELVIN, international consultant; b. Boston, July 14, 1920; s. Irving Maxwell and Selma Helen (Brodie) S.; m. Leila Feinburg, May 3, 1942; children: Patricia, Jonathan. A.B., Harvard U., 1941; LL.D. (hon.), William Penn Coll., 1979. Trainee to chmn. Sobin Chems. Inc., Boston, 1946-75; sr. v.p. Internat. Minerals & Chem. Corp., 1975-77, dir. internat. bus. devel., 1976-77, exec. cons., 1977-78; exec. v.p. IMC Chem.

Group, 1975-76; chmn. trustees Internat. Mktg. Inst., Cambridge, Mass., 1975-84; v.p. Assoc. Metals & Minerals Corp., 1978-82; dir. Comml. Solvents Corp.; exec. cons. China trade Laporte Industries U.K. and U.S.A.; lectr. in field; corporator South Boston Savs. Bank; advisor, cons. to Spl. Rep. of Pres. for Trade Negotiations, Kennedy Round of Tariff Reductions, 1962-63; mem. Pres.'s Adv. Com. Nat. Trade Policy, 1968-69; mem. adv. com. on East/West trade Dept. Commerce, 1976—; internat. trade cons. Internat. Exec. Svc. Corps to San Miguel Corp., Manila, 1984-85; mem. exec. com. Mass. Gov.'s Fgn. Bus. Coun., 1977—; cons. dir. NYBO Internat. Inc., 1987—; sr. advisor C.P. Group, Bangkokk, 1992—, Harcros Chemicals, London, 1992—. Author: (audio album) The China Trader; co-author: Ency. of China Today, The China Guide, 12th edit., 1992; mem. adv. bd. Partisan Review; contbr. numerous articles to profl. jours. Gen. chmn. New Eng. Trade Week, 1959; trustee Nat. Jewish Hosp. and Research Center, Denver, Emerson Coll.; bd. advisors Stonehill Coll., 1975-78; mem. overseers com. to visit dept. fine arts Harvard U., 1968-74; mem. Boston Com. on Fgn. Relations; bd. dirs. Nat. Council U.S.-China Trade, 1976-77; bd. dirs., mem. exec. com. Internat. Trade Ctr. New Eng. Inc.; trustee Lesley Coll., Boston U., Am. Grad. Sch. Internat. Mgmt. (Thunderbird); mem. overseers com. to visit Ctr. Internat. Affairs Harvard U., 1981—. Served to maj. F.A. AUS, 1941-46, CBI. Decorated Legion of Merit; recipient Annual Honor medal Nat. Jewish Hosp. and Rsch. Ctr., 1975; fellow Harvard U. Ctr. for Internat. Affairs, 1987-88; hon. royal consul of Nepal in Boston, 1993—. Mem. Mfg. Chemists Assn., Chemists Club of N.Y., Hong Kong-Am. C. of C., Fgn. Correspondents Club Hong Kong, Internat. Mgmt. Devel. Inst. (corp. strategic planning coun.), Soc. Am. Chem. Industry, Am. Radio Relay League, Harvard Club (Boston, N.Y.C.), Univ. Club (Boston). First Am. businessman invited to Peking, China, spring 1972. Home: 790 Boylston St Boston MA 02199-7928

SOBKOWICZ, HANNA MARIA, neurology researcher; b. Warsaw, Poland, Jan. 1, 1931; came to U.S., 1963; d. Stanislaw and Jadwiga (Ignaczak) S.; m. Jerzy E. Rose, Mar. 12, 1972. B.A., Girls State Lyceum, Gilwice, Poland, 1949; M.D, Med. Acad., Warsaw, 1954, Ph.D., 1962. Intern. 1st Internal Med. Clinic Med. Acad., Warsaw, 1954-55; resident 1st Internal Med. Clinic, Med. Acad., Warsaw, 1955-59; resident Neurol. Clinic, Med. Acad., 1959, jr. asst., 1959-61, sr. asst., 1961-63; research fellow neurology Mt. Sinai Hosp., N.Y.C., 1963-65; Nat. Multiple Sclerosis Soc. fellow Columbia U., N.Y.C., 1965-66; asst. prof. neurology U. Wis., Madison, 1966-72, assoc. prof., 1972-79, prof., 1979—. Contbr. articles to profl. jours. NIH research grantee, 1968—. Mem. Internat. Brain Rsch. Orgn., Assn. Rsch. in Otolaryngology, Soc. Neurosci., Internat. Soc. Devel. Neurosci. (editorial bd. 1984—), Electron Microscopy Soc. Am. Office: U Wis Dept Neurology 1300 University Ave Madison WI 53706-1510

SOBLE, JAMES BARRY, lawyer; b. Chgo., Apr. 14, 1942; s. Julius R. Soble and Bernyce (Morris) Rossuck; children—Debra, Jeffrey, Tony, Leslie; m. Ann S. Valenstein, June 29, 1980. B.A., Grinnell Coll., 1963; J.D., Northwestern U., 1966. Bar: Ill. 1966, Fla. 1974. Assoc. Deutsch & Peskin, Chgo., 1966-68; ptnr. Siegel & Soble, 1969-71 Peskin & Soble, 1972-73; exec. v.p., corp. counsel Millstream Corp., Sunrise, Fla., 1973-79; pvt. developer, Ft. Lauderdale, Fla., 1979-81; ptnr., shareholder Jacobs, Robbins, Gaynor, Hampp, Burns, Cole & Shasteen, P.A., St. Petersburg, Fla., 1981-83; ptnr. Taub & Williams, Tampa, Fla., 1984-88; ptnr Honigman Miller Schwartz and Cohn, 1988-97; shareholder Ruden, McCloskey, Smith, Schuster & Russell, 1997—; lectr. Law Forum, Inc., 1982-84. Pres., bd. dirs. Gulf Coast Jewish Family Services of Pinellas County, 1984-88; bd. dirs. Better Bus. Bur. West Florida, Inc.; pres. Jewish Fedn. Pinellas County, 1989-91, 93-95; pres.-elect Menorah Manor, Inc., 1996—. Mem. ABA, Ill. Bar Assn., Hillsborough County Bar Assn. Jewish. Home: 2996 Sandpiper Pl Clearwater FL 34622-3058 Office: 2700 SunTrust Fin Ctr 401 E Jackson St Tampa FL 33602

SOBOL, HAROLD, retired dean, manufacturing executive, consultant; b. Bklyn., June 21, 1930; s. Stanley and Minnie S.; m. Marion Gross, Dec. 29, 1957; children—Diane, Neil, Jessica, Martin. B.S.E.E., CUNY, 1952; M.S.E.E., U. Mich., 1956, Ph.D., 1960. Research asst. Willow Run Labs. U. Mich., 1952-55, research assoc., 1956-59; staff mem. IBM Research, Yorktown Heights, N.Y., 1960-62; with RCA Labs., Princeton, N.J., 1962-73; staff engr. RCA Labs., 1970-72, head communication tech., 1972-73; sr. mem. tech. staff Collins Radio Rockwell-Internat., Dallas, 1973-74; dir. product devel. Collins Transmission Systems div., 1974-85; dir. engring. Rockwell Telecommunications, 1985-86, v.p. engring., 1986-88, ret., 1988; prof. elec. engring., assoc. dean U. Tex., Arlington, 1988-93. Author: Advances in Microwaves Volume 8, 1974; contbr. in field. Cubmaster Tex.-Okla. council Boy Scouts Am., Dallas, 1978-80. Sperry fellow, 1955-56. Fellow IEEE (pres. microwave theory and techniques soc. 1979); mem. Am. Phys. Soc., Nat. Mgmt. Assn., Sigma Xi, Tau Beta Pi, Eta Kappa Nu. Office: U Tex PO Box 19019 Arlington TX 76019

SOBOL, LAWRENCE RAYMOND, lawyer; b. Kansas City, Mo., May 8, 1950; s. Haskell and Mary (Press) S.; m. Maureen Patricia O'Connell, May 29, 1976; children: David, Kevin. BBA, U. Tex., 1972; JD, U. Mo., 1975. Bar: Mo. 1975, U.S. Dist. Ct. (ea. dist.) Mo. 1975. Gen. counsel, gen. ptnr. Edward D. Jones & Co., Maryland Heights, Mo., 1975—; allied mem. N.Y.C. Stock Exchange, 1977—; sec. Lake Communications Corp., Conroe, Tex., 1984-86, LHC Inc., EDJ Holding Co. Inc., Unison Capital Corp., 1990—, Cornerstone Mortgage Investment Group, 1987-92; sec., bd. dirs. Cornerstone Mortgage Inc., St. Louis, 1986; v.p., bd. dirs. Tempus Corp., St. Louis, 1984—. Omar Robinson Meml. scholar U. Mo., 1974-75. Mem. ABA (securities law com. 1982—), Met. St. Louis Bar Assn. (securities law sect.), Nat. Assn. Securities Dealers (dist. bus. com., registered prin. officer, nat. arbitration com. 1991—), Securities Industry Assn. (fed. rebulation securities com. 1987-88), Forest Hills Country Club, Phi Eta Sigma. Republican. Avocations: tennis, golf. Office: Edward D Jones & Co 201 Progress Pkwy Maryland Hts MO 63043-3003

SOBOL, THOMAS, state education commissioner; b. Jan. 11, 1932; m. Harriet Sobol; three children. BA in English, Harvard U., 1953, grad., 1954; PhD, Columbia U., 1969. Head dept. English pub. sch. system Bedford, N.Y., 1961-65; dir. instrn., 1965-69; asst. supt. instrn. pub. sch. system Great Neck, N.Y., 1969-71; supt. sch. systems Scarsdale, N.Y., 1971-87; commr. N.Y. State edn. Albany, 1987—; Christian A. Johnson Prof. Columbia Univ. Teacher's College, N.Y.C. also: Columbia Univ. Teachers College 525 W 120th St New York NY 10027*

SOBOLEWSKI, JOHN STEPHEN, computer information scientist, consultant; b. Krakow, Poland, July 14, 1939; came to U.S., 1966; s. Jan Zygmund and Stefania (Zwolinska) S.; m. Helen Skipper, Dec. 17, 1965 (div. July 1969); m. Carole Straith, Apr. 6, 1974; children: Anne-Marie, Elisa, Martin. BE, U. Adelaide, Adelaide, South Australia, 1962, ME, 1966; PhD in Computer Sci., Wash. State U., 1971. Sci. officer Weapons Research Establishment, Salisbury, South Australia, 1964-66; asst. prof. computer sci. Wash. State U., Pullman, 1966-73; dir. research, assoc. prof. U. Wash., Seattle, 1973-80, dir. computer svcs., 1980-88; assoc. v.p. computing U. N.Mex., Albuquerque, 1988—; cons. govt. and industry, Seattle, 1973—; mem. bd. trustees Fisher Found., Seattle, 1984—. Author: Computers for the Dental Office, 1986; contbr. articles to profl. jours. Served as engr. with Royal Australian Army, 1957-60. Australian govt. scholar, 1954-60, Elec. Res. Bd. scholar CSIRO, Melbourne, Australia, 1961-64. Mem. IEEE, Computer Soc. Roman Catholic. Avocation: mineral collecting. Home: 8501 Northridge Ave NE Albuquerque NM 87111-2107 Office: U NMex CIRT 2701 Campus Ave NE Albuquerque NM 87131

SOBUS, KERSTIN MARYLOUISE, physician, physical therapist; b. Washington, June 16, 1960; d. Earl Francis and Dolores Jane (Gill) G.; m. Paul John Jr., March 10, 1990; children: Darlene Marie, Julieann Marie. BS in Physical Therapy summa cum laude, U. North Dakota, 1981, MD, 1987. Clinic instr. pediatric physical therapy U. North Dakota Sch. Medicine, Grand Forks, 1981-83; pediatric physical therapist Child Evaluation and Treatment Program Med. Rehab. Ctr., Grand Forks, 1981-83; asst. prof. dept. pediatrics, asst. prof. dept. physical medicine and rehab. U. Arkansas for Med. Scis., Grand Forks, 1992-96; resident internal medicine Sinai Hosp. Balt., 1987-88; resident physical medicine and rehab. Johns Hopkins Residency Program in Physical Medicine and Rehab. Sinai Hosp., Balt., 1988-91; pediatric rehab. clin. and rsch. fellow Alfred I. DuPont Inst., Wilmington, Del., 1991-92; pediatric psychiatrist Altru Health System, Grand Forks, N.D., 1997—. Contbr. articles to med. jours. Mem. Am. Acad. Cerebral Palsy and Devel. Medicine, Am. Congress of Phys. Medicine and Rehab., Alpha Omega Alpha Honor Soc. Home: 1548 30th Ave Manuel ND 48256 Office: Altru 13005 Columbia Rd PO Box 6002 Grand Forks ND 58206

SOCARIDES, CHARLES WILLIAM, psychiatrist, psychoanalyst, educator, writer; b. Brockton, Mass., Jan. 24, 1922; s. James and Theodora (Cokas) S.; m. Veronica Rak (div.); children: Richard, Daphne; m. Barbara Bonner, Jan. 28, 1973 (div. Apr. 1987); children: Alexandra, Charles Jr.; m. Claire Alford, Oct. 19, 1988; 1 child, Jacqueline Nichole. Cert., Harvard Coll., Cambridge, Mass., 1945; MD, N.Y. Med. Coll., 1947; cert., Columbia U., N.Y.C., 1952. Diplomate Am. Bd. Psychiatry and Neurology. Instr. in psychiatry Columbia U., N.Y.C., 1956-60, assoc. in psychiatry, 1960-62; clin. asst. prof. psychiatry SUNY, N.Y.C., 1955-58, clin. prof. psychiatry, 1976-78; assoc. attending psychiatrist Vanderbilt Clinic Coll. U., N.Y.C., 1960-62; assoc. clin. prof. psychiatry Albert Einstein Coll. Medicine, N.Y.C., 1969-76, clin. prof., 1976-97; clin. prof. psychiatry Montefiore Med. Ctr., N.Y.C., 1978-97; pvt. practice psychoanalysis and psychiatry, 1997—; med. cons. Armed Svcs. Dept. Def., Washington, 1978—; tng. psychiat. residents Albert Einstein Coll. Medicine, 1968-90. Author: The Overt Homosexual, 1968, Homosexuality, 1978, The Preoedipol Origin and Psychoanalytic Treatment of Sexual Perversion, 1988, Beyond Sexual Freedom, On Sexuality: Psychoanalytic Observations, 1979, The Homosexualities and the Therapeutic Process; co-author, editor (with Selma Kramer): Work and Its Inhibitions, 1996; contbr. articles to profl. jours.; numerous book reviews. Lt. USNR, 1952-54. Recipient Sigmund Freud award Am. Soc. Psychoanalytic Physicians, 1987, N.Y. Soc. for Psychoanalytic Tng., 1975, Disting. Prof. award Assn. Psychoanalytic Psychologists, Brit. Health Svc., London, 1995. Fellow Am. Psychoanalytic Assn., Am. Psychiat. Assn., Am. Coll. Psychoanalysts, Am. Soc. Psychoanalytic Physicians (hon. fellow); mem. AMA, Nat. Assn. Rsch. and Therapy of Homosexuality (pres. 1992—), N.Y. County Med. Soc., Internat. Psychoanalytic Assn., Coral Beach Club. Democrat. Greek Orthodox. Avocations: tennis, writing, professional books. Home and Office: 242 E 94th St New York NY 10128-3706

SOCHACKI, ANDRZEJ, mechanical engineer, researcher; b. Warsaw, Poland, July 26, 1948; came to U.S., 1973; s. Jerzy and Halina (Błażejczyk) S. MS, Tech. Acad., Warsaw, 1969; AAS, Maricopa Tech. Coll., Phoenix, 1983; postgrad., Ariz. State U., 1985. Sr. mech. engr. Roger Bus. Products div. Rogers Corp., Mesa, Ariz., 1986-87; sr. mech. design engr. Parker Aerospace Co., Phoenix, 1987-88; sr. project engr. Micro-Rel Inc., Tempe, Ariz., 1988-90; cons., project engr., pres., owner Design & Fabricating Co., Phoenix, 1985-96; founder, pres., chmn. The Vagabond Ctr., Phoenix, 1992; tool engr. McDonnell Douglas Aircraft Co., Mesa, Ariz., 1996—. Recipient award Medtronic Corp., Phoenix, 1989. Mem. Soc. Mfg. Engrs. (sr.). Roman Catholic. Avocations: travel, piano, research, 4 times travel around the world. Home and Office: The Vagabond Ctr 3715 E Taylor St Phoenix AZ 85008-6316

SOCHACKI, TINA MARIE, secondary education educator; b. Evergreen Park, Ill., July 10, 1967; d. Alex Wayne and Judith Anne (Zicha) Spirakes; m. Matthew Zygmunt Sochacki, June 18, 1993. BA in French and Spanish Edn., U. Ill., 1989; postgrad., Gov.'s State U., University Park, Ill., 1994-96. Cert. 6-12 tchr., Ill.; Ill. type 75 cert. Tchr. fgn. lang. Bremen H.S., Midlothian, Ill., 1989-90, Acad. of Our Lady H.S., Chgo., 1990-91, Evergreen Park H.S., 1991—. Mem. ASCD, Am. Assn. Tchrs. French, Ill. Coun. on Tchg. Fgn. Langs., U. Ill. Alumni Assn., Golden Key. Avocations: billiards, reading, spending time with family and pet pug. Office: Evergreen Park HS 9901 S Kedzie Ave Evergreen Park IL 60805-3416

SOCHEN, JUNE, history educator; b. Chgo., Nov. 26, 1937; d. Sam and Ruth (Finkelstein) S. B.A., U. Chgo., 1958; M.A., Northwestern U., 1960, Ph.D., 1967. Project editor Chgo. Superior and Talented Student Project, 1959-60; high sch. tchr. English and history North Shore Country Day Sch., Winnetka, Ill., 1961-64; instr. history Northeastern Ill. U., 1964-67, asst. prof., 1967-69, assoc. prof., 1969-72, prof., 1972—. Author: The New Woman, 1971, Movers and Shakers, 1973, Herstory: A Woman's View of American History, 1975, 2d edit., 1981, Consecrate Every Day: The Public Lives of Jewish American Women, 1981, Enduring Values: Women in Popular Culture, 1987, Cafeteria America: New Identities in Contemporary Life, 1988, Mae West: She Who Laughs Lasts, 1992; editor: Women's Comic Visions, 1991; contbr. articles to profl. jours. Nat. Endowment for Humanities grantee, 1971-72. Office: Northeastern Ill U 5500 N Saint Louis Ave Chicago IL 60625-4625

SOCIE, DARRELL FREDERICK, mechanical engineering educator; b. Toledo, Oct. 28, 1948; s. Frederick James and Emerence (Lupinski) S.; m. Pamela Sue Doll, 1977; children: Benjamin, Bethany, Michael. BS in Metall. Engring., U. Cin., 1971, MS, 1973; PhD, U. Ill., 1977. Registered profl. engr., Ill., Ohio. Research asst. dept. theoretical and applied mechanics U. Ill., Urbana, 1974-77, vis. asst. prof. dept. theoretical and applied mechanics, 1977-78; asst. prof. Dept. Mech. and Indsl. Engring. U. Ill., Urbana, 1978-81, assoc. prof., 1981-85, prof., 1986—; panelist Coopers & Lybrand Trendsetter Barometer, 1993-96; cons. Structural Dynamics, 1974-80, Owens-Corning Fiberglass, 1974-82; pres. SOMAT Corp., 1982-96. Recipient Ralph R. Teetor award Soc. Automotive Engrs., 1980, Comdr.'s award for disting. pub. svc. U.S. Army, 1990, Disting. Alumni award U. Cin., 1991; Japan Soc. for the Promotion of Sci. fellow, 1997. Mem. ASTM (Fatigue Achievement award 1992), SAE (Arch T. Colwell award 1994), ASM, Sigma Xi. Office: U Ill 144 Mech Engring Bldg 1206 W Green St Urbana IL 61801-2906

SOCOL, MICHAEL LEE, obstetrician, gynecologist, educator; b. Chgo., Oct. 3, 1949; s. Joseph and Bernice (Bofman) S.; m. Donna Kaner, Dec. 17, 1972. BS, U. Ill., 1970; MD, U. Ill., Chgo., 1974. Diplomate Am. Bd. Ob-Gyn., Am. Bd. Maternal-Fetal Medicine. Resident obstetrics and gynecology U. Ill. Hosp., Chgo., 1974-77; clin. rsch. fellow dept. obstetrics and gynecology L.A. County-U. So. Calif. Med. Ctr., 1977-79; assoc. attending physician Northwestern Meml. Hosp., Chgo., 1980-86, attending physician dept. ob-gyn., 1986—; co-dir. Northwestern Perinatal Ctr., Chgo., 1987—; head maternal-fetal medicine, chief obstetrics Northwestern U. Med. Sch., Chgo., 1987—, dir. maternal-fetal medicine fellowship program, 1987—, asst. prof. obstetrics and gynecology, 1979-84, assoc. prof., 1984-92, prof., 1992—; mem. appointment and promotions and departmental com. on clin. privileges Northwestern Meml. Hosp., Chgo., 1987—, vice-chmn. dept. ob-gyn., 1992—; mem. residency edn. com., 1987—; mem. appointments, promotions and tenure com., 1991—. Author: (with others) Clinical Obstetrics and Gynecology, 1982, 1984, Diagnostic Ultrasound Applied to Obstetrics and Gynecology, 1987, Principles and Practice of Medical Therapy in Pregnancy, 1992; peer reviewer Am. Jour. Obstetrics and Gynecology, 1980—, Obstetrics and Gynecology, 1984—; contbr. numerous articles to profl. jours. Fellow Am. Coll. Ob-Gyn., Soc., Perinatal Obstetricians, Ctrl. Assn. Ob-Gyn., Chgo. Gynecol. Soc., Soc. for Gynecol. Investigation, Am. Gynecol. and Obstetrical Soc.; mem. AMA, Assn. Profs. of Gynecology and Obstetrics, Ill. State Med. Assn., Chgo. Med. Soc. Avocation: marathon running. Office: 333 E Superior St Ste 410 Chicago IL 60611-3056

SOCOL, SHELDON ELEAZER, university official; b. N.Y.C., July 10, 1936; s. Irving and Helen (Tuchman) S.; m. Genia Ruth Prager, Dec. 26, 1959; children: Jeffrey, Steven, Sharon, Robyn, Leslie, Steven Warren. BA, Yeshiva U., 1958; JD, NYU, 1963. Asst. bursar Yeshiva U., N.Y.C., 1958-60, assoc. bursar, 1960-62, dir. student fins., 1962-70, sec., 1970—, chief fiscal officer, 1971-72, v.p. bus. affairs, 1972—; mem. N.Y. State Adv. Coun. on Fin. Assistance to Coll. Students, 1969-76; asst. dir. Tng. Inst. for Fin. Aid Officers, Hunter, Coll., CUNY, 1970-71; mem. presdl. adv. com. Temple U., 1986; mem. regents adv. task force N.Y.C. Regional Plan for Higher Edn., 1971-73; speaker Prentice Hall Law and Bus. Series, 1989, KPMG Peat Marwick Conf., 1990, Inst. for Endowment Mgmt., 1992. Pres. Minyon Park Estates, Inc. Mem. NEA, Nat. Assn. Coll. and Univ. Attys., Met. N.Y.C. Fin. Aid Adminstrs. Assn., Ea. Assn. Student Fin. Aid Officers, Am. Mgmt. Assn., Am. Assn. for Higher Edn., Nat. Assn. Coll. and Univ. Bus. Officers, Soc. Coll. and Univ. Planning, Mid. States Assn. Colls. (evaluation team Commn. on Higher Edn., U. Medicine and Dentistry N.J., 1985, Upstate Health Sci. Ctr. 1986, Carnegie-Mellon U. 1988, Albany Med. Ctr. 1989).

SOCOLOFSKY, JON EDWARD, banker; b. Chgo., Mar. 27, 1946; s. E. E. and Jane C. (Ward) S.; married; 1 child, Brian Edward. BA, DePauw U., 1968; MBA, Ind. U., 1970. Auditor No. Trust Co., Chgo., 1970-79, v.p., 1979-86, sr. v.p., 1986—. Pres. Cass Sch. Dist. # 63, Darien, Ill., 1987-93. Mem. Internat. Ops. Assn., Internat. Soc. Securities Adminstrs. Republican. Congregationalist. Avocations: water skiing, volleyball, motorcycles. Office: The Northern Trust Co 50 S La Salle St Chicago IL 60603-1003

SOCOLOW, ARTHUR ABRAHAM, geologist; b. Bronx, N.Y., Mar. 23, 1921; s. Samuel and Yetta (Solomon) S.; m. Edith S. Blumenthal, Apr. 10, 1949; children: Carl, Roy. Jeff. BS, Rutgers U., 1942; MA, Columbia U., 1947, PhD, 1955. Photogrammetrist, U.S. Army Air Corps, 1942-46; with Eagle Picher de Mexico, 1947; instr. geology So. Methodist U., 1948-50; dir. geology field camp Colo., 1948-50; asst. prof. Boston U., 1950-55; geologist Def. Minerals Exploration Authority, Alaska, 1952; assoc. prof. U. Mass., 1955-57; econ. geologist Pa. Geol. Survey, 1957-61, dir., state geologist, 1961-86; cons. geologist Gloucester, Mass., 1986—; prof. environ. geology Salem (Mass.) State Coll., 1993-95; dir. New Eng. Govs. Conf. Project on Aggregate Resources New Eng., 1990-97; mem. Outer Continental Shelf Policy Com., 1974-88, Pa. rep., 1978-88; lectr. mineral conservation Pa. State U., 1959-75; mem. conf. earth sci. source materials NSF, 1959; chmn. ann. field conf. Pa. Geologists, 1961-86; past mem. U.S. Nat. Com. on Tunnelling Tech.; mem. com. on N.Y. State low level waste program Nat. Acad. Sci.; past mem. gov.'s adv. com. Nat. Coun. on Environ. Quality; past chmn. Pa. Water Resources Coordinating Com.; geol. advisor Boston Mus. Sci., 1955-57. Former editor Pa. Geol. Bull.; mem. editorial bd. Northeastern Geol. Jour.; contbr. over 100 pubs. and papers on environ. and econ. geology to profl. jours. Served with USAAF, 1942-46. Fellow Geol. Soc. Am. (sec.-treas. N.E. sect., past nat. councilor), Mineral Soc. Am., AAAS (past pres. geography-geology sect.), Soc. Econ. Geologists; mem. AAUP, Phila. Geol. Soc. (past pres.), Am. Geol. Inst. (com. on manpower), Nat. Assn. Geology Tchrs. (past regional pres., Ralph Digman award for contbns. to geologic edn. 1980), Pa. Acad. Sci., Am. Meteoritical Soc., Am. Assn. State Geologists (past pres., editor, compiler State Geological Surveys-A History 1988), Am. Geophys. Union, Am. Commn. Stratigraphic Nomenclature (past chmn.), Harrisburg Geol. Soc., Interstate Oil Compact Commn. (rsch. com., environ. com.), Gloucester Conservation Commn. (chmn.), Fgn. Policy Assn. (past chpt. pres.), Sigma Xi. Club: Internat. Torch (past pres. chpt.). Home and Office: 26 Salt Island Rd Gloucester MA 01930-1945 *I have great respect for the individualism of man in the midst of a society and a world where there is an unavoidable interrelationship and interdependence of man upon man, and of man upon his environment. While we strive to maintain our individualism, we must share our common resources and our common aspirations. This is the challenge that makes our lives worth living.*

SOCOLOW, ROBERT HARRY, engineering educator, scientist; b. N.Y.C., Dec. 27, 1937; s. A. Walter and Edith (Gutman) S.; m. Elizabeth Anne Sussman, June 10, 1962 (div. Apr. 27, 1982); children: David, Seth; m. Jane Ries Pitt, May 25, 1986; stepchildren—Jennifer, Eric. B.A., Harvard U., 1959, M.A., 1961, Ph.D., 1964. Asst. prof. physics Yale U., New Haven, 1966-71; assoc. prof. mech. and aerospace engring. Princeton U. (N.J.), 1971-77, prof. mech. and aerospace engring., 1977—; mem. Inst. Advanced Study, Princeton, 1971; dir. Center for Energy and Environmental Studies, Princeton, 1978—. Author: (with John Harte) Patient Earth, 1971, (with K. Ford, G. Rochlin, M. Ross) Efficient Use of Energy, 1975, (with H.A. Feiveson, F.W. Sinden) Boundaries of Analysis: An Inquiry into the Tocks Island Dam Controversy, 1976, Saving Energy in the Home: Princeton's Experiments at Twin Rivers, 1979, (with C. Andrews, F. Berkhout, V. Thomas) Industrial Ecology and Global Change, 1994; editor Ann. Rev. of Energy and Environment, 1992—. Chmn. bd. Am. Coun. for Energy Efficient Econ., 1989-93; bd. dirs. Nat. Audubon Soc., 1992—. John Simon Guggenheim fellow, 1976-77; German Marshall Fund fellow, 1976-77; NSF Postdoctoral fellow, 1964-66; NSF Predoctoral fellow, 1960-64. Fellow AAAS, Am. Phys. Soc. Jewish. Home: 34 Westcott Rd Princeton NJ 08540-3060 Office: Princeton U H102 Engineering Quad Princeton NJ 08544

SOCWELL, MARGARET GERTRUDE OSBORN HARRIS, reading and language arts educator, consultant; b. Avoca, Iowa, Oct. 7, 1946; d. Fay and Mary Gertrude (Grote) Osborn; m. Richard John Socwell, Mar. 11, 1971 (div. May 1979); 1 child, Benjamin Adam. BS, Ohio State U., Columbus, 1968; MS, U. Wis., 1979. Cert. reading specialist, libr. media specialist, Spanish and French tchr., Ariz. Tchr. French Mason (Ohio) Pub. Schs., 1969-70; tchr. Spanish and French St. Matthias Cath. Girls H.S., L.A., 1970-71; tchr. French Whitewater (Wis.) Pub. Schs., 1971-72, tchr. Spanish, 1972-78; reading specialist Chilton (Wis.) Pub. Schs., 1978-79, Tolleson (Ariz.) Elem. Schs., 1979-80; tchr. reading and Spanish Deer Valley Unified Schs., Phoenix, 1980-88; tchr. reading Rio Salado C.C., Phoenix, 1987-91, tchr. lang. arts, 1989-93, tchr. social studies, 1993-96, libr. media specialist, 1996—; state forensics judge Whitewater Pub. Schs., 1974—; test designer Deer Valley Reading Curriculum Com., Phoenix, 1986-87, participant lang. arts pilot program Deer Valley Unified Sch. Dist., 1989; designer integrated social studies curriculum, 1994-96. Recipient grant Deer Valley Edn. Found., Inc., 1992. Mem. Internat. Assn. Near-Death Studies, Ariz. Reading Assn. Democrat. Avocations: reading, embroidery, cross-stitch, knitting, travel. Office: Deer Valley Pub Schs #97 20402 N 15th Ave Phoenix AZ 85027-3636

SODAL, INGVAR EDMUND, electrical engineer, scientist; b. Hemne, Norway, Feb. 12, 1934; came to U.S., 1962; s. Ingebrigt L. and Johanna (A.) Sodal; m. Sally Rollins; 1 child, Silje M. Degree in elec. engring., Trondheim Tech. Coll., Norway, 1959; BSEE, U. Colo., 1964. Engr. Fjeldseth Engring., Trondheim, 1959-61; rsch. engr. U. Norway, Trondheim, 1961-62; rsch. engr. U. Colo. Med. Ctr., Denver, 1964-66, rsch. assoc., 1966-75, instr., lectr., 1975-79; vis. rsch. assoc. dept. engring. U. Colo., Boulder, 1974-75, lectr., 1975-76; asst. prof., div. head. Ohio State U., Columbus, 1979-82, mem. grad. faculty, 1982; pres., chief exec. officer Masstron, Inc., Boulder, Colo., 1983-87; chief scientist Paradygm, Boulder, 1987-89; pres. Pacemark, Inc., Boulder, 1989-90, Med. Physics Colo., Inc., 1991—. Contbr. articles to profl. jours., chpts. to books; holder 6 patents in field. Instr. and/or program coord. in Scandinavian folklore and folk dancing for numerous groups and instns. throughout U.S., Can., and Norway, 1959—. Grantee NIH and various pvt. orgns. Mem. Assn. for Advancement Med. Instrumentation, Instrument Soc. Am., Soc. for Technology in Anesthesia, Biomed. Engring. Soc., Sons of Norway. Office: 1550 Moss Rock Pl Boulder CO 80304-1543

SODD, VINCENT JOSEPH, nuclear medicine researcher, educator; b. Toledo, Ohio, Nov. 20, 1934; s. Abraham and Sarah (Hamway) S.; m. Dorothy P. Langenderfer, Oct. 20, 1956; children: Vincent Joseph, Anthony Newman, Joseph William, Anne Marie. B.S., Xavier U., Cin., 1956, M.S., 1958; Ph.D., U. Pitts., 1964. Dep. chief nuclear medicine lab. FDA, Cin., 1974-77, acting chief, 1971-72, dir., 1974-84; assoc. prof. radiology U. Cin., 1974-77; prof. U. Cinn., 1977—; mem. radiation safety com. U. Con., 1975-86, mem. radioactive drug research com., 1979-86, mem. com. on human research, 1982-86. Author: Radiopharmaceuticals and Radiopharmaceuticals II, 1975,79, Radiation Safety in Nuclear Medicine-A Practical Guide, 1981; contbr. more than 150 articles to profl. jours.; patantee in field. Served to capt. USPHS, 1957-84. Recipient Dorst Chemistry Key Xavier U., 1956; recipient Silver award Ohio State Med. Assn., 1968. Mem. Soc. Nuclear Medicine (pres. S.E. chpt. 1979, 80, exec. dir. 1984—, exec. dir. Ctrl. chpt. 1991—, coun. 1981—, trustee 1980-81, bd. govs. Instrumentation Coun. 1982—), Internat. Commn. Radiol. Protection. Roman Catholic. Office: U Cin Coll Applied Sci ML 103 Cincinnati OH 45267

SODEN, RICHARD ALLAN, lawyer; b. Bklyn., Feb. 16, 1945; s. Hamilton David and Clara Elaine (Seale) S.; m. Marcia LaMonte Mitchell, June 7, 1969; children: Matthew Hamilton, Mark Mitchell. AB, Hamilton Coll., 1967; JD, Boston U., 1970. Bar: Mass. 1970. Law clk. to judge U.S. Ct. Appeals (6th cir.), 1970-71; assoc. firm Goodwin, Procter & Hoar, Boston, 1971-79, ptnr., 1979—; instr. Law Sch. Boston Coll., Chestnut Hill, Mass., 1973-74. Mem. South End Project Area Com.; hon. dir. United South End Settlements, pres., 1977-79; chmn. Boston Mcpl. Rsch. Bur.; bd. dirs. Greater Boston council Boy Scouts Am.; trustee Judge Baker Children's Ctr., chmn., 1994-96, pres., 1992-94; trusee, pres. New England Aquarium; trustee Boston U., Harvard Med. Ctr.; bd. visitors Boston U. Goldman Sch. Grad. Dentistry; mem. bd. overseers WGBH; mem. Mass. Minority Bus. Devel. Commn.; mem. Adv. Task Force on Securities Regulation; mem. Adv. Com. on Legal Edn.; steering com. Lawyers Com. for Civil Rights Under Law, chmn., 1992-94. Mem. ABA, Nat. Bar Assn., Mass. Bar Assn. (past vice chmn. bus. law coun., 1990-91), Boston Bar Assn. (pres. 1994-95), Mass. Black Lawyers Assn. (pres. 1980-81). Home: 42 Gray St Boston MA 02116-6210 Office: Goodwin Procter & Hoar Exchange Pl Boston MA 02109

SODER-ALDERFER, KAY CHRISTIE, counseling administrator; b. Evanston, Ill., Oct. 25, 1949; d. Earl Eugene and Alice Kathryn (Lien) Soder; m. David Luther Alderfer, May 15, 1976. BSE, No. Ill. U., 1972; postgrad., Luth. Sch. Theology, Phila., 1973; MA, Gov.'s State U., University Park, Ill., 1978; PhD, Walden U., 1985. Consecrated deaconess Luth. Ch., 1974. News reporter Suburban Life Newspaper, La Grange Park, Ill., 1972; counselor various orgns. Ill. & Pa., 1973—; parish worker Luth. Ch., De Kalb, Ill., 1973-74; pub. rels. asst. Luth. Ch. Women, Phila., 1974-76; editor Luth. Ch., Chgo., 1979—; spiritual dir. Gentle Pathways, Downers Grove, Ill., 1988—, counseling psychologist, 1990—, also bd. dirs.; cons. Evang. Luth. Ch. in Am., Chgo., 1988—, Lehigh Valley Hosp. Assn., Allentown, Pa., 1986, Luth. Social Ministry Orgns. of Pa. and N.J., 1997. Author: Gentle Journeys, 1993, With Those Who Grieve, 1995, Help! There's a Monster in My Head, 1997; editor Entree, 1988-93, Multicultural Jour., 1992—, project mgr., 1996—; graphic designs exhbn. Franklin Mus., Phila., 1981. Spokeswoman Progressive Epilepsy Network, Phila., 1980-85; chair spiritual life com. Luth. Deaconess Cmty., Gladwyne, Pa., 1990-92; founder Teens with Epilepsy and Motivation, 1995; vol. March of Dimes, Ill., 1991-93; amb. of goodwill Good Bears of the World, 1993-94; spiritual dir. Evang. Luth. Ch. in Am. Recipient Silver award Delaware Valley Neographics Soc., 1981; 50th anniversary scholar Luth. Deaconess Community, 1983. Mem. AAUW, APA (div. women and psychology, div. psychology and the arts, div. psychology and religion). Avocations: painting, mixed media, story telling, traveling, Native American studies, culture and art. Office: Gentle Pathways 1207 55th St Downers Grove IL 60515-4810

SÖDERBERG, BO SIGFRID, business executive; b. Avesta, Sweden, Mar. 22, 1939; came to U.S., 1979; s. John Sigfrid and Elisabet A. (Bjorkvall) S.; m. Kerstin Linnea Nordling; children: Monica, Mikael, Bogge, Margareta. BS in Engring., TGO, Orebro, Sweden, 1960; MBA, Fla. Inst. Tech., 1985. Mng. dir. Scandinavian Computer Systems, Stockholm, 1967-69; pres. Bror Andersson AB (BRA), Stockholm, 1969-78; exec. dir. Cap Gemini Sogeti, Paris, 1978-80, Cap Gemini Inc., Washington, 1980-82; pres. DMA Marketing Inc., Palm Bay, Fla., 1982-86; pres. Prisma Am. Inc., Vero Beach, Fla., 1986-87, also bd. dirs.; pres. Scandinavian USA Bus. Ctr., Inc., Clearwater, Fla., 1988-92, DMA Mktg. Inc., Clearwater, 1993—; seminar instr. Swedish Computer Soc., Stockholm, 1970-78; instr., lectr. Swedish Soc. for Info. Processing, Stockholm, 1972-78; lectr. Fla. Outdoor Advt. Assn., Orlando, Fla., 1986-87. Served as specialist Sweden Air Force, 1960-61. Home: 12000 4th St N Saint Petersburg FL 33716

SODERBERG, DAVID LAWRENCE, chemist; b. Evergreen Park, Ill., Jan. 28, 1944; s. Arthur Lawrence and Jean Van Norden (Freeman) S. AB in Chemistry, Ripon (Wis.) Coll., 1969. Rsch. asst. Ripon Coll., 1968-69, Pomona Coll., Claremont, Calif., 1969-70; chemist animal and plant health inspection svc. USDA, N.Y.C., 1972-73; chemist food safety and quality svc. USDA, Athens, Ga., 1974-83; supervisory chemist food safety and inspection svc. USDA, St. Louis, 1983-87; chemist, chemistry and toxicology divsn., emerging issues USDA, Washington, 1987—. Contbr. articles to profl. jours. With U.S. Army, 1965-67, Vietnam. Recipient awards USDA, 1976, 87, cert. of merit, 1980. Mem. AAAS, ASTM, Am. Chem. Soc., Assn. Official Analytical Chemists (gen. referee meat and poultry products). Office: USDA FSIS CTD E1B Rm 6912 Franklyn Ct Ste 1400 Ind Ave Washington DC 20250-3700

SODERBERG, NANCY, federal agency administrator; b. San Turce, P.R., Mar. 13, 1958; d. Lars Olof and Nancy (MacGilvrey) S. BA in French and Econs., Vanderbilt U., 1980; MS in Fgn. Svc., Georgetown U., 1984. Budget and reports analyst Bank of New England, Boston, 1980-82; rsch. asst. Brookings Inst., Washington, 1982-83; summer intern UN Devel. Program, Brazzaville, Congo, 1983; rsch. asst. Agy. Internat. Devel., Washington, 1983; del. selection asst. Mondale-Ferraro Com., Washington, 1983, fgn. policy advisor, 1984; dep. issues dir. fgn. policy Dukakis for Pres. Com., Boston, 1988; fgn. policy advisor Senator Edward M. Kennedy, Washington, 1985-88, 89-92; fgn. policy dir. Clinton/ Gore Campaign, Little Rock, 1992; dep. asst. dir. transition nat. security Clinton/ Gore Transition, Little Rock, 1992-93; dep. asst. to Pres. for nat. security affairs Nat. Security Coun., Washington, 1993—; mem. Coun. Fgn. Rels. *

SODERBERGH, STEVEN ANDREW, filmmaker; b. Atlanta, Jan. 14, 1963; s. Peter Andrew and Mary Ann (Bernard) S.; m. Elizabeth Jeanne Brantley, Dec. 1, 1989 (div. Oct. 1994). Writer, dir., editor: (film) sex, lies, and videotape, 1989 (Palme d'Or award Cannes Film Festival 1989), King of the Hill, 1993; dir., editor: (film) Kafka, 1991; exec. prodr.: (film) Suture, 1994, The Daytrippers, 1996; dir.: (film) The Underneath, 1995. Mem. AMPAS, Dirs. Guild Am. Democrat. Office: PO Box 2000 Orange VA 22960*

SODERLIND, STERLING EUGENE, newspaper industry consultant; b. Rapelje, Mont., Sept. 6, 1926; s. William John and Florence (Longbotham) S.; m. Helen Boyce, Apr. 9, 1955; children: Steven (dec.), Sarah, Lori. B.A., U. Mont., 1950; Rhodes Scholar, Oxford U., Eng., 1950-52. Reporter Mpls. Tribune, 1952-55; reporter Wall St. Jour., Chgo., 1955-56; Southeastern bur. chief Wall St. Jour., Jacksonville, Fla., 1956-57; mem. page one editing staff Wall St. Jour., N.Y.C., 1957-65, asst. mng. editor, 1966-70, mng. editor, 1970; econs. editor Dow Jones & Co., Inc., N.Y.C., 1970-77, asst. to pres., 1975-77, v.p., 1977-91; newspaper industry cons., 1992—. Served with USNR, 1944-46. Congregationalist. Home: 58 Wellington Ave Short Hills NJ 07078-3308

SODERQUIST, LARRY DEAN, lawyer, educator, consultant; b. Ypsilanti, Mich., July 20, 1944; s. Hugo E. and Emma A. (Johanson) S.; m. Ann Mangelsdorf, June 15, 1968; children: Hans, Lars. BS, Ea. Mich. U., 1966; JD, Harvard U., 1969. Bar: N.Y. 1971, Tenn. 1981. Assoc. Milbank, Tweed, Hadley & McCloy, N.Y.C., 1971-76; assoc. prof. law U. Notre Dame, South Bend, Ind., 1976-80, prof. 1980-81; vis. prof. law Vanderbilt U. Law Sch., Nashville, 1980-81, prof. 1981—, dir. corp. and securities law inst. 1993—; of counsel Tuke Yopp & Sweeney; spl. master U.S. Dist. Ct. (no. dist.) Ohio, 1977. Capt. U.S. Army 1969-71. Decorated Army Commendation medal. Mem. ABA, Am. Law Inst. Presbyterian. Author: Corporations, 1979, 4th edit., 1997, Understanding Corporation Law, 1990, Understanding the Securities Laws, 3d edit., 1993, Securities Regulation, 4th edit., 1997, Law of Federal Estate and Gift Taxation: Code Commentary, 1978, Analysis, 1980, Investor's Rights Handbook, 1993; contbr. numerous articles to legal jours. Home: 421 Sunnyside Dr Nashville TN 37205-3413 Office: Vanderbilt U Sch Law 21st Ave S Nashville TN 37240

SODERQUIST, RONALD BRUCE, minister, ministry director; b. Pine City, Minn., Mar. 16, 1943; s. Russell Eugene and Abigail Mae (Berger) S.; m. Carol Lynn Peterson, Aug. 20, 1966; children: Peter Gustav, Ingrid Ann-Marie, Anna Kristine.; BA, Northwestern Coll., 1965; MA, U. Wis., 1967; D in Ministry, Bethel Theol. Sem., 1993. Ordained min. So. Bapt. Conv., 1988. Acad. dean Kings Inst. Coll., Koronodal, Cotabato, The Philippines, 1967-69; asst. prof. English Trinity Coll., Deerfield, Ill., 1969-70; student ministry staff Campus Crusade for Christ, L.A., Mpls., Madison, 1970-77; regional dir. midwest Campus Crusade for Christ, 1977-80; internat. rep. Campus Crusade for Christ, Gothenburg, Sweden, 1980-84; spl. rep. Christian Embassy, Washington, 1984-87, dir. mil. ministry, 1987—. Avocations: travel, photography, reading. Office: Christian Embassy 2000 14th St N Ste 730 Arlington VA 22201-2573

SODERSTROM, ROBERT MERRINER, dermatologist; b. Streator, Ill., Sept. 9, 1947; s. Carl William and Virginia Rose (Merriner) S.; m. Susan Joy Nichols, Jan. 23, 1971; children: Sara, Paul, Lance. BS, U. Ill., 1969; MD, U. Mich., 1972. Dir. dermatology Hurley Med. Ctr., Flint, Mich., 1980—, Genesys Med. Ctr., Flint, Mich., 1993—; clin. prof. Mich. State U. Sch. Medicine, East Lansing, 1994—. Fellow Am. Coll. Physicians, Am. Acad. Dermatology; mem. Genesee County Med. Soc. (pres. 1993-94). Office: G-5131 W Bristol Flint MI 48507

SODOLSKI, JOHN, retired association administrator; b. Menasha, Wis., Apr. 11, 1931; s. L.V. and L.W. (Pinkowski) S.; m. C.J. Eppard. BS, U. Wis., 1953. Vice pres. Electronic Industries Assn., Washington, 1961-83; pres. U.S. Telephone Assn., Washington, 1983-93; ret., 1993. Served to 1st lt. USMC, 1955.

SOECHTIG, JACQUELINE ELIZABETH, telecommunications executive; b. Manhasset, N.Y., Aug. 12, 1949; d. Alvin Hermann and Regina Mary (Murphy) Venzke; m. James Decatur Miller, July 4, 1976 (div. Oct. 1982); M. Clifford Jon Soechtig, Oct. 19, 1983. B.A. cum laude, Coll. of New Rochelle (N.Y.), 1974; M.A. summa cum laude, U. So. Calif., 1979. Computer operator IBM, White Plains, N.Y., 1970-72, ops. job scheduler, 1972-74, various spl. assignments, 1974-75, mktg. rep., Bethesda, Md., 1975-76, Charleston, W. Va., 1979-81, adv. regional mktg. rep. Dallas, 1981-82; dist. mgr. Am. Speedy Printing Co., Dallas, 1982-83, nat. sales devel. mgr., Detroit, 1984; regional mgr. major and nat. accounts MCI Telecommunications, Southfield, Mich., 1984-85, dir. nat. accounts, 1985-86, v.p. nat. accounts, 1987-88, v.p. mktg. and customer svc., 1988-89, v.p. consumer segment, 1989-90; v.p. integrated telecommunications solutions Sprint United, Atlanta, 1990-92; pres., chief exec. officer Precision Systems, 1992-94; pres., chief exec. officer, chmn. Lasergate Sys. Inc., 1994—; interviewer, Sergio Segre, Bolonga, Italy, 1977, Radio Free Europe, Brussels, 1978, World Health Program, Rome, 1978, ITT, Brussels, 1977, Franz Josef Strauss, 1978. Recipient Golden Circle Achievement award IBM, 1980, Quar. Recognition award, 1980, 81; named New Bus. Pacesetter, 1980, 81. Republican. Club: German Am. Women's (v.p. Stuttgart, W.Ger. 1977-78). Office: Lasergate Syss Inc 28050 Us Highway 19 N Ste 502 Clearwater FL 33761-2630

SOEDERSTROM, ELISABETH ANNA, opera singer; b. Stockholm, May 7, 1927; d. Emanuel Albert and Anna (Palasova) S.; student Opera Sch., Stockholm, also pupil of Andrejewa Skilondz; m. Sverker Olow, Mar. 29, 1950; children: Malcolm, Peter, Jens. Appearances include Stockholm Opera, 1950, Salzburg Festival, 1955, Glyndebourne Opera, 1957, 59, 61, 63, 64, Met. Opera, 1959, 60, 62, 63, 83, 86-87; sang three leading roles in Rosencavalier within one year, 1959; toured USSR, 1966; others roles include Fiordiligi in Cosi Fan Tutte, Susanna and Countess in Figaro, Countess in Capriccio; radio, TV and concert appearances in U.S. and Europe; artistic leader Drottingholm Ct. Theatre, 1996, artistic dir., Drottningholm Ct. Theatre, 1993-97; author: I Min Tonart, 1978, Sjung ut, Elisabeth!, 1986. Decorated Order of Vasa (Sweden), 1997; Stelle Della Solidarieta Dell'Italia; King Olav's reward (Norway); comdr. Most Disting. Order Brit. Empire, CBE; comdr. des Arts et des Lettres; named Singer of the Court (Sweden); recipient prize for best acting Royal Swedish Acad., 1965, Literis et Artibus award, 1969. Mem. Royal Acad. Music Gt. Britain (hon.). Office: Drottningholms Theatre Mus, Box 27050, S-10251 Stockholm Sweden also: care Columbia Artists Mgmt 165 W 57th St New York NY 10019-2201

SOEJIMA, DAISUKE, international trade engineer, economist; b. Tokyo, Jan. 17, 1959; s. Aritoshi and Hiroko Soejima; m. Kiyomi Soejima, Sept. 26, 1987; children: Sayuri, Taiga, Chiaki. BS in Econs., Tokyo U., 1983; MBA, Georgetown U., 1991. Assoc. cons., mgr. coord. Mitsubishi Corp., Tokyo, 1991-95; mgr. Mitsubishi Internat. Corp., Washington, 1995-97; mgr. project and planning Mitsubishi Internat. Corp., N.Y.C., 1997—; sr. rschr. Japan Inst. for Econ. Rsch., Tokyo, 1981-83. Mem. grad. adv. bd. Georgetown U. Mem. Asian Chem. Mgmt. and Rsch. Assn., Met. Club, Beta Gamma Sigma, Alpha Mu Alpha. Home: 6328 Mori St McLean VA 22101 Office: Mitsubishi Internat Corp 520 Madison Ave New York NY 10022-4213

SOENS, LAWRENCE D., bishop; b. Iowa City, Aug. 26, 1926. Student, Loras Coll., Dubuque, Iowa, St. Ambrose Coll., Davenport, Iowa, Kenrick Sem., St. Louis, U. Iowa. Ordained priest Roman Catholic Ch., 1950, consecrated bishop, 1983. Bishop of Sioux City Iowa, 1983—. Office: Chancery Office PO Box 3379 1821 Jackson St Sioux City IA 51102-3379*

SOERGEL, KONRAD HERMANN, physician; b. Coburg, Germany, July 27, 1929; came to U.S., 1954, naturalized, 1962; s. Konrad Daniel and Erna Henrietta (Schilling) S.; m. Rosina Klara Rudin, June 24, 1955; children: Elizabeth Ann, Karen Theresa, Marilyn Virginia, Kenneth Thomas. M.D., U. Erlangen, Germany, 1954, Dr. med., 1958. Intern Bergen Pines County Hosp., Paramus, N.J., 1954-55; resident in pathology West Pa. Hosp., Pitts., 1955-56; resident in medicine Mass. Meml. Hosp., Boston, 1957-58; fellow in gastroenterology Boston U. Med. Sch., 1958-60, instr., 1960-61; mem. faculty Med. Coll. Wis., Milw., 1961—, prof. medicine, 1969—, prof. physiology, 1993—; chief sect. gastroenterology Med. Coll. Wis., 1961-93, dir. fellowship program, dept. medicine, 1993—; chmn. gastroenterology and clin. nutrition study sect. NIH, 1979-80. Contbr. articles to profl. jours., chpts. to books. Recipient Research Career Devel. award USPHS, 1963-72; Alexander von Humboldt Found. sr. fellow, 1973-74. Mem. Am. Gastroenterol. Assn., Am. Soc. Clin. Investigation, Am. Assn. Physicians, German Soc. for Digestive and Metabolic Disorders (hon.), Ger. Soc. Internal Medicine (hon.). Home: 14245 Hillside Rd Elm Grove WI 53122-1677 Office: Med Coll Wis 9200 W Wisconsin Ave Milwaukee WI 53226-3522

SOETEBER, ELLEN, journalist, newspaper editor; b. East St. Louis, Ill., June 14, 1950; d. Lyle Potter and Norma Elizabeth (Osborn) S.; m. Richard M. Martins, Mar. 16, 1974. BJ, Northwestern U., 1972. Edn. writer, copy editor Chgo. Today, 1972-74; reporter Chgo. Tribune, 1974-76, asst. met. editor, 1976-84, assoc. met. editor, 1984-86, TV and media editor, 1986, met. editor, 1987-89, assoc. mng. editor for met. news, 1989-91, dep. editor editorial page, 1991-94; mng. editor South Fla. Sun-Sentinel, Ft. Lauderdale, 1994—; fellow journalism U. Mich., Ann Arbor, 1986-87. Office: The Sun-Sentinel 200 E Las Olas Blvd Fort Lauderdale FL 33301-2248

SOETH, SARAH LAVERNE REEDY MCMILLAN, psychiatric nurse; b. Amory, Miss., Feb. 20, 1925; d. Samuel Thomas and Bessie Lee (Franklin) Reedy; m. Urshel E. McMillan, Jan. 16, 1944 (dec. 1964); children: David Thomas McMillan, Joy Laverne McMillan Keys; m. Glenn Eugene Soeth, Nov. 27, 1976 (dec. 1995). Student, Miss. State Coll. Women, 1943-44; LPN, Tupelo Sch. Nursing, 1968; MSN, U. Miss., Jackson, 1972. RN, Miss. Pvt. duty nurse Evart, Mich., 1960-64; staff nurse Aberdeen (Miss.) Monroe County Hosp., 1965-72; lic. psychiat. nurse Hinds Gen. Hosp., Jackson, Miss., 1972-78; charge nurse Tigard (Oreg.) Psychiat. Convalescent Hosp., 1978-79; staff nurse VA Med. Ctr., Reno, 1979-80, Glenn County Hosp., Willows, Calif., 1980-81; staff nurse VA Med. Ctr., Martinez, Calif., 1981-91, Fresno, Calif., 1991-93; ret., 1993; vol. Mental Health Treatment Ctr.; part-time worker Savon Photo Lab., Tupelo. Active Diabetes Assn.; dir. sr. citizen br. Faith Assembly God Presbyn. Ch., Tupelo, Miss., 1996, pres. women's ministry. Mem. Nat. Assn. Ret. Fed. Employees. Baptist. Avocations: music, reading, genealogy, hand crafts, travel.

SOFAER, ABRAHAM DAVID, lawyer, legal advisor, federal judge, legal educator; b. Bombay, India, May 6, 1938; came to U.S., 1948, naturalized, 1959; m. Marian Bea Scheuer, Oct. 23, 1977; children: Daniel E., Michael J., Helen R., Joseph S., Aaron R., Raphael J. BA in History magna cum laude, Yeshiva Coll., 1962; LLB cum laude, NYU, 1965. Bar: N.Y. 1965. Law clk. to Hon. J. Skelly Wright, U.S. Ct. Appeals, Washington, 1965-66; to Hon. William J. Brennan, Jr., U.S. Supreme Ct., Washington, 1966-67; asst. U.S. atty. So. Dist. N.Y., N.Y.C., 1967-69; prof. law Columbia U., N.Y.C., 1969-79; judge U.S. Dist. Ct. for So. Dist. N.Y., 1979-85; legal advisor Dept. State, Washington, 1985-90; ptnr. Hughes Hubbard & Reed, Washington, 1991-94; George P. Shultz disting. scholar, sr. fellow Hoover Instn., Stanford U., 1994—; hearing officer N.Y. Dept. Environ. Conservation, 1975-76. Author: War, Foreign Affairs and Constitutional Power: The Origins, 1976; contbr. articles to legal, polit., fgn. jours.; editor-in-chief: NYU Law Rev, 1964-65. Served with USAF, 1956-59. Root-Tilden scholar NYU, 1965. Mem. Fed. Bar Assn., Am. Bar Assn., N.Y. Bar Assn., Am. Law Inst. Jewish. Office: Stanford Univ The Hoover Instn Stanford CA 94305-6010

SOFFAR, WILLIAM DOUGLAS, lawyer; b. Houston, Sept. 8, 1944; s. Benjamin and Esther Goldy (Garfinkel) S.; m. Nancy Elise Axelrod, Mar. 29, 1969 (div. Sept. 1989); children: Pamela Beth, Stephanie Michelle, Jill Denise. BA, U. Houston, 1966, JD, 1969. Bar: Tex. 1969, U.S. Dist. Ct. (so. dist.) Tex. 1970, U.S. Ct. Appeals (5th cir.) 1974, U.S. Supreme Ct. 1974; cert. mediator in civil law and family law. Atty. examiner U.S. Interstate Commerce Commn., Washington, 1969-70; atty. Law Office of Adolph Uzick, Houston, 1970-72, Walsh & Soffar, Houston, 1972-73; lawyer, sole practice Law Offices of William D. Soffar, Houston, 1973-74; ptnr. Soffar & Levit, Houston, 1974—; family law and civil mediator, basic mediation and family mediation trainer Atty.-Mediator's Inst. Bd. dirs. Miller Theater Adv. Coun., Houston, 1985-90, Zina Garrison Found., Houston, 1989-91. Mem. Houston Bar Assn. (bd. dirs., family law sect. mem. 1989-90), Jewish Cmty. Ctr. (health club com. 1971—), Jewish Family Svc. (bd. dirs. 1970-71), Phi Delta Phi. Jewish. Avocations: travel, reading, raquetball. Office: Soffar & Levit 6575 West Loop S Ste 630 Bellaire TX 77401-3514

SOFIA, R. D., pharmacologist; b. Ellwood City, Pa., Oct. 8, 1942. BS, Geneva Coll., 1964; MS, Fairleigh-Dickenson U., 1969; PhD in Pharmacology, U. Pitts., 1971. Rsch. biologist Lederle Labs., N.Y., 1964-67; rsch. assoc. pharmacology Union Carbide Corp., 1967-69; sr. pharmacologist Pharmakon Labs., Pa., 1969; sr. rsch. pharmacologist Pharmakon Labs., 1971-73, dir. dept. Pharmacology and Toxicology, 1973-76, v.p. biology rsch., 1976-80, v.p. R&D, 1980-82; v.p. pre-clin. rsch. Wallace Labs., Cranbury, 1982—; cons. Pharmakon Labs., 1969-71. Mem. Am. Soc. Pharmacology and Experimental Therapeutics, Soc. Toxicology, SOc. Neuroscience, Internat. Soc. Study Pain, Am. Rheumatism Assn. Achievements include research in pharmacology and toxicology of various constituents of marijuana, development of new drugs for cardiovascular pulmonary and central nervous system diseases and pain relief. Office: Carter-Wallace Inc Half-acre Rd # 1001 Cranbury NJ 08512

SOFIA, SABATINO, astronomy educator; b. Episcopia, Italy, May 14, 1939; came to U.S., 1961; married, 1963; 2 children. BS, Yale U., 1963, MS, 1965, PhD in Astrophysics, 1966. Rsch. assoc. astrophysics Goddard Inst. Space Studies NASA, N.Y.C., 1966-67; from assoc. prof. to prof. astronomy U. South Fla., Tampa, 1967-73; vis. fellow Joint Inst. Lab. Astrophysics, Boulder, Colo., 1973-74; sr. rsch. assoc. U. Rochester, N.Y., 1974-75; adj. prof. astronomy U. Fla., 1975—; staff scientist NASA, 1975-77; sr. rsch. assoc. solar physics Nat. Acad. Sci., Nat. Rsch. Coun., 1977-79; space scientist Goddard Space Flight Ctr., Greenbelt, Md., 1979-85; mem. space and earth sci. adv. com. NASA, 1985-88; prof. astronomy Yale U., New Haven, 1985—, chmn. astronomy dept., 1993—. Mem. Am. Astron. Soc., Internat. Astron. Union, Am. Geophys. Union. Office: Yale U Dept Astronomy PO Box 208101 260 Whitney Ave New Haven CT 06520-8101

SOFTNESS, DONALD GABRIEL, marketing and manufacturing executive; b. Bklyn.; s. Burt H. and Ida (Kaiser) S.; m. Sydell Meyerson; children: Michael, Anita May, Beth. A.B., NYU, 1949, M.B.A., 1959; L.H.D., St. John's U., 1979. Chmn. Softness Group, Inc., N.Y.C., 1960-79; pres. Softness Enterprise, N.Y.C., 1979—, SecureVue, Inc., N.Y.C., 1984—; v.p., maj. prin. Radio Stas. WVNJ-AM-FM, Newark and N.Y.C.; mem. faculty Advt. Week seminars Advt. Age; prodr., sponsor Bklyn. Rollathon (skating marathon). Co-author: Cardiologists' Guide to Health and Fitness Through Exercise, 1979; contbr. articles to bus. and trade jours. Patentee in field. Served with USN. Mem. Public Relations Soc. Am., Internat. Radio TV Soc., Am. Coll. Sports Medicine. Club: N.Y. Yacht. Home and Office: 28 Trues Dr West Islip NY 11795-5139 Office: SecureVue Inc 251 E 51st St New York NY 10022-6534

SOFTNESS, JOHN, public relations executive; b. Bklyn., Nov. 7, 1930; s. Burt H. and Ida (Kaiser) S.; m. Leona Ruth Golden; children: Barney, David, Daniel. B.A., U. Miami, 1955. Reporter Miami Herald, 1953; reporter Sta. WTVJ, Miami, Fla., 1954; asso. pub. relations dir. aviation dept. Shell Oil Co., N.Y.C., 1958-60; pres., chief exec. officer The Softness Group, Inc., N.Y.C., 1960-91, chmn., 1992—; spl. counselor to Bklyn. Borough pres., 1966-76; adj. prof. communications arts St. John's U., 1981—; counselor communications com. N.Y. Heart Assn. Author: (autobiography) Boy Outta Brooklyn. Served to capt. USAF, 1955-58. Mem. Pub. Rels. Soc. Am., Pride and Alarm (chmn.), Counselors' Acad. Home: 245 E 54th St Apt 14F New York NY 10022-4719 Office: The Softness Group Inc 381 Park Ave S New York NY 10016-8806

SOGG, WILTON SHERMAN, lawyer; b. Cleve., May 28, 1935; s. Paul P. and Julia (Cahn) S.; m. Saralee Frances Krow, Aug. 12, 1962 (div. July 1975); 1 child, Stephanie; m. Linda Rocker Lehman, Dec. 22, 1979 (div. Dec. 1990); m. Nancy Rosenfield Walsh, June 2, 1991. A.B., Dartmouth Coll., 1956; J.D., Harvard U., 1959; Fulbright fellow, U. London, 1959-60. Bar: Ohio 1960, D.C. 1970, Fla. 1970, U.S. Supreme Ct., N.Y. 1985, U.S. Tax Ct. Assoc. Gottfried, Ginsberg, Guren & Merritt, 1960-63, ptnr., 1963-70; ptnr. Guren, Merritt, Feibel, Sogg & Cohen, Cleve., 1970-84; of counsel Hahn, Loeser, Freedheim, Dean and Wellman, Cleve., 1984-85; ptnr. Hahn Loeser & Parks, 1986—; trustee, pres. Cleve. Jewish News; adj. prof. Cleve. State Law Sch., 1960—; lectr. Harvard U. Law Sch., 1978-80. Author (with Howard M. Rossen); new and rev. vols. of Smith's Review Legal Gems series, 1969—; editor: Harvard Law Rev.; contbr. articles to profl. jours. Trustee Jewish Cmty. Fedn. of Cleve., 1966-72; bd. overseers Cleveland Marshall Coll. Law, Cleve. State U., 1969—; dir. Project for Improving Delivery of Legal Svcs., Case Western Res. U. Law Sch., 1991—; mem. U.S. and State of Ohio Holocaust commns. Mem. Ohio Bar Assn., Cleve. Bar Assn., Cuyahoga County Bar Assn., Fla. bar Assn., D.C. Bar Assn., N.Y. State Bar Assn., German Philatelic Soc., Oakwood Club, Union Club, Chagrin Valley Hunt, Phi Beta Kappa. Home: PO Box 0278 1834 Epping Rd Gates Mills OH 44040-0278 Office: Hahn Loeser & Parks 3300 BP America Bldg 200 Public Sq Cleveland OH 44114-2301

SOH, CHUNGHEE SARAH, anthropology educator; b. Taegu, Korea, May 1, 1947; came to U.S., 1970; d. Sang Yung and Ock Yun (Choi) S.; m. Jerry Dee Boucher. BA summa cum laude, Sogang U., 1971; postgrad., U. Calif., Berkeley, 1971; MA in Anthropology, U. Hawaii, 1983, PhD in Anthropology, 1987. Staff instr. English Korean Air Lines, Edn. & Tng. Ctr., Seoul, 1978-79; instr. anthropology Ewha Womans U., Seoul, 1985; asst. prof. U. Hawaii, 1990; asst. prof. anthropology Southwest Tex. State U., San Marcos, 1991-94; asst. prof. anthropology San Francisco State U., 1994-96, assoc. prof. anthropology, 1996—; guest lectr. Chaminade U. Honolulu, 1988; vis. asst. prof. anthropology U. Ariz., 1990-91; adj. prof. Intercultural Inst. Calif., 1997—; vis. scholar Hoovrer Inst., 1996-97; cons. in field. Author: Women in Korean Politics; contbr. articles to profl. jours. East-West Ctr. scholar, 1981-87; grantee NSF, 1985-86; fellow Korea Found., 1993, Japan Found., 1997—. Fellow Am. Anthrop. Assn.; mem. Am. Ethnological Soc., Soc. Psychol. Anthropology, Assn. Asian Studies (exec. bd. Com. Women Asian Studies), Western Social Sci. Assn., Korean Assn. Womens Studies, Royal Asiatic Soc. Korean Br. Office: San Francisco State U Dept Anthropology 1600 Holloway Ave San Francisco CA 94132-1722

SOHL, JOYCE DARLENE, religious organization administrator; b. Aurora, Ill., Dec. 15, 1935; m. Lowell Sohl (dec.); children: John, Stephen. BA, Westmar Coll., 1957; MA, U. Nebr., 1959; MBA, Fordham U., 1984. Math. tchr. Irving Jr. H.S., Lincoln, Nebr., 1959-61, Lincoln H.S., 1961-64; assoc. treas. gen. bd. global ministries women's divsn. United Meth. Ch., 1976-90, dep. gen. sec. gen. bd. global ministries women's divsn., 1991—; Author: (book) Managing Our Money, Workbook on Women and Finance; (videos) Giving: A Gift of God's Grace, 1988, Called to Mission, 1994, Managing Our Money, 1990, Count Me In, 1994; columnist: monthly column Responsively Yours, in Response, 1991—; also articles in ch. publs. and program materials for program book of Women's Soc. of World Svc. and United Meth. Women. Past mem. bd. trustees, treas. Meml. United Meth. Ch., White Plains, current lay del. to ann. conf., mem. pastor/parish rels. com., adminstrv. bd., substitute organist; mem. adv. com. United Seminary, Dayton; bd. dirs. Scarritt-Bennett Ctr.; trustee Bennett Coll., Greensboro, N.C. Mem. NAFE, Am. Mgmt. Assn. Office: Gen Bd Global Ministries United Meth Ch 475 Riverside Dr New York NY 10115-0122

SOHMER, BERNARD, mathematics educator, administrator; b. N.Y.C., July 16, 1929; s. Sol and Florence (Schonfeld) S.; m. Margot Rosette, July

27, 1952; children—Emily, Olivia. BA, NYU, 1949, MS, 1951, PhD, 1958. Lectr. CCNY, 1952-57, faculty, 1958—, prof. math., 1969—, dean students, 1969-72, v.p. student affairs, 1972-75, chmn. faculty senate, 1977-79, 85-91, ombudsman, 1991—, chmn. liberal arts and sci. faculty council, 1979-85, pres. Hillel, 1988—; asst. prof. N.Y. U., 1957-58; trustee PSC-CUNY Welfare Fund, 1982-97. Sec. Univ. Faculty Senate, 1992-94, vice chair, 1994—. Mem. AAAS, AAUP (pres. CCNY chpt. 1966-67, sec. 1977-78), Am. Math. Soc., Math. Assn. Am. (pres. elect N.Y. Met. sect. 1989-90, pres. 1992-93, past pres. 1993-94, gov. 1996—), Profl. Staff Congress (gov. CCNY chpt. 1993-96, exec. coun. 1997—). Home: 3345 92nd St Jackson Hts NY 11372-1851 Office: CCNY 139th and Convent Ave New York NY 10031

SOHN, CHANG WOOK, energy systems researcher, educator; b. Seoul, Korea, Jan. 10, 1947; parents Kye Taek and Young Bo (Koh) S.; m. Chung Hae Han Sohn, Aug. 24, 1974; children: Douglas Jemin, Sammy Sungmin. BS in Engring., Seoul Nat. U., 1969; MS in Mech. Engring., Tex. Tech. U., 1975; PhD in Mech. Engring., U. Ill., Urbana, 1980. Registered profl. engr., Ill. 1st lt. Korean Army, 1969-71; tchr. KyungGi H.S., Seoul, 1971-72; rsch. asst. Tex. Tech. U., Lubbock, 1973-74; rsch. asst. U. Ill., Urbana, 1974-79, rsch. assoc., 1979-80; rsch. engr. U.S. Army Constrn. Engring. Rsch. Lab., Champaign, Ill., 1980-84, acting. team leader, 1992, prin. investigator, 1984—, project leader, 1995—; adj. assoc. prof. U. Ill., Urbana, 1992—. Contbr. articles on fluid mechanics, heat transfer to profl. jours, ASHRAE transactions. Recipient Tech. Transfer award U.S. Army Corps of Engrs., Washington, 1991, Spl. Act award U.S. Army Yuma (Ariz.) Proving Ground, 1988; Korea Inst. Energy Rsch. fellow, 1995-96. Mem. ASME (K-19 com. 1993—), ASHRAE (com. chair Cool Storage Design Guide 1992, air conditioning rsch. ctr. industry adv. bd. mem. 1991-96). Home: 2910 Robeson Park Dr Champaign IL 61821-7609 Office: U S Army CERL PO Box 9005 Champaign IL 61826

SOHN, HONG YONG, chemical and metallurgical engineering educator, consultant; b. Kaesung, Kyunggi-Do, Korea, Aug. 21, 1941; arrived U.S., 1966; s. Chong Ku and Soon Deuk (Woo) S.; m. Victoria Bee Tuan Ngo, Jan. 8, 1972; children: Berkeley Jihoon, Edward Jihyun. BS in Chem. Engring., Seoul (Korea) Nat. U., 1962; MS in Chem. Engring., U. N.B., Can., 1966; PhD in Chem. Engring., U. Calif., Berkeley, 1970. Engr., Cheil Sugar Co., Busan, Korea, 1962-64; rsch. assoc. SUNY-Buffalo, 1971-73; research engr. DuPont Co., Wilmington, Del., 1973-74; prof. metall. engring., adj. prof. chem. engring. U. Utah, Salt Lake City, 1974—; cons. Lawrence Livermore Nat. Lab., 1976—, Kennecott Co., Salt Lake City, 1976—, Cabot Corp., 1984—, DuPont Co., 1987—, Utah Power and Light Co., 1987—. Co-author: Gas-Solid Reactions, 1976; co-editor: Rate Processes of Extractive Metallurgy, 1979, Extractive Metallurgy of Refractory Metals, 1980, Advances in Sulfide Smelting, 2 vols., 1983; Recycle and Secondary Recovery of Metals, 1985, Gas-solid Reactions in Pyrometallurgy, 1986, Flash Rection Processes, 1988, Metallurgical Processes for the Year 2000 and Beyond, 1988, Metallurgical Processes for the Early Twenty-First Century, 2 vols., 1994; patentee process for treating sulfide-bearing ores; contbr. numerous articles to sci., tech. jours. Camille and Henry Dreyfus Found. Tchr. Scholar awardee, 1977; Fulbright Disting. lectr., 1983; Japan Soc. for the Promotion of Sci. fellow, 1990. Mem. The Minerals, Metals and Materials Soc. (past dir., Extractive Metallurgy Lectr. award, 1990, Champion H. Mathewson Gold Medal award, 1993, Extractive metallurgical sci. award 1990, 94), Am. Inst. Chem. Engrs., Korean Chem. Engrs. Office: U Utah 412 Browning Building Salt Lake City UT 84112-1118 *Fortunate are those who earn a living by doing what they would rather be doing even if they do not have to do it to earn a living. Material wealth accumulated by doing what one does not enjoy doing is not worth the effort.*

SOHN, JEANNE, librarian; b. Milton, Pa.; d. Robert Wilson and Juliette Lightner (Hedenberg) Gift; m. Steven Neil Sohn, Nov. 23, 1962. BA, Temple U., 1966; MSLS, Drexel U., 1971. Lit. bibliographer Temple U., Phila., 1971-75, chief of collection devel., 1975-81; asst. dean for collection devel. U. N.Mex., Albuquerque, 1981-86, assoc. dean for libr. svcs., 1986-89; dir. libr. svcs. Cen. Conn. State U., New Britain, 1989—; cons. New Eng. Assn. Schs. and Colls., Winchester, Mass., 1991—. Mem. editorial bd. Collection Mgmt., 1984—; contbr. articles to profl. jours. Mem. Gov.'s Blue Ribbon Commn. on the Future of Libraries, 1994-96. Mem. ALA, New Eng. Libr. Assn., Conn. Libr. Assn., Assn. Coll. and Rsch. Librs., Beta Phi Mu. Home: 1820 Boulevard West Hartford CT 06107-2815 Office: Cen Conn State Univ Elihu Burritt Libr New Britain CT 06050

SOHN, LOUIS BRUNO, lawyer, educator; b. Lwów, Poland, Mar. 1, 1914; came to U.S., 1939, naturalized, 1943; s. Joseph and Fryderyka (Hescheles) S.; m. Elizabeth Mayo. LLM, Diplomatic ScM, John Casimir U., 1935; LLM, Harvard U., 1940, SJD, 1958; LLD (hon.), Free U. Brussels (Flemish sect.), 1990. Asst. to Judge M. O. Hudson, 1941-48; John Harvey Gregory teaching fellow Harvard Law Sch., 1946-47, lectr. law, 1947-51, asst. prof. law, 1951-53, John Harvey Gregory lectr. in world orgn., 1951-81, prof. law, 1953-61, Bemis prof. internat. law, 1961-81; Woodruff prof. internat. law U. Ga., 1981-91; vis. Congl. prof. George Washignton U. Law Sch., 1991-92; Disting. rsch. prof. and dir. rsch. and studies Internat. Rule of Law Inst., George Washington U. Law Sch., 1992—; Disting. fellow Jennings Randolph Program, U.S. Inst. Peace, 1991-92; cons. U.S. ACDA, 1960-70, Office Internat. Security Affairs, Dept. Def., 1963-70; asst. to del. Permanent Ct. Internat. Justice, San Francisco Conf. UN, 1945; exec. sec. legal subcom. on atomic energy Carnegie Endowment for Internat. Peace, 1946; asst. reporter on progressive devel. internat. law Am. and Canadian bar assns., 1947-48; cons. UN secretariat, 1948, 69, legal officer, 1950-51; counselor internat. law Dept. State, 1970-71; U.S. del. to UN Law of Sea Conf., 1974-82; U.S. del. head Athens Conf. on Settlement Internat. Disputes, 1984. Author: Cases on World Law, 1950, Cases on United Nations Law, 1956, 2d edit., 1967, (with G. Clark) World Peace Through World Law, 1958, 3d edit., 1966, Basic Documents of African Regional Organizations, 4 vols, 1971-72, (with T. Buergenthal) International Protection of Human Rights, 1973, (with K. Gustafson) The Law of the Sea, 1984, International Organization and Integration: student edit. 1986, (with T. Buergenthal) The Movement of Persons Across Borders, 1992, Rights in Conflict: The United Nations v. South Africa, 1994 ; also articles on legal subjects; editor devel. internat. law: Am. Bar Assn. Jour, 1947-50; editorial bd.: Am. Jour. Internat. Law, 1958—. Recipient World Peace Hero award World Federalists of Can., 1974, Grenville Clark award, 1984, William A. Owens award for creative rsch. in social and behavioral scis. U. Ga., 1985, Harry Leroy Jones award Washington Fgn. Law Soc., 1993. Mem. ABA (hon., co-rapporteur joint working group with Can. Bar Assn. on peaceful settlement of disputes 1976—, vice chmn. internat. law and practice sect. 1983-91, chmn. 1992-93, Leonard J. Theberge award 1992), Am. Soc. Internat. Law (mem. exec. coun. 1954-57, v.p. 1965-66, hon. v.p. 1980-87, 90—, pres. 1988-90, Manley O. Hudson medal 1996), World Parliament Assn. (legal advisor 1954-64), Internat. Law Assn. (v.p. Am. br.), Am. Law Inst. (assoc. reporter Fgn. Rels. Law 1978-87), Inst. Internat. Law (Geneva), Fedn. Am. Scientists (vice chmn. 1963, mem. coun. 1964-65, 68-69), Commn. Study Orgn. Peace (chmn. 1986—). Home: 801 15th St S Apt 1504 Arlington VA 22202-5023 Office: George Washington U Law Sch 720 20th St NW Washington DC 20006-4306

SOIKA, HELMUT EMIL, retirement plan executive; b. N.Y.C., May 22, 1941; s. Hubert E. and Berta Antonia (Metzger) S. BS, Fordham U., 1963, JD, 1968. Asst. trust officer Nat. Bank of N.Am., N.Y.C., 1968-71; trust officer Bank of N.Y., Westchester, 1971-72; atty. O'Neill, DiManno & Kelly, N.Y.C., 1972-76; atty. & div. mgr. Mut. of Am., N.Y.C., 1976-82; v.p., mgr. retirement plans Prudential-Bache Securities, N.Y.C., 1982-86; sr. v.p., dir. retirement plans Gruntal & Co. Inc., N.Y.C., 1986—. Office: Gruntal & Co Inc 14 Wall St New York NY 10005-2101

SOILEAU, MARION JOSEPH, engineering and physics educator; b. Simmesport, La., June 27, 1944; s. Marion and Mary Ann (Rabalais) S.; m. Cheryl A. Meche; children: Bruce, Aimee. BS in Astronomy/Physics, La. State U., 1967; MS in Physics/Optics, U. Utah, 1968; PhD in Quantum Electronics, U. So. Calif., 1979. Prof. Elec. Engring., Physics. Various positions in field to physicist Naval Weapons Ctr., China Lake, Calif., 1973-80; assoc. prof. physics North Tex. State U., 1980-84, prof. physics, 1984-87; prof. elec. engring. and physics, dir. Ctr. Rsch. and Edn. in Optics and Lasers, U. Ctrl. Fla., Orlando, 1987—. Contbr. over 100 sci. papers on nonlinear optics; contbr. articles to profl. jours. Trustee Orlando Sci. Ctr., 1991—. Capt. USAF, 1967-72. Co-recipient North Tex. State U. Pres.'s award, 1983. Fellow Optical Soc. Am., Soc. Photo-Optical and Instrumentation Engrs. (bd. govs. 1990-92), SPIE-The Internat. Optical Engring. Soc. (bd. govs. 1990-92, 94, sec. 1995, v.p. 1996, pres. 1997); mem. AAAS, IEEE (sr.), Laser Inst. Am., K.C., others. Democrat. Roman Catholic. Avocation: fishing. Home: 100 Tuskawilla Rd Winter Spgs FL 32708-2830 Office: U Cen Fla PO Box 162700 Orlando FL 32816-2700

SOJKA, GARY ALLAN, biologist, educator, university official; b. Cedar Rapids, Iowa, July 15, 1940; s. Marvin F. and Ruth Ann (Waddington) Sojka Green; m. Sandra Kay Smith, Aug 5, 1962; children: Lisa Kay, Dirk Allan. BS, Coe Coll., 1962; MS, Purdue U., 1965, PhD, 1967; LLD (hon.), Lycoming Coll., 1995. Rsch. assoc. Ind. U., Bloomington, 1967-69, asst. prof., 1969-73, assoc. prof., 1973-79, prof., 1979-84, assoc. chmn. biology, 1977-79, chmn. biology, 1979-81, dean arts and scis., 1981-84; pres. Bucknell U., Lewisburg, Pa., 1984-95; prof. biology Bucknell U., Lewisburg, 1989—; mem. higher edn. commn. Mid. States Assn. Colls. and Schs., 1992—; chmn. tax policy subcom. Nat. Assn. Ind. Colls. and Univs., 1991-93; mem. study group on internat. edn. Am. Coun. Edn., 1992-94. Chmn. bd. dirs. Stone Belt Coun. Ret. Citizens, Bloomington, 1977-78; mem. nominating com. Ind. Assn. Ret. Citizens, Indpls., 1979; mem. So. Ind. Health Sys. Agy., Bedford; bd. dirs. Geisinger Med. Found., Danville, Pa., Inst. European Studies; trustee St. Mary-of-the-Woods Coll., Ind., 1988-94; chmn. Pa. Commn. Ind. Colls. and Univs., 1989-90; dir. Suncom Industries, Northcumberland, Pa., 1991-93; mem. Pres.'s Commn. NCAA, 1993-95; bd. dirs. Bethesda Found., Lewisburg, 1996—. Recipient Ind. U. Sr. Class Tchg. award, 1975, Frederick B. Lieber award, 1977, Coe Coll. Alumni award of merit, 1982, Gary A. Sojka award Bucknell U., 1992, Cmty. Leadership award Susquahanna Valley Boy Scouts, 1994; named to Coe Coll. Athletic Hall of Fame, 1988. Mem. Am. Assn. Microbiology, Am. Acad. Microbiology, Am. Soc. Biol. Chemists, Soc. Gen. Microbiology, Nat. Assn. Independent Colls. and Univs. (subcom. chmn. 1991-93), Am. Coun. Edn. (mem. study group on internat. edn. 1992-94), Sigma Xi, Sigma Nu, Omicron Delta Kappa. Baptist. Home: Bend-in-the-Creek Farm 141 Creek Rd Middleburg PA 17842 Office: Bucknell U Dept Biology Lewisburg PA 17842

SOKAL, ROBERT REUVEN, biology educator, author; b. Vienna, Austria, Jan. 13, 1926; came to U.S., 1947, naturalized 1958; s. Siegfried and Klara (Rattner) S.; m. Julie Chen-Chu Yang, Aug. 12, 1948; children: David Jonathan, Hannah Judith. BS in Biology, St. John's U., Shanghai, Republic of China, 1947; PhD in Zoology, U. Chgo., 1952; DSc (hon.), U. Crete (Greece), 1990. From instr. to prof. U. Kans., Lawrence, 1951-69; prof., then leading prof., Disting. prof. SUNY, Stony Brook, 1969-95, dept. chmn., 1980-83, vice provost for rsch. and grad. studies, 1981-82, disting. prof. emeritus, 1995; Fulbright vis. prof. Hebrew/Tel Aviv U., Israel, 1963-64, U. Vienna, Austria, 1977, 78, 84; vis. prof. Inst. Adv. Studies, Oeiras, Portugal, 1971-80; vis. disting. prof. U. Mich., 1975-76; vis. prof. Coll. de France, Paris, 1989. Author: Principles of Numerical Taxonomy, 1963, Biometry, 1969, 3d rev. edit., 1994, Statistical Tables, 1969, 3rd rev. edit. 1994, Introduction to Biostatistics, 1973, 2d rev. edit., 1987, Numerical Taxonomy, 1973; editor Am. Naturalist Jour., 1969-84. Career investigator NIH, 1964-69; sr. fellow NSF, 1959-60, NATO fellow, 1974, Guggenheim fellow, 1975-76, 84; Ctr. Advanced Study in Behavioral Sci. fellow, 1992-93. Fellow AAAS, Am. Acad. Arts and Scis.; mem. Soc. Study Evolution (pres. 1977), Am. Soc. Naturalists (pres. 1984), The Classification Soc. (pres. 1969-71), Internat. Fedn. Classification Socs. (pres. 1988-89), Nat. Acad. Scis., Linnean Soc. London (fgn.), Soc. Systematic Zoology (hon.), Natural History Mus. (Paris, corr. mem.), B'nai Brith (pres. 1966). Democrat. Jewish.

SOKOL, MARC JEFFREY, arts administrator; b. Phila., Apr. 18, 1961; s. Arnold and Phyllis (Goldman) S. BA in Architecture and Art History, U. Pa., 1984; MFA in Arts Adminstrn., Columbia U., 1992. Instr. Am. architecture and art history Rio de Janeiro, 1984-85; exec. dir. Paris Edits., Cherry Hill, N.J., 1985-87, L'Imagerie Gallery, L.A., 1987-88; pvt. art dealer, Phila., 1988-89; exec. program dir. Sculpture in Environ., Inc. (SITE), N.Y.C., 1990-94; program officer for arts and humanities Ventures in Edn. Inc., N.Y.C, 1994—; mem. edn. adv. com. High Sch. Art and Design, N.Y.C. Contbr. articles to profl. publs. Co-founding mem. night without light com. Visual AIDS for Arts, N.Y.C.; mem. bus. coalition steering com. Walks of Life. Grantee Van Nostrand Reinhold Co., N.Y. Times Co. Found., Nat. Endowment for Arts, Dreyfus Corp. N.Y. State Coun. on the Arts, Ark. Arts Coun., Ala. State Coun. on the Arts; recipient of the Am. Inst. of Arch. N.Y. State, 1993 Pres. Citation, Traveler award Gov. Ark., 1996. Mem. AIA (learning by design com. N.Y.C. chpt., spl. citation N.Y. chpt. 1996). Avocations: travel, scuba diving, architectural walking tours. Office: Ventures in Edn 245 Fifth Ave Ste 802 New York NY 10016

SOKOL, ROBERT JAMES, obstetrician, gynecologist, educator; b. Rochester, N.Y., Nov. 18, 1941; s. Eli and Mildred (Levine) S.; m. Roberta Sue Kahn, July 26, 1964; children: Melissa Anne, Eric Russell, Andrew Ian. BA with highest distinction in Philosophy, U. Rochester, 1963, MD with honors, 1966. Diplomate Am. Bd. Ob-Gyn (assoc. examiner 1984-86), Sub-Bd. Maternal-Fetal Medicine. Intern Barnes Hosp., Washington U., St. Louis, 1966-67, resident in ob-gyn., 1967-70, asst. in ob-gyn., 1966-70, rsch. asst., 1967-68, instr. clin. ob-gyn., 1970; Buswell fellow in maternal fetal medicine Strong Meml. Hosp.-U. Rochester, 1972-73; fellow in maternal-fetal medicine Cleve. Met. Gen. Hosp.-Case Western Res. U., Cleve., 1974-75, assoc. obstetrician and gynecologist, 1973-83, asst. prof. ob-gyn., 1973-77; asst. program dir. Perinatal Clin. Rsch. Ctr., 1973-78, co-program dir., 1978-82, program dir., 1982-83, acting dir. obstetrics, 1974-75, co-dir., 1977-83, assoc. prof., 1977-81, prof., 1981-83, assoc. dir. dept. ob-gyn., 1981-83; prof. ob-gyn. Wayne State U., Detroit, 1983—, chmn. dept. ob-gyn., 1983-89, mem. grad. faculty dept. physiology, 1984—, interim dean Med. Sch., 1988-89, dean, 1989—, pres. Fund for Med. Rsch. and Edn., 1988—; chief ob-gyn. Hutzel Hosp. Detroit, 1983-89; dir. C.S. Mott Ctr. for Human Growth and Devel., 1983-89; interim chmn. med. bd. Detroit Med. Ctr., 1988-89, chmn. med. bd., 1989—, sr. v.p. med. affairs, 1992—, trustee, 1990—; past pres. med. staff Cuyahoga County Hosps.; mem. profl. adv. bd. Educated Childbirth Inc., 1976-80; sr. Ob cons. Symposia Medicus; cons. Nat. Inst. Child Health and Human Devel., Nat. Inst. Alcohol Abuse and Alcoholism, Ctr. for Disease Control, NIH, Health Resources and Services Adminstrn., Nat. Clearinghouse for Alcohol Info., Am. Psychol. Assn.; mem. alcohol psychosocial research rev. com. Nat. Inst. Alcohol Abuse and Alcoholism, 1982-86; mem. ob/gyn adv. panel U.S. Pharmacopeial Conv., 1985-90. Mem. internat. editorial bd. Israel Jour. Obstetrics and Gynecology; reviewer med. jours.; mem. editorial bd. Jour. Perinatal Medicine; editor-in-chief Interactions: Programs in Clinical Decision-Making, 1987-90; researcher computer applications in perinatal medicine, alcohol-related birth defects, perinatal risk and neurobehavioral devel.; contbr. articles to profl. jours. Mem. Pres.'s leadership council U. Rochester, 1976-80; mem. exec. com. bd. trustees Oakland Health Edn. Program, 1987—; mem. voluntary alumni admissions com. U. Rochester, 1986—. Served to maj. M.C. USAF, 1970-72. Mem. AMA, NAS (Inst. of Medicine, com. to study fetal alcohol syndrome 1994-96), ACOG (chmn. steering com. drug and alcohol abuse contract 1986-87), Am. Med. Informatics Assn., Soc. Gynecologic Investigation, Perinatal Rsch. Soc., Assn. Profs. Gyn.-Ob, Royal Soc. Medicine, Mich. Med. Soc., Wayne County Med. Soc., Detroit Acad. Medicine, Cen. Assn. Obstetricians-Gynecologists, Rsch. Soc. Alcoholism, Soc. Perinatal Obstetricians (v.p., pres.-elect 1987-88, pres. 1988-89, achievement award 1995), Am. Gynecol. and Obstet. Soc., Neurobehavioral Teratology Soc., APHA, Am. Med. Soc. on Alcoholism and Other Drug Dependencies, Soc. for Neuroscis. (Mich. chpt.), Internat. Soc. Computers in Obstetrics, Neonatology, Gynecology (v.p. 1987-89, pres. 1989-92), World Assn. Perinatal Medicine, Soc. Physicians Reproductive Choice and Health, Am. Assn. Med. Colls. (coun. of deans), Detroit Physiol. Soc. (hon.), Polish Gynecologists World Club, Phi Beta Kappa, Sigma Xi, Alpha Omega Alpha. Republican. Jewish. Home: 5200 Rector Ct Bloomfield Hills MI 48302-2654 Office: Wayne State U Sch Medicine 540 E Canfield St Detroit MI 48201-1928 *The drive for academic accomplishment was instilled early in childhood in a home environment which placed value on a multiplicity of interests in science and the arts-my parents taught me what to do. In retrospect, exposure to strong role models-professors of philosophy, pathology, psychiatry and obstetrics-gynecology-takes on increased importance-these individuals showed me how to do it. My family continues to support me in seeking and meeting new challenges. The opportunity to develop and transmit new knowledge sustains a high level of activity. I enjoy what I do.*

SOKOL, SAUL, insurance agency executive; b. Columbus, Ohio, Mar. 27, 1920; s. Nathan and Rose (Klyst) S.; m. Phyllis Davis, Jan. 15, 1950; children: Jay Bradford, Samara Sokol Fields. Student, Ohio State U., 1939-40. CLU, CPCU. Propr. Sokol Ins. Agy., Columbus, 1946—; bd. dirs. Ohio Indemnity Co., Columbus, Bancinsurance Corp., Columbus, 1946—. Author: Your Insurance Adviser, 1977; writer ins. articles The Columbus Dispatch. Mem. adv. bd. Salvation Army, Columbus, 1972—; trustee Alzheimer's Assn., Columbus, 1987-94, Wexner Heritage Village, Columbus, 1991—; trustee Syntaxis Youth Homes, Columbus, 1973. S/Sgt. Signal Corps, U.S. Army, 1942-46, ETO. Recipient Vol. Svcs. award Salvation Army, 1990. Mem. Am. Soc. CLU (Hall of Fame award 1992), Am. Soc. CPCU (pres. Columbus chpt. 1984-85), Columbus Life Underwriters Assn. (disting. hon.; pres. 1976-77; lifetime achievement award 1995), Ind. Ins. Agts. Assn., Profl. Ins. Agts. Assn., Pres Club of Ohio, Athletic Club, B'nai B'rith (pres. 1953-54). Home: 360 S Roosevelt Ave Columbus OH 43209-1832 Office: Sokol Ins Agy 3242 E Main St Columbus OH 43213-3807

SOKOL, STEPHEN M., lawyer; b. Melbourne, Australia, Jan. 14, 1945; came to U.S., 1948; s. George J. and Cynthia E. (Wilson) S.; m. Susan S. Schreiber, Jan. 23, 1973; children: Andrew, Debora. BA magna cum laude, U. Pitts., 1968; JD, Duquesne U., 1971. Bar: Pa. Staff atty. FTC, Washington, 1971-72; atty. gen. Atty.'s Gen. Office, Harrisburg, Pa., 1972-75; pvt. practice Pitts., 1975—; bd. dirs. Keystone Printing Co., Pitts. Law rev. editor Duquesne U., 1970-71. Mem. Big. Bros. of Pa., Pitts., 1994-95, Dem. Com., Pitts., 1974-80. Fellow Pa. Bar Assn., Allegheny County Bar Assn. (adv. bd. 1978-85); mem. Lions, Rotary. Avocations: oil painting, handball, tennis, hiking, travel. Office: SM Sokol 517 Frick Bldg Pittsburgh PA 15219

SOKOLOF, PHIL, industrialist, consumer advocate; b. Omaha, Dec. 14, 1922; s. Louis and Rose (Jacobson) S.; m. Ruth Rosinsky, June 1, 1947 (dec. Feb. 1982); children: Steven, Karen Sokolof Javitch. Grad. high sch., Omaha, 1939. Founder and chief exec. officer Phillips Mfg. Co., Omaha, 1955-92; founder, pres. Nat. Heart Savers Assn., Omaha, 1985—. Author: Bridge Philosophy, 1971; contbg. editor N.Y. Times, 1991; featured in Time mag., Mar. 1990, in Journal of American Medicine, Dec. 1990 as catalyst of American public's cholesterol consciousness; contbg. ed. Sunday New York Times, 1991. Designated by Congress hon. co-sponsor 1990 Nutrition Labeling and Edn. Act; conducted Poisoning of Am. nat. media campaigns against major food processors for high colesterol, high fat content in foods, 1988-93 (citation FDA 1993); activist in lowering fat content Nat. Sch. Lunch Program; conducted, funded $1 million Nutrition Facts sweepstakes quiz to educate pub. regarding nutrition food labels, 1994; ran nat. advt. campaign promoting skim milk and alerting Ams. that 2% milk is not low fat, 1995; pioneered mass cholesterol testing, Grand Island, Nebr., 1985; tested cholesterol levels 200,000 people in 16 cities, 1985-87; created, won congl. approval designating March as Nat. Know Your Cholesterol Month, 1987, Cholesterol Kills pub. svc. announcements featured on over 700 TV stas., 1987—; nat. spokesperson to create pub. awareness of danger of cholesterol and saturated fats in food products which promote heart disease. Named Person of Week, ABC News, Mar. 15, 1991; recipient Food & Drug Admin. Commr.'s Spl. Achievement citation, 1993, C. Everett Koop Health Advocate award Am. Hosp. Assn., 1994. Mem. Am. Contract Bridge League (life master), King Solomon's Cir. philanthropy,1990 (charter). Office: Nat Heart Savers Assn 9140 W Dodge Rd Omaha NE 68114-3306

SOKOLOFF, LEON, pathology educator; b. Bklyn., May 9, 1919; s. Barnet and Ray (Cohen) S.; m. Barbara Snow, June 1950 (dec. 1960); children—Michael D., Naomi B. Sokoloff Berry; m. Beverly Beinfeld Trachtenberg, July 18, 1971. BA, NYU, 1938, MD, 1944; postgrad. Columbia U., 1938-39. Diplomate Am. Bd. Pathology. Resident, Bellevue Hosp., N.Y.C., 1945-47; asst. prof. NYU, N.Y.C., 1948-52; chief, sect. on rheumatic diseases Lab. Exptl. Pathology, NIH, Bethesda, Md., 1953-73; prof. pathology SUNY-Stony Brook, 1973-91. emeritus, 1991—; vis. prof. Royal Soc. Medicine, Eng., 1985. Author: Biology of Degenerative Joint Disease, 1969. Editor: The Joints and Synovial Tissue, 1978. Contbr. articles to profl. jours. Served to capt. USPHS, 1953-73. Recipient J. van Breemen medal Dutch Rheumatism Assn., 1967, Disting. Alumnus award NYU, 1975; NIH grantee, 1973-87. Mem. Am. Coll. Rheumatol (Master 1987), Am. Soc. Investigative Pathology, Am. Coll. Veterinary Pathologists, 1992, (hon. mem.); Jewish. Avocation: medical history. Office: SUNY Dept Pathology Health Sci Ctr Stony Brook NY 11794-8691

SOKOLOV, JACQUE JENNING, health care executive, nuclear cardiologist; b. L.A., Sept. 13, 1954; s. Albert I. and Frances (Burgess) S. BA in Medicine magna cum laude, U. So. Calif., 1974, MD with hons., 1978; postgrad., Mayo Clinic, Rochester, Minn., 1978-81, U. Tex., Dallas, 1981-83. Med. diplomate. Cardiologist, nuclear cardiologist Health Sci. Ctr. U. Tex., 1981-84; chief med. officer Baylor Ctr. for Health Promotion Wellness & Lifestyle Corp., Dallas, 1985-87; v.p., dir. health care dept., corp. med. dir. So. Calif. Edison Co., Rosemead, Calif., 1987-92; CEO Advanced Health Plans, Inc./Sokolov Strategic Alliance, L.A., 1992—; chmn. bd. Coastal Physician Group, Inc., 1994—; cons. Health Care Strategic Planning Southwestern Bell, AT&T, Wang, Rosewood Corp., Dallas, 1985-87; bd. dirs. Calif. Health Decisions. Contbr. articles to profl. jours. Tech. advisor Coun. Social Security; bd. dirs. Washington Bus. Group Health. Grantee NIH, Bethesda, Md., 1983. Office: 9000 W Sunset Blvd Ste 800 Los Angeles CA 90069-5808

SOKOLOV, RICHARD SAUL, real estate company executive; b. Phila., Dec. 7, 1949; s. Morris and Estelle Rita (Steinberg) S.; m. Susan Barbara Saltzman, Aug. 13, 1972; children: Lisa, Anne, Kate. BA, Pa. State U., 1971; JD, Georgetown U., 1974. Assoc. Weinberg & Green, Balt., 1974-80, ptnr., 1980-82; v.p., gen. counsel The Edward J. DeBartolo Corp., Youngstown, Ohio, 1982-86, sr. v.p. devel., gen. coun., 1986-94; pres., CEO DeBartolo Realty Corp., Youngstown, Ohio, 1994-96, Simon DeBartolo Group, Indpls., 1996—. Mem. investment com. Jewish Fedn., Youngstown, 1992—; bd. dirs. Heritage Manor, Youngstown, United Way 1995—. Mem. Internat. Coun. Shopping Ctrs. (trustee 1994—), Urban Land Inst. (assoc.). Office: Simon DeBartolo Group 100 Debartolo Pl Youngstown OH 44512-6066

SOKOLOW, ISOBEL FOLB, sculptor; b. Bklyn.; d. Henry Folb and Betty Forshaw; m. Gilbert Sokolow; children: Helene, Cheryl. Student, Silvermine Coll. Art, 1965-68, Art Students League, Nat. Acad. Design, Westchester C.C., N.Y., Ednl. Alliance Art Sch. Tchr., art therapist Jewish Guild for the Blind, Yonkers, N.Y., 1974-76; dir. Westchester Art & Culture Assn., Ardsley, N.Y., 1984-86; coord. sculpture workshops Pietrasanta, Italy, 1984-86; coord. summer workshop Pratt U., Venice, Italy, 1987; prodr. Art Scene thru the eyes of Arthur Isobel Folb Sokolow, 1996—; artist in residence Nat. Woman's Com., Brandeis U., 1995. One-woman shows include Bell Gallery, Greenwich, Conn., 1977, River View Gallery, Dobbs Ferry, N.Y., 1978, No. Shore Sculpture Ctr., Great Neck, N.Y., 1980, Harkness House, N.Y.C., 1981, Musavi Art Ctr., N.Y.C., 1984, Atlantic Gallery, N.Y.C., 1988, 90, 92, 94, 96, Sara Lawrence Coll., 1995-96, Shelter Rock Art Gallery, 1997; exhibited in group shows at Monmouth Mus. Art, Red Bank, N.J., 1990, Westbeth Gallery, N.Y.C., 1991, Capital Bldg. Gallery, Tallahassee, 1991, Atlantic Gallery, N.Y.C., 1991, N.Y. Acad. Sci., N.Y.C., 1991, Broome St. Gallery, N.Y.C., 1991, Gallery Stendahl, N.Y.C., 1991, 97, Raleigh Gallery, Dania, Fla., 1993, Casa d'arte Gadiva Gallery, Forte dei Marmi, Italy, 1993, Bigi Art Gallery, Florence, Italy, 1993, Living Arts Gallery, Milan, Italy, 1994, Steiner Gallery, Bal Harbor, Fla., 1995, 97, Gallery, 1995; selected exhibits include Yonkers Art Assn., 1978, Audubon Artists Guild, 1978-80, N.J. Painters and Sculptors, 1980, Sculptors Allicance, 1982, Nat. Assn. Women Artists, 1984, N.Y. Soc. Women Artists, 1986, Am. Soc. Contemporary Artists, 1992; spl. exhibits include Dancer II, GM Bldg., N.Y.C., 1978-79, Torso, Schulman Realty Group, N.Y.C., 1983-85, Dancer I, Westchester C.C., Valhalla, N.Y., 1982-92, Dancer Reborn, Roosevelt H.S., Yonkers, N.Y., 1992—. Recipient Silver medal Audubon Artists, 1978, Sculpture award Mamaroneck (N.Y.) Artists Guild; Tres Jolle des Arts award Nat. Assn. Women Artists, 1984, Best in Show award, 1993. Mem. Am. Soc. Contemporary ARtists (v.p.), Artists Equity (past bd. dirs., past v.p.), Art Students League, Atlantic Gallery. Avocations: music, literature, travel. Home and Studio: 498 Winding Rd N Ardsley NY 10502-2707

SOKOLOW, MAURICE, physician, educator; b. N.Y.C., May 19, 1911; s. Alexander and Anna (Spiegelman) S.; m. Ethel Schwabacher, June 30, 1941 (dec. 1970); children: Gail Anne, Jane Carol (dec.), Anne May. A.B. cum laude, U. Calif., Berkeley, 1932; M.D., U. Calif., San Francisco, 1936. Intern San Francisco Gen. Hosp., 1935-36; resident U. Calif., San Francisco, 1936-37, research fellow, 1939-40; resident New Eng. Med. Ctr., Boston, 1937-38; research fellow Michael Reese Hosp., Chgo., 1938-39; gen. practice medicine San Francisco, 1946-62; mem. faculty cardiovascular div. Sch. Medicine, U. Calif., San Francisco, 1946—, assoc. prof. medicine, 1952-58, prof., 1958-78, prof. emeritus, 1978—, chief electrocardiograph dept., chief hypertension clinic, 1946-78, chief cardiovascular div., 1954-73; program and founding dir. cardiology tng. grant USPHS, San Francisco, 1960-73; sr. mem. Cardiovascular Rsch. Inst., 1957—; cons. in field. Author: Clinical Cardiology; Contbr. articles to med. jours., texts.; mem. editorial bd.: Jour. Cardiovascular Medicine, 1975—, Western Jour. Medicine, 1946-68. Bd. dirs. Fromm Inst Life Long Learning, U. San Francisco. Served to lt. comdr. M.C. USN, 1942-46. Nat. Heart Inst. grantee, 1950-78; named U Calif. San Francisco Alumnus of Yr., 1986. Fellow Am. Coll. Cardiology (hon.); mem. Am. Fedn. Clin. Research (v.p. 1948-49), Assn. Univ. Cardiologists, Am. Soc. Clin. Investigation, Brit. Cardiac Soc. (corr.), Am. Heart Assn., San Francisco Heart Assn. (pres. 1950-51). Club: Menlo Circus. Home: 3452 Jackson St San Francisco CA 94118-2021 Office: U Calif Sch of Medicine San Francisco CA 94143

SOKOLSKY, ROBERT LAWRENCE, journalist, entertainment writer; b. Boston, May 18, 1928; s. Henry and Lillian (Gorodetzky) S.; m. Sally-Ann Moss, Aug. 11, 1955; 1 son, Andrew E. A.B., Syracuse (N.Y.) U., 1950. Reporter Springfield (Mass.) Union, 1950; asst. dir. pub. info. ARC, Syracuse, 1952-54; entertainment editor Syracuse Herald-Jour., 1954-61, Buffalo Courier Express, 1961-72, Phila. Bull., 1972-82; entertainment writer Riverside (Calif.) Press-Enterprise, 1983—; syndicated TV columnist Ottaway News Svc., 1988-96, Scripps Howard, 1996—; radio show host; freelance writer; guest lectr. Contbr. articles to profl. jours. Bd. dirs. Brush Hollow Civic Assn., Evesham Twp., N.J. Served with U.S. Army, 1950-52. Recipient Sigma Delta Chi award for feature writing, 1950, award for entertainment coverage Twin Counties Press Club, 1984, 87. Mem. Am. Newspaper Guild (Page One award for opinion writing), Syracuse Press Club, Greater Buffalo Press Assn., TV Critics Assn., Soc. Profl. Journalists (Excellence in Journalism award 1989, 93), Pen and Pencil Club of Phila., Variety Club. Republican. Jewish. Home: 3080 Saratoga St Riverside CA 92503-5435 Office: Press-Enterprise 3512 14th St Riverside CA 92501-3814

SOLANA MADARIAGA, JAVIER, Spanish government official; b. Madrid, July 14, 1942; m. Concepción Jiménez; 2 children. Edn., Colegio del Pilar; Univ. Complutense de Madrid. Asst. to prof. U. Va., 1968-71, Univ. Autó de Madrid; prof. phys. scis. U. Complutense de Madrid; min. culture and govt. spokesman Madrid, 1982-88, min. edn., 1988-92, min. fgn. affairs, 1992-95; sec.-gen. NATO, Brussels; mem. Exec. Fedn. Socialista Madrileña and Fedn. de Trabajadores de la Enseñanza, Union Gen. de Trabajodares; mem. Congress of Deps. for Madrid, Fed. Exec. Com. Partido Socialista Obrero Español, former pres. sec and sec. rsch. and programs. Fullbright scholar. Office: NATO, 1110 Brussels Belgium*

SOLAND, NORMAN R., corporate lawyer; b. Duluth, Minn., Oct. 17, 1940; m. Carol A. Isaacson, Aug. 29, 1964; children: Kirk, Lisa, Kari, Chad. BA, U. Minn., 1963; JD, Am. Univ., 1972. Bar: Minn. 1973. Analyst CIA, 1963-73; assoc. Thompson, Hessian, Fletcher, McKasy & Soderberg, Thompson, Fletcher, Stone & Morse, 1973-79; corp. counsel Nash-Finch Co., Mpls., 1979-84, asst. sec., counsel, 1984-86, sec., gen counsel, 1986-88, v.p., sec. & gen. counsel, 1988—. Mem. ABA, Minn. State Bar Assn., Hennepin County Bar Assn., Am. Corp. Counsel Assn. Office: Nash Finch Co 7600 France Ave S PO Box 355 Minneapolis MN 55440-0355

SOLANO, CARL ANTHONY, lawyer; b. Pittston, Pa., Mar. 26, 1951; s. Nick D. and Catherine A. (Occhiato) S.; m. Nancy M. Solano, 1989; 1 child, Melanie A. BS magna cum laude, U. Scranton, 1973; JD cum laude, Vilanova U., 1976. Bar: Pa. 1976, U.S. Dist. Ct. (ea. dist.) Pa. 1978, U.S. Ct. Appeals (3rd cir.) 1980, U.S. Ct. Appeals (5th cir.) 1981, U.S. Supreme Ct. 1982, U.S. Ct. Appeals (9th cir.) 1986, U.S. Dist. Ct. (mid. dist.) Pa. 1988, U.S. Ct. Appeals (6th cir.) 1988, U.S. Ct. Appeals (Fed. cir.) 1989, U.S. Ct. Appeals (7th cir.) 1996. Law clerk Hon. Alfred L. Luongo U.S. Dist. Ct., Ea. Dist. Pa., Phila., 1976-78; assoc. Schnader, Harrison, Segal & Lewis, Phila., 1978-84, ptnr., 1985—. Mem. ABA, Am. Law Inst., Pa. Bar Assn. (statutory law com. 1980—), Phila. Bar Assn., St. Thomas More Soc., Justinian Soc., Order of Coif, Pi Gamma Mu. Roman Catholic. Home: 5 Barrister Ct Haverford PA 19041-1137 Office: Schnader Harrison Segal & Lewis 1600 Market St Ste 3600 Philadelphia PA 19103-7286

SOLAR, RICHARD LEON, banker; b. Boston, Aug. 15, 1939; s. Hervey L. and Mildred (Beckerman) S.; m. Stephanie Bennett; children: Andrew, Lisa. BA, Harvard U., 1961; MBA, Columbia U., 1963. Asst. v.p. Bankers Trust Co., N.Y.C., 1963-71; treas. Val D'Or Inds., N.Y.C., 1971-74, Diamondhead Corp., Mountainside, N.J., 1974-75, mng. dir., 1984—; sr. v.p. Bankers Trust Co., N.Y.C., 1975-84 ; chmn., dir. Bankers Trust Comml. Corp., 1983-90; sr. v.p. Gerber Childrens Wear Inc., N.Y.C., 1996—. Mem. Nat. Comml. Fin. Assn. (chmn., dir.). Club: Wyantenuck Country (Great Barrington, Mass.). Office: Gerber Childrens Wear Inc 1333 Broadway New York NY 10018-7204

SOLARI, R. C., heavy construction company executive; b. 1925; married. With Granite Construction Co., 1946—, formerly pres.; now pres., chief exec. officer, dir. Granite Construction Co., Watsonville, Calif., chmn. bd. dirs. Office: Granite Constrn Co PO Box 50085 Watsonville CA 95077-5085*

SOLARO, ROSS JOHN, physiologist, biophysicist; b. Wadsworth, Ohio, Jan. 9, 1942; s. Ross and Lena (Chuppa) S.; m. Kathleen Marie Cole, Sept. 18, 1965; children: Christopher, Elizabeth. BS, U. Cin., 1965; PhD, U. Pitts., 1971. Asst. prof. Med. Coll. Va., Richmond, 1973-77; assoc. prof. pharmacology and physiology U. Cin., 1977-81, prof. pharmacology and cell biophysics, 1981-85, prof. physiology, 1981-88; prof. physiology, head U. Ill., Chgo., 1988—; sec. gen. Internat. Soc. Heart Rsch., 1989-93, sec./treas., chmn. dept. physiology, 1995—; chmn. exptl. cardiovascular study sect. NIH, 1990-92; vice-chmn. physiology U. Cin., 1987-88. Editor: Protein Phosphorylation in Heart Muscle, 1986; contbr. articles to profl. jours. including Nature, Jour. Biol. Chemistry, Circulation Rsch. Chmn. rsch. coun. Am. Heart Assn., Met. Chgo., 1990-92. Grantee NIH, 1977—, Fogarty fellow, 1986; Brit. Am. Heart fellow Am. Heart Assn., 1974-75; Sr. Internat. fellow U. Coll. London, 1987. Mem. Am. Physiol. Soc. (chmn. subgroup), Am. Soc. Pharm. Exptl. Therapeutics, Biosphys. Soc. (chmn. subgroup 1983-84). Office: U Ill at Chgo Dept MC901 Physiology & Biophysics 835 S Wolcott Ave Chicago IL 60612-7340

SOLBERG, KATHLEEN, advertising executive. Asst. account exec. Ogilvy & Mather Direct, 1981-87, v.p., 1987-88, mgmt. supr., 1988-89, account dir., 1989-93, sr. ptnr., 1993—. Office: Ogilvy & Mather Direct 309 W 49th St New York NY 10019-7316

SOLBERG, LOREN ALBIN, state legislator, secondary education educator; b. Blackduck, Minn., Nov. 3, 1941; s. Albin Andy and Mabel Ethel (Bergen) S.; m. Joan Maxine Olsen, Aug. 9, 1969; children: Sean, John, Previn, Kjirstin. BS, Bemidji (Minn.) State U., 1965, MS, 1974; MPA, Harvard U., 1990. Tchr. math. Ind. Sch. Dist. 316, Coleraine, Minn., 1965—; mem. Minn. Ho. of Reps., St. Paul, 1983—; instr. math. Itasca C.C., Grand Rapids, Minn., 1981-83; instr. computer sci. Harvard U., Cambridge, Mass., 1988. Mayor City of Bovey, Minn., 1970-82. Democrat. Lutheran. Home: PO Box 61 Bovey MN 55709-0061 Office: Minn Ho of Reps State Office Bldg Saint Paul MN 55155-1201

SOLBERG, MYRON, food scientist, educator; b. Boston, June 11, 1931; s. Alexander and Ruth (Graff) S.; m. Rona Mae Bernstein, Aug. 26, 1956; children: Sara Lynn, Julie Sue, Laurence Michael. BS in Food Tech, U. Mass., 1952; PhD, MIT, 1960. Commd. 2d lt. USAF, 1952, advanced through grades to lt. col., 1973, ret., 1991; cons. to food industry, 1956-60, 64—; mem. rsch. staff food tech. MIT, 1954-60; quality control mgr. Colonial Provision Co., Inc., Boston, 1960-64; sci. editor Meat Processing mag., Chgo., 1968-69; mem. faculty Rutgers U., 1964—, prof. food sci., 1970—, dir. Ctr. for Advanced Food Tech., 1984—; UN expert on food product quality control, 1973-74; vis. prof. Technion, Israel Inst. Tech., Haifa, 1973-74. Co-editor Jour. Food Safety, 1977-88; contbr. articles to profl. jours. Pres. Highland Park (N.J.) Bd. Health, 1971-72. Recipient numerous research grants. Fellow AAAS, Am. Chem. Soc., Inst. Food Technologists (pres. N.Y. sect. 1971-72, Food Scientist of Yr. N.Y. sect. award 1981, Nicholas Appert award 1990); mem. Am. Soc. Microbiology, Am. Soc. Quality Control, Am. Meat Sci. Assn., N.Y. Acad. Scis., N.J. Acad. Sci. Home: 415 Grant Ave Highland Park NJ 08904-2705 Office: Rutgers U Cook Coll Food Tech Inst Ctr for Advanced Food Tech New Brunswick NJ 08903

SOLBERG, NELLIE FLORENCE COAD, artist; b. Sault Ste. Marie, Mich.; d. Sanford and Mary (McDonald) Coad; m. Ingvald Solberg, Aug. 24, 1930; children: Jeanne Elaine Solberg Unruh, Walter Eugene, Kay Louise Solberg Link. BA, Minot State U., 1930; MA, N.D. State U., 1963; postgrad. Wash. State U., 1960, U. Wyo., 1964, St. Cloud Coll., 1971. Tchr. Bismarck Elem. Schs., N.D., 1954-63, art dir. high sch., 1963-72; instr. art Bismarck Jr. Coll., 1964-67; cons. Bismarck Art Assn. Galleries, 1973-79, State Capitol Galleries, 1973-78; dir. arts festivals including Statewide Religious Arts Festival, Bismarck, 1969-85, State Treas.'s Gallery, 1977, N.D. State Capitol, Bismarck, 1973-78; co-dir. Indian Art Show, Nat. Congress Am. Indians, Bismarck, 1963. Artist: (print) Prairie Rose for N.D. centennial, 1989; one-woman shows include Minot State Coll., 1963, Dickinson State Coll., 1964, Jamestown Coll., 1964, U. N.D., Valley City State Coll., Bismarck Jr. Coll., 1963, 65, 68, 69, N.D. State U., 1970, 74, Linha Gallery, Minot N.D., 1972, 74-77, Bank of N.D., 1972-74, 76-77, Elan Gallery, 1982; exhibited in group shows at Gov. John Davis Mansion, 1960, Concordia Coll., Moorhead, Minn., 1965, N.D. Capitol, 1968, 69, Internat. Peace Gardens, 1969, Gov. William Guy Mansion, 1971, Gov. George Sinner Mansion, 1991. Mem. Indian Culture Found., 1964—, Civic Music Assn., 1942-89; works included in numerous pvt. collections U.S., Can., Europe; religious arts com. Conf. Chs., 1973; bd. dirs. Citizens for Arts, 1978-81; mem. The Statue of Liberty/Ellis Island Found., 1984-89. Recipient numerous awards including Gov.'s award for arts, 1977, Gov. Allen Olson award, 1982, Gov.'s award Bismarck Art Show, 1982, Dakota Northwestern Bank award, 1983, Dr. Shari Orser Purchase award Religious Arts Festival, 1984, William Murray award Religious Arts Festival, 1984, Mandan Art Assn. award, 1986, 18th ann. 3d prize weaving Festival of Arts, 1987, Dr. Cy Rinkel watercolor purchase award, 1987, Heritage Centennial Art award Heritage Arts, Inc., 1988; named N.D. Woman Artist of Yr., 1974, Heritage Centennial award, 1989; the New Visual Arts Gallery named the Children's Gallery in name of Nellie Solberg; Mem. Bismarck Arts and Galleries Assn. (membership com., mem. Gallery 522, mem. Visual Arts Ctr.), Bismarck Art Assn. (charter, Honor award 1960, pres. 1963-64, 71-72), Jamestown Art Assn., Linha Gallery (Minot), Nat. League Am. Pen Women (pres. N.D. 1964-66, pres. Medora br. 1972-74, treas. 1975-86), Mpls. Soc. Fine Arts, P.E.O. (pres. chpt. 1967-69), Bismarck Vets., Meml. Library (life), Soc. Preservation Gov.'s Mansion (charter, bd. dirs.), Women in the Arts Nat. Mus. (charter), Zonta, Order of Ea. Star, Sigma Sigma Sigma. Republican. Home: 925 N 6th St Bismarck ND 58501-3922

SOLBERG, NORMAN ROBERT, lawyer; b. Toledo, Aug. 28, 1939; s. Archie Norman and Margaret Jane (Olsen) S.; BA, Columbia Coll., 1961; LLB, Columbia U., 1964; postgrad. Parker Sch. Fgn. and Comparative Law, 1969; children: Eric Norman, Anne Olsen. Bar: N.Y. 1964, Mass. 1973, Mo. 1978, Ill. 1984. Japan 1992. Assoc. firm Wickes, Riddell, Bloomer, Jacobi & McGuire (now Morgan, Lewis & Bockius), N.Y.C., 1964-69; sr. atty. The Gillette Co., Boston, 1969-75; asst. internat. counsel Monsanto Co., St. Louis, 1975-79; sr. staff counsel Household Internat. Inc., Prospect Heights, Ill., 1979-87; v.p., gen. counsel Alberto-Culver Co., Melrose Park, Ill., 1987-89; pvt. practice, 1989—; pvt. practice Solberg Internat. Law Office, Osaka, Japan, 1992—. Mem. ABA (chmn. law dept. mgmt., orgns. and profl. matters, com. on corp. counsel 1983-93, chmn. Asia-Pacific law, internat. bus. law com. 1992-93, sect. bus. law), Ill. Bar Assn., Chgo. Bar Assn., Osaka Bar Assn. Republican. Lutheran. Office: Maison D'Or Michino Ste 901, 2-31 Kanzakicho Chuo-ku, Osaka 540, Japan

SOLBERG, RONALD LOUIS, investment banker, fixed-income strategist; b. Madison, Wis., May 15, 1953; s. Carl Louis and Gladys Irene Evelyn (Oen) S.; m. Anna Maria Teresa Gorgol, May 16, 1983 (div. Aug. 1992). BA in Econs. with honors, U. Wis., 1975; MA, U. Calif., Berkeley, 1977, PhD, 1984. Country risk analyst Wells Fargo Bank, San Francisco, 1978-79; asst. v.p., economist Wells Fargo Ltd., London, 1979-81; cons. RAND Corp., Santa Monica, Calif., 1982-84; acting instr. econs. U. Calif., Berkeley, 1983; 1st v.p., portfolio risk policy mgr. Security Pacific Corp., L.A., 1984-92; internat. fin. cons., 1992-94; v.p., fixed-income credit rschr. Pacific Investment Mgmt. Co., 1994-95; v.p., head Asian econ. rsch. Chase Manhattan Bank, Hong Kong, 1995—; acting head of emerging markets securities Asia, Chase Manhattan Asia Ltd., 1996—; adj. asst. prof. U. So. Calif., L.A., 1985-92. Author: (monograph with G. Grossman) The Soviet Union's Hard-Currency Balance of Payments and Creditworthiness in 1985, 1983; (book) Sovereign Rescheduling: Risk and Portfolio Management, 1988, Country Risk Analysis, 1992; contbr. articles to profl. jours. Research fellow Inst. Internat. Studies, Berkeley, 1982-84. Mem. Am. Econ. Assn., Asia Soc., Nat. Assn. for Bus. Economists, Soc. for Internat. Devel. Avocations: fly fishing, cross-country skiing, squash, billiards. Home: Borrett Mansions Apt 6B, 9 Bowen Rd, Mid-levels, Hong Kong Hong Kong Office: Chase Manhattan Bank, One Exch Sq, 39/F Central, Hong Kong Hong Kong

SOLBERG, WINTON UDELL, history educator; b. Aberdeen, S.D., Jan. 11, 1922; s. Ole Alexander and Bertha Georgia (Tschappat) S.; m. Ruth Constance Walton, Nov. 8, 1952; children—Gail Elizabeth, Andrew Walton, Kristin Ruth. A.B. magna cum laude, U. S.D., 1943, LHD (hon.), 1987; student, Biarritz (France) Am. U., 1946; A.M., Harvard, 1947, Ph.D., 1954. Instr., then asst. prof. social scis. U.S. Mil. Acad., 1951-54; instr., then asst. prof. history Yale U., 1954-58; fellow Pierson Coll., 1955-58, Morse fellow, 1958; James Wallace prof. history Macalester Coll., 1958-62; vis. prof. U. Ill., 1961-62, assoc. prof. history, 1962, prof., 1967—, chmn. dept. history, 1970-72; research fellow Ctr. Study History of Liberty in Am., Harvard U., 1962-63; summer research scholar Henry E. Huntington Library, San Marino, Calif., 1959; dir. Coe Found. Am. Studies Inst., summers 1960-62; lectr., cons. Army War Coll., 1959-62; lectr. U.S. Command and Gen. Staff Sch., 1963-64; Fulbright lectr. Johns Hopkins U. Bologna, 1967-68, Moscow (USSR) State U., 1978, U. Calcutta India, 1993; vis. prof. Konan U., Kobe, Japan, 1981; USIA Lectr., Korea and Malaysia, 1985, Korea, 1992. Author: The Federal Convention and the Formation of the Union of the American States, 1958, The Constitutional Convention and the Formation of the Union, 1990, The University of Illinois, 1867-1894, 1968, Redeem the Time: The Puritan Sabbath in Early America, 1977, History of American Thought and Culture, 1983, Cotton Mather, The Christian Philosopher, 1994; also articles. Mem. Ill. Humanities Council, 1973-75; sec. Council on Study of Religion, 1981-85. Served to maj. inf. AUS, 1943-46, 51-54; lt. col. U.S. Army Res. Recipient Faculty Achievement award Burlington No. Found., 1986, Disting. Teaching award U. Ill. Coll. Liberal Arts and Scis., 1988; NEH sr. fellow, 1974-75; NSF research grantee, 1981-82. Mem. Am. Hist. Assn., So. Hist. Assn., Orgn. Am. Historians, Am. Studies Assn. (pres. Mid-Am. 1985-86), Am. Soc. Ch. History (pres. 1985-86), AAUP (chpt. pres. 1965-66, mem. council 1969-72, 1st v.p. 1974-76), Phi Beta Kappa. Episcopalian. Home: 8 Lake Park Rd Champaign IL 61821-7101 Office: U Ill History Dept Urbana IL 61801

SOLBRIG, INGEBORG HILDEGARD, German literature educator, author; b. Weissenfels, Germany, July 31, 1923; came to U.S., 1961, naturalized, 1966; d. Reinhold J. and Hildegard M.A. (Ferchland) S. Grad. in chemistry, U. Halle, Germany, 1948; BA summa cum laude, San Francisco State U., 1964; postgrad., U. Calif., Berkeley, 1964-65; MA, Stanford U., 1966, PhD in Humanities and German, 1969. Asst. prof. U. R.I., 1969-70, U. Tenn., Chattanooga, 1970-72, U. Ky., Lexington, 1972-75; assoc. prof. German U. Iowa, 1975-81, prof., 1981-93, prof. emerita, 1993—. Author: Hammer-Purgstall und Goethe, 1973; main editor Rilke Heute, Beziehungen und Wirkungen, 1975; translator, editor; (bilingual edit.) Reinhard Goering: Seeschlacht/Seabattle, 1977, Orient-Rezeption, 1996; editor: Modulationen von Gold und Licht in Goethes Kunstmärchen: Kairoer Germanistische Studien, Vol. 10, 1997; contbr. numerous articles, revs. and transls. to profl. jours., chpts. to books. Mem. Iowa Gov.'s Com. on 300th Anniversary German-Am. Rels. 1683-1983, 1983. Recipient Hammer-Purgstall Gold medal Austria, 1974; named Ky. col., 1975; fellow Austrian Ministry Edn., 1968-69, Stanford U., 1965-66, 68-69; Old Gold fellow Iowa, 1977; Am. Coun. Learned Socs. grantee; German Acad. Exch. Svc. grantee, 1980; sr. faculty rsch. fellow in the humanities, 1983; NEH grantee, 1985; May Brodbeck fellow in the humanities, 1989; numerous summer faculty rsch. grants. Mem. MLA (life), Internat. Verein fur Germanische Sprach und Lit. Wiss., Goethe Gesellschaft, Deutsche Schiller Gesellschaft, Am. Soc. for 18th Century Studies, Can. Soc. for 18th Century Studies, Goethe Soc. N.Am., Inc. (founding mem.), Internat. Herder Soc. Prin. Rsch. Interest: transcultural, interdisciplinary studies. Avocations: horseback riding, photography. Home: 1126 Pine St Iowa City IA 52240-5711 *The circumstances of my life took me to many places and cultures. Despite the discord and problems plaguing many parts of this planet, let us not forget that it's the home of the human family, our home. Always remember: Life is, by definition, change.*

SOLDNER, PAUL EDMUND, artist, ceramist, educator; b. Summerfield, Ill.; s. Grover and Beulah (Geiger) S.; m. Virginia I. Geiger, June 15, 1947; 1 child, Stephanie. BA, Bluffton Coll., 1946; MA, U. Colo., 1954; MFA, L.A. County Art Inst., 1956; DFA (hon.), Westminster Coll., 1992. Tchr. art Medina (Ohio) County Schs., 1946-47; supr. art, asst. county supr. Wayne County Schs., Wooster, Ohio, 1951-54; tchr. adult edn. Wooster Coll., 1952-54; vis. asst. prof. ceramics Scripps Coll., 1957-66, prof., 1970-91, prof. emeritus, 1991—; prof. Claremont (Calif.) Grad. Sch., 1957-66, prof., 1970-92; prof. U. Colo., Boulder, 1966-67, U. Iowa, Iowa City, 1967-68; pres. Soldner Pottery Equipment, Inc., Aspen, Colo., 1956-77; mem. steering com. Internat. Sch. Ceramics, Rome, 1965-77; advisor Vols. for Internat. Assistance, Balt., 1966-75; craftsman, trustee Am. Craft Coun., N.Y.C., 1970-74, trustee emeritus, 1976-77; dir. U.S. sect. World Craft Coun., 1970-74; dir. Anderson Ranch Ctr. for Hand Art Sch., 1974-76; speaker 6th Internat. Ceramics Symposium Syracuse, 1989; participant Internat. Russian Artists Exchange Program, Riga, Latvia, 1989; cons. in field. Author: Kilns and Their Construction, 1965, Raku, 1964, Paul Soldner, A Retrospective View, 1991; contbr. articles to profl. jours.; subject of 5 films; 156 one-man shows including Cantini Mus. Modern Art, Marseille, France, 1981, Thomas Segal Gallery, Boston, 1982, Elements Gallery, N.Y., 1983, Louis Newman Gallery, L.A., 1985, Susan Cummins Gallery, Mill Valley, Calif., 1989, Great Am. Gallery, Atlanta, 1986, Patricia Moore Gallery, Aspen Colo., 1987, Coleg Prifysgol Cymru, Aberystwyth, Wales, 1987, Joan Hodgell Gallery, Sarasota, Fla., 1988, Esther Saks Gallery, Chgo., 1986, 88, El Camino Gallery Art, Toraance, Calif., 1987, San Antonio Art Ctr., San Angelo, Tex., 1988, traveling exhibit, 12 U.S. mus., 1992—, Besson Gallerie, London, 1996, Bernard Palissy Mus., France, 1996; 335 group shows including Nelson-Atkins Mus., Kansas City, Mo., 1983, Los Angeles Mcpl. Art Gallery, 1984, 27th Ceramic Nat. Exhibition, Everson Mus. Art, Syracuse, N.Y., 1986, Victoria & Albert Mus., London, 1986, Chicago Internat. New Art Forms Exposition, 1986, Hanover Gallery, Syracuse, N.Y., 1987, L.A. County Mus. of Art, 1987, Crain/Wolov Gallery, Tulsa, 1987, Contem Crafts Gallery, Portland, Oreg., 1988, Oakland (Calif.) Art Mus., 1988, Munson Gallery, Santa Fe, 1988, Japanese Influence on Am. Ceramics, Everson Mus., Syracuse, N.Y., 1989, traveling retrospective, 1991-93; hon. vis. artist Shigaraki Ceramic Cultural Park, Japan, 1994; works in permanent collections, Nat. Mus. Modern Art, Kyoto, Japan, Victoria and Albert Mus., London, Smithsonian Instn., Washington, Los Angeles County Mus. Art, Oakland Art Mus., Everson Mus. Art, Syracuse Australian Nat. Gallery, Taipei Fine Arts Mus.; curator Mirror Images Exhibit, Craft Alliance Gallery, St. Louis, 1989. Served with U.S. Army, 1941-46. Decorated Purple Heart; grantee NEA, 1991, Louis Comfort Tiffany Found., 1966, 72, Nat. Endowment for Arts, 1976, Colo. Gov.'s award for the Arts & Humanities, 1975; voted one of Top Twelve Potters World-Wide, Ceramics Monthly mag., 1981; Scripps Coll. Faculty Recognition award, 1985; named Hon. Mem. Coun., Nat. Coun. on Edn. for Ceramic Arts, 1989. Fellow Collequim of Craftsmen of the U.S.; mem. Internat. Acad. Ceramics, Nat. Coun. on Edn. for Ceramic Arts. Originator Am. Raku philosophy and techniques in ceramics. Home: PO Box 90 Aspen CO 81612-0090 also: 743 W Baseline Rd Claremont CA 91711-1667

SOLDO, BETH JEAN, demography educator, researcher; b. Binghamton, N.Y., Sept. 30, 1948; d. Frank E. and Ruth E. (Dayton) S.; m. T. Peter Bridge, Sept. 20, 1975. BA, Fordham U., 1970; MA, Duke U., 1973, PhD, 1977. Asst. dir. Ctr. Demographic Studies Duke U., Durham, N.C., 1974-77; sr. rsch. scholar Ctr. Population Rsch. Georgetown U., Washington, 1977, sr. rsch. fellow Kennedy Inst. Ethics, 1978—, assoc. prof. demography, 1985-92, prof., 1992—, dept. chair, 1986-95; cons. White House Conf. on Aging, Washington, co-investigator 1990—, U. Mich. Health and Retirement Survey, Survey Asset and Health Dynamics of Oldest-Old; mem. com. on population NRC/NAS, 1992—. Co-author: (with V.A. Freedman) Disability in Elderly Populations, 1994; (with L.G. Martin) Racial and Ethnic Differences in Late Life Health in the United States, 1997; contbr. articles to profl. jours. and chpts. in books. Grantee Atlantic Richfield Found., 1984, Commonwealth Fund, 1984-85, Retirement Rsch. Found., 1986-88, competitive grantee Nat. Inst. on Aging, 1986—. Fellow Gerontol. Soc. Am.; mem. Am. Sociol. Assn., Population Assn. Am. (bd. dirs. 1990-92, chair pub. affairs com. 1995—). Office: Georgetown U Dept Demography PO Box 571214 Washington DC 20057-1214

SOLÉ, MARIA JESUS (XUSCA SOLÉ), visual artist; b. Torredembarra, Spain, May 24, 1960; d. Ventura and Josefa (Ceballos) S. MFA, U. Barcelona, Spain, 1986; postgrad., Am. Leadership Coll., 1993-94, NYU, 1994, Pratt Manhattan Inst., 1994. Info. searcher La Generalitat, Barcelona, Spain, 1982-83; dir. Art Difusion, N.Y.C., 1989-93; gallery's artist Jadite Gallery, N.Y.C., 1990-97; author, tchr. Author: (graphic book) Sun and Moon, 1995, Electric Light, 1995, Different Perception of the World, vol. 1, 1995, vol. 2, 1997, The Seed Never Dies (Energy of Flowers and Plants, 1996, Light and Water (Earth Life's Origin, 1997. Mem. Dialectic Reality, Tarragona, Spain, 1976-79; vol. N.Y.C. Sch. Vol. Program, N.Y.C., 1995. Grantee Madrid's Ministry of Edn. and Sci., 1981-86, Basic Programmation, 1985. Fellow Spanish Profls. in Am.; mem. N.Y. Found. for the Arts, The Technology Assn., Invention Submission Corp.-Ideas Matter. Home: 245 W 16th St Apt A-1 New York NY 10011-6050

SOLE, MICHAEL JOSEPH, cardiologist; b. Timmins, Ont., Can., Mar. 5, 1940; s. Fred and Lillian Sole; m. Susan Karen Samuels, May 26, 1964; children: David Frederick, Leslie Meredith. BSc, U. Toronto, Ont., Can., 1962, MD, 1966. Cert. Coll. Physicians and Surgeons Ont.; diplomate Am. Bd. Internal Medicine. Rotating intern, jr. asst. resident, sr. asst. resident in internal medicine Toronto Gen. Hosp., 1966-69; cardiology fellow cardiovascular rsch. inst. U. Calif., San Francisco, 1969-71; cardiology fellow Peter Bent Brigham Hosp., Boston, 1971-73, jr. assoc. medicine, 1973-74; rsch. assoc. MIT, Cambridge, 1973-74; instr. medicine Harvard Med. Sch., 1973-74; from asst. to assoc. prof. medicine U. Toronto, 1974-83, prof. medicine and physiology, 1983—, mem. staff inst. med. sci., 1978—, dir. cardiology rsch., 1987-89, dir. centre cardiovascular rsch., 1989—; staff cardiologist Toronto Hosp., 1974-89, dir. non-invasive cardiology, 1974-79, dir. cardiology rsch., 1979-89, dir. divsn. cardiology, 1989—, dir. cardiovascular program, 1992-93, dir. Peter Munk cardiac centre, 1993—; vis. prof. Harvard U., 1975, NIH, Bethesda, Md., 1981, U. B.C., 1982, 91, 92, Capital Med. Sch. and Beijing Hosp., 1985, U. Tokyo, 1992, others; mem. Can. Govt. Task Force Diagnostic Ultrasound, 1976-78; vice-chmn. econs. com. dept. medicine Toronto Gen. Hosp., 1977, chmn., 1978, 79, chmn. emeritus, 1980, mem. various coms., 1981—, chmn. cardiology rsch. com., 1988-89, mem. cardiovascular collaborative practice group, 1989-92; rsch. assoc. Ont. Heart Found., 1979-89; assoc. rsch. inst. pediatrics Hosp. Sick Children, Toronto, 1979—; mem. med. staff Mt. Sinai Hosp., Toronto, 1979—; mem. adv. bd. Merck Pharms., 1983—, Boots Pharms., 1992-93; mem. Health Rsch. and Devel. Coun., Province of Ont., 1983-86, mem. exec. com., 1984-86; Levesque lectr. Montreal Heart Inst., 1984; mem. cardiovascular panel Med. Rsch. Coun. Can., 1985-87; mem. heart and blood vessel rsch. adv. com. Toronto Hosp., 1986-89; chmn. cardiovascular rsch. adv. com. faculty medicine U. Toronto, 1986-87, mem. various coms., 1987—, chmn. rsch. com. dept. medicine, 1987-88, mem. rsch. adv. bd., 1989—, chair life scis. com., 1990-92, chair decanal promotions com. faculty medicine, 1992-94; mem. exec. com. Centre Cardiovascular Rsch., 1988—, chmn. sci. com., 1989—, mem. exec. com. cardiovascular clin. rsch. lab., 1992—, chmn. rsch. com., 1992—; Pfizer vis. fellow Clin. Rsch. Inst., Montreal, 1988; mem. sr. adv. com. Toronto Western Hosp., 1989-90; Katz vis. prof. U. Chgo., 1989;

mem. provincial working group cardiovascular svcs. Ministry of Health, 1990-91, mem. ctrl. east region cardiovascular patient care mgmt. group, 1990-91; mem. trial devel. com. diabetes atherosclerosis intervention study WHO and Fournier Pharms., 1991-93, mem. trial exec. com., 1993—; mem. Joint Med. Rsch. Coun. Can./Pharm. Mfrs. Assn. Can. Adv. Com. Sci., 1993; mem. organizing coms. various sci. meetings; presenter in field. Mem. editl. bd. Can. Jour. Cardiology, 1988-94, Index and Revs. Congestive Heart Failure, 1988-90, Hypertension Can., 1988-90, European Jour. Pharmacology, 1992-96, Cardiosci., 1993, Jour. Heart Failure, 1994—, Circulation, 1996—, Jour. Molecular Medicine, 1996—; mem. internat. editl. bd. Cardiology Digest, 1992—; contbr. chpts. to books and articles to profl. jours.; patentee Bis Adducts of Tertiary Alcohols and Disocyanates. Grantee Heart & Stroke Found. Ont., 1969—, Med. Rsch. Coun. Can., 1982-92, 94-97; Ivan Smith Rsch. fellow U. Toronto, 1964, Hunter fellow Ont. Heart Found., 1973; Walter Watkins scholar U. Toronto, 1962. Fellow Am. Coll. Cardiology (abstract reviewer 1989, 91), Royal Coll. Physicians and Surgeons; mem. Am. Soc. Clin. Investigation, Assn. Am. Physicians, Am. Heart Assn. (fellow couns. clin. cardiology, hypertension, circulation and basic sci., mem. exec., basic sci. coun. 1986-89, mem. Katz prize selection com. 1988-90), Can. Soc. Clin. Investigation, Can. Cardiovascular Soc. (mem. young investigators award panel 1982-84, mem. student presentation award com. 1988-90, mem. nat. task force cardiovascular sci. 1992-93, Ann. Rsch. award 1975, Rsch. Achievement award 1989), Heart and Stroke Found. Can. (mem. sci. rev. bd. 1976-79, vice-chmn. 1980-83, chmn. hypertension and cardiovascular pharmacology panel 1982-83, chmn. molecular biology, biochemistry, pathology panel 1989-90), Can. Med. Assn. (mem. coun. 1982-87), Am. Fedn. Clin. Rsch., Ont. Med. Assn. (alt. del. Toronto Gen. Hosp. bd. 1988-90), Heart and Stroke Found. Ont. (mem. med. rsch. com. 1978-81, bd. dirs. 1986-92, 96—, mem. fin. com. 1986-90, 96—, mem. corp. rels. com. 1990-92, mem. rsch. policy com. 1991-93, 96—, Disting. Rsch. prof. 1989-96, Murray Robertson Meml. lectr. 1989), Internat. Soc. Heart Rsch. (exec. Am. sect. 1979-88, lectr. Latin Am. sect. 1995), Banting Rsch. Found. (hon. sec.-treas. 1979-81), Gairdner Found. (mem. rev. panel 1979-94), Alpha Omega Alpha. Office: Toronto Hosp Eaton North 13-208, 200 Elizabeth St, Toronto, ON Canada M5G 2C4

SOLECKI, R. STEFAN, anthropologist, educator; b. Bklyn., Oct. 15, 1917; s. Kazimierz John and Mary (Tarnawski) S.; m. Rose Muriel Lilien, June 24, 1955; children—John Irwin, William Duncan. B.Sc., City Coll. N.Y., 1941; M.A., Columbia, 1950, Ph.D. in Anthropology, 1958. Archaeologist Smithsonian Instn., 1948-54; archaeol. asst. anthropology Columbia U., N.Y.C., 1954-55, mem. faculty, 1959-88, prof. anthropology, 1965-88, prof. emeritus, 1988—, chmn. dept., 1975-78; adj. prof. dept. anthropology Tex. A&M Univ., College Station, 1989—; assoc. curator old world U.S. Nat. Mus., 1957-59; archael. expdns. to Alaska, 1949, 61, Iraq, 1950-51, 53, 56-57 (field dir.), 60, 78, Sudanese Nubia, 1961, Turkey, 1963, Syria, 1963, 64, 65, 88, 89, Iran, 1968, Lebanon, 1969-73, France, 1975, Ea., Midwestern and Western U.S.; collaborator in archaeology Smithsonian Instn., 1953; cons. UNESCO, 1959. Served with AUS, 1943-45. Fulbright scholar, Iraq, 1952-53; William Bayard Cutting travelling fellow Columbia, 1956-57; Fulbright-Hays faculty research awardee Syria, 1980-81; Fulbright fellow, Iraq, 1988-89. Fellow Am. Anthrop. Assn., Arctic Inst. Am., N.Y. Acad. Scis. (chmn. anthropology sect. 1977-79); mem. N.Y. Archaeol. Assn. (pres. 1960-62), N.Y. Oriental Club (pres. 1965), Profl. Archeologists of N.Y.C. (pres. 1980-81), Soc. Archaeology, Am. Schs. Oriental Research (assoc. trustee 1969-71), Prehistoric Soc., Deutsches Archaeologisches Inst., Soc. Préhistorique Français, Archaeol. Inst. Am. (exec. com. 1968-70), Assn. Field Archaeology (pres. 1972-74). Home: 500 Crescent Dr Bryan TX 77801-3713 Office: Tex A&M Univ Dept Anthropology College Station TX 77843

SOLENDER, ROBERT LAWRENCE, financial, newsprint manufacturing executive; b. Rochester, N.Y., Sept. 1, 1923; s. Samuel S. and Catherine (Goldsmith) S.; m. Ellen Van Raalte Karelsen, Nov. 25, 1948; children: Elizabeth, Jefferson, Katherine. BA, Oberlin Coll., 1943. Asst. to pres. Craven & Hedrick, Inc., N.Y.C., 1946-49; with Dallas Times Herald, 1949-75, v.p., advt. dir., 1964-69, v.p., gen. mgr., 1969-75; prin. Robert L. Solender & Assocs., Dallas, 1975—; mng. ptnr. The Devonshire Co., Dallas, 1978-95; vice chmn. Southland (Tex.) Newsprint LLC, 1996—; interim chmn., CEO, AccuBanc Mortgage Corp., 1992. Pres. Dallas Child Guidance Clinic, 1956, Dallas Assn. Mental Health, 1958, Hope Cottage Children's Bur., 1973—; bd. dirs. Dallas Theatre Center, Child Care Assn. Met. Dallas; trustee Southwestern Med. Found.; mem. adv. council Communities Found. of Tex.; assoc. Dallas Mus. Art; bd. dirs., mem. exec. com. Dallas County United Way, 1973. Served to lt. USNR, 1944-46, PTO. Mem. Dallas C. of C., Park City Club, Masons. Home: 9131 Devonshire Dr Dallas TX 75209-2411 Office: Southland Newsprint LP 5949 Sherry Ln Dallas TX 75225-6532

SOLENDER, SANFORD, social worker; b. Pleasantville, N.Y., Aug. 23, 1914; s. Samuel and Catharine (Goldsmith) S.; m. Ethel Klonick, June 19, 1935; children: Stephen, Peter, Ellen, Susan. BS, NYU, 1935; MS, Columbia U., 1937. Dir. activities Neighborhood House, Bklyn., 1935-36; asst. headworker Bronx House, N.Y., 1936-39; headworker Madison House, N.Y.C., 1939-42; exec. dir. Coun. Ednl. Alliance, Cleve., 1942-48; dir. bur. pers. and tng., also dir. Jewish community ctr. div. Nat. Jewish Welfare Bd., N.Y.C., 1948-60, exec. v.p. bd., 1960-70; exec. v.p. Fedn. Jewish Philanthropies N.Y., 1970-81, exec. cons., 1982-86; exec. v.p. United Jewish Appeal Fedn. Campaign, 1975-81; past pres. Nat. Conf. Jewish Communal Svc.; past chmn. planning com. Internat. Conf. Jewish Communal Svc.; chmn. Task Force on N.Y.C. Crisis, 1976-81. Contbr. articles to profl. jours., chpts. in books. Mem. Mt. Vernon Bd. Edn., 1953-58, pres., 1957-58, chmn. sec. HEW's ad hoc. com. to study fed. govt. social welfare programs, 1961; adv. coun. pub. welfare HEW, 1963-65; mem. Gov. Hugh Carey's Task Force on Human Svcs., N.Y. State, 1975; bd. dirs. Lavanburg Corner House, Herman Muehlstein Found.; adv. bd. Brandeis U., Hornstein Program in Jewish Communal Svc.; mem. Md. East Watch, Am.'s Watch coms. bds., Nat. Found. for Jewish Culture, 1985—, Jewish Mus., 1982—, Nat. Jewish Ctr. for Learning and Leadership, 1984—; mem. bd. Americans for Peace Now, 1995. Named Most Disting. Citizen of Mt. Vernon, 1960; recipient Joseph E. Kappel award Nat. Conf. Jewish Communal Svc., 1968, Florence G. Heller award Nat. Jewish Welfare Bd., 1972. Mem. Nat. Assn. Jewish Ctr. Workers (past pres.), Nat. Conf. Social Welfare (past pres.). Home: 1935 Gulf of Mexico Dr Seaplace G7-107 Longboat Key FL 34228 Office: 130 E 59th St New York NY 10022-1301

SOLENDER, STEPHEN DAVID, philanthropic organization executive; b. N.Y.C., Feb. 25, 1938; s. Sanford L. and Ethel (Klonick) S.; m. Elsa Adelman, June 5, 1960; children: Michael, Daniel. BA, Columbia U., 1960, MS, 1962. Dir. community ctrs., community orgn. and fundraising Am. Jewish Joint Distbn. Com., Geneva, 1969-75, dir. svcs. Muslim and Arab countries, 1969-75; dir. social planning and budgeting Assoc. Jewish Charities and Welfare Fund, Balt., 1975-79, pres., 1979-86; exec. v.p. United Jewish Appeal-Fedn. Jewish Philanthropies N.Y. Inc., N.Y.C., 1986—; mem. profl. adv. com. Brandeis U. Hornstein Ctr., Boston, 1982—; mem. health policy forum United Hosp. Fund, N.Y.C., 1987—; mem. presdl. coun., founding chmn. Human Svcs. Coun. N.Y.C., 1990-93; pres. World Coun. Jewish Communal Svc., 1994—; co-chair Human Svcs. Action Group. Bd. dirs. Jill Fox Meml. Fund, Balt., 1979-86, JCC Assn. N.A., 1984-92; bd. govs. Wurzweiler Sch. Social Work, N.Y.C., 1987—; mem. City of N.Y. Man. Boro Com., United Negro Coll. Fund, 1991—; pres. Internat. Conf. of Jewish Communal Svc., 1994—; mem. nat. adv. bd. Balt. Inst. for Jewish Communal Svc., 1995—. Office: UJA-Fedn NY 130 E 59th St New York NY 10022-1301

SOLES, ADA LEIGH, former state legislator, government advisor; b. Jacksonville, Fla., May 19, 1937; d. Albert Thomas and Dorothy (Winter) Wall; B.A., Fla. State U., 1959; m. James Ralph Soles, 1959; children—Nancy Beth, Catherine. Mem. New Castle County Library Adv. Bd., 1975-80, 95—, chmn., 1975-77; chmn. Del. State Library Adv. Bd., 1975-78; mem. Del. State Ho. Reps., 1980-92; sr. advisor Gov. of Del., 1993-94; mem. U. Del. Libr. Assocs. Bd., 1995—. Adminstrv. asst. U. Del. Commn. on Status of Women, 1976-77; acad. advisor U. Del. Coll. Arts and Scis., 1977-92. Mem. LWV (state pres. 1978-80), Phi Beta Kappa, Phi Kappa Phi, Mortar Bd., Alpha Chi Omega. Episcopalian.

SOLES, WILLIAM ROGER, insurance company executive; b. Whiteville, N.C., Sept. 16, 1920; s. John William and Margaret (Watts) S.; m. Majelle Marrene Morris, Sept. 22, 1956 (dec. 1993); children: William Roger, Majelle Janette. B.S. in Commerce, U. N.C., 1947, postgrad., 1956; LLD, Campbell U., 1981; DHL, High Point U., 1996. With Jefferson Standard Life Ins. Co., Greensboro, N.C., 1947—, v.p., mgr. securities dept., 1962-64, asst. to pres., 1964-66, exec. v.p., mgr. securities dept., 1966, pres., also dir., 1967-86; chmn., pres., chief exec. officer Jefferson-Pilot Life Ins. Co.; retired, 1993; chmn., pres. Jefferson-Pilot Corp., retired, 1993. Trustee, past chmn. High Point U.; past chmn. Wesley Long Community Hosp.; trustee, past chmn. Ind. Coll. Fund N.C.; past pres. Bus. Found. of N.C.; bd. dirs., past chmn. N.C. Ins. Edn. Found. Served with USAAF, 1941-45. Mem. N.C. Citizens for Bus. and Industry (past chmn.), Am. Council Life Ins. (past chmn., dir.), Beta Gamma Sigma. Club: Greensboro Country. Home: 604 Kimberly Dr Greensboro NC 27408-4914 Office: Jefferson-Pilot Corp PO Box 21008 Greensboro NC 27420-1008

SOLET, MAXWELL DAVID, lawyer; b. Washington, May 15, 1948; s. Leo and Pearl (Rose) S.; m. Joanne Marie Tolksdorf, Sept. 27, 1970; children: David Marc, Paul Jacob. AB, Harvard U., 1970, JD, 1974. Bar: Mass. 1974, U.S. Tax Ct. 1976, U.S. Ct. Claims 1976, U.S. Supreme Ct. 1976. Assoc. Gaston Snow & Ely Bartlett, Boston, 1974-79, Mintz, Levin, Cohn, Ferris, Glovsky & Popeo, P.C., Boston, 1979-82; ptnr. Mintz, Levin, Cohn, Ferris, Glovsky & Popeo, P.C., 1982—. Mem. ABA, Mass. Bar Assn., Boston Bar Assn. (chmn. tax sect. 1987-89), Nat. Assn. Bond Lawyers (mem. steering com. bond atty.'s workshop 1992-95). Home: 15 Berkeley St Cambridge MA 02138-3409 Office: Mintz Levin Cohn Ferris Glovsky & Popeo PC One Financial Ctr Boston MA 02111

SOLEY, ROBERT LAWRENCE, plastic surgeon; b. N.Y.C., Feb. 26, 1935; s. Max and Saide (Leader) S.; m. Judy Wasserman, June 16, 1963; children: John, Jill. BS, Yale U., 1956; MD, NYU, 1959. Diplomate Am. Bd. Surgery, Am. Bd. Plastic Surgery. Intern Bellevue Hosp., N.Y.C., 1959-60; resident in gen. surgery Mt. Sinai Hosp., N.Y.C., 1960-65; resident in plastic surgery Hosp. of U. Pa., Phila., 1967-69; practice medicine specializing in plastic surgery, White Plains, N.Y., 1969—; mem. staff, mem. med. bd. White Plains Hosp., 1985-88, chief sect. plastic surgery, 1988-94; mem. staff Westchester County Med. Ctr., St. Agnes Hosp.; clin. asst. prof. plastic surgery N.Y. Med. Coll., Valhalla, 1972—. Contbr. articles to med. jours. Capt. M.C., USAF, 1965-67. USPHS grantee, 1968-69. Fellow ACS; mem. Am. Soc. Plastic and Reconstructive Surgery, Am. Soc. Aesthetic Surgery, N.Y. State Med. Soc. (mem. ho. of dels.), Westchester County Med. Soc. (pres. 1996—, bd. dirs. 1988—), Cleft Palate Assn., Am. Burn Assn., Rotary (bd. dirs. White Plains chpt. 1982-85). Home: 30 Griffin Ave Scarsdale NY 10583-7661 Office: 170 Maple Ave White Plains NY 10601-4710

SOLGANIK, MARVIN, real estate executive; b. Chgo., Nov. 7, 1930; s. Harry and Dora (Fastoff) S.; m. Judith Rosenberg, Sept. 11, 1960; children: Randall, Janet, Robert. B.B.A., Western Res. U., 1952. Real estate broker Cleve., 1950-65, Herbert Laronge Inc., Cleve., 1965-68; sr. v.p. real estate Revco D.S., Inc., Twinsburgh, Ohio, 1968—, corp. dir., 1974—; guest lectr. Cleve. State U., Case Western Res. U., Cuyahoga Community Coll., Ohio No. U., Cleve. Real Estate Bd. Vol. jewish Welfare Fund, Shaker heights, Ohio; chmn. capital and budget coms. Jewish Fedn.; chmn. Agnon Sch. Bdlg. Com.; bd. dirs. Bellfair-J.C.B.-Home for Emotionally Disturbed Children. Recipient Appreciation award Am. Soc. Real Estate Appraisers, Akron-Cleve. chpt., 1971. Mem. Nat. Assn. Corp. Real Estate Officers, Internat. Council Shopping Ctrs. Office: D S Revco 1925 Enterprise Pky Twinsburg OH 44087-2207

SOLHEIM, JAMES EDWARD, church executive, journalist; b. Thief River Falls, Minn., May 16, 1939; s. Edward and Verna (Sagmoen) S. BA, St. Olaf Coll., 1961; MDiv, Luther Sem., 1968; MS in Journalism, Columbia U., 1975. Admissions counselor St. Olaf Coll., 1962-67; editor Am. Luth. Ch., Mpls., 1968-74; dir. communications St. Peter's Ch., N.Y.C., 1975-77; editor A.D. mag., N.Y.C., 1977-83, Luth. Ch. in Am., Phila., 1983-88; dir. communications Episcopal Diocese Mass., Boston, 1988-89; news dir. Episcopal Ch. in U.S.A., N.Y.C., 1989—. Bush Found. fellow, 1974. Mem. Assn. Ch. Press (v.p. 1987-89, Merit award 1969-89, Writing fellow 1969), Religious Pub. Rels. Coun. (v.p.), St. Olaf Alumni Assn. (pres.), Sigma Delta Chi. Democrat. Lutheran. Avocation: photography. Home: 168 W 100th St New York NY 10025-5145 Office: Episcopal Ch in USA 815 2nd Ave New York NY 10017-4503

SOLHEIM, KARSTEN, golf equipment company executive; b. Bergen, Norway, Sept. 15, 1911; came to U.S., 1913; s. Herman A. and Rogna (Koppen) S.; m. Louise Crozier, June 20, 1936; children: Louis, Sandra, Allan, John. Student, U. Wash.; student in Engring., U. Calif. Flight rsch. engr. Ryan Aero. Corp., 1945; project engr. Convair, 1951; mech. design engr. GE, Ithaca, N.Y., 1953-56; design engr. GE, Palo Alto, Calif., 1956-61, Phoenix, 1961-67; CEO Karsten Mfg. Corp., Phoenix, 1967—. Mem. Bethany Bible Ch., Phoenix. Recipient Pres.'s "E" award for export expansion Pres. Ronald Reagan, 1988. Mem. Moon Valley Country Club, Wigwam Country Club, Continental Country Club. Office: Karsten Mfg Corp PO Box 9990 Phoenix AZ 85068

SOLHEIM, WILHELM GERHARD, II, anthropologist, educator; b. Champaign, Ill., Nov. 19, 1924; s. Wilhelm Gerhard and Ragnhild Risty S.; m. Ludy Montenegro, Sept. 10, 1973; children: Gary, Kristina, Valerie, Lisa, Mei Li, Siri, Edwin. Student, U. Wis., 1943, U. Chgo., 1943-44; BS, U. Wyo., 1947; MA, U. Calif., 1949; PhD, U. Ariz., 1959. Mus. preparator Mus. Anthropology, U. Calif., Berkeley, 1947-49; research assoc. Mus. Archaeology and Ethnology, U. Philippines, 1950-54; lectr. U. East, Manila, 1950-52; provincial public affairs officer USIA, Manila, 1953-54; asst. prof. anthropology Fla. State U., Talahassee, 1960-61; mem. faculty dept. anthropology U. Hawaii, Honolulu, 1961—; prof. U. Hawaii, 1967-91, prof. emeritus, 1992—; asso. archaeologist Social Sci. Research Inst., 1963-67, archaeologist, 1967-70, editor, 1976-87; vis. prof. Inst. Advanced Studies, U. Malaya, Kuala Lumpur, Malaysia, 1979-80; v.p. R&D Transpacific Assocs., Guam, 1992; rsch. in Sarawak, The Philippines, 1983, Ea. Indonesia, 1990; dir. Ctr. for S.E. Asian Studies, U. Hawaii, 1986-89; bd. dirs. Austro-Tai Studies Inst., Guam, 1992—; cons. Irian Jaya, Indonesia archaeology program Irian Jaya Studies (a priority programme of Netherland Orgn. for Sci. Rsch.), 1994—. Author: The Archaeology of Central Philippines, 1964, (with Avelino M. Legaspi and Jaime S. Neri), Archaeological Survey in Southeastern Mindanao, 1979; founding editor Asian Perspectives, 1957-91, Asian and Pacific Archaeology Series, 1967-91, Southeast Asia and Korea from the Beginnings of Food Production to the First States, History of Humanity Vol. I, UNESCO, Paris, Prehistory and the Beginnings of Civilization, 1994, (with Charles Higham) Southeast Asia and the Pacific in History of Humanity, Vol. II From the Third Millenium to the Seventh Century B.C., UNESCO, Paris, 1996; contbr. articles to profl. jours. Trustee Hawaii Found. for History and Humanities, 1969-74, 1st v.p., 1972, 2d v.p., 1974; bd. dirs. Balik Bahay, Inc., Honolulu, 1976-93, pres., 1977-93; mem. Hawaii Com. Humanities, 1978-79. With USAF, 1943-46. Fulbright grantee, 1958-59, 83, 90; NSF grantee, 1963-66, 69-72; NEH fellow, 1967-68; Ford Found. grantee, 1972, 75-76; Vis. Scholar Exchange Program fellow Com. on Scholarly Communication with Peoples Republic of China, 1986. Fellow Philippine Assn. Advancement Sci. (founding); mem. Siam Soc., Société des Etudes Indochinoises, Royal Asiatic Soc. (Malaysian br.), Burma Research Soc., Assam Sci. Soc., Indian Archaeol. Soc., Soc. for East Asian Archaeology (hon.), Far-Eastern Prehistory Assn. (pres. 1971-76), Indo-Pacific Prehistory Assn. (pres. 1976-80, hon. mem.), Sigma Xi, Phi Kappa Phi, Phi Delta Theta. Office: U Hawaii Dept Anthropology 2424 Maile Way Honolulu HI 96822-2223

SOLIDUM, JAMES, finance and insurance executive; b. Honolulu, Mar. 12, 1925; s. Narciso and Sergia (Yabo) S.; student U. Hawaii, 1949-50; m. Vickie Mayo, Aug. 14, 1954; children: Arlin James, Nathan Francis, Tobi John, Kamomi Teresa. BA, U. Oreg., 1953. Promotional salesman Tongg Pub. Co., 1953-54; editor Fil-Am. Tribune, 1954-55; master planning technician Fed. Civil Svc., 1955-57; publs. editor Hawaii Sugar Planters Assn., 1957; field agt. Grand Pacific Life Ins. Co., 1957-59, home office asst., 1959-60, supr., 1960-62, asst. v.p., 1962-64; propr. J. Solidum & Assos., Honolulu, 1964—; pres. Fin. Devel. Inst., 1967—; contbg. writer Paradise of Pacific Mag., 1957-58, Hawaii Agrl. Mag., 1957-58; gen. ptnr. R.Z. Limited Partnership, 1981—; v.p. Grand Pacific Life Ins. Co., 1983-90; bd. dirs. Hawaii Econ. Devel. Corp., 1982-89. Mem. adv. com. Honolulu dist. SBA, 1971-77; bd. advisors Philippine Consulate of Hawaii, 1959. Pres., Keolu Elem. P.T.A., 1960-62; mem. satisfaction com. Hawaii Visitors Bur., 1963-66; chmn. budget and rev. panel IV, Aloha United Fund, 1966-72, bd. dirs., 1971-77, 82-88, chmn. bd., 1984; mem. mgmt. svcs. com., 1977, mem. cen. com., 1977-82, chmn. budget and allocations com., 1982-84; chmn. Kamehameha Dist. fin. com. Aloha coun. Boy Scouts Am., 1966; vice chmn. Businessmen's Cancer Crusade, 1965; chmn. Operation Bayanihan, Hawaii Immigration Task Force, 1970; participant Oahu Housing Workshop, State of Hawaii, Hawaii chpt. HUD, 1970; mem. task force on housing and transp. Alternative Econ. Futures for Hawaii, 1973; chmn. Bicentennial Filipiniana, 1976; chmn. SBA Bicentennial Com., 1976; campaign chmn. State Rep. Rudolph Pacarro, 1964-68; mem. exec. com. Campaign for Reelection U.S. Senator Hiram L. Fong, 1970, Gov. William Quinn for U.S. Senate, 1976; Rep. candidate for Hawaii Ho. of Reps., 1972; mem. Rep. Citizens Task Force on Housing, 1973; trustee St. Louis Alumni Found., 1970—, Kuakini Med. Ctr., 1984-86, Palama Settlement, 1975-82, v.p., 1976, treas., 1980-82; bd. mgrs. Windward YMCA, 1964-67; bd. advisers St. Louis H.S., 1963-64; bd. govs. Goodwill Industries, 1964; bd. dirs. Children's Ctr., Inc., 1975-77, Hawaii Multi-Cultural Arts Ctr., 1977-81, treas., 1979; fin. fin. chmn. St. Stephen's Parish Coun., 1974—; bd. dirs. St. Louis Fine Arts Ctr., 1985-88. With U.S. Army, 1945-47. C.L.U. Recipient Man of Year award Filipino C. of C., 1965; cert. of merit Aloha United Fund, 1971; Wisdom mag. honor award, 1974; Outstanding Alumnus honor medal St. Louis High Sch., 1976. Mem. Hawaii State C. of C. (bd. dirs. 1964-67, chmn. legis. com. 1966-67, v.p. 1970, chmn. election judges 1971, mem. ad hoc com. bus.-youth rels. 1970), Filipino C. of C. (past pres. 1965, com. chmn.), Am. Soc. CLU, Honolulu Assn. Life Underwriters (bd. dirs. 1963-66, del. nat. conv. 1967, chmn. life underwriters tng. coun. 1962-67), Hawaii Estate Planning Coun., Hawaii Plantation Indsl. Editors Assn. (sec.-treas. 1957), St. Louis Alumni Assn. (bd. dirs. 1964—, chmn. fin. 1969-75, pres. 1976, treas. 1977—), Phi Kappa Sigma. Republican. Roman Catholic. Home: 2622 Waolani Ave Honolulu HI 96817-1362 Office: 225 Queen St Apt 12-a Honolulu HI 96813-4600

SOLIMENA, MICHELE, endocrinologist, educator, researcher; b. Milan, Nov. 29, 1960. MD summa cum laude, U. Milan, 1986, PhD in Pharmacology with highest honors, 1992. Postdoctoral fellow Ctr. Cytopharmacology dept. pharmacology Sch. Medicine U. Milan, 1986-88; neurology trainee Clinica Neurologica U. Pavia (Italy) Sch. Medicine, 1986-88; postdoctoral fellow dept. cell biology Sch. Medicine Yale U., New Haven, 1988-93, asst. prof. dept. internal medicine sect. endocrinology, 1994—. Contbr. articles to profl. jours. Recipient Career Devel. award Juvenile Diabetes Found., 1994—; grantee ADA, 1996—, Donaghue Found. New Investigator grantee, 1996—; Trabucchi fellow, 1987, Levi fellow Lincei's Nat. Acad., 1988, Muscular Dystrophy Assn. fellow, 1989, Sydney Blakmer fellow, 1990-91, Juvenile Diabetes Found. fellow, 1992-93. Office: Yale U Med Sch Dept Internal Medicine 333 Cedar St New Haven CT 06510-3206

SOLIS, JORGE ANTONIO, federal judge; b. 1951. BA, McMurray Coll., 1973; JD, U. Tex., 1976. Clk. Indsl. Accident Bd., 1975-76; asst. criminal dist. atty. U.S. Attys. Office, 1976-81; with Moore & Holloway, 1981-82; criminal dist. atty. U.S. Attys. Office, 1983-87, spl. prosecutor narcotics task force, 1988; judge 350th Dist. Ct., 1989-91; fed. judge U.S. Dist. Ct. (no. dist.) Tex., 1991—. Bd. dirs. HRC Drug Abuse Treatment Ctr., Abilene, Tex., 1979—, pres. bd. dirs., 1982-83, Meals on Wheels, 1984—, Abilene (Tex.) Girls Home, 1985—; active Gov. Task Force on Drug Abuse, 1987—. Mem. State Bar Tex., Abilene Bar Assn. (past bd. dirs.), Abilene Young Lawyers Assn. (sec.-treas. 1977-78), Tex. Dist. and County Attys. Assn. Office: US Dist Ct 1100 Commerce St # 13e31 Dallas TX 75242-1027*

SOLLENBERGER, DONNA KAY FITZPATRICK, hospital and clinics executive; b. Tuscola, Ill., Jan. 13, 1949; d. Vincent Norman and Marian Louise (Mumbower) Fitzpatrick; m. Kent T. Sollenberger, Dec. 30, 1983; children: Shannon, Blake, Bradley. Student, U. Kans., 1968-70; BA in English and Chemistry, U. Ill., Springfield, 1970, MA in English, 1974. With pub. info. office Ill. Dept. Transp., Springfield, 1974-75; exec. III, dir. pub. info., strategic planning/spl. programs Ill. Dept. Conservation, Springfield, 1975-76; prof. Lincoln Land C.C., Springfield, 1980-84; chief adminstrv. officer surgery So. Ill. U. Sch. Medicine, Springfield, 1976-80, 85-91; divsn. adminstr., chief adminstrv. officer divsn. surgery U. Tex. M.D. Anderson Cancer Ctr., Houston, 1991-93, v.p. for hosps. and clinics, 1993-96; exec. v.p., COO City of Hope Nat. Med. Ctr., Duarte, Calif., 1997—; bd. dirs. svc. corp. Greater Houston Hosp. Coun. Mem. Houston Fine Arts Mus. Recipient Conservation Merit award State of Ill., 1976; named one of Outstanding Young Women in Am., 1980. Mem. Am. Coll. Healthcare Execs., Am. Hosp. Assn., Acad. Practice Assembly (instnl. membership coord. 1992—), Assn. Acad. Surgery Adminstrs. (exec. com. 1992-94, mem.-at-large so. region 1992-93, membership chairperson 1993-94), Med. Group Mgmt. Assn., Houston Area Delta Gamma Alumnae Assn. Home: 69 E Grandview Ave Duarte CA 91006 Office: City of Hope Nat Med Ctr 1500 E Duarte Rd Duarte CA 91010

SOLLENBERGER, HOWARD EDWIN, retired government official; b. N. Manchester, Ind., Apr. 28, 1917; s. Oliver Clark and Hazel (Coppock) S.; m. Agnes Hafner, Dec. 31, 1944 (dec. Nov. 20, 1995); children—David Olaf, Roger Hafner (dec.), Zoe Karin. B.A., Manchester Coll., 1941, LL.D. (hon.), 1963. Relief adminstr. Brethern Services Com., also Am. Friends Service Com., N. China, 1938-40; engaged in civilian pub. service, 1941-44; orientation officer UNRRA, 1945-46; liaison officer UNRRA, Shanghai, China, 1946-47; with Fgn. Svc. Inst., State Dept., 1947-76; dir. Chinese lang. and area sch. Fng. Service Inst., State Dept., Peiping, China, 1947-50; asso. prof. Chinese Studies Fng. Service Inst., State Dept., Washington, 1950, 55; dean Fng. Service Inst., State Dept. (Sch. Lang. and Area Studies), 1956-65; acting dir. Fng. Service Inst., State Dept. (Inst.), 1965-66, 69-71, asso. dir., 1966-69, dir., 1971-76; cons. internat. edn., 1976—; mem. adv. com. lang. and area programs NDEA, 1962-64; adv. com. Center Applied Linguistics, 1959-62; adviser Georgetown U. Sch. Langs. and Linguistics, 1964-84; Unitarian-Universalist rep. Interfaith Action for Econ. Justice, 1977-88. Author: Read Chinese Script, 1949, Chinese Newspaper Syllabus, 1949, Documentary Chinese, 1949. Pres. McLean (Va.) PTA, 1960; v.p. Fairfax Unitarian Ch., 1961-62, 66-67; pres. Fairfax Meml.Soc., 1969-74; bd. dirs. No. Va. Meml. Soc., 1989-95. Recipient Superior Honor award Dept. State, 1964, John Jacob Rogers award, Dept. State, 1976, Svc. citation Brethren Health and Welfare Assn. Mem. MLA, Linguistics Soc. Am., Assn. Asian Studies, Tau Kappa Alpha. Home: 1287 Berry Pl Mc Lean VA 22102-1503

SOLLENDER, JOEL DAVID, management consultant, financial executive; b. N.Y.C., Nov. 11, 1924; s. Samuel and Flora (Blumenthal) S.; m. Dorothy Leaf, Aug. 6, 1958; children: Jeffrey D., Jonathan L. B.S., N.Y. U., 1946. C.P.A., N.Y. Staff auditor Ernst & Young, N.Y.C., 1946-50; with United Mchts. & Mfrs., Inc., N.Y.C., 1950-86; corp. contr. United Mchts. & Mfrs., Inc., 1977—, sr. v.p., 1980—, chief acctg. officer, 1976—, also bd. dirs., officer various subs., mem. mgmt. com. parent co., 1986-88; assoc. dir. N.Y. Hist. Soc., N.Y.C.; mem. adv. coun. to Office of Charities Registration Dept. State, N.Y. State, 1986-89; v.p. fin. Piedmont Industries, N.Y.C., 1989-90; exec. v.p., CFO Earthworm Inc., 1990-95; fin. mgmt. cons., 1992-96; sr. cons. I.E.S.C., Kazakstan, 1996—. Served with U.S. Army, World War II. Decorated Combat Infantry Badge, Purple Heart with cluster, Prisoner of War medal. Mem. AICPA, N.Y. State Soc. CPAs (chief fin. officer com.), Am. Inst. Corp. Contrs., Rancho Bernardo (Calif.) Men's Club, Bailiwick Club (Greenwich, Conn.), Greenhaven Yacht Club (Rye). Clubs: Bailiwick (Greenwich, Conn.); Greenhaven Yacht (Rye).

SOLLER, R. WILLIAM, association executive, pharmacologist; b. Bronxville, N.Y., Nov. 18, 1946; s. William Henry and Barbara Mildred (Bryde) S.; m. Phyllis Sharon Hess, Jan. 12, 1979 (div. Nov. 1986); children: Adam Kipling, Eric Charles, Kyle William; m. Janet Marie Flanagan, June 11, 1988; 1 child, James Frederick. BS, Colby Coll., 1968; PhD, Cornell Grad. Sch. Med. Scis., 1975. Rsch. assoc. U. Pa. Sch. of Medicine, Phila., 1976-77, asst. prof. pharmacology, 1977-79; scientific assoc. Sterling Drug, Inc., N.Y.C., 1979-80, dir. scientific affairs, 1980-81, v.p. scientific affairs, 1982-85; v.p. product devel. Lederle Labs., Read River, N.Y., 1985; v.p., dir. scientific affairs Nonprescription Drug Mfrs. Assn., Washington, 1985-87, sr. v.p., dir. scientific affairs, 1987-90, sr. v.p., dir. of sci. and tech., 1990-92; cons. nonprescription drug industry, Washington, 1985-92. Contbr. articles to profl. jours. Vol. Christ Ch. of Alexandria (Va., 1988-92; vol. prison ministry, St. Paul's Ch., Darien, Conn., 1983-85; troop com. Boy Scouts of Am., Alexandria, 1990-92. Sr. scholar Colby Coll., Waterville, Maine, 1968; NATO fellow, Cornell U. Grad. Sch. Medicine, N.Y.C., 1971, Pharm. Mfrs. Assn. fellow, U. Pa. Sch. Medicine, 1976-77. Republican. Episcopalian. Avocation: mountaineering. Home: 9008 Chickawane Ct Alexandria VA 22309-2908 Office: Nonprescription Drug Mfrs 1150 Connecticut Ave NW Washington DC 20036

SOLLID, FAYE EISING, volunteer; b. Milw., Aug. 31, 1913; d. George Walter and Jessie Belle (Davey) Eising; m. Erik Sollid, Aug. 1, 1936 (dec. Mar. 1977); 1 child, Jon Erik. BA in Journalism, U. Wis., 1936; postgrad., U. Denver, 1947. Asst. in basic communications U. Denver, 1947. Editor Am. Hindi cookbook for Am. Woman's Club New Delhi, 1956; mem. Clearwater (Fla.) Libr. Bd., 1981-89, liaison between Libr. Bd. and Friends of Libr. Bd., 1984-89; mem. Clearwater Beautification Com., 1989-92. Recipient Citation of Sincere Appreciation for pub. svc. as mem. libr. bd. 1981-89 Mayor City of Clearwater, 1989. Mem. AAUW, Internat. Graphoanalysis Soc., Nat. Mus. Women in Arts, Upper Pinellas African Violet Soc. (v.p. 1973-74, pres. 1974-75), Sovereign Colonial Soc. Ams. Royal Descent, Plantagenet Soc., Soc. Descs. Most Noble Order Garter, Order of Crown Charlemagne in U.S.A., Colonial Order of the Crown, Suncoast Magna Charta Dames (rec. sec. 1980-83), Nat. Soc. Colonial Dames XVII Century (v.p. 1983-85, 89-93). Avocations: genealogy, handwriting analysis.

SOLLMAN, GEORGE HENRY, telecommunications company executive; b. Michigan City, Ind., Nov. 2, 1941; s. Henry Charles and Margaret Elisabeth (Gockel) S.; m. Maureen Tosh, July 12, 1968; children: Jennifer, Erich. Spl. student, MIT, 1965-66; BSEE, Northwestern U., 1964; MSEE, Northeastern U., 1967. Engring. dir. Honeywell Info. systems, Waltham, Mass., 1964-73; product line mgr. Control Data, Hawthorne, Calif., 1973-76; v.p., gen. mgr. Shugart/Xerox, Sunnyvale, Calif., 1976-84; spl. ptnr. Sand Hill Venture Group, Menlo Park, Calif., 1984; pres., chief exec. officer Centigram Corp., San Jose, Calif., 1985—; chmn. nat. bd. dirs. Am. Elec. Assn.; presdl. nomination Semicondr. Tech. Coun.; co-chmn. Alexis d'Toqueville Soc.; adv. coun. Joint Venture Silicon Valley. Patentee in field. Co-chmn. United Way of Santa Clara County; former mem. steering com. George Lucas Ednl. Found., Marin County. Home: 242 Polhemus Ave Atherton CA 94027-5439 Office: Centigram Corp 91 E Tasman Dr San Jose CA 95134-1618

SOLLON, PHILLIP BENEDICT, pharmacist, computer specialist; b. Canonsburg, Pa., Feb. 24, 1952; s. Louis Nicholas and Bernice D. (Bysick) S.; m. Margaret L. Sebelia, June 24, 1978; children: Elizabeth Ann, Phillip Louis, Louis Michael. BS, Temple U., 1974; MS in Pharmacy, Duquesne U., 1978. Lic. pharmacist, Pa. Sales and promotion profl. Aero Nat., Inc., Washington, Pa., 1970-77; pharmacist Sollon Pharmacy, Canonsburg, 1979—; cons. Steel City Software, Pitts., 1984—; exec. v.p. Jetcraft, Inc., Washington, Pa., 1985—; gen. ptnr. Sollon Bros., Canonsburg, 1984—; adj. prof. pharmacy Duquesne U., Pitts., 1982—; health officer State of Pa., Canonsburg, 1986-90. Fellow Am. Soc. Cons. Pharmacists. Roman Catholic. Avocations: horses, outdoor activities, reading.

SOLLORS, WERNER, English language, literature and American studies educator. Dr. phil., Freie Universität, Berlin, 1975. Wissenschaftlicher asst. and assistenzprofessor John F. Kennedy Inst. Freie Universität, Berlin; from asst. to assoc. prof. English and Comparative Lit. Columbia U.; Henry B. and Anne M. Cabot Prof. English Lit., prof. Afro-Am. studies Harvard U., Cambridge, Mass. Author: Amiri Baraka/LeRoi Jones: The Quest for a Populist Modernism, 1978, Beyond Ethnicity: Consent and Descent in American Culture, 1986, Neither Black Nor White Yet Both: Thematic Explorations of Interracial Literature, 1997; contbr.: Das amerikanische Drama der Gegenwart, 1976, The Harvard Encyclopedia of American Ethnic Groups, 1980, Reconstructing American Literary History, 1986, Columbia Literary History of the United States, 1988, Critical Terms for Literary Study, 1990, Looking Inward, Looking Outward: From the 1920s through the 1940s, 1990, Nationale und kulturelle Identität: Studien zur Entwicklung des kollektiven Bewusstseins in der Neuzeit, 1991, Immigrants in Two Democracies: French and American Experience, 1992, Intersecting Boundaries: The Theatre of Adrienne Kennedy, 1992, Il razzismo e le sue storie, 1992, Swedes in America: Intercultural and Interethnic Perspectives on Contemporary Research, 1993, Multiculturalism and the Canon of American Culture, 1993, Configurations de l'ethnicité aux États-Unis, 1993, History & Memory in African-American Culture, 1994, Thematics: New Approaches, 1995, New Essays on Henry Roth's Call It Sleep, 1996, Families, 1996, Cultural Difference and the Literary Text, 1996; editor: A Bibliographic Guide to Afro-American Studies, 1972, A Bibliographic Guide to Afro-American Studies Supplement I, 1974; co-editor: Bibliographie amerikanistischer Veröffentlichungen in der DDR bis 1968, 1976, Varieties of Black Experience at Harvard, 1986, The Invention of Ethnicity, 1989, The Life Stories of Undistinguished Americans As Told by Themselves, 1990, The Return of Thematic Criticism, 1993, Cane, 1993, Blacks at Harvard: A Documentary History of African-American Experience at Harvard and Radcliffe, 1993, The Black Columbiad: Defining Moments in African-American Literature and Culture, 1994, Ethnic Theory: A Classical Reader, 1996, The Promised Land, 1997; contbr. articles to profl. jours. John Simon Guggenheim Meml. fellow, Andrew W. Mellon faculty fellow Harvard U.; recipient Constance Rourke prize Am. Studies Assn., 1990. Office: Harvard U Barker Center # 259 775 Widener Library Cambridge MA 02138

SOLLOWAY, C. ROBERT, forest products company executive; b. Vancouver, B.C., Can., May 19, 1935; s. Harold Eugene and Elva Merle (McAllister) S.; m. Ila Noreen Kelly. B in Commerce, U. B.C., 1959, LLB, 1960. Bar: Can., 1961. Asst. to exec v.p., asst. to pres. West Coast Transmission Co. Ltd., Vancouver, 1962-68; corp. counsel, asst. sec. Weldwood of Can. Ltd., Vancouver, 1968-73, gen. counsel, sec., 1973-75, v.p., gen. counsel, sec., 1975—. Mem. Law Soc. B.C., Can. Bar Assn., Vancouver Bar Assn. Anglican. Clubs: Vancouver; Vancouver Lawn Tennis and Badminton. Office: Weldwood of Can Ltd, 1055 W Hastings PO Box 2179, Vancouver, BC Canada V6B 3V8

SOLMAN, JOSEPH, artist; b. Vitebsk, Russia, Jan. 25, 1909; came to U.S. 1912; s. Nathan and Rose (Peskin) S.; m. Ruth Romanofsky, Nov. 19, 1908; children: Paul, Ronni. Nat. Acad. of Design, 1927-30. Nat. Academician 1967. Easel painter WPA, N.Y.C., 1935-41; pvt. art instr. N.Y.C., 1951-66; art instr. CUNY, N.Y.C., 1967-75; artist N.Y.C., 1935—. Exhibitions: Retrospective at Phillips Mem. Mus., Washington, 1949, Retrospective at Wichita (Kansas) Mus. of Art, 1984; author: books, Joseph Solman, Crown Publishers, 1966, Monotypes of Joseph Solman, Da Capo Press, 1977, Joseph Solman, Da Capo Press, 1995; artist: several paintings. Recipient of several awards for paintings and portraits including the Nat. Inst. of Arts & Letters, 1961, and 8 prizes from the Nat. Acad. of Design Annuals, 1967-89. Mem. Nat. Acad. of Design (treas. 1979-85), Fedn. of Modern Painters & Sculptors (exec. bd. 1968-89); fellow (life) Art Student League. Home: 156 2nd Ave New York NY 10003-5716

SOLMSSEN, PETER, academic administrator; b. Berlin, Nov. 1, 1931. A.B., Harvard U., 1952; J.D., U. Pa., 1959. Atty. Ballard, Spahr, Andrews & Ingersoll, Phila., 1959-60; with U.S. Fgn. Service, 1961; vice consul Singapore, 1962-63; asst. to under sec. of state, 1963-65; 2d sec. Rio de Janeiro, 1965-67; Cultural attache U.S. Dept. State, Sao Paulo, Brazil, 1967-70; adviser on arts Washington, 1974-80, dep. ambassador at large for cultural affairs, 1981-83; pres. Phila. Coll. Art, 1983-87, U. of the Arts, Phila., 1987—. One-man photography exhbns. include: Mus. Art, Sao Paulo. Author and illustrator. Clubs: Philadelphia; Century Assn. Office: Univ Arts Office of Pres Broad And Pine St Philadelphia PA 19104

SOLNIT, ALBERT JAY, physician, commissioner, educator; b. Los Angeles, Aug. 26, 1919; s. Benjamin and Bertha (Pavin) S.; m. Martha Benedict, 1949; children—David, Ruth, Benjamin, Aaron. B.A. in Med. Scis., U. Calif., 1940, M.A. in Anatomy, 1942, M.D., 1943; M.A. (hon.), Yale U., 1964. Rotating intern L.I. Coll. Hosp., 1944, asst. resident in pediatrics, 1944-45; resident in pediatrics and communicable diseases U. Calif. div. San Francisco Hosp., 1947-48; asst. resident dept. psychiatry and mental hygiene Yale U., 1948-49, sr. resident, 1949-50, fellow in child psychiatry, 1950-52, instr. pediatrics and psychiatry, 1952-53, asst. prof., 1953-60, assoc. prof., 1960-64, prof., 1964-70, Sterling prof., 1970—, dir. Child Study Ctr., 1966-83; commr. dept. mental health and addiction svcs. State of Conn., Hartford, 1991—; tng. and supervising analyst Western New Eng. Inst. Psychoanalysis, 1962—, N.Y. Psychoanalytic Inst., 1962—; cons. Childrens Bur., HEW; mem. adv. coun. Erikson Inst. for early Childhood Edn., 1966—; nat. adviser Children, publ. of Children's Bur., 1965—; mem. com. on publs. Yale U. Press, 1971—; adv. bd. Action for Children's TV, Newtonville, Mass., 1973—; mem. div. med. scis. Assembly Life Scis., NRC, 1974—; cons. div. mental health svc. program NIMH, 1974—; Sigmund Freud Meml. prof. U. Coll. London, 1983-84; Sigmund Freud prof., dir. Freud Ctr. Psychoanalytic Studies Hebrew U., Jerusalem, 1985-87. Author: (with M.J.E. Senn) Problems in Child Behavior and Develpment, 1968), (with A. Freud, J. Goldstein) Beyond the Best Interests of the Child, 19732, (with Goldstein) Divorce and Your Child, 1983, (with R. Lord, B. Nordhaus) When Home Is No Haven, 1992; The Many Meanings of Play, 1993, The Best Interests of the Child: Least Detrimental Alternative, 1996; editor: (with S. Provence) Modern Perspectives in Child Development, 1963; mng. editor Psychoanalytic Study of the Child, 1971—; mem. editorial bd. Israel Annals Psychiatry and Related Disciplines, 1969—. WHO prof. psychiatry and human devel. U. Negev, Beer-Sheva, Israel, 1973-74. With USAAF, 1945-47. Recipient Disting. Svc. award Am. Psychiatric Assn., 1992. Mem. AAAS, Inst. Medicine of NAS, Am. Orthopsychiatric. Assn. (editorial bd. jour. 1974-82), Am. Psychoanalytic Assn. (past pres., editorial bd. jour. 1972-74), Am. Acad. Child and Adolescent Psychiatry (past pres., editorial bd. jour. 1975, Simon Wile Award, 1991), Internat. Pediatric Soc., Am. Assn. Child Psychoanalysis (past pres.), Am. Acad. Pediatrics (editorial bd. jour. 1968-76, task force pediatric edn.), Internat. Psychoanalytic Assn., Internat. Assn. Child and Adolescent Psychiatry (pres. 1974-78, hon. pres. 1990—), N.Y. Psychoanalytic Soc., Soc. Profs. Child Psychiatry. Home: 107 Cottage St New Haven CT 06511-2465 Office: 333 Cedar St New Haven CT 06510-3206 also: 410 Capitol Ave Hartford CT 06106-1308

SOLO, ALAN JERE, medicinal chemistry educator, consultant; b. Phila., Nov. 7, 1933; s. David H. and Marion J. (Gottschall) S.; m. Elma Mardirosian, Oct. 5, 1963; children: David Matthew, Julia Ann. SB, MIT, 1955; MA, Columbia U., 1956, PhD, 1959. Rsch. assoc. Rockefeller U., N.Y.C., 1958-62; asst. prof. med. chemistry SUNY, Buffalo, 1962-65, assoc. prof., 1965-70, dir. grad. studies med. chemistry, 1967-69, chmn. med. chemistry, 1969—, prof., chmn., 1970—; cons. Westwood Pharms. Inc., Buffalo, 1971-92. Predoctoral fellow NSF, 1955-56, NIH, 1957-58. Mem. Am. Chem. Soc., N.Y. Acad. Scis., Sigma Xi. Achievements include synthesis and structure-activity correlation of steroid hormone analogs and of calcium channel antagonists of the Dihydropyridine type. Office: SUNY Sch Pharmacy 439 Cooke Hall Buffalo NY 14260

SOLO, JOYCE R., volunteer; b. Buffalo, N.Y., Feb. 14, 1924; d. Jay Harry and Rose (Maisel) Rubenstein; m. Richard D. Solo, Jan. 6, 1946; children: Harry Jay Solo, Eleanor Solo, Sally Solo. BA, Wellesley Coll., 1945. Prew. LWV, Sarasota County, Fla., 1990-92; healthcare com. chair, 1988-90, 92—; sec. Sarasota County Health Care Coord. Adv. Coun., 1993-95; active Planned Approach to Comty. Health/Healthy Sarasota 2000; chair sr. adv. com. Sarasota Meml. Hosp.; vol. Reach to Recovery Breast Cancer Task Force, Manatee County Am. Cancer Soc.; pres. Beth Israel Women Bd., Temple Beth Israel, numerous other health and civic orgn. activities.

SOLO, ROBERT ALEXANDER, economist, educator; b. Phila., Aug. 2, 1916; s. Louis C. and Rebecca (Muchnick) S.; m. Roselyn Starr; 1 dau., Tova Maria. B.S., Harvard U., 1938; M.A., Am. U., 1941; Ph.D., Cornell U., 1953. Economist fed. and war agys., 1939-41; author, script chief Sta. WCAU-TV, Phila., 1949-50; mem. faculty Rutgers U., New Brunswick, N.J., 1953-55, McGill U., Montreal, Que., Can., 1955-56, CCNY, 1956-58; sr. research economist Princeton U., 1965-66; prof. dept. econs. Mich. State U., East Lansing, 1966-87, prof. emeritus, 1987—; dir. Inst. Internat. Bus. and Devel. Studies, 1966-68; mem. faculty Johns Hopkins U., Balt., summer 1953, U. Mich., Ann Arbor, summer 1957; lectr. L'Ecole Practique des Hautes Etudes, Sorbonne, Paris, 1964-65; research Institut Recherch Economique et Planification, lectr. U. Grenoble, France, 1972-73; prof. associe U. Paris IV, Dauphine, 1971, 73; cons. NASA, 1965-67, OECD, 1963-64, Commonwealth of P.R., 1959-61, U.S. Dept. Justice, 1994-96; project chmn. Study on Info. Tech., Nat. Conf. Bd., 1969-72; project dir. Nat. Planning Assn., Washington, 1961-63; U.S. del. Yugoslavian Conf. on Transfer of Tech., Belgrade, 1974; mem. Alan T. Waterman award Com., 1976-77. Author: Economics and the Public Interest, 1955, Synthetic Rubber: A Case Study in Technological Development under Public Direction, 1959 (reprinted as Across the High Technology Threshold 1980), Economic Organizations and Social Systems, 1967, (with Everett Rogers) Inducing Technological Change for Economic Growth and Development, 1973, The Political Authority and the Market System, 1974, Organizing Science for Technology Transfer in Economic Development, 1975, The Positive State, 1981, (with Charles Anderson) Value Judgement and Income Distribution, 1981, Opportunity Knocks: American Economic Policy after Gorbachev, 1991, The Philosophy of Science and Economics, 1991, also other books in field; contbr. chpts. to books, articles to profl. jours. Fulbright fellow, 1972-73. Mem. Council European Studies (steering com., exec. com., chmn. research com. 1974-77). Home: 4609 Chippewa Dr Okemos MI 48864-2009

SOLOFF, LOUIS ALEXANDER, physician, educator; b. Paris, Oct. 4, 1904; came to U.S., 1905, naturalized, 1930; s. Abraham and Rebecca (Wagenfeld) S.; m. Mathilde Robin, 1933 (dec.); 1 child, Joann Soloff Green. B.A, U. Pa., 1926; M.D., U. Chgo., 1930. Dir. pathology St. Joseph's and St. Vincent's hosps., Phila., 1933-45; dir. pathology Eagleville Sanitorium, Norristown, Pa., 1933-45; with Temple U. and Hosp., Phila., 1930—; chief div. cardiology Temple U. and Hosp., 1956-70, prof. medicine, 1966—, Blanche P. Levy disting. svc. prof., Florence P. Bernheimer prof. cardiology emeritus, 1970—; now chief cardiology emeritus Temple U. Hosp.; chief div. cardiology Episcopal Hosp., 1950-56. Mem. A.C.P., AMA, Am. Heart Assn., Am. Fedn. Clin. Research, Pa. Med. Soc., Am. Heart Assn., Council on Clin. Cardiology, AAUP, Assn. Univ. Cardiologists, Sigma Xi, Alpha Omega Alpha. Research, publs. on cardiovascular disease. Home: 1901 Walnut St Philadelphia PA 19103-4605 Office: Temple U Health Scis Center Philadelphia PA 19140

SOLOMON, AMELIA KROLL, artist; b. Zwenigo Rodka-Kiev, Russia, Nov. 24, 1908; d. Abraham Krugliak Kroll and Nora Pipco; m. Herman Lampert Solomon, July 31, 1931 (dec. 1989); children: Ernest, Suzon, Semyon T., Sheba S. Studied with Ralph Stackpole, 1947; attended, Patri Sch. Fine Art, 1960, Foothill Coll., 1969, San Miguel de Allenda Art Inst., 1970; BA magna cum laude, San Jose State U., 1979, MFA, 1986. Lectr. in field. Solo shows include Stanford (Calif.) U., 1982, 83, Oakland (Calif.) Art Assn., 1985, Open Studio, San Jose, 1989, 90, Rosicrucian Egyptian Mus., San Jose, 1989, Metro Contemporary Art Gallery, Foster City, Calif., 1989, Koret Gallery, Palo Alto, Calif., 1992; group shows include Palo Alto Art Club, 1966, 69, San Mateo Floral Fiesta, 1970, Livermore (Calif.) Art Assn., 1979, San Francisco Women Artists, 1980, 81, Ana Gardner Gallery, 1980, Soma Gallery, San Francisco, 1980, Open Studio, 1986, Fenwick's Estate Art Show, Los Altos Hills, Calif., 1987, San Jose Inst. Contemporary Arts, 1987, 94, Gallery III, San Jose, 1990, Olive Hyde Gallery, Fremont, Calif., 1990, San Jose Art League, 1993, Los Gatos (Calif.) Tait Mus., 1993, Gallery Tanantzin, San Juan Bautista, 1993. Syntex Gallery, Palo Alto, 1993, Synopsis Gallery, Mountain View, Calif., 1993, Tait Mus., Los Gatos, 1994, Solomon Dubnick Gallery, Sacramento, 1994, Seippe Gallery, Palo Alto, 1994, Koret Gallery, 1995, many others. Mem. San Jose State U. Sculptors Guild (treas. 1977-95), League Nat. PEN Women, Womens Caucus for Arts, Internat. Sculpture Ctr.

SOLOMON, ANDREW WALLACE, author; b. N.Y.C., Oct. 30, 1963; s. Howard and Carolyn Ruth (Bower) S. BA in English magna cum laude, Yale U., 1985; BA, MA in English, Jesus Coll., Cambridge U., Cambridge, Eng., 1987. Editl. intern Met. Mus. Art, N.Y.C., 1981, editl. asst., 1982, asst. editor, 1983, editor, 1986; intern dept. old master paintings Sotheby's N.Y., 1984; galleries corr., contbg. editor Harpers and Queen, London, 1987-91; contbg. writer The N.Y. Times Mag., 1989—; contbg. editor HG, 1991-93. Author: The Irony Tower: Soviet Artists in a Time of Glasnost, 1991, A Stone Boat, 1994; co-author: Novastroika, 1989; contbr. articles to profl. jours. Bd. dirs. CEC Internat. Partnership, Alliance for the Arts, The Shakespeare Project, The Moscow ICA. Jesus Coll. Travel grantee, Cambridge U., 1986; Yale Conservation Project fellow for travel, 1985, Finalist First Fiction L.A. Times award, 1995, Finalist ASMI award, 1996, Finalist Livingston award, 1994. Mem. Groucho Club, Oxford & Cambridge Club, Chelsea Arts Club, Century Assn., Nat. Arts Club, Coun. on Fgn. Rels., Conservators Coun. of N.Y. Pub. Libr. Democrat. Home and Office: 154 Kensington Park Rd, London W11 2ER, England also: 18 W 10th St New York NY 10011-8702

SOLOMON, ARTHUR CHARLES, pharmacist; b. Gary, Ind., May 30, 1947; s. Laurence A. and Dorothy B. (Klippel) S.; m. Janet Evelyn Irak, Aug. 23, 1969; children: Thomas, Michael, Mark, Jill. BS in Pharmacy, Purdue U., 1970, MS in Clin. Pharmacy, 1972; PharmD. Registered pharmacist; cert. nuclear pharmacist. Clin. prof. pharmacy U. Tex., Austin, 1972-75; v.p. Nuclear Pharmacy, Inc., Atlanta, 1975-83; exec. v.p., managed care officer Diagnostek, Inc., Albuquerque, 1983-95; pres. Health Care Svcs., Inc., 1990-95; exec. v.p., COO Value Rx, Albuquerque, 1995—; adj. prof. U. N.Mex., 1992—. Contbr. articles to profl. jours. Mem. Am. Pharm. Assn., Am. Soc. Hosp. Pharmacy, Nat. Assn. Retail Druggists, Nat. Coun. Prescription Drug Programs, Am. Managed Care Pharmacy Assn. (pres., dir.), Am. Soc. Cons. Pharmacists, Rho Chi, Pi Kappa Phi. Republican. Roman Catholic. Avocations: golf, fishing, gardening, tennis. Home: 1504 Catron Ave SE Albuquerque NM 87123-4218 Office: Value Rx 1504 Catron Ave SE Albuquerque NM 87123-4218

SOLOMON, ARTHUR KASKEL, biophysics educator; b. Pitts., Nov. 26, 1912; (married); 2 children. A.B., Princeton U., 1934; M.A., Harvard U., 1935, Ph.D. in Phys. Chemistry, 1937; Ph.D. in Physics, Cambridge U., Eng., 1947, Sc.D., 1964. Research assoc. in physics and chemistry Harvard, 1939-41; officer Brit. Ministry Supply, 1941-43; mem. staff Radiation Lab., Mass. Inst. Tech., 1945; asst. prof. phys. chemistry Med. Sch., Harvard, 1946-57, asso. prof. biophysics, 1957-68, prof., 1968-82, prof. emeritus, 1982—; assoc. in biophysics Peter Bent Brigham Hosp., Boston, 1950-72; dir. Read's Inc., Balt., 1946-77; pres. Read's Inc., 1961-77; Mem. U.S. Nat. Com. for Pure and Applied Biophysics, 1965-72, U.S. Nat. Com. for Biology, 1966-71; mem. U.S. Nat. Com. for UNESCO, 1969-74, mem. U.S. del. to gen. assembly, Nairobi, 1976; mem. vis. com. biology dept. Brookhaven Nat. Lab., 1961-65; mem. NRC com. on radiology, 1957-59, com. on growth, 1954-57; sec. Gen. Internat. Union for Pure and Applied Biophysics, 1961-72; mem. NIH radiation study sect., 1960-63, biophys. sci. tng. com., 1963-68, chmn., 1966-68; mem. U.S. del. Gen. Assembly of UNESCO, Paris, 1978; mem. adv. panel on sci., tech. and society UNESCO, 1981-84; mem. bd. internat. orgns. and programs Nat. Acad. Scis., 1973-80, chmn., 1977-79; mem. Commn. on Internat. Relations, 1977-79; mem. exec. com. Internat. Council Sci. Unions, 1966-72; U.S. del. 17th, 18th Gen. Assemblies of Internat. Council Sci. Unions, Athens, 1978, Amsterdam, 1980; chmn. disting. fellowship com. Internat. Council Sci. Unions-UNESCO, 1980-85; chmn. Harvard com. on higher degrees in biophysics, 1959-80; chmn. Harvard Med. Sch. Oral History Com.; chmn. Harvard Council on the Arts, 1973-76. Mem. editorial bds.: Quarterly Revs. of Biophysics, 1972-74, Journal Gen. Physiology, 1958-90. Trustee Inst. Contemporary Art, Boston, 1946-76, pres., 1965-71; bd. overseers Boston Mus. Fine Arts, 1978-84; mem. collectors com. Nat. Gallery Art, Washington, 1985-88. Decorated Order Andres Bello Venezuela). Fellow AAAS, Am. Acad. Arts and Scis.; mem. Am. Chem. Soc., Am. Physiol. Soc., Biophysics Soc., Soc. Gen. Physiology. Clubs: Cosmos (Washington); St. Botolph (Boston); Harvard (N.Y.C. and Boston). Home: 27 Craigie St Cambridge MA 02138-3457 Office: Harvard Med Sch Biophysics Lab 221 Longwood Ave Boston MA 02115-5822

SOLOMON, BARRY JASON, healthcare administrator, consultant; b. Boston, May 16, 1934; s. Samuel and Ethel (Fleishman) S.; m. C. Priscilla Fugate, June 29, 1958; children: R. Stephen, Jon, Julie Ellen. BS in Biology and Chemistry, Tufts U., 1955; MBA in Health Care Adminstrn., Xavier U., Cin., 1960; MPH in Health Care Adminstrn., U. N.C., 1989. Chief med. record adminstr. USPHS Hosp., Lexington, Ky., 1956-59; asst. dir. Union Meml. Hosp., Balt., 1960-61; asst. adminstr. James Lawrence Kernan Hosp., Balt., 1961-67; asst. to dean, lectr. health edn. and med. care sects. Yale U. Sch. Medicine, New Haven, 1967-70; dir. health svcs., clin. asst. prof. pharmacy adminstrn. U. R.I., Kingston, 1970-76; assoc. dir. for adminstrn. USPHS Hosp., Norfolk, Va., 1976-81; dir., COO, sr. fellow in social medicine Montefiore Hosp., Bronx, N.Y., 1981-84; assoc. v.p. for med. affairs, mem. exec. coun. of Med. Sch. U. South Fla., Tampa, 1984-89; assoc. prof., acting chmn. dept. comprehensive medicine U. So. Fla., Tampa, 1984-89, assoc. prof. Coll. Pub. Health, 1984-89; cons. in health adminstrn., Columbia, Md., 1989-93; v.p. for acad. affairs North Broward Hosp. Dist., Ft. Lauderdale, Fla., 1993-96; bd. dirs. Vis. Nurse Corp., 1987-90; bd. dirs., mem. exec. and nominating coms. Vis. Nurse Assn. Tampa Bay, 1987-90; mem. planning com. of bd. trustees Hillsborough County Hosp. Authority, 1986-88; mem. profl. affairs com. of bd. trustees H. Lee Moffitt Cancer Ctr. and Rsch. Inst., 1986-88; mem. affiliation com. S.W. Fla. Blood Bank, 1988-89; instr. hosp. adminstrn. Xavier U., 1960; course asst., instr. Am. Med. Record Assn., 1962-72; instr. Howard U. Coll. Continuing Edn., Washington, 1993; cons. St. Elizabeth Hosp., Covington, Ky., 1959, City Hosp. Ctr. at Elmhurst, 1965, Hall-Brooke Hosp., Westport, Conn., 1968-69, Conn. Mental Health Ctr., New Haven, 1969-70, South County Hosp., Wakefield, R.I., 1970-76, Centurion Hosp., Tampa, 1989, Primary Care Svcs., Tampa, 1991, Holland & Knight, Tampa, 1991, NCC Internat., Colchester, Eng., 1991, F.W. Assocs., Tampa, 1989-92, Decking Design, Norfolk, 1986-93, SMSinc., Columbia, 1993, Internat. Flooring & Protective Coatings, Inc., Norfolk, 1993—; sr. cons. Meisel Assocs., Inc., N.Y.C., 1983—. Contbr. articles to profl. jours. Trustee Montefiore-Mosholu Cmty. Ctr., 1981-84; mem. Nat. Com. on Religion and Health, 1982-84; mem., vice chmn. Chariho Sch. Bd., Richmond, R.I., 1974-76; mem. Broward Econ. Devel. Coun., Inc. Lt. USPHS, 1956-59, capt., 1976-81. Recipient citation Suncoast chpt. Am. Heart Assn., 1988. Fellow Am. Coll. Healthcare Execs.; mem. APHA. Avocation: tennis. Home: 2863 Via Venezia Deerfield Beach FL 33442

SOLOMON, CAREN GROSSBARD, internist; b. N.Y.C., Feb. 20, 1963. MD, Harvard U., 1988. Resident Brigham Womens Hosp., Boston, 1988-90, fellow in endocrinology, 1990-93, assoc. physician, 1993—; instr. medicine Harvard Med. Sch., 1993—. Recipient Clinican Scientist award Am. Heart Assn., 1995-96. Mem. ACP, Am. Diabetes Assn., Mass. Med. Soc. Office: Brigham Womens Hosp 75 Francis St Boston MA 02115-6110

SOLOMON, DAVID EUGENE, engineering company executive; b. Milton, Pa., June 22, 1931; s. Oren Benjamin and Bernardine Claire Solomon; m. Joyce Marie Hoffman, June 24, 1950; children: Timothy, Melissa, Daniel. AB, Susquehanna U., 1958; MS, Bucknell U., 1960; MBA, Ea. Mich. U., 1974. Sr. engr. Westinghouse Electric Corp., Balt., 1959-65; rsch. engr. U. Mich., 1965-67; chief engr. Electro-Optics divsn. Bendix Corp., 1967-72; v.p. ops. KMS Fusion, Inc., Ann Arbor, Mich., 1972-85; pres., CEO Solohill Engring. Inc., 1985—; bd. dirs. Ann Arbor Engring. Inc., SoloHill Labs. Inc. With USN, 1950-55. Fellow IEEE. Patentee in field. Office: 4220 Varsity Dr Ann Arbor MI 48108-2241

SOLOMON, DAVID HARRIS, physician, educator; b. Cambridge, Mass., Mar. 7, 1923; s. Frank and Rose (Roud) S.; m. Ronda L. Markson, June 23, 1946; children: Patti Jean (Mrs. Richard E. Sinaiko), Nancy Ellen (Mrs. Marvin Evans.). A.B., Brown U., 1944; M.D., Harvard U., 1946. Intern Peter Bent Brigham Hosp., Boston, 1946-47, resident, 1947-48, 50-51; fellow endocrinology New Eng. Center Hosp., Boston, 1951-52; faculty UCLA Sch. Medicine, 1952—, prof. medicine, 1966-93, vice chmn. dept. medicine, 1968-71, chmn. dept., 1971-81, assoc. dir. geriatrics, 1982-89; dir. UCLA Ctr. on Aging, 1991-96; prof. emeritus UCLA, 1993—; chief med. svc. Harbor Gen. Hosp., Torrance, Calif., 1966-71; cons. Wadsworth VA Hosp., L.A., 1952—, Sepulveda VA Hosp., 1971—; cons. metabolism tng. com. USPHS, 1960-64, endocrinology study sect., 1970-73. Editor: Jour. Am. Geriatric Soc., 1988-93; contbr. numerous articles to profl. jours. Recipient Mayo Soley award, 1986. Master ACP; mem. Assn. Am. Physicians, Am. Soc. Clin. Investigation, Western Soc. Clin. Research (councillor 1963-65), Endocrine Soc. (Robert H. Williams award 1989), Am. Thyroid Assn. (pres. 1973-74, Disting. Service award 1986), Inst. Medicine Nat. Acad. Scis., AAAS, Assn. Profs. Medicine (pres. 1980-81), Western Assn. Physicians (councillor 1972-75, pres. 1983-84), Am. Fedn. Aging Rsch. (Irving S. Wright award), Am. Geriatrics Soc. (bd. dirs. 1985-93, Milo Leavitt award 1992, Disting. Svc. award 1993), Phi Beta Kappa, Sigma Xi, Alpha Omega Alpha. Home: 2103

Ridge Dr Los Angeles CA 90049 Office: 10945 Le Conte Ave PO Box 956980 Los Angeles CA 90095

SOLOMON, DONALD WILLIAM, mathematics and computer science educator, consultant; b. Detroit, Feb. 6, 1944; s. Sidney Caesar and Bertha C. (Chaiken) S.; m. Evelyn Mae Scott, Jan. 29, 1990; 1 child, Emily. B.S. with distinction, Wayne State U., 1961, B.Medicine, 1961, M.S., 1963, Ph.D., 1966, M.D., 1968. Instr. math. Wayne State U., Detroit, 1966; asst. prof. math. U. Wis., Milw., 1966-70, assoc. prof. math., 1970-75, assoc. chmn. dept. math., 1975-78, chmn. div. natural scis., 1976-78, prof. math. scis., 1975—; cons. Lineax Corp., Milw., 1980—. Contbr. articles to profl. jours. NSF fellow, 1962, 63, 64-65; U. Wis. Grad. Sch. research grantee, 1967-68, 73-74; NSF research grantee, 1968-73. Mem. Am. Math. Soc., Math. Assn. Am., N.Y. Acad. Scis. Home: 5436 N Lydell Ave Milwaukee WI 53217-5005 Office: U Wis Dept Dept Math Scis Milwaukee WI 53201

SOLOMON, EDWARD DAVID, chain store executive; b. Paterson, N.J., Mar. 3, 1931; s. Charles and Lee (Bernstein) S.; m. Regina Ellen Purcell, Mar. 18, 1972; 1 son, David; children by previous marriage—Jerry, Susan. B.S., Wharton Sch. Fin., U. Pa., 1952. Buyer Miles Shoes div. Melville Corp., N.Y.C., 1956-59; buyer, mdse. mgr., exec. v.p., then pres. Gallenkamp Stores Co. div. Scoa Industries Inc., Los Angeles, 1959-69; pres. Karl's Shoe Stores Ltd. div. HRT Industries, Inc., Los Angeles, 1969-74; pres., chief operating officer HRT Industries, Inc., Los Angeles and N.Y.C., 1974-76; pres., chief exec. officer HRT Industries, Inc., 1977-84, chmn., 1978-84; pres., CEO Edward D. Solomon & Co., 1984-89; CEO Shoe-Town, Inc., Totowa, N.J., 1989-94; pres., CEO Edward D. Solomon and Co., 1994—. Trustee City of Hope. Served with USNR, 1953-56. Named Man of Yr., professions and fin. group City of Hope, 1973, Man of Yr. Jack Martin Fund, Mt. Sinai Hosp., N.Y.C., 1977; recipient Community Service award Brandeis U., 1979; T. Kenyon Holly humanitarian award of footwear industry, 1981. Mem. Volume Footwear Retailers Am. (bd. dirs. 1967-94, pres. 1981-82), Nat. Retail Mchts. Assn. (bd. dirs. 1981-84), Mass Retailers Inst. (dir. 1977-80). Office: Felsway Corp 66 Roberts Rd Englewd Clfs NJ 07632-2212

SOLOMON, ELDRA PEARL BROD, psychologist, educator, biologist, author; b. Phila., Apr. 9, 1940; d. Theodore and Freda Miriam (Warhaftig) Brod; m. Edwin Marshall Solomon, June 28, 1959 (div. Jan. 1985); children: Mical Kenneth, Amy Lynn, Belicia Efros. BS, U. Tampa, 1961; MS, U. Fla., 1963; MA, U. South Fla., 1987, PhD, 1989. Lic. clin. psychologist. Adj. biology prof. Hillsborough Community Coll., Tampa, Fla., 1968-86; biopsychologist Ctr. for Rsch. in Behavioral Medicine, U. South Fla., Tampa, 1985-89; dir. rsch. Advanced Devel. Systems, Tampa, 1989-92; pvt. practice clin. psychologist Tampa, 1990—; clin. dir. Ctr. for Mental Health Edn., Assessment and Therapy, Tampa, Fla., 1992—; adj. prof., mem. grad. faculty U. South Fla., 1992—; expert witness, psychol. expert county and cir. cts., 1989—; health edn. cons. Advanced Devel. Sys., Tampa, 1985-92. Author: Human Anatomy and Physiology, 1990, The World of Biology, 5th edit., 1995, Biology, 4th edit., 1996; author: (with others) Health Psychology: Individual Differences and Stress, 1988, Why Kids Kill Parents: Child Abuse and Adolescent Homicide, 1995; contbr. chpt. to book. Mem. APA, Am. Soc. Criminology, Fla. Psychol. Assn., Internat. Soc. for the Study of Dissociation (chairperson Tampa chpt., 1994-95). Democrat. Jewish. Avocations: boating, swimming, reading. Office: Ctr Mental Health Edn Assessment & Therapy 2727 W Martin Luther King Blvd Tampa FL 33607-6383

SOLOMON, ELINOR HARRIS, economics educator; b. Boston, Feb. 26, 1923; d. Ralph and Linna Harris; m. Richard A. Solomon, Mar. 30, 1957; children: Joan S. Griffin, Robert H., Thomas H. AB, Mt. Holyoke Coll., 1944; MA, Radcliffe U., 1945; PhD, Harvard U., 1948. Jr. economist Fed. Res. Bank Boston, 1945-48; economist Fed. Res. Bd. Govs., Washington, 1949-56; internat. economist U.S. State Dept., Washington, 1957-58; professorial lectr. Am. U., Washington, 1964-66; sr. economist antitrust div. U.S. Dept. Justice, Washington, 1966-82; prof. econs. George Washington U., Washington, 1982—; econ. cons., Washington, 1982—; expert witness antitrust, electronic funds transfer cases, Washington, 1988—. Author: Virtual Money, 1997; author, editor: Electronic Funds Transfers and Payments, 1987, Electronic Money Flows, 1991; contbr. articles on econs., banking and law to profl. jours. Mem. Am. Econs. Assn., Nat. Economists Club (bd. govs. 1997—). Home: 6805 Delaware St Bethesda MD 20815-4164 Office: George Washington U Dept Econs Washington DC 20052

SOLOMON, EZRA, economist, educator; b. Rangoon, Burma, Mar. 20, 1920; came to U.S., 1947, naturalized, 1951; s. Ezra and Emily (Rose) S.; m. Janet Lorraine Cameron, May 7, 1949; children—Catherine Shan, Janet Ming, Lorna Cameron. A.B. (hons.), U. Rangoon, 1940; Ph.D., U. Chgo., 1950. Instr. U. Chgo., 1948-51, asst. prof. fin., 1951-55, assoc. prof., 1955-57, prof., 1957-61; Dean Witter prof. fin. Stanford U., 1961-71, 73-90; dir. Internat. Ctr. Mgmt. Edn.; mem. Coun. Econ. Advisers, 1971-73. Author: The Theory of Financial Management, 1963, Money and Banking, 5th edit, 1968, The Management of Corporate Capital, 1959, Metropolitan Chicago: An Economic Analysis, 1958, The Anxious Economy, 1975, An Introduction to Financial Management, 2d edit, 1980, Beyond the Turning Point, 1981; editor: International Patterns of Inflation— A Study in Contrasts, 1984, Jour. Bus, 1953-57; bd. editors Jour. of Finance, 1965-66, Jour. Bus. Finance, 1969-73, Jour. Quantitative and Financial Analysis, 1969-71. Served as lt., Burma div. Royal Naval Vol. Res., 1942-47. Mem. Am. Econ. Assn. Home: 775 Santa Ynez St Stanford CA 94305-8478 Office: Stanford Univ Grad School of Busines Stanford CA 94305

SOLOMON, GAIL ELLEN, physician; b. Bklyn., May 26, 1938; d. Samuel and Estelle (Suffin) S.; m. Harvey Hecht, Oct. 28, 1962; children: Daniel, Jonathan, Elizabeth. AB, Smith Coll., 1958; MD, Albert Einstein Coll. Medicine, 1962. Diplomate Am. Bd. Pediats., Am. Bd. Psychiatry and Neurology (assoc. examiner), Am. Bd. Electroencephalography, Am. Bd. Electroencephalography and Neurophysiology, Am. Bd. Clin. Neurophysiology. Intern in pediats. Bronx Mcpl. Hosp. Ctr., 1962-63, resident in pediats., 1963-64; resident in pediats. N.Y. Hosp.-Cornell U. Med. Coll., 1964-65; NIH vis. fellow in neurology and child neurology Columbia-Presbyn. Med. Ctr., 1965-68, NIH vis. fellow in clin. neurophysiology/electroenceph.; instr. neurology Columbia U. Coll. of Physicians and Surgeons, 1968-69; instr. in neurology and pediats. Cornell U. Med. Coll., 1969-70, asst. prof. neurology and pediats., 1970-76; asst. attending in neurology and pediats. N.Y. Hosp., 1969-76, dir. electroencephalography, 1969—, assoc. attending in neurology and pediats., 1976—, assoc. attending neurologist in psychiatry, 1983—; mem. joint com. for stroke facilities NIH; mem. FDA Peripheral and CNS Adv. Com., 1979-83, chmn., 1983, cons., 1983-84; mem. med. audit com. N.Y. Hosp., mem. utilization rev. com.; mem. profl. adv. bd. N.Y. State Epilepsy Assn.; adj. attending physician in neurology Meml.-Sloan Kettering Cancer Ctr., 1982-93; assoc. attending pediatrician Hosp. Spl. Surgery, 1987—; neurology cons. Blythedale Children's Hosp., Valhalla, N.Y., 1991—, Meml.-Sloan Kettering Cancer Ctr., 1993—. Author: (with F. Plum) Clinical Management of Sergina: A Guide for the Physician, 1976, (with Plum and Kutt) 2d edit., 1983; editor: (with Kaufman and Pfeffer) Child and Adolescent Neurology for Psychiatrists, 1992; contbr. articles to profl. jours., and chpts. to med. books. Fellow Am. Acad. Neurology, Am. Acad. Pediats., Am. Electroencephalographic Soc. mem. AMA (Physician's Recognition award in Continuing Med. Edn.), N.Y. State Med. Soc., N.Y. County Med. Soc., Am. Med. Women's Assn., Am. Epilepsy Soc., Am. Acad. Clin. Neurophysiology, Eastern EEG Soc., Am. Med. EEG Assn., Child Neurology Soc., Internat. Child Neurology Assn., Tristate Child Neurology Soc., Assn. for Rsch. in Nervous and Mental Diseases, N.Y. Acad. Sci. Avocations: art museums, reading literature, French language, travel. Office: NY Hosp-Cornell U Med Coll 525 E 68th St New York NY 10021-4873

SOLOMON, GEORGE FREEMAN, academic psychiatrist; b. Freeport, N.Y., Nov. 25, 1931; s. Joseph C. and Ruth (Freeman) S.; children: Joshua Ben, Jared Freeman. A.B., Stanford U., 1952, M.D., 1955. Intern, Barnes Hosp., St. Louis, 1955-56; resident in psychiatry Langley Porter Neuropsychiat. Inst., U. Calif. Med. Sch., San Francisco, 1956-59; asst. to asso. prof. psychiatry Stanford U. Med. Sch., 1962-73; dir. med. edn. Fresno County (Calif.) Dept. Health, 1973-83; clin. prof. UCLA Med. Sch., 1974-78; clin. prof. psychiatry U. Calif. Med. Sch., San Francisco, 1976-79, prof., 1980-84, vice-chmn. dept., 1978-83; adj. prof. U. Calif., San Francisco, 1984-90; prof. psychiatry and biobehavioral sci. UCLA, 1984-95, prof. emeritus, 1995—; chief chem. dependency treatment ctr. VA Med. Ctr., Sepulveda, Calif., 1984-89; chief psychoneuroimmunology, 1989-94; chief psychiatry Valley Med. Center, Fresno, 1974-83. Co-author: The Psychology of Strength, 1975; contbr. over 170 papers and articles on psychoneuroimmunology, violence, Vietnam and other topics to profl. jours. and various publs. Capt. USAR, 1959-61. Fellow Internat. Coll. Psychosomatic Medicine, Am. Psychiat. Assn., Acad. of Behavioral Med. Research., Royal Coll. Psychiatrists. Home: 19054 Pacific Coast Hwy Malibu CA 90265-5406 Office: UCLA Sch Med Neuropsych Inst C8-258 12-138CHS Los Angeles CA 90024

SOLOMON, GEORGE M., newspaper editor; b. N.Y.C., July 19, 1940; s. Sidney and Fannie (Seidel) S.; m. Hazel Stephanie Bakst, July 23, 1967; children—Aaron, Mark, Gregory. B.S. in Journalism, U. Fla., 1963. Sports editor Sun-Sentinel, Fort Lauderdale, Fla., 1965-70; reporter, columnist Washington Daily News, 1970-72; reporter sports Washington Post, 1972-74, asst. sports editor, 1974-75, asst. mng. editor sports, 1975—. Author: Team Nobody Wanted: the Washington Redskins, 1973. Democrat. Jewish. Avocations: running; tennis. Office: Washington Post 1150 15th St NW Washington DC 20071-0001

SOLOMON, GERALD BROOKS HUNT, congressman; b. Okeechobee, Fla., Aug. 14, 1930; s. Seymour and Rlee Eugenia (Hunt) S.; m. Freda Frances Parker, Feb. 5, 1955; children: Susan, Daniel, Robert, Linda, Jeffrey. Student, Siena Coll., Albany, N.Y., 1948-49, St. Lawrence U., Canton, N.Y., 1953-54. Town supr., chief exec. Queensbury, N.Y., 1967-72; legislator Warren County, N.Y., 1968-73; mem. N.Y. State Assembly, 1972-78, 96th-97th Congresses from 29th N.Y. dist., 1979-83, 98th-105th Congresses from 24th (now 22nd) N.Y. dist., Washington, D.C., 1983—; chmn. Rules com., mem. joint com. orgn. congress 98th-105th Congresses from 24th (now 22nd) N.Y. dist., Washington; ambassador del. UN, 1985; house com. mem. Vets. Affairs Com., 1979-89, Pub. Wks. Com., 1979-83, Fgn. Affairs Com., 1983-89, 2d ranking rep. 1989—, 1st ranking rep. 1991—; founding ptnr. Assoc. of Glens Falls (N.Y.) Inc. ins. and stockbrokerage firm, 1964—. Chmn. Warren County Social Svc. Com., 1968-72; active Ea. Adirondack Heart Assn., Adirondack Muscular Dystrophy Assn.; mem. Queensbury Ctrl. Vol. Fire Co., from 1967; bd. dirs. Adirondack Park Assn., Glens Falls Area Youth Ctr.; coun. Boy Scouts Am.; mem. house rules com. U.S. Congress, 1989—, Task Force, Prisoner and Missing in S.E. Asia; former mem. Ho. Fgn. Affairs Com.; former sr. ranking rep. Vets. Affairs Com.; amb. UN, N.Y., 1985, also congl. advisor to UN session on disarmament; former congl. del. North Atlantic Assembly, vice chmn., active, 1982—; chmn. polit. fgn. affairs com. Assembly. With USMC, 1951-58, Korean War. Mem. Queensbury C. of C. (pres. 1972), Queensbury Jaycees (pres. 1964-65). Presbyterian. Lodges: Masons, Shriners, K.T, Elks, Kiwanis (bd. dir. Queensbury club 1965-69), Grange. Office: US Ho of Reps 2206 Rayburn Bldg Ofc Bldg Washington DC 20515-3222

SOLOMON, HENRY, university dean; b. Bronx, N.Y., Nov. 28, 1926; s. Max and Tillie (Gilerowitz) S.; m. Jacqueline Mona Cohen, May 31, 1953; 1 son, Michael Robert. B.A., Bklyn. Coll., 1949; M.A., NYU, 1950, Ph.D., 1960. Research assoc., then sr. staff investigator and dep. prin. investigator, logistics research project George Washington U., 1950-66, prof. econs., chmn. dept., 1962-74, 91-96; dean George Washington U. (Grad. Sch. Arts and Scis.), 1974-90, prof. and dean emeritus, 1996—; dep. asst. adminstr. econs., acting asst. adminstr. planning, research and analysis SBA, 1966-67; cons. in field. Assoc. editor: Naval Research Logistics Quar, 1957-90 . Served with U.S. Army, 1945-46. Recipient Founder's Day award N.Y. U., 1960. Mem. Am. Econ. Assn., Am. Statis. Assn. Home: 6311 Stratford Rd Chevy Chase MD 20815-5355 Office: George Washington Univ Funger 507 Washington DC 20052

SOLOMON, HOWARD, pharmaceutical company executive; b. N.Y.C., Aug. 12, 1927; s. David and Faye (Gussow) S.; m. Carolyn Ruth Bower, Dec. 17, 1961; children: Andrew Wallace, David Frederick. BSS, CCNY, 1949; LLB, Yale U., 1952. Bar: N.Y. 1952. Atty. Moses & Singer, N.Y.C., 1952-55; atty. Kay Scholer, Fierman Hays & Handler, N.Y.C., 1956-60; pres. Hildred Mgmt. Corp., N.Y.C., 1967-83; dir. Forest Labs., Inc., N.Y.C., 1964—; pres., chief exec. officer Forest Labs., Inc., 1977—; dir. Pharmax Ltd., Bexley, Kent., U.K., 1979—. Mem. Turtle Bay Music Sch., 1975-79; bd. dirs. Met. Opera, N.Y.C. Ballet. Mem. N.Y. State Bar Assn., Am. Bus. Conf. (bd. govs.), Yale Club, Harmonie Club of N.Y. Office: Forest Labs Inc 909 3rd Ave New York NY 10022-4731

SOLOMON, JACK AVRUM, lawyer, automotive distributor, art dealer; b. Omaha, Oct. 25, 1928; s. John A. and Matilda (Bienstok) S.; m. Josephine J. Kleiman, June 1948 (div. Mar. 1971); children: Debra, Alisa, Michael, Rena; m. Carolyn Summers, Dec. 1973. B.S., U. Nebr., 1950, LL.B. cum laude, 1952; LL.M. (Cook fellow), U. Mich., 1953. Bar: Nebr. 1950, Ill. 1951. Practice law Chgo., 1950—; with firm Stiefel, Greenberg, Burns, Baldridge & Solomon, 1953-66, ptnr., 1958-66; ptnr. Solomon, Rosenfeld, Elliot & Stiefel, and predecessor, 1966—, sr. ptnr., 1966—; dir. Amco Industries, Inc., Chgo., 1968—, chmn. bd., 1968-69, sec., gen. counsel, 1969—; sec., dir. Mogen David Wine Corp., Chgo., 1964-71; chmn. bd., dir. Arts and Leisure Corp., 1969-76; pres., chmn. bd., dir. Circle Fine Art Corp., 1968-95; chmn. bd. Solomon and Solomon Fine Art, Ltd., 1996—, Am.'s Gallery, Ltd., 1997—. Mem. Ill., Nebr. bar assns.; mem. Fine Art Pubs. Assn. (pres. 1982—); Mem. Order of Coif. Jewish (pres. temple 1959-61). Club: Nat. Arts (N.Y.C.). Home: 950 N Michigan Ave Chicago IL 60611 Office: 303 E Wacker Dr Ste 207 Chicago IL 60601-5212

SOLOMON, JULIUS OSCAR LEE, pharmacist, hypnotherapist; b. N.Y.C., Aug. 14, 1917; s. John and Jeannette (Krieger) S.; student Bklyn. Coll., 1935-36, CCNY, 1936-37; BS in Pharmacy, U. So. Calif., 1949; postgrad. Long Beach State U., 1971-72, Southwestern Colls., 1979, 81-82, San Diego State U., 1994—; PhD, Am. Inst. Hypnotherapy, 1988; postgrad. San Diego State U., 1994—. m. Sylvia Smith, June 26, 1941 (div. Jan. 1975); children: Marc Irwin, Evan Scott, Jeri Lee. Cert. hypnotherapist; cert. hypnoanaesthesia therapist. Dye maker Fred Fear & Co., Bklyn., 1935; apprentice interior decorator Dorothy Draper, 1936; various jobs, N.Y. State Police, 1940-45; rsch. asst. Union Oil Co., 1945; lighting cons. Joe Rosenberg & Co., 1946-49; owner Banner Drug, Lomita, 1949-53, Redondo Beach, Calif., 1953-72, El Prado Pharmacy, Redondo Beach, 1961-65; pres. Banner Drug, Inc., Redondo Beach, 1953-72, Thrifty Drugs, 1972-74, also Guild Drug, Longs Drug, Drug King, 1976-83; pres. Socoma, Inc. doing bus. as Lee & Ana Pharmacy, 1983-86, now Two Hearts Help Clinic, 1986—. Charter commr., founder Redondo Beach Youth Baseball Council; sponsor Little League Baseball, basketball, football, bowling; pres. Redondo Beach Boys Club; v.p. South Bay Children's Health Ctr., 1974, Redondo Beach Coordinating Coun., 1975; bd. dirs. So. Bay Assn. Little Theatres, 1972-75; actor in 8 shows; founder Redondo Beach Community Theater, 1975; actor Man of La Mancha Vangard Theatre, San Diego, 1995; active maj. gift drive YMCA, 1975; mem. SCAG Com. on Criminal Justice, 1974, League Calif. Environ. Quality Com., 1975; mem. Dem. State Cen. Com., Los Angeles County Dem. Cen. Com.; del. Dem. Nat. Conv., 1972; chmn. Redondo Beach Recreation and Parks Commn.; mem. San Diego County Parks Adv. Commn., 1982; mem. San Diego Juvenile Justice Commn., 1986-92; mem. San Diego County Adv. Com. Adult Detention, 1987-92; mem. human resource devel. com., pub. improvement com. Nat. League of Cities; v.p. Redondo Beach Coordinating Coun.; councilman, Redondo Beach, 1961-69, 73-77; treas. 46th Assembly Dist. Coun.; candidate 46 Assembly dist. 1966; nat. chmn. Pharmacists for Humphrey, 1968, 72; pres. bd. dirs. South Bay Exceptional Childrens Soc., Chapel Theatre; bd. dirs. so. div. League Calif. Cities, U.S.-Mex. Sister Cities Assn., Boy's Club Found. San Diego County, Autumn Hills Condominium Assn. (pres.), Calif. Employee Pharmacists Assn. (pres. 1985), Our House, Chula Vista, Calif., 1984-86; mem. South Bay Inter-City Hwy. Com., Redondo Beach Round Table, 1973-77; mem. State Calif. Commn. of Californias (U.S.-Mexico), 1975-78; mem. Chula Vista Safety Commn., 1978, chmn., 1980-81; chmn. San Diego County Juvenile Camp Contract Com., 1982-83; mem. San Diego County Juvenile Delinquency Prevention Commn., 1983-85, 89-91, San Diego County Juvenile Justice Commn., 1986-91, San Diego County Adv. Com. for Adult Detention, 1987-91; spl. participant Calif. Crime and Violence Workshop; mem. Montgomery Planning Commn., 1983-86; mem. Constnl. Observance Com., 1990-93, Troubled Teenagers Hypnosis Treatment Program, 1989—. With USCGR, 1942-45. Recipient Pop Warner Youth award, 1960, 1962, award of merit Calif. Pharm. Assn., 1962, award Am. Assn. Blood Banks, 1982. Diplomate Am. Bd. Diplomates Pharmacy Internat., 1977-81; Fellow Am. Coll. Pharmacists (pres. 1949-57); mem. South Bay Pharm. Assn. (pres.), South Bay Councilman Assn. (founder, pres.), Palos Verdes Peninsula Navy League (charter), Am. Legion, U. So. Calif. Alumni Assn. (life), Assn. Former N.Y. State Troopers (life), AFTRA, Am. Pharm. Assn., Nat. Assn. Retail Druggists, Calif. Pharmacists Assn., Calif. Employee Pharmacist Assn. (bd. dirs. 1980-81), Hon. Dep. Sheriff's Assn., San Ysidro C. of C. (bd. dirs. 1985-87), Fraternal Order of Police, San Diego County Fish and Game Assn., Rho Pi Phi (pres. alumni). Club: Trojan (life). Lodges: Elks (life), Masons (32 deg.; life), Lions (charter mem. North Redondo). Established Lee and Ana Solomon award for varsity athlete with highest scholastic average at 10 L.A. South Bay High Schs. in Los Angeles County and 3 San Diego area South Bay High Schs.

SOLOMON, MARILYN KAY, educator, consultant; b. Marshall, Mo., Oct. 16, 1947; d. John W. and Della M. (Dille) S. BS, Ctrl. Mo. State U., 1969; MS, Ind. U., 1974. Cert. in early childhood and nursery sch. edn., Mo., Ind. Tchr. Indpls. Pub. Schs., 1969-74; dir. Singer Learning Ctrs., Indpls., 1974-78; v.p. ECLC Learning Ctrs., Inc., Indpls., 1978-95; pres., CEO, owner Early Learning Ctrs., Inc., Indpls., 1995—; owner, pres., CEO, Solomon Antique Restoration, Inc., Indpls., 1996—; mem. OJT tng. task force Dept. Labor, Washington; mem. nat. task force for parenting edn. HEW, Washington; cons. to numerous corps. on corp. child care. Co-author curricula. Founding bd. dirs. Mid City Pioneer, Indpls., 1977; mem. adv. bd. Enterprise Zone Small Bus. Incubator, Indpls., 1995—; founding bd. dirs. Family Support Ctr., Indpls., 1983, pres. bd. dirs., 1985-87. Recipient Outstanding Leadership award Ind. Conf. on Social Concerns, 1975, 76, 77, Children's Mus. Edn. award, 1974; named to Outstanding Young Women of Am., 1984. Mem. Indpls. Mus. Art, Ind. Lic. Child Care Assn. (v.p. 1992, pres. 1974, 75), State of Ind. Quality and Tng. Coun. (chair 1992), Step Ahead-Marion County (rep. for child care 1992—), Ind. Alliance for Better Child Care (bd. dirs. 1992, adv. bd. 1990-95, PBS tng. 1992—, child devel. tng. com. 1996—), Order Eastern Star, Indpls. Zool. Soc. (charter). Office: Early Learning Ctrs Inc 1315 S Sherman Dr Indianapolis IN 46203-2210

SOLOMON, MARK A., lawyer; b. Cedar Rapids, Iowa, Aug. 30, 1950. BA summa cum laude, Calif. State U., San Jose, 1972; JD magna cum laude, U. Santa Clara, 1975. Bar: Calif. 1975, Nev. 1976. Mem. Lionel Sawyer & Collins, Las Vegas, Nev. Mem. ABA, State Bar Calif., State Bar Nev., Clark County Bar Assn. Office: Lionel Sawyer & Collins 1700 Bank Am Plz 300 S 4th St Las Vegas NV 89101-6014

SOLOMON, MARK RAYMOND, lawyer, educator; b. Pitts., Aug. 23, 1945; s. Louis Isadore and Fern Rhea (Josselson) S. BA, Ohio State U., 1967; MEd, Cleve. State U., 1971; JD with honors, George Washington U., 1973; LLM in Taxation, Georgetown U., 1976. Bar: Ohio, Mich., U.S. Tax Ct., U.S. Ct. Fed. Claims, U.S. Dist. (ea. dist.) Mich., U.S. Ct. Appeals (6th cir.). Tax law specialist corp. tax br. Nat. Office of IRS, 1973-75; assoc. Butzel, Long, Gust, Klein & Van Zile, Detroit, 1976-78; dir., v.p. Shatzman & Solomon, P.C., Southfield, Mich., 1978-81; prof., chmn. tax and bus. law dept., dir. MS in Taxation Program, Walsh Coll., Troy, Mich., 1981—; of counsel in tax matters Meyer, Kirk, Snyder and Safford PLLC, Bloomfield Hills, Mich., 1981—; adj. prof. law U. Detroit, 1977-81. Editor: Cases and Materials on Consolidated Tax Returns, 1978, Cases and Materials on the Application of Legal Principles and Authorities to Federal Tax Law, 1990. Mem. Mich. Bar Assn., Kiwanis (bd. dirs.), Phi Eta Sigma. Avocation: bridge (life master). Home: 2109 Golfview Dr Apt 102 Troy MI 48084-3926 Office: Meyer Kirk Snyder & Safford PLLC 100 W Long Lake Rd Ste 100 Bloomfield Hills MI 48304-2773

SOLOMON, MARTIN M., judge; b. Jan. 24, 1950; BA magna cum laude, SUNY, Albany, 1972; LLB, N.Y. Law Sch, 1975. admitted to N.Y. bar, 1976; judge N.Y.C. Civil Ct., Brooklyn, 1996—; mem. N.Y. State Senate, 1978-95, former mem. exec. com. Nat. Conf. Ins. Legislators, ranking mem. sen. ins. com., mem. health, bank, judiciary coms. Mem. Oddfellows, KP. Office: NYC Civil Ct 141 Livingston St Brooklyn NY 11201-5133

SOLOMON, MAYNARD ELLIOTT, music historian, former recording company executive; b. N.Y.C., Jan. 5, 1930; s. Benjamin and Dora (Levine) S.; m. Eva Georgiana Tevan, Jan. 22, 1951; children: Mark Jonathan, Nina Stephanie, Maury David. BA, Bklyn. Coll., 1950; postgrad., Columbia U., 1950-51. Co-founder, co-owner Vanguard Rec. Soc., Inc., N.Y.C., 1950-86; faculty grad. div. CUNY, 1979-81; vis. prof. SUNY Stony Brook, 1988, Columbia U., N.Y.C., 1990, Harvard U., Cambridge, Mass., 1992, Yale U., New Haven, 1994-95; scholarly advisor Beethoven Archives, Bonn, 1997—. Author: Marxism and Art, 1973, Beethoven, 1977 (translated into German, French, Spanish, Portuguese, Japanese, Italian, Bulgarian), Myth, Creativity and Psychoanalysis, 1978, Beethoven's Tagebuch, 1982, Beethoven's Tagebuch, German translation, 1990, Italian translation, 1992, Beethoven Essays, 1988; Mozart: A Life, 1995 (translated into Swedish, Italian, Japanese); contbg. editor: Am. Imago; mem. editl. bd. Beethovenhaus edit. Beethoven's Letters; editor: Memories of Beethoven, 1992; contbr. articles to profl. jours. Recipient Deems Taylor award ASCAP, 1978, 89, 96. Mem. PEN, Am. Musicol. Soc. (bd. dirs. 1984-86, Otto Kinkeldey award 1989), Authors Guild, N.Y. Inst. for Humanities, Phi Beta Kappa. Home: 1 W 72nd St New York NY 10023-3486

SOLOMON, MICHAEL BRUCE, lawyer; b. Chgo., Nov. 8, 1945; s. Arthur J. and Ruth H. (Halpert) S.; m. Tunny Jamri, Dec. 17, 1983. BA, U. Miami, Coral Gables, Fla., 1967, JD, 1970. Bar: Fla. 1970; U.S. Dist. Ct. (so. dist.) Fla. 1972; U.S. Ct. Appeals (5th cir.) 1989, U.S. Ct. Appeals (11th cir.) 1990. Assoc. Theodore M. Trushin P.A., Miami Beach, Fla., 1970-77; ptnr. Klein, Oshinsky & Solomon, Hallandale, Fla., 1978-87; pvt. practice Hallandale, Fla., 1988—; spl. asst., pub. defender, Dade County, Fla., 1972-78; ombudsman Dade County pub. defender's office, Miami, 1972. Contbr. article to profl. jour. Mem. ATLA, So. Dist. Fla. Trial Bar, Broward County Bar Assn. Office: Ste A 1150 E Hallandale Beach Blvd Hallandale FL 33009-4432

SOLOMON, MICHAEL ROBERT, marketing educator; b. Washington, Apr. 18, 1956. BA magna cum laude, Brandeis U., 1977; MA, U.N.C., 1979, PhD, 1981. Assoc. dir. Inst. Retail Mgmt. NYU, 1983-85, asst. prof. mktg., 1981-86, assoc. prof. mktg., 1986-87; assoc. prof., chmn. dept. mktg. Rutgers U., New Brunswick, N.J., 1987-95; human scis. prof. of consumer behavior Sch. of Human Scis. Auburn (Ala.) U., 1995—; lectr., presenter in field. Editor: The Psychology of Fashion, 1985, others; contbr. articles to profl. jours.; reviewer jours./books in field. Recipient numerous grants including Burlington Industries, 1985, Mktg. Sci. Inst., 1986, others; faculty fellow Am. Mktg. Assn. Doctoral Consortium, 1987, fellow Nat. Rsch. Svc., 1980, Fulbright fellow, 1996, others. Mem. APA, Assn. Consumer Rsch. Conf. (co-chmn. 1990), Am. Mktg. Assn. (co-chmn. mktg. educator's conf., Toronto 1987), Soc. Consumer Psychology, Ea. Psychol. Assn., Retail Rsch. Soc., Assn. Coll. Profs. Textiles and Clothing, Soc. Study Symbolic Interaction, Popular Culture Assn., others. Office: Auburn U Dept Cosumer Affairs Sch Human Scis Auburn AL 36849

SOLOMON, NEAL EDWARD, management consultant; b. San Diego, Mar. 9, 1960; s. Donald Jay and Roberta Yvonne (Recht) S. BA, Reed Coll., Portland, Oreg., 1981; AM, U. Chgo, 1982. Pres., founder Calif. Legal Search, San Francisco, 1983—; founding mem. Nat. Assn. of Legal Search Cons., 1984—. Author: Economic Constraints to Law Firm Growth, 1991, Fundamental Social Philosophy, 1991. Mem. Ctr. for the Study of Dem. Institutions, Am. Philosophical Assn. Democrat. Avocation: nature photography. Office: 1 Sansome St Ste 2000 San Francisco CA 94104-4432

SOLOMON, PAUL ROBERT, neuropsychologist, educator; b. Bklyn., Aug. 27, 1948; s. Maynard and Norma Harris (Ruben) S.; m. Suellen Zablow, Aug. 16, 1970; children: Todd, Jessica. BA in Psychology, SUNY, New Paltz, 1970, MA in Psychology, 1972; PhD in Psychology, U. Mass., 1972. Lic. psychologist, Mass. Prof. psychology and neurosci. Williams Coll, Williamstown, Mass., 1976—, neurosci. program chmn., 1990-95; dir. memory disorders clinic S.W. Vt. Med. Ctr., Bennington, 1990—; bd. dirs. No. Berkshire Mental Health Assn., North Adams, Mass. Author: Scientific Writings, 1985, Memory, 1989, Psychology 4th edit., 1993; contbr. articles to profl. jours. Bd. dirs. W. Mass. Alzheimers Assn., 1992—. Recipient Distinguished Teaching award U. Mass., Amherst, 1975; Rsch. grantee EPA, NIH, NSF, 1978—; Rsch. fellowships NIH, 1979, NSF, 1980. Fellow APA, AAAS, Am. Psychol. Soc.; mem. Soc. for Neuroscience. Home: 130 Forest Rd Williamstown MA 01267-2029 Office: Williams Coll Dept Psychology Williamstown MA 01262

SOLOMON, PHILIP MYRON, astronomer, atmospheric scientist; b. N.Y.C., Mar. 19, 1939; s. Nathan and Betty (Safer) S.; m. Sheila Movit; 1 child, Nina Beth. BS in Physics, U. Wis., 1959, MS in Astronomy, 1961, PhD, 1964. Postdoctoral fellow Princeton U., 1964-66; rsch. assoc., lectr. Columbia U., N.Y.C., 1966-71; assoc. prof. Sch. Physics and Atronomy U. Minn., 1971-73; prof. astronomy dept. earth and space scis. SUNY, Stony Brook, 1974—; vis. scientist Inst. Astronomy, Cambridge (Eng.) U., 1967-69, 72, sr. vis. scientist, 1981-82; mem. in Sch. Natural Scis., Inst. for Advanced Study, Princeton, N.J., 1973-74, 86; overseas fellow Churchill Coll., Cambridge, U., 1981-82; vis. prof. Ecole Norman Superieure, Paris, 1989, Max Plauck Inst. for Radioastronomie, Bonn, 1989, Inst. d'Astrophysique, Paris, 1993, NATO sr. scientist, 1996, vis. prof. Cambridge U., 1997. Editor: Giant Molecular Clouds in the Galaxy, 1980; contbr. numerous articles to profl. jours. Recipient Sr. Humboldt award Alexander von Humboldt Found., 1989. Mem. Am. Astron. Soc., Internat. Astron. Union. Home: 440 Riverside Dr New York NY 10027-6828 Office: SUNY Stony Book Astronomy Program Dept Earth And Scis Stony Brook NY 11794

SOLOMON, PHYLLIS LINDA, social work educator, researcher; b. Hartford, Conn., Dec. 6, 1945; d. Louis Calvin and Annabell Lee (Nitzberg) S. BA in Sociology, Russell Sage Coll., 1968; MA in Sociology, Case Western Res. U., 1970, PhD in Social Welfare, 1978. Lic. social worker, Pa. Rsch. assoc. Inst. Urban Studies Cleve. State U., 1970-71; program evaluator Cleve. State Hosp., 1971-74; project dir. Ohio Mental Health and Mental Retardation Rsch. Ctr., Cleve., 1974-75; rsch. assoc. Psychiat. Rsch. Found. of Cleve., 1975; project dir. Ohio Mental Health and Mental Retardation Rsch. Ctr., 1977-78; rsch. assoc. dirs. rsch. and mental health planning Fedn. for Community Planning, 1978-88; prof. dept. mental health scis., dir. sect. mental health svcs. and systems research Hahnemann U., Phila., 1988-94; prof. Sch. Social Work U. Pa., Phila., 1994—; secondary appointment Prof. Social Work in Psychiatry U. Pa. Sch. Medicine; adj. prof. dept. psychiatry Allegheny U. Author: (with others) Community Services to Discharged Psychiatric Patients, 1984; co-editor: New Developments in Psychiatric Rehabilitation, 1990, Psychiatric Rehabilitation in Practice, 1993; editorial adv. bd. Community Mental Health Jour., 1988—; editl. bd. Jour. Social Svc. Rsch.; contbr. articles to profl. jours. Trustee Cleve. Rape Crisis Ctr., 1981-84, CIT Mental Health Svcs., Cleve., 1985-88; mem. citizen's adv. bd. Sagamore Hills (Ohio) Children's Psychiat. Hosp., 1984-88. Named Evaluator of the Yr., Ohio Program Evaluators Group, 1987; recipient Ann. award Cuyahoga County Community Mental Health Bd., 1988. Mem. Internat. Assn. Psychosocial Rehab. Svcs. Jewish. Home: 220 E Mermaid Ln Apt 186 Philadelphia PA 19118-3215 Office: U Pa Sch Social Work 3701 Locust Walk Philadelphia PA 19104-6214

SOLOMON, RANDALL L., lawyer; b. Dayton, Ohio, June 8, 1948. BA summa cum laude, Wright State U., 1970; JD, Case Western Res. U., 1973. Bar: Ohio 1973, U.S. Dist. Ct. (no. dist.) Ohio 1973, U.S. Ct. Appeals (6th cir.) 1973, U.S. Ct. Appeals (fed. cir.) 1988. Ptnr. Baker & Hostetler, Cleve.; speaker in field. Fellow Am. Coll. Trial Lawyers; mem. ABA (mem. litigation, tort and ins. practice sects., mem. toxic and hazardous substances and environ. law coms.), Ohio State Bar Assn., Cleve. Bar Assn. (chair litigation sect. 1991-92), Nat. Inst. Trial Advocacy (mem. nat. session 1978), Def. Rsch. Inst., Master of Bench, Am. Inn of Ct. Office: Baker & Hostetler 3200 Nat City Ctr 1900 E 9th St Cleveland OH 44114-3401

SOLOMON, RICHARD HARVEY, political scientist; b. Phila., June 19, 1937; s. Bertram Harvey and Ellen (Harris) S.; m. Anne G. Keatley, Dec. 16, 1991. Part-time student, Harvard U., 1959-63, Yale U., 1961, 63-64; SB, MIT, 1960, PhD, 1966. Tech. photographer, lab. worker Photon, Inc., Cambridge, Mass., 1957; researcher Polaroid Corp., 1959-61; research assoc. Ctr. for Chinese Studies U. Mich., Ann Arbor, Mich., 1966-71, from asst prof. to prof. polit. sci., 1966-71; staff mem. NSC, Washington, 1971-76; head. polit. sci dept. The Rand Corp., Santa Monica, Calif., 1976-86, program dir. Internat. Security Policy Research, 1977-83; mem. Pres.' Commn. on Fgn. Lang. and Internat. Studies Washington, 1978-80, mem. Chief of Naval Ops. exec. panel, 1983—; dir. policy planning staff Dept. of State, Washington, 1986-89, asst. sec. of state for East Asian and Pacific affairs, 1989-92; U.S. ambassador to Philippines, 1992-93; pres. U.S. Inst. of Peace, Washington, 1993—. Author: Mao's Revolution and the Chinese Political Culture, 1971, Chinese Political Negotiating Behavior, 1986; contbr. articles to profl. jours. Office: US Inst of Peace 1550 M St NW Ste 700 Washington DC 20005-1708

SOLOMON, RICHARD JAY, architect; b. Chgo., May 20, 1943; s. Louis Richard and Jeanne (Handelman) S.; children: Aaron Louis, Jonathan Daniel, Ethan Morris Kreeger. Student, Brandeis U., 1961-63; BArch, MIT, 1967; MA in Environ. Design, Yale U., 1969. Registered architect, Ill. Pvt. practice architecture Chgo., 1974—; adj. asst. prof. archtl. design U. Ill., Chgo., 1980-89; dir. Graham Found. for Acvanced Studies in Fine Arts, Chgo., 1993—. Editor-in-chief Inland Arch. Mag., 1989-93; contbr. articles to profl. jours. Trustee Francis W. Parker Sch., Chgo., 1987—; bd. overseers Ill. Inst. Tech., Chgo., 1994—. Fellow AIA; mem. Soc. Archtl. Historians (bd. dirs. 1994—), Chgo. Archtl. Club, Arts Club, Tavern Club. Avocations: writing, collecting, drawing, polar bears. Home and Office: Apt 2N 2350 N Lincoln Park W Chicago IL 60614-3415

SOLOMON, RISA GREENBERG, video software industry executive; b. N.Y.C., June 22, 1948; d. Nathan and Frances (Guttman) Greenberg; m. Philip Howard Solomon, June 21, 1970; children: Elycia Beth, Cynthia Gayle. BA, NYU, 1969, MA, 1970. Asst. editor Redbook Mag., N.Y.C., 1969-70; assoc. editor Greenwood Press, Westport, Conn., 1970-71; mng. editor Dushkin Pub., Guilford, Conn., 1971-72; freelance editor Yale U. Press, New Haven, Conn., 1972-75; v.p. ops. Videoland, Inc., Dallas, 1980-82; v.p. Video Software Dealers Assn., Cherry Hill, N.J. and Dallas, 1981-83; pres. Videodome Enterprises, Dallas, 1983—; cons. Home Recording Rights Coalition, Washington, 1983-84. Contbr. articles to video mags. Bd. dirs. Congregation Anshai Emet, Dallas, 1985-86. Mem. Video Software Dealers Assn. (founder, dir. 1981-82). Democrat. Jewish. Avocations: world travel, tennis, water and snow skiing. Office: Videodome Enterprises 11420 Saint Michaels Dr Dallas TX 75230-2436

SOLOMON, ROBERT, economist; b. N.Y.C., May 2, 1921; s. Sol and Betty (Brownstone) S.; m. Fern Rice, Sept. 11, 1946; children: Carol Ann, Barbara Betty, Anne Eleanor. B.A., U. Mich., 1942, M.A., Harvard U., 1947, Ph.D., 1952. With Fed. Res. Bd., 1947-76, assoc. adviser research div., 1963-65, adviser research div., 1965, adviser to bd. govs., 1965-76, dir. div. internat. fin., 1966-72; sr. fellow Brookings Instn., Washington, 1976-80; guest scholar Brookings Instn., 1980—; pres. RS Assos., pub. Internat. Econ. Letter, 1981—; vice chmn. deps. of com. of 20 IMF, 1972-74; adj. prof. Am. U., 1962-67; sr. staff economist Council Econ. Advisers, 1963-64. Author: The International Monetary System, 1945-81, 1982, Partners in Prosperity, 1991, The Transformation of the World Economy, 1980-93, 1994; contbr. articles to profl. jours. Served to 1st lt. USAAF, 1942-45. Decorated D.F.C., Air medal, officier Legion of Honor France; recipient Rockefeller Pub. Service award, 1971. Mem. Am. Econ. Assn., Council on Fgn. Relations. Club: Cosmos (Washington). Home and Office: 8502 W Howell Rd Bethesda MD 20817-6827

SOLOMON, ROBERT CHARLES, philosopher, educator; b. Detroit, Sept. 14, 1942; s. Charles M. and Vita (Petrosky) S. BA, U. Pa., 1963; MA, U. Mich., 1965, PhD, 1967. Teaching fellow U. Mich., Ann Arbor, 1965-66; lectr. Princeton (N.J.) U., 1966-67, 67-68; asst. prof. U. Pitts., 1969-71, CUNY, 1971-72; assoc. prof. philosophy U. Tex., Austin, 1972-77, prof., 1977—, Quincy Lee Centennial prof., 1986—; vis. prof. U. Pa., UCLA, U. Auckland, N.Z., La Trobe U., Melbourne, Australia, U. B.C.; chmn. Phi Beta Kappa Emerson Award Com.; cons. in field. Author: From Rationalism to Existentialism, 1972, The Passions, 1976, Introducing Philosophy: Problems and Perspectives, 1977, History and Human Nature: A Philosophical Review of European History and Culture, 1750-1850, 1979, Love: Emotion, Myth and Metaphor, 1981, In the Spirit of Hegel, 1983, (with C. Calhoun) What Is an Emotion?, 1984, It's a Good Business, 1985, (with Kristine Hanson) Above the Bottom Line, 1983, From Hegel to Existentialism, 1987, Continental Philosophy After 1750, 1988, About Love, 1988, A Passion for Justice, 1990, Ethics: A Briefer Introduction, 1991, Ethics and Excellence, 1992, Entertaining Ideas, 1992, (with J. Solomon) Up the University, 1993, (with Kathleen Higgins) A Short History of Philosophy, 1996; editor: Phenomenology and Existentialism, 1972, Nietzsche, 1973, Existentialism, 1974, (with Kathleen Higins) Reading Nietzsche, 1988, From Africa to Zen, 1993, The Age of German Idealism, 1993, (with Mark A. Murphy) What Is Justice?, 1990, (With Kathleen Higgins) A Passion for Wisdom, 1997; contbr. articles to profl. jours. Recipient Outstanding Tchr. award Standard Oil Co., 1973, Pres.' Teaching Excellence award, 1985, 96. Mem. Am. Philos. Assn., N.Am. Nietzsche Soc. (exec. bd.), Internat. Soc. Research on Emotions (bd. dirs.), Soc. for Bus. Ethics.

SOLOMON, ROBERT DOUGLAS, pathology educator; b. Delavan, Wis., Aug. 28, 1917; s. Lewis Jacob and Sara (Ludgin) S.; m. Helen Fisher, Apr. 4, 1943; children: Susan, Wendy, James, William. Student, MIT, 1934-36; BS in Biochemistry, U. Chgo., 1938; MD, Johns Hopkins U., 1942. Intern John's Hopkins Hosp., 1942-43; resident in pathology Michael Reese Hosp., 1947-49; lectr. U. Ill., Chgo., 1947-50; fellow NIH pathology U. Ill., 1949-50; asst. prof. U. Md., Balt., 1955-60; assoc. prof. U. So. Calif., L.A., 1960-70; chief of staff City of Hope Nat. Med. Ctr., 1966-67; prof. U. Mo., Kansas City, 1977-78, SUNY, Syracuse, 1968-78; chief of staff The Hosp., Sidney, N.Y., 1985-86; adj. prof. U. N.C., Wilmington, 1988—; cons. VA Hosp., Balt., 1955-60, Med. Svc. Lab., Wilmington, 1989-93. Co-author: Progress in Gerontological Research, 1967; contbr. papers and profl. jours. and rsch. in biochemistry, revascular of heart, carcinogenisis, cancer chemotherapy, atherogenesis, discovery of reversibility of atherosclerosis. V.p. Rotary, Duarte, Calif., 1967; v.p. and pres. Force for an Informed Electorate. Capt. Med. Corps, AUS, 1943-46, PTO. Grantee NIH, Fleischmann Found., Am. Heart Assn., Nat. Cancer Inst., 1958-70. Fellow ACP (pres. Md. chpt.), Western Geriatrics Soc. (founding); mem. Coll. Am. Pathologists (past pres. Md. chpt.), Am. Soc. Clin. Pathologists, Assn. Clin. Scientists, Am. Chem. Soc., Royal Soc. Medicine (London). Avocations: cruising, astronomy, mathematics, fishing, stamps. Home: 113 S Belvedere Dr Hampstead NC 28443-2504

SOLOMON, RUSSELL, retail products executive; b. 1925. CEO MTS. Office: MTS PO Box 919001 West Sacramento CA 95691*

SOLOMON, SAMUEL, biochemistry educator, administrator; b. Brest Litovsk, Poland, Dec. 5, 1925; s. Nathan and Rachel (Greenberg) S.; m. Sheila R. Horn, Aug. 11, 1953 (div. 1974); children—David Horn, Peter Horn, Jonathan Simon; m. Augusta M. Vineberg, July 12, 1974. B.S. with honors, McGill U., 1947, M.S., 1951, Ph.D. in Biochemistry, 1953. Research asst. Columbia, 1953-55, asso. in biochemistry, 1958-59, asst. prof., 1959-60; asso. prof. biochemistry and exptl. medicine McGill U., 1960-66, prof., 1967-95; prof. emeritus, 1995—; prof. ob-gyn. McGill U., 1976-95; dir. endocrine lab. Royal Victoria Hosp., Montreal, Que., 1965-95, dir. research inst., 1982-85; mem. endocrinology and metabolism grants com. Med. Rsch. Coun. Can., 1967-71, regional dir. for Que., 1993-95; vis. prof. endocrinology U. Vt., 1964; cons. in field; Joseph Price orator, 1982, Am. OB-GYN Soc.; mem. steering com. Pharm. Mfg. Assn. Med. Rsch. Coun. Can. Partnership, 1993—; Med. Rsch. Coun. Can. dir. for McGill U., 1993-95. Co-editor: Chemical and Biological Aspects of Steroid Conugation, 1970; Editorial bd.: Endocrinology, 1962; asso. editor: Can. Jour. Biochemistry, 1967-71, Jour. Med. Primatology, 1971; Contbr. articles profl. jours. Mem. bd. govs. McGill U., 1975-78; mem. steering com. European Study Group on Steroid Hormones, 1974—, chmn. steering com., 1983-95, chmn. program com., 1990-91; mem. Dubin Commn. on Inquiry Drugs in Athletes, 1988-90. Recipient McLaughlin medal Royal Soc. Can., 1989. Fellow Chem. Inst. Can., Am. Ob-Gyn. Soc. (hon.), Perinatal Rsch. Soc. Am. (pres. 1976), Soc. Gynecol. Investigation (program chmn. 1980), Endocrine Soc. (publ. com. 1986-89). Home: 239 Kensington Ave 804, Montreal, PQ Canada H3Z 2H1 Office: Royal Victoria Hosp M307, 687 Pine Ave W, Montreal, PQ Canada H3A 1A1

SOLOMON, SEAN CARL, geophysicist, lab administrator; b. L.A., Oct. 24, 1945. BS geophysics, Calif. Inst. Tech., 1966; PhD geophysics, MIT, 1971. From asst. prof. to prof. geophysics Mass. Inst. Tech., Cambridge, 1972-92; dir. dept. terrestrial magnetism Carnegie Instn., Washington, 1992—; vis. scientist Lunar Sci. Inst., 1975, Jet Propulsion Lab., 1978; guest investigator Woods Hole Oceanographic Inst., 1979-92; vis. faculty Inst. Geophysics and Planetary physics, dept. earth and space scis., UCLA, 1982-83; Roland and Jane Blumberg vis. prof. planetary scis. U. Tex., Austin, 1988; vis. assoc. divsn. geol. and planetary scis. Calif. Inst. Tech., 1990-91; mem. various groups, teams, coms. NASA, 1974—, earthquake hazards reduction program peer review panel U.S. Geol. Survey, 1975, 85; lunar and planetary sci. coun. Univs. Space Rsch. Assn., 1978-80, 91-93; tech. review panel, geophysics review panel Dept. Def., 1981-86; chmn. steering com. space sci. working group Assn. Am. Univs., 1984-91; review panelist NSF, 1986, 88, 95, 96; chmn. standing com. global seismic network Inc. Rsch. Instns. Seismology, 1987-90; participant numerous oceanographic expeditions, 1967-88. Assoc. editor Proceedings of the Lunar and Planetary Sci. Conf., 1976, 78, Jour. Geophys. Rsch., 1976-78, Physics Earth and Planetary Interiors, 1977, Eos Transactions of Am. Geophys. Union, 1979-81, Geophys. Rsch. Letters, 1986-88; editor Tectonophysics, 1981; edit. bd. Physics and Chemistry of Earth, 1981-85; edit. com. Ann. Review Earth and Planetary Scis., 1993—; contbr. over 150 articles to profl. jours. Grad. fellow NSF, 1966-68, postdoctoral fellow, 1971-72; Fannie and John Hertz Found. fellow, 1968-71; Alfred P. Sloan rsch. fellow, 1977-81; John Simon Guggenheim meml. fellow, 1982-83. Fellow AAAS, Am. Acad. Arts and Scis., Am. Geophys. Union (pres. elect and pres. 1994—, pres. planetology sect. 1984-88, chmn. geophys. monograph bd. 1983-84, numerous coms.); mem. Seismological Soc. Am., Geol. Soc. Am., Am. Astron. Soc. (divsn. planetary scis.), Tau Beta Pi. Office: Carnegie Instn Dept Terrestrial Magnetism 5241 Broad Branch Rd NW Washington DC 20015-1305

SOLOMON, SOLOMON SIDNEY, endocrinologist, pharmacologist, scientist; b. N.Y.C., Dec. 2, 1936; s. Nathan and Irene (Oransky) S.; m. Linda M. Shaw, June 17, 1962 (div. 1980); children: Joan Geller, Rebecca Karen. AB in Chemistry, Harvard U., 1958; MD, U. Rochester, 1962. Intern in internal medicine New Eng. Med. Ctr., Tufts U., Boston, 1963; resident in internal medicine Boston City Hosp., 1964, 65; fellow in endocrinology and metabolism U. Wash. Sch. Medicine, Seattle, 1965-67; teaching fellow Tufts U. and Boston City Hosp., Boston, 1964-65; asst. prof., assoc. prof. then prof. medicine U. Tenn. Sch. Medicine, Memphis, 1969—, assoc. dean for rsch., 1983—, prof. pharmacology, 1986—; chief endocrinology and metabolism VA Med. Ctr., Memphis, 1971—; cons. in field; mem. merit rev. bd. VA Rsch. Svc., Washington, 1978-81. Coeditor: The Lab in Clinical Diagnosis, 1981; contbr. numerous articles and abstracts to profl. jours. Capt. MC, USAF, 1967-69. Harvard Coll. scholar, 1954-58; Whipple scholar, 1959-62; VA and NIH grantee, 1965—. recipient career and devel. award VA Ctrl. Office Rsch. Svc., 1969-71, 1st place for excellence in clin. rsch. Memphis Area Health Industry Couns., 1994. Fellow Am. Coll. Endocrinology; mem. Am. Diabetes Assn. (pres. Tenn. chpt. 1975-76, rsch. com., chmn. metabolism sect. 1982), So. Soc. Clin. Investigation (chmn. metabolism sect. 1975, 88, nominating com. 1989), Endocrine Soc., Am. Fedn. for Clin. Rsch. (counselor south sect. 1976-79), Am. Soc. Clin. Investigation, Cen. Soc. for Clin. Rsch., Am. Soc. Pharmacology and Exptl. Therapy, Fedn. Am. Soc. Exptl. Biology. Jewish. Avocations: antique furniture, history, music, tennis, running. Home: 5196 Longmeadow Dr Memphis TN 38134-4316 Office: VA Med Ctr 1030 Jefferson Ave Memphis TN 38104-2127 *At the risk of being mundane, my philosophy in life has always been to get involved...my motto is "I came to play, not to watch."*

SOLOMON, VITA PETROSKY, artist; b. Phila., Dec. 16, 1916; d. Harry and Rose (Bobrow) Petrosky; m. Charles M. Solomon, Apr. 8, 1941; children: Robert Charles, Henry Andrew, Jon David. Diploma, Moore Inst. Art, 1937; B.F.A., Tyler Sch. Fine Arts, Temple U., 1958, B.S. in Edn, 1958, M.F.A., 1960. tchr. art and art history Cheltenham High Sch.; tchr. art and English Elkins Park Jr. High Sch. Exhibited in group shows at United Soc. Artists, London, Pa. Acad. Fine Art, Phila. Art Mus., Detroit Inst. Art, Butler Inst. Art, Silvermine Guild, Conn., N.A.D., Am. Water Color Soc., Audubon Soc., Royal Acad. Arts, London, Paris Salon, Woodmere Art Gallery, Phila. Art Alliance, Royal Inst. London, Nat. Arts Club, N.Y., Met. Mus. Art , others; represented in permanent collections Nat. Portrait Gallery, Phila. Mus. Art, Fed. Res. Bank, Temple U., U. Pa., Phila. City Hall, Free Library Phila., Phila. Psychiat. Inst., Cheltenham Twp. Adminstrn. Bldg., others, including portraits on commn.; one-artist shows include Phila. Art Alliance, 1953, 54, 58, Red Door Gallery, 1959, 60, 61, Newman Gallery, 1964, Moore Coll. Art, 1974, Suzanne Gross Gallery, 1979. J.F. Lewis traveling fellow Europe, by Moore Inst., 1937; recipient Gross Meml. award Silvermine Guild, 1958, Chandler prize Allied Artists Am., 1960, Nat. Arts Club award, 1974, prizes Moore Inst., 1957, 60, 61, purchase prize Temple U., 1959 (2), 1960, painting prize, 1966, Burdine meml. prize Woodmere Gallery, 1964, painting prize Wharton Art Ctr., 1964, Lowell Painting prize C.L. Wolfe Club, Nat. Arts Club, 1966, Painting prize Silver medal Paris Salon, 1966, award Phila. Watercolor Club, 1973, Benedictine Art award, 1972, Blumenthal prize Cheltenham Art Center, 1973, Jane Peterson medal Audubon Artists, 1975, Eugenia Atwood purchase prize Phila. Print Club, 1975, Eyre medal Phila. Watercolor Club, 1977, Best Figure Painting prize Woodmere Gallery, 1977, Best in Show award Moore Coll. Art, 1980, award of excellence Ariz. Aqueous VII, 1992, 2nd prize Phila. Plastic Show, 1993, Best in Show award Tubac Ctr. Arts, Ariz., 1995, Spl. Recognition & Best of Show So. Ariz. Watercolor Guild, 1997. Mem. Am. Watercolor Soc., Cheltenham Twp. Art Centre (award for best profl. painting 1980, 83, 85), Am. Watercolor Soc., Artists Equity, Phila. Water Color Club (Pennell Meml. prize 1987, 88), Allied Artists Am., Am. Color Print Soc. (prize 1987), Western Fedn. Watercolor Socs. (award of excellence 1991), So. Ariz. Watercolor Guild (Excellence award U. Ariz. 1991, Signature mem. 1992, Past Pres.'s award 1994), So. Ariz. Tubac Ctr. Arts (award of excellence 1991, hon. mention 1993), Phila. Sketch Club (Best in Show award ann. pastel show, hon. mention 1990, 3d prize ann. print show 1993). Home: 200 Locust St Apt 24G Philadelphia PA 19106-3920 also: 6298 N Campbell Ave Tucson AZ 85718-3150

SOLOMON, WILLIAM TARVER, general construction company executive; b. Dallas, Aug. 11, 1942; s. Marion Bryant and Margaret (Moore) S.; m. Gay Ferguson, Feb. 15, 1964; children—William Tarver Jr., Meredith M. BSCE, So. Meth. U., 1965; MBA, Harvard U., 1967. With Austin Industries, Inc., Dallas, 1967—, chmn., pres., CEO, 1970—; chmn. Austin Comml., Inc., Dallas, Brit. Am. Ins. Co., Dallas; bd. dirs. A.H. Belo Corp., Chilton Corp., Fidelity Union Life, Nat. Bank Tex. Immediate past chmn. Dallas Citizens Coun.; bd. dirs. Baylor U. Med. Ctr. Found., Dallas Mus. Art; trustee Southwestern Med. Found., So. Meth. U. Recipient citation of honor Dallas chpt. AIA, 1985, Humanitarian award NCCJ, Dallas, 1982, Champion of Free Enterprise award Associated Builders and Contractors, 1985, Outstanding Alumni award Southern Meth. U., 1988. Mem. ASCE, Young Pres.'s Orgn. (past chmn. Dallas chpt.), Dallas Assembly, Salesmanship Club Dallas, Dallas C. of C. (bd. dirs.). Republican. United Methodist. Home: 3830 Windsor Ln Dallas TX 75205-1743*

SOLOMON, ZACHARY LEON, apparel manufacturing company executive; b. N.Y.C., July 22, 1934; s. Nathan and Rose Solomon; children: Lisa, Michael, Andrew, Romy; m. Susan Phillips. BA, Bklyn. Coll., 1957; MBA, NYU, 1962. Div. mdse. mgr. Abraham & Strauss, Bklyn., 1957-72; v.p., gen. mdse. mgr. Apparel Buying Svcs., Secaucus, N.Y., 1972-73; sr. v.p., gen. mdse. mgr. May Co., L.A., 1974-75, exec. v.p., 1980-82; exec. v.p. The Emporium, San Francisco, 1976-77, pres., 1978-80; exec. v.p. Manhattan Industries, N.Y.C., pres., CEO Perry Ellis, 1983-87; pres. Ellen Tracy Co., N.Y.C., 1987-90; pres., chief exec. officer Associated Merchandising Corp., N.Y.C., 1991—. Trustee Bklyn. Coll., Crown Am. R.E.I.T. Jewish. Office: Associated Merchandising 1440 Broadway New York NY 10018-2301

SOLOMONS, GUS, JR. (GUSTAVE MARTINEZ), choreographer, dancer, writer; b. Boston; s. Gustave Martinez and Olivia Mae. Student, Boston Conservatory of Music, 1956-59; BArch, MIT, 1961; postgrad., Martha Graham Sch., N.Y.C., 1961-66. Dance soloist Martha Graham Co., N.Y.C., 1964-65, Donald McKayle Co., 1961-64, Merce Cunningham Co., N.Y.C., 1965-68; artistic dir. The Solomons Dance Co., N.Y.C., 1972—; dean, artistic dir. Calif. Inst. of the Arts, Valencia, 1976-78; vis. artist-in-residence U. Calif., Santa Cruz, Calif. State U., Long Beach, others; dance panelist Nat. Endowment Arts; various other state art couns., 1983—; assoc. prof. dance numerous colls., univs., including UCLA, Un. Nev.-Las Vegas, Tex. Christian U., York, Simon Fraser, NYU; mem. faculty Tisch Sch. of Arts, 1994—; USIA cons. to Nat. Dance Co., Tanzania, East Africa, 1988, Argentina, 1994. Appearances maj. TV networks, Sta. WGBH-TV, Boston; choreographr for various univs. and dance cos.; writer dance criticism for Village Voice, Dance Mag., others. Recipient numerous grants Nat. Endowment for Arts, 1983—, N.Y. State Coun. on the Arts, 1972—; fellow Nat. Endowment for Arts, 1978-80. Studio: 889 Broadway New York NY 10003-1212 *The content of a good dance is the truth about its maker. Performing it is a confession to the audience. The dancer places himself in the position of ultimate vulnerability each time he performs; it is at once cleansing, fulfilling, and courageous.*

SOLOMONS, MARK ELLIOTT, lawyer, art dealer; b. Buffalo, Mar. 4, 1946; s. Alvin and Trude (Salant) S.; m. Jill E. Kent, Aug. 20, 1978. BA, U. Rochester, 1967; JD, U. Pa., 1970; LLM, George Washington U., 1973. Bar: N.Y. 1971, D.C. 1981. Staff atty. U.S. Dept. Labor, Washington, 1970-73, counsel coal miners benefits, 1973-77, legis. counsel, 1977-80; prin. Kilcullen Wilson & Kilcullen, Washington, 1980-86; ptnr. Arter and Hadden, Washington, 1986—, mem. exec. com., 1989—; guest lectr. law and history SUNY-Stony Brook, 1970-76, U. Mich., 1977-78, Hobart Coll., 1972-76; prin. Coun. for Excellence in Govt., 1991—; co-owner The Frogeye Co. Contr. articles to profl. jours. Vice chair Appellate Advocacy Com., 1994—. Mem. ABA (chair workers compensation and employers liability com. 1987-88, sr. vice chair 1988—, vice chair appellate advocacy com.), Fed. Bar Assn. (chair regulatory com. 1988—), D.C. Bar Assn., N.Y. Bar Assn., Am. Inn of Ct. (master 1991, counselor 1996—). Republican. Office: Arter & Hadden 1801 K St NW Washington DC 20006-1301

SOLOMONSON, CHARLES D., corporate executive; b. 1930; m. Sarah B. Auer, 1952; children: Katherine M., Charles W. B.S., Columbia U., 1954; M.B.A., Harvard U., 1956. With Denver Union Stock Yard Co., 1956-60; sec., asst. treas. G. D. Searle & Co., 1960-68; with Jos. Schlitz Brewing Co., 1968-69, treas., 1968-69; v.p. fin. Fairmont Food Co., Omaha, 1969-73, pres., 1973-74, dir., 1972-75; v.p. fin., treas. Hobart Corp., Troy, Ohio, 1975-77, v.p. fin. and Adminstrn., dir., 1977-79; sr. v.p., chief fin. officer Holiday Corp., Memphis, 1979, dir., 1980-86, exec. v.p., chief fin. and adminstrv. officer, 1981-87; ret. Trustee Nebr. Meth. Hosp., 1973-75, Miami Valley Hosp., Dayton, Ohio, 1977-79, Sta. WKNO-TV-FM, Memphis, 1983-88, Dixon Gallery and Gardens, 1985-88. Episcopalian. Home: 1030 N State St Apt 42H Chicago IL 60610-2837

SOLON, LEONARD R(AYMOND), physicist, educator, consultant; b. White Plains, N.Y., Sept. 11, 1925; s. Morris and Rebecca (Bobrov) S.; BA, Hamilton Coll., 1947; MSc, Rutgers U., 1949; PhD, NYU, 1960; m. Charlotte Rothman, June 30, 1946; children: Miriam Beth, Matthew Benjamin, Emily Lynn. Physicist, Nuc. Devel. Assos., Inc., White Plains, 1950-52; asst. chief, then chief radiation br. AEC, N.Y.C., 1952-60; dir. applied nuc. tech. Tech. Rsch. Group, Inc., Syosset, N.Y., 1960-62; cons. Burns & Roe, N.Y.C. and Servo Corp. Am., Hicksville, N.Y., 1962-64; mgr. R & D Del Electronics Corp., Mt. Vernon, N.Y., 1964-67; founder, exec. v.p., tech. dir. Hadron, Inc., Yonkers, N.Y., 1967-75; dir. bur. radiation control N.Y.C. Dept. Health, 1975-91; lectr., then adj. assoc. prof. N.Y.U. Inst. Environ. Medicine, 1955-93; environ. & radiol. health cons.; prof. health physics U.S. Mcht. Marine Acad., 1963. Served with inf. U.S. Army, 1944-46; ETO. Cert. Am. Bd. Health Physics. Mem. Am. Nuclear Soc., Health Physics Soc., Am. Phys. Soc., N.Y. Acad. Scis., Conf. Radiation Control Program Dirs., AAAS, Radiol. and Med. Physics Soc. N.Y., Phi Beta Kappa. Contbr. articles to profl. jours. Co-patentee: laser photocauterizer used in treatment of detached retina; powering lasers using nuclear sources. Home and Office: 1756 Lakefront Blvd Fort Pierce FL 34982-8003

SOLONE, RAYMOND JOSEPH, advertising executive; b. Chgo., Feb. 6, 1960; s. Arthur Romeo and Florence Marie (Kilgallon) S.; m. Denise Lynn Aaldering, Aug. 20, 1994; children: Caitlin Jean, Mitchell Joseph, Danielle Lynn. BS in Mktg., So. Ill. U., 1982, MS in Orgn. Communications, 1984.

Account mgr. Hill & Knowlton, Santa Clara, Calif., 1984-85, Carlson Assocs., Sacramento, Calif., 1985-87; mktg. communications mgr. Intel Corp., Folsom, Calif., 1987-90; v.p., ptnr. Anderson Solone Inc., Sacramento, 1990—. Bd. dirs. NorCal Ctr. on Deafness, Sacramento, 1986-87; pub. rels. cons. United Way Sacramento, 1985-87. Recipient Award of Excellence-Trademark Communication Arts Mag., 1986, Cert. Excellence Strathmore Graphics Galler, 1992, 1st Place Event Mktg. AdWeek, 1993. Mem. Am. Mktg. Assn. (exec., Bronze award 1990), Sacramento Valley Mktg. Assn., Sacramento Ad Club (Gold award direct mail 1986, Silver award newsletter 1986, Silver award advt. 1986, Delta award direct mail 1988, Silver award sales promotion campaigns 1994). Republican. Roman Catholic. Avocations: skiing, model trains, travel. Office: Anderson Solone Inc Mktg Comm 3100 Fite Cir Ste 101 Sacramento CA 95827-1805

SOLOV, ZACHARY, choreographer, ballet artist; b. Phila., Feb. 15, 1923; s. Carl Nathan and Sima (Silnutzer) S. Student, Littlefield Ballet Sch., 1937-40, U. of the Dance, 1947. Appeared with, Am. Jubilee, N.Y. World's Fair, 1940, tour with, Littlefield Ballet, 1941, Am. Ballet, S.A., 1941; with, Dance Players, summer quarters, New Hope, Pa., 1942, The Lady Comes Across, N.Y. City, 1942, Ballet Theatre, London, 1946; choreographer ballet master, Met. Opera, N.Y. City. Served as staff sgt. A.A.C., 1943-46. Recipient Capezio Dance award, 1952. Office: 200 W 58th St New York NY 10019-1406

SOLOVY, JEROLD SHERWIN, lawyer; b. Chgo., Apr. 10, 1930; s. David and Ida (Wilensky) S.; m. Kathleen Hart; children: Stephen, Jonathan. B.A., U. Mich., 1952; LL.B., Harvard U., 1955. Bar: Ill. 1955. Assoc. Jenner & Block, Chgo., 1955-63, ptnr., 1963—, chmn., 1991—; Chmn. Spl. Commn. on Adminstrn. Justice in Cook County, 1984-91, Ill. Supreme Ct. Spl. Commn. on Adminstrn. of Justice, 1992-93, Criminal Justice Project of Cook County, 1987-91. Active Cook County Jud. Adv. Council, Chgo., 1975-77, 82-89, chmn., 1989-91; trustee U.S. Supreme Ct. Hist. Soc., 1993—. Fellow Am. Coll. Trial Lawyers; mem. ABA, Chgo. Bar Assn., Ill. State Bar. Assn., Am. Law Inst. Clubs: Standard; Lake Shore Country (Chgo.). Office: Jenner & Block Bldg 4400 1 E Ibm Plz Fl 4400 Chicago IL 60611-5698

SOLOW, HERBERT FRANKLIN, film producer, writer; b. N.Y.C., Dec. 14, 1930; s. Morris David and Frances Louise (Birnbaum) S.; children: Jody, Bonnie, Jamie; m. Yvonne Fern, 1996. AB, Dartmouth Coll., 1953. Agt. William Morris Agy., N.Y.C., 1954-58; dir., exec. NBC, N.Y.C., 1958-59, Los Angeles, 1958-60, CBS, Los Angeles, 1961-63; v.p. Desilu Studios, Los Angeles, 1964-69; v.p. prodn. Paramount TV, Los Angeles, 1969; v.p. worldwide prodn. Metro-Goldwyn-Mayer, Los Angeles, 1969-73; pres. Solow Prodn. Co., Los Angeles, 1976-79; v.p. Sherwood Prodns., Los Angeles, 1980-83; ind. producer, writer Los Angeles, 1984—. Mem. Writers Guild Am., Dirs. Guild Am., Acad. Motion Picture Arts and Scis., Acad. TV Arts and Scis.

SOLOW, ROBERT MERTON, economist, educator; b. Bklyn., Aug. 23, 1924; s. Milton Henry and Hannah Gertrude (Sarney) S.; m. Barbara Lewis, Aug. 19, 1945; children: John Lewis, Andrew Robert, Katherine. BA, Harvard U., 1947, MA, 1949, PhD, 1951, DLitt (hon.), 1992; LLD (hon.), U. Chgo., 1967, Brown U., 1972, U. Warwick, 1976, Tulane U., 1983, Dartmouth Coll., 1990; DLitt (hon.), Williams Coll., 1974, Lehigh U., 1977, Wesleyan U., 1982, Boston Coll., 1986, Harvard U., 1992, Colgate U., 1990; DSc (hon.), U. Paris, 1975, U. Geneva, 1982, Bryant Coll., 1988; D of Social Sci. (hon.), Yale U., 1976, U. Mass., Boston, 1989; D Social Sci. (hon.), U. Helsinki, 1990, SUNY, Albany, 1991, U. Glasgow, 1992, Rutgers U., 1994; D honoris causa, U. Chile, 1992; Conservatoire, Nat. des Arts et Mètiers, Paris, 1994; D in Engring., Colo. Sch. Mines, 1996. Mem. faculty MIT, 1949-95, prof. econs., 1958-95, inst. prof., 1973-95, prof. emeritus, 1995—; W. Edwards Deming prof. NYU, 1996-97; sr. economist Coun. Econ. Advisers, 1961-62, cons., 1962-68; cons. RAND Corp., 1952-64; Marshall lectr., fellow commononer Peterhouse, Cambridge (Eng.) U., 1963-64; Eastman vis. prof. Oxford U., 1968-69; overseas fellow Churchill Coll., Cambridge; sr. fellow Soc. Fellows, Harvard U., 1975-89; bd. dirs. Boston Fed. Res. Bank, 1975-80, chmn., 1979-80; active President's Commn. on Income Maintenance, 1968-70, President's Com. on Tech., Automation and Econ. Progress, 1964-65, Carnegie Commn. Sci., Tech. and Govts., 1988-93, Nat. Sci. Bd., 1994—. Author: Linear Programming and Economic Analysis, 1958, (with R. Dortman, P. Samuelson) Capital Theory and the Rate of Return, 1963, The Sources of Unemployment in the United States, 1964, Growth Theory, 1970, Price Expectations and the Behavior of the Price Level, 1970, (with M. Dertouzos, R. Lester) Made in America, 1989, The Labor Market as a Social Institution, 1990, (with F. Hahn) A Critical Essay on Modern Macroeconomic Theory, 1995, Learning from "Learning by Doing", 1997. Bd. dirs., mem. exec. com. Nat. Bur. Econ. Rsch.; trustee Inst. for Advanced Study, Princeton U., 1972-78, Woods Hole Oceanographic Inst., 1988—, Alfred P. Sloan Found., 1992—, Resources for the Future, 1994—, Urban Inst., 1994—, German Marshall Fund of U.S., 1994—. With AUS, 1942-45. Recipient David A. Wells prize Harvard U., 1951, Seidman award in polit. economy, 1983, Nobel prize in Econs., 1987; fellow Ctr. Advanced Study Behavioral Scis., 1957-58, trustee, 1982-95, chmn., 1987-95. Fellow Am. Acad. Arts and Scis., Brit. Acad. (corr.); mem. AAAS (v.p. 1970), Am. Philos. Soc., Nat. Acad. Scis. (coun. 1977-80, 95), Acad. dei Lincei, Order Pour le merite (Germany), Am. Econ. Soc. (exec. com. 1964-66, John Bates Clark medal 1961, v.p. 1968, pres. 1979), Econometric Soc. (pres. 1964, mem. exec. com.). Home: 528 Lewis Wharf Boston MA 02110-3920 Office: MIT Dept Econs Cambridge MA 02139

SOLOWAY, ALBERT HERMAN, medicinal chemist; b. Worcester, Mass., May 29, 1925; s. Bernard and Mollie (Raphaelson) S.; m. Barbara Berkowicz, Nov. 29, 1953; children: Madeleine Rae, Paul Daniel, Renee Ellen. Student, U.S. Naval Acad., 1945-46; BS, Worcester Poly. Inst., 1948; PhD, U. Rochester, 1951. Postdoctoral fellow Nat. Cancer Inst. at Sloan-Kettering Inst., N.Y.C., 1951-53; research chemist Eastman Kodak Co., Rochester, N.Y., 1953-56; asst. chemist Mass. Gen. Hosp., Boston, 1956-61, asso. chemist, 1961-73; asso. prof. med. chemistry Northeastern U., Boston, 1966-68, prof. medicinal chemistry, chmn. dept., 1968-71, prof. medicinal chemistry and chemistry, chmn. dept. medicinal chemistry and pharmacology, 1971-74; dean Coll. Pharmacy and Allied Health Professions, 1975-77; dean Coll. Pharmacy Ohio State U., Columbus, 1977-88, prof. medicinal chemistry, 1977-97, Kimberly prof. pharmacy, 1997—. Author rsch. in medicinal chemistry, boron neutron caputre therapy of cancer. Recipient Disting. Achievements in Boron Sci. award Boron USA, 1994. Fellow AAAS, Acad. Pharm. Soc.; mem. Am. Chem. Soc., Am. Assn. Coll. Pharmacy, Am. Assn. Cancer Research, Am. Assn. Pharm. Sci., Am. Nuclear Soc. Office: Ohio State U 500 W 12th Ave Columbus OH 43210-1214

SOLOWAY, DANIEL MARK, lawyer; b. Buffalo, Jan. 21, 1959; s. Sol Murray and Shirley (Prashker) S.; m. Natalie Ann-Marie Chin, June 10, 1989; children: Rachel Ann, Rebecca Leigh. BA cum laude, SUNY, Buffalo, 1982; JD with hons., Fla. State U., 1985. Bar: Fla. 1985, U.S. Dist. Ct. (no. dist.) Fla. 1985, (mid. dist.) Fla. 1995, (so. dist.) Ala. 1986, U.S. Ct. Appeals (11th cir.) 1985, U.S. Supreme Ct. 1989; cert. in civil trial law. Law clk. Circuit Judge, Tallahassee, 1983-84, Douglass, Davey, Cooper & Coppins, Tallahassee, 1984-85; ptnr. McKenzie & Soloway, Pensacola, Fla., 1985—. Author: Criminal Justice: An Analysis Toward Reform, 1981; contbr. articles to profl. jours.; editor Escambia-Santa Rosa Bar Assn. newsletter, 1989-90. Profl. adv. bd. N.W. Fla. Epilepsy Soc., Pensacola, 1989—; speaker on AIDS, State of Fla. Dept. HRS, 1988—; mem. Escambia County Human Rels. Commn., 1996—. Recipient Pro Bono Svc. award Escambia-Santa Rosa Bar, 1989-90, Pro Bono Svc. Pres.'s award Fla. Bar, 1990. Mem. ABA, Assn. Trial Lawyers Am., Escambia-Santa Rosa Bar Assn. (editor newsletter 1989-90), Acad. Fla. Trial Lawyers (speaker 1993—), Nat. Orgn. Social Security Claimants Reps.. Democrat. Jewish. Avocation: writing. Office: McKenzie & Soloway 905 E Hatton St Pensacola FL 32503-3931

SOLT, ROBERT LEE, JR., surgeon; b. Bucyrus, Ohio, Dec. 28, 1931; s. Robert Lee and Grace Velma (Rinehart) S.; m. Marilyn J. Smith, June 11, 1955; children: Robert L. III, Timothy S. BS, Ohio State U., 1953, MD, 1957. Diplomate Am. Bd. Surgery. Intern White Cross Hosp., Columbus, Ohio, 1957-58; resident White Cross Hosp. (name now Riverside Meth. Hosp.), Columbus, Ohio, 1958-62; pvt. practice Bucyrus, 1962—. Contbr. articles to profl. jours. Fellow ACS, Am. Acad. of Disability Evaluating Physicians; mem. Ohio State Med. Assn., AMA. Home and Office: 1401 Home Circle Dr Bucyrus OH 44820-3441

SOLTANOFF, JACK, nutritionist, chiropractor; b. Newark, Apr. 24, 1915; s. Louis and Rose (Yomteff) S.; m. Esther Katcher, Sept. 29, 1939; children: Howard, Ruth C. Soltanoff Jacobs, Hillory Soltanoff Seaton. N.M.D. Mecca Coll. Chiropractic Medicine, 1938, U.S. Sch. Naturopathy and Allied Scis., 1951; D.Chiropractic, Chiropractic Inst. N.Y., 1956; postgrad. Atlantic States Chiropractic Inst., 1962-63, Nat. Coll. Chiropractic, 1964-65; PhD, diplomate in nutrition Fla. Natural Health Coll., 1982. Gen. practice chiropractic medicine, cons. in nutrition, N.Y.C., 1956-75, West Hurley, N.Y. and Singer Island, Fla., 1975—; lectr., cons. in field. Author: Natural Healing; pub. Warner Books; contbr. articles to profl. jours. Syndicated newspaper columnist. Fellow Internat. Coll. Naturopathic Physicians; mem. Am. Chiropractic Assn., Internat. Chiropractic Assn., Brit. Chiropractic Assn., N.Y. Acad. Scis., Am. Council on Diagnosis and Internal Disorders, Council on Nutrition, Ethical Culture Soc. Unitarian. Instrumental in instituting chiropractic care in union contracts for mems. of Teamsters Union. Home: 25 Holiday Dr West Hurley NY 12491 also: PO Box 239 West Hurley NY 12491 Office: 948 State Route 28 Kingston NY 12401-7213

SOLTERO-HARRINGTON, LUIS RUBÉN, surgeon, educator; b. San Juan, P.R., Sept. 4, 1925; s. Augusto Rafael Soltero and Anna Lila Harrington; m. Alice Joyce Carpenter, Apr. 24, 1958; children: Luis Ruben, Kathleen Ann, Susan Joyce, Robert Richard, Sharon Theresa. BS in Agr., U. P.R., Rio Piedras, 1945; BM, MD, Northwestern U., Chgo., 1949. Diplomate Am. Bd. Surgery, Nat. Be. Med. Examiners, P.R. Rd. Med. Examiners. Intern Michael Reese Hosp., Chgo., 1949-50; resident in gen. surgery Aguadilla (P.R.) Dist. Hosp., 1950-51; resident in gen. surgery, instr. Baylor U. Coll. Medicine and Affiliated Hosps., Houston, 1954-59; resident in gen. surgery Jefferson Davis, VA and M.D. Anderson Hosps., Houston, 1954-57; resident in pediatric, thoracic and cardiovasc. surgery St. Luke's-Tex. Children's Hosp., Houston, 1957-59; asst. prof. surgery U. P.R. Sch. Medicine, 1960-64, assoc. clin. prof., 1972-73, assoc. clin prof., 1973—, in charge devel. heart surgery program, 1960-64, dir. surgery residency tng. program, 1961-64; pvt. practice, San Juan, P.R., 1959—; prof. surgery U. del Caribe Sch. Medicine, Cayey, P.R., 1981—; cons. in cardiovasc. and thoracic surgery Med. Examing Bd. P.R., San Juan, 1989; chief thoracic and cardiovasc. surgery Tchrs. Hosp., San Juan, from 1959; dir. surgery residency tng. program Univ. Hosp., Rio Piedras, from 1961; cons. in thoracic and cardiovasc. surgery San Juan City Hosp., 1962—, cons. in surgery, 1964—; cons. in surgery Presbyn. Hosp., 1972—, Mimiya's Hosp., 1987—; cons. in thoracic and cardiovasc. surgery Indsl. Hosp., San Juan, 1975—, Hosp. Met., 1982—, Clinic Fernández García, 1983—; chief surgery Ruiz Arnau Hosp., Bayamon, P.R., 1978—; asst. dir. ICU, Hosp. del Maestro, 1987—; bd. dirs. Rsch. Found. Cardiovasc. Surgery Tex., 1984—, Am. Cancer Soc., 1974; mem. Nat. Adv. Cun. Mended Hearts, Inc., 1969. Contbr. articles to med. jours.; patentee partial occlusion vascular clamp to be used in small blood vessels; inventor respirator for infants based on electronic equipment. Capt., M.C., USAF, 1953-54. Recipient award for outstanding work in cardiovasc. surgery Lions Club, Hato Rey, 1961. Fellow Am. Acad. Pediat., Am. Coll. Legal Medicine (assoc.); mem. AMA (physician recognition award 1986); mem. Denton A. Cooley Cardiovasc. Surg. Soc., Michael E. De Bakey Internat. Cardiovasc. Soc., Pan Am. Med. Assn. (coun. pediatric surgery), P.R. Soc. Cardiology, Am. Heart Assn., P.R. Hear Assn., Phi Chi. Avocations: travel, horticulture, bridge. Office: 400 Domenech Ave Ste 502 San Juan PR 00918

SOLTI, SIR GEORG, conductor; b. Budapest, Hungary, Oct. 21, 1912; naturalized Brit. citizen, 1972; s. Mor Stern and Theres (Rosenbaum) S.; m. Hedi Oechsli, Oct. 29, 1946; m. Anne Valerie Pitts, Nov. 11, 1967; 2 daus. Ed., Budapest Music High Sch.; MusD (hon.), Leeds U., 1971, Oxford U., 1972, DePaul U., Yale U., 1974, Harvard U., 1979, Furman U., 1983, Sussex U., 1983, London U., 1986, Rochester U., 1987, Bologna (Italy) U., 1988, Roosevelt U., Chgo., 1990, U. Durham, 1995. Music dir. Chgo. Symphony Orch., 1969-91, music dir. laureate, 1991—. Mus. asst. Budapest Opera House, 1930-39, pianist, Switzerland, 1939-45; gen. music dir. Munich (Germany) State Opera, 1946-52, Frankfurt (Germany) City Opera, 1952-60; mus. dir. Royal Opera House Covent Garden, London, 1961-71, Orchestre de Paris, 1972-75; prin. condr. and artistic dir. London Philharm., 1979-83; condr. emeritus London Philharm., 1983-90, music dir. laureate Royal Opera House Covent Garden, London, 1992—; pianist Concours Internat., Geneva, 1942; guest condr. various orchs. including N.Y. Philharm., Vienna Philharm., Berlin Philharm., London Symphony, Bayerischer Rundfunk, Norddeutscher Rundfunk, Salzburg, Edinburgh, Glyndebourne, Ravinia and Bayreuth Festivals, Vienna State, Met. Opera; condr. concert tours with Chgo. Symphony to Europe, 1971, 74, 78, 81, 85, 89, 90, Chgo. Symphony to Japan, 1977, 86, 90, Chgo. Symphony to Australia, 1988; artistic dir. Salzburg Easter Festival and Whitsun Concerts, 1992-93; prin. guest condr. Paris Opera Bicentennial Tour, 1976, rec. artist for London Records. Recipient 31 Grammys, Lifetime Achievement Grammy award, 1996, Gold medal Royal Philharm. Soc., Gt. Britain, 1992, honored by John F. Kennedy Ctr. for Performing Arts, Washington, for lifetime achievement in music. Hon. fellow Royal Coll. Music (London). Office: care Chgo Symphony Orch 220 S Michigan Ave Chicago IL 60604-2501

SOLTYS, JOHN JOSEPH, lawyer; b. Portsmouth, Va., Feb. 4, 1942; s. John J. Sr. and Antoinette N. Soltys; children: John J. III, Amy Elaine. BS, USCG Acad., 1963; JD, Willamette U., 1970. Bar: Wash. 1970, U.S. Dist. Ct. (we. and ea. dists.) Wash. 1970. From assoc. to sr. ptnr. Karr, Tuttle, Seattle, 1970-89; sr. ptnr. Cozen & O'Connor, Seattle, 1989—. Lt. (j.g.) USCG, 1963-67. Mem. Wash. Def. Trial Lawyers (pres. 1986-87), Fedn. Ins. & Corp. Counsel. Avocations: fishing, hunting, soccer, gardening. Office: Cozen & O'Connor 1201 3rd Ave Ste 5200 Seattle WA 98101-3071

SOLURSH, LIONEL PAUL, psychiatrist; b. Toronto, Ont., Can., Jan. 14, 1936; came to U.S., 1986, naturalized, 1994; s. Coleman Bernard and Zelma Dorothy (Singer) S.; m. Marcia Persin (div.); children: Fern, Susan, Marc; m. Diane Sue Mullenax; children: Lia, Janine. MD, U. Toronto, 1959, diploma in psychiatry, 1962. Diplomate Am. Bd. Sexology; bd. cert. sex educator and clin. supr. Asst. prof. U. Toronto, 1965-73; staff psychiatrist Toronto Western Hosp., 1966-80, assoc. head psychiatry, 1973-79; outpatient psychiatrist Toronto East Gen. and Orthop. Hosp., 1980-86; assoc. prof. psychiatry U. Toronto, 1974-86; cons. psychiatrist Augusta (Ga.) Correctional Med. Inst. (name changed to Augusta State Med. Prison 1996), 1990—, chief psychiat. cons., 1992-96; dir. PTSD out-patient psychiatry VA Med. Ctr., Augusta, 1986-95, med. dir. SIPU/PTSD rehab. unit, 1991-95, med. dir. PTSD treatment team, 1995—; prof. psychiatry and health behavior Med. Coll. of Ga., Augusta, 1986—; assoc. fellow Am. Coll. Sexology, 1995—; cons. Ga. Regional Hosp., Augusta, Augusta Area Cmty. Mental Health Ctr., 1995-96; spkr. in field; telepsychiatry cons. Med. Coll. Ga. Author: (audiotape) Human Sexuality, 1967, 71, 95, (videotape) Art, Symbolism & Mental Health, 1991; contbr. chpts. to books and book revs. and more than 148 papers to profl. jours. Named R.S. McLaughlin Traveling fellow, 1966, Outstanding Young Canadian, 1974, Minister of Health Gold medalist U. Toronto, 1962. Fellow Am. Orthopsychiat. Assn., Am. Psychiat. Assn., Am. Acad. Clin. Sexologists, Royal Coll. Physicians; mem. Am. Acad. Psychiatrists in Alcoholism & Addictions, AMA, Can. Psychiat. Assn., Internat. Soc. for Traumatic Stress Studies, Am. Assn. Sex Educators, Counselors and Therapists. Jewish. Avocations: photography, scuba diving, travel, performing arts, cyberspace touring. Office: VA Med Ctr 1 Freedom Way Augusta GA 30904-6258

SOLYMOSY, EDMOND SIGMOND ALBERT, international marketing executive, retired army officer; b. Budapest, Pest, Hungary, Sept. 3, 1937; came to U.S., 1949; s. Sigmond Ladislas and Gabrielle (Lindelof) S.; m. Mary Ellen Via, Sept. 9, 1961; children: Edmond S.A. Jr., Stephan G., Philip A. BSME, Tex. A&M U., 1960, BBA, 1961, MBA, 1970; postgrad., Mich. U., 1985, Harvard U., 1991. Commd. 2d lt. U.S. Army, 1961, advanced through grades to gen., 1985; student Nat. Def. U., Washington, 1980-81; comdr. 1st Air Def. Arty. Brigade, Ft. Bliss, Tex., 1981-83; chief of staff U.S. Army Air Def. Ctr., Ft. Bliss, 1983; dir. Human Resources Directorate, Hdqrs. Dept. Army, Washington, 1983-85; dep. comdr. U.S. Army Community and Family Support Ctr., Alexandria, Va., 1985-86; chief of staff U.S. Army I Corps, Ft. Lewis, Wash., 1986-88; chief exec. U.S. Office of Def. Coop., Athens, Greece, 1988-91; ret., 1991; pres. Global Project Mgmt., Houston, 1991—; advisor Sec. of Army Panel, Washington, 1983-86, Helenic-Am. C. of C., Athens, 1988-91; bd. dirs. Am. Ikarus Inc., Maxoil, Inc.; hon. consul Republic of Hungary; chmn. Houston Com. on Fgn. Rels. Author: Continental Economic Alliances, 1981. Sponsor Spl. Olympics, Ft. Lewis, 1986; advisor Mil. Mus., Ft. Lewis, 1986-88; regional v.p. Mediterranean coun. Boy Scouts Am., Athens, 1988-91; mem. devel. com. Tex. A&M U., College Station, 1991, advisor Ctr. for Internat. Bus.; mem. bd. advisors Mosher Inst. for Internat. Policy Studies; mem. Mil. Com., Houston.; bd. dirs. Tex. A&M U. Rsch. Found. Decorated D.S.M., Def. D.S.M., Combat Infantryman's Badge, Airborne Parachutist's Badge, Army Ranger, Legion of Merit (3); recipient U.S. and Vietnamese awards for heroism, Greek Disting. Svc. award, 1991. Mem. Assn. U.S. Army (Svc. to Soldiers award 1985), VFW, Armed Forces YMCA (chmn. com. 1982, Nat. Vol. of Yr. award 1983), Internat. Propeller Club (Greece advisor 1989), Kiwanis Club Houston, Hungarian Knights Hospitaller of Order of St. John. Republican. Lutheran. Avocations: sports, jogging, sailing, fishing, hunting. Home: 2438 Stanmore Dr Houston TX 77019-3424 Office: Global Project Mgmt PO Box 27253 Houston TX 77227-7253

SOLYMOSY, HATTIE MAY, writer, publisher, storyteller, educator; b. Kew Gardens, N.Y., Apr. 1, 1945; d. Julius and Sylvia Becky (Glantz) Fuld; m. Richard Milk, June 30, 1966 (div. Feb. 1974); 1 child, Jared Marc Milk.; m. Abraham Edward Solymosy, Apr. 21, 1974 (separated Aug. 1996). BA, Queens Coll., 1966, MS in Edn., 1973. Cert. tchr., N.Y.C. and N.Y. Actress, model, 1950-60; elem. tchr. N.Y.C. Bd. of Edn., 1966—; owner Ultimate Jewelry, N.Y.C., 1976-80; tutor N.Y.C., 1983-91; children's writer N.Y., 1991—, romance writer, 1993—; owner Hatties' Tales, Cedarhurst, N.Y., 1993; storyteller Mo. flood victims, Okla. Fed. Bldg. bombing victims, various children's hosps.; exec. Hamajama Gifts. Author: (sound recs.) Delancy Dolphin, 1993, Thaddius Thoroughbred, 1993, Willie's War, 1993, Noodles-An Autobiography, 1993, (with Jared Marc Milk) Trapped With The Past, 1993, Thick Slick Tangled Webs, 1993, Cinderella Cockroach, 1993, A Christmas Tale, 1993, Chanukah Tale, 1993, Doc Simon, 1995, Mr. Music, 1996, Women on Film, 1996, Buying a Dream, 1996, Rock and Roll, 1996; owner Cigar Box Factory. Social sec., fundraiser Children's Med. Ctr., N.Y.C., 1969-79; aux. mem. St. John's Hosp., N.Y., 1987—; contbr. children's stories Okla. Bombing, Mo. Flood Victims, Children's Hosps.; assoc. mem. Mus. Natural History. Mem. Romance Writers of Am., Soc. of Children's Writers and Illustrators, Simon Wiesenthal Ctr., World Jewish Congress. Democrat. Jewish. Avocations: music, tennis, movies, gardening, dance. Home: 470 W Broadway Cedarhurst NY 11516-1531 Office: Hatties' Tales and Cigar Box Factory PO Box 24 Cedarhurst NY 11516-0024

SOLZHENITSYN, ALEKSANDR ISAYEVICH, author; b. Kislovodsk, Russia, Dec. 11, 1918; imprisoned under Joseph Stalin for critical comments, 1945-53; exiled to Soviet Cen. Asia, 1953; freed from exile, 1956; expelled from USSR, 1974; arrived back in USSR, 1994; m. Natalya Reshetovskaya, 1940 (div.), remarried, 1956 (div.); m. Natalia Svetlova, 1970; children: Yermolai, Ignat, Stephan. Corr. student in philology, Moscow Inst. History, Philosophy and Lit., 1939-41; degree in math. and physics, U. Rostov, 1941; LittD, Harvard U., 1978. Author: Odin den' Ivana Denisovicha, 1962 (pub. as One Day in the Life of Ivan Denisovich, 1963), Dlia pol'zy dela, 1963 (pub. as For the Good of the Cause, 1964), Sluchai na stantsii Krechetovka/ Matrenin dvor, 1963 (pub. as We Never Make Mistakes, 1963), Etudy i krokhotnye rasskazy, 1964 (pub. as Stories and Prose Poems, 1971, as Prose Poems, 1971, as Matryona's House and Other Stories, 1975), V kruge pervom, 1968 (pub. as The First Circle, 1968; Prix du Meilleur Livre Etranger France 1969), Rakovyi korpus, 1968 (pub. as Cancer Ward, 1968; Prix du Meilleur Livre Etranger France 1969), Le Droits de l'écrivain, 1969, Sobranie sochinenii (6 vols.), 1969-70, Six Etudes, 1971, Avgust chetyrnadtsatogo, 1971 (pub. as August 1914, 1972), Nobelevskaia lektsiia po literature, 1972 (pub. as Nobel Lecture, 1972, as One Word of Truth, 1972), Arkhipelag Gulag (3 vols.), 1973-76 (pub. as The Gulag Archipelago, 1974-78), Prusskie nochi: poema napisannaia v lagere v 1950, 1974 (pub. as Prussian Nights, 1977), Iz-pod glyb, 1974 (pub. as From Under the Rubble, 1975), Mir i nasilie, 1974, Pis'mo vozhdiam Sovetskogo soiuza, 1974 (pub. as Letter to the Soviet Leaders, 1974), A Pictorial Autobiography, 1974, Solzhenitsyn, the Voice of Freedom, 1975, Bodalsia telenok s dubom, 1975 (pub. as The Oak and the Calf, 1980), Lenin v Tsiurikhe, 1975 (pub. as Lenin in Zurich, 1976), Detente: Prospects for democracy and Dictatorship, 1975, America, We Beg You to Interfere, 1975, Amerikanskie rechi, 1975, Warning to the Western World, 1976, A World Split Apart, 1978, Alexander Solzhenitsyn Speaks to the West, 1978, Sobranie sochinenii, 1978, The Mortal Danger, 1980, East and West, 1980, Issledovaniia noveishei russkoi istorii, 1980, Publitsistika: stat'i i rechi, 1981, Krasnoe koleso: povestvovan'e v otmerennykh srokakh Uzel I: Avgust chetyrnadtsatogo, 1983 (pub. as The Red Wheel: A Narrative in Discrete Periods of Time, 1989), Krasnoe koleso: povestvovan'e v otmerennykh srokakh Uzel II: Oktiabr'shestnadtsatogo, 1984, Krasnoe koleso: povestvovan'e v otmerennykh srokakh Uzel III: Mart semnadtsatogo, 1986, Rasskazy, 1990, Kak nam obustroit' Rossiiu, 1990, Krasnoe koleso: povestvovan'e v otmerennykh srokakh Uzel IV: Aprel'semnadtsatogo, 1991, Rebuilding Russia: Toward Some Formulations, 1991, Les Invisibles, 1992, Nashi pliuralisty: otryvok iz vtorogo toma "Ocherkov literaturnoi zhizni", 1992, The Russian Question Toward the End of the Twentieth Century, 1995; (plays) Olen' i shalashovka, 1968 (pub. The Love-Girl and the Innocent, 1969), Svecha na vetru, 1968 (pub. Candle in the Wind, 1973), Pir podebitelei, 1981 (pub. as Victory Celebrations, 1983), Plenniki, 1981 (pub. as Prisoners, 1983), P'esy i kinostsenarii, 1981; editor: Russkii slovar' iazykovogo rasshireniia, 1990. Arty. officer Russian Army, World War II. Recipient Lenin prize nomination, 1964, Nobel prize for lit., 1970, Freedoms Found. award Stanford U., 1976, Templeton Found. prize, 1983. Mem. Am. Acad. Arts and Scis., Hoover Inst. War, Revolution and Peace (hon.).

SOMANI, PETER, human service administrator; b. Chirawah, India, Oct. 31, 1937; came to U.S., naturalized; m. Kamlesh; children: Anita Somani-Richardson, Jyoti, Alok. MD, Vikram U., Ujjain, India, 1960; PhD, Marquette U., Milw., 1965. Demonstrator pharmacology All India Inst. Med. Scis., New Delhi, 1960-62, external examiner PhD program, 1974, 79, 85, 86; instr. dept. pharmacology Marquette U. Sch. Medicine, Milw., 1965-66, asst. prof. dept. pharmacology, 1966-69; assoc. prof. dept. pharmacology Med. Coll. Wis., Milw., 1969-71, assoc. clin. prof. pharmacology, 1971-74; head cardiovasc. pharmacology Abbott Labs., North Chgo., Ill., 1971-72; attending physician Jackson Meml. Hosp., dir. hypertension clinic, 1978-80; attending physician U. Miami Hosps. and Clinics; dir. clin. pharmacology Med. Coll. Ohio, 1980—; dir. of health Ohio Dept. Health, Columbus, 1992—; cons. Geigy Pharms., Arduously, N.Y., 1969-70, Abbott Labs. North Chgo., 1970-71; vis. prof. Med. U. Szeged, Hungary, 1971, Christian Med. Coll., Vellore, India, 1980; Pfizer vis. prof. clin. pharmacology U. Miss. Sch. Medicine, Jackson, 1982; organizer Symposium on Antiarrhythmic Drugs, 1983; UN vis. prof. TOKTEN program Coun. Scientific and Indsl. Rsch., India, 1987; external examiner U. Western Ontario, Can., 1988. Mem. editl. bd. jour. Pharmacology and Exptl. Therapeutics, 1978, Jour. Cardiovasc. Pharmacology, 1979, Internat. Jour. Clin. Pharmacology and Biopharmacy, 1979; spkr. in field; contbr. articles to profl. jours. Achievements include research in cardiovasc. pharmacology, especially in the areas of beta-blockers, coronary circulation and myocardial hemodynamics, and antiarrhythmic drugs, regional blood flow measurements by the micro sphere techniques, cardiovasc. pharmacology and toxicology of antiarrhythmic drugs, devel. of an animal model to study the pathophysiology and pharmacology or hypertension-diabetes. Office: Ohio Dept Health PO Box 118 246 N High St Columbus OH 43266-0118

SOMASUNDARAN, PONISSERIL, surface and colloid engineer, applied science educator; b. Pazhookara, Kerala, India, June 28, 1939; came to U.S., 1961; s. Kumara Moolayil and Lakshmikutty (Amma) Pillai; m. Usha N., May 25, 1966; 1 child, Tamara. BS, Kerala U., Trivandrum, India, 1958; BE, Indian Inst. Sci., Bangalore, 1961; MS, U. Calif., Berkeley, 1962, PhD, 1964. Rsch. engr. U. Calif., 1964, Internat. Minerals & Chem. Corp., Skokie, Ill., 1965-67; rsch. chemist R.J. Reynolds Industries, Inc., Winston-Salem, N.C., 1967-70; assoc. prof. Columbia U., N.Y.C., 1970-78, prof. mineral engring., 1978-83, La Von Duddleson Krumb prof., 1983—; chmn. Henry Krumb Sch. Chem. Engring., Materials Sci. and Mining Engring., Columbia, U., 1988—, dir. Langmuir Ctr. for Colloids and Interfaces, 1987—; cons. numerous agys., cos., including NIH, 1974, B.F. Goodrich, 1974, NSF, 1974, Alcan, 1981, UNESCO, 1982, Sohio, 1984-85, IBM, 1984, Am. Cyanamd, 1988-89, Duracell, 1988-89, DuPont, 1989, Canmet, 1990-93,

Unilever, 1991—, Engelhard, 1991-94, UoP, 1991-92, Alcoa, 1991-92; mem. panel NRC; chmn. numerous internat. symposia and NSF workshops; mem. adv. panel Bur. Mines Generic Ctr., 1983-91; keynote and plenary lectr. internat. meetings; hon. prof. Ctrl. South U. Tech., China, Brahm Prakash chair in metallurgy and material sci. Indian Inst. Sci., Bangalore, 1990; hon. rsch. advisor Bejing Gen. Rsch. Inst., 1991—. Editor books, including Fine Particles Processing, 1980 (Publ. Bd. award 1980); editor-in-chief Colloids and Surfaces, 1980—; Henry Krumb lectr. AIME, 1988; contbr. numerous articles to profl. publs., patentee in field. Pres. Keralasamajam of Greater N.Y., N.Y.C., 1974-75; bd. dirs. Fedn. Indian Assocs., N.Y.C., 1974—, Vols. in Svc. to Edn. in India, Hartford, Conn., 1974—; mem. planning bd. Village of Piermont, N.Y., 1995—. Recipient Disting. Achievement in Engring. award, AINA, 1980, Antoine M. Gaudin award Soc. Mining Engrs.-AIME, 1983, Achievements in Applied Sci. award 2d World Malayalam Conf., 1985, Robert H. Richards award, AIME, 1986, Arthur F. Taggart award Soc. Mining Engrs.-AIME, 1987, honor award Assn. Indian in Am., 1988, VHP award of Excellence, Ellis Island medal of Honor, 1990, Commendations citation State of N.J. Senate, 1991; named Mill Man of Distinction, Soc. Mining Engrs.-AIME, 1983, Disting. Alumnus award Indian Inst. Sci., Bangalore, 1989, Outstanding Contbns. and Achievement award Cultural Festival India, 1991, Recognition award SIAA, 1992, Asian-Am. Heritage award Asian Am. Higher Edn. Coun., 1994. Fellow Instn. Mining and Metallurgy (U.K.); mem. AICE, NAE, Soc. Mining Engrs. (bd. dirs. 1982-85, Disting. mem. award, also others), Engring. Found. (chmn. bd. 1993-95, chmn. conf. com. 1985-88, bd. exec. com. 1985-88, bd. dirs. 1991—, Frank Aplan award 1992), Am. Chem. Soc., N.Y. Acad. Scis., Internat. Assn. Colloid and Surface Scientists (councillor 1989-92), Indian Material Rsch. Soc. (hon.), Sigma Xi.

SOMBROTTO, VINCENT R., postal union executive; b. N.Y.C., June 15, 1923; s. Raymond and Agnes (McCormick) S.; Feb. 23, 1957; children: Gloria, Vincent, Lisa, Leslie, Jacqueline, Stephen, Mara. Grad. high sch. Letter carrier N.Y.C., 1947-71; br. pres. Nat. Assn. Letter Carriers, N.Y.C., 1971-79; pres. Nat. Assn. Letter Carriers, Washington, 1979—; dir. Fund For Assuring An Ind. Retirement; v.p., mem. exec. council AFL-CIO; bd. dirs. Ctr. Nat. Policy; chmn. Employee Thrift Adv. Council of Fed. Retirement Thrift Investment Bd. Bd. adv. Sidney Harmon Program on Tech. Pub. Policy and Human Devel., Harvard U.; adv. com. Nat. Assembly Vol. Health and Social Welfare Orgns.; nat. v.p. Muscular Dystrophy Assn.; mem. adv. council Am. Diabetes Assn.; mem. President's Commn. Employment of Handicapped. Served with AUS, 1943-45. Mem. Fed. Adv. Council Occupational Safety and Health, Postal Telephone and Telegraphy Internat. (mem. exec. council). Office: Nat Assn Letter Carriers 100 Indiana Ave NW Washington DC 20001-2144*

SOMERS, ANNE RAMSAY, medical educator; b. Memphis, Sept. 9, 1913; d. Henry Ashton and Amanda Vick (Woolfolk) Ramsey; m. Herman Miles Somers, Aug. 31, 1946; children: Sara Ramsay, Margaret Ramsay. BA, Vassar Coll., 1935; postgrad., U. N.C., 1939-40; DSc (hon.), Med. Coll. Wis., 1975. Ednl. dir. Internat. Ladies Garment Workers Union, 1937-42; labor economist U.S. Dept. Labor, 1943-46; rsch. assoc. Haverford Coll., 1957-63; rsch. assoc. indsl. rels. sect. Princeton U., 1964-84; prof. U. Medicine and Dentistry of N.J.-R. Wood Johnson Med. Sch. (formerly Rutgers Med. Sch.), 1971-84, adj. prof., 1984—; adj. prof. geriat. medicine U. Pa. Sch. Medicine, 1990—; mem. Nat. Bd. Med. Examiners, 1983-86; cons. in health econs., health edn., geriats., gerontology, realted areas. Author: Hospital Regulation: The Dilemma of Public Policy, 1969, Health Care in Transition: Directions for the Future, 1971, (with H.M. Somers) Workmen's Compensation: The Prevention, Rehabilitation and Financing of Occupational Disability, 1954, Medicare and the Hospitals, 1967, Doctors, Patients and Health Insurance, 1961, Health and Health Care: Policies in Perspective, 1977, (with N.L. Spears) The Continuing Care Retirement Community: A Significant Option for Long Care?, 1992; editor: (with D.R. Fabian) The Geriatric Imperative: An Introduction to Gerontology and Clinical Geriatrics, 1981. Mem. bd. visitors. Duke U. Med. Ctr., 1972-77, U. Tex. Health Scis. Ctr., Houston, 1980-86. Recipient Elizur Wright award Am. Risk and Ins. Assn., 1962; named to Health Care Hall of Fame, 1993. Fellow Am. Coll. Hosp. Adminstrs. (hon.), Coll. Physicians Phila. (hon.); mem. Inst. Medicine of NAS, Soc. Tchrs. of Family Medicine (hon.), Nat. Acad. Social Ins. Home: Pennswood Vlg # G-205 Newtown PA 18940

SOMERS, GEORGE FREDRICK, biology educator; b. Garland, Utah, July 9, 1914; s. George Fredrick and Elizbuth (Sorenson) S.; m. Beulah Rich Morgan, June 24, 1939; children: Ralph M., Steven J., Gary F. B.S., Utah State U., 1935; B.A., Oxford U., 1938, B.Sc., 1939; Ph.D., Cornell U., 1942. Faculty Cornell U., 1941-51, asso. prof. biochemistry, 1949-51; plant physiologist U.S. Dept. Agr., 1944-51; faculty U. Del., Newark, 1951—; assoc. dir. Del. Agrl. Expt. Sta., 1951-59; assoc. dean Coll. Agr., 1954-59; chmn. dept. biol. scis. U. Del., 1959-71, H. Fletcher Brown prof. biology, 1962-81, emeritus prof., 1981—; vis. prof. U. Philippines, 1958-59. Author: (with J.B. Sumner) Chemistry and Methods of Enzymes, 3d edit, 1953, Laboratory Experiments in Biological Chemistry, 2d edit, 1949; also articles.; Editor: biochem. sect. Chem. Abstracts, 1968-75. Union Pacific scholar, 1930; Rhodes scholar, 1936; Henry Strong Denison fellow, 1939. H.C. fellow AAAS; mem. Am. Assn. Plant Physiology, Bot. Soc. Am., Sigma Xi, Phi Kappa Phi. Research on influence of environ. factors on vitamin C content of vegetables; viscoelasticity in plant tissues as related to cell wall properties; chem. properties of algal cell walls; salt-tolerant plants as food crops. Home: 22 Minquil Dr Newark DE 19713-1312

SOMERS, HANS PETER, lawyer; b. Berlin, Germany, Nov. 11, 1922; came to U.S., 1938; s. Fritz A. and Karoline E. (Neuert) S.; m. Claudia C. Schuette, May 3, 1947; children: Daniel E., Stephen A., Deborah J., Conrad S. B.A., Cornell Coll., 1946; M.A., U. Iowa, 1948; LL.B. magna cum laude, Harvard U., 1951. Bar: Mass. 1951, Pa. 1957. Assoc. Hill & Barlow, Boston, 1951-56; assoc. Morgan, Lewis & Bockius, Phila., 1956-60, ptnr., 1960-88, counsel, 1988—; lectr. law Northeastern U., Boston, 1951-53, Boston U. Law Sch., 1953-55; lectr. Villanova U. Law Sch., Phila., 1959-63; research assoc. Am. Law Inst., Cambridge, Mass., 1955-56. Editor: Harvard Law Rev., 1949-51; contbr. articles to legal jours. Served to 2d lt. AUS, 1943-46, ETO. Mem. ABA (chmn. com. tax sect. 1967-69, real property, probate and trust law 1974-77), Nat. Conf. Lawyers and Corp. Fiduciaries (chmn. 1978-81), Am. Coll. Probate Counsel (mem. editorial bd. dirs. 1976-77), Internat. Acad. of Estate and Trust Law (exec. council 1974-78, 81—). Clubs: Radnor Hunt (Malvern, Pa.) (bd. govs.); Union League (Phila.). Home: 8024 Goshen Rd Newtown Square PA 19073-1122 Office: Morgan Lewis & Bockius 2000 One Logan Sq Philadelphia PA 19103

SOMERS, HAROLD MILTON, economist, educator; b. Toronto, Ont., Can., Sept. 30, 1915; came to U.S., 1937, naturalized, 1947; s. Joseph and Elizabeth (Behr) S.; m. Claire Rosen, June 12, 1939; children: Joan, Margery, Warren. B.Com., U. Toronto, 1937; Ph.D., U. Calif., 1942; student, U. Chgo., 1940; LL.B., U. Buffalo, 1956. Teaching asst. in econs. U. Calif., 1937-39; research asst. govt. fin. U. Chgo., 1940; fellow Social Sci. Research Council, 1940-41; mem. research staff Brookings Instn., summer 1941; teaching fellow in econs. U. Mich., 1941-42, instr. in econs., summer 1942; asst. prof. econs. U. Buffalo, 1942-45, assoc. prof., 1945-46, prof., 1946-61, dean. sch. bus. adminstrn., 1947-61; lectr. U. Buffalo Sch. Law, 1957-59; prof. econs. UCLA, 1961-86, prof. emeritus, 1986—, chmn. dept. econs., 1961-66, dean div. social scis., 1967-70; vis. prof. econs. U. Calif. at Berkeley, summer 1947, Columbia, summer 1954, U. B.C., summer 1953; vis. prof. law Yale Law Sch., 1968; econ. affairs officer in fiscal div. UN, summer 1950, cons., 1950-53; cons. to research div. O.P.A., 1943; arbitrator Fed. Conciliation and Mediation Service, 1950-86, Am. Arbitration Assn., 1955-86, N.Y. State Bd. Mediation, 1952-61, Los Angeles County Employee Relations Commn. Arbitration, 1970-73; cons. U.S. Office Edn., Bur. Higher Edn., 1965-69; mem. Personnel Security bd. AEC, 1957-59; cons. N.Y. State Legis. Com. on Constn., 1957- 58; economist N.Y. State Dept. Commerce, summer 1944, cons., 1944-45; tech. adviser to mayor's full employment com., City of Buffalo, 1945-46, cons. to budget div., 1946-47; chmn. exec. com., fin. subcom. Capital Expenditures Com., 1956-57; chmn. N.Y. State Minimum Wage Bd. for Restaurant Industry, 1956-58; mem seminar adv. com. Fed. Res. Bank, N.Y., 1952; editorial cons. Blakiston Co., Phila., 1947-52; cons. Employment and Youth Opportunities Agy., Los Angeles, 1966, Calif. Adv. Commn. on Tax Reform, 1968. Author: American Policies of Postwar Readjustment (monograph), 1944, Public Finance and National Income, 1949; co-author: Industrial Conflict, 1939, Growth of the American Economy, 1944, rev. edit., 1951, Readings in Business Cycle Theory, 1944, Readings in the Theory of Income Distribution, 1946, Taxation and Business Concentration, 1952, Corporate Tax Problems, 1952, Taxation of Corporate Income in California, 1964, Taxation of Property in California, 1964, Public Finance and Welfare, 1966, A Search for City Revenue, 1968; author monographs The Sales Tax, 1964, Capital Gains, Death and Gift Taxation, 1965; editor: Estate Taxes and Business Management, 1957; editor Western Econ. Jour., 1966-69; editorial bd.: Am. Econ. Rev., 1952-54; contbr.: articles to Ency. Brit. and econ. and law jours. Mem. Am., N.Y. State bar assns., Am. Econ. Assn. (nominating com. 1969, 70), Econometric Soc. (session chmn. 1947, 51, program chmn. 1949), Am. Fin. Assn. (dir. pub. fin. 1969-71), Nat. Tax Assn. (mem. sales tax com. 1975-77, fed. taxation and fin. com. 1981-84), Phi Beta Kappa, Alpha Kappa Psi, Beta Gamma Sigma. Home: 152 N Kenter Ave Los Angeles CA 90049-2730 Office: Dept Econs U Calif Los Angeles CA 90024

SOMERS, JAMES WILFORD, information management company executive; b. Akron, Ohio, Apr. 19, 1951; s. Gilbert N. and Yvonne E. (Thuma) S.; m. Judith Field Smith, Nov. 20, 1986; children: James A., Elizabeth A. BS in Aerospace Engring., U.S. Naval Acad., 1973; MS in Aero. Engring., U.S. Naval Postgrad. Sch., 1974. Commd. ens. USN, 1973, advanced through grades to lt. comdr. select, 1981, resigned, 1981; program mgr. Office Sec. Def. Def. Nuclear Agy., Alexandria, Va., 1978-84, divsn. dir. lethality and target hardening, 1984-86, mem. sr. exec. svc., 1985; dir. staff GRC Internat., Inc./Advanced Tech. Divsn., Vienna, Va., 1986-87, group dir. engring., 1993-94, ops. dir. senser and comml. ops., 1993-94, ops. dir. mission support ops., 1994-95; pres. Info. Mgmt. Group, Great Falls, Va., 1995—. Active various Rep. Campaigns, 1988—. Capt. USNR. Mem. AIAA, Am. Def. Preparedness Assn. Lutheran. Avocations: sailing, skiing. Home: 9123 Maria Ave Great Falls VA 22066 Office: Info Mgmt Group Inc 9893 Georgetown Pike Ste 710 Great Falls VA 22066-2617

SOMERS, JOHN ARTHUR, insurance company executive; b. Cin., Feb. 24, 1944; s. Arthur Edward and Margaret Mary (Netschke) S.; m. Ann-Christin Ahlander, Dec. 28, 1968; children—Monica Ann, Christina Elizabeth, Mark Edward. B.S. in Econs., Villanova U., 1966; postgrad., Sch. Law, U. Conn., 1966-67; M.B.A. in Fin., U. Conn., 1972. Asst. town mgr. Town of Newington, Conn., 1970-72; v.p. Prudential Ins. Co. Am., Newark, 1972-81; sr. v.p. Tchrs. Ins. & Annuity Assn., N.Y.C., 1981—, exec. v.p., 1996—; bd. dirs. Cmty. Preservation Corp., Emigrant Bank, Guardian Life. Roman Catholic. Office: Tchrs Ins & Annuity Assn Am 730 3rd Ave New York NY 10017-3206

SOMERS, LOUIS ROBERT, retired food company executive; b. Pontiac, Mich., Aug. 8, 1926; s. Jay G. and Maggie (Gee) S.; m. Rynda Horinga, July 28, 1950; children: Linda, Laurie. B.S., Mich. State U., 1950. With Kellogg Co., Battle Creek, Mich., 1955-88; controller Kellogg Internat., 1967-70, 72-75; fin. dir. Kellogg Gt. Brit. Ltd., 1970-72; v.p. fin., treas. Kellogg Co., 1975-85, sr. v.p. fin., 1985-88. Trustee Alma Coll., 1982—; bd. dirs. Mich. State U. Devel. Fund, 1983-88; bd. govs. ARC, 1985-92, chmn. audit com.

SOMERS, MELVIN CLAUDE, retired mathematics educator and dean; b. Peacham, Vt., Oct. 9, 1930; s. Claude Bert and Zedena Gertrude (Magoon) S.; m. Ann Elizabeth Watkins, July 25, 1953; children: Roxanna Lynn, Steven Melvin, Sharon Lee. BS, U. Vt., 1953; MS, U. Md., 1968; EdD, Pacific States U., 1974. Cert. secondary tchr., prin., supt., Vt. Tchr., basketball and baseball coach, band dir. Danville (Vt.) H.S., 1956-63; prin. Chelsea (Vt.) H.S., 1964-70; dir. student tchg. Norwich U., Northfield, Vt., 1970-73, dir. continuing edn., 1973-74, dean admissions, 1974-81, dean student affairs, 1981-83, math. and computer prof., 1983-89; sch. evaluator Barre (Vt.) City Schs., 1981. Author: (poetry) Mack's Mountain Verses, 1994. Scoutmaster Boy Scouts Am., Albany, Ga., 1954-55, Chelsea, Vt., 1964; pres. Chelsea Fish and Game Club, 1973, Chelsea Hist. Soc., 1975, Red Mitten Crafts, Northfield, 1988; chmn. bd. dirs. Plainfield Health Clinic, 1993-94. Capt. USAF, 1953-55. Fellow Massey Ferguson, 1963, Ford Found., 1969. Mem. Am. Legion, St. Andrew's Soc. Vt. (pres.), Elks, Masons (past master). Republican. Avocations: gardening, writing poetry, antique trunk restoration, crafts. Home: RR 1 Box 98B West Danville VT 05873-9801

SOMERSET, HAROLD RICHARD, retired business executive; b. Woodbury, Conn., Sept. 25, 1935; s. Harold Kitchener and Margaret Mary (Roche) S.; m. Marjory Deborah Ghiselin, June 22, 1957 (dec. Jan. 1984); children: Timothy Craig, Paul Alexander; m. Jean MacAlpine DesMarais, Jan. 2, 1985; stepchildren: Cheryl Lyn DesMarais, James Fenelon DesMarais. B.S., U.S. Naval Acad., 1957; B.C.E., Rensselaer Poly. Inst., Troy, N.Y., 1959; LL.B., Harvard U., 1967. Bar: Mass. 1967, Hawaii 1973. Commd. ensign U.S. Navy, 1957, advanced through grades to lt., 1961; service in U.S. and Hawaii; resigned, 1964; with firm Goodwin, Procter & Hoar, Boston, 1967-72; corp. counsel Alexander & Baldwin, Inc., Honolulu, 1972-74, v.p., gen. counsel, 1974-78, group v.p.-sugar, 1978-79, exec. v.p.-agr., 1979-84; with Calif. & Hawaiian Sugar Co., San Francisco, 1984-93, exec. v.p., chief operating officer, 1984-88, pres., chief exec. officer, 1988-93, bus. cons., 1994—; bd. dirs. Longs Drug Stores Corp., Brown and Caldwell, PLM Internat., Inc., Cornnuts, Inc. Trustee San Francisco Nat. Maritime Mus., Carquinez Strait Preservation Trust (mgmt. com., pres.). Mem. St. Mary's Coll. Sch. Edn. (adv. coun.). Home and Office: 19 Donald Dr Orinda CA 94563-3646

SOMERSON, ROSANNE, artist; b. Phila., June 21, 1954; d. Herbert M. and Ileana V. (Reiver) S.; m. Alphonse Mattia, Nov. 9, 1947; 1 child, Isabel Giani. BFA, R.I. Sch. Design, 1976. Mem. staff Fine Woodworking mag., 1976-81; furniture designer and builder, 1978—; mem. faculty grad. furniture design program RISD, Providence, 1985—, prof., head program, 1992—, head furniture design dept., 1995—; instr. Boston Archtl. Ctr., 1981; teaching fellow continuing edn. sculpture and design in wood Harvard U., 1977-79; lectr. in field. Exhibited works at Brockton (Mass.) Art Mus., 1981, 84, 86, Workbench Gallery, N.Y.C., 1982, 83, Hudson River Mus., 1983, Pitts. Ctr. for Arts, 1984-85, Susan Carr Gallery, Houston, 1985, Ester Saks Gallery, Chgo., 1985, Soc. Arts and Crafts, Boston, 1986, 89, Mus. Art of RISD, 1987, Sothebys, N.Y.C., 1987, Am. Craft Mus., N.Y.C., 1986-89, Mus. Fine Arts, Boston, 1989, Oakland (Calif.) Mus., 1990, Musee des Arts Decoratifs, Paris, Oslo Mus. Applied Art, Slovak Nat. Gallery, Peter Joseph Gallery, N.Y.C., 1991-95, Pritain and Eames Gallery, N.Y.C., 1984-94, also others. Address: 771 Division Rd Westport MA 02790-1350

SOMERSTEIN, AURORA ABRERA, preschool administrator, educator; b. Manila, Feb. 17, 1943; d. Bernardo Paez and Rosalia (Sityar) Abrera; m. Jules Leon Somerstein, Dec. 10, 1967 (div. July 1995); children: Joseph, Sandra, Marc. BA in English, U. Philippines, Manila, 1964; MA in English Edn., NYU, 1978, MA in Elem. Edn., 1987; postgrad., U. Pitts., Oxford (Eng.) U., 1964-66, 86. Cert. tchr., N.Y. Instr. U. Pitts., 1965-66, U. of the East, Manila, 1968-69; tchr. Am. Internat. Sch., Manila, 1966, Domenec High Sch., Pitts., 1967-68; substitute tchr. Lakeland and Peekskill Sch. Dist., N.Y., 1975-77; exec. dir. Internat. Pre-Sch. Ctr., Inc., N.Y.C., 1977—; instr. Bd. Coop. Ednl. Svcs., N.Y.C., 1989—; exec. sec. Ctr. Ednl. TV, Manila, 1964; sec. NYU, 1973-74, UN, N.Y.C., 1975; producer, interviewer Continental Cablevision, N.Y.C., 1984—; child devel. adviser Westchester County, N.Y.C., 1989—; cons. Hudson Valley Export-Import, Inc., N.Y.C., 1988-92. Vol. Philippine Band of Mercy, Manila, 1963-93. Mem. Nat. Child Care Assn., Nat. Assn. Edn. Young Children, Nat. Coun. Tchrs. English, N.Y. Child Care Assn., Assn. Childhood Edn. Internat., Child Care Coun. Westchester, Manitoga, Peekskill/Cortlandt C. of C. (bd. dirs. 1989-92). Democrat. Avocations: reading, photography, music, travel, piano. Office: Internat Pre-Sch Ctr Inc PO Box 187 Buchanan NY 10511-0187

SOMERVILLE, DAPHINE HOLMES, elementary education educator; b. Clinton, N.C., Jan. 19, 1940; d. George Henry and Mamie Estelle (Streeter) Holmes; m. Kalford Burton Somerville, Dec. 26, 1970 (div. Sept. 1992); 1 child, Daria Lynn. AA, Blackburn Coll., 1959, BA, 1961; MS in Edn., Hofstra U., 1967; postgrad., Columbia U., 1971. Permanent teaching cert. common br. subjects grades 1-8. Tchr. East Islip (N.Y.) Sch. Dist., 1961—; mem., instr. Outcome Based/Mastery Learning/Excellence in Learning Com., East Islip, 1984-89; mentor East Islip Sch. Dist., 1987-88, mem. sch. improvement team, 1989-91, staff devel. com., 1992-96, chair Ptnrs. in Edn., 1991—. Co-author: (booklet) Baptist Training Union Study Guide, 1976; founder, co-author: (tutoring program) Adopt-A-School Child/Family, 1990. Mem. Bay Shore (N.Y.) Civic Assn. and Bay Shore Pub. Schs. Task Force for the Advancement of Equality of Ednl. Opportunity, 1967-69; sec. Islip Town NAACP, Bay Shore, 1965-90; mem. First Bapt. Ch., Bay Shore, 1951—, trustee, 1972-90; dir. Bapt. Tng. Union, 1974-81. Recipient Cmty. Svc. award Town Bd.-Town of Islip, Suffolk County, 1982, Br. Recognition award Islip Town NAACP, 1987, Disting. Svc. award L.I. Region NAACP, 1993, Dedicated Svc. award Ptnrs. in Edn. First Bapt. Ch. of Bayshore, 1995. Mem. Nat. Coun. Negro Women (life, ednl. involvement award 1993, African-Am. educator's award 1997), East Islip Tchrs. Assn. (past bldg. rep.), N.Y. State United Tchrs. Democrat. Avocations: theater, tennis, reading, working with children, traveling. Home: 130 Carman Rd Dix Hills NY 11746-5648 Office: J F Kennedy Elem Sch Woodland Dr East Islip NY 11730

SOMERVILLE, MARGARET ANNE GANLEY, law educator; b. Adelaide, Australia, Apr. 13, 1942; d. George Patrick and Gertrude Honora (Rowe) Ganley; divorced. A.u.A. (pharm.), U. Adelaide, 1963; LLB (hon. I), U. Sydney, 1973; D.C.L., McGill U., 1978; LLD (hon.), U. Windsor, Ont., 1992, Macquarie, NSW, 1993, St. Francis Xavier, Antigoush, Nova Scotia, 1996. Registered pharmacist; Bar: Supreme Ct. New South Wales 1975, Quebec 1982. New South Wales; Pharmacist NSW, Australia; atty. Mallesons, Sydney, Australia, 1974-75; cons. Law Reform Com. Can., 1976-85; asst. prof. faculty of law Inst. of Comparative Law, 1978, assoc. prof. faculty of law, 1979; prof., faculty law, faculty medicine McGill U., 1984—; founding dir. McGill Ctr. Medicine Ethics & Law, 1986-96; Gale prof. law, dir. McGill U., 1989-96; vis. prof. Sydney U., 1984, 86, 90, Ctr. for Human Bioethics, Monash U., 1985-86; cons. to numerous orgns. Editl. bd. Bioethics, 1986-96, Kennedy Inst. Ethics Jour., 1990—, Health and Human Rights, 1993—, Ecosystem Health and Medicine, 1993—; Adv. editor Social Sci. and Medicine, 1988-96; reviewer Cmty. Health Studies, Jour. Clin. Epidemiology, Can. Jour. Family Law, Jour. Pharmacy Practice, Jour. AIDS, Can. Jour. Law and Soc., Dalhousie Law Jour., Am. Jour. Law, Medicine and Ethics, Canadian Pub. Policy, Oxford U. Press; mem. adv., editl. bd. Jour. Ethics, Law and Soc.; mem. editl. bd. Humane Health Care Internat.; contbr. articles to profl. jours. Clin. ethics com. Royal Victoria Hosp., 1980-95; prin. investigator Nat. Health R&D Program, 1986-89; assoc. mem. McGill AIDS Ctr., 1990—, Nat. Adv. Com. on AIDS in Can., 1986-92; chmn. Nat. Rsch. Coun. Can., Ethics Com., 1991-95; bd. dirs. Can. Ctr. for Ethics in Sport. Australian Commonwealth scholar, McGill U., 1975; recipient U. Sydney medal, 1976, Joseph Dainow prize McGill U., 1976, Disting. Svc. award Am. Soc. Law & Medicine, 1985; named to Order of Australia. Fellow Royal Soc. Can.; mem. Am. soc. Pharm. Law, Inst. Soc., Ethics & Life Sci., Hastings Ctr., Am. Soc. Law, Medicine, and Ethics, Assn. des Prof. de Droit du Que., Can. Law Tchrs. Assn. Office: McGill Ctr Medicine Ethics & Law, 3690 Peel St, Montreal, PQ Canada H3A 1W9

SOMERVILLE, MARY ROBINSON, library director; b. Fairfield, Ala., Aug. 16, 1941; d. E. Bryce Robinson, Jr. and Margaret Allen. BA in English with honors in Writing, U. N.C., 1963; MA in English, U. Colo., 1965; MLS, U. Okla., 1971. Youth svcs. adminstr. Lincoln City (Nebr.) Librs., 1973-78; youth svcs. mgr. Louisville (Ky.) Free Pub. Libr., 1978-88, proj. dir. automation, 1985-86, grants adminstr., 1986-87, mgr. employee rels., 1987-88; youth svcs. adminstr. Broward County Libr., Ft. Lauderdale, Fla., 1988-90; youth svcs. adminstr. Miami-Dade Pub. Libr., 1990-91, asst. dir. branches and spl. svcs., 1991-93, interim dir., 1993-94, dir., 1994—. Named Outstanding Alumnus Sch. Libr. and Info. Studies U. Okla., 1995. Mem. ALA (spkr., lectr. 22 states, pres. Assn. for Libr. Svc. to children 1987-88, mem. 5 person del. to former Soviet Union 1989, cons. U.S. Dept. Edn. 1988, chair nominating com. 1992, planning and budget assembly 1992, coun. 1992, mem. exec. bd. 1993-95, pres. 1996-97, initiator projects that won H.W. Wilson Staff Devel. award and 4 John Cotton Dana awards), Phi Beta Kappa, Beta Phi Mu. Home: 800 West Ave # 735 Miami Beach FL 33139 Office: Miami Dade Pub Libr System 101 W Flagler St Miami FL 33130-1504

SOMERVILLE, MASON HAROLD, mechanical engineering educator, university dean; b. Worcester, Mass., Dec. 21, 1941; s. Harold Mervin and Eleanor Ruth (Archibald) S.; children: Mark, Matthew, Meredith, Michael, Michelle. B.S.M.E., Worcester Polytech. Inst., 1964; M.S.M.E., Northeastern U., 1966; Ph.D. in Mech. Engring., Pa. State U., 1971. Profl. engr., N.D., Ark., Tex. Grad. teaching asst Northeastern U., Boston, 1964-66; engr. Norton Co., Worcester, Mass., 1965; instr. mech. engring. dept. Pa. State U., State College, 1966-71; sr. engr. Bettis Atomic Power Lab., West Mifflin, Pa., 1971-73; prof., dir. Engring. Expt. Sta., U. N.D., Grand Forks, 1973-80; prof., head mech. engring dept. U. Ark., Fayetteville, 1980-84; prof., dean engring. Tex. Tech U., Lubbock, TX, 1984-94; dean engring. No. Ariz. U., Flagstaff, 1994—; cons. Natural Gas Pipeline, Chgo., 1974-79, Archtl. Alliance, Mpls., 1978-80; bd. dirs. Mid-Am. Solar Energy Corp., Mpls., 1978-80, Ctr. for Advanced Engring and Rsch., TTU/HSC Rsch. Found.; chmn. bd. dirs. N.D. Energy Assn., 1979-80; energy advisor State of N.D., 1978-80; mem. ABET/EAC Commn., 1987-92; speaker to pub. service groups. Author: Coal Gasification Environmental Impact, Analysis of U.S. Weather, 1980; numerous tech. papers. Mem. Lubbock Bd. City Devel., 1985-87. Recipient Ralph R. Teetor award Soc. Automotive Engrs., 1974, Haliburton award; rsch. grantee. Mem. ASME, ASHRAE, Am. Soc. Engring. Edn., Sigma Xi, Pi Tau Sigma. Republican. Episcopalian. Home: 3260 S Gillerwater Dr Flagstaff AZ 86001-8970 Office: Northern Arizona Univ Coll of Engring/Tech PO Box 15600 Flagstaff AZ 86011

SOMERVILLE, RICHARD CHAPIN JAMES, atmospheric scientist, educator; b. Washington, May 30, 1941; s. James William and Mollie (Dorf) S.; m. Sylvia Francisca Bal, Sept. 17, 1965; children: Anatol Leon, Alexander Chapin. BS in Meteorology, Pa. State U., 1961; PhD in Meteorology, NYU, 1966. Postdoctoral fellow Nat. Ctr. Atmospheric Rsch., Boulder, Colo., 1966-67; rsch. assoc. geophysical fluid dynamics lab. NOAA, Princeton, N.J., 1967-69; rsch. scientist Courant Inst. Math. Scis., N.Y.C., 1969-71; meteorologist Goddard inst. space studies NASA, N.Y.C., 1971-74; adj. prof. Columbia U., NYU, 1971-74; head numerical weather prediction sect. Nat. Ctr. Atmospheric Rsch., Boulder, 1974-79; prof. meteorology Scripps Inst. Oceanography, U. Calif.-San Diego, La Jolla, 1979—; chmn. bd. dirs. Aspen Global Change Inst.; mem. panel on climate and global change NOAA. Author: The Forgiving Air: Understanding Environmental Change, 1996. Fellow AAAS, Am. Meterol. Soc.; mem. Am. Geophysical Union, Oceanography Soc. Office: U Calif San Diego Scripps Inst Oceanography 9500 Gilman Dr Dept 0224 La Jolla CA 92093-5003

SOMERVILLE, ROMAINE STEC, arts administrator; b. Scranton, Pa., May 24, 1930; d. Michael John and Julia (Skweir) Stec; m. Frank P.L. Somerville, Sept. 29, 1962; 1 child, Julia Hooper. B.A., Marymount Coll., 1951; M.A., Columbia U., 1953; postgrad., Yale U., 1958-60. Instr. art history Marywood Coll., 1954-58; curator art Everhart Mus., Scranton, 1954-58; curator decorative arts Balt. Mus. Art, 1960-63; exec. dir. Commn. for Hist. and Archtl. Preservation, Balt., 1966-72; chief curator, asst. dir. Md. Hist. Soc., Balt., 1972-78, dir., 1978-84; field cons. Nat. Endowment for Arts, Washington, 1984-86; exec. dir. The Preservation Soc., Balt., 1993—; mem. faculty Goucher Ctr. Ednl. Resources, Johns Hopkins U. Evening Sch., 1978-80; regional advisor Am. Friends of Attingham. contbg. author, editor: exhibit catalogues Md. Hist. Soc., 1975-90. Bd. dirs. Balt. Heritage, Inc., 1975—, Corpus Christi Hist. Trust, Balt., 1976—, Hampton Hist. Site, Towson, Md., 1989—; mem. adv. bd. Soc. Colonial Dames Am. Md., 1984-88, Gov.'s House, Annapolis, 1978-86; guest curator Roman Cath. Ch. bicentennial exhibit Archdiocese of Balt., 1986-91; cons. Mother Seton House, Balt., 1980-89; pres. Balt. Coalition of Hist. Neighborhoods, 1992—; mem. gov.'s adv. com. Save Outdoor Sculpture, 1992-95; mem. collections com. Balt. Mus. of Art, 1997—. Mem. Victorian Soc. Am., Md. Hist. Soc. (gallery com. 1988—), Preservation Md., Balt. Found. for Architecture, Nat. Trust for Hist. Preservation. Office: 201 W Monument St Baltimore MD 21201-4601

SOMERVILLE, VIRGINIA PAULINE WINTERS, executive assistant; b. Jo Daviess County, Ill., Jan. 14, 1936; d. Roy and Effie Stadel Winters; m. Thomas C. Somerville, June 8, 1957; children: Tod Andrew, Ian Winter. BMus magna cum laude, U. Dubuque, 1957; MMus with honors, Roosevelt U., 1964. Music tchr. pub. sch. Jessup, Iowa, 1959-60; music tchr. pvt. sch. P.R., 1960-61; prof. music St. Andrews Presbyn. Coll., Laurinburg,

N.C., 1966-71; pvt. music tchr. Glendale, Calif., 1976-86; exec. asst. to sr. min. First Congl. Ch. L.A., 1986—; workshop and seminar leader Chapman Coll. Ch. Sec.'s Seminar, Orange, Calif., 1991, 92. Performer one-woman musical shows. Active PTA, Canoga Park, Calif., Glendale, 1972-84, Glendale Assistance League, 1975—. Recipient Citizen Appreciation award PTA-Verdugo Woodlands, Glendale, 1980, various music awards. Mem. Nat. Exec. Secs., Nat. Assn. Tchrs. of Singing. Avocations: concert going, reading, films, travel, theater. Office: First Congl Ch LA 540 S Commonwealth Ave Los Angeles CA 90020-1204

SOMERVILLE, WALTER RALEIGH, JR., government official; b. Macon, N.C., Feb. 17, 1930; s. Walter Raleigh and Bettie Lou (Hunt) S.; student Morgan State Coll., 1957-60; BA in Bus. Adminstrn., U. Md., 1970; cert. sr. exec. edn. program Fed. Exec. Inst., 1975; diploma program sr. mgrs. in govt. John F. Kennedy Sch. Govt. Harvard U., 1992; m. Jean Renwick (Nava), Sept. 12, 1975; 1 child, Thomasine A. Walker Adams; 1 stepchild, Pamela Nava-Whitter. Personnel staffing specialist FAA, Washington, 1962-65; personnel mgmt. specialist OEO, 1965-67; personnel mgmt. specialist Office Sec. Transp., 1967-70; chief civilian equal opportunity div. U.S. Coast Guard, Transp. Dept., 1970-83, dir. civil rights, 1970-83, asst. commandant civil rights, 1983—, trainee Fed. Exec. Devel. Program, 1975-76. Chmn. fin. com. Christ United Meth. Ch., Washington, 1976-85, chmn. adminstrv. coun., 1985-86; mem. human relations edn. bd. Dept. Def., 1983-85; mem. Dept. of Def. Equal Opportunity Coun.; chmn. placement and counseling com. for industry cluster Paul Quinn Coll.; bd. trustees USCG Acad., 1994—. With USAF, 1951-60. Recipient Outstanding Performance award, 1981, 82, 83, Proclamation award City Coun. of New Orleans, 1987, Key to City of Franklin, Ky., 1992, Sr. Exec. Svc. Cash Perf. award, 1993, Outstanding Contbns. to Higher Edn. Spl. award Nat. Assn. Equal Opportunity in Higher Edn., 1995; named to Nat. Assn. Equal Opportunity in Higher Edn. Registry of Disting. Individuals, 1995. Mem. Am. Mgmt. Assn., NAACP (golden heritage life mem., Roy Wilkins Meritorious Svc. award, 1987, Benjamin L. Hooks Disting. Svc. award 1993), Sr. Execs. Assn., Washington Urban League (life), U. Md. Alumni Assn. (century club), Nat. Urban League (charter mem. Pres.'s Club, mem. black exec. exch. program, vis. prof. historically black colls. and univs.). Home: 1228 4th St SW Washington DC 20024-2302 Office: 2100 2nd St SW Washington DC 20593-0001

SOMES, GRANT WILLIAM, statistician, biomedical researcher; b. Bloomington, Ind., Jan. 30, 1947; s. William Henry and Margaret Juanita (Sparks) S.; m. Brenda Sue Weddle, Sept. 2, 1967; children: Anthony William, Joshua Michael, Meghan Elizabeth. AB, Ind. U., 1968; PhD, U. Ky., 1975. Asst. prof. dept. community medicine U. Ky., Lexington, 1975-79; assoc. prof., dir. Biostats./Epidemiology Rsch. Lab. East Carolina U., Greenville, N.C., 1979-84; prof., chmn. dept. biostats. & epidemiology U. Tenn., Memphis, 1984-93; chief divsn. biostats and epidemiology dept. preventive medicine U. Tenn., Memphis, 1993—; cons. Community Health Mgmt. Info. System, Memphis, 1992—, Mid-South Found. for Med. Care, Memphis, 1992—, Cigna Health Ctr. Tenn., 1996—. Contbr. 92 articles to profl. jours.; author 100 presented papers/abstracts. Coach Little League baseball, Lexington, 1976-79, Aydon, N.C., 1979-84. Recipient Outstanding Alumni award U. Ky., 1993. Mem. Am. Statis. Assn. (v.p. West Tenn. chpt. 1985-86), Biometric Soc., Am. Soc. Hypertension, Sigma Xi, Pi Mu Epsilon. Achievements include research in cardiovascular risk factors, epilepsy, psychosocial factors and illness, smoking and behavior, dentistry and nutrition, violence (especially gun related), statistical theory mainly in categorical data analysis and nonparametric statistics.

SOMIT, ALBERT, political educator; b. Chgo., Oct. 25, 1919; s. Samuel and Mary (Rosenblum) S.; m. Leyla D. Shapiro, Aug. 31, 1947; children: Scott H., Jed L. A.B., U. Chgo., 1941, Ph.D., 1947. Prof. polit. philosophy N.Y. U., 1945-65; chmn. dept. polit. sci. State U. N.Y. at Buffalo, 1966-69, exec. v.p., 1970-80; acting pres. SUNY, Buffalo, 1976-77; pres. So. Ill. U., Carbondale, 1980-87, disting. service prof., 1987—; fellow Netherlands Inst. Advanced Study, 1978-79; Nimitz prof. polit. philosophy U.S. Naval War Coll., 1961-62. Author: (with Joseph Tanenhaus) The Development of American Political Science: From Burgess to Behavioralism, 1967, expanded edit., 1982, (with Tanenhaus) American Political Science: A Profile of A Discipline, 1964, Political Science and the Study of the Future, 1974, Biology and Politics: Recent Explorations, 1976, (with others) The Literature of Biopolitics 1963-1977, 1978, 1980, 1983, 1986, Biopolitics and Mainstream Political Science A Master Bibliography, 1990, (with Wildenmann) Hierarchy and Democracy, 1991, (with Peterson) The Dynamics of Evolution, 1992, (with Wildenmann) The Victorious Incumbent: A Threat to Democracy?, 1994, (with Peterson) The Political Behavior of Older Americans, 1994, Research in Biopolitics: Human Nature and Politics, 1995, Birth Order and Political Behavior, 1996. Served with AUS, 1950-52. Office: So Ill U Lesar Law Bldg Carbondale IL 62901

SOMJEN, GEORGE GUSTAV, physiologist; b. Budapest, Hungary, May 2, 1929; came to U.S., 1962; s. Laszlo and Margit (Ranschburg) S.; m. Eva Herman, 1952 (dec. 1974); children: Monika, Maria, Georgette, Evelyn; m. Amalia Deutsch, 1976. Grad., U. Amsterdam Med. Faculty, 1956; M.D., U. N.Z., 1962. Research asst. Pharmaco-therapeutic Lab., U. Amsterdam, 1953-56; lectr., sr. lectr. dept. physiology U. Otago, Dunedin, N.Z., 1956-62; prof. physiology Duke U., Durham, N.C., 1963—; cons. Nat. Inst. Environ. Health Scis., 1971-75. Author: Sensory Coding in the Mammalian Nervous System, 1972, Neurophysiology: The Essentials, 1983; editor: Neurophysiology Studied in Man, 1972, Mechanisms of Cerebral Hypoxia and Stroke, 1988. Recipient research grants NIH, 1964—. Mem. Am. Physiol. Soc., Soc. Neurosci., Internat. Union Physiol. Sci. (mem. com. edn. 1986-93, chmn., 1993—), Internat. Pathophysiol. Soc. (mem. com. edn.), Am. Epilepsy Soc. Office: Duke U Dept Cell Biology Div Physiology PO Box 3709 Durham NC 27710

SOMLYO, ANDREW PAUL, physiology, biophysics and cardiology educator; b. Budapest, Hungary; s. Anton and Clara Maria (Kiss) S.; m. Avril V. Russell, May 25, 1961; 1 child, Andrew Paul. BS, U. Ill., 1954, MS, 1956, MD, 1956; MS, Drexel Inst. Tech., Phila., 1963; MA (hon.), U. Pa., Phila., 1981. Asst. physician Columbia-Presbyn. Med. Ctr., N.Y.C., 1960-61; rsch. assoc. Presbyn. Hosp., Phila., 1961-67; asst. prof. pathology U. Pa., Phila., 1964-67, assoc. prof., 1967-71, prof., 1971-88, prof. physiology and pathology, 1973-88, dir. Pa. Muscle Inst., 1973-88; Charles Slaughter prof. molecular physiology-biol. physics U. Va., Charlottesville, 1988—, chmn. dept., 1988—, prof. cardiology, 1988—, dir. ctr. structural biology, 1997—; cons. NIH; Brit. Heart Found. vis. prof. Hammersmith Hosp., London, Shanghai (China) Med. U.. Author: (with others) Vascular Neuroeffector Systems, 1971, The Handbook of Physiology, Vascular Smooth Muscle, 1981, Microprobe Analysis of Biological Systems, 1981, Recent Advances in Light and Optical Imaging in Biology and Medicine, 1986; editor: Jour. Muscle Research and Cell Motility, 1987, FASEB Jour., 1996; contbr. numerous articles to jours. including Biol. Chemistry, Jour. Physiology, Am. Heart Jour., Jour. Pediatrics, Jour. Cell Biology, Cell Calcium, others; mem. editl. bd. Blood Vessels, Am. Jour. Physiology, 1979-83, Magnesium: Experimental and Clinical Rsch., Jour. Structural Biology. Recipient The Louis and Artur Lucian award for rsch. in circulatory diseases, 1996. Mem. AAAS, Soc. Gen. Physiologists, Am. Physiol. Soc. Biophys. Soc., Electron Microscopy Soc., Microbeam Analysis Soc. (Presdl. Sci. award 1996), Am. Soc. for Cell Biology, Hungarian Physiol. Soc. (hon.), Microscopy Soc. Am. (Disting. Scientist award for biol. scis. 1994), Alpha Omega Alpha Med. Soc. (CIBA-GEIGY award for Hypertension Rsch. 1991). Office: U Va Sch Medicine Dept Molecular Phys/Biol Physics PO Box 10011 449 Jordan Hall Charlottesville VA 22906-0011

SOMMA, BEVERLY KATHLEEN, medical and marriage educator; b. Bayonne, N.J., June 13, 1938; d. Leroy and Isabelle (Lysaght) Latourette; m. Louis Anthony Somma, Nov. 24, 1973; children: Francis, Keith. AS, Ocean County Coll., 1973; BA, Georgian Ct., 1977; MAT, Monmouth Coll., 1978; postgrad., U. Pa., 1980-85, 88-89. Nurse's aide Community Meml. Hosp., Toms River, N.J., 1971-72; with marriage coun. dept. psychiatry U. Pa. Sch. Medicine, Phila., 1993—; with Helene Fuld Med. Ctr. Edn., 1993—; ednl. cons. Ctr. for Cognitive Edn., Yardley, Pa., 1990—, tng. program Archdiocese Phila., Penn Found., Inc., 1993; lectr. Marriage Coun. of Phila. dept. psychiatry, sch. medicine U. Pa., 1993—; with Helene Fuld Med. Ctr. Edn., 1993—. Voter svc. chmn. LWV, Toms River, N.J., 1971-72; contact rep. Pro Life Coalition, Phila.; vol. nursing tutor Ocean County Coll., Toms River, 1972; vol. tchr.'s aide St. Michael the Archangel, Levittown, Pa., 1987-88; vol. VITA; counselor Bucks County Coun. Alcoholism and Drug Dependence, Inc., 1984-93; active World Affairs Coun. Phila. All Am. scholar; recipient U.S. Achievement Acad. Nat. award. Mem. Nat. Soc. for Fund Raising Execs., Alumni Assn. Georgian Ct. Coll., Ocean County Coll., Bucks County C.C., Sigma Tau Delta. Republican. Methodist. Avocations: cooking, tennis, golf, jogging, ice-skating. Home: 1506 Kathy Dr Yardley PA 19067-1717

SOMMER, ALFRED, medical educator, scientist, ophthalmologist; b. N.Y.C., Oct. 2, 1942; s. Joseph and Natalie Sommer; m. Jill Abramson, Sept. 1, 1963; children: Charles Andrew, Marni Jane. BS summa cum laude, Union Coll., 1963; MD, Harvard U., 1967; MHS in Epidemiology, Johns Hopkins U., 1973. Diplomate Am. Bd. Ophthalmology, Nat. Bd. Med. Examiners. Teaching fellow in medicine Harvard U. Med. Sch., Boston, 1968-69; dir. Nutritional Blindness Prevention Rsch. Program, Bandung, Indonesia, 1976-79; vis. fellow Inst. Ophthalmology U. London, Eng., 1979-80; founding dir., Dana Ctr. for Preventive Ophthalmology Johns Hopkins Med. Insts., Balt., 1980-90; assoc. prof. Johns Hopkins U., Balt., 1981-85, prof. ophthalmology, epidemiology and internat. health, 1985—, dean Johns Hopkins Sch. Hygiene and Pub. Health, 1990—; vis. prof. ophthalmology U. Padjadjaran, Indonesia, 1976-79; cons., advisor Helen Keller Internat., N.Y.C., 1973—; cons., chmn. com. NIH, Bethesda, Md., 1981—; bd. dirs. Internat. Agy. for the Prevention of Blindness, Geneva, Switzerland, 1978—; cons., com. mem. Nat. Acad. Scis., Washington, 1989; chmn. program adv. group on blindness prevention WHO, Geneva, 1989-90, com. mem., 1978-90, expert com., 1990—; chmn. steering com. Internat. Vitamin A Cons. Group, Washington, 1975—; pres. Internat. Fedn. of Tissue Banks; chmn. sci. adv. bd. Edna McConnell Clark Found.; mem. adv. com. Internat. Coun. Ophthalmology. Author: Epidemiology and Statistics for the Ophthalmologist, 1980, Nutritional Blindness: Xerophthalmia and Keratomalacia, 1982, Vitamin A Deficiency: Health, Survival and Vision, 1995, Detection and Control of Vitamin A Deficiency and Xerophthalmia, 1978, 82, 95; chmn. bd. overseers Am. Jours. Epidemiology and Epidemiologic Revs., 1990—. Charles A. Dana Found. award for Pioneering Achievement in Health, 1988, Disting. Svc. award for Contbn. to Vision Care AOHA, 1988, E.V. McCollum Internat. Lectureship in Nutrition Am. Inst. Nutrition, 1988, Second Ann. Am. Coll. Advancement in Medicine Achievement award in Preventive Medicine, 1990, Disting. Contbn. to World Ophthalmology award Internat. Fedn. Ophthalmol. Socs., 1990, Smadel award Infectious Diseases Soc. Am., 1990, Doyne Meml. award Oxford. Mem. Inst. Medicine of NAS (Food and Nutrition bd.), Am. Acad. Opthalmology (chmn. pub. health com. 1982-88, chmn. Quality of Care/Clin. Guidelines 1986-90, Hon. award 1986, blindness prevention award 1998), Nat. Soc. to Prevent Blindness (bd. dirs. 1989) Internat. Assn. to Prevent Blindness (bd. dirs. 1978—), Assn. Schs. of Pub. Health (pres.), Pa. Coll. Physicians (de Schweinitz award 1996), Chgo. Ophthalmol. Soc. (Gifford meml. award 1997). Achievements include first to detail and publish epidemiologic approach to disaster assessment; nutritional indices predict subsequent mortality in free-living children, surveillance and containment is effective intervention strategy for controlling and eradicating smallpox, vitamin A deficiency increases childhood mortality and vitamin A supplementation decreases childhood mortality, nerve fiber layer is valuable diagnostic and prognostic sign of early glaucoma; routine preventive services cost-effective in eye disease; clinical guideline development and importance of outcome assessment; research in epidemiologic and public health approaches to ophthalmology, blindness prevention, and improved health and survival. Office: Johns Hopkins Sch Hygiene and Pub Health 615 N Wolfe St Rm 1041 Baltimore MD 21205-2103

SOMMER, ALPHONSE ADAM, JR., lawyer; b. Portsmouth, Ohio, Apr. 7, 1924; s. A.A. and Adelaide (Orlett) S.; m. Storrow Cassin, June 13, 1951; children: Susan, Edward, Nancy. A.B., U. Notre Dame, 1948; LL.B., Harvard U., 1950; LL.D., Cleve. State U., 1976. Bar: Ohio 1951, D.C. 1976. Assoc. Calfee, Halter, Calfee, Griswold & Sommer, Cleve., 1950-60; ptnr. Calfee, Halter, Calfee, Griswold & Sommer, 1960-73; commr. SEC, 1973-76; ptnr. Morgan, Lewis & Bockius, Washington, 1979-94, counsel, 1994—; chmn. pub. oversight bd., AICPA. Contbr. articles to profl. jours. Chmn. pub. oversight bd. AICPA. Served with AUS, 1943-46. Mem. Nat. Assn. Securities Dealers (bd. dirs.). Home: 7105 Heathwood Ct Bethesda MD 20817-2915 Office: Morgan Lewis & Bockius 1800 M St NW Ste 925 Washington DC 20036-5802

SOMMER, BARBARA, school administrator; b. N.Y.C.; d. David and Rose (Weingarten) Melnick; m. Robert I. Sommer, Aug. 29, 1971; children: Mara, Adam. BA, Queens Coll., 1972, MS in Spl. Edn., 1975; MS in Edn. Adminstrn., Pace U., 1993. Cert. tchr. N.Y., sch. dist. adminstr. N.Y. Sub. tchr. Pub. Sch. # 20, Pub. Sch. # 21, N.Y.C., 1972; tchr. Creative Nursery Sch., N.Y.C., 1972, PS 20, N.Y.C., 1972-75; sub. tchr. PS 79, N.Y.C., 1973; tchr. PS 162, N.Y.C., 1975-78; tchr., curriculum developer Child Study Ctr. Pace U., N.Y., 1987-93, intern adminstrn. Child Study Ctr., 1991-92; dir. Westport (Conn.)-Weston Coop. Nursery Sch., 1993-95; edn. coord. White Plains (N.Y.) Child Day Care Assn., Inc., 1995—; tchr. New Castle Recreation Dept., N.Y., 1985-86; supr. Saturday Recreation Program, New Castle, N.Y., 1985; tchr. North Westchester YM-YWHA, N.Y., 1974. Chair craft fair Graffin Sch./Chappaqua PTA, 1985-86. Recipient Cert. Recognition Day Care In-Service Tng. Project, Family Support Early Intervention, N.Y. Med. Coll., MRI/Inst. for Human Devel., 1992, Cert. for Svc. Coord., Westchester Med. Ctr., 1993. Mem. NOW, AAUW, ASCD, Nat. Assn. for Edn. Young Children, Nat. Head Start Assn., Assn. for Childhood Edn. Internat., Westchester Assn. for Edn. Young Children, Westchester Edn. Coalition, Tau Delta Kappa, Phi Delta Kappa, Kappa Delta Pi.

SOMMER, HOWARD ELLSWORTH, textile executive; b. Kansas City, Mo., May 1, 1918; s. Frederick H. and Edna O. (Olsen) S.; m. Sarah Scott McElevey, June 20, 1942; children: Scott E., Paul F. BA magna cum laude, Dartmouth Coll., 1940; MBA, Harvard U., 1942. With Wolf & Co. CPAs, Chgo., 1946-76, chmn. mng. group, 1960-76; dir. Jockey Internat., Kenosha, Wis., 1959—, sr. v.p., chmn. audit com., 1979-89. Author: Procedural Routine for a Business Audit, 1947; also articles. Counsellor, Chgo. chpt. Boy Scouts Am.; vestryman, warden Episcopalian ch. Lt. col. AUS, 1942-46. Decorated Bronze Star; Croix de Guerre with palms; Medaille de la Reconnaissance (France). Mem. ASME, Assn. Cons. Mgmt. Engrs. (cert. of Award 1956, v.p. 1970-72), Inst. Mgmt. Cons. (cert. mgmt. cons., past dir.), Univ. Club (pres., dir. Chgo. chpt. 1959-61), Indian Hill Club, Harvard Bus. Sch. Club (dir. Chgo. chpt. 1958-59), North Shore Cotillion Club, Dartmouth Club, Halter Wildlife Club, Masons (32 degree), Shriners, Phi Beta Kappa, Chi Phi.

SOMMER, JEFFREY ROBERT, lawyer; b. Phila., Feb. 18, 1958; s. Joseph Robert and Janet Ann (Richards) S.; m. Lisa Marie Sievers, June 22, 1985; children: Matthew Jon, Alexander Carlton, Andrew Robert. BA, Lehigh U., 1979; JD, Widener U., 1982. Bar: Pa. 1982, U.S. Dist. Ct. (ea. dist.) Pa. 1982, U.S. Ct. Appeals (3d cir.) 1983. Law clk. Ct. of Common Pleas, Montgomery County, Pa., 1981-83; assoc. Norton A. Freedman P.C., Norristown, Pa., 1983-90; asst. pub. defender Ct. of Common Pleas, Norristown, 1982-90; ptnr. Buckley, Nagle, Gentry, McGuire & Morris, West Chester, Pa., 1990—; asst. editor Chester County Law Reporter, West Chester, 1991—. Bd. dirs. West Chester Area Day Care Ctr., 1991—, Alcohol and Drug Abuse Coun., Unionville, Pa., 1992—; mem. Mcpl. Svcs. Authority, West Whiteland Twp., 1988-89; vice chmn. Zoning Hearing Bd., Pocopson Twp., 1990—; active Chester County coun. Boy Scouts Am., 1990—. Mem. Pa. Bar Assn., Chester County Bar Assn., Lehigh U. Alumni Assn., Rotary, Masons. Republican. Presbyterian. Home: 723 Isaac Taylor Dr West Chester PA 19382-7030 Office: Buckley Nagle Gentry McGuire & Morris 304 N High St West Chester PA 19380-2614

SOMMER, JOSEPH WILLIAM, retired middle school educator; b. Jersey City, Apr. 7, 1931; s. Joseph Thomas and Frances Vetters (Boehning) S.; m. Mary Virginia Dick, Apr. 15, 1967; children: Julie, Jaimie. BA, Montclair State Coll., 1954, MA, 1956. Cert. tchr., N.J. Tchr. Parsippany (N.J.)-Troy Hills Bd. Edn., 1954-94; head dept. math., dir. student activities, musical dir. Cen. Middle Sch., Parsippany, 1958-94. Mem. NEA, N.J. Edn. Assn., Morris County Edn. Assn., Parsippany-Troy Hills Edn. Assn., Am. Assn. Math. Tchrs., N.J. Assn. Math Tchrs., N.J. Ret. Educators Assn.. Republican. Methodist. Avocations: piano, spectator sports, church choir. Home: 1512 Barnegat Ave Surf City NJ 08008-6430

SOMMERER, JOHN, accountant; b. Mt. Holly, N.J., Oct. 30, 1947; s. John Price and Barbara Elizabeth (Davis) S.; m. Diane Catherine Kuszaj, Aug. 5, 1967; children: James Peter, John Joseph, Paul Andrew, Matthew Thomas. BS, U. Hartford, 1969; MBA, U. Toronto, 1972; postgrad., Columbia U., 1972-74. CPA, Fla., N.J., N.Y. Sr. cons. Deloitte and Touche, N.Y.C., 1974-78; dir. mgmt. info. systems Pantry Pride Enterprises, Ft. Lauderdale, Fla., 1978-82; mng. ptnr. John Sommerer and Co., P.A., Coral Springs, Fla., 1982—; mayor City of Coral Springs, 1994—. Treas. Coral Springs Cmty. Chest, 1988-94. Mem. Coral Springs Kiwanis (bd. dirs. 1990, 92), Coral Springs C. of C. (pres. 1987, treas. 1986, bd. dirs. 1986-88). Roman Catholic. Home: 9501 NW 44th Pl Coral Springs FL 33065-6602 Office: John Sommerer and Co PA 3300 N University Dr Coral Springs FL 33065-6309

SOMMERFELD, NICHOLAS ULRICH, lawyer; b. Frankfurt, Fed. Republic Germany, Sept. 3, 1926; came to U.S., 1933; s. Martin and Helene (Schott) S.; m. Charlotte Ann Abrams, Sept. 11, 1954; children: Gretchen, Amy Fiore. AB, Princeton U., 1948; JD, Harvard U., 1952. Assoc. Gaston Snow & Ely Bartlett, Boston, 1954-61, ptnr., 1961-91; of counsel Hutchins Wheeler & Dittmar, Boston, 1991—. Trustee Perkins Sch. for the Blind, Watertown, Mass., 1982—. Lt. USN, 1952-54. Fellow Am. Coll. Trust Estate Counsel; mem. Boston Bar Assn. (chmn. probate com. 1986-87, chmn. steering com., lawyers com. for civil rights 1980-84), Boston Bar Found. (trustee 1994—), Internat. Acad. Estate & Trial Law (academician 1987—). Office: Hutchins Wheeler & Dittmar 101 Federal St Boston MA 02110-1817

SOMMERFELDT, JOHN ROBERT, historian; b. Detroit, Feb. 4, 1933; s. Melvin John and Virginia Zita (Gruenheck) S.; m. Patricia Natalie Levinske, Aug. 25, 1956; children: Ann, James, John, Elizabeth. AB, U. Mich., 1954, AM, 1956, PhD, 1960. Instr. history Stanford U., 1958-59; from instr. to prof. Western Mich. U., 1959-78; prof. history U. Dallas, 1978—, chmn. dept. history, 1984-87, univ. pres., 1978-80; dir. Medieval Inst., Western Mich. U., 1961-76; exec. dir. Inst. Cistercian Studies, 1973-78; dir. Center Contemplative Studies, 1976-78; pres. Cistercian Publs., 1973-79, chmn. bd., 1976-79. Author: The Spiritual Teachings of Bernard of Clairvaux, 1991; editor: Studies in Medieval Culture, 12 vols., 1964-78, Studies in Medieval Cistercian History, II 1977, Cistercian Ideals and Reality, 1978, Simplicity and Ordinariness, 1980, The Chimaera of His Age: Studies in Bernard of Clairvaux, 1980, Abba: Guides to Wholeness and Holiness, East and West, 1981, Erudition at God's Service, 1987, Bernardus Magister, 1992, Studiosorum Speculum, 1993. Fulbright scholar, 1954-55; Univ. fellow U. Mich., 1960. Mem. Mediaeval Acad. Am., Am. Hist. Assn., Am. Catholic Hist. Assn., Am. Soc. Ch. History, Phi Beta Kappa, Phi Eta Sigma, Phi Kappa Phi. Republican. Roman Catholic. Home: 2809 Warren Cir Irving TX 75062-8938 Office: U Dallas Dept History Irving TX 75062-4736

SOMMERFELT, SOREN CHRISTIAN, foreign affairs, international trade consultant, former Norwegian diplomat, lawyer; b. Oslo, May 9, 1916; s. Soren Christian and Sigrid (Nicolaysen) S.; m. Frances Bull, June 27, 1947; 1 child, Cathrine. LLD, Oslo U., 1940. Joined Norwegian Fgn. Svc., 1941; pvt. sec. to fgn. minister, UN sec. gen. Trygve Lie, 1941-44; assigned to UN Secretariat, 1946, Div. Refugees' and Displaced Persons, 1st sec. Norwegian Embassy, Copenhagen, 1948-50; counselor Norwegian del. to NATO, 1950-52; dep. head. econ. dept. Norwegian Ministry Fgn. Affairs, 1953-56, head, 1956-60; amb., head Norwegian del. to European Free Trade Assn., Gen. Agreement on Tariffs and Trade (GATT), and UN European Office, 1960-68; chmn. GATT Contracting Parties, 1968; amb. to Fed. Republic Germany, 1968-73, U.S.A., 1973-79, Italy, 1979-81; head Norwegian del. negotiating entry into European Communities, 1970-72; counsel Arent, Fox, Kintner, Plotkin & Kahn, Washington, 1982-84; ptnr. cons. firm Washington Resources, Inc., 1984-91; sr. ptnr. Sommerfelt Assocs., Washington, 1992—; bd. dirs. Nordic Enterprises, Inc. Decorated comdr. Order St. Olav, Norway, grand cross Order of Merit, Fed. Republic Germany, grand cross Order of Merit, Italy, comdr. with star Order of North Star, Sweden, comdr. Order of Leopold II, Belgium, knight Order of Falcon, Iceland, knight Order of Dannebrog, Denmark. Mem. Metropolitan Club (Washington), Chevy Chase Club (Md.), Norske Selskab Club (Oslo). Home: 2700 Calvert St NW Washington DC 20008-2621 Office: Sommerfelt Assocs 1250 24th St NW Washington DC 20037-1124

SOMMERLAD, ROBERT EDWARD, environmental research engineer; b. Jersey City, Aug. 27, 1937; s. Herman Francis and Helen Rita (Joyce) S.; m. Margaret Doreen Breen, Sept. 9, 1961; children: Sharon K., Michael E., Ellen J. BSME, N.J. Inst. Tech., 1960, MSME, 1963, postgrad., 1965. Devel. engr., rsch. assoc. Foster Wheeler Energy Corp., Livingston, N.J., 1960-71, head air pollution control sect., 1971-74; v.p. contract ops. Foster Wheeler Devel. Corp., Livingston, 1974-84; pres. Enviresponse Inc., Livingston, 1985-86; dir. bus. devel. Energy and Environ. Rsch. Corp., Edison, N.J., 1987-88; cons., 1988-89; dir. environ. bus. devel. Midwest Rsch. Inst., Falls Church, Va., 1989-90; mgr. combustion tech. Rsch.-Cottrell Cos., 1990-92, cons., 1992-93; mktg. dir. PSI Powerserve, Andover, Mass., 1993-94, cons., 1994-95; cons. Gas Rsch. Inst., Chgo., 1995—; mem. coal combustion and applications working group U.S. Dept. Energy U. San Diego, 1981-84. Patentee in field. V.p. Cranford (N.J.) Cmty. Pools Parents Assn., 1975-77, 86-87, pres., 1977-79, 84-86, 87-89; chmn. N.J. Swimming and Diving Conf., Cranford, 1986-89. Recipient Outstanding Achievement award Westfield YMCA, 1975. Fellow ASME (mem. rsch. com. indsl. and mcpl. waste 1971—, vice chmn. 1972-74, sec. 1987-91, mem. environ. affairs com. 1982-92, mem. dioxin com. 1985-92, mem. bd. performance test codes 1986-97, chmn. boiler-calorimeter com. 1986-89, numerous com. and conf. chairmanships); mem. Air and Waste Mgmt. Assn. (mem. AE-1 com. on particulate and associated acid gases, sec. 1991-94, vice chair 1996), Watchung Amateur Ski Club (mem. exec. bd. 1986-87) (Mountainside, N.J.). Roman Catholic. Home: 1368 Knottingham Dr Gurnee IL 60031-5632

SOMMERS, GEORGE R., lawyer; b. N.Y.C., Jan. 27, 1955. BA, U. So. Fla., 1975; JD, NYU, 1987. Bar: N.J. 1987, U.S. Dist. Ct. N.J. 1987, N.Y. 1988, U.S. Dist. Ct. (all dists.) N.Y. 1988, U.S. Ct. Appeals (3d cir.) 1988, U.S. Ct. Appeals (2d cir.) 1989, U.S. Supreme Ct. 1992. Assoc. Sullivan & Cromwell, N.Y.C., 1987-90; pvt. practice lawyer N.Y.C., 1990—; pres. Bill of Rights Found., N.Y.C., 1994—. Seidler scholar NYU Sch. Law, N.Y.C., 1985. Mem. Hoboken Bar Assn. (pres. 1994). Jewish. Avocations: sailing, chess. Office: 67 Wall St Ste 2411 New York NY 10005-3101

SOMMERS, GORDON L., religious organization administrator. Pres. Moravian Ch. in Am., Bethlehem, Pa., Nat. Coun. Ch. of Christ Am., 1994-95. Office: Moravian Ch in Am PO Box 1245 1021 Center St Bethlehem PA 18016-1245

SOMMERS, LAWRENCE MELVIN, geographer, educator; b. Clinton, Wis., Apr. 17, 1919; s. Emil L. and Inga (Anderson) S.; m. Marjorie Smith, Apr. 26, 1948; 1 dau., Laurie Kay. B.S., U. Wis., 1942, Ph.M., 1946; Ph.D., Northwestern U., 1950. Prof. geography Mich. State U., East Lansing, 1949—, successively instr., asst. prof. dept. geography, assoc. prof., 1949-55, prof., 1955-89, prof. emeritus, asst. provost emeritus, 1989—; chmn. dept. geography Mich. State U., East Lansing, 1955-79, mem. Environ. Quality Ctr., 1979-81, asst. provost, 1987-89; mem. adv. com. geography Office Naval Rsch. and NRC, 1958-61; fellow Am. Scandinavian Found.; bd. dirs. Am. Paytel Corp.; mem. commn. on dynamics of marginal and critical regions Internat. Geog. Union, 1996—. Co-author: Outside Readings in Geography, 1955, Introduction to Geography-Selected Readings, 1967, Cultural Geography-Selected Readings, 1967, Physical Geography-Selected Readings, 1967, Economic Geography-Selected Readings, 1970, World Regional Geography, 1976, Energy and the Adaptation of Human Settlements, 1980, Planning Issues in Marginal Areas, 1991; author: Michigan: A Geography, 1984; editor: Atlas of Michigan, 1977, Fish in Lake Michigan, 1981, Land Use: A Spatial Approach, 1981; contbr. articles on Norwegian, European, Mich., marginal areas, and econ. geography to profl. jours. Served with adj. gen. dept. AUS, 1942-45. Office Naval Rsch. grant for rsch. in Denmark, 1953, Travel grant to Europe, 1960, 82, 86, Social Sci. Rsch. Coun. and Am. Scandinavian Found. grantee for rsch. in Norway, 1948. Mem. AAAS, Am. Geog. Soc., Assn. Am. Geographers (exec. com. 1967-70, chmn. cons. svc. 1970-77, publ. com. 1968-70), Mich. State U. Acad. Coun. and Grad. Coun. (chmn. steering com. 1981-84), Am. Scandinavian Found., Scandinavian Studies Assn., Explorers Club, Sigma Xi (pres. Mich. State U. chpt. 1959-60), Phi Kappa Phi (pres. Mich. State U.

chpt. 1980-82, v.p. North Ctrl. region 1986-89, nat. pres.-elect 1989-92, exec. com. 1992—, nat. pres. 1992-95, past pres. 1995—), Phi Delta Beta. Home: 4292 Tacoma Blvd Okemos MI 48864-2734 Office: Mich State Univ Geography Dept East Lansing MI 48824

SOMMERS, LOUISE, lawyer; b. Jersey City, May 19, 1948; d. Moe and Estelle. BA with honors, Douglas Coll., 1969; JD magna cum laude, Bklyn. Law Sch., 1976. Bar: N.Y. 1977, U.S. Dist. Ct. (ea. and so. dists.) N.Y. 1977, U.S. Ct. Appeals (2d cir.). Law clk. to presiding justice U.S. Dist. Ct. (so. dist.) N.Y., N.Y.C., 1976-78; ptnr. Rogers & Wells, N.Y.C., 1978—; adj. prof. Bklyn. Law Sch., 1986—. Mem. ABA, N.Y. State Bar Assn., Assn. of Bar of City of N.Y., N.Y. Women Bar Assn.

SOMMERS, MAXINE MARIE BRIDGET, writer, educator, publisher; b. Crystal Falls, Mich., May 7, 1932; d. Francis Ernest and Irene Catherine (Raher) Munns; m. Clemens Struve, June 10, 1952 (div. 1975); children: Stephen, Joseph; m. Norval Isom Sommers (dec. 1989). Student, Milw. Downer Coll. for Women, 1948-49, U. Tex. Med. Br., Galveston, 1949-50, St. Mary's Hosp., 1950-51. Owner, operator Pound Sterling Publ., 1982—, Pound Sterling Media Svc., 1983—. Author: A Texan on the Road Again to the Far East, 1992; author 28 books and mini-books on cuisine, and travel, also children's books. Pres. Corpus Christi Symphony Guild, 1967-69, Tex. Assn. Symphony Orchestras, 1969; bd. dirs. Corpus Christi Symphony Soc., 1975—, South Tex. Health Syss. Agy., 1982-85; bd. dirs., pvt. svc. trainer Tex. divsn. Am. Cancer Soc., 1974-94; pres. Tex. Coastal Bend Mental Health Assn., 1976-78. Recipient cert. of award Byliners Tex. Wide Writers, 1992, Bus. Assoc. Night award Am. Bus. Women's Assn., 1992, cert. merit Corpus Christi Symphony Guild, 1969, cert. recognition Tex. Women's Assn. Symphony Orchestras, 1969, various awards Am. Cancer Soc. Mem. Byliners, Austin Writers League, Internat. Platform Assn. Avocations: gardening, cooking, traveling. Home: 4270 Ocean Dr Corpus Christi TX 78411-1283

SOMMERS, ROBERT THOMAS, editor, publisher, author; b. Balt., Aug. 6, 1926; s. Thomas Michael and Pearl Florence (Glendenning) S.; m. Helen Louise Ray, Oct. 19, 1952; children—Thomas Michael II, Patricia Ray. B.S., U. Md., College Park, 1950. Reporter Evening Sun, Balt., 1950-62; reporter Evening Star, Washington, 1962-66; editor U.S. Golf Assn. Jour., N.Y.C., 1966-72, Far Hills, N.J., 1972-92. Author: The Oxford Book of Golf Anecdotes, 1995, The U.S. Open: Golf's Ultimate Challenge, 1987, 2nd edit., 1996, Bobby Jones in Chapman's Library of Golf, 1992; co-author: Great Shots, 1989; contbr. articles to profl. jours. Served with U.S. Coast Guard, 1944-46, PTO. Mem. Golf Writers Assn. Am., Assn. Golf Writers Gt. Britain, Authors Guild, Plainfield (N.J.) Country Club, Ballybunion Golf Club (Ireland), Kingston Heath Golf Club (Australia), Royal and Ancient Golf Club of St. Andrews (Scotland), The Reserve Golf and Tennis Club (Fla.). Republican. Episcopalian. Avocations: reading, golf, music. Home and Office: 8083 Spendthrift Ln Port Saint Lucie FL 34986-3122

SOMMERS, WILLIAM PAUL, management consultant, think tank executive; b. Detroit, July 22, 1933; s. William August and Mary Elizabeth (Baietto) S.; m. Josephine A. Sommers; children: William F., Clare M., John C. Hughes, Joanna M. Weems, Russell L. Hughes. B.S.E. (scholar), U. Mich., 1955, M.S.E., 1956, Ph.D. (Riggs fellow, Texaco fellow, Univ. fellow), 1961. Research asso. U. Mich. Inst. Sci. and Tech., Ann Arbor, 1958-61; chief chem. propulsion space and missile systems Martin Marietta Corp., Balt., 1956-58, 61-63; v.p. Booz, Allen & Hamilton, Inc., Bethesda, Md., 1963-70; pres. Tech. Mgmt. Group Booz, Allen & Hamilton, Inc., 1973-79, sr. v.p., 1979-92; exec. v.p. Iameter, Inc., San Mateo, Calif., 1992-94; pres., CEO SRI Internat., Menlo Park, Calif., 1994—; bd. dirs. Kember Fin. Svcs., Rohr Inc., Therapeutic Discovery Corp., Litton Inc. Contbr. articles to profl. jours., also chpt. in book. Pres. Washington chpt. U. Mich. Alumni Club, 1970-71; v.p. Wildwood manor Citizens Assn., 1968-70; chief Adventure Guide program YMCA, 1971-72; bd. visitors Coll. Engring. U. Calif., Davis; mem. nat. adv. bd. Coll. Engring. U. Mich.; mem. conf. bd. Internat. Coun. on Innovation and Tech. Mem. Columbia Country Club, Willow Bend Country Club, Sigma Xi, Tau Beta Pi, Pi Tau Sigma. Republican. Roman Catholic. Home: 255 Uplands Dr Hillsborough CA 94010-6452 Office: SRI Internat 333 Ravenswood Ave Menlo Park CA 94025-3453

SOMMESE, ANDREW JOHN, mathematics educator; b. N.Y.C., May 3, 1948; s. Joseph Anthony and Frances (Lia) S.; m. Rebecca Rooze DeBoer, June 7, 1971; children: Rachel, Ruth. BA in Math., Fordham U., 1969; PhD in Math., Princeton U., 1973. Gibbs instr. Yale U., New Haven, 1973-75; asst. prof. Cornell U., Ithaca, N.Y., 1975-79; assoc. prof. U. Notre Dame, Ind., 1979-83, prof. of math., 1983—, chair dept. math., 1988-92, Vincent J. Duncan and Annamarie Micus Duncan chair math., 1994—; mem. Inst. for Advanced Study, Princeton, N.J., 1975-76; guest prof. U. Bonn, Germany, 1978-79; guest rschr. Max Planck Inst. for Math., Bonn, 1992-93; cons. GM Rsch., Warren, Mich., 1986—. Editor: Manuscripta Mathematica jour., 1986-93; contbr. articles to profl. publs. Recipient Rsch. award for Sr. U.S. Scientists Alexander Von Humboldt found., 1993; A.P. Sloan Found. rsch. fellow, 1979. Mem. Am. Math. Soc., Soc. for Indsl. and Applied Math., Phi Beta Kappa. Office: U Notre Dame Dept Math Notre Dame IN 46556

SOMORJAI, GABOR ARPAD, chemist, educator; b. Budapest, Hungary, May 4, 1935; came to U.S., 1957, naturalized, 1962; s. Charles and Livia (Ormos) S.; m. Judith Kaldor, Sept. 2, 1957; children: Nicole, John. BS, U. Tech. Scis., Budapest, 1956; PhD, U. Calif., Berkeley, 1960; D (hon.), Tech. U. Budapest, 1989, U. Paris, 1990, Free Univ Brussels, Belgium, 1992. Mem. research staff IBM, Yorktown Heights, N.Y., 1960-64; dir. Surface Sci. and Catalysis Program Lawrence Berkeley Lab., Calif., 1964—; mem. faculty dept. chemistry U. Calif.-Berkeley, 1964—, assoc. prof., 1967-72, prof., 1972—, Miller prof., 1978; Unilever prof. dept. chemistry U. Bristol, Eng., 1972; vis. fellow Emmanuel Coll., Cambridge, Eng., 1989; Baker lectr. Cornell U., Ithaca, N.Y., 1977; mem. editorial bds. Progress in Solid State Chemistry, 1973—, Jour. Solid State Chemistry, 1976-92, Nouveau Jour. de Chemie, 1977—, Colloid and Interface Sci., 1979—, Catalysis Revs., 1981, Jour. Phys. Chemistry, 1981-91, Langmuir, 1985—, Jour. Applied Catalysis, Molecular Physics, 1992—. Author: Principles of Surface Chemistry, 1972, Chemistry in Two Dimensions, 1981, Introduction to Surface Chemistry and Catalysis, 1994; editor-in-chief Catalysis Letters, 1988—; contbr. articles to profl. jours. Recipient Emmett award Am. Catalysis Soc., 1977, Kokes award Johns Hopkins U., 1976, Albert award Precious Metal Inst., 1986, Sr. Disting. Scientist award Alexander von Humboldt Found., 1989, E.W. Mueller award U. Wis., Chemical Pioneer award Am. Inst. of Chemists, 1995; Guggenheim fellow, 1969. Fellow AAAS, Am. Phys. Soc.; mem. NAS, Am. Acad. Arts and Scis., Am. Chem. Soc. (chmn. colloid and surface chemistry 1981, Surface and Colloid Chemistry award 1981, Peter Debye award 1989, Arthur W. Adamson award 1994), Catalysis Soc. N.Am., Hungarian Acad. Scis. (hon. 1990). Home: 665 San Luis Rd Berkeley CA 94707-1725 Office: U Calif Dept Chemistry D 58 Hildebrand Hall Berkeley CA 94720

SON, MUN SHIG, education educator; b. Hwanggan, South Korea, Feb. 5, 1950; came to the U.S., 1978; s. Young Hee and Jeong Poon (Park) S.; m. Ock Jhee Kim, June 7, 1978; children: Jennifer, John. BA in Statistics, Sung Kyun Kwan U., Seoul, 1975; MS in Statistics, Okla. State U., 1982, MS in Econs., 1984, PhD in Statistics, 1984. Rsch. asst. Cen. Bank Korea, Seoul, 1975-78; lectr. Okla. State U., Stillwater, 1983-84; vis. asst. prof. U. Vt., Burlington, 1984-86, asst. prof., 1986-91, assoc. prof., 1991—; cons. Green Mountain Power, Burlington, 1987, Sugarbush Ski Planning Com., Waitsfield, Vt., 1987—. With Korean Army, 1976-77. NSF grantee, 1986-91, Pak-Doo Rsch. Found. grantee, 1989—. Mem. Inst. Math. Statistics, Am. Statis. Assn., Korean Scientists and Engrs. Assn. Am., Korean Am. Univ. Profs. Assn. Home: 156 Old Stage Rd Essex Junction VT 05452-2513 Office: U Vt 16 Colchester Ave Burlington VT 05401-1455

SONDE, THEODORE IRWIN, lawyer; b. N.Y.C., Jan. 7, 1940; s. Martin and Anne (Greenbaum) S.; m. Susan Kolisch, Sept. 10, 1964; children: Andrea Martine, David Ian. BA, CCNY, 1961; LLB, NYU, 1964; LLM, Georgetown U., 1967. Bar: N.Y. 1964, D.C. 1978, U.S. Supreme Ct. With SEC, Washington, 1964-80, asst. gen. counsel, office of Gen. Counsel, 1970-74, assoc. dir. div. of enforcement, 1974-80; dir. Office of Enforcement, Fed. Energy Regulatory Commn., 1980-81; mem. Cole, Corette & Abrutyn, Washington, 1982-90, Dechert, Price & Rhodes, 1990—; adj. prof. Georgetown U. Law Sch. 1977-95, George Washington U. Nat. Law Ctr., 1976-82. Contbr. articles to legal jours. Office: Dechert Price & Rhoads 1500 K St NW Washington DC 20005-1209

SONDEL, PAUL MARK, pediatric oncologist, educator; b. Milw., Aug. 14, 1950; s. Robert F. and Audrey J. (Dworkus) S.; m. Sherie Ann Katz, Jan. 1, 1973; children: Jesse Adam, Beth Leah, Elana Rose, Jodi Zipporah. BS with honors, U. Wis., 1971, PhD in Genetics, 1975; MD magna cum laude, Harvard Med. Sch., Boston, 1977. Diplomate Nat. Bd. Med. Examiners, Am. Bd. Pediatrics; lic. physician, Wis. Postdoctoral rsch. fellow Harvard Med. Sch., Boston, 1975-77; intern in pediatrics U. Minn. Hosp., Mpls., 1977-78; resident in pediatris U. Wis. Hosp. and Clinics, Madison, 1978-80; asst. prof. pediatrics, human oncology and genetics U. Wis., Madison, 1980-84, assoc. prof., 1984-86, prof. pediatrics, human oncology and genetics, 1987—, head divsn. pediatric hematology/oncology, program leader, 1990-96; prof. U. Wis., 1996—; assoc. dir. U Wisc. Cancer Ctr., 1996—; sub-fellow pediatric oncology; Midwest Children's Cancer Ctr., Milw., 1980; vis. scientist dept. cell biology Weizmann Inst. Sci., Rehovot, Israel, 1987. Sr. editor, Clinical Cancer Rsch. 1996—, mem. editorial bd. Jour. Immunology, 1985-87, Jour. Nat. Cancer Inst., 1987—, Jour. Biol. Response Modifiers, 1990—, BLOOD, 1992—, Natural Immunity, 1992—; contbr. articles to Jour. Exptl. Medicine, Jour. Immunology, Cellular Immunology, Immunol. Revs., Med. Pediatric Oncology, Wis. State Med. Jour., Jour. Biol. Response Modifiers, Jour. Pediatrics, Jour. Clin. Oncology, Jour. Clin. Investigation, and others. State of Wis. Regents scholar, 1968; J.A. and G.L. Hartford Found. fellow, 1981-84. Mem. Am. Assn. Immunologists, Am. Assn. Clin. Histocompatibility Typing, Am. Fedn. Clin. Rsch., Am. Soc. Pediatric Hematology/Oncology, Am. Assn. Cancer Rsch., Am. Soc. Transplant Physicians, Am. Soc. Clin. Oncology, Am. Acad. Pediatrics, Leukeima Soc. Am. (bd. dirs. Wis. chpt. 1987—), Disting. Physicians Am., Am. Cancer Soc. (sci. adv. com. immunology 1992—), Midwest Soc. Pediatric Rsch., Soc. Biol. Therapy (bd. dirs. 1989—, sci. adv. bd. 1989—), Transplantation Soc., Phi Beta Kappa, others. Achievements include patent for Typing Leukocyte Antigens; research in breast cancer cells enhances resistance to doxorubicin but not lymphocyte mediated killing, clinical and immunological effects of human recombinant Interleukin-2. Home: 1114 Winston Dr Madison WI 53711-3161 Office: U Wis K4/448 Clin Sci Ctr 600 Highland Ave Madison WI 53792-0001

SONDERBY, SUSAN PIERSON, federal bankruptcy judge; b. Chgo., May 15, 1947; d. George W. and Shirley L. (Eckstrom) Pierson; m. James A. De Witt, June 14, 1975 (dec. 1978); m. Peter R. Sonderby, Apr. 7, 1990. AA, Joliet (Ill.) Jr. Coll., 1967; BA, U. Ill., 1969; JD, John Marshall Law Sch., 1973. Bar: Ill. 1973, U.S. Dist. Ct. (cen. and so. dists.) Ill. 1978, U.S. Dist. Ct. (no. dist.) Ill. 1984, U.S. Ct. Appeals (7th Cir.) 1984. Assoc. O'Brien, Garrison, Berard, Kusta and De Witt, Joliet, 1973-75, ptnr., 1975-77; asst. atty. gen. consumer protection div., litigation sect. Office of the Atty. Gen., Chgo., 1977-78; asst. atty. gen., chief consumer protection div. Office of the Atty. Gen., Springfield, Ill., 1978-83; U.S. trustee for no. dist. Ill. Chgo., 1983-86; judge U.S. Bankruptcy Ct. (no. dist.) Ill., Chgo., 1986—; adj. faculty De Paul U. Coll. Law, Chgo., 1986; spl. asst. atty. gen., 1972-78; past mem. U.S. Trustee adv. com., consumer adv. coun. Fed. Res. Bd.; past sec. of State Fraudulent I.D. com., Dept. of Ins. Task Force on Improper Claims Practices. Mem. Fourth Presbyn. Ch., Art Inst. Chgo.; past mem. Westminster Presbyn. Ch., Chgo. Coun. of Fgn. Rels.; past bd. dirs. Land of Lincoln Coun. Girl Scouts U.S.; past mem. individual guarantors com. Goodman Theatre, Chgo.; past chmn. clubs and orgns. Sangamon County United Way Capital campaign; past bd. dirs., chmn. house rules com. and legal subcom. Lake Point Tower; past mem. Family Svc. Ctr., Aid to Retarded Citizens, Henson Robinson Zoo. Master Abraham Lincoln Marovitz Inn of Ct.; fellow Am. Coll. Bankruptcy; mem. Nat. Conf. Bankruptcy Judges (legis. outreach com.), Am. Bankruptcy Inst., Comml. Law League Am. (exec. coun. bankruptcy and insolvency sect., bankrupcty com., past vice chmn. U.S. Trustee Rev. com., edn. com.), Law Club of Chgo., Legal Club of Chgo. (hon.), Nordic Law Club. Avocations: travel, flying, interior decorating. Office: US Bankruptcy Ct 219 S Dearborn St Ste 638 Chicago IL 60604

SONDEREGGER, THEO BROWN, psychology educator; b. Birmingham, Ala., May 31, 1925; d. Ernest T. and Vera M. (Sillox) Brown; children: Richard Paul, Diane Carol, Douglas Robert. BS, Fla. State U., 1946; MA in Chemistry, U. Nebr., 1948, MA in Exptl. Psychology, 1960; PhD in Clin. Psychology, U. Nebr., 1965. Lic. psychologist, Calif; clin. lic., cert. Nebr. Asst. prof. U. Nebr. Med. Ctr., Omaha, 1965-71, Nebr. Wesleyan U., Lincoln, 1965-68; asst. prof. U. Nebr., Lincoln, 1968-71, assoc. prof., 1971-76, prof., 1976-94; ret., 1994, prof. emeritus, 1995—; vol. assoc. prof. U. Nebr. Med. Ctr., 1972-77, courtesy prof. med. psychology, 1977-95. Editor: Nebr. Symposium on Motivation, 1974, 84, 91, Problems of Perinatal Drug Dependence: Research and Clinical Implications, 1986, Neurobehavioral Toxicology and Teratology vol. 8, 1988-89, Problems of Perinatal Drug Dependence, 1979, 82, 84, Feminist Therapy Interchange, 1988-89, 91, Perinatal Substance Abuse: Research and Clinical Implications, 1992, Agendas for Aging, 1994—. Mem. grant rev. coms. Nat. Inst. Drug Abuse, 1983-84, 85, 91-94. Tribute to Women award Lincoln YMCA, 1985, named Outstanding Rsch. Scientist Nebr. Chpt. Sigma Xi, 1991, Outstanding Contbn. to Status of Women, N N-L Chancellors Commn. on Status of Women, 1994, Pound Howard Disting. Career Achievement award, 1996. Fellow AAAS, Am. Psychol. Assn., Am. Psychol. Soc.; mem. Midwestern Psychol. Assn., Internat. Soc. Devel. Psychobiology, Internat. Soc. Psychoneuroendocrinolty, Nebr. Psychol. Assn. (pres. 1972), Soc. Neuroscis., Advanced Feminist Therapy Inst., Region V Adv. Coun. on Drugs, Fetal Alcohol Adv. Coun., Phi Beta Kappa (sec. Nebr. chpt. 1974), Sigma Xi (pres. 1986). Club: Altrusa YWCA. Avocations: painting, photography.

SONDHEIM, STEPHEN JOSHUA, composer, lyricist; b. N.Y.C., Mar. 22, 1930; s. Herbert and Janet (Fox) S. B.A., Williams Coll., 1950. vis. prof. contemporary theater Oxford U., England, 1990. Composer incidental music Girls of Summer, 1956, Invitation to a March, 1961, Twigs, 1971; lyrics West Side Story, 1957, Gypsy, 1959, Do I Hear A Waltz?, 1965; music and lyrics A Funny Thing Happened on the Way to The Forum, 1962, Anyone Can Whistle, 1964, Evening Primrose, 1966, Company, 1970 (Tony award 1971), Follies, 1971 (Tony award 1972), A Little Night Music, 1973 (Tony award 1973), The Frogs, 1974, Pacific Overtures, 1976, Sweeney Todd, 1979 (Tony award 1979), Merrily We Roll Along, 1981, Sunday in the Park with George, 1984 (Pulitzer prize 1985), Into the Woods, 1987 (Tony award 1988), Assassins, 1991, Passion, 1994 (Tony award 1994); additional lyrics Candide, 1973; anthologies Side by Side by Sondheim, 1976, Marry Me a Little, 1981, You're Gonna Love Tomorrow, 1983, Putting It Together, 1993; film scores Stavisky, 1974, Reds, 1981; composer songs for film Dick Tracy, 1990 (Acad. award); co-author film The Last of Sheila, 1973. Recipient Creative Arts medal Brandeis U., 1982, Grammy award, 1970, 73, 75, 79, 84, 88, Kennedy Ctr. Honor for Lifetime Achievement, 1993. Mem. Am. Acad. and Inst. Arts and Letters. *

SONDHEIMER, JUDITH MCCONNELL, pediatrician, educator; b. Englewood, N.J., Apr. 20, 1944; d. John W. and Harriet H. (Barlow) McConnell; m. Henry M. Sondheimer, June 30, 1969; 2 children. BA, Swarthmore Coll., 1966; MD, Columbia U., 1970. Diplomate Am. Bd. Pediatrics, Am. Bd. Pediatric Gastroenterology. Intern then resident U. Colo., Denver, 1970-72; pediatric GI fellow Hosp. for Sick Children, Toronto, Ont., Can., 1974-76; asst. prof. pediatrics SUNY, Syracuse, 1976-80, assoc. prof. pediatrics, 1980-85; assoc. prof. pediatrics U. Colo., Denver, 1985-89, prof. pediatrics, 1989—; chief GI/Nutrition, Children's Hosp., Denver, 1985—. Fellow Am. Acad. Pediatrics; mem. Am. Gastroenterol. Soc., N.Am. Soc. Pediatric Gastroenterology and Nutrition. Office: Childrens Hosp-GI/Nutrition 1056 E 19th Ave Denver CO 80218-1007

SONDOCK, RUBY KLESS, retired judge; b. Houston, Apr. 26, 1926; d. Herman Lewis and Celia (Juran) Kless; m. Melvin Adolph Sondock, Apr. 22, 1944; children: Marcia Cohen, Sandra Marcus. AA, Cottey Coll., Nevada, Mo., 1944; BS, U. Houston, 1959, LLB, 1961. Bar: Tex. 1961, U.S. Supreme Ct. 1977. Pvt. practice, Houston, 1961-73, 89—; judge Harris County Ct. Domestic Rels. (312th Dist.), 1973-77, 234th Jud. Dist. Ct., Houston, 1977-82, 83-89; justice Tex. Supreme Ct., Austin, 1982; of counsel Weil Gotshal and Manges, 1989-93, Houston Ctr., 1993—. Mem. ABA, Tex. Bar Assn., Houston Bar Assn., Houston Assn. Women Lawyers, Order of Barons, Phi Theta Phi, Kappa Beta Pi, Phi Kappa Phi, Alpha Epsilon Pi. Office: 2650 Two Houston Ctr 909 Fannin Houston TX 77010

SONEGO, IAN G., state assistant attorney general; b. Louisville, May 27, 1954; s. Angelo and Zella Mae (Causey) S. BA in Polit. Sci. with high honors, U. Louisville, 1976, JD, 1979. Bar: Ky. 1979, U.S. Dist Ct. (ea. dist.) Ky. 1980, U.S. Dist. Ct. (we. dist.) Ky. 1989, U.S. Ct. Appeals (6th cir.) 1989, U.S. Supreme Ct. 1990. Asst. atty. Office Commonwealth's Atty. Pike County, Pikeville, Ky., 1980, sr. asst. atty., 1988-89; assoc. John Paul Runyon Law Firm, Pikeville, 1981-87; asst. atty. gen. Office Atty. Gen., Frankfort, Ky., 1989—; lectr. criminal law Ky. Bar Assn., Jenny Wiley Park, 1981, Ky. Prosecutors Confs., 1989, 93; mem. Atty. Gen.'s task force child sexual abuse, 1992-94, Nat. Conf. on Domestic Violence, 1996. Contbg. editor Ky. Prosecuter Newsletter, 1991—. Recipient Kessleman award U. Louisville, 1975, Bd. Trustee award 1979. Outstanding Prosecutor award Ky. Atty. Mem. Ky. Commonwealth's Attys. Assn. (hon., lectr. 1987, 90, chmn. com. ethics 1984-86, bd. dirs. 1983-85, Outstanding Svc. award 1985, Spl. award 1987). Office: Office Atty Gen Criminal Appellate Divsn 1024 Capital Center Dr Frankfort KY 40601-8204

SONENBERG, DAVID A., personal manager; b. Bklyn., Mar. 22, 1947; s. Harold and charlotte (Feinberg) S.; m. Shelley Jean Marcus, May 14, 1985; 1 child, Elizabeth Cole. BA, Tufts U., 1968; JD, Harvard U., 1971. Assoc. Weisberger & Frosch, N.Y.C., 1971-73, Katz, Leavy, Rosensweig & Sindle, N.Y.C., 1973-76; pres. DAS Communications, Ltd., N.Y.C., 1977—. Producer film Dead Ringer, 1981; record I Am Siam, 1985; exec. producer TV film B.B. King Spl., 1989, Pointer Sisters Spl., 1989; mgr. records Bat Out of Hell, 1977 (golden Globe award 1982, biggest selling debut album in history), Heaven, 1988 (Grammy winner). Home and Office: 83 Riverside Dr New York NY 10024-5209

SONENBERG, JACK, artist; b. Toronto, Ont., Can., Dec. 28, 1925; s. Solomon and Leah (Saltzman) S.; m. Phoebe Helman, June 7, 1949; 1 dau., Maya. Student, N.Y. U., 1949; B.F.A., Washington U., 1951. Mem. faculty dept. art Queens Coll., 1970-72, Bklyn. Coll., 1972, Bklyn. Coll. (Sch. of Visual Arts), 1962-73; mem. faculty Pratt Inst., Bklyn., 1968—; chmn. painting and drawing dept. Pratt Inst. Bklyn., 1973—. One-man shows, Byron Gallery, N.Y.C., 1965, 68, Hampton Inst., 1968, U. No. Iowa, 1969, Grand Rapids (Mich.) Art Mus., 1968, Flint Inst. Arts, 1972, Fischbach Gallery, N.Y.C., 1973, 55 Mercer Gallery, N.Y.C., 1980, group shows include, Whitney Mus., 1967, 73, Mus. Modern Art, 1974, Art Inst. Chgo., 1975, Pratt Inst., Bklyn., 1980, Rutgers U., N.J., 1980, Nat. Gallery, Washington, 1980, Moscow Artists Union, 1989; group shows include Painting Self-Evident, Piccolo Spolete, 1992; represented in permanent collections, Guggenheim Mus., Whitney Mus., Washington U., Met. Mus., Bradley U., Nat. Gallery Can., W.Va. U. Ford Found. grantee, 1966; Guggenheim Found. grantee, 1973, N.Y. State CAPS, 1973-76, Nat. Endowment Arts grantee (sculpture), 1984-85, N.Y. Found. for the Arts grantee (painting) 1989. Office: Pratt Inst Sch Art and Design Brooklyn NY 11205

SONENBERG, MARTIN, biochemistry educator, physician; b. N.Y.C., Dec. 1, 1920; s. Berl and Nellie (Gordon) S.; m. Dellie Madeleine Ellis, Jan. 17, 1956; children: Santha, Andrea. B.A., U. Pa., 1941; M.D., NYU, 1944, PhD in Chemistry, 1952. Mem. Sloan-Kettering Cancer Center, N.Y.C., 1950, chief endocrinology, 1972-94; faculty Cornell U., 1950—, prof. biochemistry, 1967-83, prof. medicine, 1972—, prof. cell biology and genetics, 1983—. Mem. editorial bd.: Endocrinology, 1967-75; contbr. articles to profl. jours. Mem. biomed. adv. com. Population Coun., 1960; mem. adv. com. Am. Cancer Soc., 1971; chmn. endocrinology study sect. NIH, mem. adv. com. divsn. rsch. grants, 1989-91. Recipient Van Meter award Am. Thyroid Assn., 1952; Am. Cancer Soc. scholar, 1952-55; Guggenheim fellow, 1957-58; recipient Sloan award for cancer research, 1968. Mem. Am. Thyroid Assn., Am. Soc. Clin. Investigation, Am. Soc. Biol. Chemists, Endocrine Soc. Research on role of pituitary gland in normal and abnormal growth. Office: 1275 York Ave New York NY 10021-6007

SONENREICH, STEVEN DOUGLAS, hospital administrator; b. N.Y.C., Oct. 29, 1953; s. Albert and Sylvia (Hoffman) S.; m. Helen Penderakis, Feb. 5, 1983; children: Katrina, Brooke. BA, SUNY, Binghamton, 1976; MBA in Health Adminstrn., U. Miami, 1990. Dir. patient fin. svcs. Mt. Sinai Med. Ctr., Miami Beach, Fla., 1976-83, dir. mktg., 1983-86, v.p., 1986-90, exec. v.p., COO, 1990-96; CEO Columbia Cedars Med. Ctr., Miami, Fla., 1996—; bd. dirs. HMO, Healthcare Consortium Exec. Com., Dimension Health, Inc., acting CEO, 1985-87; adj. prof. Sch. Bus. Adminstrn. U. Miami, Coral Gables. Mem. Mt. Sinai Med. Ctr. Physician Hosp. Orgn. (bd. dirs., treas.), South Fla. Hosp. Assn. (bd. dirs. health consortium 1993-94, Personnel Dirs. Assn. award 1994), Am. Assn. Preferred Provider Orgns. (editl. bd., advisory dir.), Beta Gamma Sigma. Avocations: sports, music. Home: 5775 SW 131 Terrace Miami FL 33156

SONENSHEIN, ABRAHAM LINCOLN, microbiology educator; b. Paterson, N.J., Jan. 13, 1944; s. Israel Louis and Celia (Rabinowitz) S.; m. Gail Entner, Jan. 28, 1967; children: Dina Miriam, Adam Israel. AB, Princeton U., 1965; PhD, MIT, 1970. Postdoctoral fellow U. Paris, Orsay, France, 1970-72; asst. prof. Tufts U., Boston, 1972-78, assoc. prof., 1978-82, prof., 1982—. Rsch. grantee NIH, 1972—; fellow Am. Cancer Soc., 1970-72. Mem. AAAS, Am. Soc. for Microbiology, Am. Acad. Microbiology, Fedn. Am. Scientists, Sigma Xi. Office: Tufts U 136 Harrison Ave Boston MA 02111-1817

SONENSHEIN, NATHAN, marine consulting company executive, retired naval officer; b. Lodi, N.J., Aug. 2, 1915; s. H. W. and Sarah S.; m. Ila Nina Maria Baker, May 11, 1941; children: Carol Dale Manashil, William Baker. B.S., U.S. Naval Acad., 1938; M.S., MIT, 1944; grad. Advanced Mgmt. Program, Harvard U., 1964. Commd. ensign U.S. Navy, 1938, advanced through grades to rear adm., 1965; various assignments U.S. and Japan, 1938-49; dir. navy facilities div. Bur. Ships, 1949-51; engring. officer U.S.S. Philippine Sea, 1951-53; planning and estimating supt. N.Y. Naval Shipyard, 1953-56; head hull design br. Bur. Ships, 1956-60; fleet and force maintenance officer on staffs comdr.-in-chief and comdr. service force U.S. Pacific Fleet, 1960-62; dir. ship design div. Bur. Ships, 1962-64, asst. chief for design, shipbldg. and fleet maintenance, 1965; project mgr. Fast Deployment Logistics Ship Project, 1965-66; dep. chief naval material for logistic support, 1967-69; comdr. Naval Ship Systems Command, 1969-72; chmn. NMC Shipbldg. Council, 1972-73; dir. for energy Dept. Def., 1973-74, ret., 1974; asst. to pres. Global Marine Devel., Inc., Newport Beach, Calif., 1974-84; pres. Sonenshein and Assocs., marine cons. co., Moraga, Calif., 1985—; mem. nat. adv. com. Oceans and Atmosphere, 1984-86. Decorated Legion of Merit with 2 Gold stars. Mem. Am. Soc. Naval Architects and Marine Engrs. (v.p.), Am. Soc. Naval Engrs. (past pres., H.E. Saunders medal 1982), Sigma Xi. Home and Office: 1884 Joseph Dr Moraga CA 94556-2711

SONFIELD, ROBERT LEON, JR., lawyer; b. Houston, Oct. 28, 1931; s. Robert Leon and Dorothy Harriett (Huber) S.; 1 dau., Sheree. B.A., U. Houston, 1956, LL.B., J.D., 1959; Ph.D. (hon.), U. Eastern Fla., 1962; LL.D. (hon.), London Inst. Applied Research, 1973; certificate fed. taxation, NYU, 1973; certificate securities regulation, Harvard U., 1983. Bar: Tex. 1959, U.S. Supreme Ct. 1959, U.S. Dist. Ct. Tex. 1960, U.S. Tax Ct. 1960, U.S. Ct. Appeals 1960, U.S. Ct. Claims 1974. Mng. dir. Sonfield & Sonfield, Houston, 1959—; Mem. nat. adv. council Nat. Fedn. Ind. Bus. Author: Corporate Financing by Sale of Securities to the Public, 1969, Mergers and Acquisitions, 1970, Student Rights, 1971, The Limited Partnership as a Vehicle for Real Estate Investment, 1971, Integration of Partnership Offerings, 1974, The Grantor Trust Rules After The Tax Reform Act of 1986, Incentive Equity Program, Corporate Name Protection Along With Name Registration, A Guide to SEC Corporate Filing, Organizational Professionals' Residual Litigation and Investment Strategy, Comparing California, Delaware and Nevada: Corporate Laws in Light of California Corporations Code Section 2115 and Offering of Unregistered Securities Only to Accredited Investors, Disclosure Policies, Practices and Procedures For Public Companies, Regulation of Franchises, How to Become a Publicly Held Company Via the Registered Ditribution of a Percentage of Your Company's Stock to Shareholders, numerous others. Recipient St. John Garwood award, 1957, Frio-Finnegan Outstanding Alumnus award, 1970-71, citation for outstanding contbn. to legal profession, 1971. Mem. Am. Tax Lawyers Assn. (pres.), Lawyers Soc. Houson, Am. Judicature Soc., ABA, Tex. Bar

Assn. (dist. com. on admission to state bar, chmn. clients security fund com.), Houston Bar Assn. (com. chmn. council, tax sect.), Tex. Equal Access to Justice Found., Houston Bar Found., Real Estate Securities and Syndication Inst., Huguenot Soc. of London, Order Stars and Bars, SAR, Sons Confederate Vets., Mil. Order World Wars, Mil. and Hospitaller Order St. Lazarus of Jerusalem, Knightly Assn. St. George the Martyr, Smithsonian Assocs., Houston Heritage Soc., Houston Mus. Fine Arts, Newcomen Soc. N.Am., Phi Delta Phi, Delta Sigma Phi. Clubs: Metropolitan (N.Y.C.); Argyle (San Antonio); Houston, Houstonian. Office: Sonfield & Sonfield 770 S Post Oak Ln Houston TX 77056-1913

SONG, JOSEPH, pathologist, educator; b. Pyong Yang, Korea, May 11, 1927; s. Ha Ju and Hwa Soon (Koh) S.; m. Kumsan Ryu, Apr. 12, 1958; children: Patricia, Michael, Jeff. MD, Seoul (Korea) U. Sch. Medicine, 1950; MS in Pathology, U. Tenn., Memphis, 1956; MD, U. Ark. Med. Sch., Little Rock, 1965. Diplomate Am. Bd. Pathology. Pathologist in charge State Cancer Detection Survey, Providence, R.I., 1956-59; assoc. pathologist Providence Lying-In Hosp., 1959-61; assoc. prof. pathology U. Ark. Med. Ctr., Little Rock, 1961-64; dir. lab. Mercy Hosp., Des Moines, Iowa, 1965-92; cancer rschr. Mercy Hosp., Des Moines, 1993-95; clin. prof. pathology Creighton U. Sch. Medicine, Omaha, Nebr., 1968-95; med. dir. Corning Clin. Labs., Des Moines, 1995—; cons. EPA, Washington, 1975-85; pres. med. staff Mercy Hosp., Des Moines, 1981. Author: (book) The Human Uterus, 1964, Pathology of Sickle Cell Anemia, 1971 (award 1975), Beyond the Horizon, 1995. Elder Winsdor Presbyn. Ch., Des Moines, 1964; com. mem. Aldersgate Meth. Ch., Des Moines, 1995. Major Med. Corps, 1950-52, Korea. Recipient Martin Luther King Med. Achievement award, So. Christian Leadership Conf., Statesmanship award Am. Assn. Med. Adminstrs., Las Vegas, Nev., 1987. Fellow Am. Coll. of Physicians, Coll. of Am. Pathologists, Am. Soc. of Clin. Pathology, Am. Assn. for Cancer Rsch. Methodist. Avocation: classical music. Home: 2345 Park Ave Des Moines IA 50321-1505

SONG, XIAOTONG, physicist, educator; b. Taizhou, Jiangsu, People's Republic of China, Oct. 18, 1934; came to U.S., 1989; s. Hoshu Song and Jingying Wang; m. Chuchu Zhu, 1966; 1 child, Jianyang. BS in Physics, Fudan U., Shanghai, China, 1955, PhD in Physics, 1963. Rsch. fellow Dept Def., China, 1955-58; asst. prof. Hangzhou U., China, 1958-63; lectr., 1963-66, 77-83, assoc. prof., 1983-86, prof., 1986—; rsch. cons. dept. physics Inst. Nuclear and Particle Physics, U. Va., Charlottesville, 1989-90, rsch. prof., cons., 1990—; adv. com. for professorship exam., Zhejiang, China; dir. theory divsn. dept. physics Hangzhou U., China, 1984-89; referee Phys. Rev., High Energy Physics and Nuclear Physics, Nat. Natural Sci. Found., China; vis. scientist Tech. U. Munich, 1986, 88-89, European Lab. for Particle Physics, Geneva, 1986-87, Inst. Nat. Fisica Nuclear Turin Sect., Italy, 1986-88, Internat. Ctr. Theoretical Physics, Italy, 1986-88, Los Alamos Nat. Lab., 1987, Utah State U., 1987, Kans. State U., 1989, Brookhaven Nat. Lab. Contbr. articles to profl. jours. Recipient Prize of Natural Sci., Com. Sci. and Tech., Zhejiang Province, China, 1983, 84; grantee Nat. Natural Sci. Found., 1984-87. Mem. AAAS, Internat. Ctr. Theoretical Physics (sr. assoc.), Am. Phys. Soc., Chinese High Energy Physics Soc., Chinese Phys. Soc., N.Y. Acad. Sci., Sigma Xi. Achievements include research in theoretical nuclear and particle physics. Office: U Va Physics Dept Mccormick Rd Charlottesville VA 22901

SONI, MARIA HABIB, controller, treasurer; b. Kahale, Beirut, Lebanon, July 27, 1956; came to U.S., 1979; d. Habib Hanna and Sadie (Zeghondy) Abi-Khalil; divorced; 1 child, Jean-Noel. M in Child Psychology and Math, U. Lyon, 1975; BA, Beirut Bus. Sch., 1977; BA in Acctg. Tchr. Dominican Sisters, Beirut, 1974-78; adminstr. Daoud Engring., Beirut, 1978-79; v.p. Sa-Beers Jewelry, 1979-83; v.p., exec. adminstr. Gaylin Buick, Union, N.J., 1986-91; adminstr., treas., contr. Ruckstuhl USA, Union, N.J., 1992—; cons. in field. Mem. Rotary (treas. 1997-98, bd. dirs. 1995—, dir. 1997—), Interact Club (chmn.), Union Rotary (treas. 1997—). Republican. Avocations: reading, writing, painting, jewelry, art. Home: 2243 Morris Ave Union NJ 07083-5910 Office: Ruckstuhl USA Ltd 1480 Ridgeway St Union NJ 07083-5128

SONIN, AIN A., mechanical engineering educator, consultant; b. Tallinn, Estonia, Dec. 24, 1937; came to U.S., 1965; s. Elmar and Ina (Herman) S.; m. Epp Jurima, July 24, 1971; children: Juhan, Aldo. BA Sc., U. Toronto, Ont., Can., 1960, MA Sc., 1961, PhD, 1965. Rsch. fellow, teaching asst. U. Toronto, 1960-65; asst. prof. MIT, Cambridge, 1965-68, assoc. prof., 1968-74, prof. mech. engring., 1974—; sr. scientist Thermo Electron Corp., Waltham, Mass., 1981-82; cons. in field. Contbr. over 60 articles to profl. jours. in fluid and thermal sciences. Mem. ASME, AAAS, Am. Phys. Soc., Am. Nuclear Soc. Achievements include 3 patents in field. Office: MIT Rm 3-256 Cambridge MA 02139

SONKOWSKY, ROBERT PAUL, classicist, educator, actor; b. Appleton, Wis., Sept. 16, 1931; s. Paul and Loretta Stella (Nooyen) S.; m. Barbara Lou Zierke, June 8, 1956; children—Paul Victor, Steven Robert, Michael Edward. B.A., Lawrence Coll., 1954; postgrad., U. Rome, 1956-57; Ph.D., U. N.C., 1958. Instr., asst. prof. U. Tex., 1958-61; fellow Inst. Research in Humanities, U. Wis., 1961-62; asso. prof. U. Mo., 1962-63, U. Minn., Mpls., 1963-64; chmn. dept. classics U. Minn., 1964-78, prof., 1964—; disting. Marbrook vis. prof. Macalester Coll., 1987-88; actor Attic Theatre, Appleton, Wis., 1950-54, Wilderness Rd. Theater Co., Berea, Ky., The Confederacy Co. Virginia Beach, Va., summers, 1955-58, Pillsbury House and Lyric Theaters, Mpls., 1991, Looking Galss Theater, St. Paul, 1993, Theater on the Park, Mpls., 1994-96; guest artist U. Minn. Theatre, 1996. Author books; contbr. articles to profl. jours.; also recitations and recordings of classical Latin lit. in restored pronunciation; lit. recs., ednl. feature and indsl. films, TV commls. Lay reader Episc. Cathedral Ch. of St. Mark; lector Gregorian Singers, 1980-89; mem. St. Paul Sch. Com., 1971-76. Mem. AFTRA, Am. Philol. Assn., Soc. for Oral Reading of Greek and Latin Lit., Classical Assn. Mid West and South Internat. Soc. Chronobiology (nomenclature com.), Fulbright Assn. (pres. Minn. chpt. 1991-92), Phi Beta Kappa (pres. U. Minn. chpt. 1973-74, nat. senator 1976-82, pres. Minn. Assn. 1991-95, books reviewer for Key Reporter). Office: U Minn Classical & Near Ea Studies 330 Folwell Hall 9 Pleasant St SE Minneapolis MN 55455-0194

SONNABEND, ROGER PHILIP, hotel company executive; b. Boston, Sept. 17, 1925; s. Abraham M. and Esther (Lewitt) S.; m. Elsa Golub, July 17, 1949 (div.); children: Andrea, Stephanie, Jacqueline, Alan; m. Joan Snider, Feb. 18, 1971; stepchildren: Heidi Norton, Andrea Stoneman. B.A., MIT, 1946; M.B.A., Harvard U., 1949; LL.D. (hon.), U. N.H., 1969. Chief exec. officer Sonesta Internat. Hotel Corp., Boston, 1954—, chmn., 1970—. Contbr. chpts. to books and articles to profl. jours. Mem. exec. com. Nat. Alliance of Businessmen, 1968-69; bd. dirs. Bus. Execs. for Nat. Security, Inc., Washington, 1983-86; exec. com. Northeast NCCJ, 1957, regional co-chmn., nat. v.p., 1960-68; trustee Inst. Contemporary Art. Mem. World Bus. Coun., Chief Execs. Orgn., Harvard Club (Boston). Home: 350 Ocean Dr Key Biscayne FL 33149 Office: Sonesta Internat Hotels Corp 200 Clarendon St Boston MA 02116-5021

SONNE, MAGGIE LEE, travel company executive; b. Pasadena, Calif., July 14, 1958; d. Roscoe Newbold Jr. and Ann Miriam (Vierhus) S.; m. Donald Alan Blackburn, Sept. 8, 1979 (div. 1983). AS, Oreg. Inst. Tech., 1981, BS, 1983. Sales trainee NCR Corp., Dayton, Ohio, 1983-84; sales rep. NCR Corp., Portland, Oreg., 1984-86; account mgr. NCR Corp., Seattle, 1986-87; sr. account mgr. NCR Corp., Portland, 1987-88; sr. account rep. Wang Labs., Portland, 1988-91; account exec. Tandem Computers, Portland, 1991-94; sr. acct. exec. Fin. Svcs., L.A., 1994-96; pres. Travel Club Adventures, Surfside, Calif., 1996—. Active Emily's List, Project Vote Smart, Ams. for Change, Presdl. Task Force, Pres. Coun., Tandem Computers, Inc. Mem. Soc. Advancement Mgmt., Costeau Soc., Alpha Chi. Avocations: sailing, diving, skiing, biking, golf. Home: PO Box 323 Surfside CA 90743-0323

SONNEBORN, HENRY, III, former chemical company executive, business consultant; b. Balt., Mar. 11, 1918; s. Henry, Jr. and Lillian B. (Hamburger) S.; m. Clara Louise Lauer, Nov. 12, 1942; 1 child, Peter. A.B., Johns Hopkins U., 1938, Ph.D., 1941; doctorate (hon.), Hebrew U., Jerusalem, 1976. V.p., bd. dirs. Sonneborn Chem. and Refining, N.Y.C., 1950-60; bus. cons., Larchmont, N.Y.; bus. cons. Contbr. articles to profl. jours. Mem. PMI-Strang Clinic, 1969-72; trustee Hosp. for Joint Diseases, 1961—, chmn. bd., 1985-88; pres. Am. Friends Hebrew U., 1974-77; trustee Johns Hopkins U., 1978—. Served to lt. USNR, 1942-46. Jewish. Home: 5006 Theall Rd Rye NY 10580

SONNECKEN, EDWIN HERBERT, management consultant; b. New Haven, July 22, 1916; s. Ewald and Pauline (Halfmann) S.; m. Elizabeth Gregory, June 3, 1939; children: William H., Richard G., Paul D. B.S., Northwestern U., 1938; M.B.A., 1940. With Montgomery Ward & Co., Chgo., 1940-42; price adminstr. OPA, Chgo., 1943; mgr. sales B.F. Goodrich Co., Akron, Ohio, 1943-53; dir. planning Ford Motor Co., Dearborn, Mich., 1953-57; pres. Market Planning Corp., N.Y.C., 1957-61; from dir. corp. planning and research to v.p. corp. bus. planning Goodyear Tire & Rubber Co., 1961-80; chmn. Mktg. Sci. Inst., Cambridge, Mass., 1980-84; also trustee, chmn. research policy com. Mktg. Sci. Inst.; mgmt. cons., Akron, 1985—; Pres. Akron (Ohio) chpt. Am. Mktg. Assn., 1950, v.p. Detroit chpt., 1955, nat. v.p., dir., 1957, nat. pres., 1964-65, mem. global mktg. coun., 1986—. Pres. YMCA, Akron, 1978; chmn. trustees First Congl. Ch., Akron, 1985, chmn. endowment trust, 1987—. Served with AUS, 1945-46. Mem. Am. Statis. Assn., Am. Assn. Pub. Opinion Research, Nat. Assn. Bus. Economists, Am. Mktg. Assn., Internat. Mktg. Fedn. (pres.), European Soc. for Opinion and Market Research, Beta Gamma Sigma, Portage Country (Akron). Avocation: golf. Home: 736 Hampton Ridge Dr Akron OH 44313-5024

SONNEDECKER, GLENN ALLEN, historian of pharmacy; b. Creston, Ohio, Dec. 11, 1917; s. Ira Elmer and Letia (Linter) S.; m. Cleo Bell, Apr. 3, 1943; 1 child, Stuart Bruce. BS, Ohio State U., 1942; MS, U Wis., 1950, PhD, 1952; Dr. Sci. honoris causa, Ohio State U., 1964, Phila. Coll. Pharmacy and Sci., 1989; PharmD honoris causa, Mass. Coll. Pharmacy, 1974. Lic. pharmacist. Mem. editorial staff Sci. Service, Washington, 1942-43; editor Jour. Am. Pharm. Assn. (practical pharmacy edit.), Washington, 1943-48; asst. prof. U. Wis., 1952-56, asso. prof., 1956-60, prof., 1960-81, Edward Kremers prof., 1981-86; sec. Am. Inst. History of Pharmacy, 1949-57, dir., 1957-73, 81-85, hon. dir. life, chmn. bd., 1988-89; editor-in-chief RPh, 1978-80; sec., bd. dirs. Friends of Hist. Pharmacy, 1945-49; chmn. Joint Com. on Pharmacy Coll. Librs., 1960-61; U.S. del. Internat. Pharm. Fedn., 1953, 55, 62; U.S. rep. to Mid. East Pharm. Congress, Beirut, 1956; sec. sect. history of pharmacy and biochemistry Pan-Am. Congress Pharmacy and Biochemistry, 1957. Co-author books; contbr. to pharm. and hist. publs. Recipient Edward Kremers award (for writings), 1964, Nat. award Rho Chi, 1967, Schelenz plaquette Internat. Soc. for History of Pharmacy, 1971, Remington honor medal Am. Pharm. Assn., 1972, Urdang medal, 1976, Folch Andreu prize, Spain, 1985, Profile award Am. Found. Pharm. Edn., 1994; Am. Found. fellow, 1948-52, Guggenheim fellow, 1955, Fulbright Rsch. scholar, Germany, 1955-56. Mem. Am. Pharm. Assn. (life mem.; sec. sect. history of pharmacy 1949-50, vice chmn. 1950-51, chmn. 1951-52, rsch. assoc. 1964-65, chmn. joint task force with Acad. Pharm Scis. 1985, hon. chmn. bd. trustees 1985), Internat. Acad. History Pharmacy (1st v.p. 1970-81, pres. 1983-91, hon. pres. 1991—), Am. Assn. History of Medicine (exec. coun. 1966-69), Internat. Gesellschaft fur Geschichte der Pharmazie (exec. bd. 1965-89), hon. mem. socs. for history of pharmacy of Italy, Benelux, pan-Arab, Spain; mem. Sigma Xi, Rho Chi (mem. nat. exec. coun. 1957-59), Phi Delta Chi. Unitarian. Home: 2030 Chadbourne Ave Madison WI 53705-4047 Office: Univ Wis Pharmacy Bldg Madison WI 53706

SONNEMAN, EVE, artist; b. Chgo., 1946; d. Eric O. and Edith S. BFA, U. Ill., 1967; MFA, U. N.Mex., 1969. One-woman shows include Castelli Gallery, N.Y.C., 1976, 78, 80, 82, 84-86, Tex. Gallery, Houston, 1976, 78, 80, 82, 85, Galerie Farideh Cadot, Paris, 1978, 80, 83, François Lambert Gallery, Milan,Italy, 1980, 87, Mpls. Inst. Arts, 1980, La Noveau Musée, Lyon, France, 1980, Musée de Toulon (France), 1983, Centre Georges Pompidou, Paris, 1984, Circus Gallery, L.A., 1989, Jones Troyer Fitzpatrick, Washington, 1989, Zabriskie Gallery, N.Y., 1990, Gloria Luria Gallery, Miami, 1990, Grand Central Terminal, N.Y.C., 1991, Charles Cowles Gallery, 1992, Sidney Janis Gallery, N.Y.C., 1996, La Geode Mus., Paris, 1996; author: America's Cottage Gardens, 1990, Where Birds Live, 1992; photographs subject of book Real Time, 1976. Grantee Nat. Endowment Arts, 1971, 78, Polaroid Corp., 1978; Cartier fellowship, France, 1989. Address: 446 W 47 St 5C New York NY 10036

SONNEMANN, HARRY, electrical engineer, consultant; b. Munich, Germany, Sept. 3, 1924; came to U.S., 1938, naturalized, 1944; s. Leopold and Emmy (Markus) S.; m. Shirley E. Battles, Nov. 25, 1949; children: Carol Jean, Joyce Elaine, Patricia Ann. B.S., Poly. Inst. Bklyn., 1954. Research electroence-phalography, 1944-47; asst. to dir. electronics dept. AEC contract, Columbia U., 1947-50; supr. electronics shop Columbia Hudson Labs., 1951-53, head electronics dept., 1954-59; asst. dir. Project Artemis, 1959-64, Project Artemis (Hudson labs.), 1961-64; asst. dir. field engring. Advanced Research Projects Agy., Nuclear Test Detection Office, 1964-67; acting dep. dir. Nuclear Test Detection Office, 1967-68; spl. asst. in electronics to asst. sec. navy for research and devel. Navy Dept., 1968-76, spl. asst. to asst. sec. navy for research and devel., 1976-77; asst. to chief engr. NASA, 1977-78, dep. chief engr., 1978-84, asst. chief engr., 1984-86, cons., 1986—; pres. SBC Assocs. Inc., McLean, Va., 1988-95; chmn. Dept. Def. Tactical Satellite Exec. Steering Group, 1968-69, chmn. Dept. Def. nav. satellite exec. steering group, 1969-70, 72-73. Treas. Art League. No. Va., 1967-68; pres. Rotonda Condominium Unit Owners Assn., 1982-84. Clubs: Washington Figure Skating (dir. 1968-73, treas. 1969-72), Ice of Washington (pres. 1974-76). Home and Office: 8360 Greensboro Dr Apt 907 Mc Lean VA 22102-3514

SONNENBERG, BEN, playwright, poet, editor, producer; b. N.Y.C., Dec. 30, 1936; s. Benjamin and Hilda (Caplan) S.; m. Dorothy Gallagher, Mar. 10, 1981; children by previous marriages: Susanna, Emma, Saidee. Literary advisor Oxford (Eng.) Playhouse, 1963-65; lit. mgr. Repertory Theatre of Lincoln Ctr., N.Y.C., 1971-72; lectr. drama ctr. Juilliard Sch., N.Y.C., 1977-78; editor Grand Street, N.Y.C., 1981-90; pub. Grand Street Books, N.Y.C., 1990—. Author: Jane Street, The Courtship of Rita Hayworth, Mole Wedding, (plays) Poems of Anna Comnena and More Poems, 1990, Lost Property, Memoirs and Confessions of a Bad Boy, 1991; editor: Grand Street Reader, 1986, Performance and Reality: Essays from Grand Street; prodr. Westbeth Growing Up, 1995, Breadman, 1996, Lavender Lake, 1997; contbr. articles to The Nation, London mag., Yale Rev., Raritan, Harper's/Queen (Eng.), The Paris Rev. Fellow Royal Soc. of Lit.; mem. PEN. Office: Grand Street Pubs Inc 50 Riverside Dr New York NY 10024-6555

SONNENBERG, HARDY, data processing company research and development executive, engineer; b. Schoensee, Fed. Republic Germany, Apr. 12, 1939; s. Gustav and Wanda (Neumann) S.; m. Doris Linda Adam, June 20, 1964; children: Kevin, Denise. BS, U. Alta., 1962; MS, Stanford U., 1964, PhD, 1967. Registered profl. engr., Ont. Advanced devel. engr. GTE Sylvania, Mountain View, Calif., 1966-68, engring. specialist, 1968-70, sect. mgr., 1970-73; dir. rsch. Optical Diodes Inc., Palo Alto, Calif., 1973-74; mem. rsch. staff Xerox Rsch. Centre Can., Mississauga, Ont., 1975-78, area mgr., 1978-80, lab. mgr., 1980-86, mgr. rsch. ops., 1986-87, mgr. tech. and engring. systems, 1987-94, v.p. rsch. and tech., 1994-96; pres. Calisco Cons., Freelton Outreach, 1997—; chmn. indsl. adv. coun. McMaster U., Hamilton, Ont., 1990-93, active, 1987-94. Contbr. articles to profl. jours. Patentee in field. Chmn. bd. dirs. local ch., Hamilton, Ont., 1983-85, 89-93; pres. Sheridan Park Assn., Mississauga, 1988-89; chmn. Conf. Bd. Can. Rsch. Mgrs. Forum, 1991-93. Recipient cert. of recognition for invention NASA, 1973, 74, Achievement award Xerox Corp., 1981, Charles E. Ives Engring. award, 1983. Mem. IEEE, Am. Phys. Soc., Assn. Profl. Engrs. Ont., Soc. for Imaging Sci. and Tech., Soc. Photographic Scientists and Engrs., Sigma Xi. Avocations: outdoor activities, singing, church participation. Home: 900 Hwy 97 Box 126, Freelton, ON Canada L0R 1K0 Office: Xerox Graphic Systems, 2660 Speakman Dr, Mississauga, ON Canada L5K 2L1

SONNENFELD, BARRY, cinematographer, film director. Cinematographer: (films) Blood Simple, 1984, Compromising Positions, 1985, Three O'Clock High, 1987, Raising Arizona, 1987, Throw Momma from the Train, 1987, Big, 1988, When Harry Met Sally..., 1989, Miller's Crossing, 1990, Misery, 1990, (TV movies) Out of Step, 1984 (Emmy award best cinematography 1984); dir.: (films) The Addams Family, 1991, Addams Family Values, 1993, Get Shorty, 1995, Men In Black, 1997; dir., co-prodr.: For Love or Money, 1993. Office: Creative Artists Agy 9830 Wilshire Blvd Ste 807 Beverly Hills CA 90212 also: United Talent Agency 9560 Wilshire Blvd Beverly Hills CA 90212*

SONNENFELD, MARION, linguist, educator; b. Berlin, Feb. 13, 1928; d. Kurt and Sibylla (Lemke) S. BA with high honors, Swarthmore Coll., 1950; MA, Yale U., 1951, PhD, 1956. Instr., asst. prof. Smith Coll., Northampton, Mass., 1954-62; assoc. prof. Wells Coll., Aurora, N.Y., 1962-67, German chmn., dir. German sch., 1965-67; assoc. prof., prof. SUNY Coll., Fredonia, 1967-77, SUNY disting. teaching prof., 1977-93, emerita, 1993, acting dean arts and humanities, 1980-81; mem. com. on learning assessment Fund for the Improvement of Post Secondary Edn., 1988-90, nat. screening com. for Fulbright grants, 1989-91; bd. mem. Adams Gallery, Dunkirk, N.Y., 1995—. English translator of German books and plays. Active Literacy Vols. Am., 1994—. Yale U. Jr. Sterling fellow, 1951-53, NEH postdoctoral fellow Ind. U., 1977; SUNY faculty exch. scholar, 1984—. Mem. MLA, AAUP. Office: SUNY Dept Fgn Langs Lit Fredonia NY 14063

SONNENFELDT, HELMUT, former government official, educator, consultant, author; b. Berlin, Germany, Sept. 13, 1926; came to U.S., 1944, naturalized, 1945; s. Walter H. and Gertrud (Liebenthal) S.; m. Marjorie Hecht, Oct. 4, 1953; children—Babette Sonnenfeldt Lubben, Walter H., Stewart H. A.B., Johns Hopkins, 1950, M.A., 1951. With Dept. State, Washington, 1952-77; formerly dir. Office Rsch. and Analysis for USSR and Eastern Europe, 1965-69; lectr. Sch. Advanced Internat. Studies, Johns Hopkins U., 1958-69, vis. scholar, 1977-78; guest scholar Brookings Instn., Washington, 1978—; sr. mem. Nat. Security Coun., 1969-74; counselor Dept. State, 1974-77. Former gov. UN Assn. of U.S.; dir. Atlantic Coun. of U.S., World Affairs Coun. Washington; trustee Johns Hopkins U. With AUS, 1945-46. Mem. Inst. Strategic Studies (London) (mem. exec. com.), Coun. on Fgn. Rels. N.Y., Pi Delta Epsilon. Home: 4105 Thornapple St Chevy Chase MD 20815-5129 Office: Brookings Instn 1775 Massachusetts Ave NW Washington DC 20036-2188

SONNENFELDT, MARJORIE HECHT, public relations executive, consultant; b. Balt., Feb. 8, 1931; d. Stewart Emanuel and Sylvia (Cahn) Hecht; m. Helmut Sonnenfeldt, Oct. 4, 1953; children: Babette Sonnenfeldt Lubben, Walter H., Stewart H. AB with honors magna cum laude, Smith Coll., 1952. Adminstr. U.S. Dept. State, Washington, 1952-54; rschr./writer Dem. Nat. Com., Washington, 1954-56, Robert L. Spivack, Journalist, Washington, 1956-59; writer, editor Com. Nat. Trade Policy, Washington, 1959-63; freelance writer, cons., editor Washington, 1964-69; mem. coun. staff Montgomery County Coun., Rockville, Md., 1970-71; community rels. adviser Montgomery County Planning Bd., Silver Spring, Md., 1971-73; chmn. Montgomery County Bd. Appeals, Rockville, 1973-81; exec. dir. Consumers World Trade, Washington, 1978-80; dir. internat. govt. affairs, v.p. Hill and Knowlton Inc., Washington, 1981-87; v.p. Fleishman-Hillard, Inc., Washington, 1987—. Bd. dirs. D.C. chpt. Am. Jewish Com., 1982—; bd. dirs. Lourie Ctr. Infants & Young Children, Rockville, 1993—. Office: Fleishman-Hillard Inc 1301 Connecticut Ave NW Washington DC 20036-1815

SONNENFELDT, RICHARD WOLFGANG, management consultant; b. Berlin, July 3, 1923; s. Walter H. and Gertrude (Liebenthal) S.; m. Shirley C. Aronoff, Dec. 23, 1949; m. Barbara A. Hausman, Mar. 8, 1981; children: Ann Elizabeth, Lawrence Alan, Michael William. BSEE, Johns Hopkins U., 1949; postgrad., U. Pa., 1953-56. Mgr. engring. and prodn. RCA, 1949-62; gen. mgr. digital systems div. Foxboro Co., 1962-65; chief exec. officer, pres., dir. Digitronics Corp., 1965-70; v.p. RCA Corp., 1970-79; chmn. bd. dirs., CEO Electronic Indsl. Engring. Corp., 1972-75; exec. v.p. ops. NBC, N.Y.C., 1979-82; dean Sch. Mgmt. Poly Inst. N.Y., Bklyn., 1982-84, prof. mgmt., 1982—; chmn. bd. dirs., CEO NAPP Systems, Inc., 1987-90; lectr. Harvard U. Bus. Sch., Sloan Sch., MIT; cons. in field; bd. dirs. Tetktronix, Inc., Foxboro Co., Lee Enterprises, Decision Industries Corp., Compuflight Corp., Biospherics Inc., Deerpark Baking Co., Tridex Corp., Internat. Harvest Group, Comm. Satellite Network Corp., Medlife Software Inc., Solar Outdoor Lighting Inc. Contbr. articles to profl. jours.; patentee in field. Fellow IEEE; mem. Am. Coun. Germany, Coun. Fgn. Rels., Tau Beta Pi, Omicron Delta Kappa. Home and Office: 4 Secor Dr Port Washington NY 11050-3418

SONNENSCHEIN, ADAM, lawyer; b. N.Y.C., Oct. 15, 1938; s. Harry D. and Sybil (Reinus) S.; m. Phyllis Cokin, Oct. 25, 1968; children: Andrew, Michael. BA, Amherst Coll., 1960; LLB, Columbia U., 1965. Bar: N.Y. 1965, Mass. 1970. Assoc. Berlack, Israels & Liberman, N.Y.C., 1965-70; ptnr. Sprague Assocs., Boston, 1970-72, Walter & Sonnenschein, Boston, 1972-78, Hausserman, Davison & Shattuck, Boston, 1978-83, Foley, Hoag & Eliot, Boston, 1983—. Mem. ABA, Mass. Bar Assn., Boston Bar Assn., Assn. of Bar of City of N.Y. Office: Foley Hoag & Eliot 1 Post Office Sq Boston MA 02109

SONNENSCHEIN, HUGO FREUND, academic administrator, economics educator; b. N.Y.C., Nov. 14, 1940; s. Leo William and Lillian Silver S.; m. Elizabeth Gunn, Aug. 26, 1962; children: Leah, Amy, Rachel. AB, U. Rochester, 1961; MS, Purdue U., 1963, PhD, 1964, PhD (hon.), 1996; PhD (hon.), Tel Aviv U., 1993; D (hon.), U. Autonoma Barcelona, Spain, 1994; PhD (hon.), Lake Forest Coll., 1995. Mem. faculty dept. econs. U. Minn., 1964-70, prof., 1968-70; prof. econs. U. Mass., Amherst, 1970-73, Northwestern U., 1973-76; prof. econs. Princeton (N.J.) U., 1976-87, Class of 1926 prof., 1987-88, provost, 1991-93; dean and Thomas S. Gates prof. Sch. Arts and Scis. Sch. Arts & Scis., U. Pa., Phila., 1988-91; pres., prof. dept. econs. and Coll., U. Chgo., 1993—; vis. prof. U. Andes, Colombia, 1965, Tel Aviv U., 1972, Hebrew U., 1973, U. Paris, 1978, U. Aix-en-Provence, France, 1978, Stanford U., 1984-85. Editor Econometrica, 1977-84; assoc. editor Jour. Econ. Theory, 1972-75; mem. bd. editors Jour. Math. Econs, 1974—, SIAM Jour, 1976-80; contbr. articles to profl. jours. Trustee U. Rochester, 1992, U. Chgo., 1993—. Fellow, Social Sci. Rsch. Coun., 1967-68, NSF, 1970—, Ford Found., 1970-71, Guggenheim Found., 1976-77. Fellow Am. Acad. Arts and Scis., Econometric Soc. (pres. 1988-89); mem. NAS.

SONNENSCHEIN, RALPH ROBERT, physiologist; b. Chgo., Aug. 14, 1923; s. Robert and Flora (Kieferstein) S.; m. Patricia W. Niddrie, June 21, 1952; children—David, Lisa, Ann. Student, Swarthmore Coll., 1940-42, U. Chgo., 1942-43; B.S., Northwestern U., 1943, B.M., 1946, M.S., 1946, M.D., 1947; Ph.D., U. Ill., 1950. Research asst. in physiology Northwestern U. Med. Sch., 1944-46; intern Michael Reese Hosp., Chgo., 1946-47; successively research fellow clin. sci., research asst. psychiatry, research asso. psychiatry U. Ill. Med. Sch., Chgo., 1947-51; mem. faculty U. Calif. Med. Sch., Los Angeles, 1951-88, prof. physiology, 1962-88, prof. emeritus, 1988—; liaison scientist Office Naval Research, London, 1971-72. Author papers on pain, innervation of skin, peripheral circulation. Served with AUS, 1943-46. Spl. research fellow USPHS, 1957-58; fellow Swedish Med. Research Council, 1964-65; grantee USAF; grantee Office Naval Research; grantee NIH; grantee NSF. Mem. Am. Physiol. Soc., Microcirculatory Soc., Soc. Exptl. Biology and Medicine, AAAS, Hungarian Physiol. Soc. (hon.). Home: 18212 Kingsport Dr Malibu CA 90265-5636 Office: U Calif Sch Medicine Dept Physiology Los Angeles CA 90095-1751

SONNHALTER, CAROLYN THERESE, physical therapist, consultant; b. Bedford, Ohio, Apr. 26, 1942; d. Gabriel Edward Jr. and Josephine Irene (Kubera) Farkas; m. Donald Joseph Lippert, June 11, 1966 (div. June 1981); 1 child, Kevin Michael; m. Robert Louis Sonnhalter, Aug. 31, 1985. BS, Ohio State U., 1964. Lic. phys. therapist, Ohio. Staff and sr. phys. therapist Akron (Ohio) City Gen. Hosp., 1964-69; asst. dir. phys. therapy Akron Gen. Med. Ctr., 1975-82; dir. phys. therapy Litchfield Rehab. Ctr., Akron, 1983-87; phys. therapist HMO Health Ohio, Akron, 1987-97, Phoenix-Hudson Corp., Middleburg Heights, Ohio, 1993—; dir. phys. therapy Tri-County Home Nursing, Mogadore, Ohio, 1997—; devel. phys. therapy first outpatient Chronic Pain Mgmt. Program, Ohio, 1983; cons. video animation on mechanism of whiplash for use by med. and legal profls., Ohio, 1996. Mem. Am. Phys. Therapy Assn., Alpha Gamma Delta. Avocations: traveling Ohio and nearby states in search of antiques, gardening. Home: 3631 Oak Rd Stow OH 44224-3934 Office: Tri County Home Nursing Home 725 S Cleveland Ave Mogadore OH 44260-1521

SONNINO, CARLO BENVENUTO, electrical manufacturing company executive; b. Torino, Italy, May 12, 1904; came to U.S., 1952, naturalized, 1959; s. Moise and Amelia S.; m. Mathilde Girodat, Jan. 21, 1949; children—Patricia, Frederic, Bruno. Ph.D., U. Milano, Italy, 1927, LL.B., 1928. Dir. research Italian Aluminum Co., Milano, 1928-34; pres. Laesa Cons. Firm, Milano, 1934-43; tech. adviser Boxal, Fribourg, Switzerland, 1944-52, Thompson Brand, Rouen, France, 1972-76; materials engrng. mgr. Emerson Electric Co., St. Louis, 1956-72; staff scientist Emerson Electric Co., 1973—; prof. metall. engrng. Washington U., St. Louis, 1960-68, U. Mo., Rolla, 1968—; cons. Monsanto Chem. Co., Wagner Co., other maj. firms, U.S., Europe. Decorated knight comdr. Italian Republic. Fellow Am. Soc. Metals, ASTM (hon.), Alpha Sigma Mu. Patentee process for synthetic cryolite; patentee in field of metallurgy, corrosion; mfr. 1st aluminum cans in world, 1940. Home: 7206 Kingsbury Blvd Saint Louis MO 63130-4140 Office: Emerson E and S Div Emerson Electric Co 8100 W Florissant Ave Saint Louis MO 63136-1417 *I have always been guided by the highest ethical standards in professional, business, and civic life, even in the most difficult moments, and by strong dislike for hypocrisy and greed.*

SONNTAG, BERNARD H., agrologist, research executive; b. Goodsoil, Sask., Can., June 27, 1940; s. Henry R. and Annie (Heesing) S.; m. Mary L. Ortman, Aug. 10, 1963; children: Calvin, Galen, Courtney Anne. BSA, Sask. U., Saskatoon, 1962, MSc, 1965; PhD, Purdue U., 1971. Economist Agriculture Can., Saskatoon, 1962-66; cons. D.W. Carr & Assoc., Ottawa, Ont., Can., 1966-68; economist Agriculture Can., Lethbridge, Alta., 1968-79, Saskatoon, 1979-80; dir. rsch. sta. Agriculture Can., Brandon, Man., 1980-86, Swiftcurrent, Sask., 1986-89, Lethbridge, 1989-95; dir. gen. Prairie Farm Rehab. Adminstrn., Regina, Sask., Can., 1996—; pres. Man. Inst. Agrologists, Brandon, 1984. Recipient Leadership award Bell Can., 1993. Fellow Agrl. Inst. Can.; mem. Rotary. Roman Catholic. Home: 3123 Winchester Rd, Regina, SK Canada S4V 2T4 Office: Agriculture Can PFRA, 1800 Hamilton St, Regina, SK Canada S4P 4L2

SONS, LINDA RUTH, mathematics educator; b. Chicago Heights, Ill., Oct. 31, 1939; d. Robert and Ruth (Diekelman) S. AB in Math., Ind. U., 1961; MS in Math., Cornell U., 1963, PhD in Math., 1966. Teaching asst. Cornell U., Ithaca, N.Y., 1961-63, instr. math., summer 1963, rsch. asst., 1963-65; asst. prof. No. Ill. U., De Kalb, 1965-70, assoc. prof., 1970-78, prof., 1978—; presdl. tchg. prof. No. Ill. U., DeKalb, 1994—; vis. assoc. prof. U. London, 1970-71; dir. undergrad. studies math. dept. No. Ill. U., 1971-77, exec. sec. univ. coun., 1978-79; chair faculty fund No. Ill. U. Found., De Kalb, 1982—. Author: (with others) A Study Guide for Introduction to Mathematics, 1976, Mathematical Thinking in a Quantitative World, 1990; contbr. articles to profl. jours. Mem. campus ministry com. No. Ill. Dist. Luth. Ch./Mo. Synod, Hillside, 1977—; mem. ch. coun. Immanuel Luth. Ch., De Kalb, 1978-85, 87-89; pres. Luth. Women's Missionary League, 1974-87; bd. dirs., treas. De Kalb County Migrant Ministry, 1967-78. NSF Rsch. grantee, 1970-72, 74-75; recipient 1988 Award for Disting. Svc. of Ill. Sect. of the Math Assn. Am., 1991 Award for Excellence in Coll. Teaching of Ill. Coun. Tchrs. Math. Mem. Am. Math. Soc., Assn. for Women in Math., Math. Assn. Am. (mem. nat. bd. govs. 1989-92, mem. com. undergrad. program in math. 1990-96, Disting. Svc. to Ill. Sect. award 1988, Disting. Coll. or U. Tchg. of Math. award 1995), Ill. Math. Assn. (v.p. sect., pres.-elect, pres., then past pres. 1982-87, bd. dirs. 1989-92), London Math. Soc., Phi Beta Kappa (pres. No. Ill. assn. 1981-85), Sigma Xi (past. chpt. pres.). Achievements include research in classical complex analysis--especially value distribution for meromorphic functions with unbounded characteristic in the unit disc. Office: No Ill U Dept Math Scis De Kalb IL 60115

SONS, RAYMOND WILLIAM, journalist; b. Harvey, Ill., Aug. 25, 1926; s. William Henry and Gladys Lydia (Steinko) S.; m. Bettina Dieckmann; children: David, Pamela Sons Clarke, Ronald. B.A., U. Mich., 1950. Reporter, mng. editor Murphysboro (Ill.) Daily Ind. edit. So. Illinoisan newspaper, 1950-52; assoc. news editor Middletown (Ohio) Jour., 1952-53; reporter, asst. city editor, sportswriter, sports editor Chgo. Daily News, 1953-78; sports editor, columnist Chgo. Sun-Times, 1978-92. Served with USAAF, 1945-46. Recipient Best Sports Story in Ill. award U.P.I., 1970, Marshall Field award for outstanding editorial contbn. to Chgo. Daily News, 1972; Best Sports Column award AP Sports Editor, 1979, Best Sports Column award Ill. AP, 1987, Chgo. Journalism Hall of Fame, 1996. Roman Catholic. Home: 4100 Torrington Ct Fort Collins CO 80525-3419

SONTAG, FREDERICK EARL, philosophy educator; b. Long Beach, Calif., Oct. 2, 1924; s. M. Burnett and Cornelia (Nicholson) S.; m. Carol Furth, June 10, 1950; children: Grant Furth, Anne Burnett Karch. BA with great distinction, Stanford U., 1949; MA, Yale U., 1951, PhD, 1952; LLD (hon.), Coll. Idaho, 1971. Instr. Yale U., 1951-52; asst. prof. philosophy Pomona Coll., Claremont, Calif., 1952-55, assoc. prof., 1955-60, prof., 1970—, Robert C. Denison prof. philosophy, 1972—, chmn. dept. philosophy, 1960-67, 76-77, 80-84; chmn. coordinating com. in philosophy Claremont Grad. Sch. and Univ. Ctr., 1962-65; vis. prof. Union Theol. Sem., N.Y.C., 1959-60, Collegio di Sant' Anselmo, Rome, 1966-67, U. Copenhagen, fall 1972; theologian-in-residence Am. Ch. in Paris, fall 1973; Fulbright regional vis. prof., India, East Asia, Pacific areas, 1977-78; mem. nat. adv. council Kent Fellowship Program of Danforth Found., 1963-66. Author numerous books, the most recent being: Love Beyond Pain: Mysticism Within Christianity, 1977; Sun Myung Moon and the Unification Church, 1977, also German, Japanese and Korean transl.; (with John K. Roth) God and America's Future, 1977; What Can God Do?, 1979; A Kierkegaard Handbook, 1979; The Elements of Philosophy, 1984, (with John K. Roth) The Questions of Philosophy, 1988, Emotion, 1989, The Return of the Gods, 1989, Willgenstein and the Mystical, 1995, Uncertain Truth, 1995, The Descent of Women, 1997, The Acts of the Trinity, 1996, Pres. bd. dirs. Claremont Family Svc., 1960-64; trustee The Coro Found., Los Angeles and San Francisco, 1967-71; bd. dirs., chmn. ways and means com. Pilgrim Place, Claremont, 1970-77. Served with AUS, 1943-46. Vis. scholar Ctr. for Study Japanese Religions, Kyoto, Japan, spring 1974; vis. fellow East-West Ctr., Honolulu, summer 1974. Wig Disting. Prof. award, 1970, 76; Fulbright regional vis. prof. India, East Asia, Pacific Areas, 1977-78. Mem. Am. Philos. Assn., Metaphys. Soc. Am., Soc. on Religion in Higher Edn. (Kent fellow 1950-52), Am. Acad. Religion, Phi Beta Kappa. Congregationalist. Office: Pomona Coll 551 N College Ave Claremont CA 91711-4410

SONTAG, JAMES MITCHELL, cancer researcher; b. Denver, Dec. 8, 1939; s. Samuel Henry and Rose Hazel (Silverman) S.; m. Elizabeth Crockett Tunis; children: Ariella, Eythan. BS, Lamar State Coll. Tech., Beaumont, Tex.; MS, U. Ill., 1967; PhD, Weizmann Inst. Sci., Rehovot, Israel, 1971; MPH, Harvard U., 1982. Damon Runyon Meml. Fund Cancer Research postdoctoral fellow, 1971-72; guest worker Nat. Cancer Inst., NIH, Bethesda, Md., 1972-73; staff fellow Nat. Cancer Inst., NIH, 1973-74, exptl. oncologist, 1973-76, mgr. carcinogen bioassay program, 1973-76, asst. to divsn. dir. cancer cause and prevention, 1976-80; exec. sec. Clearinghouse on Environ. Carcinogens, 1976-80, asst. dir. for interagy. affairs Office of Dir., 1980-82, spl. asst. epidemiology and biostatistics program, 1982-96; chief office divsn. ops. & analysis divsn. cancer epidemiology and genetics Nat. Cancer Inst., 1996—. Author, editor in field. Served with AUS, 1956-59. Beaumont LWV scholar, 1963-65. Mem. Beta Beta Beta. Home: 10500 Rockville Pike Apt 610 Rockville MD 20852-3341 Office: Nat Cancer Inst Exec Plaza North Room 543 Bethesda MD 20892

SONTAG, PETER MICHAEL, travel management company executive; b. Vienna, Austria, Apr. 25, 1943; came to U.S., 1960; s. Otto Schiedeck and Maria Katharina (Schmidt) Cigalle; m. Eleanor Ann Alexander, Jan. 24, 1971; children: Alicia Alexandra, Julie Katherine. Diploma in hotel mgmt., Schule fuer Gastgewerbe, Vienna, 1960; BS magna cum laude, West Liberty State Coll., 1969, LLD, 1991; MBA, Columbia U., 1971. Steel worker Weirton (W.Va.) Steel Co., 1965-69; fin. analyst Citicorp, N.Y.C., 1970-71; ops. staff exec. ITT, N.Y.C., 1971-73; asst. v.p. Sun Life Ins. Co. Am., Balt., 1974-75; exec. v.p. Travel Guide, Inc., Balt., 1975-76; pres. Travelwhirl, Inc., Balt., 1976-78; founder Gelco Travel Services, Mpls., 1978-83; chmn., chief exec. officer Sontag, Annis & Assocs., Washington, 1983-86, US Travel Systems, Inc., Washington, 1986—; CEO Travelogue Inc., Washington, 1997, Crown Mktg. Group, Clearwater, Fla., 1997—; prin. CORVES Cons., Inc., Rockville, Md., 1983-86; pub. Travel Bus. Mgr., 1983-86; speaker in field, 1983—. With Austrian Air Force, 1963-64. Named one of Twenty Five Most Influential Execs. in Travel Industry Travel Bus. News, 1985, 87, 88, 89; named Delta Sigma Pi scholar. Mem. Alpha Phi Sigma, Delta Mu Delta (charter), Lakewood Country Club. Republican. Avocations: skiing, sailing, photography, collecting antique cars. Office: Crown Mktg Group 17755 US Hwy 19N Clearwater FL 34624*

SONTAG, SUSAN, writer; b. N.Y.C., Jan. 16, 1933; m. Philip Rieff, 1950 (div. 1958); 1 son, David. BA, U. Chgo., 1951; MA in English, Harvard U., 1954, MA in Philosophy, 1955. Instr. English U. Conn., Storrs, 1953-54; editor Commentary, N.Y.C., 1959; lectr. philosophy City Coll., N.Y.C., 1959-60, Sarah Lawrence Coll., Bronxville, 1959-60; instr. dept. religion Columbia U., N.Y.C., 1960-64; writer in residence Rutgers U., 1964-65. Author: (novels) The Benefactor, 1963, Death Kit, 1967, The Volcano Lover: A Romance, 1992; (plays) Alice in Bed: A Play in Eight Scenes, 1993; (stories) I, etcetera, 1978, The Way We Live Now, 1991; (essays) Against Interpretation, 1966 (Mat. Book award nomination 1966), Styles of Radical Will, 1969, Trip to Hanoi, 1969, On Photography, 1977 (Nat. Book Critics Circle award for criticism 1978), Illness as Metaphor, 1978, Under the Sign of Saturn, 1980, AIDS and Its Metaphors, 1989; (anthology) A Susan Sontag Reader, 1982; screenwriter, dir.: (films) Duet for Cannibals, 1969, Brother Carl, 1971; dir.: (films) Promised Lands, 1974, Unguided Tour, 1983; editor, author of introduction: Antonin Artaud: Selected Writings, 1976, A Roland Barthes Reader, 1982, Danilo Kis's Homo Poeticus: Essays & Interviews, 1995. Guggenheim fellow, 1966, 75, Rockefeller Found. fellow, 1965, 74, MacArthur fellow, 1990-95; recipient George Polk Meml. award, 1966, Ingram Merrill Found. award in lit. in field of Am. Letters, 1976, Creative Arts award Brandeis U., 1976, Malaparte prize, 1992; named Officier de l'Ordre des Arts et des Lettres, France, 1984. Mem. Am. Acad. Arts and Scis. (elected 1993), Am. Acad. Arts and Letters (Arts and Letters award 1976), PEN (pres. Am. Ctr. 1987-89).

SOO, SHAO LEE, mechanical engineer, educator; b. Peking, China, Mar. 1, 1922; came to U.S., 1947, naturalized, 1962; s. Hsi Yi and Yun Chuan (Chin) S.; m. Hermia G. Dan, June 7, 1952; children: Shirley A. Soo Gorman, Lydia M., David D. BS, Nat. Chiaotung U., 1945; MS, Ga. Inst. Tech., 1948; ScD, Harvard U., 1951. Engr. China Nat. Aviation, Calcutta and Shanghai, 1945-47; lectr. Princeton (N.J.) U., 1951-54, asst. prof., 1954-57, assoc. prof. mech. engring., 1957-59; prof. mech. engring. U. Ill., Urbana, 1959-93, prof. emeritus, 1993—; cons. NASA, NIH, ANL, Dept. Energy, EPA, NATO, Nat. Inst. Standards and Tech.; mem. sci. adv. bd. EPA, 1976-78; adv. energy transp. World Bank, 1979; China, UNDP, 1985, 92, NATO AGARD lectr.; Fulbright-Hays Disting. lectr., 1974—, lectr. Chinese Acad. Sci., 1980; guest lectr. China-Japan Conf. Fluidized Beds, 1985, 88, 91, bd. dirs. S.L. Soo Assocs., Ltd., Urbana; vis. prof. Delft Tech. U., The Netherlands, 1993. Author 7 books on thermodynamics, energy conservation and multiphase flow; mem. editorial bd. Internat. Jour. Multiphase Flow, 1972—, Jour. Pipelines, 1980—, Internat. Jour. Sci. and Engring., 1983, Jour. Engring. Chem. and Metallurgy China, 1990—; contbr. numerous articles to profl. jours. Recipient Applied Mechanics Rev. award, 1972, Disting. Lecture award Internat. Pipeline Assn., 1981, Alcoa Found. award, 1985, NASA award for creative devel., 1992. Fellow ASME; mem. ASEE, AIChE (Particle Tech. Forum), Combustion Inst., Fine Particle Soc. (chmn. fluidized beds com.), Chinese Acad. Sci. (hon. prof.), Internat. Freight Pipeline Soc. (Plaque of Appreciation 1995), Sigma Xi, Pi Tau Sigma (hon.), Phi Kappa Phi. Methodist. Patentee in field (6). Home: 2020 Cureton Dr Urbana IL 61801-6226 Office: 1206 W Green St Urbana IL 61801-2906

SOOKNE, HERMAN SOLOMON (HANK SOOKNE), human services executive; b. Far Rockaway, N.Y., June 30, 1932; s. Harry Martin Sookne and Sarah (Kopolov) Sterenstein; m. Joan Gilman, Apr. 12, 1954 (div. Apr. 9, 1971); children: Charles Michael, David Howard, Susan Frances; m. Polly Henry Johnson, Mar. 1972. Student, Georgetown U., 1949-50; BS in Bus. & Econs., NYU, 1953. Pres., owner Gilclan Bldg. Corp., Merrick, N.Y., 1955-68; divsn. mgr. Boise Cascade Bldg. Corp., Freehold, N.J., 1968-70; dir. property mgmt. and engring. Amprop, Inc., Miami, Fla., 1970-73; pres., CEO Bowman Property Investors, Dallas, 1973-79; gen. mgr. Fidinam, Inc., Houston, 1979-82; mktg. cons. Cooper Communities, Inc., Bella Vista, Ark., 1982-88; v.p. mktg. and ops. Epworth Villa Retirement Ctr., Oklahoma City, 1988—. Scoutmaster Boy Scouts Am., L.I., N.Y., 1955-60; bd. dirs., pres. Copperchase Condo's Inc., Oklahoma City, 1991-95; chmn. trustees United Meth. Ch. of the Servant, 1997. With U.S. Army, 1953-55, Korea. Mem. Ark. Bd. Realtors, Nat. Soc. for Fund Raising Execs., Soc. for Advancement of Mgmt., Nat. Assn. Home Builders, Nat. Soc. Heat, Refrigeration & Air Conditioning Engrs. Republican. Methodist. Avocations: sailing, tennis, ch. affairs, woodworking, reading. Home: 11300 N Pennsylvania Ave # 152 Oklahoma City OK 73120-7774 Office: 14901 N Pennsylvania Ave Oklahoma City OK 73134-6069

SOONG, TSU-TEH, engineering science educator; b. Honan, China, Feb. 10, 1934; s. Tung and Yu-Hsieh (Lee) S.; m. Dorothy Yen-Ling Tsai, June 5, 1959; children—Karen, Stephen, Susan. B.S., U. Dayton, 1955; postgrad., U. Ill., 1955-56; M.S., Purdue U., 1958, Ph.D., 1962. Instr. engring. sci. Purdue U., 1958-62; sr. research engr. Jet Propulsion Lab., Pasadena, Calif., 1962-63; asst. prof. engring. sci. State U. N.Y. at Buffalo, 1963-66, assoc. prof., 1966-68, prof., 1968-89; Samuel P. Capen prof., 1989—; part-time lectr. engring. U. Calif. at Los Angeles, 1962-63; part-time research mathematician Cornell Aero. Lab., Buffalo, 1964-67, prin. research mathematician, 1967-70. NSF Sci. Faculty fellow Tech. U. Delft, Netherlands, 1966-67; Humboldt Sr. Scientist, U. Hanover, Fed. Republic of Germany, 1987-88. Mem. ASCE, NSPE, Earthquake Engring. Rsch. Inst., Sigma Xi, Tau Beta Pi. Research in stochastic processes and structural control in engring. Home: 249 Wellingwood Dr East Amherst NY 14051-1750

SOPER, ANNE MARIE, psychologist; b. Indpls., Feb. 19, 1951; d. William and Helen (Starost) Speicher; m. Dan Allen Soper, Nov. 19, 1978; children: Thomas, Mark, Elise. Student, Butler U., 1969-70; BA summa cum laude, Mich. State U., 1973; MA, Ball State U., 1977; MEd, Harvard U., 1982; EdD, Boston U., 1990. Cert. sch. psychologist, Ind. Sch. psychologist Logansport (Ind.) Pub. Schs., 1977-78, Indpls. Pub. Schs., 1978-80; vocat. rehab. counselor Morgan Meml. Goodwill, Boston, 1980-81; psychology intern Simmons Coll., Boston, 1982-83, West-Ros-Park Mental Health, Boston, 1984-86; counselor Resolve, Arlington, Mass., 1986-90; psychology intern South End. Cmty. Health, Boston, 1995-96; psychologist Metrowest Mental Health, Marlborough, Mass., 1995—, Tri City Mental Health, Medford, Mass., 1995—; tchg. asst. Boston U., 1983-84. Butler U. scholar, 1969. Mem. APA, Mass. Psychol. Assn., Phi Beta Kappa. Avocations: reading, music, travel.

SOPER, JAMES HERBERT, botanist, curator; b. Hamilton, Ont., Can., Apr. 9, 1916; s. Herbert Armitage and Anna Eliza Gertrude (Cooper) S.; m. Jean Elizabeth Morgan, Aug. 17, 1946; children: Nancy Elizabeth, Mary Florence, Daphne Evans, Ian Morgan. B.A., McMaster U., 1938, M.A., 1939; Ph.D. (Harris fellow, Austin fellow), Harvard U., 1943. Mem. faculty U. Toronto, 1946-67, curator, 1946-67, prof. botany, 1966-67; chief botanist Can. Mus. Nature, Ottawa, Ont., 1967-81, curator emeritus, 1981—, rsch. assoc., 1993-95. Author: Mt. Revelstoke National Park Wildflowers, 1976, Shrubs of Ontario, 1982; contbr. articles to profl. jours. Served with RCAF, 1943-45. Recipient Royal Jubilee medal, 1978. Mem. Royal Canadian Inst. (life) (pres. 1962-63), Canadian Bot. Assn. (pres. 1982-83), Ottawa Field Naturalists Club, Fedn. Ont. Naturalists (hon.).

SOPER, QUENTIN FRANCIS, chemist; b. Buhl, Minn., Dec. 3, 1919; s. Claude E. and Dessie E. (Zern) S.; m. Genevieve Landreth, Oct. 5, 1946; children—John, Julia, Dan, Jean. B.Chem., U. Minn., 1940; Ph.D. in Organic Chemistry, U. Ill., 1943. Sr. organic chemist Eli Lilly & Co., Indpls., 1944-62; research scientist Eli Lilly & Co., 1962-66; head agrl. organic chemistry research Eli Lilly & Co., Greenfield, Ind., 1965-72, sr. agrl. assoc., 1972-76, research adviser, 1976-84; ret., 1984. Co-inventor Penicillin V; inventor herbicides Treflan, Balan, Paarlan, Surflan, Sonalan, Dipan. Recipient Outstanding Achievement award U. Minn., 1977, John Scott award City of Phila., 1980, Pioneer award Am. Inst. Chemists, 1981. Mem. Am. Chem. Soc., Weed Sci. Soc., N.Y. Acad. Scis. Presbyterian. Home: 2120 W 38th St Indianapolis IN 46228-3202

SOPINKA, JOHN, Canadian supreme court justice; b. Broderick, Sask., Can., Mar. 19, 1933; s. Metro and Nancy (Kikcio) S.; m. Marie Wilson, 1956; children: Randall, Melanie. BA, U. Toronto, 1955, LLB, 1958; JD (hon.), Ukrainian Free U., Munich. Bar: Nfld. 1973, N.B. 1975, Sask. 1984, Alta. 1987, Y.T. 1987, N.W.T.1987. Assoc. Fasken & Calvin, Barristers and Solicitors, Toronto, 1960-66, ptnr., 1966-77; ptnr., head litigation dept. Stikeman, Elliott, Barristers & Solicitors, Toronto, 1977-88; puisine judge Supreme Ct. of Can., Ottawa, Ont., 1988—; apptd. Queen's Counsel, 1975; lectr. civil procedure Osgoode Hall Law Sch., 1974-82, U. Toronto Law Sch., 1976-84; mem. Commns. of Inquiry into Royal Can. Mounted Police relationship with Dept. Nat. Revenue, into Certain Deaths Hosp. for Sick Children and Related Matters, into Facts of Allegations of Conflict of Interest Concerning Hon. Sinclair M. Stevens; chief counsel Commn. on Aviation Safety; counsel Commn. of Inquiry into Cessation of Ops. Can. Comml. Bank and Northland Bank; mem. Task Force on Equality of Opportuniy in Athletics; former bencher Law Soc. Upper Can., frequent lectr. continuing edn. series. Author: (with Lederman and Bryant) The Law of Evidence in Canada, 1992, The Trial of an Action, 1981, (with Gelowitz) The Conduct of an Appeal, 1993; contbr. articles to profl. jours. Bd. dirs. Hockey Can., 1960—; mem. Bd. Edn. Town of Oakville, 1967-69; co-chmn. Acad. Tribunal U. Toronto, 1975-80; mem. Police Complaints Bd. Met. Toronto; mem. bd. fgn. advisors Ukranian Legal Found. Fellow Am. Coll. Trial Lawyers (jud.); mem. Advocate's Soc. (bd. dirs., chmn. subcom. adminstrn. Ont. cts., lectr.), Can. Bar Assn. (chmn. Ont. subsect. comparative law sect. 1967-68, nat. chmn. of sect. 1970, lectr.), County of York Law Assn., Univ. Club, Blvd. Club, Lawyer's Club. Avocations: squash, skiing, tennis, music. Home: 161 Carleton St, Rockcliffe Pk, Ottawa, ON Canada K1M 0G6 Office: Supreme Ct Can, Wellington St, Ottawa, ON Canada K1A 0J1*

SOPKIN, GEORGE, cellist, music educator; b. Chgo., Apr. 3, 1914; s. Isador and Esther (Sopkin) S.; m. Thelma Friedman, July 5, 1936; children—Monica, Paula; m. Carol Borchard Durham, Aug. 30, 1956; children—Edwin, Anthony. Student with, Daniel Saidenberg, Am. Conservatory Music, 1930-32; with, Emmanuel Feurermann, Chgo., Mus. Coll., 1932-34; D.Mus. (hon.), Northland Coll., 1977. Assoc. prof. music U. Wis., 1940-42, artist-in-residence, 1963-79, prof., 1967-77, Disting. prof., 1977-85; prof. Carnegie Mellon U., 1985—, formed trio concert tour of Europe, 1985; staff ABC, Chgo., 1946-52; artist-in-residence Northwestern U., 1952-55, U. Wisconsin-Milw., Cleve. Inst.; founder New Eng. Piano Quartette, 1980. Mem., Kansas City (Mo.) Philharmonic Orch., 1933-34, Chgo. Symphony Orch., 1934-40, Pro Arte String Quartet, 1940-42, founder, 1946, since mem., Fine Arts Quartet, Chgo., soloist, Kansas City (Mo.) Philharmonic Orch., Chgo. Symphony Orch., Ill. Symphony Orch., Milw. Chamber Orch., Saidenberg Symphonette, frequent TV appearances; artist of film for, Ency. Brit. films, Nat. Ednl. TV films; recording artist for, Mercury, Decca, Concert-disc, Everest, numerous tours, Europe. Bd. dirs. Contemporary Concerts, Inc., Chgo. Served with USAAF, 1943-45. Mem. Lincoln Acad. Address: Newbury Neck Rd Surry ME 04684

SOPKO, MICHAEL D., mining company executive; b. Montreal, Jan. 22, 1939; s. John and Mary Sopko; m. Mary Raatikainen, Dec. 28, 1979; children: David, Stuart, Andrew. B Metall. Engring., McGill U., 1960, M Metall. Engring., 1961, PhD, 1964. Jr. engr., mgr. Ont. divsn. Inco Ltd., Copper Cliff, 1964-73; mgr. Iron Ore Recovery Plant, Inco, Copper Cliff, Ont., 1973; ops. mgr. Exmibal (Inco), Guatemala, 1973-78; from mgr. copper refinery to pres. Inco Ltd.-Ont. Div., Copper Cliff, 1978-89; from v.p. human resources to pres. Inco Ltd., Toronto, Ont., 1989-92; chmn., CEO Inco Ltd., Toronto, 1992—, also bd. dirs.; bd. dirs. Inco Ltd., The Toronto Dominion Bank, Voisey's Bay Nickel Co., Co-Steel, Inc., Conf. Bd. Can.; mem. Toronto Bd. Trade. Mem. Mining Assn. Can. (bd. dirs. 1991-95, chmn. 1995—), Nickel Devel. Inst. (bd. dirs. 1991-95), Credit Valley Golf and Country Club. Office: Inco Ltd, 145 King St W Ste 1500, Toronto, ON Canada M5H 4B7

SOPKO, THOMAS CLEMENT, lawyer; b. Warren, Ohio, Mar. 21, 1945; s. Clement and Mary (Sroka) S.; m. Joyce Ann Deffenbaugh, Aug. 5, 1967; children: Amy L., Kathleen A. BS in History, Xavier U., 1967; JD, U. Notre Dame, 1970. Bar: Ind. 1970, U.S. Dist. Ct. (no. dist.) Ind. 1970, U.S. Dist. Ct. (so. dist.) Ind. Assoc. Edward Kalamaros and Assocs., South Bend, Ind., 1970-75; ptnr. Hardig & Sopko, South Bend, 1976-85; pvt. practice South Bend, 1986-91; ptnr. Sopko & Firth, South Bend, 1991—; dep. prosecutor County of St. Joseph, South Bend, 1976-79; town atty. Town of Osceola, Ind., 1975-82; gen. counsel Notre Dame Fed. Credit Union, 1986—, Holy Cross Coll., Notre Dame, 1989—, speaker for continuing legal edn. seminars on civil litigation, trial practice and procedure, family law and mediation matters. Chmn. profl. divsn. United Way St. Joseph County; bd. dirs. St. Joseph County Alcoholism Coun., South Bend; active Jud. Nominating Com., St. Joseph County, 1985-88; chmn. St. Anthony's Parish Coun., South Bend, 1991-93. Scholar U. Notre Dame Law Sch., 1967-70. Fellow Ind. Bar Assn. Found.; mem. St. Joseph County Bar Assn. (pres. 1994-95, bd. govs. 1990—, pres.-elect 1993-94, v.p. 1992-93, chmn. continuing legal edn. 1992-94), Ind. Trial Lawyers Assn. (dist. chmn. 1979-80), Assn. Trial Lawyers Am., ABA. Republican. Roman Catholic. Avocations: downhill skiing, tennis, golf, jogging. Home: 1418 E Washington St South Bend IN 46617-3343 Office: Sopko & Firth 5th Fl Plaza Bldg 210 S Michigan St South Bend IN 46601-2017

SOPPELSA, GEORGE NICHOLAS ANGELO, artist; b. Youngstown, Ohio, July 16, 1939; s. Joseph and Rose (Gaiarsa) S. BFA, Ohio State U., 1961. One-man shows include Mulvane Art Mus., Washburn U., Topeka, 1985, John Szoke Gallery, N.Y.C., 1989, Homer Babbidge Libr., U. Conn., Storrs, 1990, The Gallery, St. Mary's Coll. Md., St. Mary's City, 1991, Inter Art Galerie Reich, Cologne, Germany, 1994, Randall Tuttle Fine Arts, Woodbury, Conn., 1996; exhibited in group shows at John Szoke Gallery, N.Y.C., 1989, Art at 100 Pearl, Hartford, Conn., 1989, Butler Inst. Am. Art, Youngstown, Ohio, 1990, Hurlbutt Gallery, Greenwich, Conn., 1993, Mattatuck Mus., Waterbury, Conn., 1995, Aldrich Mus., Ridgefield, Conn., 1995; represented in permanent collections at Mulvane Art Ctr., Topeka, Conn. Collection, Hartford. Fellow Nat. Endowment for Arts, 1987, Vt. Studio Colony, 1988; grantee Conn. Commn. on Arts, 1991, vis. artist Weir Farm Nat. Hist. Site, Wilton, Conn., 1994-95. Office: Brairton & Tubbs Art Agts 135 Central Ave East Hartford CT 06108-3103

SOPPELSA, JOHN JOSEPH, decal manufacturing company executive; b. Cleve., Apr. 23, 1948; s. Anthony Joseph and Elizabeth Ann (McCarthy) S.; m. Nikki Lynn Stevens, Sept. 7, 1968. Student, Cleve. State U., 1966-68, Baldwin-Wallace Coll., Berea, Ohio, 1985. Sales rep. Manning Studios, Inc., Cleve., 1967-70, Pitney-Bowes, Inc., Stamford, Conn., 1970-72, Wampole Chem., Stamford, 1972-75; pres. Sun Art Decals Inc., Cleve., 1975—. Office: Sun Art Decals Inc 885 W Bagley Rd Berea OH 44017-2903

SOPRANOS, ORPHEUS JAVARAS, manufacturing company executive; b. Evanston, Ill., Oct. 4, 1935; s. James Javaras and Marigoula (Papalexatou) S.; m. Angeline Buches, Dec. 31, 1959; children—Andrew, Katherine. A.B., U. Chgo., 1957, M.B.A., 1957. Mgmt. trainee Ford Motor Co., Chgo., 1958-59; with Amsted Industries, Chgo., 1959—; dir. bus. research Amsted Industries, 1966-70, treas., 1970-80, v.p., 1980—; pres. Amsted Internat., 1991-93, corp. v.p., 1993—. Served with U.S. Army, 1958, 61-62. Mem. Am. Inst. C.P.A.s, Ill. Soc. C.P.A.s. Clubs: Univ. (Chgo.), Skokie Country, Mid-Am. Office: 205 N Michigan Ave Chicago IL 60601

SORA, SEBASTIAN ANTONY, business machines manufacturing executive, educator; b. N.Y.C., June 29, 1943; s. Joseph Louis and Angelina Maria (Maletta) S.; m. Janet Lee Dietz, Apr. 11, 1970 (dec. July 1972); 1 child, Joseph Walter; m. Mary Frances Elizabeth Boscketti, Oct. 12, 1974; children: Joseph Walter, Sebastian Nicholas, Frances Ann, Jenny Concetta. BS, Bklyn. Coll., 1964; MBA, Iona Coll., 1974, PMC, 1976; DPS, Pace U., 1989. Math. modeller Assoc. Univs. Inc., 1964-66; with U.S. Coast and Geodetic Survey, Washington, 1967-70; mgr. programming IBM, Yorktown, N.Y., 1966-67, 70-75, programmer, modeller, 1970-72; mgr. program system and design IBM, Fishkill, N.Y., 1971-77; analyst on market models IBM, Harrison, N.Y., 1977-81; sr. programmer IBM, Boeblingen, Fed. Republic Germany, 1981-82; mgr. rsch. staff 1st Josephson system IBM, Yorktown, 1982-84; program dir. Systems Rsch. Inst. IBM, N.Y.C., 1984-87; mgr. edn. program World Trade Corp. IBM, North Tarrytown, N.Y., 1989-90; mgr. promotional-artificial intelligence systems IBM, White Plains, N.Y., 1990—; assoc. prof. MIS Montclair State Coll., Upper Montclair, N.J., 1992-95; pres. Bus. Edn. Systems Tech., 1992-95; assoc. prof. info. sci. Pace U., White

Plains, N.Y., 1977-96; asst. prof. telecommunications Iona Coll., New Rochelle, N.Y., 1986; asst. prof. mgmt. Manhattan Coll., Bronx, N.Y., 1988; cons. AID, Washington, 1989. Editor Jour. Value Based Mgmt., 1987—, Jour. Cross Cultural Mgmt., Jour. of Am. Mgmt., 1994-95; contbr. articles to profl. jours.; patentee fluxless solder, also others. Mem. IEEE (technol. leadership com. 1986—, info. policy com. 1986-95), Data Processing Mgmt. Assn. Roman Catholic. Home: 1 Christie Ct Somers NY 10589 Office: Internat Bus Edn Sys Techs 1 Christie Ct Somers NY 10589-2430

SORBER, CHARLES ARTHUR, academic administrator; b. Kingston, Pa., Sept. 12, 1939; s. Merritt Walter and Marjory (Roachford) S.; m. Linda Ellen Babcock, Feb. 20, 1972; children: Kimberly Ann, Kingsley Charles. BS in Sanitary Engring., Pa. State U., 1961, MS in Sanitary Engring., 1966; PhD, U. Tex., 1971. Sanitary engr. U.S. Army, France and Fed. Republic Germany, 1961-65; chief gen. engring. br. U.S. Army Environ Hygiene Agy., Edgewood Arsenal, Md., 1966-69; comdr. U.S. Army Med. Environ. Research Unit, Edgewood Arsenal, 1971-73; dir. environ. quality div. U.S. Army Med. Bioengring. R&D Lab., Frederick, Md., 1973-75; asst. dean coll. scis. and math. U. Tex., San Antonio, 1976-77, acting dir. div. earth & phys. scis., 1977-80, dir. Ctr. Applied Research & Tech., 1976-80; assoc. dean coll. engring. U. Tex., Austin, 1980-86, L.B. (Preach) Meaders prof., 1985; dean sch. engring. U. Pitts., 1986-93; pres. U. Tex.-Permian Basin, Odessa, 1993—; bd. dirs. Tex. Commerce Bank-Odessa, Wilkes U. Coun.; cons. various cos. and agys. Author, co-author more than 140 papers, book chpts., reports on land application of wastewater and sludges, water and wastewater reuse, water and wastewater disinfection, and higher edn. Recipient Disting. Alumnus award Wilkes Coll., 1987, Disting. Grad. award Coll. of Engring., U. Tex., Austin, 1994, Outstanding Engring. Alumnus award Pa. State U., 1994; John A. Focht teach fellow U. Tex.-Austin, 1982. Fellow ASCE; mem. NSPE, Am. Acad. Environ. Engrs. (trustee 1994—, diplomate, Gordon Maskew Fair award 1993), Water Environ. Fedn. (com. chmn. 1983-85, 86-89, 93—, bd. control 1988-94, Svc. award 1985, 89, 90, 96, v.p. 1990-91, pres.-elect 1991-92, pres. 1992-93), Am. Soc. Engring. Edn., Am. Water Works Assn., Coun. Pub. Univ. Pres. and Chancellors (exec. com. Tex. 1994-95), Odessa Country Club, Club at Mission Dorado, Petroleum Club (Midland), Horseshoe Bay Resort and Conf. Club. Office: U Tex Permian Basin 4901 E University Blvd Odessa TX 79762-8122

SORBY, DONALD LLOYD, university dean; b. Fremont, Nebr., Aug. 12, 1933; s. Lloyd A. and Orpha M. (Simmons) S.; m. Jacquelyn J. Burchard, Nov. 7, 1959; children: Thomas, Sharon. B.S. in Pharmacy, U. Nebr., 1955; M.S., U. Wash., 1958, Ph.D., 1960. Dir. pharm. services U. Calif., San Francisco, 1970-72; chmn. dept. pharmacy practice Sch. Pharmacy, U. Wash., Seattle, 1972-74; dean Sch. of Pharmacy, U. Mo., Kansas City, 1974-84; dean Sch. of Pharmacy, U. Pacific, Stockton, Calif., 1984-95, dean emeritus, 1995—; bd. dirs. Longs Drugstores Inc. Contbr. articles in field to profl. jours. Mem. Am. Pharm. Assn. (Linwood F. Tice award 1995), Am. Assn. Colls. of Pharmacy (pres. 1980-81), Calif. Pharm. Assn., Acad. Pharm. Rsch. and Scis., Calif. Soc. Health-sys. Pharmacists, Sigma Xi, Phi Kappa Phi, Rho Chi. Home: 4362 Yacht Harbor Dr Stockton CA 95204-1126 Office: U Pacific Sch Pharmacy Stockton CA 95211

SOREFF, STEPHEN MAYER, artist; b. N.Y.C., Feb. 2, 1931; s. Joseph and Jeanne (Goldring) S.; m. Almeda Helen Soreff; children: Alexander, Zachary. BA, Bklyn. Coll., 1954; AA, Pratt Inst., Bklyn., 1960. Engring. designer Slocum & Fuller, N.Y.C., 1954-58; indsl. designer George Kress Assocs., Newark, 1958-62, Walter Darwin Teague Assocs., N.Y.C., 1962-68; prof. art U. Wash., Seattle, 1968-70, C.W. Post Ctr. L.I. U., Greenvale, N.Y., 1970-95; pvt. practice artist N.Y.C., 1965—. exhibited works include Crystall Art, Mus. Hudson Highlands, 1988, Star Lake, Emporia Coll., 1988, The Infinite Painting, U. Md., 1988, The Artists Tomb, W&J Coll., 198, The Information Shower, 1992, Richard Humphrey Gallery, N.Y.C., 1995, Reading (Pa.) Mus., 1996, Eighth Flr. Gallery, N.Y.C., 1996; works in collections of Mus. of Modern Art, N.Y.C., Whitney Mus., Guild Hall Mus. Recipient award Art Quest, Inc., Los Angeles, 1987, Metro Art, Inc., Scarsdale, N.Y., 1987, N.Y. chpt. Nat. Drawing Assn., 1987; fellow Macdowell, Va. Ctr., Altosde Chavon, Cite des Arts Internat. Home: 79 Mercer St New York NY 10012-4430

SOREL, CLAUDETTE MARGUERITE, pianist; b. Paris; d. Michel M. and Elizabeth S. Grad. with top honors, Juilliard Sch. Music, 1947, post-grad., 1948; student of, Sigismund Stojowski, Sari Biro, Olga Samaroff Stokowski, Mieczyslaw Horszowski, Rudolf Serkin; ensemble with, Felix Salmond; musicology with, Dr. Robert Tangeman; music history with, Marian Bauer; grad., Curtis Inst. Music, 1953; B.S. cum laude in Math., Columbia U., 1954. music faculty, vis. prof. Kans. U., 1961-62; assoc. prof. music Ohio State U., 1962-64; prof. music, head piano dept. SUNY Fredonia, 1964—, Disting. Univ. prof., 1969—, univ. artist, 1969—, faculty exchange scholar, 1976—; mem. internat. jury Van Cliburn Internat. Piano Competition, Tex., 1966, Que. and Ont. Music Festivals, 1967, 75; chmn. music panel Presdl. Scholars in Arts Program, 1979—; juror numerous nat. and internat. music competitions; cons. Ednl. Testing Service, Princeton. Author: Compendium of Piano Technique, 1970, 2d edit., 1987, Japanese edit., 1987, Mind Your Musical Manners - Off and On Stage, 1972, 3d revised edit., 1995, The 24 Magic Keys, 3 vols., 1974, The Three Nocturnes of Rachmaninoff, 1974, 2d edit., 1975, 3d edit. with cassette in compact disc, 1988, Fifteen Smorgasbord Studies for the Piano, 1975, 2d edit., 1995, 17 Little Piano Studies, 1995, Arensky Piano Etudes, 1976; spl. editor: Music Insider; painter of oil portraits; contbr. articles to profl. mags.; compiler: The Modern Music of Today, 1974, Serge Prokofieff - His Life and Works, 1947, The Ornamentations in Mozart's Music, 1984; debut at Town Hall, N.Y.C., 1943; since appeared in leading cities of U.S.; performed with N.Y. Philharm., London Philharm., Zurich, Boston, San Antonio, Milw., NBC, Phila., New Orleans and Cin. symphony orchs., Youth Orch. of Am., 200 others; appeared at Aspen, Berkshire, Chautauqua, other festivals, European concert tours, 1956, 57, 58, to Eng., Sweden, Holland, Germany, Switzerland, France; appeared on various radio, TV programs; made recs. for RCA Victor Rec. Co., Monitor Records, Mus. Heritage; compact disc MacDowell Piano Concerto #2 with N.Y. Philharm. Orch., 1993; 2000 solo appearances, U.S. and Europe. Bd. dirs. Olga Samaroff Found.; Jr. com. aux. bd. N.Y. Philharmonic Symphony Orch., N.Y. State Nat. Fedn. Music Clubs; mem. adv. bd. Univ. Library Soc.; pres. Shelton Apartments, Inc. Fulbright fellow, 1951; Ford Found. Concert grantee, 1962; winner Phila. Orch. Youth Auditions, 1950, to appear with orch. under direction of Eugene Ormandy; U.S. Senatorial Bus. Adv. Com. Fulbright scholar, 1951; recipient Harry Rosenberg Meml., Frank Damrosch prizes, 1947, Nat. Fedn. Music Clubs Young Artist award, 1951; citation svc. to Am. music Nat. Fedn. Music Clubs, 1966, citations Nat. Assn. Composers & Condrs., 1967, Mu Phi Epsilon, 1968, Freedom medal U.S. Senatorial Com., 1994; nominated Kyoto Japan Humanitarian award, 1989, 92; Claudette Sorel Scholarship for Women Ctr. in Music created by NYU. Mem. Nat. Music Coun. (dir. 1973—, chmn. performance com.), Nat. Arts Club, Music Critics Assn., Broadcast Music Incorp., Columbia Univ. Club (N.Y.C.), Nat. Arts Club, Pi Kappa Lambda, Mu Phi Epsilon (dir. Meml. Found., nat. chmn. Sterling Staff Concert Series, citation 1968). Home: 333 W End Ave New York NY 10023-8131 *The most difficult achievement in life is to try to reach one's goals while keeping one's highest idealism and integrity. If these aims can also be maintained in an atmosphere of freedom and respect for quality in all aspects of life, then the individual is most fortunate.*

SOREL, EDWARD, artist; b. N.Y.C., Mar. 26, 1929; s. Morris and Rebecca (Kleinberg) Schwartz; m. Nancy Caldwell, May 29, 1965; children: Jenny, Katherine; children by previous marriage: Madeline, Leo. Diploma, Cooper Union, 1951. Co-founder Pushpin Studio, 1953; free-lance artist, 1956—; syndicated Sorel's News Service, 1969-70, King Features. Author, illustrator: Making the World Safe for Hypocrisy, 1972; exhibited in, Pushpin Studio retrospective at the Louvre, 1970, other European galleries, 1970-71; exhibited one-man show, Graham Galleries, N.Y.C., 1973, 78, Galerie Bartsch & Chariau, Munich, 1986, Retrospective Exhibition Cooper Union, 1987, Susan Conway Galleries, Washington, 1992, Soc. Illustrators Am. Mus. Illustration, N.Y.C., 1993, Davis and Langdale Galleries, N.Y.C., 1994; illustrator: Pablo Paints a Picture, 1961, Gwendolyn the Miracle Hen, 1963 (N.Y. Herald Tribune Book award for illustration 1962), What's Good for a Five-Year-Old, 1969, The Duck in the Gun, 1969, Word People, 1970, Magical Storybook, 1972, Superpen, 1978, The Zillionaire's Daughter, 1990, First Encounters, 1994; contbr. to The Nation, The New Yorker, American Heritage and The Atlantic mags. Recipient awards Soc. Illustrators, Art Dirs. Club N.Y.; Augustus St. Gauden's medal Cooper Union; George Polk award for satiric drawing, 1981; Page One award Newspaper Guild of N.Y. for best editorial cartoon (magazines), 1988, Hamilton King award Soc. Illustrators, 1990.

SORELLE, RUTH DOYLE, medical writer, journalist; b. Port Arthur, Tex., Oct. 9, 1948; d. Richard Thomas and Ruth Elaine (Droddy) D.; m. Paul Charles SoRelle, Apr. 10, 1970; children: Danielle Amanda, Richard Paul. BJ, U. Tex., 1971; MPH, U. Tex., Houston, 1988. Reporter Port Arthur News, summer 1968, 69, Univ. and Info. Svc., Austin, Tex., 1970-71; med. editor U. Tex. MD Anderson Hosp., Houston, 1973-74; editor Resources Devel. Corp., Houston, 1974-76; med. editor Baylor Coll. Medicine, Houston, 1977-78; copy editor Houston Chronicle, Houston, 1978-79; med. writer Houston Chronicle, 1979—; instr. U. Houston, 1986, 87, 89. Leader Presbyn. Youth Fellowship, Houston, 1989. Recipient John P. McGovern award Am. Med. Writers Assn., Community Svc. award Tex. Assoc. Press, 1993, Katie award Dallas Press Club, 1992, 93, Anson Jones award Tex. Med. Assn., 1981, 83, 85, 86, 88, 90, 92, Francis C. Moore award Harris County Med. Assn., 1984-94, Silver Star Tex. award Tex. Hosp. Assn., 1984, 86, 89, 92, Tex. Pub. Health Assn. award, 1981, 89, 90, 91, 94, Houston Area Health Care Coalition's Health Policy Leadership award, 1990, Paul Ellis award Am. Heart Assn., 1988, 95, others. Mem. Am. Med. Writer's Assn. (bd. dirs. southwest chpt. 1994-95), Press Club of Houston (Deadline Coverage award 1984, Investigative Series award 1990, Mag. Feature award 1994). Home: 5814 Warm Springs Rd Houston TX 77035-2428*

SOREN, DAVID, archaeology educator, administrator; b. Phila., Oct. 7, 1946; s. Harry Friedman and Erma Elizabeth (Salamon) Soren; m. Noelle Louise Schattyn, Dec. 22, 1967. B.A., Dartmouth Coll., 1968; M.A., Harvard U., 1972, Ph.D., 1973. Cert. Rome Classics Ctr. Curator of coins Fogg Art Mus., Cambridge, Mass., 1972; asst. prof. U. Mo., Columbia, 1972-76, assoc. prof., dept. head, 1976-81; prof. archaeology U. Ariz., Tucson, 1982-97, Regents prof., 1997—, dept. head, 1984-89; guest curator Am. Mus.. Natural History, N.Y.C., 1983-90, lectr., 1993—; creator/dir. Kourion Excavations, Cyprus, 1982-89, Portugal, 1983-84, Am. Excavations at Lugnano, Italy, 1988-93; pot cons., field dir. Tunisia Excavations, Chgo. Oriental Inst./Smithsonian Instn., 1973-78; bd. dirs. humanities program U. Ariz., 1992-94; dir. excavations Chianciano Terme, Italy, 1995—; subject of The Learning Channel TV program: series "Archaeology", 1995. Author: (books) Unreal Reality, 1978, Rise and Fall of Fantasy Film, 1980, Carthage, 1990, French edit., 1994; co-author: Kourion: Search for a Lost Roman City, 1988, Corpus des Mosaiques de Tunisie, 1972, 3rd rev. edit., 1986, Carthage: A Mosaic of Ancient Tunisia, 1987; editor: Excavations at Kourion I, 1987; producer: (film) Carthage: A Mirage of Antiquity, 1987; creator and guest curator: (internat. traveling exhbn.) Carthage: A Mosaic of Ancient Tunisia, 1987-92; editor, founder Roscius, 1993—; creative cons. TV miniseries Lost Civilizations, 1994; contbr. articles to profl. jours. Subject of National Geographic spl. Archeological Detectives, 1985; work subject of feature articles in Newsweek, Conoisseur, National Geographic and others; recipient Cine Golden Eagle, 1980, Angenieux Film award Industrial Photography mag., 1980, Outstanding American Under 40 award C. Johns Hopkins-Britain's Royal Inst. Internat. Affairs, 1985; named Outstanding American Under 40 Esquire mag., 1985, hon. Italian citizen Lugnano, Italy, 1989; grantee NEH, 1979, 87, Fulbright, Lisbon, 1983. Mem. Nat. Geog. Soc. (project dir. 1983-84), Am. Sch. Oriental Rsch. (dept. rep. 1981-85), Archaeol. Inst. Tucson (pres. 1983-86), Luso-Am. Commn. (citation 1983-84), Explorer's Club. Office: U Ariz Dept Classics 371 MLB Tucson AZ 85721

SOREN, TABITHA L., television newscaster, writer; b. San Antonio, Aug. 19, 1967; d. John Thomas and Mary Jane (Quinn) Sornberger. BA cum laude in Journalism, NYU, 1989. Intern Cable News Network, N.Y.C., Sta. WNBC TV, N.Y.C.; desk asst. ABC TV, N.Y.C.; news anchor, statehouse correspondent ABC Sta. WVNY-TV, Vt.; news reporter, anchor MTV News Dept., N.Y.C., 1991—; contbg. corr. NBC News, N.Y.C., 1992—; columnist N.Y. Times Syndication Sales Corp., N.Y.C.; cons. editor Elle, N.Y.C. Contbr. articles to various periodicals. Recipient Peabody Journalism award U. Ga., 1993, Leadership award Nat. League Women Voters, 1993. Office: MTV News 1515 Broadway New York NY 10036*

SORENSEN, ALLAN CHRESTEN, service company executive; b. Edson, Alta., Can., Apr. 27, 1938; came to U.S., 1962, naturalized, 1965; s. Henry and Vivien A. (Howie) S.; children: Scott, Jody. B.S. in Pharmacy, Drake U., 1961. Salesman Hoffman LaRoche Pharm. Co., Kitchener, Ont., Can., 1961-62; salesman Personnel Pool of Am., Inc., Chgo., 1962-63; sales mgr. Personnel Pool of Am., Inc., 1963-67, dir., pres., 1967-89, chief exec. officer, 1978-91; chmn. interim svcs. Personnel Pool of Am., Inc. (name changed to Interim Svcs. Inc. 1992), 1989—; dir., vice chmn. Let's Talk Cellular & Wireless, 1994—; dir. The Apple Tree Cos., Inc., 1996—. Bd. dirs. Broward Workshop. Mem. Nat. Assn. Temp. Svcs. (past pres., bd. dirs.), Exec. Assn. Ft. Lauderdale, Home Health Svcs. and Staffing Assn. (past chmn., bd. dirs.). Republican. Club: Rotary. Home: 1500 S Ocean Dr Fort Lauderdale FL 33316-3242 Office: Interim Svcs Inc 2050 Spectrum Blvd Fort Lauderdale FL 33309-3008

SORENSEN, ANDREW AARON, academic administrator; b. Pitts., July 20, 1938; s. Albert Aaron and Margaret (Lindquist) S.; m. Donna Ingemie, Aug. 4, 1968; children: Aaron Ashley, Benjamin Samuel. BA, U. Ill., 1959; BDiv, Yale U., 1962, MPh, 1970, PhD, 1971; MPH, U. Mich., 1966. Asst. prof. Cornell U., Ithaca, N.Y., 1971-73; asst. prof. U. Rochester, N.Y., 1973-76, assoc. prof., 1976-83; prof., dean U. Mass., Amherst, 1983-86; prof., dean Johns Hopkins U., Balt., 1986-90, exec. dir. AIDS Inst.; provost, v.p. acad. affairs U. Fla., Gainesville, 1990-96; pres. U. Ala., Tuscaloosa, 1996—; chmn. adminstrv. bd. Whitney Marine Biol. Lab., 1990-96; chmn. editl. bd. Univ. Press Fla., 1990-96; vis. fellow U. Cambridge, 1979-80. Author 5 books; contbr. over 100 articles to profl. jours. Exec. dir. Johns Hopkins AIDS Inst., Balt., 1987-90; bd. dirs. Ala. Shakespeare Festival, 1996—, Blount, Internat., 1997—. U.S. Dept. Edn. fellow Lincoln U., 1966-67, NSF fellow Harvard U., 1975-76. Presbyterian. Office: Office of Pres U Ala 203 Rose Adminstrn Bldg Box 870100 Tuscaloosa AL 35487-0100

SORENSEN, BURTON ERHARD, investment banker; b. Chgo., Oct. 28, 1929; s. Soren Kirsten and Christine (Petersen) S.; m. Linda Graf, Aug. 28, 1954 (div. 1970); children: Debra, Jack, Peter, Janice; m. France Elizabeth Pepinger, Dec. 28, 1972. Student, Northwestern U., 1949; B.A., Wheaton Coll., 1955. Vice pres. Kidder, Peabody & Co., N.Y.C., 1956-71; v.p. Goldman, Sachs & Co., N.Y.C., 1972-76, ptnr., 1977-84; chief exec. officer, chmn. Lord Securities Corp., N.Y.C., 1984—; dir. Provident Companies, Inc., Chattanooga, Tenn., Servicemaster Industries Inc. Served to cpl. USMC, 1951-53, Korea. Mem. City Midday Club (N.Y.C.), Morris County Golf Club (Covent, N.J.), Grandfather Golf and Country Club (Linville, N.C.), The Sanctuary Golf Club (Sanibel Island, Fla.). Republican. Office: Lord Securities Corp 2 Wall St New York NY 10005-2001

SØRENSEN, ERIK, international company executive; b. Randers, Denmark, July 19, 1944; s. Christen and Erna Sørensen; m. Brigitte Berg; children: Anne Marie, Thomas, Anne Louise, Anne Mette, Anne Sophie. MS in Chemistry, Tech. U. Denmark, 1968; MBA in Internat. Fin., Cph Sch. Econs., 1971. Sr. economist Novo Industri A/S, Bagsvaerd, Denmark, 1970-71, mgr. econs. and planning, 1972-74, v.p. sales and mktg., 1974-80; pres. bioindsl. group Novo Industri A/S, Denmark, 1980-88; pres. Health Care Grp Novo Nordisk A/S, Denmark, 1988-1995; pres., CEO Christian Hansen Group, Denmark, 1995—. Lt. Danish Army, 1968-70. Office: Chr. Hansen Group, Bøge Allé 10, 2970 Hoersholm Denmark

SORENSEN, GILLIAN MARTIN, United Nations official; b. Columbus, Ohio, Mar. 4, 1941; d. John Butlin and Helen (Hickam) Martin; m. Theodore C. Sorensen, June 28, 1969; 1 child, Juliet. BA, Smith Coll., 1963. Commr. N.Y.C. Commn. for UN and Consular Corps, 1978-90; pres. Nat. Conf., 1990-93; undersec gen., spl. advisor for pub. policy UN, N.Y.C., 1993-97, asst. sec. gen. for external rels., 1997—. Del. Dem. Nat. Conv., 1976, 84, 88. Mem. Coun. on Fgn. Rels., Bus. Coun. for UN (bd. dirs. 1990—), Women's Forum. Avocations: skiing, tennis, jogging. Office: UN Rm S-3840 New York NY 10017

SORENSEN, HENRIK VITTRUP, electrical engineering educator; b. Skanderborg, Denmark, Jan. 17, 1959; came to U.S. 1983; s. Evan Anton and Anne Marie (Vittrup) S.; m. Karen Ann Taylor, Mar. 5, 1988; 1 child, Amanda Elisabeth. MS, Aalborg U. Ctr., 1983; PhD, Rice U., 1988. Asst. prof. Dept. Electrical Engring. U. Pa., Phila., 1988-95; v.p. Ariel Corp., Cranbury, N.J., 1995—; cons. AT&T Bell Labs., Murray Hill, N.J., 1990-95. Author: Handbook for Digital Signal Processing, 1992, The FFT Bibliography, 1995, A Digital Signal Processing Laboratory, 1997; contbr. articles to profl. jours. Fellow Rotary; mem. IEEE (editor 1990-94, vice chmn. Phila. sect. 1991-94), Sigma Xi, Eta Kappa Nu. Lutheran. Achievements include development of fast algorithms for the split radix fast Fourier transform and for the fast Hartley transform. Home: 75 Franklin Dr Plainsboro NJ 08536-2310 Office: Ariel Corp 2540 Us Highway 130 Cranbury NJ 08512-3507

SORENSEN, JACKI FAYE, choreographer, aerobic dance company executive; b. Oakland, Calif., Dec. 10, 1942; d. Roy C. and Juanita F. (Bullon) Mills; m. Neil A. Sorensen, Jan. 3, 1965. BA, U. Calif., 1964. Cert. tchr., Calif. Ptnr., Big Spring Sch. Dance, 1965; tchr. Pasadena Ave. Sch., Sacramento, 1968; founder, pres., choreographer Jacki's Inc., DeLand, Fla., 1990—; cons., lectr. on phys. fitness. Author: Aerobic Dancing, 1979, Jacki Sorensen's Aerobic Lifestyle Book, 1983; choreographer numerous dance exercises for records and videocassettes. Trustee Women's Sports Found. Recipient Diamond Pin award Am. Heart Assn., 1979, Individual Contbn. award Am. Assn. Fitness Dirs. in Bus. and Industry, 1981, Spl. Olympics Contbn. award, 1982, Contbn. to Women's Fitness award Pres.'s Coun. Phys. Fitness and Sports, 1982, Healthy Am. Fitness Leader award U.S. Jaycees, 1984, Lifetime Achievement award Internat. Dance Exercise Assn., 1985, New Horizons award Caldwell (N.J.) Coll., 1985, Legend of Aerobics award City Sports mag., 1985; Pres. Coun. award Calif. Womens' Leadership Conf., 1986, Hall of Fame award Club Industry mag., 1986, IDEA, 1992. Mem. AAHPERD, AFTRA, Am. Coll. Sports Medicine, Nat. Intramural and Recreation Assn. Office: Jacki's Inc PO Box 289 Deland FL 32721-0289

SORENSEN, JOHN FREDERICK, retired minister; b. Cadillac, Mich., Apr. 4, 1923; s. Neil Thomas and Helga S. (Anderson) S.; m. D. Marieta Moore, Mar. 16, 1944; children: Jack, Keith, Robert. BA, Mich. State U., 1957; MDiv, Garrett Theol. Sem., 1962; DD (hon.), Holy Trinity Coll., 1996. Ordained to ministry United Meth. Ch. as deacon, 1960, as elder, 1962. Pastor Mulliken (Mich.) United Meth. Ch., 1951-55, Upton Ave. United Meth. Ch., Battle Creek, Mich., 1955-64, Haven United Meth. Ch., Jackson, Mich., 1964-67, Ithaca (Mich.) United Meth. Ch., 1967-72, 1st United Meth. Ch., Lansing, Mich., 1972-78; assoc. pastor Community United Meth. Ch., Holiday, Fla., 1985-93; mem. various coms. for Conf. Dist., United Meth. Ch., 1962-85; summer exch. pastor to Loughton, Eng., 1975. Contbr. columns to newspapers, 1967-72. Founder Free Health Clinic. With USN, 1942-46. Recipient Spl. Tribute Gov. Mich., 1985, Ionia Hospice award, 1986; named Rural Pastor of Yr. United Meth. Ch., Mich., 1955, Amb., Ionia C. of C., 1983-85; commd. Ky. Col., 1995. Fellow Designate Acad. Parish Clergy (edn. com. 1982-84, state sec. 1994-97), West Pasco Ministerial Assn. Shriners (past master 1972), Masons; mem. Fla. Naval Sailors Assn. (chaplain 1996-97, 97—), Polish Legion Am. (chaplain post 184 1996-97, 97—). Home: 4427 Pelorus Dr New Port Richey FL 34652-5810

SORENSEN, JOHN NOBLE, mechanical and nuclear engineer; b. Mpls., Jan. 2, 1934; s. Alfred Noble and Helen Viola (Baker) S.; m. Joan Elizabeth Reiche, Sept. 15, 1954; children: Laura Elizabeth, Nancy Helen, Karen Lynn. BSME, U. N.D., 1955; MSME, U. Pitts., 1958. Cert. engr. Sr. engr. Westinghouse Electric, Pitts., 1955-67; v.p., gen. mgr. NUS Corp., Rockville, Md., 1967-86; v.p., dir. Grove Engring., Inc., Rockville, 1986-93; tech. asst. to commr. U.S. NRC, Washington, 1993—. Mem. ASME, NSPE, Am. Nuclear Soc., Sigma Xi. Home: 629 Crocus Dr Rockville MD 20850-2046 Office: US NRC Washington DC 20555

SORENSEN, LEIF BOGE, physician, educator; b. Odense, Denmark, Mar. 25, 1928; came to U.S., 1955, naturalized, 1963; s. Henry V. and Mary (Nielsen) S.; m. Janice D. Nolan; 1 child, Heidi. BS, Odense Katedralskole, 1946; MD, U. Copenhagen, Denmark, 1953, PhD in Biochemistry, 1960. Intern Copenhagen County Hosp., Hellerup, Denmark, 1954; resident Copenhagen Municipal Hosp., 1955, U. Chgo. Hosp., 1957-60; mem. faculty, scientist U. Chgo. and Franklin McLean Meml. Research Inst., 1956—; prof. medicine U. Chgo., 1970—; attending physician dept. medicine, assoc. chmn. dept. Pritzker Sch. Medicine, U. Chgo., 1976—; cons. FDA, 1972—. Mem. editorial bd.: Jour. Lab. and Clin. Medicine, 1964-70, Arthritis and Rheumatism, 1965-72; Contbr. articles to profl. jours. With M.C. Danish Army, 1951. Fulbright scholar, 1955; Ill. Arthritis Found. grantee, 1970-72; NIH Fogarty Internat. Center sr. fellow, 1980. Mem. AAAS, Am. Rheumatism Soc., Am. Soc. Clin. Investigation, Central Soc. Clin. Research, N.Y. Acad. Scis., Danish Med. Assn., Ill. Acad. Gen. Practice., Am. Geriatrics Soc., Gerontologic Soc. Am., Am. Fedn. Aging Research. Home: 1700 E 56th St Apt 2801 Chicago IL 60637-1935

SORENSEN, PETER ALAN, employee benefits consultant; b. Red Wing, Minn., June 26, 1957; s. Milton Leroy and Rosemary Martha (Anderson) S.; m. Debra Lea Warwick, July 29, 1978 (div. May 1985); children: Kathryn Lea, Karisa Lynn; m. Peggy Jean Hanisch, May 30, 1987. Student, U. Wis., Green Bay, 1975-76, U. Wis., River Falls, 1976-77. CLU, ChFC, life underwriters tng. coun. fellow. Agt. Nat. Guardian Life, Madison, Wis., 1978-82, spl. agt., 1982-85, sales mgr., 1985-88, spl. sales mgr., 1988-90, assoc. gen. agt., 1990-91, gen. agt., 1991—. Town chmn., Bay City, Wis., 1991-93; mem. First Luth. Ch. Mem. ChFC, Am. Soc. CLU, Nat. Assn. Life Underwriters (pres. Hiawatha Valley Life Underwriters, Red Wing 1982-83, Nat. Sales Achievement award 1980-87, Nat. Quality award 1984-91), U.S. Jaycees, Elks (chaplain lodge 845 1988-93, Loyal Knight 1993-94, Leading Knight 1994-95, Exalted Ruler 1995-96). Republican. Avocations: golf, hunting, fishing, billiards, reading. Home: RR 35 Bay City WI 54723 Office: Sorensen Fin Svcs PO Box 45 318 Plum St Red Wing MN 55066-2530

SORENSEN, RAYMOND ANDREW, physics educator; b. Pitts., Feb. 27, 1931; s. Andrew J. and Dora (Thuesen) S.; m. Audrey Nickols, Apr. 2, 1953; 1 dau., Lisa Kirsten. B.S., Carnegie Inst. Tech., 1953, M.S., 1955, Ph.D., 1958. Mem. faculty Columbia, 1959-61; asst. prof. Carnegie-Mellon U., Pitts., 1961-65, assoc. prof., 1965-68; prof. physics Carnegie-Mellon U., 1968—, chmn. dept., 1980-89. NSF sr. postdoctoral fellow, 1965-66. Fellow AAAS, Am. Phys. Soc. Home: 1235 Murdoch Rd Pittsburgh PA 15217-1234

SORENSEN, ROBERT C., marketing executive, educator; b. Lincoln, Nebr., Sept. 7, 1923; s. Christian Abraham and Annis Sarah (Chaikin) S.; m. Marjorie Joyce Mattson, Sept. 11, 1943; children: Robert C.A., Katherine M., David W.M. Student, U. Nebr., 1940-42, Northwestern U., 1942-43; AB, U. Chgo., 1944, MA, 1948, PhD, 1954. Field examiner Chgo. regional office NLRB, 1945-46; indsl. rels. dir. Scott Radio Labs., Chgo., 1946-48; dir. prelegal div. John Marshall Law Sch., Chgo., 1947-48; asst. prof. law U. Nebr. Coll. Law, Lincoln, 1948-52; ops. analyst Ops. Rsch. Office, Johns Hopkins U., Chevy Chase, Md., 1952-54; dir. audience analysis dept. Radio Free Europe, Munich, 1954-59; dir. rsch. This Week Mag., N.Y.C., 1959-61; v.p., dir. rsch. D'arcy Advt. Co., N.Y.C., 1961-65; exec. dir. Ctr. for Advanced Practice, McCann-Erickson Inc., N.Y.C., 1965-67; pub. Psychology Today Mag., N.Y.C., 1967-68;pres. Robert C. Sorensen & Assocs. Inc., N.Y.C., 1968-85; v.p., dir. mktg. Warner Comm. Inc., N.Y.C., 1972-74; prof. mktg. Grad. and Undergrad. Sch. Bus. Adminstrn., Rider Univ., Lawrenceville, N.J., 1981-93; prof. emeritus, 1993—; pres. Sorensen Mtkg./Mgmt. Corp., N.Y.C., 1979—; cons. behavior and mktg. mgmt., market rsch., intellectual property, unfair competition and anti-trust, juror selection and litigation dynamics. Author: Adolescent Sexuality in Contemporary America. 1973, (with Viggo Mortensen) Free Will and Determinism, 1987, (monograph) Preparing and Proving Survey Research in Trademark Litigation, 1990; assoc. editor: Zygon: Jour. of Religion and Sci.; mem. editorial bd. The Trademark Reporter, 1990-92; contbr. articles to profl. jours. Past v.p., councilor Inst. on Religion in an Age of Sci.; bd. dirs., past chmn. Foster Parents Plan Internat., Foster Parents Plan U.S.A.; bd. dirs. Scandinavian Seminar, Inc., Scandinavian Seminar Coll. (Copenhagen), Childreach Inc., Ctr. Adv. Studies in Religion and Sci. Recipient UN award for civilian work in Korea, 1953. Mem. AAAS, Market Rsch. Coun., Am.

Sociol. Assn., Am. Assn. Pub. Opinion Rsch., Am. Mktg. Assn., Internat. Trademark Assn., The Coffee House, Univ. Club. Democrat. Unitarian. Address: Carlyle House 50 E 77th St New York NY 10021

SORENSEN, SHEILA, state senator; b. Chgo., Sept. 20, 1947; d. Martin Thomas Moloney and Elizabeth (Koehr) Paulus; m. Wayne B. Slaughter, May, 1969 (div. 1976); 1 child, Wayne Benjamin III; m. Dean E. Sorensen, Feb. 14, 1977; (stepchildren) Michael, Debbie, Kevin, Dean C. BS, Loretto Heights Coll., Denver, 1965; postgrad. pediatric nurse practicioner, U. Colo., Denver, 1969-70. Pediatric nurse practicioner Pub. Health Dept., Denver, 1970-71, Boise, Idaho, 1971-72; pediatric nurse practicioner Boise (Idaho) Pediatric Group, 1972-74, Pediatric Assocs., Boise, 1974-77; mem. Idaho State Ho. Reps., 1987-92; mem. Idaho Senate, 1992—, chair senate health and welfare com., 1992-94, chair senate majority caucus, vice chair state affairs com., 1994—; state chair Am. Legis. Exchange Coun. Precinct committeeman Ada County Rep. Ctrl. Com., Boise, 1982-86, dist. vice chair, 1985-88; polit. chair Idaho Med. Assn. Aux., 1984-87, Ada County Med. Assocs., 1986-87; bd. dirs. Family Practice Residency Program, 1992-94, Univ./Cmty. Health Sci. Assn., Bishop Kelly Found., 1993—; chair Senate Majority Caucus, 1995, vice chair state affairs com. Recipient AMA Nathan Davis award for Outstanding State Legislator, 1994. Mem. Nat. Conf. State Legislators, Nat. Orgn. Women Legislators (state chair), Am. Legis. Exch. Coun. Roman Catholic.

SORENSEN, THEODORE CHAIKIN, lawyer, former special counsel to President of United States; b. Lincoln, Nebr., May 8, 1928; s. Christian Abraham and Annis (Chaikin) S.; m. Gillian Martin, June 28, 1969; 1 child, Juliet Suzanne; children from previous marriage: Eric Kristen, Stephen Edgar, Philip Jon. B.S. in Law, U. Nebr., 1949, LL.B., 1951, LL.D. (hon.), 1969; LL.D. (hon.), U. Canterbury, 1966, Alfred U., 1969, Temple U., 1969, Fairfield U., 1969. Bar: Nebr. 1951, N.Y. 1966, U.S. Supreme Ct. 1966, D.C. 1971. Atty. Fed. Security Agy., 1951-52; mem. staff joint com. r.r. retirement U.S. Senate, 1952; asst. to Sen. John F. Kennedy, 1953-61; sec. New Eng. Senators' Conf., 1953-59; spl. counsel to pres. U.S., 1961-64; mem. firm Paul, Weiss, Rifkind, Wharton & Garrison, N.Y.C., 1966—; mem. Pres.'s Adv. Com. Trade Negotiations, 1978; chmn. Gov.'s panel on N.Y. State Export Credit Agy., 1982. Editor: Nebr. Law Rev, 1950-51; author: Decision Making in the White House, 1963, Kennedy, 1965, The Kennedy Legacy, 1969, Watchmen in the Night: Presidential Accountability After Watergate, 1975, A Different Kind of Presidency, 1984, (with Ralf Dahrendorf) A Widening Atlantic? Domestic Change and Foreign Policy, 1986; editor: Let the Word Go Forth: The Speeches, Statements and Writings of John F. Kennedy, 1988. Dem. candidate for U.S. Senate, 1970; chmn. Dem. Nat. Com. task force on polit. action, 1981-82, mem. task force on fgn. policy, 1986; mem. Internat. Trade Roundtable, 1985; chmn., 1994—, dir. Twentieth Century Fund, 1984—, Coun. on Fgn. Rels., 1993—, Central Asian-Am. Enterprise Fund ,(1995—), Nat. Dem. Inst. for Internat. Affairs, 1993—; trustee N.Y. Acad. Medicine, 1991—; advisor Russian-Am. Press and Info. Ctr., 1993—, pres's Commd. on White Ho. Fellows, 1996—. Named by Jr. C. of C. as one of ten Outstanding Young Men of Year, 1961. Mem. Order of Coif, Phi Beta Kappa. Office: Paul Weiss Rifkind Wharton & Garrison 1285 Avenue Of The Americas New York NY 10019-6028

SORENSEN, THOMAS CHAIKIN, retired financial executive; b. Lincoln, Nebr., Mar. 31, 1926; s. Christian and Annis (Chaikin) S.; m. Mary Barstler (div.); children: Ann Christine Sorensen Ketter, Alan Thomas, Jens Christian.; m. Pamela A. Berse; children—Matthew Thomas, Adam Lincoln. B.A., U. Nebr., 1947, LHD (hon.), 1996. Radio announcer, 1943-44, newspaper reporter, 1945-46; asst. night editor Nebr. State Jour., 1946-49; dir. news and pub. affairs radio sta. KLMS, Lincoln, 1949-51; instr. U. Nebr. Sch. Journalism, 1948-50; info. officer, press attaché Am. Embassy, Beirut, Lebanon, 1952-56, Baghdad, Iraq, 1956, Cairo, Egypt, 1957-59; program officer for Near East USIA, Washington, 1959-61; dep. dir. for policy USIA, 1961-65; v.p. U. Calif., 1966-68; sr. fellow Adlai Stevenson Inst., 1968-69; v.p. Leasco Corp., 1969-70; ptnr. Sartorius & Co., N.Y.C., 1971-74; sr. v.p., dir. Advest Inc., 1974-80; v.p. Capital Rsch. Internat., 1980-90; cons. Capital Group Inc., 1990-96; lectr. govt. and fgn. affairs U. Va., 1995-96. Author: The Word War, 1968. Named one of 10 Outstanding Young Men in Fed. Service, 1961. Mem. Washington Inst. of Fgn. Affairs, Va. Inst. Polit. Leadership, Phi Beta Kappa, Sigma Delta Chi, Delta Sigma Rho. Home: Matfield 2725 Hunt Country Ln Charlottesville VA 22901-8989

SORENSEN, W. ROBERT, clergy member, church administrator. BA, Concordia Coll., Moorhead, Minn., 1956; MDiv, Luther Theol. Sem., 1959; PhD, U. Iowa, 1978. Exec. dir. Divsn. Higher Edn. and Schs., Evang. Luth. Ch. in Am., Chgo. Office: Evangelical Lutheran Church Am 8765 W Higgins Rd Chicago IL 60631-4101

SORENSON, JAMES ROGER, public health educator; b. Yakima, Wash., Feb. 9, 1943; s. Paul Olaf and Helen Leona (Anderson) S.; m. Nancy Ellen O'Neal, May 24, 1968;1 child, Peter Matthew. BA in Sociology, U. Wash., 1965, MA in Sociology, 1966; PhD in Sociology, Cornell U., 1970. Asst. prof. Princeton (N.J.) U., 1969-74; assoc. prof. Boston U. Sch. of Medicine, 1974-84, Boston U. Sch. of Pub. Health, 1979-84; prof. Boston Univ. Schs. of Medicine and Pub. Health, 1984-85; prof. Sch. Pub. Health U. N.C., Chapel Hill, 1985—; cons. NIMH (Changing Role of Women Com.), 1971, Rutgers U. Ednl. Decision Making Project, 1970-74, Nat. Inst. Child Health and Human Devel., 1977-79, Nat. Heart , Lung and Blood Inst., Sickle Cell Br., 1977-80, 1991-92, Boston Comprehensive Sickle Cell Ctr., 1979-85, Nat. Ctr. for Human Genome Rsch., 1990-91; com. mem. Ea. Sociol. Soc. Papers Com., 1970-73, Genetics Core Group, Inst. for Soc., Ethics and the Life Scis., 1971-76, NYU com. on Med. and Ethical Issues in Treating Spina Bifida, 1973-74, Nat. Found. March of Dimes Clin. Rsch. (Human) adv. com. 1974-75; sci. assoc. Boston City Hosp., 1975-85, N.E. Group on Med. Edn., 1976-77; also many coms. at U. N.C. including Dean's Cabinet Sch. of Pub. Health, 1985—; dir. and chair steering com. Sch. of Pub. Health Promotion/Disease Prevention Program, 1986-89; adv. bd. Injury Prevention Rsch. Ctr., many others. Author: (with others) In Sickness and in Health: Social Dimensions of Medical Care, 1981, Reproductive Pasts, Reproductive Futures: Genetic Counseling and Its Effectiveness, 1981; also numerous articles to profl. jours. and chpts. to books; reviewer Am. Jour. Med. Genetics, Am. Jour. Preventive Medicine, Am. Jour. Pub. Health, Archives of Pathology and Laboratory Medicine, Human Relations, Jour. of Health and Social Behavior, Jour. Am. Geriatrics Soc., Milbank Meml. Fund Quarterly, New Eng. Jour. of Medicine, Patient Edn. and Counseling, Prenatal Diagnosis, Sci., Tech. and Human Values, Social Sci. and Medicine; exec. editor: Health Edn. Rsch., 1996—. Mem. adv. coun. Com. to Combat Huntington's Disease, Mass. chpt., 1979-85, edn. and comty. adv. bd. Am. Heart Assn., N.C. affiliate, 1986-89. Named fellow NIMH, Cornell U., 1967-69, Inst. of Soc., Ethics and Life Scis; named Falk lectr. Ea. Sociol. Soc., 1975-76; recipient Disting. Alumnus award Yakima Valley Coll., 1985; grantee; Mass. Dept. Pub. Health, Nat. Found., March of Dimes, NIDA, Nat. Cancer Inst. and others (19 grants in all). Mem. Am. Pub. Health Assn., Soc. Profl. Health Educators, N.C. Soc. Profl. Health Educators, Coun. on Health Edn. in Higher Edn., N.C. Pub. Health Assn., Phi Beta Kappa, Delta Omega. Avocations: music, theatre. Home: 21 Wysteria Way Chapel Hill NC 27514 Office: U NC Sch Pub Health 326 Rosenau CB 7400 Chapel Hill NC 27599

SORENSON, LIANE BETH MCDOWELL, women's affairs director, state legislator; b. Chgo., Aug. 13, 1947; d. Harold Davidson McDowell and Frances Elanor (Williams) Daisey Van Kleeck; m. Boyd Wayne Sorenson, June 30, 1973; children: Nathan, Matthew, Dana. BS in Edn., U. Del., 1969, M in Counseling with honors, 1986. Tchr. Avon Grove Sch. Dist., West Grove, Pa., 1969-70, Alexis I. duPont Sch. Dist., Wilmington, Del., 1970-73, Barrington (Ill.) Sch. Dist., 1973-75; counseling intern Medill Intensive Learning Ctr.-Christina Sch. Dist., Newark, Del., 1985; counselor Family Violence Shelter CHILD, Inc., Wilmington, 1985, 86-87, dir. parent edn. programs, 1987-88; dir. Office Women's Affairs, exec. dir. Commn. on Status of Women U. Del., Newark, 1988—; mem. Del. Legislature, Dover, 1992—; chair Del. Ho. Edn. Com., 1992—; commr. Edn. Commn. State Del.; mem. tng. com. Nat. Conf. State Legislatures; mem. joint sunset com. Del. Legislature, Del. House of Reps., 1992-94, Del. Senate, 1994—, Del. Legis. Joint Fin. Com. Del. Legis., 1994—. Presenter papers various meetings & confs. Pres. bd. dirs. Nursing Mothers, Inc., 1980-81; trustee Hockessin Montessori Sch., 1982-84, enrollment chair, 1982-83; trustee Hockessin Pub. Libr., 1982-84, pres. bd., 1982-84; bd. dirs. Del. Coalition for Children, 1986-88; bd. dirs. Children's Bur. Del., 1984-87, sec., 1985-87; pres. Jr. League Wilmington, 1986-87, rsch. coun. v.p., 1985-86; bd. dirs. YWCA New Castle County, 1989-91; pres. Del. Women's Agenda, 1986-88; vice-chair Women's Leadership Ctr., 1992—; mem. Del. Work Family Coalition; bd. dirs. Del. divsn. Am. Cancer Soc., 1993—. Grantee Del. Dept. Svcs. to Children, Youth and Their Families, 1987-88, 1988, State of Del. Gen. Assembly, 1992; recipient Disting. Legis. Svc. award Del. State Bar Assn., 1997. Mem. Am. Assn. for Higher Edn. (chair women's caucus 1991-92, program chair women's caucus 1990-91, pre-conf. workshop coord. women's caucus 1990 Ann. Conf.), Del. Greenway and Trails Coun., Rotary (charter mem. Hackessin Pike Creek club 1994—), Del. Alliance for Arts in Edn., Del. Family Law Commn. Republican. Methodist. Avocations: camping, hiking. Office: State of Delaware Legislative Hall Dover DE 19901

SORENSON, PERRY, resort facility executive; m. Sally Slagle; children: Eric, Karin, Bjorn. MBA with honors, U. Utah. Dist. dir. Holiday Inns, Hawaii, 1980-83, regional v.p., 1983-86; v.p., chief operating officer Embassy Suites, Inc.; chief operating officer Outrigger Hotels and Resorts. Avocations: reading, running, tennis. Office: Outrigger Hotels and Resorts 2375 Kuhio Ave Honolulu HI 96815-2939

SORENSTAM, ANNIKA, professional golfer; b. Stockholm, Sweden, Oct. 9, 1970; m. David Esch. Student, U. Ariz. With Women's Profl. Golf European Tour, 1992—, LPGA, 1993—, Swedish Nat. Team, 1987-92, Solheim Cup Team, 1994, 96. Tournaments won include: Australian Ladies Open, 1994, U.S. Women's Open, 1995, 96, Australian Ladies Masters, 1995, GHP Heartland Classic, 1995, Betsy King LPGA Classic, 1996, Samsung World Championship of Women's Golf, 1995, 96, Michelob Light Classic, 1997, Chrysler-Plymouth Tournament of Champions, 1997, others. Office: LPGA 100 Internat Golf Dr Daytona Beach FL 32124*

SORGEN, ELIZABETH ANN, retired educator; b. Ft. Wayne, Ind., Aug. 21, 1931; d. Lee E. and Miriam N. (Bixler) Waller; m. Don DuWayne Sorgen, Mar. 8, 1952; children: Kevin D., Karen Lee Sorgen Hoeppner, Keith Alan. BS in Edn., Ind. U., 1953; MS in Edn., St. Francis Coll., Ft. Wayne, 1967. Tchr. East Allen County Schs., Monroeville, Ind., 1953-94, also bldg. rep. and math. book adoption rep., 1953-94. Founder nursery sch., choir mem. St. Marks Luth. Ch., Monroeville, 1960—; active Allen County Local Edn. Fund; vol. Sci. Ctrl. Recipient Golden Apple award East Allen County Schs., 1976, Monroeville Tchr. of Yr. award, 1993. Mem. AAUW, East Allen County Educators Assn., Ft. Wayne Retired Tchrs. Assn., Ind. Two Steppers, Delta Kappa Gamma. Avocations: square and line dancing, camping, gardening. Home: 25214 Lincoln Hwy E Monroeville IN 46773-9710

SORGENTI, HAROLD ANDREW, petroleum and chemical company executive; b. Bklyn., May 28, 1934; s. Louis J. and Lucille (Sisti) S.; m. Ann Rusnack, June 30, 1962; children: Elizabeth, Lucille. B.S.Ch.E., CCNY, 1956; M.S., Ohio State U., 1959. Research engr. Battelle Meml. Inst., Columbus, Ohio, 1956-59; with Atlantic Richfield Co., 1959-91, v.p. research and engring., products div., 1975-76; sr. v.p. chem. devel. Arco Chem. Co. subs. Atlantic Richfield Co., Phila., 1977-79, pres., 1979-87, pres., CEO, 1987-90, vice chmn. bd., 1991; ptnr. Freedom Group Partnership, Phila., 1991-92; chmn. Freedom Chem. Co., Phila., 1992-96; gen. ptnr. Sorgenti Investment Ptnrs., Phila., 1996—; bd. dirs. Provident Mut. Life Ins. Co., Crown Cork & Seal. Bd. dirs. Phila. Orch. Assn., Pa. Acad. Fine Arts. Mem. Am. Chem. Soc., Am. Inst. Chem. Engrs., Soc. Chem. Industry, Ohio State U. Alumni Assn., CCNY Alumni Assn., Union League. Office: Sorgenti Investment Ptnrs 1735 Market St Ste 1313 Philadelphia PA 19103-7501

SORGI, DEBORAH BERNADETTE, educational software company executive; b. N.Y.C., May 2, 1955; d. Waldo L. and Maria N. (Santo) S.; m. Philip A. Keith, Dec. 24, 1991. BAin Elem. Edn., St. Francis Coll., 1976; MS in Reading, St. John's U., 1979. Cert. tchr., N.Y. Adminstrv. asst. Will Darrah and Assoc., N.Y.C., 1976-77; classroom tchr. St. Rita Sch., Bklyn., 1977-80; ednl. cons. Jostens Learning Corp. (formerly, Prescription Learning Corp.), Phoenix, 1980-82, regional dir., 1982-86, regional mktg. mgr., 1986-90, sr. mktg. mgr., 1990-91, area sales mgr., 1991-92; v.p. Simon & Schuster Tech. Group/CCC, Sunnyvale, Calif., 1992; pres. EduStar Am., Inc., Orlando, Fla., 1992-93; gen. mgr. edn. Wang Labs., Inc., Billerica, Mass., 1994-95, bus. devel. mgr. pub. sector, 1995-96; regional v.p. Jostens Learning Corp., San Diego, Calif., 1996—, 1997. Republican. Roman Catholic. Avocations: piano, golf, reading, opera and classical music, tennis.

SORKIN, ALAN LOWELL, economist, educator; b. Decatur, Ill., Nov. 2, 1941; s. Martin and Sally Eileen (Steinberg) S.; m. Sylvia Jean Smardo, Sept. 9, 1967; children: David, Suzanne. BA, Johns Hopkins U., 1963, MA, 1964, PhD, 1966. Rsch. assoc. Brookings Instn., Washington, 1967-69; asst. prof. internat. health and econs. Johns Hopkins U., Balt., 1969-72, assoc. prof. internat. health and econs., 1972-74, adj. prof. dept. internat. health Sch. Hygiene and Pub. Health, 1986—; prof., chmn. dept. econs., 1974—; also adj. prof. preventive and social medicine Med. Sch., U. Md., 1974—. Author: Education, Unemployment and Economic Growth, 1974, Health Economics: An Introduction, 1975, 2d edit., 1983, 3d edit., 1992. The Urban American Indian, 1978, Economic Aspects of Natural Hazards, 1982, Health Care and the Changing Economic Environment, 1986, Monetary and Fiscal Policy and Business Cycles in The Modern Era, 1988, Public Health and Development, 1988, (with others) Female Labor Force and Development, 1990, Nutrition, Food Policy and Development, 1995, others; contbr. articles to profl. jours. Mem. Am. Econs. Assn., Phi Beta Kappa, Delta Omega. Republican. Lutheran. Home: 1694 Campbell Rd Forest Hill MD 21050-2342 Office: U Md Dept Econ 5401 Wilkens Ave Baltimore MD 21228-5334 *Personal relationships are more important than material possessions. Persons with many friends have a sense of well-being that can never be embodied in materialism.*

SORKIN, LAURENCE TRUMAN, lawyer; b. Bklyn., Oct. 20, 1942; s. Sidney and Lilly (Kowensky) S.; m. Joan Carol Ross, June 25, 1972; children: Andrew Ross, Suzanne Ross. AB summa cum laude, Brown U., 1964; LLB, Yale U., 1967; LLM, London Sch. Econs. and Polit. Sci., 1968. Bar: N.Y. 1968, D.C. 1972, U.S. Supreme Ct. 1973. Law clk. to Judge J. Joseph Smith U.S. Ct. Appeals (2d cir.), 1968-69; assoc. Cahill Gordon & Reindel, N.Y.C., 1969-75, ptnr., 1975—; vis. lectr. Yale U., 1972, 73; lectr. various profl. orgns.; rsch. asst. to Lester and Bindman for book Race and Law in Great Britain, 1972. Contbr. to State Antitrust Law (Lifland), 1984; author (with Lifland, Sorkin and Van Cise): Understanding the Antitrust Laws, 1986. Fulbright scholar, 1967-68. Bd. dirs. The Legal Aid Soc., N.Y.C., 1988-94, N.Y. Lawyers for Pub. Interest, 1990-93. Mem. ABA (antitrust law sect. 1978—), N.Y. State Bar Assn. (antitrust sect., chmn. com. on legis. 1978-79, sec. 1979-80, chmn. com. on mergers 1987-89, chmn. Clayton Act com.1989-94, exec. com. 1989-94, comml. & fed. litigation sect. chmn. com. antitrust 1996—), Assn. of Bar of City of N.Y. (mem. com. trade regulation 1974-77, 95—, com. on electronic funds transfer 1979-80), Phi Beta Kappa. Office: Cahill Gordon & Reindel 80 Pine St New York NY 10005-1702

SORO, MAR BAWAI, bishop; b. Kirkuk, Iraq, Mar. 3, 1954; s. Andrew Athniel and Souria (Sada) S. MA in Theology, Cath. U. Am., 1994. Ordained priest Holy Apostolic Cath. Assyrian Ch. of the East. Parish priest Assyrian Ch., Toronto, Ont., Can., 1982-85; diocesian bishop Diocese of Western U.S. Assyrian Ch., San Jose, Calif., 1985-95; gen. sec. Assyrian Ch. of East Commn. on Inter-ch. Rels. and Edn. Devel., Seattle, 1995—; mem. Ctrl. Com., W.C.C., Geneva, 1982-91; mem. official dialogue with Roman Cath. Ch., Vatican City, 1984—, with Middle East Coun. Chs., Limassol, Cypress, 1991—. Pub. The Messenger, 1993—. Avocations: reading, computer applications. *

SOROKA, CYNTHIA ANNE, writer, photographer; b. N.Y.C., Sept. 28, 1967; d. George E. and Diane (Feldman) S. AS in Broadcasting, Bergen C.C., Paramus, N.J., 1987; BA in Comm., SUNY, New Paltz, 1989. Payroll clk., audit clk., receptionist Howard Johnson Hotel, Saddle Brook, N.J., 1987-88; intern WPDH, Poughkeepsie, N.Y., 1989; disc jockey WALL-AM/WKOJ-FM, 1989; weekend anchor and newscaster WGNY-FM Radio, Newburgh, N.Y., 1989-90; disc jockey WCZX-FM, Poughkeepsie, N.Y., 1990; disc jockey, traffic dir., producer WRKL-AM 91, Pomona, N.Y., 1990-91; disc jockey, accts. payable, traffic dir. WVIP-AM&FM, Mt. Kisco, N.Y., 1991; from photo asst. to v.p. Expressions Photography, Closter, N.J., 1982-96; pres. Ariel Starr Prodns., Closter, 1991—; v.p. Flash Blasters Inc., Closter, 1992-95, Charles Atlas Ltd., 1997—. Author: The Dark Chronicles, vol. 1, 1993, vol. 2, 1994, vol. 3, 1995, The Dark Chronicles The Light Years Part 1, 1996, Part 2, 1997; poems included: Distinguished Poets of Am., 1991-93, Outstanding Poets of 1995, 96; contbr. articles to publs. including Renaissance mag. Vol. Englewood (N.J.) Hosp., 1982-83. Mem. Nat. Assn. Broadcast Employees, Authors Guild Am., Bergen County Sci. Fiction Assn., Horror Writers Assn. Home: PO Box 767 Closter NJ 07624 Office: Ariel Starr Prodns Ltd PO Box 767 Closter NJ 07624

SOROKIN, PETER PITIRIMOVICH, physicist; b. Boston, July 10, 1931; s. Pitirim Alexandrovich and Elena Petrovna (Baratynskaya) S.; m. Anita J. Schell, Oct. 1, 1977; children: Elena P., Paul P. A.B., Harvard U., 1952, M.S., 1953, Ph.D., 1958. Staff physicist IBM Watson Rsch. Ctr., Yorktown Heights, N.Y., 1957-68, fellow, 1968—. Contbr. articles in quantum electronics to profl. jours. Recipient Michelson medal Franklin Soc., 1974; R.W. Wood award Optical Soc. Am., 1978; Harvey prize, 1984; IBM fellow, 1968—; APS Schawlow prize, 1991. Mem. Nat. Acad. Sci. (Comstock award 1983), Am. Acad. Sci., N.Y. Acad. Sci. Patentee laser devices. Home: 5 Ashwood Rd South Salem NY 10590 Office: IBM T J Watson Rsch Ctr PO Box 218 Yorktown Heights NY 10598-0218

SOROS, GEORGE, fund management executive; b. Budapest, Hungary, Aug. 12, 1930; came to U.S., 1956; s. Tivadar and Elisabeth (Szucs) S.; m. Annaliese Witschak, Sept. 17, 1960 (div. June 1983); children: Robert, Andrea, Jonathan; m. Susan Weber, June 19, 1983; children: Alexander, Gregory. BS, London Sch. Econs., 1952; LLD (hon.), New Sch. for Social Rsch., 1990; D. Civil Law, U. Oxford, Eng., 1990; LHD (hon.), Yale U., 1991. Arbitrage trader F.M. Mayer, N.Y.C., 1956-59; analyst Wertheim & Co., N.Y.C., 1959-63; v.p. Arnhold and S. Bleichroeder, N.Y.C., 1963-73; pres. Soros Fund Mgmt., N.Y.C., 1973—. Author: The Alchemy of Finance, 1987, 2nd edit., 1994, Opening the Soviet System, 1990, Underwriting Democracy, 1991. Mem. Coun. on Fgn. Rels., N.Y.C., 1988—, Royal Inst. Internat. Affairs, London, 1990—, Bretton Woods Com., Washington, 1989; mem. exec. com. Helsinki Watch, N.Y.C., 1982—; mem. com. Americas Watch, N.Y.C., 1982—; chmn., founding pres. Ctrl. European U., Prague, Budapest, 1991; chmn. Open Soc. Fund, 1981, Open Soc. Inst., 1993, founds. in Albania, Belarus, Bosnia and Herzegovina, Bulgaria, Croatia, Czech Republic, Estonia, Georgia, Hungary, Kazakhstan, Kyrgyestan, Latvia, Lithuania, Macedonia, Moldova, Poland, Romania, Russia, Slovakia, Slovenia, South Africa, Rroma, Ukraine, Yugoslavia. Recipient honor Lawyers Co. for Human Rights, N.Y.C., 1990. Mem. Brooks' London, Queens Club (London), N.Y. Athletic Club, Town Tennis, Meadow Club (Southampton, N.Y.). Avocations: tennis, skiing, chess, backgammon. Office: Soros Fund Mgmt 888 7th Ave Ste 3300 New York NY 10106

SOROS, SUSAN WEBER, educational administrator; b. Bklyn., Apr. 15, 1955; d. Murray and Iris (Horowitz) Weber; m. George Soros, June 19, 1983; children: Alexander George, gregory James. BA, Barnard Coll., N.Y.C., 1977; MA, Parsons Sch. Design, N.Y.C., 1987. Asst. dir. New York: The State of Art Exhbn., Albany, 1977; assoc. prodr. The Big Picture (film), 1978, In Search of Rothko (film), 1979; dir. Philip Colleck of London, Ltd., N.Y.C., 1988—; exec. dir. The Open Soc. Fund, Inc., N.Y.C., 1985-92; pub. Source: Notes in the History of Art, N.Y.C., 1980—; dir. The Bard Grad. Ctr. for Studies in Decorative Arts, N.Y.C., 1991—. Trustee Am. Fedn. of the Arts, N.Y.C., 1995—, the Bklyn. Mus., 1992—, Bard Coll., Annandale, N.Y., 1991—; mem. vis. com. European sculpture and decorative arts Met. Mus. Art, 1995—, Mus. of Fine Art, 1994—. Recipient Woman of Achievement award Women in Fin. Devel., 1996, Bard medall for outstanding svc. Bard Coll., 1995, Award for Achievements in Art Edn., AWED, 1993. Mem. Am. Assn. Mus. (applied art com. 1992—), Furniture History Soc., Internat. Coun. Mus. Office: The Bard Grad Ctr for Studies in Decorative Arts 18 W 86th St New York NY 10024-3602

SORREL, WILLIAM EDWIN, psychiatrist, educator, psychoanalyst; b. N.Y.C., May 27, 1913; s. Simon and Lee (Lesenger) S.; m. Rita Marcus, July 1, 1950; children: Ellyn Gail, Joy Shelley, Beth Mara. BS, NYU, 1932; MA, Columbia U., 1934, MD, 1939; PhD, NYU, 1963. Diplomate Am. Bd. Med. Psychotherapists (profl. adv. coun. 1992—); qualified psychiatrist, also cert.examiner N.Y. State Dept. Mental Hygiene. Intern Madison (Tenn.) Sanitarium and Hosp., 1939; resident physician Alexian Bros. Hosp., St. Louis, 1940; officer instrn. St. Louis U. Sch. Medicine, 1940-41; asst. psychiatrist Central State Hosp., Nashville, 1941; assoc. psychiatrist Eastern State Hosp., Knoxville, 1942-44; assoc. attending neuropsychiatrist, chief clin. psychiatry Jewish Meml. Hosp., N.Y.C., 1946-59; assoc. attending neuropsychiatrist, chief clin. child psychiatry Lebanon Hosp., Bronx, N.Y., 1947-65; psychiatrist-in-chief Psychiatry Clinic, Yeshiva U., 1950-66, asst. prof. psychiatry, 1952-54, assoc. prof., 1954-58, prof., 1959-62, psychiatrist-in-chief, assoc. dir. Psychol. Center,, 1957-67; prof. human behavior Touro Coll., 1974—; attending psychiatrist St. Clare's Hosp., N.Y.C., 1983—; asst. prof. clin. psychiatry Albert Einstein Coll. Medicine, 1986—; psychiat. cons. SSS, 1951, N.Y. State Workmens Compensation Bd., 1951—, Bronx-Lebanon Med. Ctr., 1985—; vis. psychiatrist Fordham Hosp., N.Y.C., 1951; attending neuropsychiatrist, chief mental hygiene svc. Beth-David Hosp., 1950-60; attending neuropsychiatrist Grand Central Hosp., 1958-66, Morrisania Hosp., 1959-72; psychiatrist-in-chief Beth Abraham Hosp., 1954-60; psychiat. cons. L.I. U. Guidance Ctr., 1955-60, Daytop Village, 1970-71; assoc. psychiatrist Seton City Hosp., 1955; guest lectr. U. London, 1947; vis. prof. Jerusalem, Israel Acad. Med., 1960, Hebrew U., 1960; mem. psychiat. staff Gracie Sq. Hosp., 1960—; chief psychiatry Trafalgar Hosp., 1962-72; vis. prof. psychiatry Tokyo U. Sch. Medicine, 1964; adj. prof. N.Y. Inst. Tech., 1968; vis. lectr. in psychiatry N.Y. U., 1971-73; Am. del. Internat. Conf. Mental Health, London, 1948; mem. Am. Psychiat. Commn. to USSR, Poland and Finland, 1963, Empire State Med., Sci. and Ednl. Found. Author: (booklets) Neurosis in a Child, 1949, A Psychiatric Viewpoint on Child Adoption, 1954, Shock Therapy in Psychiatric Practice, 1957, The Genesis of Neurosis, 1958, The Prejudiced Personality, 1962, The Schizophrenic Process, 1962, The Prognosis of Electroshock Therapy Success, 1963, Psychodynamic Effects of Abortion, 1967, Violence Towards Self, 1971, Basic Concepts of Transference in Psychoanalysis, 1973, A Study in Suicide, 1972, Masochism, 1973, Emotional Factors Involved in Skeletal Deformities, 1977, Cults and Cult Suicide, 1979, Further Viewpoints on the Genesis of Neurosis, 1996; assoc. editor Jour. Pan Am. Med. Assn., 1992—; contbr. articles on the psychoses. Vice pres. Golden Years Found.; N.Y.C. chmn. Com. Med. Standards in Psychiatry, 1952-54. Recipient Sir William Osler Internat. Honor Med. Soc. Gold Key; 3d prize oil paintings N.Y. State Med. Art Exhibit, 1954; NYU Founders Day award, 1963; Presdl. Achievement award, 1984, medal for med. excellence Pan Am. Med. Assn., 1997, others. Fellow Am. Psychiat. Assn. (life, pres. Bronx dist. 1960-61, other offices, Gold medal 1974, 94), Am. Assn. Psychoanalytic Physicians (pres. 1971-72, bd. govs. 1972—); mem. AMA, Ea. Psychiat. Assn., N.Y. State Soc. Med. Rsch., Am. Med. Writers Assn., N.Y. Med. Soc., N.Y. County Med. Soc., N.Y. Soc. for Clin. Psychiatry, Pan Am. Med. Assn. (various offices including pres. 1989—, assoc. editor jour. 1992—, Disting. Med. Svc. award 1997), Assn. for Advancement Psychotherapy, Bronx Soc. Neurology and Psychotherapy (pres. 1960-61, Silver medal 1970), Mensa. Home: 23 Meadow Rd Scarsdale NY 10583-7642 Office: 263 West End Ave New York NY 10023-2612 *Very meaningful to me is the matter of professionalism in the practice of my discipline. A helping service to individuals is to add and enhance their contentment of living; especially in a world of turmoil. Medical science has added greatly to the art of my training; and I apply it daily.*

SORRELL, MARTIN STUART, advertising and marketing executive; b. London, Feb. 14, 1945; s. Jack and Sally (Goldberg) S.; m. Sandra Carol Ann Finestone, Apr. 25, 1971; children: Mark, Robert, Jonathan. BA, Cambridge (Eng.) U., 1966, MA, 1970; MBA, Harvard U., 1968. Cons. Glendinning Assocs., Conn., 1968-70; v.p. Mark McCormack Orgn., London, 1970-74; dir. James Gulliver Assocs., London, 1975-77; group fin. dir. Saatchi & Saatchi, London, 1977-86; group chief exec. WPP Group PLC, London, 1986—; non-exec. dir. Storehouse, London, 1994—. Trustee U. Cambridge Found., Princess Royal Trust for Carers; mem. governing body London Bus Sch.; mem. adv. bd. Instituto de Estudios Superiores de la Empresa, Judge

Inst. Mgmt. Studies. Avocation: cricket, skiing. Office: WPP Group PLC, 27 Farm St, London W1X 6RD, England

SORRELL, WILLIAM H., state official; b. Burlington, Vt., Mar. 9, 1947; s. Marshal Thomas and Esther Sorrell; m. Mary Alice McKenzie; children: McKenzie, Thomas. AB, U. Notre Dame, 1970; JD, Cornell U., 1974. Dep. state's atty. Chittenden County State of Vt., 1975-77, state's atty. gen. Chittenden County, 1977-78, 89-92; ptnr. McNeil, Murray & Sorrell, 1978-89, sec. adminstrn., 1992-97, atty. gen., 1997—. Pres. United Cerebral Palsy Vt.; sec. Vt. Coalition Handicapped; bd. dirs. Winooski Valley Pk. Dist. Office: Office Atty Gen 109 State St Montpelier VT 05609-1001*

SORRELLS, FRANK DOUGLAS, mechanical engineer, consultant; b. Toccoa, Ga., May 14, 1931; s. Ralph Price and Ila B. (Freeman) S.; m. Alma M. West, June 19, 1954; 1 child, Desiree G. BSME, U. Tenn., 1957, MS, 1968. Registered profl. engr., Tenn. Chief engr. Formex Co., Greeneville, Tenn., 1960-67; exec. v.p. Charles Lee Assoc., Knoxville, Tenn., 1967-76; pvt. practice consulting engr. Knoxville, Tenn., 1976-78, 83-88; dir. engring. Cole Nat. Corp., Knoxville, Tenn., 1978-83; mgr. tech. transfer Valmet Paper Machinery div. Valmet-Enerdry, Knoxville, Tenn., 1988-93; pres. PEPE Software LLC, Knoxville, Tenn., 1996—; cons., Knoxville, 1976—; mem. Advanced Toroidal Facility Design Team, cons. Oak Ridge (Tenn.) Nat. Lab., 1984-85. Inventor, patentee of 8 patents and co-inventor, patentee of 14 patents in fields of filtration, web processing, plastic forming and lens processing. Staff sgt. USAF, 1950-54. Mem. NSPE, ASME (Energy Resources Rech. award 1987), Tenn. Soc. Profl. Engrs. Avocations: fishing, boating. Home and Office: 5516 Timbercrest Trl Knoxville TN 37909-1837

SORRELS, RANDALL OWEN, lawyer; b. Va., Dec. 11, 1962; s. Charles Vernon and Marjorie Elaine (Jones) S.; m. Cheryl Ann Casas, June 29, 1985; children: Ashley Michelle, Stephanie Leigh. BA in Polit. Sci.and Speech Comm. magna cum laude, Houston Bapt. U., 1984; JD magna cum laude, South Tex. Coll. Law, 1987. Bar: Tex. 1987, U.S. Dist. Ct. (so. dist.) Tex.; bd. cert. in civil trial law and personal injury trial law tex. Bd. Legal Specialization. Assoc. Fulbright & Jaworski, Houston, 1987-90; ptnr. Abraham, Watkins, Nichols, & Friend, Houston, 1990—. Fellow Houston Bar Found., Tex. Bar Found.; mem. ABA, ATLA, State Bar Tex. (bd. dirs. 1994—, bd. advisor pattern jury charge comm. Vol. 1 1994—, Vol. 4, 1995—, chmn. profl. devel. com. 1996—, vice chair legis. com. 1996—), Tex. Trial Lawyers Assn. (sustaining life mem., bd. dirs.), Houston Bar Assn., Houston Trial Lawyers Assn. (bd. dirs., v.p., chmn. CLE com. 1993—), Houston Young Lawyers Assn., Tex. Young Lawyers Assn., Coll. of the State Bar of Tex., Assn. of Civil Trial and Appellate Specialists, Am. Inns of Ct., Million Dollar Adv. Forum. Home: 4524 Palmetto St Bellaire TX 77401-3710 Office: Abraham Watkins Nichols & Friend 800 Commerce St Houston TX 77002-1707

SORRENTINO, GILBERT, English language educator, novelist, poet; b. Bklyn., Apr. 27, 1929; s. August E. and Ann Marie (Davis) S.; m. Victoria Ortiz; children: Jesse, Delia, Christopher. Student, Bklyn. Coll., 1949-51, 54-56. In various positions, 1947-70; including reins. clk. Fidelity and Casualty Co., N.Y.C., 1947-48; freight checker Ace Assembly Agy., N.Y.C., 1954-56; packer Bennett Bros. Inc., N.Y.C., 1956-57; messenger Am. Houses, Inc., N.Y.C., 1948-49; shipping-room supr. Thermo-fax Sales, Inc., Queens, N.Y., 1957-60; editor Grove Press, N.Y., 1965-70; tchr. Columbia U., 1966, Aspen Writers Workshop, 1967, Sarah Lawrence Coll., 1972, The New Sch. for Social Rsch., 1976—; NEH chairperson in lit. U. Scranton, 1979; prof. English Stanford (Calif.) U., 1982—; editorial cons. Contemporary Lit., 1989—. Author: The Darkness Surrounds Us, 1960, Black and White, 1964, The Sky Changes, 1966, The Perfect Fiction, 1968, Steelwork, 1970, Imaginative Qualities of Actual Things, 1971, Corrosive Sublimate, 1971, Splendide-Hotel, 1972, Flawless Play Restored, 1974, A Dozen Oranges, 1976, White Sail, 1977, Sulpiciae Elegidia/Elegiacs of Sulpica, 1977, The Orangery, 1978, Mulligan Stew, 1979, Aberration of Starlight, 1980, Selected Poems, 1958-80, 1981, Crystal Vision, 1981, Blue Pastoral, 1983, Something Said: Essays, 1984, Odd Number, 1985, Rose Theatre, 1987, Misterioso, 1989, Under the Shadow, 1991, Red the Fiend, 1995. With U.S. Army, 1951-53. Recipient Samuel Fels award in fiction Coord. Coun. Lit. Mags., 1974, John Dos Passos prize, 1981, Am. Acad. and Inst. Arts and Letters award in lit., 1985, Lannan Lit. award for fiction, 1992; John Simon Guggenheim Meml. fellow, 1973-74, 87-88; grantee Creative Artists Pub. Svc. Program, 1974-75, Nat. Endowment for Arts, 1974-75, 78-79, 83-84. Mem. PEN Am. Ctr. Office: Stanford U Dept English Stanford CA 94305

SORRENTINO, RENATE MARIA, illustrator; b. Mallnitz, Carinthia, Austria, June 21, 1942; came to the U.S., 1962; d. Johann and Theresia (Kritzer) Weinberger; m. Philip Rosenberg, Nov. 22, 1968 (dec. 1982); m. Francis J. Sorrentino, Sept. 4, 1988. Grad. gold and silversmith artist, Höhere Technische Lehranstalt, Austria, 1961. Draftswoman Elecon Inc., N.Y.C., 1962-65; jr. designer Automatics Metal Prod. Corp., N.Y.C., 1965-70; designer, art dir. Autosplice, Inc., Woodside, N.Y., 1970-90; freelance artist Jupiter, Fla., 1990—. Patentee Quick Disconnect from Continuous Wire, 1977. Home: 2301 Marina Isle Way Apt 404 Jupiter FL 33477-9423 Office: Autosplice Inc 10121 Barnes Canyon Rd San Diego CA 92121-2725

SORTE, JOHN FOLLETT, investment firm executive; b. Boston, June 30, 1947; s. Martin Eugene and Elizabeth Foster (Bradley) S.; m. Colleen Sarah Costello, July 28, 1979; children: Bradley Follett, Laura Elizabeth, Kathryn Clare. BA in Chem. Engring., Rice U., 1969, M in Chem. Engring., 1970; MBA, Harvard U., 1972. Assoc. Shearson Hammill & Co., Inc., N.Y.C., 1972-74; v.p. Shearson Hayden Stone, Inc., N.Y.C., 1974-79; 1st v.p. Shearson Loeb Rhoades, Inc., N.Y.C., 1979-80; 1st v.p. Drexel Burnham Lambert, Inc., N.Y.C., 1980-82, mng. dir., 1982-88, exec. v.p., 1989-90, pres., chief exec. officer, dir., 1990-92; pres., chief exec. officer New Street Capital Corp., N.Y.C., 1992-94; pres. New Street Advisors L.P., N.Y.C., 1994—; chmn. N.Y. Media Group, Inc., 1995—; bd. dirs. Vail Resorts, Inc., WestPoint Stevens, Inc. V.p., bd. dirs. DBL Found., Inc., N.Y.C., 1991-95; bd. trustees Rippowam Cisqua Sch. Office: New Street Advisors LP Ste 1703 99 Park Ave Rm 1703 New York NY 10016-1601

SORTER, BRUCE WILBUR, federal program administrator, educator, consultant; b. Willoughby, Ohio, Sept. 1, 1931; s. Wilbur David and Margaret Louise (Palmer) S.; m. Martha Ann Weirich, Sept. 2,1960 (div. 1967); 1 child, David Robert. *Great-grandparents Jacob and Catherine Sortore left France-Germany and arrived in New Jersey about 1720. A grandson,Henry Sortore, fought in the Revolutionary War. The family moved to upper state New York near Belmont. One branch of the family, my great-grandparent, Charles N., as a child, came to Mayfield, Ohio in 1831 by covered wagon with a few possessions including a cow. They subsequently became prosperous farmers. Charles' brother became a state senator and medical doctor*. BA, U. Md., 1967; MCP, Howard U., 1969; PhD, U. Md., 1972. Cert. community developer. Commd. USAFR, 1967, advanced through grades to lt. col., 1964; sr. planner, cons. Md. Nat. Capital Park and Planning Com., 1968-71; instr. psychology, sociology Howard and P.G. C.C., Columbia and Largo, Md., 1971-72; cmty. resource devel. dept. Md. Coop. Extension Svc., U. Md., College Park, Md., 1972-92; coord. rural info. ctr. Md. Coop. Ext. Svc., U. Md., College Park, 1989-92; affiliate prof. U. Md., 1985-92, ret., 1996; ext. advisor USDA Internat. Programs, Washington, 1991-96; co-author, co-dir. Dept. Edn. Coun. Effectiveness Tng. Program, 1979-81; author First County Energy Conservation Plan, Prince George's County, 1978-85. Author, co-author 12 books; contbr. articles to profl. publs., chpts. to books. Developer, dir. teamwork tng. programs U.S. Dept. Edn., U.S. Dept. Agriculture, Brazil, Poland, Nat. Grange, 1972-92; cons. Fed. Power Commn. U.S., 1973-75, State Dept. Natural Resources, Md., 1978-79, Dept. Edn., Brazil, 1981-82, Nat. Grange, 1987, Edn. Ext. Svcs., Poland, 1991-92. Urban Planning fellow Howard U., 1968, Human Devel. fellow U. Md., 1970; recipient Meritorious Svc. award Dept. Def., 1983, Disting. Community Svc. award Md. Community Resource Devel. Assn., 1983, Citation for Outstanding Svc., Ptnrs. of Am., 1983, Excellence in Ednl. Programs award Am. Express, 1984, Project of Yr. award Am. Psychol. Assn., 1976, Award of Yr. Am. Vol. Assn., 1976, Achievement award Nat. Assn. of Counties, 1980. Mem. Internat. Cmty. Devel. Soc. (bd. dirs., Achievement award for outstanding contbn. to cmty. devel. 1985, Disting. Svc. award 1990), Md. Cmty. Resource Devel. Assn. (sec.-treas. 1979, pres. 1980, 88-89). Republican. Methodist. Avocations: volunteer work, tennis, sailing, skiing. *Decide where you want to go. Ask yourself, is it worth the cost? If the answer is yes, then go with determination for time is in short supply.*

SORTER, GEORGE HANS, accounting and law educator, consultant; b. Vienna, Austria, Dec. 2, 1927; came to U.S., 1938; s. Alfred and Hertha (Kohn) S.; m. Dorienne Lachman, Aug. 18, 1966; children: David, Ivan, Adrienne. Ph.B., U. Chgo., 1953, M.B.A., 1955, Ph.D., 1963. C.P.A., N.Y. Instr. U. Chgo., 1955-58, asst. prof., 1959-63, assoc. prof., 1963-65, prof., 1966-74; Vincent C. Ross prof. acctg., prof. of law NYU, N.Y.C., 1974—; Arthur Young prof. U. Kans., 1969; Coopers & Lybrand prof. Tuck Sch. Dartmouth Coll., 1982; bd. dirs. NYU Credit Union, 1982-85; dir. Greater N.Y. Savs. Bank, N.Y.C., 1983—; audit com. City of N.Y., 1985—. Author: Accounting Theory, 1963, Accounting Thoughts of W.W. Werntz, Boundaries of Accounting Universe, 1978, Relevant Financial Statements, 1978, Financial Accounting: An Events and Cash Flow Approach, 1990, The Mix-Max Co., 1990. Mem. Ill. Sch. Bd. Dist. 233, Flossmoor, 1970-74; bd. dirs. Sch. Emotionally Disturbed Children, Chgo., 1960-74, Renaissance Soc., 1956-74, Found. Acctg. Edn., N.Y.C., 1975-79. Erskine fellow U. Canterbury, 1979. Mem. Am. Acctg. Assn. (v.p 1980-81 Outstanding Acctg. Educator), N.Y. State Soc. C.P.A.s (dir. 1980-82), Am. Inst. C.P.A.s, Fin. Acctg. Standard Adv. Com. Home: 37 Washington Sq W New York NY 10011 Office: NYU Tisch Hall 40 W 4th St New York NY 10012-1106

SORTLAND, PAUL ALLAN, lawyer; b. Powers Lake, N.D., July 30, 1953; s. Allan Berdette and Eunice Elizabeth (Nystuen) S.; m. Carolyn Faye Anderson, June 23, 1979; children: Joseph Paul, Martha Marie, Nicholas John, Benjamin David. BA, St. Olaf Coll., 1975; JD, U. Minn., 1978. Bar: Minn. 1978, N.D. 1981, U.S. Dist. Ct. Minn. 1979, U.S. Dist. Ct. N.D. 1980, U.S. Ct. Appeals (8th cir.) 1987, U.S. Supreme Ct. 1991. Assoc. Alderson & Ondov, Austin, Minn., 1978-80, Qualley, Larson & Jones, Fargo, N.D., 1980-83; ptnr. Holand, Lochow & Sortland, Fargo, 1983-85; pres. Sortland Law Office, Fargo, 1985-88; ptnr. Messerli & Kramer, Mpls., 1988-92; Sortland Law Office, Mpls., 1993—; adj. prof. bus. law Moorhead State U., 1987. Mem. ATLA, N.D. Bar Assn., Minn. Bar Assn. (cert. civil trial specialist), Kiwanis, Million Dollar Advocates Forum, Gamma Eta Gamma. Lutheran. Home: 120 Quebec Ave S Minneapolis MN 55426-1509 Office: 701 4th Ave S Ste 1700 Minneapolis MN 55415-1818

SORTLAND, TRUDITH ANN, speech and language therapist, educator; b. Butte, Mont., Dec. 3, 1940; d. Kenneth Hjalmer Sortland and Sigrid V. (Kotka) Strand. BS, Minot (N.D.) State U., 1965. Tchr. Westby (Mont.) Sch., 1960-61, Glasgow (Mont.) Southside Sch., 1962-65, Glasgow AFB, Mont., 1965-80; tchr., speech and lang. pathologist Mineral County Sch. Dist., Hawthorne, Nev., 1965-68, 78—; kindergarten tchr. Mineral County Sch. Dist., Mina, Nev., 1968-72; elem. tchr. Mineral County Sch. Dist., Mina, 1978-80; speech, language pathologist Mineral County Sch. Dist., Mina, Republic of Korea, 1980—; tchr. Dept. Def., Pusan, Republic of Kores, 1972-73, Illesheim, Fed. Republic Germany, 1973-78; tchr. Mohall (N.D.) Pub. Sch., 1964-65; cons. Mary Kay Cosmetics, tchr. Glasgow AFB, 1965-68. Supt. Sunday sch. Bethany Luth. Ch., Hawthorne, 1987—, sec. Ladies Aid, 1987—. Mem. NEA, Nev. Edn. Assn., AAUW (past sec., pres.), Pair O Dice Square Dance Club (sec. 1989—), Delta Kappa Gamma. Avocations: square and round dancing, photography. Home: PO Box 816 Hawthorne NV 89415-0816 Office: Mineral County Sch Dist A St Hawthorne NV 89415

SORTOR, HAROLD EDWARD, financial executive; b. Craig, Nebr., Jan. 18, 1925; s. Harold E. and Ruth (Oldham) S.; m. Dorothy M. Johnson, Oct. 9, 1954; 1 child, Georgia Lynn. B.S., U. Ill., 1949, J.D., 1950. Bar: Ill. bar 1950; C.P.A., Ill. Tax supr. Ernst & Ernst, Chgo., 1950-56; mem. firm McDermott, Will & Emery, Chgo., 1956-59; tax mgr. Amphenol-Borg Electronics Corp. (name changed to Amphenol Corp. 1965), Oak Brook, Ill., 1959-62; asst. controller Amphenol-Borg Electronics Corp. (name changed to Amphenol Corp. 1965), 1962-63, treas., 1963-68; treas. Bunker Ramo Corp., 1968, Montgomery Ward & Co., Chgo., 1968-73; sr. v.p. corporate finance CNA Financial Corp., 1973-75; group v.p. finance Pennzoil Co., 1975-85; lectr. Northwestern U., 1954-59. Mem. Sch. Bd. Dist. 25, Cook County, Ill., 1962-67, pres., 1965-67; bd. dirs. United Charities Chgo., 1971-75, Ill. sect. Am. Cancer Soc., 1972-75. Served with AUS, 1943-46. Mem. AICPA. Home: 11 Little Comfort Rd Savannah GA 31411-1446

SORVINO, MIRA, actress; b. 1968; d. Paul S. AB, Harvard U., 1990. Appeared in films including Amongst Friends, 1993, The Second Greatest Story Ever Told, 1993, Quiz Show, 1994, Parallel Lives, 1994, Barcelona, 1994, Tarantella, 1995, Sweet Nothing, 1995, Mighty Aphrodite, 1995 (Oscar for Best Supporting Actress), The Dutch Master, 1995, Blue in the Face, 1995, Beautiful Girls, 1996, (TV) The Buccaneers, 1995, Norma Jean and Marilyn, 1996, Jake's Women, 1996, Romy and Michele's High School Reunion, 1997, The Replacement Killers, 1997, Mimic, 1997; assoc. prodr. Amongst Friends, 1993. Office: The William Morris Agy 151 S El Camino Dr Beverly Hills CA 90212-2704*

SOSA, ERNEST, philosopher, educator; b. Cardenas, Cuba, June 17, 1940; s. Ernesto and Maria (Garriga) S.; m. Sara Mercedes, Dec. 21, 1961; children: E. David, Adrian J. BA, U. Miami, 1961; MA, U. Pitts., 1962, PhD, 1964. Instr. U. Western Ontario, London, Ontario, Can., 1963-64, U. Pitts., 1964; postdoctoral fellow Brown U., Providence, 1964-66; asst. prof. U. Western Ontario, London, Ontario, 1966-67; asst. prof. to full prof. Brown U., Providence, 1967-74, chmn. of philosophy, 1970-76, full prof., 1974—, Romeo Elton prof., 1981—; vis. prof. U. Miami, 1970, Nat. U. Mexico, 1979, 80, 81, Harvard U., Cambridge, Mass., 1982. Author: Knowledge in Perspective, 1991; gen. editor book series, Cambridge Univ. Pres., 1990—, Blackwell Publishers, 1991—; contbr. numerous articles to profl. jours. Grantee NSF, 1970-72, Exxon Ednl. Found., 1980-82; recipient Sr. fellowship NEH, 1988-89. Mem. Am. Philos. Assn. (sec.-treas. 1974-82, chair internat. coop. com. 1984-89, ea. divsn. rep. 1995—), Am. Coun. Learned Socs./Soviet Acad. Commn., Internat. Fedn. Philos. Soc. (steering com. mem. 188-89, v.p. 1988-93), Institut Internat. de Philosophie (exec. com. 1993—). Avocations: running, travel. Office: Brown U Dept Philosophy Providence RI 02912

SOSA, SAMUEL (SAMMY SOSA), professional baseball player; b. San Pedro de Macoris, Dominican Republic. With Tex. Rangers, 1989; outfield Chgo. Cubs, 1989—. Selected to N.L All-Star Team, 1995. Office: Chgo Cubs 1060 W Addison St Chicago IL 60613-4305*

SOSHNIK, JOSEPH, investment banking consultant; b. Omaha, Feb. 14, 1920; s. Ben Nathan and Clara (Lehman) S.; m. Miriam Saks, June 29, 1941; children—David, Allan (dec.), Robert. B.S.C. summa cum laude, Creighton U., 1941; M.S. (Alfred P. Sloan fellow), U. Denver, 1943; student, U. Colo., 1943-44; Ph.D., U. Nebr., 1952, LHD (hon.), 1988. Instr., asst. prof., assoc. prof. Creighton U., 1946-57, auditor, budget cons., 1952-57; with U. Nebr., 1957-71, prof. bus. adminstrn., 1966-71, comptroller, 1957-62, vice chancellor, 1962-68, pres. Lincoln campuses and outstate activities, 1968-71; v.p. Kirkpatrick, Pettis, Smith, Polian, Inc., 1971-73, exec. v.p., 1973-90, chmn. exec. com., 1973-85, also bd. dirs.; investment banking cons. Omaha, 1990—. Contbr. articles to profl. jours. Chmn. Nebr. Commn. Higher Edn. Facilities Act, 1964-71; chmn. Omaha Tomorrow, 1981-82; trustee Nebr. Council Econ. Edn., 1969—, chmn., 1974-75, 83; trustee Nebr. Ednl. TV Council Higher Edn., 1969-71, Omaha Indsl. Found., 1979-91, v.p., 1986-91; trustee U. Nebr. Found., 1978—; mem. higher edn. adv. com. Midwest Regional Conf. Council State Govts., 1963-71; mem. Citizens Adv. Com. Omaha Pub. schs., 1954-57; trustee Lincoln Gen. Hosp. and Lincoln Gen. Hosp. Assn., 1962-71, treas., 1963-67; nat. trustee NCCJ, 1978-83, co-chmn. Midlands exec. bd., 1973-80, bd. govs., 1989—; bd. dirs. Lincoln Hosp. and Health Council, 1962-69, sec. treas., 1962-64; bd. dirs. Lincoln Community Chest, 1963-69, Child Guidance Center, 1960-63, Nebraskans for Pub. TV, 1972-76, Jewish Fedn. Omaha, 1975-78, Father Flanagan's Boys Home, 1978-88, Jr. Achievement Omaha, 1981-83, Met. Arts Coun. Omaha, 1987-95, treas., 1989-93, Nebr. Found. for the Humanities, 1993-96; mem. Boys Town Nat. Coun. Friends, 1989—; bd. govs. Omaha Boys' Clubs, 1972-76; mem. Lincoln Found., 1968-71; mem. council bus. execs. Creighton U. Coll. Bus. Adminstrn., 1972-77, chmn., 1973-77; mem. pres.'s council Creighton U., 1973—; trustee Temple Israel, 1973-75, 91-93; mem. citizens assembly United Way Midlands, 1975—; bd. visitors Creighton Inst. Bus., Law and Social Research, 1976-78; mem. pres.'s adv. council U. Nebr., 1977-87; mem. Nebr. Com. for Higher Edn., 1986—; treas., mem. exec. com. St. Joseph Health Care Found., 1982-84; chmn. Leadership Omaha, 1986-88. Served with USNR, 1943-46. Recipient Bus. Leadership award Alumni Assn. U. Nebr., Spl. Charter award Nebr. Council Econ. Edn., Disting. Svc. award; John P. Begley award Creighton U., Alumni Achievement citation Creighton U., Alumni Merit award Creighton U. Mem. Nebr. Assn. Commerce and Industry (dir. 1982-88), Am. Council Edn., Nat. Assn. State Univs. and Land-Grant Colls. (senate joint com. bus. officers 1959-66), Nat. Assn. Coll. and Univ. Bus. Officers, Nebr. Securities Industry Assn. (pres. 1986-87), Greater Omaha C. of C. (bd. dirs. 1980-90, dir. emeritus 1991—, v.p. 1986-88, dir. found. 1985—), Innocents Soc., Order of Artus, Beta Gamma Sigma., Alpha Sigma Nu, Pi Lambda Phi, Delta Sigma Pi, Delta Sigma Rho. Home: 834 S 112th Plz Omaha NE 68154-3310

SOSLOWSKY, LOUIS JEFFREY, bioengineering educator, researcher; b. Bklyn., Apr. 4, 1964; s. Martin and Phyllis (Popowitz) S. BS, Columbia U., 1986, MS, 1987, PhD, 1991. Rsch. asst. Bioengring. Inst., Columbia U., N.Y.C., 1983-86, rsch. fellow, 1986-91; asst. prof. bioengring., mech. engring., orthopedic surgery U. Mich., Ann Arbor, 1991—; reviewer Jours. Biomech. Engring., Biomechanics, Orthopaedic Rsch., Surg. Rsch., 1991—; panelist Shoulder Workshop, Am. Acad. Orthopaedic Surgeons-ASES, NIH, Vail, Colo., 1992. Contbr. numerous articles to Biorheology Jour., Biomechanics Jour. Orthopaedic Rsch., Clinics in Sports Medicine, numerous chpts. in Biomechanics of Diarthrodial Joints, Basic Orthopedic Biomechanics, also others. Grantee Orthopaedic Rsch. and Edn. Found., 1991—, NSF, 1992—, Whitaker Found., 1992—. Mem. ASME, AAUP, Orthopaedic Rsch. Soc., Am. Soc. Biomechanics, Sigma Xi, Tau Beta Pi, Chi Epsilon. Office: U Mich Orthopaedic Rsch Labs Rm G-161 400 N Ingalls St Ann Arbor MI 48109-2003

SOSOKA, JOHN RICHARD, consulting firm executive, engineer; b. L.A., Nov. 30, 1929; s. John and Mary (Kovach) S.; m. Audrey T. Trezona, Apr. 26, 1952; children: John Richard Jr., Cathie Ann, Karen Elizabeth. BS in Gen. Engring., UCLA, 1952; MBA, Calif. State U., 1975. Registered mech., elec., fire protection, metallurgy, control systems and civil engr., Calif. Project engr. Stathem Instrument, L.A., 1954-55; staff engr. Aerojet Gen., Azusa, Calif., 1955-60; tech. dir. Unitek Corp., Monrovia, Calif., 1960-65; staff engr. TRW Systems, Redondo Beach, Calif., 1965-69; engr. mgr. Allen-Jones Electronics, Gardena, Calif., 1969-70; sect. head City of Long Beach, Calif., 1970-79; pres. Sosoka & Assoc.s, Los Alamitos, Calif., 1979-90; exec. v.p. Sparvan, Inc., Long Beach, Calif., 1990-91; pres. PSI Engrs., Inc., Long Beach, Calif., 1991—. Fellow ASHRAE (dir. and regional chair 1990-93, Disting. Svc. award 1988); mem. Assn. Energy Engrs. (v.p. 1980-81, Energy Engr. of Yr. award 1985). Republican. Episcopalian. Achievements include patent in Welding. Home: 848 Roxanne Ave Long Beach CA 90815-5013 Office: PSI Engrs Inc 5000 E Spring St Ste 800 Long Beach CA 90815-1275

SOSSI, ANTHONY, medical administrator; b. Bklyn., Dec. 1, 1935; s. Alfred and Mary (Mendolia) S.; m. Barbara Schauler, May 19, 1962; children: Barbara, Marion, Jacqueline, Andrea, Maureen. BA, Columbia Coll., 1956; MD, N.J. Med. Sch., 1960. Lic. N.Y. Internist Howard Beach Med. Assocs., Queens, N.Y., 1966-87; dir. of medicine Cath. Med. Ctr. (formerly Mary Immaculate Hosp.), Jamaica, 1987-96; acting chmn. medicine Cath. Med. Ctr., Jamaica, 1996—. Lt. USN, 1962-64. Avocations: music, computers, reading. Office: Cath Med Ctr 88-25 153d St Jamaica NY 11432

SOSTILIO, ROBERT FRANCIS, office equipment marketing executive; b. Boston, Nov. 17, 1942; s. Natale J. and Louise (Caruso) S.; m. Gail Marie McGuinness, Apr. 17, 1966. Student, U. Maine, 1960-61, Broward Jr. Coll., Ft. Lauderdale, 1967-70, Miami-Dade Jr. Coll., 1979. Product assurance engr. Saxon Copystatics, Miami, Fla., 1970-77; internat. svc. mgr. Saxon Export Corp., Miami, 1977-80; nat. svc. mgr. Cybernet Internat., Warren, N.J., 1980-81; mgr. nat. copier svc. Monroe Systems for Bus., Morris Plains, N.J., 1981-82; nat. OEM mgr. Panasonic Indsl. Co., Secaucus, N.J., 1982-86; assoc. dir. copier rsch. Dataquest, San Jose, Calif., 1987-90; mgr. product program Ricoh Corp., West Caldwell, N.J., 1986-87, dir. copier mktg., 1990-94, dir. strategic planning, 1994-96; dir. converging digital peripherals Cap Ventures, 1996—. Editor newsletter Multifunctionality, 1987, Color Copiers, 1989. Block capt. Meadow Ridge Civic Assn., Basking Ridge, N.J., 1985-87; sgt.-at-arms UNICO Nat., San Jose, 1990. With USN, 1964-67. Roman Catholic. Avocations: woodworking, home remodeling, dog training, travel, cooking. Office: Ricoh Corp One Snow Rd Marshfield MA 02050

SOTER, GEORGE NICHOLAS, advertising executive; b. Chgo., May 16, 1924; s. Nicholas A. and Emily (Damascus) S.; m. Effie Hartocollis, Feb. 7, 1949; children: Nicholas, Thomas, Peter. Student, U. Chgo., 1947-51. Writer McCann-Erickson, Chgo., 1951-53; with Needham, Louis & Brorby, Chgo., 1954-62; v.p., creative dir. Needham, Louis & Brorby, N.Y.C., 1958-62; v.p., assoc. creative dir. Lennen & Newell Inc., N.Y.C., 1962-67; v.p., co-dir. creative svcs., mgmt. supr. Kenyon & Eckhardt Inc., N.Y.C., 1968-73; exec. v.p., creative dir. Pampuzac-Soter Assocs. Inc., N.Y.C., 1974-76; sr. writer Marsteller Inc., N.Y.C., 1980-82; v.p., creative Lord, Geller, Federico, Einstein, Inc., N.Y.C., 1982-87; sr. v.p., creative dir. Great Scott Advt. Co. Inc., N.Y.C., 1987-93; dir. Soter Advt. & Mktg. Consulting Svcs., N.Y.C., 1993—; founder, pres. Greek Island Ltd., N.Y.C., 1963—; dir. Interpub. Product Devel. Workshop, N.Y.C., 1967. With U.S. Army, 1943-47, ETO. Home: 404 Riverside Dr New York NY 10025-1861

SOTH, LAUREN KEPHART, journalist, economist; b. Sibley, Iowa, Oct. 2, 1910; s. Michael Ray and Virginia Mabel (Kephart) S.; m. Marcella Shaw Van, June 15, 1934; children: John Michael, Sara Kathryn, Melinda. BS in Journalism, Iowa State U., 1932, MS in Econs., 1938; LHD (hon.), Grinnell Coll., 1990. From instr. to assoc. prof. journalism and econs. Iowa State U., Ames, 1933-46; from editorial writer to editorial page editor Des Moines Register and Des Moines Tribune, 1947-75; columnist Des Moines Register/Extra Newspaper Features syndicate, 1976-94; chmn. agr. com., bd. dirs. Nat. Planning Assn., Washington, 1953-76; bd. dirs. Resources for the Future, Washington, 1956-76; mem. Am. Soc. Newspaper Editors, 1954-75. Author: Farm Trouble, 1957, An Embarrassment of Plenty, 1965, The Farm Policy Game--Play by Play, 1989. Maj. U.S. Army, 1942-46, PTO. Decorated Bronze star medal; recipient Pulitzer prize for editorial writing, 1956. Mem. Nat. Conf. Editorial Writers (pres. 1961), Am. Agrl. Econs. Assn. Episcopalian. Avocations: golf, fishing. Home: 907 Ashworth Rd West Des Moines IA 50265-3673

SOTIR, THOMAS ALFRED, healthcare executive, retired shipbuilder; b. Marlboro, Mass., July 8, 1936; s. Nisi and Pauline Violet (Theodore) S.; m. Sandra Losano, Oct. 2, 1960; children: Laura Jean, Mark Joseph, Christine Marie. BS in Indsl. Engring., Northeastern U., 1959; MBA, Xavier U., Cin., 1966. Employee rels. generalist GE, Cin., 1959-66, mgr. incoming materials, 1966-67, mgr. adminstrn., 1967-68, mgr. employee rels., Arkansas City, Kans., 1968-71, mgr. grievance negotiations, Lynn, Mass., 1971-77; with Electric Boat div. Gen. Dynamics Corp., Groton, Conn., 1977-91, dir. labor rels., 1977-79, v.p. human resources, 1979-89, dir. total quality mgmt., 1989-91; cons. human resources R.A. Flath Assocs., New London, Conn., 1991-92; v.p. human resources Kennebec Health System, Augusta, Maine, 1992—; mem. faculty U. New Haven Bus. Sch., 1979-91; adv. panel job evaluation State of Conn., 1985-91. Trustee, exec. com. Thames Sci. Ctr., New London, Conn., 1987-89; bd. dirs. United Way, Groton, 1979-87. Capt. USAR, 1959-69. Mem. Shipbuilders Coun. Am. (chmn. indsl. rels. com. Washington chpt. 1987-88), Kennebec Valley C. of C. (bd. dirs.), Rotary. Republican. Roman Catholic. Avocations: hunting, fishing, cooking. Home: 21 Sewall St Augusta ME 04330-5531

SOTIRHOS, MICHAEL, ambassador; b. N.Y.C., Nov. 12, 1928; m. Estelle Manos; 2 children. B.B.A., CCNY, 1950. Ptnr. Ariston Sales Co., Ltd., 1948, founder, chmn., 1958—; chmn. bd. Ariston Interior Designers, Inc., 1973-85; U.S. amb. to Jamaica, 1985-89; U.S. amb. to Greece Athens, 1989-93; bd. dirs. Atlantic Bank of N.Y., Alexander S. Onassis Found.; cons. various internat. shipping & pharm. firms. Former mem. Nat. Vol. Service Adv. Council; former chmn. Internat. Ops. Com., Peace Corps; mem. nat. adv. council SBA, 1976; former chmn. Nat. Republican Heritage Groups Council. Decorated comdr. Order of Distinction (Jamaica); recipient Man of Yr. award Nat. Rep. Heritage Groups Coun.

SOTIRIOS OF TORONTO See ATHANASSOULAS, SOTIRIOS

SOTO, JOCK, dancer; b. Gallup, N.M., 1965. Student, Phoenix Sch. Nallet, Sch. Am. Ballet. Mem. corps de ballet N.Y.C. Ballet, 1981-84, soloist, 1984-85, prin. dancer, 1985—. Appeared in The Magic Flute, 1981, Bagaku, The Nutcracker, Mozartiana, Rubies, Symphony in C, The Four Temperaments, Western Symphony, Stravinsky Violin Concerto, Symphony in Three Movements, Cortege Hongrois, Liebeslieder Walzer, A Midsummer Night's Dream, Brahms/Handel, Glass Pieces, Moves, The Four Seasons, In The Night, Opus 19/The Dreamer, I'm Old Fashioned, Delibes Divertissement, A Schubertiad, Concerto for Two Solo Pianos, Celebration, Allegro Brillante, A Schubert Sonata, X-Ray; N.Y.C. Ballet's Balanchine Celebration, 1993. Office: NYC Ballet NY State Theater Lincoln Ctr Plz New York NY 10023*

SOTOMAYOR, SONIA, federal judge; b. N.Y.C., June 25, 1954; d. Juan Luis and Celina (Baez) S.; m. Kevin Edward Noonan, Aug. 14, 1976 (div. 1983). AB, Princeton (N.J.) U., 1976; JD, Yale U., 1979. Bar: N.Y. 1980, U.S. Dist. Ct. (ea. and so. dists.) N.Y. 1984. Asst. dist. atty. Office of Dist. Atty. County of N.Y., N.Y.C., 1979-84; assoc., ptnr. Pavia & Harcourt, N.Y.C., 1984-92; fed. judge U.S. Dist. Ct. (so. dist.) N.Y., N.Y.C., 1992—. Editor Yale U. Law Rev., 1979. Bd. dirs. P.R. Legal Def. and Edn. Fund, N.Y.C., 1980-92, State of N.Y. Mortgage Agy., N.Y.C., 1987-92, N.Y.C. Campaign Fin. Bd., 1988-92; mem. State Adv. Panel on Inter-Group Rels., N.Y.C., 1990-91. Mem. Phi Beta Kappa. Office: US Courthouse 500 Pearl St New York NY 10007-1316

SOTOMORA-VON AHN, RICARDO FEDERICO, pediatrician, educator; b. Guatemala City, Guatemala, Oct. 22, 1947; s. Ricardo and Evelyn (Von Ahn) S.; m. Eileen Marie Holcomb, May 9, 1990. M.D., San Carlos U., 1972; M.S. in Physiology, U. Minn., 1978; m. Victoria Monzon, Nov. 26, 1971; children—Marisol, Clarisa, Ricardo, III, Charlotte Marie. Rotating intern Gen. Hosp. Guatemala, 1971-72; pediatric intern U. Ark., 1972-73, resident, 1973-75; fellow in pediatric cardiology U. Minn., 1975-78; research assoc. in cardiovascular pathology United Hosps., St. Paul, 1976; fellow in neonatal-perinatal medicine St. Paul's Children's Hosp., 1977-78, U. Ark., 1981-82; instr. pediatrics U. Minn., 1978-79; pediatric cardiologist, unit cardiovascular surgery Roosevelt Hosp., Guatemala City, 1979-81; asst. prof. pediatrics (cardiology and neonatology), U. Ark., Little Rock, 1981-83; practice medicine specializing in pediatric cardiology-neonatology, 1983—. Diplomate Am. Bd. Pediatrics, Sub-Bd. Pediatric Cardiology, Neonatal-Perinatal Medicine. Fellow Am. Acad. Pediatrics, Am. Coll. Cardiology, Am. Coll. Chest Physicians, Am. Coll. Angiology; mem. AMA, AAAS, Ark. Med. Soc., N.Y. Acad. Scis., Am. Heart Assn., Soc. Pediatric Echocardiography, Guatemala Coll. Physicians and Surgeons, Central Ark. Pediatric Soc., So. Soc. Pediatric Research, Soc. Critical Care Medicine. Clubs: Pleasant Valley Country (Little Rock). Home: 25 River Ridge Cir Little Rock AR 72227 Office: 5 Office Park Dr Ste 105 Little Rock AR 72211-3865

SOTT, HERBERT, lawyer; b. Detroit, Jan. 26, 1920; s. Harry and E. Helen (Nalven) S.; m. Elaine D. Davidson, Oct. 14, 1987; children by previous marriage; Lesley Sott Geary, Lynne Sott Jackson. A.B., U. Mich., 1940, M.B.A., 1942, J.D. with distinction, 1943. Bar: Mich. 1946. Since practiced in Detroit; ptnr. Friedman, Meyers & Keys, 1951-68; partner Barris, Sott, Denn & Driker, 1968—. Active Founders Soc. Detroit Inst. Arts, Detroit Grand Opera Assn., Detroit Symphony Assn., Detroit Zool. Assn.; bd. dirs. Detroit Symphony Orch., Mich. Heart Assn., Mich. Cancer Found., Jewish Home for Aged, Jewish Family and Children's Service, Jewish Vocat. Service. Served as lt. (j.g.) USNR, 1943-46. Mem. Detroit, Mich., Am. bar assns. Clubs: Detroit, Franklin Hills. Office: Barris Sott Denn & Driker 15th Flr 211 W Fort St Ste 15 Detroit MI 48226-3211

SOUDER, MARK EDWARD, congressman; b. Ft. Wayne, Ind., July 18, 1950; s. Edward Getz and Irma (Fahling) S.; B.S., Ind. U., Ft. Wayne, 1972; M.B.A., U. Notre Dame, 1974; m. Diane Kay Zimmer, July 28; children—Brooke Diane, Nathan Elias. Mgmt. trainee Crossroads Furniture Co., Houston, 1974; mktg. mgr. Gabberts Furniture & Studio, Mpls., 1974-76; mktg. mgr., exec. v.p. Souder's Furniture & Studio, Grabill, Ind., 1976-80, pres., 1981-84; econ. devel. liaison for U.S. Rep. Dan Coats, 1983—; U.S. congressman, Ind. 4th Dist., 1995—, mem. edn. and workforce com., govt. reform and oversight com., small bus. com. Publicity chmn. Grabill County Fair, 1977—; advisor Dan Coats for Congress Com., 1980-81; mem. Ind. Area Devel. Council; mem. bus. alumni adv. com. Ind. U.-Ft. Wayne. Mem. Midwest Home Furnishings Assn. (dir. 1976-84, past treas., exec. v.p.), Ft. Wayne, Grabill chambers commerce, Allen County Hist. Soc., Alumni Assn. Ind. U. at Ft. Wayne (dir., past pres.), Alumni Assn. U. Notre Dame. Republican. Mem. Apostolic Christian Ch. Home: 13733 Ridgeview Ct Grabill IN 46741 Office: US House Reps 418 Cannon House Office Bldg Washington DC 20515-1404*

SOUDERS, JEAN SWEDELL, artist, educator; b. Braham, Minn., July 13, 1922; d. John Almond and Frances Johanna (Alm) Swedell; m. Robert Livingston Souders, Sept. 22, 1945 (dec. 1985). BA, Duluth (Minn.) State Coll., 1944; postgrad., Minn. Sch. of Art, 1944, Walker Sch. of Art, Minn., 1948; MA, U. Iowa, 1955, MFA, 1956. Instr. art St. Olaf Coll., Northfield, Minn., 1947-50; instr. craft U. Minn., 1951; prof. art history painting Calif. State U., Chico, Calif., 1957-74; prof. art history Calif. State U., Chico, 1959-60; faculty gen. studies Calif. State U., Chico, Calif., 1971-73. Exhbn. Creative Art Ctr., 1975, Des Moines Art Ctr., Crocker Mus. of Art, and various others. Mem. Nat. Archives, Mus. of Women in the Arts, Washington, Women Artists Assn. San Francisco. Lutheran. Avocations: photography, hiking, backpacking, classical music.

SOUHAM, GÉRARD, communications executive; b. Paris, May 30, 1928; s. Lucien and Mary-Françoise (Husson) S.; m. Eliane Meyrat, June 23, 1951; children: Glenn (dec.), Yan, Philip. Diploma, Am. Community Sch., Paris, 1948; cert., Ecole Commerciale de Paris. Chargé de mission State Dept., Europe, 1950-52; pub. info. officer Allied Air Forces NATO, Fontainebleau, 1953-55; chmn. bd., chief exec. officer J. Walter Thompson, Paris, 1955-75; v.p. J. Walter Thompson, N.Y.C., 1970-75; prin. S3C Gerard Souham Group Communication Cos., Paris and Lausanne, Switzerland, 1975—, SC3 Gerard Souham Group Communication Cos., N.Y.C., 1979—; chmn., CEO CERAMERIC, 1997—; bd. dirs. Am. Overseas Meml., I.T. Fin., AVON, France, Color Stone, Internat. Inc., Image Axis, Inc.; bd. dirs. Turner Prodn. S.A., chmn., 1994—; chmn. bd. Turner Prodn. Europe, 1994. Author: Général Souham Comte de l'Empire, 1964, Impressions sur..., 1970, Souham, 1989, Sur les Champs de Bataille de la Révolution et de l'Empire, 1990. Mem. pvt. sector internat. and pub. rels. coms. USIA, 1985; mem. world bd. govs. USO, Washington, 1984, chmn. fundraising com., 1989—, pres., Paris, 1995. Decorated Knight of Legion of Honor (France); Officer Order of Leopold (Belgium), Knight of Belgian Crown. Mem. Internat. Advt. Assn. (v.p. pub. svc., bd. dirs.), Internat. Inst. Strategic Studies London, France, USA (bd. dirs.), Am. Overseas Meml. Assn. (bd. dirs. 1988—). Roman Catholic. Clubs: HM Guards Polo (Windsor, Eng.) (life); Polo de Bagatelle (Paris); N.Y. Athletic; Yacht of Monaco. Avocation: collecting fine bindings. Office: Souham Group Comm 500 5th Ave New York NY 10110

SOULE, GARDNER BOSWORTH, writer; b. Paris, Tex., Dec. 16, 1913; s. Edgar Huckabee and Floy DeVore (Perfect) S.; m. Janie Lee McDowell, Sept. 20, 1940 (dec.); m. Mary Muir Downing, Apr. 23, 1994. B.A., Rice Inst., 1933; B.S., Columbia U., 1935, M.S., 1936. With A.P., N.Y.C., 1936-41, Newspaper PM, 1942; mng. editor Better Homes and Gardens, Des Moines, 1946-50. Free-lance writer articles, books, N.Y.C., 1950—; Author: The Maybe Monsters, 1963, Tomorrow's World of Science, 1963, Gemini and Apollo, 1964, The Mystery Monsters, 1965, Trail of the Abominable Snowman, 1966, The Ocean Adventure: Science Explores the Depths of the Sea, 1966, Sea Rescue, 1966, UFO's and IFO's, 1967, Undersea Frontiers, 1968, Under the Sea, 1969, Strange Things Animals Do, 1970, Wide Ocean, 1970, The Greatest Depths, 1970, Surprising Facts, 1971, New Discoveries in Oceanography, 1974, Wide Ocean, Brit. edit, 1974, Remarkable Creatures of the Seas, 1975, Men Who Dared The Sea: The Ocean Adventures of the Ancient Mariners, 1976, German edit., 1978, The Long Trail: How Cowboys and Longhorns Opened The West, 1976, Mystery Monsters of the Deep, 1981, Mystery Creatures of the Jungle, 1982, Antarctica, 1985, Christopher Columbus, 1988; Contbr.: articles to mags. including Boys' Life. Served to lt. USNR, 1943-46. Mem. Authors League, Columbia University Club (N.Y.C.), Sigma Delta Chi, Sigma Nu. Address: 85 River Rd Apt 13 Essex CT 06426-1343

SOULE, GEORGE ALAN, literature educator; b. Fargo, N.D., Mar. 3, 1930; s. George Alan and Ruth Georgia (Knudsen) S.; m. Carolyn Richards, Nov. 24, 1961; 1 child, Katherine. BA, Carleton Coll., 1947; postgrad., Corpus Christi Coll., Cambridge (Eng.) U., 1952-53; MA, Yale U., 1956, PhD, 1960. Instr. English lit. Oberlin (Ohio) Coll., 1958-60; asst. prof. U. Wis., Madison, 1960-62; from asst. prof. to prof. Carleton Coll., Northfield, Minn., 1962-95, prof. emeritus, 1995—, dir. Centennial, 1965-67; chair English dept. Carleton Coll., Northfield, 1980-83; dir. summer writing program Carleton Coll., Northfield, Minn., 1980-86; cons. Ednl. Testing Svc., Princeton, N.J., 1967-84, 94—. Editor (book) Theatre of the Mind, 1974; contbr. articles, revs. to profl. jours. With U.S. Army, 1954-55. Internat. fellow Rotary, 1952-53, Sterling pre-doctoral fellow Yale U., 1957-58. Mem. Johnson Soc. of Lichfield, Boswell Soc. of Auchinleck, Friends of Dove Cottage, The Charles Lamb Soc., Rotary, The Iris Murdock Soc. Episcopalian. Avocations: cooking, traveling, Jeopardy (Champion Sr. Tournament 1990). Home: 313 Nevada St Northfield MN 55057-2346 Office: Carleton Coll 1 N College St Northfield MN 55057-4001

SOULE, LUCILE SNYDER, pianist, music educator; b. Fargo, N.D., Sept. 21, 1922; d. Roy Henry and Gene (McGhee) Snyder; m. Leon Cyprian Soule Jr., Sept. 1, 1954 (dec. Dec. 1994); children: Robert Leon, Anne Lucile. MusB, MusB in Edn., MacPhail Coll. Music, 1943; MA, Smith Coll., Northampton, Mass., 1945; postgrad. diploma, Juilliard Sch. Music, 1948. Organist various chs., Mont., La., and Ohio, 1935-68; instr. Smith Coll., Northampton, 1945-46; freelance pianist, accompanist Juilliard Sch. Music, also pvt. groups and individuals, N.Y.C., 1946-49; from instr. to asst. to assoc. prof. Newcomb Coll., Tulane U., New Orleans, 1949-51, 52-61; staff pianist, soloist New Orleans Symphony, 1954-61; guest artist Contemporary Music Festival La. State U., Baton Rouge, 1953-61; lectr. Lakewood br. Ohio State U., 1964-66; music tchr. East Cleveland (Ohio) Pub. Schs., 1969-85; music dir. East Cleveland Theater, 1985—; accompanist Zhao Rongchun, Cleve., 1995—; pres. New Orleans Music Tchrs. Assn., 1958-59; bd. dirs., publicity chair Rocky River (Ohio) Chamber Music Soc., 1963-67; v.p. Cleve. chpt. Am. Orff Schluwerk Assn., Cleve., 1974-75, presenter nat. conf., 1982. Pianist (CD with Zhao) Master of the Erhu, 1996. Mem. Citizens Adv. Group, East Cleveland, 1967-69. Woolley Found. fellow, 1950-51, tchg. fellow Case Western Res. U., 1967-68, tchg. fellow Smith Coll., 1943-45; scholar Juilliard Sch. Music, 1946-48. Mem. Darius Millhaud Soc. (bd. dirs. 1984—), Fortnightly Mus. Club (corr. sec. 1996—), Lecture Recital Club (bd. dirs. 1993-95), Mu Epsilon. Democrat. Christian Scientist. Avocations: church work, gourmet cooking, travel, art. Home and Office: 15617 Hazel Rd East Cleveland OH 44112-2904

SOULE, ROBERT D., safety and health educator, administrator; b. DeTour Village, Mich., July 8, 1941; s. Harold M. and Mildred M. (Abear) S.; m. Mary Ann Kretzschmar, June 13, 1964; children: Dawn Marie, Robert John, Rebecca Ann. BS, Mich. State U., 1963; MS in Chem. Engring., Purdue U., 1965; EdD in Higher Edn. Adminstrn., U. Pitts., 1993. Cert. safety profl. cert in indsl. hygiene; registered profl. engr., Mich., Ind., Tex. Calif. Environ. health engr. Dow Chem. Co., Midland, Mich., 1965-69; sr. indsl. hygienist Dow Chem. Co., Freeport, Tex., 1969-70; v.p. Clayton Environ. Cons., Southfield, Mich., 1970-77; prof. safety and health Indiana U. of Pa., 1977—; cons. in pvt. practice, Indiana, Pa., 1977—. Contbr. chpts. to books; mem. editorial bd. Am. Indsl. Hygiene Assn. Jour., 1979-85, Occupational Hazards, 1992—. Fellow Am. Indsl. Hygiene Assn.; mem. Am. Conf. Govtl. Indsl. Hygienists, Am. Soc. Safety Engrs. (profl.), Am. Acad. Indsl. Hygiene (sec.-treas.). Office: Indiana U Pa Dept Safety Scis 117 Johnson Hall Indiana PA 15705

SOULE, SALLIE THOMPSON, retired state official; b. Detroit, May 13, 1928; d. Hayward Stone and Elizabeth Robinson Thompson; A.B., Smith Coll., 1950; M.A., U. Vt., Burlington, 1952; m. Gardner Northup Soule, July 26, 1958; stepchildren: Gardner Northup, Nancy Soule Brown; children: Sarah Goodwin, Trumbull Dickson. Sec. trade sales dept. Macmillan Pub. Co., N.Y.C., 1952-57; tech. writer sales svc. div. Eastman Kodak Co., Rochester, N.Y., 1957-58; feature writer Brighton-Pittsford Post, Pittsford, N.Y., 1958-68; v.p., gen. mgr. F. H. Horsford Nursery, Inc., Charlotte, Vt., 1968-76; ptnr., pres. Bygone Books, Inc., Burlington, Vt., 1978—; mem. Vt. Ho. of Reps., 1976-80, mem. ways and means com., 1976-80; mem. Vt. Senate, 1980-84, mem. appropriation com., energy and natural resources com. 1980-84; commr. Vt. Dept. Employment and Tng., Montpelier, 1985-88; chmn. Vt. Employment Security Bd., 1985-88.

SOULTOUKIS, DONNA ZOCCOLA, library director; b. Princeton, N.J., July 28, 1949; d. Peter Joseph and Josephine (Taraschi) Zoccola; m. Dimitrios Athanasios Soultoukis, July 26, 1980. AB, Georgian Ct. Coll., Lakewood, N.J., 1971; MS, Drexel U., 1976; Cert., Italian U. for Foreigners, Perugia, 1974. Libr. asst. Geology Libr. Princeton U., 1971-73; libr. Friends Hosp., Phila., 1976-86, dir. libr. svcs., 1986—; bd. dirs. Mental Health Materials Ctr., N.Y.C., 1996—; cons. Lower Bucks Hosp., Bristol, Pa., 1991-95. Vol. outreach program Old St. Joseph's Ch., Phila., 1992-95, sanctuary min., 1993—, mem. pastoral coun., 1995—, bd. dirs., 1997—; bd. dirs. Mental Health Matereal Ctr., 1996—. Mem. Med. Libr. Assn. (chair mental librs. divsn. 1991-93), Spl. Librs. Assn. (Phila. chpt. bd. dirs. 1985-88, pres. 1982-84, chmn. long-range planning 1993, mem. adv. bd. 1995—, chair profl. devel. com. Solo divsn., 1995—, mem. strategic planning com. Solo divsn.). Avocations: travel, cooking. Home: 290 Cinnabar Ln Yardley PA 19067 Office: Friends Hosp 4641 Roosevelt Blvd Philadelphia PA 19124-2343

SOUNEY, PAUL FREDERICK, pharmacist; b. Bristol, Conn., Mar. 29, 1947; s. Frederick Raymond and Julia Yvonne (Weeks) S.; m. Billie Lorraine Petersen, Apr. 7, 1972; children: Jared Paul, Jeremy Christian. BS, Northeastern U., 1971, MS, 1984. Drug info. pharmacist Hartford (Conn.) Hosp., 1971-77; pharmacy supervisor Boston Hosp. for Women, 1977-81; clin. rsch. pharmacist Channing Labs./Harvard Med. Sch., Boston, 1981-92; med. info. scientist Astra Merck Inc., Providence, R.I., 1992—; dir. drug info. Brigham and Women's Hosp., Boston, 1981-90, dir. clin. pharmacy, 1985-92; cons. in field. Editor: Comprehensive Pharmacy Review, 3d edit., 1996; contbr. articles to profl. jours.; editl. adv. panelist Internat. Pharm. Abstracts, Pharmacy Practice News. Treas. men's club First Congl. Ch., 1993—; vol. Mansfield (Mass.) Animal Shelter, 1990-94. Mem. Am. Coll. Clin. Pharmacy, Am. Soc. Health Sys. Pharmacists, Am. Pharmaceutical Assn., Acad. Managed Case Pharmacy, New Eng. Coun. Hosp. Pharmacists, Northeastern Univ. Alumnae Assn. Office: Astra Merck Inc One Citizens Plz Providence RI 02903

SOURBIER, JAMES HENRY, IV, police chief; b. Waynesboro, Pa., Sept. 11, 1962; s. James H. III and Martha Louise (Reed) S.; m. Karen Louise Palmer, Feb. 18, 1984; children: James H. V, Rebekah Margaret. BS, Shippensburg U., 1983. Police officer Wash. Twp., Waynesboro, 1985-88; investigator Franklin County Dist. Atty. Office, Chambersburg, Pa., 1989—; conservation officer Pa. Game Commn., Harrisburg, 1992—; chief of police Pa. State U., Mont Alto, 1985—, chmn. safety com., 1986—; expert witness in latent fingerprints and motor vehicle accidents; investigator motor vehicle accident reconstructionist. Mem. Internat. Narcotic Enforcement Officers Assn., Nat. Criminal Justice Assn., Pa. Chiefs of Police Assn., Franklin County Law Enforcement Officers Assn. (pres. 1990-92), Pi Sigma Alpha. Republican. Avocations: farming, hunting. Office: Pa State U Police Svcs Mont Alto Campus Mont Alto PA 17237

SOURIAN, PETER, writer, educator; b. Boston, Apr. 7, 1933; s. Zareh Missak and Zabelle (Bayentz) S.; m. Eve Jeanne Pocquet, Sept. 25, 1971; children: Mark, Delphine. BA, Harvard U., 1955. Lectr. ext. divsn. NYU, N.Y.C., 1963-65; instr. English English Bard Coll., Annandale-on-Hudson, N.Y., 1965-66, asst. prof., 1966-68, assoc. prof. English, 1968-75, prof. English, 1975—, dept. chair, 1984-86, 90-94; mem. faculty New Sch. Social Rsch., N.Y.C., 1975—; TV critic The Nation mag., N.Y.C., 1975-81; mem. editorial bd. Ararat Quarterly, N.Y.C., 1975—. Author: (novels) Miri, 1957, The Best and Worst Times, 1961, The Gate, 1965, (essays and criticism) At The French Embassy in Sofia, 1992; contbr. articles to profl. jours. Bd. dirs. Armenian Ctr. Columbia U., N.Y.C., 1988—. With U.S. Army, 1957-59. Lilly Endowment grantee, 1976, Kellogg Found. grantee, 1977. Mem. MLA, PEN, Nat. Book Critics Circle, Century Assn. Home: 30 E 70th St New York NY 10021-4942 Office: Bard Coll Annandale on Hudson New York NY 12504

SOURKES, THEODORE LIONEL, biochemistry educator; b. Montreal, Que., Can., Feb. 21, 1919; s. Irving and Fannie (Golt) S.; m. Shena Rosenblatt, Jan. 17, 1943; children: Barbara, Myra. B.Sc., McGill U., 1939, M.Sc. magna cum laude, 1946; Ph.D., Cornell U., 1948; D.U. honoris causa, U. Ottawa, Can., 1990. Asst. prof. pharmacology Georgetown U. Med. Sch., 1948-50; research asso. dept. enzyme chemistry Merck Inst. Therapeutic Research, Rahway, N.J., 1950-53; sr. research biochemist Allan Meml. Inst., Montreal, 1953-65; dir. lab. neurochemistry Allan Meml. Inst. Psychiatry, 1965—; mem. faculty McGill U., Montreal, 1954—; prof. biochemistry McGill U., 1965—, prof. psychiatry, assoc. dean of medicine for research Faculty Medicine, 1972-75; prof. pharmacology, 1990—, emeritus, 1991; Mem. Que. Med. Research Council, 1971-77; sr. fellow Parkinson's Disease Found., N.Y.C., 1963-66; assoc. mem. McGill Ctr. for Medicine, Ethics and Law, 1991. Author: Biochemistry of Mental Disease, 1962, Nobel Prize Winners in Medicine and Physiology, 1901-1965, 1967; sect. editor Internat. Jour. of the History of Neuroscis., 1996—. Decorated Officer Order of Canada. Fellow Royal Soc. Can.; mem. Canadian Biochem. Soc., Pharmacol. Soc. Can., Canadian Coll. Neuropsychopharmacology (Heinz Lehmann award 1982, medal 1990), Am. Soc. Biol. Chemists, Am. Soc. Pharmacology and Exptl. Therapeutics, Am. Soc. Neurochemistry, Internat. Soc. Neurochemistry, Internat. Brain Research Orgn., Venezuelan Order Andrés Bello, Sigma Xi. Research and publs. on drugs for treatment high blood pressure; 1st basic research on methyldopa; elucidation of role of dopamine and other monamines in nervous system; first trials of L-dopa in Parkinson's disease, biochemistry of mental depression, pathways of stress in the nervous system, imaging serotonin in brain, history of biochemistry. Home: 3033 Sherbrooke St W # 303, Montreal, PQ Canada H3Z 1A3

SOURS, JAMES KINGSLEY, association executive, former college president; b. Corydon, Iowa, Sept. 16, 1925; s. James N. and Virginia (Kantor) S.; m. Alice Hyde, July 11, 1947; children—James W., Mary Jan. David Bryan. Student, Phillips U., 1943; BA, U. Wichita, 1949; MPA, Harvard U., 1951, PhD, 1954. Adminstrv. aid City Mgr.'s Office, Wichita, 1947-49; mem. faculty Wichita State U., 1951-65; prof. polit. sci., head dept., 1958-62; dean Fairmount Coll. Arts and Scis., 1962-65; chmn. Fairmount Coll. Arts and Scis. (Center Urban Studies), 1957-63; pres. So. Oreg. State Coll., Ashland, 1969-79; ednl. cons. Dankook U., Seoul, 1979-80, dir. Inst. Asian Studies and Cultures, 1990—; ednl. cons. Korean Ministry Edn., 1979-80; exec. v.p. Am. Coll. Testing Program, Iowa City, 1965-68; vis. prof. polit. sci. U. Istanbul, Turkey, 1968-69; vis. prof. Dankook U., Seoul, Korea, 1976, 79-80; dir. devel. Oreg. Shakespearean Festival Assn., 1980-85; v.p., bd. dirs. Dankook U. Am., 1990—; bd. dirs. Oreg. Partnership for Internat. Edn., Internat. Wildlife Recovery Ctr., Eagle Point, Oreg., Rogue Valley Manor Found.; chmn. bd. dirs. Aletheia Psycho-Phys. Found., 1988-96. Author: series Some Observations on the Management of Large Cities, 1957; also numerous articles. V.p. NCAA, 1959-64; founding pres. Urban League Wichita, 1953-56, Wichita City Commn. Human Rels., 1962; trustee Carpenter Found., 1983-87, v.p., 1984-87; chmn. Sedgwick County chpt. ARC, 1964, Jackson County chpt., 1973-75; bd. dirs. So. Oreg. Hist. Soc., 1987-89; mem. Oreg. Am. Revolution Bicentennial Commn., 1972-76; chmn. com. nursing edn. Wesley Med. Ctr., Wichita, 1962-64. Served with USNR, 1943-46. Adminstn. fellow Harvard U., 1949-51. Democrat. Unitarian. Home: 3100 Payne Rd Medford OR 97504-9407

SOUTAS-LITTLE, ROBERT WILLIAM, mechanical engineer, educator; b. Oklahoma City, Feb. 25, 1933; s. Harry Glenn and Mary Evelyn (Miller) Little; m. Patricia Soutas, Sept. 3, 1982; children: Deborah, Catherine, Colleen, Jennifer, Karen. B.S. in Mech. Engring, Duke U., 1955; M.S., U. Wis., 1959, Ph.D., 1962. Design engr. Allis Chalmers Mfg. Co., Milw., 1955-57; instr. mech. engring. Marquette U., 1957-59; instr. U. Wis., Madison, 1959-62; asst. prof. U. Wis., 1962-63, Okla. State U., 1963-65; prof. Mich. State U., 1965—, chmn. dept. mech. engring., 1972-77, chmn. dept. biomechanics, 1977-90; dir. biomechanics evaluation lab., 1989—; Cons. A. C. Electronics Co., Ford Motor Co., CBS Research Lab., B. F. Goodrich Co.; lectr. AID, India, 1965. Author: Elasticity, 1973; Contbr. articles to profl. jours. Vice pres. Okemos (Mich.) Sch. Bd., 1967-72; mem. Meridian Twp. (Mich.) Charter Commn., 1969-70, Meridian Twp. Zoning Bd. Appeals, 1969-71. Recipient award for excellence in instrn. engring. students Western Electric Co., 1970-71, Disting. Faculty award, 1996; NSF grantee, 1964-69, 79, NIH grantee, 1973-75, 79—. Fellow ASME; mem. Soc. Engring. Sci., Am. Soc. Biomechanics, Internat. Soc. Biomechanics, N.Am. Soc. Clin. Gait and Movement Analysis, Sigma Xi, Pi Tau Sigma, Ta Beta Pi. Home: 2402 Hulett Rd Okemos MI 48864-2512 Office: Mich State U Dept Matls Sci Mechani East Lansing MI 48824

SOUTER, DAVID HACKETT, United States supreme court justice; b. Melrose, Mass., Sept. 17, 1939; s. Joseph Alexander and Helen Adams (Hackett) S. BA, Harvard U., 1961, LLB, 1966; Rhodes scholar, Oxford U., 1961-63, MA, 1989. Bar: N.H. Assoc. firm Orr & Reno, Concord, 1966-68; asst. atty. gen. N.H., 1968-71, dep. atty. gen., 1971-76, atty. gen., 1976-78; assoc. justice Superior Ct. N.H., 1978-83, N.H. Supreme Ct., 1983-90; judge U.S. Ct. Appeals (1st cir.) N.H., 1990; assoc. justice U.S. Supreme Ct., Washington, 1990—. Trustee Concord Hosp., 1973-85, pres. bd. trustees, 1978-84; bd. overseers Dartmouth Med. Sch., 1981-87. Mem. N.H. Bar Assn., N.H. Hist. Soc. (v.p. 1980-85, trustee 1976-85), Phi Beta Kappa. Republican. Episcopalian. *

SOUTER, ROBERT TAYLOR, retired banker; b. Melrose, Mass., Feb. 17, 1909; s. Walter Wilson and Mary (Taylor) S.; m. Barbara P. Claybourne, Sept. 7, 1935; children—Scott C., Pamela (Mrs. Darroll Hanssen). Student, Harvard, 1934. Treas. Braintree Coop. Bank, Mass., 1937-42; v.p. U.S. Savs. and Loan League, 1942-47; v.p., dir. Coast Fed. Savs. & Loan Assn., Los Angeles, 1947-55; pres., dir. World Savs. and Loan Assn., Oakland, Calif., 1955-86. Republican. Methodist. Home: 4 Windsor Dr Hillsborough CA 94010-6359

SOUTH, FRANK EDWIN, physiologist, educator; b. Norfolk, Nebr., Sept. 20, 1924; s. Frank Edwin and Gladys (Brinkman) S.; m. Berna Deane Phyllis Casebolt, June 23, 1946; children: Frank Edwin, Robert Christopher. AB, U. Calif., Berkeley, 1949, PhD, 1952. Asst. prof. physiology U. P.R. Sch. Medicine, 1953-54, U. Ill. Coll. Medicine, 1954-61; asso. prof. Colo. State U., 1961-62, prof., 1962-65; prof. U. Mo., 1965-76; prof., dir. Sch. Life and Health Scis., U. Del., Newark, 1976-82; prof. emeritus U. Del., Newark, 1989, Sch. Life and Health Scis., U. Del., Newark, 1989—; mem. governing bd., dir. Hibernation Info. Exchange, 1959—. Mem. editorial bd. Cryobiology, 1989; contbr. numerous articles on physiology of hibernation, temperature regulation, renal function, marine mammals, artificial atmospheres, and sleep to profl. jours. Bd. dirs. Del. Lung Assn., 1976-82, Del. Cancer Network, 1977-82; mem. research com. Del. Heart Assn., 1977-82; mem. N.E. regional research com. Am. Heart Assn.; mem. med. adv. bd. A.I. DuPont Inst., Wilmington, Del., 1978-83. Served with AUS, 1943-45. Decorated Purple Heart with oak leaf cluster, Bronze Star with oak leaf cluster, Pres. unit citation, Croix de Guerre (unit); NIH career devel. awardee, 1961-65; recipient European African Mid East campaign medal with bronze spear head and silver star, World War II victory medal, Army of Occupation medal with Germany clasp, combat med. badge. Fellow AAAS, Sigma Xi; mem. Am. Physiol. Soc., Soc. Hist. Preservation. Episcopalian. Clubs: Ranger Battalions Assn. World War II, Haven Yacht Club.

SOUTH, MARY ANN, pediatrics educator; b. Portales, N.Mex., May 23, 1933; d. John Anderson and Carrie (Schumpert) S.; m. Allard W. Loutherback, Dec. 29, 1983 (dec. June 1985); children: George Louie, Linda Lee Loutherback Putnam. Student, Baylor U., Waco, Tex., 1951-53; BA, Ea. N.Mex. U., 1955; MD, Baylor U., Houston, 1959. Diplomate Am. Bd. Pediatrics. Intern Presbyn.-St. Luke's Hosp., Chgo., 1959-60, resident in pediatrics, 1960-62; fellow in infectious diseases Baylor U., 1962-64; fellow in immunology, instr. in pediatrics U. Minn., Mpls., 1964-66; asst. prof., assoc. prof. Baylor U. Coll. Medicine, 1966-73; assoc. prof. U. Pa., Phila., 1973-77; prof., chmn. dept. pediatrics Tex. Tech U. Health Scis. Ctr., Lubbock, 1977-79, rsch. prof., 1979-83; med. officer Nat. Inst. Neurol.-Communicative Disorders and Stroke, NIH, Bethesda, Md., 1982-85; vis. scientist Gallaudet Coll., Washington, 1984-85; prof. pediatrics Meharry Med. Coll., Nashville, 1986-89, W.K. Kellogg disting. prof., 1989—. Contbr. over 140 articles to med. jours., chpts. to books. Recipient Disting. Alumnus award Ea. N.Mex. U., 1969, rsch. career devel. award NIH, 1968-73. Fellow Infectious Diseases Soc. Am.; mem. Am. Pediatric Soc., Am. Assn. Immunology, Assn. for Gnotobiology, Am. Med. Women's Assn., Pediatric Infectious Diseases Soc., Alpha Omega Alpha. Home: 9479 New Hwy 96 W Franklin TN 37064 Office: Meharry Med Coll 1005 DB Todd Blvd Nashville TN 37208

SOUTH, STEPHEN A., academic administrator. Pres. Knoxville (Tenn.) Bus. Coll. Office: Knoxville Bus Coll Office of the President 720 N 5th Ave Knoxville TN 37917-6721

SOUTHALL, IVAN FRANCIS, author; b. Melbourne, Victoria BNA, Australia, June 8, 1921; s. Francis Gordon and Rachel Elizabeth (Voutier) S.; m. Joy Blackburn, Sept. 8, 1945; children—Andrew John, Roberta Joy, Elizabeth Rose, Melissa Frances; m. Susan Helen Westerlund, Nov. 11, 1976. Ed., pub. schs., Victoria. Free-lance writer, 1947—. Author over 60 books in 22 langs., including: Ash Road, 1965 (Book of Yr. 1966), To the Wild Sky, 1967 (Book of Yr. 1968), Bread and Honey, 1970 (Book of Yr. 1971), Josh, 1971 (Carnegie medal 1971), Fly West, 1975 (Book of Yr. 1976), The Long Night Watch, 1983 (Nat. Children's Book award 1986). Found. pres. Knoxbrooke Day Tng. Centre for Intellectually Handicapped, Victoria, 1967-69. Served as flight lt. Royal Australian Air Force, 1942-47, Europe. Decorated D.F.C., RAF, Order Australia; recipient emeritus fellowship award Australia Coun., 1993. Methodist. Home: PO Box 25, Healesville, 3777 Victoria Australia Office: Farrar Straus & Giroux Inc 19 Union Sq W New York NY 10003-3304

SOUTHAM, ARTHUR M., insurance company executive. Pres. Care Am. So. Calif., Chatsworth, Calif., 1988-96; pres., CEO Health Net, Woodland Hills, Calif., 1996—. Office: Health Net 21600 Oxnard St Ste 1700 Woodland Hills CA 91367-4972

SOUTHARD, WILLIAM G., lawyer; b. Toledo, Ohio, May 6, 1953; s. James Theodore and Dorothy (Fergusson) S.; m. Martha Donelan, Aug. 14, 1976; children: Abigail, Margaret, Michael. BA, Williams Coll., 1975; JD, Columbia U., 1978. Bar: Ill. 1978, U.S. Dist. Ct. Ill. 1979, Mass. 1981, U.S. Dist. Ct. Mass. 1981, U.S. Ct. Appeals (1st cir.) 1985. Assoc. Schiff Hardin & Waite, Chgo., 1978-81; assoc. Bingham, Dana & Gould, Boston, 1981-85, ptnr., 1985—; dep. chmn. litigation, 1994—. Assoc. editor Columbia Jour. Transnat. Law, 1978; contbr. articles to profl. jours. Mem. ABA, ASTM, Boston Bar Assn. Office: Bingham Dana & Gould 150 Federal St Boston MA 02110

SOUTHARD-RITTER, MARCIA, nursing administrator; b. Cape Girardeau, Mo., Dec. 12, 1942; d. Leebert Melton and Katherine Louise (Goslin) Loyd; m. C. John Ritter, Dec. 20, 1986; children: Robin Hacket, Emilie Clardy, Stephen Southard, Benjamin Ritter, Daniel Southard. Diploma, Jewish Hosp. Sch. Nursing, St. Louis, 1963; BS in Health Care Adminstrn., St. Joseph Coll., North Windham, Maine, 1984; MS in Health Sci. Adminstrn., Cen. Mich. U., 1986. RN, Mo.; cert. nursing adminstr., healthcare exec.; lic. nursing home adminstr. Head nurse, staff nurse S.E. Mo. Hosp., Cape Girardeau, 1963-69; cardiovascular nurse Internal Medicine Group, Cape Girardeau, 1969-72; staff nurse, head nurse St. Francis Hosp., Cape Girardeau, 1972-76, dir. critical care, 1976-82, dir. patient care adminstrv. svcs., 1982, v.p. patient care, 1982—. Contbr. articles to profl. jours. Mem. NAFE, AACN, ANA, Mo. Nurses Assn., Am. Coll. Health Care Execs., Am. Orgn. Nurse Execs. Office: St Francis Med Ctr 211 Saint Francis Dr Cape Girardeau MO 63703-5049

SOUTHERLAND, S. DUANE, manufacturing company executive; b. Durham, N.C., Apr. 24, 1949; s. Sydney Duane and Beatrice Marie (Carver) S.; m. Linda F. Lewis, Jan. 5, 1974, 1 child, S. Duane III. BSE, Duke U., 1971, MS in Engring., 1973, MBA, 1974. Ops. analyst Cooper Group Div. Cooper Industries, Apex, N.C., 1974-78; planning analyst Cooper Industries, Houston, 1978-81; dir. fin. Cooper Electronics Div. Cooper Industries, Nashua, N.H., 1981-83; gen. mgr. Conn. ops. Kirsch Div. Cooper Industries, Beacon Falls, Conn., 1983-87; pres. Kirsch Div. Cooper Industries, Sturgis, Mich., 1987-94; pres., CEO Conso Products Co., Union, S.C., 1995—. Republican. Baptist.

SOUTHERN, EILEEN (MRS. JOSEPH SOUTHERN), music educator; b. Mpls., Feb. 19, 1920; d. Walter Wade and Lilla (Gibson) Jackson; m. Joseph Southern, Aug. 22, 1942; children: April, Edward. A.B., U. Chgo., 1940, M.A., 1941; Ph.D., NYU, 1961; M.A. (hon.), Harvard U., 1976; D.A. (hon.), Columbia Coll., Chgo., 1985. Instr. Prairie View U., Hempstead, Tex., 1941-42; asst. prof. So. U., Baton Rouge, 1943-45, 49-51; tchr. N.Y.C. Bd. Edn., 1954-60; instr. Bklyn. Coll., CUNY, 1960-64, asst. prof., 1964-69; assoc. prof. York Coll., CUNY, 1969-71, prof., 1972-75; prof. music Harvard U., Cambridge, Mass., 1976-87, chmn. dept. Afro-Am. studies, 1976-79, prof. emeritus, 1987—. Concert pianist, 1940-55; author: The Buxheim Organ Book, 1963, The Music of Black Americans: A History, 1971, 3d edit., 1997, Readings in Black American Music, 1971, 2d edit., 1983, Anonymous Chansons in MS El Escorial Biblioteca del Monasterio, IV a 24, 1981, Biographical Dictionary of Afro-American and African Musicians, 1982, African-American Traditions in Song, Sermon, Tale, and Dance, 1630-1920; An Annotated Bibliography, 1990 (with Josephine Wright); editor: The Black Perspective in Music (1973-90), Nineteenth Century African-American Musical Theater, 1994; contbr. articles to profl. jours. Active Girl Scouts U.S.A., 1954-63; chmn. mgmt. com. Queens Area YWCA, 1970-73. Recipient Alumni Achievement award U. Chgo., 1970, Deems Taylor award ASCAP, 1973, Peabody medal Johns Hopkins U., 1991; NEH grantee, 1979-83. Mem. NAACP, Internat. Musicol. Soc., Am. Musicol. Soc. (hon., bd. dirs. 1974-76), Sonneck Am. Music Soc. (bd. dirs. 1986-88), Renaissance Soc., Phi Beta Kappa (hon. Radcliffe Coll.), Alpha Kappa Alpha. Home: PO Box 1 Jamaica NY 11411-0001 Office: Harvard U Cambridge MA 02138

SOUTHERN, HUGH, performing arts consultant; b. Newcastle-on-Tyne, Eng., Mar. 20, 1932; came to U.S., 1955; s. Norman and Phyllis Margaret (Hiller) S.; m. Jane Rosemary Llewellyn, Dec. 18, 1954 (div.); children: Hilary, William Norman; m. Kathy Ayers Dwyer, Dec. 10, 1989; 1 child, Jaime Andres. B.A., King's Coll., Cambridge, Eng., 1956. Assoc. account exec. Fuller & Smith & Ross, N.Y.C., 1956-58; treas. Westport Country Playhouse Conn., 1958; adminstrv. mgr. Theatre Guild-Am. Theatre Soc., N.Y.C., 1959-62; asst. dir. Repertory Theatre, Lincoln Ctr., N.Y.C., 1962-65; gen. mgr. Nat. Repertory Theatre, N.Y.C., 1965-67; mgmt. assoc. San Francisco Opera, 1967-68; exec. dir. Theatre Devel. Fund, N.Y.C., 1968-82; dep. chmn. programs Nat. Endowment for Arts, Washington, 1982-89, acting chmn., 1989; gen. mgr. Met. Opera Assn. Inc., N.Y.C., 1989-90; dir. Va. Festival of Am. Film, Charlottesville, Va., 1995-96; acting dir. performing arts program N.Y. State Council on Arts, N.Y.C., 1974-75, acting exec. dir., 1976; dir. New Dramatists, N.Y.C., 1978-82, Film Forum, N.Y.C., 1978-82; trustee Actor's Fund Am., N.Y.C., 1978-85. Trustee Manhattan Country Sch., N.Y.C., 1970-82, chmn., 1971-74; mem. Mayor's Com. on Cultural Policy, N.Y.C., 1974-75; dir. Vol. Cons. Group, Inc., N.Y.C., 1976-82, 92—. Home: 204 Tunbridge Rd Baltimore MD 21212

SOUTHERN, ROBERT ALLEN, lawyer; b. Independence, Mo., July 17, 1930; s. James Allen and Josephine (Ragland) S.; m. Cynthia Agnes Drews, May 17, 1952; children: David D., William A., James M., Kathryn S. O'Brien. B.S. in Polit. Sci., Northwestern U., 1952, LL.B., 1954. Bar: Ill. 1955. Assoc. Mayer, Brown & Platt, Chgo., 1954-64, ptnr., 1965-96, mng. ptnr., 1978-91; mng. ptnr. Mayer, Brown & Platt, L.A., 1991-96; CEO So. Assocs., Gurnee, Ill., 1997—. Editor in chief Northwestern U. Law Rev., 1953-54. Trustee, v.p., gen. counsel LaRabida Children's Hosp. and Rsch. Ctr., Chgo., 1974-89; trustee Kenilworth (Ill.) Union Ch., 1980-88; pres. Joseph Sears Sch. Bd., 1977-79; trustee Rush-Presbyn.-St. Luke's Med. Ctr., 1983-91, life trustee, 1991—; bd. dirs. Boys and Girls Clubs Chgo., 1986-91; governing mem. Orchestral Assn. Chgo., 1988-93. With U.S. Army, 1955-57. Mem. ABA, Chgo. Bar Assn., Law Club Chgo., Legal Club Chgo., Order of Coif, Indian Hill Club, Chgo. Club. Office: 7600 Bittersweet Dr Gurnee IL 60031-5110

SOUTHERN, RONALD D., diversified corporation executive; b. Calgary, Alta., Can., July 25, 1930; s. Samuel Donald and Alexandra (Cuthill) S.; m. Margaret Visser, July 30, 1954; children: Nancy, Linda. BSc, U. Alta., Edmonton, 1953; LLD (hon.), U. Calgary, 1976, U. Alberta, 1991. Pres., CEO ATCO Ltd., Calgary, 1954-85, dep. chmn., CEO, 1985-91, chmn., pres., CEO, 1985-93; chmn., CEO ATCO Ltd. and Can. Utilities Ltd., Calgary, 1994—, ATCO Ltd., Calgary, 1994—, Can. Utilities Ltd., Calgary, 1994—; chmn. Akita Drilling Ltd.; bd. dirs. Fletcher Challenge Can. Ltd., Can. Airlines Corp., Can. Pacific Ltd., Chrysler Can. Ltd., IMASCO Ltd., LaFarge, Royal Ins. Ltd., Xerox of Can. Inc., Fletcher Challenge Ltd., New Zealand; co-chmn. Spruce Meadows Tournaments; chmn. Spruce Meadows Round Table. Recipient Holland Trade award Gov. of The Netherlands, 1985, (with wife) Sportsmen of Yr. award Calgary Booster Club, Internat., Disting. Entrepreneur award U. Man. Faculty Mgmt., 1990; inducted into Can. Bus. Hall, 1995; named Businessman of Yr. U. Alta., 1986, to Order of Can. Brit. Empire, 1986, Comdr. Brit. Empire, 1995, CEO of the Yr. Fin. Post, 1996. Mem. Ranchmen's Club. Calgary Golf and Country Club. Home: 67 Massey Pl SW, Calgary, AB Canada T2V 2G7 Office: ATCO Ltd & Can Utilities Ltd, 1600 909-11 Ave SW, Calgary, AB Canada T2R 1N6

SOUTHWARD, GLEN MORRIS, statistician, educator; b. Boise, Idaho, Oct. 8, 1927; s. Glen P. and Emma M. (Martin) S.; m. M. Lorraine Kissack, Oct. 3, 1974; children from previous marriage: Judith Ann, Richard Todd. BS, U. Wash., 1949, MS, 1956, PhD, 1966. Asst. prof. stats. Wash. State U., Pullman, 1967-71; biometrician Internat. Pacific Halibut Commn., Seattle, 1971-75; assoc. prof. stats. N.Mex. State U., Las Cruces, 1975-80, prof., 1980-93, prof. emeritus, 1993—. Contbr. articles to profl. jours. Fellow Am. Inst. Fishery Rsch. Biologists; mem. Am. Statis. Assn., Biometric Soc. (sec., treas. Western N.Am. region 1984-91), Sigma Xi. Avocations: photography, cooking. Office: NMex State U Stats and Rsch Support Inst PO Box 3130 Las Cruces NM 88003-8003

SOUTHWICK, ARTHUR FREDERICK, legal educator; b. Pitts., Nov. 22, 1924. BA, Coll. of Wooster, 1947; MBA, U. Mich., 1950, JD, 1951. Bar: Ohio 1951. Atty. trust dept. Nat. City Bank, Cleve., 1951-56; asst. prof. law U. Mich., Ann Arbor, 1956-61, assoc. prof., 1961-66, prof. bus. law, health svcs. mgmt. and policy, 1966-90, prof. emeritus, 1990—. Author: The Law of Hospital and Health Care Administration, 1988; contbr. articles to legal publs. and med. jours. Elder 1st Presbyterian Ch., Ann Arbor, 1963—. Mem. Am. Acad. Health Care Attys., Acad. of Legal Studies in Bus., Nat. Health Lawyers Assn., Am. Soc. Law, Medicine and Ethics. Home: 26 Southwick Ct Ann Arbor MI 48105-1410 Office: U Mich Sch Bus Adminstrn Ann Arbor MI 48109

SOUTHWICK, CHARLES HENRY, zoologist, educator; b. Wooster, Ohio, Aug. 28, 1928; s. Arthur F. and Faye (Motz) S.; m. Heather Milne Beck, July 12, 1952; children: Steven, Karen. B.A., Coll. Wooster, 1949; M.S., U. Wis., 1951, Ph.D., 1953. NIH fellow, 1951-53; asst. prof. biology Hamilton Coll., 1953-54; NSF fellow Oxford (Eng.) U., 1954-55; faculty Ohio U., 1955-61; assoc. prof. pathobiology Johns Hopkins Sch. Hygiene and Pub. Health, Balt., 1961-68; prof. Johns Hopkins Sch. Hygiene and Pub. Health, 1968-79; assoc. dir. Johns Hopkins Internat. Ctr. for Med. Rsch. and Tng., Calcutta, India, 1964-65; chmn. dept. environ., population and organismic biology U. Colo., Boulder, 1979-82, prof. biology, 1979—, prof. emeritus, 1993—; researcher and author publs. on animal social behavior and population dynamics, influences animal social behavior on demographic characteristic mammal populations, primate ecology and behavior, estuarine ecology and environmental quality; mem. primate adv. com. Nat. Acad. Sci.-NRC, 1963-75, com. primate conservation, 1974-75; mem. Gov.'s Sci. Adv. Com. State of Md., 1975-78; mem. com. on rsch. and exploration Nat. Geog. Soc., 1979—; mem. adv. bd. Caribbean Primate Rsch. Ctr., 1987—, Wis. Primate Rsch. Ctr., 1990—; mem. Integrated Conservation Rsch., 1989—. Editor, author: Primate Social Behavior, 1963, Animal Aggression, 1970, Nonhuman Primates in Biomedical Research, 1975, Ecology and the Quality of Our Environment, 1976, Global Ecology, 1985; Ecology and Behavior of Food-Enhanced Primate Groups, 1988; author: Global Ecology in Human Perspective, 1996. Recipient Fulbright Rsch. award India, 1959-60. Fellow AAAS, Acad. Zoology, Animal Behavior Soc.; mem. Am. Soc. Zoologists, Ecol. Soc. Am., Am. Soc. Mammalogists, Am. Soc. Primatology (Disting. Primatologist award 1994), Internat. Primatology Soc., Am. Inst. Biol. Scis., Primatology Soc. Gt. Britain, Internat. Soc. Study Aggression.

SOUTHWICK, DAVID LEROY, geology researcher; b. Rochester, Minn., Aug. 30, 1936; m. 1959; 3 children. BA, Carleton Coll., 1958; PhD in Geology, Johns Hopkins U., 1962. Geologist U.S. Geol. Survey, 1962-68; asst. prof. to prof. geology Macalester Coll., 1968-77; sr. geologist Minn. Geol. Survey, St. Paul, 1977-89, asst. dir., rsch. assoc., 1989-93, acting dir., 1993-94, dir., 1994—; adj. assoc. prof. U. Minn., 1983-94, prof., 1994—. Fellow Geol. Assn. Can., Geol. Soc. Am.; mem. Am. Geophys. Union. Office: Minnesota Geological Survey 2642 University Ave W Saint Paul MN 55114-1032

SOUTHWICK, E. MICHAEL, diplomat; b. Willits, Calif., 1945; m. Susan Obee; children: Edward, Andrew, Katherine. Grad., Stanford U., 1966. Consular officer, staff asst. to amb. Carol Laise U.S. Dept. State; adminstr., consular officer Kigali, Rwanda; dep. chief of mission Bujumbura, Burundi & Niamey, Niger; assignments officer for Africa Bu. Pers.; exec. dir. Bur. Intel & Rsch.; dep. chief of mission Nairobi, Kenya, 1990-94; U.S. amb. to Uganda, 1994—. Recipient Meritorious Honor award, Order of Merit Govt. of Niger. Office: US Ambassador Kampala Uganda US Dept of Washington Washington DC 20521-2190*

SOUTHWICK, LAWRENCE, JR., management educator; b. Northampton, Mass., Sept. 5, 1938; s. Lawrence Sr. and Caroline (Ingram) S.; m. Patricia A. Matthews, Oct. 21, 1961; children: Lawrence III, Rebecca A., Catherine A. BS in Math., Case Western Res. U., Cleve., 1960; MBA, Western Mich. U., 1963; MS in Indsl. Adminstrn., Carnegie-Mellon U., 1965, PhD in Econs., 1967. Cert. mgmt. acct., fin. mgmt. Asst. prof. mgmt. SUNY, Buffalo, 1966-70, assoc. prof., 1970—; chmn. dept. mgmt. SUNU, Buffalo, 1976-81, 91-94; cons. in field. Author: Managerial Economics, 1985. Councilman Town of Amherst, 1972-91. Mem. NAFE, Am. Law and Econ. Assn., Am. Econ. Assn., Seneca Nation of Indians Econ. Devel. Corp. (bd. dirs.), Restoration Soc. (bd. dirs., pres.), Friendship Found. (bd. dirs.). Republican. Unitarian. Home: 100 Oakland Rd Williamsville NY 14221-6816 Office: SUNY Sch Mgmt Buffalo NY 14260

SOUTHWICK, PAUL, retired public relations executive; b. West Newton, Mass., Mar. 27, 1920; s. Alfred and Pauline (Winkler) S.; m. Susan Barbara Heider, Feb. 24, 1947; children: Thomas Paul, Peter Alfred, Linda Susan. AB in Econs. cum laude, Harvard Coll., 1943. Coor. AP, Concord, N.H., 1947-49; UP UPI, Washington, 1949-57; mem. profl. staff govt. info. subcom. U.S. Ho. Reps., 1957-59; legis. asst., adminstrv. asst. U.S. Senator Long of Hawaii, 1959-62; dep. adminstr. charge accelerated pub. works program Area Redevel. Adminstrn., 1962-63; spl. asst. The White House, 1963-65; spl. asst. for congl. rels. Office of U.S. Sec. Commerce, 1965-67; v.p. Newmyer Assocs., Inc., Washington, 1967-87; ind. cons., 1987-93, ret., 1993. With USNR, 1941-45, PTO. Mem. Nat. Press Club (Washington), Bethesda (Md.) Country Club. Democrat. Presbyterian. Home: 4012 Underwood St Bethesda MD 20815-5028

SOUTHWORTH, HORTON COE, educational educator, education scholar; b. Monroe, Mich., Apr. 2, 1926; s. Frederick Osgood and Bertha Southworth; m. Jannene MacIntyre, Apr. 1971; children: Sueann, Nancy, Jim, Janet, Jaye, Bradford, Alexandra. BS, Mich. State U., East Lansing, 1950, MA, 1953, EdD, 1962. Cert. K-8 tchr., elem. prin., Mich. Mid. sch. tchr. Bellevue (Mich.) Pub. Schs., 1950-51, elem. prin., 1951-53, supervising prin., 1953-55; elem. prin. Pontiac (Mich.) Pub. Schs., 1955-59; coord. Macomb Tchr. Ctr. Mich. State U., Warren, 1959-67, asst. prof., 1962-64, assoc. prof., 1964-67; prof. edn., chmn. elem. edn. dept. U. Pitts., 1967-91; scholar-in-residence Duquesne U., Pitts., 1990—, cons., 1991-92; cons. Pa. Dept. Edn., Harrisburg, 1968-91; treas. Learning Tree Assocs. Pitts., 1974—. Chmn. Three Rivers dist. Boy Scouts Am., Pitts., 1980-90; pres. Univ. Childrens Sch., California, Pa., 1988—, mem. adv. com. grad. program in Pa., Nova Southeastern U., Harrisburg, 1989—; invited participant Leadership Conf., Oxford U., 1995, 97. With USNR, 1944-46, PTO. Recipient Chancellor's Disting. Tchr. award U. Pitts., 1988, Prof. Emeritus award, 1991, Presdl. citation Merit, 1997. Mem. Assn. Tchr. Educators (33 Yr. Mem. award 1991), Pa. Assn. Colls. and Tchr. Educators (exec. bd. 1985-91), Masons (life), Kappa Delta Pi (5 Yr. Chpt. Counselor award 1989), Phi Delta Kappa (25 Yr. Mem. award 1985, 40 Yr. Mem. award 1996), Theta Chi. Democrat. Presbyterian. Avocations: skiing, reading, gardening. Home: 619 S Linden Ave Pittsburgh PA 15208-2812 Office: Learning Tree Schs Corp Penn West Bldg Pittsburgh PA 15221

SOUTHWORTH, JAMIE MACINTYRE, education educator; b. Ironton, Ohio, Oct. 16, 1931; d. Gaylord and Lydia Marcum (Adkins) MacIntyre; m. Horton C. Southworth; children: Jaye, Brad, Alexandra, Sueann, Janet, Jim. BS, Ball State U., 1952, MA, 1961; EdD, U. Pitts., 1981; attended, Oxford (Eng.) U., 1997. Cert. adminstr. and tchr., reading specialist, Pa. Instr. Mich. State U., East Lansing, 1964-67; instr., coord. U. Minn., Mpls., 1967-71; rsch. assoc. Pitts. Pub. Schs., 1971-80; assoc. prof. California U. Pa., 1988; prof. edn. California U., Pa., 1993—; state grants educator, 1990-95; mem. univ. faculty devel. com. California U., 1992—, co-chairperson faculty devel., 1997—, chairperson dept. promotion and tenure com., 1993—, mem. the evaluation com., 1994—, mem. faculty devel. state com., 1997—; chancellor State Adv. Com., Calif. Univ. rep., 1994—; invited participant Oxford (Eng.) U. Leadership Studies, 1995, 97; dir. leadership tng. proposal, 1996—. Contbr. articles to profl. jours. U.S. Office of Edn. title III & IVC grantee; grantee Pa. Vocat. Tech. State, 1990-91, 93, Bibliotherapy Project California Univ. Pa., 1992, Pa. State, 1993, Pa. Campus Compac, 1993. Mem. Am. Assn. Colls. Tchr. Edn., NEA Young Children, Kappa Delta Pi (counselor), Phi Delta Kappa.

SOUTHWORTH, LINDA JEAN, artist, critic, educator; b. Milw., May 11, 1951; d. William Dixon and Violet Elsie (Kuehn) S.; m. David Joseph Roger, Nov. 16, 1985 (div. July 1989). BFA, St. John's U., Queens, N.Y., 1974; MFA, Pratt Inst., Bklyn., 1978. Printmaker, still life and portrait painter, collage artist, photographer self-employed, N.Y.C., 1974—; art critic Resident Publs., N.Y.C., 1993-95; adj. prof. art history St. Francis Coll., Bklyn., 1985-94; artist-in-residence Our Saviour's Atonement Luth. Ch., N.Y.C., 1993-95. Exhibited in solo shows at Galimaufry, Croton-on-Hudson, N.Y., 1977, Kristen Richards Gallery, N.Y.C., 1982, Gallery 84, N.Y.C., 1990, The Bernhardt Collection, Washington, 1991, The Netherland Club, N.Y.C., 1992, Chuck Levitan Gallery, Soho, 1996; group shows include Union St. Graphics, San Francisco, 1974, Nuance Gallery, Tampa, 1987, 88, Soc. Illustrators Ann. Drawing Show, N.Y.C., 1989, 90, Salmagundi Club, N.Y.C., 1991, 92, Henry Howells Gallery, N.Y.C., 1992, 93, Mus. Gallery, N.Y.C., 1994, Cavalier Gallery, Greenwich, Conn., 1995, Carib Gallery, N.Y.C., 1995, Chuck Levitan Gallery, N.Y.C., 1996, N.Y. State Mus., 1997; artist Christmas card/UNICEF, 1992; represented in permanent collections at Peltz, Walker & Dubinsky, Valois of Am. Avocations: ballroom dancing, old inns and architecture, cycling. Home: 106 Cabrini Blvd Apt 5D New York NY 10033-3422

SOUTHWORTH, R. MORRISON, development counsel; b. Charlottesville, Va., Jan. 2, 1951; s. Richard Spencer Southworth and Geneva (James) Sutphin; m. Diana Page Dunbar, Sept. 21, 1981 (div. Aug. 1983). BA in Econs. and Bus., Emory and Henry Coll., 1975; postgrad., George Washington U., 1988; MEd in Instnl. Advancement, Vanderbilt U., 1991. Account exec. Clay Media, Charlottesville, 1979-82, Wilson and Peck Advt., Balt., 1982-84, WHRO Pub. Broadcasting, Norfolk, Va., 1985-86, Forrsberg Advt., Virginia Beach, Va., 1986-87; ind. fundraising cons. Virginia Beach, 1987-89; edn. libr. Vanderbilt U., Nashville, 1989-91; asst. dir. devel. Fisk U., Nashville, 1990-91; pvt. practice Palmyra, Va., 1991—; dir. for devel. Horizon Inst. for Policy Solutions. Contbg. editor to regional publs.; profl. drummer, vocalist, actor. Vol. Soc. for Prevention Cruelty to Animals, Back Bay Nat. Wildlife Refuge; docent Va. Life Saving Mus., 1986-88; mem. Tenn. Hist. Soc., 1993—, Friends of Fluvanna Libr., 1989, 94—; rep. Vanderbilt U. Press for Va. Festival of the Book and So. Festival of the Books; player/mgr. Men's Sr. Baseball League. Mem. Virginia Beach Writers (founding), Sigma Iota, Alpha Phi Omega. Republican. Avocations: writing, animal welfare, equitation, dogs. Office: Ct Green PO Box 476 Palmyra VA 22963-0476

SOUTHWORTH, ROD BRAND, computer science educator; b. Binghampton, N.Y., Aug. 24, 1941; s. William Tanner Southworth and Ruth Evelyn (Brabham) Woods; m. Patrice Marie Gapen, Jan. 10, 1978; children: Suzi Lynn, Judi Leigh, Megan Marie, Robin Ashley. BS in Bus., U. Ariz., 1965; MS in Mgmt. Sci. and Info Systems, Colo. State U., 1978. Mktg. rep. IBM, Denver, 1966-69; system analyst Colo. State U., Fort Collins, 1969-73, grad. teaching asst., 1978-79; project mgr. Systems and Computer Tech., Portland, Oreg., 1973-75; asst. dir. Systems and Computer Tech., Fairbanks, Alaska, 1975-77; instr. in computer info. systems Laramie County C.C., Cheyenne, Wyo., 1979—. Author: (software) PC-DOS/MS-DOS Simplified, 1st edit. 1988, 3rd edit. 1992, DOS Complete and Simplified, 1990, DOS Essentials, 1991, DOS 5 Simplified, 1992, DOS 6.2 Simplified, 1994. Mem. Civil Air Patrol, Cheyenne, 1991. Mem. Data Processing Mgmt. Assn. (mem. assoc. level model curriculum 1984-85), Assn. Computing Machinery (mem. assoc. level computer info. processing model curriculum 1991-92). Avocations: boating, water skiing, fishing, stamp collecting, tennis. Home: PO Box 5457 Cheyenne WY 82003-5457 Office: Laramie County Comm Coll 1400 E College Dr Cheyenne WY 82007-3204

SOUTHWORTH, WILLIAM DIXON, retired education educator; b. Union City, Tenn., Dec. 28, 1918; s. Thomas and Gertrude (Dyer) S.; m. Violet Kuehn, July 22, 1944; children: Geoffrey Scott, Linda Jean. PhB, Marquette U., 1948, MEd, 1950; PhD, NYU, 1961. Tchr., coach La Follette Sch., Milwaukee County, Wis., 1948-51; teaching dist. prin. Grand View Sch., Milwaukee County, 1951-56; supervising dist. prin. Maple Dale Sch., Milwaukee County, 1956-58; bldg. prin. Main St. Sch., Port Washington, N.Y., 1958-65; asst. supt. for elem. edn. Huntington (N.Y.) pub. schs., 1965-67; assoc. prof., acting head dept. adminstrn. and supervision St. John's U., Jamaica, N.Y., 1967, chmn. dept., 1968-73, prof., 1968-84; adj. prof. Berne U., St. Kitts; parliamentarian for 35 internat., nat. regional orgns., expert witness, pub. moderator, and workshop leader. Author: Care and Nurture of the Doctoral Candidate, 1968, 74, Q The Story of Captain Quimby Scott, U.S. Navy WWII, 1997, The Art of Successful Meetings, 1997; contbg. editor Condominium Times; contbr. numerous articles to edni. jours., condominium and parliamentary publs. Served with USN, 1938-44. Lutheran. Home: Apt 608 7100 Sunshine Skyway Ln Saint Petersburg FL 33711-4926
In the conflicting demands of self and society, one must strike a balance by retaining the uniqueness of one's individuality while serving the society that nurtured that uniqueness. It is in the balance thus struck that the complete person evolves—self-esteeming, and socially involved.

SOUTTER, THOMAS DOUGLAS, retired lawyer; b. N.Y.C., Nov. 1, 1934; s. Thomas G. and Hildreth H. (Callanan) S.; m. Virginia Hovenden; children: Alexander D., C. Anson, Hadley H. BA, U. Va., 1955, LL.B., 1962; postgrad., Advanced Mgmt. Program, Harvard U., 1980. Bar: N.Y. 1962, R.I. 1969. Atty. Breed, Abbott & Morgan, N.Y.C., 1962-68; with Textron Inc., Providence, 1968-95; gen. counsel Textron Inc., 1970-95, v.p., 1971-80, sr. v.p., 1980-85, exec. v.p., gen. counsel, 1985-95; cons., 1995—; mem. adv. bd. Internat. and Comparative Law Ctr., 1975-95; mem. Assn. Gen. Counsel; bd. dirs. Avco Fin. Svcs., Inc., 1985-95, Paul Revere Corp. 1993-95; trustee New England Legal Found. Nat. chmn. ann. giving campaign U. Va. Law Sch., 1992-94; former trustee Providence Preservation Soc., Providence Performing Arts Ctr.; mem. U. Va. Arts and Scis. Alumni Coun.; mem. Narragansett coun. Boy Scouts Am. Lt. USNR, 1955-59. Mem. ABA, N.Y. State Bar Assn., R.I. Bar Assn., Internat. Bar Assn. Office: PO Box 878 40 Westminster St 17th Fl Providence RI 02903-2525

SOUVEROFF, VERNON WILLIAM, JR., business executive, author; b. L.A., Aug. 12, 1934; s. Vernon William Sr. and Aileen (Young) S.; m. Aileen Patricia Robinson; children—Gail Kathleen, Michael William, Kirk Laron. B.S. in E.E., Stanford U., 1957; postgrad., Ohio State U., 1958-59. With Litton Industries, Beverly Hills, Calif., 1960-75; with ITT Corp., N.Y.C., 1975-87; prin. Bus. Acquisitions and Investments, 1988—; corp. v.p. ITT Corp., N.Y.C., 1983-84, sr. v.p., 1984-87; pres. ITT Gilfillan, 1979-83; group exec. ITT Def. Space Group, 1983-84; dir. ITT Telecom and Electronics N.Am., 1984-86; pres., chief exec. officer ITT Def. Tech. Corp., 1986-87; exec. dir. Nat. Ctr. for Career Change, 1990—; mem. U.S. Def. Policy Adv. Com. on Trade, Washington, 1984-88; bd. advisors, investor Venture Resources, Venture Capital, 1988-92; bd. dirs. Elanix, Inc., Formida Holdings Ltd., Australia; chmn. bd. dirs. Formida Software Corp., San Jose, Calif., 1996—. Author books on def. downsizing. Served as officer USAF, 1957-60. Recipient Exec. Salute award Los Angeles C. of C., 1981; Ring of

Quality ITT Corp., 1983. Mem. IEEE, Nat. Contracts Mgmt. Assn., Electronics Industries Assn., Am. Def. Preparedness Assn. (former dir.), Nat. Security Indsl. Assn., Air Force Assn., Navy League, Assn. U.S. Army. Presbyterian.

SOUW, BERNARD ENG-KIE, physicist, consultant; b. Pekalongan, Java, Indonesia, Jan. 7, 1942; came to U.S., 1984, naturalized citizen, 1990; s. Tjwan-Ling and Pek-Liang (Kwee) S.; m. Martha Tjoei-Lioe Lim, July 17, 1967; children: Victor, Verena. Diploma in Physics, Tech. U. of Clausthal, Zellerfeld, Fed. Republic of Germany, 1972; D in Natural Scis., U. Duesseldorf, Fed. Republic of Germany, 1981. Rsch. assoc. U. Duesseldorf, 1973-83; rsch. scientist Isotope Rsch. Inst., Haan, Fed. Republic of Germany, 1983; univ. asst. Free U. of Berlin, 1984; vis. scientist A. F. Wright Aero. Labs., Dayton, Ohio, 1984-85; rsch. scientist Brookhaven Nat. Lab., Upton, N.Y., 1985—; cons. cvd-diamond, plasma and laser applications; adj. prof. N.J. Inst. Tech., 1994—. Contbr. articles to Jour. Applied Physics, Jour. Quantitative Spectroscopy, Jour. Plasma Physics, Plasma Physics and Controlled Fusion, Physica, Jour. Vac. Sci. Tech., Diamond and Related Materials, Nuclear Instruments and Methods in Physics Rsch. Mem. Am. Phys. Soc., L.I. Optical Soc., Materials Rsch. Soc. Office: Brookhaven Nat Lab Bldg 701 M Upton NY 11973

SOVENYHAZY, GABOR FERENC, surgeon; b. Budapest, Hungary, Apr. 7, 1947. MD, SUNY, 1975. Diplomate Am. Bd. of Colon and Rectal Surgeons. Intern Maimonides Med. Ctr., Bklyn., 1974-75, resident in gen. surgery, 1976-79; resident in colon and rectal surgery Grant Hosp., Columbus, 1979-80; pvt. practice, 1980—; hosp. appt. Spartanburg Gen. Hosp., S.C.; asst. prof. colon and rectal surgery U. S.C. Fellow ACS, Am. Soc. Colorectal Surgery, Piedmont Colorectal Assn., Am. Soc. Gastrointestinal Endoscopy, Am. Soc. Colon and Rectal Surgeons. Office: 11 Doctors Park Ste 210 Spartanburg SC 29307

SOVERN, MICHAEL IRA, law educator; b. N.Y.C., Dec. 1, 1931; s. Julius and Lillian (Arnstein) S.; m. Lenore Goodman, Feb. 21, 1952 (div. Apr. 1963); children: Jeffrey Austin, Elizabeth Ann, Douglas Todd; m. Eleanor Leen, Aug. 25, 1963 (div. Feb. 1974); 1 child, Julie Danielle; m. Joan Wit, Mar. 9, 1974 (dec. Sept. 1993); m. Patricia Walsh, Nov. 12, 1995. AB summa cum laude, Columbia U., 1953, LLB (James Ordronaux prize), 1955, LLD (hon.), 1980; PhD (hon.), Tel Aviv U., 1982; LLD (hon.), U. So. Calif., 1989. Bar: N.Y. 1956, U.S. Supreme Ct. 1976. Asst. prof., then assoc. prof. law U. Minn. Law Sch., 1955-58; mem. faculty Columbia Law Sch., 1957—, prof. law, 1960—, Chancellor Kent prof., 1977—, dean Law Sch., 1970-79; chmn. exec. com. faculty Columbia U., 1968-69, provost, exec. v.p., 1979-80, univ. pres., 1980-93, pres. emeritus, 1993; rsch. dir. Legal Restraints on Racial Discrimination in Employment, Twentieth Century Fund, 1962-66; spl. counsel to gov. N.J., 1974-77; cons. Time Mag., 1965-80; bd. dirs. Chem. Bank, 1981-96, Chase Manhattan Bank, 1996, AT&T, GNY Ins. Group, Warner Lambert, Sequa; mem. panel of arbitrators N.J. Bd. Mediation, Fed. Mediation and Conciliation Svc.; bd. dirs. Asian Cultural Coun., Shubert Orgn., Sta. WNET-TV, NAACP Legal Def. Fund, Freedom Forum Newseum; chmn. N.Y.C. Charter Revision Commn., 1982-83; co-chmn. 2d Cir. Commn. on Reduction of Burdens and Costs in Civil Litigation, 1977-80; chmn. Commn. on Integrity in Govt., 1986; pres. Italian Acad. Advanced Studies in Am., 1991-93, Shubert Found., 1996—; chmn. Japan Soc., 1993—, Am. Acad. Rome, 1993—; chmn. nat. adv. coun. Freedom Forum Media Studies Ctr., 1993—. Author: Legal Restraints on Racial Discrimination in Employment, 1966, Law and Poverty, 1969, Of Boundless Domains, 1994; host Sta. WNET-TV series Leading Questions. Mem. Pulitzer Prize Bd., 1980-93, chmn. pro tem, 1986-87; trustee Kaiser Family Found., Presdl. Legal Expense Trust. Commendatore in the Order of Merit of the Republic of Italy, 1991; recipient Alexander Hamilton medal Columbia Coll., 1993, Citizens Union Civic Leadership award, 1993. Fellow Am. Acad. Arts and Scis.; mem. ABA, Coun. Fgn. Rels., Assn. Bar City N.Y., Am. Arbitration Assn. (panel arbitrators), Am. Law Inst., Econ. Club, Nat. Acad. Arbitrators. Office: Columbia U Sch Law 435 W 116th St New York NY 10027-7201

SOVIE, MARGARET DOE, nursing administrator, educator; b. Ogdensburg, N.Y., July 7, 1934; d. William Gordon and Mary Rose (Bruyere) Doe; m. Alfred L. Sovie, May 8, 1954; 1 child, Scot Marc. Student, U. Rochester, 1950-51; diploma in nursing, St. Lawrence State Hosp. Sch. Nursing, Ogdensburg, 1954; student, St. Lawrence U., 1956-60; BSN summa cum laude, Syracuse U., 1964, MS in Edn., 1968, PhD in Edn., 1972; DSc (hon.), Health Sci. Ctr. SUNY, Syracuse, 1989; MSN, U. Pa., 1995, adult health nurse practitioner, 1996. Cert. post-masters gerontol. nurse practitioner. Staff nurse, clin. instr. St. Lawrence State Hosp., Ogdensburg, 1954-55, instr. nursing, 1955-62; staff nurse Good Shepherd Hosp., Syracuse, 1962; nursing supr. SUNY Upstate Med. Ctr., Syracuse, 1963-65, insvc. instr., 1965-66, edn. dir. and coord. nursing svc., 1966-71, asst. dean Coll. Health Related Professions, 1972-84, assoc. prof. nursing, 1973-76, dir. continuing edn. in nursing, 1974-76, assoc. dean and dir. div. continuing edn. Coll. Health Related Professions, 1974-76; spl. assignment in pres.'s office SUNY Upstate Med. Ctr. and Syracuse U., 1972-73; assoc. dean for nursing U. Rochester, N.Y., 1976-88, assoc. prof. nursing, 1976-85, prof., 1985-88; assoc. dir. for nursing Strong Meml. Hosp., U. Rochester Med. Ctr., 1976-88; chief nursing officer Hosp. U. Pa., Phila., 1988-96, assoc. exec. dir., 1988-94, assoc. dean for nursing practice Sch. Nursing, 1988-96, Jane Delano prof. nursing adminstrn. Sch. Nursing, 1988—; sr. fellow Leonard Davis Inst. Health Econs. U. Pa., Phila., 1992—; trustee bd. U. Pa. Health Sys., Phila., 1993-96; nursing coord. and project dir. Cen. N.Y. Regional Med. Program, Syracuse, 1968-71; mem. edn. dept. State Bd. Nursing, Albany, N.Y., 1974-84, chmn., 1981-83, chmn. practice com., 1975-80, mem. joint practice com., 1975-80, vice chmn., 1980-81; mem. adv. com. to clin. nurse scholars program Robert Wood Johnson found., Princeton, N.J., 1982-88; adj. assoc. prof. Syracuse U. Sch. Nursing, 1973-76, chmn. vis. com. Coll. Nursing, 1996—; mem. Gov.'s Health Adv. Panel N.Y. State Health Planning Commn., 1976-82, task force on health manpower policy, 1978, informal support networks sect. steering com., 1980; mem. health manpower tng. and utilization task force State N.Y. Commn. on Health Edn.and Illness Prevention, 1979; mem. task force on nursing personnel N.Y. State Health Adv. Coun., 1980; mem. adv. panel on nursing svcs. U.S. Pharm. Conv. Inc., Washington, 1985-90; cons. Nat. Ctr. for Svcs. Rsch. and Health Care Tech. Assessment, Rockville, Md., 1987; mem. nursing stds. task force Joint Commn. Accreditation Health Care Orgns., 1988-90; mem. various other adv. coms.; lectr. in field. Mem. editl. bd. Health Care Supr., 1982-87, Nursing Econs., 1983—, Best Practices and Benchmarking in Health Care, 1995—; manuscript rev. panel Nursing Outlook, 1987-91; mem. editorial bd. Seminars for Nurse Mgrs., 1994—; contbr. articles to profl. jours., chpts. to books. Mem. bd. visitors Sch. Nursing U. Md., Balt., 1984-89; mem. bd. mgrs. Strong Meml. Hosp., Rochester, 1983-88; bd. dirs. Monroe County Assn. for Hearing, Rochester, 1979-82, Vis. Nurse Svc., Rochester and Monroe County, 1978, Southeastern Pa. chpt. ARC, 1991—. Ann. Margaret D. Sovie lectureship inaugurated Strong Meml. Hosp. U. Rochester, 1989; spl. nurse rsch. fellow NIH, 1971-72; grantee various orgns.; recipient Dean's Outstanding Alumni award Coll. of Nursing, Syracuse U., 1994. Fellow Am. Acad. Nursing (program com. 1980-81, task force on hosp. nursing 1981-83, chair expert panel on quality health 1994—); mem. ANA (nat. rev. com. for expanded role programs 1975-78, site visitor to programs requesting accreditation 1976-78, cabinet on nursing svcs. 1986-90, cert. bd. nursing adminstrn. 1983-86, Ad Hoc com. on advanced practice 1992-95), Am. Orgn. Nurse Execs. (stds. task force 1987), N.Y. State Nurses Assn. (med. surg. nursing group, chmn. edn. com. dist. 4, 1974-76, chmn. cmty. planning group for nursing dist. 4, 1974-75, coun. on regional planning in nursing 1974-76, del. to conv. 1978, Nursing Svc. Adminstrn. award 1985), Inst. Medicine (com. design strategy for quality rev. and assurance in Medicare 1988-90), Sigma Theta Tau, Pi Lambda Theta. Republican. Roman Catholic. Avocations: golf, cross-country skiing, swimming, dancing. Office: U Pa Sch Nursing 420 Guardian Dr Philadelphia PA 19104-6096

SOVIERO, DIANA BARBARA, soprano; b. Jersey City, Mar. 19, 1946; d. Amerigo and Angelina Catani; student Juilliard Sch. Music, Hunter Coll. Opera Workshop. Appearances with opera cos. including Tulsa Opera, Houston Grand Opera, San Diego Opera, Ottawa (Ont., Can.) Opera, Zurich Opera, Goldovsky Opera Theatre, Lake George Opera, New Orleans Opera, Hamburg (W.Ger.) Opera, Dallas Opera, Chgo. Opera, Rome Opera, Paris Opera, Nice Opera, Avignon Opera, San Francisco Opera, Montreal (Que., Can.) Opera, Toulouse, France, Caracas, Venezuela, Vienna Opera, Parma Opera, Italy, Munich Opera, W.Ger., Edmonton (Alta., Can.) Opera, Winnipeg (Man., Can.) Opera, Calgary (Alta.) Opera, Madrid Opera, Greater Miami Opera, Bastille Opera, Montreal Opera, Covent Garden, Florence Opera, Opera Pacific at Costa Mesa; with Met. Opera, 1986—, now leading soprano; instr. master classes The Faculty, sch. for actors, Los Angeles. Recipient Richard Tucker award. Mem. AFTRA, Am. Guild Musical Artists, SAG. Office: Columbia Artists Zemsky Green Div 165 W 57th St New York NY 10019-2201 Office: care Royal Opera House-Contracts, Convent Gardens, London WC2, England*

SOVIERO, JOSEPH C., chemical company executive; b. 1938. BS, Polytech. Inst. Bklyn., 1960; MS, NYU, 1965. With Union Carbide Corp., Danbury, Conn., 1965—, corporate v.p. Office: Union Carbide Corp 39 Old Ridgebury Rd Danbury CT 06810-5108

SOVIK, EDWARD ANDERS, architect, consultant; b. Honan, China, June 9, 1918; s. Edward Anderson and Anna (Tenwick) S.; m. Genevieve Elaine Hendrickson, June 29, 1946; children: Rolf, Martin, Peter. BA, St. Olaf Coll., 1939; student, Art Students League N.Y., 1939-40, Luther Theol. Sem., 1940-42; MArch, Yale U., 1949; DFA (hon.), Concordia Coll., 1981. Ret. chmn. SMSQ, Architects and predecessors, Northfield, Minn.; prof. art emeritus St. Olaf Coll., Northfield; lectr. on ch. design at various confs., schs., univs.; participant, planner, del. numerous domestic and fgn. confs. on religion and architecture; mem., officer various profl., religious and pub. bds. and commns. Author: Architecture for Worship; Contbr. numerous articles to mags., anthologies.; works include chs., coll. and univ. bldgs., instns. With USMC, 1942-45; maj. Res. Decorated D.F.C., Purple Heart, Air medal. Fellow AIA; mem. AIA Minn. (pres. 1977, Gold medal 1981), Phi Beta Kappa. Republican. Lutheran. Home: 711 Summit Ave Northfield MN 55057-1568

SOWADA, ALPHONSE AUGUSTUS, bishop; b. Avon, Minn., June 23, 1933; s. Alphonse B. and Monica (Pierskalla) S. Student, Onamia (Minn.) Sem., 1947-53; grad., Crosier House of Studies, Ft. Wayne, Ind., 1959; M.A., Cath. U. Am., 1961. Ordained priest Roman Cath. Ch., 1958; arrived in Irian Jaya to work among Asmat, 1961, selected as mission superior, 1966; ordained bishop Diocese Agats-Asmat, 1969—; mem. exec. com. Indonesian Conf. of Bishops, 1991—. Contbr. to: Nat. Geog. Yearbook, 1968, other publs. Mem. Order of Alhambra, Crosier Order, Kappa Delta Gamma. Office: Kantor Keuskupan Agats, Asmat Agats 99677, Irian Jaya Indonesia*

SOWALSKY, PATTI LURIE, author; b. Hartford, Conn., Oct. 16, 1940; d. Joseph Aaron and Mildred (Weisinger) Lurie; m. Jerome Saul Sowalsky, Oct. 22, 1961; children: Richard, John, Susan. Cert. dental hygiene, U. Pa., 1960. Author, publisher On Exhibit Fine Art Publs., Potomac, Md., 1992—. Author, publisher: (art travel guide) On Exhibit: The Art Lover's Travel Guide to American Museums, 1992-96. Docent Corcoran Mus., Washington, 1985-90; cert. in Braille, Libr. of Congress, Washington, Golden Circle mem. Kennedy Ctr., Washington, 1988—. Recipient Docent of Yr. award Corcoran Mus., Washington, 1989. Avocations: art collector, rosearian. Home: 8613 Chateau Dr Potomac MD 20854 Office: On Exhibit Fine Art Publs PO Box 59734 Potomac MD 20859

SOWD, DAVID HOWARD, writer; b. Canton, Ohio, Jan. 15, 1946; s. William Howard and Ruth Geiger (Smith) S.; m. Judith Ann Kovacs, Sept. 16, 1967 (div. May 1980); children: Aaron, Hannah. BA in Philosophy, Ohio State U., 1967; MA in English, Kent State U., 1970; PhD in English, Bowling Geen State U., 1973. Clk. U.S. Postal Svc., Canton, Ohio, 1974-81; instr. Kent State U. and U. Akron, Ohio, 1981-84; libr., br. head Stark County Dist. Libr., Canton, 1984-87; reporter The Plain Dealer, Cleve., 1987-91; mem. mktg. com. Ohio Ballet, Akron, 1989-90; cons. Booksellers, Cleve., 1991-93. Free-lance writer Cleve. Plain Dealer, Cleve. Mag., Radio World, Libr. Jour., 1984—, Akron Beacon Jour., Scene Entertainment Weekly, Sun Newspapers, Akron and Cleve., 1991—; reviewer books. Sigma Delta Chi scholar, 1963-67. Mem. Cleve. Music Group (bd. dirs. 1989), Stark County Arab-Am. Assn. (sec. 1987), Canton Fedn. Musicians, Soc. Profl. Journalists, Jazz Journalists Assn., Press Club Cleve. Home and Office: 1309 Fulton Rd NW Apt 5 Canton OH 44703-1430

SOWDER, DONALD DILLARD, chemicals executive; b. Rocky Mt., Va., Mar. 28, 1937; s. Roman Dillard and Virginia (Dowdy) S.; m. Beverly Reid, Nov. 29, 1957; children: Reid Dillard, Susan Allison, Donald Stuart. BS, Va. Tech., 1959; cert. in sales mgmt., Columbia U., 1976, cert. in fin., 1984; diploma, U.S. Army Command & Gen. Staff Coll., 1978; cert. in mgmt., U. Va., 1993. Sales rep. Sealtest Foods, Norfolk, Va., 1962-64; med. sales rep. Lederle Labs. div. Am. Cyanamid Co., Norfolk, 1964-69; dist. sales mgr. Lederle Labs. div. Am. Cyanamid Co., Washington, 1969-74; nat. mgr. sales tng. Lederle Labs. div. Am. Cyanamid Co., Pearl River, N.Y., 1974-76; mgr. fed. govt. affairs Lederle Labs. div. Am. Cyanamid Co., Washington, 1976-81; nat. sales mgr. hosp. div. Lederle Labs. div. Am. Cyanamid Co., Wayne, N.J., 1981-85, nat. sales mgr. oncology div., 1985-88; dir. govt. sales Lederle Labs. div. Am. Cyanamid Co., Fairfax, Va., 1988-95; pharmaceutical mktg. cons., 1995—; instr. U.S. Army Command & Gen. Staff Coll., Washington, 1977-81; govt. sales advisor Nat. Wholesale Drug Assn., Alexandria, Va., 1991; mem. Health Industry Fed. Adv. Coun., 1994. Editorial reviewer Mil. Medicine, 1992—; contbr. articles to profl. jours. Bd. dirs. Shadow Walk Devel. Assn., 1990—. Col. USAR. Instr. of Yr. USAR, 1979. Mem. Assn. Mil. Surgeons U.S. (chmn. sustaining mems. 1980-81, lectr. 1989), Am. Soc. Hosp. Pharmacists, Res. Officers Assn., Va. Tech. Corps of Cadets Alumni Assn. (bd. dirs.), Mil. Dist. of Washington Officers Club System. Republican. Methodist. Avocations: golf, tennis, water sports. Home and Office: 10415 Dominion Valley Dr Fairfax VA 22039-2415

SOWDER, FRED ALLEN, foundation administrator, alphabet specialist; b. Cin., July 17, 1940; s. William Franklin and Lucille (Estes) S.; m. Sandra Ann Siegman, July 15, 1961 (div. Sept. 1963); 1 child, William. Student, Cin. Sch. Ct. Reporting, 1975; diploma Self-Health Insts., Sch. of Med. Masso-Therapy, 1985; diploma, Cin. Sch. Hypnosis, 1989. Founder World Union Universal Alphabet, Cin., 1981—, Internat. Assn. Sch. Massage, Cin., 1988—. Inventor of hundreds of published and unpublished alphabets and writing systems, including light wave, color and musical tone systems and tactile systems for the blind; author: Sowder Shorthand, 1980, Universal Alphabet: What and Why, 1981, Your Intimacy Quotient: The Symptoms, Causes & Consequences of Intimacy Deprivation, 1996; contbr. numerous articles to mags. State dir. Soc. Separationists, Cin., 1967-70; bd. dirs. ACLU of Ohio, ACLU Found., 1984-89, sec., Cin. chpt., 1984-89. Mem. AAAS, Amnesty Internat., Ohio Com. to Abolish Capital Punishment, Assn. for Humanistic Psychology, Internat. Soc. for Gen. Semantics, Am. Sunbathing Assn., The Naturist Soc., Am. Massage Therapy Assn., Urban Appalachian Coun. Democrat. Home: PO Box 252 Cincinnati OH 45201-0252 Office: World Union Universal Alphabet PO Box 252 Cincinnati OH 45201-0252

SOWDER, ROBERT ROBERTSON, architect; b. Kansas City, Kans., Dec. 29, 1928; s. James Robert and Agnes (Robertson) S.; m. Joan Goddard, July 26, 1954; 1 dau., Lisa Robertson Lee. B.A., U. Wash., 1953; B.Arch., U. Va., 1958; grad. diploma in Architecture, Ecole Des Beaux Arts, Fontainebleau, France, 1952. Designer Architects Collaborative, Boston, 1958-59, Peirce & Pierce (architects), Boston, 1959-63; asso. Fred. Bassetti & Co. (architects), Seattle, 1963-67; partner Naramore, Bain, Brady & Johanson (architects), Seattle, 1967-81; pres. NBBJ Internat., 1976-81; architect TRA, Seattle, 1981-83; v.p. Daniel, Mann, Johnson & Mendenhall, San Francisco, 1983-93; prin. RRS Consulting, 1993—; archtl. design critic Boston Archtl. Ctr., 1961-62. Important works include Ridgeway III Dormitories, Bellingham, Wash. (Dept. Housing and Urban Devel. Honor award), Seattle Rapid Transit (HUD Excellence award), Safeco Ins. Co. Home Office Complex, Seattle, King County Stadium, Balt. Conv. Ctr., Oreg. Conv. Ctr., San Francisco (Moscone) Conv. Ctr. Expansion, Honolulu Conv. Ctr., Wilmington (Del.) Conv. Ctr. Served with CIC U.S. Army, 1954-56. Recipient Premier Prix D'Architecture Ecole Des Beaux Arts, Fontainebleau, 1951, 52, Prix D'Remondet Fontainebleau, 1952. Mem. AIA, Internat. Assn. Assembly Mgrs., Seattle Tennis Club, Scarab, Sigma Chi. Episcopalian. Home and Office: 17032 NE 135th Ct Redmond WA 98052-1715

SOWERS, WESLEY HOYT, lawyer, management consultant; b. Whiting, Ind., Aug. 26, 1905; s. Samuel Walter and Bertha E. (Spurrier) S.; m. Gladys Krueger, Jan. 21, 1929; children: Penny (Mrs. David Buxton), Wesley Hoyt. BS, Purdue U., 1926, MS, 1927; JD, DePaul U., 1941; grad., Advanced Mgmt. Program, Harvard, 1960. Bar: Ill. 1940; registered patent atty. and practitioner ICC. Chemist Shell Oil Co., East Chicago, Ind., 1927-29; sales engr. Nat. Lead Co., St. Louis, 1929-31; lab. supr. patent atty. Pure Oil Co., Chgo., 1932-42; v.p. Bay Chem. Co., New Orleans, 1942-50, Frontier Chem. Co., Wichita, Kans., 1950-57; pres. Frontier Chem. div. Vulcan Materials Co., 1957-65; exec. v.p., dir. Vulcan Materials Co., Birmingham, 1958-65; mgmt. counsel, 1965—; mem. health professions vis. com. Wichita State U. Patentee in field. Past chmn. Met. Planning Commn., Wichita and Sedgwick County, 1958; commr. Kans. Econ. Devel. Bd.; chmn. Kansas Com. for Constitutional Revision, Sedgwick County U.S. Savs. Bonds Sales; past chmn. Kans. Radio Free Europe; past mem. adv. com. Kans. Geol. Survey; mem. Kans. Senate, 1970-81; former mem. engring. adv. council Sch. Engring. and Architecture, Kans. State U.; regent, trustee Wichita State U., HCA/Wesley Med. Ctr., Wichita; bd. dirs. Health Systems Agy. of Southeast Kans., Bd. of Health Sedgwick County, Inst. Logopedics, Quivira council Boy Scouts Am., YMCA, Health Systems Agy. S.E. Kans.; past trustee Midwest Research Inst.; mem. adv. bd. Kans. U. Bus. Sch.; vis. com. Coll. Health Profession, Wichita State U.; chmn. Kans. Health Care Providers Malpractice Commn.; mem. Kans. Health Care Costs Commn., Kans. Health Coordinating Council, Wichita/Sedgwick County Bd. Health; mem. gov.'s adv. commn. Kans. Dept. Health and Environment. Mem. AAAS, Kans. C. of C. (past pres., past dir.), Wichita C. of C. (past pres. 1959, past dir., Uncommon Citizen award 1988), Kans. Assn. Commerce and Industry (past pres., dir.), Am. Chem. Soc., AAAS, Smithsonian Assocs., Soc. Chem. Industry, Ill. Bar Assn., Wichita Bar Assn., Phi Delta Theta. Lodge: Rotary. Home and Office: care Canterbury Assisted Liv Ctr 1402 NW 122nd St Oklahoma City OK 73114

SOWERS, WILLIAM ARMAND, civil engineer; b. Willis, Va., Apr. 23, 1923; s. Harry Cline and Effie Vivian (Slusher) S.; m. Gale Johnson, May 20, 1978; children: Jane Dixon, Jean Marie. Student, Roanoke Coll., 1940-42; BCE, Va. Poly. Inst., 1947, BS in Archtl. Engring., 1948. Registered profl. engr., Va. Assoc. Brown, Wells & Meagher, Roanoke, Va., 1948-50; ptnr. R.L. Brown and Assocs., Roanoke, 1950-53, Sowers, Knowles & Rodes, Roanoke, 1953-59, Sowers, Rodes & Whitescarver, Roanoke, 1959-84, Sowers & Assocs., Roanoke, 1984-94; DJG Sowers, Mann Sowers-Mann, Roanoke, 1994-96; McKinney, Sowers-Mann, 1996—. Trustee ACEC Health Life Ins., St. Louis, 1975-83; commr. city planning City of Roanoke, 1976-92. Mem. Am. Cons. Engrs. (nat. pres. 1970-72), Cons. Engrs. Coun. Va. (svc. award 1972), Va. Soc. Profl. Engrs. (Svc. to Profession award 1972), Illuminating Engring. Soc., Hunting Hills Country Club, Masons. Office: PO Box 4038 Roanoke VA 24015-0038

SOWLE, DONALD EDGAR, management consultant; b. Mt. Pleasant, Mich., May 27, 1915; s. Sidney Edgar and Mary Agnes (West) S.; m. Gretchen Elizabeth MacRae, July 4, 1942 (dec. Feb. 1993); children: Lisa Sowle Cahill, Mary Ann Sowle Messing; m. Catherine Taggart Lewis, Nov. 25, 1995. B.S., Central Mich. U., 1940; postgrad., Harvard U., 1942, M.I.T., 1942; M.B.A., U. Chgo., 1950. Sales rep. Armour & Co., Grand Rapids, Mich., 1940-41; commd. 2d lt. USAF, advanced through grades to col., 1958; asst. dir. Jet Propulsion Lab., Calif. Inst. Tech., Pasadena, 1965-68; group v.p. Gulf & Western Industries, Los Angeles, 1968-69; dir. studies Congl. Commn. on Govt. Procurement, Washington, 1970-73; pres., chmn. bd. dirs. Don Sowle Assocs., Inc., Arlington, Va., 1973-81; adminstr. Fed. Procurement Policy, Exec. Office of The Pres. of The U.S., Washington, 1981-85; mgmt. cons., 1985—; dir. Procurement Round Table, 1985; mem. adv. bd. Fed. Contracts Report, Bur. Nat. Affairs, 1965-91; nat. regent Inst. Cost Analysis, 1981; instr. Georgetown U., 1961-65; adj. prof. and mem. adv. council procurement mgmt. program Kogod Coll. Am. U., Washington. Mem. adv. coun. Sch. Bus. Marymount U., 1985-94. Recipient Dept. Def. Joint Svc. Commendation medal, 1963, Legion of Merit award Sec. Def., 1964, Pub. Svc. award Los Angeles County, 1969, award Cen. Mich. U., 1968, 92. Fellow Nat. Contract Mgmt. Assn. (cert. profl. contract mgr., bd. advisers, Herbert Roback Meml. award 1990); mem. U.S. C. of C. (procurement coun. 1985), Nat. Security Indsl. Assn. (hon. life), Nat. Assn. Uniforms Svcs. (life mem., bd. dirs. 1984-88), Ret. Officers Assn. (life), Ronald Regan Alumni Assn., Am. Legion, Capitol Hill Club, Officers Club, NASA Alumni League, Beta Gamma Sigma. Republican. Roman Catholic. Home: 2795 N Quebec St Arlington VA 22207

SOWMAN, HAROLD GENE, ceramic engineer, researcher; b. Murphysboro, Ill., July 21, 1923; s. Harold Thomas and Thelma (Crombar) S.; m. Gladys May Wright, Dec. 8, 1945; children—Letitia Ann, Daniel Patrick. B.S. in Ceramic Engring., U. Ill., 1948, M.S. in Ceramic Engring., 1949, Ph.D. in Ceramic Engring., 1951. Assoc. ceramist Titanium Alloy, Niagara Falls, N.Y., 1951-52; research assoc. Knolls Atomic Power Lab., Gen. Electric Co., Schenectady, 1952-57; various supervisory and mgmt. positions in nuclear materials research and devel. 3M Co., St. Paul, 1957-65; research specialist 3M Co., 1965-67, sr. research specialist, 1967-70, corp. scientist, 1970-87; Friedberg Meml. lectr. Nat. Inst. Ceramic Engrs., 1988. Author articles, govt. reports on research and devel. of ceramic and nuclear materials; patentee in field. Served to 2d lt. AUS, 1943-46. Recipient Hon. Alumni award for disting. service in engring. U. Ill. Coll. Engring., 1983. Fellow Am. Ceramic Soc. (John Jeppson medal 1985, Samuel Geijsbeek award 1989); mem. Nat. Acad. Engring., Acad. of Ceramics, 3M Carlton Soc., Sigma Xi, Tau Beta Pi (chpt. Eminent Engr. award 1983). Home: 855 Towne Cir Stillwater MN 55082-4131

SOX, HAROLD CARLETON, JR., physician, educator; b. Palo Alto, Calif., Aug. 18, 1939; s. Harold Carleton and Mary (Griffiths) S.; m. Carol Helen Hill, Aug. 26, 1962; children: Colin Montgomery, Lara Katherine. BS, Stanford U., 1961; MD cum laude, Harvard U., 1966. Diplomate Am. Bd. Internal Medicine (pretest writing com. 1992-94). Intern and resident Mass. Gen. Hosp., Boston, 1966-68; clin. assoc. Nat. Cancer Inst., Bethesda, Md., 1968-70; instr. Dartmouth Med. Sch., Hanover, N.H., 1970-73; asst. prof. medicine to prof. Stanford U. Sch. Medicine, Calif., 1973-88; Joseph Huber prof., chmn. dept. medicine Dartmouth Med. Sch., 1988—; panel mem. Nat. Bd. Med. Examiners, Physicians Assts. Nat. Certifying Exam., 1973-76, chair com. on priority-setting for health tech. assessment Inst. Medicine, 1990-91, chair U.S. preventive svcs. task force, 1990-95, chair Inst. Medicine com. on HIV and U.S. blood supply, 1994-95; chair task force to revise internal medicine residency curriculum Federated Coun. Internal Medicine, 1993-97. Author: Medical Decision Making, 1988; editor: Common Diagnostic Tests, 1987, 2d edit., 1990; mem. editorial bd. Med. Decision Making, 1980-87, Jour. Gen. Internal Medicine, 1985-87, New Eng. Jour. Medicine, 1990-97; cons. assoc. editor Am. Jour. Medicine, 1988-95; assoc. editor Sci. Am. Medicine, 1995—; contbr. chpts. to books and articles to profl. jours. Fellow ACP (clin. efficacy assessment subcom. 1985-92, bd. regents, 1991—, chmn. ednl. policy com. 1994—, pres.-elect 1997—); mem. Soc. for Gen. Internal Medicine (coun. 1980-83), Soc. for Med. Decision Making (trustee 1980-83, pres. 1983-84), Am. Fedn. Clin. Rsch., Assn. Am. Physicians, Assn. Profs. Medicine (bd. dirs. 1996—), Inst. Medicine of NAS, Alpha Omega Alpha. Home: Faraway Ln Hanover NH 03755-2312 Office: Darthmouth-Hitchcock Med Ctr Dept Lebanon NH 03756

SOXMAN, JANE ANN, pediatric dentist; b. Pitts., Aug. 19, 1948; d. Don Germain and Rose Bayonne (Dunkel) S.; m. John F. Buzzatto, Apr. 28, 1984; children: Zachary Harrison, Bailey Ann. BS cum laude, U. Rochester, 1970; DDS, Med. Coll. Va., 1980; Cert., Children's Hosp. Pitts., 1983. RN, N.Y.; Diplomate Am. Bd. Pediat. Dentistry. Nurse ICU Strong Meml. Hosp., Rochester, N.Y., 1970-71; flight attendant Pan Am. World Airways, Washington, 1971-74; nurse ICU/CCU St. Mary's Hosp., Richmond, Va., 1972-80; faculty mem. Med. Coll. Va. Sch. Dentistry, Richmond, 1980-81; resident in pediat. dentistry Children's Hosp. Pitts., 1981-83; pvt. practice Allison Park, Pa., 1983—; staff mem. Children's Hosp. Pitts., 1984—; spkr., writer in field. Author, prodr.: (video) Prenatal and Infant Dental Care, 1995; radio and TV appearances, 1997; author numerous poems. Religious edn. tchr. St. Mary's Ch., Glenshaw, Pa., 1995—. Named one of Outstanding Young Women of Am., 1983. Mem. ADA, Am. Acad. Pediat. Dentistry, Tri-State Acad. Pediat. Dentists, Pa. Dental Assn., Dental Soc. Western Pa., Sigma Zeta. Avocations: dance, tennis, horseback riding. Office: 3960 William Flynn Hwy Allison Park PA 15101-3603

SOYER, DAVID, cellist, music educator; b. Phila., Feb. 24, 1923; s. Samson and Esther (Faggin) S.; m. Janet Putnam, June 23, 1957; children: Daniel, Jeffrey. Student pub. schs., N.Y.C.; D.F.A. (hon.), U. South Fla., 1976, SUNY, 1983. Prof. cello Curtis Inst. Music, 1967; prof. music U. Md. Cellist with, Bach Aria Group, 1948-49, Guilet Quartet, 1949-51, New Music Quartet, 1954-55, Guarneri String Quartet, N.Y.C., 1964—, (Recipient 5 Grammy awards for Guarneri Quartet recs. 1965-74). Served with USNR, 1942-46. Mem. Century Assn. Jewish. Home: 6 W 77th St New York NY 10024-5125 also: RR 4 Box 903 Brattleboro VT 05301-9512 Office: Herbert Barrett Mgmt care H Beall Mgmt 1776 Broadway New York NY 10019-2002

SOYKE, JENNIFER MAE, emergency and family physician; b. McKeesport, Pa., Feb. 2, 1952; d. Edgar Arthur and Phyllis Jean (Parks) S.; m. Jeff Willensky, Sept. 25, 1977; 1 child, Jordana Soyke-Willensky. BA in Biology, U. Oreg., 1983; MD, Oreg. Health Scis. U., 1988. Diplomate Am. Bd. Family Practice. Resident Madigan Army Med. Ctr., Tacoma, Wash., 1988-91; staff physican U.S. Army Blanchfield Army Cmty. Hosp., Fort Campbell, Ky., 1991-95; pvt. practice Springfield, Oreg., 1995-96; with Good Shepherd Cmty. Hosp. Emergency Dept., Hermiston, Oreg., 1996-97, Cottage Grove Hosp. Emergency Dept., 1997—; chair family practice quality improvement Blanchfield Army Cmty. Hosp., Fort Campbell, 1992-94; White Primary Care Clinic, 1993-95, patient edn. coord., 1993-95; emergency room part-time, Smith County Meml. Hosp., Carthage, Tenn., 1992-95, Sumner Regional Med. Ctr., Gallatin, Tenn., 1992-95, Trinity Hosp., Erin, Tenn., 1994-95; staff physician Miller Med Group and Edgefield Hosp., Nashville, part time emergency rm., urgent care clinic, 1992. Contbr. articles to profl. jours. Chair, bd. dirs. Amazon Coop. Pre-sch. Amazon U. of Oreg. Housing, Eugene, 1981-82; mem. bd. dirs. and newsletter editor Lake Louise Elem. Sch. Parent Tchr. Student Assn., 1989-90. Major U.S. Army Med. Corps, 1988-95. Recipient Nurses Choice award Dept. Family Practice, Madigan Army Med. Ctr., 1989; Mead Johnson award for excellence in family practice, 1990. Fellow Am. Acad. Family Physicians (many coms., chair com. on spl. constituencies 1996, convenor nat. conf. of women, minority and new physicians, 1996; also active during residency and student period); mem. AMA, (alt. del. to young physician sect. 1993, Army del. to young physician sect. 1993, 94, Am. Acad. Family Physicians del. to young physician sect. 1995, 96), Oreg. Acad. Family Physicians (bd. dirs. student mem. 1985-86), Doctors Ought to Care (founding mem. Oreg. chpt. 1987-88, bd. trustees Wash. chpt. 1989-91), Uniformed Svcs. Acad. Family Physicians (chair membership com. 1993-95). Avocations: family time, gardening, rosaria, walking, reading.

SOYSTER, MARGARET BLAIR, lawyer; b. Washington, Aug. 5, 1951; d. Peter and Eliza (Shumaker) S. AB magna cum laude, Smith Coll., 1973; JD, U. Va., 1976. Bar: N.Y. 1977, U.S. Dist. Ct. (so. and ea. dists.) N.Y. 1977, U.S. Ct. Appeals (2nd cir.) 1979, U.S. Supreme Ct. 1981, U.S. Ct. Appeals (4th cir.) 1982, U.S. ct. Appeals (11th cir.) 1987, U.S. Ct. Appeals (7th cir.) 1991, U.S. Ct. Appeals (3d cir.) 1992. Assoc. Rogers & Wells, N.Y.C., 1976-84, ptnr., 1984—. Mem. ABA, Assn. of Bar of City of N.Y., Nat. Assn. Coll. and Univ. Attys., Phi Beta Kappa. Office: Rogers & Wells 200 Park Ave Ste 5200 New York NY 10166-0005

SOZEN, METE AVNI, civil engineering educator; b. Turkey, May 22, 1930; m. Joan Bates; children: Timothy, Adria, Ayshe. BCE, Roberts Coll., Turkey, 1951; MCE, U. Ill., 1952, PhD in Civil Engring., 1957; hon. doctorate, Bogazici U., Istanbul, Turkey, 1988. Registered structural engr., Ill. Jr. engr. Kaiser Engrs., Oakland, Calif., 1952; structural engr. Hardesty and Hanover, N.Y.C., 1953; research asst. civil engring. U. Ill., Urbana, 1953-55, research assoc., 1955-57, asst. prof. civil engring., 1957-59, assoc. prof., 1959-63, prof., 1963-94; prof. Purdue U., 1994—; cons. problems related to earthquake-resistant constrn. VA, various firms Europe, S.Am., U.S., UNESCO, UN Devel. Programs; cons. criteria for mass housing projects P.R.; adv. com. structural safety VA, rsch. project NSF, Applied Tech. Coun., Los Alamos and Sandia Nat. Labs.; chief investigator various NSF contracts and grants. Contbr. over 125 tech. papers, monographs, procs., reports to profl. jours.; presenter numerous papers to profl. meetings U.S.A, Japan, Italy, India, Turkey, Mexico. Recipient Drucker award U. Ill., 1986, Howard award, 1987, Boase award, 1988, Parlar Sci. and Tech. prize Mid. East Tech. U., Ankara, Turkey, 1995. Mem. NAE, ASCE (hon., Rsch. prize 1963, Raymond C. Reese award 1971, 94, Moiseiff award 1972, Howard award 1987, Raymond C. Reese Rsch. award 1994), Am. Concrete Inst. (Kelly award 1975, Bloem award 1985, Lindau award 1993), Am. Arbitration Assn. (nat. panel) Seismological Soc. Am., Swedish Royal Acad. Engring. Office: Purdue Univ Sch of Civil Engring 4149 Civil Engring Bldg West Lafayette IN 47907-1284

SPACE, THEODORE MAXWELL, lawyer; b. Binghamton, N.Y., Apr. 3, 1938; s. Maxwell Evans and Dorothy Marie (Boone) S.; m. Susan Shultz, Aug. 18, 1962 (div. Apr. 1979); children: William Schuyler, Susanna; m. Martha Collins, Apr. 6, 1991. AB, Harvard U., 1960; LLB, Yale U., 1966. Bar: Conn., 1966, U.S. Dist. Ct. Conn., U.S. Tax Ct., U.S. Ct. Appeals (2d, 6th and 11th cirs.), U.S. Ct. Appeals. Assoc. Shipman & Goodwin, Hartford, Conn., 1966-71, ptnr., 1971—, mng. ptnr., 1984-87, adminstv. ptnr., 1988-91. Mem. Bloomfield (Conn.) Bd. Edn., 1973-85, chmn., 1975-85; treas. Citizens Scholarship Found., Bloomfield, 1971-73, bd. dirs., 1973-91; mem. Bloomfield Human Rels. Commn., 1973-75; mem. Bloomfield Town Dem. Com., 1976-83; corporator Hartford Pub. Libr., 1976—; libr. com. Conn. Hist. Soc., 1990—, chair, 1993—; chair fin. com., coun. mem. Unitarian Soc. Hartford, 1988-91. Lt. (j.g.) USN, 1960-63. Mem. ABA, Conn. Bar Assn. (exec. com. adminstrv. law sect. 1980—), Hartford County Bar Assn., Am. Law Inst., Nat. Health Lawyers Assn., Conn. Health Lawyers Assn., Swift's Inn, Hartford Club. Democrat. Unitarian Universalist. Avocations: reading, classical music. Home: 59 Prospect St Bloomfield CT 06002-3038 Office: Shipman & Goodwin One American Row Hartford CT 06103-2833

SPACEK, SISSY (MARY ELIZABETH SPACEK), actress; b. Quitman, Tex., Dec. 25, 1949; d. Edwin S. and Virginia S.; m. Jack Fisk, 1974; children: Schuyler Elizabeth, Virginia Madison. Student, Lee Strasberg Theatrical Inst. Motion picture appearances include Prime Cut, 1972, Ginger in the Morning, 1972, Badlands, 1974, Carrie, 1976 (Acad. award nomination for best actress 1976), Three Women, 1977, Welcome to L.A., 1977, Heartbeat, 1980, Coal Miner's Daughter, 1980 (Acad. award for best actress 1980), Raggedy Man, 1981, Missing, 1982 (Acad. award nomination for best actress), The River, 1984 (Acad. award nomination for best actress), Marie, 1985, 'Night Mother, 1986, Crimes of the Heart, 1986 (Acad. award nomination for best actress), Violets Are Blue, 1986, JFK, 1991, The Long Walk Home, 1990, Hard Promises, 1992, Trading Mom, 1994, The Grass Harp, 1995, Streets of Laredo, 1995, If These Walls Could Talk, 1996; TV movie appearances include The Girls of Huntington House, 1973, The Migrants, 1973, Katherine, 1975, Verna: USO Girl, 1978, A Private Matter, 1992, A Place for Annie, 1994, The Good Old Boys, 1995; guest host TV show Saturday Night Live, 1977; appeared in episode TV show The Waltons. Named Best Actress for Carrie, Nat. Soc. Film Critics, 1976, Best Supporting Actress, N.Y. Film Critics, 1977. Office: care Creative Artists 9830 Wilshire Blvd Beverly Hills CA 90212-1804

SPACEY, KEVIN, actor; b. South Orange, N.J., July 26, 1959. Student, Juilliard Sch., 1979-81. Stage appearances include Henry IV, part I, 1981, Barbarians, 1982, Hurlyburly, 1985, Long Days Journey into Night, 1986, National Anthems, 1988, Lost in Yonkers, 1991 (Tony award for Best Featured Actor, 1991, Drama Desk award, 1991), Playland, 1993; TV appearances include (series) Wiseguy, 1987-88, (films) The Murder of Mary Phagan, 1988, Will You Remember Me, 1990, Fall From Grace, 1990, Darrow, 1991; films include Heartburn, 1986, Working Girl, 1988, Rocket Gibraltar, 1988, Dad, 1989, See No Evil, Hear No Evil, 1989, A Show of Force, 1990, Henry and June, 1990, Glengarry Glen Ross, 1991, Consenting Adults, 1992, The Ref, 1994, Outbreak, 1995, Swimming With Sharks, 1995, The Usual Suspects, 1995 (Acad. award for best supporting actor 1996), Seven, 1995. Office: Altman Greenfield & Selvaje 36th Fl 120 W 45th St Fl 36 New York NY 10036-4041

SPACH, JULE CHRISTIAN, church executive; b. Winston-Salem, N.C., Dec. 21, 1923; s. Jule Christian and Margaret Stockton (Coyner) S.; m. Nancy Clendenin, Sept. 18, 1948; children: Nancy Lynn Lane, Margaret Cunningham, Ann Thomerson, Cecelia Welborn, Robert. Student, Va. Mil. Inst., 1942-43; BSChemE, Ga. Inst. Tech., 1949; postgrad., Union Theol. Sem., Richmond, Va., 1951-52, Duke U., 1955-56; MA in Ednl. Adminstrn., U. N.C., Greensboro, 1976; LHD (hon.), Stillman Coll., Tuscaloosa, Ala., 1977; LittD (hon.), Belhaven Coll., Jackson, Miss., 1977; LLD, King Coll., Bristol, Tenn., 1977. Salesman Mengle Corp. subs. Internat. Container Corp., Winston-Salem, 1950-52; from prof. scis., athletic dir. to pres. Quinze de Novembro Coll., Garanhuns, Pernanbuco, Brazil, 1952-64; edn. dir. Cruzada ABC-Recife, Pernanbuco, 1965-70; pres. Cruzada ABC-Recife, 1969-70; exec. sec. Parliamentary Christian Leadership, Brasilia, Fed. Dist., Brazil, 1970-73; exec. dir. Presbyn. Mission in Brazil, Campinas, Sao Paulo, 1973-75; moderator Gen. Assembly of Presbyn. Ch. in U.S., Atlanta, 1976-77; exec. dir. Triad United Meth. Home, Inc., Winston-Salem, 1977—; dir. First Home Fed. Savs. and Loan. Author: (biography) Every Road Leads Home. Bd. dirs. Instituto Gammon, Presbyn. Ch. U.S., Forsyth County Coun. on Aging Forsyth County Sr. Svcs. Forsyth County, Covenent Fellowship of Presbyns., William Black Lodge, Synod of N.C., Presbyn. Ch. U.S.A.; bd. visitors Lee's McRae Coll., Montreat Anderson Coll.; mem. cabinet United Way, 1987; chmn. Winston-Salem Forsyth County Coun. on Svcs. to Homeless; chmn. bd. dirs. Sr. Svcs., Inc., Winston-Salem. With USAAF, 1943-45, prisoner of war, Poland. Decorated Purple Heart; recipient Jefferson award, 1991. Mem. Sertoma Club (3 Svc. awards), Lions, Rotary. Republican. Home: Arbor Acres 1244 Arbor Rd Apt 197 Winston Salem NC 27104 Office: 1240 Arbor Rd Winston Salem NC 27104 *The Christian faith teaches us that the greatest of all gifts is love. This gift comes from God, and it is ours through the presence of His spirit dwelling in us. This love gives man peace within and with his fellow man.*

SPACH, MADISON STOCKTON, cardiologist; b. Winston-Salem, N.C., Nov. 10, 1926; s. Jule Christian and Margaret (Stockton) S.; m. Cecilia Goodson, June 25, 1949; children: Madison Jr., Joyce, Susan, David. AB, Duke U., 1950, MD, 1954. Diplomate Am. Bd. Pediatrics, Am. Bd. Pediatric Cardiology. Intern and resident dept. pediatrics Duke U., Durham, N.C., 1954-57, resident, 1955-56, fellow cardiology, 1956-57; prof. pediatrics Duke U. Sch. Medicine, Durham, N.C., 1968—, James B. Duke prof. pediatrics, 1977, prof. physiology, 1978-88, chief pediatric cardiology, 1986-91, prof. cell biology, 1988—; pres. Soc. for Pediatric Rsch., 1974; chmn. Sub-Board of Pediatric Cardiology, 1975-77, Nat. Heart, Lung, Blood Inst. Manpower Com., 1982-85. Author 167 published papers on cardiovascular rsch.; mem. editorial bd. Circulation, 1981-91. With USN, 1944-46, PTO. Fellow Am. Coll. Cardiology, Am. Inst. for Med. and Biomed. Engring.; mem. N.Y. Acad. Scis., Internat. Soc. for Heart Rsch. (Am. sect.), Am. Physiol. Soc., Phi Beta Kappa, Alpha Omega Alpha. Democrat. Presbyterian. Office: Duke U Sch Medicine PO Box 3475 Durham NC 27702-3475

SPACKMAN, THOMAS JAMES, radiologist; b. Oak Park, Ill., Apr. 24, 1937; s. Thomas Frederick and Louise Mary (Kaiser) S.; m. Donna S. Stewart, June 25, 1960; children—Kirsten, Thomas James, Victoria. BA, DePauw U., 1959; MD, Western Res. U., 1964; Diploma in Bus. Studies, London Sch. Econs., 1987. Intern, then resident in internal medicine Yale-New Haven Med. Center, 1964-66, resident in diagnostic radiology, 1966-68, fellow clin. research tng. unit, 1968-69; instr., then asst. prof. radiology Yale U. Med. Sch., 1969-74; asso. prof. U. Pa. Med. Sch., 1974-78; prof. radiology U. Conn. Med. Sch., Farmington, 1978—; head dept. U. Conn. Med. Sch., 1978-90; dir. radiology St. Francis Hosp. and Med. Ctr., Hartford, Conn., 1992-93; pres. Elscint, Inc., Hackensack, N.J., 1993—; sr. v.p. Elscint, Ltd., Haifa, Israel, 1993—; mem. Conn. Med. Exam. Bd., 1980-86; bd. dirs. Elscint, Inc. Mem. editorial adv. bd. Diagnostic Imaging, 1989-92; author articles in field, chpts. in books. Fellow Am. Coll. Radiology; mem. AMA, Assn. Univ. Radiologists, Soc. Pediatric Radiology, Radiol. Soc. N.J. Office: Elscint Inc 505 Main St Hackensack NJ 07601-5900

SPACKS, PATRICIA MEYER, English educator; b. San Francisco, Nov. 17, 1929; d. Norman B. and Lillian (Talcott) Meyer; 1 child, Judith Elizabeth Spacks. BA, Rollins Coll., Winter Park, Fla., 1949, DHL, 1976; MA, Yale U., 1950; PhD, U. Calif., Berkeley, 1955. Instr. English Ind. U., Bloomington, 1954-56; instr. humanities U. Fla., Gainesville, 1958-59; from instr. to prof. Wellesley Coll., Mass., 1959-79; prof. English Yale U., New Haven, 1979-89, chmn. dept., 1985-88; Edgar F. Shannon prof. English U. Va., 1989—, chmn. dept., 1991-97. Author: The Poetry of Vision, 1967, The Female Imagination, 1975, Imagining a Self, 1976, The Adolescent Idea, 1982, Gossip, 1985, Desire and Truth, 1990, Boredom: The Literary History of a State of Mind, 1995. Fellow Guggenheim Found., 1969-70, NEH, 1974, Am. Council Learned Socs., 1978-79, Nat. Humanities Ctr., 1982-83, 89. Mem. MLA (2nd v.p. 1992, 1st v.p. 1993, pres. 1994, mem. adv. com. 1976-80, mem. exec. coun. 1986-89), Am. Acad. Arts and Scis., Am. Coun. Learned Socs. (mem. bd. trustees 1992—, vice chair 1994-97, chair 1997—), Am. Philos. Soc. Home: 1830 Fendall Ave Charlottesville VA 22903-1614 Office: U Va Dept English 219 Bryan Hall Charlottesville VA 22903

SPADA, JAMES, author, publisher; b. S.I., N.Y., Jan. 23, 1950; s. Joseph Vincent and Mary (Ruberto) S. Student, Wagner Coll., 1968-71, Calif. State U., 1979-80. Pres., Spada Pubs, Los Angeles, pub. Barbra Quar., Los Angeles, 1980-83. Mem. Authors Guild, ACLU. Democrat. Author: Barbra: The First Decade-The Films and Career of Barbra Streisand, 1974, The Films of Robert Redford, 1977, The Spada Report, 1979, Streisand-the Woman and the Legend, 1981, Monroe-Her Life in Pictures, 1982, Judy and Liza, 1983, Hepburn: Her Life in Pictures, 1984, The Divine Bette Midler, 1984, Fonda: Her Life in Pictures, 1985, Shirley and Warren, 1985, Grace: The Secret Lives of a Princess, 1987, Peter Lawford: The Man Who Kept the Secrets, 1991, More Than a Woman: An Intimate Biography of Bette Davis, 1993, Streisand: Her Life, 1995; book packager The 1984 Marilyn Monroe Pin-Up Calendar, 1983, The Telephone Book, 1984, Elizabeth Taylor: A Biography in Photographs, 1984, Bette Davis: A Biography in Photographs, 1985, Natalie Wood: A Biography in Photographs, 1986.

SPADER, JAMES, actor; b. Mass., Feb. 7, 1960. Student, Phillips Acad., Michael Chekhov Studio. Appeared in pictures Endless Love (debut 1981), The New Kids, 1985, Tuff Turf, 1985, Pretty in Pink, 1986, Mannequin, 1987, Wall Street, 1987, Less Than Zero, 1987, Baby Boom, 1987, Jack's Back, 1988, The Rachel Papers, 1989, sex, lies and videotape (Best actor award Cannes Festival 1989), 1989, Bad Influence, 1990, White Palace, 1990, True Colors, 1991, Storyville, 1992, Bob Roberts, 1992, Music of Chance, 1993, Dream Lover, 1994, Wolf, 1994, Stargate, 1994, Two Days in the Valley, 1996, Crash, 1997, Keys to Tulsa, 1997, Critical Care, 1997; TV movies, Cocaine: One Man's Seduction, 1983, A Killer in the Family, 1983, Family Secrets, 1984, Starcrossed, 1985; TV series The Family Tree, 1983. Office: care Toni Howard/ICM 8942 Wilshire Blvd Beverly Hills CA 90211-1934

SPAEDER, ROGER CAMPBELL, lawyer; b. Cleve., Dec. 20, 1943; s. Ferd N. and Luceil (Campbell) S.; m. Frances DeSales Sutherland, Sept. 7, 1968; children: Michael, Matthew. BS, Bowling Green U., 1965; JD with honors, George Washington U., 1970. Bar: D.C. 1971, U.S. Dist. Ct. D.C. 1971, U.S. Ct. Appeals (D.C. cir.) 1971, U.S. Supreme Ct. 1976, U.S. Ct. Claims 1979, U.S. Dist. Ct. Md. 1984, U.S. Ct. Appeals (2d and 4th cirs.) 1985. Asst. U.S. atty. D.C., Washington, 1971-76; ptnr. Zuckerman, Spaeder, Goldstein, Taylor & Kolker, Washington, 1976—; faculty Atty. Gen. Advocacy Inst., 1974-76, Nat. Inst. Trial Adv., 1978-79; adj. faculty Georgetown U. Law Ctr., 1979-80, Am. U. Ctr. Adminstrn. Justice, 1976-79; lectr. D.C. Bar Continuing Legal Edn. Programs, 1980—. Recipient Spl. Achievement award Dept. Justice, 1971. Mem. ABA (co-chair com. on complex crimes litigation 1989-92, divsn. co-dir. sect. litigation 1992—), Bar Assn. D.C. (lectr. Criminal Practice Inst. 1977-80), D.C. Bar (com. criminal jury instrns. 1972, div. courts, lawyers, adminstrn. of justice, 1976-78; adv. com. continuing legal edn. 1986), Def. Rsch. Inst., Assn. Trial Lawyers Am., Assn. Plaintiffs' Trial Attys., Nat. Assn. Criminal Def. Lawyers, Omicron Delta Kappa. Contbr. articles to profl. jours. and chpts. to books. Home: 7624 Georgetown Pike Mc Lean VA 22102-1412 Office: Zuckerman Spaeder Goldstein Taylor & Kolker 1201 Connecticut Ave NW Fl 12 Washington DC 20036-2638

SPAEH, WINFRIED HEINRICH, retired banker; b. Essen, Fed. Republic of Germany, Dec. 23, 1930; came to U.S., 1961; s. Josef and Anna (Belker) S.; m. Waltraut Schab, Aug. 15, 1964; children: Andrea, Olivier. Abitur, Gymnasium Essen-Werden, 1951; postgrad. Columbia U., 1961-62; With Dresdner Bank, Essen and Düsseldorf, 1951-60; with internat. banking div. Morgan Guaranty Trust Co. of N.Y., N.Y.C., 1961-66, v.p. German offices, Frankfurt, 1969, gen. mgr., 1972; exec. mgr. Dresdner Bank AG, Frankfurt/Main., 1975, dep. of mng. dirs., 1979-82, sr. officer, N.Y.C., 1982-95; ret. 1995; dir. Dresdner (SE Asia) Ltd., Singapore, 1978-80, Aseambankers Malaysia Berhad, Kuala Lumpur, 1977-80, P.T. Asian and Euro-Am. Capital Corp. Ltd., Jakarta, 1977-80; chmn. Conf. State Bank Suprs./Fgn. Bankers Adv. Coun., Washington, 1993-96. Chmn. exec. com., bd. dirs. Friends of Dresden, Inc. Mem. Am. Inst. Contemporary German Studies (bd. dirs. 1983—), Bankers Assn. Fgn. Trade (chmn. 1982-90, internat. adv. coun. 1982-95), Inst. Internat. Bankers (bd. dirs. 1989-92), German-Am. C. of C. (bd. dirs. 1985-93), N.Y. C. of C. (bd. dirs.), N.Y.C. Partnership (bd. dirs., internat. bus. coun.), Muenchener Herren Club, Union Internat. Club (Frankfurt), Belle Haven Club (Greenwich, Conn.). Home: 25 Turner Dr Greenwich CT 06831-4415

SPAEPEN, FRANS AUGUST, applied physics researcher, educator; b. Mechelen, Belgium, Oct. 29, 1948; came to U.S., 1971; s. Jozef F.M. and Ursula (Roppe) S.; m. Moniek Steemans, Aug. 21, 1973; children: Geertrui M., Elizabet U., Hendrik J.L. Burgerlijk Metaalkundig Ingenieur, U. Leuven, Belgium, 1971; PhD, Harvard U., 1975. IBM postdoctoral fellow Harvard U., Cambridge, Mass., 1975-77; asst. prof. applied physics Harvard U., 1977-81, assoc. prof., 1981-83, Gordon McKay prof. applied physics, 1983—; vis. prof. U. Leuven, 1984; chmn. Gordon Conf. on Phys. Metallurgy, 1988; dir. Harvard Materials Rsch. Lab., 1990—; NRC com. on solid state scis., 1990-93, condensed matter and materials physics, 1996-97; Krengel lectr. Technion, Israel, 1994. Co-editor: Solid State Physics; mem. editl. bd. Jour. Applied Physics, Applied Physics Letters, 1990-93, Applied Physics Revs., 1991—, Phys. Rev., 1994—, Jour. Non-Crystalline Solids, 1990-94; contbr. numerous articles to profl. publs., chpts. to books, Fulbright, 1971. Recipient Best Paper award Acta Metallurgica, 1994. Fellow Am. Phys. Soc. (chmn. divsn. materials physics 1992), AIME-The Metall. Soc.; mem. Am. Soc. Metals (lectr.), Materials Rsch. Soc. (councillor 1986-88, 90-92, co-chmn. fall meeting Boston 1990, chmn. program com. 1993—), Koninklijke Vlaamse Ingenieurs Vereniging, Böhimische Physikalische Gesellschaft, Orde van den Prince. Office: Harvard U Div Engring and Applied Scis 29 Oxford St Cambridge MA 02138-2901

SPAETH, C. EDMOND, library media specialist; b. Yonkers, N.Y., May 3, 1945; s. Camille and Ida Mae (Therrien) S.; m. Merrill Hunting, Sept., 1973; 1 child, Erin Elise. BA, Mich. State U., 1974; MS, L.I. U., 1981. Cert. sch. libr. specialist, N.Y. Libr. media specialist West Park (N.Y.) Union Free Sch., Valley Central Schs., Kingston (N.Y.) City Schs.; reference libr. Newburgh (N.Y.) Free Libr.; freelance storyteller. Reviewer ABC/CLIO Video Rating Guide for Librs.; contbr. entries premier edit. Hudson River Almanac; contbr. articles to JeMe Souviens. Chairperson Town of Fishkill Parks Bd.; trustee Mt. Gulian Historic Site. With USN, 1967-71. Recipient Storybook Garden grant. Mem. SLMSSENY (pres., v.p., editor newsletter), Ulster County Sch. Libr. System Bd., Kingston City Schs. Libr. Bd., Beta Phi Mu.

SPAETH, EDMUND BENJAMIN, JR., lawyer, law educator, former judge; b. Washington, June 10, 1920; s. Edmund B. and Lena (Link) S. AB magna cum laude, Harvard U., 1942, LLB, 1948. Bar: Pa. 1949. Judge Ct. of Common Pleas, Phila., 1964-73; judge Superior Ct of Pa., 1973-86, pres. judge, 1983-86; of counsel Pepper, Hamilton & Scheetz, Phila., 1986—; adj. prof. U. Pa. Law Sch., 1986-97; chair Pennsylvanians for Modern Cts., 1987—. Bd. dirs. Pub. Interest Law Ctr. of Phila. Fellow Am. Bar Found. (life); mem. ABA, Am. Law Inst. (life), Pa. Bar Assn., Phila. Bar Assn., Am. Judicature soc., Order of Coif, Phi Beta Kappa. Home: Cathedral Village Apt L-206 600 E Cathedral Rd Philadelphia PA 19128-1933 Office: 3000 Two Logan Sq Philadelphia PA 19103

SPAETH, GEORGE LINK, physician, ophthalmology educator; b. Phila., Mar. 3, 1932; s. Edmund Benjamin and Lena Marie (Link) S.; m. Ann Ward, May 17, 1955; children: Kristin Lea Crowley, George Link Jr., Eric Edmund. BA magna cum laude, Yale U., 1954; MD cum laude, Harvard U., 1959; postgrad., U. Mich., 1960, U. Pa., 1971. Diplomate Am. Bd. Ophthalmology. Resident surgeon Wills Eye Hosp., Phila., 1960-63, attending surgeon, 1970—, dir. glaucoma svc., 1968—; clin. fellow NIH, Bethesda, Md., 1963-65; instr. U. Pa., Phila., 1965-68; pvt. practice Phila., 1965-68; prof. ophthalmology Temple U. Med. Sch., Phila., 1968-75, Jefferson Med. Coll., Phila., 1975—; ophthalmologist Chestnut Hill Hosp., Phila., 1975—; attending surgeon, Graduate Hosp.; cons., Bryn Mawr Hosp. Author: 14 books in ophthalmology and surgery, 1970—; contbr. over 500 articles to profl. jours.; editor: Ophthalmic Surgery jour., 1985-96; patentee differometer, tonometer tip cover. Pres. Chestnut Hill Cmty. Assn., Phila., 1970-72; trustee, treas. Thomas Harrison Found., 1975—; founder, pres. E.B. Spaeth and The Eye Disease Found., 1978—, Profls. for Nuclear Army Control, 1985-88; interviewer Yale Alumni Schs. Com., Phila., 1965—; Yale Class coun., 1968—, Yale Assn. Alumni Reps., 1996—; curriculum com. Jefferson Med. Coll., 1987-90; institutional review bd. Jefferson Med. Coll., 1990-95. Lt. comdr. USPHS, 1963-68. Recipient Pub. Svc. award Chestnut Hill Coll., 1972, Sir Stuart Duke Elder Glaucoma award Internat. Glaucoma Soc., 1986, Newberg award Lawyers Alliance for World Security, 1995, Derrick Vail award Ill Soc. Prevention of Blindness, 1996; NIH grantee, 1968—. Fellow Am. Acad. Ophthalmology (chmn. ethics com. San Francisco 1987-95, coun. 1980-93, vice chmn. residency rev. com. Chgo. 1982-88, Sr. honor award 1988), Am. Assn. Rsch. in Vision and Ophthalmology, Royal Coll. Ophthalmologist, United Kingdom, Danish Ophthalmological Soc., Ind. Soc. of Ophthalmology; mem. Am. Glaucoma Soc. (pres. 1983-85), Coll. Physicians Phila. (sec. 1976-84), Phila. County Med. Soc., Pa. Acad. Ophthalmology (pres. coun.), Physicians for Social Responsibility (pres. emeritus Phila. chpt.), ACS (bd. govs., chmn. adv. coun., chmn. subcom. monitoring), Phila. Club, Phila. Cricket Club, Phi Beta Kappa, Alpha Omega Alpha. Democrat. Episcopalian. Avocations: playing piano, sports, photography, gardening, poetry writing. Office: Wills Eye Hosp 900 Walnut St Philadelphia PA 19107-5509

SPAETH, KARL HENRY, retired chemical company executive, lawyer; b. Phila., Mar. 12, 1929; s. Edmund Benjamin and Lena Marie (Link) S.; m. Ann Dashiell Wieland, Sept. 14, 1963; children—Karl Henry, Edmund Alexander, Christopher Philip. AB, Haverford Coll., 1951; postgrad. Oxford U., 1955; JD, Harvard U., 1958. Bar: Pa. 1959, U.S. Ct. (ea. dist.) Pa. 1959, U.S. Ct. Appeals (3d cir.) 1959. Assoc. MacCoy, Evans & Lewis, Phila., 1959-62; counsel for fgn. ops. Scott Paper Co., Phila., 1962-69; v.p., corp. sec. Quaker Chem. Corp., Conshohocken, Pa., 1969-95, ret. v.p., 1995; bd. dirs. Greater Phila. Internat. Network, 1991-94, Cen. Phila. Devel. Corp., 1991—; bd. dirs., sec.-treas. Edmund B. Spaeth Clin. Rsch. Found., 1982—; chmn. bd. dirs. Pa. Chem. Industry Coun., 1984-86. Chmn. bd. trustees Quaker Chem. Found., 1982—; bd. overseers Univ. Mus., U. Pa., Phila., 1983-89, 90-96, dir. coun. U. Mus. U. Pa., 1996—; bd. dir. Opera Co. Phila., 1988—; vestry Ch. St. James the Less, Phila., 1992—; bd. dirs. Chestnut Hill Acad., Phila., 1976-83, pres., 1979-83; mem. Whitemarsh Twp. Bd. Suprs., Pa., 1969-75, chmn., 1972-74; mem. Com. of Seventy, Phila., 1984-96; internat. adv. com. Phila. First Partnership Econ. Devel., 1994—. Comdr. USNR, 1952-55. Mem. Am. Soc. Corp. Secs., Pa. Bar Assn. (chmn. sect. on internat. and comparative law 1980-92), Montgomery Bar Assn., Phila. Com. on Fgn. Rels. (exec. com., sec. 1984-94), Phila. Club, Phila. Athenaeum, Libr. Co. of Phila., Phila. Cricket Club. Republican. Anglican. Oxford Union, Univ. Barge (sec. 1988-94), Mil. Order Fgn. Wars (registrar 1989-91, vice commdr. 1991-93). Home: 2129 Harts Ln Conshohocken PA 19428

SPAETH, NICHOLAS JOHN, lawyer, former state attorney general; b. Mahnomen, Minn., Jan. 27, 1950. A.B., Stanford U., 1972, J.D., 1977; B.A., Oxford U., Eng., 1974. Bar: Minn. 1979, U.S. Dist. Ct. (Minn.) 1979, U.S. Ct. Appeals (8th cir.) 1979, N.D. 1980, U.S. Dist. Ct. (N.D.) 1980, U.S. Supreme Ct. 1984. Law clk. U.S. Ct. Appeals (8th cir.), Fargo, N.D., 1977-78; law clk. to Justice Byron White U.S. Supreme Ct., Washington, 1978-79; pvt. practice, 1979-84; atty. gen. State of N.D., Bismarck, 1984-93; ptnr. Dorsey & Whitney, Fargo, 1993—; adj. prof. law U. Minn., 1980-83. Rhodes scholar, 1972-74. Democrat. Roman Catholic. Office: Dorsey & Whitney PO Box 1344 Fargo ND 58107-1344

SPAETH, STEVEN MICHAEL, lawyer; b. Janesville, Wis., Oct. 10, 1963; s. Herman Joseph and Lonna Rae (Weeks) S. BS in Econs., Ea. Mich. U.,

1986; JD, Northwestern U., 1989. Bar: Wis. 1989. Gen. atty. FCC, Washington, 1989—. Contbr. articles to profl. jours. Mem. Wis. Bar Assn. Republican. Lutheran. Office: FCC 1919 M St NW Washington DC 20036-3521

SPAFFORD, MICHAEL CHARLES, artist; b. Palm Springs, Calif., Nov. 6, 1935. BA, Pomona Coll., 1959; MA, Harvard U., 1960. One man shows include Seattle Art Mus., 1982, 86, Reed Coll., 1984, Whtcom county Mus., 1987, U. Puget Sound, Tacoma, Wash., 1973, Tacoma Art Mus., 1975, 86, Utah Mus. Fine Arts, Salt Lake City, 1975, Francine Seders Gallery, Seattle, 1965—, Bellevue Art Mus., 1991, Cheney-Cowles Mus., Spokane, Wash., 1994; exhibited in group shows at Wilcox Gallery, Swarthmore Coll., Pa., 1977, Seattle Art Mus., 1977, 80, 84, Am. Acad. and Inst. Arts and Letters, N.Y.C., 1980, 83, 89, 95, Kobe, Japan, 1981, Eastern Wash. U., 1982, Henry Art Gallery, 1982, 86, Bellevue Art Mus., 1987, 95, Cheney Cowles Mus., 1988, Holter Mus. of Art, Helena, Mont. Recipient Rome Prize Am. Acad. in Rome, 1967-69, award Am. Acad. and Inst. Arts and Letters, 1983; Louis Comfort Tiffany Found. grantee, 1965-66; Neddy fellow, 1996. Home: c/o Francine Seders Gallery 6701 Greenwood North Seattle WA 98103

SPAGNOLO, SAMUEL VINCENT, internist, pulmonary specialist, educator; b. Pitts., Sept. 3, 1939; s. Vincent Anthony and Mary Grace (Culotta) S.; m. Lucy Aleta Weyandt, June 20, 1961 (div. Feb., 1992); children: Samuel, Brad, Gregg. BA, Washington & Jefferson Coll., 1961; MD, Temple U., 1965. Diplomate Am. Bd. Internal Medicine, Bd. of Pulmonary Disease; active lic. physician in Fla., Calif., Md., D.C.; inactive Pa., Mass. Sr. resident in medicine VA Med. Ctr., Boston, 1969-70, chief resident in medicine, 1970-71; Harvard Clin. and Rsch. fellow in pulmonary diseases Mass. Gen. Hosp., Boston, 1971-72; asst. chief med. svc. VA Med. Ctr., Washington, 1972-75, acting chief med. svc., 1975-76, chief pulmonary disease sect., 1976-94; instr. in medicine Boston U. Sch. of Medicine, Tufts u. Sch. Medicine, Boston, 1970-71; clin. and rsch. fellow in pulmonary diseases Harvard U. Sch. of Medicine, Mass. Gen. Hosp., Boston, 1971-72; clin. asst. prof. medicine Georgetown U., Washington, 1975-77; asst. prof. medicine George Washington U. Sch. of Medicine and Health Scis., Washington, 1972-75, assoc. prof., 1975-81, prof. medicine, 1981—, dir. divsn. pulmonary diseases and allergy, 1978-93; assoc. chmn. dept. medicine George Washington U. Med. Ctr., Washington, 1986-89; cons. in pulmonary diseases The Washington Hosp. Ctr., Washington, D.C., 1977—, Will Rogers Inst., White Plains, N.Y., 1980—, U.S. Dept. Labor, Washington, 1980—, Walter Reed Army Med. Ctr., Washington, 1987; rep. Am. Coll. Chest Physicians to Am. Registry Pathology, Washington, 1981-92; numerous radio tv appearances on Health Oriented Programs; invited lectr. in U.S., Russia, Jordan; chmn., mem. many coms. George Washington U. Sch. of Medicine, George Washington Med. Ctr., VA Med. Ctr., Washington; med. chest cons. in attempted assasination of former Pres. Regan. Author: (books): Clinical Assessment of Patients with Pulmonary Disease, 1986; co-author: (with A.E. Medinger) Handbook of Pulmonary Emergencies, 1986, (with others) Handbook of Pulmonary Drug Therapy, 1993, (with Witorsch, P.) Air Pollution and Lung Disease in Adults, 1994; contbr. numerous articles to profl jours. including Med. Clin. N. Am., Chest, So. Med. Jour., Am. Jour. Cardiology, Jour. Am. Med. Assn., Clin. Rsch., Am. Rev. Respiratory Disease, Am. Lung Assn. Bull., Clin. Notes on Respiratory Diseases, Jour. Nuclear Medicine, Drug Therapy; presented abstracts at over 13 profl. meetings; reviewer for Chest, Am. Review Respiratory Diseases. Lt. cmmdr. U.S. Pub. Health Svc., 1966-68. Decorated Cavaliere in Order of Merit, Republic of Italy, 1983; nominated for Golden Apple award by med. students Geo. Washington Sch. of Medicine, Phila., 1977; recipient cert. appreciation D.C. Lung Assn., 1983. Fellow Am. Coll. Physicians (coun. critical care 1983-85), Am. Coll. Chest Physicians (gov. D.C., coun. of govs. 1989-96); mem. Am. Thoracic Soc. (exec. com. D.C. chpt. 1978, 85, 89, mem. adv. com. tuberculosis control, 1978-84, pres. D.C. chpt. 1981-83), Nat. Assn. VA Physicians (sec. 1987-89, v.p. 1989-91, pres. 1992—), Internat. Lung Found. (pres. 1991—). Achievements include first major review of patient outcome during early history of intensive care units; an analysis of mechanisms of hypoxemia in patients with chronic liver disease; first report of Pneumocystis Carinii Pneumonitis in patients with lung cancer; first prospective evaluation of short course therapy reported in U.S. using Isoniazid and Rifampin; first American report using laser through fiberoptic bronchoscope to treat lung cancer; first report to evaluate continuous intravenous morphine to control pain in cancer patients; description of a simple technique to measure the total lung volume non-invasively using the routing chest x-ray. Avocations: reading, swimming, stamp collecting, gardening, chess. Office: Geo Washington U 2150 Pennsylvania Ave NW Washington DC 20037-3201

SPAGNUOLO, PASQUALINA MARIE, rehabilitation nurse; b. Phila., Jan. 21, 1942; d. Charles and Lena (Damiano) Caruolo; children: Louis, Charles, Jason. Lic. practical nurse diploma, Salem (N.J.) Community Coll., 1985; BSN, Widener U., Chester, Pa., 1989. Lic. practical nurse, Del., N.J., Pa.; RN, Del., N.J., Pa. Practical nurse A.I. Dupont Rehab. Hosp., Wilmington, Del.; med. sec. Underwood Meml. Hosp., Woodbury, N.J., nurse's aide; pvt. duty nurse, Mt. Ephraim, N.J. Merit scholar Widener U., 1985-86, Charlotte Newcomb scholar, 1986-87; recipient Eleanore O. Dower award, 1988.

SPAHN, GARY JOSEPH, lawyer; b. N.Y.C., July 23, 1949; s. Harry G. and Mary (Hopkins) S.; m. Lois Luttinger, Aug. 9, 1975; children: Gary J. Jr., Lori J. BA, L.I. U., 1971, MA, 1976; JD, U. Richmond, 1975. Bar: Va. 1975, U.S. Ct. Appeals (4th cir.) 1975, U.S. Supreme Ct. 1980. Law clk. to Hon. Judge Dortch U.S. Dist. Ct. (ea. dist.) Va., Richmond, 1975-77; from assoc. to ptnr. Mays & Valentine, Richmond, 1977—, now ptnr., chmn. products liability and ins. sect.; lectr. in field, 1980—; mem. judicial conf. U.S. Ct. Appeals (4th cir.). Co-author: Virginia Law of Products Liability, 1990. Pres. Southhampton Citizens Assn., Richmond, 1982-85; dir. Southhampton Recreation Assn., Richmond, 1983; mem. coun. Southside Montessori Sch., Richmond, 1983-85. With USAF, 1967-73. Mem. ABA (litigation and tort and ins. sects.), Internat. Assn. Def. Counsel, Am. Assn. Ins. Attys., Assoc. Def. Trial Attys., Def. Rsch. Inst., Va. Assn. Def. Attys., Va. Mfrs. Assn., Products Liability Adv. Counsel, Va. Power Boat (commodore). Avocations: boating, basketball, racquetball. Office: Mays & Valentine PO Box 1122 1111 E Main St Richmond VA 23208-1122

SPAHN, MARY ATTEA, retired educator; b. Buffalo, July 16, 1929; d. George H. and Madeline Barbara (Bitar) Attea. A.B., Nazareth Coll., Rochester, N.Y., 1950; Ed.M., SUNY, Buffalo, 1952, Ed.D., 1966. Tchr. Clarence (N.Y.) Cen. Schs., 1951-65; tchr. reading Sweet Home Cen. Schs., Amherst, N.Y., 1965-68; assoc. prof. elem. edn. D'Youville Coll., Buffalo, 1970-75; prof. curriculum and supervision SUNY Coll., Buffalo, 1975-85, prof. emeritus, 1985—; part time tchr. creativity East Aurora Schs., N.Y., 1988; coordinator Sweet Home secondary sch. summer reading program, 1968-70; cons. to Niagara Wheatfield, Clarence Central, Sweet Home schs. Author: Turning Students on Through Creative Writing, 2d edit., 1979; (poetry) Weep Willow Weep, 1974; Fragments, 1979, Busy Bodies, 1975, Flutterbyes, A Collection of Easy Readings, 1985, (with others) Flutterbyes II, 1992; contbr. articles to profl. jours. Vol. Creative Edn. Found., Creative Problem Solving Inst., Ministry of Care, McCauley House, 1988—; leader Bishop's Com., 1987. Mem. NEA, Internat. Reading Assn. (pres. 1968 Niagara Frontier coun.), N.Y. State Reading Assn. (sec. 1970), Am. Ednl. Rsch. Assn., United Univ. Profs., Nat. Coun. Tchrs. English, East Aurora Writers Guild, Southtown's Quilters Club, Bernina Club, Penwomen, Grief Counselling, Phi Delta Kappa. Home: 58 Buffalo Rd East Aurora NY 14052-1628 *Persistence, determination, sensitivity, sharing, willingness to take risks and give of myself, plus a faith in God...these are the qualities which have helped me on the road to success.*

SPAHN, WARREN, retired baseball player; b. Buffalo, N.Y., Apr. 23, 1921. Pitcher Boston Braves, 1946-52, Milw. Braves, 1953-64, N.Y. Mets, 1965, San Francisco Giants, 1965. Recipient Cy Young award, 1957; named to Baseball Hall of Fame, 1973. Achievements include led or tied for most wins in Nat. League 1949, 50, 53, 57-61, led Nat. League strikeouts 1949, 50, 52, led Nat. League ERA 1947, 53, 61, led Nat. League in complete games, 1949, 51, 57-59, no-hitters against Phila., 1960, San Francisco, 1961, All-star game, 1947, 49-54, 56-63, mem. World Series Champions, 1957, winningest left-hander in game's history with 363 victories. Office: c/o Nat Baseball Hall Fame Mus PO Box 590 Cooperstown NY 13326-0590

SPAHR, FREDERICK THOMAS, association executive; b. South Bend, Apr. 27, 1939; s. Ervin Leonard and Elizabeth Mary (Layden) S.; m. Patricia Margaret McGraw, Aug. 6, 1966; children—Susan, John, Kathryn, Joseph. B.A., Ind. U., Bloomington, 1961; M.Ed., Boston U., 1963; Ph.D., U. So. Calif., 1968. Asst. prof. Pa. State U., 1968; dep. exec. sec. Am. Speech Lang. Hearing Assn., Rockville, Md., 1971-79; exec. dir. Am. Speech Lang. Hearing Assn., 1980—; treas. Nat. Com. for Rsch. in Neurol. and Communication Disorders, 1983-89. Bd. dirs. People-to-People Com. for Handicapped, Friends of Nat. Inst. for Deafness and Other Communication Disorders. Fellow Am. Speech-Lang.-Hearing Assn.; mem. Nat. Student Speech, Lang. and Hearing Assn. (hon.), Am. Soc. Assn. Execs. (Key award 1987, bd. dirs. 1995—), Greater Washington Soc. Assn. Execs. (chmn. bd. dirs.), Washington Assn. Rsch. Found. (chmn. bd. trustees), Assn. Ambassadors Club (Montgomery County, Md.) (pres.), World Future Soc., Phi Delta Kappa. Office: Am Speech-Language-Hearing Assn 10801 Rockville Pike Rockville MD 20852-3226

SPAIDE, RICHARD FREDERICK, ophthalmologist; b. Allentown, Pa., Nov. 19, 1955; s. Frederick and Dorothy Spaide; m. Wai Chang Ho, May 25, 1985; children: Theodore, Christopher, Emily. BS, Muhlenberg U., 1977; MD, Jefferson Med. Coll., 1981. Diplomate Am. Bd. Ophthalmology. Resident in ophthalmology St. Vincent's Hosp., N.Y.C., 1982-85; chief ophthalmologist Landstuhl (Germany) Army Regional Med. Ctr., 1986-89; fellow in retina Manhattan Eye, Ear, Throat Hosp., N.Y.C., 1989-90; pvt. practice ophthalmologist N.Y.C., 1990—; ophthalmologist Vitreous, Retina, Macula Cons. of N.Y., N.Y.C., 1994—; clin. asst. prof. N.Y. Med. Coll., N.Y.C., 1993—. Med. advisor Jour. Ophthalmic Photography; contbr. chpts. to books and articles to profl. jours.; inventor in field. Named one of the best ophthalmologist in N.Y. The Best Doctors N.Y. Metro Area, 1994, 96. Fellow ACS, Am. Acad. Ophthalmology; mem. Am. Uveitis Soc., Macula Soc., Vitreous Soc., Nat. Assn. for Visually Handicapped (bd. med. dirs. 1995—), Assn. for Rsch. in Vision and Ophthalmology, N.Y. Soc. Clin. Ophthalmology, N.Y. Med. Soc., N.Y. Ophthalmol. Soc. Avocation: photography. Home: 1365 York Ave New York NY 10021 Office: 519 E 72nd St Ste 203 New York NY 10021-4028

SPAIN, JACK HOLLAND, JR., lawyer; b. Greenville, N.C., Jan. 24, 1939; s. Jack Holland and Lucy Marie (Hardee) S.; m. Mary Elizabeth Rhamstine, May 9, 1964; children: John Hardee, Sidney Holland. AB, U. N.C., 1960; JD, Harvard U., 1963. Bar: Va. 1964, U.S. Dist. Ct. (ea. dist.) Va. 1964. Assoc. Hunton & Williams, Richmond, Va., 1964-71; ptnr. Hunton & Williams, Richmond, 1971—. Bd. dirs. Maymount Found., Richmond, 1975—, pres., 1980-82; mem. bd. elders 2d Presbyn. Ch., Richmond, City Dem. Com., Richmond; spl. counsel Local Govt. Com., Va. Constl. Revision Com. Lt. comdr. USN. Mem. ABA (chmn. taxation com., local govt. sect.), Va. Bar Assn., Richmond Bar Assn., Am. Coll. Bond Lawyers, Harvard U. Law Sch. Assn. Va. (pres.), Downtown Club (Richmond), Harvard Club (N.Y.C.), Phi Beta Kappa, Phi Eta Sigma, Phi Alpha Theta. Avocations: spectator sports, antiques, Chinese art, farming. Office: Hunton & Williams River Front Pla E Twr 951 E Byrd St Richmond VA 23219-4040

SPAIN, JAMES DORRIS, JR., biochemist, educator; b. Washington, Feb. 3, 1929; s. James Dorris and Frances (Pitkin) S.; m. Patricia Mann, Oct. 3, 1952; children: James Williamson, Caryn Ann, Mary Alisa. Student, Tulane U., 1947-48; B.S., Mich. Technol. U., 1951; M.S., Med. Coll. Va., 1953; Ph.D., Stanford, 1956. Research fellow biochemistry U. Tex.-M.D. Anderson Hosp. and Tumor Inst., 1955-56; assoc. prof. dept. chemistry Mich. Technol. U., Houghton, 1956-62; head dept. biol. scis. Mich. Technol. U., 1962-68, prof. biochemistry, 1962-84, prof. emeritus, 1985—; dir. Ctr. for Instrnl. Computing, Ea. Mich. U., Ypsilanti, 1984-85; vis. prof. Clemson U., S.C., 1985-94; pres. Electronic Homework Sys., Inc., 1994—; cons. Computer Applications in Biology and Chemistry; dir. SUMIT Courseware Devel. Project, 1979-82. Author: Some Computer Programs for Biology, 1970, Biological Simulation Techniques, 1972, Lake Superior Basin Bibliography, 1976, BASIC Computer Models in Biology, 1978, BASIC Microcomputer Models in Biology, 1982, Developing Chemical Skills with Computerized Instruction, 1990, Computer Simulation in Biology: A BASIC Introduction, 1992, CHEMI-SKILL-BILDR Electronic Homework System, 1994; contbr. articles to profl. jours. Chmn. adv. council St. Josephs Hosp. Sch. Nursing, 1967; Trustee, pres. Portage Twp. Sch. Bd., 1968-76; trustee Copper Country Intermediate Sch. Dist., 1975-78. Recipient Faculty Research award Mich. Technol. U., 1965. Mem. Am. Chem. Soc. (past sect. v.p., chmn.), Sigma Xi, Phi Lambda Upsilon. Episcopalian. Clubs: Miscowaubik (gov. 1971-74, 79-82), Boscobel Country; Lodge: Rotary. Home: 129 Leslie Ln Pendleton SC 29670-9697

SPAIN, JAMES WILLIAM, political scientist, writer, investor; b. Chgo., July 22, 1926; s. Patrick Joseph and Mary Ellen (Forristal) S.; m. Edith Burke James, Feb. 21, 1951; children: Patrick, Sikandra, Stephen, William. M.A., U. Chgo., 1949; Ph.D., Columbia U., 1959. Cons. sec. army, 1949-50; with U.S. Fgn. Service, 1951-53; researcher, lectr. Columbia, 1955-62; mem. policy planning council State Dept., 1963-64; dir. Office Research and Analysis for Near East and South Asia, 1964-66; country dir. for Pakistan and Afghanistan, 1966-69; charge d'affaires Am. embassy, Rawapindi, 1969; consul gen. Istanbul, Turkey, 1970-72; minister Am. embassy, Ankara, 1972-74; diplomat-in-residence, vis. prof. history and govt. Fla. State U., Tallahassee, 1974-75; amb. to Tanzania Dar es Salaam, 1975-79; amb., dep. permanent rep. UN, N.Y.C., 1979; amb. to Turkey, Ankara, 1980-81; amb. to Sri Lanka, Colombo, 1985-89; fgn. affairs fellow Carnegie Endowment for Internat. Peace and Rand Corp., Washington, 1982-84; guest resident investor Colombo, Sri Lanka, 1991—; chmn. Lanka Infrastructure Ltd.; bd. dirs. Hawk Mountain Fed. Express, Ltd., Lanka Internat. Bus. Svcs., Ltd.; adj. prof. polit. sci. Am. U., Washington, 1965-67. Author: The Way of the Pathans, 1962, The Pathan Borderland, 1963, American Diplomacy in Turkey, 1984, Pathans of the Latter Day, 1995, Innocents of the Latter Day, 1997. Pres. bd. trustees Joseph Frazer Meml. Hosp.; bd. dirs. Rainbow Found. With U.S. Army, 1946-47. Fellow Ford Found., 1953-55; recipient Presdl. Exec. award, 1983, Wilbur I. Carr award for Disting. Diplomacy, 1989. Mem. Coun. Fgn. Rels., Washington Inst. Fgn. Affairs, Am. Fgn. Svc. Assn., Assn. Diplomatic Studies and Tng., Cosmos Club. Home: Galle Face Ct II # 42, Colombo 3, Sri Lanka

SPAIN, JAYNE BAKER, corporate executive, educator; b. San Francisco; d. Lawrence Ian and Marguerite (Buchanan) Baker; student U. Calif. at Berkeley, 1944-47, Music U. Cin., 1947-50; LL.D., Edgecliff Coll., Cin., 1969; Dr. Pub. Service, George Washington U., 1970; LL.D., U. Cin., 1971, Dumbarton Coll., 1972, Springfield (Mass.) Coll., 1973, Gallaudet Coll., Washington, 1973; L.H.D. Bryant Coll., 1972, Russell Sage Coll., Troy, N.Y., 1973, Loyola Coll., Balt., 1975; m. John A. Spain, July 14, 1952; children—Jeffry Alan, Jon Kimberly. Pres., Alvey-Ferguson Co., Cin., 1952-66, pres. Alvey-Ferguson Operations div. Litton Industries, Inc., 1966-70, also dir. parent co., 1970-94; vice chmn. CSC, 1971-75 ; sr. v.p. Gulf Oil Corp., Pitts., from 1975; Disting. vis. prof. and exec.-in-residence George Washington U., Washington, 1979-88; dir. Beatrice Foods, Chgo., Ohio Nat. Life Ins., Cin. Vice chmn. Pres.'s Com. on Employment Handicapped, 1966-82; participant internat. trade fairs U.S. Depts. State, Commerce, Europe, North Africa, 1961-66, mem. trade and investment mission, India, 1965; mem. U.S. com. Internat. Council Social Welfare; mem. Pres.'s Adv. Com. on Productivity; dir. Pvt. Sector Council, Washington, Dean's Adv. com. Coll. of Bus. U. Cin.; mem. Internat. Soc. Rehab. Disabled; mem. adv. com. sheltered workshops U.S. sec. labor; mem. Ohio Gov.'s Commn. on Status of Women; mem. bldg. com. Children's Med. Center, Cin. Bd. dirs., past pres. Convalescent Hosp. Children, Cin., Greater Cin. Hosp. Council, Children's Neuromuscular Diagnostic Center, Cin., Cin. Sci. Center; bd. dirs. President's Commn. on Personnel Interchange; chmn. bd. trustees Fed. Women's Award; mem. dean's adv. council Coll. Bus. Adminstrn. U. Cin.; chmn. Found. of Ams. for the Handicapped; bd. dirs. Recs. for the Blind. Recipient Distinguished Service award for work overseas blind People Com., Washington, 1965; Migel medal Am. Found. Blind, N.Y., 1966; Gold Plate award industry Acad. Achievement, Dallas, 1967; Top Hat award Bus. and Profl. Women's Clubs. Am., N.Y., 1967; named to Cin. Bus. Hall Fame, 1994. Mem. Conveyor Equipment Mfrs. Assn. (sec., treas., dir. 1960-63), Machinery and Allied Products Inst., Am. Mgmt. Assn., Internat. Platform Assn. Episcopalian. Contbr. articles to profl. jours.

SPAIN, RICHARD COLBY, lawyer; b. Evanston, Ill., Nov. 17, 1950; s. Richard Francis and Anne Louise (Brinckerhoff) S.; m. Nancy Lynn Mavec, Aug. 3, 1974; children: Catherine Day, Sarah Colby. BA cum laude, Lawrence U., 1972; JD, Case Western Reserve U., 1975; LLM in taxation, John Marshall Law Sch., 1985. Bar: Ohio 1975, Ill. 1982, U.S. Dist. Ct. (no. dist.) Ohio 1977, U.S. Dist. Ct. (no. dist.) Ill. 1982, Mass. 1996. Ptnr. Spain & Spain, Cleve., 1975-82, Whitted & Spain, P.C., Chgo., 1985-89, Spain, Spain & Varnet P.C., Chgo., Northborough, Mass., 1989—; assoc. Canel Whitted & Aronson, Chgo., 1982-85; dir., sec. Stone Perforating Co., Chgo., 1988—, Chgo. EDM, Inc., Chgo., Highland Park, Ill., 1994—. Contbr. articles to profl. jours. Dir., chair resource devel. com. ARC Ill., 1993—; dir., pres. Hanover Condominium Assn., Chgo., 1992—; dir. Chgo. Youth Symphony Orch., 1983—; dir. Combined Health Appeal of Ill., 1992—. Mem. Chikaming Country Club, The Winter Club Lake Forest, The Charlton Club (Chgo.). Home: 1780 Bowling Green Dr Lake Forest IL 60045-3504 Office: Spain Spain & Varnet PC 33 N Dearborn St Ste 2220 Chicago IL 60602-3109

SPAIN, STEVE RANDALL, secondary school educator; b. South Boston, Va., May 16, 1968; s. Steve Randall Sr. and Gloria Gale (Adcock) S. Student, Campbell U., 1986-88; BA in English, Longwood Coll., 1990, MA in English, 1992. Cert. tchr., Va. English instr., forensic coach Mecklenburg County Pub. Schs., Boydton, Va., 1992-93, libr., debate coach, 1994; adj. prof. English Southside Va. C.C., Alberta, 1992-93, Ctrl. Tex. Coll., Norfolk, Va., 1995—; English instr. Randolph-Macon Acad., Front Royal, Va., 1994-95; English instr., forensic judge Colonial Heights (Va.) City Schs., 1995—; forensic judge Va. H.S. League, Charlottesville, 1992-94. Contbr. poetry to profl. publs. All-Am. scholar USAA, 1990; Lee-Jackson Found. grantee, 1996. Mem. MLA, Nat. Coun. Tchrs. English, Nat. Adj. Faculty Guild, Mable Powell English Club (projects chair 1987), Lambda Iota Tau (pres. 1990, life mem.), Alpha Phi Omega (pub. rels. com. 1987-88, projects chair 1987, life mem.). Avocations: collecting books and stamps, photography, travel.

SPAINHOWER, JAMES IVAN, retired college president; b. Stanberry, Mo., Aug. 3, 1928; s. Elmer Enoch and Stella Irene (Cox) S.; m. Joanne Steanson, June 10, 1950; children: Janet Dovell, James Jeffrey. BA, Phillips U., Enid, Okla., 1950, LLD (hon.), 1967; BD, Lexington (Ky.) Theol. Sem., 1953; MA in Polit. Sci., U. Mo., Columbia, 1967, PhD, 1971; U. Ark., 1954; diploma, U. Pacific Sch. Religion, Berkeley, Calif., 1958; DPA (hon.), Culver-Stockton Coll., 1973; LL.D. (hon.), Maryville Coll., St. Louis, 1976; Litt.D. (hon.), Kirksville (Mo.) Coll. Osteo. Medicine, 1977; D.H.L. (hon.), Mo. Valley Coll., 1984; LLD (hon.), Eureka Coll., 1989, Lynchburg Coll., 1993. Ordained to ministry Christian Ch. (Disciples of Christ), 1950; pastor chs. in Ark. and Mo., 1953-70; mem. Mo. Ho. of Reps. from, Saline County, 1963-70; pres. Asso. Med. Schs. Mo., Jefferson City, 1970-72; part-time prof. polit. sci. Lincoln U., Jefferson City, 1970-72; treas. State of Mo., 1973-80; pres. Sch. of Ozarks, Point Lookout, Mo., 1981-82, Lindenwood Coll., St. Charles, Mo., 1983-89; pres. divsn. higher edn. Christian Ch. (Disciples of Christ), 1989-93. Author: Pulpit, Pew and Politics, 1979. Chmn. Mo. del. Dem. Nat. Conv., 1976; elected mem. Acad. Squires, 1981; 1st chmn. Mo. Children's Trust Fund, 1984-86. Recipient Mental Health award Mo. Mental Health Assn., 1967, Meritorious Service award St. Louis Globe Dem., 1968, Harry S. Truman award Saline County Young Democrats, 1970, citation of merit Alumni Assn. U. Mo., 1975; named Mo. Lay Educator of Year Mo. chpt. Phi Delta Kappa, 1968. Home and Office: 8067 Old White River Rd Rogers AR 72756-7662

SPAKE, NED BERNARR, energy company executive; b. Montpelier, Ohio, Sept. 18, 1933; s. Lewis W. and Gertrude E. (Foley) S.; m. Marilyn Rae Faulk, July 14, 1956; children: Julie Ann Spake Scott, Cynthia Ann Spake Lovern. B. Indsl. Engring., U. Fla., Gainesville, 1957; MBA, Rollins Coll., Winter Park, Fla., 1967. Mgr. Fla. Power Corp., Winter Park, Fla., 1962-72; dir. Fla. Power Corp., St. Petersburg, Fla., 1972-76, asst. v.p., 1976-78, v.p., 1978-83; v.p. Fla. Progress Corp., St. Petersburg, 1983-86; pres., chief exec. officer, dir. Progress Technologies Corp., St. Petersburg, Fla., 1985-89; pres., chief exec. officer, chmn. bd. Advanced Separation Technologies, Inc., St. Petersburg, Fla., 1985-89, Rein Energy Corp., Alachua, Fla., 1989-92; pres., CEO The Nouveau Group Inc., Winter Park, Fla., 1992—, also bd. dirs. Patentee in field. Mem. adv. coun. Engring. Sch. U. Fla., Gainesville, 1978—; bd. dirs. U. Fla. Rsch. Found., Inc., 1986-94; dir. GelTech, Inc., 1986-87. Lutheran. Home and Office: The Nouveau Group Inc 500 Osceola Ave Apt 401 Winter Park FL 32789

SPALDING, ANDREW FREEMAN, lawyer; b. Toledo, June 24, 1951; s. Dean and Shirley Louise (Maitland) S.; m. Adele Taylor, May 17, 1980; children: Amy Louise, Adam Freeman, Audrey Wade, Abigail Maitland. BA, U. Calif.-Berkeley, 1973; JD, So. Meth. U., 1977. Bar: Tex. 1977, U.S. Dist. Ct. (so., ea., and we. dists.) Tex. 1978, U.S. Ct. Appeals (5th cir.) 1978; bd. cert. Civil Trial Law, Personal Injury Trial Law, Tex.. Bd. Legal Specialization. Assoc. Bracewell & Patterson, Houston, 1977-84, ptnr., 1984—. Notes and comments editor Southwestern Law Jour., Dallas, 1976-77. Fellow Tex. Bar Found., Houston Bar Found.; mem. State Bar Tex., Tex. Assn. Def. Counsel, Houston Bar Assn., Def. Rsch. Inst., Knights Momus, Krewe Maximilian. Clubs: Houston. Office: Bracewell & Patterson 2900 S Tower Pennzoil Pla 711 Louisiana St Houston TX 77002-2716

SPALDING, JAMES STUART, retired telecommunications company executive; b. Edinburgh, Scotland, Nov. 23, 1934; arrived in Can., 1957, permanent resident, 1962; Student, Edinburgh U., 1951-52, Glasgow U., 1953. Gen. mgr., dir. United Corps. Ltd., Montreal, Que., Can., 1970-72; pension fund mgr. BCE, Inc., Montreal, 1972-74, sr. asst. treas., 1974-76, treas., 1976-79, v.p., 1979-83, v.p. fin., 1983-84, exec. v.p. fin., 1984-90; ret., 1990; pub. gov. Can. Investor Protection Fund. Mem. Inst. Chartered Accts. Scotland, Order Chartered Accounts Que., Fin. Execs. Inst. Can. (past chmn.). Home: 53 Country Club Pl, Brockville, PQ Canada H3Y 3A4

SPALTY, EDWARD ROBERT, lawyer; b. New Haven, Oct. 1, 1946; s. Kermit and Elinor (Phelan) Turgeon; m. Suzy Clune; children: Thomas John, Kathleen Tess. AB, Emory U., 1968; JD, Columbia U., 1973. Bar: Mo. 1975, U.S. Dist. Ct. (we. dist.) Mo. 1975, U.S. Ct. Claims 1977, U.S. Ct. Appeals (8th cir.) 1984, U.S. Supreme Ct. 1994. Assoc. Webster & Sheffield, N.Y.C., 1973-74; mng. atty. Armstrong, Teasdale, Schlafly & Davis, Kansas City, Mo., 1974—. Contbr. articles to profl. jours. Chmn. bd. dirs. Mo. Easter Seals Soc., 1990-92; bd. dirs. Nat. Easter Seal Soc., former chmn. rules, agenda and resolutions com., former chmn. membership and orgnl. structure com. ho. of dels.; founding mem. Heartland Franchise Assn. With U.S. Army, 1968-70. Mem. ABA (litigation sect., franchising forum com.), Mo. Bar Assn. (civil rules and procedures com.), Kansas City Met. Bar Assn. (chmn. antitrust and franchise law com., co-chair 14th and 16th ann. Nat. Franchise Law Inst.), Lawyers Assn. Kansas City, Mo. Orgn. Def. Attys., Def. Rsch. Inst., Am. Judicature Soc., Internat. Rels. Coun. Kansas City, Am. Arbitration Assn. (nat. panel arbitrators 1987, arbitrator U.S. Dist. Ct. we. dist. Mo. 1986—), Kansas City (Mo.) Club, Columbia Club (v.p.), Sigma Nu, Pi Sigma Alpha, Phi Delta. Home: 13703 NW 73rd St Parkville MO 64152-1120 Office: Armstrong Teasdale et al 2345 Grand Blvd Ste 2000 Kansas City MO 64108-2625

SPANDER, ART, sportswriter; b. L.A., Aug. 30, 1938; m. Elizabeth Newman, June 17, 1962; children: Debbie, Wendy. BA in Polit. Sci., UCLA, 1960. With UPI, 1960; joined Santa Monica (Calif.) Evening Outlook, 1963-65, San Francisco Chronicle, 1965-79; columnist San Francisco Examiner, 1979—. Author: Golf: The Passion and the Challenge, 1978, The Art Spander Collection, 1989. Recipient AP Sports Editors awards, Profl. Football Writers Am. awards, 1st place awards San Francisco Press Club, 1st Place Golf Writers Assn. Am. awards, Hayward-Newland Lifetime Achievement award Calif. Golf Writers. Office: San Francisco Examiner 110 5th Ave San Francisco CA 94118-1310*

SPANDORFER, MERLE SUE, artist, educator, author; b. Balt., Sept. 4, 1934; d. Simon Louis and Bernice P. (Jacobson) S.; m. Lester M. Spandorfer, June 17, 1956; children: Cathy, John. Student, Syracuse U., 1952-54; BS, U. Md., 1956. Mem. faculty Cheltenham (Pa.) Sch. Fine Arts, 1969—; instr. printmaking Tyler Sch. Art Temple U., Phila., 1980-84; faculty Pratt Graphics Ctr., N.Y.C., 1985-86. One women shows include Richard Feigen Gallery, N.Y.C., 1970, U. Pa., 1974, Phila. Coll. Textiles and Sci., 1977,

Ericson Gallery, N.Y.C., 1978, 79, R.I. Sch. Design, 1980, Syracuse U., 1981, Marian Locks Gallery, Phila., 1973, 78, 82, Temple U., 1984, Tyler Sch. Art, 1985, University City Sci. Ctr., 1987, Gov.'s Residence, 1988, Wenninger Graphics Gallery, Provinceton, Mass., 1989, Widener U. Art Mus., 1995, Gloucester County Coll., 1996, Mangel Gallery, 1992, 97; group shows Bklyn. Mus. Art, 1973, San Francisco Mus. Art, 1973, Balt. Mus. Art, 1970, 71, 74, Phila. Mus. Art, 1972, 77, Fundacio Joan Miro. Barcelona, Spain, 1977, Del. Mus. Art, Wilmington, 1978, Carlsberg Glyptotek Mus., Copenhagen, 1980, Moore Coll. Art, Phila., 1982, Tyler Sch. Art, 1983, William Penn Meml. Mus., Harrisburg, Pa., 1984, Ariz. State U., 1985, Tiajin Fine Arts Coll., China, 1986, Beaver Coll., Phila., 1988, The Port of History Mus., Phils., 1987, Sichuan Fine Arts Inst., Chong Qing, China, 1988, Glynn Vivian Mus., Swansea, Wales, 1989, Phila. Mus. Art, 1990, Fgn. Mus., Riga, Latvia, 1995; represented in permanent collections Met. Mus. Art, N.Y.C., Whitney Mus. Am. Art, N.Y.C., Mus. Modern Art, N.Y.C., The Israel Mus., Balt. Mus. (gov.'s prize and purchase award 1970), Phila. Mus. Art (purchase award 1977), Toyoh Bijutsu Gakko, Tokyo, Library of Congress, Temple U.; commd. works represented in U. Pa. Inst. Comtemporary Art, 1991; co-author: Making Art Safely, 1993. Recipient award Balt. Mus. Art/Md. Inst. Art, 1971, Govs. prize and Purchase award Balt. Mus. Art, 1970, Outstanding Art Educators award Pa. Art Edn. Assn., 1982, Purchase award Berman Mus., 1995; grantee Pa. Coun. Arts, 1989. Mem. Am. Color Print Soc., Pa. Art Edn. Assn. Jewish. Studio: 307 E Gowen Ave Philadelphia PA 19119-1023

SPANEL, HARRIET ROSA ALBERTSEN, state senator; b. Audubon, Iowa, Jan. 15, 1939; m. Leslie E. Spanel, June 3, 1961; 3 children. BS in Math., Iowa State U., 1961. Rep. Wash. State, 1987-93, senator, 1993—. Home: 901 Liberty St Bellingham WA 98225-5632 Office: PO Box 40482 Olympia WA 98504-0482

SPANGLER, ARNOLD EUGENE, investment banker; b. Ft. Dodge, Iowa, Aug. 1, 1948; s. Kermit Charles and Cora (Buroos) S.; m. Penelope Angell, Nov. 8, 1980; children: Christopher Paul, Allison Elizabeth. BS, Iowa State U., 1970; MBA, Harvard U., 1972. Assoc. Hornblower & Weeks-Hemphill, Noyes, N.Y.C., 1972-74; product officer Citibank, N.Y.C., 1974-76; with Lazard Freres & Co., N.Y.C., 1976-89, gen. ptnr., 1983-89; mng. dir. mergers and acquisitions Paine Webber Inc., N.Y.C., 1989-91; sr. advisor Bentley Assocs., L.P., N.Y.C., 1992-93; mng. dir. Mancuso & Co., N.Y.C., 1993—; bd. dirs. Syncor Internat. Corp., L.A. Home: 1165 Park Ave New York NY 10128-1210

SPANGLER, ARTHUR STEPHENSON, JR., psychologist; b. Boston, June 20, 1949; s. Arthur Stephenson and Barbara Louise (Fellows) S.; m. Deborah A. Kauders, Nov. 27, 1971; children: Heather Anita, Rebecca Haley. BS, Hobart Coll., 1971; MEd, Boston Coll., 1974; ScD, Boston U., 1985. Diplomate Am. Acad. Pain Mgmt.; Nat. bd. cert. counselor; lic. psychologist, Mass.; lic. clin. social worker, Mass.; lic. rehab. counselor, Mass. Mass. Counselor Met. State Hosp., Waltham, Mass., 1971-73; with J.T. Berry Rehab. Ctr., North Reading, Mass., 1974-75; program coord. Shore Collaborative, Medford, Mass., 1975-76; dir. instl. sch. programs So. Shore Collaborative, North Weymouth, Mass., 1976-79; dir. mental retardation program South Shore Mental Health Ctr., Quincy, Mass., 1979-85; coord. outpatient clinic Boston Pain Ctr., Spaulding Rehab. Hosp., Quincy, Mass., 1985-86; v.p., dir. behavioral medicine svcs. Mass. Bay Counseling, Quincy, Mass., 1985—; dir. indsl. disability mgmt. svcs., psychologist chronic pain program Miriam Hosp., Providence, Mass., 1987-88; psychologist John Graham Headache Ctr. Faulkner Hosp., Boston, 1992-94; adj. prof. Sargent Coll., Boston U., 1990—. Vol. counselor Multi-Svc. Ctr., Newton, Mass., 1973-75; bd. dirs. Newton-Wellesley-Weston-Needham Community Mental Health and Mental Retardation Ctr., Newton, 1976-80, pres. 1979-80; mem. Boston Symphony Assn. Vols. Recipient award Nat. Assn. Retarded Citizens, 1974. Mem. APA (assoc.), ACA, Assn. for Study of Pain, Soc. Behavioral Medicine, New England Pain Assn. Episcopalian. Home: 151 Tremont St Apt 11P Boston MA 02111-1110 Office: 1 Billings Rd Quincy MA 02171-2456

SPANGLER, CLEMMIE DIXON, JR., business executive; b. Charlotte, N.C., Apr. 5, 1932; s. Clemmie Dixon and Veva C. (Yelton) S.; m. Meredith Jane Riggs, June 25, 1960; children: Anna Wildy, Abigail Riggs. BS, U. N.C., 1954; MBA, Harvard U., 1956; LHD (hon.), Queens Coll., 1985; LLD (hon.), Davidson Coll., 1986, Furman U., 1993. Pres. C.D. Spangler Constrn. Co., Charlotte, 1958-86, Golden Eagle Industries, Inc., 1968-86; chmn. bd. Bank of N.C., Raleigh, 1973-82; dir. NCNB Corp., 1983-86; chmn. N.C. Bd. Edn., 1982-86; pres. U. N.C., Chapel Hill, 1986-97; bd. dirs. BellSouth Corp., Atlanta; chmn. bd. dirs. Nat. Gypsum Co., Charlotte. Past deacon Myers Park Bapt. Ch., vice-chmn. Charlotte-Mecklenburg Bd. Edn., Charlotte, 1972-76; past trustee Charlotte Nature Mus., Charlotte Symphony Orch., Crozer Theol. Sem.; past chmn. Charlotte adv. bd. Salvation Amry; past bd. dirs. YMCA, Equitable Life Assurance Soc., Jefferson-Pilot Corp.; pres. bd. trustees Mint Mus. Art; bd. dirs. Union Theol. Sem., 1985-90, Assocs. Harvard Bus. Sch. With U.S. Army, 1956-58. Recipient Liberty Bell award Mecklenburg County Bar Assn., 1985, Alumni Achievement award Harvard Bus. Sch., 1988. Mem. Assn. Am. Univs., Bus. Higher Edn. Forum, Harvard Club (N.Y.C.), Univ. Club (N.Y.C.), Quail Hollow Country Club (Charlotte). Office: U NC Gen Adminstrn Office of President PO Box 2688 Chapel Hill NC 27515-2688

SPANGLER, DAVID ROBERT, college administrator, engineer; b. Flint, Mich., Aug. 17, 1940; s. John Solomon and Margaret Inger (McKinley) S.; m. Sally Jeanne Henry, Aug. 28, 1965; children: Timothy David, Megan Marie. BS, U.S. Mil. Acad., 1962; MS in Engring., U. Ill., 1966, PhD in Structural Dynamics, 1977. Registered profl. engr. Commd. 2d lt. U.S. Army, 1962, advanced through grades to lt. col., 1979; prof. math. U.S. Mil. Acad. U.S. Army, West Point, N.Y., 1968-71; engr. Korea Support Command U.S. Army, 1972-73; dep. dist. engr. C.E. U.S. Army, Walla Walla, Wash., 1973-74; research coordinator Def. Nuclear Agy. U.S. Army, Washington, 1976-79; bn. comdr. U.S. Army, Hawaii, 1979-81; inspector C.E. U.S. Army, San Francisco, 1981-82; ret. U.S. Army, 1982; prof. engring. St. Martin's Coll., Lacey, Wash., 1982-84, pres., 1984—; mem. Nat. Com. for Tunnelling Tech., Washington, 1977-79; cons. Thurston County, Olympia, Wash., 1982-84. Contbr. articles to profl. jours. Bd. dirs. Econ. Devel. Coun., Thurston County, 1985-88, Wash. State Capitol Mus., 1988-91. Decorated Bronze Star with 2 oak leaf clusters, Meritorious Service medal, Def. Nuclear Agy. Joint Service medal. Mem. Soc. Mil. Engrs. (v.p. 1980-81, pres. 1973-74), Nat. Assn. Ind. Colls. and Univs. (bd. dirs. 1992-95, treas. 1994), Ind. Colls. Wash. (bd. dirs.), Assn. Benedictine Colls. and Univs. (pres. 1994-95), Rotary (mem. gov.'s oversight com. on tech. 1996). Roman Catholic. Avocation: running. Office: St Martin's Coll Office of Pres Lacey WA 98503

SPANGLER, DENNIS LEE, physician; b. Akron, Ohio, Nov. 8, 1947; s. Wesley Daniel and Florence Adele (Smith) S.; m. July 7, 1972; children: Mathew Brian, Adam Christopher. BS, U. Akron, 1969; MD, Ohio State Med. Sch., 1973. Diplomate Am. Bd. Pediatrics, Am. Bd. Allergy and Immunology. Intern U. Fla. Med. Sch., Gainesville, 1973-74; resident U. Fla. Med. Sch., 1974-75, fellow allergy and clin. immunology, 1975-77; pvt. practice Atlanta Allergy Clinic, P.A., 1977—; chief med. officer Atlanta Allergy and Asthma Clinic, 1995—; dir. chronic lung clinic Ga. Bur. Crippled Children; asst. clin. prof. pediatrics Med. Coll. of Ga. Past pres., bd. dirs. midwest branch Ga. Lung Assn., Atlanta, 1981-82, med. adv. com., 1978—; pres. Fla. Pediatric Alumni Assn., Gainesville, 1985-86. Fellow Am. Acad. Pediatrics, Am. Acad. Allergy and Immunology, Am. Coll. Allergy (therapeutics com. 1983-88, chmn. drug and anaplylaxis Com. 1988—, chmn. com. 1987—), Am. Assn. Cert. Allergists (bd. govs. 1988—, bd. sec.); mem. Am. Thoracic Soc., Am. Coll. Allergy and Asthma (bd. regents 1996—), Ga. Med. Assn., Cobb County Med. Soc., Southeastern Allergy Assn., Cherokee Country Club. Roman Catholic. Avocations: scuba diving, creating stain glass windows. Office: Atlanta Allergy Clinic 1965 N Park Pl NW Atlanta GA 30339-2001

SPANGLER, DOUGLAS FRANK, state legislator; m. Mary Clare Spangler. BS, Kans. State U., 1985; MPA, U. Kans., 1993. Small bus. owner; mem. from dist. 36 Kans. State Ho. of Reps., Topeka. Dem. precinct committeeman, Wyco Dem. Ctrl. Com., 1986-88. Address: 3026 N 54th St Kansas City KS 66104-2117

SPANGLER, LORNA CARRIE, pharmacy technician; b. San Jose, Calif., Feb. 4, 1938; d. Earl Albert and Elsie Carol (Lincoln) LaPorte; children: Kirk Earl, Eric Clair, David Paul, Linda Jean Spangler-Whiting. AA, Monterey Peninsula Coll., 1958; AS in Pharmacy Tech., Santa Ana (Calif.) Coll., 1982; BSBA, Calif. State U., Long Beach, 1986, MS in Vocat. Edn., 1992. Registered pharmacy technician, Calif.; cert. Pharmacy Technician Certification Bd., 1995; cert. C.C. instr., Calif. Pharmacy technician Meml. Med. Ctr., Long Beach, Calif., 1976-78, technician coord., 1979-87; pharmacy technician Hoag Meml. Hosp., Newport Beach, Calif., 1987-92, Sharp Health Care, Murrieta, Calif., 1992—; preceptor Pharmacy Technician Interns, 1992—; accreditation team Am. Bur. Health Edn. Schs., 1987-91; adv. com. Cerritos (Calif.) Coll., 1982—, Calif. Paramed. Tech. Coll., 1996—; spkr. in field. Mem. ctrl. com. Libertarian Party, Riverside County, 1996—, treas., 1997—. Mem. Assn. of Pharmacy Technicians (founder, treas. 1989-91), Valley Computer Soc. (founder 1991), So. Calif. Assn. Pharmacy Technicians (treas. 1990-92, sec. 1992-96, pres. 1996—), Am. Vocat. Assn., Calif. Soc. of Hosp. Pharmacy (task force mem. 1982, nominating com. technician div., 1988), Omicron Tau Theta (Nu chpt. 1988). Avocations: hiking, reading, gardening. Office: Sharp Health Care Murrieta 25500 Medical Center Dr Murrieta CA 92562-5965

SPANGLER, MILLER BRANT, science and technology analyst, planner, consultant; b. Stoyestown, Pa., Sept. 1, 1923; s. Elbert Bruce and Raye Isabel (Brant) S.; m. Claire Labin Kussart, Sept. 20, 1947; children: Daryl Claire, Philip Miller, Coreen Sue. BS with honors, Carnegie-Mellon U., 1950; MA, U. Chgo., 1953, PhD, 1956. Chem. engr. Gulf Rsch. Corp., Harmarville, Pa., 1950-51; assoc. engr. rsch. corp. IBM, Yorktown Heights, N.Y., 1956-60; mgr., market rsch. fed. systems div. IBM, Rockville, Md., 1960-63; program economist U.S. Agy. for Internat. Devel., Turkey, India, 1963-66; dir. ctr. for techno-econ. studies Nat. Planning Assn., Washington, 1966-72; chief, cost benefit analysis br. U.S. Atomic Energy Commn., Washington, 1972-75; spl. asst. policy devel. U.S. Nuclear Regulatory Commn., Washington, 1975-89; pres. Techno-Planning, Inc., Bethesda, Md., 1989-94; freelance author Bethesda, 1994—; mem. adv. bd. NSF Sea Grant Program, Washington, 1969, Environ. Profl. Jour., L.A., 1981-88. Author: New Technology and the Supply of Petroleum, 1956, New Technology and Marine Resource Development, 1970, The Role of Research and Development in Water Resources Planning, 1972, U.S. Experience in Environmental Cost-Benefit Analysis, 1980; contbr. numerous articles and papers to profl. jours. Recipient Planning Rsch. award Program Edn. and Rsch. in Planning U. Chgo., 1953. Mem. N.Y. Acad. Scis., Am. Assn. for the Advancement Sci., Nat. Assn. Environ. Profls., Soc. for Risk Analysis, Internat. Assn. for Impact Assessment., Tau Beta Pi. Republican. Methodist. Avocations: oriental gardening, traveling, photography. Home: 9115 Mcdonald Dr Bethesda MD 20817-1941

SPANGLER, RONALD LEROY, retired television executive, aircraft executive; b. York, Pa., Mar. 5, 1937; s. Ivan L. and Sevilla (Senft) S.; children: Kathleen, Ronald Jr., Beth Anne. Student U. Miami (Fla.), 1955-59. Radio announcer Sta. WSBA, York, 1955-59; TV producer Sta. WBAL-TV, Balt. and NBC TV, 1958-65; pres., chmn. bd. LewRon Television, N.Y.C., Hollywood, Calif., 1965-78; pres., chmn. bd. Spanair Inc., distbr. Rockwell bus. aircraft, 1975-85; owner Prancing Horse Farm. Mem. Video Tape Producers Assn. N.Y.C., Rolls Royce Owners Club, Ferrari Clubs Am. and Italia, Mercedes Benz Club Am., Porsche Club Am. Avocations: racing Ferrari automobiles, collecting and dealing in vintage Ferrari automobiles. Home: Prancing Horse Farm 3710 Ady Rd Street MD 21154

SPANGLER, SCOTT MICHAEL, private investor; b. Toledo, Aug. 4, 1938; s. Walter James and Martha Zoe (Hirscher) S.; m. Jean Galt Schmonsees, June 10, 1963; children—Karen Elizabeth, Scott Michael, Andrew Galt. B.M.E., U. Cin., 1961; M.B.A., Harvard U., 1963. Research asso. M.I.T., 1963-65; fin. exec. Cooper Industries, Inc., Mt. Vernon, Ohio, 1965-68; v.p. indsl. group White Motor Corp., Cleve., 1968-70; pres. Spangler and Co., Houston, 1970-73; dir., pres., chief exec. officer AZL Resources, Inc. (and affiliates), Phoenix, 1973-84; pres., chief exec. officer First Phoenix Capital, Inc., Scottsdale, Ariz., 1984-90; assoc. adminstr. AID, Washington, 1990-93; pres. First Phoenix Capital Inc., Phoenix and Washington, 1993—; bd. dirs. First So. Capital Corp., Alamosa Nat. Bank, Cen. Ariz. Bank, New London Oil Inc. Mem. World Pres.' Orgn., Chief Execs. Orgn., Harvard Club, Paradise Valley Country Club, Met. Club. Republican. Presbyterian. Office: 700 New Hampshire Washington DC 20037-2406

SPANGLER, VERA MAE, mental health nurse; b. Montebello, Va., Jan. 21, 1939; d. Roy Hall and Flora May (Smiley) Allen; m. Jerry Cleveland Utt, Jan. 20, 1956 (div. June 1981); 1 child, Sherry Lynn; m. Danny Eugene Spangler, Apr. 16, 1994. AAS, Piedmond Va. C.C., 1984. RN, Va. Staff nurse, RN Kings' Daughter's Hosp., Staunton, Va., 1984-87; nurse supr., unit mgr. Liberty House Nursing Home, Waynesboro, Va., 1987-90; quality assurance nurse supr. Walnut Hills Convalescent Ctr., Petersburg, Va., 1990-92; RN, clinician A Ctrl. State Hosp., Petersburg, 1992—. Republican. Presbyterian. Avocation: doll collecting. Home: 4607 Woodstream Ct Petersburg VA 23803-8856 Office: Ctrl State Hosp PO Box 4030 Petersburg VA 23803-0030

SPANIER, GRAHAM BASIL, academic administrator, family sociologist, demographer, marriage and family therapist; b. Capetown, South Africa, July 18, 1948; s. Fred and Rosadele (Lurie) S.; m. Sandra Kay Whipple, Sept. 11, 1971; children: Brian Lockwood, Hadley Alison. BS, Iowa State U., 1969, MS, 1971; PhD, Northwestern U., 1973. Assoc. dean, prof. in charge Pa. State U., University Park, 1973-82, pres., 1995—; vice provost, prof. SUNY, Stony Brook, 1982-86; provost, v.p. for acad. affairs Oreg. State U., Corvallis, 1986-91; chancellor U. Nebr., Lincoln, 1991-95; pres. Pa. State U., 1995—; bd. dirs. Acad. Health Cts. Author 10 books and 100 articles to profl. jours. Pres., chmn. bd. dirs. Christian Children's Fund, Richmond, Va., 1985-94; del. White House Conf. on Families, Washington, 1980; host Pub. Broadcast TV programs, 1973-76; bd. dirs. Nat. 4H Coun., 1997—. Recipient Moran award Am. Assn. Family and Consumer Scis., 1987; named Outstanding Young Alumnus Iowa State U., 1982; Am. Assn. Marriage and Family Therapy fellow, 1983—, Woodrow Wilson fellow, 1972. Mem. Nat. Coun. Family Rels. (pres. 1987-88, Outstanding Grad. Student award 1972), Population Assn. Am., Am. Sociol. Assn. (family sect. chmn. 1983-84), Internat. Sociol. Assn., Am. Assn. Higher Edn., Am. Assn. Family and Consumer Scis., Nat. Assn. State Univs. and Land Grant Colls. (exec. com. coun. on acad. affairs 1990-91, bd. pres. commn. on info. technologies 1993-96, chair, 1996—), Am. Coun. on Edn. (commn. on women 1992-95), Nat. Collegiate Athletic Assn. (pres. commn. 1995), Am. Assn. State Colls. (joint commn. on accountability report 1993-95), Acad. Health Ctrs. (bd. dirs. 1996—). Democrat. Avocations: aviation, magic, athletics. Office: Pa State Univ Office of Pres 201 Old Main University Park PA 16802-1503

SPANN, GEORGE WILLIAM, management consultant; b. Cuthbert, Ga., July 21, 1946; s. Glinn Linwood and Mary Grace (Hiller) S.; B.S. in Physics with honors, Ga. Inst. Tech., 1968, M.S., 1970, M.S. in Indsl. Mgmt., 1973; m. Laura Jeanne Nason, June 10, 1967; children: Tanya Lynne, Stephen William. Engr., Martin Marietta Corp., Orlando, Fla., 1968-70; research scientist Engring. Expt. Sta., Ga. Inst. Tech., 1970-75; v.p., dir. Metrics, Inc., mgmt. and engring. cons., Atlanta, 1973-78, pres., dir., 1978—; v.p., dir. Exec. Data Systems, Inc., 1981—; mem. Ga. Energy Policy Council, Ga. Metrication Council, NASA applications survey group for Landsat follow-on; mem. com. on practical applications of remote sensing from space Space Applications Bd. Nat. Research Council; market research cons. NOAA, NASA, pvt. cos. Regents scholar, 1964. Mem. Am. Soc. Photogrammetry, Urban and Regional Info. Systems Assn., Atlanta Jaycees, Tau Beta Pi, Phi Kappa Phi, Sigma Pi Sigma. Author papers, reports. Home: 3475 Clubland Dr Marietta GA 30068-2509 Office: 1640 Powers Ferry Rd SE Bldg 27 Marietta GA 30067-5491

SPANN, KATHARINE DOYLE, marketing and communications executive; b. Holton, Kans.; d. Edward James and Josephine (Hurla) Doyle; m. Hugh J. Spann; 1 dau., Susan Katharine. BS, Emporia State Coll., V.p. Bozell & Jacobs Advt. (formerly L.C. Cole Co.), San Francisco, 1951-76; pres. Katharine Doyle Spann Assos., 1977—; propr. Kate's Vineyard, Napa Valley, Calif. Bd. dirs. No. Calif. Am. Inst. Wine and Food, Napa Valley Opera House. Named Advt. Woman of Yr., 1962; recipient El Capitan award Peninsula chpt. Pub. Relations Soc. Am., 1962, 66, Am. Silver Anvil award, Pub. Relations Soc. Am., 1962, 66, Excellence award Publicity Club of Bay Area, 1966. Trustee, bd. dirs., mem. exhbn. com., audience devel. com. Fine Arts Mus. San Francisco. Mem. Am. Soc. Enology, Am. Inst. Wine and Food, Napa Valley Women in Wine, Calif. Vintage Wine Soc. (wine com.), Officier Commandeur, Conferie des Chevaliers du Tastevin (events com.), Delta Sigma Epsilon. Club: Metropolitan (San Francisco). Home: 1447 Whitehall Ln Saint Helena CA 94574-9684

SPANNAGEL, ALAN WAYNE, physiologist; b. Harlingen, Tex., May 9, 1958; s. Billy Wayne and Ersel Lou (Jones) S.; m. Kathy Lynn Lang, 1980 (div. 1982); m. Maristella Partin, 1987 (div. 1988). BS in Marine Biology, Tex. A&M U., 1980; MS in Biology, U. Houston, Clear Lake City, 1985; postgrad., U. Tex. Health Sci. Ctr., San Antonio. Rsch. technician dept. surgery U. Tex. Med. Br., Galveston, 1981-85, rsch. assoc., 1985-87; grad. rsch. asst. dept. physiology U. Tex. Health Sci. Ctr., San Antonio, 1987—; instr., lectr. Physiology for Occupl. Therapy Students, 1990-93; reviewer and cons. on Physiol. Studies. Contbr. articles to profl. sci. jours. Mem. Am. Pancreatic Assn. Achievements include isolation, purification and physiological studies on a novel gastrointestinal peptide, the luminal CCK-releasing factor; demonstration that adapted changes in pancreatic juice composition have physiological effects on gastrointestinal hormone secretion and gastrointestinal function; showed that dietary peptides, not intact protein, stimulated pancreatic secretion during a meal. Home: 154 Barbara Bend Universal City TX 78148 Office: Univ Tex Health Sci Ctr Dept of Physiology 7703 Floyd Curl Dr San Antonio TX 78284-6200

SPANNINGER, BETH ANNE, lawyer; b. Bucks County, Pa., July 3, 1950; d. Feryl Louis and Nancy Elizabeth (Hendricks) S. AB magna cum laude, Muhlenberg Coll., 1972; MA, MEd, Lehigh U., 1975; JD, Temple U., 1979. Bar: Pa. 1979. Asst. dist. atty. Phila. Dist. Atty.'s Office, 1979-81; assoc. Bolger, Picker, Hankin & Tannenbaum, Phila., 1981-86, ptnr., 1986-88; sr. counsel SmithKline Beecham Corp., Phila., 1988-96, v.p., assoc. gen. counsel, 1996—. Mem. ABA, Pa. Bar Assn., Phila. Bar Assn., Del. Valley Assn. Corp. Counsel, Animal Health Inst. (law com. 1992—), Phi Beta Kappa. Avocations: literature, jogging, theater, piano.

SPANNUTH, JOHN ROY, aquatics association executive; b. Reading, Pa., Oct. 7, 1933; s. John R. and Virginia Spannuth; children: John III, Virginia. BA in Health and Phys. Edn., West Chester U., 1961. Aquatics dir. YMCA, Reading, 1956-59; swimming coach West Chester (Pa.) U., 1959-61; aquatics dir. Phillips Petroleum Co., Bartlesville, Okla., 1961-68; exec. dir. Amarillo (Tex.) Aquatic Club, 1968-69; nat. aquatics adminstr. Nat. AAU, Indpls., 1970-74; exec. dir. Spl. Olypmics Kennedy Found., Washington, 1974-75; nat. swimming coach Country of Bahrain, 1980-83; dir. recreation Saudi Arabian Air Force, Riyadh, 1984-86; sr. aquatics dir. Cleve. County Family YMCA, Norman, Okla., 1986-89; pres., CEO U.S. Water Fitness Assn., Boynton Beach, Fla., 1989—; bd. dirs. Internat. Swimming Hall of Fame; spkr. in field. Recipient C. Carson award Health & Fitness Leaders, Ranson Arthur award U.S. Masters Swimming Assn. Mem. Am. Swimming Coaches Assn. (past pres.). Office: US Water Fitness Assn PO Box 3279 Boynton Beach FL 33424-3279

SPANOGLE, ROBERT WILLIAM, marketing and advertising company executive, association administrator; b. Lansing, Mich., Nov. 13, 1942; s. William P. and Mary A. (Lenneman) S.; m. Ruth Ann Long, Jan. 14, 1967; children: John Paul Stephen Donald, Amy Lynn. AA, Lansing C.C., 1969; BA, Mich. State U., 1971; postgrad., U. Pa., 1985. Cons. Nat. League Cities, Washington, 1971-72; cons. Am. Legion, Indpls., 1972-75, dir. membership, 1975-79; exec. dir. Am. Legion, Washington, 1975-81, nat. adjutant, 1981—; chmn. HP Direct, Inc., Indpls., 1985—; chmn. exec. com. HP Direct, Inc., Washington, 1989—; mem. individual investors adv. com. N.Y. Stock Exch., N.Y.C., 1989-92. Bd. govs. USO, Washington, 1986-92; trustee St. Mary of the Woods Coll., Terre Haute, Ind., 1991—; treas. Civil War Battle Flags Commn. State of Ind., Indpls., 1994—; sec. 500 Festival Assocs., Indpls., 1985-91; mem. Vet.'s Day Coun., Indpls., 1989; bd. dirs. Indpls. Athletic Club, Crossroads Coun. Boy Scouts Am., 1985-92. With U.S. Army, 1962-65. Mem. Am. Legion of Mich. (Hon. Comdr. 1985), Kiwanis (exec. com. 1989-92). Roman Catholic. Avocations: golf, hunting, reading. Home: 672 Yosemite Dr Indianapolis IN 46217-3962 Office: Am Legion 700 N Pennsylvania St Indianapolis IN 46204-1129

SPANOS, ALEXANDER GUS, professional football team executive; b. Stockton, Calif., Sept. 28, 1923; m. Faye Spanos; children: Dean, Dea Spanos Berberian, Alexis Spanos Ruhl, Michael. LLD (hon.), U. Pacific, 1984. Chmn. bd. dirs. A.G. Spanos Constrn. Inc., Stockton, Calif., 1960—; chmn. bd. dirs. A.G. Spanos Properties Inc., Stockton, Calif., 1960—, A.G. Spanos Mgmt. Inc., Stockton, Calif., 1967—, A.G. Spanos Enterprises Inc., Stockton, Calif., 1971—, A.G. Spanos Devel. Inc., Stockton, Calif., 1973—, A.G. Spanos Realty Inc., Stockton, Calif., 1978—, A.G. Spanos Jet Ctr. Inc., Stockton, Calif., 1980—, A.G.S. Fin. Corp., Stockton, Calif., 1980—; pres., chmn. bd. dirs. San Diego Chargers, 1984—; Chmn. bd. dirs. A.G.S. Spanos Land Co., Stockton, Calif., 1982—. Former trustee Children's Hosp., San Francisco, San Francisco Fine Arts Mus.; trustee Eisenhower Med. Ctr., Rancho Mirage, Calif.; hon. regent U. Pacific, Stockton, 1972-82; gov. USO, , Washington, 1982—. Served with USAF, 1942-46. Recipient Albert Gallatin award Zurich-Am. Ins. Co., 1973, Horatio Alger award Horatio Alger Found., 1982, medal of Honor Statue of Liberty-Ellis Islan Found., 1982. Mem. Am. Hellenic Ednl. Progressive Assn., Calif. C. of C. (bd. dirs. 1980-85). Republican. Greek Orthodox. Avocation: golfing. Office: San Diego Chargers Jack Murphy Stadium PO Box 609609 San Diego CA 92160-9609 also: A G Spanos Constrn Co 1341 W Robinhood Dr Stockton CA 95207-5515*

SPANOS, POL DIMITRIOS, engineering educator; b. Messini, Peloponnesus, Greece, Feb. 27, 1950; came to U.S., 1973; s. Dimitrios Constandin Spanos and Aicaterine Polychronis Bonaros; children: Demetri, Eudokia. Diploma in mech. engring., Nat. Tech. U., Athens, 1973; MS in Civil Engring., Calif. Inst. Tech., 1974, PhD in Applied Mechanics, 1976. Registered profl. engr., Tex., Greece. Rsch. asst. Calif. Inst. Tech., Pasadena, 1973-76, rsch. fellow, 1976-77; from asst. prof. to assoc. prof. U. Tex.-Austin, 1981-84, P.D. Henderson assoc. prof. engring., 1983-84; prof. mech. engring. and civil engring. Rice U., Houston, 1984-88, L.B. Ryon endowed chair in engring., 1988—; cons. on analytical and numerical applications of theory of dynamics and vibrations, worldwide. Author: Random Vibrations, Probabilistic Offshore Mechanics, Probabilistic Methods in Civil Engineering, Random Vibration and Statistical Linearization, Dynamic Analysis of Non-Linear Structures by the Method of Statistical Quadratization, Stochastic Finite Elements: A Spectral Approach, Computational Stochastic Mechanics, Probabilistic Structural Mechanics: Advances in Structural Reliability Methods, Random Vibrations: A Broad Perspective; contbr. to profl. jour. issues devoted to dynamics and vibrations; mem. editl. bd. 8 jours.; editor-in chief or co-editor 2 primary jours. on mechanics. Recipient European award of sci. N.V. Phillipps Co., Eindhoven, Netherlands, 1969, Presdl. Young Investigator award in earthquake engring. NSF, 1984-89, Cert. merit McDonnell Douglas Astronautics Co., Houston, 1987, G.R. Brown award for superior tchg. Rice U., 1995, 96. Fellow ASME (participant tech. confs. and coms., Pi Tau Sigma Gold medal 1982, G.L. Larson Meml. award 1991), ASCE (participant tech. confs. and coms., W.L. Huber Civil Engring. Rsch. prize 1989, Alfred M. Freudenthal medal 1992, Humboldt Rsch. award for sr. scientists, from Alexander von Humboldt Found., Germany, 1995), Am. Acad. Mechanics; mem. Earthquake Engring. Rsch. Inst., Internat. Assn. for Structural Safety and Reliability, Hellenic Profl. soc. (sponsor scholarship com.). Office: Rice U Dept Mech Engring MS 321 6100 Main St Houston TX 77005-1827

SPANOVICH, MILAN, civil engineer; b. Steubenville, Ohio, Feb. 19, 1929; s. Stanley and Katherine (Komazec) S.; m. Sylvia J. Tomko, Apr. 16, 1971. B.S. Civil Engring, Carnegie-Mellon U., 1956, M.S. Civil Engring., 1957. Registered profl. engr., Pa., N.Y., Ohio, Va., W.Va., Mich., N.Mex., Ky., Md., Colo., N.J., Del., N.C., Fla. Instr. Carnegie-Mellon U., 1957-60; charter assoc., v.p. E. D'Appolonia Assocs., 1957-61; mem. civil engring. staff U. N.Mex., 1961-63; founder, sr. cons. Engring. Mechs., Inc., Pitts., 1963-96. Contbr. articles on soil mechs. to tech. jours. Bd. dirs. Carnegie Mellon U. Andrew Carnegie Soc. Recipient Pitts. Young Civil Engr. of Yr. award, 1969. Fellow ASCE (Pitts. Civl Engr. of the Yr. 1987, chmn. numerous coms.), Am. Cons. Engrs. Council; mem. Cons. Engrs. Council

Greater Pitts. (pres. 1972-74), Engring. Soc. Western Pa. (dir. 1972, 77-83), Nat. Soc. Profl. Engrs., Pa. Soc. Profl. Engrs. (pres. Pitts. chpt. 1971, Hornfeck award Pitts. chpt. 1979, state dir. 1976-79, Disting. Service award Pitts. chpt. 1985, Pa. Engr. of the Yr. 1988, Profl. Devel. award 1989, Outstanding Svc. award Pitts. chpt. 1993), ASTM (chmn. task com. on relative density of granular soils 1959-63), Am. Concrete Inst., Hwy. Research Bd., Internat. Soc. Soil Mechs. and Found. Engring., Pitts. Geol. Soc., Am. Arbitration Assn., Profl. Engrs. in Pvt. Practice (chmn. 1970-71), Pitts. Builders Exchange, Soc. Explosives Engrs., Am. Soc. Hwy. Engrs., Carnegie-Mellon U. Alumni Assn. (mem. planning com.), Chi Epsilon Nat. Civil Engring. Honor Soc. Patentee found. systems. Home: 216 Eton Rd Pittsburgh PA 15205-1733

SPAR, EDWARD JOEL, demographer; b. N.Y.C., Jan. 2, 1939; s. Max and Dora (Miller) S.; m. Rosalind Getzoff, June 10, 1962; 1 dau., Zoe; m. 2d Elizabeth A. Harrington, Sept. 10, 1977; children: Melissa, Daniel, Matthew. B.B.A., CCNY, 1961. Statistician Alfred Politz Research, N.Y.C., 1962-65; sr. statistician Computer Users Co., N.Y.C., 1965-68; v.p. Daniel Starch, Mamaroneck, N.Y., 1968-71; pres. Market Statistics, N.Y.C., 1971—; demographic cons. N.Y. Times, 1982—; exec. dir. Coun. Profl. Assns. on Fed. Stats.; dir. Bill Comms., Strategy Rsch., Miami, Fla., Dualabs, Arlington, Va. Mem. Assn. Pub. Data Users, Am. Statis. Assn., Coun. Profl. Assocs. Fed. Statistics, (exec. dir.), Am. Mktg. Assn. Democrat. Jewish. Home: 5400 Bradley Blvd Bethesda MD 20814-1002 Office: 633 3d Ave 1429 Duke St Alexandria VA 22314-3461

SPARANO, VINCENT THOMAS, editor; b. Newark, Apr. 7, 1934; s. Gaetano and Agnes (Martucci) S.; m. Elizabeth Frances Rooney, Nov. 21, 1959; children: Donna Marie, Michael Thomas, Matthew John, Ellen Elizabeth. Student, Newark Coll. Engring., 1952-53; BS, NYU, 1959. Assoc. editor Sports Afield Mag., N.Y.C., 1959-60; editor Outdoor Life Mag., N.Y.C., 1960-95; outdoor life, editor emeritus, sr. field editor Gannett News Svc., 1996—. Author: Complete Outdoors Encyclopedia, 1972 (Library Assn. Outstanding Reference Work award 1973), The Outdoor Sportsman's Illustrated Dictionary, 1980, The American Fisherman's Fresh and Salt Water Guide, 1976; editor: Shooting-Why We Miss, 1977, Greatest Hunting Stories Ever Told, 1983, Classic Hunting Tales, 1986, Tales of Woods and Waters, 1989, Hunting Dangerous Game, 1992, Game Birds and Gun Dogs, 1992. editor-in-chief, pub. Northeast Guides to Saltwater Fishing and Boating, Southeast Guides to Saltwater Fishing and Boating. Committeeman Boy Scouts Am., 1970; chmn. Fairfield Fishing Derby, 1971—; trustee Camp Wyanokie Commn., Fairfield, 1976; bd. dirs. Catch and Release Found. Served to cpl. U.S. Army, 1954-56. Recipient Conservation Svc. award U.S. Dept. of Interior, 1996. Mem. Outdoor Writers Assn. Am. (bd. dirs.), Rod and Gun Editors Assn. Met. N.Y. (pres. 1977-78), Nat. Rifle Assn. (cert. firearms instr.), Fairfield Conservation and Sportsman's Assn. (pres. 1983-85), Sigma Delta Chi, Theta Chi. Roman Catholic. Lodges: Elks, K.C. Avocations: hunting; fishing; boating. Home: 17 Henning Dr Fairfield NJ 07004-1744 also: PO Box 821 190 Arnold Blvd, Barnegat Light Long Beach Island NJ 08008

SPARBERG, ESTHER B., chemist, educator; b. N.Y.C., June 17, 1922; d. Abraham and Sarah (Kurnick) Braun; m. Lester S. Sparberg, Dec. 31, 1944; children—Andrew, Alice. B.S. in Chemistry, U. N.C., 1943; M.A., Columbia U., Tchrs. Coll., 1945, Ed.D., 1958. Chemist Interchem. Corp., 1943; technician Rockefeller Inst. Med. Research, 1943-44; tchr. chemistry Julia Richman High Sch., N.Y.C., 1946-47; mem. faculty Hofstra U., 1959-95, prof. chemistry, 1977-89, prof. emerita, 1989; also dir. NSF projects for tchrs. Sci. Co-author: A Laboratory Manual of Concepts in Chemistry, 1968, Chemical Quantitative Analysis: A New Approach, 1972, Ideas, Investigation and Thought, A General Chemistry Laboratory Manual, 1978, The Physical Sciences: the Search for Order and Harmony, 1997; contbr. articles to profl. jours. Sci. manpower fellow Columbia U., 1956-57. Mem. Am. Chem. Soc., History Sci. Soc., Am. Sci. Tchrs. Assn., Kappa Delta Pi. Democrat. Jewish. Office: Hofstra U Hempstead NY 11550

SPARBERG, MARSHALL STUART, gastroenterologist, educator; b. Chgo., May 20, 1936; s. Max Shane and Mildred Rose (Haffron) S.; m. Eve Gaymont Enda, Mar. 15, 1987. B.A., Northwestern U., 1957, M.D., 1960. Intern Evanston Hosp., Ill., 1960-61; resident in internal medicine Barnes Hosp., St. Louis, 1961-63; fellow U. Chgo., 1963-65; practice medicine specializing in gastroenterolgy Chgo., 1967—; asst. prof. medicine Northwestern U., 1967-72, assoc. prof., 1972-80, prof. clin. medicine, 1980—; instr. Washington U., St. Louis, 1961-63, U. Chgo., 1963-65. Author: Ileostomy Care, 1969, Primer of Clinical Diagnosis, 1972, Ulcerative Colitis, 1978, Inflammatory Bowel Disease, 1982; contbr. numerous articles to profl. jours. Pres. Fine Arts Music Found., 1974-76, Crohn's Disease and Colitis Found. of Am., pres. Ill. chpt., 1994-97; bd. dirs. Lyric Opera Guild, 1974-94, Chamber Music Soc. North Shore Chgo., 1984—; physician to Chgo. Symphony Orch., 1981-97. With USAF, 1965-67. Named Outstanding Tchr. Northwestern U. Med. Sch., 1972. Mem. AMA, ACP, Am. Gastroent. Assn., Am. Coll. Gastroent. (bd. govs.), Chgo. Med. Soc., Chgo. Soc. Internal Medicine, Chgo. Soc. Gastroenterology (pres.), Chgo. Soc. Gastrointestinal Endoscopy (pres.). Democrat. Jewish. Office: 676 N Saint Clair St Ste 1525 Chicago IL 60611-2995

SPARGO, BENJAMIN H., educator, renal pathologist; b. Six Mile Run, Pa., Aug. 11, 1919; s. Benjamin H. and Lillian (Rankin) S.; m. Barbara Scollard, Mar. 12, 1942; children—Janet, Patricia. B.S. in Biol. Scis, U. Chgo., 1948, M.S. in Pathology, 1952, M.D. with honors, 1952. Intern Univ. Hosp., Ann Arbor, Mich., 1953-54; resident pathology U. Chgo. Med. Sch., 1954-55, mem. faculty, 1954—, prof. renal pathology, 1964-95; prof. pathology emeritus, 1995—, assoc. chmn. dept., 1974-80; cons. Armed Forces Inst. Pathology, 1975-79, Midwest Regional Organ Bank of Ill., 1989-94. Served with USAAF, 1941-46. Recipient Research Career award Nat. Heart Inst., 1964. Mem. Internat. Acad. Pathology (chmn. edn. com. 1975-77). Home: 5550 S South Shore Dr Chicago IL 60637-5057

SPARK, DAME D. B. E. MURIEL SARAH, writer; b. Edinburgh, Scotland, Feb. 1, 1918; d. Bernard and Sarah Elizabeth Maud (Uezzell) Camberg; m. S.O. Spark, (marriage dissolved); 1 son. Student, Heriot Watt Coll., Edinburgh, James Gillespie Sch., Edingburgh; DLitt (hon.), Strathclyde U., 1971, U. Edinburgh, 1989, Aberdeen U., 1995; DUniv. (hon.), Heriot-Watt U., 1995. Gen. sec. Poetry Soc., 1947-49; editor Poetry Rev., 1949. Author: (non-fiction) Child of Light: A Reassessment of Mary Wollstonecraft Shelley, 1951 (rev. as Mary Shelley, 1987), Emily Brontë: Her Life and Work, 1953, John Masefield, 1953, revised, 1992, The Essence of the Brontës, 1993; (poetry) The Fanfarlo and Other Verse, 1952, Collected Poems I, 1967, Going Up to Sotheby's and Other Poems, 1982; (autobiography) Curriculum Vitae, 1992; (fiction) The Comforters, 1957, Robinson, 1958, The Go-Away Bird and Other Stories, 1958, Memento Mori, 1959, The Ballad of Peckham Rye, 1960, The Bachelors, 1960, Voices at Play, 1961, The Prime of Miss Jean Brodie, 1961, The Girls of Slender Means, 1963, The Mandelbaum Gate, 1965 (James Tait Black Meml. prize 1966, Yorkshire Post Book of Yr. award 1965), Collected Stories I, 1968, The Public Image, 1968, (juvenile) The Very Fine Clock, 1968, The Driver's Seat, 1970, Not to Disturb, 1971, The Hothouse by the East River, 1973, The Abbess of Crewe, 1974, The Takeover, 1976, Territorial Rights, 1979, Loitering with Intent, 1981, Bang-Bang You're Dead and Other Stories, 1982, The Only Problem, 1984, The Stories of Muriel Spark, 1985, A Far Cry from Kensington, 1988, Symposium, 1990, (juvenile) The French Window and the Small Telephone, 1993; (play) The Doctors of Philosophy, 1962; (radio plays) The Party Through the Wall, 1957, The Interview, 1958, The Dry River Bed, 1959, The Ballad of Peckham Rye, 1960 (Prix Italia 1962), The Danger Zone, 1961; editor: A Selection of Poems by Emily Brontë, 1952, My Best Mary: The Letters of Mary Shelley, 1953, The Letters of the Brontës: A Selection, 1954, Letters of John Henry Newman, 1957. Decorated Officier de l'Ordre des Arts et des Lettres (France), Dame Order Brit. Empire, 1993; recipient Observer short story prize, 1951, Ingersoll T.S. Eliot award, 1992. Fellow Royal Soc. Edinburgh; mem. AAAL (hon. 1978). Address: care David Higham Assocs Ltd, 5-8 Lower John St, London W1R 4HA, England

SPARKES, CHERYL FLOWERS, accountant; b. Texarkana, Ark., July 31, 1956; d. Charles Glendon and Mary Carolyn (Caldwell) Flowers; m. Jay Bedford Sparkes, July 14, 1984. BSBA, U. Ark., 1978. CPA, Tex., CMA. Staff acct. Ernst & Ernst, Dallas, 1978-80; sr. acct. Ernst & Whinney, Dallas, 1980-82, mgr., 1983-84, sr. mgr., 1984-89; sr. mgr. Ernst & Young, Dallas, 1989-94, fin. adv. svcs. regional dir. human resources, 1993-95, cons. ptrn., market leader, dispute resolution, litigation, 1994-95; with Ernst & Young, N.Y.C., 1995—. Chmn. Nat. Edn. Com., 1996—; neighborhood capt. Am. Cancer Soc., Dallas, 1990-92; active Dallas Mus. Art, 1985-95, Jr. League Dallas, 1990-95. Mem. AICPA, Inst. Mgmt. Accts., Tex. Soc. CPAs, Delta Delta Delta. Avocations: weight training, traveling. Home: 250 E 54th St Apt 9C New York NY 10022 Office: Ernst & Young LLP 787 7th Ave New York NY 10019-6018

SPARKMAN, BRANDON BUSTER, educator, writer, consultant; b. Hartselle, Ala., Aug. 2, 1929; s. George Olen and Mary Louise (Jones) S.; m. Wanda Phillips, Sept. 13, 1952; children—Ricky Brandon, Rita Sharon, Robert Lee. B.S., U. North Ala., 1952; M.A., U. Ala., 1958, Ednl. Specialist, 1961; Ed.D., Auburn (Ala.) U., 1970. Tchr., asst. prin. Phllips High Sch., Bear Creek, Ala., 1954-57; prin. Tuscumbia, Ala., 1957-65; asst. supt., 1965-69; ednl. cons. Auburn Center, 1969-70; mem. faculty dept. sch. adminstrn. Auburn U., 1970; asst. supt. for staff personnel devel. Jackson (Miss.) Pub. Schs., 1970-71, supt., 1971-73; sch. supt. Richland County Sch. Dist. 1, Columbia, S.C., 1973-75; asst. supt. instruction Hartselle (Ala.) City Schs., 1975-80; supt. Guntersville (Ala.) City Schs., 1980-88; adj. prof. Auburn U., 1988—; pres., chief exec. officer The Right Combination Pub. & Ednl. Svcs. Corp., Guntersville, Ala., 1984-93; writer, cons. in field. Sr. author: Blueprint for a Brighter Child, 1973, STEPS (System for Teacher Evaluation of Pre-reading Skills), 1974; co-author: Preparing Your Preschooler for Reading, 1977, Competency Tests for Basic Reading Skills, 1978, Soaring High with Science, 1985, Soaring High with Social Studies, 1985; author: How Well Does Your Child Read, 1979, Writing Composition Made Easy, 1991, Blueprint for Expository Writing, 1993; editor: The In-Between Years, 1979; creator: CORE (Program Management Through Computer Systems), 1975; editor, contbg. author: The Advantaged, A Preschool Program for the Disadvantaged, 1969; contbr. articles to profl. jours. Bd. dirs. Morgan County chpt. ARC, United Givers Fund, Colbert-Lauderdale Child Study Center, Sheffield-Tuscumbia Credit Union; bd. govs. Jackson Symphony Orch.; adv. bd. Jackson Mental Health Center. Served with AUS, 1952-54. Recipient Human Relations award Jackson. Mem. Am., Ala assns. sch. adminstrs. (past pres.), Ala. Council Sch. Adminstrn. and Supervision (past pres.), Assn. Supervision and Curriculum Devel., Ala. Assn. Supervision and Curriculum Devel. (past pres.), Florence State U. Alumni Assn. (past pres.). Methodist (ch. sch. tchr., supt., vice chmn. ofcl. bd., chmn. commn. edn.). Home and Office: PO Box 961 Guntersville AL 35976-0961

SPARKMAN, ROBERT SATTERFIELD, retired surgeon, educator; b. Brownwood, Tex., Feb. 18, 1912; s. Ellis Hugh and Ola (Stanley) S.; m. Willie Ford Bassett, Feb. 21, 1942. B.A., Baylor U., 1935, M.D., 1935, LL.D., 1974. Diplomate Am. Bd. Surgery. Intern Cin. Gen. Hosp., 1935-36, resident in surgery, 1938-40; intern Good Samaritan Hosp., Lexington, Ky., 1936-37; resident in pathology Baylor Hosp., Dallas, 1937-38; practice medicine specializing in surgery Dallas, 1946—; chief dept. surgery Baylor U. Med. Center, Dallas, 1969-81; emeritus chief Baylor U. Med. Center, 1982-97; mem. staff Parkland Meml. Hosp., Dallas; clin. prof. surgery U. Tex. Southwestern Med. Sch., Dallas, 1963-97; chief civilian surg. cons. 5th U.S. Army Area, 1950-73. Editor, also prin. author: The Texas Surgical Society—The First Fifty Years, 1965; editor: Essays of a Louisiana Surgeon, 1977, Minutes of the American Surgical Association, 1880-68, 1972, The Southern .Surgical Association; The First 100 Years, 1887-1987, 1989—; mem. editorial bd.: Am. Jour. Surgery; Contbr. articles to profl. jours. Bd. dirs. Friends of Dallas Pub. Libr., 1968—. Served to col. M.C. AUS, 1940-46, PTO. Decorated Bronze Star medal; recipient Disting. Alumnus award Baylor U., 1976, Disting. Alumnus award Coll. Medicine, 1976, Disting. Alumnus award Tex. Beta chpt. Alpha Epsilon Delta, A.C. Greene award Friends of Dallas Pub. Libr., 1993; commd. hon. Ky. col., 1980. Fellow ACS (bd. govs. 1962-70); mem. AMA, Am. Surg. Assn. (2d v.p. 1977-78), So. Surg. Assn. (pres. 1978, hon. mem. 1983), Okla. Surg. Assn. (hon.), Tex. Surg. Soc. (pres. 1965), Dallas Gen. Surgeons Soc. (pres. 1961), Internat. Soc. Surgery, Tex. Med. Assn., Soc. Med. Cons. to Armed Forces, James D. Rives Surg. Soc., Soc. Surgery Alimentary Tract, Internat. Biliary Assn., Philos. Soc. Tex., Parkland Surg. Soc. (hon. mem.), Petroleum Club, Dallas Country Club, Phi Beta Kappa, Alpha Omega Alpha. Home: 5351 Wenonah Dr Dallas TX 75209-5517

SPARKMAN, STEVEN LEONARD, lawyer; b. Sarasota, Fla., May 30, 1947; s. Simeon Clarence and Ursula (Wahlstrom) S.; m. Terry Jeanne Gibbs, Aug. 23, 1969; children: Joanna Jeanne, Kevin Leonard. BA, Fla. State U., 1969, JD, 1972. Bar: Fla. 1972, U.S. Dist. Ct. (mid. dist.) Fla. 1974, U.S. Ct. Appeals (5th cir.) 1975. Legal rsch. asst. Office Gen. Counsel, Fla. Dept. Revenue, Tallahassee, 1971; legis. intern com. on community affairs Fla. Ho. of Reps., Tallahassee, 1971-72; jud. rsch. aide Fla. 2d Dist. Ct. Appeals, Lakeland, 1972-73; asst. county atty. Hillsborough County, Tampa, Fla., 1973-75; assoc. Carlton, Fields, Ward, Emmanuel, Smith & Cutler, P.A., Tampa, 1975-80, sr. atty., 1980—; mem. Fla. State U. Coll. Law Bd. Visitors, 1994—. Sec., bd. dirs. Bapt. Towers Plant City, Inc., 1981-84; deacon 1st Bapt. Ch., Plant City, 1980—. 1st lt. USAFR, 1973. Mem. ABA, Fla. Bar Assn. (exec. coun. local govt. law sect. 1978-79), Hillsborough County Bar Assn., Tampa Kiwanis (bd. dirs. 1980-82, 96—, Layman of Yr. 1984, 89). Democrat. Office: Carlton Fields Ward Emmanuel Smith & Cutler PA 777 S Harbour Island Blvd Tampa FL 33602

SPARKS, DAVID STANLEY, university administrator; b. Phila., Dec. 8, 1922; s. Richard Frederick and Grace Dorothy (Tuttle) S.; m. Phyllis Ann Bate, June 12, 1949; children: Robert F., E. Anne. A.B., Grinnell (Iowa) Coll., 1944; M.A., U. Chgo., 1945, Ph.D., 1951. Instr., asst. prof., assoc. prof. U. Md., College Park, 1947-65; prof. history U. Md., 1965—, assoc. dean grad. studies and research, 1967-70, dean, 1970-77, acting vice chancellor for acad. affairs, 1976-77, acting v.p. grad. studies and research, 1978-79, v.p. grad. studies and research, 1979-87, acting v.p. for acad. affairs, 1982-83, v.p. acad. affairs, grad. studies and research, 1987-88, vice chancellor for acad. affairs, 1988-91, vice chancellor emeritus, 1991; vis. professorial lectr. dept. history Johns Hopkins, 1965. Co-editor, author: American Civilization: A History of the United States, 1960, The Making of American Democracy, Readings and Documents, 2 vols, 1962; Editor: Inside Lincoln's Army: The Diary of General Marsena Rudolph Patrick, 1964. Recipient research awards Am. Philos. Soc., 1958, Social Sci. Research Council, 1957. Mem. Am., So. hist. assns., Orgn. Am. Historians, Am. Assn. U. Profs. (pres. U. Md. chpt.), Nat. Acad. Univ. Research Adminstrs., Phi Kappa Phi. Club: Cosmos (Washington). Home: 10500 Rockville Pike Apt 1309 Rockville MD 20852-3350

SPARKS, DONALD EUGENE, interscholastic activities association executive; b. St. Louis, May 26, 1933; s. Lloyd Garland and Elsie Wilma (Finn) S.; m. Gloria Helle, Sept. 22, 1951; children: Robert, Michael, Donna Lyn. BS in Edn., Truman State Univ., 1956, MA, 1959, postgrad., 1962-63. Cert. tchr. and principal, Mo. High sch. coach, athletic dir. The Parkway Sch. Dist., Chesterfield, Mo., 1959-77; assoc. dir. Mo. High Sch. Activity Assn., Columbia, 1977-81; asst. dir. Nat. Fedn. State High Sch. Assns., Kansas City, Mo., 1981—. Recipient spl. Nat. Athletic Dir.'s citation Nat. Fedn. State High Sch. Assns., 1972. Mem. Nat. Interscholastic Adminstrs. Assn. (Disting. Service award 1979), Athletics Hall of Fame. Home: 5204 NW 84th Ter Kansas City MO 64154-1420 Office: Nat Fedn State High Sch Assns 11724 NW Plaza Cir Kansas City MO 64153-1158

SPARKS, DONALD LEWIS, soil chemistry educator; b. Paris, Ky., June 26, 1953; s. Elmer Johnston and Christine (McKenzie) S.; m. Joy Lynn Gooden, Sept. 14, 1984. BS, U. Ky., 1975, MS, 1976; PhD, Va. Poly. Inst. and State U., Blacksburg, 1979. Asst. prof. soil chemistry U. Del., Newark, 1979-83, assoc. prof., 1983-87, prof., 1987—, chmn. dept. plant and soil scis., 1989—, disting. prof., 1994—, Francis Alison prof., 1996—; cons. DuPont Corp., Wilmington, Del., 1981—. Author: (book) Kinetics of Soil Chemical Processes, 1989, Environmental Soil Chemistry, 1995; editor: (book) Soil Physical Chemistry, 1986, Rates of Soil Chemical Processes, 1991, Method of Soil Analysis: Chemical Methods, 1996; editorial bd.: (publs.) Am. Jour. Soil Sci. Soc., 1984—, Geoderma, 1986—, Soil Sci., 1987—; editor: Advances in Agronomy, 1990—; contbr. over 90 articles and 26 book chpts. to profl. publs. Pres. Torch Club of Del., Newark, 1989—. Fellow Soil Sci. Soc. of Am. (Soil Sci. Rsch. award 1994), Am. Soc. of Agronomy (N.E. br. rsch. award 1986, Francis Alison award 1996, Marion L. and Christye M. Jackson Soil Sci. award 1991); mem. AAAS, Am. Chem. Soc., Clay Minerals Soc. Mem. Christian Ch. (Disciples of Christ). Achievements include pioneering application of chemical kinetics to soil systems. Office: U Del Dept Plant And Scis Newark DE 19717-1303

SPARKS, HARVEY VISE, JR., physiologist; b. Flint, Mich., June 22, 1938; s. Harvey Vise and Ellen Louise (Paschall) S.; m. Barbara M. Taylor, Jan. 17, 1969; children—Matthew Taylor, Catherine Elliott, Wendy Sue, Harvey Vise. Student, U. Mich., 1956-59, M.D., 1963. Postdoctoral fellow dept. physiology Harvard Med. Sch., Boston and; U. Goteborg, Sweden; instr. U. Mich., 1966-67, asst. prof. physiology, 1967-70, assoc. prof., 1970-74, prof., 1974-78; asst. to dean U. Mich. (Med. Sch.), 1970-71, asst. dean, 1971-72; prof. physiology Mich. State U., East Lansing, 1978—, chmn. dept., 1978-89, vice provost human health programs, 1989-93, univ. disting. prof., 1997—; Fulbright lectr. U. Zimbabwe, 1986-87; vis. prof. U. Zimbabwe, 1995; mem. survey team, liaison com. on med. edn. AMA Am. Assn. Med. Colls.; mem. rev. teams NIH. Author: Casebook of Physiology, 1973, Essentials of Cardiovascular Physiology, 1987; contbr. numerous articles to profl. jours.; editor: (with others) Handbook of Physiology, 1979. Recipient Meritorious Service award Mich. Heart Assn., 1962, Borden award for med. student research, 1963, Merit award NIH, 1988; Mich. Heart Assn. student fellow, 1962-63; John and Mary Markle scholar, 1967-72; USPHS postdoctoral fellow, 1963-66; U. Mich. student research fellow, 1960-61; USPHS grantee, 1963—. Fellow Royal Soc. Medicine; mem. AAAS, Am. Physiol. Soc. (pres. 1987-88, editl. bd. Am. Jour. Physiology 1974-88), Microcirculatory Soc., Am. Heart Assn. (coun. on circulation, editl. bd. Circulation Rsch.), Mich. Pub. Health Inst. (bd. dirs. 1989-94), Internat. Union Physiol. Scis. (treas. 1990—), Coun. Internat. Exch. Scholars (Africa area com. 1988-91), Russian Acad. Sci. (fgn.), Victor Vaughn Soc., Alpha Omega Alpha, Phi Kappa Phi, Phi Zeta. Home: 8122 W Lovejoy Rd Perry MI 48872-8902 Office: Mich State U Dept Physiology East Lansing MI 48824

SPARKS, JOHN EDWARD, lawyer; b. Rochester, Ind., July 3, 1930; s. Russell Leo and Pauline Anna (Whittenberger) S.; m. Margaret Joan Snyder, Sept. 4, 1954; children: Thomas Edward, William Russell, Kathryn Chapman. A.B., Ind. U., 1952; LL.B., U. Calif., Berkeley, 1957; postgrad., London Sch. Econs., 1957-58. Bar: Calif. 1958. Assoc. Brobeck, Phleger & Harrison, San Francisco, 1958-66, ptnr., 1967-95, of counsel, 1995—; adj. prof. law U. San Francisco, 1967-69; pres. Legal Aid Soc. San Francisco, 1978-79, dir., 1971-81; trustee Pacific Legal Found., Sacramento, 1975-80. Editor U. Calif. Law Rev., 1956-57. Served to 1st lt. Q.M.C. U.S. Army, 1952-54, Korea. Recipient Wheeler Oak Meritorious award U. Calif., Berkeley, 1986. Fellow Am. Bar Found., Am. Coll. Trial Lawyers; mem. State Bar Calif., Bar Assn. San Francisco (bd. dirs. 1974-75), ABA, Am. Judicature Soc., Boalt Hall Alumni Assn. (pres. 1983-84), Pacific Union Club (San Francisco),. Democrat. Office: Brobeck Phleger & Harrison Spear St Tower 1 Market Plz San Francisco CA 94105

SPARKS, MORGAN, physicist; b. Pagosa Springs, Colo., July 6, 1916; s. Harry Lysinger and Pearl (Morgan) S.; m. Elizabeth MacEvoy, Apr. 30, 1949; children: Margaret Ellen, Patricia Rae, Morgan MacEvoy, Gordon K. B.A., Rice U., 1938, M.A., 1940; Ph.D., U. Ill., 1943. With Bell Telephone Labs., Murray Hill, N.J., 1943-72; exec. dir. semicondr. components Bell Telephone Labs., 1968-69, v.p. tech. info. and personnel, 1969-71, v.p. electronic tech., 1971-72; pres. Sandia Nat. Labs., Albuquerque, 1972-81; dean Anderson Sch. Mgmt., U. N.Mex., Albuquerque, 1981-84. Contbr. articles on transistors, pn junctions and properties of semicondrs. to profl. jours. Rockefeller Found. fellow U. Ill., 1940-43. Fellow Am. Phys. Soc., IEEE (Jack A. Morton award 1977), Am. Inst. Chemists; mem. Am. Chem. Soc., Nat. Acad. Engring., Phi Beta Kappa, Sigma Xi, Phi Lambda Upsilon. Patentee semicondr. electronics. Home: 904 Lamp Post Cir SE Albuquerque NM 87123-4119

SPARKS, ROBERT DEAN, medical administrator, physician; b. Newton, Iowa, May 6, 1932; s. Albert John and Josephine Emma (Kleinendorst) S.; children: Steven, Robert, Ann Louise, John James. BA, U. Iowa, 1955, MD, 1957; D of Humanitarian Service, Creighton U., 1978. Diplomate Am. Bd. Internal Medicine. Intern Charity Hosp. of La., New Orleans, 1957-58, resident in internal medicine, 1958-59; asst. in medicine Charity Hosp. of La., 1958-59; fellow in gen. medicine and gastroenterology Tulane U. Sch. Medicine, 1959-62, instr. medicine, 1959-63, asst. prof., 1963-64, assoc. prof., 1964-68, prof., 1968-72, asst. dean, 1964-67, assoc. dean, acting dean, 1967-68, vice dean, 1968-69, dean, 1969-72, chief sect. gastroenterology, 1968-72; chancellor Med. Ctr. U. Nebr., 1972-76, prof. medicine, 1972-76; v.p. U. Nebr. System, 1972-76; health program dir. W.K. Kellogg Found., Battle Creek, Mich., 1976-81, v.p. programming, 1981-82, sr. v.p., 1982, pres., chief programming officer, 1982-86, pres., 1982-88, trustee, 1988, pres. emeritus, cons., 1988-92; pres., CEO, Calif. Med. Assn. Found., San Francisco, 1995—; cons. U. Tenn. Health Sci. Ctr., 1988-90, Boston U. Health Policy Inst., 1989-90; bd. dirs., mem. sci., compensation and trust rev. coms. Syntex Corp., Palo Alto, Calif., 1987-91, v.p. product safety and compliance, 1991-93; mem. overseers com. to visit Harvard U. Med. and Dental Schs., 1984-90; mem. vis. com. U. Miami Sch. Medicine, 1982-86; assoc. med. dir. for addiction treatment svcs., dir. for edn. and rsch., Battle Creek Adventist Hosp., 1990-91; v.p. Howe-Lewis Internat Inc., Menlo Park, N.Y., 1993-94, cons., 1994-95. Contbr. articles to profl. jours. Bd. dirs. Nat. Coun. on Alcoholism and Drug Dependence, N.Y.C., 1982-93, treas., 1986-88, chmn., 1989-90, past chmn., 1991-92; bd. dirs. Battle Creek Symphony Orch., 1981-88, Lakeview Sch. Dist., Battle Creek, 1979-83, 88-91; trustee Monsour Med. Found., Jeannette, Pa., 1976-90, interim pres., 1989, chmn. bd., pres., 1989-90; mem. Pres. Reagan's Adv. Bd. Pvt. Sector Initiatives, Washington, 1986-89; chmn. bd. dirs. Bard Coll. Health Policy and Practice Inst., 1988—, Consumer Health Info. Rsch. Inst., 1990-95, Chelsea-Arbor Treatment Ctr., 1990-91, Calhoun County Bd. Health, 1988-91, chmn., 1989-91; mem., bd. dirs. Mental Health and Addictions Found. of Mich., Battle Creek, 1991-93. Recipient Harvard Dental award Harvard U. Sch. Dental Medicien, 1992. Fellow ACP; mem. AMA, Nat. Acad. Scis. Inst. Medicine (com. study of treatment and rehab. svcs. for alcoholism and alcohol abuse, bd. mental health and behavioral medicine), Coun. Mich. Founds. (trustee 1986-88), Assn. Am. Med. Colls. (disting. svc. mem. 1975—), Phi Eta Sigma, Alpha Omega Alpha. Republican. Presbyterian. Avocations: tennis, bridge, reading, travel. Home: 7 Robert S Dr Menlo Park CA 94025-5543 Office: Calif Med Assn Found PO Box 7690 221 Main St San Francisco CA 94120-7690

SPARKS, ROBERT WILLIAM, retired publishing executive; b. Seattle, Dec. 30, 1925; s. James Donald and Gladys (Simmons) S. Student, U. Wash., 1947-50; B.A., U. Hawaii, 1954, M.A., 1965. Editor, various publs., 1947-64; mng. editor U. Hawaii Press, 1964-66, dir., 1967-87; cons. East-West Ctr., Jour. Hawaiian History, Japanese and Chinese book pubs., 1987-92; advisor New World Press, Beijing, 1986; mem. adv. bd. to pres. Kamehameha Schs. Author: Seattle, Sitka, San Francisco, 1955, Letters From an Island, 1962, New Endings, 1989; contbr. articles to internat. pub. jours. Served with AUS, 1944-46, PTO. Recipient McInerny editorship, 1953; Pacific House citation Pacific and Asian Affairs Council, 1974. Mem. Assn. Am. Univ. Presses, Assn. Am. Publishers, Internat. Assn. Scholarly Publishers, Soc. for Scholarly Pub., Hawaiian Hist. Soc., Hawaii Found. History and Humanities, Honolulu Acad. Arts, Bishop Mus. Assn. Home: 3634 Nihipali Pl Honolulu HI 96816-3307

SPARKS, SAM, federal judge; b. 1939. BA, U. Tex., 1961, LLB, 1963. Aide Rep. Homer Thornberry, 1963; law clk. to Hon. Homer Thornberry U.S. Dist. Ct. (we. dist.) Tex., 1963-65; assoc. to ptnr., shareholder Hardie, Grambling, Sims & Galatzan (and successor firms), El Paso, Tex., 1965-91; dist. judge U.S. Dist. Ct. (we. dist.) Tex., 1991—. Fellow Am. Coll. Trial Lawyers, Tex. Bar Found. (life); mem. Am. Bd. Trial Advocates (advocate), State Bar Tex. Office: US Dist Ct Judge 200 W 8th St Ste 100 Austin TX 78701-2333

SPARKS, THOMAS E., JR., lawyer; b. Little Rock, Jan. 11, 1942; s. Thomas E. and Marie Christine Lundgren, Sept. 11, 1976; children: Thomas Gunnar, Erik Richard, Andrew Pal. BS, Washington and Lee U., 1963; JD, U. Ark., 1968; LLM, Harvard U., 1970. Bar: Ark. 1968, Calif. 1970. Assoc.

Pillsbury Madison & Sutro, San Francisco, 1970-76; ptnr. Pillsbury, Madison & Sutro, San Francisco, 1977-84, Baker & McKenzie, San Francisco, 1984-87, Pillsbury Madison & Sutro, San Francisco, 1987—. Trustee Grace Cathedral, San Francisco. 1st lt. U.S. Army, 1965. Mem. ABA, Calif. Bar Assn., Olympic Club (San Francisco). Office: Pillsbury Madison Sutro LLP 235 Montgomery St San Francisco CA 94104-2902

SPARKS, WALTER CHAPPEL, horticulturist, educator; b. New Castle, Colo., Aug. 22, 1918; s. Lester Elroy and Jean Ivene (Murray) S.; m. Barbara Ferne Gardner, May 31, 1942; children: Robert, Richard, Eugene. Student, Western State Coll., 1936-37; BS, Colo. State U., 1941, MS, 1943; postgrad., U. Minn., 1945, Wash. State U., 1949, 56-57; DSc (hon.), U. Idaho, 1984. Instr., head dept. agr. Pueblo Jr. Coll., 1941; grad. asst. Colo. State U., 1941-43, instr. horticulture, 1943-44, asst. prof., 1944-47, assoc. prof., 1947; assoc. horticulturist U. Idaho, Aberdeen, 1947-57; acting supt. Aberdeen br. Agrl. Expt. Sta., 1951, 57, 65, horticulturist, 1957—, research prof. horticulture, 1968—, prin. liaison coordinator for potato program, 1976—; exchange prof. Research Inst., Kolding, Denmark, 1972-73; adviser and lectr. on potato problems to various fgn. govts.; cons., adv., Israel, 1980, Philippines, 1981, Jamaica, 1988; dir. Postharvest Inst. Perishables, 1980—. Contbr. articles to profl. jours. Recipient 50th Anniversary medal Fed. Land Banks, 1967, Disting. Svc. in Potato Industry award Gov. of Idaho, 1967, Alumni Svc. award 1980, Disting. Faculty award Phi Kappa Phi, 1980, Disting. Svc. award for rsch. in potato postharvest storage tech., 1987, Cert. of Appreciation Nat. Potato Rsch. Edn. Found., 1986, Agriculture Svc. award N.W. Food Processor Field Reps., 1987; named to Hall of Fame Potato Mus. Brussels, 1977, Idaho Agrl. Hall of Fame, 1983, Idaho Potato Hall of Fame for outstanding contbn. to Idaho Potato Industry, 1996; Eldred Jenne Rsch. fellow, 1957; named 1 of 100 "People Make the Difference" in Idaho, 1990. Mem. AAAS, Am. Inst. Biol. Scis., Am. Soc. Hort. Sci. (life), European Assn. Potato Research, N.W. Assn. Horticulturists, Entomologists and Plant Pathologists, Idaho Acad. Sci., Nat. Potato Research and Edn. Found. (cert. appreciation seed potato storage tech. 1986), N.W. Food Processors Assn. (Disting. Service award, 1987), N.W. Fieldman's Assn. (Disting. Agrl. Service award, 1987), Potato Assn. Am. (life mem., past pres., dir.), Western Regional Potato Improvement Group (past pres.), C. of C., Scabbard and Blade, Sigma Xi (Outstanding Research Paper award 1974), Gamma Sigma Delta (Outstanding Research Worker award 1977, award of merit 1978), Alpha Zeta, Beta Beta Beta, Epsilon Rho Epsilon. Club: Rotary. Home: 1100 Burnett Dr Apt 513 Nampa ID 83651-7578 Office: U Idaho Rsch and Extension Ctr Aberdeen ID 83210 *If the food losses occurring from the farmer to the consumer (including storage) could be minimized or completely eliminated, the food supply could be significantly increased without bringing one more acre of land into production, or using one more pound of fertilizer, or using one additional gallon of fuel. Proper handling and storage can accomplish this goal.*

SPARLING, MARY CHRISTINE, foundation executive; b. Collingwood, Ont., Can., July 8, 1928; d. Alexander and Catherine Henrietta (MacDonald) Malcolm; m. Wintfield Henry Sparling, June 17, 1950; children: Margaret, John. BA, Queen's U., Kingston, Ont., 1949; BEd (Gold medal 1970), St. Mary's U., Halifax, N.S., 1970; MA in Edn., Dalhousie U., 1978; DFA (hon), Nova Scotia Coll. Art & Design, 1994. Curator edn. N.S. Mus., Halifax, 1968-73; dir. art gallery Mt. St. Vincent U., Halifax, 1973-94; v.p. Neptune Theatre Found., Halifax, 1994—; cons. in field; bd. mem. Pier 21 Soc.; Atlantic regional coord. Can.'s Yr. of Asia Pacific, 1997. Recipient Ohio State award for film script The Artist in Nova Scotia, 1977, Queen's Silver Jubilee medal, 1977, Outstanding Cultural Exec. award N.S. Cultural Fedns., 1991; Warner-Lambert award for disting. arts adminstrn. in Can., 1993. Fellow Can. Mus. Assn. (pres. 1974-76, coun. 1972-78); mem. N.S. Coalition on Arts and Culture. Unitarian. Home: 6030 Jubilee Rd, Halifax, NS Canada B3H 2E4

SPARLING, PETER DAVID, dancer, dance educator; b. Detroit, June 4, 1951; s. Robert Daniel and Emily Louise (Matthews) S. BFA, Juilliard Sch., N.Y.C., 1973. Dancer José Limón Co., N.Y.C., 1971-73; co. instr. London (Eng.) Contemporary Dance Theatre, 1983-84; prin. dancer Martha Graham Dance Co., N.Y.C., 1973-87; asst. prof. dance U. Mich., Ann Arbor, 1984-87, chmn. dance dept., assoc. prof., 1987-94, prof. of dance, 1994—; artistic dir. Peter Sparling Presents Solo Flight, N.Y.C., 1977-82, Peter Sparling Dance Co., N.Y.C., 1980-84; co-dir. Ann Arbor Dance Works, 1984—; guest choreographer Victorian Coll. Arts, 1981, 84, Dance Uptown, Am. Ballet Theatre II, Cloud Dance Theatre, Taiwan, Ballet Gulbenkian, Lisbon, Utah Repertory Dance Theatre, Joseph Holmes Dance Theatre, Corning Dances, Fla. State U. Choreographer Divining Rod, 1973, Little Incantations, 1974, Three Farewells, 1977, Suite to Sleep, 1978, A Thief's Progress or The Lantern Night, 1979, Excursions of Chung Kuei, 1978, Nocturnes for Eurydice, 1978, Once in a Blue Moon, 1978, Harald's Round, 1979, Hard Rock, 1979, What She Forgot He Remembered, 1979, Sitting Harlequin, 1979, In Stride, 1979, Elegy, 1979, The Tempest, 1980, Orion, 1980, Landscape with Bridge, 1980, Nocturnes, Modern Life, Bright Bowed River, A Fearful Symmetry, Alibi, Rounding the Square, De Profundis, Rondo, Wings, Witness, The Boy Who Played With Dolls. Louis Horst Meml. scholar Juilliard Sch., 1973; Nat. Endowment for the Arts fellow 1971, 79, 83; grantee U. Mich., 1985-86, 89, Mich. Coun. for the Arts, 1986; recipient Choreographer's award Mich. Dance Assn., 1988, Artist's award Arts Found. Mich., 1989. Office: Univ of Michigan Dept of Dance Dance Bldg Ann Arbor MI 48109*

SPARR, DANIEL BEATTIE, federal judge; b. Denver, June 8, 1931; s. Daniel John and Mary Isabel (Beattie) S.; m. Virginia Sue Long Sparr, June 28, 1952; children: Stephen Glenwood, Douglas Lloyd, Michael Christopher. BSBA, U. Denver, 1952, JD, 1966. Bar: Colo. U.S. Dist. Ct. Assoc. White & Steele, Denver, 1966-70; atty. Mountain States Telephone & Telegraph Co., Denver, 1970-71; ptnr. White & Steele, Denver, 1971-74; atty. Wesley H. Doan, Lakewood, Colo., 1974-75; prin. Law Offices of Daniel B. Sparr, Denver, 1975-77; judge 2d dist. Colo. Dist. Ct., Denver, 1977-90; judge U.S. Dist. Ct. Colo., Denver, 1990—. Mem. Denver Bar Assn. (trustee 1975-78), Denver Paralegal Inst. (bd. advs. 1976-88), William E. Doyle's/Am. Inns of Ct., Am. Bd. Trial Advs., ABA, Colo. Bar Assn. Office: US Dist Ct 1929 Stout St Denver CO 80294-0001*

SPARROW, EPHRAIM MAURICE, mechanical engineering scientist, educator; b. Hartford, Conn., May 27, 1928; s. Charles and Frieda (Gottlieb) S.; m. Ruth May Saltman, Nov. 2, 1952; 1 child, Rachel Bernarr. BS, MIT, 1948, MS, 1949; MA, Harvard Coll., 1950, PhD, 1956; Doutor Honoris Causa, U. Brazil, 1967. Heat transfer specialist Raytheon Mfg. Co., 1952-53; rsch. specialist Lewis Rsch. Ctr., NASA, Cleve., 1953-59; prof. mech. engring. U. Minn., 1959—, Inst. prof., 1994—, chmn. fluid dynamics program, 1968-80, Morse alumni disting. tchg. prof., 1980—; program dir. NSF, 1986-87, dir. chem., biochem. and thermal engring. divsn., 1986-88; vis. prof., chief AID mission U. Brazil, 1966-67; adv. prof. Xi'an Jiaotong U., 1984—; cons. in field, 1960—; pres. 1st Brazilian Symposium on Heat Transfer and Fluid Mechanics, 1966; mem. solar energy panel Fed. Coun. on Sci. and Tech., 1972; U.S. sci. committeeman 5th Internat. Heat Transfer Conf., 1973-74. Author: (with R.D. Cess) Radiation Heat Transfer, 1966, 2nd edit., 1978; editor: Handbook of Numerical Heat Transfer, Advances in Numerical Heat Transfer; hon. mem. editorial bd. Internat. Jour. Heat Mass Transfer, 1964—, Internat. Comm. in Heat Mass Transfer, 1975—; sr. editor Jour. Heat Transfer, 1972-80; editor Series in Computational and Phys. Processes in Mechanics and Thermal Scis., 1980—; chmn. editorial adv. bd. Numerical Heat Transfer, 1978—; contbr. over 560 tech. articles to profl. jours. Recipient Ralph Coates Roe award Am. Soc. Engring. Edn., 1978, Outstanding Teaching award U. Minn., 1985, Fed. Engr. of Yr. award NSF, 1988, Sr. Rsch. award Am. Soc. Engring. Edn., 1989, Horace T. Morse award for outstanding contbns. to undergraduate teaching, 1993; named George Hawkins Disting. lectr. Purdue U., 1985. Fellow ASME (Meml. award for outstanding contbn. to sci. heat transfer 1962, Max Jakob award for eminent contbn. 1976, Centennial medal 1980, Disting. Svc. award heat transfer div. 1982, Charles Russ Richards Meml. award 1985, Worcester Reed Warner medal 1986, 50th Anniversary award heat transfer div. 1988, Disting. lectr. 1986-91, 93-94); mem. NAE, Biomed. Engring. Soc. (faculty advisor 1994—), Sigma Xi (Monie A. Ferst medal for contbn. to rsch. through edn. 1993), Pi Tau Sigma. Home: 2105 Hoyt Ave W Saint Paul MN 55108-1314 Office: U Minn Dept Mech Engring Minneapolis MN 55455-0111

SPARROW, HERBERT GEORGE, III, lawyer; b. Ft. Bragg, N.C., May 26, 1936; s. Herbert George and Virginia (Monroe) S.; m. Nancy Woodruff, Mar. 4, 1962; children: Amy Winslow, Edward Harrison, Herbert G. IV, Alison Kidder. AB cum laude, Princeton U., 1958; JD, U. Mich., 1961. Bar: Mich. 1961, Calif. 1964, D.C. 1979, U.S. Ct. Claims 1982, U.S. Tax Ct. 1983, U.S. Ct. Mil. Appeals 1962, U.S. Supreme Ct. 1976. Assoc. Dickinson, Wright, Moon, Van Dusen & Freeman, Detroit, 1965-70, ptnr., 1970—; adj. prof. Detroit Coll. Law, 1977—. Author numerous articles environ. law.; speaker in field. Bd. dirs. Family Life Edn. Coun., Grosse Pointe, Mich., 1982-88, Adult Well-Being Svcs., Inc., Detroit, 1995—. Capt. JAGC, U.S. Army, 1962-65. Mem. ABA, Mich. Bar Assn. (rep. assembly 1979-85, environ. law sect. coun. 1985-91), Calif. Bar Assn., D.C. Bar Assn., Detroit Bar Assn., Am. Arbitration Assn. (panel arbitrators 1975—), Mich. State Bar Found. (fellow 1989—), Environment Law Inst. (assoc.), Phi Delta Phi (pres. Kent Inn Assn., Ann Arbor 1985—). Office: Dickinson Wright Moon 500 Woodward Ave Ste 4000 Detroit MI 48226-3423

SPARTZ, ALICE ANNE LENORE, retired retail executive; b. N.Y.C., May 14, 1925; d. John Francis and Alice Philomena (Murray) Rattenbury; m. George Eugene Spartz, Oct. 29, 1949; children: Mary Elizabeth, James, Barbara, Anne, Thomas, William, Michael, John, Matthew, Clare, Robert, Richard. Student, Wright Coll., 1945-47, No. Ill. U., 1950; AA, Triton Coll., 1987. Svc. rep. Ill. Bell Tel., Chgo., 1945-46; stewardess United Airlines, Denver, 1947-49; ret. mgr. Family Life League Resale Shop, Oak Park, Ill., 1987-95; retired, 1995. Mem. Cicero (Ill.) Cmty. Coun., 1967-69; mem. Park Dist. Oak Park Com., 1973-74; active Ill. Right to Life Com., Chgo., 1971—, Com. Pro-Life Caths., Chgo., 1992—; former bd. dirs. Ill. Pro-Life Coalition, Family Life League; vol. canteen workers ARC, Chgo., 1942-45. Mem. St. Edmunds Womens Club. Democrat. Roman Catholic. Avocations: travel, sewing, reading, swimming, pro-life activist. Office: 226 N Ridgeland Ave Oak Park IL 60302-2323

SPATT, ARTHUR DONALD, federal judge; b. 1925. Student, Ohio State U., 1943-44, 46-47; LLB, Bklyn. Law Sch., 1949. Assoc. Davidson & Davidson, N.Y.C., 1949, Lane, Winard, Robinson & Schorr, N.Y.C., 1950, Alfred S. Julien, N.Y.C., 1950-52, Florea & Florea, N.Y.C., 1953; pvt. practice N.Y.C., 1953-67, Spatt & Bauman, N.Y.C., 1967-78; justice 10th judicial cir. N.Y. State Supreme Ct., 1979-82; adminstrv. judge Nassau County, 1982-86; assoc. justice appellate div. Second Judicial Dept., 1986-89; dist. judge U.S. Dist. Ct. (ea. dist.) N.Y., Bklyn., 1989-90, Uniondale, N.Y., 1990—. Active Jewish War Vets. Mem. ABA, Assn. Supreme Ct. Justices State of N.Y., Bar Assn. Nassau County, Assn. of Bar of City of N.Y., Jewish Lawyers Assn. Nassau County, Bklyn. Law Rev. Assn., Long Beach Lawyers Assn., Theodore Roosevelt Am. Inn of Ct., Master of the Bench. Office: US Dist Ct 2 Uniondale Ave Uniondale NY 11553-1259

SPATTA, CAROLYN DAVIS, mediator, consultant; b. Gauhati, Assam, India, Jan. 20, 1935; d. Alfred Charles and Lola Mildred (Anderson) Davis; m. John Robert Spatta, June 2, 1957 (div. Feb. 1964); children: Robert Alan, Jennifer Lynn Spatta-Harris; m. S. Peter Karlow, July 25, 1981. AB, U. Calif., Berkeley, 1964; MA, U. Mich., 1968, PhD, 1974. Rsch. asst. U. Calif., Berkeley, 1963-65; instr. Schoolcraft Coll., Livonia, Mich., 1968-74; corp. sec. Oberlin (Ohio) Coll., 1974-78; pres. Damavand Coll., Tehran, Iran, 1978-79; cons. pvt. practice, Washington, 1979-80; v.p., adminstr. E. Mich. U., Ypsilanti, Mich., 1980-81; Dir. Inst. grants programs and adv. svc. Assn. Am. Colls., Washington, 1982-84; v.p., adminstrn. and bus. affairs Calif. State U., Hayward, 1984-92, prof. geography and environ. studies, 1992-94; ind. mediator, cons. higher edn., 1995—; vis. lectr. E. Mich. U., Ypsilanti, 1969, 1970; mem. accreditation team Western Assn. Schs. Colls.; Fulbright scholar, Malaysia, 1994; bd. dirs. Ada Mabel, Inc., 1995—. Contbr. articles to profl. jours. Bd. dirs. Wellness, Inc.; mem. Trinity Parish, Menlo Pk., Calif. (pers., bldg. coms.), U. Mich. Alumni Assn., St. John's Episc. Ch. (pastoral care commn.), Chevy Chase, Md., Oberlin Open Space Com., Tenaya Guild, John Muir Hosp., Walnut Creek, Calif. (pres.), steering com. Ann Arbor Citizens for Good Schs.; trustee Pacific Sch. of Religion, 1992—. Recipient fellowship Nat. Defense Foreign Lang., 1966-68; Fulbright scholar, Malaysia, 1994—. Mem. Asian Studies on Pacific Coast, Assn. Asian Studies, Assn. Am. Geographers, Soc. Profls. in Dispute Resolutions, No. Calif. Mediation Assn., Acad. Family Mediators. Avocations: travel, reading, walking, cooking and entertaining, golf, art, music.

SPATZ, HUGO DAVID, film producer; b. Zanesville, Ohio, Nov. 29, 1913; s. Charles Edwin and Mary Jane (Elias) S.; m. Ruth D. Wallie, Nov. 26, 1945. BA, Ohio State U., 1933, MA, 1935; PhD, Columbia Pacific U., San Pedro, Calif., 1986. Buyer Schiff Shoe Corp., Columbus, Ohio, 1936-39; gen. mgr. Zenith Precision Optics Corp., Wheeling, W.Va., 1940-42; v.p. Fredrick Optical Co., Cleve., 1945-56; pres. The House of Hugo Opticians, Cleve., 1957-73, Away to Adventure Travelogues, Port Charlotte, Fla., 1974—. Columnist weekly column "Profiles". Pres. Charlotte County (Fla.) Civic Coalition, 1985-86; v.p. The Alliance of th e Arts; adv. bd. Cultural Ctr., Charlotte County; pres. Home Owners, N.Y. Area, Port Charlotte, 1984-85; chmn. Water & Sewer Bd., Charlotte County, 1988; mem. Comprehensive Land Plan Com., Charlotte County, 1987; pub. mem. Polit. Sign Com., 1988. With U.S. Army, 1942-45. Named Citizen of Yr., Citizens of University Heights, 1975; commd. Ky. col., 1987. Mem. Masons (master 1968-69). Republican. Home: 22525 Nyack Ave Pt Charlotte FL 33952-7116

SPAULDING, FRANK HENRY, librarian; b. Danielson, Conn., July 12, 1932; s. Jacob Lindhurst and Frances (Upham) S.; m. Eugenia Jenewicz, May 25, 1963; children—Geoffrey Michael, Jennifer Anne. A.B., Brown U., 1957; M.S.L.S., Case Western Res. U., 1961. Supr. info. ctr. Colgate-Palmolive Co., Piscataway, N.J., 1961-65; group supr. library tech. processes Bell Labs., Holmdel, N.J., 1965-70, head library ops., 1970-84; mgr. library services AT&T Bell Labs., Holmdel, 1985-87, mgr. mktg. library network, 1984-86; library/info. cons., 1987—; pres. Sp. Libraries. Assn. 1986-87; treas. Am. Soc. for Info. Sci., 1983-86; pres. Documentation Abstracts, N.Y.C., 1983-85; dir. Universal Serials and Book Exchange, Washington, 1983-85, Palinet, Phila., 1979-81. Compiler: Managing the Electronic Library, 1983; author: Today's Information Specialist Tomorrow's Knowledge Technician, Knowledge Counselor in 2006, International Information: International Librarianship; creator: Task Force on the Value of the Informational Professional. Mem. Buten Mus. Wedgwood. Served to lt. USN, 1957-60. Mem. ALA (com. on accreditation 1989-93), Spl. Librs. Assn. (del. to Internat. Fedn. Libr. Assn. and Inst. 1987-89).

SPAULDING, JOHN PIERSON, public relations executive, marine consultant; b. N.Y.C., June 25, 1917; s. Forrest Brisbine and Genevieve Anderson (Pierson) S.; m. Eleanor Rita Bonner, Aug. 18, 1947; children: Anne Spaulding Balzhiser, John F., Mary T. Spaulding Calvert; m. 2d, Donna Alene Abrescia, May 15, 1966. Student Iowa State Coll., 1935-36, Grinnell Coll., 1936-38, U. Chgo., 1938-39. Reporter, Chgo. City News Bur., UPI, 1939-40; editor Cedar Falls (Iowa) Daily Record, 1940-41; picture editor Des Moines Register & Tribune, 1941-42, 47-50; pub. relations dir. Motor Club Iowa, Davenport, 1950-51; commd. 2d. lt. USAF, 1942, advanced through grades to maj., 1947, recalled, 1951, advanced through grades to lt. col.; ret., 1968; v.p. Vacations Hawaii, Honolulu, 1969-70; dir. pub. relations, mgr. pub. relations services Alexander & Baldwin, Inc., Honolulu, 1970-76; mgr. community relations Matson Navigation Co., Honolulu, 1976-81. Pres., Econ. Devel. Assn., Skagit County, Wash., 1983-85; pres., chmn. Fidalgo Island Endl. Youth Found.; mem. Anacortes (Wash.) Sch. Bd., 1982-88; mem. Gov.'s Tourism Devel. Council, 1983-85; mem. adv. com. State Ferry System, 1982—, productivity coun., 1990—; chmn. Everett chpt. S.C.O.R.E., 1984-86, Bellingham chpt., 1991—; mem. citizens adv. com. Skagit County Transit, 1995—. Decorated Air medal. Mem. Pub. Relations Soc. Am. (pres. Hawaii chpt. 1974), Hawaii Communicators (pres. 1973), Nat. Def. Transp. Assn. (pres. Aloha chpt. 1980-81, Disting. Service award 1978-79), Air Force Assn., Can. Inst. Internat. Affairs, Anacortes C. of C., Sigma Delta Chi (life). Clubs: Propeller (pres. Port of Honolulu 1979-80), Honolulu Press, Fidelgo Yacht, Hawaii Yacht, Royal Hawaiian 400 Yacht (comdr. 1977-81), Rotary (sec. 1996—), Elks. Home: 6002 Sands Way Anacortes WA 98221-4015

SPAULDING, WILLIAM ROWE, investment consultant; b. Cambridge, Mass., Nov. 26, 1915; s. William Rowe and Jennie Jane (Gillam) S.; m. Gertrude Ellen Mowry, June 7, 1947; children: Edward Albert, William Mathews. BS, U. N.H., 1938; MBA, Harvard U., 1940. Trader Kidder Peabody & Co., N.Y.C., 1940-41; asst. exec. v.p. Mut. Savs. Cen. Fund, Inc., Boston, 1946-58; v.p. Vance Sanders & Co., Boston, 1959-63; trustee Century Shares Trust, Boston, 1963-71, mng. trustee, chmn., 1969-71; chmn. bd., chief exec. officer Wakefield Savs. Bank (Mass.), 1971-81, trustee, 1959-84, hon. trustee, 1994—; ind. dir., trustee Fidelity Group of Mut. Funds, Boston, 1972-87, active emeritus, 1988-89; ret., 1989; dir. Mass. Congl. Fund, 1970-96; active Initiative for Edn., Sci. and Technology to the Republic of South Africa, 1995; spkr. Investment Analyst Soc. of South Africa, Johannesburg Stock Exch. Auditorium, 1995. Trustee Melrose-Wakefield Hosp., 1973-84, Lakeside Cemetery Corp., Wakefield, 1973—; dir., fin. v.p. Citizens Scholarship Found., Wakefield, 1962—; mem. nat. adv. bd. Citizens' Scholarship Found. Am., 1989-92; mem. fin. com., mem. ho. of dels. Mass. Easter Seal Soc., v.i.p. telethon, 1990—; trustee Laudholm Farm Trust, Wells Nat. Estuarine Rsch. Res., 1982-94, hon. trustee, 1994—; exec. vol. Internat. Exec. Svc. Corps., Kingston, Jamaica, 1989, shirtsleeve amb., 1994—; citizen amb. People to People, 1994—; with Securities Industry Delegation to China, 1994; mem. Wakefield Hist. Commn., 1984-86; co-chmn. bd. advisors U. New Eng., Biddeford, Maine/Westbrook Coll., Portland, Maine. With AUS, 1942-45, MTO, ETO, lt. col. Decorated Bronze Star; Croix de Guerre (Belgium); named to Eagle Scout Boy Scouts Am., 1928; named Grand Marshall, Independence Day Parade, Wakefield, Mass., 1994. Mem. Pres.'s Coun. U. N.H., Fin. Analysts Fedn. (Boston chpt.), Assn. Investment Mgmt. and Rsch. (mem. initiative for edn., sci. and tech. South Africa 1995), Phi Kappa Phi. Congregationalist. Home and Office: 35 Yale Ave Wakefield MA 01880-2337 also: Drakes Island Box 1999 Wells ME 04090

SPEAKER, SUSAN JANE, lawyer; b. Dallas, Dec. 25, 1946; d. William R. and Jane E. (Aldrich) Turner; m. David C. Speaker, Dec. 21, 1968; children: David Allen, Melissa. BA, U. Ark., 1970, JD, 1985. Bar: Okla. 1985, U.S. Dist. Ct. (no., ea. and we. dists.) Okla. 1985. Assoc. Hall, Estill, Hardwick, Gable, Golden & Nelson, P.C., Tulsa, 1985-91; atty. Resolution Trust Corp., 1991-92; shareholder Speaker & Matthews, P.C., 1992-96; atty. Comml. Fin. Svcs., Inc., Tulsa, 1996—. Editor U. Ark. Law Rev., 1983-85. Mem. ABA, Okla. Bar Assn., Tulsa Bar Assn., Assn. Trial Lawyers Am., Phi Beta Kappa, Delta Theta Phi.

SPEAKES, LARRY MELVIN, public relations executive; b. Cleveland, Miss., Sept. 13, 1939; s. Harry Earl and Ethlyn Frances (Fincher) S.; m. Laura Christine Crawford, Nov. 3, 1968; children: Sondra LaNell, Barry Scott, Jeremy Stephen. Student, U. Miss., 1957-61; Litt. D. (hon.), Ind. Central U., 1982. News editor Oxford (Miss.) Eagle, 1961-62; news editor Bolivar Comml., Cleveland, 1962-63; mng. editor Bolivar Comml., 1965-66; dep. dir. Bolivar County Civil Def., 1963-65; gen. mgr. Progress Pubs., Leland, Miss., 1966-68; editor Leland Progress, Hollandale Herald, Bolivar County Democrat, Sunflower County News; press sec. U.S. Senator J.O. Eastland of Miss., 1968-74; staff asst. Exec. Office of Pres., Mar.-May 1974; press asst. to spl. counsel to Pres., May-Aug. 1974; asst. White House press sec., 1974-76, asst. press sec. to Pres., 1976-77; press sec. to Gerald R. Ford, 1977; v.p. Hill & Knowlton, Inc., internat. pub. relations and pub. affairs counsel, Washington, 1977-81; prin. dep. press sec. and asst. to Pres. of U.S., Washington, 1981-87; sr. v.p. Merrill Lynch & Co., Inc., N.Y.C., 1987-88; v.p. comm. No. Telecom Ltd., Washington and Toronto, Ont., Can., 1991-93; sr. v.p. corp. and legis. affairs U.S. Postal Svc., Washington, 1994—; corp. comm. cons., lectr. on press and politics, 1988-91; mem. pub. rels. seminar. Author: Speaking Out: The Reagan Presidency From Inside the White House; contbr. Crisis Repsponse: Inside Stories on Managing Image Under Siege. Recipient Presdl. Citizens medal, 1987, Gen. Excellence award Miss. Press Assn., 1988, Disting. Journalism Alumni award U. Miss., 1981, Hall of Fame, 1985, Silver Em. Miss. Scholastic Press Assn., 1988, Spl. Achievement award Nat. Assn. Govt. Communications, 1983, Silver Anvil award Pub. Rels. Soc. Am., 1988. Mem. Arthur Page Soc. (trustee), Sigma Delta Chi, Kappa Sigma (Man of Yr. 1982), Lambda Sigma, Omicron Delta Kappa. Methodist. Home: 4800 Thiban Ter Annandale VA 22003-4250

SPEAR, ALLAN HENRY, state senator, historian, educator; b. Michigan City, Ind., June 24, 1937; s. Irving S. and Esther (Lieber) S. BA, Oberlin Coll., 1958, LLD (hon.), 1997; MA, Yale U., 1960, PhD, 1965. Lectr. history U. Minn., Mpls., 1964-65, asst. prof., 1965-67, assoc. prof., 1967—; mem. Minn. State Senate, St. Paul, 1973—, chmn. jud. com., 1983-93; chmn. crime prevention com., 1993—; pres. Minn. State Senate, 1993—; vis. prof. Carleton Coll., Northfield, Minn., 1970, Stanford U., Palo Alto, Calif., 1970. Author: Black Chicago, 1967. Mem. Internat. Network Gay and Lesbian Offcls., Com. on Suggested State Legislation of Coun. of State Govts.; bd. dirs. Family and Children's Svc. of Mpls. Mem. Dem. Farm Labor Party. Avocations: cooking, travel, reading, classical music. Home: 2429 Colfax Ave S Minneapolis MN 55405-2942 Office: Minn State Senate 120 State Capitol Saint Paul MN 55155

SPEAR, HARVEY M., lawyer; b. Providence, May 24, 1922; s. Alfred and Esther (Marcus) S.; m. Ruth Abramson, June 27, 1965; children: Jessica Tjernberg, Elizabeth Anne. A.B., Brown U., 1942; LL.B., Harvard, 1948; M.A., George Washington U., 1949, LL.M., 1952, S.J.D., 1955. Bar: Mass. 1948, D.C. 1948, N.Y. 1954, U.S. Supreme Ct. 1954; CPA, Md. Asst. U.S. atty. D.C., 1948; legal asst. to chmn., asst. to vice chmn. SEC, 1948-50; spl. asst. to atty. gen. Dept. Justice, 1951-54; pvt. practice law N.Y.C. and Washington, 1956—; counsel Cadwalader Wickersham & Taft, N.Y.C., 1996—. Contbr. articles to legal jours. Founding trustee Harlem Prep. Sch., 1967; mem. Met. Opera Assn., 1961—. Served to maj. USMCR, 1942-45. Mem. ABA, Assn. of Bar of City of N.Y. Home: 765 Park Ave New York NY 10021-4254 also: 78 Hither Ln East Hampton NY 11937-2635 Office: 100 Maiden Ln New York NY 10038-4818

SPEAR, KATHLEEN KELLY, lawyer; b. Cinco Bayou, Fla., June 4, 1949; d. John Francis and Alma (Cancian) Kelly; m. Brian Blackburn Spear, June 17, 1972; children: Matthew, Olivia. AB magna cum laude, Smith Coll., 1971; MA, Brown U., 1973; JD cum laude, Northwestern U., 1979. Bar: Ill. 1979, U.S. Ct. Appeals (7th cir.) 1979, U.S. Dist. Ct. (no. dist.) Ill. 1979, U.S. Ct. Appeals (7th cir.) 1980, U.S. Ct. Appeals (8th cir.) 1982, U.S. Ct. Appeals (10th cir.) 1983. Assoc. Kirkland & Ellis, Chgo., 1979-84; antitrust and litigation counsel Kraft Inc., Glenview, Ill., 1984-85; sr. counsel bus. devel. and venture Kraft, Inc., Glenview, Ill., 1985-88, group counsel frozen foods, 1988-92, v.p., dep. gen. counsel; mem. bd. dirs. Am. Frozen Food Inst. Mem. bd. dirs. Shakespeare Repertory Theatre., Chgo. Bot. Gardens; mem. vis. com. Northwestern U. Law Sch. Mem. ABA, Ill. Bar Assn., Chgo. Bar Assn., Chgo. Council Lawyers, North Shore Smith Club. Roman Catholic. Office: Kraft Foods Inc 3 Lakes Dr Northfield IL 60093

SPEAR, LAURINDA HOPE, architect. BFA, Brown U., 1972; MArch, Columbia U., 1975. Registered architect, Fla., N.Y., Colo.; cert. Nat. Coun. Archtl. Registration. Founding prin. Arquitectonica, Coral Gables, Fla.; mem. faculty U. Miami; lectr. in field. Prin. works include Pink Ho., Miami, Fla., 1978, The Palace, Miami, 1982 (Honor award Miami chpt. AIA 1982), Overseas Tower (Honor award Fla. chpt. AIA 1982, Honor award Miami chpt. 1982), The Atlantis, Miami, 1982 (Miami chpt. AIA award 1983), The Sq. at Key Biscayne (Honor award Miami chpt. AIA 1982), The Imperial, Miami, 1983, Casa los Andes (Record Hos. award Archtl. Record 1986), North Dade Justice Ctr., Miami, 1987 (Honor award Miami chpt. AIA 1989), Rio, Atlanta, 1988 (Honor award Miami chpt. AIA 1989), Banco de Credito del Peru, Lima, 1988 (Honor award Miami chpt. AIA 1989), The Ctr. Innovative Tech., Herndon, Va., 1988 (Honor award Va. chpt. AIA 1989, Honor award Miami chpt. 1990, Merit award Fairfax, Va., County Exceptional Design Awards Program 1990), Sawgrass Mills (Merit award Miami chpt. AIA 1990, Honor award Fla. chpt. 1991), Miracle Ctr. (Honor award Miami chpt. AIA 1989), Internat. Swimming Hall of Fame, Ft. Lauderdale, Fla., 1991, Banque de Luxembourg, 1993, Disney All-Star Resorts, Orlando, Fla., 1994, Foster City (Calif.) Libr., 1994, U.S. Embassy, Lima, 1994, USCG Family Housing, Bayamon, P.R., 1994, Altamira Ctr., Caracas, Venezuela, 1994. Mem. beaux arts support group Lowe Art Mus., Miami; bd. dirs. Miami Youth Mus. Recipient Design Awards citation Progressive Architecture, 1975, 80, Rome Prize in Architecture, 1978, Award of Excellence, Atlanta Urban Design Commn., 1989. Fellow AIA. Office: FAIA 550 Brickell Ave Ste 200 Miami FL 33131-2521

SPEAR, RICHARD EDMUND, art history educator; b. Michigan City, Ind., Feb. 3, 1940; s. Irving S. and Esther Marion (Lieber) S.; m. Athena Tacha, June 11, 1965. B.A., U. Chgo., 1961; M.F.A., Princeton U., 1963;

Ph.D., 1965. Mem. faculty Oberlin (Ohio) Coll., 1964—, prof. art history, 1975-83, Mildred Jay prof. art history, 1983—; dir. Allen Meml. Art Mus., 1972-83; Harn Eminent Scholar prof. U. Fla., 1997-98; disting. vis. prof. George Washington U., Washington, 1983-84; trustee Intermuseum Conservation Assn., 1972-83, pres., 1975-77. Author: Caravaggio and His Followers, 1971, 75, Renaissance and Baroque Paintings from the Sciarra and Fiano Collections, 1972, Domenichino, 1982; editor-in-chief Art Bull., 1985-88; contbr. articles to profl. jours. Regional exec. bd. ACLU, 1974-76. Recipient Premio Daria Borghese Gold medal, 1972; Fulbright scholar Italy, 1966-67; Am. Coun. Learned Socs. fellow, 1971-72; NEH fellow, 1980-81, sr. fellow Ctr. Advanced Study in Visual Arts Nat. Gallery Art, 1983-84, Guggenheim fellow, 1987-88; Nat. Humanities Ctr. fellow, 1992-93. Mem. Coll. Art Assn. Am. Democrat. Home: 291 Forest St Oberlin OH 44074-1509 Office: Oberlin Coll Dept Art Oberlin OH 44074

SPEAR, ROBERT CLINTON, environmental health educator, consultant; b. Los Banos, Calif., June 26, 1939; s. Clinton Wentworth Spear and Maytie Izetta (Patten) Gill; m. Patricia Warner, Dec. 15, 1962; children: Andrew Warner, Jennifer Ellen. BS, U. Calif., Berkeley, 1961, MS, 1962; PhD, Cambridge U., 1968. Registered profl. engr., Calif. Sys. engr. U.S. Naval Weapons Ctr., China Lake, Calif., 1962-65, 68-69; from asst. prof. to assoc. prof. environ. health U. Calif. Sch. Pub. Health, Berkeley, 1970-81, prof., 1981—, dir. No. Calif. Occupational Health Ctr., 1980-89, assoc. dean, 1988-91, dir. Environ. Engring. and Health Scis. Lab., 1991-96; assoc. dean U. Calif. Coll. Engring., Berkeley, 1994-96; dir. Ctr. for Occupational and Environ. Health U. Calif.-Berkeley, Berkeley, 1992. Contbr. articles on engring. aspects of environ. health to profl. jours. Mem. Nat. Adv. Com. on Occupational Safety and Health, U.S. Dept. Labor, 1986-88. NSF grad. fellow Cambridge U., 1965-68, sr. internat. fellow Fogarty Ctr., NIH, Australian Nat. U., 1977-78, research grantee Nat. Inst. Occupational Safety and Health NIH, State of Calif., 1971—. Mem. ASME, AAAS, Am. Indsl. Hygiene Assn., Assn. Univ. Programs in Occupational Health and Safety (pres. 1984-85). Democrat. Avocation: sailing. Home: 1963 Yosemite Rd Berkeley CA 94707-1631 Office: U Calif Sch Pub Health Berkeley CA 94720

SPEAR, ROBERT NEWELL, JR., museum director; b. Burlington, Vt., Feb. 21, 1920; s. Robert Newell and Dorothy Irene (Moorby) S.; m. Sally Stalker, FEb. 22, 1958 (div. 1978); 1 child, Karen. Grad., high sch., 1937. Dairy farmer Colchester, Vt., 1937-51; tech. specialist Gen. Electric Co., Burlington, 1952-72; nature ctr. dir. Green Mountain Audubon Soc., Huntington, Vt., 1972-78; founding dir., carver, curator Birds of Vt. Museum, Huntington, 1978—. Author: Birds of Vermont, 1976. Served with USN, 1945-46. Recipient Wildlife Conservation award Nat. Wildlife Fedn./Vt. Fedn. Sportsmen Clubs, 1966, Sci. Educators award Vt. Sci. Tchrs. Assn., 1979. Avocations: birding, travel, hiking, canoeing. Office: Birds of Vt Mus 900 Sherman Hollow Rd Huntington VT 05462-9420

SPEAR, THOMAS TURNER, history educator; b. Coral Gables, Fla., Dec. 23, 1940. BA, Williams Coll., 1962; MA, U. Wis., 1970, PhD, 1974; postgrad., Sch. Oriental and African Studies, 1976-77. Sr. lectr. La Trobe U., Melbourne, Australia, 1973-80; Charles R. Keller prof. Williams Coll., Williamstown, Mass., 1981-92; prof. U. Wis., Madison, 1993—, dir. African studies program, 1995—; reviewer NEH, Social Sci. Rsch. Coun./Am. Coun. Learned Socs. Author: The Kaya Complex: A History of the Mijikenda Peoples of the Kenya Coast to 1900, 1978, Kenya's Past: An Introduction to Historical Method in Africa, 1981, (with Derek Nurse) The Swahili: Reconstructing the History and Language of and African Soc., 800-1500, 1985, Mountain Farmers: Moral Economics of Land and Agricultural Development in Aracha and Meru, 1997; editor: (with Richard Waller) Being Maasai: Ethnicity and Identity in East Africa, 1993; contbr. articles to profl. jours. Grantee Williams Coll., 1984, 87-89, 91-92, NEH, 1984, Am. Coun. Learned Socs., 1982, La Trobe U., 1976-77; recipient A.C. Jordan prize U. Wis., 1972, Fgn. Area fellowship Social Sci. Rsch. Coun./Am. Coun. Learned Socs., 1970-72, Coll. Tchrs. fellowship NEH, 1987-88, Guggenheim fellowship, 1995-96, U. Wis., 1995—. Mem. Am. Hist. Soc. (contbr. Guide to Hist. Lit.), African Studies Assn., African Studies Assn. Australia (founder, exec. sec. 1978-80), Internat. African Inst. Office: U Wis Dept History 3211 Humanities 455 N Park St Madison WI 53706-1405

SPEARING, ANTHONY COLIN, English literature educator; b. London, Jan. 31, 1936; came to U.S., 1987; s. Frederick and Gertrude (Calnin) S. MA, Cambridge U., Eng., 1960. W.M. Tapp rsch. fellow Gonville-Caius Coll. Cambridge U., 1959-60, asst. lectr. in English, 1960-64, official fellow Queens' Coll., 1960-87, life fellow, 1987—, dir. studies in English, 1967-85, lectr. in English, 1964-85, reader in medieval English lit., 1985-87; vis. prof. English U. Va., Charlottesville, 1979-80, 84, prof. English, 1987-89, Kenan prof. English, 1989—; William Matthews lectr. Birkbeck Coll., London, 1983-84; invited lectr. numerous colls. and univs. in U.K., Europe, Can. and U.S.; Lansdowne vis. fellow U. Victoria, 1993. Author: Criticism and Medieval Poetry, 1964, rev. edit., 1972; (with Maurice Hussey and James Winny) An Introduction to Chaucer, 1965; The Gawain-Poet: A Critical Study, 1970, Chaucer: Troilus and Criseyde, 1976, Medieval Dream-Poetry, 1976, Medieval to Renaissance in English Poetry, 1985, Readings in Medieval Poetry, 1987, The Medieval Poet as Voyeur, 1993; editor: The Pardoner's Prologue and Tale (Chaucer), 1965, rev. edit., 1994, The Knight's Tale (Chaucer), 1966, rev. edit., 1995, The Franklin's Prologue and Tale (Chaucer), 1966, rev. edit., 1994; co-editor: (with Elizabeth Spearing) Shakespeare: The Tempest, 1971, Poetry of the Age of Chaucer, 1974, The Reeve's Prologue and Tale (Chaucer), 1979, Julian of Norwich: Revelations of Divine Love, 1997; contbr. numerous articles to profl. jours. Mem. Medieval Acad. Am., Internat. Assn. U. Profs. English, New Chaucer Soc. (trustee 1986-90). Office: Univ Va Dept English Bryan Hall Charlottesville VA 22903

SPEARING, KAREN MARIE, physical education educator, coach; b. Chgo., Apr. 17, 1949; d. John Richard and Naomi (Allen) Miller; m. Edward B. Spearing III, Apr. 28, 1973. BS in Phys. Edn., U. Wis., Whitewater, 1972; MS in Outdoor Edn., No. Ill. U., 1978. Cert. phys. edn. tchr., Ill.; cert. CPR instr., hunter safety instr., boating safety instr., master snowmobile instr., Ill. Tchr., coach Glenside Mid. Sch., Glendale Heights, Ill., 1973—, athletic dir., 1981-92, 95—, dept. chairperson, 1992-93; hunter safety instr. State of Ill., 1988—, water safety instr., 1989—, snowmobile instr., 1990—, master snowmobile instr., 1995, CPR instr., 1996—. Awards chairperson U.S. Power Squadron, Chgo., 1987-93, mem. exec. com. DuPage br., 1993-96, edn. officer, 1996—; mem. com. Ill. Hunting and Fishing Days, Silver Springs State Pk., 1993—; amb. People to People Citizen Amb. Program, Russia and Belarus, 1993; mem. Outdoor Wilderness Leadership Class, 1997. Mem. AAHPERD, Ill. Assn. Health, Phys. Edn., Recreation and Dance, Ill. H.S. Assn. (volleyball referee). Avocations: clock collecting, hunting, fishing, boating. Office: Glenside Mid Sch 1560 Bloomingdale Rd Glendale Heights IL 60139-2734

SPEARMAN, DAVID HAGOOD, veterinarian; b. Greenville, S.C., Nov. 16, 1932; s. David Ralph and Elizabeth (Hagood) S.; student Clemson Coll., 1950-52, BS, 1975; DVM, U. Ga., 1956; m. Patsy Lee Cordle, Dec. 18, 1954; children: Kathleen Elizabeth, David Hagood. With Cleveland Park Animal Hosp., Greenville, 1956-57; individual practice vet. medicine, Easley, S.C., 1957—, Powdersville, S.C., 1957-96. Mem. S.C. State Bd. Vet. Examiners, 1981-87, chmn. 1987, Pickens County Planning and Devel. Bd., 1972—; pres. Northside Parent-Tchr. Orgn., 1965-67; mem. adv. bd. vet. technicians program Tri-County Tech., 1975-76; mem. admissions com. Vet. Coll., U. Ga., 1975; mem. adv. com. Pre-Vet Club, Clemson U.; chmn. Easley Zoning Bd., 1980-83; mem. S.C. Bd. Vet. Examiners, 1982-89, chmn., 1987. Mem. AVMA (alt. del. 1992-95, S.C. del. 1996—), Blue Ridge Veterinary Med. Assn. (founder, pres., sec.), S.C. Assn. Veterinarians (pres. 1974-75, publicity chmn. 1975—, chmn. animal health technician com., Veterinarian of Yr. 1985), Am. Animal Hosp. Assn. (assoc.), S.C. Wildlife, Pickens County Horse, Cattle, and Fair Assn. (pres.), Jr. C. of C. (past officer, Key Man award 1959), Trout Unltd. (state dir.), Pickens County Foxhunters Assn., Clemson U. Tiger Lettermen Assn., Easley Boosters Club, Easley C. of C., World Wildlife Fund, Nat. Wildlife Fedn., Audubon Soc., Nature Conservancy, Internat. Platform Assn., Pickens County Hist. Soc., Lions (pres., internat. del. 1971, 73) Pendelton Farmers Soc., Alpha Psi, Alpha Zeta. Presbyterian (deacon, elder, youth leader 1972-74, chmn. orgn. com. 1973-75, 83-85, pulpit com.), Nursery Bldg. com., Stewardship com. Avocations: photography, fly fishing. Home: Burdine Springs 505 Asbury Cir PO Box 327 Easley SC 29640-1343 Office: 6714 Calhoun Memorial Hwy Easley SC 29640-3672

SPEARMAN, DAVID LEROY, elementary education educator, administrator; b. Chgo., June 4, 1959; s. Lee Roy and Florida Lee (Gordon) S.; m. Tina R. Smith, Aug. 20, 1994; 1 child, David Gordon. Student, Loyola U., Chgo., 1977-78, Moody Bible Inst., 1978-81; BA in Comm., Columbia Coll., Chgo., 1986; postgrad., DePaul U., 1987-89, Chgo. City Wide Colls., 1988—, Chgo. State U., 1992-93; MA in Ednl. Adminstrn., Governor's State U., 1994. Cert 03 tchr., lang. arts endorsement K-8, adminstrv. 020 endorsement, speech endorsement, Ill. Prodr., announcer, talk show host Sta. WYCA, Hammond, Ind., 1983-88; music dir., announcer Sta. WCFJ, Chicago Heights, Ill., 1988-89; tchr. Evangelical Christian Sch., Chgo., 1987-89; truant officer Chgo. Bd. of Edn., 1990-92; tchr. Truth Elem. Sch., Chgo., 1992—; 4th grade facilitator Truth Elem. Sch., Chgo., 1994-95, 3rd grade facilitator, 1995-97, chair dept. sci., 1993—, chair social com., 1994-95, dir. summer sch., 1994, coord. social ctr., 1994; freelance camera operator Sta. WCFC-TV, Chgo., 1989—, Ctrl. City Prodns., Chgo., 1992—, Chgo. Cable Acess Prodns., 1992—; CEO Dana Prodns. Inc. Author: (booklet) Teacher's Opinions of the Security and Safety Climate in Chicago Public Schools at Cabrini Green, 1993; contbr. articles to profl. jours., mags. and newspapers. Youth counselor Cook County Juvenile Detention Ctr., 1979-80; scout leader Boy Scouts Am., Chgo., 1992—, asst. scoutmaster Chgo. Housing Authority scouting program, 1992—; bd. dirs. ISO Aeronautics Chgo. Bd. Edn., 1994—. Recipient Tchr. Incentive award Oppenheimer Found., 1993-94, 95-96, Rochelle Lee Found. award, 1993-94, 96-97; named one of Outstanding Young Men of Am., 1989; Chgo. Found. for Edn. grnatee, 1993-94, 94-95, 95-96; tchr. honoree Chgo. State of City Address Dinner by Mayor Richard Daley, 1995; honored by visitation by U.S. Sec. of Edn. Richard Riley and Chgo. Pub. Schs. CEO Paul Vallas, 1995. Mem. Chgo. Tchrs. Union, Moody Bible Inst. Alumni, Columbia Coll. Alumni Govs. State U. Alumni, Internat. Platform Assn. Evangelical Pentecostal. Avocations: video editing and producing, freelance filmmaking. Office: Sojourner Truth Elem Sch 1443 N Ogden Ave Chicago IL 60610-1007

SPEARS, ALEXANDER WHITE, III, tobacco company executive; b. Grindstone, Pa., Sept. 29, 1932; s. Alexander White and Eva Marie (Elliott) S.; m. Shirley Pierce; 1 child, Craig Stewart. BS, Allegheny Coll., Meadville, Pa., 1953; PhD, SUNY, 1960. Research asso., then research fellow SUNY, Buffalo, 1956-58; instr. Millard Fillmore Coll., Buffalo, 1958-59; with Lorillard Corp., Greensboro, N.C., 1959—, v.p. R & D, 1971-74, sr. v.p. ops. and rsch., 1975-79, exec. v.p. ops. and rsch., 1979-91, vice chmn., COO, 1991-95; also bd. dirs., 1991—, chmn., CEO, 1995—; asst. prof. Guilford Coll., 1961-65, mem. bd. assocs., 1990, 91, trustee, 1995—; chmn. bd. visitors Greensboro Coll., 1990-94. Patentee in field; past editor: Tobacco Sci. Jour. Chmn. Coun. on Edn., 1974, mem. exec. com., 1987; chmn. model sch. task force Greensboro Bd. Edn. and Greensboro C. of C., 1975; mem. N.C. Humanities Coun., 1978-81, Piedmont Triad Airport Authority, 1993—; bd. dirs. United Way of Greensboro, 1980-85, N.C. Bus. Com. on Edn., 1983-84, Greensboro Devel. Corp., 1985—, pres., 1992-94; chmn. Greensboro Area United Negro Coll. Fund, 1982, N.C. AT&T St. U., Focus on Excellence campaign, 1984-86, Greensboro Pub. Sch. Fund, 1987; capital campaign chmn. Greensboro Area Girl Scouts U.S., 1987; bd. dirs. N.C. A&T U. Found., 1985-93, trustee, 1990—; bd. dirs. Greensboro NCCJ, 1990-92, chmn. ann. dinner, 1991, N.C. Citizens for Bus. and Industry, 1984-88, YMCA, 1989—, chmn., 1993-95; chmn. Hayes-Taylor Capital Campaign, 1990; bd. dirs. Ctr. Indoor Air Rsch., 1988—, chmn., 1991-95, Coun. for Tobacco Rsch., 1990—; mem. U.S. Tech. Study Group Cigarette Safety Act of 1984, U.S. Study CPSC Tech. Adv. Group Cigarette Safety Act. of 1990; adv. bd. U. N.C., Greensboro, 1988-94; chmn. fundraiser campaign Greensboro Hist. Mus., 1988-89, trustee, 1989—. Recipient Disting. Achievement award in tobacco sci. Philip Morris, 1970; named to Jr. Achievement Bus. Leaders Hall of Fame, 1994, and YMCA Hall of Fame, 1994. Mem. AAAS, Am. Chem. Soc., Soc. Applied Spectroscopy, Am. Mgmt. Assn., N.Y. Acad. Scis., Internat. Coop. Ctr. Sci. Rsch. Relative to Tobacco (sci. com. 1972), Greensboro C. of C. (bd. dirs. 1974-75, 86-87, 96—, chmn. 1997, Nathaniel Greene award 1975, hon. chmn. 1994 Kmart Greater Greensboro Open). Presbyterian. Office: Lorillard Tobacco Co 714 Green Valley Rd Greensboro NC 27408-7018 also: PO Box 10529 Greensboro NC 27404-0529

SPEARS, DIANE SHIELDS, fine arts coordinator, educator; b. Seattle, May 21, 1942; d. Richard Keene McKinney and Dorothy Jean (Shields) Thacker; m. Howard Truman Spears, Sept. 3, 1977; 1 child, Truman Eugene. BA in Art, English, Edn., Trinity U., 1964; MA in Christian Counseling, San Antonio Theol. Sem., 1986, D of Christian Edn., 1988. Cert. tchr. secondary edn., elem. edn. Instr. ESL Dliel-Geb (Def. Lang. Inst.), San Antonio, 1973-74, Ceta/Ace Bexar County Sch. Bd., San Antonio, 1975-78; tchr. elem. edn., art, music New Covenant Faith Acad., San Antonio, 1983-89; instr. ESL Jewish Family Svc., San Antonio, 1991; tchr. elem. art Edgewood Ind. Sch. Dist., San Antonio, 1992-93, dist. art specialist, 1993-95, fine arts coord., 1995—; owner, operator Art for Kings, San Antonio, 1985—; mem. adv. bd. Zion Arts Inst., San Antonio, 1995—. Illustrator teacher-created materials-lit. activities for young children, 1989-90; author: (art curriculum) Art for Kings, 1987; editor: (art curriculum) Edgewood Ind. Sch. Dist. Elem. Art Curriculum, 1993; exhibited in group shows Charles and Emma Frye Mus., Seattle, 1966, 68. Dir. intercessory prayer New Covenant Fellowship, San Antonio, 1980-90. Mem. NEA, Nat. Mus. for Women in Arts (charter), Colored Pencil Soc. Am. (charter), Tex. Art Edn. Assn. (1st pl. graphics divsn. 1995), San Antonio Art Edn. Assn. (1st pl. 1995), Hill Country Arts Found., Coppini Acad. Fine Arts. Republican. Avocations: water skiing, motorcycle riding, sewing, writing. Home: 4823 Chedder San Antonio TX 78229 Office: Edgewood Ind Sch Dist Guerra Devel Ctr 1931 Herbert Ln San Antonio TX 78227-2253

SPEARS, GEORGANN WIMBISH, marketing executive; b. Ft. Worth, Apr. 21, 1946; d. George Vardeman and Lela Ellon (Clifton) Wimbish. BA in Govt. and History, Tex. Christian U., 1969. Cert. secondary govt. and history tchr., Tex. V.p., gen. mgr. Sports Today Mag., Arlington, Tex., 1982-83; editor corp. newsletter Amason Internat. Mktg., Dallas, 1983-85; supply mgr., dir. Am. Photocopy, Arlington, 1985-92; v.p. Mineral Wells (Tex.) Clay Products, Inc., 1993-96; v.p. mktg., vice chmn. bd. dirs. Educators Industries, Inc., Ft. Worth, 1993-96, chmn. bd. dirs., 1995—; v.p., vice chmn., bd. dirs. Superior Properties, Inc., 1995—. Features editor mag. Sports Today, 1982. Active Jewel Charity Ball, Ft. Worth, 1979—, Rep. Party of Tex., Austin, 1983—, PETA, 1992—; vol. ICU and CCU Arlington Meml. Hosp., 1983-86; vol. John Peter Smith Hosp., 1980-82. Mem. U. North Tex. Athletics (trustee 1994—), People for Ethical Treatment of Animals. Republican. Episcopalian. Avocations: creative writing, decorating, horseback riding. Home: 1909 Rockbrook Dr Arlington TX 76006-6615 Office: Educators Industries Inc 1909 Rockbrook Dr Arlington TX 76006-6615

SPEARS, JAE, state legislator; b. Latonia, Ky.; d. James and Sylvia (Fox) Marshall; m. Lawrence E. Spears; children: Katherine Spears Cooper, Marsha Spears-Duncan, Lawrence M., James W. Student, U. Ky. Reporter Cin. Post, Cin. Enquirer newspapers; rschr. Stas. WLW-WSAI, Cin.; tchr. Jiya Gakuen Sch., Japan; lectr. U.S. Mil. installations East Anglia, Eng.; del. State of W.Va., Charleston, 1974-80; mem. W.Va. Senate, Charleston, 1980-1993; mem. state visitors com. W.Va. Extension and Continuing Edn., Morgantown, 1977-91, W.Va. U. Sch. Medicine, 1992—; with state sen., 1980-93; reapptd. to Jud. Hearing Bd., 1997, others. Chmn. adv bd. Sta. WNPB, 1992-94; congl. liaison Am. Pub. TV Stas. and Sta. WNPB-TV, 1992—; mem. coun. W.Va. Autism Task Force, Huntington, 1981-90; mem. W.Va. exec. bd. Literacy Vols. Am., 1986-90, 94—, pres., 1990-92; mem. Gov.'s State Literacy Coun., 1991—; bd. dirs. Found. Ind. Colls. W.Va., 1986—; mem. regional adv. com. W.Va. Gov.'s Task Force for Children, Youth and Family, 1989; mem. USS W.Va. Commn., 1989; mem. exec. com. W.Va. Employer Support Group for Guard and Res., 1989, mem. steering com., 1990—. Recipient Susan B. Anthony award NOW, 1982, nat. award Mil. Order Purple Heart, 1984, Edn. award Profl. Educators Assn. W.Va., 1986, Ann. award W.Va. Assn. Ret. Sch. Employees, 1985, Meritorious Service award W.Va. State Vets. Commn., 1984, Vets. Employment and Tng. Service award U.S. Dept. Labor, 1984, award W.Va. Vets. Council, 1984; named Admiral in N.C. Navy, Gov. of N.C., 1982, Hon. Brigadier Gen. W.Va. N.G., 1984. Mem. Bus. and Profl. Women (Woman of Yr. award 1978), Nat. League Am. Pen Women (Pen Woman of Yr. 1984), Nat. Order Women Legislators, DAR, VFW (aux.), Am. Legion (aux.), Delta Kappa Gamma, Alpha Xi Delta. Democrat. Home and Office: PO Box 2088 Elkins WV 26241-2088

SPEARS, JAMES GRADY, small business owner; b. Port Arthur, Tex., July 20, 1941; s. John Grady and Dorothy Nell (Haney) S. Grad. high sch., Port Arthur. Adminstr. Child Health & Devel. Studies, Oakland, Calif., 1962-69; sales mgr. Sunshine Biscuits Inc., Houston, 1969-75; owner, pres. S.W. Tookie Inc./Tookie's Restaurant, Seabrook, Tex., 1975—. Mem. Greater Houston Convention & Visitors Bur., Clear Lake Convention & Visitors Bur. With USN, 1959-62. Mem. Tex. Restaurant Assn., Houston Restaurant Assn., Seabrook Assn., Old Seabrook Assn. Republican. Roman Catholic. Avocations: collectibles, fine art, antiques, listening to records, self improvement. Home: 16310 Hickory Knoll Dr Houston TX 77059-5311 Office: SW Tookie Inc/Tookie's Restaurant 1202 Bayport Blvd Seabrook TX 77586-3406

SPEARS, KENNETH GEORGE, chemistry educator; b. Erie, Pa., Oct. 23, 1943. BS, Bowling Green State U., 1966; MS, PhD in Phys. Chemistry, U. Chgo., 1970. NIH predoctoral fellow U. Chgo., 1968-70; NRC-NOAA postdoctoral fellow NOAA, Boulder, Colo., 1970-72; prof. dept. chemistry Northwestern U., 1972—, mem. biomedical engring. dept., 1987—. Bd. editors The Rev. Scientific Instruments, 1980-83; conbtr. articles to profl.jours. Alfred P. Sloan Found. fellow, 1974-76. Fellow AAAS; mem. Am. Phys. Soc., Am. Chem. Soc., Midwest Bio-Laser Inst. (adv. bd. 1985—). Office: Northwestern U Dept Chemistry Evanston IL 60208-3113

SPEARS, MARIAN CADDY, dietetics and institutional management educator; b. East Liverpool, Ohio, Jan. 12, 1921; d. Frederick Louis and Marie (Jerman) Caddy; m. Sholto M. Spears, May 29, 1959. BS, Case Western Res. U., 1942, MS, 1947; PhD, U. Mo., 1971. Chief dietitian Bellefaire Children's Home, Cleve., 1942-53; head dietitian Drs. Hosp., Cleve., 1953-57; assoc. dir. dietetics Barnes Hosp., St. Louis, 1957-59; asst. prof. U. Ark., Fayetteville, 1959-68; assoc. prof. U. Mo., Columbia, 1971-75; prof., head dept. hotel, restaurant, instn. mgmt. and dietetics Kans. State U., Manhattan, 1975-89; cons. dietitian small hosps. and nursing homes; cons. dietetic edn. Author: Foodservice Organizations Textbook, 3d edit., 1995; contbr. articles to profl. jours. Mem. Am. Dietetic Assn. (Copher award 1989), Am. Sch. Foodsvc. Assn., Food Systems Mgmt. Edn. Coun., Soc. Advancement of Foodsvc. Rsch., Nat. Restaurant Assn., Coun. Hotel, Restaurant, Inst. Mgmt. Edn., Manhattan C. of C., Sigma Xi, Gamma Sigma Delta, Omicron Nu, Phi Kappa Phi. Home: 1522 Williamsburg Dr Manhattan KS 66502-0408 Office: Kans State U 105 Justin Hall Manhattan KS 66506-1400

SPEARS, MONROE KIRK, English educator, author; b. Darlington, S.C., Apr. 28, 1916; s. James Monroe and Lillian (Fair) S.; m. Betty Greene, Sept. 3, 1941; 1 dau., Julia Herndon. A.B., A.M., U. S.C., 1937; Ph.D., Princeton U., 1940; D. Letters (hon.), U. of South, 1983. Instr. English U. Wis., 1940-42; asst. prof., then assoc. prof. English Vanderbilt U., 1946-52; prof. English U. South, 1952-64; Libbie Shearn Moody prof. English Rice U., 1964-86, prof. emeritus, 1986—; vis. prof. U. Wash., summer 1960, U. Mich., summer 1961, Swarthmore Coll., 1961-62; mem. adv. council dept. English Princeton U., 1960-66, Christian Gauss lectr., 1975; dir. NEH Seminars for Coll. Tchrs. Rice U., 1975, 78. Author: The Poetry of W.H. Auden: The Disenchanted Island, 1963, Hart Crane, 1965, Dionysus and the City: Modernism in Twentieth Century Poetry, 1970, Space Against Time in Modern American Poetry, 1972, The Levitator and Other Poems, 1975, American Ambitions: Selected Essays on Literary and Cultural Themes, 1987, Countries of the Mind: Literary Explorations, 1992, One Writer's Reality, 1996; editor: (with H.B. Wright) The Literary Works of Matthew Prior, 2 vols., 1959, W.H. Auden: A Collection of Critical Essays, 1964, The Narrative Poetry of Shakespeare, 1968, Sewanee Rev., 1952-61, adv. editor., 1961-73. Served to capt. AUS and USAAF, 1942-46, ETO. Am. Philos. Soc. and Carnegie Found. grantee, 1949; Rockefeller fellow, 1956, Guggenheim fellow, 1965-66, 72-73, Brown Found. fellow, U. South, 1988. Fellowship So. Writers, S.C. Acad. Authors. Democrat. Episcopalian. Home: 117 Carruthers Rd Sewanee TN 37375-2007

SPEARS, SALLY, lawyer; b. San Antonio, Aug. 29, 1938; d. Adrian Anthony and Elizabeth (Wylie) S.; m. Tor Hultgreen, July 15, 1961 (div. Jan. 1983); children: Dagny Elizabeth, Sara Kirsten, Kara Spears. BA, U. Tex., 1960, LLB, 1965. Bar: Tex. 1961, Ill. 1971. Practice law Stamford, Conn., 1966-67, Chgo., 1970-71, Northbrook, Ill., 1972-73, Toronto, Ont., Can., 1973-81; assoc. firm Cummings & Lockwood, Stamford, 1966-67, Kirkland & Ellis, Chgo., 1970-71; sr. atty. Allstate Ins. Co., Northbrook, Ill., 1971-73; gen. counsel, sec. Reed Paper Ltd., Reed Ltd., Toronto, 1973-78, Denison Mines Ltd., Toronto, 1978-81; pvt. practice law San Antonio, 1981—; apptd. by Sec. of Def. to serve on Def. Adv. Com., Women in the Svcs., 1997. Mem. Tex. Bar Assn., San Antonio Bar Assn., Bankruptcy Bar Assn., Bexar County Women's Bar Assn., San Antonio Country Club, The Club at Sonterra. Home: 433 Evans Ave San Antonio TX 78209-3725 Office: Ste 211 4600 Broadway San Antonio TX 78209-6262

SPEAS, CHARLES STUART, personnel director; b. Phila., Jan. 1, 1944; s. Austin LeRoy and Peggy Elaine (Drake) S.; m. Julie Ellen Royce, Apr. 10, 1965; children: Eric S. Speas, Robert Austin Speas. Student, Tri-State Coll., U. Notre Dame, Purdue U. Lic. agt. in life, accident and health ins., Ind. Sr. scheduling coord. Excel Industries, Elkhart, Ind., 1966-73; corp. dir. pers. EFP Corp., Elkhart, 1973—; cons. various Elkhart, Goshen area bus., 1980—. Contbr. articles profl. jours. Participant Soviet/Am. Conf. on Trade and Econ. Cooperation, Kremlin, 1991. With USAF, 1962-66. Mem. Ind. Pers. Assn., Goshen Indsl. Club (recipient cert. of appreciation 1990), Soc. for Human Resources Mgmt., Elkhart C. of C. (task force on healthcare availability/cost). Republican. Avocations: woodworking, fishing, gardening, golf. Home: 23683 River Dr Goshen IN 46526-9000 Office: EFP Corp 223 Middleton Run Rd Elkhart IN 46516-5429

SPEAS, RAYMOND AARON, retired insurance company executive; b. Lynneville, Iowa, Feb. 10, 1925; s. Harold H. and Susie B. Speas; m. Betty Jane Welshhons, Apr. 27, 1945; children: Raymond D., Gaylynn J. BS in Bus. Adminstrn., Drake U., 1951. CLU. With Equitable Life Ins. Co. of Iowa, Des Moines, 1951—, v.p., contr., 1967-76; sr. v.p., adminstrn. Equitable of Iowa Cos., Des Moines, 1976-77, sr. v.p., treas., 1977-82, exec. v.p., treas., 1982-92, also bd. dirs.; bd. dirs. E.I. Sales Inc.; exec. v.p., treas. Equitable Am. Life Ins. Co. Mem. Internat. Youth Coun. YMCA, 1966-74, bd. dirs. Des Moines, 1960-63; exec. bd. Iowa Soc. Christian Chs., 1977; past pres., bd. dirs. Des Moines Jr. Achievement. With U.S. Army, 1943-46. Fellow Life Office Mgmt. Assn.; mem. Life Ins. Agy. Mgmt. Assn., Des Moines Golf and County Club. Home: 3524 Grand Ave Des Moines IA 50312-4300 Office: Equitable of Iowa Cos 604 Locust St Des Moines IA 50309-3705 also: Equitable of Iowa Cos 699 Walnut Hub Tower PO Box 9107 Des Moines IA 50306

SPEAS, ROBERT DIXON, aeronautical engineer, aviation company executive; b. Davis County, N.C., Apr. 14, 1916; s. William Paul and Nora Estelle (Dixon) S.; m. Manette Lansing Hollingsworth, Mar. 4, 1944; children: Robert Dixon, Jay Hollingsworth. BS, MIT, 1940; Air Transport Pilot rating, Boeing Sch. Aero., United Air Lines, 1938; DBA in Aviation (hon.), Embry Riddle Aero. U., 1995. Aviation reporter Winston Salem Jour., 1934; sales rep. Trans World Airlines, 1937-38; engr. Am. Airlines, 1940-44, asst. to v.p., 1944-46, dir. maintenance and engring., cargo div., 1946-47, spl. asst. to pres., 1947-50; U.S. rep. A.V. Roe Can., Ltd., 1950-51; pres., chmn. bd. R. Dixon Speas Assocs., Inc. (aviation cons.), 1951-76; chmn., chief exec. officer Speas-Harris Airport Devel., Inc., 1974-76; chmn. bd., pres. Aviation Consulting, Inc., 1976-82, chmn. bd., 1982-84; pres. PRC Aviation, 1984-97; founder, dir. R. Dixon Speas Assocs. (subs. Arthur D. Little), 1997—; mem. aeros. and space engring. bd. Nat. Rsch. Coun., 1980-84. Author: Airplane Performance and Operations, 1945, Pilots' Technical Manual, 1946, Airline Operation, 1949, Technical Aspects of Air Transport Management, 1955, Financial Benefits and Intangible Advantages of Business Aircraft Operations, 1989. Recipient 1st award Ann. Nat. Boeing Thesis Competition, 1937, rsch. award Am. Transport Assn., 1942, William A. Downes Airport Operators Coun. Internat. award, 1992; inductee Ariz. Aviation Hall of Fame, 1995, William Littlewood Memorial lecture Am. Inst. of Aeronautics and Astronautics, 1994. Fellow AIAA (treas. and coun. 1963-64, chmn. ethics com. 1989-92, AIAA-SAE William Littlewood lectr. 1994), Royal

Aero. Soc., Soc. Automotive Engrs. (v.p. 1955, coun. 1964-66); mem. ASME, Flight Safety Found. (bd. govs. 1958-71, 79-90, exec. com. 1979-90), Inst. Aero Scis. (past treas., coun. 1959-62, exec. com. 1962), Coll. Aeronautics (trustee 1967—), Soc. Aircraft Investigators, Manhasset C. of C. (pres. 1962), Wings Club (pres. 1968-69, coun. 1966-71, 73-90, 92-95, chmn. devel. com. 1989—, Sight lectr. 1992), Skyline Country Club. Home: 4771 E Country Villa Dr Tucson AZ 85718-2640 Office: 6262 N Swan Rd Tucson AZ 85718-3600

SPEASE, LOREN WILLIAM, chiropractor; b. Luverne, Minn., Sept. 15, 1930; s. Chester Clair and Ethelwyn Mary (Coon) S.; m. Darlene Mae Braa, Apr. 15, 1953; children: Bryce, Craig, Laura, Julie. D of Chiropractic, Northwestern Coll. Chiropractic, 1958. Enlisted USMC, 1948, advanced through grades to staff sgt., discharged, 1952; ptnr. Spease Tire Shop, Luverne, Minn., 1952-55; founder, owner Spease Chiropractic Back Care Ctr., Brookings, S.D., 1958—. Judge advocate Dakota Marine Detachment, USMC League, Sioux Falls, 1992—. 2d lt. Minn. Nat. Guard and USAR. Mem. S.D. Chiropractors Assn. (chmn., resolutions com. 1958—, Golden Svc. award 1997), Sioux Valley Chiropractic Soc. (past pres.), Habitat for Humanity, Elks, Am. Legion, Chi Omega Phi. Republican. Baptist. Avocations: flying, reading, travel, music, bird watching. Home: 404 W Wye Mesa Brookings SD 57006-4533 Office: Spease Chiropractic Back Care Ctr 406 4th St Brookings SD 57006-2003

SPECHT, ALICE WILSON, library director; b. Caracus, Venezuela, Apr. 3, 1948; (parents Am. citizens) d. Ned and Helen (Lockwood) Wilson; m. Joe W. Specht, Dec. 30, 1972; 1 child, Mary Helen. BA, U. Pacific, 1969; MLS, Emory U., 1970; MBA, Hardin-Simmons U., 1983. Libr. social scis. North Tex. State U., Denton, 1971-73; reference libr. Lubbock (Tex.) City and County Libr., 1974-75; system coord. Big Country Libr. System, Abilene, Tex., 1975-79; assoc. dir. Hardin-Simmons U., Abilene, 1981-88, dir. univ. librs., 1988—; apptd. Mayor's Task Force Libr. Svcs., 1995-96. Author bibliog. instrn. aids, 1981-90; editor; The College Man, For Pilots Eyes Only. Mem. mayor's task force Abilene Pub. Libr., 1995-96. Recipient Boss of Yr., Am. Bus. Women's Assn., 1994. Mem. ALA, Tex. Libr. Assn. (chair com. 1978-84, sec.-treas. coll. and univ. librs. divsn. 1993-94, legis. com. 1994—), Abilene Libr. Consortium (chair adminstrv. coun. 1990, 93, coord. nat. conf. 1991, 93), Rotary (chair com. 1989-90). Home: 918 Grand Ave Abilene TX 79605-3233 Office: Hardin-Simmons U PO Box 16195 2200 Hickory Abilene TX 79698-0001

SPECHT, GORDON DEAN, retired petroleum executive; b. Garner, Iowa, June 3, 1927; s. Reuben William and Gladys (Leonard) S.; m. Cora Alice Emmert, May 24, 1952; children: Mary Ellen, Grant. BS in Chem. Engring., Iowa State U., 1950, MS in Chem. Engring., 1951; SM in Chem. Engring., MIT, 1954. Engr. Exxon Corp. Bayway Refinery, Linden, N.J., 1951-59, systemn services div. mgr., 1960-61, engring. services div. mgr., 1962-63, chem. coordination div. mgr., 1964; mgr. systems dept. Exxon Corp.-Exxon Chem. Co., N.Y.C., 1965-70; sr. advisor communications and computer scis. dept. Exxon Corp., Florham Park, N.J., 1971-76, assoc. cons., 1977-85; retired, 1986. Patentee in field. Asst. scoutmaster Boy Scouts Am., Westfield, N.J., 1986—; sr. qualified observer Sperry Obs., Cranford, N.J., 1986—; celestial navigation instr. U.S. Power Squadrons, 1990—. With U.S. Army, 1945-46, 1st lt. C.E., 1952-53, Korea. Decorated Bronze Star. Mem. Am. Inst. Chem. Engrs., Amateur Astronomers, Inc., No. N.J. Power Squadron, MIT Club of No. N.J., MIT Club of Princeton, Nat. Eagle Scout Assn., Tau Beta Pi, Phi Lambda Upsilon, Phi Kappa Phi, Tau Kappa Epsilon. Republican. Methodist. Avocations: astronomy, sailing, canoeing, swimming, bicycling. Home: 15 Normandy Dr Westfield NJ 07090-3431

SPECIALE, RICHARD, bank executive; b. N.Y.C., Aug. 16, 1945. B.S.B.A., Georgetown U., 1967; M.B.A., NYU, 1976. Sr. acct. Price Waterhouse & Co., N.Y.C., 1969-74; sr. v.p. J.P. Morgan and Co. Inc., N.Y.C., 1974—; bd. dirs. instnl. owners divsn. Real Estate Bd. N.Y., 1984—, chmn., 1991—, mem. bd. govs., 1988-90, 92—; bd. dirs. Downtown-Lower Manhattan Assn., Inc., N.Y.C., Grand Ctrl. Partnership Inc.; mem. adv. bd. Real Estate Inst., NYU, 1984—; dir. Realty Found. of N.Y., 1994—. Bd. dirs. Children's Arts and Scis. Workshops, N.Y.C., 1978-84; trustee Dance Theatre Found., N.Y.C., 1984—, Alvin Ailey Am. Dance Theatre, N.Y.C., 1984—; mem. real estate and constrn. coun. Lincoln Ctr., 1985—. Mem. AICPA, N.Y. State Soc. CPAs, Industrial Devel. Rsch. Coun. Office: JP Morgan & Co Inc 60 Wall St New York NY 10005-2836

SPECK, EUGENE LEWIS, internist; b. Boston, Dec. 17, 1936; s. Robert A. and Anne (Rosenberg) S.; m. Rachel Shoshana; children: Michael Robert, Keren Sara. AB, Brandeis U., Waltham, Mass., 1958; MS, U. Mass., 1961; PhD, George Washington U., 1966, MD, 1969. Diplomate Am. Bd. Internal Medicine with subspecialty in infectious diseases. Intern N.Y. Hosp.-Cornell, 1969-70; rsch. assoc. NIH, Bethesda, Md., 1970-72; resident Barnes Hosp.-Washington U., 1972-73; instr. medicine Washington U., St. Louis, 1972-73; fellow Strong Meml. Hosp.-U. Rochester, 1973-75; instr. medicine U. Rochester, N.Y., 1973-75, asst. prof. medicine, 1975-80; asst. prof. medicine U. Nev., Las Vegas, 1980-85, assoc. prof., 1985-95, prof. medicine, 1995—; dir./co-dir. infectious disease unit U. Med. Ctr. of So. Nev., Las Vegas, 1980—; ptnr. Infectious Diseases Consultants, 1983—; cons. Clark County Health Dept., Las Vegas, 1980—, U. Med. Ctr. So. Nev., Las Vegas, 1980—, Sunrise Hosp., Las Vegas, 1980—, Valley Hosp., Las Vegas, 1980—. Contbr. articles to profl. jours., chpts. to books. Fellow ACP; mem. Am. Soc. Microbiology, Infectious Disease Soc. Am., Alpha Omega Alpha. Avocations: tennis, skiing, racquetball. Home: 2228 Chatsworth Ct Henderson NV 89014-5309 Office: Infectious Diseases Cons 3006 S Maryland Pkwy Ste 780 Las Vegas NV 89109-2246

SPECK, LAWRENCE W., architect; b. Houston, Apr. 22, 1949; s. H.K. and Esther (Elliot) S.; m. Cynthia Alexander, Jan. 2, 1971 (div. 1988); children: Sloan Garret, Harrison Alexander; m. Amanda Mayhew Dealey, Oct. 3, 1992. BS in Mgmt., MIT, 1971, BS in Art and Design, 1971, MArch, 1972. Registered architect, Mass., Tex. Instr. MIT, Boston, 1972-75; asst. prof. U. Tex., Austin, 1975-79, assoc. prof., 1979-84, prof., 1984—, dean Sch. Arch., 1993—; prin. Lawrence W. Speck Assocs., Austin, 1975—; dir. Ctr. Study Am. Architecture U. Tex. at Austin; adj. curator architecture Dallas Mus. Art, 1985-87. Editor: Architecture for the Emerging American City, 1985; author: Landmarks of Texas Architecture, 1986; co-editor: New Regionalism, 1987. Bd. dirs. Buell Ctr. Columbia U., N.Y.C., 1985-87. Fulbright sr. scholar Council for Internat. Exchange Scholars, 1978. Fellow AIA (5 design awards Austin chpt. 1984-87); mem. Tex. Soc. of Architects (3 design awards 1986), Soc. Arch. Historians, Sigma Chi. Avocations: athletics, children's literature. Home: 1402 Hardouin Ave Austin TX 78703-2517 Office: 3209 Tarryhollow Dr Austin TX 78703-1638 Address: 3209 Tarryhollow Dr Austin TX 78703-1638

SPECK, MARVIN LUTHER, microbiologist, educator; b. Middletown, Md., Oct. 6, 1913; s. John Luther and Pearl Lighter (Wilhide) S.; m. Jean Moler Critchlow, Sept. 11, 1940; children: Linda Jean, Martha Loraine, Susan Carol. B.S., U. Md., 1935, M.S., 1937; Ph.D., Cornell U., 1940. Instr. microbiology U. Md., 1940-41; asst. chief bacteriologist Nat. Dairy Research Labs., Balt., 1941-47; mem. faculty N.C. State U. at Raleigh, 1947—, prof. food microbiology, 1951-79, William Neal Reynolds prof. food sci., 1957-79, prof. emeritus, 1979—; lectr. Am. Inst. Chem. Engrs., 1978-79; spl. con. USPHS, 1950-62, HEW, 1967-70. Author: (with others) Dairy Microbiology, 1957; editor: Methods for the Microbiological Examination of Foods, 1976, 84; mem. editorial bd. Jour. Dairy Sci, 1953-68. Recipient J.M. Jarrett award N.C. Pub. Health Assn.; Nordica Internat. Research award Am. Cultured Dairy Products Inst., 1981; Nat. Award for Agrl. Excellence Nat. Agri-Mktg. Assn., 1984. Fellow Am. Acad. Microbiology (bd. govs. 1976), Inst. Food Technologists (nat. lectr. 1968); mem. Am. Soc. Microbiology (vice chmn. 1976-77, chmn. sect. 1977-79), Am. Dairy Sci. Assn. (Borden award dairy mfg. 1959, Pfizer-Lewis award for rsch. on cheese 1967), N.C. Dairy Products Assn. (Disting. Svc. award 1976), Sigma Xi, Phi Kappa Phi, Gamma Sigma Delta, Alpha Zeta. Presbyterian (elder). Home: 3204 Churchill Rd Raleigh NC 27607-6806

SPECK, SAMUEL WALLACE, JR., academic administrator; b. Canton, Ohio, Jan. 31, 1937; s. Samuel Wallace Sr. and Lois Ione (Schneider) S.; m. Sharon Jane Anderson, Jan. 20, 1962; children: Samuel Wallace III, Derek Charles. BA, Muskingum Coll., 1959; postgrad., U. Zimbabwe, Harare, 1961; MA, Harvard U., 1963, PhD, 1968. Prof. polit. sci. Muskingum Coll., New Concord, Ohio, 1964—, asst. to pres., 1986-87, exec. v.p., 1987, acting pres., 1987-88, pres., 1988—; mem. Ohio Ho. of Reps., 1971-76; state senator from Ohio 20th Dist., 1977-83; assoc. dir. Fed. Emergency Mgmt. Agy., 1983-86; bd. dirs. Camco Fin. Corp., Cambridge, Ohio, Cambridge (Ohio) Savs. Bank; pres. Eastern Ohio Devel. Alliance, 1990-92; Fund for Improvement of Postsecondary Edn., 1990-92, chmn. 1991. Contbr.: Southern Africa in Perspective, 1972; also numerous articles on African and Am. govt. and pub. policy. Bd. dirs. Ohio Tuition Trust Authority, 1991-93, Internat. Ctr. for Preservation Wild Animals. Recipient Outstanding Legislator award VFW/DAV/Am. Legion, Conservation Achievement award State of Ohio. Mem. Assn. Ind. Colls. and Univs. of Ohio (chmn. 1992-94). Republican. Presbyterian. Home: 57 College Pl New Concord OH 43762-1101 Office: Muskingum Coll Office of Pres New Concord OH 43762

SPECTER, ARLEN, senator; b. Wichita, Kans., Feb. 12, 1930; s. Harry and Lillie (Shanin) S.; m. Joan L. Levy, June 14, 1953; children: Shanin, Stephen. Student, U. Okla., 1947-48; BA Internat. Rels., U. Pa., 1951; LL.B., Yale U., 1956. Asst. counsel Warren Commn., Washington, 1964; magisterial investigator Commn. of Pa., 1965; asst. dist. atty. City of Phila., 1959-63, dist. atty., 1966-74; ptnr. Dechert Price & Rhoads, Phila., 1956-66, 74-80; U.S. senator from Pa., 1981—; lectr. law Temple U., 1972-75, U. Pa., 1968-72; chmn. Appropriations Subcom. on Labor, Health and Human Svcs., sel. com. in intelligence, judiciary subcom. on terrorism, tech. and gov. info., spec. com. on aging, vet. affaors, sen. rep. policy com. Bd. editors Law Jour.; contbr. articles to profl. jours. Served to 1st U.S. Army, 1951-53. Recipient Youth Svcs. award B'nai B'rith, 1966; recipient Sons of Italy award, 1968, Community Humanitarian award Bapt. Ch., 1969, man of Yr. award, Temple Beth Ami, 1971, N.E. Cath. High Sch. Outstanding Achievement award, 1973. Mem. Phi Beta Kappa. Republican. Jewish. Office: US Senate 711 Senate Hart Bldg Washington DC 20510-3802*

SPECTOR, ABRAHAM, ophthalmic biochemist, educator, laboratory administrator; b. Nyack, N.Y., Jan. 14, 1926; s. Benjamin and Eva (Kaplovitz) S.; m. Joan Gruden, June 25, 1950 (dec. Jan. 1981); children: David Julian, Paul Joseph; m. Marguerite B. Filson, May 27, 1983. AB, Bard Coll, 1947, DS (hon.), 1985; PhD, NYU, 1957; MD (hon.), U. of the Republic, Uruguay, 1981. Rsch. chemist Lederle Lab., Pearl River, N.Y., 1948-52; instr. ophthalmic rsch. Harvard U., Boston, 1958-64, assoc. ophthalmic rsch., 1964-65; lectr. biol. chemistry Northeastern U., Boston, 1959-62; asst. prof. ophthalmic biochemistry Columbia U., N.Y.C., 1965-67, assoc. prof., 1967-73, prof., 1973—, dir. lab. biochemistry and molecular biology, 1976—, rsch. dir., dept. ophthalmology, 1989, 1996—, Malcolm P. Aldrich rsch. prof. ophthalmology, 1996—; mem. Vision Research and Tng. Com., Nat. Eye Inst., 1970-71, chmn. cataract workshop, 1973, mem. visual scis. study sect., 1976-80, chmn., 1978-80, bd. sci. advisors, 1982-85, chmn., 1983-85. mem. sci. adv. com. Fight for Sight, Inc., 1980-84; bd. sci. advisors Inst. Biol. Scis. Oakland U., 1982—; vis. prof. ophthalmology U. P.R., 1982—; vis. prof. biochemistry Med. U. Shanghai, 1986—. Assoc. editor Archives of Ophthalmology, 1968-70; sect. editor Experimental Eye Rsch., 1985-92; mem. editorial bd. Investigative Ophthalmology and Visual Sci., 1968-82, 87-92, Experimental Eye Rsch., 1974-85; contbr. numerous articles to profl. jours. Recipient Bausch & Lomb Sci. medal, 1944, Merit award NIH, 1987, Japanese Coop. Cataract Rsch. Group Internat. award, 1987, Sr. Scientific Investigators award Rsch. to Prevent Blindness, 1987, 94, Alcon Rsch. Inst. award, 1994; Guggenheim fellow, 1971-72, Fulbright fellow, 1981. Mem. AAAS, Assn. for Rsch. in Vision and Ophthalmology (pres. 1976, trustee 1970-75, Proctor medal 1983), Am. Soc. Biol. Chemistry, Am. Chem. Soc., Am. Soc. for Cell Biology, Harvey Soc., Marine Biol. Lab., Oxygen Soc. Home: 808 Broadway Apt 612 New York NY 10003-4806 Office: Columbia U Dept Ophthalmology Eye Research Addition 5th Fl 630 W 168th St New York NY 10032-3702

SPECTOR, ANITA FROHMANN, buyer; b. N.Y.C., Apr. 26, 1943; d. Ira and Minnie (Glazer) Friedman; m. Robert Frohmann, Dec. 24, 1961; 1 child, Edward Frohmann; m. Boris Spector, Apr. 21, 1985; stepchildren: Jeffrey Spector, Lori Spector Krein. BS, Adelphi U., 1984; MA, SUNY, 1992; PhD, Walden U., 1997. Buyer furniture/furnishings Colgate Palmolive Co., N.Y.C., 1983-87, buyer office supplies/forms, 1987-90, buyer fabric care packaging/household surface care packaging, 1990-95, materials sourcing project analyst, 1995-97, buyer point of sale and packaging, 1997—. Mem. AAUW, The Doctorate Assn. N.Y. Educators. Avocations: reading, travel, bicycling, music, decorating. Home: 4 Park Ave Apt 16C New York NY 10016-5311 Office: Colgate Palmolive Co 300 Park Ave New York NY 10022-7402

SPECTOR, ARTHUR JAY, federal judge; b. N.Y.C., Sept. 10, 1949; s. Nathan and Yetta (Ehrlich) S.; m. Kayla Dee Jaffe, Aug. 3, 1974; children: Joel, Andrew. BA, CCNY, 1971; JD cum laude, Boston U., 1974. Bar: N.Y. 1975, U.S. Ct. Appeals (2d cir.) 1975, U.S. Dist. Ct. (ea. dist.) N.Y. 1975, U.S. Dist. Ct. (so. dist.) N.Y. 1975, Mich. 1976, U.S. Dist. Ct. (ea. dist.) Mich. 1976, U.S. Ct. Appeals (6th cir.) 1981, U.S. Supreme Ct. 1979. Asst. dist. atty. N.Y. County, N.Y.C., 1974-76; assoc. Isackson and Neering, Bay City, Mich., 1976-79; ptnr. Pergande, Shaw and Spector, Bay City, Mich., 1980; equity owner, assoc. Pergande, Shaw and Spector, later Pergande, Shaw, Spector and Wenzloff, Bay City, Mich., 1980-84; judge U.S. Bankruptcy Ct., Bay City and Flint, Mich., 1984—. Contbg. editor: Norton Bankruptcy Law and Practice 2nd Edit. With U.S. Army, 1970-71. Mem. Nat. Conf. Bankruptcy Judges (mem. jud. ethics com. 1987-88), Am. Bankruptcy Inst. Office: US Bankruptcy Ct 111 First St PO Box 911 Bay City MI 48707-0911

SPECTOR, DAVID M., lawyer; b. Rock Island, Ill., Dec. 20, 1946; s. Louis and Ruth (Vinikour) S.; m. Laraine Fingold, Jan. 15, 1972; children: Rachel, Laurence. BA, Northwestern U., 1968; JD magna cum laude, U. Mich., 1971. Bar: Ill. 1971, U.S. Dist. Ct. (no. dist.) Ill. 1971, U.S. Ct. Appeals (7th cir.) 1977, U.S. Ct. Appeals (4th cir.) 1984, U.S. Dist. Ct. (cen. dist.) Ill. 1984. Clk. Ill. Supreme Ct., Chgo., 1971-72; ptnr., assoc. Isham, Lincoln & Beale, Chgo., 1972-87; ptnr. Mayer, Brown & Platt, Chgo., 198-97, Hopkins & Sutter, Chgo., 1997—; chmn. ABA Nat. Inst. on Ins. Co. Insolvency, Boston, 1986; co-chmn. ABA Nat. Inst. on Internat. Reins.: Collections and Insolvency, N.Y., 1988; chmn. ABA Nat. Inst. on Life Ins. Co. Insolvency, Chgo., 1993; spkr. in field. Editor: Law and Practice of Insurance Company Insolvency, 1986, Law and Practice of Life Insurer Insolvency, 1993; co-editor: Law and Practice of International Reinsurance Collections and Insolvency, 1988; contbr. articles to profl. jours. Mem. ABA (chair Nat. Inst. on Life Insurer Insolvency 1993), Chgo. Bar Assn., Legal Club of Chgo. Home: 2100 N Lincoln Park W Chicago IL 60614 Office: Hopkins & Sutter Three First National Plz Chicago IL 60602-4205

SPECTOR, ELEANOR RUTH, government executive; b. N.Y.C., Dec. 2, 1943; d. Sidney and Helen (Kirschenbaum) Lebost; m. Mel Alan Spector, Dec. 10, 1966; children: Nancy, Kenneth. BA, Barnard Coll., 1964; postgrad. sch. pub. adminstrn., George Washington U., 1965-67; postgrad sch. edn., Nazareth Coll., 1974. Indsl. investigator N.Y. State Dept. Labor, White Plains, 1964-65; mgmt. intern Navy Dept., Washington, 1965, contract negotiator, 1965-68, contract specialist, 1975-78, contracting officer/br. head, 1978-82, dir. div. cost estimating, 1982-84; dep. asst. sec. def. for procurement Washington, 1984-91; dir. Def. Procurement, Washington, 1991—; advisor Nat. Contract Mgmt. Assn., 1984—. Recipient Def. Meritorious Civilian Svc. medal, 1986, 93, 96, Meritorious Svc. Presdl. award, 1989, 94, Disting. Civilian Svc. Presdl. award, 1990, Def. Disting. Civilian Svc. medal, 1991, 94. Office: Office Under Sec Defense Acquisition & Technology 3060 Def Pentagon Rm 3E144 Washington DC 30301-3060

SPECTOR, GERSHON JERRY, physician, educator, researcher; b. Rovno, Poland, Oct. 20, 1937; came to U.S., 1949; naturalized, 1956; m. Patsy Carol Tanenbaum, Aug. 28, 1966. BA, Johns Hopkins U., 1960; MD cum laude, U. Md., 1964. Intern Beth Israel Hosp., Boston, 1964-65; resident in surgery Sinai Hosp., Balt., 1965-66; resident in otolaryngology Mass. Eye and Ear Infirmary, Boston, 1966-69, Peter Bent Brigham Hosp., Boston, 1968-69; teaching fellow in otolaryngology Harvard U. Med. Sch., Boston, 1968-69; assoc. physician Ill. Crippled Children's Svc., Carbondale, 1971; mem. faculty Washington U. Med. Sch., St. Louis, 1971—, assoc. prof. otolaryngology, 1974-76, prof., 1976—; chief dept. otolaryngology St. Louis County Hosp., 1971-77; mem. staff Washington U. Med. Ctr., Barnes Hosp.; dir. temporal bone bank, 1971-81; guest examiner Am. Bd. Otolaryngology, 1975-77; rsch. cons. neurosci. group, G.D. Searle Pharm. Corp. Mem. editl. bd. Laryngoscope, 1978, editor-in-chief, 1984-94; contbr. articles to med. jours. With U.S. Army, 1969-71. Hancock scholar, 1962. Fellow ACS; mem. AAAS, AMA, Am. Acad. Ophthalmology and Otolaryngology (Honor award 1979), St. Louis Med. Soc., St. Louis County Med. Soc., Am. Coun. Otolarygology, St. Louis Ear, Nose and Throat Club (pres. 1986), So. Med. Assn., Deafness Rsch. Found., Pan. Am. Assn. Otorhinolaryngology and Broncho Esophagology, Am. Soc. Head and Neck Surgery, Soc. Univ. Otolaryngologists, Am. Laryngological, Rhinological and Otological Soc. (Edmund Prince Fowler award 1974), Am. Soc. Cell Biology, Electron Microscopy Soc., N.Y. Acad. Scis., Am. Assn. Anatomists, Am. Acad. Facial Plastic and Reconstructive Surgery, Am. Neuro-Otology Soc., Gesellschaft fur Neurootologie und Aequilibrimoetrie A.V., Barany Soc., Am. Radium Soc., Assn. Acad. Surgery, Am. Fedn. Clin. Oncologic Socs., Am Otological Soc., Acoustical Soc. Am., Soc. for Neurosci., Internat. Skull Base Soc. (founding), Brazilian Skull Base Soc. (hon.), Centurion Club, Alpha Omega Alpha, Psi Chi. Home: 7365 Westmoreland Dr Saint Louis MO 63130-4241 Office: Washington U Med Sch Saint Louis MO 63110

SPECTOR, HARVEY M., osteopathic physician; b. Phila., July 10, 1938; s. Philip and Sylvia (Rischall) S.; m. Rochelle Fleishman, June 16, 1963; children: Jill, Larry. DO, Phila. Coll. Osteo. Medicine, 1963. Osteopathic physician Phila., 1964—; preceptor Hershey (Pa.) Med. Sch., 1987—, Phila. Coll. Osteopathic Medicine, 1989—; assoc. prof. medicine Med. Coll. Pa., 1991—. Recipient Humanitarian award, Chapel of Four Chaplains, Phila., 1984. Mem. Am. Osteo. Assn. (del.), Pa. Osteo. Med. Assn. (del.), Am. Acad. Osteo. Gen. Practitioners, Phila. County Osteo Med. Soc., Med. Club Phila., Abington Dolphins Aquatic Club (pres. 1984-86), B'nai B'rith. Jewish. Avocations: golf, swimming. Office: 1220 Cottman Ave Philadelphia PA 19111-3650

SPECTOR, JOSEPH ROBERT, retired diversified manufacturing executive; b. N.Y.C., Apr. 16, 1923; s. Benjamin and Julia (Wagner) S. A.B., Dartmouth Coll., 1946; LL.B., Cornell U., 1952. Bar: N.Y. bar 1952, Fla. bar 1953. Asst. counsel Equitable Life Assurance Soc., N.Y.C., 1956-64; asst. gen. counsel Gen. Precision Co., Tarrytown, N.Y., 1964-68; corp. counsel Singer Co., N.Y.C., 1968-70; v.p., gen. counsel, sec. UMC Industries, Inc., Stamford, Conn., 1970-81, ret., 1981. Trustee Morocco-Am. Cultural Assn. Charitable Trust, No. Dispemsar, 1974-90; pres. 20 East 11 Owners Corp. With USNR, 1942-46. Mem. ABA, Am. Soc. Corp. Secs., Fla. Bar Assn., Assn. of Bar of City of N.Y., Yale Club. Home: 236 Loch Rd Columbia SC 29210-4406 also: 1 Blvd Mohammed V, Tangier Morocco

SPECTOR, LOUIS, retired federal judge, lawyer, arbitrator, consultant; b. Niagara Falls, N.Y., Apr. 4, 1918; s. Jacob and Gussie (Yochelson) S.; children: Gale Anne Spector Pasternack, Arthur George, James Aland. Student (N.Y. State scholar), Niagara U., 1936-37; LL.B. with honors, U. Buffalo (later State U. N.Y.), 1940. Bar: N.Y. bar 1940, D.C. bar 1972, U.S. Supreme Ct. bar 1971, U.S. Ct. Claims bar 1968. Assoc. firm Saperston, McNaughton & Saperston, Buffalo, 1941-42; asst. chief legal div. U.S. Army C.E., Buffalo Dist., 1942-43; chief sect. claims appeals and litigation U.S. Army C.E. (Great Lakes Div.), Chgo., 1946; chief legal br. and real estate div. U.S. Army C.E. (Great Lakes Div.), Buffalo Dist., 1946-53; exec. dir. Buffalo Port Authority, 1953-54; mem. Bd. Contract Appeals, Washington, 1954-59; chmn. Army panel Armed Services Bd. Contract Appeals, Washington, 1959-62, Unified Armed Services Bd. Contract Appeals, 1962-68; trial judge U.S. Ct. Claims, Washington, 1968-82, judge, 1982-85; cons., arbitrator, mediator Falls Church, Va., 1985—; lectr., speaker, writer public contracts; Congressional appearances, 1953, 66, 69, 77. Contbr. articles to profl. publs. Served with C.E. U.S. Army, 1943-46. Recipient Freshman medal Niagara U., 1936, Sophomore medal, 1937. Fellow Am. Bar Found.; mem. ABA (chmn. sect. pub. contract law 1967-68); Fellow Nat. Contract Mgmt. Assn. (nat. bd. advisers 1967—); mem. ABA (ho. of dels. 1968-70), Fed. Bar Assn. (gen. editor jour. 1960-74, nat. chmn. com. govt. contracts and procurement law 1961-63, Distinguished Service award D.C. chpt. 1974), Lincoln Law Soc. (alumni pres. 1951). Club: Cosmos. Home: 6219 Beachway Dr Falls Church VA 22041-1425 *The concept of justice has been a central concern of my life. It is not a unique concern. Daniel Webster described it as "the great interest of man on earth . . . the ligament which holds civilized beings and nations together." And Reinhold Neibuhr reflected that: "Man's capacity for justice makes democracy possible; but man's inclination to injustice makes democracy necessary.".*

SPECTOR, MARSHALL, philosophy educator; b. Chgo., Feb. 11, 1936; s. Israel Hayyim Spector and Pauline (Futorian) Axelrood; m. Nan Shipman, Dec. 26, 1959; children: Anthony, Jessica. BS in Physics, Ill. Inst. Tech., 1957; MS in Physics, U. Chgo., 1959; PhD in Philosophy, Johns Hopkins U., 1963. Asst. prof. philosophy Duke U., Durham, N.C., 1963-68; assoc. prof. SUNY, Stony Brook, 1968-74, prof., 1974—. Author: Methodological Foundations of Relativistic Mechanics, 1972, Concepts of Reduction in Physical Science, 1978. NSF grantee. Office: SUNY Stony Brook Dept Philosophy Stony Brook NY 11794-3750

SPECTOR, MELBOURNE LOUIS, management consultant; b. Pueblo, Colo., May 7, 1918; s. Joseph E. and Dora (Bernstein) S.; m. Louise Vincent, Nov. 23, 1948; 1 son, Stephen David. B.A. with honors, U. N.Mex., 1941. Intern U.S. Bur. Indian Affairs, 1941, Nat. Inst. Pub. Affairs, 1941; personnel asst. Office Emergency Mgmt., 1941-42; chief classification div. War Relocation Authority, 1942-43, Hdqrs. USAAF, 1943-45; employment officer UNRRA, 1945-46; pvt. employment, 1946-47; personnel officer Dept. State, 1947-49; detail Econ. Coop. Adminstrn., 1948; dep. dir. personnel Econ. Coop. Adminstrn., Marshall Plan, Paris, 1949-51; dep. dir., acting dir. personnel Econ. Coop. Adminstrn., Mut. Security Adminstrn., FOA, 1951-54; asst., dep. dir. Mission to Mexico, ICA, 1954-57, acting dir., 1957-59; chief C. Am., Mex. and Caribbean div. ICA, 1959-61; dir. Office Personnel Mgmt., AID, 1961-62; exec. dir. Bur. Inter-Am. Affairs, Dept. State, 1962-64; commd. fgn. service officer, 1964; counselor for adminstrv. affairs Am. embassy, New Delhi, India, 1964-66; seminarian Sr. Seminar Fgn. Policy, Dept. State, 1966-67; exec. dir. U.S.-Mex. Commn. for Border Devel. and Friendship, 1967-69, Am. Revolution Bicentennial Commn., 1969-71; mem. mgmt., policy and coordination staffs Dept. State, 1971-73; ret., 1973, cons., 1973—; mem. Fgn. Svc. Grievance Bd., 1976-77; exec. dir. Am. Consortium for Internat. Pub. Adminstrn., 1980-84, 93-94, dir. Marshall Plan Oral History Project, 1987—. Mem. Cosmos Club, Am. Soc. Pub. Adminstrn., Pi Kappa Alpha, Phi Kappa Phi. Home: 6414 Bannockburn Dr Bethesda MD 20817-5430

SPECTOR, MICHAEL JOSEPH, agribusiness executive; b. N.Y.C., Feb. 13, 1947; s. Martin Wilson and Dorothy (Miller) S.; BS in Chemistry, Washington and Lee U., 1968; m. Margaret Dickson, Sept. 14, 1977. Research chemist Am. Viscose, Phila., 1968-69; pres. MJS Entertainment Corp., Miami, Fla., 1970-84, also MJS Internat., Inc.; ptnr. Old Town Key West Devel. Ltd. (Fla.), 1977—; mem. bd. dirs. Plz. Bank of Miami, Fla., 1979-84, founder; pres. MJS Entertainment of Can. Inc., Toronto, Ont., Margo Farms, MJS Prodns., Inc., N.Y.C.; chmn., pres., CEO Margo Nursery Farms, Inc., Dorado, P.R., 1981—, also bd. dirs.; bd. dirs. Goodwill Industries So. Fla., v.p. fin., 1980, bd. dirs. Plz. Bank of Miami. Served with AUS, 1969-70. Recipient Robert E. Lee rsch. grant Washington and Lee U., 1967-68. Mem. Nat. Assn. Record Merchandisers (dir. Nova div., chmn. one-stop distbn. com. 1982-83), Country Music Assn., Dorado Beach, Golf and Tennis Club, Bankers Club of San Juan. Patentee synthetic stretching process. Home: Hyatt Dorado Beach Box 8 Dorado PR 00646-0008

SPECTOR, PHIL, record company executive; b. Bronx, N.Y., Dec. 25, 1940; m. Veronica Bennett, 1968 (div. 1974); children: Gary Phillip and Louis Phillip (twins), Donte Phillip, Nicole and Phillip (twins). Student, UCLA. Producer with Atlantic Records, 1960-61; founder Philles Records, 1962; now pres. Warner-Spector Records, Inc.; also Mother Bertha Music. Mem. mus. group: Teddy Bears, 1958-59; producer records for Gene Pitney, Ike and Tina Turner, Ben E. King, the Beatles, Righteous Bros., Checkmates, Crystals, Ronettes, John Lennon, George Harrison, The Ramones, Yoko Ono, others; producer album A Concert for Bangladesh (Grammy award); composer songs including You've Lost That Lovin' Feelin' (7 million performances; named most performed song in U.S. broadcasting history 1997), others; appeared in films Tami, Easy Rider; prod., TV documentary film A Giant Stands 5 Ft. 7 In.; prod. film That Was Rock. Named to Rock and Roll Hall of Fame, 1989; named Country Music Song of Yr. Songwriter and Pub. for To Know Him Is To Love Him, 1989; recipient lifetime achievement award U. Calif., Berkeley, 1994, Phila. award Phila. Music Alliance, 1994 (includes star on Phila.'s Walk of Fame); inducted into Songwriters Hall of Fame, 1996. Office: care Warner-Spector Records Inc 686 S Arroyo Pky Pasadena CA 91105-3233

SPECTOR, ROBERT DONALD, language professional, educator; b. N.Y.C., Sept. 21, 1922; s. Morris and Helen (Spiegel) S.; m. Eleanor Helen Luskin, Aug. 19, 1945; children: Stephen Brett, Eric Charles. BA, L.I. U., 1948, DHL, 1994; MA, NYU, 1949; PhD, Columbia U., 1962. Instr. L.I. U., Bklyn., 1948-59; asst. prof. L.I. U., 1959-62, asso. prof., 1962-65, prof. English, 1965-94, chmn. senate, 1966-67, 69-70, chmn. dept., 1970-75, dir. humanities and comm. arts, 1975-84, coord. div. of humanities and div. of comms. and performing arts, 1990—, dir. humanities, 1984-90; prof. emeritus L.I. U., 1994—, 1993—; editor, cons. Johnson Reprint Corp., 1967-84. Author: English Literary Periodicals, 1966, Tobias George Smollett, 1968, updated edit., 1989, Pär Lagerkvist, 1973, Arthur Murphy, 1979, Tobias Smollett: A Reference Guide, 1980, The English Gothic, 1983, Backgrounds to Restoration and Eighteenth-Century English Literature, 1989, Political Controversy, 1992, Smollett's Women, 1994, Samuel Johnson and the Essay, 1997; editor: Essays on the Eighteenth Century Novel, 1965, Great British Short Novels, 1970, 9 other vols. English and Am. lit., revs. and articles, poetry. Trustee L.I. U., 1969-70; chmn. George Polk Award Com., 1977—. Served with USCGR, 1942-46. Recipient L.I. U. Trustee award for scholarly achievement, 1978, Tristram Walker Metcalfe Alumnus of Year, 1981; Swedish Govt. travel and research grantee, 1966; fellow Huntington Library, 1974; fellow Folger Library, 1975; fellow Newberry Library, 1976. Mem. MLA, Am.-Scandinavian Found. (publs. com. 1962-84), P.E.N. Home: 1761 E 26th St Brooklyn NY 11229-2405

SPECTOR, STANLEY, historian, foreign language educator; b. N.Y.C., June 10, 1924; s. Irving and Sophie (Braun) S.; m. Betty Peishan Yue, Mar. 8, 1963; children—Pat Lee, Stephanie Spector Van Denberg, Lee Paul, Jon Marc. B.S., Coll. City N.Y., 1945; Ph.D., U. Wash., 1953; postgrad., London Sch. Oriental and African Studies, 1950-51. Instr. history CCNY, 1946; instr. Far Eastern history U. Wash., Seattle, 1951-52, asst. prof., 1955; lectr. history UCLA, 1953; lectr. in history, post-certificate class Chung Cheng Chung Hsueh Singapore, 1954; asst. prof. Far Eastern history Washington U., St. Louis, 1955-58, assoc. prof., 1959-64, assoc. prof. Chinese history, 1964-65, prof. emeritus Asian studies, 1965-89, prof. emeritus, 1989—; chmn. dept. Chinese and Japanese studies, 1964-72, dir. East Asian Lang. and AreaCtr., 1964, Office Internat. studies, 1969; vis. prof. Chinese and Japanese history Columbia U., 1962; vis. prof. U. Singapore, summers 1967-69, 71-73, Waseda U., Tokyo, 1966-67, Ikip U., Bandung, Indonesia, summer 1969. Author: Li Hung-chang and the Huai Army, 1964; co-editor: Guide to the Memorials of Seven Leading Officials of the 19th Century China, 1955. Chmn. Seattle chpt. Am. Vets. Com., 1948-49; co-chmn. Citizens for Stevenson, Seattle, 1952; chmn. St. Louis-Nanjing (Peoples Republic China) Sister City Com. Served with USNR, 1942-43. Social Sci. Research Council fellow, 1950-51, 58-59; Ford Found. fellow, 1953-55; Social Sci. Research Council, Toyo Bunko, 1966-67; Fulbright research scholar Japan, People's Republic of China, Hong Kong, Singapore, Malaysia, 1966-67; Fulbright research scholar USSR, 1975-76. Mem. AAUP, Midwest Conf. on Asian Studies (pres. 1967-68), Chinese Lang. Tchrs. Assn. (pres. 1971—), Am. Polit Sci. Assn., Assn. Asian Studies, Am. Hist. Assn., Internat. Studies Assn. Home: 50 Arundel Pl Saint Louis MO 63105-2278 Office: Washington U PO Box 1088 Saint Louis MO 63130

SPEDALE, VINCENT JOHN, manufacturing executive; b. Chgo., Dec. 2, 1929; s. Joseph and Mildred (Satarino) S.; m. Joan Deeny, Apr. 11, 1953; children: Kathleen, Joseph, Barbara, Judith, Robert, Anthony. BSME, Ill. Inst. Tech., 1952; MS in Indsl. Engring., Wayne State U., 1959; postgrad. in mgmt., MIT, 1977. With Chrysler Corp., 1952-70; v.p. mfg. solar gas turbine div. Internat. Harvester Co., San Diego, 1971-73; v.p. mfg. truck div. Internat. Harvester Co., Chgo., 1973-78, v.p., gen. mgr. engine div., 1978-81; pres. machine tool div. ACME Precision Products, Inc., Detroit, 1982-87; v.p. ops. ICM Industries, Inc., Chgo., 1987-91; CEO Forum Group, Indpls., 1991-92, Union City (Ind.) Body Co., 1992-93, K-Whit Inc., Fishers, Ind., 1993-94; mfg. cons. Kamaz Truck and Diesel Mfg., Naberezhniye-Chelny, Russia, 1995; CEO Blue Lustre, Inc., Fishers, 1996-97, Vinco Mgmt. Cons., Wheaton, Ill., 1997—. Mem. Soc. Automotive Engrs. Roman Catholic. Home: 1260 Shady Ln Wheaton IL 60187-3722

SPEECE, RICHARD EUGENE, civil engineer, educator; b. Marion, Ohio, Aug. 23, 1933; s. Irvin Ward S. and Desta May (Speece); m. Jean Margaret Edscorn, Nov. 15, 1969; children: Eric Jordan, Lincoln Dana. BCE, Fenn. Coll., 1956; M of Engring., Yale U., 1958; PhD, MIT, 1961. Assoc. prof. civil engring. U. Ill., Urbana, 1961-65; prof. N.Mex. State U., 1965-70, U. Tex., Austin, 1970-74; Betz chair prof. environ. engring. Drexel U., Phila., 1974-88; Centennial prof. Vanderbilt U., Nashville, 1988—; vis. scholar Cambridge (Eng.) U., 1994; cons. to govt., industry. Contbr. articles to profl. jours.; patentee in field. Recipient hon. mention for best paper Trans. Am. Fisheries Soc., 1973. Mem. Assn. Environ. Engring. Profs. (Disting. Faculty award 1970, disting. lectr. 1978, trustee 1981-83, Engring. Sci. award 1982), ASCE (J. James Cross medal 1983), Am. Soc. Microbiologists, Water Environ. Fedn. (Harrison Prescott Eddy medal 1966), U.S. ANC (Founder's award 1991), Internat. Assn. on Water Pollution Rsch. and Control. Office: Vanderbilt U Civil Engring Dept Nashville TN 37203

SPEED, BILLIE CHENEY (MRS. THOMAS S. SPEED), retired editor, journalist; b. Birmingham, Ala., Feb. 21, 1927; d. John J. and Ruby (Petty) Cheney; m. Thomas S. Speed, July 7, 1968; children: Kathy Lovell Windham Williams, Donna Lovell Adams, Melanie Lovell Wright. Grad., W.Ga. Coll. Reporter, sports writer Birmingham News, 1945; sports writer, gen. assignment reporter, ch. editor Atlanta Jour., 1947-53, with promotion dept., 1955-57, religion editor, 1965-89; feature editor Coach and Athlete Mag., 1958, So. Outdoors, 1958. Recipient Sharp Tack award Cumberland dist. Seventh Day Adventists; Spl. Service award Christian Council of Metro Atlanta, 1974, award for outstanding personal ministry, 1986, personal service award, 1986; Arthur West award for religious feature writing United Meth. Ch., 1977; Alumni Achievement award West Ga. Coll., 1985; Trustee award Protestant Radio & TV Ctr., 1986; Faith & Freedom award Religious Heritage of Am., 1986. Fellow Religious Pub. Relations Council; mem. Nat. Religion Newswriters Assn., Nat. Fedn. Press Women, Theta Sigma Chi. Methodist. Home: 559 Rays Rd Stone Mountain GA 30083-3142

SPEED, LAKE, professional race car driver; b. Jackson, Miss., Jan. 17, 1948; m. Rice Speed; children: Chambers, Sara Ann, Maurie. Winner 6 U.S. Nat. Kart Championships, World Karting Assn. World Championship, LeMans, France, 1978; race car driver NASCAR Winston Cup races, 1980—, with win in 1988 TranSouth 500. Office: c/o NASCAR PO Box 2875 Daytona Beach FL 32120-2875

SPEED, LESLIE BOKEE, lawyer; b. Balt., Jan. 19, 1949; d. William George and Jean Alice (LaVine) Speed. BA, U. Colo., 1972; JD, U. Denver, 1977. Bar: Colo. 1978. Assoc. Holland and Hart, Denver, 1978-84, ptnr., 1984-93; dir., shareholder Parcel, Mauro, Hultin & Spaanstra P.C., Denver, 1993—. Author: Corporate Powers, 1990; gen. editor U. Denver Law Rev., 1977. Bd. dirs. Denver Broncos Charities Fund, 1993—, Colo. Lawyers Health Program, 1994—; mem., sec. Colo. state adv. com. to U.S. Commn. on Civil Rights, Denver, 1974-77; sec. Denver Broncos Youth Found., 1984—. Mem. ABA, Colo. Bar Assn. (co-chmn. gaming, entertainment and sports law com. 1994-95), Denver Bar Assn., Sports Lawyers Assn. (bd. dirs. 1988—), Order of St. Ives. Democrat. Episcopalian. Home: 1201 Williams St Apt 15C Denver CO 80218-2678 Office: Parcel Mauro Hultin & Spaanstra 1801 California St Ste 3600 Denver CO 80202-2636

SPEED, TERENCE PAUL, statistician, educator; b. Victor Harbor, Australia, Mar. 14, 1943; came to U.S., 1987; s. Harold Hector and Jeanette Elisabeth (Hacklin) S.; m. Freda Elizabeth Pollard, Dec. 22, 1964. BS, Melbourne U., Victoria, Australia, 1965; PhD, Monash U., Victoria, 1969. Tutor Monash U., 1965-67, lectr., 1967-69; lectr. U. Sheffield, United Kingdom, 1969-73; prof. U. Western Australia, 1974-82; chief CSIRO Div. Math. and Statistics, Canberra, Australia, 1983-87; prof. U. Calif., Berkeley, 1987—. Home: 1830 Arch St Berkeley CA 94709-1310 Office: U Calif Dept Statistics Berkeley CA 94720

SPEEDY, ERIC DAWSON, laboratory technician; b. York, Pa., July 11, 1969; s. Harry Wilson and Janet Patricia (Roney) S.; m. Melissa Ann Rao, May 5, 1995. BS, Allegheny Coll., 1991. Biology technician Allegheny Coll., Meadville, Pa., 1991-93; lab. technician Hilltop Lab. Animals, Inc., Scottdale, Pa., 1994—. Bd. dirs. Greater Latrobe Recreation Soccer Assn, Latrobe, Pa., 1995. Mem. Am. Assn. Lab. Animal Sci., Nat. Ski Patrol Systems. Avocations: skiing, golf, outdoor activities, reading. Home: 2955 Seminary Dr Greensburg PA 15601

SPEER, DAVID JAMES, retired public relations executive; b. Mpls., Apr. 30, 1927; s. Ray Patterson and Grace Elizabeth (Kane) S.; m. Nancy How Girouard; children: Robert J. Girouard, Mark J. Girouard. B.A. in Polit. Sci., U. Minn., 1950. Sports reporter Mpls. Tribune, 1945-50; night radio editor AP, Mpls., 1950-51; ptnr. Speer's Publicity Service, Mpls., 1950-59; pres. Sullivan & Speer Inc., Mpls., 1959-61; sr. v.p. Padilla, Sarjeant, Sullivan & Speer, Inc., Mpls., 1961-71, pres., sec., 1971-77; pres., chief operating officer Padilla and Speer, Inc., Mpls., 1977-86; Minn. commr. Trade and Econ. Devel., 1987-91; cons. Padilla Speer Beardsley Inc., Mpls., 1991-93; exec. dir. Friends of the Communication Ctr., St. Paul, Minn., 1993—; cons. pub. relations, Mpls., N.Y.C., 1961-86; dir. pub. relations Minn. State Fair, 1961-68, St. Paul Winter Carnival Assn., 1952-68. Past chmn. Minn. Multiple Sclerosis Soc.; bd. dirs. St. Paul Chamber Orch.; consul of Finland in Minn. Served with USN, 1945-46. Mem. Pub. Rels. Soc. Am. (pres. chpt. 1967), U. Minn. Alumni Assn. (pres. 1975-76), Mpls. Club. Home: 23235 Saint Croix Trl N Scandia MN 55073-9725

SPEER, GLENDA O'BRYANT, middle school educator; b. Uvalde, Tex., Mar. 30, 1956; d. Harvey Glen and Mary (Miller) O'Bryant; m. Weldon Michael Speer, July 12, 1975; children: Janena Lea, Jon Michael. BS, Sul Ross State U., Alpine, Tex., 1978; MA, U. Tex., San Antonio, 1984. Tchr. math. Jackson Middle Sch., San Antonio, 1978-82; tchr. math., computers Bradley Middle Sch., San Antonio, 1982-86, chmn. dept. math., 1986—; computer edn. tchr. trainer N.E. Ind. Sch. Dist., San Antonio, 1984—; acad. pentathlon coach Bradley Middle Sch., 1988-92; software reviewer Nat. Coun. Tchrs. Math., Reston, Va., 1994. Editor Math Matters newsletter, 1989—; writer curriculum guide: Computer Literacy Guide for Teachers, 1992. Black belt Karate and self-defense instr. Tang So Do Karate Assn., San Antonio, 1994—. Recipient Supt.'s award N.E. Ind. Sch. Dist., 1990, 92, 93, Red Apple Tchrs. award St. Mary's U., San Antonio, 1992. Mem. Nat. Coun. Tchrs. Math., Tex. Coun. Tchrs. Math., Bradley Middle Sch. PTA. Avocations: genealogy, Southwest history. Office: Bradley Middle Sch 14819 Heimer Rd San Antonio TX 78232-4528

SPEER, JACK ATKESON, publisher; b. Wichita, Kans., July 3, 1941; s. Jack Shelley and Shannon Speer; m. Judith Ann Fuller, Aug. 5,1967; children: Martin Fuller, Elizabeth Fuller. BS in Bus. Adminstrn., Kansas. State U., 1966, ML, 1967; postgrad., U. Mo., 1967, U. So. Calif., 1969; IBM Pres.'s Class, Harvard U., 1980. Mem. advt., editorial, mech. staffs Wichita Eagle-Beacon, 1954-64; editorial asst. Emporia (Kans.) Gazette, 1964-65; supr. libr. data processing Kans. State U., Emporia, 1965-67; mgr. data processing ctr. Kans. State U., Manhattan, 1967-69; mgr. systems and programming John Wiley Inc.-Becker & Hayes Inc., Bethesda, Md., 1969-72; dir. libr. info. systems Informatics Inc. Info. Systems Group, Rockville, Md., 1972-77; v.p. ops. Arcata Real Estate Data Inc., Miami, Fla., 1977-79; mgr. electronic info. systems Arcata Publs. Group, Norwalk, Conn., 1979-83; v.p. mktg./sales, data imaging group The William Byrd Press, Richmond, Va., 1983-84; sr. v.p. ops. NewsBank Inc., New Canaan, Conn., 1984-85; pres., pub. Buckmaster Pub., Mineral, Va., 1986—; mem. faculty Cath. U. Am. Libr. Sch., Kans. State U. Libr. Sch.; customer adv. coun. U.S. Postal Svc., 1996—. Author: Amateur Radio Call Directory, 1982—, Buckmaster's Ann. Stockholder Reports, 1986—, Front-Page-News (CD-ROM), 1989, HamCall (CD-ROM), 1988—; compiler Libraries and Automation: A Bibliography, 1967, The Living Bible Concordance, 1972. Trustee Jefferson-Madison Regional Libr., 1990-91; commr. Louisa County Planning Commn. Mem. ALA, NRA, Am. Radio Relay League, Nat. Info. Standards Orgn. (CD-ROM com), D.C. Libr. Assn. (pres.), Rotary, Sigma Tau Gamma. Office: Buckmaster Pub 6196 Jefferson Hwy Mineral VA 23117-3425

SPEER, JAMES, religious organization administrator. Dir. Daniel Springs Encampment, Gary, Tex. Office: Daniel Springs Encampment PO Box 310 Gary TX 75643-0310*

SPEER, JOHN ELMER, freelance paralegal, reporter; b. Conrad, Mont., Mar. 19, 1956; s. Elmer Constant and Mildred Saphronia (LaBelle) S.; m. Sharron D. Knotts, May 23, 1982 (div. Mar. 1986); 1 child, Jeremy Keith; 1 foster child, Casey. Paralegal assoc., Coll. of Great Falls, Mont., 1994. Bar: Mont. 1996; Constrn. Law CLE, 1997. Farmer Valier, Mont., 1956-73; janitor Shelby (Mont.) pub. schs., 1974-75; freelance news reporter Sta. KSEN, Shelby, 1980—, various TV stas., newspapers, Great Falls, 1980-90; office cleaner Parkdale Housing Authority, Great Falls, 1990-95; freelance paralegal, Great Falls, 1993—; law clk., paralegal Mont. State Dist. Judge Thomas McKittrick, Great Falls, 1993; rschr. line-up identification appeal binder to U.S. Supreme Ct., 1993; trial assistance atty. Chas. Joslyn, spring 1996. Contbr. victim-witness assistance program operating manual, 1992. Counselor and adv. Victim-Witness Assistance Svcs., Great Falls, 1991-93. Mem. Mont. Big Sky Paralegal Assn., Am. Counseling Assn. Jehovah's Witness. Avocations: hiking, fishing, cooking, travel, swimming. Home: 3308 Lower River Rd Trlr 19 Great Falls MT 59405-7273

SPEER, MAX MICHAEL, special education educator; b. Granite City, Ill., Nov. 10, 1949; s. Max J. and Betty L. (Butler) S.; m. Anita Christine Patton, June 12, 1971; children: Michael, Max. BS in Edn., So. Ill. U., Edwardsville, 1973. Cert. tchr. elem. social and emotional disorders. cert. tchr. learning disabled and educable mentally handicapped, Ill. Tchr. jr. high spl. edn. Granite City Sch. Dist., 1973—. With U.S. Army, 1969-70. Mem. Coun. for Exceptional Children. Episcopalian. Avocations: tennis, bridge.

SPEER, NANCY GIROUARD, educational administrator; b. Mankato, Minn., Sept. 14, 1941; d. Jared and Katherine (Schmitt) How; m. Robert L. Girouard, Aug. 29, 1964 (dec. Mar. 1983); children: Robert James Girouard, Mark Jared Girouard; m. David J. Speer, Dec. 21, 1985. BA, Wellesley Coll., 1963; MA in Tchg., Wesleyan U., 1965; cert. mgmt., Smith Coll., 1985. Tchr. secondary sch. Bunnell H.S., Stratford, Conn., 1964-65; tchr., class advisor Lincoln Sch., Providence, 1965-69; substitute tchr. Mankato, 1972-74; pub. info. dir. City of Mankato, 1974-78; univ. editor, dir. pub. affairs forum Mankato State U., 1978-79; comms. mgr. Humphrey Inst., U. Minn., Mpls., 1980-83, dir. external rels., 1983-87, dir. devel. and external rels., 1987-95; dir. devel. Breck Sch., Mpls., 1996—; mem. steering com. Minn. Meeting, Mpls., 1990-96. Contbr. articles to mags. and periodicals; photographer for publs. and newspapers. Bd. dirs. Minn. Newspaper Found., St. Paul, 1985-91, chairperson, 1990-91bd. dirs., vice-chairperson Cabrini House, Mpls., 1993—; bd. dirs., sec. Minn. Ctr. for Book Arts, Mpls., 1990—; bd. dirs. Minn. Landmark Ctr., St. Paul, 1994—; dir. Minn. Women's Campaign Fund, Mpls., 1994—, co-pres. bd., 1997; mem. Leadership Mpls., Mpls. C. of C., 1982. Bush Leader fellow, 1985-87. Avocations: horseback pack trips, appreciation of nature, books. Home: 23235 Saint Croix Trl N Scandia MN 55073-9725 Office: Breck Sch 123 Ottawa Ave N Minneapolis MN 55422-5124

SPEER, WILLIAM THOMAS, JR., banker, investor, consultant, rancher; b. Boston, Feb. 17, 1936; s. William Thomas and Marie Dorothy (DeWolfe) S.; m. Glenda Jane Farris, Nov. 15, 1972; children: Jason Farris, Tyson DeWolfe, Courtland Conley, William Thomas III. AA, Marin Jr. Coll., Kentfield, Calif., 1955; BA in Bus., Calif. State U.-Fullerton, 1962; postgrad. U. Calif.-San Francisco, 1955-56. Bank examiner Fed. Res. Bank, 1962-67, 68-70; exec. v.p. First Nat. Bank, Cañon City, Colo., 1967-68; v.p., then sr. v.p. Bank of Idaho, Boise, 1970-74; sr. v.p. Bank of N.Mex., Albuquerque, 1975; prin. organizer, founder, pres., CEO, chmn. bd. Am. Bank of Commerce, Boise, 1975-94; exec. cons. First Security Bank, N.A., 1994-95, cons., 1995—; developer Willowgrove Estates, Meridian, Idaho, Rivers Bend Condominiums, McCall, Idaho, Snake Riverview Ranches, Inc. (pres.), King Hill, Idaho; guest lectr. Boise State U.; cons. in field. Contbr. articles to profl. jours. Bd. dirs. Idaho chpt. Am. Heart Assn., 1983, chmn. bd., 1985; bd. dirs. Boise Philharm., 1984, Boise Better Bus. Bur., 1994, Boise Sr. Citizens, 1994; active Pub. TV Sta., 1981-83. With U.S. Army, 1957-61. Recipient gov.'s appreciation award Idaho-Oreg. Lions Club, 1982. Mem. Am. Bankers Assn., Idaho Bankers Assn. (exec. coun.), BBB, Western Ind. Bankers Assn., Idaho Ind. Bankers Assn. (pres. 1986), Robert Morris Assocs., Nat. Assn. Home Builders, U.S. Indsl. Council, Greater Boise C. of C., Nat. Fedn. Ind. Bus., Idaho Water Users Assn., Boise State U. Club, Ducks Unltd., Pheasants Forever, Hillcrest Country Club, Centurion Club, Bronco Boosters Club, Elks. Home: PO Box 7566 Boise ID 83707-1566

SPEERING, ROBIN, educator, computer specialist; b. Athens, Ga., Apr. 23, 1937; s. Harry and Effie (Adams) S. BS, U. Ga., 1962, MEd, 1970, EdS, 1974; MRE, Southwestern Bapt. Sem., 1964. Cert. tchr., Ga. Ind. audiovisual equipment specialist Athens, 1957-69; mgr. Speering Printing Co., Athens, 1965-67, asst. mgr., computer specialist, 1986—; tchr. Oconee County H.S., Watkinsville, Ga., 1968-69, Barrow County Schs., Winder, Ga., 1970-73, Comer (Ga.) Elem. Sch., 1974-76, Tadmore Elem. Sch., Hall County, Ga., 1976-77, Richmond County Schs., Augusta, Ga., 1977-85, Truett-McConnell Coll., Watkinsville, Ga., 1995-96; freelance writer, Athens, 1986—. Contbr. articles to newsletters, area newspapers. Tchr. Christian Fellowship Ch., Athens, 1990—. Mem. ASCD, NEA, Ga. Assn. Educators, Printing Industry Assn. Ga., Kappa Delta Pi. Avocations: music, photography, electronics. Home: PO Box 6943 Athens GA 30604-6943 Office: Speering Printing Co 278 Hodgson Dr Athens GA 30606-2962

SPEERS, ROLAND ROOT, II, lawyer; b. Jacksonville, Fla., Oct. 8, 1933; s. Roland Root and Alice (Calkins) S.; m. Florence Briscoe, Dec. 18, 1954; children: Kirsten, Guy, Gina Marie. B.A. cum laude, UCLA, 1955, J.D., 1958. Bar: Calif. 1958, D.C. 1978. Dep. commr. corps. Calif. Dept. Corps., Los Angeles, 1958-59; sec., gen. counsel Suburban Cos., Pomona, Calif., 1959-64, Amcord, Inc., Los Angeles, 1964-67; asst. to pres. Amcord, Inc., 1967, v.p. corp. devel., 1968; v.p., gen. counsel Amcord, Inc., Newport Beach, Calif., 1970; sr. v.p. Amcord, Inc., 1971, exec. v.p., 1972-75, pres., 1975-94; ptnr. Speers, Dana, Teal Balfour & MacDonald, Costa Mesa, Calif., 1977-94; dir. Logicon, Inc., Torrance, Calif., Twelve Eleven Priss, Newport Beach, Calif. Trustee Pitzer Coll., Pomona, 1975-80; bd. councillors Center Pub. Affairs U. So. Calif., 1976-81; bd. dirs. Newport Harbor Art Mus., 1977-82; sr. warden St. James Episcopal Ch., 1993. Mem. D.C. Bar Assn., State Bar Assn. Calif., UCLA Alumni Assn., UCLA Law Sch. Alumni Assn., Phi Alpha Delta. Clubs: Big Canyon Country (Newport Beach).

SPEERT, ARNOLD, college president, chemistry educator; b. Bronx, N.Y., June 19, 1945; s. David Jack and Dorothy Bernice (Feldman) S.; m. Myrna Goldstein, June 11, 1967; children: Alan Michael, Debra Beth. BS, CCNY, 1966; PhD, Princeton U., 1971. Asst. to dean grad. and rsch. program William Paterson Coll., Wayne, N.J., 1970-71, from asst. to assoc. prof. chemistry, 1970-80, prof., 1980—, asst. to v.p. acad. affairs, 1971-78, assoc. dean acad. affairs, 1978-79, v.p. acad. affairs, 1979-85, pres., 1985—; bd. dirs. State Farm Indemnity Co. Vice chair, trustee Barnert Hosp., Paterson, 1986—, Jewish Fedn. North Jersey, Wayne, 1986-96, YM & YWHA No. N.J., Wayne, 1988—, Respiratory Health Assn., 1990-93; bd. dirs. William Paterson Coll. Found., 1985—. Mem. Am. Assn. State Colls. and Univs. (bd. dirs. 1993-95), Tri-County C. of C. (bd. dirs. 1986-94), N.J. State Bd. Examiners, N.J. Pres.'s Coun. (chair 1996—). Home: 48 Brandon Ave Wayne NJ 07470-6032 Office: William Paterson Coll 300 Pompton Rd Wayne NJ 07470-2103

SPEICHER, CARL EUGENE, pathologist; b. Carbondale, Pa., Mar. 21, 1933; s. William Joseph and Elizabeth Marcella (Connolly) S.; m. Mary Louise Walsh, June 21, 1958; children: Carl E. Jr., Gregory, Erik. BS in Biology, King's Coll., 1954; MD, U. Pa., 1958; primary course in aeroship medicine, Sch. of Aerospace Medicine, Brooks AFB, Tex., 1969; fellowship in med. chemistry, SUNY, Syracuse, 1970-71. Diplomate Am. Bd. Pathology. Intern U. Pa. Hosp., Phila., 1958-59, resdient, 1959-63; chief lab. svcs. USAF Hosp., London, Eng., 1963-66, USAF Med. Ctr. Wright Patterson, Dayton, Ohio, 1966-70; dir. clin. labs. and chmn. dept. pathology Wilford Hall USAF Med. Ctr., San Antonio, Tex., 1971-77; prof. dept. pathology Ohio State U., Columbus, 1977—; co-dir. James Cancer Club James Hosp. and Rsch. Ctr., Columbus, 1990—; vice chair dept. pathology Ohio State Univ., Columbus, 1992—; dir. clin. svcs. Ohio State U. Med. Ctr., Columbus, 1977—. Co-author: Choosing Effective Laboratory Tests, 1983; author: (book) The Right Test 1st edit., 1990, 2d rev. edit., 1993. Col. USAF, 1963-77. Decorated Legion of Merit, 1977, USAF; fellowship in med. chemistry SUNY, Syracuse, 1970-71. Mem. AMA (Physicians Recognition award), Ohio Soc. Pathologists, Ctrl. Ohio Soc. Pathologists, Royal Soc. of Medicine (Eng.), Coll. of Am. Pathologists, Am. Soc. Clin. Pathologists, Alpha Omega Alpha. Office: Ohio State U Med Ctr 410 W 10th Ave Columbus OH 43210-1240

SPEIDEL, DAVID HAROLD, geology educator; b. Pottsville, Pa., Aug. 10, 1938; s. Harold O. and Edith M. (Rosser) S.; m. Margaret Helen Liebrecht, Sept. 8, 1962. B.S., Franklin and Marshall Coll., Lancaster, Pa., 1960; Ph.D., Pa. State U., 1964. Research asso. Pa. State U., 1964-66; asst. prof. to prof. dept. geology Queens Coll., CUNY, Flushing, 1966—; chmn. dept. Queens Coll., CUNY, 1980-88, dean faculty sci., 1970-79, chmn. faculty senate, 1992-96; maj. projects sect. head, earth scis. NSF, 1988-89; vis. scholar Sr. Specialists div. Congl. Research Service, Washington, 1977-78. Author: (with A.F. Agnew) Natural Geochemistry of Our Environment; editor (with L. Ruedisili and A.F. Agnew) Perspectives on Water: Uses and Abuses; contbr. articles to profl. jours. Fellow Geol. Soc. Am.; mem. AAAS, Seismol. Soc. Am., Am. Ceramic Soc., Mineral. Soc. Am., Am. Geophys. Union, Am. Inst. Profl. Geologists, Nat. Hazards Soc., N.Y. Acad. Scis., Soc. Environ. Geochemistry and Health, Sigma Xi. Office: Queens Coll Dept Geology Flushing NY 11367

SPEIDEL, JOHN JOSEPH, physician, foundation officer; b. Iowa City, Iowa, Sept. 17, 1937; s. Thomas Dennis and Edna (Warweg) S.; divorced; 1 child, Sabrina Brett. A.B. cum laude, Harvard U., 1959, M.D., 1963, M.P.H., 1965. Diplomate: Nat. Bd. Med. Examiners, Am. Bd. Preventive Medicine. Intern St. Luke's Hosp., N.Y.C., 1963-64; resident N.Y.C. Dept. Health, 1965-67, dep. dir. maternal and infant care project, 1966-67; chief research div. Office of Population, AID, Dept. State, Washington, 1969-76; assoc. dir. Office of Population, 1977, dep. dir., acting dir. office, 1978-83; v.p. Population Action Internat. (formerly Population Crisis Com.), 1983-87, pres., 1987-95; program officer for population Hewlett Found., 1995—; lectr. population and family planning Georgetown U., 1973-75. Contbr. articles to profl. jours.; Editor: (with others) Female Sterilization, 1971, Hysteroscopic Sterilization, 1974, Intrauterine Devices, 1974, Control of Male Fertility, 1975, Advances in Female Sterilization Technology, 1976, Risks, Benefits and Controversies in Fertility Control, 1978, Reversal of Sterilization, 1978, Pregnancy Termination, 1979, Vaginal Contraception, 1979. Served to maj. U.S. Army, 1967-69. Recipient Meritorious Unit citation Office of Population, 1969-71, Arthur S. Flemming award Washington Downtown Jaycees, 1972. Mem. Am. Pub. Health Assn. (Carl S. Shultz award 1982), Population Assn. Am. Office: William & Flora Hewlett Found 525 Middlefield Rd Ste 200 Menlo Park CA 94025-3448

SPEIER, JOHN LEO, JR., retired chemist; b. Chgo., Sept. 29, 1918; s. John L. and Mary Jane (Dickman) S.; m. A. Louise Kimmel, Oct. 21, 1944; children—Susan, Genevieve, Dorothy, Margaret, John L. III, Thomas J. B.Sc., St. Benedict's Coll., 1941; M.Sc., U. Fla., 1943; Ph.D., U. Pitts., 1947. Naval Stores research fellow U. Fla., 1941-43; research fellow Mellon Inst., Pitts., 1943; sr. fellow Mellon Inst., 1947-56; mgr. organic research Dow Corning Corp., Midland, Mich., 1956-69; scientist in corp. research Dow Corning Corp., 1969-75, sr. scientist in corp. research, 1975-93; retired, 1994. Contbr. numerous articles to profl. jours., 1950—; holder 100 patents prodn. organosilicon compounds and allied products. Named Indsl. Research and Devel. Scientist of Yr. Indsl. Research/Devel. mag., 1978. Mem. AAAS, Am. Chem. Soc. (Frederick Stanley Kipping award 1990), Sigma Xi.

SPEIGHT, JAMES GLASSFORD, research company executive; b. Murton, Eng., June 24, 1940; came to U.S., 1980; s. George Madison and Elizabeth (Glassford) S.; m. Sheila Elizabeth Stout, Dec. 28, 1963; 1 child, James. BSc in Chemistry with honors, Manchester U., Eng., 1961, PhD in Organic Chemistry, 1965. Research fellow Manchester U., 1965-67; research officer Research Council, Edmonton, Alta., Can., 1967-80; research assoc. Exxon

Corp., Linden, N.J., 1980-84; chief sci. officer Western Rsch. Inst., Laramie, Wyo., 1984-89, chief exec. officer, 1990—; adv. com. Grant McEwan Community Coll., Edmonton, 1975-80; chmn. petroleum-natural gas research task force, Alta. Research Council, 1978-79; search com. V.P. for Research and Grad. Studies, U. Wyo., 1985; external mem. promotions com. U. Mosul, Iraq, 1985; thesis examiner, Indian Inst. Techn., Bombay, 1974, U. Mosul, 1976, 77, 78; vis. lect. petroleum sci., U. Mosul, Iraq, 1978; lectr. petroleum sci., U. Alberta, Edmonton, Can., 1976-80, U. Calgary, Alta., 1979-80. Editor Fuel Sci. and Tech. Internat., 1983—, Energy Sources, 1983—; referee numerous jours., manuscripts; contbr. more than 200 sci. articles to profl. jours. Fellow Am. Inst. Chemists, Royal Soc. Chemistry (chartered chemist), Chem. Inst. Can. (treas. Edmonton sect. 1971-78, editor newsletter 1975-77); mem. Am. Chem. Soc. (program com. petroleum divsn. 1981-91, 94—, bus. mgr. petroleum divsn. 1982-85), Sigma Xi. Office: Western Rsch Inst 365 N 9th St Laramie WY 82072-3380

SPEIGHT, VELMA RUTH, alumni affairs director; b. Snow Hill, N.C., Nov. 18, 1932; d. John Thomas and Mable Lee (Edwards) S.; m. Howard H. Kennedy, 1953 (div. 1961); 1 child, Chineta. BS, N.C. A&T U., 1953; MEd, U. Md., 1965, PhD, 1976. Cert. counselor, tchr., Md. Tchr. math., French Kennard High Sch., Centreville, Md., 1954-60; counselor Kennard High Sch., Centreville, 1960-66; coord. guidance dept. Queen Anne's County High Sch., Centreville, 1966-69; adv. specialist in civil rights Md. State Dept. Edn., Balt., 1969-72, supr. guidance, 1972-76, dep. asst. state supt., 1976-82, asst. state supt., 1982-86; dir. EEO recruitment U. Md., College Park, 1972; coord. guidance and counseling U. Md. Ea. Shore, Princess Anne, 1986-87; assoc. prof. counselor edn. East Carolina U., Greenville, 1989; chmn. dept. edn., coord. grad. prog. guidance and counseling U. Md., Eastern Shore, Greenville, 1989-93, chmn. dept. edn., 1990-94; dir. alumni affairs N.C. A&T U., Greensboro, 1993—; adj. prof. Loyola U., Balt., 1976-80, Johns Hopkins U., Balt., 1980; cons., 1987—; speaker numerous seminars. Mem. Nat. Coalition for Chpt. I Parents, Washington, 1980-87, Human Rights Commn., Howard County, Md., 1987—; chmn. Gov.'s com. Studying Sentencing Alternatives for Women, Annapolis, Md., 1987; founder, chmn. Mothers to Prevent Dropouts, Centreville. Recipient Early Childhood Edn. award Japanese Govt., 1984, Md. State Tchrs'. Assn. Minority award Black Chs. for Excellence in Edn.; Fulbright Hayes scholar, 1991. Mem. Am. Counseling Assn., Nat. Alliance Black Educators, Assn. for Supervision and Curriculum Devel., Assn. Tchr. Edn., Md. Assn. Coll. Tchr. Edn., Md. Counseling Assn., N.C. A&T U. Alumni Assn. (nat. pres. 197983, Excellence award 1983), Tchr. Edn. and Profl. Standards Bd. Democrat. Presbyterian. Club: Community Action (Centreville). Avocations: reading, cooking, sewing, bicycling. Home: 11 Carissa Ct Greensboro NC 27407-6366 Office: NC A&T State U Off of Dir Alumni Affairs Greensboro NC 27411

SPEILLER-MORRIS, JOYCE, English composition educator; b. Utica, N.Y., Nov. 11, 1945; d. Arnold Leonard Speiller and Sybil (Sall) McAdam; m. Joseph Raymond Morris, Mar. 17, 1984. BS, Syracuse U., 1968; MA, Columbia U., 1969. Cert. tchr., N.Y., Fla. Chmn. upper sch. social studies dept., tchr. grade 6 social studies and English Cathedral Heights Elem. Sch., N.Y.C., 1969-74; adj. prof. Broward Community Coll., Hollywood, Davie and Pompano, Fla., 1982-90, Biscayne Coll., Miami, Fla., 1983, Miami-Dade Community Coll., 1983, Nova U., Miami and Davie, 1983-84; adj. prof., semester lectr. U. Miami, Coral Gables, 1985—; master tchr. U. Miami, 1990, 92, 94, faculty fellow, 1990-94, mem. curriculum devel., 1991-94; contbr. presentation to Fla. Coll. English Assn., 1991-92, Wyo. Conf. English, 1991; guest spkr. in field of svc.-learning, 1992-94; cons. svc.-learning curriculum design, 1994; acad. advisor U. Miami, 1994, 95, 96. Reviewer textbook McGraw Hill, 1993; contbr. instr.'s manual of textbook, 1994; contbr. poetry to revs., articles to profl. jours. Founder, dir. Meet the Author program, Coral Gables, 1989—. Recipient V.P. award U. Miami, 1992, cert. recognition West Palm Beach, Fla., TV sta., 1992; grantee Fla. Office for Campus Vols., 1992, Dade Community Found., 1992. Mem. MLA, Nat. Soc. Experiential Edn., Fla. Coll. English Assn., Coll. English Assn., Nat. Coun. Tchrs. English, Fla. Chpt. of Tchrs. of English to Spkrs. of Other Langs. (spkr. conf. 1992), Conf. on Coll. Composition and Comm., Am. Correctional Assn., Phi Delta Kappa, Phi Lambda Theta. Avocations: reading, community svc. Home: Tower 200 Apt 806 19101 Mystic Pointe Dr North Miami Beach FL 33180 Office: U Miami Office English Composition PO Box 248145 Coral Gables FL 33124-8145

SPEIRS, DEREK JAMES, diversified corporation financial executive; b. Montreal, Que., Can., Dec. 21, 1933; s. James B. and Marie C. (Hunt) S.; m. Carol Alice Cumming, Dec. 8, 1967 (div. Feb. 1989); children: Lara Marie, Gregory Ross, Scott Lawrence Gordon. B. Commerce with honors in Econs., McGill U., 1954, M.B.A., 1959. Chartered acct., Can., chartered corp. sec. Devel. dir. fine papers, corp. acctg. dir. Domtar, Inc., Montreal, 1970-72, dir. corp. devel., 1976-78, v.p. fin., corp. devel., 1978-89, sr. v.p. fin. and corp. devel., 1989-91; v.p., sec. fin. Consoltex, Montreal, 1972-76, bus. cons., 1991—; pres. Speirs Cons. Inc. Mem. Can. Inst. Chartered Accts., Fin. Execs. Inst., C.D. Howe Inst., Lac Marois Country Club, St. James Club, Montreal Amateur Athletic Assn. Avocations: travel, skiing. Home: 365 Stanstead Ave, Ville Mont-Royal, Montreal, PQ Canada H3R 1X5 Office: Ste 1100, 2 Pl Alexis Nihon, Montreal, PQ Canada H3Z 3C1

SPEISER, THEODORE WESLEY, astrophysics, planetary and atmospheric sciences educator; b. Del Norte, Colo., Nov. 23, 1934; s. Alfred Theodore and Virginia Melva (Pickens) S.; m. Patricia Jane McCrummen, June 10, 1956; children: Tanya Lee, Kelly Ann, Tertia Ava. BS, Colo. State U., 1956; MS, Calif. Inst. Tech., 1959; PhD, Pa. State U., 1964. Asst. prof. U. Colo., Boulder, 1969-74, assoc. prof., 1974-85, prof. astrophysics, planetary and atmospheric scis., 1985—; cons. NOAA, Boulder, 1970—. Contbr. articles to profl. jours. Served to capt. U.S. Army, 1960-61. Recipient U.S. Sr. Scientist award A.V. Humboldt Found., 1977; Fulbright fellow, 1956. Mem. Am. Geophys. Union (local br. v.p. 1986-87, pres. 1987). Avocations: photography, hiking, cross-country skiing, tennis. Home: 2335 Dartmouth Ave Boulder CO 80303-5209 Office: U Colo Dept of Astrophysics Planetary & Atmospheric Scis C Box 391 Boulder CO 80309

SPEITEL, GERALD EUGENE, consulting environmental engineer; b. Phila., Feb. 4, 1930; s. Edmond Joseph and Lillian M. (Kohlschreiber) S.; m. Rosemarie Noller, Aug. 22, 1953; children: Gerald Eugene, Edmond C. BS, Drexel Evening Coll., 1963; M.S. in Engring. Mgmt, Drexel U., 1967. With Dept. Water, City of Phila., 1948-51, Day & Zimmerman, Phila., 1953-54; with John G. Reutter Assos., Camden, N.J., 1954-72, v.p., 1970-72; pres. Speitel Assos., Marlton, N.J., 1972-88; dir. Environ. Measurements and Analysis, Hammonton, N.J., 1979-86; sr. v.p. BCM Engrs., Inc., 1986-90; prin. Gerald E. Speitel, Forensic Engr., 1991—. Served with C.E. U.S. Army, 1951-53. Named Honor Man of Yr. Drexel Evening Coll., 1983, 90; recipient Del. Valley Engr. of Yr. award, 1989, Disting. N.J. Civil Engr. award ASCE, 1989, Penjerdel award, 1989, Mary S. Irick Drexel medal, 1991. Fellow ASCE (life, pres. South Jersey br. 1978-79, N.J. sect. 1979-80, nat. dir. dist. 1 1981-84, v.p. 1987-89, N.J. Engr. of Yr. 1984), Am. Cons. Engrs. Coun.; mem. NSPE (life), N.J. Soc. Profl. Engrs. (Disting. Svc. award 1993), Nat. Acad. Forensic Engrs. (diplomate), Am. Acad. Environ. Engrs. (diplomate), Cons. Engrs. Coun. N.J. (pres. 1967-68, Engring. Excellence award 1979, 80, Grand award 1980), KC, Atlantic City Country Club. Roman Catholic. Home and Office: 921 Third St Ocean City NJ 08226-4019

SPEJEWSKI, EUGENE HENRY, physicist, educator; b. East Chicago, Ind., Sept. 15, 1938; s. Henry Louis and Carrie Jane (Fuss) S.; m. Norma Beverly Seekins, June 8, 1963; children: Maria Suzanne, Beverly Anne, Andrew John, Jeannette Michelle. B.S., U. Notre Dame, 1960; Ph.D., Ind. U., 1966. Research assoc. Ind. U., Bloomington, 1965-67; research assoc. Princeton U., 1967-69, instr., 1969-71; asst. prof. Oberlin Coll., Ohio, 1971-72; dir. UNISOR, Oak Ridge Assoc. Univs., 1972-85, mgr. SDS program, 1985-86, chmn. spl. projects div., 1986-89; v.p., dir. tng. and mgmt. systems div. Oak Ridge Inst. for Sci. and Edn., 1989-95, assoc. dir. for edn. and tng. group, 1995—; vis. prof. physics U. Tenn., Knoxville, 1981-84; mem., chmn. HHIRF Users Exec. Com., Oak Ridge Nat. Lab., 1982-84; referee U.S. Dept. Energy, various profl. jours. Co-editor: Future Directions in Studies of Nuclei Far from Stability, 1980; contbr. articles to profl. jours. Referee U.S. Soccer Fedn.; bd. dirs. Oak Ridge Community Playhouse, 1985-88, 95—. Mem. AAAS, Am. Phys. Soc., Am. Mgmt. Assn., Oak Ridge Sertoma Club (sec., treas., pres., chair bd. dirs.), Sigma Xi.

SPELLACY, WILLIAM NELSON, obstetrician, gynecologist, educator; b. St. Paul, May 10, 1934; s. Jack F. and Elmyra L. (Nelson) S.; m. Lynn Larsen; children: Kathleen Ann, Kimberly Joan, William Nelson. B.A., U. Minn., 1955, B.S., 1956, M.D., 1959. Diplomate: Am. Bd. Ob-Gyn, subsplty. cert. in maternal and fetal medicine. Intern Hennepin County Gen. Hosp., Mpls., 1959-60; resident U. Minn., Mpls., 1960-63; practice medicine specializing in ob-gyn. Mpls., 1963-67, Miami, Fla., 1967-73, Gainesville, Fla., 1973-79, Chgo., 1979-88; prof., head dept. U. Ill. Coll. Medicine, Chgo., 1979-88; prof., chmn. dept. U. So. Fla. Coll. Medicine, Tampa, 1988—; prof. dept. obstetrics and gynecology U. Miami, 1967-73; prof., chmn. dept. U. Fla., 1973-79. Contbr. articles to med. jours. Mem. AMA, Am. Gynecol. Soc., Am. Assn. Obstetricians and Gynecologists, Am. Gynecol. and Obstet. Soc., Soc. Gynecol. Investigation, Am. Coll. Obstetricians and Gynecologists, Endocrine Soc., Am. Fertility Soc., Assn. Profs. Gynecology and Obstetrics, Am. Diabetes Assn., Perinatal Research Soc., South Atlantic Soc. Obstetrics and Gynecology, Central Assn. Obstetrics and Gynecology, Soc. Perinatal Obstetricians, Ill. Med. Soc., Inst. of Medicine. Episcopalian. Club: Rotary. Home: 845 Seddon Cove Way Tampa FL 33602-5704 Office: U South Fla Coll Medicine Dept OBGYN 4 Columbia Dr Ste 514 Tampa FL 33606-3589

SPELLER, ROBERT ERNEST BLAKEFIELD, publishing executive; b. Chgo., Jan. 19, 1908; s. John Ernest and Florence (Larson) S.; m. Maxine Elliott Watkins; children: Robert Ernest Blakefield, Jon Patterson. Student Columbia U., 1929. Mng. editor Fgn. Press Service, 1930-31; pres. Mohawk Press, 1931-32, Robert Speller Pub. Corp., 1934-52, Record Concerts Corp., 1940-53, Robert Speller & Sons, Pubs., Inc., 1955—, Norellyn Press, Inc., 1960-83, Transglobal News Service, Inc., 1960—; corresp. Raleigh News & Observer, 1949-53; pub. Hough's Ency. Am. Woods, 1957—, mng. editor 1964-75; chmn. bd., pres., chief exec. officer Nat. Resources Publs., Inc., 1968-84; pres., dir. Transglobal Resources Devel. Corp., 1983—; owner, operator, prodr. Concert Theatre, N.Y.C., 1939-43, mgr. Otto Klemperer, Leon Barzin, Margaret Speaks, others; pub. East Europe Mag., 1970—; sec., dir. Encoder Research & Devel. Corp., 1971—, Pecos Internat., Inc., 1974-77; v.p., dir. Pecos Western Corp. of Del., 1973-83; pres., chmn. bd. VTL Corp., 1986-87; pres. Contender Corp., 1986-87; dir. Gen. Research Corp., Fashion Form Mfg. Corp. Mem. founding bd. USO; trustee Philippa Schuyler Meml. Found. Served with Signal Corps, AUS, 1944-45. Mem. Gourmet Soc. (founder), Am. Legion, Columbia U. Club (N.Y.C.), Delta Chi. Office: 115 E 9th St New York NY 10003-5414

SPELLING, AARON, film and television producer, writer, actor; b. Dallas, Apr. 22, 1923; s. David and Pearl (Wall) S.; m. Carole Gene Marer, Nov. 23, 1968; children: Victoria Davey, Randall Gene. Student, Sorbonne, U. Paris, France, 1945-46; B.A., So. Meth. U., 1950. Actor Thomas-Spelling Prodns., L.A., 1953-69; screenwriter Zane Grey Series, L.A., 1972-76; prodr. Zane Grey Theater, L.A., 1977-86, The Dick Powell Show, L.A., 1986—; co-owner with Danny Thomas Thomas-Spelling Prodns., L.A., 1969-72; co-pres. Spelling-Goldberg Prodns., L.A., 1972-76; pres. Aaron Spelling Prodns., Inc., L.A., 1977-86, chmn., CEO, 1986—. Writer numerous TV plays and movies; producer over 58 TV series including The Mod Squad, The Rookies, Family, Nightingales, Dynasty, The Colbys, Love Boat, Hotel, Beverly Hills 90210, Charlie's Angels, Fantasy Island, Starsky and Hutch, T.J. Hooker, Matt Houston, Hart to Hart, Melrose Place, 7th Heaven, Savannah, Sunset Beach, Pacific Palisades; also 130 TV movies for ABC, CBS, NBC; producer 10 theatrical films including Mr. Mom, Knight Mother, Surrender, Loose Cannons, Cross My Heart, Soapdish; author: Aaron Spelling-A Prime Time Life, 1996. Bd. dirs. Am. Film Inst. Served with USAAF, 1942-45. Decorated Bronze Star medal, Purple Heart with oak leaf cluster; recipient Eugene O'Neill awards, 1947, 48, NAACP Image awards 1970, 71, 73, 75, Winston Churchil medal of Wisdom, 1988, Lifetime Achievement award People's Choice Awards, 1996, Courage to Dream award Fulfillment Fund, 1996, GLADD award; named Man of Yr., Publicists Guild Am., 1971, Man of Yr. B'nai B'rith, Beverly Hills chpt., 1972, 85, NAACP Humanitarian of Yr., 1983, Man of Yr. Scopus award Am. Friends of Hebrew U., 1993; 1st prodr. honored by Mus. of Broadcasting, honored for contbns. to victims' rights by City of Las Vegas; inducted into TV Acad.'s Hall of Fame. Mem. Writers Guild Am. (award 1962), Prodrs. Guild Am., The Caucus of Prodrs., Writers and Dirs., Hollywood Radio and TV Soc., Hollywood TV Acad. Arts and Scis., Acad. Motion Picture Arts and Scis., Friars, Big Brothers of Am. Democrat. Jewish. Office: Spelling Television Inc 5700 Wilshire Blvd Ste 575 Los Angeles CA 90036-3659

SPELLMAN, GEORGE GENESER, SR., internist; b. Woodward, Iowa, Sept. 11, 1920; s. Martin Edward and Corinne (Geneser) S.; m. Mary Carolyn Dwight, Aug. 26, 1942; children: Carolyn Anne Spellman Rambow, George G. Jr., Mary Alice, Elizabeth Spellman-Chrisinger, John Martin Pile-Spellman, Loretta Suzanne Spellman Hoffman. BS, St. Ambrose Coll., 1940; MD, State U. Iowa, 1943. Diplomate Am. Bd. Internal Medicine. Intern Providence Hosp., Detroit, 1944; resident in internal medicine State U. Iowa, Iowa City, 1944-46; pvt. pactice Mitchell, S.D., 1948-50, Sioux City, Iowa, 1950-91; instr. U. Iowa Coll. Medicine, 1975-77; clin. assoc. U. Iowa Coll Medicine, 1977-95; ret. U. Iowa, 1995; mem. Iowa Bd. Med. Examiners, 1989-95; instr. schs. nursing St. Vincent Hosp. and Luth. Hosp.; staff St. Joseph Mercy Hosp. (merged with St. Vincent's Hosp. into Marian Health Ctr.), 1950-91, chief of staff, 1963; clin. assoc. prof. medicine State U. Iowa; bd. dirs. Mid-Step Svcs. Mentally Handicapped, Hospice of Siouxland, Marian Health Ctr., 1974-80, 89-91, also co-founder, 1st pres., chmn. dependency unit, founder renal dialysis unit, 1964, St. Joseph Mercy-St. Vincent's Hosps., 1977-89. Contbr. articles to med. jours. Ordained deacon Cath. Ch., 1988; vol. cons. Siouxland Community Health Ctr., 1993—. Capt. M.C., U.S. Army, 1946-48. Decorated Knight of St. Gregory (Vatican); named Internist of Yr., Iowa Soc. Internal Medicine, 1987; recipient Laureate award Iowa Chpt. ACP, 1991, Humanitarian award Siouxland Community, 1991. Fellow ACP; mem. AMA, Iowa State Med. Soc., Woodbury Med. Soc., Am. Soc. Internal Medicine, Iowa Soc. Internal Medicine, Alpha Omega Alpha. Home: 3849 Jones St Sioux City IA 51104-1447 *I've loved the practice of medicine. The challenge presented by a difficult patient's illness, to diagnosing then witnessing the patient's response to your treatment are rewards experienced in no other profession. In medicine also, one is always thankful for the help of the divine healer.*

SPELLMAN, MITCHELL WRIGHT, surgeon, academic administrator; b. Alexandria, La., Dec. 1, 1919; s. Frank Jackson and Altonette Beulah (Mitchell) S.; m. Billie Rita Rhodes, June 27, 1947; children: Frank A., Michael A., Mitchell A., Maria A., Melva A., Mark A., Manly A., Rita A. A.B. magna cum laude, Dillard U., 1940, LL.D. (hon.), 1983; M.D., Howard U., 1944; Ph.D. in Surgery (Commonwealth Fund fellow), U. Minn., Mpls., 1955; D.Sc. (hon.), Georgetown U., 1974, U. Fla., 1977. Intern Cleve. Met. Gen. Hosp., 1944-45, asst. resident in surgery, 1945-46; asst. resident in surgery Howard U. and Freedmen's Hosp., Washington, 1946-47; chief resident in thoracic surgery Howard U. and Freedmen's Hosp., 1947-48, teaching asst. in physiology, 1948-49, chief resident in surgery, 1949-50, teaching asst. in surgery, 1950-51; asst. prof. surgery Howard U., 1954-56, assoc. prof., 1956-60, prof., 1960-68; dir. Howard surgery service at D.C. Gen. Hosp., 1961-68; fellow in surgery U. Minn., 1951-54; sr. resident in surgery U. Minn. Med. Sch. and Hosp., 1953-54; dean Charles R. Drew Postgrad. Med. Sch., Los Angeles, 1969-77; prof. surgery Charles R. Drew Postgrad. Med. Sch., 1969-78; asst. dean, prof. surgery Sch. Medicine, U. Calif. at Los Angeles, 1969-78; clin. prof. surgery Sch. Med., U. So. Calif., 1969-78; dean for med. svcs., prof. surgery Harvard Med. Sch., Boston, 1978-90, dean emeritus for med. svcs., 1990—, dean emeritus for internat. projects, 1990—, prof. surgery emeritus, 1990—; dir. internat. exch. programs Harvard Med. Internat., 1995—; exec. v.p. Harvard Med. Ctr., 1978-90; fellow Ctr. for Advanced Study in Behavioral Scis.; vis. prof. Stanford, 1975-76; bd. dirs. Kaiser Found. Hosps., Kaiser Found. Health Plan, 1971-89; mem. D.C. Bd. Examiners in Medicine and Osteopathy, 1955-68; mem. Nat. Rev. Com. for Regional Med. Programs, 1968-70; mem. spl. med. adv. group, nat. surg. cons. VA, 1969-73; mem. Commn. for Study Accreditation of Selected Health Ednl. Programs, 1970-72; chmn. adv. com. br. med. devices Nat. Heart and Lung Inst., 1972; Am. health del. to visit People's Republic of China, 1973; hon. dir. State Mut. Cos., 1990—; mem. com. mandatory retirement in higher edn. NAS/NRC, 1989-91; mem. panel on internat. programs Nat. Libr. Medcine, 1996, 97. Mem. editorial bd.: Jour. Medicine and Philosophy, 1977-90; Contbr. articles on cardiovascular physiology and surgery, measurement of blood volume, and radiation biology to profl. jours. Past bd. dirs. Sun Valley Forum on Nat. Health; mem. ethics adv. bd. HEW, 1977-81; bd. dirs. Harvard Comty. Health Plan, 1979-84; former trustee Occidental Coll.; former bd. overseers com. to visit univ. health svc. Harvard, bd. overseers Harvard Comty. Health Plan, 1984-95; former regent Georgetown U.; former vis. com. U. Mass. Med. Ctr.; mem. bd. visitors UCLA Sch. Medicine; mem. corp. MIT; adv. bd. PEW Scholars Program in Biomed. Scis., 1984-86; bd. dirs. Med. Edn. for South African Blacks, 1985—. Markle scholar in med. scis., 1954-59; recipient Distinguished Alumnus award Dillard U., 1963; Distinguished Postgrad. Achievement award Howard U., 1974; Outstanding Achievement award U. Minn., 1979. Mem. AMA, AAAS, AAUP, ACS, Nat. Med. Assn. (William A. Sinkler Surgery award 1968), Soc. Univ. Surgeons, Am. Coll. Cardiology, Am. Surg. Assn., Inst. of Medicine of Nat. Acad. Scis. (chmn. program com. 1977-79, governing coun. 1978-80), Nat. Acad. Practice in Medicine, Am. Assn. Sovereign Mil. Order of Malta (Knights and Dames of Malta), MIT Corp. (life mem. emeritus), Cosmos Club. Roman Catholic. Office: 138 Harvard St Ste 300 Brookline MA 02146-6418

SPELLMAN, THOMAS JOSEPH, JR., lawyer; b. Glen Cove, N.Y., Nov. 11, 1938; s. Thomas J. and Martha H. (Erwin) S.; m. Margaret Mary Barth, June 23, 1962; children: Thomas Joseph, Kevin M., Maura N. BS, Fordham U., 1960, JD, 1965. Bar: N.Y. 1966, U.S. Dist. Ct. (so. and ea. dist.) N.Y. 1968, U.S. Ct. Appeals (2nd cir.) 1980, U.S. Supreme Ct. 1981. Staff atty. Allstate Ins. Co., N.Y.C., 1966-69; trial atty. Hartford Ins. Co., Hauppauge, N.Y., 1969-71; ptnr. Wheller & Spellman, Farmingville, N.Y., 1971-76, Devitt Spellman Barrett Callahan Leyden & Kenney LLP and predecessors, Smithtown, N.Y., 1976—; mem. grievance com. 10th Jud. Dist., Westbury, N.Y., 1984-92. Capt. USAR, 1960-68. Fellow Am. Bar Found., N.Y. Bar Found; mem. Suffolk County Bar Assn. (bd. dirs., sec.-treas., v.p. 1982, pres. 1992-93), N.Y. State Bar Assn. (Ho. of Dels. 1989—, nominating com. 1992-93, v.p. 1996—). Home: 8 Highwoods Ct Saint James NY 11780-9610 Office: Devitt Spellman et al 50 Route 111 Smithtown NY 11787-3700

SPELLMIRE, GEORGE W., lawyer; b. Oak Park, Ill., June 10, 1948. Attended, Brown U.; BA, Ohio State U., 1970; JD, De Paul U., 1974. Bar: Ill. 1974, U.S. Dist. Ct. (no. dist.) Ill. 1974, U.S. Tax Ct. 1984, U.S. Ct. Appeals (7th cir.) 1984, U.S. Supreme Ct. 1994. Ptnr. Hinshaw & Culbertson, Chgo. Author: Attorney Malpractice: Prevention and Defense, 1988; co-author: Accountants' Legal Liability Guide, 1990, Illinois Handbook on Legal Malpractice, 1982, Associates Primer for the Prevention of Malpractice, 1987. Mem. ABA, Am. Coll. Trial Lawyers, Soc. Trial Lawyers, Fed. Trial Bar, Internat. Assn. Def. Counsel (legal malpractice com., def. counsel practice mgmt. com.), Ill. State Bar Assn., Chgo. Bar Assn., Trial Lawyers Club Chgo. Office: Hinshaw & Culbertson 222 N La Salle St Ste 300 Chicago IL 60601-1013

SPELTS, RICHARD JOHN, lawyer; b. Yuma, Colo., July 29, 1939; s. Richard Clark and Barbara Eve (Pletcher) S.; children: Melinda, Meghan, Richard John Jr.; m. Gayle Merves, Nov. 14, 1992. BS cum laude, U. Colo., 1961, JD, 1964. Bar: Colo. 1964, U.S. Dist. Ct. Colo. 1964, U.S. Supreme Ct. 1968, U.S. Ct. Appeals (10th cir.) 1970, U.S. Dist. Ct. (ea. dist.) Mich. 1986. With Ford Motor Internat., Cologne, Germany, 1964-65; legis. counsel to U.S. Senator, 89th and 90th Congresses, 1967-68; minority counsel U.S. Senate Subcom., 90th and 91st Congresses, 1968-70; asst. U.S. atty., 1st asst. U.S. atty. Fed. Dist. of Colo., 1970-77; pvt. practice Denver, 1977-89; risk mgr. sheriff's dept. Jefferson County, Golden, Colo., 1990-91; owner Video Prodn. for Lawyers, 1991—. Selected for Leadership Denver, 1977; recipient cert. for outstanding contbns. in drug law enforcement U.S. Drug Enforcement Adminstrn., 1977, spl. commendation for criminal prosecution U.S. Dept. Justice, 1973, spl. commendation for civil prosecution U.S. Dept. Justice, 1976. Mem. Fed. Bar Assn. (chmn. govt. torts seminar 1980), Colo. Bar Assn. (bd. govs. 1976-78), Denver Bar Assn., Colo. Trial Lawyers Assn., Denver Law Club, Order of Coif. Republican. Methodist. Home and Office: 6697 W Hinsdale Ave Littleton CO 80123-4511

SPENCE, ANDREW, artist, painter; b. Bryn Mawr, Pa., Oct. 4, 1947; s. Thomas and Elizabeth Spence; m. Mary Stewart Stoll, June 24, 1977. BFA, Temple U., 1969; MFA, U. Calif., Santa Barbara, 1971. One-man shows include TransAvant Garde Gallery, Austin, Tex., 1989, Barbara Krakow Gallery, Boston, 1989, Barbara Toll Fine Arts, N.Y.C., 1982-83, 85, 87-88, 90, Compass Rose Gallery, Chgo., 1990, James Corcoran Gallery, L.A., 1990, Max Protetch Gallery, N.Y.C., 1992-93, Barbara Scott Gallery, Miami, 1993, 96, Worcester (Mass.) Art Mus., 1991, Morris Healy Gallery, N.Y.C., 1996; exhibited in group shows including Corcoran Gallery of Art, Washington, 1987, Hirshhorn Mus. and Sculpture Garden, Smithsonian Instn., Washington, 1989, Whitney Mus. Am. Art, N.Y., 1989, 91-92, Met. Mus. Art, N.Y.C., 1993; represented in permanent collections including Balt. Mus. Art, Cleve. Mus. Art, Cin. Art Mus., Hirshhorn Mus. and Sculpture Garden, Laguna Gloria Art Mus., Met. Mus. Art, N.Y.C., San Diego Mus. Contemporary Art, Walker Art Ctr., Whitney Mus. Am. Art, N.Y.C. Painting grantee Nat. Endowment for Arts, 1987; Guggenheim fellow, 1994.

SPENCE, ANDREW MICHAEL, dean, finance educator; b. Montclair, N.J., 1943. BA in Philosophy summa cum laude, Princeton U., 1966; BA, MA in Maths., Oxford U., 1968; PhD in Econs. with honors, Harvard U., 1972. Asst. prof. polit. econ. Kennedy Sch. Govt. Harvard U., Cambridge, Mass., 1971-75, prof. econs., 1977-83, prof. bus. adminstrn., 1979-83, George Gund prof. econs. and bus. adminstrn., 1983-86, vis. prof. econs. dept., 1976-77, chmn. bus. econs. PhD program, 1981-83; chmn. econs. dept. Harvard U., 1983-84, dean Faculty Arts and Scis., 1984-90; assoc. prof. dept. econs. Stanford (Calif.) U., 1973-75, Philip H. Knight prof., dean Grad. Sch. Bus., 1990—; bd. dirs. BankAm. Corp., Gen. Mills, Inc., Nike, Inc., Siebel Syss., Sun Microsyss., VeriFone, Inc.; chmn. Nat. Rsch. Coun. Bd. on Sci., Tech. and Econ. Policy. Author: 3 books; mem. editl. bd. Am. Econs. Rev., Bell. Jour. Econs., Jour. Econ. Theory and Pub. Policy; contbr. over 50 articles to profl. jours. Mem. econs. adv. panel NSF, 1977-79; mem. econs. adv. com. Sloan Found., 1979—. Danforth fellow, 1966; Rhodes scholar, 1966; recipient J.K. Galbraith prize for excellence in tchg., 1978. Fellow AAAS, Econometric Soc.; mem. Am. Econ. Assn. (John Bates Clark medal 1981). Office: Stanford U Grad Sch Bus Bldg 350 Memorial Way Stanford CA 94305-5015

SPENCE, BARBARA E., publishing company executive; b. Bryn Mawr, Pa., July 8, 1921; d. Geoffrey Strange and Mary (Harrington) Earnshaw; m. Kenneth M. Spence Jr., June 29, 1944; children: Kenneth M. III, Christopher E., Hilary B. Grad. high sch. Movie, radio editor Parade Mag., N.Y.C., 1941-45; with Merchandising Group, N.Y.C., 1946-47; exec. dir. Greenfield Hill Congl. Ch., Fairfield, Conn., 1958-74, dir. religious edn., 1968-74; assoc. Ten Eyck-Emerich Antiques, 1974-76; personnel dir. William Morrow & Co., Inc., N.Y.C., 1976-91; ret., 1991. Chmn. pub. relations, bd. dirs. ARC, 1951-56, Family Service Soc., Fairfield, 1956-57, 61-63; chmn. pub. relations Citizens for Eisenhower, 1952, Fairfield Teens Players, 1968-71; bd. dirs. Fairfield Teens, Inc., 1965-70, Planned Parenthood of Greater Bridgeport, 1969-75, chmn. pub. affairs, 1971-72, chmn. personnel, 1972-73, chpt. vice chmn., 1973-75; pres. steering com. Am. Playwrights Festival Theatre, Inc., Fairfield, 1969-70, v.p., bd. dirs., 1971—; bd. govs. Unquowa Sch., Fairfield, 1963-69; bd. dirs. Fairfield U. Playhouse, 1971-73, Downtown Cabaret Theatre, Bridgeport, 1975-76. Mem. AAP (compensation survey com.), Fairfield Women's Exch. (bd. dirs. 1993). Home: 101 Twin Brook Ln Fairfield CT 06430-2834

SPENCE, CLARK CHRISTIAN, history educator; b. Great Falls, Mont., May 25, 1923; s. Christian Edward and Lela (Killian) S.; m. Mary Lee Nance, Sept. 12, 1953; children: Thomas Christian, Ann Leslie. B.A., U. Colo., 1948, M.A., 1951; Ph.D, U. Minn., 1955. Instr. Carleton Coll., Northfield, Minn., 1954-55; instr., then assoc. prof. Pa. State U., 1955-60; vis. lectr. U. Calif.-Berkeley, 1960-61; mem. faculty U. Ill., Champaign, 1961—; prof. history U. Ill., 1964-90, prof. emeritus, 1990—, chmn. dept., 1967-70, assoc. mem. Ctr. for Advanced Study, 1975; vis. lectr. Yale, summer 1964; vis. prof. U. Colo., summer 1967; disting. vis. prof. Ariz. State U., spring 1988. Author: British Investment and the American Mining Frontier, 1958, God Speed the Plow: The Coming of Steam Cultivation to Great Britain, 1960, Sinews of American Capitalism: An Economic History, 1964, The American West, 1966, Mining Engineers in the American West, 1970, Territorial Politics and Government in Montana, 1864-89, 1975, Montana: A Bicentennial History, 1978, The Rainmakers: American Pluviculture to World War II, 1980, The Salvation Army Farm Colonies,

1985, The Conrey Placer Mining Company, 1989, The Northern Gold Fleet: Twentieth Century Gold Dredging in Alaska, 1996. Served with USAAF, 1943-46. Fulbright fellow Eng., 1953-54; Ford Found. fellow, 1963-64; Guggenheim fellow, 1970-71; recipient ann. book award Agrl. History Soc., 1959. Mem. Western History Assn. (pres. 1969-70), Mining Hist. Assn. (pres. 1990-91), Phi Beta Kappa, Phi Alpha Theta. Home: 1107 Foley St Champaign IL 61820-6326

SPENCE, DIANNA JEANNENE, software engineer, educator; b. Mountain View, Calif., June 5, 1964; d. Ronald Kenneth and Susan (Durham) S.; m. James Paul Blyn. BA, Coll. William and Mary, 1985; MS, Ga. State U., 1996. Tchr. math. and computers Woodward Acad., College Park, Ga., 1985-90; software engr. Computer Comm. Specialists, Inc., Norcross, Ga., 1990—; tutor, 1994—. Mem. Pi Kappa Phi, Pi Mu Epsilon. Universalist. Avocations: travel, writing, music, theater.

SPENCE, DONALD POND, psychologist, psychoanalyst; b. N.Y.C., Feb. 8, 1926; s. Ralph Beckett and Rita (Pond) S.; m. Mary Newbold Cross, June 2, 1951; children: Keith, Sarah, Laura, Katherine. AB, Harvard U., 1949; PhD, Columbia U., 1955. Lic. psychologist, N.Y., N.J. From rsch. asst. to prof. psychology NYU, 1954-74; prof. psychiatry Robert Wood Johnson Med. Sch., Piscataway, N.J., 1974-95; ret., 1995; vis. prof. psychology Stanford (Calif.) U., 1971-72, Princeton (N.J.) U., 1975-95, Louvain-le-Neuve, Belgium, 1980, William Alanson White Inst., N.Y.C., 1992; mem. personality and cognition rsch. rev. com. NIMH, 1969-73. Author: Narrative Truth and Historical Truth, 1982, The Freudian Metaphor, 1987, The Rhetorical Voice of Psychoanalysis, 1994; mem. editl. bd. Psychoanalysis and Contemporary Thought, Psychol. Inquiry, Theory and Psychology; contbr. articles to profl. jours. With U.S. Army, 1944-46, ETO. Recipient rsch. scientist award NIMH, 1968-74; decorated 2 battle stars. Mem. APA (pres. theoretical and philos. divsn. 1992-93), Am. Psychoanalytic Assn., N.Y. Acad. Sci., Sigma Xi. Democrat. Home: 9 Haslet Ave Princeton NJ 08540-4913

SPENCE, DOUGLAS RICHARD, educational consultant; b. Pittsburg, Calif., Apr. 8, 1947; s. Thomas C. and Jeane (Ramey) S.; m. Doretta Kaump, Mar. 21, 1970; children: Larame Douglas, Shiane S., Maverick R. (dec.), Devony D., Shilon C. BS in Computer Sci., Fla. Inst. Tech., Melbourne, 1972. Lic. pilot and insgt.; cert. residential real estate appraiser; PADI instr. In mgmt. Radio Shack div. Tandy Corp., Ft. Worth, 1972-75; ret. air traffic control, automation, contract oversight FAA, Denver Air Rt. Traffic Controller, 1975-89; sr. cons., ptnr. Cross and Assocs., Boulder, Colo., 1989—; officer, bd. dirs., cons. Pure Water Place, Longmont, Colo., 1980—; owner, operator Desiderata Ranch, Berthoud, Colo., 1981—; cons. in fields of market devel., fund raising, passive and active solar and earth shelter design, alternative edn. programs. Designer, cons., builder solar earth shelter, 1981. Bd. dirs. Desiderata Schs. (K-12), Berthoud, 1988—; founding mem. Up With People, Inc., Broomfield, Colo., 1966—. With U.S. Army, 1967-69, Vietnam. Named among Top 30 Young Scientists in Am., Nat. Sci. Tchrs. Assn./NASA, 1965. Mem. Up With People Alumni Assn. Avocation: scuba. Home and Office: Desiderata Ranch 4617 W County Rd 2 Berthoud CO 80513-8620

SPENCE, EDWARD LEE, publisher, historian, archaeologist; b. Munich, Germany, Nov. 6, 1947; s. Judson Cauthen and Mary Virginia (Truett) S.; m. Mary Tabb Gildea, Sept. 11, 1979 (div. Feb. 1981); 1 child, Matthew Lee. BA in Marine Archeology, U. S.C., 1967, postgrad., 1977; D of Marine Histories, Coll. of Marine Arts, 1972; PhD (hon.), Sea Rsch. Soc., 1976, Colombian Rsch. Inst., 1993. Pres. Shipwreck Cons., Sullivan's Island, S.C., 1976-94; marine archeology cons. Coll. Charleston, S.C., 1983-84; underwater archeologist Shipwrecks Inc., Munhall, Pa., 1985-87; archeol. dir. Ocean Enterprises, Ltd., Nassau, The Bahamas, 1986-87; underwater archeologist Freedom Marine Ltd., Vancouver, B.C., Can., 1988-89; pub., sr. editor Shipwreck Press Inc., Sullivan's Island, 1988-91; chief underwater archeology Old Providence Island, Colombia, 1992-94; pub., sr. editor Narwhal Press Inc., Miami, Fla., 1994—; curator Mus. Sunken Treasure, Cape Canaveral, Fla., 1980; mem. adv. bd. Contemporary U., U. S.C., Columbia, 1971; cons. Seahawk Deep Ocean Tech., Tampa, Fla., 1991—. Author: Shipwrecks of South Carolina and Georgia 1521-1865, 1985, Shipwrecks of the Civil War, 1994, Romance on the Confederate Coast, 1994, Treasures of the Confederate Coast: The Real Rhett Butler & Other Revelations, 1995, Shipwrecks, Pirates, and Privateers: Sunken Treasuers of the Upper South Carolina Coast, 1521-1865, 1995. Co-founder Hot Line, Charleston, 1971; mem. maritime subcom. S.C. Bi-Centennial Comm., Charleston, 1975-76; co-founder S.C. Underwater Archeol. Rsch. Coun., 1971; 2d vice comdr. Am. Legion, 1997—. Grantee S.C. Com. for Humanities, 1983-84, NEH, 1983-84; Nat. Honors scholar U. Miami, 1966. Mem. Sea Rsch. Soc. (pres., pres. emeritus 1970—), Intertel, French Honor Soc. (alumnus), Mensa, Order of De Molay (alumnus, chaplain, historian), Tau Kappa Epsilon (alumnus), Mu Alpha Theta (alumnus). Republican. Avocations: sailing, photography, fishing, hunting, numismatics. Home: 1750 I'on Ave Sullivans Island SC 29482 Office: Narwhal Press Inc 1629 Meeting St Charleston SC 29405-9408

SPENCE, FLOYD DAVIDSON, congressman; b. Columbia, S.C., Apr. 9, 1928; s. James Wilson and Addie (Lucas) S.; m. Deborah Williams, July 3, 1988; children from previous marriage: David, Zack, Benjamin, Caldwell. A.B., U. S.C., 1952, J.D., 1956. Bar: S.C. 1956. Former partner firm Callison and Spence, West Columbia, S.C.; mem. S.C. Ho. Reps., 1956-62; mem. S.C. Senate, 1966-70, minority leader, 1966-70, chmn. joint com. internal security, 1967-70; mem. 92nd-105th Congresses from 2nd S.C. dist., Washington, D.C., 1971—; chmn. nat. security com. 105th Congress, mem. subcom. mil. procurement; ranking minority mem. Armed Svcs. com., 1992-94; mem. Ho. of Reps. com. on coms. 103d Congress; mem. Rep. policy com. 104th Congress; mem. Vietnam Era Vets in Congress. Editor S.C. Law Quarterly. Past chmn. Indian Waters Coun. S.C. Boy Scouts Am., 1965-66, exec. bd., 1963—; chmn. Lexington County Mental Health Assn., 1959; former mem. bd. visitors U.S. Naval Acad. Served as capt. USNR, ret. Recipient Watchdog of the Treasury award, Order of the Palmetto award. Mem. ABA, U.S. Supreme Ct. Bar Assn., Lexington County Bar Assn., Am. Legion, VFW, Res. Officers Assn., Navy League, Kappa Alpha Order, Phi Alpha Delta (former chief justice), Kappa Sigma Kappa, Omicron Delta Kappa. Lutheran. Office: US Ho Reps 2405 Rayburn Bldg Ofc Bldg Washington DC 20515-4002*

SPENCE, FRANCIS JOHN, archbishop; b. Perth, Ont., Can., June 3, 1926; s. William John and Rose Anna (Jordan) S. BA, St. Michael's Coll., Toronto, 1946; postgrad., St. Augustine's Sem., Toronto, 1946-50; JCD, St. Thomas U., Rome, 1955. Ordained to priest Roman Cath. Ch., 1950. Consecrated bishop, 1967; diocesan sec. Kingston, Ont., 1950-52; parish asst., 1955-61; mem. Marriage Tribunal, 1961-66; diocesan dir. hosp. and charities, 1961-66; pastor Sacred Heart Ch., Marmora, Ont., 1966-67; aux. bishop Mil. Vicar Canadian Forces, 1967-70; bishop of Charlottetown P.E.I., 1970-82; archbishop of Kingston Ont., 1982—; mil. vicar of Can., 1982-88. Office: Catholic Diocesan Centre, 390 Palace Rd, Kingston, ON Canada K7L 4T3

SPENCE, GERALD LEONARD, lawyer, writer; b. Laramie, Wyo., Jan. 8, 1929; s. Gerald M. and Esther Sophie (Pfleeger) S.; m. Anna Wilson, June 20, 1947; children: Kip, Kerry, Kent, Katy; m. LaNelle Hampton Peterson, Nov. 18, 1969. BSL, U. Wyo., 1949, LLB, 1952, LLD (hon.), 1990. Bar: Wyo. 1952, U.S. Ct. Claims 1952, U.S. Supreme Ct. 1982. Sole practice Riverton, Wyo., 1952-54; county and pros. atty. Fremont County, Wyo., 1954-62; ptnr. various law firms, Riverton and Casper, Wyo., 1962-78; sr. ptnr. Spence, Moriarty & Schuster, Jackson, Wyo., 1978—; lectr. legal orgns. and law schs. Author: (with others) Gunning for Justice, 1982, Of Murder and Madness, 1983, Trial by Fire, 1986, With Justice for None, 1989, From Freedom to Slavery, 1993, How To Argue and Win Every Time, 1995, The Making of a Country Lawyer, 1996. Mem. ABA, Wyo. Bar Assn., Wyo. Trial Lawyers Assn., Assn. Trial Lawyers Am., Nat. Assn. Criminal Def. Lawyers. Office: Spence Moriarty & Schuster PO Box 548 Jackson WY 83001-0548

SPENCE, GLEN OSCAR, clergyman; b. Willow Springs, Mo., Jan. 20, 1927; s. John Oscar and Emma Adelia (Kentch) S.; m. Margaret Carolyn Hunter, Sept. 10, 1948; children: Rodney Glen, Randall Eugene. B.S. in Agr, U. Mo., 1950; B.A. in Bible, Oakland City (Ind.) Coll., 1957, D.Div. (hon.), 1982. Tchr. agr. Mountain View, Mo., 1950-55; instr. biology Oakland City Coll., 1955-57; ordained to ministry Gen. Bapt. Ch., 1954; pastor chs. in Evansville, Ind., 1958-65, 73-76; dir. denominational affairs Oakland City Coll., 1965-72; exec. dir. Gen. Assn. Gen. Bapts., Poplar Bluff, Mo., 1977-92; moderator Gen. Assn. Gen. Bapts., 1961, pres. gen. bd., 1963-64. Served with USNR, 1945-46. Recipient Alumnus of Yr. award Oakland City Coll., 1996. Mem. Kiwanis (lt. gov. Mo.-Ark. dist. divsn. 15 1992-93, chmn. human and spiritual values com. Mo.-Ark. dist. 1993-94, Man of Yr. award 1996), Poplar Bluff Club.

SPENCE, JAMES ROBERT, JR., television sports executive; b. Bronxville, N.Y., Dec. 20, 1936; s. James Robert and Mary Jeffery (Grant) S.; m. Betsy Jo Viener, June 16, 1992. B.A., Dartmouth Coll., 1958. Prodn. asst. ABC Sports, Inc. (known as Sports Programs, Inc. through 1966), N.Y.C., 1960-63; asst. to exec. producer ABC's Wide World of Sports, 1963-66, coordinating producer, 1966-70; v.p. program planning ABC Sports, Inc., 1970-78, sr. v.p., 1978-86; pres. Sports Television Internat. Inc., N.Y.C., 1986—. Author: Up Close and Personal - The Inside Story of Network Television Sports, 1988. Served with U.S. Army, 1958-60. Club: Westchester Country (Rye, N.Y.). Office: Sports TV Internat Inc 545 Madison Ave New York NY 10022-4219

SPENCE, JONATHAN DERMOT, historian, educator; b. Surrey, Eng., Aug. 11, 1936; came to U.S., 1959; s. Dermot Gordon Chesson and Muriel (Crailsham); m. Helen Alexander, Sept. 15, 1962 (div. 1993); children: Colin Chesson, Ian Alexander; m. Chin Annping, Aug. 12, 1993. B.A., Cambridge (Eng.) U., 1959; Ph.D., Yale U., 1965; L.H.D. (hon.), Knox Coll., 1984, U. New Haven, 1989; DLitt. (hon.), Wheeling Coll., 1985, Chinese U. Hong Kong, 1996, Gettysburg Coll., 1996. Asst. prof. history Yale U., New Haven, 1966-71; prof. Yale U., 1971—, chmn. dept. history, dir. div. humanities.; Wiles lectr. Queens's U., Belfast, 1985; Gauss lectr. Princeton U., 1987; vis. prof. Peking U., 1987; chmn. Council on East Asian Studies; bd. govs. Yale U. Press, 1988—; hon. prof. Nanjing U., 1993. Author: Ts'Ao Yin and the K'Ang-Hsi Emperor, 1966, To Change China, 1969, Emperor of China, 1974, The Death of Woman Wang, 1978, The Gate of Heavenly Peace, 1981, The Memory Palace of Matteo Ricci, 1984, The Question of Hu, 1988, The Search for Modern China, 1990, Chinese Roundabout, 1992, God's Chinese Son, 1996; editor: Ch'ing-Shih We'T'I, 1965-73, (with others) From Ming to Ch'ing, 1979; mem. editorial bd. Am. Hist. Rev., 1990-93, Yale Jour. Criticism, 1989, Yale Rev., 1991, China Quar., 1992. Served with Brit. Army, 1954-56. Recipient John Adison Porter prize, 1965, Christopher award, 1975, Devane teaching medal, 1978, L.A. Times book award, 1982, Vursell prize Am. Acad. and Inst. Arts and Letters, 1983, Comisso prize (Italy), 1987, Gelber prize (Can.), 1990; named to Coun. of Scholars, Libr. of Congress, 1988—; Yale fellow in East Asian Studies, 1962-65, 68-70, Guggenheim fellow, 1979-80, John D. and Catherine T. MacArthur Found. fellow, 1988-93. Mem. Am. Acad. Arts and Scis., Am. Philos. Soc., Assn. Asian Studies. Home: 691 Forest Rd New Haven CT 06515-2520 Office: Yale U History Dept PO Box 208324 New Haven CT 06520

SPENCE, MARY LEE, historian; b. Kyle, Tex., Aug. 4, 1927; d. Jeremiah Milton and Mary Louise (Hutchison) Nance; m. Clark Christian Spence, Sept. 12, 1953; children: Thomas Christian, Ann Leslie. BA, U. Tex., 1947, MA, 1948; PhD, U. Minn., 1957. Instr., asst. prof. S.W. Tex. State U., San Marcos, 1948-53; lectr. Pa. State U., State College, 1955-58; mem. faculty U. Ill., Urbana-Champaign, 1973—, asst. prof., assoc. prof., 1973-81, 81-89, prof. history, 1989-90, prof. emerita, 1990—. Editor (with Donald Jackson) The Expeditions of John Charles Fremont, 3 vols., 1970-84, (with Clark Spence) Fanny Kelly's Narrative of Her Captivity Among the Sioux Indians, 1990, (with Pamela Herr) The Letters of Jessie Benton Fremont, 1993, The Arizona Diary of Lily Fremont, 1878-1881, 1997; contbr. articles to profl. jours. Mem. Children's Theater Bd., Urbana-Champaign, 1965-73. Grantee Nat. Hist. Pub. and Records Commn., Washington, 1977-78, 87-90, Huntington Libr., 1992; recipient Excellent Advisor award Liberal Arts and Sci. Coll./U. Ill., 1986. Mem. Western History Assn. (pres. 1981-82), Orgn. Am. Historians, Phi Beta Kappa (exec. sect. Gamma chpt. 1985-89, pres. 1991-92), Phi Alpha Theta. Episcopalian. Home: 1107 S Foley St Champaign IL 61820-6326 Office: U Ill Dept History 810 S Wright St Urbana IL 61801-3611

SPENCE, PAUL HERBERT, librarian; b. Geraldine, Ala., Dec. 25, 1923; s. John Clardy and Leila (Carrell) S.; m. Ruth Schmidt, May 9, 1954; children—John Carrell, Peter Schmidt, Robert McCollough. A.B., Emory U., 1948, M.A., 1956; Ph.D., U. Ill., 1969. Asst. reference librarian Emory U., Atlanta, 1950-53; periodical reference librarian Air U., Maxwell AFB, 1953-56; dir. library Air Force Inst. of Tech., Wright-Patterson AFB, Ohio, 1957-58; asst. dir. social studies U. Notre Dame, South Bend, Ind., 1959-60, U. Nebr., Lincoln, 1960-63; history and polit. sci. librarian U. Ill., Urbana, 1963-66; assoc. dir. libraries U. Ga., Athens, 1966-70; dir. libraries U. Ala., Birmingham, 1970-84, collection devel. librarian, 1985-89, prof. emeritus, 1989—, libr. cons., 1990—. Bd. dirs. Southeastern Library Network, Atlanta, 1973-75. Served with U.S. Army, 1943-46, ETO. Mem. ALA (council mem. 1976-78), Ala. Library Assn. (treas. 1975-76), Southeastern Library Assn. (pres. 1980-82). Democrat. Presbyterian. Home: 614 Warwick Rd Birmingham AL 35209-4426 Office: U Ala at Birmingham 172 Sterne Libr Birmingham AL 35294

SPENCE, RICHARD DEE, paper products company executive, former railroad executive; b. Tucumcari, N.Mex., Apr. 7, 1925; s. Andrew Doke and Myrtle Hannah (Roach) S.; m. Mary Ames Kellogg, July 24, 1976; children: Mary B., Ames T., Richard T.; children from previous marriage: Diana, Richard N. BS, UCLA, 1949; grad., Transp. Mgmt. Program, Stanford U., 1956, Sr. Execs. Program, MIT, 1962. With So. Pacific Transp. Co., San Francisco, 1946-75, asst. v.p. ops., 1967-69, v.p. ops., 1969-75; pres., chief oper. officer Consol. Rail Corp., Phila., 1975-78; pres. L&N R.R. Co., Louisville, 1978-80; exec. v.p. ops. Family Lines Rail System, 1980-84; cons. in field, 1984-90; dir., prin. Skippingdale Paper Products, England, 1986—. With USN, 1943-46. Mem. Ponte Vedra Club, Tournament Players Club, Sawgrass Club, Bohemian Club, Golf House Club of Elie (Scotland), Phi Kappa Sigma. Republican. Episcopalian. Home and Office: 339 Ponte Vedra Blvd Ponte Vedra Beach FL 32082-1813

SPENCE, ROBERT DEAN, physics educator; b. Bergen, N.Y., Sept. 12, 1917; s. La Vergne Robert and Jennie (Waterman) S.; m. Helen Holbrook, June 14, 1942; children—John, Elizabeth, Janet, Barbara. B.S., Cornell U., 1939; M.S., Mich. State U., 1942; Ph.D., Yale, 1948. Asst. prof. physics Mich. State U., East Lansing, 1947-49, assoc. prof., 1949-52, prof., 1952-86, emeritus, 1986—; vis. prof. U. Bristol, Eng., 1955-56, Technische Hogesch., Eindhoven, Netherlands, 1964, Rijks universiteit, Leiden, Netherlands, 1970-71. Recipient Distinguished Faculty award Mich. State U., 1963; Guggenheim fellow, 1955-56. Mem. Nat. Soc. Profl. Engrs., Sigma Xi, Phi Kappa Phi. Research and publs. on math. physics, chem. physics, magnetism. Home: 1849 Ann St East Lansing MI 48823-3707

SPENCE, ROBERT LEROY, publishing executive; b. Carlisle, Pa., Sept. 13, 1931; s. Leroy Oliver and Esther Helen (Lau) S.; m. Barbara Amelia Hunter, Sept. 1, 1954 (div. Sept. 1978); children—Robert Roy, Bonnie Leigh; m. 2d, Maryanne Elizabeth Yacono, Jan. 10, 1979. B.A., Dickinson Coll., 1953; postgrad. Temple U., 1955-57, Rutgers U., 1956, 59-60, U. Pa., 1960. Cert. tchr., N.J. Chmn. dept. math. Haddon Heights High Sch., N.J., 1954-62; sr. editor Silver Burdett Co., Morristown, N.J., 1962-64; editor-in-chief Harcourt Brace Jovanovich, Inc., N.Y.C., 1964-81; v.p., pub. Harper & Row Publishers, Inc., N.Y.C., 1981-85, Scribner Ednl. Pubs. div. Macmillan, Inc., N.Y.C., 1985; pres. R&M Spence, Inc., Sparta, N.J., 1985—. Author textbook series: Growth in Mathematics, 1978, Excel in Mathematics, 1989-90, Mathematics Plus: Multicultural Projects, 1993. Mem. Assn. Am. Pubs. (mem. exec. com. 1981-84), Nat. Council Tchrs. Math., Internat. Reading Assn., Am. Numismatic Assn. Avocations: rare coin collecting; coin newsletter author and publisher; artist; writer. Home and Office: 37 Heather Ln Sparta NJ 07871-3538

SPENCE, ROY, advertising executive. Pres. Gurasich, Spence, Darilek & McClure, Austin, Tex. Office: Gurasich Spence Darilek & McClure 1250 Capital of Tex Hwy F14 Austin TX 78746

SPENCE, SANDRA, professional administrator; b. McKeesport, Pa., Mar. 25, 1941; d. Cedric Leroy and Suzanne (Haudenshield) S. BA, Allegheny Coll., 1963; MA, Rutgers U., 1964. With Pa. State Govt., Harrisburg, 1964-68, Appalachian Regional Commn., Washington, 1968-75; legis. rep. Nat. Assn. Counties, Washington, 1975-77; fed. rep. Calif. Dept. Transp., Washington, 1977-78; dir. congl. affairs Amtrak, Washington, 1978-81, corp. sec., 1981-83; dir. computer svcs. Nat. R.R. Passenger Corp., Washington, 1983-84; co-owner Parkhurst-Spence Inc., 1985; owner The Spence Group, 1986-90; v.p. Bostrom Corp., Washington, 1990-92; exec. dir. Soc. Glass and Ceramic Decorators, 1992—; chmn. legis. com. Womens Transp. Seminar, 1977-79, dir., 1982-83, v.p., 1983-84, chmn. edn. com., 1982-83; com. on edn. and tng. Transp. Rsch. Bd., 1982-85; mng. ptnr. Cambio Capital Club, 1996. Contbr. articles to profl. jours. Commr., sec. D.C. Commn. for Women, 1983-88; del. Ward III Dem. Com., 1982-90, 1st vice chmn., 1987-88. Fellow Eagleton Inst. Politics, 1963-64; recipient Achievement award Transp. Seminar, 1982, 83. Mem. Greater Washington Soc. Assn. Execs. (vice-chair law and legis. com. 1989-90, chmn. 1990-91, chmn. scholarship com. 1992-93, bd. dirs. 1993-96, Rising Star award 1989, Chmn.'s award for Govt. Rels. 1991), Am. Soc. Assn. Execs. (mgmt. cert. 1987), Phi Beta Kappa. Home: 3701 Appleton St NW Washington DC 20016-1807 Office: Soc Glass and Ceramic Decorators 1627 K St NW Ste 800 Washington DC 20006-1702

SPENCE, WILLIAM ALLEN, lawyer; b. LaCrosse, Wis., Sept. 17, 1942; s. William Allen and Ann Lorraine (Samuels) S.; m. Lavern D. Gaynor, Feb. 19, 1977; children: Kelly, Tyler, Ryan. BA in English, Northwestern U., 1965; JD, Loyola U., Chgo., 1971. Bar: Ill. 1971, U.S. Dist. Ct. (no. dist.) Ill. 1971, U.S. Ct. Appeals (7th cir.) 1971. Law clk. Ill. Appellate Ct., Chgo., 1971-73; assoc. Pope, Ballard, Sheperd & Fowle, Chgo., 1973-78; asst. U.S. atty. U.S. Dept. Justice, Chgo., 1979-87; ptnr. Isham, Lincoln & Beale, Chgo., 1987-88, Freeborn & Peters, Chgo., 1988—; prof. law E. China U. Politics and Law, Shanghai, 1994; profl. advisor State Pharm. Adminstrn. China. Trustee Chgo. City Day Sch., 1985—; pres. 1130 Lake Shore Dr. Corp., Chgo., 1986—; co-chmn. Chgo. Sister Cities China Com. Mem. ABA, Chgo. Bar Assn., Union League Club, Saddle and Cycle Club. Avocations: architecture, sailing, skiing, tennis.

SPENCER, ALBERT FRANKLIN, physical education and education educator; b. Pitts., Dec. 31, 1943; s. Albert Clair and Ann Mary (Kielbas) S. BS in Edn., Slippery Rock (Pa.) State, Coll., 1966; MS, Clarion (Pa.) State Coll., 1981; PhD in LS, Fla. State U., Tallahassee, 1985, PhD in Phys. Edn., 1992. Phys. edn. tchr., libr., coach St. John's Indian Sch., Komatke, Ariz., 1976-77, Duncan (Ariz.) H.S., 1977-79; tchr. math. and sci. Army and Navy Acad., Carlsbad, Calif., 1979-80; phys. edn. tchr., libr., coach Baboquivari H.S., Sells, Ariz., 1980-81; asst. men's intercoll. basketball coach Fla. State U., Tallahassee, 1981-83; asst. prof. phys. edn., dir. audiovisual svcs. St. Leo (Fla.) Coll., 1983-86; asst. prof. Atlanta U. and Emory U., Atlanta, 1986-87; assoc. prof. phys. edn./athletics, libr. dir., coach Ga. Mil. Coll., Milledgeville, 1987-90; asst. prof. edn. U. Nev., Las Vegas, 1991-94; asst. prof. phys. edn., dept. human performance/health scis. Rice U., Houston, 1994—; cons. ednl. tech. Atlanta Pub. Schs., 1986-87; profl. basketball scout Bertka Agy. and L.A. Lakers, 1985-91; deptl. dir. KMart, New Kensington, Pa., 1972-74; dir. athletics YMCA, Kittanning, Pa., 1969. Contbg. author: Twentieth-Century Young Adult Writers, 1994; contbr. articles and revs. to profl. jours. Fundraiser KC, Las Vegas; vol. coach for youth league St. Anthony Elem. Sch., San Antonio, Fla.; scoutmaster Boy Scouss Am., New Kensington. Mem. AAHPERD, ALA, Am. Libr. and Info. Sci. Educators, Fla. Assn. for Health, Phys. Edn., Recreation and Dance, Tex. Assn. for Health, Phys. Edn., Recreation and Dance, U.S. Phys. Edn. Assn., Tex. Faculty Assn., Beta Phi Mu, Omicron Delta Kappa. Roman Catholic. Avocations: writing, golf, basketball, hiking. Office: Rice U Dept Human Perf/Hlth Svcs PO Box 1892 Houston TX 77251

SPENCER, CAROL BROWN, association executive; b. Normal, Ill., Aug. 26, 1936; d. Fred William and Sorado (Gross) B.; m. James Calvin Spencer, Dec. 18, 1965 (div. July 1978); children: James Calvin Jr., Anne Elizabeth. BA in English, Calif. State U., Los Angeles, 1964, MA in Pub. Adminstrn., 1986. Cert. secondary edn. tchr., Calif. Tchr. English Seneca Vocat. High Sch., Buffalo, 1966-70; pub. info. officer City of Pasadena, Calif., 1979-90, City of Mountain View, Calif., 1990-93; exec. dir. Calif. Assn. for the Gifted, 1993—; owner PR to Go, 1994—. Sec., bd. dirs. Calif. Music Theatre, 1987-90; bd. dirs. Pasadena Beautiful Found., 1984-90, Pasadena Cultural Festival Found., 1983-86, Palo Alto-Stanford Heritage, 1990-93; mayoral appointee Strategic Planning Adv. Com., Pasadena, 1985-86; active Mountain View Lib. Found., 1997—. Mem. NOW, Pub. Rels. Soc. Am., Calif. Assn. Pub. Info. Ofcls. (exec. bd., Paul Clark Achievment award 1986, award for mktg. 1990), City/County Comms. and Mktg. Assn. (bd. dirs. 1988-90, Savvy award for mktg. 1990), Nat. Assn. for Gifted Children. Democrat. Episcopalian. Home: 426 Escuela Ave Apt 19 Mountain View CA 94040-2022

SPENCER, CONSTANCE MARILYN, secondary education educator; b. New York, Jan. 2, 1942; d. Edward Bennett and Blanche Lloyd (Miller) Asbury; m. Robert William Spencer, Dec. 30, 1966; children: Keane Thomas, Keith Lyle. BA, U. Calif., Santa Barbara, 1964; MA in English, U. West Fla., 1974. Cert. lang. devel. specialist, preliminary adminstr. Tchr. Valley Stream (N.Y.) N. H.S., Workman Jr. H.S., Pensacola, Fla., Imperial Beach (Calif.) Elem. Sch.; substitute tchr. South Bay Union Sch., Imperial Beach; mgr. Geni, Inc., Pasadena, Calif., Avon Products, Inc., Pasadena; tchr. Walnut (Calif.) H.S., 1985—; pres. Am. Computer Instrn. Inc., Upland, Calif.; grant writer Walnut Valley Unified Sch. Dist., 1986-97, mentor tchr., 1988-97; accreditation co-chair Walnut H.S., 1993-94. Mem., sec. Toastmistress, Ontario, Calif., 1977-86. Grantee Calif. Dept. Edn., 1987, Walnut Valley Unified Sch. Dist., 1988, Diamond Bar (Calif.) Rotary, 1994. Republican. Roman Catholic. Avocation: writing. Home: 2238 Coolcrest Way Upland CA 91784-1290 Office: Walnut HS 400 Pierre Rd Walnut CA 91789-2535

SPENCER, DAVID MILLS, library administrator; b. Eugene, Oreg., Dec. 7, 1950; s. Richard J. and Adelaide (Marsh) S. BA in English Lit., Lewis & Clark Coll., 1973; M in Urban and Regional Planning, U. Oreg., 1978; MLS, Cath. U. Am., 1988. Asst. planner Linn County Planning Dept., Albany, Oreg., 1979-80; from asst. planner to dir. Benton County Devel. Dept., Corvallis, Oreg., 1980-87; from reference libr. to br. libr. Nat. Air & Space Mus. Br. Libr. Smithsonian Instn. Librs., Washington, 1989-97. vestryman St. Thomas Episcopal Ch., Washington, 1993-95, jr. warden, 1995-97. Mem. Spl. Libr. Assn., Nat. Trust for Hist. Preservation. Democrat.

SPENCER, DONALD CLAYTON, mathematician; b. Boulder, Colo., Apr. 25, 1912; s. Frank Robert and Edith (Clayton) S.; m. Mary Jo Halley (div.); children: Maredith (dec.), Marianne; m. Natalie Robertson (dec.); 1 child, Donald Clayton Jr. BA, U. Colo., 1934; BS, MIT, 1936; PhD, Cambridge (Eng.) U., 1939, ScD, 1963; ScD (hon.), Purdue U., 1971. Instr. MIT, Cambridge, 1939-42; assoc. prof. Stanford (Calif.) U., 1942-46, prof., 1946-50, 63-68; assoc. prof. Princeton (N.J.) U., 1950-53, prof., 1953-63, 68-78, Henry Burchard Fine prof. emeritus, 1978—. Co-author: (with A.C. Schaeffer, monograph) Coefficient Regions for Schlicht Functions, 1950, (with M. Schiffer) Functionals of Finite Riemann Surfaces, 1954, (with A. Kumpera) Lie Equations, vol. I: General Theory, 1972, (with H.K. Nickerson and N.E. Steenrod, textbook) Advanced Calculus, 1959. Recipient Bocher prize Am. Math. Soc., 1948, Nat. medal of sci. Pres. of U.S., 1989, George Norlin award U. Colo., 1990. Fellow Am. Acad. Arts and Scis.; mem. NAS. Home: 943 County Rd 204 Durango CO 81301-8547

SPENCER, DONALD SPURGEON, historian, academic administrator; b. Anderson, Ind., Jan. 29, 1945; s. Thomas E. and Josephine (Litz) S.; m. Pamela Sue Roberts, June 19, 1965; 1 child, Jennifer Wynne. BA, Ill. Coll., 1967; PhD, U. Va., 1973. Asst. prof. history Westminster Coll., Fulton, Mo., 1973-76, Ohio U., Athens, 1976-77; from asst., assoc. to full prof., assoc. dean, asst. provost U. Mont., Missoula, 1977-90; provost SUNY, Geneseo, 1990-93; pres. Western Ill. U., Macomb, 1994—. Author: Louis Kossuth and Young America, 1978, The Carter Implosion: Jimmy Carter and the Amateur Style of Diplomacy,1989; contbr. articles to jours. in field. With U.S. Army, 1968-71, Korea. Woodrow Wilson Found. fellow, 1968; Danforth Found. univ. teaching fellow, 1971. Mem. Phi Beta Kappa. Congregationalist. Home: 2001 Wigwam Hollow Rd Macomb IL 61455-9336 Office: W Ill Univ Office of the President Sherman Hall Macomb IL 61455

SPENCER, EDGAR WINSTON, geology educator; b. Monticello, Ark., May 27, 1931; s. Terrel Ford and Allie Belle (Shelton) S.; m. Elizabeth Penn Humphries, Nov. 26, 1958; children: Elizabeth Shawn, Kristen Shannon. Student, Vanderbilt U., 1949-50; B.S., Washington and Lee U., 1953; Ph.D., Columbia U., 1957. Lectr. Hunter Coll., 1954-57; mem. faculty Washington and Lee U., 1957—, prof. geology, head dept., 1962-95, Ruth Parmly prof.; pres. Rockbridge Area Conservation Coun., 1978-79, 95-97; NSF sci. faculty fellow, New Zealand and Australia; dir. grant for humanities and pub. policy on land use planning Va. Found., 1975; dir. grant Petroleum Rsch. Fund, 1981-82; leader field trip Ctrl. Appalachian Mts. Internat. Geol. Congress, 1989. Author: Basic Concepts of Physical Geology, 1962, Basic Concepts of Historical Geology, 1962, Geology: A Survey of Earth Science, 1965, Introduction to the Structure of the Earth, 1969, 3d edit., 1988, The Dynamics of the Earth, 1972, Physical Geology, 1983, Geologic Maps, 1993. Recipient Va. Outstanding Faculty award Va. Coun. of Higher Edn., 1990. Fellow Geol. Soc. Am., AAAS; mem. Am. Assn. Petroleum Geologists (dir. field seminar on fold and thrust belts 1987, 88-91), Am. Inst. Profl. Geologists, Am. Geophys. Union, Nat. Assn. Geology Tchrs., Yellowstone-Bighorn Rsch. Assn., Phi Beta Kappa (hon.), Sigma Xi. Home: PO Box 1055 Lexington VA 24450-1055

SPENCER, ELIZABETH, author; b. Carrollton, Miss., 1921; d. James Luther and Mary James (McCain) S.; m. John Arthur Blackwood Rusher, Sept. 29, 1956. BA, Belhaven Coll., 1942; MA, Vanderbilt U., 1943; LittD (hon.), Southwestern U. at Memphis, 1968; LLD (hon.), Concordia U. at Montreal, 1988; LittD (hon.), U. of the South, 1992. Instr. N.W. Miss. Jr. Coll., 1943-44, Ward-Belmont, Nashville, 1944-45; reporter The Nashville Tennessean, 1945-46; instr. U. Miss., Oxford, 1948-51, 52-53; vis. prof. Concordia U., Montreal, Que., Can., 1976-81, adj. prof., 1981-86; vis. prof. U. N.C., Chapel Hill, 1986-92. Author: Fire in the Morning, 1948, This Crooked Way, 1952, The Voice at the Back Door, 1956, The Light in the Piazza, 1960, Knights and Dragons, 1965, No Place for an Angel, 1967, Ship Island and Other Stories, 1968, The Snare, 1972, The Stories of Elizabeth Spencer, 1981, Marilee, 1981, The Salt Line, 1984, Jack of Diamonds and Other Stories, 1988, (play) For Lease or Sale, 1989, On the Gulf, 1991, The Night Travellers, 1991; contbr. short stories to mags. and anthologies. Recipient Women's Democratic Com. award, 1949, recognition award Nat. Inst. Arts and letters, 1952, Richard and Hinda Rosenthal Found. award Am. Acad. Arts and Letters, 1957; Guggenheim Found. fellow, 1953, 1st McGraw-Hill Fiction award, 1960, Henry Bellamann award for creative writing, 1968; Award of Merit medal for the short story Am. Acad. Arts and Letters, 1983, Salem award for lit., 1992, Dos Passos award for fiction, 1992, N.C. Gov.'s award for lit., 1994, Corrington awrd for lit., 1997, Richard Wright award for lit., 1997; Kenyon Rev. fellow in fiction, 1957; Bryn Mawr Col. Donnelly fellow, 1962; Nat. Endowment for Arts grantee in lit., 1983, Sr. Arts Award grantee Nat. Endowment for Arts, 1988. Mem. Am. Acad. Arts and Letters, Fellowship of So. Writers (charter; vice chancellor 1993—). Home: 402 Longleaf Dr Chapel Hill NC 27514-3042

SPENCER, FOSTER LEWIS, newspaper editor; b. Putnam, Conn., Dec. 18, 1932; s. Ralph Washburn and Helen (Thompson) S.; m. Dorothy Virginia Purda, Aug. 18, 1956; children: Faith Elizabeth, Beth Mary. B.A., U. Mass., 1960. News editor Palmer (Mass.) Jour.-Register, 1956-60; Sunday feature editor Springfield (Mass.) Republican, 1960-65; mng. editor Buffalo News, 1966—; chmn. N.Y. State adv. bd./UPI, 1980-86. Served with USAF, 1952-56, Korea. Recipient Spl. award AP, 1979. Mem. N.Y. AP Assn. (pres. Albany 1976-77), N.Y. State Soc. Newspaper Editors (pres. 1983). Democrat. Congregationalist. Home: 292 Summer St Buffalo NY 14222-2114 Office: Buffalo News 1 News Plz Buffalo NY 14203-2930

SPENCER, FRANCIS MONTGOMERY JAMES, pharmacist; b. St. John's, Antigua, Mar. 11, 1943; came to U.S., 1974; s. Stanley M. and Sarah Jane Elizabeth (Spencer) James; m. Jean V. Cole, May 9, 1981; children: David, Frances, Weslie. BS in Pharmacy, Northeastern U., Boston, 1982. Registered pharmacist, Mass., N.H., Fla.; registered cons. pharmacist, pharmacy preceptor, Fla. Sr. dispensing drugist Holberton Hosp., Antigua, 1968-73, lectr. in pharmacy, 1970-73; pharmacist, intern Mount Auburn Hosp., Cambridge, Mass., 1978-82; staff pharmacist Centro-Asturiano Hosp., Tampa, Fla., 1986-90, Dr.'s Hosp., Tampa, Fla., 1991—; pharmacy mgr. Eckerd Drug Co., Tampa, Fla., 1983—; co-founder, pres., chief exec. officer Spenscott, Inc., Bronx, N.Y., 1989—; assoc. mem. Delta Search, Inc., Tampa, 1987—. Mem. profl. adv. panel Drug Topics mag., Oradell, N.J., 1987—. Fellow Am. Soc. Cons. Pharmacists (registered cons. Fla.), Internat. Biog Assn. (life, dept. dir. gen.); mem. AASA, Fla. Pharmacy Assn., Am. Biog. Inst. Inc. (dep. gov., hon. mem. rsch. bd. advisors), N.Y. Acad. Scis., Am. Soc. Pharmacy Law, Mass. State Pharmacy Assn., N.H. Pharmacy Assn., Am. Coll. Heatlh Care Adminstrs. Methodist. Avocations: reading, travel, classical music. Home: PO Box 245 Mango FL 33550-0245

SPENCER, FRANK COLE, medical educator; b. Haskell, Tex., 1925. MD, Vanderbilt U., 1947. Intern Johns Hopkins U., Balt., 1947-48, fellow in surgery, 1947-48, asst. resident in surgery, 1953-54; resident in surgery Johns Hopkins Sch. Medicine, Balt., 1954-55; surgeon, outpatient dept. Johns Hopkins Hosp., 1955; resident in surgery Wadsworth VA Ctr. Hosp., 1949-50; fellow cardiovascular surgery USPHS, Los Angeles, 1951; asst. prof. surgery Johns Hopkins U., 1955-59, assoc. prof., 1959-61; prof. surgery U. Ky.; now chmn. dept. surgery, George David Steward prof. surgery NYU. Served to lt. M.C., USN, 1951-53. John and Mary R. Markle scholar in med. sci. Johns Hopkins U., 1956. Office: NYU Sch of Medicine Dept of Surgery 550 1st Ave New York NY 10016-6481*

SPENCER, HARRY IRVING, JR., retired banker; b. Worcester, Mass., Feb. 3, 1925; s. Harry Irving and Bertha (Johnson) S.; m. Violet Virginia Bergquist, Sept. 16, 1950; children—Nancy Elaine, Harry Irving III, Carol Helen. B.A., Clark U., 1950. With Worcester County Nat. Bank, 1950-82, asst. treas., 1954-58, cashier, 1958-82, v.p., 1966-69, sr. v.p., 1969-77, exec. v.p., cashier, 1977-82, clk., dir., 1980-82; exec. v.p., cashier, sec. Shawmut Worcester County Bank, N.A., 1982-88, also bd. dirs.; sec., treas., dir. Nobility Hill Realty Corp.; dir. Worcester Capital Corp., Wornat Leasing Corp. Bd. dirs. Worcester Taxpayers Assn. Methodist (trustee). Clubs: Kiwanis; Economic (Worcester, Mass.), Plaza (Worcester, Mass.). Home: 79 Birchwood Dr Holden MA 01520-1939 Office: 446 Main St Worcester MA 01608-2302

SPENCER, IVAN CARLTON, clergyman; b. nr. West Burlington, Pa., July 8, 1914; s. Ivan Quay and Annie Minnie (Back) S.; m. Elizabeth Garate, Apr. 14, 1935 (dec. May 1995); children: David Carlton, Esther Elizabeth (Mrs. Saied Adour), John Wesley; m. Margaret Alderman, July 12, 1996. Grad., Elim Bible Inst., 1933; D.D., Am. Bible Coll., 1966. Ordained to ministry Elim Missionary Assemblies. Pastor various chs., 1935-38; instr. Elim Bible Inst., 1938, campus pastor, 1938-44, pres., 1949-82; gen. sec. Elim Missionary Assemblies (now Elim Fellowship), 1940-54, gen. chmn., 1954-85; bd. dirs. Nat. Assn. Evangs., 1958-85, Pentecostal Fellowship of N. Am., 1961-86, treas., 1963-65, 73-81. Address: 7245 College St Lima NY 14485

SPENCER, JAMES CALVIN, SR., humanities educator; b. Detroit, Oct. 21, 1941; s. Donald and Beulah S.; m. Linda J. Voloshen, Nov. 21, 1987; children: James, Anne. BA, Calif. State U., 1966; MA, SUNY, 1970, PhD in Philosophy, 1973. NDEA fellow SUNY, Buffalo, 1968-70, SUNY fellow, 1970-71; instr. Cuyahoga C.C., Parma, Ohio, 1971-73, asst. prof., 1973-77, assoc. prof., 1977-81, prof. philosophy and art, 1981—; cons. continuing edn. divsn. Kans. State U., 1986, Case Western U., Cleve., 1973, Ford Motor Co., Brookport, Ohio, 1990, Campus Planning Inst., Cleve., 1991-94, PBS Nat. Faculty Referral Network, 1996—; pres. Spencer Enterprises, Brecksville, Ohio, 1991—; reviewer manuscripts for Wadsworth Pub. and McGraw-Hill Pub. Author: The Nightmare Never Ends, 1992; co-author: Instructor's Manual for the Voyage of Discovery: A History of Western Philosophy, 1996; contbr. articles to profl. jours. Ward com. Democratic Party, Ashland, Brecksville, Ohio, Libertarian Party, Buffalo, N.Y.; Chevalier de la Chaine des Rotisseurs, Chevalier Ordre Mondial, 1996—. Grantee Nat. Sci. Found., 1979. Mem. French Food Soc., French Wine Soc., Am. Wine Soc. Office: Cuyahoga Community College 11000 W Pleasant Valley Rd Cleveland OH 44130-5114 *My life has demonstrated the correctness of what the wise have known since Mesopotamia as the formula for success: Hard work, much luck and enough intelligence to know when to take advantage of them both.*

SPENCER, JAMES H., art director, production designer. Prodn. designer: (TV movies) Friendly Persuasion, 1975, Red Alert, 1977, King, 1978, Some Kind of Miracle, 1979, Son Rise: A Miracle of Love, 1979, Not in Front of the Children, 1982, Journey to the Center of the Earth, 1993, (films) Fire Sale, 1977, Die Laughing, 1980, King of the Mountain, 1981, Stripes, 1981, Poltergeist, 1982, The Sender, 1982, Gremlins, 1984, Innerspace, 1987, The 'Burbs, 1989, Gremlins 2: The New Batch, 1990, Lethal Weapon 3, 1992; art dir.: (films) Bound for Glory, 1976, Rocky, 1976, Twilight Zone-The Movie ("Nightmare at 20,000 Feet"), 1983, (TV-movie) Journey to the Center of the Earth, Richie Rich, 1994. Office: c/o Art Directors 11365 Ventura Blvd # 315 North Hollywood CA 91604*

SPENCER, JAMES R., federal judge; b. 1949. BA magna cum laude, Clark Coll., 1971; JD, Harvard U., 1974, MDiv, 1985. Staff atty. Atlanta Legal Aid Soc., 1974-75; asst. U.S. atty. Washington, 1978, U.S. Dist. Ct. (ea. dist.) Va., 1983; judge U.S. Dist. Ct. (ea. dist.) Va., Richmond, 1986—; adj. prof. law U. Va., 1987—. Capt. JAGC, U.S.Army, 1975-78, res. 1981-86. Mem. ABA, Nat. Bar Assn., State Bar Ga., D.C. Bar, Va. State Bar, Richmond Bar Assn., Washington Bar Assn., Old Dominion Bar Assn., Omega Psi Phi, Sigma Pi Phi. Office: US Courthouse 1000 E Main St Richmond VA 23219-3525

SPENCER, JEFFREY PAUL, art educator; b. Omaha, Oct. 31, 1962; s. James Stanley and Darlene (Rahe) S. BFA, U. Nebr., 1987; MFA, U. Tenn., 1990. Instr. Met. C.C., Omaha, 1990—, U. Nebr., 1996—. Mem. Young Dems., Omaha, 1993—. NEA grantee, 1991. Mem. Coll. Art Assn. Home: 815 S 46th Ave Omaha NE 68106-2008

SPENCER, JIMMY, professional race car driver; b. Berwick, Pa., Feb. 15, 1957; m. Pat Spencer; children: Jimmy, Katrina. Profl. race car driver NASCAR Winston Cup, 1989—; 2-time NASCAR Modified nat. champion, 1986, 87; winner 1994 Diehard 500. Office: Jimmy Spencer Fan Club PO Box 1626 Mooresville NC 28115

SPENCER, JOHN HEDLEY, biochemistry educator; b. Stapleford, Eng., Apr. 10, 1933; emigrated to Can., 1956; s. Thomas and Eva (Johnson) S.; m. Magdeliene Vera Kulin, Sept. 16, 1958; children—Robin Anne, David Thomas, Mark Stewart. BSc, U. St. Andrews, Scotland, 1955, BSc with honors, 1956; student, Montreal Cancer Rsch. Soc., 1956-59; PhD, McGill U., 1960. Damon Runyon Meml. Fund postdoctoral fellow Columbia U., N.Y.C., 1959-61; mem. faculty McGill U., Montreal, 1961-78, assoc. prof. biochemistry, 1966-71, prof., 1971-78; prof. biochemistry Queen's U., Kingston, Ont., 1978—, head biochemistry, 1978-90; vis. prof. U. Montreal, 1992-93. Author: The Physics and Chemistry of DNA and RNA, 1972; co-editor: Planet Earth: Problems and Prospects, 1995. Recipient Ayerst award Can. Biochem. Soc., 1972. Fellow Royal Soc. Can.; mem. AAAS, Can. Biochem. Soc. (treas. 1966-69, pres. 1979-80), Can. Fedn. Biol. Socs. (pres. 1981-82), Biochem. Soc., Am. Soc. Biochemistry and Molecular Biology, Royal Soc. Can., Sigma Xi. Home: 36 Kenwoods Cir, Kingston, ON Canada K7K 6Y1

SPENCER, LAVAL WING, physician; b. Lehi, Utah, Apr. 12, 1928; s. Lawrence Valdor and Mary Georgia (Wing) S.; m. Betty Jean Robertson, Nov. 10, 1950; children: Scott, Kelly, James, Debra Jean. AS, Weber Coll., 1956; BS, U. Utah, 1959, MD, 1963. Charter Diplomate Am. Bd. Family Practice. Amateur radio operator Extra Class, K7MD. Electronic technician Hill AFB, Ogden, Utah, 1950-53, med. officer, 1985-88; resident in gen. practice Dee Hosp., Ogden, 1963-66; pvt. practice Ogden, 1966-85; hon. med. staff McKay-Dee Hosp., 1988—; mem. Utah emergency and comm. com. Utah Med. Assn., Salt Lake City, 1970-77; chmn. med. edn. and rsch. com. McKay-Dee Hosp., Ogden, 1972-73, pres. med. staff, 1973; clin. instr. U. Utah, Salt Lake City, 1978-88. Contbr. articles and essays to profl. publs. Sgt. USAAF, 1946-49, PTO. Recipient honoree award Women's Coun., 1995, Stewart Rehab. Ct., McKay-Dee Found. Fellow Am. Acad. Family Physicians (charter), Royal Soc. Health; mem. AMA, Utah Med. Assn., Weber County Med. Soc., Ogden Surg.-Med. Soc. (treas. 1970-75). Avocation: amateur radio operator. Home: 1365 Lark Cir Ogden UT 84403-2141

SPENCER, LEWIS DOUGLAS, lawyer; b. Frankfort, Ind., Feb. 6, 1917; s. Clarence D. and Hazel (Ghormley) S.; m. Marcia Jane Maish, Jan. 29, 1947; children: Karen Jane Spencer Redman, Margo Linn Spencer Estruth. AB, DePauw U., 1939; LLB, Columbia, 1942; student, Motorola Exec. Inst., 1969. Bar: N.Y. 1942, Ind. 1943, Ill. 1947. Assoc. firm Carter, Ledyard and Milburn, N.Y.C., 1942-43, Barnes, Hickam, Pantzer & Boyd, Indpls., 1943-44, O'Connor & Farber, N.Y.C., 1944-47, Peterson, Rall, Barber, Ross & Seidel, Chgo., 1947-51; atty. Motorola, Inc. (and subsidiaries), 1951-77, asst. sec., 1956-74, sec., 1974-77, gen. atty., 1959-73, gen. counsel, 1973-77, v.p., 1965-77; lectr. sch. law Loyola U., Chgo., 1978-79, prof. sch. law, 1979-86. Contbr. articles to profl. jours. Mem. Park Ridge (Ill.) Bd. Fire and Police Commrs., 1964-67; mem. Park Ridge Zoning Bd. Appeals and Zoning Commn., 1967-75, chmn., 1968-75; bd. dirs. Park Ridge United Fund, 1966-69, pres., 1968. Mem. Chgo. Tax Club (bd. dirs. 1965-71, pres. 1969), The Nat. Soc., SAR. Mem. Park Ridge Community Ch. (bd. dirs. 1964-72, chmn. congregation 1970-71). Home: 5555 N Sheridan Rd Apt 1602 Chicago IL 60640-1628

SPENCER, LONABELLE (KAPPIE SPENCER), political agency administrator, lobbyist; b. Owatonna, Minn., Aug. 3, 1925; d. Reuben Alvin and Florence Elizabeth (Wells) Kaplan; m. Mark Rodney Spencer, Sept. 14, 1947 (dec. May 1986); children: Gregory Mark, Gary Alan, Carol Ann (Spencer) Glumac, Dane Kaplan. BA, Grinnell Coll., 1947. State bd. legis. chair Am. Assn. Univ. Women, Des Moines, Iowa, 1978-82; nat. legis. com. Am. Assn. Univ. Women, Washington, 1980-83, nat. bd. legis. chair, 1982-83, nat. legis. and program coms., 1985-89, nat. bd. dir. for women's issues, 1985-89; founder, dir. Nat. Gender Balance Project, Sarasota, Fla., 1988—; bd. dirs., nat. steering com. Nat. Women's Political Caucus, Washington, 1992—; lobbyist, cmty. activist state legis. and congress, Fla. Iowa, Washington, 1974—; pub. policy cons. women's orgns., nationwide, 1978—; rep. Fla. women's pol. caucus ERA summit, Washington, 1992—. Author: (pub. policy manuals) Don't Leave It All to the Experts, 1981, Take An Unratified State to Launch, 1981, It's a Man's World Unless Women Vote, 1983, Woman Power: It's a Capitol Idea, 1995, Gender Balance Project-USA: Politics and Decision Making, 1995; exhibitor, presenter in field. U.S. rep. World Assn. Girl Guides Girl Scouts U.S., Acapulco, Mex., 1965, bd. dirs. Moingona Coun. Girl Scouts U.S., 1965-75; Rep. candidate Iowa senate, Des Moines, 1976; del., workshop presenter Internat. Fedn. Univ. Women, Netherlands, New Zealand, Finland, Sweden, 1983, 86, 89, workshop presenter U.S./China Joint Conf. on Women's Issues, Beijing, China, 1995, Nongovernmental Orgn. Forum, Huairou, China, 1995; trustee Grinnell (Iowa) Coll., 1993—; Iowa del. to Nat. Women's Conf., 1977. Recipient Girl Scout awards Moingona Girl Scout Coun., Des Moines, 1969, 73, 78, Christine Wilson medal for Equality and Justice, Iowa Women's Hall of Fame, Des Moines, 1990; named gift honoree Am. Assn. Univ. Women, Des Moines and Sarasota, Fla. branches, Iowa and Vt. divsns., 1980, 82, 87, 92. Mem. AAUW (leader corps, various coms. 1975—), UN Fund for Women (UNIFEM), Nat. Assn. Commns. for Women, Vet. Feminists of Am., Women in Senate and House WISH-LIST (founder 1992—), Fla. Women's Consortium (founder, bd. dirs. 1989—). Republican. Avocations: travel. Home: 3735 Beneva Oaks Way Sarasota FL 34238-2524

SPENCER, MARGARET GILLIAM, lawyer; b. Spokane, Wash., Aug. 30, 1951; d. Jackson Earl and Margaret Kathleen (Hindley) Gilliam; m. John Bernard Spencer, Feb. 21, 1993. BA in Sociology, U. Mont., 1974, MA in Sociology, 1978, JD, 1982. Bar: Mont. 1982, Colo. 1982. Assoc. Holland & Hart, Denver, 1982-84; assoc. Roath & Brega, P.C., Denver, 1984-88, shareholder, dir., 1988-89; spl. counsel Brega & Winters, P.C., Denver, 1989; corp. counsel CH2M Hill, Inc., Denver, 1989—. Democrat. Episcopalian. Avocations: skiing, scuba diving. Office: CH2M Hill Inc PO Box 22508 Denver CO 80222-0508

SPENCER, MARY MILLER, civic worker; b. Comanche, Tex., May 25, 1924; d. Aaron Gaynor and Alma (Grissom) Miller; 1 child, Mara Lynn. BS, U. North Tex., 1943. Cafeteria dir. Mercedes (Tex.) Pub. Schs., 1943-46; home economist coordinator All-Orange Dessert Contest, Fla. Citrus Commn., Lakeland, 1959-62, 64; tchr. purchasing sch. lunch dept. Fla. Dept. Edn., 1960. Clothing judge Polk County (Fla.) Youth Fair, 1951-68, Polk County Federated Women's Clubs, 1964-66; pres. Dixieland Elem. Sch. PTA, 1955-57, Polk County Council PTA's, 1958-60; chmn. public edn. com. Polk County unit Am. Cancer Soc., 1959-60, bd. dirs., 1962-70; charter mem., bd. dirs. Lakeland YMCA, 1962-72; sec. Greater Lakeland Community Nursing Council, 1965-72; trustee, vice chmn. Polk County Eye Clinic, Inc., 1962-64, pres., 1964-82; bd. dirs. Polk County Scholarship and Loan Fund, 1962-70; mem. exec. com. West Polk County (Fla.) Community Welfare Council, 1960-62, 65-68; mem. budget and audit com. Greater Lakeland United Fund, 1960-62, bd. dirs., 1967-70, residential chmn. fund drive, 1968; mem. adv. bd. Polk County Juvenile and Domestic Relations Ct., 1960-69; worker children's services div. family services Dept. Health and Rehab. Services, State of Fla., 1969-70, social worker, 1970-72, 74-82, social worker OFR unit, 1977-81, with other pers. svcs., 1981-82; supr. OFR unit 1982-83, pub. assistance specialist IV, 1984-89; with other pers. svcs. Emergency Fin. Assistance Housing Program, 1990-96. Mem. exec. com. Suncoast Health Council, 1968-71; mem. Polk County Home Econs. Adv. Com., 1965-71; sec. bd. dirs. Fla. West Coast Ednl. TV, 1960-81; bd. dirs. Lake Region United Way, Winter Haven, 1976-81; mem. Polk County Community Services Council, 1978-88. Mem. Nat. Welfare Fraud Assn., Fla. Congress Parents and Tchrs. (hon. life; pres. dist. 7 1961-63, chmn. pub. relations 1962-66), AAUW (pres. Lakeland br. 1960-61), Polk County Mental Health Assn., Fla. Health and Welfare Council, Fla. Health and Social Service Council, U. North Tex. Alumni Assn. Democrat. Methodist. Lodge: Order of Eastern Star. Home and Office: PO Box 2161 Lakeland FL 33806-2161

SPENCER, MELVIN JOE, hospital administrator, lawyer; b. Buffalo Center, Iowa, Jan. 2, 1923; s. Kenos W. and Jennie (Michaelson) S.; m. Dena Joyce Butterfield, Mar. 1, 1952; children: Dennis Norman, Gregory Melvin, Shelly Lynn Spencer Goodnight. AB, U. Mich., 1948, JD, 1950. Bar: Iowa 1950, Mo. 1950, Okla. 1961. Practiced in Kansas City, Mo., 1950-61, Oklahoma City, 1961—; assoc., then ptnr. Watson, Ess, Marshall & Enggas, 1950-61; ptnr. Miller & Spencer (and predecessor firm), 1961-75, of counsel, 1975-80; adminstr. Deaconess Hosp., 1975-92, cons., 1992-93; dir. Union Bank & Trust Co., Oklahoma City, 1977-88, 89-96, adv. dir., 1996—; dir., sec. Hosp. Casualty Co., 1977-92; dir., treas. VHA of Okla., Inc., 1986-92. Assoc. editor Mich. Law Rev., 1949-50. Mcpl. judge City of Roeland Park, Kans., 1952, mem. city coun., 1954; area Rep. precinct chmn., 1968-69; del. Rep. State Conv., 1968, 96; bd. dirs. Deaconess Hosp., Oklahoma City, Christian Counseling Ctr., 1973-75; trustee Okla. Hosp. Assn., 1978-84, chmn. bd. trustees, 1983; trustee, vice chmn. bd. dirs. Ctrl. Coll., McPherson, Kans., 1972-86; trustee Okla. Ambulance Trust, 1984-87; mem. adv. bd. Okla. State U. Tech. Inst., 1980-92; mem. Okla. Hist. Soc.; bd. dirs. Emergency Med. Svcs. Ctrl. Okla., 1975-78, FMC Ministries, Inc.; mem. const. coun. Free Meth. Ch. World Fellowship; chmn. Free Meth. Found.; gen. counsel Free Meth. Ch. N.Am., 1969-95, sec., mem. bd. adminstrn., chmn. investment com., 1986-88. Capt. USAAF, 1943-46. Named Layman of Yr., Free Meth. Ch. N.Am., 1984; recipient W. Cleveland Rodgers Disting. Svc. award Okla. Hosp. Assn., 1985; fellow Cen. Coll. Acad. of Achievers, 1990. Mem. Okla. Bar Assn., Oklahoma County Bar Assn., Men's Dinner Club, Order of Coif, Phi Beta Kappa, Phi Kappa Phi. Home: 5910 N Shawnee Ave Oklahoma City OK 73112-1627

SPENCER, MILTON HARRY, economics and finance educator; b. N.Y.C., Mar. 25, 1926; m. Roslyn Pernick; children: Darcy, Robin, Cathy. BS, NYU, 1949, MA, 1950; PhD, Cornell U., 1954. Instr. econs., fin. Queens Coll., N.Y.C., 1949-52; research asst. Cornell U., Ithaca, N.Y., 1952-54; economist Armour & Co., Chgo., 1954-55; assoc. prof. Wayne State U., Detroit, 1955-62, prof., 1962-91, prof. emeritus, 1991—; vis. prof. U. Hawaii, Honolulu, 1965-66; lectr., U.S., Australia, Europe, Asia, Africa, South Am.; cons. U.S. Dept. State, Washington, 1959—, govts. of Chile, Israel, Eng., France, Italy, Australia, Hong Kong, Japan, Rep. of China and various domestic and fgn. corps. Author: Basic Economics, 1951, Economic Thought, 1954, Business and Economic Forecasting, 1958, Managerial Economics, 3 edits., 1959-68, Contemporary Economics, 8 edits., 1971-93; various monographs; contbr. numerous articles to profl. jours. Served as cpl. U.S. Army, 1943-45. Recipient Disting. Service awards from U.S. Dept. State, Govts. of Chile, Israel, France, Spain, England, Italy, Belgium. Mem. Am. Econ. Assn., Am. Fin. Assn., Nat. Assn. Bus. Economists. Avocations: piloting vintage planes, hang gliding.

SPENCER, PETER LEVALLEY, SR., editor; b. Panama, Jan. 15, 1962; s. Cannon Peter L. and Eugenia (Bruno) S.; m. C. Ashley Jackson, Feb. 29, 1988; children: Piers, Jackson. BA, U. South, 1984. Ordained priest Episcopal Ch. Assoc. editor Consumers' Rsch., Washington, 1985-87, mng. editor, 1988-90, exec. editor, 1990-91, editor, 1992—. Episcopalian.

SPENCER, PRISCILLA JAMES, physical education educator; b. Boston, Aug. 21, 1960; d. Richard P. and Gwendolyn (Williams) S. BA in Psychology, Bates Coll., Lewiston, ME, 1983; MS in Phys. Edn. Recreation, Southern Conn. State U., 1990. Conn. Profl. Educator in Phys. Edn. and Health. Counselor Youth and Family Svcs., Westfield, Mass., 1983-85; phys. edn. tchr. Clark Elem. Sch., Hartford, Conn., 1988-89, Pleasant Valley Elem. Sch., South Winds, Conn., 1989—; cons. Pub. Schs., Conn., 1991—. Co-author: Popcorn's Travels Across America, 1992; author: Gymnastics for All, 1994. Cmty. instr. ARC, Farmington, Conn., 1989—. Named Outstanding Elem. Phys. Edn. Program Conn. Assn. Health, Phys. Edn. and Recreation, 1991; recipient Celebration of Excellence award State Conn. Dept. Edn., 1992. Mem. Nat. Orgn. Health Phys. Edn. and Recreation, Conn. Assn. Health, Phys. Edn., Recreation and Dance, Assn. for Exptl. Edn., Am. Youth Hostels Inc. (trip leader 1989—). Home: 4314 Dobson St Philadelphia PA 19129

SPENCER, RICHARD HENRY, lawyer; b. Kansas City, Mo., Nov. 29, 1926; s. Byron Spencer and Helen Elizabeth (McCune) Hockaday; m. Barbara G. Rau, Aug. 2, 1952 (div. 1955); 1 chlid, Christina G. Cuevas; m. Katherine Graham, Dec. 28, 1957; children: Elisabeth M., Katherine S. Rivard. BS in Engring., Princeton U., 1949; LLB, U. Mo., 1952. Bar: Mo. 1952, U.S. Dist. Ct (we. dist.) Mo. 1955. Assoc. Spencer, Fane, Britt & Browne, Kansas City, 1952-59, ptnr., 1959-94; ret. ptnr., 1995—; bd. dirs., sec. Daniels-McCray Lumber Co., Kansas City, 1975—, First Am. Ins. Co., Kansas City, 1971—. Co-author: Fiduciary Duties, Rights and Responsibilities of Directors, 1985. Sec. Kansas City Symphony, 1983—; sec., bd. dirs. Met. Performing Arts Fund, Kansas City, 1984—. Mem. ABA, Mo. Bar Assn., Lawyers Assn. Kansas City, Kansas City Club (pres. 1974), Kansas City Country Club (pres. 1986), Rotary. Republican. Episcopalian. Avocations: hunting, golf, traveling. Home: 77 Le Mans Ct Shawnee Mission KS 66208-5230 Office: Spencer Fane Britt & Browne 1400 Commerce Bank Bldg 1000 Walnut St Kansas City MO 64106-2107

SPENCER, RICHARD PAUL, biochemist, educator, physician; b. N.Y.C., June 7, 1929; s. David E. and Frances (Fried) S.; m. Gwendolyn Enid Williams, Apr. 7, 1956; children: Carolyn Roberts, Jennifer Holt, Priscilla James. AB, Dartmouth Coll., 1951; MD, U. So. Calif., 1954; MA (NSF fellow, Helen Hay Whitney fellow), Harvard U., 1958, PhD, 1961. Intern Beth Israel Hosp., Boston, 1954-55; practice medicine specializing in nuclear medicine; mem. faculty biophysics U. Buffalo, 1961-63; chief radioisotope service VA Hosp., Buffalo, 1961-63; asso. prof. nuclear medicine Yale Sch. Medicine, 1963-68, prof., 1968-74; prof., chmn. dept. nuclear medicine U. Conn. Health Center, 1974—. Author: The Intestinal Tract, 1960, (with others) Biophysical Principles, 1965, Radionuclide Studies of the Spleen, 1975, Clinical Focus on Nuclear Medicine, 1977, Handbook of Nuclear Medicine, 1977, Therapy in Nuclear Medicine, 1978, Radiopharmaceuticals: Structure-Activity Relationships, 1981, Interventional Nuclear Medicine, 1984, New Procedures In Nuclear Medicine, 1988; contbr. (with others) articles to profl. jours. Mem. Am. Physiol. Soc., AAAS, Soc. Nuclear Medicine, Biophys. Soc. Achievements include discovery of functional asplenia; developed first complete description of relationship of food intake to reproductive success and to longevity in a species. Office: U Conn Health Ctr Farmington CT 06030

SPENCER, RICHARD THOMAS, III, healthcare industry executive; b. Oak Park, Ill., Mar. 18, 1936; s. Richard Thomas Jr. and Lois Anne (Pollock) S.; m. Andrea B. Schlickeiser, June 29, 1962; 1 child, Richard Thomas IV. BA, U. Mich., 1959; postgrad., U. Pa., 1976, Stanford U., 1984, Clemson U., 1985. Mktg. group Mobil Oil Co., Detroit, 1962; internat. trade specialist U.S. Dept. Commerce, Detroit, 1963-64; account exec. J.

Walter Thompson Co., Detroit, 1965-66; sales mgr. Sarns Inc., Ann Arbor, Mich., 1967-69; v.p. mktg. Cordis Dow Corp., Miami, Fla., 1970-81; pres. mktg. divsn. Cordis Corp., Miami, Fla., 1982-87; pres., CEO Uni-Med Internat. Corp., Miami, Fla., 1988—; exec. v.p., COO, bd. dirs. World Med. Mfg. Corp., Sunrise Fla.; cons. in field. Contbr. articles to profl. jours. With U.S. Army, 1959-61. Republican. Avocations: skiing, scuba diving, running, stereo equipment, geopolits. Office: Uni-Med Internat Corp PO Box 331120 Miami FL 33233-1120

SPENCER, ROBERT C., political science educator; b. Chgo., Mar. 28, 1920; m. Edith Maxham McCarthy, Sept. 13, 1941; children: Margaret, Catherine, Anne, Thomas More, David. AB, U. Chgo., 1943, MA, 1952, PhD in Polit. Sci. (Univ. fellow 1952-53), 1955. Instr. polit. sci. and sociology St. Michaels Coll., 1949-51, asst., then assoc. prof. polit. sci., 1953-60, prof. govt., 1960-63, dir. summer sessions, 1960-61, asst. to pres., 1963-65; prof. polit. sci., chmn. dept., dean summer sessions U. R.I., 1965-67; grad. dean U. R.I. (Grad. Sch.), 1967-69; founding pres. Sangamon State U., Springfield, Ill., 1969-78; prof. govt. and public affairs Sangamon State U., 1978-88, prof. emeritus, 1988—; research assoc. Indsl. Relations Center, U. Chgo., 1952-53; extension lectr. N.Y. State Sch. Indsl. and Labor Relations, Cornell U., 1956-57; vice chmn. West Central Ill. Ednl. Telecommunications Consortium, 1975-77, chmn., 1977-78; chmn. task force personnel Vt. Little Hoover Commn., 1957-58; mem. Ill. adv. com. U.S. Commn. on Civil Rights, 1979-87; bd. mgrs. Franklin Life Variable Annuity Funds, 1974—; vis. prof. polit. sci., sr. rsch. assoc. local govt. ctr. Mont. State U., Bozeman, 1985, 89, 90—. Author: (with Robert J. Huckshorn) The Politics of Defeat, 1971. Bd. dirs. City Day Sch., Springfield, 1979-83, Gt. Am. People Show Repertory Co., 1980-90; vice chmn. Petersburg Libr. Bd., 1982-88; chmn. Petersburg Zoning Bd. Appeals, 1984-90; mem. Vt. Senate, 1959-63; faculty fellow Ford Found.'s Nat. Ctr. for Edn. in Politics, rsch. dir. Dem. Nat. Com., 1962-63; mem. adv. bd. Landmark Preservation Coun. Ill., 1986-89; mem., treas. Gallatin County Coun. on Aging, 1993—. Roman Catholic. Home: 2303 S 3rd Ave Bozeman MT 59715-6009

SPENCER, ROGER FELIX, psychiatrist, psychoanalyst, medical educator; b. Vienna, Austria, Apr. 19, 1934; s. Eugene S. Spitzer and Santa (Kurz) Spencer; m. Barbara Ann Houser, Aug. 18, 1958; children—Geoffrey, Jennifer, Rebecca. B.S., Yale Coll., 1956; M.D., Harvard Med. Sch., 1959. Diplomate Am. Bd. Psychiatry. Intern, N.C. Meml. Hosp., Chapel Hill, 1959-60, resident in psychiatry, 1960-63; instr. U. N.C. Sch. Medicine, 1963-66, asst. prof., 1966-69, assoc. prof., 1969-76, prof., 1976—, dir. of liaison and cons., 1967-77, dir. out patient psychiatry, 1977-95. Recipient Career Tchr. award NIMH, 1965-67. Fellow Am. Psychiat. Assn., Am. Psychoanalytic Assn.; mem. N.C. Psychoanalytic Soc., N.C. Neuropsychiat. Assn., U. N.C. Recreation Assn. "The Farm." Contbr. articles to profl. jours. Office: UNC Hosps Psychiatry Dept CB 7160 Chapel Hill NC 27599

SPENCER, SAMUEL, lawyer; b. Washington, Dec. 8, 1910; s. Henry Benning and Katharine (Price) S.; children from previous marriage: Henry B., Janet Spencer Dougherty, Richard A.; m. June Byrne, May 29, 1982. Student, Milton (Mass.) Acad., 1924-29; A.B. magna cum laude, Harvard U., 1932, LL.B., 1935. Bar: N.Y. 1937, D.C 1938, U.S. Supreme Ct 1950. Assoc. Shearman & Sterling, N.Y.C., 1935-37, Covington, Burling, Rublee, Acheson & Shorb, Washington, 1937- 40, 45-47; ptnr. Spencer, Graham & Holderman, 1947—; pres. bd. commrs., D.C., 1953-56; pres., chmn. bd. Tenn. R.R. Co., 1956-73. Bd. dirs. Nat. Symphony Orch., 1949-51, Garfield Hosp., 1947-53, 56-62; bd. dirs. Children's Hosp., 1948-53, sec., 1951-53; trustee Potomac Sch., 1947-53; pres. Washington Hosp. Ctr., 1958-60, bd. dirs., 1958-65; mem. Washington Nat. Monument Soc., 1958-91. Served to comdr. USNR, 1940-45. Decorated Bronze Star with combat V. Mem. ABA, Bar Assn. D.C., Am. Cancer Soc. (trustee D.C. chpt. 1951-53), AIA (hon.), Washington Inst. Fgn. Affairs (bd. dirs. 1961-89, sec. 1961-81), Jud. Council D.C. Circuit (com. on adminstrn. of justice 1966-70), Soc. of Cincinnati, Phi Beta Kappa. Episcopalian (sr. warden). Clubs: Metropolitan of Washington (bd. govs. 1949-53, 56-61, pres. 1959-60); Chevy Chase (Md.). Home: 5904 Cedar Pky Bethesda MD 20815-4251 Office: 2000 Massachusetts Ave NW Washington DC 20036-1022

SPENCER, SAMUEL REID, JR., educational consultant, former university president; b. Rock Hill, S.C., 1919; m. Ava Clark; 1948; children: Samuel Reid, Ellen Spencer Henschen, Clayton, Frank. AB summa cum laude, Davidson Coll., 1940, LLD (hon.), 1964; MA, Harvard U., 1947, PhD, 1951; LHD (hon.), Oglethorpe U., 1977, Queens Coll., 1983, Bridgewater Coll., 1986, Marymount U., 1988, Hollins Coll., 1991, Mary Baldwin Coll., 1992; LittD (hon.), Washington and Lee U., 1991. With Vick Chem. Co., N.Y.C., 1940; research asst. to Grenville Clark, Dublin, N.H., 1947-48; asst. to pres. Davidson Coll., 1951-54, dean of students, asso. prof. history, 1954, dean of students, prof. history, 1955-57; pres. Mary Baldwin Coll., 1957-68; pres. Davidson (N.C.) Coll., 1968-83, pres. emeritus, 1983—; pres. Va. Found. for Ind. Colls., Richmond, 1983-88; sr. cons. Acad. Search Consultation Svc., 1989—; interim pres. Hollins Coll., 1990-91; dir. Piedmont Bank & Trust Co.; Fulbright lectr. U. Munich, 1965-66; mem. Bd. Fgn. Scholarships, 1980-83, chmn., 1982-83; bd. dirs. Assn. Am. Colls., 1976-83, chmn. assn., 1981-82; pres. So. Univ. Conf., 1979-80; mem. commn. govtl. relations Am. Council Edn., 1973-76. Author: Decision for War, 1917, 1953, Booker T. Washington and the Negro's Place in American Life, 1955, (with J. Garry Clifford) The First Peacetime Draft, 1986. Bd. dirs. Grenville Clark Fund, Dartmouth Coll., 1973—, Charlotte-Mecklenburg chpt. Urban League, 1979-83; trustee Agnes Scott Coll., 1975-91, Mary Baldwin Coll., 1996—; trustee Union Theol. Sem., Richmond, Va., 1985-94, chmn., 1988-94. Maj. AUS, 1940-45. Austin fellow Harvard, 1947-48; Rosenwald fellow, 1948-49; Kent fellow Nat. Council on Religion in Higher Edn., 1949-51. Mem. Fulbright Assn. (bd. dirs. 1989-92), Phi Beta Kappa, Omicron Delta Kappa. Presbyterian (bd. Christian edn.). Address: PO Box 1117 Davidson NC 28036-1117

SPENCER, WILLIAM A., physician, educational administrator; b. Oklahoma City, Feb. 16, 1922. B.S. cum laude, Georgetown U., 1942; M.D., Johns Hopkins U., 1946. Diplomate Am. Bd. Pediatrics. Intern Johns Hopkins Hosp Harriet Lane Home, Balt., 1946-47, resident, 1947-48; med. dir. Southwestern Poliomyelitis Respiratory Ctr., Houston, 1950-59; dir. Tex. Inst. Rehab. and Research, Houston, 1959-77; pres. Inst. for Rehab. and Research, Houston, 1977-88; instr. dept. pediatrics Baylor Coll. Medicine, Houston, 1950-55, asst. prof. dept. pediatrics, 1955-57, asst. prof. dept. physiology, 1954-57, prof., chmn. dept. rehab. medicine, 1957-88; vis. mem. grad. faculty Tex. A&M U., College Station; cons. staff VA Hosp., Houston; cons. spinal injury service and phys. medicine and rehab. VA Hosp., Houston; cons. dept. biomath. and phys. medicine and rehab. M.D. Anderson Hosp. and Tumor Inst., Houston; asst. attending physician Ben Taub Gen. Hosp., Houston; mem. active staff Tex. Children's Hosp., Houston, Inst. for Rehab. and Research, Houston; mem. courtesy staff St. Anthony's Ctr., Houston; Horowitz vis. prof. Inst. Phys. Medicine and Rehab., NYU Med. Ctr., 1964; mem. U. Houston Ctr. for Pub. Policy Adv. Council, 1981—; mem. VA Rehab., Research and Devel., Sci. Merit Rev. Bd., 1981—; mem. sci. adv. bd. Paralyzed Vets. Am. Tech. and Research Found., 1981—; mem. com. on health care of racial/ethnic minorities and handicapped persons Nat. Acad. Sci., 1980-81; mem. panel on testing of handicapped Nat. Acad. Sci., 1980-81; intermittent cons. Nat. Inst. Handicapped Research, Washington, 1979—; mem. Inst. Medicine, Nat. Acad. Scis., 1971—; mem. phys. medicine services adv. com. Joint Commn. on Accreditation of Hosps., 1972—; mem. med. commn. Rehab. Internat., 1977—; ad hoc mem. VA Sci. Rev. and Evaluation Bd. for Rehab. Engring. Research and Devel., 1981—. Cons. editor Jour. Am. Phys. Therapy Assn., 1965-71; mem. editorial bd. Med. Informatics Jour., Health Services Hosp. Research and Ednl. Trust, 1967-73, Computer Programs in Biomedicine, 1968—, Stroke-A Jour. of the Cerebral Circulation, 1969-70, Computers and Human Concern, 1973—, Am. Jour. Phys. Medicine, 1975—, Informatique Medicine, 1975—, Bull. Prosthetics Research, 1982—. Served to capt., M.C., U.S. Army, 1948-50. Recipient Physician's award Pres. Commn. on Employment of Handicapped, 1964, Gold medal 6th Internat. Congress Phys. Medicine, 1972, Disting. Citizens award Goodwill Industries, 1976. Mem. AMA, Am. Physiol. Soc., Am. Congress Rehab. Medicine (Gold Key 1972, Culter award 1978), AAAS, Tex. Med. Assn., Harris County Med. Soc., Houston Pediatric Soc., Nat. Rehab. Assn., N.Y. Acad. Scis., So. Med. Assn., So. Soc. Pediatric Research, Soc. Advanced Med. Systems, Assn. Computing Machinery, Am. Assn. Med. Systems and Informatics, Am. Documentation Inst., Internat. Rehab. Medicine Assn., Am. Acad. Orthopedics (assoc.), Am. Acad. Phys. Medicine (hon.), Am. Coll. Physicians in Computation, Tex. Soc. Profl. Engrs. (hon.), Nat. Assn. Rehab. and Research Ctrs. (exec. com. of bd. 1982—), Houston C. of C., Sigma Xi, Phi Beta Kappa, Alpha Omega Alpha. Office: Tex Inst Rehab & Rsch 1333 Moursund St Houston TX 77030-3405

SPENCER, WILLIAM COURTNEY, foundation executive, international business executive; b. Uniontown, Pa., Sept. 15, 1919; s. Clarence Ashley and Hazel (Stark) S.; m. Evelyn Van Cleve Bailey, Aug. 6, 1942; children: Courtney Lloyd, Henry Bailey, Edward Ashley. AB, Drew U., 1941; AM, Columbia U., 1946, EdD, 1952. Tchr. Scarsdale (N.Y.) Pub. Schs., 1946-49; dir. Univ. Sch. Columbia, 1949-52; prof. edn. and adminstrn. U. Del., 1952-55; prof., dir. grad. program tchr. edn. NYU, 1955-59, prof. higher edn. and internat. affairs, 1960-61; prof. adminstrn. U. Chile, Santiago, 1959-60; dir. Interam. affairs Inst. Internat. Edn. and asst. sec. gen. Coun. Higher Edn. in Am. Republics, 1961-65; assoc. dean Grad. Sch. Bus. Columbia U., 1965-67, spl. asst. to pres., 1967-69; pres. Western Coll., Oxford, Ohio, 1969-74, The Lindenwood Colls., 1974-79, Fund for Peace, 1979-80; v.p. Trans Internat. Mgmt. Corp., 1979-88; spl. adviser Fund for Higher Edn., 1979-82, pres., 1982-86; spl. asst. to pres. Internat. Exec. Svc. Corps, Stamford, Conn., 1988; dir. internat. devel. svcs. Nippon Manpower Ltd, Tokyo, 1988-91; pres. Trans Internat Exec. Svcs., 1988—; cons. UNESCO Latin Am. major project in edn., Chile, 1959-60, project edn. and econ. planning, India, 1962; cons. Am. Coun. Edn., 1960-61; del. Pan-Am Assembly on Population, 1965; mem. standing com. on internat. edn. Coll. Entrance Exam. Bd., 1972-74; cons. Am. Med. Internat. Inc., 1980, McGraw Hill Internat. Book Co., 1981, AID, Indonesia, 1982, Thermo-Electron Corp., China, 1984, Internat. Exec. Svc. Corps, Jamaica, 1989, Costa Rica, 1991, 93, Hungary, 1991. Author: Education and World Responsibility, 1965, also articles; editor: Art and the University, 1964, University and National Development, 1965, Agriculture and the University, 1965. Bd. dirs. Internat. Sch. Svc., 1963-69, chmn., 1967-69; mem. Mo. master planning com. Coordinating Bd. Higher Edn., 1975-79; pres. Ind. Colls. and Univs. of Mo., 1977-79; bd. dirs. St. Louis Coun. on World Affairs, 1977-79; mem. scholarship bd. Timken Co. Ednl. Fund, 1971-76; bd. dirs. Internat. Inst. Energy Conservation, 1984-89, Conn. River Mus., 1988—. Lt. comdr. USNR, 1942-46. Decorated Purple Heart; commendation medals from Royal Navy, U.S. Navy. Mem. Coun. Fgn. Relations, N.Y. Yacht Club, Essex (Conn.) Yacht Club, North Cove Yacht Club. Home: 100 Dudley Ave Apt C-11 Old Saybrook CT 06475-2336

SPENCER, WILLIAM FRANKLIN, SR., soil scientist, researcher; b. Carlinville, Ill., Mar. 4, 1923; s. Jesse H. and Mayme (Wohlert) S.; m. Marjorie Ann Hall, June 2, 1946; children: Barbara Annette, William Franklin Jr., Gary Alan. BS in Agr., U. Ill., 1947, MS in Chemistry, 1950, PhD in Agronomy, 1952. Asst. chemist U. Fla., Lake Alfred, 1951-54; soil scientist USDA Agrl. Rsch. Svc., Laramie, Wyo., 1954-55, Brawley, Calif., 1955-57; assoc. soil chemist U. Fla., Lake Alfred, 1957-62; rsch. leader USDA Agrl. Rsch. Svc., Riverside, Calif., 1962-95; mem. Western Soil & Water Rsch. Com., Riverside, 1965-75; cons. Cen. U., Maracay, Venezuela, 1959. Contbr. over 105 articles to profl. jours. With U.S. Army, 1943-46, PTO. Fellow AAAS, Am. Soc. Agronomy, Soil Sci. Soc. Am.; mem. Soc. Environ. Toxicology and Chemistry, Internat. Soil Sci. Soc., Gamma Sigma Delta, Sigma Xi. Methodist. Achievements include research on behavior and fate of pesticides. Home: 2935 Arlington Ave Riverside CA 92506-4450 Office: U Calif USDA Agrl Rsch Svc Riverside CA 92521

SPENCER, WINIFRED MAY, art educator; b. Tulsa, Oct. 7, 1938; d. Len and Madge (Scofield) S. BA in Comml. Art, U. Tulsa, 1961, Cert. in Tchg., 1962. Cert. comml. art, K-12 art, English/journalism tchr. Freelance comml. artist Tulsa, 1962-63; art/sci. educator Pleasant Porter Elem. Tulsa Pub. Schs., 1963-65, art educator, supervising tchr. Kendall Elem., 1965-70, art educator, team leader pilot program Bunche Elem., 1970-75, art educator Carnegie Elem., 1975-81, art educator, fine arts dept. chair Foster Jr. High, 1982-83, art educator, fine arts dept. chair Foster Mid. Sch., 1983—; judge Okla. Wildlife Arts Festival, Okla. Wildlife Assn., Tulsa, 1988; supervising tchr., tchr. tng. U. Tulsa, 1965-70, Northeastern State U., Tahlequah, Okla, 1965-70; pres. Tulsa Elem. Art Tchrs., Tulsa Pub. Schs., 1967-68, curriculum writing/curriculum cons., 1970-75, 91—; coord. summer arts/artists in the schs. program Tchr. Adv. Bd., Summer Arts Tulsa Arts and Humanities Coun., 1986-94. Exhibited in group shows at Tulsa City-County Ctrl. Libr., 1989, Philbrook Art Mus., 1993, 94. Mem. Rep. Nat. Com., 1994-96; art adv. PTA, Tulsa, 1970—; mem. Christian Sci. Ch., Tulsa, 1960—; mem. city of Tulsa goals for tomorrow task force on cultural affairs, 1995—. Invited U.S. China Joint Conf. on Edn., Citizen Amb. Program People to People Internat., 1992, U.S. Spain Joint Conf. on Edn., Citizen Amb. Program People to People Internat., 1995. Mem. AAUW, NEA, ASCD, Okla. Edn. Assn., Tulsa Classroom Tchrs. Assn., Okla. Mid. Level Edn. Assn. (del. 1994), Nat. Art Edn. Assn. (del. 1992, 94, 96), Okla. Art Edn. Assn. Avocation: travel. Home and Office: 439 S Memorial Dr Tulsa OK 74112-2203

SPENCER-DAHLEM, ANITA JOYCE, medical, surgical and critical care nurse; b. Weirton, W.Va., Aug. 26, 1961; d. Carlas A. and Evelyn Faye (Miller) Spencer; m. Terry Dahlem. BS, Alderson-Broaddus Coll., Philippi, W.Va., 1984. Cert. ACLS, ANCC. Staff nurse, orthopedic unit Charleston (W.Va.) Area Med. Ctr., 1984-86; ICU staff nurse Ohio Valley Hosp., Steubenville, Ohio, 1986—; nurse on cardiac catheterization unit Ohio Valley Hosp., Steubenville, 1994-97. Mem. Ohio Nurses Assn.

SPENGLER, DAN MICHAEL, orthopedic surgery educator, researcher, surgeon; b. Defiance, Ohio, Feb. 25, 1941; s. Harold A. and Wilhelmina Spengler; m. Cynthia Niswonger; children: Christina, Craig. BS, Baldwin-Wallace Coll., 1962; MD, U. Mich., 1966. Diplomate Am. Bd. Orthopaedic Surgery (bd. dirs. 1988-97). Rotating intern King County Hosp., Seattle, 1966-67; resident in orthopedics U. Mich., Ann Arbor, 1970-73; asst. prof. U. Wash., Seattle, 1974-78, assoc. prof., 1978-83; bd. dirs. Am. Bd. Orthopaedic Surgery. Author: Low Back Pain, 1982. Fellow Am. Acad. Orthopaedic Surgeons; mem. Am. Orthopaedic Assn., ACS, Am. Bd. Orthopaedic Surgeons (pres. 1993-94), Assn. Bone and Joint Surgeons, Internat. Soc. for Study of Lumbar Pain, U. Nashville Club. Avocations: flying, golf, running, skiing. Office: Vanderbilt U Dept Orthopedic Rehab 1211 21st Ave S # D-4208 Nashville TN 37212-2717

SPENSER, IAN DANIEL, chemist educator; b. Vienna, Austria, June 17, 1924; m. Anita Fuchs, Sept. 5, 1951; children: Helen Ruth, Paul Andrew. B.Sc. with honors, U. Birmingham (Eng.), 1948; Ph.D. in Biochemistry, U. London, 1952, D.Sc. in Organic and Biochemistry, 1969. Demonstrator in biochemistry King's Coll., U. London, 1948-52, asst. lectr. in biochemistry Med. Coll. St. Bartholomew's Hosp., 1952-54, lectr., 1954-57; postdoctoral fellow div. pure chemistry NRC Can., Ottawa, Ont., 1953-54; asst. prof. biochemistry McMaster U., Hamilton, Ont., Can., 1957-59; assoc.prof. McMaster U., 1959-64, prof., 1964-68, prof. chemistry, 1968-89, prof. emeritus, 1989—; Akademischer Gast Laboratorium für Organische Chemie/Eidgenössische Technische Hochschule, Zürich, Switzerland, 1971, 89; vis. prof. Inst. Organic Chemistry, Tech. U. Denmark, Lyngby, 1977, Inst. Organische Chemie/Univ. Karlsruhe, Fed. Republic Germany, 1981, Institut für Pharmazeutische Biologie, Universität Bonn, Federal Republic of Germany, 1989. Research in biosynthesis of alkaloids, biosynthesis of vitamin Bl and vitamin B6. Recipient Sr. Scientist award NATO, 1980; recipient Can.-Japan Exchange award, 1982-83, Univ. Club of Hamilton award, 1990. Fellow Royal Soc. Can., Chem. Inst. Can. (John Labatt Ltd. award 1982-83), Royal Soc. Chemistry (U.K.); mem. Biochem. Soc., Am. Soc. Biochemistry Molecular Biol., Am. Soc. Pharmacognosy, Phytochem. Soc. N. Am. Office: McMaster U, Dept Chemistry, Hamilton, ON Canada L8S 4M1

SPERAKIS, NICHOLAS GEORGE, artist; b. N.Y.C., June 8, 1943; s. George and Cathren (Cokatas) S.; m. Yolanda de Carmen Mesa, Feb. 1, 1983. Student, Pratt Inst., 1960, NAD, 1960-61, Art Students League N.Y., Pratt Graphic Art Center, 1961-63. Instr. Sumitt (N.J.) Art Center, 1971, New Sch. Social Research, N.Y.C., 1972—, Fashion Inst. Tech., N.Y.C., 1977—. Exhibited one-man shows at Paul Kessler Gallery, 1963, 64, Provincetown, Mass., Hinckley and Brohel Art Gallery, Washington, 1964, N.Y.C., 1965, Mari Galleries, Woodstock, N.Y., 1966, 67, 68, Larchmont, N.Y., 1967, Eric Schindler Galleries, 1965, Richmond (Va.) Art Gallery, N.Y. U. Student Loeb Center, 1969, L.I. U., 1971, Pratt Inst., 1971, Bienville Gallery, New Orleans, 1972, 74, Pace U., N.Y.C., 1972, Lerner-Heller Gallery, N.Y.C., 1975, 76, Daedal Gallery, Balt., 1976, Reading Mus. Art, (Pa.), 1977, Bklyn. Mus., 1977, Washington Irving Gallery, N.Y.C., 1982, Museo Universitario Del Chopo, Mexico City, 1984, Forum Gallery, N.Y.C., Mus. Contemporary Art, Bogota, The Atler Gallery, Munich, 1989, Galerieverein Blankenese, Hamburg, Fed. Republic Germany, 1988, Galeria Sextante, Bogota, 1989, La Francia, Centro de Arte, Medellin, Colombia, 1989, various woodcut exhbns., , Alexander S. Onassis Ctr. N.Y.U., 1995, others; exhibited group shows, Mercy Hurst Coll., Erie, Pa., 1963, 64, Bklyn. Mus., 1964, 77, Jewish Mus., 1964, Chrysler Mus., 1964, 65, Assoc. Am. Artists Galleries, N.Y.C., 1965, Norfolk (Va.) Mus. Arts Scis., 1965, Long Beach (Calif.) Coll., 1969, Am. Acad. and Nat. Inst. Arts and Letters, 1969, 75, Mid West Mus-Am-Art, 1981, numerous others, print exhbns., France, Italy, Spain, other European Countries, Far East, 1970-71, Lerner-Heller Gallery, 1973, 76, Amherst Coll., 1974, Worcester (Mass.) Mus. Fine Art, 1977, Reading (Pa.) Mus. Art, 1977, Galeria El Museo Santate de Bogota, Colombia, 1992, Mus. Modern Art, Rio de Janeiro, Brazil, 1992, travel Ams., Europe, 1992, Rhino Horn, N.Y.C., 1994, WhiteHall, N.Y.C., 1993, 94, Barnard/Biderman Fine Art, N.Y.C., 1994; represented in permanent collections Bklyn. Mus., Walter P. Chrysler Mus., Norfolk, Va., Norfolk Mus. Arts and Scis., N.Y.C. Public Library, Phila. Mus. Fine Arts, Worcester Mus. Fine Art, Flint (Mich.) Art Inst., Mus. Modern Art, N.Y.C., U. Conn., Storrs, Amherst Coll., Okla. Fine Arts Center Mus., Am. Acad. and Nat. Inst. Arts and Letters, Detroit Inst. Fine Art, Corcoran Gallery of Art, Midwest Mus. Am. Art, Exeter Acad., Conn., Mus. Modern Art, N.Y.C., print collections Nat. Mus. Am. Art Smithsonian Instn., DeHunter Mus. Art, Chattanooga, Libr. of Congress, Washington, High Mus. Art, Atlanta, Free Libr., Phila., Kunst Mus., Fine Arts Mus. Bern Switzerland, Australian Nat. Gallery, Canberra, Snite Mus. Art, U. Notre Dame, Ind., Bibliotheque Royale Albert/ER, Bruxelles, Belgium, Museo Rayo, Roldanillo, Colombia, Stedelijk Mus., Amsterdam, The Netherlands, Hirshhorn Mus., Washington, Mus. Modern Art Santa Fe de Bogota, Nordjyllands Kunstmus., Aalborg, Denmark, Banco Bozano Simonsen, Rio de Janeiro, Mus. Modern Art, Bogota, Rose Art Mus. Brandeis U., Conn.; organized (with others), Rhino Horn artist group, N.Y.C., 1970. Recipient First Prize Purchase award Mercy Hurst Coll., 1964; Lawrence and Hinda Rosenthal award Am. Acad. and Nat. Inst. Arts and Letters, 1969; Guggenheim graphics fellow, 1970; McDowell Colony summer residency, 1976. Mem. Soc. Am. Graphic Artists. Address: 245 W 29th St Floor 12A New York NY 10001 *Art doesn't bring out the voters for candidates X or Z. Art brings forth an experience and enters the knowledge of the viewer, so it helps the individual consider new channels and modes of behavior. One of the reasons there is so much censorship of art is due to the power art has to transform people at the roots not into some action but in a more generalized manner in terms of understanding institutions and traditions for what they really are. I think art changes emotions more than it changes specific ideas.*

SPERANDIO, GLEN JOSEPH, pharmacy educator; b. Glen Carbon, Ill., May 8, 1918; s. Henry A. and Marjorie (Dunstedter) A.; m. Dorys Bell, June 21, 1946; 1 child, James Glen. B.S., St. Louis Coll. Pharmacy, 1940; M.S., Purdue U., 1947, Ph.D., 1950. Pharmacist, 1936-41; analytical chemist Grove Labs., St. Louis, 1941-43, 45; mfg. pharmacist William R. Warner Co., St. Louis, 1944; instr. Purdue U., 1946-50, asst. prof. pharmacy, 1950-53, assoc. prof., 1953-62, prof., 1962—, head dept., 1966-78, assoc. dean, 1978-83, assoc. dean emeritus, 1984—; exec. dir. Ind. Soc. Hosp. Pharmacists, 1984—; indsl. cons., 1955-81; pharm. cons. VA Hosp., Indpls., 1963-69; mem. blue ribbon com. on standardized bd. exams. Nat. Assn. Bds. Pharmacy, 1969; cons. on clin. pharmacy Surgeon Gen., U.S. Army, 1973-80. Author: Laboratory Manual of Cosmetics, 1956, (with others) Scoville's Art of Compounding, 1959, (with others) Clinical Pharmacy, 1966; author, editor: (with others) Hosp. Pharmacy Notes, 1959-74. Served with USCGR, 1944. Named 1st prof. clin. pharmacy in U.S., Distinguished Alumnus St. Louis Coll. Pharmacy, 1969, Indian Sagamore of the Wabash, 1997. Mem. AMA, Am. Soc. Hosp. Pharmacists, Parenteral Drug Assn. (regional v.p. 1965-67), Nat. Formulary, Ind. Soc. Hosp. Pharmacists (pres. 1955-57, hon. mem., disting. educator 1980), Am. Pharm. Assn. (sec.-treas. sect. practical pharmacy 1956), Ind. Pharm. Assn., Tipp County Pharm. Assn., Internat. Fedn. Pharmacists, Soc. Cosmetic Shemists, Am. Legion, Masons (32 deg.), Golden Key, Sigma Xi, Kappa Psi (nat. svc. award 1967, nat. pres. 1963-67), Rho Chi, Phi Lambda Upsilon. Research in drug, cosmetic formulation. Home: PO Box 2509 West Lafayette IN 47906-0509 Office: Purdue U Sch Pharmacy Lafayette IN 47907 *A great help in solving problems is to look at the situation from the other person's point of view.*

SPERANZA, PAUL SAMUEL, JR., lawyer; b. Rochester, N.Y., May 12, 1947; s. Paul Samuel and Rosemary Gloria (Patti) S.; m. Cheryl Ann Amering, June 27, 1969; children: Sarah, Martha. BS, Syracuse U., 1969; JD, U. San Francisco, 1971; LLM in Taxation, NYU, 1972. Bar: N.Y., Calif., Pa., U.S. Supreme Ct., U.S. Tax Ct., U.S. Ct. Appeals (2d cir.). Assoc. Martin, Dutcher, Cooke, Mousaw & Vigdor, Rochester, 1972-73; ptnr. Wegman, Mayberry, Burgess, Feldstein & Speranza, Rochester, 1973-76; gen. counsel, sec., bd. dirs. Wegmans Food Markets, Inc., Rochester, 1976—; chmn. fin. and acctg., tax and human resources com., audit retirement plan com. Wegmans Food Markets, Inc.; mem. govt. rels. tax and steering coms. N.Y. State Bus. Coun., Albany, 1984—; bd. dirs., counsel, sec. Wegmans Fed. Credit Union, Rochester, 1984—. Contbr. articles to profl. publs. Bd. dirs., chmn. various coms. Our Lady of Mercy H.S., Rochester, 1988-94, chmn. bd., 1990-93; bd. dirs. Blue Cross Blue Shield of the Rochester Area, 1995—; capt. fund raiser Syracuse U. Capital Fund, 1988. Mem. ABA (sects. on adminstrv. law, antitrust, closely held corps., tort and ins. practice, labor and employment law, real property, probate and trust law, taxation), Tax Execs. Inst., Food Mktg. Inst. (chmn. lawyers and economists com. 1991-93, mem. govt. rels., tax, lawyers and economists coms. 1983—), Am. Corp. Counsel Assn., N.Y. State Bar Assn. (sects. on labor, taxation, corp., negligence, antitrust, estates and trusts), Pa. Bar Assn., Monroe County Bar Assn. (corp. counsel sect.), Internat. Coun. Shopping Ctrs., Nat. Assn. Real Estate Execs., Urban Land Inst., Syracuse U. Soc. of Fellows. Republican. Roman Catholic. Avocations: charities, helping economically disadvantaged youth, running, travel, food. Home: 45 Grosvenor Rd Rochester NY 14610-2513 Office: Wegmans Food Markets Inc 1500 Brooks Ave # 844 Rochester NY 14624-3512

SPERBER, DANIEL, physicist; b. Vienna, Austria, May 8, 1930; came to U.S., 1955, naturalized, 1967; s. Emanuel and Nelly (Liberman) S.; m. Ora Yuval, Nov. 29, 1963; 1 son, Ron Emanuel. M.Sc., Hebrew U., 1954; Ph.D., Princeton U., 1960. Tng. and rsch. asst. Israel Inst. Tech., Haifa, 1954-55, Princeton U., 1955-60; sr. scientist, rsch. adviser Ill. Inst. Tech. Rsch. Inst., Chgo., 1960-67; assoc. prof. physics Ill. Inst. Tech., 1964-67, Rensselaer Poly. Inst., Troy, N.Y., 1967-72; prof. Rensselaer Poly. Inst., 1972—; Nordita prof. Niels Bohr Inst., Copenhagen, 1973-74, NATO research fellow, vis., prof., 1974-77; vis. prof. G.S.I., Darmstadt, Fed. Republic Germany, 1983; sr. Fulbright research scholar, Saha Inst. Nuclear Physics, Calcutta, India, 1987-88. Contbr. over 100 sci. papers to profl. jours. Served to capt. Israeli Army, 1948-51. Fellow Am. Phys. Soc.; mem. Israel Phys. Soc., N.Y. Acad. Scis., Sigma Xi. Jewish. Home: 1 Taylor Ln Troy NY 12180-7162 Office: Rensselaer Poly Inst Dept Physics Troy NY 12180-3590 *My goals are to further an understanding of nature by basic research in nuclear theory and to introduce a new generation to this research.*

SPERBER, MARTIN, pharmaceutical company executive, pharmacist; b. N.Y.C., Aug. 6, 1931; s. David and Gertrude (Besen) S.; m. Ellen Claire Marx, June 7, 1953; children—Steven Jay, Susan Barbara Parnes. B.S., Columbia U., N.Y.C., 1952. Registered pharmacist. Pharmacist, dir. sales and mktg. Henry Schein, Inc., N.Y.C., 1953-65, v.p., 1965-80; pres., chief oper. officer Henry Schein, Inc., Port Washington, N.Y., 1980-89, vice chmn., 1989—, also bd. dirs.; pres., chief oper. officer Schein Pharm., Inc., Port Washington, 1985-89, chmn., chief exec. officer, 1989—, also bd. dirs.; chmn., chief exec. officer Danbury Pharm. Inc., Carmel, N.Y., 1989—, also bd. dirs.; chmn., chief exec. officer Steris Labs., Inc., Phoenix, 1989—, also bd. dirs. Mem. coun. of overseers Arnold and Marie Schwartz Coll. Pharmacy, L.I. U. Mem. Am. Pharm. Assn. Office: Schein Pharm Inc 100 Campus Dr # 375 Florham Park NJ 07932-1006*

SPERDUTO, LEONARD ANTHONY, mathematics educator; b. Philadelphia, Jan. 19, 1958; s. Anthony and Lena (Maio) S. AAS, Camden County Coll., Blackwood, N.J., 1982, 87; BA, Rutgers U., 1989. Cert. tchr. math., N.J. Math. tutor Rutgers U., Camden, N.J., 1987-89; substitute tchr. Maple Shade (N.J.) Bd. Edn., 1989-90; math. tutor Camden County Coll.,

Blackwood, 1992-94, adj. instr. basic skills math., 1992—. Mem. Nat. Coun. Tchrs. Math. Home: 6849 Clark Ave Camden NJ 08105-3101 Office: Camden County Coll PO Box 200 Blackwood NJ 08012

SPERELAKIS, NICHOLAS, SR., physiology and biophysics educator, researcher; b. Joliet, Ill., Mar. 3, 1930; s. James and Arestia (Kayadakis) S.; m. Dolores Martinis, Jan. 28, 1960; children: Nicholas Jr., Mark, Christine, Sophia, Thomas, Anthony. BS in Chemistry, U. Ill., 1951; diploma, U.S Navy & Marine Corps Electronics Sch., 1952; MS in Physiology, U. Ill., 1955, PhD in Physiology, 1957. Teaching asst. U. Ill., Urbana, 1954-57; instr. Case Western Res. U., Cleve., 1957-59, asst. prof., 1959-66, assoc. prof., 1966; prof. U. Va., Charlottesville, 1966-83; Joseph Eichberg prof. physiology Coll. Medicine U. Cin., 1983-96, chmn. dept., 1983-93, Eichberg prof. emeritus, 1996—; cons. NPS Pharm., Inc., Salt Lake City, 1988-95, Carter Wallace, Inc. Cranbury, N.J., 1988-91; vis. prof. U. St. Andrews, Scotland, 1972-73, U. San Luis Potosi, Mex., 1986, U. Athens, Greece, 1994; Rosenblueth prof. Centro de Investigacion y Avanzades, Mex., 1972; mem. sci. adv. com. several internat. meetings, editorial bd. numerous sci. jours. Co-editor: Handbook of Physiology: Heart, 1979; editor: Physiology and Pathophysiology of the Heart, 1984, 2d edit., 1988, 3d edit., 1995, Calcium Antagonists: Mechanisms of Action on Cardiac Muscle and Vascular Smooth Muscle, 1984, Cell Interactions and Gap Junctions, vols. I and II, 1989, Frontiers in Smooth Muscle Research, 1990, Ion Channels in Vascular Smooth Muscle and Endothelial Cells, 1991, Essentials of Physiology, 1992, 2d edit., 1996, Cell Physiology Source Book, 1995 (Outstanding Acad. Book, Choice Am. Libr. Assn. 1996), Electrogenesis of Biopotentials, 1995; assoc. editor Circulation Rsch., 1970-75, Molecular Cellular Cardiology; contbr. articles to profl. jours.; author/co-author over 500 rsch. publs. and book chpts. Lectr. Project Hope, Peru, 1962. Sgt. USMC, 1951-53, Res., 1953-59. Recipient Disting. Alumnus award Rockdale (Ill.) Pub. Schs., 1958; U. Cin. Grad. fellow, 1989; NIH grantee, 1959—. Mem. Am. Physiol. Soc. (chair steering com. sect. 1981-82), Biophys. Soc. (coun. 1990-93), Am. Soc. Pharmacology and Exptl. Therapeutics, Internat. Soc. Heart Rsch. (coun. 1980-89, 92—), Am. Heart Assn. (established investigator 1961-66, Rsch. Merit award 1995, Sam Kaplan Rsch. award, 1996), Am. Hellenic Ednl. Progressive Assn. (pres. Charlottesville chpt. 1980-82), Ohio Physiol. Soc. (pres. 1990-91), Phi Kappa Phi. Democrat. Greek Orthodox. Avocations: ancient coins, stamp collecting. Office: U Cin Coll Medicine 231 Bethesda Ave Cincinnati OH 45229-2827 *One of the most important contributions to society and civilization that we can make is to express our serious and urgent concern for the well-being of planet Earth, the environment, plants, animals, and humans, and to educate the public worldwide accordingly.*

SPERING, MARK ANDREW, optometrist; b. Montrose, Pa., Oct. 1, 1969; s. Henry L. and Mary Ann (Sipe) S.; m. Kimberly Ann Scherer, July 9, 1994. BS in Natural Sci., Indiana U. Pa., 1991; BS in Optometry, Pa. Coll. Optometry, 1992, OD, 1994. Pvt. practice, Erie, Pa., 1994-95, Allentown, Pa., 1995—. Mem. Am. Optometric Assn. (specialist in contact lens divsn.), Pa. Optometric Assn., Lehigh Valley Optometric Soc. Avocations: tennis, reading, travel, music. Office: Allentown Eye Assocs PC 2004 W Allen St Allentown PA 18104-5053

SPERLING, ALLAN GEORGE, lawyer; b. N.Y.C., Dec. 10, 1942; s. Saul and Gertrude (Lober) S.; m. Susan Kelz, June 27, 1965; children: Matthew Laurence, Stuart Kelz, Jane Kendra. Bar: N.Y. 1969, U.S. Ct. Appeals (2d cir.) 1975. Law clk. to presiding justice U.S Dist Ct., New Haven, 1967-68; assoc. Cleary, Gottlieb, Steen & Hamilton, N.Y.C., 1968-75, ptnr., 1976—. Editor Yale Law Jour. Chmn. bd. Merce Cunningham Dance Found., N.Y.C., 1992—, vice-chmn., 1985-92; chmn. bd. Rye (N.Y.) Arts Ctr. Inc., 1985-88, bd. dirs., 1990-94; bd. dirs. Friends of the Neuberger Mus., Purchase, N.Y., 1989—. Mem. ABA, N.Y. State Bar Assn., Order of Coif, Phi Beta Kappa. Home: Kirby Ln Rye NY 10580 Office: Cleary Gottlieb Steen & Hamilton 1 Liberty Plz New York NY 10006-1404

SPERLING, ELLIOT HARRIS, history educator; b. N.Y.C., Jan. 4, 1951; s. Solomon and Edith (Kantor) S.; m. Annie Joly, Apr. 10, 1982; 1 child, Coline Joly. BA, Queens Coll., CUNY, 1973; MA, Ind. U., 1980, PhD, 1983. Vis. asst. prof. of history U. So. Miss., Hattiesburg, 1984-85; asst. prof. of Tibetan studies dept. of Uralic and Altaic studies Ind. U., Bloomington, 1986-93; vis. asst. prof. of Tibetan and Himalayan studies, dept. Sanskrit and Indian studies Harvard U., Cambridge, Mass., 1992-93; assoc. prof. of Tibetan studies, dept. ctrl. Eurasian studies Ind. U., 1993—; vis. lecturer U. Delhi, India, 1994-95. Contbr. articles to profl. jours. John D. & Catherine T. MacArthur Found. fellow, 1984-89, Fulbright scholar, 1994-95. Mem. The Tibet Soc., The Mongolia Soc., The Am. Oriental Soc., The Assn. for Asian Studies. Democrat. Jewish. Office: Ind U Dept Ctrl Eurasian Studies Goodbody Hall Bloomington IN 47405

SPERLING, GEORGE, cognitive scientist, educator; s. Otto and Melitta Sperling. BS in Math., U. Mich., 1955; MA in Psychology, Columbia U., 1956; PhD in Psychology, Harvard U., 1959. Rsch. asst. in biophysics Brookhaven Nat. Labs., Upton, N.Y., summer 1955; rsch. asst. in psychology Harvard U., Cambridge, Mass., 1957-59; mem. tech. rsch. staff Acoustical and Behavioral Rsch. Ctr., AT&T Bell Labs., Murray Hill, N.J., 1958-86; prof. psychology and neural sci. NYU, N.Y.C., 1970-92; disting. prof. cognitive scis. and psychobiology U. Calif., Irvine, 1992—; instr. psychology Washington Sq. Coll., NYU, 1962-63; vis. assoc. prof. psychology Duke U., spring 1964; adj. assoc. prof. psychology Columbia U., 1964-65; acting assoc. prof. psychology UCLA, 1967-68; hon. rsch. assoc. Univ. Coll., U. London, 1969-70; vis. prof. psychology U. Western Australia, Perth, 1972, U. Wash., Seattle, 1977; vis. scholar Stanford (Calif.) U., 1984; mem. sci. adv. bd. USAF, 1988-92. Recipient Meritorious Civilian Svc. medal USAF, 1993; Gomberg scholar U. Mich., 1953-54; Guggenheim fellow, 1969-70. Fellow AAAS, APA (Disting. Sci. Contbn. award 1988), Am. Acad. Arts and Sci., Optical Soc. Am.; mem. NAS, Assn. for Rsch. in Vision and Ophthalmology, Ann. Interdisciplinary Conf. (founder, organizer 1975—), Eastern Psychol. Assn. (bd. dirs. 1982-85), Soc. for Computers in Psychology (steering com. 1974-78), Psychonomic Soc., Soc. Exptl. Psychologists (Warren medal 1996), Soc. for Math. Psychology (chmn. 1983-84, exec. bd. 1979-85), Phi Beta Kappa, Sigma Xi. Office: U Calif SS Plz A Dept Cognitive Scis Irvine CA 92697

SPERLING, GEORGE ELMER, JR., lawyer; b. Phila., Feb. 5, 1915; s. George E. and Margaret Ethel (Fulton) S.; m. Elizabeth Ruth Smollett, Feb. 3, 1945; children: Mary Elizabeth, Doris Fulton, Patricia Anne. A.B., Pa. State Coll., 1936, M.A., 1937; J.D., U. Mich., 1940. Bar: Mich. 1940. Practice in Ann Arbor, 1940-42; counsel Standard Oil Co., Cleve., 1943-45, Carnation Co., Los Angeles, 1946-82; asst. sec. Carnation Co., 1951-63, sec., 1963-82, mem. jr. bd. dirs., 1952-62; v.p. Buckley & Sperling, Monterey, Calif., 1982-85; ptnr. Buckley, Sperling & Frey, Monterey, 1985-87; ptnr. Buckley & Sperling, Santa Monica, 1987—, pres., 1992—. Chmn. Wilshire YMCA, 1952—; pres. Brentwood Protective Assn., 1958-60; trustee Bel Air Town and Country Sch.; mem. pres.' coun. San Francisco Theol. Sem., San Anselmo, Calif., 1993—; pres. Clara Schmidt Found., 1992—. Mem. Navy League, Pa. State Coll. Alumni Assn. of So. Calif. (v.p.), Mich., Ohio, Calif., Wis. bar assns., Brentwood Youth Council (pres. 1959). Presbyn. Clubs: Toastmasters, Riviera Country, President's (U. Mich.). Lodge: Miracle Mile Kiwanis (pres. dir.). Home: 347 25th St Santa Monica CA 90402-2521 *The most important thing for a person to do is to keep your mind alert at all times. You will never get old if you keep thinking of ways to help your country, your neighbors, your friends, and yourself.*

SPERLING, GODFREY, JR., journalist; b. Long Beach, Calif., Sept. 25, 1915; s. Godfrey and Ida (Bailey) S.; m. Betty Louise Feldmann, June 22, 1942; children—Mary (Mrs. John H. McAuliffe), John Godfrey. B.S., U. Ill., 1937; J.D., U. Okla., 1940. Bar: Ill. bar 1940. Practice in Urbana, Ill.; also reporter Champaign-Urbana News-Gazette, 1940-41; mem. staff Christian Sci. Monitor, 1946—, Midwest bur. chief, 1957-62, N.Y. bur. chief, 1962-65, news mgr., asst. chief Washington bur., 1965-73, nat. polit. corr., 1970-83, chief Washington Bur., 1973-83, sr. Washington columnist, 1984—; lectr. nat. affairs, 1955—, Woodrow Wilson vis. fellow, 1976—. Served to maj. USAAF, 1941-46; col. Res. Recipient Alumnus Achievement award U. Ill., 1987, Spl. Citation, Nat. Press Found. for unique contbns. to Am. journalism, 1994. Mem. Okla. Bar Assn., Ill. Bar Assn., Mass. Bar Assn., Congl. Press Corr. Assn., White House Press Corr. Assn., Nat. Press Club (Washington), Overseas Writers Club (Washington), Gridiron of Washington (pres. 1991), Sperling Breakfast Group (host 1966—), Navy Officers Club (Bethesda), Cosmos Club (Washington), Sigma Delta Chi. Christian Scientist. Home: 8101 Connecticut Ave N500 Chevy Chase MD 20815 Office: Christian Science Monitor 910 16th St NW Washington DC 20006-2903

SPERLING-ORSECK, IRENE, publishing company executive. V.p., pub. Tradeshow Week, L.A. Office: Tradeshow Week 5700 Wilshire Blvd Los Angeles CA 90036-3659*

SPERO, BARRY MELVIN, medical center executive; b. Richmond, Va., July 13, 1937; s. Stanley Leo and Jean (Marmorstein) S.; m. Merle Burns, May 29, 1960; children: Amy, Robin, Melissa. BA, U. Richmond, 1959; MHA, Med. Coll. Va., 1961. Asst. adminstr. Bapt. Hosp., Nashville, 1963-66, adminstrv. dir., 1966-68; v.p., dir. hosp. adminstrn. Hosp. Affiliates, Inc., Nashville, 1968-71; exec. dir. Bon Secours Hosp., Grosse Pointe, Mich., 1971-77; pres. The Mt. Sinai Med. Ctr., Cleve., 1977-85; pres., pres. NeWell Health Care System Newton-Wellesley Hosp., 1985-90; pres. Maimonides Med. Ctr., Bklyn., 1990-95, Masonicare, Wallingford, Conn., 1995—. Mem. pers. practice com. Combined Jewish Philanthropies; chmn. United Way, West Suburban Hosp. Div.; regional bd. Bay Bank Middlesex; mem. Perpetual Benevolent Fund Com., Blue Print 2000, Commonwealth Mass.; bd. dirs. Premier Health Alliance, chmn., 1981-84, Premier Preferred Care, Healthfirst; trustee Villa Maria Nursing Ctr./Bon Secours Hosp., 1974-94, chmn., bd. dirs., 1988-94; bd. dirs. Conn. Assn. Not-for-Profit Providers for the Aging, 1995—, League Vol. Hosps. and Homes, 1991-95, chmn.-elect, 1992-95; mem. State of Ohio Gov.'s Commn. on Health Care Cost, 1984-85; mem. various coms. Coun. Tchg. Hosps., 1992-95; treas. Vol. Hosps. Am., Mass., 1986-90; chmn. hosp. adv. com. Blue Cross N.E. Ohio, 1983-85; trustee Med. Instrumentation Sys., 1978-84; mem. various coms. Am. Assn. Homes and Svcs. for the Aging, 1995—. Fellow Am. Coll. Healthcare Execs.; mem. Greater N.Y. Hosp. Assn. (bd. govs. 1992-94), Am. Hosp. Assn. (com. on Medicare payment for outpatient svcs. 1989-90), Mass. Hosp. Assn. (bd. trustees 1987-90, com. on Medicare payment for outpatient svcs. 1989-90), Mass. Hosp. Assn. (bd. trustees 1987-90, com. on health systems 1986-90, Met. Boston Hosp. Coun. (chmn. 1988-90), New Eng. Healthcare Assembly (Blue Ribbon com. 1985-90), Ohio Hosp. Assn. (exec. coun., bd. trustees 1981-85), Greater Cleve. Hosp. Assn. (exec. coun., bd. trustees 1978-85), Coun. Tchg. Hosps. (various coms. 1992-94), Conn. Hosp. Assn. (bd. dirs. 1997—). Jewish. Avocations: golf, tennis, scuba diving. Office: Masonicare PO Box 70 Wallingford CT 06492

SPERO, JOAN EDELMAN, foundation president; b. Davenport, Iowa, Oct. 2, 1944; d. Samuel and Sylvia (Halpern) Edelman; m. C. Michael Spero, Nov. 9, 1969; children: Jason, Benjamin. Student, L'Inst. d'Etudes Politiques, Paris, 1964-65; BA, U. Wis., 1966; MA, Columbia U., 1968, PhD, 1973. Asst. prof. Columbia U., N.Y.C., 1973-79; ambassador of U.S. to UN Econ. and Social Council, N.Y.C., 1980-81; v.p. Am. Express Co., N.Y.C., 1981-83, sr. v.p. internat. corp. affairs, 1983-89; treas., sr. v.p., 1989-91; exec. v.p. corp. affairs and communications Am. Express Co., 1991-93; under sec. for econ., bus. and agrl. affairs Dept. of State, Washington, 1993-97; pres. Doris Duke Charitable Found., N.Y.C., 1997—; vis. scholar Fed. Res. Bank N.Y., 1976-77. Author: The Politics of International Economic Relations, 5th edit., 1997, The Failure of the Franklin National Bank, 1980; contbr. articles to profl. jours. Trustee Amherst Coll.; bd. dirs. French-Am. Found.; mem. Coun. Am. Ambassadors. Named to Acad. Women Achievers, YWCA, 1983; named Fin. Woman of Yr., Fin. Women's Assn., 1990; recipient George Washington Disting. Statesperson award, 1994; Woodrow Wilson fellow. Mem. Coun. on Fgn. Rels. (Internat. Affairs fellow), The Trilateral Commn., Svcs. Policy Adv. Com., Phi Beta Kappa. Democrat. Jewish. Avocations: writing; swimming. Office: Doris Duke Charitable Found 39th Fl 1585 Broadway Fl 39 New York NY 10036-8200

SPERO, NANCY, artist; b. Cleve., 1926. BFA, Sch. Art Inst. Chgo., 1949; student, Ecole des Beaux-Arts, Paris, 1950, Atelier Andre l'Hote, Paris, 1950. One-woman shows include Hewlett Gallery, Carnegie-Mellon U., Pitts., 1989, Rhona Hoffman Gallery, Chgo., 1986, Inst. Contemporary Art, London, 1987, Everson Mus. Art, Syracuse, N.Y., 1987, Mus. Contemporary Art, L.A., 1988, Smith Coll. Mus. Art, Northampton, Mass., 1990, Haus am Walsee, Berlin, Germany, 1990, Barbara Gross Galerie, Munich, Salzburger Kunstverein, Austria, 1991, Christine König Gallery, Vienna, Austria, 1992, Ulmer Mus., Ulm, Germany, 1992, Josh Baer Gallery, N.Y.C., 1993, Nat. Gallery Can., Ottowa, 1993, Greenville (S.C.) County Mus. Art, 1993, Rhona Hoffman Gallery, Chgo., 1994, Printworks, Chgo., 1994, Kunststichting Kanaal Art Found., Kortrijk, Belgium, 1994, Malmö (Sweden) Konsthall, 1994, Am. Ctr., Paris, MIT List Visual Arts Ctr., Cambridge, 1994, Arthur M. Sackler Mus., Harvard U., 1995, Fine Arts Gallery, U. Md. Baltimore County, 1995, Barbara Gross Galerie, Munich, 1995, N.Y. Kunsthalle, 1996, Vancouver Art Gallery, 1996, Hiroshima City Mus. Contemporary Art, 1996, Jüdisches Mus. der Stadt Wien, 1996, Heeresspital, Innsbruck, Tyrol, 1996, Jack Tilton Gallery, N.Y.C., 1996, PPOW Gallery, N.Y.C., 1996, others; exhibited in group shows at The Biennial of Sydney, Australia, 1986, Mus. Modern Art, N.Y.C., 1988, The Bertha and Karl Leubsdorf Art Gallery, Hunter Coll., N.Y.C., 1988, Le Grande Halle de La Villette, Paris, 1989, Bullet Space, N.Y.C., 1989, Ctr. Internat. d'Art Contemporain, Montreal, 1990, Dum Umeni Mesta Brna, Brünn, Czechoslowakia, 1991, Boston (Mass.) U. Art Gallery, 1991, Mus. der Stadtentwässerung, Zurich, 1994, Stichting Artimo, Beurs van Berlage, Amsterdam, 1994, Sch. Art Inst. Chgo., Betty Rymer Gallery, Chgo., 1994, MIT List Visual Arts Ctr., Cambridge, 1995, Southeastern Ctr. for Contemporary Art, Winston-Salem, N.C., 1995, Ctr. Georges Pompidou, Paris, 1995, Uffizi Gallery, Florence, Italy, 1995, Mus. Modern Art, N.Y.C., 1996, numerous others.

SPERTUS, PHILIP, investment company executive; b. Chgo., 1934; grad. MIT, 1956. With Intercraft Industries Corp., Chgo., pres., 1969-79, chmn. bd., 1979-92, also chief exec. officer and dir. Office: 3321 Bee Caves Rd Ste 333 Austin TX 78746-6769

SPERZEL, GEORGE E., JR., personal care industry executive; b. 1951. BS in Bus. Adminstrn./Mgmt., U. Louisville, 1977. With General Electric Co., 1977-93; with Andrew Jergens Co., Cin., 1993—, now v.p., CFO; v.p., CFO Kao Corp. of Am., Wilmington, Del., 1995—. Office: Andrew Jergens Co 2535 Spring Grove Ave Cincinnati OH 45214-1729 also: Kao Corp Am Ste 404 902 Market St Wilmington DE 19801

SPETH, JAMES GUSTAVE, United Nations executive, lawyer; b. Orangeburg, S.C., Mar. 4, 1942; s. James Gustave and Amelia St. Clair (Albergotti) S.; m. Caroline Cameron Council, July 3, 1965; children: Catherine Council, James Gustave, Charles Council. BA summa cum laude, Yale U., 1964, LLB, 1969; MLitt, Oxford U., 1966; LLD (hon.), Clark U., 1995. Bar: D.C. 1969. Law clk. to Justice Hugo L. Black U.S. Supreme Ct., 1969-70; sr. staff atty. Natural Resources Def. Council, Washington, 1970-77; mem. Council Environ. Quality, Washington, 1977-79, chmn., 1979-81; prof. law Georgetown U. Law Ctr., Washington, 1981-82; pres. World Resources Inst., Washington, 1982-93; adminstr. UN Devel. Program, N.Y.C., 1993—; founded World Resources Inst.; organized Western Hemisphere Dialogue environ. and devel., 1990; chaired U.S. Task Force internat. devel. and environ. security. Contbr. articles to profl. jours.; speaker in field. Bd. dirs. World Resources Inst., Nat. Resources Def. Coun., Woods Hole Rsch. Ctr., Keystone Ctr., Leadership award 1994. Recipient Resources Def. award Nat. Wildlife Fedn., 1976, Barbara Swain award of honor Nat. Resources Coun. Am., 1992; named to Global 500 Honor Role United Nations Environ. Program, 1988; Rhodes scholar, 1964-66. Mem. Coun. on Fgn. Rels. (N.Y.C.), China Coun. for Internat. Coop. on Environment and Devel. Episcopalian. Office: UNDP 1 United Nations Plz New York NY 10017-3515

SPETRINO, RUSSELL JOHN, retired utility company executive, lawyer; b. Cleve., Apr. 22, 1926; s. John Anthony and Madeline Spetrino; m. Marilyn Folk, July 17, 1954 (dec.); children: Michael J., Ellen A. Spetrino Raines; m. Mildred Pilkton, June 26, 1993. B.S., Ohio State U., 1950; LL.B., Western Res. U., 1954. Bar: Ohio 1954. Asst. atty. gen. Ohio, 1954-57; atty.-examiner Public Utilities Commn. of Ohio, Columbus, 1957-59; atty. Ohio Edison Co., Akron, 1959-69, sr. atty., 1970-73, gen. counsel, 1973-78, v.p., gen. counsel, 1978-87, exec. v.p., gen. counsel, 1987-89, ret., 1989. Served with inf. U.S. Army, 1944-46. Mem. Portage Country Club. Republican. Home: 333 N Portage Path Unit 34 Akron OH 44303-1252 *The importance of—and the strength that can be derived from—simple intellectual honesty never ceases to amaze me. It is so much easier to deal successfully with others when every effort is made to understand their views, and your own views are based upon thoughtful, honest conviction.*

SPEVACK, MARVIN, English educator; b. N.Y.C., Dec. 17, 1927; s. Nathan and Miriam (Propper) S.; m. Helga Husmann, May 28, 1962; 1 child, Edmund Daniel. B.A., CCNY, 1948; M.A., Harvard U., 1950, Ph.D., 1953. Instr. English CCNY, 1955-61; asst. prof. City Coll. N.Y., 1961-63; prof. English, U. Muenster, Germany, 1963-89, dir. English seminar, 1964-89, dir. Inst. Erasmianum, 1974-89; Fulbright lectr. U. Münster, Germany, 1961-62; vis. prof. U. Munich, 1962-63, NYU, summer 1966, Harvard U., summer 1973, U. N.Mex., 1985-86, Bowling Green State U., fall 1989; fellow Folger Shakespeare Libr., 1970; hon. rsch. fellow Univ. Coll., London, 1980-81, 95—; vis. fellow Wolfson Coll., Cambridge (Eng.) U., 1984; scholar-in-residence Ctr. for Renaissance and Baroque Studies, U. Md., spring 1989; vis. rsch. fellow Inst. for Advanced Studies in Humanities, U. Edinburgh, Scotland, 1991. Author: Harvard Concordance to Shakespeare, 1973, A Complete and Systematic Concordance to the Works of Shakespeare, 9 vols., 1968-80, Robert Burton, Philosophaster, 1984, Shakespeare: The second, Third, and Fourth Folios, 1985, New Cambridge Julius Caesar, 1988, Shakespeare-Text, Language and Criticism: Essays in Honor of Marvin Spevack, 1988, New Variorum Antony and Cleopatra, 1990, A Shakespeare Thesaurus, 1993; also articles and editions. Served with AUS, 1953-55. Guggenheim fellow, 1973-74, Andrew W. Mellon Found. fellow Huntington Libr., 1992, Ctr. for Book fellow Brit. Libr., London, 1994-95. mem. MLA, Internat. Assn. Univ. Profs. English, Internat. Shakespeare Assn., The Bibliog. Soc., Deutsche Shakespeare Gesellschaft W., Shakespeare Assn., Soc. Textual Scholarship, Harvard Club (N.Y.C.), Harvard of Rhein-Ruhr Club (Germany, Phi Beta Kappa. Home: 14 Potstiege, 48161 Münster Germany Office: 12-20 Johannisstrasse, 48143 Münster Germany

SPEWOCK, THEODOSIA GEORGE, reading specialist, educator; b. Canton, Ohio, Sept. 11, 1951; d. George Eleftherios and Despina George (Ilvanakis) Sideropoulos; m. Michael Andrew Spewock, Aug. 23, 1974. BS, Kent State U., 1974; MEd in reading, Pa. State U., 1978; cert. in early childhood edn., Ind. U. of Pa., 1989, cert. elem. prin., 1994; postgrad., Pa. State U. Tchr. Winnisquam Regional Sch. Dist., Tilton, N.H., 1974-77; reading specialist Tyrone (Pa.) Area Sch. Dist., 1978-80, home-sch. liaison, 1980—, title 1 coord., 1994—; chair adv. bd. Family Ctr., Tyrone, 1994; steering com. Altoona Reading Inst., Altoona, Pa., 1991—; chair state reading conf. Keystone Reading Assn., 1994-96. Creator and host (weekly radio story hour): Mrs. Spewock & Friends, 1990—; author: Just for Five's, 1995, Just for Four's, 1995, Just for Three's, 1995, Just for Two's, 1995, Just for One's, 1995, Just for Babies, 1995, Getting Ready to Read, 1996; contbr. articles to profl. jours. Assoc. contbr. Altoona Symphony Orch., 1994; mem. adv. bd. strategic planning Tyrone Area Sch. Dist., 1994; rep. Pa. in Washington D.C., 1992. Recipient Dist. Svc. award Tyrone Area Cmty. Orgn., 1992, Outstanding Employee award, 1989. Mem. Keystone State Reading Assn. (pres. 1995), Internat. Reading Assn., Blair County Reading Coun. (pres. 1986-88), Assn. Supervision and Curriculum Devel., Nat. Assn. Edn. Young Children, Pa. Assn. Fed. Program Coords., Phi Delta Kappa. Avocations: piano, reading, folk dancing, cross-country skiing, walking for fitness. Office: Tyrone Area Sch Dist 1317 Lincoln Ave Tyrone PA 16686-1415

SPEYRER, JUDE, bishop; b. Leonville, La., Apr. 14, 1929. Ed., St. Joseph Sem., Covington, La., Notre Dame Sem., New Orleans, Gregorian U., Rome. Ordained priest Roman Cath. Ch., 1953. Consecrated bishop Lake Charles, La., 1980—. Office: PO Box 3223 414 Iris St Lake Charles LA 70602*

SPEZIALE, A. JOHN, organic chemist, consultant; b. Rocky Hill, Conn., Nov. 3, 1916; s. Antonio and Giovina (DiMarco) S.; m. Dorothy Baumeister, May 2, 1942; children: Dona Speziale Luedde, Karen Speziale Hutcheson, Wendy Speziale Tarson. B.S. in Pharmacy, U. Okla., 1942, M.S., 1943; Ph.D., U. Ill., 1948. With Monsanto Co., St. Louis, 1948-79; sr. scientist agrl. div. Monsanto Co., 1960-63; dir. research Monsanto Agrl. Products Co., 1963-79; chem., agrl. and indsl. cons., 1979—; vis. lectr. Washington U., St. Louis, 1950-53; bd. dirs. Mycogen Corp., EOSystem, Inc. Author publs. Served with U.S. Army, 1944-46. Recipient Kenneth A. Spencer award, 1981. Mem. AAAS, Am. Chem. Soc. (exec. com. organic div. 1974-76, mem. editorial bd. Jour. Organic Chemistry 1964-69, lectr. 1970-74, St. Louis sect. award 1973), Weed Sci. Soc. Am. (hon.), Sigma Xi. Patentee synthesis and mechanism action pesticides, phosphorus chemistry, enamines, epoxides, heterocyclics, haloamides. Home: 2635 Saklan Indian Dr Apt 2 Walnut Creek CA 94595-3020

SPEZIALE, JOHN ALBERT, lawyer; b. Winsted, Conn., Nov. 21, 1922; s. Louis and Mary (Avampato) S.; m. Mary Kocsis, Aug. 12, 1944; children: John Albert, Marcia Jean. BA in Econs., Duke U., 1943, JD, 1947. Bar: Conn. 1948. Clk. Judiciary Com. of Conn. Gen. Assembly, 1949; judge Mcpl. Ct., Torrington, Conn., 1949-51; dir. CD, 1951-52; fed. atty. OPS, 1951-52; mem. Conn. State Jud. Council, 1955-59; sr. partner firm Speziale, Mettling, Lefebre & Burns, Torrington, 1958-61; city atty. Torrington, 1957-59; treas. State of Conn., 1959-61; judge Conn. Ct. Common Pleas, 1961-65, Conn. Superior Ct., 1965-77; presiding judge Conn. Superior Ct. (Appellate div.), 1975-77, chief judge, 1975-77, mem. exec. com., 1975-84, chmn. exec. com., 1977-81; justice Conn. Supreme Ct., 1977-81, chief ct. adminstr., 1978-81, chief justice, 1981-84; sr. ptnr. Cummings & Lockwood, Hartford, 1984-92; of counsel, 1992—; state trial referee Conn., 1986—; mem. exec. com. Nat. Conf. State Trial Judges, 1970-74; faculty advisor grad. session Nat. Coll. State Judiciary, U. Nev., 1973; mem. Conn. Jud. Rev. Coun., 1975-77; co-chmn. planning commn. criminal adminstrn. Conn. Justice Commn., 1975-78; mem. Conn. Commn. on Adult Probation, 1976-77, Adv. Coun. on Ct. Unification, 1976-78, Conn. Bd. Pardons, 1977-78; mem. exec. com. Nat. Bd. Trial Advocacy, 1983-88, dir. 1988—; mem. mediation com. Ctr. Pub. Resources, 1985—. chmn. State-Fed. Relations Com. Conf. of Chief Justices, 1983-84; chmn. adv. bd. Use of Vol. Lawyers to Supplement Jud. Resources, Nat. Inst. Justice and Nat. Ctr. for State Ctrs., 1983-87; mem. lawyers com. Nat. Ctr. for State Cts., 1985-88; chmn. subcom. jud. decisions Nat. Assn. Ins. Commrs. adv. Com. Environ. Liability Ins., 1985-87; mem. Panel of Trial and Appellate Judges, Asbestos Claims Facility, 1986—;l arbitrator Ins. Arbitration Forums, Inc., 1986—; others. Trustee Conn. Jr. Republic, 1975-83; bd. dirs. Newington Children's Hosp. 1983-86, corporator 1983—; chmn. awards com. Freedoms Found. at Valley Forge, 1982, trustee Nat. Council, 1986—; fellow Pvt. Adjudication Found. Duke U. Sch. Law, 1986—. Lt. (j.g.) USNR, 1942-46, PTO. Recipient Conn. Trial Lawyers Jud. award, 1977; 1st Unico Nat. Disting. Key award, 1977; Citizen of Yr. award Elks, 1982; Alva P. Loiselle lifetime achievement award, 1984; Disting. Service award Nat. Ctr. for State Cts., 1985; Significant Practical Achievement award Ctr. for Pub. Resources Legal Program, 1985; Conn. Law Rev. award, 1985. Fellow Am. Bar Found. (life), Conn. Bar Found. (charter life fellow, chmn. James W. Cooper fellows 1994—); mem. ABA (vice chmn. 1984-86, com. on stds. jud. adminstrn. jud. adminstrn. divsn.), Inst. Jud. Adminstrn., Am. Judicature Soc. (dir. 1978-82), Conn. Bar Assn. (com. on alternative dispute resolution 1985-87, com. on liaison with state cts. 1986-92), Hartford Bar Assn., Litchfield County Bar Assn., Supreme Ct. Hist. Soc., Am. Arbitration Assn. (comml. panel arbitrators 1987—, panelist large complex case program 1993—), Am. Fedn. Musicians (life), Sons of Italy of Am., Conn. State Srs. Golf Assn., Inc., Litchfield Country Club, Torrington Country Club, Union Club (life), Bear Lakes Country Club (Fla.), K.C., Phi Beta Kappa. Roman Catholic. Home: 278 Wind Tree Torrington CT 06790-7904 Office: Cummings & Lockwood City Place 1 Hartford CT 06103

SPEZZANO, VINCENT EDWARD, newspaper publisher; b. Retsof, N.Y., Apr. 3, 1926; s. Frank and Lucy S.; m. Marjorie Elliott, Dec. 18, 1948; children: Steve, Judy, Mark, Christine (dec.). BA in Journalism, Syracuse (N.Y.) U., 1950. Reporter Livingston Republican, Geneseo, N.Y., 1950-51, Lynchburg (Va.) News, 1951-54, St. Louis Globe-Democrat, 1954-55; polit. writer, then dir. public service and research Rochester (N.Y.) Times Union, 1955-68; dir. public service, then dir. promotion and public service Gannett Co., Inc., 1968-75; pres., publisher Cape Publs., Inc., Cocoa, Fla., 1975-84; chmn. Cape Publs., Inc., 1984-91; asst., then v.p. Gannett/South, Gannett Co., Inc., 1977-79; pres. Gannett Southeast Newspaper Group, Gannett Co.,

Inc., 1979-82; exec. v.p. USA Today, 1982-83, pres., 1983; sr. v.p. communications Gannett Co., 1983-84, bd. dirs.; pres., pub. Gannett Rochester Newspapers, 1984-90, chmn., 1990-91; pres. Gannett N.E. Div., 1984-86; past mem. journalism endowment adv. com. U. Fla.; bd. dirs. Marine Midland Bank. Editor handbook. Past trustee St. John Fisher Coll., Rochester; trustee Brevard Art Ctr. and Mus., Melbourne, Fla.; bd. dirs. Cape Canaveral Hosp., 1991—, Fla. Inst. Tech., 1991—, Astronauts Meml. Found., 1991—, vice-chmn., space camp adv. bd.; bd. vice-chmn. Rochester Conv. Bur., 1986-91; mem. Founder's Com. The Rochesterians, 1986—; mem. adv. bd. Space Pioneers, Inc. With A.C., USNR, 1944-46. Recipient News Ariting award Va. Press Assn., 1953, Citizen of Yr. award Citizens Club Rochester, 1960, Disting. Svc. award for non-members Kiwanis Club, 1960, Pub. Svc. Reporting award Am. Polit. Sci. Assn., 1963; named NE Kiwanis Citizen of Yr., 1987, Boss of Yr. Coca Beach chpt. Nat. Secretaries Assn., 1977, Rochester Communicator of Yr., 1987, Rochester Citizen of Yr., 1987, Cavaliere (Knight) in Order of Merit Republic of Italy, 1994. Mem. Internat. Newspaper Promotion Assn. (pres. 1970-71, Silver Shovel award 1975), Am. Newspapers Pubs. Assn., So. Newspaper Pubs. Assn. Found. (chmn.), Fla. Press Assn. (bd. dir., pres. 1984), N.Y. Newspaper Pubs. Assn. (bd. dirs.), Cocoa Beach Area C. of C., Rochester Area C. of C. (bd. dir. 1985—, chmn. bd. 1989-90). Roman Catholic. Home: 855 S Atlantic Ave Cocoa Beach FL 32931-2424 Office: 1 Gannett Plz Melbourne FL 32940 also: Cape Pubs Inc PO Box 363000 Melbourne FL 32936

SPHEERIS, PENELOPE, film director; b. New Orleans, 1945. MFA, UCLA Film Sch. Producer: TV series of shorts for Saturday Night Live; films include: The Decline of Western Civilization II: The Metal Years, 1988, Real Life, 1979; dir. (documentary) the Decline of Western Civilization, 1981, (films) Suburbia, 1984, (also screenwriter) The Boys Next Door, 1985, Hollywood Vice Squad, 1986, Dudes, 1987, Wayne's World, 1992, The Beverly Hillbillies, 1993, The Little Rascals, 1994; screenwriter: Summer Camp Nightmare, 1987; actress: Wedding Band, 1990; tv films directed include: Prison Stories: Women on the Inside, 1990, Black Sheep, 1996. Office: The Gersh Agency Inc 232 N Canon Dr Beverly Hills CA 90210-5302*

SPHIRE, RAYMOND DANIEL, anesthesiologist; b. Detroit, Feb. 12, 1927; s. Samuel Raymond and Nora Mae (Allen) S.; m. Joan Lois Baker, Sept. 5, 1953; children—Suzanne M., Raymond Daniel, Catherine J. BS, U. Detroit, 1948; MD, Loyola U., Chgo., 1952. Diplomate Am. Bd. Anesthesiology. Intern Grace Hosp., Detroit, 1952-53; resident Harvard Anesthesia Lab.-Mass. Gen. Hosp., 1953-55; attending anesthesiologist Grace Hosp., Detroit, 1955-72, dir. dept. inhalation therapy, 1968-70; sr. attending anesthesiologist, dir. dept., dir. dept. respiratory therapy Detroit-Macomb Hosps. Assn., 1970—, trustee, 1978—, chief of staff, 1980—; clin. asst. prof. Wayne State U. Sch. Medicine, 1967—; clin. prof. respiratory therapy Macomb Community Coll., Mount Clemens, Mich., 1971—; examiner Am. Registry Respiratory Therapists, 1972—; insp. Joint Rev. Com. Respiratory Therapy Edn., 1972—. Co-author: Operative Neurosurgery, 1970, First Aid Guide for the Small Business or Industry, 1978. With AUS, 1944-45; 1st lt. M.C., USAF, 1952. Fellow Am. Coll. Anesthesiologists, Am. Coll. Chest Physicians; mem. AMA, Am. Soc. Anesthesiologists, Wayne County Soc. Anesthesiologists (pres. 1967-69), Am. Assn. Respiratory Therapists, Soc. Critical Care Medicine, Detroit Athletic Club, Country Club of Detroit, Cumberland Club (Portland, Maine), Severance Lodge. Roman Catholic. Home: 19874 Westchester Dr Clinton Township MI 48038-6417 Office: 119 Kercheval Ave Grosse Pointe MI 48236-3618

SPICE, DENNIS DEAN, investment banking and financial consultant; b. Rochester, Ind., Feb. 7, 1950; s. Donnelly Dean and Lorene (Rhodes) S.; m. Linda Kay Buehler, Oct. 1, 1971; children: Kristie Lorene, Danielle Deanne. AA, SUNY, Albany, 1974; BA, Eastern Ill. U., 1978; MBA, U. Ill., Urbana, 1985. Employee benefits mgr. Eastern Ill. U., Charleston, 1977-80; disbursements officer State Univs. Retirement System, Champaign, Ill., 1980-81, asst. dir. adminstrn., 1981-85, assoc. exec. dir., 1985-90, exec. dir., 1991-95; pres., CEO Instnl. Advisors, Ltd., Champaign, 1995—; mem. dean's adv. bd. Ea. Ill. U. Lumpkin Coll. Bus. and Applied Scis.; bd. dirs. Ea. Ill. Univ. Found. Staff sgt. USMC, 1968-77; Vietnam. Mem. Econ. Club Chgo., Champaign C. of C., Execs. Club of Chgo. Office: Instnl Advisors Ltd 5008 W Bluebill Rd Ste 200 Champaign IL 61821-9512

SPICER, HOLT VANDERCOOK, speech and theater educator; b. Pasadena, Calif., Feb. 1, 1928; s. John Lovely and Dorothy Eleanor (Clause) S.; m. Marion Arel Gibson, Aug. 16, 1952; children: Mary Ellen, Susan Leah, Laura Alice, John Millard. BA, U. Redlands, 1952, MA, 1957; PhD, U. Okla., 1964. From instr. speech and theatre to prof. Southwest Mo. State Coll., 1952-93, emeritus prof., 1993—, head dept. speech and theatre, 1967-71, dean Sch. Arts and Humanities, 1971-85; chmn. Dist. 4 Nat. Debate Tournament Com., 1955, 58, 64, 68. Bd. dirs. Springfield Community Ctr., Mo., 1981—. Named Debate Coach of Decade U.S. Air Force Acad., 1965, Holt V. Spicer Debate Forum, 1988; recipient Alumni Achievement award in Speech and Debate U. Redlands, 1991; team won CEDA Nat. Debate championship, 1992. Mem. Speech Communication Assn., Am. Forensic Assn., AAUP. Episcopalian (vestryman 1981-85). Home: 2232 E Langston St Springfield MO 65804-2646 Office: SW Mo State U 901 S National Ave Springfield MO 65804-0027

SPICER, JOHN AUSTIN, physicist; b. Rock Springs, W.Va., Sept. 25, 1930; s. Ernest Marvin and Ruth (Stevens) S.; m. Erika Gruendig, 1959; children: Cynthia, Michael, Marilynn. BS, U. Wyoming, 1956, MS, 1957; PhD, U. Freiburg, Germany, 1962. Mathematician Geotech. Corp., Laramie, Wyo., 1956-57; physicist Goodyear Aerospace Corp., Litchfield, Ariz., 1962-63; head engr. Aerojet Gen. Corp., Azusa, Calif., 1963-64; mathematical analyst North Am. Aviation Info. Systems Div., Downey, Calif., 1973-76; program mgr. Chrysler Space Systems Div., New Orleans, La., 1966-68; sr. research mathematician U. Dayton Research Inst., Ohio, 1968-70; ops. research analyst U. McCall Printing Corp. Systems Dept., Dayton, 1970-71; mathematician Systems Dyamics Br. AF Flight Dynamics La., 1971-72; physicist Radar and Microwave Tech. Br. AF Avionics lab., 1972-74, Analysis and Evaluation Br. AF Avionics Lab., 1974-89; physicist tech group, target recognition br. AF Avionics Lab., Dayton, Ohio, 1989—. Contbr. articles on neural networks, wavelets and fractal methodology to profl. jours.; presenter in field. Achievements include inventing "exact stability," which is a numerical integration routine that yields a dead beat response, that is, always stable and controllable, reaches equilibrium in minimum time, and is always stable. Home: 4666 N State Route 235 Conover OH 45317-9601 Office: WL/AACR Bldg 620 WL/ACCR Dayton OH 45433-7001

SPICER, WILLIAM EDWARD, III, physicist, educator; b. Baton Rouge, Sept. 7, 1929; s. William Edward II and Kate Crystal (Watkins) S.; m. Cynthia Stanley, June 12, 1951 (div. 1969); children: William Edward IV, Sally Ann; m. Diane Lubarsky, Apr. 24, 1969; 1 dau., Jacqueline Kate. B.S., Coll. William and Mary, 1949, MIT, 1951; M.A., U. Mo., 1953, Ph.D., 1955; D.Tech. (hon.), U. Linköping, Sweden, 1975. Scientist RCA Labs, 1955-61, Lawrence Radiation Lab., U. Calif.-Livermore, 1961-62; mem. faculty Stanford U., 1962—, prof. elec. engring. and materials sci. engring., 1965—, prof. by courtesy applied physics, 1976—, Stanford Ascherman prof. engring., 1978—, prof. Stanford Synchrotron Radiation Lab, 1992—; dir. Acad. Skills, Inc., Los Altos, Calif., 1971-73; dep. dir. Stanford Synchrotron Radiation Lab., 1973-75, cons. dir., 1975—, prof., 1992—; cons. to govt. and industry, 1962—; mem. solid state sci. panel Nat. Acad. Sci.-NRC, 1965-73; cons., lectr. Chinese Univ. devel. project World Bank-Fudan U., 1983; mem. panel atomic and molecular physics div. Nat. Bur. Standards, 1966-73, chmn., 1971-73; mem. adv. group election devices Dept. Def., 1975-82; fellow Churchill Coll., Cambridge U., Eng., 1979; mem. panel Japanese tech. evaluation program U.S. Dept. Commerce and NSF, 1983-84; acting dir. Stanford Photon. Lab., 1972; chmn. affiliated faculty Stanford Syncrotron Radiation Lab., 1988-92. Mem. editorial bd. Jour. Crystal Growth, 1981-85; author publs. theory and experiment solid state and surface physics and chemistry, photoemission, optical properties solids, electronic structure metals, semiconductors, insulators, high temperature superconductors. Bd. dirs. Princeton (N.J.) YMCA, 1960-62. Recipient Achievement award RCA, 1957, 60, mentor award Nat. Conf. Black Phys. Students, 1992; named Scientist of Yr., Indsl. Research and Devel. mag., 1981; Guggenheim fellow, 1978-79. Fellow IEEE, Am. Phys. Soc. (Oliver Buckley Solid State Physics prize 1980), Am. Vacuum Soc. (chmn. electronics material div. 1978-79, dir. 1979-80, trustee 1981-82, Medard W. Welch award 1984); mem. Phi Beta Kappa. Home: 785 Mayfield Ave Palo Alto CA 94305-1043 Office: Stanford U Mccullough Bldg Stanford CA 94305

SPIEGEL, DANIEL LEONARD, lawyer; b. Balt., Sept. 5, 1945; s. William and Anna (Stiffman) S.; m. Marianne Albertson; 1 child, Anna. AB, Washington U., St. Louis, 1967; MPA, Harvard U., 1969; JD, Georgetown U., Washington, 1979. Legis. asst. U.S. Senate, Washington, 1969-76; spl. asst. to Sec. of State Dept. of State, Washington, 1977-78, mem. policy planning staff, 1978-79; ptnr. Akin, Gump, Strauss, Hauer, LLP, Washington, 1983-90, dir. internat. practice, 1991-93, head internat. policy practice, 1997—; amb., permanent rep. U.S. Mission to UN, Geneva, 1993-96. Sr. advisor Clinton-Gore transition Dept. of State, Washington, 1992-93. Office: US Mission to UN, Rt de Pregny 11, 1292 Chambesy Switzerland

SPIEGEL, EVELYN SCLUFER, biology educator, researcher; b. Phila., Mar. 20, 1924; d. George and Helen (Laurantos) Sclufer; m. Melvin Spiegel, Apr. 16, 1955; children: Judith Ellen, Rebecca Ann. BA, Temple U., 1947; MA, Bryn Mawr Coll., 1951; PhD, U. Pa., 1954. Asst. program dir. for regulatory biology NSF, Washington, 1954-55; instr. in biology Colby Coll., Waterville, Maine, 1955-59; rsch. assoc. Dartmouth Coll., Hanover, N.H., 1961-74, rsch. assoc. prof. biology, 1974-78, rsch. prof. biology, 1978-91; rsch. prof. biology emerita, 1991—; vis. scholar Calif. Inst. Tech., Pasadena, 1964-65, U. Calif.-San Diego, La Jolla, 1970, Nat. Inst. for Med. Rsch., Mill Hill, Eng., 1971, NIH, Washington, 1975-76, U. Basel (Switzerland) Bicocenter, 1979, 80, 81, 82, 85. Contbr. numerous articles to profl. jours., chpts. to books and book reviews. Mem. Soc. for Devel. Biology, Marine Biol. Lab. Corp. (trustee 1981-86, 88-92). Office: Dartmouth Coll Dept Biol Scis Hanover NH 03755

SPIEGEL, HART HUNTER, retired lawyer; b. Safford, Ariz, Aug. 30, 1918; s. Jacob B. and Margaret (Hunter) S.; m. Genevieve Willson, Feb. 12, 1946; children: John Willson, Claire Margaret Spiegel Brian, Jennifer Emily Spiegel Grellman. BA, Yale U., 1940, LLB, 1946. Bar: Calif. 1946, D.C. 1960. Assoc. Brobeck, Phleger & Harrison, San Francisco, 1947-55, ptnr., 1955-90; chief counsel IRS, Washington, 1959-61, mem. adv. group to commr., 1975. Served to lt. USMC, 1942-46, PTO. Mem. ABA (coun. mem. tax sect. 1966-68), Am. Law Inst., Bar Assn. San Francisco (pres. 1983), Pacific Union Club, Berkeley Tennis Club (pres. 1964-65). Home: 3647 Washington St San Francisco CA 94118-1832 Office: Brobeck Phleger & Harrison 1 Market Pla Spear St Tower San Francisco CA 94105

SPIEGEL, HERBERT, psychiatrist, educator; b. McKeesport, Pa., June 29, 1914; s. Samuel and Lena (Mendlowitz) S.; m. Natalie Shainess, Apr. 24, 1944 (div. Apr. 1965); children: David, Ann; m. Marcia Greenleaf, Jan. 29, 1989. B.S., U. Md., 1936, M.D., 1939. Diplomate: Am. Bd. Psychiatry. Intern St. Francis Hosp., Pitts., 1939-40; resident in psychiatry St. Elizabeth's Hosp., Washington, 1940-42; practice medicine specializing in psychiatry N.Y.C., 1946—; attending psychiatrist Columbia-Presbyn. Hosp., N.Y.C., 1960—; faculty psychiatry Columbia U. Coll. Physicians and Surgeons, 1960—; adj. prof. psychology John Jay Coll. Criminal Justice, CUNY, 1983—; mem. faculty Sch. Mil. Neuropsychiatry, Mason Gen. Hosp., Brentwood, N.Y., 1944-46. Author: (with A. Kardiner) War Stress and Neurotic Illness, 1947, (with D. Spiegel) Trance and Treatment: Clinical Uses of Hypnosis, 1978; subject of book: (by Donald S. Connery) The Inner Source: Exploring Hypnosis with Herbert Spiegel, M.D.; Mem. editorial bd.: Preventive Medicine, 1972; Contbr. articles to profl. jours. Mem. profl. advisory com. Am. Health Found.; mem. pub. edn. com., smoking and health com. N.Y.C. div. Am. Cancer Soc.; mem. adv. com. Nat. Aid to Visually Handicapped. Served with M.C. AUS, 1942-46. Decorated Purple Heart. Fellow Am. Psychiat. Assn., Am. Coll. Psychiatrists, Am. Soc. Clin. Hypnosis, Am. Acad. Psychoanalysis, Internat. Soc. Clin. and Exptl. Hypnosis, William A. White Psychoanalytic Soc., N.Y. Acad. Medicine, N.Y. Acad. Scis.; mem. Am. Orthopsychiat. Assn., Am. Psychosomatic Soc., AAAS, AMA, N.Y. County Med. Soc. Office: 19 E 88th St New York NY 10128-0557

SPIEGEL, JERROLD BRUCE, lawyer; b. N.Y.C., Apr. 11, 1949; s. Seymour S. and Estelle (Minsky) S.; m. Helene Susan Cohen, Mar. 3, 1972; children: Dana Sean, Amy Barrett, Evan Tyler. BS, Queens Coll., 1970; JD cum laude, NYU, 1973. Bar: N.Y. 1974. Assoc. Austrian, Lance & Stewart, N.Y.C., 1973-75, Gordon Hurwitz Butowsky Baker Weitzen & Shalov, N.Y.C., 1975-79; ptnr. Shapiro Spiegel Garfunkel & Driggin, N.Y.C., 1979-86, Frankfurt, Garbus, Klein & Selz P.C., N.Y.C., 1986—. Editor Ann. Survey Am. Law, 1972-73,. Mem. ABA (corp. law sect.), Order of the Coif, Omicron Delta Epsilon. Office: Frankfurt Garbus Klein & Selz PC 488 Madison Ave New York NY 10022-5702

SPIEGEL, JOHN WILLIAM, banker; b. Indpls., Mar. 14, 1941; s. William Sordon and Elizabeth (Hall) S.; children: W. Robert, John F., Bradley H.; m. Elizabeth Devereux Morgan, Aug. 16, 1986; stepchildren: David P. Adams III, Morgan G. Adams, Devereux Socas. BA, Wabash Coll., 1963; MBA, Emory U., 1965; postgrad., Nova U., 1993-97. Rsch. assoc. IMEDE (Mgmt. Inst.), Lausanne, Switzerland, 1965-66; mgmt. trainee Trust Co. Bank, Atlanta, 1966-67, bond portfolio mgr., 1967-72; data processing mgr. Trust Co. Ga., Atlanta, 1972-78, treas., 1978-85; exec. v.p., chief fin. officer SunTrust Banks Inc., Atlanta, 1985—; mem. exec. com. CFO divsn. ABA, 1987-90, chair, 1989-90; former instr. Morehouse Coll. and Banking Schs. Mem. exec. com., bd. dirs. Alliance Theatre, Atlanta, 1985-92, pres., 1989-91; bd. dirs. High Mus. Art, Atlanta, 1985—; pres. Young Audiences Atlanta Inc., 1981-84, bd. dirs., 1985, mem. adv. bd., 1986—; pres. bd. visitors Grady Meml. Hosp., Atlanta, 1983-90; v.p. exec. bd. Atlanta Area coun. Boy Scouts Am., 1983-92, treas., 1989-91, mem. adv. bd., 1992; mem. adv. coun. Ga. State U. Sch. Accountancy, 1981-85, chmn. curriculum subcom., 1983-84; mem. exec. com., trustee Morehouse Sch. Medicine, 1984-93, chmn. fin. com., 1987-90, chmn., 1990-92; mem. Leadership Atlanta, 1976—, trustee, 1990-94; trustee, mem. exe. com. Robert W. Woodruff Arts Ctr. Inc., 1976—, treas., 1976-83, chmn. fin. com., 1984-89, 93—; chmn. fin. com., bd. dirs. Schenck Sch., Atlanta, 1986-88; exec. vice chmn. bd. trustees Holy Innocents Episcopal Sch., Atlanta, 1976-79, bd. dirs., treas., 1987-90; bd. dirs. Atlanta Opera, 1986—, United Way Met. Atlanta, Inc., 1994—, Rock Tenn. Co., Sallie Mae, Conti Fin. Corp., Suburban Lodges Am., Inc.; mem. Emory U. Bd. Visitors, 1991-95. Episcopalian. Home: 3043 Nancy Creek Rd NW Atlanta GA 30327-1901 Office: SunTrust Banks Inc PO Box 4418 Atlanta GA 30302-4418

SPIEGEL, LAWRENCE HOWARD, advertising executive; b. N.Y.C., Oct. 9, 1942; s. Melvin Arthur and Rose (Black) S.; m. Christy Mansfield; children from previous marriage: Robert, David. BA, NYU, 1963. Print buyer William Esty Co., N.Y.C., 1964-65, broadcast buyer, 1965-66; media planner Batten, Barton, Durstine & Osborn, Inc., N.Y.C., 1966-67, media supr., 1967-68, assoc. media dir., 1969-72, v.p., 1972-74; media group head Jack Tinker & Ptnrs., N.Y.C., 1968-69; v.p. Tracy-Locke, Dallas, 1974-80, sr. v.p., 1980-84, exec. v.p., 1984-89; prin. The Richards Group, Dallas, 1989—; pres. Tex. Coun. Advt., 1991—. Guest editor Mktg. and Media Decision mag., June 1982. Mem. Dallas Cable Bd., 1983-86; chmn. mktg. com. U. Tex., Dallas, 1984-89; pres. Cable Access Dallas, Inc., 1985-86; trustee Dallas Symphony Assn., 1978—; bd. dirs. Equest Inc., 1991-92; bd. dirs. I Have a Dream Found., 1994-96. Mem. Assn. Broadcasting Execs. Tex. (pres. 1975-76), Am. Women in Radio and TV, Inc. (bd. dirs. 1992-93). Republican. Avocations: skiing, sailing. Office: The Richards Group 8750 N Central Expy Ste 1200 Dallas TX 75231-6430

SPIEGEL, MARILYN HARRIET, real estate executive; b. Bklyn., Apr. 3, 1935; d. Harry and Sadie (Oscher) Unger; m. Murray Spiegel, June 12, 1954; children: Eric Lawrence, Dana Cheryl, Jay Barry. Grad. high sch., Bklyn. Exec. sec. S & W Paper Co., N.Y.C., 1953-54, Japan Paper Co., N.Y.C., 1954-58; salesperson Red Carpet Realtors, Los Alamitos, Calif., 1974-75, Coll. Park Realtors, Garden Grove, Calif., 1975-79; owner, broker S & S Properties, Los Alamitos, Calif., 1979—. Named Realtor of Yr., 1989. Mem. Calif. Assn. Realtors (bd. dirs. 1984—), West Orange County Bd. Realtors (bd. dirs. 1984—, 1st v.p. 1987, pres. 1988), Million Dollar Sales Club, Long Beach C. of C., Seal Beach C. of C., Orange County C. of C., Summit Orgn., Toastmasters (pres. founders group Garden Grove, Calif. 1990). Home: 1371 Oakmont Rd Apt 150D Seal Beach CA 90740-3732 Office: S & S Properties 3502 Katella Ave Ste 208 Los Alamitos CA 90720-3115

SPIEGEL, MELVIN, retired biology educator; b. N.Y.C., Dec. 10, 1925; s. Philip Edward and Sadie (Friedman) S.; m. Evelyn Sclufer, Apr. 16, 1955; children: Judith Ellen, Rebecca Ann. B.S., U. Ill., 1948; Ph.D., U. Rochester, 1952; M.A. (hon.), Dartmouth Coll., 1967. Research fellow U. Rochester, 1952-53, Calif. Inst. Tech., 1953-55, 64-65; asst. prof. Colby Coll., 1955-59; mem. faculty Dartmouth Coll., Hanover, N.H., 1959—, prof. biology, 1966-93; prof. emeritus Dartmouth Coll, Hanover, N.H.; chmn. dept. biol. scis. Dartmouth Coll., Hanover, N.H., 1972-74; summer investigator Marine Biol. Lab., Woods Hole, Mass., 1954—; sr. research biologist U. Calif.-San Diego, 1970-71; vis. prof. biochemistry Nat. Inst. Med. Research, Mill Hill, London, 1971; vis. prof. Biocenter, U. Basel, 1979-82, 85; Wilson Meml. lectr. U. N.C., 1975; program dir. developmental biology NSF, 1975-76; mem. cell biology study sect. NIH, 1966-70. Editorial bd.: Biol. Bull., 1966-70, 71-75, Cell Differentiation, 1979-88 ; contbr. articles to profl. jours. Trustee Marine Biol. Lab. Corp.; mem. exec. com., trustee Marine Biol. Lab., 1976-80. Served with AUS, 1943-46, ETO. Decorated Purple Heart with 2 oak leaf clusters, Combat Inf. badge. Fellow AAAS; mem. Am. Soc. Cell Biology, Am. Soc. Devel. Biology, Internat. Soc. Devel. Biologists (sec.-treas. 1977-81, bd. dirs. 1981-85). Home: 15 Barrymore Rd Hanover NH 03755-2401

SPIEGEL, PHYLLIS, public relations consultant, journalist; b. Bronx, N.Y.; d. Bernard and Lillian (Horowitz) Finkelberg; m. Stanley Spiegel, Sept. 20, 1959 (div. 1981); children: Mark, Adam. BA, NYU. Feature writer various newspapers, pubs., 1960's-70's; dir. pub. rels. Mort Barish Assocs., Princeton, N.J., 1975-80; account exec. pub. rels. Keyes Martin, Springfield, N.J., 1980-84; pres. Phyllis Spiegel Assocs., Plainsboro, N.J., 1984—. Pub. rels. dir., founder Red Oak Coop. Nursery Sch., Middletown, N.J., 1960's, MStudent Enrichment Program, Matawan, N.J., 1960's-70's; pub. rels. cons., event organizer New Philharm. of N.J., Morristown, 1991-93; advocate Child Placement Rev. Bd. of Family Ct., Mercer County, N.J., 1994—. Recipient Commendation from Gov. N.J. for U. Med. and Dentistry of N.J. campaign, 1983, Commendation for N.J. Pharm. Assn. campaign Pub. Rels. News Assn., 1979. Mem. Soc. for Humanistic Judaism (bd. dirs. 1983-85). Avocations: film and theatre, classical music, reading, travel, walks. Office: Phyllis Spiegel Assocs PO Box 243 Plainsboro NJ 08536-0243

SPIEGEL, S. ARTHUR, federal judge; b. Cin., Oct. 24, 1920; s. Arthur Major and Hazel (Wise) S.; m. Louise Wachman, Oct. 31, 1945; children: Thomas, Arthur Major II, Andrew, Roger Daniel. BA, U. Cin., 1942, postgrad., 1949; LLB, Harvard U., 1948. Assoc. Kasfir & Chalfie, Cin., 1948-52; assoc. Benedict, Bartlett & Shepard, Cin., 1952-53, Gould & Gould, Cin., 1953-54; ptnr. Gould & Spiegel, Cin., 1954-59; assoc. Cohen, Baron, Druffel & Hogan, Cin., 1960; ptnr. Cohen, Todd, Kite & Spiegel, Cin., 1961-80; judge U.S. Dist Ct. Ohio, Cin., 1980—; sr. status, 1995—. Served to capt. USMC, 1942-46. Mem. ABA, FBA, Ohio Bar Assn., Cin. Bar Assn., Cin. Lawyers Club. Democrat. Jewish. Office: US Dist Ct 838 US Courthouse 5th Walnut St Cincinnati OH 45202

SPIEGEL, SIEGMUND, architect; b. Gera, Germany, Nov. 13, 1919; s. Jakob and Sara (Precker) S.; ed. Coll. City N.Y., 1939-40, Columbia, 1945-50; m. Ruth Josias, Apr. 13, 1945; children: Sandra Renee, Deborah Joan. Came to U.S., 1938, naturalized, 1941. DHL (hon.) Hofstra U., 1993. Draftsman, Mayer & Whittlesey, architects, N.Y.C., 1941-47, office mgr., 1947-55; pvt. practice architecture, East Meadow, N.Y., 1956—. Served with AUS, 1941-45; ETO. Decorated Purple Heart, Bronze Star, Croix de Guerre with palme (Belgium); recipient grand prize for instnl. bldgs. (for Syosset Hosp.), L.I. Assn., 1963; grand prize Human Resources Sch., 1966; grand prize Stony Brook Profl. Bldg., 1966; Beautification award, Town Hempstead, N.Y., 1969; Archi award for Harbour Club Apts., L.I. Assn., 1970, for Birchwood Blue Ridge Condominiums, 1974; Dr. Martin Luther King Jr. award Nassau County, 1986; Louis E. Yavner award N.Y. State Bd. Regents, 1992. Fellow Acad. Marketing Sci., L.I.U., 1971. Registered architect, N.Y., N.J., Mass., Md., Va., Pa., Conn., Ga., Vt., Tenn., N.H., Fla.; lic. profl. planner, N.J. Mem. AIA, N.Y. State Assn. Archs., East Meadow C. of C. (pres. 1966). Club: Kiwanis. Author: The Spiegel Plan. Contbr. articles to Progressive Architecture. Prin. works include: Syosset (N.Y.) Hosp., 1962; Reliance Fed. Savs. and Loan Assn. Bank, Queens, N.Y., 1961; Louden Hall Psychiat. Hosp., 1963; Human Resources Sch., Albertson, N.Y., 1964; Nassau Center for Emotionally Disturbed Children, 1968; Harbor Club Apt., Babylon, N.Y., 1968; Reliance Fed. Bank, Albertson, 1967; North Isle Club and Apt. Cmty., Coram, N.Y., 1972; County Fed. Savs. & Loan Assn., Commack, N.Y., 1972; Birchwood Glen Apt. Cmty., Holtsville, N.Y., 1972; Bayside Fed. Savs. & Loan Bank Plaza, Patchogue, N.Y., 1973; L.E. Woodward Sch. for Emotionally Disturbed Children, Freeport, N.Y., 1974, Birchwood Sagamore Hills, Blue Ridge and Bretton Woods Condominium Cmtys., Coram, N.Y., 1975, Maple Arms Condos, Westbury, N.Y., 1982, Dept. Pub. Works, Freeport, N.Y., Nuc. Molecular Resonance Bldg., 1983. Home: Carlton Terr 6-D 10245 Collins Ave Bal Harbour FL 33154

SPIEGELBERG, EMMA JO, business education educator; b. Mt. View, Wyo., Nov. 22, 1936; d. Joseph Clyde and Dorcas (Reese) Hatch; BA with honors, U. Wyo., 1958, MEd, 1985; EdD Boston U., 1990; m. James Walter Spiegelberg, June 22, 1957; children: William L., Emory Walter, Joseph John. Tchr. bus. edn. Laramie (Wyo.) High Sch., 1960-61, 65-93, adminstr., 1993—. Bd. dirs. Cathedral Home for Children, Laramie, 1967-70, 72—, pres., 1985-88, Laramie Plains Mus., 1970-79. Author: Branigan's Accounting Simulation, 1986, London & Co. II, 1993; co-author: Glencoe Computerized Accounting, 1993, 2nd edit., 1995, Microcomputer Accounting: Daceasy, 1994, Microcomputer Accounting: Peachtree, 1994, Microcomputer Accounting: Accpac, 1994, Computerized Accounting with Peachtree, 1995, Glencoe Computerized Accounting: Peachtree, 1995. Named Wyo. Bus. Tchr. of Yr., 1982, Wyo. Asst. Prin. of Yr., 1997. Mem. Am. Vocat. Assn. (policy com. region V 1984-87, region V Tchr. of Yr. 1986), Wyo. Vocat. Assn. (exec. bd. 1978-80, pres. 1981-82, Outstanding Contbns. to Vocat. Edn. award 1983, Tchr. of Yr. 1985, exec. sec. 1986-89), Nat. Bus. Edn. Assn.(bd. dirs. 1987-88, 1991-96, Sec. Tchr. of the Yr. 1991), Mt. Plains Bus. Edn. Assn. (Wyo. rep. to bd. dirs. 1982-85, pres. 1987-88, Sec. Tchr. of the Yr. 1991, Leadership award 1992), Internat. Soc. Bus. Edn., Wyo. Bus. Edn. Assn. (pres. 1979-80), NEA, Wyo. Edn. Assn., Albany County Edn. Assn. (sec. 1970-71), Nat. Assn. Secondary Sch. Prins., Wyo. Assn. Secondary Sch. Prins., Laramie C. of C. (bd. dirs. 1985-88), U. Wyo. Alumni Assn. (bd. dirs. 1985-90pres. 1988-89), Kappa Delta Pi, Phi Delta Kappa, Alpha Delta Kappa (state pres. 1978-82), Chi Omega, Pi Lambda Theta, Delta Pi Epsilon. Mem. United Ch. of Christ. Club: Zonta. Home: 3301 Grays Gable Rd Laramie WY 82070-5031 Office: Laramie High Sch 1275 N 11th St Laramie WY 82072-2206

SPIEGELBERG, HANS LEONHARD, medical educator; b. Basel, Switzerland, Jan. 8, 1933; came to U.S., 1961; s. Hans G. S.; m. Elizabeth von der Crone, May 19, 1962; children: Franzi, Daniel, Markus. MD, U. Basel, Basel, 1958. Med. diplomate, Switzerland. Intern and resident in pediatric allergy and immunology Dept. of Medicine, U. of Basel, Switzerland; intern and resident in allergy and immunology NYU, N.Y.C., 1961-63; with Scripps Rsch. Inst., La Jolla, Calif., 1963-90; prof. U. Calif., San Diego, 1990—; cons. VA Med. Ctr., L.A., 1966-90. Editor (jour.) Seminars in Immunopathology, 1988—. Home: 2234 Paseo Dorado La Jolla CA 92037-3208 Office: U Calif San Diego 9500 Gilman Dr La Jolla CA 92093-5003*

SPIEGELBERG, HARRY LESTER, retired paper products company executive; b. New London, Wis., Apr. 24, 1936; s. Harry Henry and Gladys Louise (Kalt) S.; m. Bonnie Faye Ludden, Jan. 23, 1960; children: Susan Faye Spiegelberg Schuldes, Sharon Louise Spiegelberg Kozlowski, Stephen Harry, Scott Charles. BSChemE, U. Wis., 1959; MS, Inst. Paper Chemistry, Appleton, Wis., 1963, PhD, 1966; MBA, U. Chgo., 1980. Teaching asst. U. Wis. Coll. Engring., Madison, 1957-59; engr. Kimberly-Clark Corp., Neenah, Wis., 1959-61, rsch. scientist, 1965-68, mgr. new concepts, 1968-73, dir. R & D, 1973-84, v.p. consumer tissue rsch., 1985-92; v.p. tech. and patent strategy Kimberly-Clark Corp., 1992-93, v.p. tech. transfer, 1993-96, ret., 1996; mem., past chmn. vis. com. dept. chem. engring. U. Wis., 1985—, mem., past chmn. indsl. liaison coun. Coll. Engring., 1987-93; founder, vice chmn. Paper Industry Hall of Fame; past pres. Ctr. Project Inc. Contbr.

chpt. to book; patentee in nonwovens and tissue fields. Capt. C.E. USAR, 1959-67. Recipient Disting. Svc. citation U. Wis., 1986. Congregationalist. Avocations: bicycling, backpacking. Home: 3624 S Barker Ln Appleton WI 54915-7038

SPIEGEL-HOPKINS, PHYLLIS MARIE, psychotherapist; b. Chgo., Oct. 28, 1947; d. Joseph Frank and Marie Ann (Hejhal) Spiegel; m. Daniel Mark Hopkins, Jan. 14, 1984. BSE, Chgo. State U., 1968, MA in History, 1972; MA in Clin. Psychology, Ill. Sch. Profl. Psychology, Chgo., 1988; D in Clin. Hypnotherapy, Am. Inst. Hypnotherapy, Santa Ana, Calif., 1991. Cert. tchr., Ill; cert. clin. hypnotherapist. Tchr. Holy Cross Grammar Sch., Chgo., 1968-69, Chgo. Bd. Edn., 1969-81, Mt. Asissi Acad., Lemont, Ill., 1981-82; police officer Chgo. Police Dept., 1982—; psychotherapist pvt. practice Chgo., 1988—; mem. Am. Bd. Hypnotherapy. Mem. ACA, Nat. Guild Hypnotists, S.W. Hypnosis Soc., Assn. for Study Dreams, Internat. Med. and Dental Hypnotherapy Assn., C.G. Jung Inst. Chgo., Assn. Past-Life Therapy and Rsch. (life), Internat. Assn. Counselors and Therapists (life), Am. Psychotherapy and Med. Hypnosis Assn., Fraternal Order Police. Avocations: watercolor painting, acrylic painting. Office: PO Box 185 Bedford Park IL 60499-0185

SPIEGELMAN, ART, author, cartoonist; b. Stockholm, Feb. 15, 1948; s. Wladek and Andzia (Zylberberg) S.; m. Francoise Mouly, July 12, 1977; children: Nadja, Dashiell. Student, Harpur Coll. (now SUNY), Binghamton, N.Y. Creative cons., artist, designer, editor, writer Topps Chewing Gum, Inc., Bklyn., 1966-88; editor Douglas Comix, 1972; contbg. editor Arcade, the Comics Revue, 1975-76; founding editor Raw, 1980—; artist, contbg. editor New Yorker, 1992—; instr. San Francisco Acad. Art, 1974-75, N.Y. Sch. Visual Arts, 1979-87. Author, illustrator: The Complete Mr. Infinity, 1970, The Viper Vicar of Vice, Villainy, and Vickedness, 1972, Ace Hole, Midge Detective, 1974, The Language of Comics, 1974, Breakdowns: From Maus to Now: An Anthology of Strips, 1977, Work and Turn, 1979, Every Day Has Its Dog, 1979, Two-Fisted Painters Action Adventure, 1980, Maus: A Survivor's Tale, 1986 (Joel M. Cavior award for Jewish Writing 1986, Nat. Book Critics Cir. nomination 1986, Pulitzer prize 1992), Maus, Part Two, 1992 (Nat. Book Critics Cir. nomination 1992, Pulitzer prize 1992), The Wild Party, 1994, (with F. Mouly) Read Yourself Raw, 1987; contbr. The Apex Treasury of Underground Comics, 1974; compiling editor (with B. Schneider) Whole Grains: A Book of Quotations, 1972; exhbns. include N.Y. Cultural Ctr., Inst. Contemporary Art, London, Seibu Gallery, Tokyo, Mus. Modern Art, N.Y.C., 1991, Galerie St. Etienne, N.Y.C., 1992, Ft. Lauderdale Mus. Art, 1993; creator Wacky Packages, Garbage Pail Kids and other novelties; contbr. to numerous underground comics. Recipient Playboy Editorial award for best comic strip, 1982, Yellow Kid award for best comic strip author, 1982, Regional Design award Print mag., 1983, 84, 85, Inkpot award San Diego Comics Conv., 1987, Stripschappening award for best fgn. comics album, 1987, Alpha Art award Angoulerne, France, 1993. Office: Raw Books & Graphics 27 Greene St New York NY 10013-2537

SPIEKERMAN, JAMES FREDERICK, lawyer; b. The Dalles, Oreg., Feb. 13, 1933; s. Oscar Frederick and Anne (Hesketh) S.; m. Rosalind Lee Somers, Dec. 27, 1962; children: Tim, Cynthia, Peter. BS, U. Oreg., 1955, LLB, 1961. Bar: Oreg. 1961. Law clk. U.S. Fed. Dist. Ct., Portland, Oreg., 1961-62; assoc., then ptnr. and sr. ptnr. Schwabe, Williamson & Wyatt, Portland, 1962-96; retired, Aug. 1995. Capt. USAF, 1956-58. Mem. ABA, Oreg. State Bar (bd. govs. 1988-91, v.p. 1989-90), Multnomah Bar Assn. (pres. 1973), Oregon Assn. of Def. Counsel (pres. 1982), Fed. Ins. and Corp. Counsel, City Club of Portland, Multnomah Athletic Club (Portland). Republican. Episcopalian. Avocations: fly fishing, tennis.

SPIELBERG, STEVEN, motion picture director, producer; b. Cin., Dec. 18, 1947; m. Amy Irving, Nov. 27, 1985 (div.); 2 children: Max Samuel, Sasha; m. Kate Capshaw; 1 dau. BA, Calif. State Coll., Long Beach; Hon. Doctorate in Creative Arts, Brandeis U., 1986. Founder Amblin Entertainment (Universal Studios), Dreamworks SKG (with Jeffrey Katzenberg and David Geffen); directed segments of TV series Columbo; dir. TV movies Night Gallery, 1969, Duel, 1971, Savage, 1972, Something Evil, 1972; exec prodr. series: Steven Spielberg's Amazing Stories, Tiny Toon Adventures, Family Dog, seaQuest DSV; films include (dir.): The Sugarland Express, 1974 (also story), Jaws, 1975, Close Encounters of the Third Kind, 1977 (also co-writer), 1941, 1979, Raiders of the Lost Ark, 1981, Indiana Jones and the Temple of Doom, 1984, Indiana Jones and the Last Crusade, 1989, Hook, 1991, Jurassic Park, 1993, Men in Black, 1996; (dir., prodr.): E.T. The Extra-Terrestrial, 1982, The Color Purple, 1985, Empire of the Sun, 1987, Always, 1989, Schindler's List, 1993 (Best Drama & Best Dir. Golden Globe awards, Best Picture & Best Dir. Acad. awards); (dir., exec. prodr.): Twilight Zone: The Movie, 1983; (prodr.): Poltergeist, 1982 (also co-writer), An American Tail: Fievel Goes West, 1991, Casper, 1995; (exec. prodr.): I Wanna Hold Your Hand, 1978, Used Cars, 1980, Continental Divide, 1981, Gremlins, 1984, The Goonies, 1985, Back to the Future, 1985, Young Sherlock Holmes, 1985, The Money Pit, 1986, An American Tail, 1986, Innerspace, 1987, *batteries not included, 1987, Who Framed Roger Rabbit?, 1988, The Land Before Time, 1988, Dad, 1989, Back to the Future Part II, 1989, Joe Verses the Volcano, 1990, Back to the Future Part III, 1990, Gremlins 2: The New Batch, 1990, Arachnophobia, 1990, Cape Fear, 1991, We're Back!: A Dinosaur's Story, 1993, The Flintstones, 1994, The Little Rascals, 1994, Balto, 1995, Twister, 1996, The Lost World, 1997, Amistad, 1997; (actor): The Blues Brothers, 1980. Recipient Man of Yr. award Hasty Pudding Theater, Harvard U., 1983, Outstanding Directorial Achievement award for feature films Dirs. Guild Am., 1985, Film award Brit. Acad. Film and TV Arts, 1986, Irving Thalberg Mem. award Acad. Motion Picture Arts and Scis., 1987, Golden Lion award for career achievement Venice Film Festival, 1993, Life Achievement award Am. Film Inst., 1995. Fellow Brit. Acad. Film and TV Arts. Won film contest with 40-minute war movie, Escape to Nowhere, at age 13; made film Firelight at age 16, and made 5 films while in coll.; became TV dir. at Universal Pictures at age 20. Office: CAA 9830 Wilshire Blvd Beverly Hills CA 90212-1804*

SPIELMAN, BARBARA HELEN NEW, editor, consultant; b. Canton, Ohio, June 28, 1929; d. Arthur Daniel and Helen Barbara (Rickenmann) New; m. David Vernon Spielman, Nov. 24, 1956; children: Daniel Bruce, Linda Barbara. BS in English and History Edn. cum laude, Miami U., Oxford, Ohio, 1951. Cert. tchr., Ohio, Tex. Tchr. Canton Pub. Schs., 1951-53; vets. aide U. Tex., Austin, 1954-57; copy editor, mng. editor U. Tex. Press, Austin, 1964-91; ret., 1991; editorial cons. Chicago Manual of Style, 13th edit., 1975, Amon Carter Mus., Ft. Worth, 1970—, Ctr. for Mex. Am. Studies, Austin, 1980, Archer M. Huntington Art Gallery, Austin, 1975—, 64 Beds Project for Homeless and Hungry, Austin, 1989—; mem. search com. for dir., U. Tex. Press, 1991. Troop leader Girl Scouts Am., Austin, 1970-73; officer PTA, Austin, 1964-73. Mem. Am. Assn. Univ. Presses, Smithsonian Instn., Nat. Geog. Soc., Althenoi, Seton Med. Ctr. Aux., Phi Beta Kappa, Kappa Delta Pi, Sigma Sigma Sigma. Democrat. Presbyterian. Avocations: reading, gardening, piano, painting, drawing. Home: 3301 Perry Ln Austin TX 78731-5330

SPIELMAN, CHRIS, professional football player; b. Canton, Ohio, Oct. 11, 1965. Student, Ohio State U. With Detroit Lions, 1988-95, Buffalo Bills, 1996—. Recipient Lombardi award, 1987; named to Sporting News Coll. All-Am. team, 1986, 87, Pro Bowl team, 1989-91. Office: Buffalo Bills 1 Bills Rd Orchard Park NY 14127*

SPIELMAN, JOHN PHILIP, JR., historian, educator; b. Anaconda, Mont., June 16, 1930; s. John Philip and Lewanna (Coleman) S.; BA, U. Mont., 1951; MA, U. Wis., 1953, PhD, 1957; m. Danila B. Cole, Sept. 14, 1955. Instr., U. Mich., Ann Arbor, 1957-59; asst. prof. history Haverford (Pa.) Coll., 1959-65, assoc. prof., 1965-70, prof., 1970-85, Audrey Dusseau meml. prof. humanities, 1985—, dean, 1966-68. Served with U.S. Army, 1953-55. Mem. Am. Hist. Assn., Soc. French Hist. Studies, Soc. Austrian and Habsburg Historians. Author: Leopold I of Austria, 1977, The City and the Crown, 1993; co-author 2 textbooks; translator: Simplicissimus (Grimmelshausen), 1981. Home: 749 Millbrook Ln Haverford PA 19041-1210

SPIELVOGEL, SIDNEY MEYER, investment banker; b. N.Y.C., July 14, 1925; s. Hyman and Rae (Mandel) S.; m. Beverly Anne Gold, Dec. 18, 1960; 1 son, Peter James. B.S.S., CCNY, 1944; A.M., Harvard U., 1946, M.B.A., 1949. Economist Treasury Dept., Washington, 1946-47; assoc. dept. mgr. Alexander's Dept. Stores, 1949-53; asst. to mdse. mgr., dept. mgr. Bloomingdale's Dept. Store, 1953-56; with Prudential-Bache Securities Inc., 1956-88, 1st v.p., 1971-75, sr. v.p., 1975-85, mng. dir., 1986-88; dir. MoneyMart Assets Inc., 1976-96, pres., 1981-87; lectr. Hunter Coll., N.Y.C., 1963-68, The New Sch., 1993-96. Bd. dirs. Emanu-el Midtown YM-YWHA, N.Y.C., 1975-91; mem. Harvard Grad. Soc. Coun., 1983-88, 89-92, 94—, chmn., 1985-87. Mem. Phi Beta Kappa. Clubs: Harvard (N.Y.C.), Harvard Bus. Sch. (N.Y.C.), World Trade Center (N.Y.C.). Home: 245 E 19th St New York NY 10003-2639 Office: Corp Capital Cons Inc 1185 Avenue Of The Americas New York NY 10036-2601

SPIER, PETER EDWARD, artist, author; b. Amsterdam, Netherlands, June 6, 1927; came to U.S., 1952, naturalized, 1958; s. Joseph Eduard and Albertine Sophie (Van Raalte) S.; m. Kathryn M. Pallister, July 12, 1958; children: Thomas P., Kathryn E. Student, Ryks Academie Voor Beeldende Kunsten, Amsterdam, 1945-47. Jr. editor Elsevier's Weekly, Amsterdam, 1950-51, Elsevier Pub. Co., Houston, 1952. Free-lance author, illustrator, N.Y.C., 1952—, speaker, lectr. schs. and libraries.; author, illustrator: 38 books, including: The Star-Spangled Banner, 1973, Fast-Slow, High-Low, 1972, Crash! Bang! Boom!, 1972, Tin Lizzie, 1975, Noah's Ark, 1977, Oh, Were They Ever Happy!, 1978, Bored—Nothing to Do, 1978, The Legend of New Amsterdam, 1979, People, 1980, Peter Spier's Village Books, 1981, Rain, 1982, Christmas!, 1983, The Book of Jonah, 1985, Dreams, 1986, We The People, 1987, Peter Spier's Circus, 1992, Father, May I Come?, 1993; illustrator over 150 books; contbr., illustrator many nat. mags. Historian Village of Shoreham, N.Y. Lt. Royal Netherlands Navy, 1947-58. Runner-up for Caldecott medal, 1960; recipient Christopher award, 1970, Boston Globe award, 1967, Caldecott medal, 1978, Christopher award, 1978, Nat. Religious Book award, 1978, Lewis Carroll Shelf award, 1978, Media award NCCJ, 1980, David McCord award, 1989. Mem. Shoreham Country Club (N.Y.). Address: PO Box 566 5 Wardencliff Rd Shoreham NY 11786-0566

SPIERINGS, EGILIUS LEONARDUS HENDRICUS, neurologist, headache specialist, pharmacologist; b. Helmond, The Netherlands, Aug. 16, 1953; came to U.S., 1986; s. Egilius L.H. and Johanna A. (Schellekens) S.; m. Maria K.B. Zarska, Dec. 27, 1976; children: Sven E.J., Natalia M.K. BS cum laude, Erasmus U., Rotterdam, The Netherlands, 1974, MD, 1978, PhD in Experimental Pharmacology, 1980. Registered in medicine, cert. in neurology The Netherlands; lic. physician Mass. Intern in neurosurgery Univ. Hosp., Rotterdam, The Netherlands, 1980-81; resident in neurology Univ. Hosp., Rotterdam, 1982-84; fellow in headache mgmt. Headache Rsch. Found., Boston, 1981-82; resident in psychiatry Hippolytus Hosp., Delft, The Netherlands, 1985; asst. prof. neurology Tufts U. Sch. Medicine, Boston, 1986-90; dir. John R. Graham Headache Ctr., Boston, 1987-90; dir. headache sect. Brigham & Women's Hosp., Boston, 1990-94, dir. headache rsch. dept. neurology, 1994-96; dir. Clin. Headache Rsch. Ctr., Wellesley Hills, 1996—; lectr. neurology Harvard Med. Sch., 1990—; spkr. over 350 meetings nationally. Author: The Pathophysiology of the Migraine Attack, 1980, Migraine, 1986, Migraine Questions & Answers, 1995, Management of Migraine, 1996; co-author: Hoofdpijn, 1984; sect. editor Office Practice of Nuerology, 1996; editor: De Pathogenesevan Migraine, 1982; contbr. over 140 articles to profl. jours. and chpts. to books, over 40 radio and TV appearances. Edn. dir. Headache Consortium New Eng., 1991—. Fellow Am. Assn. Study of Headache; mem. Netherlands Migraine Found. (bd. dirs. 1980-85), Netherlands Soc. Migraine Patients (bd. dirs. 1982-86), Internat. Headache Soc. (bd. dirs. 1985-86, assoc. editor Cephalagia, 1986-89). Home: 30 Circuit Ave Westwood MA 02090-2807 Office: 25 Walnut St Ste 102 Wellesley Hills MA 02181-2106

SPIERS, RONALD IAN, diplomat; b. Orange, N.J., July 9, 1925; s. Thomas Hoskins and Blanca (De Ponthier) S.; m. Patience Baker, June 11, 1949; children: Deborah Wood, Peter, Martha, Sarah. BA, Dartmouth Coll., 1948; M in Pub. Affairs, Princeton U., 1950. With U.S. Atomic Energy Commn., 1950-54; officer-in-charge disarmament and arms control Dept. State, 1955-61; dir. NATO Affairs, 1962-66; polit. counselor London, 1966-69; asst. sec. for Bur. Politico-Mil. Affairs U.S. Dept. State, Washington, 1969-73; U.S. ambassador Nassau, Bahamas, 1973-74; dep. chief-of-mission Am. Embassy, London, 1974-77; U.S. permanent rep. to Cento Coun., 1977-79; U.S. ambassador Ankara, Turkey, 1977-80; asst. sec. for intelligence and rsch., mem. U.S. Intelligence Bd. U.S. Dept. State, Washington, 1980-81; U.S. ambassador Islamabad, Pakistan, 1981-83; under-sec. for mgmt. U.S. Dept. State, Washington, 1983-89; under-sec. gen. for polit. affairs UN, N.Y.C., 1989-92; internat. affairs cons. U. S. Dept. State, Washington, 1992—; career ambassador U.S. Fgn. Svc., 1984. Served to lt. (j.g.) USN, 1943-46, PTO. Woodrow Wilson fellow Princeton U., 1948. Fellow Nat. Acad. of Pub. Adminstrn.; mem. Am. Fgn. Svc. Assn., Internat. Inst. Strategic Studies, Coun. on Fgn. Rels., Am. Acad. of Diplomacy, Washington Inst. Fgn. Affairs. Home: RR 1 Box 54A South Londonderry VT 05155-9801

SPIERS, TOMAS HOSKINS, JR., architect; b. Paris, Jan. 26, 1929; s. Tomas Hoskins and Blanca Genevive (DePonthier) S. (parents Am. citizens); m. Nancy M. Fenold, Aug. 10, 1952; children: Merrick David, Jordan Henry, Corey Albert. Student Mohawk Coll., 1946-48; BA, Hobart Coll., 1951; MArch, Yale U., 1960. Registered architect, Pa., N.J., N.Y., Mass., Md., Ohio, Conn., S.C., R.I., Ind., Va., W.Va., Fla., Ga., Vt. Archtl. designer Pederson & Tilney, New Haven, 1955-60; mng. dir. Pederson & Tilney Italia SpA, Milan, Italy, 1960-66; v.p. European ops. Pederson/Tilney/Spiers, Milan, 1963-66; v.p. S.E. Asia, Louis Berger, Inc., Bangkok, Thailand, 1966-68; v.p. architecture Benatec Assos., Harrisburg, Pa., 1968-75, v.p. design, 1975-78, sr. v.p., 1979-87; pres., 1987-91, chief exec. officer, 1991-94, pres. Spiers, McDonald, Bharucha & Royal, Inc., 1994—; lectr. archtl. restoration Pa. State U., 1975-80; cons. Pa. Hist. & Mus. Commn., Bur. Historic Sites; mem. Pa. State Hist. Preservation Bd., 1980-84, chmn. 1986-88. Prin. works include restoration of Gen. Knox quarters, Valley Forge, Pa., Eagle Hotel, Waterford, Pa., The Highlands, Whitemarsh, Pa., Washington Monument, Balt. Bd. dirs. Urban League of Harrisburg, Inc., 1977-84. Served with USN, 1951-55. Mem. AIA (elected to Coll. of Fellows 1996, com. on hist. resources 1977-94, exec. com. 1980-82, chmn. 1983), ASCE, Am. Arbitration Assn. (arbitrator 1974—), Assn. Preservation Tech. (bd. dirs., editor bull. 1979-82, v.p. 1984-87, pres. 1988-92), Soc. Am. Mil. Engrs. Home: 357 N 27th St Camp Hill PA 17011-3629 Office: Spiers McDonald Bharucha & Royal Inc 150 Corporate Center Dr Ste 101 Camp Hill PA 17011-1759

SPIES, CLAUDIO, composer, educator; b. Santiago, Chile, Mar. 26, 1925; came to U.S., 1942, naturalized, 1966; s. Mauricio and Gertrudis (Heilbronn) S.; m. Emmi Vera Tobias, June 10, 1953 (div. 1986); children: Caterina, Michael, Tatiana, Leah, Susanna. AB, Harvard, 1950, MA, 1954. Instr. music Harvard U., 1953-57; lectr. music Vassar Coll., 1957-58; asst. prof. music, condr. orch. Swarthmore Coll., 1958-63, assoc. prof., 1964-69, prof., 1969-70; prof. music Princeton U., 1970-95, prof. music emeritus, 1995—. Conducted 1st performances of new works, Stravinsky, Boston, 1954, Santiago, 1954, Swarthmore Coll., 1963-68, Harvard, 1968, cond. own works, Composer's Forum, N.Y.C., 1961, Los Angeles County Museum, 1965, Columbia U. Group for Contemporary Music, 1966 (recipient prize for composition U. de Chile 1948, 54, 56); (Brandeis U. Creative Arts citation 1967); composer: orch. Music for a Ballet, 1955, Descanso en jardin; woodwind quartet, tenor and baritone; text by Jorge Guillén, 1957, Il Cantico di Frate Sole; bass. and orch., 1958, Five Psalms; soprano, tenor and 6 instruments; commd. by Harvard Mus. Assn., 1959, Verses from the Book of Ruth; women's voices and piano; commd. by Phila. Art Alliance, 1959, Tempi; music 14 instruments; commd. by Fromm Music Found., 1962, Proverbs on Wisdom; male voices, piano and organ; commd. by Colgate U., 1964, Animula Vagula, Blandula; 4 parts, a cappella, 1964, Viopiacem; duo for viola and keyboard instruments, 1965, LXXXV, Eights and Fives; strings and clarinets, 1967, Times Two; horns, 1968, Three Songs on Poems by May Swenson, 1969, Bagatelle for piano, 1970, 7 Enzensberger-Lieder; baritone, 4 instrumentalists, 1972, Shirim le Hathunatham; soprano, 5 instruments, 1975, Five Sonnet-Settings; Shakespeare; vocal quartet and piano, 1976-77; 5 Dádivas, occasional pieces for piano, 1977-81, Half-Time; for clarinet and trumpet, 1981, Rilke: Rühmen; soprano, clarinet, trumpet, piano, 1981, Tagyr for baritone, flute, clarinet, bassoon, horn and viola, 1983, Seven Sonnets; Shakespeare/Celan; soprano, bass, clarinet, bass clarinet, string trio, 1989; Lament and a Complementary Envoi, Dylan Thomas, baritone, piano, 1990, Dreimal Sieben, oboe and piano, 1991, Insieme, flute and violin, 1994, Beisammen, 2 oboes, also English horns, 1995, Bis, Oboe and Piano, 1996, Coniunctim, oboe and violin, 1996, Facing the Music, Pearl Auster, for chamber chorus piano four-hands, 1996, A la Vez, oboe-English horn and clarinet, bass clarinet, eb clarinet, 1997; contbr. numerous articles and revs. to Perspectives of New Music, Mus. Quarterly, Notes, Tempo, Coll. Music Symposium, Jour. of Arnold Schoenberg Inst., vols. essays Berg, Brahms, Mendelssohn, Stravinsky; mem. editorial bd. Perspectives of New Music. Recipient Bohemian Club prize Harvard, 1950; John K. Paine Traveling fellow, 1950-51; Lili Boulanger Meml. Fund award, 1956; grantee The Ingram Merrill Found., 1966; sr. fellow Council Humanities, Princeton, spring 1966, fall 1966-67; award Nat. Inst. Arts and Letters, 1969; fellow Nat. Endowment Arts, 1975. Mem. Am. Soc. U. Composers (mem. founding bd.), Internat. Alban Berg/Soc. Ltd. (mem. founding bd.), Phila. Composers' Forum (exec. com. 1966-67), League-ISCM (mem. bd. 1970-73), Am. Brahms Soc., Phi Beta Kappa. Office: Princeton U Music Dept Woolworth Ctr Mus Stud Princeton NJ 08544-1007

SPIES, DENNIS J., editor; b. Hays, Kans., Dec. 20, 1941; s. Joseph A. and Germaine A. (Giebler) S.; (widowed Apr. 1985); children: Quentin, Tracy, Angie; m. Linda Yarbrough, Feb., 1990. BA, West Tex. State U., 1970. Draftsman Jeppesen and Co., Denver, 1963-65; tech. illustrator Emerson Electric, St. Louis, 1965-66; reporter Amarillo (Tex.) Globe-News, 1966-68, copy editor, 1968-80, news editor, 1980-84, night city editor, 1984-86, mng. editor, 1986—. Author: (poetry) Sharing, 1984, Kansas Moon, 1989, Road Kill, 1995. Bd. dirs. Adult Literacy Coun., Amarillo, 1987-91, Goodwill Industries, 1987-93, United Way, 1989-90; mem. steering com. Leadership Amarillo, 1989-90. With USAF, 1960-63. Mem. AP Mng. Editors, Lions. Avocations: poetry, cooking, music, cars, motorcycles. Office: Amarillo Globe-News 907 S Van Buren St Amarillo TX 79101-3329

SPIES, JACOB JOHN, health care executive; b. Sheboygan, Wis., Jan. 27, 1931; s. Jacob Alfred and Julia Effie (Wescott) S.; m. Donna Dolores Jerale, June 17, 1954; children: Gary, Joni, Shari. BBA, U. Wis., 1955. V.p. health care systems Wausau (Wis.) Ins. Cos., 1972-77, v.p. mgmt. systems, 1977-79; dep. dir. Health Policy Inst. Boston U., 1979-85; pres., chief exec. officer Co-Med, Inc., Columbus, Ohio, 1984-85; sr. v.p. PARTNERS Nat. Health Plans, Irving, Tex., 1985-90; chmn. PARTNERS Health Plans of Colo., Denver, 1986-90; prin. The Furst Group, Dallas, 1990—; pres., CEO Dallas/Ft. Worth Health Industry Coun., 1994—; bd. dirs. Integrated Healthcare Corp.; adv. bd. Healthcare Adminstrn.; chmn. Tex. Women's U. Co-author: A Corporations Experience with IPA-HMO, 1981, Health Care Cost Containment, 1983. Sgt. U.S. Army, 1952-54, Korea. Decorated Bronze Star, 1953. Mem. Group Health Assn. Am. (com. mem. 1988, 91), Am. Managed Care and Rev. Assn. (bd. dirs.), Nat. Assn. Employers on Health Care Actions (chmn.), North Tex. Med. Edn. Consortium (bd. trustees 1995—), LaCima Club, Denton Country Club. Episcopalian. Home and Office: The Furst Group 1492 Rockgate Rd S Bartonville TX 76226

SPIESICKE, MARGRIT HERMA, counselor; b. Hannover, L. Saxonia, Germany, Dec. 29, 1925; came to U.S. 1960; d. Louis Adolf Otto Fritz and Else Herma (Meier) Becker; m. Horst Guenther Spiesicke, Nov. 9, 1949; 1 child, Marc Anthony. Cert. English/German Interpreter, Hannover (Germany) Lang. Coll., 1947; AA with hons., Broward C.C., Hollywood, Fla., 1983; BA in Humanities, Fla. Internat. U., 1989; postgrad., Nova U., 1992—. State interpreter British Mil. Govt., Hannover, 1947-49; sec., office mgr. Townsend Co., Montreal, Can., 1950-60; sec., adminstrv. asst. Wometco Enterprises, Miami, 1960-85; adminstrv. sec. Barry U., Miami, 1985-88; med. sec. Broward Correctional Instn., Pembroke Pines, Fla., 1988-90, instl. counselor, 1990—. Vol. group counselor Mancy Figueredo, M.D., Miami, 1988-89. Mem. Phi Kappa Phi. Republican. Lutheran. Avocations: music, reading, creative writing.

SPIESS, FRED NOEL, oceanographer, educator; b. Oakland, Calif., Dec. 25, 1919; s. Fred Henry and Elva Josephine (Monck) S.; m. Sarah Scott Whitton, July 25, 1942; children: Katherine Spiess Dallaire, Mary Elizabeth Spiess DeJong, John Morgen Frederick, Helen Spiess Shamble, Margaret Josephine Deligio-Spiess. A.B., U. Calif., Berkeley, 1941, Ph.D., 1951; M.S., Harvard U., 1946. With Marine Phys. Lab., U. Calif., San Diego, 1952—; dir. Marine Phys. Lab., U. Calif., 1958-80, U. Calif. Inst. Marine Resources, 1980-88; dir. Scripps Inst. Oceanography, La Jolla, 1964-65, prof. oceanography, 1961—; chair U. Calif. Acad. Coun. and Assembly U. Calif. Bd. Regents, 1988-90; Mem. Naval Research Adv. Commn., 1978-81; mem. com. on geodesy Nat. Acad. Scis., 1980-84; mem. Def. Sci. Bd., 1976-79. Capt. USNR, 1941-79. Decorated Silver Star medal, Bronze Star medal; recipient John Price Wetherill medal Franklin Inst., 1965; Compass Disting. Scientist award Marine Technol. Soc., 1971; Robert Dexter Conrad award U.S. Sec. of Navy, 1974, Navy Disting. Pub. Svc. award, 1990; Newcomb Cleveland prize AAAS, 1981. Fellow Acoustical Soc. Am. (Pioneers of Underwater Acoustics medal 1985), Am. Geophys. Union (Maurice Ewing award 1983), Marine Tech. Soc. (Lockheed award 1985); mem. Nat. Acad. Engring., Phi Beta Kappa, Sigma Xi. Home: 9450 La Jolla Shores Dr La Jolla CA 92037-1137 Office: U Calif San Diego Scripps Inst Oceanogra La Jolla CA 92093

SPIKINGS, BARRY PETER, film company executive, producer; b. Boston, Eng., Nov. 23, 1939; came to U.S., 1986; children from previous marriage: Nicolas, Rebecca. Student, Boston (Eng.) Grammar Sch. Dir. Great Western, 1969-72; ptnr. Brit. Lion Films Holdings Ltd., Eng., 1972-75; chmn. Shepperton Studios, Eng., 1972-75; joint mng. dir., chmn., chief exec. officer E.M.I. Film & Theater Corp., 1975-82, chm., chief exec., 1982-85; ind. producer, 1982-85; dir. Galactic Films, 1985-86; pres., chief oper. officer Nelson Entertainment Group Inc., Beverly Hills, Calif., 1986-91; ptnr. Pleskow Spikings Partnership, Beverly Hills, 1991-95, Spkings Entertainment, Beverly Hills, 1995—. Prodr. The Deer Hunter, 1978 (Oscar for best picture). Office: Spikings Entertainment 335 N Maple Dr Ste 135 Beverly Hills CA 90210-3858

SPIKOL, ART, editor, writer, illustrator; b. Phila., Mar. 22, 1936; s. Emanuel and Yetta (Levy) S.; m. Rosalind Noshay, Jan. 12, 1958 (div.); 1 child, Victoria; m. Linda Parent, May 28, 1967; 1 child, Elizabeth. Student, Phila. Coll. Art, 1959-62. Art dir. Phila. mag., 1969-74, exec. editor, 1975-78, editor, 1980-82; art dir. Boston mag.; v.p. communications Einstein Med. Ctr., Phila., 1982-85; pres. Art Spikol, Inc., Phila., 1985—. Author: Magazine Writing: The Inside Angle, 1979, The Physalia Incident, 1988; columnist Writer's Digest, 1976-94, contbg. editor, 1994—. Recipient Best Feature Writing award Sigma Delta Chi, 1972, Penney-Mo. Mag. award U. Mo., 1974, Nat. Mag. Editor award Columbia Sch. Journalism, 1982. Jewish. Avocations: sketching, painting, pocket billiards. Office: Art Spikol Inc 751 S 5th St Philadelphia PA 19147-3042

SPILHAUS, ATHELSTAN, meteorologist, oceanographer; b. Cape Town, Union of South Africa, Nov. 25, 1911; came to U.S., 1931, naturalized, 1946; s. Karl Antonio and Nellie (Muir) S.; m. Kathleen Fitzgerald, 1978; children by previous marriage: Athelstan F., Mary Muir, Eleanor (dec.), Margaret Ann, Karl Henry. B.Sc., U. Cape Town, 1931, D.Sc., 1948; M.S., Mass. Inst. Tech., 1933; D.Sc., Coe Coll., 1961, Hahnemann Med. Coll., 1968, U. R.I., 1968, Phila. Coll. Pharmacy and Sci., 1969, Hamilton Coll., 1970, U. S.E. Mass., 1970, U. Durham, Eng., 1970, U. S.C., 1971, Southwestern U. at Memphis, 1972; LL.D., Nova U., 1970, U. Md., 1978. Research asst. Mass. Inst. Tech., 1934-35; asst. dir. tech. services Union of South Africa Def. Forces, Pretoria, 1935-36; research asst. Woods Hole (Mass.) Oceanographic Instn., and Cambridge, Mass., 1936-37; investigator in phys. oceanography Woods Hole (Mass.) Oceanographic Instn., and Cambridge, 1938, phys. oceanographer, 1940—; asst. prof. meteorology N.Y. U., 1937, asso. prof., 1937-42, prof., 1942, dir. research, 1946; meteorol. adviser to Union S. Africa Govt., 1947; dean Inst. Tech. U. Minn., 1949-66, prof. physics, 1966-67; pres. Franklin Inst., Phila., 1967-69, Aqua Internat. Inc., 1969-70; fellow Woodrow Wilson Internat. Center for Scholars, 1971-74; with NOAA, Dept Commerce, Washington, 1974-80; disting. scholar Annenberg Center, U. So. Calif., 1981; vis. scholar Inst. Marine and Coastal Studies, U. So. Calif., 1982-83; pres. Pan Geo, Inc., 1984—; Dir. Sci. Service, Inc., Am. Dynamics Corp., Donaldson Co., Minn.; trustee Aerospace Corp., Los Angeles; U.S. commr. Seattle World's Fair, 1961-62; chmn. nat. fisheries center and aquariam adv. bd. U.S. Dept. Interior; mem. adv. coms. for armed forces; mem. nat. com. IGY; mem. com. on oceanography, com. on polar research Nat. Acad. Scis.; mem. exec. bd. UNESCO, 1955-58; mem.

sci. adv. com. Am. Newspapers and Pubs. Assn.; sr. summer fellow Woods Hole Oceonographic Instn., 1990. Contbr.: numerous articles to profl. jours. including Jour. of Meterology; author: numerous articles to profl. jours. including The Ocean Laboratory. Trustee Woods Hole Oceanographic Instn., St. Paul Inst.; mem. Nat. Sci. Bd., 1966-72; vice chmn. Invest-in-America. Served from capt. to lt. col. USAAF, 1943-46. Decorated Legion of Merit, Exception Civilian Service medal USAF; recipient Patriotic Civilian Service award Dept. Army. Fellow AAAS (pres. 1970, chmn. 1971), Am. Geog. Soc., Geog. Soc., Royal Meteorol. Soc., Am. Geophys. Union; mem. AIAA, NAS (mem. com. pollution), Am. Philos. Soc. Episcopalian. Clubs: Cosmos (Washington); Bohemian (San Francisco). Inventor of Bathythermograph, 1938. Home: PO Box 1063 Middleburg VA 22117-1063 Office: Pan Geo Inc PO Box 2000 Middleburg VA 22117-2000

SPILHAUS, ATHELSTAN FREDERICK, JR., oceanographer, association executive; b. Boston, May 21, 1938; s. Athelstan F. and Mary (Atkins) S.; m. Sharon Brown, June 11, 1960; children—Athelstan F. III, Ruth Emily, Mary Christina. S.B. in Chem. Engring., MIT, 1959, S.M. in Geology and Geophysics, 1960, Ph.D. in Oceanography, 1965. Cert. meeting profl. Phys. scientist U.S. Govt., Washington, 1965-67; asst. exec. dir. Am. Geophys. Union, Washington, 1967-70, exec. dir., 1970—; bd. dirs. Renewable Natural Resources Found., Washington. editor newspaper EOS. Chmn. Conv. Liaison Council, Washington, 1981-82. Fellow AAAS, Washington Acad. Sci., Am. Geophys. Union (hon.), Indian Geophys. Union, Geol. Assn. Canada; mem. Am. Soc. Limnology and Oceanography, Council Biology Editors, Am. Inst. Physics (mem. gov. bd. 1988—), Geol. Soc. Am., Philos. Soc. Washington (pres. 1982-83), Geol. Soc. Washington (2nd v.p. 1975), Soc. Exploration Geophysicists, Am. Soc. Assn. Execs., Assn. Am. Pubs. (div. exec. com. 1980-82, 94-97), Assn. Earth Sci. Editors (dir. 1972-78, pres. 1977), Council Engring. and Scientific Soc. Execs. (dir. 1976-82, pres. 1980-81), Internat. Union Geodesy Geophysics (mem. fin. com. 1987—), Canadian Geophys. Union, European Geophys. Soc. Clubs: Cosmos (Washington, pres. 1992-93); Chesapeake Yacht (Md.). Home: 10900 Picasso Ln Rockville MD 20854-1710 Office: Am Geophys Union 2000 Florida Ave NW Washington DC 20009-1231

SPILHAUS, KARL HENRY, textiles executive, lawyer; b. N.Y.C., July 19, 1946; s. Athelstan Frederick and Mary (Atkins) S.; m. Constance DeLaMater, Dec. 30, 1989; stepchildren: Mary Alexis Welch, Antonia Morrow Welch. BA, U. Pa., 1971; JD, New Eng. Sch. Law, 1975. Bar: Mass. 1975. Staff atty. Legal Svcs., Cape Cod and the Islands, 1975-76; with No. Textile Assn., 1976—, pres., 1982—; pres. No. Textile Export Trading Co., Boston, 1992-95; pres. Cashmere and Camel Hair Mfrs. Inst., 1984—; U.S. del. Internat. Labor Orgn. Textiles Com.; mem. adv. coun. U. Mass., Dartmouth, 1979—. Trustee Mus. Am. Textile History; mem. Eliot Ch. of South Natick. With USMC, 1966-69, Vietnam. Mem. Textile Club Boston (pres.), Soc. King's Chapel, Phi Psi (hon.). Office: No Textile Assn 230 Congress St Boston MA 02110-2409

SPILKA, MARK, retired English language educator; b. Cleve., Aug. 6, 1925; s. Harvey Joseph and Zella (Fenberg) S.; m. Ellen Potter, May 6, 1950 (div. Dec. 1965); children: Jane, Rachel, Aaron; m. Ruth Dane Farnum, Jan. 18, 1975 (div. May 1993); stepchildren: Betsy, Polly; m. Shelly Regenbaum, July 4, 1993; stepchildren: Shir, Livi. BA magna cum laude, Brown U., 1949; MA, Ind. U., 1953, PhD, 1956. Editl. asst. Am. Mercury, 1949-51; instr. U. Mich., 1954-58, asst. prof., 1958-63; assoc. prof. Brown U., Providence, 1963-67, prof., 1967-95, prof. emeritus, 1995—, Israel J. Kapstein prof. English, 1990, chmn. English dept., 1968-73; Summer seminar dir. Nat. Endowment for Humanities, 1974; pres. Conf. Editors of Learned Jours., Modern Lang. Assn., 1974-75; vis. prof. Grad. Inst. Modern Letters U. Tulsa, summer 1975, Hebrew U., Jerusalem, 1972, Ind. U., summer 1976. Author: The Love Ethic of D.H. Lawrence, 1955, Dickens and Kafka: A Mutual Interpretation, 1963, Virginia Woolf's Quarrel with Grieving, 1980, Hemingway's Quarrel with Androgyny, 1990, Renewing the Normative D.H. Lawrence: A Personal Progress, 1992; editor: D.H. Lawrence: A Collection of Critical Essays, 1963, Towards a Poetics of Fiction: Essays from Novel: A Forum on Fiction, 1967-76, 1977, (with Caroline McCracken-Flesher) Why the Novel Matters: A Postmodern Perplex, 1990; mng. editor: Novel: A Forum on Fiction, 1967-77; editor, 1978—. Served with USAAF, 1944-46. Named Harry T. Moore Disting. D.H. Lawrence scholar MLA and D.H. Lawrence Soc., 1988; Ind. Sch. Letters fellow, 1961, 63; Guggenheim fellow, 1967-68; Nat. Endowment for Humanities fellow, 1978-79, 87. Mem. MLA (pres. Dickens Soc. 1986), AAUP, Phi Beta Kappa. Home: 294 Doyle Ave Providence RI 02906-3355

SPILLANE, MICKEY (FRANK MORRISON SPILLANE), author; b. Bklyn., Mar. 9, 1918; s. John Joseph and Catherine Anne S.; m. Mary Ann Pearce, 1945 (div.); children: Kathy, Ward, Mike, Carolyn; m. Sherri Malinou, Nov. 1964 (div.); m. Jane Rodgers Johnson, Oct. 1983. Attended, Kans. State Coll. Scripter, asst. editor Funnies, Inc., in 1940's; co-founder Spillane-Fellows Prodns., Nashville, 1969. Author: (mystery-suspense novels) I, the Jury, 1947, Vengeance is Mine!, 1950, My Gun Is Quick, 1950, The Big Kill, 1951, One Lonely Night, 1951, The Long Wait, 1951, Kiss Me, Deadly, 1952, Tough Guys, 1960, The Deep, 1961, The Girl Hunters, 1962, Day of the Guns, 1964, The Snake, 1964, Bloody Sunrise, 1965, The Death Dealers, 1965, The Twisted Thing, 1966, The By-Pass Control, 1967, The Delta Factor, 1967, Body Lovers, 1967, Killer Mine, 1968, Me. Hood!, 1969, Survival: Zero, 1970, Tough Guys, 1970, The Erection Set, 1972, The Last Cop Out, 1973, The Flier, 1973, Tomorrow I Die, 1984, The Killing Man, 1989, (children's books) The Day the Sea Rolled Back, 1979 (Junior Literary Guild award 1979), The Ship That Never Was, 1982, Black Alley, 1986; screenwriter, actor: (films) The Girl Hunters, 1963; creator: (TV series) Mike Hammer, 1984-87; editor: Murder Is My Business, 1994; appeared in Miller Lite Beer commls. Served to capt. USAAF, World War II. Address: care E P Dutton 375 Hudson St New York NY 10014*

SPILLENKOTHEN, MELISSA J., federal agency administrator. Asst. sec. for adminstrn. U.S. Dept. Transp., Washington, 1995—. Office: US Dept Transp Office of Adminstrn 400 7th St SW Washington DC 20590-0001*

SPILLER, EBERHARD ADOLF, physicist; b. Halbendorf, Ger., Apr. 16, 1933; came to U.S., 1968; s. Walter Richard and Ruth Elfriede (Radzey) S.; m. Marga Dietz, Dec. 18, 1964; children—Michael, Bettina. Diploma, U. Frankfurt, Ger., 1960, Ph.D., 1964. Asst. U. Frankfurt, 1960-68, mem. faculty, 1966-68; physicist IBM Research Center, Yorktown Heights, N.Y., 1968-93; emeritus physicist IBM, 1993—; guest prof. Tech. U. Denmark, 1994-95, U. Ctrl. Fla., 1996, U. Md., 1997—; vis. scientist Nat. Inst. Stds. and Tech., 1997—, Lawrence Livermore Lab., Calif., 1997—. Author: Soft X-Ray Optics, 1994. Fellow AAAS, Am. Optical Soc.; mem. German Phys. Soc., Photo-Optic Instrumentation Soc. Research in solid state physics, laser and coherence optics, nonlinear optics, thin films, soft x-rays, x-ray microscopy, lithography; inventor multilayer x-ray optics, x-ray astronomy, x-ray lithography. Home: 60 Lakeside Rd Mount Kisco NY 10549 Office: IBM Corp TJ Watson Research Ctr Yorktown Heights NY 10598

SPILLERS, WILLIAM RUSSELL, civil engineering educator; b. Fresno, Calif., Aug. 4, 1934; s. William Horton and Marguerite Ester (Johnson) S.; m. Priscilla Watson, Sept. 10, 1960 (div. 1981); children: Sarah, William, Lars; m. Sandra Lynn Newsome, July 15, 1983 (div. 1995). Student, Fresno State Coll., 1951-53; BS, U. Calif., Berkeley, 1955, MS, 1956; PhD, Columbia U., 1961. Registered profl. engr., N.Y., N.J. Structural engr. John Blume Assocs., San Francisco, 1956-57; teaching asst. Columbia U., N.Y.C., 1957-61, prof. civil engring. and engring. mechanics, 1961-76; prof. civil engring. Rensellaer Poly. Inst., Troy, N.Y., 1976-90; prof., chmn. civil and environ. engring. N.J. Inst. Tech., Newark, 1990—; disting. prof. civil and environ. engring. N.J. Inst. Tech., 1995—; cons. Weidlinger Assoc., N.Y.C., 1957-76, Geiger Berger Assoc., N.Y.C., 1957-76, DeLeuw Oh Eocha, Manchester, Eng., 1974, Parsons Hawaii, Los Angeles, 1983, Horst Berger Ptnrs., N.Y.C., 1980; organizer NSF workshop on design theory, Troy, N.Y., 1988. Author: Automated Structural Analysis, 1972, Iterative Structural Design, 1975, Intro Structures, 1985, (with R. Levy) Analysis of Geometrically Nonlinear Structures, 1995; editor 4 books including Design Theory, 1988; contbr. more than 135 articles to profl. jours. NSF fellow, 1976, Guggenheim fellow, 1968. Mem. ASCE (numerous coms., chmn. exec. com. TCCP, 1987), Internat. Assn. Bridge & Structural Engrs. Democrat. Achievements include contribution to the development of fabric structures; initiated the science of design theory; participated in development of applications of digital computers to large structural systems. Home: 571 Parker St Newark NJ 07104-1523 Office: NJ Inst Tech Dept Civil & Environ Engring Newark NJ 07102

SPILLIAS, KENNETH GEORGE, lawyer; b. Steubenville, Ohio, Nov. 8, 1949; s. George and Angeline (Bouyoucas) S.; m. Monica Mary Saumweber, May 10, 1975; children: Geoffrey David, Alicia Anne, Stephanie Marie. BA, Pa. State U., 1971; JD magna cum laude, U. Pitts., 1974. Bar: Pa. 1974, Fla. 1978, U.S. Supreme Ct. 1978, U.S. Ct. Appeals (2d, 3d, 4th, 5th, 6th cirs.) 1975, (11th cir.) 1981, U.S. Dist. Ct. (mid. dist.) Fla. 1979, U.S. Dist. Ct. (so. dist.) Fla. 1978. Trial atty. U.S. Dept. Justice, Washington, 1974-76; asst. dist. atty. Dist. Atty. of Allegheny County, Pitts., 1976-78; asst. atty. gen. Fla. Dept. Legal Affairs, West Palm Beach, Fla., 1978-79; ptnr. Spillias & Mitchell, West Palm Beach, 1979-82, Considine & Spillias, West Palm Beach, 1982-83, Schneider, Maxwell, Spillias et al, West Palm Beach, 1984-86, Wolf, Block, Schorr et al, West Palm Beach, 1986-88, Shapiro & Bregman, West Palm Beach, 1988-91; of counsel Greenberg, Traurig et al, West Palm Beach, 1991; pvt. practice West Palm Beach, 1991—; instr. bus. law Coll. of the Palm Beaches, West Palm Beach, 1980-81; CLE lectr. Palm Beach County Bar Assn., 1983—. County commr. Bd. County Commrs., Palm Beach County, 1982-86; co-founder, mem. Children's Svcs. Coun., Palm Beach County, 1986-91; steering com. Fla. Atlantic U. Inst. of Govt., Boca Raton, 1983-94; bd. dirs. The Literacy Coalition of P.B.C., West Palm Beach, 1990—, health and human svcs. Fla. Dist. IX, 1995—, Ctr. for Family Svc., West Palm Beach, 1992-96, Palm Beach County Coun. of Arts, 1985-86; mem. policy coun. Fla. Inst. Govt., Tallahassee, 1985-86; fund raising chmn. United Cerebral Palsey Telethon, West Palm Beach, 1984-85; judge Palm Beach Post Pathfinders Awards, 1992-96. Recipient Cmty. Svc. award Downtown Civitan Club, West Palm Beach, 1983, Man of the Day award United Cerebral Palsey, 1986, Spl. Honoree award Palm Beach County Child Advocacy Bd., 1986, Children's Trust award Exch. Club/Dick Webber Ctr. for Prevention Child Abuse, 1991, Up and Comers Award in Law, South Fla. Bus. Jour./Price Waterhouse, 1988, Achievement award Nat. Assn. Counties, 1986; named to Outstanding Young Men of Am., U.S. Jaycees, 1975, 84. Mem. ABA, Acad. Fla. Trial Laywers, Assn. Trial Lawyers Am. (judge student trial competition 1995-96), Allegheny County Bar Assn., Palm Beach County Bar Assn. (appellate practice com. 1990—), Order of the Coif. Avocations: sports, scuba diving, theater, reading, music. Home: 147 Gregory Rd West Palm Beach FL 33405 Office: 250 S Australian Ave Ste 1504 West Palm Beach FL 33401-5016

SPILLMAN, JANE SHADEL, curator, researcher, writer; b. Huntsville, Ala., Apr. 30, 1942; d. Marvin and Elizabeth (Russell) Shadel; m. Don Lewis Spillman, Feb. 18, 1973; children: K. Elizabeth, Samuel Shadel. AB, Vassar Coll., 1964; MA, SUNY, 1965. Rsch. asst. Corning (N.Y.) Mus. Glass, 1965-70, asst. curator, 1971-73, assoc. curator Am. glass, 1974-77, curator, 1978—, head of curatorial dept., 1994—; cons. New Bedford (Mass.) Glass Mus., 1986, The White House Curator's Office, Washington, 1987-90. Author: Complete Cut and Engraved Glass of Corning, 1979, rev. edit., 1997, Knopf Collectors Guide to Glass, Vol. 1, 1982, Vol. 2, 1983, White House Glassware, 1989, Masterpieces of American Glass, 1990, The American Cut Glass Industry: T.G. Hawkes and His Competitors, 1996, also 6 other books, numerous articles. Mem. Am. Assn. Mus. (chairperson curators com. 1989-93), Nat. Early Am. Glass Club (bd. dirs. 1989-95), Glass Circle of London. Office: Corning Mus Glass 1 Museum Way Corning NY 14830-2253

SPILLMAN, ROBERT ARNOLD, architect; b. Bethlehem, Pa., May 21, 1931; s. Otto Henry and Ruth Meredith (Miller) S.; m. Cidney Jane Brandon, July 7, 1956; children—Catherine, Sarah, Peter. B.Arch., Cornell U., 1954. Registered profl. architect Pa., N.J. Archl. designer office Douglass Orr, New Haven, 1956-58; ptnr. Lovelace & Spillman, Architects, Bethlehem, 1959-70; sr. ptnr. Spillman Farmer Architects, Bethlehem, 1971-82; pres. Spillman Farmer Shoemaker Pell Whildin, P.C, Bethlehem, 1983-96. Trustee, Laros Found., Bethlehem, 1970—; pres. Bethlehem Library Bd., 1970-74, United Way Northampton and Warren Counties, 1979-81, Lehigh River Found., 1992-95; v.p. Lehigh Valley Indsl. Parks, 1985-96, pres. 1996—; chmn. City of Bethlehem Bd. Historic Archl. Rev., 1961-82; Olympic torchbearer, 1996. Fellow AIA (pres. Ea. Pa. chpt. 1969-70); mem. Pa. Soc. Architects (disting. bldg. awards 1971, 76, 78, 94), Soc. Coll. and Univ. Planners. Democrat. Episcopalian. Served as 1st lt. USAF, 1954-56. Clubs: Bethlehem; Bay Head Yacht (N.J., rear commodore 1985-87). Office: Spillman Farmer Shoemaker Pell 1 Bethlehem Plz Ste 1000 Bethlehem PA 18018-5716

SPILMAN, RAYMOND, industrial designer; b. Wichita, Kans., Jan. 12, 1911; s. Robert Bruce and Willa (Wood) S.; m. Mary Jordan, May 15, 1937; children: Susan, Alden. Student, Kans. State U., 1933. Stylist GM Corp., 1935-39; staff designer Walter Dorwin Teague, N.Y.C., 1940-42; chief designer Johnson Cushing & Nevell, N.Y.C., 1942-46; propr. Raymond Spilman Indsl. Design, N.Y.C., 1946, Stamford, Conn., 1963, Darien, Conn., 1983—; ednl. adviser, lectr. design and design curriculums, color applications in design. Mem. edit. bd., Color Rsch. and Applications Quar., 1976-80; producer films on color and design; collections included in Archives of Domestic Life Smithsonian Inst., 1950—. Recipient Elec. Mfg. Design award Gates Pub. Co., 1950, award U.S. Trade Fair Exhbns., Yugoslavia, 1955, Italy, 1957, Peru, 1959 and 63, Poland, 1964, Graphis award, Graphis mag. Italy, 1957, Internat. Triennale award Undicesima Triennale di Milano, Milan, Italy, 1957, Wescon award of merit West Cost Elec. Prodn. Mfg. Assn., 1959, Design USA award Indsl. Design Soc. Am., 1965, Product Engring. Master Design awards, 1959, 66, Housewares Design award, 1967, 68, citation for design in steel Am. Iron and Steel Inst., 1974, John Vassos award Indsl. Design Soc. Am., 1985, Personal Recognition award Indsl. Designers Soc. Am., 1993; Endowment Arts design project fellow Nat. Endowment Arts, 1977; Design Advancement grantee Nat. Endowment Arts, 1989-90. Fellow Indsl. Design Soc. Am. (Personal Achievement award 1993, Personal Recognition award 1993); mem. Am. Soc. Indsl. Designers (pres. 1960-62, chmn. bd. dirs. 1963-64), Am. Inter-Soc. Color Coun. (bd. dirs. 1970-72, 76-77), Phi Delta Theta. Home and Office: Raymond Spilman Indsl Design 1 Althea Ln Darien CT 06820-2501

SPINA, ANTHONY FERDINAND, lawyer; b. Chgo., Aug. 15, 1937; s. John Dominic and Nancy Maria (Ponzio) S.; m. Anita Phyllis, Jan. 28, 1961; children—Nancy M. Spina Okal, John D., Catherine M. Spina Samatas, Maria J. Spina Samatas, Felicia M. B.S. in Social Sci., Loyola U., Chgo., 1959; J.D., DePaul U., 1962. Bar: Ill. 1962. Assoc. Epton, Scott, McCarthy, & Bohling, Chgo., 1962-64; sole practice, Elmwood Park, Ill., 1964-71; pres. Anthony & Spina, P.C., 1971-84, Spina, McGuire & Okal, P.C., 1985—; atty. Leyden Twp., Ill., 1969-89, Village of Rosemont, Ill., 1971; counsel for Pres. and dir. Cook County Twp. Ofcls. of Ill., 1975-96; counsel for exec. dir. Ill. State Assn. Twp. Ofcls., 1975-96; counsel Elmwood Park Village Bd., 1967-89, Norwood Park St. Lighting Dist., 1988—, various Cook County Twps. (including DuPage, 1980-82, Maine, 1981—, Norwood Park, 1982—, Wayne, 1982-84), all Cook County Hwy. Commrs. Traffic Fine Litigation, 1974-96, Hanover Twp. Mental Health Bd., 1991—, Glen Edens Assn., 1994—; mem. Elmwood Park Bldg. Code Planning Commn. Bd. Appeals. Recipient Lacodaire medal, Dean's Key Loyola U.; Loyola U. Housing awards, 1965, 71, 76; award of appreciation Cook County Twp. Ofcls., av rating Martindale-Hubbel. Mem. Ill. Bar Assn., ABA, Chgo. Bar Assn., West Suburban Bar Assn. of Cook County (past chmn. unauthorized practice of law sect.), Am. Judicature Soc., Justinian Soc. Lawyers, Ill. State Twp. Attys. Assn. (past v.p., pres. 1982-86, dir. 1986—), Nat. Inst. Town and Twp. Attys. (past v.p., pres. 1993-95, Ill. del.), Montclare/Leyden C. of C., Edgebrook C. of C. (past bd. dirs.), Nat. Assn. Italian Am. Lawyers, World Bocce Assn. (dir. 1994—), Blue Key, Delta Theta Phi, Tau Kappa Epsilon, Pi Gamma Mu. Roman Catholic. St. Rocco Soc. of Simbario, KC (scribe, trustee, past grand knight, bldg. corp. dir. 1967—, Calabresi in Am. Orgn. (bd. dirs. 1990—), Fra Noi Ethnic Publ., dir., 1995— Author Rosemont Village Ordinances, 1971; Elmwood Park Bldg Code, 1975, Leyden Twp. Codified Ordinances, 1987. Office: 7610 W North Ave Elmwood Park IL 60707-4142

SPINA, HORACIO ANSELMO, physician; b. Buenos Aires, Mar. 19, 1939; came to U.S., 1970; s. Antonio and Rosa Palma S.; m. Patricia Anne Duffy, Apr. 4, 1985; children: Alicia V., Cristina V., Mario A. Student, Nat. U. Cordoba, Argentina, 1968; MD in Psychiatry, U. Pitts., 1974. Diplomate Am. Bd. Psychiatry and Neurology. Resident U. Pitts., 1971-74; rotating intern Shadyside Hosp., Pitts., 1970-71; med. dirs. psychiat. svcs. and chem. dependence program St. Clair Mem. Hosp., Pitts., 1980—; clin. asst. prof. psychiatry U. Pitts.; med. dir. gero-psychiat. svcs. St. Clair Meml. Hosp., Pitts., 1996—. Mem. APA, Nat. Depressive Manic Depressive Assn., InterAm. Coll. Physicians and Surgeons, Psychiat. Physicians Pa., Cordoba Soc. Pharmacology and Therapeutics, N.Y. Acad. Scis., Am. Soc. Clin. Psychopharmacology, Acad. Psychosomatic Medicine, Nat. Alliance for Mentally Ill. Avocations: cooking, gardening, music, computers. Office: 1050 Bower Hill Rd Ste 303 Pittsburgh PA 15243-1869

SPINCIC, WESLEY JAMES, oil company executive, consultant; b. New Castle, Pa., Aug. 6, 1945; s. Edward and Mary Louise (Ferk) S.; m. Gayle Sharon Burnett, June 14, 1975; children: John Reginold, Sheri Diane. BS in Engring., U.S. Mil. Acad., 1967; postgrad. in bus., U. So. Calif., 1973. Account rep. Dupont Glore-Forgon, L.A., 1973-74; drilling engr. Mobil Oil Co., Dallas, 1974-77; drilling supt. Ranger Oil Co., Houston, 1977; drilling and engring. mgr. Kilroy Co. Tex., Houston, 1977-81;, 1981-95; bd. dirs. Humble (Tex.) Nat. Bank, Avanti Internat., Avanti Cons., Inc., 1996—; chmn. bd. Consumer Direct Mortgage, Inc.; chmn. bd., CEO Consumer Direct Mortgage Corp., 1996—. Organizer Kingwood (Tex.) Emergency Med. Assn., 1978. Capt. U.S. Army, 1967-73. Mem. Soc. Petroleum Engrs., Am. Petroleum Inst., Internat. Assn. Drilling Contractors, Tex. Ind. Producers and Royalty Owners Assn., Assn. West Point Alumni, Internat. Gamefish Assn., Billfish Assn. Republican. Roman Catholic. Avocations: golf, hunting, fishing, boating. Home: 4714 Breezy Point Kingwood TX 77345 Office: Ste 220 15600 John F Kennedy Blvd Houston TX 77032-2343

SPINDEL, ROBERT CHARLES, electrical engineering educator; b. N.Y.C., Sept. 5, 1944; s. Morris Tayson and Isabel (Glazer) S.; m. Barbara June Sullivan, June 12, 1966; children—Jennifer Susan, Miranda Ellen. B.S.E.E., Cooper Union, 1965; M.S., Yale U., 1966, M.Phil., 1968, Ph.D., 1971. Postdoctoral fellow Woods Hole Oceanographic Instn, Mass., 1971-72, asst. scientist, 1972-76; assoc. scientist Woods Hole Oceanographic Instn., Mass., 1976-82; sr. scientist Woods Hole Oceanographic Instn, Mass., 1982-87, chmn. dept. ocean engring., 1982-87; dir. applied physics lab. U. Wash., 1987—. Contbr. articles to profl. jours.; patentee on underwater nav. Recipient A.B. Wood medal Brit. Inst. Acoustics, 1981, Gano Dunn medal The Cooper Union, 1989. Fellow IEEE (assoc. editor jour. 1982—), Acoustical Soc. Am. (exec. coun. 1985-86), Marine Tech. Soc. (pres. elect 1991-93, pres. 1993-95). Independent. Jewish. Avocations: automobile restoration, hiking. Home: 14859 SE 51st St Bellevue WA 98006-3515 Office: U Wash Applied Physics Lab 1013 NE 40th St Seattle WA 98105-6606

SPINDEL, WILLIAM, chemist, consultant; b. N.Y.C., Sept. 9, 1922; s. Joseph and Esther (Goldstein) S.; m. Sara Lew, 1942 (div. 1966); children: Robert Andrew, Lawrence Marshall; m. Louise Phyllis Hoodenpyl, July 30, 1967. B.A., Bklyn. Coll., 1944; M.A., Columbia U., 1947, Ph.D., 1950. Jr. scientist Los Alamos Lab, Manhattan Dist., 1944-45; instr. Poly. Inst., Bklyn., 1949-50; assoc. prof. State U. N.Y., 1950-54; rsch. assoc., vis. prof. Columbia, 1954-57, vis. prof., sr. lectr., 1962-74; assoc. prof., then prof. Rutgers U., 1957-64; prof., chmn. dept. chemistry Belfer Grad. Sch. Sci., Yeshiva U., 1964-74; exec. sec., office chemistry and chem. tech. NAS-NRC, 1974-81, also staff dir. bd. on chem. scis. and tech., prin. staff officer commn. phys. scis., math. and resources, 1982-90, sr. cons., 1990—; vis. Am. scientist, Yugoslavia, 1971-72. Contbr. articles to profl. jours. Served with AUS, 1943-46. Recipient prof. staff award NRC, 1985; Guggenheim fellow, 1961-62; Fulbright Research scholar, 1961-62. Fellow AAAS; mem. Am. Chem. Soc. Club: Cosmos. Achievements include research on separation of stable isotopes, isotope effects on chemical and biological processes; developed chemical exchange process for concentrating nitrogen-15. Home: 6503 Dearborn Dr Falls Church VA 22044-1116 *Working at and for the sciences has yielded a most fulfilling professional life.*

SPINDLER, GEORGE DEARBORN, anthropologist, educator, author, editor; b. Stevens Point, Wis., Feb. 28, 1920; s. Frank Nicholas and Winifred (Hatch) S.; m. Louise Schaubel, May 29, 1942; 1 dau., Sue Carol Spindler Coleman. B.S., Central State Tchrs. Coll., Wis., 1940; M.A., U. Wis., 1947; Ph.D., U. Calif. at Los Angeles, 1952. Tchr. sch. in Wis., 1940-42; research asso. Stanford, 1950-51, mem. faculty, 1951—, prof. anthropology and edn., 1960-78, exec. head dept., 1963-67, 84; vis. prof. U. Wis., Madison, 1979, 80, 81, 82, 83, 84, 85; editor Am. Anthropologist, 1962-66; cons. editor Holt, Rinehart & Winston, 1965-91, Harcourt, Brce, 1991—; vis. prof. U. Calif., Santa Barbara, 1986-91. Author: Menomini Acculturation, 1955, (with A. Beals and L. Spindler) Culture in Process, 1967, rev. edit., 1973, Transmission of American Culture, 1959, (with L. Spindler) Dreamers Without Power, 1971, rev. edit., 1984, Burgbach: Urbanization and Identity in a German Village, 1973, (with Louise Spindler) The American Cultural Dialogue and its Transmission, 1990; editor: Education and Anthropology, 1955, (with Louise Spindler) Case Studies in Cultural Anthropology, 1960—, Methods in Cultural Anthropology, 1965—, Case Studies in Education and Culture, 1966—, Basic Units in Anthropology, 1970; editor, contbr.: Education and Culture, 1963, Being An Anthropologist, 1970, Education and Cultural Process, 1974, rev. edit., 1987, The Making of Psychological Anthropology, 1978, 2nd edit., 1994, Doing the Ethnography of Schooling, 1982, Interpretive Ethnography of Schooling at Home and Abroad, 1987, Pathways to Cultural Awareness: Cultural Therapy with Students and Teachers, 1994. Pres. Peninsula Sch. Bd., Menlo Park, Calif., 1954-56. Served with AUS, 1942-45. Recipient Lloyd W. Dinkelspell award Stanford U., 1978, Disting. Svc. award Soc. Internat. Diplomacy and Third World Anthropologists, 1984, Disting. Career Contbn. award Com. on Role and Status of Minorities, Am. Edn. Rsch. Assn., Nat. Acad. Edn., 1994; fellow Ctr. Advanced Study of Behavioral Scis., 1956-57; subject of Vol. 17 Psychoanalytic Study of Soc. essays, 1992. Fellow Am. Anthrop. Assn.; mem. Southwestern Anthrop. Assn. (pres. 1962-63), Coun. for Anthropology and Edn. (pres. 1982, George and Louise Spindler award for outstanding contbns. to ednl. anthropology 1987), Nat. Acad. Edn. Home: 489 Kortum Canyon Rd Calistoga CA 94515-9703 Office: Ethnographics PO Box 38 Calistoga CA 94515-0038 *My major aims as a professional observer and interpreter of human behavior are to acquire knowledge by research and disseminate understanding to others by teaching, writing, and editing. As a person I try to keep love, work, play in balanced relationship to each other, and strive for tolerance at least, and hopefully appreciation for others who are different than myself.*

SPINDLER, JOHN FREDERICK, lawyer; b. Milw., Aug. 23, 1929; s. Howard L. and Margaret (Knauf) S.; m. Martha Murdoch, June 26, 1952; children: Susan Spindler Nelson, Elizabeth Spindler, John F. Jr., Robert P. BA, U. Mich., 1951, JD, 1953. Bar: Mich. 1953, Pa. 1954, U.S. Ct. Claims 1955, U.S. Ct. Mil. Appeals 1955, Conn. 1956, U.S. Supreme Ct. 1956, U.S. Dist. Ct. Conn. 1960, U.S. Tax Ct. 1967, Fla. 1977. Assoc. Cummings & Lockwood, Stamford, Conn., 1956-63, ptnr., 1963—. Bd. dirs. Stamford YMCA, 1987-93, Stamford Hist. Soc., 1984-90. 1st lt. JAGC, U.S. Army, 1953-56. Home: 175 Saddle Hill Rd Stamford CT 06903-2306 Office: Cummings & Lockwood Four Stamford Plz PO Box 120 Stamford CT 06904-0120

SPINDLER, PAUL, public relations executive; b. Chgo., May 2, 1931; s. Isaac Edward and Sophia (Stein) S.; m. Gail Klynn; children from previous marriage: Kevin, Makayla, Sydney, Jeffrey. BA in Journalism, Temple U., 1952. Reporter Akron Beacon Jour., Akron, Ohio, 1955-58, San Francisco Examiner, 1958-59; editor Santa Clara (Calif.) Daily Jour., 1959-63; dir. pub. affairs Litton Industries, Inc., Beverly Hills, Calif., 1963-68; dir. pub. relations Internat. Industries, Beverly Hills, 1968-70; pres. Paul Spindler & Co., L.A., 1970-75; exec. v.p. Manning Selvage & Lee, Inc., N.Y.C., 1975-85; pres. The Spindler Co., L.A., 1985-87; pres. Western div. GCI Group, L.A., 1987-91; pres. GCI Spindler, L.A., 1991-96; cons. GCI Group Inc., L.A., 1997—; chmn. Bristol Tech. Sys., Inc., Irvine, Calif., 1997—; bd. dirs. Phoenix House Calif., Inc.; vis. com. mem. Sch. Bus. Adminstrn. U. So. Calif. Cpl. U.S. Army, 1952-54. Mem. Pub. Relations Soc. Am., Mountain Gate Country Club (L.A.). Democrat. Jewish. Office: Bristol Tech Sys Inc 18201 Von Karman Ave Ste 305 Irvine CA 92612-1005

SPINELLA, J(OSEPH) JOHN, insurance company executive; b. Queens, N.Y., Jan. 13, 1946; s. Peter Paul and Catherine (Vecchio) S.; m. MaryAnn D. Spinella, Feb. 1, 1969; children: Donna, Debra. BS in Math., SUNY, Cortland, 1972. Actuarial asst. Aetna Life & Casualty, Hartford, Conn., 1971-77; assoc. actuary INA Ins. Co., Phila., 1977-82; exec. v.p., chief operating officer Med. Mut. Liability Insurance Soc. of Md., Towson, 1982-85; pres., COO Med. Mut. Liability Soc. of Md., Towson, 1985, pres., CEO, 1986-87; pres. Spinella & Assocs., Inc., Balt., 1987-92, 95—; pres. med. profl. liability divsn. Great Am. Ins. Co., Hunt Valley, Md., 1992-95; mem. Gov.'s commn. on health care providers profl. liability ins., 1983-85, Gov.'s joint exec. legis. task force on med. malpractice, 1985, Annapolis, Md.; bd. dirs. Med. Mid-Atlantic Ins. Soc. of Md., Mid-Atlantic Med. Ins. Co., Interstate Automobile Ins. Co. Mem. Md. Hosp. Assn. tort reform task force, Towson, 1985. Roman Catholic. Avocations: golf, tennis, squash. Home: 11 David Luther Ct Cockeysville Hunt Valley MD 21030-1741 Office: Spinella & Assocs Inc 11 David Luther Ct Cockeysville MD 21030-1741

SPINELLA, JUDY LYNN, healthcare administrator; b. Ft. Worth, Apr. 8, 1948; d. Gettis Breon and Velrea Inez (Webb) Prothro; children: Scott Slater, Jennifer. BS, U. Tex., 1971; MS, Tex. Woman's U., 1973; MBA, Vanderbilt U., 1993. RN, Tex., Calif., Tenn. Asst. prof. U. Tex., Arlington, 1976-81; dir. emergency svcs. San Francisco Gen. Hosp., 1981-84, assoc. adminstr. for clin. svcs., 1984-88; exec. dir. for nursing svcs. Vanderbilt U. Med. Ctr., Nashville, 1988-93, dir. patient care svcs., 1993-94; dir., COO Vanderbilt U. Hosp., Nashville, 1994-96; healthcare cons. APM, Inc., N.Y.C., 1996—. Wharton fellow Johnson & Johnson, 1987. Mem. Am. Orgn. Nurse Execs., Emergency Nurses Assn. (bd. dirs., treas. 1979-86), Tenn. Orgn. Nurse Execs. (bd. dirs. 1989-91), Sigma Theta Tau. Avocations: hiking, skiing, travel. Home: 431 Prestwick Ct Nashville TN 37205

SPINELLI, ANNE CATHERINE, elementary education educator; b. Chgo., Dec. 19, 1943; d. Stanley J. and Lucy A. (Schmidt) Malaski; m. Joseph P. Spinelli Jr., May 28, 1966. BS in Edn., Ohio U., 1965; postgrad., Ashland U., 1989—. Lic. tchr. kindergarten - 8th grade. Tchr. K-3 North Olmsted (Ohio) City Schs., 1965-70, master tchr., 1970-71, kindergarten tchr., 1971-74; kindergarten tchr. Cloverleaf Schs., Lodi, Ohio, 1974—; seminar presenter sci. dept. Ednl. Rsch. Coun. Am., Cleve., 1969-74, State of Ohio Supr. Assn., Columbus, 1986, Great Lakes Internat. Reading Assn., Chgo., 1993; panelist Ohio Coun. Elem. Sch. Sci. Conv., Akron, 1969; speaker Nat. Sci. Tchrs. Assn. Great Lakes Conf., Cleve., 1971, State of Ohio Proficiency Conf., Cleve., 1996. Co-author: North Olmsted Schools Motor Perception Book for Kindergarten, 1970, Kingergarten Home Activities Book, 1991. Mem. Zoning Commn., Westfield Twp., Medina County, Ohio, 1978-90; area coord. Cancer Soc., Medina County, 1983, 85, 89; mem. Zoning Bd. Appeals, Westfield Twp Medina County, Ohio, 1996—. Jennings scholar Jennings Found., N.E. Ohio, 1987-88; named Outstanding Educator/Acad. Subjects Mid East Ohio/Spl. Edn. Regional Resouce Ctr., 1994, Medina County (Ohio) Tchr. of the Year, 1995; finalist Tchr. of Yr. for Ohio, 1996. Mem. ASCD, NEA, Ohio Edn. Assn., No. Ohio Edn. Assn., N.E. Ohio Edn. Assn., Cloverleaf Edn. Assn. (bldg. reps. 1985-94), Internat. Reading Assn., Lizotte Reading Coun., Elem., Kindergarten, Nursery Sch. Educators. Avocations: travel, gardening. Office: Westfield Elem Sch 9055 S LeRoy Rd Westfield Center OH 44251

SPINELLI, JERRY, writer; b. Norristown, Pa., Feb. 1, 1941; s. Louis Anthony and Lorna Mae (Bigler) S.; m. Eileen Mesi, May 24, 1977; children: Kevin, Barbara, Lana, Jeffrey, Molly, Sean, Benjamin. BA, Gettysburg (Pa.) Coll., 1963; MA, Johns Hopkins U., 1964. Editor Chilton Co., Radnor, Pa., 1966-89. Author: Space Station Seventh Grade, 1982, Who Put That Hair in My Toothbrush?, 1984, Night of the Whale, 1985, Jason and Marceline, 1986, Dump Days, 1988, Maniac Magee, 1990 (Newbery medal 1991, Boston Globe/Horn Book award 1991), Bathwater Gang, 1990, There's a Girl in My Hammerlock, 1991, Dump Days, 1991, Fourth Grade Rats, 1991, Bathwater Gang Get Down to Business, 1992, Do the Funky Pickle, 1992, Report to the Principal's Office!, 1992, Who Ran My Underwear Up the Flagpole?, 1992, Picklemania, 1993, Tooter Pepperday, 1995, Crash, 1996. Avocations: tennis, reading, country music, travel. *

SPINGOLA, JEANNIE SAUNDRA, college, special education and adult educator, counselor; b. San Francisco, June 17; d. Frank and Camella Regina (Mazzaferro) S.; m. Peter William Connolly. BA, San Francisco Coll. Women, 1970; MA, U. San Francisco, 1974; student, Dominican Coll., 1971. Counselor Dept. Store Local 1100, San Francisco; cons. ESL Am. Fgn. Studies, San Francisco; counselor, instr. San Francisco Coll. Dist.; cons. Fgn. Lang. Inst., San Francisco. Composer and vocal performer classical and musical comedy Macy's California. Mem. ASCD, ICF, MEA/OSIA, CABE, Am. Fedn. Tchrs., AMA, CAMP, Nat. Assn. Hist. Preservation, Am. CB Radio Assn., Calif. Psychol. Assn., Friends of J. Paul Libr.

SPINK, FRANK HENRY, JR., association manager, publisher, urban planner,; b. Chgo., Sept. 23, 1935; s. Frank Henry and Madeline Imogene (Ryan) S.; m. Barbara Jean Westbrook, June 30, 1962; children: Christina Jean, Suzan Josette. BArch, U. Ill., 1958; M of Urban Planning, U. Wash., 1963. Planner City of Bellevue, Wash., 1961-62, City of Fremont, Calif., 1963-66; planning dir. City of Pleasanton, Calif., 1966-67; community builders coun. dir. ULI-The Urban Land Inst., Washington, 1967-72; program div. dir. ULI-The Urban Land Inst., 1972-74, tech. publs. div. dir., 1974-75, publs. dir., 1976-80, publs. v.p., pub., 1981—; founding mem. and trustee emeritus Partners for Liveable Places, Washington. Creator/pub.: (subscription svc.) Project Reference File, 1971—; creator (reference book series) Community Builders Handbook Series, 1975—; contbr. numerous books by ULI, 1975—. Lt. USNR, 1958-61. Mem. Am. Inst. of Cert. Planners, Va. Watercolor Soc. (founder artist), Sumi'e Soc. of Am. (gold medal 1990, Best of Show 1991), Potomac Valley Watercolorists (pres.), Fremont Artist Assn. (pres.), Soc. of Western Artists, Lambda Alpha Internat. (pres. George Washington chpt. 1990-91, v.p. East 1992-95, 1st v.p. 1996—). Republican. Episcopal. Avocations: watercolorist, oriental watercolorist. Home and Studio: 5158 Piedmont Pl Annandale VA 22003-5527 Office: ULI-The Urban Land Inst 1025 Thomas Jefferson St NW Washington DC 20007-5201

SPINKS, JOHN LEE, retired engineering executive; b. Central City, Ky., June 19, 1924; s. William Lee and Lucy Susan (Greenwood) S.; m. Marion Louisa Mutz, Dec. 24, 1951; children—Susan Marie, Douglas John. B.S.M.E., U. Ky., 1951; postgrad., U. So. Calif., 1951-52, UCLA, 1957-58; grad., Res. Police Acad., 1977; Ph.D. (hon.), World U., 1984. Registered profl. engr., Calif., La., Tex., Del., Wis., N.H., Okla., Ky., Miss.; diplomate Am. Acad. Environ. Engrs. Aerodynamicist Rockwell Internat., Los Angeles, 1951-52, Downey, Calif., 1954-55; engr. Bell Telephone Labs., Burlington, N.C., 1952-54, Mobil Oil Corp., Torrance, Calif., 1955-56; supervising engr. II S. Coast Air Quality Mgmt. Dist., El Monte, Calif., 1956-83; pres. Environ. Emissions Engring. Co., Palos Verdes Peninsula, Calif., 1983-95; ret., 1995; dep. dir. civil engring. divsn., space divsn. USAFR, L.A. AFB, 1961-73; past cons. nat. and internat. govt. air quality agys. Co-author: Air Pollution Engineering Manual, 1967, 2d edit., 1973. Former res. police officer Hermosa Beach Police Dept.; mgr. Little League Baseball, 1966-70; instr. rock and ice mountaineering dir. AQMD Golf League, 1968-81; formre lectr. marathon running; usher St. Francis Episcopal Ch., Palos Verdes Estates, 1968-81. Lt. col. USAAF, 1943-46. Decorated Air Force Commendation medal; recipient U.S. Presdl. Sports award in running, 1977, Sierra Peaks emblem; named to Hon. Order Ky. Cols. Fellow Inst. for Advancement Engring.; mem. Am. Assn. Engring. Socs., Sierra Club, Triangle. Clubs: Srs. Track, Pacific Crest. Home: 26856 Eastvale Rd Palos Verdes Peninsula CA 90274-4007 *The achievement of one's personal goals in itself has little meaning. Complete fulfillment comes with guiding youngsters in their formative years, helping them reach higher levels of motivation and social behavior to insure saneness for tomorrow.*

SPINKS, MICHAEL, retired professional boxer; b. 1956; s. Leon and Kay S.; m. Sandy (dec.); 1 child, Michelle. Profl. boxer, 1976—. World Boxing Assn. Light-Heavyweight champion, 1981-86; World Boxing Council Light-Heavyweight champion, 1983-85; Internat. Boxing Fedn. Heavyweight champion, 1985-87; Gold medalist 1976 Olympics, Montreal, Can. Office: care Butch Lewis 250 W 57th St New York NY 10019-3700*

SPINKS, PAUL, retired library director; b. London, Mar. 7, 1922; came to U.S., 1952; m. Clarice Ada Goode, Jan. 27, 1946 (dec. May 1996); 1 child, Philip Andrew. B.A., U. Okla., Norman, 1958; M.L.S., U. Okla., 1959. Catalog asst. Brit. Mus. Library, London, 1939-52; research reports librarian Naval Postgrad. Sch., Monterey, Calif., 1959-61; assoc. librarian Naval Postgrad. Sch., 1961-74, dir. libraries, 1975-93; prof. emeritus, 1993—. Author studies in field. Recipient Civilian Svc. Meritorious award USN, 1993. Mem. ALA, Spl. Libraries Assn., Am. Soc. Info. Sci. Episcopalian. Club: Brit.-Am. (sec. Monterey 1982-85). Home: 855 Capistrano Dr Salinas CA 93901-2420

SPINNATO, JOSEPH ANTHONY, II, obstetrician; b. Ketchikan, Alaska, May 10, 1949; s. Joseph Anthony and Ann Spinatto; m. Diane Dusak, Apr. 26, 1969; children: Joseph Anthony III, Mark Andrew, Julie Anne. BS, U. Dayton, 1970; MD, U. Louisville, 1974. Diplomate Am. Bd. Obstetricians and Gynecologists. Resident on ob/gyn U. Louisville, 1974-77; asst. prof. ob/gyn Sch. Medicine Tex. Tech U., Lubbock, 1979-82; nutrition intern Montreal (Can.) Diet Dispensary, 1980; fellow in maternal-fetal medicine U. Tenn. Ctr. for Health Scis., Memphis, 1982-84, clin. instr. dept. ob/gyn, 1982-84; assoc. prof. divsn. maternal-fetal medicine dept. ob/gyn Coll. Medicine U. South Ala., 1984-88; dir., prof. divsn. maternal-fetal medicine dept. ob/gyn. Sch. Medicine/U. Louisville, 1988—; mem. ob/gyn staff Lubbock Gen. Hosp., 1979-82, City of Memphis Hosps., 1982-84, U. South Ala. Med. Ctr., Mobile, 1984-88, Norton Hosp., Louisville, 1988—, U. Louisville Hosp., 1988—; mem. birth defects adv. com., human resources dept. Commonwealth of Ky., 1992; dir. maternal transport North Hosp., 199-92, dir. women's reproductive testing cir., 1988—; dir. improved pregnancy outcome project U. Louisville, 1988-92, 96—; dir. Fetal Rev. Bd., 1990-92; presenter, lectr., rschr. in field. Spl. reviewer jours. in field; contbr. articles, abstracts to profl. publs. Dir. teenage parent program Emerson Sch., Louisville, 1988-92, 96—. Lt. comdr. Med. Corps USN, 1977-79. Nutrition intern March of Dimes, 1980; grantee Smith Kline French Labs., 1986, NIH, 1986, NKC Cmty. Trust Fund, 1988, 95-96, WHAS Crusade for Children, 1989-90, 92, Ky. Human Resources Dept., 1990, 93-94; recipient Outstanding Tchr. award, 1991, 93, APGO Excellence in Tchg. award U. Louisville, 1994. Mem. Am. Coll. Obstetricians and Gynecologists, Assn. Profs. of Gynecology and Obstetrics (Excellence in Tchg. award 1994), Soc. Perinatal Obstetricians, So. Perinatal Assn., Nat. Perinatal Assn., Jefferson County Med. Soc., Louisville Obgyn Soc., Am. Inst. Ultrasound in Medicine. Avocations: tennis, golf, music, basketball. Office: U Louisville Dept Ob/Gyn Louisville KY 40292

SPINNER, ROBERT JAY, orthopedic surgeon; b. N.Y.C., Dec. 8, 1961; s. Morton and Paula (Lerner) S. SB, MIT, 1984; M of Studies, Oxford (Eng.) U., 1985; MD, Mayo Clinic, 1989. Rsch. fellow, Luce scholar Prince of Wales Hosp., Hong Kong, 1989-90; intern in surgery Duke Univ., Durham, N.C., 1990-91, jr. resident in surgery, 1991-92, resident in orthopaedic surgery, 1992-96; resident in neurosurgery Mayo Clinic, Rochester, Minn., 1996—. Recipient Davison Teaching award Duke U. Med. Sch., 1993, Goldner Rsch. award in Orthopaedic Surgery Duke U. Med. Ctr., 1996; Schilling scholar Mayo Found., 1984-86. Mem. Phi Beta Kappa, Sigma Xi, Alpha Chi Sigma. Avocations: travel, reading.

SPINOLA, JOHN, broadcast executive; married; 2 children. B, U. Notre Dame; M, UCLA. V.p., gen. mgr. WPCQ-TV, Charlotte, N.C., WJZ-TV, Balt., WBZ-AM, Boston, WBZ-TV, Boston; v.p. ops. Group W TV Co., Boston; pres., gen. mgr. WJBK-TV FOX 2, Southfield, Mich., 1995—. Office: WJBK-TV Box 2000 Southfield MI 48037-2000

SPINOTTI, DANTE, cinematographer. Cinematographer: (films) Sotto, Sotto, 1984, The Berlin Affair, 1985, Manhunter, 1986, Choke Canyon, 1986, Crimes of the Heart, 1986, From the Hip, 1987, Illegally Yours, 1987, Beaches, 1988, Mamba, 1988, The Legend of the Holy Drinker, The Comfort of Strangers, 1989, Torrents of Spring, 1989, Hudson Hawk, 1990, True Colors, 1991, Frankie and Johnny, 1992, (with Doug Milsome) The Last of the Mohicans, 1992, Blink, 1993, The Quick and the Dead, 1994, Nell, 1994, The Man of the Stars, 1994, Heat, 1995. Office: Smith/Gosnell/Nicholson & Assoc PO Box 1166 1515 Palisades Dr Pacific Palisades CA 90272*

SPINRAD, BERNARD ISRAEL, physicist, educator; b. N.Y.C., Apr. 16, 1924; s. Abraham and Rose (Sorrin) S.; m. Marion Eisen, June 29, 1951; children: Alexander Abraham, Mark David, Jeremy Paul, Diana Esther; m. Lois Ringston Helton, Jan. 28, 1983. BS with honors, Yale, 1942, MS, 1944, PhD in Phys. Chemistry, 1945, Sterling fellow postdoctoral research, 1945-46. Physicist Oak Ridge Nat. Lab., 1946-48; mem. staff Argonne Nat. Lab., 1949-67, 70-72, dir. reactor engring. div., 1957-63, sr. physicist applied physics div., 1963-67, 70-72; dir. div. nuclear power and reactors IAEA, Vienna, Austria, 1967-70; prof. nuclear engring. Oreg. State U., Corvallis, 1972-82, prof. emeritus, 1983—; prof., chmn. dept. nuclear engring. Iowa State U., Ames, 1983-90, prof. emeritus, 1990—; adviser and participant U.S. delegation Internat. Conf. Peaceful Uses Atomic Energy, Geneva, 1955, 58; cons. IAEA, 1961, 63, 72, 74; chmn. European-Am. Com. Reactor Physics, 1962-64; mem. com. nuclear and alternative energy systems NRC, 1974-79, com. innovative concepts and approaches to energy conservation, 1984-85, com. univ. research reactors, 1986-88; vis. researcher Internat. Inst. Applied Systems Analysis, Vienna, 1978-79, chmn. nuclear engring. dept. head orgn., 1986-87. Author books, papers and reports in field; mem. editorial bd. Annals of Nuclear Energy. Named Man of Year Chgo., 1956, Man of Year Hinsdale, Ill., 1958. Fellow Am. Phys. Soc., Am. Nuclear Soc. (past dir.); mem. AAAS, Am. Chem. Soc., UN Assn. Am., Sigma Xi. Address: 18803 37th Ave NE Seattle WA 98155-2713 *I have lived by trying to understand the rich fabric of the world and our lives, and I love the richness. All the elements should be in it, and this means that apparent contradictions are to be harmonized and resolved, rather than set against each other. I find that I have to be selectively moderate, aggressively opposing the nonsense which is bound up with the valid points in polarized ideologies. It is an attitude which is a bit lonely, for it rejects blind loyalty and blind faith, but I value the dignity of it.*

SPINRAD, HYRON, astronomer; b. N.Y.C., Feb. 17, 1934; s. Emanuel B. and Ida (Silverman) S.; m. Bette L. Abrams, Aug. 17, 1958; children—Michael, Robert, Tracy. A.B., U. Calif. at Berkeley, 1955, M.A., 1959, Ph.D. (Lick Obs. fellow), 1961. Studied galaxies U. Calif. at Berkeley, 1960-61; planetary atmospheres work Jet Propulsion Lab., Pasadena, Calif., 1961-63; investigation atmospheres of coolest stars U. Calif. at Berkeley, 1964-70. Mem. Am. Astron. Soc., Astron. Soc. Pacific. Spl. research water vapor on Mars, molecular hydrogen on Jupiter, Saturn, Uranus and Neptune, temperature measurements on Venus atmosphere, spectra of galaxies and near-infrared observations, 71-72, location of faint radio galaxies, redshifts of galaxies, galaxy evolution and cosmology, 1973, spectroscopic observations of volatile gases in comets. Home: 7 Ketelsen Ct Moraga CA 94556-1814 Office: Univ California Dept Astronomy Berkeley CA 94720

SPINRAD, ROBERT JOSEPH, computer scientist; b. N.Y.C., Mar. 20, 1932; s. Sidney and Isabel (Reiff) S.; m. Verna Winderman, June 27, 1954; children: Susan Irene, Paul Reiff. B.S., Columbia U., 1953, M.S. (Bridgham fellow), 1954; Ph.D. (Whitney fellow), MIT, 1963. Registered profl. engr., N.Y. Project engr. Bulova Research & Devel. Lab., N.Y.C., 1953-55; sr. scientist Brookhaven Nat. Lab., Upton, N.Y., 1955-68; v.p. Sci. Data Systems, Santa Monica, Calif., 1968-69; v.p. programming Xerox Corp., El Segundo, Calif., 1969-71; dir. info. scis. Xerox Corp., 1971-76, v.p. systems devel., 1976-78; v.p. research Xerox Corp., Palo Alto, 1978-83; dir. systems tech. Xerox Corp., 1983-87, dir. corp. tech., 1987-92, v.p. tech. analysis and devel., 1992-94; v.p. technology strategy, 1994—; cons. Contbr. articles to profl. jours. Mem. Nat. Acad. Engring., Calif. Coun. on Sci. and Tech., Sigma Xi, Tau Beta Pi. Achievements include patents in field. Office: Xerox Corp 3333 Coyote Hill Rd Palo Alto CA 94304-1314

SPIOTTA, RAYMOND HERMAN, editor; b. Bklyn., Feb. 24, 1927; s. Michael Joseph and Olga Elizabeth (Schmidt) S.; m. Maria Theresa Attanasio, Apr. 17, 1949; children: Robert, Michael, Ronald, Mark, Sandra. B.M.E., Pratt Inst., 1953. Mfg. engr. Arma div. Am. Bosch Arma Corp., Garden City, N.Y., 1948-53; mng. editor Machinery mag., N.Y.C., 1953-65; editor Machine and Tool Blue Book, Wheaton, Ill., 1965-89; editorial dir. Machine and Tool Blue Book & Mfg. Systems, Carol Stream, Ill., 1989-90; cons. editor Cutting Tool Engring., Northbrook, Ill., 1992-95; acquisitions editor Hanser Gardner Publs., Cin., 1995—. Contbr. to Am. Peoples Ency. Yearbook; contbr. articles to profl. jours. Mem. DuPage County (Ill.) area council Boy Scouts Am., 1966-73. Served with AC USNR, 1944-48. Mem. Numerical Control Soc. of AIM-Tech., Soc. Am. Value Engrs., Soc. Mfg. Engrs., Am. Inst. Indsl. Engrs., Robotics Internat., Computer and Automated Sys. Assn. Roman Catholic. Home and Office: 1484 Aberdeen Ct Naperville IL 60564-9796

SPIOTTO, JAMES ERNEST, lawyer; b. Chgo., Nov. 25, 1946; s. Michael Angelo and Vinnetta Catherine (Henninger) S.; m. Ann Elizabeth Humphreys, Dec. 23, 1972; children: Michael Thomas, Mary Catherine, Joan Elizabeth, Kathryn Ann. AB, St. Mary's of the Lake, 1968; JD, U. Chgo., 1972. Bar: Ill. 1972, U.S. Dist. Ct. (no. dist.) Ill. 1973, U.S. Ct. Appeals (3rd and 7th cir.) 1974, U.S. Supreme Ct. 1978, U.S. Ct. Appeals (9th cir.) 1984, U.S. Dist. Ct. (so. dist.) Calif. 1984. Exclusionary rule study-project dir. Law Enforcement Assistance Agy. Grant, Chgo., 1972; law clk. to presiding justice U.S. Dist. Ct., Chgo., 1972-74; assoc. Chapman and Cutler, Chgo., 1974-80, ptnr., 1980—; chmn. program on defaulted bonds and bankruptcy Practising Law Inst., 1982—, chmn program on troubled debt financing, 1987—. Author: Defaulted Securities, 1990; contbr. numerous articles to profl. jours. With USAR, 1969-75. Mem. Assn. Bond Lawyers, Law Club of City of Chgo., Union League, Econs. Club Chgo. Roman Catholic. Office: Chapman and Cutler 111 W Monroe St Chicago IL 60603

SPIRA, JOEL SOLON, electronics company executive; b. N.Y.C., Mar. 1, 1927; m. Ruth Rodale, Nov. 7, 1954; children: Susan, Lily, Juno. BS in Physics, Purdue U., 1948. Project engr. Reeves Instrument Corp., Paramus, N.J., 1952-59; prin. systems analyst ITT Communications Systems, Paramus, 1959-61; pres., dir. rsch. Lutron Electronics Co., Inc., Coopersburg, Pa., 1961-90, chmn., 1990—. Mem. Nat. Acad. Engring. Office: Lutron Electronics Co Inc 7200 Suter Rd Coopersburg PA 18036-1249

SPIRA, MELVIN, plastic surgeon; b. Chgo., July 3, 1925; s. Samuel and Jessie (Tivin) S.; m. Rita Silver, Nov. 27, 1952; children—Mary Ann, Joel Bennett, Pamela Beth. Student, Wright Jr. Coll, Chgo., 1942-43, Franklin and Marshall Coll., Lancaster, Pa., 1943-44; DDS, Northwestern U., 1947, MSD, 1951; MD, Med. Coll. of Ga., 1956. Diplomate Am. Bd. Plastic Surgery (chmn. 1984-85). Intern Duke U. Hosp., Durham, N.C., 1956-57, jr. asst. resident, 1958-59, asst. resident, 1959-60; resident Jefferson Davis Hosp, Houston, 1960-61, asst. in surgery and plastic surgery; sr. attending physician Ben Taub Gen. Hosp, Houston, chief of plastic surgery; attending physician Tex. Children's Hosp., Houston; chief plastic surgery St. Lukes Episcopal Hosp., Houston; prof. Baylor Coll. Medicine, Houston, past head divsn. plastic surgery. Served with USN, 1943-45, 48-50. Fellow ACS; mem. Houston Surg. Soc., Am. Soc. Maxillofacial Surgeons (pres. 1974-75), Am. Soc. Plastic and Reconstructive Surgeons, Harris County Med. Soc., Plastic Surgery Research Council, So. Med. Assn., Tex. Med. Assn., Am. Trauma Soc., G.V. Black Soc., Internat. Soc. for Burn Injuries, Am. Burn Assn., Am. Cleft Palate Assn., Am. Assn. Plastic Surgeons (pres. 1992-93), Acad. Plastic Surgery Forum, Internat. Soc. Reconstructive Microsurgery, Tex. Surg. Soc., Michael E. DeBakey Internat. Cardiovascular Soc., Baron Hardy Soc., Am. Soc. for Aesthetic Plastic Surgery, Alpha Omega Alpha, Sigma Xi. Avocations: snow skiing; photography; painting; tennis. Office: Baylor Coll Medicine Div Plastic Surgery 6560 Fannin St Ste 800 Houston TX 77030-2725

SPIRA, PATRICIA GOODSITT, performing arts association executive; b. Milw.; d. Lawrence Manfred and Ruth Pauline (Miller) Goodsitt; m. Marvin Alfred Spira, July 12, 1952; children: David, James, Ann, Ellen. BA in History, U. Wis., Milw., 1967. Dir. group sales Swan Theatre and Supper Club, Milw., 1962-63; mgr. box office Performing Arts Ctr., Milw., 1969-80; dir. devel. St. Louis Conservatory and Schs., 1980-81; pres. Box Office Mgmt. Internat., N.Y.C., 1981—; tchr. Creative Dramatics, Milw., 1962-66; adv. coun. Town Hall, N.Y.C., 1989—; bd. dirs. Theatre and Dance Co., N.Y.C., 1986-89. bd. dirs. Milw. Chamber Music Soc., 1974-80. Mem. Am. Soc. Assn. Execs. (cert.), N.Y. Soc. Assn. Execs. Avocations: reading, travel, theater. Office: The Internat Ticketing Assn 250 W 57th St Ste 722 New York NY 10107-0799

SPIRER, JUNE DALE, marketing executive, clinical psychologist; b. N.Y.C., May 14, 1943; d. Leon and Gloria (Wagner) Spirer; BA, Adelphi U., 1965; MS, Yeshiva U., 1980, PhD in Psychology, 1984, postgrad. NYU, 1997. Diplomate Am. Coll. Forensic Examiners. TV/radio buyer BBD&O, 1965-66, SSC&B, 1966-68; sr. media planner Norman, Craig & Kummel, N.Y.C., 1968-71; assoc. media dir. Ted Bates Co., 1971-72; v.p., account supt. C.T. Clyne Co., N.Y.C., 1972-74; dir. advt. Am. Express, 1974-75; corp. dir. advt. Del Labs., Farmingdale, N.Y., 1975-79; pres. J. Spirer & Assocs., Inc., N.Y.C., 1978-96; pres., CEO Media Placement Svcs., Inc., 1985-95, Tactics, Inc., 1988-95; CEO 75 Main St. Restaurant, Southampton, N.Y., 1990—; Mem. Am. Psychol. Assn. Home: PO Box 490 Southampton NY 11969-0490 Office: 2 Horatio St New York NY 10014-1608

SPIRES, ROBERT CECIL, foreign language educator; b. Missouri Valley, Iowa, Dec. 1, 1936; s. Roy C. and Ellen M. (Epperson) S.; m. Roberta A. Hyde, Feb. 2, 1963; children: Jeffrey R., Leslie Ann. BA, U. Iowa, 1959, MA, 1963, PhD, 1968. Asst. prof. Ohio U., Athens, 1967-69; asst. prof. dept. Spanish and Portuguese U. Kans., Lawrence, 1969-72, assoc. prof., 1972-78, prof., 1978—, chmn. dept., 1983-92. Author: La novela española, 1978, Beyond the Metafictional Mode, 1984, Transparent Simulacra, 1988, Post-Totalitarian Spanish Fiction, 1996; contbg. editor SigloXX/20th Century; editl. bd. Jour. of Interdisciplinary Literary Studies, 1993—, Ind. Jour. of Hispanic Lit., 1992—. Served with U.S. Army, 1959-61. NEH fellow, 1981-82, U.S.-Spain Joint Com. fellow, 1985-86, Hall Ctr. for Humanities fellow, 1992, Program Cultural Coop. fellow, 1993. Mem. Revista de Estudios Hispánicos (editorial bd. 1985—), Anales de Literatura Contemporánea (editorial bd. 1981—), Letras Peninsulares (editorial bd. 1987—), MLA (del. assembly 1989-91), MLA 20th Century Spain (exec. com. 1983-89), 20th Century Spanish Assn. Am. (v.p. 1989-92). Home: 2420 Orchard Ln Lawrence KS 66049-2710 Office: U Kans Dept Spanish & Portuguese Lawrence KS 66045-0239

SPIRN, MICHELE SOBEL, communications professional, writer; b. Newark, Jan. 26, 1943; d. Jack and Sylvia (Cohen) Sobel; m. Steven Frederick Spirn, Jan. 27, 1968; 1 child, Joshua. BA, Syracuse U., 1965. Creative dir. Planned Communications Svcs., N.Y.C., 1966-72, EDL Prodns., N.Y.C., 1972-73; free-lance writer Bklyn., 1973-83; dir. pub. rels. Nat. Coun. Jewish Women, N.Y.C., 1983-90, dir. communications, 1990-95; freelance writer Bklyn., 1995—; adj. lectr. CUNY, Bklyn., 1977-81. Author: The Fast Shoes, 1985, The Boy Who Liked Green, 1985, The Know-Nothings, 1995; co-author: A Man Can Be..., 1981, A Know-Nothing Birthday, 1997, Racing to the Light, 1997, Wait Till The Midnight Hour, 1997; editor, columnist Children's Entertainment Rev. mag., N.Y.C., 1982; columnist The Phoenix newspaper, Bklyn., 1983. Pres. Tenth St. Block Assn., Bklyn., 1989-91; vol. Model Media Program, Bklyn., 1985—. Recipient Silver medal for pub. svc. film N.Y. Internat. Film and TV Festival, 1972. Mem. Editl. Freelancers Assn., Soc. Children's Book Writers and Illustrators. Avocations: reading, gardening.

SPIRNAK, JOHN PATRICK, urologist, educator; b. Cleve., Mar. 17, 1951; s. John Joseph and Mary Barbara (Mancos) S.; m. Diane Lynne Miller, Sept. 15, 1979; children: Jennifer, Patrick, Christopher. BS in Zoology, Ohio U., 1973; MD, Emory U., 1977; degree in Urology, Case Western Reserve U., 1983. Diplomate Am. Bd. Urology. Intern, gen. surg. resident Univ. Hosp., Cleve., 1977-79, urology resident, 1980-83; nephrology rsch. resident Metro Health Med. Ctr., Cleve., 1979-80, dir. urology, 1987—; sr. instr. divns. urology Case Western Reserve U., Cleve., 1983-85, asst. prof. urology, 1985-91, assoc. prof. urology, 1991—; adv. panel mem. U.S. Pharmacopeia Urology, Washington, 1986—. Editor Urologic Decision Making, 1991, New Diagnostic Tests, 1996; manuscript reviewer Jour. Endourology, 1989—, Urology, 1993—, Jour. Urology, 1994—; contbr. articles to profl. jours. and chpts. to books. Named One of Top Doctors Cleve. Mag., 1996. Fellow ACS; mem. AMA, Am. Assn. Surgery Trauma, Am. Urol. Assn., Cleve. Urol. Soc. (sec./treas. 1986-88, pres. 1988-89). Avocations: sports, gardening. Home: 2178 Silveridge Trl Westlake OH 44145-1797 Office: Metro Health Med Ctr 2500 Metrohealth Dr Cleveland OH 44109-1900

SPIRO, HERBERT JOHN, political scientist, politician, educator, ambassador; b. Hamburg, Germany, Sept. 7, 1924; came to U.S., 1938, naturalized, 1944; s. Albert John and Marianne (Stiefel) S.; m. Elizabeth Anna Petersen, June 7, 1958 (div.); children: Peter John, Alexander Charles Stiefel; m. Marion Ballin, July 22, 1985. Student, San Antonio Jr. Coll., 1942-43; AB summa cum laude, Harvard U., 1949, MA, 1950, PhD, 1953; MA (hon.), U. Pa., 1971. Adminstrv. asst. U.S. War Dept., Vienna, Austria, 1945-46; mem. faculty Harvard U., Cambridge, Mass., 1950-61, asst. prof., 1957-61; assoc. prof. polit. sci. Amherst (Mass.) Coll., 1961-65; prof. polit. sci. U. Pa., Phila., 1965-73; mem. policy planning staff Dept. State, Washington, 1970-75; ambassador to Cameroon, 1975-77; amb. to Equatorial Guinea, 1975-76; fellow Woodrow Wilson Internat. Ctr. for Scholars, Smithsonian Instn., Washington, 1978; vis. prof. polit. sci. Def. Intelligence Sch., Washington, 1979-80; univ. prof. polit. sci. John F. Kennedy Inst. for N.Am. Studies, Free U. Berlin, 1980-89; Fulbright sr. research prof. U. Coll. Rhodesia and Nyasaland, 1959-60; cons. Brit. Commn. to Rev. Constn., Fedn. Rhodesia and Nyasaland, 1960, Japanese Commn. on Revision Constn., 1962; vis. assoc. prof. U. Chgo., 1961, Stanford (Calif.) U., 1963; chmn. Asian and African Studies program, Amherst-Smith-Mt. Holyoke Colls., U. Mass., 1964-65; vis. prof. internat. affairs Woodrow Wilson Sch., Princeton (N.J.) U., 1966; mem. adv. council polit. sci. Haverford Coll., 1966-71; affiliated with Nuffield Coll., Oxford (Eng.) U., 1967-68; resident scholar Rockefeller Found. Study Ctr., Bellagio, Italy, 1968, 78; vis. prof. govt., guest scholar Ctr. for Internat. Affairs, Harvard U., 1983; vis. scholar U. Tex., Austin, 1984-89; life mem. Brit. studies faculty seminar U. Tex., Austin, 1983—; researcher Lyndon Baines Johnson Presdl. Library, 1985-86; fellow Aspen (Colo.) Inst. Humanistic Studies, 1986; adj. prof. govt. U. Tex., Austin, 1989-91; participant internat scholarly and diplomatic confs.; lectr. various univs. Author: Politics of German Codetermination, 1958, (with others) Patterns of Government, 1958, 2d edit., 1962, Government by Constitution, 1959, Politics in Africa, 1962, 2d edit., 1975, Five African States, 1963, World Politics: The Global System, 1966, (with others) Authority, Nomos I, 1958, Responsibility, Nomos III, 1960, Privacy Nomos XIII, 1971, Why Federations Fail, 1968, Responsibility in Government, 1969, The Dialectic of Representation 1619-1969, 1969, Politics as the Master Science: From Plato to Mao, 1970, Theory and Politics, 1971, Between Sovereignty and Integration, 1974, A New Foreign Policy Consensus?, 1979, (with others) The Legacy of the Constitution, 1987, (with others) Anti-Americanism, 1988; editor, contbr.: (with others) Africa: The Primacy of Politics, 1966, Patterns of African Development, 1967, 'Privatization' of U.S. Foreign Relations, 1995; contbr. to: World Book Ency., Ency. Britannica, Intern. Ency. of the Social Scis.; host Spiro's Conversations, Austin Community TV, 1992—; contbr. articles to profl. jours. Del. Tex. State Rep. Conv., 1990-92; precinct chmn. Travis County; Rep. cand. for Tex. Ho. of Reps., 1991, U.S. House of Reps., 1992, 94, U.S. Senate, 1993. Decorated Bronze Star with oak leaf cluster, Purple Heart; grand officer Legion of Valor Cameroon, 1977; recipient Detur prize Harvard Coll., 1948, Bowdoin prize, 1952; John Harvard scholar, 1949-51, Holzer scholar, 1949-51; Guggenheim fellow, 1959-60, Social Sci. Research Council faculty fellow, 1962, 67-68, Rockefeller Found. fellow, 1958, Sheldon travelling fellow Harvard U., also Fulbright fellow, 1953-54; Moody grantee Lyndon Baines Johnson Found., 1985. Fellow Assn. for Diplomatic Studies; mem. African Studies Assn., Am. Polit. Sci. Assn. (coun. 1968-70, chmn. election com. 1969), Internat. Polit. Sci. Assn., Am. Soc. Polit. and Legal Philosophy, Coun. Fgn. Rels., Am. Coun. on Germany, Coun. Am. Ambs., Am. Fgn. Svc. Assn., Retired Fgn. Svc. Assn. of Cen. Tex. (v.p. programs 1997—), Mil. Order Purple Heart, Austin Com. Fgn. Affairs (dir.), Harvard Alumni Assn. (appointed regional dir. Tex. 1994-97), Wissenschaftliche Gesellschaft Berlin, Signet Soc., Harvard U. Faculty Club, Harvard Club (N.Y.C.), Harvard Club Berlin (pres. 1985-89), Harvard Club Austin (pres. 1990-92), Phi Beta Kappa. Republican. Address: USAA Towers Apt 713 1 Towers Park Lane San Antonio TX 78209

SPIRO, HOWARD MARGET, physician, educator; b. Cambridge, Mass., Mar. 23, 1924; s. Thomas and Martha (Marget); m. Marian Freelove Wagner, Mar 11, 1951; children—Pamela Marget, Carolyn Standish, Philip Marget, Martha Standish. B.A., Harvard, 1944, M.D., 1947; M.A., Yale, 1967. Intern Peter Bent Brigham Hosp., Boston, 1947-48; resident Peter Bent Brigham Hosp., 1948-51, Mass. Gen. Hosp., 1953-55; practice medicine, specializing in gastroenterology New Haven, 1955—; chief gastrointestinal unit Yale Sch. Medicine, 1955-82, prof. medicine, 1967—, dir. program for humanities in medicine, 1983—. Author: Clinical Gastroenterology, 1970, 4th edit., 1993, Doctors, Patients and Placebos, 1986; editor: Jour. Clin. Gastroenterology, 1979—, (with others) When Doctors Get Sick, 1987, Empathy and the Practice of Medicine, 1993, Facing Death--Where Culture, Religion and Medicine Meet, 1996. Served with USNR, 1943-45; Served with AUS, 1951-53. Mem. ACP (master). Club: Madison Beach. Home: 89 Middle Beach Rd Madison CT 06443-3006 Office: Box 208019 333 Cedar St New Haven CT 06520-8019

SPIRO, MELFORD ELLIOT, anthropology educator; b. Cleve., Apr. 26, 1920; s. Wilbert I. and Sophie (Goodman) S.; m. Audrey Goldman, May 27, 1950; children: Michael, Jonathan. B.A., U. Minn., 1941; Ph.D., Northwestern U., 1950. Mem. faculty Washington U., St. Louis, 1948-52, U. Conn., 1952-57, U. Wash., 1957-64; prof. anthropology U. Chgo., 1964-68; prof., chmn. dept. anthropology U. Calif., San Diego, 1968—; Bd. dirs. Social Sci. Research Council, 1960-62. Author: (with E.G. Burrows) An Atoll Culture, 1953, Kibbutz: Venture in Utopia, 1955, Children of Kibbutz, 1958, Burmese Supernaturalism, 1967, Buddhism and Society: A Great Tradition and Its Burmese Vicissitudes, 1971, Kinship and Marriage in Burma, 1977, Gender and Culture: Kibbutz Women Revisited, 1979, Human Nature and Culture, 1993; editor: Context and Meaning in Culture Anthropology, 1965, Oedipus in the Trobriands, 1982, Burmese Brother or Anthropological Other?, 1992. Fellow Am. Acad. Arts and Scis., Nat. Acad. Scis.; mem. Am. Anthrop. Assn., Am. Ethnol. Soc. (pres. 1967-68), AAAS, Soc. for Psychol. Anthropology (pres. 1979-80). Home: 2500 Torrey Pines Rd La Jolla CA 92037

SPIRO, ROBERT HARRY, JR., foundation and business executive, educator; b. Asheville, N.C., Dec. 5, 1920; s. Robert Harry and Eoline Peterson (Shaw) S.; m. Terrie C. Gay, May 17, 1980; children by previous marriage: Robert Timothy, Elizabeth Susan, James Monroe. BS, Wheaton (Ill.) Coll., 1941; postgrad. Navy Supply Sch., Harvard U., 1943; postgrad., U. N.C., 1945-46; PhD, U. Edinburgh, Scotland, 1950; student, Union Theol. Sem., summers 1951-53; postdoctoral, Duke U., summer 1956; ScD (hon.), Fla. Inst. Tech. Assoc. prof. King Coll., Bristol, Tenn., 1946-50; prof. history Miss. Coll., 1950-57; pres. Blue Ridge Assembly, Black Mountain, N.C., 1957-60; dean Coll. Liberal Arts Mercer U., prof. history, 1960-64; pres. Jacksonville U., Fla., 1964-79; under sec. of Army, 1980-81; cons. to bus., 1981-84, 86—; nat. exec. dir. Res. Officers Assn. U.S., 1984-86; chmn. RHS Imprinted Products Inc., 1988—; past bd. mgrs. Voyager Variable Annuity of Fla., 1972-79; v.p. Am. Sec. Coun. Found., 1991—; past pres. Fla. Assn. Colls. and Univs.; mem., past chmn. Ind. Colls. and Univs., 1964-79, chmn., 1967; sec.-treas. Assn. Urban Univs., 1968-76; past mem. Fla.-Columbia Ptnrs.; gen. chmn. Jacksonville Sesquicentennial Commn., 1970-72; mem. N.C. Tricentennial Commn., 1959-65; past mem. adv. coun. Robert A. Taft Inst. Govt., Inst. Internat. Edn. Contbr. articles to profl. pubis. and encys. Trustee Southwestern Bapt. Theol. Sem., 1968-78; mem. Fla.-Colombia Ptnrs.; chmn. bd. Bapt. Coll. and Sem., Washington, 1989—. Lt. USNR, 1941-45; ret. rear adm. USNR, 1978. Decorated Palmes Academique (France); recipient Disting. Civilian Svc. award Dept. of Army, 1981. Mem. Navy League U.S. (former pres. Jacksonville coun.), Naval Res. Assn. (nat. adv. coun.), Res. Officers Assn. U.S. Naval Inst., Ret. Officers Assn., Am. Legion, Kiwanis (pres. Clinton, Miss. 1956-57; pres. Georgetown, D.C. club 1991-92), Army-Navy Country Club (Arlington, Va.), Army and Navy Club (Washington), Phi Delta Kappa, Alpha Kappa Psi, Phi Alpha Theta, Phi Kappa Phi. Home: 105 Follin Ln SE Vienna VA 22180-4957 *Esse Quam Videre—"To Be Rather than to Seem" —is an eloquent apothegm I learned in high school Latin classes. For me it has been a demanding goal for daily living, a worthy aspiration for each task in life and a challenging vision of what I wish and ought to be.*

SPIRO, THOMAS GEORGE, chemistry educator; b. Aruba, Netherlands Antilles, Nov. 7, 1935; s. Andor and Ilona S.; m. Helen Handin, Aug. 21, 1959; children—Peter, Michael. BS, UCLA, 1956; PhD, MIT, 1960. Fulbright rschr. U. Copenhagen, Denmark, 1960-61; NIH fellow Royal Inst. Tech., Stockholm, 1962-63; research chemist Calif. Research Corp., LaHabra, 1961-62; mem. faculty Princeton U., 1963—, prof. chemistry, 1974—, head dept., 1979-88, Eugene Higgins prof., 1981—. Author: (with William M. Stigliani) Environmental Issues in Chemical Perspective, 1980, Chemistry of the Environment, 1996; contbr. articles to profl. jours. Recipient Bomem-Michelson award Bomem Corp., 1986; NATO sr. fellow, 1972, Guggenheim fellow, 1990. Fellow AAAS; mem. Am. Chem. Soc., Phi Beta Kappa, Sigma Xi. Office: Princeton U Dept Chemistry Princeton NJ 08544

SPIRTOS, NICHOLAS GEORGE, lawyer, financial company executive; b. Youngstown, Ohio, Mar. 19, 1950; s. George Nicholas Spirtos and Tulla (Palaologos) Waldron; m. Andrea Carel DeFrane, Aug. 19, 1979. BA in Physics, Philosophy, UCLA, 1969, MA in Biochemistry, 1974, JD, 1978. Bar: Calif., 1978; cert. rape crisis counselor, Calif. Intelligence analyst, 1969-72; dir. product devel. Adolph's Food Products, Burbank, Calif., 1972-73; asst. to pres. Eckel Research and Devel., San Fernando, Calif., 1973-74; dep. State Public Defender Los Angeles, 1977-82; sole practice Palm Desert, Calif., 1982—; co-founder Tekni-Query Cons., 1990; appellate lawyer Calif. and U.S. Supreme Ct., 1982; exec. v.p. Gen. Counsel Compensation Strategies Group, Santa Ana, Calif., 1988-89; pro bono legal counsel Junipero Serra H.S., Gardena, Calif., 1987-88; cons. to U.S. Govt., 1982—; bd. dirs. Myelin Project, Washington, 1993-95. Patentee solubilization of Sodium CMC at room temperature, 1972. Founder, fund raiser Pacific Multiple Sclerosis Research Found., Beverly Hills, Calif., 1982—, coordinator with Reed Neurology Ctr. at UCLA; bd. dirs. John F. Kennedy Ctr. Performing Arts, Very Spl. Arts for Cachella Valley, 1996—. Westinghouse Sci. scholar, 1965; recipient Gregor Mendell award in genetics, 1962; named Jr. Engr. of Yr. Am. Assn. Aero. Engrs., 1963, Outstanding Speaker U. So. Calif., 1965. Mem. State Bar Calif., Internat. Platform Assn. Republican. Greek Orthodox. Avocation: classic automobiles. Office: 44489 Town Center Way # D-404 Palm Desert CA 92260-2723

SPISAK, JOHN FRANCIS, environmental company executive; b. Cleve., Mar. 27, 1950; s. Ernest Lawrence and Adele Marie (Chipko) S.; m. Barbara Ann Heisman, June 10, 1972; children: John Stefan, Theresa Rose. BS in Chemistry, Purdue U., 1972, BS in Biology with honors, 1972. Rsch. engr. Anaconda Minerals, Tucson, 1972-79; chief metallurgist Fed. Am. Uranium, Riverton, Wyo., 1979-80; v.p. ops. Anschutz Mining Corp., Denver, 1980-87; chmn. bd. dirs. Warrenton Refining (subs. of Anschutz Corp.), Denver, 1987-89; CEO Terranext, Inc., Denver, 1989—; mem. Western States-U.S. Senate Coalition for Superfund Reform. Contbr. articles to profl. pubis.; patentee sequential flotation of sulfide ores. Named One of Fifty Colo. Top Bus. Leaders, Colo. Assn. Commerce and Industry. Mem. AIME, Soc. Mining, Metallurgy and Exploration, Nat. Assn. Environ. Mgrs. (co-founder, bd. dirs. Washington chpt., co-chmn. govt. liaison and advocacy com.), Denver Petroleum Club, Elks. Republican. Roman Catholic. Avocations: classical piano, cycling, model railroads. Home: 9570 Lacosta Ln Littleton CO 80124-8909 Office: Terranext Union Tower 165 S Union Blvd Ste 1000 Lakewood CO 80228-2214

SPITALERI, VERNON ROSARIO, newspaper publisher, manufacturing company executive; b. Pelham, N.Y., Aug. 2, 1922; s. Rosario S. and Martha (Landerer) S.; m. Marjorie A. Ferrar, Oct. 14, 1952; children: Marc, Eric, Kris, Lynn. B.S., Carnegie Mellon U., 1942. Mgr. mech. dept. Am. Newspaper Pubs. Assn., N.Y.C., 1946-53; research dir., gen. adminstr. Miami Herald and Knight Newspapers (Fla.), 1953-57; chmn. bd., pres. Sta-Hi Corp., Newport Beach, Calif., 1957-74; v.p. Republic Corp., 1974-76, Sun Chem. Corp., 1976-79; chmn. bd. Sta-Hi Color Service, Sta-Hi Europe, Brussels, Concrete Floats-Huntington Engring. Corp., Huntington Beach, Calif.; editor, pub. Laguna Beach (Calif.) News-Post, 1967-81; pres. Laguna Pub. Co., Nat. Newspaper Found.; dir. Suburban Newspapers Am. ; chmn. bd. Victory Profl. Products, Mango Surfware. Pres., Boys Club, Laguna Beach; mem. citizens adv. com. Laguna Beach; pres. Laguna Beach Library Bd., Laguna Playhouse, Laguna Coordinating Council; bd. dirs. Sta-Hi Found.; dir. Opera Pacific. Served to lt. comdr. USNR, 1942-46. Decorated Purple Heart. Mem. Am. Mgmt. Assn., Nat. Newspaper Assn. (dir.), Calif. Newspaper Pubs. Assn. (dir.), Laguna Beach C. of C. (bd. dir.), Alpha Tau Omega. Republican. Roman Catholic. Club: Dana Point Yacht.

SPITLER, LEE WILLIAM, banker; b. Racine, Wis., Feb. 14, 1919; s. Marion Albert and Agnes Elizabeth (Lowe) S.; m. Helen Deloris Krejci, Mar. 19, 1949; children—Susan D., Lee William, Anne M., James E. B.S., U. Md., 1956; M.B.A., George Washington U., 1962; postgrad. advanced mgmt. program, Harvard U., 1963; grad., U.S. Air Force War Coll., 1959, U.S. Air Force Command and Staff Coll., 1955. Commd. 2d lt. U.S. Air Force, 1943, advanced through grades to col., 1954; chief personnel stats. div. Hdqrs. U.S. Air Force, Washington, 1950-54; asst. dir. statis. services U.S. Air Force, 1958-63; asst. comptroller Hdqrs. U.S. European Command U.S. Air Force, Paris, 1955-58; asst. comptroller Hdqrs. Air Tng. Command U.S. Air Force, Randolph AFB, Tex., 1963-64; ret. U.S. Air Force, 1964; v.p. Computax Corp., El Segundo, Calif., 1965-69; exec. v.p. Irving Bank Corp., N.Y.C., 1969-84; sr. exec. v.p. Irving Trust Co., N.Y.C., 1969-84; ret., 1984; pres. Spitler Fin. Svcs., Monterey, Calif., 1985—; dir. Turkiye Tutunculer Bankasi AS, Izmir, Turkey, 1984-87. mem. nat. adv. bd. Am. Security Council. Decorated Legion of Merit. Mem. Internat. Assn. Fin. Planning, Am. Bankers Assn., Am. Mgmt. Assn., Soc. for Mgmt. Info. Systems, Ret. Officers Assn., Nat. Assn. Uniformed Services, Mil. Order World Wars, Am. Assn. Mil. Comptrollers, Am. Legion, Veterans of Fgn. Wars, Am. Assn. Ret. Personnel, Inst. Cert. Planners, Air War Coll. Alumni Assn., First Fighter Group Assn. Clubs: Harvard, West Point Officers. Home: 1690 Jubilee Dr Brentwood CA 94513-6747 Office: 200 Glenwood Cir Monterey CA 93940

SPITZ, BARBARA SALOMON, artist; b. Chgo., Jan. 8, 1926; d. Fred B. and Sadie (Lorch) Salomon; m. Lawrence S. Spitz, Mar. 19, 1949; children—Thomas R., Linda J., Joanne L. A.B., Brown U., 1947; student, Art Inst. Chgo., 1942-43, R.I. Sch. Design, 1945. One-woman exhbns. include Benjamin Galleries, Chgo., 1971, 73, Kunsthaus Buhler, Stuttgart, Germany, 1973, Van Straaten Gallery, Chgo., 1976, 80, Elca London Studio, Montreal, Que., Can., 1977, Loyola U. Chgo., 1988, Schneider, Bluhm, Loeb gallery, Chgo., 1993, The Ctr. Gallery, 1994; group exhibitions include Am. Acad. Arts and Letters, Library of Congress traveling print exhbn., Tokyo Cen. Mus. Arts, Nat. Acad. Design, N.Y.C., Pratt Graphic Ctr., Honolulu Acad. Arts, Wadsworth Atheneum, Nat. Aperture, 1986—, Laguna Art Mus., others; represented in permanent collections, Phila. Mus. Art, DeCordova Mus., Okla. Art Ctr., Milw. Art Ctr., Los Angeles County Mus. Art, Art Inst. Chgo., Portland Mus. Art. Vice-chmn. Chgo. area Brown U. Bicentennial Drive; treas. Hearing and Speech Rehab. Ctr., Michael Reese Hosp., 1960; fine arts patron bd. Newport Harbor Art Mus. Mem. Print Club Phila., Boston Printmakers, Arts Club of Chgo., Soc. Am. Graphic Artists. Address: 1106 Somerset Ln Newport Beach CA 92660-5629

SPITZ, CHARLES THOMAS, JR., clergyman; b. Hazard, Nebr., May 26, 1921; s. Charles Thomas and Magdalene (Schneemann) S.; m. Dorothy O. Gross, June 11, 1944 (dec. 1982); children: Charles Thomas III, Gretchen Ann.; m. Karen Ankener Lucas, Aug. 25, 1983; 1 child, Garrett Richard. Grad., St. Paul's Coll., Concordia, Mo., 1939; AB, Concordia Sem., St. Louis, 1944, DD, 1965; DD, Capital U., Columbus, Ohio, 1967, Muhlenberg Coll., 1967, Gettysburg Coll., 1970; LHD, Luther Coll., Decorah, Iowa, 1967. Ordained to ministry Lutheran Ch., 1944; pastor in Waterloo, Iowa, 1944-46, Marengo, Iowa, 1947-53; dir. broadcasting Luth. Laymen's League, St. Louis, 1953-66; gen. sec. Luth. Council U.S., 1966-73; pastor in Manhasset, L.I., N.Y., 1974-84; exec. assoc. Fuchs, Cuthrell & Co., 1984-85; sr. ptnr. Corp. Exec. Outplacement, 1986-91; pres. Creative Energetics, 1985—; exec. assoc. Evang. Lutheran in Mission, 1974-76; pres. Luth. Ch. in Mission, 1975-78; dir. Assn. Evang. Luth. Chs., 1976-83; mem. Commn. Luth. Unity, 1978-83; mem. commn. on faith and order Nat. Council Chs., 1977-83, vice chmn., 1979-82. Trustee Eger Luth. Home, 1987-92; bd. dirs., treas. Licensing Link, 1995—. Home: 21 Deepdale Dr Manhasset NY 11030-3303

SPITZ, LEWIS WILLIAM, historian, educator; b. Bertrand, Nebr., Dec. 14, 1922; s. Lewis William and Pauline Mary (Griebel) S.; m. Edna Marie Huttenmaier, Aug. 14, 1948; children: Stephen Andrew, Philip Mathew. AB, Concordia Coll., 1944; MDiv, Concordia Sem., 1946; MA, U. Mo., 1947; PhD, Harvard U., 1954; DD (hon.), Concordia Theol. Sem., 1977; LLD (hon.), Valparaiso (Ind.) U., 1978; LittD (hon.), Wittenberg U., 1983; DLitt (hon.), Concordia Coll., 1988. With U. Mo., Columbia, 1953-60, assoc. prof. history, 1958-60; Fulbright prof. U. Mainz, Fed. Republic of Germany, 1960-61; prof. history Stanford (Calif.) U., 1960—, William R. Kenan Jr. prof., 1974—, assoc. dean humanities and scis., 1973-77; vis. prof. Harvard U., Cambridge, Mass., 1964-65; dir. rsch. Ctr. for Reformation Rsch., Clayton, Mo., summer 1964, mem. bd. control, 1973—; sr. fellow South Eastern Medieval and Renaissance Inst., Duke U., summer 1968; vis. prof. Barnard Coll., 1980-81; sr. fellow Inst. Advance Study Princeton U., 1979-80; vis. prof. Institut für Europäische Geschichte, Mainz, 1992. Author: Conrad Celtis: The German Arch-Humanist, 1957, The Religious Renaissance of the German Humanists, 1963, Life in Two Worlds: A Biography of William Sihler, 1968, The Renaissance and Reformation Movements, 2 vols., 1987, Humanismus und Reformation in der Deutschen Geschichte, 1980, The Protestant Reformation, 1517-1559, 1985; contbr. The Harvest of Humanism in Central Europe: Essays in Honor of Lewis W. Spitz, 1992; co-author (with Barbara Sher Tinsley): Johann Sturm on Education, 1995, Luther and German Humanism, 1996; mem. editl. bd. Soundings, 1973-79; mng. editor: Archive for Reformation History, 1968-76. Recipient Harbison award for tchg. Danforth Found., 1964; Guggenheim fellow, 1956; Nat. Endowment for Humanities sr. fellow, 1965; Am. Coun. Learned Socs. fellow, 1971; Huntington Libr. fellow, 1959; Inst. Advanced Study Princeton fellow, 1979-80; Pew Found. fellow, 1983. Fellow Am. Acad. Arts and Scis.; mem. Am. Soc. Reformation Rsch. (pres. 1963-64), Am. Hist. Assn., No. Calif. Renaissance Soc. (pres. 1964-65), Am. Soc. Ch. History (pres. 1976-77). Home: 827 Lathrop Dr Stanford CA 94305-1054 Office: Stanford U Dept History Stanford CA 94305 *College teaching has enabled me to develop a career which coincides perfectly with my inner needs and goals in life, which have more to do with service than with ambition, more with love of people than wish to dominate, more with mind and spirit than with material things.*

SPITZ, SEYMOUR JAMES, JR., retired fragrance company executive; b. Milw., Nov. 17, 1921; s. Seymour James and Marie (Spinette) S.; m. Elizabeth Taylor Parks, Feb. 7, 1948 (div. Aug. 1967); children: William Taylor, Elizabeth Seymour, Anne Bellin; m. Ellen C. Flynn, July 25, 1969; 1 dau., Ellen Christina. SB, MIT, 1943. With Newport Industries div. Heyden Newport Chem. Corp., Pensacola, Fla., 1946-65; asst. chief engr., 1955-57, asst. v.p., 1957-58; v.p. Newport Industries div. Heyden Newport Chem. Corp., 1959-60, exec. v.p., 1960-61, pres., 1961-65; v.p. parent co. Heyden Newport Chem. Corp., 1962-65, became group v.p., 1965; exec. v.p. Heyden Newport Chem. Corp. (name now Tenneco Chems., Inc.), 1966; pres. Tenneco Chems., Inc., 1967-69; sr. v.p. parent co. Tenneco Inc.; pres. and dir. Internat. Flavors & Fragrances Inc., N.Y.C., 1970-85. Mem. MIT Corp. Devel. Com., 1977-86; trustee Spence Sch., 1982-88, Savannah (Ga.) Symphony, 1990-95, Telfair Mus. Art, Savannah, 1993-96. With USN, WWII, 1943-46. Mem. Univ. Club (N.Y.C.), Larchmont Yacht Club (N.Y., trustee 1986-89), Landings Club, Oglethorpe Club (Savannah, bd. dirs. 1995—), Chatham Club. Home: 6 Brandenberry Rd Savannah GA 31411-2201

SPITZBERG, IRVING JOSEPH, JR., lawyer, corporate executive; b. Little Rock, Feb. 9, 1942; s. Irving Joseph and Marie Bettye (Seeman) S.; m. Roberta Frances Alprin, Aug. 21, 1966 (div. 1988); children—Edward Storm, David Adam; m. Virginia V. Thorndike, Dec. 24, 1988. B.A., Columbia U., 1964; B.Phil., Oxford U., 1966; J.D., Yale U., 1969. Bar: Calif. 1969, D.C. 1985, Va. 1995. Asst. prof. Pitzer Coll., Claremont, Calif., 1969-71; fellow Inst. Current World Affairs, N.Y.C., 1971-74; vis. lectr. Brown U., Providence, 1973; assoc prof. SUNY, Buffalo, 1974-80; dean of coll. SUNY, 1974-78; gen. sec. AAUP, Washington, 1980-84; exec. dir. Coun. for Liberal Learning of Assn. Am. Colls., Washington, 1985-89; pres. The Knowledge Co., Fairfax, Va., 1985—; ptnr. Spitzberg & Drew, Washington, 1990-92; of counsel Spirer & Goldberg, Washington, 1993—; coord. Alvan Ikoku Coll., Nigeria, 1979-80; cons. Bd. Adult Edn., Kenya, 1973-74, Philander Smith Coll., Little Rock, 1978-80; co-dir. nat. study on campus life for Carnegie Found. for Advancement Teaching, 1989-90. Author and editor: Exchange of Expertise, 1978, Universities and the New International Order, 1979, Universities and the International Exchange of Knowledge, 1980; author: Campus Programs on Leadership, 1986, Racial Politics in Little Rock, 1987; co-author: (with Berdahl and Moodie), Quality and Access in Higher Education, 1991, (with Virginia Thorndike) Creating Community on College Campuses, 1992. Founder Coalition for Ednl. Excellence, Western N.Y., 1978-80; founding mem. Alliance for Leadership Devel., Washington, 1985; counsel GASP, Pomona, Calif., 1969-71; Dem. Committeeman, Erie County, N.Y., 1978-80; founding pres. Internat. Found. for St. Catherine's Coll., Oxford, 1986—; founder Coun. for Liberal Learning. Nat. winner Westinghouse Sci. Talent Search, 1960; Kellett scholar Trustees of Columbia U., 1964-66. Mem. Internat. Soc. Ednl., Am. Immigration Lawyers Assn., Nat. Acad. Elder Law Attys., Assn. Study Higher Edn., Cultural, and Sci. Exchs., Washington Ethical Soc. Jewish. Clubs: Columbia, Yale (Washington). Avocations: kids, the InterNet. Office: The Knowledge Co 10301 Democracy Ln Ste 403 Fairfax VA 22030-2545

SPITZE, ROBERT GEORGE FREDERICK, agricultural economics educator; b. Berryville, Ark., Oct. 12, 1922; s. Wesley Henry and Nora Catherine (Stullken) S.; m. Hazel Cleo Taylor, Mar. 4, 1944; children—Glenna Dean Spitze Franklin, Ken Rollin. Student, Columbia U., 1944; BS (Sears Roebuck nat. fellow), U. Ark., 1947; PhD (Knapp research fellow), U. Wis., 1954. Instr. U. Wis., Madison, 1950; asst. prof. to prof. U. Tenn., Knoxville, 1951-60; prof. agrl. econs. U. Ill., Urbana, 1960-93; vis. prof. Wye Coll., U. London, 1967-68; vis. research prof. policy U.S. Dept. Agr., Washington, 1975; vis. lectr. various univs., U.S. and Eng.; cons. Fed. Intermediate Credit Bank, 1958-59, Ill. Gen. Assembly Commn. on Revenue, 1963, Tex. A&M U., 1970, Am. Farm Bur. Fedn., Chgo., 1971, Ill. Gov.'s Commn. on Farm Income, 1972, Nat. Agrl. Research Policy Adv. Com., 1975, U.S. Dept. Agr. Econs. Research Service, 1976, Wharton Econometric Forecasting Inc., 1977, Nat. Rural Center, Washington, 1979-80, Nat. Public Policy Com., 1980, Okla. State U., 1986; mem. Ill. Gov.'s Council Econ. Advisers, 1974-76. Co-author: Food and Agricultural Policy, Economics and Politics, 1994; co-editor Policy Rsch. Notes, 1975-92, Food, Agriculture, and Rural Policy into the Twenty-first Century, 1994; editor: Agricultural and Food Policy: Issues and Alternatives for the 1990s, 1990; contbr. articles to profl. jours., chpts. to books. Lt. USNR, 1943-47. Recipient Funk recognition award, 1973, Excellence in Teaching award U. Ill., 1977, Outstanding Agr. Coll. Alumni award U. Ark., 1994. Mem. AAAS, Am. Econ. Assn., Am. Agrl. Econs. Assn. (Disting. Policy award 1981, Disting. Teaching award 1972, travel study grantee to France 1964), Internat. Assn. Agrl. Econs., Agrl. Econs. Soc. (U.K.), AAUP, Blue Key, Sigma Xi, Omicron Delta Kappa, Gamma Sigma Delta, Phi Eta Sigma, Alpha Zeta, Phi Sigma. Office: U Ill Dept Agr Econ 1301 W Gregory Dr Urbana IL 61801-3608

SPITZER, ADRIAN, pediatrician, medical educator; b. Bucharest, Rumania, Dec. 21, 1927; came to U.S., 1963, naturalized, 1968; s. Osias and Sophia S. S.; m. Carole Zelter, Oct. 31, 1951; 1 son, Vlad. B.S., Matei Basarab Lyceum, Bucharest, 1946; M.D., Med. Sch. Bucharest, 1952. Diplomate: Am. Bd. Pediatrics. Intern White Plains (N.Y.) Hosp., 1964; resident Hosp. Med. Coll. Pa., 1965-66; postdoctoral fellow pediatric nephrology Albert Einstein Coll. Medicine, 1966-67; postdoctoral fellow in renal physiology Cornell U. Med. Sch., 1967-68; practice medicine specializing in pediatric nephrology Bronx, N.Y., 1968—; asst. prof. pediatrics Albert Einstein Coll. Medicine, 1968-72, assoc. prof., 1972-76, prof., 1976—, dir. div. nephrology, 1973—; mem. staff Bronx Mcpl. Hosp. Ctr., Hosp. Albert Einstein Coll. Medicine/Montefore Med. Ctr.; mem. Medicine B Study sect.-NIH, 1976-80; Prof. C. Dunders rotating chmn. U. Utrecht, The Netherlands, 1990—; vis. fellow St. Catherine's Coll.; vis. fellow dept. biochemistry Oxford U., 1981-82; coord. Internat. Study Kidney Disease in Children; chmn. organizing com. 1st-6th Internat. Workshop on Devel. Renal Physiology, 1980-95; mem. renal adv. com. N.Y.C. Dept. Health; sci. adv. bd. rsch. and grant com. Nat. Kidney Found., 1982; chmn. pediatric nephrology bd. Am. Bd. Pediat., 1982-83. Mem. editorial bd.: Pediatric Nephrology, Seminars in Nephrology; assoc. editor: Pediatric Renal Disease, 1979, 2d edit., 1992; editor: The Kidney Development, 1982. NIH spl fellow, 1967; John E. Fogarty Sr. Internat. fellow, 1981-82; grantee NIH, N.Y. State Health Research Council, Nat. Kidney Found.; recipient Bela Schick medal for extraordinary achievements in acad. and clin. pediatrics. Mem. Am. Soc. Nephrology, Am. Soc. Pediatric Nephrology (council 1977-80, pres. 1981-82), Am. Fedn. Clin. Research, Am. Physiol. Soc., Soc. Pediatric Research, Salt and Water Club, Am. Acad. Pediatrics, Am. Pediatrics

Soc., Intersoc. Council for Kidney and Urinary Tract Research (sec.-treas. 1984-89). Office: Albert Einstein Coll Medicine 1410 Pelham Pkwy S Bronx NY 10461-1101

SPITZER, CARY REDFORD, avionics consultant, electrical engineer; b. New Hope, Va., July 31, 1937; s. Clyde Burke and Marion Jeanette (Redford) S.; m. Carrie Laura Ruth Logan, June 18, 1960; 1 child, Stiegel Logan. BSEE, Va. Poly. Inst. & State U., 1959; MS in Engring. Mgmt., George Washington U., 1970. Rsch. engr., engring. mgr. Langley Rsch Ctr., NASA, Hampton, Va., 1962-94; founder, pres. AvioniCon, Inc., 1993—; lectr. UCLA, 1989—, George Washington U., 1994. Author: Viking Orbiter Views of Mars, 1981, Digital Avionics Systems, 1987, 2d edit., 1993, Avionics Handbook, 1997; contbr. articles to sci. publs. 1st lt. USAF, 1959-62. Recipient Volare award Airline Avionics Inst., 1988; named Va. Peninsula Engr. of Yr., 1993; recipient Digital Avionics award Am. Inst. of Aeronautics and Astronautics, 1994. Fellow AIAA (assoc., Digital Avionics award 1994), IEEE (Centennial medal 1984), Aerospace and Electronic Systems Soc. of IEEE (pres. 1973-74, editor-in-chief Trans. 1996—), Exch. Club (pres. Williamsburg 1985). Methodist. Avocations: kite flying, car mechanics. Home and Office: 3409 Foxridge Rd Williamsburg VA 23188-2499

SPITZER, HUGH D., lawyer; b. Seattle, Feb. 14, 1949; s. George Frederick and Dorothy Lea (Davidson) S.; m. Ann Scales, Oct. 14, 1983; children: Johanna Spitzer, Claudia Spitzer, Jenny Spitzer. BA, Yale U., 1970; JD, U. Wash., 1974; LLM, U. Calif., 1982. Bar: Wash. 1974, U.S. Dist/ Ct. (ea. and we. dists.) Wash. 1975, U.S. Ct. Appeals (9th and D.C. cirs.) 1975, U.S. Supreme Ct. 1980. Program analyst N.Y.C. Health and Hosp. Corp., 1970-71; labor lawyer Hafer, Cassidy & Price, Seattle, 1974-76; legis. asst. Seattle City Coun., 1976-77; legal counsel to mayor City of Seattle, 1977-81; mcpl. bond lawyer Foster Pepper & Shefelman, Seattle, 1982—; affiliated prof. sch. law U. Wash. Contbr. articles to profl. jours. bd. dirs. King County Housing Ptnrship, Seattle; vice chair Puget Sound Water Quality Authority Wash. State, 1989-96; chair Seattle Law Income Housing Levy Oversight com., 1988-96. Mem. Nat. Assn. Bond Lawyers. Democrat. Avocations: hiking, skiing. Office: Foster Pepper & Shefelman 1111 3rd Ave Bldg Ste 3400 Seattle WA 98101

SPITZER, JACK J., banker; b. N.Y.C., Sept. 11, 1917; s. Ira I. and Jennie (Brody) S.; m. Charlotte May Braunstein, Dec. 21, 1941; children: Jil Spitzer-Fox, Robert Braunstein. BA, UCLA, 1938; LLD (hon.), Adelphi U., 1980, Ben-Gurion U.of the Negev, 1991. Pres., CEO Spitzer Co., L.A., 1951-59; pres., chief exec. officer Brentwood Savs. & Loan, L.A., 1959-66, Sterling Savs. & Loan, Riverside, Calif., 1966-72, Security Savs. & Loan, Seattle, 1972-78; chmn. bd. dirs. Cert. Reports, Kinderhook, N.Y., 1967—; chmn. bd. dirs., chief exec. officer Covenant Mortgage, Mercer Island, Wash., 1982—, Pacific Linen, Bothell, Wash., 1984—; chmn. Vitritek Environ., Inc., Columbia, Md., 1993—. Pres. United Way, Riverside, 1970; nat. chmn. David Ben-Gurion Centennial Com. of the U.S., Inc., 1985-87; mem. U.S. Del. to Inauguration of Pope John Paul II, apptd. by Pres. Carter, 1978; 1st v.p. Dem. County Ctrl. Com., L.A., 1953-62; Vice chmn., bd. govs. Ben-Gurion Univ. of Negev, 1984—, pres. Am. Assocs., 1985; founder, chmn. Seattle-Beer Sheva (Israel) Sister City Com., 1977; exec. committeeman Am. Jewish Joint Distbn. Com., 1985-96; v.p. Conf. on Jewish Material Claims, 1978—; vice chmn. bd. trustees Med. Edn. for South African Blacks, 1984—; chmn. bd. trustees B'nai B'rith Youth Orgn., 1996—; chmn. adv. coun. Cath. U. Am.-Internat. Ctr. for Aging. Served to 2d lt. U.S. Army, 1943-46. Spitzer dept. of Social Work at Ben-Gurion Univ. named in his honor, 1986; recipient Outstanding Communal Svc. award Wurtzweiler Sch. Social Work, 1987, Gold medal for Humanitarian Svc., B'nai B'rith, 1994. Mem. Meml. Found. for Jewish Culture (treas. 1978—, chmn. exec. com. 1990—, pres. 1994-96, hon. life pres. 1996—), Alexis de Tocqueville Soc., United Way, Rainier Club (Seattle), A.Z.A. of B'nai Brith (internat. pres. 1938-39, Harry Lapidus Communal Svc. award 1936, Sam Beber Outstanding Alumnus award 1970), B'nai Brith (west coast pres. 1968-69, internat. pres. 1978-82, hon. pres. 1982—, internat. chmn. susquicentennial celebration 1992-94), Rotary (World Cmty. Svc. award 1994). Avocation: ping pong. Home: PO Box 2008 Kirkland WA 98083-2008 Office: Covenant Mortgage Corp 9725 SE 36th St Ste 304 Mercer Island WA 98040-3840

SPITZER, JOHN BRUMBACK, lawyer; b. Toledo, Mar. 6, 1918; s. Lyman and Blanche (Brumback) S.; m. Lucy Ohlinger, May 10, 1941 (dec. Oct. 13, 1971); children: John B., Molly (Mrs. Edmund Frost), Lyman, Adelbert L.; m. Vondah D. Thornbury, July 3, 1972; stepchildren: Vondah, Barbara, James R. Thornbury. Grad., Phillips Andover Acad., 1935; B.A., Yale, 1939, LL.B., 1947. Bar: Ohio 1947. Since practiced in Toledo; law clk. to U.S. Supreme Ct. Justice Stanley Reed, 1947-48; ptnr. Marshall, Melhorn, Cole, Hummer & Spitzer, Toledo, 1955-86, Hummer & Spitzer, Toledo, 1986-89; with Hummer Legal Svcs. Corp., Perrysburg, Ohio, 1990—; pres. Spitzer Box Co., 1955-63; v.p. Spitzer Bldg. Co., 1960-91, pres. 1992—. Pres. Toledo Symphony Orch., 1956-58, v.p., sec., 1958-86. Maj. AUS, World War II. Mem. Belmont Country Club. Congregationalist. Home: 29620 Gleneagles Rd Perrysburg OH 43551-3515 Office: Hummer Legal Svcs Corp 4841 Monroe St Ste 205 Toledo OH 43623-4352

SPITZER, LYMAN, JR., astronomer; b. Toledo, June 26, 1914; s. Lyman and Blanche C. (Brumback) S.; m. Doreen D. Canaday, June 29, 1940; children: Nicholas, Dionis, Lutetia, Lydia. AB, Yale U., 1935, DSc, 1958; Henry Fellow, Cambridge (Eng.) U., 1935-36; PhD, Princeton U., 1938; Nat. Rsch. fellow, Harvard U., 1938-39; DSc, Case Inst. Tech., 1961, Harvard U., 1975, Princeton U., 1984; LLD, Toledo U., 1963. Instr. physics and astronomy Yale U., 1939-42; scientist Spl. Studies Group, Columbia U. Div. War Research, 1942-44; dir. Sonar Analysis Group, 1944-46; assoc. prof. astrophysics Yale U., 1946-47; prof. astronomy, chmn. dept. and dir. obs. Princeton U., 1947-79, Charles A. Young prof. astronomy, 1952-82, chmn. rsch. bd., 1967-72, dir. project Matterhorn, 1953-61, chmn. exec. com. Plasma Physics Lab., 1961-66, sr. rsch. astronomer, 1982-97—; trustee Woods Hole Oceanographic Inst., 1946-51; mem. Com. on Undersea Warfare, NRC, 1948-51; mem. Yale U. Council, 1948-51; chmn. Scientists Com. on Loyalty Problems, 1948-51; chmn. Space Telescope Inst. Council, Assoc. Univs. Rsch. Astronomy, 1981-90. Author: monograph Physics of Fully Ionized Gases, 1956, rev., 1962; Diffuse Matter in Space, 1968, Physical Processes in the Interstellar Medium, 1978, Searching Between The Stars, 1982, Dynamical Evolution of Globular Clusters, 1987, Dreams, Stars and Electrons-Selected Writings of L. Spitzer, 1997; editor: Physics of Sound in the Sea, 1946; contbr. articles to Astrophysical Jour., Physics of Fluids, Phys. Rev., others. Recipient Rittenhouse medal, 1957, Exceptional Sci. Achievement medal NASA, 1972, Bruce Gold medal, 1973, Henry Draper Gold medal, 1974, James C. Maxwell prize, 1975, Karl Schwarzschild medal, 1975, Disting. Pub. Svc. medal NASA, 1976, Gold medal Royal Astron. Soc., 1978, Nat. medal sci., 1980, Janssen medal, 1980, Franklin medal Franklin Inst., 1980, Crafoord prize Royal Swedish Acad. Scis., 1985, Madison medal Princeton U., 1989, Franklin medal Am. Philos. Soc., 1991. Mem. NAS, Am. Acad. Arts and Scis., Am. Philos. Soc., Am. Astron. Soc. (past pres.), Royal Soc. (London, fgn.), Royal Astron. Soc. (assoc.), Royal Soc. Scis. Liège (fgn. corr.), Am. Phys. Soc., Astron. Soc. Pacific, Am. Alpine Club, Alpine Club (London). Unitarian. Research on interstellar matter, space astronomy, stellar dynamics, broadening of spectral lines, conductivity of ionized gases, controlled release of thermonuclear energy.

SPITZER, T. QUINN, management consultant company executive; married; 5 children. Grad., U. Va.; postgrad., U. Ga. Group mgr. N.Am. ops. Kepner-Tregoe, Princeton, N.J., 1978-90, pres., chmn., CEO, 1990—; dep. dir. Ariz. Dept. Corrections, 1983; cons. in field. TV and radio appearances include CNN, NPR, CNBC, Can. Broadcasting Corp.; spkr. in field. Mem. Young Presidents' Orgn., nat. Alliance Bus. (bd. dirs.). Office: Kepner & Tregoe Inc Rsch Rd PO Box 704 Princeton NJ 08542

SPITZER, WALTER OSWALD, epidemiologist, educator; b. Asuncion, Paraguay, Feb. 19, 1937; Canadian citizen; MD, U. Toronto, 1962; MHA, U. Mich., 1966; MPH, Yale U., 1970. Gen. dir. Internat. Christian Med. Soc., 1966-69; asst. prof. clin. epidemiology McMaster U., Hamilton, Ont., Can., 1969-73, assoc. prof., 1973-75; prof. epidemiology McGill U., Montreal, 1975-95, prof. medicine, 1983-95, Strathcona prof. and chmn. dept. epidemiology and biostats., 1984-93, prof. emeritus, 1996—; sr. epidemiologist Genentech Inc.; clin. prof. medicine Stanford U., 1996—; rsch. prof. obgyn. and cmty. medicine U. Calif., San Francisco, 1997—; cons. PanAm. Health Orgn., Washington, 1975, 77, Aga Khan Found., Geneva, 1983-84. Editor Jour. Clin. Epidemiology, 1981-95; contbr. articles to biomed. jours. Named Nat. Health Scientist of Can., 1981. Fellow Royal Coll. Physicians and Surgeons Can., Am. Coll. Epidemiology; mem. Inst. Medicine of Nat. Acad. Scis. (U.S.). Avocations: music, sailing, photography. Home: 10707 La Honda Rd Woodside CA 94062-3751 Office: 460 Point San Bruno Blvd South San Francisco CA 94080-4918

SPITZER, WILLIAM GEORGE, university dean, physicist, educator, researcher; b. L.A., Apr. 24, 1927; s. Max and May Lea (Axleband) S.; m. Jeanette Dorothy Navsky, June 23, 1949; children—Matthew Laurence, Margaret Ilene. B.A., UCLA, 1949; M.S., U. So. Calif., 1952; Ph.D., Purdue U., 1957. Mem. tech. staff Bell Telephone Lab., Murray Hill, N.J., 1957-62; mem. tech. staff Bell & Howell Research Ctr., Pasadena, Calif., 1962-63; prof. material sci. and physics U. So. Calif., Los Angeles, 1963—, chmn. dept. material sci., 1967-69, chmn. dept. physics, 1969-72, 78-81, vice provost, dean Grad. studies, 1983-85; dean Letters, Arts and Scis. U. So. Calif., 1985-89; retired, 1992; acting provost U. So. Calif., 1993. Contbr. chpts. to books, articles to profl. jours. Served with U.S. Army, 1945-46. Hon. DHL awarded by Hebrew Union Coll., Jewish Inst. of Religion, 1992. Fellow Am. Phys. Soc.; mem. IEEE (sr.). Home: 4995 Lamia Way Oceanside CA 92056-7431 Office: U So Calif Material Sci Dept Vivian Hall Engring University Park Los Angeles CA 90089

SPITZNAGEL, JOHN KEITH, microbiologist, immunologist; b. Peoria, Ill., Apr. 11, 1923; s. Elmer Florian and Anna S. (Kolb) S.; m. Anne Moulton Sirch, Feb. 2, 1947; children: John, Jean, Margaret, Elizabeth, Paul. B.A., Columbia U., 1943, M.D., 1946. Diplomate Nat. Bd. Med. Examiners, Am. Bd. Internal Medicine. Intern Johns Hopkins Hosp., Balt., 1946-47; resident in internal medicine Barnes Hosp., St. Louis, 1949-51; vis. investigator Rockefeller Inst., N.Y.C., 1952-53, Nat. Inst. Med. Research, London, 1967-68; mem. faculty U. N.C., Chapel Hill, 1957-79; prof. microbiology and infectious diseases U. N.C., 1957-79; cons. N.C. Meml. Hosp., Chapel Hill, 1974-79; ad hoc adviser NIH, 1971—; prof. microbiology and immunology, chmn. dept. Emory U., Atlanta, 1979-93, prof. emeritus microbiology and immunology, 1993—; mem. study sect. bacteriology and mycology NIH, 1975-79, 85-89, chmn., 1977-79. Editor: Infection and Immunity, 1970-80, Jour. Immunology, 1973-80, Jour. Reticuloendothelial Soc, 1973-80. Served with M.C. AUS, 1947-57. Recipient Research Career Devel. award USPHS, 1957-67, Disting. Service award Sch. Medicine U. N.C., Chapel Hill, 1987; USPHS postdoctoral fellow, 1968; USPHS and AEC grantee. Fellow ACP, Infectious Disease Soc.; mem. AAAS, AAUP, Am. Soc. Microbiology (div. group councilor 1977-79), Am. Assn. Immunologists, Reticuloendothelial Soc. (pres. 1982), Infectious Disease Soc., So. Soc. Clin. Rsch., Assn. Am. Med. Sch. Microbiology and Immunology Chmn. (pres. 1990-91), Sigma Xi. Research on cell biology of human neutrophil polymorphonuclear leukocytes, and oxygen ind. mechanisms of antimicrobial phagocytoses; first to demonstrate cationic antimicrobial proteins of polymorphonuclear leukocytes granules; co-discoverer of a cationic protein of polymorph granules with antimicrobial action and a powerful attractant for mononuclear phagocytes. Home: 2251 Brianwood Ct Decatur GA 30033-1715 Office: 1440 Clifton Rd NE Atlanta GA 30322-1053

SPITZNAGEL, JOHN KEITH, periodontist, researcher; b. St. Louis, Feb. 22, 1951; s. John Keith and Anne Moulton (Sirch) S.; m. Susan Victoria Lipton, Jan. 2, 1981; children: Matthew, Katya. BS in Biology, U. N.C., 1977, DDS, 1982, cert. in Periodontology, 1992, PhD in Microbiology, 1994. Postdoctoral fellow Forsyth Dental Ctr., Boston, 1983-85; cons. in bioinformatics, 1984—; periodontic resident U. Tex. Health Sci. Ctr., San Antonio, 1985-91, dentist-scientist fellow, 1987-93; asst. prof. periodontology U. Tenn., Memphis, 1993—. Contbr. articles to profl. jours. Scout leader Boy Scouts Am., Chapel Hill, N.C., 1978-81, Memphis, 1995—. With USCG, 1971-75. Recipient Dentist Scientist award Nat. Inst. Dental Rsch., 1987. Mem. ADA, AAAS, Am. Acad. Periodontology, Am. Soc. for Microbiology, Internat. Assn. Dental Rsch., Delta Sigma Delta. Episcopalian. Avocations: computers/electronics, amateur radio, sailing, fishing, golf. Office: U Tenn Coll of Dentistry 875 Union Ave Memphis TN 38103-3513

SPIVACK, FRIEDA KUGLER, psychologist, administrator, educator, researcher; b. N.Y.C., Aug. 21, 1932; d. David and Anna (Steir) Kugler; married; children: Alizah Brozgold, Ely. MA with honors, Hunter Coll., 1963; PhD, NYU, 1971. Prof. Manhattan Coll., N.Y.C., 1971-74, Queens Coll., Flushing, N.Y., 1974-76, Lehman Coll., N.Y.C., 1976-92; bd. dirs., v.p. HCHC, Inc., Bklyn.; keynote spkr. N.Y. State Edn. Conf., N.Y.C., 1996, N.Y. Divsn. of Early Childhood Conf., 1997. Contbr. articles to profl. jours., chpts. to textbooks; author family guidance program curriculum in field, infant abecedary program, children's devel. assessments; editor, author: Learning to Function in Life, 1996; author: Perspective of Conductive Education, Infants and Young Children, Young Children's Journal. Mem. exec. bd. N.Y. State Divsn. Early Childhood, 1981—; del. Coun. for Exceptional Children, 1981-88; bd. dirs., pres. Inter-Am. Conductive Edn. for Motor Disabled, Family Diagnostic Treatment Ctr., Bklyn.; chmn. Empire State Consortium of Early Childhood Grants, 1990-91; bd. dirs., exec. dir. ACE Integration Head Start, 1994—; bd. dirs. sponsoring bd. coun. N.Y.C. Head Start. Mem. AAUP, Nat. Assn. Sch. Psychologists, Internat. Coun. Psychologists, Coun. for Exceptional Children (lectr., keynoter 1994, 95, 96, 97), Am. Fedn. Tchrs.-Profl. Staff Congress, Assn. Edn. Young Child, Internat. Coll. Pediatrics (mem. exec. bd. 1986—), N.Y.C. Reggio Emilia Program. Avocations: sculpture, writing, travel. Office: ACE Integration Head Start 1419 Broadway Brooklyn NY 11221 also: HCHC Inc at Kingsbrook Jewish Med Ctr DMRI Rm 219C Schenectady Ave Brooklyn NY 11203

SPIVACK, GORDON BERNARD, lawyer, lecturer; b. New Haven, June 15, 1929; s. Jacob and Sophie (Ocheretianski) S.; m. Dolores Olivia Traversano, Jan. 16, 1956; children—Michael David, Paul Stephen. B.S. with philosophic orations and honors with exceptional distinction, Yale U., 1950, LL.B. magna cum laude, 1955. Bar: Conn. 1955, U.S. Supreme Ct. 1962, N.Y. 1970. Trial atty. antitrust div. Dept. Justice, Washington, 1955-60; asst. chief field ops. antitrust div. Dept. Justice, 1961-64, chief field ops. antitrust div., 1964-65, dir. ops. antitrust div., 1965-67; assoc. prof. law Yale U., New Haven, 1967-70; vis. lectr. Yale U., 1970-78; ptnr. Lord, Day & Lord, N.Y.C., 1970-86, Coudert Bros., N.Y.C., 1986—; speaker on antitrust law; mem. Pres.'s Nat. Commn. for Rev. Antitrust Law and Procedures, Washington, 1978-79. Contbr. numerous articles on antitrust law to profl. jours. Served with U.S. Army, 1950-52. Recipient Sustained Superior Performance award Dept. Justice, 1955-60. Fellow Am. Coll. Trial Lawyers; mem. ABA, N.Y. State Bar Assn., Bar Assn. City N.Y., Yale Club (N.Y.C.), Pine Orchard Yacht and Country Club (Conn.). Jewish. Avocation: detective stories. Home: 118 Townsend Ter East Haven CT 06512-3129 Office: Coudert Bros 1114 Avenue Of The Americas New York NY 10036-7703

SPIVACK, HENRY ARCHER, life insurance company executive; b. Bklyn., Apr. 15, 1919; s. Jacob and Pauline (Schwartz) S.; m. Sadie Babe Meiseles, Jan. 1, 1941; children: Ian Jeffrey, Paula Janis. Student CCNY, 1936-42; BBA, Am. Coll., Bryn Mawr, Pa., 1965. CLU. Comptroller Daniel Jones, Inc., N.Y.C., 1947-59; field underwriter Union Cen. Life Ins. Co., N.Y.C., 1959-79, mgr. programming dept., 1966-69, assoc. agy. mgr., 1977-79; pension dir. Bleichroeder, Bing & Co., N.Y.C., 1975-77, sr. v.p. NCA Agy., Inc. (formerly New Confidence Agy.), 1979-90, Bentley Agy., Inc., 1990-92; Luxco & Assocs., 1990—; pension dir., employee benefit plan cons., estate and fin. planning, pres. Profl. Benefit Planners Inc. N.J.; instr. N.Y. State Ins. Dept., C.W. Post Coll., L.I. U., N.Y. Ctr. for Fin. Studies; coord. Ins. Dept. Yeshiva U., N.Y.; ins. courses instr.; also lectr., moderator. Contbr. articles to publs. Served with USN, 1943-46. Mem. Life Underwriters Assn. N.Y. (past chmn. blood bank), Am. Soc. CLU's (past chmn. N.Y. chpt. pension sect., past chmn. profl. liaison com.), Am. Soc. Pension Actuaries, Pensioneers at C.W. Post Coll., C.W. Post Coll. Tax Inst. and Fin. Planning Inst., Practising Law Inst., Internat. Assn. Fin. Planners, Internat. Assn. Registered Fin. Cons. (registered fin. cons.), Internat. Platform Assn., Greater N.Y. Brokers Assn. Lodge: K.P. (life; past dep. grand chancellor N.Y. state). Office: 500 N Broadway Jericho NY 11753-2111

SPIVAK, ALVIN A., retired public relations executive; b. Phila., Nov. 30, 1927; s. Herman and Bella (Haimovitz) S.; m. Martha Barry, Nov. 26, 1965; 1 dau., Denise. B.S., Temple U., 1949. With I.N.S., 1949-58; Senate reporter, also mem. gen. staff I.N.S., Washington, 1951-58; with U.P.I., 1958-67, White House reporter, 1960-67; pub. affairs dir. Nat. Adv. Commn. on Civil Disorders, 1967-68, Democratic Nat. Com., 1968-70; corp. pub. affairs dir. Gen. Dynamics Corp., 1970-94, ret., 1994. Served with USAAF, 1946-47. Mem. Nat. Press Club, Beta Gamma Sigma. Home: 9201 Fernwood Rd Bethesda MD 20817-3315

SPIVAK, JOAN CAROL, medical public relations specialist; b. Phila., May 12, 1950; d. Jack and Evelyn Lee (Copelman) S.; m. John D. Goldman, May 17, 1980; children: Jesse, Marcus. AB, Barnard Coll., 1972; M of Health Scis., Johns Hopkins U., 1980. Freelance writer N.Y.C., 1980-84; project dir. Impact Med. Communication, N.Y.C., 1984-87; exec. v.p. Daniel J. Edelman Inc., N.Y.C., 1987—. Co-author: (pamphlet) Lead: New Perspectives on an Old Problem, 1978; contbr. The Book of Health, 1981. Bd. dirs. May O'Donnell Dance Co., N.Y.C., 1983-85, Chamber Ballet U.S.A., N.Y.C., 1985-87, Nat. Child Labor Commn., 1991—, Cases, 1995—. Mem. N.Y. Acad. Sci. Democrat. Jewish. Avocations: pottery, sailing. Office: Daniel J Edelman Inc 1500 Broadway New York NY 10036-4015

SPIVAK, JONATHAN M., journalist; b. Boston, Sept. 2, 1928; s. Lawrence E. and Charlotte (Ring) S.; m. Dorothy A. Amendt, Jan. 10, 1953 (div.); children: Jennifer Lee, Timothy L.A.; m. 2d Micheline Aler, Dec. 18, 1980. B.A. magna cum laude, Harvard U., 1950. Reporter Hollister Evening Free Lance, Calif., 1954-55, UP, San Francisco, 1955, San Francisco Call Bull., 1956-57; staff corr. Wall St. Jour., San Francisco, 1957-58, Washington, 1959-78, London, 1978-83, N.Y.C., 1984; writer Paris. Served to 2d lt. U.S. Army, 1951-53. Recipient several writing awards. Mem. Inst. Medicine, Acad. Scis., Phi Beta Kappa, Athenaeum Club (London), Harvard Club (N.Y.C.). Jewish. Home: Ferme le Gres, Lauris France 84360

SPIVAK, ROBERT ELLIOT, financial consultant; b. Phila., Dec. 30, 1936; s. Philip and Helen (Kramer) S.; m. Willa Cohen, June 21, 1958 (div. 1973); children: Michael, Merri, Gregory; m. Ann Taylor Hogge, Sept. 11, 1976. BSBA, Muhlenburg Coll., 1958; postgrad., U. Pa., 1960-61; degree in fin. cons., Am. Coll., 1987. Fin. cons. CMS Cos., Phila., 1968—; lectr. in field. Contbr. articles to profl. jours. Pres. U.S. Com. Sports for Israel, 1981—; chmn. So. N.J. Cystic Fibrosis, 1975; mem. Drug Edn. Info. Clinic, Cherry Hill, N.J., 1972; bd. dirs. Internat. Jewish Sports Hall of Fame, Israel, 1981—, Wingate Inst. for Phys. Fitness, 1981—, Phila. JCC Coun., 1980-88; bd. dirs. Phila. chpt. ADL, 1996, Boys' Town Jerusalem, 1995-96; del. U.S. Olympic Com., 1989; bd. dirs. Einstein Med. Ctr., 1992. Honoree Phila. Office Israel Bonds, 1988; named Man of Yr., U.S. Com. Sports for Israel, 1995. Mem. Nat. Assn. Security Dealers, Million Dollar Round Table, Assn. Advanced Life Underwriting, Am. Soc. CLUs, Woodcrest Country Club (pres. 1975), B'rith Shalom (v.p. 1970-72), B'nai B'rith. Democrat. Jewish. Home: 2330 Pine St Philadelphia PA 19103-6415 Office: CMS Cos 2330 Pine St Philadelphia PA 19103-6415

SPIVEY, BRUCE E., integrated healthcare delivery systems management executive; b. Cedar Rapids, Iowa, Aug. 29, 1934; s. William Loranzy and Grace Loretta (Barber) S.; children: Lisa, Eric; m. Patti Amanda Birge, Dec. 20, 1987. B.A., Coe Coll., 1956; M.D., U. Iowa, 1959, M.S., 1964; M.Ed., U. Ill., 1969; hon. doctorate Sci., Coe Coll., 1978. Diplomate Am. Bd. Ophthalmology (fellow, bd. dirs. 1975-83). Asst. prof. U. Iowa Coll. Medicine, Iowa City, 1966, assoc. prof., 1968-71; dean Sch. Med. Scis. U. Pacific, San Francisco, 1971-76; prof., chmn. dept. ophthalmology Pacific Med. Ctr. (now Calif. Pacific Med. Ctr.), San Francisco, 1971-87, pres., CEO, dir., 1976-91; exec. v.p., CEO Am. Acad. Ophthalmology, San Francisco, 1978-93; pres., CEO Calif. Healthcare System, Bay area, 1986-92, Northwestern Healthcare Network, Chgo., 1992—; bd. dirs. Ophthalmic Pub. Co., Chgo., 1977—, pres., 1993—; v.p. Am. Bd. Med. Specialties, 1978-82, pres., 1980-82; chmn. bd. dirs. Vol. Hosps. of Am.-No. Calif., 1985-87, nat. bd. dirs., 1991-96; mem. nat. adv. eye coun. NEI, NIH, 1987-92; mem. spl. med. advisors group Dept. Vets. Affairs, 1987-93; trustee, bd. dirs., sec. bd. Ophthal. Mut. Ins. Co., 1988-96, Phoenix Alliance, Inc., 1993—, Primesight, 1996—. Contbr. over 110 articles to profl. jours.; inventor instruments for eye surgery. Bd. dirs. Pacific Vision Found., San Francisco, 1978—, U.S.-China Ednl. Inst., 1979—; trustee Coe Coll., 1985—, Found. AAO, 1981—. Served to capt. U.S. Army, 1964-66. Decorated Bronze Star; recipient Emile Javal Gold medal Internat. Contact Lens Council, San Francisco, 1982, Gradle medal Pan-Am. Assn. Ophthalmol., others. Fellow ACS, Am. Acad. Ophthalmology (Disting. Svc. award 1972, Sr. Honor award 1986, Guest of Honor 1996); mem. AMA, Am. Ophthal. Soc. (Howe medal 1993, bd. dirs. 1986-91, pres. 1994-95), Academia Ophthal. Internat., Soc. Med. Adminstrs., Internat. Congress Ophthalmology (sec.-gen. 1978-82), Internat. Coun. Ophthalmology (sec.-gen. 1994—, trustee 1986—), Pacific-Union Club. (San Francisco), Chgo. Club, Chevy Chase Club, Racquet Club Chgo., Glen View Club, Cosmos Club. Republican. Presbyterian. Office: Northwestern Healthcare Network 980 N Michigan Ave Chicago IL 60611-4501

SPIVEY, TED RAY, English educator; b. Fort Pierce, Fla., July 1, 1927; s. Theodore Roosevelt and Etty Pearl (Sumner) S.; m. Julia Brannon Douglass, June 30, 1962; children—Mary Leta, John Andrew. A.B., Emory U., 1949; M.A., U. Minn., 1951, Ph.D., 1954. Reporter Greenville Reporter, S.C., 1949-50; instr. Emory U., Atlanta, 1954-56; mem. faculty Ga. State U., Atlanta, 1956-89, assoc. prof. English, 1960-64; prof. Ga. State U., 1964-89, Regents' prof., 1984-89, emeritus, 1989—. Author: (with Kenneth M. England) A Manual of Style, 1960, The Renewed Quest, 1969, The Coming of the New Man, 1971, The Journey Beyond Tragedy, 1980, Revival: Southern Writers in the Modern City, 1986, The Writer as Shaman: The Pilgrimages of Conrad Aiken and Walker Percy, 1986, To Die in Atlanta: Poems of the Civil War and After, 1987, Beyond Modernism: Toward a New Myth Criticism, 1988, A City Observed: Poems of the New Age, 1988, (with Arthur Waterman) Conrad Aiken: A Priest of Consciousness, 1989, Flannery O'Connor: The Woman, The Thinker, the Visionary, 1995, Airport: America Rediscovered, 1997, Time's Stop in Savannah: Conrad Aiken's Inner Journey, 1997. Served with USN, 1945-46. Urban Life Center grantee, 1977-80. Mem. So. Atlantic Modern Lang. Assn. Democrat. Episcopalian. Club: Brittany. Home: 3181 Frontenac Ct NE Atlanta GA 30319-2414

SPLANE, RICHARD BEVERLEY, social work educator; b. Calgary, Alta., Can., Sept. 25, 1916; s. Alfred William and Clara Jane (Allyn) S.; m. Verna Marie Huffman, Feb. 22, 1971. BA, McMaster U., 1940, LLD (hon.), 1990; cert. social sci. and adminstrn., London Sch. Econs., 1947; MA, U. Toronto, 1948, MSW, 1951, PhD, 1961; LLD (hon.), Wilfrid Laurier U., 1988, U. B.C., Can., 1996. Exec. dir. Children's Aid Soc., Cornwall, Ont., Can., 1948-50; with Health and Welfare Can., Ottawa, 1952-72; exec. asst. to dep. minister nat. welfare Health and Welfare Can., 1959-60, dir. unemployment assistance, 1960-62, dir. gen. welfare assistance and services, 1960-70, asst. dep. minister social allowances and services, 1970-72; vis. prof. U. Alta., Edmonton, 1972-73; prof. social policy Sch. Social Work, U. B.C., Vancouver, 1973—; cons. Govt. Can., Govt. Alta., UNICEF. Author: The Development of Social Welfare in Ontario, 1965; (with Verna Huffman Splane) Chief Nursing Officers in National Ministries of Health, 1994, 75 Years of Community Service to Canada: Canadian Council on Social Development, 1920-1995. Served with RCAF, 1942-45. Recipient Centennial medal Govt. Can., 1967, Charles E. Hendry award U. Toronto, 1981, Commemorative medal for 125th anniversary of Confedn. of Can., 1992, Disting. Svc. award Internat. Coun. on Social Welfare, 1996. Mem. Can. Assn. Social Workers (Outstanding Nat. Svc. award 1985), Can. Inst. Pub. Adminstrn., Can. Hist. Assn., Can. Coun. on Social Devel. (Lifetime Achievement award 1995), Internat. Assn. Schs. Social Work, Internat. Confs. Social Devel. (pres.), World Federalists of Can. (pres. Vancouver br.), Vancouver Club, Order of Can. Mem. United Ch. Can. Office: U BC Sch Social Work, 208 West Mall, Vancouver, BC Canada V6T 1Z2

SPLETE, ALLEN PETERJOHN, association executive, educator; b. Carthage, N.Y., June 24, 1938; s. Howard Henry and Minnie Bertha (Peterjohn) S.; m. Marilyn Lois Detweiler, June 18, 1966; children—Heidi, Michael. BA, St. Lawrence U., 1960; MA with distinction, Colgate U., 1962; PhD, Syracuse U., 1968; LHD, Campbellsville Coll., 1990; LLD, Davis and Elkins Coll., 1990; LHD, Mt. Union Coll., 1992, St. Thomas Aquinas Coll., 1992, U. Indpls., 1994, Juniata Coll., 1994, Hastings Coll., 1994; EdD, Marywood Coll., 1995; LHD, Holy Family Coll., 1996.

Adminstrv. asst. to v.p. acad. affairs Syracuse U., N.Y., 1965-68, assoc. dean, exec. asst. to provost, 1968-70; v.p. for acad. planning St. Lawrence U., Canton, N.Y., 1970-82; pres. Westminster Coll., New Wilmington, Pa., 1982-85; exec. v.p. Coun. Ind. Colls., Washington, 1985-86, pres., 1986—; dir. Nat. Prepaid Tuition Plan, 1988-91; cons. York Coll., Pa., 1974; mem. planning and research com. N.Y. State Com. on Ind. Colls. and Univs., 1975-82; mem. statewide higher edn. adv. com. N.Y. State Senate Com. on Higher Edn., 1979-82; mem. nat. adv. bd. Flaming Rainbow U., 1989—; mem. adv. bd. Assn. Gov. Bds. Presdl. Search Consultation Svc., 1987-94, Academic Search Consultation Svc., 1989—, mem. Harvard Sem. for new pres. adv. bd., 1990—; bd. dirs. Am. Coun. on Edn., 1991-92; mem. oversight and review com. leadership and orgnl. devel. program United Negro Coll. Fund, 1991-96, SCT adv. coun., 1996—, Eric Nat. Adv. Bd. Co-author: Frederic Remington-Selected Letters, 1988, A Good Place To Work: Sourcebook for the Academic Workplace, 1991; editor: (with others) Confs. on Adirondack Park, 1972-82, Can.-Am. Relations, 1974-75; contbr. articles to profl. jours. Chmn. planning bd. Village of Canton, 1974-81; elder Neelsville Presbyn. Ch., 1986-89; trustee Adirondack Conservancy, Wilsboro, N.Y., 1980-82. Served to 1st lt. U.S. Army, 1960-62. Recipient Alumni citation St. Lawrence U., 1987; John Ben Snow Found. grantee, 1981. Mem. Pa. Assn. Colls and Univs. (govt. relations com. 1983-85), Middle States Assn. (team chmn. com. on higher edn. 1976-78, 81), Assn. Am. Colls. (project rev. cons. 1981-82), Soc. Educators and Scholars (bd. editors), Assn. Am. Colls. (pres. adv. com. 1977-78, reviewer Quill project 1978-79), St. Lawrence County Hist. Assn. (pres. 1977-82), Frederic Remington Mus. Assn., Beta Theta Pi (v.p. 1980-83). Republican. Home: 10821 Longmeadow Dr Damascus MD 20872-2240 Office: Coun Ind Colls 1 Dupont Cir NW Ste 320 Washington DC 20036-1137

SPLIETHOFF, WILLIAM LUDWIG, chemical company executive; b. Matamoras, Pa., Apr. 8, 1926; s. Oscar and Louisa (Rummel) S.; m. Dorothy Coffman, June 11, 1949; children: Christina Spliethoff Hansen, Karen Spliethoff Walker, William Mark; m. Marjorie Ann Johnson, Nov. 15, 1971. BS in Chemistry, Pa. State U., 1946, MS, 1948; PhD in Organic Chemistry, Mich. State U., 1953. Rsch. chemist E.I. duPont de Nemours & Co., Wilmington, Del., 1952-60; dir. market rsch. chem. divsn. Gen. Mills, Inc., Kankakee, Ill., 1960-62, mgr. comml. devel., 1962-67; asst. mng. dir. Polymer Corp., Sydney, Australia, 1967-69; v.p. Gen. Mills Chems., Inc., Mpls., 1969-77; exec. v.p. Henkel Corp., Mpls., 1977-86; mgmt. cons. Chanhassen, Minn., 1986—; bd. dirs. Princess Soft Toys, Inc.; sr. v.p. Henkel of Am., N.Y.C., 1981-86; chmn. Habib-Gen., Ltd., Karachi, Pakistan, 1970-79, Nutralgum, S.P.A., Milan, 1972-85, Henkel Ireland Ltd., Cork, 1975-86; v.p. Chem-Plast, S.P.A., Milan, 1977-86, Poliamidas de Venezuela, S.A., Caracas, 1975-86, Gemisa, S.A. de C.V., Mexico City, 1979-86. Mem. bd. edn., Kankakee, 1964-67. Mem. Am. Chem. Soc., Chem. Market Rsch. Assn., Comml. Devel. Assn. (honor award 1982), Sigma Xi, Phi Lambda Upsilon.

SPLINTER, WILLIAM ELDON, agricultural engineering educator; b. North Platte, Nebr., Nov. 24, 1925; s. William John and Minnie (Calhoun) S.; m. Eleanor Love Peterson, Jan. 10, 1953; children: Kathryn Love, William John, Karen Ann, Robert Marvin. BS in Agrl. Engring., U. Nebr., 1950; MS in Agrl. Engring., Mich. State U., 1951, PhD in Agrl. Engring., 1955. Instr. agrl. engring. Mich. State U., East Lansing, 1953-54; assoc. prof. biology and agrl. engring. N.C. State U., Raleigh, 1954-60, prof. biology and agrl. engring., 1960-68; prof., chmn. dept. agrl. engring. U. Nebr., Lincoln, 1968-84, George Holmes Disting. prof., 1984—, head dept. agrl. engring., 1984-88, assoc. vice chancellor for rsch., 1988-90, intermim vice chancellor for rsch., dean grad. studies, 1990-92, vice chancellor for rsch., 1992-93, George Holmes Disting. prof. emeritus, 1993-94; interim dean Coll. of Engring. and Tech., 1995—; cons. engr. Mem. exec. bd. Am. Assn. Engring. Socs.; hon. prof. Shengyang (People's Republic of China) Agrl. U. Contbr. articles to tech. jours.; patentee in field. Served with USNR, 1946-51. Recipient Massey Ferguson gold medal, 1978, John Deere gold medal, 1995, Kiwanis award for disting. svc., 1994; named to Nebr. Hall of Agrl. Achievement. Fellow AAAS, Am. Soc. Agrl. Engrs. (pres., adminstrv. council, found. pres.); mem. Nat. Acad. Engring., Soc. Automotive Engrs., Am. Soc. Engring. Edn., Nat. Soc. Profl. Engrs., Sigma Xi, Sigma Tau, Sigma Pi Sigma, Pi Mu Epsilon, Gamma Sigma Delta, Phi Kappa Phi, Beta Sigma Psi. Home: 4801 Bridle Ln Lincoln NE 68516-3436 Office: U Nebr 202 Biol Systems Engring Labs Lincoln NE 68583-0832

SPLITSTONE, GEORGE DALE, retired hospital administrator; b. Sharon, Pa., Oct. 10, 1925; s. Paul R. and Rose (Kelly) S.; divorced; children by previous marriage: David, Scott. B.A., Westminster Coll., 1951; M.S., Columbia U., 1953. Asst. adminstr. Denver Gen. Hosp., 1953-56, Reid Meml. Hosp., Richmond, Ind., 1956-59; adminstr. Reid Meml. Hosp., 1959-68; pres. Univer. Community Hosp., Tampa, Fla., 1968-87. Dist. dir. Boy Scouts Am., 1983. Served with U.S. Army, 1943-46. Kellogg Found. grantee, 1977. Mem. Am. Coll. Hosp. Adminstrs., Fla. Hosp. Assn. (dir. 1973), Tampa Area Hosp. Council (v.p. 1980-83). Democrat.

SPLITTSTOESSER, WALTER EMIL, plant physiologist; b. Claremont, Minn., Aug. 27, 1937; s. Waldemar Theodore and Opal Mae (Young) S.; m. Shirley Anne O'Connor, July 2, 1960; children: Pamela, Sheryl, Riley. BS with distinction (univ. fellow), U. Minn., 1958; MS, S.D. State U., 1960; PhD, Purdue U., 1963. Plant breeder U. Minn., 1956-58; weed scientist S.D. State U., 1958-60; plant physiologist Purdue U., 1960-63, Shell Oil Co., Modesto, Calif., 1963-64; biochemist U. Calif., Davis, 1964-65; mem. faculty U. Ill., Urbana, 1965-97; prof. plant physiology U. Ill., 1974-97, head vegetable crops div., 1972-82; vis. prof. Unov. Coll., Dublin, Ireland, 1987, Univ. Coll., London, 1972, La Trobe U., Melbourne, Australia, 1995; biologist Parkland Coll., Champaign, Ill., 1974; vis. rsch. assoc. Rothamsted Exptl. Sta., Herpenden, England, 1980; disting. vis. prof. Nagoya (Japan) U., 1982; biotechnologist U. Coll., Dublin, 1987. Author: Vegetable Growing Handbook, 1979, 2d edit., 1984, 3d edit., 1990; contbr. numerous articles to sci. jours.; rev. editor: Analytical Biochemistry, 1969-78, NSF, 1978-79; numerous others. Recipient J.H. Gourley award Am. Fruit Grower-Am. Soc. Hort. Sci., 1974, Outstanding Grad. Educator award, 1990; NIH fellow, 1964-65. Fellow Am. Soc. Hort. Sci. (rev. editor jour. 1969-98), Japanese Soc. Promotion of Sci.; mem. Am. Soc. Plant Physiologists, Sigma Xi (pres. 1990-91), Alpha Zeta, Gamma Sigma Delta, Delta Theta Sigma, Phi Kappa Phi. Home: 2006 Cureton Dr Urbana IL 61801-6226 Office: U Ill 1102 S Goodwin Ave Urbana IL 61801-4730

SPOCK, ALEXANDER, pediatrician, professor; b. Shamokin, Pa., May 5, 1929; m. Diana Stafford; children: Christopher, Karen, Diana, Alexander. BS, Loyola Coll., 1951; MD, U. Md., 1955. Intern Geisinger Meml. Hosp., Danville, Pa., 1955-56, resident, 1956-58; fellow in pediats. and allergy Duke U. Med. Ctr., Durham, N.C., 1960-62, assoc. prof. in pediatrics, 1962-66; prof. in pediatrics, 1967—; dir. pediatric chest and cystic fibrosis clinic Duke U. Med. Ctr., Durham, N.C., 1964—; cons. pediatrician Project Hope, Columbia, 1967, Tunisia, 1969-70, mem. med. bd., 1970—, med. coord., Pediatric Inst., Krakow, Poland, 1977—. Contbr. articles to profl. jours. Mem. com. Am. Lung Assn., N.Y.C., 1975—, Nat. Cystic Fibrosis Rsch. Found., Bethesda, Md. Capt. U.S. Army, 1958-60. Mem. Am. Acad. Pediatrics, N.C. Thoracic Soc. (pres. 1981-82), Am. Acad. of Allergy, Thoracic Soc., AMA. Roman Catholic. Home: 9 Bentgrass Ln Durham NC 27705-1848

SPOCK, BENJAMIN MCLANE, physician, educator; b. New Haven, Conn., May 2, 1903; s. Benjamin Ives and Mildred Louise (Stoughton) S.; m. Jane Davenport Cheney, June 25, 1927 (div. 1976); children: Michael, John Cheney; m. Mary Morgan Councille, Oct. 24, 1976. B.A., Yale U., 1925, student Med. Sch., 1925-27; M.D., Columbia U., 1929. Intern in medicine Presbyn. Hosp., N.Y.C., 1929-31; in pediatrics N.Y. Nursery and Child's Hosp., 1931-32; in psychiatry N.Y. Hosp., 1932-33; practice pediatrics N.Y.C., 1933-44, 46-47; instr. pediatrics Cornell Med. Coll., 1933-47; asst. attending pediatrician N.Y. Hosp., 1933-47; cons. in pediatric psychiatry N.Y. City Health Dept., 1942-47; cons. psychiatry Mayo Clinic and Rochester Child Health Project, Rochester, Minn.; asso. prof. psychiatry Mayo Found., U. Minn., 1947-51; prof. child devel. U. Pitts., 1951-55, Western Res. U., 1955-67. Author: Baby and Child Care, 1946, (with J. Reinhart and W. Miller) A Baby's First Year, 1954, (with M. Lowenberg) Feeding Your Baby and Child, 1955, Dr. Spock Talks with Mothers, 1961, Problems of Parents, 1962, (with M. Lerrigo) Caring for Your Disabled Child, 1965, (with Mitchell Zimmerman) Dr. Spock on Vietnam, 1968, Decent and Indecent, 1970, A Teenagers Guide to Life and Love, 1970, Raising Children in a Difficult Time, 1974, Spock on Parenting, 1988, (with Mary Morgan) Spock on Spock: A Memoir of Growing Up With the Century, 1989, A Better World for Our Children, 1994. Presdl. candidate Peoples Party, 1972, advocator Nat. Com. for a Sane Nuclear Policy (SANE), co-chmn., 1962 . Served to lt. comdr. M.C., USNR, 1944-46. Home: PO Box 1268 Camden ME 04843-1268 *In pediatric practice I was trying, with difficulty, to reconcile concepts gained in psychoanalytic training with what mothers told me about their children. After ten years of that, I was able to write Baby & Child Care, which, in turn, brought invitations to research and teaching jobs. To save children from radiation I became a public supporter of a test ban treaty and co-chairman of SANE in 1962, which led, eventually to full-time opposition to the Vietnam war, conviction for conspiracy, conversion to socialism.*

SPODAK, MICHAEL KENNETH, forensic psychiatrist; b. Bklyn., Nov. 5, 1944; s. Harry and Betty (Rahn) S.; children: Lisa Beth, Brett David. B.S., Union Coll., 1966; M.D., SUNY-Syracuse, 1970. Diplomate: Nat. Bd. Med. Examiners, Am. Bd. Neurology and Psychiatry. Intern Mary Imogene Bassett Hosp., Cooperstown, N.Y., 1970-71; resident John Hopkins Hosp., Balt., 1974-77; practice medicine specializing in civil and criminal forensic psychiatry Towson, Md., 1977—; chief dept. psychiatry Balt. County Gen. Hosp., Randallstown, 1978-85; mem. staff Clifton T. Perkins Hosp. Ctr., Jessup, Md., 1977-92; clin. asst. prof. psychiatry U. Md. Hosp., Balt., 1983—; psychiat. cons. Bur. Disability Ins., Social Security Adminstrn., Workmen's compensation Commn., Balt., 1981—; dir. community forensic services Mental Hygiene Adminstrn., Md., 1982-92; faculty Nat. Jud. Coll., 1988—; mem. Md. Task Force on Somatic Therapies. Contbr. numerous articles on forensic psychiatry to profl. jours., chpt. to book. Served with M.C. USN, 1972-74. Mem. Am. Acad. Psychiatry and Law, Am. Psychiat. Assn., Md. Psychiat. Soc., Md. Med. Soc. (chmn. occupational health com. 1983-90), Baltimore County Med. Soc. Office: 26 W Pennsylvania Ave Towson MD 21204-5001

SPODEK, BERNARD, early childhood educator; b. Bklyn., Sept. 17, 1931; s. David and Esther (Lebenbaum) S.; m. Prudence Debb, June 21, 1957; children: Esther Yin-ling, Jonathan Chou. BA, Bklyn. Coll., 1952; MA, Columbia U., 1955, EdD, 1962. Cert. early childhood edn. tchr., N.Y. Tchr. Beth Hayeled Sch., N.Y.C., 1952-56, N.Y. City Pub. Schs., Bklyn., 1956-57, Early Childhood Ctr., Bklyn. Coll., 1957-60; asst. prof. elem. edn. U. Wis.-Milw., 1961-65; assoc. prof. early childhood edn. U. Ill., Champaign, 1965-68, prof. dept. curriculum and instrn., 1968-97, dir. dept. grad. programs, 1986-87, chair dept., 1987-89, dir. hons. program, Coll. Edn., 1984-86, mem. faculty Bur. Ednl. Rsch., 1981-85, prof. emeritus, 1997—; dir. insts. Nat. Def. Edn. Act, 1965-67, dir. experienced tchr. fellowship program, 1967-69, co-dir. program for tchr. trainers in early childhood edn., 1969-74; vis. prof. Western Wash. State U., 1974, U. Wis., Madison, 1980; vis. scholar Sch. Early Childhood Studies, Brisbane (Australia) Coll. Advanced Edn., Delissa Inst. Early Childhood Studies, S. Australia Coll. Advanced Edn., 1985, Beijing Normal U., Nanjing Normal U., E. China Normal U., Shangai, People's Republic China, 1986; rsch. fellow Kobe U., Japan, 1996. Author or co-author 28 books including: (with others) A Black Studies Curriculum for Early Childhood Education, 1972, 2d edit., 1976, Teaching in the Early Years, 1972, 3d edit., 1985, Early Childhood Education, 1973, Studies in Open Education, 1975 (Japanese trans.), Early Childhood Education: Issues and Perspectives, 1977, (with Nir-Janiv and Steg) International Perspectives on Early Childhood Education, 1982 (Hebrew trans.), with Saracho and Lee (Mainstreaming Young Children, 1984, (with Saracho and Davis) Foundations of Early Childhood Education, 1987, 2d edit. (Japanese trans.), 1991, (with Saracho) Right from the Start, 1994, Dealing with Individual Differences in the Early Childhood Classroom, 1994; editor: Handbook of Research in Early Childhood Education, 1982, Today's Kindergarten, 1986, (with Saracho and Peters) Professionalism and the Early Childhood Practitioner, 1988, (with Saracho) Early Childhood Teacher Education, 1990, Issues in Early Childhood Curriculum, 1991, Educationally Appropriate Kindergarten Practices, 1991, Issues in Childcare, 1992, Handbook of Research on the Education of Young Children, 1993, (with Saracho) Language and Literacy in Early Childhood Education, 1993; (with Sufford and Saracho) Early Childhood Special Education, 1994; (with Garcia, McLaughlin & Saracho) Meeting the Challenge of Cultural and Linguistic Diversity, 1995; series editor Yearbook in Early Childhood Education, early childhood edn. publs., 1971-79; guest editor Studies in Ednl. Evaluation, 1982, Early Education and Child Development, 1995; also contbr. chpts to books, articles to profl. jours. Mem. Assn. for Childhood Edn. Internat. (nursery sch. com. 1964-66), Am. Ednl. Rsch. Assn. (chair early childhood and child devel. spl. interest group 1983-84, publs. com. 1984-86), AAUP, Nat. Assn. Edn. Young Children (sec. 1965-68, bd. govs. 1968-72, pres. 1976-78, editorial adv. bd. 1972-76, book rev. editor, 1972-74, cons. editor, 1985-87 Young Children jour., mem. tchr. edn. commn. 1981-88, chair commn. on appropriate edn. 4-5 yr. old children, 1984-85, cons. editor Early Childhood Rsch. Quar. 1987-90), Nat. Soc. for Study of Edn. (1972 yearbook com.), Soc. Rsch. Child Devel. Office: U Ill Dept Curriculum & Instrn 1310 S 6th St Champaign IL 61820-6925

SPODICK, PEARL BLEGEN, counselor, medical psychotherapist; b. Mpls., June 4, 1927; d. Harry Cornelius and Vera Maude (Kidder) Blegen; m. Robert Casper Spodick, Nov. 1, 1955; children: Michael, Peter, Russell, Edward, Rebecca. BA, Albertus Magnus Coll., 1978; MA in Psychology and Art Therapy, Goddard Coll., 1980; postgrad., Simmon's Coll., 1977. Cert. med. psychotherapist, clin. mental health counselor; nat. cert. counselor; CHAMPUS (Civilian Health and Med. Program for Uniformed Svcs.) authorized marriage and family therapist, Conn. Cons., art psychotherapist Conn. D.C.Y.S., 1978—, Conn. Sexual Trauma Tratment Program, 1978-79, Arden House Long Term Care Facility, Hamden, Conn., 1979-82, Ctr. for Study of Normative Behavior, Hamden, 1982-85, Curtis Home Children's Residential Treatment Ctr., Meriden, Conn., 1982-93; instr. psychology Albertus Magnus Coll., Hamden, 1988-90; med. psychotherapist, counselor The Psychotherapy Ctr., Woodbridge, Conn., 1980-93, Hamden, Conn., 1993—; med. psychotherapist, counselor Art Psychotherapy and Counseling Ctr., Woodbridge, 1980-93, Hamden, 1993—. Fellow Am. Bd. Med. Psychotherapists (diplomate); mem. ACA (cert.), Nat. Bd. Cert. Clin. Hypnotherapists (cert.), Am. Art Therapy Assn. (ATR, legis. rep. 1983-89), Am. Assn. Study Mental Imagery, Am. Assn. Cert. Clin. Mental Health Counselors (cert.), Am. Bd. Behavioral Therapists (cert.), Am. Mental Health Counselors Assn. Democrat. Jewish. Avocations: painting, drawing, sculpture, crocheting, reading. Office: The Psychotherapy Ctr 1890 Dixwell Ave Ste 208 Hamden CT 06514-3171

SPOELHOF, JOHN, consumer products company executive. CEO Prince Corp. Office: Prince Corp 1 Prince Ctr Holland MI 49423-5407 Office: One Prince Ctr Holland MI 49423*

SPOERI, RANDALL KEITH, healthcare company executive; b. Cleve., June 12, 1946; s. Theodore Warren and Marion (Barrick) S.; m. Kathleen Loma Bryden Hayes, Aug. 31, 1968 (div. Mar. 1981); 1 child, Jennifer Anne; m. Deborah Jean Hammett, June 20, 1981; 1 child, Jason Randall. BS, Calif. Polytech. State U., 1968; MS, Tex. A&M U., 1970, PhD, 1976. Math. statistician U.S. Bur. of the Census, Suitland, Md., 1976-80; assoc. prof. U.S. Naval Acad., Annapolis, 1980-83; assoc. exec. dir. Am. Statis. Assn., Alexandria, Va., 1983-88; sr. corp. statistician Humana, Inc., Louisville, Ky., 1988-92; chief program coord., info. branch Health Care Fin. Adminstrn., Balt., 1993; asst. v.p. Nat. Com. for Quality Assurance, Washington, 1994-95; sr. dir. of health care analysis NYLCare Health Plans, Inc., N.Y.C., 1995—. Author: Quantitative Methods In Quality Management, 1991; contbr. articles to profl. jours. Mem. adv. com. Health Care Fin. Adminstrn., Balt., 1990-92, bur. dir. citation, 1993, adv. bd. Juran Inst., Wilton, Conn., 1995—. 1st lt. U.s. Army, 1970-72. Recipient Svc. award Am. Statis. Assoc., Alexandria, 1994. Mem. AAAS, Am. Statis Assn., Am. Soc. for Quality Control (health care divsn. chair 1995-96), Inst. Indsl. Engring. Avocations: sports, music. Home: 504 Thistledown Ct Millersville MD 21108

SPOFFORD, ROBERT HOUSTON, advertising agency executive; b. N.Y.C., Apr. 3, 1941; s. Robert Knowlton and Linda Prieber (Houston) S.; m. Susan Proctor Allerton; children: Margaret, Robert Christopher. B.E.E., Cornell U., 1964. Account exec. Batten, Barton, Durstine & Osborn, Inc., N.Y.C., 1964-71, v.p., 1971-84, sr. v.p., 1984-88, exec. v.p., dir. strategic planning, 1988—. Contbr. articles to advt. and data processing jours. Mem. Westchester County Democratic Com. N.Y. 1974-78; ch. organist. First recipient Founder's medal Batten, Barton, Durstine & Osborn, Inc., 1985. Unitarian. Home: 39 Glenside Way San Rafael CA 94903 Office: BBDO LA 10960 Wilshire Blvd Los Angeles CA 90024-3702

SPOFFORD, SALLY HYSLOP, artist; b. N.Y.C., Aug. 20, 1929; d. George Hall and Esther (McNaull) Hyslop; m. Gavin Spofford, Mar. 11, 1950 (dec. Jan. 1976); children: Lizabeth Spofford Smith, Leslie Spofford Russell. Student, The China Inst., N.Y.C., 1949, The Art Students League, N.Y.C., 1950; BA with high honors, Swarthmore Coll., 1952. Instr. Somerset Art Assn., Peapack, N.J., 1978-95, Hunterdon Art Ctr., Clinton, N.J., 1985—; adv. bd., lectr. Apollo Muses, Inc., Gladstone, N.J.; bd. trustees Artshowcase, Inc. One-man show Riverside Studio, Pottersville, N.J., 1985, Morris Mus., Morristown, N.J. 1989, Schering-Plough Gallery, Madison, N.J., 1989, Phoenix Gallery, N.Y.C., 1990, Robin Hutchins Gallery, Maplewood, N.J., 1992, Berlex Labs. Corp. Office, Wayne, N.J., 1992, Hunterdon Art Ctr., Clinton, N.J., 1993, The Williams Gallery, Princeton, N.J., 1997; exhibited in group shows at Hickory (N.C.) Mus., 1983, Purdue U., 1983, Monmouth (N.J.), 1984, Nabisco Brands Gallery, E. Hanover, N.J., 1985, 89, Hunterdon Art Ctr., Clinton, N.J., 1988, 93, Schering-Plough Gallery, Madison, 1988, Morris Mus., Morristown, 1989, Montclair (N.J. State U., 1995; represented in permanent collections N.J. State Mus., Trenton, Newark Mus. Painting residency fellow Vt. Studio Ctr., 1992. Mem. Assoc. Artists N.J. (pres. 1985-87), N.J. Watercolor Soc., Federated Art Assns. of N.J. (panel mem. 1985, demonstrator 1991). Home: PO Box 443 Bernardsville NJ 07924-0443

SPOHN, HERBERT EMIL, psychologist; b. Berlin, Germany, June 10, 1923; s. Herbert F. and Bertha S.; m. Billie M. Powell, July 28, 1973; children—Jessica, Madeleine. B.S.S., CCNY, 1949; Ph.D., Columbia U., 1955. Research psychologist VA Hosp., Montrose, N.Y., 1955-60; chief research sect. VA Hosp., 1960-64; sr. research psychologist Menninger Found., Topeka, 1965-80; dir. hosp. research Menninger Found., 1979-94, dir. research dept., 1981-94; ret., prof. emeritus for rsch., 1994—; mem. mental health small grant com. NIMH, 1972-76, mem. treatment assessment rev. com., 1983-86, chmn. 1986-87. Author: (with Gardner Murphy) Encounter with Reality, 1968; assoc. editor: Schizophrenia Bull, 1970-87, 91—; contbr. articles to profl. jours. Served with AUS, World War II. USPHS grantee, 1964—. Fellow Am. Psychopath. Assn.; mem. AAAS, N.Y. Acad. Sci., Soc. Psychopath. Research, Phi Beta Kappa, Sigma Xi. Office: Menninger Found PO Box 829 Topeka KS 66601-0829

SPOHN, JANICE, elementary education educator, consultant; b. Pitts., Jan. 12, 1952; d. James Arthur and Jean Edna (Smithyman) Rowan; m. Chester Michael Spohn II, Oct. 23, 1972; children: Chester M. III, Lisa Marie. BE, Clarion U., 1973; ME, Slippery Rock U., 1989; supervisory cert., Duquesne U., 1992. Cert. reading specialist, gifted edn., supervisor reading, Pa. Group supr. Butler County (Pa.) Children Ctr., 1974-87; temp. instr. Slippery Rock U., Slippery Rock, Pa., 1989; reading specialist North Allegheny Schs., Pitts., 1990—; coord. Pa. Framework Network, North Allegheny Schs., 1991—; inservice com. Allegheny Intermediate Unit, 1993—; Pa. Framework steering com. Allegheny Intermediate Unit, 1993—. Co-author/editor: (book) Pennsylvania Framework-Portfolio Implementation Guide, 1993. Mem. ASCD, Nat. Coun. Tchrs. of English, Internat. Reading Assn., Keystone State Reading Assn., Three Rivers Reading Coun., Butler County Reading Coun. Avocations: reading, crafts, camping. Home: 520 Herman Rd Butler PA 16001-9157 Office: Peebles Elem N Allegheny Schs 8526 Peebles Rd Pittsburgh PA 15237-5720

SPOHR, ARNOLD THEODORE, artistic director, choreographer; b. Rhein, Sask., Can., Dec. 26, 1927. Student, Winnipeg (Can.) Tchrs. Coll., 1942-43; Assocs., Royal Conservatory Music, Toronto, Can.; cert., Royal Acad. Dance; LLD (hon.), U. Man., Can., 1970, U. Winnipeg, 1984; DFA (hon.), U. Victoria, Can., 1987. Cert. tchr. pub. schs. Tchr. piano, 1946-51; prin. dancer Winnipeg Ballet (now Royal Winnipeg Ballet), 1945-58, artistic dir., tchr. dance, 1958-88, artistic dir. emeritus, 1988—; choreographer, performer Rainbow Stage Sta. CBC-TV, 1957-60; dir. dept. dance Nelson Sch. Fine Arts, 1964-67; artistic dir. dept. dance Banff Sch. Fine Arts, 1967-81; bd. dirs. Can. Theatre Centre; vice chmn. Bd. Dance Can.; adjudicator Can. Council, Can. Dance Tchrs. Assn., N.Y. Internat. Ballet Competitions. Choreographer Ballet Premier, 1950, Intermede, 1951, E Minor, 1959, Hansel and Gretal, 1960, also 18 musicals for Rainbow Stage. Decorated Order of Can., 1970; recipient Centennial medal Govt. of Can., 1967, Manitoba's Order of Buffalo, 1969, Molson prize, 1970, Can. Actor's Equity Assn. Champagne award, 1979, Dance mag. Ann. award, 1981, Diplome D'honneur Can. Conf. of Arts, 1983, Can. Tourism medal, 1985, Royal Bank award, 1987. Mem. Dance in Can. Assn. (bd. dirs., Can. Dance award 1986). Office: Canada's Royal Winnipeg Ballet, 380 Graham Ave, Winnipeg, MB Canada R3C 4K2*

SPOKANE, ROBERT BRUCE, biophysical chemist; b. Cleve., Aug. 5, 1952; s. Herbert Norman and Marjorie Ellen (Firsten) S.; m. Linda Carol Wright, June 20, 1976; children: Lea, Hannah, Tara. BS in Chemistry, Ohio U., 1975; MS in Biophys. Chemistry, U. Colo., 1978, PhD in Biophys. Chemistry, 1981. Cert. full cave diver. Teaching asst. Dept. Chemistry, U. Colo., Boulder, 1975-77, rsch. asst., 1977-81; staff scientist Procter & Gamble Co., Cin., 1981-84; rsch. scientist Dept. Neurophysiology, Children's Hosp., Cin., 1984-90, YSI Co., Rsch. Ctr., Yellow Springs, Ohio, 1990—; cons. Synthetic Blood Internat., Yellow Springs, 1992. Contbr. articles to profl. jours. Rescuer, treas. Boulder Emergency Squad, 1980; rescue diver Kitty Hawk Scuba, Dayton, Ohio, 1992. Recipient Merck Index award Ohio U., 1975. Mem. Am. Chem. Soc., N.Y. Acad. Sci., Am. Physiol. Soc., Nat. Speleological Soc. (cave diving sect.), Sigma Xi. Achievements include research in implantable glucose sensors; oxygen tonometer for peritoneal oxygen measurements; interferant removal system for biosensors, water chemistry in submerged caves. Home: 1715 Garry Dr Bellbrook OH 45305-1362 Office: YSI Co 1725 Brannum Ln Yellow Springs OH 45387-1107

SPOLAN, HARMON SAMUEL, banker; b. Phila., Dec. 12, 1935; s. Jay and Edythe (Greenberg) S.; m. Betty Jane Evnitz, Mar. 30, 1958; children: Michael, Suzanne. AB, Temple U., 1957, LLB, 1959; postgrad. Oxford U., 1966. Bar: Pa. 1960. Ptnr. Ravetz & Shuchman, Phila., 1960-68, Blair & Co., N.Y.C., 1968-72; v.p. Butcher & Singer, Phila., 1972-74; pres. Capital First Corp., Phila., 1974-75, State Nat. Bank, Rockville, Md., 1975-78, Jefferson Bank, Phila., 1978—; pres., bd. dirs. JeffBanks, Inc., Phila., Bryn Mawr Resources, Phila.; lectr. law U. Pa., Phila., 1964-68. Author: Federal Aids to Financing, 1970; contbr. articles to profl. jours. Former chmn. bd. Huntingdon Hosp., Willow Grove, Pa., 1982-89; bd. dirs. YMHA, Phila., 1978—; dir. Anti-Defamation League, 1982. Named Man of the Yr., Nat. Assn. Women Bus. Owners, 1978; Disting. Alumnus, Central High Sch., 1975. Mem. ABA, Phila. Bar Assn., Locust Club, Oxford and Cambridge Club (London). Republican. Jewish. Office: Jefferson Bank 250 S 18th St Philadelphia PA 19103-6140

SPONG, JOHN SHELBY, bishop; b. Charlotte, N.C., June 16, 1931; s. John Shelby and Doolie Boyce (Griffith) S.; m. Joan Lydia Ketner, Sept. 5, 1952 (dec. 1988); children: Ellen Elizabeth, Mary Katharine, Jaquelin Ketner; m. Christine Mary Bridger, Jan. 1, 1990. A.B., U. N.C., 1952; M.Div., Va. Theol. Sem., 1955; D.D., St. Paul's Coll., 1976, Va. Theol. Sem., 1977. Ordained to ministry Episcopal Ch., 1955, bishop, 1976; rector St. Joseph's Ch., Durham, N.C., 1955-57, Calvary Ch., Tarboro, N.C., 1957-65, St. John's Ch., Lynchburg, Va., 1965-69, St. Paul's Ch., Richmond, Va., 1969-76; bishop Diocese of Newark, 1976—; mem. governing body Nat. Episc. Ch., 1973-76. Author: Honest Prayer, 1973, This Hebrew Lord, 1974, Dialogue--In Search of Jewish-Christian Understanding, 1975, Christpower, 1976, The Living Commandments, 1977, The Easter Moment, 1980, Into the Whirlwind: The Future of the Church, 1983, Beyond Moralism, 1986, Survival and Consciousness, 1987, Living in Sin? A Bishop Rethinks Human Sexuality, 1988, Rescuing the Bible from Fundamentalism--A Bishop Rethinks the Meaning of Scripture, 1991, Born of a Woman, 1992, Resurrection: Myth or Reality?, 1994, Liberating the Gospels, Reading the Bible with Jewish Eyes, 1996. Mem. Richmond Human Relations Commn. Club:

Rotary. Home: 43 Ogden Pl Morristown NJ 07960-5248 Office: 24 Rector St Newark NJ 07102-4512

SPONG, WILLIAM BELSER, JR., lawyer, educator; b. Portsmouth, Va., Sept. 29, 1920; s. William Belser and Emily (Nichols) S.; m. Virginia Wise Galliford, June 3, 1950 (dec. May 1993); children: Martha Kingman, Thomas Nichols. Student, Hampden-Sydney Coll., 1937-40, LLD (hon.), 1968; LLB, U. Va., 1947; postgrad., U. Edinburgh, Scotland, 1947-48; LLD (hon.), Roanoke Coll., Washington and Lee U. and Coll. William and Mary. Bar: Va. 1947. Lectr. law Coll. William and Mary, 1948-49, 75-76; practice law Portsmouth, 1949-76; mem. Va. Ho. Dels., 1954-55, Va. Senate, 1956-66, U.S. Senate, 1966-73; gen. counsel Comm. for Conduct Fgn. Policy, 1973-75; dean Marshall-Wythe Sch. Law Coll. William and Mary, 1976-85, Woodbridge prof. emeritus, 1985—; pres. Old Dominion U., 1989-90; spl. master Va. Electric & Power Co., et al vs. Westinghouse Corp., 1977-80, re Dalkon Shield litigation, 1983-85, Smith vs. Morton-Thiokol, 1988; ptnr. Cooper, Spong & Davis, Portsmouth, 1990—; guest scholar Woodrow Wilson Center Smithsonian Instn.; vis. scholar U. Va. Sch. Law, 1973; adj. prof. law U. Richmond, 1974-75, Salzburg Seminar, 1979; sr. visitor Inst. Advanced Legal Studies, U. London, 1985; vis. prof. Washington and Lee U., 1986; Ewald Disting. vis. prof. U. Va. Sch. Law, 1987; Menzies lectr. Australian Nat. U., 1990. Chmn. Va. Commn. Pub. Edn., 1958-62, Gov.'s Commn. on Va.'s Future, 1982-84; mem. Va. Coun. Higher Edn., 1985-89; trustee Hampden-Sydney Coll., 1951-72, Va. Hist. Soc., 1990-96; mem. bd. visitors Air Force Acad., 1970, Naval Acad., 1971, Coll. William and Mary, 1992-96. With USAAF, 1942-45. Mem. Va. Bar Assn. (pres. 1976), Portsmouth Bar Assn. (past pres.), Order of Coif, Phi Beta Kappa, Phi Alpha Delta, Omicron Delta Kappa, Pi Kappa Alpha. Home: 351 Middle St Portsmouth VA 23704-2826 Office: Cooper Spong & Davis PO Box 1475 Portsmouth VA 23705-1475

SPONSLER, GEORGE CURTIS, III, research administrator, lawyer; b. Collingswood, N.J., Dec. 2, 1927; s. George Curtis and Mary Grace (Hollinberger) S.; m. Bridget Ruth Butcher, Sept. 3, 1955; children: Freda Grace, Naomi Margaret Bride, Curtis Alexander. B.S. in Engring., Princeton U., 1949, M.A., 1951, Ph.D., 1952; J.D., George Washington U., 1981. Bar: Md. 1981, D.C. 1982, U.S. Ct. Appeals (4th cir.) 1982, U.S. Ct. Appeals (fed. cir.) 1984. U.S. Supreme Ct. 1986. With Lincoln Lab., MIT, 1952-56; liaison officer Office Naval Research, London, 1956-58; head spl. projects br. Office Naval Research, Washington, 1958-59; sr. scientist Hoffman Sci. Center, Santa Barbara, Calif., 1959-60; chief sci., dir. tech, analysis and ops. research U.S. Navy Bur. Ships, 1960-63; dir. advanced planning, fed. systems div. IBM, 1963-66, dir. center exploratory studies, 1966-68; exec. sec. div. engring. Nat. Acad. Sci.-NRC, 1968-70; pres. Law Math. and Tech. Inc., 1970—; on leave, Congl. fellow U.S. Senate, Washington, 1987-88; mem. adv. com. to Office Emergency Planning, Nat. Acad. Sci., 1967-72, chmn. subcom. automation, 1966-68, mem. joint adv. com. on electromagnetic pulse, 1970-74; cons. Exec. Office of Pres., 1971-73. Contbr.: Tech. Innovation, Harper Ency. of Sci.; author articles in field. Fellow AAAS (electorate nominating com. 1980-83, chmn.-elect sect. X, 1983-84, chmn. 1984-85, mem. coun. 1985-86), Am. Physics Soc.; mem. IEEE (sr., chmn. subcom. on privacy of communications and info. policy com. 1982-85, aerospace R&D policy com. 1990-92), Phi Beta Kappa, Sigma Xi. Democrat. Episcopalian. Club: Cosmos (Washington). Home: 7804 Old Chester Rd Bethesda MD 20817-6280

SPOOLSTRA, LINDA CAROL, minister, educator, religious organization administrator; b. Hillsdale, Mich., July 11, 1947; d. Jay Carroll and Carol Elsa (Linstrom) Lehmann; m. Gerald William Spoolstra, Feb. 17, 1973. BA, Bethel Coll., 1969; MA, Fla. State U., 1970; M of Div., McCormick Theol. Sem., Chgo., 1978; DD (hon.), Cen Bapt. Theol. Sem., Kansas City, Kans., 1988. Ordained Am. Bapt. Clergywoman. Tchr. Dade County Pub. Schs., Miami, Fla., 1970-71; ins. claims adjustor Safeco Ins. Co., Chgo., 1971-72; dir. of community outreach and edn. N. Shore Bapt. Ch., Chgo., 1972-78, assoc. pastor, 1978; pastor First Bapt. Ch., Swansea, Mass., 1978-84; exec. dir. commn. on the ministry Am. Bapt. Chs. U.S.A., Valley Forge, Pa., 1984-90; exec. minister Am. Bapt. Chs. Mass., Dedham, 1990—; mem. Nat. Coun. Chs. Profl. Ch. Leadership, N.Y.C., 1984-90; mem. commn. on pastoral leadership Bapt. World Alliance, McLean, Va., 1986-90; mem. gen. bd. Nat. Coun. Chs. of Christ, 1990-96. Trustee Andover-Newton Theol. Sch., 1990—. Avocations: sailing, tennis, travel, classical music. Office: Am Bapt Chs Mass 20 Milton St Dedham MA 02026-2915

SPOON, ALAN GARY, communications and publishing executive; b. Detroit, June 4, 1951; s. Harry and Mildred (Rudman) S.; m. Terri Alper, June 3, 1975; children: Ryan, Leigh, Randi. B.S., MIT, 1973, M.S., 1973; J.D., Harvard U., 1976. Cons. The Boston Cons. Group, 1976-79, mgr., 1979-81, v.p., 1981; v.p. The Washington Post Co., 1984-85; v.p., contr. Washington Post, 1985-86, v.p. mktg., 1986-87; v.p. fin., CFO The Washington Post Co., 1987-89; pres. Newsweek mag., 1989-91; COO The Washington Post Co., 1991—, pres., 1993—; dir. Info. Industry Assn., Washington, 1982-83, 88-89; bd. dirs., trustee WETA-Pub. Broadcasting, 1986-92; bd. dirs. The Riggs Nat. Bank of Washington, 1991-93. Dir. Norwood Sch., 1989-93, chmn., 1993-95; dir. Internat. Herald Tribune, 1991—, Smithsonian Nat. Mus. Natural History, 1994—, Am. Mgmt. Sys., Inc., 1996—. Recipient award for scholarship and athletics Eastern Coll. Athletic Conf. and MIT, 1973. Home: 7300 Loch Edin Ct Potomac MD 20854-4835 Office: The Washington Post Co 1150 15th St NW Washington DC 20071-0001

SPOONER, ED THORNTON CASSWELL, geology educator and researcher; b. Blandford, Dorset, Eng., June 16, 1950; m. 1972; two children. BA, U. Cambridge, 1971, MA, 1975; MA, Oxford U., 1975; PhD in Geology, U. Manchester, 1976. Demonstrator mineralogy Oxford U., 1973-77; lecr. geology Oriel & Pembroke Colls., Oxford U., 1974-77; asst./assoc. prof. geology U. Toronto, 1977-90, prof., 1990—, grad. coord. geology, 1990-95. Natural Sci. and Engring. Rsch. Coun. Can. grantee, 1978—. Mem. Soc. Econ. Geology. Office: University of Toronto, Dept Geology/22 Russell St, Toronto, ON Canada M5S 3B1

SPOONER, ERIC WARBASSE, pediatric cardiologist; b. Ann Arbor, Mich., May 7, 1945; s. Charles W. and Vera (Warbasse) S.; m. Maria A., June 21, 1969; children: Emily, Molly. BS, U. Mich., 1967; MD, Wayne State U., 1971. Instr. pediatrics U. Mich. Sch. Medicine, Ann Arbor, 1976-77; asst. prof. pediatrics Albany Med. Ctr., 1977-81, clin. asst. prof. pediatrics, 1981-96, assoc. prof. pediatrics, 1996—; sec., treas. Shaher, Farina, Spooner, Albany, 1980-96, chief sect. pediatric cardiology, 1996—; v.p., sec. Capital Dist. Pediatric Cardiology Assocs., 1996—. Fellow Am. Coll. Cardiology, Am. Acad. Pediatrics, Am. Soc. Echo Cardiology; mem. N.Y. Coll. Cardiology, Upstate N.Y. Cardiac Soc. Avocations: sailing, skiing, bicycling, singing, rollerblading. Office: 319 S Manning Blvd Ste 203 Albany NY 12208-1743

SPOONER, RICHARD EDWARD, aerospace company executive; b. Dayton, Ohio, Sept. 15, 1946; s. LaVoy and Marie (Brooks) S.; m. Cora Marie Waugh, June 4, 1969; children: Angela Loada, Tracey Elizabeth. BS, USAF Acad., Colorado Springs, 1969; MS, U. Utah, 1977; grad., Nat. Def. U., 1970. Served in USAF, various locations; dir. intelligence programs Lockheed Martin Corp., Arlington, Va.; data analyst Gen. Elec. Co., Springfield, Va.; dir. mil. programs Martin Marietta Corp., Springfield. Col. USANG. Mem. Tuskegee Airmen, Inc., Air Force Assn., Air Traffic Control Assn., Am. Astronautical Soc., Nat. Mil. Intelligence Assn. Baptist. Avocatins: running, aerobic exercise, golf, basketball. Home: 15447 Silvan Glen Dr Dumfries VA 22026-1009 Office: Lockheed Martin Corp 1425 Jefferson Davis Hwy Arlington VA 22202-3229

SPOONHOUR, JAMES MICHAEL, lawyer; b. San Antonio, Mar. 24, 1946; s. Robert W. and Marie C. (Schulze) S.; m. Terri Walker; children: Taylor, Erin, Whitney, Michael. BA, U. Nebr., 1968, MA, 1970; JD, Georgetown U., 1974. Bar: Fla. 1974, U.S. Dist. Ct. (mid. dist.) Fla. 1974. Assoc. Lowndes, Piersol, Drosdick & Doster, Orlando, Fla., 1974-76; asst. prof. law Loyola U., New Orleans, 1976-77; ptnr. Lowndes, Drosdick, Doster, Kantor & Reed, P.A., Orlando, 1977—. Contbr. to profl. publs. Bd. dirs. Vis. Nurse Assn., Orlando, 1979-89; chmn. sch. bd. The First Acad., Orlando, 1986-89. With USAF, 1970-72. Mem. ABA, Assn. Trial Lawyers Am., Fla. Bar, Orange County Bar Assn. Republican. Office: Lowndes Drosdick Doster Kantor & Reed PA 215 N Eola Dr Orlando FL 32801-2028

SPOOR, WILLIAM HOWARD, food company executive; b. Pueblo, Colo., Jan. 16, 1923; s. Charles Hinchman and Doris Field (Slaughter) S.; m. Janet Spain, Sept. 23, 1950; children: Melanie G., Cynthia F., William Lincoln. BA, Dartmouth Coll., 1949; postgrad., Denver U., 1949, Stanford U., 1965. Asst. sales mgr. N.Y. Export divsn. Pillsbury Co., 1949-53; mgr. N.Y. office Pillsbury Co., 1953-62; v.p. export divsn. Pillsbury Co., Mpls., 1962-68, v.p., gen. mgr. internat. ops., 1968-73, CEO, 1973-85, also bd. dirs., chmn. exec. com., 1987, pres., CEO, 1988, past chmn. bd. dirs.; bd. dirs. Coleman Co. Mem. regional export expansion coun. Dept. Commerce, 1966-74; bd. dirs. exec. Coun. Fgn. Diplomats, 1976-78; mem. bd. visitors Nelson A. Rockefeller Ctr., Dartmouth Coll., 1992-95; Minn. Orchestral Assn., United Negro Coll. Fund, 1973-75; chmn. Capitol City Renaissance Task Force, 1985; trustee Mpls. Found., 1985-92; mem. sr. campaign cabinet Carlson Com. U. Minn., 1985; mem. corps. rels. com. Nature Conservancy, 1985; mem. Nat. Cambodia Crisis Com., pres. pvt. sector Dept. Transp. task force, 1982, pres. pvt. sector survey on cost control, 1983; chmn. YWCA Tribute to Womwn in Internat. Industry. 2d lt. inf. U.S. Army, 1943-46. Recipient Golden Plate award, Am. Acad. Achievement, Disting. Bus. Leadership award, St. Cloud State U., Miss. Valley World Trade award, Outstanding Achievement award, Dartmouth Coll., Horatio Alger award, 1986, Medal of Merit, U.S. Savs. Bond Program; honored with William H. Spoor Dialogues on Leadership, Dartmouth Coll., honored Fair Player Minn. Women's Polit. Caucus, 1989. Mem. Grocery Mfrs. Am. (treas. 1973-84), Nat. Fgn. Trade Coun., Minn. Hist. Soc. (mem. exec. com. 1983, bd. dirs.), Minn. Bus. Partnership, River Club N.Y.C., Woodhill Country Club, Lafayette Club (Wayzata, Minn.), Mpls. Club (bd. govs. 1985, pres. 1986), Little Club, Gulf Stream Bath and Tennis Club, Delray Beach Yacht Club, Gulf Stream Golf Club, Old Baldy Club (Saratoga, N.Y.), Alta Club (Salt Lake City), Phi Beta Kappa. Home: 622 Ferndale Rd W Wayzata MN 55391-9628 Office: 4900 IDS Ctr Minneapolis MN 55402

SPORE, RICHARD ROLAND, III, lawyer, educator; b. Memphis, May 28, 1962; s. Richard R. Jr. and Melba (Cullum) S.; m. Patricia Ann Witherspoon, Aug. 15, 1987; 1 child, Caroline Dare. BA, U. of the South, 1984; JD, U. Va., 1987; MBA, Christian Bros. U., 1992. Bar: Tenn. 1987. Assoc. Burch, Porter & Johnson, Memphis, 1987-94, ptnr., 1995—; adj. prof. bus. law Christian Bros. U., Memphis, 1992—. Author: The Partnering Paradigm: An Entrepreneur's Guide to Strategic Alliances, 1994, Business Organizations in Tennessee, 1995. Mem. Pro Bono Panel for Sr. Citizens, Memphis, 1987—; chmn. small bus. coun. Memphis Area C. of C., 1993; pres. Sewanee Club of Memphis, 1989. Recipient Disting. Svc. award Pro Bono Panel for Sr. Citizens, 1992. Mem. ABA, Tenn. Bar Assn., Memphis Bar Assn. Republican. Methodist. Office: Burch Porter & Johnson 130 Court Ave Memphis TN 38103-2217

SPORES, RONALD MARVIN, anthropology educator, ethnohistorian; b. Eugene, Oreg., Jan. 25, 1931; s. Marvin C. and Marie (Norwood) S.; children: Lisa France, Ronald Jonathan. B.S., U. Oreg., 1953; M.A., Mexico City Coll., 1960; Ph.D., Harvard U., 1964. Asst. prof. anthropology U. Mass., Amherst, 1964-65; prof. anthropology Vanderbilt U., Nashville, 1965-93, dir. anthropology program, 1967-77, prof. emeritus, 1993—. Author: The Mixtec Kings and Their People, 1967, The Mixtecs, 1984; co-author: The Cloud People, 1983; series editor: Vanderbilt Publications in Anthropology, 1971—. Served with U.S. Army, 1953-55, Korea. Mem. Am. Soc. for Ethnohistory (pres. 1978-79). Republican. Methodist. Home: 3415 W End Ave Nashville TN 37203-1077 Office: Vanderbilt U Anthropology Dept Nashville TN 37235

SPORKIN, STANLEY, federal judge; b. Phila., 1932; m. Judith Sally Imber, Sept. 30, 1955; children: Elizabeth Michael, Daniel Paul, Thomas Abraham. AB, Pa. State U., 1953; LLB, Yale U., 1957. Bar: Del. 1958, Pa. 1958, U.S. Dist. Ct. D.C. 1963, U.S. Supreme Ct. 1964, U.S. Ct. Appeals (2d cir.) 1975, U.S. Ct. Appeals (4th cir.) 1978. Law clk. to presiding justice U.S. Dist. Ct. Del., 1957-60; assoc. Haley Woolenberg & Bader, Washington, 1960-61; staff atty. spl. study securities markets U.S. SEC, Washington, 1961-63, atty., 1963, chief atty. enforcement br., 1963-66, chief enforcement atty., 1966, asst. dir., 1967, assoc. dir., 1968-72, dep. dir. div. trading and markets, 1972-73, dir. div. enforcement, 1973-81; gen. counsel CIA, Washington, 1981-86; judge U.S. Dist. Ct. D.C., Washington, 1985—; adj. prof. Antioch Law Sch., 1974-81, Howard U., 1981—; mem. exec. com. U. Calif. Securities Regulation Inst., 1977—. Contbr. articles to profl. jours. Recipient Nat. Civil Svc. League's Spl. Achievement award, 1976, Rockefeller Pub. Svc. award, 1978, Pres.' Disting. Fed. Civilian Svc. award, 1979, Pa. State U. Almunus of Yr. award, 1979, William O. Douglas award for lifetime achievement Assn. Securities and Exch. Commn. Alumni, 1994; honored by B'nai B'rith Hall of Fame; named Alumni Fellow Coll. Bus. Administrn. Pa. State U., 1990. Fellow Am. Bar Found.; mem. ABA, Fed. Bar Assn. (exec. council securities law sect. 1978—), Del. Bar Assn., Bar Assn. of D.C., Am. Law Inst., Am. Inst. CPA's, Fed. Legal Council, Adminstrv. Conf. of U.S., Phi Beta Kappa, Phi Kappa Phi. Office: US Dist Ct US Courthouse Rm 2428 333 Constitution Ave NW Washington DC 20001-2802*

SPORN, MICHAEL BENJAMIN, cancer researcher; b. N.Y.C., Feb. 15, 1933; married; 2 children. MD, U. Rochester, 1959. Intern U. Rochester Sch. Medicine, 1959-60; mem. staff lab. neurochemistry Nat. Inst. Neurol. Diseases and Blindness, 1960-64; mem. staff Nat. Cancer Inst., Bethesda, Md., 1964-70, head lung cancer unit, 1970-73, chief lung cancer br., 1973-78, chief lab. chemoprevention, 1978-95; prof. pharmacology Dartmouth Med. Sch., Hanover, N.H., 1995—. Recipient Am. Cancer Soc. Medal of Honor, 1994. Mem. Am. Assn. Cancer Rsch. (B.F. Cain Meml. award 1991), Am. Soc. Biol. Chemistry. Achievements include research in nucleic acids and cancer, vitamin A and related compounds, carcinogeneisis studies, retinoids and cancer prevention, peptide growth factors and transforming growth factor-beta. Office: Dept Pharmacology Dartmouth Med Sch Hanover NH 03755-3835

SPORN, STANLEY ROBERT, retired electronic company executive; b. N.Y.C., Dec. 10, 1928; s. Max and Mollie (Thau) S.; m. Audrey Brandfield, June 29, 1952; children: Lawrence (dec.), David, Howard. BEE, CCNY, 1950; MSEE, U. Tenn., 1951. Devel. engr. Arma div. AMBAC Industries, N.Y.C., 1951-55, sr. engr., 1958-60, supr., then sect. head, 1960-76, dir. engring., 1976-78; sr. devel. engr. Norden Labs., White Plains, N.Y., 1955-58; dir. engring. Gull Airborne Equipment, Smithtown, N.Y., 1978-81, v.p. engring., 1981-86; v.p. advanced tech. Gull Electronic Systems Divsn. Parker Hannifin Corp., Smithtown, 1986-95; ret., 1995. Author: (with others) Mechanical Design and Systems Handbook, 1964; patentee accelerometers, servos, electronics. Mem. Tau Beta Pi, Eta Kappa Nu. Office: Gull Inc Electronic Systems Divsn 300 Marcus Blvd Smithtown NY 11788-2044

SPOSITO, JAMES A., lawyer, consultant; b. Carbondale, Pa., Jan. 11, 1943; s. Anthony James and Hortense (Talarico) S.; m. Karen Mascelli, Nov. 25, 1966 (div. Nov. 1976); children: James A. Jr., Angela. BS in History, U. Scranton, 1964; MS, Marywood Coll., Scranton, 1969; JD, George Mason U., 1980; D Law, Strasburg (France) U., 1980. Bar: Pa. 1980, U.S. Dist. Ct. (mid. dist.) Pa. 1980, U.S. Ct. Appeals (3d cir.) 1983; cert. tchr., Pa. Tchr. elem. and secondary schs., Pa., 1966-76; aide to Congressman Phil Sharp U.S. Ho. of Reps., Washington, 1977-78; pres. James A. Sposito & Assocs., Scranton, 1980—; pres. Spo-Jac Enterprises, Carbondale, 1964—; pres., owner, broker Sposito Realty Co., Carbondale, 1965—. Advisor 114th legis. dist. State Rep.'s Office, Pa., 1978—. Acting 2d lt. U.S. Army N.G., 1964-71. Mem. ATLA, Pa. Bar Assn., Pa. Trial Assn., Susquehanna County Bar Assn., Lackawanna Bar Assn., Thunderbird Investment Club (pres. 1966-70), Elkview Country Club. (sr. golf mem.). Roman Catholic. Avocations: golf, hunting, fishing. Home: RR 1 Box 1155 Carbondale PA 18407-9016 Office: 547 Hickory St Scranton PA 18505-1322

SPOTO, ANGELO PETER, JR., internist, allergist; b. Tampa, Fla., Mar. 25, 1933; s. Angelo Peter and Zillah Marie (Renfroe) S.; m. Carolyn Jeanette Barbee, Aug. 30, 1958; children: Keith Peter, Elizabeth Anne, Jacqueline Marie. AA, U. Fla., 1953; BS in Medicine, Duke U., 1956, MD, 1957. Diplomate Am. Bd. Internal Medicine, Am. Bd. Allergy and Immunology. Intern Duke U. Med. Ctr., Durham, 1957-58, fellow in medicine (allergy), 1958-59; resident in internal medicine USAF Hosp., Lackland AFB, Tex., 1960-62; resident in allergy Walter Reed Army Med. Ctr., Washington, 1962-63; staff allergist Watson Clinic LLP, Lakeland, Fla., 1966—; ptnr., 1968—; med. staff Lakeland Reg. Med. Ctr., 1966—; bd. dirs. Watson Clinic Found., 1984—, pres., 1984-93; clin. assoc. prof. medicine U. South Fla., Tampa, 1973-77; chmn. bd. dirs. Polk Internat., Inc., 1986—; bd. dirs. Am. Group Practice Corp., 1991-94, chmn., 1992-94. Contbr. articles to profl. jours. Ruling elder Presbyn. Ch., 1970—. Maj. USAF, 1959-66. Decorated Air Force Commendation medal. Fellow ACP, Am. Acad. Allergy, Am. Coll. Allergy; mem. AMA (alt. del. 1992), Polk County Med. Assn. (exec. com. 1971), Fla. Med. Assn., Fla. Allergy Soc. (pres. 1973-74, exec. com. 1972-78), Southeastern Allergy Assn., So. Med. Assn., Am. Group Practice Assn. (trustee 1985-94, pres. 1991-92), Assn. Cert. Allergists (bd. govs. 1971-75), Lakeland C. of C. (bd. dirs. 1987-89). Republican. Presbyterian. Avocation: tennis. Home: 2515 Hollingsworth Hill Ave Lakeland FL 33803-3236 Office: Watson Clinic LLP 1600 Lakeland Hills Blvd Lakeland FL 33805-3019

SPOTO, DONALD, writer, educator; b. New Rochelle, N.Y., June 28, 1941; s. Michael George and Anne Hortense (Werden) S. BA summa cum laude, Iona Coll., New Rochelle, 1963; MA, Fordham U., 1966, PhD, 1970. Instr. Fairfield U., Conn., 1966-68; prof. Coll. New Rochelle, 1968-74; mem. faculty CUNY, N.Y.C., 1974-75, New Sch. for Social Rsch., N.Y.C., 1975-86; adj. prof. U. So. Calif., L.A., 1987-89; vis. lectr. Brit. Film Inst., Nat. Film Theatre, London, 1980-86; nat. lectr. Am. Film Inst., Washington, 1979-82. Author: The Art of Alfred Hitchcock, 1976, 2d edit., rev., 1992, Camerado, 1978, Stanley Kramer: Film Maker, 1978, The Dark Side of Genius: The Life of Alfred Hitchcock, 1983 (Edgar award Mystery Writers Guild 1984), The Kindness of Strangers: The Life of Tennessee Williams, 1985, Falling In Love Again, 1985, Lenya: A Life, 1989, Madcap: The Life of Preston Sturges, 1990, Laurence Olivier: A Biography, 1991, Blue Angel: The Life of Marlene Dietrich, 1992, Marilyn Monroe: The Biography, 1993, A Passion for Life: The Biography of Elizabeth Taylor, 1995, The Decline and Fall of the House of Windsor, 1995, Rebel: The Life and Legend of James Dean, 1996, Notorious: The Life of Ingrid Bergman, 1997; author numerous revs., essays; contbr. articles to mags. and newpapers. Mem. Authors Guild Am., Writers Guild Am. Roman Catholic. Office: care Elaine Markson Literary Agy 44 Greenwich Ave New York NY 10011-8347

SPOTSWOOD, ROBERT KEELING, lawyer; b. Balt., July 11, 1952; s. William Syson and Helen Marie (Fairchild) S.; m. Ashley Hayward Wiltshire, Aug. 19, 1978; children: Robert Keeling, Mary Hayward. BS with highest distinction in Applied Math., U. Va., 1974, JD, 1977. Bar: Ala. 1977, U.S. Dist. Ct. (no. dist.) Ala. 1979, U.S. Dist. Ct. (so. dist.) Ala. 1980, U.S. Ct. Appeals (5th cir.) 1979, U.S. Ct. Appeals (11th cir.) 1981, U.S. Dist. Ct. (mid. dist.) Ala. 1986, U.S. Supreme Ct. 1987. Ptnr. Bradley, Arant, Rose & White, Birmingham, Ala., 1977—. Mem. Birmingham Bar Assn., ABA. Club: Mountain Brook. Home: 3865 Cove Dr Birmingham AL 35213-3801 Office: Bradley Arant Rose & White PO Box 830709 Birmingham AL 35283-0709

SPOTTSVILLE, SHARON ANN, counselor; b. St. Louis; d. Robert F. and Elberta M. (Thompson) Hunter; children: Raymon L., Rodney L. BA, Cleve. State U., 1980, MEd, 1984. Lic. clin. counselor, Ohio. Counselor asst. pvt. practice psychiatry Cleve., 1980-84; counselor, social worker Harambee Svcs. to Black Families, Cleve., 1984-89; coord. parenting devel. rsch. projects Child Guidance Ctr., Cleve., 1989-94; case mgr. supr. Murtis H. Taylor-Multi Svcs. Ctr., Cleve., 1994—; presenter workshops; cons. and trainer in field. Co-author: Parenting Plus. Mem. ACA, Assn. Multi-Cultural Counseling and Devel., Ohio Mental Health Counselors Assn. Home: 19014 Winslow Rd Shaker Hts OH 44122-4868 Office: Murtis H Taylor Multi Svcs Ctr 13422 Kinsman Rd Cleveland OH 44120-4410

SPRABARY, LARRY DREW, military analyst; b. Lewisville, Tex., Sept. 24, 1946; s. H. L. and Frankie Charlene (Lester) S.; m. Glenda Kay Baggett, Feb. 28, 1970; 1 child, Christopher Lain. BS in Mgmt., Embry-Riddle Aero. U., 1979; MS in Human Resources, U. Ctrl. Tex., 1990. Commd. 2d lt. U.S. Army, 1967, advanced through grades to maj., 1977; inspector gen. HQ U.S. Army Europe and 7th Army U.S. Army, Heidelberg, Germany, 1979-82; test officer Tng. and Doctrine Command U.S. Army, Ft. Hood, Tex., 1982-87; spl. asst. to CG Test and Experimentation Command U.S. Army, Ft. Hood, 1987-88; ret. U.S. Army, 1988; staff analyst BDM Corp., Killeen, Tex., 1988-89; mil. plans analyst Test and Experimentation Command, Ft. Hood, 1989-91, 1991—. Decorated Air medal, Bronze Star, Army Commendation medal, Meritorious Svc. medal; named U.S. Army Civilian Tester of Yr., 1993. Baptist. Avocations: golfing, skiing, water sports. Office: Hdqs TEXCOM CSTE-TCC-A Fort Hood TX 76544-5065

SPRABERY, CAROL ANN, mental health service professional; b. North Island, Calif., July 6, 1945; d. Thomas Eugene and Dorothy Frances (Grimes) Forister; div.; children: Scott Ellis, Cynthia Anne. BS, U. Miss., 1967; MEd, Miss. State U., 1986, PhD, 1990. Lic. profl. counselor, Miss.; cert. profl. counselor, Md.; cert. psychometrist, nat. counselor. Adolescent counselor Laurelwood Psychiat., Meridian, Miss.; counselor Lamar Sch., Meridian; tchr. counselor edn. Weems Cmty. Mental Health Ctr., Meridian, 1990-95; pvt. practice Glen Burnie, Md., 1995—; mem. adj. faculty Miss. State U., 1990—. Mem. ACA, Miss. Counselors Assn., Md. Counselors Assn., Assn. Mental Health Counselors, Assn. Sch. Counselors, Lauderdale County Mental Health Bd. Office: 1600 Crain Hwy S Ste 601 Glen Burnie MD 21061-5555

SPRACHER, JOHN C., banking executive; b. Bluefield, W.Va., Oct. 7, 1954; s. David E. and Maryanne (Cole) S.; m. Pamela S. Yost, July 2, 1983. BSBA, Va. Tech., 1976; MBA, W.Va. Coll. Grad. Studies, 1983. V.p. First Cmty. Bank of Mercer County, Inc., Princeton, W.Va., 1983-95, CEO, 1995—; mem. EDP steering, benefits, and sr. credit com. FCFT, Inc.; bd. dirs., v.p., supr. exec. mgr. First Fed. Savs. Bank. Mem. Va. Tech. Found.; former chmn. bd. dirs., past pres., past treas. Greater Bluefield Jaycees; former assoc. dir. Greater Bluefield C. of C.; bd. dirs. Princeton-Mercer County C. of C.; fundraiser United Way of the Vas., Mountain Dominion Dist. Boy Scouts Am.; lay pres., mem. ch. coun., fin. com., usher, past chmn. centennial celebration Immanuel Luth. Ch.; dir. Main St. Bluefield; treas., mem. exec. com., chmn. bd. dirs. Hist. Crab Orchard Mus. and Pioneer Park, Inc. Capt. U.S. Army. Mem. W.Va. Bankers Assn. (trustee ins. trust), Va. Tech. Alumni Assn. (bd. dirs., former pres., v.p., sec., treas. Black Diamond chpt.), Fincastle Country Club, Platinum Hokie Club, Univ. Club (past pres., v.p.). Avocations: antiques and collectibles, genealogy, history. Home: 822 Albemarle St Bluefield WV 24701 Office: First Cmty Bank 1001 Mercer St Princeton WV 24740-3027

SPRAGENS, WILLIAM CLARK, public policy educator, consultant; b. Lebanon, Ky., Oct. 1, 1925; s. Thomas Eugene and Edna Grace (Clark) S.; m. Elaine Jean Dunham, June 14, 1964. AB in Journalism, U. Ky., 1947, MA, 1953; PhD, Mich. State U., 1966. Instr. U. Tenn., Knoxville, 1962-64; part-time instr. Mich. State U., East Lansing, 1964-65; asst. prof. Millikin U., Decatur, Ill., 1965-67, Wis. State U., Oshkosh, 1967-69; assoc. prof. Bowling Green (Ohio) State U., 1969-82, prof., 1982-86, prof. emeritus, 1986—; pres. Spragens and Darnes Assocs., Reston, Va., 1996—. Author: Electronic Magazines, 1995; editor-in-chief: Popular Images of American Presidents, 1988. Del. candidate McGovern for pres. campaign, Bowling Green, 1972; co-dir. Nat. Convs. Program, 1972, 76, 80, 84. Lyndon Baines Johnson Found. grantee, 1977, 78. Mem. World Affairs Coun. Washington, Am. Polit. Sci. Assn., Internat. Soc. for Polit. Sociology, Am. Soc. for Pub. Adminstrn. Democrat. Presbyterian. Avocations: collectibles, psychology. Home and Office: PO Box 410 Herndon VA 20172-0410

SPRAGUE, ANN LOUISE, space scientist; b. Bellfonte, Pa., Feb. 25, 1946; d. David Carpenter and Opal (Wheat) S. BA in Geology, Syracuse U., 1969; MA, Boston U., 1980; PhD, U. Ariz., 1990. Sci. tchr. Selinsgrove Mid. Sch., 1970-79; space scientist Lunar and Planetary Lab. U. Ariz., Tucson, 1990—. Contbg. author: Caloris Basin: An Enhanced Source for Potassium in Mercury's Atmosphere, 1990, The Moon: Mid:Infrared (7.4-11.4) Spectroscopy of Selected Regions, 1992, Sulfur at Mercury, Elemental at the Poles and Sulfides in the Regolith, 1995, Water Brought In to Jupiter's Atmosphere by Fragments R and W of Comet SL-9, 1996. Mem. AAAS, Internat. Astron. Union, Am. Astron. Soc., Am. Geophys. Union. Office: U Ariz Lunar and Planetary Lab Tucson AZ 85721

SPRAGUE, CHARLES CAMERON, medical foundation president; b. Dallas, Nov. 14, 1916; s. George Able and Minna (Schwartz) S.; m. Margaret Frederica Dickson, Sept. 7, 1943; 1 dau., Cynthia Cameron. BBA, BS, DSc, So. Meth. U.; MD, U. Tex. Med. Branch, Galveston, 1943; DSc (hon.), U. Dallas, 1983, Tulane U., 1991. Diplomate Am. Bd. Internal Medicine. Intern U.S. Naval Med. Center, Bethesda, Md., 1943-44; resident Charity Hosp., New Orleans, 1947-48, Tulane U. Med. Sch., 1948-50; Commonwealth research fellow in hematology Washington U. Sch. Medicine, St. Louis, also Oxford (Eng.) U., 1950-52; mem. faculty Med. Sch. Tulane U., 1952-67, prof. medicine, 1959-67; dean Med. Sch. Tulane U. (Sch. Medicine), 1963-67; prof., dean U. Tex. Southwestern Med. Sch., Dallas, 1967-72; pres. U. Tex. Health Sci. Center, Dallas, 1972-86; pres. SW Med. Found., 1987-88, chmn. bd., CEO, 1988-95; pres. emeritus U. Tex. SW Med. Ctr., 1988-95; chmn. emeritus SW Med. Found., 1995—; Mem. Nat. Adv. Council, 1966-70; mem. adv. com. to dir. NIH, 1973—; chmn. Gov.'s Task Force Health Manpower, 1981, Gov.'s Med. Edn. Mgmt. Effectiveness Com.; chmn. allied health edn. adv. com., coordinating bd. Tex. Coll. and Univ. System.; mem. coordinating bd., Tex. Higher Edn., 1989—, vice chmn., 1990—. Adv. com. Ctr. Sci. and Soc., U. Tex., Dallas, 1991—. With USNR, 1943-47. Recipient Ashbel Smith Disting. Alumnus award U. Tex. Med. Br., 1967; Disting. Alumnus award So. Meth. U., 1965; recipient Sports Illustrated Silver Anniversary award, 1963. Mem. Assn. Am. Med. Colls. (chmn. council deans 1970, chmn. exec. council and assembly 1972-73), Am. Soc. Hematology (pres. 1966), Assn. Acad. Health Ctrs. (bd. dirs. 1982—, chmn. bd. 1985-86). Office: Southwestern Medical Found PO Box 45708 5323 Harry Hines Blvd Dallas TX 75245-0708*

SPRAGUE, EDWARD AUCHINCLOSS, retired association executive, economist; b. N.Y.C., Oct. 9, 1932; s. Irvin Auchincloss and Maude Browning (Fisher) S.; m. Patricia Ivy Cannon, Apr. 27, 1957; children: James Edward, Elizabeth Mary, Jennifer Ann. BA, Princeton U., 1954; MA, NYU, 1961. Rsch. analyst N.J. State C. of C., Newark, 1957-59; assoc. economist F.W. Dodge Corp., N.Y.C., 1959-62; economist Lehman Bros., N.Y.C., 1962-67; v.p. Nat. Assn. Mfrs., N.Y.C. and Washington, 1967-77; dir. tax policy The Tax Found., Washington, 1977-82, sr. v.p., 1985-89; exec. dir. Tax Exec. Inst., 1982-85; v.p., exec. dir. The Tax Coun., 1979-82, 86-91, cons., 1991-92; cons. Employers Coun. on Flexible Compensation, Washington, 1992-93; ret., 1993. Editor: Building Business, 1961-62; jour. The Tax Executive, 1983-85. With U.S. Army, 1955-57. Mem. Nat. Tax Assn. Republican. Home: 47921 Tranquility Ln Lexington Park MD 20653

SPRAGUE, GEORGE FREDERICK, geneticist; b. Crete, Nebr., Sept. 3, 1902; s. Elmer Ellsworth and Lucy Kent (Manville) S. B.S., U. Nebr., 1924, M.S., 1926, D.Sc., 1958; Ph.D., Cornell U., 1930. With Dept. Agr., 1924-72, leader corn and sorghum investigations, 1958-72; mem. faculty U. Ill., Urbana, 1973-86; prof. emeritus U. Ill., 1986-93. Editor: Corn and Corn Improvement, 3d edit, 1989; contbr. articles to profl. jours. Recipient Superior Svc. award USDA, 1960, Disting. Svc. award, 1970, Wolf Found. award, Nat. Coun. Plant Breeders award, DeKalb Career award; inducted into USDA-Agrl. Rsch. Svc. Sci. Hall of Fame. Fellow AAAS, Washington Acad. Scis., Am. Soc. Agronomy (pres. 1960, Crops Rsch. award 1957); mem. NAS, Crops Sci. Soc. (pres. 1951), Am. Genetics Assn., Genetics Soc. Am., Am. Soc. Plant Physiologists, Am. Naturalists, Biometrics Soc. Home: 494 W 10th Ave Apt 208 Eugene OR 97401-2880

SPRAGUE, JAMES MATHER, medical scientist, educator; b. Kansas City, Mo., Aug. 31, 1916; s. James P. and Lelia (Mather) S.; m. Dolores Marie Eberhart, Nov. 25, 1959; 1 son, James B. B.S., U. Kans., 1938, M.A., 1940; Ph.D., Harvard U., 1942; A.M. (hon.), U. Pa., 1971. From asst. to asst. prof. anatomy Hopkins Med. Sch., 1942-50; asst. prof. to prof. anatomy U. Pa. Med. Sch., Phila., 1950-83; chmn. dept. U. Pa. Med. Sch., 1967-76, Joseph Leidy prof. anatomy, 1973-83, emeritus Joseph Leidy prof., 1983—, dir. Inst. Neurol. Sci., 1973-80, chmn. univ. faculty senate, 1963; vis. prof. Northwestern U., 1948, U. Oxford, 1949, Rockefeller U., 1955, Cambridge U., 1956, U. Pisa, 1966, 74-75, U. Leuven, 1984—, Kyushu U., 1988; sci. cons. NIH, 1957-60. Co-editor: Progress in Psychobiology and Physiological Psychology, 1966-84; asso. editor: Acta Neurobiol. Exper., 1976; contbr. articles to profl. jours. Recipient Macy faculty award, 1974-75, Disting. Tchg. award Lindbach Found., 1965; Guggenheim fellow, 1948-49. Mem. NAS, Am. Assn. Anatomists (v.p. 1976-78), Japanese Assn. Anatomists (hon.), Soc. Neurosci. (founding coun.). Democrat. Home: 410 Lantern Ln Berwyn PA 19312-2011 Office: Dept Cell & Devel Biology Dept Neurosci Sch Medicine U Pa Philadelphia PA 19104-6058

SPRAGUE, JO ANN, state legislator; b. Nashville, Ind., Nov. 3, 1931; m. Warren G. Sprague; 6 children. BA, U. Mass., 1980. Mem. Mass. Ho. of Reps., Boston, 1992—, mem. capital budget com., 1990-92; mem. Walpole Prison Adv. Com., 1970-92, Rep. Town Meeting, 1979—. Bd. trustees Walpole Scholar Found., 1990-92. 2d lt. U.S. Army, 1950-53. Mem. Walpole Vis. Nurses Assn. (bd. dirs. 1989-92), Walpole LVW, Norfolk Am. Legion (Post No. 335). Republican. Home: 305 Elm St Walpole MA 02081-1903 Office: Mass Ho of Reps State Capitol Boston MA 02133

SPRAGUE, JOHN LOUIS, management consultant; b. Boston, 1930; s. Robert Chapman and Florence Antoinette (van Zelm) S.; m. Mary-Jane Whitney, June 19, 1952; children—John Louis, William Whitney, Catherine van Zelm, David Hyatt. A.B., Princeton, 1952; Ph.D., Stanford, 1959. With Sprague Electric Co., North Adams, Mass., 1959-87; co-dir. engring. labs., sr. v.p. engring. Sprague Electric Co., 1964-65, v.p. research and devel., 1965-66, sr. v.p. semi-condr. div., 1967-76, pres., 1976-87, chief exec. officer, 1981-87; pres. John L. Sprague Assocs. Inc., 1988—; bd. dirs. Sipex Corp., Allmerica Fin., Aerovox, Inc., MRA Labs., Inc., Calif. Micro Devices, Aerospace Coating Sys., Inc., Boyd Converting Co. Chmn. Williamstown United Fund-ARC Campaign, 1961; trustee Pine Cobble Sch., 1978, Middlesex Sch., 1994-96. Lt. (j.g.) USNR, 1952-55. Mem. IEEE, Electrochem. Soc., Am. Chem. Soc., Sci. Research Soc. Am., Confrerie des Chevaliers du Tastevin, Confrerie de la Chaine des Rotisseurs, Mayflower Hist. Soc., Sigma Xi, Phi Lambda Upsilon. Club: Princeton (N.Y.C.). Home: 175 Bee Hill Rd Williamstown MA 01267-0548

SPRAGUE, NORMAN FREDERICK, JR., surgeon, educator; b. L.A., June 12, 1914; s. Norman F. and Frances E. (Ludeman) S.; m. Caryll E. Mudd, Dec. 27, 1941 (dec. Apr. 1978); children: Caryll (Mrs. Mingst), Norman Frederick III, Cynthia Sprague Connolly, Elizabeth (Mrs. Day); m. Erlenne Estes, Dec. 31, 1981. AB, U. Calif., 1933; MD, Harvard U., 1937. Intern Bellevue Hosp., N.Y.C., 1937, house surgeon, 1938-39; pvt. med. practice L. A., 1946—; mem. hon. staff Hosp. of Good Samaritan, L. A.; mem. staff St. Vincent Med. Ctr., L. A.; asst. clin. prof. surgery UCLA, 1951—; dir. emeritus Western Fed. Savs. & Loan Assn.; chmn. bd. dirs. Western Pioneer Co., 1961-63, Pioneer Savs. & Loan Assn., 1959-63; dir. Arden-Mayfair, Inc., 1966-69; also chmn. exec. com.; dir., mem. exec. com. Cyprus Mines Corp., 1959-79; trustee Mesabi Trust, 1964-76. Chmn. exec. com., v.p. Harvard Sch., 1954-65; mem. Cmty. Redevel. Agy. City of L.A., 1966-69, vice-chmn., 1967-69; mem. Calif. Regional Med. Programs Area IV Coun., 1970-75; bd. dirs., v.p. Calif. Inst. Cancer Rsch., 1974-80, pres., 1980-82; bd. dirs. Cancer Assoc., 1975-80; trustee UCLA Found., Marlborough Sch., 1981-90, Mildred E. and Harvey S. Mudd Found., Hollywood Bowl Assn., 1962-66; hon. trustee Calif. Mus. Found.; mem. exec. com.; trustee Youth Tennis Found., 1960-70; trustee, pres., mem. exec. com. S.W. Mus.; founding trustee Harvey Mudd Coll.; chmn. bd. trustees Caryll and Norman Sprague Found., 1957—, Harvard Sch.; mem. bd. visitors UCLA Med. Sch.; nat. bd. dirs. Retinitis Pigmentosa Internat.; mem. adv. com. Univs. Space Rsch. Assn., Divsn. Space Biomedicine, 1982-94. Maj. M.C. AUS, 1941-46. Decorated Bronze Star; recipient Bishop's award of Merit Episc. Diocese L.A., 1966, Highest Merit award So. Calif. Pub. Health Assn., 1968. Mem. AMA, SAR, Calif. Med. Assn., L.A. County Med. Assn., Univ. Space Rsch. Assn. (mem. adv. com. divsn. space biomedicine 1982-94), Am. Cattlemen's Assn., Symposium Soc., Tennis Patrons Assn. (dir. 1960-70), Calif. Club, Harvard Club, L.A. Country Club, Delta Kappa Epsilon. Home: 550 S Mapleton Dr Los Angeles CA 90024-1811 Office: 2049 Century Park E Ste 2760 Los Angeles CA 90067-3202

SPRAGUE, PETER JULIAN, software company executive, lecturer; b. Detroit, Apr. 29, 1939; s. Julian K. and Helene (Coughlin) S.; m. Tjasa Krofta, Dec. 19, 1959; children: Carl, Steven, Kevin, Michael. Student, Yale U., 1961, MIT, 1961, Columbia U., 1962-66. Chmn. Wave Sys., Inc.; bd. dirs. Enlightened Software Inc. Trustee Strang Clinic. Mem. Yale Club. Home: 399 Under Mountain Rd Lenox MA 01240-2036 Office: Wave Sys Corp 540 Madison Ave New York NY 10022-3213

SPRAGUE, WILLIAM DOUGLAS, lawyer, company executive; b. Houston, Dec. 23, 1941; s. William Douglas and Helen (Mims) S.; m. Marilyn Wells, Aug. 7, 1965; children: William Douglas III, Anne W., Robert L. BS, U. Wis., 1964; JD, Harvard U., 1967. Bar: Mich. 1972, Ind. 1978, Pa. 1991. Assoc. Reinhart, Boerner, Van Deuren, Norris & Rieselbach, Milw., 1967-71; lawyer Ford Motor Credit Co., Dearborn, Mich., 1971-77; various legal positions to sr. v.p. adminstrn. AMAX Coal Co., Indpls., 1977-87; assoc. gen. counsel Alumax Inc., San Mateo, Calif., 1987-88; v.p., gen. counsel Lukens Inc., Coatesville, Pa., 1988—. Chmn. bd. dirs. United Way Chester County, Exton, Pa., 1990. Mem. ABA, Phi Kappa Phi, Phi Eta Sigma. Avocations: golf, bridge. Office: Lukens Inc 50 S 1st Ave Coatesville PA 19320-3418

SPRAGUE, WILLIAM WALLACE, JR., retired food company executive; b. Savannah, Ga., Nov. 11, 1926; s. William Wallace and Mary (Crowther) S.; m. Elizabeth Louise Carr, Oct. 3, 1953; children: Courtney, Lauren Duane, William Wallace III, Elizabeth Louise. BSME, Yale U., 1950. With Savannah Foods & Industries, Inc., 1952-94, ret., 1994, sec., 1961-62, v.p., 1962-72, pres., chief exec. officer, 1972-92, chmn. bd. dirs., CEO, 1993-94, also bd. dirs.; bd. dirs., pres. Adeline Sugar Factory Co., Ltd., Savannah, Coastal Mgmt. Corp., Savannah. Trustee Savannah Bus. Group; chmn. emeritus Youth Futures Authority, Savannah. With USN, 1945-46. Named Sugar Man of Yr. and recipient Dyer Meml. award B.W. Dyer & Co., 1985; named Industrialist of Yr. Internat. Mgmt. Coun., 1988. Mem. World Sugar Rsch. Orgn. (chmn. 1982-85), The Sugar Assn. (bd. dirs.),Carolina Plantation Soc., St. Andrews Soc., Oglethorpe Club, Century Club (Savannah). Office: Savannah Foods & Industries PO Box 339 Savannah GA 31402-0339

SPRAINGS, VIOLET EVELYN, psychologist; b. Omaha, Aug. 1, 1930; d. Henry Elbert and Straunella (Hunter) S.; A.B., U. Calif., Berkeley, 1948, M.A., 1951, postgrad., 1960-64, Ph.D., San Francisco, 1982. Tchr., Oakland (Calif.) Public Schs., 1951-58; psychologist Med. Edn. Diagnostic Ctr., San Francisco, 1959-62; dir. psychol. edn. and lang. services Calif. Dept. Edn., 1963-71; asst. prof. San Francisco State U., 1964-71; assoc. prof. edn. psychology Calif. State U., Hayward, 1971-79; dir. Spraings Acad., Orinda, Lafayette and Walnut Creek, 1967—; psychologist in pvt. practice, 1962—; dir. Western Women's Bank; mem. adv. bd. Bay Area Health Systems Agy.; instr. U. Calif., Berkeley extension, 1964—; mem. oral bd. for Edn. Psychologists, 1972—; mem. Calif. Dept. Task Force on Psychol. Assessment, 1987—. Mem. adv. com. Foothill Jr. Coll. Dist.; cons. Psychol. Casey Family Program, 1986—. Recipient Phoebe Apperson Heart award San Francisco Examiner, 1968. Mem. Am. Psychol. Assn., Internat. Neuropsychol. Assn. (charter), Calif. Psychol. Assn., Calif. Assn. Sch. Psychologists and Psychometrists, Western Psychol. Assn., Nat. Council Negro Women, AAUW, Delta Sigma Theta, Psi Chi, Pi Lambda Theta. Contbr. articles to profl. jours. Home: 170 Glorietta Blvd Orinda CA 94563-3543 Office: 89 Moraga Way Orinda CA 94563-3023

SPRALEY, JUDITH ANN, nursing educator, administrator; b. Gross Point, Mich., Jan. 11, 1936; d. Leonard Joseph and Margaret (McCloskey) S. BSN, Mount St. Joseph Coll., 1958; MEd, U. Cin., 1986. RN, Ohio; CNOR. Dir. nursing svc. Otto C. Epp Meml. Hosp., Cin.; nursing instr. Deaconess Hosp. Sch. Nursing, Cin.; nursing administr. U. Hosp., Cin.; chair surg. tech. program Cin. State Tech. Coll. and C.C.; author, instr. operating rm. courses for nurses & surg. technologists; acute and long term patient advocate; cons. in field. Mem. AAUP, Assn. Oper. Rm. Nurses, Assn. Surg. Technologists (liaison com. on cert for surg. technologist). Home: 8034 Mildmay Ct Cincinnati OH 45239-4012

SPRANG, MILTON LEROY, obstetrician, gynecologist, educator; b. Chgo., Jan. 15, 1944; s. Eugene and Carmella (Bruno) S.; m. Sandra Lee Karabelas, July 16, 1966; children: David, Christina, Michael. Student, St. Mary's Coll., 1962-65; MD, Loyola U., 1969. Diplomate Am. Bd. Ob-gyn; Nat. Bd. Med. Examiners; CME accreditation. Intern St. Francis Hosp., Evanston, Ill., 1969-70, resident, 1972-75, sr. attending physician, 1985—; assoc. attending phsycian Evanston Hosp., 1975-79, attending physician, 1980-84, sr. attending physician, 1985—, v.p. med. staff, 1990-91, pres.-elect, 1991-92, pres., 1992-93; also bd. dirs., 1991-94; sec. exec. com. Evanston Hosp., 1993-94; chmn. ob-gyn Cook County Grad. Sch. Medicine,, Chgo., 1983-91; instr. Northwestern U. Med. Sch., Chgo., 1975-78, asst. prof., 1984-95, assoc. prof., 1995—; pres. Northwestern Healthcare Network Physician Leadership, 1994; lectr. acad. and civic groups OB-Gyn. Nat. Ctr. Advanced Med. Edn., 1991—; bd. dirs. Ill. Found. Med. Rev.; bd. trustees Ill. State Ins. Svcs., 1992—; bd. govs. Ill. State Med. Inter-Inst. Exch., 1987-92. Editor: Profl. Staff News, 1992-93; chmn. editorial bd. Jour. Chgo. Medicine, 1986-91; contbr. articles to profl. jours. Bd. dirs. Am. Cancer Sooc., chmn. profl. edn. com. North Shoore unit, 1982-85; bd. dirs. Chgo. Community Info. Network, 1994-95; mem. Nat. Rep. Congrl. Com., 1981—, Ill. Med. Polit. Action Com. With USN, 1970-72. Fellow ACS, Am. Coll.Ob-Gyn. (chmn. Ill. sect. 1975-76), Am. Soc. Colposcopy and Cervical Pathology; mem. AMA (Physician Recognition award 1977, 80, 83), Ill. Med. Soc. (del. to AMA 1987, 91—, ho. dels., govt. affairs com. 1988—, chmn. reference com. 1989, chmn. bd. trustees 1996—, chmn. fin. com. 1992-94, sec.-treas. 1994-96), Chgo. Med. Soc. (v.p. 1984-85, adv. com. advt. stds. 1978-84, counselor, physician's rev. com. 1980-85, chmn. 1985, exec. coun. north suburban br. 1981-82, 86, chmn. 1985, trustee ins. bd. 1982—, nominating com. 1985—, trustee 1986-92, treas. 1986-89, sec. 1989-90, pres.-elect 1990-91, pres. 1991-92, chmn. fin. com. 1986-89, chmn. ethical rels. com. 1994—, chmn. bd. trustees 1990-91), Chgo. Found. Med. Care (nominating com. 1980-84, med. care evaluation and edn. com. 1980-83, practice guidelines com. 1984), Physician Benefit Trust (chmn. fin. com. 1993-97). Roman Catholic. Avocations: reading, raising fish, swimming. Home: 4442 Concord Ln Skokie IL 60076-2606 Office: AGSO 1000 Central St Evanston IL 60201

SPRATT, JOHN MCKEE, JR., congressman, lawyer; b. Charlotte, N.C., Nov. 1, 1942; s. John McKee and Jane Love (Bratton) S.; m. Jane Stacy, May 31, 1968; children: Susan Elizabeth, Sarah Stacy, Catherine Bratton. A.B., Davidson Coll., 1964; M.A., Corpus Christi Coll., Oxford U., 1966; LL.B., Yale U., 1969. Ops. analyst Office of Asst. Sec. of Def., 1969-71; ptnr. Spratt, McKeown & Spratt, Mork, S.C., 1971-83; pres. Spratt Ins. Agy., Ft. Mill, 1973-82, Bank of Ft. Mill, S.C., 1973-82; mem. 98th-105th Congresses from 5th S.C. dist., Washington, D.C., 1983—; mem. Armed Svcs. com., subcoms. oversight and investigations, military acquisitions, govt. opns. com., subcom. commerce, consumer, monetary affairs, joint com. orgn. congress, budget com., nat. security-mil. procurement com., house dem. policy com.; former dir. Bank of York. Chmn. bd. trustees Divine Saviour Hosp., York, 1980-82; bd. dirs. Piedmont Legal Services, Inc., 1978-82; bd. visitors Davidson Coll., 1978-80; chmn. bd. visitors Winthrop Coll., 1976. Served to capt. JAGC, U.S. Army, 1969-71. Mem. S.C. Bar Assn. (ho. of dels.), ABA. Democrat. Presbyterian. Office: US Ho of Reps 1536 Longworth Bldg Ofc Bldg Washington DC 20515-4005*

SPRATT, JOHN STRICKLIN, surgeon, educator, researcher; b. San Angelo, Tex., Jan. 3, 1929; s. John Stricklin and Nannie Lee (Morgan) S.; m. Beverly Jane Winfiele, Dec. 27, 1951; children: John Arthur, Shelley Winfiele, Robert Stricklin. AS, U. Tex.-Arlington, 1947; BS with high honors, So. Methodist U., 1949; MD, U. Tex.-Dallas, 1952; MSPH, U. Mo., 1970; postgrad. Washington U., St. Louis, 1961. Asst. in physiology Southwestern Med. Sch., U. Tex., Dallas, 1952; intern, Barnes Hosp., Washington U., St. Louis, 1952-53, asst. resident in surgery, 1955-57, resident, Am. Cancer Soc. fellow in surgery, 1958-59; USPHS Cancer Research fellow in radiotherapy and surgery Mallinckrodt Inst. Radiology, St. Louis, 1957-58, chief resident, 1958-59; mem. surg. faculty Washington U., 1952-76; chief surgeon Ellis Fischel State Cancer Hosp., Columbia, Mo., 1961-76; practice medicine specializing in surgery, Louisville, 1976—; mem. staffs U. Louisville Hosp., Norton-Kosair Children's Hosp., VA Hosp., Bapt. Hosp. East, Jewish Hosp.; prof. surgery U. Mo.-Columbia, 1961-76; prof. surgery U. Louisville, 1976—, prof. health systems, 1980—; clin. prof. surgery F. Edward Hebert Sch. Medicine Uniformed Svcs. U. Health Scis., Bethesda, Md., 1988. Contbr. numerous articles in cancer, surgery and med. edn. fields to sci. publs. Mem. editorial bd. Cancer mag., 1964-91, Am. Jour. Surgery, Jour. Surg. Oncology. Editor, editor-in-chief Louisville Medicine mag., 1979-82, Jour. Pelvic Surgery, 1995—, served to capt. USNR, 1952-93, (ret.). Grantee Nat. Cancer Inst., Am. Cancer Soc., recipient St. George medal, 1997. Fellow ACS, Am. Acad. Med. Adminstrs. (editl. bd. The Executive, diplomate), Royal Soc. Health; mem. AMA, Am. Coll. Physician Execs., Am. Surg. Assn., Soc. Surg. Oncology, Res. Officers Assn., Naval Res. Assn., Assn. Mil. Surgeons U.S., Soc. Med. Cons. Armed Forces, Soc. Pelvic Surgeons, Ctrl. Surg. Assn., Soc. Surgery Alimentary Tract, Cell Proliferation Soc., Am. Assn. Cancer Edn., Soc. Univ. Surgeons, Am. Coll. Physician Execs., Alpha Omega Alpha. Democrat. Baptist. Club: Cosmos (Washington). Lodge: Rotary. Home: 2206 Bell Tavern Ct Louisville KY 40207-1215 Office: 529 S Jackson St Louisville KY 40202-3229

SPRAY, PAUL ELSWORTH, surgeon; b. Wilkinsburg, Pa., Apr. 9, 1921; s. Lester E. and Phoebe Gertrude (Hull) S.; m. Mary Louise Conover, Nov. 28, 1943; children: David C., Thomas L., Mary Lynn (Mrs. Thomas Branham). BS, U. Pitts., 1942; MD, George Washington U., 1944; MS, U. Minn., 1950. Diplomate Am. Bd. Orthopedic Surgery. Intern U.S. Marine Hosp., S.I., 1944-45; resident Mayo Found., Rochester, Minn., 1945-46, 48-50; practice medicine specializing in orthopedic surgery Oak Ridge, Tenn., 1950—; mem. active staff Oak Ridge Hosp., Knoxville, Roane County Hosp.; courtesy staff Park West and Harriman Hosp., Tenn.; vol. vis. cons. CARE Medico, Jordan, 1959, Nigeria, 1962, 65, Algeria, 1963, Afghanistan, 1970, Bangladesh, 1975, 77, 79, Peru, 1980, U. Ghana, 1982; AMA vol. physician, Vietnam, 1967, 72; vis. assoc. prof. U. Nairobi, 1973; mem. tchg. team Internat. Coll. Surgeons to Peru, 1979, 84 ; vis. prof. orthop. surgery U. Khartoum, 1976; hon. prof. San Luis Gonzaga U., Ica, Peru, 1979; AmDoc vol. cons. U. Biafra Tchg. Hosp., 1969; vis. prof. Mayo Clinic, 1988; sec. orthops. overseas divsn. CARE Medico, 1971-76, sec. Medico adv. bd., 1974-76, vice chmn., 1976, chmn., 1977-79, v.p. CARE, Inc., 1977-79, pub. mem. CARE bd. dirs., 1980-90, mem. bd. overseers, 1991—; chmn. Orthops. Overseas, Inc., 1982-86, treas., 1986-88, emeritus mem., 1994; mem. U.S. organizing com. 1st Internat. Acad. Symposium on Orthops., Tianjin, China, 1983; mem. CUPP Internat. Adv. Coun., 1986—; invited guest spkr. Japan Orthop. Assn., 1994. Mem. editorial bd. Contemporary Orthopedics, 1984-96. V.p. Anderson County Health Coun., 1975, pres., 1976-77, hon. bd. dirs., 1991—; pres. health commn. Coun. So. Mountains, 1958-65, sec., bd. dirs., 1965-66; Tenn. pres. UN Assn., 1966-67; vice-chmn. bd. Camelot Care Ctr., Tenn., 1979-82, chmn., 1982-86; chmn. bd. dirs. Camelot Found., 1986-87; hon. mem. World Orthopedic Concern, 1990; with del. to Vietnam People to People, 1993, citizen amb. to Vietnam, 1993; del. to Oak Ridge's Sister City, Obinsk, Russia, 1993; trustee Vietnam Am. Scholarship Fund, 1992-95. Recipient Svc. to Mankind award Sertoma, 1967, Humanitarian award Lions Club, 1968, Freedom Citation Sertoma, 1978, Amb. Goodwill Lions Club, award 1979, Medico Disting. Svc. award, 1990, 1st Ann. Vocat. Svc. award Oak Ridge Rotary, 1979, Tech. Communication award East Tenn. chpt. Soc. for Tech. Communication, 1983, Individual Achievement award Meth. Med. Ctr. of Oak Ridge, 1991, Humanitarian award Orthopaedics Overseas, 1992; Melvin Jones fellow Lions Club, 1993. Fellow ACS, Internat. Coll. Surgeons (Tenn. regent 1976-80, bd. councillors 1980-84, hon. chmn. bd. turstees 1981-83, trustee 1983-84, v.p. U.S. sect. 1982-83, mem. surg. teams com. 1983-90, Humanitarian award 1992); mem. AMA (Humanitarian Svc. award 1967, 72), Sociètè International Chirugie Orthopèdique et de Traumuatologie, So. Orthopedic Assn., Western Pacific Orthopedic Assn., Am. Fracture Assn., Am. Acad. Orthopedic Surgeons (mem. com. on injuries 1980-86), Tenn. Med. Assn. (com. on emergency med. svcs. 1978-97), Peru Acad. Surgery (corr.), Peruvian Soc. Orthopedic Surgery and Traumatology (corr.), Clin. Orthopedic Soc., Mid-Am. Orthopaedic Soc., Rotary Club (Oak Ridge chpt., Paul Harris fellow). Home: 507 Delaware Ave Oak Ridge TN 37830-3902 Office: 160 W Tennessee Ave Ste C Oak Ridge TN 37830-6501

SPRAYBERRY, ROSLYN RAYE, secondary school educator; b. Newnan, Ga., June 29, 1942; d. Henry Ray and Grace (Bernhard) S. BA, Valdosta State Coll., 1964; MA in Teaching, Ga. State U., 1976, EdS in Spanish, 1988; EdD, Nova U., 1993. Cert. tchr., Ga. Tchr. history Griffin (Ga.) High Sch., 1964-65; tchr. 6th grade Beaverbrook Elem Sch., Griffin, 1965-66; tchr. Spanish, chair fgn. lang. dept. Forest Park (Ga.) High Sch., 1966-77; chair fgn. lang. dept. Spanish Forest Park (Ga.) High Sch., 1969-77; tchr. Spanish, chair fgn. lang. dept. Riverdale (Ga.) High Sch., 1977—; correlator Harcourt, Brace, Jovanovich, 1989; adv. bd. So. Conf. Lang. Teaching, 1992—; lectr. and speaker in field. Contbr. articles to The Ednl. Resource Info. Ctr. Clearinghouse on Langs. and Linguistics, Ctr. for Applied Linguistics, Washington; designed courses for the Gifted, Ga. Dept. of Edn. Cnvener Acad. Alliances-Atlanta II, Clayton County, Ga., 1982—; advisor, workshop leader Ga. Fgn. Lang. Camp, Atlanta, 1983; dir. Clayton County Fgn. Lang. Festival, 1990-91. Recipient STAR Tchr. award Ga. C. of C., 1982; Fulbright-Hays scholar, 1978; NEH grantee, 1977, 84. Mem. NEA, Am. Coun. Tchrs. Fgn. Langs., Am. Assn. Tchrs. Spanish and Portuguese, Ga. Assn. Educators, Fgn. Lang. Assn. Ga. (treas. 1977-85, assoc. editor jour. 1981-86, Tchr. of Yr. award 1976), Clayton County Edn. Assn., So. Conf. Lang. Teaching, KPS Leadership Specialists (co-founder 1993). Methodist. Avocations: quilt playing, traveling, reading, writing. Home: 9261 Brave Ct Jonesboro GA 30236-5110

SPRECHER, DAVID A., university administrator, mathematician; b. Saarbrucken, Fed. Republic Germany, Jan. 12, 1930; s. Wolfgang and Karolina (Jung) S.; children: Lorrie, Jeannie. Student, Hebrew U., 1952-54; A.B., U. Bridgeport, 1958; Ph.D., U. Md., 1963. Instr. math. U. Md., 1961-63; asst. prof. Syracuse U., 1963-66; asso. prof. math. U. Calif.-Santa Barbara, 1966-71, prof., 1971-92, prof. emeritus, 1993—, chmn. dept., 1972-75, assoc. dean Coll. of Letters and Sci., 1975-78, dean Coll. of Letters and Sci., 1978-81, provost/dean, 1981-91. Author: Elements of Real Analysis, 1970, 2nd edit., 1987, Precalculus Mathematics, 1974, Finite Mathematics, 1976; (with P. Frank and A. Yaqub) A Brief Course in Calculus With Applications, 1971, 2nd edit., 1976; (with P. Frank) Calculus, 1975; contbr. articles to profl. jours. Served with Israeli Army, 1948-50. Mem. Am. Math. Soc., Math. Assn. Am. Office: U Calif 6607 South Hall Santa Barbara CA 93106

SPRECHER, BARON WILLIAM GUNTHER, pianist, composer, conductor, diplomat; b. Saarbrucken, Germany, Jan. 20, 1924; came to U.S., 1952.; s. Wolf and Karoline (Jung) Sprecher; m. Blossom Tag, Aug. 6, 1952. Studied piano with Prof. Wittels, Tel Aviv; studied piano with Madame Vengerova, N.Y.C.; studied composition with Paul Ben-Haim, Tel Aviv, studied conducting with Georg Singer; hon. degree, Inst. of Vocal Arts, 1957; Dr. honoris causa in Philosophy of Music, World Univ. Roundtable, 1988; MusD (hon.), London Inst. Applied Rsch., 1991, DFA (hon.), 1993, HHD, 1993; MusD (hon.), Australian Inst. Coord. Rsch., 1991; diploma, Gran Premio Am., 1990, Paladino del Tricolore, 1990; D Musicology, Somerset U.; D Music (hon.), Atlantic Southeastern U.; Diploma, Acad. Argentina de Diplomacia; Assoc. (hon.), Inst. Affairs Internat., Paris, 1993; DD (hon.), The Christian Congregation; D rerum politicarum (hon.), LittD, U. Aeterna Lucina Vitama, 1991; DD (hon.), LittD, Eng., 1994; PhD (hon.), Germany, 1994. Korrepetitor Israel Folk Opera, Tel-Aviv, 1940-43; piano soloist Israel Philharm. Orch., Tel-Aviv, 1946-48; pres., music dir. Bronx Philharm., N.Y.C., 1971-83; music dir. Sta. WEVD, N.Y.C., 1969-85; asst. pianist accompanying Lotte Lenya, Richard Tucker, Jan Peerce, Itzhak Perlman, Jan Kiepura, Ilona Massey; prof. Inst. Hautes Etudes Economiques et Sociales; rsch. prof. Alliance Universelle Paix Connaissance, Paris, 1991; prof. Haute Ecole de Recherche, Inst. des Hautes Etudes Economiques et Sociales; mem. coun. Inst. de Documentation et D'Etudes Europeennes; dep. mem., diplomat Internat. State Parliament. Composer: (Song Book) Yinglish, piano soloist 1st performance of Gershwin's Concerto in F in Israel; composer Piano Sonata, 1945, Jerusalem Concerto for Piano and Orch., 1967, (TV spl.) Great is Thy Faith, 1970; pianist-condr. 24 record albums; mem. The First Piano Quartet (Acad. award nomination, Peabody award). Consul Sovereign State Aeterna Lucina for State and City of N.Y.; comdr. fgn. rels. Island Du Caricom, 1995; diplomat World Jewish Congress; senator Coun. of States for Protection of Life and Human Rights, Palermo, Italy; del. at large Rep. Presdl. Task Force; active Nat. Rep. Senatorial Com. Decorated noble knight Noble House of Amena, knight order Knight Templars of Jerusalem, knight comdr. Lofsensis Ursinius Order, baron Order of Bohemian Crown, comdr. Order of Golden Lance (Australia), Capt. Légion de L'Aigle Mer, Baron of Montsalvat, knight Holy Grail, count San Ciriaco, comdr. fgn. rels. Island du Caricom, 1995, Sen Maison Internationale Des Intellectuels, Sen European Parliament, Internat. Parliament for Safety and Peace, diplomat World

Jewish Congress, Laird-Lord of Camster, Caithness, Scotland, 1995; recipient Diplomatic medal Internat. Parliament for Safety and Peace, 1995, Gold Cross of Honour, Albert Schweitzer Soc. Austria, Albert Einstein medal, Circulo Nobiliario Caballeros Universales, 1992, Swan Knight (Chevalier du Cygne), Order of the Swan, Knight of Yr. award Internat. Writers and Artists Assn., 1995, Noble Conquistador, Internat. Chivalric Order of the Knights of Justice, and other.s. Fellow United Writers' Assn. India; mem. ASCAP, Maison Internat. des Intellectuels, Internat. Parliament for Safety and Peace, World Parliament Confedn. of Chivalry (Grand Coun.), World Acad. Assn. of the Universe (life), Bronx Philharm. Symphony Soc., Inc. (founder, pres.), Internat. Platform Assn., Am. Fedn. Musicians, Robert Stolz Soc. Gt. Britain, World Univ. Roundtable (trustee, founder), Internat. Cultural Corr. Inst., Circulo Nobiliario de los Caballeros Universales (grandmaster U.S.), Royal Order Bohemian Crown (baron), Lègion de L'Aigle de Mer (capt.), USA United Srs. Assn. Inc. Avocations: walking, chivalry and heraldry, cats, collecting rare musical books and recordings, collecting rare medieval coins and antique Coptic Ethiopian Crosses. Home and Office: Res Montsalvat 1D 2235 Cruger Ave Bronx NY 10467-9411

SPREITER, JOHN ROBERT, engineering educator, space physics scientist; b. Oak Park, Minn., Oct. 23, 1921; s. Walter F. and Agda E. (Hokanson) S.; m. Brenda Owens, Aug. 7, 1953; children: Terry A., Janet L., Christine P., Hilary M. B Aero. Engring., U. Minn., 1943; MS, Stanford U., 1947, PhD, 1954. Research scientist Ames Research Ctr. NASA, Moffett Field, Calif., 1943-69, chief theoretical studies br., 1962-69; prof. applied mechanics, mechanical engring. and aeros. and astronautics Stanford (Calif.) U., 1968-92, prof. emritus, 1992—; lectr. Stanford U., 1951-68; cons. Nielsen Engring. and Research Inc., Mountain View, Calif., 1968-85, RMA Aerospace, Mountain View, 1985—. Contbr. numerous articles to profl. jours. and books. Served with USN, 1944-46. Fellow AIAA, Royal Astron. Soc., Am. Geophys. Union; mem. AAAS, Am. Phys. Soc., The Planetary Soc., Saratoga Tennis Club (treas. 1955-65), Fremont Hills Country Club (Los Altos Hills, Calif.), Stanford Faculty Club, Sigma Xi, Tau Beta Pi, Tau Omega. Democrat. Achievements include pioneering studies in transonic aerodynamics; numerous contributions to studies of solar terrestrial relations, solar wind interaction with the earth, moon, other planets, and the local interstellar medium. Home: 1250 Sandalwood Ln Los Altos CA 94024-6739 Office: Stanford U Div Mechs & Computation Stanford CA 94305

SPRENGER, CURTIS DONALD, choir conductor, educator; b. Loveland, Colo., Feb. 3, 1934; s. Fred John and Frieda Louise (Bangert) S.; m. Marlene Marian Banek, June 5, 1963; 1 child, Branden B. A.B., U. No. Colo., 1959, M.A., 1962, Ed.D. in Music, 1969. Dir. choral activities Greeley High Sch., Colo., 1961-65, Dickinson State Coll., N.D., 1966-68, Santa Rosa Jr. Coll., Calif., 1972—; condr. Sonoma County Chorus, Santa Rosa, 1969-76, No. Calif. Chamber Chorale, Santa Rosa, 1971—, China Tour, 1985, Europe Tours, 1974, 76, 78, 82, 83, 85, 87, 88, 90, 92, 95, 97; lectr. Shanghai Conservatory of Music, 1985. Served with U.S. Army, 1953-56. Recipient Am. Choir Rep. award to French Celebration of Am. Bi-Centennial in Lyon, France, 1976; 5th prize Spittal Internat. Festival of Music, Austria, 1976; 1st prize Gdansk Festival of Music, Poland, 1978, Cmty. Coll. Performance award Western br. conv. Am. Choral Dirs. Assn., Sacramento, 1994; named Outstanding Music Prof. Santa Rosa Jr. Coll., 1980-81. Mem. State Am. Choral Dirs. Assn. (v.p. Calif. 1971-75, community choir rep. Western br. 1986—), Calif. Music Assn. Community Colls. (choral rep. 1980-89, choral judge 1973—), Music Educators Assn. Theta Xi. Republican.

SPRENKLE, CASE MIDDLETON, economics educator; b. Cleve., Aug. 18, 1934; s. Raymond E. and Helen K. (Middleton) S.; m. Elaine Elizabeth Jensen, June 22, 1957; children: David, Peter, Amy. B.S., U. Colo., 1956; M.A., Yale U., 1957, Ph.D., 1960. Instr. econs. Yale U., New Haven, 1959-60; mem. faculty U. Ill., Urbana, 1960—, prof. econs., 1970—, chmn. dept. econs., 1976-80, acting head dept. econs., 1995-96, asst. dean Coll. Commerce, 1962-65; dir. U. Ill.-U. Warsaw MBA program, 1991—; faculty Econs. Inst., Boulder, Colo., 1965, 72, 81; vis. scholar London Sch. Econs., 1967, 74, 81, 88; vis. lectr. City of London U., 1981; cons. Ill. Revenue Commn., 1962—; bd. dirs. Aggregate Equipment co. Contbr. articles to profl. jours. Bd. dirs. Champaign-Urbana Symphony, treas., 1972-74, pres., 1975-77; bd. dirs. Champaign County Arts and Humanities Coun., 1977-79; bd. dirs. Champaign-Urbana Mass Transit Dist., 1983—, vice chmn., 1985, 93-94. Am. Bankers Assn. grantee, 1970-71. Mem. Am. Econs. Assn., Am. Fin. Assn., Omicron Delta Epsilon. Presbyterian. Home: 3403 S Persimmon Cir Urbana IL 61802-7128 Office: U Ill Dept Econs 1201 S 6th St Champaign IL 61820

SPRICK, DENNIS MICHAEL, critic, copy editor; b. Passaic, N.J., Sept. 2, 1956; s. Frederick Vincent and Jeannette Mary (Claudepierre) S. BA, Lehigh U., 1978. Copy editor Daily Advance, Roxbury, N.J., 1978-80; film and Broadway critic, copy editor Times Herald-Record, Middletown, N.Y., 1980—. Mem. Phi Beta Kappa. Roman Catholic. Avocations: yoga, singing, vegetarian cooking, massage. Office: Times Herald-Record 40 Mulberry St PO Box 2046 Middletown NY 10940-6302

SPRIESTERSBACH, DUANE CARYL, university administrator, speech pathology educator; b. Pine Island, Minn., Sept. 5, 1916; s. Merle Lee and Esther Lucille (Stucky) S.; m. Bette Rae Bartell, Aug. 31, 1946; children: Michael Lee, Ann. B.Ed., Winona State Tchrs. Coll., 1939; M.A., U. Iowa, 1940, Ph.D., 1948. Asst. dir. pers. rels. Pacific Portland Cement Co., San Francisco, 1946-47; prof. speech pathology U. Iowa, Iowa City, 1948-89, prof. emeritus, 1989—, dean. Grad. Coll., v.p. ednl. devel. and rsch., 1965-89, v. pres. and dean emeritus, 1989—, acting pres., 1981-82; v.p. ops. Breakthrough, Inc., Oakdale, Iowa, 1993-94; cons., 1994—; com. mem. Nat. Inst. Neurol. Disease and Blindness; chmn. dental tng. com. Nat. Inst. Dental Research, 1967-72, chmn. spl. grants rev., 1978-82; chmn. bd. Midwest Univs. Cons. Internat. Activities, Columbus, 1978-87. Author: Psychosocial Aspects of Cleft Palate, 1973, (with others) Diagnostic Methods in Speech Pathology, 1978; co-editor: Cleft Palate and Communication, 1968, Diagnosis in Speech Language Pathology, 1994. Pres. Iowa City Community Theater, 1964, 77, 83. Served to lt. col. U.S. Army, 1941-46, ETO. Decorated Bronze Star; Nat. Inst. Dental Rsch. fellow, 1971. Fellow AAAS; mem. Assn. Grad. Schs. (pres. 1979-80), Am. Speech and Hearing Assn. (pres. 1965, honor award), Am. Cleft Palate Assn. (pres. 1961-62, disting. service award), Midwestern Assn. Grad. Schs. (chmn. 1979-80), Mortar Board, Sigma Xi. Episcopalian. Club: Cosmos (Washington). Home: 2 Longview Knl NE Iowa City IA 52240-9148 Office: Univ Iowa M212 Oakdale Hall Oakdale IA 52319

SPRIGGS, DAVID, healthcare administrator, educator; b. Chgo., May 12, 1950; s. H. Randall and Mary N. (Sievert) S.; m. Nancy J. Gerlach, Jan. 22, 1973. BS, U. Wis., 1973, MD, 1977. Cert. Am. Bd. Internal Medicine; lic., N.Y. Fellow Dana Farber Cancer Inst., Boston, 1982-85; from instr. to assst. prof. Harvard U., Boston, 1985-89; asst. prof. U. Wis., Madison, 1989-93; assoc. mem., chief devel. chemotherapy Meml. Sloan-Kettering Cancer Ctr., N.Y.C., 1993—. Sr. editor: (jour.) Clin. Cancer Rsch., 1996. Grantee Nat. Cancer Inst., 1994—. Mem. AAAS, Am. Assn. for Cancer Rsch., Am. Soc. Clin. Oncology. Avocations: golf, science fiction. Office: Meml Hosp 1275 York Ave New York NY 10021-6007

SPRIGGS, RICHARD MOORE, ceramic engineer, research center administrator; b. Washington, Pa., May 8, 1931; s. Lucian Alexander and Kathryn (Aber) S.; m. Patricia Anne Blaney, Aug. 1, 1953; children—Carolyn Elizabeth Spriggs Muchna, Richard Moore, Alan David. BS in Ceramics, Pa. State U., 1952; MS in Ceramic Engring., U. Ill., 1956, PhD, 1958. Sr. research engr. Ferro Corp., Cleve., 1958-59; sr. staff scientist, group leader, ceramics rsch. AVCO Corp., Wilmington, Mass., 1959-64; assoc. prof. metall. engring. Lehigh U., Bethlehem, Pa., 1964-67, prof. metallurgy and materials sci. and engring., 1967-80, adminstrv. asst. to pres., 1970-71, asst. v.p. for adminstrn., 1971-72, v.p. for adminstrn., 1972-78, dir. phys. ceramics lab., 1964-70, assoc. dir. Materials Research Ctr., 1964-70; vis. sr. staff assoc. Nat. Materials Adv. Bd. NRC, Washington, 1979-80, sr. staff officer, staff scientist, 1980-87, staff dir. bd. on assessment of NBS programs, 1984-87; J.F. McMahon prof. ceramic engring., dir. NYS Ctr. Advanced Ceramic Tech. N.Y. State Coll. Ceramics, Alfred (N.Y.) U., 1987—, dir. office of sponsored programs, 1988—; affiliate staff scientist Pacific Northwest Lab., 1994—. Contbr. articles to profl. publs. Co-patentee in field. Pres., bd. dirs. YMCA, Bethlehem, Pa., 1978-79. Served to lt. USNR, 1952-56. Fellow Armco Steel Corp., 1956-58, Am. Council on Edn., 1970-71; Centennial fellow Coll. Earth and Mineral Scis., Pa. State U., 1996. Fellow Am. Ceramic Soc. (disting. life, pres. 1984-85, Ross Coffin Purdy award 1965, Hobard M. Kraner award Lehigh Valley sect. 1980, trustee pension trust fund 1979-84, Orton lectr. 1988, McMahon lectr. 1988, Mueller lectr. 1996, coord. programs and meetings 1991-92), Ceramic Soc. Japan (Centennial medal 1991), Brit. Inst. Ceramics; mem. AAAS, N.Y. Acad. Scis., Internat. Inst. for Sci. of Sintering, Nat. Inst. Ceramic Engrs., Materials Rsch. Soc. Japan (hon.), Ceramic Ednl. Coun., Brit. Ceramic Soc., Internat. Acad. Ceramics (trustee 1988-96), Am. Soc. Engring. Edn., Materials Rsch. Soc., Fed. Materials Socs. (trustee 1978-84), Ceramic Assn. N.Y. (sec.-treas. 1988—), Serbian Acad. Scis. and Arts (fgn.), Rotary (dir. 1982-87, pres. 1985-86). Office: Alfred U Ctr Advanced Ceramic Tech NY State College of Ceramics Alfred NY 14802

SPRINCZ, KEITH STEVEN, financial services company professional; b. Whitewater, Wis., Mar. 8, 1956; s. Steven B. Sprincz and Mary Lou (Crotte) Zolli; m. Renee Michele Werner, Sept. 11, 1982; children: Nicholas, Cameron. BS in Mktg., Colo. State U., 1978; student, Am. Coll., 1985-86. CLU, ChFC. Agt. Prudential, Denver, 1978-83; ins. broker Nolen/Western, Denver, 1983-88, ptnr., 1988—; tchr. Life Underwriters Tng. Coun., Bethesda, Md., 1991-92. Chmn. bd. elders Bethlehem Luth. Ch., Lakewood, Colo., 1989; campmaster coord. Boy Scouts Am., Denver, 1989—, scoutmaster, 1983—; capt. March of Dimes, Denver, 1981, Big Bros., Denver, 1984; pres. Centennial Assn. Life Underwriters, 1986-87; sch. bd. mem., 1993—, pres., 1995—. Recipient Outstanding Family award Boy Scouts Am., 1986. Avocations: stamp collecting, fishing, softball, gardening. Office: Nolen Western 5690 Dtc Blvd Ste 140 Englewood CO 80111-3233

SPRING, MICHAEL, editor, writer; b. N.Y.C., Oct. 14, 1941; s. Sol and Muriel (Roth) S.; m. Marjorie Hornblower Bauer, Mar. 1965 (div. 1980); children: Declan, Evan; m. Janis Abrahms, 1993. B.A., Haverford Coll., Pa., 1964; M.A., Columbia U., N.Y.C., 1970. Reporter Bergen Record, Hackensack, N.J., 1969-71; editor Scholastic Inc., N.Y.C., 1971-87; editorial dir. Fodor's Travel Publs., 1987-94, v.p., 1989-94; pub. Macmillan Travel, N.Y.C., 1994—; broadcaster, writer WNCN-FM, N.Y.C., 1983-84. Author: Great Weekend Escape Book, 1982, 4th rev. edit. 1990, Student's Guide to Julius Caesar, 1984; editor: American Way of Working, 1980, 50 vol. Barron's Book Notes series, 1984, Scholastic Literature Anthologies, 4 vols., 1985, 87, Great European Itineraries, 1987, Touring Europe, 1990, 3d edit. 1994; contbg. editor Conde Nast's Traveler, 1987—; travel expert CNN Travel Show, 1991-94. Democrat. Jewish. Home: 20 Country Rd Westport CT 06880-2525 Office: Macmillan Travel 1633 Broadway New York NY 10019-6708

SPRING, PAULL E., bishop. Bishop Northwestern Pa. Evang. Luth. Ch. in Am., Oil City. Office: Evang Luth Ch in Am PO Box 338 Rte 257 Salina Rd Seneca PA 16346-0338*

SPRING, RAYMOND LEWIS, legal educator; b. Warsaw, N.Y., Aug. 5, 1932. AB, Washburn U., 1957, JD, 1959. Bar: Kans. 1960, U.S. Ct. Appeals (10th cir.) 1960. Assoc. Crane, Martin, Claussen & Ashworth, Topeka, 1959-65; examiner workmen's compensation program State of Kans., 1961-62; asst. prof. law Washburn U., Topeka, 1965-68, assoc. prof., 1968-71, acting dean Sch. Law, 1970-71, prof., dean Sch. Law, 1971-78, disting. prof., 1978—, interim v.p. for acad. affairs, 1988-91; faculty Karl Menninger Sch. Psychiatry and Mental Health Scis., 1987—; mem. cts. subcom. Kans. Gov.'s Com. on Criminal Adminstrn., 1970-79; dir. Century Savs. Assn., Shawnee Mission, Kans., 1978-84, chmn., 1980-82. Author: (with Ryan) Vernon's Kansas Criminal Code Annotated, 1971, Vernon's Kansas Code of Criminal Procedure, 1973; The End of Insanity, 1983; (with Lacoursiere and Weissenberger) Patients, Psychiatrists and Lawyers: Law and the Mental Health System, 1989, 2d edit., 1997. Bd. dirs. Topeka Welfare Planning Coun., 1964-66, Kans. Adv. and Protective Svcs., Inc., 1987-96, Shawnee Coun. Campfire Girls, 1965-68; chmn. Shawnee County Young Reps., 1962-64; leader edn. divsn. Topeka United Fund, 1972; deacon Ctrl. Congrl. Ch., 1972-74, 79-80, 85-87, trustee, 1980-81, moderator, 1988; mem. Kans. Bd. Admissions of Attys., 1979-86, Kans. Gov.'s adv. com. mental Health and Retardation Svcs., 1983-90; mem. human studies commn. Colmery-O'Neil VA Med. Ctr., 1982-89; mem. pattern instrns. (criminal) adv. com. Kans. Jud. Coun., 1996—. Recipient Disting. Svc. award Washburn Law Sch. Assn., 1987, William O. Douglas Outstanding Prof. award, 1980. Mem. ABA, Kans. Bar Assn. Topeka Bar Assn., Kans. Hist. Soc. (bd. dirs. 1980-93), Nat. Eagle Scout Assn., Barristers, Phi Kappa Phi, Delta Theta Phi, Phi Sigma Kappa. Home: 1616 SW Jewell Ave Topeka KS 66604-2737 Office: 1700 SW College Ave Topeka KS 66621-0001

SPRINGER, CHARLES EDWARD, state supreme court justice; b. Reno, Feb. 20, 1928; s. Edwin and Rose Mary Cecelia (Kelly) S.; m. Jacqueline Sirkegian, Mar. 17, 1951; 1 dau., Kelli Ann. BA, U. Nev., Reno, 1950; LLB, Georgetown U., 1953; LLM, U. Va., 1984; student Grad. Program for Am. Judges, Oriel Coll., Oxford (Eng.), 1984. Bar: Nev. 1953, U.S. Dist. Ct. Nev. 1953, D.C. 1954, U.S. Supreme Ct. 1962. Pvt. practice law Reno, 1953-80; atty. gen. State of Nev., 1962, legis. legal adv. to gov., 1958-62; legis. bill drafter Nev. Legislature, 1955-57; mem. faculty Nat. Coll. Juvenile Justice, Reno, 1978—; juvenile master 2d Jud. Dist. Nev., 1973-80; justice Nev. Suprem Ct., Carson City, 1981—; vice-chief justice, 1987, chief justice, 1988; mem. Jud. Selection Commn., 1981, Nev. Supreme Ct. Gender Bias Task Force, 1981—; trustee Nat. Coun. Juvenile and Family Ct. Judges, 1983—; mem. faculty McGeorge Sch. Law, U. Nev., Reno, 1982—; mem. Nev. Commn. for Women, 1991-95. With AUS, 1945-47. Recipient Outstanding Contbn. to Juvenile Justice award Nat. Coun. Juvenile and Family Ct. Judges, 1989, Midby-Byron Disting. Leadership award U. Nev., 1988. Mem. ABA, Am. Judicature Soc., Am. Trial Lawyers Assn., Phi Kappa Phi. Office: Nev Supreme Ct Capitol Complex 201 S Carson St Carson City NV 89701-4702

SPRINGER, DAVID EDWARD, lawyer; b. Chgo., Jan. 20, 1952; s. Edward W. and Mildred (Bergmark) S. AB summa cum laude, Yale U., 1974, JD, 1977. Bar: Ill. 1977, U.S. Ct. Appeals (5th cir.) 1978, U.S. Dist. Ct. (no. dist.) Ill. 1978, U.S. Ct. Appeals (7th cir.) 1981, U.S. Supreme Ct. 1981, U.S. Ct. Appeals (4th cir.) 1982, U.S. Ct. Appeals (fed. cir.) 1983, Wis. 1990, U.S. Dist. Ct. (D.C. cir.) 1991, U.S. Ct. Appeals (8th cir.) 1992. Atty., ptnr. Kirkland & Ellis, Chgo., 1977-86, Skadden, Arps, Slate, Meagher & Flom, Chgo., 1986—. Mem. Chgo. Club, City Club Chgo., Phi Beta Kappa. Republican. Protestant. Office: Skadden Arps Slate 333 W Wacker Dr Ste 2100 Chicago IL 60606-1226

SPRINGER, DOUGLAS HYDE, retired food company executive, lawyer; b. Englewood, N.J., Jan. 31, 1927; s. Arthur Hyde and Melicent Katherine (Messenger) S.; m. Virginia Helen Chouinard, Nov. 23, 1949; children: Susan Compton, Debora Lee. Student, Wesleyan U., 1944-45; AB, Yale U., 1947; LLB, Columbia U., 1950. Bar: N.Y. 1950. Atty. Port of N.Y. Authority, 1950-52; legal counsel Worthington Corp., Harrison, N.J., 1953-61, asst. sec., 1956-61; asst. counsel Campbell Soup Co., Camden, N.J., 1961-65, asst. sec., 1965, spl. assignments, 1966, dir. spl. studies, corp. planning, 1966-69, dir. corp. planning frozen foods, 1969-70, asst. treas., 1970-71, treas., 1971-73, v.p. fin. planning, 1973-75, v.p., controller, 1975-78, v.p., treas., 1978-88, v.p. investment mgmt., 1988-90; trustee Meml. Health Allience; mem. adv. bd. Pa. Liberty Mut. Ins. Co., 1971-88; mem. Eastern regional adv. bd. Arkwright-Boston Mfrs. Mut. Ins. Co., 1985-90; exec. sec. Gov.'s Interstate Adv. Com., 1966; asst. to mem. Pres.'s Commn. on Postal Orgn., 1967-68; spl. asst. to chmn South Jersey Port Corp., 1969-71; mem. N.J. Econ. Devel. Council, 1972-76; mem. adv. coun. Tax Found., 1980-89. Trustee Nat. Food Processors Assn. Retirement Plan and Trust Indenture Fund, 1976-89, Perkins Ctr. for Arts, 1979-88, Ind. Coll. Fund, N.J., 1982-88; mem. exec. bd., v.p. fin. Camden County coun. Boy Scouts Am., 1978-90; mem. Y's Men's Club, Moorestown, N.J., 1990—, v.p., 1992-94, pres., 1994-95; mem. found. bd. Family "Y" of Burlington County, 1995—. With USNR, 1944-46. Mem. Nat. Assn. Corp. Treas. (bd. dirs. 1982-88), Phila. Treas. Club, Internat. Bus. Forum (bd. dirs. 1980-88), Phi Nu Theta, Phi Delta Phi, N.J. Soc. Pa. (pres. 1992-93, treas. 1994—). Clubs: Yale (Phila., N.Y.C.); Nassau (Princeton, N.J.), Laurel Creek (Mt. Laurel, N.J.). Home: 735 Mill St Moorestown NJ 08057-1803

SPRINGER, FLOYD LADEAN, architect; b. Goodrich, N.D., Feb. 1, 1922; s. George Roy Springer and Louise Baumbach; m. Dorothy Mae Shepard (dec. Sept. 1995); children: Debra Louise, Tami June. Student, U. Denver, 1948-51; BS in Archtl. Engring., U. Colo., 1952; postgrad., U. Wash., 1953-54, U. Utah, Portland, Oreg., 1980. With Seattle Delta Investment Group, 1984—. Cpl. inf. U.S. Army, 1941-44, PTO. Decorated Silver Star. Presbyterian. Avocations: photography, landscaping, leaded art glass, oil painting, writing. Home and Office: 18548 60th Ave NE Seattle WA 98155-4453

SPRINGER, FRED EVERETT, federal agency administrator; b. Washington, June 30, 1945; s. Sidney and Janet L. (Bushlow) Kurland; m. Lola Weinberg Springer, Aug. 3, 1946; children: Eileen Gerri Frazier, Michelle Sherrie, Paul Louis. BSCE, U. Md., 1967; postgrad., George Washington U. Civil engr. Naval Facilities Engring. Command, Bur. of Stds., 1967-70, FPC, Washington, 1970-76; chief project mgmt. br. Divsn. of Lic. Projects, Office of Elec. PowerRegulation FPC/FERC, Washington, 1976-83; dep. dir. project mgmt. divsn. hydropower lic. Office of Elec. Power Regulation FERC, Washington, 1983-84; dir. divsn. project mgmt. FERC, Washington, 1984-87, dir. Office Hydropower Licensing, 1987-96; tchr. specialty courses to numerous fed. and state agys.; mem. steering com. Hydrovision 94, 96; mem. exec., steering coms. Waterpower 97; spkr. numerous nat. specialty confs. Pres., v.p. Highland of Olney (Md.) Civic Assn.; v.p., treas. B'nai Shalom of Olney; coach Olney Boys and Girls Club. Mem. ASCE, Tau Beta Pi, Chi Epsilon. Democrat. Jewish. Office: OHL-FERC 888 First St NE Rm 62-09 Washington DC 20426

SPRINGER, GEORGE STEPHEN, mechanical engineering educator; b. Budapest, Hungary, Dec. 12, 1933; came to U.S., 1959; s. Joseph and Susan (Grausz) S.; m. Susan Martha Flory, Sept. 15, 1963; children: Elizabeth Anne, Mary Katherine. B in Engring., U. Sydney, Australia, 1959; M in Engring., Yale U., 1960, MSc in Engring., 1961, PhD, 1962. Registered profl. engr., Mass. Asst. prof. mech. engring. MIT, Cambridge, Mass., 1962-67; prof. mech. engring. U. Mich., Ann Arbor, 1967-83; Paul Pigott prof., chmn. dept. aeronautics and astronautics Stanford (Calif.) U., 1983—. Author: Erosion by Liquid Impact, 1975; co-author, co-editor 12 books; contbr. over 150 articles to scholarly and profl. jours. Recipient Pub. Svc. Group Achievement award, NASA, 1988. Fellow AIAA (Engr. of Yr. 1995), ASME (Worcester Reed Warner medal 1994), Soc. Advancement Materials and Process Engring. (Delmonte award 1991); mem. Am. Phys. Soc., Soc. Automotive Engrs. (Ralph Teetor award 1978), Nat. Acad. Engring., Hungarian Nat. Acad. Sci. (fgn. mem.). Achievements include patent in field. Office: Stanford U Dept Aeronautics and Astronautics Stanford CA 94305

SPRINGER, JAMES VAN RODEN, lawyer; b. N.Y.C., July 9, 1934; s. Charles Meredith and Jeanne (Nehrbas) S.; m. Carol Murphy, Mar. 31, 1962; children: Stephen, Catherine. AB, Harvard U., 1955, LLB, 1961. Bar: N.Y. 1962, D.C. 1962, U.S. Ct. Appeals (D.C. cir.) 1963, U.S. Ct. Appeals (10th cir.) 1972, U.S. Ct. Appeals (2d cir.) 1973, U.S. Ct. Appeals (5th cir.) 1976, U.S. Ct. Appeals (6th and 7th cirs.) 1977, U.S. Ct. Appeals (11th cir.) 1981, U.S. Ct. Appeals (1st cir.) 1984, U.S. Ct. Appeals (4th cir.) 1986, U.S. Ct. Appeals (9th cir.) 1990, U.S. Ct. Appeals (fed. cir.) 1991, U.S. Supreme Ct. 1968. Law clk. to chief judge U.S. Ct. Appeals for 2d Cir., N.Y.C., 1961-62; assoc. Covington and Burling, Washington, 1962-67; asst. legal advisor U.S. Dept. State, Washington, 1967-68; dep. solicitor gen. U.S. Dept. Justice, Washington, 1968-71; ptnr. Dickstein Shapiro Morin & Oshinsky, LLP, Washington, 1972—. Pres. Harvard Law Rev., 1960-61; contbr. articles to profl. jours. With U.S. Army, 1955-58, Korea. Mem. ABA, D.C. Bar. Democrat. Home: 3017 44th Pl NW Washington DC 20016 Office: Dickstein Shapiro & Morin & Oshinsky LLP 2101 L St NW Washington DC 20037-1526

SPRINGER, JOHN K., securities representative; b. Brownsville, Tenn., Nov. 18, 1942; s. Hosea H. Springer and Mary C. (Nunnally) Boyer; m. Julia Wright, June 28, 1975; children: Rachel Lee, Mary N., Esther K. BS, U. Tenn., 1969. CLU; registered prin. Life ins. agt. Aetna Life, Knoxville, Tenn., 1974-77; mgr., gen. agt. Ky. Cen. Life, Knoxville, 1977-92; regional dir. Western Res. Life, Knoxville, 1990—; br. mgr. InterSecurities, Inc., Knoxville, 1991—, registered prin., 1991—; investment advisor rep. Inter Securities, Inc. Radio host: (talk show/WRJZ) Dealing with Money, 1984-85, Family Lifestyles, 1993—; host Family Lifestyles-Family Finances, 1993—. Bd. dirs. Christian Acad. of Knoxville, 1986-93, East Tenn. Christian Conciliation Svc., Knoxville, 1985, Knox Area Rescue Ministries, 1993-96, CPC of Knoxville, 1996-99; Sunday Sch. tchr. Calvary Bapt. Ch., Knoxville, 1978-92; local dir. Billy Graham's Worldwide Pictures, Knoxville, 1982-87. 1st lt. U.S. Army, 1969-70. Mem. Nat. Assn. Life Underwriters (bd. dirs. 1988, Nat. Quality awards 1980-92, numerous Nat. Sales Achievement awards), Am. Soc. CLU and ChFc. Republican. Avocations: golf, swimming, hiking. Home: 1610 Winding Ridge Trl Knoxville TN 37922-5748

SPRINGER, JOHN SHIPMAN, public relations executive; b. Rochester, N.Y., Apr. 25, 1916; s. Wilfred A. and Alice Jane (Grosjean) S.; m. June Alicia Reimer, June 3, 1953; children: Gary John, Alicia Ann, Cynthia Lynn. Student, U. Toronto, Ont., Can., 1935-37; Ph.B., Marquette U., 1939. Feature writer Rochester Democrat and Chronicle, 1940-41; sgt. USAF, 1942-45; head mag. publicity RKO Radio Pictures, N.Y.C., 1946-57, 20th Century-Fox Films, N.Y.C., 1957-59; v.p. Arthur Jacobs, Pub. Relations, 1959-60; ptnr. Jacobs & Springer (pub. relations), 1960-62; pres. John Springer Assos., Inc., N.Y.C., Los Angeles, London, Paris and Rome, 1964—. Author: All Talking! All Singing! All Dancing!, 1966, The Fondas, 1970, They Had Faces Then, 1975, Forgotten Films to Remember, 1980, They Sang, They Danced, They Romanced, 1991; contbr. to: Close Ups, Conversations with Joan Crawford; author mag. articles and newspaper features.; creator/producer "Film Segments" Night of 100 Stars; producer/host stage-screen shows starring Bette Davis, Myrna Loy, Sylvia Sidney, Joan Crawford, Rosalind Russell, Debbie Reynolds, Joanne Woodward, Lana Turner, Henry Fonda, others in, N.Y.C., U.S. tour, Australia, Gt. Britain; writer/producer Ann. Am. Mus. Moving Image ann. tributes to Sidney Lumet, Elia Kazan, James Stewart, Sidney Poitier, Mike Nichols, Robert DeNiro, Al Pacino; prodr., dir. three films/live events at 92d St. Y, New York, with in person guest stars including Ginger Rogers, Liv Ullmann, Tony Randall, Sylvia Sidney, Van Johnson, Geraldine Fitzgerald, Farley Granger, Betty Comden, Adolph Green, etc., 1991; prodr. Players Club Pipe Nights, Tribute to John Steinbeck; prodr., moderator: Forgotten Films to Remember series. Bd. dirs. Actors Studio, Nat. Theatre of Deaf. Recipient Byline award Coll. Journalism, 1970, By-line award Marquette U., 1970. Mem. Players Club (honored with Pipe Night 1995). Democrat. Roman Catholic. Home and Office: 130 E 67th St New York NY 10021-6136

SPRINGER, MARLENE, university administrator, educator; b. Murfreesboro, Tenn., Nov. 16, 1937; d. Foster V. and Josephine Jones; children: Ann Springer, Rebecca Springer. BA in English & Bus. Adminstrn., Centre Coll., 1959; MA in Am. Lit., Ind. U., 1963, PhD in English Lit., 1969. Chair English dept. U. Mo., Kansas City, 1980-81, acting assoc. dean grad. sch., 1982; Am. Coun. of Edn. Adminstrn. fellow U. Kans., Laurence, 1982-83; dean of grad. sch. U. Mo., Kansas City, 1983-84, assoc. vice chancellor for acad. affairs & grad. studies, 1985-89; vice chancellor for acad. affairs East Carolina U., Greenville, N.C., 1989-94; pres. CUNY Coll. S.I., 1994—. Author: What Manner of Woman: Essays, 1977, Thomas Hardy's Use of Allusion, 1983, Plains Woman: The Diary of Martha Farnsworth, 1986 (Choice award 1986), Ethan Frome: A Nightmare of Need, 1993. Huntington Libr. fellow, 1988. Mem. Am. Coun. on Edn. (profl. devel. com. 1991—, invited participant Nat. Forum 1984), Am. Assn. State Colls. & Univs. (exec. com. 1992-94), Acad. Leadership Acad. (exec. com. 1992-94), Assn. Tchr. Educators (chair 1992), Coun. Grad. Schs. (chair 1986-88). Office: Coll Staten Island 2800 Victory Blvd Staten Island NY 10314-6609

SPRINGER, MICHAEL LOUIS, federal agency administrator; b. Sarasota, Fla., Jan. 28, 1938; s. Stewart and Vergie (Fayard) S.; m. Afife Camila Chamas, Aug. 31, 1963; children: Elizabeth Karime, Michele Renee, John David. BA, George Washington U., 1964; MPA, The Am. U., 1978. With fin. mgmt. office Nat. Libr. Medicine, Bethesda, Md., 1969-71; dep. dir. mgmt. and orgn. div. U.S. EPA, Washington, 1971-73, dir. mgmt. info. and data systems div., 1973-75; sr. mgmt. assoc. mgmt. improvement and evaluation U.S. Office Mgmt. and Budget, Washington, 1977-82; dep. dir. Office Adminstrn. U.S. NRC, Washington, 1982-86; staff dir. Office Consolidation, Washington, 1987-88; dir. Office Consolidation U.S. Nuclear Regulatory Commn., Washington, 1988-94, dir. divsn. facilities and property mgmt., 1994-96; dep. dir. Office of Adminstrn. U.S. Nuc. Regulatory Commn., Washington, 1997—; bd. dirs. Transp. Action Partnership North Bethesda and Rockville, Md., 1988—. Mem. Citizens Adv. Com. for North Bethesda Master Plan, Montgomery County, 1990-91. Roman Catholic. Office: Nuclear Regulatory Commn Mail Stop T-7D59 Washington DC 20555

SPRINGER, PAUL DAVID, lawyer, motion picture company executive; b. N.Y.C., Apr. 27, 1942; s. William W. and Alma (Markowitz) S.; m. Mariann Frankfurt, Aug. 16, 1964; children: Robert, William. BA, U. Bridgeport, 1963; JD, Bklyn. Law Sch., 1967. Bar: N.Y. 1968, U.S. Dist. Ct. (so. and ea. dists.) N.Y. 1968, U.S. Ct. Appeals (2d cir.) 1970, U.S. Supreme Ct. 1973, Calif. 1989. Assoc. Johnson & Tannenbaum, N.Y.C., 1968-70; assoc. counsel Columbia Pictures, N.Y.C., 1970; assoc. counsel Paramount Pictures, N.Y.C., 1970-79, v.p., theatrical distbn. counsel, 1979-85, sr. v.p., chief resident counsel East Coast, 1985-87; sr. v.p., asst. gen. counsel Paramount Pictures, L.A., 1987—; Bar: N.Y. 1968, U.S. Dist. Ct. (so. and ea. dists.) N.Y. 1968, U.S. Ct. Appeals (2d cir.) 1970, U.S. Supreme Ct. 1973, Calif. 1989. Trustee West Cunningham Park Civic Assn., Fresh Meadows, N.Y., 1978—. Mem. ABA, Assn. of Bar of City of N.Y., L.A. Copyright Soc., Acad. Motion Picture Arts and Scis., Motion Picture Pioneers.

SPRINGER, ROBERT DALE, retired air force officer, consultant, lecturer; b. Millheim, Pa., Jan. 17, 1933; s. Simon Peter and Ruth Olive (McCool) S.; m. Bonnie Joan Brubaker, Aug. 30, 1953; children: Robert Dale Jr., Debra K. Springer Miller, Curtis A., Michele L. Demmy, Tania. BA in Social Sci., George Washington U., 1964, MS in Internat. Affairs, 1969. Cert. command pilot. Commd. 2d lt. U.S. Air Force; advanced through grades to lt. gen.; comdr. 435th Tactical Airlift Wing, Rhein-Main Air Base, Federal Republic Germany, 1978-80, 322d Airlift Div, Ramstein Air Base, Federal Republic Germany, 1980-81, Air Force Manpower and Personnel Ctr., Randolph AFB, Tex., 1982-84, 21 A.F., McGuire AFB, N.J., 1984-85; insp. gen. USAF, Washington, 1985-87; with DCS-personnel Mil. Airlift Command, Scott AFB, Ill., 1981-82, vice comdr.-in-chief, 1987-88; ret., 1988; media cons., lectr., 1989—; dir. Air Force Commissary Svc., San Antonio, 1982-84, Army-Air Force Exch. Svc., Dallas, 1982-84; chmn. bd. dirs. Air Force Welfare Bd., San Antonio, 1982-84. Exec. dir Air Force Meml. Found., 1992—; trustee Aerospace Edn. Found., 1992-94, The Falcon Found., 1996—; adv. bd. First Bank. Mem. Air Force Assn. (Presdl. Citation 1984), Airlift-Tanker Assn. (life mem., sr. v.p. 1989-94), Arnold Air Soc. (exec. dir. 1990-93, trustee 1993—), Ret. Officers Assn. (life), Daedalians (life). Lutheran. Lodge: Masons. Avocations: tennis; golf; reading.

SPRINGER, WAYNE RICHARD, medical center safety director; b. Milw., Nov. 16, 1946; s. Richard Andrew and Irma Edna (Richter) S.; m. Jane Bradley, Aug. 19, 1972; children: Matthew Bradley, Katherine Jane. BA, Northwestern U., 1968; PhD, U. Calif., Berkeley, 1977. Vol. Peace Corps, Somalia, Antigua, 1969-72; postdoctoral fellow U. Calif., San Diego, 1977-79, rsch. biochemist, 1979-92; assoc. project biochemist, 1992—; rsch. biochemist VA Med. Ctr., San Diego, 1979—, chem. hygiene officer, 1992-94, dir. environ., health and safety, 1994—. Coach Little League, Bobby Sox. Mem. Am. Soc. Biochem. Molecular Biology, Am. Biol. Safety Assoc., Am Soc. Healthcare Engr. Avocations: travel, gardening. Office: VA San Diego Healthcare Sys 138S 3350 La Jolla Village Dr San Diego CA 92161-0002

SPRINGFIELD, JAMES FRANCIS, retired lawyer, banker; b. Memphis, Nov. 5, 1929; s. C.L. and Mildred (White) S.; m. Shirley Burdick, June 1, 1951 (div.); children: Sidney, Susan, James Francis; m. Nancy Hardwick Ragan, Feb. 8, 1987 (dec. Jan. 1988); m. Donna Thomas Moore, Feb. 22, 1989. BA with distinction in econs., Southwestern at Memphis (now Rhodes Coll.), 1951; LLB, U. Memphis, 1960. Bar: Tenn. 1960. With Union Planters Nat. Bank, Memphis, 1951-94; exec. v.p., sr. trust officer, head trust dept. Union Planters Nat. Bank, 1968-85, gen. counsel, sec. bd., 1985-94; sec. bd., exec. v.p., gen. counsel Union Planters Corp., 1985-94; ret., 1994. Mem. president's coun. Rhodes Coll., Memphis, chmn., 1991-92, internat. chmn. ann. fund, 1995-96; chmn. bd. trustees So. Coll. Optometry, 1978-80; trustee Plough Found., Memphis Conf. United Meth. Ch. Found., 1978-85, U. Tenn. Med. Units Found., 1975-82, MidSouth Pub. Comm. Found., 1985-87; chmn. fin. com. Hutchinson Sch.; sec. bd. trustees Vision Edn. Found., 1977-78; bd. regents Tenn. Trust Sch., chmn., 1977; mem. president's adv. coun. Lambuth Coll., 1982-85; mem. exec. bd. Chickasaw coun. Boy Scouts Am., 1983-87; bd. visitors Memphis State U. Cecil C. Humphreys Sch. Law, treas. Balmoral Civic Club, 1967-68. Lt. (j.g.) USNR, 1951-54. Mem. Tenn. Bar Assn. (chmn. interprofl. rels. com. 1976), Memphis and Shelby County Bar assn. (chmn. moral fitness com. 1972), Tenn. Bankers Assn. (chmn. legis.com. trust div. 1976-77, treas. 1972-73, pres. 1976-77, bd. dirs. 1976-77), Bank Adminstrn. Inst. (chmn. trust comm. 1981-82), Estate Planning Coun. Memphis (pres. 1973-74), Sigma Nu (div. comdr. 1967-68, treas., bd. dirs. House Corp. 1966-81), Omicron Delta Kappa (Rhodes Coll. chpt.). Republican. Home: 1692 Village Ridge Rd Collierville TN 38017-9785

SPRINGGATE, CLARK FRANKLIN, physician, researcher; b. Champaign, Ill., Nov. 14, 1946; s. William F. and Marjorie E. (Fitch) S.; children from a previous marriage: Elizabeth, Benjamin; m. Diane Louise Rotnem, Oct. 19, 1991. AB in Biology, Boston U., 1967; PhD in Biochemistry, Boston Coll., 1972; MD, U. Miami, 1983. Diplomate Nat. Bd. Med. Examiners, Am. Bd. Pathology. Med. dir. Richardson Vicks Pharm., Shelton, Conn., 1989-91; v.p., med. dir. TSI Biomed. Rsch. Group, Medford, Mass., 1992-94; v.p. Scicor, Indpls., 1988-89; pres. Springgate Biotech, Guilford, Conn., 1991—, Biotech Regular Cons., Guilford, 1994—. Contbr. articles to jours. Heart Transplant, Am. Soc. Hist. Immunogey. Bd. dirs. AIDS Protect New Haven, 1994-95; funding bd. Leap Youth Program, New Haven, 1991-92. Leukemia Soc. Am. fellow, 1972-74. Mem. AAAS, ACP Execs., Conn. State Med. Soc. Achievements include research in immune monitoring of heart transplant patients to prevent rejection and infection, diagnostic flow cytometry-oncology. Home: 1320 Little Meadow Rd Guilford CT 06437-1659

SPRINGSTEEN, BRUCE, singer, songwriter, guitarist; b. Freehold, N.J., Sept. 23, 1949; s. Douglas and Adele S.; m. Julianne Phillips, May 13, 1985 (div. 1988); m. Patti Scialfa; children: Evan James, Jessica Rae. Attended community coll. Performed in N.Y. and N.J. nightclubs; signed with Columbia Records in 1972; first album Greetings from Asbury Park, New Jersey, 1973; nationwide concert tours with The E-Street Band, 1974-92; albums include The Wild, The Innocent and the E-Street Shuffle, 1974, Born to Run, 1975 (Gold Record award), Darkness on the Edge of Town, 1978, The River, 1980, Nebraska, 1982, Born in the U.S.A., 1984 (Best Pop/Rock Album of Yr., Downbeat Readers Poll 1984), Bruce Springsteen and the E-Street Band Live/1975-1985, 1986, Tunnel of Love, 1987, Chimes of Freedom, 1988, Human Touch, 1992, Lucky Town, 1992, Bruce Springsteen Greatest Hits, 1995. The Ghost of Tom Joad, 1995; songs composed include Thunder Road, Glory Days, Rosalita, Pink Cadillac, Jersey Girl, Hungry Heart, Streets of Philadelphia (Golden Globe award for Best Original Song in a Film, 1994, Acad. award for best original song in a film 1994, MTV Best Video from a Film award 1994), Dead Man Walking (Acad. award nominee for best original song in a film 1996); appears on Patti Scialfa's album, Rumble Doll, 1993. Recipient Grammy award for best male rock vocalist, 1984, 87, 94. Office: care Premier Talent Agy 3 E 54th St New York NY 10022-3108*

SPRINGSTEEN, DAVID FOLGER, retired financial consultant; b. N.Y.C., Mar. 29, 1932; s. Nelson J. and Gwendolyn (Folger) S.; BS, MIT, 1954; MBA, Harvard U., 1958; m. Nancy Neller, Oct. 22, 1955; children: Susan S. Jamieson, Page S. Vanatta. Aero. rsch. scientist Lewis Flight Propulsion Lab. NASA, Cleve., 1955-57; with Chase Manhattan Bank, N.Y.C., 1958-71, asst. treas., 1961-64, 2d v.p., 1964-68, v.p. Energy div., 1969-71; v.p. corp. fin. Stone & Webster Securities Corp., 1971-74; v.p. corp. fin. E.F. Huttons & Co., Inc., N.Y.C., 1974-78; fin. cons., corp. fin. David F. Springsteen Co., Greenwich, Conn., 1978-97. Bd. dirs. Eastman Cmty. Assn., 1992—. Served to lt. USAF, 1955-57. Mem. Holland Soc. Home: PO Box 248 4 Lakeview Pl Grantham NH 03753 Office: PO Box 248 Grantham NH 03753-0248

SPRINKEL, BERYL WAYNE, economist, consultant; b. Richmond, Mo., Nov. 20, 1923; s. Clarence and Emma (Schooley) S.; m. Lory Kiefer, Aug. 29, 1993; children: Gary L., Kevin G. Student, N.W. Mo. State U., 1941-43, U. Oreg., 1943-44; BS, U. Mo., 1947; MBA, U. Chgo., 1948, PhD, 1952; LHD (hon.), DePaul U., 1975; LLD (hon.), St. Michael's Coll., 1981, U. Mo., 1985, U. Rochester, 1985, Govs. State U., 1988, U. Nebr., 1988; Doctor of Pub. Adminstrn., Marion Coll., 1988. Instr. econs. and fin. U. Mo., Columbia, 1948-49, U. Chgo., 1950-52; with Harris Trust & Savs. Bank, Chgo., 1952-81, v.p., economist, 1960-68, dir. rsch., 1963-69, sr. v.p., 1968-74, economist, 1968-81, exec. v.p., 1974-81; undersec. monetary affairs Dept. Treasury, Washington, 1981-85; chmn. Coun. Econ. Advisers, The White House, Washington, 1985-89, mem. Pres.'s Cabinet, 1987-89; pvt. cons. economist, 1989—; cons. Fed. Res. Bd., 1955-59, Bur. of Census, 1962-70, Joint Econ. Com. U.S. Congress, 1958, 62, 67, 71, Ho. of Reps. Banking and Currency Com., 1963, Senate Banking Com., 1975; econ. adv. bd. to sec. commerce, 1967-69; bd. economists Time mag., 1968-80; bd. dirs. US Life Corp., Duff and Phelps Utilities Income Fund, Inc. Author: Money and Stock Prices, 1964, Money and Markets-A Monetarist View, 1971; co-author: Winning with Money, 1977;. Pres. Homewood-Flossmoor (Ill.) Community High Sch., 1959-60. With AUS, 1943-45. Recipient Hamilton Bolton award Fin. Analysts Assn., 1968, Alexander Hamilton award U.S. Treasury, 1985. Fellow Nat. Assn. Bus. Economists; mem. Am. Econ. Assn., Nat. Assn. Bus. Economists, Beta Gamma Sigma. Home: 20140 Saint Andrews Dr Olympia Fields IL 60461-1169

SPRINKLE, ROBERT LEE, JR., podiatrist; b. Winston-Salem, N.C., July 13, 1932; s. Robert Lee and Elton Elizabeth Sprinkle; children: Robert III, Karen, Ralph, Richard, Roy, Randy, Drouin; m. Nancy House Dixon. Student Salem Coll., 1952; BS, Ohio Coll. Podiatry, 1956; DPM, Pa. Coll. Podiatry, 1970. Practice medicine specializing in podiatry, Winston-Salem, 1957—; chmn. N.C. Bd. Podiatry Examiners, 1968-74; clin. assoc. prof. Dr. William M. School Coll. Podiatric Medicine; researcher reconstructive surgery human foot and ankle. Chmn. Mayor's Com. on Hiring the Handicapped, 1963-64; commr. Old Hickory council Boy Scouts Am., 1970-71, v.p., 1973-74, Silver Beaver award, 1969, mem. adv. bd. Old North State coun.; pres. St. Leo's Parochial Sch. PTA, 1969-70; dir. Half Way House, 1965-66; chmn. Bishop McGuiness PTA, 1976; adv. bd. Old North Sate Coun. Paul Harris fellow Rotary Internat., 1971-72; grantee Schering, Inc., 1972-74; recipient St. George medal, 1971. Mem. Am. Podiatry Assn., N.C. Podiatry Assn. (past pres.), Piedmont Podiatry Assn., Am. Pub. Health Assn., Internat. Analgesia Soc., KC (4th degree), Forsyth Country Club, Colonial Country Club, Twin City Club, Rotary (dist. gov. 1976-77). Democrat. Roman Catholic. Home: 10 Mock St Thomasville NC 27360 Office: ABC Family Foot and Ankle Clinic PO Box 5442 17 W Main St Thomasville NC 27360

SPRINKLE, WILLIAM MELVIN, engineering administrator, audio-acoustical engineer; b. Washington, Sept. 2, 1945; s. Melvin Cline and Gladys Virginia (Miller) S.; div.; children: Timothy William, Allison Anne. BS in Chemistry, Randolph-Macon Coll., 1967; M in Engring. Adminstrn., Va. Poly. Inst. & State U., 1990. Registered profl. engr., Va. Sr. cons. Sprinkle & Assocs., Kensington, Md., 1973-76; audio systems engr. Robertshaw Controls Co., Richmond, Va., 1976-80; sr. engr. TDFB-Engrs. & Architects, Richmond, Va., 1980-85; property mgmt. officer Signet Bank, Richmond, Va., 1985-87; asst. dir. engring. Va. Dept. Corrections, Richmond, 1987—; mem. summer adj. faculty Eastman Sch. Music, Rochester, N.Y., 1974-83. Editor newsletter Richmond Area Bicycling Assn.; contbr. Time Saver Standards for Architectural Design Data, 1982. Scoutmaster Boy Scouts Am., 1970-72, unit commr., 1990-92. Named Eagle Scout Boy Scouts Am. Mem. Acoustical Soc. Am., Pi Delta Epsilon (v.p.). Methodist. Office: Dept of Corrections 6900 Atmore Dr Richmond VA 23225-5644

SPRINSON, DAVID BENJAMIN, biochemistry educator; b. Raigorod, Ukraine, Apr. 5, 1910; came to U.S., 1921; s. Moses and Rebecca (Skolnick) S.; m. Helen Evans Yeargain, Oct. 8, 1943; children: Joan, Mary, John. BS, CCNY, 1931; MS, NYU, 1936; PhD, Columbia U., 1946, DSc (honoris causa), 1991. Rsch. assoc. Columbia U., N.Y.C., 1946-51, asst. prof. biochemistry, 1951-54, assoc. prof., 1954-58, prof., 1958-78, prof. biochemistry and molecular biology emeritus, 1978—; prof. biochemistry and molecular biology emeritus St. Luke's/Roosevelt Hosp. Ctr., N.Y.C., 1979—; career investigator Am. Heart Assn., 1958-75. Contbr. articles to sci. jours. Grantee NIH, NSF, Am. Heart Assn., Am. Cancer Soc., 1950-91; recipient Disting. Svc. award Coll. Physicians and Surgeons, 1995. Mem. NAS, AAAS, Am. Soc. for Biochemistry and Molecular Biology. Office: St Luke's/Roosevelt Hosp Ctr 1000 10th Ave New York NY 10019-1147

SPRINTHALL, NORMAN ARTHUR, psychology educator; b. Attleboro, Mass., Aug. 19, 1931; s. William Archie and Edith Jarvis (Clark) S.; m. Lois May Thies; children: Douglas, Jane, Carolyn. AB magna cum laude, Brown U., 1954, MA, 1959; EdD, Harvard U., 1963. Dir. fin. aid Brown U., 1955-60; asst. prof., then assoc. prof. psychology, program chmn. counseling Harvard U., 1963-72; mem. faculty U. Minn., Mpls., 1972-82; prof. ednl. psychology U. Minn., 1973-82, program chmn. counseling, 1972-74; prof., head counselor edn. program N.C. State U., Raleigh, 1982-87, prof., counselor, educator, 1987-95, prof. emeritus; cons. Bur. Educationally Handicapped; co-dir. Ethical Reasoning Project in Pub. Adminstrn., U.S. and Poland, 1993-95. Author: Educational Psychology: Readings, 1969, Guidance for Human Growth, 1971, Educational Psychology: A Developmental Approach, 6th edit., 1994, Value Development as the Aim of Education, 2d edit., 1981, Adolescent Psychology: A Developmental View, 1984, 2d rev. edit., 1988, 3d edit., 1995; co-author: Stewart-Sprinthall Management Survey (SSMS) Ethics and Public Administration; mem. editorial bd. profl. jours. Bd. dirs. Josephson Inst. Advancement of Ethics, 1986-90, mem. bd. advisors Character Counts Coalition, 1994—. Fellow APA; mem. Phi Beta Kappa.

SPRITZER, RALPH SIMON, lawyer, educator; b. N.Y.C., Apr. 27, 1917; s. Harry and Stella (Theuman) S.; m. Lorraine Nelson, Dec. 23, 1950; children: Ronald, Pamela. B.S., Columbia U., 1937, LL.B., 1940. Bar: N.Y. bar 1941, U.S. Supreme Ct. bar 1950. Atty. Office Alien Property, Dept. Justice, 1946-51; anti-trust div. Dept. Justice, 1951-54, Office Solicitor Gen., 1954-61; gen. counsel FPC, 1961-62; 1st asst. to solicitor gen. U.S., 1962-68; prof. law U. Pa., Phila., 1968-86, Ariz. State U., Tempe, 1986—; gen. counsel AAUP, 1983-84; Adj. prof. law George Wasington U., 1967; cons. Adminstrv. Conf. U.S., Ford Found., Pa. Gov.'s Justice Commn. Served with AUS, 1941-46. Recipient Superior Service award Dept. Justice, 1960; Tom C. Clark award Fed. Bar. Assn., 1968. Mem. Am. Law Inst. Home: 1024 E Gemini Dr Tempe AZ 85283-3004 Office: Ariz State Univ Coll Law Tempe AZ 85287

SPRIZZO, JOHN EMILIO, federal judge; b. Bklyn., Dec. 23, 1934; s. Vincent James and Esther Nancy (Filosa) S.; children—Ann Esther, Johna Emily Sprizzo Bolka, Matthew John. BA summa cum laude, St. John's U., Jamaica, N.Y., 1956; LLB summa cum laude, St. John's U., 1959. Bar: N.Y. 1960. Atty. U.S. Dept. Justice, 1959-63; asst. U.S. atty. so. dist. N.Y. Dept. Justice, N.Y.C., 1963-68, chief appellate atty., 1965-66, asst. chief criminal div., 1966-68; assoc. prof. Fordham U. Law Sch., N.Y.C., 1968-72; ptnr. Curtis, Mallet-Prevost, N.Y.C., 1972-81; dist. judge U.S. Dist. Ct. (so. dist.) N.Y., N.Y.C., 1981—; cons. Nat. Com. for Reform of Criminal Laws, N.Y.C., 1971-72; mem. Knapp Commn., 1971-72; assoc. atty. Com. of Ct. on Judiciary, N.Y.C., 1971-72. Co-contbr. articles to profl. law revs. Mem. ABA, D.C. Bar Assn., Assn. of Bar of City of N.Y. Office: US Dist Ct US Courthouse Foley Sq New York NY 10007-1501

SPROAT, JOHN GERALD, historian; b. L.A., Apr. 1, 1921; s. John Gerald and Grace (Elwell) Drummond S.; m. Ruth Christensen, Mar. 18, 1967; 1 child by previous marriage, Barbara. B.A., San Jose State Coll., 1950; M.A., U. Calif.-Berkeley, 1952, Ph.D., 1959. Instr. Mich. State U., 1956-57; asst. prof. Williams Coll., 1957-63; prof. Lake Forest Coll., Ill., 1963-74; prof. history U. S.C., Columbia, 1974-92, chmn. dept., 1974-83; dist. prof. emeritus, 1992—; sr. fellow Inst. for So. Studies, 1992—; Fulbright prof. Hamburg U., Fed. Republic Germany, 1961-62; vis. fellow Cambridge U., Eng., 1970; vis. prof. U. Calif.-Berkeley, 1972; Fulbright prof. U. Munich, Fed. Republic Germany, 1982, Indonesia, 1993-94; Am. participant lectr. USIA, India, Pakistan, 1987; mem. S.C. Commn. Archives and History, 1974-83, chmn., 1979-83; mem. S.C. Bd. Rev. Hist. Places, 1974-86, chmn., 1978-83; del. Am. Council Learned Socs. Author: The Best Men: Liberal Reformers in the Gilded Age, 1988; (with others) The Shaping of America, 1972, Making Change: South Carolina Banking in the 20th Century, 1990; contbr. chpts. to books; exec. producer A Bond of Iron, S.C. ETV, 1979; gen. editor So. Classics Series. Past pres., trustee Columbia Mus. Art; pres. Historic Columbia Found., 1997—. Served with USAAF, 1941-45. NEH grantee, 1976, 77, 79, 85; Shell Found. grantee, 1967, 70, 73; Lilly Endowment grantee, 1966-67. Mem. Am. Hist. Assn., Orgn. Am. Historians, So. Hist. Assn. Episcopalian. Clubs: Capital City (Columbia). Home: 1686 Woodlake Dr Columbia SC 29206-4647 Office: U SC Inst For So Studies Columbia SC 29208

SPROGER, CHARLES EDMUND, lawyer; b. Chgo., Feb. 18, 1933; s. William and Minnette (Weiss) S. BA (David Himmelblau scholar), Northwestern U., 1954, JD, 1957. Bar: Ill. 1957. Practiced in Chgo., 1958—; assoc. Ehrlich & Cohn, 1958-63, Ehrlich, Bundesen, Friedman & Ross, 1963-72; partner Ehrlich, Bundesen, Broecker & Sproger, 1972-77; pvt. practice, 1977—; mem. adv. com. curriculum Ill. Inst. Continuing Legal Edn., Chgo., 1976—; v.p. Mediation Coun. of Ill., 1986-87; arbitration panelist for Cir. Ct. Cook County, 1990—. Editor: Family Lawyer, 1962-63; contbr. articles to legal publs. Mediator Pastoral Psychotherapy Inst., 1982-86. Fellow Am. Acad. Matrimonial Lawyers (bd. examiners 1972-86, chmn. Law Day U.S.A. 1975); mem. ABA, Ill. Bar Assn. (chmn. coun. family law 1970-71), Chgo. Bar Assn. (matrimonial law com. 1958—), Am. Arbitration Assn. (divorce mediation com. 1983—), Decalogue Soc., U. Mich. Club Chgo. (pres. 1988-89), Phi Alpha Delta. Office: 155 N Michigan Ave Chicago IL 60601

SPROLE, FRANK ARNOTT, retired pharmaceutical company executive, lawyer; b. Bklyn., Sept. 13, 1918; s. Frank Newland and Eleanor Arnott (Greenberg) S.; m. Sarah Louise Knapp, Sept. 23, 1944; children—Wendy Sprole Bangs, Frank J., Anne Sprole Mauk, Jonathan K., Sarah Sprole Obregon. B.A., Yale U., 1942; LL.B., Columbia U., 1949. Bar: N.Y. 1949. Assoc. firm Winthrop Stimson, Putnam & Roberts, N.Y.C., 1949-50; atty. Bristol-Myers Co., N.Y.C., 1950-52, asst. sec., 1952-55, sec., 1955-67, v.p., 1965-73, sr. v.p., 1973-77, vice chmn. bd., 1977-84; bd. dirs., officer Proprietary Assn., Washington, 1978-84; dir., officer Knapp Fund, N.Y.C., 1960-93. Pres. bd. trustees Hotchkiss Sch., Lakeville, Conn., 1980-85; trustee Internat. Inst. Rural Reconstrn., N.Y.C., and Manila, 1983-87. Served to lt. comdr. USNR, 1942-45, PTO. Mem. Assn. of Bar of City of N.Y., Yale Club of N.Y.C., Wee Burn Country Club, Bohemian Club, Mid Ocean Club, John's Island Club, Riomar Country Club. Republican. Episcopalian. Avocation: golf. Home: 394 Mansfield Ave Darien CT 06820-2112

SPROTT, DAVID ARTHUR, statistics and psychology educator; b. Toronto, Ont., Can., May 31, 1930; s. Arthur Frederick and Dorothy (Barry) S.; m. Muriel Doris Vogel; children: Anne, Jane. BA, U. Toronto, 1952, MA, 1953, PhD, 1955. Rsch. asst. Galton Lab., London, 1955-56; biogeneticist, clin. tchr. dept. psychiatry U. Toronto, 1956-58; assoc. prof. stats. U. Waterloo, Ont., 1958-61, prof., 1961-96; disting. prof. emeritus U. Waterloo, 1996—; prof. psychology U. Waterloo, Ont., 1964-96, dean math., 1966-72, chmn. dept. stats., 1966-75; prof. Centro de Investigacion en Matematicas, Guanajuato, Mex., 1993—; vis. prof. various univs. and colls. Contbr. numerous articles to profl. jours. Recipient Gold medal Statis. Soc. Can., 1988. Fellow Am. Statis. Assn., Inst. Math. Stats., Royal Soc. Can., Royal Photog. Soc.; mem. Internat. Statis. Inst., Statis. Soc. Can. (hon.). Avocations: photography, wine making. Office: U Waterloo Math Faculty, Waterloo, ON Canada N2L 3G1

SPROTT, JOHN T., ambassador; b. Phoenix, Apr. 6, 1933; m. Jeanne S.; 5 children. B.A., Northern Ariz. Univ.; Ph.D., Univ. of Colorado. Econ. instructor Univ. of Colorado, 1960-61; asst. econ. prof. Duquesne Univ., Penn., 1962-65; chmn., Econ. & Comml. Study Prog. Frn. Svc. Inst., 1966-67; sr. econ. adviser U.S. Econ. Mission to Chile, 1968-71; dep. coord., then coord. Econ. & Comml. Studies div. Fgn. Svc. Inst., 1971-75, dean, Sch. of Profl.Studies, 1975-81, dep. dir., 1981-93; U.S. amb. to Swaziland Mbabane, 1993—; lect. Johns Hopkins Univ., 1967-68. with U.S. Navy 1951-55. Mem. Sr. Exec. Svc. Assn., Aircraft Owners and Pilots Assn. Office: Am Embassy Mbabane Dept State Washington DC 20521-2350*

SPROTT, RICHARD LAWRENCE, government official, researcher; b. Tampa, Fla., Aug. 9, 1940; s. Joseph Albert and Marie Marguerite (Goaper) S.; m. Margaret Ann Weidel, June 19, 1965; children—Lynn Marie, Deborah Ann. Student, Franklin and Marshall Coll., 1958-60; B.A., U. N.C., 1962, M.A. in Psychology, 1964, Ph.D. in Psychology, 1965. Asst. prof. Oakland U., Rochester, Mich., 1967-69; assoc. staff scientist Jackson Lab., Bar Barbor, Maine, 1969-71, staff scientist, 1971-80; health scientist adminstr. Div. Research Resources, NIH, Bethesda, Md., 1980-81; br. chief Nat. Inst. on Aging, Bethesda, 1981-84, assoc. dir., 1984—. Editor: Hormonal Correlates of Behavior, 1975, Age, Learning Ability and Intelligence, 1980; mem. editorial bd. Exptl. Aging Research jour., 1978—; contbr. articles to profl. jours. Mem. Bar Harbor Town Council, 1975-79, chmn., 1978-79; mem. bd. appeals Town of Bar Harbor, 1972-75, mem. warrant com., 1972-75. NIH fellow, 1965-67; NIH grantee, 1969-79. Fellow Am. Psychol. Assn.; mem. Behavior Genetics Assn. (membership chmn. 1979). Home: 11514 Regency Dr Potomac MD 20854-3733 Office: Nat Inst on Aging 7201 Wisconsin Ave Rm 2c231 Bethesda MD 20814-4810

SPROUL, JOAN HEENEY, elementary school educator; b. Johnstown, Pa., July 17, 1932; d. James L. and Grace M. (Dunn) Heeney; m. Robert Sproul, July 31, 1957; 1 child, Mary Claire. BS, Clarion U., 1954; MA, George Wash. U., 1963; postgrad., U. Va., 1966-88. Cert. tchr., Va. Kindergarten tchr. Jefferson Sch., Warren, Pa., 1954-55; primary grades tchr. Alexandria (Va.) Pub. Schs., 1955-64; elem. tchr. Fairfax County Schs., Springfield, Va., 1965—; math. lead tchr. West Springfield (Va.) Sch., 1987—. Contbr. (with others) Virginia History, 1988. Advisor Springfield Young Organists Assn., 1971-83; mem. Fairfax County Dem. Com., 1988-94, West Springfield Civic Assn., 1965—. Grantee Impact II, 1985-86. Mem. NEA, Nat. Fedn. Bus. and Profl. Women (pres., dir. dist. VIII 1984—, Woman of Yr. 1985, 88), Delta Kappa Gamma (2d v.p. Va. chpt. 1963—), Phi Delta Kappa. Episcopalian. Avocations: reading, music, gardening, fashion design. Home: 8005 Greeley Blvd West Springfield VA 22152-3036 Office: West Springfield Elem Sch 6802 Deland Dr Springfield VA 22152-3009

SPROUL, JOHN ALLAN, retired public utility executive; b. Oakland, Calif., Mar. 28, 1924; s. Robert Gordon and Ida Amelia (Wittschen) S.; m. Marjorie Ann Hauck, June 20, 1945; children: John Allan, Malcolm J., Richard O., Catherine E. A.B., U. Calif., Berkeley, 1947, LL.B., 1949. Bar: Calif. 1950. Atty. Pacific Gas & Electric Co., San Francisco, 1949-52, 56-62, sr. atty., 1962-70, asst. gen. counsel, 1970-71, v.p. gas supply, 1971-76, sr. v.p., 1976-77, exec. v.p., 1977-89; gen. counsel Pacific Gas Transmission Co., 1970-73, v.p., 1973-79, chmn. bd., 1979-89, also bd. dirs.; atty. Johnson & Stanton, San Francisco, 1952-56; bd. dirs. Oreg. Steel Mills, Inc. Bd. dirs. Hastings Coll. of Law. Served to 1st lt. USAAF, 1943-46. Mem. Calif. Bar Assn. (inactive), Pacific Coast Gas Assn., World Trade Club, Pacific-Union Club, Orinda Country Club. Home: 8413 Buckingham Dr El Cerrito CA 94530-2531 Office: Pacific Gas and Electric Co Mail Code H17F PO Box 770000 San Francisco CA 94177

SPROULE, BETTY ANN, computer industry strategic planning manager; b. Evanston, Ill., Dec. 30, 1948; d. Harold Fletcher and Lois (Reno) Mathis; m. J. Michael Sproule, Mar. 3, 1973; children: John Harold, Kevin William. BS, Ohio State U., 1969, MS, 1970, PhD, 1972. Mem. tech. staff Bell Telephone Labs., Columbus, Ohio, 1973-74; asst. prof. U. Tex., Odessa, 1974-77; analyst bus. systems Maj. Appliance Bus. div. GE, Louisville, 1977-78; dir. forecasting and analysis Brown and Williamson Tobacco, Louisville, 1978-86; strategic planning mgr. Hewlett-Packard Co., Santa Clara, Calif., 1986—. Contbr. articles to profl. jours.; patentee in field. Sr. mem. IEEE, Soc. Women Engrs. Home: 4135 Briarwood Way Palo Alto CA 94306-4610 Office: Hewlett-Packard Co 5301 Stevens Creek Blvd Santa Clara CA 95051-7201

SPROULL, ROBERT LAMB, retired university president, physicist; b. Lacon, Ill., Aug. 16, 1918; s. John Steele and Chloe Velma (Lamb) S.; m. Mary Louise Knickerbocker, June 27, 1942; children: Robert F., Nancy

M. AB, Cornell U., 1940, PhD, 1943; LLD (hon.), Nazareth Coll., 1983. Research physicist RCA labs., 1943-46; faculty Cornell U., 1946-63, 65-68, prof. physics, 1956-63, dir. lab. atomic and solid state physics, 1959-60, dir. materials sci. center, 1960-63, v.p. for acad. affairs, 1965-68; dir. Advanced Research Projects Agy., Dept. Def., Washington, 1963-65; v.p., provost U. Rochester, N.Y., 1968-70; pres. U. Rochester, 1970-84, pres. emeritus, 1984—; prin. physicist Oak Ridge Nat. Lab., 1952; physicist European Rsch. Assoc., Brussels, 1958-59; lectr. NATO, 1958-59; past bd. dirs., John Wiley & Sons, Charles River Labs., United Technols. Corp., Xerox Corp., Bausch & Lomb; mem. sci. adv. com. GM Corp., 1971-80, chmn., 1973-80; mem. Def. Sci. Bd., 1966-70, chmn., 1968-70; mem. Naval Rsch. Adv. Com., 1974-76, Sloan Commn. Higher Edn., 1977-79, N.Y. Regents Commn. Higher Edn., 1992-93. Author: Modern Physics, 1956; Editor: Jour. Applied Physics, 1954-57. Trustee Deep Springs Coll., 1967-75, 83-87, Cornell U., 1972-77. Ctr. for Advanced Study in Behavioral Scis. fellow, 1973; Meritorious Civilian Svc. medal Sec. of Def., 1970. Fellow Am. Acad. Arts and Scis.; mem. Telluride Assn. (pres. 1945-47), Inst. of Def. Analysis (trustee 1984-92). Home: 16910 Bay St Jupiter FL 33477-1206

SPROUSE, EARLENE PENTECOST, educational diagnostician; b. Hopewell, Va., Apr. 23, 1939; d. Earl Paige and Sophia Marlene (Chairky) Pentecost; m. David Andrew Koren, July 3, 1957 (div. Jan. 1963); children: David Andrew Jr., Elysia Marlene, Merri Paige; m. Wayne Alexender Sprouse, Sept. 2, 1964; 1 child, Michael Wayne. AS, Paul D. Camp C.C., Franklin, Va., 1973; BS in Comm. Disorders, Old Dominion U., 1975, MEd in Spl. Edn., 1977. Tchg. cert. with endorsement in speech lang. pathology, learning disabilities and emotional disturbance, Va. Speech lang. pathologist Southampton County Schs., Va., 1975-76; learning disabled tchr. itinerant Franklin (Va.) City Pub. Schs., 1976-78, emotionally disturbed/learning disabled tchr., 1978-85, speech lang. pathologist, 1986-91, edml. diagnostician, 1992—; com. mem. The Childrens Ctr., Franklin, 1986—, Early Childhood Coun., Franklin, 1992—; needs assessment com. Juvenile Domestic Rels. Ct., Franklin, 1993—; project leader curriculum guide Listening and Lang. Processing Skills, 1990-91. Com. mem. Dem. Com., Suffolk, Va., 1985-92, Family Fair, Franklin, 1993—, Career Edn. Adv. Com. Va. Dept. Edn., 1995—. Recipient Excellence in Edn. award C. of C., Hampton Roads, Va., 1988-89; grantee Va. Edn. Assn., Richmond, 1994—, Project UNITE Dept. Edn., Richmond, 1994—. Mem. ASCD, Coun. for Exceptional Children (com. mem.), Speech and Hearing Assn. Va., Franklin City Edn. Assn. (pub. rels. com., pres. 1980, 91), Orton Dyslexia Soc. Presbyterian. Avocations: fishing, music. Home: 319 Gray's Creek Ln Surry VA 23883 Office: Franklin City Pub Schs 800 W 2nd Ave Franklin VA 23851-2162

SPROUSE, JAMES MARSHALL, retired federal judge; b. Williamson, W.Va., Dec. 3, 1923; s. James and Garnet (Lawson) S.; m. June Dolores Burt, Sept. 25, 1952; children: Tracy Sprouse Ferguson, Jeffrey Marshall, Andrew Michael, Sherry Lee Sprouse Shinholser, Shelly Lynn Sprouse Schneider. AB, St. Bonaventure (N.Y.) U., 1947; LLB, Columbia U., 1949; postgrad. in internat. law, U. Bordeaux, France, 1950. Bar: W.Va. Asst. atty. gen. State of W.Va., 1949; with W.Va. CIA, 1952-57; pvt. practice W.Va., 1957-72, 75-79; justice W.Va. Supreme Ct. Appeals, 1972-75; judge U.S. Ct. Appeals (4th cir.), Lewisburg, W.Va., 1979-92, sr. cir. judge, 1992-95, ret., 1995; pvt. practice, 1995—. With AUS, 1942-45. Fulbright scholar. Mem. ABA, W.Va. State Bar, W.Va. Bar Assn., W.Va. Trial Lawyers Assn., Kanawha County Bar Assn., VFW, Am. Legion, Shriners, Aheppa. Democrat. Presbyterian. Office: PO Box 159 Union WV 24983-0159

SPROUSE, ROBERT ALLEN, II, retail chain executive; b. Portland, Oreg., Dec. 25, 1935; s. John Alwyn and Mary.Louise (Burpee) S.; m. Frances Carolyn Russell, June 22, 1957. Student, Williams Coll., 1953-57. With Sprouse-Reitz Stores Inc., Portland, 1957—; buyer, sec. Sprouse-Reitz Stores Inc., 1963-69, v.p., 1969-73, pres., 1973—, chief exec. officer, 1986-91, also bd. dirs., chmn., 1991-94; chmn. Windermere Comml. Real Estate, 1996—. Mem. Chief Execs. Orgn., Multnomah Athletic Club, Arlington Club, Rotary. Republican. Episcopalian.

SPROUSE, SUSAN RAE MOORE, human resources specialist; b. Amsterdam, N.Y., Feb. 23, 1948; d. Charles Franklin and Alice Rae (Lawson) Moore; m. Richard D. Sprouse, May 5, 1973; children: Jennifer Lynn, Melinda Rae. BS, U. So. Miss., 1970, MBA, 1971. Spl. non-exempt employee rels. GE Co., Owensboro, Ky., 1972-74; from instr. entry level tng. to spl. profl. rels. and EEO GE Co., Chgo., 1974-78; from employee rels. clk. to material control specialist GE Co., Ft. Smith, Ark., 1978-82; employee rels. rep. Mason Chamberlain Inc., Stennis Space Ctr., Miss., 1982-90; human resource specialist Inst. for Naval Oceanography, Stennis Space Ctr., 1990-92; program coord. Ctr. for Ocean and Atmospheric Modeling, Stennis Space Ctr., 1992-95; human resources specialist Computer Scis. Corp., Stennis Space Ctr., 1995—; co. rep. Jr. Achievement, Owensboro, 1972-74. Libr., Am. flag chair DAR, Picayune, Miss., 1967-92; bd. dirs. Picayune On Stage, v.p., sec., 1982—. Named Outstanding Jr. Mem. DAR, Picayune, 1970; profiled in Picayune Item, 1988. Mem. Nat. Soc. Magna Charta Dames, Sigma Sigma Sigma, Phi Delta Rho. Republican. Church of Christ. Avocations: community theater, reading. Office: CSC Bldg 3205 Bay Saint Louis MS 39529

SPROW, HOWARD THOMAS, lawyer, educator; b. Atlantic City, Dec. 4, 1919; s. Howard Franklin and Elizabeth B. (Riley) S.; m. Mildred J. Fiske, July 22, 1945; children—Howard Hamilton, Mildred Elizabeth (Mrs. Wilson), Matthew Thomas. A.B. cum laude, Colgate U., 1942; J.D., Columbia, 1945; LLD (hon.), St. Lawrence U., 1987. Bar: N.Y. 1946. Assoc. Brown, Wood, Fuller, Caldwell & Ivey, N.Y.C., 1945-53; ptnr. Brown, Wood, Fuller, Caldwell & Ivey, 1954-70; gen. counsel, v.p. corporate and pub. affairs, sec. Merrill Lynch, Pierce, Fenner & Smith Inc., N.Y.C., 1970-77, Merrill Lynch & Co., Inc., 1973-77; ptnr. Rogers & Wells, N.Y.C., 1977-80; of counsel Rogers & Wells, 1980-87; prof. law Albany Law Sch., Union U., 1980-90, prof. emeritus, 1990—; of counsel Crane & Mackrell, Albany, 1990-92; sr. counsel Whiteman Osterman & Hanna, Albany, 1992—; adj. prof. law Fordham U., 1974-80; mem. adv. panel to Law Revision Commn. on Recodification N.Y. State Ins. Law, 1973-84, chmn., 1976-80; bd. dirs. Farm Family Holdings, Inc., Glenmont, N.Y. Mem. editorial bd. Columbia Law Rev, 1944-45; editor: Financing in the International Capital Markets, 1982. Mem. ABA, N.Y. State Bar Assn., Assn. of Bar of City of N.Y. Home: 55 Marion Ave Albany NY 12203-1820 Office: Whiteman Osterman & Hanna One Commerce Plz Albany NY 12260

SPROWL, CHARLES RIGGS, lawyer; b. Lansing, Mich., Aug. 22, 1910; s. Charles Orr and Hazel (Allen) S.; m. Virginia Lee Graham, Jan. 15, 1938; children: Charles R., Robert A., Susan G., Sandra D. A.B., U. Mich., 1932, J.D., 1934. Bar: Ill. 1935. Pvt. practice, 1934—; of counsel Taylor, Miller, Sprowl, Hoffnagle & Merletti, 1986—; dir. Simmons Engring. Corp., Petersen Aluminum Corp. Mem. Bd. Edn., New Trier Twp. High Sch., 1959-65, pres. 1962-65; mem. Glencoe Zoning Bd. Appeals, 1956-76, chmn., 1966-76; mem Glencoe Plan Commn., 1962-65; bd. dirs. Glencoe Pub. Libr., 1953-65, pres. 1955-56; trustee Highland Park Hosp., 1959-69; bd. dirs. Cradle Soc., 1968-92. Fellow Am. Coll. Trial Lawyers; mem. Chgo. Bar Assn. (bd. mgrs. 1949-51), Ill. Bar Assn., ABA, Juvenile Protective Assn. (dir. 1943-53), Northwestern U. Settlement (pres. 1963-70, dir.), Soc. Trial Lawyers, Delta Theta Phi, Alpha Chi Rho. Presbyn. Clubs: Law (pres. 1969-70), Legal (pres. 1953-54), Univ, Monroe, Skokie Country. Home: 380 Green Bay Rd Winnetka IL 60093-4004 Office: 33 N La Salle St Chicago IL 60602-2607

SPROWLS, ROBERT WAYNE, veterinarian, laboratory administrator; b. Phillips, Tex., Mar. 19, 1946; s. Charlie and Nettie Elizabeth (Green) S.; m. Linda Sue Rhoades, Aug. 11, 1966; children—Kimberly, Kari. B.S. in Vet. Sci., Tex. A&M U., 1968, D.V.M., 1969, Ph.D., 1973. NIH fellow pathology Tex. A&M U., College Station, 1969-73; asst. prof. Med. Ctr., U. Ark., Little Rock, 1973-75; pathologist Nat. Ctr. Toxicological Research, Jefferson, Ark., 1973-75; head pathologists Tex. Vet. Med. Diagnostic Lab., Amarillo, 1975-81; dir. Tex. Vet. Med. Diagnostic Lab., 1981—. Contbr. articles to profl. jours. Bd. sec. Valley View Nazarene Ch., Amarillo, 1994—. Mem. AVMA, Am. Assn. Vet. Lab. Diagnosticians (mem. exec. bd. 1992—, mem. accreditation com. 1990—), Acad. Vet. Cons. (corr. sec. 1992—), Tex. Vet. Medicine Assn., High Plains Vet. Medicine Assn. (sec.-treas. 1980-81, 90—), Am. Assn. Bovine Practitioners. Office: Tex A&M Vet Med Diagnostic Lab PO Box 3200 Amarillo TX 79116-3200

SPRUGEL, GEORGE, JR., ecologist; b. Boston, Sept. 26, 1919; s. George and Frances Emily (Strong) S.; m. Catharine Bertha Cornwell, Oct. 27, 1945; 1 son, Douglas George. B.S., Iowa State U., 1946, M.S., 1947, Ph.D., 1950. Instr., then asst. prof. zoology and entomology Iowa State U., 1946-54; asst. head biology br. Office Naval Research, 1951-53; spl. asst. to asst. dir., div. biology and medicine NSF, 1953-54, program dir. environ. biology, 1954-64; chief scientist Nat. Park Service, 1964-66; chief Ill. Natural History Survey, 1966-80, chief emeritus, 1980—; Cons. in field; mem. adv. com. environ. biology NSF, 1965; dir. program conservation of ecosystems U.S. Internat. Biol. Program, 1969-72; mem. study group on role lunar receiving lab. NASA, 1969-70, mem. life scis. com., 1972-78; mem. ecology adv. com. Bur. Reclamation, 1972-74; mem. Gov. of Ill. Sci. Adv. Com., 1967-80, Ill. Environ. Quality Council, 1970-73; mem. environ. studies bd. com. to devel. protocol for toxic substances Nat. Acad. Scis.-Nat. Acad. Engring., 1972-73; mem. NRC, 1968-72. Served as officer USNR, 1940-45, 51-53. Fellow AAAS (council 1961-73, v.p., chmn. sect. biol. scis. 1971); mem. Am. Inst. Biol. Scis. (mem.-at-large gov. bd. 1969-72, exec. com. 1972-75, pres. 1974), Ecol. Soc. Am. (council 1961-78, v.p. 1968), Am. Soc. Zoologists (sec. 1970-72, chmn. div. ecology 1971), Sci. Research Soc. Am., Sigma Xi. Home: 2710 S 1st St Champaign IL 61821-7114

SPRUIELL, VANN, psychoanalyst, educator, editor, researcher; b. Leeds, Ala., Oct. 16, 1926; s. Vann Lindley and Zada (Morton) S.; m. Iris Taylor, Sept. 20, 1951 (div. Oct. 1966); children: Graham, Fain, Garth; m. Joyce Ellis, Feb. 11, 1967; stepchildren: Sidney Reavey, Catherine Ellis, Matson Ellis. BS, U. Ala., Tuscaloosa, 1948; MD, Harvard U., 1952. Resident Bellevue Hosp., N.Y.C., 1952-53, N.Y. Hosp., N.Y.C., 1953-55; fellow Tulane Sch. Medicine, New Orleans, 1955-57; pvt. practice New Orleans, 1957—; vis. rschr. Anna Freud Ctr., London, 1972-73; co-pub. JOURLIT and BOOKREV; pres. and founding mem. Psychoanalytic Archives CD-ROM Texts (PACT), New Orleans, 1993—; clin. prof. psychiatry La. State U. Sch. Medicine, Tulane U. Sch. Medicine; sec. Ctr. for Advanced Studies in Psychoanalysis, 1989—. Editl. bd. Psychoanalytic Quarterly, 1973—; N.Am. editor Internat. Jour. Psychoanalysis, London, 1988-93; editor Psychoanalysis South, 1996—; mem. various other editl. bds.; contbr. articles to profl. jours. and books. Sgt. U.S. Army, 1944-46. Mem. Am. Psychoanalytic Assn. (sec. bd. on profl. stds. 1979-92), Wyvern Club. Avocations: interdisciplinary studies, sailing. Home: 215 Iona St Metairie LA 70005-4137

SPRUNG, DONALD WHITFIELD LOYAL, physics educator; b. Kitchener, Ont., Can., June 6, 1934; s. Lyall MacAulay and Doreen Bishop (Price) S.; m. Hannah Sueko Nagai, Dec. 12, 1958; children: Anne Elizabeth, Carol Hanako. BA, U. Toronto, Ont., 1957; PhD, U. Birmingham, Eng., 1961, DSc, 1977. Asst lectr. U. Birmingham, Eng., 1960-61; instr. Cornell U., Ithaca, N.Y., 1961-62; rsch. staff lab. nuclear sci. MIT, Boston, 1964-65; asst. prof. McMaster U., Hamilton, Ont., 1962-66, assoc. prof., 1966-71, physics prof., 1971—, dean faculty sci., 1975-84, mem. bd. govs., 1986-90, chair dept. physics and astronomy, 1991-97; vis. prof. U. Barcelona, Spain, 1991-92, 95. Contbr. articles to profl. jours. C.D. Howe fellow, 1969-70. Fellow Royal Soc. Can.; mem. Can. Assn. Physicists (Herzberg medal 1972, medal for outstanding achievement 1997), Am. Phys. Soc.; mem. Inst. Physics. Avocations: bicycling, cabinet making. Office: McMaster Univ Dept Physics and Astronomy, 1280 Main St W, Hamilton, ON Canada L8S 4M1

SPRUNGL, KATHERINE LOUISE, nurse; b. Sandusky, Ohio, May 29, 1961; d. Karl William and Patricia Carol (Addy) Steuk; m. Jeffery Alan Sprungl; children: Diana Kristine, Alixandra Marie. AA, Cuyahoga Community Coll., 1982; BS, Bowling Green State U., 1986. RN, Ohio; cert. inpatient obstetric nurse. Med. technician Fairview Gen. Hosp., Cleve., 1983-84; staff nurse labor, delivery Fairview Gen. Hosp., 1984-86; office staff nurse Dr. T. J. Wasserbauer, M.D., Inc., Cleve., 1984-85; counselor, instr. Far West Ctr. Project Find, Westlake, Ohio, 1986—; instr. Am. Heart Assn., Cleve., 1983—, Well Aware, Westlake, Ohio, 1986-88; staff nurse-labor, delivery SW Gen. Hosp., Middleburg Heights, Ohio, 1987, St. Joseph Hosp., Lorain, Ohio, 1988, Cleve. Metrohealth System, 1988-95; nurse Profl. Nursing Svc., Cuyahoga Falls, Ohio, 1995—; cons. Well Aware, 1985, Far West Ctr., 1986. Author: Living with Arthritis, 1986, Teen Contact, 1991. Project founder, dir. Teen Contact, 1991. Mem. Assn. Women's Health, Obstetrics and Neonata Nurses. Avocations: raising, showing riding quarter horses. Home: 1545 King Rd Hinckley OH 44233-9773

SPULBER, NICOLAS, economics educator emeritus; b. Brasov, Romania, Jan. 1, 1915; m. Pauline, Aug. 5, 1950; 1 son, Daniel Francis. MA, New Sch. Social Rsch., 1950, PhD magna cum laude, 1952. Rsch. assoc. Ctr. Internat. Studies, Mass. Inst. Tech., 1952-54; mem. faculty Ind. U., Bloomington, 1954—; prof. econs. Ind. U., from 1961, acting chmn. Inst. East European Studies, 1956-59, Disting. prof. econs., 1974-80, Disting. prof. emeritus, 1980—; vis. prof. City Coll., City U. N.Y., 1963-64. Author: The Economics of Communist Eastern Europe, 1957, reissued 1976, The Soviet Economy: Structure, Principles, Problems, 2d edit, 1969, Soviet Strategy for Economic Growth, 1964, The State and Economic Development, 1966, Socialist Management and Planning, 1971, Organizational Alternatives in Soviet-Type Economies, 1979, Managing the American Economy from Roosevelt to Reagan, 1989, Restructuring The Soviet Economy: In Search of the Market, 1991, The American Economy: The Struggle for Supremacy in the 21st Century, 1995, Redefining the State: Privatization and Welfare Reform in Industrial and Transitional Economies, 1997; co-author: Quantitative Economic Policy and Planning, 1976, Economics of Water Resources: From Regulation to Privatization, 1994; editor, co-editor 5 books; contbr. numerous articles to profl. jours. in, U.S. and fgn. countries. Halle fellow, 1951-52; grantee Am. Philos. Soc., 1956; grantee Ford Found., 1962-63; rsch. fellow Ford Faculty Found., 1960-61; sr. fellow Internat. Devel. Rsch. Ctr., Ind. U., 1969-71. Mem. Am. Econ. Assn. Office: Ind U Dept Econs Bloomington IN 47405

SPUNT, SHEPARD ARMIN, real estate executive, management and financial consultant; b. Cambridge, Mass., Feb. 3, 1931; s. Harry and Naomi (Drooker) S.; B.S., U. Pa., 1952, M.B.A., 1956; m. Joan Murray Fooshee, Aug. 6, 1961 (dec. June 1969); children—Erica Frieda and Andrew Murray (twins). Owner, Colonial Realty Co., Brookline, Mass., 1953—, Cambridge, 1960—; sr. assoc. Gen. Solids Assocs., 1956—; chmn. bd. Gen. Solids Systems Corp., 1971-74; trustee Union Capital Trust, Boston; incorporator Liberty Bank & Trust Co., Boston; dir., clerk The Computer Co., Inc., Cambridge, Mass., 1986—. Chmn., Com. for Fair Urban Renewal Laws, Mass., 1965—; Boston Area assoc. trustee U. Pa.; treas. Ten Men of Mass., 1980. Pres., New Eng. Council of Young Republicans, 1964-67, 69-71; vice chmn. Young Rep. Nat. Fedn., 1967-69, dir. region I, 1964-67, 69-71; mem. Brookline Rep. Town Com., 1960—, treas., 1996—; del. Atlantic Conf. Young Polit. Leaders, Brussels, 1973; bd. dirs. Brookline Taxpayers Assn., 1964—, v.p., 1971-72, pres., 1972—. Registered profl. engr., Mass. Mem. Nat. Soc. Profl. Engrs., Rental Housing Assn., Greater Boston Real Estate Bd., Navy League, Boston Athenaeum, Copley Soc. Boston. Lodges: Masons, Shriners. Author: (with others) A Business Data Processing Service for Small Business Practitioners, 1956; A Business Data Processing Service for Medical Practitioners, 1956, rev. edit., 1959. Author, sponsor consumer protection and election law legislation Mass. Gen. Ct., 1969—. Patentee in field of automation, lasers, dielectric bonding. Home: 177 Reservoir Rd Chestnut Hill MA 02167-1426 Office: 21 Elmer St Cambridge MA 02138-6107

SPURGEON, EDWARD DUTCHER, law educator; b. Newton, N.J., June 2, 1939; s. Dorsett Larew and Mary (Dutcher) S.; m. Carol Jean Forbes, June 17, 1963; children: Michael Larew, Stephen Edward. AB, Princeton U., 1961; LLB, Stanford U., 1964; LLM in Taxation, NYU, 1968. Bar: Calif. 1965. Assoc. atty. Stammer McKnight et al, Fresno, Calif., 1964-67; assoc. atty. Paul Hastings Janofsky and Walker, L.A., 1968-70, ptnr., 1971-80; prof. law U. Utah, Salt Lake City, 1980-90, Wm. H. Leary prof. law and policy, 1990-93, assoc. dean acad. affairs Coll. Law, 1982-83, dean Coll. Law, 1983-90; dean, prof. Sch. of Law U. Ga., Athens, 1993—; pres., dir. Albert and Elaine Borchard Found., L.A., 1983—; vis. prof. law Univ. Coll. London, fall 1990, Stanford U. Law Sch., spring 1991; ex-officio mem. Utah State Bar Commn., 1984-90; cons. devel. office U. Utah, 1991-93. Co-author: Federal Taxation of Trusts, Grantors and Beneficiaries, 1st edit., 1978, 2d edit., 1989, 3d edit., 1997. Mem. Utah Gov.'s Task Force Officers and Dirs. Liability Ins., 1985-87, Utah Dist. Ct. Reorgn. Commn., 1986-87, Justice in 21st Century Commn., Utah, 1989-91; bd. visitors, exec. com. Stanford U. Law Sch., 1988-93. Mem. ABA (Commn. on Legal Problems of the Elderly 1991-95, spl. advisor 1995—), Am. Bar Found. Office: U of Ga Law School Athens GA 30602

SPURLING, EVERETT GORDON, JR., architect, construction specifications consultant; b. Fallston, N.C., Sept. 5, 1923; s. Everett Gordon and Vera Mae (Lattimore) S.; m. Margaret Ball Duckworth, Sept. 9, 1944; children: David Steven, Diana Lynn, Norman Kent. AS, Mars Hill Coll., 1940-42; B in Archtl. Engring. with high honors, N.C. State U., 1947, postgrad., 1948. Registered architect, N.C., Va., Md. Inspector aircraft Glenn Martin Co., Balt., 1942; draftsman, architect F. Carter Williams, Architect, Raleigh, N.C., 1947-52; staff architect C.E. Silling and Assocs., Charleston, W.Va., 1952-53, Greife and Daley, Architects, Charleston, 1953-55; ptnr. Hunter and Spurling, Architects, Charleston, 1955-57; project architect, assoc. McLeod and Ferrara, Architects, Washington, 1957-64; owner, cons. E.G. Spurling Jr., Architect, Washington and Bethesda, Md., 1964—; guest lectr. Montgomery Coll., Cath. U., U. Mo.-Rolla, George Washington U.; guest speaker, panelist numerous constrn. orgns. Contbr. articles to profl. jours. Served as sgt. C.E., U.S. Army, 1944-46, ETO. Recipient Design award GSA, 1990. Fellow AIA, Constrn. Specifications Inst. (hon. mem. 1995, cert. of appreciation 1971, 93, Ben John Small Meml. award 1979, edn. commendation 1979, Master Format spl. award 1983, Mid-Atlantic Region cert. of appreciation 1990, 92); mem. Am. Arbitration Assn. (panelist 1979-96), Specifications Cons. in Ind. Practice (pres. 1977-80), Tau Beta Pi, Phi Kappa Phi. Democrat. Baptist. Avocations: fishing, woodworking, art, fgn. travel. Home and Office: 6312 Marjory Ln West Bethesda MD 20817-5804

SPURR, HARVEY W., JR., plant pathology research administrator; b. Oak Park, Ill., June 8, 1934; m. Idamarie Thome, 1956; 3 children. BS, Mich. State U., 1956; PhD in Plant Pathology, U. Wis., 1961. Fellow plant pathology NIH U. Wis., Madison, 1961-63; plant pathologist agrl. rsch. sta. Union Carbide Corp., N.C., 1963-69; assoc. prof. plant pathology N.C. State U., Oxford, 1969-74, prof. plant pathology, 1974—; rsch. plant pathologist Oxford (N.C.) Tobacco Lab. USDA, 1969—, rsch. leader, lab. dir., 1988-94; ret. USDA, 1994; Prof. emeritus, Plant Pathology North Carolina U. Mem. Am. Phytopath Soc. Office: Oxford Plant Protection Ctr 901 Hillsboro St Oxford NC 27565 also: USDA Crops Rsch Lab PO Box 1168 Oxford NC 27565

SPURRIER, MARY EILEEN, investment advisor, financial planner; b. Mpls., Sept. 16, 1943; d. Charles Joseph and Ruth Eileen (Rowles) Dickman; m. Joseph Leo Spurrier, Jan. 16, 1965 (div. Aug. 1976); 1 child, Christopher Jude; m. Gary Albert Gutfrucht, July 8, 1988. BS, U. Minn., 1965. CFP; registered prin., registered investment advisor. Rsch. fellow, libr. Sch. Bus. Adminstrn. U. Minn., Mpls., 1965-68; exec. dir. Zero Population Growth, N.Y., 1972-76; fin. cons. Merrill Lynch, Rochester, N.Y., 1977-84, Shearson/Smith Barney, 1984-89; investment cons. CitiCorp, Rochester, 1989-91; assoc. v.p. Essex Investment, Rochester, 1991-95; pres. M. Spurrier Fin. Svcs., Rochester, 1995—; bd. dirs. Micro Bus. Alliance, Rochester; cons. Fund Devel. Rochester Women's Network, 1995—, Women's Coun. C. of C., Rochester, 1992—; spkr. in field. Contbr. articles to newspapers. Chmn. endowment campaign YWCA, Rochester, 1994—, bd. dirs., mem. fin. com. 1997—; mentor Wilson Commencement Park, Rochester, 1993—; v.p., bd. dirs. N.Y. State Environ. Planning Lobby, 1973-75; bd. dirs. N.Y. State Family Planning Coalition, 1973-75; fin. dir. LWV, Rochester, 1989-90. Recipient Eminent Rochester Women award Upstate Mag., 1974. Mem. NAFE (spkr. 1990-95), Women's Network, Rochester Women's Network, Women's Coun. C. of C., Nat. Assn. Women Bus. Owners (bd. dirs. Greater Rochester chpt. 1997—). Avocations: gardening, reading, walking, canning and preserving, volunteer work. Office: 315 Westminster Rd Rochester NY 14607-3230

SPURRIER, PATRICIA ANN, executive director; b. El Paso, Tex., Feb. 27, 1943; d. James Ray and Lucile Gray (Lafferty) Spurrier; m. Martin Oliver Bright, Sept. 18, 1964 (div. 1967); 1 child, James R. Student, Frederick Coll., 1962-64. Planning technician Reston Va, Inc./Gulf Reston, Inc., 1966-75; adminstrv. asst. Gulf Oil, Tulsa, 1975-79; planner Conde Engring., El Paso, Tex., 1979-82; adjutant U.S. Horse Cavalry Assn., Ft. Bliss, Tex., 1983-91; exec. dir. U.S. Cavalry Assn., Ft. Riley, Kans., 1991—; sec. U.S. Cavalry Meml. Found., Fort Riley, 1994—; trustee Spurrier Trust, El Paso, 1990—; mem. Bigheart Cemetery Found., Barnsdale, Okla., 1989—. Editor The Cavalry Jour., 1990—. Mem. U.S. Army Daus. Republican. Avocations: research, painting, genealogy. Home: 1517 Leavenworth St Manhattan KS 66502-4154 Office: US Cavalry Assn PO Box 2325 Fort Riley KS 66442-0325

SPURRIER, STEVE, university athletic coach, former professional football player. Quarterback San Francisco 49'ers, 1967-75, Tampa Bay Buccaneers, 1976; head football coach Duke U., 1987-89, U. Fla. Gators, 1990—. Winner Heisman Trophy, U. Fla., 1966. Office: Univ Fla PO Box 14485 Gainesville FL 32604-2485*

SPYERS-DURAN, PETER, librarian, educator; b. Budapest, Hungary, Jan. 26, 1932; came to U.S., 1956, naturalized, 1964; s. Alfred and Maria (Almasi-Balogh) S-D; m. Jane F. Cumber, Mar. 21, 1964; children: Kimberly, Hilary, Peter. Certificate, U. Budapest, 1955; M.A. in L.S, U. Chgo., 1960; Ed.D., Nova U., 1975. Profl. asst. libr. adminstrn. div. ALA, Chgo., 1961-62; assoc. dir. librs., assoc. prof. U. Wis., 1962-67; dir. librs., prof. Western Mich. U., 1967-70; dir. librs., prof. libr. sci. Fla. Atlantic U., 1970-76; dir. libr. Calif. State U., Long Beach, 1976-83; prof. libr. and info. sci., dir. libr. Wayne State U., Detroit, 1983-86, dean, prof. libr. and info. sci. program, 1986-95, dean and prof. emeritus, 1995—; cons. Spyers-Duran Assocs., 1995—; acting univ. libr. Nova Southeastern U., Ft. Lauderdale, Fla., 1996-97; vis. prof. State U. N.Y. at Geneseo, summers 1969-70; cons. publs., libr. and info. scis.-related enterprises; chmn. bd. internat. confs., 1970—. Author: Moving Library Materials, 1965, Public Libraries - A Comparative Survey of Basic Fringe Benefits, 1967; editor: Approval and Gathering Plans in Academic Libraries, 1969, Advances in Understanding Approval Plans in Academic Libraries, 1970, Economics of Approval Plans in Research Libraries, 1972, Management Problems in Serials Work, 1973, Prediction of Resource Needs, 1975, Requiem for the Card Catalog: Management Issues in Automated Cataloging, 1979, Shaping Library Collections for the 1980's, 1981, Austerity Management in Academic Libraries, 1984, Financing Information Systems, 1985, Issues in Academic Libraries, 1985; mem. editorial bd. Jour. of Library Adminstration, 1989-95. Mem. Kalamazoo County Library Bd., 1969-70; Bd. dirs. United Fund. Mem. ALA, Mich. Libr. Assn., Internat. Fed. Libr. Assns., Assn. Info. Sci., Fla. Libr. Assn., Calif. Libr. Assn., Fla. Assn. Community Colls., Boca Raton C. of C., U. Chgo. Grad. Libr. Sch. Alumni Club (pres. 1973-75), Mich. Libr. Consortium (bd. dirs. 1983-87), Detroit Area Libr. Network (pres. bd. dirs. 1985-95), Mich. Ctr. for Book (pres. 1988-89), Am. Soc. Info. Sci., Assn. Libr. and Info. Sci. Edn. Republican. Methodist. Home: 7295 Maiden Cane Ct Largo FL 33777 Office: Wayne State Univ Librs Detroit MI 48202

SQUARCIA, PAUL ANDREW, school superintendent; b. Yukon, Pa., Nov. 17, 1939; s. Paul and Lucy (Nardonne) S.; m. Gena Maria Porreca, Aug. 18, 1962; children: Paul, Stephanie, Suzanne. BS, Boston U., 1961, cert. advanced studies, 1974; EdD, Boston Coll., 1987; MEd, U. N.H., 1967. Sci. tchr. Berlin (N.H.) Sch. Dept., 1961-63, asst. prin., 1963-66; prin. Oxford Hills High Sch., South Paris, Maine, 1967-70; prin. Silver Lake Regional Dist., Kingston, Mass., 1970-72, asst. supt. schs., 1972-78, supt. schs., 1978—; adj. prof. Bridgewater (Mass.) State Coll., 1980—, Lesley Coll., Cambridge, Mass., 1980—. Recipient Nat. Superintendent of the Yr. awd., Massachusetts, Am. Assn. of School Administrators, 1993. Mem. ASCD, Am. Assn. Sch. Adminstrs., Mass. Assn. Sch. Supts. (pres. 1992-93). Roman Catholic. Avocations: reading, traveling, spectator sports. Home: 28 Holmes Ter Plymouth MA 02360-4013 Office: Silver Lake Regional Dist 250 Pembroke St Kingston MA 02364*

SQUIBB, SAMUEL DEXTER, chemistry educator; b. Limestone, Tenn., June 20, 1931; s. Benjamin Bowman and Lou Pearl S.; m. JoAnn Kyker, Dec. 15, 1951; children—Sandra Lavanne, Kevin Dexter. B.S., E. Tenn. State U., 1952; Ph.D., U. Fla., 1956. Assoc. prof., dir. chemistry Western Carolina U., Cullowhee, N.C., 1956-60; asst. prof., dir. chemistry Eckerd

Coll., St. Petersburg, Fla., 1960-63; asso. prof. Eckerd Coll., 1963-64; prof. chemistry U. N.C., Asheville, 1964-94, prof. emeritus, 1994—, chmn. dept., 1964-94; vis. prof. U. N.C., Chapel Hill, 1976-81, 83-87, 92-95, Clemson U., S.C., 1982; cons. So. Assn. Colls. and Schs., State of W.Va. Author: Experimental Organic Chemistry, 1972, Understanding Chemistry One, 1979, rev. 1990, Two, 1981, rev. 1991, Three, 1981, rev. 1992, Four, 1981, rev. 1992, Five, 1981, rev. 1989, Six, 1984, Chemistry One, 1976, rev. 1987, Two, 1980, rev. 1990, Experimental Chemistry One, 1976, rev. 1988, Two, 1981, rev. 1991; contbr. articles to profl. jours. Mem. Grose United Meth. Ch. Disting. Tchr. award U. N.C.-Asheville, 1983. Fellow Am. Inst. Chemists (life, nat. publs. bd. 1988-92); mem. Am. Chem. Soc. (Charles H. Stone award Carolina Piedmont sect. 1979, Disting. Chemist award Western Carolinas sect. 1993, chmn. Tampa Bay subsect. 1963, Western Carolina sect. 1981, editor Periodic News Western Carolina sect. 1980—, Disting. Chemist award 1993), N.C. Inst. Chemists (pres. 1977-79, sec. 1975-77, 85-91, Disting. Chemist award 1986), Skyland Twirlers Square Dance Club, Silver Spurs Advanced Square Dance Club, Skylark Round Dance Club, Phi Beta Kap.

SQUIBB, SANDRA HILDYARD, special education educator; b. Kansas City, Mo., May 23, 1943; d. Victor Herbert and Vivian Aline (Henderson) Hildyard; children: Jason, Trevor. BA, So. Meth. U., 1966; MS, FHSU, 1984. Cert. early childhood, spl. edn. tchr., Kans., Tex., cert. bldg. adminstr. K-12. Speech pathologist Edinburg (Tex.) Consolidated Sch. Dist., 1971-74; owner, audiologist Northwest Kans. Hearing Svc., Colby, Kans., 1976—; supr. Northwest Kans. Ednl. Svc. Ctr., Colby, 1980-87; coord. Northwest Kans. Ednl. Svc. Ctr., Oakley, Kans., 1987-92; treas. Kans. Div. of Early Childhood, 1987-89. Precinct chmn. Dem. Party, Thomas County, 1980—, party chmn., 1988-90; mem. Parent Adv. Coun., Colby, 1984-87; mem. bd. Alcohol and Drug Abuse Coun.; cmty. rep. Head Start Policy Coun., 1994—. Recipient grants in field. Mem. Coun. for Exceptional Children (award of excellence 1991). Roman Catholic. Avocations: skiing, golf. Home: 425 La Hacienda Dr Colby KS 67701-3914 Office: NW Kans Hearing Svcs 175 S Range Ave Colby KS 67701-2931

SQUIER, DAVID LOUIS, manufacturing executive; b. Buffalo, Oct. 30, 1945; s. Clayton L. and Ruth H. Squier; m. Sue Sampson, Aug. 12, 1967; children: Jennifer, Allison. BS in Mech. Engring., Lehigh U., 1967; MBA, Wharton Sch., U. Pa., 1971. With mfg. mgmt. program GE, various cities, 1967-70; mgr. corp. planning Howmet Corp., Greenwich, Conn., 1971-73; mgr. corp. and bus. planning Howmet Corp., Muskegon, Mich., 1973-75; plant mgr. Howmet Corp., Hampton, Va., 1976-78; gen. mgr. Howmet Corp., Wichita Falls, Tex., 1979-82; v.p. Howmet Corp., Greenwich, 1983-87, sr. v.p., 1987-89, exec. v.p., 1989-91, COO, 1991-92, pres., CEO, 1992—, also bd. dirs. Mem. rev. and prioritization bd. Iacocca Inst., Bethlehem, Pa., 1990—. Home: 56 Laurel Rd New Canaan CT 06840-3206 Office: Howmet Corp 475 Steamboat Rd Greenwich CT 06830-7144

SQUIER, JACK LESLIE, sculptor, educator; b. Dixon, Ill., Feb. 27, 1927; s. Leslie Lee and Ruth (Barnes) S.; m. Jane Bugg, June 9, 1950. Student, Oberlin Coll., 1945-46; B.S., Ind. U., 1950; M).F.A., Cornell U., 1952. Instr. Cornell U., 1952, asst. prof. art, 1958-61, assoc. prof., 1961-65, prof., 1965—; designer Howatt Pottery Co., N.Y.C., 1953; account exec. Jamian Advt. Co., N.Y.C., 1954-58; asst. prof. U. Calif., Berkeley, 1960; mem. Internat. Assn. Art, UNESCO, 1964-72, mem. exec. com., 1966-69, v.p., 1969-72. One-man shows include Alan Gallery, N.Y.C., 1956, 59, 62, 64, White Mus., Cornell U., 1959, 68, Instituto de Arte Contemporaneo, Lima, Peru, 1963, Landau-Alan Gallery, N.Y.C., 1966, 69, Herbert F. Johnson Mus., Cornell Univ. (retospective of work , 1953-93); exhibited in group shows at Mus. Modern Art, N.Y.C., 1957, Whitney Mus., N.Y.C., 1952, 54, 56, 58, 62, 67, 78, Hirshhorn Mus., Washington, 1978, Mus. Fine Arts, Boston, 1958, Chgo. Art Inst., 1960, Brussel's Worlds Fair, 1956, competition, Auschwitz, Poland, 1957, Albright-Knox Mus., Buffalo, 1968, Claude Bernard Gallery, Paris, 1957, Hanover Gallery, London, 1958; represented in permanent collections Mus. Modern Art, N.Y.C., Whitney Mus. Art, Hirshhorn Mus., Instituto de Arte Contemporaneo, Everson Mus., Syracuse, N.Y., Stanford U. Mus., St. Lawrence U. Mus., SUNY at Potsdam, Ithaca Coll., Johnson Mus. at Cornell U., Houston Mus., Hood Mus.-Dartmouth (N.H.) U.; retrospective exhbn. Herbert F. Johnson Mus. Cornell U., 1993; work pub. in various, books, mags., newspapers, slide collections, catalogs. Served with AC USN, 1945-47. Home: 221 Berkshire Rd Ithaca NY 14850

SQUIRE, ALEXANDER, management consultant; b. Dumfrieshire, Scotland, Sept. 29, 1917; s. Frederick John and Lillian (Ferguson) S.; m. Isabelle L. Kerr, June 23, 1945; children: Jonathan, David, Deborah, Stephen, Philip, Martha, Timothy, Rebecca, Elizabeth. B.S., MIT, 1939. Research metallurgist Handy and Harman, Fairfield, Conn., 1939-41; devel. metallurgist Sullivan Machinery Co., Michigan City, Ind., 1941-42; head powder metallurgy br. Watertown Arsenal Lab., Mass., 1942-45; mgr. metall. devel. Westinghouse Electric Corp., Pitts., 1945-50; project mgr. Bettis Atomic Power Lab., Pitts., 1950-62; gen. mgr. plant apparatus div. Westinghouse, 1962-69; dir. purchases and traffic Westinghouse Electric Corp., 1969-71; pres. Westinghouse Hanford Co., Richland, Wash., 1971-79; bus. cons. Richland, 1979-80; dep. mng. dir. Wash. Public Power Supply System, 1980-85, cons., 1985—. Mem. Nat. Acad. Engring., Am. Nuclear Soc., Am. Soc. Metals, AIME, Am. Def. Preparedness Assn. Address: 2415 Winburn Ave Durham NC 27704-5145

SQUIRE, ANNE MARGUERITE, religious leader; b. Amherstburg, Ont., Can., Oct. 17, 1920; d. Alexander Samuel and Coral Marguerite Park; m. William Robert Squire, June 24, 1943; children: Frances, Laura, Margaret. BA, Carleton U., Ottawa, 1972, BA with honors, 1974, MA, 1975; LLD (hon.), Carleton U., 1988; DD (hon.), United Theol. Coll., 1979, Queen's U., 1985. Cert. tchr., Ont. Adj. prof. Carleton U., 1975-82; sec. div. ministry personnel and edn. United Ch. Can., Toronto, 1982-85, moderator, 1986-88. Author curriculum materials, 1959—; contbr. articles to profl. jours. Mem. bd. mgmt. St. Andrew's Coll., Saskatoon, Sask., 1982, Queens Theol. Coll., Kingston, Ont., 1980-82; founding mem. Muslim-Christian Dialogue Group. Recipient Senate medal Carleton U., 1972. Mem. Can. Research Inst. for Advancement Women, Delta Kappa Gamma (pres. 1978-79). Office: 731 Weston Dr, Ottawa, ON Canada K1G 1W1

SQUIRE, JAMES ROBERT, retired publisher, consultant; b. Oakland, Calif., Oct. 14, 1922; s. Harry Edwin and Ruby (Fulton) S.; m. Barbara Lyman, Jan. 20, 1946; children: Kathryn Elizabeth, Kevin Richard, David Whitford. BA, Pomona Coll., 1947, DLitt, 1966; MA, U. Calif., Berkeley, 1949, PhD, 1956. Tchr. secondary sch. Oakland, Calif., 1949-54; supr., lectr. English edn. U. Calif. at Berkeley, 1951-59; prof. English U. Ill., Urbana, 1959-67; exec. sec. Nat. Council Tchrs. English, 1960-67; editor-in-chief, sr. v.p. Ginn & Co., Lexington, Mass., 1968-74; sr. v.p., pub. Ginn & Co., 1975-80, sr. v.p., dir. research and devel., 1980-82, sr. v.p., sr. cons., 1983-84; cons., 1984-94; lectr. grad. sch. edn. Harvard U., 1990-97; sr. rsch. assoc. Boston U., 1996-97; pres. Nat. Conf. Rsch. in English, 1982-83; pres. Hall of Fame in Reading, 1995-96; sr. rsch. assoc. Boston U., 1996—. Author: (with W. Loban, M. Ryan) Teaching Language and Literature, 1961, 69, (with R.K. Applebee) High School English Instruction Today, 1968, (with B.L. Squire) Greek Myths and Legends, 1967, Teaching English in the United Kingdom, 1969, A New Look at Progressive Education, 1972; editor: Teaching of English, 76th Yearbook Nat. Soc. Study Edn., 1977, Dynamics of Language Learning, 1987, Writing K-12 Exemplary Programs, 1987, (with J. Jensen, D. Lapp, J. Flood) Handbook of Research on Teaching the English Language Arts, 1991, (with E.J.. Farrell) Transactions in Literature: A Fifty Year Perspective; section editor: Ency. of English Studies and Language Arts, 1994. Bd. dirs. Am. Edn. Publ. Inst., 1968-70. With AUS, 1943-45. Recipient Creative Scholarship award Coll. Lang. Assn., 1961, Lifetime Rsch. award Nat. Conf. Rsch. in English, 1992; named Ky. col., 1966; named to Hall of Fame in reading, 1987. Mem. MLA (pres. 1995), Assn. Am. Pubs. (vice chmn. sch. divsn. 1971-73, chmn. 1974-76, 81-82, Mary McNulty award 1983), Nat. Coun. Tchrs. English (Exec. Com. award 1967,l Disting. Svc. award 1991), Internat. Reading Assn., Coll. Conf. on Composition and Communication, Phi Delta Kappa. Home: 1 Nubanusit Rd Marlborough NH 03455-4503 Office: Harvard Grad Sch Edn 209 Larsen Hall Cambridge MA 02138

SQUIRE, LARRY RYAN, neuroscientist, psychologist, educator; b. Cherokee, Iowa, May 4, 1941; s. Harold Walter and Jean (Ryan) S.; m. Mary Fox.; 2 children. BA, Oberlin Coll., 1963; PhD in Psychology, MIT, 1968; postgrad., Albert Einstein Med. Coll., 1968-70. With U. Calif., San Diego, 1973—, prof., 1981—; rsch. career scientist VA Med. Ctr., San Diego, 1980—; lectr. in field. Editor, author: Memory and Brain, 1987; mem. editorial adv. bd. numerous profl. jours.; editor Behavioral Neuroscience, 1990-95; contbr. articles to profl. jours., chpts. to books. Recipient Charles A. Dana Award for Pioneering Achievements in Health and Education, 1993, Disting. Sci. Contbn. award APA, Lashley prize Am. Philosophical Soc., McGovern award AAAS; William James fellow Am. Psychol. Soc. Mem. NAS, Am. Acad. Arts and Scis., Soc. Neurosci. (pres. 1994). Address: 2402 Carmel Valley Rd Del Mar CA 92014-3802 Office: U California San Diego Dept Psychiatry La Jolla CA 92093

SQUIRE, RUSSEL NELSON, musician, emeritus educator; b. Cleve., Sept. 21, 1908. B.Mus. Edn., Oberlin Coll., 1929; A.M., Case Western Res. U., 1939; Ph.D., NYU, 1942; postgrad. U. So. Calif. Dir. Oberlin Summer Music Sch., Ohio, 1929; dir. instrumental music instrn. Chillicothe Pub. Schs., Ohio, 1929-37; faculty Pepperdine U., Malibu, Calif., 1937-56, prof. music, 1937-56, now prof. emeritus, also chmn. fine arts div., 1940-56; faculty Calif. State U.-Long Beach, 1956-72, prof. music, 1964-72, now prof. emeritus; vis. prof. Pacific Christian Coll., 1970-74; prof. philosophy Sch. Edn., Pepperdine U., 1972-78; profl. theater orch. pianist, 1926-28; founder/propr./dir. Ednl. Travel Service involving study residencies in Europe, the Near East, China, India, Australia, Africa; Service: Agoura, Calif., 1958-84. Author: Studies in Sight Singing, 1950; Introduction to Music Education, 1952; Church Music, 1962; Class Piano for Adult Beginners, 1964, 4th edit., 1990; also contbr. articles to profl. jours. Founder/pres. Council for Scholarship Aid to Fgn. Students, Inc.; mem. Los Angeles County Music Commn., 1948-60; bd. dirs. Opera Guild So. Calif., 1948-60; pres. Long Beach Symphony Assn., 1963-64 (bd. dirs 1961-64). Mem. Music Tchrs. Assn. Calif. (br. pres. 1948-51), AAUP (chpt. founding pres. 1948-49), Rotary, Phi Mu Alpha Sinfonia (life). Club: Twenty (Los Angeles), Bohemians (Los Angeles). Home: 350 Robin Rd Waverly OH 45690-1521

SQUIRE, WALTER CHARLES, lawyer; b. N.Y.C., Aug. 5, 1945; s. Sidney and Helen (Friedman) S.; m. Sara Jane Abamson; children: Harrison, Russell, Zachary, Andrew. BA, Yale U., 1967; JD, Columbia U., 1971. Bar: N.Y. 1971, U.S. Dist. Ct. (so. and ea. dists.) N.Y. 1975, U.S. Ct. Appeals (2d cir.) 1974, U.S. Supreme Ct. 1977. Ptnr. Jones Hirsch Connors & Bull, N.Y.C., 1986—. Bd. govs. Arthritis Found. N.Y., Inc., 1993—; bd. dirs. MedicAlert Found., N.Y., 1990—. Mem. ABA, N.Y. State Bar Assn., Assn. of Bar of City of N.Y., Internat. Bar Assn., Licensing Execs. Soc., Am. Arbitration Assn. (arbitrator 1975—, mediator 1993—), Am. Acad. Hosp. Attys., Risk Ins. Mgmt. Soc. (lectr. 1983, 84). Office: Jones Hirsch Connors & Bull 101 E 52nd St New York NY 10022-6018

SQUIRES, ARTHUR MORTON, chemical engineer, educator; b. Neodesha, Kans., Mar. 21, 1916; s. Charles Loren and Vera Amber (Moore) S. A.B. with distinction in Chemistry, U. Mo., 1938; Ph.D, Cornell U., 1947. Design engr. M.W. Kellogg Co., N.Y.C., 1942-46; asst. dir. process devel. Hydrocarbon Research, Inc., N.Y.C., 1946-51, dir. process devel., 1951-59; cons. chem. process industries N.Y.C., 1959-67; prof. chem. engring. CUNY, 1967-74, disting. prof., 1974-76, chmn. dept. chem. engring., 1970-73; Vilbrandt prof. chem. engring. Va. Poly. Inst. and State U., Blacksburg, 1976-82, disting. prof., 1978-86, disting. prof. emeritus, 1986—. Author: The Tender Ship, 1986; editor: (with D.A. Berkowitz) Power Generation and Environmental Change, 1971; contbr. articles to profl. jours.; patentee in field. Mem. N.Y. Pro Musica, 1953-60. Fellow Am. Acad. Arts and Scis., AAAS; mem. Nat. Acad. Engring., Am. Inst. Chem. Engrs. (inst. lectr.), Am. Chem. Soc. (Henry H. Storch award 1973), ASME, Sigma Xi, Tau Beta Pi. Avocation: performing medieval and Renaissance music. Home: 2710 Quincy Ct Blacksburg VA 24060-4124 Office: Va Poly Inst and State U Dept Chem Engring Blacksburg VA 24061

SQUIRES, JOAN H., orchestra executive. Exec. dir. Milwaukee Symphony Orchestra, Wis. Office: Milw Symphony Orch 330 E Kilbourn Ave Ste 900 Milwaukee WI 53202-3141

SQUIRES, JOHN HENRY, judge; b. Urbana, Ill., Oct. 21, 1946; s. Henry Warrick and Nell Catherine (McDonough) S.; m. Mary Kathleen Damhorst, June 7, 1969; children: Jacqueline Marie, Mary Elizabeth, Katherine Judith, Emily Jean, Grace Dorothy. AB cum laude, U. Ill., 1968, JD, 1971. Bar: Ill. 1971, U.S. Dist. Ct. (cen. dist.) Ill. 1972, U.S. Tax Ct. 1978. Assoc. Brown, Hay & Stephens, Springfield, Ill., 1971-76, ptnr., 1977-87; judge U.S. Bankruptcy Ct. No. Dist. of Ill., ea. div., 1988—; trustee in bankruptcy, 1984-87; adj. prof. law The John Marshall Law Sch., Chgo., 1994, DePaul U., Chgo., 1996; lectr. Chgo. Bar Assn., Ill. Inst. Continuing Legal Edn. , Comml. Law League Am., Ill. Credit Union League; mem. lay adv. bd. St. Joseph's Home, Springfield, 1980-84, sec., 1982-83, v.p., 1983-84. With USAF, 1969. Mem. Chgo.-Lincoln Am. Inn of Ct., Am. Bus. Club, Union League of Chgo., Nat. Conf. of Bankruptcy Judges. Office: US Bankruptcy Ct No Dist Ill Ea Div Rm 656 219 S Dearborn St Chicago IL 60604

SQUIRES, RICHARD FELT, research scientist; b. Sparta, Mich., Jan. 15, 1933; s. Monas Nathan and Dorothy Lois (Felt) S.; m. Else Saederup, 1 child, Iben. BS, Mich. State U., 1958; postgrad., Calif. Inst. Tech., 1961. Rsch. biochemist Pasadena Found. for Med. Rsch., 1961-62; chief biochemistry sect. rsch. dept. A/S Ferrosan, Soeborg, Denmark, 1963-78; neurochemistry group leader CNS Biology sect. Lederle Labs. div. Am. Cyanamid Co., Pearl River, N.Y., 1978-79; prin. rsch. scientist The Nathan S. Kline Inst. for Psychiat. Rsch., Orangeburg, N.Y., 1979—. Contbr. 83 articles to profl. jours.; patentee in field. Nat. Inst. Neurol. and Communication Disorders and Stroke grantee, 1981-84. Mem. Soc. Neurosci., Collegium Internat. Neuro-Psychopharmacologicum, Internat. Soc. Neurochemistry, European Neurosci. Assn., Am. Soc. Neurochemistry, Am. Soc. Biochemistry and Molecular Biology, Am. Soc. Pharmacology and Exptl. Therapeutics. Home: 10 Termakay Dr New City NY 10956-6434 Office: Nathan S Kline Inst Psychiat Rsch Orangeburg NY 10962

SQUIRES, SCOTT WILLIAM, special effects expert, executive. With Indsl. Light & Magic, San Rafael, Calif., 1975-79, visual effects supr., 1985—; co-founder, pres. Dreamquest Visual Effects, 1979-85. Asst. cameraman (film) Close Encounters of the Third Kind, 1977; cameraman (film) Buck Rogers and the Battleship Galactica, 1977; rsch. designer (film) Star Trek I, 1979; spl. effects supr. films including Blue Thunder, Buckeroo Bonzai, Deal of the Century, One From the Heart, Blade Runner, Dentsu, 1988, Micronauts, 1988; tech. dir. Witches of Eastwick, 1986, Willow, 1987, Who Framed Roger Rabbit, 1988; visual effects supr. (film) The Hunt for Red October, 1990; dir. visual effects (film) Showscan, 1991; effects supr. (comml.) Disney Coke. Recipient Acad. Tech. award pioneering work on input scanners, 1995, several effects awards as effects supr. Brit. Petroleum Elevator comml. Office: Indsl Light & Magic PO Box 2459 San Rafael CA 94912-2459*

SQUIRES, WILLIAM RANDOLPH, III, lawyer; b. Providence, Sept. 6, 1947; s. William Randolph and Mary Louise (Gress) S.; m. Elisabeth Dale McAnulty, June 23, 1984; children: Shannon, William R. IV, Mayre Elisabeth, James Robert. BA in Econs., Stanford U., 1969; JD, U. Tex., 1972. Bar: Wash. 1973, U.S. Dist. Ct. (we. dist.) Wash. 1973, U.S. Dist. Ct. (ea. dist.) Wash. 1976, U.S. Ct. Appeals (9th cir.) 1976, U.S. Supreme Ct. 1976, U.S. Claims Ct. 1982. Assoc. Oles, Morrison, Rinker, Stanislaw, & Ashbaugh, Seattle, 1973-78; ptnr., chmn. litigation group Davis Wright Tremaine (formerly Davis, Wright, Todd, Riese & Jones), Seattle, 1978-97; mem. Summit Law Group, Seattle, 1997—. Mem. ABA, Wash. State Bar Assn., Seattle-King County Bar Assn. Episcopalian. Clubs: Wash. Athletic, Rainier (Seattle). Home: 5554 NE Penrith Rd Seattle WA 98105-2845 Office: Summit Law Group 1505 W Lake Ave N Ste 300 Seattle WA 98109

SRAGOW, ELLEN, gallery owner; b. N.Y.C., 1943. BA, Hofstra U., 1964; MA, NYU, 1966. Registrar art collection NYU, N.Y.C., 1967-71; dir. Sragow Gallery, N.Y.C., 1974—. Mem. Internat. Fine Print Dealers Assn., Art Table. Office: Sragow Gallery 73 Spring St New York NY 10012-5800

SREEBNY, LEO M., oral biology and pathology educator; b. N.Y.C., Jan. 8, 1922; s. Morris and Lillie (Bogdanoff) S.; m. Mathilda H. Sternfeld, Mar. 9, 1945; children—Oren, Daniel. B.A., U. Ill., 1942, D.D.S., 1945, M.S., 1950, Ph.D., 1954. With dept. periodontics U. Ill., 1948-57, asso. prof., 1956-57; asso. prof., chmn. dept. oral biology U. Wash., Seattle, 1957-60; prof. U. Wash., 1960-75; dir. U. Wash. (Center for Research Oral Biology), 1967-75; dean Sch. Dental Medicine, SUNY-Stony Brook, 1975-79, prof. dept. oral biology and pathology, 1979—; cons. VA Hosp., Seattle, 1960—; mem. dental study sect. NIH, 1964-68, chmn., 1967-68; mem. com. on sci. policy Nat. Acad. Sci., 1973-74. Author: (with Julia Meyer) Secretory Mechanisms in Salivary Glands, 1963, The Salivary System, 1987, (with I. Van der Waal) Diseases of the Salivary Glands, 1997; contbr. numerous articles to sci., biol. jours. Served with AUS, 1942-45; with USNR, 1946-48. Recipient Internat. Assn. for Dental Research Sci. award, 1969; Silver medal for contbns. to dental sci. and art City of Paris, 1979; Salivary Research Group Award, 1987. Mem. Fedn. Dentaire Internat. (chmn. sci. assembly com. 1973—, rep. UN Conf. on Youth 1983-84), Internat. Assn. Dental Research (bd. govs. 1981), Fedn. Dentaire Internat. (list of honor 1988), Am. Assn. Dental Research, ADA. Home: 35 Gnarled Hollow Rd East Setauket NY 11733-2929 Office: SUNY Stony Brook Sch Dental Medicine Stony Brook NY 11794

SREENIVASAN, KATEPALLI RAJU, mechanical engineering educator; b. Kolar, India, Sept. 30, 1947; married 1980; 2 children. BE, Bangalore U., 1968; ME, Indian Inst. Sci., 1970, PhD in Aeronautical Engring., 1975. JRD Tata fellow Indian Inst. Sci., 1972-74, project asst., 1974-75; fellow U. Sydney, Australia, 1975, U. Newcastle, 1976-77; rsch. assoc. Johns Hopkins U., Balt., 1977-79; from asst. prof. to assoc. prof. Yale U., New Haven, 1982-85, prof. mech. engring., 1985—, Harold W. Cheel prof. mech. engring., 1988—, prof. physics, 1990—, prof. applied physics, 1993—; vis. scientist Indian Inst. Sci., 1979, vis. prof., 1982, Calif. Inst. Tech., Pasadena, 1986, Rockefeller U., 1989, Jawaharlala Nehru Ctr. Advancement Sci. Studies, 1992, chmn. mech. engring. dept., 1987-92; vis. sci. DFVLR, Gottingen, Germany, 1983; mem. Inst. for Advanced Study, Princeton, N.J., 1995. Recipient Narayana Gold medal Indian Inst. Sci., 1975, Disting. Alumnus award, 1992; Humboldt Found. fellow, 1983, Guggenheim fellow, 1989. Fellow ASME, Am. Phys. Soc. (Otto Laporte award 1995), AIAA (assoc.); mem. Am. Math. Soc., Conn. Acad. Sci. and Engring., Sigma Xi. Achievements include research in origin and dynamics of turbulence; control of turbulent flows; chaotic dynamics; fractals.

SRERE, BENSON M., communications company executive, consultant; b. Rock Island, Ill, Aug. 13, 1928; s. Jacob H. and Margaret (Weinstein) S.; m. Betty Ann Cerruti, June 20, 1957; children: David Benson, Anne Michele, Peter John. BA magna cum laude, U. So. Calif., 1949. Newsman U.P., Los Angeles, 1948-56; assoc. editor Good Housekeeping mag., N.Y.C., 1956-59; sr. editor Good Housekeeping mag., 1959-67, asst. mng. editor, dir. spl. publs. div., 1967-68, mng. editor, 1968-72, exec. editor, v.p., 1972-75, v.p., editorial dir., 1975-76; v.p., gen. mgr. King Features Syndicate, 1976-81; v.p. Hearst Metrotone News, 1976-81; exec. asst. to pres. Hearst Corp., 1981—, v.p., 1983-94; dir. Hearst/ABC Video Svcs., Hearst/ABC Viacom Entertainment Svcs., A&E Cable Network, Lifetime Cable Network. Trustee Optometric Center of N.Y. Found., 1978-79. Served with U.S. Army, 1950-52. Mem. Soc. Profl. Journalists, Phi Beta Kappa, Phi Kappa Phi, Phi Eta Sigma. Home: 11 Lafayette Ct Greenwich CT 06830-5324

SRINIVASA, VENKATARAMANIAH, engineer; b. Mysore, India, Aug. 30, 1941; came to U.S., 1968; s. Venkataramaniah and Gowramma S.; m. Janakimala Muthiah, June 1972; children: Supreeth, Suman. BSc, Mysore U., 1962, MSc, 1964; MS, Rutgers U., 1972, PhD, 1975. Rsch. fellow CFTRI, Mysore, 1964-67; tech. officer Indian Inst. Packaging, Bombay, 1967; rsch. intern, rsch. and tching. asst. Rutgers U., New Brunswick, N.J., 1972-75, rsch. intern, tching. asst., rsch. fellow Bur. Engring. Rsch., 1970-75; sr. packaging engr. Abbott Labs., Abbott Park, Ill., 1975-78, sr. project engr., 1978-83, mgr., 1983—. Mem. Inst. Packaging Profls., Soc. Plastics Engrs., Am. Chem. Soc., Sigma Xi. Home: 2729 Sallmon Ave Waukegan IL 60087-3514

SRINIVASACHARI, SAMAVEDAM, chemical engineer; b. Visakhapatnam, India, Oct. 5, 1926; came to U.S., 1958; s. Appalachari Srinivasa and Chudamani Samavedam; m. Vasanta S. Chari, Feb. 11, 1955; children: Sarita, Roger. M of Chem. Engring., NYU, 1959; PhD in Chem. Engring., Poly. Inst. Bklyn., 1967. Registered profl. engr., Pa. Teaching fellow Poly. Inst. Bklyn., 1960-63; sr. process devel. engr. Internat. Latex & Chemical, Dover, Del., 1966-73; prin. process engr. Catalytic, Inc., Phila., 1973-75; sr. process engr. Coalcon/Union Carbide, N.Y.C., 1976-77, Foster Wheeler Energy Corp., Livingston, N.J., 1977-82; chemical and environ. engr. Duro-Test Corp., Clifton, N.J., 1987-92, mgr. environ. engring., 1992—. Mem. AICE, Am. Chem. Soc. Democrat. Hindu. Achievements include design of chem. and petroleum plants, design of synthetic fuels plants; rsch. in environ. and regulatory problems of indsl. plants, environ. clean up of indsl. plant sites. Home: 12 The Ter Rutherford NJ 07070-2028 Office: Duro-Test Corp 185 Scoles Ave Clifton NJ 07012-1125

SRINIVASAN, VENKATARAMAN, marketing and management educator; b. Pudukkottai, Tamil Nadu, India, June 5, 1944; came to U.S., 1968; s. Annaswamy and Jambagalakshmi Venkataraman; m. Sitalakshmi Subrahmanyam, June 30, 1972; children: Ramesh, Mahesh. B Tech., Indian Inst. Tech., Madras, India, 1966; MS, Carnegie-Mellon U., 1970, PhD, 1971. Asst. engr. Larsen & Toubro, Bombay, 1966-68; asst. prof. mgmt. and mktg. U. Rochester, N.Y., 1971-73, assoc. prof., 1973-74; assoc. prof. Stanford (Calif.) U., 1974-76, prof., 1976-82, dir. PhD program in bus., 1982-85, Ernest C. Arbuckle prof. mktg. and mgmt. sci., 1982—; mktg. area coord., 1976-78, 88-93; cons. in field. Mem. editorial bd. Jour. Mktg. Rsch., 1988—, Mktg. Sci., 1980—, Mgmt. Sci., 1974-91; contbr. articles to profl. jours. Mem. Am. Mktg. Assn., Inst. Ops. Rsch./Mgmt. Scis. Hindu. Avocation: classical music.

SROGE, MAXWELL HAROLD, marketing consultant, publishing executive; b. N.Y.C., Oct. 9, 1927; s. Albert N. and Goldie (Feldman) S.; children: Roberta, David, Marc, Sarah. Student, CCNY, 1946-48, NYU, 1948, New Sch. Social Research, 1948. Dir. sales Bell & Howell Co., Chgo., 1950-60; dir. prodn. planning Bell & Howell Co., 1961-62, pres. Robert Maxwell div., 1962-63; pres. Maxwell Sroge Co., Inc., Chgo., 1965—, Telespond, Inc., Chgo., 1971—, Maxwell Sroge Pub., Inc., Chgo., 1976—; chmn. JUF Comm. Industry, 1974-75, Transatlantic Catalogue Corp.; chmn. Direct Mktg. Svcs., Inc.; pub. Non-Store Mktg. Report, Inside Leading Mail Order Houses, Mail Order Industry Ann. Report, Best in Catalogs, How to Create Successful Catalogs, The Catalog Marketer, 101 Ideas for More Profitable Catalogs; bd. dirs. Tools Direct, DMSI; chmn. Telespond Inc. Mem. New Ill. Com., 1965; speakers bur. Percy for Gov., 1964, Citizens for Percy, 1972; co-chmn. Percy for Pres. Exploratory Com., 1974; mem. regional adv. bd. Nat. Jewish Hosp., 1974-75; mem. devel. com. WTTW-Channel 11, 1975-76, NCCJ; founder Save the Tarryall, Inc., 1982. Served with USNR, World War II. Mem. Direct Mail Mktg. Assn. (Gold Mail Box award 1978, Internat. Gold Carrier Pigeon award 1979), Nat. Retail Merchants Assn., Retail Advt. Conf., World Futures Soc. *To succeed man must stretch himself, his mind, his heart, his grasp. Our capabilities far exceed our accomplishments. Within each of us there is the potential for greatness if we will dig deep enough to find it. Those of us who have been blessed to have discovered success owe a special responsibility to the world around us to make it a better place for all men to live.*

SROKA, JOHN WALTER, trade association executive; b. Perth Amboy, N.J., July 24, 1946; s. John and Mary (Teliszewski) S.; m. Paula J. Devitt, Aug. 17, 1968; children: Amanda, Alexandra. BA in Psychology, Fairleigh Dickinson U., 1968, postgrad., 1968-69; postgrad. in law, Am. U., 1972-73. Asst. exec. dir. Associated Gen. Contractors of Am., Washington, 1973-87; exec. v.p. Nat. Assn. Sheet Metal and Air Conditioning Contractors, Chantilly, Va., 1987—. Sgt. U.S. Army, 1969-71. Mem. Am. Soc. Assn. Execs. Roman Catholic. Office: SMACNA 4201 Lafayette Center Dr Chantilly VA 20151-1209

STAAB, MICHAEL JOSEPH, lawyer; b. Hays, Kans., Oct. 12, 1955; s. Robert Joseph and Beatrice Agnes (Schenk) S.; m. Kathy Lee Brock, Jan. 11, 1986; children: Colton Brock, Matthew Michael. BA magna cum laude, Ft. Hays State U., 1978; JD, Drake U., 1981; LLM in Health Law, DePaul U., 1993. Bar: Idaho 1981, U.S. Dist. Ct. Idaho 1981, Utah 1986, U.S. Dist. Ct. Utah 1986, Ill. 1990, U.S. Dist. Ct. (no. dist.) Ill. 1990. Assoc. Quane,

Smith, Howard and Hull, Boise, Idaho, 1981-83, Meuleman & Miller, Boise, Idaho, 1983; pvt. practice Boise, Idaho, 1983-85; ptnr. Biele, Haslam & Hatch, Salt Lake City, 1985-89, Parsons, Behle & Latimer, Salt Lake City, 1989-90; assoc. Steinberg, Polacek & Goodman, Chgo., 1990-93, Ruff, Weldenaar and Reidy, Ltd., Chgo., 1994-96, Gardner, Carton and Douglas, Chgo., 1996—; legal advisor Ill. Pediatric Brain Injury Resource Ctr., Algonquin, Ill., 1991-96; mem. Chgo. adv. bd. Drake U., 1996—. Contbr. articles to legal publs. Bd. dirs. Winnetka Village Caucus, 1992-94, Big Bros./Big Sisters, Salt Lake City, 1985-89, Utah Head Injury Assn., Salt Lake City, 1988-90, Pediat. Brain Injury Assn., Salt Lake City, 1988-90. Mem. ABA, Ill. Bar Assn., Chgo. Bar Assn., Nat. Health Lawyers Assn., Nat. Order of Barristers, Order of Omega, K.C., Phi Kappa Phi, Phi Alpha Theta, Phi Eta Sigma. Roman Catholic. Avocations: bicycling, reading, basketball, baseball, antiques. Home: 173 De Windt Rd Winnetka IL 60093-3708 Office: 321 N Clark St Chicago IL 60610

STAAB, THOMAS EUGENE, chemist; b. Peoria, Ill., Jan. 26, 1941; s. Leo Reuben and Mary Blanche (Griffin) S.; BS in Chemistry, St. Louis U., 1963; m. Donna Marie Murnighan, May 30, 1967; children: Lynn Anne, Thomas Patrick. Rsch. and devel. chemist for elastomers Victor Products div. Dana Corp., Chgo., 1963-65, application engr. for oil seals, 1965-68, application engring. supr. for oil seals, 1968-70, chief product engr. for oil seals, 1970-72, mgr. sales and engring., Ft. Wayne, Ind., 1972-73, chief product engr. for oil seals, Chgo., 1973-75, prodn. supr., 1975-77, materials engr. for gaskets, 1977-79, mgr. oil seal engring., Lisle, Ill., 1979-82, chief devel. engr. materials, 1982-83, prodn. area mgr. 1983-84, mgr. materials devel., 1984-86, mgr. tech. svcs., 1986-90, environ. mgr., 1990-92, sen. tech. svc. engr. 1992—. Alliance chief Y Indian Guides, 1975-76; mgr./coach Little League, 1978-81. Mem. Rubber Mfrs. Assn. (past chmn. oil seal tech. com.), Soc. Automotive Engrs. (past mem. adv. bd. of sealing com.), Am. Chem. Soc. Roman Catholic. Patentee hydrodynamic shaft seal, rotary shaft seals, antistick, non-liquid absorbing gasket, reinforced core heavy duty gasket. Home: PO Box 393 Hinsdale IL 60522-0393 Office: 1945 Ohio St Lisle IL 60532-2169

STAAB, THOMAS ROBERT, textile company financial executive; b. Beaver Falls, Pa., Apr. 23, 1942; s. Henry Louis and Margaret Constance (Clarke) S.; m. Angela Maria Simon, Aug. 5, 1965; children: Thomas II, Jennifer, Thea. BBA, U. Pitts., 1964, MBA, 1965. CPA, Pa. Sr. audit mgr. Price Waterhouse & Co., Pitts., 1970-77; practice fellow Fin. Acctg. Standards Bd., Stamford, Conn., 1978-80; dir. corp. acctg. and taxes Fieldcrest Cannon Inc., Eden, N.C., 1981-85, asst. contr., 1985-86, contr., 1986-92, v.p. fin., 1992-93; CFO, 1994—; mem. adv. bd. Arkwright Mut. Ins. Co. Served to lt. USN, 1966-70. Mem. Am. Inst. CPA's, Pa. Inst. CPA's, N.C. Textile Mfrs. Assn., Am. Textile Mfrs. Inst. Republican. Roman Catholic. Avocation: farming. Home: 3726 Nc # 65 Reidsville NC 27320 Office: Fieldcrest Cannon Inc 326 E Stadium Dr Eden NC 27288-3523

STAAR, RICHARD FELIX, political scientist; b. Warsaw, Poland, Jan. 10, 1923; s. Alfred and Agnes (Gradalska) S.; m. Jadwiga Maria Ochota, Mar. 28, 1950; children: Monica, Christina. B.A., Dickinson Coll., 1948; M.A. (Univ. fellow), Yale, 1949; Ph.D., U. Mich., 1954. Research analyst U.S. Dept. State, Washington, 1951-54; prof. polit. sci. Ark. State Coll., Jonesboro, 1957-58; lectr. overseas program U. Md., Munich, Germany, 1958-59; assoc. prof. to prof., chmn. dept. polit. sci. Emory U., 1959-69; sr. fellow Hoover Instn. on War, Revolution and Peace at Stanford, 1969—, prin. assoc. dir., 1969-81, dir. internat. studies program, 1975-81, 85-91; U.S. ambassador to Mut. and Balanced Force Reductions Negotiations, Vienna, 1981-83; Nimitz chair Naval War Coll., 1963-64; prof. polit. affairs Nat. War Coll., 1967-69; cons. Office Sec. Def., 1969-73; adj. prof. USMC Command and Staff Coll., 1971-81; sr. advisor to Comdg. Officer Politico-Mil. Affairs USNR, Treasure Island, Calif., 1975-81; disting. vis. prof. nat. security affairs Naval Postgrad. Sch., 1979; cons. U.S. ACDA, 1983-86, Sandia Nat. Labs., 1991—; mem. bd. visitors Def. Language Inst., 1988—. Author: Poland, 1944-62, The Sovietization of a Captive People, 1962, reprinted, 1975, Communist Regimes in Eastern Europe, 5th edit., 1988, USSR Foreign Policies After Detente, 1985, rev. edit., 1987, Foreign Policies of the Soviet Union, 1991, The New Military in Russia, 1996; co-author: Soviet Military Policies Since World War II, 1986; contbg. author and editor: Aspects of Modern Communism, 1968; editor: Yearbook on International Communist Affairs, 1969-91, Arms Control: Myth Versus Reality, 1984, Public Diplomacy: USA Versus USSR, 1986, Future Information Revolution in the USSR, 1988, United States - East European Relations in the 1990's, 1989, East-Central Europe and the USSR, 1991, Transition to Democracy in Poland, 1993; mem. editl. bd. Current History, Orbis, Strategic Rev., Mediterranean Quar.; contbr. articles to profl. jours. Asst. dist. commr. Quapaw Area council Boy Scouts Am., 1954-57; active Profs. for Goldwater, 1964; mem. Reagan for Pres. Com., 1980; dir. for nat. security affairs Office of Pres.-Elect, 1980-81; mem. Academicians for Reagan, 1984. Served to col. USMCR, 1960-83. Decorated Legion of Merit. Mem. Am. Polit. Sci. Assn., Internat. Studies Assn., Am. Assn. Advancement Slavic Studies, Phi Beta Kappa, Kappa Sigma. Republican. Methodist. Home: 36 Peter Coutts Cir Stanford CA 94305-2503 Office: Hoover Instn Stanford CA 94305-6010

STAATS, DEAN ROY, retired reinsurance executive; b. Somerville, N.J., Sept. 18, 1924; s. Roy Theodore and Mabel Ellen (Rhodes) S.; m. Marilyn Ann Hockenbury, 1947 (div. 1956; 1 child, Barry Clinton; m. Marilyn Lee Truitt, Dec. 16, 1961. B.Sc., Brown U., 1946, M.A., 1948. Asst. actuary N.Am. Reassurance Co., N.Y.C., 1959-67, data processing officer, 1967-69, v.p., actuary, 1969-71, sr. v.p., 1971-84, exec. v.p., 1984-86; pres., dir. NARe Life Mgmt. Co., N.Y.C., 1985-86; rep. Life Ins. Guaranty Corp, 1977-86; U.S. mgr. Can. Reassurance Co., 1984-86; cons. actuary, 1986-89. Served to lt. (j.g.), USN, 1943-46, PTO. Fellow Soc. Actuaries; mem. Am. Acad. Actuaries N.Y. Jr. Actuaries Club (pres. 1960-61), Soc. Actuaries (reins. adminstrn. com. 1984-85). Republican. Clubs: Anchor and Saber (pres. 1959-60). Avocations: art collectibles; tennis; gardening; travel. Home and Office: 234 Hansell Rd Newtown Square PA 19073-2509

STAATS, ELMER BOYD, foundation executive, former government official; b. Richfield, Kans., June 6, 1914; s. Wesley F. and Maude (Goodall) S.; m. Margaret S. Rich, Sept. 14, 1940; children: David Rich, Deborah Rich Staats Sanders, Catharine Rich Staats Taubman. AB, McPherson (Kans.) Coll., 1935, LLD (hon.), 1966; MA, U. Kans., 1936; PhD, U. Minn., 1939; D. in Pub. Service (hon.), George Washington U., 1971; D. in Adminstrn. (hon.), U. S.D., 1973; LLD (hon.), Duke U., 1975, Nova U., 1976, U. Pa., 1981, Lycoming Coll., 1982; LHD (hon.), Ohio State U., 1982. Research asst. Kans. Legis. Council, 1936; teaching asst. U. Minn., 1936-38; staff Pub. Adminstrn. Service, Chgo., 1937-38; staff mem. U.S. Bur. Budget, Exec. Office Pres., 1939-47, asst. to dir., 1947, asst. dir. charge legis. reference, 1947-49, exec. asst. dir., 1949-50, dep. dir., 1950-53, 58-66; comptroller gen. U.S. Washington, 1966-81; pres. Harry S. Truman Scholarship Found., 1981-84, chmn., 1984—; bd. dirs. rsch. dir. Marshall Field & Co., Chgo., 1953; exec. dir. ops. coord. bd., Nat. Security Coun., 1953-58; professorial lectr. pub. adminstrn. George Washington U., 1944-49; mem. bd. visitors Nat. Def. U., 1981-90; mem. vis. com. John F. Kennedy Sch. Govt., Harvard U., 1974-80, Grad. Sch. Mgmt., UCLA, 1976—; mem. Com. on Pub. Policy Studies U. Chgo., 1976—; trustee Nat. Inst. Pub. Affairs, 1969-77; mem. Conf. Bd., 1966; mem. dir.'s adv. coun. Met. Life Ins. Co., 1985-94, emeritus mem., 1994—; dir. Computer Data Systems, Inc., 1981—; bd. advisors Alexander Proudfoot & Co., 1981-85; mem. pub. rev. bd. Arthur Andersen & Co., 1981-91; bd. dirs. Air Products and Chems., 1981-85, Met. Life Ins. Co., 1981-85, Nat. Intergroup Inc. (formerly Nat. Steel Corp.), 1981-86; chmn. congl. panel on social security orgn., 1983-84; mem. nat. commn. on pub. svc., 1987-90; mem. commn. to rev. honor code of West Point U.S. Mil. Acad., 1988-89; mem. Govt. Acctg. Standards Bd., 1984-90; chmn. Fed. Acctg. Standards Adv. Bd., 1991—. Author: Personnel Standards in the Social Security Program, 1939; contbr. to: Am. Polit. Sci. Rev. Trustee Am. U., 1969-80; trustee McPherson Coll., 1969-79, mem. bd. trustees and research and policy com., com. for econ. devel., 1981—; bd. govs. Internat. Orgn. of Supreme Audit Instns., 1969-80; trustee Kerr Found., 1981—; bd. dirs. George C. Marshall Found., 1984—. Recipient Rockefeller Pub. Service award, 1961, Alumni achievement award U. Minn., 1964, Disting. Service citation U. Kans., 1966, Warner D. Stockberger Achievement award, 1973, Abraham O. Smoot Pub. Service award Brigham Young U., 1975, Person of Yr. award Washington chpt. Inst. Internal Auditors, 1975, Thurston award Inst. Internal Auditors, 1988, medal of honor Am. Inst. CPAs, 1980, Engr. of Yr. award San Fernando Valley Engrs. Council, 1980, Presdl. Citizens medal, 1981, Hubert Humphrey medal, 1981, Pub. Service Achievement award Common Cause, 1981; fed. exec. award Evaluation Research Soc., 1980; named to Acctg. Hall of Fame, 1981; fellow Brookings Instn., 1938-39. Mem. Nat. Acad. Pub. Adminstrn., Assn. Govt. Accountants, Am. Acad. Polit. and Social Sci. (dir. 1966—), Am. Soc. Public Adminstrn. (pres. Washington 1948-49, nat. coun. 1958-65, nat. pres. 1961-62), Am. Mgmt. Assns. (gen. mgmt. coun. 1966-85, trustee 1981-85), Cosmos Club (Washington), Chevy Chase (Md.), Phi Beta Kappa, Pi Sigma Alpha, Beta Gamma Sigma, Alpha Kappa Psi. Methodist. Office: Harry S Truman Scholarship Found 712 Jackson Pl NW Washington DC 20006-4901*

STAATS, THOMAS ELWYN, neuropsychologist; b. Marietta, Ohio; s. Percy Anderson and Julia (Bourmorck) S.; m. Debra R.; children: Lauren Malu, Kara Kristyn, Stacy Rhnea, Ronald Derek. B.A. cum laude, Emory U., 1970; M.A., U. Ala., 1972, Ph.D., 1974; postgrad. U. Tex., Tyler, 1992. Diplomate Am. Bd. Profl. Disability Cons.; lic. psychologist. Dir., chief psychologist Caddo Parish Diagnostic Ctr., Shreveport, La., 1974-81; exec. dir. Doctors Psychol. Ctr., Shreveport, 1979-91, Comprehensive Assessments, 1991—; cons. to Charter Forest Hosp., Shreveport Impairment and Disability Evaluation Ctr.; neuropsychol. cons. La. State U. Med. Ctr.; clin. assoc. prof. psychology La. State U., Shreveport, 1977—, clin. assoc. prof. psychiatry Sch. Medicine, 1980—; mem. faculty Am. Acad. Disability Evaluating Physicians. Author: Manual For the Stress Vector Analysis Test Series, 1983, The Doctors Guide to Instant Stress Relief, 1987; Stress Management and Relaxation Training System Handbook. Contbr. articles to profl. jours. and popular mags. Mem. Gov's. Com. of 1000, La., 1979. U. Ala. Grad. Research Council fellow, 1974; recipient AADEP award 1991. Fellow Am. Inst. Stress; mem. APA, Nat. Acad. Neuropsychology. Republican, Nat. Register of Health Svc. Providers in Psychology. Episcopalian. Avocations: scuba diving, gun collecting, camping, boating, stress, malingering and chronic pain research. Home: 10816 Sunrise Pointe Shreveport LA 71106 Office: Comprehensive Assessments Inc 1532 Irving Pl Shreveport LA 71101-4604

STABA, EMIL JOHN, pharmacognosy and medicinal chemistry educator; b. N.Y.C., May 16, 1928; s. Frank and Marianna T. (Mack) P.; m. Joyce Elizabeth Ellert, June 19, 1954; children—Marianna, Joanna, Sarah Jane, John, Mark. B.S. cum laude, St. John's U., 1952; M.S., Duquesne U., 1954; Ph.D., U. Conn., 1957. Asst. prof. U. Nebr., 1957-60, prof., chmn. dept., 1968; prof. dept. pharmacognosy U. Minn., 1968—; interim dir. R&D Tom's of Main, Kennebunk, 1996—; cons. econs. plants and plant tissue culture U.S. Army Q.M.C.; cons. on drug plants and plant tissue culture NASA; cons. N.C.I. at NIH on anti-cancer natural product prodn., 1991-92; cons. Govt. of Korea, food and pharm. industry cons. NSF-Egyptian Acad. Sci. Rsch. Tech., 1984—; internat. vis. prof. Dalhousie U., 1983; cons. on Indonesia biotech. devel. World Bank-Midwestern Univs. Consortium for Internat. Activities, 1985-90, Thailand, 1989; mem. natural products revision com. U.S. Pharmacopeia, 1980—, chair subcom. natural products, 1995-2000; mem. adv. coun. on life scis. NASA, 1984-87. Mem. editorial bd.: Jour. Plant Cell, Tissue and Organ Culture, 1980-86, plant cellular and developmental biology sect. of In Vitro, 1988—. Served with USNR, 1945-46, PTO. Sr. fgn. fellow NSF, Poland, 1969; Fulbright fellow, Germany, 1970; Coun. Sci. and Indsl. Rsch.-NSF fellow, India, 1973, Pakistani Coun. Sci. and Indsl. Rsch.-NSF fellow, Pakistan, 1978; fellow U.K. Sci. Engring. Rsch. Coun., 1989. Fellow AAAS; mem. Am. Soc. Pharmacognosy (pres. 1971-72), Am. Assn. Colls. Pharmacy (chmn. tchrs. sect. 1972-73, dir. 1976-77), Tissue Culture Assn. (pres. plant sect. 1972-74), Am. Pharm. Assn. and Acad. (chmn. pharmacognosy and nat. products 1977), Soc. Econ. Botany, Am. Soc. Pharmacognosy. Home: 2840 Stinson Blvd Minneapolis MN 55418-3127 Office: U Minn Coll Pharmacy Unit F-9106 Minneapolis MN 55455

STABENOW, DEBORAH ANN, congresswoman; b. Gladwin, Mich., Apr. 29, 1950; d. Robert Lee and Anna Merle (Hallmark) Greer; children: Todd Dennis, Michelle Deborah. BS magna cum laude, Mich. State U., 1972, MSW magna cum laude, 1975. With spl. svcs. Lansing (Mich.) Sch. Dist., 1972-73; county commr. Ingham County, Mason, Mich., 1975-78; state rep. State of Mich., Lansing, 1979—; mem. 105th Congress from 8th Michdist. Founder Ingham County Women's Commn.; co-founder Council Against Domestic Assault; mem. Dem. Bus. and Profl. Club, Mich. Dem. Women's Polit. Caucus, Grance United Meth. Ch. (past lay leader, chair Social Concerns Task Force, Sunday Sch. music tchr., Lansing Boys' Club, profl. adv. com. Lansing Parents Without Ptnrs., adv. com. Ctr. Handicapped Affairs, Mich. Council Family and Divorce Mediation Adv. Bd., Nat. Council Children's Rights, Big Bros./Big Sisters Greater Lansing Adv. Bd., Mich. Child Study Assn. Bd. Advisors, Mich. Women's Campaign Fund. Recipient Service to Children award Council for Prevention of Child Abuse and Neglect, 1983, Disting. Service to Mich. Families award Mich. Council Family Relations, 1983, Outstanding Leadership award Nat. Council Community Mental Health Ctrs., 1983, Snyder-Kok award Mental Health Assn. Mich., Awareness Leader of Yr. award Awareness Communications Team Developmentally Disabled, 1984, Communicator of Yr. award Woman in Communications, 1984, Lawmaker of Yr. award Nat. Child Support Enforcement Assn., 1985, Disting. Service award Lansing Jaycees, 1985, Disting. Service in Govt. award Retarded Citizens of Mich., 1986; named One of Ten Outstanding Young Ams. Jaycees, 1986. Mem. NAACP, Lansing Regional C. of C., Delta Kappa Gamma. Home: 2709 S Deerfield Ave Lansing MI 48911-1783 Office: US House Of Reprs 1516 Longworth Washington DC 20515-2208

STABILE, BENEDICT LOUIS, retired academic administrator, retired coast guard officer; b. Bklyn., Dec. 13, 1927; s. Domenic and Vita (Grillo) S.; m. Barbara Adele Thompson, June 10, 1951; children: Janet T., Bennett R., Gale V., Roderick T. BS, USCG Acad., 1950; naval engring. degree, MIT, 1956. Commd. USCG, 1950, advanced through grades to vice admiral; served aboard USCG cutters Eastwind, Unimak, Castle Rock, Reliance & Mellon; comdg. officer USCG Yard, Curtis Bay, Md., 1975-77; chief engr. USCG, Washington, 1977-79; dist. comdr. USCG (7th Dist.), Miami, Fla., 1979-82; vice comdt. USCG, Washington, 1982-86; ret. USCG, 1986; coll. pres. Webb Inst. Naval Architecture, Glen Cove, N.Y., 1986-90, ret., 1990. Decorated Meritorious Service medal (3), D.S.M. (2), Legion of Merit, Order of Merit of Italian Republic. Mem. Am. Soc. Naval Engrs., Soc. Naval Architects and Marine Engrs.

STABILE, BRUCE EDWARD, surgeon; b. Monterey Park, Calif., Apr. 14, 1944; s. Edward Emilio and Angela (Cramandozzi) S.; m. Caroline Graston, Sept. 18, 1967; children: Jessica, Drew. BA, UCLA, 1966; MD, U. Calif., San Francisco, 1970. Diplomate Am. Bd. Surgery. From asst. prof. to assoc. prof. UCLA Sch. Medicine, 1977-85; from assoc. prof. to prof. surgery U. Calif. San Diego Sch. Medicine, 1985-93; prof. surgery UCLA Sch. Medicine, 1993—; chmn. dept. surgery Harbor-UCLA Med. Ctr., Torrance, 1993—; med. expert Med. Bd. Calif., 1980—. Fellow Am. Coll. Surgeons, Am. Surg. Assn.; mem. Soc. Univ. Surgeons, Assn. Acad. Surgery, Am. Gastroenterol. Soc., San Diego Soc. Gen. Surgeons (pres. 1992-93). Office: Harbor-UCLA Med Ctr 1000 W Carson St Torrance CA 90502-2004

STABLER, DONALD BILLMAN, business executive; b. Williamsport, Pa., Dec. 23, 1908; s. George William and Etta Mae (Billman) S.; m. Dorothy Louise Witwer, Aug. 10, 1952; 1 dau., Beverly Anne. B.S., Lehigh U., 1930, M.S., 1932, LL.D., 1974; LL.D., Dickinson Law Sch., 1981; LHD, Susquehanna Univ., 1995. Owner Donald B. Stabler (Contractor), Harrisburg, Pa., 1940-55; chmn. bd., chief exec. officer Stabler Cos. Inc., 1955-91, Stabler Constrn. Co., 1955-91, Protection Services Inc., 1955—, State Aggregates Inc., DBS Transit, Inc., 1964—, Stabler Cos. Inc., 1976—, Stabler Devel. Co., Harrisburg, Pa., 1983—, Stabler Land Co., Harrisburg, Pa., 1984—, Ea. Industries, Inc., Elco-Hausman Constrn. Corp., 1976—, The Center Valley (Pa.) Club Inc., 1992—, Work Area Protection Corp., St. Charles, Ill., 1986—, Precision Solar Controls Inc., Garland, Tex., 1990—; bd. dirs. Millers Mut. Ins. Co., Harrisburg., Road Info. Program, Washington, pres., 1970-74, chmn. bd., 1975-78, chmn. emeritus, 1979—. Bd. dirs. Miami Heart Rsch. Inst.; trustee Lehigh U. Recipient silver hard hat award Constrn. Writers Assn., 1973, Humanitarian award Lions, 1973, Nat. Automobiler Dealers award, 1978, Man & Boy award Boys' Club, 1984, Man of Yr. March of Dimes, 1994, real estate award, 1994, rebuilding Am. award CIT, 1985, master entrepreneur of yr. award Cen. Pa. 1994; named man of yr. Pa. Hwy. Info. Assn., 1992. Mem. Am. Rd. and Transp. Builders Assn. (dir., ARBA award 1974, Nello L. Teer, Jr. award 1994), Associated Pa. Constructors (dir., adv. bd., pres. 1949-50), Nat. Asphalt Pavement Assn., Pa. Asphalt Pavement Assn., U.S. C. of C., Pa. C. of C., Harrisburg C. of C. (adm. 1960), Am. Soc. Hwy. Engrs. (Industry Man of Year 1975), Harrisburg Builders Exchange, Nat. Soc. Profl. Engrs., Pa. Soc. Profl. Engrs. (Engr. of Yr. Harrisburg chpt. 1981), Com. of 100 Miami Beach (dir.), Pa. Soc. N.Y., Lehigh U. Alumni Assn. (pres. 1965-66, L-in-Life award 1972), Navy League, Chi Epsilon, Pi Delta Epsilon. Presbyterian. Clubs: Tall Cedars; Surf (Miami Beach) (pres. 1974-76, chmn. bd. of govs. 1976-78, bd. govs. 1974—); Bal Harbour (Miami); Harrisburg Country (Harrisburg); Saucon Valley Country (Bethlehem, Pa.). Lodges: Masons, Shriners, Jesters, Elks, Rotary. Home: Stray Winds Farm 4001 Mcintosh Rd Harrisburg PA 17112-1927 also: 236 Bal Bay Rd Bal Harbour FL 33154 Office: 635 Lucknow Rd Harrisburg PA 17110-1635

STABLER, LEWIS VASTINE, JR., lawyer; b. Greenville, Ala., Nov. 5, 1936; s. Lewis Vastine and Dorothy Daisy Stabler; m. Monteray Scott, Sept. 5, 1958; children: Dorothy Monteray Scott, Andrew Vastine, Monteray Scott Smith, Margaret Langston. BA, Vanderbilt U., 1958; JD with distinction, U. Mich., 1961. Bar: Ala. 1961. Assoc. firm Cabaniss & Johnston, Birmingham, Ala., 1961-67; assoc. prof. law U. Ala., 1967-70; ptnr. Cabaniss, Johnston, Gardner, Dumas & O'Neal (and predecessor firms), Birmingham, 1970-91, Walston, Stabler, Wells, Anderson and Bains, Birmingham, 1991-97, L. Vastine Stabler Attorney at Law, Birmingham, 1997—; Mem. com. of 100 Candler Sch. Theology, Emory U. Bd. editors: Mich. Law Rev, 1960-61. Fellow Am. Bar Found.; mem. Am. Law Inst., Ala. Law Inst. (mem. council, dir. 1968-70), ABA, Ala. Bar Assn., Birmingham Bar Assn., Am. Judicature Soc., Am. Assn. Railroad Trial Counsel, Order of Coif. Methodist (cert. lay speaker). Clubs: Country of Birmingham, Rotary. Home: 3538 Victoria Rd Birmingham AL 35223-1404 Office: Attorney at Law PO Box 53-1161 Birmingham AL 35253-1161

STABLER, ROSE BURCH, meteorologist; b. Mobile, Ala., July 27, 1958; d. Clyde Addison and Kazuko (Ikegami) B.; m. Ken Stabler, Dec. 25, 1945; children: Alexa, Marissa. Student, West Point, 1976; BS, U. South Ala., 1980, MBA, 1984; cert. broadcast meteorology, Miss. State U., 1995; postgrad., Portland State U. Mktg. rep. IBM, Mobile, 1980-81; grad. rsch. asst. U. South Ala., Mobile, 1982-84; weathercaster, reporter Sta. WALA-TV, Mobile and Pensacola, Fla., 1987-90; talk show host Sta. WPMI-TV, Mobile and Pensacola, 1990-96; meteorologist, weathercaster Sta. WDSU-TV, New Orleans, 1993—. Appeared in movies including French Silk, Future Force, also numerous commls.; spokesmodel for Casino Rouge. Named Miss Ala., Miss. USA Pageant, 1979. Mem. AFTRA, Nat. Weather Assn. (broadcast seal of approval), Am. Meteorological Assn. Office: Sta WDSU-TV 520 Royal St New Orleans LA 70130-2114

STACEY, WESTON MONROE, JR., nuclear engineer, educator; b. Birmingham, Ala., July 23, 1937; s. Weston Monroe and Dorothy (Toole) S.; m. Penny Smith; children: Helen Lee, Weston Monroe III, Lucia Katherine. BS in Physics, Ga. Inst. Tech., 1959, MS in Nuclear Sci., 1963; PhD in Nuclear Engring., MIT, 1966. Nuclear engr. Knolls Atomic Power Lab., Schenectady, N.Y., 1962-64, 66-69, Argonne Nat. Lab., Chgo., 1969-77; Callaway Regents prof. Ga. Inst. Tech., Atlanta, 1977—. Author 5 books; contbr. more than 170 articles to profl. jours. Recipient Cert. Appreciation Dept. Energy, Disting. Assoc. award Dept. Energy, 1990. Fellow Am. Phys. Soc., Am. Nuclear Soc. (bd. dirs. 1974-77, Outstanding Achievement award 1981, 96); mem. AAAS, Am. Soc. Engr. Educators. Office: Ga Inst Tech Nuclear Engring Dept 0225 Atlanta GA 30332

STACHOWSKI, MICHAEL JOSEPH, lawyer, consultant; b. Buffalo, Feb. 27, 1947; s. Stanley Joseph and Pearl (Wojcik) S.; children: Lisa Ann, Evan Michael, Crystal Lee; m. Deborah Ann Jakubczak, Oct. 19, 1979. BA, Canisius Coll., 1970; JD, SUNY-Buffalo, 1973; cert. Hague Acad. Internat. Law, Netherlands, 1976. Bar: N.Y. 1974, U.S. Dist. Ct. (we. dist.) N.Y. 1974, U.S. Ct. Appeals (2d cir.) 1974. Atty. Sportservice, Inc., Buffalo, 1973-74; assoc. Siegel & McGee, Buffalo, 1974-75; confidential clk. 8th dist. N.Y. Supreme Ct., Buffalo, 1975-77; rsch. counsel N.Y. State Assembly, Albany, 1977-80; sole practice, Buffalo, 1976-86, dep. atty. Town of Cheektowaga, N.Y., 1986—, spl. prosecutor; Michael J. Stachowski P.C., 1987—. Campaign mgr. various jud. candidates, Buffalo, 1977—; fund raiser Erie County Democrats, Buffalo, 1979—, vice chmn. 1988-97, com.; bd. dirs. Buffalo Columbus Hosp., 1988—, sec., 1991-92, treas., 1993-95, chmn. merger com. with Buffalo Gen.; mem. N.Y. State Dem. Com., 1988—. Fellow Am. Acad. Matrimonial Lawyers; mem. N.Y. State Bar Assn., Erie County Bar Assn., East Clinton Profl. Businessmen's Assn. (v.p. 1976—, pres. 1985). Roman Catholic. Home: 12 Beaverbrook Ct Depew NY 14043-4242 Office: 2025 Clinton St Buffalo NY 14206-3311

STACHOWSKI, WILLIAM T., state senator; b. Buffalo, Feb. 14, 1949; s. Stanley J. and Pearl (Wojcik) S. BA in Polit. Sci., Coll. Holy Cross, 1972. Legislator Erie County Legislature, Buffalo, 1974-81; senator N.Y. State Legislature, Albany, 1981—; mem. U.S. Rte. 19 Assn., Western N.Y., 1982—, U.S. Rte. 62 Assn., Western N.Y., 1985—, City of Buffalo Auditorium Task Force. Recipient Friend of Law Enforcement award N.Y. State Sheriffs, 1990, Fellow Medal Hilbert Coll., 1993. Mem. Erie County Dem. Party, 1967—. Roman Catholic. Avocations: sports. Home: 2030 Clinton St Buffalo NY 14206-3312 Office: NY State Senate State Capital Albany NY 12247

STACK, EDWARD WILLIAM, business management and foundation executive; b. Rockville Centre, N.Y., Feb. 1, 1935; s. Edward Henry and Helen Margaret (Leitner) S.; m. Christina Carol Hunt, Aug. 19, 1967; children: Amy Alison, Kimberly Anne, Suzanne Gail. BBA, Pace U., 1956; LLD (hon.), Hartwick Coll., 1982; LHD (hon.), Pace U., 1991, L.I. U., 1994. Sec., dir. Clark Estates, Inc., fin. and bus. mgmt., N.Y.C., 1956-90, pres., bd. dirs., 1990—; v.p., dir. Leatherstocking Corp., hotels and real estate, Cooperstown, N.Y., 1961-92, pres., bd. dirs., 1992—; sec.-treas., dir. The New Republic, Inc., mag., Washington, 1974—; regional adv. bd. Chase Banking Corp., N.Y.C., 1993—. Sec., trustee N.Y. State Hist. Assn., Cooperstown, 1961—; vice chmn., trustee Mary Imogene Bassett Hosp., 1961—; sec. Nat. Baseball Hall of Fame and Mus., Inc., Cooperstown, 1961-77, pres., chmn., 1977-93, chmn., 1993—; v.p., bd. dirs. Farmers' Mus., Inc., Cooperstown, 1964—; sec. Clark Found., N.Y.C., 1963-90, v.p., bd. dirs. 1990—; v.p., bd. dirs. Scriven Found., N.Y.C., 1976—; trustee Hartwick Coll., Oneonta, N.Y.; trustee, treas. Bethany Deaconess Soc., Bklyn.; bd. dirs. United Meth. City Soc. of Meth. Ch., N.Y.C.; adv. bds. Salvation Army Nassau County and Greater N.Y. Mem. Downtown Assn. (N.Y.C.), Mohican Club (Cooperstown, N.Y.). Republican. Home: 25 Waverly St Glen Head NY 11545-1004 Office: 30 Wall St New York NY 10005-2201

STACK, GEOFFREY LAWRENCE, real estate developer; b. Trinidad, British West Indies, Sept. 16, 1943; s. Gerald Francis and V. Louise (Bell) S.; m. Victoria Hammack, 1970 (div. 1986); 1 child, Kathryn; m. Nancy J. Haarer, Apr. 19, 1987; children: Alexandra, Natalie. BA, Georgetown U., 1965; MBA, U. Pa., 1972. Dir. acquisitions J.H. Snyder Co., L.A., 1972-75; from project mgr. to exec. v.p. Richards West, Newport Beach, Calif., 1975-77; pres. Regis Homes Corp., Newport Beach, 1977-93; mng. dir. Sares-Regis Group, Irvine, Calif., 1993—; bd. dirs. Arral & Ptnrs., Hong Kong, Calif. Housing Coun., Sacramento. Mem. adv. bd. Coro So. Calif., Santa Ana, 1991—; bd. regents Franciscan Sch. of Theology, Berkeley, Calif., 1991—; bd. advisors Grad. Sch. Bus., U. Calif., Irvine, 1992; bd. dirs. Nat. Multihousing Coun., 1987—. Capt. USMC, 1967-70. Decorated 2 Bronze Stars, 20 Air medals, Navy Commendation medal, Purple Heart. Mem. Young Pres. Orgn., Big Canyon Country Club, Pacific Club, Ctr. Club. Democrat. Roman Catholic. Office: Sares Regis Group 18802 Bardeen Ave Irvine CA 92612-1521

STACK, GEORGE JOSEPH, philosophy educator; b. N.Y.C.; s. George Francis and Elizabeth (Sullivan) S.; m. Claire Avena (dec.); children: Diane Joan, Christopher George. B.A., Pace U., 1960; M.A., Pa. State U., 1962, Ph.D., 1964. Instr. humanities Pa. State U., 1962-63; instr. philosophy L.I. U., 1963-64, asst. prof., 1964-67; asst. prof. SUNY, Brockport, 1967-68, asso. prof., 1968-70, prof., chmn., 1970-77, prof., 1977-95, prof. emeritus, 1995—, also advisor Center for Philosophic Exchange, 1970-82; cons. to Choice. Author: Berkeley's Analysis of Perception, 1970, 2d edit., 1992, On Kierkegaard: Philosophical Fragments, 1976, Kierkegaard's Existential Ethics,

1977, 2d edit., 1992, Japanese transl., 1985, Sartre's Philosophy of Social Existence, 1978, reprinted 1992, Lange and Nietzsche, 1983; contbg. author: Nietzsche and Modern German Thought, 1991, Nietzsche and Emerson, 1992, Nietzsche: Man, Knowledge, Will to Power, 1994; editorial advisor: Folia Humanistica, Filosofia Oggi; contbr. over 180 philos. articles to profl. jours. Home: PO Box 92 Grapevine TX 76099

STACK, J. WILLIAM, JR., management consultant; b. Lansing, Mich., July 13, 1918; s. Joseph William and Helen (Dodge) S.; m. Wolcott Rorick, Sept. 25, 1948; children: Christopher D., Nathan S., Joseph W., David R., Peter S. B.A., Yale U., 1940. With Gen. Motors Corp, 1945-57; dir. mktg. Gen. Motors Corp (AC Electronics div.), 1955-57; v.p. Kurth Malting Co., Milw., 1957-59; gen. sales mgr. Massey Ferguson, Inc., Toronto, Can., 1960-62; pres., founder Stancor Ltd., Toronto, 1963-68; pres. William Stack Assocs. Inc., N.Y.C., 1968—; mem. Navy and Marine Corps Acquisition Rev. Com., 1974-75. Active Rep. Town Com. Lt. comdr. USNR, 1940-45. Mem. Yale Club of N.Y.C., New Canaan Country Club. Episcopalian. Home: 31 Lakeview Ave New Canaan CT 06840-5947 Office: Stack Assocs 31 Lakeview Ave New Canaan CT 06840-5947 *Success is measured by what you give back; not what you take. To help one person, to advance one worthy cause is the mark of total achievement.*

STACK, JOHN WALLACE, lawyer; b. Chgo., May 30, 1937; s. Wallace and Irma Evelyn (Anderson) S.; divorced; children: James Randolph, Linnea Claire, Theodore. BBA, U. Wis., 1960; JD, U. Calif., Berkeley, 1963. Bar: Ill. 1963, D.C. 1972, U.S. Ct. Appeals (7th cir.) 1963, U.S. Supreme Ct. 1972. Assoc. Pattishall, McAuliffe & Hofstetter, Chgo., 1963-64; assoc. Winston & Strawn, Chgo., 1964-70, ptnr., 1970—. Contbg. editor U. Calif. Law Rev., 1963. Mem. ABA (antitrust and corp., banking and bus. law sects.), W Club of U. Wis. (Madison), Order of Coif, Phi Delta Phi, Beta Gamma Sigma. Republican. Lutheran. Avocations: sports, gardening, reading. Home: 2906 Lincoln St Evanston IL 60201-2047 Office: Winston & Strawn 35 W Wacker Dr Chicago IL 60601-1614

STACK, MAURICE DANIEL, retired insurance company executive; b. N.Y.C., Dec. 15, 1917; s. Maurice E. and Margaret (Brooks) S.; m. Catherine T. O'Connor, Nov. 25, 1943; children: Mary Jane, Eileen, Peter, Clare. Student, U. Notre Dame, 1935-36; BBA, Manhattan Coll., 1939; MBA, Harvard, 1941. Investment analyst Carnegie Corp., N.Y.C., 1946-48; adminstrv. asst. Tchrs. Ins. & Annuity Assn., 1948-49; investment analyst First Nat. Bank N.Y., 1949-54; fin. sec. Atlantic Mut. Ins. Co., N.Y.C., 1954-56; v.p. Atlantic Mut. Ins. Co., 1957-60, fin. v.p., trustee, 1961-66, chmn. fin. com., 1966-83; trustee emeritus Atlantic Mutual Ins. Co. Trustee emeritus, adviser St. Vincent's Hosp.; trustee emeritus YWCA. Served to maj. C.E., AUS, 1941-46. Mem. Soc. for Propagation of the Faith (dir.), K.M. Club (N.Y.C.), Harvard Club (N.Y.C.). Home: 85 Lynbrook Ave Point Lookout NY 11569-0095

STACK, MAY ELIZABETH, library director; b. Jackson, Miss., Nov. 10, 1940; d. James William and Irene Thelma (Baldwin) Garrett; m. Richard Gardiner, Apr. 15, 1962; children: Elinor, Harley David. BS, Miss. State Coll. for Women, 1962; MBA, Western New Eng. Coll., 1981; MLS, So. Conn. State U., 1989. Clk. Western New Eng. Coll., Springfield, Mass., 1965-66; acquisitions staff Western New Eng. Coll., Springfield, 1966-72, cataloger, 1972-84, asst. dir., 1984-89, acting dir., 1989-90, dir., 1990—; chair Ctrl./Western Mass. Automated Resource Sharing Collection Devel. Com., Paxton, Mass., 1993-95, exec. bd., 1993-96. mem. East Longmeadow (Mass.) Hist. Soc., 1989-92. Mem. ALA, Mass. Libr. Assn., Assn. Coll. and Rsch. Librs., Libr. and Mgmt. Assn., Libr. Info. and Technology Assn. Methodist. Avocations: horseback riding, show dogs. Office: Western New Eng Coll D'Amour Libr 1215 Wilbraham Rd Springfield MA 01119-2612

STACK, PAUL FRANCIS, lawyer; b. Chgo., July 21, 1946; s. Frank Louis and Dorothy Louise Stack; m. Nea Waterman, July 8, 1972; children: Nea Elizabeth, Sera Waterman. BS, U. Ariz., 1968; JD, Georgetown U., 1971. Bar: Ill. 1971, U.S. Ct. Claims 1975, U.S. Tax Ct. 1974, U.S. Ct. Internat. Trade 1977, U.S. Supreme Ct. 1975. Law clk., U.S. Dist. Ct., Chgo., 1971-72; Asst. U.S. Atty. No. Dist. Ill., Chgo., 1972-75; mng. dir. Stack & Filpi, Chgo., 1976—. Bd. dirs. Riverside (Ill.) Pub. Libr., 1977-83, Suburban Libr. Sys., Burr Ridge, Ill., 1979-82; mem. Mayor's ad hoc adv. com. on Ctrl. Libr., Chgo., Ill., 1987-88; mem. bd. edn. Twp. H.S. Dist. 208, Riverside, Ill., 1989-97; pres. Village of Riverside, 1997—. Mem. Chgo. Zool. Soc. (gov. 1980, planned giving adv. com. 1996—), Chgo. Bar Assn., Union League Club of Chgo. (bd. dirs. 1986-89). Presbyterian. Home: 238 N Delaplaine Rd Riverside IL 60546-2035 Office: 140 S Dearborn St Ste 411 Chicago IL 60603-5202

STACK, ROBERT LANGFORD, actor; b. Los Angeles, Jan. 13, 1919; s. James Langford and Elizabeth (Wood) S.; m. Rosemarie Bowe, Jan. 23, 1956; children: Elizabeth Langford, Charles Robert. Student, U. So. Calif., 1937-38. Pres. St. Pierre Prodns., Los Angeles, 1959—. Actor, co-producer: (TV series) The Untouchables, 1959-63 (2 nominations, 1 Emmy award); actor: The Name of the Game, 1968-71, Most Wanted, 1976-77, Strike Force, 1982-83, Unsolved Mysteries, 1986—; actor: (TV movies) The Strange and Deadly Occurence, 1974, The Adventure of the Queen, 1975, Murder on Flight 502, 1975, Undercover with the KKK, 1979 (narrator), Perry Mason: The Curse of the Sinister Spirit, 1987, The Return of Elliot Ness, 1991; (TV miniseries) George Washington, 1984, Hollywood Wives; (films) including First Love, 1940, When the Daltons Rode, 1940, Mortal Storm, 1940, Nice Girl, 1941, Badlands of Dakota, 1941, To Be or Not To Be, 1942, Eagle Squadron, 1942, Men of Texas Fighter Squadron, 1948, Date with Judy, 1948, Miss Tatlock's Millions, 1948, Mr. Music, 1950, The Bullfighter and the Lady, 1950, My Outlaw Brother, 1951, Bwana Devil, 1952, War Paint, 1953, The High and the Mighty, 1953, Iron Glove, 1954, Written on the Wind, 1956 (Acad. Award nomination for best supporting actor), The Last Voyage, 1959, John Paul Jones, 1959, The Caretakers, 1963, The Corrupt Ones, 1967, Story of a Woman, 1970, '1941', 1979, Airplane!, 1980, Uncommon Valor, 1983, Big Trouble, 1984, Glory Days, 1987, Caddyshack II, 1988, Joe Verses the Volcano, 1990. Served with USN, WWII. Recipient Emmy award Acad. TV Arts and Scis. Office: care Camden Artists 409 N Camden Dr Beverly Hills CA 90210-4417

STACK, STEPHEN S., manufacturing company executive; b. DuPont, Pa., Apr. 25, 1934; s. Steve and Sophie (Baranowski) Stasenko; m. Lois Sims Agnew, May 25, 1996. BSME, Case Western Res. U., 1956; postgrad. Syracuse U. Registered profl. engr., Ill. Mech. engr. Kaiser Aluminum, Erie, Pa., 1956-58; instr. Gannon U., Erie, 1958-60, Syracuse (N.Y.) U., 1960-61; engring. supr. A. O. Smith Corp., Erie and Los Angeles, 1961-66; gen. mgr. Am. Elec. Fusion, Chgo., 1966-67; mgr. new products Maremont Corp., Chgo., 1967-69; dir. market planning Gulf and Western Ind., Bellwood, Ill., 1969-71; mgmt. and fin. cons. Stack & Assos., Chgo., 1971-76; pres. Seamcraft, Inc., Chgo., 1976—; mem. Ill. Legis. Small Bus. Conf., 1980, Gov.'s Small Bus. Adv. Commn., 1984-94, Ill. State House Conf. on Small Bus., 1984, 86; chmn. West Cell, 1988—, Bridge Pers. Svcs. Corp., 1989—; v.p. Ind. Bus. Assn. Ill., 1993-94; mem. small bus. adv. coun. Fed. Res. Bank of Chgo., 1989-91; del. White House Conf. on Small Bus., 1986. Patentee in liquid control and metering fields. Treas. Sem. Townhouse Assn., 1993-94; active Lincoln Park Conservation Assn., Sheffield Neighbors Assn. Recipient Am. Legion award, 1948, Case Western Res. U. Honor key, 1956, Eagle Scout award, 1949. Mem. Ill. Mfrs. Assn. (bd. dirs. 1986—, vice chmn. 1996—), Small Mfrs. Action Council (vice chmn. 1986-87, chmn. 1988-89), Mfrs. Polit. Action Com. (exec. com. 1987—, vice chmn. 1993-95, chmn. 1996—), Am. Mgmt. Assn., Ind. Bus. Assn. Ill. (v.p. 1993), Pres.' Assn., Blue Key, Beta Theta Pi, Theta Tau, Pi Delta Epsilon. Clubs: Chgo. Yacht, Chgo. Execs., East Bank, Singapore (Mich.) Yacht, Capitol Hill (Washington), Fullerton Tennis (pres. 1971-79, treas. 1979-83, bd. dirs. 1983-86), Lake Shore Ski (v.p. 1982, 91), Lincoln Park Tennis Assn., Oak Park Tennis Club. Office: 932 W Dakin St Chicago IL 60613-2922

STACKABLE, FREDERICK LAWRENCE, lawyer; b. Howell, Mich., Dec. 4, 1935; s. Lawrence Peter and Dorothea R. (Kiney) S. BA, Mich. State U., 1959; JD, Wayne State U., 1962. Bar: Mich. 1962, U.S. Dist. Ct. (ea. and we. dists.) Mich. 1964; U.S. Supreme Ct. 1968. Lawyer Ingham County Cir. Ct. Commnr.; v.p. Mich. Assn. Cir. Ct. Commrs., 1963, pres., 1967-70; 18th dist. rep. Ingham County Bd. Suprs.; mem. Com. on Mich. Law Revision Commn.; state rep. 58th House Dist., 1971, 72, 73, 74. County del. Rep. Party, Ingham County, Mich., 1969-70, state del., Mich., 1971-74; Lansing city atty., 1975. Recipient Disting. Alumni award Wayne State U. Sch. Law, Detroit, 1987. Mem. Mich. Bar Assn., Ingham County Bar Assn., Nat. Conf. Commrs. Uniform State Laws, Mich. Trail Riders Assn. (dir., past pres.), Mich. Internat. Snowmobile Assn., Sportsman's Alliance Mich., Cycle Conservation Club, Am. Judicature Soc. Avocations: horseback riding, snowmobiling, skiing, traveling. Office: 300 N Grand Ave Lansing MI 48933-1214

STACKELBERG, JOHN RODERICK, history educator; b. Munich, May 8, 1935; came to U.S., 1946; s. Curt Freiherr and Ellen (Biddle) von Stackelberg; m. Steffi Heuss, Oct. 10, 1965 (div. Apr. 1983); m. Sally Winkle, Mar. 30, 1991; children: Katherine Ellen, Nicholas Olaf, Emmet Winkle. AB, Harvard U., 1956; MA, U. Vt., 1972; PhD, U. Mass., 1974. Reading instr. Baldridge Reading Svcs., Greenwich, Conn., 1957-62; lang. tchr. Hartnackschule, Berlin, 1963-67; English and social studies tchr. Lake Region Union High Sch., Orleans, Vt., 1967-70; lectr. history San Diego State U., 1974-76; asst. prof. history U. Oreg., Eugene, 1976-77, U. S.D., Vermillion, 1977-78; asst. prof. history Gonzaga U., Spokane, Wash., 1978-81, assoc. prof. history, 1981-88, prof. history, 1988—. Author: Idealism Debased, 1981; contbr. articles to profl. jours. Pres. Spokane chpt. UN Assn., 1986-90. With U.S. Army, 1958-60. Leadership Devel. fellow Ford Found., 1969-70. Avocations: chess, tennis. Home: 9708 E Maringo Dr Spokane WA 99206-4429 Office: Gonzaga U Dept History Spokane WA 99258

STACKELBERG, OLAF PATRICK VON, mathematician; b. Munich, Germany, Aug. 2, 1932; came to U.S., 1946, naturalized, 1947; s. Curt Frhrr. and Ellen (Biddle) von Stackelberg; m. Cora Elizabeth Sleighter, Sept. 4, 1954; children: John Sleighter, Peter Olaf, Paul Emmet. B.S. in Math, M.I.T., 1955; M.S., U. Minn., 1960, PhD. in Math, 1963. Asst. prof. math. Duke U., Durham, N.C., 1963-68; asso. prof. Duke U., 1968-76; prof. Kent (Ohio) State U., 1976—, chmn. dept. math, 1976-96; vis. asso. prof. U. Ill., 1969-70, U. London, Eng., 1974, Wesleyan U., summers 1965-76. Mng. editor: Duke Math. Jour, 1971-74; contbr. articles U.S. and fgn. jours. Mem. State of Ohio Steering Com., Project Discovery. Served with Chem. Corps AUS, 1956-58. Alexander von Humboldt research fellow U. Stuttgart, Germany, 1965-66; NSF research grantee. Mem. AAAS, AAUP, Am. Math. Soc., Math. Assn. Am. (nat. bd. govs. 1991-94), Inst. Math. Stats., Fedn. Am. Scientists, Assn. Computer Machinery, London Math. Soc. Home: 1411 Aurora Hudson Rd Aurora OH 44202-8408 Office: Kent State U Dept Math and Computer Sci Kent OH 44242

STACKHOUSE, JOHN WESLEY, publishing executive; b. South Bend, Ind., Feb. 12, 1940; s. Zeno Walter and Mildred Ellen (Delcamp) S.; m. Patsy Ann Erickson, Sept. 14, 1963; children: John E. Joseph W., David P., Katherine A., Jason A., Ryan E., Patricia M. BS in Acctg. and Econs., U. Indpls., 1962. Auditor Ernst & Ernst (now Ernst & Young), Indpls., 1962-65; mgr. gen. acctg. Lake Cen. Airlines, Indpls., 1965-68; from mgr. gen. acctg. to dir. fin. svcs. Howard W. Sams & Co., Inc., Indpls., 1968-73; from sr. fin. analyst to asst. comptr. ITT Pub., Indpls., 1973-81; v.p. fin., treas., CFO Nixon Newspapers, Inc., Peru, Ind., 1981—, also bd. dirs. Bd. dir. Peru/Miami County Econ. Devel. Corp., 1993—; bd. dirs. Grissom AFB Cmty. Coun., 1996—. With USAR, 1963-69. Mem. Internat. Newspaper Fin. Execs. (bd. dirs. 1991-97), Peru C. of C. (bd. dirs. 1991-96, pres. elect 1992, pres., 1993, 94), Rotary (pres. Peru club 1989-90). Presbyterian. Avocations: photography, reading, fishing. Office: Nixon Newspapers Inc 35 W 3rd St Peru IN 46970-2154

STACKHOUSE, ROBERT, sculptor; b. Bronxville, N.Y., 1942. BA, U. South Fla., 1965; postgrad., U. Md., 1967. Vis. artist and lectr., U. Hawaii, Manoa, 1990, U. South Fla., Tampa, 1991, U. Denver, 1992. One-man shows Corcoran Gallery Art, Washington, 1973, 88, Honolulu Acad. Arts, 1990, Va. Mus. Fine Arts, Richmond, 1990, U. Denver Art Gallery, 1993, Struve Gallery, Chgo., 1993, Morgan Gallery, Kansas City, Mo., 1993, Baumgartner Galleries, Washington, 1993; exhibited in group shows Corcoran Gallery Art, 1970, Balt. Mus. Art, 1970, Walker Art Ctr., Mpls., 1977, Art Inst. Chgo., 1977, Hunter Mus. Art, Chattanooga, 1981, Bklyn. Mus., 1986, 89, Nat. Mus. Am. Art, Smithsonian Inst, Washington, 1989, William A. Farnsworth Libr. and Art Mus., Rockland, Maine, 1990, Am. Acad. and Inst. Arts and Letters, N.Y.C., 1991, U. Wyo. Art Mus., 1993, numerous others; travelling exhbns. Corcoran Gallery Art, 1975, 87, Ft. Worth Art Mus., 1975, Huntsville (Ala.) Mus. Art, Hunter Mus. Art, Chattanooga, 1984, Okla. Mus. Art, Oklahoma City; represented in permanent collections Mus. Modern Art, N.Y.C., Art Inst. Chgo., Mus. Contemporary Art, Chgo., Walker Art Ctr., Balt. Mus. Art, Hirshhorn Mus. and Sculpture Garden, Corcoran Gallery Art, also corp. collections; commns. include bronze On the Beach Again, Australia Nat. Gallery, Canberra; painted wood St. Louie Bones, Laumeier Sculpture Park, St. Louis, Oliver Ranch Project/Russian River Bones, Geyserville, Calif., 1989; extruded red brass Delaware Passage, Del. Art Mus., Wilmington, 1991, Divers, Marine Sci. Bldg., U. Hawaii, 1991. *

STACY, BILL WAYNE, academic administrator; b. Bristol, Va., July 26, 1938; s. Charles Frank and Louise Nelson (Altwater) S.; m. Sue Varnon; children: Mark, Sara, James. B.S.Ed., S.E. Mo. State U., 1960; M.S., So. Ill. U., 1965, Ph.D., 1968. Tchr. Malden High Sch., Mo., 1960-64; faculty Southeast Mo. State U., Cape Girardeau, 1967-89, dean Grad. Sch., 1976-79, interim pres., 1979, pres., 1980-89; pres. Calif. State U., San Marcos, 1989—; dir. Boatmen's Nat. Bank. Bd. dirs. San Diego United Way. Mem. Am. Assn. state Colls. and Univs. (dir.), Am. Assn. Higher edn., PIC Policy Bd., San Diego Rotary, Pvt. Industry Coun. Presbyterian. *

STACY, CHARLES BRECKNOCK, lawyer; b. Charleston, W.Va., Sept. 2, 1924; s. George Palmer and Patti (Hubbard) S.; m. Judith Cook Willner, June 14, 1947 (dec. Jan. 1996); 1 child, Charles Brecknock. B.S., Yale U., 1948, LL.B., 1951. Bar: W.Va. 1951. Assoc. firm Spilman, Thomas & Battle, 1951-58; v.p. Lewis-Hubbard Corp., 1957; ptnr. Spilman, Thomas & Battle, Charleston, 1958—; mem. U.S. Circuit Ct. Judge Nominating Commn., 4th Circuit, 1977-79. Contbr. articles to law and tax publs. Pres. Kanawha-Charleston Vis. Nursing Assn., 1966-67; bd. dirs. Charleston Symphony Orch., 1960-70, pres., 1962-63; bd. trustees Woodberry Forest (Va.) Sch., 1970-76; pres. Woodberry Forest Alumni Assn., 1972-74; bd. dirs. Community Council of Kanawha Valley, Inc., 1971-79, pres., 1975-77; bd. dirs. United Way of Kanawha Valley, Inc., 1973-77, exec. com., 1975-77; trustee Greater Kanawha Valley Found., 1968-72, adv. bd., 1972—, chmn. bd., 1970-72; bd. dirs. W.Va. Tax Inst., 1958-67, pres., 1959-60. Served with USAAF, 1943-46. Fellow Am. Bar Found., Am. Coll. Trust and Estate Counsel, Am. Coll. Tax Counsel; mem. ABA (coun. 1977-83, vice chmn. adminstrn. sect. taxation 1980-83), Kanawha County Bar Assn., W.Va. State Bar (chmn. standing com. on state and fed. taxation 1959-70), W.Va. Bar Assn., Am. Law Inst., Am. Judicature Soc., Edgewood Country Club Charleston (gov. 1973-75, 83-86), Sea Pines Country Club (Hilton Head, S.C.), Yale Club N.Y.C., Rotary (bd. dirs. Charleston club 1979-80, 83-91, pres. 1989-90). Democrat. Presbyterian. Home: 1560 Thomas Cir Charleston WV 25314-1623 Office: Spilman Ctr 300 Kanawha Blvd E Charleston WV 25301-2531

STACY, DENNIS WILLIAM, architect; b. Council Bluffs, Iowa, Sept. 22, 1945; s. William L. and Mildred Glee (Carlsen) S.; BArch., Iowa State U., 1969; postgrad. U. Nebr., 1972. Registered architect, Iowa, Tex., Colo., Mo.; m. Judy Annette Long, Dec. 28, 1968; 1 child, Stephanie. Designer Troy & Stalder Architects, Omaha, 1967, Architects Assocs., Des Moines, 1968-69, Logsdon & Voelter Architects, Temple, Tex., 1970; project architect Roger Schutte & Assos., Omaha, 1972-73; architect, assoc. Robert H. Burgin & Assocs., Coun. Bluffs, 1973-75, Neil Astle & Assocs., Omaha, 1975-78; owner, prin. Dennis W. Stacy, AIA, Architect, Glenwood, Iowa, 1978-81, Dallas, 1981—. Mem. City of Dallas Urban Design Adv. Com., 1992-96, chmn., 1995-96, dir. Greater Dallas Planning Coun., 1997; chmn., Glenwood Zoning Bd. Adjustment, 1979-81; chmn. Mills County Plant Iowa Program, 1979-81; mem. S.W. Iowa Citizen's Adv. Com., Iowa State Dept. Transp., 1977-81; regional screening chmn. Am. Field Svc. Internat./Intercultural Programs, 1974-79, Iowa-Nebr. rep., 1978-80. With U.S. Army, 1969-71. Decorated Nat. Def. Svc. medal, Vietnam Svc. medal, Vietnam Campaign medal, Army Commendation medal. Mem. AIA (recipient Iowa Design Honor award 1981, Dallas AIA commendation awards (2) 1990, 92, 95, citation of honor award 1991, 92, Dallas Design awards (2) 1991, 96, Texas Design Honor award 1992, Dallas AIA Firm of Yr. award 1992, Dallas commr. design, 1991, chmn. Dallas design awards 1992, pres Dallas AIA 1996), Nat. Coun. Archtl. Registration Bds., Tex. Soc. Archs. (environ. resource com. 1994-95, chmn., Tex. arch. pub. com., 1992-97, chmn. 1997), The 500 Inc. (outstanding mem. 1985), Glenwood Optimist (Disting. Svc. award 1982, pres. 1980-81), Masons. Archtl. Works include: Davies Amphitheater, 1980, Addison Nat. Bank Bldg., 1985, Fairview Recreation Complex, 1984, Computer Lang. Rsch. Corp. Learning Ctr., 1987., Villa Roma, 1988, C.U. Performing Arts Ctr., 1989, Mercedes-Benz Distbn. Ctr., 1987, Dallas Chpt. AIA Offices, 1990, Janadria Festival Arena, 1994, Surg. Ctr. Pain Mgmt. Inst., 1995, Physicians Consultants Clinic, 1994, Horizon Pain Mgmt. Ctr., 1995, Rheumatology Assoc. Clinic, 1996, Addison Nat. Br. Bank, 1996. Home: 4148 Cobblers Ln Dallas TX 75287-6725 Office: 4222 Trinity Mills Rd Ste 270 Dallas TX 75287-7605

STACY, RICHARD A., administrative law judge; b. Eldorado, Ark., Mar. 7, 1942; s. Jack Leonard S. and Estelle (Mabry) Carrier; m. Karen Kay King, Aug. 20, 1961; children: Mark L., Andrea L. BA, U. Wyo., 1965, JD, 1967. Bar: Wyo. 1967, Colo. 1967, U.S. Supreme Ct. 1972. Revisor Wyo. Statute Revision Com., Cheyenne, 1967-69; asst. atty. gen. State of Wyo., 1969-72; asst. U.S. atty. Dept. Justice, Cheyenne, 1972-75; U.S. atty. Dis. Wyo., Cheyenne, 1981-94; adminstrv. law judge Office of Hearing & Appeals, San Jose, Calif., 1994—; mem. atty. gen's adv. com. of U.S. attys. Dept. Justice, 1981-84. Mem. Gov.'s Statewide Drug Alcohol Adv. Bd., 1988-94. Mem. ABA, Wyo. Bar Assn., Colo. State Bar, Santa Clara County Bar Assn. (hon., com. on bench, bar, media, police relationships 1995—). Republican. Episcopalian. Club: Kiwanis (charter pres. Wheatland 1977). Office: Hearings & Appeals 280 S 1st St San Jose CA 95113-3002

STADDON, JOHN ERIC RAYNER, psychology, zoology, neurobiology educator; b. Grayshott, Hampshire, Eng.; came to U.S., 1960; s. Leonard John and Dulce Norine (Rayner) S.; m. Lucinda Paris. BSc, Univ. Coll., London, 1960; PhD, Harvard U., 1964. Asst. prof. psychology U. Toronto, Ont., Can., 1964-67; from asst. prof. to prof. Duke U., Durham, N.C., 1967-72, prof., 1972-83, J.B. Duke prof. psychology, prof. neurobiology and zoology, 1983—. Author: Adaptive Behavior and Learning, 1983, Behaviorism, 1993; editor: Behavioral Processes, 1979; cons. editor Behavior and Philosophy, 1993; assoc. editor Jour. Exptl. Analysis of behavior, 1979-82. Recipient von Humboldt prize, 1985. Fellow AAAS, N.Y. Acad. Scis., Soc. Exptl. Psychologists; mem. Phi Beta Kappa (hon.), Sigma Xi. Avocations: history, philosophy of science, public policy. Office: Duke U Dept Exptl Psychology PO Box 90086 Durham NC 27708-0086

STADE, GEORGE GUSTAV, humanities educator; b. N.Y.C., Nov. 25, 1933; s. Kurt Herman and Eva Bergit (Aronson) S.; m. Dorothy Louise Fletcher, Dec. 16, 1957; children: Bjorn, Eric, Nancy, Kirsten. B.A., St. Lawrence U., 1955; M.A., Columbia U., 1958, Ph.D., 1965. Tchr. Collegiate Sch., N.Y.C., 1957-58; instr. Bernard Baruch Sch. Bus., N.Y.C., 1958-59, Bklyn. Poly. Inst., 1959-60, Rutgers U.-Newark, 1960-62; instr. Columbia U., N.Y.C., 1962, asst. prof., 1965, assoc. prof., 1968, prof. English, 1971—; cons. various law firms, N.Y.C., 1960—. Author: Robert Graves, 1967, Confessions of a Lady-Killer, 1979; editor: European Writers, 13 vols., Selected Letters of E.E. Cummings, 1968, Six Modern British Writers, 1974, Six Contemporary British Writers, 1976, European Writers: Selected Authors, 3 Vols., 1992, British Writers Supplement II, 1992, British Writers Supplement III, 1995; contbr. over 100 articles to profl. jours. Mem. PEN, N.Y. Book Critics Circle, Popular Culture Assn., MLA. Home: 430 W 116th St New York NY 10027-7239 Office: Columbia U 604 Philosophy Hall New York NY 10027

STADELMAN, WILLIAM RALPH, chemical institution executive; b. Ont., Can., July 18, 1919; s. John Joseph and Lillian (Trachsell) S.; m. Jean MacLaren, Nov. 2, 1951; 1 child, Mary Laren. B.A.Sc., U. Toronto, 1941; M.B.A., U. Pa., 1949. Chief process engr. Can. Synthetic Rubber, Ltd., 1943-47; lectr. mktg. U. Pa., 1948-49; asst. to mgr. Pa. Salt Mfg. Co., 1950; sec.-treas. Ont. Research Found., Mississauga, 1950-64, pres., 1964-84; pres. WRS Assocs., 1984—; dir., sr. exec. Inst. Chem. Sci. and Tech., 1985-89; dir. Med. Tech. Investment Corp. Fellow World Acad. Art and Sci.; mem. Assn. Profl. Engrs. Ont., Can. Rsch. Mgmt. Assn., Bd. Trade Met. Toronto, Club of Rome, Caledon Ski Club. Home and Office: WRS Assocs, 31 Rykert Crescent, Toronto, ON Canada M4G 2T1

STADELMANN, EDUARD JOSEPH, plant physiologist, educator; b. Graz, Austria, Sept. 24, 1920; s. Eduard Joseph and Josefa (Eigner) S.; m. Ok Young Lee, Mar. 22, 1975. BS, Bundesrealgymnasium, Graz, Austria, 1939; PhD, U. Innsbruck, Austria, 1953; Pvt. Docent, U. Freiburg, Switzerland, 1957; PhD (hon.), Agrl. U. Vienna, 1989. Sr. asst. U. Freiburg, 1962-63; rsch. assoc. U. Minn., Mpls., 1963, asst. prof., 1964-66, assoc. prof., 1966-72, prof. hort. sci., 1972-91, prof. emeritus, 1991—. Muellhaupt Scholar in Biology, Ohio State U., 1958-59; Humboldt Found. awardee, 1974-75; Fulbright award, Coun. Internat. Exchange, 1979-80, 87-88. Mem. Am. Inst. Biology, Am. Soc. Plant Physiologists, German Bot. Soc., Swiss Bot. Soc., Sigma Xi. Roman Catholic. Office: Univ Minn Dept Hort Sci 1970 Folwell Ave Saint Paul MN 55108-6007

STADLER, CRAIG ROBERT, professional golfer; b. San Diego, June 2, 1953; s. Donald Edwin and Betty M. (Adams) S.; m. Susan Barrett, Jan. 6, 1979; children: Kevin Craig, Christopher Barrett. Student, U. So. Calif. Profl. golfer Palm Beach Gardens, Fla.; winner Hope Classic, 1980, Greater Greensboro Open, 1980, Kemper Open, 1981-82, Tucson Open, 1982, Masters, 1982, World Series of Golf, 1982, 92, Tour Championship, 1991. U.S. amateur champion, 1973; mem. U.S. Walker Cup team, 1975; leading money winner PGA Tour, 1982. Mem. Golf Mag. (Player of Yr. 1982). *

STADTER, PHILIP AUSTIN, classicist, educator; b. Cleve., Nov. 29, 1936; s. John M. and Mary Louise (Jones) S.; m. Lucia Angela Ciapponi, July 6, 1963; children: Paul, Maria, Mark. B.A., Princeton U., 1958; M.A., Harvard U., 1959, Ph.D., 1963. Instr. U. N.C., Chapel Hill, 1962-64, asst. prof., 1964-67, assoc. prof., 1967-71, prof., 1971—, chmn. dept. classics, 1976-86, prof. comparative lit., 1991—, Falk prof. humanities, 1991—. Author: Plutarch's Historical Methods, 1965, The Public Library of Renaissance Florence, 1972, Arrian of Nicomedia, 1980, A Commentary on Plutarch's Pericles, 1989; editor: The Speeches of Thucydides, 1973, Plutarch and the Historical Tradition, 1992. Fulbright fellow Rome, 1960-61; Guggenheim fellow Florence, Italy, 1967-68; NEH fellow, 1974-75; fellow Am. Council Learned Socs., Oxford, Eng., 1982-83. Fellow Nat. Humanities Ctr.; mem. Am. Philol. Assn. (dir. 1977-80), Am. Assn. Ancient Historians, Soc. Promotion of Hellenic Studies, Classical Assn. Middle West and South. Democrat. Roman Catholic. Office: U NC Dept Classics Chapel Hill NC 27599-3145

STADTLER, BEATRICE HORWITZ, author; b. Cleve., June 26, 1921; d. David and Minnie (Gorelick) Horwitz; m. Oscar Stadtler, Jan. 31, 1945; children—Dona Stadtler Rosenblatt, Sander, Miriam Stadtler Rosenbaum. MS in Religious Edn., John Carroll U., 1983, M Judaic Studies, 1988. Sec. Cleve. Dept. Pub. Health and Welfare, 1940; sec., dept. mgr. Fed. Pub. Housing Authority, Cleve., 1943; primary supr. Temple Beth Shalom Religious Sch., Cleve., 1953; registrar Cleve. Coll. Jewish Studies, 1958-83; asst. editor Israel Philatelist, 1975—; speaker on holocaust, lectr. at writer's confs. and classes; scholar-in-residence various cities; tchr. Cleve. Hebrew Schs., 1992—. Author: Once Upon a Jewish Holiday, 1963, The Story of Dona Gracia, 1969, The Adventures of Gluckel of Hamlen, 1967, Rescue From the Sky (in Hebrew), 1972, Personalities of the Jewish Labor Movement, 1972, The Holocaust: A History of Courage and Resistance, 1975 (prize outstanding juvenile book, Jewish Book Coun. Nat. Jewish Welfare Bd. 1975), The History of Israel Through Her Postage Stamps, 1993 (Silver medals Can. Nat. Philatelic Lit. Competition and Nat. Philatelic Lit. Competition); also stories and articles for children in Chattanooga Shofar newspaper; poems in book Women Speak to God; film strip The Adventures of Mirkee Pirkee and Danny Dollar, 1963 (prize Nat. Coun. Jewish Audio Visual Materials 1963); libertto rock opera Solomon the King; contbr. articles to Shofar mag., Uoung Judean; contbr. articles on Holocaust to New Book of Knowledge, Holocaust Literature: a Handbook of Critical Historical and Literary Writings, 1993; author weekly column Cleve. Jewish News, 1964-70, Boston Jewish Advocate, 1970-92; contbr. articles to pubs. Adviser youth group United Synagogue, 1967-70; mem. Holocaust task force

Jewish Community Fedn. Cleve.; mem. Educator's Assembly, Pioneer Women., Edn. Council N. Am.; mem. U.S. Holocaust Meml. Council, chmn. adv. panel Holocaust edn., judge writing contest for students 9th-12th grades.; mem. Gov.'s commn. of the State of Ohio on Holocaust Edn.; mem. State of Ohio Holocaust Commn., Cleve. Holocaust Ctr. (chmn. edn.), Bd. Cleve. Hebrew Schs. (chmn. edn.); bd. dirs. Women's Div. Jewish Nat. Fund. Recipient Leslie Reggel award for outstanding contbns. to Israel Philately, 1994, prizes Fedn. and Welfare Funds Audio Visual Coun. of Am. Assn. Jewish Edn., prize by Judah Magnes Mus., Berkeley, Calif. Democrat. Home: 24355 Tunbridge Ln Cleveland OH 44122-1631

STADTMAN, EARL REECE, biochemist; b. Carrizozo, N.Mex., Nov. 15, 1919; s. Walter William and Minnie Ethyl (Reece) S.; m. Thressa Campbell, Oct. 19, 1943. B.S., U. Calif., Berkeley, 1942, Ph.D, 1949. With Alcan Hwy. survey Pub. Rds. Adminstrn., 1942-43; rsch. asst. U. Calif., Berkeley, 1938-49, sr. lab. technican, 1949; AEC fellow Mass. Gen. Hosp., Boston, 1949-50; chemist lab. cellular physiology Nat. Heart Inst., 1950-58, chief enzyme sect., 1958-62, chief lab. biochemistry, 1962—; biochemist Max Planck Inst., Munich, Germany, Pasteur Inst., Paris, 1959-60; faculty dept. microbiology U. Md.; prof. biochemistry grad. program dept. biology Johns Hopkins U.; adv. com. Life Scis. Rsch. Office, Am. Fedn. Biol. Sci., 1974-77; bd. dirs. Found. Advanced Edn. Scis., 1966-70, chmn. dept. biochemistry, 1966-68; biochem. study sect. rsch. grants NIH, 1959-63. Editor Jour. Biol. Chemistry, 1960-65, Current Topics in Cellular Regulation, 1968—, Circulation Rsch., 1968-70; exec. editor Archives Biochemistry and Biophysics, 1960—, Life Scis., 1973-75, Procs. NAS, 1975-81, Trends in Biochem. Rsch., 1975-78; mem. editorial adv. bd. Biochemistry, 1969-76, 81—. Recipient medallion Soc. de Chemie Biologique, 1955, medallion U. Pisa, 1966, Presdl. Rank award as Disting. Sr. Exec., 1981, Welch Found. Award in Chemistry, 1991, Rsch. award Am. Aging Assn., 1992, Paul Glen award Am. Gerontology Soc., 1993. Mem. Am. Chem. Soc. (Paul Lewis Lab. award in enzyme chemistry 1952, exec. com. biol. div. 1959-64, chmn. div. 1963-64, Hillebrand award 1969), Am. Soc. Biol. Chemists (publs. com. 1966-70, coun. 1974-77, 82-84, pres. 1983—, Merckaward 1983), Nat. Acad. Sci. (award in microbiology 1970), Am. Acad. Arts and Scis., Am. Soc. Microbiology, Washington Acad. Scis. (award biol. chemistry 1957, Nat. medal sci. 1979, meritorious exec. award 1980, Robert A. Welch award in chemistry 1991, Paul Glenn award in aging, 1993). Office: Nat Heart and Lung Inst 9000 Rockville Pike Bethesda MD 20814-1436

STADTMAN, THRESSA CAMPBELL, biochemist; b. Sterling, N.Y., Feb. 12, 1920; d. Earl and Bessie (Waldron) Campbell; m. Earl Reece Stadtman, Oct. 19, 1943. BS, Cornell U., 1940, MS, 1942; PhD, U. Calif.-Berkeley, 1949. Rsch. assoc. U. Calif., Berkeley, 1942-47; Rsch. assoc. med. sch. Harvard U., Boston, 1949-50; biochemist Nat. Heart, Lung and Blood Inst. NIH, USPHS, HHS, Bethesda, Md., 1950—; mem. Burroughs-Wellcome Fund Toxicology Adv. Commn., 1994—; pres.-elect Internat. Soc. Vitamins and Related BioFactors, 1995—. Editor Jour. Biol. Chemistry, Archives Biochemistry and Biophysics, Molecular and Cellular Biochemistry; editor-in-chief Bio Factors; contbr. articles on amino acid metabolism, methane biosynthesis, vitamin B12 biochemistry, selenium biochemistry to profl. jours. Helen Haye Whitney fellow Oxford U., Eng., 1954-55; Rockefeller Found. grantee U. Munich, 1959-60; recipient Rose award, 1987, Klaus Schwarz medal, 1988. Mem. NAS, Am. Soc. Microbiology, Biochem. Soc., Soc. Am. Biochemists, Am. Chem. Soc., Am. Acad. Arts and Scis., Sigma Delta Epsilon (hon.). Home: 16907 Redland Rd Derwood MD 20855-1954

STADTMAN, VERNE AUGUST, former foundation executive, editor; b. Carrizoso, N.Mex., Dec. 5, 1926; s. Walter William and Minnie Ethel (Reece) S.; m. Jackolyn Carol Byl, Aug. 26, 1949; children: Kristen Karen, Rand Theodore, Judith Dayna, Todd Alan. A.B., Calif.-Berkeley, 1950. AUS, 1945-47; mng. editor Calif. Monthly, Calif. Alumni Assn., Berkeley, 1950-64; centennial editor U. Calif., Berkeley, 1964-69; assoc. dir., editor Carnegie Commn. on Higher Edn., Berkeley, 1969-73, Carnegie Council on Policy Studies in Higher Edn. Berkeley, 1973-80; v.p. gen. services Carnegie Found. for Advancement Teaching, Princeton, N.J., 1980-89; trustee Editorial Projects Edn., Inc., 1957-91, pres., 1962-63, chmn. bd., 1980-86; guest scholar Hiroshima U., Japan, 1978. Author: California Campus, 1960, University of California, 1868-1968, 1970, Academic Adaptations, 1980; editor: (with David Riesman) Academic Transformation: Seventeen Institutions Under Pressure, 1973 (Book of Yr. award Am. Council Edn.); compiler-editor: Centennial Record of the University of California, 1967. Served with AUS, 1945-47. Recipient Alumnus Service award Calif. Alumni Assn., 1970. Mem. Am. Alumni Council (pres. 1963-64). Home: 182 Saint James Dr Sonoma CA 95476-8336

STADTMUELLER, JOSEPH PETER, federal judge; b. Oshkosh, Wis., Jan. 28, 1942; s. Joseph Francis and Irene Mary (Kilp) S.; m. Mary Ellen Brady, Sept. 5, 1970; children: Jeremy, Sarah. B.S. in Bus. Adminstrn., Marquette U., 1964, J.D., 1967. Bar: Wis. 1967, U.S. Supreme Ct. 1980. with Kluwin, Dunphy, Hankin and McNulty, 1968-69; asst. U.S. atty. Dept. Justice, Milw., 1969-74; 1st. asst. U.S. atty. Dept. Justice, 1974-75; with Stepke, Kossow, Trebon and Stadtmueller, Milw., 1975-76; asst. U.S. atty. Dept. Justice, 1977-78, dep. U.S. atty., 1978-81, U.S. atty., 1981-87; judge U.S. Dist. Ct. (ea. dist.) Wis., Milw., 1987—, chief judge, 1995—. Recipient Spl. Commendation award Atty. Gen. U.S., 1974, 80. Mem. ABA, State Bar Wis. (bd. govs. 1979-83, exec. com. 1982-83), Am. Law Inst., Fed. Judges Assn. (bd. dirs. 1995—), Univ. Club (Milw.). Republican. Roman Catholic. Club: University (Milw.). Office: 471 US Courthouse 517 E Wisconsin Ave Milwaukee WI 53202-4504*

STAEHELIN, LUCAS ANDREW, cell biology educator; b. Sydney, Australia, Feb. 10, 1939; came to U.S., 1969; s. Lucas Eduard and Isobel (Malloch) S.; m. Margrit Weibel, Sept. 17, 1965; children: Daniel Thomas, Philip Roland, Marcel Felix. Dipl. Natw., Swiss Fed. Inst. Tech., Zurich, 1963, Ph.D. in Biology, 1966. Research scientist N.Z. Dept. Sci. and Indsl. Research, 1966-69; research fellow in cell biology Harvard U., Cambridge, Mass., 1969-70; asst. prof. cell biology U. Colo., Boulder, 1970-73, assoc. prof., 1973-79, prof., 1979—; vis. prof. U. Freiburg, 1978, Swiss Fed. Inst. Tech., 1984, 92; mem. cellular biology and physiology study sect. NIH, Bethesda, Md., 1980-84; mem. DOE panel on rsch. directions for the energy bioscis., 1988, 92; mem. NSF adv. panel for cellular orgn., 1994-96. Editor Jour. Cell Biology, 1977-81, European Jour. Cell Biology, 1981-90, Plant Physiology, 1986-92, Plant Jour., 1991—, Biology of the Cell, 1996—; editor: (with C.J. Antzen) Encyclopedia of Plant Physiology, Vol. 19, Photosynthesis III, 1986; contbr. numerous articles to sci. jours. Recipient Humboldt award Humboldt Found., 1978, Sci. Tchr. award U. Colo., 1984; grantee NIH, 1971—, USDA, 1994—, NASA, 1997—. Mem. AAAS, Am. Soc. Cell Biology, Am. Soc. Plant Physiology, German Acad. Natural Scis. Leopoldina. Home: 2855 Dover Dr Boulder CO 80303-5305 Office: U Colo Dept Molecular Cell/Devel Biology Campus Box 347 Boulder CO 80309-0347

STAEHLE, ROBERT L., foundation executive; b. Rochester, N.Y., Apr. 22, 1955; s. Henry Carl and Isabel Montgomery S. BS in Aero. and Astronautic Engring., Purdue U., 1977. Prin. investigator Skylab Expt. ED-31 (bacteria aboard Skylab), NASA/Marshall Space Flight Center, Huntsville, Ala., 1972-74; student trainee engring. Skylab Expt. ED-31 (bacteria aboard Skylab), NASA/Marshall Space Flight Center, 1974-77; sci. observation analyst Caltech/Jet Propulsion Lab., Pasadena, Calif., 1977-78; engr. advanced projects group, 1978-83, mem. tech. staff system integration sect. of Space Sta., 1983-87, mem. tech. staff and space sta., user ops. team leader, 1987-88; tech. mgr. Jet Propulsion Lab., Pasadena, Calif., 1988—, mgr. space sta. Freedom support office Pasadena ops., 1990-92, Pluto team leader, 1992-93, mgr. Pluto Express preproject, 1993-96; mgr. Ice and Fire preprojects Jet Propulsion Lab., Pasadena, 1996—; prin. founder, pres. World Space Found., South Pasadena, Calif., 1979—; founding dir. So. Calif. Space Bus. Roundtable, 1987-95. Co-author: Project Solar Sail, New Am. Libr., 1990; contbr. articles to profl. jours. Mem. Cmty. Leaders Adv. Bd. for Irvine Scholars, Occidental Coll., L.A., 1996—; bd. dirs. Caltech Y, 1987-93. Nat. Space Club Goddard scholar, 1977; Charles A. Lindbergh Fund grantee, 1986. Fellow Brit. Interplanetary Soc.; mem. AIAA, Tau Beta Pi, Sigma Gamma Tau. Avocations: photography, hiking. Office: Jet Propulsion Lab Pasadena CA 91109

STAELIN, DAVID HUDSON, electrical engineering educator, consultant; b. Toledo, May 25, 1938; s. Carl Gustav and Margaret E. (Hudson) S.; m. Ellen Mahoney, June 16, 1962; children: Carl H., Katharine E., Paul H. SB, MIT, 1960, SM, 1961, ScD in Elec. Engring., 1965. Instr. elec. engring. MIT, Cambridge, 1965, asst. prof., 1965-69, assoc. prof., 1969-76, prof., 1976—; asst. dir. Lincoln Lab. MIT, Lexington, 1990—; vis. asst. scientist Nat. Radio Astronomy Obs., Charlottesville, Va., 1968-69; cons. Jet Propulsion Lab., Pasadena, Calif., 1969, Wellesley, Mass., 1965—; dir. Environ. Rsch. and Tech., Inc., Concord, Mass., 1969-78; co-founder, chmn. PictureTel Corp., Peabody, Mass., 1984-87; mem. com. on radio frequency requirements for rsch., NAS, Washington, 1980-86, chmn. 1983-86; chmn. advanced microwave sounder working group NASA, Washington, 1981-82, mem. space applications adv. com.,NASA, 1983-86. Co-author: Made in America, 1989, Electromagnetic Waves, 1994; also articles; patentee grinding and polishing sheet glass, display of dynamic images, ribbon-beam cathode ray tube. Fellow IEEE, AAAS; mem. Am. Geophys. Union, Am. Meteorl. Soc., Internat. Union for Radio Sci. Office: MIT Rm 26-341 Cambridge MA 02139

STAELIN, RICHARD, business administration educator; b. Larchmont, N.Y., Aug. 3, 1939; s. Richard Carl and Dorothy (Potts) S.; m. Julie Ann Fischer, Aug. 24, 1963; children: Adam, Kate. BSME, U. Mich., 1961, BS in Math., 1962, M.B.A., 1963, Ph.D., 1969. Market planner IBM, Harrison, N.Y., 1963-66; prof. Carnegie-Mellon U., Pitts., 1969-82; Edward and Rose Donnell prof. Duke U., Durham, N.C., 1982—, assoc. dean faculty affairs, 1982-91, mng. dir., 1995—; exec. dir. Mktg. Sci. Inst., Cambridge, Mass., 1991-93; vis. prof. Australian Grad. Sch., Kensington, Australia, 1980-81. Author: Consumer Protection Legislation and the U.S. Food Industry, 1980; mem. editorial bd. Jour. Mktg. Rsch., 1974-82, Jour. Consumer Rsch., 1976-87; area editor Mktg. Sci., 1983-88; editor-in-chief Mktg. Sci., 1995—. Mem. Pitts. Exec. Bd.; treas. Pitts. Arts and Crafts Ctr., 1976-79; bd. dirs. Dispute Settlement Ctr., Chapel Hill, N.C.; bd. vis. drama dept. Duke U., 1990—. Recipient Best Mktg. Paper award Inst. Mgmt. Sci., 1985, hon. mention, 1986, AMA/Irwin Disting. Mktg. Educators award, 1996; HEW grantee, 1972-74; NSF grantee, 1973-79. Mem. Am. Mktg. Assn., Assn. Consumer Research, Inst. Mgmt. Sci. Office: Fuqua School of Business Science Dr Rm 339 Durham NC 27706-2597

STAFF, CHARLES BANCROFT, JR., music and theater critic; b. Franklin, Ind., July 2, 1929; s. Charles Bancroft and Clara Margaret (Jennings) S. AB, Franklin Coll., 1951; BM, Ind. U., 1955. Copy editor Indpls. News, 1955-58, movie, TV critic, 1958-65, music, drama critic, 1965—; pianist dance band, Franklin, 1943-46. Composer numerous musical pieces string quartet, 1954, wind quintet, 1954, violin sonata, 1955, Deat Under A Tree, Wicked Tales for Evil Children, 1980. Organist Presbyn. Ch., Franklin, 1945-48, Bapt. Ch. Franklin, 1948-51. Recipient Best Critical Writing award Indpls. Press Club, 1977, 78. Democrat. Office: Indpls News 307 N Pennsylvania St Indianapolis IN 46204-1811*

STAFFIER, PAMELA MOORMAN, psychologist; b. Passaic, N.J., Dec. 7, 1942; d. Wynant Clair and Jeannette Frances (Rentzsch) Moorman; B.A., Bucknell U., 1964; M.A. in Psychology, Assumption Coll., Worcester, Mass., 1970, C.A.G.S., 1977; Ph.D., Union Inst., 1978; m. John Staffier, Jr., Apr. 5, 1975; children—M. Anthony, C. Matthew. Psychologist, Westboro (Mass.) State Hosp., 1965, prin. psychologist, also asst. to supt., 1973-76; psychologist Moriarty Mental Health Clinic; psychiat. cons. local gen. hosp.; research psychologist Wrentham (Mass.) State Sch., 1966, Cushing Hosp., Framingham, Mass., 1967; prin. psychologist, also asst. to supt. Grafton (Mass.) State Hosp., 1967-72; dir. Staffier Psychol. Assocs., Inc., 1978—. Mem. Am. Psychol. Assn. (assoc.), Am. Psychol. Practitioners Assn. (founding mem.), Mass. Psychol. Assn., Nat. Register Health Service Providers in Psychology. Research, publs. on state hosp. closings, biochem. basis of Schizophrenia. Home: 68 Adams St PO Box 1103 Westborough MA 01581 Office: 57 E Main St Westborough MA 01581-1464

STAFFORD, DONALD GENE, chemistry educator; b. Valliant, Okla., Oct. 9, 1930; s. Otto Lewis and Rose Lavelle (Osterdock) S.; m. Jane Wright, July 5, 1951; children—Michael Royce, Robert Gene, Joel Dan. B.S., U. Okla., 1957, Ph.D., 1969; M.S., Okla. State U., 1961. Prof. sci. edn. East Cen. U., Ada, Okla., 1961-73, prof. chemistry, 1973—; adj. prof. U. Okla., Norman, 1970—. Author: The Improvement of Science in Oklahoma (7-12), 1970, Guidelines and Successful Practices in Elementary Edn, 1970, Wings for a Dinosaur, 1972, Early Childhood Resource Book, 1972, Teaching Science in the Elementary School, 1973, 3d edit., 1979, Teaching Science in the Secondary School, 1973, Research, Teaching, and Learning with the Piaget Model, 1976, Investigations in Physical Science, 1976, The Learning Science Program K-6 (7 children's books and 7 tchr.'s guides), 1976, TOP, The Oklahoma Project, Chemistry, 1987, The Learning Cycle, 1988. Served with AUS, 1948-53. Mem. Am. Chem. Soc., Nat. Sci. Tchrs. Assn., Okla. Sci. Tchrs. (pres. 1973-74, 78-79), Sigma Xi. Home: 2202 Fullview Dr Ada OK 74820-4436

STAFFORD, EARL, conductor. Began piano studies at age 8; profl. and solo debut with Thunder Bay Symphony at age 10; studied at Faculty of Music, U. Toronto, with Milton Kaye in N.Y.C., at Paris Conservatory with Franco Ferrara and Aldo Ciccolini; joined Royal Winnipeg Ballet as prin. pianist, 1975, appointed assoc. music dir., 1982, now music dir. and condr.; also music dir. dance div. Banff Ctr. Fine Arts. Orchestrator numerous ballets for Royal Winnipeg Ballet, including Five Tangos, Bluebird Pas De Deux, Giselle Pas De Deux, Tchaikovsky Pas De Deux, Nuages; guest condr. various Can. orchs. including Vancouver Symphony, Calgary Philharmonic, Regina Symphony, Winnipeg Symphony, Saskatoon Symphony Orch., Nat. Arts Ctr. Orch., Thunder Bay Symphony. Recipient Gold medal for accompanying, Internat. Ballet Competition, Varna, Bulgaria, 1980. Office: EML Internat Artist Mgmt Inc, 219 Baseline Rd East, London, ON Canada N6C 2N6*

STAFFORD, FRANK PETER, JR., economics educator, consultant; b. Chgo., Sept. 17, 1940; s. Frank Peter and Ida Gustava (Tormala) S.; m. Lilian Elisabeth Lundin, Aug. 8, 1964; children: Craig Peter, Jennifer Elisabeth, Christine Anna. BA, Northwestern U., 1962; MBA, U. Chgo., 1964, PhD, 1968. Asst. prof. econs. U. Mich., 1966-71, assoc. prof., 1971-73, 74-75, prof., 1976—, chmn. dept. econs., 1980—, rsch. scientist Inst. Social Rsch., 1995—, chair budget study com., 1995—; vis. assoc. prof. Grad. Sch. Bus.-Stanford U., 1973-74; spl. asst. for econ. affairs U.S. Dept. Labor, Washington, 1975-76; vis. prof. dept. econs. U. Saarlandes, Fed. Republic Germany, 1986; faculty rsch. assoc. Inst. Social Rsch., Ann Arbor, 1979—; vis. scholar Indsl. Inst. for Econs. and Social Rsch., Stockholm, 1979, 83, 90, Worklife Study Ctr., Stockholm, 1988, 90; Tinbergen Found. prof. U. Amsterdam, 1992, 94; panel mem. Social Sci. Rsch. Coun., N.Y.C., 1979—; rsch. assoc. Nat. Bur. Econ. Rsch., Cambridge, Mass., 1983—; prof. econs. Tinbsrgne Found. U. Amsterdam, 1992; vis. scholar U. Stockholm, 1994. Author, editor: Time Use Goods and Well Being, 1986, Studies in Labor Market Behavior: Sweden and the United States, 1981; mem. editorial bd.: Am. Econ. Rev., 1976-78; contbr. articles to profl. jours. Co-dir. Panel Study of Income Dynamics, 1995—. Grantee NSF, 1973, 80, 95—, NICHD, 1995—. Mem. Am. Econs. Assn. Home: 3535 Daleview Dr Ann Arbor MI 48105-9686 Office: U Mich Dept Econs Lorch Hall Rm 312 Ann Arbor MI 48105

STAFFORD, JOHN ROGERS, pharmaceutical and household products company executive; b. Harrisburg, Pa., Oct. 24, 1937; s. Paul Henry and Gladys Lee (Sharp) S.; m. Inge Paul, Aug. 22, 1959; children—Carolyn, Jennifer, Christina, Charlotte. AB, Dickinson Coll., 1959; LLB with distinction, George Washington U., 1962, Degree (hon.), 1994. Bar: D.C. 1962. Assoc. Steptoe & Johnson, Washington, 1962-66; gen. atty. Hoffman-LaRoche, Nutley, N.J., 1966-67, group atty., 1967-70; gen. counsel Am. Home Products Corp., N.Y.C., 1970-74, v.p., 1972-77, sr. v.p., 1977-80, exec. v.p., 1980-81, pres., 1981—, chmn., chief exec. officer, 1986—; bd. dirs. The Chase Manhattan Corp., Allied Signal Inc., Grocery Mfrs. Am., Inc., Nynex Corp. Bd. dirs. Ctrl. Park Conservancy, Project Hope, Am.-China Soc., Am. Paralysis Assn. Recipient John Bell Larner 1st Scholar award George Washington U. Law Sch., 1962, Outstanding Achievement Alumnus award, 1981. Mem. ABA, D.C. Bar ASsn., Nat. Assn. Mfrs. (bd. dirs.), Sky Club (N.Y.C.), Essex Fells (N.J.) Country, Links Club (N.Y.C.), Baltusrol (N.J.), Robert Trent Jones (Va.). Office: American Home Products Corp 5 Giralda Farms Madison NJ 07940-1027

STAFFORD, PATRICK MORGAN, biophysicist; b. Roanoke, Va., June 3, 1950; s. Jess Woodrum and Georgine Elna (Morgan) S.; m. Kristina Lee Troyer, July 10, 1976; children: Kathryn Lee, Jess Walter. BS in Physics, Va. Poly. Inst., 1972; M Med. Sci. in Medical Physics, Emory U., 1979; PhD in Biophysics, U. Tex., Houston, 1987. Diplomate Am. Bd. Radiology. Assoc. engr. Duke Power Co., Charlotte, N.C., 1973-78; rsch. scientist U. N.Mex., Los Alamos, 1979-81; asst. physicist U. Tex., Houston, 1981-87; asst. prof. U. Pa., Phila., 1987-91; v.p. Radiation Care, Inc., Atlanta, 1991-95, Oncology Therapies, Inc., 1995—; adj. prof. Ga. Inst. Tech., 1993—; lectr. in field. Author: Dynamic Treatment with Pions at Lampf, 1980, Critical Angle Dependance of CR-39, 1986, Real-Time Portal Imaging; jour. reviewer Medical Physics, Internat. Jour. Radiation Oncology, Biology and Physics. Active Atlanta Emory Symphony, 1978; deacon Crabapple Bapt. Ch., Alpharetta, Ga., 1992. Rosalie B. Hite fellow U. Tex., 1983. Mem. Am. Assn. Physicists in Medicine (radiation therapy com. 1989-92, liaison from ASTRO 1995—, continuing edn. com. 1995—), Am. Coll. Med. Physics (commn. on comm. 1991-94), Am. Coll. Radiology, Am. Soc. for Therapeutic Radiology and Oncology. Home: 430 Kensington Farms Dr Alpharetta GA 30201-3740 Office: Oncology Therapies Inc 1155 Hammond Dr NE Ste A Atlanta GA 30328-5332

STAFFORD, REBECCA, academic administrator, sociologist; b. Topeka, July 9, 1936; d. Frank C. and Anne Elizabeth (Larrick) S. AB magna cum laude, Radcliffe Coll., 1958, MA, 1961; PhD, Harvard U., 1964. Lectr. dept. sociology Sch. Edn., Harvard U., Cambridge, Mass., 1964-70, mem. vis. com. bd. overseers, 1973-79; assoc. prof. sociology U. Nev., Reno, 1970-73, prof., 1973-80, chmn. dept. sociology, 1974-77, dean Coll. Arts and Scis., 1977-80; pres. Bemidji (Minn.) State U., 1980-82; exec. v.p. Colo. State U., Ft. Collins, 1982-83; pres. Chatham Coll., Pitts., 1983-91, Monmouth U., West Long Branch, N.J., 1993—; bd. dirs. First Union North, N.J. Contbr. articles to profl. jours. Trustee Monmouth Med. Ctr.; bd. dirs. Univ. Presbyn. Hosp., 1985-93, Pitts. Symphyony, 1984-93, Winchester-Thurston Sch.; chmn. Harvard U. Grad. Sch. Coun., 1987-93. Recipient McCurdy-Rinkle prize for rsch. Eastern Psychiat. Assn., 1970; named Woman of Yr. in Edn., City of Pitts., 1986, Woman of Yr. in Edn., YWCA Tribute to Women, 1989; grantee Am. Coun. Edn. Inst. Acad. Deans, 1979, Inst. Ednl. Mgmt., Harvard U., 1984. Mem. Harvard U. Alumni Assn. (bd. dirs. 1985-87), Phi Beta Kappa, Phi Kappa Phi. Office: Monmouth University West Long Branch NJ 07764

STAFFORD, ROBERT THEODORE, lawyer, former senator; b. Rutland, Vt., Aug. 8, 1913; s. Bert L. and Mable R. (Stratton) S.; m. Helen C. Kelley, Oct. 15, 1938; children—Madelyn, Susan, Barbara, Dianne. B.S., Middlebury Coll., 1935, LL.D., 1960; postgrad., U. Mich., 1936; LL.B., Boston U., 1938, LL.D., 1959; LL.D., Norwich U., 1960, St. Michaels Coll., 1967, U. Vt., 1970. Bar: Vt. bar 1938. City prosecutor Rutland, 1939-42; state's atty. Rutland County, 1947-51; dep. atty. gen. Vt., 1953-54, atty. gen., 1954-56, lt. gov., 1957-58, gov., 1959-60; mem. 87th to 92d Congresses, Vt.-at-large; apptd. U.S. Senate, 1971, mem., 1972-89, chmn. com. on environment and public works, 1981-87, chmn. edn. subcom., 1981-87, ranking mem., 1987-89; ptnr. Stafford, Abiatell & Stafford, 1938-46; sr. ptnr. Stafford & LaBrake, 1946-51. Chmn. UN-U.S.A. Assn. Panel UNESCO, 1989—. Lt. comdr. USNR, 1942-46, 51-52; capt. Res. Named Disting. Scholar U. Vt., 1989, Disting. Prof. Pub. Affairs Castleton State Coll., 1989. Mem. V.F.W., Am. Legion. Club: Elk. Home and Office: 1 Sugarwood Hill Rd RR 1 Box 3954 Rutland VT 05701 Office: Castleton Coll Coolidge Libr Bldg Castleton VT 05735

STAFFORD, SHANE LUDWIG, lawyer; b. Camden, N.J., Mar. 10, 1955; s. Joseph and Victoria Stafford; m. Connie, Jan. 19, 1980; children: Courtney, Ashley and Shaun (twins). BS, Calif. State U., 1977; JD, Southwestern U., L.A., 1980; LLD, U. Miami, 1980. Bar: Fla. 1980, U.S. Dist. Ct. (so. dist.) Fla. 1981. Intern Ins. Co. North Am., Miami, Fla., 1980-81; assoc. Miami, Fla., 1981-83; ptnr. Varner & Stafford, Lake Worth, Fla., 1983-85, Varner, Stafford & Seaman, Lake Worth, 1985—. Mem. Assn. Trial Lawyers Am., Acad. Trial Lawyers Fla., Palm Beach County Bar Assn., Phi Delta Phi. Avocations: golf, family. Office: Varner Stafford & Seaman 2328 10th Ave N Ste 2B Lake Worth FL 33461-6606

STAFFORD, THOMAS PATTEN, retired military officer, former astronaut; b. Weatherford, Okla., Sept. 17, 1930; m. Linda A. Dishman; children: Dionne, Karin. BS, U.S. Naval Acad., 1952; student, USAF Exptl. Flight Test Sch., 1958-59; DSc (hon.), Oklahoma City U., 1967; LLD (hon.), Western State U. Coll. Law, 1969, U. Cordoba, Argentina; D Communications (hon.), Emerson Coll., 1969; D Aero. Engring. (hon.), Embry-Riddle Aero. Inst., 1970; LHD (hon.), U. Okla., 1994; M of Humane Letters (hon.), Southwestern U., 1994; HHD (hon.), Oklahoma Christian U. Commd. 2d lt. USAF, 1952; advanced through grades to lt. gen.; chief performance br. Aerospace Research Pilot Sch., Edwards AFB, Calif.; with NASA, Houston, 1962-75; assigned Project Gemini, pilot Gemini VI, 1965, command pilot Gemini IX, 1966, comdr. Apollo X, 1969, chief astronaut office, 1969-71; dep. dir. flight crew operations, comdr. Apollo-Soyuz flight, 1975; comdr. Air Force Flight Test Ctr., Edwards AFB, 1975; lt. gen., dep. chief staff Research, Devel. and Aquisition, 1979; ret., 1979; chair The White House/NASA Com. to Independently Advise NASA How to Return to Moon and Explore Mars, 1990-91; chmn. bd. Omega Watch Co. Am.; dir. start F-117A Stealth Fighter, B-2 Stealth Bomber program, 1978; co-founder tech. cons. firm, Stafford, Burke, Hecker, Inc., Alexandria, Va.; adv. numerous govtl. agys. including NASA, Air Force Systems Command; defense advisor to Ronald Reagan during presdl. campaign; bd. dirs. numerous cos. Co-author: Pilot's Handbook for Performance Flight Testing, Aerodynamics Handbook for Performance Flight Testing. Decorated DFC with oak leaf cluster, D.S.M. (3), Disting. Flying Cross (2); recipient NASA Disting. Svc. medal (2), NASA Exceptional Svc. medal (2), Air Force Command Pilot Astronaut Wings; Chanute Flight award AIAA, 1976, VFW Nat. Space award, 1976; Gen. Thomas D. White USAF Space trophy Nat. Geog. Soc., 1976; Gold Space medal Fedn. Aeronautique Internationale, 1976, Laurel Award, Space/Missiles, Aviation Week & Space Tech., 1991, Congl. Space medal honor V.P. Dan Quayle, 1993, Rotary Nat. award Space Achievement, 1993, Goddard award Astronaut Hall of Fame, 1993, Pub. Svc. award NASA, 1994; co-recipient AIAA, 1966, Harmon Internat. Aviation trophy, 1966, Spl. Trustees award NATAS, 1969. Fellow Am. Astronautical Soc., Soc. Exptl. Test Pilots; mem. AIAA, AFTRA (hon. life). Holder all-time world speed record for space flight, 24,791.4 miles per hour. Address: 1006 Cameron St Alexandria VA 22314-2427 *As we move through life, each of us has an opportunity to make a contribution to humanity. In this respect, I have been extremely fortunate as I have been privileged to help explore new frontiers in space and aviation technology. But, it is clear to me that the most important element in a successful program is people. Their willingness to discipline their efforts and to work together to achieve important objectives remains the most important factor in a successful operation.*

STAFFORD, WILLIAM HENRY, JR., federal judge; b. Masury, Ohio, May 11, 1931; s. William Henry and Frieda Gertrude (Nau) S.; m. Nancy Marie Helman, July 11, 1959; children: William Henry, Donald Helman, David Harrold. B.S., Temple U., 1953, LL.B., 1956; J.D., 1968. Bar: Fla. 1961, U.S. Ct. Appeals (5th cir.) 1969, U.S. Supreme Ct. 1970. Assoc. firm Robinson & Roark, Pensacola, 1961-64; individual practice law Pensacola, 1964-67, state atty., 1967-69, U.S. atty., 1969-75; U.S. dist. judge U.S. Dist. Ct. for No. Dist. Fla., Tallahassee, 1975—, U.S. dist. judge, chief judge, 1981-93, sr. judge, 1996—; instr. Pensacola Jr. Coll., 1964, 68; mem. judicial council U.S. Ct. Appeals (11th cir.), 1986-89; apptd. com. on intercircuit assignments, 1987-92, subcom. on fed. jurisdiction, 1983-87. Lt. (j.g.) USN, 1957-60. Mem. Fla. Bar (mem. numerous coms., bench/bar commn. 1991-92, bench/bar implementation commn. 1993), Dist. Judges Assn. 11th Cir. (pres. 1984-85), State Fed. Judicial Council Fla., Am. Inns of Ct., Tallahassee Bar Assn., Tallahassee Inn (pres. 1989-91), Masons, Shriners, Rotary, Sigma Phi Epsilon, Phi Delta Phi. Republican. Episcopalian. Office: US Dist Ct 110 E Park Ave Tallahassee FL 32301-7750*

STAGE, THOMAS BENTON, psychiatrist; b. Marietta, Ohio, July 23, 1926; s. John Douglas and Grace (Shawhan) S.; m. Doris Jeane Weinstock, Dec. 22, 1951; children: Samuel Ray, Amy Elizabeth, James Robert; m.

Alicia Anderson Marsh, June 7, 1993. B.A. cum laude, Marietta Coll., 1949; M.D., Ohio State U., 1952. Diplomate: Am. Bd. Psychiatry and Neurology. Intern Detroit Receiving Hosp., 1952-53; psychiat. resident, fellow Menninger Sch. Psychiatry, Topeka, 1953-56; sect. chief, chief psychiatry VA Hosp., Topeka, 1956-62; adminstr. VA Hosp., Sheridan, Wyo., 1962-66; dir. VA Hosp., Salem, Va., 1967-72; dep. asst. chief med. dir. for ambulatory care VA Central Office, Washington, 1972-74; dir. No. Va. Mental Health Inst., Falls Church, 1974-78; asst. commr. for mental health State of Va., Richmond, 1978-79; dir. clin. services Fairfax-Falls Church Community Services Bd., Vienna, Va., 1979-82, psychiat. cons. for med. affairs, 1982—; instr. Menninger Sch. Psychiatry, 1958-62, U. Wyo. Sch. Nursing, 1963-66; assoc. prof. U. Va. Med. Sch., 1972-74; cons. surveyor Joint Commn. on Accreditation of Hosps., 1976—; cons. Crow-No. Cheyenne USPHS Hosp., 1963-66, Ala. Dept. Mental Health (Wyatt Com.), 1986-91; psychiatric cons. on accreditation Commonwealth of Va. Dept. Mental Health, Mental Retardation and Substance Abuse, 1982—; mem. Comprehensive Mental Health Ctr. Com., 1968-73, Gov.'s Adv. Commn. on Mental Health, 1971-74; chmn. Drug Abuse Rehab. Com., 1970-73; cons. adminstrv. psychiatry NIMH, 1975-78; chmn. steering com. Asso. Faculties Program Community Psychiatry, Washington, 1975-77; mem. State Health Coordinating Coun., 1976-89. Contbr. articles to profl. jours. Served wtih USNR, 1944-46, PTO. Fellow Am. Psychiat. Assn. (life); mem. Am. Assn. Psychiat. Adminstrs., Washington Psychiat. Soc., Psychiat. Soc. Va., Am. Assn. Community Psychiatrists. Home: 11410 Hollow Timber Way Reston VA 20194-1906 Office: Fairfax-Falls Ch Comty Svcs Ste 800 12011 Government Center Pkwy Fairfax VA 22035-1100

STAGEBERG, ROGER V., lawyer. B of Math. with distinction, U. Minn., 1963, JD cum laude, 1966. Assoc. Mackall, Crounse & Moore, Mpls., 1966-70, ptnr., 1970-86; shareholder and officer Lommen, Nelson, Cole & Stageberg, P.A., Mpls., 1986—; bd. dirs. Astrocom Corp., Mpls. Mem. U. Minn. Law Rev. Bd. dirs. Mpls. Legal Aid Soc., 1970—, treas., 1973, pres., 1977, dir. of fund, 1980—; chmn. bd. trustees Colonial Ch. of Edina, 1975, chmn. congregation, 1976, pres. found., 1978; officer, trustee Mpls. Found, 1983-88. Mem. Minn. State Bar Assn. (numerous offices and coms., pres. 1994), Hennepin County Bar Assn. (chmn. securities law sect. 1979, chmn. attys. referral svc. com. 1980, sec. 1980, treas. 1981, pres. 1983), Order of Coif. Office: Lommen Nelson Cole & Stageberg PA 1800 IDS Center 80 S 8th St Minneapolis MN 55402-2100

STAGER, DONALD K., construction company executive. Chmn. Dillingham Constrn. Holdings Inc., Pleasanton, Calif. Recipient, Roebling award Am. Soc. of Civil Engineers, 1995. Office: Dillingham Constrn Corp 5960 Inglewood Dr Pleasanton CA 94588-8535

STAGER, LAWRENCE E., archaeologist, educator; b. Kenton, Ohio, Jan. 5, 1943; married; 2 children. BA, Harvard U., 1965, MA, 1972, PhD in Syro-Palestinian Archeology and History, 1975. Instr. Oriental Inst., U. Chgo., 1973-74, asst. prof., 1974-75, assoc. prof. Syro-Palestinian archaeology, 1976-87; Dorot prof. archeology of Israel, Dept. Near Eastern Langs. and Civilizations and Anthropology Harvard U., Cambridge, Mass., 1986—; fellow Inst. for Advanced Study, Hebrew U., 1983-84; co-dir. Am. Expdn., Idalion, Cyprus, 1972-74; dir. UNESCO Save Carthage Project, Am. Punic Archaeol. Expdn., 1975-80, Harvard Semitic Mus., 1987—, Leon Levy Expdn. to Ashkelon, Israel, 1985—. Author: Ashkelon Discovered, 1991, A Heap of Broken Images: Essays in Biblical Archaeology, 1997; co-author: Idalion I, Idalion II; contbr. articles to profl. jours. Mem. Am. Schs. Oriental Rsch. (editor newsletter 1975-76, assoc. trustee 1977-80, trustee 1987-90, assoc. editor bull. 1978—), Archaeol. Inst. Am. (v.p. 1986-88, trustee 1989-91), Am. Orient Soc., Soc. Bibl. Lit. Rsch. in economy, society and religion of ancient Israel; archaeology of Philistines, Canaanites and Phoenicians. Office: Harvard U Semitic Mus Dept Near Ea Langs/Civil Cambridge MA 02138-2091

STAGG, LOUIS CHARLES, English language and literature educator; b. New Orleans, Jan. 3, 1933; s. Louis Anatol and Gladys (Andrews) S.; BA in English, La. Coll., 1955; MA in English U. Ark., 1957, PhD in English, 1963; m. Mary Casner, June 5, 1959; children: Robert Charles, Helen Marie. Teaching asst. English U. Ark., 1955-59; asst. prof. William Jewell Coll., 1959-60; instr. Stephen F. Austin State U., 1960-62; asst. prof. Memphis State U. (name changed to U. Memphis), 1962-69, assoc. prof., 1969-77, prof. English language and literature 1977—, dir. grad. studies in English, 1985-88, dir. English Drama Players, 1968—, dir undergrad. advising for English, 1970-80, 88-91, chair policies and procedures com. for English, 1983-95, tenure and promotion com. for English, 1978-80, 82-86, 89-97; chmn. acad. policies com. Memphis State U. Senate, 1981-82, 88-90, 93-94, 95-96, mem. exec. com. senate, 1987-91, 93-96, parliamentarian of senate, 1987-88, 90-91, 94-95, humanities rep. budget adv. com. dean coll. arts and scis., 1992-93, mem. steering com., chair of schedules, originator Alliance Creative Theatre, Edn. and Rsch. series, 1986,89, 90, 92, 94, 96; cons. NEH, 1975, 76, 78, Ohio State U. Press, summer 1985, 86, U. Jordan, Aman, 1985; chair policies and procedures subdivsn. Eng. Dept. so. assn. colls., schs. self study, mem. steering com., 1992-93; cons. Memphis State U. Learning Media-Ctrs. catalogue Shakespeare holdings, 1992-93, rev., 1993-94, 94-95. Mem. Memphis Oratorio Soc. Chorus, 1969-92, diction coach, 1987, Memphis Symphony Chorus, 1993—, Memphis in May Tattoo Chorus, 1993, Memphis in May Sunset Symphony Choir, 1996, Martin Luther King Tribute Concert Choir, 1995, 96. Recipient summer stipend NEH, 1967; Memphis State U. grantee, 1965; travel grantee to U.S. Library of Congress, summer 1971. Mem. MLA, So. Humanities Coun. (sec.-treas. 1974-76, exec. com. 1976-83, 94-96, chmn. coun. 1993-94, chmn. sect. humanities in pluralistic society 1984, ad hoc com. on crisis in teaching humanities 1977, chmn. local arrangements for convs. 1975, 94, chmn. sect. on Thomas Hardy, 1996), Tenn. Philol. Assn. (pres. 1976-77, exec. com. 1977, local arrangements chmn. 1965, 69, 75, 87, chmn. Shakespeare sect. 1996), Marlowe Soc. Am. (book reviewer 1984, 86, 87, 88, 93), Am. Soc. for Theatre Rsch., Samuel Beckett Soc., Conf. on Christianity and Lit., South Cen. Conf. on Christianity and Lit. Soc. for Study of Works of Harold Pinter (asst. constitution revision 1988, asst. with planning 1992, treas. 1994—, mem. exec. com. 1994—), Ark. Philol. Assn., Shakespeare Assn. Am. (local arrangements host com. 1985), Stratford-Upon-Avon Shakespeare Festival, Eng.; Eugene O'Neill Soc., Alliance for Creative Theatre, Edn. and Rsch. (chmn. schedules com., rep. for English, mem. steering com., originator of proposal 1986, 89, 90, 92, 94, 96, cons. residency S.E. Mo. State U. 1997), Internat. Shakespeare Assn., Am. Soc. Theatre Rsch., Internat. Soc. Theatre Rsch., Medieval and Renaissance Drama Soc., Renaissance Soc. Am., South Cen. Renaissance Conf. (chmn. nominations 1976, exec. com. 1978-80, program com. 1981-83, chmn. sect. Shakespeare 1981, 85, 95, 16th Century lit. 1982, chmn. local arrangements 1983, symposium on humanism 1984, chmn. Shakespeare on film and the teaching of Brit. Drama 1986, chmn. music in Shakespeare's plays 1987, chmn. sect. Thematic Approaches to Tudor/Stuart Drama 1988, chmn. sect. Medieval influences on Renaissance drama 1993, chmn. Shakespeare's Villains: Stage and Page 1995, Adaptations of Renaissance Drama, 1996, chmn. local arrangements for convention 1990, chmn. spl. session 1989, 95, Shakespeare II sect. 1996), South Cen. MLA (assoc. editor for English, South Cen. Bull. 1982-84, nominations com. 1985-86, 95-96, book reviewer South Cen. Rev. 1983, 85, 86, sec. English I.B. Renaissance, 1986, chair, 1987, sec. spl. sect. Renaissance Drama, 1988, chair Shakespeare's Tragi-comedies and tragi-comic romances, 1989, co-chair local arrangements 1980, 92, chair panel on renaissance drama criticism 1995, sec. renaissance drama sect. 1997), South Atlantic MLA, South Cen. Coll. English Assn. (sec.-treas. 1980-81, v.p. 1981-82, pres. 1982-83, exec. com. 1983-90, co-host 1982, com. constitution revision 1989), Coll. English Assn., Internat. Patristic Medieval and Renaissance Conf. (sect. chmn. Medieval drama 1977, chair Shakespeare session 1994, chair Renaissance drama section 1995, chmn. 17th century Brit. lit. sect. 1996, chmn. Milton sect. 1996), Am. Theatre Assn. (chmn. sect. combining Brit. lit. and theatre in teaching of drama 1983, chmn. Shakespeare sect. 1994), The Stratford Can. Shakespeare Festival, AAUP (sec. treas. Memphis State U. chap. 1982-86, v.p. 1986-88, pres. 1988-90), Phi Beta Kappa (pres. Memphis alumni assn. 1985-88, mem. spl. panel The Soc. and the New Scholarship at 37th triennial coun. '94), Alpha Chi. Democrat. Episcopalian (lay reader 1969-86). Author: (with J. Lasley Dameron) Poe's Critical Vocabulary, 1966; author series: Index To The Figurative Language of John Webster's Tragedies, 1967, of Ben Jonson's Tragedies, 1967, of Thomas Heywood's Tragedies, 1967, of George Chapman's Tragedies, 1970, of John Marston's Tragedies, 1970, of Thomas Middleton's Tragedies, 1970, of Cyril Tourneur's Tragedies, 2d edit. all 7 under title Index to the Figurative Language of the Tragedies of Shakespeare's Chief 17th Century Contemporaries 1977), 3d edit., 1982; Index to the Figurative Language of the Tragedies of Shakespeare's Chief 16th Century Contemporaries, 1984; contbr. to Great Writers of the English Language: Dramatists, 1979, 87; circulation editor Interpretations, 1976-80; contbr. articles on English and American drama to profl. jours., publs. on Shakespeare, other lit. publs. Home: 5219 Mason Rd Memphis TN 38117-2104 Office: U Memphis Dept English PO Box 526176 Memphis TN 38152-6176 *It's time—past time— we realized we all belong to one race, human, and that we have only one world, this one, only one ecological system, this one, if we want humanity to survive beyond our own life times.*

STAGG, TOM, federal judge; b. Shreveport, La., Jan. 19, 1923; s. Thomas Eaton and Beulah (Meyer) S.; m. Margaret Mary O'Brien, Aug. 21, 1946; children: Julie, Margaret Mary. B.A., La. State U., 1943, J.D., 1949. Bar: La. 1949. With firm Hargrove, Guyton, Van Hook & Hargrove, Shreveport, 1949-53; pvt. practice law Shreveport, 1953-58; sr. ptnr. firm Stagg, Cady & Beard, Shreveport, 1958-74; judge U.S. Dist. Ct. (we. dist.) La., 1974-84, 91-92, chief judge, 1984-90, sr. judge, 1992—; Pres. Abe Meyer Corp., 1960-74, Stagg Investments, Inc., 1964-74; mng. partner Pierremont Mall Shopping Center, 1963-74; v.p. King Hardware Co., 1955-74; Mem. Shreveport Airport Authority, 1967-73, chmn., 1970-73; chmn. Gov.'s Tidelands Adv. Council, 1969-70; del. La. Constl. Conv., 1973-74; chmn. rules com., com. on exec. dept.; mem. Gov.'s Adv. Com on Offshore Revenues, 1972-74. Active Republican party, 1950-74, del. convs., 1956, 60, 64, 68, 72; mem. Nat. Com. for La., 1964-72, mem. exec. com., 1964-68; Pres. Shreveport Jr. C. of C., 1955-56; v.p. La. Jr. C. of C., 1956-57. Served to capt., inf. AUS, 1943-46, ETO. Decorated Bronze Star, Purple Heart with oak leaf cluster. Mem. Am., La., Shreveport bar assns., Photog. Soc. Am. Office: US Dist Ct 300 Fannin St Ste 4100 Shreveport LA 71101-3121*

STAGGERS, KERMIT LEMOYNE, II, history and political science educator, state senator; b. Washington, Pa., Nov. 2, 1947; s. Kermit LeMoyne and Christine Ruby (Scherich) S.; m. June Ann Wenda, Aug. 22, 1970; children: Ayn Kristen, Kyle Lee. BS, U. Idaho, 1969, MA, 1975; PhD, Claremont Grad. Sch., 1986. Instr. history Troy (Ala.) State U., 1975-76, U. Idaho, Moscow, 1977, Northwestern Coll., Orange City, Iowa, 1979-80, Coll. Lake County, Grayslake, Ill., 1981-82; lectr. history Chapman Coll., Orange, Calif., 1979, U. Md.-Europe, Heidelberg, Germany, 1988-89; vis. instr. history Trinity Coll., Deerfield, Ill., 1980; ad. instr. history Coll. St. Francis, Joliet, Ill., 1982; assoc. prof. history and polit. sci. U. Sioux Falls (S.D.), 1982—; mem. S.D. Senate, 1995—; expert analyst on polit. and social issues for local radio and TV. Contbr. to profl. pubs. Chair Senate Transp. Com., 1997—; mem. Forward Sioux Falls Devel. Coun. Capt. USAF, 1970-76. Recipient Guardian Small Bus. award Nat. Fedn. Ind. Bus., 1996; Malone Faculty fellow, 1993. Mem. Orgn. Am. Historians, Conf. on Faith and History, Federalist Soc., Am. Legis. Exch. Coun., Kiwanis, Phi Alpha Theta, Phi Kappa Phi. Republican. Disciples of Christ. Avocations: book collecting, travel. Home: 1135 S Walts Ave Sioux Falls SD 57105-0543 Office: U Sioux Falls Dept History/Polit Sci 1101 W 22nd St Sioux Falls SD 57105-1600

STAGLIN, GAREN KENT, finance and computer service company executive; b. Lincoln, Nebr., Dec. 22, 1944; s. Ramon and Darlene (Guilliams) S.; m. Sharalyn King, June 8, 1968; children: Brandon Kent, Shannon King. BS in Engring. with honors, UCLA, 1966; MBA, Stanford U., 1968. Treas. Stanco, Inc., 1968—; assoc. Carr Mgmt. Co., N.Y.C., 1971-75; v.p. Crocker Nat. Bank, San Francisco, 1975-76; dir. fin. Itel Corp., San Francisco, 1976-77, pres. ins. services div., 1977-79; corp. v.p., gen. mgr. ADP Automotive Svcs. Group, San Ramon, Calif., 1978-91; chmn., chief exec. officer Safelite Glass Corp., Columbus, Ohio, 1991—; owner Staglin Family Vineyard, Rutherford, Calif., 1985—; bd. dirs. Grimes Aerospace Corp., Cyber Cash Corp. Bd. dirs. Peralta Hosp. Cancer Inst., 1977-78, Berkeley Reportory Theatre, 1979-85, Summa Care, Inc., 1988-90, Quick Response Svcs., Inc., 1991—, First Data Corp., 1992—; trustee Justin Sienna H.S., Napa, Calif., 1995—; chmn. major gifts program Ea. Bay region Stanford (Calif.) U., 1989-92. Lt. USN, 1968-71. Mem. Stanford Assocs. (bd. govs. 1985-92), World Pres. Orgn., Internat. Inst. Soc. (bd. govs. 1985-92), Stanford Bus. Sch. (adv. bd. 1995—). Democrat. Lutheran. Home: PO Box 680 1570 Bella Oaks Ln Rutherford CA 94573

STAHELI, DONALD L., grain company executive; b. 1931. BS, Utah State U., 1953; MS, U. Ill., 1954, PhD, 1956. With Swift & Co., 1958-69, Allied Mills (now World Meat and World Milling Groups of Continental Grain Co., 1969—; dir. Continental Grain Co., N.Y.C., 1977—, exec. v.p., 1977-84, pres., COO, 1984-88, CEO, chmn., 1988—. With USAF, 1956-58. Office: Continental Grain Co 277 Park Ave New York NY 10172

STAHELI, LYNN TAYLOR, pediatric orthopedist, educator; b. Provo, Utah, Nov. 13, 1933; s. Harvey Roulin and Letha (Taylor) S.; m. Ann Lee Smith, June 4, 1957 (div. 1976); children: Linda Ann, Diane Kay, Todd Kent; m. Lana Ribble, June 11, 1977. BS, Brigham Young U., 1956; MD, U. Utah, 1959. Intern U. Utah, Salt Lake City, 1960; resident in orthopedic surgery U. Wash., 1964-68; dir. rsch. and edn. Children's Hosp., Seattle, 1968-77, dir. dept. orthopedics, 1977-92; prof. dept. orthopedics U. Wash., Seattle, 1968—; mem. med. exec. com. Children's Hosp. and Med. Ctr., Seattle, 1977-92; cons. Fircrest Sch., Seattle, 1968-80, Boyer Children's clinic, Seattle, 1968-80, Seattle Pub. Schs. Spl. Edn. Program, 1968-80; invited speaker for more than 1000 individual presentations in 30 countries, 1960—; founder Duncan Seminar for Cerebral Palsy, 1980. Editor: Jour. Pediatric Orthopedics, 1981—; author: Med. Writing and Speaking, 1986, Fundamentals of Pediatric Orthopedics, 1992; contbr. articles to numerous profl. jours. Founding mem. bd. N.W. Inst. Ethics and Life Scis., Seattle, 1974—; bd. dirs. Rainier Found., Seattle, 1988—; founder Internat. Scholarship for Pediatric Orthopedics, Seattle, 1988-93. Capt. USAF, 1960-63. Mem. Pediatric Orthopedic Soc. N.Am., Am. Acad. Orthopedic Surgeons (pediatric orthopedics com. 1980-86), Am. Acad. Pediatrics (chmn. com. on shoewear 1985—, Disting. Svc. award 1995), Am. Acad. Cerebral Palsy and Devel. Medicine (chmn. instrnl. course com. 1982—), Alpha Omega Alpha. Avocations: flying, sailing, boating, canoeing, photography. Home: 4116 48th Ave NE Seattle WA 98105-5116 Office: Childrens Hosp Dept Orthopedics 4800 Sand Point Way NE Seattle WA 98105-3901

STAHL, ALAN MICHAEL, curator; b. Providence, Aug. 7, 1947; s. Benjamin and Evelyn (Miller) S.; m. Pamela McAbee Dec. 28, 1968 (div. 1976). BA, U. Calif., Berkeley, 1968; MA, U. Pa., 1973, PhD, 1977. Asst. curator Am. Numismatic Soc., N.Y.C., 1980-82, assoc. curator, 1982-86, curator, 1986—; visiting prof. Universita di Venezia, Venice, Italy, 1987-88. Author: Merovingian Coinage/Metz, 1982, Venetian Tornesello, 1985, Medal in America, 1988. Recipient Research Grant G.K. Delmas Found., 1981, 83, 85. Mem. Fed. Internat. de la Medaille (USA del.), Am. Medallic Sculpture Assn., Nat. Sculpture Soc. (councillor), Medieval Acad. Am., N.Y. Numismatic Club. Home: 11 Fairview Pl Ossining NY 10562 Office: Am Numismatic Soc Broadway at 155th St New York NY 10032

STAHL, ALICE SLATER, psychiatrist; b. Vienna, Austria, Jan. 28, 1913; came to U.S., 1938; d. Sam and Helen (Bluman) Slater; widowed; chidlren: Kenneth Lee, June Audrey. Baccalaureate, Gymnasium, Vienna, 1932; Med. Dr., U. Vienna Med. Sch., 1938. Intern Williamsport (Pa.) Gen. Hosp., 1939-40; resident in psychiatry Gallinger Mcpl. Hosp., Washington, 1940-41, Independence State Hosp., 1941-42; resident in psychiatry Bellevue Hosp., N.Y.C., 1942-43, attending psychiatry, 1945-48; staff psychiatrist Jewish Bd. of Guardians, N.Y.C., 1943-45; attending psychiatrist Jamaica Hosp., Queens, N.Y., 1948-52; dir. adolescent psychiatry Hillside Hosp., Glen Oaks, N.Y., 1954-62, attending staff psychiatrist, 1962-97; supervising psychiatrist Bergen Pines County Hosp., Paramus, N.J.; asst. prof. clin. psychiatry Yeshiva U. Med. Sch., 1978-96. Fellow AMA (life), Am. Psychiat. Assn. (life); mem. Am. Psychoanalytic Assn. (life), Am. Soc. for Adolescent Psychiatry (life). Avocations: swimming, hiking, gardening, grandmotherhood. Home and Office: 305 Joan Pl Wyckoff NJ 07481-2818

STAHL, DAVID EDWARD, trade association administrator, retired; b. Chgo., Apr. 10, 1934; s. Archie Edward and Dorothy (Berning) S.; m. Carolyn Downs Stahl, June 23, 1956; children: Stephen, Michael, Kurt, Thomas. BS, Miami U., 1956. Exec. v.p. Republic Realty Mortgage Corp., Chgo., 1963-66; dep. mayor City of Chgo., 1966-70, city comptroller, 1971-73; exec. v.p. Urban Land Inst., Washington, 1973-76, Nat. Assn. Home Builders, Washington, 1977-84; pres. Nat. Forest Products Assn., Washington, 1984-87; exec. v.p. Urban Land Inst., Washington, 1987-92; exec. dir. Young Pres.'s Orgn., Irving, Tex., 1992-95; ret., 1995; del. 6th Ill. Constl. Conv., Springfield, 1970. Served to lt. USAF, 1956-59. Mem. Am. Soc. Assn. Execs., Econ. Club (Chgo.), Wayfarers Club, Annapolis Yacht Club, Ocean Reef Club, Lambda Alpha. Roman Catholic. Home: 100 Severn Ave # 607 Annapolis MD 21403

STAHL, FRANK LUDWIG, civil engineer; b. Fuerth, Germany, 1920; came to U.S., 1946, naturalized, 1949; s. Leo E. and Anna (Regensburger) S.; m. Edith Cosmann, Aug. 31, 1947; children—David, Robert. BSCE, Tech. Inst. Zurich, Switzerland, 1945. With Ammann & Whitney, Cons. Engrs., N.Y.C., 1946-93, project engr., 1955-67, assoc., 1968-76, sr. assoc., 1977-81, chief engr. Transp. div., 1982-93; pvt. cons., 1994—; author and lectr. in field. Prin. works include: Verrazano-Narrows Bridge, Throgs Neck Bridge, Walt Whitman Bridge, Improvements to Golden Gate Bridge, rehab. of Williamsburg Bridge, N.Y.C. Royal Gorge Bridge, Colo., Interstate-10 Deck Tunnel, Phoenix, Ariz.; contbr. articles to profl. jours. on bridge design and construction. Recipient Gold award The James F. Lincoln Arc Welding Found., 1986, John A. Roebling medal Internat. Bridge Conf., 1992. Fellow ASCE (Thomas Fitch Rowland prize 1967, Innovation in Civil Engring. award of merit 1983, Metro. Civil Engr. of Yr. award 1987, Roebling award 1990), ASTM (vice chmn. com. A-1 on steel, stainless steel and related alloys 1978-83, chmn. steel reinforce-subcom. 1971-82, award of merit 1982); mem. Am. Inst. Steel Constrn. (Prize Bridge award 1986), Engring. Found. (rsch. coun. on structural connections), Internat. Assn. Bridge and Structural Engring., Internat. Bridge Tunnel and Turnpike Assn. Home: 20911 28th Rd Flushing NY 11360-2412

STAHL, GARY EDWARD, neonatologist; b. N.Y.C., Mar. 19, 1951; s. Louis and Susan (Stein) S.; m. Deborah Susan Levy, July 1, 1973; children: Adam Louis, Eric Alexander. B.S., B.S.E.E., MIT, 1973; M.D., U. Rochester, 1977. Diplomate Am. Bd. Pediatrics, subbd. neonatal-perinatal medicine. Pediatric resident Children's Hosp., Phila., 1977-80; neonatal fellow U. Pa., Phila., 1980-83; asst. prof. pediatrics U. Pa. Sch. Medicine, Phila., 1983-90; assoc. prof. pediatrics Hahnemann U. Sch. Medicine, Phila., 1991-93, U. Med. Dentistry N.J., Camden, 1991-93; dir. neonatal svcs., vice chief dept. pediats. Children's Regional Hosp., Camden, 1993—. Contbr. articles to profl. jours. Fellow Am. Acad. Pediatrics; mem. Nat. Perinatal Soc., Pa. Perinatal Soc., Phila. Perinatal Soc., Physicians for Social Responsibility, Sigma Xi. Office: Children's Regional Hosp at Cooper 1 Cooper Plz Camden NJ 08103-1461

STAHL, JACK LELAND, real estate company executive; b. Lincoln, Ill., June 28, 1934; s. Edwin R. and Edna M. (Burns) S.; m. Carol Anne Townsend, June 23, 1956; children: Cheryl, Nancy, Kellea. BS in Edn., U. N.Mex., 1957. Tchr. Albuquerque Public Schs., 1956-59; pres. House Finders, Inc., Albuquerque, 1959-65; v.p. N.Mex. Savs. & Loan Assn., Albuquerque, 1965-67; chmn. bd. Hooten-Stahl, Inc., Albuquerque, 1967-77; mem. N.Mex. Ho. of Reps., 1969-70; pres. The Jack Stahl Co., Albuquerque, 1977—; mem. N.Mex. Senate, 1981-86; lt. gov. State of N.Mex., 1987-90. Mem. N. Mex. Ho. of Reps., 1969-70, exec. bd. Gr. S.W. Coun. Boy Scouts Am, 1982-89; bd. dirs. BBB N. Mex., 1968-82, pres. 1975-76; trustee Univ Heights. Hosp.,1980-85; vice chmn. N. Mex. Bd. Fin., 1987-90, N. Mex. Cmty. Devel. Coun., 1987-90; bd. dirs. Ctr. for Entrepreneurship and Econ. Devel., 1994—; mem. Gov.'s Bus. Adv. Coun., 1995—. Named Realtor of Yr., Albuquerque Bd. Realtors, 1972. Mem. Nat. Assn. Realtors, Nat. Homebuilders Assn., N.Mex. Amigos, 20-30 Club (pres. 1963-64), Rotary. Republican. Methodist. Office: 1911 Wyoming Blvd NE Albuquerque NM 87112-2865

STAHL, LADDIE L., electrical engineer, manufacturing company executive; b. Terre Haute, Ind., Dec. 23, 1921; s. Edgar Allen and Martha (Llewellyn) S.; m. Thelma Mae Beasley, Dec. 11, 1942; children: Stephanie, Laddie L., Craig. B.S. in Civil Engring., Purdue U., 1942; M.S. in Engring., Johns Hopkins U., 1950. With GE, 1954-90; mgr. planning and resources, electronics sci. and engring., corp. research and devel. GE, Schenectady, N.Y., 1974-76, mgr. electronics systems programs ops., elec. sci. and engring., 1976-84, mgr. spl. programs and project devel. operation, 1984-90; dir. tech. transfer program Data Storage Systems Ctr. Carnegie Mellon U., Pitts., 1990—; chmn. adv. group U.S. Army Electronics Command, 1971-74; mem. U.S. Army Sci. Bd., 1978-87; cons. in field. Contbr. articles to profl. pubs. Mem. alumni bd. dirs. Purdue U., 1979-82. Served with U.S. Army, 1942-54, ETO; maj. gen. Res. (ret.), 1954-77. Decorated D.S.M., Legion of Merit. Mem. AIAA (sr.), IEEE (life), Am. Def. Preparedness Assn., Tau Beta Pi, Chi Epsilon. Clubs: Mohawk (Schenectady); Army and Navy (Washington). Home: 29 Fairway Ln Rexford NY 12148-1213 Office: Carnegie Mellon U Hamerschlag Hall A206 ECE Dept Hamburg Hall 2505 Pittsburgh PA 15213-3890

STAHL, LESLEY R., journalist; b. Lynn, Mass., Dec. 16, 1941; d. Louis and Dorothy J. (Tishler) S.; m. Aaron Latham; 1 dau. BA cum laude, Wheaton Coll., Norton, Mass., 1963. Asst. to speechwriter Mayor Lindsay's Office, N.Y.C., 1966-67; rschr. N.Y. Election unit CBS News, 1967-68; rschr. London-Huntley Brinkley Report, NBC News, 1969; producer, reporter WHDH-TV, Boston, 1970-72; news corr. CBS News, Washington, from 1972; White House corr. CBS News, 1979-91; moderator Face the Nation, 1983-91; co-editor, corr. CBS News, 60 Minutes, 1991—. Trustee Wheaton Coll. Recipient Tex. Headliners award, 1973, Dennis Kauff award for lifetime achievement in journalism, Fifth Estate award Broadcasting Mag. Hall of Fame, 1992, Fred Friendly First Amendment award, 1996; named Best White House Corr., Washington Journalism Rev., 1991. Office: CBS News 60 Minutes 555 W 57th St New York NY 10019-2925*

STAHL, LOUIS A., lawyer; b. Oct. 31, 1940; s. Louis A. and Dorothy (Cox) S.; m. Mary Kathleen Quinn, Apr. 4, 1960; children: Lisa, Suzanne, Gretchen, Nicole. BA magna cum laude, Wheeling Jesuit U., 1962; postgrad., Duquesne U., 1965-66; JD summa cum laude, Notre Dame U., 1971. Bar: Ariz. 1971, U.S. Dist. Ct. Ariz. 1971, U.S. Ct. Appeals (9th cir.) 1974, U.S. Supreme Ct. 1975. Ptnr. Streich Lang P.A., Phoenix, 1971—; mem. Maricopa County Superior Ct. Rule 26.1 Study Com., 1992—; Frances Lewis lawyer in residence Washington & Lee Univ. Law Sch., 1986; seminar panelist Ariz. Bankers Assn., 1987, Profl. Ednl. Systems, Inc., 1989; mediator, arbirtator U.S. Arbitration and Mediation of Ariz., Nev. and N. Mex., 1993—. Contbg. author: Arizona Attorneys' Fees Manual, 1987, Arizona Professionalism Manual, 1992; contbr. papers to law revs. and jours. Active Phoenix and Maricopa County Young Reps., Ariz. Rep. Party's Lawyers' Ballot Security Com., 1980, Vols. for Reagan-Bush, 1980, Re-elect Rep. Ernest Baird Fin. Com., 1992, Ariz. Rep. Caucus.; founding mem., v.p., dir., legal counsel Performing Arts Combined Talent; pres., bd. dirs. Make a Wish Found. Ctrl. & So. Ariz., 1995—. Mem. ABA (vice-chmn. health ins. com., sect. ins., negligence and compensation law 1973-79, contbg. editor The Forum 1976-79), State Bar Ariz. (mem. profl. liability com. 1979-86, chmn. 1983-86, mem. com. on rules of profl. conduct ethics com. 1981-93, com. on professionalism 1989-91, discipline task force 1991-92, co-chmn. peer rev. com. 1991—), Def. Rsch. Inst., Ariz. Assn. of Def. Counsel, Ariz. Bar Found., Phoenix C. of C. (military affairs com.), Am. Numismatic Assn., Phoenix Coin Club. Office: Streich Lang PA 2 N Central Ave Ste 200 Phoenix AZ 85004-2322

STAHL, NORMAN H., federal judge; b. Manchester, N.H., 1931. BA, Tufts U., 1952; LLB, Harvard U., 1955. Law clk. to Hon. John V. Spalding Mass. Supreme Ct., 1955-56; assoc. Devine, Millimet, Stahl & Branch, Manchester, N.H., 1956-59, ptnr., 1959-90; dist. judge U.S. Dist. Ct. (N.H. dist.), 1990-92; cir. judge U.S. Ct. Appeals (1st cir.), Concord, N.H., 1992—. Del. to Rep. Nat. Conv., 1988. Mem. N.H. Bar Assn. Office: US Ct Appeals 55 Pleasant St Rm 220 Concord NH 03301-3938

STAHL, O(SCAR) GLENN, writer, lecturer, former government official; b. Evansville, Ind., Apr. 30, 1910; s. Oscar and Mayme (Wittmer) S.; m. Marie Jane Rueter, June 26, 1934; children: Elaine Marie, Alan G. A.B., U. Evansville, 1931, LL.D., 1984; M.A., U. Wis., 1933; Ph.D., N.Y. U., 1936. Instr. govt. NYU, 1933-35; personnel officer TVA, 1935-41; with Fed. Security Agy. (later HEW), 1941-51; dir. personnel, 1948-51; with U.S. CSC (now OPM), 1951-69, dir. bur. policies and standards, 1955-69; adj. prof.

public adminstrn. Am. U., 1949-69; part time prof. U. Tenn., 1939, Dept. Agr. Grad. Sch., 1941-49; vis. lectr. various univs., U.S. and abroad; lectr. Salzburg Seminar in Am. Studies, 1965; tech. assistance adviser to Venezuela UN, 1958-59, 72; U.S. rep. UN Conf., Ethiopia, 1964; Ford Found. cons. to, India, 1968-69, 71, Nepal, 1969, Pakistan, 1974; AID adviser, Pakistan, 1969, 71; U.S. rapporteur Internat. Congress Adminstrv. Scis., Dublin, 1968; U.S. rep. UN Seminar, Tashkent, Uzbekistan, 1969; spl. advisor to W. Ger., 1971; spl. cons. Public Adminstrn. Service-Govtl. Affairs Inst. and Internat. Personnel Mgmt. Assn., 1973-76; dir. Internat. Symposium on Public Personnel Adminstrn., Salzburg, 1973, 75; speaker Latin Am. Conf. on Civil Service Tng., Venezuela, 1982. Author: Training Career Public Servants for the City of New York, 1936, Public Personnel Administration, 8th edit, 1983, The Personnel Job of Government Managers, 1971, Frontier Mother, 1979, The Need for a Public Philosophy, 1987, Standing Up for Government, 1990; editor: Personnel Adminstrn, 1945-55, Improving Public Services, 1979, (with others) Police Personnel Administration, 1974; contbr. numerous articles to jours. Mem. Arlington County (Va.) Sch. Bd., 1948-50; pres. Arlington Com. to Preserve Public Schs., 1958-61. Recipient Disting. Service award CSC, 1960; Stockberger award Soc. Personnel Adminstrn., 1962; Career Service award Nat. Civil Service League, 1967; medal of Honor U. Evansville, 1981; hon. fellow Nat. Acad. Pub. Adminstrn., 1988. Mem. Am. Polit. Sci. Assn., Am. Soc. Public Adminstrn. (editorial bd. 1955-58), Internat. Inst. Adminstrv. Sci., Internat. Personnel Mgmt. Assn. (hon. life mem., exec. com. Public Personnel Assn. 1951-54, pres. 1965-66, Washington rep. 1971-73). Presbyterian. Home: 3600 N Piedmont St Arlington VA 22207-5333

STAHL, RICHARD G. C., journalist, editor; b. Chgo., Feb. 22, 1934; m. Gladys C. Weisbecker; 1 child, Laura Ann. Student, Northwestern U., U. Ill., Chgo. Editor Railway Purchases and Stores Mag., Chgo., 1960-63; editor pub. rels. dept. Sears Roebuck & Co., Chgo., 1963-68; dir pub. rels. dept. St. Joseph's Hosp. Med. Ctr., Phoenix, 1968-72; v.p. pub. rels. Consultation Svcs., Inc., Phoenix, 1972-73; creative dir. Don Jackson and Assoc., Phoenix, 1973; editor, pub. rels. mgr. Maricopa County Med. Soc., Phoenix, 1974-76; sr. editor Ariz. Hwys. mag., Phoenix, 1977—. Regional editor: (travel guides) Budget Travel, 1985, USA, 1986, Arizona, 1986; free-lance writer and editor. Mem. Soc. Profl. Journalists. Avocation: woodworking. Office: Ariz Hwys Mag 2039 W Lewis Ave Phoenix AZ 85009-2819 *Personal philosophy: Follow your dream and fulfill your potentialities.*

STAHL, STEPHEN LEE, theater director, writer, producer; b. Phila., Mar. 15, 1949; s. Myer and Fridel (Goldstein) S.; m. Cornell DeFanis, Dec. 29, 1969 (div. May 1976); 1 child, Meredith. Student, Lee Strasburg Actors Studio, 1981. Artistic dir. Studio 3 Prodns., Phila., 1979-82; artistic dir., tchr. drama Actors Ctr., Phila., 1982-85; dir. Troyvay Internat., Paris, London, 1985-87, Theatre of Living Arts, Phila., 1987—, Theatre on the Sq., San Francisco; tchr. drama Freez Frame Inc., Phila., 1987—; dir., writer, prodr. Music Found. Awards, 1989-93; instr. Duality Playhouse, N.Y.C., 1995-96. Writer, dir. plays Lady Day, 1986-87 (Bay City award 1987, Creative Drama award 1987), Philly's Beat, 1985 (citation City of Phila. 1985); dir. plays Hosanna, 1981, Coupla White Chicks, 1983, He Plays Piano, 1984, Danny and the Deep Blue Sea, 1984, Sister Mary ... etc., 1985-87, Tallulah, 1987, Psycho Beach Party, 1994, Sophie, Totie and Belle, 1994, We Love Lucy, 1994, P.S. Bette Davis, 1994, 30,000 Pigs Roamed the City, 1995-96, Judy at the Wall Inn, 1995-96, Lenny, 1995-96, The Passion, 1995-96, Skirts, 1995-96; co-producer play Heart Strings, 1990, Jerker, 1993, Women Behind Bars, 1993, Chicago's Gangsters, 1996-97. Bd. dirs. Max Goldstein Outreach, Phila., 1979-82, Young Persons Apprenticeship Program, Phila., 1979-82. Democrat. Avocations: art, design, tennis. Home: 17 N Main St New Hope PA 18938-1314

STAHL, WILLIAM MARTIN, professional training director; b. Danbury, Conn., Dec. 13, 1945; s. William M. and Mary Elizabeth (Barrett) S.; m. Elizabeth Larkin, 1968 (div. 1979); 1 child, Nathaniel Edward; m. Pamela Putnam, July 13, 1984; 1 child, Julia Barrett. BA, Bard Coll., 1968; MS, Bank Street Coll., 1975. Asst. tchr., tchr. Willowbrook State Sch., S.I., 1968-70; tchr., supr. Bronx (N.Y.) Children's Hosp., 1970-75; sch. cons. Washington County Mental Health, Inc., Montpelier, Vt., 1975-80; behavioral cons. Peabody (Mass.) Pub. Schs., 1980-86; founder, dir. profl. tng., treas. Ctr. for Applied Spl. Tech., Inc., Peabody, 1984—; grad. faculty Goddard Coll., Plainfield, Vt., 1977-80; clinician, supr. North Shore Children's Hosp., Salem, Mass., 1981-86, asst. dir. Med. Ednl. Evaluation Ctr. Clinic, 1986-88; dir. New Tools Inst., Harvard U./Ctr. for Applied Spl. Tech.d, 1989—; presenter in field. Mem. Nat. Assn. Sch. Psychologists, Nat. Assn. MacIntosh Trainers. Office: CAST Inc 39 Cross St Peabody MA 01960-1628

STAHLMAN, MILDRED THORNTON, pediatrics and pathology educator, researcher; b. Nashville, July 31, 1922; d. James Geddes and Mildred (Thornton) S. AB, Vanderbilt U., 1943, MD, 1946; MD (hon.), U. Goteborg, Sweden, 1973, U. Nancy, France, 1982. Diplomate Am. Bd. Pediatrics, Am. Bd. Neonatology. Cardiac resident La Rabida Sanitarium, Chgo., 1951; instr. pediatrics Vanderbilt U., Nashville, 1951-58, instr. physiology, 1954-60, asst. prof. pediatrics, 1959-64, asst. prof. physiology, 1960-62, assoc. prof. pediatrics, 1964-70, prof., 1970—, prof. pathology, 1982—, Harvie Branscomb Disting. prof., 1984, dir. div. neonatology, 1961-89. Editor: Respiratory Distress Syndromes, 1989; contbr. over 140 articles to profl. publs. Recipient Thomas Jefferson award Vanderbilt U., 1980, Apgar award Am. Acad. Pediatrics, 1987; NIH grantee, 1954—. Mem. AAAS, Am. Pediatric Soc. (pres. 1984), Soc. Pediatric Rsch., Am. Physiology Soc., So. Soc. Pediatric Rsch. (pres. 1961-62), Royal Swedish Acad. Scis., Inst. of Medicine of the Nat Acad. of Scis. Episcopalian. Home: 538 Beech Creek Rd S Brentwood TN 37027-3421 Office: Vanderbilt U Med Ctr A0109 Med Ctr N 21st Ave Nashville TN 37232-2370*

STAHMANN, ROBERT F., education educator; b. Peoria, Ill., Nov. 26, 1939; s. Fred Soeffner and Mary Emma (Thompson) S.; m. Kathleen Cook, Dec. 21, 1965; children: Benjamin C., John C., Paul C., Mark C., Anne. BA, Macalester Coll., 1963; MS, U. Utah, 1965, PhD, 1967. Research fellow U. Utah, 1966-67; sr. counselor U. Iowa, Iowa City, 1967-71; coordinator counseling service U. Iowa, 1971-72, dir. counseling service, 1972-75, asst. prof. edn., 1967-71, asso. prof., 1971-75; prof. family scis. Brigham Young U., Provo, Utah, 1975—, chmn. dept. family scis., 1983-89, dir. Marriage and Family Counseling Clinic, 1976-83, coordinator program in marriage and family therapy, 1977-83; vis. prof. sex and marital therapy clinic Coll. Medicine, U. Utah, 1980-81; mem. Utah State Marriage and Family Therapy Licensing Bd., 1982-92; mem. Commn. Accreditation for Marriage and Family Therapy Edn., 1989-94, chair, 1990-94. Co-author: Premarital Counseling, 1980, 2d edit., 1987, Dynamic Assessment in Couples Therapy, 1993, Premarital and Remarital Counseling, 1997; co-editor: Ethical and Professional Issues for Marital and Family Therapists, 1980; co-editor, contbr.; Counseling in Marital and Sexual Problems: A Clinician's Handbook, 1977, 3d edit., 1984; assoc. editor: Jour. Coll. Student Pers., 1971-77; editor: Jour. Assoc. Mormon Counselors and Psychotherapists, 1977-78; contbr. chpts. to books., articles to profl. jours. Scoutmaster Boy Scouts Am., 1969-72, 83-87, cubmaster, 1976-79; mem. Orem City Beautification Commn., 1986-87; mem. adv. bd. Ret. Sr. Vol. Program for Utah County, 1987-89. Fellow Am. Assn. Marriage and Family Therapy (bd. dirs. 1977-79); mem. ACA, Am. Assn. Sex Educators, Counselors and Therapists (cert.), Am. Assn. Christian Counselors, Utah Assn. Marriage and Family Counselors (pres. 1978-80), Nat. Coun. on Family Rels., Utah Coun. on Family Rels. (pres. 1987-88), Sigma Xi, Phi Kappa Phi. Mem. LDS Ch. Office: Brigham Young Univ 240 TLRB Provo UT 84602

STAHR, ELVIS J(ACOB), JR., lawyer, conservationist, educator; b. Hickman, Ky., Mar. 9, 1916; s. Elvis and Mary Anne (McDaniel) S.; m. Dorothy Howland Berkfield, June 28, 1946; children: Stephanie Ann, Stuart Edward Winston, Bradford Lanier. AB, U. Ky., 1936; BA (Rhodes scholar), U. Oxford, Eng., 1938; BCL, 1939, MA, 1943; diploma in Chinese Lang., Yale U., 1943; LL.D., W.Va. Wesleyan Coll., Waynesburg Coll., 1959, Concord Coll., 1960, U. Md., U. Pitts., 1961, La. State U., Tex. Christian U., U. Ky., 1962, U. Notre Dame, 1964, Ind. State U., 1966, Brown U., 1967, Northwestern U., U. Fla., 1968, U. Tampa, 1972, Ind. U., 1976, Cumberland Coll., 1990; D.Environ. Sci., Rollins Coll., 1973; D in Mil. Sci., Northeastern U., 1962; D.Pub. Adminstrn., Bethany Coll., 1962; D.H.L., DePauw U., 1963, Rose Hulman Inst., 1965, Transylvania U., 1973; Litt.D., U. Cin., 1966, U. Maine, 1976; Pd.D., Culver-Stockton Coll., 1966; D.Sc., Norwich U., 1968, Hanover Coll., 1975. Bar: N.Y. State 1940, Ky. 1948, U.S. Supreme Ct. 1950, U.S. Ct. Mil. Appeals 1952, D.C. 1983. Practiced as assoc. Mudge, Stern, Williams & Tucker, N.Y.C., 1939-41; sr. assoc. Mudge, Stern, Williams & Tucker, 1946-47; assoc. prof. law U. Ky., 1947-48, prof. law, 1948-56; dean U. Ky. (Coll. Law), 1948-56, provost, 1954-56; exec. dir. Pres. Eisenhower's Com. on Edn. Beyond High Sch., 1956-57; vice chancellor professions U. Pitts., 1957-58; pres. W.Va. U., Morgantown, 1958-61; spl. asst. Sec. Army, Washington, 1951-52, cons., 1953; Sec. of the Army Dept. Def., Washington, 1961-62; pres. Ind. U., 1962-68, Nat. Audubon Soc., N.Y.C., 1968-79; sr. counselor Nat. Audubon Soc., 1979-81, pres. emeritus, 1981—; ptnr. Chickering & Gregory, San Francisco, 1982-85; of counsel Chickering & Gregory P.C., San Francisco, 1986—; dir. Acacia Mut. Life Ins. Co., 1968-85; pres. Univ. Assocs., Inc., 1981-90; exec. v.p. Pub. Resource Found., 1982—; sr. cons. Cassidy & Assocs., Inc., 1984—; chmn. Washington Conservation Roundtable, 1986-87; dir. Chase Manhattan Corp. and Bank, 1976-79, Fed. Res. Bank Chgo., 1966-68, dep. chmn., 1967, 68; Mem. Constn. Rev. Commn. Ky., 1949-56, Ind., 1967-68; mem. U.S. del. UN Conf. on Human Environment, Stockholm, 1972, Joint U.S.-USSR Com. on Cooperation for Protection of Environment, 1973, Internat. Whaling Commn., London, 1975, 78; mem. U.S. Aviation Adv. Commn., 1970-73, Nat. Commn. for World Population Yr., 1974; nat. chmn. U.S.O., 1973-76; pub. mem. Nat. Petroleum Council, 1974-79; mem. Summit Conf. on Inflation, 1974. Author: (with others) Economics of Pollution, 1971. Mem. Nat. Commn. on Accrediting, 1963-68; trustee Transylvania U., 1969-76, mem. founders bd. 1978-80; pres. Midwestern Univs. Rsch. Assn., 1963-66; incorporator Argonne Univs. Assn., 1965, trustee, 1965-67; trustee Univs. Rsch. Assn., 1965, mem. coun. pres' 1965-68, chmn. 1968; bd. dirs. Alliance to Save Energy, 1977-88, Resolve, 1977-81, Coun. Fin. Aid to Edn., 1966-69; chmn. higher edn. adv. com. Edn. Commn. States, 1966-68; mem. bd. Govtl. Affairs Inst., 1968-72, Inst. Svcs. to Edn., 1965-67; chmn. Commn. on Fed. Rels., Am. Coun. on Edn., 1966-68; mem. exec. com. Nat. Assn. State Univs. and Land Grant Colls., 1965-68; mem. at-large bd. dirs. Am. Cancer Soc., 1970-76; trustee Com. Econ. Devel., 1964-82, hon.trustee, 1982—; mem. exec. bd. Nat. Assn. Ednl. Broadcasters, 1969-72; adv. coun. Elec. Power Rsch. Inst., 1971-77, Gas Rsch. Inst., 1977-83, Population Inst., 1981—, FAIR, 1982—; mem. Govtl. Affairs Com. of Ind. Sector, 1980-91; bd. dirs. Regional Plan Assn. Greater N.Y., 1970-75; evaluation panel Nat. Bur. Standards, 1975-77; adv. coun. Nat. Energy Project, Am. Enterprise Inst. Pub. Policy Rsch.1974-76; chmn. Coalit. Concerned Charities, 1972-78; mem. exec. bd. Am. Com. for Internat. Conservation, 1978-80; bd. dirs. World Environ. Ctr., 1978-85, Environ. and Energy Study Inst., 1983-90, mem. chmn.'s coun. 1990—; Green Fire Cnserv. Assn., 1988-91, bd. dirs. com. Constnl. System, 1985—, Nat. Water Alliance, 1983-86, Land Betwen the Lakes Assn., 1986-89, Pvt. Trust for Pub. Edn., 1990-92, Pub. Mems. Assn. of Fgn. Svc., 1991-94. Lt. col. AUS, 1941-46, N. Africa, China. Decorated Spl. Breast Order of Yun Hui (2), Army Navy Air Force medal 1st class (China), Bronze Star medal with oak leaf cluster (U.S.), Order of Grand Cross (Peru); recipient Algernon Sydney Sullivan medallion of N.Y. So. Soc., 1936, Meritorious Civilian Svc. medal Dept. Army, 1953, Disting. Civilian Svc. medal, 1971, Disting. Svc. award U. Ky. Alumni Assn., 1961, Disting. Svc. award Res. Officers Assn. U.S., 1962, Kentuckian of Yr. award Ky. Press Assn., 1961, WHAS (Louisville), 1968, Conservation Svc. award Dept. Interior, 1979, Conservation Achievement award Nat. Wildlife Fedn., 1978, Barbara Swain Award of Honor Natural Resources Coun. of Am., 1988, Sesquicentennial medal U. Mich., 1967, Centennial medal U. Ky., 1965; named one of Am.'s Ten Outstanding Young Men U.S. Jr. C. of C., 1948, named Ky. Col. and Gen., U. Ky. Hall of Disting. Alumni, Tennis Hall of Fame, ROTC Hall of Fame, named hon. citizen of Tex., Ind., Sagamore; awarded keys to cities of San Francisco, San Juan, New Orleans, Orlando, others. Mem. Assn. U.S. Army (life, pres. 1965-68, chmn. coun. trustees 1969-74), Ind. Soc. of Chgo. (hon. life), Jr. C. of C. Internat. (hon. life senator), Assn. Am. Rhodes Scholars, ABA, Fed. Bar Assn., Kentuckians (pres. N.Y.C. 1976-79, life trustee), S.R., SAR, Ky. Bar Assn., D.C. Bar Assn., Ind. Bar Assn. (hon.), Disciples of Christ Hist. Soc. (life mem.), Army-Navy (Washington), Field (Greenwich), Pilgrims of U.S., Boone and Crockett, Order of Coif, Phi Beta Kappa, Sigma Chi (mem. founding bd. 1974-91, Balfour Nat. award 1936, Significant Sig 1961, Order of Constantine 1981), Omicron Delta Kappa (dir. found. 1984-90, Laurel Crowned Circle award), Phi Delta Phi, Tau Kappa Alpha (Dist. Alumni award 1966), Merton Soc. (Oxford, Eng.), Oxford Soc.: hon. mem. Blue Key, Beta Gamma Sigma, Alpha Kappa Psi, Kappa Kappa Psi. Presbyterian. Home: 16 Martin Dl N Greenwich CT 06830-4719 Office: Chickering & Gregory PC 1815 H St NW # 650 Washington DC 20006-3604 *Focus on getting good results rather than on getting credit for them.*

STAINE, ROSS, lawyer; b. El Paso, Tex., July 13, 1924; s. Adelbert Claire and Dennie Joe (Stowe) S.; m. Mary Louise Sibert, Aug. 15, 1947; children: Martha Louise, Julie Ann, Ross. B.A., Tex. A&M U., 1947; LL.B., U. Tex., 1950. Bar: Tex. Assoc. Baker & Botts, Houston, 1947, ptnr., 1962—. Served with AUS, 1943-46; served to 1st lt. U.S. Army, 1950-52, PTO. Mem. State Bar Tex., Houston Bar Assn., Tex. Law Rev. Assn., Order of Coif, Phi Delta Phi. Baptist. Clubs: Forest (Houston), Coronado (Houston), Univ. (Houston). Home: 5555 Del Monte Dr Apt 807 Houston TX 77056-4117 Office: Baker & Botts 3000 One Shell Plaza Houston TX 77002

STAINES, DAVID MCKENZIE, English educator; b. Toronto, Aug. 8, 1946; s. Ralph McKenzie and Mary Rita (Hayes) S. BA, U. Toronto, 1967; AM, Harvard U., 1968, PhD, 1973. Asst. prof. English Harvard U., Cambridge, Mass., 1973-78, vis. assoc. prof., summers 1980, 82; assoc. prof. English U. Ottawa, Ont., 1978-85, prof., 1985—; vice-dean faculty of Arts U. Ottawa, Ont., 1994-95, dean faculty of arts, 1995—. Author: Tennyson's Camelot, 1982, Beyond the Provinces: Literary Canada at Century's End, 1995; contbr. articles and revs. Arthurian lit., medieval drama and romance to profl. jours.; editor: The Canadian Imagination, 1977, The Forty-ninth and Other Parallels, 1986; editor Jour. Can. Poetry, 1984—; gen. editor New Can. Libr., 1988—; translator The Complete Romances of Chrétien de Troyes, 1990; co-editor Elements of Literature, 1990, The Short Story in English, 1991. Ind. study fellow NEH, London, 1977-78, fellow Huntington Libr., San Marino, Calif., 1979. Mem. Medieval Acad. Am. (chmn. com. on ctrs. and regional assn. 1981-87), MLA, Internat. Arthurian Soc., Assn. Can. Univ. Tchrs. English. Roman Catholic. Avocations: theater, bridge. Home: 12 Galt St, Ottawa, ON Canada K1S 4R4 Office: Univ Ottawa, Office of Dean Faculty Arts, Ottawa, ON Canada K1N 6N5

STAINES, MAVIS AVRIL, artistic director, ballet principal; b. Cownsville, Que., Can., Apr. 9, 1954; d. David Russell and Betty (Knott) S.; m. Jyrki Virsunen, Feb. 4, 1988. Student, Nat. Ballet Sch., 1968-73, 81-83. Dancer Nat. Ballet of Can., 1973-78, 1st soloist, 1975-78; dancer Dutch Nat. Ballet, 1978-81; artistic dir. Nat. Ballet Sch., Toronto, Ont., Can., 1989—; mem. artistic staff Nat. Ballet Sch., 1982, assoc. artistic dir., 1984; juror Prix de Lausanne, Switzerland, 1993, 94, 95, guest spkr., 1997; presenter Prix de Lausanne Internat. Symposium, 1997; mem. task force on classicl ballet tng. DANCE/USA, Phila., 1994; mem. dance adv. com. The Can. Coun.; mem. Dance 20/20 Com., mem. DAN/CE--The Dance Comty. of Educators; bd. dirs. Kala Nidhi Fine Arts of Can. Office: The Nat Ballet Sch, 105 Maitland St, Toronto, ON Canada M4Y 1E4

STAINES, MICHAEL LAURENCE, oil and gas production executive; b. Guildford, Eng., May 30, 1949; came to U.S., 1958; s. John Richard and Myrra (Smith) S.; m. Laura Catherine Terdoslavich, May 11, 1974; children: Leslie Myrra, Claire Alexandra, Julia Wallis, Cameron Sutton. BS, Cornell U., 1971; MBA, Drexel U., 1976. Asst. comptr. grants U. Pa., phila., 1976-78; sr. analyst Sun Co., Radnor, Pa., 1978-80, Penn Cen. Energy Group, Radnor, 1980-83; v.p., sec. Bryn Mawr Energy Co., Bala Cynwyd, Pa., 1983-88; sr. v.p., dir., sec. Resource Am., Inc., Phila. and Akron, Ohio, 1988—. Chmn. stewardship com. St. Mary's Episc. Ch., Radnor, 1990. Winner Silver medal in coxless pair rowing, 1976 Olympic Games, Montreal; named Oarsman of Yr. Schuylkill Navy, Phila., 1976; U.S. Nat. Rowing Champion, 1971, 72, 73. Mem. Soc. Corp. Secs., Ohio Oil and Gas Assn., Oil and Gas Assn. N.Y., Havre de Grace (Md.), Yacht Club, Bachelors Barge Club (Phila.), Vesper Boat Club (capt. 1973). Avocations: classic automobiles and motorcycles, sailing. Office: Resource Am Inc 2876 S Arlington Rd Akron OH 44312-4716

STAINROOK, HARRY RICHARD, banker; b. Phila., Jan. 11, 1937; s. Millward M. and Janet (Cruickshank-Smith) S.; m. Judith Ann Swann, May 21, 1966; children: Jennifer, Eric. B.A., Rutgers U., 1970. Mgr. bank ops. First Pa. Bank, Phila., 1956-61, asst. v.p. br. dept., 1964-73, v.p., mgr. London office, 1973-75, v.p. internat. dept., 1975-78; sr. v.p. comml. group First Pa. Bank, 1978-81, exec. v.p., trust and investments, 1981-85; exec. v.p. trust and investments Mfrs. and Traders Trust Co., Buffalo, 1985—. Chmn., bd. dirs. Greater Buffalo Opera Co.; bd. dirs. Buffalo Philharm. Orch., U. Buffalo Found.; adv. bd. Buffalo Coun. on World Affairs. With U.S. Army, 1961-64. Mem. N.Y. State Bankers Assn., Buffalo C. of C., English Speaking Union, Saturn Club. Lutheran. Office: Mfrs and Traders Trust Co One M and T Pla Buffalo NY 14240

STAIR, FREDERICK ROGERS, retired foundation executive, former seminary president; b. Knoxville, Tenn., Mar. 7, 1918; s. Fred Rogers and Cristyne (Miller) S.; m. Martha Osborne, Dec. 19, 1942; children: Mary Miller, Thomas Osborne. B.S., Davidson Coll., 1939, D.D., 1960; postgrad., U. Edinburgh, 1945-46; B.D., Union Theol. Sem., Va., 1947, Th.M., 1948; LL.D., Davis and Elkins Coll., 1969; postgrad., Advanced Mgmt. Program, Harvard, 1972-73. Ordained to ministry Presbyn. Ch., 1943; asst. to pres. Union Theol. Sem., Va., 1948-53; pastor Central Presbyterian Ch., Hickory, N.C., 1953-59, Atlanta, 1959-67; pres. Union Theol. Sem., Va., 1967-81; exec. dir. Presbyn. Ch. (U.S.A.) Found., Charlotte, N.C., 1981-88. Trustee Davidson Coll., 1954-59, 74-85, chmn. bd., 1980-85; program coord. Inst. for Theol. Edn. Mgmt. Served with inf. AUS, 1942-46. Moses D. Hoge fellow, 1948, rsch. fellow Yale Divinity Sch., 1973, Ecumenical Inst., U. Salamanca, Spain, 1979. Mem. Phi Beta Kappa, Phi Gamma Delta, Omicron Delta Kappa, Sigma Upsilon. Home: 5150 Sharon Rd Charlotte NC 28210-4799

STAIR, GOBIN, publishing executive, painter, graphic designer; b. S.I., N.Y., July 30, 1912; s. Gobin and Elsie (Wilson) S.; m. Julia Sitterly, Oct. 5, 1933; children—Adrian, Charlotte. A.B., Dartmouth, 1933; L.H.D., Starr King Sch. for Ministry, 1975. With Beacon Press, Boston, 1956-75, dir., 1962-75. Illustrator: Gulliver's Travels (Swift), 1967, Middle Passage (Coxe), 1960, Old Quotes at Home (Darling), 1965, The King Lear Experience, 1976, Old Tales for a new Day (Fahs and Cobb), 1980, True to Form, 1988; creator: Alphabet Mural, Kingston Mass. Pub. Libr., 1994; creator: Evolution of Spirituality Mural, Unitarian Universalist Ch., Kingston, 1996. Mem Bookbuilders of Boston (pres. 1961-62, William A. Dwiggins award 1965), Boston Soc. Printers. Home: 9 Wapping Rd PO Box 123 Kingston MA 02364

STAIR, THOMAS OSBORNE, physician, educator; b. Richmond, Va., Jan. 10, 1950; s. Frederick Rogers Jr. and Martha (Osborne) S.; m. Lucy Caldwell, Dec. 28, 1973; children: Rebecca Caldwell, Peter Caldwell. AB, U. N.C., 1971; MD, Harvard U., 1975. Diplomate Am. Bd. Emergency Medicine (examiner 1982-88). Residency dir. emergency dept. Georgetown U. Hosp., Washington, 1979-85, asst. dir. emergency dept., 1979-89; asst. dean for continuing med. edn. Georgetown U. Sch. Medicine, Washington, 1985-89; chair dept. emergency medicine, 1989-95; prof. U. Md., Balt., 1995—. Co-author: Common Simple Emergencies, 1985, 2d edit., 1997. Recipient Excellence in Teaching award Emergency Medicine Residents Assn., 1986. Fellow Am. Coll. Emergency Physicians; mem. Soc. Acad. Emergency Medicine, Am. Med. Informatics Assn. Home: 4822 Quebec St NW Washington DC 20016-3229 Office: Univ Maryland Baltimore MD 21228

STAIRS, DENIS WINFIELD, political science educator; b. Halifax, N.S., Can., Sept. 6, 1939; s. Henry Gerald and Freda (Winfield) S.; m. Valerie Downing Street, Aug. 10, 1963 (div. Dec. 1986); children: Robert Woodliffe, Christopher Winfield; m. Jennifer Smith, July 18, 1987. BA, Dalhousie U., 1961, Oxford U., 1964, MA, Oxford U., 1968; PhD, U. Toronto, 1969. Asst. prof. dept. polit. sci. Dalhousie U., 1966-70, assoc. prof., 1970-75, dir. Centre Fgn. Policy Studies, 1971-75, prof. polit. sci., 1975—, McCulloch prof., 1995—, chmn. dept., 1980-85, mem. adv. com. acad. relations, dept. external affairs, 1978—, v.p., acad. and research, 1988-93; bd. dirs. Atlantic Coun. Can., 1979—; mem. coun. Social Sci. and Humanities Rsch. Coun. Can., 1981-87; mem. rsch. coun. Can. Inst. Advanced Rsch., 1986—; bd. dirs. Orgn. for Study of Nat. History of Can. Author: The Diplomacy of Constraint: Canada, the Korean War, and the United States, 1974. Rhodes scholar, 1961; J.W. Dafoe postgrad. fellow internat. studies, 1965-66; Can. Council leave fellow, 1972-73; Social Scis. and Humanities Research Council Can. leave fellow, 1979-80. Fellow Royal Soc. Can.; mem. Can. Polit. Sci. Assn. (pres.), Can. Inst. Internat. Affairs, Internat. Studies Assn. Club: Royal N.S. Yacht Squadron. Office: Dalhousie U, Dept Polit Sci, Halifax, NS Canada B3H 4H6

STAKER, ROBERT JACKSON, senior federal judge; b. Kermit, W.Va., Feb. 14, 1925; s. Frederick George and Nada (Frazier) S.; m. Sue Blankenship Poore, July 16, 1955; 1 child, Donald Seth; 1 stepson, John Timothy Poore. Student, Marshall U., Huntington, W.Va., W.Va. U., Morgantown, U. Ky., Lexington; LL.B, W.Va. U., 1952. Bar: W.Va. 1952. Practiced in Williamson, 1952-68; judge Mingo County Circuit Ct., Williamson, 1969-79; U.S. dist. judge So. Dist. W.Va., Huntington, 1979-95, sr. U.S. dist. judge, 1995—. Served with USN, 1943-46. Democrat. Presbyterian.

STAKGOLD, IVAR, mathematics educator; b. Oslo, Dec. 13, 1925; came to U.S., 1941, naturalized, 1947; s. Henri and Rose (Wishengrad) S.; m. Alice Calvert O'Keefe, Nov. 27, 1964 (dec. Jan. 1994); 1 dau., Alissa Dent. BME, Cornell U., 1945, MME, 1946; PhD, Harvard U., 1949. Instr., then asst. prof. Harvard, 1949-56; head math. and logistics brs. Office Naval Research, 1956-59; faculty Northwestern U., 1960-75, prof. math. and engrng. scis., 1964-75, chmn. engrng. scis., 1969-75; prof. math. U. Del., 1975—, chmn., 1975-91; dir. Washington office Am. Math. Soc., 1994-95; mem. U.S. Army basic rsch. com. NRC, 1977-80, MS 2000 oversight com., 1989-91; mem. com. on applications of math. NAS-NRC, 1982-86; mem. adv. panel on computational and applied math. Nat. Inst. Standards and Tech., 1990-95; vis. faculty Math. Inst., Oxford (Eng.) U., 1973, 92, Univ. Coll., London, 1978, Victoria U., Wellington, N.Z., 1981, Ecole Polytechnique Federale de Lausanne, Switzerland, 1981, Bari U., 1987, U. Complutense, Madrid, 1987, 92, U. Milan, 1992. Author: Boundary Value Problems of Mathematical Physics, Vols. I and II, 1967, Green's Functions and Boundary Value Problems, 1978; mem. editl. bd. Am. Math. Monthly, 1975-80, Jour. Applicable Analysis, 1977-90, Internat. Jour. Engrng. Sci., 1977—, Jour. Integral Equations, 1978—, Jour. Math. Analysis and Applications, 1988-94, SIAM Rev., 1989-94. Mem. Soc. Indsl. and Applied Math. (trustee 1976-85, chmn. 1979-85, pres. 1989-90, past pres. 1991), Conf. Bd. Math. Sci. (chmn. 1990-92), Coun. Sci. Soc. Pres. (exec. bd. 1990), Am. Math. Soc. (dir. Washington office 1995-96), Delaware Maths. Coalition (dir. 1996—). U.S. rep. World Bridge Championships, 1959, 60; holder 7 nat. bridge championships. Home: 19 Wood Rd Wilmington DE 19806

STAKIAS, G. MICHAEL, lawyer; b. Norfolk, Va., Feb. 2, 1950; s. George and Gloria May (Hoggard) S. BA, William & Mary, 1972; JD, Thomas M. Cooley Law Sch, 1976; LLM, NYU, 1977. Bar: Mich., 1976, D.C. 1980, Pa. 1980, N.Y. 1994. Atty. U.S. SEC, Washington, 1977-80; ptnr. Blank, Rome, Comisky & McCauley, Phila., 1980—, chmn. bus. and corp. dept., 1996—. Bd. dirs. Thomas M. Cooley Law Sch., Lansing, Mich., 1988—. Mem. ABA (bus. law sect., chmn. small bus. capital formation subcom. 1988—), Patrons Found. Office: Blank Rome Comisky & McCauley 1200 Four Penn Ctr Plz Philadelphia PA 19103

STALBERG, ZACHARY, newspaper editor; b. Phila., Apr. 6, 1947; m. Deborah Lock, Sept. 2, 1990. Student polit. sci., Temple U., 1968. Reporter Bucks County Courier Times, Levittown, Pa., 1970-71; reporter Phila. Daily News, 1971-75, city editor, 1975-77, mng. editor, 1977-79, exec. editor, 1979-84, editor, 1984—. Served with U.S. Army, 1968-70. Mem. Am. Soc. Newspaper Editors. Home: 413 S 49th St Philadelphia PA 19143-1709 Office: Philadelphia Daily News 400 N Broad St Philadelphia PA 19130-4015*

STALCUP, JOE ALAN, lawyer, clergyman; b. Hooker, Okla., Feb. 13, 1931; s. Herbert I. and Ruby (Gantt) S.; m. Nancy Jo Vaughn, Sept. 3, 1950; children: Melinda, Sondra Jo, Cheri Ann. B.B.A. cum laude, So. Methodist U., 1951, J.D. magna cum laude, 1959, M.Th. magna cum laude, 1978. Bar: Tex. 1959. Tchr. Dallas Ind. Sch. Dist., 1951-57; assoc. mem. firm Locke, Purnell, Boren, Laney & Neely, Dallas, 1959-66; assoc. atty., partner firm Geary, Brice & Lewis, Dallas, 1966-67; founder, sr. partner firm Stalcup,

Johnson, Meyers & Miller (and predecessor firm), Dallas, 1968-75; dean Sch. Theology for the Laity, 1978-80, 92-96. Pres. Dallas County Young Democrats, 1952-54; Bd. dirs., mem. exec. com. N. Tex. Christian Communications Commn., 1972-78; bd. dirs., v.p. Greater Dallas Council Chs., 1972-75; bd. dirs., chmn. Christian Ch. Found., 1976-84, 86-91, Christian Bd. Publ., 1991—. Mem. ABA, Tex. Bar Assn., Dallas Bar Assn., Am. Judicature Soc., Phi Alpha Delta. Mem. Christian Ch. (minister). Home: 7594 Benedict Dr Dallas TX 75214-1903 Office: 6510 Abrams Rd Dallas TX 75231-7217

STALDER, FLORENCE LUCILLE, secondary education educator; b. Fairmont, W.Va., Jan. 3, 1920; d. Brooks Fleming and Sally May (Odewalt) Clayton; m. Bernard Nicholas Stalder, Sept. 14, 1946; children: Kathryn Lynn Stalder Mirto, Susan May Stalder Woodard. BA in Edn. with honors, Fairmont State Coll., 1966; MA, W.Va. U., 1973; postgrad., Kent State U., 1973, U. Va., Charlottesville, 1981. Cert. elem. tchr., W.Va. Sec. to mgr. Hall Agy., Inc., Fairmont, W.Va., 1941-43; sec. to supt. Westinghouse Electric Corp., Fairmont, 1943-47; sec. to purchasing agt. Fairmont Supply Co., 1947-48; sec. to dist. mgtr. Ea. Gas & Fuel Assoc., Gen. Stores Div., Grant Town, W.Va., 1948-50; sec. to pres., v.p. Hutchinson Coal Co., Fairmont, 1950-52; sec. to personnel mgr. Consolidation Coal Co., Fairmont, 1957-61; sec. and asst. to adminstr. Fairmont Clinic (Monongahela Valley Assoc. Health Ctrs.), 1965-70; instr. Fairmont Jr. High, Miller Jr. High Schs., 1968-85; instr., dir. W.Va. Univ. Younger Youth Sci. Camps, Fairmont, 1966-72; workshop instr. W.Va. State Bd. Edn. Energy Workshops, Fairmont, 1973-74; adult edn. instr., Fairmont, 1985—; sec., exec. bd. mem. Score. Pres. PTA, 1958-61; troop leader Girl Scouts USA, 1961-64; sec., mem. League of Women Voters, Fairmont, 1968-97; charter mem. Lifelong Learners Fairmont State Coll.; counselor, charter mem. Mil. Order Fgn. Wars U.S. Mem. AAUW (pres. 1972-74), NEA, DAR (1st v.p. regent 1986-92, regent 1992-95, state good citizen chmn.), Marion County Edn. Assn., W.Va. Edn. Assn., W.Va. Adult Edn. Assn., Daus. of Founders and Patriots of Am. (pres. 1979-85, nat. officers club 1985—), Daus. of Am. Colonists (vice regent 1988-91, regent 1991-94), Daus. Am. Pioneers, Alpha Delta Kappa (pres. 1979-81). Republican. Methodist. Avocations: ecology and conservation issues, humane education, food preservation, gardening. Home: 1208 Bell Run Rd Fairmont WV 26554-1400

STALERMAN, RUTH, civic volunteer, poet; b. N.Y.C., Mar. 18, 1919; d. Samuel and Minnie (Weckstein) Kosson; m. Joseph Stalerman, June 5, 1949 (dec. Aug. 1986); children: Helene, Enid. Student, Modern Machines Bus. Sch. Various bookkeeping positions, to 1951. Poetry pub. Am. Anthology Contemporary Poetry, Nat. Libr. Poetry, A Far Off Place, Songs on the Wind, Tears of Fire, numerous other pubs. and jours. Co-editor, then editor newsletter PTA; dist. dir. Girl Scouts U.S., 1958-62; pres. White Plains chpt. B'nai B'rith, cons. on membership, programming; mem. White Plains Hosp. Aux., mem. instnl. rev. bd. Recipient Editor's choice awards for outstanding achievement in poetry, 1994, 95, 96. Mem. Jewish War Vets. (chaplain, contbr. to newsletter), Internat. Soc. Poets. Home: 50 Lawrence Dr North White Plains NY 10603

STALEY, DELBERT C., telecommunications executive; b. Hammond, Ind., Sept. 16, 1924; s. Eugene and Nellie (Downer) s.; m. Ingrid Andersen, Mar. 16, 1946; children—Crista Staley Ellis, Cynthia, Clifford, Corinn. Student, Rose Poly. Inst., Hammond, 1943-44; grad. advanced mgmt. program, Harvard U., 1962; D. Engring. (hon.), Rose Hulman Inst. Tech., 1981; LL.D. (hon.), Skidmore Coll., 1983. With Ill. Bell Telephone, 1946-76, v.p. ops., 1972-76; pres. Ind. Bell, 1976-78; v.p. residence mktg. AT&T, 1978-79; pres. N.Y. Telephone, 1979-83, chmn. bd., chief exec. officer, 1983; chmn. bd., chief exec. officer NYNEX Corp., White Plains, N.Y., 1983-89, chmn., dir. internat. mgmt. com., 1989-91; chmn. bd. dirs. Alcatel Network Systems, Inc.; prin. East Haven Investments Ltd.; bd. dirs. Polaroid Corp., Digital Equipment Corp., Maynard, Mass. With U.S. Army, 1943-46; ETO. Recipient Puerto Rican Legal Def. and Edn. Fund award, 1981, Cleveland Dodge award YMCA Greater N.Y., 1983, New Yorker for N.Y. award Citizens Com. for N.Y., 1984, Leadership in Mgmt. award Pace U., 1988, Albert Schweitzer Leadership award Hugh O'Brian Youth Found., 1988, Hammond Achievement award The Hammond Hist. Soc., 1988, Gold Medal award USO, 1988, Am. Vocation Success award Pres. George Busch, 1989. Mem. Ind. Acad. (hon.), Telephone Pioneers Am. (pres. 1983-84), Westchester Country Club, Blind Brook Club, Royal Poinciana Club. Presbyterian. Home: 32 Polly Park Rd Rye NY 10580-1927 Office: NYNEX Corp 1095 Avenue Of The Americas New York NY 10036-6797

STALEY, FRANK MARCELLUS, JR., mathematics educator; b. Columbia, S.C., July 21, 1930; s. Frank Marcellus and Sarah (Ryan) S.; m. Valeria Howard, June 9, 1956; children: Frank Howard, Elisa Claire. Student, Morehouse Coll., Atlanta, 1946-48; BS, S.C. State U., 1951; MA, Columbia U., 1958; postgrad., various colls. Tchr. math. Ft. Valley (Ga.) State Coll., 1955-57, Va. State Coll., Petersburg, 1957-58; assoc. prof. math. S.C. State Coll., Orangeburg, 1958-90. Active Boy Scouts Am., Den Leader award, Silver Beaver award, Vigil award, mem. exec. bd. 1971-74, Dist. Award of Merit; chmn. bd. Orangeburg County Dept. Social Svcs., ARC; vol. Orangeburg Regional Hosp., Dist. 5 Sch. Sys., Orangeburg Recreation Department. Decorated Army Commendation medal, Purple Heart, Army Res. medal, Korean Svc. medal, others; life mem. Basketball Hall of Fame; names to ROTC Hall of Fame, S.C. State U. Mem. AAUP, Math. Assn. Am., Nat. Coun. Tchrs. Math., Am. Legion (past vice comdr.), VFW (past post comdr.), Res. Officers Assn. (life), Ret. Officers Assn., Assn. U.S. Army, Scabbard and Blade, Omega Psi Phi (life, Man of the Yr. 1975), Alpha Kappa Mu, Kappa Delta Pi, Phi Delta Kappa, Kappa Mu Epsilon, Masons, Shriner. Democrat. Home: 1756 Belleville Rd NE Orangeburg SC 29115-3809 Office: SC State Coll Box 1947 300 College St NE Orangeburg SC 29117-0001

STALEY, HARRY L., fund raising executive; b. Kansas City, Kans., Aug. 10, 1930; s. Harry W. and Irene O. (Lee) S.; m. Jayne Rothschild, Oct. 15, 1955; 1 child, Harriet Joseph. BA, Bucknell U., 1952; JD, NYU, 1960. Pers. asst. E.I. duPont & Co., 1952-54; editor USGA Jour. US Golf Assn., 1956-57; law clk. Jay Leo Rothschild, 1957-60, assoc., 1960-65; sr. cons. and dir. Marts and Lundy, Inc., 1965-74; exec. dir. Westchester Med. Found., 19074-76; founding ptnr. Staley-robeson, Inc., 1976—; bd. dirs. Am. Assn. Fund-Raising Counsel & AAFRC Trust for Philanthropy; exec. dir. Westchester Health Fund. Mem. ABA, Nat. Soc. Fund-Raising Execs.. Home: 90 Donizetti Rd Westerley RI 02891 Office: 3010 Westchester Ave Purchase NY 10577-2524

STALEY, HENRY MUELLER, manufacturing company executive; b. Decatur, Ill., June 3, 1932; s. Augustus Eugene, Jr. and Lenore (Mueller) S.; m. Violet Lucas, Feb. 4, 1955; children—Mark Eugene, Grant Spencer. G-rad., Governor Dummer Acad., 1950; B.S. in Psychology, Northwestern U., 1954, M.B.A. in Finance, 1956. Salesman Field Enterprises, Chgo., 1953; salesman A.E. Staley Mfg. Co., 1951, mgmt. trainee, 1956-57, ins. mgr., 1957-59, asst. treas., 1959-65, treas., asst. sec., 1965-73, v.p., treas., asst. sec., 1973-77, v.p. bus. and econ. analysis, 1977-87, also dir., 1969-85; pvt. investor Decatur, 1987—; dir. Staley Continental, Inc., 1985-88. Crusade chmn. Macon County unit Am. Cancer Soc., 1964-65, mem. bd. dirs., 1965-71, vice chmn. bd., 1965-66, chmn. bd., 1966-69; bd. dirs. United Way Decatur and Macon County, 1972-74; mem. adv. council Millikin U., 1968—, chmn. adv. council, 1970-71; mem. Decatur Meml. Hosp. Devel. Council, 1969-71, mem. finan. com., bd. dirs., 1970-79, mem. long-range planning com., 1976-77, mem. devel. and community relations com., 1977-78. Mem. Decatur C. of C. (dir. 1967-72), Sigma Nu. Clubs: Decatur, Decatur Country. Home and Office: 276 N Park Pl Decatur IL 62522-1952 also: 74 Ironwood Ln Lahaina HI 96761-9062

STALEY, JOHN FREDRIC, lawyer; b. Sidney, Ohio, Sept. 26, 1943; s. Harry Virgil and Fredericka May (McMillin) S.; m. Sue Ann Bolin, June 11, 1966; children—Ian McMillin, Erik Bolin. A.B. in History, Fresno State Coll., 1965; postgrad. in pub. adminstrn. Calif. State U.-Hayward, 1967-68; J.D., U. Calif. 1972. Bar: Calif. 1972. Ptnr. Staley, Jobson & Wetherell, Pleasanton, Calif., 1972—; lectr. Hastings Coll. Law, 1973-74; founding mem., Bank of Livermore; bd. dirs. Xscribe Corp. (NASOAQ XSCR)' del. U.S.-China Joint Conf. on Law, Beijing, 1987. Mem. Livermore City Coun., 1975-82, vice mayor, 1978-82; bd. dirs. Alameda County Tng. and Employment Bd., Alameda-Contra Costa Emergency Med. Svcs. Agy., Valley Vol. Ctr. With M.I., U.S. Army, 1966-67. Fellow Am. Acad. Matrimonial Lawyers; mem. ABA, Calif. State Bar, Alameda Bar Assn., Contra Costa Bar Assn., Amador Valley Bar Assn., Calif. Assn. Cert. Family Law Specialists (pres. 1988-89, Hall of Fame award, 1994), Lawyer Friends of Wine. Office: Staley Jobson & Wetherell 5776 Stoneridge Mall Rd Ste 310 Pleasanton CA 94588-2838

STALEY, LYNN, English educator; b. Madisonville, Ky., Dec. 24, 1947; d. James Mulford and Florine (Hurt) Staley. AB, U. Ky., 1969; MA, PhD, Princeton U., 1973. Grad. asst. Princeton (N.J.) U., 1971-73; instr. English Colgate U., Hamilton, N.Y., 1974-75, from asst. to assoc. prof., 1975-86, prof., 1986—. Author: The Voice of the Gawain-Poet, 1984, The Shepheardes Calendar: An Introduction, 1990, Margery Kempe's Dissenting Fictions, 1994, (with David Aers) The Powers of the Holy: Religion, Politics and Gender in Late MEdieval English Culture, 1996; editor: The Book of Margery Kempe, 1996; contbr. articles to profl. jours. Mem. MLA, Medieval Acad. Am., Renaissance Soc. Am., New Chaucer Soc., Spenser Soc. Office: Colgate U Dept English 13 Oak Dr Hamilton NY 13346-1338

STALEY, MARSHA LYNN, elementary school educator; b. California, Mo., July 19, 1950; d. David D. and Jenny L. (Howard) Hutchison; children: Timothy Jay Turley, Damon Andrew Turley; m. Richard Lynn Staley, June 30, 1989. AA, State Fair C.C., Sedalia, Mo., 1982; BS in Edn., Drury Coll., 1984; MS in Elem. Adminstrn., S.W. Mo. State U., 1993; doctoral student, U. Mo., 1994—. Cert. tchr. grades 1-8, Mo. Tchr. grade 5 Newburg (Mo.) Elem. Sch., 1986-88; tchr. grades 1, 4, 5 and 6 Sherwood Elem. Sch., Springfield, Mo., 1988-93, Westport Elem. Sch., Springfield, 1993—. Mem. Pi Delta Kappa, Pi Lambda Theta (v.p. Alpha chpt. 1995—). Avocations: reading, horseback riding, bicycling, hiking. Office: U Mo 209C Townsend Columbia MO 65211

STALEY, THOMAS FABIAN, language professional, academic administrator; b. Pitts., Aug. 13, 1935; s. Fabian Richard and Mary (McNulty) S.; m. Carolyn O'Brien, Sept. 3, 1960; children: Thomas Fabian, Caroline Ann, Mary Elizabeth, Timothy X. A.B., Regis Coll., 1957, B.S., 1957; M.A., U. Tulsa, 1958; Ph.D., U. Pitts., 1962; D.H.L., Regis Coll., 1979. Asst. prof. English Rollins Coll., 1961-62; mem. faculty U. Tulsa, 1962-88, prof. English, 1969-88, dean Grad. Sch., 1969-77; dir. Grad. Inst. Modern Letters, Trustees prof. modern lit. U. Tulsa (Grad. Sch.), 1977—; dean Coll. Arts and Scis. U. Tulsa, 1981-83, provost, v.p. acad. affairs, 1983-88, McFarlin prof. modern lit., 1988—; prof. English, dir. Ransom Humanities Rsch. Ctr. U. Tex., Austin, 1988—, Chancellor's Centennial prof. of the Book, 1989-92, Harry Huntt Ransom chair liberal arts, 1992—; Fulbright prof., Italy, 1966-67; Fulbright lectr., 1971; Danforth assoc., 1962-67; chmn. Internat. James Joyce Symposium; dir. Grad. Inst. Modern Letters, 1970-81. Author: James Joyce Today, 1966, James Joyce's Portrait of the Artist, 1968, Italo Svevo: Essays on His Work, 1969, (with H.J. Mooney) The Shapeless God: Essays on the Modern Novel, 1968, (with B. Benstock) Approaches to Ulysses: Ten Essays, 1970, Approaches to Joyce's Portrait: Ten Essays, 1977, Jean Rhys: A Critical Study, 1979; editor: Il Punto Su Joyce, 1973, Dorothy Richardson, 1975, Ulysses: Fifty Years, 1974, Twentieth-Century Women Novelists, 1982, British Novelists, 1890-1929, Traditionalists, Dictionary of Lit. Biography, Vols. 34, 36, 70, 77, An Annotated Critical Bibliography of James Joyce, 1989, Joyce Studies: An Annual edit., 1990—, Studies in Modern Literature Series, 1990, Reflections on James Joyce: Stuart Gilbert's Paris Journal, 1993, James Joyce Quar., 1963-89; adv. editor Twentieth-Century Lit., 1966—; bd. dirs. Eighteenth-Century Short Title Catalogue/North America, 1990; contbr. articles to profl. jours. Bd. dirs. Tulsa Arts Coun., 1969-76, NCCJ, 1979—; pres. James Joyce Found., 1968-72; chmn. bd. Undercroft Montessori Sch., 1968-70, Marquette Sch., 1969-70; bd. dirs. Cascia Hall Prep. Sch.; chmn. disting. authors com. Tulsa Libr. Trust, 1984; mem. bd. commrs. Tulsa City-County Libr., chmn., 1980-82; mem. adv. coun. Tex. Inst. for Humanities; trustee Regis U., 1992—; bd. dirs. Libr. of Am., 1994—, Harlick Trust, 1994—; mem. symposium com. Lyndon Baines Johnson Presdl. Libr., 1993—. Recipient Am. Council Learned Socs. award, 1969, 80. Mem. MLA, Internat. Assn. Univ. Profs. English, Anglo-Irish Studies Assn., Am. Com. for Irish Studies, Assn. Internat. de Bibliophilie, James Joyce Soc., Hopkins Soc., Tex. Philos. Soc. (bd. dirs. 1991—), U.S. Tennis Assn., Tulsa Tennis Club, Westwood Country Club, The Athenaeum Club (London), Grolier Club (N.Y.), Edgecomb Tennis Club (Kennebunk, Maine), Tarry House, Phi Beta Kappa. Home: 2528 Tanglewood Trl Austin TX 78703-1540

STALFORT, JOHN ARTHUR, lawyer; b. Balt., June 9, 1951; s. John Irving and Libby Jean (Adams) S.; m. Rebecca Higgins, Aug. 21, 1976 (div. 1984); m. Anne Cheesman, July 19, 1985. BA, U. Va., 1973, MBA, JD, 1977. Bar: Md. 1977. Assoc. Miles & Stockbridge, Balt., 1977-84, ptnr., 1984—. Author: Commercial Financing Forms-Maryland, 1986. Sec. Roland Pk. Rds. and Maintenance Corp., Balt., 1978-83. Mem. ABA, Md. State Bar Assn. (chmn. sect. bus. law 1995-96), Nat. Assn. of Bond Lawyers, Roland Pk. Civic League, Balt. Country Club, Ctr. Club, Md. Club, Talbot Country Club, Phi Beta Kappa. Republican. Presbyterian. Avocations: skiing, tennis, golf, lacrosse, running. Office: Miles & Stockbridge 10 Light St Baltimore MD 21202-1435

STALKER, JACQUELINE D'AOUST, academic administrator, educator; b. Penetang, Ont., Can., Oct. 16, 1933; d. Phillip and Rose (Eaton) D'Aoust; m. Robert Stalker; children: Patricia, Lynn, Roberta. Teaching cert., U. Ottawa, 1952; tchr. music, Royal Toronto Conservatory Music, 1952; teaching cert., Lakeshore Tchrs. Coll., 1958; BEd with honors, U. Manitoba, 1977, MEd, 1979; EdD, Nova U., 1985. Cert. tchr. Ont., Man., Can. Adminstr., tchr., prin. various schs., Ont. and Que., 1952-65; area commr. Girl Guides of Can., throughout Europe, 1965-69; administr., tchr. Algonquin Community Coll., Ottawa, Ont., 1970-74; tchr., program devel. Frontenac County Bd. Edn., Kingston, Ont., 1974-75; lectr., faculty advisor dept. curriculum, edn. U. Man., Can., 1977-79; lectr. U. Winnipeg, Man., Can., 1977-79; cons. colls. div. Man. Dept. Edn., 1980-81, sr. cons. programming br., 1981-84, sr. cons. post secondary, adult and continuing edn. div., 1985-88, dir. post secondary career devel. br. and adult and continuing edn. br., 1989; asst. prof. higher edn., coord. grad. program in higher edn. U. Man., 1989-92, assoc. prof., coord. grad. program in higher edn., 1992-95; cons. lectures, seminars, workshops throughout Can. Contbr. articles to profl. jours.; mng. editor Can. Jour. of Higher Edn., 1989-93. Mem. U. Man. Senate, 1976-81, 86-89, bd. govs., 1979-82; Can. rep. Internat. Youth Conf., Garmisch, Fed. Republic of Germany, 1968; vol. Can. Cancer Soc.; mem. Assn. RN Accreditation Coun., 1980-85; chair Child Care Accreditation Com., Man., 1983-90; chair Task Force Post-Secondary Accessibility, Man., 1983; vol. United Way Planning and Allocations; provincial dir., mem. nat. bd. Can. Congress for Learning Opportunities for Women. Recipient award for enhancing the Outreach activities of the univ. U. Man., 1994. Mem. Can. Soc. Study Higher Edn., Man. Tchrs. Soc., U. Man. Alumni Assn., Women's Legal Edn. and Action Fund, Am. Assn. Study Higher Edn. Home: 261 Baltimore Rd, Winnipeg, MB Canada R3L 1H7

STALLINGS, CHARLES HENRY, physicist; b. Durham, N.C., Dec. 28, 1941; s. Henry Harroll and Dorothy (Powers) S.; m. Elizabeth Bright, Sept. 4, 1965; children: Deborah, Sharon. BS, N.C. State U., 1963, MS, 1964; PhD, U. Wis., 1970. Sr. physicist Physics Internat. Co., San Leandro, Calif., 1970-73, dep. dept. mgr., 1974-76, dept. mgr., 1976-79, dir. satellite X-ray test facility office, 1979-81, dir. bus. devel., 1981-83, v.p., dir. rsch. devel., v.p., gen. mgr., 1983—. Contbr. articles to tech. jours. Patentee in field. Mem. Gen. Plan Rev. Com., Pleasanton, Calif., 1983. Mem. Am. Phys. Soc., IEEE (assoc.). Home: 1717 Courtney Ave Pleasanton CA 94588-2692 Office: PRIMEX Physics Internat 2700 Merced St San Leandro CA 94577-5602

STALLINGS, HENRY E., II, state legislator; b. Dec. 30, 1950. BA, Western Mich. U.; JD, Detroit Coll. Law. Prin. Preferred Food Stamp Distributors, Inc.; congl. fellow Congl. Black Caucus, 1983; dir. divsn. of minority and women-owned bus. enterprises Dept. of Commerce, 1984-85; v.p., gen. mgr. First Independence Nat. Bank, 1986; senator Dist. 3 Mich. State Senate, 1995—, mem. econ. devel., internat. trade, regulator affairs coms., mem. human resources, fin., labor and vets. affairs coms., asst. Dem. whip.

STALLINGS, (CHARLES) NORMAN, lawyer; b. Tampa, Fla., Apr. 3, 1914; s. Otto Pyromus and Minnie Henderson (Mitchell) S.; m. Mary Phillips Powell, Feb. 6, 1943; children: Charles Norman, Jean Katherine, Mary Anne. A.B., U. Fla., 1935; J.D., Harvard U., 1938, LL.M., 1940. Bar: Mo. 1939, Fla. 1940, D.C. 1941, Ga. 1946. Asso. firm Ryland, Stinson, Mag & Thomson, Kansas City, Mo., 1938-39, Sutherland, Tuttle & Brennan, Washington, 1940-41, Atlanta, 1946-49; mem. firm Shackleford, Farrior, Stallings & Evans, Tampa, Fla., 1949-84, of counsel, 1984—. Vice chmn. Hillsborough County (Fla.) Aviation Authority, 1955-61. Served to lt. col. U.S. Army, 1941-46, ETO. Decorated Bronze Star; Croix de Guerre avec Palma, Belgium). Fellow Am. Coll. Trial Lawyers; mem. ABA, Hillsborough County Bar Assn. (past pres.), Fla. Bar Assn. (past gov.), Univ. Club (past pres.), Tampa Yacht and Country Club (past gov.), Ye Mystic Krewe of Gasparilla (past capt. and king), Phi Delta Phi, Kappa Alpha. Republican. Episcopalian. Home: 1901 S Ardsley St Tampa FL 33629-5930 Office: PO Box 3324 Tampa FL 33601-3324

STALLINGS, RONALD DENIS, lawyer; b. Evansville, Ind., Feb. 22, 1943; s. Denis and Gertrude (Tong) S.; m. Vicki Lee Chandler, Aug. 21, 1965; children: Courtnay, Claire, Ryan. B in Indsl. Engring., Ga. Inst. Tech., 1965; LLB, U. Va., 1968. Bar: Ga. 1968. Assoc. Powell, Goldstein, Frazer & Murphy, Atlanta, 1968-75, ptnr., 1976—. Co-author: Georgia Corporate Forms, 1988. Mem. ABA, Ga. Bar Assn., Atlanta Bar Assn., Nat. Assn. Bond Lawyers, Phoenix Soc. Atlanta (trustee 1987-93). Roman Catholic. Home: 4601 Polo Ln NW Atlanta GA 30339-5345 Office: Powell Goldstein Frazer & Murphy 191 Peachtree St NE Fl 16 Atlanta GA 30303-1740

STALLINGS, VIOLA PATRICIA ELIZABETH, systems engineer, educational systems specialist; b. Norfolk, Va., Nov. 6, 1946; d. Harold Albert and Marie Blanche (Welch) S.; m. (div. Oct. 1984); 1 child, Patricia N.P. Stallings. BS in Psychology, Va. State U., 1968; MBA with distinction, U. Pa., 1975; postgrad., Temple U., 1972-74, Calif. State U., San Francisco, 1973; EdD with specialization in tech., Nova Southeastern U., Ft. Lauderdale, Fla., 1996. Cert. project mgr. Tchr., supr. Peace Corps, Liberia, West Africa, 1968-71; tchr. Day Care Ctr., disruptive h.s. students Tioga Comm. Youth Ctr., 1972-73; tchr. Phila. Sch. Dist., 1972-76; bus. cons. Phila., 1976; sr. sys. engr./sr. industry svcs. specialist, project mgr. IBM/K-12 Edn., Mt. Laurel, N.J., 1976Ó; bd. dirs. Woodrock, Inc., Phila., 1974-84, 87-95; mem. nat. edn. rsch. fund com.; task force leader IBM Corp., 1990-91. Bd. dirs., v.p. Unity Ch. of Christ, 1993-95. Recipient Outstanding Svc. award IBM Black Workers Alliance, Washington, 1984. Mem. AAUW, ASCD, Assn. for Ednl. Comm. and Tech., Beta Gamma Sigma. Baptist. Avocations: reading, writing, drawing, gardening, cooking, dancing, sewing. Home: 105 Burnamwood Ct Mount Laurel NJ 08054-3106 Office: IBM EduQuest 1000 Atrium Way Mount Laurel NJ 08054-3902

STALLKNECHT-ROBERTS, CLOIS FREDA, publisher, publicist; b. Birmingham, Ala., Dec. 31, 1934; d. August and Sadie Bell (Wisener) Anton; m. Randall Scott Roberts; children: Yvonne Denise, April O'dell, Kurt William. Publicist Ms. Clois Presents, L.A., 1968—; advt. Engineered Magic, Advt., Santa Ana, Calif., 1976, 77, 81; pub. Internat. Printing, L.A., 1981—. Editor: Nostradamus, William Bartram, Apuleious, 1990-92, Metamorphoses L.A., 1996-97. Home and Office: PO Box 165 Inyokern CA 93527-0165 Office: Engineered Magic 510 De La Estrella San Clemente CA 92672

STALLMAN, DONALD LEE, corporate executive; b. Rochester, N.Y., Feb. 20, 1930; s. William F. and Clara Elizabeth (Boulle) S.; m. Dolores Anita Putney, Nov. 8, 1958; stepchildren: Nancy, Terri, Jeff. Student, Hobart Coll., Geneva, N.Y., 1948-49, U. Rochester, 1953-54. V.p. Kolstad Assocs., Inc., Rochester, N.Y., 1954—; pres. Water Treatment Assocs., Latham, N.Y., 1975—, KB Fabrications, Latham, N.Y., 1977—; dir. Kolstad Assocs., Inc.; chmn. bd. Water Treatment Assocs.; vice chmn. bd. K.B. Fabrications; adv. bd., pres. Bruner Corp., Milw., 1982-83. Designer Chock-o-Lette Spl. Aircraft Wheel Chock, 1978, Water Treatment Skid for Oil Field Applications, 1980; inventor in field. Cons. Capital Dist. Planning Commn., Albany, 1980-81. With U.S. Army, 1951-53. Decorated Bronze Star medal, Purple Hearts (2). Mem. Am. Soc. Plumbing Engrs., Water Quality Assn., Quiet Birdman Soc., Latham Area C. of C. (mem. transport com. 1985—), Sigma Chi. Republican. Roman Catholic. Avocations: flying, boating, golf. Home: 16 Hillcrest Rd Latham NY 12110-4133 also (winter): 111 Royal Park Dr Fort Lauderdale FL 33309 Office: Water Treatment Assocs PO Box 367 Latham NY 12110-0367

STALLMEYER, JAMES EDWARD, engineer, educator; b. Covington, Ky., Aug. 11, 1926; s. Joseph Julius and Anna Catherine (Scheper) S.; m. Mary Katherine Davenport, Apr. 11, 1953; children: Cynthia Marie, James Duncan, Michael John, Catherine Ann, John Charles, Gregory Edward. BS, U. Ill., 1947, MS, 1949, PhD, 1953. Jr. engr. So. Ry. System, 1947; research asst. U. Ill., Urbana, 1947-49; research asso. U. Ill., 1951-52, asst. prof. civil engring, 1952-57, assoc. prof., 1957-60, prof., 1960-91, prof. emeritus, 1991—; cons. on structural problems various indsl. and govt. agys. Author: (with E.H. Gaylord Jr.), Design of Steel Structures; editor: (with E.H. Gaylord Jr.) Structural Engineering Handbook; contbr. to Shock and Vibration Handbook. Served with USN, 1944-46. Standard Oil fellow, 1949-51; recipient Adams meml. award, 1964, Everitt award for teaching excellence, 1981. Mem. ASCE, Am. Concrete Inst., Am. Ry. Engring. Assn., ASTM, Am. Welding Soc., Am. Soc. Metals, Soc. Exptl. Stress Analysis, Scabbard and Blade, Sigma Xi, Chi Epsilon, Sigma Tau, Tau Beta Pi, Phi Kappa Phi. Republican. Roman Catholic. Club: KC. Office: Newmark Civil Engring 205 N Mathews Ave Urbana IL 61801-2350

STALLONE, SYLVESTER ENZIO, actor, writer, director; b. N.Y.C., July 6, 1946; s. Frank and Jacquline (Labofish) S.; m. Sasha Czack, Dec. 28, 1974 (div.); children: Sage, Seth; m. Brigitte Nielsen, Dec. 15, 1985 (div. 1987). Student, Am. Coll. of Switzerland, 1965-67, U. Miami, 1967-69. Formerly, usher, fish salesman, horse trainer, delicatessen worker, truck driver, bouncer, zoo attendant, short order cook, pizza demonstrator, phys. edn. tchr., motel supt., bookstore detective. Appeared in motion pictures Lords of Flatbush, 1973, Capone, 1974, Rocky, 1976, (Oscar for Best Picture 1976, Golden Globe award for best picture 1976, Donatello award for best actor in Europe 1976, Christopher Religious award 1976, Bell Ringer award Scholastic Mag. 1976, Nat. Theatre Owners award 1976) F.I.S.T, 1978, Paradise Alley, 1978, Rocky II, 1979, Nighthawks, 1981, Victory, 1981, Rocky III, 1982, First Blood, 1982, Rhinestone, 1984, Rambo: First Blood Part II, 1985, Rocky IV, 1985, Cobra, 1986, Over the Top, 1987, Rambo III, 1988, Lock Up, 1989, Tango and Cash, 1989, Rocky V, 1990, Cliffhanger, 1993, Demolition Man, 1993, The Specialist, 1994, Judge Dredd, 1995, Assassins, 1995, Firestorm, 1996, Daylight; producer, dir. film Staying Alive, 1983; author: Paradise Alley, 1977, The Rocky Scrapbook, 1977, Rocky II, Copland, 1997. Recipient Star of the Year award 1977, named Show West actor of the year 1979, Artistic Achievement award Nat. Italian Am. Found., 1991, Order of Arts and Letters, French Ministry, 1992, Caesar award for Career Achievement, 1992. Mem. Screen Actors Guild, Writers Guild, Stuntmans Assn. (hon.), Dirs. Guild. Nomination for two Oscars (acting and writing) in same year (1976) occurred for only 3d time in history. Office: William Morris Agency 151 El Camino Dr Beverly Hills CA 90212 *Once in one's life, for one mortal moment, one must make a grab for immortality; if not, one has not lived.*•

STALLONE, THOMAS MICHAEL, clinical psychologist; b. N.Y.C., Dec. 5, 1952; s. Vito Joseph and Mary Ellen (Kearney) S.; m. Bonnie Elizabeth Wenk, May 30, 1982; 1 child, Thomas Lucius. B of Profl. Studies, N.Y. Inst. Tech., 1987; MA, Spalding U., 1991; D of Psychology, Pacific U., 1994. Lic. psychologist, Wash.; cert. psychol. assoc. in clin. psychology, rational emotive therapy; diplomate Am. Bd. Forensic Examiners; registered Nat. Register Health Providers in Psychology. Internat. banker Sumitomo Bank, Ltd., N.Y.C., 1980-82; pvt. practice hypnosis cons. LaGrange, Ky. and N.Y.C., 1982—; internat. banker Bank of N.Y., N.Y.C., 1982-87; rehab. specialist Goodwill Industries Ky., Louisville, 1989; psychol. assoc. div. mental health Ky. Corrections Cabinet, La Grange, 1989-91; teaching asst. Pacific U., Forest Grove, Oreg., 1991-93; psychotherapist Portland, Oreg., 1991-95; clin. psychologist Vancouver, Wash., 1995—; Author: The Boke of Taliesyne, 1979, The Effects of Psychodrama on Inmates Within a Structured Residential Behavior Modification Program, 1993, Rational Emotive Behavior Therapy and Subpersonalities, 1997. Author: The Boke of Taliesyne, 1979, The Effects of Psychodrama on Inmates Within a Structured Residential Behavior Modification Program, 1993. Cons. Hist. Arms, Ltd., N.Y.C., 1983-87, N.Y. Medieval Festival, 1984-86; dir., cons. Whitestone

(N.Y.) Creative Arts Workshop, 1977, Ky. Shakespeare Festival, Louisville, 1987-88; treas., advisor 4H Exec. Coun., La Grange, 1988-91. Decorated Grant of Arms Chief Herald of Ireland; named to Honorable Order of Ky. Col. Mem. APA, Am. Soc. Group Psychotherapy and Psychodrama, Internat. Soc. for Profl. Hypnosis, Wash. State Psychol. Assn., Ancient Order Hibernians, Mensa. Avocations: hypnosis, meditation, Martial Arts, Medieval history, teaching.

STALLWORTH, ANNE NALL, writer, writing educator; b. Birmingham, Ala., Sept. 30, 1935; d. John Martin and Lida Lucille (Crump) Nall; m. Clarke J. Stallworth Jr., Mar. 23, 1925; children: Carole Anne Stallworth, Clarke J. Stallworth III. Student, Birmingham-So. Coll., 1952-53. Tchr. U. Ala., Birmingham; tchr. Birmingham. Author: This Time Next Year, 1972 (Best Fiction award), Where the Bright Lights Shine, 1977, Go, Go, Said the Bird, 1984 (movie rights pending); (short story) Waiting (McCall's mag.), 1976. All had fgn. publ. Editor Found. for Women's Health newsletter, Birmingham; publicity dir. Birmingham Music Club. Recipient Best Fiction award Ala. Libr., 1972. Avocations: speaking at libraries, women's clubs; presenting workshops for writers. Home: 4316 Wilderness Rd Birmingham AL 35213-2212

STALLWORTH-BARRON, DORIS A. CARTER, librarian, educator; b. Ala., June 12, 1932; d. Henry Lee Carter and Hattie Belle Stallworth; m. George Stallworth, 1950 (dec.); children: Annette LaVerne, Vanzette Yvonne; m. Walter L. Barron, 1989. BS, Ala. State U., 1955; MLS, CUNY, 1968; postgrad., Columbia U., St. John's U., NYU. Cert. supr. and tchr. sch. libr. media, N.Y. Libr. media specialist N.Y.C. Bd. Edn.; head libr. Calhoun County High Sch., Hobson City, Ala.; cons. Libr. Unit, N.Y.C. Bd. Edn.; cons. evaluator So. Assn. Secondary Schs., Ala.; supr., adminstr., liason rep. Community Sch. Dist. #24 N.Y.C. Sch. System; previewer libr. media Preview Mag., 1971-73; mem. ednl. svcs. adv. coun. Sta. WNET, 1987-89; mem. coun. N.Y.C. Schs. Libr. System, 1987-90; turn-key tchr. trainer N.Y. State Dept. Edn., 1988; spl. guest speaker and lectr. Queens Coll., City U., Community Sch. Dist. #24, PTA, N.Y. City Sch. System, Libr. unit, 1980-90; curriculum writer libr. unit N.Y.C. Bd. Edn., 1985-86. Contbr. articles to ednl. publs. Mem. State of Ala. Dem. Exec. Com., 1994—; active A+ for Kids. Mem. NAFE, ALA, Am. Assn. Sch. Librs. (spl. guest speaker and lectr. for conv. 1987), Am. Sch. Libr.'s Assn., Nat. Assn. Black Pub. Adminstrs., N.Y. State Libr. Assn., N.Y.C. Sch. Librs. Assn., Nat. Forum for Black Pub. Adminstrs., N.Y. Coalition 100 Black Women, Lambda Kappa Mu Sorority, Inc., Alpha Kappa Alpha Sorority Inc.

STALNAKER, JOHN HULBERT, physician; b. Portland, Oreg., Aug. 29, 1918; s. William Park II and Helen Caryl (Hulbert) S.; m. Louise Isabel Lucas, Sept. 8, 1946; children: Carol Ann, Janet Lee, Mary Louise, John Park, Laurie Jean, James Mark. Student, Reed Coll., Portland, 1936-38; AB, Willamette U., Salem, Oreg., 1941; MD, Oreg. Health Scis. U., 1945. Diplomate Am. Bd. Internal Medicine. Intern Emanuel Hosp., Portland, 1945-46; resident in internal medicine St. Vincent Hosp., Portland, 1948-51; clin. instr. U. Oreg. Med. Sch., 1951-54, 60-62; staff physician VA Hosp., Vancouver, Wash., 1970-79; cons. in internal medicine, 1951-79. Contbr. articles to profl. jours. Pianist various civic and club meetings, Portland; leader Johnny Stalnaker's Dance Orch., 1936-39. Lt. (j.g.) USNR, 1946-48. Fellow ACP; mem. AMA, Multnomah County Med. Soc., Oreg. State Med. Assn., N.Am. Lily Soc., Am. Rose Soc. Avocations: music, photography, horticulture. Home: 2204 SW Sunset Dr Portland OR 97201-2068

STALOFF, ARNOLD FRED, financial executive; b. Dover, N.J., Dec. 12, 1944; s. William and Ida (Greenberg) S.; m. Sharon Marcia Teplitsky, June 10, 1967; children: Kimberly, Lindsay. BBA, U. Miami, 1967. Statistician U.S. Census Bur., Washington, 1967-68; fin. analyst SEC, Washington, 1968-71; sr. v.p. Phila. Stock Exch., 1971-78; v.p. Securities Industry Automation Corp., N.Y.C., 1978-80; pres. Fin. Automation Corp., Phila., 1980-83, Phila. Bd. Trade, 1983-89; pres., CEO Commodity Exch., Inc. (COMEX), N.Y.C., 1989-90; CEO Bloom Staloff Corp., Phila., 1990—; bd. dirs. Phila. Stock Exch., Lehman Bros. Fin. Products, Inc. Bd. dirs. Variety Club for Handicapped Children, Phila., 1987-92; mem. adv. bd. Phila. Internat. Airport, 1988—. Mem. Nat. Futures Assn. (bd. dirs. 1987-90). Avocations: fly fishing, golf, skiing. Office: Bloom Staloff Corp 2000 Market St Philadelphia PA 19103-3231

STALON, CHARLES GARY, retired economics educator, institute administrator; b. Cape Girardeau, Mo., Oct. 26, 1929; s. Charles Douglas and Lucy Idell (Row) S.; m. Marie Allene Hitt, Mar. 15, 1952; children: Connie Lucille Stalon Babbitt, Donna Jean Stalon Williams. Student, Ohio State U., 1955-56; BA, Butler U., 1959; MS, Purdue U., 1963, PhD, 1966. Econs. instr. Purdue U., Lafayette, Ind., 1962-63; econs. prof. So. Ill. U., Carbondale, 1963-77; rsch. economist Fed. Power Commn., Washington, 1969-70; commr. Ill. Commerce Commn., Springfield, 1977-84, Fed. Energy Regulatory Commn., Washington, 1984-89; dir. Putnam, Hayes & Bartlett, Inc., Washington, 1989-91; dir. Inst. Pub. Utilities, prof. econs. Mich. State U., East Lansing, 1991-93; pres. Mid-Am. Regulatory Commn., Chgo., 1983-84; mem. adv. coun. Gas Rsch. Inst., 1982-84, 91—; bd. dirs. N.J. Resources Corp., New Eng. ISO Corp. Author: (book chpt.) Papers in Quantitative Economics, 1968, The Future of Electrial Energy, 1986; contbr. articles to profl. jours. With USN, 1948-49, 52-54. Mem. Am. Econ. Assn., Transp. and Pub. Utility Group, Nat. Soc. Rate of Return Analysts (bd. dirs. 1982-90), Nat. Assn. Regulatory Utilities Commns., Nat. Regulatory Rsch. Inst. (bd. dirs. 1983-84, 91-94), Inst. for Study of Regulation (bd. dirs. 1984-87).

STAM, DAVID HARRY, librarian; b. Paterson, N.J., July 11, 1935; s. Jacob and Deana B. (Bowman) S.; m. Deirdre Corcoran, May 15, 1963; children—Julian, Wendell, Kathryn. AB, Wheaton Coll., 1955; postgrad., New Coll., U. Edinburgh, 1955-56; MLS, Rutgers U., 1962; postgrad., CUNY, 1963-64; PhD, Northwestern U., 1978. Asst. editor library publs., reference librarian, manuscript cataloguer New York Pub. Library, 1959-64; librarian Marlboro (Vt.) Coll., 1964-67; head tech. services dept. Newberry Library, Chgo., 1967-71; assoc. librarian Newberry Library, 1969-73; librarian Milton S. Eisenhower Library, Johns Hopkins U., Balt., 1973-78; Andrew W. Mellon dir. rsch. libraries N.Y. Pub. Library, N.Y.C., 1978-86; Univ. librarian Syracuse U., 1986—; trustee Gladys K. Delmas Found. Author: Wordsworthian Criticism 1964-1973: An Annotated Bibliography, 1974, (with Rissa Yachnin) Turgenev in English: A Checklist of Works by and about Him, 1960; Contbr. articles to profl. jours. Served with USNR, 1956-58. Brit. Acad. Overseas fellow, 1975, Brit. Libr. fellow, 1995-96. Mem. Am. Hist. Assn., Am. Antiquarian Soc., Caxton Club (Chgo.), Princeton Club N.Y., Grolier Club (N.Y.C.). Home: 2400 Euclid Ave Syracuse NY 13224-1811 Office: Syracuse U E S Bird Libr 222 Waverly Ave Syracuse NY 13210-2412

STAMAS, STEPHEN, investment executive; b. Salem, Mass., Apr. 26, 1931; s. Theodore and Georgia (Fotopulos) S.; m. Elaine Heidi Zervas, Apr. 24, 1955; children: Heidi, Theodore. A.B., Harvard, 1953, Ph.D., 1957; B.Phil. (Rhodes scholar), Oxford U., 1955. Budget examiner Bur. Budget, Washington, 1957-59; loan officer Devel. Loan Fund, Washington, 1959-60; mgr. internat. div. treasurer's dept. Standard Oil Co. (N.J.), N.Y.C., 1960-63; dep. European financial rep. Standard Oil Co. (N.J.), London, Eng., 1963-64; govt. relations mgr. Esso Europe, 1964-67; petroleum planning mgr. Esso Internat., 1967-68; dep. asst. sec. for financial policy Dept. Commerce, Washington, 1968-69; chief economist Standard Oil Co. (N.J.), N.Y.C., 1969-70; dep. mgr. pub. affairs dept. Standard Oil Co. (N.J.), 1971; v.p., pub. affairs Exxon Corp., N.Y.C., 1973-86; pres. Wallace Funds, N.Y.C., 1986-87; pres. N.Y. Philharm., 1984-89, chmn., 1989-96; pvt. investment exec. Windcrest Ptnrs., N.Y.C., 1992—. Trustee, pres. Am. Ditchley Found.; trustee, vice chmn. Rockefeller U.; chmn. Am. Assembly, Columbia U., Marlboro Sch. Music; mem. bd. overseers Harvard Coll., 1979-85; bd. dirs. N.Y. Philharm.-Symphony Soc.; bd. dirs. emeritus Lincoln Ctr. for the Performing Arts; chmn., bd. dirs. The Greenwall Found., BNY Hamilton Funds, Inc., Seacor Holdings Inc. Mem. Coun. Fgn. Rels., Acad. Polit. Sci., Am. Coun. on Germany, Phi Beta Kappa. Clubs: Harvard (N.Y.C.), Century Assn. (N.Y.C.), Manursing Island (Rye, N.Y.). Home: 325 Evandale Rd Scarsdale NY 10583-1505 Office: Windcrest Ptnrs 122 E 42nd St New York NY 10168-0002

STAMATAKIS, CAROL MARIE, state legislator, lawyer; b. Canton, Ohio, Apr. 27, 1960; d. Emmanuel Nicholas and Catherine Lucille (Zam) S.; m. Michael Charles Shklar, Mar. 23, 1985. BA in Criminology and Criminal Justice, Ohio State U., 1982; JD, Case Western Res., 1985. Bar: N.H. 1985, U.S. Dist. Ct. N.H. 1985. Atty. Law Office Laurence F. Gardner, Hanover, N.H., 1985-87, Law Office William Howard Dunn, Claremont, N.H., 1987-90, Elliott, Jasper & Stamatakis, Newport, N.H., 1990-93; state rep. N.H. State Legislature, 1988-94; of counsel Law office of Michael C. Shklar, Newport, 1994—; staff atty. N.H. Dept. Health and Human Svcs., Keene, 1994—; instr. Am. Inst. Banking, Claremont, 1987-88, 91-92, 95. Asst. editor: (jours.) Health Matrix: The Jour. of Health Services Mangement, 1983-85. Treas., mem. Town of Lempster N.H. Conservation Commn., 1987—; bd. dirs. Orion House, Inc., Newport, N.H., 1987-91; town chair N.H. Dem. Party, 1987—; mem. Town of Lempster Recycling Com., 1988—, Community Task Force on Drug and alcohol Abuse, 1988. Mem. N.H. Bar Assn., Sierra Club, Upper Valley Group (former vice chair and solid waste chair). Avocations: drawing, painting. Home: PO Box 807 Newport NH 03773-0807

STAMATY, CLARA GEE KASTNER, artist; b. Piqua, Ohio, May 15, 1919; d. Sam and Dina (Glad) Kastner; m. Stanley Stamaty, Apr. 27, 1944 (dec. Sept. 1979); 1 child, Mark Alan; m. Milton Ziment, Aug. 12, 1984. Grad. high sch., Piqua, Ohio; grad., Cin. Art Acad., 1943; postgrad., Art Students League, N.Y.C., 1959, Pratt Graphic Workshop, N.Y.C., 1968-69, Prints Divsn. Libr., N.Y.C., 1969-70. Artist Air Svc. Command/Paterson Field, Dayton, Ohio, 1943-45; tchr. Stamaty Studios, Elberon, N.J., 1962-80; mem. graphic design adv. com. Brookdale C.C., Lincroft, N.J., 1974-80; guild del. to ann. sems. Federated Art Assns. N.J., Westfield, 1974-80. One person shows include Monmouth County Libr., Monmouth YM-YWHA, West Long Branch Libr., Long Branch Libr., Temple Beth Miriam; exhibited in group shows at Jewish Cmty. Ctr. Greater Monmouth County, Guild of Creative Art, Am. Watercolor Soc., N.Y.C. Nat. Acad. Galleries, Cin. Art Mus., Dayton Art Inst., Butler Art Inst., Ohio U., Massillon Mus., Monmouth Coll., N.J. Watercolor Soc., Morris Mus., Brookdale Coll., Garden State Watercolor Soc., Princeton, Monmouth Mus., Garden State Art Ctr. Celebrity House; represented in permanent collections Ford Co., Detroit, United Meth. Ch., Red Bank, N.J., Ranney Sch., Rumson, N.J., others; author, editor, illustrator: What's Cookin?, 1957; author, illustrator: Ginny, 1967; contbr. cartoons and illustrations to over 50 nat. mags., hardcover books and paperbacks; contbr. cartoon feature series to various mags. including Christian Sci. Monitor, Catholic Miss, Co-Ed Mag., Better Homes & Gardens, Am. Mag., others. Recipient 8 1st prize awards Three Arts Club, 1939-42, Spl. award Dayton Art Inst., 1945, Gold medal Long Branch Cmty. Ctr., 1962, Purchase award Meth. Ch., Red Bank, 1965. Mem. Nat. Cartoonist Soc. (hon. life), Guild of Creative Art (exhibiting artist 1960—, sec. 1967-68, gallery dir. 1968-70, publicity dir. 1972-75, v.p. 1974-75), Art Alliance N.J., Monmouth Arts Found., Monmouth County Arts Coun. (adv. bd., guild del. 1996), Eastern Star. Avocations: writing poetry, yoga, walking, reading, dancing. Home and Office: Stamaty Studios 1019 Woodgate Ave PO Box 2075 Long Branch NJ 07740-2075

STAMATY, MARK ALAN, cartoonist, author, artist; b. Bklyn., Aug. 1, 1947; s. Stanley and Clara Gee (Kastner) S. B.F.A., The Cooper Union, 1969. Mem. faculty Parson's Sch. Design, N.Y.C., 1977-81. Author-illustrator: (children's books) Who Needs Donuts, 1973 (Bklyn. Art Books For Children award 1974), Small in the Saddle, 1975, Minnie Maloney & Macaroni, 1976, Where's My Hippopotamus?, 1977, (comic strip collections) Macdoodle St., 1981, Washingtoon, 1983; cartoonist: Macdoodle St., Village Voice newspaper, 1978-79, Carrrttoooonnn, Village Voice newspaper, 1980-81, (Washington Post and syndication) Washingtoon, 1981—; polit. cartoonist TIME mag., 1994-96, Doodlennium, Slate Mag., 1996—; illustrator various publs., including: (children's book) Yellow Yellow, 1971, (Bklyn. Art Books for Children award). Recipient Purchase award N.J. State Mus., about 1969, Gold medal Soc. Illustrators, 1974. Mem. PEN Am. Ctr. Avocations: impersonating Elvis Presley; watching the world; softball; swimming. Office: care Village Voice 36 Cooper Sq New York NY 10003-7118

STAMBAUGH, ARMSTRONG A., JR., restaurant and hotel executive; b. Cleve., Nov. 1, 1920; s. Armstrong Alexander and Beatrice (Snyder) S.; m. Janet Turley Marting, July 26, 1943 (div. 1958); children—Susan Reed (Mrs. Roy H. Beaton, Jr.), Sally Russell (Mrs. Michael H. Huber), Elizabeth Renshaw (Mrs. James W. Ewing); m. Aagot Hinrichsen Cain, June 10, 1972. B.A., Dartmouth, 1942; Indsl. Adminstr., Harvard, 1943, M.B.A., 1946. Research asst., then instr. bus. adminstrn. Harvard Grad. Sch. Bus. Adminstrn., 1946-48; with Gulf Oil Corp., 1948-66; coord. sales devel. mktg. hdqrs. Gulf Oil Corp., Houston, 1962-63; v.p. Eastern marketing region Gulf Oil Corp., Phila., 1963-66; exec. v.p. adminstrn. Howard Johnson Co., Inc., 1966-70, exec. v.p. ops. and adminstrn., 1970-79, exec. v.p., asst. to pres., 1979-81, dir., 1969-81; operator, developer food and lodging facilities, 1981—. Pres. trustees Fox Chapel Country Day Sch., Pitts., 1955-57; div. vice chmn. Boston United Fund, 1961; bd. dirs. Houston Internat. Trade and Travel Fair, 1962-63, World Affairs Coun. Phila., 1964-65; dir. Phila. C. of C., 1964, 65, 66; bd. overseers Hanover Inn, Dartmouth Coll., 1979-85, chmn., 1984-85; trustee Old Sturbridge Village, Mass., 1979—. Served to lt. (j.g.) USNR, 1943-46. Mem. Pine Valley Golf Club (N.J.), Weston (Mass.) Golf Club, Kittansett Golf Club (Mass.), Boston Skating Club, Harvard Club (Boston), Vineyard Haven Yacht Club (Mass.), Paradise Valley Country Club (Ariz.), Delta Tau Delta. Home and Office: 474 Concord Rd Weston MA 02193-1313

STAMBAUGH, JOHN EDGAR, oncologist, hematologist, pharmacologist, educator; b. Everrett, Pa., Apr. 30, 1940; s. John Edgar and Rhoda Irene (Becker) S.; B.S. cum laude in Chemistry, Dickinson Coll., 1962; M.D., Jefferson Med. Coll., 1966, Ph.D., 1968; m. Shirley Louise Fultz, June 24, 1961; 4 children. Intern, Thomas Jefferson U. Hosp., Phila., 1968-69, resident, 1969-70; oncology fellow Jefferson Med. Coll., 1970-72, instr. pharmacology, 1969-70, asst. prof., 1970-74, assoc. prof., 1974-82, prof., 1982—, asst. prof. medicine, 1976—; pvt. practice medical oncology Hematology and Chronic Pain, Woodbury, N.J.; staff physician Cooper Med. Center, Camden, N.J., 1972—, Underwood Meml. Hosp., Woodbury, 1972—, West Jersey Hosp., 1973—, J.F. Kennedy Hosp., 1978—, Our Lady of Lourdes Hosp., 1990—. Fellow Am. Coll. Clin. Pharmacology, Am. Acad. Pain Mgmt., Am. Soc. Pain Mgmt.; mem. ABA, AMA, Am. Soc. Clin. Pharmacology, N.J. Med. Soc., Gloucester County Med. Soc., Camden County Med. Soc., Am. Soc. for Pharmacology and Exptl. Therapeutics, Am. Soc. Clin. Oncology, Am. Assn. for Cancer Research, Internat. Assn. for Study of Pain, Am. Pain Soc., Am. Assn. Clin. Research, Sigma Xi. Contbr. articles to profl. jours. Office: 17 W Red Bank Ave Ste 101 Woodbury NJ 08096-1630

STAMBERG, SUSAN LEVITT, radio broadcaster; b. Newark, Sept. 7, 1938; d. Robert I. and Anne (Rosenberg) Levitt; m. Louis Collins Stamberg, Apr. 14, 1962; 1 child, Joshua Collins. BA, Barnard Coll, 1959; DHL (hon.), Gettysburg Coll., 1982, Dartmouth Coll., 1984, Knox Coll., U. N.H., SUNY, Brockport. Editorial asst. Daedalus, Cambridge, Mass., 1960-62; editorial asst. The New Republic, Washington, 1962-63; host, producer, mgr., program dir. Sta. WAMU-FM, Washington, 1963-69; host All Things Considered Washington, 1971-86; host Weekend Edition Nat Pub. Radio, Washington, 1987-89; spl. corr. Nat. Pub. Radio, 1990—; bd. dirs. AIA, Washington, 1983-85, PEN/Faulkner Fiction Award Found., 1985—. Author: Every Night at Five, 1982, The Wedding Cake in the Middle of the Road, 1992, Talk: NPR's Susan Stamberg Considers All Things, 1993. Recipient Honor award Ohio U., 1977, Edward R. Murrow award Corp. for Pub. Broadcasting, 1980; named Woman of Yr., Barnard Coll., 1984; fellow Silliman Coll. Yale U., 1984—; inducted Broadcasting Hall of Fame, 1994, Radio Hall of Fame, 1996. Avocations: sketching; piano; knitting. Office: Nat Pub Radio 635 Massachusetts Ave NW Washington DC 20001-3752

STAMELMAN, RICHARD HOWARD, French and humanities educator; b. Newark, Mar. 7, 1942; s. Louis Robert and Golda (Senzer) S.; children: Emily, Gibson, Jeremy White. B.A., Hamilton Coll.; Ph.D., Duke U. Asst. prof. French and humanities Wesleyan U., Middletown, Conn., 1967-74, assoc. prof., 1974-79, prof., 1979-93, William R. Kenan Jr. prof. humanities, 1983-92, dean humanities, 1986-89, dir. Ctr. for the Humanities, 1976-82, dir. humanities devel., 1982-85; dir. Weston Ctr. for Fgn. Langs., Lits. and Cultures Williams Coll., Williamstown, Mass., 1992—, prof. Romance langs., lit. studies, 1992—; chair dept. French and Italian U. Colo., Boulder, 1991-92; organizer (study group) Ecrire le Livre: Autour d'Edmond Jabès, Cerisy-la-Salle, France, 1987; co-dir. Edouard Morot-Sir Summer Inst. for French Cultural Studies, Hanover, N.H., 1994. Author: The Drama of Self in Guillaume Apollinaire's Alcools, 1976, Claude Garache: Prints, 1965-85, 1985, Lost Beyond Telling: Representations of Death and Absence in Modern French Poetry, 1990; editor: Contemporary French Poetry, Studies in 20th Century Literature, 1989, Ecrire le Livre: Autour d'Edmond Jabès, 1989, Italian transl., 1991, French Poetry since the War, L'Esprit Créateur, 1992; editor, prin. translator: The Lure and the Truth of Painting, Selected Essays by Yves Bonnefoy, 1995; translator: The Grapes of Zeuxis and Other Fables by Yves Bonnefoy, 1987, Once More the Grapes of Zeuxis by Yves Bonnefoy, 1989, The Last Grapes of Zeuxis by Yves Bonnefoy, 1993; mem. editorial bd. French Forum; contbr. articles to profl. jours. Recipient Chevalier dans l'ordre des Palmes Académiques award French Govt., 1993; NEH fellow, 1973; Am. Council Learned Socs. grantee, 1983. Mem. MLA (regional del. 1987-90, mem. program com. 1996—), Am. Assn. Tchrs. French, Acad. Lit. Studies. Home: 432 South St #C-6 Bennington VT 05201 Office: Williams Coll Weston Ctr Fgn Langs Lits Culture Williamstown MA 01267

STAMES, WILLIAM ALEXANDER, realtor, cost management executive; b. Douglas, Ariz., Mar. 26, 1917; s. Alex Basil and Teresa (Ruis) S.; AA, Long Beach Coll., 1941; postgrad. U. Calif., Berkeley, 1962-64; cert. mgmt. practices Naval Officers CIC Sch., Glenview, Ill., 1955; grad. Real Estate Inst., Calif.; m. Marguerite Winifred Nelson, June 11, 1943; 1 child, Wynn Lorain. Owner, Stames Beverage Co., Brawley, Calif., 1945-50; liaison engr. Lockheed Missiles & Space Co., Sunnyvale, Calif., 1958-60, liaison engr. sr., 1960, adminstr., 1960-62, staff adminstr., 1962-63, liaison engr., sr., design engr. sr., 1965-76; owner, mgr. Cost Reduction Equipment Sales & Tech., Sunnyvale, 1967-76; realtor Cornish & Carey, 1988—. Dir. ret. activities office Naval Amphibious Base, Coronado, Calif. Comdr. USNR, 1941-69, ret., World War II, Korea, Vietnam. Decorated D.F.C., Air medal with four gold stars, Presdl. citation; inductee D.F.C. Soc. Honor Roll. Mem. Am. Mgmt. Assn., Mountain View Real Estate Bd. (pres.), Calif. Assn. Realtors (bd. dirs.), Tailhook Assn. Clubs: Commonwealth San Francisco, Ret. Officers (past pres. Peninsula chpt.), Lions. Author: Polaris Electrical Subsystems Design History, 1964; Poseidon Subsystem Invention, 1971. Home: 1060 Coronado Ave Coronado CA 92118-2439

STAMEY, THOMAS ALEXANDER, physician, urology educator; b. Rutherfordton, N.C., Apr. 26, 1928; s. Owen and Virginia (Link) S.; m. Kathryn Simmons Dec. 1, 1973; children: Fred M., Charline, Thomas A. III, Allison, Theron. BA, Vanderbilt U., 1948; MD, Johns Hopkins U., 1952. Diplomate Am. Bd. Urology. Intern, then resident Johns Hopkins Hosp., 1952-56; asst. prof. urology Johns Hopkins U. Sch. Medicine, Balt., 1958-60, assoc. prof., 1960-61; assoc. prof. Stanford (Calif.) U., 1961-64, 1964-90, prof., chmn. dept., 1991-94, chmn. divsn. urology, 1961-90. Author: Renovascular Hypertension, 1967, Pathogenesis and Treatment of Urinary Tract Infections, 1980, Urinalysis and Urinary Sediment: A Practical Guide for the Health Science Professional, 1985; editor: Campbell's Urology, Monographs in Urology, 1980—. Capt. M.C., USAF, 1956-58. Recipient Sheen award ACS, 1990, Ferdinand C. Valentine award N.Y. Acad. Medicine, 1991. Mem. Am. Urol. Assn. (Ramon Guiteras award 1995), Am. Surg. Assn. (sr.), Inst. Medicine of NAS. Avocations: fishing, astronomy. Office: Stanford U Med Ctr Urology Dept Rm S287 300 Pasteur Dr Stanford CA 94305-5118*

STAMM, ALAN, lawyer; b. Galesburg, Ill., Nov. 22, 1931; s. Gustave Frederick and Miriam (Simon) S.; m. Shelley Lynn Ramage, Mar. 19, 1978; 1 child, Lucinda Anne. Student, Universidad Nacional de Mex., summer 1950; AB, Yale U., 1952; JD, Harvard U., 1957. Bar: Calif. 1957, U.S. Supreme Ct. 1963. Assoc. Thelen, Marrin, Johnson & Bridges, San Francisco, 1957-60; staff atty. Litton Industries Inc., Beverly Hills, Calif., 1960-66; asst. sec. Litton Industries Inc., Beverly Hills, 1963-66; sec., gen. counsel Internat. Rectifier Corp., L.A., 1966-69, v.p., 1968-69; v.p., gen. counsel Republic Corp., L.A., 1969-71, also bd. dirs., 1970-71; v.p., gen. counsel Sat. Rev. Industries, N.Y.C., 1971-72; v.p., gen. counsel Mattel Inc., Hawthorne, Calif., 1972-74, staff cons., 1974-75; of counsel Long & Levit, L.A., 1975-82, O'Donnell & Gordon, L.A., 1983-87, Hedges, Powe & Caldwell, L.A., 1988-90; pvt. practice L.A., 1990—; judge pro tem Mcpl. Ct. L.A. Jud. Dist., 1977—; arbitrator L.A. Superior Ct. 1979—, judge pro tem L.A. Superior Ct. 1989—, arbitrator Nat. Assn. Securities Dealers, 1981—. Founding trustee Ctr. for Law in the Pub. Interest; adv. trustee L.A. Ctr. for Photog. Studies; trustee Marlborough Sch., L.A. Lt. (j.g.) USNR, 1952-54; lt. comdr. Res.; ret. Mem. ABA, Calif. Bar Assn., L.A. Bar Assn., Am. Jewish Com., Harvard Law Sch. Assn., L.A. County Art Mus., Am. Arbitration Assn. (nat. panel arbitrators), NAACP, Sierra Club, Nat. Assn. Yale Alumni (former bd. govs.), Yale Club of So. Calif. (former dir.), Harvard Club of So. Calif., Phi Beta Kappa. Home: 422 Denslow Ave Los Angeles CA 90049-3507 Office: 1840 Century Park E Fl 8 Los Angeles CA 90067-2101

STAMM, CHARLES H., lawyer. Exec. v.p., gen. counsel Tchrs. Ins. & Annuity Assn., N.Y.C. Office: Tchrs Ins & Annuity Assn 730 3rd Ave New York NY 10017-3206

STAMM, GEOFFREY EATON, arts administrator; b. Washington, July 30, 1943; s. George Edward Stamm and Dorothy Bourne (Baden) Elliott; m. Florence Theresa Ryan, Nov. 19, 1983. AB, Hamilton Coll., 1965; diploma in arts adminstrn., Harvard U., 1974. Mus. tech. Indian Arts and Crafts Bd., Washington, 1965-67, rsch. asst., 1967-69, coord. spl. projects, 1969-74, asst. to gen. mgr., 1974-78, asst. gen. mgr., 1978-93, gen. mgr., 1993-94, dir., 1994—. Chmn. Foggy Bottom and West End Adv. Neighborhood Commn., Washington, 1983-86; pres. St. Mary's Ct. Housing Devel. Corp., Washington, 1988-93. Mem. Am. Assn. Mus., Am. Craft Coun., Native Am. Art Studies Assn. Office: Indian Arts and Crafts Bd 1849 C St NW Washington DC 20240-0001

STAMM, JOHN WILLIAM RUDOLPH, dentist, educator, academic dean; b. Germany, Nov. 3, 1942; married; 2 children. DDS, U. Alta., Can., 1967; DDPH, U. Toronto, Can., 1969, MScD, 1971. Diplomate Am. Bd. Dental Pub. Health. Dental dir. Baffin region Nat. Health & Welfare, 1967; pvt. dental practice Fort Saskatchewan, Alta., 1968; rsch. asst. & biometrics Sch. Hygiene & Faculty Dentistry U. Toronto, 1968-71; asst. prof. Faculty Dentistry McGill U., 1971-74, assoc. prof., 1974-80, chmn., 1974-84, prof., 1980-84; dir. Dental Rsch. Ctr. U. N.C., 1985-89, prof. Sch. Dentistry, 1985—, asst. dean, 1985-89, dean, 1989—; vis. prof. U. Riyadh, Saudi Arabia, 1980; mem. expert adv. panel oral health WHO, 1984-90; mem. study sect. oral biology & medicine NIH, 1988-90; cons. Quebec Ministry Social Affairs, 1974-76, Alta. Health Unit Assn., 1977-79, Can. Electrolytic Zinc, 1978-82, Can. Dental Assn., 1980, Am. Fund Dental Health, 1980-83, Dental Health St. Regis Indians N.Y. State Dept. Health, 1980. Editl. bd. Jour. Dental Edn., 1980-83, Jour. Cmty. Dentistry & Oral Epidemiology, 1988—, Oral Diseases, 1994—; assoc. editor Caries Rsch., 1995—; contbr. articles to profl. jours. Grantee Ont. Dept. Health, 1969, McGill U., 1973, Quebec Health Sci. Rsch. Coun., 1973, Ministry Social Affairs Quebec, 1972-74, Nat. Inst. Dental Rsch., 1976-78, 85, Med. Rsch. Coun., 1981-84, Nat. Health & Welfare, 1982-85, NIH, 1985—, Robert Wood Johnson Found., 1986-91. Fellow AAAS, Royal Coll. Dentists Can. (chief examiner 1980-82), Internat. Coll. Dentists, Am. Coll. Dentists, Acad. Dentistry Internat.; mem. Am. Assn. Dental Schs., Am. Assn. Pub. Health Dentists, Am. Bd. Dental Pub. Health, Am. Assn. Dental Rsch., Can. Dental Assn., Can. Soc. Pub. Health Dentists (pres. 1979-81), Internat. Assn. Dental Rsch., Omicron Kappa Upsilon. Office: U NC Sch Dentistry CB #7450 Chapel Hill NC 27599-7450

STAMM, ROBERT JENNE, building contractor, construction company executive; b. Albuquerque, Nov. 17, 1921; s. Roy Allen and Elizabeth C. (Baldridge) S.; m. Florence I. Bradbury, May 14, 1943; children—R. Brad, Susan Stamm Evans. BSCE, U. N.Mex., 1942; postgrad. in Naval Architecture, U.S. Naval Acad., 1943. Registered profl. engr. and surveyor, N.Mex. With Bradbury & Stamm Constrn. Co., Albuquerque, 1946—; chmn., chief exec. officer Bradbury & Stamm Constrn. Co., 1975—, former pres. Mem. U. N.Mex. Found., 1982-94, N.Mex. Commn. on Higher Edn.,

1986-95; mem. centennial exec. com. U. N.Mex., chmn. devel. fund, 1984-85, 89-94; trustee Albuquerque Cmty. Found., 1983—; trustee Albuquerque Mus., 1993—, chmn. 1995-97; bd. dirs. N.Mex. Mus. Natural History, 1995—; bd. dirs., pres. Albuquerque Bus.-Edn. Compact, 1987-88, Albuquerque Mus. Found., 1986-91, 96-97, Indsl. Found. Albuquerque; past bd. dirs., officer United Way, Girl Scouts U.S.A., Boy Scouts Am., Presbyn. Hosp. Ctr. Found., Presbyn. Heart Inst., Greater Albuquerque Cmty. Ednl. Alliance, N.Mex. First, Albuquerque Econ. Forum, Albuquerque YMCA, Anderson-Abruzzo Internat. Balloon Mus. Comdr. USNR, 1943-69, ret. Recipient Regents Recognition medal U. N.Mex., 1986, Zimmerman award, 1988, U. N.Mex. Centennial Alumnus awrad Nat. Assn. State Univ. and Land Grant Colls., 1987, Disting. Pub. Svc. award State N.Mex., 1990, Award of Excellence, Presbyn. Helath Fedn., 1991, Disting. Citizen award Boy Scouts-Great S.W. Coun., 1994; named Most Admired Co., N.Mex. Pvt. 100, 1990, 92, 94, 95, 96; named to Albuquerque Sr. Citizen Hall of Fame, 1994; named for N.Mex. Outstanding Philanthropic Leadership, 1994. Mem. NSPE (Albuquerque Engr. of Yr. 1987, N.Mex. Lifetime Svc. award 1995), Assoc. Gen. Contractors N.Mex. (pres. bldg. br. 1962), Econ. Forum Albuquerque, Exec. Assn. Greater Albuquerque, Albuquerque country Club (bd. dirs. 1972-76, 87-89), Albuquerque Tennis Club (bd. dirs. 1978-80). Episcopalian. Clubs: Albuquerque Country (bd. dirs. 1972-76, 87-89), Albuquerque Tennis (bd. dirs. 1978-80). Lodge: Elks. Avocations: tennis; skiing; golf. Home: 1524 Las Lomas Rd NE Albuquerque NM 87106-4532 Office: Bradbury & Stamm Constrn Co PO Box 25027 Albuquerque NM 87125-0027

STAMOS, JOHN JAMES, judge; b. Chgo., Jan. 30, 1924; s. James S. and Katherine (Manolopoulos) S.; m. Helen Voutiritsas, Sept. 3, 1955 (dec. 1981); children—James, Theo, Colleen, Jana; m. Mary Sotter, March 21, 1986. LL.B., DePaul U., 1948. Bar: Ill. 1949. Since practiced in Chgo.; asst. corp. counsel City Chgo., 1951-54; asst. states atty. Cook County, 1954-61; chief criminal div. States Attys. Office, 1961-64, 1st asst. states atty., 1964-66, states atty., 1966-68; judge Appellate Ct. of State of Ill., 1968-88; Judge Ill. Supreme Ct., Springfield, 1988-90; ret., 1990; of counsel Stamos and Trucco, Chgo., 1991—. Served with AUS, 1943-45.

STAMP, FREDERICK PFARR, JR., federal judge; b. Wheeling, W.Va., July 24, 1934; s. Frederick P. Sr. and Louise (Aul) S.; m. Joan A. Corson, Sept. 20, 1975; children: Frederick Andrew, Joan Elizabeth. BA, Washington and Lee U., 1956; LLB, U. Richmond, 1959. Bar: W.Va. 1959, Va. 1959, Pa. 1986, U.S. Supreme Ct. 1973, U.S. Ct. Appeals (4th cir.) 1962, U.S. Dist. Ct. (no. dist.) W.Va. 1960, U.S. Dist. Ct. (so. dist.) W.Va. 1975, U.S. Dist. Ct. (we. dist.) Pa., U.S. Tax Ct. 1973, W.Va. Supreme Ct. Appeals 1966, Va. Supreme Ct. Appeals 1959. Assoc., then ptnr. Schrader, Stamp, Byrd, Byrum & Companion and predecessor firms, Wheeling, 1960-90; judge U.S. Dist. Ct. (no. dist.) W.Va., Wheeling, 1990-94, apptd. chief judge, 1994—; mem. ho. of dels. W.Va. Legislature, Charleston, 1966-70. Mem. W.Va. Bd. Regents, Charleston, 1970-77; trustee Linsly Sch., Wheeling, 1977—. Fellow Am. Bar Found., Am. Coll. Trial Lawyers; mem. W.Va. Bar Assn. (pres. 1981-82), W.Va. Commn. on Uniform State Laws, Nat. Conf. Commrs. on Uniform State Laws. *

STAMP, NEAL ROGER, lawyer; b. Watkins Glen, N.Y., Sept. 19, 1918; s. Nelson Mathews and Mae Emma (Broderick) S.; m. Maja Stina Cavetz, Apr. 24, 1946; children: Thomas G., Gayle E. AB, Cornell, 1940, JD, 1942. Bar: N.Y. 1943. Pvt. practice Rochester, 1946-47; asst. sec. corp., asso. legal counsel Cornell U., Ithaca, N.Y., 1947-59; sec. corp., asso. legal counsel Cornell U., 1959-62, sec. corp., 1959-79, univ. counsel, 1962-79, sr. counsel, 1979-84, univ. counsel emeritus, 1979—, dir. aero. lab., research found.; higher edn. cons., 1979—; lectr. Practicing Law Inst.; dir. First Bank & Trust Co., Ithaca, 1971-84, chmn., 1978-84. Trustee Tompkins County Meml. Hosp., 1959-66, pres., 1961-62; bd. dirs. Challenge Industries, 1986-94, Vis. Nurse Svc. Tompkins County, 1996—, Sr. Citizens Coun. Tompkins County, 1997—. 1st lt. inf. AUS, 1942-46, MTO. Mem. ABA (ho. of dels. 1977-79), N.Y. State Bar Assn., Tompkins County Bar Assn., Assn. of Bar of City of N.Y., Nat. Assn. Coll. and U. Attys. (exec. bd. 1964-68, 72-79, life mem., pres. 1976-77). Home: Apt 14-2-F PO Box 4508 700 Warren Rd Ithaca NY 14852-4508

STAMP, ZACHARY LAYNE, state agency administrator; b. Burlington, Iowa, Nov. 12, 1953; s. Ronald Eugene and Edna Joan (Hustead) S.; m. Debra Ann Melvin, Dec. 20, 1975 (div. Nov. 1982); 1 child Zachary Layne Jr. (dec.); m. Diane K. Ford, Oct. 23, 1983; children: Perry Ford, Nathan Ford. BA, Western Ill. U., 1975; JD, So. Ill. U., 1980. Bar: Ill. 1980, U.S. Dist Ct. (cen. dist.) Ill. Dep. sheriff McDonough County Sheriff's Office, Macomb, Ill., 1975-76; asst. scheduler Office of Gov. Ill., Springfield, 1977, senate liaison, 1985-86, dir. legis. affairs, 1986-89; legal counsel senate Rep. staff Ill. Gen. Assembly, Springfield, 1980-81, asst. to Rep. leader, 1981-83, gen. counsel, 1985-86; pvt. practice Stronghurst, Ill., 1983-85; dir. of legislative affairs Office of the Gov., 1986-91; dir. Ill. Dept. Ins., Springfield, 1989-91; assoc. Peterson and Ross, Springfield, 1991—; legal counsel Ill. Rep. State Cen. Com., Springfield, 1983-85. Regional dir. Citizens for Thompson, Chgo., 1976, office mgr. 1978. Mem. Western Ill. U. Alumni Council (v.p. 1986-87), Sigma Phi Epsilon. Republican. Home: RR 1 Box 90b-10 New Berlin IL 62670-9450 Office: Zack Stamp Ltd. 500 S 2nd St Springfield IL 62701-1705

STAMPER, JAMES M., retired English language educator; b. Roxana, Ky., Sept. 26, 1917; s. Marion and Amanda (Combs) S.; m. Diane C. Mahoney, Aug. 12, 1967. BS in Edn., Union Coll., 1941; MA in English, U. Ky., 1946. Subs. tchr. Ermine Elem. Sch., Dry Fork Elem. Sch., 1936-37; elem. tchr. various schs., 1937-41; h.s. Eng. tchr. Whitesburg H.S., Ky., 1941-46; instr. English U. Ky., Lexington, 1946-49, U. Md., College Park, 1949-52; instr. bus. English DePaul U., Chgo., 1952-62; English tchr., cons. in high sch. English Bd. Edn., Chgo., 1962-72; ret. Chgo. Area Schs., 1972; subst. tchr. Chgo. Area schs., 1972-82; vis. instr. in English Jacksonville (Fla.) U. Co-author: A Handbook on Oral Reading Diagnosis, Resource Materials for Essential English in the Secondary Schools, A Syllabus in Basic English; contbr. articles to profl. jours. Scholar Knights of Columbus, Union Coll., U. Ky. Mem. AARP. Home: 1448 N Picadilly Cir Mount Prospect IL 60056-1028

STAMPER, JOE ALLEN, lawyer; b. Okemah, Okla., Jan. 30, 1914; s. Horace Allen and Ann (Stephens) S.; m. Johnnie Lee Bell, June 4, 1936; 1 child, Jane Allen (Mrs. Ernest F. Godlove). B.A., U. Okla., 1933, LL.B., 1935, J.D., 1970. Bar: Okla. bar 1935. Practice in Antlers, 1935-36, 46—; mem. firm Stamper, Burrage & Hadley, 1974—; atty. Pushmataha County, 1936-39; spl. justice Okla. Supreme Ct., 1948. Mem. Okla. Indsl. Commn., 1939-40; pres. Antlers Sch. Bd., 1956-67, Pushmataha Found., 1957—; mem. Okla. Bicentennial Com., 1971—; vice chmn. bd. U. Okla. Law Center, 1975-78; mgr. Okla. Democratic party, 1946, dist. chmn., 1946-50; alt. del. Dem. Nat. Conv., 1952. Served to col. AUS, 1935-46, E O. Decorated Bronze Star. Fellow Am. Bar Found., Am. Coll. Trial Lawyers, Am. Bd. Trial Advocates (advocate); mem. ABA (del. 1974-91, state del. 1975-86, mem. com. on law book pub. practices 1974-76, bd. govs. 1986-89, standing com. on fed. jud. improvement 1989-92), SAR, Okla. Bar Assn. (bd. govs. 1969-73, Pres.'s award 1977, 80, 93), Okla. Bar Found. (pres. 1977), Mil. Order World Wars, Pi Kappa Alpha. Baptist (deacon). Clubs: Petroleum (Oklahoma City). Lodges: Masons, Shriners, Lions. Home: 1000 NE 2nd St Antlers OK 74523-2822 Office: PO Box 100 112 N High St Antlers OK 74523-2250

STAMPER, MALCOLM THEODORE, aerospace company executive; b. Detroit, Apr. 4, 1925; s. Fred Theodore and Lucille (Cayce) S.; m. Marion Philbin Guinan, Feb. 25, 1946; children: Geoffrey, Kevin, Jamie, David, Mary, Anne. Student, U. Richmond, Va., 1943-44; BEE, Ga. Inst. Tech., 1946; postgrad., U. Mich., 1946-49; DHumanities, Seattle U., 1994. With Gen. Motors Corp., 1949-62; with Boeing Co., Seattle, 1962-90; mgr. electronics ops., v.p., gen. mgr. turbine div. Boeing Co., 1964-66; v.p., gen. mgr. Boeing Co. (747 Airplane program), 1966-69, v.p., gen. mgr. comml. airplane group, 1969-71, corp. sr. v.p. ops., 1971-72; pres. Boeing Co., 1972-85, vice chmn., 1985-90; chief exec. officer Storytellers Ink Pub., Seattle, 1990—, also chmn. bd. dirs.; bd. dirs. Esterline Co., Chrysler Co., Pro-Air Inc., Whittaker Corp., Pro-Air Airline; trustee The Conf. Bd., 1988—. Candidate for U.S. Ho. of Reps., Detroit, 1952; trustee, chmn. Seattle Art Mus.; nat. bd. dirs. Smithsonian Assocs. With USNR, 1943-46. Named Industrialist of Year, 1967; recipient Educator's Golden Key award, 1970, Elmer A. Sperry award, 1982, AIEE award, Ga. Inst. Tech. award, Sec. Dept. Health and Human Services award, Silver Beaver award Boy Scouts Am., 1989, Literary Lions award, 1995; named to Engring. Hall of Fame. Mem. Nat. Alliance Businessmen, Phi Gamma Delta.

STAMPER, ROBERT LEWIS, ophthalmologist, educator; b. N.Y.C., July 27, 1939; m. Naomi T. Belson, June 23, 1963; children: Juliet, Marjorie, Alison. BA, Cornell U., 1957-61; MD, SUNY-Downstate, 1965. Diplomate Am. Bd. Ophthalmology (assoc. examiner 1976-92, bd. dirs. 1992—, mem. glaucoma panel 1993—); lic. physician, Calif. Intern Mt. Sinai Hosp., N.Y.C., 1965-66; resident in ophthalmology Washington U.-Barnes Hosp., St. Louis, 1968-71; Nat. Eye Inst.-NIH fellow dept. ophthalmology Washington U., St. Louis, 1971-72, from instr. ophthalmology to asst. prof. dept. ophthalmology, 1971-72; asst. prof. dept. ophthalmology Pacific Presbyn. Med. Ctr., San Francisco, 1972-76, assoc. prof. ophthalmology, 1976-87; chmn. dept. ophthalmology Calif. Pacific Med. Ctr. (formerly Pacific Presbyn. Med. Ctr.), San Francisco, 1987-96; asst. opthalmologist Barnes Hosp., St. Louis, 1971-72, Harkness Hosp., San Francisco, 1973-74; dir. ophthalmic photography and fluorescin angiography, dept. ophthalmology Washington U., St. Louis, 1969-72; dir. resident tng. Pacific Presbyn. Med. Ctr., 1972-89, dir. glaucoma svc., vice-chmn. dept. ophthalmology, 1974-87; chief ophthalmology svc. Highland Hosp., Oakland, Calif., 1974-76; clin. instr. dept. ophthalmology U. Calif., San Francisco, 1974-77; clin. asst. prof. ophthalmology U. Calif., Berkeley, 1974-78, asst. clin. prof. ophthalmology, 1978-85; sr. rsch. assoc. Smith-Kettlewell Inst. Visual Scis., San Francisco, 1972-89; project co-dir. ophthalmic curriculum for med. students Nat. Libr. Medicine, 1973-75; commr. Joint Commn. on Allied Health Pers. in Ophthalmology, 1975-87, bd. dirs., 1978-88, sec., 1980, v.p., 1982-83, pres., 1984-85; provisional asst. chief dept. ophthalmology Mt. Zion Hosp., San Francisco, 1976-87, assoc. chief dept. ophthalmology, 1982-86; ophthalmic cons. Ft. Ord, Calif., 1976—, Oakland (Calif.) Naval Hosp., 1978-83; instr. Stanford (Calif.) U., 1977—; glaucoma cons. U. Calif., Davis, 1978-84; vis. lectr. dept. ophthalmology Hadassah Hebrew U. Med. Ctr., Jerusalem, 1978, Oxford (Eng.) U. Eye Hosp., 1986; ind. med. examiner State of Calif., 1979—; mem. appeals hearing panel Accreditation Coun. for Grad. Med. Edn., 1986-93, mem. residency rev. com. for ophthalmology, 1993—; mem. provisional courtesy staff Peralta Hosp., Oakland, 1988-92; mem. ophthalmic devices adv. panel USFDA, 1989-92; presenter, lectr. in field. Editor Ophthalmology Clinics of North Am., 1988—; mem. editl. adv. com. Ophthalmology, 1982-89, mem. editl. bd., 1983-94; contbr. articles to profl. jours. Chmn. bd. Agy. for Jewish Edn., Oakland, 1986-89; bd. dirs. Jewish Fedn. Greater East Bay, Oakland, 1992-94; bd. dirs. Found. for Glaucoma Rsch.; mem. glaucoma adv. com. Nat. Soc. to Prevent Blindness, 1981—; mem. Am. Diabetes Assn. Surgeon USPHS, 1966-68. Recipient Nat. Soc. for Performance and Instrn. award for self-instrnl. material in ophthalmology, 1975, Honor award Am. Acad. Ophthalmology, 1982, Sr. Honor award, 1992, Statesmanship award Joint Commn. on Allied Health Pers. in Ophthalmology, 1989; N.Y. State Regents scholar, 1961, N.Y. State scholar in medicine, 1965; Blalock student fellow UCLA Sch. Medicine, 1961, Fight for Sight student fellow dept. ophthalmology N.Y. Hosp. and Cornell Med. Ctr., 1962, 63, 64. Fellow Am. Acad. Ophthalmology and Otolaryngology (rep. to joint commn. on allied health pers., faculty home study course sect. X, chmn. sect. VIII 1983-85, bd. councilors, editl. adv. com. Opthalmology jour. 1982-89, editl. bd. Ophthalmology jour. 1983-94, and many others), ACS; mem. AMA (Physician's Recognition award 1989), Am. Ophthalmologic Soc., Assn. for Rsch. in Vision and Ophthalmology, Calif. Med. Assn. (asst. sec. sect. ophthalmology, chmn., sci. bd. rep. adv. panel on ophthalmology 1985-91), Nat. Soc. Prevent Blindness (mem. glaucoma adv. com. 1981—, bd. dirs. 1986—), No. Calif. Soc. Prevent Blindness, Calif. Assn. Ophthalmology, Pan Am. Ophthalmological Soc., N.Y. Acad. Scis., Las Vegas Ophthalmological Soc. (hon.), Am. Glaucoma Soc. (v.p. 1997—). Office: Calif Pacific Med Ctr 2100 Webster St Ste 214 San Francisco CA 94115-2375

STAMPFLI, JOHN FRANCIS, logistics consultant; b. Dhahran, Saudi Arabia, Oct. 27, 1957; s. Edmund Francis and Luisa Marie (Saucedo) S.; m. Susan Frances Thiel, Mar. 1992. BA in History, Calif. State U., Fullerton, 1980. Substitute tchr. East Whittier (Calif.) City Sch. Dist., 1980-81; customshouse broker LAX/Port of Long Beach, Calif., 1981-87; mgr. logistics Unisys Corp., Blue Bell, Pa., 1987-93; cons. Irvine, Calif., 1993—; field dir. U.S. Naval Inst., 1992—; participant NASA Landsat Adv. Process, 1995. Contbr. articles to profl. jours. Olympic Torch Relay Marshal, 1984; staff mem. to Congressman William E. Dannemeyer, 39th Dist., Calif., 1977-78. Mem. Am. Def. Preparedness Assn., Armed Forces Comm. and Electronics Assn., Assn. Old Crows, Navy League of U.S., U.S. Naval Inst., Phi Alpha Theta. Republican. Home: 26191 La Real Mission Viejo CA 92691-2834

STAMPLEY, NORRIS LOCHLEN, former electric utility executive; b. Bentonia, Miss., Dec. 21, 1920; s. Orville K. and Norma Eloise S.; m. Mary Virginia Russum, May 28, 1942; children: Mary Lynn, Virginia Kaye. Registered profl. engr., Miss. Engr. U.S. Navy Dept., Washington, 1942-45; with Miss. Power & Light Co., Jackson, 1947-84, chief engr., 1968-72, v.p., 1972-80, sr. v.p., 1980-84; now ret. Miss. Power & Light Co. Pres. Met. YMCA, Jackson, 1980, 85; trustee Mcpl. Separate Sch. Dist., 1980-90, Miss. Baptist Found., 1981-85, 87-92; chmn. So. Baptist Conv. Brotherhood Commn., 1985-86. Served with Signal Corps, U.S. Army, 1945-47. Named Alumnus of Yr. Hinds Jr. Coll., 1980. Mem. Nat. Soc. Profl. Engrs., Miss. Engring. Soc. (Engr. of Yr. 1974), IEEE, Am. Nuclear Soc., Jackson C. of C. (dir.), Phi Theta Kappa (Alumnus of Yr. 1977). Clubs: Exchange (pres. 1975). Home: 156 Pavilion Dr Brandon MS 39042-4333

STAMPS, THOMAS PATY, lawyer, consultant; b. Mineola, N.Y., May 10, 1952; s. George Moreland and Helen Leone (Paty) S.; children: Katherine Camilla, George Belk, Elizabeth Margaret, Carley Lynn; m. Diana Lynn Whittaker, Dec. 11, 1993. BA, U. Ill., 1973; postgrad., Emory U., 1975-76; JD, Wake Forest U., 1979. Bar: Ga. 1979, N.C. 1979. Pers. dir. Norman Jaspan, N.Y.C., 1973-74; assoc. Macey & Zusmann, Atlanta, 1979-81; prin. Zusmann, Small, Stamps & White PC, Atlanta, 1981-85; cons. GMS Cons., Oxford, Ga., 1975—; ptnr. Destin Enterprises, Atlanta, 1983-85. Author: Study of a Student, 1973, History of Coca-Cola, 1976; asst. editor Ga. Jour. So. Legal History, 1991-94. Chmn. Summer Law Inst., Atlanta, 1981-85; mem. Dem. Party Ga., Atlanta, 1983—; atty. Vol. Lawyers for Arts, Atlanta, 1981-94, Atlanta Vol. Lawyers Found.; panel mem. U.S. Bankruptcy Trustees No. Dist. Ga., 1982-89; mem. Bench and Bar Com., State Bar Ga., 1996—; active High Mus. Art, 1986—, Atlanta Hist. Soc., Atlanta Bot. Gardens, Atlanta Symphony Orch., Ga. Trust Hist. Preservation, Ind.; sec. Friends of Woodrow Wilson, 1988—, chmn. dinner, 1990—; trustee Ga. Legal History Found., 1989—. Named to Honorable Order of Ky. Colonels; recipient Svc. award Inst. Continuing Legal Edn., Athens, Ga., 1981, 86. Mem. ABA, Atlanta Bar Assn. (com. chmn. 1981-85), N.C. Bar Assn., Lawyers Club, Phi Alpha Delta (justice, Atlanta 1982-83, emeritus 1983). Office: 7715 Jett Ferry Rd Atlanta GA 30350-5419

STAMSTA, JEAN F., artist; b. Sheboygan, Wis., Nov. 2, 1936; d. Herbert R. and Lucile Caroline (Malwitz) Nagel; m. Duane R. Stamsta, Aug. 18, 1956; children: Marc, David. BS, BA, U. Wis., 1958. guest curator Milw. Art Mus., 1986; resident artist Leighton Artist Colony, Banff, Alta., Can., 1987. One-woman shows Am. Craft Mus., N.Y.C., 1971, Winona (Minn.) State U., 1986, Lawrence U., Appleton, Wis., 1990, Walkers Point Ctr. Arts, Milw., 1990, U. Wis. Ctr., Waukesha, 1995; exhibited in group shows, incuding Cleve. Mus. Art, 1977, Milw. Art Mus., 1986, 88, Nat. Air and Stace Mus., Smithsonian Instn., Washington, 1986, Madison (Wis.) Art Ctr., 1987, 90, Paper Press Gallery, Chgo., 1988, North Arts Ctr., Atlanta, 1990, Dairy Barn Cultural Arts Ctr., Athens, Ohio, 1991, Paper Arts Festival, Appleton, 1992, Fine Arts Mus., Budapest, Hungary, 1992, Tilburg Textile Mus., The Netherlands, 1993, U. Wis. Union Gallery, 1994, Holland Area Arts Coun. Gallery, U. Mich., Ann Arbor, 1996; Self-Portraits: Wisconsin Artists, Charles Allis Art Mus., Milw., 1996. NEA craftsman fellow, 1974. Avocations: swimming, travel. Home and Studio: 9313 Center Oak Rd Hartland WI 53029

STANALAJCZO, GREG C., computer services executive; b. 1959. Degree, Oakland U. With CDI Computer Svcs., Inc., Troy, Mich., 1986—, pres., 1993-95; exec. v.p., COO Tech. Teammates Inc., 1996. Office: Technology Teammates Inc 1111 Rosedale Ct Detroit MI 48211-1076

STANAWAY, LORETTA SUSAN, small business owner; b. Selfridge AFB, Mich., Jan. 1, 1954; d. Vincent Carl and Carolyn Jane (Grasser) Pizzo; m. Thomas Lee Stanaway, Apr. 23, 1983; stepchildren: Todd Richard, Toni Marie. Student, Ctrl. Mich. U., 1972-75. Intern, reporter Daily Times-News, Mt. Pleasant, Mich., 1974; editorial asst. Bar Jour. Mich., Lansing, 1975-76; with prodn. control dept. Dart Container Corp., Mason, Mich., 1976-80; mgr. Payless Shoes, Lansing, 1980; shift supr. Greyhound Food Mgmt., Lansing, 1980-82; owner, mgr. L.S. Distbg., Lansing, 1982-89, Send Out Svcs. S.O.S., Lansing, 1989—; owner, mgr. lawn care divsn., snow removal divsn. Send Out Svcs., 1993—; mem. focus group on customer svc. Small Bus. Devel. Ctr., Lansing, 1991—. Treas. Mich. Coalition on Smoking or Health, Lansing, 1987-89; bd. dirs. Am. Cancer Soc. Mich., Lansing, 1988-89; mem. custodial svcs. com. Ingham Intermediate Sch. Dist., 1991—; mem. adminstrv. bd., council on ministries, sunday sch. supt., Grovenburg United Meth. Ch., 1994—. Recipient Outstanding Svc. award Am. Cancer Soc. Mich., 1988. Mem. NAFE, Nat. Assn. Self-Employed, Nat. Fedn. Ind. Bus., Internat. Platform Assn. Republican. Methodist. Avocations: camping, fishing, gardening, birdwatching, travel. Home and Office: 546 Armstrong Rd Lansing MI 48911-3811

STANBERRY, DOSI ELAINE, English literature educator, writer; b. Elk Park, N.C.; m. Earl Stanberry; 1 child, Anita St. Lawrence. Student in Bus. Edn., Steed Coll. Tech., 1956; BS in Bus. and English, East Tenn. State U., 1961, MA in Shakespearean Lit., 1962; EdD, Tex. A & M Univ., 1975; postgrad., North Tex. State U., U. South Fla., NYU, Duke U., U. N.C. Prof. Manatee Jr. Coll., Bradenton, Fla., 1964-67, Dickinson State U., N.D., 1967-81; retired, 1981. Author: Poetic Heartstrings, Mountain Echoes, Love's Perplexing Obsession Experienced by Heinrich Heine and Percy Bysshe Shelley, Poetry from the Ancients to Moderns: A Critical Anthology, Finley Forest, Chapel Hill's Tree-lined Tuck, (plays) The Big Toe, The Funeral Factory; contbr. articles, poetry to jours., mags. Recipient Editor's Choice award Nat. Libr. Poetry, 1988, 95, Distinguished Professorof English Award, Dickinson State U., 1981; included in Best Poems of 1995. Mem. Acad. Am. Poets, N.C. Writers Network, N.C. Poetry Soc. (Carl Sandburg Poetry award 1988), Poetic Page, Writers Jour., Poets and Writers, Friday-Noon Poets, Delta Kappa Gamma. Home: Finley Forest 193 Summerwalk Cir Chapel Hill NC 27514-8642

STANBERY, RUTH BLOMQUIST, computer company executive, educator; b. Chgo., Feb. 12, 1949; d. Roy Theodore and Ruth Theresa (Johnson) Blomquist; m. Frankie D. Gunning (div. June 1975); children: Elyn Blomquist, Dena Blomquist, Lukas Brock Theodore Stanbery; m. Donald Loran Stanbery, Aug. 16, 1985. BA, Elmhurst Coll., 1979; MEd, Nat. Coll. Edn., 1980, No. Ill. U., 1981. Tchr. DuPage City (Ill.) Sch. Dist., 1979-83; tchr., headmistress D.A.E.S., Downer's Grove, Ill., 1983-86, The Learning Ctr., Rochelle, 1996—; product coord. Del Monte, DeKalb, Ill., 1986-91, Suter Co., Sycamore, Ill., 1991-93; owner, CEO Stanbery Computer Svcs., Rochelle, 1993—; cons., seminar leader D.A.E.S., student advocate. Contbr. articles to profl. jours. Mem. long range planning com. Sch. Dist. #231, Rochelle, 1995-96. Mem. Nat. Assn. Tchrs. English, Assn. Curriculum & Supervision, Assn. Women Students (v.p. 1976), Ill. Edn. Assn. (v.p. 1977), Job's Daughters (officer), Order Ea. Star (oofficer), Am. Legion Aux., Omicron Delta Kappa, Kappa Delta Epsilon. Avocations: mind puzzles, crafts, reading, gardening, camping. Home: PO Box 55 Malta IL 60150-0055 Office: Stanbery Computer Svcs Box 546 Rochelle IL 61068

STANBURY, JOHN BRUTON, physician, educator; b. Clinton, N.C., May 15, 1915; s. Walter A. and Zula (Bruton) S.; m. Jean F. Cook, Jan. 6, 1945; children: John Bruton, Martha Jean, Sarah Katherine, David McNeill, Pamela Cook. A.B., Duke U., 1935; M.D., Harvard U., 1939; M.D. (hon.), U. Leiden (Netherlands), 1975; postgrad., U. Pisa, Italy, 1994. House officer Mass. Gen. Hosp., 1940-41, asst. resident, 1946, chief med. resident, 1948, mem. med. staff, 1949—; research fellow pharmacology Harvard Med. Sch., 1947; vis. prof. medicine U. Leiden, 1955; prof. exptl. medicine MIT, Cambridge, 1966-80; emeritus MIT, 1980—; cons. Pan Am. Health Orgn., WHO, UNICEF, U.S. AEC. Author: Endemic Goiter: The adaptation of man to iodine deficiency, 1954, Metabolic Basis of Inherited Disease, 5th edit., 1984, The Thyroid and Its Diseases, 5th edit., 1984, Endemic Goiter, 1969, Human Development and the Thyroid, 1972, Endemic Goiter and Endemic Cretinism, 1980, Prevention and Control of Iodine Deficiency Disorders, 1987, A Constant Ferment, 1991, The Damaged Brain of Iodine Deficiency, 1994, The Inborn Errors of the Thyroid System, 1994. Served from lt. (j.g.) to comdr. USNR, 1941-45. Recipient Delmar S. Fahrney medal Franklin Inst., 1993, Prince Mahidol award, Thailand, 1994. Mem. Am. Assn. Physicians, Soc. Clin. Investigation, Am. Thyroid Assn. (pres. 1969), Am. Acad. Arts and Scis., Endocrine Soc., Endocrine Socs. Finland, Colombia, Peru, Ecuador and Argentina, Internat. Coun. for Control of Iodine Deficiency Disorders. Democrat. Episcopalian. Home: 43 Circuit Rd Chestnut Hill MA 02167-1802

STANBURY, ROBERT DOUGLAS GEORGE, lawyer, executive; b. Exeter, Ont., Can., Oct. 26, 1929; s. James George Stuart and Elizabeth Jean (Hardy) S.; m. Miriam R. Voelker, June 21, 1952; children: Susan Meloff, Carol Vivian, Ian, Duncan. BA in Journalism, U. Western Ont., 1950; grad., Osgoode Hall Law Sch., 1955; LLB, York U., 1991. Bar: Ont. 1955, Queen's counsel 1974. Acct. exec. Public and Indsl. Relations Ltd., Toronto, 1950-51; ptnr. Hollingworth & Stanbury, Toronto, 1955-65; mem. Can. Parliament, 1965-77; minister of citizenship and info., 1969-71, of comm., 1971-72, of nat. revenue, 1972-73; del. to UN Gen. Assembly, 1974-76; from v.p., gen. counsel, sec. to chmn., CEO Firestone Can. Inc., Hamilton, Ont., 1977-85; sec., dir. Dayton Tire Can. Ltd., 1977-83; dir. Workers Compensation Bd. (Ont.), 1985-88; counsel Inch Easterbrook & Shaker Barristers & Solicitors, Hamilton, Ont., 1986—; pres., CEO Can. Coun. for Native Bus., 1988-91; vice chmn. bd. dirs. Workers Compensaton Bd., Ont., 1991-94. Mem. N.Y. Bd. Edn., 1961-64, chmn., 1963-64; mem. Met. Toronto Sch. Td., 1963-64, Met. Toronto Planning Bd., 1963; bd. dirs. Hamilton and Dist. C. of C., 1979-85, pres., 1983-84; bd. dirs. Hamilton Found., 1980-84, pres., 1982-83; bd. dirs. Art Gallery Hamilton, 1980-88, v.p., 1984-86, pres., 1986-87, bd. govs., 1988—; bd. dirs. Art Gallery Hamilton Found., 1996—, Can. C. of C., 1982-86, exec. com., 1983-86; bus. adv. coun. McMaster U., 1983-89, chmn., 1987-88; bd. dirs., v.p. Inst. Corp. Dirs. in Can., 1986-87, pres., 1987-88, vice-chmn., 1988-91; bd. govs. Jr. Achievement Hamilton-Wentworth, 1988-91; mem. Can. Broadcast Stds. Coun., Ont., 1990—, vice chmn., 1996—; mem. adv. coun. U. Western Ont. Grad. Sch. Journalism, 1994—; mem. Nunavut Arbitration Bd., 1994—; chmn. Employers' Coun. on Workers Compensation, 1996—. Recipient Can. Centennial medal, 1967, Queen's Jubilee medal, 1977, Confedn. medal, 1993; apptd. mem. for life Queen's Privy Coun. for Can., 1969; hon. mem. InterParliamentary Union. Fellow Inst. Dirs. (U.K.); mem. Law Soc. Upper Can., Internat. Commn. Jurists, Can. Coun. Adminstrv. Tribunals, Soc. Ont. Adjudicators and Regulators, Can. Club of Hamilton (bd. dirs. 1986-89), Kappa Alpha, Phi Delta Phi. Liberal. Presbyterian. Home: 607 Edgewater Cres, Burlington, ON Canada L7T 3L8 Office: 1 King St W Ste 1500, Hamilton, ON Canada L8P 4X8

STANCIL, IRENE MACK, family counselor; b. St. Helena Island, Sept. 29, 1938; d. Rufus and Irene (Wilson) Mack; m. Nesby Stancil, Dec. 29, 1968; 1 child, Steve Lamar. BA, Benedict Coll., 1960, CUNY, 1983; MA, New World Bible Coll., 1984; SSD, United Christian Coll., 1985. Supr. City of New York; tchr. local bd. edn., S.C. Mem. Am. Ctr. for Law & Justice.

STANCILL, JAMES MCNEILL, finance educator, consultant; b. Orange, N.J., July 30, 1932; s. James Sr. and Anne Jeanne (Sauter) S.; m. Catherine Jackson, Sept. 25, 1954; children: Martha A., Mary C., Christine E. AB, George Washington U., 1954, MBA, 1957; PhD in Fin. and Econs., U. Pa., 1965. Buyer Melpar Inc., Falls Church, Va., 1954-59; instr., adminstrv. officer U. Pa., Phila., 1959-64; prof. fin. U. So. Calif., Los Angeles, 1964—; prin. Stancill & Assocs., Pasadena, Calif., 1964—. Author: Management of Working Capital, 1970; contbr. numerous articles to Harvard Bus. Rev., 1977—. Avocations: genealogy, sailing. Office: Grad Sch Bus Univ Of So Calif Los Angeles CA 90089-1421

STANCZAK, JULIAN, artist, educator; b. Borownica, Poland, Nov. 5, 1928; came to U.S., 1950, naturalized, 1957; s. Victor and Elizabeth (Cwynar) S.; m. Barbara M. Meerpohl, June 10, 1963; children: Danuta M., Christopher. B.F.A., Cleve. Inst. Art., 1954; M.F.A., Yale U., 1956. Tchr. Art Acad. Cin., 1957-64, Cleve. Inst. Art, 1965—. One-man shows include

Dayton Art Inst., 1964, Martha Jackson Gallery, N.Y.C., 1964, 65, 68, 71, 72, 75, 77, 79, Miami U., Oxford, Ohio, 1965, Feingarten Galleries, Los Angeles, 1966, Kent State U., 1968, Dartmouth, 1968, Akron (Ohio) Art Inst., 1969, Cleve. Inst. Art, 1971, London Arts Gallery, 1971, Cin. Art Mus., 1972, 80, Corcoran Gallery Art, Washington, 1972, Canton (Ohio) Art Inst., 1974, Pollack Gallery, Toronto, 1975, Ohio State U., 1976, IMF and CARE, Washington, 1978, Butler Inst. Am. Art, Youngstown, Ohio, 1980, Nat. Mus., Warsaw, Poland, 1981, Alice Simsar Gallery, Ann Arbor, Mich., 1982, 88, New Gallery, Cleve., 1983, Charles Foley Gallery, Columbus, Ohio, 1984, 88, Walker Gallery, Chgo., 1986, Carl Solway Gallery, Cin., Jane Haslem Gallery, Washington, 1986, Standard Oil Co. Hdqrs., Cleve., 1987, Alice Simsar Gallery, Ann Arbor, Mich., Boca Raton Mus. Art, Fla., 1989, Carl Solway Gallery, Cin., Charles Foley Gallery, Columbus, Ohio, Ctr. for Contemporary Art, Cleve., 1990; one man retrospective David Anderson Gallery, Buffalo, N.Y., Dennos Mus.,Traverse City, Mich.; exhibited in group shows: Mus. Modern Art, N.Y.C., 1965, Albright Knox Art Gallery, Buffalo, 1965, 68, Detroit Art Inst., 1965, Larry Alrich Mus., 1965, U. Ill., 1965, Gallery Moos, Toronto, 1965, Kranert Art Mus., Urbana, Ill., 1965, San Francisco Mus. Art, 1965, Flint (Mich.) Inst. Art, 1966, Carnegie Inst., Pitts., 1967, Japan Cultural Forum, 1967, Smithsonian Instn., Washington, 1967, 69, 85, Dept. State, Washington, 1968, Cin. Art Mus., 1968, 83, Del. Art Ctr., 1970, Seibu, Tokyo, 1971, Mansfield (Ohio) Art Ctr., 1973, Butler Art Inst., Youngstown, Ohio, 1973, Minn. Art Mus., Mpls., 1973, Akron Art Inst., 1975, Indpls. Mus. Art, 1976, Bklyn. Mus. Art, 1976, 80, Cleve. Mus. Art, 1976, 77, 83, Memphis Acad. Art, 1981, Nat. Gallery Art, 1981, 85, Hirshhorn Mus. Art, 1981, Montclair Art Mus., N.J., 1982, Art Acad. Cin., 1986, Embassies Travelling Exhbn., Madrid, 1987, Warsaw, Poland, 1991; represented in permanent collections: Nat. Mus. Am. Art, Albright Knox Art Gallery, Larry Aldrich Mus., Mus. Modern Art, Dayton Art Inst., Hirshhorn Mus., Washington, Butler Inst. Am. Art, Youngstown, Ohio, Rufino Tomajo Mus., Mex., Cleve. Art Assn., Milw. Art Inst., Canton (Ohio) Art Inst., USIA, N.Y.C., Balt. Mus. Art, San Francisco Mus. Art, Herron Mus. Art, Indpls., Okla. Art Ctr., Oklahoma City, Pa. Acad. Fine Arts, Phila., Carnegie Inst., Pitts., Cleve. Mus. Art, Cin. Art Mus., Tulsa Mus. Fine Arts, Columbus (Ohio) Art Mus., Akron Art Inst., Corcoran Art Mus., Nat. Gallery, Washington, Lowe Art Mus., Coral Gables, Fla., Contemporary Art Mus., Houston, Winnipeg Fine Arts Ctr., Man., Can., Dracket Fine Art Collection, Cin., Kalamazoo Inst. Arts, Worcester Art Mus., Phoenix Art Mus., Indpls. Mus. Art, Wasserman Devel. Corp., Cambridge, Dartmouth Coll., Hanover, N.H., Etzold Sammlung, Cologne, Fed. Republic Germany, Johnson & Johnson Fine Art Collection, Conn., Nelson Rockefeller Collection, N.Y., Chase Manhattan Bank, N.Y., Mus. Fine Arts, Los Angeles, Newport Harbor Mus., Newport Beach, Calif., N.Y. State U. at Buffalo. Recipient 1st prize Dayton Art Inst., 1964; recipient Butler Inst. Am. Art award, 1966, Cleve. Fine Arts prize, 1970, Ohio Arts Council award, 1972, Best of Show award Internat. Platform Assn., 1973-76. Mem. Abstract Artists Am., Internat. Platform Assn. Pioneer optical art. Address: 6229 Cabrini Ln Seven Hills OH 44131-2848

STANCZYK, BENJAMIN CONRAD, judge; b. Detroit, Apr. 4, 1915; s. Bruno and Josephine (Tarczynski) S.; m. Stephanie W. Wojsowski, June 4, 1946; children: Benjamin Conrad Jr., Kathy Jo Thibault. AB, Wayne State U., 1936; JD, U. Mich., 1939. Bar: Mich. 1939, U.S. Dist. Ct. (ea. and we. dists.) Mich. 1939, U.S. Ct. Appeals (6th and 10th cir.) 1943. Pvt. practice Detroit, 1939-49, asst. pros. atty., 1949-57; judge Common Pleas Ct., Detroit, 1957-75; vis. judge State of Mich., Detroit, 1975-97; chair Income Tax Study Commn., Detroit, 1960-62; adv. bd. Madonna Coll., 1961-65; chair Tri-County Dental Health Coun., Detroit, 1962-68, pres., 1962-65; judge advocate Am. Legion Mich., 1962-63, DAV Dept. of Mich. 1966-70; Nat. Legis. Officer, Polish Legon of Am. Vets., 1961-63. Pub. Poles in Michigan. Pres. Polish Nat. Alliance 167, Detroit, 1949-57, Ctrl. Citizens Commn., Polish Coordinating Coun., Detroit, 1951-58, Cass Tech H.S. Assn., 1964-65; spokesmen Detroit's Polish Cmty. in Pol. and Cult. Matters, 1950-75, mem. Adv. Com. on Sch. Needs, Detroit, 1956-58; trustee Hist. Soc. Mich., 1988-96; adv. dem. Platform Comm. of Fgn. Affairs, 1952, 56; mem. exec. bd. Detroit's 250th Birthday Com., 1951; mem. Mich. Soccer and Football Commn., 1956-58; pres., mem. adv. bd. Vols. Am., 1977-80; organizer family music concerts Detroit Symphony Orch., 1954; active NAACP. With U.S. Army, 1942-46. Mem. ABA, NRA, NAACP, Grosse Point Camera Club (pres. 1993-94, 96-97), Detroit Press Club (charter), Lions (pres. Detroit chpt. 1966-67, 96-97), Pi Sigma Alpha, Delta Sigma Rho. Democrat. Roman Catholic. Avocations: travel, photography, horology, firearms, numismatics. Office: 22811 Mack Ste 211 Saint Clair Shores MI 48080

STANDBERRY, HERMAN LEE, school system administrator, consultant; b. Oran, Mo., Feb. 22, 1945; s. Willie Standberry and Bettie Mae (Thompson) Standberry-Taylor; m. Barbara Irene Palmer, July 1, 1942; children: Donna, Debra, Nina, Miriam, Miranda, Gretchen, Charles, Mary, Dwayne, Helena, Regina, Lakesha. BS, So. Ill. U., 1968; MA, Newport U., 1981, LHD (hon.), 1990; EdD, Walden U., 1992; D Ministry, U. Bibl. Studies and Sem., 1997; MEd, Ind. Wesleyan U., 1997. Cert. supt., gen. adminstr., curriculum, tchr. Tchr. Community H.S. Dist. 428, Blue Island, Ill., 1968-70; exec. dir. Kane County Coun. for Econ. Opportunity, Batavia, Ill., 1970-75; dep. dir./program planner, HeadStart dir., casemgr., youth supr., educator State of Ill., Dept. Pub. Aid., Dept. Corrections, Chgo., Joliet and St. Charles, Ill., 1975-85; adminstrv. asst. to prin. Bloom High Sch. Dist. 206, Chicago Heights, Ill., 1992-93; asst. prin. Rogers High Sch., Michigan City, Ind., 1994-95; prin. Mich. City (Ind.) Area Alternative H.S., 1995—; chmn. bd. dirs. Greater Chgo. Coun. of Religious Orgns., 1985-89; mem. George Bush's Rep. Presdl. Task Force, Washington, 1989; nominated mem. U.S. Rep. Senatorial Inner Cir., Washington, 1989. Author (curriculum) Business Law I & II, 1968, Career Counseling and Survival, 1978. Bd. dirs. United Way, Elgin, Ill, 1972, City of Elgin-Fremont Youth Orgn., 1971-72; host agy. rep. Dept. Human Svcs., Chgo., 1985-90; sustaining mem. Ill. Rep. Party, Springfield, 1989; host agy. Percy Julian High Sch., Chgo., 1989-90, Ill. Dept. Pub. Aid, Chgo., 1987. Recipient grant Ill. Dept. Pub. Aid, 1984-87, hon. award Christian World Affairs Conf., 1985-86. Mem. Internat. Assn. Police and Community Rel. Officers, United Evangelistic Consulting Assn. (chmn. bd. dirs., pres. 1985—). Home: 803 E 193rd St Glenwood IL 60425-2011 Office: United Evangelistic Assn 1236 W 103rd St Chicago IL 60643-2361

STANDBRIDGE, PETER THOMAS, retired insurance company executive; b. Norristown, Pa., Mar. 30, 1934; s. Henry Kay and Helen Margaret (Ballard) S.; m. Jean Ann Sire, Sept. 29, 1956; children: Kevin Scot, Keith Alan, Kathryn Ann, Steven Todd. A.B., Lafayette Coll., Easton, Pa., 1955. Regional mgr. Kemper Group, Richmond, Va., 1961-63; div. sales mgr. Kemper Group, Syracuse, Summit, N.Y., N.J., 1963-73; spl. planning officer Kemper Group, Long Grove, Ill., 1973; v.p. mktg. Kemper Group, 1973-86, sr. v.p., 1986-87, exec. v.p., 1988-96; dir. Kemper County Mut. Ins., Garland, Tex., 1978-85, Am. Protection Ins. Co., Long Grove, 1976-96, Acord Corp., Oradell, N.J., 1978-82. Mem. Henrico County (Va.) Rep. Com., 1960-64; trustee Village of Manlius, N.Y., 1966-68; bd. govs. Good Shepherd Hosp., Barrington, Ill., 1983-92; chmn. Marquis Soc. Lafayette Coll., 1984-86; bd. dirs. Buehler YMCA, Palatine, Ill., 1989-92; trustee Lafayette Coll., 1991-93. Mem. Lake Zurich (Ill.) Golf Club, The Landings Club (Ga.). Republican. Episcopalian. Home: 5 Moonrise Circle Savannah GA 31411

STANDEL, RICHARD REYNOLD, JR., lawyer, communications executive; b. N.Y.C., Nov. 20, 1936; s. Richard Reynold and Antoinette (Pfinder) S.; m. Elizabeth Hughes, Dec. 5, 1963. AB, Columbia U., 1956, JD, 1959; LLM, NYU, 1972. Bar: N.Y. 1960, Colo. 1974, Tenn. 1978. Assoc. Wickes, Riddell, Bloomer, Jacobi & McGuire, N.Y.C., 1959-64; assoc. gen. counsel Manville Corp., Denver, 1964-71, dir. acquisitions and divestments, 1972-76; v.p., gen. counsel, sec. No. Telecom Inc., Nashville and Dallas, 1976—. Bd. dirs. Nashville Urban League, 1984-86. Ford Found. scholar, 1952-56; Columbia U. Law Sch. scholar, 1956-59. Mem. Tenn. Bus. Roundtable (bd. dirs. 1985-92), Richland Country Club. Presbyterian. Office: No Telecom Inc Dept 8473 MS C-1531 2221 Lakeside Blvd Richardson TX 75082-4305

STANDER, JOSEPH WILLIAM, mathematics educator, former university official; b. Covington, Ky., Dec. 2, 1928; s. Charles G. and Rosa (Kerner) S. B.S., U. Dayton, Ohio, 1949; M.S., Cath. U. Am., 1957, Ph.D. in Math, 1959. Joined Soc. of Mary Roman Cath. Ch., 1946; tchr. Hamilton (Ohio) Cath. High Sch., 1949-50, Colegio Ponceno, Ponce, P.R., 1950-55; mem. faculty U. Dayton, 1960—, prof. math., 1970—; dean U. Dayton (Grad. Sch.), 1968-74, v.p. acad. affairs, 1974-89, prof. math. dept., 1990—. Mem. Math. Assn. Am. Office: U Dayton Math Dept 300 College Park Ave Dayton OH 45469-0001

STANDFAST, SUSAN J(ANE), state official, research, consultant, educator; b. Callicoon, N.Y., July 2, 1935; m. Theodore P. Wright Jr., 1967; children: Henry S., Margaret S., Catherine B. AB in Biology and Chemistry, Wells Coll., 1957; MD, Columbia U., 1961; MPH In Epidemiology, U. Calif., Berkeley, 1965. Cert. Am. Bd. Preventive Medicine. Intern King County Hosp., Swedish Hosp, Seattle, 1961-62; pediatric resident U. Wash., Seattle, 1963; sr. resident in epidemiology N.Y. State Health Dept., 1965-67; instr. dept. community health Albany (N.Y.) Med. Coll., 1965-67, asst. prof. dept. preventive and community medicine, 1968-72, cons. in epidemiology, 1968-72, adj. asst. prof. preventive and community medicine, 1975-80, adj. assoc. prof., 1980-91, cons. preventive medicine dept. family practice, 1983-91; research physician bur. cancer control, div. epidemiology N.Y. State Dept. Health, Albany, 1975-83, dir. cancer surveillance unit cancer control sect. bur. chronic disease prevention, 1983-85, asst. to dir. div. epidemiology, 1985-86, dir. injury control program div. epidemiology, 1986-90; physician pub. health Albany, 1983-95; retired, 1995, dir. disability prevention program, 1988-91; cons. epidemiologist div. family health N.Y. State Dept. Health, Albany, 1991-95; vis. lectr. G.S. Med. Coll., Bombay, 1969-70, London Sch. Hygiene, 1974-75, Coll. Cmty. Medicine, Lahore, Pakistan, 1991; cons. in epidemiology Bombay Cancer Registry Tata Meml. Hosp., Albany, 1968-72; cons. infectious diseas sect. VA Med. Ctr., Albany, 1979; mem. ad hoc task force on data resource devel. for dir. epidemiology and biometry rsch. program Nat. Inst. Child Health and Human Devel., Bethesda, Md., 1979-80; assoc. prof. epidemiology Sch. Pub. Health, SUNY, 1987—, co-dir. master's pub. health program, 1991—; instr. AARP 55 Alive, 1996—; lectr. in field. Contbr. numerous articles to profl. jours. Mem. med. adv. bd. Hudson-Mohawk chpt. Nat. Found. SIDS, 1976-84; mem. med. adv. bd coun. on human sexuality Planned Parenthood, Albany, 1971-88; mem. Physicians for Social Responsibility, 1984—, Doctors Ought to Care, 1984—, also numerous pub. health task forces and coms.; bd. dirs. Eddy Cmty. Care, Troy, N.Y.; vol. Colonie Sr. Svcs. Ctr., Newtonville, N.Y., 1996—. Recipient Disting. Alumnae award Wells Coll., 1994. Fellow Am. Coll. Preventive Medicine, Am. Coll. Epidemiology; mem. APHA, Am. Assn. for Automotive Medicine. Home: 27 Vandenburg Ln Latham NY 12110-1190

STANDING, KIMBERLY ANNA, educational researcher; b. Hagerstown, Md., Mar. 24, 1965; d. Thomas Townsend and Ruth Annadeane (Powell) Stone; m. Christopher G. Standing, May 20, 1989; 1 child, Iain Christopher. BA in Math., St. Mary's Coll., 1988; MA in Higher Edn. Adminstrn., George Washington U., 1996. Rsch. analyst Westat, Inc., Rockville, Md., 1988—. Mem. Am. Ednl. Rsch. Assn., Assn. Study Higher Edn. Home: 11545 Brundidge Ter Germantown MD 20876-5500 Office: Westat Inc 1650 Research Blvd # Tb243 Rockville MD 20850-3195

STANDISH, JOHN SPENCER, textile manufacturing company executive; b. Albany, N.Y., Apr. 17, 1925; s. John Carver and Florence (Spencer) S.; m. Elaine Joan Ritchie, Oct. 20, 1962 (div. 1984); children: John Carver, Christine Louise; m. Patricia Hunter, Nov. 9, 1985. BS, MIT, 1945. Asst. to prodn. mgr. Forstmann Woolen Co., Passaic, N.J., 1945-52; various positions Albany Internat. Corp., 1952-72, v.p., 1972-74, exec. v.p., 1974-76, vice chmn., 1976-84, chmn., 1984—; bd. dirs. Berkshire Life Ins. Co., Pittsfield, Mass. Bd. dirs. Albany chpt. ARC, 1966-92, chpt. chmn., 1971-74, bd. govs., Washington, 1980-86; bd. dirs. United Way Northeastern N.Y., Albany, 1980-97, pres., 1984-85; trustee Albany Med. Coll. and Ctr., 1984-93, Sienna Coll., Loudonville, N.Y., 1987—; chmn. U. Albany Fund, 1982-87, 89-92; pres. U. Albany Found., 1992—. Sgt. U.S. Army, 1945-46. Mem. Am. Mgmt. Assn., World Econ. Forum, Ft. Orange Club, Wolferts Roost Country Club, Schuyler Meadows Country Club, John's Island Club (Fla.). Republican. Episcopalian. Avocations: bridge, tennis, golf. Home: 1 Schuyler Meadow Club Rd Loudonville NY 12211-1423 Office: Albany Internat Corp PO Box 1907 Albany NY 12201-1907

STANDISH, ROBERT C., professional sports team executive. BSBA, U. Conn. Past gen. mgr., CEO Ruidoso Downs Race Track, Ruidoso, N.Mex.; exec. dir. U.S. Equestrian Team, Gladstone, N.J., 1989—; accredited ofcl. judge Am. Quarter Horse Assn.; former gen. mgr. Sheepfields Farm, New Vernon, N.J./directed and managed the campaigns of 18 AQHA Champions and one World Champion horse; previously gen. mgr. of The Heritage Place, Inc., Oklahoma City. Office: US Equestrian Team Pottersville Rd Gladstone NJ 07934

STANDISH, SAMUEL MILES, oral pathologist, college dean; b. Campbellsburg, Ind., July 6, 1923; s. Irvin Arthur and Etta May (Smedley) S.; m. Gertrude Elizabeth Eberle, Aug. 6, 1949; children—Nancy Jo, Linda Sue. D.D.S., Ind. U., 1945, M.S., 1956. Diplomate: Am. Bd. Oral Pathology (dir. 1973-80), Am. Bd. Forensic Odontology. Practice dentistry, specializing in oral pathology Indpls., 1948-58; mem. faculty Sch. Dentistry Ind. U., 1958-88, emeritus prof. oral pathology, 1967-88, chmn. div. clin. oral pathology, 1967-77, asst. dean sch., 1969-74, asso. dean, 1974-88; cons. Nat. Cancer Inst., 1969-73, Nat. Bd. Dental Examiners, 1966-74, ADA, 1971-77. Author: (with others) Oral Diagnosis/Oral Medicine, 1978, Maxillofacial Prosthetics: Multidisciplinary Practice, 1972, Outline of Forensic Dentistry, 1982. Served with USNR, 1945-47. Fellow Am. Acad. Oral Pathology (pres. 1972-73); mem. ADA, Internat. Assn. Dental Research, Am. Acad. Forensic Sci., Sigma Xi, Omicron Kappa Upsilon, Xi Psi Phi. Home: 4548 Manning Rd Indianapolis IN 46228-2768 Office: Ind U Sch Dentistry Indianapolis IN 46202

STANDISH, WILLIAM LLOYD, judge; b. Pitts., Feb. 16, 1930; s. William Lloyd and Eleanor (McCargo) S.; m. Marguerite Oliver, June 12, 1963; children: Baird M., N. Graham, James H., Constance S. Bar: Pa. 1957, U.S. Supreme Ct. 1967. Assoc. Reed, Smith, Shaw & McClay, Pitts., 1957-63, ptnr., 1963-80; judge Ct. Common Pleas of Allegheny County (Pa.), 1980-87; judge U.S. Dist. Ct., Pa. we. dist., 1987—; solicitor Edgeworth Borough Sch. Dist., 1963-66. Bd. dirs. Sewickley (Pa.) Community Ctr., 1981-83, Staunton Farm Found., mem, 1984—, trustee, 1984-92; corporator Sewickley Cemetery, 1971-87; trustee Mary and Alexander Laughlin Children's Ctr., 1972-90; trustee Leukemia Soc. Am., 1978-80, trustee western Pa. chpt., 1972-80, Western Pa. Sch. for the Deaf, YMCA of Sewickley, 1996—. Recipient Pres. award Leukemia Soc. Am., 1980. Mem. ABA, Pa. Bar Assn., Allegheny County Bar Assn., Am. Judicature Soc., Acad. Trial Lawyers Allegheny County (treas. 1977-78, bd. dirs. 1979-80), Am. Inn of Ct. (Pitts. chpt. 1993—). Office: US Dist Ct 605 US Courthouse Pittsburgh PA 15219

STANDRING, JAMES DOUGLAS, real estate developer; b. Fresno, Calif., Dec. 2, 1951; s. James Robert Pusey and Jacquelin (Moore); m. Paula Jean Monson, Oct. 27, 1972; children: Craig Douglas, Ryan Scott, Melinda Jean, Kevin Paul. BS, Calif. State U., Fresno, 1975. Pres. Westland Industries, Inc., Portland, Oreg., 1976—; ptnr. Aloha Land and Cattle, Inc., Portland, 1982—; bd. dirs. Homebuilders Assn. Metro Portland, v.p. 1988-90, pres. 1990-91; bd. dirs. Oreg. Bldg. Industry Assn., v.p. 1993-96, pres. 1996-97; bd. dirs. Nat. Assn. Homebuilders, Washington, Oreg. trustee BUILD-PAC, 1992—, exec. com., 1994—. Bd. dirs. Tualitin Valley Econ. Devel. Corp., Portland, 1988-95; co-founder, bd. dirs. People for Washington County Charities, Beaverton, Oreg., 1985-88; mem. Tualitin Valley Econ. Devel. Commn., 1000 Friends of Oreg.; steering com. Oreg. Med. Laser Ctr., 1995—. Named Portland Metro. Builder of Yr., 1992, Oregon Builder of Yr., 1992. Mem. Multnomah Athletic Club, Portland City Club, Portland Golf Club, Sierra Club, Univ. Club, Elks. Republican. Episcopalian. Home: 5 Nansen Smt Lake Oswego OR 97035-1029 Office: Westland 6655 SW Hampton St Ste 100 Portland OR 97223-8358

STANEK, ALAN EDWARD, music educator, performer, music administrator; b. Longmont, Colo., July 3, 1939; s. Edward Thomas Stanek and Mary Rose (Hicks) Stanek MacDougall; m. Janette Elizabeth Swanson, Aug. 23, 1963; children: Michael Alan, Karen Leigh. B in Mus. Edn., U. Colo., 1961; MusM, Eastman Sch. Music, 1965; MusD, U. Mich., 1974. Dir. instrumental music Ainsworth Pub. Sch., Nebr., 1961-64, Cozad Pub. Sch., Nebr., 1965-67; asst. prof. music Hastings Coll., Nebr., 1967-76; prof., chmn. dept. music Idaho State U., Pocatello, 1976—. . Contbr., editor, reviewer for profl. jours. including Clarinet, Idaho Music Notes, Nebr. Music Educator. Mem. Music Educators Nat. Conf., Idaho Music Educators Assn. (chmn. higher edn. 1978-86, 96—, pres. 1988-90, chair state solo contest 1990-92), Internat. Clarinet Assn. (sec. 1978-84, v.p. 1986-88, pres. 1996—), Coll. Music Soc., Nat. Assn. Coll. Wind and Percussion Instrs. (chmn. Idaho 1978-88), Nat. Assn. Schs. Music (sec. N.W. region 1979-82, vis. evaluator 1990—, chair N.W. region 1991-94), Rotary (pres. Gate City chpt. 1994-95). Office: Idaho State U Dept Music PO Box 8099 Pocatello ID 83209

STANFILL, DENNIS CAROTHERS, business executive; b. Centerville, Tenn., Apr. 1, 1927; s. Sam Broome and Hattie (Carothers) S.; m. Therese Olivieri, June 29, 1951; children: Francesca (Mrs. Peter Tufo), Sara, Dennis Carothers. BS, U.S. Naval Acad., 1949; M.A. (Rhodes scholar), Oxford U., 1953; LHD (hon), U. S.C. Corporate finance specialist Lehman Bros., N.Y.C., 1959-65; v.p. finance Times Mirror Co., Los Angeles, 1965-69; exec. v.p. 20th Century-Fox Film Corp., 1969-71, pres., 1971, chmn. bd., chief exec. officer, 1971-81; pres. Stanfill, Bowen & Co., 1981-90; chmn. bd. dirs., chief exec. officer AME, Inc., 1990-91; co-chmn., co-CEO Metro-Goldwyn-Mayer, Inc., 1992-93; sr. advisor Credit Lyonnais, 1993-95; pres. Dennis Stanfill Co., 1995—; bd. dirs. Dial Corp., Weingart Found. Trustee Calif. Inst. Tech. Served to lt. USN, 1949-59; politico-mil. policy div. Office Chief Naval Ops., 1956-59.

STANFILL, SHELTON G., performing arts administrator; m. Brigitte. BA in History and Social Scis., Colo. State U., postgrad. Exec. dir. Hopkins Ctr. Dartmouth Coll.; dir. cultural programs Colo. State U.; dir. Nat. Arts Festival 12th Winter Olympic Games; ptnr. Brown, Stanfill & Brown; pres., CEO Wolf Trap Found. for Performing Arts, Vienna, Va.; pres. Music Ctr. L.A. County, 1994—; chair panels, cons. Nat. Endowment for Arts, Lincoln. Ctr., Bklyn. Acad. Music, UCLA; advisor Telluride Film Festival. Avocations: reading, wine, dancing, film, medieval history. Office: Nicholas T Goldsborough 400 W Temple St Los Angeles CA 90012-2716

STANFORD, DENNIS JOE, archaeologist, museum curator; b. Cherokee, Iowa, May 13, 1943; s. William Erle and Mary L. (Fredenburg) S.; m. Margaret Brierty, June 4, 1988; 1 dau., Brandy L. BA, U. Wyo., 1965; MA, U. N.Mex., 1967, PhD, 1972. Archeologist, curator Smithsonian Instn., Washington, 1972—, head div. archeology, 1990-92, chmn. dept anthropology, 1992—; v.p., dir. Taraxacum Press, 1981—; mem. adv. bd. Ctr. for the Study of the First Americans, 1985—; rsch. assoc. Denver Mus. Natural History, 1989—. Author: The Walakpa Site, Alaska, 1975; editor: (with Robert L. Humphrey) Pre-Llano Cultures of the Americas, 1979, (with George C. Frison) The Agate Basin Site, 1982, (with Jane Day) Ice Age Hunters of the Rockies, 1992. Mem. Anthrop. Soc. Washington (gov. 1974-77), Soc. Am. Archeology, Am. Quaternary Assn. Research, publs. on Paleo-Indian Studies, N.Am., S.Am., N.E. Asia, especially Western U.S., Arctic. Home: 1350 Massachusetts Ave SE Washington DC 20003-1556 Office: Smithsonian Instn Washington DC 20560

STANFORD, DONALD ELWIN, English educator, editor, poet, critic; b. Amherst, Mass., Feb. 7, 1913; s. Ernest Elwood and Alice (Carroll) S.; m. Edna Goodwin, July, 1937 (div. 1946); 1 child, Don David; m. Maryanna Peterson, Aug. 14, 1953 (dec. Mar. 1992). B.A., Stanford U., 1933, Ph.D., 1953; M.A., Harvard U., 1934. Instr. La. State U., Baton Rouge, 1949-50, asst. prof. English, 1953-54, assoc. prof., 1954-62, prof., 1962-79, Alumni prof. English, 1979-83, Alumni prof. emeritus, 1983—; vis. prof. Duke U., Durham, N.C., 1961-62, Tex. A&M U., College Station, 1984. Author: New England Earth, 1941, The Traveler, 1955, In the Classic Mode: The Achievement of Robert Bridges, 1978, Revolution and Convention in Modern Poetry, 1983; editor: The Poems of Edward Taylor, 1960, Dictionary of Literary Biography, vol. 19, 1981, Dictionary of Literary Biography, vol. 20, 1983, Selected Letters of Robert Bridges, 2 vols., 1983, Humanities Series, 1963-66, The So. Rev., 1963-83, cons. editor The So. Rev., 1987—; mem. adv. bd.: Hopkins Quar., 1981—. Recipient Disting. Research Master award La. State U., 1982; Guggenheim Found. fellow, 1959-60; La. State U. Disting. Faculty fellow, 1973-74; NEH research scholar, summers 1972, 78. Mem. PEN, MLA, South Atlantic MLA, Phi Beta Kappa, Phi Kappa Phi. Democrat. Club: Athenaeum (London). Home: 776 Delgado Dr Baton Rouge LA 70808-4730

STANFORD, HENRY KING, college president; b. Atlanta, Apr. 22, 1916; s. Henry King and Annie Belle (Callaway) S.; m. Laurie Ruth King, Sept. 19, 1936; children: Henry, Lowry, Rhoda, Peyton. AB, Emory U., 1936, MA, 1940, LLD, 1961; postgrad., U. Heidelberg, Germany, 1936-37; MS in Govt. Mgmt. (Alfred P. Sloan Found. fellow 1941-43), U. Denver, 1943, LLD, 1962; PhD (Tax Found. fellow 1943-44), NYU, 1949; DCL Jacksonville (Fla.) U, 1963; LLD, Loyola U., New Orleans, 1968, U. Akron, Kyung Hee U., Seoul, Korea, 1968, Rollins Coll., 1977, Barry Coll., 1979; DHL, U. Tampa, 1969; DLitt, U. R.I., 1970; D in Higher Edn., U. Miami, 1981; DHL, Birmingham-So. Coll., 1987. Instr., Emory U., 1937-40; asst. prof. Ga. Inst. Tech., 1940-41; instr. NYU, 1943-46; prof. pub. adminstrn., also dir. sch. pub. adminstrn. U. Denver, 1946-48; pres. Ga. Southwestern Coll., Americus, 1948-50; dir. U. Center in Ga., 1950-52; asst. chancellor U. System of Ga., 1952-53; pres. Ga. State Coll. for Women, Milledgeville, 1953-56; chief of party NYU-Internat. Cooperation Adminstrn. Contract, Ankara, Turkey, 1956-57; pres. Birmingham-So. Coll., 1957-62, U. Miami, Fla., 1962-81; pres. emeritus U. Miami, 1981—; interim pres. U. Ga., 1986-87, pres. emeritus, 1987—; bd. dirs. Avatar Holdings, 1980—, DWG, Southeastern Pub. Service, Wilson Bros., 1982-86, Fischbach Corp., 1985-86, NVF, 1985-86, So. Bell, 1969-85; research asst. Tax Found., N.Y.C., 1943-44; staff N.A.M. com. exec., 1944-46; mem. bd. dirs. Birmingham br. Fed. Res. Bank Atlanta, 1960-62, Jacksonville br., Atlanta, 1967-72, chmn., 1969, 72. Trustee Knight Found., 1982-97; vice chmn. Invest-in-Am., 1984-86, chmn. 1986-87; chmn. Dade County Community Relations Bd., 1969-71; bd. visitors Air U., Maxwell AFB, Ala., 1963-66; trustee Caribbean Resources Devel. Found., 1978—, pres., 1978-83, chmn., 1983-84; chmn. Jimmy Carter Hist. Site Adv. Commn., 1990—. Decorated Star of Africa medal Liberia; officer Order of Merit Fed. Republic of Germany; recipient Eleanor Roosevelt-Israel Humanitarian award, 1965, Outstanding Civilian Svc. award U.S. Army, 1966, Silver Medallion Fla. Region NCCJ, 1968, Ga. Region, 1987, Disting. Svc. award Ga. Coll., 1979, hon. alumnus, 1996, C.H.I.E.F. award Ind. Colls. and Univs. Fla., 1983, Sibley award Ga. Mil. Coll., 1991, Emory medal, 1991, Adrian Dominican Ednl. Leadership award Barry U., 1991, Atlanta Boys' High Alumnus award, 1992, James Blair Humanitarian award Americus, Ga., 1993, Westmeyer award pub. svc. NYU, 1993. Mem. So. Assn. Colls. and Schs. (chmn. commn. colls. 1960-62, pres. 1972-73), Nat. Assn. Ind. Colls. and Univs. (dir. 1976-80), Assn. Caribbean Univs. and Rsch. Insts. (v.p. 1965-79), Golden Key Honor Soc. (bd. dirs. 1982-91), Internat. Assn. Univ. Pres. (exec. com. 1977-81), Delta Phi Alpha, Phi Beta Kappa, Omicron Delta Kappa, Phi Sigma Iota, Alpha Kappa Psi, Phi Mu Alpha, Phi Kappa Phi, Rotary. Methodist. Lodge: Rotary (Americus, Ga.) (pres. 1984-85). Office: PO Box 1065 510 W Lamar St Americus GA 31709-3443 *The greatest literary influence on my life has been Goethe's Faust, Part I. Reading it in the original German as a college student, I was struck immediately with the demands Faust made of himself in concluding the contract with Mephistopheles: he would lose his soul if he ever chose a "bed of ease," succumbed to flattery, opted for pleasure alone, or said to any one moment, "Linger awhile; you are so nice!" In other words, whenever he ceased striving, he was lost.*

STANFORD, JACK ARTHUR, biological station administrator; b. Delta, Colo., Feb. 18, 1947; s. LeRoy and Wilma (Tucker) S.; children: Jake, Chriss. BS in Fisheries Sci., Colo. State U., 1969, MS in Limnology, 1971; PhD in Limnology, U. Utah, 1975. Fisheries biologist Alaska-Fish and Game, Dillingham, 1968-69; rsch. biologist and limnologist instr. U. Mont., Missoula, 1973-74; dir. Flathead Lake Biol. Sta. U. Mont., Polson, 1980—; research prof. zoology U. Mont., Missoula, 1983-86; Jessie M. Bierman prof. U. Mont., Missoula, Mont., 1986—; prof. N. Tex. State U., Denton, 1974-81; panelist div. biotic system NSF, Washington, 1985—. Editor: Ecology of Regulated Streams, 1979, Groundwater Ecology, 1994; editor: Regulated Rivers: Research and Management, 1985—; contbr. over 100 articles to profl. jours. Advisor Nature Conservancy, Boulder, Colo., 1982—. Named Bierman Prof. Ecology U. Mont., 1986—; grantee EPA, U.S. Army, U.S. Bur. Reclamation, NSF, U.S. Nat. Park Svc.; disting. scholar U. Mont., 1997. Mem. Mont. Acad. Aci., Am. Soc. Limnology and Oceanography, Ecol. Soc. Am. (pub. affairs com., 1984—), N.Am. Benthological Soc. (exec. com. 1979, 1988-89, pres. 1997), AAAS. Avocation: fly fishing, skiing.

Office: U Mont Flathead Lake Biol Sta 311 Bio Station Ln Polson MT 59860-9659

STANFORD, JANE HERRING, business administration educator; b. Lockhart, Tex., Dec. 17, 1939; d. John William and Frances Argyra (Cheatham) H. Jr.; m. Rube Valton Stanford, Sept. 17, 1966; children: Steven Scott, Lisa Ann. BS in Secondary Edn., Texas A&M U., Kingsville, 1965; MS in Counseling, Texas A&M U., Corpus Christi, 1982; MBA, Texas A&M U., Kingsville, 1988; PhD in Orgn. Theory and Policy, U. North Tex., 1992. Cert. secondary sch. tchr., coun., Tex. English tchr. Robstown (Tex.) H.S., 1965-67; Bus. tchr. Miller H.S., Corpus Christi, 1967-78; owner, mgr. The Cottage, Portland, Tex., 1978-81; instr. Del Mar Coll., Corpus Christi, 1981-83, Bee County Coll., Beeville, Tex., 1984-88; tching. fellow U. North Tex., Denton, 1988-90; assoc. prof. bus. policy and internat. mgmt. Texas A&M U., Kingsville, 1990—, chair dept. mgmt. and marketing, 1994—; mem. grad. faculty Tex. A&M U., Kingsville, chair faculty senate, 1995-96, mem. exec. com. of senate, 1993—, chair Univ. Assessment, Budgeting and Planning Com., 1997—; cons., internat. lectr. on strategic mgmt. within internat. context, workshop leader and participant in acad. issues for various groups, including S.W. Fedn. Adminstrv. Disciplines, Houston, 1992-95. Author: Building Competitiveness: U.S. Expatriate Management Strategies in Mexico, 1995; co-editor Tex. A&M U. System Internat. Bus. Newsletter, 1993; contbr. articles to profl. jours. Co-author Best Conf. Paper, Richard d. Irwin, Inc., Houston, 1991; grantee SBA for Women in Bus. Conf., 1993; nominated to S.W. Acad. of Mgmt. Doctoral Consortium, S.W. Fedn. Adminstrv. Disciplines, 1990; Tex. A&M U. Sys. Chancellor's fellow in leadership in higher edn. program, 1997, finalist Disting. Svc. award, 1997. Mem. Am. Assn. Higher Edn. (conf. panel presenter 1997), Bus. Assn. Latin Am. Studies, Acad. Internat. Bus. (track chair 1994-95), Acad. Mgmt., So. Mgmt. Assn., S.W. Acad. Mgmt., S.W. Case Rsch. Assn. (track chair 1992), Exec. Women in Tex. Govt., Kappa Delta Pi (life), Delta Sigma Pi. Presbyterian. Avocations: book collecting, photography, art, travel. Home: 13526 Carlos Fifth Ct Corpus Christi TX 78418 Office: Texas A&M Univ Campus Box 187 Kingsville TX 78363

STANFORD, JOSEPH STEPHEN, diplomat, lawyer, educator; b. Montreal, Que., Can., May 7, 1934; s. Walter Albert and Geraldine (O'Loghlin) S.; m. Agnes Mabelle Walker, Nov. 16, 1957; children: Kevin, Karen, Michael. BA, U. Montreal, 1953; LLB, U. Alta., Edmonton, Can., 1956. Bar: Alta. 1957; called to Queen's Counsel 1984. Mem. Greenan, Cooney & Stanford, Calgary, Alta., 1957-60; joined Fgn. Svc., Dept. External Affairs, Govt. of Can., 1960; amb. to Israel Tel Aviv, 1979-82; also Can. high commr. to Cyprus; asst. dep. min. for Africa and Mid. East Dept. External Affairs, Ottawa, Ont., 1983-85, asst. dep. min. for Europe, 1985-87, assoc. undersec. of state for external affairs, 1987-88; dep. solicitor gen. Govt. of Can., Ottawa, 1988-93; ret., 1994; sr fellow, conflict mgr. Canadian Center Mgmt. Devel., Ottawa, 1993-96; assoc., bd. dirs. Conflict Mgmt. Group, Cambridge, Mass., 1994—. Contbr. articles on internat. law, fgn. investment and conflict resolution to profl. jours. Roman Catholic. Avocations: wilderness canoeing, tennis, skiing. Home: 58 Amberwood Cres, Nepean, ON Canada K2E 7C3

STANFORD, MELVIN JOSEPH, retired dean, educator; b. Logan, Utah, June 13, 1932; s. Joseph Sedley and Ida Pearl (Ivie) S.; m. Yvonne Watson, Feb. 8, 1951 (div. 1956); children: Connie Stanford Tendick, Cheryl Stanford Bohn; m. Linda Barney, Sept. 2, 1960; children: Joseph Barney Stanford, Theodore Barney Stanford, Emily Stanford Schultz, Charlotte Stanford Vaughan, Charles Barney Stanford, Sarah Stanford. B.S. (First Security Found. scholar), Utah State U., 1957; M.B.A. (Donald Kirk David fellow), Harvard U., 1963; Ph.D., U. Ill., 1968. CPA, Utah. Asst. audit supr. Utah Tax Commn., 1959-61, auditor, 1958-59; acct. Haskins & Sells, C.P.A.s, Boston, 1961-62; acctg. staff analyst Arabian Am. Oil Co., Dhahran, Saudi Arabia, 1963-66; teaching and rsch. asst. U. Ill., Urbana, 1966-68; mem. faculty Brigham Young U., Provo, Utah, 1968-82; dir. mgmt. devel. programs Brigham Young U., 1970-73, prof. bus. mgmt., 1974-82; dean Coll. Bus., Mankato (Minn.) State U., 1982-89, prof. mgmt., 1989-94, prof. emeritus, 1994—; mem. adv. bd. M.L. Bigelow & Co., Inc., Organ Builders; cons. Strategic Planning, Decision Case Mgmt., New Enterprise Mgmt.; vis. prof. mgmt. Boston U., Europe, 1975-76; vis. prof. agrl. mgmt. U. Minn., 1991-92. Author: Business Plan Guidebook, 1995, 97, New Enterprise Management, 1975, 82, Management Policy, 1979, 83; co-author: Cases in Business Policy and Strategy, 1990, Decision Cases for Agriculture, 1992; also articles, mgmt. cases; founder Midwestern Jour. Bus. and Econs., 1985. Bishop, Mankato ward LDS Ch., 1987-91. With USAF, 1951-55, USAR, 1956-80. Named Amb. of City of Mankato, 1988. Fellow N.Am. Case Rsch. Assn. (v.p. for rsch. 1985-86, pres. 1987-88, Curtis E. Tate Jr. Outstanding Case Writer award 1992); mem. SAR (pres. Utah 1978-79, nat. trustee 1979-81, Meritorious Svc. medal 1981, Patriot medal 1991), Kiwanis, Sons of Utah Pioneers, Alpha Kappa Psi, Phi Kappa Phi. Home: 1754 Cobblestone Dr Provo UT 84604-1155

STANG, PETER JOHN, organic chemist; b. Nürnberg, Germany, Nov. 17, 1941; came to U.S., 1956; s. John Stang and Margaret Stang Pollman; m. Christine Schirmer, 1969; children: Antonia, Alexandra. BS, DePaul U., Chicago, 1963; Ph. D., U. California, Berkeley, 1966; hon. degr., Moscow State Lomonossov U., 1992, Russian Academy of Sciences, 1992. Instr. Princeton (N.J.) U., 1967-68; from asst. to assoc. prof. U. Utah, Salt Lake City, 1969-79, prof., 1979-92, Disting. prof. chemistry, 1992—. Co-author: Organic Spectroscopy, 1971; author: (with others) Vincy Cations, 1979; editor: (with F. Diederich) Modern Acetylene Chemistry, 1995; contbr. 300 articles to sci. publs. Humboldt-Forschungspreis, 1977; JSPS Fellowship, 1985; Fulbright-Hays Sr. Scholarship, 1988. Fellow AAAS; mem. Am. Chem. Soc. (assoc. editor Jour. Am. Chem. Soc. 1982—). Office: Univ Utah Dept Chemistry Salt Lake City UT 84112

STANGE, JAMES HENRY, architect; b. Davenport, Iowa, May 25, 1930; s. Henry Claus and Norma (Ballhorn) S.; m. Mary Suanne Peterson, Dec. 12, 1954; children: Wade Weston, Drew Dayton, Grant Owen. BArch, Iowa State U., 1954. Registered architect, Iowa, Nebr., Kans., Mo., Okla. Designer Davis & Wilson, Lincoln, Nebr., 1954-62, v.p., 1962-68; v.p., sec. Davis, Fenton, Stange, Darling, Lincoln, Nebr., 1977-92, pres., 1976-93, chmn., 1978-94; mem. State Bd. Examiners for Engrs. and Architects, 1989-92, chmn. region V NCARB, 1991. Prin. works include Lincoln Airport Terminal, Sq. D Mfg. Plant, Lincoln, Bryan Meml. Hosp. (masterplans and additions), 1970, 80, 90, Bryan Ambulatory Care Ctr. Med. Office Bldg., Same Day Surgery Conf. Ctr., Parking Garage, 1993-95, Nebr. Wesleyan Theatre, Lincoln, Hasting (Nebr.) YMCA, various structures U. Nebr., Lincoln, ctr. and br. offices Am. Charter Fed. Savs & Loan, Southeast High Sch. (addition), 1984, U. Nebr. Animal Sci. Bldg., 1987, Beadle Ctr., UNL, 1991. Pres. Lincoln Ctr. Assn., 1979, Capitol Assn. Retarded Citizens, 1972-96; chmn. United Way Campaign, 1986, chmn. bd., 1988; chmn. Bryan Hosp. Found. Endowment Com., 1988-90; bd. dirs. Delta Dental, 1987-92, Downtown Lincoln Assn., 1985-94, steering com. 1989, v.p. Nebr. Jazz Orch., 1995, Nebr. Art Assn., 1996—; mem. mayor's com. Study Downtown Redevel., 1989, pub. bldg. commn., masterplan rev. com., 1994; deacon Presbyn. Ch., 1960, chmn. bd. trustees, 1968-90, elder, 1972-87, 97—. Recipient Honor award Conf. on Religious Architecture-1st Plymouth Ch. Addition, 1969, also numerous state and nat. awards from archtl. orgns. Mem. AIA (Nebr. bd. dirs. 1964-65, treas. 1965, sec. 1966, v.p. 1967, pres. Nebr. 1968, mem. com. on architecture for health, 1980-94, Regional Design award 1976, 88, 96), Am. Assn. Health Planners, Interfaith Forum on Religion, Art, Architecture, Lincoln C. of C. (bd. dirs. 1982). Republican. Clubs: Exec. (pres. 1972), Crucible, 12, Hillcrest Country (pres. 1977), Lincoln Univ. (sec. 1992—, bd. dirs. 1991-97, pres. 1995, 96). Avocations: travel, photography, golf. Home: 3545 Calvert St Lincoln NE 68506-5744 Office: Davis/Fenton/Stange/Darling Inc 211 N 14th St Lincoln NE 68508-1616

STANGEL, IVAN, biomaterials scientist, educator; b. Kosice, Czechoslovakia, Sept. 8, 1946; came to U.S., 1949; s. Louis and Hermina (Aibester) S.; m. Cynthia Susan Palmer, Apr. 25, 1985; 1 child, Jacob Louis. DMD, U. Pa., 1970. Resident U. Coll. Hosp. U. London, 1970-71; clin. staff Luth. Med. Ctr./Sunset Park Family Health Ctr., Bklyn., 1971-72; clin. staff Polyclinique dentaire U. Lausanne, Switzerland, 1973; instr. dept. operative dentistry Sch. Dental Medicine Tufts U., Boston, 1974; pvt. practice Burlington, Vt., 1974-77; lectr. dept. operative dentistry McGill U., Montreal, 1977-78, asst. prof. dept. clin. dentistry, 1978-80, asst. prof. sect. operative dentistry divsn. prosthodontics, 1980-82, assoc. prof., 1982—, assoc. prof., dir. biomaterials sci., 1995—; guest rschr. ADA Health Found., Gaithersburg, Md., 1992-95; cons. in field, 1990—; vis. prof. Dept. Biomaterials Boston U., 1983-84; asst. dental surgeon, Montreal Gen. Hosp., 1978—. Editl. bd. Operative Dentistry; editl. cons. Jour. Dental Rsch., Dental Materials; contbr. numerous articles to profl. jours. Fellow Acad. Dental Materials; mem. Adhesion Soc., Acad. Dental Materials, Am. Acad. Operative Dentistry, Can. Soc. biomaterials, Coun. Physicians and Dentists, Dental Materials Group, Internat. Assn. Dental Rsch., Internat. Coll. Dentists, Order Dentists Quebec. Avocations: sailing, running, skiing, mountaineering. Home: 4990 Grosvenor Ave, Montreal, PQ Canada H3W 2M1 Office: McGill U Faculty Divsn, 740 Docteur Penfield Ave, Montreal, PQ Canada H3A 1A4

STANGELAND, ROGER EARL, retail chain store executive; b. Chgo., Oct. 4, 1929; s. Earl and Mae E. (Shaw) S.; m. Lilah Fisher, Dec. 27, 1951; children: Brett, Cyndi Stangeland Meili, Brad. Student, St. Johns Mil. Acad., 1943-47, Carleton Coll., 1947-48; B.S., U. Ill., 1949-51. With Coast to Coast Stores, Mpls., 1960-78, pres., 1972-77; sr. v.p., exec. v.p. Household Merchandising, Chgo., 1978-84; chief exec. officer, chmn. bd. Vons Grocery Co., Los Angeles, 1984-85; past CEO The Vons Cos., Inc., Arcadia, Calif., chmn., 1986—, now chmn. emeritus. Chmn. Wauconda (Ill.) Bd. Edn., 1957-60, Hopkins (Minn.) Bd. Edn., 1968-74; bd. fellows Claremont (Calif.) U. Ctr. and Grad. Sch., 1986; bd. dirs. L.A. area Boy Scouts Am.; trustee Hugh O'Brian Youth Found.; mem. CEO bd. advisors U. So. Calif. Sch. Bus. Adminstrn.; trustee St. John's Mil. Acad; bd. visitors Peter F. Drucker Grad. Mgmt. Ctr. Mem. Am. Inst. Wine and Food (bd. dirs.), Food Mktg. Inst. (chmn. bd. dirs.), Food Employers Coun. (exec. com., bd. dirs.), Mchts. & Mfrs. Assn. (bd. dirs.), L.A. Area C. of C. (bd. dirs.), Jonathan Club (L.A.), Calif. Club. Home: 842 Oxford Rd San Marino CA 91108-1214 Office: Vons Grocery Co PO Box 3338 618 Michillinda Ave Arcadia CA 91007-6300*

STANGER, ABRAHAM M., lawyer; b. N.Y.C., Sept. 25, 1921; s. Joseph I. and Tillie (Rothfeld) S.; m. Claire Y. Schwebel, Sept. 18, 1948; children: Richard, Jordan, Hope. BA cum laude, CCNY, 1941; LLB, NYU, 1948, LLM, 1952, Dr. Jud. Sci., 1958. Bar: N.Y. 1949, U.S. Tax Ct. 1951, U.S. Dist. Ct. (so. dist.) N.Y. 1951, U.S. Dist. Ct. (ea. dist.) N.Y. 1953, U.S. Supreme Ct. 1958, U.S. Ct. Appeals (2d cir.) 1960, U.S. Ct. Claims 1984; CPA, N.Y. Sr. ptnr. corp. fin. reporting, disclosure issues and tax matters Stanger, Robson & Rothstein, N.Y.C., 1960-72; sr. ptnr. corp. div. fin. reporting, disclosure issues and tax matters Trubin Sillcocks Edelman & Knapp, N.Y.C., 1972-83; sr. ptnr. corp. fin. reporting, disclosure issues and tax matters Seyfarth, Shaw, Fairweather & Geraldson, N.Y.C., 1983—; adj. prof. law NYU, 1958—; mem. Fin. Acctg. Standards Adv. Council, 1979-83. Contbr. numerous articles on fin. reporting and disclosure to profl. jours; edit. staff NYU Law Rev., 1947-48; columnist Corp. Law Rev., 1978-86. Recipient Scroll Appreciation award, NYU. Fellow Am. Bar Found.; mem. AICPA (futures issues com. 1985-88), ABA (chmn. com. law and acctg. sect. bus. law 1980-85, chmn. subcom. lawyers replies to auditors 1985—, chmn. subcom. acctg. methods of com. tax acctg. problems sect. of taxation 1982-86, vice chmn. com. tax acctg. problems 1986-90, mem. nat. conf. of lawyers and CPA's 1988-91), N.Y. State Bar Assn., Assn. of Bar of City of N.Y., N.Y. County Lawyers Assn., Internat. Bar Assn. (rep. on consultative group internat. acctg. stds. com. 1987—, rep. on consultative group internat. auditing practices com. 1995—), Am. Judicature Soc. Home: 605 Park Ave New York NY 10021-7016 Office: Seyfarth Shaw Fairweather & Geraldson 900 3rd Ave New York NY 10022-4728

STANGER, ILA, writer, editor; b. N.Y.C.; d. Jack Simon and Shirley Ruth (Nadelson) S. B.A., Bklyn. Coll., 1961. Feature and travel editor Harpers Bazaar, N.Y.C., 1969-75; exec. editor Travel and Leisure mag., N.Y.C., 1975-85; editor in chief Food and Wine Mag., N.Y.C., 1985-89, Travel and Leisure mag., N.Y.C., 1990-93; contbg. editor Town and Country and Quest mag., 1993—; writer on arts, features and travel; consulting editor Internat. Masters Pubs., London. Mem. N.Y. Travel Writers., Am. Soc. Mag. Editors. Home and Office: 115 W 71st St New York NY 10023-3838

STANGER, ROBERT HENRY, psychiatrist, educator; b. N.Y.C., N.Y., May 19, 1937; s. Sidney and Mary (Strassner) S.; m. Andrea Rogin, Aug. 28, 1960; children: Lee Ann, David Neal. AB, Guilford Coll., 1959; MD, Emory U., 1964. Intern in internal medicine Wake Forest U., 1964-65; resident in gen. psychiatry U. Pitts., 1967-70; resident in psychiatry; pvt. practice gen. psychiatry Monroeville, Pa., 1970—; med. dir. Allegheny Valley Mental Health-Mental Retardation Ctr., New Kensington, Pa., 1970-76; dir. psychiat. svcs. Allegheny Valley Hosp., Natrona Heights, Pa., 1984-96; chmn. dept. psychiatry and behavioral medicine Allegheny Valley Hosp., 1984-96; pvt. practice Natrona Heights, Pa., 1996—; clin. instr. psychiatry U. Pitts. Sch. Medicine, 1970-79, clin. asst. prof., 1980—; cons. Westinghouse Elec. Corp., East Pitts., 1977-87; mem. ethics com. human rsch. Allegheny Valley Hosp., 1976—; chmn. dept. psychiatry Citizens Gen. Hosp., 1978-88. Capt. M.C., U.S. Army, 1965-67, Vietnam. Mem. AMA, Am. Psychiat. Assn. (del. 1986-88), Pa. Psychiat. Soc. (councilor 1976-79, treas. 1979-80, sec. 1980-81, v.p. 1981-82, pres.-elect 1982-83, pres. 1983-84), Pitts. Psychiat. Soc. (councilor 1974-76, sec. 1977-78, pres.-elect 1978-79, pres. 1979-80), Allegheny County Med. Soc. Home: 120 Daugherty Dr Monroeville PA 15146-2710 Office: 805 Jefferson Ave Natrona Heights PA 15065-2413

STANIAR, LINDA BURTON, insurance company executive; b. Glen Ridge, N.J., July 6, 1948; d. Harold Burton and Helen (Kintzing) Staniar; m. William Glasgow Bergh, Jan. 21, 1978; 1 child, Courtney Christian Bergh. BA, Briarcliff Coll., 1970; MA, NYU, 1974. Pub. rels. asst. N.Y. Life Ins. Co., N.Y.C., 1977-78, pub. rels. assoc., 1978-80, dir., 1981-84, asst. v.p., 1984-86, corp. v.p., 1986-88, v.p. pub. rels. and advt., 1988-93, v.p. corp. comms., 1993-96, sr. v.p. corp. comm., 1996—. Mem. Advt. Women of N.Y., PRSA and YWCA Acad. of Women Achieves. Office: NY Life Ins Co 51 Madison Ave New York NY 10010-1603

STANISCI, THOMAS WILLIAM, lawyer; b. Bkln., Nov. 16, 1928; s. Vito and Angela Marie (Martino) S.; m. Catherine Ellen Cullen, June 4, 1955; children: Thomas, Marianne, Ellen, William, Peter. BA, St. John's Coll. Men, 1949, JD, 1953, postgrad., 1954. Bar: N.Y. 1953, U.S. Dist. Ct. (so. and ea. dists.) N.Y. 1956, U.S. Supreme Ct., 1981; diplomate Am. Bd. Profl. Liability Attys. (trustee). Assoc. Diblasi Marasco & Simone, White Plains, N.Y., 1954-60; mem. Simone Brant & Stanisci, White Plains, 1960-66, Shayne Dachs Stanisci & Harwood, Mineola, N.Y., 1966-83; sr. mem. Shayne Dachs Stanisci Corker & Sauer, Mineola, 1983—; lectr. Practising Law Inst., 1975-79; instr., lectr. Am. Mgmt. Assn., 1976-77, N.Y. State Bar Assn., 1993, 94; guest lectr. Adelphi U., Hofstra U., 1975-79; guest speaker, panelist network and local TV programs. Contbr. articles in field. With U.S. Army, 1950-52. Mem. ATLA, Am. Arbitration Assn., Am. Bd. Trial Advs., Nassau Suffolk Trial Lawyers Assn. (bd. dirs. 1978-90, treas. 1991, sec. 1992, vice chmn. 1993-94, chmn. 1995—), Nassau County Bar Assn. (bd. dirs. 1993-96, lectr. acad. law), Columbian Lawyers. Office: 250 Old Country Rd Mineola NY 11501-4253

STANISLAO, JOSEPH, consulting engineer, educator; b. Manchester, Conn., Nov. 21, 1928; s. Eduardo and Rose (Zaccaro) S.; m. Bettie Chloe Carter, Sept. 6, 1960. BS, Tex. Tech. U., 1957; MS, Pa. State U., 1959; Eng.ScD, Columbia U., 1970. Registered profl. engr., Mass., Mont. Asst. engr. Naval Ordnance Research, University Park, Pa., 1958-59; asst. prof. N.C. State U., Raleigh, 1959-61; dir. research Darlington Fabrics Corp., Pawtucket, R.I., 1961-62; from asst. prof. to prof. U. R.I., Kingston, 1962-71; prof., chmn. dept. Cleve. State U., 1971-75; prof., dean N.D. State U., Fargo, 1975-94, acting v.p. agrl. affairs, 1983-85, asst. to pres., 1983—; dir. Engrng. Computer Ctr. N.D. State U., 1984—; prof. emeritus indsl. engring. and mgmt. N.D. State U., Fargo, 1994—; pres. XOX Corp., 1984-90; chmn. bd., chief exec. officer ATSCO, 1989-94, chief engr., 1993—; prof. emeritus N.D. State U., 1994; adj. prof. Mont. State U., 1994—, dir. indsl. and mgmt. engrng. program, 1996—, mfg. rsch., sponsored by Nat. Sci. Found. 1997—. Contbr. chpts. to books, articles to profl. jours.; patentee pump apparatus, pump fluid housing. Served to sgt. USMC, 1948-51. Recipient Sigma Xi award, 1968; Order of the Iron Ring award N.D. State U., 1972, Econ. Devel. award, 1991; USAF recognition award, 1979, ROTC appreciation award, 1982. Mem. Am. Inst. Indsl. Engrs. (sr.; v.p. 1964-65), ASME, Am. Soc. Engrng. Edn. (campus coord. 1979-81), Acad. Indsl. Engrs. Tex. Tech U., Lions, Elks, Am. Legion, Phi Kappa Phi, Tau Beta Pi (advisor 1978-79). Roman Catholic. Home: 8 Park Plaza Dr Bozeman MT 59715-9343

STANKEY, SUZANNE M., editor; b. Grand Rapids, Mich., Apr. 4, 1951; d. Robert Michael and Elizabeth (Rogers) Stankey; m. Homer Brickey, Jr. B.A., Ohio U., Athens, 1973; B.J., U. Mo., Columbia, 1977. Editor Living Today, The Blade, Toledo, 1980-82, Toledo Mag., The Blade, 1982-92, Living Today, Toledo, 1992—. Mem. Toledo Press Club, Toledo Sailing Club, Toledo Rowing Club. Home: 2510 Kenwood Blvd Toledo OH 43606-3601 Office: The Blade 541 N Superior St Toledo OH 43660-1000

STANKIEWICZ, WLADYSLAW JOZEF, political philosopher, educator; b. Warsaw, Poland, May 6, 1922; s. Jozef Edmund and Helena Kamilla (Pawlowicz) S. M.A., U. St. Andrews, Scotland, 1944; Ph.D., London Sch. Econs. and Polit. Sci., 1952. Lectr. Polish U. Coll., London, 1947-52; research asso. Mid-European Studies Center, N.Y.C., 1952-54; vis. postdoctoral fellow Princeton U., 1954-55; economist Govt. of Ont., Can., 1956-57; mem. faculty U. B.C., Vancouver, 1957-87; prof. polit. sci. U. B.C., 1965-87, prof. emeritus, 1987—; lectr. in over 60 univs. in, Europe, N.Z., Australia, Africa, and Asia. Author numerous books, 1955—, latest being Canada-U.S. Relations and Canadian Foreign Policy, 1973, Aspects of Political Theory: Classical Concepts in an Age of Relativism, 1976, Approaches to Democracy, 1980, Am. edit., 1981, In Search of a Political Philosophy: Ideologies at the Close of the Twentieth Century, 1993, Jottings: Thoughts & Aphorisms, 1995; editor books, 1964—, latest being In Defense of Sovereignty, 1969, British Government in an Era of Reform, 1976, The Tradition of Polish Ideals, 1981. Served with Polish Army, 1940-46. Fellow Can. Council, 1968-69, 74-75; Social Scis. and Humanities Research Council Can., 1979-80; I.W. Killam Sr. fellow, 1969-70, 71-72, 77-78. Mem. Am. Soc. Polit. and Legal Philosophy, Am. Polit. Sci. Assn. Office: Univ BC, Dept Polit Sci, Vancouver, BC Canada V6T 1Z1 *I think it is important to believe in a hierarchy of values; to eschew what is merely practical or popular; to shape one's thoughts into a coherent system of ideas reflecting a Weltanschauung; to pursue long-range goals; not to commit oneself to secondary objectives; to see a project through all its stages; to avoid the distinction between working and living; to preserve a sense of the joy of life.*

STANLEY, ARTHUR JEHU, JR., federal judge; b. nr. Lincoln, Kans., Mar. 21, 1901; s. Arthur and Bessie (Anderson) S.; m. Ruth Willis, July 16, 1927; children: Mary Louise Stanley Andrews, Carolyn Stanley Lane, Constance Stanley Yunghans, Susan Stanley Hoffman. LL.B., Kansas City Sch. Law (U. Mo.), Kansas City, 1928. Bar: Kans. bar 1928. County atty. Wyandotte County, Kans., 1935-41; U.S. dist. judge Dist. of Kans., Leavenworth, 1958-71; chief judge Dist. of Kans., 1961-71, sr. U.S. dist. judge, 1971—; mem. Jud. Conf. U.S., 1967-70, chmn. com. on operation jury system, 1973-78, mem. bicentennial com., 1975-78. Mem. Kans. Senate, 1941. Served with 7th U.S. Cav. Can. Army, World War I; with USN, 1921-25; Yangtze Patrol Force 1923-25; 9th Air Force USAAF, 1941-45; disch. to Inf. Res. as lt. col. Fellow Am. Bar Found.; mem. ABA, Kans. Bar Assn., Wyandotte County Bar Assn. (past pres.), Leavenworth County Bar Assn., Am. Judicature Soc., Kans. Hist. Soc. (pres. 1974-75), Am. Legion. Anglican. Home: 501 N Esplanade St Leavenworth KS 66048-2027 Office: US Dist Ct 235 Fed Bldg Leavenworth KS 66048 *My goal in life has been to have and deserve the affection of my family and the respect of my professional colleagues.*

STANLEY, BOB, artist; b. Yonkers, N.Y., Jan. 3, 1932; s. Robert and Margaret (Druitz) S.; m. Marylin Herzka, 1970. B.A., Oglethorpe U., 1953; postgrad., Columbia U., 1953, Bklyn. Mus. Art Sch., 1954-56. faculty Sch. Visual Arts, N.Y.C., 1970-72, 84—; vis. artist La. State U., 1976, Syracuse U., 1978, Princeton U., 1979-80, St. Lawrence U., Canton, N.Y., 1978, New Arts Program, Kutztown, Pa., 1984. One man exhbns. include Bianchini Gallery, N.Y.C., 1965, 66, Internat. Gallery Orez, The Hague, Holland, 1966, Contemporary Art Center, Cin., 1966, Galerie Ricke, Kassel, Germany, 1966, 67, Gegenverkehr, Aachen, Germany, 1969, On 1st, N.Y.C., 1969, Warren Benedek Gallery, 1972, N.Y. Cultural Center, 1974, La. State U. Union Gallery, Baton Rouge, 1976, Hal Bromm Gallery, N.Y.C. & Elizabeth Weiner Gallery, 1978, 80, Bucklew Goehring Gallery, Tampa, Fla., 1983, Centre d'Art Contemporain, Dijon, France, 1986, John Davis Gallery, N.Y.C., 1986, 87, Galerie G. Lavrov, Paris, 1987, 88, Gallerie Bébert, Rotterdam, The Netherlands, 1989, The Painted Bride Gallery, Phila., 1990, The Greenville County (S.C.) Art Mus., 1991, Barbierato Arte Contemporanea, Asiago, Italy, 1992, Moderne Künst Dietmar Werle, Köln, Germany, 1992, Conde Gallery, N.Y.C., 1996; retrospective exhibit at Holly Keenberg-Contemporary Art, Winnipeg, Man., Can., 1980; group exhbns. include 2 man show, P.S.I. Long Island City, 1977, Antisensitivity Show, Ohio U., 1964, Pop and Circumstance, Four Seasons, N.Y.C., 1965, Contemporary Americans, Art Inst. Chgo., 1965, John G. Powers Collection, Larry Aldrich Mus., Ridgefield, Conn., 1966, Hanford Yang Collection, Larry Aldrich Mus., Ridgefield, 1968, 29th Ann., Art Inst. Chgo., 1969, Aspects of a New Realism, Milw. Art Center, 1969, Ann. Exhbn, Whitney Mus. Am. Art, N.Y.C., 1967, 69, 72, 73, 17th, Nat. Print Exhbn, Bklyn. Mus., 1970, Monumental Art, Contemporary Arts Center, Cin., 1970, Recent Aquisitions, Washington U. Mus., St. Louis, 1967, Obsessive Image, Inst. Contemporary Art, London, Eng., 1968, Documenta 68, Kassel, Germany, Another Aspect of Pop, P.S.I. Long Island City, 1978, Milw. Art Center, 1969, Corcoran Gallery Art, 1980, Parrish Art Mus., Southampton, N.Y., 1980, Des Moines Art Center, 1980, Krannert Art Mus., Champaign-Urbana, Ill., 1980, William Paterson Coll., Wayne, N.J., 1980, Worcester Art Mus., Mass., 1981, Orozco Gallery, Mexico City, 1981, Am. Acad. and Inst. Arts and Letters, 1982, Daniel Wolf Gallery, N.Y.C., 1982, Ft. Worth Art Mus., 1984, Harcus Gallery, Boston, 1984, Fuji I, Tokyo, 1985, U. R.I. Fine Arts Ctr., 1985, Art Mus. Princeton, N.J., 1985, White Columns, N.Y.C., 1987, Lyman Allyn Mus., New London, Conn., 1987, High Mus. Art, Atlanta, 1988, Lehigh U., Bethlehem, 1988, Nelson-Atkins Mus. Art, Kansas City, 1989, Contemporary Arts Ctr., Cin., 1990, Centro Cultural La Gerneral Granada, Spain, 1990, Greenville County Mus. Art., 1995, Shardin Art Gallery, Kutztown (Pa.) U., 1996, numerous others. Recipient Casandra Found. award, 1969, Igor Found. award, 1987. Address: 95 Vandam St Apt 2R New York NY 10013-1020

STANLEY, DANIEL JEAN, geological oceanographer, senior scientist; b. Metz, France, Apr. 14, 1934; came to U.S., 1941, naturalized, 1946; s. Paul Emile and Madeleine (Simon) Streisguth; m. Adrienne N. Ellis, Mar. 5, 1988; children: Marc Michel, Eric Paul, Brian, Natalie Anne, Susan. B.Sc., Cornell U., 1956; M.Sc., Brown U., 1958; D.Sc., U. Grenoble, France, 1961. Rsch. geologist French Petroleum Inst., Paris, 1958-61; asst. to dir. U.S. Waterways Expt. Sta., Vicksburg, Miss., 1961-63; asst. prof. geology Ottawa U., Ont., Can., 1963-64; rsch. assoc. prof. Dalhousie U., Halifax, N.S., Can., 1964-66; sr. scientist, oceanographer, dir. Deltas-Global Change Program div. sedimentology Smithsonian Instn., Washington, 1966—; adj. prof. U. Québec, 1992—; cons. to govts. Mediterranean countries; sci. expert Internat. Ct. Justice, 1981—; curator Smithsonian Instn., Washington. Editor: New Concepts of Continental Margin Sedimentation, 1969, Mediterranean Sea: A Natural Sedimentation Laboratory, 1972, Marine Sediment Transport and Environmental Management, 1976, Sedimentation in Submarine Canyons, Fans and Trenches, 1978, The Shelfbreak: A Critical Interface on Continental Margins, 1983, Geological Evolution of the Mediterranean Basin, 1985; contbr. chpts to books, articles to profl. jours. Bd. dirs. Mediterranean Basin and Deltas Programs. Served to capt. C.E., U.S. Army, 1961-63. Recipient médaille Alpes Maritimes, France, 1976, F.P. Shepard medal Soc. for Sedimentary Geology, 1990; named Hon. Prof., East China U., 1995; grantee in field. Fellow Geol. Soc. Am., AAAS, Geol. Soc. Belgium; mem. Internat. Assn. Sedimentologists, Am. Assn. Petroleum Geologists, Soc. Econ. Paleontologists and Mineralogists, Geol. Soc. Washington, Sigma Xi. Republican. Club: Cosmos (Washington). Office: Smithsonian Instn Sedimentology Dv Washington DC 20560

STANLEY, DAVID, retail company executive; b. Kansas City, Mo., 1935; married. Grad., U. Wis., 1955; LLB, Columbia U., 1957. Assoc. Paul, Weiss, Rifkind, Wharton & Garrison, N.Y.C., 1957-60; assoc. Faegre & Benson, Mpls., 1960-64, ptnr., 1964-71; exec. v.p. Piper, Jaffray & Hopwood, Mpls., 1971-80; pres. Payless Cashways, Inc., Kansas City, 1980-86, CEO, 1982—, chmn., 1985—, also bd. dirs.; bd. dirs. Local Initiatives, Support Corp., Nat. Equity Fund, Inc., Piper Jaffray Cos., Inc., Best Buy Co., Inc.,

DIGI Internat., Inc. Bd. dirs. Dole Found. Office: Payless Cashways Inc PO Box 419466 2300 Main St Kansas City MO 64108-2415

STANLEY, EDWARD ALEXANDER, geologist, forensic scientist, technical and academic administrator; b. N.Y.C., Apr. 7, 1929; s. Frank and Elizabeth (Wolf) S.; m. Elizabeth Ann Allison, June 7, 1958; children: Karen (dec.), Scott. B.S., Rutgers U., 1954; M.S., Pa. State U., 1956, Ph.D., 1960. Geologist, Amoco Petroleum Co., Tulsa, 1960-62; prof. U. Del., 1962-64, U. Ga., 1964-77; assoc. dean rsch., chmn. geology dept. Indiana (Pa.) U. , 1977-81; supr. Phillips Petroleum Co., Bartlesville, Okla., 1981-86, dir., comdg. officer N.Y.C. Police Dept. Crime Lab., 1986-94, cons. geology, forensic sci., microscopy 1994—; cons. geology, Athens, Ga., 1963-77, Indiana, Pa., 1977-81. Contbr. articles to profl. jours. Served to sgt. USAF, 1947-50. NSF grantee 1965-68, 74, Office Water Resources Rsch. grantee, 1965-68; NAS exch. prof. Soviet Union, 1968-69, 73; invited guest Moscow Forensic Labs., 1990; invited speaker FBI Internat. Symposium on Forensic Trace Evidence, 1991. Fellow AAAS, Geol. Soc. Am., Royal Microscopical Soc.; mem. Am. Assn. Petroleum Geologists, Am. Acad. of Forensic Sci., Am. Soc. Crime Lab Dirs., Internat. Assn. for Identification, , Am. Assn. Stratigraphic Palyologists, N.Y. Microscopical Soc., Sigma Xi. Presbyterian. Avocations: photography, music, firearms. Home: 2004 Haverford Rd Ardmore PA 19003-3010

STANLEY, ELAINE GERBER, government official. BAS in Polit. Sci., Goucher Coll., Balt., 1970; M in Environ. Planning, U. N.C., 1972. With various state and local environ. planning agys.; with EPA, 1978-88; with enforcement and superfund programs Resource Conservation and Recovery Act; dep. dir. Office Waste Programs Enforcement Office Solid Waste and Emergency Response, 1988-94; dir. Office Enforcement & Compliance Assurance, Office Compliance, Washington, 1994—. Office: Office Enforcement & Compliance Assurance 401 M St SW Washington DC 20460-0001

STANLEY, ELLEN MAY, historian, consultant; b. Dighton, Kans., Feb. 3, 1921; d. Delmar Orange and Lena May (Bobb) Durr; m. Max Neal Stanley, Nov. 5, 1939; children: Ann Y. Stanley Epps, Janet M. Stanley Horsky, Gail L. Stanley Peck, Kenneth D., Neal M., Mary E. Stanley McEniry. BA in English and Journalism, Ft. Hays (Kans.) State U., 1972, MA in History, 1984. Pvt. practice local/state historian, cons., writer local history Dighton, 1973—, cons. genealogy, 1980—; vice chmn. State Preservation Bd. Rev., Kans., 1980-87; area rep. Kans. State Mus. Assn., 1978-84. Author: Early Lane County History: 12,000 B.C.—A.D. 1884, 1993 (cert. of commendation Am. Assn. State and Local History), Cowboy Josh: Adventures of a Real Cowboy, 1996; contbr. articles to profl. jours. Precinct woman com. Alamota Township, Kans., 1962-86; mem. Dem. State Affirmative Action Com., 1975. Recipient hon. mention for photography Ann. Christian Arts Festival, 1974, Artist of Month award Dane G. Hansen Mus., 1975. Mem. Kans. State Hist. Soc. (pres. 1990-91), Lane County Hist. Soc. (sec. 1970-78). Methodist. Avocations: fossil hunting, walking, photography, antiques. Home: 100 N 4th Dighton KS 67839 Office: 116 E Long St Dighton KS 67839

STANLEY, H(ARRY) EUGENE, physicist, educator; b. Norman, Okla., Mar. 28, 1941; s. Harry Eugene and Ruth S.; m. Idahlia Dessauer, June 2, 1967; children: Jannah, Michael, Rachel. BA in Physics (Nat. Merit scholar), Wesleyan U., 1962; postgrad. (Fulbright scholar), U. Cologne, W. Ger., 1962-63; PhD in Physics, Harvard U., 1967; PhD (hon.), Bar-Ilan U., Ramat-Gan, Israel, 1994, Roland Eötvös U., Budapest, Hungary, 1997. NSF predoctoral rsch. fellow Harvard U., 1963-67; mem. staff Lincoln Lab MIT, 1967-68, asst. prof. physics, 1969-71, assoc. prof., 1971-73; Miller rsch. fellow U. Calif., Berkeley, 1968-69; Hermann von Helmholtz assoc. prof. health scis. and tech. Harvard U.-MIT Program in Health Scis. and Tech., 1973-76; vis. prof. Osaka (Japan) U., 1975; univ. prof., prof. physics, prof. physiology Sch. Medicine, dir. Ctr. Polymer Studies Boston U., 1976—; Joliot-Curie vis. prof. Ecole Superieure de Physique et Chimie, Paris, 1979; vis. prof. Peking U., 1981, Seoul Nat. U., 1982, 30th Ann. Saha Meml. Lecture, 1992; dir. NATO Advanced Study Inst., Cargese, Corisca, 1985, 88, 90; dir. IUPAP Internat. Conf. on Thermodynamics and Statis. Mechanics, 1986; dir. Enrico Fermi Sch., Varenna, Italy, 1996; cons. Sandia Nat. Lab., 1983-94, Dowell Schlumberger Co., 1982-92, Elscint Co., 1983-85; nat. co-chmn. Com. of Concerned Scientists, 1974-76. Author: Introduction to Phase Transitions and Critical Phenomena, 1971, From Newton to Mandelbrot: A Primer in Theoretical Physics, 1990, Fractal Forms, 1991, Fractal Concepts in Surface Growth, 1995; editor: Biomedical Physics and Biomaterials Science, 1972, Cooperative Phenomena Near Phase Transitions, 1973, On Growth and Form: Fractal and Non-Fractal Patterns in Physics, 1985, Statistical Physics, 1986, Random Fluctuation and Pattern Growth, 1988, Correlations and Connectivity: Geometric Aspects of Physics, Chemistry and Biology, 1990, Fractals in Science, 1994, Disordered Materials and Interfaces, 1996, Physics of Complex Systems, 1997; assoc. editor Phys. A., 1988-91, editor, 1991—. Recipient Choice award Am. Assn. Book Pubs., 1972, Macdonald award, 1986, Venture Rsch. award British Petroleum, 1989, Mass. Prof. of Yr. award Coun. Advancement and Support of Edn., 1992, Floyd K. Richtmyer prize, 1997; John Simon Guggenheim Meml. fellow, 1979-80. Fellow AAAS, Am. Phys. Soc. (chmn. New Eng. sect. 1982-83); mem. Non-Linear Sci. Panel of Nat. Acad. Sci., Hungarian Phys. Soc. (hon.). Home: 50 Metacomet Rd Newton MA 02168-1465 Office: Boston U Ctr for Polymer Studies Boston MA 02215 *The greatest joy of my professional life is to share in the excitement of learning something new—however minor—about the workings of Nature. The greatest joy of my personal life is to be able to imagine that I've done my very best to meet the needs of my family and my co-workers. The greatest obstacle to happiness is the persistent feeling that it is impossible to find that tortuous path whereby both joys may occasionally be experienced.*

STANLEY, HUGH MONROE, JR., lawyer; b. Ft. Lewis, Wash., Oct. 25, 1944; s. Hugh Monroe Sr. and Rita (McHugh) S.; m. Patricia Page, Aug. 17, 1968; children: Allison Michelle, Matthew Monroe, Trevor Marshall. BA magna cum laude, U. Dayton, 1966; JD, Georgetown U., 1969. Bar: Ohio 1969, U.S. Ct. Appeals (6th cir.) 1983, U.S. Supreme Ct. 1979. Assoc. Arter & Hadden, Cleve., 1969-76, ptnr., 1976—, chmn. litigation dept., 1983-96. Staff editor Georgetown Law Jour., bd. editors. Fellow Am. Bar Found., Bar Assn. Greater Cleve., Am. Coll. Trial Lawyers, Internat. Acad. Trial Lawyers, Internat. Soc. Barristers, Nat. Assn. R.R. Trial Counsel; mem. ABA, Fed. Bar Assn., Def. Rsch. Inst., Cleve. Assn. Civil Trial Attys., Ohio Assn. Civil Trial Attys. Republican. Roman Catholic. Avocation: reading. Office: Arter & Hadden 1100 Huntington Bldg 925 Euclid Ave Cleveland OH 44115

STANLEY, JAMES PAUL, printing company executive; b. Montreal, Que., Can., Aug. 15, 1915; s. Paul Garton and Florence May (Tooke) S.; m. Anne Seymour Raynsford ; children—Marie, Susan, James, Sarah. B.Engring., McGill U., Montreal, 1938. Staff engr. Stevenson, Kellogg Ltd., 1938-41; plant mgr. Dow Brewery Ltd., 1947-53; v.p., then pres. Ronalds-Federated Ltd., Montreal, 1954-77; chmn. bd., chief exec. officer Ronalds-Federated Ltd., 1977-80. Gov. Montreal Gen. Hosp. Served with RCAF, 1941-46. Fellow Graphic Arts Tech. Found. Mem. Ch. of Eng. Clubs: St. James's. Home: 799 Wartman Ave, Kingston, ON Canada K7M 4M3

STANLEY, JANICE FAYE, special education educator; b. Montgomery, Ala., Nov. 21, 1953; d. Holley Moring and Miriam Elizabeth (Long) S. BS in Edn., Auburn U., 1977, EdS, 1992; M of Spl. Edn., Troy State U., 1982. Spl. edn. tchr. Fews Elem. Sch., Montgomery, 1977-79, Vaughn Rd. Elem. Sch., Montgomery, 1979-81, Dunbar Elem. Sch., Montgomery, 1981-91, Catoma Elem. Sch., Montgomery, 1991-95, Chisholm Elem. Sch., 1995—. Edn. mgr. Civitan Club, Montgomery, 1992-93, bd. dirs., 1992—, sec. edn. meeting, 1996—. Mem. Kappa Delta Pi. Methodist. Avocations: reading, swimming, attending plays. Home: 8500 English Oak Loop Montgomery AL 36117-6822 Office: Chisholm Elem Sch 307 E Vandiver Blvd Montgomery AL 36110-1815

STANLEY, JULIAN CECIL, JR., psychology educator; b. Macon, Ga., July 9, 1918; s. Julian Cecil and Ethel (Cheney) S.; m. Rose Roberta Sanders, Aug. 18, 1946 (dec. Nov. 1978); 1 child, Susan Roberta Willhoft; m. Barbara Sprague Kerr, Jan. 1, 1980. B.S., Ga. So. U., 1937; Ed.M., Harvard U., 1946, Ed.D., 1950; D of Ednl. Excellence (hon.), U. North Tex., 1990; hon. doctorate, State U. of West Ga., 1997. Tchr. Fulton and West Fulton high schs., Atlanta, 1937-42; instr. psychology Newton (Mass.) Jr. Coll., 1946-48; instr. edn. Harvard U., 1948-49; asso. prof. ednl. psychology George Peabody Coll. Tchrs., 1949-53; assoc. prof. edn., 1953-57, prof. edn., 1957-62, prof. ednl. psychology, 1962-67, chmn. dept., 1962-63; dir. lab. exptl. design U. Wis., Madison, 1961-67; prof. edn. and psychology Johns Hopkins U., 1967-71, prof. psychology, 1971—, dir. study mathematically precocious youth, 1971—; mem. rsch. adv. coun. Coop. Rsch. Br., U.S. Office Edn., 1962-64; mem. com. examiners for aptitude tests Coll. Entrance Exam. Bd., 1961-65, chmn., 1965-68; mem. rsch. com. Ednl. Testing Svc., 1962-67; fellow Social Sci. Rsch. Coun. Inst. Math. for Social Scientists, U. Mich., summer 1955; postdoctoral fellow statistics U. Chgo., 1955-56; Fulbright rsch. scholar U. Louvain, Belgium, 1958-59; Fulbright lectr. New Zealand and Australia, 1974; cons. U. Western Australia, 1980; fellow Ctr. for Advanced Study in Behavioral Sci., 1965-67, vis. scholar, 1983; hon. prof. Shanghai (People's Republic of China) Tchrs. U.; disting. tchr. Commn. on Presdl. Scholars, 1987, 92; disting. vis. prof. U. Ga., 1947, U. Hawaii, 1960, Harvard U., 1963, U. North Tex., 1990, U. NSW, Australia, 1992; mem. adv. bd. Tex. Acad. Maths. and Sci., 1988—; trustee Ctr. for Excellence in Edn., 1989-93. Author: Measurement in Today's Schools, 4th edit., 1964, (with D.T. Campbell) Experimental and Quasi-Experimental Designs for Research, 1963, 66, (with Gene V. Glass) Statistical Methods in Education and Psychology, 1970, (with K.D. and B. Hopkins) Educational and Psychological Measurement and Evaluation, 3d edit., 1990, (with K.D. Hopkins, G.H. Bracht) Perspectives in Educational and Psychological Measurement, 1972; editor: Improving Experimental Design and Statistical Analysis, 1967, Preschool Programs for the Disadvantaged, 1972, Compensatory Education for Children, Ages 2-8, 1973, (with D.P. Keating, L.H. Fox) Mathematical Talent: Discovery, Description, and Development, 1974, (with W.C. George, C.H. Solano) The Gifted and the Creative: A Fifty-Year Perspective, 1977, Educational Programs and Intellectual Prodigies, 1978, (with W.C. George, S.J. Cohn) Educating the Gifted: Acceleration and Enrichment, 1979, (with C.P. Benbow) Academic Precocity: Aspects of Its Development, 1983; adv. editor jours. Served with USAAC, 1942-45. Julian C. Stanley chair in ednl. psychology created U. Wis., Madison, 1995. Fellow APA (pres. div. ednl. psychology 1965-66, div. evaluation and measurement 1972-73, Thorndike award for disting. psychol. contbns. to edn. 1978, divsn. evaluation and measurement Lifetime Contbn. award 1997), AAAS, Am. Statis. Assn., Am. Psychol. Soc. (J. McKeen Cattell award 1994); mem. Nat. Council Measurement Edn. (pres. 1963-64), Am. Ednl. Research Assn. (pres. 1966-67, award for disting. contbns. to research in edn. 1980), Nat. Assn. for Gifted Children (2d v.p. 1977-79, Disting. Scholar award 1982), AAUP (past pres. chpt.), Psychometric Soc. (past dir.), AAUP (past chpt. pres.), Tenn. Psychol. Assn. (past pres.), Nat. Acad. Edn., Phi Beta Kappa (past chpt. pres.), Phi Beta Kappa Assocs., Sigma Xi, Phi Delta Kappa. Office: Johns Hopkins U 351 Bloomberg Ctr Baltimore MD 21218-2686 *I am deeply indebted for my graduate education to the G.I. Bill following World War II.*

STANLEY, KAREN FRANCINE MARY LESNIEWSKI, human resources professional; b. Amsterdam, N.Y., Oct. 10, 1948; d. Francis Raymond and Genievive Mary (Klementowski) Lesniewski; m. Mark Anthony Stanley, Nov. 11, 1972. BA, Alliance Coll., 1970; MA, The Coll. St. Rose, 1976, CAS, 1987. English tchr. Middle Country Sch., Centereach, N.Y., 1970-71; English and social studies tchr. Mt. Carmel, Gloversville, N.Y., 1971-72; English tchr. Bishop Scully H.S., Amsterdam, 1972-80, Shenendehowa Ctrl., Clifton Park, N.Y., 1980-82; English tchr., head dept. Broadalbin (N.Y.) Ctrl. Sch., 1982-86; adminstrv. intern Saratoga Springs (N.Y.) City Sch. Dist., 1986-87, dir. for human resource svcs., 1987—; bd. dirs. N.Y. State Staff Devel. Coun., 1990-92. Mem. Am. Soc. for Human Resource Mgrs., N.Y. State Assn. Women Adminstrs., Nat. Assn. Schs., Colls. and Univs., Nat. Assn. Ednl. Negotiators, Soroptimist Internat. (sec. Saratoga County chpt. 1991-92, del. Dist. I 1992-93, 96-97, asst. treas. 1994-95, treas. 1995-96, del. 1996—), Ednl. Adminstrn. Assn./Coll. St. Rose (bd. dirs., sec. 1986-89, pres. 1989-92). Republican. Roman Catholic. Avocations: gardening, reading, sailing, golf. Office: Saratoga Springs City Schs 5 Wells St Saratoga Springs NY 12866-1205

STANLEY, MARGARET KING, performing arts administrator; b. San Antonio, Tex., Dec. 11, 1929; d. Creston Alexander and Margaret (Haymore) King; children: Torrey Margaret, Jean Cullen. Student, Mary Baldwin Coll., 1948-50; BA, U. Tex., Austin, 1952; MA, Incarnate Word Coll., 1959. Tchg. cert. 1953. Elem. tchr. San Antonio Ind. Sch. Dist., 1953-54, 55-56, Arlington County Schs., Va., 1954-55, Ft. Sam Houston Schs., San Antonio, 1955-57; art, art history tchr. St. Pius X Sch., San Antonio, 1959-60; English tchr. Trinity U., 1963-65; designer-mfr., owner CrisStan Clothes, Inc., San Antonio, 1967-73; founder, exec. dir. San Antonio Performing Arts Assn., 1976-92, founder Arts Council of San Antonio, 1962; founding chmn. Joffrey Workshop, San Antonio, 1979; originator, founding chairwoman Student Music Fair, San Antonio, 1963; radio program host On Stage, San Antonio, 1983—. Originator of the idea for a new ballet created for the City of San Antonio, "Jamboree," commd. from the Joffrey Ballet, world premiere in San Antonio, 1984. Pres. San Antonio Symphony League, 1971-74; v.p. Arts Council of San Antonio, 1975; bd. govs. Artists Alliance of San Antonio, 1982; v.p. San Antonio Opera Guild, 1974-76, founder Early Music Festival, San Antonio, 1990-92; mem. adv. bd. Hertzberg Circus Mus. Recipient Outstanding Tchr. award Arlington County Sch. Dist., 1954, Today's Woman award San Antonio Light Newspaper, 1980, Woman of Yr. in Arts award San Antonio Express News, 1983, Emily Smith award for outstanding alumni Mary Baldwin Coll., 1973, Erasmus medal The Dutch Consulate, 1992, Mary Baldwin Sesquicentennial medallion, 1992; named to Women's Hall of Fame, San Antonio, 1984, Disting. Alumnae, St. Mary's Hall, 1995; teaching fellow Trinity U., San Antonio, 1964-66. Mem. Internat. Soc. for the Performing Arts (regional rep. 1982-85, bd. dirs. 1991-97), Met. Opera Nat. Coun., Assn. Performing Arts Presenters, Women in Comm. (Headliner award 1982, San Antonio chpt.), Jr. League of San Antonio, Battle of Flowers Assn., S.W. Performing Arts Presenters (chmn. 1988-92). Avocations: traveling, reading.

STANLEY, PETER WILLIAM, academic administrator; b. Bronxville, N.Y., Feb. 17, 1940; s. Arnold and Mildred Jeanette (Pattison) S.; m. Joan Olivia Hersey, Sept. 14, 1963 (div. 1978); m. Mary-Jane Cullen Cosgrove, Sept. 2, 1978; 1 dau., Laura. B.A. magna cum laude, Harvard U., 1962, M.A., 1964, Ph.D., 1970; LHD (hon.), Occidental Coll., 1994. Asst. prof. history U. Ill., Chgo., 1970-72; asst. prof. history Harvard U., 1972-78, lectr. history, 1978-79; dean of coll. Carleton Coll., Northfield, Minn., 1979-84; program officer in charge edn. and culture program Ford Found., 1984-87, dir. edn. and culture program, 1987-91; pres. Pomona Coll., Claremont, Calif., 1991—; lectr. Fgn. Service Inst., Arlington, Va., 1977-89. Author: A Nation in the Making: The Philippines and the United States, 1974; co-author: Sentimental Imperialists: The American Experience in East Asia, 1981; editor, contbr.: Reappraising an Empire: New Perspectives on Philippine-American History, 1984; contbr. numerous articles to scholastic jours., 1966—. Trustee The Coll. Bd., 1991—, vice chair, 1993-94, chair, 1994-96; dir. The James Irvine Found., 1997—, The Hitachi Found., 1993—, Assn. Am. Colls. and Univs., 1995—; bd. fellows Claremont U. Ctr., 1991—; active humanities and scis. coun. Stanford U., 1986—; nat. adv. coun. Nat. Fgn. Lang. Ctr., 1992—; mem. exec. com. Consortium Financing Higher Edn., 1992—; bd. dirs. Nat. Assn. Latino Elected Ofcls. Edn. Fund, Commn. on Internat. Edn., Am. Coun. Edn., 1992-95. Fellow Charles Warren Ctr. for Studies in Am. History-Harvard U., 1975-76; Frank Knox Meml. fellow Harvard U., 1962-63. Mem. Am. Hist. Assn., Assn. Asian Studies, Coun. on Fgn. Rels., Phi Beta Kappa. Home: 345 N College Ave Claremont CA 91711-4408 Office: Pomona Coll Pres Office Claremont CA 91711-6301

STANLEY, RALPH, bluegrass musician; b. Stratton, Va., Feb. 25, 1927. Founder (with Carter Stanley) band, Stanley Bros. and Clinch Mountain Boys, 1946; albums include: Old Country Church, Hills of Home, Old Home Place, The Stanley Sound Around The World, Plays Requests, A Man and His Music, I Want to Preach the Gospel, Cry From the Cross, Let Me Rest on Peaceful Mountain, Banjo in the Hills, Best of Bluegrass, Folk Song Festival, In Person, 1983, Collector's Edition Vols. 1-6, Long Journey Home, Rank Strangers, Together for the Last Time; appeared at Royal Albert Hall, London, 1966. Grammy nomination, Best Country Vocal Collaboration for Miner's Prayer" (with Dwight Yoakam), 1994. Office: Rebel Records PO Box 3057 Roanoke VA 24015-1057

STANLEY, RICHARD HOLT, consulting engineer; b. Muscatine, Iowa, Oct. 20, 1932; s. Claude Maxwell and Elizabeth Mabel (Holthues) S.; m. Mary Jo Kennedy, Dec. 20, 1953; children: Lynne Elizabeth, Sarah Catherine, Joseph Holt. BSEE and BSME, Iowa State U., 1955; MS in Sanitary Engring., U. Iowa, 1963. Lic. profl. engr., Iowa, other states. With Stanley Cons. Inc., Muscatine, Iowa, 1955—, pres., 1971-87, chmn., 1984—; also bd. dirs. Stanley Cons. Inc.; bd. dirs. Dover Resources, Inc., HON Industries, Inc., vice-chmn., 1979—; chmn. Nat. Constrn. Industry Coun., 1978, Com. Fed. Procurement Archtl.-Engring. Svcs., 1979; pres. Ea. Iowa C.C., Bettendorf, 1966-68; mem. indsl. adv. coun. Iowa State U. Coll. Engring., Ames, 1969—, chmn., 1979-81. Contbr. articles to profl. jours. BD. dirs. N.E.-Midwest Inst., 1989-95, treas., 1991-93, chmn., 1993-95; bd. dirs. Stanley Found., 1956—, pres., 1984—; bd. dirs. Muscatine Health Support Found., pres., 1984—; bd. dirs. Muscatine United Way, 1969-75, Iowa State U. Meml. Union, 1968-83, U. Dubuque, Iowa, 1977-93, Inst. Social and Econ. Devel., 1992-; bd. govs. Iowa State U. Achievement Found., 1982-96. Recipient Young Alumnus award Iowa State U. Alumni Assn., 1966, Disting. Svc. award Muscatine Jaycees, 1967, Profl. Achievement citation Coll. Engring., Iowa State U., 1977, Anson Marston medal Iowa State U., 1991; named Sr. Engr. of Yr., Joint Engring. Com. Quint Cities, 1973. Fellow ASCE, Am. Cons. Engrs. Coun. (pres. 1976-77), Iowa Acad. Sci.; mem. IEEE (sr.), ASME, Am. Soc. Engring. Edn., Nat. Soc. Profl. Engrs., Cons. Engrs. Coun. Iowa (pres. 1967), Iowa Engring. Soc. (pres. 1973-74, John Dunlap-Sherman Woodward award 1967, Disting. Svc. award 1980, Voice of Engr. award 1987, Herbert Hoover Centennial award 1989), Muscatine C. of C. (pres. 1972-73), C. of C. of U.S. (constrn. action coun. 1976-91), Tau Beta Pi, Phi Kappa Phi, Pi Tau Sigma, Eta Kappa Nu. Presbyterian (elder). Club: Rotary. Home: 601 W 3rd St Muscatine IA 52761-3119 Office: Stanley Cons Inc Stanley Bldg Muscatine IA 52761

STANLEY, ROBERT ANTHONY, artist, educator; b. Defuniac Springs, Fla., Mar. 10, 1942; m. Jane Tumosa, May 11, 1973; children: Daiva, Thomas, Daniel. BA cum laude, U. Dayton, 1964; MS, Pratt Inst., N.Y.C., 1969. Dir. art program Upward Bound project Earlham Coll., Richmond, Ind., 1967-68; lectr. art dept. U. Dayton, Ohio, 1967-68; asst. prof. art and humanities Harrisburg (Pa.) C.C., 1969-71; prof. art Oakton Coll., Des Plaines, Ill., 1971—; mem. com. League for Humanities Study Grant, Des Plaines, 1988-89; assoc. dir. Inst. for Environ. Response, N.Y.C., 1968-70; presenter League for Innovation Conf., 1994, Mid-Am. Art Conf., 1997. Author: Exploring the Film, 1968 (Maxi award 1969), (interactive multimedia) VisLang, 1994; contbr. articles to profl. jours.; shows include William Penn Mus., Harrisburg, Pa., New Horizons in Art Chgo., 1974, Internat. All on Paper, Buffalo, 1979, Zaner Gallery, Rochester, N.Y., 1983, Germanow Art Gallery, Rochester, 1985, Joy Horwich Gallery, Chgo., 1988, 95, U. Oreg., Portland, 1991, Atrium Gallery, N.Y.C., 1991, Shelter Gallery, Chgo., 1992, Matrix Gallery, Chgo., 1994, Ctr. for Visual and Performing Arts, Munster, Ind., 1994, Museé d'Art Contemporain, Chamalieres, France, 1994, 97. Vol. Ctr. of Concern, Park Ridge, Ill., 1993—; bd. dirs. Kloempken Prairie Restoration, Des Plaines, 1987-89. Grantee OCC Ednl. Found., 1989; recipient 2d Place Paragon award for video Nat. Coun. Cmty. Rels., 1985, 1st place Gold award for graphics Art Ctr. Show, Dayton Art Inst., 1969, award of merit Internat. Works on Paper, 1979. Mem. NEA, Ill. Higher Art Edn. Assn. (founding mem., bd. dirs. 1975-76, 83-84). Office: Joy Horwich Gallery 226 E Ontario St Chicago IL 60611

STANLEY, ROBERT MICHAEL, professional baseball player; b. Fort Lauderdale, Fla., June 25, 1963. Degree, U. Fla. With Tex. Rangers, 1987-91; catcher N.Y. Yankees, 1992-95; with Boston Red Sox, 1996—. Named to The Sporting News Am. League All-Star Team, 1993, The Sporting News Am. League Silver Slugger Team, 1993. Office: Boston Red Sox 4 Yawkey Way Boston MA 02215*

STANLEY, ROBERT WARREN, association executive; b. Washington, Oct. 26, 1941; s. Herbert Homer and Ida Virginia S. B.A., U. Md., 1963. Editorial asst. personnel services Washington Gas Light Co., 1963-68; asst. coordinator Project Interchange, NEA, Washington, 1968-70; advt. and promotions mgr., membership dir. Assn. Supervision and Curriculum Devel., Washington, 1970-71; exec. dir. Nat. Assn. Floor Covering Installers, Washington, 1971-74; exec. v.p. Nat. Glass Dealers Assn., Washington, 1974-82; v.p. Orgn. Mgmt. Services Internat., 1982-83; exec. dir. Nat. Assn. Dental Labs., 1983—; v.p., sec. Robwood Interiors/Desks etc., Leesburg, Va., 1991-94; v.p. Table Works Plus, Leesburg, 1994—; mem. nat. adv. coun. Am. Subcontractors Assn., 1974-82; bd. dirs. Glass and Metal Inst., 1974-82, Nat. Constrn. Employees Coun., 1975-82; chmn. Consumer Safety Glazing Com., 1974-75, sec.-treas., 1978-82; sec. Auto Glass Industry Com. Hwy. Safety, 1975-82; co-chmn. Constrn. Industry Nat. Legis. Conf., 1975-82; chmn. task force U.S. C. of C.-sponsored Insts. Orgn. Mgmt., 1978-79; bd. dirs., trustee advisor Am. Fund for Dental Health, 1983-95, bd. dirs. Oral Health Am., 1995—; advisor Nat. Found. for Dentistry for Handicapped, 1988—. Author booklets, articles in field. Served with USAR, 1965. Recipient cert. of merit Nat. Glass Dealers Assn., 1975, Spl. Leadership Achievement award Nat. Assn. Dental Labs., 1987, 88, Merit award , 1988. Mem. Am. Soc. Assn. Execs., Nat. Assn. Exposition Mgrs., Nat. Assn. Execs. Club, Greater Washington Soc. Assn. Execs., Found. for Internat. Meetings (founding mem., bd. dirs. 1972-76, exec. com. 1977-82). Democrat. Episcopalian. Clubs: Masons, Shriners. Home: 9303 Clanbrook Ct Fairfax VA 22031-1910 Office: 555 E Braddock Rd Alexandria VA 22314-2161

STANLEY, SCOTT, JR., editor; b. Kansas City, Kans., July 11, 1938; s. Winfield Scott and Irene Mae (Flint) S.; m. Janice Johns, Aug. 30, 1959 (div. July 1992); children: Leslie, Scott, Margaret; m. Cynthia Ward, Dec. 30, 1995. BA, Earlham Coll., 1960. Mng. editor Am. Opinion mag., Boston, 1961-85; editor Rev. of The News mag., Boston, 1965-85; editor-in-chief Conservative Digest, Washington, 1985-88, Am. Press Internat., Washington, 1987—; pres. USA Tech., 1991-92; mng. editor Nutrition and Healing, 1994—; dep. editor Insight on the News, Washington, 1995—; mem. nat. bd. dirs. Young Ams. for Freedom, 1960-62; public speaker and univ. lectr., 1962—. Keynote speaker Am. Party Nat. Conv., 1976; pres. Ams. Legal Def. Fund, 1977—; bd. govs. Council for Nat. Policy, 1981—; bd. dirs. Free Congress Polit. Action Com. Recipient award of merit Young Ams. for Freedom, Freedom award Nat. Congress for Freedom. Episcopalian. Clubs: Nat. Press, Meganset Yacht. Home: 1211 S Eads Arlington VA 22202

STANLEY, STEVEN MITCHELL, paleobiologist, educator; b. Detroit, Nov. 2, 1941; s. William Thomas and Mildred Elizabeth (Baker) S.; m. Nell Williams Gilmore, Oct. 11, 1969. AB with highest honors, Princeton U., 1963; PhD, Yale U., 1968. Asst. prof. U. Rochester, 1967-69; asst. prof. paleobiology Johns Hopkins U., 1969-71, assoc. prof., 1971-74, prof., 1974, chmn. dept. Earth and planetary Scis., 1987-88; assoc. in rsch. Smithsonian Instn., 1972—; mem. bd. earth scis. NRC, 1985—, vice chmn., 1988, mem. bd. earth scis. resources, 1988-88, com. on solid earth scis., exec. and steering com., 1988, com. on geoscis., environ, and resources, 1990—. Author: Relation of Shell Form to Life Habits in the Bivalvia, 1970, (with D.M. Raup) Principles of Paleontology, 1971, Macroevolution: Pattern and Process, 1979, The New Evolutionary Timetable: Fossils, Genes, and the Origin of species, 1981, Earth and Life Through Time, 1986, Extinction, 1987, Exploring Earth and Life Through Time, 1992, Children of the Ice Age: How a Global Catastrophe Allowed Humans to Evolve, 1996; mem. editl. bd. Am. Jour. Sci., 1975—, Paleobiology, 1975-82, 88—, Evolutionary Theory, 1973—. Recipient Outstanding Paper award Jour. Paleontology, 1968, Allan C. Davis medal Md. Acad. Scis., 1973, Outstanding Tech. Paper award Washington Geol. Soc., 1986; Guggenheim fellow, 1981. Fellow NAS, Am. Acad. Arts and Scis., Geol. Soc. Am. (chmn. Penrose com. 1978); mem. Paleontol. Soc. (councilor 1976-77, sr. councilor 1991-93, pres. 1993-94, Charles Schuchert award 1977), Soc. for Study Evolution (councilor 1982-84), Am. Geophys. Union, Paleontol. Rsch. Inst., Am. Geol. Inst. (mem. exec. com.). Office: Johns Hopkins U Dept Earth Planetary Sciences Baltimore MD 21218

STANLEY, THOMAS BAHNSON, JR., investor; b. Martinsville, Va., Jan. 9, 1927; s. Thomas B. and Anne (Bassett) S.; m. Ruth Barnes, Sept. 10, 1949; children: Thomas Bahnson III, Susan Walker, Andrew. B.S. in C.E., Va. Mil. Inst., 1946; B.S.C., U. Va., 1948; grad., Advanced Mgmt. Program, Harvard U., 1970. With Stanley Furniture Co., Stanleytown, Va., 1948-79, dir., 1950-79, exec. v.p., 1952-62, pres., 1962-71, chmn., 1971-79; pres. Mead Interiors, Stanleytown, 1969-74; group v.p. Mead Corp., Dayton, Ohio,

1969-74; also dir. Mead Corp.; bd. dirs. Main Street Bank Group, Martinsville, Va., Stanley Land & Lumber Co., Drakes Branch, Va. Mem. Henry County Sch. Bd., 1957-80; chmn. bd. trustees Ferrum Coll., 1977-79. Mem. So. Furniture Mfrs. Assn. (dir., pres. 1966, chmn. 1967). Methodist. Lodge: Masons (32 deg.). Home: Land's End 100 Hunter's Green Dr Stanleytown VA 24168 Office: PO Box 26 Stanleytown VA 24168-0026

STANLEY, TIMOTHY WADSWORTH, economist; b. Hartford, Conn., Sept. 28, 1927; s. Maurice and Margaret Stowell (Sammond) S.; m. Nadia Leon, June 7, 1952; children: Timothy Wadsworth III, Alessandra Maria, Christopher Maurice, Flavia Margaret. Student, Choate Sch., 1943-45; B.A., Yale, 1950; LL.B., Harvard, 1955, Ph.D., 1957. Bar: Conn. 1956, U.S. Supreme Ct. 1971. Mem. staff Office Sec. Def., 1955; teaching fellow Harvard U., 1955-56; spl. asst. White House staff, 1957-59, spl. asst. to asst. sec. def. for internat. security affairs, 1959-62; vis. research fellow Council on Fgn. Relations, N.Y.C., 1962-63; div. dir. policy planning staff Office Sec. Def., 1963-64; asst. to sec. def. for NATO force planning, Paris, 1965-67; def. adviser (minister) U.S. Mission to NATO, Paris and Brussels, 1967-69; vis. prof. internat. relations Johns Hopkins Sch. Advanced Internat. Studies, 1969-70; exec. v.p. Internat. Econ. Policy Assn., Washington, 1970-74; pres. Internat. Econ. Policy Assn., 1974-84, chmn., 1984-87; pres. Internat. Econ. Studies Inst., 1974-96; profl. lectr. George Washington U., 1957-60; cons. to various govt. agys., univs., bus. orgns., 1969-70; spl. rep. ACDA in negotiations for East-West Mut. Balanced Force Reductions, 1973-74, cons., 1974-80; mem. U.S. Govt. Adv. Com. on Investment, Tech. and Devel., 1974-93; mem. Nat. Strategic Materials and Minerals Program Adv. Com., 1984-88. Author: American Defense and National Security, 1955, NATO in Transition, 1965, Detente Diplomacy, 1970; co-author: U.S. Troops in Europe, 1971, The United States Balance of Payments, 1972, Raw Materials and Foreign Policy, 1977, Technology and Economic Development, 1979, U.S. Foreign Economic Strategy for the Eighties, 1982, Mobilizing U.S. Industry: A Vanishing Option for National Security?, 1987, To Unite our Strength: Enhancing the United Nations Peace and Security System, 1992; contbr. articles to profl. jours. Bd. dirs. Atlantic Coun. U.S., UN Assn. U.S., Nat. Capital Area, v.p., 1992-96; mem. transition team Pres.-elect George Bush, 1988-89. Served to 1st lt. AUS, 1946-48, 51-52. Recipient Distinguished Civilian Service medal Dept. Def., 1969. Mem. Met. Club. Congregationalist. Home: 3028 O St NW Washington DC 20007-3107

STANLEY, WOODROW, mayor; b. Schlater, Miss., June 12, 1950; s. Sam and Bessie S.; m. Reta James, July 19, 1974; children: Heather, Jasmine. AA, Mott C.C., 1971; BA in Polit. Sci., U. Mich., 1974, postgrad., 1986—. Counselor Urban League St. Acad., Flint, Mich., 1974-77; coord. Opportunities Industrialization Ctr., Flint, 1977-90; svcs. dir. Human Investment Corp., Flint, 1990-91; mayor City of Flint, 1991—; mem. City Coun., Flint, 1983-91; speaker numerous civic, ethnic, urban, ednl., bus. orgns., 1974—. Chmn. Econ. Devel. Corp., 1991—, bd. dirs. 1983-91; former chair Citizens Adv. Com. Ombudsman's Office City of Flint; vol. United Negro Coll. Fund Annual Telethon; mem. Nat. Coun. Negro Women, Flint chpt., Priorities '90 Com., Cancer is Colorblind Com. Am. Cancer Soc., Flint Black Leadership Dialogue, Doyle Ryder Elem. Sch. Parent Adv. Coun., Longfellow Middle Sch. Parent Adv. Coun., Citizens Adv. Coun. New Paths, Inc., Citizens Adv Com. Criminal Justice Program Mott C.C., adv. com. Coalition for Positive Youth Devel., Saginaw Valley Consistory #71, 32 degrees, Eureka Lodge PHA, adv. com. Edgar B. Holt Scholarship U. Mich., Flint, steering com. African Relief Fund Coalition Greater Flint, Citizens Adv. Com. African Afro Am. History Program, U. Mich. Flint, 1983—, Flint Human Rels. Commn., 1973-76; former mem. REACH Program, Citizens Adv. Com. Mott C.C., NAACP Credit Union; bd. dirs. Foss Ave Christian Sch., YMCA, 1976-77; chmn. bd. trustees Valley Area Agency on Aging, 1982-91; pres. bd. trustees McCree Theatre, 1975-90; convener Tri-County Coun. Mayors, 1992—. Recipient numerous awards including Outstanding Young Man of Am. U.S. Jaycees, 1976, Cert. Appreciation ESL Program Mott C.C., 1983, Cert. Recognition Nat. League Cities, 1989, Mich. Mcpl. League, 1990, NAACP Flint chpt. Die Hard award 1990, Appreciation award Am. Cancer Soc., 1990, Cert. Appreciation Nat. League Cities, 1990, Disting. Alumni U. Mich., Flint Alumni Soc., 1992, Donald Riegle Community Svc. award Flint Jewish Fedn., 1993, others. Mem. Nat. League of Cities (bd. dirs. 1992—), Mich. Mcpl. League (bd. dirs.), Mich. Assn. Mayors (bd. dirs. 1992—), NAACP, U. Mich. Alumni Soc., Assn. Black Social Workers (Flint chpt.), Nat. Forum Black Pub. Adminstrs. Democrat. African Methodist Episcopalian. Office: Office of the Mayor City Hall 1101 S Saginaw St Flint MI 48502-1416

STANN, JOHN ANTHONY, investment banker; b. San Francisco, Nov. 10, 1947; s. John Peter and Mary Jane (Erny) S.; m. Judith Darlene Knapp, Apr. 27, 1973; children: John Andrew, Theodore Joseph, Rebecca Marie. BA in Econs. and Math., U. Mo., 1969. Cost acct. Monsanto Co., St. Louis, 1971-73, acctg. supr., 1973-76; salesman Monsanto Co., Brighton, Mo., 1976-79; market mgr. Monsanto Co., St. Louis, 1979-81; mfr's. rep. Farbenfabriken, Bayer, Davos & Others, St. Louis, 1981-82; corp. valuations officer, v.p. A.G. Edwards & Sons, Inc., St. Louis, 1982-92; investment banking advisor to numerous pvt. cos., utility corp. finance corp.; v.p. A.G. Edwards and Sons, Inc., St. Louis, 1993—, Dev. Comm. of Neriny Hall H.S., 1994—. Fundraiser Archdiocese of St. Louis, 1981-84, 87-92, YMCA, St. Louis, 1987; chmn. fin. com. St. Clare Parish, St. Louis, 1982-84; mem. Assumption Parish Coun., 1988-90, chmn., 1989-90; youth baseball mgr. Affton Athletic Assn., St. Louis, 1985-86; poll worker Danforth for Senate, St. Louis, 1982. Lt. USNR, 1969-71. Named Man of Yr. St. John's Men's Club, 1978. Mem. Fox Run Golf Club. Republican. Roman Catholic. Avocations: handball, golf. Home: 9148 Fox Bridge Dr Saint Louis MO 63127-1362 Office: AG Edwards & Sons Inc 1 N Jefferson Ave Saint Louis MO 63103-2205

STANNARD, JAN GREGORY, academic administrator; b. Detroit, Dec. 30, 1953; s. Frank Kempster and Edith (Olmsted) S.; m. Roberta A. Salay, Sept. 5, 1981; children: Salay Robyn, Ivan Frank, Jazna Olmsted. BS, U. Mich., 1976, MS, 1978, PhD, 1981; EdD, Northeastern U., 1989. Chemist Dow Chem. Co., Midland, Mich., 1969-71; praktikant F. Hoffman LaRoche, Basel, Switzerland, 1975; prof. U. Nebr., Lincoln, 1981-83, Tufts U., Boston, 1983-91; exec. dir. Endicott Coll., Beverly, Mass., 1991-96; v.p. Mass. Bay C.C., 1996—; owner Denali R&D, Hanover, Mass., 1985—; cons. Hanover Pub. Libr., 1994—, Pulpdent Corp., Watertown, Mass., 1985-92, Johnson & Johnson Co., New Brunswick, N.J., 1990; lifetime faculty appointment King of Thailand, Chiang Mai U., 1994; adv. bd. A.S.E.P., C.A.P. Author: Materials in Dentistry, 1986, 2d edit., 1988; mem. editl. rev. bd. Jour. Dental Materials, 1994—. Active Flint Area (Mich.) Sci. Fair Com., 1985-90, Girls Inc. Eureka Project, Beverly, 1991-93; writer Small Cities Grant Program, Beverly, 1992; ptnr. PALMS-Beverly Pub. Schs., 1993—. Recipient Westinghouse Sci. award Westinghouse Corp., 1972, Rsch. Svc. award NIH, 1977-81. Fellow Nebr. Acad. Sci.; mem. Internat. Assn. Dental Rsch., New England Assn. Schs. and Colls. Accreditation Team, Sigma Xi, Phi Delta Kappa. Avocations: mountain climbing, volleyball, tennis, antique restoration. Office: Mass Bay CC 50 Oakland St Wellesley MA 02181-5307

STANNERS, CLIFFORD PAUL, molecular and cell biologist, biochemistry educator; b. Sutton, Surrey, Eng., Oct. 19, 1937; married; 3 children. BSc, McMaster U., 1958; MSc, U. Toronto, 1960, PhD, 1963. Fellow molecular biology MIT, Cambridge, Mass., 1962-64; from asst. prof. to prof. med. biophysics U. Toronto, Can., 1964-82; sr. sci. biol. rsch. Ont. (Can.) Cancer Inst., 1964-82; prof. biochemistry McGill U., Montreal, 1982—, dir. McGill Cancer Ctr., 1988—; mem. grants Med. Rsch. Coun. & Nat. Cancer Inst. Can., 1965—, U.S. Nat. Cancer Inst., 1973-79. Assoc. editor Jour. Cell Physiology, 1973-92, Cell, 1975-84. Mem. AAAS, Can. Biochem. Soc., Can. Soc. Cell Biology, Am. Assn. Cancer Rsch. Achievements include rsch. in growth control of animal cells; protein synthesis somatic cell genetics; cell virus interactions; intercellular adhesion molecules; human cancer; human carcinoembryonic antigen cloning and function. Office: McGill Cancer Ctr, 3655 Drummond St, Montreal, PQ Canada H3G 1Y6

STANNETT, VIVIAN THOMAS, chemical engineering educator; b. Langley, Eng., Sept. 1, 1917; came to U.S., 1947, naturalized, 1957; s. Ernest and Dorothy Grace (Rustell) S.; m. Flora Susanne Sulzbacher, May 30, 1946; 1 dau., Rosemary Anthia. B.S., London Poly., 1939; Ph.D., Poly. Inst. Bklyn., 1950. Chemist, govt. and industry Eng., 1939-47; research assoc. Mellon Inst., Pitts., 1950-51; research chemist Koppers Co., Pitts., 1951-52; prof. polymer chemistry State U. Coll. Forestry, Syracuse, N.Y., 1952-61; asso. dir. Camille Dreyfus Labs., Research Triangle Inst., Durham, N.C., 1961-67; Camille Dreyfus prof. chem. engring. N.C. State U., Raleigh, 1967—; vice provost, dean Grad. Sch., N.C. State U., 1975-82. Author: Cellulose Acetate Plastics, 1950, Handbook of Chemical Technology, 1953; contbr. articles to profl. jours. Recipient Borden award Am. Chem. Soc., 1974, Anselm Payen award, 1974, O. Max Gardner award U. N.C., 1984, Polymer Chemistry award Am. Chem. Soc., 1987. Onley medal Am. Assn. Textile Chemists and Colorists, 1995. Fellow Royal Soc. Chemistry, TAPPI (Silver medal synthetic divsn. 1967), N.Y. Acad. Scis., Soc. Plastics Engrs. (Internat. award and gold medal 1978, N.C. Sci. medal 1981); mem. NAE. Home: 1105 Bancroft St Raleigh NC 27612-4701

STANNFE, HELEN, writer; b. Dayton, Apr. 10; d. Robert Jay and Florence Ellen Millekin; m. Wayne B. Stannfe, Oct. 17, 1971; children: Robert, Linda, Brooke. BL, Ohio State U., 1963, MLitt., 1965. With Women's Circle magazine, 1964-72; Speaker in field. Author: The Children's Place, 1980, Jennifer Jumps!, 1982, The 5 Senses, 1988, Here We Are!, 1990, Eileen Learns To Cook, 1991, The Day We Moved, 1993, Rebecca And The Ring, 1997, and numerous others. Mem. League Women Voters, Literacy Volunteers of America. Mem. Boxwood Garden Club, Lake Shore Womens' Club, Writers Guild. Home and office: Werik Publications, Inc 3424 Helen Road Cleveland OH 44122-3871

STANS, MAURICE HUBERT, retired business consultant, former government official; b. Shakopee, Minn., Mar. 22, 1908; s. J. Hubert and Mathilda (Nyssen) S.; m. Kathleen Carmody, Sept. 7, 1933 (dec. Oct. 1984); children: Steven, Maureen (dec.), Theodore, Terrell. Student, Northwestern U., 1925-28, Columbia U., 1929-30; LL.D., Ill. Wesleyan U., 1954, Northwestern U., 1960, DePaul U., 1960; D.P.A., Parsons Coll., 1960; LL.D., Grove City Coll., St. Anselm's Coll., 1969, U. San Diego, Gustavus Adolphus Coll., 1970, Pomona Coll., 1971, Maryville Coll., 1971, Rio Grande Coll., 1972, Nat. U., 1979, Pepperdine U., 1984. C.P.A. With Alexander Grant & Co. (C.P.A.'s), Chgo., 1928, exec. ptnr., 1940-55; pres., dir. Moore Corp. (stove mfrs.), Joliet, Ill., 1938-45; dir., mem. exec. com. James Talcott, Inc., N.Y.C., 1941-55; fin. cons. to postmaster gen. U.S., 1953-55, dep. postmaster gen. U.S., 1955-57; dep. dir. U.S. Bur. Budget, 1957-58, dir., 1958-61; pres. Western Bancorp., Los Angeles, 1961-62; also vice chmn. United Calif. Bank; sr. ptnr. William R. Staats & Co., 1963-64; pres. William R. Staats Co., Inc., 1964-65, Glore Forgan, William R. Staats, Inc., N.Y.C., 1965-69; syndicated columnist, 1961-62; sec. of Commerce Washington, 1969-72; Bd. dirs. Uniglobe Travel (Internat.), Vancouver; pres., bd. dirs. Farmont Corp., L.A.; bd. dirs., treas. Electronic Town Hall Meetings, Inc., 1992-93; bd. dirs., chmn. AT&D Inc., 1992-93; bus. cons., L.A., 1975-92; chmn., bd. dirs. Weatherby, Inc., 1986-91. Author: The Terrors of Justice, 1978, One of the Presidents' Men, Twenty Years With Eisenhower and Nixon, 1995; contbr. numerous articles on govt. fin., fgn. trade and bus. to profl. publs. Founder, past pres., dir. Stans Found., Chgo.; chmn. Nixon Finance Com., 1968, Republican Nat. Finance Com., 1968-69, 72-73, Finance Com. to Re-Elect Pres., 1972-73; fin. chmn., bd. dirs. Nixon Presdl. Library, 1985—; trustee Pomona Coll., 1962-69; bd. dirs. Huntington Med. Rsch. Inst.; bd. dirs. Arnold and Mabel Beckman Found., Irvine, Calif., 1988-92, Eisenhower World Affairs Inst., Washington, 1991-93; chmn. Minority Enterprise Devel. Adv. Coun., Washington, 1989-91; founding dir. African Wildlife Found., Washington, 1958. Recipient Great Living Am. award U.S. C. of C., 1961, Tax Found. award, 1960, Free Enterprise award Internat. Franchise Assn., 1988; named to Acctg. Hall of Fame, 1968; creator Stans African Halls sect. Mus. York County, Rock Hill, S.C., 1980; financed and constructed Stans Hist. Ctr. Shakopee, Minn., 1988, deeded to Scott County Hist. Soc. Mem. NAM (dir. 1968-69), AICPA (pres. 1954-55, Pub. Service award 1954), Ill. Soc. CPAs (dir. 1944-46), D.C. Soc. CPAs (hon.), Hawaii Soc. CPAs (hon.), Am. Acctg. Assn. (nat. Alpha Kappa Psi award 1952), Fed. Govt. Accts. Assn., Nat. Assn. Postmasters (hon.), Iron Molders and Foundry Workers Union (hon.). Clubs: Union League, Adventurers (Chgo.), California (Los Angeles), Athenaeum (Pasadena), Shikar-Safari Club Internat. (founding 1952, trustee internat. found.), Safari Club Internat., East African Profl. Hunters (hon.), Explorers (N.Y.C.), African Safari (Washington, founding bd. dirs. 1957), Jamhuri of Garissa (Kenya) (hon.), Valley Hunt (Pasadena).

STANSBERRY, JAMES WESLEY, air force officer; b. Grafton, W.Va., Dec. 29, 1927; s. William Adrian and Phyllis Gay (Robinson) S.; m. Audrey Mildred Heinz, May 7, 1950; children: Nora G. Fitzpatrick, Amy G. Stansberry Goodhand, Lisa Stansberry De Regis. BS, U.S. Mil. Acad., 1949; MBA, Air Force Inst. Tech., 1956. Advanced through grades from pvt. to lt. gen. USAF; chief prodn. (Kawasaki Gifu Contract Facility), Gifu, Japan, 1956-57; dep. asst. to Sec. of Def. for atomic energy Washington, 1970-71; dep. dir. procurement policy U.S. Air Force, 1972-73; dep. chief staff contracting and mfg. (Hdqrs. Air Force Systems Command), Andrews AFB, Md., 1977-81; comdr. Electronic Systems Div. Hanscom AFB, Mass., 1981-84; pres. Stansberry Assocs. Inc., 1984—. Decorated DSM with oak leaf cluster, Legion of Merit with oak leaf cluster; named Disting. grad. Lancaster (N.Y.) H.S. Methodist. Home: 43 Monadnock Dr Westford MA 01886-3021 *The real secrets are enthusiasm, competence and good luck; and it helps immensely to marry a good woman. Work and persistence define us, accomodating various levels of talent, intelligence and luck. Work and persistence prevail, buttressed by discipline and determination, and perhaps supported by a sense of humor.*

STANSBURY, HARRY CASE, state commissioner. BS in Gen. Studies, La. State U., 1968; JD, Loyola U., New Orleans, 1971; student, Oxford (Eng.) U., 1985, Harvard U., 1988. Bar: La., N.Y., D.C., U.S. Supreme Ct., U.S. Ct. Appeals (1st-11th cirs., D.C. cir., fed. cir.), U.S. Ct. Mil. Appeals, U.S. Ct. Fed. Claims, U.S. Ct. Internat. Trade, U.S. Tax Ct., U.S. Dist. Ct. (ea., mid. and we. dists.) La., U.S. Dist. Ct. (ea., no., so. and we. dists.) N.Y., U.S. Dist. Ct. D.C. Staff atty. La. Securities Commn., New Orleans, 1971-75, dep. commr. securities, 1975—; mem. liaison com. fed. securities code project Am. Law Inst.-ABA, 1974-80; speaker, expert witness in field. Contbr. articles to profl. jours. Mem. ABA (sect. bus. law, sect. internat. law and practice, sect. legal edn. and admissions to bar, mem. subcom. derivative instruments fed. regulation securities com. 1993—), N.Am. Securities Adminstrs. Assn. (mem. registration exemption com. 1991—), La. State Bar Assn. (sect. corp. and bus. law, mem. internat. law com. 1991-92), N.Y. State Bar Assn. (banking, corp. and bus. law sect.), D.C. Bar Assn. (corp., fin. and securities law divsn.), Assn. of Bar of City of N.Y., Assn. of Bar of D.C., New Orleans Bar Assn. (vice chair corps. and bus. law com. 1992-94, chair 1994—), Fed. Bar Assn. (fin. instns. and economy sect.), Internat. Bar Assn. (sect. bus. law, mem. issues and trading in securities com. 1991—), La. State U. Alumni Assn., Loyola Law Alumni Assn., Harvard Law Sch. Assn., Am. Friends Rewley House, Supreme Ct. Hist. Soc. Office: La Office Securities 3445 N Causeway Blvd Ste 509 Metairie LA 70002-3723

STANSBURY, PHILIP ROGER, lawyer; b. Milw., May 7, 1931; s. Carroll and Margaret (Manning) S.; m. Daviette Clagett Hill, Dec. 5, 1959; children: Henry Tayloe, Catherine Contee. AB, Haverford (Pa.) Coll., 1953; JD, Harvard U., 1956. Bar: D.C. 1956, U.S. Ct. Appeals (D.C. crct.) 1956. Assoc. Covington & Burling, Washington, 1958-66, ptnr., 1966—. Contbr. articles to profl. jours. Mem. Southwestern Legal Found. (adv. bd.). Republican. Roman Catholic. Office: Covington & Burling 1201 Pennsylvania Ave NW PO Box 7566 Washington DC 20044

STANSEL, JAMES W., agricultural research administrator; b. Angleton, Tex., Apr. 8, 1934; married, 1954; 2 children. BS, Tex. A&M U., 1956, MS, 1959; PhD in Plant Breeding and Genetics, Purdue U., 1965. Asst. geneticist Tex. A&M U., Beaumont, 1960-66, asst. prof. genetics, 1966-70, asst. prof. agronomy Agrl. Rsch. and Ext. Ctr., 1970-77, assoc. prof. genetics/environ., scientist in charge we. div., 1972-77, prof. agronomy, 1978-82, resident dir., prof. agr. Tex. Agrl. Exptl. Sta., 1982—. Mem. Am. Soc. Agronomy, Crop Sci. Soc. Am., Rice Tech. Working Group. Office: Tex A&M U Agrl Rsch & Extension Ctr Rte 7 Box 999 Beaumont TX 77713-8530

STANSELL, RONALD BRUCE, investment banker; b. Hammond, Ind., Apr. 9, 1945; s. Herman Bruce and Helen Rose S.; m. Kathie Van Atta, Oct. 2, 1976; children: Kelsey, Kymberlie. BA, Wittenberg U., 1967; MA, Miami U., Oxford, Ohio, 1969. Investment officer First Nat. Bank, Chgo., 1969-73; mgr. investments Chrysler Corp., Detroit, 1973; asst. v.p. A.G. Becker, Chgo., 1973-76; v.p. Blyth Eastman Dillon, Chgo., 1976-79; v.p. Dean Witter Reynolds Inc., Chgo., 1979-82; v.p. First Boston Corp., 1982-88; sr. v.p. Prudential-Bache Securities, Chgo., 1988-90; ptnr. William Blair & Co., 1991—. Mem. Mettawa (Ill.) Zoning Bd., 1978-80; trustee Village of Mettawa, 1980-91, village treas., 1977-78. With USMCR, 1968-74. Named to Pres.'s Club, Blyth Eastman Dillon, 1977, 78, 79. Mem. Bond Club Chgo., Investment Analyst Soc., Fixed Income Group, Exmoor Country Club, Bob O'Link Golf Club, Grandfather Golf Club, John's Island Country Club, LaSalle Club, Forest Creek Golf Club, Belfair Golf Club.

STANSFIELD, CHARLES W., educational administrator; m. Charlene Rivera, Sept. 6, 1989. BA in Spanish, Fla. State U., 1968, MA in Fgn. Lang. Edn., 1969, MS in Teaching English as Second Lang., 1970, PhD in Fgn. and Second Lang. Edn., 1973. Tchr. English, Centro Colombo-Americano, Bogota, Colombia, 1966; 2jr. high sch. tchr. Spanish Fla. State U. Demonstration Sch., 1968-69; instr. Spanish, U. Colo., Boulder, 1970-73, asst. prof., 1973-80, assoc. prof., 1980-81; assoc. program dir. lang. programs Ednl. Testing Svc., Princeton, N.J., 1981-86; dir. fgn. lang. edn. and testing div. Ctr. for Applied Linguistics, Washington, 1986-94, dir. ERIC Clearinghouse Lang. and Linguistics, 1986-94; pres. Second Lang. Testing, Inc., Bethesda, Md., 1994—; dir. Peace Corps Tng. Ctr., Managua, Nicaragua, 1978; mem. exec. com. Joint Nat. Com. on Langs., 1988-93; conf. coord. Interagy. Lang. Roundtable Invitational Symposium on Lang. Aptitude Testing, Rosslyn, Va., 1988; mem. adv. bd. Nat. Fgn. Lang. Resources Ctr., U. Hawaii, 1991-93; numerous presentations at profl. meetings, 1970—. Author: Cuaderno de ejercicios, 1976, rev. edit., 1981; co-author: Manual de laboratorio, 2d rev. edit., 1981, The Test of Spoken English as a Measure of Communicative Ability in the Health Professions,: Validation and Standard Setting, 1983, (with others) Multiple-Choice Cloze Items and the Test of English as a Foreign Language, 1988; co-editor: Second Language Proficincy Assessment: Current Issues, 1988, Language Aptitude Reconsidered, 1990; also numerous articles. Named Outstanding Alumnus Fla. State U., 1994; Colo. Congress Fgn. Lang. Tchrs. scholar, 1981. Mem. Am. Assn. Tchrs. Spanish and Portuguese (life), Am. Coun. on Teaching Fgn. Langs. (Paul Pinsleur award 1984), Am. Ednl. Rsch. Assn., Internat. Assn. Applied Linguistics, Nat. Assn. for Bilingual Edn., Nat. Coun. on Measurement in Edn., Internat. Lang. Testing Assn. (pres. 1992-93), Tchrs. English to Speakers Other Langs., Washington Area Tchrs. English to Speakers Other Langs., Colo. Tchrs. English to Speakers Other Langs. (Gladys Doty award 1987). Home and Office: 10704 Mist Haven Ter Rockville MD 20852

STANSKY, PETER DAVID LYMAN, historian; b. N.Y.C., Jan. 18, 1932; s. Lyman and Ruth (Macow) S. B.A., Yale U., 1953, King's Coll., Cambridge (Eng.) U., 1955; M.A., King's Coll., Cambridge (Eng.) U., 1959; Ph.D., Harvard U., 1961; D.L. (hon.), Wittenburg U., 1984. Teaching fellow history and lit. Harvard U., 1957-61, instr., then asst. prof. history, 1961-68; assoc. prof. history Stanford U., 1968-73, prof., 1973-74, Frances and Charles Field prof., 1974—, chmn. dept. history, 1975-78, 79-82, 89-90, assoc. dean humanities and scis., 1985-88; chmn. publs. com. Conf. Brit. Studies, 1970-78; pres. Pacific Coast Conf. Brit. Studies, 1974-76, N. Am. Conf. Brit. Studies, 1983-85; vis. fellow Wesleyan Center Humanities, Middletown, Conn., 1972, All Soul's Coll., Oxford (Eng.) U., 1979, St. Catherine's Coll., Oxford (Eng.) U., 1983. Author: Ambitions and Strategies, 1964, England Since 1867, 1973, Gladstone, 1979, William Morris, 1983, Redesigning the World, 1985, On or About December 1910, 1996; co-author: Journey to the Frontier, 1966, The Unknown Orwell, 1972, Orwell: The Transformation, 1979, London's Burning, 1994. Guggenheim fellow, 1966-67, 73-74; Am. Council Learned Socs. fellow, 1978-79; NEH fellow, 1983, Royal Hist. Soc. fellow Ctr. for Advanced Study Behavioral Scis., 1988-89. Fellow Am. Acad. Arts and Scis. (coun. 1994—); mem. Am. Hist. Assn. (pres. Pacific Coast br. 1988-89), Conf. on Brit. Studies, Victorian Soc., William Morris Soc., AAUP, Century Assn. Home: 375 Pinehill Rd Hillsborough CA 94010-6612 Office: Stanford U Dept History Stanford CA 94305

STANTON, DONALD SHELDON, academic administrator; b. Balt., June 8, 1932; s. Kenneth Gladstone and Dorothy Erma (Hettrick) S.; m. Barbara Mae Hoot, June 25, 1955; children: Dale Richard, Debra Carol, Diane Karen. AB, Western Md. Coll., 1953, LLD, 1981; MDiv magna cum laude, Wesley Theol. Sem., 1956; MA, Am. U., 1960; Ed.D., U. Va., 1965; L.H.D., Columbia Coll., 1979; Litt.D., Albion Coll., 1983. Ordained to ministry United Methodist Ch., 1956; pastor Balt. and Va. confs. United Meth. Ch., 1953-59; dir. Richmond (Va.) Area Wesley Found., 1959-63; chaplain, dean of students Greensboro Coll., 1963-65; chaplain Wofford Coll., 1965-69; dir. office coll. services United Meth. Div. Higher Edn., Nashville, 1969-75; v.p. for devel. Wesleyan Coll., 1975-78; pres. Adrian Coll., 1978-88, Oglethorpe U., Atlanta, 1988—; adminstr., prof. European internat. ednl. programs, summers 1960, 69-71, 73; chmn. pres.'s assn. Mich. Intercollegiate Athletic Assn., 1986-87. Contbr. articles, revs. to profl. publs. in U.S., Japan, Argentina, chpts. to books; editor: Faculty Forum, 1972-74; bass-baritone soloist. Bd. dirs. Toledo (Ohio) Symphony, 1980-83, Lewanee County Jr. Achievement, 1980-83, Found. Ind. Higher Edn., 1996—, Nat. Conf. Christians and Jews, Atlanta Region, Atlanta Area Coun. Boy Scouts Am.; chair bd. trustees U. Ctr. Ga., 1994-96; chair So. Collegiate Athletic Conf., 1994-95. Adminstrn. bldg. at Adrian Coll. named in honor of Stanton and his wife, 1988. Mem. Am. Assn. Univ. Adminstrs. (bd. dirs. 1990-93), Ga. Assn. Colls. (pres. 1992), Soc. Wesley (Disting. Alumni Recognition award 1988), Ga. Found. for Ind. Colls. (vice chair 1992), Nat. Assn. Ind. Colls. and Univs. (past mem. pub. rels. com.), Assn. Pvt. Colls. and Univs. Ga. (treas. 1996-97), Commerce Club, Rotary, Omicron Delta Kappa, Order of Omega, Tau Kappa Epsilon, Psi Chi, Phi Eta Sigma. Home: 1571 Windsor Pky NE Atlanta GA 30319-2740 Office: Oglethorpe U Office of Pres 4484 Peachtree Rd NE Atlanta GA 30319-2737

STANTON, GEORGE BASIL, JR., engineering executive, chemical engineer; b. Bklyn., Nov. 3, 1926; s. George B. and Despina Stanton. B in Chem. Engring., Poly. Inst., Bklyn., 1945, M in Chem. Engring., 1948; MBA, NYU, 1971, MA in Safety and Health, 1975. Registered profl. engr., N.J., cert indsl. hygienist, safety profl. Chief occupl. health Dept. Labor State of N.J., 1971-74; cons. engr. N.J., 1974-79; pres. Am. Hazard Control Cons., Inc., Caldwell, N.J., 1979—; adj. prof. N.J. Inst. Tech., 1974-92, Ctr. for Safety NYU, 1977-84; organizer, pres. Essex Fells Found. for Ednl. Excellence, Inc., 1994-95; ASME rep. Joint Coun. for Health, Safety and Environ. Edn. of Profls., 1995—. Fellow Royal Soc. Health; mem. ASME (Centennial medal 1980), Am. Soc. Safety Engrs. (award 1980). Office: Am Hazard Control Cons Inc PO Box 231 Caldwell NJ 07006-0231

STANTON, JOHN JEFFREY, editor, broadcast journalist, government programs director, analyst, professional society administrator; b. Wichita Falls, Tex., July 19, 1956; s. John Joseph Jr. and Joan (Marley) S.; m. Scylla Maria Silva, Jan. 6, 1981; 1 child, Damien Kristian. BS in Pub. Adminstrn. and Bus. Adminstrn., Nichols Coll., 1978; M in Pub. Adminstrn., U. Detroit, 1980. Rsch. asst. Am. Enterprise Inst., Washington, 1977; rep. aide R.I. Ho. of Reps., Providence, 1977-78; mng. editor Am. Politics, Washington, 1982, assoc. editor, 1983, corp. advisor, 1984, sr. editor, 1985-87; editor, govt. programs mgr. ENTEK, Alexandria, Va., 1988-90; govt. programs dir., cons. Tuckerman Group, Springfield, Va., 1991; comm. industry writer Arlington, Va., 1991—; program dir. TeleStrategies, McLean, Va., 1991-93; Washington corr., mem. editl. bd. Tech. Transfer Jour., 1994—; editor Tech. Transfer Newsletter; asst. to pres., info. transfer specialist Am. Def. Preparedness Assn., Arlington, 1994-97; adminstrn. dir. Am. Def. Preparedness Assn.-Nat. Security Indsl. Assn., Arlington, 1997—; creator, co-host (radio programs) Power Breakfast, Sta. WNTR, Washington, 1987, Am. Politics Radio, 1987; frequent guest broadcast journalist Stas. WNTR, WAMU-NPR, Washington, WBAL, Balt. and Washington areas; contbr. Nat. Def. Mag., 1996—. Contbr. Nat. Def. mag. Polit. campaign cons. to Glenn Tenney, 1992—; commr. Arlington Little League Baseball, 1993; mentor Arlington County Ct. Sys., 1997. Recipient Doers Honoree The Washington Times, 1988. Roman Catholic. Avocations: coaching youth league sports programs.

STANTON, MARSHALL P., academic administrator, minister; b. Satanta, Kans., Oct. 15, 1935; s. Vernon and Julia (Beatrice) S.; m. Janice Marie Duryee, Dec. 20, 1956; children: Eric, Kirsten, Nathan. BA, Friends U., 1957, DD, 1986; BD, Asbury Theol. Sem., 1960; ThM, Princeton Theol. Sem., 1961. Ordained minister United Meth. Ch. Pastor United Meth. Ch.,

Laurel, Ohio, 1958-60, Jewell, Kans., 1961-66, Salina, Kans., 1966-67, Colby, Kans., 1971-78; dist. supt. United Meth. Ch., Hutchinson, Kans., 1978-84; pres. Kans. Wesleyan U., Salina, 1984—, also bd. dirs. Bd. dirs. Southwestern Coll., Winfield, Kans., 1978-84. Mem. Kans. Ind. Coll. Assn. (chmn. bd. dirs. 1989-90), Assoc. Colls. Ctrl. Kans. (chmn. bd. dirs. 1988-89, 95-96), Ministerial Assn. (pres. Salina chpt. 1969-70, pres. Colby chpt. 1973-74), Salina C. of C. (bd. dirs. 1986-99), vice chmn. 1996). Avocations: jogging, bicycling, radio-control model aircraft. Home: 151 Aspen Rd Salina KS 67401-3609 Office: Kans Wesleyan U Office of Pres 100 E Claflin Ave Salina KS 67401-6146

STANTON, MICHAEL JOHN, newspaper editor; b. New Britain, Conn., Mar. 30, 1944; s. John Martin and Helen (McNally) S.; m. Barbara Ann Mucha, Aug. 27, 1966; 1 child, Sean. A.B. in English, Holy Cross Coll., 1966. Reporter, editor Providence (R.I.) Jour., 1968-72; press sec. Gov. R.I., Providence, 1972-77; asst. news editor St. Louis Globe-Dem., 1977-81; news copy desk chief Detroit Free Press, 1981-83, exec. news editor, 1983-85, asst. to exec. editor, 1985-86; exec. news editor Seattle Times, 1986—. Office: The Seattle Times PO Box 70 Fairview Ave N & John St Seattle WA 98111*

STANTON, PATRICK MICHAEL, lawyer; b. Phila., Sept. 8, 1947; s. Edward Joseph and Helen Marie (Coghlan) S.; m. Kathleen Ann Fama, Aug. 22, 1970; children: Cheryl Marie, Susan Elizabeth. BS in History, St. Joseph's U., 1969; JD, U. Va., 1972; MBA, Fairleigh Dickinson, 1984. Bar: Ohio 1972, U.S. Dist. Ct. (so. dist.) Ohio 1972, N.J. 1982, U.S. Dist. Ct. N.J. 1982, N.Y. 1984. Assoc. Taft, Stettinius & Hollister, Cin., 1972-80; labor counsel Union Camp Corp., Wayne, N.J., 1980-83; dir. labor relations, equal employment oppurtunity programs W.R. Grace & Co., N.Y.C., 1983-86; of counsel Shanley & Fisher, P.C., Morristown, N.J., 1986-89, ptnr., chmn. labor and employment group, 1989-95; Stanton, Hughes, Diana, Zucker & Salsberg P.C., Florham Park, N.J., 1995—; adj. prof. bus. law Fairleigh Dickinson Univ.; exec. dir. Sidney Reitman employment law Am. Inn. Ct., 1993—. Pres., bd. dirs. N.Y. State Adv. Coun. on Employment Law, Inc., N.Y.C., 1985-86. DuPont scholar U. Va., 1970. Mem. ABA, N.J. State Bar Assn. (exec. com. labor employment law sect. 1989—, rec. sec. 1995—), Phi Alpha Theta, Delta Mu Delta. Roman Catholic. Home: 292 Forest Ave Glen Ridge NJ 07028-1808 Office: Stanton Hughes Diana Zucker & Salsberg PC 30A Vreeland Rd Ste 340 Florham Park NJ 07932-1901

STANTON, ROBERT JAMES, JR., geologist, educator; b. L.A., June 17, 1931; s. Robert James and Audrey (Franke) S.; m. Patricia Ann Burns, Sept. 13, 1953; children—John, Carol. B.S., Calif. Inst. Tech., 1953; Ph.D., 1960; M.A., Harvard U., 1956. Research geologist Shell Devel. Co., Houston, 1959-67; mem. faculty Tex. A&M U., 1967—, prof. geology, 1972-86, Ray C. Fish prof. geology, 1986—, head dept., 1979-83; vis. prof. U. Nuremburg-Erlangen, Germany, 1984. Co-author: Paleoecology: Principles and Applications, 1981, 2d edit., 1990. Served with AUS, 1953-55. Fellow Geol. Soc. Am.; mem. Internat. Paleontol. Union, Paleontol. Soc., Paleontol. Research Inst., Soc. Econ. Paleontologists and Mineralogists (Outstanding Paper award 1970), Sigma Xi, Tau Beta Pi. Home: 3609 Sunnybrook Ln Bryan TX 77802-3922 Office: Tex A&M U Dept Geology College Station TX 77843

STANTON, ROBERT JOHN, corporate bank executive, lawyer; b. Coffeyville, Kans., Jan. 25, 1913; s. William P. and LaVeta (Reilly) S.; m. Mary Locke, June 4, 1938; children: Robert John Jr., James Locke, William Clark. AB, U. Okla., 1935, LLB, 1937. Bar: Okla. 1937. Assoc., firm mem. Martin, Logan, Finney, Stanton and Moyers, Tulsa, Okla., 1937-54; gen. counsel, sr. v.p., dir. Amerada Petroleum Corp., Tulsa, N.Y.C., 1954-69; sr. v.p., dir. Amerada Hess Corp., N.Y.C., 1969-71; chmn. trust com. First Nat. Bank and Trust, Co., Tulsa, 1971-79; rsch. fellow Southwestern Legal Found. Chmn. William K. Warren Found., Tulsa, 1973-91. Capt. (JAGD) U.S. Army, 1944-46. Mem. ABA, Okla. Bar Assn., Order of Coif, Phi Beta Kappa. Republican. Roman Catholic.

STANTON, ROBERT JOHN, JR., English language educator; b. Manhattan, N.Y., July 7, 1942; s. Robert John Stanton and Mary McGinty; m. Felicia Lena Giancola, Nov. 15, 1959; children: Robert III, Sharon. BA, Hofstra U., 1970; MA, U. Mass., Amherst, 1972, postgrad., 1974-79. Instr. English Flagler Coll., St. Augustine, Fla., 1972-74; tchg. asst. U. Mass., Amherst, 1974-77, lectr. in Rhetoric, 1979-81; English tchr. Bishop Kenny H.S., Jacksonville, Fla., 1982-83, Duval County Pub. Schs., Jacksonville, 1984-87; asst. prof. English Jacksonville U., 1987-91, assoc. prof. English, 1992-96, chmn. divsn. humanities, 1993—. Author: Seventeen British Novelists, 1978, Gore Vidal, 1978, Truman Capote, 1980, Views From A Window: Conversations with Gore Vidal, 1980; co-author: Beneath Mad River Mansion, 1992, Noah's Orbella, 1994, The Devil's Road, 1996. Mem. MLA, Nat. Assn. Tchrs. English, Fla. Assn. Depts. English (pres. 1996), Swift River (Mass.) Hist. Soc. Democrat. Avocations: astronomy, reading, writing, observing the universe. Home: 614 15th Ave South Jacksonville Beach FL 32250 Office: Jacksonville Univ Jacksonville FL 32211

STANTON, ROGER D., lawyer; b. Waterville, Kans., Oct. 4, 1938; s. George W. and Helen V. (Peterson) S.; m. Judith L. Duncan, Jan. 27, 1962; children: Jeffrey B., Brady D., Todd A. AB, U. Kans., 1960, JD, 1963. Bar: Kans. 1963, U.S. Dist. Ct. Kans. 1963, U.S. Ct. Appeals (10th cir.) 1972, U.S. Supreme Ct. 1973. Assoc. Stanley, Schroeder, Weeks, Thomas & Lysaught, Kansas City, Kans., 1963-68; ptnr. Weeks, Thomas, Lysaught, Bingham & Johnston, Kansas City, 1968-72, Weeks, Thomas & Lysaught, 1969-80, also bd. dirs., chmn. exec. com., 1981-82, Stinson, Mag & Fizzell, 1983-96; chmn. products practice group, also bd. dirs., 1993-95; ptnr. Berkowitz, Feldmiller, Stanton, Brandt, Williams & Stueve, Prairie Village, Kans., 1997—. Active Boy Scouts Am., 1973-79; pres. YMCA Youth Football Club, 1980-82; co-chmn. Civil Justice Reform Act com. Dist. of Kans., 1991-95. Fellow Am. Coll. Trial Lawyers (state chmn. 1984-86); mem. Internat. Assn. Def. Counsel, Exec. cmte. East Kansas/West Miss. Cptr., Am. Bd. Trial Adv., Def. Rsch. Inst. (state co-chmn. 1979-90, Exceptional Performance award 1979), Kans. Bar Assn. (Pres.'s award 1982), Johnson County Bar Found. (pres. elect, trustee), Chmn. Bench/Bar Cmte. of Johnson Co. Bar Assn., Kans. Assn. Def. Counsel (pres. 1977-78), Kans. Inn. Ct., U. Kans. Sch. Law Alumni Assn. (bd. dirs. 1972-75). Chmn. bd. editors Jour. Kans. Bar Assn., 1975-83; contbr. articles to legal jours. Office: Berkowitz Feldmiller Stanton et al 4121 W 83rd St Ste 227 Prairie Vlg KS 66208-5323

STANTON, RONALD P., export company executive. Chmn. Transammonia, Inc., N.Y.C., 1965—. Office: Transammonia Inc 350 Park Ave New York NY 10022-6022*

STANTON, SARA BAUMGARDNER, retired secondary school educator; b. Johnstown, Pa., Sept. 11, 1930; d. Emmanuel Boyd and Ethel Leora (Shaffer) Baumgardner; m. George Welles Stanton, June 20, 1953; children: David Mark, Frederick George. BS in Edn., Bucknell U., 1952. Tchr. Adams-Summerhill High Sch., Sidman, Pa., 1952-53, Waymart (Pa.) High Sch., 1953-55, Honesdale (Pa.) High Sch., 1955-57; substitute tchr. Wayne County Sch. Dist., 1957-77; tchr. Honesdale High Sch., 1977-90; ret., 1990; leadership instr. Pa. Assn. Hosp. Auxs., Harrisburg, Pa., 1976-97. Den mother Cub Pack 104, 1965-69; bd. dirs. Health Systems Agy., Wilkes-Barre, Pa., 1983-86; adv. bd. Pa. State U.-Scranton Campus, 1977-85; trustee Wayne County Meml. Hosp., Honesdale, 1974-86. Recipient Leader's Fellowship award Nat. Bd. YMCA, 1964, B'nai B'rith Citizenship Citation, 1974 (co-recipient with husband). Mem. AAUW (br. pres. 1980-81), Pa. Assn. Hosp. Auxs. (mem. leadership tng. team 1975-80, 91-97, chmn. state ann. conv. 1985, pres. 1986-88), Pa. Assn. Sch. Retirees, Hosp. Assn. Pa. (mem. cmty. concerns com. 1974-75, ex officio 1986-88), Wayne County Hist. Soc. (bd. dirs. 1991-92, 95—, sec. 1995-97), Woman's Club Honesdale (pres. 1958-60). Republican. Methodist. Avocation: music. Home: 1512 West St Honesdale PA 18431-1764

STANTON, THOMAS MITCHELL, lawyer, educator; b. Vicksburg, Miss., Sept. 30, 1922; s. John Francis and Hazel Florence (Mitchell) S.; m. Jean Aldrich Herron, Oct. 31, 1953; children: Lucinda S. Duddy, Amy S. Conklin, Thomas Herron. BS, Harvard U., 1943, JD, 1948. Bar: Ohio 1949, Wis. 1962. Pvt. practice law Cin., 1949-56; corp. atty. Kroger Co., Cin., 1957-61; with Kimberly-Clark Corp., Neenah, Wis., 1962-86; v.p., gen. counsel Kimberly-Clark Corp., Neenah, 1971-84, v.p., internat. counsel, 1985-86; ret. Kimberly-Clark Corp., 1986; lectr. litigation decision analysis Boston U., Northwestern U., U. Wis., 1986—; pvt. practice law Neenah, 1987—; v.p., sec., bd. dirs. Tango, Inc.; pres., dir. Dataphon Co. of S.C. Trustee Friends of Bronze Age Archeology in the Aegean Area. Capt. AUS, 1943-46. Mem. ABA, Wis. Bar Assn., Am. Corp. Counsel Assn. (internat. legal affairs com.), North Shore Golf Club, Univ. Club. Home: 390 Park St Menasha WI 54952-3428 Office: 101 W Canal St Ste 25 Neenah WI 54956-3093

STANTON, VIVIAN BRENNAN (MRS. ERNEST STANTON), retired educator; b. Waterbury, Conn.; d. Francis P. and Josephine (Ryan) Brennan; B.A., Albertus Magnus Coll.; M.S., So. Conn. State Coll., 1962, 6th yr. degree, 1965; postgrad. Columbia U.; m. Ernest Stanton, May 31, 1947; children—Pamela L., Bonita F., Kim Ernest. Tchr. English, history, govt. Milford (Conn.) High Sch., 1940-48; tchr. English, history, fgn. Born Night Sch., New Haven, 1948-54, Simon Lake Sch., Milford, 1960-62; guidance counselor, psychol. examiner Jonathan Law High Sch., Milford, 1962-73, Nat. Honor Soc. adv., 1966-73, mem. Curriculum Councils, Graduation Requirement Council, Gifted Child Com., others, 1940-48, 60-73; guidance dir. Foran High Sch., Milford, 1973-79, career center coordinator, 1976-79, ret., 1979. Active various community drives; mem. exec. bd. Ridge Rd PTA, 1956-59; mem. Parent-Tchr. council Hopkins Grammer Sch., New Haven; mem. Human Relations Council, North Haven, 1967-69; vol., patient rep. surg. waiting rm. Fawcett Meml. Hosp., P.C., Sun City Ctr. Emergency Squad, Good Samaritans. Mem. Nat. Assn. Secondary Schs. and Colls. (evaluation com.; chmn. testing com.), AAUW, LWV, Conn. Personnel and Guidance Assn., Conn. Sch. Counselors Assn., Conn. Assn. Sch. Psychol. Personnel, Conn., Milford (pres. 1945-47) edn. assns. Clubs: Univ., Charlotte Harbor Yacht, Sun City Ctr. Golf and Racquet. Home: 237 Courtyard Blvd Apt 202 Sun City Center FL 33573-5779

STANTON, WILLIAM JOHN, JR., marketing educator, author; b. Chgo., Dec. 15, 1919; s. William John and Winifred (McGann) S.; m. Imma Mair, Sept. 14, 1978; children by previous marriage: Kathleen Louise, William John III. BS, Ill. Inst. Tech., 1940; MBA, Northwestern U., 1941, PhD, 1948. Mgmt. trainee Sears Roebuck & Co., 1940-41; instr. U. Ala., 1941-44; auditor Olan Mills Portrait Studios, Chattanooga, 1944-46; asst. prof., asso. prof. U. Wash., 1948-55; prof. U. Colo., Boulder, 1955-90; prof. emeritus, 1990—; head mktg. dept. U. Colo., 1955-71, acting dean, 1963-64; assoc. dean U. Colo. (Sch. Bus.), 1964-67. Author: Economic Aspects of Recreation in Alaska, 1953; (with Richard H. Buskirk and Rosann Spiro) Management of a Sales Force, 9th edit., 1995 (also Spanish transl.), (with others) Challenge of Business, 1975, (with M. Etzel and B. Walker) Fundamentals of Marketing, 11th edit., 1997 (also Spanish, Portuguese and Indonesian transls.), (with M.S. Sommers and J.G. Barnes) Can. edit. Fundamentals of Marketing, 7th edit., 1995, (with K. Miller and R. Layton) Australian edit., 3d edit., 1994, (with R. Varaldo) Italian edit., 2d edit., 1990, (with others) South African edit., 1992; monographs on Alaska Tourist Industry, 1953-54; contbr. articles to profl. jours. Mem. Am. Mktg. Assn., Western Mktg. Assn., Beta Gamma Sigma. Roman Catholic. Home: 1445 Sierra Dr Boulder CO 80302-7846

STANTON-HICKS, MICHAEL D'ARCY, anesthesiologist, educator; b. Adelaide, Australia, June 3, 1931; came to U.S., 1972; s. Cedric Stanton-Hicks and Florence (Haggett) Perrin; m. Kristina Litsmark, Aug. 4, 1969 (div. Aug. 1984); children: Erik Michael, Leif Neal; m. Ursula Koch, Aug. 27, 1985. MB, BChir, Adelaide U., 1962; MD, U. Dusseldorf, 1984. Bd. equivalent Am. Bd. Anesthesiology; diplomate Am. Bd. Pain Medicine. Intern Queen Elizabeth Hosp., Adelaide, 1961-62, tutor, staff anesthesiologist, 1970-72; resident Royal Postgrad. Med. Sch., London and Lasarettet Köping, 1966-68; asst. dir. anesthesiology intensive care Södersjükhuset, Stockholm, 1968-69; instr. anesthesiology U. Wash. Med. Sch., Seattle, 1969-70, asst. prof., 1972-75; prof., chmn. dept. U. Mass. Med. Sch., Worcester, 1975-83; prof. U. Colo. Health Scis. Ctr., Denver, 1983-86, vice chmn. dept., 1983-85, acting chmn., 1985-86; prof., dir. pain clinic and rsch. Johannes Gutenberg U., Mainz, Germany, 1986-88, prof., 1986—; dir. pain mgmt. ctr. Cleve. Clinic Found., 1988—; med. examiner Indsl. Commn. Ohio; mem. Gov.'s Ohio Pain Initiative, Dept. Health. Author, editor: Regional Anesthesia: Advances and Selected Topics, 1978; (with Boas) Chronic Low Back Pain, 1982; author: (with Raj and Nolte) Illustrated Manual of Regional Anesthesia, 1988 (Most Beautiful Book of Yr. award Frankfurt, Fed. Republic Germany Pubs. Book Conv. 1989), Pain and Sympathetic Nervous System, 1989; (with Janig and Boas) Reflex Sympathetic Dystrophy, 1989; (with Janig) Reflex Sympathetic Dystrophy: A Reappraisal, 1996. Squadron leader res. Royal Australian Air Force, 1962-65. Australian Univs. Commn. mature age scholar, 1953-60. Fellow Royal Coll. Surgeons (faculty anesthetists), Royal Coll. Anesthetists, Am. Acad. Pain Medicine; mem. Internat. Assn. Study Pain (chmn. spl. interest group on sympathetically maintained pain 1990—), Am. Soc. Regional Anesthesia (bd. dirs. 1979-91, pres. 1989-90, Disting. Svc. award, 1998), Am. Soc. Anesthesiologists, Assn. Anesthetists Gt. Britain and Ireland, Ohio State Med. Assn., Cleve. Acad. Medicine, Am. Acad. Med. Infrared Imaging (bd. dirs. 1991—, pres. 1994-95), Am. Pain Soc., Am. Acad. Pain Medicine, Am. Neuromodulation Soc. (pres. 1994—), Army-Navy-Air Force Club. Republican. Anglican. Avocations: skiing, photography, travel, flying. Home: 198 Woodsong Way Chagrin Falls OH 44023-6703 Office: Cleve Clinic Found 9500 Euclid Ave Cleveland OH 44195-0001

STANWICK, TAD, retired systems engineer; b. Severn, Md., May 4, 1916; s. Walter L. and Mary Ann (Pfeiffer); m. Wickliffe Shackleford, Dec. 16, 1941; children: Covington Philip, Wickliffe Mary, Wells Thomas. Student, St. John's Coll., Annapolis, Md., 1935, U.S. Naval Acad., 1936. Asst. to pres. and chmn. bd. Am. Machine & Foundry Co., N.Y.C., 1952-55, v.p., 1955-57; v.p., dir. Cleve. Pneumatic Industries, Inc., 1957-62; pres. Pneumo Dynamics Corp., 1959-62; pres., chmn. bd. Stanwick Corp., 1962-92. Author: Lacrosse, 1939. Bd. dirs. U.S. Bus. and Indsl. Council. Served as comdr. USNR, 1940-53. Mem. Philos. Soc. Washington, Soc. Naval Architects and Marine Engrs., Internat. Oceanographic Found., Def. Orientation Conf. Assn., Internat. Christian Union Bus. Execs., Metaphys. Soc. Am., IEEE, Philos. Soc. Am., Holy Name Soc., Phi Sigma Kappa. Clubs: U.S. Yacht Racing Union, Chesapeake Bay Yacht Racing Assn, Annapolis Yacht, CIMAV Yacht, Army and Navy. Home: 4715 Upton St NW Washington DC 20016-2369

STANZLER, JORDAN, lawyer. AB, Harvard U., 1967; JD, U. Chgo., 1972; LLM in Taxation, NYU, 1987. Bar: Calif. 1972, R.I. 1975, N.Y. 1981. Asst. U.S. atty. So. Dist. N.Y., 1982-88, chief tax unit, 1987-88; ptnr. Anderson Kill & Olick, San Francisco, 1988—; lectr. ins. coverage matters. Contbr. articles to profl. jours. Office: Anderson Kill & Olick CitiCorp Ctr 1 Sansome St San Francisco CA 94104-4448

STAPLES, EDWARD TAYLOR, reporter; b. St. Louis, Feb. 12, 1945; s. George Edward and Virginia (How) S.; m. Deborah Jane Moore, June 1990; 1 child, Andrew James. BA, So. Meth. U., 1967; MA in Journalism, U. Mo., Columbia, 1973; cert. Grad. Sch. Journalism, Columbia U., 1991. Polit. reporter The Columbia Tribune, 1972; columnist Civil Svc. Jour., Washington, 1975-78; spokesman, speech writer Civil Svc. Commn., Office Pers. Mgmt., 1973-78; newswriter Hwy. Users Found., 1979-80; writer Media Monitor syndicated radio commentary, 1981-86; mem. staff Accuracy in Media, Reed Irvine Syndicated Newspaper column, 1981-86; editor Trend Watch, Alexandria, Va., 1986-88; staff writer U.S. English, Washington, 1989; editor Am. Banker Newsletter Divsn., Washington, 1990-91; sr. reporter Real Estate Fin. Today, Washington, 1991-97; Washington editor Mortgage Backed Securities Letter, others, 1997—; subeditor Washington Inquirer, 1981-86. Contbr. Global Asset Monitor, London, 1990-91; contbr. articles to profl. jours. and major newspapers in U.S. and abroad (Eng., Scotland and Sweden). With U.S. Army, 1969-70. Selected for Young Am. Polit. Leaders Conf., U.S. State Dept., 1982, 83. Mem. Nat. Assn. Real Estate Editors, Soc. Profl. Journalists, Soc. Am. Bus. Editors and Writers. Avocation: squash. Home: 2919 Wellington Rd Alexandria VA 22308 Office: IDD 1130 17th St NW Ste 430 Washington DC 20036-4641

STAPLES, JOHN NORMAN, III, lawyer; b. Durham, N.C., Aug. 1, 1946; s. Norman Appleton Staples and Elizabeth (Stewart-Richardson) Smith; m. Lila Banks James, May 18, 1968; children: Susan Banks, John William, James Nicholas. BA in English, Trinity Coll., 1968; JD, Pepperdine U., 1976. Bar: Calif. 1976. Former ptnr. Millard, Morris & Staples, Carmel; head of adv. svcs. West Coast Alex Brown Capital Adv. Trust Co., San Francisco, Calif.; bd. dirs. Household Credit Svcs., Salinas, Calif. Bd. dirs. Monterey Peninsula United Way, 1980-83, Planned Parenthood Monterey County, 1986-90; chmn. bd. dirs. All Sts. Episcopal Day Sch., Carmel Valley, Calif., 1986-89; trustee Monterey Peninsula Mus. Art; trustee Calif. Assn. Ind. Schs., 1986-89. Capt. USMC, 1968-73, lt. col. USAFR, Ret. Mem. ABA, Monterey County Bar Assn., Calif. Bar Assn. Office: Alex Brown Adv Trust Co 101 California St Fl 46 San Francisco CA 94111-5802

STAPLES, O. SHERWIN, orthopedic surgeon; b. Boston, May 19, 1908; s. Oscar S. and Nellie E. (Barnes) S.; m. Mable Hughes, Dec. 11, 1945; children—Katherine E., Thomas H. A.B., Harvard, 1930, M.D., 1935. Diplomate: Am. Bd. Orthopaedic Surgery (examiner 1964-69). Intern Boston City Hosp., 1935-37; resident Mass. Gen., Children's hosps., Boston, 1937-39; asst. orthopaedic surgery (Mass. Gen. Hosp.), 1939-46; asst. orthopaedic surgeon New Eng. Peabody Home Crippled Children, 1939-46; chmn. orthopaedic surgery sect. Hitchcock Clinic and Mary Hitchcock Meml. Hosp., 1946-73; cons. VA Hosp., White River Junction, Vt., 1947-73, chief, orthopedic sect., 1973-81, cons. orthopedics, 1981-92; asst. orthopaedic surgery Harvard Med. Sch., 1939-46; mem. faculty, chmn. orthopaedic sect. Dartmouth Med. Sch., 1946-73, clin. prof. surgery, 1967-73, emeritus, 1973—. Asso. editor: Jour. Bone and Joint Surgery, 1961-67; Contbr. articles to med. jours. Served from capt. to lt. col. M.C. AUS, 1942-45, MTO. Mem. Aesculapian Club, N.H. Med. Soc., Grafton County Med. Soc. (pres. 1963), Boylston Med. Soc., Boston Orthopaedic Club (pres. 1960-61), Am. Acad. Orthopaedic Surgeons, A.C.S., Am. Orthopaedic Assn., New Eng. Surg. Soc., Soc. Internat. de Chirurgie Orthopedique et de Traumatologie, Am. Orthopaedic Foot Soc. (founding), Assn. Orthopaedic Chmn. (founding). Home: Hemlock Rd Hanover NH 03755

STAPLES, RICHARD FARNSWORTH, lawyer; b. Providence, Nov. 24, 1919; s. Harold E. and Margaret (Smith) S.; m. Mary Kingsbury, June 20, 1942; children: Richard Farnsworth, Jr., Benjamin T., Edward K. A.B., Harvard U., 1941, LL.B., 1949. Bar: R.I. 1949. Ptnr. Tillinghast, Collins & Graham, Providence, 1949-81; ptnr. Hinckley, Allen & Snyder, Providence, 1981-87, of counsel, 1987—; mem. commn. on jud. tenure and discipline, 1987-93; mem. ethics adv. panel R.I. Supreme Ct., 1995—. Chmn. sch. com. Town of Barrington (R.I.), 1956-62, mem., 1957-62; mem. State Bd. Edn., Providence, 1964-69, chmn., 1968-69; pres. R.I. Hist. Soc., 1981-83. Served to 1st lt. U.S. Army, 1943-46. Decorated Bronze Star. Mem. ABA, R.I. Bar Assn., Soc. Colonial Wars, Providence Art Club, Harvard Club. Home: 180 Slater Ave Providence RI 02906-5723 also: Loon Lake Rd Freedom NH 03836-0298

STAPLETON, HARVEY JAMES, physics educator; b. Kalamazoo, Dec. 22, 1934; s. Herbert James and Viola Delia (Early) S.; m. Joan Eilleen Sylvander, June 22, 1957; children: Patricia Lynne, Susan Joan, Jeffrey Denis. B.S., U. Mich., 1957; Ph.D., U. Calif., Berkeley, 1961. Faculty physics U. Ill., Urbana, 1961—, prof., 1969-95, prof. emeritus, 1995—, assoc. dean Grad. Coll., 1980-95, assoc. vice chancellor for rsch., 1987-95; interim dean Grad. Coll., 1992; interim vice chancellor for rsch. U. Ill., 1992; Alfred P. Sloan fellow, 1962-64. Contbr. articles to profl. jours. Fellow Am. Phys. Soc.; mem. Phi Beta Kappa, Sigma Xi, Phi Sigma Kappa, Phi Kappa Phi, Phi Eta Sigma. Roman Catholic. Home: 3806 Gulf Of Mexico Dr # 310 Longboat Key FL 34228-2706

STAPLETON, JAMES FRANCIS, lawyer; b. Bridgeport, Conn., June 30, 1932; s. James M. and Lucy V. (Moran) S.; m. Margaret M. Daly, July 13, 1957; children: James F., Mark T., Paul and Kathleen. BSS, Fairfield U., 1954; LLB, Boston Coll., 1957; LLM, Georgetown U., 1958. Bar: Conn. 1957, U.S. Dist. Ct. (ea. and so. dists.) N.Y. 1979, U.S. Ct. Appeals (2d cir.) 1966, U.S. Dist. Ct. Conn. 1961, Mass. 1957, U.S. Supreme Ct. 1965, U.S. Ct. Appeals, (D.C. cir.) 1958. Atty., Appellate Sect., Antitrust Div., U.S. Dept. Justice, 1957-58; assoc., ptnr. Marsh, Day & Calhoun, Bridgeport, Conn., 1958-73; city atty. City of Bridgeport, 1971-73; legis. counsel Conn. Bankers Assn., 1971-73; judge Conn. Superior Ct., 1973-78; chmn. Criminal Justice Commn., State of Conn., 1991-95; ptnr. Day, Berry & Howard, Stamford, Conn., 1978—. Mem. Bridgeport Bd. Edn., 1960-69. Fellow Am. Bar Found., Am. Coll. Trial Lawyers (chmn. state com. 1994-96, regent 1996—); mem. Am. Bd. Trial Advocates, Conn. Bar Assn. (bd. govs., ho. of dels., v.p., pres.), Fed. Bar Coun. Found. for 2d Circuit (chmn.), ABA, Bridgeport Bar Assn., Stamford-Darien Bar Assn. Home: 225 Winton Rd Fairfield CT 06430-3858 Office: Day Berry & Howard One Canterbury Green Stamford CT 06901

STAPLETON, JAMES HALL, statistician, educator; b. Royal Oak, Mich., Feb. 8, 1931; s. James Leo and Dorothy May (Hall) S.; m. Alicia M. Brown, Apr. 3, 1963; children: James, Lara, Sara. B.A., Eastern Mich. U., 1952; M.S., Purdue U., 1954, Ph.D., 1957. Statistician Gen. Electric Co., 1957-58; asst. prof. stats. and probability Mich. State U., East Lansing, 1958-63; asso. prof. Mich. State U., 1963-72, prof., 1972—, chmn. dept., 1968-75, grad. dir., 1985-96; cons. Gen. Telephone Co. of Ind.; vis. prof. U. Philippines, 1978-79. Mem. USS-Mich. Swim Com., AAU, 1976-84, chmn., 1976-78; mem. Mich. AAU Exec. Bd., 1976-81. NSF fellow, 1966-67. Mem. Inst. Math. Stats., Am. Statis. Assn. Office: Mich State U Dept Statistics East Lansing MI 48823

STAPLETON, JEAN, journalism educator; b. Albuquerque, June 24, 1942; d. James L. and Mary (Behrman) S.; m. John Clegg, Apr. 15, 1965 (dec. Sept. 1972); m. Richard Bright, Jan. 13, 1973 (div. 1985); children: Lynn, Paul, Bright; m. William Walter Farran, Nov. 9, 1996. BA, U. N.Mex., 1964; MS in Journalism, Northwestern U., 1968. Reporter Glenview (Ill.) Announcements, 1967-68, Angeles Mesa News Advertiser, L.A., 1968-69, City News Svc., Radio News West, L.A., 1969-71; press sec. polit. campaign, 1972; instr. journalism East L.A. Coll., 1973-75, prof., dept. chair, 1975—. Author: Equal Marriage, 1975, Equal Dating, 1979. Mem. NOW (pres. L.A. chpt. 1973-74), Women in Comm., Soc. Profl. Journalists, Ninety Nines, Am. Yankee Assn. Democrat. Methodist. Home: 3232 Philo St Los Angeles CA 90064-4719 Office: East LA Coll 1301 Avenida Cesar Chavez Monterey Park CA 91754-6001

STAPLETON, JEAN (JEANNE MURRAY), actress; b. N.Y.C.; d. Joseph E. and Marie (Stapleton) Murray; m. William H. Putch (dec.); 2 children. Student, Hunter Coll., N.Y.C., Am. Apprentice Theatre, Am. Actors Co., Am. Theatre Wing; student with, Harold Clurman; LHD (hon.), Emerson Coll.; hon. degree, Hood Coll., Monmouth Coll. Opera debut in Candide with Balt. Opera Co.; appeared in The Italian Lesson with Balt. Opera; first N.Y. stage role in The Corn is Green, Equity Library Theatre; starred as mother in Am. Gothic, Circle-in-the-Sq.; Broadway debut with Judith Anderson In The Summer House; also appeared on Broadway in Damn Yankees, Bells Are Ringing, Juno, Rhinoceros and Funny Girl, Arsenic & Old Lace, Bwax & On Tour; first major break in comic ingenue role as Myrtle Mae with Frank Fay in Harvey on-tour; played with nat. tour of Come Back, Little Sheba starring Shirley Booth; starred in tour of Morning's at Seven, The Show-Off, Daisy Mayme; appeared in motion pictures including Damn Yankees, 1958, Bells Are Ringin, 1960, Up the Down Staircase, 1967, Cold Turkey, 1971, The Buddy System, 1984, Klute; appeared in numerous TV shows including Studio One, Naked City, Armstrong Circle Theatre, The Defenders, Jackie Gleason show, PBS-TV appearances Grown-ups; performances include Trying Times Shakespeare Co. D.C., 1994, Night Seasons, Signature Theatre N.Y., 1994, Blithe Spirit, Costa Mesa, Calif., Mrs. Piggle-Wiggle on Showtime; guest star Grace Underfire (Emmy nomination), Caroline in the City, Murphy Brown, The Matchmaker at A.C.T., S.F., Guest: Everybody Loves Raymond "The Entertainer" at CSC, N.Y., Film: "Michael" with John Travolta; stepmother in N.Y.C. Opera's Cinderella, 1995, The Habitation of Dragon's on TNT, Roads to Home, Eleanor: First Lady of the World, The Birthday Party, MOuntain Language; CD-Rom Grandma Ollie's Morphabet Soup, 1996. U.S. commr. to Internat. Woman's Yr. Commn. and Nat. Conf. Women, Houston, 1977; bd. dirs. Women's Rsch. and Edn. Inst.; trustee Actors' Fund Am. Recipient Emmy award for best performance in comedy series All in the Family 1970-71, 71-72, 78, Golden Globe awards Hollywood Fgn. Press Assn. 1972, 73, Obie award, 1990. Mem. AFTRA, SAG, Actors Equity Assn. Office: care Bauman & Hiller 5757 Wilshire Blvd Los Angeles CA 90036-3635

STAPLETON, KATHARINE HALL (KATIE STAPLETON), food broadcaster, author; b. Kansas City, Mo., Oct. 29, 1919; d. William Mabin and Katharine (Hall) Foster; m. Benjamin Franklin Stapleton, June 20, 1942; children: Benjamin Franklin, III, Craig Roberts, Katharine Hall. BA, Vassar Coll., 1941. Cookbook reviewer Denver Post, 1974-84; producer, writer, host On the Front Burner, daily radio program Sta. KOA-CBS, Denver, 1976-79, Cooking with Katie, live one-hour weekly, Sta. KOA, 1979-89; guest broadcaster Geneva Radio, 1974, London Broadcasting Corp., 1981, 82; tour leader culinaries to Britain, France and Switzerland, 1978-85. Eng., 1978. Chmn. women's div. United Fund, 1955-56; founder, chmn. Denver Debutante Ball, 1956, 57; hon. chmn. Nat. Travelers Aid Assn., 1952-56, 93-96; commr. Denver Centennial Authority, 1958-60; trustee Washington Cathedral, regional v.p., 1967-73; trustee, Colo. Women's Coll., 1975-80; sole trustee Harmes C. Fishback Found. Decorated chevalier de L'Etoile Noire (France); recipient People-to-People citation, 1960, 66, Beautiful Activist award Altrusa Club, 1972, Gran Skillet award Colo./Wyo. Restaurant Assn., 1981, Humanitarian of Yr. award Arthritis Found., 1995, Disting. Woman of Yr. award Rocky Mountain News, 1996; named Chevalier du Tastevin, 1989, Outstanding Vol. Fundraiser Nat. Philanthropy Day, 1995, Disting. Woman of Yr., Rocky Mountain News. Republican. Episcopalian. Clubs: Denver Country, Denver. Author: Denver Delicious, 1980, 3d. edit., 1983; High Notes, 1984. Home: 8 Village Rd Cherry Hills Village CO 80110

STAPLETON, KATHARINE LAURENCE, English literature educator, writer; b. Holyoke, Mass., Nov. 20, 1911; d. Richard Prout and Frances (Purtill) S. A.B., Smith Coll., 1932; postgrad., U. London, Eng., 1932-33. Registrar Mass. Pub. Employment Service, 1933-34; mem. faculty Bryn Mawr Coll., 1934—, prof. English and polit. theory, 1948-64, chmn. dept. English, 1954-65, Mary E. Garrett prof. English, 1964-80, prof. emeritus, 1980—. Author: Justice and World Society, 1944, The Design of Democracy, 1949, H.D. Thoreau: A Writer's Journal, 1960, Yushin's Log and Other Poems, 1969, The Elected Circle: Studies in the Art of Prose, 1973, Marianne Moore: The Poet's Advance, 1978, Some Poets and Their Resources: The Future Agenda, 1995. Mem. bd. sponsors Nat. Com. for an Effective Congress. Recipient Lindback Found. award, 1980; Smith Coll. Alumnae fellow, 1932-33; Guggenheim fellow, 1947-48; Nat. Endowment for Arts fellow, 1972-73. Mem. MLA, Renaissance Soc., Thoreau Soc., Assn. Lit. Scholars and Critics, Four Chaplains Legion of Honor, Phi Beta Kappa. Home: 229 N Roberts Rd Bryn Mawr PA 19010-2817

STAPLETON, MAUREEN, actress; b. Troy, N.Y., June 21, 1925; d. John P. and Irene (Walsh) S.; m. Max Allentuck, July 1949 (div. Feb. 1959); children: Daniel, Katharine; m. David Rayfiel, July, 1963 (div.). Student, Siena Coll, 1943. Debut in Playboy of the Western World, 1946; toured with Barretts of Wimpole Street, 1947; plays include Anthony and Cleopatra, 1947, Detective Story, The Bird Cage, Rose Tattoo, 1950-51, The Sea Gull, Orpheus Descending, The Cold Wind and the Warm, 1959, Toys in the Attic, 1960-61, Plaza Suite, 1969, The Gingerbread Lady, 1970 (Tony award 1970), 27 Wagons Full of Cotton, Country Girl, 1972, Secret Affairs of Mildred Wild, 1972, The Gin Game, 1977-78, The Little Foxes, 1981; motion pictures include Lonely Hearts, 1959, The Fugitive Kind, 1960, A View from the Bridge, 1962, Bye Bye Birdie, 1963, Trilogy, 1969, Airport, 1970, Plaza Suite, 1971, Interiors, 1978, The Runner Stumbles, 1979, Reds, 1981 (Oscar award as best supporting actress), The Fan, 1981, On the Right Track, 1981, The Electric Grandmother, 1982, Mother's Day, 1984, Johnny Dangerously, 1984, Cocoon, 1985, The Money Pit, 1986, Nuts, 1987, Made in Heaven, 1987, Cocoon: The Return, 1990, Passed Away, 1992, Trading Mom, 1994, The Last Good Time, 1995; TV films include Tell Me Where It Hurts, 1974, Cat On a Hot Tin Roof, 1976, All the King's Men, 1958, For Whom the Bell Tolls, 1959, Save Me a Place at Forest Lawn, 1966, Mirror, Mirror, Off the Wall, 1969, Queen of the Stardust Ballroom, 1975, The Gathering, 1977, Part II, 1979, Letters From Frank, 1979, Little Gloria ... Happy at Last, 1982, Sentimental Journey, 1984, Private Sessions, 1985, Liberace: Behind the Music, 1988, Last Wish, 1992, Miss Rose White, 1992. Recipient Nat. Inst. Arts and Letters award, 1969. *

STAPLETON, NIGEL JOHN, multinational information publishing executive; b. London, Nov. 1, 1946; s. Frederick Ernest John and Katie Margaret (Tyson) S.; m. Johanna Augusta Molhoek, Dec. 20, 1982; children: Henry James, Elizabeth Jane. BA with honors, Cambridge U., Eng., 1968; MA, Cambridge U., 1971. Internal auditor Unilever, Ltd., London, 1968-70; group mgr. internal audit Unilever, Ltd., 1970-73, sr. auditor, 1973-75; corp. planning mgr. Bocm Silcock, Hampshire, Eng., 1975-77; devel. dir. Bocm Silcock, 1977-80; comml. mem. N.Am. office Unilever PLC, London, 1980-82; v.p. fin. Unilever U.S., Inc., N.Y.C., 1982-86; fin. dir. Reed Internat. P.L.C., London, 1986-96; dep. chmn. Reed Internat., London, 1994-96; CFO Reed Elsevier PLC, London, 1994-96, chmn., 1997—. Fellow Chartered Inst. Mgmt. Accts.; mem. United Oxford and Cambridge Club. Avocations: tennis, opera, classical music. Office: Reed Elsevier PLC, 25 Victoria St, London SW1H 0EX, England

STAPLETON, WALTER KING, federal judge; b. Cuthbert, Ga., June 2, 1934; s. Theodore Newton and Elizabeth Grantland (King) S.; m. Georgianna Duross Stapleton; children: Russell K., Theodore N., Teryl J. B.A., Princeton, 1956; LL.B., Harvard, 1959; LL.M., U. Va., 1984. Bar: Del. Assoc. mem. firm Morris, Nichols, Arsht & Tunnell, Wilmington, Del., 1959-65; dep. atty. gen. State of Del., 1963; partner Morris, Nichols, Arsht & Tunnell, 1966-70; judge U.S. Dist. Ct. Del., Wilmington, 1970-85; chief judge U.S. Dist. Ct. Del., 1983-85; judge U.S. Ct. Appeals (3d cir.), 1985—; Dep. atty. gen., Del., 1964; mem. Jud. Conf. U.S., 1984-85. Bd. dirs. Am. Bapt. Chs., U.S.A., 1978. Baptist. Office: US Ct Appeals 844 N King St Wilmington DE 19801-3519

STAPP, DAN ERNEST, retired lawyer, utility executive; b. New Orleans, July 1, 1934; s. James Frank, Jr. and Marguerite Edna (Joubert) S.; m. Barbara Allan Wilmot, June 10, 1961; children: Marguerite Wilmot (dec.), Mary Darby, Paul Wilmot, James Andrew. B.B.A., Loyola U., New Orleans, 1955, LL.B., 1957. Bar: La. 1957. With New Orleans Pub. Service Inc., 1958-68, asst. to v.p., 1965-68; with Entergy Svcs. (formerly MSU System Svcs. Inc.), New Orleans, 1968-92; v.p., sec., asst. treas. Entergy Svcs., 1968-80; sr. v.p., 1980-92; sec. System Fuels, Inc., New Orleans, 1972-92, Entergy Corp. (formerly Middle South Utilities, Inc.), New Orleans, 1974-92, Systems Energy Resources, Inc., Jackson, Miss., 1974-91, Electec, Inc., 1984-91, Entergy Ops., Inc., 1990-91, Enterg Power, Inc., 1990-92. Trustee Mercy Hosp., New Orleans, 1973-80, pres., 1975, chmn. bd. devel., 1971-72; mem. pres.'s coun. Loyola U., 1975-85, chmn., 1980-82; adv. coun. Coll. Bus. Adminstrn., 1969-70; mem. adv. bd. Asso. Cath. Charities, 1979-82; gen. chmn. United Way Greater New Orleans, 1978, trustee, 1978-84; mem. exec. bd. New Orleans Area coun. Boy Scouts Am., 1980-85, pres., 1984-85. 2d lt. AUS, 1957. Mem. ABA, La. Bar Assn., New Orleans Country Club, Pickwick Club, Blue Key (past chpt. pres.), Alpha Sigma Nu, Delta Theta Phi. Republican. Roman Catholic. Home: 401 Bellaire Dr New Orleans LA 70124-1014

STAPP, JOHN PAUL, flight surgeon, retired air force officer; b. Bahia, Brazil, July 11, 1910; s. Charles Franklin and Mary Louise (Shannon) S.; m. Lillian Lanese, Dec. 23, 1957. B.A., Baylor U., 1931, M.A. cum laude, 1932, D.Sc., 1956; Ph.D., U. Tex., 1939; M.D., U. Minn., 1943; grad., Army Field Service Sch., 1944, Sch. Aviation Medicine, 1945, Indsl. Med. Course, 1946; D.Sc., N.Mex. State U., 1979. Diplomate Am. Bd. Preventive Medicine, Am. Bd. Aerospace Medicine. Intern St. Mary's Hosp., Duluth, Minn., 1944; commd. 1st lt. U.S. Army, 1944; advanced through grades to col. M.C. USAF, 1957; resident Lincoln Army AC Regional, 1944-45; research project officer (Aero Med. Lab.), Wright Field, Ohio, 1946; chief lab. (Aero Med. Lab.), 1958-60; chief scientist aerospace med. div. Brooks AFB, Tex., 1960-65; chief impact injury br. (Armed Forces Inst. Pathology), Washington, 1965-67; chief med. scientist Nat. Hwy. Safety Bur., 1967-70; cons. N.Mex. State U. Phys. Sci. Lab., La Cruces; cons. Dept. Transp., Washington, 1970-72; adj. prof. Safety and Sys. Mgmt. Ctr., U. So. Calif., 1972-76, Sys. Mgmt. Ctr., L.A., 1973-76; cons. accident epidemiology and pathology Armed Forces, Bur. Stds., NIH, Nat. Acad. Scis., Gen. Svcs. Adminstrn.; chief Aero Med. Field Lab., Holloman AFB, Alamogordo, N.Mex., 1953-58; cons. N.Mex. State U. Phys. Scis. Lab., Las Cruces, 1972—; mem. subcom. on flight safety NACA; permanent chmn. SAE Ann Stapp Car Crash Conf.; chmn. Gov.'s Commn. Internat. Space Ctr., 1986; pres. N.Mex. Rsch. Inst., 1987. Contbr. chpts. to books, articles to profl. jours. Mem. N.Mex. Gov.'s Commn. Internat. Space Hall of Fame, 1974—; mem. N.Mex. Planning Bd., 1975—; Bd. dirs. Kettering Found.; v.p. Internat. Astronautical Fedn., 1959-60. Decorated DSM with bronze oak leaf, Legion of Merit (for crash rsch.) with bronze oak leaf; recipient award for outstanding rsch. by Air Force officer Nat. Air Coun., 1951, John Jeffries award for med. rsch. Inst. Aero. Sci., 1953, Air Power award for sci. Air Force Assn., 1954, Flight Safety Found. award for contbns. Air Transp. Safety, 1954, Air Force Cheney award, 1955, Gorgas award Assn.. Mil. Surgeons, 1956, Med. Tribune award for automotive safety, 1965, award for contbns. to automotive safety Am. Assn. for Automotive Medicine, 1972, Cresson medal Franklin Inst., 1973, Excalibur award safety rsch., 1975, Cert. of Achievement, Nat. Space Club, 1976, Lovelace award NASA Assn. Flight Surgeons, 1982, Outstanding Svc. award Aviation/Space Writers Assn., 1984, Honda medal ASME, 1984, Disting. Alumnus award Baylor U., 1986, Nat. medal for tech. Pres. Bush, 1991, Nat. Medal Tech., 1991; elected to Internat. Space Hall of Fame, 1979, Nat. Aviation Hall of Fame, 1985, Safety and Health Hall of Fame, Internat., 1991, Disting. Pub. Svc. award Nat. Aviation and Space Writers Assn., 1994; ann. John Paul Stapp medal biomechanics Aerospace Med. Assn., 1993—; dedicated Stapp Found., Soc. Automotive Engrs., 1995. Fellow Aero. Med. Assn. (Liliencrantz award for deceleration research 1957), Am. Astronautical Soc., Am. Rocket Soc. (pres. 1959, Wyld award 1955, Leo Stevens medal 1956), Soc. Automotive Engrs.; mem. U.S. Mil. Surgeons Assn., Internat. Acad. Astronautics, Internat. Acad. Aviation Medicine, Civil Aviation Medicine Assn. (pres. 1968), Am. Soc. Safety Engrs. (hon.), Order Daedalians (hon.), Sigma Xi. Achievements include research rocket sled experiments reproducing aircraft crash forces to determine human tolerance limits, 1947-51. Home: PO Box 553 Alamogordo NM 88311-0553 Office: NMex Rsch Inst PO Box 454 Alamogordo NM 88311-0454 *Life is consciousness involved in thinking and doing; it is valued in terms of the quality of resulting contributions to the stream of human advancement. I live in hopes of always doing better and producing more.*

STAPP, OLIVIA BREWER, opera singer; b. N.Y.C., May 31, 1940; d. Henry and Jean Brewer; m. Henry Stapp III; 1 child, Henry. BA, Wagner Coll; studied with, Marjorie Mayer Steen, Ettore Campogalliani, Rodolfo Ricci and Oren Brown; Dr. honoris causa, Wagner Coll., 1988. Artistic dir. Festival Opera, N.Y.C. Appeared as leading soprano in Turandot, Idomeno at La Scala, Milano; Tosca, Elektra, Macbeth, Tabarro at Met. Opera, N.Y.C.; Ernani, Macbeth, Il Tabarro at Liceo Barcelona; Macbeth, Madame Butterfly, Tosca, Aida, Fanciulla del West, Lohengrin at Deutche Oper Berlin; Vespre Siciliani at Grand Theater, Geneva; Nabucco, Attila, Macbeth at Zurich Oper; Salome at The Colon Theater, Buenos Aires; Cavalleria Rusticana, Anna Bolena, Tosca, Nabucco at San Francisco; Elektra Cavalleria Rusticana at Vienna Staatsoper; Idameneo at Munich Staatsoper; Carmen, The Consul, Ariadne auf Naxos, Anna Bolena, Roberto Deveraux, Cavalleria Rusticana at City Opera, N.Y.C.; Lady Macbeth, Nabucco, Turandot at Hamburg Staatsoper; Fanciulla del West, Aida, Nabucco, Turandot at the Arena de Verona; Turandot at Seoul, Korea; Turandot in N.H.K. Tokyo; Norma in Winnipeg, Edmonton, Montreal and Vancouver, Can.; Lady Macbeth in Chatelet Theater, Paris, others. Recipient Puccini award Vissi d'Arte, 1991; Fulbright scholar. Address: Columbia Artist Mgmt Inc Zemsky Green Div 165 W 57th St New York NY 10019-2201

STAPRANS, ARMAND, electronics executive; b. Riga, Latvia, Feb. 28, 1931; s. Theodore and Elvira (Ulmanis) S.; m. Vija Spalvins, Sept. 25, 1955; children: Silvija, Armin, Erik. Student, Willamette U., 1949-52; BSEE, U. Calif., Berkeley, 1954, MSEE, 1955, PhDEE, 1959. Rsch. asst. dept. elec. engring. U. Calif., 1955-57; engr. microwave tube div. Varian Assocs., Palo Alto, Calif., 1957-60, engring. mgr., 1960-68, ops. mgr., 1978-78, 86-89, chief engr., 1978-86, gen. mgr. coupled cavity tube divsn., 1989-92, v.p., 1990-95; gen. mgr. microwave power tube products, 1992-95; pres. microwave power tube products divsn. Comms. and Power Inds., Palo Alto, Calif., 1995—. Contbr. articles to profl. jours., chpt. to book; patentee microwave tubes field. Fellow IEEE (electron device adminstrv. com. 1983-88). Home: 445 Knoll Dr Los Altos CA 94024-4732 Office: Comm and Power Inds M/S B-110 Microwave Power Tube Prod Divsn 811 Hansen Wax Box 50750 Palo Alto CA 94303-0750

STARBIRD, LONNIE DARRYL, producer of custom car shows, designer and builder of custom automobiles; b. Topeka, Aug. 7, 1933; s. Austin Tyler and Lucy Marie (Campbell) S.; m. Donna Mae Gray, July 5, 1953; children: Debra Marie, Clifford Dean, Cristy Mae, Rick Alan. Student, Wichita State U., 1951-54. Owner Starbird Custom Autos, Wichita, Kans., 1955-86, Starbird Prodns., Wichita, 1957-83; pres. Nat. Rod & Custom Assn., Mulvane, Kans., 1970-84, Dickens Christmas Exposition, Mulvane, 1982-83, Nat. Show Prodn., Inc., Mulvane, 1983—, Nat. Ad Agy. Inc., Mulvane, 1983—; design cons. Monogram Models, Morton Grove, Ill., 1963-67; freelance photographer leading auto mags., 1957-86; builder, curator Nat. Rod and Custom Care Hall of Fame Mus., 1996—. Starbird creations featured in Stern Mag. in Germany, 1986, Custom Car mags. in England and Australia, 1979, 83; L & M Custom Car tour of Europe - 6 Starbird creations over 20 major cities, 1986. Named Custom Car Builder of Yr., Nat. Hot Rod Assn., 1960, Constructer of Yr., Internat. Show Car Assn., 1986; recipient Master Builder award Grand Nat. Roadster Show, 1963; winner of 500 trophies in leading auto shows throughout US. Mem. Internat. Auto Show Producers Assn. (v.p. 1986). Roman Catholic. Home: RR 3 Box 180 Afton OK 74331-9003 Office: Nat Show Producers Inc RR 3 Box 180 Afton OK 74331-9003

STARCHMAN, DALE EDWARD, medical radiation biophysics educator; b. Wallace, Idaho, Apr. 16, 1941; s. Hubert V. and Lottie M. (Alford) S.; m. Erlinda Socrates, Dec. 13, 1969; children: Ann, Cindy, Julie, Mark. Student, Rockhurst Coll., 1959-61; BS in Physics, Pitts. (Kans.) State U., 1963; MS in Radiation Biophysics, U. Kans., 1965, PhD in Radiation Biophysics, 1968. Cert. Radiol. Physicist, Health Physicist, Med. Physicist. Chief health physicist ITT Rsch. Inst., Chgo., 1968-71; radiol. physicist Mercy Hosp. Inst. of Radiation Therapy, Chgo., 1968-71; prof., head radiation biophysics Northeast Ohio U. Coll. of Medicine, Rootstown, Ohio, 1971—; pres. Med. Physics Svcs., Inc., Canton, Ohio, 1971—. Author: (with Wayne R. Hedrick and David L. Hykes) Ultrasound Physics and Instrumentation, 3rd edit., 1995; contbr. numerous articles in profl. jours., chpts. in books, monographs. Fellow Am. Coll. Radiology; mem. Am. Assn. Physicists in Medicine (bd. mem. at large 1984-86, pres. Penn-Ohio chpt. 1975-76, rec. sec. midwest chpt. 1970, mem. edn. coun. 1980-83, chmn. Am. assn. med. dosimetrists task group 1976-78, mem. diagnostic radiology task group on quality control 1975—, mem. numerous other coms. 1975-83), Health Physics Soc. (chmn. summer sch. sub. com. 1977-78), Radiol. Soc. N.Am. (assoc. scis. com. 1976-86, task force chmn. 1983-86, mem. 1975-86), Sigma Xi, Kappa Mu Epsilon. Achievements include research areas including selection, quality assurance and acceptance testing of diagnostic x-ray units, design of radiology facilities; effects of tissue inhomogeneities on electron therapy, radiation atrophy in bone, large field therapy swing technique, polymer dosimetry, photon spectra through thick shields, fetal effects, ultrasound. Home and Office: 5942 Easy Pace Cir NW Canton OH 44718-2216

STARE, FREDRICK JOHN, nutritionist, biochemist, physician; b. Columbus, Wis., Apr. 11, 1910; s. Fredrick Arthur and Susan (Seidell) S.; m. Joyce Allen, Sept. 14, 1935 (dec. May 1957); children: Fredrick Allen, David, Mary; m. Helen Haxton Foreman, June 9, 1959 (dec. Feb. 1974); m. Mary Bartlett Bade, Dec. 30, 1976 (div. 1983); m. Irene Mackey Kinsey, Sept. 15, 1984. B.S., U. Wis., 1931, M.S., 1932, Ph.D., 1934; M.D., U. Chgo., 1941; MA (hon.), Harvard U., 1945; D.Sc., Suffolk, 1963, Trinity Coll., Dublin, 1964, Muskingum Coll., 1977. Asst. biochemist U. Wis., 1931-34; Nat. Research fellow Washington U. Sch. Medicine, St. Louis, 1934-35; Gen. Edn. Bd. fellow Cambridge (Eng.) U., 1935-36, Szeged, Hungary, 1936, Zurich, 1937; research assoc. Bowman Cancer Found., Wis., 1937-39; intern Barnes Hosp., St. Louis, 1941-42; asst. prof. nutrition Harvard Med. Sch. and Sch. Pub. Health; prof. nutrition, chmn. dept. nutrition, 1942-76; prof. nutrition emeritus Harvard Sch. Pub. Health, 1976—; jr. asso. medicine Peter Bent Brigham Hosp., 1942-44, asso. in medicine, 1944-50, sr. asso. medicine, 1950-60, cons. medicine, 1960-70; co-founder syndicated radio program Healthline; dir. Continental Group; former mem. food and nutrition bd. NRC; cons. nutrition Sec. War, USPHS; mem. health adv. com. Fgn. Operations Adminstrn.; com. health Commn. on Inter-govtl. Relations; mem. Nat. Health Edn. Com. Author: Living Nutrition, Scope Manual on Nutrition, Eat OK-Feel OK, Food for Today's Teens, Food for Fitness After Fifty; The Executive Diet, Panic in the Pantry, Your Basic Guide to Nutrition, Dear Dr. Stare: What Shall I Eat?, The Harvard Square Diet; Nutrition for Good Health, The 100% Natural, Purely Organic, Cholesterol-Free, Megavitamin, Low-carbohydrate Nutrition Hoax, Balanced Nutrition Beyond The Cholesterol Scare, Adventures in Nutrition, Your Guide to Good Nutrition; nat. syndicated columnist: Food and Your Health; former editor: Nutrition Revs. Overseer emeritus New Eng. Conservatory Music; bd. dir. Lown Cardiovascular Found., Pathfinder Internat.; co-founder, bd. dirs. Am. Coun. Sci. and Health. Recipient Pub. Svc. award U. Chgo., 1982, medal of honor Internat. Found. for Nutrition Rsch. and Edn., 1989, Disting. Svc. award U. Chgo. Med. and Biol. Scis. Alumni Assn., 1992, Excellence in Med. Nutrition Edn. award Am. Soc. Clin. Nutrition, 1993, Disting. Emeritus Prof. award Harvard Sch. Pub. Health, 1993, citation for 50 yrs. of svc. Harvard U., 1993, Am. Coun. Sci. and Health award, 1994; Fredrick John Stare professorship of nutrition established by Harvard U., 1991; John Harvard fellow, 1996. Fellow APHA, Royal Irish Coll. Physicians (hon.); mem. AMA (Goldberger award 1961), Am. Acad. Arts and Scis., Mass. Med. Soc., Am. Chem. Soc., Am. Soc. Biol. Chemists, Am. Inst. Nutrition (Elvehjem award 1969), Biochem. Soc. (Eng.), Am. Soc. Clin. Investigation, Am. Soc. Arteriosclerosis, Am. Dietetic Assn. (hon.), Group of European Nutritionists (hon.), Soc. Nutrition Edn., Harvard Club (Boston, N.Y.C.), Cosmos Club, Sigma Xi. Home: 267 Cartwright Rd Box 812085 Wellesley MA 02181-0013 Office: Harvard U Sch Pub Health 665 Huntington Ave Boston MA 02115-6021 *I never expect anyone to work any harder than I do. Be overly generous in giving credit to others. Never ask anyone to do anything you are not willing to do yourself.*

STARER, BRIAN D., lawyer; b. Utica, N.Y., 1945. BS, U.S. Merchant Marine Acad., 1967; JD, Union U., 1972. Bar: N.Y. 1972, U.S. Dist. Ct. (no., so. and ea. dists.) N.Y., U.S. Ct. Appeals (2nd, 3rd and 5th cirs.) 1973, U.S. Ct. Appeals (9th cir.) 1976, U.S. Supreme Ct. 1977, U.S. Ct. Internat. Trade 1977, U.S. Ct. Customs and Patent Appeals 1980. Mem. Haight, Gardner, Poor & Havens, N.Y.C. Mng. editor Albany Law Rev., 1971-72; contbr. articles to profl. jours. Mem. ABA, Maritime Law Assn. U.S., Internat. Bar Assn., N.Y. State Bar Assn. Office: Haight Gardner Poor & Havens 195 Broadway New York NY 10007-3100

STARER, ROBERT, composer; b. Vienna, Austria, Jan. 8, 1924; came to U.S., 1947, naturalized, 1957; s. Nison and Erna (Gottlieb) S.; m. Johanna Herz, Mar. 27, 1942; 1 child, Daniel. Student, State Acad., Vienna, 1938-39, Jerusalem Conservatory, 1939-42; postgrad. diploma, Juilliard Sch. Music, 1949. mem. faculty Juilliard Sch. Music, 1949-74; assoc. prof. Bklyn. Coll., 1963-66, prof., 1966-91, Disting. prof., 1986-91, ret., 1991. Composer: Symphony 1, 1950, Symphony 2, 1951, Piano Concerto 1, 1947, Piano Concerto 2, 1952, Concerto a Tre, 1954, Viola Concerto, 1958, Ariel, 1959, Joseph and His Brothers, 1966; opera The Intruder, 1956, Concerto for Violin Cello and Orch, 1967, Six Variations with Twelve Notes, 1967, On The Nature of Things (chorus), 1968, Symphony 3, 1969; ballets The Dybbuk, 1960, Samson Agonistes, 1961, Phaedra, 1963, Mutabili, 1965, Third St. Overture, 1970, (opera), Pantagleize, 1971, Concerto Piano 3, 1972, Images of Man, 1973, Stone Ridge Set, Mandala, Profiles in Brass, 1974, The Last Lover (opera), 1975, Journals of a Songmaker; text by Gail Godwin, 1975, The People, Yes; text by Carl Sandburg, 1976, Piano Quartet, 1977; song cycle Transformations, 1978; operas Apollonia, 1978, Anna Margarita's Will, 1979; chorus Voices of Brooklyn, 1980, Evanescence, 1981; Violin Concerto, 1982, Hudson Valley Suite, 1983, Concerto a Quattro, 1984, Piano Trio, 1985, Remembering Felix, 1986, Kaaterskill Quartet, 1987, Cello Concerto, 1987, Duo for violin and piano, 1988, Angel Voices for brass and organ, 1989, Night Thoughts for chorus and synthesizer, 1990, Yizkor and Anima Eterna for flute and harpsichord, 1991, Clarinet Quintet, 1992, Episodes for Viola, Cello and Piano, 1993, Concerto for Two Pianos, 1994, String Quartet No. 2, 1995, String Quartet No. 3, 1996; also chamber music, choral, piano music, songs.; author: Rhythmic Training, 1969, Continuo: A Life in Music, 1987, The Music Teacher, 1997; Symphonic works premiered by N.Y. Philharmonic condrs., other leading condrs. in, U.S., abroad, ballets commd. by Martha Graham, 1961-63, CBS TV for Anna Sokolow, 1964, Lincoln Center for John Butler, 1967. With Royal Air Force, 1943-46. Recipient award Am. Acad. and Inst. Arts and Letters, 1979; Guggenheim fellow, 1957, 63; Fulbright postdoctoral research grantee, 1964; Nat. Endowment for Arts grantee, 1974, 77. Mem. ASCAP, Am. Music Ctr. (dir. 1962-64), Am. Acad. Arts and Letters.

STARFIELD, BARBARA HELEN, physician, educator; b. Bklyn., Dec. 18, 1932; d. Martin and Eva (Illions) S.; m. Neil A. Holtzman, June 12, 1955; children: Robert, Jon, Steven, Deborah. AB, Swarthmore Coll., 1954; MD, SUNY, 1959; MPH, Johns Hopkins U., 1963. Teaching asst. in anatomy Downstate Med. Ctr., N.Y.C., 1955-57; intern in pediatrics Johns Hopkins U., 1959-60, resident, 1960-62, dir. pediatric med. care clinic, 1963-66, dir. community staff comprehensive child care project, 1966-67, dir. pediatric clin. scholars program, 1971-76, prof. health policy, joint appointment in pediatrics, 1975—, disting. univ. prof., 1994—; mem. Nat. Com. Vital Stats., 1994—; cons. DHHS; mem. nat. adv. coun. Agy. for Health Care Policy and Rsch., 1990-94; adv. subcom. on Health Systems and Svcs. Rsch. Pan Am. Health Orgn., 1988-92, 1995—; cons. Health Care Fin. Adminstrn., 1980—. Mem. editl. bd. Med. Care, 1977-79, Pediatrics, 1977-82, Internat. Jour. Health Svcs.,1978—, Med. Care Rev., 1980-84, Health Svc. Rsch., 1996—; assoc. editor Annual Rev. Pub. Health, 1996—; contbr. articles to profl. jours. Recipient Dave Luckman Meml. award, 1958; HEW Career Devel. award, 1970-75, Am. Pub. Health Assn. Martha May Eliot award, 1995, Disting. Investigator award, Assn. for Health Svcs. Rsch., 1995, 1st Primary Care Achievement award, Pew Charitable Trust Fund, 1994, 1st Annual Rsch. award of Ambulatory Pediatric Assn., 1990. Fellow Am. Acad. Pediat.; mem. APHA (Martha May Eliot award 1995), NAS Inst. Medicine (governing coun. 1981-83), Am. Pediat. Soc., Soc. Pediat. Rsch., Internat. Epidemiologic Assn., Ambulatory Pediat. Assn. (pres. 1980), Sigma Xi, Alpha Omega Alpha. Office: Johns Hopkins Sch Hygiene 624 N Broadway Baltimore MD 21205-1900

STARGELL, WILLIE (WILVER DORNEL STARGELL), professional sports team coach, former baseball player; b. Earlsboro, Okla., Mar. 6, 1941. Student, Santa Rosa Jr. Coll. Player Pitts. Pirates, 1962-82, coach, 1982-85; coach Atlanta Braves, 1985-88, special assistant; asst. gen. mgr. Pittsburgh Pirates, 1997—; player All-Star Game, 1964-66, 71-73, 78. Named Sportsman of Yr. Sports Illus. mag., 1979, co-Most Valuable Player Nat. League, 1979, Major League Player of Yr. Sporting News, 1979; inducted into Baseball Hall of Fame, 1988. Office: Pittsburgh Pirates 600 Stadium Cir Pittsburgh PA 15212-5731*

STARING, GRAYDON SHAW, lawyer; b. Deansboro, N.Y., Apr. 9, 1923; s. William Luther and Eleanor Mary (Shaw) S.; m. Joyce Lydia Allum-Poon, Sept. 1, 1949; children: Diana Hilary Agnes, Christopher Paul Norman. A.B., Hamilton Coll., 1947; J.D., U. Calif.-Berkeley, 1951. Bar: Calif. 1952, U.S. Supreme Ct. 1958. Atty. Office Gen. Counsel, Navy Dept., San Francisco, 1952-53; atty. admiralty and shipping sect. U.S. Dept. Justice, San Francisco, 1953-60; assoc. Lillick & Charles, San Francisco, 1960-64, ptnr., 1965—; titulary mem. Internat. Maritime Com.; bd. dirs. Marine Exchange at San Francisco, 1984-88, pres. 1986-88; instr. pub. speaking Hamilton Coll., 1947-48; adj. prof. Hastings Coll. Law, 1996—. Author: Law of Reinsurance, 1993; assoc. editor Am. Maritime Cases, 1966-92, editor, 1992—; contbr. articles to legal jours. Mem. San Francisco Lawyers Com. for Urban Affairs, 1972-90; bd. dirs. Legal Aid Soc., San Francisco, 1974-90, v.p., 1975-80, pres., 1980-82. With USN, 1943-46, comdr. USNR. Fellow Am. Bar Found., Am. Coll. Trial Lawyers; mem. ABA (chmn. maritime ins. com. 1975-76, mem. standing com. admiralty law 1976-82, 86-90, chmn. 1990, ho. dels. 1986-90), Fed. Bar Assn. (pres. San Francisco chpt. 1968), Bar Assn. San Francisco (sec. 1972, treas. 1973), Calif. Acad. Appellate Lawyers, Maritime Law Assn. U.S. (exec. com. 1977-88, v.p. 1980-84, pres. 1984-86), Brit. Ins. Law Assn., Brit.-Am. C. of C. (bd. dirs. 1987—), World Trade Club San Francisco, Tulane Admiralty Inst. (permanent adv. bd.), Assocs. Maritime Mus. Libr. (dir. 1990-92, pres. 1992-94). Home: 195 San Anselmo Ave San Francisco CA 94127-1513 Office: 2 Embarcadero Ctr Ste 2600 San Francisco CA 94111-3900 *"How small, of all that human hearts endure,/That part which laws or kings can cause or cure!".*

STARK, BRUCE GUNSTEN, artist; b. Queens, N.Y., Feb. 17, 1933; s. Richard M. and Karen (Gunsten) S.; m. Joan Patricia Lauer, Nov. 19, 1960; children: Robert, Ronald. Student, Sch. Visual Arts, N.Y.C., 1955-58. Artist, cartoonist N.Y. Daily News, N.Y.C., 1961—. One-man shows Art Inst., Pitts., 1968, U. Kutztown, Pa., 1970, N.Y. Bank for Savs., N.Y.C., 1971; group shows Nat. Art Mus. Sport, N.Y.C., 1971; represented in permanent collections Everett Dirksen Library, L.D. Johnson Library, Baseball Hall Fame, Cooperstown, N.Y., Basketball Hall Fame, Mass. Served with USN, 1952-54. Recipient Nat. Cartoonist Soc.'s Rueben Catagory awards for sports, 1966, 75, spl. features, 1968; Page One award for best sports cartoon, 1970, 73 N.Y.C., 71; 3d, 4th, 6th prizes Internat. Salon de Caricatures Montreal, 1966, 68, 69; Most Outstanding Achievement award Sch. Visual Arts, 1982. Original cartoons requested by Pres. Nixon, Johnson; 1st color cartoon appearing on front page of N.Y. Daily News. Home: 1715 Clarendon Ave Lakeland FL 33803 *My goals, ideas, principles and standards of conduct are all helpfully outlined for me by God in His holy word—the Bible. I really need no other source. Whatever success has come to me, I think, is because of this, and what God has done for me, through His Son, Jesus Christ.*

STARK, DENNIS EDWIN, banker; b. Springfield, Ill., Dec. 24, 1937; s. Edwin C. and Ida (Fentem) S. B.S., Ill. Wesleyan U., 1959; Sanxay fellow practical ethics, Princeton U., 1959-60; M.B.A., Harvard U., 1962. Adminstrv. asst. to chmn. bd. Industrial Valley Bank, Phila., 1962-64; fin. analyst E.I. DuPont de Nemours, Wilmington, Del., 1964-65; asst. treas. Old Stone Bank, Providence, 1965-68, treas., 1968-71; sr. v.p., treas., sec. Old Stone Bank and Old Stone Corp., Providence, 1971-76; exec. v.p., chief fin. officer Old Stone Corp., Old Stone Bank, 1976-86, Dime Bank, N.Y.C., 1986-88; ptnr. Bank Mgmt. Ptnrs., N.Y.C., 1988-90; sr. v.p., CFO, corp. sec. Cen Fed Bank, Pasadena, Calif., 1990-92; exec. v.p., CFO, corp. sec. Ea. Bank, Lynn, Mass., 1995; ptnr. Fin. Mgmt. Ptnrs., Cranston, R.I., 1996—. Mem. bd. overseers Peabody Essex mus., Salem, Mass.; mem. fin. com. St. Stephen's Ch., Providence; mem. bd. visitors Ill. Wesleyan U., Bloomington; trustee Gilbert Stuart Meml., Saunderstown, R.I. Mem. Fin. Execs. Inst., Fin. Mgrs. Soc., Am. Soc. Corp. Secs., Harvard Bus. Sch. Assn. of R.I., Acacia (co-founder Ill. Wesleyan U. chpt.), Providence Art Club, Hope Club, Harvard Club (N.Y.C., Boston), Agawam Hunt, Dunes club. Republican. Episcopalian. Avocations: philately, numismatics. Home (summer): 41 Courtway St Narragansett RI 02882-3610 Office: 21 Hersey Rd Cran Finance RI 02910-6010

STARK, DIANA, public relations and promotion executive; b. N.Y.C., July 1; d. Benjamin and Sara (Zelasny) S.; BA, Hunter Coll. Promotion mgr. TV Guide mag., N.Y.C., 1950-61; promotion mgr. Show Bus. Illustrated, N.Y.C., 1961-62; broadcast specialist Young & Rubicam, N.Y.C., 1962-69; pres. Stark Communications, Inc., N.Y.C., 1969-76; pub. svc. publicity account exec. Y & R E, N.Y.C., 1976-77; pres. Stark Communications, Internat., N.Y.C., 1978—; pub. rels. workshop leader Chgo. Econ. Devel. Corp., 1973-76; cons. to Asahi Shimbun for English Language Newsletter. 1991-92. Columnist Host mag., 1960-65; writer, producer programs for women's TV shows, 1962—; coord. We Have Arrived, Portraits at Ellis Island, Augustus Sherman Photographs 1902-1924; book developer Ellis Island: The First Experience With Liberty, 1991. Mem. Pub. Rels. Soc. Am., NATAS (trustee 1974-78, publicity com. chmn., chpt. gov. 1972-76, 82-86, 87-91, editor N.Y. TV Directory 1987-90), Internat. Radio and TV Soc., Fgn. Policy Assn.

STARK, FORTNEY HILLMAN (PETE STARK), congressman; b. Milw., Nov. 11, 1931; s. Fortney Hillman Sr. and Dorothy M. (Mueller) S.; children: Jeffrey Peter, Beatrice Ann, Thekla Brumder, Sarah Gallun, Fortney Hillman Stark III; m. Deborah Roderick. BS, MIT; MBA, U. Calif. Teaching asst. MIT, Cambridge, 1953-54; prin. Skaife & Co., Berkeley, Calif., 1957-61; founder Beacon Savs. & Loan Assn., Antioch, Calif., 1961; pres., founder Security Nat. Bank, Walnut Creek, Calif., 1963-72; mem. 93d-102nd Congresses from 9th Calif. dist., 1973—; chmn. ways and means subcom. on health 93d-103d Congresses from 13th dist. Calif., 1973—; mem., chmn. D.C. com., Ways and Means com., subcom. Health, Select Revenue Measures, joint econ. com. Bd. dirs. ACLU, 1971, Common Cause, 1971, Starr King Sch.; del. Dem. State Cen. Com.; trustee Calif. Dem. Coun. Capt. USAF, 1955-57. Mem. Delta Kappa Epsilon. Office: House of Representatives 239 Cannon Bldg Washington DC 20515-0513

STARK, FRANCIS C., JR., horticulturist, educator; b. Drumright, Okla., Mar. 19, 1919; s. Francis C. and Maude Salena (Crowder) S.; m. Dorothy Lucille Moore, Sept. 14, 1941; children: Carolyn P. Stark Reich, Francis C. III. B.S., Okla. A&M Coll., 1940; M.S., U. Md., 1941, Ph.D., 1948. Asst. prof. horticulture U. Md., College Park, 1945-49; asso. prof. U. Md., 1949-51, prof., 1951-80, prof. emeritus, 1980—, head dept. horticulture, 1964-74, chmn. food sci. program, 1966-73, provost agr. and life scis., 1974-80, acting vice chancellor acad. affairs, 1981-82, spl. asst. to v.p., 1982—. Contbr. articles to profl. jours. Mem. Md. Gov.'s Commn. on Migratory Labor, 1959-79, chmn., 1963-76; bd. dirs. Capital Area Christian Ch., 1961-66, 89-94, pres., 1963-66; bd. dirs. Christian Ch. Facilities for aging, 1965-96, pres., 1975-80; trustee Lynchburg (Va.) Coll., 1970-79. With USAAF, 1942-45. Recipient Hon. State Farmer award Md. Future Farmers Assn., 1966. Fellow Am. Soc. Hort. Sci., AAAS. Club: Rotary. Office: U Md Dept Horticulture College Park MD 20742

STARK, HELEN MORTON, secondary education educator; b. Kearny, N.J., Nov. 27, 1935; d. Alexander and Alexanderina (Campbell) Morton; m. Frederick John Stark, May 7, 1960; children: Deborah K., Edward J. II. BA in Math., Montclair (N.J.) State Coll., 1957; postgrad., West Chester (Pa.) U., 1976, Villanova U., 1977, St. Joseph's U., Pa., 1990-91, Drexel U., 1991. Cert. math. tchr., Pa. Tchr. N.J. Sch. for Deaf, Trenton, 1957-58; tchr. math. Radnor (Pa.) Sch. Dist., 1975-96; ret., 1996; del. math.-science com. U.S.-China Conf. on Women's Issues, 1995. Mem. M.S. Theater Group, Wayne, Pa., 1982—. Recipient Edyth May Sliffe award for Disting. Math. Teaching Math. Assn. Am., 1991. Mem. Nat. Coun. Tchrs. Math., Assn. Tchrs. Math. Phila. and Vicinity, LWV. Avocations: golf, travel, dance.

STARK, JACK LEE, academic administrator; b. Urbana, Ind., Sept. 26, 1934; s. Lynn C. and Helen (Haley) S.; m. Jil Carolyn Harris, June 14, 1958; children: Janet, Jeffrey, Jennifer, Jonathan. BA, Claremont McKenna Coll., 1957; hon. degree, Redlands U., LDH, 1973. Asst. to pres. Claremont (Calif.) McKenna Coll., 1961-70, pres., 1970—. Active Pomona Valley Cmty. Hosp.; bd. dirs. Thacher Sch., Ojai, Calif. Capt. USMCR, 1957-60. Mem. Assn. Ind. Calif. Colls. and Univs. (chmn.), Ind. Colls. So. Calif. (bd. dirs.), Western Coll. Assn. (bd. dirs.). Club: California (Los Angeles). Home: 1679 Tulane Rd Claremont CA 91711-3426 Office: Claremont McKenna Coll Office of Pres 500 E 9th St Claremont CA 91711-5903

STARK, JOAN SCISM, education educator; b. Hudson, N.Y., Jan. 6, 1937; d. Ormonde F. and Myrtle Margaret (Kirkey) S.; m. William L. Stark, June 28, 1958 (dec.); children: Eugene William, Susan Elizabeth, Linda Anne, Ellen Scism; m. Malcolm A. Lowther, Jan. 31, 1981. B.S., Syracuse U., 1957; M.A. (Hoadly fellow), Columbia U., 1960; Ed.D., SUNY, Albany, 1971. Tchr. Ossining (N.Y.) High Sch., 1957-59; free-lance editor Holt, Rinehart & Winston, Harcourt, Brace & World, 1960-70; lectr. Ulster County Community Coll., Stone Ridge, N.Y., 1968-70; asst. dean Goucher Coll., Balt., 1970-73; asso. dean Goucher Coll., 1973-74; assoc. prof., chmn. dept. higher postsecondary edn. Syracuse (N.Y.) U., 1974-78; dean Sch. Edn. U. Mich., Ann Arbor, 1978-83, prof., 1983—; dir. Nat. Ctr. for Improving Postsecondary Teaching and Learning, 1991-96. Editor: Rev. of Higher Edn., 1991-96; contbr. articles to various publs. Leader Girl Scouts U.S.A., Cub Scouts Am.; coach girls Little League; dist. officer PTA, intermittently, 1968-80; mem. adv. com. Gerald R. Ford Library, U. Mich., 1980-83; trustee Kalamazoo Coll., 1979-85; mem. exec. com. Inst. Social Research, U. Mich., 1979-81; bd. dirs. Mich. Assn. Colls. Tchr. Edn., 1979-81. Mem. Am. Assn. for Higher Edn., Am. Ednl. Rsch. Assn., Assn. Study Higher Edn. (dir. 1977-79, v.p. 1983, pres. 1984, Rsch. Achievement award 1992), Assn. Innovation Higher Edn. (nat. chmn. 1974-75), Assn. Instl. Rsch. (disting. mem.), Assn. Colls. and Schs. Edn. State Univs. and Land Grant Colls. (dir. 1981-83), Acctg. Edn. Change Commn., Phi Beta Kappa, Phi Kappa Phi, Sigma Pi Sigma, Eta Pi Upsilon, Lambda Sigma Sigma, Phi Delta Kappa, Pi Lambda Theta. Office: Univ Mich 2002 Sch of Edn Ann Arbor MI 48109-1259

STARK, JOEL, speech language pathologist; b. N.Y.C., Nov. 18, 1930; s. Jacob William and Naomi (Peck) S.; m. Muriel Weiner, Dec. 16, 1950 (div. 1967); children: Holly, James; m. Arlene Kraat, Mar. 2, 1992. BA, L.I. U., 1950; MA, Columbia U., 1951; PhD, NYU, 1956. Instr. L.I. U., Bklyn., 1951-54; asst. prof. CCNY, 1954-62; assoc. prof. Stanford (Calif.) U., 1965-68; prof. speech/lang. pathology Queens Coll., Flushing, N.Y., 1968—; cons. Nassau County Med. Ctr., East Meadow, N.Y., 1968—. Contbr. articles to profl. jours. Fellow Am. Speech Lang. Hearing Assn. Office: Queens Coll Speech & Hearing Ctr Flushing NY 11367-1597

STARK, MATTHEW, higher education and civil rights administrator; b. N.Y.C., Jan. 27, 1930; s. Edward and Frieda S.; m. Terri L. BA, Ohio U., 1951, BS in Edn., 1951; MA in Ednl. Psychology, U. Minn., 1959; PhD in Ednl. Adminstrn. & Counseling, Western Reserve U., 1963. Counselor jr. coll. counseling office U. Minn., 1953-54, coord. residence counseling program, 1954-60; dean of students Moorhead State U., 1962-63; asst. prof., coord. human rels. programs U. Minn., 1963-70, asst. prof., coord. ednl. programs, 1970-73; exec. dir. Minn. Civil Liberties Union, 1973-87; ret., 1987; cmty. legal edn. bd. dirs. U. Minn.; v.p. Friends of Pub. Edn.; mem. bd. dirs. ACLU. Pres., bd. dirs. Minn. affiliate ACLU; mem. Minn. Farm. and Migratory Labor Com.; chmn. Minn. state adv. com. U.S. Commn. Civil Rights; mem. Bicentennial of U.S. Constitution Com., State of Minn.; mem. curriculum devel. task force Minn. State Bd. Edn.; mem. Gov.'s Blue Ribbon Task Force on Human Rights Dept.; founder, mem. ERA Coalition Minn., Minn. Coalition Against Censorship, Minn. Coalition Orgns. on Sex Equity in Edn., Minn. Gay and Lesbian Legal Assistance. Mem. Am. Personnel & Guidance Assn., Freedom to Read Found. (bd. dirs.). Home: 444 Penn Ave S Minneapolis MN 55405-2059

STARK, NATHAN J., medical administrator, consultant, lawyer; b. Mpls., Nov. 9, 1920; s. Harold and Anna (Berlow) S.; m. Lucile D. Seidler, Nov. 28, 1943; children: Paul S., David H., Robert, Margaret J. AA, Woodrow Wilson Jr. Coll., Chgo., 1940; BS, U.S. Mcht. Marine Acad., 1943; JD, Ill. Inst. Tech., 1948; LLD (hon.), Park Coll., 1969, U. Mo., 1980; DHL, Scholl Coll., Hahnemann U., 1987. Bar: Ill. 1947, Mo. 1952. Plant mgr. Englander Co., Inc., Chgo., 1949-51; partner law firm Downey, Abrams, Stark & Sullivan, Kansas City, Mo., 1952-53; v.p. Rival Mfg. Co., Kansas City, 1954-59; sr. v.p. ops. Hallmark Cards, Inc., Kansas City, 1959-74; dir. Hallmark Cards, Inc., 1960-74; pres., chmn. Crown Center Redevel. Corp., 1971-74; sr. vice chancellor health scis. Schs. Health Professions, U. Pitts., until 1984, sr. vice chancellor emeritus, 1984—, also pres. Univ. Health Center, 1974-79, 81—, also prof. Grad. Sch. Public Health; undersec. HEW, Washington, 1979-81; of counsel Fort & Schlefor, Washington; lawyer, treas., pres., CEO Nat. Acad. of Social Ins., 1992-95; dir. ERC Corp., 1970-79, Hallmark Continental Ltd., Ireland, 1971-73; mem. exec. bd. Nat. Bd. Med. Contbr. articles to profl. and bus. jours. Legal counsel Lyric Opera Theatre, Kansas City, Mo., 1958-72; mem. com. undergrad. med. edn. AMA, 1966-73; vice chmn. health ins. benefits adv. com. NEW, 1965-70; sec. task force on Medicaid, 1960-70, chmn. adv. commn. incentive reimbursement experimentation, 1968-70; chmn. capital investment conf. HEW-HRA, 1976; mem. liaison com. Am. Assn. Med. Colls.-AMA, 1970-74; chmn. task force lifelong learning opportunities Kellogg Found., 1975-77; chmn. cmty. hosp.-med. staff group practice program Robert Wood Johnson Found., 1974-79; mem.-at-large Nat. Bd. Med. Examiners; mem. bd. Blue Cross Western Pa., 1975-79, Am. Nurses Found., 1975-77, Health Sys. Agy. SW Pa., 1976—; v.p. Kansas City Philharm. Assn., 1954; sec. Eddie Jacobson Meml. Found., 1960—; mem. tech. bd. Milbank Meml. Fund, 1976-78; pres., chmn. Kansas City Gen. Hosp. and Med. Ctr., 1962-74; trustee Allegheny Found., 1975—, Pitts. Ballet Theater, 1977-79, Pitts. Chamber Opera Theater, 1978—; mem. VA Scholars Bd. Governance, 1979—; hon. fellow, trustee Hastings Ctr., 1981; v.p. Pitts. Opera; adv. bd. of trustees St. Joseph Coll., trustee, 1994. Recipient Chancellor's medal U. Mo. at Kansas City, 1969; Pro-Meritus award Rockhurst Coll., 1967; Layman award; AMA, 1974. Fellow Am. Acad. Pediatrics (hon.); mem. Inst. Medicine of NAS (coun. 1973-76), Am. Hosp. Assn. (hon. mem., Trustee award 1968), Am. Coll. Hosp. Adminstrs., Nat. Acad. Social Ins. (bd. trustees, pres. 1992-94). Home: 4343 Westover Pl NW Washington DC 20016-5554

STARK, NELLIE MAY, forest ecology educator; b. Norwich, Conn., Nov. 20, 1933; d. Theodore Banjamin and Dorothy Josephine (Pendleton) Beetham; m. Oscar Elder Stark, Oct. 1962 (dec.). BA, Conn. Coll., 1956; AM, Duke U., 1958, PhD, 1962. Botanist Exptl. Sta., U.S. Forest Svc., Old Strawberry, Calif., 1958-66; botanist, ecologist Desert Rsch. Inst., Reno, Nev., 1966-72; prof. forest ecology Sch. Forestry, U. Mont., Missoula, 1972-92; pvt. cons. Philomath, Oreg.; pres. Camas Analytical Lab., Inc., Missoula, 1987-92. Contbr. articles to profl. jours. Named Disting. Dau. Norwich, Conn., 1985; recipient Conn. award Conn. Coll., 1986, 54 grants. Mem. Ecol. Soc. Am. (chair ethics com. 1974, 76), Soc. Am. Foresters (taskforce 1987-88).

STARK, PATRICIA ANN, psychologist, educator; b. Ames, Iowa; d. Keith C. and Mary L. (Johnston) Moore. BS, So. Ill. U., Edwardsville, 1970, MS, 1972; PhD, St. Louis U., 1976. Counselor to alcoholics Bapt. Rescue Mission, East St. Louis, 1969; researcher alcoholics Gateway Rehab. Center, East St. Louis, 1972; psychologist intern Henry-Stark Counties Spl. Edn. Dist. and Galesburg State Research Hosp., Ill., 1972-73; instr. Lewis and Clark Community Coll., Godfrey, Ill., 1973-76, asst. prof., 1976-84, assoc. prof., 1984, coordinator child care services, 1974-84; mem. staff dept. psychiatry Meml. Hosp., St. Elizabeth's Hosp., 1979—; supr. various workshops in field, 1974—; dir. child and family services Collinsville Counseling Center, 1977-82; clin. dir., owner Empas-Complete Family Psychol. and Hypnosis Services, Collinsville, 1982—; cons. community agys., 1974—; mem. adv. bd. Madison County Council on Alcoholism and Drug Dependency, 1977-80. Mem. Am. Psychol. Assn., Ill. Psychol. Assn., Midwestern Psychol. Assn., Nat. Assn. Sch. Psychologists, Am. Soc. Clin. Hypnosis, Internat. Soc. Hypnosis. Office: 2802 Maryville Rd Maryville IL 62062-5424

STARK, RAY, motion picture producer. Student, Rutgers U. Publicity agt., lit. agt.; talent agt. Famous Artist Agy., to 1957; co-founder Seven Arts Prodn. Co., 1957; ind. film producer, 1966—. Producer : (films) The World of Suzie Wong, 1960, The Night of the Iguana, 1964, Reflections in a Golden Eye, 1967, Funny Girl, 1968, The Owl and the Pussycat, 1970, Fat City, 1972, The Way We Were, 1973, Funny Lady, 1975, The SUnshine Boys, 1975, Murder By Death, 1976, Smokey and the Bandit, 1977, The Goodbye Girl, 1977, The Cheap Detective, 1978, California Suite, 1978, Chapter Two, 1979, The Electric Horseman, 1979, Seems Like Old Times, 1980, Annie, 1982, Blue Thunder, 1983, Nothing in Common, 1986, Peggy Sue Got Married, 1986, The Secret of My Success, 1987, Biloxi Blues, 1988. Steel Magnolias, 1989, Revenge, 1990, Lost in Yonkers, 1993, Barbarians at the Gate, 1993 (Emmy award Outstanding Made to Television Movie 1993), Mr. Jones, 1993, Dr. Jekyll and Ms. Hyde, 1995, Mariette in Ecstacy, 1996, To Gillian on Her 37th Birthday, 1996, Harriet the Spy, 1996. Recipient Thalberg award Acad. Motion Picture Arts and Scis., 1980. Office: Hepburn Bldg W 10202 W Washington Blvd Culver City CA 90232-3119

STARK, RICHARD BOIES, surgeon, artist; b. Conrad, Iowa, Mar. 31, 1915; s. Eugene and Hazel (Carson) S.; m. Judy Thornton, Oct. 31, 1967. A.B., Stanford U., 1936; postgrad., U. Heidelberg, 1936-37; M.D., Cornell U., 1941. Diplomate Am. Bd. Plastic Surgery (pres. 1967-68). Intern Peter Bent Brigham Hosp., Boston, 1941-42; asst. resident surgery Childrens Hosp., Boston, 1942; plastic surgeon Northington Gen. Hosp., Ala., 1945-46, Percy Jones Gen. Hosp., Mich., 1946; postwar fellow anatomy and embryology Stanford U., 1946-47; from asst. resident to resident in head and neck surgery VA Hosp., Bronx, N.Y., 1947-50; asst. resident, resident surgery, plastic, head and neck and gen. surgery N.Y. Hosp., 1947-50; instr. surgery Cornell U., 1950-52, asst. prof., 1952-55, assoc. prof., 1955; asst. attending surgeon N.Y. Hosp., 1950-55; asst. prof. surgery Columbia U., 1955-58, assoc. prof., 1958-73, prof. clin. surgery, 1973—; assoc. attending surgeon St. Luke's Hosp., N.Y.C., 1955-58, founding attending surgeon dept. plastic surgery, 1958—; founder dept. plastic surgery, 1955; cons. Walter Reed Med. Ctr., 1970-77. Author: Plastic Surgery, 1962, Cleft Palate, 1968, Plastic Surgery at the New York Hospital 100 Years Ago, 1952, Aesthetic Plastic Surgery, 1980, Total Facial Reconstruction, 1985, Plastic Surgery of the Head and Neck, 1986; contbr. numerous chpts. to books, articles to profl. jours.; assoc. editor: Plastic Reconstructive Surgery, 1977-82; founding editor: Annals Plastic Surgery, 1978-81; 20 one-person art shows, 1946—. Chmn. Medico Adv. Bd., 1976-77; mem., v.p. CARE Bd.; v.p. Wellborn Found., N.Y.C. Served with AUS, 1943-46. Decorated Bronze Star (U.S.); Medal of Honor (2) (Vietnam); cavallero Order of San Carlos (Colombia), Dieffenbach medal (Berlin), Gold medal Nat. Inst. Social Scis. Fellow ACS; mem. Am. Assn. Plastic Surgeons, Am. Soc. Plastic and Reconstructive Surgery (pres. 1966, Spl. Achievement award), Found. Am. Soc. Plastic and Reconstructive Surgery (pres. 1961-65), Am. Surg. Assn., Soc. Univ. Surgeons, French Soc. Plastic Surgeons, Brasilian Soc. Plastic Surgeons, Colombian Soc. Plastic Surgeons, Argentina Soc. Plastic Surgeons, Brit. Assn. Plastic Surgery, Peruvian Acad. Surgeons, N.Y. Surg. Soc., N.Y. Acad. Medicine (pres. Friends Rare Book Room), Plastic and Reconstructive Surgery (sec., pres. 1966), N.Y. State Med. Soc. (pres., sec., med. history), N.Y. Regional Soc. Plastic and Reconstructive Surgery (pres. 1064-65), Halsted Soc. (pres. 1973-74), James IV Assn. Surgeons, Am. Soc. Aesthetic Plastic Surgery (pres. 1974-75), Nat. Arts Club (exhibiting mem.), Century Club (profl. artist), Artist Fellowship. Home: 35 E 75th St New York NY 10021-2761

STARK, ROBERT MARTIN, mathematician, civil engineer, educator; b. N.Y.C., Feb. 6, 1930; s. Alexander and Julia (Gross) S.; m. Carol LaSage, Jan. 13, 1955 (dec. Mar. 1988); children: Bradley R., Timothy D., Steven M., Candice B. AB, Johns Hopkins U., 1951; MA, U. Mich., 1952; PhD, U. Del., 1965. Rsch. scientist Bausch and Lomb, Rochester, N.Y., 1955; instr. Rochester Inst. Tech., 1956-57; asst. dean engring., asst. prof. math. Cleve. State U., 1957-62; instr. U. Del., 1962-64, asst. prof. civil engring. and ops. rsch., 1964-68, assoc. prof., 1968-76, prof., 1976—; pres., cons. applied sci. R.M. Stark & Co., Inc.; vis. assoc. prof. MIT, 1972-73; chmn. grad. program in ops. rsch.; cons. in field. Author: (with R.L. Nicholls) Mathematical Foundations for Design: Civil Engineering Systems, 1972; (with R.H. Mayer, Jr.) Quantitative Construction Management: Uses of Linear Optimization, 1983; (with R. Engelbrecht-Wiggans and M. Shubik) Auctioning, Bidding and Contracting, 1983; (with C. Sloyer, et al) Contemporary Applied Mathematics Series, 1987, Mathagrams, 1996. Bd. dirs. Geriatrics Svcs. Del., Inc., 1989—, Wilmington Sr. Ctr., 1994—, Meals on Wheels Found.; bd. dirs. Del. Acad. Sci., 1990—, pres., 1994-96; bd. dirs., v.p. White Clay Watershed Assn., 1992—; commr. Del. Heritage Commn., 1990—. Grantee Office Naval Rsch., 1974-81, NSF, 1969-70, U.S. Army Rsch. Office, 1966-68. Mem. AAAS, ASCE, Nat. Coun. Tchrs. Math., Inst. Mgmt. Sci., Ops. Rsch. Soc. Am., Phila. Ops. Rsch. Soc. (pres. 1970). Avocations: research, publs. ops. rsch., applied probability. Home: One Fox Ln Newark DE 19711 Office: U Del Dept Math Sci Newark DE 19716

STARK, ROBIN CARYL, psychotherapist, consultant; b. Yonkers, N.Y., Apr. 16, 1953; d. Louis and Bernice (Cooper) S. BA cum laude Psychology, Hunter Coll., 1979; MSW, NYU, 1982. Diplomate Am. Bd. Clin. Social Work; lic. social worker, N.Y.; cert. psychoanalytic psychotherapy, psychotherapy of eating disorders. Pvt. practice psychotherapy N.Y.C., 1983—; mem. adj. field faculty Grad. Sch. Social Svc., Fordham U., N.Y.C., 1986-87, Grad. Sch. Social Work, Hunter Coll., N.Y.C., 1987-88; coord. patient care svcs. Achievement and Guidance Ctrs. Am., Inc., N.Y.C., 1988-89; staff psychotherapist Ctr. for Study of Anorexia and Bulimia, 1990-94, facilitator wellness support chronic & life-challenging illness, 1993—. Recipient service award Young Adult Inst., 1987; N.Y.C. Youth Bur. grantee, 1983-85. Mem. NASW, Acad. Cert. Social Workers. Office: 410 E 57th St Ste 1A New York NY 10022-3059

STARK, ROHN TAYLOR, professional football player; b. Mpls., May 4, 1959; m. Ann Stark; 1 child, Rohn Jr. BS in Finance, Fla. State U., 1982. With Indpls. Colts, 1982-84; punter Indpls. Colts (formerly Balt. Colts), 1984-94, Pitts. Steelers, 1994—. Punter on the Sporting News Coll. All-Am. Team, 1981, NFL All-Pro team, 1992; played in Pro Bowl 1985, 86, 90, 92. Office: Pitts Steelers 300 Stadium Cir Pittsburgh PA 15212*

STARK, S. DANIEL, JR., convention and visitors bureau executive; b. Port Hueneme, Calif., Mar. 26, 1953; s. S. Daniel and Eloise Marie (Fisher) S.; m. Pauline Laube Finley, July 19, 1997; 1 child, Kaitlyn Elizabeth. BS, Calif. Poly. U., Pomona, 1981; cert. in exec. mgmt., Claremont Grad. Sch., 1989, MA in Mgmt., 1992. Driver-guide San Diego Wild Animal Pk./Zool. Soc. San Diego, Escondido, Calif., 1974-76; attractions host Disneyland divsn. The Walt Disney Co., Anaheim, Calif., 1976-80, mgmt. intern, 1981, supr. ops., 1981-82, area supr. ops., dept. mgr., 1982-87; mgmt. cons. S.D. Stark, Jr., Redlands, Calif., 1987—; dir. mktg. Ramada Express Hotel & Casino, Laughlin, Nev., 1988-89; exec. dir. San Bernardino (Calif.) Conv. and Visitors Bur., 1989—; part-time instr. mgmt. and mktg. So. Calif. campus U. Phoenix, 1997—; cons. Hemmeter Devel. Corp., Honolulu, 1985, Calif. Authority Racing Fairs, Sacramento, 1987-88, USIA for Latvian Ministry Transp., tourism divsn., 1992, U.S. Bur. Land Mgmt., tourism mgmt. project U. Alaska Sch. Mgmt.; adj. prof. Sch. Bus. and Pub. Admisntrn., Calif. State U., San Bernardino, 1992-93. Bd. dirs. Leadership So. Calif., 1993—, grad. pub. affairs tng., 1993; congl. appointee del. White House Conf. on Travel & Tourism, 1995; mem. regional econ. strategies consortium So. Calif. Assn. Govts. Recipient resolution Calif. Assembly, 1989, San Bernardino County Bd. Suprs., 1989, City of San Bernardino Mayor and Coun., 1989, Calif. Senate, 1989; selected as one of 1991 Up and Coming Young Bus. Leaders in San Bernardino County; named one of Inland Empire Bus. All Stars, 1991; recipient World Champion Trail Horse award Am. Jr. Quarter Horse Assn., 1972, Calif. Tourism award for Best Spl. Event-Rt. 66 Rendevouz, 1997. Mem. Am. Horse Shows Assn. (life), Am. Quarter Horse Assn (life), Assn. Travel Mktg. Execs., Internat. Assn. Conv. and Visitors Burs. (cert. comm., conv. mktg., tourism mktg.), Pub. Rels. Soc. Am. (bd. dirs. Calif. Inland Empire chpt. 1990-95, Polaris award 1997), Travel Industry Assn. Am., Calif. Festivals and Events Assn. (pres. 1997—, bd. dirs. 1994—), Inland Empire Tourism Coun. (bd. dirs. 1996—, exec. com. 1996—, treas. 1997-98), Calif. Travel Industry Assn., Tourism Assn. So. Calif. (bd. dirs. 1990-95, vice chair 1992-95), Western Assn. Convs. and Vis. Bur. (chmn. Calif. coun. 1992-94), FarmHouse Fraternity (internat. bd. dirs. 1986-94, v.p. 1990-92, Snyder Alumni award 1984). Avocations: boating, fishing, films, equestrian competition. Office: San Barnardino Conv and Visitors Bur 201 N E St Ste 103 San Bernardino CA 92401-1520

STARK, SUSAN R., film critic; b. N.Y.C., July 9, 1940; d. Albert A. and Lillian H. (Landau) Rothenberg; m. Allan F. Stark, June 26, 1968 (div. 1983); children: Allana Fredericka, Paula-Rose. B.A., Smith Coll., 1962; M.A.T., Harvard U., 1963. Film critic Detroit Free Press, 1968-79, Detroit News, 1979—. Mem. Phi Beta Kappa. Office: Detroit News 615 W Lafayette Blvd Detroit MI 48226-3124*

STARK, THOMAS MICHAEL, state supreme court justice; b. Riverhead, N.Y., Feb. 13, 1925; s. John Charles and Mary Ellen (Gaynor) S.; m. Jane Claire Crabtree, Dec. 30, 1954; children: Elizabeth Mary, Ellen Gaynor. BS cum laude, Holy Cross Coll., 1945; LLB, Harvard U., 1949. Bar: N.Y., 1950. Assoc. Zaleski & Jablonka, Riverhead, 1949-51; sole practice Riverhead, 1951-63, town atty., 1953, justice of peace, mem. town bd., 1956-57; mem. Riverhead Bd. Edn., Riverhead, 1960-63; judge county ct. County of Suffolk, Riverhead, 1963-68; justice 10th Jud. Dist. Supreme Ct. N.Y., Riverhead, 1969—, assoc. justice appellate term, 1985—; supervising judge Suffolk County Superior Criminal Cts., Riverhead, 1978-92; panel discussion leader Ann. Conf. N.Y. State Trial Judges, 1970-81; chmn. criminal law subcom. N.Y. State Trial Judges Benchbook, 1970-75; vice chmn. com. on criminal jury instrns. N.Y. State Office Ct. Adminstrn., 1975—; lectr. N.Y. State Office Ct. Adminstrn., 1977-87; mem. N.Y. State Ct. Facilities Task Force, 1980-84. Mem. exec. bd., v.p. Suffolk County council Boy Scouts Am., 1955-58; mem. exec. com., co-leader Riverhead, Suffolk County Republican Com., 1961-62. Served as ensign USNR, World War II. Recipient Silver Beaver award Boy Scouts Am., 1957, Disting. Eagle Scout, 1974; named Judge of Yr., Suffolk County Criminal Bar Assn., 1984. Mem. ABA (jud. adminstrn. sect.), N.Y. State Bar Assn. (presiding officer jud. sect. 1988-89, ho. dels. 1989-90), Suffolk County Bar Assn. (sec. 1959-62, 3d v.p. 1962-63). Home: Bay Woods Aquebogue NY 11931 Office: Suffolk County Criminal Bldg Riverhead NY 11901

STARKE, HAROLD E., JR., lawyer; b. Richmond, Va., Aug. 1, 1944. BA, Randolph-Macon Coll., 1967; JD, U. Richmond, 1971; LLM in Taxation, NYU, 1973. Bar: Va. 1971, D.C. 1981. Mem. Mays & Valentine, Richmond. Assoc. editor U. Richmond Law Rev., 1970-71. Bd. trustees Randolph-Macon Coll., 1983-85, 94-96. Fellow Am. Coll. Tax Counsel; mem. ABA (taxation, bus. law, real property, probate and trust law sects),

Va. State Bar (chmn. taxation sect. 1985-86), Va. Bar Assn. (com. on taxation), D.C. Bar, Richmond Bar Assn., Richmond Estate Planning Coun., Randolph-Macon Estate Planning Coun. (chmn. 1985—), McNeill Honor Soc., Phi Delta Phi. Office: Mays & Valentine NationsBank Center PO Box 1122 Richmond VA 23218-1122

STARKMAN, GARY LEE, lawyer; b. Chgo., Sept. 2, 1946; s. Oscar and Sara (Ordman) S. AB, U. Ill., 1968; JD cum laude, Northwestern U., 1971. Bar: Ill. 1971, U.S. Dist. Ct. (no. dist.) Ill. 1972, U.S. Ct. Appeals (7th cir.) 1972, U.S. Supreme Ct. 1974, Trial Bar U.S. Dist. Ct. (no. dist.) Ill. 1982, U.S. Ct. Appeals (3d cir.) 1984, U.S. Ct. Appeals (D.C. cir.) 1984. Asst. U.S. Atty. No. Dist. Ill., 1971-75; gen. counsel, dir. research Citizens for Thompson Campaign Com., 1975-77; counsel to Gov. of Ill., 1977-81; ptnr. Ross & Hardies, Chgo.; mem. admissions com. U.S. Dist. Ct. (no. dist.) Ill. Chmn. state agys. divsn. Jewish United Fund Met. Chgo., 1978-81; chmn. Ill. Racing Bd., 1991-96; bd. dirs. Internat. Assn. Racing Commn., 1992-94; mem. community adv. bd. Jr. League of Chgo., 1979-83. Recipient John Marshall award for appellate litigation, Atty. Gen. U.S., 1974, Nat. Svc. award Tau Epsilon Phi, 1968; named to Ten Outstanding Young Citizens, Chgo. Jr. C. of C., 1978. Mem. ABA (litigation sect.), Chgo. Bar Assn. (constl. law com.), Decalogue Soc., Northwestern U. Law Alumni Assn. Co-author textbook: Cases and Comments on Criminal Procedure, 1974, 2d edit., 1980, 4th edit., 1992; contbr. writings to profl. publs., book revs. to periodicals. Office: Ross & Hardies 150 N Michigan Ave Ste 2500 Chicago IL 60601-7524

STARKS, FLORENCE ELIZABETH, retired special education educator; b. Summit, N.J., Dec. 6, 1932; d. Edward and Winnie (Morris) S. BA, Morgan State U., 1956; MS in Edn., CUNY, 1962; postgrad., Fairleigh Dickinson U., 1962-63, Seton Hall U., 1963, Newark State Coll. Cert. blind and visually handicapped and social studies tchr., N.J. Tchr. adult edn. Newark Bd. of Edn.; ret., 1995; tchr. N.Y. Inst. for Edn. of the Blind, Bronx; developer first class for multiple handicapped blind children in pub. sch. system, Newark, 1960; ptnr. World Vision Internat. Mem. ASCD, AFL-CIO, AAUW, Coun. Exceptional Children, Nat. Assn. Negro Bus. and Profl. Women's Club Inc., N.J. Edn. Assn., Newark Tchrs. Assn., Newark Tchrs. Union-Am. Fedn. Tchrs., World Vision Internat. (ptnr.). Home: 4 Park Ave Summit NJ 07901-3942

STARKS, FRED WILLIAM, chemical company executive; b. Millford, Ill., Aug. 16, 1921; s. Otis Earl and Evelyn Viola S.; m. Minnie Jane Reynolds, Sept. 4, 1946; children: David F., Steven J., Daniel J. B.S., U. Ill., 1943, M.S., 1947; Ph.D., U. Nebr., 1950. Supr., U.S. Rubber Co., Torrance, Calif., 1943-44; supr. DuPont, Niagara Falls, N.Y., 1950-57; pres. Starks Assocs., Inc., Buffalo, N.Y., 1957-89, chmn., 1989—; spl. lectr. U. Buffalo, 1959-63. Lt. (j.g.) USNR, 1944-46. Avery fellow, 1948-49; USPHS fellow, 1949-50. Mem. Am. Chem. Soc., N.Y. Acad. Sci., Am. Inst. Chemists, Sigma Xi. Clubs: Buffalo, Cosmos, Chemists. Patentee in field. Home: 742 Highland Ave Buffalo NY 14223-1645 Office: Starks Assocs Inc 1280 Niagara St Buffalo NY 14213-1503

STARKS, ROSALYN JUNE, physical education and health educator; b. Phoenix, June 17, 1952; d. Ross Owen and Maribel Louise (Barnes) S. BS in Edn., U. Ariz., 1974; MA in Edn., No. Ariz. U., 1991. Tchr. Phys. Edn. K-12, Ariz. Phys. edn. tchr. Santa Cruz Valley Union High Sch., Eloy, Ariz., 1975-84; phys. edn., health tchr. Phoenix Union High Sch. Dist., 1985—; coach Santa Cruz Valley Union H.S. and So. Mountain H.S., Phoenix, 1975—, facilitator student assistance program, 1987—; Phoenix 5A Metro Region Rep. State Softball Adv. Bd., 1990-94; mem. HIV/AIDS articulation com. Phoenix Union H.S. Dist., 1994—; mem. crisis intervention team South Mountain H.S., 1995—, dir. studies com., 1993—, title I literacy strategies cadre, 1995—. Del. People to People Internat. Citizen Amb. Program, Berlin Reflections, 1994; del. Sports Devel. Delegation to South Africa, 1997. Named Softball Coach of Yr., A Ctrl. Divsn., 1980. Mem. AAHPERD, NEA, Ariz. Edn. Assn., Ariz. AHPERD, Phoenix Union H.S. Dist. Classroom Tchrs. Assn. Avocation: bowling. Home: 4406 N 111th Dr Phoenix AZ 85037-5333 Office: S Mountain High School 5401 S 7th St Phoenix AZ 85040-3104

STARKS, WILLIAM EDWARD (SKIP STARKS), investment consultant; b. Pennsacola, Fla., Apr. 6, 1965; s. William Leroy and Sherry Lynne (Barkhau) S.; m. Susanne Badgett, Oct. 17, 1992. BA in Psychology and Fin., U. Conn., 1987. Asst. mgr. Stuart James & Co., Inc., Charlotte, N.C., 1987-89; mgr., prin. Edward D. Jones & Co., Mystic, Conn., 1989-91; fin. cons. Smith Barney, New London, Conn., 1991-94; assoc. v.p. investments Morgan Stanley Dean Witter, 1994—. Co-author newsletter: Individual Point of View, 1990. Bd. dirs. Stonington Youth Svcs. Program, 1991—, Mystic Cmty. Ctr., 1996—; treas. Mystic Congl. Ch., 1993-95. Phil Skalandunas Meml. scholar, Newtown (Conn.) Ednl. System, 1983, Zeta Psi Ednl. scholarship 1986. Mem. U. Conn. Alumni Assn., Southeastern C. of C., Mystic C. of C., Mystic Rotary (sec. 1990—), Zeta Psi (v.p. 1987, Ednl. scholar 1987). Avocations: softball, basketball, cycling, travel, outdoor sports, golf. Office: Morgan Stanley Dean Witter 47 Water St Mystic CT 06355-2521

STARKWEATHER, TERESA MADERY, artist, educator; b. L.A., June 12, 1950; d. Earl and Maureen Madery; m. Lee A. Starkweather, May 29, 1977; children: Ashley, Chelsea. Student, Art Ctr. Coll. Design, L.A., 1970-72; BFA, Atlanta Coll. Art, 1973; credential, Calif. State U., Northridge, 1994-96. artist Chaleur, Torrance, Calif., 1991, Prestige Graphics, L.A., 1993-95; artist, designer Zarah Co., Topanga, Calif., 1991-95. Artistic dir. Echoes Cards, Topanga, Calif., 1991-94; fine arts tchr. Santa Monica (Calif.) H.S., 1996—. Contbg. artist Am. Artist Mag., spring 1991, The Best of Watercolor, 1995, Splash 4 The Splendor of Light, 1996; exhibited Madison Nat. Watercolor, Edgewood Coll., Wis., 1988, Woodstock Artists Assn., Hudson River Regional Watercolor, 1989, Lankershim Arts Ctr., Calif., 1990, L.A. City Hall, 1990, Orlando Gallery, Sherman Oaks, Calif., 1991, Watercolor West Nat. Exhbn., Calif., 1991, Century Gallery, L.A., 1992, L.A. Mcpl. Art Gallery, 1993, Artspace Gallery, L.A., 1993, Springfield Art Mus., Mo., 1994, Foothills Art Ctr., Colo., 1994, Orlando Gallery, Sherman Oaks, 1996. Recipient Bronze medal Art Calif. Mag. Discovery Awards, 1992, 93, 1st pl. award Valley Watercolor Assn., Artspace Gallery, L.A., 1993, Patron Purchase award Watercolor U.S.A., Springfield, Mo., 1994, 2d pl. award Nat. Watercolor Soc. Show, 1997; finalist The Artist's Mag. Awards, 1996. Avocations: horseback riding, tennis.

STARLING, JAMES LYNE, university administrator, retired; b. Ridgeway, Va., Aug. 16, 1930; s. Leonard Anderson and Florine (Anderson) S.; m. Martha Elizabeth Lewis, Mar. 17, 1968; 1 child, Elizabeth Anne. B.S., Va. Polytech. Inst. & State U., Blacksburg, 1951; M.S., Pa. State U., 1955, Ph.D., 1958. Instr. agronomy Pa. State U., University Park, 1957-58, asst. prof. agronomy, 1958-63, assoc. prof. agronomy, 1963-69, prof., head dept. agronomy, 1969-85, assoc. dean for adminstrn., Coll. Agr., 1985-93, sr. assoc. dean, 1993-95; interm dean Pa. State U., 1996—. Served to 1st lt. U.S. Army, 1951-53, Korea. Fellow AAAS; mem. Am. Soc. Agronomy (pres. N.E. br. 1980-81), Crop Sci. Soc. Am., Am. Forage and Grassland Council, Pa. Grassland Council (pres. 1968), Pa. Plant Food and Protectant Edn. Soc. (pres. 1974-75), Phi Kappa Phi, Gamma Sigma Delta, Phi Epsilon Phi, Phi Sigma. Democrat. Methodist. Club: Kiwanis (State College, pres. 1982-83). Home: 1736 Princeton Dr State College PA 16803-3261 Office: Pa State U 201 Agr Adminstrn Bldg University Park PA 16802

STARNER, BARBARA KAZMARK, marketing, advertising and export sales executive; b. Detroit, Sept. 2, 1940; d. Eugene Anthony and Lucille Ann (Marcinkowski) Kazmark; m. G. Frederick Starner, June 30, 1962; 1 child, Natasha Lucienne. BA with honors, U. Mich., 1962; BS, Ohio State U., 1965. Tchr. art Columbus (Ohio) Pub. Schs., 1965-68, Mt. Olive Pub. Schs., Budd Lake, N.J., 1968-71; stained glass designer Barbara Designs, LaCrosse, Wis., 1975-87; from trade show mgr. to v.p. advt., mktg., export sales Kart-A-Bag divsn. Remin, Joliet, Ill., 1978—; advt. and mktg. cons. Starner Mktg., L.A., 1987-95. Mem., pres. East Bank Artists, LaCrosse, 1979-86; co-founder, dir. crafts Great River Traditional Music & Crafts Festival, LaCrosse, 1975-87; chmn. Spiritual Frontiers Fellowship, Mpls., 1979-85, 85-87; co-chmn. Spiritual Sci. Fellowship, 1985-87; fund raiser, mem./cook 1st crew Sloop Clearwater Restoration, Maine-N.Y., 1969 (Hudson River pollution clean-up). Mem. NAFE. Democrat. Mem. Universalist Ch. Avocations: landscape and portrait painting, jewelry design. Office: Kart-A-Bag 510 Manhattan Rd Joliet IL 60433-3099

STARNES, EARL MAXWELL, urban and regional planner, architect; b. Winter Haven, Fla., Sept. 14, 1926; s. Thomas Lowe and Kathryn Maxwell (Gates) S.; m. Dorothy Jean Prather, Aug. 21, 1949; children: Tom, Will, Janet, Patricia. Student, Fla. So. Coll., 1946-48; BArch cum laude, U. Fla., 1951; MS in Urban and Regional Planning, Fla. State U., 1973, PhD, 1977. Registered architect, Fla. Assoc. Courtney Stewart (Architect), Ft. Lauderdale, Fla., 1951-52, William Bigoney, Architect, Ft. Lauderdale, 1952-53, William T. Vaughn, Architect, Ft. Lauderdale, 1953, Alfred B. Parker, Architect, Miami, Fla., 1953-55, Rufus Nims, Architect, Miami, 1955-57; ptnr. Starnes & Rentscher, Architects, Miami, 1957-63, Starnes, Rentscher & Assocs., Architects, Miami, 1963-71; dir. div. mass transp. Fla. Dept. Transp., Tallahassee, 1971-72; dir. div. state planning Fla. Dept. Adminstrn., 1972-75; engaged in research and cons. service Tallahassee, 1975; prof., chmn. urban and regional planning Coll. Architecture U. Fla., Gainesville, 1976-88; prof. urban and regional plan coordination, doctorial studies Coll. of Architecture U. Fla., 1989-93, prof. emeritus, 1993—; instr. architecture U. Miami, 1953; adj. asst. prof. dept. urban and regional planning Coll. Social Scis., Fla. State U., 1971-74; mem. adv. panel B8-15, Nat. Coop. Hwy. Research Program, Transp. Research Bd., NRC-Nat. Acad. Scis., 1974—; mem. adv. bd. Pub. Tech., Inc., 1974—; mem. North Central Fla. Regional Planning Com., 1980-85, Fla. Substate Dist. Com., 1985-87; co-chmn. Joint Liaison Com. on Div. Responsibility for Urban Services, Dade County, Fla., 1965-71; chmn. joint policy com. U. Miami-Dade County Jackson Med. Center, 1966-71; chmn. Cape Fla. State Park Adv. Council, 1966-69, Dade County Landscape Ordinance Study Com., 1967-70, South Fla. Everglades Area Planning Council, 1969-71; vis. lectr. Calif. Poly. State U., San Luis Obispo, 1988-89; cons. Urban Planning Fla. and Caribbean. Prin. works include 1st Unitarian Ch., Miami; contbr. article on archtl. planning relationship Ency. Architecture Planning, 1987, chpt. to Growth Management, 1992, chpt. and preface (with Ivonne Audinal) to Rural Sustainability in America, 1996; contbr. chpts. to books, articles on land use and urban devel. policies, wetland protection, state planning, greeways and rural sustainability to profl. jours. Active South Dade Mental Health Soc., 1967-68, Cape Fla. Acquisition Com., 1966, Dade County Downtown Govtl. Center Com., 1967-71, Miami Downtown Devel. Authority, 1970, Gov.'s Task Force on Resource Mgmt., 1971-72, Nat. Task Force on Natural Resources and Land Use Info. and Tech., 1973-74, Fla. Gov.'s Commn. on Property Rights, 1993-94; county commr. Dist. 7, Dade County, 1964-71; vice mayor, 1964, 68; mem. adv. com. Legis. Council Subcom. on Constrn. Industry Study, 1966-68; bd. dirs., chmn. retirement and compensation com. State Assn. County Commrs., 1968-71; mem. Alachua County Budget Study Com., 1978, Fla. Land Use Adv. Com. for Phosphate Lands, 1978-80, Suwanee River Water Mgmt. Bd., 1982-87, 91—, chmn. 1987-88; chmn. Fla. Inst. Phosphate Research, 1984-87; bd. dirs. 1000 Friends of Fla, 1986—; gov.'s adv. commn. on coastal mgmt., 1997. With USCG, 1944-46. Fellow AIA (urban design com. 1976-80); mem. Am. Inst. Cert. Planners, Nat. Inst. Bldg. Scis. (steering com. for rsch. 1979-80), Assn. Collegiate Schs. of Planning (bd. dirs. 1986-88), Gargoyle Soc., Phi Kappa Phi. Democrat. Unitarian. Office: PO Box 234 Cedar Key FL 32625-0234

STARNES, JAMES WRIGHT, lawyer; b. East St. Louis, Ill., Apr. 3, 1933; s. James Adron and Nell (Short) S.; m. Helen Woods Mitchell, Mar. 29, 1958 (div. 1978); children: James Wright, Mitchell A., William B. II; m. Kathleen Israel, Jan. 26, 1985. Student St. Louis U., 1951-53; LLB, Washington U., St. Louis, 1957. Bar: Mo. 1957, Ill. 1957, Fla. 1992. Assoc. Stinson, Mag & Fizzell, Kansas City, Mo., 1957-60, ptnr., 1960-90; ptnr. Mid-Continent Properties Co., 1959-90, Fairview Investment Co., Kansas City, 1971-76, Monticello Land Co., 1973—, of counsel Yates, Mauck, Bohrer, Elliff, Croessmann & Wieland, P.C., Springfield, Mo., 1995—; sec. Packaging Products Corp., Mission, Kans., 1972-89; chmn., treas. Galerie of Naples (Fla.), Inc., 1990-92. Bd. dirs. Mo. Assn. Mental Health, 1968-69, Kansas City Assn. Mental Health, 1966-78, pres., 1969-70; bd. dirs. Heed, 1965-73, 78-82, pres., 1966-67, fin. chmn. 1967-68; bd. dirs. Kansas City Halfway House Found., exec. com., 1966-69, pres., 1966; bd. dirs. Joan Davis Sch. for Spl. Edn., 1972-88, v.p., 1972-73, 79-80, pres., 1980-82; bd. dirs. Sherwood Ctr. for Exceptional Child, 1977-79, v.p., 1978-79. Served with AUS, 1957. Mem. ABA, Mo. Bar, Fla. Bar, Springfield Bar Assn., Kansas City Bar Assn., Washington U. Law Alumni Assn. (bd. govs. 1990-92). Presbyterian (deacon). Mem. adv. bd. Washington U. Law Quar., 1957-90. Home: 2657 E Wildwood Rd Springfield MO 65804-5271 Office: Yates Mauck Bohrer Elliff Croessmann & Wieland 3333 E Battlefield St Ste 1000 Springfield MO 65804-4048

STARNES, SUSAN SMITH, elementary education educator; b. Grinnell, Iowa, Oct. 8, 1942; d. Edwin Fay Smith Jr. and Miriam Jane (Spaulding) Smith Simms; m. Wayman J. Starnes, Apr. 25, 1964; children: Michele Ann Starnes Hoffman, Mary Shannon Starnes Zornes. BS in Edn. summa cum laude, Mo. Bapt. Coll., 1991. Cert. early childhood tchr., elem. tchr. 1-8. Adminstr. Presbyn. Ch. in Am. Hist. Ctr., St. Louis, 1985-90; tchr. 3rd grade Ctrl. Christian Sch., St. Louis, 1991—; mem. chapel com. Ctrl. Christian Sch., St. Louis, 1991—. Children's dir. Canaan Bapt. Ch., St. Louis, 1991-96, Bible study fellowship children's leader, 1986-89, mission trip vol., 1992, 93; camp counselor Youth for Christ, Kansas City, 1992, 93, Awana leader, 1996—. Mem. Kappa Delta Pi. Avocations: recreational vehicling, swimming, scuba diving.

STARNES, WILLIAM HERBERT, JR., chemist, educator; b. Knoxville, Tenn., Dec. 2, 1934; s. William Herbert and Edna Margaret (Osborne) S.; m. Maria Sofia Molina, Mar. 4, 1986. BS with honors, Va. Poly Inst., 1955; PhD, Ga. Inst. Tech., 1960. Rsch. chemist Esso Rsch. & Engring. Co., Baytown, Tex., 1960-62, sr. rsch. chemist, 1962-64, polymer additives sect. head, 1964-65, rsch. specialist, 1965-67, rsch. assoc., 1967-71; instr. and rsch. assoc. dept. chemistry U. Tex., Austin, 1971-73; mem. tech. staff AT&T Bell Labs., Murray Hill, N.J., 1973-85; prof. chemistry Poly. U., Bklyn., 1985-89, head dept. chemistry and life scis., 1985-88, assoc. dir. polymer durability ctr. 1987-89, Floyd Dewey Gottwald Sr. prof. chemistry Coll. William and Mary, Williamsburg, Va., 1989—, prof. applied sci., 1990—; invited lectr. several fgn. countries and U.S.; ofcl. guest U.S.S.R. Acad. Scis., 1990, Russian Acad. Scis., 1992; dist. vis. prof., Beijing Inst. of Tech., China, 1996; vis. scientist Tex. Acad. Scis., 1964-67; mem. bd. doctoral thesis examiners Indian Inst. Tech., New Delhi, 1988, McGill U., Montreal, 1989, MacQuarie U., Sydney, 1991, McMaster U., Hamilton, Can., 1994; panelist, reviewer NSF Acad. Rsch. Facilities Modernization Program, 1990; channel program mentor U. Cairo, 1994-95; mem. opinion leader panel Wall St. Jour., 1995—; sci. advisor European Multinational Environ. Rsch. Project on PVC in Landfills, 1996—; cons. numerous indsl. cos., govtl. and pvt. agys.; course dir. continuing edn. Mem. adv. bd. and bd. reviewers Jour. Vinyl Tech., 1981-83; mem. editl. bd. Jour. of Chemical and Biochemical Kinetics, 1992-95, Polymer Degradation and Stability, 1997—; contbr. articles to profl. jours., chpts. to books; patentee in field. NSF fellow 1958-60; recipient Profl. Progress award Soc. Profl. Chemists and Engrs. 1968, Disting. Tech. Staff award AT&T Bell Labs. 1982, Polymer Sci. Pioneer award Polymer News, 1988, Honor Scroll award N.J. Inst. Chemists, 1989; NSF grantee, 1989—, Nat. Bur. Standards Ctr. for Fire Rsch. grantee, Internat. Copper Rsch. Assn. grantee, Va. Ctr. Innovative Tech. grantee, GenCorp Found. grantee. Fellow AAAS (Project 2061 1985-86, chmn. chemistry subpanel 1985-86, mem. panel on phys. scis. and engring., 1985-86), Am. Inst. Chemists (life); mem. Am. Chem. Soc. (bd. dirs. southeastern Tex. sect. 1970, speakers bur. div. polymer chemistry 1976—, mem.-at-large exec. com. Va. sect. 1995), Soc. Plastics Engrs. (thesis advisor award Vinyl Plastics divsn. 1996), N.Y. Acad. Scis. (life), Va. Acad. Sci., Sigma Xi (M.A. Ferst award Ga. Inst. Tech. chpt. 1960), Phi Kappa Phi, Phi Lambda Upsilon (pres. Va. Poly. Inst. chpt. 1954-55). Current work: Degradation, stabilization, flammability, microstructures, and polymerization mechanisms of synthetic polymers, especially poly (vinyl chloride); free radical chemistry; carbon-13 nuclear magnetic resonance and organic synthesis. Subspecialties: Organic chemistry; Polymer chemistry. Office: Coll William and Mary Dept Chemistry PO Box 8795 Williamsburg VA 23187-8795

STARR, CHAUNCEY, research institute executive; b. Newark, Apr. 14, 1912; s. Rubin and Rose (Dropkin) S.; m. Doris Evelyn Debel, Mar. 20, 1938; children: Ross M., Ariel E. E.E., Rensselaer Poly. Inst., 1932, Ph.D., 1935, D.Engring. (hon.), 1964; D.Engring. (hon.), Swiss ETH, 1980; D. Sci. (hon.), Tulane U., 1986—. Research fellow physics Harvard, 1935-37; research asso. Mass. Inst. Tech., 1938-41; research physicist D.W. Taylor Model Basin, Bur. Ships, 1941-42; staff radiation lab. U. Calif., 1942-43, Tenn. Eastman Corp., Oak Ridge, 1943-46, Tenn. Eastman Corp. (Clinton Labs.), 1946; chief spl. research N. Am. Aviation, Inc., Downey, Calif., 1946-49; dir. atomic energy research dept. N. Am. Aviation, Inc., 1949-55, v.p., 1955-66; gen. mgr. N. Am. Aviation, Inc. (Atomics Internat. div.), 1955-60, pres. div., 1960-66; dean engring. U. Calif. at Los Angeles, 1966-73; cons. prof. Stanford, 1974—; pres. Electric Power Research Inst., 1973-78, vice chmn., 1978-87, pres. emeritus, 1987—; Dir. Atomic Indsl. Forum. Contbr. sci. articles to profl. jours. Decorated Legion of Honor (France); recipient Henry D. Smyth award Atomic Indsl. Forum, 1983. Fellow Am. Nuclear Soc. (past pres.), Am. Phys. Soc., AAAS (dir.); mem. AIAA (sr.), Am. Power Conf., Nat. Acad. Engring., Am. Soc. Engring. Edn., Royal Swedish Acad. for Engring. Scis., Eta Kappa Nu, Sigma Xi. Home: 95 Stern Ln Atherton CA 94027-5422

STARR, CHESTER G., history educator; b. Centralia, Mo., Oct. 5, 1914; s. Chester Gibbs and Nettie (Glore) S.; m. Gretchen Daub, July 15, 1940; children: Jennifer (Mrs. Michael Johnson), Richard G., Thomas J.J. A.B. with distinction, U. Mo., 1934, LL.D., 1981; M.A., 1935; Ph.D., Cornell U., 1938; LLD (hon.), U. Ill., 1987, St. Michaels Coll., 1992. Faculty U. Ill. at Urbana, 1940-70, prof. history, 1953-70, chmn. div. humanities, 1953-55, chmn. dept. history, 1960-61; prof. U. Mich., Ann Arbor, 1970-85; Bentley prof. U. Mich., 1973-85, Hudson prof., 1981-82; Cons. World Book, 1963-67, Ency. Americana, 1966—. Author: Roman Imperial Navy, 1941, From Salerno to the Alps, 1948, Emergence of Rome, 1950, Civilization and the Caesars, 1954, Origins of Greek Civilization, 1961, History of Ancient World, 1965, Rise and Fall of Ancient World, 1965, Awakening of the Greek Historical Spirit, 1968, Athenian Coinage, 480-449 B.C, 1970, Ancient Greeks, 1971, Ancient Romans, 1971, Early Man, 1973, Political Intelligence in Classical Greece, 1974, 94, Economic and Social Growth of Early Greece, 1977, Essays on Ancient History, 1979, Beginnings of Imperial Rome, 1980, The Roman Empire: A Study in Survival, 1982, Individual and the Community: The Rise of the Polis, 1986, Past and Future in Ancient History, 1987, Influence of Sea Power on Ancient History, 1988, The Birth of Athenian Democracy, 1990, 93, The Aristocratic Temper of Greek Civilization, 1991. Served from 1st lt. to lt. col. AUS, 1942-46, MTO. Decorated Bronze Star; Croce di Guerra Italy).; Recipient certificate as distinguished grad. U. Mo., 1963; Am. Acad. in Rome fellow, 1938-40; Guggenheim fellow, 1950-51, 58-59. Fellow Am. Acad. Arts and Scis.; mem. Am. Hist. Assn. (chmn. com. on ancient history 1961-67, Disting. scholar 1991), AAUP (chpt. pres. 1956-57), Socs. for Promotion Roman and Hellenic Studies, Royal Numis. Soc., Assn. Ancient Historians (pres. 1974-78), Phi Beta Kappa, Phi Mu Alpha. Home: 2301 Blueberry Ln Ann Arbor MI 48103-2212

STARR, DARLENE R., special education educator, education educator; b. Bucyrus, Ohio, Aug. 25, 1943; d. Dale H. and Helen J. (Rettig) Laipply; m. Douglas K. Rudy, Sept. 12, 1987; children: Kris, Kim, Kirk, Shane, Aubry. BS in Elem. Edn., St. Cloud State U., 1976; reading specialist, Avila Coll., 1981; MS in Spl. Edn., Kans. U., 1987. Cert. grades K-9 elem. reading/learning disabilities. Tchr. Wright Devel. Ctr., Monticello, Minn., 1977-78; tchr., dir. chpt. 1 Maple Lake (Minn.) Dist. Schs., 1978-80; chpt. 1 tchr. Olate (Kans.) Dist. Schs., 1980-82; first grade tchr. Spring Hill (Kans.) Dist. Schs., 1982-85; kindergarten tchr. Marietta (Ga.) City Schs., 1985-86; learning disabilites tchr. Louisburg (Kans.) Dist. Schs., 1987-90, tchr. grade 2, 1990-91; learning disabilities tchr. Olathe (Kans.) Dist. Schs., 1991—; adj. prof. Ottawa U., Overland Park, Kans., 1993—; learning disabilities cons., Olathe, 1992—. Mem. Nat. Coun. for Tchrs. Math., Coun. for Learning Disabilities, Internat. Reading Assn., Kans. Reading Assn. (chair parents and reading com.), Delta Kappa Gamma. Lutheran. Avocations: golf, tennis, antiquing, reading. Home: 9230 Lichtenauer Dr # 47 Lenexa KS 66219

STARR, DAVID, newspaper editor, publisher; b. N.Y.C., Aug. 1, 1922; s. Aaron and Helen (Simon) S.; m. Marjorie Giffen, Aug. 3, 1943; children: Pamela, Peter. B.A., Queens Coll., 1942. Reporter, rewriteman L.I. Daily Press, 1942-50; exec. editor Nassau Daily Rev. Star, 1950-53; asst. editor Newark Star-Ledger, 1954-56; asso. editor L.I. Press, 1953-54, 56-62, mng. editor, 1962-69, editor, 1969-77; sr. editor Newhouse Newspapers, 1971—; pub. Springfield Union-News, Sunday Republican, 1977—, now pres. and pub.; pres. Springfield Ctrl., Inc., 1978-88, chmn., 1989-95. Trustee Nassau Community Coll., SUNY, 1959-66; bd. dirs. Springfield Libr. and Mus. Assn., chmn., 1988-90; mem. Mass. Cultural Coun., 1980—; bd. dirs. Am. Arts Alliance, 1988-92, chmn., 1989-92. Mem. Am. Soc. Newspaper Editors, Am. Newspaper Pubs. Assn.

STARR, FREDERICK BROWN, furniture manufacturing executive; b. Westfield, Mass., Dec. 11, 1932; s. Frederick Rickaby and Virginia (Brown) S.; m. Sue Zook, June 1958; children: Jonathan, Curtis, Anne. BA in English, Trinity Coll., Hartford, Conn., 1955. Archtl. ceilings salesman Armstrong World Industries, Inc., Indpls., 1958-63, mktg. mgmt., Lancaster, Pa., 1963-73, v.p., gen. sales mgr. subs. co. Thomasville Furniture Industries, Inc., (N.C.), 1973-77, sr. v.p., gen. sales mgr., 1977-82, pres., CEO, 1982—, also dir.; bd. dirs. Furniture Libr., High Point, N.C. vice-chair U. N.C., Greensboro, 1985—, Reynolds House Mus., 1988—; pres. N.C. Shakespeare Theatre, 1987—; bd. dirs. Community Hosp., Thomasville, 1984—; chmn. TFI Found., Thomasville, 1984—. Served with U.S. Army, 1955-57. Mem. Internat. Home Furnishings Market Assn. (chmn. 1995—). Republican. Episcopalian. Home: 5506 E Rockingham Rd Greensboro NC 27407-7242 Office: Thomasville Furniture 401 E Main St Thomasville NC 27360-4152

STARR, HARVEY, political scientist; b. N.Y.C., Nov. 11, 1946; s. Nathan and Betty (Brand) S.; m. Madonna Kissel, June 1, 1969 (div. Dec. 1979); m. Dianne C. Luce, July 2, 1994. BA, SUNY, Buffalo, 1967; M of Philosophy, Yale U., 1970, PhD, 1971. Acting instr. Dept. Polit. Sci., Yale U., New Haven, Conn., 1970-71; visiting fellow in politics Dept. Politics, U. Aberdeen, Scotland, 1971-72, 78-79; asst. prof. Dept. Polit. Sci., Ind. U., Bloomington, 1972-77, assoc. prof., 1977-83, prof., 1983-89; prof. in internat. affairs Dept. Govt. & Internat. Studies, U. S.C., Columbia, 1989—; editl. bd. Am. Polit. Sci. Rev., 1985-89, 91-95, Internat. Studies Quar., 1985-90, Jour. of Politics, 1988-97, Comparative Polit. Studies, 1979-92, Internat. Interactions, 1985-91, editor, 1991—; assoc. editor Teaching Polit. Sci., 1978-81. Author: Henry Kissinger: Perceptions of International Politics, 1984, Anarchy, Order, and Integration, 1997; co-author: Inquiry, Logic and International Politics, 1989, World Politics: Menu for Choice, 1981, 85, 89, 92, 96, The Diffusion of War: A Study of Opportunity and Willingness, 1991, Agency, Structure and International Politics, 1997; contbr. articles to profl. jours. Grantee NSF, 1982-84. Mem. Peace Sci. Soc. Midwest (pres. 1978-80), Ind. Consortium for Security Studies (dep. dir. 1980-89), Data Devel. in Internat. Rsch. (exec. coun. 1986-87, 89-92), Conflict Processes Sect., Am. Polit. Sci. Assn. (exec. coun. 1989-91, pres. 1992-95, v.p. 1995-96), So. Polit. Sci. Assn. (exec. coun. 1991-94). Office: U SC Dept Govt Internat Studies Columbia SC 29208

STARR, ISIDORE, law educator; b. Bklyn., Nov. 24, 1911. BA, CCNY, 1932; MA, Columbia U., 1939; LLB, St. John's U., Jamaica, N.Y., 1936; JSD, Bklyn. Law Sch., 1942; PhD, New Sch. Social Rsch., 1957. Bar: N.Y. 1937. Tchr. N.Y.C. high schs., 1934-61; assoc. prof., prof. edn. Queens Coll., 1961-75, emeritus, 1975—; dir. Inst. on Law-Related Edn., Lincoln-Filene Ctr., Tufts U., 1963; dir. Law Studies Inst., N.Y.C., 1974; adv. on Our Living Bill of Rights Film Series (6 films) Encyclopedia Britannica Ednl. Corp.; mem. Ariz. Ctr. for Law-Related Edn.; cons. in field. Bd. dirs. Phi Alpha Delta Juvenile Justice Program, 1981—. 1st lt. U.S. Army, 1943-46. John Hay fellow, 1952-53. Recipient Outstanding Citizen award Philip Morris Cos., 1992. Mem. ABA (hon. chair adv. commn. on Youth Edn. for Citizenship, Isidore Starr award for Spl. Achievement in Law Studies, Leon Jaworski award 1989), Am. Judicature Soc., Am. Soc. for Legal History, Am. Legal Studies Assn., Nat. Coun. Social Studies (past pres.), Phi Beta Kappa, Phi Alpha Delta (cert. of appreciation 1981). Author: The Lost Generation of Prince Edward County, 1968, The Gideon Case, 1968, The Feiner Case, 1968, The Mapp Case, 1968, The Supreme Court and Contemporary Issues, 1968, Human Rights in the United States, 1969, The American Judicial System, 1972, The Idea of Libery, 1978, Justice: Due Process of Law, 1981; co-editor Living American Documents, 1971.. Address: 6043 E Harvard St Scottsdale AZ 85257

STARR, JOHN ROBERT, retired newspaper editor, political columnist; b. Lake Village, Ark., Dec. 29, 1927; s. John Philip and Thelma (Russell) S.; m. Norma Wilson, Nov. 14, 1948; children—John P., Linda Sharon, Robert Russell. B.A. in French, Southwestern U.-Memphis, 1952; postgrad., U. Tenn., 1977-78. Sports writer The Comml. Appeal, Memphis, 1952-57; newsman A.P., Little Rock, 1957-66, bur. chief, 1966-76; writer in residence U. Ark.-Little Rock, 1976-77; mng. editor Ark. Democrat, 1978-92. Author: Yellow Dogs and Dark Horses, 1987. Served with U.S. Army, 1946-47. Recipient Ark. Journalist award U. Ark., 1981. Avocation: writing. Home: 8 Daven Ct Little Rock AR 72209-2924 Office: Little Rock Newspapers Inc 121 E Capitol Ave Little Rock AR 72201-3819

STARR, KEVIN, librarian, educator. BA, U. San Francisco, 1962; MA, Harvard U., 1965, PhD, 1969; MLS, U. Calif., Berkeley, 1974; postgrad., Ch. Div. Sch. Pacific, Berkeley, 1983-84. From asst. to assoc. prof. Am. lit. Harvard U., Cambridge, Mass., 1969-74; city libr. San Francisco, 1973-76; prin. Kevin Starr Assocs., San Francisco, 1983-85; prof. comm. arts U. San Francisco, 1981-89; prof. Sch. Planning and Devel. U. So. Calif., 1989—; state libr. Calif., 1994—; Allston Burr sr. tutor Eliot House Harvard U., Cambridge, 1970-73; cons. Beyl and Boyd, Inc., San Francisco, 1979-83; sr. cons. Hill and Knowlton USA, San Francisco, 1983-84; vis. assoc. prof. English U. Calif., Berkely, 1974, vis. lectr. polit. sci., 1976, lectr. librarianship, 1978; adj. prof. humanities San Francisco State U., 1975-76; Regent's lectr. polit. sci. U. Calif., Riverside, 1977; adj. prof. English Santa Clara (Calif.) U., 1977-78; vis. prof. history U. Calif., Davis, 1985-86; vis. scholar, media fellow Hoover Inst., 1986-88; vis. fellow Ctr. Humanistic Studies, Claremont McKenna Coll., 1987; faculty master Embassy Residential Coll., 1990-94. Sr. editor New West Mag., 1977; vatican corr. Hearst Newspapers, Rome, 1978; columnist Examiner, San Francisco, 1977-83; contbng. editor L.A. Times, 1994—; contbr. articles to profl. jours., chpts. to books. Exec. aide to mayor San Francisco, 1973; bd. trustees Am. Issues Forum, 1975-76, Calif. Hist. Soc., 1992—; co-chmn. sister city com., San Francisco and Sydney, Australia, 1981-86; advisor Jr. League San Francisco, 1982-84; canidate San Francisco Bd. Suprs., 1984; councilor Am. Antiquarian Soc., 1996—; mem. Calif. Coun. Humanities, 1996—; regent Cathedral St. Mary Assumption, San Francisco, 1996—. Lt. German Army, 1962-64. Office: Calif State Lib 914 Capitol Mall Lib and Cts Bldg PO Box 942837 Sacramento CA 94237-0001*

STARR, LEON, retired chemical research company executive; b. Bronx, N.Y., May 2, 1937; s. Michael and Bella (Foux) S.; m. Joan Gail Linett, June 19, 1960; children—Michael Jason, Jennifer Nicole. B.S., Poly. Inst., Brooklyn, 1958; Ph.D., U. Mo., 1962. Teaching asst. U. Mo., Columbia, 1958-62; chem. researcher Mobil Chem. Co., Edison, N.J., 1962-67; various mgmt. positions then dir. tech. Celanese Corp., N.Y.C., 1967-83, corp. v.p. tech., 1983-86; pres. Celanese Research Co., N.Y.C., 1983-90; pres., corp. v.p. tech. Hoechst Celanese Corp., Chatham, N.J., 1986-90, ret., 1990; pres. Lee Starr Assocs., 1991—; adv. bd. U. Pa. 1988-90; adv. coun. Hampton U., 1988—; nat. adv. coun. Synthesis Coalition on Engring. Edn. 1991—; ptnr. Internat. Think-Tank Group, 1995—. Contbr. chpt. to book; patentee in field. Fellow Phillips Corp., U. Mo., 1961-62, Poly. Inst. N.Y., 1985. Mem. AAAS, Assn. Rsch. Dirs. (bd. dirs. 1995—), Am. Chem. Soc. (corp. assoc. 1983-90, bd. govs.), Natural Sci. Assn., N.Y. Acad. Scis., Soc. Chem. Industry, Chem. Mfrs. Assn. (chmn. chem. regulations and adv. com. 1977-82), Am. Inst. Chemists, Sales and Mktd. Execs. Internat. (v.p. 1972-73), STAR Residential (bd. dirs. 1994—), Sigma Xi. Avocations: tennis; sailing; collecting antique scientific instruments.

STARR, MARTIN KENNETH, management educator; b. N.Y.C., May 21, 1927; s. Harry and Melanie (Krauss) S.; m. Polly Exner, Apr. 3, 1955; children: Christopher Herschel, Loren Michael. BS, MIT, 1948; MS, Columbia U., 1951, PhD, 1953. Ptnr., dir. M.K. Starr Assocs., 1956-61; prof. mgmt. sci. Columbia U., N.Y.C., 1961-96; dir. Ctr. for the Study of Ops. Columbia U., 1980-95, dir. Ctr. for Enterprise Mgmt., 1995-96, vice dean Grad. Sch. Bus., 1974-75; Disting. prof. ops. mgmt. Crummer Grad. Sch. Bus. Rollins Coll., Winter Park, Fla., 1996—, dir. Ctr. for Enterprise Mgmt., 1996—; guest lectr. Am. U., Beirut, 1964, MIT, 1964-67, U. Cape Town, S. Africa, 1976, 80, 82, 84, 86, 88; cons. GE, E.I. duPont de Nemours & Co., Eastman Kodak Co., Lever Brothers, TRW, R.J. Reynolds, Young & Rubicam, IBM. Author: The Structure of Human Decisions, Inventory Control-Theory and Practice, 1972, Product Design and Decision Theory, 1963, (with David W. Miller) Executive Decisions and Operations Research, 2d edit., 1969, Systems Management of Operations, 1971, Management: A Modern Approach, 1971, Production Management: Systems and Synthesis, 2d edit., 1972, (with Irving Stein) The Practice of Management Science, 1976, Operations Management, 1978, (with G. Dannebring) Management Science: An Introduction, 1981, (with Earl K. Bowen) Statistics for Business and Economics, 1982, (with Marion Sobol) Statistics for Business and Economics: An Action Learning Approach, 1983, Managing Production and Operations, 1989, Global Corporate Alliances and the Competitive Edge, 1991, (with Marion Sobol) Introduction to Statistics for Executives, 1993, Operations Management: A Systems Approach, 1996; editor: Executive Readings in Management Science, 1965, (with Milan Zeleny) Multiple Criteria Decision Making, 1977, Global Competitiveness: Getting the U.S. Back on Track, 1988; editor-in-chief Mgmt. Sci., 1967-82; mem. editl. bd. Behavioral Sci., 1970—; editl. adviser Operational Rsch. Quar., 1970-85; cons. editor: Columbia Jour. World Business: Focus: Decision Making, fall, 1977, Quantitative Methods in Mgmt., McGraw-Hill Book Co., N.Y.C.; contbr. articles to profl. jours. Mem. Inst. Mgmt. Scis. (pres. 1974-75), Prodn. and Ops. Mgmt. Soc. (pres.-elect 1994—, pres. 1995, past pres., bd. dirs. 1996—), Beta Gamma Sigma. Home: 100 S Interlachen Ave # 304 Winter Park FL 32789 Office: Rollins Coll 317 Crummer Grad Sch Bus Winter Park FL 32789 *The ability to manage complex systems has become the most pressing requirement as we move to and through the year 2000. Remarkable growth of strong systems interdependencies has occurred since 1990. Global connectivity through the Internet is altering established patterns for living and doing business. Management science using the systems approach combines art and logic with advancing computer-linked technology to rationalize transitions to achieve social benefit. Perhaps a new name is needed to describe this effort. By whatever name it is called, the impact of systems-oriented management science will determine the character of the 21st century and will, in turn, be changed by it.*

STARR, MELVIN LEE, counseling organization executive; b. N.Y.C., Mar. 17, 1922; s. Herman and Martha (Aberman) S.; m. Eileen Ferne Kagan, Sept. 7, 1947; children: Marianne, Lisa Caren. BBA, U. Miami, 1947; postgrad. Columbia U., 1949-53, U. Denver, 1955-56, Ariz. State U., 1956-57; MA, U. Ariz., 1950; EdD, Western Colo. U., 1974. Faculty, adminstrn. Tucson Pub. Schs., 1950—; tchr. Doolen Jr. High Sch., 1951-53, counselor high sch., 1953-62, asst. prin. Alice Vail Jr. High Sch., 1962-64, Catalina High Sch., 1964-68; prin. Rincon High Sch., 1968-71, Tucson High Sch., 1971-74; asst. supt. Tucson Pub. Schs., 1974-78, assoc. supt., 1978-82; pvt. practice family counseling; pres., CEO Psychol. Engring. for Bus. and Industry, Tucson, 1984—. Mem. Tucson Mayor's Com. on Human Relations, 1969—; mem. Ariz. state com. Anti Defamation League, 1971; Ariz. state adv. bd. Good Shepherd Sch. for Girls, 1971; mem. Dem. Cen. Com., Pima City, Ariz., 1968—; bd. dirs., Mobile Meals of Tucson, Pima County Bd. Health, So. Arix. Girl Scouts U.S. Council; chmn. Tucson Community Ctr. Commn.; bd. dirs. Amigos de los Americanos, AnyTown, Ariz., Lighthouse YMCA, Beacon Found., Big Bros., NCCJ, Jr. Achievement, Tucson Community Center, Pacific Western region Anti-Defamation League, Handmaker Nursing Home Pima County, United Way, CODAC, Planned Parenthood, Girl Scouts Am., Ariz. Mobile Meals, Epilepsy Soc. So. Ariz., Drug Abuse and Alcohol Consortium; adv. bd. Tucson Free Med. Clinic; bd. dirs. Los Ninos Crisis Ctr., 1995—. Mem. Ariz. Assn. Student Teaching (state treas.), NEA, Ariz. Interscholastic Assn. (pres. conf. 1971, legis. council), Ariz. Personnel and Guidance Assn., Nat. Assn. Secondary Sch. Prins., Am. Assn. Sch. Adminstrs., Assn. Supervision and Curriculum Devel., Ariz. Sch. Adminstrs., Phi Epsilon Pi, Phi Delta Kappa. Home: 7101 E River Canyon Rd Tucson AZ 85750-2111 Office: PO Box 30163 Tucson AZ 85751-0163 also: 482 Elm Dr Ste E Las Vegas NV 89109

STARR, PAUL ELLIOT, sociologist, writer, editor, educator; b. N.Y.C., May 12, 1949; s. Saul and Sarah Marion (Buzen) S.; m. Sandra Lurie Stein, Apr. 12, 1981. BA, Columbia U., 1970; PhD, Harvard U., 1978. Jr. fellow Harvard Soc. Fellows, 1975-78; asst. prof. Harvard U., Cambridge, Mass., 1978-82, assoc. prof., 1982-85; prof. sociology Princeton (N.J.) U., 1985—; founder, co-editor The Am. Prospect; founder The Electronic Policy Network, 1995. Author: The Discarded Army: Veterans After Vietnam, 1974, The Social Transformation of American Medicine, 1983 (C. Wright Mills award 1983, Pulitzer prize 1984, Bancroft award 1984), The Logic of Health-Care Reform, 1992. Guggenheim Found. fellow, 1981-82. Democrat. Office: Princeton U Dept of Sociology Green Hall Princeton NJ 08544-1010

STARR, RICHARD CAWTHON, botany educator; b. Greensboro, Ga., Aug. 24, 1924; s. Richard Neal and Ida Wynn (Cawthon) S. BS in Secondary Edn., Ga. So. Coll., 1944; MA, George Peabody Coll., 1947; postgrad. (Fulbright scholar), Cambridge (Eng.) U., 1950-51; PhD, Vanderbilt U., 1952. Faculty Ind. U., 1952-75, prof. botany, 1960-76; founder, head culture collection algae U. Tex., Austin, prof. botany, 1976—; Head course marine botany Marine Biol. Lab., Woods Hole, Mass., 1959-63. Algae sect. editor: Biol. Abstracts, 1959—; editorial bd.: Jour. Phycology, 1965-68, 76-78; assoc. editor: Phycologia, 1963-69; Contbr. articles to profl. jours. Trustee Am. Type Culture Collection, 1962-68, 80-85. Guggenheim fellow, 1959; sr. fellow Alexander von Humboldt-Stiftung, 1972-73; recipient Disting. Tex. Scientist award Tex. Acad. Sci., 1987. Fellow AAAS, Ind. Acad. Sci.; mem. NAS (Gilbert Morgan Smith Award 1985), Am. Inst. Biol. Scis. (governing bd. 1976-77, exec. com. 1980), Bot. Soc. Am. (sec. 1965-69, v.p. 1970, pres. 1971, Darbaker prize 1955), Phycological Soc. Am. (past pres., v.p., treas.), Soc. Protozoologists, Internat. Phycological Soc. (sec. 1964-68), Brit. Phycological Soc., Akademie Wissenschaft zu Göttingen (corr.), Sigma Xi. Office: U Tex Dept Botany Austin TX 78713

STARR, RICHARD WILLIAM, retired banker; b. Phila., Oct. 7, 1920; s. Edwin Bell and Bertha (Aurand) S.; student U. Buffalo, 1946-50; BS, U. So. Calif., 1952-58; grad. Am. Inst. Banking, 1942, Pacific Coast Sch. Banking, U. Wash., 1968, Stanford Grad. Sch. Credit and Fin. Mgmt., 1958; Harvard U. Grad. Sch. Advanced Mgmt. Program, 1975; m. Evelyn Irene Johnson, Aug. 3, 1943; children: David Richard, Daniel Robert. With Marine Trust Co. of Buffalo, 1939-50, mgr. credit dept., 1947-50; with Calif. Bank, L.A., 1952-61, with United Calif. Bank (formerley Calif. Bank), 1961-79, with First Interstate Bank (formerly United Calif. Bank), 1979-83; installment credit officer, 1952-53, mgr. credit dept., 1953-58, comml. lending officer, loan adminstr., 1958-61, br. mgr., 1961, asst. cashier, 1955, asst. v.p., 1956-63, v.p., 1963-71, sr. v.p., 1971-83, area adminstr. nat. div., 1969-70, br. adminstr., 1970-73, mgr. state div. corp. banking dept., 1973-74, mgr. so. div. Calif. Banking Group, L.A., 1974-76, adminstr. spl. credits divsn., 1976-79, with First Interstate Bank, exec. v.p., adminstr. Calif. divsn., 1979-80, sr. credit adminstr. bank credit policy and supervision div., 1980-83, also chmn. credit policy worldwide, pvt. practice cons., Orange, Calif., 1983-94; dir. I.C.N. Pharms., Inc., Costa Mesa, Calif. Served with USCGR, 1942-45, USNR, 1947-52. Mem. Mortgage Banking Assn. (chmn. Orange County 1962—), Robert Morris Assocs., Calif. Bankers Assn. (exec. com. 1972), Masons, Santa Ana Country Club, Jonathan Club, Beta Gamma Sigma. Republican. Home: 2849 N Rustic Gate Way Orange CA 92867-1709

STARR, RINGO (RICHARD STARKEY), musician, actor; b. Liverpool, Eng., July 7, 1940; s. Richard and Elsie (Gleave) Starkey; m. Maureen Cox, Feb. 11, 1965 (div. 1975); children: Zak, Jason, Lee; m. Barbara Bach, Apr. 27, 1981. Drummer, vocalist mus. group, The Beatles, 1962-69; musician with Rory Storme's Hurricanes, 1959-62; solo performer, 1970-77; toured with All-Starr Band, 1992; recs. include Sentimental Journey, 1970, Beaucoups of Blues, 1970, Ringo, 1973, Goodnight Vienna, 1974, Blast From Your Past, 1975, Starrstruck: Ringo's Best, 1989, Ringo's Rotogravure, 1976, Ringo the Fourth, 1977, Bad Boy, 1978, Stop and Smell the Roses, 1981, Time takes Time, 1992; solo albumn It Don't Come Easy, 1971, Only You, 1975, No No Song, 1975, (with the Beatles) A Hard Day's Night, 1964, Rubber Soul, 1965, Sgt. Pepper's Lonely Hearts Club Band, 1967, Magical Mystery Tour, Yellow Submarine, 1969, The Beatles, Abbey Road, Let It Be, 1969, Hey Jude, 1970, Reel Music, 1982, numerous others; film appearances with the Beatles include A Hard Day's Night, 1964, Help!, 1965, Yellow Submarine, 1968, Let It Be, 1970, TV film Magical Mystery Tour, 1967; individual film appearances include Candy, 1968, The Magic Christian, 1969, 200 Motels, 1971, Blindman, 1971, Tommy, 1972, That'll Be the Day, 1973, Born to Boogie, also dir., producer, 1974, Son of Dracula, also producer, 1975, Lisztomania, 1975, Ringo Starrs, 1976, Caveman, 1981, The Cooler, 1982, Give My Regards to Broad Street, 1984; appeared in TV miniseries Princess Daisy, 1983; star TV series Shining Time Station, PBS, 1989—. Decorated Order Brit. Empire; recipient numerous Grammy awards with The Beatles; inducted with The Beatles into Rock and Roll Hall of Fame, 1988. Office: 2 Glynde Mews, London SW3 1SB, England*

STARR, ROSS MARC, economist, educator; b. Oak Ridge, Nov. 14, 1945; s. Chauncey and Doris E. S.; m. Susan S. Strauss, July 2, 1967; children: Daniel, Diana. B.S., Stanford U., 1966, Ph.D., 1972. Cons. Rand Corp., summers 1966, 67, Western Mgmt. Sci. Inst., Grad. Sch. Mgmt., UCLA, summers 1967, 71; Cowles Found. staff research economist Yale U., New Haven, 1970; faculty Yale U., 1970-74, assoc. prof. econs., 1974; assoc. prof. econs. U. Calif.-Davis, 1975-76, prof. econs., 1976-80; prof. econs. U. Calif.-San Diego, 1980—, chmn. dept., 1987-90; vis. lectr. London Sch. Econs., 1973-74; vis. scholar U. Calif.-Berkeley, 1978-80; vis. lectr. Peoples U. of China, Beijing, 1987. Author: General Equilibrium Theory: An Introduction, 1997; co-editor: Essays in Honor of Kenneth J. Arrow, 1986: v.1, Social Choice and Public Decision Making, v.2, Equilibrium Analysis, v.3, Uncertainty, Information and Communication; editor: Gen. Equilibrium Models of Monetary Economies, 1989; contbr. articles to profl. jours. NDEA fellow, 1966-69; Yale jr. faculty fellow, 1973-74; Guggenheim fellow, 1978-79; NSF grantee, 1979-81, 83-85. Office: U Calif San Diego Dept Econs 0508 9500 Gilman Dr La Jolla CA 92093-5003

STARR, STEPHEN FREDERICK, academic administrator, historian; b. N.Y.C., Mar. 24, 1940; s. Stephen Z. and Ivy (Edmondson) S.; children: Anna, Elizabeth. B.A. in Ancient History, Yale U., 1962; M.A. in Slavonic Langs. and Lit., King's Coll., Cambridge U., 1964; Ph.D. in History, Princeton U., 1968. Assoc. prof. dept. history Princeton U., 1968-74; sec. Kennan Inst. for Advanced Russian Studies, Woodrow Wilson Internat. Center for Scholars, Washington, 1974-79; v.p. acad. affairs Tulane U., New Orleans, 1979-82; prof. history, adj. prof. architecture Tulane U., 1979-83; scholar-in-residence Historic New Orleans Collection, 1982-84; pres. Oberlin (Ohio) Coll., 1983-94, The Aspen Inst., Washington, 1994—; spl. cons. President's Commn. Fgn. Langs. and Internat. Studies, 1978-81; v.p. Nat. Council for Soviet and East European Rsch., 1978-80. Author: Decentralization and Self Government in Russia, 1830-1870, 1972, Konstant in Melnikov: Solo Architect in a Mass Society, 1978, 2nd edit., 1981, Il padiglione di Melnikov, 1979, Bamboula! The Life and Times of Louis Moreau Gottschalk, 1994, (with Hans von Herwarth) Against Two Evils, 1981, The Russian Avant-Garde, 1981, Red and Hot: The Fate of Jazz in the USSR, 1983, New Orleans Unmasqued, 1985, Southern Comfort, The Garden District of New Orleans, 1800-1900, 1990. Mem. Greater New Orleans Found., 1983-91, La. Repertory Jazz Ensemble, 1980—; bd. dirs. Rockefeller Bros. Fund, 1984-94; trustee Eurasia Found., 1997—. Mem. Am. Assn. Advancement Slavic Studies, Coun. Fgn. Rels., Internat. Rsch. and Exch. Bd. (trustee), Nat. Fgn. Lang. Ctr. (bd. advisers). Office: Chm Ctrl Asia Inst Nitze Sch Adv Intl Studies/Johns Hopkins Univ 1619 Massachusetts Ave NW Washington DC 20036-2213

STARR, STEVEN DAWSON, photographer; b. Albuquerque, Sept. 6, 1944; s. Richard Vernon and Carol (Harley) S.; m. Marilynne Sue Anderson, Aug. 6, 1965; 1 child, Stephen Richard. Student, Antioch Coll., 1962-63, Bethel Coll., 1963-64; B.A., San Jose State Coll., 1967. Photographer San Jose Mercury-News, Calif., 1966-67; photographer, picture editor A.P., 1968-73; audiovisual producer Starr Productions, Inc., Coral Gables, Fla., 1974-85; photographer Picture Group Agy., 1986-88, Saba Press, N.Y.C., 1988—. Recipient Pulitzer prize for spot news photography, 1970, Nat. Headliners award, 1970, George Polk Meml. award, 1970, Pictures of Year hon. mention, 1970. Office: Saba Press 116 E 16th St Fl 8 New York NY 10003-2112

STARRETT, FREDERICK KENT, lawyer; b. Lincoln, Nebr., May 23, 1947; s. Clyde Frederick and Helen Virginia (Meyers) S.; m. Linda Lee Jensen, Jan. 19, 1969; children: Courtney, Kathryn, Scott. BA, U. Nebr., 1969; JD, Creighton U., 1976. Bar: Nebr. 1976, Kans. 1977, U.S. Dist. Ct. Nebr. 1976, Mo. 1987, U.S. Dist. Ct. Kans. 1977, U.S. Ct. Appeals (8th and 10th cirs.) 1983, U.S. Supreme Ct. 1993. Pvt. practice law Great Bend, Kans., 1976-77, Topeka, 1977-86; ptnr. Miller, Bash & Starrett, P.C., Kansas City, Mo., 1986-90, Lathrop Norquist & Miller, 1990-91, Lathrop and Norquist, Overland Park, Kans., 1991-95, Lathrop & Gage L.C., Overland Park, Kans., 1996—. Lt (j.g.) USNR, 1969-72. Mem. ABA, Kans. Bar Assn. (pres. litigation sect. 1985-86), Am. Bd. Trial Advs., Mo. Orgn. Def. Lawyers, Civitan Club (pres. 1985-86, Disting. Pres. award 1985-86). Democrat. Presbyterian. Avocations: aviation, scuba diving. Office: Lathrop & Gage LC 1050/40 Corporate Woods 9401 Indian Creek Pkwy Overland Park KS 66210-2005

STARRFIELD, SUMNER GROSBY, astrophysics educator, researcher; b. L.A., Dec. 29, 1940; s. Harold Ernest and Eve (Grosby) S.; m. Susan Lee Hutt, Aug. 7, 1966; children: Barry, Brian, Sara. BA, U. Calif., Berkeley, 1962; MA, UCLA, 1965, PhD, 1969. From lectr. to asst. prof. Yale U., New Haven, 1967-71; rsch. scientist IBM, Yorktown Heights, N.Y., 1971-72; asst. prof. Ariz. State U., Tempe, 1972-75, assoc. prof., 1975-80, prof., 1980—; vis. assoc. prof. Steward Observatory, Tucson, 1978-79; vis. staff mem. Los Alamos (N.Mex.) Nat. Lab., 1974-94. Author numerous scientific papers. Grantee Ariz. State U., 1973, NSF, 1974—, NASA, 1981—; Los Alamos summer fellow, 1974, 86; Joint Inst. Lab. Astrophysics fellow, 1985-86. Fellow Royal Astron. Soc.; mem. Internat. Astron. Union, Am. Astron. Soc. (high energy astrophyics div., mem. pubis. bd. 1978-81), Am. Physical Soc. (astrophysics div.). Achievements include discovery of thermonuclear runaway theory of nova outburst; co-discovery of hottest known class of pulsating variable stars and the cause of their pulsations, ultraviolet studies of nova cygni, 1992. Office: Ariz State U Dept Physics/Astronomy PO Box 871504 Tempe AZ 85287-1504

STARRS, JAMES EDWARD, law and forensics educator, consultant; b. Bklyn., July 30, 1930; s. George Thomas and Mildred Agatha (Dobbins) S.; m. Barbara Alice Smyth, Sept. 6, 1954; children: Mary Alice, Monica, James, Charles, Liam, Barbara, Siobhan, Gregory. BA and LLB, St. John's U., Bklyn., 1958; LLM, NYU, 1959. Bar: N.Y. 1958, D.C. 1966, U.S. Ct. Mil. Appeals 1959, U.S. Dist. Ct. (so. and ea. dists.) N.Y. 1960. Assoc. Lawless & Lynch, N.Y.C., 1958; teaching fellow Rutgers U., Newark, 1959-60; asst. prof. law DePaul U., Chgo., 1960-64; assoc. prof. law George Washington U., Washington, 1964-67, prof. law, 1967—, prof. forensic scis., 1975—; cons. Nat. Commn. Reform Fed. Criminal Laws, Washington, 1968, Cellmark Diagnostics, Germantown, Md., 1987—, Time-Life Books, 1993; participant re-evaluation sci. evidence and trial of Bruno Richard Hauptmann for Lindbergh murder, 1983; participant reporting sci. re-analysis of firearms evidence in Sacco and Vanzetti trial, 1986; project dir. Alfred G. Packer Victims Exhumation Project, 1989, A Blaze of Bullets: A Sci. Investigation into the Deaths of Senator Huey Long and Dr. Carl Austin Weiss, 1991, Meriwether Lewis Exhumation Project, 1992—, Frank R. Olson Exhumation Project, 1994, Jesse W. James Exhumation Project, 1995. Author: (with Moenssens and Inbau) Scientific Evidence in Criminal Cases, 1986, (with Moenssens, Inbau and Henderson) Scientific Evidence in Civil and Criminal Cases, 1995; editor: The Noiseless Tenor, 1982; co-editor: (review) Scientific Sleuthing, 1976—; mem. editl. bd. Jour. Forensic Sci., 1980—; contbr. articles to profl. jours. Served to sgt. U.S. Army, 1950-53, Korea. Recipient Vidocq Soc. award, 1993; Ford Found. fellow, 1963; vis. scholar in residence USMC, 1984. Fellow Am. Acad. Forensic Sci. (chmn. jurisprudence sect. 1984, 94, 95, bd. dirs. 1986-89, Jurisprudence Sect. award 1988, Disting. fellow 1996); mem. ABA, Mid-Atlantic Assn. Forensic Sci., Assn. Trial Lawyers Am., Internat. Soc. Forensic Sci. (chmn. jurisprudence sect. 1988—). Roman Catholic. Home: 8602 Clydesdale Rd Springfield VA 22151-1301 Office: George Washington U Nat Law Ctr 720 20th St NW Washington DC 20006-4306

STARRY, DONN ALBERT, former aerospace company executive, former army officer; b. N.Y.C., May 31, 1925; s. Don Albert and Edith (Sortor) S.; m. Leatrice Hope Gibbs, June 15, 1948; children: Michael, Paul, Melissa, Melanie. B.S., U.S. Mil. Acad., 1948; M.S. in Internat. Affairs, George Washington U., 1966. Commd. 2d lt. U.S. Army, 1948, advanced through grades to gen., 1977; svc. in Europe, Korea and Vietnam; comdr. 11th armored cavalry rgt. Vietnam, Cambodia, 1969-70; assigned Dept. Army Staff, 1970-72; comdr. Armor Center and Ft. Knox, Ky., 1973-76, V Corps, Europe, 1976-77; comdr. Tng. and Doctrine Command Ft. Monroe, Va., 1977-81; comdr. in chief U.S. Readiness Command, 1981-83, ret., 1983; v.p. mission analysis and tech. affairs Ford Aerospace and Communications Corp., Detroit, 1983-84, v.p., gen. mgr. space missions group, 1984-86; exec. v.p. Ford Aerospace Corp., Arlington, Va., 1987-90; spl. asst. to pres. BDM Internat., McLean, Va., 1988-90; chmn. bd. Maxwell Techs. Inc., San Diego, 1996—; author, lectr., counselor to govt. and industry. Mem. Def. Sci. Bd., 1985-93, Order of Aaron and Hur, Friends of Fifth of May; trustee Eisenhower Found., 1995—; chmn. bd. U.S. Cavalry Meml. Found., 1995—. Decorated Def. D.S.M., Army D.S.M. with oak leaf cluster, Silver Star, Bronze Star with V, Soldier's medal, Purple Heart, Legion of Merit with 2 oak leaf clusters, French Ordre Nationale du Merite, German Knight Commdr.'s Cross of Order of Merit with Badge and Star, Disting. Flying Cross, Air Medal with 9 oak leaf clusters; named to U.S. Army Ft. Leavenworth Command and Gen. Staff Coll. Hall of Fame, 1993. Mem. U.S. Armor Assn., Assn. U.S. Army. Episcopalian. Office: 11401 Lilting Ln Fairfax Station VA 22039-1717

STARTUP, CHARLES HARRY, airline executive; b. Middletown, N.Y., Feb. 24, 1914; s. Charles H. and Laura Beatrice (Langan) S.; m. Jane Butler Williams, June 26, 1942; children—Charles Alan, Ann Elizabeth, Thomas Andrew. A.B., Middlebury Coll., 1936; postgrad., U. Cin., 1937-39. With Am. Airlines, N.Y.C., 1939-63, asst. v.p. customer service, 1957-59; v.p. passenger sales Am. Airlines, 1959-61, v.p. passenger sales, 1961-63; v.p. mktg. Nat. Car Rental System, 1963-64. Adminstr. Light Opera of Manhattan, 1981-84. Mem. Cin. Sales Execs. Council (pres. 1955), Soc. Consumer Affairs Profls. (dir.), Chi Psi. Club: Skal (N.Y.C.). Home: 221 W College St Oberlin OH 44074-1533

STARTUP, WILLIAM HARRY, chemist; b. Port Jervis, N.Y., Oct. 24, 1945; s. William George and Robina Victoria (Sutherland) S.; m. Frances Williams, Nov. 6, 1976; 1 child, Elizabeth. BS in Chemistry, SUNY, Cortland, 1974. Sr. flavor analyst PFW-Hercules, Middletown, N.Y., 1975-91; analytical supr. Tastemaker, Cin., 1991-96; analytical chemistry mgr. Alex Fries and Bros., 1996—. Bd. dirs. Humane Soc. Middletown N.Y., 1985-91. Sgt. USAF, 1966-70. Mem. Am. Chem. Soc., Assn. of Ofcl. Analytical Chemists. Home: 892 Sabino Ct Cincinnati OH 45231-4905 Office: Alex Fries & Bros 10311 Chester Rd Cincinnati OH 45215-1224

STARTZELL, DAVID N., sports association executive; b. Washington, June 16, 1949; s. James Startzell; m. Judith L. Jenner. BA in Sociology, Miami U., Oxford, Ohio, 1971; MS in Planning, U. Tenn., 1976. Planning com. Tech. Assistance Ctr., U. Tenn., Knoxville; asst. planning dept. City of Oxnard, Calif.; dir. trail mgmt. svcs. Appalachian Trail Conf., Harpers Ferry, W.Va., 1978-79, dir. resource protection, 1979-81, assoc. dir., 1981-86, exec. dir., CEO, 1986—; active various trails and conservation group coalitions; chmn. task force producing Trails for All Americans; former planning cons. Office of Mayor, Knoxville. Recipient Conservation Svc. award U.S. Dept. Interior, 1995. Office: Appalachian Trail Conf PO Box 807 799 Washington St Harpers Ferry WV 25425-0807*

STARYK, STEVEN S., violinist, concertmaster, educator; b. Toronto, Ont., Can., Apr. 28, 1932; s. Peter and Mary Staryk; m. Ida Elisabeth Busch, May 17, 1963; 1 child, Natalie. Student, Royal Conservatory of Music, Toronto, 1942-48, Harbord Collegiate Inst., Toronto, 1945-48; LittD (hon.), York U., Toronto, 1980. Soloist, concertmaster CBC-Radio Can., Toronto, 1951-55, Royal Philharmonic Orch., London, 1956-59; 1st concertmaster, tchr. Concertgebouw Orch. and Amsterdam Conservatory, 1960-63; concertmaster Chgo. Symphony Orch., 1963-67; prof. of violin Oberlin (Ohio) Coll. Conservatory, 1968-72, Acad. of Music, Vancouver, B.C., Can., 1972-75, Royal Conservatory of Music, Toronto, 1975-87; concertmaster Toronto Symphony, 1982-87; prof. of violin, chair string div. U. Wash. Sch. Music, Seattle, 1987—; faculty music U. Toronto, 1980-87; vis. prof. U. Victoria, 1972, U. Ottawa, 1975, Northwestern U., 1965-66; founding mem. Quartet Can., 1975-80. Soloist, recitalist, N.Am., Europe and the Far East; recording artist on EMI-HMV, CBC, Everest, Orion, other labels. Recipient

2 Arts awards Can. Council, Ottawa, 1968, 75, Queen's Silver Jubilee medal Govt. of Can., Toronto, Shevchenko medal, Winnipeg, Man., Can. Home: 5244 17th Ave NE Seattle WA 98105-3408 Office: U Wash Sch Music Mail Stop DN-10 Box 353450 Seattle WA 98195

STARZINGER, VINCENT EVANS, political science educator; b. Des Moines, Jan. 12, 1929; s. Vincent and Genevieve (Evans) S.; m. Mildred Hippee Hill, June 16, 1953; children: Page Hill, Evans. AB summa cum laude, Harvard U., 1950, LLB, 1954, PhD, 1959; AM (hon.), Dartmouth Coll., 1968. Bar: Iowa 1954. Practice with firm Bannister, Carpenter, Ahlers & Cooney, Des Moines, 1954; teaching fellow, then instr. govt. Harvard, 1957-60; mem. faculty dept. govt. Dartmouth, 1960-94, chmn. dept. govt., 1972-77, 83-85, Joel Parker prof. law and polit. sci., 1976-94, prof. emeritus, 1994—. Author: Middlingness: Juste Milieu Political Theory in England and France, 1815-48, 1965, repub. as The Politics of the Center, 1991; also articles. Served with AUS, 1955-56. Sheldon traveling fellow, 1950-51; Social Sci. Research Council fellow, 1958-59; Dartmouth faculty fellow, 1963-64; Am. Philos. Soc. award and Earhart Found. fellow, 1970-71. Mem. ABA, Am. Polit. Sci. Assn., Iowa Bar Assn., Am. Alpine Club, Cambridge (Mass.) Boat Club, Phi Beta Kappa.. Home: Elm St Norwich VT 05055 Office: PO Box 981 Hanover NH 03755-0981

STARZYNSKI, CHRISTINE JOY, secondary educator; b. Chgo.; d. Stanley J. and Lottie (Wnek) Dudek; children: Karolyn, Katherine, Jeanne. BA, Northeastern U.; MA in Teaching, Webster U. Tchr. Des Plaines (Ill.) Dist. 62 Schs.; tchr. Spanish, Dist. 211 Schs., Hoffman Estates, Ill., dept. chmn.; with Spanish program Schaumburg (Ill.) Schaumburg Pub. Libr., 1984-92; bd. dirs. Kohl Internat. Teaching Awards, 1992-94. Recipient Kohl Exemplary Teaching award, 1986; inducted into Adminstr's. Acad.; named Vol. of Yr. Schaumburg Twp., 1996. Mem. Am. Assn. Tchrs. Spanish and Portuguese (conv. presenter), Am. Coun. Tchrs. Fgn. Langs., Ill. Coun. Tchrs. Fgn. Langs. Avocation: travel. Home: 319 Mendon Ln Schaumburg IL 60193-1037 Office: Hoffman Estates High Sch 1100 W Higgins Rd Hoffman Estates IL 60195

STASACK, EDWARD ARMEN, artist; b. Chgo., Oct. 1, 1929; s. Clifford Clement and Elizabeth Frances (Mallek) S.; m. Mary Louise Walters, June 20, 1953 (div. 1972); children: Caren Marie, Jennifer Elizabeth, John Armen, Michael Clifford; m. Diane Miura Hirsch, June 26, 1993. BFA with high honors, U. Ill., Urbana, 1955, MFA, 1956. Instr. in art U. Hawaii, 1956-61, prof. art, chmn. dept. art, 1969-72, program chmn. in printmaking, 1975-83, prof. emeritus, 1988; affiliate Downtown Gallery, N.Y.C., 1960-70. Author: (with J. Halley Cox) Hawaiian Petroglyphs, 1970, (with Georgia Lee) Petroglyphs of Kaho'olawe, 1993, Ka'upulehu Petroglyphs, 1994; one-man shows include Honolulu Acad. Arts, 1961, 66, 69, 76, 87, U.S. embassies Istanbul and Izmir, Turkey, 1976, Am. Cultural Ctr., Bucharest, Romania, 1976, Cleve. Inst. Art, 1976, Hilo (Hawaii) Coll. Gallery, 1976, Amfac Plaza Gallery, 1978, Ryan Gallery, 1981, Art Loft, Honolulu, 1983, Commons Gallery, U. Hawaii, 1996, Hawaii Volcano Nat. Park Art Ctr., 1996; group shows include Carnegie Inst., Pitts., 1964, Krakow (Poland) Biennial, 1966, 68, Smithsonian Instn., Washington, 1967, Mexico City Mus. Modern Art, 1968, Leicester Gallery, London, 1965, Art Mus. Manila, The Philippines, 1982, 2d Internat. Biennial Print Exhibit Republic of China, 1986, Yuma Art Ctr., 1990; represented in permanent collections Mus. Modern Art, N.Y.C., Met. Mus. Art, N.Y.C., Chgo. Art Inst., Bklyn. Mus., Honolulu Acad. Arts, Hawaii State Found. Culture and the Arts, Libr. of Congress, Phila. Mus. Art, Boston Pub. Libr. Served with U.S. Army, 1952-54. Recipient numerous prizes, including; Boston Printmakers Mems. prize, 1967; Juror's awards Honolulu Printmakers, 1957, 58, 59, 62, 63, 66, 67, 68, 74, 77, 87; Soc. Am. Graphic Artists prizes, 1956, 57, 61, 62, 63, 68, 73, 78, 79, 80, 91; Tiffany Found. fellow, 1958, 62; Rockefeller Found. grantee, 1959; MacDowell Colony fellow, 1971, 75; Hawaii State and U.S. Bicentennial Commns. fellow, 1975. Mem. Soc. Am. Graphic Artists, Australian Rock Art Rsch. Assn., Rock Art Assn. Hawaii (emeritus pres.), Am. Rock Art Rsch. Assn. Office: 1878 Paradise Ln Prescott AZ 86301-5282

STASHEFF, JAMES DILLON, mathematics educator; b. N.Y.C., Jan. 15, 1936; s. Edward and Evelyn Columbia (Maher) S.; m. Ann Helen Pekarik; children: Steven, Kim. BA, U. Mich., 1956; MA, Princeton (N.J.) U., 1958, PhD, 1961; DPhil, Oxford (Eng.) U., 1961. Moore instr. MIT, Cambridge, Mass., 1960-62; asst. prof. Notre Dame U., South Bend, Ind., 1962-64, assoc. prof., 1964-68, prof., 1968-70; prof. Temple U., Phila., 1970-78, U. N.C., Chapel Hill, 1976—; vis. prof. Princeton U., 1968-69, U. Pa., Phila., fall 1983 and fall 1992, Rutgers U., New Brunswick, N.J., spring 1987, Lehigh U., spring 1993. Author: H-Spaces from a Homotopy Point of View, 1970, (with others) Characteristic Classes, 1974. Danforth fellow, 1956-60, Sloan fellow, 1967-69; Marshall scholar, 1958-60; NSF grantee 1964-84, 85-88, 89—. Mem. Am. Math. Soc., London Math. Soc., Math. Assn. Am., Phi Beta Kappa. Roman Catholic. Avocations: dancing. Office: U NC Math CB # 3250 Chapel Hill NC 27599

STASHOWER, MICHAEL DAVID, retired manufacturing company executive; b. Cleve., July 15, 1926; s. Joseph G. and Tillie (Mirlevitz) S.; m. Gloria Goodstein, Oct. 29, 1950; children—Susan, Deborah Missal, Jon. B.A., Cornell U., 1947, M.B.A., 1949. With Ford Motor Co., 1949-57; contr. Dodge assembly plant Chrysler Corp., 1958-62; asst. contr. Am. Machine & Foundry Co., 1962-67; comptr. Perkin-Elmer Corp., 1967-76, v.p., comptr., 1976-79, sr. v.p. fin., 1979-85; v.p. fin. Softstrip, Inc., Waterbury, Conn., 1985-87, exec. v.p., 1987-90; sr. v.p., CFO Data Switch Corp., Shelton, Conn., 1990-93, exec. v.p., CFO, 1993-94, ret., 1994; dir. Data Switch Corp. Past pres. United Jewish Appeal/Fedn. Westport-Wilton-Norwalk, Conn.; v.p., treas., hon. dir. Temple Israel of Westport, Conn., 1984-91; bd. dirs. Coun. Jewish Fedns.; bd. dirs., treas. Jewish Home for the Elderly; treas. Guidance Clin. Fairfield County, Conn. With USNR, 1944-46. Mem. Cedar Point Yacht Club. Home: 14 Cardinal Ln Westport CT 06880-1714

STASHOWER, SARA ELLEN, advertising executive; b. Cleve., Sept. 6, 1954; d. David Lippmann and Sally Carol (Weiss) S. BA cum laude, Macalester Coll., 1976; MEd, Harvard U., 1982. Lower sch. instr., curriculum supr. St. Paul Acad., 1976-81; cons. 3M Co., St. Paul, 1979-81; promotions dir. Robinson Broadcasting, Cleve., 1982-83; account exec. Liggett-Stashower Advt., Cleve., 1984-89, v.p., account supr., 1989-94, sr. v.p., 1994—; sr. v.p., gen. mgr. Liggett Stashower Consulting, Cleve., 1994; cons. Ctr. for Contemporary Art, Cleve., 1993-94; co-founder, pres. First Person Edn., 1996—. Trustee Playhouse Square Found., Cleve., 1993—, Cleve. Film Soc., 1990-96, Cleve. Children's Mus., 1996-97; trustee, com. chair Montefiore Home, Cleve., 1991-97; co-founder, co-chair exec. com. Playhouse Square Ptnrs., 1990-93; trustee New Orgn. for Visual Arts, 1991-96; Ohio co-chair, alumni rep. Macalester Coll. Alumni Admissions, 1981—; trustee Ohio Motorists, 1996—. Recipient Achievement award No. Ohio Live Mag., 1992, 93; named one of Outstanding Young Women in Am., 1986. Mem. Cleve. Advt. Club (instr. 1990—), Jr. League Cleve. (community advisor 1990-94). Jewish. Home: 11 Mornington Ln Cleveland Heights OH 44106 Office: Liggett-Stashower Advt 1228 Euclid Ave Cleveland OH 44115-1831

STASIOR, WILLIAM F., engineering company executive; b. 1941. BSEE, Northwestern U., MSEE. With Booz Allen & Hamilton Inc., N.Y.C., 1967—, pres., COO, 1990—; CEO, chmn. bd. dirs. Booz Allen & Hamilton Inc., McLean, Va., 1991—. Office: Booz Allen & Hamilton Inc 8283 Greensboro Dr Mc Lean VA 22102-3802*

STASIUKAITIS, BRENDA HODGE, physical therapist; b. Winston-Salem, N.C., July 29, 1960; d. George McLeod and Marie (Tanner) Hodge; m. Robert Joseph Stasiukaitis, May 22, 1982; children: David Michael, Brian Patrick. BS in Phys. Therapy, East Carolina U., 1982. Lic. phys. therapist, S.C. Staff phys. therapist Roper Hosp., Charleston, S.C., 1982-83, team leader, phys. therapist, 1982-85; clinic dir. Phys. Rehab. Svcs., Mt. Pleasant, S.C., 1985-87; pres. Summerville (S.C.) Phys. Therapy, 1987—; mem. adv. bd. St. Francis Home Health, Charleston, 1987—, Interim HealthCare, North Charleston, 1987—, Home Health Svcs., Charleston, 1987-93, Med. Pers. Pool, North Charleston, 1987-94. Mem. Am. Phys. Therapy Assn., Summerville C. of C. Republican. Methodist. Avocations: travel, water sports, youth ministry, interactive distribution. Home: 123 Huckleberry Ln Summerville SC 29485-8017 Office: Summerville Phys Therapy PA 128 W Richardson Ave Summerville SC 29483-6072

STASSEN, JOHN HENRY, lawyer; b. Joliet, Ill., Mar. 22, 1943; s. John H. and Florence C. (McCarthy) S.; m. Sara A. Gaw, July 6, 1968; children: John C., David A. BS, Northwestern U., 1965, JD, Harvard U., 1968. Bar: Ill. 1968. Assoc. Kirkland & Ellis, Chgo., 1968, 73-76, ptnr. 1977—. Contbr. articles to legal jours. Gov. Northwestern U. Libr. Bd. Govs.; bd. dirs. Landmark Preservation Coun. Ill. Lt. comdr., JAGC, USNR, 1969-72. Mem. ABA (past chmn. com. on futures regulation), Ill. Bar Assn., Chgo. Bar Assn., Phila. Soc., Mid America Club. Home: 1310 N Astor St Chicago IL 60610-2114 Office: Kirkland & Ellis 200 E Randolph St Ste 5900 Chicago IL 60601-6436

STASZESKY, FRANCIS MYRON, electric company consultant; b. Wilmington, Del., Apr. 16, 1918; s. Frank J. and Ruth (Jones) S.; m. Barbara F. Kearney, May 30, 1943; children—Francis Myron, John B., Barbara J., Faith A., Paul D. BSME, MIT, 1943; MSME, Mass. Inst. Tech., 1943. Mech. engr. Union Oil Co. Calif., L.A., 1943-45; with E.I. duPont de Nemours Co., Wilmington, Del., 1946-48; joined Boston Edison Co., 1948, supervising engr. design and constrn., 1948-57, supt. engring. and constrn. dept., 1957-64, v.p., asst. to pres., 1964-67, exec. v.p., 1967-79, pres., chief operating officer, 1979-83; cons., 1983—; dir. Boston Edison Co., 1968-83. Fellow ASME (life); mem. IEEE (sr., life), Nat. Acad. Engring., Engring. Soc. New Eng. (pres. 1961-62), Palm Valley Country Club (Palm Desert, Calif.), Brae Burn Country Club (West Newton, Mass.). Address: 166 Bank St Harwich Port MA 02646-1321

STATEN, DONNA KAY, elementary art educator; b. Temple, Tex., Apr. 17, 1958; d. Paul James and Doris Mary (Kleypas) Hoelscher; 1 child, Ryan. BS in Edn., U. Mary Hardin-Baylor, Belton, Tex., 1980. Cert. tchr. in art, elem. edn., health, phys. edn. and recreation, Tex. Art tchr. Meridith Magnet Sch., Temple, 1980-84; bank officer mktg. Tex. Am. Bank, Houston, 1985-88; pvt. practice art tchr., designer art tchr. and designer, Houston, 1989; tchr. ESL Aldine Ind. Sch. Dist., Houston, 1990; art tchr. Meridith Magnet Sch., 1991—; exec. dir. Visual Arts Friends of the Cultural Activities Ctr., Temple, 1993-95, Temple Sister Cities Corp., Temple, 1994—; chmn. fine arts team Meridith Campus, 1993-96; state rev. panelist Tex. Edn. Agy., 1997. Curator Internat. Children's Art Exhbn., 1996, art exhibit From Russia with Love, 1992-95. Mem. The Contemporaries, Temple, 1994—; singer St. Luke's Ch. Choir, Temple, 1991—, mem. St. Luke's Women's Soc., 1993—; treas. Oaks Homeowners Assn., Temple, 1994-95, sec. bd. dirs., 1997—. Recipient honorable mention in Christmas Decorating Contest Women's Day mag., 1989, cert. of recognition Crayola/Binney & Smith, 1993-94, 95-96. Mem. ASCD, AAUW, Fine Arts Network, Internat. Soc. for Edn. Through Art, Nat. Art Edn. Assn., Tex. Classrm. Tchrs. Assn., Am. Craft Coun., Soc. Craft Designers, Tex. Computer Edn. Assn., Tex. Fine Arts Assn., Tex. Art Edn. Assn., Nat. Mus. of Women in the Arts, Cultural Activities Ctr., Temple Assn. for the Gifted, Electronic Media Interest Group, Tex. Alliance Edn. and the Arts., Friends of the Temple Libr., Tex. Assn. Gifted and Talented. Roman Catholic. Avocations: exercise, painting and drawing, singing. Home: 3927 River Oaks Cir Temple TX 76504-3566 Office: Meridith Magnet Sch 1717 E Avenue J Temple TX 76501-8414

STATHIS, NICHOLAS JOHN, lawyer; b. Calchi, Dodecanese Islands, Greece, Feb. 27, 1924; s. John and Sylvia (Koutsonouris) S. Student Columbia U., 1942-43, 44-48, AB, 1946, JD, 1948. Bar: N.Y. 1949. Assoc. James Maxwell Fassett, N.Y.C., 1948-50; asst. counsel to spl. com. to investigate organized crime in interstate commerce U.S. Senate, Washington, 1951; trial atty. Fidelity & Casualty Co. N.Y., N.Y.C., 1952; law sec. to Harold R. Medina, judge U.S. Ct. Appeals (2d cir.), N.Y.C., 1952-54; spl. dep. atty. gen. N.Y. State Election Frauds Bur., Dept. Law, 1956; assoc. Watson, Leavenworth, Kelton & Taggart, N.Y.C., 1954-60, ptnr., N.Y.C., 1961-81; ptnr. Hopgood, Calimafde, Kalil, Blaustein & Judlowe, N.Y.C., 1981-84, Botein, Hays & Sklar, N.Y.C., 1984-89; of counsel White & Case, N.Y.C., 1989-93; corp. coun., dir. intellectual property, Aphton Corp., N.Y.C., 1993—; lectr. Practising Law Inst., 1968-69. Contbr. articles to profl. jours. on trademarks. Pres., exec. dir., chmn., bd. dirs. Found. Classic Theatre and Acad., 1973—; bd. dirs. Concert Artists Guild, 1974-91, Pirandello Soc., 1976—, Bklyn. Philharm. Orch., 1986-91, Orpheon, Inc., 1986—. Served with AUS, 1943-44. Mem. ABA, Assn. of Bar of City of N.Y., N.Y. State Bar Assn., Fed. Bar Coun., Am. Intellectual Property Law Assn., N.Y. Intellectual Property Law Assn. Democrat. Greek Orthodox. Home: 1885 John F Kennedy Blvd Jersey City NJ 07305-2113 Office: 220 W 42nd St Fl 18 New York NY 10036-7211

STATKUS, JEROME FRANCIS, lawyer; b. Hammond, Ind., June 13, 1942; s. Albert William and Helen Ann (Vaicunas) S.; children: Wesley Albert, Nicholas Jerome. BA, So. Ill. U., 1964; JD, U. Louisville, 1968; MA, U. Wyo., 1974. Bar: Wyo. 1971, U.S. Dist. Ct. Wyo. 1971, Wis. 1989, D.C. 1977, U.S. Ct. Claims 1973, U.S. Supreme Ct. 1974, U.S. Ct. Appeals (10th and 7th cirs.) 1975. Law clk. U.S. Dist. Ct., So. Dist. Ill., Peoria, 1968-69; asst. atty. gen. State of Wyo., Cheyenne, 1971-75; legis. asst. to U.S. Senator Clifford Hansen, Washington, 1975-76; asst. U.S. atty. U.S. Dept. Justice, Dist. of Wyo., 1976-77; sole practice, Cheyenne, 1978-79; assoc. Horisky, Bagley & Hickey, Cheyenne, 1979-81; ptnr. Rooney, Bagley, Hickey Evans & Statkus, Cheyenne, 1981-88; exec. dir. Wyo. State Bar, 1988-89; trustee Village of Germantown, Wis., 1991-93; office share Ladewig and Rechlicz, 1990-93; pvt. practice, Douglas, Wyo., 1993-96, Germantown, 1996—; asst. pub. defender State of Wyo., Douglas, 1993-96. Pres. Ret. Sr. Vol. Program, Cheyenne, 1982-83; treas. Pathfinder (drug rehab.), Cheyenne, 1982-85; bar commr. 1st Jud. Dist., 1985-87; mem. Future Milw., 1991; chair Waukesha County Devel. Disability Adv. Coun., 1996—. Served with USNR, 1969-70. Mem. VFW, Wyo. Bar Assn., D.C. Bar Assn., Wis. State Bar Assn., Wyo. Trial Lawyers Assn. (bd. dirs. 1984-85), Wis. Vietnam Vets., KC. Republican. Roman Catholic. Home: PO Box 14 Germantown WI 53022 Office: W156n11340 Pilgrim Rd Germantown WI 53022-3465

STATLER, IRVING CARL, aerospace engineer; b. Buffalo, N.Y., Nov. 23, 1923; s. Samuel William and Sarah (Strauss) S.; m. Renee Roll, Aug. 23, 1953; children—William Scott, Thomas Stuart. B.S. in Aero. Engring., U. Mich., 1945, B.S. in Engring. Math., 1945; Ph.D., Calif. Inst. Tech., 1956. Research engr. flight research dept. Cornell Aero. Lab., Inc., Buffalo, 1946-53; prin. engr. flight research dept. Cornell Aero. Lab., Inc., 1956-57, asst. head aero-mechanics dept., 1957-63, head applied mechanics dept., 1963-70, sr. staff scientist aeroscis. div., 1970-71; research scientist U.S. Army Air Mobility Research and Devel. Lab., Moffett Field, Calif., 1971-73; dir. Aeromechanics Lab. U.S. Army Air Mobility Research and Devel. Lab., 1973-85, dir. AGARD, 1985-88; sr. staff scientist NASA Ames Rsch. Ctr., 1988-92, chief Human Factors Rsch. Divsn., 1992—; research scientist research analysis group Jet Propulsion Lab., Pasadena, Calif., 1953-55; chmn. flight mechanics panel adv. group aerospace research and devel. NATO, 1974-76; lectr. U. Buffalo, Millard-Fillmore Coll., Buffalo, 1957-58. Served with USAAF, 1945-46. Fellow AIAA (Internat. Cooperation in Space Sci. medal 1992), AAAS, German Aerospace Soc., Royal Aero Soc.; mem. Am. Helicopter Soc., Sigma Xi. Home: 1362 Cuernavaca Circulo Mountain View CA 94040-3571 Office: NASA Ames Rsch Ctr MS 262-7 Moffett Field CA 94035

STATLER, OLIVER HADLEY, writer; b. Chgo., May 21, 1915; s. Oliver Isaiah and Alice Mae (Hadley) S. BA, U. Chgo., 1936; LHD (hon.), Nat. Coll. Edn., Evanston, Ill., 1966. Administr. U.S. Civil Svc., Japan, 1947-54; writer, 1954—; tchr. U. Hawaii, Honolulu, 1977, adj. prof., 1977—. Sgt. U.S. Army, 1940-45, PTO. Guggenheim Found. fellow, 1973; Ctr. for Asian and Pacific Studies, U. Hawaii scholar-in-residence fellow, 1981; Japan Found. fellow, Tokyo, 1986. Mem. PEN, Authors Guild, Assn. for Asian Studies. Democrat. Home and Office: 1212 Nuuanu Ave #909 Honolulu HI 96817

STATMAN, JACKIE C., career consultant; b. Kingman, Kansas, June 15, 1936; d. Jack Carl and Dorothy E. (Kendall) Pulliam; m. Jerome Maurice Statman, Dec. 29, 1959; children: David Alan, Susan Gail Piotrowski. BA, U. Kans., 1958. Reg. music therapist Topeka State Hosp., Kans., 1958-59; caseworker Child Welfare, Pensacola, Fla., 1960-61; devel. rsch. tester The Children and Youth Project, Dallas, 1973-74; middle sch. counselor The Hockaday Sch., Dallas, 1981-84; career cons. Career Design Assocs., Inc., Garland, Tex., 1984-86; owner Career Focus Assocs., Plano, Tex., 1987—; pres. Assn. Women Entrepreneurs of Dallas, Inc., 1991-93; mem. career edn. adv. com. Plano Ind. Sch. Dist., 1993—. Author: (newspaper column) "Career Forum", 1991-92. Mem. Cmty. Svcs. Commn., City of Plano, 1993—, chmn., 1997; mem. Leadership Plano Alumnae Assn., 1990—; bd. dirs. Mental Health Assn. in Tex., 1989-93; founding pres. Mental Health Assn. Collin County, 1988-90. Recipient Child Advocacy award Mental Health Assn. of Greater Dallas, 1985, Golden Rule award JC Penney Comp., Inc., 1986, Humanitarian Vo. of the Yr. award Vol. Ctr. Collin County, 1990. Mem. Am. Counseling Assn., Nat. Assn. Women Bus. Owners (mem. Dallas/Ft. Worth bd. dirs. 1992-93), Nat. Career Devel. Assn., Plano C. of C. Avocations: community and civic volunteering. Office: Career Focus Assocs 1700 Coit Rd Ste 220 Plano TX 75075-6138

STAUB, AUGUST WILLIAM, drama educator, theatrical producer, director; b. New Orleans, Oct. 9, 1931; s. August Harry and Laurel (Elfer) S.; m. Patricia Gebhardt, Nov. 22, 1952; 1 child, Laurel Melicent. BA, La. State U., 1952, MA, 1956, PhD, 1960. Instr., tech. dir. La. State U., 1955; instr. Ea. Mich. U., 1956-58; assoc. dir. Dunes Summer Theatre, Michigan City, Ind., summers 1957-60; asst. prof., assoc. dir. univ. theatre U. Fla., 1960-64; assoc. prof. U. New Orleans, 1964-66, prof., chmn. dept. drama and communications, 1966-76; prof., head drama dept. U. Ga., 1976-95; exec. producer Jekyll Island Mus. Comedy Festival, 1984-88, Highlands (N.C.) Playhouse, 1989—, Ga. Repertory Theatre, 1991-95; staff dir. Theatre in the Square, Ga.; exec. sec. Theatres of La.; v.p. New Orleans Internat. Jazz Festival, 1967-69; pres. S.W. Theatre Conf., 1973-74. Author: Lysistrata, 1968, The Social Climber, 1969, A Small Bare Space, 1970, Introduction to Theatrical Arts, 1971, Creating Theatre, 1973, Varieties of Theatrical Arts, 1980, 83, 94; gen. editor: Artists and Ideas in the Theatre (Peter Lang), 1989—; assoc. editor Speech Tchr., 1966-68, So. Speech Comm. Jour., 1974-77, Quar. Jour. Speech, 1977-79. Bd. dirs. Friends Ga. Mus., Ga. Symphony, Coun. Arts for Children, New Orleans, New Orleans Ctr. Creative Arts, Athens Arts. Commn., Ga. Alliance Arts Edn. Lt. AUS, 1952-54. Recipient Creativity in Rsch. medallion U. Ga., 1987, Disting. Svc. award S.W. Theater Conf., 1985; La. State U. Found. Disting. Faculty fellow, 1970-71. Fellow Coll. of Fellows of Am. Theatre, Coll. of Fellows of the S.W. Theatre Assn.; mem. Am. Theatre Assn. (pres. 1985-86, bd. dirs.), Univ. and Coll. Theatre Assn. (pres. 1974-75), Nat. Assn. Schs. Theatre (pres. 1981-83), Univ. Resident Theatre Assn. (bd. dirs.), Inst. European Theatre, Nat. Theatre Conf., Am. Soc. Theatre Rsch., Internat. Fedn. Theatre Rsch. Home: 400 Ponderosa Dr Athens GA 30605-3324 *How good it is to be able to earn a living doing what one loves to do.*

STAUB, W. ARTHUR, health care products executive; b. Detroit, Dec. 25, 1923; s. Edward Elmer and Emma Josephine (Fleury) S.; m. Alla Elizabeth Edwards, June 26, 1948; children: James Randall, Sally Ann, David Scott. BS, Dartmouth Coll., 1944; MD, Temple U., 1947. Intern Muhlberg Hosp., Plainfield, N.J., 1947-48; resident in pediatrics Abington (Pa.) Meml. Hosp., 1950-51; practice medicine specializing in pediatrics Westfield (N.J.) Med. Group, 1948-63; assoc. med. dir. Ciba Pharm. Co., Summit, N.J., 1963-66; med. dir., v.p. life sci. div. Becton-Dickinson and Co., Rutherford, N.J., 1966-70; v.p. med. affairs C. R. Bard Co., Murray Hill, N.J., 1970-88, also bd. dirs.; bd. dirs. Crestmont Fed. Savs. and Loan Assn., Edison, N.J., Colonial Trust Nat. Bank, North Palm Beach, Fla.; cons. Children's Specialized Hosp., Westfield, 1948-88, Overlook Hosp., Summit, 1948-88. Contbr. articles to profl. jours. Sec., treas. Westfield Med. Soc., 1961; deacon Presbyn. Ch., Westfield, 1959—. Served to capt. USAF, 1951-53. Fellow Am. Coll. Physician Execs.; mem. AAAS, Assn. Advancement Med. Instrumentation, Health Industry Mfrs. Assn. (chmn. med. and sci. steering com.). Republican. Presbyterian. Clubs: Echo Lake Country (Westfield) (bd. trustees 1984—); Lost Tree (North Palm Beach, Fla.); Skytop (Pa.). Avocations: golf, physical fitness, reading, sailing, travel. Home: 810 Village Rd North Palm Beach FL 33408-3334

STAUBER, DONNA BETH, education educator; b. Belton, Tex., Dec. 18, 1955; d. William R. and Pansy Joan (Bell) Parmer; 1 child, Chassati Thiele; m. George Russell Stauber, July 25, 1987; children: Blake, Michal. BS, Tex. A & M U., 1978; MS in Edn., Baylor U., 1983; PhD in Health Edn., Tex. Woman's U., 1993. Cert. health edn. specialist. Tchr., coach Sand Springs (Okla.) Ind. Sch. Dist., 1978-80, McGregor (Tex.) Ind. Sch. Dist., 1980-82, Leander (Tex.) Ind. Sch. Dist., 1983-87; grad. asst. Baylor U., Waco, Tex., 1982-83, lectr., 1987-94; lectr. Baylor U., 1994; product devel. coord. WRS Group, Inc., Waco; lectr. at various confs. on self-esteem, body image, and emotional healing to educators. Vol. Multiple Sclerosis Soc. Mem. AAHPERD, Tex. Assn. Health, Phys. Edn., Recreation and Dance, Soc. Pub. Health Edn., Nat. Wellness Assn., Assn. for Worksite Health Promotion, Am. Coll. Health Assn., Internat. Coun. Health, Phys. Edn., Recreation, Sport and Dance (health edn. commn. 1995). Home: 9601 Bryce Dr Waco TX 76712-3218

STAUBER, MARILYN JEAN, secondary and elementary school; b. Duluth, Minn., Feb. 5, 1938; d. Harold Milton and Dorothy Florence (Thompson) Froehlich; children: Kenneth D. and James H. Atkinson; m. Lawrence B. Stauber Sr., Jan. 11, 1991. BS in Edn., U. Minn., Duluth, 1969, MEd in Math., 1977. Cert. elem. and secondary reading tchr., remedial reading specialist, devel. reading tchr., reading cons. Sec. div. vocat. rehab. State Minn., Duluth, 1956-59; sec. Travelers Ins. Co., Duluth, 1962-66; lead tchr. Title 1 reading and math. Proctor, Minn., 1969—. Mem. choirs and Choral Soc. John Duss Music, chairperson Outreach, Forbes Meth. Ch., proctor. Mem. NEA, VFW, Internat. Reading Assn., Nat. Reading Assn., Minn. Arrowhead Reading Coun., Elem. Coun. (pres. 1983-84, 86-87), Proctor Fedn. Tchrs. (recert. com. 1980—, treas. 1981-86), Proctor Edn. Assn. (chairperson recert. com.), Am. Legion, Phi Delta Kappa. Home: 6713 Grand Lake Rd Saginaw MN 55779-9782

STAUBITZ, ARTHUR FREDERICK, lawyer, healthcare products company executive; b. Omaha, Nebr., Mar. 14, 1939; s. Herbert Frederick Staubitz and Barbara Eileen (Dallas) Alderson; m. Linda Medora Miller, Aug. 18, 1962; children: Michael, Melissa, Peter. AB cum laude, Wesleyan U., Middletown, Conn., 1961; JD cum laude, U. Pa., 1964. Bar: Ill. 1964, U.S. Dist. Ct. (no. dist.) Ill. 1964, U.S. Ct. Appeals (7th cir.) 1964, Pa. 1972. Assoc. Sidley & Austin, Chgo., 1964-71; sr. internat. atty., asst. gen. counsel, dir. Japanese ops. Sperry Univac, Blue Bell, Pa., 1971-78; from asst. to assoc. to dep. gen. counsel Baxter Internat. Inc., Deerfield, Ill., 1978-85, v.p., dep. gen. counsel, 1985-90; v.p. Baxter Diagnostics, 1990-91; sr. v.p., sec., gen. counsel Amgen, Inc., Thousand Oaks, Calif., 1991-92; v.p., gen. mgr. Ventures Group Baxter World Trade Corp., Deerfield, Ill., 1992-93; v.p., sec., gen. counsel Baxter Internat. Inc., Deerfield, Ill., 1993, sr. v.p., gen. counsel, 1993—. Mem. Planning Commn., Springfield Twp., Montgomery County, Pa., 1973-74, mem. Zoning Hearing Bd., 1974-78; bd. dirs. Twp. H.S. Dist. 113, Deerfield and Highland Park, Ill., 1983-91, pres., 1989-91; trustee Food and Drug Law Inst., 1991-92, 93—, Carthage Coll., Kenosha, Wis., 1996— ; bd. dirs. Music of the Baroque, 1994—, also vice-chmn. planning. Mem. ABA, Chgo. Bar Assn. Episcopalian. Home: 232 Deerfield Rd Deerfield IL 60015-4412 Office: Baxter Internat Inc 1 Baxter Pky Deerfield IL 60015-4625

STAUBUS, GEORGE JOSEPH, accounting educator; b. Brunswick, Mo., Apr. 26, 1926; s. George Washington and Florence Lidwina (Pittman) S.; m. Sarah Mayer, Apr. 11, 1949; children: Lindsay, Martin, Paul, Janette. B.S., U. Mo., 1947; M.B.A., U. Chgo., 1949, Ph.D., 1954. C.P.A., Ill. Instr. U. Buffalo, 1947-49, U. Chgo., 1950-52; asst. prof. then assoc. prof. acctg. U. Calif.-Berkeley, from 1952, now Michael N. Chetkovich prof. emeritus; vis. prof. NYU, 1965, London Grad Sch. Bus. Studies, 1966-67, U. Kans., 1969-70; Erskine lectr. U. Canterbury, New Zealand, 1972, 91. Author: A Theory of Accounting to Investors, 1961, Activity Costing and Input-Output Accounting, 1971, Making Accounting Decisions, 1977, An Accounting Concept of Revenue, 1980, Activity Costing for Decisions, 1988, Economic Influences on the Development of Accounting in Firms, 1995—. Served with USN, 1944-46. Recipient Disting. prof. Calif. Soc. C.P.A.s, 1981. Fellow Acctg. Researchers Internat. Assn. (treas. 1981-83); mem. Am. Acctg. Assn. (disting. internat. lectr. 1982), Am. Inst. C.P.A.s, Fin. Execs. Inst. Office: UC Berkeley Acctg Dept Berkeley CA 94720

STAUDENMAIER, MARY LOUISE, banker, lawyer; b. Marinette, Wis., Apr. 13, 1938; d. Louis W. and Hildegarde C. (Schmit) S. BA, Mt. Mary

Coll., Milw., 1960; JD, Marquette U., 1971; postgrad. in banking, U. Wis., 1980; postgrad. in bus., Harvard U., 1980. Bar: Wis., 1971. Tchr. math. Milw. High Sch., 1960-66; security analyst 1st Wis. Trust, Milw., 1966-68, trust adminstr., 1968-70; v.p. Am. City Bank & Trust, Milw., 1970-75; trust officer Marine Nat. Exchange Bank, Milw., 1975; v.p., trust officer Heritage Trust Co., Milw., 1975-77; pres., chief exec. officer, trust officer Stephenson Nat. Bank and Trust, Marinette, 1977—, also bd. dirs., chmn.; bd. dirs., chmn.; speaker on estate planning; bd. dirs. TYME Corp.; bd. dirs. Bar Examiners State of Wis. Bd. dirs. Marinette Area Econ. Devel. Corp.; mem. fin. coun. and investment com. Cath. Diocese Green Bay, Wis.; mem. Marinette Downtown Revitalization Com.; past chmn. Marinette Downtown Adv. Com.; past pres. Marinette Voyageurs Com.; chair fin. com. Holy Family Congregation; past bd. dirs. Marinette Area Indsl. Devel. Corp., United Way Marinette and others; bd. dirs. Woolsack Soc. Marquette U. Law Sch. Recipient Touhey award Marinette Cath. Cen. High Sch., 1988, Mary Neville Bielefeld award Marquette U., 1989, Madonna medal for Profl. Excellence, Mount Mary Coll., 1990. Mem. Wis. Bar Assn. (past bd. dirs. corp., banking and bus. law com.), Wis. Bankers Assn. (br. banking task force), Marinette County Bar Assn. (past pres.), Wis. Trustees Assn. (past mem. legis. com.), Ind. Bankers Assn., Marinette Area C. of C. (past bd. dirs.), Marquette U. Law Alumni Assn. (past bd. dirs.), Assn. Marquette U. Women (past bd. dirs.). Home: 2411 Riverside Ave Marinette WI 54143 Office: Stephenson Nat Bank & Trust 1820 Hall Ave Marinette WI 54143

STAUDER, WILLIAM VINCENT, geophysics educator; b. New Rochelle, N.Y., Apr. 23, 1922; s. William P. and Margaret (Boll) S. A.B., St. Louis U., 1943, M.S. in Physics, 1948; S.T.L., St. Mary's (Kans.) Coll., 1953; Ph.D. in Geophysics, U. Calif. at Berkeley, 1959. Joined S.J., 1939, ordained priest Roman Catholic Ch., 1952. Faculty St. Louis U., 1959-92, prof. geophysics, 1966-92, prof. emeritus, 1992—, rector Jesuit community, 1967-73, 88-91, chmn. dept. earth and atmospheric scis., 1972-75, acting dean Grad. Sch., 1974-75, dean Grad. Sch., 1975-87, dir. univ. rsch., 1975-87, assoc. acad. v.p., 1989—; vis. research assoc. U. Calif.-Berkeley, 1984-85. Contbr. articles to profl. jours. Trustee Marquette U., 1978-90. Fellow Am. Geophys. Union; mem. Seismol. Soc. Am. (bd. dirs. 1962-68, pres. 1965, chmn. Eastern sect. 1964), Phi Beta Kappa, Sigma Xi. Home: 3601 Lindell Blvd Saint Louis MO 63108-3301

STAUDERMAN, BRUCE FORD, advertising executive, writer; b. Jersey City, Mar. 17, 1919; b. Herbert Henry and Helen Ann (Jacobus) S.; m. Claude Outhier, Mar. 23; 1946. Student, Syracuse U., 1936-38, TV Workshop, N.Y.C., 1949-50, Sch. TV Technique, 1950. V.p. TV, radio, films Meldrum & Fewsmith, Inc. (advt. agy.), Cleve., 1954-62; exec. v.p., chmn. plans bd., exec. creative dir. Meldrum & Fewsmith, Inc. (advt. agy.), 1973-79; v.p., creative dir. Ogilvy & Mather (advt. agy.), N.Y.C., 1962-69, Kenyon & Eckhardt, Inc. (advt. agy.), N.Y.C., 1979-83, Barnhart & Co. (advt. agy.), Denver, 1983-84; pres. Stauderman Advt., 1984—; v.p., creative dir. Mktg. Resources Group (advt. agy.), 1985-88; dir. TV, advt. cons. Intermarco-Elvinger (advt. co.), Paris, 1969-73; TV cons. gov., Ohio, 1958; council mem., judge C.L.I.O. Festival, 1960—; chmn. Paris jury, 1969-73; jury mem. Internat. Advt. Film Festival, Cannes, Venice, 1976—. Radio, TV program writer: House of Mystery, 1946-51; writer, producer, dir., WXEL-TV, Cleve., 1951-54. Mem. men's com. Cleve. Playhouse, 1958-62; chmn. TV com. Cleve. United Fund, 1958-59. Served from pvt. to 2d lt. AUS, 1941-46; to 1st lt. N.G. Essex Troop AUS, 1948-50. Mem. Am. Assn. Advt. Agys. (TV and radio adminstrs. com. 1958-62), Am. Fedn. TV and Radio Artists, Naval Club (London). Home: 8647 Falcon Green Dr West Palm Beach FL 33412

STAUFF, WILLIAM JAMES, commitment systems manager; b. Providence, Mar. 2, 1949; s. William A. and Charlotte A. (Thorpe) S.; m. Bertha Nichols, Jan. 22, 1972; children: William J., Heidi A., Anneliese C. BS in Bus. Adminstrn., Northeastern U., Boston, 1977; MBA, Suffolk U., 1983; ABS, Moody Bible Inst. Chgo., 1992-97; ThD, Bethany Theol. Sem., Dothan, Ala., 1997. Process writer, indsl. engr. Rockwell Internat., Hopedale, Mass., 1972-77; bus. mgr., acct. Luth. Svc. Assn. New Eng., Framingham, Mass., 1977-80; mgr. acctg. and fin. Office Info. Tech. Harvard U., Cambridge, Mass., 1980-89; dir. bus. ops. facilities mgmt. U. Va., Charlottesville, Va., 1989-97; mgr. commitment sys. Billy Graham Evangelistic Assn., Mpls., 1997—; pub. acctg. auditor Charles Murphy/Paul Haggerty, CPAs, Framingham, 1977-80. Mem. Assn. Higher Edn. Facilities Officers. Avocations: gardening, music, teaching. Home: 1150 Hennepin Ave #1401 Minneapolis MN 55403 Office: Billy Graham Evang Assn PO Box 9313 Minneapolis MN 55440

STAUFFER, CHARLES HENRY, retired chemistry educator; b. Harrisburg, Pa., Apr. 17, 1913; s. Charles C. and Hannah (Henry) S.; m. Eleanor Ramsdell, July 8, 1939; children—Charles R., Anne Elizabeth, John E. A.B., Swarthmore Coll., 1934; M.A., Harvard U., 1936, Ph.D., 1937. Instr. Worcester (Mass.) Poly. Inst., 1937-43, asst. prof., 1943-52, assoc. prof., 1952-58; assoc. prof. affiliate Clark U., Worcester, 1941; prof., chmn. dept. chemistry St. Lawrence U., Canton, N.Y., 1958-65; prof. chemistry, chmn. div. natural scis. math. Bates Coll., Lewiston, Maine, 1965—, Charles A. Dana prof. chemistry, 1968-77, prof. emeritus, 1977—; dir. chem. kinetics data project Nat. Acad. Scis., 1954-64; mem. adv. com. Office Critical Constants, 1961-64. Fellow AAAS, Am. Chem. Soc. (sec., chmn. No. N.Y. sect., councilor Maine sect.); mem. Sigma Xi, Phi Beta Kappa (Swarthmore Coll. chpt.). Clubs: Mason, Searsport Yacht. Home: 10 Champlain Ave Lewiston ME 04240-5217

STAUFFER, ERIC P., lawyer; b. Tucson, Feb. 1, 1948; s. Robert D. and Jeanne E. (Catlin) S.; m. Jane F. Snyder, Aug. 2, 1969; children: Curtis Austen, Marcus Elias, Laura Afton. BA, U. South Fla., 1969; JD, Yale U., 1972. Bar: Ariz. 1972, Maine 1974, D.C. 1979. Spl. asst. to gov., fed. state coord. State of Maine, 1973-75; Maine alt. to New England Regional Commn., 1973-75; gen. counsel Maine State Housing Auth., 1976-77; adminstrv. asst. to chmn. Dem. Nat. Com., 1977-78; mem. Preti, Flaherty, Beliveau & Pachios, Portland, Maine, 1978—. Bd. dirs. Jr. Achievement Maine, Inc., 1995—, Maine Real Estate Devel. Assn.; pres. Goodwill Industries, Maine, 1981-82, bd. dirs., 1979-93. Recipient Pub. Svc. award Maine Real Estate Devel. Assn., 1992. Mem. Nat. Health Lawyers Assn., Maine State Bar Assn., Ariz. State Bar, D.C. Bar, Maine Real Estate Devel. Assn. (bd. dirs. 1991—, Pub. Svc. award 1992). Office: Preti Flaherty Beliveau & Pachios LLC PO Box 11410 443 Congress St Portland ME 04104-7410

STAUFFER, ROBERT ALLEN, former research company executive; b. Dayton, Ohio, Jan. 26, 1920; s. John G. and Verna G. (Theobald) S.; m. Justine M. Wells, Mar. 20, 1943 (div. 1969); children—Susan, Nancy; m. Ruth Stanley Munro, Oct. 30, 1969. B.A. in Chemistry, Harvard, 1942. With Nat. Research Corp., Cambridge, 1942-67; gen. mgr. research div. Nat. Research Corp., 1949-63, dir., 1954-67, v.p., 1949-67; with Norton Co., Worcester, Mass., 1963-71; v.p. research Norton Co., 1963-71; v.p., gen. mgr. Norton Research Corp., Cambridge, 1968-71; v.p. NRC Metals Corp., 1955-56, Environ. Research and Tech., Concord, Mass., 1971-80. Patentee in field. Home: 3208 Heatherwood at Kings Way Yarmouth Port MA 02675

STAUFFER, RONALD EUGENE, lawyer; b. Hempstead, N.Y., Jan. 22, 1949; s. Hiram Eugene and Florence Marie (Hintz) S.; m. Vicki Lynn Hartman, June 12, 1973; children: Eric Alan, Craig Aaron, Darren Adam. SB, MIT, 1970; JD magna cum laude, Harvard U., 1973. Bar: D.C. 1973, U.S. Ct. Mil. Appeals 1976, U.S. Tax Ct. 1979. Ptnr. Hogan & Hartson, Washington, 1977-87, Sonnenschein Nath & Rosenthal, Washington, 1988—. Contbr. articles to profl. publs. Capt. U.S. Army, 1970-77. Mem. ABA (chair TIPS Employee Benefits Com. 1977—), D.C. Bar Assn., Tau Beta Pi, Sigma Gamma Tau. Avocations: running, water skiing. Home: 10207 Woodhaven Pond Dr Fairfax Station VA 22039-1658 Office: Sonnenschein Nath & Rosenthal 1301 K St NW Ste 600 Washington DC 20005-3317

STAUFFER, STANLEY HOWARD, retired newspaper and broadcasting executive; b. Peabody, Kans., Sept. 11, 1920; s. Oscar S. and Ethel L. (Stone) S.; m. Suzanne R. Wallace, Feb. 16, 1945 (div. 1961); children: Peter, Clay, Charles; m. Elizabeth D. Priest, July 14, 1962 (div. 1991); children: Elizabeth, Grant; m. Madeline A. Sargent, Nov. 27, 1992. AB, U. Kans., 1942. Assoc. editor Topeka State Jour., 1946-47; editor, pub. Santa Maria (Calif.) Times, 1948-52; rewrite and copy editor Denver Post, 1953-54; staff mem. AP (Denver bur.), 1954-55; exec. v.p. Stauffer Publs., Inc., 1955-69; gen. mgr. Topeka Capital-Jour., 1957-69; pres. Stauffer Comm., Inc., 1969-86, chmn., 1986-92; bd. dirs. Topeka/Shawnee County Devel. Corp.; chmn. Stauffer Comm. Fnd. Past pres. Topeka YMCA; past chmn. adv. bd. St. Francis Hosp.; past chmn. Met. Topeka Airport Authority; trustee William Allen White Found., Menninger Found., Midwest Rsch. Inst., Washburn U. Endowment Assn. With USAAF, 1942-45. Named Chpt. Boss of Yr. Am. Bus. Women's Assn., 1976, Outstanding Kans. Pub. Kappa Tau Alpha, 1980, Legion of Honor De Molay, Topeka Phi of Yr., 1971. Mem. Kans. Press Assn. (past pres.), Inland Daily Press Assn. (past dir.), Air Force Assn. (past pres. Topeka), Kans. U. Alumni Assn. (past dir.), Kans. C. of C. and Industry (past chmn.), Def. Orientation Conf. Assn., Topeka Country Club, Top of the Tower Club, Garden of the Gods Club, La Quinta (Calif.) Country Club, Masons (32d deg.), Shriners, Phi Delta Theta (past chpt. pres.), Sigma Delta chi (past chpt. pres.). Episcopalian (past sr. warden). Office: Stauffer Comm Inc 6th & Jefferson St Topeka KS 66607

STAUFFER, THOMAS GEORGE, hotel executive; b. Akron, Ohio, Mar. 4, 1932; s. Caldwell E. and Rose C. (Ortscheidt) S.; m. Lois Campsey, June 18, 1960. B.S., Case Western Res. U., 1954. Cert. hotel adminstr. Pres. Renaissance Hotels Internat. (Ams.), 1954—. Recipient Legion of Honor, Order of DeMolay. Mem. Am. Hotel and Motel Assn., Urban Land Inst., Nat. Restaurant Assn. (dir.), Rolling Rock Club, Clifton Club, Lakewood Country Club, Masons, Shriners, Sigma Chi (Significant Sigma Chi). Home: 10701 Estill Dr Cleveland OH 44107-1418 Office: Renaissance Hotels Internat 29800 Bainbridge Rd Solon OH 44139-2202

STAUFFER, THOMAS MICHAEL, university president; b. Harrisburg, Pa., Dec. 5, 1941; s. John Nisley and Louise Lee Stauffer; m. Marion Walker, Aug. 26, 1966 (div. Dec. 1989); children: Amity Juliet, Courtney Amanda, Winston Thomas; m. Deborah Whisnand, May 16, 1993; 1 stepchild, Elizabeth Stinson. Student, Juniata Coll., 1959-61; BA cum laude, Wittenberg U., Ohio, 1963; Cert. in E. European Politics, Freie U. Berlin, 1964; MA, PhD, U. Denver, 1973. Asst. dean coll., asst. prof. polit. sci. Keene State Coll., 1968-72; dir. fellows in acad. adminstrn., office leadership devel. Am. Coun. Edn., 1972-78; v.p., dir. div. external relations Am. Council on Edn., Washington, 1978-82; exec. sec. Fedn. of Assn. of the Acad. Health Care Professions, 1975-80; chmn. task force on the future of Am. Coun. on Edn., 1978; exec. dir. Bus.-Higher Edn. Forum, 1978-81, Nat. Commn. on Higher Edn. Issues, 1980-81; pres., prof. pub. policy U. Houston, Clear Lake, 1982-91; pres., prof. pub. policy and internat. rels. Golden Gate U., 1992—; spl. asst. to adminstr. NASA, 1992; cons. NSF, Dept. State, Coun. for Internat. Exch. Scholars, Japan External Trade Orgn.; mem. commn. on credit and credentials, Am. Coun. Edn., Bay Area Internat. Forum; chair nat. bd. Challenger Ctr. for Space Sci. Edn., 1987-89, Ctr. for Advanced Space Studies, 1990-94; mem. dels. on higher edn. and econ. devel. to People's Republic of China, S.E. Asia, Japan, Rwanda, Sri Lanka, United Arab Emirates, 1978-96. Exec. editor Ednl. Record and Higher Edn. and Nat. Affairs, 1978-82; contbr. articles to profl. jours., newspapers, monographs, chpts. to books. Chmn. com. advanced tech. Tex. Econ. Devel., 1984, Houston Com. on Econ. Diversification Planning, 1984, Houston World Trade Ctr. Task Force, 1985, East Tex. 2000 Com. on Econ. Devel., S.E. Tex. Higher Edn. Coun., 1989, Clear Lake Area Econ. Devel. Found.; v.p. Inter-Am., U. Coun. for Econ. and Social Devel., Houston World Trade Assn.; vice chmn. Tex. Sci. and Tech. Coun., 1986; pres. St. John Hosp.; chmn. San Francisco Consortium on Higher Edn.; bd. dirs. Houston Hosp. Coun. Found., Tex. Coun. on Econ. Edn., Tex. Senate Space Industry Tech. Commn., Tex. Innovation Info. Network Sys., San Francisco C. of C.; vice-chair San Francisco World Trade Assn.; chair San Francisco Consortium on Higher Edn.; mem. steering com. Houston Econ. Devel. Coun., Calif. Ind. Edn. Coun., blue ribbon com. City Coll., Bay Area Coun., Calif. Invention Ctr., Silicon Valley Mfgs. Assn.; chair San Francisco Mayor's Blue Ribbon Com. on Econ. Devel. Recipient Disting. Alumni award Grad. Sch. Internat. Studies U. Denver, 1989, Tex. Senate Resolution of Commendation, 1991, Challenger Ctr. Nat. award, 1990, ACE Fellow Anniversary award, 1990; Am. Coun. on Edn. fellow in acad. adminstrn., 1971, Ford Found. and Social Sci. Found. fellow, 1963-68, sr. fellow Am. Leadership Forum. Mem. AAAS, Internat. Studies Assn. (co-chmn. ann. meeting 1978), Am. Hosp. Assn., Policy Studies Orgn., Internat. Assn. Univ. Pres., San Francisco Com. on Fgn. Rels., Oakland C. of C., Sacramento C. of C., San Francisco C. of C. (econ. devel. com., bd. dirs.), Commonwealth Club, San Francisco World Trade Club, City Club, Univ. Club San Francisco. Home: 1806 Green St San Francisco CA 94123-4922 Office: Golden Gate U Office of Pres 536 Mission St San Francisco CA 94105-2921

STAUFFER, WILLIAM ALBERT, insurance company executive; b. Maryville, Mo., June 9, 1930; s. Marion W. and Louise (Mangelsdorf) S.; m. Jean VanSlyck Shanley, Apr. 11, 1953; children—Rebecca, John, Rachel. B.J., U. Mo., 1952. Gen. mgr. York (Nebr.) Daily News-Times, 1955-61, Grand Island (Nebr.) Daily Ind., 1961-63; with Northwestern Bell Telephone Co., 1963-83, sec.-treas., 1970-72; v.p., chief exec. officer Northwestern Bell Telephone Co., Fargo, N.D., 1972-74; v.p., chief exec. officer-Iowa Northwestern Bell Telephone Co., Des Moines, 1974-83; exec. v.p., chief operating officer Blue Cross-Blue Shield Iowa, Des Moines, 1984-87; bus. cons. Des Moines, 1987-95; bd. dirs. Hubbell Realty Co., Des Moines, Iowa-Des Moines Nat. Bank, Life Care Retirement Community, Inc., Nat. By-Products, Inc., Des Moines, POP Radio Corp., N.Y.C., Cable Com., Inc., Lithonia, Ga. Pres. Convalescent Home Children, Des Moines, 1969; v.p. Mid-Iowa council Boy Scouts Am.; pres. Hospice of Ctrl. Iowa Found., Regional Health Care Corp., Omaha, 1971, Mercy Hosp. Found., 1979-81; mem. adv. bd. Mercy Hosp., Des Moines.; Bd. dirs., sec. Omaha Symphony Orch. Assn., 1970, Iowa Coll. Found., Des Moines Symphony Orch. Assn., YMCA, Des Moines; bd. dirs. Blue Shield Iowa, Living History Farms; trustee Drake U., Des Moines; trustee devel. coun. U. Mo., pres. 1986-90. Served with USAF, 1952-54. Named to Mo. Basketball Hall of Fame, 1990, U. Mo. Intercollegiate Athletics Hall of Fame, 1991; recipient Faculty-Alumni award U. Mo., 1976, Disting. Svc. award, 1996. Mem. C. of C. Des Moines (pres. 1981), Greater Des Moines Com., Phi Delta Theta. Clubs: Wakonda (pres. 1989), Des Moines. Home: 3920 Grand Ave Ste 301 Des Moines IA 50312-3525

STAUP, JOHN GARY, safety engineer; b. Cleve., May 10, 1931; m. Ellsworth Leroy and May Ann (Weisgerber) S.; m. Elizabeth Louise Friemoth, Jan. 10, 1953; children: Michael Steven, Valerie Elysa Staup Gerdemann, Timothy Karl. BA, Dayton U., 1949; student, U. Mich. Design engr. Gramm Trailer, Delphos, Ohio, 1955-57, F.C. Russell Co., Pandora, Ohio, 1957-59, Ins. Svc. Office, Lima, Ohio, 1959-65, Ctrl. Mut. Ins., Van Wert, Ohio, 1965-76, Mid. Am. Tech. Svcs., Delphos, 1980—; adminstr. safety programs and security programs for various firms. Sgt. USAF, 1951-55. Mem. Am. Single Shot Rifle Assn. (sec.-treas. 1991—), Maumee Valley Soc. Safety Engr., Optimist Club (v.p.). Avocations: gun collecting, civic involvement, public speaking, target shooting, travel. Home: 709 Carolyn Dr Delphos OH 45833-1316

STAUTBERG, SUSAN SCHIFFER, communications executive; b. Bryn Mawr, Pa., Nov. 9, 1945; d. Herbert F. and Margaret (Berwind) Schiffer; m. T. Aubrey Stautberg, Jr., Dec. 10, 1979. BA, Wheaton Coll., 1967; MA, George Washington U., 1970. Nat. TV corr., Washington, 1970-74; White House fellow, 1974-75; dir. communications U.S. Consumer Products Safety Commn., Washington, 1976-78, McNeil Consumer Products Co., 1978-80; v.p. Fraser/Assos., Washington, 1980; exec. asst. to pres. Morgan Stanley & Co., N.Y.C., 1980-82; dir. comm. Deloitte & Touche, N.Y.C., 1982—. pres. MasterMedia Ltd., 1986—; with PartnerCom, N.Y.C.; bd. dirs. States, Inc.; Author: Making It in Less Than an Hour, 1976, Pregnancy Nine to Five: The Career Woman's Guide to Pregnancy and Motherhood, 1985, The Pregnancy and Motherhood Diary: Planning the First Year of your Second Career, 1988, Managing it All, 1989, Balancing Act, 1992. Mem., nat. chmn. adv. coun. Ctr. for Study of the Presidency, 1976—; mem. Phila. Regional Panel for Selection White House Fellows; bd. dirs. Schiffer Pub., The Berwind Found.; mem. Reagan-Bush Presdl. Transition Team; mem. Commn. Presdl. Scholars; State Dept. speaker various countries. Selected as one of Wheaton's 10 Most Outstanding Grads., Alumnae Assn., Wheaton Coll., 1982. Mem. Pub. Rels. Soc. Am. (bd. dirs.), Pub. Affairs Profls., Nat. Soc. Colonial Dames, Acorn Club, City Tavern Club, Cosmopolitan Club, Colony Club, Radnor Hunt Club. Office: PartnerCom 9 W 57th St Fl 20 New York NY 10019-2602

STAUTH, ROBERT EDWARD, food service executive; b. 1945. Grad., Kans. State U.; student, Stanford U. Exec. Program, 1989. Joined Fleming Cos., Inc., Oklahoma City, 1977, various mgmt. positions, 1977-93, pres., COO, bd. dirs., 1993, CEO, 1993—, chmn.,CEO, 1994; bd. dirs. IGA, Inc. Adv. bd. Coll. Bus. Adminstrn., Okla. U.; mem. Okla. State Fair Bd. Mem. Food Distbrs. Internat., Food Mktg. Inst. (exec. steering com. on efficient consumer response, industry rels. com.), Okla. State C. of C. (bd. dirs.), Okla. Bus. Roundtable (bd. dirs., state fair bd.). Office: Fleming Cos Inc PO Box 26647 6301 Waterford Blvd Oklahoma City OK 73126

STAVELY, KEITH WILLIAMS FITZGERALD, librarian; b. New Brunswick, N.J., May 13, 1942; s. Homer Eaton and Elizabeth (Williams) S.; m. Kathleen Fitzgerald, Aug. 19, 1978; 1 child, Jonathan Keith. BA, Yale U., 1964, PhD, 1969; MLS, Simmons Coll., 1980. Asst. prof. English Boston U., 1969-74, Ohio State U., 1990-91; lectr. in English Boston Coll., 1975-80; adult svcs. libr. Watertown (Mass.) Free Pub. Libr., 1979-89, br. libr., 1984-89, head adult svcs., 1989-90; reference libr. Somerville (Mass.) Pub. Libr., 1991-92; asst. adminstr. Fall River (Mass.) Pub. Libr., 1992—. Author: Puritan Legacies: Paradise Lost and the New England Tradition, 1630-1890, 1987, paperback edit., 1990, The Politics of Milton's Prose Style, 1975; co-author: Family Man: What Men Feel About Their Wives, Their Children, Their Parents, and Themselves, 1978; contbr. articles and revs. to profl. pubis. Fellow Fulbright Found., India, 1964-65, Am. Coun. Learned Socs., 1988-89, John Simon Guggenheim Meml. Found., 1989. Mem. MLA (Prize for Ind. Scholars 1987), ALA, Mass. Libr. Assn., Phi Beta Kappa.

STAVER, LEROY BALDWIN, banker; b. Portland, Oreg., Oct. 1, 1908; s. Herbert LeRoy and Grace (Baldwin) S.; m. Helen M. Matschek, Oct. 16, 1937 (dec. Mar. 1995); 1 son, Roger. J.D., Northwestern Coll. Law, 1930; grad., Rutgers U. Grad. Sch. Banking, 1937-39. Bar: Oreg. bar 1929. With U.S. Nat. Bank of Oreg., 1925-74, asst. trust officer, 1936-42, trust officer, 1942-58, v.p., trust officer, 1958—, trust officer, 1959-63, exec. v.p., exec. trust officer, 1963-66, pres., 1966-72, chmn., 1971-74, also dir.; chmn. Commerce Mortgage Co., 1967-74; chmn., chief exec. officer U.S. Bancorp., 1969-74, also dir. Hon. trustee Med. Rsch. Found. Oreg., pres., 1975-76; life trustee Willamette U., St. Vincent Med. Rsch. Found., Oreg. Grad. Inst. Sci. and Tech.; hon. bd. dirs. World Forestry Ctr. Named to Oreg. Bankers Assn. Hall of Fame, 1989. Mem. Am., Oreg. bar assns., C. of C. (pres. 1975), Oreg. Hist. Soc. (bd. dirs. 1978-91), Delta Theta Phi. Clubs: Arlington, Waverley Country. Home: 9908 SE Cambridge Ln Milwaukie OR 97222-7402 Office: US Nat Bank Oreg PO Box 4412 Portland OR 97208-4412

STAVERT, ALEXANDER BRUCE, bishop; b. Montreal, Que., Can., Apr. 1, 1940; s. R. Ewart and Kathleen H. (Rosamond) S.; m. Diana Greig, June 26, 1982; children: Kathleen, Rosamond, Timothy. Student, Lower Can. Coll., Montreal, 1957; BA, Bishop's U., 1961; STB, U. Toronto, Ont., Can., 1964, ThM, 1976, DD (hon.), 1986. Ordained to ministry Anglican Ch. as deacon, 1964, as priest, 1965. With Mission of Schefferville, Que., 1964-69; fellow, tutor in div. Trinity Coll., U. Toronto, 1969-70, chaplain, 1970-76; with St. Clement's Mission East, St. Paul's River, Que., 1976-81; chaplain Champlain Regional Coll., Bishop's U., 1981-84; dean, rector St. Alban's Cathedral, Prince Albert, Sask., Can., 1984-91; consecrated bishop Anglican Diocese of Que., Quebec, 1991—. Address: Diocese of Que, 31 rue des Jardins, Quebec, PQ Canada G1R 4L6

STAVES, SUSAN, English educator; b. N.Y.C., Oct. 5, 1942; d. Henry Tracy and Margaret (McClernon) S. AB, U. Chgo., 1963; MA, U. Va., 1964, PhD, 1967. Woodrow Wilson intern Bennett Coll., Greensboro, N.C., 1965-66; from asst. prof. to prof. Brandeis U., Waltham, Mass., 1967—, Paul Proswimmer prof. of Humanities, 1993—; dept. chair Brandeis U., Waltham, 1986-89, 95—; Clark prof. UCLA, 1989-90. Author: Players' Scepters: Fictions of Authority in the Restoration, 1979, Married Women's Separate Property in England, 1660-1833, 1990; co-author: (with John Brewer) Early Modern Conceptions of Property, 1994; co-editor: (with Cynthia Ricciardi) Elizabeth Griffith's Delicate Distress, 1997; also articles in Modern Philology, 18th-Century Studies, Studies in Eng. Lit., Studies in Eighteenth Century Culture, Law and History, Prose Studies, others. Assoc. mem. Belmont (Mass.) Dem. Town Com.; mem. ACLU, 1967—. Woodrow Wilson fellow, 1963-64, Woodrow Wilson Dissertation fellow, 1966-67, Harward Liberal Arts fellow, 1980-81, John Simon Guggenheim fellow, 1981-82. Mem. MLA (exec. com. div. on late-18th century English lit. 1984-86), Am. Soc. for 18th-Century Studies (exec. bd. 1987-90), Am. Soc. for Legal History, AAUP, English Inst. Episcopalian. Avocations: tennis, squash. Office: Brandeis U Dept English Waltham MA 02254

STAVIG, MARK LUTHER, English language educator; b. Northfield, Minn., Jan. 20, 1935; s. Lawrence Melvin and Cora (Hjertaas) S.; m. Donna Mae Ring, July 3, 1957; children—Anne Ragnhild, Thomas Edward, Rolf Lawrence. B.A., Augustana Coll., 1956, Oxford U., 1958; M.A., Oxford U., 1962; Ph.D., Princeton U., 1961. Instr. to asst. prof. English U. Wis., Madison, 1961-68; from assoc. prof. to prof. English Colo. Coll., Colorado Springs, 1968—. Author: John Ford and the Traditional Moral Order, 1968, The Forms of Things Unknown: Renaissance Metaphor in Romeo and Juliet and A Midsummer Night's Dream, 1995; editor: Ford, 'Tis Pity She's a Whore, 1966. Fellow Danforth Found., 1956-61, Woodrow Wilson Found., 1956-57; Fulbright scholar Oxford U., 1956-58. Mem. MLA, Shakespeare Assn. Am. Democrat. Home: 1409 Wood Ave Colorado Springs CO 80907-7348 Office: Colo Coll Dept English Colorado Springs CO 80903

STAVITSKY, ABRAM BENJAMIN, immunologist, educator; b. Newark, May 14, 1919; s. Nathan and Ida (Novak) S.; m. Ruth Bernice Okney, Dec. 6, 1942; children: Ellen Barbara, Gail Beth. AB, U. Mich., 1939, MS, 1940; PhD, U. Minn., 1943; VMD, U. Pa., 1946. Research fellow Calif. Inst. Tech., 1946-47; faculty Case Western Res. U., 1947—, prof. microbiology, 1962—, prof. molecular biology, 1983-89, emeritus, 1989; mem. expert com. immunochemistry WHO, 1963-83; mem. microbiology fellowship com. NIH, 1963-66; mem. microbiology test com. Nat. Bd. Med. Examiners, 1970-73; chmn. microbiology test com. Nat. Bd. Podiatry Examiners, 1978-82. Mem. editl. bd. Jour. Immunological Methods, 1979-88, Immunopharmacology, 1983-96. Vice pres. Ludlow Community Assn., 1964-66. Fellow AAAS; mem. Am. Assn. Immunologists, Am. Soc. Microbiology, Sigma Xi. Home: 14604 Onaway Rd Cleveland OH 44120-2845 Office: 2119 Abington Rd Cleveland OH 44106-2333

STAVRO, STEVE A., professional hockey team executive. Chmn. bd., chief exec. officer Toronto Maple Leafs, Ont., Can. Office: Toronto Maple Leafs, 60 Carlton St, Toronto, ON Canada M5B 1L1*

STAVROPOULOS, WILLIAM S., chemical executive; b. Bridgehampton, N.Y., May 12, 1939; m. Linda Stavropoulos; children: S. William, Angela D. BA in Pharm. Chemistry, Fordham U.; PhD in Medicinal Chemistry, U. Washington. Research chemist in pharm. research Dow Chem. Co., Midland, Mich., 1967, research chemist for diagnostics product research, 1970, research mgr. diagnostics product research, 1973, bus. mgr. diagnostics product research, 1976, bus. mgr. polyolefins, 1977, dir. mktg. plastics dept., 1979; comml. v.p. Dow Chem. Co. Latin Am., Coral Gables, Fla., 1980; pres. Dow Latin Am., 1984; comml. v.p., basics and hydrocarbons Dow Chem. Co. U.S.A., Midland, 1985-87; group v.p. Dow Chem. Co. U.S.A., 1987-90; pres. Dow U.S.A., 1990—; v.p. The Dow Chemical Co., 1990; sr. v.p. The Dow Chem. Co., 1991; pres., 1992; pres., CEO, bd. dirs. The Dow Chem. Co., Midland, 1993—; bd. dirs. Dow Corning Corp., The Dow Chem. Co., Marion Merrel Dow Inc.; CEO Essex Chem Corp, 1988-92. Office: Dow Chem Co 2030 Dow Ctr Midland MI 48674

STAVROU, NIKOLAOS ATHANASIOS, political science educator; b. Griazdani-Delvino, Albania, May 5, 1935; came to U.S., 1956, naturalized, 1962; s. Athanasios Haritos and Aristoula F. (Laiou) S.; married. BA, Hunter Coll., 1963; MA in Internat. Affairs, George Washington U., 1965, PhD in Polit. Sci, 1970. Research fellow Inst. Sino-Soviet Studies, George Washington U., 1963-64; lectr. govt. Howard U., Washington, 1968-70; asst. prof. Howard U., 1970-72, assoc. prof. polit. sci., 1972-77, prof. polit. sci. and internat. affairs, 1978-79, assoc. chmn. dept. polit. sci., 1979-82; adj. professorial lectr. George Washington U., 1983; guest lectr. Fgn. Service Inst. State Dept.; coordinator Eastern Mediterranean Study Group; area specialist on Yugoslav, Albanian and Greek affairs; polit. commentator on

TV and radio. Author: Allied Politics and Military Interventions: The Political Role of the Greek Military, 1977, Albanian Communism and the Red Bishop, 1996; contbg. author: Political Parties of Europe; contbg. author: Yearbook on International Communism; editor: Edvard Kardelj: The Historical Roots of Non-Alignment, 1980, Greece under Socialism, 1988; author, editor Greece Under Socialism, 1988; editor Mediterranean Quar., 1991—; contbr. more than 200 articles to profl. jours., chpts. to books. Howard U. Research grantee, 1973-74, 77-78, 88-89. Mem. Internat. Studies Assn. (v.p. Mediterranean affairs), Cosmos Club (Washington). Eastern Orthodox. Office: Howard Univ Dept Polit Sci Washington DC 20059

STAW, BARRY MARTIN, business and psychology educator; b. Los Angeles, Sept. 13, 1945; s. Harold Paul and Shirley C. (Posner) S.; m. Adrienne McDonnell; 1 child, Jonah Martin. BS, U. Oreg., 1967; MBA, U. Mich., 1968; PhD, Northwestern U., 1972. Asst. prof. bus. adminstrn. U. Ill., Urbana, 1972-75; assoc. prof. Northwestern U., Evanston, Ill., 1975-77, prof., 1977-80; prof. U. Calif., Berkeley, 1980—, Mitchell prof. Leadership and communication, 1986—; researcher in organizational psychology. Editor: Psychological Dimensions of Organizational Behavior; co-editor: New Directions in Organizational Behavior, (book series) Research in Organizational Behavior; mem. editl. bd. Adminstrv. Sci. Quar., Organizational Behavior and Human Decision Processes, 1974—, Basic and Applied Social Psychology, Motivation & Emotion; contbr. numerous articles to profl. jours. Fellow APA, Am. Psychol. Soc., Acad. Mgmt. Soc. for Organizational Behavior. Democrat. Jewish. Avocations: basketball, tennis, skiing. Office: Univ of Calif Haas Sch Bus Adminstrn Berkeley CA 94720

STAY, BARBARA, zoologist, educator; b. Cleve., Aug. 31, 1926; d. Theron David and Florence (Finley) S. A.B., Vassar Coll., 1947; M.A., Radcliffe Coll., 1949, Ph.D., 1953. Entomologist Army Research Center, Natick, Mass., 1954-60; vis. asst. prof. Pomona Coll., 1960; asst. prof. biology U. Pa., 1961-67; asso. prof. zoology U. Iowa, Iowa City, 1967-77; prof. U. Iowa, 1977—. Fulbright fellow to Australia, 1953; Lalor fellow Harvard U., 1960. Mem. Am. Soc. Zoologists, Am. Inst. Biol. Scis., Am. Soc. Cell Biology, Entomol. Soc. Am., Iowa Acad. Scis., Sigma Xi. Office: U Iowa Dept Biological Scis Iowa City IA 52242

STAYIN, RANDOLPH JOHN, lawyer; b. Cin., Oct. 30, 1942; s. Jack and Viola (Tomin) S.; children: Gregory S., Todd R., Elizabeth J. BA, Dartmouth Coll., 1964; JD, U. Cin., 1967. Bar: Ohio 1967, U.S. Dist. Ct. (so. dist.) Ohio 1968, U.S. Dist. Ct. D.C. 1977, U.S. Ct. Appeals (6th cir.) 1968, U.S. Ct. Appeals (fed. cir.) 1986, U.S. Supreme Ct. 1974, U.S. Ct. Appeals (D.C. cir.) 1976, U.S. Ct. Internat. Trade, 1985. Assoc. Frost & Jacobs, Cin., 1967-72; exec. asst., dir. of legislation U.S. Sen. Robert Taft, Jr., Washington, 1973-74, chief of staff, 1975-76; assoc. Taft, Stettinius & Hollister, Washington, 1977, ptnr., 1978-88; ptnr. Barnes & Thornburg, Washington, 1988—; bd. dirs. W.J.S. Holdings Ltd., W.J.S. Inc.; mem. adv. coun. U.S. and FGN. Comml. Svc., U.S. Dept. Commerce. Chmn., mem. numerous coms., chmn., worker campaigns for local politicians Rep. Party state and local orgns.; mem. Citizens to Save WCET-TV, 1967-72, Fine Arts Fund, 1970-72, Cancer Soc., 1970-72; chmn. agy. rels. com. Hamilton County Mental Health and Mental Retardation Bd., 1969-71, vice chmn., 1971, chmn., 1971-72; v.p. Recreation Commn., City of Cin., 1970-72; mem. funds mgmt. com. Westwood 1st Presbyn. Ch., 1968, v.p., 1969, pres., 1970, trustee, 1970, elder, 1971-72; bd. dirs. Evans Mill Pond Owners Assn., v.p., 1986, pres., 1987; active Washington Nat. Cathedral Fund Com. Mem. ABA (sect. on internat. law and practice, vice chmn. com. on nat. legislation 1977-79, internat. sect., anti-trust sect.), Am. Soc. Assn. Execs. (legal sect., internat. sect.), Internat. Bar Assn., D.C. Bar Assn. (com. on internat. law). Avocations: theater, tennis, skiing, travel, reading. Office: Barnes & Thornburg 1401 I St NW Ste 800 Washington DC 20005-2225

STAYTON, THOMAS GEORGE, lawyer; b. Rochester, Minn., May 1, 1948; m. Barbara Joan Feck, Aug. 8, 1970; children: Ryan, Megan. BS, Miami U., Oxford, Ohio, 1970; JD, U. Mich., 1973. Bar: Ind. 1973, U.S. Dist. Ct. (so. dist.) Ind. 1973, U.S. Ct. Appeals (7th cir.) 1977. Ptnr. Baker & Daniels, Indpls., 1973—. Recipient Sagamore of the Wabash Gov. of Ind., 1988. Mem. ABA, Ind. State Bar Assn., Indpls. Bar Assn. Club: Indpls. Athletic. Office: Baker & Daniels 300 N Meridian St Ste 2700 Indianapolis IN 46204-1750

STEAD, EUGENE ANSON, JR., physician; b. Atlanta, Oct. 6, 1908; s. Eugene Anson and Emily (White) S.; m. Evelyn Selby, June 15, 1940; children: Nancy White, Lucy Ellen, William Wallace. B.S., Emory U., 1928, M.D., 1932. Med. intern Peter Bent Brigham Hosp., Boston, 1932-33; surg. intern Peter Bent Brigham Hosp., 1934-35, assoc. medicine, 1939-42, acting physician-in-chief, 1942; research fellow medicine Harvard, 1933-34; asst. resident medicine Cin. Gen. Hosp., 1935-36, resident, 1936-37; instr. medicine U. Cin., 1935-37; resident phys. Thorndike Meml. Lab.; asst. medicine Harvard and Boston City Hosp., 1937-39; instr. medicine Harvard, 1938-41, assoc., 1941-42; prof. medicine Emory U.; physician-in-chief Grady Hosp., Atlanta, 1942-46; dean Emory U., 1945-46; physician in chief Duke Hosp., 1947-67; prof. medicine Duke U. Sch. Medicine, 1947-78; disting. physician VA, 1978-85. Editor: Circulation, 1973-78, N.C. Med. Jour., 1983-92; Contbr. numerous articles on various aspects of circulation to med. jours. Mem. N.C. Med. Soc., Am. Fedn. Clin. Research, Assn. Am. Physicians, Am. Soc. Clin. Investigation, Alpha Omega Alpha, Sigma Xi, Phi Beta Kappa. Methodist. Home: 5113 Townsville Rd Bullock NC 27507-9438 Office: Duke U Dept Medicine Durham NC 27710

STEAD, FRANCESCA MANUELA LEWENSTEIN, natural health care consultant, massage therapist; b. Bklyn., May 2, 1949; d. Robert Gottschalk Lewenstein and Shirley Winifred (Goodman) Lewenstein Ozgen; m. Thomas David Stead, May 28, 1975; children: Chandra Dharani, Thomas Robert. Student, Case Western Res. U., 1967-69; BA in Govt. cum laude, Ohio U., 1973; cert. in Massage Therapy, Cen. Ohio Sch. Massage, Columbus, 1978. Lic. massage therapist; cert. sports massage therapist. Youth service coordinator Adams-Brown Community Action Agy., Decatur, Ohio, 1973; child welfare worker Scioto Children's Services, Portsmouth, Ohio, 1975-77; project dir. youth services Scioto County Community Action Agy., Portsmouth, Ohio, 1978-79; co-owner Stead Enterprises, Otway, Ohio, 1978—; self employed massage therapist Portsmouth, Ohio, 1979—; owner Total Health Care Cons., Portsmouth, 1985-95, Jade Star Sys., Otway, Ohio, 1995—; drug and alcohol counselor Coun. on Alcoholism, West Union, Ohio, 1982; instr. Yoga, Cradtal, Shawnee State U., Portsmouth, 1985—; staff mem. Area Psychiatric and Psychotherapy Group, Health Ctr. One, Huntington, W.Va., 1986-90; instr. summer career edn. prog. Shawnee State U., 1986; reimbursement officer Ohio Dept. Mental Health, Columbus, 1982-85; cons. Portsmouth Dept., 1977; cons. drug abuse Aberdeen Sch., Ohio, 1982; Yoga instr. YMCA, Portsmouth, 1979-80, 85-87. Dem. campaign worker Ohio, 1968—; organizer So. Ohio Task Force on Domestic Violence, 1976; organizer campus ministry Shawnee State U., Portsmouth, 1976-77; organizer Portsmouth Food Coop., 1975. Flora Stone Mather scholar Case Western Res. U., 1967. Mem. Portsmouth Area Women's Network (adv. bd. 1988—), Am. Massage Therapy Assn. (govt. affairs com. Nat. Sports Massage Team Ohio chpt. 1990—, Ohio del. nat. conv. 1991, 93, sports massage team strategic planning com. 1995—), Women in Networking, Pi Gamma Mu. Democrat. Kagyupa Buddhist. Avocations: weaving, science fiction, painting, skiing, gardening, ethnology. Home and Office: 1211 3rd St Portsmouth OH 45662-4336

STEAD, JAMES JOSEPH, JR., securities company executive; b. Chgo., Sept. 13, 1930; s. James Joseph and Irene (Jennings) S.; m. Edith Pearson, Feb. 13, 1954; children: James, Diane, Robert, Caroline. BS, DePaul U., 1957, MBA, 1959. Asst. sec. C. F. Childs & Co., Chgo., 1957-62; exec. v.p., sec. Koenig, Keating & Stead, Inc., Chgo., 1962-66; 2d v.p., mgr. midwest mcpl. bond dept. Hayden, Stone Inc., Chgo., 1966-69; sr. v.p., nat. sales mgr. Ill. Co. Inc., 1969-70; mgr. instl. sales dept. Reynolds and Co., Chgo., 1970-72; partner Edwards & Hanly, 1972-74; v.p., instnl. sales mgr. Paine, Webber, Jackson & Curtis, 1974-76; v.p., regional instl. sales mgr. Reynolds Securities, Inc., 1976-78; sr. v.p., regional mgr. Oppenheimer & Co., Inc., 1978-88; sr. v.p., regional mgr. fixed income Tucker Anthony, 1988—; instr. Mcpl. Bond Sch., Chgo., 1967—. With AUS, 1951-53. Mem. Security Traders Assn. Chgo., Nat. Security Traders Assn., Am. Mgmt. Assn., Mcpl. Fin. Forum Washington. Clubs: Execs., Union League, Mcpl. Bond, Bond (Chgo.); Olympia Fields Country (Ill.); Wall Street (N.Y.C.). Home: 1005 Hickory Ridge Ct Frankfort IL 60423-2114 Office: 1 S Wacker Dr Chicago IL 60606-4614

STEAD, WILLIAM WHITE, physician, educator, public health administrator; b. Decatur, Ga., Jan. 4, 1919; s. Eugene Anson and Emily (White) S.; m. Ethel Barnett, June 14, 1947 (div.); 1 child, Richard Barnett; m. Joan Jordan DeVore, Apr. 22, 1975. AB, Emory U., 1940, MD, 1943. Intern Grady Meml. Hosp., Atlanta, 1944; resident in medicine Emory U., 1944-45, U. Cin., 1946-48; resident in medicine U. Minn., 1948-49, faculty med. schs. 1949-57; faculty med. schs. U. Fla., 1957-60; prof. medicine Med. Coll. Wis., Milw. County Gen. Hosp., Milw., 1960-72; med. dir. Muirdale Sanatorium, Milw., 1963-72; prof. medicine U. Ark. Med. Sch., 1972—; chief pulmonary diseases service VA Hosp., Little Rock, 1972-73; cons. VA Hosp., 1973—; dir. Tb control Ark. Health Dept., Little Rock, 1973—; Cons. VA Hosp., Wood, Wis., 1960-72. Author 3 books on Tb, also numerous articles. Served to lt. (j.g.) M.C. USNR, 1945-46; capt. M.C. AUS, 1953-54. Recipient Tom T. Ross award Ark. Public Health Assn., 1981; Robert S. Abernathy award for excellence in medicine Am. Coll. Physicians, 1984, James D. Bruce award Am. Coll. Physicians, 1988; research grantee in pulmonary emphysema, 1957-65. Master ACP; mem. AAAS, Am. Fedn. for Clin. Rsch. (nat. sec. 1955-58, v.p. 1958-59, pres. 1959-60), Ctrl. Soc. Clin. Rsch., Am. Soc. Clin. Investigation, Am. Thoracic Soc. (Trudeau medal 1988), Am. Coll. Chest Physicians. Research on unitary concept of Tb and epidemiology of Tb in prison and among elderly in nursing homes; chemotherapy of Tb; variation in susceptibility to Tb infection; history of Tb as a global epidemic; suggestion for genetic engineering of material to enhance resistance to initial infection with Tb. Office: Ark Dept of Health 4815 W Markham St Little Rock AR 72205-3866

STEADMAN, CHARLES WALTERS, lawyer, corporate executive, writer; b. Falls City, Nebr., July 25, 1914; s. William Sherman and Marie (Walters) S.; m. Dorothy Marie Fawick, Feb. 14, 1942 (dec. Sept. 1974); children: Suzanne Louise Steadman Hoerr (dec.), Carole Elaine Steadman Kinney, Charles T. W., Dorothy M. (Diana); m. Consuelo Matthews Artini, May 10, 1986. A.B., U. Nebr., 1935; J.D., Harvard U., 1938. Bar: Ohio 1939, D.C. 1956, U.S. Supreme Ct. 1950, U.S. Ct. Claims 1958. Partner Marshman, Hornbeck, Hollington, Steadman & McLaughlin, Cleve., 1946-65, Steadman, Jones & Baxter, 1956-70; chmn. bd. St. Regis Hotel Corp., 1960-63; vice chmn. Leaseway Intercontinental, 1961-65; prin. Charles W. Steadman Counselor-at-Law, 1970; chmn. com. to end govt. waste Nat. Taxpayers Union, 1979; chmn. bd., pres. Steadman Security Corp., Steadman Technology and Growth Fund, Steadman Investment Fund, Steadman Associated Fund, Steadman American Industry Fund; chief counsel Select U.S. Senate Com., 1956; spl. master commr. Matter of Dissolution of Cleve. Savs. Soc., 1959-62; spl. presdl. rep. to Oman, 1980. Author: Steadman's Revision of the Ohio Civil Practice Manual, 1950, The National Debt Conclusion: Establishing the Debt Repayment Plan, 1993; also legal and econ. articles.; editor: Charles W. Steadman Economic Review. Bd. govs. Investment Co. Inst., 1969-72; chmn. Washington met. area Rep. Nat. Fin. Com., 1980-81; mem. exec. com. Presdl. Inaugural Com., 1981; founder Presdl. Trust, 1981; trustee Tex. Wesleyan Coll., 1982-84; founder, chmn. Nat. Debt Repayment Found, 1982. Served as lt. col. AUS, World War II; chief counsel legal div. Cleve. Ordnance Dist. Recipient Disting. Service award U. Nebr., 1960. Mem. ABA (coun. corp., banking and bus. law 1958-60), Ohio Bar Assn., Cleve. Bar Assn., Ohio Bar, Bar Assn. D.C., Internat. Bar Assn., Am. Law Inst. (life), Am. Judicature Soc., 1925 F Street Club, Union Club (Cleve.), Beach Club (Palm Beach, Fla.), Everglades Club (Palm Beach, Fla.), Racquet and Tennis Club (N.Y.C.), Sky Club (N.Y.C.). Home: 425 Worth Ave Palm Beach FL 33480 also: 700 New Hampshire Ave NW Washington DC 20037 Office: 1730 K St NW Washington DC 20006

STEADMAN, DAVID ROSSLYN AYTON, business executive, corporate director; b. Wembley, Eng., June 7, 1937; came to U.S., 1980; s. Eric and Iris Sina (Smith) S.; m. Beryl Ellen Giles, Jan. 5, 1963 (div.); children: Michael, Christopher, Timothy. B.Sc. in Engring. with honors, City U., London, 1960. Mng. dir. Cossor Electronics, Harlow, Eng., 1974-78; chmn. EMI med. Electronics, London, 1978-80; pres. Raytheon Data Systems, Norwood Mass., 1980-84, Raytheon Ventures, Lexington, 1985-87; chmn., chief exec. officer GCA Corp., Andover, Mass., 1987-88; pres. Atlantic Mgmt. Assocs., Inc., Bedford, N.H., 1988—; chmn., CEO Integra-Hotel & Restaurant Co., 1990-94; chmn. Brookwood Cos., Inc., 1989—, Aavid Thermal Techs., Inc., 1993-96, Tech. Svc. Group, Inc., 1994—; bd. dirs. Vitronics Corp., Telequip Corp., Wahlco Environ. Sys., Inc., chmn. 1996—; bd. dirs. Kurzweil Applied Intelligence, Inc. Fellow Instn. Elec. Engrs. (U.K.); mem. Inst. Mgmt. (U.K.; companion), Inst. Mech. Engrs. (U.K.). Avocations: music; sailing. Office: Atlantic Mgmt Assocs Inc PO Box 10670 Bedford NH 03110

STEADMAN, DAVID WILTON, museum official; b. Honolulu, Oct. 24, 1936; s. Alva Edgar and Martha (Cooke) S.; m. Kathleen Carroll Reilly, Aug. 1, 1964; children: Alexander Carroll, Kate Montague. B.A., Harvard U., 1960, M.A.T., 1961; M.A., U. Calif.-Berkeley, 1966; Ph.D., Princeton U., 1974. Lectr. Frick Collection, N.Y.C., 1970-71; asst. dir., acting dir., assoc. dir. Princeton U. Art Mus., 1971-73; dir. galleries Claremont Colls., (Calif.), 1974-80; art cons. Archtl. Digest, L.A., 1974-77; rsch. curator Norton Simon Mus., Pasadena, Calif., 1977-80; dir. Chrysler Mus., Norfolk, Va., 1980-89, Toledo Mus. Art, Ohio, 1989—. Author: Graphic Art of Francisco Goya, 1975, Works on Paper 1900-1960, 1977, Abraham van Diepenbeeck, 1982. Chester Dale fellow Nat. Gallery Art, Washington, 1969-70. Mem. Coll. Art Assn., Am. Assn. Mus. Dirs. Episcopalian. Office: Toledo Mus Art PO Box 1013 Toledo OH 43697-1013

STEADMAN, JACK W., professional football team executive; b. Warrenville, Ill., Sept. 14, 1928; s. Walter Angus and Vera Ruth (Burkholder) S.; m. Martha Cudworth Steinhoff, Nov. 24, 1949; children: Thomas Edward, Barbara Ann, Donald Wayne. B.B.A., So. Methodist U., 1950. Accountant Hunt Oil Co., Dallas, 1950-54; chief accountant W.H. Hunt, Dallas, 1954-58, Penrod Drilling Co., Dallas, 1958-60; gen. mgr. Dallas Texans Football Club, 1960-63; gen. mgr. Kansas City Chiefs Football Club, 1963-76, exec. v.p., 1966-76, pres., 1976-88; also chmn. bd., 1988—; chmn. benefit com. NFL; chmn. Hunt Midwest Enterprises, Inc., Kansas City; dir. Commerce Bank of Kansas City, Pvt. Industry Coun.; former chmn. Full Employment Coun. Former bd. dirs. Children's Mercy Hosp., bd. dirs. Civic Council, Starlight Theatre Assn., Kansas City, Am. Royal Assn.; pres. Heart of Am. United Way, 1981; adv. trustee Research Med. Ctr., Kansas City; trustee Midwest Research Inst.; mem. Village Presbyn. Ch.; past chmn. C. of C. of Greater Kansas City. Recipient Kans. Citian of Yr. award, 1988. Mem. Indian Hills Country Club, Kansas City Club (pres. 1988), 711 Inner, River, Carriage, Man-of-the-Month Fraternity. Home: 6436 Wenonga Ter Shawnee Mission KS 66208-1732 Office: Kansas City Chiefs 1000 Walnut St Ste 1528 Kansas City MO 64106-2146

STEADMAN, JOHN MARCELLUS, III, English educator; b. Spartanburg, S.C., Nov. 25, 1918; s. John Marcellus and Medora Rice (Rembert) S. AB, Emory U., 1940, MA, 1941, DHL (hon.), 1976; MA (T.W. Hunt scholar), Princeton U., 1948, PhD, 1949. Instr. English Ga. Inst. Tech., 1941-42; asst. prof. U. N.C., 1949-51; ind. study and rsch. in English lit., 1953-61; from rsch. assoc.to sr. rsch. assoc. Henry E. Huntington Libr., San Marino, Calif., 1962—; mem. faculty U. Calif., Riverside, 1966—; prof. English U. Calif., 1967—, faculty rsch. lectr., 1977, prof. emeritus, 1989—; vis. disting. prof. City U. N.Y., fall, 1974. Author numerous books including Disembodied Laughter: Troilus and the Apotheosis Tradition, 1972, The Lamb and The Elephant: Ideal Imitation and the Context of Renaissance Allegory, 1974, Epic and Tragic Structure in Paradise Lost, 1976, Nature into Myth: Medieval and Renaissance Moral Symbols, 1979, Milton's Biblical and Classical Imagery, 1984, The Hill and the Labyrinth: Discourse and Certitude in Milton and His Near-Contemporaries, 1984, The Wall of Paradise: Essays on Milton's Poetics, 1985, Milton and the Paradoxes of Renaissance Heroism, 1987, Redefining a Period Style: "Renaissance," "Mannerist," and "Baroque" in Literature, 1990, Ryoanji Temple and Other Poems, 1993, Moral Fiction in Milton and Spenser, 1995, Reconnaissances: Poems, 1996, Winter Harvest, A Retrospective, 1996; co-editor latest being A Milton Ency., vols. I-IX, 1978-83; editor: latest being Huntington Libr. Quar., 1962-81. Capt. USAAF, 1942-46; capt. USAF, 1951-52. Grantee Huntington Libr., 1961-62; Procter fellow Princeton U., 1949, Guggenheim fellow, 1979. Mem. Milton Soc. Am. (pres. 1973, honored scholar 1976), So. Calif. Renaissance Conf., Phi Beta Kappa, Chi Phi, Fine Arts Club. Democrat. Home: 250 S Oak Knoll Ave Apt 109 Pasadena CA 91101-2923 Office: Henry E Huntington Libr San Marino CA 91108

STEADMAN, JOHN MONTAGUE, judge; b. Honolulu, Aug. 8, 1930; s. Alva Edgar and Martha (Cooke) S.; m. Alison Storer Lunt, Apr. 8, 1961; children—Catharine N., Juliette M., Eric C. Grad., Phillips Acad., Andover, Mass., 1948; BA summa cum laude, Yale U., 1952; LLB magna cum laude, Harvard U., 1955. Bar: D.C. 1955, Calif. 1956, U.S. Supreme Ct. 1964, Hawaii 1977. Assoc. Pillsbury, Madison & Sutro, San Francisco, 1956-63; atty. Dept. Justice, 1963-64; dep. under sec. army for internat. affairs, 1964-65; spl. asst. to sec. and dep. sec. def. Dept. Def., 1965-68; gen. counsel Dept. Air Force, 1968-70; vis. prof. law U. Pa. Law Sch., 1970-72; prof. law Georgetown U. Law Ctr., Washington, 1972-85, assoc. dean, 1979-84; assoc. judge D.C. Ct. Appeals, 1985—; instr. Lincoln Law Sch., San Francisco, 1961-62, San Francisco Law Sch., 1962-63; vis. prof. U. Mich. Sch. Law, 1976, U. Hawaii Sch. Law, 1977; of counsel firm Pillsbury, Madison & Sutro, Washington, 1979-85. Editor: Harvard Law Rev, 1953-55. Sinclair-Kennedy Traveling fellow, 1955-56. Mem. Am. Law Inst., Phi Beta Kappa, Delta Sigma Rho, Zeta Psi. Episcopalian. Home: 2960 Newark St NW Washington DC 20008-3338 Office: DC Ct Appeals 500 Indiana Ave NW Washington DC 20001-2131

STEADMAN, LYDIA DUFF, elementary school educator, symphony violinist; b. Hollywood, Calif., Dec. 31, 1934; d. Lewis Marshall and Margaret Seville (Williams) Duff; m. John Gilford Steadman, Apr. 14, 1961 (dec.). Student, Pepperdine U., 1952-55; BA in Music Edn., U. So. Calif., 1957. Cert. spl. secondary music, edn. tchr., Calif. Instrumental music tchr. Lancaster (Calif.) Sch. Dist., 1957-62; instrumental music tchr. Simi Sch. Dist., Simi Valley, Calif., 1962-70, elem. tchr., 1970—; tchr. Polynesian culture, dances, games, 1970—; hist. play wright for elem. grades, organizer elem. sch. dance festivals; dir. All Dist. Orch., Lancaster, Simi Valley Schs., 1957-70; compile Japanese Culture Study Unit for elem. grades Ventura County. 1st violinist San Fernando Valley Symphony, Sherman Oaks, Calif., 1962-75, Conejo Valley Symphony, Thousand Oaks, 1975-81, tour concert mistress, 1980; 2d violinist Ventura County Symphony, Santa Susana Symphony, 1981-95; 1st violinist Simi Valley's Santa Susana Symphony. Pres. San Fernando Cmty. Concerts, Van Nuys, Calif., 1982-94; free lancing with pit orch. Cabrillo Music Theatre, Conejo Players Theater, Moorpart College Theatre; organizer ann. sch. Jump Rope-a-Thon for Am. Heart Assn., Nat. Geog. Geography Bee; bd. dirs. East Ventura County Cmty. Concert Assn. Mem. AAUW, NAFE, Bus. and Profl. Women of Conejo Valley (pres. Golden Triangle chpg. 1988-90, 95-96, issues and mgmt. chair 1990, ways and means chair Coast chpt. 1990, editor Golden Triangle newsletter 1988-90, treas. 1992-93, sec. 1993-94, v.p. 1994—), Pacific Asia Mus., Armand Hammer Mus., Sigma Xi. Republican. Mem. Ch. of Christ. Avocations: hula dancing, walking, collecting world coins, world traveling, violin. Home: 32016 Allenby Ct Westlake Vlg CA 91361-4001

STEAMER, ROBERT JULIUS, political science educator; b. Rochester, N.Y., Oct. 14, 1920; s. William August and Lotte (Becker) S.; m. Jean Worden, Apr. 12, 1947; children: Gregg Robert, James Worden. B.A. in Social Sci., Bucknell U., 1947; M.A. in Polit. Sci., U. Va., 1952; Ph.D., Cornell U., 1954; postgrad. law, Oxford (Eng.) U., 1968-69. Asst. prof. Oglethorpe U., 1952-55, U. Mass., 1955-56; assoc. prof. La. State U., 1956-62; prof. polit. sci., chmn. dept. Lake Forest (Ill.) Coll., 1962-72; prof. U. Mass., Boston, 1972-88, dean Coll. II, 1974-76, vice chancellor for acad. affairs, provost, 1976-79; vis. summer prof. Tulane U., 1958, Cornell U., 1960, UCLA, 1965; staff cons. La. sect. U.S. Commn. Civil Rights, 1961. Author: The Constitution: Cases and Comments, 1959, The Supreme Court in Crisis, 1971, The Supreme Court: Constitutional Revision and the New Strict Constructionism, 1973, Chief Justice: Leadership and the Supreme Court, 1986; sr. co-author: American Constitutional Law: Cases and Commentary, 1991; contbr. articles to profl. jours. Served with USAAF, 1942-46. Recipient Gt. Tchr. award Lake Forest Coll., 1965; Lilly Found. Research award, 1967; Major Research award Project 87, 1981; hon. research fellow U. Exeter, Eng., 1981. Mem. Am. Polit. Sci. Assn., Midwest Polit. Sci. Assn. (v.p. 1970-71), New Eng. Polit. Sci. Assn. (pres. 1979-80). Home: 439 Kilbourn Rd Rochester NY 14618-3635

STEANS, PHILLIP MICHAEL, lawyer; b. Oak Park, Ill., May 23, 1943; s. William B. and Evelyn A. (Leonetti) S.; m. Randi R. Solberg, Sept. 17, 1966; children: Erik, Joshua, Molly. BA summa cum laude, Ripon (Wis.) Coll., 1965; JD, U. Chgo., 1968. Bar: Wis. 1968, Ill. 1968, Minn. 1986, U.S. Dist. Ct. (we. dist.) Wis. 1968. Ptnr. Solberg & Steans, Menomonie, Wis., 1968-85; mng. ptnr. Steans, Skinner, Schofield & Higley, Menomonie, 1985-91; shareholder Bakke-Norman, S.C., Menomonie, 1991-94; pres. Phillip M. Steans, S.C., Menomonie, 1994—; dist. atty. Dunn County, Wis., Menomonie, 1969-74; asst. city atty. City of Menomonie, 1969-86; asst. family ct. commr. Dunn County, 1993. NCAA scholar, 1965. Mem. Nat. Bd. Trial Advocacy (mem. civil and criminal sects.). Avocations: racquetball, reading. Home: E 5745 708th Ave Menomonie WI 54751 Office: 393 Red Cedar St Ste 6 Menomonie WI 54751-2267

STEAR, EDWIN BYRON, corporate executive; b. Peoria, Ill., Dec. 8, 1932; s. Edwin Joseph and Juanita Blanche (Hoffman) S.; married; children—Brian Douglas, Linnea Susan. B.S. in Mech. Engring, Bradley U., 1954; M.S., U. So. Calif., 1956; Ph.D. (Hughes Staff fellow), UCLA, 1961. Mem. tech. staff Hughes Aircraft Co., Culver City, Calif., 1954-59; asst. research engr. U. Calif., Los Angeles, 1959-61; asst. prof. engring. U. Calif., 1964-68, assoc. prof., 1968-69; mgr. guidance and control research lab. Lear Siegler, Inc., Santa Monica, Calif., 1963-64; assoc. prof. elec. engring. U. Calif., Los Angeles and Santa Barbara, 1969-73; prof. U. Calif., 1973-79, chmn. dept., 1975-79; chief scientist USAF, 1979-82; dir. Wash. Technology Ctr., 1983-90; prof. elec. engring. U. Wash., Seattle, 1983-90, assoc. dean research Coll. Engring., 1983-85; corp. v.p. tech. assessment Boeing Co., Seattle, 1990-97, with Boeing Def. and Space Group, 1997—; mem. sci. adv. bd. USAF, 1971-79, 84-92, vice chmn., 1986-89, chmn., 1989-90; mem. aeros. adv. com. NASA, 1984-90; cons. to industry and govt., 1964-79, 82—; mem. SAE Tech. Stds. Bd., 1994—, chair, 1996—; mem. Industry Adv. Coun. Accreditation Bd. Engring. and Tech., Inc., 1994—; mem. Ctr. for Strategic Internat. Studies, 1995-96; trustee Analytical Svcs., Inc., 1984-90; mem. guidance and control panel NATO Adv. Group Aerospace R&D, 1981-92, dep. chmn. panel, 1988-90, chmn. 1990-92; lectr. Xerox Disting. Lecture Series, 1996; mem. adv. bd. Coll. Engring. Bradley u., Peoria, Ill., 1990—, U. Ill., Champagne-Urbana, 1996—. Editor: (with A. Kadish) Hormonal Control Systems, 1969; mem. editorial bd. Aircraft jour. AIAA, 1974-77; contbr. articles to profl. lit. Served to 1st lt. USAF, 1961-63. Named Disting. Alumnus Bradley U., 1980; recipient civilian exceptional svc. medals USAF, 1982, 92; Arnold D. Beckman lectr. on rsch. and innovation U. Ill., Urbana, 1993; Mental Health Tng. Program fellow UCLA, 1972-74. Fellow IEEE, AIAA, AAAS; mem. Internat. Fedn. Automation Control, Sigma Xi, Eta Kappa Nu, Pi Mu Epsilon, Tau Beta Pi, Phi Eta Sigma, Tau Sigma. Home: 14010 SE 44th Pl Bellevue WA 98006-2331 Office: The Boeing Co PO Box 3707 MS 13-43 Seattle WA 98124-2207

STEARLEY, ROBERT JAY, retired packaging company executive; b. Brazil, Ind., Sept. 6, 1929; s. Melvin George and Hila Mona (Bolin) S.; m. Helen Louise Dellacca, Nov. 25, 1950; children: Rhonda Jo, Robert Thomas. B.S. in Mech. Engring., Rose Hulman Inst. Tech., 1957; postgrad., Harvard U., 1979. Gen. mgr. Poly Tech Corp., Mpls., 1961-63; gen. mgr. plastics Gt. Plains Bag Corp., Stamford, Conn., 1963-66, v.p., 1966-71, v.p. ops., 1971-75, pres., 1975-84, dir., 1966-84; v.p. Jefferson Smurfit Corp., Alton, Ill., 1984—. Mem. Paper Shipping Sack Mfg. Assn. (dir. 1980-82), Am. Legion. Republican. Methodist. Club: Norwood Hills Country (St. Louis). Lodge: Elks. Home: 2 Country Estate Pl Saint Louis MO 63131-3411

STEARN, TODD, federal government official. Asst. to pres., staff sec. Office of Staff Sec., Washington, 1995—. Office: Office of Staff Sec 1600 Pennsylvania Ave NW Washington DC 20502-0001*

STEARNS, CLIFFORD BUNDY, congressman, business executive; b. Washington, DC, Apr. 16, 1941; s. Clifford Robert and Emily Elizabeth (Newlin) S.; m. Joan Bette Moore; children: Douglas Moore, Clifford Bundy Jr., Scott Newlin. BSEE, George Washington U., 1963. Mgr. Control Data

Systems, Inc., L.A., 1967-69; sr. contract adminstr. CBS, Inc., Stamford, Conn., 1969; account exec. Kutola Advt. Agy., Greenwich, Conn., 1970-71, Images 70/Wilson Leigh Welch, Inc., Greenwich, 1971-72; motel owner Hatfield, Mass., 1972-77; pres., motel mgr. Stearns House, Inc., Silver Springs, Fla., 1977-88; mem. 101st-103rd Congresses from 6th Fla. dist., 1989—; mem. banking, fin. and urban affairs com., vets. affairs com. 101st Congress from 6th Fla. dist., mem. energy and commerce com., subcoms. energy and power, commerce, consumer protection and competetiveness; 104th Congress, mem. commerce and vets. coms., subcoms. telecom. and fin., healthcare, energy and power; broker Silver Springs (Fla.) Real Estate, 1981-88. Trustee, vice chmn. Monroe Regional Hosp., Ocala, Fla., 1984-89; bd. dirs. Boys Club of Ocala, 1980-84; pres. Toastmaster Club L.A., 1962. Capt. USAF, 1963-67. Mem. Am. Hotel/Motel Assn., Fla. Hotel/Motel Assn., Am. Assn. Realtors, Fla. Assn. Realtors, Marion County Motel Assn. (pres. 1979), Marion C. of C. (bd. dirs. 1987—), Kiwanis (pres. Ocala club 1984). Republican. Presbyterian. Avocations: basketball, swimming, computers. Home: 2071 SE 54th Ter Ocala FL 34471-8702 Office: US Ho of Reps 332 Channing St NE Bldg Washington DC 20002-1028 Office: Ho of Reps 2352 Rayburn Office Bldg Washington DC 20515 also: 115 SE 25th Ave Ocala FL 34471-9179

STEARNS, ELLIOTT EDMUND, JR., retired surgeon; b. Cleve., Jan. 11, 1923; s. Elliott Edmund and Sarah (Hoyt) S.; m. Martha Hudson Small, June 26, 1945; children: Michael Elliott, Philip Hoyt, Daniel Arthur. Student, Williams Coll., 1941-43; BS, U. Calif., Berkeley, 1945; MD, U. Calif., San Francisco, 1948. Diplomate Am. Bd. Urology. Intern U.S. Pub. Health Hosp., San Francisco, 1949-50; resident Sonoma Co. Hosp., Santa Rosa, Calif., 1950-51; fellow urology Cleve. Clinic, 1952-54; chief resident urology Cin. (Ohio) Gen. Hosp., U. Cin., 1954-56; med. staff St. Mary's Hosp., Tucson, 1956-87, St. Joseph's Hosp., Tucson, 1956-87, Tucson (Ariz.) Med. Ctr., 1956-87, Pima County Hosp., Tucson, 1956-87; ret., 1987; exec. com. mem. Pima County Med. Soc., Tucson, 1970s; chief of surgery St. Joseph's Hosp., Tucson, 1980s. Author: Catapult, 1994. Capt. USAF, 1954-56. Fellow ACS. Home: 2926 N Cascade Cir Tucson AZ 85715

STEARNS, JAMES GERRY, retired securities company executive; b. Lapine, Oreg., Jan. 29, 1922; s. Carey Summer and Betty (Hunt) S.; m. June Elizabeth Speer, Nov. 21, 1943; children: Robert Sumner, Katherine Inga, Gerry Marshall. Student, Oreg. State U. Flight instr. U.S. AAC, 1942-45; supr. Modoc County (Calif.), Alturos, 1951-67; dir. Calif. Dept. Conservation, Sacremento, 1967-72; sec. Calif. Agr. and Services Agy., Sacremento, 1972-75; dir. office alcohol fuels U.S. Dept. Energy, Washington, 1981-82; chmn., chief exec. officer Securities Investor Protection Corp., Washington, 1982-94; ret., 1994. With USAAC, 1942-45. Republican. Lodges: Masons; Shriners; Jesters. Office: Securities Investor Protection Corp 805 15th St NW Ste 800 Washington DC 20005-2207

STEARNS, LLOYD WORTHINGTON, investment adviser, Oriental artifact consultant; b. Somerville, Mass., Feb. 16, 1910; s. Charles Victor and Flora D. (Liscom) S.; B.S. in Indsl. Engring., N.Y. U., 1934; m. Adelaide Church, Nov. 23, 1932; 1 child, Adelaide Liscom Stearns McRae. Indsl. security analyst Adminstrv. and Research Corp., 1934-38; asst. to treas., v.p. Northam Warren Corp., 1938-41; with Met. Life Ins. Co., 1941-75, sr. procedure analyst, mgmt. cons., exec. asst. to sr. v.p., to exec. v.p., 1941-60, to pres., 1960, sec., emergency com., 1950-75; coll. relations cons.; dir. Soundscriber, Inc.; pres., dir. Dispoz Sani Products, Ltd. Bd. dirs. Mil. Pub. Inst., Inc.; sec. N.Y. State Life Ins. Civil Def. Adv. Com., 1954-64; corp. mem. N.Y. World's Fair 1964-65 Corp.; mem. nat. def. com. U.S. C. of C. and NAM; mem. joint com. emergency operation Am. Life Conv.-Life Ins. Assn. Am.; mem. corps com. Lincoln Center for Performing Arts, 1959-62; v.p., treas., dir., vice chmn. N.Y. com. Nat. Strategy Seminars, Inc.; dir. Nat. Inst. Disaster Moblzn., Inc., Battery Park Colonnade Assocs., Inc.; sec. French-Polyclinic Fund, Inc. Trustee French Hosp., N.Y.C., N.Y. Polyclinic Med. Sch. and Hosp. Served to col. AUS, 1933-70; sec. gen. to chief commr. Allied Commn. Rome, Mediterranean Theater Opers., WWII, 1941-46, NATOUSA; with Res. 1946-70. Decorated Legion of Merit; recipient Outstanding Civilian Service medal U.S. Army; decorated comdr. Crown of Italy, comdr. Sts. Maurice and Lazarus (Italy); War Cross Commemorative Royal Yugoslav Army. Mem. Am. Ordnance Assn. (dir., chmn. programs), Am. Legion, Vet. Fgn. Wars, Soc. Colonial Wars (council), SAR (bd. mgrs.), N.Y. Soc. Mil. and Naval Officers World Wars (sec.), Mil. Order of World Wars, Assn. U.S. Army (pres. N.Y. chpt. 1961-62, regional pres. 1963-64), Def. Orientation Conf. Assn., N.Y. Chamber Commerce, Newcomen Soc., New Eng. Hist. and Geneal. Soc., U.S. Naval Inst., Statue of Liberty Found., Gateway Civic Assn (pres., sec., treas. 1983—), Phi Gamma Delta. Episcopalian. Clubs: University (N.Y.C.); Army and Navy (Washington); Masons. Home and Office: 410 Main St Keene NH 03431-4180

STEARNS, MILTON SPRAGUE, JR., financial executive; b. N.Y.C., June 3, 1923; s. Milton Sprague and Katherine (Stieglitz) S.; m. Virginia McCormick; children—Virginia Parker Stearns King, John Brackett, Barbara Ellison Stearns Terry, Kathryn Trowbridge Stearns Sergio, Elizabeth Sprague (dec.). Grad., Phillips Exeter Acad., 1942; BS cum laude, Harvard U., 1946, MBA, 1948. With The Fidelity Bank, Phila., 1948-72; group v.p. nat. lending div. The Fidelity Bank; pres. Charter Fin. Co., Radnor, Pa., 1972—; chmn., chief exec. officer Judson Infrared, Inc., 1976-87; bd. dirs. CFM Tech. Corp., Inc., West Chester, Pa., Infocore, King of Prussia, Pa.; ret. dir. The West Co., Phoenixville, Pa. Trustee Franklin Inst., Bryn Mawr Presbyn. Ch., pres. 1993-95. Served with USNR, WWII; lt. (j.g.) Res. ret. Mem. Robert Morris Assoc. (pres. Phila. chpt. 161-62), Spee Club Cambridge, Mass., Merion Golf Club, Merion Cricket Club, Phila. Skating and Humane Soc., Union League Club of Phila., Delray Beach (Fla.) Club, Delray Beach Yacht Club, Country Club of Fla., Gulfstream Bath and Tennis Club, Pine Tree Golf Club. Home: 43 Righters Mill Rd Gladwyne PA 19035-1548 Office: 290 King Of Prussia Rd Ste 300 Radnor PA 19087

STEARNS, NEELE EDWARD, JR., diversified holding company executive; b. Chgo., Apr. 2, 1936; s. Neele Edward Sr. and Grace (Kessler) S.; m. Bonnie Ann Evans; children: Katherine Grace, Kendra Ann. BA magna cum laude, Carleton Coll., 1958; MBA with distinction, Harvard U., 1960. Audit staff Arthur Andersen Co., 1962-66, audit mgr., 1966-67; asst. gen. mgr. internat. divsn. Imperial-Eastman Corp., 1967-68; asst. treas. Allied Products Corp., 1968-69, treas., 1969-72; v.p. Henry Crown (Ill.) and Co., 1972-75, v.p., controller, 1975-79; exec. v.p., chief oper. officer Henry Crown and Co., 1979-86; pres., chief exec. officer CC Industries, Inc., Chgo., 1986-95; chmn. exec. com. Barnes Internat., Inc., Northbrook, Ill., 1996—; dir. Maytag Corp., 1989—, Wallace Computer Svcs., Inc., 1990—. Trustee, chmn. fin. com. Ravinia Festival Assn.; trustee, chmn. Lakeland Health Svcs. (Highland Park Hosp.). Mem. Commercial Club Chgo., Econ. Club Chgo., Univeristy Club Chgo., Chgo. Club, Skokie Country Club, Phi Beta Kappa. Office: Barnes Internat Inc 707 Skokie Blvd Northbrook IL 60062-2857

STEARNS, PETER NATHANIEL, history educator; b. London, Mar. 3, 1936; (parents Am. citizens); s. Raymond P. and Elizabeth (Scott) S.; m. Nancy Driessel (div. 1976); children: Duncan, Deborah; m. Carol Zisowitz, Mar. 26, 1978; children: Clio Elizabeth, Cordelia Raymond. AB, Harvard U., 1957, MA, 1959, PhD, 1963. Instr. to assoc. prof. U. Chgo., 1962-65; prof., chmn. history dept. Rutgers U., New Brunswick, N.J., 1965-74; Heinz prof. history Carnegie Mellon U., Pitts., 1974—, chmn. dept. history, 1986-92, dean Coll. Humanities and Social Scis., 1992—; co-dir. Pitts. Ctr. for Social History, 1986-92; chmn. acad. adv. coun. N.Y.C. Coll. Bd., 1982-85; chmn. Pacesetter World History commn., Coll. Bd., 1992-95, Coll. Bd. Advanced Placement World History. Author: European Society in Upheaval: Social History since 1800, 1967 (trans. Swedish), rev. edit., 1975, 3d edit., 1991, Priest and Revolutionary: Lamennais and the Dilemma of French Catholicism, 1967 (trans. Polish), Modern Europe, 1789-1914, 1969, Revolutionary Syndicalism and French Labor: a cause without rebels, 1971, (with Harvey Mitchell) Workers and Protest: The European Labor Movement, The Working Classes and the Rise of Socialism, 1890-1914, 1971, The European Experience since 1815, 1972, 1848: The Revolutionary Tide in Europe, 1974 (pub. in Eng. as The Revolutions of 1848), Lives of Labor: Work in Maturing Industrial Society, 1975 (trans. German), Old Age in European Society, 1977, Face of Europe, 1977, Paths to Authority: Toward the Formation of Middle Class Consciousness, 1978, Be A Man! Males in Modern Society, 1979, rev. edit., 1990, (with Linda Rosenzweig) Themes in Modern Social History, 1985, (with Carol Stearns) Anger: The Struggle for Emotional Control in America's History, 1986, World History: Patterns of Change and Continuity, 1987, rev. edit., 1994, (with others) Makers of Modern Europe, 1987, rev. edit., 1994, (with others) Readings in World History, Vol. 1: The Great Tradition and Vol. 2: The Modern Centuries, 1987, Expanding the Past: A Reader in Social History, 1988, Life and Society in the West, The Modern Centuries, 1988, World History: Traditions and New Directions, 1988, rev. edit., 1994, (with C. Stearns) Emotion and Social Change, Toward a New Psychohistory, 1988, (with Andrew Barnes) Social History and Issues in Consciousness and Cognition, 1989, Jealousy: Evolution of an Emotion in American History, 1989, Interpreting the Industrial Revolution, 1991, (with Michael Adas and Stuart Schwartz) World Civilizations, 1991, rev. edit., 1995, Meaning Over Memory: Issues in Humanities Education, 1993, The Industrial Revolution in World History, 1993, (translated into Swedish), American Cool: Developing a 20th Century Emotional Style, 1994, Turbulent Passage: A Global History of the 20th Century, 1994, (with Ron Harre) Discursive Psychology in Practice, 1995, Millenium III, Century XXI, 1996, (with Hinshaw) Encyclopedia of the Industrial Revolution, 1996, Fat History: Bodies and Beauty in the West, 1997, Starting School: Comparative Educational History in France, US, Japan, 1997; editor: Century for Debate, 1969, The Impact of the Industrial Revolution, 1972, (with Walkowitz) Workers in the Industrial Revolution, 1974, The Other Side of Western Civilization, 1979, rev. edit., 1984, 4th edit., 1991, The Rise of Modern Women, 1977, (with Michael Weber) The Spencers of Amberson Avenue: A Turn-of-the-Century Memoir, 1983, (with Van Tassel) Old Age in a Bureaucratic Society, 1986; editor in chief Jour. Social History, 1967—; editor: Encyclopedia of Social History, 1993, Ency. World Hist., 1995, 5th edit. Encyclopedia World History rev.; contbg. editor history of emotions series NYU Press; contbr. over 150 articles to profl. and popular jours. Guggenheim Found. fellow, 1973-74; NEH grantee, 1981-84, 86, 90, Rockefeller Found. grantee, 1982-83. Fellow Internat. Soc. for Rsch. on Emotion; mem. Am. Hist. Soc., World History Assn., Am. Hist. Assn. (v.p., head teaching div. 1995—), Nat. Bd. Profl. Teaching Standards. Democrat. Avocations: racquet sports, travel. Home: 509 S Linden Ave Pittsburgh PA 15208-2846 Office: Carnegie Mellon U History Dept Pittsburgh PA 15213-3890

STEARNS, RICHARD GAYLORE, judge; b. L.A., June 27, 1944; s. Gaylore Rhodes and Jeannetta Viola (Hofheinz) S.; m. Patricia Ann McElligott, Dec. 21, 1975. BA, Stanford U., 1968; MLitt, Oxford U., Eng., 1971; JD, Harvard U., 1976. Bar: Mass. Dep. campaign mgr. McGovern for Pres., Washington, 1970-72; spl. asst. U.S. Senate, Washington, 1972-73; asst. dist. atty. Norfolk County, Dedham, 1976-79, 80-82; del. dir. Kennedy for Pres., Washington, 1979-80; asst. U.S. atty. U.S. Dept. Justice, Boston, 1982-90; assoc. justice Superior Ct. Mass., Boston, 1990-94; U.S. dist. judge U.S. Dist. Ct. Mass., Boston, 1994—. Author: Massachusetts Criminal Law: A Prosecutor's Guide, 16th edit., 1996. Mem. jud. conf. com. on federal-state jurisdiction; trustee Vincent Meml. Hosp., Boston. Rhodes scholar, 1968. Mem. ABA, Mass. Bar Assn., Phi Beta Kappa. Office: US Dist Ct 707 PO & Courthouse Bldg Boston MA 02109

STEARNS, ROBERT LELAND, curator; b. L.A., Aug. 28, 1947; s. Edward Van Buren and Harriett Ann (Hauck) S.; m. Sheri Roseanne Lucas, Oct. 2, 1982 (div. 1994); children: Marissa Hauck, Caroline Lucas. Student, U. Calif., San Diego, 1965-68, BFA, 1970; student, Calif. Poly. State U., San Luis Obispo, 1968. Asst. dir. Paula Cooper Gallery, N.Y.C., 1970-72; prodn. asst. Avalanche Mag., N.Y.C., 1972; dir. Kitchen Ctr. for Video/Music, N.Y.C., 1972-77, Contemporary Arts Ctr., Cin., 1977-82; dir. performing arts Walker Art Ctr., Mpls., 1982-88; dir. Wexner Ctr. for Arts, Columbus, Ohio, 1988-92; mem. Wexner Ctr. Found., Columbus, 1990-92; dir. Stearns & Assocs./Contemporary Exhbn. Svcs., Lancaster, Ohio, 1992—; adj. prof. dept. art, assoc. dean Coll. Art, Ohio State U., Columbus, 1988-92; cons. McKnight Found., St. Paul, 1978, Jerome Found., 1978-79; chmn. Artists TV Workshop, N.Y.C., 1976-77; bd. dirs., chmn. Minn. Dance Alliance, Mpls., 1983-88; bd. dirs. Haleakala, Inc., N.Y.C.; mem. various panels Nat. Endowment for Arts, Washington, 1977— ; mem. pub. arts policy Greater Columbus Arts Coun., 1988-90; adv. coun. Bklyn. Acad. Music, 1982-84, Houston Grand Opera, 1991-93. Author, editor: Robert Wilson: Theater of Images, 1980, Photography and Beyond in Japan, 1995; author: Mexico Now: Point of Departure, 1997, Robert Wilson: Scenografie e Installazioni, 1997; editor: Dimensions of Black, 1970; exec. editor: Breakthroughs, 1991; author and editor numerous catalogues. Decorated chevalier Order of Arts and Letters (France); Jerome Found. travel grantee, 1986, Japan Found. travel grantee, 1991.

STEARNS, STEPHEN RUSSELL, civil engineer, forensic engineer, educator; b. Manchester, N.H., Feb. 28, 1915; s. Hiram Austin and Elisabeth Scribner (Brown) S.; m. Eulalie Moody Holmes, Jan. 1 1939; children: Marjorie Elisabeth, Stephen James, Jonathan David. A.B., Dartmouth Coll., 1937; C.E., Thayer Sch. Engring., 1938; M.S., Purdue U., 1949. Civil engr. Gannett, Eastman, Fleming, Harrisburg, Pa., 1938-40; marine egr. Bur. Ships, Phila. Navy Yard, 1940-41; engr. Dry Dock Assocs., Phila Navy Yard, 1941-43; instr. Thayer Sch. Engring., Dartmouth, 1943-45, asst. prof., 1945-53, prof. civil engring., 1953-80; UN cons., Poland, 1974, 78; engr. Ops. Research, Inc., Washington., 1962-64; phys. reconnaisance in Alaska Boston U. Phys. Research Labs., 1953; chief applied snow and ice research br. Snow, Ice, Permafrost Research Establishment, U.S. Army Engrs., 1954-55; Mem. Sch. Bd., Hanover, N.H., 1951-60, chmn., 1957-59; mem. N.H. Gov.'s Transp. Com., 1966-67, Task Force, 1969; chmn. Lebanon (N.H.) Regional Airport Authority, 1966-69; mem. N.H. Bd. Registration Profl. Engrs., 1975-83. Mem. ASCE (dir. 1978-81, pres. 1983-84), NSPE, Am. Soc. Engring. Edn., Nat. Soc. Profl. Engrs., Dartmouth Soc. Engrs. (Robert Fletcher award), Sigma Chi. Congregationalist. Home: 10 Barrymore Rd Hanover NH 03755-2402

STEARNS, SUSAN TRACEY, lighting design company executive, lawyer; b. Seattle, Oct. 28, 1957; d. Arthur Thomas and Roberta Jane (Arrowood) S.; m. Ross Alan De Alessi, Aug. 11, 1990; 1 child, Chase Arthur. AA, Stephens Coll., 1977, BA, 1979; JD, U. Wash., Seattle, 1990. Bar: Calif. 1990, U.S. Ct. Appeals (9th cir.) 1990, U.S. Dist. Ct. (no. dist.) Calif 1990, U.S. Dist. Ct. (we. dist.) Wash. 1991, Wash. 1991. TV news prodr. KOMO, Seattle, 1980-86; atty. Brobeck, Phleger & Harrison, San Francisco, 1990-92; pres. Ross De Alessi Lighting Design, Seattle, 1993—. Author periodicals in field. Alumnae Assn. Coun. Stephens Coll., Columbia, Mo., 1995—. Named Nat. Order of Barristers U. Washington, Seattle, 1990. Mem. ABA (mem. state labor and employment law subcom.), Wash. State Bar Assn. (mem. bench-bar-press com.), State Bar Calif., King County Bar Assn., Bar Assn.San Francisco, Wash. Athletic Club. Avocations: travel, dance. Office: Ross De Alessi Lighting Design 2815 2nd Ave Ste 280 Seattle WA 98121-1261

STEBBINS, RICHARD HENDERSON, electronics engineer, peace officer, security consultant; b. Pittsburgh, Pa., Dec. 2, 1938; s. Earl Carlos and Esther Frances (Kusluch) S.; m. Rosemary Tanneberger, Aug. 12, 1984; children from previous marriage: Richard Earl, Susan Elizabeth. BSEE with high honors, U. Md., 1965; postgrad., Trinity U., 1973-74. cert. peace officer, Tex. Engring. tech. Nat. Security Agy., Ft. Meade, Md., 1960-65; design engr. Page Communications Engr., Washington, 1965-66, Electromechanical Rsch., Inc., College Park, Md., 1966-67, Honeywell, Inc., Annapolis, Md., 1967-68; electronics engr., intelligence rsch. specialist Fed. Civil Svc., San Antonio, 1968-91; pvt. cons. San Antonio, 1991—; comdr.'s advisor Air Force Cryptologic Support Ctr., San Antonio, 1988-91; deputy dir. countermeasures ops., intelligence rsch. specialist USAF HQ Electronic Security Command, San Antonio, 1981-88; mem. blue ribbon com. on ops. security & comm. security roles & relationships for command and svc. Author, lectr. in field; contbr. articles to profl. jours. With USN, 1956-59. Mem. NRA, Tau Beta Pi, Eta Kappa Nu, Phi Kappa Phi. Republican. Episcopalian. Avocations: hunting, fishing, target shooting, family history rsch. Home: 9602 Clear Falls San Antonio TX 78250-5067

STEBBINS, ROBERT ALAN, sociology educator; b. Rhinelander, Wis., June 22, 1938; s. William Nelson and Dorothy May (Guy) S.; m. Karin Yvonne Olson, Jan. 11, 1964; children: Paul, Lisa, Christi. B.A., Macalester Coll., 1961; M.A., U. Minn., 1962, Ph.D., 1964. Assoc. prof. Presbyterian Coll., Clinton, S.C., 1964-65; assoc. prof.to prof. Meml. U. Nfld., St. John's, Can., 1965-73; prof. U. Tex.-Arlington, 1973-76; prof. sociology U. Calgary, Alta., Can., 1976—, dept. head, 1976-82; head dept. sociology and anthropology Meml. U. Nfld., 1968-71. Author: Commitment to Deviance, 1971, The Disorderly Classroom: Its Physical and Temporal Conditions, 1974, Teachers and Meaning, 1975, Amateurs, 1979, The Magician, 1984, Sociology: The Study of Society, 2d edit., 1990, Canadian Football: The View from the Helmet, 1987, Deviance: Tolerable Differences, 1988, The Laugh-Makers: Stand-Up Comedy as Art, Business, and Life-Style, 1990, Amateurs, Professionals and Serious Leisure, 1992; co-editor: Fieldwork Experience, 1980, The Sociology of Deviance, 1982, Experiencing Fieldwork, 1991, Career, Culture, and Social Psychology in a Variety Art, 1993, Predicaments: Moral Difficulty in Everyday Life, 1993, The Franco-Calgarians: French Language, Leisure and Linguistic Lifestyle in an Anglophone City, 1994, The Connoisseur's New Orleans, 1995, The Barbershop Singer: Inside the Social World of a Musical Hobby, 1996, Tolerable Differences: Living with Deviance, 2d edit., 1996. Pres. St. John's Orch., 1967-68; mem. Dallas Civic Symphony, 1973-76, Orch. Soc. of Calgary, 1978—. Can. Coun. Sabbatical Leave fellow, 1972-72, Calgary Inst. for Humanities fellow, 1987-88, Killam resident fellow, 1990; NEH summer stipend, 1976; Acad. Leisure Scis. fellow, 1996—. Mem. Leisure Studies Assn., Can. Sociology and Anthropology Assn. (pres. 1988-89), Internat. Sociol. Assn., Assn. for Can. Studies, World Leisure and Recreation Assn., Social Sci. Fedn. Can. (pres. 1991-92), Can. Assn. for Leisure Studies (v.p. 1993-96), Internat. Soc. bassists Club (Ann Arbor, Mich., chmn. amateur divsn. 1974-84). Home: 144 Edgemont Estates Dr NW, Calgary, AB Canada T3A 2M3 Office: U Calgary Dept Sociology, 2500 University Dr NW, Calgary, AB Canada T2N 1N4

STEBBINS, THEODORE ELLIS, JR., museum curator; b. N.Y.C., Aug. 11, 1938; s. Theodore Ellis and Mary Emma Flood S.; children: Michael Morgan, Theodore Samuel, Susan Ellis. B.A., Yale U., 1960; J.D., Harvard U., 1964, Ph.D., 1971. Chester Dale fellow Nat. Gallery Art, Washington, 1967; instr. Smith Coll., 1968; assoc. prof. art history and Am. studies, curator Am. painting and sculpture Yale U., New Haven, 1969-77; John Moors Cabot curator Am. paintings Mus. Fine Arts, Boston, 1977—; lectr. fine arts Harvard U., 1979-81; prof. art history Boston U., 1982—; mem. governing bd. Yale U. Art Gallery; trustee Inst. Contemporary Art, Boston. Author: Life and Works of Martin Johnson Heade, 1975, American Master Drawings and Watercolors, 1976, The Oil Sketches of Frederic Edwin Church, 1978, Drawings of Washington Allston, 1979, Luminism in Context, 1980, The Lane Collection, 1983, A New World: Masterpieces of American Painting, 1983, intro. to The Bostonians, 1986, Boston Collects Contemporary Painting and Sculpture, 1986, Charles Sheeler: The Photographs, 1987, Weston's Westons: Portraits and Nudes, 1989, The Lure of Italy: American Artists and the Italian Experience (Winner Minda de Gunzberg prize 1993), 1992, Weston's Westons: California and the West, 1994, Driftwood Winslow Homer's Final Painting, 1996. Trustee Howard Heinz Endowment; pres. Stebbins Fund; chmn. John Heinz for Senate, 1976. Recipient Joseph Coolidge Shaw medal Boston Coll., 1983. Club: Century Assn. Office: Mus Fine Arts 465 Huntington Ave Boston MA 02115-5523

STEBBINS, VRINA GRIMES, elementary school educator, counselor; b. Columbus, Ohio, Aug. 24, 1939; d. Marion Edward and Vrina Elizabeth (Davis) Grimes; m. Gary Frank Stebbins, Dec. 23, 1959; 1 child, Gregory Gary. Student, Ohio U., 1957-59; BS in Edn., Miami U., Oxford, Ohio, 1965; MS in Edn., St. Francis Coll., 1971; Counseling Endorsement, Ind.-Purdue U., Ft. Wayne, 1988. Cert. elem. classroom educator K-6, sch. counselor, social worker, Ind. 1st grade tchr. Greenville (Ohio) Pub. Schs., 1963-68; elem. educator East Allen County Schs., New Haven, Ind., 1969-84; elem. sch. counselor East Allen County Schs., New Haven, 1984—; presenter at Ind. profl. orgns., 1985-92, 1st Presbyn. Ch., Ft. Wayne, 1984—, Project 2000, Ft. Wayne, 1992—; participant Bus.-Edn. Exchange, Ft. Wayne C. of C., 1993. Mem. ACA, Ind. Counseling Assn. (com. mem. 1992-93, Ind. Elem. Counselor of Yr. 1991), East Allen Educators' Assn. (chair com. 1989—, East Allen County Schs. Elem. Educator of Yr. 1989, 95), Arts United, Phi Delta Kappa, Delta Kappa Gamma (1st v.p. Ind. state 1993-95, Ind. state pres. 1995-97). Democrat. Presbyterian. Avocations: travel, collecting antiques and angels. Home: 5712 Sandra Lee Ave Fort Wayne IN 46819-1118 Office: Village Elem Sch 4625 Werling Dr Fort Wayne IN 46806-3410

STEC, JOHN ZYGMUNT, real estate executive; b. Stalowawola, Poland, Jan. 21, 1925; Came to U.S.A. 1947.; s. Valenty and Maria (Madej) S. m. Wanda G. Baca, Oct. 13, 1956; children: David, Maria, Monica. Student, Poland, 1941-44, Kent St. U., Oh., 1965-66, Kent St. U., Oh., 1966-67. Cert. Master of Corporate Real Estate. With The Singer Co., Cleve., 1952-54, dis. mgr., 1954-60, sales supr., 1960-67; dir. real estate The Singer Co., Detroit and Chgo., 1967-73; v.p. Fabri Center of Am., Beachwood, Ohio, 1973—; sr. v.p. real estate Fabri-Centers of Am., Inc., Beachwood, Ohio, 1987—; With U.S. Army 1950-52. With U.S. Army, 1950-52. Mem. Nat. Assoc. of Corporate Real Estate (speaker, organizer 1974-77, audit Com. 1977-79, bd. dirs. 1970-82, Outstanding Achievement award 1982). Chagrin Valley Club. Repulican. Roman Catholic. Avocations: swimming, hiking, reading. Home: 9630 Stafford Rd Chagrin Falls OH 44023-5302 Office: Fabri-Ctrs Am Inc 5555 Darrow Rd Hudson OH 44236-4011 *Personal philosophy: Think success and you'll be successful. Perseverence of any goal leads to achievement. Learning is knowledge. Knowledge is the most powerful key that leads to greatness.*

STECK, THEODORE LYLE, biochemistry and molecular biology educator, physician; b. Chgo., May 3, 1939; s. Irving E. and Mary L. S.; children: David B., Oliver M. B.S. in Chemistry, Lawrence Coll., 1960; M.D., Harvard U., 1964. Intern Beth Israel Hosp., Boston, 1964-65; fellow Beth Israel Hosp., 1965-66; research assoc. Nat. Cancer Inst., NIH, Bethesda, Md., 1966-68, Harvard U. Med. Sch., Boston, 1968-70; asst. prof. medicine U. Chgo., 1970-74, asst. prof. biochemistry and medicine, 1973-74, assoc. prof., 1974-77, prof., 1977-84, chmn. dept. biochemistry, 1979-84, prof. biochemistry and molecular biology, 1984—, chair environ. studies program, 1993—. Office: 920 E 58th St Chicago IL 60637-1432

STECK, WARREN FRANKLIN, chemical company executive, former biochemistry researcher; b. Regina, Sask., Can., May 10, 1939; m. 1963; 2 children. B in Eng., McGill U., 1960; PhD in Organic Chemistry, U. Sask., 1964. Rsch. assoc. Rsch. Inst. Okla. U., 1963-64; asst. rsch. officer Nat. Rsch. Coun. Can., 1964-70, assoc. rsch. officer, 1970-76, sr. rsch. officer, 1976-80, asst. dir., 1980-81, assoc. dir., 1982-83, dir. Plant Biotech. Inst., 1983-90, dir. gen. Plant Biotech Inst., 1991-94; pres. Fytokem Inc., Saskatoon, Sask., 1995—. Mem. Phytochemical Soc. N.Am., Internat. Assn. Plant Tissue Culture. Achievements include rsch. in insect sex attractants and pheromones, chem. ecology. Office: Fytokem Inc, 102-111 Research Dr, Saskatoon, SK Canada S7N3R2

STECKEL, BARBARA JEAN, city financial officer; b. L.A., Mar. 9, 1939; d. John Herschel and Bernice Evelyn (Selstad) Webb Banta; m. Jimmie Raeburn Lugenbeel, Feb. 16, 1957 (div. 1962); Leanna Virgina, Debra Lynn; m. Dale Robert Steckel, Mar. 16, 1962; 1 child, Richard Alan. AA in Bus., Anchorage Community Coll., 1975; BBA, U. Alaska, Anchorage, 1980. City clk., treas. City of Kotzebue, Alaska, 1973-74, city mgr., treas., 1974-76; grants adminstr. Municipality of Anchorage, Alaska, 1976-79, contr., 1979-82, mcpl. mgr., 1982-84, chief fiscal officer, 1984-87; fin. dir., treas. City of Riverside, Calif., 1988—; bd. dirs. Riverside Cmty. Health Svcs. Corp.; chmn. Cmty. Health Corp. Mem. adv. coun. sch. bus. and pub. adminstrn. U. Alaska, Anchorage, 1982-85; bd. dirs. Anchorage Parking Authority, 1984-87, ICMA Retirement Corp., 1985-93, Police and Fire Retirement Sys. Mcpl. of Anchorage, 1982-87, chmn., 1986; devel. com. mem. Am. Heart Assn., Anchorage, 1987. Mem. Govt. Fin. Officers U.S. and Can. (bd. dirs. 1984-87), Mcpl. Fin. Officers Alaska (pres. 1981-82), Nat. Assn. Accts. (bd. dirs. 1986-87), Am. Soc. Women Accts., Calif. Soc. Mcpl. Fin. Officers (chmn. cash mgmt. com. 1989-91, bd. dirs. 1992-95, pres. elect 1995-96, pres. 1996-97), Mcpl. Treas. Assn. (R.E. Phillips award, Svc. award, debt com. chmn. 1992-95), Calif. Mcpl. Treas. Assn., Internat. City Mgrs. Assn., U. Alaska Alumni Assn., Rotary, Elks. Avocations: reading, sewing. Office: City of Riverside 3900 N Main St Riverside CA 92522-0001

STECKEL, RICHARD J., radiologist, academic administrator; b. Scranton, Pa., Apr. 17, 1936; s. Morris Leo and Lucille (Yellin) S.; m. Julie Raskin, June 16, 1960; children: Jan Marie, David Matthew. BS magna cum laude, Harvard U., 1957, MD cum laude, 1961. Diplomate: Am. Bd. Radiology.

Intern UCLA Hosp., 1961-62; resident in radiology Mass. Gen. Hosp., Boston, 1962-65; clin./rsch. assoc. Nat. Cancer Inst., 1965-67; mem. faculty UCLA Med. Sch., 1967—, prof. radiol. scis. and radiation oncology, dir. Jonsson Comprehensive Cancer Ctr., 1974-94; chair dept. radiol. scis. UCLA Med. Ctr., 1994—; pres. Assn. Am. Cancer Insts., 1981. Author/editor 3 books; contbr. over 130 articles on radiology and cancer diagnosis to profl. publs. Fellow Am. Coll. Radiology; mem. Radiol. Soc. N. Am., Am. Roentgen Ray Soc., Assn. Univ. Radiologists. Office: UCLA Med Ctr Dept Radiol Scis 10833 Le Conte Ave Los Angeles CA 90095-3075

STECKLER, LARRY, publisher, editor, author; b. Bklyn., Nov. 3, 1933; s. Morris and Ida (Beekman) S.; m. Catherine Coccozza, June 6, 1959; children: Gail Denise, Glenn Eric, Kerri Lynn, Adria Lauren. Student, CCNY, 1951. Assoc. editor Radio-Electronics mag., N.Y.C., 1957-62, editor, 1967-85; pub., editor in chief Radio Electronics mag., 1985-92; electronics editor Popular Mechanics mag., N.Y.C., 1962-65; assoc. editor Electronic Products mag., Garden City, N.Y., 1965-67; editorial dir. Merchandising 2-Way Radio mag., N.Y.C., 1975-77; v.p., dir. Gernsback Publs., N.Y.C., 1975-84, pres., dir., 1984—; pub., editorial dir. Spl. Projects mag., 1980-84, Radio-Electronics Ann., 1982-84; pub., editor in chief Hands-On Electronics, 1984-88, Computer Digest, 1985-90, Experimenters Handbook, 1986-96, Modern Short Stories, 1987-90, Video/Stereo Digest, 1989-91, Popular Electronics Mag., 1988—, GIZMO, 1988—, Hobbyists Handbook, 1989-96, Sci. Probe! mag., 1989-93, StoryMasters, 1989—, Electronics Shopper, 1990, Electronics Market Ctr., 1991—, Electronics Now Mag., 1992—, Radio Craft, 1993-96, Poptronix Handbook, 1996—; pres. Claggk, Inc., 1986-97, Silicon Chip, 1993-94, Sci. Probe Inc., 1989-93, Poptronix Inc., 1997—; pub., editor-in-chief Poptronix online, 1997—; mem. electronics adv. bd. Bd. Coop. Ednl. Services, Nassau County, N.Y., 1975-77; pres. Electronics Industry Hall of Fame, 1985—; bd. dirs. Pub. Hall of Fame, 1987-89. Author books, handbooks; pub.; contbr. articles to profl. jours. Bd. dirs. Nassau County council Camp Fire Girls, 1971-72. Served with U.S. Army, 1953-56. Recipient Coop. award Nat. Alliance TV and Electronic Services Assns., 1974, 75; inducted into Electronics Industry Hall of Fame, 1985. Mem. IEEE, Internat. Soc. Cert. Electronic Technicians (chmn. 1974-76, 79-81, 93-95, Chmn.'s award 1985, dir.-at-large 1991-93, rep. to NESDA bd. 1991-93, Region 9 dir. 1995—), Nat. Electronics Sales and Svc. Dealers Assn. (rec. sec. N.Y. state 1976-78, Man of Yr. award 1975, 85, treas. 1991-94, M.L. Finneyberg Excellence award 1994), Am. Mgmt. Assn., Radio Club Am., Internat. Underwater Explorers Soc., Am. Soc. Bus. Press Editors (sr.), Internat. Performing Magicians (exec. dir.), Soc. Profl. Journalists, L.A. Press. Home: 9072 Lawton Pines Ave Las Vegas NV 89129 Office: Gernsback Pub Inc 500 BiCounty Blvd Farmingdale NY 11735-3918 *Do not be afraid to try the unaccepted. Do not be afraid to do the undesirable. Do what you enjoy. . .do it well. . .and after it is done. . .never regret having done it. . .only regret what you have not yet done.*

STECKLER, PHYLLIS BETTY, publishing company executive; b. N.Y.C.; d. Irwin H. and Bertha (Fellner) Schwartzbard; m. Stuart J. Steckler; children: Randall, Sharon Steckler-Slotky. BA, Hunter Coll.; MA, NYU. Editorial dir. R.R. Bowker Co., N.Y.C., Crowell Collier Macmillan Info. Pub. Co., N.Y.C., Holt Rinehart & Winston Info. Systems, N.Y.C.; pres., CEO Oryx Press, Scottsdale, Ariz., 1973-76, Phoenix, 1976—; adj. prof. mktg. scholarly publs. Ariz. State U., Tempe; mem. president's adv. coun. Hunter Coll. Past chmn. Info. Industry Assn.; pres. Ariz. Ctr. for the Book; bd. dirs. Contemporary Forum of Phoenix Art Mus., Phoenix Pub. Libr. Friends; past pres. Friends of the Librs., U.S.A.; mem. edn. adv. coun. Senator John McCain; mem. Ariz. Women's Forum. Recipient Women Who Make a Difference award The Internat. Women's Forum, 1995, Excellence in Pub. award Ariz. Book Pub. Assn., 1997 ; elected to Hunter Coll. Hall of Fame. Mem. ALA, Spl. Librs. Assn., Am. Soc. Info. Soc., Ariz. Libr. Assn., Univ. Club of Phoenix (v.p., bd. dirs.). Home: 5104 N 32d St Phoenix AZ 85018 Office: Oryx Press 4041 N Central at Indian School Rd Phoenix AZ 85012

STECKLING, ADRIENNE See ADRI

STEDGE-FOWLER, JOYCE, retired clergywoman; b. Spring Valley, N.Y., Mar. 2, 1926; d. Sidney and Lila Mae (Joyce) Kearsing; m. Leland Stedge, Sept. 4, 1948 (div. Apr. 1978); children: Leland Jr., Deborah Stedge-Stroud, David, Donald, Claudia, Douglas; m. Joseph Charles Fowler, June 23, 1985. B Liberal Arts, U. Iowa, 1947; MDiv, Union Theol. Sem., N.Y.C., 1973. Ordained to ministry Ref. Ch. in Am., 1973; cert. elem. tchr., N.Y. Elem. tchr. Ramapo I Sch. Dist., Suffern, N.Y., 1966-68, Ramapo II Sch. Dist., Spring Valley, 1968-69; pastor Rochester Ref. Ch., Accord, N.Y., 1973-76; NIMH clin. pastoral intern in mental health St. Elizabeths Hosp., Washington, 1976-77, clin. pastoral resident in supervision and consultation, 1977-79; pastor-at-large New Castle Presbytery, Wilmington, Del., 1979-82; interim pastor Coop. Parish St. George's, Port Penn, Del. City, Pencader Presbyn. chs., 1980; interim pastor 1st and Olivet Presbyn. Ch., Wilmington, 1980, Hanover Presbyn. Ch., Wilmington, 1981, Ocean City (Md.) Presbyn. Ch., 1982; pastor Christ Presbyn. Ch., Martinsville, N.J., 1982-85; min. to elderly United Presbyn. Ch., Plainfield, N.J., 1985-91, ret., 1991; chaplain Robert Wood Johnson Health Care Ctr., Plainfield, 1985-91; cons., clin. pastoral educator and therapist, 1975-95; mem. task force on abortion Nat. Coun. Chs., 1970-73, mem. Commn. on Women in Ministry, 1973-80, mem. women's ecumenical coordinating group, 1973-79; mem. justice for women com. Elizabeth Presbytery, 1982—, mem. social issues com., 1986-91, moderator, 1991-92, mem. gen. coun., 1990-91, mem. pers. com., 1991-95; del. to Gen. Assembly, Presbyn. Ch. (U.S.A.), 1985, 91. Former leader Rockland County coun. Girl Scouts U.S.A.; former treas., fin. chmn., bd. dirs.. LWV; com. mem. Water, Sewer and Fgn. Policy Rockland County Study, 1955-73; former program chmn. Women's Assn., former adult edn. chmn. Spring Valley Ref. Ch.; former mem. coun. and edn. chmn. Ctrl. Rockland Ecumenical Witness, Spring Valley. Democrat. Achievements include becoming the 1st woman ordained in the Reformed Church in America by Rockland-Westchester Classis. Avocations: reading, swimming, walking, children and grandchildren. Home: 1352 New Brunswick Ave Piscataway NJ 08854-2081

STEDMAN, RICHARD RALPH, lawyer; b. Columbus, Ohio, July 18, 1936; s. Ralph Dale and Kathleen (Smith) S.; m. Elizabeth Ann Witschey, Dec. 18, 1965; children: Gretchen Kathleen, Richard Ralph II, Patrick Christopher Raymond. BBA, Ohio State U., 1958, JD, 1964. Bar: Ohio 1964; CPA, Ohio. Staff acct. Price Waterhouse & Co., Columbus, 1958-60; salesman Royal McBee Co., Columbus, 1960; ptnr. Vorys, Sater, Seymour & Pease, Columbus, 1964—. Contbr. articles to profl. jours. trustee, counsel Found. Cath. Diocese of Columbus, 1985—; trustee Ohio Dominican Coll., 1990-96, St. Charles Prep. Sch., 1990—, Edward Orton, Jr. Ceramic Found., 1994—. Merson fellow Ohio State U., 1963-64. Mem. Columbus Bar Assn., Fin. Execs. Inst., Athletic Club Columbus, Columbus Club, Brookside Golf and Country Club, Zanesfield Rod and Gun Club, Equestrian Order of Knights Holy Sepulchre of Jerusalem. Republican. Avocations: golfing, tennis, fishing. Office: Vorys Sater Seymour & Pease 52 E Gay St # 1008 Columbus OH 43215-3108

STEED, CONNIE MANTLE, nurse; b. Ft. Riley, Kans., Oct. 6, 1956; d. Ronald James Jr. and Ivey Coene (Jenkins) Mantle; m. Thomas Joseph Steed, Jr., Aug. 27, 1979; children: Christopher Michael, Robert James. ADN, Columbus Coll., 1976; postgrad. RN, S.C.; cert. in infection control. Nurse aide Bradley Ctr. Psychiatric Hosp., Columbus, Ga., 1975-76; staff nurse West Ga. Med. Ctr., LaGrange, 1976-78, nurse epidemiologist, 1978-87, nurse edn. coord., 1987-88; employee health coord. Spartanburg Regional Med. Ctr., S.C., 1988-89; nurse epidemiologist Greenville Meml. Hosp., S.C., 1989—; nat. infection control adv. bd. mem. SmithKline and Beecham, Inc., 1991-92; nat. adv. com. mem. Standard Textiles, Inc., Cin., 1993-94; cons. Kimberly Clark Healthcare Divsn., Roswell, Ga., 1992, B. Braun, Inc., Bethlehem, Pa., 1992-93; mem. regulatory affairs com. S.C. Hosp. Assn., 1995, 96; chmn. S.C. TB Task Force, 1993-96. Co-author: Home Health Infection Control Manual, 1988; contbr. articles to profl. jours. Recipient scholarship for abstract devel. Palmetto Hosp. Trust, Inc., 1995. Mem. Am. Heart Assn. (dist. 4 chmn. 1984-87, Ray Johnson award for edn. achievement Ga. affiliate 1987), Assn. for Profls. in Infection Control and Epidemiology, Inc. (Horizon award Palmetto chpt. 1995, nat. govt. affairs com. mem. 1994, 95), Nat. Assn. for Profls. in Infection Control and Epidemiology, Ga. Infection Control Network (mem. of yr. award 1988), Inc. (chmn. bd. 1982-91, award 1988). Republican. Avocations: reading, softball. Office: Greenville Meml Hosp 701 Grove Rd Greenville SC 29605-5601

STEED, EMMETT D., hotel executive; b. Logan, Utah, July 14, 1950; s. Dale R. and Elizabeth (Emmett) S.; m. Jana Carol Jones, July 31, 1976; 3 children. BA in Journalism, Utah State U., 1974; M in Internat. Mgmt., Am. Grad. Sch., 1975. Asst. contr. Marriott Hotels Camelback Inn, Scottsdale, Ariz., 1975-76, Marriott Hotels Essex Ho., N.Y.C., 1976-78; contr. Marriott Mexicana, Acapulco, Mex., 1978-80, Marriott Hotel, L.A., 1980-82; regional contr. Marriott Hotels, Plantation, Fla., 1982-85; resident mgr. Marriott Hotels, Panama City, Panama, 1985-89, Scottsdale, Ariz., 1985-89; v.p. Red Lion Hotels and Inns, Vancouver, Wash., 1989-92; gen. mgr. Red Lion Hotel/Orange County Airport, 1992—; bd. dirs. South Coast Metro Alliance. Bd. govs. Orange Garde; dir. LDS Ch. Employment, Ft. Lauderdale, 1984-85; pres. Costa Mesa Tourism and Promotion Coun.; dist. chmn. Orange County Coun., Boy Scouts Am.; bd. dirs. Costa Mesa C. of C. Mem. Am. Mgmt. Assn. (treas.), Am. Grad. Sch. of Internat. Mgmt. Alumni Assn., Sigma Chi (life). Republican. Avocations: jogging, skiing, basketball, tennis, archery, photography. Office: Red Lion Hotel Orange County Airport 3050 Bristol St Costa Mesa CA 92626-3036

STEEDMAN, DORIA LYNNE SILBERBERG, organization executive; b. L.A.; d. Mendel B. and Dorothy H. (Howell) Silberberg; m. Richard Cantey Steedman, Feb. 19, 1966; 1 child, Alexandra Loren. BA summa cum laude, UCLA. Producer EUE/Screen Gems, N.Y.C., 1963-66, Jack Tinker & Ptnrs., N.Y.C., 1966-68, Telpac Mgmt., N.Y.C., 1968-72; v.p. broadcast prodn. Geer DuBois Advt., N.Y.C., 1973-78, account mgr., dir. ops., 1979-92; exec. v.p., dir. creative devel. Partnership for a Drug-Free America, N.Y.C., 1992—. Recipient Andy award Art Dirs. Club, 1968, 71; named one of 100 Best and Brightest Women in Advt., Advt. Age mag., 1988; named Advt. Woman of Yr., 1996. Mem. Advt. Women N.Y. (pres. 1993-95), Advt. Women N.Y. Found. (pres. 1994-97), Phi Beta Kappa. Office: Partnership for a Drug-Free Am 405 Lexington Ave New York NY 10174-0002

STEEL, DANIELLE FERNANDE, author; b. N.Y.C., Aug. 14, 1947; d. John and Norma (Stone) Schuelein-Steel. Student, Parsons Sch. Design, 1963, NYU, 1963-67. Vice pres. pub. relations and new bus. Supergirls Ltd., N.Y.C., 1968-71; copywriter Grey Advt., San Francisco, 1973-74. Author novels Going Home, 1973, Passion's Promise, 1977, Now and Forever, 1978, The Promise, 1978, Season of Passion, 1979, Summers End, 1979, To Love Again, 1980, The Ring, 1981, Loving, 1980, Love, 1981, Remembrance, 1981, Palomino, 1981, Once in a Lifetime, 1982, Crossings, 1982, A Perfect Stranger, 1982, Thurston House, 1983, Changes, 1983, Full Circle, 1984, (non-fiction) Having A Baby, 1984, Family Album, 1985, Secrets, 1985, Wanderlust, 1986, Fine Things, 1987, Kaleidoscope, 1987, Zoya, 1988, Star, 1988, Daddy, 1989, Message from Nam, 1990, Heartbeat, 1991, No Greater Love, 1991, Jewels, 1992, Mixed Blessings, 1992, Vanished, 1993, Accident, 1994, The Gift, 1994, Wings, 1994, Lightning, 1995, Five Days in Paris, 1995, Malice, 1996; (children's) Martha's Best Friend, Martha's New School, Martha's New Daddy, Max's New Daddy, Max and The Babysitter, Max's Daddy Goes To The Hospital; contbr. poetry to mags., including Cosmopolitan, McCall's, Ladies Home Jour., Good Housekeeping. Home: PO Box 1637 New York NY 10156-1637 Office: care Dell Publishing 1540 Broadway New York NY 10036-4039*

STEEL, DAWN, motion picture producer; b. N.Y.C., Aug. 19; m. Charles Roven; 1 child, Rebecca. Student in mktg., Boston U., 1964-65, NYU, 1966-67. Sportswriter Major League Baseball Digest and NFL, N.Y.C., 1968-69; editor Penthouse Mag., N.Y.C., 1969-75; pres. Oh Dawn!, Inc., N.Y.C., 1975-78; v.p. merchandising, cons. Playboy mag., N.Y.C., 1978-79; v.p. merchandising Paramount Pictures, N.Y.C., 1979-80; v.p. prodn. Paramount Pictures, L.A., 1980-83, sr. v.p. prodn., 1983-85, pres. prodn., 1985-87; pres. Columbia Pictures, 1987-90; formed Steel Pictures, 1990—; (with Charles Raven and Bob Cavallo) formed Atlas Entertainment (with exclusive movie prodn. agreement with Turner Pictures), 1994. Bd. dirs. Claremont Coll., Home Edn. Network; mem. dean's adv. bd. UCLA Sch. Theater, Film and TV, 1993—. Recipient Crystal award Women in Film, L.A., 1989. Mem. Acad. Motion Picture Arts and Scis., Am. Film Inst. (bd. dirs. 1988-90), NOW Legal Def. Fund. Democrat. Jewish. Avocations: skiing, tennis, gardening. Office: Atlas Entertainment 9169 Sunset Blvd Los Angeles CA 90069-3129

STEEL, DUNCAN GREGORY, physics educator; b. Cleve., Jan. 11, 1951; s. Robert John and Mildred (Graham) S.; m. Nancy Elizabeth Harknett, May 3, 1975; children: Adam, Benjamin. BA, U. N.C., 1972; MS, U. Mich., 1973, 75, PhD, 1976. Physicist Exxon Rsch. and Engring., Linden, N.J., 1977-78, Hughes Rsch. Labs., Malibu, Calif., 1975-85; prof. U. Mich., Ann Arbor, 1985—; scientist Inst. Gerontology Sch. Medicine, U. Mich., Ann Arbor, 1986—, rsch. assoc. biophys. rsch. divsn., 1992—; topical editor Jour. Optical Soc., Washington, 1986-92. Contbr. articles to profl. jours. Fellow Optical Soc. Am., Am. Phys. Soc.; mem. IEEE (sr.). Achievements include first phase conjugate laser, first high resolution nonlinear laser spectroscopy of semiconductor heterostructures; demonstration of collision induced resonances in atoms; demonstration of low noise (below the standard quantum limit) room temperature semiconductor lasers; demonstration of in vitro tryptophan phosphorescence for studies of protein structure in solution; discovery of structural annealing in proteins during protein folding. Office: U Mich Physics Dept 500 E University Ave Ann Arbor MI 48109-1120

STEEL, HOWARD HALDEMAN, pediatric orthopedic surgeon; b. Phila., Apr. 17, 1921; s. Howard Hinchman and Elizabeth (Haldeman) S.; m. Joan Elizabeth Clack, Aug. 16, 1964; children—Michael, Celia, Turner, Kathleen, Patrick, Townsend, Anna, Howard H. III. A.B., Colgate U., 1942; M.D., Temple U., 1945, M.S., 1951; Ph.D. in Anatomy, U. Wash., 1966. Enlisted U.S. Navy, 1941, advanced through grades to lt. comdr. M.C., 1955; ret., 1956; intern Temple U. Med. Center, Phila., 1945-46; resident in orthopaedic surgery Temple U. Med. Center, 1948-51; prof. orthopaedic surgery U. Wash., Seattle, 1965-66, Temple U., 1966—; endowed chair, prof. pediatric orthopaedics Temple U. Hosp., 1989—; clin. prof. orthopaedic surgery Med. Coll. Pa., 1985—; chief surgeon Shriners Hosp. for Crippled Children, Phila., 1966-86, emeritus chief of staff, 1986—; pres. Steel Fudge Shops, Inc., Atlantic City, 1958—; chmn. bd. Steels Fudge, Inc.; Hunterian lectr., London, 1958; med. cons. U.S. Army Med. Corps, USN, 1965-85; clin. prof. emeritus U. Pa., 1985—; prof. emeritus orthopaedic surgery Temple U., 1985—. Contbr. articles to profl. jours. Mem. Pine Barrens Conservation com. N.J. Legislature, Trenton, 1973-75; v.p. Colgate U. Alumni Corp., 1965-78; trustee Colgate U., 1972-78; hon. mem. Nat. Treasure of Japan, 1992. Recipient Apple Tchg. awards Sr. Class U. Wash., 1966, Temple U. Med. Sch., 1976, Disting. Alumnus award Colgate U., 1975, Humanitarian award City of Phila., 1978, Presdl. citation for rsch. in Berrylium, 1942, Humanitarian award Chapel of Four Chaplains, 1981. Fellow A.C.S.; mem. AMA (Billings Gold medal), Am. Orthopaedic Assn., Phila. Orthopaedic Soc. (pres. 1970), Am. Acad. Orthopaedic Surgeons, Pediatric Orthopaedic Soc., Orthopaedic Research Soc., Scoliosis Research Soc., Phila. Acad. Surgeons, Phila. Coll. Medicine, Eastern Orthopaedic Assn. (founder, 1st pres., Disting. Service award 1978), Jefferson Orthopaedic Soc., Phila. Roentgen Ray Soc., Am. Spinal Injury Assn., Hon. Nat. Treasure Japan, Phi Beta Kappa, Alpha Omega Alpha. Clubs: Phila. Country, Phila. Skating & Humane Soc., Merion Cricket, Merion Golf, The Courts Gladwyne, Wissahickon Skating, Wissahickon Ski, Confrerie des Chevalier du Tastevin, Union League Phila., Orpheus Club Phila., Ocean City Yacht, Corinthian Yacht, Masons (columbia 91 award 1981), Shriners. Researcher, developer orthopaedic procedures. Office: Shriners Hosp for Crippled Children 8400 Roosevelt Blvd Philadelphia PA 19152-1212

STEEL, KUNIKO JUNE, retired artist; b. San Francisco, June 3, 1929; d. Jirohei and Moriyo (Shiraishi) Nakamura; m. John Schulein-Steel, Jan. 26, 1963 (dec. May 1978). Student, U. Calif., 1948-49; diploma, Am. Acad. Art, Chgo., 1951; student, Academic Julian, Paris, 1952-53, Art Inst. Chgo., 1954-55, Art Students League, N.Y.C., 1959-62, 79-85. Exhibited in group shows at Rafilson Gallery, Chgo., 1954, Arts of N.E., Silvermine, Conn., 1966, 79, 90, 92, Modern Maturity Traveling Exhibit, 1990-92, Schoharie Exhibit, Cobleskill, N.Y., 1993-94, Mus. of Modern Art, Miami, Coral Gables, Fla., 1993, 37th Chautaqua Nat. Exhibit of Am. Art, 1994, Montclair State U., 1994, 95. Vol., crafts tchr. Hosp. for Spl. Surgery, N.Y.C., 1967-84; vol. Japanese Gallery Met. Mus., 1994; past vol. costume conservation Met. Mus., N.Y.C., 1979-94. Recipient scholarship Palo Alto Quota Club, 1948, Art Students League, 1960. Mem. N.Y. Artists Equity. Avocations: designing arts and crafts, painting.

STEEL, RONALD LEWIS, author, historian, educator; b. Morris, Ill., Mar. 25, 1931. BA magna cum laude, Northwestern U., 1953; MA, Harvard U., 1955. Vice consul U.S. Fgn. Service, 1957-58; editor Scholastic mag., N.Y.C., 1959-62; sr. assoc. Carnegie Endowment for Internat. Peace, 1982-83; fellow Woodrow Wilson Internat. Ctr. Scholars, 1984-85; prof. internat. relations U. So. Calif., Los Angeles, 1986—; fellow Wissenschaftskolleg zu Berlin, Federal Republic of Germany, 1988; vis. fellow Yale U., 1971-73; vis. prof. U. Tex., 1977, 79, 80, 85, Wellesley Coll., 1978, Rutgers U., 1980, UCLA, 1981, Dartmouth Coll., 1983, Princeton U., 1984; Shapiro prof. internat. rels. George Washington U., 1995-96. Author books including: The End of Alliance: America and the Future of Europe, 1964, (with G. Kimble) Tropical Africa Today, 1966, Pax Americana, 1967, Imperialists and Other Heroes, 1971, Walter Lippmann and the American Century, 1980, Temptations of a Superpower, 1995; editor various publs. for H.W. Wilson Co., 1961-67; contbr. to N.Y. Rev. Books; contbg. editor New Republic. Served with U.S. Army, 1954-56. Recipient Sidney Hillman award, 1968, Washington Monthly book award, 1980, Los Angeles Tims book award for nonfiction, 1980, Nat. Book Critics Circle award, 1981, Bancroft prize Columbia U., 1981, Am. History Bancroft prize, 1980, Am. Book award for biography, 1982; Guggenheim fellow, 1973-74. Mem. Council on Fgn. Relations. Office: U So Calif Sch Internat Rels Los Angeles CA 90089-0043

STEELE, ANA MERCEDES, government official; b. Niagara Falls, N.Y., Jan. 18, 1939; d. Sydney and Mercedes (Hernandez) S.; m. John Hunter Clark, June 2, 1979. AB magna cum laude, Marywood Coll., 1958. Actress, 1959-64; sec. Nat. Endowment for Arts, Washington, 1965-67, dir. budget and research, 1968-75, dir. planning, 1976-78, dir. program coordination, sr. exec. service, 1979-81, assoc. dep. chmn. for programs, dir. program coordination, sr. exec. service, 1982-93, acting chmn., acting sr. dep. chmn., 1993, sr. dep. chmn., sr. exec. svc., 1993-96; dep. chmn. for mgmt. and budget, sr. exec. svc., 1996—; guest lectr. George Washington U., 1987; trustee Marywood Coll., 1989—. Author, editor report: History of the National Council on the Arts and National Endowment for the Arts During the Johnson Administration, 1968; editor: Museums USA (Fed. Design Council award of Excellence 1975), 1974; National Endowment Arts 1965-1985; A Brief Chronology of Federal Involvement in the Arts, 1985. Former reader Rec. for the Blind, N.Y.C.; former tutor Future for Jimmy, Washington. Named Disting. Grad. in Field of Arts, Marywood Coll., 1976; recipient Sustained Superior Performance award Nat. Endowment for Arts, Washington, 1980, Disting. Service award, 1983, 84, 85, 89, 92, 96. Mem. Actors' Equity Assn., Screen Actors Guild, Delta Epsilon Sigma, Kappa Gamma Pi. Office: Nat Endowment for Arts Nancy Hanks Ctr 1100 Pennsylvania Ave NW Washington DC 20004-2501

STEELE, ANITA MARTIN (MARGARET ANNE MARTIN), law librarian, legal educator; b. Haines City, Fla., Dec. 30, 1927; d. Emmett Edward and Esther Majulia (Phifer) Martin; m. Thomas Dinsmore Steele, June 10, 1947 (div. 1969); children: Linda Frances, Roger Dinsmore, Thomas Garrick, Carolyn Ann; m. James E. Beaver, Mar. 1980. BA, Radcliffe Coll., 1948; J.D., U. Va., 1971; M.Law Librarianship, U. Wash., 1972. Asst. prof. law U. Puget Sound, Tacoma, 1972-74, assoc. prof. law, 1974-79, prof. law, 1979—, dir. law library, 1972-94; prof. law, dir. law libr. Seattle U., Tacoma, 1994—. Author: (book) Martin and Carmichael Descendants in Georgia, 1811-1994, 1994; contbr. articles to profl. jours.; mem. editorial adv. bds. various law book pubs., 1980—. Treas., Congl. Campaign Orgn., Tacoma, 1978, 80; mem. adv. bd. Clover Park Vocat.-Tech. Sch., Tacoma, 1980-82. Mem. Am. Assn. Law Libraries, Internat. Assn. Law Libraries, Am. Soc. Internat. Law. Republican. Home: 1502 S Fernside Dr Tacoma WA 98465-1305 Office: Seattle U Sch Law 950 Broadway Tacoma WA 98402-4405

STEELE, BETTY LOUISE, retired banker; b. Sigourney, Iowa, Nov. 20, 1920; d. Otto Orville and Freda Marie Christina (Strohman) Utterback; m. David L. Steele, Jan. 17, 1942; 1 child, David Leroy. Student pub. schs., Iowa. With N.W. Des Moines Nat. Bank, 1959-68, v.p., 1966-68; v.p., sec. Brenton Banks, Inc., Des Moines, 1968-86; mem. pension com. Brenton Banks, Inc., 1980-86, vice chmn. investment com., 1983-86, dir., 1976-83; sec. Brenton Found., 1970-83; mem. State Banking Bd., 1977-81. Author articles. Bd. dirs. Ctrl. Iowa chpt. ARC, 1984-90, mem. exec. com., asst. treas., 1984-90, mem. fin. audit com., 1985-93; mem. dean's com. Iowa State U. Coll. Home Econs., 1982-84; mem. Iowa Pub./Pvt. Sector Task Force, Gov.'s Com. for Volunteerism, 1984. Mem. Des Moines C. of C. (Nat. Leadership award 1976), Fin. Women Internat. (nat. pres. 1976-77, bd. dirs. 1970-78, trustee ednl. found. 1974-76, (Betty L. Steele award given in her honor Iowa chpt.), Am. Bankers Assn. (govt. relations council 1977-79), Iowa Bankers Assn. (legis. com. 1975-76). Republican. Home: 1914 S 11th St Oskaloosa IA 52577

STEELE, BRUCE CARL, editor; b. York, Pa., Sept. 9, 1959; s. William Melvin and Kaye Marilyn (Meyer) S.; m. Christopher Cornell Oakley, Feb. 14, 1987. BA, U. Ala., 1981; MFA, Columbia U., 1987. Staff editor Alexandria (La.) Daily Town Talk, 1982-85; sr. editor Cahners Pub., N.Y.C., 1987-92; mng. editor Out Mag., N.Y.C., 1992-95, exec. editor, 1995—. Office: Out Pub Inc 110 Greene St Apt 600 New York NY 10012-3838

STEELE, CARL LAVERN, academic administrator; b. Patoka, Ill., Aug. 22, 1934; s. Boyd Alfa and Effie Jane (Corson) S.; m. Lula Irene Saliba, June 11, 1961; children: Jeffrey Van, Gregory Michael, Douglas Alan. BEd, So. Ill. U., 1956, MEd, 1960; MLS, No. Ill. U., 1971. Tchr. Shawneetown (Ill.) Community High. Sch., 1956-57; GED instr. U.S. Army, Ft. Hood, Tex. and Ulm, Fed. Republic of Germany, 1957-59; tchr. Forrest-Strawn-Wing Unit Dist., Forrest, Ill., 1959-61, Richwoods Community High Sch., Peoria, Ill., 1961-66; asst. dir. instructional materials Sauk Valley Coll., Dixon, Ill., 1966-68; dir. Ednl. Resources Ctr., Rock Valley Coll., Rockford, Ill., 1968-93; ret., 1993; part-time traffic safety instr. Rock Valley Coll., 1992—. Asst. World Record sec. Nat. Fresh Water Fishing Hall of Fame, Hayward, Wisc., 1977-79. Served with U.S. Army, 1957-59. Mem. ALA, Assn. Ednl. Communications and Technology, Ill. Assn. Ednl. Communications and Technology (conv. chmn. 1976), No. Ill. Media Assn. (conv. chmn.), Learning Resource Commn. ICCCA (chmn. 1981). Democrat. Presbyterian. Avocations: fishing, travel, reading, woodworking, gardening. Home: 5758 Weymouth Dr Rockford IL 61114-5569

STEELE, CHARLES GLEN, retired accountant; b. Faulkton, S.D., July 24, 1925; s. Clifford D. and Emily O. (Hanson) S.; m. Shirley June Ferguson, Nov. 9, 1947; children: Richard Alan (dec.), Deborah Ann Steele Most. B.B.A., Golden Gate U., San Francisco, 1951, M.B.A., 1962. With Deloitte Haskins & Sells, 1951-86, partner, 1963-86, partner charge Chgo. office, 1973-76; partner charge personnel and adminstrn. Deloitte Haskins & Sells, N.Y.C., 1976-78; chmn., chief exec. officer Deloitte Haskins & Sells, 1978-86; instr. evening program Golden Gate U., 1952-58. Served with USNR, 1943-48. Recipient Elijah Watts Sells Gold medal for highest grade in U.S. for C.P.A. exam., 1951. Mem. Am. Inst. C.P.A.s. Home and Office: 26349 Rio Ave Carmel CA 93923-9101

STEELE, CHARLES RICHARD, biomedical and mechanical engineering educator; b. Royal, Iowa, Aug. 15, 1933; married, 1969; 4 children. BS, Tex. A&M U., 1956; PhD in Applied Mechanics, Stanford U., 1960. Engring. specialist aircraft structure Chance-Vought Aircraft, Dallas, 1959-60; rsch. scientist shell theory Lockheed Rsch. Lab., Palo Alto, 1960-66; assoc. prof. Stanford (Calif.) U., 1966-71, prof. applied mechanics, 1971—; lectr. U. Calif., Berkeley, 1964-65; vis. prof. Swiss Fed. Inst. Technology, Zurich, 1971-72, U. Luleå, Sweden, 1982, Chung Kung U., Taiwan, 1985; tech. dir. Shelltech Assoc. Editor-in-chief: Internat. Jour. Solids Structures, 1985—. Fellow ASME (chmn. exec. com. applied mechanics divsn. 1983-84), Am. Acad. Mechanics (pres. 1989-90); mem. AIAA, NAE, Acoustical Soc. Am. Achievements include research in asymptotic analysis in mechanics; thin shell theory; mechanics of the inner ear; noninvasive determination of bone stiffness. Office: Stanford University Dept Applied Mech & Engin Durand Bldg 355A Stanford CA 94305-4040*

STEELE, DIANA ALEXANDER, lawyer; b. Phila., Oct. 3, 1946; d. Joseph Middleton and Martha Cynthia (Pound) S.; m. Eric John Heyer, June 8, 1980. BA, Wellesley Coll., 1968; JD, NYU, 1971, LLM in Taxation, 1982. Bar: N.Y., 1971. Staff atty. Appeals Bur. Legal Aid Soc., N.Y.C., 1971-74, sr. supervising atty., 1974-78; staff counsel ACLU, N.Y.C., 1978-81; assoc. Reid & Priest, N.Y.C., 1982-86, ptnr., 1986—. Office: Reid & Priest 40 W 57th St New York NY 10019-4001

STEELE, EARL LARSEN, electrical engineering educator; b. Denver, Sept. 24, 1923; s. Earl Harold and Jennie (Larsen) S.; m. Martha C. Hennessey, June 27, 1953; children: Karl Thomas, Earl Robert, Karen Lynn, Kevin Douglas, Lisa Louise, Colleen Carol. B.S. with honors, U. Utah, 1945; Ph.D., Cornell U., 1952. Research physicist Gen. Electric Co., 1952-56; chief device devel. Motorola, Inc., 1956-58; mgr. devel. lab. Hughes Aircraft Co., 1958-64; research scientist N.Am. Rockwell Corp., 1964-69; prof. elec. engring. U. Ky., Lexington, 1969-90, prof. emeritus, 1991—; chmn. dept. U. Ky., 1971-80, 1988-89; Affiliate prof. Ariz. State U., 1956-58, U. Calif.-Irvine, 1966-69; adviser So. Calif. Coll., Costa Mesa, 1963-64; charter mem. Orange County Academic Decathlon (Calif.); bd. dirs. Southeastern Center for Elec. Engring. Edn., 1975—, treas., 1980-81, v.p., 1981-82, resident dir., 1981-82, 89-90, pres., 1982-83, mem. coun. of pres.', 1983—. Author: Optical Lasers in Electronics; contbr. articles to profl. jours. Fellow IEEE; mem. Am. Soc. Engring. Edn. (U. Ky. Coll. Engring. rep. to ASEE, 1988-90), Am. Phys. Soc., Internat. Soc. Hybrid Microelectronics, Sigma Xi, Tau Beta Pi, Eta Kappa Nu (dir. 1974-76, v.p. 1983-84, pres. 1984-85). Mem. LDS Ch. Home: 313 Blueberry Ln Lexington KY 40503-2004

STEELE, ELIZABETH MEYER, lawyer; b. San Mateo, Calif., Jan. 12, 1952; d. Bailey Robert and Kathryn Steele (Horrigan) Meyer; m. Gene Dee Fowler, Aug. 9, 1975 (div. Apr. 1985); 1 child, Steele Sternberg. BA, Kirkland Coll., 1974; JD, U. N.Mex., 1977. Counsel U.S. Dept. Energy, Los Alamos, N.Mex., 1977-78; law clk. to judge Howard C. Bratton U.S. Dist. Ct., Albuquerque, 1978-80; assoc. Davis, Graham & Stubbs, Denver, 1980-84, ptnr., 1985-87; v.p., gen. counsel Jones Intercable, Inc., Englewood, Colo., 1987—. Office: Jones Intercable Inc 9697 E Mineral Ave Englewood CO 80112-3408

STEELE, ERNEST CLYDE, retired insurance company executive; b. Corbin, Ky., May 11, 1925; s. J. Fred and Leona (McFarland) S.; m. Cora Jones, June 17, 1944 (dec. Nov. 1988); children: Gerald R., David. P.; m. Helen LeCoultre, July 7, 1990. BS with honors, U. Ky., 1948, MS, 1950. Asst. actuary Peninsular Life Ins. Co., Jacksonville, Fla., 1950-54; actuary Pioneer Life & Casualty Co., Gadsden, Ala., 1955; v.p., actuary Guaranty Savs. Life Ins. Co., Montgomery, Ala., 1956-57; exec. v.p., actuary Am. Investment Life Ins. Co., Nashville, 1958-59; pres., actuary Appalachian Nat. Life Ins. Co., Knoxville, Tenn., 1959-67; sr. v.p., chief investment officer, ops. analyst Coastal States Life Ins. Co., Atlanta, 1968-71; exec. v.p., dir. Coastal States Life Ins. Co., 1971-74, pres., dir., 1974-79; pres., dir. Occidental Life Ins. Co. of N.C., 1979-85, chmn., 1986-88; pres., dir. Peninsular Life Ins. Co., 1981-83, chmn., 1986-88; exec. v.p. investments MCM Corp., 1985-88; past pres. Ga. Assn. Life Inst. Cos., 1976-77. Mem. devel. coun. U. Ky. Served to 2d lt. U.S. Army, 1943-45. Fellow Life Mgmt. Inst.; mem. Life Office Mgmt. Assn. (past chmn. bd.), Am. Council Life Ins. (past dir.), U. Ky. Alumni Assn. (past bd. dirs.), Am. Acad. Actuaries, Pi Mu Epsilon. Republican. Baptist. Home: 103 Newell Village Dr Seymour TN 37865-5931 *My success in life is measured by the success of those with whom I have been associated.*

STEELE, GLENN DANIEL, JR., surgical oncologist; b. Balt., June 23, 1944; m. Diana; 1 child, Joshua; m. Lisa; children: Kirsten, Lara. AB magna cum laude, Harvard Coll., 1966; MD, NYU, 1970; PhD, Lund U., Sweden, 1975. Intern, then resident Med. Ctr. U. Colo., Denver, 1970-76; fellow NIH in immunology Univ. Lund, Sweden, 1973-75; asst. surgeon Sidney Farber Cancer Inst., Boston, 1976-78; cons. surgeon Boston Hosp. for Women, 1977-80; clin. assoc. surgical oncology Sidney Farber Cancer Inst., 1978-79; jr. assoc. in surgery Peter Bent Brigham Hosp., Boston, 1976-82; instr. surgery Med. Sch. Harvard, Boston, 1976-78; asst. prof. surgery Med. Sch. Harvard Coll., 1978-81; asst. physician surgical oncology Sidney Farber Cancer Inst., 1979-82; assoc. prof. surgery Med. Sch. Harvard Coll., 1981-84; surgeon Brigham & Women's Hosp., 1982-84; assoc. physician surgical oncology Dana-Farber Cancer Inst., 1982-84, physician surg. oncology, 1984-95; chmn. dept. surgery, deaconess Harvard Surg. Svc. New England Deaconess Hosp., Boston, 1985-95; William V. McDermott prof. surgery Med. Sch. Harvard Coll., 1985-95; prof. Univ. Chgo., dean biological scis. divsn. and Pritzker Sch. Medicine; v.p. medical affairs Pritzker Sch. Medicine. assoc. editor Jour. of Clin. Oncology, 1986—, Jour. of Hepatobiliary-Pancreatic Surgery, 1993—; mem. editorial bd. Annals of Surgery, Annals of Surg. Oncology, British Jour. of Surgery, Surgery, Surgical Oncology; contbr. numerous articles to profl. jours. Recipient NIH fellow 1973-75, Am. Cancer Soc. fellow 1972-73, 76-79, various other rsch. grants. Fellow Am. Coll. Surgeons (chmn. patient care and rsch. com. commn. on cancer 1989-91, mem. bd. govs. 1991-95, chmn. commn. on cancer 1991-93, mem. exec. com. commn. on cancer 1992-93); mem. Am. Assn. Immunologists, Am. Bd. Surgery (dir. 1993—), Ill. Surgical Soc., Am. Bd. Med. Specialties, Am. Soc. Clin. Oncology, Am. Surg. Assn., Assn. Program Dirs. in Surgery, Assn. for Surgical Edn., Internat. Fedn. Surg. Colls., Internat. Surg. Group, Soc. Surg. Oncology (treas. 1994-97, v.p. 1997), New England Cancer Soc., and numerous other mems. Office: Univ Chicago 5841 S Maryland Ave # Mc1000 Chicago IL 60637-1463

STEELE, HOWARD LOUCKS, government official; b. Pitts., Jan. 27, 1929; s. Howard Bennington and Ruby Alberta (Loucks) S.; B.S., Washington and Lee U., 1950; M.S., Pa. State U., 1952; Ph.D., U. Ky., 1962; m. Sally E. Funk, June 6, 1952 (div. 1977); children: John F., David A., Patricia A.; m. 2d, Jane R. Cornelius, July 30, 1977 (div. 1996); 1 dau., Jennifer L. Sales mgr. Greenville (Pa.) Dairy Co., 1952-56; owner H.L. Steele Bulk Milk Hauling, Greenville, Pa., 1955-60; asst. prof. Clemson (S.C.) U., 1956-57, asso. prof., 1957-64; assoc. prof. Ohio State U., Columbus, 1964-71; with Fgn. Agrl. Svc./Internat. Cooperation and Devel. U.S. Dept. Agr., Washington, 1971—, project mgr. AID, Guatemala, 1976-77, Bolivia, 1977-80, Honduras, 1980-82, Sri Lanka, 1982-84, Bur. Latin Am. and Caribbean AID, Washington, 1984-88, office of the dir. tech. assistance div., 1988-90, with Office of the Dep. Adminstr., 1990—; USDA liaison officer Inter-Am. Inst. for Cooperation in Agr., 1993—; instr. U. Md., College Park, 1974-76; vis. prof. U. Sao Paulo, Piracicaba, Brazil, 1964-66; partner Kingwood Acres Farm, Rockwood, Pa., 1966—. Recipient Nat. Forensic Union award; named One of Outstanding Young Men in U.S., U.S. Jaycees, 1965; cert. of merit Dept. Agr., 1975, 1992. Mem. Am. Agrl. Econs. Assn., Internat. Assn. Agrl. Economists, Internat. Agribus. Mgmt. Assn., Sons Am. Revolution, Gamma Sigma Delta, Sigma Nu. Lodges: Masons, Shriners. Author: Comercialização Agrícola; contbr. to Agriculture, Lincoln Library of Essential Information; contbr. articles to profl. jours. Home: 5204 Holden St Fairfax VA 22032-3418 Office: USDA/FAS/ICD 14th St and Independence Ave South Bldg Rm 3117 Washington DC 20250-1083

STEELE, JAMES HARLAN, former public health veterinarian, educator; b. Chgo., Apr. 3, 1913; s. James Hahn and Lydia (Nordquist) S.; m. Aina Oberg, 1941 (dec. 1969); children: James Harlan, David Michael; m. Maria-Brigitte Meyer, 1969. DVM, Mich. State Coll., 1941; MPH, Harvard U., 1942. With Ohio Dept. Health, 1942-43; with USPHS, 1943-71; advancing through grades to asst. surgeon gen. for vet. affairs and chief vet. officer; chief vet. pub. health activities Communicable Disease Center, Atlanta, 1947-71; prof. environ. health U. Tex. Sch. Pub. Health, Houston, 1971-83, prof. emeritus, 1983—; cons. WHO, 1950—, Pan-Am. Health Orgn., 1945—, FAO, UN, 1960, German Health Svc., 1986-93; vis. prof. Tex. A&M U., 1976—, all univ. prof., 1981-82. Author: Bovine Tuberculosis Control in Man and Animals, 1969, rev. (with Charles Thoen), 1995; editor-in-chief Zoonoses Handbooks, 1979-84, cons. editor, 1994; contbr. articles to profl. jours. and sects. to books on food hygiene and irradiation. Recipient Mich. State U. Alumni award, 1958, USPHS Order of Merit, 1963, Karl F. Meyer Gold Head Cane award, 1966, Disting. Svc. award USPHS, 1971, Mich. State U. Coll. Vet. Medicine award, 1972, hon. mem. Epidemic Intelligence Svc., 1975, Centennial award U. Pa., 1984, Am. Vet. Med. Assn. Internat. Vet. award, 1984, Pub. Svc. award, 1993; James H. Steele Vet. Pub. Health award World Vet. Epidemiology Soc., 1975, Disting. Svc. award Am. Vet. History Soc., 1995; James H. Steele ann. lectr. established in his honor U. Tex. Health Sci. Ctr., 1993, James H. Steele Pub. Health Professorship, 1996. Fellow Am. Pub. Health Assn. (emeritus, 1984; Bronfman award 1971, Centennial award 1972), Am. Coll. Epidemiology (founding fellow); mem. Conf. Pub. Health Vets. (founder), Am. Soc. Tropical Medicine (emeritus), Am. Coll. Vet. Preventive Medicine (founder, hon. diploma 1983, Pres.'s award 1994), Nat. Acad. Health Practitioners, World Vet. Epidemiology Soc. (founder, pres. 1971), Am. Vet. Epidemiology Soc. (pres. 1966-88), World Vet. Assn. (hon.), Philippines Vet. Med. Assn. (hon.), Peru Vet. Med. Assn. (hon.), Hellenic Vet. Soc. (Athens Greece, hon. diploma, 1977), U.S. Animal Health Assn. (life), U.S.-Mex. Pub. Health Assn. (hon., life), Mil. Surgeons Assn. (hon. life), Infectious Disease Soc. Am. (emeritus), Internat. Epidemiology Soc. (emeritus), XXI World Vet. Congress (Moscow, hon. diploma 1979), German Health Svc. (hon. diploma, 1988, Order of Merit 1993), Harvard U. Alumni Assn., Mich. State U. Alumni Assn., Alpha Psi. Episcopalian. Home: 10722 Riverview Way Houston TX 77042-1391 Office: School of Public Hlth University of Texas Houston TX 77225 *I have believed firmly throughout my career that I should share my knowledge and expertise with my fellow man, be he American or citizen of the world. Those of us who are more fortunate to be endowed with intellectual advantages have an even greater responsibility to share.*

STEELE, JOHN HYSLOP, marine scientist, oceanographic institute administrator; b. Edinburgh, U.K., Nov. 15, 1926; s. Adam and Annie H.; m. Margaret Evelyn Travis, Mar. 2, 1956; 1 son, Hugh. B.Sc., Univ. Coll., London U., 1946, D.Sc., 1964. Marine scientist Marine Lab., Aberdeen, Scotland, 1951-66; sr. prin. sci. officer Marine Lab., 1966-73, dep. dir., 1973-77; dir. Woods Hole Oceanographic Instn., Mass., 1977-89, pres., 1986-91; mem. NAS/NRC Ocean Sci. Bd., 1978-88, chmn., 1986-88; mem. rsch. and exploration com. Nat. Geog. Soc.; mem. Arctic Rsch. Commn., 1988-92; trustee U. Corp. Atmospheric Rsch., 1987-91, Bermuda Biol. Sta., R.W. Johnson Found.; del. Internat. Coun. Exploration Sea; bd. dirs. Exxon Corp.; hon. prof. U. Aberdeen. Author: The Structure of Marine Ecosystems, 1974; Contbr. articles to profl. jours. Served with Brit. Royal Air Force, 1947-49. Recipient Alexander Agassiz medal Nat. Acad. Sci., 1973. Fellow Royal Soc. London, AAAS, Royal Soc. Edinburgh, Am. Acad. Arts and Scis. Home: PO Box 25 Woods Hole MA 02543-0025 Office: Woods Hole Oceanographic Inst Woods Hole MA 02543

STEELE, JOHN LAWRENCE, journalist; b. Chgo., June 9, 1917; s. Leo M. and Helen (Schuhmann) S.; m. Louise V. Stein, June 27, 1940; children: Deborah, John Lawrence, Scott. Grad., Lake Forest Acad., 1935; A.B., Dartmouth Coll., 1939; Nieman fellow, Harvard U., 1951-52. With Chgo. City News Bur., 1939; staff Chgo. bur. U.P.I., 1939-41; bur. legislative corr. U.P., Washington, 1941-42, 45-53; legis. polit. corr. Time mag., 1953-55; White House corr., 1955-58; chief Washington bur.; Time-Life News Svc., 1958-69; sr. corr. Time-Life News Service, 1969-79; v.p. Time Inc., Washington, 1979-82, cons., 1982-84, pub. policy cons., 1985—. Collaborator: (with A.H. Vandenberg, Jr. and Joe A. Morris) The Private Papers of Senator Vandenberg, 1952; contbr. articles to mags. and jours., chpts. to books. Mem. Dartmouth Coll. Alumni Coun., 1971-74; mem. Native Am. Vis. Com., 1973-78, chmn., 1975-78; bd. dirs. Mag. Pubs. Assn., 1979-81; participant TV news interview programs NBC, CBS, BBC, 1950-79. Recipient The Dartmouth Alumni award for disting. svc. in journalism and pub. affairs. Mem. Burning Tree Club, Met. Club, Sigma Delta Chi (Hall of Fame 1979). Home and Office: 3100 Newark St NW Washington DC 20008-3343

STEELE, JULIUS RAYNARD, special education educator; b. Little Rock, Ark., Oct. 18, 1952; s. D. J. Steele and Juanita (Thomas) Gilbert; children: Misty N., Sara M. BS, Northwestern U., Natchitoches, La., 1974; MA, La. Tech. U., 1978; EdS, Point Loma Nazarene Coll., 1992; EdD in Ednl. Leadership, No. Ariz. U., 1995. Cert. tchr. handicapped, severely handicapped, counseling, physical edn., edn. adminstrn, Calif. Tchr. learning handicapped Caddo Parish Schs., Shreveport, La., 1974-81; tchr. severely handicapped Pulaski County Schs., Little Rock, 1988-89, San Diego City Schs., 1989-93; asst. prin. Oxnard Union High Sch. Dist., 1993—; cons. Point Loma Nazarene Coll., San Diego, 1992-93. Mem. adv. bd. San Diego Parks & Recreation Disabled Svcs., 1992-93, adv. com. Lincoln Prep. High Sch., San Diego, 1992-93. Mem. Assn. Calif. Sch. Adminstrs., Omega Psi Phi (treas.). Democrat. Avocations: cycling, wood carving. Home: PO Box 2765 Oxnard CA 93034-2765

STEELE, KAREN DORN, journalist; b. Portland, Oreg., Oct. 27, 1943; d. Ronald Gottche and Margaret Elizabeth (Cates) Moxness; m. Charles Stuart Dorn, Oct. 30, 1965 (div. Oct. 1982); children: Trilby Constance Elizabeth Dorn, Blythe Estella Dorn; m. Richard Donald Steele, July 4, 1983. BA, Stanford U., 1965; MA, U. Calif., Berkeley, 1967. Prodr. Sta. KSPS-TV, Spokane, Wash., 1970-72, dir. news and pub. affairs, 1972-82; reporter Spokesman-Rev., Spokane, 1982-87, environ./spl. projects reporter, 1987—. Contbr. articles to sci. publs. (Olive Br. award NYU Ctr. War, Peace & The Media 1989). Bd. dirs. Women Helping Women, Spokane, 1994; trustee St. George's Sch., Spokane, 1988-92. Mid-career fellow Stanford Knight Fellowship Program, 1986-87, Arms Control fellow Ctr. for Internat. Security and Arms Control, Stanford U., 1986-87; Japan Travel grantee Japan Press Found., Tokyo, 1987, rsch. grantee John D. and Catherine T. MacArthur Found., 1992; recipient Gerald Loeb award Anderson Sch. Mgmt. UCLA, 1995, George Polk award L.I. U., 1995, William Stokes award U. Mo., 1988; inductee State Hall of Journalistic Achievement, Wash. State U., Pullman, 1995. Unitarian. Avocations: literature, poetry, cooking, hiking, travel. Office: Spokesman-Rev PO Box 2160 W 999 Riverside Ave Spokane WA 99210-1615

STEELE, KAREN KIARSIS, state legislator; b. Haverhill, Mass., Sept. 26, 1942; d. Victor and Barbara (McFee) Kiarsis; m. Edward E. Steele, Apr. 16, 1966; children: Shawn Robert, Gretchen Garvey. BA, U. Vt., 1964. Tchr. Waterbury Sch. System, 1964-65, Burlington (Vt.) Sch. System, 1965-67; legislator State of Vt., Montpelier, 1982—. Trustee Ctrl. Vt. Hosp., Berlin, Woodridge Nursing Home, Berlin. Mem. Am. Legis. Exch. Coun. (nat. chmn. health and human svcs. task force). Republican. Avocations: golf, swimming, reading. Home: RR 2 Box 796 Waterbury VT 05676-9713 Office: State House Montpelier VT 05602

STEELE, KENNETH FRANKLIN, JR., hydrology educator, resource center director; b. Statesville, N.C., Jan. 16, 1944; s. Kenneth Franklin and Ruth Virginia (Wilhelm) S.; m. Sheila Kay Stumpf, Sept. 3, 1966; children: Krista Robin, Celisa Anne. BS in Chemistry, U. N.C., 1966, PhD in Geology, 1971. Registered profl. geologist, Ark., registered hydrogeologist. From instr. to assoc. prof. geology U. Ark., Fayetteville, 1970-83, prof., 1983—, dir. Ark. Water Resources Ctr., 1988—; cons. in field. Contbr. numerous articles to profl. jours., chpts. to books; editor: Animal Waste and the Land-Water Interface. Summer faculty fellow Oak Ridge Associated Univs., 1981, 83, 85. Mem. Assn. Ground-Water Scientists and Engrs., Geol. Soc. Am. (regional bd. dirs. 1980-82, 84-86), Am. Water Resources Assn. (bd. dirs. 1991-94), Ark. Ground Water Assn. (bd. dirs. 1988-90, 93-95, v.p. 1991, pres. 1992), Nat. Assn. Water Inst. Dirs. (counselor 1990-93). Achievements include research on the importance of rainstorms on spring water chemistry, nitrate and pesticide contamination of ground water. Home: 1115 Valley View Dr Fayetteville AR 72701-1603 Office: U Ark Water Resources Ctr 113 N Ozark Ave Fayetteville AR 72701-4040

STEELE, KURT D., publishing company executive; b. 1945; married. BA, Colgate U., 1967; JD, Columbia U., 1971. Assoc. Brown & Wood, 1971-74; atty. McGraw & Hill Inc., N.Y.C., 1974-85, v.p., assoc. gen. counsel, 1981-86; sr. v.p., gen. counsel, sec. Standard & Poor's Corp., N.Y.C., 1986-90; exec. v.p., gen. counsel Rand McNally & Co., Skokie, Ill., 1990—. Office: Rand McNally Inc 8255 Central Park Ave Skokie IL 60076-2908

STEELE, LENDELL EUGENE, research scientist; b. Kannapolis, N.C., May 5, 1928; s. Robert Lee and Ina (Chapman) S.; m. Rowena Miller, Jan. 29, 1949; children—Joyce Lee Steele McCartney, Carol Ann Steele, Pamela Jane Steele Nelson, Linda Kay Steele Miller. B.S. in Chemistry, George Washington U., 1950; M.A. in Econs, Am. U., 1959. Registered profl. engr., Calif. Chemist U.S. Geol. Survey, Washington, 1949, U.S. Dept. Agr. Research Center, Beltsville, Md., 1949-50; chemist U.S. Naval Research Lab., Washington, 1950-51, chemist-research physicist, 1953-58, mgr. sci. research, 1958-86; metall. engr. AEC, Germantown, Md., 1966; cons. U.S. Metal Properties Council, 1968-70, 75-85; pvt. practice tech. cons. Springfield, Va., 1986—; U.S. rep. to IAEA, Vienna, Austria, 1967-93. Author: Analysis of Reactor Vessel Radiation Effects Surveillance Programs, 1970, Neutron Irradiation Embrittlement of Reactor Pressure Vessel Steels, 1975; Editor, contbg. author: Structural Integrity of Lightwater Reactor Components, 1983, Status of U.S.A. Nuclear Reactor Pressure Vessel Surveillance, 1983, Radiation Embrittlement and Surveillance of Nuclear Reactor Pressure Vessels: An International Study, Vol. I, 1983, Vol. II, 1986, Vol. III, 1989, Vol. IV, 1993; Light Water Reactor Structural Integrity, Vol. I, 1984, Vol. II, 1988, Component Repair, Replacement and Failure Prevention in Light Water Reactors, 1986; contbr. articles to profl. jours. Served with USAF, 1951-53. Recipient Superior Civilian Service medal U.S. Navy, 1976. Fellow Am. Soc. Metals, D.C. Acad. Sci. (Engring. Sci. award 1966), ASTM (life, Dudley award and medal 1972, bd. dirs. 1980-82, vice chmn. bd. 1983-84, chmn. bd. 1985, award of merit 1979); mem. Rsch. Soc. Am. (Applied Sci. award 1962), Am. Nuclear Soc. (Spl. award and prize 1972), Fedn. Materials Socs. (pres. 1984), Sigma Xi. Home and Office: 7624 Highland St Springfield VA 22150-3931

STEELE, NANCY EDEN ROGERS, educator; b. Elgin, Ill., Aug. 18, 1946; d. Vance Donald and Barbara Marie (Yarwood) Rogers; m. James Frederick Steele, Apr. 12, 1976; children: Justin Vance Jabari, Barbara Marie Noni. BS, Centenary Coll., 1968; MA, U. Nebr., 1971. Program asst. Head Start & Follow Through, Lincoln, Nebr., 1971-74; K-12 resource tchr. Nantucket (Mass.) Pub. Schs., 1975-77; kindergarten lead tchr. Parkville Sch., Guaynabo, P.R., 1977-79; instr. in gen. psychology L.A. C.C., Sebana Seca, P.R., 1978-79; lang. arts and parent edn. tchr. Sweetwater Union H.S. Dist., Chula Vista, Calif., 1980-86; upper grade team leader park View Elem. Sch., Chula Vista, 1986-91; upper grade tchr. Clear View Elem. Sch., Chula Vista, 1991-94; mentor tchr. Chula Vista Elem. Sch. Dist., 1990-94; acad. dir. Nat. Civilian Cmty. Corps, San Diego, 1994-96; asst. prin. Harborside Elem. Sch., Chula Vista, 1996—; cons. in field. Author: Peace Patrol: A Guide for Creating a New Generation of Problem Solvers, 1994 (Golden Bell award 1993); co-author: Power Teaching for the 21st Century, 1991. Mem. Friends of Odawara, Japan, 1994-96. Recipient Peacemaker of Yr. award San Diego Mediation Ctr., 1993, Champion for Children award Children's Hosp. and San Diego Office of Edn., 1994. Mem. NEA, ASCD, AAUW, Nat. Coun. for Social Studies, Calif. Edn. Assn., Assn. Calif. Sch. Adminstrs., Chula Vista Aquatics Assn. (v.p. bd. dirs. 1986-96), Optimist Club (bd. dirs. 1991-96). Home: 1551 Malibu Point Ct Chula Vista CA 91911-6116

STEELE, OLIVER, English educator; b. Birmingham, Ala., May 13, 1928; s. Oliver L. and Mary Lucile (Abernethy) S.; m. Joy Cogdell, Dec. 23, 1950; children—Christopher, Mark, Eleanor, Andrew, Paul. B.S. in English, Auburn U., 1949, M.S. in English, 1951; Ph.D., U. Va., 1965. Instr. English U. Va., Charlottesville, 1959-65, asst. prof. English, 1965-67; assoc. prof. English U. Iowa, Iowa City, 1967-74, prof. English, 1974-92, prof. emeritus English, 1992—; Editor: Ellen Glasgow: a Bibliography, 1964, The Faerie Queene: Book I & II, 1965. Served with U.S. Army, 1953-55; Germany. Mem. Renaissance Soc. Am., Bibliographical Soc. U. Va., Raven Soc. Democrat. Avocation: music. Home: 1120 E Court St Iowa City IA 52240-3232 Office: Univ Iowa Dept English Iowa City IA 52240

STEELE, RICHARD J., management consultant; b. Elkhart, Ind., Sept. 27, 1925; s. Cornelius H. and Harriett (Poel) S.; m. Martha J. Micko, July 8, 1950; children: Barbara, Cheryl, Patricia, Thomas, Richard Jr., Marjorie, Gregory, Susan, Kathleen. SB, MIT, 1946; MBA, Ind. U., 1949. Cert. mgmt. cons. V.p. Fry Cons.'s, Inc., Chgo., 1950-70; pres. Richard Steele and Ptnrs., Inc., N.Y.C., 1970-72, Richard Steele Cons.'s, Inc., Columbia, Md., 1978-96; group v.p. Macro Systems, Inc., Silver Spring, Md., 1972-78; sr. v.p. Birch & Davis Assocs., Inc., Silver Spring, 1979-94; counselor Nat. Health Coun., N.Y.C., 1971-94. Author: (with others) Determinants of HMO Success, 1988. Trustee Village of Riverwoods, Ill., 1967. Lt. USNR, 1943-75, WWII, Korea. Recipient Award of Merit Am. Heart Assn., 1974. Mem. World Future Soc., Inst. Mgmt. Cons. Republican. Unitarian. Home and Office: 5122 Durham Rd E Columbia MD 21044-1423

STEELE, ROBERT EDWIN, orthopedic surgeon; b. Kansas City, Mo., Jan. 8, 1937; s. Robert Edwin and Margaret Jane (Levens) S.; m. Emily Wells Stephens, May 9, 1964; children: Edward Stephen, Thomas McKewon, Linda Katherine. AB, U. Mo., 1959; MD cum laude, Harvard U., 1963. Diplomate Am. Bd. Orthopedic Surgery; cert. Am. Acad. Orthopedic Surgeons, Assn. Arthritic Hip and Knee Surgery. Intern Mass. Gen. Hosp., Boston, 1963-64; resident in orthopedics Harvard U., 1966-71; instr. in orthopedic surgery Harvard Med. Sch., Boston, 1971; mem. med. staff Good Samaritan Hosp., Corvallis, Oreg., 1971—; bd. dirs. Good Samaritan Hosp., 1984-88, pres. med. staff, 1985, chmn. peer rev. com., 1994. Author: Studies on Osteonecrusis, 1979. Lt. USNR, 1964-66, Vietnam. Recipient Kappa Delta award for Outstanding Orthopedic Rsch., Am. Acad. Orthopedic Surgeons, 1978. Mem. Corvallis Orthopedic Surgeons (pres. 1990). Achievements include performance of total knee replacement. Avocations: camping, cycling, hiking, skiing, white water boating. Office: Corvallis Orthopedic Surg 3640 NW Samaritan Dr Corvallis OR 97330-3738

STEELE, RODNEY REDFEARN, judge; b. Selma, Ala., May 22, 1930; s. C. Parker and Miriam Lera (Redfearn) S.; m. Frances Marion Blair, Aug. 1, 1964; children: Marion Scott, Claudia Redfearn, Parker Blair. AB, U. Ala., 1950, MA, 1951; LLB, U. Mich., 1954. Bar: Ala. 1954, U.S. Dist. Ct. (mid. dist.) Ala. 1959, U.S. Ct. Appeals (5th cir., now 11th cir.) 1981. Law clk. Ala. Ct. Appeals, 1956-57; assoc. Knabe & Nachman, Montgomery, Ala., 1957-61; asst. U.S. atty. Dept. Justice, Montgomery, 1961-66; staff atty. So. Bell T&T Co., Atlanta, 1966-67; judge U.S. Bankruptcy Ct., Mid. dist. Ala., Montgomery, 1967—, chief judge, 1985—; adj. prof. Jones Law Sch. Served with U.S. Army, 1954-56, Korea. Mem. ABA, Ala. State Bar, Montgomery County Bar Assn. Democrat. Episcopalian. Office: US Bankruptcy Ct PO Box 1248 1 Court Sq Montgomery AL 36102-1248

STEELE, SARAH JANE, elementary school educator; b. Scottsbluff, Nebr., May 28, 1947; d. Earl Roe and Mary Eleanor (Blakey) Cherry; m. Gary Gene Steele, May 19, 1968; children: Jason Linn, Sally Suzanne. BS, Chadron State Coll., 1970, MS, 1994. Tchr. k., 1, 2 grades Chadron (Nebr.) Elem. Sch., 1970-71; tchr. 6th grade Morrill (Nebr.) Elem. Sch., 1971—. Mem. NEA, Nebr. State Edn. Assn., Morrill Edn. Assn. (pres. 1983-84), Alpha Delta Kappa (pres. 1994-96), Phi Delta Kappa. Republican Congregationalist. Avocations: reading, sporting events, crafts. Home: 100777 County Road D Morrill NE 69358-2105 Office: Morrill Pub Schs Box 486 Morrill NE 69358

STEELE, SHELBY, writer, educator; b. Chgo., 1946; s. Shelby Sr. and Ruth S. Grad., Coe Loll., 1968; M in Sociology, So. Ill. U., 1971; PhD in English, U. Utah, 1974. Prof. dept English Calif. State U., San Jose. Author: The Content of Our Character: A New Vision of Race in America, 1991 (Nat. Book Critics Circle award 1991); contbr. essays to profl. jours. Office: San Jose State U Dept English 1 Washington Sq San Jose CA 95192-0090*

STEELE, VICTORIA LEE, librarian; b. L.A., Feb. 24, 1952; d. John Wilms and Marjorie (Lee) Erpelding; m. Timothy Reid, Jan. 14, 1979. BA, UCLA, 1974, MLS, 1981; MA, U. So. Calif., 1993. Libr. Belt Libr. of Vinciana UCLA, 1981-82, head history and spl. collections Biomed. Libr., 1983-86, dir. devel. librs., 1986-88; head spl. collections U. So. Calif., L.A., 1988—; fundraising cons. Author: Becoming a Fundraiser, 1992; prodr. film: Every time I See a Patient..., 1994; contbr. articles to profl. publs. Mem. adv. bd. Fulbright Program for So. Calif., 1995—; mem. adv. coun. Annenberg Sch. for Communication U. So. Calif., 1994—; founder L.A. Preservation Network; vol. Save Outdoor Sculpture, 1995—. U. Calif. rsch. grantee, 1979, U. So. Calif. rsch. grantee, 1995; Fulbright fellow (U.K.), 1995. Mem. ALA (3M/JMRT award 1982, G.K. Hall award 1995). Office: U So Calif Doheny Libr University Park Los Angeles CA 90089-0182

STEELMAN, FRANK (SITLEY), lawyer; b. Watsonville, Calif., June 6, 1936; s. Frank S. Sr. and Blossom J. (Daugherty) S.; m. Diane Elaine Duke, June 27, 1960; children: Susan Butler, Robin Thurmond, Joan Bentley, David, Carol. BA, Baylor U., 1958, LLB, 1962. Spl. agt. IRS, Houston, 1962-64, atty. for estate tax, 1964-68; trust officer First City Nat. Bank, Houston, 1968-71; sr. v.p., trust officer First Bank & Trust, Bryan, Tex.,

1971-73; assoc. Goode, Skrivanek & Steelman, College Station, Tex., 1973-74; pvt. practice Bryan, 1974—; vis. lectr. Tex. A&M U., College Station, 1974-75; mcpl. judge City of Bryan, 1986-88. Bd. dirs. Bryan Devel. Found., 1994—; mem. Bryan Zoning Bd. Adjustments, 1992-94; pres. Brazos Valley Estate Planning Coun., 1973-74, Am. Heart Assn., 1975-76; deacon, mem. ch. choir, Sunday sch. tchr. So. Bapt. Ch. Mem. Rotary (bd. dirs. Bryan club 1973-74). Avocations: walking, golf. Office: 1810 Greenfield Plz Bryan TX 77802-3408

STEEN, CARLTON DUANE, private investor, former food company executive; b. Walnut Grove, Minn., June 12, 1932; s. Conrad Wendell and Hilda (Eng) S.; m. Dorothy Corinne Sorknes, Aug. 16, 1953; children: James, Craig, Jennifer. BA in Econs. cum laude, St. Olaf Coll., 1954; MA in Indsl. Relations, U. Minn., 1957. Job analyst Exxon Corp., Roselle, N.J., 1958-59; personnel adminstr. Kraft Inc., Chgo., 1959-65, compensation mgr., 1965-69; plant mgr. Kraft Inc., Decatur, Ga., 1969-70, Champaign, Ill., 1971-74; v.p. prodn. Kraft Inc., Chgo., 1974-76; pres. Indsl. Foods div., Memphis, 1976-82, Indsl. Foods Group, 1982-87. Served to capt. USAF, 1955-57. Republican. Lutheran.

STEEN, JOHN THOMAS, JR., lawyer; b. San Antonio, Dec. 27, 1949; s. John Thomas and Nell (Donnell) S.; m. Ida Louise Clement, May 12, 1979; children: John T. III, Ida Louise Larkin, James Higbie Clement. AB cum laude, Princeton U., 1971; JD, U. Tex., 1974. Bar: Tex. 1974, U.S. Dist. Ct. (we. dist.) Tex. 1976, U.S. Ct. Appeals (5th cir.) 1989. Assoc. firm Matthews & Branscomb, San Antonio, 1977-82; ptnr. firm Soules, Cliffe & Reed, San Antonio, 1982-83; sr. v.p., gen. counsel, dir. Commerce Savs. Assn., San Antonio, 1983-88; pvt. practice, San Antonio, 1988—; bd. dirs. North Frost Bank, San Antonio, 1982-84. Trustee San Antonio Acad., 1976-81, 87-93, chmn. bd., 1989-91; adv. coun. San Antonio Acad., 1991—; v.p. Bexar County Easter Seal Soc., San Antonio, 1976-77; trustee, vice chmn. San Antonio C.C. Dist., 1977-82; bd. dirs. Tex. Easter Seal Soc., Dallas, 1977-80, San Antonio Rsch. and Planning Coun., 1978-81, Community Guidance Ctr., 1983-84; vice-chmn. Leadership San Antonio, 1978-79; dir. Fiesta San Antonio Commn., 1982-83, 93-96; Bexar County commr., San Antonio, 1982, Tex. Commn. on Economy and Efficiency in State Govt., 1985-89; Coliseum Adv. Bd., 1985-91, chmn. bd., 1990-91; pres. San Antonio Performing Arts Assn., 1984-85; bd. trustees World Affairs Coun. San Antonio, 1982—, chmn. bd., 1984-86; trustee United Way San Antonio, 1985-92; bd. dirs. Accord Med. Found., 1987-92; mem. adv. bd. U. Tex., San Antonio, 1987—; trustee, Austin Coll, 1996—, Tex. Cavaliers Charitable Found., 1994-97; active Pan-Tex. Assembly, 1985—. 1st lt. USAR, 1973-81. Fellow San Antonio Bar Found., Tex. Bar Found. (life); mem. Tex. Bar. Assn., San Antonio Acad. Alumni Assn. (pres. 1976-77), Pan-Tex. Assembly, Ivy Club (Princeton, N.J.), San Antonio German Club (pres. 1982-83), Order of Alamo, Tex. Cavaliers (bd. dirs. 1989-92, 94-97, comdr. 1994-95, King Antonio LXXIV 1996-97, mem. King's coun. 1997—), San Antonio Country Club (bd. govs. 1990-93, v.p. 1992-93), Argyle Club, Conopus Club (bd. dirs. 1989-90), Princeton Club San Antonio and South Tex. (pres. 1980-81), Chevalier, Confrérie des Chevaliers du Tastevin, Sous-Commanderie de Southern Tex., 1994—. Phi Delta Phi. Home: 207 Ridgemont Ave San Antonio TX 78209-5431 Office: 300 Convent St Ste 2440 San Antonio TX 78205-3710

STEEN, LOWELL HARRISON, physician; b. Kenosha, Wis., Nov. 27, 1923; s. Joseph Arthur and Camilla Marie (Henriksen) S.; m. Cheryl Ann Rectanus, Nov. 20, 1969; children—Linda C., Laura A., Lowell Harrison Jr., Heather J., Kirsten M. B.S., Ind. U., 1945, M.D., 1948. Intern Mercy Hosp.-Loyola U. Clinics, Chgo., 1948-49; resident in internal medicine VA Hosp., Hines, Ill., 1950-53; pvt. practice, Highland, Ind., 1953—; pres., chief exec. officer Whiting Clinic, 1960-85; mem. sr. staff St. Catherine Hosp., East Chicago, Ind.; staff Community Hosp., Munster, Ind.; bd. commrs. Joint Commn. Accreditation of Hosps. Served with M.C., AUS, 1949-50, 55-56. Recipient Disting. Alumni Service award Ind. U., 1983. Fellow ACP; mem. AMA (trustee 1975, chmn. bd. trustees 1979-81), Ind. Med. Assn. (pres. 1970, chmn. bd. 1968-70), World Med. Assn. (dir. 1978-82, chmn. 1981-82, del. world assembly), Ind. Soc. Internal Medicine (pres. 1963), Am. Soc. Internal Medicine (Disting. Internist award 1981), Lake County Med. Soc., Ind. U. Sch. Medicine Alumni Assn. (pres. 1989-90, Disting. Alumnus award 1981). Presbyterian. Home: 8800 Parkway Dr Hammond IN 46322-1520 also: Gateway 8800 Parkway Dr Highland IN 46322-1520 Office: 3641 Ridge Rd Hammond IN 46322-2064

STEEN, LYNN ARTHUR, mathematician, educator; b. Chgo., Jan. 1, 1941; s. Sigvart J. and Margery (Mayer) S.; m. Mary Elizabeth Frost, July 7, 1940; children: Margaret, Catherine. BA, Luther Coll., 1961; PhD, MIT, 1965; DSc (hon.), Luther Coll., 1986, Wittenberg U., 1991, Concordia Coll., Minn., 1996. Prof. math. St. Olaf Coll., Northfield, Minn., 1965—; vis. scholar Inst. Mittag-Leffler, Djursholm, Sweden, 1970-71; writing fellow Conf. Bd. Math. Sci., Washington, 1974-75; exec. dir. Math. Sci. Edn. Bd., Washington, 1992-95. Author: Counterexamples in Topology, 1970, Everybody Counts, 1989; editor: Mathematics Today, 1978, On the Shoulders of Giants, 1990, Math. Mag., 1976-80, Why Numbers Count, 1997; contbg. editor: Sci. News, 1976-82. NSF Sci. faculty fellow, 1970-71, Danforth Found. grad. fellow, 1961-65. Fellow AAAS (sec. math. sect. 1982-88); mem. Am. Math. Soc., Math. Assn. Am. (pres. 1985-86, Disting. Svc. award 1992), Coun. Sci. Soc. Pres. (chmn. 1989), Sigma Xi (Bd. Dirs. Spl. award 1989). Home: 716 Saint Olaf Ave Northfield MN 55057-1523 Office: St Olaf Coll Dept of Math Northfield MN 55057

STEEN, NANCY, artist; b. Denver, Feb. 7, 1949; d. John and Petrita (Pino) Ciddio; m. Charles A. Steen, Nov. 13, 1968 (div. June 1976); children: Monica Lee Steen, Charles A. Steen III; m. Ben Q. Adams, Dec. 31, 1985. BA cum laude, Gonzaga U., 1973; postgrad., N.Mex. State U., 1973-74, U. N.Mex., 1974-76. Pub., owner New Leaf Press, Walnut Creek, Calif., 1974-79, The Leaf Press, Santa Monica, Calif., 1974-79, New Leaf Press, Albuquerque, 1974-79; rsch. adminstr. Taos Editions, Albuquerque, 1981-89; asst. dir. Western Graphics, Albuquerque, 1983—, R.C. Gorman pub., 1983-91. Author: R.C. Gorman: The Graphic Works, 1988, Who is R.C. Gorman?: An Insiders Portrait, 1996; exhibited in one-woman and group shows including Art Outdoors, Albuquerque, 1980, Mus. of Art, Albuquerque, 1980, 81, Susanne Brown, Scottsdale, Ariz., 1981, Mus. of Art, Santa Fe, 1982, Am. Design, Dallas, 1983, Phoenix Art Mus., 1983, Nabisco World Headquarters, East Hanover, N.J., 1984, Gallery One, Dallas, 1986, Gallery One, Denver, 1986, 87, Gallery Mach, Seattle, 1988, Mus. of the Permain Basin, Odessa, Tex., 1989, Silver City (N.Mex.) Mus., 1990, Santa Fe Style, Madison, Wis., 1990, Denver Art Mus., 1993, Dartmouth Street Gallery, 1994, Fiesta Del Carazon Creative Response to AIDS, Albuquerque, 1994, Live at the KIMO, Albuquerque, 1994; exhibited in numerous permant collections include L.A. County Mus. of Art, Oakland Mus. of Art, San Jose Mus. of Art, Phoenix Art Mus., U. Nev., Koofenay Sch. of Art, U. Calgary, U. Wash., N.Mex. State U., Maderia Sch., Tamarind Inst., Crocker Gallery, Western Graphics Collection, Mus. of Fine Art, Monterey Peninsula Mus. of Art, many others. Chairperson NAMES Project-Quilt Dis., Albuquerque, 1994; bd. dirs. NMAPLA-N.Mex. Assn. of People Living with AIDS, Albuquerque, 1993-94; fundraiser Make A Wish, Denver, 1994, Am. Heart Assn., Honolulu, Albuquerque, 1994-97. Grantee N.Mex. State U., 1973. Mem. Pi Beta Phi. Democrat. Roman Catholic. Avocations: gardening, reading, music. Home: PO Box 373 Corona NM 88318 Office: Western Graphics Workshop PO Box 373 Corona NM 88318-0373

STEEN, PAUL JOSEPH, retired broadcasting executive; b. Williston, N.D., July 4, 1932; s. Ernest B. and Inez (Ingebrigtson) S.; m. Judith Smith; children—Michael M., Melanie. BA, Pacific Luth. U., 1954; MS, Syracuse U., 1957. Producer, dir. Sta. KNTV, San Jose, Calif., 1957-58, Sta. KVIE, Sacramento, 1958-60; asst. prof. telecommunications Pacific Luth. U., Tacoma, 1960-67; dir. ops. Sta. KPBS San Diego State U., 1967-74; gen. mgr., 1974-93, prof. telecommunications and film, 1974-93, dir. univ. telecommunications; co-chmn. Office of New Tech. Initiatives. Dir. (tel. program) Troubled Waters (winner Nat. Ednl. TV award of excellence 1970). With AUS. Named Danforth Assoc. Mem. Pacific Mountain Network (bd. dirs., chmn., bd. of govs. award 1993), NATAS, Assn. Calif. Pub. TV Stas. (pres.), Pi Kappa Delta. Home: 4930 Campanile Dr San Diego CA 92115-2331

STEEN, WESLEY WILSON, former bankruptcy judge, lawyer; b. Abbeville, La., Feb. 15, 1946; s. John Wesley and Margaret (Chauvin) S.; m. Evelyn Finch, Aug. 29, 1970; children: Anna Frances, John Wesley, Lee Wilson. BA in English, U. Va., 1968; JD, La. State U., 1974. Bar: La. 1974, Tex. 1988. Assoc. Sanders, Downing, et al, Baton Rouge, 1974-77, ptnr., 1977-80; solo practice law, Baton Rouge, 1980-83; pres., atty. Steen, Rubin, et al, Baton Rouge, 1983-84; bankruptcy judge U.S. Bankruptcy Ct., Middle Dist. La., part time, 1983-84, full time, Baton Rouge, 1984-87; mem. Winstead, Sechrest & Minick, Houston, 1988—; mem. La. State Law Inst. Continuous Revision Com., La. Trust Code, 1980-87; mem. Baton Rouge Estate and Bus. Planning Council, 1980-87, State Bar Com. on Bar Admissions, Baton Rouge, 1981-85; adj. asst. prof. law La. State U., 1979-87, So. U. Law Sch., 1981; congl. page U.S. Ho. of Reps., 1963-64. Adv. editor Am. Bankruptcy Law Jour.; contbr. articles to profl. jours. Vestryman, St. James Episcopal Ch., 1980-83; bd. dirs., pres. Baton Rouge Symphony Assn., 1976-87, St. James Place, 1985-87, Cerebral Palsy Ctr., 1981, Baton Rouge Gallery, 1982. Fellow Am. Coll. Bankruptcy; mem. Baton Rouge Bar Assns., La. Bar Assn., Order of Coif, Omicron Delta Kappa. Republican. Episcopalian. Avocations: jogging, computers. Office: Winstead Sechrest & Minick 910 Travis St Ste 1700 Houston TX 77002-5807

STEENBURGEN, MARY, actress; b. Newport, Ark., Feb. 8, 1953; m. Malcolm McDowell, 1980 (div. 1990); children: Lilly, Charlie; m. Ted. Danson, Oct. 7, 1995. Student, Neighborhood Playhouse. Films: Goin' South, 1978, Time After Time, 1979, Melvin and Howard, 1980 (Academy Award, Best Supporting Actress), Ragtime, 1981, A Midsummer Night's Sex Comedy, 1982, Cross Creek, 1983, Romantic Comedy, 1983, One Magic Christmas, 1985, Dead of Winter, 1987, End of the Line, 1987 (also exec. prodr.), The Whales of August, 1987, Miss Firecracker, 1989, Parenthood, 1989, Back to the Future III, 1990, The Long Walk Home, 1990 (narrator), The Butcher's Wife, 1991, Philadelphia, 1993, What's Eating Gilbert Grape, 1993, Clifford, 1994, It Runs in the Family, 1994, Pontiac Moon, 1994, Powder, 1995, Nixon, 1995, My Family, 1995, The Grass Harp, 1995; appeared in Showtime TV's Faerie Tale Theatre prodn. of Little Red Riding Hood and (miniseries) Tender Is the Night, 1985, Gulliver's Travels, 1996; TV series: Ink, 1996; TV films: The Attic: The Hiding of Anne Frank, 1988; theater appearances include: Holiday, Old Vic, London, 1987, Candida, Broadway, 1993. Office: William Morris Agy Inc 151 S El Camino Dr Beverly Hills CA 90212-2704

STEENHAGEN, ROBERT LEWIS, landscape architect, consultant; b. Grand Rapids, Mich., July 11, 1922; s. Abraham and Rena (Vanden Broek) S.; m. Doris Brisentine, Aug. 2, 1952; children: Deborah, Cynthia, James. A.S., Grand Rapids Jr. Coll., 1942; B.S., Mich. State U., 1949. Chief landscape design Eastern design office Nat. Park Service, Phila., 1963-66; capt. planning team Nat. Park Service, Washington, 1966-70; asst. mgr. N.E. area Design Office Nat. Park Service, Denver, 1971-77, assoc. mgr., 1978-80; cons. landscape architecture Lakewood, Colo., 1980—. Served to sgt. U.S. Army, 1942-45, PTO. Recipient Meritorious Service award Nat. Park Service, 1971; recipient Performance award for Nat. Bicentennial Program, 1976. Fellow Am. Soc. Landscape Architects. Home: 2473 S Carr Ct Denver CO 80227-3104

STEENSGAARD, ANTHONY HARVEY, federal agent; b. Rapid City, S.D., Mar. 21, 1963; s. Harvey Hans and Dorothy Lorraine (Hansen) S. Student, U. Alaska, 1981-83, Anchorage C.C., 1983-84; AAS in Indsl. Security, C.C. Air Force, 1989; BS in Criminal Justice, Wayland U., 1989; MS in Computer Systems Engring., U. Calif., San Diego, 1996. Lic. pilot, radio operator. Bookseller B. Dalton Bookseller, Rapid City, S.D., 1978-81, Anchorage, Alaska, 1981-83; warehouseman Sears, Roebuck & Co., Anchorage, 1983-85; security specialist Alaska Air N.G., Anchorage, 1985-88; agt., draftsman, engring. cons. U.S. Border Patrol, El Centro, Calif., 1988—; pvt. computer cons., 1994—. Author: Unit Security Manager's Guide Book, 1988. Vol. U.S. Senator George McGovern's Campaign, Rapid City, 1980, Congressman Tom Daschle's Campaign, Rapid City, 1980, Spl. Olympics, Rapid City, 1981; observer CAP, Anchorage, 1981; public affairs officer Civil Air Patrol, Rapid City, S.D., 1996. With USMC, 1981-85, USAFR, 1985-95. Recipient Hon. Sci. award Bausch and Lomb, 1984. Mem. Am. Legion, Air Force Assn., VFW, Fraternal Order Eagles, Fraternal Order of Police. Democrat. Lutheran. Avocations: reading, computers, aviation, history, wargaming. Office: US Border Patrol 1111 N Imperial Ave El Centro CA 92243-1739

STEENSLAND, RONALD PAUL, librarian; b. Dothan, Ala., Dec. 16, 1946; s. Maurice John and Claire Folkes S.; m. Nancy Hollister, Dec. 20, 1970; 1 child, Ronald Paul. B.A., Fla. State U., 1969, M.S., 1970; postgrad., Miami (Ohio) U., 1972, U. Md., 1980, U.S. Army War Coll., 1995. Dir. Davidson County Pub. Libr., Lexington, N.C., 1970-73, Hidalgo County Libr. System, McAllen, Tex., 1973-76, Los Alamos County Libr., 1976-77, Lexington (Ky.) Pub. Libr., 1977—; chmn. John Cotton Dana Library Public Relations Awards, 1977. Treas. Hildago County chpt. ARC, 1975. Served to col. USAR, 1969-70. Recipient Service award United Way. Mem. Res. Officers Assn. (sec.-treas. chpt. 100), Assn. U.S. Army (sec. Bluegrass chpt.), U.S. Chess Fedn., ALA, Southeastern Library Assn., Ky. Library Assn., Lexington C. of C., Alpha Tau Omega. Baptist. Clubs: Lafayette, Pres.'s, Lexington Chess, Rotary. Office: Lexington Pub Libr 140 E Main St Lexington KY 40507-1318

STEENSMA, ROBERT CHARLES, English language educator; b. Sioux Falls, S.D., Nov. 24, 1930; s. Anton Charles and Martha (Johnson) S.; m. Sharon Hogge, Sept. 5, 1964; children: Craig, Michael, Laura, Kathryn, Rebecca. BA, Augustana Coll., Sioux Falls, 1952; MA, U. S.D., 1955; PhD, U. Ky., 1961. Instr. English Augustana Coll., 1955-57; asst. prof. U. S.D., 1959-62; asst. prof., then asso. prof. Utah State U., Logan, 1962-66; mem. faculty U. Utah, 1966—, prof. English, 1971—; lectr. Utah Humanities Coun., 1992-94, 97—. Author: Sir William Temple, 1970, Dr. John Arbuthnot, 1979; Editor: On The Original and Nature of Government (Sir William Temple), 1965; Contbr. articles to profl. jours. Served to capt. USNR, 1948-83. Mem. Rocky Mountain MLA, U.S. Naval Inst., Am. Soc. 18th Century Studies, South Cen. Soc. for 18th Century Studies (pres. 1994-95), Western Lit. Assn., S.D. Hist. Soc., Utah Hist. Soc. Republican. Lutheran. Office: U Utah Dept English Salt Lake City UT 84112

STEEPLES, DOUGLAS WAYNE, university dean, consultant, researcher; b. Great Bend, Kans., Mar. 30, 1935; s. Marion Wayne and Dorothy Augusta (King) S.; children from previous marriage: Donald Bruce, John Douglas, Sheila Margaret; m. Christine Marie Webster, Dec. 8, 1990. B.A. summa cum laude, U. Redlands, 1957; M.A., U. N.C., 1958, Ph.D., 1961; cert., Inst. Ednl. Mgmt., Harvard U., 1981. Asst. prof. history Calif. State U.-Northridge, 1961-64; prof. history Earlham Coll., Richmond, Ind., 1963-80; acad. v.p. Wartburg Coll., Waverly, Iowa, 1979-80; exec. v.p. Westminster Coll., Salt Lake City, 1980-83; provost Ohio Wesleyan U., Delaware, Ohio, 1983-85, acting pres., winter 1984; dean Coll. Liberal and Fine Arts, U. So. Colo., Pueblo, 1985-89; v.p. for acad. affairs Aurora (Ill.) U., 1989-94; dean Coll. Liberal Arts, Mercer U., Macon, Ga., 1994—; cons. higher edn. mgmt.; cons., reader advanced placement program Ednl. Testing Service, Princeton, N.J., 1976—; cons., evaluator North Central Assn. Schs. and Colls., Chgo., 1985—; bd. dirs. Western Ind. Colls. Fund, Salt Lake City, 1980-83; bd. dirs. Am. Con. of Acad. Deans, 1995; bd. trustees Econ. and Bus. Hist. Soc., 1995-98. Editor, contbg. author: Institutional Revival: Case Histories, 1986, Successful Strategic Planning Case Studies, 1989, Managing Change in Higher Education, 1990; assoc. editor Bus. Libr. Rev., 1996-98; contbr. articles to various publs. Pres. Luth. Inter-parish Coun., Richmond, 1975-78; bd. dirs. Soc. for Use and Preservation of Resources, Richmond, 1976-79; mem. adv. bd. Pueblo Symphony Orch., 1987-89; mem. allocations coms. United Way Richmond, 1976-79, Pueblo, 1988-89, Aurora, 1990-94. Scholar U. Redlands, Calif., 1953-57; Danforth fellow, 1957-61; Woodrow Wilson fellow, 1957-58; Found. for Econ. Edn. fellow in bus., 1963; Am. Philos. Soc. grantee, 1966. Mem. Am. Hist. Assn., Orgn. Am. Historians, So. Hist. Assn., Sierra Club, Phi Beta Kappa (senator united chpts. 1973-79), Omicron Delta Kappa. Republican. Lodges: Rotary (bd. dirs. 1983-84). Avocations: mountaineering, running, bagpiping. Office: Mercer U Coll Liberal Arts 1400 Coleman Ave Macon GA 31207-0001

STEER, ALFRED GILBERT, JR., foreign language educator; b. Lansdowne, Pa., May 30, 1913; s. Alfred Gilbert and Selma Elizabeth (Taber) S.; m. Elizabeth Jean Kell, Sept. 6, 1947; children: Susan Elizabeth, John Thomas. A.B., Haverford Coll., 1935; M.A., Duke U., 1938; Ph.D., U. Pa., 1954. Instr. Washington and Lee U., 1937-41, Haverford Coll., U. Pa., 1947-55; head lang. div Internat. Mil. Tribunal, Nurnberg, Germany, 1945-46; asst. prof., then assoc. prof. SUNY-Binghamton, 1955-59; assoc. prof. Columbia U., 1959-67; prof. Germanic and Slavic langs., head dept. Germanic and Slavic langs U. Ga., Athens, 1967-83, prof. emeritus, 1983—, chmn. linguistics com., 1969-83. Author: (with W.W. Pusey III and B.Q. Morgan) Readings in Military German, 1943, Goethe's Science in the Structure of the Wanderjahre, 1979, Goethe's Elective Affinities the Robe of Nessus, 1990, Interesting Times: A Memoir, 1992; contbg. author: Jahrbuch des Freien Deutschen Hochstifts, 1965, Approaches to Teaching Goethe's Faust, 1986, Science Skeleton of Goethe's Works, 1987; also articles. Bd. dirs. Univ. System of Ga. Studies Abroad Programs, 1969-70, Prospective Tchr. Fellowship Program, HEW. Served with USNR, World War II. Fellow Am. Philos. Soc., 1965-66; fellow Columbia Council for Research in Humanities, 1965-66. Mem. MLA, Am. Assn. Tchrs. German (v.p., pres. chpt. 1970-71). Home: 335 Beechwood Athens GA 30606-4013 Office: U Ga Dept Germanic Slavic L Athens GA 30602

STEER, MAX DAVID, speech pathologist, educator; b. N.Y.C., June 14, 1910; s. Charles and Sadie (Hisiger) S.; m. Ruth Pittelman, Aug. 25, 1942. B.S., L.I. U., 1932, LL.D., 1957; A.M., U. Iowa, 1933, Ph.D., 1938. Diplomate: in clin. psychology Am. Bd. Examiners in Profl. Psychology. Student tchr. N.Y.C. Pub. Schs., 1931-32; research asst. psychol. and speech clinic U. Iowa, 1934-35; instr. speech, dir. speech clinic Purdue U., 1935-37, asst. prof., 1938-40, asso. prof., 1940-46, prof. speech, dir. speech and hearing clinic, dir. voice sci. lab., dir. Purdue Naval voice communications research program, supr. pub. sch. hearing t, 1946—, head dept. audiology and speech scis., 1963-70, Hanley disting. prof. audiology and speech scis., 1970-76, disting. prof. emeritus, 1976—; Cons. speech, hearing problems Ind. Bd. Health, 1954-55, chmn. hearing and speech adv. com., 1956; cons. neurol. and sensory diseases service program USPHS; cons. Ind. Sch. for Deaf, Muscatatuck State Sch. for Retarded, Ft. Wayne State Sch. for Retarded, Pan Am. Health Orgn., WHO, 1972—, U. Bogota, 1974—; mem. nat. research adv. com. Bur. Edn. for Handicapped, U.S. Office Edn., HEW, 1972—; cons., vis. lectr. Nat. Rehab. Inst., Panama, 1974—; cons. various govt. agys., 1965—; mem. Ind. Hearing Commn., chmn., 1958-60, 67—. Contbr. research reports to psychol., speech jours. Bd. dirs. Ind. Soc. Crippled Children, 1947-49, v.p., 1950-51; bd. dirs. Purdue Research Found., 1974—; Pres. Am. Speech and Hearing Found. Served as lt. comdr. USNR, 1942-46. Recipient citation as hon. old master Purdue U., 1975; Kephart award for disting. service to handicapped, 1974; Sagamore of Wabash citation Gov. Ind., 1976; M.D. Steer Audiology and Speech-Lang. Ctr. dedicated at Purdue U., 1986. Mem. Am. Speech and Hearing Assn. (pres. 1951), Internat. Assn. Logopedics and Phoniatrics (v.p. 1959-65, 68-80, exec. v.p. 1980—), Speech Assn. Am. (chmn. speech sci. com. 1948), Acoustical Soc. Am., Am. Psychol. Assn., AAAS, Ind. Speech Correction Assn. (pres. 1938, exec. council 1946-49), Ind. Clin. Psychol. Assn., AAUP, Latin Am. Fedn. Logopedics, Phoniatrics and Audiology (cons. 1972—, hon. mem. exec. bd. 1973—, award 1973), Sigma Xi. Home: 342 Westview Cir West Lafayette IN 47906-1662

STEER, REGINALD DAVID, lawyer; b. N.Y.C., July 16, 1945; s. Joseph D. and Rozica (Yusim) S.; m. Marianne Spizzy, July 22, 1983; children: Derek B., Trevor A. BA, U. Minn., 1966, JD, 1969. Bar: Minn. 1969, Calif. 1973, U.S. Dist. Ct. (no., ea. and cen. dists.) Calif., U.S. Ct. Mil. Appeals 1969, U.S. Ct. Appeals (9th cir.), U.S. Ct. Appeals (11th cir.), U.S. Supreme Ct. 1981, U.S. Ct. Internat. Trade, 1994. Assoc. Pillsbury, Madison & Sutro, San Francisco, 1973-79, ptnr., 1979—; mem. exec. com., 1997-98; lectr. Calif. Continuing Edn. of Bar, San Francisco, 1981, Petroleum Attys. Meeting, Washington, 1996. Capt. U.S. Army, 1969-73. Served to Capt. U.S. Army, 1969-73. Mem. ABA (antitrust and litigation sects.). Club: Olympic (San Francisco). Avocations: piano, tennis, photography. Office: Pillsbury Madison & Sutro 235 Montgomery St San Francisco CA 94104-2902

STEERE, ALLEN CARUTHERS, JR., physician, educator; b. Apr. 11, 1943; m. Margaret Mercer, 1969; children: Allen Caruthers III, Margaret Hamilton, Samuel Mercer, John Summers. BA, Columbia U., 1965, MD, 1969; DSc. (hon.), Indiana U., 1992, SUNY, 1997. Diplomate Am. Bd. Internal Medicine; lic. rheumatologist, N.Y., Ga., Ct., Mass. Intern St. Luke's Hosp., N.Y.C., 1969-70, asst., sr. resident, 1970-72, chief resident, instr. medicine, 1972-73; chief resident, instr. medicine Coll. Physicians and Surgeons Columbia U., N.Y.C., 1972-73; clin. instr. medicine Hosp. for Spl. Surgery Cornell U., N.Y.C., 1972-73; clin. instr. medicine Grady Meml. Hosp. Emory U., Atlanta, 1973-75; clin. fellow in rheumatology Yale U., New Haven, 1975-77, asst. prof. medicine, epidemiology and pub. health, 1977-81, assoc. prof. medicine, 1981-87; prof. medicine, chief rheumatology and immunology New Eng. Med. Ctr. Tufts U., Boston, 1987—. With USPHS, 1973-75. Recipient Citation for Elucidation of Lyme disease Infectious Diseases Soc. Am., 1984, Ciba-Geigy Rheumatology prize Internat. League Against Rheumatism, 1985, award for discovery of Lyme disease Nat. Inst. Arthritis and Musculoskeletal Skin Diseases, 1988, Richard and Hinda Rosenthal award ACP, 1990, Joseph Mather Smith prize Coll. Physicians and Surgeons, Columbia U., 1990, Zucker Faculty prize Tufts U., 1990, award for studies Lyme disease Nat. Health Coun., 1990, Lee C. Howley Sr. prize Arthritis Found., 1993; Rsch. fellow Arthritis Found., 1977-80, Sr. fellow, 1981-86. Mem. Am. Soc. Clin. Investigation, Am. Fedn. Clin. Rsch., Am. Coll. Rheumatology (Howard and Martha Holley rsch. prize in rheumatology 1995). Office: Tufts U Sch Medicine New Eng Med Ctr # 406 750 Washington St Boston MA 02111-1526

STEERE, ANNE BULLIVANT, retired student advisor; b. Phila., July 27, 1921; d. Stuart Lodge and Elizabeth MacCuen (Smith) B.; m. Richard M. H. Harper Jr., Nov. 14, 1942 (div. Oct. 1967); children: Virginia Harper Kliever, Richard M. H. Harper III, Patricia Harper Flint, Stuart Lodge Harper, Lucy Steere, Grace Steere Johnson; m. Bruce Middleton Steere, July 5, 1968. BS in Sociology, So. Meth. U., 1978, M in Liberal Arts, 1985. Asst. to dir. Harvard Law Sch. Fund, Cambridge, Mass., 1958-68; advisor to older students So. Meth. U., Dallas, 1976-85. Contbr. articles to profl. jours. Trustee, Pine Manor Coll., Chestnut Hill, Mass., 1983—; bd. dirs. Planned Parenthood, Dallas, 1975-85. Mem. New Eng. Hist. and Geneal. Soc., Alpha Kappa Delta. Episcopalian. Clubs: Chilton (Boston); Jr. League. Avocations: reading, needlepoint, sailing. Home (winter): 369 S Lake Dr # 5D Palm Beach FL 33480

STEERE, WILLIAM CAMPBELL, JR., pharmaceutical company executive; b. Ann Arbor, Mich., June 17, 1936; s. William Campbell and Dorothy (Osborne) S.; m. Lynda Gay Powers, Jan. 29, 1957; children: William, Mark, Christopher. BS, Stanford U., 1959. Sales rep. Pfizer & Co., Modesto, Calif., 1970-72; v.p., dir. ops. Pfizer Labs, N.Y.C., 1982-84; sr. v.p., dir. ops. Pfizer Pharms., N.Y.C., 1982-84, exec. v.p., 1984-86, pres., 1986-91; pres., CEO Pfizer Inc., 1991-92, chmn. bd., CEO, 1992—, also bd. dirs.; bd. dirs. Texaco Inc., NYU Med. Ctr., Minerals Techs. Inc., Fed. Res. Bank of N.Y., Sta. WNET-TV. Trustee N.Y. Bot. Garden; bd. overseers Meml. Sloan-Kettering Cancer Ctr. Mem. Pharm. Rsch. and Mfrs. Am. (bd. dirs.), Bus. Coun. (bd. dirs.), Bus. Roundtable, Univ. Club, N.Y. Yacht Club. Avocations: sailing, skiing. Office: Pfizer Inc 235 E 42nd St New York NY 10017-5703*

STEERS, GEORGE W., lawyer; b. N.Y.C., Jan. 29, 1941. BA, Yale U., 1963; LLB cum laude, Columbia U., 1966. Bar: Wash. 1970. Law clk. U.S. Ct. Appeals (2d cir.), 1966-67; mem. Stoel Rives, LLP, Seattle, Wash. Mem. ABA, Wash. State Bar Assn., Seattle-King County Bar Assn. Office: Stoel Rives LLP 600 University St Ste 3600 Seattle WA 98101-4109

STEEVES, ERIC WILLIAM, school administrator; b. Millinocket, Maine, June 8, 1958; s. William John and Helen Rose (Vitchner) S. BA, U. South Fla., 1981; MS, Husson Coll., 1984; diploma, Maine State Prins.' Acad., 1992; MEd, U. Maine, 1995. Cert. social studies, bus. edn. tchr., guidance counselor, prin., Maine. Asst. mgr. hardware div. C.R. Steeves & Sons Plumbing & Hardware, Millinocket, Maine, 1981-86; social studies tchr. Penobscot Valley High Sch., Howland, Maine, 1986-88, Katahdin High Sch., Sherman Station, Maine, 1988-91; vice prin. Katahdin Jr./Sr. High Sch., Sherman Station, 1991-93; guidance counselor Millinocket (Maine) Elem.

Sch., 1994—, Stearns H.S., 1995—. Mem. MSAD (peer support tng. instr. 1989—, chmn. computer curriculum com. 1991—), ACA, Aroostoock County Athletic Dirs. Assn. (chmn. 1991-92, chmn. budget com. 1992—), Nat. Assn. Secondary Sch. Prins., Maine State Prins.' Assn., Maine Sch. Counselor's Assn., Katahdin Area Crisis Intervention Team, Millinochet Alcohol and Drug Edn. and Info. Team. Republican. Avocations: softball, basketball, golf, fishing, hunting. Home: 92 Massachusetts Ave Millinocket ME 04462-2316 Office: Stearns H S Guidance Office Millinocket ME 04462

STEFANCICH, DONNA LEE, information security specialist; b. West Islip, N.Y., Jan. 13, 1961; d. Stanley Frank and Irene Eleanor (Soullard) S. AAS in Archtl. Tech., SUNY, Farmingdale, 1981; BS in Computer Sci. summa cum laude, NY Inst. of Tech., 1985, postgrad., 1993—. Programmer, analyst Fairchild Republic Co., Farmingdale, N.Y., 1985-87; sr. computer security analyst Grumman Data Systems, Bethpage, N.Y., 1987-94; mgr. data security and controls Nationar, Woodbury, N.Y., 1994-95; mgr. network security Cablevision Systems Corp., Woodbury, 1995—. Mem. Nat. Computer Security Assn., Computer Security Inst., Nu Ypsilon Tau. Avocations: golf, in-line skating, jogging, gardening. Home: 17 Taca Blvd Deer Park NY 11729 Office: Cablevision Systems Corp 150 Crossways Park Dr W Woodbury NY 11797-2051

STEFANE, CLARA JOAN, business education secondary educator; b. Trenton, N.J., Apr. 8; d. Joseph and Rose M. (Bonfanti) Raymond; m. John E. Stefane, July 19, 1975. BS in Bus. Adminstrn., Georgian Ct. Coll., Lakewood, N.J., 1968. Cert. tchr. gen. bus. and secretarial studies, N.J. Tchr. bus. Camden Cath. High Sch., Cherry Hill, N.J., 1960-68, Cathedral High Sch., Trenton, 1970-72; tchr., bus., chair dept. McCorristin Cath. High Sch., Trenton, 1972-95—; mem. Mercer County Task Force for Bus. Edn., Trenton, 1989-90. Sustaining mem. Rep. Nat. Com.; del. mem. 1992 Presdl. Trust; mem. Rosary Altar Soc., Incarnation Ch. Named Tchr. of Yr., The Cittone Inst., Princeton, N.J., 1991. Mem. ASCD, N.J. Bus. Edn. Assn., Nat. Cath. Edn. Assn., Sisters of Mercy of the Ams. (assoc.). Roman Catholic. Avocations: reading, creative writing, attending operas and Yankee baseball games. Home: 278 Weber Ave Trenton NJ 08638-3638 Office: McCorristin Cath High Sch 175 Leonard Ave Trenton NJ 08610-4807

STEFANIAK, NORBERT JOHN, business administration educator; b. Milw., Jan. 12, 1921; s. Peter Stephen and Mary Ann (Schlaikowski) S.; m. Elizabeth Jean Horning, Aug. 27, 1949; children—John, Mary, Jane, Beth, Joel, Peter, James, Thomas, Anne, Jean. B.B.A., U. Wis., 1948, M.B.A., 1950, Ph.D., 1960. C.P.A. Instr. U. Wis., Milw., 1950-53; treas., controller Wauwatosa (Wis.) Realty Co., 1953-56; prof. bus. adminstrn. U. Wis., Milw., 1957-75, prof. emeritus. Author: Real Estate Marketing, monograph and articles in field. Past commr. West Allis (Wis.) Planning Commn.; bd. dirs. Internat. Exch. Found.-Poland and Milw. County, Wis.; condemnation commr. Milw. County; bd. review City of West Allis, Wis. With USAAF, WWII. Named Polish-Am. Man of Yr., Polish Nat. Alliance (Milw. Soc.), 1990. Mem. Am. Real Estate and Urban Econs. Assn. (past pres.), Wis. Realtors Assn. (past dir.), Wis. Real Estate Exam. Bd. (past vice chmn.), Am. Soc. Real Estate Counselors (emeritus), Polish Nat. Alliance. Home: 865 S 76th St Milwaukee WI 53214-3026 Office: S63w13680 Janesville Rd Muskego WI 53150-2713

STEFANICS, ELIZABETH T. (LIZ STEFANICS), state legislator. BA, Eastern Ky. U.; MS, U. Wis.; PhD, U. Minn. Mem. N.Mex. Senate, 1996; mem. conservation com., judiciary com., chmn. health and human svcs. com., adminstr. health and human svcs.; exec. dir. Oppeham, Santa Fe, 1996—. Democrat. Address: PO Box 10127 Santa Fe NM 87504-6127 Office: Oppeham PO Box 4625 Santa Fe NM 87502*

STEFANIK, JEAN MARIANNE, educator, naturalist; b. Springfield, Mass., June 10, 1949; d. Edward Carl and Suzanne Florence (Chelkonas) S. BS in Elem. Edn.; MEd, Am. Internat. Coll.; postgrad. Norwich U., U. Vt., Merrimack Valley Coll., Franklin Pierce Coll., U. Mass., U. Hawaii. Reading specialist Easthampton (Mass.) Schs., 1973-74; dir. curriculum Barre Town (Vt.) Sch. Dist., 1974-80; extended edn. program dir., Amherst Sch. Dist., N.H., 1980—; part-time educator Computer Ctr., Tandy Corp., Manchester, N.H., 1981-82; part-time instr. Notre Dame Coll., Manchester, 1981-83, Merrimack Valley Coll., 1981-86, U. N.H. Coll. for Lifelong Learning, 1982-87, 92—, sabbitical including work for Smithsonian Inst. Marine Systems Lab. and New England Aquarium's Right Whale Rsch. Team, 1987-88; mem. Alaska Oil Spill and Ecology Info. Ctr., Juneau, 1989; mem. Earthwatch/Rsch. Teams Giant Clams of Tonga, 1988, Fijian Coral Reefs, 1993, field svc. rep., 1993-95. Mem. ASCD (internat., bd. dirs. 1979-80, 82—, mem. elem. global edn. pilot project 1992-94, issues com. 1995-96), Vt. Assn. Supervision and Curriculum Devel. (pres. 1979-80, treas. 1977-79), N.H. Assn. Supervision and Curriculum Devel. (pres. 1982-84, 86-87, bd. dirs. 1981—), New Eng. Aquarium Self Contained Underwater Breathing Apparatus Club (pres. 1990-93), United Divers N.H. (pres. 1996—), N.H. Orchid Soc. (bd. trustees 1994—), Seamark (chmn. 1993), Mensa, Phi Delta Kappa, Alpha Chi. Home: 285 Beaver St Manchester NH 03104-5569

STEFANILE, LAWRENCE VINCENT, management counsulting company executive; b. Jersey City, N.J., Jan. 24, 1939; s. Angelo Anthony and Agnes Antoinette (Altomonte) S.; m. Margaret Ann Marzell, Apr. 2, 1967. AB, Seton Hall U., 1961; MA, Niagara U., 1962; doctoral equivalency, St. John's U., 1968; EdD, U. Am., 1991. Cert. sch. adminstr., N.J.; cert. Am. Coll. Hosp. Adminstrs. Coord. internat. tchr. devel. program at Ohio U. U.S. Dept. State, 1963-64; vice prin. Marist High Sch., Bayonne, N.J., 1964-68; dir. coll. rels. St. peter's Coll., Jersey City, 1968-72; COO St. Francis Hosp., Jersey City, 1972-81; pres. Vanguard Mgmt. Svc., Short Hills, N.J., 1981—; with U.S. Dept. Vets. Affairs, N.Y.C., 1993—, Phila., 1993—; cons. Village of Ridgefield Park, N.J., 1968—, U.S. Dept. Vets. Affairs, Newark, 1992—, Borough of Little Ferry, N.J., 1992—. Author: The Art of The Search: A Guide to Successful Job Placement, 1991, A Systems Approach to Job Search and Placement, 1992. Trustee St. Francis Hosp., Jersey City, 1978; bd. dirs. Hudson chpt. ARC, Jersey City, 1978; commr. Manpower Commn.-Hudson, Jersey City, 1979; mem. Hosp. Reimbursement coun. N.J. Dept. Health, Princeton, 1980. Seton Hall U. scholar, 1957; fellow Niagara U., 1961, Fulbright Found., 1962, Ohio U., 1962; named to Internat. Tchr. Devel. Program, Fulbright Exch., 1962. Mem. Seton Hall U. Alumni, Niagara U. Alumni Assn., U. Am. Alumni Assn. Office: Vanguard Mgmt Svc Mountainside Crossing 1108 Springfield Ave Mountainside NJ 07092-2906

STEFANO, GEORGE B., neurobiologist, researcher; b. N.Y.C., Sept. 11, 1945; s. George and Agnes (Hendrickson) S.; m. Judith Mary Stefano, Aug. 24, 1968; 1 child, Michelle Laura. Ph.D., Fordham U., 1973. Mem. faculty N.Y.C. C.C., 1972-79, Medgar Evers Coll., CUNY, 1979-82; prof. cell biology, chmn. dept. biol. sci. SUNY, Old Westbury, 1982-86, asst. v.p. rsch., 1985-89, dir. Old Westbury Neurosci. Inst. and Gerontology Ctr., 1986—; pres., dir. East Coast Neurosci. Found., Dix Hills, N.Y., 1977-82; rsch. coord. dept. anesthesiology St. Joseph Hosp. and Med. Ctr., Paterson, N.J., 1979-82; disting. teaching prof. SUNY, 1991; adj. prof. surgery, dir. cardiac rsch. program SUNY, Stony Brook, 1995—; rsch. assoc. dept. psychiatry Harvard Med. Sch., 1995—. cons. NIDA. Co-founder, mem. editl. bd. Molecular Cellular Neurobiology and Prog. Neuro Endcini Immunology; editor Advances in Neuroimmunology; contbr. over 240 papers to sci. jours. Named CASE Prof. N.Y., 1991. Nat. Acad. Scis. grantee, 1978, 80; NIMH grantee, 1979—; NSF grantee, 1989—; Nat. Inst. Drug Abuse grantee 1993—. project dir. NIMH-COR, 1983—. Mem. AAAS, Soc. Neurosci. (pres. Old Westbury chpt.), Assn. Immuno-Neurobiologists (exec. pres. 1991—), N.Y. Acad. Sci., Gerontol. Soc. Am.

STEFANO, JOSEPH WILLIAM, film and television producer, author; b. Phila., May 5, 1922; s. Dominic and Josephine (Vottima) S.; m. Marilyn Epstein, Dec. 5, 1953; 1 son, Andrew Dominic. Ed. pub. schs. Pres. Villa di Stefano Prodns., 1962—. Toured as song and dance man in Student Prince, 1945, Merry Widow, 1946; composer music and lyrics popular songs, night club revues, indsl. shows, others, 1946-57; author screenplays The Black Orchid, 1958, The Naked Edge, 1960, Psycho, 1960, Anna di Brooklyn, 1962, Eye of the Cat, 1969, Futz, 1970, The Kindred, 1986, Blackout, 1989, Psycho IV: The Beginning, 1990, Two Bits, 1995; TV drama Made in Japan, 1959, movies for TV, 1970-78; prodr., author TV series The Outer Limits, 1963-64, Swamp Thing, 1990; exec. con. The Outer Limits, 1995—. Recipient Robert E. Sherwood award for Made in Japan, Fund for Republic, 1959, Edgar Allen Poe award for Psycho, Mystery Writers Am., 1960, Columbia award Federated Italo-Ams. Calif., 1964, Pres.'s award Acad. Sci.-Fiction Fantasy and Horror Films, 1987, Movieguide commendation for Two Bits, One of Ten Best Films of 1995; inducted into Cultural Hall Fame, South Phila. H.S. Mem. ASCAP, Writers Guild Am., Dirs. Guild Am., Producers Guild Am., Acad. Motion Pictures Arts and Scis., Mystery Writers Am. Home: 10216 Cielo Dr Beverly Hills CA 90210-2035 *For me it has always been important to succeed first in my own eyes. This personal sense of success seems warmer and surer and more likely to maintain the spirit during those moments when worldly success dances to tunes other than my own. Goals are golden. Guidelines are lines on a street map; they show how many different ways there are to go from where to when.*

STEFANO, ROSS WILLIAM, business executive; b. Cortland, N.Y., June 18, 1955; s. Nicola Sebastian and Gloria Maria (Saltarez) S.; m. Janet Stapleton, Apr. 2, 1977; children: Nicolas J.J., Christian A., Mari Elizabeth. BS, Cornell U., 1977, MBA, 1978. CPA, Calif. CPA Coopers & Lybrand, San Francisco, 1978-81; fin. mgr. Genstar Corp., San Francisco, 1981-83; v.p., treas., v.p. mktg. CIS Corp., Syracuse, N.Y., 1983-92; cons., 1992-94; pres. Pietrafesa Co., Liverpool, N.Y., 1994—. Bd. dirs., exec. dir. FM Soccer Club, 1984—; bd. dirs. Syracuse YMCA, 1986-89; fund raiser Boy Scouts Am., Syracuse, 1986-89, Cath. Charities, Syracuse, 1991. Mem. AICPA, Cavalry Club. Office: Peitrafesa Co 7400 Morgan Rd Liverpool NY 13090-3902

STEFANSCHI, SERGIU, dancer; b. Komralid, Romania, Mar. 2, 1941; emigrated to Can., 1971, naturalized, 1977; s. Alexander and Lidia S. Diploma, Acad. Dance, Leningrad, 1960. Tchr. Nat. Ballet Sch. and Nat. Ballet of Can., Toronto, 1978—. Prin. dancer, Bucharest (Romania) Opera, 1960-68, Jeunesse Musicale de France, 1969-70, Theatre Francaise de la Dance, Paris, 1970, Nat. Ballet of Can., Toronto, Ont., 1971-78, appeared with, Belgrade (Yugoslavia) Opera, 1966, 68, Coob Marieta (Ga.) Ballet, 1976 (Recipient Silver medal I, Internat. Ballet Concourse, Varna, Bulgaria 1964), Internat. Guest Theater. Mem. Actors Equity Can. Mem. Romania Orthodox Ch. Home: 319 Ave Keewatin, Toronto, ON Canada M4P 2A4 Office: 111 Maitland St, Toronto, ON Canada M4Y 1E4

STEFENELLI, GEORGE EDWARD, physician; b. Bklyn., Sept. 27, 1948; s. George Edward and Ann Marie (Mandel) S.; m. Rosemary Elizebeth Stefenelli, June 16, 1973; children: Stephanie, Rory, George, Samantha. BSN, SUNY, Stony Brook, 1975; DO, Phila. Sch. Osteo. Medicine, 1986. Diplomate Am. Bd. Ob-Gyn.; lic. physician, N.J., Pa., Md. Intern Interfaith Med. Ctr., Bklyn., 1986-87; resident U. Medicine and Dentistry of N.J., Stratford, 1987-91; asst. prof. clin. ob-gyn. U. Medicine and Dentistry N.J., Stratford, 1992—; ptnr. Potomac Ob-Gyn., Waynesboro, Pa., 1993—. Capt. U.S. Army, 1976-82. Mem. Am. Osteo. Assn., Am. Coll. Osteo. Ob-Gyn., Am. Coll. Ob-Gyn., Pa. Med. Soc., Franklin County Med. Soc., Pa. Osteo. Med. Soc., Am. Soc. Colposcopy and Cervical Pathology, Am. Assn. Gynecologic Laparoscopists, Am. Soc. for Reproductive Medicine. Home: 11681 Dellwood Dr Waynesboro PA 17268

STEFFAN, WALLACE ALLAN, entomologist, educator, museum director; b. St. Paul, Aug. 10, 1934; m. Sylvia Behler, July 16, 1966; 1 child, Sharon. B.S., U. Calif.-Berkeley, 1961, Ph.D., 1965. Entomologist dept. entomology Bishop Mus., Honolulu, 1964-85, head diptera sect., 1966-85, asst. chmn., 1979-85; dir. Idaho Mus. Natural History, Idaho State U., Pocatello, 1985-89, U. Alaska Mus., 1989-92; prof. biology U. Alaska Fairbanks, 1989-92; exec. dir. Great Valley Mus. Natural History, 1992-94; dir. Sun Cities Mus. Art, Sun City, Ariz., 1995-97, Burpee Mus. of Natural History, 1997—; mem. grad. affiliate faculty dept. entomology U. Hawaii, 1969-85; reviewer NSF, 1976—; mem. internat. editorial adv. com. World Diptera Catalog, Systematic Entomology Lab., U.S. Dept. Agr., 1983-85; mem. affiliate faculty biology, Idaho State U., 1986-89; bd. dirs. Idaho State U. Fed. Credit Union, 1986-89; mem. adv. coun. Modesto Conv. & Visitors Bureau, 1992-95; mem. Ft. Hall Replica Commn., 1986-89. Acting editor Jour. Med. Entomology, 1966; assoc. editor Pacific Insects, 1980-85. Judge Hawaii State Sci. and Engring. Fair, 1966-85, chief judge sr. display div., 1982, 83, 84; advisor to bd. Fairbanks Conv. and Visitors Bur., 1989-91; mem. vestry St. Christophers Episcopal Ch., 1974-76, St. Matthew's Episcopal Ch., Fairbanks, 1990-91; pres. Alaska Visitors Assn., Fairbanks, 1991; advisor Fairbanks Conv. Visitors Bur. Bd., 1989-91; bd. dirs. Kamehameha Fed. Credit Union, 1975-77, chmn., mem. supervisory com., 1980-84. Served with USAF, 1954-57. Grantee NIH, 1962, 63, 67-74, 76-81, 83-85. U.S. Army Med. Research and Devel. Command, 1964-67, 73-74, NSF, 1968-76, 83-89, City and County of Honolulu, 1977, U.S. Dept. Interior, 1980, 81. Mem. Entomol. Soc. Am. (mem. standing com. on systematics resources 1983-87), Am. Mosquito Control Assn., Pacific Coast Entomol. Soc., Soc. Systematic Zoology, Hawaiian Entomol. Soc. (pres. 1974, chmn. coms. 1966-85, editor procs. 1966), Hawaiian Acad. (councillor 1976-78), Entomol. Soc. Wash., Fairbanks C. of C. (adv. bd. Conv. Visitors Bur. 1989), Alaska Visitors Assn. (pres. Fairbanks chpt. 1991), Sigma Xi (pres. San Joaquin chpt. 1994-95, mem. bd. cultural connections 1994-95). Office: Burpee Mus Natural History 737 N Main St Rockford IL 61103-6903

STEFFEL, SUSAN ELIZABETH, English language and literature educator; b. Muskegon, Mich., Feb. 9, 1951; d. Sherman Burgess and Geraldine (Westerman) Bos; m. Andrew John Steffel, July 12, 1975. BA, Hope Coll., 1973; MA in English, Mich. State U., 1978, PhD in English, 1993. Tchr. secondary English Maple Valley Schs., Vermontville, Mich., 1973-91; assoc. prof. English Ctrl. Mich. U., Mt. Pleasant, 1991—; supr. secondary student tchrs. dept. English Ctrl. Mich. U., 1991—, vice-chair profl. educators, 1994-95, chair profl. educators coun., 1995—. Co-author: High School English: A Process for Curriculum Development, 1985, 20th Century Children's Authors, 1994. Recipient Excellence in Edn. award Lansing Regional C. of C., 1985, 86, 88, 89, 90, Excellence in Teaching award Ctrl. Mich. U., 1996. Mem. ASCD, AAUW, Am. Assn. Colls. for Tchr. Edn., Am. Ednl. Rsch. Assn., Nat. Coun. Tchrs. English (guest reviewer 1993—), Mich. Coun. Tchrs. English (mem. steering com. 1985—, asst. editor jour. 1993—), Assembly Lit. for Adolescents, Conf. English Edn., Golden Key Honor Soc. (hon.), Phi Kappa Phi, Phi Delta Kappa (sec. 1995—). Avocations: reading, gardening, pets, needlework. Office: Ctrl Mich U 242 Anspach Hall Mount Pleasant MI 48859

STEFFEN, LLOYD HOWARD, minister, religion educator; b. Racine, Wis., Nov. 27, 1951; s. Howard C. and Ruth L. (Rode) S.; m. Emmajane S. Finney, Feb. 14, 1981; children: Nathan, Samuel, William. BA, New Coll., 1973; MA, Andover Newton Theol. Sch., 1978; MDiv, Yale U., 1978; PhD, Brown U., 1984. Ordained to ministry United Ch. of Christ, 1983. Chaplain Northland Coll., Ashland, Wis., 1983—, assoc. prof., 1982-90; assoc. prof. Lehigh U., Bethlehem, Pa., 1990—, chaplain, 1990—; mem. theol. com. Wis. Conf. United Ch. of Christ, Madison, 1985-87, mem. div. ch. and ministry NW assn. Wis. Conf., Eau Claire, 1987-90; mem. ecumenical commn. Penn N.E. Conf., 1994—; mem. Common Ground, Bethlehem, 1994—, chair, 1995—. Author: Self-Deception and the Common Life, 1986, Life/Choice: The Theory of Just Abortion, 1994, Abortion: A Reader, 1996; contbr. articles to profl. jours. Town supr. Town of La Pointe, Wis., 1984-87. Recipient NEH Inst. award Harvard U., 1988, East-West Ctr., 1995; Univ. fellow Brown U., 1982; faculty devel. grantee Northland Coll., 1986, 90, Lehigh U., 1994. Mem. Soc. Christian Ethics, Am. Acad. Religion, Assocs. for Religion and Intellectual Life, Assn. for Coordination of Univ. Religious Affairs. Home: 224 W Packer Ave Bethlehem PA 18015-1518 Office: Lehigh U Johnson Hall # 36 Bethlehem PA 18015

STEFFEN, PAMELA BRAY, secondary school educator; b. Bessemer, Ala., Mar. 9, 1944; d. James Ernest and Margaret Virginia (Parsons) Bray; m. Ted N. Steffen, June 17, 1972; children: Elizabeth, Thor. BA, U. Louisville, 1966; MA, Spalding U., 1975. Cert. tchr., gifted tchr., Ky. Tchr. English and German Louisville (Ky.) Pub. Schs., 1967-73; tchr. English to fgn. students Internat. Ctr., U. Louisville, 1970-78; bookkeeper T.N. Steffen PSC, Louisville, 1978-85; tchr. of adults Jefferson County Pub. Schs., Louisville, 1985-87, tchr. English and German, 1987—; network participant, bd. dirs. Foxfire, Louisville, 1990—; spokesperson Coalition Essential Schs., Providence, 1990—, Ctr. for Leadership in Sch. Reform, Louisville, 1990—; group leader AAUW, Louisville, 1983-88; presenter seminars; 94 AATG summer Austrian Inst. Graz; participant Austrian Landeskunde Internat., 1994. Bd. dirs. Jefferson County Med. Soc. Aux., Louisville, 1984-88, Highland Cmty. Ministries, Louisville, 1980-87, Highland Ct. Apts. for Elderly, Louisville, 1984-87; nat. v.p. Deafness Rsch. Found. Aux., 1984-88; mem. vestry and rector search com. St. Andrew's Episcopal Ch., Louisville, 1985-88; active Louisville Fund for Arts campaign, 1980-93; Louisville Orch. Assn. fundraiser. Fullbright fellow Goethe Inst., Munich, 1969; grantee Ky. Arts Coun., 1991-92, artist-in-residence, 1992—; grantee Ky. Humanities Coun. CES, 1993, fall forum presenter; named to Ky.'s Commonwealth Inst. Tchrs. and Vis. Tchrs. Inst.; selected for Landeskunde in Österreich, 1994; summer study scholar Goethe Inst., Freiberg, Germany, 1996. Mem. ASCD, Nat. Coun. Tchrs. English, Coalition Essential Sch., Greater Louisville Coun. Tchrs. English, Am. Assn. Tchrs. German. Avocations: swimming, travel, beagling, writing, reading. Home: 2404 Park Boundary Rd Louisville KY 40205-1620 Office: Fairdale High Sch 1001 Fairdale Rd Fairdale KY 40118-9731

STEFFENS, DONNA IRENE, gifted and talented education coordinator; b. Akron, Ohio, July 23, 1945; d. Harry Lee and Hazel Irene (Jay) Dye; m. Donald William Steffens, Dec. 18, 1971; children: Buddy Burgy, Jyl, Scott. BS in Edn., U. Akron, 1968, MS in Ednl. Adminstrn., 1972, post-grad., 1974. Cert. tchr., prin., supr./coord./dir. instrn., Wis. Tchr. elem. Copley (Ohio) Pub. Schs., 1966-74; inservice cons. Summit County Svcs., Akron, Ohio, 1973; tchr. Title 1 Cedarbur (Wis.) Pub. Schs., 1975, middle sch. tchr., 1988-90, dist. coord. gifted programming, 1990—, dir. summer enrichment acad., 1996—; pvt. tutor Columbia, Md., 1978; day care operator Ellicott City, Md., 1978-79; instr. Cardinal Stritch Coll. of Edn., 1995 (curriculum coun. for dist., 1993-95, staff devel. com., 1993-95, assessment com., 1993-95); Christian edn. coord. Alliance Bible Ch., Cedarburg; adv. coun. chair Gifted Program, Cedarburg, 1988-92; enrichment program adv. com. U. Washington County. Mem. Libr. Bd., 1991, Cedarburg Cmty. Scholarship Bd., 1991, Jaycettes, 1979-81; bd. dirs. Workforce 2010, WATG; chair Parents Supporting Parents; mem. bldg. and scholarship coms. Alliance Bible Ch., chmn. Christian edn. com. Recipient Meritorious Svc. award Wis. Assn. Edn. Gifted and Talented, 1991, Jennings grant Copley Pub. Schs. Mem. ASCD, Wis. Coun. Gifted and Talented, Wis. Assn. Edn. Gifted and Talented. Avocations: singing, crafts, travel. Office: Cedarburg Sch Dist W68n611 Evergreen Blvd Cedarburg WI 53012-1847

STEFFENS, DOROTHY RUTH, political economist; b. N.Y.C., May 5, 1921; d. Saul M. and Pearl Y. (Reiter) Cantor; m. Jerome Steffens, Nov. 19, 1940; children: Heidi Sue, Nina Ellen. BBA, CCNY, 1941; MEd, Temple U., 1961; PhD, Anthony U., 1981. Economist Nat. War Labor Bd., Washington, 1941-44, United Elec. Radio Machine Workers, Phila., 1944-46; instr. group dynamics Temple U., Phila., 1955-57; seminar program dir. Soc. Friends, Washington, 1958-61; tng. dir. Nat. Coun. Negro Women, Washington, 1967-68; edn. cons. Peace Corps, Nigeria, 1969-70; exec. dir. Women's Internat. League for Peace and Freedom, Phila., 1971-77, Fund for Open Info. and Accountability, Inc., 1978-80; conf. dir. Haverford Coll., 1980-84; exec. sec. Nigerian Women's Com., 1968-69; del. African Women's Seminar UN, Accra, Ghana, 1969; mem. Africa panel Am. Friends Svc. Com., 1976-88, mem. internat. divsn. exec. com., 1977-84; resource lectr. Internat. Women's Seminar, Lillehammer, Norway, 1991. Author: The Day after Summer, 1966; editorial bd. The Churchman, 1977—; mem. nat. bd. Gray Panthers, 1989-91; contbr. articles to profl. jours., newspapers, mags. N.Y. C. of C. scholar, N.Y. State Regents scholar CCNY, 1941. Quaker. *Women, minorities and the economically disadvantaged have the wisdom and the capacity to bring about a world of peace and social justice and to do it non-violently.*

STEFFENS, JOHN LAUNDON, brokerage house executive; b. Cleve., July 7, 1941; m. Louise Cullen, Nov. 25, 1967; children: Drew, Julie, Wesley. B in Econs., Dartmouth Coll., 1963. Various positions Merrill Lynch, 1963—; exec. v.p. Pvt. Client Group, 1990-97, vice-chmn. bd., 1997—. Office: Merrill Lynch & Co Inc World Fin Ctr N Tower 250 Vesey St New York NY 10281-1012

STEFFER, ROBERT WESLEY, clergyman; b. Spokane, Wash., June 24, 1934; arrived in Can., 1987; s. Harold Wesley and Kathryne (Trumble) S.; m. Diane De'Moisey, Aug. 19, 1960; children: Erika Kirsten, Beauregard Gregory Robert. BA, Whitworth Coll., 1956; BD, Lexington Theol. Sem., 1959; MA, Ind. U., 1966, PhD, 1967. Ordained to ministry Christian Ch. (Disciples of Christ), 1959. Civilian dir. religious edn. U.S. Army Armor Ctr., Ft. Knox, Ky., 1960-64; assoc. min. Christian Ch. (Disciples of Christ), Oklahoma City, 1967-71; prof. Phillips U., Enid, Okla., 1971-76; fraternal worker div. overseas ministries Christian Ch. (Disciples of Christ), Barrow-in-Furness, Cumbria, Eng., 1976-79; Lilly vis. prof. religious edn. Christian Theol. Sem., Indpls., 1979-81; dir. edn. for mission div. homeland ministries Christian Ch. (Disciples of Christ), Indpls., 1981-87; exec. regional min. Christian Ch. (Disciples of Christ) in Can., Guelph, Ont., 1987-97; sr. minister Eureka (Ill.) Christian Ch., 1997—; sec. Coll. Chs. of Christ in Can., Guelph, 1987-97. Contbr. articles to religious publs. and ency. Col. USAR, 1964—. Lilly Found. fellow in adult edn. Ind. U., 1964-66. Mem. Disciples of Christ Hist. Soc. (life, trustee 1990-94), Religious Edn. Assn. (bd. dirs. 1994-97), Conf. Regional Mins. and Moderators (2nd v.p.), Ch. Fin. Coun. (bd. dirs. 1995-96, exec. com. 1995). Democrat. Avocations: gardening, reading, travel, music. Home: RPO Park Mall, PO Box 30013 2 Quebec St, Guelph, ON Canada N1H 8J5 Office: Eureka Christian Ch 302 S Main St Eureka IL 61530-1312

STEFFES, DON CLARENCE, state senator; b. Olpe, Kans., Jan. 13, 1930; s. William A. and Marie M. (Dwyer) S.; m. Janie L. Steele, Oct. 10, 1953; children: Michael, Steve, David, Andrew, Nancy, Terrence, Jennifer. BS, Kans. State Tchrs. Coll., 1952, MS, 1958. Mgr. Abilene C. of C., Kans., 1955-57; mem. staff Topeka C. of C., 1957-60; mgr. McPherson C. of C., Kans., 1960-65; exec. v.p. Kans. Devel. Credit Corp., Topeka, 1965-68, McPherson Bank & Trust, 1968-73; pres., CEO BANK IV McPherson (formely McPherson Bank & Trust), 1973-91; mem. Kans. State Senate, Topeka, 1992—; chmn. Fin. Instns. and Ins. Cos., Topeka, 1997—. Mem. Kans. Main St. Adv. Counsel, Topeka, 1978-82; pres., bd. dirs. Mingenback Found., McPherson, Kans., 1970—; vice chmn. Nat. Commn. Agrl. Fin., Washington, 1987-89; v.p. McPherson Indsl. Devel. Co., 1970-75. Named Man of Yr. McPherson Coll., 1989. Mem. Kans. Bankers Assn. (pres. 1985), KC. Roman Catholic. Home: 1008 Turkey Creek Dr Mc Pherson KS 67460-9763

STEFFES, KENT, volleyball player; b. Pacific Palisades, Calif., June 23, 1968. Student, Stanford U.; BA in Econ., UCLA, 1993. Profl. volleyball tour player. Named AVP Rookie of Yr., 1989, Up & Coming Player of Yr., 1988, AVP Most Valuable Player by Volleyball Monthly Mag., 1992. Mem. Assn. Volleyball Profls. (sec., bd. dirs.). First and only AVP mem. to win with 3 different ptnrs. in same yr., 1990; won 8 Miller Lite Opens, 1991; first and only AVP mem. to win 2 Joe Cuervo Gold Crown Series Events with different ptnrs. in same yr., 1991; won Miller Lite Tournament of Champions with Karch Kiraly, 1992, Miller Lite U.S. Championships, 1992, Miller Lite Grand Prix, 1992, with Karch Kiraly, 1993, first-ever Olympic Beach Volleyball Competition, with Karch Kiraly, 1996; compiled record 18 AVP Open wins, 1992; tied all-time consecutive open wins, 1992. Office: Assn Volleyball Profls 6th Fl Ste 600 330 Washington Blvd Marina Del Rey CA 90292-5147*

STEFFEY, EUGENE PAUL, veterinary medicine educator; b. Reading, Pa., Oct. 27, 1942; s. Paul E. and Mary M. (Balthaser) S.; children: Michele A., Bret E., Michael R., Brian T. Student, Muhlenberg Coll., 1960-63; D in Vet. Medicine, U. Pa., 1967; PhD, U. Calif., Davis, 1973. Diplomate Am. Coll. Vet. Anesthesiologists (pres. 1980). NIH spl. research fellow U. Calif., San Francisco, 1973; asst. prof. U. Calif., Davis, 1974-77, assoc. prof., 1977-80, prof. vet. medicine, 1980—, also chmn. dept. vet. surgery, 1980-93; mem. scientific reviewers Am. Jour. Vet. Research, Schaumburg, Ill., 1984-87. Contbr. numerous articles to profl. jours. Mem. AVMA, Am. Coll. Vet. Anesthesiologists, Am. Physiol. Soc., Am. Soc. Pharmacology Exptl. Therapeutics, Am. Soc. Anesthesiologists, Assn. Vet. Anaesthetists, Calif. Soc. Anesthesiologists, Comparative Respiratory Soc., Internat. Anesthesia Rsch. Soc., Pa. Vet. Med. Assn., Royal Coll. Vet. Surgeons (hon. assoc.), Sigma Xi, Phi Zeta. Office: U Calif Dept Surg/Radiol Scis School of Vet Medicine Davis CA 95616

STEFFY, JOHN RICHARD, nautical archaeologist, educator; b. Lancaster, Pa., May 1, 1924; s. Milton Grill and Zoe Minerva (Fry) S.; m. Esther Lucille Koch, Oct. 20, 1951; children: David Alan, Loren Craig. Student, Pa. Area Coll., Lancaster, 1946-47, Milw. Sch. Engring., 1947-49. Ptnr. M.G. Steffy & Sons, Denver, Pa., 1950-72; ship reconstructor Kyrenia Ship Project, Cyprus, 1972-73, Inst. Nautical Archaeology, College Station, Tex., 1973—; from lectr. to prof. anthropology Tex. A&M U., College Station, 1976-88, Sara W and George O. Yamani prof. nautical archaeology, 1989-90, prof. emeritus, 1990—; lectr. on ship constrn. Author: Wooden Shipbuilding and the Interpretation of Shipwrecks, 1994; co-editor: The Athlit Ram, 1991; contbr. chpts. to books and articles to profl. jours. Sec. Denver Borough Authority, Pa., 1962-72. Served with USN, 1942-45. MacArthur Found. fellow, 1985. Mem. Archaeol. Inst. Am., Soc. Nautical Research, N.Am. Soc. Oceanic History. Republican. Methodist. Office: Tex A&M U Inst Nautical Archaeology College Station TX 77843

STEFFY, MARION NANCY, state agency administrator; b. Fairport Harbor, Ohio, Sept 23, 1937; d. Felix and Anna (Kosaber) Jackopin; 1 child, Christopher C. BA, Ohio State U., 1959; postgrad. Butler U., 1962-65, Ind. U., 1983. Exec. sec. Franklin County Mental Health Assn., Columbus, Ohio, 1959-61; caseworker Marion County Dept. Pub. Welfare, Indpls., 1961-63, supr., 1963-66, asst. chief supr., 1966-73; dir. div. pub. assistance, Ind. Dept. Pub. Welfare, Indpls., 1973-77, asst. adminstr., 1977-85; regional adminstr. Adminstrn. Children and Families Ill. Dept. Health and Human Svcs., Chgo., 1985—; lectr. Ball State U., Lockyear Coll., Ind. U. Grad. Sch. Social Work; mem. Ind. Devel. Disabilities Coun., 1979-81, Ind. Cmty. Svc.s Adv. Coun., 1978-81; Ind. Child Support Adv. Coun., 1976-82, Welfare Svc. League, 1968—; chmn. rules com. Ind. Health Facilities Coun., 1974-81. Chmn. Lawrence Twp. Roundtable, 1983—. Mem. Nat. Assn. State Pub. Welfare Adminstrs., Am. Pub. Welfare Assn., Network of Women in Bus. Roman Catholic. Office: Adminstrn for Children & Families 105 W Adams St Chicago IL 60603-4102

STEG, LEO, research and development executive; b. Vienna, Austria, Mar. 30, 1922; came to U.S., 1941, naturalized, 1946; s. Jacob and Clara (Gellert) S.; m. Doreen Ethel Ray, June 12, 1947; children: Paula Jamie, Ellen Leslie, Audrey Leigh. B.S., City Coll. N.Y., 1947; M.S., U. Mo., 1948; Ph.D., Cornell U., 1951. Registered profl. engr., Pa. Chief engr. Fed. Design Co., N.Y.C., 1946-47; instr. mech. engring. U. Mo., Columbia, 1947-48; instr. applied mechanics and materials Cornell U., Ithaca, N.Y., 1948-51, asst. prof., 1951-55; systems engr., missile and space div. GE, Phila., 1955-56, mgr. space sci. lab., 1956-79, chief scientist, 1980-81; sr. v.p. University City Sci. Center, Phila., 1981-82; pres. Steg, Ray & Assocs., Villanova, Pa., 1980—; sci. and pub. policy fellow Brookings Inst., Washington, 1982-84; pres. Technical Applications Internat., Inc., McLean, Va., 1990—; adj. prof. Drexel U.; cons. to space scis. bd. Nat. Acad. Scis., other govt. agencies. Contbr. articles to profl. jours.; editor 2 books. Asso. trustee U. Pa. Named Engr. of Yr. Phila., 1965. Fellow AIAA (editor-in-chief jour. 1963-67), AAAS; mem. Phila. Acad. Scis. (founding), Franklin Inst. Phila. (past mem. bd. mgrs.), Long Beach Island Found. Arts and Scis. (past chmn. bd.), Sigma Xi, Phi Kappa Phi. Clubs: Cosmos, Cornell of N.Y. Home: 1616 Hepburn Dr Villanova PA 19085-2005

STEGEMEIER, RICHARD JOSEPH, oil company executive; b. Alton, Ill., Apr. 1, 1928; s. George Henry and Rose Ann (Smola) S.; m. Marjorie Ann Spess, Feb. 9, 1952; children: Richard Michael, David Scott, Laura Ann, Martha Louise. BS in Petroleum Engring., U. Mo., Rolla, 1950, cert. petroleum engr. (hon.), 1981; MS in Petroleum Engring., Tex. A&M U., 1951; D of Engring. (hon.), U. Mo., Rolla, 1990. Registered profl. engr., Calif. Various nat. and internat. mgmt. positions with Unocal Corp. (formerly Union Oil Co.), L.A., 1951—, pres. sci. and tech. div., 1979-80, sr. v.p. corp. devel., 1980-85, pres., COO, 1985-88, CEO, also chmn. bd. dirs., 1988-94; bd. dirs. First Interstate Bancorp, Found. Health Corp., Halliburton Co., Northrop Corp., Outboard Marine Corp. Patentee in field. Bd. dirs. Calif. Econ. Devel. Corp.; bd. govs. Town Hall of Calif., The Music Ctr. of L.A. County; bd. overseers Exec. Coun. on Fgn. Diplomats, Huntington Libr.; chmn. L.A. World Affairs Coun., 1990-94; pres. World Affairs Coun. of Orange County, 1980-82; chmn. Brea (Calif.) Blue Ribbon Com., 1979-80 ; trustee Com. for Econ. Devel., U. So. Calif., Harvey Mudd Coll., Loyola Marymount U.; mem. adv. bds. Northwestern U. Kellogg Grad. Sch. of Mgmt.; bd. vis. UCLA Anderson Grad. Sch. of Mgmt., U. Mo., Rolla; mem. adv. bd. Calif. State U., Fullerton, adv. coun., Long Beach; bd. dirs. YMCA of L.A., L.A. Philharm. Assn., John Tracy Clinic; chmn. L.A. area coun. Boy Scouts of Am., Calif. C. of C. chmn., 1994; gen. campaign chmn. United Way of Greater L.A., 1990-91; trustee and immediate past pres. Hugh O'Brian Youth Found., 1993-94, L.A. Archidiocese Edn. Found. Recipient Merit award Orange County Engring. Coun., 1980, Outstanding Engr. Merit award Inst. Advancement Engring., 1981, Disting. Achievement medal Tex. A&M U., Hugh O'Brian Youth Found. Albert Schweitzer Leadership award, 1990, Human Rels. award Am. Jewish Com., 1990. Mem. AIChE (Disting. Career award So. Calif. sect. 1989), NAM (bd. dirs.), Nat. Acad. Engring., Am. Petroleum Inst. (bd. dirs.), Soc. Petroleum Engrs. (lectr. 1978), Nat. Petroleum Coun., 25 Yr. Club Petroleum Industry (past pres.), Calif. Bus. Roundtable, Calif. Coun. on Sci. and Tech., Calif. Club. Republican. Roman Catholic. Office: Unocal Corp 376 Valencia Ave Brea CA 92823-6345*

STEGENGA, PRESTON JAY, international education consultant; b. Grand Rapids, Mich., July 9, 1924; s. Miner and Dureth (Bouma) S.; m. Marcia Jean DeYoung, July 28, 1950; children: James Jay, Susan Jayne. BA, Hope Coll., 1947; MA, Columbia U., 1948; PhD, U. Mich., 1952; LHD (hon.), Northwestern Coll., Iowa, 1989. Instr. history, polit. sci. Berea Coll., Ky., 1948-50; asoc. prof. Berea Coll., 1952-55; assistantship U. Mich., 1950-52; pres. Northwestern Coll., Orange City, Iowa, 1955-66; chief Cornell U. Project, U. Liberia-U.S. AID Program, Monrovia, W. Africa, 1966-68; coordinator internat. program Calif. State U., Sacramento, 1968-71; dir. Calif. State U. (Internat. Center), 1971-88; acting v.p. acad. affairs Calif. State U., 1974-75; spl. asst. to pres. Calif. State U., Sacramento, 1988-92; mem. Calif. State Liaison Com. for Internat. Edn.; ednl. cons. to Pres., Republic of Liberia, 1973-74; cons. internat. programs Am. Assn. State Colls. and Univs., 1975-89; cons. UN Devel. Programme, 1975-88; internat. edn. cons., 1992—; v.p. Sacramento chpt. UN Assn., U.S.A., 1969-71, pres., 1971-73, bd. dirs.; mem. Calif. UN Univ. Adv. Coun., 1976-80, internat. trade com. C. of C., 1984—, chair coll.-U. com., 1995—; pres. Tri-State Coll. Conf., 1963-64; dir. Fulbright project for Chinese scholars, 1985; cons. internat. projects Calif. State Fair, 1990—. Author: Anchor of Hope, 1954; asst. to editor History of Edn. Jour.; contbr. articles to profl. jours. Trustee Western Sem., Mich., Northwestern Coll., Iowa, 1955-66, 91-96, New Brunswick Sem., N.J., 1955-66, Global Calif. Coun., 1991-93; trustee, v.p. World Affairs Coun., 1976-77, 85-90, pres., 1990-92, trustee, 1993-98; mem. Task Force for Improving Am. Competence in World Affairs, 1980-89; mem. internat. bd. Los Rios Coll. Found., 1980-85; mem. Am. Coun. for UN U., 1979-85, Interfaith Svc. Bd., 1985-90; bd. dirs. New Zealand-Sacramento Sister City, 1989—. With AUS, 1942-45. Decorated Purple Heart; named hon. chief Kpelle Tribe, West Africa, 1973, hon. commodore Port of Sacramento, 1983, Multi-Cultural Educators Hall of Fame, 1996; recipient Disting. Svc. award UN Assn., 1971, Republic of Venezuela Edn. award, 1979, Outstanding Svc. award Fed. Republic of Germany, 1985, Disting. Svc. award Calif. State U. Chancellor, 1988, Citation of Achievement, Calif. Sec. of State, 1988, U.S. Congl. Register Recognition Citation, 1988, President's Award, World Affairs Coun., 1992, Gov.'s award Calif. State Fair, 1993, Internat. award Sacramento C. of C., 1993, Disting. Svc. award Assn. Citizens & Friends of Liberia, 1995; Ministry of Edn. scholar Republic of China, 1981; German Acad. Exch. Svc. fellow U. Bonn, 1981; Hon. Legis. Resolutions, Calif. State Senate and Assembly, 1988. Mem. Assn. Iowa Coll. and Univ. Pres. (v.p. 1965-66), NEA, Calif. State Univ. Student Personnel Assn., Am. Acad. Polit. and Social Sci., Assn. for Advancement of Dutch-Am. Studies, Phi Delta Kappa, Phi Kappa Phi, Phi Beta Delta. Mem. Reformed Ch. Am. Home: 545 Mills Rd Sacramento CA 95864-4911

STEGER, CHARLES WILLIAM, university administrator; b. Richmond, Va., June 16, 1947; s. Charles William and Virginia Belle (Garrett) S.; m. Janet Grey Baird, Sept. 13, 1969; children: Christopher B., David C. BArch, Va. Poly. Inst. & State U., 1970, MArch, 1971, PhD, 1978. Registered architect, Va. Project planner, architect Wiley & Wilson Inc., Lynchburg, Va., 1971-72, mgr. urban planning dept., 1973-74; dir. Environ. Design Consortium Inc., Blacksburg, Va., 1974-85; inst. grad. urban design program Coll. Architecture and Urban Studies , Va. Poly. Inst. and State U., Blacksburg, 1974-76, chmn. grad. urban design program, 1976-81; dean Coll. Architecture and Urban Studies, Va. Poly. Inst. and State U., Blacksburg, 1981-93; acting v.p. for pub. svc. Va. Poly. Inst. and State U., Blacksburg, 1990-93, v.p. for devel. and univ. rels., 1993—; bd. dirs. Va. Found. Architecture, Richmond. Contbr. articles to jours. in field. Bd. dirs. Va. Chamber Music Acad., Blacksburg, 1989—, Hollins Coll., Roanoke, Va., 1987—, Boswil (Switzerland) Found., 1986—, Ctr. in the Square, Roanoke, 1993—; v.p. Va. Tech. Found., Inc., 1993—; adv. coun. Va. Ctr. on Rural Devel., 1992—; commr. Govs. Commn. on Population Growth and Devel., Richmond, 1989-94. Fellow AIA (bd. dirs. ACSA Health Facilities Rsch. Program, Washington 1989—, ACSA Coun. on Arch. Rsch., 1987—); mem. Am. Planning Assn., Am. Inst. Cert. Planners, Commonwealth Club (Richmond, Va.), Shenandoah Club (Roanoke, Va.). Avocations: cattle farming, golf, canoeing. Office: Va Poly Inst and State U VP Devel Univ Rels 315 Burruss Hall Blacksburg VA 24061

STEGER, EDWARD HERMAN, chemist; b. New Orleans, Dec. 11, 1936; s. Herman Christoph and Katherine (Walther) S.; m. Amy Patricia Duvall, July 29, 1960; children: David B., Sandra E. BS, Tulane U., 1958. Analytical chemist Atlantic Rsch. Corp., Gainesville, Va., 1960-64, head control lab., 1964—; presenter at profl. confs. Contbr. articles to Fine Particle Soc. Jour. Lt. USNR, 1958-60. Mem. Am. Chem. Soc., N.Y. Acad. Scis., Phi Beta Kappa, Phi Eta Sigma, Alpha Chi Sigma. Baptist. Home: 4311 Alta Vista Dr Fairfax VA 22030-5302 Office: Atlantic Rsch Corp 5945 Wellington Rd Gainesville VA 20155-1633

STEGER, EVAN EVANS, III, lawyer; b. Indpls., Oct. 24, 1937; s. Charles Franklin and Alice (Hill) S.; m. Suzy Gillespie, July 18, 1964; children—Cynthia Anne, Emily McKee. A.B., Wabash Coll., 1959; J.D., Ind. U., 1962. Bar: Ind. 1962, U.S. Dist. Ct. (so. dist.) Ind. 1962, U.S. Ct. Appeals (7th cir.) 1972, U.S. Tax Ct. 1982, U.S. Supreme Ct. 1982. Assoc. Ice, Miller, Donadio and Ryan, and predecessor firm Ross, McCord, Ice and Miller, Indpls., 1962-69, ptnr., 1970-96, mng. ptnr., 1996— . Fellow Am. Coll. Trial Lawyers; mem. ABA, Ind. Bar Assn., Indpls. Bar Assn., Internat. Assn. Def. Counsel. Democrat. Presbyn. Office: Ice Miller Donadio & Ryan Box 82001 1 American Sq Indianapolis IN 46282

STEGER, JOSEPH A., university president. Formerly sr. v.p. and provost U. Cin., pres., 1984—. Office: U Cin PO Box 210063 Cincinnati OH 45221-0063

STEGER, RALPH JAMES, chemist; b. Meridian, Okla., Jan. 24, 1940; s. Daniel Bose and Opal Creola (Brothers) S. BS in Chemistry and Math., Langston U., 1962. Cartographer Aeronautical Chart and Info. Ctr. ACIC USAF, St. Louis, 1962-63; lab. technician Sigma Chem. Co., St. Louis, 1963; phys. scientist U.S. Army Chem. Corps, Edgewood Arsenal, Md., 1963-65; rsch. chemist Chem. Rsch., Devel. and Engring. Ctr. SMCCR Rsch. Lab., Analytical Div., Aberdeen Proving Ground, Md., 1965-86; chemist Chem. Rsch., Devel. and Engring. Ctr. SMCCR-Detection, Detection Technology, Aberdeen Proving Ground, 1986—; adv. com. Garrison Gents, Balt., 1980—; ACOR monitoring govt. contracts, Balt., 1987—. Contbr. articles to profl. publs. Mem. Okla. Hist. Soc. Mem. AAAS, N.Y. Acad. Sci., Okla. Hist. Soc. Office: CBDCOM-RTE Aberdeen Proving Ground MD 21010-5423

STEGER, WILLIAM MERRITT, federal judge; b. Dallas, Aug. 22, 1920; s. Merritt and Lottie (Reese) S.; m. Ann Hollandsworth, Feb. 14, 1948; 1 son, Merritt Reed (dec.). Student, Baylor U., 1938-41; LL.B., So. Meth. U., 1950. Bar: Tex. 1951. Pvt. practice Longview, 1951-53; apptd. U.S. dist. atty. Eastern Dist. Tex., 1953-59; mem. firm Wilson, Miller, Spivey & Steger, Tyler, Tex., 1959-70; U.S. dist. judge Ea. Dist. Tex. Tyler, 1970—. Republican candidate for gov. of Tex., 1960; for U.S. Ho. of Reps., 1962; mem. Tex. State Republican Exec. Com., 1966-69; chmn. Tex. State Republican Party, 1969-70. Pilot with ranks 2d lt. to capt. USAAF, 1942-47. Mem. ABA, State Bar Tex., Masons (32 degree, Shriner). Home: 801 Meadowcreek Dr Tyler TX 75703-3524 Office: US Courthouse PO Box 1109 Tyler TX 75710-1109

STEGMAN, MICHAEL ALLEN, city and regional planning educator; b. Bklyn., Oct. 12, 1940; s. Robert and Natalie (Ohrbach) S.; m. Nancy Weiss, Aug. 12, 1962; children—Laurie Michelle, Karen Jill. B.A. in Polit. Sci., Bklyn. Coll., 1962; M. City Planning, U. Pa., 1964, Ph.D. in City Planning, 1966. Asst. to assoc. prof. U. N.C., Chapel Hill, 1966-74; prof. city and regional planning U. N.C., 1974—, dept. chmn., 1983—; asst. sec. policy, devel. & rsch. HUD, Washington; dep. asst. sec. research HUD, Washington, 1979-81. Author: Housing Investment in the Inner City, 1972, Dynamics of Rental Housing in New York City, 1982, Housing in New York: Study of a City, 1985, Cases in Housing Finance and Public Policy; editor: Housing and Economics: The American Dilemma, 1971. Chmn. Mayor's Task Force on Human Services, Chapel Hill, N.C., 1982; mem. Housing Policy Com. Legis. Task Force on Housing, 1981-83; mem. Govs. Commn. on Housing Options for Older Adults, N.C., 1981; chmn. Chapel Hill Housing Authority, 1973-75, Chapel Hill Redevelopment Authority, 1971-73. Mem. Am. Planning Assn., Nat. Housing and Redevel. Ofcls., Nat. Low Income Housing Coalition. Office: HUD Policy Devel and Rsch 451 7th St SW Washington DC 20410 Office: Dept Housing & Urban Devel Policy Devel & Rsch 451 7th St SW Washington DC 20410-0001*

STEGMAYER, JOSEPH HENRY, housing industry executive; b. Teaneck, N.J., Jan. 4, 1951; s. Arthur Harry and Alicia (Ward) S.; m. Delene Russell. BS in Fin., U. Louisville, 1973. Spl. projects Worthington Industries Inc., Columbus, Ohio, 1973-75, dir. investor rels., 1975-77, dir. corp. rels., 1977-80, v.p. corp. devel., 1980-82, v.p., CFO, 1982-93, treas., 1983-93, also bd. dirs.; pres. Clayton Homes, Inc., Knoxville, Tenn., 1993—, also bd. dirs.; bd. dirs. Cardinal Funds Inc., Columbus, First Enterprise Fin. Group, Inc. Editor: We've Only Scratched the Surface, 1981. Chmn. YMCA, Columbus, 1981-83; pres. Columbus Zoo, 1987-90, chmn., 1990-93; bd. dirs. Muskingum Coll., 1984-93, Knoxville Zoo, Found. of Diocese of Columbus, United Way Knoxville; fin. chmn. Ronald McDonald House, Columbus; mem. chancellor's assocs. bd. U. Tenn. Named Citizen of Yr., Columbus Jaycees, 1984; recipient Outstanding Achievement in Fin. award Phi Beta Kappa, 1984. Mem. Fin. Execs. Inst., Knoxville C. of C. (bd. dirs.), Athletic Club, U. Tenn. Faculty Club. Roman Catholic. Avocations: scuba diving, travel, investing. Office: Clayton Homes Inc PO Box 15169 Knoxville TN 37901-5169

STEHLE, EDWARD RAYMOND, secondary education educator, school system administrator; b. Pitts., May 30, 1942; s. Edward August and Mary Josephine (Veverka) S.; m. Alberta McConnell; 1 child, Christian Dollison. BA, U. Pitts., 1964; MA, Columbia U., 1966, doctoral student, 1966-68. Instr. European history C.W. Post Coll., Long Island U., Greenville, N.Y., 1967-68, Middlebury (Vt.) Coll., 1968-69; history master The Lawrenceville Sch., Lawrenceville, N.J., 1969—, dir. day students, 1978-83, asst. dir. coll. counseling, 1983-88, chmn. history dept., 1988-94; asst. dir. The N.J. Scholars Program, Lawrenceville, 1981; vis. scholar Cambridge (Eng.) U., 1996; cons. U. Del. Sea Grant Coll., Newark, 1981-82; cons. on history of migrations Statue of Liberty-Ellis Island Found., N.Y.C., 1985-88; mem. selection com. Morris County (N.J.) Summer Opportunities for Tchrs. Program, Morristown, 1985-86; bd. mem. N.J. Scholars Program, Lawrenceville, 1988—; trustee Craftsbury Chamber Players, Greensboro, Vt., 1985-89; chmn. bd. N.J. Scholar Program, 1988-96. Co-author: A Guide to Programming in Basic Plus, 1975; contbr. Harper's Encyclopedia of the Modern World, 1972. Vice pres. Assoc. Mems., Ch. of Christ, Greensboro, 1974-76, pres., 1976-78. Mem. Am. Hist. Assn., Nassau Club (Princeton, N.J.), Mountainview Country Club (Greensboro, Vt.). Democrat. Episcopalian. Avocation: painting. Home: 2810 Main St Lawrenceville NJ 08648-1017 Office: The Lawrenceville Sch Main St Lawrenceville NJ 08620-2310

STEHLI, FRANCIS GREENOUGH, geologist, educator; b. Upper Montclair, N.J., Oct. 16, 1924; s. Edgar and Emily (Greenough) S.; m. Irene Comfort, June 19, 1948; children: Anne, Robert, John, Edgar. B.S., St. Lawrence U., 1949, M.S., 1950; Ph.D., Columbia U., 1953. Asst. prof. invertebrate paleontology Calif. Inst. Tech., 1953-56; tech. group supr. research dept. Am. Petroleum Corp., 1956-60; prof. geology, chmn. dept. Case Western Res. U., 1960-73, Samuel St. John prof. earth scis., 1973-80, acting dean sci., 1975, acting dean sci. and engring., 1976, dean sci. and engring., 1977-80; dean grad. studies and research U. Fla., Gainesville, 1980-82; dean Coll. Geoscis. U. Okla., Norman, 1982-86; chmn. sci. adv. com. DOSECC, Inc., 1986—; rsch. assoc. Archeol. Rsch. Team, 1993—; geol. cons., 1960—. Author articles in field. Served with USNR, 1943-46. Fellow Geol. Soc. Am., AAAS; mem. Geochem. Soc., Paleontol. Soc. (pres.), Am. Soc. Engring. Edn., No. Ohio Geol. Soc. Home: 11240 Stratford Ridge Dr Chardon OH 44024-8652 Office: 5561 SW 91st Ter Gainesville FL 32608-4369 also: Archeol Rsch Team 1519 NW 25 Terrace Gainesville FL 32605

STEHLIN, JOHN SEBASTIAN, JR., surgeon; b. Brownsville, Tenn., June 16, 1923; s. John Sebastian and Princess (King) S.; m. Mary Elizabeth Cleary, Sept. 19, 1950 (div. 1962); 1 child, Mary Cleary. Student, Vanderbilt U., 1941-42, Notre Dame U., 1943-44; M.D., Med. Coll. Wis., 1947. Diplomate: Am. Bd. Surgery. Intern Milw. Hosp., 1947-48; resident pathology Bapt. Hosp., Memphis, 1948-49; resident surgery Milw. Hosp., 1949-52; fellow surgery Lahey Clinic, Boston, 1952-53; sr. fellow surgery U. Tex., M.D. Anderson Hosp. and Tumor Inst., Houston, 1955-56; fellow surgery Lahey Clinic, Boston, 1956; mem. surg. staff U. Tex., M.D. Anderson Hosp. and Tumor Inst., Houston, 1957-67; asst. surgeon U. Tex., M.D. Anderson Hosp. and Tumor Inst., 1957-60, asso. surgeon, 1961-67; asst. prof. surgery U. Tex. Postgrad. Sch. Medicine, Houston, 1957-60; asso. prof. U. Tex. Postgrad. Sch. Medicine, 1961-63; asso. prof. surgery U. Tex. Postgrad. Sch. Medicine (Grad. Sch. Biomed. Scis.), 1963-67; clin. asso. prof. surgery Baylor Coll. Medicine, Houston, 1967—; mem. surg. staff St. Joseph Hosp., Houston, 1967—; hon. prof. faculty medicine U. Republic Uruguay, 1965; founder, sci. dir. Stehlin Found. Cancer Research, Houston, 1969—. Contbr. over 100 articles to sci. jours. Served to capt. USAF, 1953-55. Recipient humanitarian award B'nai B'rith, 1982; named to City of Houston Hall of Fame, 1985. Fellow ACS; mem. Am. Assn. Cancer Research, AAAS, AMA, Cancer Assn. Argentina (hon.), Cancer Soc. Chile (hon.), Internat. Platform Assn., Soc. Surg. Oncology, Inc., Pan Am. Med. Assn., Soc. Dermatology Uruguay (hon.), Surg. Soc. Chile (hon.), Royal Soc. Medicine, Western Surg. Assn., Southwestern Surg. Congress, So. Med. Assn., Tex. Med. Assn., Tex. Surg. Soc., N.Y. Acad. Scis., Salem Surg. Soc. (hon.), Phoenix Surg. Soc. (hon.), Harris County Med. Soc., Houston Surg. Soc., Am. Judicature Soc. Office: 1315 Calhoun St Ste 1800 Houston TX 77002-8232

STEHMAN, FREDERICK BATES, gynecologic oncologist, educator; b. Washington, July 20, 1946; s. Vernon Andrew and Elizabeth Coats (Bates) S.; m. Helen Sellinger, July 17, 1971; children—Christine Renee, Eileen Patricia, Andrea Kathleen, Lara Michelle. A.B., U. Mich., 1968, M.D., 1972. Diplomate Am. Bd. Ob-gyn. Resident in ob-gyn. U. Kans. Med. Ctr., Kansas City, 1972-75, resident in surgery, 1975-77; fellow in gynecol. oncology UCLA, 1977-79; asst. prof., attending staff Ind. U. Med. Ctr., Indpls., 1979-83, assoc. prof., 1983-87, prof., 1987—, chief gynecol. oncology, 1984-88, interim chmn., 1992-94, chair 1994—; chief ob-gyn service Wishard Meml. Hosp., Indpls., 1987-95. Author: (with B.J. Masterson and R.P. Carter) Gynecologic Oncology for Medical Students, 1975; also articles. Nat. Cancer Inst. grantee, 1981-89. Fellow Am. Coll. Obstetricians and Gynecologists, ACS (chpt. dir. 1984-92); mem. AMA, Am. Soc. Clin. Oncology, Am. Cancer Soc., Am. Gynecology and Obstetrics Soc., Ind. Med. Assn., Assn. Profs. Gynecology and Obstetrics, Central Assn. Obstetricians and Gynecologists, Gynecol. Oncology Group, K.E. Krantz Soc., Marion County Med. Soc., Soc. Gynecol. Oncologists, Western Assn. Gynecol. Oncologists, Phi Chi. Office: Ind U Med Ctr 550 University Blvd # 2440 Uh Indianapolis IN 46202-5149

STEHN, LORRAINE STRELNICK, physician; b. Richmond, Ind., Aug. 27, 1950; d. Daniel H. and Eleanor Gayle (Robertson) Strelnick; m. Thomas Veasey Stehn, June 16, 1973; children—Alexander Veasey, Andrew Thomas. BA, Carleton Coll., 1972; DO, Coll. Osteo. Medicine and Surgery, 1976. Diplomate Am. Bd. Family Practice. Intern, Pontiac Osteo. Hosp., Mich., 1976-77; vol. med. officer U.S. Peace Corps, Swaziland, 1977-79; resident in family practice St. Mary's Hosp., Port Arthur, Tex., 1980-82; family practice osteo. medicine, Aransas Pass, Tex., 1982—; med. adv. Christian Service Ctr., Aransas Pass, 1983—; chief staff Coastal Bend Hosp., Aransas Pass, 1985, 90, 95. Pres. bd. dirs. Corpus Christi (Tex.) Chorale, 1995-96. Recipient Service award Aransas Pass Jr. High 1984. Fellow Am. Acad. Family Practice (pres. bd. dirs. profl. counseling services); mem. Tex. Med. Assn. Democrat. Home: 1613 S Saunders St Aransas Pass TX 78336-3107

STEIB, JAMES TERRY, bishop; b. May 17, 1940. Ordained priest Roman Cath. Ch., 1967. Titular bishop Fallaba, 1983; aux. bishop St. Louis, 1983; consecrated bishop, 1984; bishop Diocese of Mempis, 1993—. Address: Diocese of Memphis PO Box 341669 Memphis TN 38134-1669

STEIER, MICHAEL EDWARD, cardiac surgeon; b. N.Y.C., Mar. 22, 1942; s. Philip and Gertrude S.; m. Sheila Elaine Finkelstein, June 9, 1963; children: Douglas, James, Lauren. BA, Long Island U., 1964; MD, Univ. Health Scis., Chgo., 1968. Resident in gen. surgery St. Vincent's Hosp., N.Y.C., 1969-73; resident in thoracic surgery Mayo Clinic, Rochester, Minn., 1973-75; cardiac surgeon S.W. Fla. Regional Med. Ctr., Ft. Myers, Fla., 1975—, Lee Meml. Hosp., Ft. Myers, 1975—, Cape Coral (Fla.) Hosp., 1977—, Naples (Fla.) Cmty. Hosp., 1996—; chief surgery, S.W. Fla. Regional Med. Ctr., Ft. Myers, 1980-82, pres. med. staff, 1982; cons. Naples Cmty. Hosp., 1996—. Fellow Am. Coll. Surgeons, Am. Coll. Chest Physicians, Am. Coll. Cardiology; mem. Soc. for Thoracic Surgeons, N.Y. Acad. Scis., Cardiac Surg. Assn. S.W. Fla. (pres. 1993—), Explorers Club. Office: Cardiac Surgical Assocs SW Fla 2675 Winkler Ave Fort Myers FL 33901-9342

STEIGBIGEL, ROY THEODORE, infectious disease physician and scientist, educator; b. Bklyn., Nov. 23, 1941; s. Samuel and Lillian I. (Parker) S.; m. Julia Ann Enterline, June 10, 1967 (div. 1983), children: Keith D., Glenn N.; m. Sidonie Ann Morrison, Oct. 15, 1985; 1 child, Andrew M. BA, Carleton Coll., 1962; MD, U. Rochester, 1966. Diplomate Am. Bd. Internal Medicine, Am. Bd. Infectious Disease. Resident U. Rochester, N.Y., 1966-68; resident Stanford U., Palo Alto, Calif., 1970-71, fellow, 1971-73; from asst. to assoc. prof. U. Rochester, N.Y., 1973-83; prof. SUNY, Stony Brook, 1983—; mem. adv. bd. infectious disease U.S. Pharmacopea, Rockville, Md., 1980—; mem. adv. panels NIH, Bethesda, Md., 1985-87. Contbr. over 10 chpts. to books and over 95 articles to profl. jours. Served in USPHS, 1968-70. Fellow NIH, 1971-73, grantee, 1985—. Fellow ACP, Infectious Disease Soc. Am. Office: SUNY Stony Brook School of Medicine HSC-T-15-080 Stony Brook NY 11794-8153

STEIGER, DALE ARLEN, publishing executive; b. LaCrosse, Wis., May 14, 1928; s. Walter Elmer and Doris Adeline (Howe) S.; m. Alyce Ann Dyrdahl, Oct. 8, 1949; children: Christine Ann, Marta Louise. Student U. Wis., LaCrosse, 1945-46, 48-49; BA, Chgo. Acad. Fine Arts, 1951; postgrad. Drake U., 1958-62, Iona Coll., 1968. Art dir. Trane Co., LaCrosse, 1955, Look mag., Des Moines, 1956, promotions mgr. Cowles Subscription div., 1957-67, exec. v.p. Cowles Communications subdiv., 1960-71; v.p. mktg., asso. pub. Curtis Publs. Co., N.Y.C., 1971-72; pres. Dale Steiger Assocs., N.Y.C., 1972—, Blue Ribbon Reading Svc., Rye, N.Y., 1979, DASCO, Darien, Conn., 1991; pres., pub. Videofinder mag., 1981—, Pulling mag., 1981—; pres. SUBCO, 1986; chmn. Hair and Beauty Inc.; pub. Hair and Beauty News, 1988—; chief exec. officer Mktg. Group SMC Publs.; pres., chief exec. officer DASCO, Inc., Darien, Conn.; lectr. direct mail and mktg. Author: (with others) The Handbook of Circulation Management, 1980. Served with AUS, 1946-48. Recipient Industry Achievement award Fulfillment Mgmt. Assn., 1979; Lee C. Williams award for outstanding contbns. to periodical pub. field, 1982. Mem. Mag. Publs. Assn., Audit Bur. Circulations, Fulfillment Mgmt. Assn. (pres., chmn. bd.), Nat. Soc. Art Dirs., VFW, Am. Legion, Cornell Club, Westchester Country Club. Republican. Presbyterian (elder).

STEIGER, GRETCHEN HELENE, marine mammalogist, research biologist; b. Williamsport, Pa., May 7, 1960; d. Robert Folk and Helene (Moltz) S.; m. John Calambokidis, July 29, 1989; 1 child, Alexei Steiger Calambokidis. BS in Zoology, U. N.C., 1982. Rsch. biologist Cascadia Rsch. Collective, Olympia, Wash., 1982—, also bd. dirs.; pres. Cascadia Rsch., 1988—; whale census technician, Barrow, Alaska, 1988; rsch. assoc. U. Alaska, Fairbanks, 1991; presenter in field. Author (with others) numerous govt. reports and publs.; contbr. articles to profl. jours. Instr. Feminists Self-def. Tng., Olympia, 1984-92. Mem. Soc. Northwestern Vertebrate Biology, Soc. Marine Mammalogy (charter), Wildlife Soc. (Wash. chpt.). Office: Cascadia Research Collective 218 1/2 4th Ave W Olympia WA 98501-1004

STEIGER, JANET DEMPSEY, government official; b. Oshkosh, Wis., June 10, 1939; 1 child, William Raymond. BA, Lawrence Coll., 1961; postgrad., U. Reading, Eng., 1961-62, U. Wis., 1962-63; LLD (hon.), Lawrence U., 1992. Legis. aide Office of Gov., Wis., 1965; v.p. The Work Place, Inc., 1975-80; commr. Postal Rate Commn., Washington, 1980-89, acting chmn., 1981-82, chmn., 1982-89; commr. FTC, Washington, 1989—; U.S. del. OECD, Paris, 1989—. Author: Law Enforcement and Juvenile Justice in Wisconsin, 1965; co-author: To Light One Candle, a Handbook on Organizing, Funding and Maintaining Public Service Projects, 1978, 2d edit., 1980. Chmn. Commn. on Vets. Edn. Policy, 1987-90. Woodrow Wilson scholar; Fulbright scholar, 1961. Mem. Phi Beta Kappa. Office: FTC Office of Chmn 6th & Pennsylvania Ave NW Washington DC 20580-0002*

STEIGER, PAUL ERNEST, newspaper editor, journalist; b. N.Y.C., Aug. 15, 1942; s. Ernest and Mary Agnes (Walsh) S.; children: Erika Maren, Laura Arlene, Isabelle Amanda, William Ernest. B.A., Yale U., 1964. Staff reporter Wall Street Jour., San Francisco, 1966-68; asst. mng. editor Wall Street Jour., N.Y.C., 1983-85, dep. mng. editor, 1985-92, mng. editor, 1991—, also v.p.; bus. writer Los Angeles Times, 1968-71, econ. corr. Washington bur., 1971-78, bus. editor L.A., 1978-83. Co-author: The 70's Crash, 1970. Recipient G.M. Loeb award UCLA, 1971, 74, 78, John Hancock award, 1971. Office: Wall Street Journal Dow Jones & Co Inc 200 Liberty St New York NY 10281-1003*

STEIGERWALDT, DONNA WOLF, clothing manufacturing company executive; b. Chgo., Apr. 2, 1929; d. Harry Hay and Donna (Currey) Wolf; m. William Steigerwaldt, Dec. 31, 1969; children: Debra, Linda. BA, U. Colo., Colo. Springs, 1950, LHD (hon.), 1987. Ins. broker Conn. Mut. Life Ins. Co., Chgo., 1950-53; vice chmn. Jockey Internat., Inc., Kenosha, Wis., 1978-80, chmn., chief exec. officer, 1980—. Pres. Donna Wolf Steigerwaldt Found., Inc.; mem. Infant Welfare Soc., Evanston Hosp.-Glenbrook Hosp. Corp., N.W. Cmty. Hosp. Aux., Aid to Animals No. Ill., Inc.; vice chmn. Carthage Coll., 1982-92, chmn., 1992—. Paul Harris fellow, Rotary, 1984. Mem. Am. Apparel Mfrs. Assn., Navy League U.S., Glenview Hist. Soc., Exec. Women Internat. (hon.), Rotary (Paul Harris fellow 1984). Republican. Epsicopalian. Clubs: North Shore Country, Plaza, Valley Lo Sports; Meadows Country (Sarasota, Fla.). Office: Jockey Internat Inc PO Box 1417 2300 60th St Kenosha WI 53140-3822

STEIGMAN, ANDREW L., academic dean; b. N.Y.C., Aug. 30, 1933; s. Nathan and Sarah (Levine) S.; m. Meryl Fialka, June 20, 1959; children: Daria H., Jonathan S. AB summa cum laude, Princeton U., 1954; postgrad., London Sch. Econs., 1954-55, Am. U., Washington, 1958-60. Fgn. svc. officer Dept. State, various locations, 1958-69; first sec. Dept. State, U.S. Embassy, Paris, 1969-72; polit. counselor Dept. State, U.S. Embassy, Lagos, Nigeria, 1972-75; U.S. ambassador to Gabon Dept. State, U.S. Embassy, Libreville, Gabon, 1975-77; dir. nat. intelligence tasking office Intelligence Community Staff, Washington, 1978-80; dep. asst. sec. for personnel Dept. State, Washington, 1981-84; asst. dean/prof. internat. relations Georgetown U., Washington, 1985—; vis. fellow Woodrow Wilson Fellowship Found., Princeton, 1987-93; mem. edn. com. Atlantic Council, Washington, 1989—. Author: The Foreign Service of the United States, 1985. With U.S. Army, 1955-57. Wilbur Carr award, U.S. Dept. State, 1985. Mem. Am. Polit. Sci. Assn., Am. Hist. Assn., Am. Fgn. Svc. Assn., Phi Beta Kappa. Avocation: philately. Office: Georgetown U Sfs Icc # 301 Washington DC 20057

STEIGMAN, CARMEN KAY, pathologist; b. Dallas, May 14, 1956; d. Walter Benjamin and Margaret Louise (Patton) S. BS, N.E. La. U., 1977; MD, La. State U., 1983; MPH, St. Louis U., 1994. Diplomate Am. Bd. Pathology; cert. anatomic, clin. and pediatric pathology. Pathology resident Fairfax Hosp., Falls Church, Va., 1983-87; pediatric pathology fellow Children's Hosp. of Phila., 1987-89; pathologist Sparrow Hosp., Lansing, Mich., 1989-90; asst. prof. pathology St. Louis U. Sch. Medicine, 1990-96; pathologist Cardinal Glennon Childrens Hosp., 1990-96; dir. Pub. Health Lab. City of St. Louis Dept. Health and Hosps., 1996—. Fellow Coll. Am. Pathologists; mem. Soc. for Pediatric Pathology, Am. Assn. Clin. Chemistry, Am. Coll. Physician Execs., Am. Pathology Found. Office: Pub Health Lab 634 N Grand Blvd Saint Louis MO 63103-1002

STEIL, GEORGE KENNETH, SR., lawyer; b. Darlington, Wis., Dec. 16, 1924; s. George John and Laura (Donahoe) S.; m. Mavis Elaine Andrews, May 24, 1947; children: George Kenneth, John R., MIchelle Steil Bryski, Marcelaine Steil-Zimmermann. Student, Platteville State Tchrs. Coll., 1942-43; JD, U. Wis., Madison, 1950. Bar: Wis. 1950, U.S. Tax Ct. 1971, U.S. Dist. Ct. (western dist.) Wis. 1950. Assoc. J. G. McWilliams, Janesville, 1950-53; ptnr. McWilliams and Steil, Janesville, 1954-60, Brennan, Steil, Ryan, Basting & MacDougall (S.C., and predecessor), Janesville, 1960-72; pres. Brennan, Steil, Basting & MacDougall (S.C., and predecessor), 1972—; lectr. law U. Wis., 1974; bd. dirs. Heritage Mut. Ins. Co., Sheboygan, Wis., Blain Supply Inc., Blain's Farm & Fleet Stores; trustee, bd. dirs. Roman Cath. Diocese of Madison; mem. Wis. Supreme Ct. Bd. Atty. Profl. Responsibility, 1982-87, chmn., 1984-87; chmn. Gov.'s Adv. Coun. Jud. Selection, State of Wis., 1987-92; chmn. Wis. Lottery Bd., 1987-90. Bd. dirs. St. Coletta Sch. for Exceptional Children, Jefferson, Wis., 1972-76, 78-84, 86-89, chmn., 1982-83; bd. regents U. Wis., 1990—, pres., 1992-94; bd. dirs. U. Wis. Hosp. Authority, 1996—, U. Wis. Med. Fround., 1996—. Recipient Disting. Svc. award U. Wis. Law Alumni, 1991. Fellow Am. Bar Found. (life), Am. Coll. Trust and Estate Counsel; mem. ABA, Jamesville Area C. of C. (pres. 1970-71), State Bar Wis. (pres. 1977-78), Wis. Bar Found. (bd. dirs. 1976—, Charles L. Goldberg Disting. Svc. award 1990). Roman Catholic. Home: 2818 Cambridge Ct Janesville WI 53545-2797 Office: Brennan Steil Basting & MacDougall 1 E Milwaukee St Janesville WI 53545-3011

STEILEN, JAMES R., lawyer; b. Mitchell, S.D., Apr. 17, 1949; s. Ronald and Gladys M. (Aulner) S.; m. Carol Jane Scoonover, June 6, 1970; children: Matthew, Jennifer, Katherine, Daniel. BA, U. Iowa, 1971; JD, Harvard U., 1974. Bar: Minn. 1974. Shareholder Popham, Haik, Schnobrich & Kaufman Ltd., Mpls., 1974—. Capt. U.S. Army, 1971-76. Mem. Wayzata Country Club. Office: Popham Haik Schnobrich & Kaufman Ltd 3300 Piper Jaffray Tower 222 S 9th St Minneapolis MN 55402-3389

STEIN, ALLAN MARK, lawyer; b. Montreal, Quebec, Can., Oct. 18, 1951; came to U.S., 1977; s. Boris and Beatrice (Fishman) S. B in Commerce, Sir George Williams, 1972; BA, Loyola, Montreal, 1973; B in Civil Law, McGill U., 1976, LLB, 1977; JD, Nova U., 1979. Bar: Fla. 1979, U.S. Dist. Ct. (so. dist.) Fla. 1979, U.S. Ct. Appeals (5th cir.) 1980, U.S. Ct. Appeals (11th cir.) 1983, U.S. Dist. Ct. Ariz. 1993. Assoc. Law Offices of Paul Landy Beiley, Miami, Fla., 1980, Heitner & Rosenfeld, Miami, 1980-85, Rosenfeld & Stein, Miami, 1985-90, Rosenfeld, Stein & Sugarman, Miami, 1990-94, Rosenfeld & Stein P.A., Miami, 1994—. Mem. North Dade Bar Assn. (bd. dirs. 1985-90). Republican. Jewish. Avocation: photography. Office: 18260 NE 19th Ave Ste 202 Miami FL 33162-1632

STEIN, BARRY EDWARD, medical educator. Prof. dept. physiology Med. Coll. Va.-Va. Commonwealth U., Richmond, 1982-94, affil. prof., 1994—; prof., chmn. dept. neurobiology and anatomy Bowman Gray Sch. Medicine-Wake Forest U., Winston-Salem, N.C., 1994—; bd. trustees The Gwendolyn Hardy Williams and Oliver Williams Found., Inc., 1992—; lectr. in field. Co-author: The Merging of the Senses, 1993; contbr. chpts. to books including The Cognotive Neurosciences, 1995, Electrophysiology of Vision, 1991, The Development of Intersensory Perception: Comparative Perspectives, 1994, others; contbr. numerous articles to profl. pubs. including Experimental Neurology, Jour. Experimental Psychology, Vision Rsch., others; mem. editl. bd. Somatosensory and Motor Rsch., Jour. Cognitive Neuroscience, The Behavioral and Brain Sciences. Home: 1825 Georgia Ave Winston Salem NC 27104 Office: Bowman Gray Sch Med Anatomy and Neurobiology Med Ctr Blvd Winston Salem NC 27157-1010*

STEIN, BENNETT MUELLER, neurosurgeon; b. N.Y.C., Feb. 2, 1931; s. Walter Charles and Marjorie Clare (Bennett) S.; m. Doreen Holmes, May 28, 1955 (dec. 1984); children: Susan, Marjorie; m. Bonita Soontit, Sept. 19, 1987; 1 child, Bennett Charles. A.B., Dartmouth Coll., 1952; M.D., C.M., McGill U., Montreal, Que., Can., 1955. Diplomate: Am. Bd. Neurol. Surgery, Nat. Bd. Med. Examiners. Rotating intern U.S. Naval Hosp., St. Albans, N.Y., 1955-56; Fulbright scholar Inst. Neurology, Nat. Hosp., London, 1958-59; asst. resident in surgery Presbyn. Hosp., N.Y.C., 1959-60; asst. resident in neurosurgery Presbyn. Hosp., 1960-63, chief resident, 1963-64; spl. fellow neuroanatomy Nat. Inst. Neurol. Diseases and Blindness, 1964-66; asso. in neurol. Surgery Columbia U. Coll. Phys. and Surgeons, 1964-68, mem. faculty, 1968—, Byron Stookey prof. neurol. surgery, 1980-96; dir. service neurol. surgery Presbyn. Hosp., 1980-96; prof. neurol. surgery, chmn. dept. Tufts-New Eng. Med. Center, Boston, 1971-80; dir. Am. Bd. Neurol. Surgeons, 1988—. Author articles in field; mem. editorial bds. profl. jours. Served as officer M.C. USNR, 1956-58. Fellow A.C.S.; mem. Am. Assn. Anatomists, AMA, Acad. Neurol. Surgeons, Congress Neurol. Surgeons, Am. Assn. Neurol. Surgeons, Am. Acad. Neurol. Surgeons, Soc. Neurol. Surgeons, Cajal Club, Brazilian Neurol. Soc. (corr.), N.Y. State Neurosurg. Soc., New Eng. Neurosurg. Soc., Mass. Med. Soc., Boston Surg. Soc., Boston Soc. Psychiatry and Neurology, Sigma Xi, Alpha Omega Alpha, Alpha Kappa Kappa. Lutheran. Office: Presbyn Hosp Columbia-Presbyn Med Ctr 710 W 168th St New York NY 10032-2603

STEIN, BERNARD, stockbroker; b. N.Y.C., Nov. 24, 1913; s. Abraham and Fannie (Zoob) S.; m. Marion Charlotte Holtsberg, Feb. 24, 1946; children: Robert Frederick, Ellen Frances (Mrs. Howard Lazarus). Student, Sch. Commerce, NYU, 1930-32. Ptnr. firm Ralph E. Samuel & Co., N.Y.C., 1947-70, Neuberger & Berman, Inc., 1970—; sr. v.p., treas., dir. Energy Fund, N.Y.C., 1962-80, pres., 1980-91, dir. emeritus; former vice chmn. Neuberger & Berman Mgmt. Co., N.Y.C. Served with USAAF, 1942-45. Clubs: Quaker Ridge Golf (Scarsdale); Beach Point (Mamaroneck, N.Y.). Home: 8 Split Tree Rd Scarsdale NY 10583-7900 Office: Neuberger & Berman 605 3rd Ave New York NY 10158

STEIN, BERNARD ALVIN, business consultant; b. Winnipeg, Can., June 4, 1923; s. Herman Louis and Rebecca (Harris) S.; m. Dorothy Lock, Jan. 1, 1942; 1 dau., Marilynn Stein Lakein. Vice-pres. food drug div. Giant Food, Inc., Washington, 1951-69; v.p., gen. mgr. Read Drug Stores, Balt., 1969-70; pres. Scotty Stores div. Sav-A-Stop, Jacksonville, Fla., 1970-71; pres., gen. mgr. Liberal Markets, Dayton, Ohio, 1971-72; pres. Pueblo Supermarkets, San Juan, P.R., 1972-74, Hills Supermarkets, Brentwood, N.Y., 1974-75, Allied Supermarkets, Detroit, 1976-78, Chatham Supermarkets, Detroit, 1978-81; CEO Network Assocs., Chgo., 1981-92; bus. cons. Balt., 1992—. Mem. Presdl. Com. for Emergency Food Controls, 1969. Served with USAAF, 1943-45. Decorated Air medal. Home: 43 Stone Pine Ct Baltimore MD 21208 Office: 43 Stone Pine Ct Baltimore MD 21208-1038

STEIN, DALE FRANKLIN, retired university president; b. Kingston, Minn., Dec. 24, 1935; s. David Frank and Zelda Jane S.; m. Audrey Dean Bloemke, June 7, 1958; children—Pam, Derek. B.S. in Metallurgy, U. Minn., 1958; Ph.D., Rensselaer Poly. Inst., Troy, N.Y., 1963. Metallurgist rsch. lab. GE, Schnectady, N.Y., 1958-67; assoc. prof. U. Minn., 1967-71; prof. metall. engring., head dept. Mich. Technol. U., Houghton, 1971-77; head mining engring. Mich. Technol. U., 1974-77, v.p. acad. affairs, 1977-79, pres., 1979-91; pres. emeritus, 1991—; cons. NSF, Dept. of Energy, 1972-90; trustee Rensselaer Poly. Inst., 1989-95; chmn. com. on decontamination and decommissioning uranium enrichment facilities NRC, 1993-96; active Nat. Materials Adv. Bd., 1987-93; chmn. adv. com. Ctr. for Nuclear Waste Regulatory Analyses. Contbr. articles to profl. jours. Paul Harris fellow. Fellow Metall. Soc. (pres. 1979, inst. Hardy Gold medal 1965), Am. Soc. Metals (Geisler award Eastern N.Y. chpt. 1967); mem. AIME, AAAS, NAE, Sigma Xi, Phi Kappa Phi, Tau Beta Pi, Alpha Sigma Nu.

STEIN, DAVID FRED, investment executive; b. N.Y.C., May 17, 1940; s. William Howard and Phoebe Louise (Hockstader) S.; m. Susan Vail Beresford, June 17, 1963 (div. 1970); 1 child, Jeremy Vail; m. Ellen Gail Cohen, Sept. 16, 1973; children: Katharine Ellen, Nicholas David. BA, Harvard U., 1962; MBA, Harvard Grad. Sch. Bus. Adminstrn., 1965. Assoc. Bache & Co., N.Y.C., 1965-68; assoc., then gen. ptnr. Kuhn Loeb & Co., N.Y.C., 1969-77; mng. dir. Lehman Brothers Kuhn Loeb, N.Y.C., 1977-83, Shearson Lehman Am. Express, N.Y.C., 1983-86; sr. exec. v.p., dir. Am. Express Bank, N.Y.C., 1986-87; mng. dir. Shearson Lehman Hutton, N.Y.C., 1987-89; mng. dir., mem. exec. com. The Stamford Co., N.Y.C., 1989-90; mng. dir. J & W Seligman & Co., N.Y.C., 1990-96; vice chmn., 1997—; co-chmn. Seligman, Henderson Co., N.Y.C., 1991—; mem. Internat. Com. of Nat. Assn. Security Dealers, 1970-85. Trustee P.R. Traveling Theatre, N.Y.C., 1970-72, Altro Health and Rebab. Ctr., Bronx, N.Y., 1975-82, Blythedale Children's Hosp., Valhalla, N.Y., 1977—, Montefiore Med. Ctr., Bronx, 1990—; trustee, chmn. fin. com. Riverdale Country Sch., Bronx, 1988—; mem. Coun. on Fgn. Rels. With U.S. Army, 1962-63. Mem. Century Country Club (Purchase, N.Y.), River Club (N.Y.C.), Harvard Club (N.Y.C.), Edgartown (Mass.) Yacht Club, Mill Reef Club (Antigua, B.V.I.), Chappaquiddick Beach Club (Edgartown). Democrat. Avocations: reading, sailing, fishing, skiing. Home: 875 Park Ave New York NY 10021-0341 Office: J & W Seligman 100 Park Ave New York NY 10017-5516

STEIN, ELLIOT, JR., media executive; b. St. Louis, Jan. 31, 1949; s. Elliot and Mary Ann (Bleiweiss) S. BA, Claremont McKenna Coll., 1971. Assoc. Lehman Bros., N.Y.C., 1972-79; chmn. Caribbean Internat. News Corp., San Juan, P.R., 1985—; ptnr. Commonwealth Capital Ptnrs., N.Y.C., 1988—, TCS TV Ptnrs., LP, N.Y.C., 1990—; Bd. dirs. ACX Pacific, Inc., Softplay, Inc., Horizon Music, Inc., Capital USA, Inc., Alliance Tech. Fund, Inc. Trustee Claremont U. Ctr., 1980—, New Sch. Social Rsch., 1990—; dir. Citizens Budget Commn., 1991—; active Coun. Fgn. Rels., 1990—, Found. Econ. Trends, 1990—. Democrat. Office: Commonwealth Capital Ptnrs 444 Madison Ave New York NY 10022-6903

STEIN, ERIC, retired law educator; b. Holice, Czechoslovakia, July 8, 1913; came to U.S., 1940, naturalized, 1943; s. Zikmund and Hermina (Zalud) S.; m. Virginia Elizabeth Rhine, July 30, 1955. JUD, Charles U., Prague, Czechoslovakia, 1937; JD, U. Mich., 1942; Dr. honoris causa, Vrije U., Brussels, 1978, U. Libre, Brussels, 1979. Bar: Ill. 1946, D.C. 1953. Practiced law Prague, 1937; with State Dept., 1946-55; acting dep. dir. Office UN Polit. Affairs, 1955; mem. faculty U. Mich. Law Sch., Ann Arbor, 1956, prof. internat. law and orgn., 1958-76; Hessel E. Yntema prof. law U. Mich. Law Sch., 1976-83, emeritus prof., 1983—; co-dir. internat. legal studies, 1958-76, dir., 1976-81; vis. prof. Stanford Law Sch., 1956, 77, Law Faculties, Stockholm, Uppsala and Lund, Sweden, 1969, Inst. Advanced Legal Studies U. London, 1975, U. Ariz., 1991, 92; lectr. Hague Acad. Internat. Law, summer 1971; vis. lectr. European U. Inst., Florence, Italy, 1983, Beijing, Shanghai, Wuhan, 1986, U. Tokyo, Kyoto, 1986, Coll. of Europe, Bruges, Pontificia, Madrid, 1988; Jean Monnet prof. European U. Inst., Florence, Italy, 1991, Henry Morris lectr. Kent Coll. of Law, Chgo., 1992, Jeanne Kiewit Taylor disting. vis. lectr. U. Ariz., winter 1993; adviser U.S. delegation UN Gen. Assembly, 1947-55; mem. adv. panel, cons. Bur. European Affairs, State Dept., 1966-73; cons. U.S. rep. for trade negotiations, 1979; vice chmn. com. Atlantic studies Atlantic Inst., 1966-68; mem. adv. council Inst. European Studies, Free U., Brussels, Belgium, 1965-70; mem. U.S. Com. for Legal Edn. Exchange with China, 1983-91; lectr. Acad. of European Law, Florence, Italy 1990. Author: (with others) American Enterprise in the European Common Market-A Legal Profile, vols. I, II, 1960, (with H.K. Jacobson) Diplomats, Scientists and Politicians: The United States and the Nuclear Test Ban Negotiations, 1966, Harmonization of European Company Law: National Reform and Transnational Coordination, 1971, Impact of New Weapons Technology on International Law-Selected Aspects, 1971, Un Nuovo Diritto per l'Europa, 1991; editor: (with Peter Hay) Law and Institutions in the Atlantic Area Readings, Cases and Problems, 1967, (with Peter Hay and Michel Waelbroeck) European Community Law and Institutions in Perspective, 1976; co-author, co-editor: Courts and Free Markets-Perspectives From the United States and Europe, 1982; bd. editors: Am. Jour. Internat. Law, 1965—; mem. adv. bd. Common Market Law Rev., 1964—, Legal Issues of European Integration, 1974—, Rivista di Diritto Europeo, 1978—, Columbia Jour. East European Law, 1994—, Columbia Jour. European Law, 1994—; contbr. articles to profl. jours. Mem. Internat. Com. for Revision Czechoslovak Constn., 1990-92. With AUS, 1943-46. Decorated Bronze Star, Order Italian Crown, Italian Mil. Cross; Guggenheim fellow, 1962-63; Social Sci. Rsch. Coun. grantee; Rockefeller Found. scholar-in-residence, 1965, 73; Alexander von Humboldt Stiftung awardee, 1982; fellow Inst. Advanced Study, Berlin, 1984-85, IREX rsch. grant, 1995. Mem. ABA (co-chmn. European law com. 1982, mem. coun. sect. on internat. law and practice 1983-84), Internat. Law Assn., Coun. Fgn. Rels., Am. Soc. Internat. Law (exec. coun. 1954-57, bd. rev. and devel. 1965-67, 70-75, hon. v.p. 1982—), Brit. Inst. Internat. and Comparative Law, Internat. Acad. Comparative Law (assoc.). Home: 2649 Heatherway St Ann Arbor MI 48104-2850

STEIN, GARY S., state supreme court associate justice; b. Newark, June 13, 1933; s. Morris J. and Mollie (Goldfarb) S.; married, July 1, 1956; children—Jill, Carrie, Michael, Terri, Jo; m. Et Tilchin, July 1, 1956. A.B., Duke U., 1954, LL.B. with distinction, 1956; D.H.L. (hon.), N.J. Inst. Tech., 1985. Bar: D.C. 1956, Ohio 1957, N.Y. 1958, N.J. 1963. Research asst. U.S. Senate AntiTrust and Monopoly Subcom., Washington, 1955; assoc. Kramer, Marx, Greenlee & Backus, N.Y.C., 1956-65; sole practice Paramus, N.J., 1966-72; ptnr. Stein & Kurland, Esquires, Paramus, N.J., 1972-82; dir. Gov.'s Office of Policy and Planning, Trenton, N.J., 1982-85; assoc. justice Supreme Ct. N.J., Hackensack, 1985—; mcpl. atty., Paramus, 1967-71; counsel N.J. Election Law Revision Commn., 1970; atty. Bd. Adjustment, Teaneck, N.J., 1973-82. Mem. editorial bd. Duke Law Jour., 1954-56, assoc. editor, 1955-56. Mem. Dist. Ethics Com. for Bergen County, N.J., 1977-80, chmn. 1981. Served with U.S. Army, 1957-58, 61-62. Mem. ABA, N.J. State Bar Assn. (com. on state legislation 1973-79, chmn. 1973-76, jud. selection com. 1976-81, Constl. amendment com. 1977-79, court modernization com. 1976-79), Bergen County Bar Assn., Order of Coif. Jewish. Avocation: tennis. Office: NJ Supreme Ct 25 Main St Hackensack NJ 07601-7015

STEIN, GEORGE HENRY, historian, educator, administrator; b. Vienna, Austria, May 18, 1934; came to U.S., 1939, naturalized, 1948; m. Dorothy Ann Lahm, Nov. 22, 1963; 1 child, Kenneth. B.A. with honors (N.Y. State Regents scholar), Bklyn. Coll., 1959; M.A. in History (Regents fellow), Columbia U., 1960, Ph.D. in History (Pres.'s fellow), 1964. Lectr. history City Coll., CUNY, 1962-63; instr. dept. history Columbia U., N.Y.C., 1963-65; asst. prof. Columbia U., 1965-66; assoc. prof. dept. history SUNY-Binghamton, 1966-70, prof., 1970—, disting. teaching prof., 1973—, vice chmn. grad. affairs, 1974-76, v.p. acad. affairs, 1976-87, provost, 1985-87, acting pres., 1986-87; manuscript evaluator and cons. to numerous publishers, 1964—. Author: The Waffen SS: Hitler's Elite Guard at War, 1939-45, 1966, paperback edit., 1984 (transl. into German, 1967, French, 1967, Spanish, 1973, Portuguese, 1970); contbr. articles on modern European history to scholarly publs.; editor: Hitler, 1968; contbr. book revs. to hist. jours. Served with USAF, 1953-57. NEH fellow, 1970-71. Mem. Am. Hist. Assn. (mem. conf. group on cen. European history, conf. group for use of psychology in history), Acad. Polit. Sci., Assn. of Contemporary Historians, Am. Assn. Higher Edn., Nat. Assn. State Univs. and Land Grant Colls. (mem. council acad. affairs 1976-87), Am. Counc. Edn. (exec. com. nat. coun. chief acad. officers 1983-85), Com. Internat. d'Histoire de la Deuxieme Guerre Mondiale (mem. Am. com. on history of WWII). Office: SUNY Dept History Binghamton NY 13901

STEIN, HERBERT, economist; b. Detroit, Aug. 27, 1916; s. David and Jessie (Segal) S.; m. Mildred Fishman, June 12, 1937; children: Rachel (Epstein), Benjamin. AB, Williams Coll., 1935, LLD (hon.), 1980; PhD, U. Chgo., 1958; LLD (hon.), Rider Coll., 1971, Hartford U., 1973, Roanoke Coll., 1984, New Haven U., 1987, Hofstra U., 1994. Economist FDIC, 1938-40, Nat. Def. Adv. Commn., 1940-41, WPB, 1941-44, Office War Moblzn. and Reconversion, 1945; economist Com. Econ. Devel., 1945-48, assoc. dir. research, 1948-56, dir. research, 1956-66, v.p., chief economist, 1966-67; sr. fellow Brookings Instn., 1967-69; mem. Pres.'s Council Econ. Advisers, Washington, 1969-72; chmn. Pres.'s Council Econ. Advisers, 1972-74; A. Willis Robertson prof. econs. U. Va., Charlottesville, 1974-84; weekly columnist The Economy Today, Scripps-Howard and other newpapers, 1974-80; bd. contbrs. Wall St. Jour., 1974—; cons. Congl. Budget Office, 1976-89; mem. Adv. Com. Nat. Growth Policy Processes, 1976-77, Pharm. Reimbursement Adv. Bd., 1976-77; adj. scholar Am. Enterprise Inst., 1975-77, sr. fellow, 1977—; cons. U.S. Dept. State, 1983-92; mem. Pres.'s Econ. Policy Adv. Bd., 1981-89; mem. Pres.'s Blue Ribbon Commn. on Def. Mgmt., 1985-86. Author: U.S. Government Price Policy during the World War, 1938, (with de Chazeau, Hart, Means, Myers, Yntema) Jobs and Markets, 1946, The Fiscal Revolution in America, 1969, rev. edit., 1990, Economic Planning and the Improvement of Public Policy, 1975, (with W. Leontief) The Economic System in an Age of Discontinuity, 1976, (with Benjamin Stein) On the Brink, 1977, (with Benjamin Stein) Money Power, 1980, Presidential Economics, 1984, rev. edit., 1994, Washington Bedtime Stories, 1986, Governing the $5 Trillion Economy, 1989, (with M. Foss) An Illustrated Guide to the American Economy, 1992, A New Illustrated Guide to the American Economy, 1995, On the Other Hand..., 1995; editor: Policies to Combat Depression, 1956, Tax Policy for the Twenty-First Century, 1988, AEI Economist, 1977-88; contbr. to: Agenda for the Nation, 1968, Contemporary Economic Problems, 1976, 77, 78, 79, 80; columnist: Slate Mag. Co-chmn. Economists for Ford, 1976; founding mem. Ams. for An Effective Presidency, 1980; mem. vis. com. econs. dept. Harvard U., 1979-80; mem. Group of 30, 1978-81. Served as ensign USNR, 1944-45. Recipient 1st prize Pabst Post-War Employment awards, 1944, Frank Seidmam award polit. economy Rhodes Coll., Memphis, 1989; Center Advanced Study in Behavioral Scis. fellow, 1965-66. Mem. Am., Va. econ. assns., So. Econ. Assn. (pres. 1983-84), Nat. Economists Club (chmn., bd. govs. 1969-70), Am. Acad. Arts and Scis., Phi Beta Kappa. Club: Cosmos. Office: Am Enterprise Inst 1150 17th St NW Washington DC 20036-4603

STEIN, HERMAN DAVID, social sciences educator, past university provost; b. N.Y.C., Aug. 13, 1917; s. Charles and Emma (Rosenblum) S.; m. Charmion Kerr, Sept. 15, 1946; children: Karen Lou Gelender, Shoshi Stein Bennett, Naomi Elizabeth. B.S.S., CCNY, 1939; M.S., Columbia U., 1941, D. Social Welfare, 1958; L.H.D., Hebrew Union Coll.-Jewish Inst. Religion, Cin, 1969; LLD, Jewish Theol. Sem., 1995. Family case worker, dir. pub. relations Jewish Family Service, N.Y.C., 1941-45; mem. faculty Sch. Social Work, Columbia U., N.Y.C., 1945-47, 50-64, prof. social scis., 1958-64, dir. rsch. ctr., 1959-62; dean Sch. Applied Social Scis. Case Western Res. U., Cleve., 1964-68, provost for social and behavioral scis., 1967-71, John Reynolds Harkness prof., social adminstr., 1972-89, univ. provost, v.p., 1969-72, 86-88, univ. prof. and provost emeritus, 1990—, univ. prof., faculty Ctr. for Internat. Health, 1989—; founder, dir. Global Currents Lectures, 1983-88; vis. prof. Sch. Social Work, U. Hawaii, Honolulu, winter 1971-72; fellow ctr. for Advanced Study in Behavior Scis., 1974-75, 78-79; Dep. dir. budget and rsch. dir. welfare dept. Am. Joint Distbn. Com. (European Hdqrs.), Paris, 1947-50; sr. adviser to exec. dir. UNICEF, 1974-83; cons. UNICEF, UN Social Devel. Div., 1960-83; adv. com. NIMH, 1959-71; mem. Bd. Human Resources, Nat. Acad. Scis., 1972-74; lectr. Sch. Social Work, Smith Coll., 1951-62, Harvard U. Sch. Pub. Health, 1971-85; cons. indsl. and nonprofit orgns. Author: The Curriculum Study of the Columbia University School of Social Work, 1960; co-author: The Characteristics of American Jews, 1965; Editor: (with Richard A. Cloward) Social Perspectives on Behavior, 1958, Planning for the Needs of Children in Developing Countries, 1965, Social Theory and Social Invention, 1968, The Crisis in Welfare in Cleveland, 1969, Organization and the Human Services, 1981; mem. editorial bd.: Adminstr. in Social work, 1976—; contbr. to profl. jours. Chmn. Mayor's Commn. on Crisis in Welfare in Cleve., 1968. Recipient Disting. Svc. award Coun. on Social Work Edn., 1970, René Sand award Internat. Coun. on Social Welfre, 1984, Univ. medal Case Western Res. U., 1994. Mem. NASW (chmn. commn. internat. social welfare 1964-65, Lifetime Achievement award 1996), Am. Sociol. Assn., Soc. Applied Anthropology, Coun. Social Work Edn. (pres. 1966-69, Significant Lifetime Achievement award 1996), Internat. Assn. Schs. Social Work (pres. 1968-76, Katherine A. Kendall award 1996), Internat. Conf. Social Welfare (exec. com. 1976-80, internat. adv. bd. 1986—, bd. dirs. coun. internat. programs 1965-92), Club of Rome (assoc. 1988—), Phi Beta Kappa. Office: Case Western Res U 436 Pardee Hall Cleveland OH 44106

STEIN, HOWARD S., banker; b. N.Y.C., Dec. 27, 1939; s. J. Zachary and Adele (Epstein) S. B.A., U. Mich., 1961; M.B.A., Harvard U., 1963. Mem. treas.'s staff Gen. Motors Corp., N.Y.C., 1963-69; dep. dir., dir. fiscal ops. Human Resources Adminstrn., City of N.Y., 1969-71, dep. adminstr., 1972-74, 1st dep. adminstr., 1974-78; asst. commr. Manpower and Career Devel.

Agy., N.Y.C., 1971-72; dep. commr. rent and housing maintenance Housing and Devel. Adminstrn., City of N.Y., 1972; v.p. Citicorp Credit Services Inc., N.Y.C., 1979-86; sr. v.p. Citicorp Retail Services Inc., N.Y.C., 1986-87; exec. dir. Landmark Mut. Funds Group of Citibank, N.A., N.Y.C., 1987-88; v.p. br. banking sect. devel. div. Citibank NA, 1989-91; sr. credit officer worldwide securities svcs. div. Fin. Instns. Group Citibank NA, N.Y.C., 1991-94; group risk mgr. Global Transaction Svcs., N.Y.C., 1995—; lectr. human resources policy Nova U., Ft. Lauderdale, Fla., 1973-74; field instr. adminstrn. specialization NYU Sch. Social Work, 1976-77; mem. risk mgmt. com. Participants Trust Co., 1995—. Past Bd. dirs., chmn. program com. Vol. Urban Cons. Group, Inc.; chmn. bd. dirs. Nova Inst; past treas., past pres., bd. dirs. Child Study Assn. Am./Wel-Met, Inc., 1963-85; past treas., bd. dirs. Career Center for Social Services Greater N.Y., Inc.; past treas., past pres. bd. dirs. Cavalier King Charles Spaniel Club U.S.A., Inc.; past bd. dirs., past sec. Child Welfare Info. Services; treas., bd. dirs., chmn. fin. com. WNYC Found.; bd. dirs. Senate Residence Owners Inc., New Goddard-Riverside Housing Devel. Fund Co., N.Y.C. Health and Hosps., Corp., 1976, Homes for the Homeless; mem. corp. Children's Mus., Boston; bd. dirs., treas., mem. fin. com. Goddard Riverside Neighborhood Houses; mem. Dept. Disciplinary com. Supreme Ct. State N.Y. Appellate Divsn. 1st Jud. Dept. Club: Harvard (N.Y.C., past mem. admissions com.). Home: 1158 5th Ave New York NY 10029-6917 Office: 399 Park Ave New York NY 10022

STEIN, IRVIN, orthopedic surgeon, educator; b. Fayetteville, N.C., Oct. 17, 1906; s. Kalman and Fannie (Berman) S.; m. Dorothy Bluthenthal, Aug. 21, 1934 (dec. Sept. 1985); children: Jane (Mrs. Gerard Finerman), Margery (Mrs. Frederich Schab), Katherine (Mrs. Keith Sachs); m. Bernice Hutzler, July 1986. AB, U. N.C., 1926; MD, Thomas Jefferson U., Phila., 1930. Diplomate Am. Bd. Orthopedic Surgery. Intern Sinai Hosp., Balt., 1930-31; resident surg. pathology Johns Hopkins, 1931-32; resident Phila. Orthopaedic Hosp., 1932-33; resident orthopedic surgery Johns Hopkins Hosp. and Children's Hosp. Sch., 1933-34; chief orthopedic surgery Phila. Gen. Hosp., 1941—; dir. chmn. dept. orthopedic surgery Albert Einstein Med. Center, Phila., 1962-72; emeritus chmn. Albert Einstein Med. Center, 1972—; clin. prof. orthopedic surgery emeritus U. Pa. Sch. Medicine, Phila.; cons. dept. health svcs. Phila. Sch. System. Co-author: Living Bone in Health and Disease, 1955; contbr. numerous articles to profl. jours. Chmn. Phila. Chamber Orch. Soc., 1967-70; bd. dirs. emeritus Phila. Orch.; bd. dirs. Lifelong Learning Soc., Fla. Atlantic U. Recipient Rehab. Physician of Year award Phila. Easter Seal Soc., 1971. Fellow ACS, N.Y. Acad. Scis., Coll. Physicians Phila., Am. Med. Writers Assn., Internat. Coll. Surgeons (pres. Pa. div. 1971, regent), Phila. Orthopedic Soc. (pres. 1970), Am. Acad. Orthopedic Surgery, Am. Geriatric Assn., Am. Acad. Surgery. Club: Broken Sound Golf. Home and Office: 2066 N Ocean Blvd Boca Raton FL 33431-7802

STEIN, JAY, retail executive; m. Cynthia Greener; 2 children. With Stein Mart, Inc., Greenville, Miss., 1966-79, pres., 1979-89; chmn., CEO Stein Mart, Inc., Greenville, 1989—; bd. dirs. Promus Hotel Corp., Barnett Bank Jacksonville, Bolles Sch., Nat. Conf. Christians and Jews, Am. Heritage Life Ins. Co.; trustee, mem. exec. com. John F. Kennedy Ctr. for Performing Arts; vice chmn. bd. govs. Hebrew Union Coll.; founding mem. The Holocaust Mus., Washington. Pres. Jacksonville Symphony Orch.; past mem. Mayor's Select Com. on Ethics in City Govt. Recipient Humanitarian award Nat. Conf. Christians and Jews, 1993. Office: 1200 Riverplace Blvd Jacksonville FL 32207-9046

STEIN, JAY M., planning and design educator, consultant; b. N.Y.C., Dec. 21, 1946; s. Samuel and Helen (Hershkowitz) S.; m. Karen Lee Klenberg, Aug. 18, 1987; children: Danielle Eva, Melissa Ilana. BA, Harpur Coll., 1968; MA, York U., Toronto, Ont., Can., 1971; PhD, U. Mich., 1976. Cert. planner. Lectr. U. Mich., Ann Arbor, 1974-76; asst. prof. planning Ga. Inst. Tech., Atlanta, 1976-81, assoc. prof., 1981-86; prof., chmn. dept. SUNY, Buffalo, 1986-89, acting dean, 1988; prof., chmn. dept. urban and regional planning U. Fla., 1989—; vis. prof. Stanford (Calif.) U., 1984-85; prin. Jay M. Stein Assocs.; cons. Legal Svcs. Corp. Ga., Atlanta, 1980-84, Atlanta Regional Commn., 1982, Legal Svcs. Corp. Ala., Montgomery, 1983-84, New Orleans Legal Svcs., 1988-89. Editor: Public Infrastructure, 1988, Growth Management: The Planning Challenge of the 1990s, 1992, Classic Readings in Urban Planning, 1995, Classic Readings in Real Estate and Development, 1996, (with Kent Spreckelmeyer) Classic Readings in Architecture, 1997; editl. bd. Jour. Arch. and Planning Rsch., Jour. Infrastructure Sys., Jour. Pub. Works Mgmt. and Policy; contbr. chpts. to books, articles to profl. jours. Mem. Am. Inst. Cert. Planners, Am. Planning Assn. (mem. jour. editorial bd. 1984-88, 95—), Assn. Collegiate Schs. Planning (exec. com. 1980-82), Urban Land Inst. (affiliate), Assn. Collegiate Schs. of Architecture (affiliate), Fla. Planning and Zoning Adminstrn., Urban Affairs Assn. Avocations: tennis, photography. Office: Univ Fla Coll Architecture Dept Urban & Regional Planning Gainesville FL 32611

STEIN, JAY WOBITH, legal research and education consultant, mediator arbitrator; b. Sauk Centre, Minn., June 19, 1920; s. Julius A. and Emaline (Wobith) S.; children: Holly Jayne, Navida Carol, April Jae, Andrew John, John Henry. BA cum laude, U. Minn., 1942; MA, Stanford U., 1949, Syracuse U., 1960; MS, Columbia U., 1950, PhD, 1952. Dir. CIA rsch. team, 1947-49; dir. library, asst. prof. social studies Southwestern U., Memphis, 1954-57; asst. dir. librs., adminstv. assoc. to v.p. Syracuse (N.Y.) U., 1958-61; faculty Maxwell Sch., Syracuse, 1959-61; asst. to pres. Drake U., Des Moines, Iowa, 1961-64; dir. State Higher Edn. Commn., Des Moines, 1964-67; dean Coll. Arts and Scis., prof. polit. sci. Western Ill. U., Macomb, 1967-69, prof. polit. sci. and edn., 1969-87; rsch. libr. John Marshall Law Sch. Libr., Chgo., 1989-94; ind. rsch. cons. law, libr., edn. Columbus, Ohio, 1995—; founder Rsch. & Resolution, Columbus, Ohio, 1996—; catalogue planner, econs. and govt., N.Y. Pub. Library, 1953; proposal reviewer U.S. Dept. Edn. Fund for the Improvement of Post-secondary Edn., 1982. Author: The Mind and the Sword, 1961, How Society Governs Education, 1975, Mass Media, Education and a Better Society, 1979, Society, Culture and Education, 1984, others; editor Scholar and Educator jour., 1977-85; contbr. articles to profl. jours. Mem. Coun. of Faculties of Bd. Govs. State Colls. and Univs., 1980-86, chmn., 1984-85; Family Cultural Ensemble, 1968-71; active with ch. and civic groups. With USN, 1942-46. Coolidge Found. fellow, 1984; grantee Univ. Rsch. Coun., others; recipient various overseas grants, 1970-80, including U. Bonn Acad. Exch., Germany, Internat. Recreation Assn., Switzerland, U.S. Dept. Edn., Europe and Egypt, also Iran, USSR. Mem. ABA (assoc.), ALA (life), ASPA, Am. Arbitration Assn. (panel of arbitrators), Am. Judicature Soc., Soc. Educators and Scholars (founder 1976, exec. dir. 1976-82, chmn. bd. 1980-88), Rotary, Phi Beta Kappa, Phi Kappa Phi, Phi Delta Kappa, Alpha Mu Gamma, Pi Sigma Alpha, Lambda Alpha Psi. Avocations: books, swimming, running. Office: 518 E Town St Apt 510 Columbus OH 43215-4831

STEIN, JEROME LEON, economist, educator; b. Bklyn., Nov. 14, 1928; s. Meyer and Ida (Shapiro) S.; m. Hadassah Levow, Aug. 27, 1950; children: Seth, Gil, Ilana. B.A. summa cum laude, Bklyn. Coll., 1949; M.A., Yale U., 1950, Ph.D., 1955. Instr. Brown U., Providence, 1953-56; asst. prof. Brown U., 1956-60, assoc. prof., 1960-62, prof., 1962-70, Eastman prof. polit. economy, 1970-94; prof. emeritus Brown U., Providence, 1994—; vis. prof. Hebrew U., Jerusalem, 1965-66, 72-73, 78; Ford Found. rsch. prof. econs. U. Calif., Berkeley, 1979-80, Sorbonne, U. Paris, 1982, Tohoku U., Sendai, Japan, 1983, Haute Etudes Comml., France, 1987, Monash U., Melbourne U., Australia, 1989, U. Aix-en-Provence, Marseille, France, 1992, 95, 96, 97, U. Munich, 1994, La Sapienza, Rome, 1994; vis. prof. applied math. Brown U., 1996—. Author: Essays in International Finance, 1962, (with G.M. Borts) Economic Growth in a Free Market, 1964, Money and Capacity Growth, 1971, Monetarism, 1976, Monetarist, Keynesian and New Classical Economics, 1982, Economics of Futures Markets, 1986, International Finance Markets, 1991, Fundamental Determinants of Exchange Rates, 1995; bd. editors Am. Econ. Rev., 1974-80; assoc. editor Jour. Fin., 1964-70. Ford Found. faculty fellow, 1961-62; Social Sci. Research Council grantee, 1965-66; Guggenheim fellow, 1972-73. Mem. Am. Econ. Assn. Home: 77 Elton St Providence RI 02906-4505 Office: Brown U 79 Waterman St Providence RI 02912-9079

STEIN, JOSEPH, playwright; b. N.Y.C.; s. Charles and Emma S.; m. Elisa Loti, Feb. 7, 1975; children by previous marriage: Daniel, Harry, Joshua; children of present marriage: John, Jenny Lyn. BSS, CCNY, 1934; MSW, Columbia U., 1937. Psychiat. social worker N.Y.C., 1938-45. Writer: radio shows, including Raleigh's Room, 1948-49, Henry Morgan Show, 1949-52; TV shows, including Your Show of Shows, 1952-54; Sid Caesar Show, 1954-55; playwright Plain and Fancy, 1955; Mr. Wonderful, 1957, Juno, 1959, Take Me Along, 1959, Enter Laughing, 1963, Fiddler on the Roof, 1964 (Am. Theatre Wing Tony award for best musical, 1965, N.Y. Drama Critics Circle award Best Musical 1965), Zorba, 1968 (Tony nomination), Irene, 1975, King of Hearts, 1978, Carmelina, 1979, The Baker's Wife, 1983, (Olivier award nomination London 1989), Rags, 1986 (Tony nomination); screenplays Enter Laughing, 1970; Fiddler on the Roof, 1972 (Screen Actors Guild award). Mem. Authors League, Screen Writers Guild (award recipient), Dramatists Guild Coun. Home: 1130 Park Ave New York NY 10128-1255 Office: 250 W 57th St New York NY 10102-0158

STEIN, LAWRENCE A., lawyer; b. Balt., Mar. 18, 1965; s. Hersh and Ellen (Hart) S.; m. Diane Wells, June 23, 1991; children: Joshua A., Julie E. AB, U. Chgo., 1988; JD, No. Ill. U., 1993. Bar: Ill. 1993, U.S. Dist. Ct. (no. dist.) Ill. 1993, U.S. Ct. Appeals (7th cir.) 1993, Md. 1994, U.S. Dist. Ct. Md. 1994. Assoc. Huck, Bouma, Martin, Charlton & Bradshaw, Wheaton, Ill., 1993—; advisor Prairie State Legal Svcs., Carol Stream, Ill., 1993—. Commr. Glen Ellyn (Ill.) Architecture Review Commn., 1994—. Recipient Am. jurisprudence award for excellence in appellate advocacy Lawyers Coop., 1991. Mem. ABA, Ill. Trial Lawyers Assn., DuPage County Bar Assn., Ill. State Bar Assn., Am. Inns Ct., Phi Delta Phi. Republican. Jewish. Home: 69 Ott Ave Glen Ellyn IL 60137 Office: Huck Bouma Martin Charlton & Bradshaw 1755 S Naperville Rd # 200 Wheaton IL 60187-8132

STEIN, MARK RODGER, allergist; b. Phila., Apr. 24, 1943; s. Eli and Norma Ruth (Berman) S.; m. Phyllis Mary Feinstein, Dec. 27, 1964; children: Amy Lynn, Philip Warren. BA, LaSalle Coll., Phila., 1964; MD, Jefferson Med. Coll., Phila., 1968. Diplomate Nat. Bd. Med. Examiners, Am. Bd. Internal Medicine, Am. Bd. Allergy and Immunology. Intern Abington (Pa.) Meml. Hosp., 1968-69; resident internal medicine Letterman Army Med. Ctr., San Francisco, 1972-75; fellow allergy and clin. immunology Fitzsimons Army Med. Ctr., Denver, 1975-77; pvt. practice West Palm Beach, Fla., 1979—; asst. prof. depts. medicine and pediat. Uniformed Svcs. U. Health Scis., Sch. Medicine, Bethesda, Md., 1978-79; clin. asst. prof. dept. internal medicine U. South Fla. Coll. Medicine, Tampa, 1979-83, 97; clin. care cons. Clin. Ctr., NIH, Bethesda, 1978-79; mem. active staff, chief dept. allergy, Good Samaritan Hosp., West Palm Beach, St. Mary's Hosp., West Palm Beach, 1985—; mem. active staff Palm Beach Gardens Med. Ctr., Jupiter Med. Ctr. Contbr. articles to profl. jours. Trustee Am. Lung Assn., West Palm Beach, 1984-93, 95—. Fellow ACP, Am. Acad. Allergy, Asthma and Immunology, Am. Coll. Allergy, Asthma and Immunology (chmn. geriatric com. 1988-90), Am. Assn. Cert. Allergists; mem. Am. Thoracic Soc., Mil. Allergists, Fla. Med. Assn., Palm Beach County Med. Assn., Asthma and Allergy Found. Am., Fla. Allergy and Immunology Soc. (pres. 1987-88), Southeastern Allergy Assn., B'nai B'rith. Jewish. Avocations: tennis, golf. Office: 840 US Highway 1 North Palm Beach FL 33408

STEIN, MARSHALL DAVID, lawyer; b. Greensboro, N.C., Dec. 17, 1941; s. Joseph and Celia (Feuer) S.; m. Helene Sue Weiner, Mar. 20, 1965; children: Lisa D., Daniel R. BA, Brandeis U., 1964; LLB, Boston U., 1967. Bar: Mass. 1968, U.S. Dist. Ct. Mass. 1970, U.S. Ct. Appeals (1st cir.) 1971, U.S. Dist. Ct. Vt. 1978, U.S. Supreme Ct 1981. Asst. U.S. Atty. Office of U.S. Atty., U.S. Dist. Ct. Mass., 1974-76; chief staff atty. U.S. Ct. Appeals (1st cir.), Boston, 1976-78; ptnr. Cherwin, Glickman & Theise, LLP, Boston, 1982-96, Sherwin, Glickman & Theise, LLP, Boston, 1996—. Assoc. editor Mass. Law Rev., Boston, 1980-90; contbr. articles to profl. jours. Panelist issues in housing discrimination U.S. Commn. Civil Rights, Washington, 1985. Mem. Mass. Bar Assn., Boston Bar Assn. (chmn. jud. pay raise subcom. 1993-96). Jewish. Office: Cherwin, Glickman & Theise, LLP 1 International Pl Boston MA 02110-2602

STEIN, MARVIN, psychiatrist, historian; b. St. Louis, Dec. 8, 1923; s. Samuel G. and Dora (Kline) S.; m. Ann Hackman, May 5, 1950; children: Leslie, David, Lisa. BS, MD, Washington U., St. Louis, 1949; grad., Phila. Psychoanalytic Inst., 1959. Intern St. Louis City Hosp., 1949-50; asst. resident in psychiatry Barnes Hosp., St. Louis, 1950-51; fellow in psychiatry Hosp. U. Pa., 1953-55; asst. prof., then assoc. prof. psychiatry U. Pa. Med. Sch., 1956-63; prof. psychiatry Cornell U. Med. Sch., N.Y.C., 1963-66; prof., chmn. dept. psychiatry SUNY Downstate Med. Ctr., Bklyn., 1966-71; chmn. dept. psychiatry Mt. Sinai Sch. Medicine, N.Y.C., 1971-87, Esther and Joseph Klingenstein prof., 1971-94, Esther and Joseph Klingenstein prof. emeritus, 1994—; mem. fellowships rev. panel NIMH, 1961-64, chmn. mental health extramural rsch. adv. com., 1968-71, chmn. rev. com. Mental Health Aspects of AIDS, 1988-90; mem. rsch. adv. com. VA, 1965-68, mem. rsch. svc. merit rev. bd. in behavioral sci., 1972-75; chmn. Mental Health Rsch. Career Award Com., 1963-67; chmn. bd. dirs. Founds. Fund for Rsch. in Psychiatry, 1967-70; mem. behavioral medicine study sect. NIH, 1981-83, geriatric rev. com., 1986-88. Contbr. articles on brain and behavior and immune function to med. jours. USPHS postdoctoral fellow, 1951-53; mental health career investigator, 1956-61; sr. fellow grantee, 1961-63. Mem. Am. Psychiat. Assn. (chmn. rsch. coun. 1981-84), N.Y. Acad. Medicine (Salmon com. 1984—). Home: 5700 Arlington Ave Bronx NY 10471-1503 Office: Mt Sinai Sch Medicine 1 Gustave L Levy Pl New York NY 10029-6504

STEIN, MICHAEL ALAN, cardiologist; b. Chgo., May 31, 1958; s. Harold Marc and Carlyne Mae (Skirow) S.; m. Ann Palmer Coe, June 9, 1984; children: Sara Elizabeth, David Benjamin. BA magna cum laude, Lawrence U., 1980; MD, U. Ill., 1984. Diplomate in internal medicine and cardiovascular diseases Am. Bd. Internal Medicine. Intern, resident in medicine U. Ill., Chgo., 1984-87; fellow in cardiology, then interventional cardiology U. Iowa, Iowa City, 1987-91; asst. prof. Emory U., Atlanta, 1991-95; med. dir. CCU Atlanta VA Med. Ctr., Decatur, Ga., 1991-95; med. dir. cardiac catheterization lab., Dunwoody Med. Ctr., Atlanta, 1994-95; staff cardiologist Cardiology Cons., Pensacola, Fla., 1995-96; staff cardiologist So. Med. Group, Key West, Fla., 1996—. Recipient clin. investigator award NIH, 1990-95. Fellow Am. Coll. Cardiology, Am. Heart Assn. (coun. clin. cardiology); mem. AAAS, Soc. for Cardiac Angiography & Interventions. Avocations: sailing, sailboat racing, hiking, scuba diving, fishing. Home: 7 Amaryllis Dr Key West FL 33040-6204 Office: 1111 12th St Key West FL 33040-4088

STEIN, MILTON MICHAEL, lawyer; b. N.Y.C., Sept. 18, 1936; s. Isidore and Sadie (Lefkowitz) S.; m. Jacqueline Martin, June 17, 1962; children: April, Alicia. AB, Columbia U., 1958, LLB, 1961. Bar: N.Y. 1962, Pa. 1971, U.S. Supreme Ct. 1971. Asst. dist. atty. N.Y. County, 1962-67; sr. counsel Nat. Commn. for Reform of Fed. Criminal Law, Washington, 1967-70; asst. dist. atty., chief of appeals City of Phila., 1970-73; asst. dir. Nat. Wire Tapping Commn., Washington, 1973-75; dir. D.C. Law Revision, Washington, 1975-77; spl. asst. HUD, Washington, 1977-79; asst. gen. counsel U.S. Commodity Futures Trading Commn., Washington, 1979-83; v.p. N.Y. Futures Exch., N.Y.C., 1983-89, N.Y. Stock Exch., N.Y.C., 1989—. Mem. ABA, N.Y. State Bar Assn., Assn. of Bar of City of N.Y. Democrat. Jewish. Home: Hudson House PO Box 286 Ardsley On Hudson NY 10503-0286

STEIN, MYRON, internist, educator; b. Boston, May 27, 1925; s. Isador and Sara Esther (Zimble) S.; m. Pauline June Alpert, June 21, 1953 (dec. 1992); children: Lisa Jayne, Susan Jo Stein-Matthews, Amy Stein Weinberg, Laurie Jennifer. BA, Dartmouth Coll., 1948; MD, Tufts U., 1952. Diplomate Am. Bd. Internal Medicine. Assoc. medicine Med. Sch. Harvard U., Boston, 1957-65; assoc. prof. med. sci. Brown U., Providence, 1965-68, prof. med. sci., 1968-73; pvt. practice medicine Beverly Hills, Calif.; prof. medicine Sch. Medicine, UCLA, 1973-75, clin. prof., 1975—; cons. VA Hosp., Providence, 1965-73, L.A., 1975-89, Wadsworth VA Med. Ctr.; mem. pulmonary study sect. NIH, Bethesda, Md., 1971-95. Editor: Pulmonary Embolic Disease, 1965, Pulmonary Thromboembolism, 1973, New Directions in Asthma, 1975, Bronchial Asthma, 1985, 3d edit., 1993; contbr. 120 articles to med. jours. Mem. bd. corp. vis. com. Sch. Medicine Tufts U., Medford, Mass., 1986; bd. overseers, 1987. With AUS, 1943-46. Recipient Maimonides award Govt. of Israel, 1982. Fellow Am. Coll. Chest Physicians (sr. editor 1971-79); mem. Calif. Thoracic Soc. (sec.-treas. 1978, pres. 1981), L.A. Trudeau Soc., New Eng. Pulmonary Soc., Calif. Lung Assn. (chmn. edn. com. 1978-82, bd. dirs. 1981, Calif. medal 1989). Democrat. Jewish. Avocations: tennis, jogging, collecting lead soldiers. Office: 414 N Camden Dr Ste 1100 Beverly Hills CA 90210-4532

STEIN, OTTO LUDWIG, botany educator; b. Augsburg, Germany, Jan. 14, 1925; came to U.S., 1939, naturalized, 1944; s. Julius and Margaret (Haas) S.; m. Diana Borut, June 15, 1958; children: Deborah Lee, Judith Ann, Suzanne Beth, Jonathan Henri Richard. B.S. with distinction, U. Minn., 1949, M.S., 1952, Ph.D., 1954. Instr. botany U. Mo. at Columbia, 1955; USPHS research fellow Brookhaven Nat. Lab., 1955-57, research collaborator, 1958-68; asst. prof. botany U. Mont., Missoula, 1957-63; asso. prof. U. Mont., 1963-64; asso. prof. botany U. Mass., Amherst, 1964-70; prof. botany U. Mass., 1970-90, prof. emeritus, 1990—, head dept., 1969-74; dir. U. Mass./U. Freiburg (Germany) Exchange Program, 1979; vis. asst. prof. botany U. Calif., Berkeley, 1961-62. Served with AUS, 1944-46. NATO sr. research fellow Imperial Coll., London, Eng., 1971-72. Fellow Linnean Soc. (London), AAAS; mem. Bot. Soc. Am. (chmn. developmental sect. 1963-65), Soc. Developmental Biology, Soc. Exptl. Biology, Sigma Xi., Gamma Sigma Delta, Alpha Zeta, Gamma Alpha. Home: 140 Red Gate Ln Amherst MA 01002-1845 Office: U Mass Dept Biology Amherst MA 01003

STEIN, PAUL DAVID, cardiologist; b. Cin., Apr. 13, 1934; s. Simon and Sadie (Friedman) S.; m. Janet Louise Tucker, Aug. 14, 1966; children: Simon, Douglas, Rebecca. BS, U. Cin., 1955, MD, 1959. Intern Jewish Hosp., Cin., 1959-60, med. resident, 1961-62; med. resident Gorgas Hosp., C.Z., 1960-61; fellow in cardiology U. Cin., 1962-63, Mt. Sinai Hosp., N.Y.C., 1963-64; rsch. fellow Harvard Med. Sch., Boston, 1964-66; asst. dir. cardiac catheterization lab. Baylor U. Med. Ctr., Dallas, 1966-67; asst. prof. medicine Creighton U., Omaha, 1967-69; assoc. prof. medicine U. Okla., Oklahoma City, 1969-73; prof. rsch. medicine U. Okla. Coll. Medicine, Oklahoma City, 1973-76; dir. cardiovascular rsch. Henry Ford Hosp., Detroit, 1976-94, med. dir. cardiovascular rehab., 1994—; adj. prof. physics Oakland U., Rochester, Mich., 1985—; prof. medicine (Henry Ford) Case Western Res. U., Cleve., 1994—. Author: A Physical and Physiological Basis for the Interpretation of Cardiac Ausculation: Evaluations Based Primarily on Second Sound and Ejection Murmurs, 1981, Pulmonary Embolism, 1996; contbr. articles to profl. jours. Coun. on Clin. Cardiology fellow Am. Heart Assn., 1971, Coun. on Circulation fellow, 1972. Fellow ACP, ASME, Am. Coll. Cardiology, Am. Coll. Chest Physicians (pres. 1993), Internat. Acad. Chest Physicians and Surgeons (pres. 1993); mem. Am. Physiol. Soc., Ctrl. Soc. Clin. Rsch. Office: Henry Ford Health System Cardiac Wellness Ctr 6525 Second Ave Detroit MI 48202-3006

STEIN, PAUL E., superintendent; m. Carol Mannin; children: Christine, John, James. BS in polit. sci., U.S.A.F. Acad., Colo., 1966; MBA, Fla. State U., 1973; attended, Air War Coll., Maxwell Air Force Base, Ala., 1986. Commd. 2d lt. USAF, 1966, advanced through grades to lt. gen., 1994; asst. football coach USAF, Colo., 1966-67; chief personnel svcs. 7149th combat support group USAF, Spangdahlem Air Base, Germany, 1967-69; chief spl. svcs. divsn. 36th combat support group USAF, Bitburg Air Base, Germany, 1969-71; chief, spl. svcs. divsn. 2d comabt support group USAF, Barksdale Air Force Base, La., 1971-72; ops. analyst AWACS Test Ops. The Boeing Co., Washington, 1974-80; requirements program officer USAF, Washinton, 1980, tactical fighter requirements officer, 1980-82, 86-91; comdr. Keesler Tech. Training Ctr., Miss., 1991-92; dir., legislative liaison Office of the Sec., Washington, 1992-94; supr. USAF Acad., Colo., 1994—. Decorated Disting. Svc. medal, Legion of Merit with one bronze oak leaf cluster. Office: USAF Legislative Liason SAF/LL Washington DC 20330 Office: USAF Academy 2304 Cadet Dr Ste 342 U S A F Academy CO 80840-5001*

STEIN, PAULA JEAN ANNE BARTON, hotel real estate consultant; b. Chgo., July 29, 1929; m. Marshall L. Stein; children: Guy G., George L. BA, Lake Forest (Ill.) U., 1951; postgrad., Roosevelt U., Chgo., 1955-77, UCLA, 1978-79. Lic. internat. hotel and mgmt. cons./broker, Ill. Adminstrv. asst. publicity Kefauver for Pres., Chgo., 1951; adminstrv. asst. Wells Orgns., Chgo., 1952; rschr., writer Employers Assn. Am., Chgo.; writer Woodworking Jobbers Assn., Chgo., 1953; cons. L.A., 1978-80; founder, pres., ptnr., cons. internat. hotel real estate Steinvest, Inc., Chgo., 1980—; cons., hotels Nat. Diversified Svcs., Inc., Chgo., 1990—, Chatmar, Inc., Bayview Hotels, Monterey, Calif., Sunrise Ptnrs., Chgo. IBA fellow, 1990. Mem. World Future Soc. (profl.). Avocations: oil painting, grandparenting, social services causes, citizen-diplomacy. Home and Office: Steinvest Inc City Commons House 202 641 W Willow St Chicago IL 60614-5176

STEIN, PAULA NANCY, psychologist, educator; b. N.Y.C., Aug. 23, 1963; d. Michael and Evelyn (Graber) S.; m. Andreas Howard Smoller, Sept. 2, 1991; 1 child, Rebecca Leigh Smoller. BA, Skidmore Coll., 1985; MA with distinction, Hofstra U., 1986, PhD, 1989. Lic. clin. psychologist, N.Y.; cert. in sch. psychology, N.Y. Intern NYU Med. Ctr.-Rusk Inst., N.Y.C., 1988-89; instr. Mt. Sinai Med. Ctr., N.Y.C., 1989-93, asst. prof. rehab. medicine, 1993—; chief psychologist Fishkill (N.Y.) Consultation Group, 1991—. Contbr. chpt. to book, articles to profl. jours. Kraewic scholar Skidmore Coll., 1985. Mem. APA, Am. Congress Rehab. Medicine (subcom. on tng.), Assn. for Advancement of Behavior Therapy, Hudson Valley Psychol. Assn., Phi Beta Kappa. Jewish. Avocations: skiing, swimming, tennis. Office: Fishkill Consultation Group Box 446 90 Main St Fishkill NY 12524

STEIN, RICHARD PAUL, lawyer; b. New Albany, Ind., Sept. 2, 1925; s. William P. and Lillian M. (Russell) S.; m. Mary Charlotte Key, June 22, 1959; children: Richard Paul, William, Patricia. Student, Miligan (Tenn.) Coll., 1943-44, Duke, 1944-45; J.D., U. Louisville, 1950. Bar: Ind., 1950. With labor relations Goodyear Engring. Co., Charlestown, Ind., 1952-54; ptnr. Naville & Stein, New Albany, 1954-61; pros. atty. 52d Jud. Circuit Ind., 1956-61; U.S. atty. So. Dist. Ind., 1961-67; chmn. Pub. Service Commn. of Ind., 1967-70; legis. counsel Eli Lilly Co., Indpls., 1970-74; v.p. pub. affairs Pub. Service Co. Ind., 1974-90; atty., pub. affairs cons., 1990—; dir. Indpls. Indians; Co-counsel New Albany-Floyd County Bldg. Authority, 1960-62; mem. State Bd. Tax Commrs. Adv. Bd., Jud. Study Commn. Sec. New Albany Dist. Dem. Com., 1956-61; chmn. New Albany United Way, 1957. Served to lt. USNR, 1943-46, 50-51; lt. Res. Named Floyd County Young Man of Yr. Floyd County Jr. C. of C., 1955, Outstanding Young Man of Yr. New ALbany Jaycees, 1958. Mem. Ind. Bar Assn., Marion County Bar Assn., Ind. Prosecutors Assn. (pres. 1960-61), Ind. Electric Assn. (dir.), Am. Legion, Pi Kappa Alpha, Phi Alpha Delta. Roman Catholic. Clubs: Highland Country, Skyline. Lodge: K.C. Avocations: tennis, golf, reading. Home: 12414 Medalist Pkwy Carmel IN 46033

STEIN, RICHARD STEPHEN, chemistry educator; b. N.Y.C., Aug. 21, 1925; s. Isidor and Florence (Lewengood) S.; m. Judith Elma Balise, May 27, 1951; children: Linda Ann, Anne Marie, Carol Joan, Lisa Jean. BS, Poly. Inst. Bklyn., 1945; MA, Princeton U., 1948, PhD, 1949; DS (hon.), U. Ulm, Fed. Republic Germany, 1989; DSc (hon.), U. Mass., 1992. Postdoctoral fellow Cambridge U., 1948-49; research assoc. Princeton U., 1949-50; asst. prof. U. Mass., Amherst, 1950-57; asso. prof. U. Mass., 1957-59, prof., 1959-61, Commonwealth prof., 1961-80, Goessman prof. chemistry, 1980-92; Goessman prof. emeritus, 1992—; founder, dir. Polymer Research Inst. U. Mass., 1961—; cons. Procter and Gamble. Co-editor: Electromagnetic Scattering, 1967, Structure and Properties of Polymer Films, 1973; contbr. numerous articles to profl. jours. Recipient Internat. award Soc. Plastics Engrs., 1969, Bingham award Rheology Soc., 1972, Award for Disting. svc. for Advancement of Polymer Sci., Soc. Polymer Sci. Japan, 1988, Gordon Res. Conf. Huggins award, 1987. Mem. NAS, NAE, AAAS, AAUP, Am. Acad. Arts and Scis., Am. Chem. Soc. (Bordon award 1972, Polymer Chemistry award 1983), Am. Phys. Soc. (award in high polymer physics 1976), Rheology Soc., Sigma Xi. Founder sci. rheo-optics of polymers. Home: 5 Berkshire Ter Amherst MA 01002-1301

STEIN, ROBERT A., writer; b. Duluth, Minn., Aug. 5, 1933; s. Abe A. and Grace (Wichterman) S.; m. Betty Lou Pavlik, Nov. 5, 1955; children: Robert Jr., David K., Steven J. BS in Commerce, U. Iowa, 1956, MA in Counselor Edn., 1968, MA in Writing, 1986. Cert. tchr. Iowa; cert. profl. counselor. Commd. 2d lt. USAF, 1956, advanced through grades to col.; ret., 1977; dir., safety and security U. Iowa Hosps./Clinics, Iowa City, 1977-85; ret., 1985; writer, tchr. Iowa City, 1985—; writer, tchr. Iowa City/Johnson County Sr.

Citizens Ctr., Iowa City, 1994—. Author: (novel) Appollyon: A Novel, 1985, The Chase, 1988, The Black Samaritan, 1997, (fiction) Death Defied, 1988 (Internat. Literary award 1988). Decorated Bronze star 1969. Mem. Authors Guild, Authors League Am., Air Force Assn. (life), Military Affairs Assn. (charter), Daedalians, Nat. Iowa Lettermen's Club (past pres.), Rotary (Paul Harris fellow), Phi Delta Kappa. Avocations: flying, international travel, sports announcer U. Iowa, swimming. Home and Office: 2020 Ridgeway Dr Iowa City IA 52245

STEIN, ROBERT ALAN, electronics company executive; b. Chgo., Oct. 18, 1930; s. Manfred and Mildred (Rosenfield) S.; m. Frances Roslyn Berger, Dec. 25, 1960; 1 dau., Marcia Beth. B.A., U. Chgo., 1950, M.B.A., 1953. C.P.A., Ill. Sr. auditor Scovell, Wellington & Co., Chgo., 1955-63; supr. corp. acctg. Mack Trucks, Inc., Montvale, N.J., 1963-65; v.p. fin., treas. Lionel Corp., N.Y.C., 1965-82; pres. ITI Electronics, Inc., Fairfield, N.J., 1982—. Served with U.S. Army, 1953-55. Mem. Am. Inst. CPAs. Home: 32 Stonewall Dr Livingston NJ 07039-1822 Office: 12 Kulick Rd Fairfield NJ 07004-3308

STEIN, ROBERT ALLEN, legal association executive, law educator; b. Mpls., Sept. 16, 1938; s. Lawrence E. and Agnes T. (Brynildson) S.; m. Sandra H. Stein; children: Linda Stein Routh, Laura Stein Conrad, Karin Stein O'Boyle. BS in Law, U. Minn., 1960, JD summa cum laude, 1961; LLD (hon.), Uppsala U., Sweden, 1993. Bar: Wis. 1961, Minn. 1967. Assoc. Foley, Sammond & Lardner, Milw., 1961-64; prof. law sch. U. Minn., Mpls., 1964—; assoc. dean U. Minn., 1976-77, v.p. adminstrn. and planning, 1978-80, dean law sch., 1979-94, faculty rep. men's intercollegiate athletics, 1981-94; of counsel Mullin, Weinberg & Daly, P.A., Mpls., 1970-80, Gray, Plant, Mooty, Mooty & Bennett, Mpls., 1980-94; exec. dir. ABA, Chgo., 1994—; vis. prof. UCLA, 1969-70, U. Chgo., 1975-76; commr. Uniform State Laws Commn. Minn., 1973—; v.p. Nat. Uniform Laws Com., 1991-93, exec. comm. 1993—; acad. fellow Am. Coll. Trusts and Estates Counsel, 1975—; vis. scholar Am. Bar Found., Chgo., 1975-76; mem. trust com. Northwestern Nat. Bank St. Paul, 1977-81; trustee Gt. No. Iron Ore Properties, 1982—; advisor Restatement of Law Second, Property, 1977—, Restatement of Law Trusts (Prudent Investor Rule), 1989-90. Author: Stein on Probate, 1976, 3d edit., 1995, How to Study Law and Take Law Exams, 1996, Estate Planning Under the Tax Reform Act of 1976, 2d edit, 1978, In Pursuit of Excellence: A History of the University of Minnesota Law School, 1980, others; contbr. articles to legal jours. Founding bd. dirs. Park Ridge Ctr., 1985-95; co-chair Gov.'s Task Force on Ctr. for Treatment of Torture Victims, 1985, bd. dirs., 1985-87. Fellow Am. Bar Found (bd. dirs. 1987-94), Am. Coll. Tax Counsel; mem. ABA (coun. sect. of legal edn. and admission to bar 1986-91, vice chairperson 1991-92, chair-elect 1992-93, chair 1993-94), Internat. Acad. Estate and Trust Law (academician), Am. Judicature Soc. (bd. dirs. 1984-88), Am. Law Inst. (coun. mem. 1987—), Minn. Bar Assn. (bd. govs. 1979-94, exec. coun., probate and trust law sect. 1973-77), Hennepin County Bar Assn. Home: 990 N Lake Shore Dr #7A Chicago IL 60611-1353 Office: American Bar Assn 750 N Lake Shore Dr Chicago IL 60611-4403

STEIN, ROBERT BENJAMIN, biomedical researcher, physician; b. Buffalo, Oct. 28, 1950; s. Frank and Eleanor (Bankoff) S.; m. Marcia Joan Lieberman, Aug. 10, 1975 (div.); children: Rebecca Anne, Joshua David; m. Sophia Anne Rose, Dec. 29, 1989; children: Susan Claire, Stephanie Michelle. BS, Ind. U., 1972; MD, PhD, Duke U., 1979. Diplomate Am. Bd. Anatomic and Clin. Pathology. House staff Duke U. Med. Ctr., Durham, N.C., 1980-83; sr. research fellow Dept. Virus and Cell Biology Merck Sharp & Dohme Rsch. Labs., West Point, Pa., 1983-87, assoc. dir. molecular and cardiovascular pharmacology, 1987-89, sr. dir., head dept. pharmacology, 1989-90; v.p. rsch. Ligand Pharms., Inc., San Diego, 1990-92, v.p. rsch. and preclin. devel., 1992-93, sr. v.p., CSO, 1993-96; exec. v.p., rsch. and preclin. devel. DuPont Merck, Wilmington, Del., 1996—. Contbr. articles to profl. jours., chpts. to books. Ins. Med. scholar, 1977-79; James B. Duke scholar, 1976-78; Lang Med. Pub. award, 1979; NIH grantee, 1974-75. Fellow Am. Soc. Clin. Pathologists, N.Y. Acad. Scis., Am. Physiol. Soc., AAAS, Sigma Xi, Phi Beta Kappa, Alpha Omega Alpha. Avocations: piano, history, literature, windsurfing. Office: DuPont Merck E400-2426 PO Box 80400 Wilmington DE 19880-0400

STEIN, RONALD JAY, artist, airline transport pilot; b. N.Y.C., Sept. 15, 1930; s. William and Ruth (Krasner) S. Diploma, The Cooper Union, 1953; BFA, Yale U., 1955; MFA, Rutgers U., 1960; grad., FAA Acad. Pilot Examiner Sch., 1980. Cons. Aviation Assocs., 1988—; mem. faculty Worcester Mus. Fine Arts, Rutgers U., 1960-63; aviation cons.; pilot examiner, accident prevention safety counselor FAA. One man shows sculpture and paintings include, Mirski Gallery, Boston, 1956, Inst. Contemporary Art, Boston, 1958, Irving Gallery, Milw., 1960, 71, Mayer Gallery, N.Y.C., 1960, 61, Rigelhaupt Gallery, Boston, 1966, Tibor Denagy Gallery, N.Y.C., 1964, N.Y. World's Fair, 1964, Marlborough Gallery, London, 1967, Kind Gallery, Chgo., 1969, Hokin Gallery, Palm Beach, Fla., 1974, Benson Gallery, L.I., N.Y., 1988, Benton Gallery, South Hampton, N.Y., 1988, 89, Odeon Gallery, Sag Harbor, N.Y., 1993; exhibited in group shows, Inst. Contemporary Art, Boston, Corcoran Gallery, Washington, Contemporary Arts Mus., Houston, U. N.C., Raleigh, Mus. Contemporary Art, Chgo., Benton Gallery, South Hampton, N.Y., Mus. Modern Art, N.Y.C., Cornell U., Ithaca, N.Y., Finch Coll. Mus. Fine Arts, N.Y.C.; represented in permanent collections, Am. Fedn. Art, N.Y.C., Guggenheim Mus., N.Y.C., Carnegie Inst., Chgo., Tenn. Fine Arts Ctr., Nashville, Mus. Contemporary Art, Chgo., Wadsworth Athenaeum, Hartford, Conn., Finch Coll. Mus. Art, N.Y.C., Guild Hall, East Hampton, N.Y., Mus. Modern Arts, N.Y.C., Smithsonian Instn., others. Commd. spl. min. of eucharist Most Holy Trinity Roman Cath. Ch., East Hampton, N.Y., 1992—. Capt. U.S. Mcht. Marine, 1976-81. Mem. NRA, Yale Club. Republican. Home: 836 Fireplace Rd East Hampton NY 11937-1512

STEIN, RUTH ELIZABETH KLEIN, physician; b. N.Y.C., Nov. 2, 1941; d. Theodore and Mimi (Foges) Klein; m. H. David Stein, June 9, 1963; children: Lynn Andrea Stein Melnick, Sharon Lisa, Deborah Michelle. AB, Barnard Coll., 1962; MD, Albert Einstein Coll. Medicine, 1966. Diplomate Am. Bd. Pediatrics. Intern, then resident Bronx Mcpl. Hosp. Ctr., 1966-68; sr. resident, fellow; instr. dept. pediatrics George Washington U., Washington, 1969-70; with Albert Einstein Coll. of Medicine, Bronx, 1970—, assoc. prof. pediatrics, 1977-83, prof., 1983—; vice chmn. dept. pediatrics Albert Einstein Coll., 1992—; pediatrician-in-chief, dir. pediatrics Jacobi Med. Ctr. (formerly Bronx Mcpl. Hosp. Ctr.), 1992—; vis. prof. pub. health dept. epidemiology Yale U. Sch. of Medicine, New Haven, 1986-87; scholar-in-residence United Hosp. Fund, N.Y., 1995—; dir., prin. investigator Preventive Intervention Rsch. Ctr. for Child Health, N.Y., Nat. Child Health Assessment Planning Project, N.Y., Behavioral Pediatric Tng. Program, N.Y.; dir. gen. pediatrics Pediatric Divsn., N.Y.; apptd. to Montefiore Med. Ctr., North Ctrl. Bronx Hosp. Editor: Caring for Children with Chronic Illness: Issues and Strategies, 1989, Health Care for Children: What's Right, What's Wrong, What's Next, 1997; mem. editorial bd. Jour. Behavioral and Devel. Pediatrics; contbr. articles to profl. jours. Recipient Rsch. award Ambulatory Pediatric Assn., 1995. Fellow Am. Acad. Pediatrics; mem. APHA, Am. Pediatric Soc., Soc. for Pediatric Rsch., Ambulatory Pediatric Assn. (bd. dirs. 1982-89, pres. 1987-88), Soc. for Behavioral Pediatrics, Alpha Omega Alpha. Jewish. Home: 91 Larchmont Ave Larchmont NY 10538-3748 Office: Albert Einstein Coll Medicine 1300 Morris Park Ave Bronx NY 10461-1926

STEIN, SANDRA LOU, educational psychologist, educator; b. Freeport, Ill., Oct. 6, 1942; d. William Kenneth and Marien Elizabeth Stein. BS, U. Wis., Madison, 1964; MS in Edn., No. Ill. U., 1967, EdD, 1969. Tchr. English Rockford (Ill.) Sch. Dist., 1964-65; tchr. Russian Jefferson County Sch. Dist., Lakewood, Colo., 1965-66; asst. prof. edn. U. S.C., Columbia, 1969-71, No. Ill. U., DeKalb, 1971-72, Rider U., Lawrenceville, N.J., 1972-75; assoc. prof. edn. Rider Coll., Lawrenceville, N.J., 1975-81, prof. edn., 1981—, dept. chair, 1983-91; cons. on measurement and evaluation, women's edn., 1973—. Contbr. articles to ednl. publs. Treas. Lawrenceville Men's Breakfast Club, 1983-85; deacon Presbyn. Ch. Lawrenceville, 1984-87; contest judge N.J. Fedn. Bus. and Profl. Women, 1989; vol. Habitat for Humanity, Trenton, N.J., 1989. Recipient Disting. Teaching award Rider Coll. and Lindback Found., 1981. Mem. AAUP (Outstanding Achievement award Rider Coll. chpt. 1988), Am. Ednl. Rsch. Assn., Am. Psychol. Assn., Phi Delta Kappa (chpt. pres. 1986-87, Svc. Key award 1991, faculty advisor 1994—). Office: Rider U 2083 Lawrenceville Rd Trenton NJ 08648-3001

STEIN, SEYMOUR, electronics executive, scientist; b. Bklyn., Apr. 4, 1928; s. Louis Harry and Clara (Roth) S.; m. Corinne Leader, Sept. 14, 1954; children: Paul M., Emily L. BEE, CCNY, 1949; MS in Applied Physics, Harvard U., 1950, PhD in Applied Physics, 1955. Sr. engring. specialist Applied Rsch. Lab., GTE Sylvania, Waltham, Mass., 1954-56, sr. scientist, 1959-64, assoc. dir., 1964-66; dir. Communications Systems Lab., GTE Sylvania, Waltham, 1966-69; staff mem. Hermes Electronics, Cambridge, Mass., 1956-59; pres. Stein Assocs. div. Adams-Russell Co. Waltham, 1969-79; pres. SCPE, Inc., Newton Centre, Mass., 1979—. Co-author: Communications Systems and Techniques, 1966, 2nd edit., 1995, Modern Communication Principles, 1967. Fellow IEEE. Jewish. Office: SCPE Inc 56 Great Meadow Rd Newton MA 02159-2748

STEIN, SOL, publisher, writer, editor in chief; b. Chgo., Oct. 13, 1926; s. Louis and Zelda (Zam) S.; m. Patricia Day, Mar. 31, 1962; children: Kevin David, Jeffrey Lewelyn, Leland Dana, Robert Bruce, Andrew Charles, David Day, Elizabeth Day. BSS, CCNY, 1948; MA, Columbia U., 1949, post-grad., 1949-51. Lectr. social studies CCNY, 1948-51; sr. editor, ideological adv. staff Voice of Am., U.S. State Dept., 1951-53; gen. editor, originator Beacon Press Paperbacks, Boston, 1954—; cons. to pres. Harcourt, Brace, Jovanovich, N.Y.C., 1958-59; exec. v.p. The Mid-Century Book Soc., N.Y.C., 1959-62; pres., editor in chief Stein & Day Pubs., Briarcliff Manor, N.Y., 1962-89; pres. The Colophon Corp., Scarborough, N.Y., 1983-95, The WritePro Corp., 1989—, The Stein Software Corp., 1993—; lectr., playwright Columbia U., 1958-60, Dialogue for Writers, Pub., U. Calif., Irvine, 1990-93; treas. The Forensic Found., N.Y.C., 1959-62; founding mem. Playwrights Group, The Actors Studio, 1957. Author: (plays) The Illegitimist, 1953 (1st prize Dramatists Alliance), A Shadow of My Enemy, 1957, (novels) The Husband, 1969, The Magician, 1971. Living Room, 1974, The Childkeeper, 1975, Other People, 1979, The Resort, 1980, The Touch of Treason, 1985, A Deniable Man, 1989, The Best Revenge, 1991 (computer software) WritePro, The Stein Creative Writing Program, 1989—, FirstAid for Writers, 1991, FictionMaster, 1993, WritePro for Business, 1996; (non-fiction) A Feast for Lawyers, 1989, Stein on Writing, 1995; also articles, revs. poetry. Exec. dir. Am. Com. for Cultural Freedom, 1953-56; mem. exec. com. Am. Friends of Captive Nations. Served to 1st lt. AUS, 1945-47. Fellow Yaddo Found., 1952, MacDowell Colony, 1952-56. Recipient Disting. Instr. award U. Calif. at Irvine, 1992. Mem. New Dramatists Com. (coun. mem.), Internat. Brotherhood Magicians (hon. life), Writers Guild Am. East, Phi Beta Kappa. Avocations: tennis, inventing computer software programs. Home: 43 Linden Cir Scarborough NY 10510-2009 Office: The WritePro Corp 43 S Highland Ave Ossining NY 10562-5226

STEIN, STEPHEN WILLIAM, lawyer; b. N.Y.C., Apr. 12, 1937; s. Melvin S. and Cornelia (Jacobowitz) S.; m. Judith N., Jan. 22, 1966. AB, Princeton U., 1959; LLB, Columbia U., 1962; LLM, NYU, 1963. Bar: N.Y. 1962, Fla. 1962. Assoc. White & Case, N.Y.C., 1963-67; atty. advisor U.S. Agy. Internat. Devel., Washington, 1967-69; regional legal advisor Mission to India U.S. Agy. Internat. Devel., New Delhi, 1969-71; asst. gen. counsel U.S. Agy. Internat. Devel., Washington, 1971-73; assoc. ptnr. Delson & Gordon, N.Y.C., 1973-87; ptnr. Kelley Drye & Warren, N.Y.C., 1987—; mem. U.S. exec. com. Indonesian Trade, Tourism & Investment Promotion Program, 1990-92; mem. U.S.-Indonesia Trade & Investment Adv. Com., 1989-92; vis. instr. internat. Devel. Law Inst., 1993; lectr. Internat. Law Inst., Washington, 1984, 85; spkr. in field. Mem. ABA (mem. sect. internat. law, mem. various coms.), Internat. Bar Assn. (mem. sect. energy resources law, sect. bus. law, mem. various coms.), Assn. Bar of City of N.Y. (mem. com. internat. security affairs 1995-97, mem. com. Asian affairs 1992—, former mem. others), Am. Indonesian C. of C. (bd. dirs. 1986—, pres. 1989-96). Home: 320 Central Park W New York NY 10025-7659 Office: Kelley Drye & Warren 101 Park Ave New York NY 10178

STEIN, THOMAS HENRY, social science educator; b. Elmhurst, Ill., May 17, 1949; s. Peter Leonard and Marion Edith (Zirbel) S.; m. Alberta Piazza, July 10, 1971; 1 child, Heather. BA in Polit. Sci., Loyola U., Chgo., 1971; postgrad., Loyola U., 1972-76; MS in Edn., Pacific Western U., 1988, PhD in Edn., 1989. Cert. tchr., Ill. Budget analyst U.S. Dept. Def., Gt. Lakes Naval Sta., Ill., 1971-72; tchr. social sci., coach bowling, softball Mother Guerin High Sch., River Grove, Ill., 1972—; tchr. Highland Park (Ill.) High Sch., 1981-84; instr. Franklin Park (Ill.) Park Dist., 1977—; tchr. Triton Coll., River Grove, 1990-91; evaluator Chgo. Met. History Fair, 1980-89; faculty adviser Scholastic, Inc., N.Y.C., 1990—; dir. Students Against Animal Cruelty, River Grove, 1991—; mod. Nat. Honor Soc., 1993—. With Ill. N.G., 1971-77. Recipient Outstanding Achievement award Am. Express/Assn. Am. Geographers, 1989. Fellow Acad. Polit. Sci.; mem. ASCD, Nat. Coun. Social Studies, Nat. Hist. Soc., Ctr. Study of the Presidency, Nat. Cath. Edn. Assn., Orgn. History Tchrs., Am. Polit. Sci. Assn. Democrat. Roman Catholic. Avocations: bowling, politics, baseball, animal activism, fitness training. Home: 3601 Emerson St Franklin Park IL 60131-1713 Office: Mother Guerin High Sch 8001 W Belmont Ave River Grove IL 60171-1012

STEIN, WILLIAM WARNER, anthropology educator; b. Buffalo, Oct. 9, 1921; s. Carl and Blanche (Gutman) S.; m. Rhoda Ruth Spector, June 12, 1949 (dec. 1993); children: Daniel Julian, Susan Isabel. AB, U. Buffalo, 1949; PhD, Cornell U., 1955. Asst. prof. U. Miami, Coral Gables, Fla., 1956-61, U. Alta., Calgary, Can., 1961-63; from asst. to assoc. prof. U. Kans., Lawrence, 1963-65; from assoc. prof. to prof. SUNY, Buffalo, 1965-94, prof. emeritus, 1994. Author: Hualcan: Life in the Highlands of Peru, 1961, El levantamiento de Atusparia, 1988, Mariátegui y Norka Rouskaya, 1989, El caso de los becerros hambrientos y otros ensayos de antropologia económica peruana, 1991, A Peruvian Psychiatric Hospital, 1995; editor: Peruvian Contexts of change, 1985. Served with U.S. Army, 1941-45, ETO. Home: 2423 23rd St Lubbock TX 79411

STEINBACH, ALICE, journalist; b. Balt.. Student, U. London. Feature writer Balt. Sun, 1981—; formerly dir. pub. info. Balt. Mus. Art. Recip. Pulitzer Prize for feature writing, 1985. Office: Balt Sun Calvert At Centre St Baltimore MD 21278

STEINBACH, TERRY LEE, professional baseball player; b. New Ulm, Minn., Mar. 2, 1962. Student, U. Minn. Catcher Oakland (Calif.) Athletics, 1986-96, Minn. Twins, 1997—. Named Southern League MVP, 1986, selected to Am. League All-Star Team, 1988, 89, 93, MVP All-Star Game, 1988. Office: Minn Twins 34 Kirby Puckett Pl Minneapolis MN 55415*

STEINBACK, ROBERT LAMONT, newspaper columnist; b. N.Y.C., Nov. 20, 1955; s. Robert Lee Jr. and Trudy Marcella (Miller) S. BA in Econs., U. Rochester, 1977; MS in Journalism, Northwestern U., 1983. Comml. credit analyst Chem. Bank N.Y. N.Am., Rochester, N.Y., 1977-81; stockbroker Merrill Lynch Pierce Fenner & Smith, Rochester, 1981-82; intern reporter Green Bay (Wis.) Press Gazette, 1982; reporter, editor, columnist Miami (Fla.) Herald, 1983—. Recipient Explanatory Journalism award Fla. Soc. Newspaper Editors, 1990, Green Shade award for best serious commentary Soc. Profl. Journalists, 1991. Office: Miami Herald 1 Herald Plz Miami FL 33132-1609*

STEINBAUM, ROBERT S., publisher, lawyer; b. Englewood, N.J., Oct. 13, 1951; s. Paul S. and Esther R. (Rosenberg) S.; m. Rosemary Konner, May 26, 1982; children: Marshall, Elliot. BA, Yale U., 1973; JD, Georgetown U., 1976. Bar: D.C. 1976, N.J. 1980, N.Y. 1982. Atty. Cole & Groner P.C., Washington, 1976-79; asst. U.S. atty. U.S. Atty.'s Office, Newark, 1979-84; atty. Scarpone & Edelson, Newark, 1984-87; publ. N.J. Law Jour., Newark, 1987—; trustee Met. West Jewish News, Whippany, N.J., 1990-95, 96—. Trustee North Jersey Blood Ctr., East Orange, N.J., 1987-93, Leadership N.J., 1990. Office: NJ Law Jour PO Box 20081 238 Mulberry St Newark NJ 07102-3528

STEINBERG, ALAN WOLFE, investment company executive; b. Bklyn., Oct. 26, 1927; s. Benjamin F. and Gertrude (Wolfe) S.; m. Suzanne Nichols, Oct. 12, 1958; children: Carol Albanese, Laura Frohman, Benjamin T. AB with honors and spl. distinction in math, Columbia U., 1947, MS, 1950. Indsl. engr. USDA, Washington, 1948-50; ops. rschr. Port of N.Y. Authority, 1950-55; prof. engring. NYU, 1956-63; pres. Am. Computing Ctrs., N.Y.C., 1962-66; v.p., dir. TBS Computer Ctrs., N.Y.C., 1967-76; mng. ptnr. Alan W. Steinberg Partnership, N.Y.C. and South Miami, Fla., 1974—. Contbr. articles to profl. jours. Nat. advisor automation United Jewish Appeal, N.Y.C., 1965-75; trustee Fla. Nature Conservancy, Winter Park, 1990—, treas., 1990—; bd. dirs., treas. Fla. Audubon Soc., Casselberry, 1984-95, Defenders of Wildlife, Washington, 1985-95, chmn. bd. dirs. 1995—; 1st v.p. Tropical Audubon Soc., South Miami, 1983-93. Recipient Chmn.'s award Fla. Audubon Soc., 1989, 93; funded named scholarship Columbia Coll. Fellow Fairchild Tropical Garden; mem. Columbia Coll. Alumni Assn. (bd. dirs. 1992-93, sustaining), Phi Beta Kappa (sustaining South Fla.). Home: 5522 Riviera Dr Coral Gables FL 33146-2747 Office: 7800 S Red Rd Ste 203 Miami FL 33143-5523

STEINBERG, AMY WISHNER, dermatologist; b. N.Y.C., Nov. 19, 1959; d. Arnold Blaine and Sylvia Fay (Bernoff) Wishner; m. Alan Lloyd Steinberg, June 15, 1986; children: Joshua Darren, Arielle Dana, Natalie Tara. BS, Northwestern U., Evanston, Ill., 1981; MD, Northwestern U., Chgo., 1983. Clin. instr. Univ. Hosp., Stony Brook, N.Y., 1987—; pvt. practice Stony Brook, 1987—. Fellow Am. Acad. Dermatology; mem. AMA, Suffolk Dermatology Soc. Office: 2500 Rt 347 Bldg 5 Stony Brook NY 11790

STEINBERG, ARTHUR G(ERALD), geneticist; b. Port Chester, N.Y., Feb. 27, 1912; s. Bernard Aaron and Sarah (Kaplan) S.; m. Edith Wexler, Nov. 22, 1939; children: Arthur E., Jean E. Strimling. B.S., CCNY, 1933, M.A., Columbia U., 1934, Ph.D. (Univ. fellow), 1941. Mem. genetics dept. McGill U., Montreal, Que., Can., 1940-44; chmn. dept. genetics Fels Research Inst., asso. prof. genetics Antioch Coll., Yellow Springs, Ohio, 1946-48; cons. div. biometry and med. stats. Mayo Clinic, Rochester, Minn., 1948-52; geneticist Children's Cancer Research Found. and research assoc. Children's Hosp., Boston, 1952-56; prof. biology Case Western Res. U., Cleve., 1956-72; asst. prof. human genetics, dept. preventive medicine Case Western Res. U., 1956-60, asso. prof., 1960-70, prof. human genetics, dept. reproductive biology, 1970—, Francis Hobart Herrick prof. biology, 1972-82, emeritus, 1982—, prof. human genetics, dept. medicine, 1975-82; lectr. genetics dept. orthodontics Harvard Sch. Dental Medicine, 1956-58; dir. heredity clinic Lakeside Hosp., Cleve., 1958-76; vis. prof. Albert Einstein Med. Coll., N.Y.C., 1962, 64, 66, Ind. U., Bloomington, 1972, N.Y. U. Sch. Medicine, 1977; XIIth Ann. Raymond Dart lectr. U. Witwatersrand, Johannesburg, S.Africa, 1975; mem. permanent com. to arrange Internat. Congresses Human Genetics; mem. med. adv. bd. Cystic Fibrosis Found. Cleve., 1957-69; mem. sci. adv. bd. Nat. Cystic Fibrosis Research Found., 1961-63; cons. to expert adv. panel on human genetics WHO, 1961, mem. expert adv. panel, 1965-85; mem. research adv. com. United Cerebral Palsy Found., 1962-65; mem. med. adv. bd. Nat. Genetics Found., 1966-68, chmn., 1968-80; dir. WHO Collaborating Centre for Reference and Research on Genetic Factors of Human Immunoglobulins, 1966-78; cons. study of diabetes in Pima Indians NIH, 1970—. Editor: Am. Jour. Human Genetics, 1956-61; sr. editor: Progress in Med. Genetics, 1960-83; mem. internat. bd. editors: Human Genetics Abstracts, 1962—; cons. editor: Transfusion, 1964—; contbg. editor: Vox Sanguinis, 1965-79; contbr. articles to sci. jours. Bd. dirs. Cleve. Zoo; mem. Cleve. Inst. Art, Cleve. Mus. Art, Cleve. Health Mus., Mus. Natural History. Fellow Australian Acad. Sci. (sr.), AAAS; mem. Am. Soc. Human Genetics (pres. 1964, dir. 1954-66), Genetics Soc. Am., Am. Assn. Immunologists, Japanese Soc. Human Genetics (hon.), Societe Francaise d'Anthropologie et d'Ecologie Humaine (fgn. mem. sci. counsel 1972), Sigma Xi. Home: 20300 N Park Blvd Apt 4B Cleveland OH 44118-5026 Office: 405Nc Millis Sci Center Case Western Res U Cleveland OH 44106

STEINBERG, ARTHUR IRWIN, periodontist, educator; b. Pitts., Sept. 16, 1935; s. Ben and Sylvia (Jacobs) S.; B.S. in Microbiology, U. Pitts., 1957, D.M.D. cum laude, 1963, postgrad. in radiobiology, 1957-59; diploma in periodontology-immunology (USPHS fellow), Harvard U., 1966; m. Barbara Fay Ehrenkranz, May 23, 1959; children: Sharon Jill, Mindy Ruth, Michael Eli. Asst. prof. periodontology SUNY, Buffalo, 1966-67; assoc. prof. periodontology Temple U., Phila., 1967-68, assoc. prof. grad. periodontology, 1968-70; attending periodontist Phoenixville (Pa.) Hosp., 1971—, now mem. infections control com., by-laws com., religious affairs com., 1977—, credentials com., 1982—; mem. staff Suburban Gen. Hosp., Norristown, Pa., 1972—, Phoenixville Hosp., 1976—; asst. prof. periodontics U. Pa., 1973-82, clin. assoc. prof., 1982—; lectr. continuing edn., off-campus program U. Pitts., 1973—; Fulbright-Hays lectr. Nat. U. Ireland, Cork, 1970-71; vis. prof. Cork Dental Sch. and Hosp., 1971—; lectr. Periodontology Soc. Madrid, Spain, 1980, 5th region Soc. Periodontology Viña Del Mar, Chile, 1985; dentist in pediatrics Charlestown (Mass.) Boys Club, 1965-66; speaker Periodontists Conv., Chgo., 1966, N.J. Coll. Medicine and Dentistry, Conn. Dental Assn., 1967, U. Ind. Schs. Dentistry and Medicine, Phila. Ann. Dental Sci. Session, 1969, N.J. Dental Assn., 1970, Wilmington chpt. Sigma Epsilon Delta, 1974, Lehigh Valley Dental Soc., 1974, Inst. Medicine, Bucharest, Rumania, 1976, Irish Dental Assn., 1992, other confs. and convs.; participant Project Head Start, Childrens Hosp., Boston, 1966; mem. fundraising subcom. Harvard U. Sch. Dental Medicine, 1980—; mem. faculty U. Pitts, 1988—; commencement speaker U. Pa. Sch. Dental Medicine, 1988, Harcum Coll. Dental Hygiene Program, 1994-95; presentor Phila. County Dental Soc. Ann. Meeting Liberty Dental Conf., 1988, 90, Acad. Gen. Dentistry Ann. Meeting, 1988; judge medicine and healthcare divsn. Del. Valley Sci. Fair, 1997. Contbg.-author The Fulbright Experience. Inducted into Phoenixville Hosps. Hall of Honor, 1996; mem. Legion Honor Chapel Four Chaplains, Valley Forge, Pa. Fellow Am. Coll. Dentists, Coll. Physicians Phila., Pierre Fauchard Acad., Acad. Dentistry Internat., Internat. Acad. Dental Studies; mem. AMA, Am. Dental Assn., AAUP, Harvard Dental, Fulbright (dir. 1977-79, mem. fin. resources com. 1983—) alumni assns., Pa. Soc. Periodontists (chmn. ins. com. 1967-69), Harvard Odontological Soc., Fulbright Assn., Nat. Fulbright-Alumni Assn. (a founder 1976, v.p. fin. affairs 1976-79), Am. Acad. Periodontology (ins. com. 1969, hosp. care com. 1973-74, continuing edn. speaker 1976 conv., 1983 conv.; nominating com. chmn. Pa. region to exec. council 1975, nat. clin. affairs com., 1984), Am. Coll. Clin. Pharmacology, Northeastern Soc. Periodontists, Acad. Stomatology Phila., Phila. Acad. Scis., Sigma Xi, Omicron Kappa Upsilon, Psi Omega (dep. councillor Zeta chpt. 1977-79). Clubs: Masons (32 deg., Shriner), Rotary (dir. 1973-76, chmn. found. com., chmn. internat. svc. 1974-76), B'nai B'rith, Harvard of Phila., Pottstown (Pa.) Area Study (pres. 1976-77). Contbg. author: Dentistry and the Allergic Patient, 1973; contbr. numerous articles to profl. jours. Home and Office: 1681 Pheasant Ln Norristown PA 19403-3331

STEINBERG, CHARLES ALLAN, electronics manufacturing company executive; b. Bklyn., June 7, 1934; s. Joseph and Rose (Graff) S.; m. Helen Greene, June 16, 1956; children—Ruth, Steven, Bruce. B.S.E.E., CCNY, 1955; M.S.E.E., M.I.T., 1958. Mem. tech. staff Bell Telephone Labs., Whippany, N.J., 1955; research and teaching asst. MIT, 1955-58; engring. sect. mgr. Airborne Instruments Lab. div. Eaton Corp., Deer Park, N.Y., 1958-63; exec. v.p. Ampex Corp., Redwood City, Calif., 1963-86, pres., chief exec. officer, 1986-88; pres. bus. and profl. group Sony Corp. Am., Montvale, N.J., 1988—. Contbr. numerous articles on med. electronics and diagnosis, info. systems to profl. jours.; patentee computer techniques in medicine. Bd. dirs. Santa Clara County (Calif.) United Fund, 1969-71. Mem. IEEE, CCNY Alumni Assn., M.I.T. Alumni Assn., Sigma Xi, Tau Beta Pi, Eta Kappa Nu. Office: Sony Electronics Inc 3 Paragon Dr Montvale NJ 07645-1725

STEINBERG, DANIEL, preventive medicine physician, educator; b. Windsor, Ont., Can., July 21, 1922; came to U.S., 1922; s. Maxwell Robert and Bess (Krupp) S.; m. Sara Murdock, Nov. 30, 1946 (dec. July 1986); children: Jonathan Henry, Ann Ballard, David Ethan; m. Mary Ellen Stratthaus, Aug. 11, 1991; 1 stepchild: Katrin Seifert. B.S. with highest distinction, Wayne State U., 1941, M.D. with highest distinction, 1944; Ph.D. with distinction (fellow Am. Cancer Soc. 1950-51), Harvard U., 1951; M.D. (hon.), U. Gothenburg, 1991. Intern Boston City Hosp., 1944-45; physician Detroit Receiving Hosp., 1945-46; instr. physiology Boston U. Sch. Medicine, 1947-48; joined USPHS, 1951, med. dir., 1959; research staff lab. cellular physiology and metabolism Nat. Heart Inst., 1951-53, chief sect. metabolism, 1956-61, chief of lab. metabolism, 1962-68; lectr. grad. program NIH, 1955, mem. sci. adv. com. ednl. activities, 1955-61, com. chmn., 1955-60; mem. metabolism study sect. USPHS, 1959-61; chmn. heart and lung research rev. com. B Nat. Heart, Lung and Blood Inst., 1977-79; vis. scientist Carlsberg Labs., Copenhagen, 1952-53, Nat. Inst. Med. Research, London, 1960-61, Rockefeller U., 1981; pres. Lipid Research Inc., 1961-64, adv. bd., 1964-73; prof. medicine, head div. metabolic disease Sch. Medicine, U. Calif., San Diego and La Jolla; also program dir. basic scis. medicine Sch. Medicine, U. Calif., 1968—. Former editor Jour. Lipid Research; mem. editorial bd. Jour Clin. Investigation, 1969-74, Jour. Biol. Chemistry, 1980-84, Arteriosclerosis, 1980—; exec. editor Analytical Biochemistry, 1978-80; contbr. articles to profl. jours. Bd. dirs. Found. Advanced Edn. in Scis., 1959-68, pres., 1956-62, 65-67. Served to capt. M.C. AUS, World War II. Mem. Nat. Acad. Scis., AAAS, Am. Acad. Arts and Scis., Am. Heart Assn. (mem. exec. com. coun. on arteriosclerosis 1960-63, 65-73, chmn. coun. arteriosclerosis 1967-69), Fedn. Am. Scientists (exec. com. 1957-58), Am. Soc. Biol. Chemists, Am. Soc. Clin. Investigation, Assn. Am. Physicians, Am. Fedn. Clin. Rsch., European Atherosclerosis Discussion Group, Alpha Omega Alpha. Home: 7742 Whitefield Pl La Jolla CA 92037-3810 Office: U Calif San Diego Dept Medicine 0682 9500 Gilman Dr La Jolla CA 92093-5003

STEINBERG, DAVID, comedian, author, actor; b. Winnipeg, Man., Can., Aug. 9, 1942; s. Jacob and Ruth S.; married; 2 children: Sasha, Rebecca. Student, Hebrew Theol. Coll., U. Chgo. Writer, actor Second City, Chicago; actor: Broadway appearances include Carry Me Back to Morningside Heights, Little Murders, (TV shows) Music Scene, The David Steinberg Show; dir.: (films) Paternity, 1981, Going Berserk, 1983, also The Richard Belzer Show, (TV shows) Newhart, Designing Women, Seinfeld, It Had To Be You, (commls.) Pizza Hut (with Roseanne Barr, Clio award 1987), NCR (with Dom deLuise), Jell-O (with Bill Cosby), Bartles & Jaymes; author spl. Return of Smothers Bros; rec. David Steinberg Disguised as a Normal Person; starred in film Something Short of Paradise, 1979. Office: care Hightlights Commercialsc 1049 N Las Palmas Los Angeles CA 90038*

STEINBERG, DAVID ISAAC, economic development consultant, educator; b. Cambridge, Mass., Nov. 26, 1928; s. Naaman and Miriam (Goldberg) S.; m. Isabel Maxwell, 1951 (div. 1962); 1 child, Christopher; m. Ann Myongsook Lee, May 15, 1964; children: Alexander L., Eric D. BA, Dartmouth Coll., 1950; MA, Harvard U., 1955; DLitt (hon.), Sungkunkwan U., Seoul, Republic of Korea. Analyst Nat. Security Coun., Washington, 1951-53; program officer Asia Found., N.Y.C., 1956-58; asst. rep. Asia Found., Burma, 1958-62, Hong Kong, 1962-63; rep. Asia Found., Republic of Korea, 1963-68, Washington, 1968-69; cons., sr. fgn. svc. officer AID, Washington and Bangkok (Thailand), 1969-86; ret., 1986; pres. Mansfield Ctr. for Pacific Affairs, Helena, Mont., 1986-87, Sr. Resources Internat., 1989-94; disting. prof. Korea Studies Georgetown U., Washington, 1990-94; rep. The Asia Found., Seoul, Republic of Korea, 1994—; pvt. cons., Washington, 1987—, World Bank, 1987—, Woodrow Wilson Ctr. for Scholars of the Smithsonian Instn., Dept. of State and the Agy. for Internat. Devel., the Can. Internat. Devel. Agy., Devel. Assocs., Inc., and others; founding mem. Burma Studies Found., De Kalb, Ill., 1987. Author: Burma's Road Toward Development, 1981, Burma, 1982, The Republic of Korea Economic Transformation and Social Change, 1988, The Future of Burma, 1990. 1st lt. U.S. Army, 1953-55. Fellow Lingnan U., Canton, China, 1948, Dartmouth Coll., 1950; named Disting. Prof. of Korea Studies, Georgetown U. Mem. Assn. Asian Studies, Oriental Ceramic Soc., Asia Devel. Roundtable (chmn. 1984-86, 87—), Siam Soc., Royal Asiatic Soc. (life Korea br.), Burma Rsch. Soc. (life), Asia Soc. (cons. 1988—), Cosmos Club, Royal Bangkok (Thailand) Sports Club. Home: 6207 Goodview St Bethesda MD 20817 Office: The Asia Found, KPO Box 738, Seoul 110-607, Republic of Korea

STEINBERG, DAVID JOEL, academic administrator, historian, educator; b. N.Y.C., Apr. 5, 1937; s. Milton and Edith (Alpert) S.; m. Sally Levitt (div. Dec., 1986); children: Noah, Jonah; m. Joan Diamond, Aug. 28, 1987. BA magna cum laude, Harvard U., 1959, MA, 1963, PhD, 1964; LittD, Kyung Hee U., Seoul, Korea, 1989; LLD (hon), Keimyung U., Daegu, Korea. Prof. history U. Mich., 1964-73; exec. asst. to pres. Brandeis U., Waltham, Mass., 1973-77, v.p., univ. sec., 1977-83; pres. L.I. U., Brookville, N.Y., 1985—; testified before Com. on Fgn. Affairs, U.S. Ho. of Reps., Fgn. Affairs Com. of U.S. Senate; cons. The Ford Found., UN Fund for Population Activities. Author: Philippine Collaboration in World War II, 1967 (Univ. Press award 1969), The Philippines: A Singular and a Plural Place, 1982, rev. edit., 1994; author (with others) In Search of Southeast Asia: A Modern History, 1970, rev. edit., 1987, Asia in Western and World History: A Guide for Teaching, 1993. Trustee Commn. Ind. Colls. and Univs.; bd. dirs. L.I. Assn.; past pres. Cambridge (Mass.) Ctr. for Adult Edn., chmn. L.I. Group. English Speaking Union Exchange scholar, Malvern Coll., NDEA scholar, Fulbright Found. exchange scholar. Mem. Council Fgn. Relations, Assn. Asian Studies (chmn. fin. com.), Phi Beta Kappa. Democrat. Jewish. Club: Harvard (N.Y.C.). Office: LI U Northern Blvd Greenvale NY 11548

STEINBERG, HOWARD ELI, lawyer, holding company executive, public official; b. N.Y.C., Nov. 19, 1944; s. Herman and Anne Rudel (Sinnreich) S.; m. Judith Ann Schucart, Jan. 28, 1968; children: Henry Robert, Kathryn Jill. A.B., U. Pa., 1965; J.D., Georgetown U., 1969. Bar: N.Y. 1970, U.S. Dist. Ct. (so. and ea. dists.) N.Y. 1973, U.S. Ct. Appeals (2d cir.) 1976. Assoc. Dewey, Ballantine, Bushby, Palmer & Wood, N.Y.C., 1969-76, ptnr., 1977-83; sr. v.p., gen. counsel, corp. sec. Reliance Group Holdings Inc., N.Y.C., 1983—; chmn. N.Y. State Thruway Authority, 1996—. Editor case notes: Georgetown Law Jour., 1968-69. Bd. dir. Puerto Rican Legal Def. and Edn. Fund. Inc., 1993-95; bd. overseers U. Pa. Sch. Arts and Scis., 1989—. Capt. JAGC, USAR, 1972-74. Mem. ABA, N.Y. State Bar Assn., Assn. of Bar of City of N.Y. (com. on securities regulation 1984-87, com. on corp. law 1987-90, com. on fed. legis. 1990-93, chair ad hoc com. on Senate Confirmation Process 1991-92), Univ. Club. Jewish. Office: Reliance Group Holdings Inc 55 E 52nd St New York NY 10055-0002 also: NY State Thruway Authority 200 Southern Blvd Albany NY 12209

STEINBERG, JACK, lawyer; b. Seattle, Jan. 6, 1915; s. Solomon Reuben and Mary (Rashall) S.; widower; children: Roosevelt, Mary Ann Steinberg Shulman, Quentin. BA, U. Wash., 1936, JD, 1938. Bar: Wash. 1938, U.S. Dist. Ct. (we. dist.) Wash. 1938, U.S. Ct. Appeals (9th cir.) 1938. Ptnr. Steinberg & Steinberg, Seattle, 1938—. Former editor and pub. The Washington Examiner; contbr. numerous articles to legal jours. Judge pro tem Seattle Mcpl. Ct., Seattle, 1952; past pres. Emanuel Congregation, Seattle, Seattle chpt. Zionist Orgn. Am. Recipient Scrolls of Honor award (3) The State of Israel. Mem. Assn. Trial Lawyers Am., Am. Judicature Soc., Wash. Bar Assn., Wash. Assn. Trial Lawyers, Seattle-King County Bar Assn. Jewish Orthodox. Avocation: outdoor activities. Office: Steinberg & Steinberg 1210 Vance Bldg Seattle WA 98101

STEINBERG, JAMES IAN, marketing executive; b. N.Y.C., Oct. 2, 1957; s. S. Sherman and Marian Steinberg; m. Andrea F.C. Hacquoil, Feb. 28, 1984. Student, U. London, 1978; BA, Columbia Coll., 1979; MBA, NYU, 1984. Account exec. Grey Advt., N.Y.C., 1984-86; sr. product mgr. Sterling Drug Co., N.Y.C., 1986-91; mktg. dir. Revlon Consumer Products, N.Y.C., 1991-93; bus. devel. Gannett Corp., N.Y.C., 1995-97; v.p. mktg., sales Apple Designsoute, 1997—. Mem. Am. Mktg. Assn., Columbia Club. Avocation: squash. Home: 4 River House Irvington NY 10533-1540

STEINBERG, JAMES JONAH, medical administrator, educator; b. Winnipeg, Man., Can., Aug. 4, 1935; s. Abraham David and Goldie (Berg) S.; m. Norma Sheila Fishman, Aug. 17, 1958; children: Deborah, Rebecca. BS in Medicine, MD, U. Man., 1959, MS in Physiology, 1962. Diplomate Am. Bd. Internal Medicine. Rsch. fellow U. Man., Winnipeg, 1961-62; sr. resident in medicine Boston City Hosp., 1962-63; fellow in metabolics VAMC Boston, 1963-64; rsch. fellow Harvard Med. Sch., Boston, 1964-67; rsch. assoc. New Eng. Deaconess Hosp., Boston, 1969-74; dir. orthopedic rsch. Robert Breck Brigham Hosp., Boston, 1974-89; chief endocrine sect. VAMC West Roxbury, Boston, 1974-89; chief med. svc. VAMC Bedford, Mass., 1989—; prof. medicine Sch. Medicine Boston U., 1989—; asst., assoc. prof. medicine Harvard Med. Sch., Boston, 1974-89; lectr. in medicine Harvard Med. Sch., Boston, 1989—; investigator NIH, 1974-89. Fellow Med. Rsch. Coun., Can., 1961-62. Avocations: chamber music, gardening, languages. Office: VAMC Bedford 200 Springs Rd Bedford MA 01730-1114

STEINBERG, JANET ECKSTEIN, journalist; b. Cin.; d. Charles and Adele (Ehrenfeld) Eckstein; m. Irvin S. Silverstein, Oct. 22, 1988; children: Susan Carole Steinberg Somerstein, Jody Lynn Steinberg Lazarow. BS, U. Cin., 1964. Free-lance writer; guest appearances Braun and Co., Sta.-WLW-TV, Sta. WMKV-TV; guest lectr. Tri State Travel Sch., 1994—; travel cons., 1994—; Contbr. numerous articles to newspapers, mags. and books, U.S., Can., Singapore, Australia, N.Z.; travel columnist Am. Israelite, 1996—, Jewish News, 1996—, Cin. Post, 1978-86, Ky. Post, 1978-86, Cin. Enquirer, 1986-94, MetroWest Jewish News, New Orleans, 1996—; travel editor S. Fla. Single Living, 1988-92; contbr. Singles Scene and Cin. Mag., 1980-94; travel columnist Eastside Weekend Mag., 1994-96; contbg. editor Travel Agt., 1986-88, Birnbaum Travel Guides, 1988—, The Writer, 1988-92, Entree, 1986-97; travel columnist Northeast mag., 1986-88, South Fla. Single Living, 1984-92. Recipient Lowell Thomas travel journalism award, 1985, 86, 91, Henry E. Bradshaw Travel Journalism award, 1st place, best of show, 1988, Buckeye Travel award Ohio Divsn. Travel & Tourism, 1992. Mem. Am. Soc. Journalists and Authors, Soc. Am. Travel Writers (1st place award for best newspaper story 1981, 3d place award for best mag. story 1981, 91, 1st place award for best newspaper article award 1984, 91, 96, best mag. article 1985, 96, 2d place award best pathos article, 1984, 88, 2d place award specific category, 1989, 96, 1st place award best mag. series 1996, 2d place best mag. article, 1st and 2nd place best consumerism articles 1996), Midwest Travel Writers Assn. (Best Mag. Story award 1981, 95, Best Series award 1981, 84, 94, 96, Cipriani award 1981, 1st place award best article 1989, 2d place award for best article 1982-84, 89, 95, 3d place award best article 1992, Mark Twain award 1992, 96, best mag. series), Am. Soc. Journalists and Authors, Soc. Am. Travel Writers, Midwest Travel Writers Assn., Soc. Profl. Journalists, Losantiville Country Club, Travelers Century Club, Circumnavigators Club. Home: 900 Adams Crossing # 9200 Cincinnati OH 45202-1666

STEINBERG, JOAN EMILY, retired middle school educator; b. San Francisco, Dec. 9, 1932; d. John Emil and Kathleen Helen (Montgomery) S. BA, U. Calif.-Berkeley, 1954; EdD, U. San Francisco, 1981. Tchr., Vallejo (Calif.) Unified Sch. Dist., 1959-61, San Francisco Unified Sch. Dist., 1961-93, elem. tchr., 1961-78, tchr. life and phys. sci. jr. high sch., 1978-85, 87-93, sci. cons., 1985-87; lectr. elem. edn. San Francisco State U., 1993-94; ind. sci. edn. cons., 1993—. Contbr. articles to zool. and edn. books and profl. jours. Fulbright scholar U. Sydney (Australia), 1955-56; recipient Calif. Educator award, 1988, Outstanding Educator in Teaching award U. San Francisco Alumni Soc., 1989. Mem. ASCD, San Francisco Zool. Soc., Exploratorium, Astron. Soc. Pacific, Am. Fedn. Tchrs., Calif. Acad. Scis., Calif. Malacozool. Soc., Nat. Sci. Tchrs. Assn., Elem. Sch. Sci. Assn. (sec. 1984-85, pres. 1986-87, newsletter editor 1994—), Calif. Sci. Tchrs. Assn., Sigma Xi. Democrat.

STEINBERG, JONATHAN ROBERT, judge; b. Phila., Jan. 3, 1939; s. Sigmund Hopkins and Hortense B. (Gottlieb) S.; m. Rochelle Helene Schwartz, May 30, 1963; children: Andrew Joshua, Amy Judith. BA, Cornell U., 1960; LLB cum laude, U. Pa., 1963. Bar: D.C. 1963, U.S. Ct. Appeals (D.C. cir.) 1964. Law clk. to judge U.S. Ct. Appeals (D.C. cir.), 1963-64; atty. advisor, then dep. gen. counsel Peace Corps, Washington, 1964-69; com. on labor and pub. welfare, counsel subcom. on vets. affairs, U.S. Senate, 1969-71, counsel subcom. on R.R. retirement, 1971-73, counsel spl. subcom. on human resources, 1972-77, chief counsel com. on vets. affairs, 1977-81, minority chief counsel and staff dir. com. on vets. affairs, U.S. Senate, 1981-87, chief counsel and staff dir. com. on vets. affairs, 1987-90; assoc. judge U.S. Ct. of Vets. Appeals, 1990—. Contbr. to legal jours. Bd. dirs. Bethany West Recreation Assn., Bethany Beach, Del., 1973-84, 86-90. Mem. aba, D.C. Bar Assn., Order of Coif. Democrat. Jewish. Home: 11204 Hawhill End Potomac MD 20854-2039 Office: US Ct Vets Appeals 625 Indiana Ave NW Ste 900 Washington DC 20004-2901

STEINBERG, JOSEPH SAUL, investment company executive; b. Chgo., Feb. 5, 1944; s. Paul S. and Sylvia (Neikrug) S.; child from previous marriage, Sarah Aliza; m. Diane L. Heidt, 1987; children: Paul Steven, Rachel Catherine. A.B., NYU, 1966; M.B.A., Harvard U., 1970. Vol. Peace Corps, Kingston, Jamaica, 1966-68; v.p. Carl Marks & Co., Inc. (investment bankers), N.Y.C., 1970-78; pres. Leucadia Nat. Corp., N.Y.C., 1979—; also bd. dirs.; bd. dirs. Empire Ins. Group, MK Gold Co. Trustee NYU. Clubs: Harvard, Nat. Arts (N.Y.C.). Office: Leucadia Nat Corp 315 Park Ave S New York NY 10010-3607

STEINBERG, LAURA, lawyer; b. Phila., Feb. 3, 1948; d. Leonard and Pearl (Zeid) S.; m. William A. Zucker, Apr. 1, 1972; children: Seth, Adam, Bree. BA magna cum laude with honors, Bryn Mawr Coll., 1968; JD cum laude, Harvard U., 1972. Bar: Mass. 1972, U.S. Dist. Ct. Mass. 1972, U.S. Dist. Ct. R.I. 1974, U.S. Ct. Appeals (1st cir.) 1973, U.S. Ct. Appeals (10th and D.C. cirs.) 1986, U.S. Ct. Appeals (4th cir.) 1988, U.S. Claims Ct. 1979, U.S. Supreme Ct. 1988. Assoc. Sullivan & Worcester, Boston, 1972-79, ptnr., 1979—, mem. mgmt. com., head litigation dept., 1988—; dir. Greater Boston Legal Svcs., 1987-90. Bd. dirs. Law Firm Resources Project, Boston, 1980-86; pres. Peirce Extended Day Program, Inc., West Newton, Mass., 1983-86. Spl. career fellow U. Calif., Berkeley, 1968-69; Fulbright scholar, 1968. Mem. Boston Bar Assn. (vice-chmn. litigation sect. 1992-94, chmn. 1994-95). Avocations: reading, tennis. Office: Sullivan & Worcester 1 Post Office Sq Boston MA 02109

STEINBERG, LAWRENCE EDWARD, lawyer; b. Dallas, Nov. 25, 1935; s. Oscar J. and Pearl L. (Soloman) S.; children: Adam Joseph, Ilana Sara. B.B.A., U. Tex., 1958; J.D., So. Methodist U., 1960. Bar: Tex. 1960. Since practiced in Dallas; partner firm Steinberg Soloman & Meer, 1971-88, Johnson & Steinberg, Dallas, 1988-93; of counsel Jenkins & Gilchrist, Dallas, 1994—. Mem. Urban Rehab. Stds. Bd., Dallas, 1975-76; mem. adv. com. affirmative action program Dallas Ind. Sch. Dist., 1974-76; regional bd. chmn. Anti-Defamation League of B'nai Brith, 1974-77, nat. exec. com., 1977—, nat. law com., 1974-87; trustee Edna Gladney Home, 1975-92, Shelton Sch., 1987-90, Temple Emanu-El, 1992-94; bd. dirs. Jewish Fedn. Greater Dallas, 1984-87, 91-94. Mem. Lincoln City Club, Columbian Club, Masons, Shriners, Zeta Beta Tau., Phi Delta Phi, Beta Gamma Sigma, Pi Tau Pi (nat. pres.). Home: 10131 Hollow Way Rd Dallas TX 75229-6634 Office: 1445 Ross Ave Ste 3200 Dallas TX 75202-2770

STEINBERG, LEO, art historian, educator; b. Moscow, July 9, 1920; came to U.S., 1945; s. Isaac N. and Anna (Esselson) S. PhD, NYU Inst Fine Arts, 1960; PhD (hon.), Phila. Coll. Art, 1981, Parsons Sch. Design, 1986, Mass. Coll. Art, 1987, Bowdoin Coll., 1995. Assoc. prof. art history Hunter Coll., CUNY, N.Y.C., 1961-66, prof., 1966-75; prof. Grad. Ctr. CUNY, 1969-75; Benjamin Franklin prof. art. history U. Pa., Phila., 1975-91, prof. emeritus, 1991—; Charles Eliot Norton lectr. Harvard U., 1995-96. Author: Other Criteria, 1972, Michelangelo's Last Paintings, 1975, Borromini's San Carlo alle Quattro Fontane, 1977, The Sexuality of Christ in Renaissance Art and in Modern Oblivion, 1983, 2d enlarged edit., 1996. Recipient award in lit. Am. Acad. and Inst. Arts and Letters, 1983; fellow Am. Acad. Arts and Scis., 1978, Univ. Coll., London U., 1979, MacArthur Found., 1986; recipient Frank Jewett Mather award, 1956, 84. Mem. Coll. Art Assn. Am. Home: 165 W 66th St New York NY 10023-6508

STEINBERG, MALCOLM SAUL, biologist, educator; b. New Brunswick, N.J., June 1, 1930; s. Morris and Esther (Lerner) S.; children—Jeffery, Julie, Eleanor, Catherine; m. Marjorie Campbell, 1983. B.A., Amherst Coll., 1952; M.A., U. Minn., 1954, Ph.D., 1956. Postdoctoral fellow dept. embryology Carnegie Instn., Washington, 1956-58; asst. prof. Johns Hopkins, Balt., 1958-64; assoc. prof. Johns Hopkins, 1964-66; prof. biology Princeton U., 1966-90, Henry Fairfield Osborn prof. biology, 1975—, prof. molecular biology, 1990—; instr.-in-charge embryology course Marine Biol. Lab., 1967-71, trustee, 1969-77; chmn. Gordon Research Conf. on Cell Contact and Adhesion, 1985; appointed to NAS/NRC Bd. on Biology, 1986-92. Mem. editorial bd. Bioscience, 1976-82; contbr. articles to profl. jours. Fellow AAAS; mem. AAUP, Soc. Comparative Internat. Biology (program officer divsn. developmental biology 1966-69, chmn. elect, then chmn. 1982-85), Am. Soc. Cell Biology, Internat. Soc. Developmental Biologists, Internat. Soc. Differentiation (bd. dirs. 1995—), Soc. Developmental Biology (trustee, sec. 1970-73), Sigma Xi. Home: 86 Longview Dr Princeton NJ 08540-5642

STEINBERG, MARCIA IRENE, science foundation program director; b. Bklyn., Mar. 7, 1944; d. Solomon and Sylvia (Feldman) S.; 1 child, Eric Gordon. BS, Bklyn. Coll., 1964, MA, 1966; PhD, U. Mich., 1973. Rsch. scientist Meth. Hosp. Bklyn. Dept. Pathology, Bklyn., 1966-67, U. Mich. Dept. Surg. Rsch., Ann Arbor, Mich., 1967-68; post doctoral fellow Syracuse U. Dept. Biology, Syracuse, N.Y., 1973-76; from post doctoral fellow to assoc. prof. SUNY, Syracuse, N.Y., 1976-89; with NSF, Washington, 1990—; reviewer NATO fellowship NSF, San Francisco, 1988, Ad Hoc NSF, Syracuse, N.Y., manuscripts in field; vis. scientist Weizmann Inst. Renal Rsch. Fund, Weizmann Inst., Israel, 1987, 1988. Contbr. articles to profl. jours. Recipient Wellcome Rsch. Travel Grant, Wellcome Found. Cambridge U., U.K., 1985, Regents scholarship SUNY Bd. Regents, Bklyn., 1960-64. Mem. AAAS, Am. Soc. Biochemistry Molecular Biology, Assn. Women Sci. Office: 1800 G St NW Washington DC 20006-4407

STEINBERG, MARSHALL, toxicologist; b. Pitts., Sept. 18, 1932; s. Harry Lionel and Eva (Goldstein) S.; m. Patricia Louise Zobac, Nov. 3, 1962; children: Leslie Renee, Michael Allan, Maureen Sara. BS, Georgetown U., 1954; MS, U. Pitts., 1956; PhD, U. Tex., 1966. Commd. U.S. Army, 1956, advanced through grades to col., 1957-74, ret., 1976; prin. investigator Tracor Jitco, Rockville, Md., 1977, v.p., chief ops., 1977-78; v.p., dir. life scis. Hazleton Labs. Am., Vienna, Va., 1978-83; v.p., sci. dir. Hazleton Labs. Corp., Vienna, Va., 1983-87, v.p. Asian ops., 1987-90; v.p. health and environment Hercules, Inc., Wilmington, Del., 1990—; chmn. safety panel Fed. Working Group on Pest Mgmt., Washington, 1973-74; cons. Office of Pesticide Programs; EPA, Washington, 1975-77; mem. expert in pharmacology and toxicology French Govt., 1985-90; chmn.-elect safety com. Internat. Pharm. Excipients Coun., 1990—, also bd. dirs.; bd. dirs. Global Environ. Svcs., Inc. Author articles, govt. reports. book chpts. Bd. dirs. Del. chpt. Am. Lung Assn.; trustee Health Environ. Scis. Inst.; mem. sci. adv. bd. Digene, 1986-89. Decorated Legion of Merit. Mem. Soc. Toxicology (sec. 1983, 85), Am. Coll. Toxicology (pres. 1986), Am. Indsl. Hygiene Assn., Toxicology Lab. Accreditation Bd. (sec. 1985-91), Acad. Toxicological Scis. (fellow, councillor 1982-85, v.p. 1990-91), Royal Soc. Medicine, Internat. Soc. Regulatory Toxicology and Pharmacology, Brandywine Valley Assn. (bd. dirs.). Jewish. Avocation: hunting. Office: Hercules Inc Hercules Plz Wilmington DE 19894

STEINBERG, MARTY, lawyer; b. Balt., May 13, 1945. BS cum laude in Pharmacy, U. Pitts., 1968; JD cum laude, Ohio State U., 1971. Bar: Ohio 1971, Fla. 1974; U.S. Supreme Ct. 1981; Registered Pharmacist Ohio 1968. Atty. U.S. Dept. Justice, Washington, 1972-78, atty. in charge N.Y. regional offices, 1978-79; chief counsel, permanent subcommittee on investigations U.S. Senate, Washington, 1979-82; ptnr. Holland & Knight, Miami, Fla.; inst. Canisius Coll. Buffalo, N.Y. 1978-79, SUNY Buffalo 1978-79, Am. U. Washington D.C. 1980-81. Contbr. to profl. jours. Bd. dirs. Miami Citizens Against Crime 1984—. Recipient Am. Jurisprudence award. Mem. ABA, Fla. Bar Assn., Ohio State Bar Assn., Am. Pharm. Assn., Am. Assn. Corp. Counsel, Am. Law Inst. (chmn. civic justice adv. com.). Office: Holland & Knight 1200 Brickell Ave PO Box 15441 Miami FL 33101

STEINBERG, MARVIN EDWARD, orthopaedic surgeon, educator; b. New Brunswick, N.J., Aug. 31, 1933; s. David and Fannie (Karshmer) S.; m. Delores Gusky White, Nov. 22, 1956; children: David, James, Susan, Julie. BA, Princeton U., 1954; MD, U. Pa., 1958; MA (status pro tem), U. Oxford, Eng., 1964. Cert. Am. Bd. Orthopaedic Surgery, re-cert.; lic. Pa., N.J. Asst. prof. orthopaedic surgery dept. orthopaedic surgery U. Pa., Phila., 1968-73, assoc. prof., 1973-80, vice-chmn., 1977—, prof. orthopaedic surgery, 1980—, prof. orthopaedic surgery in medicine, 1988—, interim chmn., 1994-95; dir. Joint Reconstrn. Ctr., Hosp. U. of Pa., Phila., 1987—; examiner Am. Bd. Orthpaedic Surgeons, Chgo., 1977—. Editor, author: The Hip & Its Disorders, 1991; guest editor: Orthopaedic Clinics of N.America, 1982, (jour.) Seminars in Arthroplasty, 1991; editl. cons. Clin. Orthopaedics and Related Rsch., 1987; assoc. editor Jour. Bone & Joint Surgery, 1992—; contbr. numerous articles to jours. and textbooks. Named one of The Best Drs. in Phila., Phila. Mag., 1984, 87, 94; Fulbright scholar, Oxford, 1963-64; fellow Arthritis Found., Oxford, 1963-64. Fellow ACS, Am. Acad. Orthopaedic Surgeons; mem. AMA, Assn. for Acad. Surgery, Ea. Orthopaedic Assn. (pres. 1975-76), Orthopaedic Rsch. Soc., Internat. Soc. for Orthopaedic Surgery and Traumatology (sec.-treas. 1996—), Am. Orthopaedic Assn., The Hip Soc., Arthritis Found., Girdlestone Soc., Assn. Rsch. Circulation Osseuse, Lupus Found. Jewish. Avocations: traveling, sailing, boating, photography. Home: 221 Winding Way Merion PA 19066 Office: Hosp of U of Pa 3400 Spruce St Philadelphia PA 19104

STEINBERG, MELVIN ALLEN, lieutenant governor, lawyer; b. Balt., Oct. 4, 1933; s. Irvin and Julia (Levenson) S.; m. Anita Akman, 1958; children: Edward Bryan, Susan Renee, Barbara Ellen. AA, U. Balt., 1952, JD, 1955. Bar: Md. 1955. Ptnr. Steinberg Lichter Coleman & Rogers, Towson, Md., 1978-86, Levin Gann & Hankin, Towson, 1986—; atty. with Rifkin, Livingston, Levitan & Silver, Baltimore; mem. Md. State Senate, 1967-87, vice chmn. jud. process, 1975-79; chmn. fin. com., 1979-82, pres. of senate, 1983-87, lt. gov., Md., 1987—. Del. Dem. Nat. Conv., 1968. Mem. Am. Judicature Soc., ABA, Md. Bar Assn., Balt. Bar Assn., Nu Beta Epsilon. Democrat. Jewish. Lodges: B'nai B'rith, Masons. *

STEINBERG, MEYER, chemical engineer; b. Phila., July 10, 1924; s. Jacob Louis and Freda Leah S.; m. Ruth Margot Elias, Dec. 24, 1950; children: David Martin, Jay Louis. BSChemE, Cooper Union, 1944; MSChemE, Bklyn. Poly. Inst., 1949. Registered profl. engr. N.Y. Jr. chem. engr. Manhattan dist., Kellex Corp., Oak Ridge, Los Alamos, 1944-46; asst. chem. engr. Deutsch & Loonam, 1947-50; chem. engr. Guggenheim Brothers, Mineola, N.Y., 1950-57; head process sci. div. Brookhaven Nat. Lab., Upton, N.Y., 1957—; expert in fossil and nuclear energy. Contbr. articles to profl. jours. Served with AUS, 1944-46. Recipient IR-100 award, 1970; Wasson award Am. Concrete Inst., 1972, Engr. of Year award, 1985, Ind. award Quest, 1985. Fellow Am. Nuclear Soc., Am. Inst. Chem. Engrs. (dir. L.I. sect.); mem. Am. Chem. Soc., AAAS, Am. Concrete Inst., Inst. Assos. Hydrogen Energy, Sigma Xi. Democrat. Jewish. Research on nuclear and fossil energy. Home: 15 Alderfield Ln Melville NY 11747-1724 Office: Brookhaven Nat Lab Upton NY 11973

STEINBERG, MICHAEL, music critic, educator; b. Breslau, Germany, Oct. 4, 1928; came to U.S., 1943, naturalized, 1950; s. Siegfried and Margarethe (Cohn) S.; m. Jane Bonacker, July 26, 1953 (div. 1983); children: Peter Sebastian, Adam Gregory; m. Jorja Fleezanis, July, 1983. A.B., Princeton U., 1949, M.F.A., 1951; Mus. D. (hon.), New Eng. Conservatory Music, 1966. Free-lance writer, 1952—; head history dept. Manhattan Sch. Music, N.Y.C., 1957-64; music critic Boston Globe, 1964-76; dir. publs. Boston Symphony Orch., 1976-79; artistic adviser San Francisco Symphony, 1979-89, program annotator, lectr., 1989—; artistic adviser Minn. Orch., 1989-92; artistic dir. Minn. Sommerfest, 1990-92; program annotator, lectr. N.Y. Philharmonic, 1995—; vis. mem. faculty Hunter Coll., 1954, U. Sask. (Can.), 1959, Smith Coll., 1964, Brandeis U., 1964-65; faculty New Eng. Conservatory Music, 1968-71, Wellesley Coll., 1971-72, Brandeis U., 1971-72, Mass. Inst. Tech., 1973; disting. vis. prof. McMaster U., Hamilton, Ont., 1982; cons. NEH, Nat. Endowment for Arts, Mass. Council of Arts and Humanities, Calif. Arts Council, Rockefeller Found. Author: The Symphony: A Listener's Guide, 1995. Served with U.S. Army, 1955-57. Recipient Sang prize for criticism in arts, 1969; citation for Excellence in Criticism Am. Guild Organists, 1972. Mem. Am, Internat. musicological socs. Home: 6828 Valley View Rd Minneapolis MN 55439-1646 Office: Davies Symphony Hall San Francisco CA 94102

STEINBERG, MORTON M., lawyer; b. Chgo., Feb. 13, 1945; s. Paul S. and Sylvia (Neikrug) S.; m. Miriam C. Bernstein, Aug. 25, 1974; children: Adam Michael, Shira Judith. AB with honors U. Ill., 1967; JD, Northwestern U., 1971. Bar: Ill. 1971, U.S. Dist. Ct. (no. dist.) Ill. 1971, U.S. Ct. Appeals (7th cir.) 1971, U.S. Supreme Ct. 1974; DC, 1994, Colo. 1995. Assoc. Caffarelli & Wiczer, Chgo., 1971-73; assoc. Arnstein, Gluck, Lehr, Barron & Milligan, Chgo., 1974-76, ptnr., 1977-86; ptnr., Rudnick & Wolfe, 1986—; speaker in field. Sr. editor Jour. Criminal Law and Criminology, Northwestern U., 1969-71; Bd. dirs. Camp Ramah in Wis., Inc., Chgo., 1974—, sr. v.p., 1992-94, pres., 1994—; bd. dirs., v.p. Camp Ramah in Wis. Endowment Corp., 1993—; bd. dirs. North Suburban Synagogue Beth-El, Highland Park, Ill., 1978—, corp. sec., 1983-87, pres. 1989-91, chmn. bd. trustees, 1991-93, trustee, 1991—; mem. Nat. Ramah Commn., 1987—, v.p. 1994—; bd. dirs. Found. Conservative Judaism in Israel, 1985-90; Midwest region bd. dirs. United Synagogue of Conservative Judaism, 1989-91, 94—; charter mem. U.S. Holocaust Meml. Mus., 1992; pro bono counsel Frank

Lloyd Wright Home and Studio Found., Oak Park, Ill., 1996—. Served with USAR, 1969-75. Recipient Youth Leadership award Nat. Fedn. Jewish Men's Clubs, N.Y.C., 1963; cert. of merit U.S. Dist. Ct. Fed. Defender Program, Chgo., 1969. Mem. ABA, Internat. Wine Lawyers Assn., Ill. State Bar Assn., Chgo. Bar Assn., D.C. Bar. Jewish. Home: 1320 S Lincoln Ave Highland Park IL 60035-3459 Office: Rudnick & Wolfe 203 N La Salle St Chicago IL 60601-1210

STEINBERG, PAUL, allergist, immunologist; b. N.Y.C., Nov. 5, 1937; s. Harry and Mary Steinberg; m. Vivian Claire Gallo, June 26, 1960; children: David Charles, Douglas Allen. BS, CCNY, 1959; MD, Johns Hopkins U., 1963. Diplomate Am. Bd. Allergy and Immunology. Intern, resident dept. medicine Strong Meml. Hosp., Rochester, N.Y., 1963-65; epidemic intelligence svcs. officer Nat. Communicable Disease Ctr., Atlanta, 1965-67; staff assoc. NIH, Bethesda, Md., 1967-70; spl. fellow div. clin. immunology Johns Hopkins U., Balt., 1970-72; asst. prof. dept. medicine U. Mich., Ann Arbor, 1972-76; dir. allergy sect. Park Nicollet Med. Ctr., Mpls., 1980-85; clin. prof. dept. medicine U. Minn., Mpls., 1983—; dir. allergy and immunology div. Hennepin County Med. Ctr., Mpls., 1985—. Contbr. numerous articles to profl. jours. and chpt. to book. Exec. bd. dirs. Minn. chpt. Asthma and Allergy Found. of Am., Mpls., 1984-88. Served to surgeon USPHS, 1965-67. Fellow Am. Acad. Allergy and Immunology, Am. Coll. Allergy and Immunology; mem. Minn. Allergy Soc. (pres. 1983-84, 87-89), Minn. Med. Assn. (Interspecialty Coun. rep. 1987—), Sigma Xi, Phi Beta Kappa. Avocations: fishing, book collecting. Office: Hennepin County Med Ctr 701 Park Ave Minneapolis MN 55415-1623

STEINBERG, ROBERT PHILIP, lawyer; b. Danville, Ill., Apr. 4, 1931; s. Frederick Philip and Beulah Iona (Olmsted) S.; m. Doris Elizabeth Blank, May 10, 1958; children: Susan Elizabeth, Mary Louise. BA, DePauw U., 1953; LLB, N.Y. U., 1956. Bar: N.Y. 1956, Pa. 1959. Assoc. Shearman & Sterling, N.Y.C., 1956; assoc. Drinker Biddle & Reath, Phila., 1958-65, ptnr., 1965-97, chmn., 1992-94, of counsel, 1997—. V.p. Germantown Hist. Soc., Phila., 1991-95, The Phila. Theatre Co., 1992—. Mem. Phila. Bar Assn. (treas. 1970-72). Home: 3906 W Netherfield Rd Philadelphia PA 19129-1014 Office: Drinker Biddle & Reath LLP Phila Nat Bank Bldg 1345 Chestnut St Philadelphia PA 19107-3426

STEINBERG, SAUL PHILLIP, holding company executive; b. N.Y.C., Aug. 13, 1939; s. Julius and Anne (Cohen) S.; m. Barbara Herzog, May 28, 1961 (div. 1977); children: Laura, Jonothan, Nicholas; m. Laura Sconocchia, Dec. 21, 1978 (div. Dec. 1983); 1 child, Julian; m. Gayfryd McNabb, Jan. 22, 1984; children: Rayne, Holden. BS, Wharton Sch., U. Pa., 1959. Founder, chmn., chief exec. officer, dir. Reliance Group Holdings Inc., N.Y.C.; bd. dirs. Symbol Techs. Inc., Zenith Nat. Ins. Corp. Chmn. bd. overseers Wharton Sch. U. Pa.; mem. bd. overseers Cornell U. Med. Coll., N.Y.C.; trustee Jewish Med. Ctr., N.Y.C., U. Pa., N.Y. Pub. Libr. Jewish. Home: 740 Park Ave New York NY 10021-4251 Office: Reliance Group Holdings Inc 55 E 52nd St New York NY 10055-0002

STEINBERG, STEPHEN ARTHUR, information systems executive; b. Hartford, Conn., June 15, 1944; s. Morris and Irene (Lebon) S.; m. Lois Shapiro, Apr. 21, 1974; children: Beth, Meredith, Genna. B Elec. Engring., Rensselaer Poly. Inst., 1966; MBA, U. Chgo., 1968. Sr. systems cons. Mobil Oil Corp., N.Y.C., 1968-71; v.p. systems and tech. Citibank, N.A., N.Y.C., 1972-88; v.p., dir. info. systems Capital Markets Assurance Corp., N.Y.C., 1989—, sr. v.p. Mem. IEEE Computer Soc. Avocation: jazz drummer. Office: Capital Markets Assurance Corp 885 3rd Ave New York NY 10022-4834

STEINBERG, WARREN LINNINGTON, school principal; b. N.Y.C., Jan. 20, 1924; s. John M. and Gertrude (Vogel) S.; student U. So. Calif., 1943-44, UCLA, 1942-43, 46-47, BA, 1949, MEd, 1951, EdD, 1962; m. Beatrice Ruth Blass, June 29, 1947; children: Leigh William, James Robert, Donald Kenneth. Tchr., counselor, coach Jordan High Sch., Watts, Los Angeles, 1951-57; tchr. athletic coordinator Hamilton High Sch., Los Angeles, 1957-62; boys' vice prin. Univ. High Sch., Los Angeles, 1962-67, Crenshaw High Sch., Los Angeles, 1967-68; cons. Ctr. for Planned Change, Los Angeles City Sch., 1968-69; instr. edn. UCLA, 1965-71; boys' vice prin. LeConte Jr. High Sch., Los Angeles, 1969-71, sch. prin., 1971-77; adminstrv. cons. integration, 1977-81, adminstr. student to student interaction program, 1981-82; prin. Gage Jr. High Sch., 1982-83, Fairfax High Sch., 1983-90. Pres. Athletic Coordinators Assn., Los Angeles City Schs., 1959-60; v.p. P-3 Enterprises, Inc., Port Washington, N.Y., 1967-77, Century City (Calif.) Enterprises, 1966-88. V.p. B'nai B'rith Anti-Defamation League, 1968-70; mem. adv. com. Los Angeles City Commn. on Human Relations, 1966-71, 72-76, commr., 1976—, also chmn. edn. com.; pres. Los Angeles City Human Relations Commn., 1978-87; mem. del. assembly Community Relations Conf. of So. Calif., 1975-91; mem. citizens adv. com. for student integration Los Angeles Unified Sch. Dist., 1976-79; chmn. So. Calif. Drug Abuse Edn. Month com., 1970. Bd. dirs. DAWN, The Seedling, 1993-95, Project ECHO - Entrepreneurial Concepts, Hands-On, 1996—. Served with USMCR, 1943-46. Recipient Beverly Hills B'nai B'rith Presdl. award, 1965, Pres.'s awardCommunity Rels. Conf. So. Calif., 1990, Lifetime Achievement award L.A. City Human Rels. Commn., 1996, award Bd. Edn. L.A. Unified Sch. Dist., 1997; commended Los Angeles City Council, 1968, 88. Mem. West Los Angeles Coordinating Council (chmn. case conf., human relations), Beverly-Fairfax C. of C. (bd. dirs. 1986-88). Lodges: Lions (dir. 1960-62), Kiwanis. Contbr. articles on race relations, youth behavior to profl. jours. and newspapers. Home: 2737 Dunleer Pl Los Angeles CA 90064-4303

STEINBOCK, JOHN THOMAS, bishop; b. L.A., July 16, 1937. Student, L.A. Diocesan sems. Ordained priest Roman Cath. Ch., 1963. Aux. bishop Diocese of Orange, Calif., 1984-87; bishop Diocese of Santa Rosa, Calif., 1987-91; titular bishop of Midila, 1984; bishop Diocese of Fresno, Calif., 1991—. Office: Diocese of Fresno 1550 N Fresno St Fresno CA 93703-3711

STEINBRENNER, GEORGE MICHAEL, III, professional baseball team executive, shipbuilding company executive; b. Rocky River, Ohio, July 4, 1930; s. Henry G. and Rita (Haley) S.; m. Elizabeth Joan Zieg, May 12, 1956; children: Henry G. III, Jennifer Lynn, Jessica Joan, Harold Zeig. BA, Williams Coll., 1952; postgrad., Ohio State U., 1954-55. Asst. football coach Northwestern U., 1955, Purdue U., 1956-57; treas. Kinsman Transit Co., Cleve., 1957-63; pres. Kinsman Marine Transit Co., Cleve., 1963-67, dir., 1965—; pres., chmn. bd. Am. Ship Bldg. Co., Cleve., 1967-78, chmn. bd., 1978—; prin. owner N.Y. Yankees, Bronx, 1973-90, 93—; limited ptnr. N.Y. Yankees, 1990-93; owner Bay Harbor Inn, Tampa, Fla., 1988—; bd. dirs. Gt. Lakes Internat. Corp., Gt. Lakes Assocs., Cin. Sheet Metal & Roofing Co., Nashville Bridge Co., Nederlander-Steinbrenner Prodns. Mem. Cleve. Little Hoover Com., group chmn., 1966; chmn. Cleve. Urban Coalition; vice chmn. Greater Cleve. Growth Corp., Greater Cleve. Jr. Olympic Found.; founder Silver Shield Found., N.Y.C.; chmn. Olympic Overview Commn.; v.p. U.S. Olympic Com., 1989—. Served to 1st lt. USAF, 1952-54. Named Outstanding Young Man of Yr. Ohio Jr. C. of C., 1960, Cleve. Jr. C. of C., 1960; Chief Town Crier, Cleve., 1968; Man of Yr., Cleve. Press Club, 1968. Mem. Greater Cleve. Growth Assn. (bd. dirs.). Office: NY Yankees Yankee Stadium E 161st St & River Ave Bronx NY 10451*

STEINBRONN, RICHARD EUGENE, lawyer; b. Chgo., Oct. 16, 1941; s. Eugene Frederick and Harriet (Slominski) S.; m. Patricia Burckell, June 13, 1964; children: Jeanne L., Nanette C., Richard Eugene Jr. BA in Philosophy, St. John's U., Collegeville, Minn., 1963; LLB, U. Notre Dame, 1966. Bar: Ind. 1966, U.S. Dist. Ct. (no. dist.) Ind. 1969, U.S. Ct. Appeals (7th cir.) 1969. Assoc. Thornburg, McGill & Deahl, Elkhart, Ind., 1968-72; ptnr. Thornburg, McGill & Deahl, Elkhart, 1973-81; ptnr. Barnes & Thornburg, Elkhart, 1982-85, Ft. Wayne, Ind., 1986—. Rsch. editor Notre Dame Lawyer (law rev.), 1965-66. Chmn. United Way, Elkhart, 1978-85; bd. dirs., pres. Jr. Achievement Elkart County, 1971-85; adv. bd. Leadership Ft. Wayne, 1991—. Capt. U.S. Army, 1963-68. Mem. ABA, Nat. Health Lawyers Assn., Def. Rsch. Inst., Ind. Bar Assn. (bd. dirs. litigation sect. 1984-86), Elkhart County Bar Assn. (chmn. com. 1968-85), Allen County Bar Assn. (bd. dirs. 1986-88, jud. selection com. 1987-88, sec. 1989-90), 7th Cir. Bar Assn., Greater Ft. Wayne C. of C. (bd. dirs.), Rotary (dist. 6540 youth exch. com. Ft. Wayne club 1986-91, chmn. internat. affairs 1991, dist. chmn. 1992-95, dir. ctrl. states youth exch. inc. exec. 1994—), Anthony Wayne Rotary Club (bd. dirs., pres. 1996-97). Republican. Roman Catholic. Avocations: Civil War history, fly fishing. Office: Barnes & Thornburg 1 Summit Sq Ste 600 Fort Wayne IN 46802

STEINBRUCKNER, BRUNO FRIEDRICH, foreign language educator; b. Linz/Donau, Austria, Aug. 22, 1941; came to U.S., 1965, naturalized, 1973; s. Bruno and Michaela Maria (Wimberger) S.; m. Claudia Jane Frey, Mar. 9, 1973. Ph.D., U. Innsbruck, 1965. Asst. U. Innsbruck, spring 1965; mem. faculty Am. U., 1965—, prof. German studies, 1973—, chmn. dept. lang. and fgn. studies, 1975-79; dir. The Am. U. Ctr., Vienna, 1985-96. Author: Dialektographie des oberen Mühlviertels, 1976, Ludwig Thoma, 1978; also articles.; contbg. author: Encyclopedic Dictionary of Religion, 1979; Contbg. author: Die deutsche Literatur, Germany in World Politics, 1979; contbg. author: Federal Republic of Germany, 2d edit., 1982, Germany, 1996. Mem. Am. Goethe Soc. (pres. 1971-73), Am. Assn. Tchrs. German (chpt. corr. sec. 1965-66), Nat. Humanities Faculty. Home: PO Box 747 Mc Lean VA 22101-0747 Office: PO Box 314, A-1191 Vienna Austria

STEINDLER, HOWARD ALLEN, lawyer; b. Cleve., June 12, 1942; s. Sidney and Lois Jean (Rosenberg) S.; m. Shirley Weinstein, Oct. 26, 1973; children: Rebecca, Allison, Daniel. B.S., Miami U.-Oxford, Ohio, 1964; J.D., Ohio State U., 1967. Bar: Ohio 1967. Mem. firm Benesch, Friedlander, Coplan & Aronoff, Cleve., 1967—. Pres. bd. trustees Cleve. Scholarship Program, 1987—. Office: Benesch Friedlander Coplan & Aronoff 2300 BP America Bldg 200 Public Sq Cleveland OH 44114-2301

STEINDLER, MARTIN JOSEPH, chemist; b. Vienna, Austria, Jan. 3, 1928; came to U.S., 1938; s. J.P. and M.G. S.; m. Joan Long, Aug. 16, 1952; children: M.H., T.P. PhB, U. Chgo., 1947, BS, 1948, MS, 1949, PhD, 1952. Chemist Argonne (Ill.) Nat. Lab., 1953-74, sr. chemist, 1974—, assoc. dir. div. chem. engring., 1978-84, dir. chem. tech. div., 1984-93, sr. tech. advisor, 1993—; mem. adv. com. on nuclear waste NRC, Washington, 1988-96, chmn. 1995; adminstrv. judge ASLBP, 1973-90. Contbr. articles to profl. publs.; patentee in field. Pres. Matteson-Park Forest (Ill.) Sch. Bd., 1959-78. Recipient Disting. Performance medal U. Chgo., 1992. Mem. AAAS, Am. Nuclear Soc., Am. Inst. Chem. Engrs. (Robert E. Wilson award 1990), Sigma Xi. Office: Argonne Nat Lab 9700 Cass Ave Argonne IL 60439-4803

STEINEM, GLORIA, writer, editor, lecturer; b. Toledo, Mar. 25, 1934; d. Leo and Ruth (Nuneviller) S. BA, Smith Coll., 1956; postgrad. (Chester Bowles Asian fellow), India, 1957-58; D. Human Justice, Simmons Coll., 1973. Co-dir., dir. ednl. found. Ind. Rsch. Svc., Cambridge, Mass. and N.Y.C., 1959-60; contbg. editor Glamour Mag., N.Y.C., 1962-69; co-founder, contbg. editor New York Mag., 1968-72; feminist lectr., 1969—; co-founder, editor Ms. Mag., 1971-87, columnist, 1980-87, cons. editor, 1987—; Active various civil rights and peace campaigns including United Farmworkers, Vietnam War Tax Protest, Com. for the Legal Def. of Angela Davis (treas., 1971-72); active polit. campaigns of Adlai Stevenson, Robert Kennedy, Eugene McCarthy, Shirley Chisholm, George McGovern; Co-founder, bd. dirs. Women's Action Alliance, 1970—; convenor, mem. nat. adv. com. Nat. Women's Polit. Caucus, 1971—; co-founder, pres. bd. dirs. Ms. Found. for Women, 1972—; founding mem. Coalition of Labor Union Women, 1974; mem. Internat. Women's Year Commn., 1977; editorial cons. Conde Nast Publications, 1962-69, Curtis Publishing, 1964-65, Random House Publishing, 1988—, McCall Publishing. Author: The Thousand Indias, 1957, The Beach Book, 1963, Wonder Woman, 1972, Outrageous Acts and Everyday Rebellions, 1983, Marilyn: Norma Jeane, 1986, Revolution from Within: A Book of Self-Esteem, 1992, Moving Beyond Words, 1994; contgb. corr. NBC Today Show, 1987-88; contbr. to various anthologies. Pres. Voters for Choice, 1979—. Recipient Penney-Missouri Journalism award, 1970, Ohio Gov.'s award for Journalism, 1972, Bill of Rights award ACLU of So. Calif., 1975; named Woman of the Yr. McCall's mag., 1972; Woodrow Wilson Internat. Ctr. for Scholars fellow, 1977; inducted into Nat. Women's Hall of Fame, 1993. Mem. NOW, AFTRA, Nat. Press Club, Soc. Mag. Writers, Authors' Guild, Phi Beta Kappa. Office: Ms Magazine 230 Park Ave Lbby 7 New York NY 10169-0099

STEINER, CHARLES HARRIS, sports broadcaster, journalist; b. N.Y.C., July 17, 1949; s. Howard Stanley and Gertrude (Harris) S. Student, Bradley U., Peoria, Ill., 1967-71. Newscaster WIRL, Peoria, 1969-70, KSTT, Davenport, Iowa, 1970-74; news dir. WAVZ Radio, New Haven, 1972-73, All-News WPOP Radio, Hartford, Conn., 1973-77, All-News WERE Radio, Cleve., 1977-78; sports broadcaster WOR Radio, N.Y.C., 1978-86; sports dir. RKO Radio Network, N.Y.C., 1980-86; play-by-play announcer N.Y. Jets WABC Radio, N.Y.C., 1986-88; anchorman ESPN, Bristol, Conn., 1988—. Recipient Emmy award Nat. Acad. TV Arts and Scis., 1993, Cable Ace award Nat. Acad. Cable Programming, 1994, Clarion award Women in Comm., 1993; named to Bradley U. Hall of Fame, 1995. Office: ESPN ESPN Pla Bristol CT 06010

STEINER, DONALD FREDERICK, biochemist, physician, educator; b. Lima, Ohio, July 15, 1930; s. Willis A. and Katherine (Hoegner) S. BS in Chemistry and Zoology, U. Cin., 1952; MS in Biochemistry, U. Chgo., 1956, MD, 1956; D Med. Sci. (hon.), U. Umea, 1973, U. Ill., 1984, Technische Hochschule, Aachen, 1993, U. Uppsala, 1993. Intern King County Hosp., Seattle, 1956-57; USPHS postdoctoral research fellow, asst. medicine U. Wash. Med. Sch., 1957-60; mem. faculty med. sch. U. Chgo., 1960—, chmn. dept. biochemistry, 1973-79, A.N. Pritzker prof. biochemistry, molecular biology and medicine, 1985—, sr. investigator Howard Hughes Med. Inst., 1986—; Jacobaeus lectr., Oslo, 1970; Luft lectr., Stockholm, 1984. Co-editor: The Endocrine Pancreas, 1972, discoverer proinsulin. Recipient Gairdner award Toronto, 1971, Hans Christian Hagedorn medal Steensen Meml. Hosp., Copenhagen, 1970, Lilly award, 1969, Ernst Oppenheimer award, 1970, Diaz-Cristobal award Internat. Diabetes Fedn., 1973, Banting medal Am. Diabetes Assn., 1976, Banting medal Brit. Diabetes Assn., 1981, Passano award, 1979, Wolf prize in medicine, 1985, Frederick Conrad Koch award Endocrine Soc., 1990. Mem. Nat. Acad. Scis., Am. Soc. Biochemists and Molecular Biologists, AAAS, Am. Diabetes Assn. (50th Anniversary medallion 1972), European Assn. Study Diabetes, Am. Acad. Arts and Scis., Sigma Xi, Alpha Omega Alpha. Home: 2626 N Lakeview Ave Apt 2508 Chicago IL 60614-1821

STEINER, ERICH ERNST, botany educator; b. Thun, Canton Bern, Switzerland, Apr. 9, 1919; came to U.S., 1922; s. Gotthold and Emmy (Schmid) S.; m. Dorothy Aileen White, July 8, 1944; children: Kurt Edric, Karl Rolf, Kim Eric. BS, U. Mich., 1940; PhD, Ind. U., 1950. Instr. botany dept. of botany U. Mich., Ann Arbor, 1950-53, asst. prof. dept. of botany, 1953-56, assoc. prof. dept. of botany, 1956-61, prof. dept. of botany, 1961-88, prof. emeritus, 1988—, chmn. dept. botany, 1968-71, dir. Matthaei Bot. Gardens, 1971-77, 89-91. Author: Botany Laboratory Manual, 1957m 65; translator: Genetics of Fungi, 1967; mem. editorial bd. Plant Sci. Bull., 1959-71. Sec. Mich. Acad. Sci., 1957-58. 2d lt. Med. Adminstrv. Corps, U.S. Army, 1943-46; ETO. NSF Postdoctoral fellow, 1960-61. Mem. Bot. Soc. Am., Genetics Soc. Am., Am. Soc. Naturalists, Soc. for Study of Evolution, Am. Assn. Bot. Gardens and Arboreta (bd. dirs. 1979-82), Sigma Xi, Phi Beta Kappa. Avocations: gardening, woodworking, photography; achievements include research in the genetics and evolution of Oenothera. Office: U Mich Dept Of Biology Ann Arbor MI 48109

STEINER, GEORGE (FRANCIS STEINER), author, educator; b. Paris, Apr. 23, 1929; s. Frederick George and Elsie (Franzos) S.; m. Zara Shakow, 1955; children—David Milton, Deborah Tarn. BA, U. Chgo., 1949; MA, Harvard U., 1950; PhD, Oxford U., 1955; DLitt (hon.), Trinity Coll., Dublin, 1996; LittD (hon.), Louvain U., 1980, Mount Holyoke Coll., 1983, Durham U., 1995; D honoris causa, U. Bristol, 1989; DLitt (hon.), U. Glasgow, 1990, U. Liége, 1990, U. Ulster, 1993, U. Durham, 1995, Kenyon Coll., 1996. Mem. staff Economist, London, 1952-56; mem. staff Inst. Advanced Study Princeton (N.Y.) U., N.J., 1956-58, Gauss lectr., 1959-60; Massey lectr., 1974; First Lord Weidenfeld prof. Comp. Lit. Oxford U., 1994—; cons. and lectr. in field; Maurice lectr. U. London, 1984, Leslie Stephen lectr. Cambridge U., 1985, W.P. Ker lectr. U. Glasgow, 1986; lectr. Page-Barbour Lectures U. Va., 1987, Gifford lectr., 1990; vis. prof. Coll. France, 1992; First Lord Weidenfield vis. prof. comparative lit., Oxford U., 1994—. Author: Tolstoy or Dostoevsky, 1958, The Death of Tragedy, 1960, Anno Domini, 1964, Language and Silence, 1967, Extraterritorial, 1971, In Bluebeard's Castle, 1971, The Sporting Scene: White Knights in Reykjavik, 1973, After Babel, 1975 (adapted for TV as The Tongues of Men, 1977), Heidegger, 1978, On Difficulty and Other Essays, 1978, The Portage to San Cristobal of A.H., 1981, Antigones, 1984, George Steiner: A Reader, 1984, Real Presences, 1989, Proofs and Three Parables, 1992, Homer in English, 1996, No Passion Spent, 1996, The Deeps of the Sea, 1996; editor: The Penguin Book of Modern Verse Translation, 1966, Homer: A Collection of Critical Essays (with Robert Flagles), 1962. Decorated chevalier de la Legion d'Honneur (France); Churchill Coll. fellow, 1961—; Hon. fellow Balliol Coll., Oxford, Eng., 1995; Fulbright prof., 1958-69; recipient O. Henry Short Story award, 1958, Guggenheim fellowship, 1971-72, Zabel award Nat. Inst. Arts and Letters, U.S., 1970, King Albert medal Royal Belgian Acad., 1982, P.E.N. Internat. Fiction prize, 1993; Faulkner Fiction grantee P.E.N., 1983; Le Prix du Souvenir, 1974. Mem. Am. Acad. Arts and Scis. (hon.), English Assn. (pres. 1975), German Acad. Lit. (corr.). Office: Churchill Coll, Cambridge England

STEINER, GILBERT YALE, political scientist; b. Bklyn., May 11, 1924; s. Isidor Aaron and Fannie (Gelbtrunk) S.; m. Louise King, July 27, 1950; children: Charles King, Daniel Tod, Paula Amy. A.B., Columbia U., 1945; A.M., 1948; Ph.D., U. Ill., 1950. Faculty U. Ill., Urbana, 1950-66; prof. govt., pub. affairs U. Ill., 1959-66; asst. dean U. Ill. (Grad. Coll.), 1956-58; dir. Inst. Govt. and Pub. Affairs, 1958-66; sr. fellow Brookings Instn., Washington, 1966—; dir. govtl. studies Brookings Instn., 1968-76, acting pres., 1976-77; staff dir. Chgo. Home Rule Commn., 1954-55; research dir. Northeastern Ill. Local Govt. Area Commn., 1957-63; vis. prof. polit. sci. U. Calif.-Berkeley, 1964-65; Kimball lectr. Brigham Young U., 1985; study dir. Commn. to Recommend Plan for Pub. Higher Edn. in, Ill., 1960; spl. asst. to gov., Ill., 1961-63; cons. Bush Found., Edna McConnell Clark Found. Author: The Congressional Conference Committee, 1951, Legislation by Collective Bargaining, 1951, (with others) Chicago's Government, 1954, (with S.K. Gove) Legislative Politics in Illinois, 1960, Social Insecurity, 1966, The State of Welfare, 1971, The Children's Cause, 1976, The Futility of Family Policy, 1981, Constitutional Inequality, 1985; editor: The Abortion Dispute and the American System, 1983. Bd. dirs. Found. for Child Devel., Manpower Demonstration and Research Corp., Governance Inst. Served with AUS, 1943-46. Social Sci. Research Council fellow, 1957; Ford Found. fellow, 1961-62. Home: 5408 Center St Chevy Chase MD 20815-7101 Office: Brookings Institute Washington DC 20036

STEINER, HENRY JACOB, law and human rights educator; b. Mt. Vernon, N.Y., 1930; s. Meier and Bluma (Henigson) S.; m. Pamela Pomerance, Aug. 1, 1982; stepchildren: Duff, Jacoba. BA magna cum laude, Harvard U., 1951, MA, 1955, LLB magna cum laude, 1955. Bar: N.Y. 1956, Mass. 1963. Law clk. to Hon. John M. Harlan, U.S. Supreme Ct., 1957-58; assoc. Sullivan and Cromwell, N.Y.C., 1958-62; asst. prof. sch. law Harvard U., Cambridge, Mass., 1962-65, prof., 1965—, Jeremiah Smith, Jr. prof. law, 1986—, founder, dir. law sch. Human Rights Program, 1984—; chair Human Rights Studies Com., Harvard U., 1994—; vis. prof. CEPED, Rio de Janeiro, Brazil, 1968-69; vis. prof. Yale U., New Haven, 1972-73, Stanford U., 1965; cons. AID, 1962-64, Ford Found., 1966-69. Co-author: (textbook) Transnational Legal Problems, 4th edit., 1994, Tort and Accident Law, 2d edit., 1989, International Human Rights in Context: Law, Politics, Morals, 1996; author: Moral Argument and Social Vision in the Courts, 1987, Diverse Partners: Non-Governmental Organizations in the Human Rights Movement, 1991; author, editor: Ethnic Conflict and the UN Human Rights System, 1997; former devels. editor Harvard Law Rev.; contbr. articles to profl. jours. Office: Harvard Law Sch Cambridge MA 02138

STEINER, HERBERT MAX, physics educator; b. Goeppingen, Germany, Dec. 8, 1927; came to U.S., 1939, naturalized, 1944; s. Albert and Martha (Epstein) S. B.S., U. Calif., Berkeley, 1951, Ph.D., 1956. Physicist Lawrence Berkeley Lab., Berkeley, Calif., 1956—; mem. faculty U. Calif., Berkeley, 1958—, prof. physics, 1966—, William H. McAdams prof. physics, chmn. dept., 1992-95; vis. scientist European Center Nuclear Research, 1960-61, 64, 68-69, 82-83, Max Planck Inst. Physics and Astrophysics, Munich, 1976-77; vis. prof. Japanese Soc. Promotion Sci., 1978; vis. prof. physics U. Paris, 1989-90; vis. scientist Deutsches Electron Synchrotron Lab., 1995-96. Author articles in field. Served with AUS, 1946-47. Recipient Sr. Am. Scientist award Alexander von Humboldt Found., 1976-77; Guggenheim fellow, 1960-61. Fellow Am. Phys. Soc. Office: U Calif Berkeley Dept Physics Berkeley CA 94720

STEINER, JEFFREY JOSEF, industrial manufacturing company executive; b. Vienna, Austria, Apr. 3, 1937; came to U.S., 1958; s. Beno and Paula (Bornstein) S.; m. Claude Angel, Apr. 11, 1957 (div. 1972); children: Eric, Natalia, Thierry; m. Linda Schaller, Mar. 6, 1976 (div. June 1983); children: Benjamin, Alexandra; m. Irja Bonnier, Mar. 19, 1987. Student textile design, U. London, 1956; student textile mfg., Bradford Inst. Tech., London, 1957; HHD (hon.), Yeshiva U., 1994. Mgmt. trainee Metals and Controls div. Tex. Instruments, Attleborough, Mass., 1958-59, mgr. internat., 1959-60; pres. Tex. Instruments, Argentina, Brazil, Mex., Switzerland, France, 1960-66, Burlington Tapis, Paris, 1967-72; chmn., pres. Cedec S.A. Engring. Co., Paris, 1973-84; chmn., CEO Fairchild Corp., N.Y.C., 1985—, Banner Aerospace, 1993—; vice chmn. Shared Techs., Inc.; bd. dirs. Copley Fund, Fall River, Mass., Franklin Corp., N.Y.C.; vice chmn. Shared Technologies Fairchild, Inc. Trustee Montefiore Med. Ctr., N.Y.C.; bd. dirs. Israel Mus., Yeshiva U. Bus. Sch. Decorated Knight of Arts (France), knight Indsl. Merit of France, chevalier de L'Ordre des Arts et des Lettres, 1990, chevalier de L'order National du Merite (France), commandatore de la Republica (Italy); recipient mayor's medal City of Paris, 1990. Mem. City Athletic Club, Racing Club, Polo Club. Jewish. Avocations: tennis, sailing. Office: Fairchild Corp 110 E 59th St Ste 31 New York NY 10022-1304

STEINER, KENNETH DONALD, bishop; b. David City, Nebr., Nov. 25, 1936; s. Lawrence Nicholas and Florine Marie (Pieters) S. B.A., Mt. Angel Sem., 1958; M.Div., St. Thomas Sem., 1962. Ordained priest Roman Catholic Ch., 1962, bishop, 1978; assoc. pastor various parishes Portland and Coos Bay, Oreg., 1962-72; pastor Coquille Ch., Myrtle Point, Powers, Oreg., 1972-76, St. Francis Ch., Roy, Oreg., 1976-77; aux. bishop Diocese of Portland, Oreg., 1977—; pastor St. Mary's Ch., Corvallis, Oreg., 1986—; adminstr. Archdiocese Portland, 1995-96. Democrat. Office: Saint Marys Ch 501 NW 25th St Corvallis OR 97330-5415

STEINER, MARY ANN, nursing administrator, consultant; b. Spokane, Wash., Nov. 12, 1946; d. John Anthony and Mildred Ann (Costello) S.; m. Michael Moloney; 1 child, Christine Hutton. Vacat. nurse (cum laude), Coll. San Mateo, 1970; RN, NYU, 1980. Staff nurse Mills Meml. Hosp., San Mateo, Calif., 1970-73; charge nurse emergency dept. Grande Ronde Hosp., LaGrande, Oreg., 1973-76; charge nurse CCU, SCU Mills Meml. Hosp., San Mateo, 1976-90; pres. Maids, Etc., San Mateo, 1990-92; supr. advice nurse Mills-Peninsula Homecare, Burlingame, Calif., 1992-94; home health nursing educator Age Ctr. Alliance, Burlingame, 1992-94; home health nurisng educator Age Ctr. Alliance, Menlo Park, Calif., 1993—; nurse mgr. telemedicine dept. MidPeninsula Homecare & Hospice, Mountainview, Calif., 1994-96; nurse mgr. Home Health Plus, Burlingame, Calif., 1997—; pub. speaker League of Women Voters, San Mateo, 1985-95, Calif. State dir. of speakers No. On Prop. 128, Burlingame, 1990, telemedicine cons. Hosp. Consortium of San Mateo Co., Burlingame, 1993—. Bd. dirs. League of Women Voters, San Mateo, 1985-95, vice chair Libertarian party, San Mateo, 1995-97; chairwoman Libertarian Party, San Mateo. Roman Catholic. Home: 815 N Humboldt St San Mateo CA 94401-1471

STEINER, MICHAEL LOUIS, pediatrician; b. Youngstown, Ohio, Jan. 27, 1937; s. Morris Louis and Blanche Evelyn Steiner; m. Diane W. Martin, Dec. 24, 1961; children: Jocelyn, Mindy, Susan. AB, U. Pa., 1958; MD, St. Louis U., 1962. Diplomate Am. Bd. Pediatrics. Intern U. Fla. Teaching Hosp., Gainesville, 1962-63, resident in pediatrics, 1963-65, instr. pediatrics, 1965; practice medicine specializing in pediatrics and pediatric cardiology Palm Beach Gardens, Fla., 1967—; cons. cardiology div. children's med. services State of Fla., 1968—. Contbr. articles to profl. jours. Served to capt. U.S. Army, 1965-67. Recipient Physician Recognition award AMA, 1970-97. Fellow Am. Acad. Pediats.; mem. Am. Heart Assn. (rsch. com. 1970—), Fla. Pediat. Soc., Palm Beach County Med. Soc. Republican. Jewish.

STEINER, PAUL ANDREW, retired insurance executive; b. Woodburn, Ind., Feb. 17, 1929; s. Eli Gerig and Emma Mae (Yaggy) S.; m. Ruth Edna Henry, Sept. 1, 1950; children: Mark, Nancy, Jonathan, David. AB, Taylor

U., 1950. C.P.C.U. Owner feed and grain, lumber and constrn. firms, Bluffton, Ohio, 1951-64; home office rep. Brotherhood Mut. Ins. Co., Ft. Wayne, Ind., 1964-65, dir. claims, 1966-71, v.p., treas., 1968-71, pres., 1971-94, chmn. bd., 1974—. Past treas., bd. trustees Nat. Assn. Evangels.; tristee Am. Bible Soc., World Relief Corp.; past chmn. Summit Christian Coll.; trustee Taylor U. Named Layman of Yr., Nat. Assn. Evangelicals, 1977. Mem. Nat. Assn. Mut. Ins. Cos. (past chmn. bd.; Merit award 1973), DEVCO Mut. Assn. (past chmn.) Conf. Casualty Ins. Cos. (past pres.), Mut. Ins. Cos. Assn. Ind. (past pres.), Soc. C.P.C.U.s (past nat. ethics com. past pres. No. Ind. chpt.), Ft. Wayne Rotary (past pres.). Republican. Evang. Mennonite. Club: Christian Bus. Men's Com. (Ft. Wayne). Home: 1825 Florida Dr Fort Wayne IN 46805-5036 Office: Brotherhood Mut Ins Co 111 E Ludwig Rd Ste 100 Fort Wayne IN 46825-4240

STEINER, PETER OTTO, economics educator, dean; b. N.Y.C., July 9, 1922; s. Otto Davidson and Ruth (Wurzburger) S.; m. Ruth E. Riggs, Dec. 20, 1947 (div. 1967); children: Alison Ruth, David Denison; m. Patricia F. Owen, June 2, 1968. A.B., Oberlin Coll., 1943; M.A., Harvard, 1949, Ph.D., 1950. Instr. U. Calif., Berkeley, 1949-50, asst. prof. econs., 1950-57; assoc. prof. U. Wis., Madison, 1957-59, prof., 1959-68; prof. econs. and law U. Mich., Ann Arbor, 1968-91, prof. emeritus, 1991—, chmn. dept. econs., 1971-74, dean Coll. Lit., Sci. and Arts, 1981-89; vis. prof. U. Nairobi, Kenya, 1974-75; Cons. U.S. Bur. Budget, 1961-62, Treasury Dept., 1962-63, various pvt. firms, 1952—. Author: An Introduction to the Analysis of Time Series, 1956, (with r. Dorfman) The Economic Status of the Aged, 1957, (with R.G. Lipsey) Economics, 10th edit., 1993, On the Process of Planning, 1968, Public Expenditure Budgeting, 1969, Mergers: Motives, Effects, Policies, 1975, Thursday Night Poker: Understand, Enjoy and Win, 1996; contbr. articles to profl. publs. Served to lt. USNR, 1944-46. Social Sci. Research Council Faculty Research fellow, 1956; Guggenheim fellow, 1960; Ford Faculty Research fellow, 1965. Mem. Am. Econ. Assn., Econometric Soc., AAUP (chmn. com. Z 1970-73, pres. 1976-78). Home: 502 Heritage Dr Ann Arbor MI 48105-2556 Office: U Mich Law Sch 625 S State St Ann Arbor MI 48109-1215

STEINER, RICHARD RUSSELL, linen supply company; b. Chgo., Feb. 26, 1923; s. Frank Gardner and Ruth (Cowie) S.; m. Colleen M. Kearns, Dec. 6, 1949; children—Robert C., Kevin K., Sheila M. B.A., Dartmouth Coll., 1948. With Steiner Corp., Salt Lake City, 1948—; divisonal dir., v.p. Steiner Corp., 1951-59, pres., 1959—; dir. Am. Uniform Co. Served with USAAF, 1942-46. Decorated D.F.C. Mem. Phi Beta Kappa. Clubs: Alta, Salt Lake Country. Office: 505 E South Temple Salt Lake City UT 84102-1004

STEINER, ROBERT FRANK, biochemist; b. Manila, Philippines, Sept. 29, 1926; came to U.S., 1933; s. Frank and Clara Nell (Weems) S.; m. Ethel Mae Fisher, Nov. 3, 1956; children: Victoria, Laura. A.B., Princeton U., 1947; Ph.D., Harvard U., 1950. Chemist Naval Med. Research Inst., Bethesda, Md., 1950-70; chief lab. phys. biochemistry Naval Med. Research Inst., 1965-70; prof. chemistry U. Md., Balt., 1970—, chmn. dept. chemistry, 1974—; prof. emeritus, 1996—; dir. grad. program in biochemistry U. Md., Balt., 1985; mem. biophysics study sect. NIH, 1976. Author: Life Chemistry, 1968, Excited States of Proteins and Nucleic Acids, 1971, The Chemistry of Living Systems, 1981, Excited States of Biopolymers, 1983; editor Jour. Biophys. Chemistry, 1972—, Jour. Fluorescence, 1991; contbr. more than 160 articles to profl. jours. Served with AUS, 1945-47. Recipient Superior Civilian Achievement award Dept. Def., 1966; NSF rsch. grantee, 1971-77, NIH, 1973-93. Fellow Washington Acad. Sci., Japan Soc. for Promotion Sci.; mem. Am. Soc. Biol. Chemists. Club: Princeton (Washington). Achievements include development of fluorescence techniques for studying proteins. Home: 2609 Turf Valley Rd Ellicott City MD 21042-2021 Office: 5401 Wilkens Ave Baltimore MD 21228-5334

STEINER, ROBERT LISLE, language consultant, retired; b. Tehran, Iran, May 21, 1921; s. Robert Lisle and Lois (Foresman) S.; m. Margaret S. Sherrard, June 4, 1944; children—Patricia Jean, Robert Lisle III, William Sherrard, John Scott. Grad., Mercersberg (Pa.) Acad., 1938; B.A., Wooster (O.) Coll.; M.I.A., Columbia, 1948. Cons. Commn. Chs. on Internat. Affairs, 1948-49; cultural attache Am. embassy, Iran, 1950-52; educationist U.S. Office Edn., 1952-54; program dir. Am. Friends of Middle East, 1954-59; v.p. Vershire Co., Vt., 1959-62; dir. Peace Corps, Kabul, Afghanistan, 1962-66; regional dir. North Africa, Near East and South Asia, 1966-69; dir. Washington office Devel. & Resources Corp., 1969-70; dir. Ctr. for Cross-Cultural Tng. and Research, adviser to univ. pres. on internat. affairs U. Hawaii, Honolulu, 1971-72; dir., gen. mgr. Hawaii Pub. Broadcasting Authority, 1972-73; exec. dir. N.J. Edn. Consortium, Princeton, 1973-78; pres. InterLink Lang. Ctrs., Princeton, 1979-91, chmn., 1992—; tchr. U. Kansas City, Mo., 1957, Bradford (Vt.) Acad., 1961; poultry cons. Middle East Tech. U., Ankara, Turkey, 1963. Councilman, v.p. Shanks Village Assn., Orangeburg, N.Y., 1948; chmn. Kabul Sch. Bd., 1965. Served as pilot USNR, 1943-46. Mem. Princeton Mid. East Soc. (sec. 1986-88, treas. 1993-95). Democrat. Presbyterian. Home: 1898 Villa Ct Lancaster PA 17603 Office: Interlink Lang Ctrs 1898 Villa Ct Lancaster PA 17603-2386

STEINER, ROBERT S., psychologist; b. Newark, N.J., Feb. 20, 1952; s. Henry and Hilda (Eisenberg) S.; m. Pamela Nadine Abrams, Oct. 11, 1984; children: Michael, James. BA cum laude, Clark U., 1973, MA, 1974; post-grad., The Merrill-Palmer Inst., Detroit, 1978; PsyD with distinction, Yeshiva U., 1987. Lic. psychologist, N.Y. Staff psychologist Elmcrest Psychiat. Inst., Portland, Conn., 1980-82; sch. psychologist N.Y. City Pub. Schs., Bklyn., 1982-85; instr. and tutor SUNY Empire State Coll., N.Y.C., 1983-86; adj. asst. prof. psychology L.I. U., Bklyn. Ctr., 1983-88; psychotherapist Comprehensive Counseling Ctr., Rego Park, N.Y., 1988—; sch. psychologist The Lowell Sch., Bayside, N.Y., 1985-89, clin. dir., 1989-92; sr. psychologist Luth. Med. Ctr., Bklyn., 1992-95; clinic adminstr. Canarsie Mental Health Clinic, Bklyn., 1995—; pvt. practice psychology Bklyn., 1995—; Reviewer books, Small Press Mag., 1992. Editl. bd. Humanistic Psychology Inst. Rev., 1977. Mem. Am. Psychol. Assn., Psychologists for Social Responsibility, Phi Beta Kappa. Avocation: music, fiction. Home: 86 Prospect Park West Brooklyn NY 11215

STEINER, ROGER JACOB, linguistics educator, author, researcher; b. South Byron, Wis., Mar. 27, 1924; s. Jakob Robert and Alice Mildred (Cowles) S.; m. Ida Kathryn Posey, Aug. 7, 1954 (dec. May 1992); children: David Posey, Andrew Posey. BA, Franklin & Marshall Coll., 1945; MDiv, Union Theol. Sem., 1947; MA, U. Pa., 1958, PhD, 1963. Ordained to ministry, Meth. Ch., 1947. Clergyman United Meth. Ch., N.Y., Wis., Pa., 1945-61; lectr. U. Bordeaux, France, 1961-63; instr. dept. langs. & lit. U. Del., Newark, 1963-64, asst. prof., 1964-71, assoc. prof., 1971-80, prof., 1980-85; prof. dept. linguistics U. Del., Newark, 1985-96; cons. Charles Scribner's Sons, N.Y.C., 1972-75, Larousse, N.Y.C., 1981-84, Houghton-Mifflin, Boston, 1981-84, Macmillan, 1994—. Author: Two Centuries of Spanish and English Bilingual Lexicography (1590-1800), 1970, New College French and English Dictionary, 1972, rev. 2nd edit. 1988. Recipient fellowship Am. Philos. Soc., Phila., 1971, Lilly Found., Phila., 1979-81. Mem. MLA (founder lexicography group 1974-75, chmn. 1976, 77, 80, 85), Dictionary Soc. N.Am., Del. Coun. for Internat. Visitors, Phi Beta Kappa (pres. chpt. 1975-76). Republican. Avocations: languages, photography. Office: U Del Dept Linguistics Newark DE 19716-2551

STEINER, STUART, college president; b. Balt., July 24, 1937; s. Louis and Lillian (Block) S.; m. Rosalie Weiner, Sept. 12, 1962; children—Lisa, Susan, David, Robyn. AA, Balt. Jr. Coll., 1957; B.S., U. Md., 1959; grad. cert., Fla. State U., 1962; M.S.W., U. Pa., 1963; J.D., U. Balt., 1967; M.A., Tchrs. Coll., Columbia U., 1972; EdD, Columbia U., 1987. Caseworker, then supr. and dir. juvenile ct. services Balt. Dept. Social Services, 1960-64; dir. referral center Health and Welfare Council Met. Balt., 1964; dir. admissions and placement Harford Jr. Coll., Bel Air, Md., 1965-67; dean of students Genesee Community Coll., Batavia, N.Y., 1967-68; dean of coll. Genesee Community Coll., 1968-75, pres., 1975—; pres. SUNY West; mem. coun. of pres.'s SUNY, acting dep. to chancellor for community colls., 1985, pres. of assn. Pres. of Pub. Community Colls. Contbr. articles to profl. jours. Bd. dirs. St. Jerome Hosp., Genesee County Community Chest, Health Sci. Agy., Western N.Y., N.Y. Spl. Olympicsd Com., Girl Scouts Genesee Valley, 1989-90; trustee Villa Maria Coll.; trustee, v.p. N.Y. Chiropractic Coll.; pres. Genesee County United Way, Community Coll. of Balt. Hall of Fame. Named Sigma Delta scholar, 1958-59, Heisler scholar, 1960-61, Kellogg fellow, 1971-72; recipient CEO award Assn. of C.C. Trustees (N.E. region) 1997. Mem. Am. Assn. Higher Edn., Assn. Pres. Pub. C.C.s (pres.), Pvt. Indsl. Coun. (bd. dirs.). Home: 33 Woodcrest Dr Batavia NY 14020-2721 Office: Genesee Community Coll One College Rd Batavia NY 14020

STEINER, ULRICH ALFRED, chemist; b. Bombay, India, Mar. 26, 1922; came to the U.S., 1957; s. Jakob Alfred and Mathilde (Gass) S.; m. Ingeborg Maria Lauber, June 2, 1949 (dec. 1959); children: Gabriele Gertsch, Beat Ulrich; m. Claire Beulah Koss, Jul. 15, 1961. Diploma in chemistry, Federal Inst. Tech., Zurich, Switzerland, 1946, Dr. SC, 1948. Rsch. chemist Emser Werke, Domat/Ems, Switzerland, 1948-53, asst. dept. head, 1953-57; rsch. chemist Union Carbide, Boundbrook, N.J., 1957-86; rsch. assoc. Amoco Performance Products, Inc., Boundbrook, N.J., 1986-91; ret. Patentee in field. Recipient Thomas Alva Edison Patent award R&D Coun. N.J., 1992. Home: 237 Jefferson Ave North Plainfield NJ 07060

STEINER-HOUCK, SANDRA LYNN, interior designer; b. Columbia, Pa., May 29, 1962; d. Howard Jr. and Mary Louise Steiner; m. Paul Harry Houck, Sept. 14, 1990; children: Brandon Paul, Brittany Leigh. AA in Interior Design, Bauder Fashion Coll., 1981. Cert. kitchen designer. Designer Bob Harry's Kitchen Ctr., Inc., York, Pa., 1982-87, Leggett, Inc., Camp Hill, Pa., 1987-90, Mother Hubbard's Kitchen Ctr., Mechanicsburg, Pa., 1990-93; owner ind. design svc., 1994—. Designer: Bath Industry Technical Manuals Vol.3, 1993; contbr. designs to profl. jours. Recipient 1st pl. award and Best of Show Resdl. Bath Design, 1986, Showroom Design, 1989, 3d pl. award Resdl. Kitchen, 1992, Resdl. Bath Design, 1992, Heritage Custom Kitchens Mfr.'s Design award, 1986, 94, 3 Nat. Design. awards Resdl. Kitchen, 1994, Kasmar Kitchen Design award 1994, 95, 96, 2d pl. Nat. Design award Kitchen Design, 1997, 1st pl. Nat. Design award Bath Design, 1997. Mem. Am. Soc. Interior Design, Soc. Cert. Kitchen Designers. Home and Office: 515 Mockingbird Dr Columbia PA 17512

STEINFELD, ALLAN, sports association administrator. M in Elec. Enging. and Radio Astronomy, Cornell U. Staff mem. N.Y. Road Runners Club, N.Y.C., 1978-92, pres., 1992; chief referee of men's and women's marathons, 1984 L.A. Olympics; adviser several TV broadcasts; race dir. Fifth Ave Mile, the Advil Mini Marathon, the Trevira Twosome, N.Y. Games; mem. exec. com. TAC's Men's Long Distance Running Com. Office: NY Road Runners Club 9 E 89th St New York NY 10128-0602

STEINFELD, JEFFREY IRWIN, chemistry educator, consultant, writer; b. Bklyn., July 2, 1940; s. Paul and Ann (Ravin) S. B.Sc., MIT, 1962; PhD, Harvard U., 1965. Postdoctoral fellow U. Sheffield, Yorkshire, Eng., 1965-66; asst. prof. chemistry MIT, Cambridge, 1966-70; assoc. prof. MIT, 1970-79, prof., 1980—. Author: Molecules & Radiation, 1974; co-author: Chemical Kinetics and Dynamics, 1989; editor: Laser and Coherence Spectroscopy, 1977, Laser-Induced Chemical Processes, 1981; co-editor: Spectrochimica Acta, 1983—; contbr. articles to profl. jours. Treas. Ward 2 Democratic Com., Cambridge, 1972-73. NSF fellow Harvard U., Cambridge, 1962-65; NSF fellow Sheffield U., 1965-66; Alfred P. Sloan Found. research fellow MIT, 1969-71; Guggenheim fellow, 1972-73. Fellow Am. Phys. Soc.; mem. AAAS, Union Concerned Scientists, Fedn. Am. Scientists, Sigma Xi, Phi Lambda Upsilon. Jewish. Office: MIT Room 2-221 Cambridge MA 02139

STEINFELD, MANFRED, furniture manufacturing executive; b. Josbach, Germany, Apr. 29, 1924; s. Abraham and Paula (Katten) S.; m. Fern Goldman, Nov. 13, 1949; children: Michael, Paul, Jill. Student U. Ill., 1942; BS in Commerce, Roosevelt U., 1948. Research analyst State of Ill., 1948-50; v.p. Shelby Williams Industries, Inc., Chgo., 1954-63, pres., 1964-72; chmn. bd., 1973-96, chmn. exec. com., 1996—; bd. dirs. Amalgamated Trust & Savs. Bank. Mem. adv. bd. Sch. Human Ecology, U. Tenn., 1981-87, devel. council, 1982-87; mem. adv. bd. dept. interior design Fla. Internat. U., 1981-85. Life trustee Roosevelt U., Chgo.; past pres. Roosevelt U. Bus. Sch. Alumni Council; hon. governing mem. Art Inst. Chgo., mem. com. 20th century decorative art; bd. dirs. Jewish Fedn. Chgo., 1986-90; gen. chmn. Jewish United Fund, 1987, 97; nat. vice chmn. United Jewish Appeal, 1988-94. Served to 1st lt. AUS, 1942-45, 50-52. Decorated Bronze Star, Purple Heart; named Small Bus. Man of Yr., Central Region, 1967; established Manfred Steinfeld Hospitality Mgmt. Program at Roosevelt U., Chgo., 1988; established Fernand Manfred Steinfeld Chair Judaic Studies U. Tenn., Knoxville, 1995; recipient Horatio Alger award of disting. Ams., 1981, Outstanding Bus. Leader award Northwood Inst., 1983. Mem. Horatio Alger Assn. (bd. dirs. 1986-92), Standard Club, Bryn Mawr Country Club, Bocaire Country (Boca Raton, Fla.), Beta Gamma Sigma. Home: 1300 N Lake Shore Dr Apt 34D Chicago IL 60610-2195 Office: Mdse Mart Rm 11-111 Chicago IL 60654 also: Shelby Williams Industries Inc 150 Shelby Williams Dr Morristown TN 37813

STEINFELD, PHILIP S., pediatrician; b. Bronx, Mar. 4, 1932; s. Samuel and Sarah (Frishman) S.; m. Ruth L. Hyman, Aug., 1961 (div. June 1977); children: Andrea, Melissa, David; m. Sherry Lynn Rubinroit, Jan. 15, 1978; 1 child, Sara. BS, Queens Coll., 1953; MD, U. Basle, Switzerland, 1960. Diplomate Am. Bd. Pediatrics. Rotating intern Kings County Hosp. Ctr., Bklyn., 1960-61; resident pediatrics Mt. Sinai Hosp., N.Y.C., 1961-63, jr. clin. asst. pediatrics, 1963-65, sr. clin. asst., 1965-68; attending pediatrician L.I. Jewish Hosp., 1968—, North Shore Univ. Hosp., 1970—; clin. instr. pediatrics Cornell U., N.Y.C., 1986-90, clin. asst. prof. pediatrics, 1991—; mem. adv. bd. TEMPO, Woodmere, N.Y., 1975—, Five Town Adolescent Ctr., Woodmere, 1975—. Fellow Am. Acad. Pediatrics. Office: 1573 Broadway Hewlett NY 11557-1428

STEINFELD, RAY, JR., food products executive; b. Portland, Oreg., Nov. 21, 1946; s. Ray and June Catherine (Cox) S.; m. Janis Bowen, Nov. 11, 1978; children: Erik, Blair. Student, Wheaton Coll., 1964-66, Drew U., 1967; BS in Polit. Sci., Lewis and Clark Coll., 1968. Sales rep. Continental Can Co., L.A., 1969-72; co-chmn. bd., CEO, Steinfeld's Products Co., Portland, Oreg., 1972—; chmn. Oreg. Mus. Sci. in Industry, 1992-94. Treas., bd. dirs. Portland Recycling Team, 1973—; pres. exec. bd. Stop Oreg. Litter and Vandalism, 1973-92, pres., 1976; chmn., exec. com. Oreg. Landmark of Quality, 1985-87, Oreg. Ballet Theatre, 1994—, bd. dirs., 1995—, v.p. devel., 1997—; pres. exec. com. William Temple House, 1985-91; vestry mem. Trinity Episcopal Ch., 1987-90; chmn. Oregn. Strategic Plan Agrl. Dept., 1988, World Trade Week, Portland, 1989; mem. Gov. Robert's Task Force, Salem, Oreg., 1991-92; bd. dirs. Oreg. Enterprise Forum, 1992—, chmn., 1995. Mem. Pickle Packers Internat. (chmn. mdse. com.), Portland C. of C. (bd. dirs. 1995—). Democrat. Espiscopalian. Avocations: tennis, golf, bridge, handball. Office: 10001 N Rivergate Blvd Portland OR 97203-6526

STEINFELD, THOMAS ALBERT, publisher; b. N.Y.C., June 17, 1917; s. Albert and Marjorie (Lesser) S.; m. Joan Rollinson, July 29, 1945 (dec. Nov. 1973); children: Geoffrey T., Jill R.; m. Viviane Barkey, June 20, 1977. Student, G. Phillips Exeter Acad., 1934, Harvard U., 1934-35. Salesman John Orr Products, N.Y.C., 1935-36; asst. advt. mgr. Bloomingdale's, N.Y.C., 1936-37; with Playbill mag., N.Y.C., 1937—; pub. Playbill mag., 1962-65, pres., 1962-68; now v.p., nat. sales dir. Playbill. Served to capt. AUS, 1942-46, CBI. Mem. English Speaking Union, Aspetuck Valley Country Club (Weston, Conn.), The Wings Club (N.Y.C.). Home: 83 W Meadow Rd Wilton CT 06897-4722 Office: 52 Vanderbilt Ave New York NY 10017-3808

STEINFELS, PETER FRANCIS, newspaper correspondent, writer; b. Chgo., July 15, 1941; s. Melville Philip and Margaret Mary (Hollahan) S.; m. Margaret Mary O'Brien, Aug. 31, 1963; children: Gabrielle, John Melville. AB, Loyola U., 1963; MA, Columbia U., 1964, PhD, 1976. Editorial asst. Commonweal Mag., N.Y.C., 1964-65, asst. editor, 1965-67, assoc. editor, 1967-71, exec. editor, 1978-84, editor, 1984-88; sr. religion corr. N.Y. Times, 1988—; assoc. for humanities Inst. of Soc., Ethics and Life Scis., Hastings-on-Hudson, N.Y., 1972-77; co-editor (with Margaret O'Brien Steinfels) Hastings Ctr. Report, Hastings-on-Hudson, 1973-77. Author: The Neoconservatives, 1979; editor (with Robert M. Veatch) Death Inside Out, 1975. Roman Catholic. Home: 924 W End Ave New York NY 10025-3534 Office: NY Times 229 W 43rd St Fl 3 New York NY 10036-3913*

STEINFINK, HUGO, chemical engineering educator; b. Vienna, Austria, May 22, 1924; s. Mendel and Malwina (Fiderer) S.; m. Cele Intrator, Mar. 21, 1948; children: Dan E., Susan D. BS, CCNY, 1947; MS, Columbia U., 1948; PhD, Bklyn. Poly. Inst., 1954. Rsch. chemist Shell Devel. Co., Houston, 1948-51, 53-60; T. Brockett Hudson prof. chem. engring. U. Tex., Austin, 1960—. Contbr. articles to profl. jours. With AUS, 1944-46. Fellow Am. Mineral Soc.; mem. AIChE, Am. Chem. Soc., Am. Crystallographic Assn. (pres.-elect 1994, pres. 1995, past pres. 1996), Materials Rsch. Soc., Phi Beta Kappa, Sigma Xi, Phi Lambda Epsilon. Home: 3811 Walnut Clay Dr Austin TX 78731-4011 Office: U Tex Coll Engring Austin TX 78712

STEINFORT, JAMES RICHARD, university program director; b. Grand Rapids, Mich., Oct. 1, 1941; s. Gerald Gene and Harriett Lois (Stauffer) S.; m. Elizabeth Ann O'Laughlin, Mar. 14, 1964; children: Dawn, Robin, Susan, Troy, Ginger. AA in Computer Sci., San Jacinto Coll., Pasadena, Tex., 1973; BS in Tech. Mgmt. cum laude, Regis Coll., 1987. Chartered cons., Am. Cons. League. Customer engr. Control Data Corp., Mpls., 1964-65; computer engr. GE, Phoenix, 1965-69; tech. analyst Manned Spacecraft Ctr., Houston, 1969-73, systems analyst, 1973-75; tech. support mgr. Ohio Med. Products, Houston, 1975-79; prodn. regional mgr. Johnson & Johnson Co., Denver, 1979-83; prin., internat. cons. J.R. Steinfort & Assocs., Boise, Idaho, 1983-90; dir. TIES (Tech. and Indsl. Ext. Svc.) Boise State U., 1990-95; exec. dir. Idaho Mfg. Alliance, Boise, 1995-97, Assn. of Idaho Mfrs., 1997—; cons. The Timberline Group, Boise, 1996—. Author: (non-fiction) Conspiracy in Dallas, 1975, rev. edit., 1992, 96; (tech. manuals) Medical/EDP Design Applications, 1985, Factory Quality Audit, 1991; editor newsletter Industry TIES, 1992-94, ISO-9000 Guidelines & Checklist, 1994. Chmn. subcom. Gov.'s Prayer Breakfast Commn., Boise, 1988-92; v.p. Full Gospel Businessman's Internat., Boise, 1990. With USAF, 1960-64. Univ. Ctr. grantee Econ. Devel. Adminstrn., Boise, 1990-96. Mem. Am. Soc. for Quality Control (sr.), Nat. Assn. Mgmt. and Tech. Assistance Ctrs. (bd. dirs. 1990-96), Am. Mgmt. Assn., Am. Cons. League (chartered cons.), Idaho Total Quality Inst. (bd. dirs. 1991-96, trustee 1995—, Idaho Quality award), Tech. Transfer Soc. Avocations: hiking, camping, photography, writing, hunting. Home: 11934 Ginger Creek Dr Boise ID 83713-3677 Office: Assn of Idaho Mfrs PO Box 829 Boise ID 83701 also: The Timberline Group # 281 3355 N Five Mile Rd Boise ID 83713

STEINGLASS, PETER JOSEPH, psychiatrist, educator; b. N.Y.C., Mar. 1, 1939; s. Sam and Bella Sarah (Bernstein) S.; m. Abbe Stahl, July 1, 1962; children: Matthew Aaron, Joanna Eowyn. AB, Union Coll., 1960; MD, Harvard U., 1965. Diplomate, Am. Bd. Psychiatry and Neurology. Head clin. rsch. program Nat. Inst. Alcohol Abuse and Alcoholism, Washington, 1971-74; asst. prof. psychiatry George Washington U., Washington, 1974-77; assoc. prof. psychiatry George Washington U., 1977-81, prof. psychiatry and behavioral sci., 1981-90; exec. dir. Ackerman Inst. for the Family, N.Y.C., 1990—; vis. prof. psychiatry Hebrew U., Jerusalem, 1981-82; clin. prof. psychiatry Cornell U. Med. Coll., 1993—. Author: The Alcoholic Family, 1987; contbr. articles to sci. publs. Lt. comdr. USPHS, 1969-71. Fellow Am. Psychiat. Assn., Am. Assn. Marriage and Family Therapy (cumulative contbn. award 1992), Assn. Clin. Psychosocial Rsch.; mem. Am. Family Therapy Acad. (charter, bd. dirs. 1987-89, v.p. 1989-91, Disting. Contbn. award 1987), Aesculapian Soc., Phi Beta Kappa. Democrat. Jewish. Avocations: photography, classical music. Office: Ackerman Inst for the Family 149 E 78th St New York NY 10021-0405

STEINGRABER, FREDERICK GEORGE, management consultant; b. Mpls., July 7, 1938; s. Frederick F. and Evelyn (Luger) S.; m. Veronika Agnes Wagner, Aug. 9, 1974; children—Karla, Frederick. B.S., Ind. U., 1960; MBA, Beta Gamma Sigma, U. Chgo., 1964. Cert. mgmt. cons. Internat. banker Harris Trust, Chgo., 1960-61; with comml. loan and credit No. Trust Co., Chgo., 1963; assoc. A.T. Kearney, Chgo., 1964-69, prin., 1969-72, officer/ptnr., 1972—, pres., chief ops. officer, 1981, chief exec. officer, 1983—, chmn. bd., 1986-95; also bd. dirs.; bd. dirs. Lawter Internat., Mercury Fin. Co.; mem. Inst. for Ill., 1986; bd. dirs. Maytag Corp., Southeastern Thrift & Bank Fund, The Conf. Bd. Chief Crusader United Way-Crusade of Mercy, Chgo., 1983-90, div. chmn., 1988; bd. dirs. Ill. Coalition, 1989, Northwestern Healthcare Network, 1989—, fin. rsch. and adv. com. City of Chgo., 1989—; mem. Chgo. Com., 1994; mem., past chmn. dean's adv. coun. Ind. U., 1985—, bd. dirs. Ind. U. Found.; mem. coun. of Grad. Sch. Bus. U. Chgo.; mem. Northwestern U. Assocs.; bd. dirs. Children's Meml. Hosp., Chgo., 1985—; exec. com. Mid.-Am. Com., 1985—. Recipient Disting. Alumnus award U. Chgo., 1996, Disting. Corp. Exec. award U. Chgo., 1996. Mem. NAM (bd. dirs.), Inst. Mgmt. Cons., Chgo. Coun. Fgn. Rels. (bd. dirs.), Ill. State C. of C. (bd. dirs. 1982-88, exec. com. 1984-88, chmn. Ill. Alliance for Econ. Initiatives), Exec. Club Chgo., Acad. Alumni Fellows Ind. U. (award), Chgo. Club, Econ. Club (bd. dirs.), Comml. Club, Met. Club, Glenview Club, others. Home: 615 Warwick Rd Kenilworth IL 60043-1149 Office: AT Kearney Inc 222 W Adams St Chicago IL 60606-5307

STEINHARDT, HENRY, photographer; b. N.Y.C., Nov. 15, 1920; s. Maxwell and Ruth (Davis) S.; m. Elizabeth Smith, 1946 (dec. 1955); children: Elizabeth, Maxwell; m. Helene Fleck, Feb. 1, 1958; 1 child, Henry III. AB, Harvard U., 1942, MArch, 1949. Registered architect. Office mgr. R.H. Cutting, Architect, N.Y.C., 1951-53; ptnr., architect Steinhardt & Thompson, Architects, N.Y.C., 1953-61; architect The Cerny Assocs., St. Paul, 1961-63, John Graham & Co., Seattle, 1963-67, Morse/Kirk, Seattle, 1967-68, N.G. Jacobson & Assocs., Seattle, 1968-69; pvt. practice Mercer Island, Wash., 1969-75; architect USN, Bremerton, Wash., 1975-78; photographer Mercer Island, 1979—. Prin. works exhibited at Washington, Seattle and Andover, Mass.; contbr. articles to fgn. archtl. jours. 1st lt. U.S. Army, 1943-46; capt. USAF, 1950-52. Recipient Design award Progressive Architecture, 1959, Archtl. award Fifth Ave. Assn., 1960. Fellow AIA. Democrat. Home and Office: 7825 SE 63rd Pl Mercer Island WA 98040-4813

STEINHART, DEAN RAYMOND, education administrator; b. Allentown, Pa., May 6, 1930; s. Raymond Charles and Zelia (Johns) S.; BS Kutztown U., 1957; MA, Franklin and Marshall Coll., 1963; MEd, Pa. State U., 1962, EdD, 1980; m. Norma Myers, Ar. 20, 1952; children: Eric Charles, Carl David. Tchr. sci. Elizabethtown (Pa.) Area H.S., 1957-59; tchr. biology, sci. coordinator, 1960-67, secondary sch. prin., 1968-73, dir. secondary edn., middle sch. and high sch., 1973-75, asst. supt. schs., 1975-80; supt. schs. No. Lebanon Sch. Dist., Fredericksburg, Pa., 1980-83; nat. sales mgr. Continental Press, Inc., Elizabethtown, 1984-85; advisor environ. edn. Pa. Dept. Edn., 1985-93; chmn., sch. svcs. adv. Dept. Edn., 1993—; bd. suprs. Mt. Joy Twp., Lancaster County, 1984-90. Bd. dirs. No. Lancaster County Med. Center, Lancaster County Conservatory, 1995—. Served with USMC, 1948-52. NSF fellow, 1960-62; Kettering Found. fellow, 1978; recipient Freedoms Found. award, 1979. Republican. Clubs: Rotary (treas.), Masons, Shriners. Address: 2059 Cloverleaf Rd Mount Joy PA 17552-8702

STEINHAUER, GILLIAN, lawyer; b. Aylesbury, Bucks, Eng., Oct. 6, 1938; d. Eric Frederick and Maisie Kathleen (Yeates) Pearson; m. Bruce William Steinhauer, Jan. 2, 1960; children: Alison (Humphrey) Eric, John, Elspeth. AB cum laude, Bryn Mawr (Pa.) Coll., 1959; JD cum laude, U. Mich., 1976. Bar: Mich. 1976, Mass. 1992, U.S. Dist. Ct. (ea. dist.) Mich. 1976, U.S. Ct. Appeals (6th cir.) 1982. Assoc. Miller, Canfield, Paddock & Stone, Detroit, 1976-82, sr. ptnr., 1983-92; dir. Commonwealth of Mass. Workers' Compensation Litigation Unit, Boston, 1992—; mem. Atty. Gen.'s Task Force to Reduce Waste, Fraud and Abuse in the Workers' Compensation System, 1992—. Chancellor Cath. Ch. St. Paul, Detroit, 1976-83, 91; pres. bd. trustees Cath. Cmty. Svcs. Inc., 1989-92; bd. dirs. Spaulding for Children, 1991-92, Davenport House, 1992-96, chair 1995-96, mem. Vestry St. Michael's Ch., Marblehead, Mass., 1994-97. Mem. Mich. State Bar Found. (life), Fed. Jud. Conf. 6th Cir. (life). Home: 510 Hale St Prides Crossing MA 01965 Office: 100 Cambridge St Rm 1801 Boston MA 02202-0044

STEINHAUS, JOHN EDWARD, physician, medical educator; b. Omaha, Feb. 23, 1917; s. Emil F. and Pearl (Haynie) S.; m. Mila Jean Pinkerton, Feb. 21, 1943; children: Kathryn, Carolyn, Barbara, William, Elizabeth. B.A., U. Neb., 1940, M.A., 1941; M.D., U. Wis., 1945, Ph.D., 1950. Diplomate: Am. Bd. Anesthesiologists. Pvt. practice specializing in anesthesiology Madison,

Wis., 1951-58, Atlanta, 1958—; faculty U. Wis., 1951-58; mem. faculty Emory U., Atlanta, 1958—; prof. anesthesiology Emory U., 1959-87, prof. emeritus, 1987—, chmn. dept., 1959-85; chief anesthesiology service Grady Meml. Hosp., 1959-77, Emory U. Hosp., 1958-85. Author: Medical Care Divided; contbr. articles to profl. jours. Pres. Anesthesia Found. Mem. Am. Soc. Anesthesiologists (past pres., Disting. Service award 1982), So. Soc. Anesthesiologists (past pres.), AMA, AAAS, Assn. U. Anesthetists (past pres.), Anesthesiology History Assn. (pres), Soc. Pharm. Exptl. Therapeutics, Phi Beta Kappa, Sigma Xi, Alpha Omega Alpha. Home and Office: 836 Castle Falls Dr NE Atlanta GA 30329-4114

STEINHERZ, LAUREL JUDITH, pediatric cardiologist; b. N.Y.C., Jan. 5, 1947; d. Bernard and Adeline Weinberger; m. Peter Gustav Steinherz, July 4, 1967; children: Jennifer, Jonathan, Daniel, David. Student, Hebrew U., Jersualem, 1966; BA with distinction, U. Rochester, 1967; MD, Albert Einstein Coll. Medicine, 1970. Diplomate Am. Bd. Pediatrics, sub-bd. pediatric cardiology. Intern in pediatrics N.Y. Hosp.-Cornell Med. Ctr., N.Y.C., 1970-71; pediatric cardiology fellow N.Y. Hosp. Cornell U. Med. Ctr., N.Y.C., 1973-75, asst. attending pediatrician, 1978-85, assoc. attending pediatrician, 1985—; resident in pediatrics St. Louis Children's Hosp., 1971-72; attending pediatrician State U. Hosp. and King County Med. Ctr., Bklyn., 1975-77; asst. prof. pediatrics Cornell U. Med. Coll., N.Y.C., 1977-85, assoc. prof. pediatrics, 1985—; from asst. to assoc. attending pediatrician Meml. Sloan Kettering Cancer Ctr., N.Y.C., 1977—, dir. pediatric cardiology, 1977—. Contbg. author: Adolescent Medicine II, 1976, Principles and Practice of Oncology, 1992; contbr. articles to profl. jours. Hutzler Found. grantee, 1987. Fellow Am. Acad. Pediatrics, Am. Coll. Cardiology; mem. Am. Heart Assn., Children's Cancer Group (chair cardiology discipline com.). Avocations: photography, swimming, Star Trek. Office: Meml Sloan Kettering Cancer Ctr 1275 York Ave New York NY 10021-6007

STEINHOFF, HAROLD WILLIAM, retired research institute executive; b. Ft. Morgan, Colo., Mar. 9, 1919; s. Lawrence Henry and Helen Grace (Morse) S.; m. Marian Andelea Towne, Jan. 19, 1944; children: Richard Terrell, David Lee. BS in Forestry, Colo. A&M Coll., 1941; MS in Forest Zoology, Syracuse U., 1947, PhD in Wildlife Biology, 1957. Grad. teaching asst. Syracuse (N.Y.) U., 1941-42, 46-47; timber estimator U.S. Forest Svc., Ft. Collins, Colo., 1944; ranger U.S. Nat. Park Svc., Estes Park, Colo., 1947; prof. Colo. State U., Ft. Collins, 1947-74, Centennial prof., 1970—, regional adminstr., 1974-77, dist. dir., 1977-81; project leader Four Corners Rsch. Inst., Durango, Colo., 1977—, pres., 1981-92; cons. Devel. Rsch. Assocs., Denver, 1971, Stanford Rsch. Inst., Menlo Park, Calif., 1971; project leader Huddelston & Buck, Denver, 1972. Author: Wildlife Ecology, 1961, Ecosystem Biology, 1976; editor: Ecological Impact of Snowpack Augmentation, 1976; contbr. The Values of the Wildlife Resource, 1987. Dean Teaching Inst. Ft. Collins Coun. Chs., 1952-56; chmn. environ. com. Durango C. of C., 1977; chmn. LaPlata County Energy Coun., Durango, 1977, Durango Uranium Tailings Task Force, 1978-91. Capt. C.E. U.S. Army, 1942-46, ETO. Recipient Oliver Pennock Disting. Svc. award Colo. State U., 1968. Mem. The Wildlife Soc. (coun. 1966-71), Coll. Forestry Alumni Assn. (pres. 1964-64, Honor Alumnus award 1976), Soc. Am. Foresters, Am. Inst. Biol. Sci., Nat. Wildlife Fedn., Toastmasters (pres. Durango chpt. 1980-81), Phi Kappa Phi (pres. Ft. Collins 1965). Avocations: photography, family history and genealogy. Home: 2705 N College Dr Durango CO 81301-4410

STEINHOFF, RAYMOND O(AKLEY), consulting geologist; b. Hart, Mich., Apr. 22, 1925; m. Anne M. Steinhoff, 1952; 1 child, Kirk O. BS, So. Meth. U., 1948, MS, 1948; PhD in Geology, Tex. A&M, 1965. Instr. geology Tex. A&M U., Coll. Sta., Tex., 1948-51; geologist Atlantic Rich., Coll. Sta., 1951-53, Humble Oil and Refining Co., Coll. Sta., 1953-57; asst. prof. geology Tulane U., New Orleans, 1957-65, assoc. prof., 1965-70, chmn. dept., 1969-70; prof. and dept. head geology Stephen F. Austin State U., Nacogdoches, Tex., 1970-78; divsn. geologist Buttes, 1978-79; cons. geologist Graham, Tex., 1979-81; cons. Trinexco, 1964-69. Sgt. U.S. Army, 1944-46; 1st lt. USAF, 1952-53, Korea. Mem. Am. Assn. Petroleum Geologists (emeritus), New Orleans Gol. Soc., Phi Kappa Phi. Home: Rte 4 Box 562 Enterprise AL 36330

STEINHOFF, WILLIAM RICHARD, English literature educator; b. Chgo., Feb. 13, 1914; s. William Richard and Nellie (Mulligan) S.; m. Rosannah Jenne Cannon, Jan. 6, 1940; m. Marilyn Mason Brown, May 8, 1993. A.B., Calif.-Berkeley, 1938, M.A., 1940, Ph.D., 1948. Mem. faculty U. Mich., Ann Arbor, 1948—; prof. English lit. U. Mich., 1963—, prof. emeritus, 1985—; vis. prof. U. Aix-Marseilles, France, 1964-65; mem. exec. com. Coll. Conf. Composition and Communications, 1959-60. Author: George Orwell and the Origins of 1984, 1975 (pub. in Eng. as The Road to 1984); editor: (with others): Modern Short Stories, 1951, (with others) The Image of the Work, 1952, (With A. Carr) Points of Departure, 1960. Chmn. Mich. Commn. Tchr. Certification, 1961-62. 2d lt. AUS, 1943-46. Ford fellow, 1954-55; Fulbright lectr., Indonesia, 1984-85, Bratislava, Czechoslovakia, 1987-88. Home: 2108 Scottwood Ave Ann Arbor MI 48104-4511

STEINHORN, IRWIN HARRY, lawyer, educator, corporate executive; b. Dallas, Aug. 13, 1940; s. Raymond and Libby L. (Miller) S.; m. Linda Kay Shoshone, Nov. 30, 1968; 1 child, Leslie Robin. BBA, U. Tex., 1961, LLB, 1964. Bar: Tex. 1964, U.S. Dist. Ct. (no. dist.) Tex. 1965, Okla. 1970, U.S. Dist. Ct. (we. dist.) Okla. 1972. Assoc. Oster & Kaufman, Dallas, 1964-67; ptnr. Parness, McQuire & Lewis, Dallas, 1967-70; sr. v.p., gen. counsel LSB Industries, Inc., Oklahoma City, 1970-87; v.p., gen. counsel USPCI, Inc., Oklahoma City, 1987-88; ptnr. Hastie & Steinhorn, Oklahoma City, 1988-95; mem., officer, dir. Conner & Winters, Oklahoma City, 1995—; adj. prof. law Oklahoma City U. Sch. Law, 1979—; lectr. in field. Mem. adv. com. Okla. Securities Commn., 1986—. Served to capt. USAR, 1964-70. Mem. ABA, Tex. Bar Assn., Okla. Bar Assn. (bus. assn. sect., sec.ptreas. 1986-87, chmn. 1988-89), Com. to Revise Okla. Bus. Corp. Act, Oklahoma City Golf and Country Club, Rotary, Phi Alpha Delta. Republican. Jewish. Home: 6205 Avalon Ln Oklahoma City OK 73118-1001 Office: Conner & Winters One Leadership Sq 211 N Robinson Ave Ste 1700 Oklahoma City OK 73102-7101

STEINKAMP, FREDRIC, film editor. Editor: (films) The Adventures of Huckleberry Finn, 1960, Where the Boys Are, 1960, Two Loves, 1961, All Fall Down, 1962, Period of Adjustment, 1962, It Happened at the World's Fair, 1963, Sunday in New York, 1963, Quick, Before It Melts, 1964, The Unsinkable Molly Brown, 1964, Once a Thief, 1965, Duel at Diablo, 1966, Grand Prix, 1966 (Academy award best film editing 1966), Mister Buddwing, 1966, Doctor, You've Got to Be Kidding, 1967, Charly, 1968, The Extraordinary Seaman, 1969, The Shoot Horses, Don't They?, 1969 (Academy award nomination best film editing 1969), (with Marjorie Fowler and Roger J. Roth) The Strawberry Statement, 1970, The Marriage of a Young Stockbroker, 1971, (with Donald Guidice) A New Leaf, 1971, Nightmare Honeymoon, 1972, (with Michael McLean) Freebie and the Bean, 1974, (with Guidice) Three Days of the Condor, 1975, (with Thomas Stanford and Guidice) The Yakuza, 1975, (with David Bretherton and Guidice) Harry and Walter Go to New York, 1976, Bobby Deerfield, 1977, Fedora, 1979, (with Karl F. Steinkamp) Bound by Honor, 1993; (films; with William Steinkamp) Hide in Plain Sight, 1980, Tootsie, 1982 (Academy award nomination best film editing 1982), Against All Odds, 1984, (also with Pembroke Herring and Sheldon Kahn) Out of Africa, 1985 (Academy award nomination best film editing 1985), White Nights, 1985, Adventures in Babysitting, 1987, Burglar, 1987, Scrooged, 1988, Havana, 1990, The Firm, 1993, Sabrina, 1995. Office: c/o Paul Hook ICM 8942 Wilshire Blvd Beverly Hills CA 90210*

STEINKAMP, ROBERT THEODORE, lawyer; b. St. Louis, Sept. 11, 1945; s. William P. and Leona M. (Kraus) S.; m. Cheryl Sue Dunlop, Aug. 19, 1967; children: Theodore Bewick, Rebecca Anne. BA, William Jewell Coll., Liberty, Mo., 1967; JD, U. Mo., Kansas City, Mo., 1971; postgrad., U. Mo., Kansas City, 1971-72. Bar: Mo. 1971, U.S. Dist. Ct. (we. dist.) Mo. 1971, U.S. Tax Ct. 1971, U.S. Ct. Appeals (8th cir.) 1971. Assoc. Morris, Foust, Moudy & Beckett, Kansas City, 1971-76; ptnr. Morris, Foust & Beckett, Kansas City, 1976-78, Beckett & Steinkamp, Kansas City, 1978-90; v.p., gen. counsel, sec. Applebee's Internat., Inc., Kansas City, 1990—. Mem. Downtown, Inc., Kansas City, 1978-84, Friends of Art, Nelson Art Gallery, Kansas City, 1985—, Nat. Hist. Preservation Found., 1985—; bd. dirs., committeeman Kappa Alpha Order Nat. Fraternity Housing Corp., Lexington, Va., 1984-92; bd. dirs., pres. ADKASHA, Liberty, Mo., 1977—; bd. dirs. Liberty Symphony Orch., Inc., 1982-87, pres. 1984-86; Clay County Fine Arts Coun., 1991-93; sec. Heartland Franchising Assn., 1991-93; nat. co-chmn. William Jewell Coll., Ann. Fund. 1995-96, 96-97. Mem. ABA (forum on franchising, corp. and tax sects.), Kansas City Bar Assn. (vice-chmn. bus. law com. 1996, chmn. 1997), Lawyer's Assn. Kansas City, Mo. Bar Assn., Clay County Bar Assn., Kans. City Club, Liberty Hills Country Club (bd. dirs. 1985-87). Republican. Methodist. Avocations: golf, tennis, reading, travel. Office: Applebees Internat Inc 4551 W 107th St Ste 100 Overland Park KS 66207-4037

STEINKAMP, WILLIAM, film editor. Editor: (films) King of the Mountain, 1981, The Fabulous Baker Boys, 1989 (Academy award nomination best film editing 1989), (with Michael Tronick and Harvey Rosenstock) Scent of a Woman, 1992, Man Trouble, 1992; (films; with Fredric Steinkamp) Hide in Plain Sight, 1980, Tootsie, 1982 (Academy award nomination best film editing 1982), Against All Odds, 1984, (also with Pembroke Herring and Sheldon Kahn) Out of Africa, 1985 (Academy award nomination best film editing 1985), White Nights, 1985, Adventures in Babysitting, 1987, Burglar, 1987, Scrooged, 1988, Havana, 1990, The Firm, 1993. Office: care Motion Picture Editors 7715 W Sunset Blvd Ste 200 Los Angeles CA 90046-3912*

STEINKE, BETTINA, artist; b. Biddeford, Maine, June 25, 1913; d. William and Alice Mary (Staples) S.; m. Don Blair, Mar. 21, 1946. Student, Sch. Fine Arts, Newark, 1930, Cooper Union, 1931-33, Phoenix Art Sch., 1934-35. Represented in permanent collections Indpls. Mus., Ft. Worth Mus., Nat. Cowboy Hall of Fame and Western Heritage; artist original drawings of Toscanini, 1938, Paderewski, 1939 (both now in Smithsonian Inst.); charcoal portraits NBC book on Toscanini and Orch., 1938; many portraits of well known personalities; retrospective shows Palm Springs Desert Mus., Gilcrease Mus., Tulsa, Okla., Nat. Cowboy Hall of Fame, 1995; subject of biography Bettina. Pres. bd. dirs. Harwood Found. U. N.Mex.; exec. bd. Nat. Cowboy Hall of Fame and Western Heritage. Recipient Gold and Silver medals Nat. Cowboy Hall of Fame, Oklahoma City, 1973-89, Gold medal award for Outstanding Contbn. to Painting, 1995, N.Mex. Gov.'s award, 1996, John Singer Sargant award Portrait Soc. (East Coast), 1996, others; scholar Phoenix Art Sch., N.Y.C., 1934-35. Mem. Nat. Acad. Western Artists (Prix de West award, Cowboy Hall of Fame). Home: PO Box 2342 Santa Fe NM 87504-2342

STEINMAN, LISA MALINOWSKI, English literature educator, writer; b. Willimantic, Conn., Apr. 8, 1950; d. Zenon Stanislaus and Shirley Belle Malinowski; m. James A. Steinman, Apr. 1968 (div. 1980); m. James L. Shugrue, July 23, 1984. BA, Cornell U., 1971, MFA, 1973, PhD, 1976. Asst. prof. English Reed Coll., Portland, Oreg., 1976-82, assoc. prof., 1982-90, prof., 1990—, Kenan prof. English lit. and humanities, 1993—; cons. NEH, Washington, 1984-85. Author: Lost Poems, 1976, Made in America, 1987, All That Comes to Light, 1989, A Book of Other Days, 1992, Ordinary Songs, 1996; editor Hubbub Mag., 1983—; editl. bd. Williams Rev., 1991—, Stevens Jour., 1994—; contbr. articles to profl. jours. Fellow Danforth Found., 1971-75, NEH, 1983, 96, Oreg. Arts Commn., 1984-84, Nat. Endowment for Arts, 1984; Rockefeller Found. scholar, 1987-88; recipient Pablo Neruda award, 1987, Oreg. Inst. Lit. Arts award, 1993. Mem. MLA, Poets and Writers, PEN (N.W. chpt., co-founder, officer 1989-93). Home: 5344 SE 38th Ave Portland OR 97202-4208 Office: Reed Coll Dept English 3203 SE Woodstock Blvd Portland OR 97202-8138

STEINMAN, ROBERT CLEETON, accountant; b. Phila., June 11, 1931; s. George Curtis and Kathryn Agnes (Johnstone) S.; m. Nancy Badri Pourian, Sept. 24, 1960; children: Shirley Kathryn, Susan Soraya, Robert Mark. B.Sc. in Bus. Adminstrn, Drexel U., 1954, M.B.A., 1970. C.P.A., Pa. Accountant Main Lafrentz & Co. (C.P.A.'s), Phila., 1956-58; asst. treas. Ostheimer and Co., Inc., Phila., 1958-62; controller Biol. Abstracts, Inc., Phila., 1962-64; budget, cost and fin. analysis mgr. PQ Chems. Co., 1964-70; v.p., group controller 1st Pa. Bank, Phila., 1970-78; sr. v.p., comptroller Phila. Savs. Fund Soc., 1978-87; controller Kravco Co., 1987-88, spl. asst. to the pres., 1988-91; chief fin. officer Lorel Mktg. Group Inc., King of Prussia, Pa., 1991-92; adj. asso. prof. Grad. Sch., Drexel U., Phila. Co-founder Briarlin Civic Assn., 1969, treas., 1969-72, pres., 1975—; Bd. dirs. Sigma Pi Nat. Found., treas. frat. Served with AUS, 1954-56. Mem. Pa. Bankers Assn. (faculty trust tng. sch.), Fin. Execs. Inst., Pa. Inst. CPAs, Sigma Rho, Sigma Pi, Overbrook Golf Club. Republican. Methodist. Home: 804 Lawrence Ln Newtown Square PA 19073-2610

STEINMETZ, DAVID CURTIS, religion educator, publisher, minister; b. Columbus, Ohio, June 12, 1936; s. Walter Curtis and Lucy Margaret (Binderbasen) S.; m. Virginia Ruth Verploegh, June 20, 1959; children: Claire Elise, Matthew Eliot. BA with highest honor, Wheaton Coll., 1958; BD summa cum laude, Drew U., 1961; postgrad., U. Goettingen, Federal Republic of Germany, 1964-65; ThD, Harvard U., 1965. Ordained to ministry United Meth. Ch., 1959. Asst. and assoc. prof. Lancaster (Pa.) Theol. Sem., 1966-71; prof. Duke U., Durham, N.C., 1971-88, Amos Ragan Kearns prof. history of Christianity, 1988—; pres., pub. The Labyrinth Press, Inc., 1981-96; vis. prof. Harvard U., 1977; adv. coun. Interpretation, Richmond, Va., 1979-84, 87-92. Author: Misericordia dei, 1968, Reformers in the Wings, 1971, Luther and Staupitz, 1980, Luther in Context, 1986, Calvin in Context, 1995; editor Oxford Studies in Historical Theology; mem. editorial bd. Archiv für Reformationsgeschichte, 1977-93, Duke U. Monographs in Medieval and Renaissance Studies, 1972—, Brill Studies in Medieval and Reformation Thought, Leiden, Netherlands, 1981—. Named Scholar-Tchr. of Yr. Duke U., 1986; Rockefeller doctoral fellow Rockefeller Found., 1964-66, faculty fellow Assn. Theol. Schs., 1970, 77-78, Guggenheim fellow Guggenheim Found., 1977-78, NEH summer fellow, 1990. Mem. Medieval Acad. Am., Am. Soc. Ch. History (pres. 1985), Renaissance Soc. Am., Soc. for Reformation Rsch., Soc. for Scholarly Pub., Am. Friends of the Herzog August Bibliothek (founding pres.). Office: Duke U Div Sch Durham NC 27706

STEINMETZ, JOHN CHARLES, geologist, paleontologist; b. St. Paul, Sept. 26, 1947; s. Charles Leonard and Ruth Naomi (Osteraas) S.; m. Sarah Cook Tristán, May 29, 1982; children: Katherine Ruth, Elizabeth Margaret. BS, U. Ill., 1969, MS, 1975; PhD, U. Miami, 1978. Asst. prof. U. South Fla., St. Petersburg, 1977-82; advanced rsch. geologist Marathon Oil Co., Littleton, Colo., 1982-86, sr. geologist, 1986-90, advanced sr. geologist, 1990-94; dir. state geologist Mont. Bur. of Mines and Geology, 1994—. Mem. bd. advisors Micropaleontology Press, N.Y.C., 1986—. Trustee Paleontol. Rsch. Instn., Ithaca, N.Y., 1990—, v.p., 1992-94, pres. 1994-96. Mem. Assn. Am. State Geologists, Am. Assn. Petroleum Geologists, Geol. Soc. Am., Internat. Nannoplankton Assn. (U.S. treas. 1982-92), Mont. Geol. Soc., Paleontol. Soc., Soc. Econ. Paleontologists and Mineralogists.

STEINMETZ, JON DAVID, mental health executive, psychologist; b. N.Y.C., June 4, 1940; s. Lewis I. and Rose (Josefsberg) S.; m. Jane Audrey Hilton, Dec. 24, 1964; children: Jonna Lynn, Jay Daniel. BA, NYU, 1962; MA, Bradley U., 1963. Lic. psychologist, Ill. Intern in psychology Galesburg (Ill.) State Rsch. Hosp., 1963-64; staff psychologist Manteno (Ill.) State Hosp., 1964-68, program dir., 1968-70, asst. dir., 1970-72; dep. dir. Manteno Mental Health Ctr., 1972-80, Tinley Park (Ill.) Mental Health Ctr., 1980-88; dir. Chgo. Read Mental Health Ctr., 1988-91; ret., 1991; clin. dir. Jane Addams Hull House Assn., 1992—. Trustee Village of Park Forest, Cook and Will Counties, Ill.; officer, bd. dirs. various civic orgns., Park Forest. Home: 200 Hickory St Park Forest IL 60466-1016

STEINMETZ, MICHAEL, biochemist; b. Luebeck, Germany, July 4, 1947; s. Ludwig Max and Anne-Marie (Wiemann) S.; m. Cornelia Wessel, Mar. 10, 1972; children: Lars, Stephanie, Silja, Thomas. Diploma in Chemistry, U. Hamburg, 1973; Dr. Rer. Nat., U. Munich, 1977. Scientific asst. Inst. Physiol. Chemistry, Munich, 1971-80; rsch. fellow Calif. Inst. Tech., Pasadena, 1980-83; mem. Basel Inst. for Immunology, 1983-86; assoc. dir., head biology dept. F. Hoffmann-La Roche, Ltd., Basel, 1986-91; v.p. dept. biotechnology rsch. F. Hoffmann-La Roche, Inc., Nutley, N.J., 1991-92, v.p. preclin. rsch., 1992-94; v.p. pre-clin. R&D Hoffmann-La Roche, Inc., Nutley, N.J., 1994-97; mng. dir. Venture Asset Mgmt., LLC, Cambridge, Mass., 1997—. Contbr. numerous articles to profl. jours. Lievre fellow Am. Cancer Soc.; recipient Young Investigator award Am. Assn. for Clin. Histocompatibility Testing, 1983; Venia Docendi, U. Basel, 1985. Mem. Acad. Europaea, European Molecular Biology Orgn., European Network of Immunology Institutes, The Human Genome Orgn. Avocations: reading, skiing, swimming, windsurfing. Office: Venture Asset Mgmt c/o MPM Capital 1 Cambridge Ctr Cambridge MA 02142-1605

STEINMETZ, RICHARD BIRD, JR., lawyer; b. Orange, N.J., Mar. 27, 1929; s. Richard Bird and Charlotte (Quinby) S.; m. Merriam Holly Miller, June 9, 1956; children: Richard Blair, Jonathan Bird, Edward Quinby. BA, Yale U., 1950; JD, Harvard U., 1955. Bar: N.Y. 1955. Assoc. Chadbourne and Parke, N.Y.C., 1955-59; with Anaconda Co., N.Y.C., 1959-79, v.p., gen. counsel, 1971-79; v.p. Colt Industries Inc., N.Y.C., 1979-82; v.p., gen. counsel Pittston Co., Greenwich, Conn., 1982-84; exec. v.p. Case, Pomeroy and Co., N.Y.C., 1984-94; bd. dirs. Case, Pomeroy and Co. Served to capt. USMC, 1950-52. Mem. ABA, Assn. of Bar of City of N.Y., Assn. of Gen. Counsel. Republican. Episcopalian. Home: 78 Zaccheus Mead Ln Greenwich CT 06831-3752

STEINMETZ, ROBERT CHARLES, architect; b. Charleston, W.Va., Oct. 16, 1951; s. Charles and Bernadine Steinmetz; m. Deborah Susan Toselle, Dec. 29, 1974. BArch, La. State U., 1974. Architect Pound Flower & Dedyler, Columbus, Ga., 1974-75, David Allan Grinnell, Atlanta, 1975, Maxwell & Lebreton, New Orleans, 1975-77; architect, assoc. Mathes Group, New Orleans, 1977-84; architect, prin. Steinmetz & Assocs., New Orleans, 1984—; value added reseller computers, software Integrated Facility Systems Corp., New Orleans, 1991—. Mem. New Orleans Mus. Art, New Orleans Preservation Res. Ctr., Nat. Trust for Hist. Preservation. Mem. AIA (chair interiors com. 1995), La. Architecture Assn., La. Landmarks Soc., Nat. Coun. Archtl. Registration Bds. (cert.), Internat. Facility Mgmt. Assn. Office: 225 Baronne St Ste 1720 New Orleans LA 70112-1772*

STEINMETZ, SEYMOUR, pediatrician; b. Czechoslovakia, Oct. 6, 1934; s. Nathan and Gisela (Perl) S.; m. Ronnie P. Simons, June 24, 1973. BA, Yeshiva U., N.Y.C., 1956; MD, Albert Einstein Coll. Medicine, Bronx, N.Y., 1960. Diplomate Am. Bd. Pediatrics. Intern UCLA Hosp., L.A., 1960-61, resident pediatrician, 1961-62; chief resident pediatrician Montefiore Hosp., Bronx, N.Y., 1964-65; fellow in child psychiatry Jacobi Hosp., Bronx, N.Y., 1965-66; pvt. practice, Gt. Neck, N.Y., 1966-74; pvt. practice Fremont (Calif.) Pediatric Med. Group, 1974—, pres., 1984—. With USAF, 1962-64. With M.C., USAF, 1962-64. Fellow Am. Acad. Pediatrics. Office: Fremont Pediatric Med Group 3755 Beacon Ave Fremont CA 94538-1411

STEINMILLER, JOHN F., professional basketball team executive; b. Mt. Prospect, Ill.; m. Corinne Steinmiller; children: John Henry, Mary Kate. V.p. bus. ops. Milw. Bucks, 1977—. Bd. dirs. M.W. Athletes Against Childhood Cancer Fund, Milw. Big Bros.-Big Sisters, Metro Milw. YMCA, Milw. Convention Visitors Bur.; mem. Greater Milw. Com. Recipient Contardi Commitment award MACC Fund, 1991. Office: Milw Bucks 1001 N 4th St Milwaukee WI 53203-1314

STEINRUCK, CHARLES FRANCIS, JR., management consultant, lawyer; b. Phila., Apr. 25, 1908; s. Charles Francis and Laura (Crutchley) S.; m. Esther Sophia Schramm, June 1, 1936 (dec. Oct. 1962); children—Carol, Lisa.; m. Alice Bignell Marchese, Nov. 22, 1967. Student, U. Pa., 1925-28; LL.B., South Jersey Law Sch. (now Rutgers U.), 1937, J.D., 1972. Bar: D.C. bar 1938. Accountant J.S. Timmons, Inc., Phila., 1926-28; merged with Philco Corp., 1928, asst. to sec., 1937-41, asst. sec., 1941-42, sec., 1942-61; asst. sec. Philco-Ford Corp., 1962-68; cons., 1962—; resident v.p. Togotechnique, S.A.R.L., Republique Togolaise, 1979—. Author: An Anecdotal History, 1988. Mem. John W. Westcott Law Soc., Night Watch Sr. Soc. (U. Pa.), Am. Bar Assn., Sigma Kappa Phi, Delta Sigma Pi. Republican. Presbyterian. Clubs: Germantown Cricket (Phila.); Seaview Country (Absecon, N.J.). Home: 614 E Mcdevitt Dr Absecon NJ 08201-6000

STEINWACHS, DONALD MICHAEL, public health educator; b. Boise, Idaho, Sept. 9, 1946; s. Don Peter and Emma Bertha (Weisshaupt) S.; m. Sharon Kay Carlson, Aug. 25, 1972. MS, U. Ariz., 1970; PhD, Johns Hopkins U., 1973. Asst. prof. health svcs. adminstrn. Johns Hopkins U., Balt., 1973-79, assoc. prof. health policy and mgmt., 1979-86, dir. Health Svcs. Rsch. & Devel. Ctr., 1982—, prof. health policy and mgmt., 1986—, chairperson health policy and mgmt., 1994—; sec. adv. com. Dept. Vets. Affairs, Washington, 1991-92; mem. Inst. Medicine, NAS, Washington, 1993—; bd. dirs. Health Outcomes Inst., Inc., Mathematica Policy Rsch., Inc. Contbr. articles to profl. jours. Mem. Gov.'s Commn. on Health Policy Rsch. and Fin., Md., 1988-90. Capt. U.S. Army, 1973. Grantee NIMH, Agy. for Health Care Policy and Rsch., Robert Wood Johnson Found. Mem. Ops. Rsch. Soc. Am., Assn. Health Svc. Rsch. (bd. dirs., pres.), Found. for Health Svc. Rsch. (bd. dirs., pres.). Achievements include development of methods for using management information systems to examine patterns of medical care, costs, and indicators of the quality of care. Office: Johns Hopkins U Dept Healthcare Policy & Mgmt 624 N Broadway Rm 482 Baltimore MD 21205-1900

STEIR, PAT IRIS, artist; b. Newark, Apr. 10, 1940. Studies, Pratt Inst., 1956-58, 60-62; BFA, Boston U., 1961, studies, 1958-60; DFA (hon.), Pratt Inst., 1991. Art dir. Harper & Row, N.Y.C., 1968-69; tchr. Calif. Art Inst., 1973-75. One woman shows include Terry Dintenfass Gallery, N.Y., 1964, Bienville Gallery, N.Y., 1969, Graham Gallery, N.Y., 1971, Fourcade, Droll, Inc., N.Y., 1975, John Doyle Gallery, Paris, 1975, Galerie Farideh Cadot, Paris, 1976, 78, 79, 80, Morgan Thomas Gallery, Santa Monica, Calif., 1976, Otis Art Inst., L.A., 1976, Xavier Fourcade, Inc., N.Y., 1976, Carl Solway Gallery, Cin., 1977, Galeria Marilena Bonomo, Bari, Italy, 1978, Galerie d'Art Contemporain, Geneva, 1980, Art Mus. U. So. Fla., Tampa, 1990, Galerie Montenay, Paris, 1990, N.J. Ctr. for Visual Arts, Summit, 1990, Musée d'Art Contemporain, Lyon, France, Victoria Miro Gallery, London, 1990, Dennis Ochi Gallery, Sun Valley and Boise, Idaho, 1990, Robert Miller Gallery, N.Y.C., 1990, Landfall Press, Chgo., 1990, Gallerie Thaddeus Ropac, Paris, 1990, Tate Gallery, London, 1990, Linda Cathcart Gallery, Santa Monica, Calif., 1991, Galerie Franck & Schulte, Berlin, 1991, MacKenzie Art Gallery, Regina, Can., 1991, K. Kimpton Gallery, San Francisco, 1991, Bellas Artes, Sante Fe, 1991, Thaddeus Ropac, Salzburg, Austria, 1991, Whitney Mus. N.Y.C., 1991, Nina Freudenheim Gallery, Buffalo, 1991, The Bklyn. Mus., 1992, Documenta IX, Kassel, Germany, 1992; installation show Le Magazine, Grenoble, Switzerland, 1990; group exhbns. include Ben Shahn Gallery William Patterson Coll., Wayne, N.J., 1990, Ecole Des Beaux Arts, Tourcoing, France, 1990, 91, Mus. Art R.I. Sch. Design, 1990, Marc Richards Gallery, L.A., 1990, Louver Gallery, N.Y., 1990, Norah Haime Gallery, N.Y., 1990, Nat. Gallery of Art, Washington, 1990; represented in permanent collections including Kunstmuseum, Bern, Switzerland, Walker Art Ctr., Mpls., Bklyn. Mus., Musee d'art Contemporain, Lyons, France, Met. Mus. Art, N.Y., Mus. Modern Art, N.Y., Nat. Gallery, Washington, Nat. Mus. Am. Art, Washington, Whitney Mus. Am. Art, N.Y. Studio: c/o Robert Miller Gallery 41 E 57th St New York NY 10022-1908*

STEISS, ALAN WALTER, research administrator, educator; b. Woodbury, N.J., Feb. 15, 1937; s. Walter and Martha (Schreeder) S.; m. Patricia Foster McClintock, June 13, 1959; children: Carol Jean, Darren C., Todd A. BA in Sociology and Psychology, Bucknell U., 1959; MA in Urban Planning, U. Wis., 1966, PhD, 1969. Statewide planning dir. State of N.J., Trenton, 1960-65; mem. faculty Va. Poly. Inst. and State U., Blacksburg, 1967-69, program chmn. environ. and urban systems, 1969-78, assoc. dean architecture, 1974-78, assoc. dean rsch. div., 1978-83, assoc. provost, 1983-88; dir. div. rsch. devel. and adminstrn. U. Mich., Ann Arbor, 1988-96, coord. rsch. info. mgmt. sys., 1996, prof. urban planning, prof. pub. health, 1988-96, coord. m-pathways project, 1996—; cons. various state and local govts., 1960—, Trust Territory of the Pacific, Micronesia, 1968. Author numerous book including: Management Control in Government, 1982, Governmental Accounting and Control, 1984, Strategic Management and Organizational Decision Making, 1985, Financial Management in Public Organizations, 1989, Management Planning and Control, 1991. Chair Montgomery (Va.) Pub. Svc. Authority, 1978-83; bd. dirs. Mich. Pub. Health Inst., 1990-95; mem. policy and planning bd. Mich. Consortium for Enabling Tech., 1991-95; hon. chair region V United Way Campaign, 1991-92. Univ. fellow U. Wis., 1959-60, NDEA fellow, 1966-67. Mem. AAUP, ASPA, Am. Inst. of Planners (prog. chmn. 1964), Assn. Collegiate Schs. of Planning (mem. exec. com. 1970-71, sec. 1971-73), Assn. Collegiate Schs. in Architecture, Nat. Assn. Schs. Pub. Affairs and Adminstrn. (inst. rep. 1975-76), Coun. of Univ. Insts. for Urban Affairs, N.J. Fed. of Planning Officials (sec. 1960-64), Urban America Inc., Nat. Urban Coalition, Psi Chi, Tau Sigma Delta, Lambda Alpha. Home: 4419 Corey Cir Ann Arbor MI 48103-9036 Office: U Mich 3036 Adminstrv Srvs Bldg Ann Arbor MI 48109-1432

STEITZ, JOAN ARGETSINGER, biochemistry educator; b. Mpls., Jan. 26, 1941; d. Glenn D. and Elaine (Magnusson) Argetsinger; m. Thomas A. Steitz, Aug. 20, 1966; 1 child, Jonathan Glenn. B.S., Antioch Coll., 1963; Ph.D., Harvard U., 1967; D.Sc. (hon.), Lawrence U., Appleton, Wis., 1982, Rochester U. Sch. Medicine, 1984, Mt. Sinai Sch. Medicine, 1989, Bates Coll., 1990; DSc (hon.), Trinity Coll., 1992, Harvard U., 1992. Postdoctoral fellow MRC Lab. Molecular Biology, Cambridge, Eng., 1967-70; asst. prof. molecular biophysics and biochemistry Yale U., New Haven, 1970-74; assoc. prof. Yale U., 1974-78, prof. molecular biophysics and biochemistry, 1978—; investigator Howard Hughes Med. Inst., 1986—. Recipient Young Scientist award Passano Found., 1975, Eli Lilly award in biol. chemistry, 1976, U.S. Steel Found. award in molecular biology, 1982, Lee Hawley, Sr. award for arthritis rsch., 1984, Nat. Medal of Sci., 1986, Dickson prize for Sci. Carnegie-Mellon U., 1988, Warren Triennial prize Mass. Gen. Hosp., 1989, Christopher Columbus Disc. award in biomed. rsch., 1992, Weizmann Women and Sci. Awd., 1994, City of Medicine award, 1996. Fellow AAAS; mem. Am. Acad. Arts and Sci., Nat. Acad. Arts and Sci., Am. Phil. Soc., NY Acad. of Scis., (Weizmann Women & Sci. Awd, 1994). Home: 45 Prospect Hill Rd Branford CT 06405-5711 Office: Yale U Sch Medicine Dept Blochem & Biophysics 295 Congress Ave New Haven CT 06519-1418

STEJSKAL, JOSEPH FRANK, JR., carbohydrate chemist; b. Oak Park, Ill., Jan. 16, 1932; s. Joseph Frank and Bertha Helen (Urban) S.; m. Dorothy May Milas, Nov. 28, 1953; children: Patricia Anne, Joseph Frank III. BS, Wheaton Coll., 1953. Chemist Corn Products Refining Co., Argo, Ill., 1953-89; phys. sci. asst. U.S. Army Food Container Inst., Chgo., 1955-57; chemist Am. Maize Products Co., Hammond, Ind., 1987-96; ret. Cerestar USA, Inc., Hammond, 1996. Mem. Brookfield (Ill.) Hist. Commn., 1993-96; elder, treas. Presbyn. Ch. USA, gen. assembly del., 1951-96, nat. del. 1970); instnl. rep. Boy Scouts Am., 1961-90, cmty. svc. award 1978, silver beaver award 1987. Mem. Hollywood Citizens Assn. (historian). Republican. Presbyn. Holder patents in field. Avocations: golf, chess, local history, church and community activities. Home: 3611 Rosemear Ave Brookfield IL 60513-1738

STELCK, CHARLES RICHARD, geology educator; b. Edmonton, Alta., Can., May 20, 1917; s. Robert Ferdinand and Florella Maud (Stanbury) S.; m. Frances Gertrude McDowell, Apr. 24, 1945; children—David, Brian, Leland, John (dec.). B.Sc., U. Alta., 1937, M.Sc., 1941; Ph.D., Stanford U., 1951. Registered profl. geologist, Alta. Field geologist B.C. Dept. Mines, Victoria, Can., 1939-41; field geologist Canol Project, Norman Wells, N.W.T., Can., 1941-43, Imperial Oil Co., Calgary, Alta., 1943-49; from lectr. to prof. emeritus geology U. Alta., Edmonton, 1946—. Contbr. numerous articles principally on biostratigraphy of Cretaceous to sci. publs. Fellow Royal Soc. Can.; mem. Assn. Profl. Engrs., Geologists and Geophysicists Alta. (Centennial award 1979), Geol. Assn. Can. (Logan medal 1982), Geol. Soc. Am., Can. Soc. Petroleum Geologists (Douglas medal 1994), Order of Can. (officer 1997). Conservative. Office: U Alta, Dept Earth/Atmospheric Scis, Edmonton, AB Canada T6G 2E3

STELL, WILLIAM KENYON, neuroscientist, educator; b. Syracuse, N.Y., Apr. 21, 1939; arrived in Can., 1980; dual citizenship with Can., 1992; s. Henry Kenyon and Edith Doris (Lawson) S.; m. Judith Longbotham, June 27, 1974 (div. 1996); children: Jennifer Susan, Sarah Ruth; m. Kathie L. Roller, Oct. 26, 1996. B.A. in Zoology with high honors, Swarthmore Coll., 1961; Ph.D. in Anatomy, U. Chgo., 1966, M.D. with honors (E. Gellhorn prize 1967), 1967. Staff fellow, then sr. staff fellow Nat. Inst. Neurol. Diseases and Stroke, NIH, 1967-72; asso. prof., then prof. ophthalmology and anatomy UCLA Med. Sch., 1972-80; assoc. dir. Jules Stein Eye Inst., UCLA, 1978-80; prof. anatomy U. Calgary (Can.) Faculty Medicine, 1980—, prof. surgery/ophthalmology, 1992—, head dept., 1980-85, prof. surgery and ophthalmology, 1992—; dir. Lions Sight Ctr., Calgary, 1980—; guest rschr. in physiology Lab. Physiologie Nerveuse, Ctr. Nat. de la Recherche Scientifique, Gif-sur-Yvette, France, 1985-86; vis. fellow Vision Scis. Ctr. Rsch. Sch. Biol. Scis. Australian Nat. U., Canberra, 1996. Served with USPHS, 1967-69. Grantee USPHS, Med. Rsch. Coun. Can., Alta. Heritage Found. Med. Rsch., Natural Scis. and Engring. Rsch. Coun. Can., NATO, Human Frontier Sci. Program; William and Mary Greve Internat. research scholar, 1979-80. Mem. Assn. Rsch. in Vision and Ophthalmology, Soc. Neurosci. Home: 2020 17th Ave NW, Calgary, AB Canada T2M 0S6 Office: Univ of Calgary, 3330 Hospital Dr NW, Calgary, AB Canada T2N 4N1

STELLA, FRANK DANTE, food service and dining equipment executive; b. Jessup, Pa., Jan. 21, 1919; s. Facondino and Chiara (Pennoni) S.; m. Martha Theresa Yetzer (dec. Apr. 1994); children: Daniel (dec.), Mary Anne, William J., Philip J., Marsha, James C., Stephen P. Student, U. Detroit, 1937-41, Washington and Lee, 1944; D in Bus. and Industry (hon.), Gentium Pacem U., Rome, 1979; D in Sci. and Bus. Adminstn. (hon.), Cleary Coll., 1985. Pres., chmn., CEO F.D. Stella Products Co., Detroit, 1946—; founding ptnr. The Fairlane Club (sold to Club Corp. Am., 1979); chmn. bd., CEO Stella Internat., N.Y.C.; mem. Mich. Higher Edn. Facilities Commn., Area-Wide Water Quality Bd., Fed. Statis. Commn., White House Fellows Commn. and others; chmn. Detroit Income Tax Rev. Bd.; instr. orgn. and mgmt. small bus. U. Detroit; vice chmn., bd. dirs. Met. Realty Corp.; bd. dirs. Fed. Home Loan Bank Indpls., Computer Bus. Solutions Inc. Chmn. Internat. Inst. of Friends. Recipient over 35 awards from local, nat. and internat. civic and profl. orgns. including Ellis Island medal of Honor, 1995; named Michiganian of Yr., 1997. Mem. Alliance for Mich. (bd. dirs. 1984—), Detroit Ctrl. Bus. Dist. Assn., Nat. Comml. Refrigerator Sales Assn. (bd. dirs., pres. 1953-54, adv. bd. 1954—), Nat. Assn. Wholesaler-Distbrs. (del. 1982—), Wholesale Distbrs. Assn. (bd. dirs. 1973—, v.p. 1976, pres. 1977-79), Bus. Edn. Alliance (various offices), Mich. Restaurant Assn., Food Svc. Execs. Assn., Italian-Am. C. of C. Mich., Nat. Italian-Am. Found. (charter, bd. dirs., exec. com., pres. 1979—), Hispanos Organized to Promote Entrepreneurs (bd. dirs. 1976-81), Econ. Club Detroit (bd. dirs. 1982—), Air Force Assn. (charter), Am. Soc. Legion Merit, Greater Detroit C. of C. (chmn. 1980-81, bd. dirs.), Wayne County C.C. Found. (pres.), Young Pres.'s Orgn., Detroit Club, Detroit Athletic Club, Detroit Golf Club, The Fairlane Club, Capitol Hill Club, Skyline Club (Southfield). Home: 19180 Gainsborough Rd Detroit MI 48223-1344 Office: 7000 Fenkell St Detroit MI 48238-2052

STELLA, JANET LOUISE, special education educator; b. Pitts., Oct. 11, 1961; d. Adam John and Patricia Jean (Mitchell) S. BS in Child Devel./Child Care magna cum laude, U. Pitts., 1983; MEd in Mentally and/or Physically Handicapped, California U. Pa., 1992. Cert. tchr. mentally and/or physically handicapped, Pa. Devel. care specialist Allegheny Valley Sch., Pitts., 1983; tchr. Parents Anonymous Pitts. Therapeutic Children's Ctr., 1983-84; substitute child devel. specialist Craig House Technoma, Pitts., 1984-85; resident advisor, asst. site supr., then site supr. Chartiers Mental Health-Mental Retardation Ctr., Pitts., 1985-88; case mgr. for mentally retarded adults Allegheny East Mental Health and Mental Retardation Ctr., Pitts., 1989-93; spl. edn. tchr. Allegheny Intermediate Unit, Pitts., 1993—; cons. on family and child support svcs. subcom. Pa. Protection and Advocacy, Inc., Pitts., 1987-89. Vol. Children's Hosp. Pitts., 1980-81. Presdl. scholar California U. Pa., 1992. Mem. Coun. for Exceptional Children, South Park Runners Club, Sigma Pi Epsilon Delta. Roman Catholic. Home: 3145 Belleville St Pittsburgh PA 15234-2739 Office: Allegheny Intermediate Unit 4 Station Sq Fl 2 Pittsburgh PA 15219-1119

STELLA, JOHN ANTHONY, investment company executive; b. Jessup, Pa., Feb. 3, 1938; s. John Anthony and Alda (Parri) S.; m. Aurelia M. Arre, Feb. 20, 1965; children—John C., Matthew A., Krista R. B.S., U. Detroit, 1960; M.B.A., NYU, 1965. Bus. evaluation cons. Allied Chem. Co., N.Y.C., 1965-70; treas. Spinnerin Yarn Co., Hackensack, N.J., 1970-72, Penn-Dixie Cement Corp., N.Y.C., 1972-74; v.p. finance Halecrest Co., 1974-76; treas. Rsch.-Cottrell, 1976-84, v.p., contr./treas., 1984-88; pres. John A. Stella & Assocs., Plainfield, N.J., 1988-91; sr. v.p. Investment Support Systems, Inc., Bloomfield, N.J., 1991-95; pres. State Tax Auditing and Rsch., Inc., Plainfield, 1993—. Served with AUS, 1960. Office: State Tax Auditing & Rsch Inc 925 Madison Ave Plainfield NJ 07060-2336

STELLER, ARTHUR WAYNE, educational administrator; b. Columbus, Ohio, Apr. 12, 1947; s. Fredrick and Bonnie Jean (Clark) S. BS, Ohio U., 1969, MA, 1970, PhD, 1973. Tchr., Athens (Ohio) City Schs., 1969-71; curriculum coord., tchr. Belpre (Ohio) City Schs., 1971-72; prin. elem. schs., head tchr. learning disabilities South-Western City Schs., Grove City, Ohio, 1972-76; dir. elem. edn. Beverly (Mass.) Pub. Schs., 1976-78; adj. prof. Lesley Coll., Cambridge, Mass., 1976-78; coord. spl. projects and systemwide planning Montgomery County Pub. Schs., Rockville, Md., 1978-80; asst. supt. Shaker Heights (Ohio), 1980-83; supt. schs. Mercer County Pub. Schools., Princeton, W. Va., 1983-85; supt. schs. Oklahoma City Pub Schs., 1985-92; supt. schs. Cobb County, Ga., 1992-93; dep. supt. Boston Pub. Schs., 1993-95, acting supt., 1995-96; supt. Kingston Sch. Dist., N.Y., 1996—; adj. faculty Harvard U., 1992-93. Author: Educational Planning for Educational Success, Effective Schools Research: Practice and Promise; editor: Effective Instructional Management; cons. editor, book rev. editor Jour. for Ednl. Pub. Rels.; mem. editl. bd. Jour. for Curriculum & Supervision, Reading Today's Youth; contbr. articles to profl. jours. Bd. govs. Kirkpatrick Ctr.; mem. Oklahoma City Com. for Econ. Devel.; founding bd. dirs. Oklahoma Alliance Against Drugs, Oklahoma Zool. Soc. Inc.; selected for Leadership Okla. City, 1986; bd. dirs. Leadership Oklahoma City, ARC; bd. dirs. Okla. Centennial Sports Inc., Rip Van Winkle Coun. BSA; mem. Oklahoma Acad. for State Goals, State Supt.'s Adv. Coun.; mem. clin. experiences adv. com. U. Okla. Coll. Edn.; trustee Arts Coun. Oklahoma City, Omniplex Sci. and Arts Mus., Oklahoma City Area Vocat.-Tech. Dist. 22 Found.; mem. Urban Ctr. Ednl. Adv. Bd., U.S. Dept. Edn. Urban Supt. Network, Coun. Great City Schs. Bd., Urban Edn. Clearing House Adv. com., U. Okla. Adminstrn. cert. program com., Cmty. Literacy Coun. Bd.; chmn. bd. dirs. Langston U.; chairperson United Way Greater Okla., Sch. Mgmt. Study Group, Okla. Reading Coun. (Okla. literacy coun. reading award 1989), Okla. City PTA; bd. dirs. Oklahoma County chpt. ARC, Jr. Achievement Greater Oklahoma City Bd., Oklahoma State Fair Bd., Horace Mann League Bd., Last Frontier Coun. Bd. Charles Kettering Found. IDEA fellow, 1976, 78, 80; Nat. Endowment Humanities fellow, Danforth Found., 1987-88; recipient Silver Beaver award Boy Scouts Am., 1990, Amb. award Horace Mann League, 1995, 96, 97. Mem. ASCD (exec. coun., pres.-elect 1993-94, pres. 1994-95, rev. coun. 1997—), World Coun. Curriculum and Instrn. (life), Nat. Orgn. Legal Problems in Edn., Nat. Policy Bd. Ednl. Adminstrn., Am. Assn. Sch. Adminstrs. (life, Leadership for Learning award, 1991, Coll. Bd. Advanced Placement Spl. Recognition award 1991), Nat. Assn. Elem. Sch. Prins. (life), Nat. Assn. Edn. Young Children (life), Nat. Sch. Pub. Rels. Assn. (Honor award 1991), Internat. Soc. Ednl. Planning, Nat. Soc. Study Edn., Nat. Planning Assn., Coun. Basic Edn., Am. Edn. Fin. Assn., Ohio Assn. Elem. Sch. Adminstrs., Buckeye Assn. Sch. Adminstrs., Ohio ASCD, Ohio U. Coll. Edn. (disting. alumnus award 1991), Okla. ASCD (Publ. award 1989), Okla. Assn. Sch. Adminstrs., Mass. Assn. Sch. Adminstrs., Mass. ASCD, Okla. Coalition for Pub. Edn., Okla. Commn. for Ednl. Leadership, Urban Area Supts. (Oklahoma br.), Ohio U. Alumni Assn. (nat. dir. 1975-78, pres. Cen. Ohio chpt. 1975-76, pres. Mass. chpt. 1976-78, life mem. trustee's acad.), World Future Soc. (life), Greater Oklahoma City C. of C. (exec. bd. dirs.), South Oklahoma City C. of C. (bd. dirs.), Oklahoma Heritage Assn., Heritage Hills Assn. (bd. dirs.), Victorian Soc. (New England chpt.), Nat. Eagle Scout Assn., Aerospace Found. (hon. bd. dirs.), Am. Bus. Card Club, Coca Cola Collectors Club, Internat. Club, Rotary (Boston), Mgmt. Consortium (bd. advisors), Tau Kappa Epsilon Alumni Assn. (regional officer Mass. 1976-78, named Alumni Nat. Hall of Fame 1986, Nat. Alumnus of Yr. 1993, Excellence in Edn. award 1993), Kappa Delta Pi (life, advisor Cen. Okla. chpt., nat. publs. com.), Phi Delta Kappa (life). Methodist. Home: 225 N Manor Ave Kingston NY 12401

STELLWAGEN, ROBERT HARWOOD, biochemistry educator; b. Joliet, Ill., Jan. 6, 1941; s. Harwood John and Alma Dorothy (Handorf) S.; m. Joanne Kovacs, June 15, 1963; children: Robert Harwood, Alise Anne. AB, Harvard U., 1963; PhD, U. Calif.-Berkeley, 1968. Staff fellow NIH, Bethesda, Md., 1968-69; postdoctoral scholar U. Calif.-San Francisco, 1969-70; asst. prof. biochemistry U. So. Calif., L.A., 1970-74, assoc. prof., 1974-80, prof., 1980—, chmn. dept., 1981-86, vice chmn. dept., 1993—; vis. scientist Nat. Inst. for Med. Research, Mill Hill, Eng., 1979. Contbr. articles to profl. jours. Recipient Henderson prize Harvard U., 1963; NSF fellow, 1963-67; NIH grantee, 1971-84. Mem. AAAS, Am. Soc. Biochemistry and Molecular Biology, Sierra Club, Phi Beta Kappa. Democrat. Office: U So Calif 2011 Zonal Ave Los Angeles CA 90033-1034

STELPSTRA, WILLIAM JOHN, minister; b. Paterson, N.J., Nov. 1, 1934; s. Duke and Nellie (Stapert) S.; m. Anna Rizkovsky, Sept. 6, 1958; 1 child, Linda Mae. BA, Alma White Coll., 1957; B. of Religion, Zarephath Bible Sem., 1958. Ordained to ministry Pillar of Fire Ch., 1954. Pastor Pillar of Fire Ch., Little Falls, N.J., 1956-60; evangelist Wesleyan Meth. Ch., 1960-64; founder, dir. Bethel Children's Home, Paterson, N.J., 1964-71, Bethel Ranch Rehab. for Men, West Milford, N.J., 1971—; founder, pres. World for Christ Crusade, Inc., N.J., Fla., 1960—; dir. fgn. missions World for Christ Crusade, Inc., Haiti, Ghana, India, 1980—; adminstr. Fellowship House, Bloomfield, N.J., 1979—, Bright Side Manor, Teaneck, N.J., 1978—. Mem. Ocean Grove C. of C. Republican. Wesleyan Ch. Avocations: painting with oils, swimming, boating, travel, gardening. Home: 1005 Union Valley Rd West Milford NJ 07480-1220 Office: World for Christ Crusade 1005 Union Valley Rd West Milford NJ 07480-1220

STELZEL, WALTER TELL, JR., accountant, financial company executive; b. Chgo., Aug. 23, 1940; s. Walter Tell and Kathryn (Evans) S.; m. Sarah Rauen, Jan. 5, 1963; children: William, Susan, Michael. BSBA, Xavier U., 1962; MBA, U. Chgo., 1983. CPA, Ill. Sr. acct. Ernst & Ernst, 1962-69; contr. U.S. Reduction Co., 1969-74; asst. corp. contr. Am. Nat. Can. Co. (formerly Nat. Can. Corp.), Chgo., 1974-76, corp. contr., 1976-78, v.p., contr., 1978-81, v.p., asst. to pres., 1981-84, exec. v.p. fin., 1984-93, sr. exec. v.p., bd. mem., CFO, 1993—. 1st lt. U.S. Army, 1962-65, Germany. Office: Am Nat Can Co 8770 W Bryn Mawr Ave Chicago IL 60631-3515

STELZER, IRWIN MARK, economist; b. N.Y.C., N.Y., May 22, 1932; s. Abraham and Fanny (Dolgins) S.; m. Marian Faris Stuntz, 1981. BA cum laude, NYU, 1951, MA, 1952; PhD, Cornell U., 1954. Fin. analyst Econometric Inst., 1952; teaching fellow Cornell U., 1953-54; instr. U. Conn., 1954-55; researcher Twentieth Century Fund, 1953-55; economist W.J. Levy, Inc., 1955-56; sr. cons., v.p. Boni, Watkins, Jason & Co., Inc., 1956-61; lectr. NYU, 1955-56, CCNY, 1957-58; researcher Brookings Instn., 1956-57; pres. Nat. Econ. Rsch. Assocs., Inc., 1961-85, I.M. Stelzer Assocs. Inc., 1986—; chmn. bd. Putnam, Hayes & Bartlett, Inc., N.Y.C., 1989-91; dir. regulatory policy studies Am. Enterprise Inst., 1990—; adv. coun. Electric Power Rsch. Inst.; adv. com. revision of rules of practice and procedure FERC; chmn. com. on adequate power supply FPC; bd. dirs. The Energy Adv. Group of the Keystone Ctr; past dir. The Energy and Environ. Policy Ctr., Harvard U.; mng. dir. Rothschild, Inc.; assoc. mem. Nuffield Coll., Oxford U.; mem. publs. com. The Pub. Interest; others. Author: Selected Antitrust Cases: Landmark Decisions, 1955, The Antitrust Laws: A Primer, 1993; econ. columnist The Sunday Times, London, 1986—; columnist N.Y. Post, Courier Mail, Australia; contbr. articles to econs. field; mem. publ. com. The Pub. Interest. Mem. Mayor's Energy Policy Adv. Group for N.Y.C.; adv. panel Pres.'s Nat. Commn. for Rev. of Antitrust Laws and Procedures; mem. Gov.'s Adv. Panel on Telecom., bd. governing trustees Am. Ballet Theatre; bd. dirs. U.S. Nat. Com., World Energy Conf.; mem. Fed. Energy Regulatory Com. Task Force on Pipeline Competition. Mem. Am. Econ. Assn., Reform Club, Cosmos Club, Phi Beta Kappa. Home: PO Box 1008 Aspen CO 81612-1008 Office: Am Enterprise Inst 1150 17th St NW Washington DC 20036-4603

STEM, CARL HERBERT, business educator; b. Eagleville, Tenn., Jan. 30, 1935; s. Marion Ogilvie and Sara Elizabeth (Jones) S.; m. Linda Marlene Wheeler, Dec. 28, 1963; children: Anna Elizabeth, Susan Kathleen, John Carl, David Leslie. BA, Vanderbilt U., 1957; AM (Woodrow Wilson fellow, Harvard scholar), Harvard U., 1960, PhD, 1969. Internat. fin. economist, bd. govs. Fed. Res. System, Washington, 1963-70; prof. econs. Tex. Tech. U., Lubbock, 1970-73; prof. internat. fin., chmn. area of fin., adminstr. grad. programs, assoc. dean, dean Coll. Bus. Adminstrn. Tex. Tech U., Lubbock, 1970—; sr. econ. adviser Office Fgn. Direct Investments, U.S. Dept. Commerce, Washington, 1973-74; cons. U.S. Dept. Treasury, 1974-75; mem. faculty Grad. Sch. Credit and Fin. Mgmt., Lake Success, N.Y., 1974-87; adj. scholar Am. Enterprise Inst. Public Policy Rsch., Washington, 1974-88; treas. Mission Jour., Inc., 1969-88. Editor (with Makin and Logue) Eurocurrencies and The Interational Monetary System; contbr. articles to profl. jours. Trustee St. Mary Plains Hosp., Lubbock, Tex., 1987-92, chmn., 1992; v.p. Tex. Coun. of Collegiate Edn. for Bus., 1977-78, pres., 1978-79; mem. acad. adv. coun. United Arab Emirates U., Al Ain, 1996—. Capt. Security Agy. AUS, 1961-62. Fulbright scholar U. Reading, Eng., 1957-58. Mem. Southwestern Bus. Adminstrn. Assn. (pres. 1982-83), Nat. Assn. Bus. Economists, So. Bus. Adminstrn. Assn. (v.p. 1985-86, pres. 1986-87), Lubbock Econ. Coun. (pres. 1973), Am. Assembly Collegiate Schs. Bus. (stds. com. 1981-84, bd. dirs. 1993-96, bus. accreditation com. 1997—), Lubbock Club (pres. 1986-87), Phi Beta Kappa, Omicron Delta Kappa, Phi Kappa Phi, Beta Gamma Sigma, Tau Kappa Alpha. Mem. Ch. of Christ. Home: 6218 Louisville Dr Lubbock TX 79413-5429 Office: Tex Tech U Bus Adminstrn Lubbock TX 79409 *Most important to me are the ever timely values of our Judeo-Christian heritage- faith in God and a deep appreciation for the inherent value of man. These values have underpinned my aspirations and sustained me through disappointments. They have generated the perseverance and continual hope so vital to me as I have worked for self-growth and to make a contribution to the institutions and people with which I have been associated in various periods of my life.*

STEMBERG, THOMAS GEORGE, retail executive; b. Newark, Jan. 18, 1949; s. Oscar Michael and Erika (Ratzer) S.; m. Dola Davis Hamilton, Sept. 24, 1988. Student, Am. Internat. Sch., Vienna, 1962-67; AB, Harvard U., 1971, MBA, 1973. With Jewel Cos., Star Market, Cambridge, Mass., 1973-82, v.p. sales and merchandising, 1982; sr. v.p. sales and merchandising First Nat. Supermarkets, Hartford, Conn., 1982-83, pres., 1983-84; pres. Staples, Inc., Newton, Mass., 1986-88, chmn., 1988—. Baker scholar Harvard Bus. Sch., 1973; R.H. Macy fellow Harvard Bus. Sch., 1973. *

STEMBRIDGE, VERNIE A(LBERT), pathologist, educator; b. El Paso, Tex., June 7, 1924; s. Vernie Albert and Anna Marie (Lawless) S.; m. Aileen Cofer Marston, June 14, 1944; children—Shirley (Mrs. J.P. Watkins), Ann (Mrs. Donald M. Connell), Vivian (Mrs. Lance E. Porter). B.A., U. Tex. at El Paso (formerly Tex. Coll. Mines), 1943; M.D., U. Tex., Galveston, 1948. Diplomate: Am. Bd. Pathology (trustee 1969-80, sec. 1976-79, pres. 1980). Intern U.S. Marine Hosp., Norfolk, Va., 1948-49; resident in pathology Med. Br., U. Tex., Galveston, 1949-52; asst. prof. pathology Med. Br., U. Tex., 1952-54, asso. prof., 1954-56; asso. prof. Southwestern Med. Sch., Dallas, 1959-61; prof. Southwestern Med. Sch., 1961—, Ashbel Smith prof., 1991—, chmn. dept. pathology, 1966-88; chmn. emeritus Southwestern Med. Sch., Dallas, 1992—; interim dean Sch. Allied Health Scis. U. Tex. Southwestern Med. Sch., 1988-91; assoc. dir. clin. labs. U. Tex. Med. Br. Hosps., 1952-56; sr. pathologist, chief aviation pathology sect. Armed Forces Inst. Pathology, Washington, 1956-59; dir. pathology labs. Parkland Hosp., Dallas, 1966-85; cons. VA Hosp., Dallas; cons. to surgeon gen. USAF; civil air surgeon FAA; chmn. sci. adv. bd. Armed Forces Inst. Pathology; mem. State of Tex. Radiation Adv. Bd., 1987-94. Contbr. articles to med. jours. Served with USAF, 1956-59. Decorated Legion of Merit; named Outstanding Alumnus U. Tex. at El Paso, 1978, Hon. Alumnus, U. Tex. Southwestern Med. Sch., 1964, Ashbel Smith outstanding alumnus U. Tex. Med. Br., 1982; recipient Joint Disting. Service award Am. Soc. Clin. Pathologists/Coll. Am. Pathologists, 1987. Mem. Internat. Acad. Pathology (counselor 1970-73), Am. Soc. Clin. Pathologists (bd. dirs. 1973-79, pres. 1977-78, bd. registry, gov. 1983-90, Ward Burdick award for outstanding contbns. 1981, Bd. Registry Disting. Svc. award 1995), AMA (residency rev. com. of pathology 1972-78, chmn. 1977-78, residency rev. com. nuclear medicine 1972-78), Intersoc. Pathology Coun. (sec. 1979-84), Coll. Am. Pathologists, Am. Assn. Pathologists, Assn. Pathology Chairmen (mem. coun., pres. 1979, Disting. Svc. award 1996), Am. Assn. Blood Banks, Tex. Soc. Pathologists (pres. 1966, Caldwell award 1967, annual lectureship established in honor), Tex. Med. Assn. (ho. of dels. 1966-86), Dallas County Med. Soc. (pres. 1985, Max Cole Leadership award 1991), Am. Registry Pathology (bd. dirs. 1986-91, chmn. 1989-90, Disting. Svc. award 1995), Phi Rho Sigma, Mu Delta, Alpha Omega Alpha. Home: 10424 Marsh Ln Dallas TX 75229-5223 Office: 5323 Harry Hines Blvd Dallas TX 75235-7208

STEMMER, EDWARD ALAN, surgeon, educator; b. Cin., Jan. 20, 1930; s. Edward Purcell and Helen Marie (Smith) S.; m. Lois Jean Mess, May 1, 1954; children: Susan Helen, Linda Diane, Paul Frederick, Nancy Joan, Carol Jean. BA, U. Chgo., 1949, MD, 1953. Diplomate Am. Bd. Surgery, Am. Bd. Thoracic Surgery. Resident in surgery U. Chgo., 1953-60; chief resident in surgery Stanford U., Palo Alto, Calif., 1960-62, instr. surgery, 1962-64; asst. prof. surgery U. Utah, Salt Lake City, 1964-65; from asst. prof. surgery to prof. surgery U. Calif., Irvine, 1966—; acting chmn. surgery U. Calif., Irvine, 1978-80; chief surg. svc. VA Hosp., Long Beach, Calif., 1965—. Editor: Vascular Disease in the Elderly, 1997; contbr. articles to profl. jours., chpts. to books. Capt. USAF, 1955-57, maj. USAFR, 1957-72. Grantee NIH, Am. Heart Assn., 1962-90; recipient disting. svc. award Am. Heart Assn., 1971. Mem. Am. Assn. Thoracic Surgery, Assn. VA Surgeons (pres. 1979-80, disting. svc. award 1995), Am. Surg. Assn., Am. Coll. Surgeons (pres. So. Calif. chpt. 1974-75), L.A. Surg. Soc. (pres. 1986-87), Sigma Xi. Avocations: carpentry, gardening, electronics. Home: 135 College Park Dr Seal Beach CA 90740 Office: VA Med Ctr 5901 E 7th St Long Beach CA 90822-5201

STEMMLER, EDWARD JOSEPH, physician, retired association executive, retired academic dean; b. Phila., Feb. 15, 1929; s. Edward C. and Josephine (Heitzmann) S.; m. Joan C. Koster, Dec. 27, 1958; children: Elizabeth, Margaret, Edward C., Catherine, Joan. B.A., La Salle Coll., Phila., 1950, Sc.D. (hon.), 1983; M.D., U. Pa., 1960; Sc.D. (hon.), Ursinus Coll., 1977, Phila. Coll. Pharmacy and Sci., 1989; L.H.D. (hon.), Rush U., 1986, Med. Coll. Pa., 1994; ScD (hon.), SUNY, Syracuse, 1994. Diplomate Am. Bd. Internal Medicine. Intern U. Pa. Hosp., 1960-61, med. resident, 1961-63, fellow in cardiology, 1963-64, chief med. resident, 1964-65, chief med. outpatient dept., 1966-67; chief of medicine U. Pa. Med. Svc., VA Hosp., Phila., 1967-73; mem. deans com. VA Hosp., 1974-88; instr. medicine Grad. Div. Medicine, U. Pa., 1964-66, NIH postdoctoral rsch. trainee, dept. physiology, 1965-67, assoc. in medicine, 1966-67; assoc. in physiology Grad. Div. Medicine, 1967-72, asst. prof. medicine, 1967-70, assoc. prof., 1970-74, prof., 1974—, Robert G. Dunlop prof., 1981-91, prof. emeritus, 1991—; assoc. dean Univ. Hosp. (Sch. Medicine), 1973, assoc. dean student affairs, 1973-75, acting dean, 1974-75, dean, 1975-88, dean emeritus, 1989—; exec. v.p. U. Pa. Med. Ctr., 1986-89; exec. v.p. Assn. Am. Med. Colls., 1990-94, sr. adv. to pres., 1994-95; mem. Nat. Bd. Med. Examiners, 1974-76, nominating and ad hoc governance coms., 1985, vice chmn., 1987-89, treas., 1989-91, chmn., 1991-95; mem. exec. com.; mem. ednl. policy com. Nat. Fund for Med. Edn., 1975-77; mem. deans com. VA Hosp., 1974-89; trustee Dorothy Rider Pool Healthcare Trust, 1991—, Ursinus Coll., 1991—, Wintergreen Nature Found., 1996—. Contbr. articles to profl. jours. Chmn. Pa. Deans Com., 1976-87; bd. govs. Mid-Ea. Regional Med. Libr. Svcs., 1977-81, chmn., 1978-81; bd. visitors U. Pitts. Sch. Medicine, 1980-85, U. Md. Sch. Medicine, 1991-94; mem. bd. overseers Dartmouth Med. Sch. and C. Everett Koop Inst., 1992—; mem. adv. com. dept. medicine U. Ala., Birmingham, 1985-89; mem. vis. com. Tufts U. Sch. Medicine, 1990-94, Med. U. S.C., 1990—, U. Calif., Davis, 1993—. Decorated Commendation medal; recipient Frederick A. Packard award, 1960, Albert Einstein Med. Ctr. staff award, 1960, Roche award, 1960. Master ACP (treas., chmn. investment com. 1975-80, Laureate award Ea. Pa. region 1986); mem. AMA (health policy agenda), Inst. Medicine NAS, Assn. Am. Med. Colls. (ad hoc external exam. rev. com. 1980-82, exec. coun. 1980-85, coun. of deans adminstrv. bd. 1980-85, chmn. 1983-84, nat. chmn.-elect 1985-86, chmn. assembly 1986-87), Coll. of Physicians of Phila. (bd. censors 1979-85, coun. 1979-85, 90-92), Am. Clin. and Climatological Soc., Alpha Omega Alpha. Republican. Mem. Christian Ch. Home: Rt #1 Box 676 Roseland VA 22967

STEMPEL, ERNEST EDWARD, insurance executive; b. N.Y.C., May 10, 1916; s. Frederick Christian and Leah Lillian S.; m. Phyllis Brooks (dec. Mar. 1993); children: Diana Brooks Bergquist, Calvin Pinkcomb, Neil Frederick, Robert Russell. A.B., Manhattan Coll., 1938; LL.B., Fordham U., 1946; LL.M., NYU, 1949, D.J.S., 1951; LL.D. (hon.), Manhattan Coll., 1986. Bar: N.Y. 1946. With Am. Internat. Underwriters Corp., N.Y.C., 1938-53; v.p., dir. Am. Internat. Co. Ltd., Hamilton, Bermuda, 1953-63, chmn. bd., from 1963; chmn., dir. Am. Internat. Assurance Co. (Bermuda) Ltd., Am. Internat. Reins. Co. Ltd., Bermuda, Philippine Am. Life Ins. Co., Manila, Australian Am. Assurance Co., Ltd., Am. Internat. Assurance Co., Ltd., Hong Kong, AIG Life Ins. Co., Del. Am. Life Ins. Co., Wilmington, Del., Am. Internat. Life Assurance Co. of N.Y.; pres., dir. Starr Internat. Co. Inc.; sr. advisor Am. Internat. Group Inc.; dir. C.V. Starr & Co. Inc., N.Y.C., Am. Life Ins. Co., Wilmington, Seguros Interamericana (S.A.), Mexico, Mt. Mansfield Co., Inc., Stowe, Vt., Seguros Venezuela (C.A.), Caracas, dir. Am. Internat. Underwriters (Latin Am.), Inc., Bermuda, Am. Internat. Underwriters Mediterranean, Inc., Bermuda, Pacific Union Assurance Co., Calif., Underwriters Adjustment Co., Panama. Served to lt. (s.g.) USNR, 1942-46. Mem. Am. Bar Assn., N.Y. State Bar. Clubs: Marco Polo (N.Y.C.), Royal Bermuda Yacht (Bermuda), Mid-Ocean (Bermuda), Coral Beach & Tennis Club (Bermuda), Riddell's Bay Golf and Country (Bermuda). Office: Am Internat Co Ltd, PO Box HM 152, Hamilton HM AX, Bermuda

STEMPEL, GUIDO HERMANN, III, journalism educator; b. Bloomington, Ind., Aug. 13, 1928; s. Guido Hermann Jr. and Alice Margaret (Menninger) S.; m. Anne Elliott, Aug. 30, 1952; children: Ralph Warren, Carl William, Jane Louise. Student, Carnegie Tech., 1945-46; AB in Journalism, Ind. U., 1949, AM in Journalism, 1951; PhD in Mass Communication, U. Wis., 1954. Sports editor Frankfort (Ind.) Times, 1949-50; instr., asst. prof. Sch. Journalism, Pa. State U., University Park, 1955-57; from assoc. prof. to prof. Dept. Journalism, Cen. Mich. U., Mt. Pleasant, 1957-65; assoc. prof. Sch. Journalism, Ohio U., Athens, 1965-68, prof., 1968-82, Disting. prof., 1982-97, dir., 1972-79, Disting. prof. emeritus, 1997—; rsch. cons. Ohio Newspaper Assn., Columbus, 1985—; chmn. rsch. com. Coll. Media Advisors, 1963-69, 79-84; mem. adv. bd. dept. comm. arts U. West Fla., 1987—; survey coord. Scripps Howard News Svc., 1992—. Co-author: The Media in the 1984 and 1988 Presidential Campaigns, 1991; assoc. editor, Newspaper Rsch. Jour., 1992—; co-editor Web Jour. of Mass Comm. Rsch., 1997—; editor, co-author: The Practice of Political Communication, 1994; co-editor, co-author: Research Methods in Mass Communications, 1981, 2d edit., 1989; editor: Journalism Quar., 1972-89; contbr. articles to profl. jours. Mem. bd. visitors Def. Info. Sch., Ft. Meade, 1985-96. Recipient Chancellor's award U. Wis., 1977. Mem. Assn. for Edn. in Journalism and Mass Communication (chmn. rsch. com. 1968-71; Eleanor Blum award 1989), Soc. Profl. Journalists, Rotary (pres. Athens unit 1984-85). Democrat. Methodist. Home: 7 Lamar Dr Athens OH 45701-3730 Office: Ohio Univ Sch of Journalism Athens OH 45701

STEMPLE, JOEL GILBERT, computer company executive; b. Bklyn., Feb. 3, 1942; s. Max David and Helen (Nechamkin) S.; m. Sharon Claire Schneider, Apr. 6, 1968; children—Tracy, Allyson. BS, Bklyn. Coll., 1962; MA, Yale U., 1964, PhD, 1966. Asst. prof. Queens Coll., Flushing, N.Y., 1966-70, assoc. prof. math., 1970-82; v.p. Manchester Equipment Co. Inc., Hauppauge, N.Y., 1982—. Office: Manchester Equipment Co Inc 50 Marcus Blvd Hauppauge NY 11788-3730

STEMPLER, JACK LEON, government and aerospace company executive; b. Newark, Oct. 30, 1920; s. Morris and Ida (Friedman) S.; m. J. Adelaide Williams, Oct. 28, 1950; children: Mark N., Sandra J., Carrie B. B.A., Montclair (N.J.) State Coll., 1943; LL.B., Cornell U., 1948. Bar: N.Y., D.C. 1949. Atty. com. uniform code mil. justice Dept. Def., 1948-49, atty. adviser legis. div., 1949-50; asst. counsel Munitions Bd., 1950-53; counsel Armed Forces Housing Agy., 1952-54, Advanced Research Projects Agy., 1958-65; asst. gen. counsel logistics Dept. Def., 1953-65, asst. to sec. def. for legislative affairs, 1965-70; gen. counsel Dept. Air Force, 1970-77; asst. to sec. of def. for legis. affairs, 1977-81; v.p. legis. affairs LTV Aerospace, Washington, 1982-92; ret., 1992; cons. in field. Served to 1st lt. USMCR, 1942-46, PTO. Recipient Outstanding Civilian Performance award Dept. Def., 1959, Distinguished Civilian Service award, 1965, Distinguished Civilian Service award with palm, 1969, with 2d bronze palm, 1970; Exceptional Civilian Service award USAF, 1973, 75, 77; awarded Presdl. rank of Disting. Exec., 1980; recipient Disting. Public Service award Dept. Def., 1981. Mem. Fed., D.C. bar assns., Cornell Law Sch. Assn., Air Force Aid Soc. (trustee). Home: 4701 Newcomb Pl Alexandria VA 22304-1506

STEN, JOHANNES WALTER, control systems engineer, consultant; b. Balt., Aug. 1, 1934; s. Johannes Adolf and Aili Augusta (Bohm) S.; m. Elizabeth Eleanore Mackey, May 6, 1961; children: Nathan Allen, Curtis John, Theresa Jean, David Hal. B Engring. Sci., Johns Hopkins U., 1957; postgrad., u. Pa., 1962-65. Elec. engr. Johns Hopkins Physics Lab., Silver Spring, Md., 1957-58; R&D engr. E.I DuPont de Nemours Co., Wilmington, Del., 1960-64; instruments engr. E.I DuPont de Nemours Co., Newark, Del., 1964-74, sr. instruments engr., 1974, systems cons., 1974-79, project engr., 1979-90, sr. cons. polymers engring., 1990-93; ret.; ind. controls sys. cons. North East, Md., 1993—. Contbr. to profl. publs. 1st lt. U.S. Army, 1958-60. Mem. Instrument Soc. Am. (charter mem. batch standards com., cited as pioneer in computer-based control 1992), Delaware Valley Finnish Am. Soc. Lutheran. Achievements include establishing method of defining chemical batch process characteristics and complexity for controls system configuration, hardware and software.

STENBERG, CARL W(ALDAMER), III, academic program director, educator; b. Pitts., July 8, 1943; s. Carl W. and Mildred (Baggs) S.; m. Kirstin D. Thompson; children: Erik Anders, Kerry Cathryn, Kaameran Baird. BA, Allegheny Coll., 1965; MPA, SUNY, Albany, 1966, PhD, 1970. Research asst. N.Y. State Div. Budget, Albany, 1967; analyst, then sr. analyst U.S. Adv. Commn. on Intergovtl. Relations, Washington, 1968-77, asst. dir. for policy implementation, 1977-83, acting exec. dir., 1982; exec. dir. Council of State Govts., Lexington, Ky., 1983-89; prof., dir. Weldon Cooper Ctr. for Pub. Svc. U. Va., Charlottesville, 1989-95, Disting. prof. pub. svc., 1991-95; prof., dean Yale Gordon Coll. Liberal Arts U. Balt., 1995—; mem. Am. Part Program USIA, 1987; adj. prof. George Washington U., 1971, 81, Am. U., 1972-80, 82, U. Md., 1976, U. So. Calif., 1984-87; v.p. Bureaucrat Inc., Washington, 1973-77, mng. editor, 1973-77. Feature editor Pub. Mgmt. Forum Pub. Adminstrn. Rev., 1977-83, editor U. of Va. newsletter, 1994-95. Pres. Reston Home Owners' Assn., Va., 1973-74; mem. U.S. del. Ad Hoc Group on Urban Problems, OECD, 1980-82. Vivien Stewart vis. fellow Cambridge U., Eng., 1980; recipient Disting. Alumni award Polit. Sci. Dept. Rockefeller Coll., 1985. Mem. Am. Soc. Pub. Adminstrn. (pres. 1990-91, Marshall E. Dimock and Louis Brownlow awards), Va. Alliance for the Pub. Svc. (pres. 1991-92). Home: 501 Edgevale Rd Baltimore MD 21210 Office: Univ Baltimore U Balt 1420 N Charles St Baltimore MD 21201-5720

STENBERG, DONALD B., state attorney general; b. David City, Nebr., Sept. 30, 1948; s. Eugene A. and Alice (Kasal) S.; m. Susan K. Hoegemeyer, June 9, 1971; children: Julie A., Donald B. Jr., Joseph L., Abby E. BA, U. Nebr., 1970; MBA, Harvard U., 1974, JD cum laude, 1974. Bar: Nebr. 1974, U.S. Dist. Ct. Nebr. 1974, U.S. Ct. Appeals (fed. cir.) 1984, U.S. Ct. Claims 1989, U.S. Ct. Appeals (8th cir.) 1989, U.S. Supreme Ct., 1991. Assoc. Barlow, Watson & Johnson, Lincoln, Nebr., 1974-75; ptnr. Stenberg and Stenberg, Lincoln, 1976-78; legal counsel Gov. of Nebr., Lincoln, 1979-82; sr. prin. Erickson & Sederstrom, Lincoln, 1983-85; pvt. practice law Lincoln, 1985-90; atty. gen. State of Nebr., Lincoln, 1991—. Mem. Phi Beta Kappa. Republican. Office: Office of Atty Gen 2115 State Capitol Lincoln NE 68509

STENCER, MARK JOSEPH, academic administrator, consultant; b. Pitts., Mar. 19, 1955; s. Frank C. and Ramona (Calabrese) S. BFA, Carnegie-Mellon U., 1976; BA in Liberal Arts, U. Mich., 1979; MA in Mgmt., NYU, 1982. Asst. dir. NYU Office Acad. Devel., N.Y.C., 1980-82; program dir. John B. Cummings Co., Inc., Fundraising and Pub. Rels. Cons., N.Y.C., 1982-84; assoc. dir. The Statue of Liberty, Ellis Island Found., N.Y.C., 1984-86; dir. devel. Fordham U., N.Y.C., 1986-91; exec. v.p. Cambridge U., England, 1991-95; exec. campaign dir. Cmty. Counselling Svc. Co., Inc., Jersey City, N.J., 1995—. Named one of Outstanding Young Men Am., 1985, 86. Mem. Nat. Assn. Fundraising Execs., Coun. Advancement and Support of Edn. Republican. Roman Catholic. Avocation: pianist. Home: 201 St Pauls Ave #11-k Jersey City NJ 07306

STENCHEVER, MORTON ALBERT, physician, educator; b. Paterson, N.J., Jan. 25, 1931; s. Harold and Lena (Suresky) S.; m. Diane Bilsky, June 19, 1955; children: Michael A., Marc R., Douglas A. A.B., NYU, 1951; M.D., U. Buffalo, 1956. Diplomate Am. Bd. Ob-Gyn. (bd. dirs. 1988—, v.p. 1990-92, treas. 1992-96, chmn. 1996—, mem. resident rev. com. 1993—, chmn. divsn. urogynecology of reconstructive pelvic surgery). Intern Mt. Sinai Hosp., 1956-57; resident obstetrics and gynecology Columbia-Presbyn. Med. Center, N.Y.C., 1957-60; asst. prof., Oglebey research fellow Case-Western Res. U., Cleve., 1962-66; asso. prof. dept. reproductive biology Case-Western Res. U., 1967-70, dir. Tissue Culture Lab., 1965-70, coordinator Phase II Med. Sch. program, 1969-70; prof., chmn. dept. obstetrics-gynecology U. Utah Med. Sch., Salt Lake City, 1970-77; prof. ob-gyn. U. Wash. Sch. Medicine, Seattle, 1977—, chmn. dept., 1977-96; chmn. test com. for ob-gyn. Nat. Bd. Med. Examiners, 1979-82. Author: Labor: Workbook in Obstetrics, 1968, 2d edit., 1993, Human Sexual Behavior: A Workbook in Reproductive Biology, 1970, Human Cytogenics: A Workbook in Reproductive Biology, 1973, Introductory Gynecology: A Workbook in Reproductive Biology, 1974; co-author: Comprehensive Gynecology, 1987, 2d edit., 1992, 3d edit., 1997, Caring for the Older Woman, 1991, 2d edit., 1996, Health Care for the Older Woman, 1996, Office Gynecology, 1992, 2d edit., 1996; assoc. editor Ob-Gyn., 1986—, Ob-Gyn. Survey; mem. editorial bd. Western Jour. Medicine; contbr. articles to profl. jours. Served to capt. USAF, 1960-62. Fellow Am. Coll. Obstetricians and Gynecologists (com. on residency edn. 1974-80, learning resource commn. 1980-86, vice chmn. 1982-83, chmn. prolog self-assessment program 1982-86, vice chair com. health care for the underserved women 1995—), Am. Assn. Obstetricians and Gynecologists, Am. Gynecol. Soc., Am. Soc. Ob-Gyn., Pacific Coast Ob-Gyn. Soc.; mem. AAAS, AMA, Assn. Profs. Gynecology and Obstetrics (chmn. steering com. teaching methodis in ob-gyn. 1970-79, v.p. 1975-76, pres. 1983-84, v.p. Found. 1986-87, pres. Found. 1987-91), Pacific N.W. Ob-Gyn. Soc., Wash. State Med. Assn., Seattle Gynec. Soc. (v.p. 1981, pres.-elect 1982, pres. 1982-83), Pacific Coast Ob-Gyn. Soc., Am. Soc. Human Genetics, Ctrl. Assn. Ob-Gyn., Soc. Gynecologic Investigation, Wash. State Obstet. Soc., Tissue Culture Assn., N.Y. Acad. Sci., Utah Ob-Gyn. Soc., Utah Med. Assn., Teratology Soc., Am. Fertility Soc. Home: 8301 SE 83rd St Mercer Island WA 98040-5644 Office: U Wash Dept Ob-Gyn 1959 NE Pacific St Seattle WA 98195-0004

STENDAHL, KRISTER, retired bishop; b. Stockholm, Sweden, Apr. 21, 1921; came to U.S., 1954, naturalized, 1967; s. Olof and Sigrid (Ljungquist) S.; m. Brita Johnsson, Sept. 7, 1946; children: John, Anna, Daniel. Teol. kand., U. Uppsala, Sweden, 1944, teol. lic., 1949, teol.dr., 1954; Litt. D. (hon.), Upsala Coll., 1963; D.D., St. Olaf Coll., 1971, Harvard U., 1985, St. Andrews U., 1987, Calif. Luth. U., 1995; LL.D., Susquehanna U., 1973; L.H.D. (hon.), Hebrew Union Coll./Jewish Inst. Religion, 1980, Brandeis U., 1981, Loyola U., New Orleans, 1992. Ordained priest Ch. of Sweden, 1944. Chaplain to students Uppsala U., 1948-50, instr. O.T., N.T. exegesis, 1951-54, docent, 1954; asst. prof. N.T., 1954-56; asso. prof. Harvard U. Div. Sch., 1956-58, John H. Morison prof. N.T. studies, 1958-63, Frothingham prof. Bibl. studies, 1963-68, dean, John Lord O'Brian prof. div., 1968-79, Andrew W. Mellon prof. div., 1981-84; pastor Luth. Ch. Am., 1968-84; bishop of Stockholm Ch. of Sweden, 1984-88; Robert and Myra Kraft and Jacob Hiatt Disting. prof. Christian studies Brandeis U., 1991-93; moderator consultation on ch. and Jewish people World Council Chs., 1975-85; co-dir. Osher Ctr. for Tolerance and Pluralism Shalom Hartman Inst., 1994—. Author: The School of St. Matthew, 1954, 2d edit., 1968, The Bible and the Role of Women, 1966, Holy Week, 1974, Paul Among Jews and Gentiles, 1976, Meanings, 1984, Energy for Life, 1990, Final Account, 1995. Recipient Disting. Service award Assn. Theol. Schs., 1988. Fellow Am. Acad. Arts and Scis.; mem. Nathan Soederblom Soc.

STENEHJEM, WAYNE KEVIN, state senator, lawyer; b. Mohall, N.D., Feb. 5, 1953; s. Martin Edward and Marguerite Mae (McMaster) S.; m. Tama Lou Smith, June 16, 1978 (div. Apr. 1984); 1 child, Andrew; m. Beth D. Bakke, June 30, 1995. AA, Bismarck (N.D.) Jr. Coll., 1972; BA, U. N.D., 1974, JD, 1977. Bar: N.D. 1977. Ptnr. Kuchera & Stenehjem, Grand Forks, N.D., 1977—; spl. asst. atty. gen. State of N.D., 1983-87; mem. N.D. Ho. Reps., 1976-80, N.D. State Senate, 1980—; chmn. Senate Com. on Social Svcs., 1985-86, Senate Com. on Judiciary, Interim Legis. Judiciary Com., 1995—, Legis. Coun., 1995—; mem. Nat. Conf. Commrs. on Uniform State Laws, 1995—; mem. Gov.'s Com. on Juvenile Justice. Chmn. Dist. 42 Reps., Grand Forks, 1986-88; bd. dirs. N.D. Spl. Olympics, 1985-89, Christus Rex Luth. Ch., pres., 1985-86. Named Champion of People's Right to Know, Sigma Delta Chi, 1979, Outstanding Young Man of N.D., Grand Forks Jaycees, 1985, N.D. Friend of Psychology, N.D. Psychol. Assn., 1990; recipient Excellence in County Govt. award N.D. Assn. Counties, 1991, Legis. Svc. award State Bar Assn. N.D., 1995. Mem. N.D. State Bar Assn. (Legis. Svc. award), Grand Forks County Bar Assn., Mental Health Assn. (bd. dirs.). Home: 2204 12th Ave N Grand Forks ND 58203-2251 Office: Kuchera Stenehjem & Walberg PO Box 6352 212 S 4th St Grand Forks ND 58206-6352

STENGEL, ROBERT FRANK, mechanical and aerospace engineering educator; b. Orange, N.J., Sept. 1, 1938; s. Frank John and Ruth Emma (Geidel) S.; m. Margaret Robertson Ewing, Apr. 8, 1961; children: Brooke Alexandra, Christopher Ewing. SB, MIT, 1960; MS in Engring., Princeton U., 1965, MA, 1966, PhD, 1968. Aerospace technologist NASA, Wallops Island, Va., 1960-63; tech. staff group leader C.S. Draper Lab., Cambridge, Mass., 1968-73, Analytic Scis. Corp., Reading, Mass., 1973-77; assoc. prof. Princeton (N.J.) U., 1977-82, prof. mech. and aerospace engring., 1982—, assoc. dean engring., 1994-97; cons. GM, Warren, Mich., 1985-94; mem. com. strategic tech. U.S. Army NRC, 1989-92; vice chmn. Congl. Aero. Adv. Com., Washington, 1986-89; mem. com. on trans-atmospheric vehicles USAF Sci. Adv. Bd., 1984-85; mem. com. on low altitude wind shear and its hazard to aviation Nat. Rsch. Coun., 1983. Author: Stochastic Optimal Control: Theory and Application, 1986, reprinted as Optimal Control and Estimation, 1994; N.Am. editor Cambridge Aerospace Series, 1993—, Cambridge Univ. Press, 1993—; contbr. over 100 tech. papers to profl. publs.; patentee wind probing device. Lt. USAF, 1960-63. Recipient Apollo Achievement award NASA, 1969, Cert. of Commendation, MIT, 1969. Fellow IEEE, AIAA; mem. Soc. Automotive Engrs. (mem. aerospace guidance and control systems com.). Avocations: photography, music, bicycling. Home: 329 Prospect Ave Princeton NJ 08540-5330 Office: Princeton U D202 Engineering Quadrangle Princeton NJ 08544

STENGEL, RONALD FRANCIS, management consultant; b. Lock Haven, Pa., Oct. 18, 1947; s. Elmer S. and Elizabeth (Heivley) S.; m. Margaret Linda Dezack, Aug. 23, 1969. BSME, U. Pa., 1969, MBA, 1976. Mfg. engr. Control Data Corp., Valley Forge, Pa., 1969-70; mgr. mfg. svcs. Knoll Internat., East Greenville, Pa., 1970-75; ptnr. mgmt. cons. Touche Ross & Co., Phila., 1976-85; pres. RF Stengel & Co. Inc., Valley Forge, 1985—.

STENGER, JUDITH ANTOINETTE, middle school educator; b. Camp Blanding, Fla., Dec. 20, 1942; d. Jack Joseph DiSalvo and Judith Lorraine (Donnelly) DiSalvo-Kohser; m. Harry Richard Stenger, Feb. 4, 1967; children: Scott Joseph, Christopher Richard. BS in Art Edn., Indiana U. Pa., 1965; postgrad., Trinity Coll., 1983-84, Western Md. Coll., 1983-84. Tchr. art elem. sch. Elizabethtown (Pa.) Schs., 1965, Freedom (Pa.) Area Schs., 1966; tchr. art elem. and mid. schs. Carroll County (Md.) Schs., 1967-69; spl. educator Montgomery County (Md.) Schs., 1980-92, tchr. art mid. sch., 1992—; co-leader Md. Student Assistance Program (drug intervention), Rockville, 1995—, mem., 1993—. Represented in 17 group shows. Named Outstanding Tchr. Coun. Exceptional Children, 1986. Mem. NEA, Md. State Tchrs. Assn., Montgomery County Tchrs. Assn., Nat. Art Edn. Assn., Nat. Artists Equity, Md. Art Edn. Assn., Rockville Arts Place. Avocations: printmaking, sculpture, painting. Office: Montgomery County Pub Schs Parkland Mid Sch 4610 W Frankfort Dr Rockville MD 20853-2721

STENGER, VERNON ARTHUR, analytical chemist, consultant; b. Mpls., June 11, 1908; s. Laurence Arthur and Effie Harriet (Dahlberg) S.; m. Ruth Luella Day, Aug. 2, 1933 (dec. Oct. 1994); children: Robert, Emilie, Alan, Gordon, David; m. Eleanor Miller, Sept. 19, 1996. BS, U. Denver, 1929, MS, 1930; PhD, U. Minn., 1933; DSc (hon.), U. Denver, 1971. Chemist Eastman Kodak Co., Rochester, N.Y., 1929-30, N.W. Rsch. Inst., U. Minn., Mpls., 1933-35; chemist Dow Chem. Co., Midland, Mich., 1935-40, tech. expert, 1940-53, asst. lab. dir., 1954-61, rsch. scientist, 1961-73, cons., 1973—; chmn. subcom. on magnesium alloy analysis ASTM, Phila., 1941-54. Author: (with I.M. Kolthoff) Volumetric Analysis, Vol. I, 1942, Vol. II, 1947, (with Kolthoff and R. Belcher) Volumetric Analysis, Vol. III, 1957; contbr. 10 encyclopedia articles, 6 chpts. to books and articles to profl. jours. Bd. mem. Midland Symphony Orch., hon. mem. 1990—. Recipient Anachem award Soc. Analytical Chemists, Detroit, 1970. Fellow Am. Inst. Chemists, N.Y. Acad. Scis.; mem. Am. Chem. Soc. (chmn. com. on analytical reagts. 1967-73, mem. adv. bd. Analytical Chemistry 1953-56, Midland sect. award 1979), Geochem. Soc., Sigma Xi. Baptist. Achievements include patent for apparatus for instrumental determination of total organic carbon (TOC), widely used in water analysis, various analytical methods in industry. Home: 1108 E Park Dr Midland MI 48640-4275

STENGLER, RON JOSEPH, gaming corporation executive; b. Mankota, Sask., Can., Aug. 18, 1948; s. Marcus Stengler and Amy Mary Selenski; m. Coleen Schonhofler, Dec. 28, 1968 (div. 1982); children: Erica Stengler Young, Ingrid. B Adminstrn., U. Sask., Saskatoon, 1971. Various mgmt. positions Sask. Provincial Govt.; gen. mgr. Western Can. Summer Games, Regina, Sask.; v.p. Westbridge Computer Corp., Regina; pres. R.Mac Inc., Regina, 1991—; pres., CEO Sask. Gaming Corp., Regina, 1994—. Home: 307 Avon Dr, Regina, SK Canada S4V 1L8 Office: Sask Gaming Corp, 1880 Saskatchewan 3d Fl, Regina, SK Canada S4P 0B2

STENHOLM, CHARLES W., congressman; b. Stamford, Tex., Oct. 26, 1938; m. Cynthia Ann Watson; children: Chris, Cary, Courtney Ann. Card., Tarleton State Jr. Coll., 1959; B.S. in Agrl. Edn., Tex. Tech U., 1961, M.S. in Agrl. Edn., 1962; LL.D. (hon.), McMurry Coll., 1983, Abilene Christian U., 1991. Farmer Tex.; past pres. Rolling Plains Cotton Growers and Tex. Electric Coops.; mem. 96th-105rd Congresses from 17th Tex. dist., Washington, D.C., 1979—; apptd. deputy whip 96th-105d Congresses from 17th Tex. dist., 1989—; former mem. state Dem. Exec. Com.; dep. whip Washington, 1989—; Dem mem. agrl. subcom.; co-chmn. Congl. Leaders United for a Balanced Budget. Active Bethel Luth. Ch., Ericksdahl, Tex.; charter trustee Cotton Producer Inst. Recipient Gerald W. Thomas Outstanding Agriculturalist award Tex. Tech U., 1979, Am. Farmer Degree Future Farmers Am., 1979, Disting. Alumnus award Tarleton State U., 1979, Pres. Coun. award Tex. Future Farmers Am., 1981, Disting. Alumnus award Tex. Tech U., 1987, MORE Common Sense Sound Dollar awards, 1988, 90, Guardian of Small Bus. awards, 1980-92, Watchdogs of the Treasury awards, 1980-92, Legis. award Nat. Rural Health Assn., 1991, Disting. Svc. award Tex. Soc. Biomed. Rsch., 1993, Disting. Svc. award Tex. Med. Assn., 1993, Dr. Nathan Davis award AMA, 1993, Leadership in Advocacy for Children's Health award Nat. Assn. Children's Hosps., 1996, Meritorious Health Svc. award Nat. Assn. Cmty. Health Ctrs., 1997, Golden Plow award Am. Farm Bur. Fedn., 1988, 92, 96, golden Triangle award Nat. Fermers Union, 1994, Thomas Jefferson award Food Distbn. Industry, 1994, 95, Progressive Fermer Man of Yr. award, 1993, Econ. Patriot award, 1997; named Legislator of Yr. Chem. Prodrs. and Distbrs. Assn., 1992, Man of Yr. Progressive Farmer, 1993. Mem. Tex. State Soc. (Washington, past pres.), Tex. Breakfast Club (Washington, past pres.), Rolling Plains Cotton Growers (past pres.), Stamford C. of C. (past pres.). Democrat. Lutheran. Office: 1211 Longworth Bldg Washington DC 20515-4317

STENHOUSE, EVERETT RAY, clergy administrator; b. Minco, Okla., May 15, 1931; s. George E. and Jessie Loraine (Dean) S.; m. Alice Irene English, Aug. 22, 1948; children: Brenda Jones, Judy Lundberg, Stephen, Andrew. Student, U. Calif. Berkeley, U. Athens, 1969-71. Ordained to ministry Assemblies of God, 1955. Pastor Wayside Chapel, Bakersfield, Calif., 1955-59, Bethel Temple, Bakersfield, 1960-63; dist. dir. youth So. Calif. Dist. Assemblies of God, Costa Mesa, Calif., 1963-67; assoc. pastor 1st Assembly of God, San Diego, 1968-69; missionary Assemblies of God Fgn. Missions, Athens, Greece, 1969-73; pastor Bethany Ch., Alhambra, Calif., 1974-79; supt. So. Calif. Dist., Assemblies of God, Costa Mesa, 1979-85; asst. gen. supt. Gen. Coun. Assemblies of God, Springfield, Mo., 1986-94; bd. adminstrn. Nat. Assn. Evangs., Wheaton, Ill., 1986-94, Pentecostal Fellowship of No. Am., Ont., Can., 1986-94; chmn., bd. dirs. Assemblies of God Theol. Sem., Springfield, 1991-94, Ministers Benefit Assn., Springfield, 1986-94. Contbr. articles to various mags. Home: 19 Durango Cir Rancho Mirage CA 92270-4801

STENNETT, WILLIAM CLINTON (CLINT STENNETT), radio/TV station executive, state senator; b. Winona, Minn., Oct. 1, 1956; s. William Jessie and Carole Lee (Halsey) S. BA in Journalism, Idaho State U., 1979. Gen. mgr. Wood River Jour., Hailey, Idaho, 1979-85, pres., pub., 1985-87; pres. Sta. KWRV-TV, Ketchum, Idaho, Sta. KSKI-FM, Sun Valley, Idaho; mem. Idaho Ho. of Reps., Boise, 1990-94, state senator, 1995—. Recipient Gen. Excellence award Idaho Newspaper Assn., 1985, 96, 97; named Legislator of the Yr. Idaho Soil Conservation Dists., 1994, Idaho Wildlife Found., 1996. Mem. Idaho Broadcasters (bd. dirs.), Ketchum Sun Valley C. of C. (bd. dirs. 1990-95), Rotary. Democrat.

STENT, GUNTHER SIEGMUND, molecular biologist, educator; b. Berlin, Germany, Mar. 28, 1924; came to U.S., 1940, naturalized, 1945; s. George and Elizabeth (Karfunkelstein) S.; m. Inga Loftsdottir, Oct. 27, 1951; 1 son, Stefan Loftur. BS, U. Ill., 1945, PhD, 1948; DSc (hon.), York U., 1984. Research asst. U. Ill., 1945-48; research fellow Calif. Inst. Tech., 1948-50, U. Copenhagen, Denmark, 1950-51, Pasteur Inst., Paris, France, 1951-52; asst. research biochemist U. Calif., Berkeley, 1952-56; faculty U. Calif., 1956—, prof. molecular biology, 1959-94; prof. emeritus, 1994—; prof. arts and scis. U. Calif., 1967-68, chmn. molecular biology, 1980-86, chmn. molecular and cell biology, 1987-92, dir. virus lab., 1980-86; document analyst U.S. Field Info. Agy. Tech., 1946-47; mem. genetics panel NIH, 1959-64, NSF, 1965-68; fellow Inst. Advanced Studies, Berlin, 1985-90. Author: Papers On Bacterial Viruses, 2d edit., 1966, Molecular Biology of Bacterial Viruses, 1963, Phage and the Origin of Molecular Biology, 1966, The Coming of the Golden Age, 1969, Function and Formation of Neural Systems, 1977, Morality as a Biological Phenomenon, 1978, Paradoxes of Progress, 1978, Molecular Genetics, 2d edit., 1978; mem. editl. bd. Jour. Molecular Biology, 1965-68, Genetics, 1963-68, Zeitschrift für Vererbungslehre, 1962-68, Ann. Revs. Genetics, 1965-69, Ann. Revs. Microbiology, 1966-70, Jour. Neurosci., 1988-96; contbr. numerous sci. papers to profl. lit. Merck fellow NRC, 1948-56; sr. fellow NSF, 1960-61; Guggenheim fellow, 1969-70; Fogarty Resident Scholar NIH, 1990-92. Mem. NAS, Am. Acad. Arts and Scis., Soc. Neurosci., Am. Philos. Soc., Acad. Scis. and Lit. of Mainz (Germany), European Acad. Scis. and Arts, Cosmos Club. Home: 145 Purdue Ave Kensington CA 94708-1032

STENWICK, MICHAEL WILLIAM, internist, geriatric medicine consultant; b. Red Wing, Minn., Nov. 12, 1941; s. Vincent Ferdinand and Geraldine Frances (Veith) S.; m. Judith Ann Nelson, June 10, 1961; children: Scott Michael, Gregg William. BS cum laude, Hamline U., 1963; MD, U. Minn., 1969. Diplomate Am. Bd. Internal Medicine. Fellow dept. pharmacology U. Minn., Mpls., 1966-68; intern in internal medicine Northwestern Hosp., Mpls., 1969-70, resident in internal medicine, 1970-73; sr. internist internal medicine sect. Bloomington Lake Clinic, Mpls., 1973—; bd. dirs. Bloomington Lake Clinic, Mpls., pres. 1977, v.p. 1989—, fin. com., 1987—, chmn. properties, 1984—, chmn. trustees profit sharing; med. adviser Kimberly Quality Care, St. Paul, 1990-94; internal medicine cons. Fairview Multiple Sclerosis Ctr. and Rehab. Unit, Mpls., 1986—; informal adviser internal medicine sect. Minn. Relative Value Index, Mpls., 1971; mem. task force Riverside Med. Ctr., Mpls., 1988-91, chmn. critical care com., 1986-91, reviewer quality assurance subcom., 1989-90. Contbr. articles to profl. jours. Mem., co-organizer, 1st pres. Cyrus Barnum Soc., U. Minn. Med. Sch., Mpls.; bd. dirs. Signal Inn Beach and Racquetball Club, Sanibel Island, Fla., 1983-84, 89—, Signal Inn Condominium Assn., Sanibel Island, 1983-84, 89—; co-emcee Nursing Talent Show, Northwestern Hosp., Mpls., 1969; 1st med. dir. Beltrami Health Ctr., Mpls., 1970-72. Recipient scholarship Charles and Alora Allis Found., 1960-63, Walter Kenyon award, 1963, grant U. Minn., 1963. Fellow Am. Coll. Physicians; mem. AMA, Am. Soc. Internal Medicine, Minn. Med. Assn., Hennepin County Med. Assn., Mpls. Soc. Internal Medicine. Republican. Lutheran. Achievements include research in drug specificity that could be defined even in an alkylating agent. Office: Bloomington Lake Clinic 3017 Bloomington Ave Minneapolis MN 55407-1715

STENZEL, KURT HODGSON, physician, nephrologist, educator; b. Stamford, Conn., Nov. 3, 1932; s. Alfred B. and Aurelie C. (Hodgson) S.; m. Carolyn Briggs, Dec. 21, 1957; children—Matthew, Jennifer, Mary. BA magna cum laude, N.Y. U., 1954; M.D., Cornell U., 1958. Intern Bellevue

Hosp., N.Y.C., 1958-59; resident, 1959-60, 62-63; asst. in medicine Cornell U. Med. Coll., N.Y.C., 1959-60; asst. prof. medicine Cornell U. Med. Coll., 1965-68, asso. prof. biochemistry and surgery, 1969-75, prof. biochemistry, medicine and surgery, 1976—, chief div. nephrology (medicine), 1979-92, dir. Rogosin Kidney Ctr., 1970—; attending physician, surgeon N.Y. Hosp., N.Y.C., 1976—; Diplomate Am. Bd. Internal Medicine and Nephrology. contbr. articles to profl. publs. Served to lt., M.C. USNR, 1960-62. Recipient Nat. Kidney Found. Hoenig award for excellence in renal medicine. Fellow ACP; mem. Am. Soc. Biol. Chemists, Am. Soc. Nephrology, Transplantation Soc., Am. Fedn. Clin. Research, Am. Assn. Immunologists, Am. Soc. for Artificial Internal Organs, Phi Beta Kappa. Research on cell biology, cellular immunology, transplantation and dialysis. Office: The Rogosin Inst 505 E 70th St New York NY 10021-4872

STENZEL, WILLIAM A., consulting services executive; b. Cambridge, Mass., Jan. 21, 1923; s. Herman Rheinhold and Helen (Proskurniak) S.; m. Pallie Jean Bottorff, July 25, 1952; children: Jeffrey Rheinhold, Anne Virginia, Peter Deane, Christopher James. B.A. cum laude, Harvard U., 1944, M.B.A., 1948. Advt. mgr. Waltham Watch Co., Mass., 1948-54; v.p. Tracer Lab. Inc., Waltham, 1954-62; sr. v.p. Premier Indsl. Corp., Cleve., 1962-85, Mex. Info. and Cons. Svcs., Inc., 1985—; v.p. Edn. Techs. and Cons., Inc. Bd. dirs. Greater Cleve. chpt. ARC, 1983-86, bd. dirs., mem. exec. com. Orange City chpt., Calif.; fundraiser Cleve. Orch., 1977-81; trustee Mid Town Corridor, 1985-87, Dunham Tavern Mus., 1985-87; bd. dirs., mem. fin. devel. com. Orange City chpt. ARC; bd. dirs. Blood, tissue svcs. So. Calif. region ARC, 1992-95; pres. San Clemente Friends of the Libr., 1995—; treas. Friends of the Libr. Found., Orange County, 1997—;. Fellow Rowfant Club, 1985—. Clubs: Harvard Bus. Sch., Rowfant (Cleve.). Home and Office: 124 Avenida Cota San Clemente CA 92672-3327

STEP, EUGENE LEE, retired pharmaceutical company executive; b. Sioux City, Iowa, Feb. 19, 1929; s. Harry and Ann (Keiser) S.; m. Hannah Scheuermann, Dec. 27, 1953; children—Steven Harry, Michael David, Jonathan Allen. BA in Econs., U. Nebr., 1951; MS in Acctg. and Fin., U. Ill., 1952. With Eli Lilly Internat. Corp., London and Paris, 1964-69; dir. Elanco Internat. Eli Lilly Internat. Corp., Indpls., 1969-70, v.p. marketing, 1970-72, v.p. Europe, 1972; v.p. mktg. Eli Lilly and Co., Indpls., 1972-73, pres. pharm. div., 1973-86, exec. v.p., 1986—, also dir.; bd. dirs. Scios-Nova Cell-Genesys, Medco Rsch. Pathogenesis, Guidant Corp. 1st lt. U.S. Army, 1953-56. Mem. Pharm. Mfrs. Assn. (bd. dirs. 1980-92), Internat. Pharm. Mfrs. Assn. (pres. 1991-92). Home: 741 Round Hill Rd Indianapolis IN 46260-2917

STEPAN, FRANK QUINN, chemical company executive; b. Chgo., Oct. 24, 1937; s. Alfred Charles and Mary Louise (Quinn) S.; m. Jean Finn, Aug. 23, 1958; children: Jeanne, Frank Quinn, Todd, Jennifer, Lisa, Colleen, Alfred, Richard. A.B., U. Notre Dame, 1959; M.B.A., U. Chgo., 1963. Salesman Indsl. Chems. div. Stepan Chem. Co., Northfield, Ill., 1961-63, mgr. internat. dept., 1964-66, v.p. corporate planning, 1967-69, v.p., gen. mgr., 1970-73, pres., 1973-84; pres., chmn., chief exec. officer Stepan Co., Northfield, Ill., 1984—, also bd. dirs. Mem. liberal arts council Notre Dame U., South Bend, Ind., 1972—; bd. dirs. Big Shoulders, Chgo. Served to 1st lt. AUS, 1959-61. Mem. Chem. Mfrs. Assn. (bd. dirs.), Soap and Detergent Assn. (bd. dirs.), Ill. Bus. Roundtable, Econ. Club Chgo., Exmoor Country Club, Bob O'Link Golf Club, Everglades Club. Home: 200 Linden St Winnetka IL 60093-3862 Office: Stepan Co Edens & Winnetka Rds Northfield IL 60093

STEPANEK, DANIEL P., public relations executive. BS, Marquette U.; MA in Journalism, U. Iowa; MBA in Fin., Loyola U., Chgo. Previously with Combustion Enging., Borg Warner, RJR Industries; v.p., gen. mgr. CMF&Z Pub. Rels., N.Y.C.; mng. ptnr. KCSA Pub. Rels., N.Y.C., 1992—. Office: KCSA Pub Rels 820 2nd Ave New York NY 10017-4504

STEPANIAN, IRA, banking executive; b. Cambridge, Mass., Nov. 14, 1936; s. Sarkis H. and Armenoohi (Kupelian) S.; m. Jacquelynne McLucas, Aug. 6, 1961; children: Philip, Alisa, Steven. B.A., Tufts U., 1958; M.B.A., Boston Coll., 1971. Credit investigator Dun & Bradstreet, Boston, 1958-59; rsch. assoc. Ernst Assocs., Inc., Arlington, Mass., 1959-63; with First Nat. Bank Boston, 1963-95, exec. v.p., 1980, vice chmn., from 1981, pres., from 1983, chmn., CEO, dir., 1989-95; vice chmn. Bank of Boston Corp., 1981—, pres., 1983—, COO, dir., 1983-87, CEO, 1987-95; bd. dirs. NYNEX-New Eng., NYNEX-N.Y., Chem. Group, Blue Eagle Golf Cos., Tad Resources Internat. Trustee emeritus Tufts U., Medford, Mass.; chmn. Boston Mus. Sci.; trustee Boston Mus. Fine Arts, Gen. Hosp. Office: First Bank of Boston 100 Federal St PO Box 2016 Boston MA 02106-2016

STEPANICH, FRED CHARLES, civil and water resources engineer; b. Neodesha, Kans., Aug. 4, 1931; arrived in The Philippines, 1972; s. Joe and Agnes (Sustar) S. BSCE cum laude, U. Notre Dame, 1959; MSCE, Colo. State U., 1963. Cons. engr. Henningson Durham Richardson, Taipei, Taiwan, 1966, Seoul, Korea, 1967-68; cons. engr. Camp Dresser McKee, Bangkok, 1969-70, Manila, 1974-75; cons. engr. Harza Enging., Jakarta, Indonesia, 1971-72, Daniel Mann Johnson Mendenhall, Manila, 1974, United Rice Mills, San Juan, P.R., 1978, King and Gavaris, Kuala Lumpur, Malaysia, 1980; cons. engr. Enging. Sci. Engrs., Madras, India, 1976-77, Cairo, 1978, Aleppo, Syria, 1980, Kota Kinabalu, Malaysia, 1981, Colombo, Sri Lanka, 1982, Aqaba, Jordan, 1986; cons. engr. Internat. Fund for Agrl. Devel., Rome, 1987; cons. engr. Aquaculture Hatcheries, Manila, 1988, Bangkok, 1989; cons. engr. Asian Devel. Bank, Manila, Pakistan, 1973, Khushab, Pakistan, 1989, Lahore, Pakistan, 1990; cons. engr. dept. pub. works and hwys. Asian Devel. Bank, Manila, 1991-94; cons. engr. Bur. Cen. d'Etudes pour les Equipments d'Outre Mer Engrs., Jatiluhur, Indonesia, 1990-91, Berger Internat. Engrs., Jakarta, Indonesia, 1991; cons. Asian Devel. Bank, Thimpu, Bhutan, 1984, Lahore, Pakistan, 1982, Enging. Sci. Engrs., Medan, Indonesia, 1983, Manila, 1982, Henningson Durham Richardson, Taipei, Taiwan, 1966, Seoul, Korea, 1967-68, Camp Dresser McKee, Bangkok, 1969-70, Manila, 1974-75, Harza Enging., Jakarta, Indonesia, 1971-72, King and Gavaris, Kuala Lumpur, Malaysia, 1980, Daniel Mann Johnson Mendenhall, Manila, 1974, United Rice Mills, San Juan, P.R., 1978, Madras, India, 1976-77, Cairo, 1978, Aleppo, Syria, 1980, Kota Kinabalu, Malaysia, 1981, Colombo, Sri Lanka, 1982. Contbr. articles to profl. jours. Charitable activity mem. Am. Legion, Manila, 1988. With USN, 1951-54. Fellow ASCE; mem. Am. Water Resources Assn., Internat. Commn. for Irrigation & Drainage, Soc. Am. Mil. Engrs., Am. Legion. Roman Catholic. Avocations: computers, sports, choir and chorus groups. Office: PO Box 1546, Manila 1099, The Philippines

STEPANSKI, ANTHONY FRANCIS, JR., computer company executive; b. Jersey City, N.J., June 29, 1941; s. Anthony Francis and Gertrude Stepanski; m. Jane Ellen Schuler, Sept. 5, 1965; children—Matthew A.W., Melinda Kate. BA in Physics, Clark U., 1963. Sales rep. IBM Corp., N.Y.C., 1964-68; from sales rep. to sr. v.p. AGS Computers, Inc., N.Y.C. and Mountainside, N.J., 1968-82; exec. v.p. AGS Computers, Inc., Mountainside, 1982-93; pres., chief exec. officer AGS Info. Services, Inc., Mountainside, 1986-93; also bd. dirs. AGS Computers, Inc., a NYNEX Co., Mountainside; pres., CEO, Origin Technology, N.A. (subs. Origin/Eindhoven, The Netherlands). Trustee Clark U., Worcester, Mass., 1987, Children's Specialized Hosp. Found., Mountainside, 1989-96; bd. dirs. Westchester Artificial Kidney Ctr., Valhalla, N.Y., 1982, Westfield Symphony Orch., N.J., 1983-96. Served with USAR, 1965-66. Office: Origin Tech 430 Mountain Ave New Providence NJ 07974-2732

STEPHAN, ALEXANDER F., German language and literature educator; b. Lüdenscheid, Fed. Republic Germany, Aug. 16, 1946; came to U.S., 1968; s. Eberhard and Ingeborg (Hörnig) S.; m. Halina Konopacka, Dec. 15, 1969; 1 child, Michael. MA, U. Mich., 1969; PhD, Princeton U., 1973. German instr. Princeton U., N.J., 1972-73; asst. prof. German UCLA, 1973-77, assoc. prof., 1977-83, prof., 1983-85; prof. German U. Fla., Gainesville, 1985—, chmn., 1985-93. Author: Christa Wolf, 1976, 4th edit., 1991, Die deutsche Exilliteratur, 1979, Christa Wolf (Forschungsbericht), 1981, Max Frisch, 1983, Anna Seghers im Exil, 1993, Im Visier des FBI, 1995, Anna Seghers: Das siebte Kreuz. Welt und Witkung eines Romans, 1997; editor: Peter Weiss, Die Asthetik des Widerstands, 1983, 3d edit., 1990, Exilliteratur und die Kunste, 1990, Exil-Studien, 1993—, Christa Wolf: The Author's Dimension, 1993, 1995; co-editor: Studies in GDR Culture and Society, 1981-90, Schreiben im Exil, 1985, (TV documentary) Im Visier des FBI, 1995; editl. bd. Germanic Rev., Humanities Monograph Series, U. Fla., 1985-93. Peter Weiss Jahrbuch, 1994—; fellow Humboldt Found., 1988, 94, Guggenheim Found. fellow, 1989, VG Wort fellow, 1992, UCLA faculty fellow, 1984, U. Fla., 1986, 92; grantee Internat. Rsch. and Exchs. Bd., 1993, German Acad. Exch. Svcs., 1993, 97, NEH, 1974, 84, 97, Am. Coun. Learned Socs., 1976, 77, 84, Sch. Theory and Criticism, 1978, Am. Philos. Soc., 1979, 81, 92. Mem. Internat. Vereinigung fur Germanische Sprach und Literaturwissenschaften, Soc. for Exile Studies, German Studies Assn., German PEN, Internat. Anna Seghers Soc. (founding). Home: 2402 NW 27th Terr Gainesville FL 32605-2829 Office: U Fla Dept Germanic & Slavic Langs/Lit 263 Dauer Gainesville FL 32611

STEPHAN, CHARLES ROBERT, retired ocean engineering educator, consultant; b. N.Y.C., Sept. 30, 1911; s. Charles Albert and Ella (Wallendorf) S.; m. Eleanor Grace Storck, Feb. 14, 1937 (dec. July 1992); children: Yvonne Stephan Brown, Joan Stephan Cathcart, Charles Royal, Robert W. BS in Enging., U.S. Naval Acad., 1934; D Enging. (hon.), Fla. Atlantic U., 1978. Commd. ensign U.S. Navy, 1934, advanced through grades to capt.; served various capacities including WWII, South Pacific and Korean war areas U.S. Navy, various locations, 1941-52; ret. U.S. Navy, 1963; prof. ocean enging. Fla. Atlantic U., Boca Raton, 1964-76; prof. emeritus Fla. Atlantic U., 1976—; assoc. prof. naval sci., Rensselaer Poly. Inst., Troy, N.Y., 1944-46. Contbr. articles to various publs. Bd. dirs. Legion of Valor of U.S.A., 1985-92, membership chair, 1985-93, nat. comdr., 1995-96. Capt. USN. Decorated Navy Cross, 2 Bronze Star medals. Fellow Marine Technology Soc.; mem. U.S. Naval Inst., U.S. Navy League (v.p. Delray Beach coun.), Pearl Harbor Survivors (pres. Fla. Gold Coast chpt.), Kiwanis. Republican. Lutheran. Avocations: photography, travel, swimming, bowling. Home and Office: 1st Colonial Inn Apt 259 845 1st Colonial Rd Virginia Beach VA 23451-3816

STEPHAN, EDMUND ANTON, lawyer; b. Chgo., Oct. 7, 1911; s. Anton Charles and Mary Veronica (Egan) S.; m. Evelyn Way, July 3, 1937; children: Miriam, Edmund Anton, Martha (Mrs. Robert McNeill), Donald, Christopher, Evelyn, Gregory, Joan (Mrs. David Nelson). AB, U. Notre Dame, 1933; LLB, Harvard, 1939. Bar: N.Y. 1940, Ill. 1945. Assoc. Carter, Ledyard & Milburn, N.Y.C., 1939-42; atty. charge N.Y. office U.S. Alien Property Custodian, 1943-45; assoc. Mayer, Brown & Platt (and predecessors), Chgo., 1945-47; ptnr. Mayer, Brown & Platt (and predecessors), 1947-90, sr. counsel, 1991—; dir. (hon.) Brunswick Corp., Marsh & McLennan Cos. Emeritus chmn. bd. trustees U. Notre Dame. Mem. ABA, Ill. Bar Assn., Chgo. Bar Assn., Legal Club, Mid-Day Club, Chgo. Club, Law Club, Michigan Shores Club, Westmoreland Country Club, Harvard Club (N.Y.C.), Bob-O-Link Golf Club (Highland Park, Ill.). Roman Catholic. Home: 1410 Sheridan Rd Wilmette IL 60091-1840 Office: Mayer Brown & Platt 190 S La Salle St Chicago IL 60603-3410

STEPHAN, JOHN JASON, historian, educator; b. Chgo., Mar. 8, 1941; s. John Walter and Ruth (Walgreen) S.; m. Barbara Ann Brooks, June 22, 1963. B.A., Harvard U., 1963, M.A., 1964; Ph.D., U. London, 1969. Rsch. assoc. Social Sci. Ctr., Waseda U., Tokyo, 1969-70; mem. faculty U. Hawaii, Honolulu, 1970—, prof. history, 1977—, chmn. East Asian studies program, 1973-74, dir. program on Soviet Union in Pacific-Asia region, 1986-88; rsch. prof. Japan Found.; fellow U. Hokkaido, 1976-77; vis. prof. Inst. of Far East, Moscow, 1982, Inst. Econ. Rsch., Khabarovsk, USSR, 1982-83, Stanford U., 1986, Kennan Inst. for Advanced Studies, 1987; adj. rsch. assoc. East-West Ctr., 1988-92; Sanwa disting. lectr. Tufts U. Fletcher Sch. Law and Diplomacy, 1989. Author: Sakhalin: A History, 1971, The Kuril Islands: Russo-Japanese Frontier in the Pacific, 1974, The Russian Fascists, 1978, Hawaii Under the Rising Sun, 1984, Soviet-American Horizons on the Pacific, 1986, The Russian Far East, 1994. Sr. assoc. mem. St. Antony's Coll., Oxford (Eng.) U., 1977; Bd. dirs. Library Internat. Relations, Chgo., 1976-87; Hawaii rep. U.S.-Japan Friendship Commn., 1980-83. Recipient Kenneth W. Baldridge prize Hawaii chpt. Phi Alpha Theta, 1996; Fulbright fellow, 1967-68; Asia Found. grantee, 1974. Mem. AAUP, Am. Hist. Assn., Am. Assn. Advancement Slavic Studies, Assn. Asian Studies, Authors Guild, Internat. House of Japan, Can. Hist. Assn. Home: 4334 Round Top Dr Honolulu HI 96822-5021

STEPHANI, NANCY JEAN, social worker, journalist; b. Garden City, Mich., Feb. 19, 1955; d. Ernest Helmut Schulz and Margaret Mary Fowler Thompson; m. Edward Jeffrey Stephani, Aug. 29, 1975; children: Edward J., Margaret J., James E. AA, Northwood Inst., Midland, Mich., 1975; student in theology, Boston Coll., 1991; BS summa cum laude, Lourdes Coll., Sylvania, Ohio, 1992; MSW, Ohio State U., 1995. Lic. social worker. Profl. facilitator Parents United, Findlay, Ohio, 1989-94; contbg. writer Cath. Chronicle, Toledo, 1988-95; mem. ministry formation faculty Cath. Diocese of Toledo, 1992-96; crisis intervention specialist John C. Hutson Ctr., 1994—; contbg. writer Sunset Gazette, 1996—; social work clinician Family Svc. Hancock County, Blanchard Valley Home Health Social Svc.; trustee, bd. dirs. Hope House for the Homeless, Findlay, 1990—, v.p. 1996-97, pres. 1997-98; mem. Hancock County Cluster on Elderly; adult edn. coord. St. Michael Parish, Findlay, 1986-93, mem. strategic plan core com., 1989-91, v.p., pres. parish coun., 1985-89; program planning com. Family Life Conf., Cath. Diocese, 1994-95, mem. accreditation com. ministry formation dept.; profl. facilitator Hope Plus Program through Hancock County Common Pleas Ct., 1996—; mem. Crit. Incident Stress Debriefing team, Hancock County, 1997—; profl. facilitator, Hancock County Survivors of Suicide group, 1997—; field instr. dept. social work U. Findlay, 1996—. Founder Food Coop., MPBA, Findlay, 1981; founding mem. Chopin Hall, Findlay, 1983; mem. Hancock County AIDS Task Force, 1994—; strategic planning com. mem., co-chair goal setting com. Findlay Pub. Schs., 1994. Nat. Inst. Food Svcs. grantee, 1974; Diocese of Toledo grantee, 1991; Ohio State U. Coll. Social Work grantee, 1994. Mem. NOW, NASW, Am. Assn. on Child Abuse, Transpsychol. Assn., Friends of Creation Spirituality, Cognitive/Behavioral Profl. Soc., Call to Action, Pax Christi. Avocations: jogging, hiking, cooking, travel. Home: 2615 Goldenrod Ln Findlay OH 45840-1025

STEPHANICK, CAROL ANN, dentist, consultant; b. South Amboy, N.J., Feb. 5, 1952; d. Edward Eugene and Gladys (Pionkowski) S. BS, Rutgers U., 1974; MS, Med. Coll. Pa., 1980; DMD, Temple U., 1984. Lic. dentist, Pa., N.J., Vt. Med. technologist Jersey Shore Med. Ctr., Neptune, N.J., 1975-76, South Amboy Meml. Hosp., 1976-78, Smith-Kline Clin. Labs., King of Prussia, Pa., 1981; instr. dept. biology St. Peter's Coll., Jersey City, 1976-78; instr., edn. coord. Coll. Allied Health, Hahnemann U., Phila., 1978-80; instr. dept. oral radiology Sch. Dentistry, Temple U., Phila., 1984-87; assoc. dentist Personal Choice Dental Assocs., South Amboy, 1985-86, Marcucci and Marcucci, P.C., Phila., 1986-90, Gwynedd Dental Assocs., Springhouse, Pa., 1990-92; spl. events coord. Liberty Dental Conf., Phila., 1990—. Neighbor patrol Sprague St. Neighbors Town Watch, Phila., 1986-93. Named to Legion of Honor, Chapel of Four Chaplains, 1987. Mem. ADA, Pa. Dental Assn., Philadelphia County Dental Soc. (publicity coord. 1990—, pub. info. coord. 1991, semi-finalist judge sr. smile contest 1990—, com. on concerns of women dentists, select com. 1988—), Delaware Valley Assn. Women Dentists, Am. Assn. for Functional Orthodontics, Am. Soc. Clin. Pathologists (med. technologist), Delta Sigma Delta. Roman Catholic. Avocations: reading, weight training, walking, sailing, dog training. Home: PO Box 386 Haddonfield NJ 08033-0310 Office: 777 White Horse Pike S Hammonton NJ 08037-2029

STEPHANOPOULOS, GEORGE ROBERT, federal official; b. Fall River, Mass., Feb. 10, 1961; s. Robert and Nikki C. Stephanopoulos. AB Polit. Sci. summa cum laude, Columbia U., 1982; M Theology, Oxford U., 1986. Adminstrv. asst. rep. Edward Feighan, Washington; dep. comm. dir. Dukakis Bentsen campaign, 1988; exec. floor mgr. to House Majority leader Gephardt, Washington; dir. comm. Clinton/Gore campaign, Little Rock; dir. comm. The White House, Washington, 1997—, sr. advisor to the Pres. of U.S., 1993-96; vis. prof. polit. sci. Columbia U., N.Y.C., 1997—. Contbr. to ABC News and Newsweeks Mags., 1997—. Recipient medal of Excellence Columbia U., 1993; Rhodes scholar Oxford U. Mem. Phi Beta Kappa. Democrat. Greek Orthodox. Office: The White House 1600 Pennsylvania Ave NW Washington DC 20502-0001 also: Internat Affairs Bldg 420 W 118th St Rm 1315 New York NY 10027

STEPHANOPOULOS, GREGORY, chemical engineering educator, consultant, researcher; b. Kalamata, Greece, Mar. 10, 1950; came to U.S., 1973; s. Nicholas and Elizabeth (Bitsanis) S.; m. Maria Flytzani; children—Nicholas-Odysseas, Alexander, Rona-Elisa. BS, Nat. Tech. U., Athens, Greece, 1973; MS, U. Fla., Gainesville, 1975; PhD, U. Minn., Mpls., 1978. Registered profl. engr., Greece. Asst. prof. chem. enging. Calif. Inst. Tech., Pasadena, 1978-83, assoc. prof. chem. enging., 1983-85; prof. chem. enging. MIT, Cambridge, 1985—. Editor: Kinetics and Thermodynamics of Biological Systems, 1983, Biotechnology/Bioprocessing Vol. 3, 1993; Mem. editorial bd. Mathematical Biosciences, 1984—, Biotech. Progress, 1984—. Contbr. 145 articles to profl. jours. Dreyfus Tchr. scholar Camille and Henry Dreyfus Found., 1982; recipient Pres. Young Investigator award NSF, 1984; NSF grantee, 1980—. Fellow AIMBE (founding); mem. Am. Inst. Chem. Engrs. (programming coordinator 1983, Computing in Chem. Egring. award 1993), Am. Chem. Soc. Greek Orthodox. Avocations: chess; music; travel. Office: Mass Inst Tech Dept Chem Engring 56-469C 77 Massachusetts Ave Cambridge MA 02139-4301

STEPHEN, DENNIS JOHN, financial planner; b. Allentown, Pa., Apr. 25, 1948; s. Martin Paul and Bernice Evelyn (Baumer) S.; m. Constance Rose Wilcox, Jan. 20, 1996; children: Christopher Matthew, Erin Marie. BS in Edn., Millersville U., 1970; postgrad., Marywood Coll., 1971-72, Pa. State U., 1971-73, Coll. Fin. Planning, Denver, 1981-83. CFP; registered investment advisor. Tchr., coach Boyertown (Pa.) Area Sch., 1970-77; ins. cons. W.H. Seward Agy., Reading, 1973-84; registered rep. First Buffalo Corp., 1973-89, Keogler Morgan & Co. Inc., 1989-97, Royal Alliance, 1997—; insr. cons. J.K. Lengel and Assocs., Reading, 1985-90; owner, fin. cons. Dennis J. Stephen CFP, Boyertown, 1977-88; pres., registered investment advisor Dennis J. Stephen Assocs. Ltd, Boyertown, 1988—; owner, ins. cons. Wyomissing (Pa.) Fin. Group, 1989—. Guest WBC-TV, 1985. Fin. chmn. St. Columbkill Roman Cath. Ch., Boyertown, 1985—; adv. bd. Helping Hands, Inc., Bechtelsville, Pa., 1979—; bd. v.p. Boyertown Area Sch. Bd., 1983-85, bd. dirs., singer Hosanna Music Ministry, Boyertown, 1983-84; singer, mem. Alpha Music Ministry, Boyertown, 1985-95; cubmaster, dist. com. Cub Scouts and Explorers, Boy Scouts Am., Boyertown, 1970—. Recipient Disting. Sales award Sales and Mktg. Execs., 1981, Life Quality award Investment Guaranty Life, 1979. Mem. Am. Bus. Clubs, Inst. Cert. Fin. Planners, Northeastern Pa. Soc. Inst. Cert. Fin. Planners (pres. 1992), Boyertown Lions Club (com. chmn. 1977—), Full Gospal Businessmen's Fellowship, Boyertown Area Bus. Assn. (pres. 1982, bd. dirs. 1977-81, 82-88). Democrat. Avocations: hunting, toy train collecting. Home: 1480 Orchard Ln Boyertown PA 19512-8934 Office: Wyomissing Fin Group 875 Berkshire Blvd Ste 103 Wyomissing PA 19610-1246 also: Dennis Stephen Assoc Ltd 1260 E Philadelphia Ave Gilbertsville PA 19525

STEPHEN, JOHN ERLE, lawyer, consultant; b. Eagle Lake, Tex., Sept. 24, 1918; s. John Earnest and Vida Thrall (Klein) S.; m. Gloria Yzaguirre, May 16, 1942; children: Vida Leslie Stephen Renzi, John Lauro Kurt. JD, U. Tex., 1941; postgrad., Northwestern U., 1942, U.S. Naval Acad. Postgrad. Sch., Annapolis, 1944; cert. in internat. law, U.S. Naval War Coll., Newport, R.I., 1945; cert. in advanced internat. law, U.S. Naval War Coll., 1967. Bar: Tex. 1946, U.S. Ct. Appeals (D.C. cir.) 1949, U.S. Tax Ct. 1953, U.S. Supreme Ct. 1955, U.S. Dist. Ct. D.C. 1956, U.S. Ct. Appeals (2nd cir.) 1959, U.S. Ct. Appeals (7th cir.) 1964, U.S. Dist. Ct. (so. dist.) N.Y. 1964, D.C. 1972, U.S. Dist. Ct. (no. dist.) Ill. 1974, U.S. Dist. Ct. (we. dist.) Wash. 1975, Mich. 1981, U.S. Dist. Ct. (we. dist.) Mich. 1981, U.S. Dist. Ct. (so. dist.) Tex. 1981. Gen. mgr., corp. counsel Sta. KOPY, Houston, 1946; gen. atty., exec. asst. to pres. Tex. Star Corp. and affiliated cos., Houston, 1947-50; ptnr. Hofheinz & Stephen, Houston, 1950-57; v.p., gen. counsel TV Broadcasting Co., Tex. Radio Corp., Gulf Coast Network, Houston, 1953-57; spl. counsel, exec. asst. Mayor, City of Houston, 1953-57; spl. counsel Houston C. of C., 1953-56; sr. v.p., gen. counsel Air Transp. Assn. Am., Washington, 1958-70; v.p., gen. counsel Amway Corp. and affiliated cos., Ada, Mich., 1971-82; counsellor, cons. Austin, Tex., 1983—; chief protocol City of Houston, 1953-56; advisor Consulates Gen. of Mex., San Antonio, Houston, New Orleans, Washington, 1956-66; mem. adv. bd. Jour. of Air Law and Commerce, 1966-72; vis. lectr. Harvard Bus. Sch., Pacific Agribus. Conf., Southwestern Legal Found., Inter-Am. Law Conf.; apptd. by Pres. legal advisor, del. U.S. Diplomatic Dels. to Internat. Treaty Confs., Paris, London, Rome, Tokyo, Madrid, Bermuda, Guadalajara, Dakar, 1961-71, Internat. Air-Rte. Dels. to U.K., France, Spain, Portugal, Belgium, The Netherlands, Japan, Rep. of Korea, Mex., Australia, Argentina, Soviet Union, and Brazil, 1960-70; legal advisor, del. U.S. dels. to United Nations Specialized Orgns., Montreal, Geneva, 1964-71; U.S. rep. Internat. Conf. on Aircraft Noise, London, 1967; hon. faculty mem. sch. of law, sch. of bus., U. Miami, 1968—; accredited corr. United Nations, Rep. and Dem. Nat. Convs. Author, editor in field. Chmn. legal com. Nat. Aircraft Noise Abatement Coun.; bd. dirs. Houston Mus. Fine Arts, 1953-57, Contemporary Arts Assn., 1952-57, Tex. Transp. inst., 1964-72. Comdr. USNR, 1941-46, PTO and S.E. Asia; mem. staff Supreme Allied Command, NATO, 1952. Recipient Jesse L. Lasky award RKO Pictures-CBS, Hollywood, Calif., 1939, H.J. Lutcher Stark award U. Tex., 1939, 40, Walter Mack award Pepsico, U. Tex., 1941, Best U.S. Pub. Svc. Broadcasts award CCNY, 1946. Mem. ABA (past chmn., mem. coun. sect. pub. utility, comms. and transp. law, standing com. on aero. law), Am. Law Inst., World Peace Through Law Ctr. Geneva (past chmn. internat. aviation law com.), Fed. Bar Assn. (exec. com. transp. coun., comms. coun.), D.C. Bar, State Bar Tex., State Bar Mich., Fed. Comms. Bar Assn., Assn. ICC Practitioners, Am. Judicature Soc., Washington Fgn. Law Soc. (vis. lectr. 1967-68), Japanese Air Law Soc. (hon. mem. 1966—), Venezuelan Air and Space Law Soc. (hon.), Internat. Club (Washington), Explorers (Washington), Houston Polo Club, Lakeshore Club (Chgo.), Nat. Aviation Club (Washington), Saddle & Cycle Club (Chgo.), Breakfast Club (Houston), Execs. (Houston), Ky. Cols., Ark. Travelers, Tex. Adms. Home: 6904 Ligustrum Cv Austin TX 78750-8352

STEPHEN, MICHAEL, psychologist. BA in Psychology, U. Okla., 1973; MS, Okla. State U., 1977, PhD in Counseling Psychology, 1986. Lic. psychologist. Pvt. practice psychology, 1991—; mem. univ. faculty; lectr. in field. Author: Cherry Lane: The Power of Abuse; Sex, Love, and God; and Healing, a woman's story; The Mental States Examination for Beginning and Advanced Professionals, Hypoglycemia: A Disease of the Mind. Vol. child abuse prevention and related polit. issues. Fellow Christian Athletes Assn., Okla. Thoroughbred Assn.; mem. APA, Okla. Psychol. Assn., Christian Assn. Psychologists. Avocations: athletics, race horse training, ranching, film and acting. Home: Unit G 14309 N Pennsylvania Ave Oklahoma City OK 73134-6007

STEPHENS, BART NELSON, former foreign service officer; b. Norfolk, Va., May 29, 1922; s. Bart Dannelly and Lura Lee (Cannon) S.; m. Barrett Krausz, Jan. 7, 1950; children: Tracey Rainier, Schuyler Barrett, Holly Cannon, Sinah Kendall Lee. A.B., Duke, 1943; A.M., Harvard, 1947; lang. tng., Fgn. Service Inst., 1962, 66, 76. Divisional asst. Greece-Turkey-Iran sect., pub. affairs overseas program staff Dept. State, 1948-49; asst. pub. affairs officer Thessaloniki, Greece, 1950; asst. info. officer Athens, 1950-51; pub. affairs officer Patras, Greece, 1951-54 and, Thessaloniki, 1954; dir. Amerika Haus, Nuernberg, Germany, 1955-59; mem. cultural council City of Nuernberg, 1958-59; mgmt. analyst USIA, Washington, 1959-61; cultural attache Am. Embassy, Warsaw, Poland, 1963-65; dir. Am. Cultural Center, Saigon, Vietnam, 1967-68; 1st sec., regional projects officer Am. Embassy, Vienna, Austria, 1968-70; consul, pub. affairs officer Am. consulate gen. Stuttgart, Germany, 1970-73; area coordinator (Europe) USIA, Washington, 1973; seminar-conf. Programming officer USIA, 1973-74; dep. dir. Office Internat. Arts Affairs, Dept. State, 1974-76; counselor cultural affairs officer Am. Embassy, Bangkok, 1977-82; counselor Sr. Fgn. Service. Contbr. articles to profl. jours. Vice chmn., bd. dirs. Thailand-U.S. Ednl. Found., 1977-82; bd. dirs. John F. Kennedy Found., Thailand, 1977-82, John E. Peurifoy Found., 1979-82, Lynchburg Symphony Orch., 1992-93; exec. sec. Eisenhower Exch. Fellowship Selection Com., Thailand, 1977-82; mem. winter forums com. Sweet Briar Coll., 1990-96. Lt. (j.g.) USNR, 1944-46, PTO. Decorated Bronze Star with combat V, Purple Heart.; recipient Meritorious Svc. award USIA, 1956, medal for civilian service in Vietnam, 1968, Civilian award U.S. European Command, 1973. Mem. Am. Fgn. Svc. Assn., Soc. Lees of Va., Siam Soc., Westwood Country Club (Vienna, Va.), Boonsboro Country Club, Phi Beta Kappa, Omicron Delta Kappa, Phi Eta Sigma, Pi Kappa Phi. Home: 201 St James Pl Lynchburg VA 24503-4226 *Personal responsibility should be an essential principle for all of us, in the family, job and community. My 34 years in the U.S. Foreign Service gave me a wonderfully stimulating and rewarding career and a profound belief: the diplomatic service is America's first line of defense.*

STEPHENS, BOBBY GENE, college administrator, consultant; b. Glendale, S.C., Mar. 8, 1935; s. Dewey and Bertha Cordelia (Mott) S.; m. Sandra Elizabeth White, June 27, 1957; children: Elaine, Ward, Todd, Adam. B.S., Wofford Coll., 1957; M.S., Clemson U., 1961, Ph.D., 1964; LHD (hon.), MacMurray Coll., 1987. Textile chemist Reeves Bros., Fairforest, S.C., 1957-58; grad. asst. Clemson (S.C.) U., 1960-63; instr. chemistry Wofford Coll., Spartanburg, S.C., 1963-64, asst. prof., 1964-67, assoc. prof., 1967-72, prof., v.p. acad. affairs, 1972-80; pres. MacMurray Coll., Jacksonville, Ill., 1980-86; v.p. research and enrollment Wofford Coll., Spartanburg, S.C., 1986-91, v.p. sci. and tech., 1991—; project dir. Howard Hughes Med. Inst., 1992—; cons. colls. and industry. Contbr. articles to sci. jours.; inventor extractions with propylene carbonate, 1975; producer: TV series The Psychology of Interpersonal Behavior, 1974. Co-chmn. Daniel Morgan Restoration Com., 1986-88; vice chmn. Spartanburg County Pollution Control Authority, 1970-74; bd. dirs. S.C. Lung Assn., Spartanburg, 1970-75, Comms. Svcs., Inc., 1977-80; sect. maj. United Way, 1975-77. 1st lt. U.S. Army, 1958-60. Recipient Jefferson award S.C. Acad. Sci., 1969; recipient 1st prize graphics div. 2d Edit. Art Contest, 1971, 2d and 3d prizes Lawson's Fork Creek Photography Contest, 1978; USPHS grantee; NSF grantee. Mem. Am. Chem. Soc., Nat. Assn. Gifted Children, Assn. Ednl. Communications and Tech., Phi Beta Kappa. Methodist. Home: 131 Henry Ct Spartanburg SC 29306-6901 Office: Wofford College 429 N Church St Spartanburg SC 29303-3612

STEPHENS, C. MICHAEL, service executive; b. Wichita Falls, Tex., Feb. 4, 1949; s. W. Wesley and Mildred Ruth (Smith) S.; m. Janet Kay Speare, Dec. 28, 1971 (div. 1996); children: Kelley Michelle, Suzanne Janelle. BA, Okla. State U., 1971; postgrad., U. Okla., 1971-72. V.p. sales Arrowlite Industries, Tulsa, 1972-76; v.p., regional mgr. Top Value Motivation, Dayton, Ohio, 1976-86; v.p. S&H Citadel, Inc. (formerly S&H Motivation and Travel), Chgo., 1986-96; v.p., regional mgr. Meridian Enterprises Corp., St. Louis, 1996—. Recipient Presdl. Achievement award, 1986. Mem. Am. Mgmt. Assn., Motivation Masters Coun., Kappa Sigma, Cedar Ridge Country Club, Pres. Club. Presbyterian. Avocations: golf, racquetball, martial arts.

STEPHENS, CARSON WADE, minister; b. San Angelo, Tex., Mar. 12, 1950; s. Allison Carson and Betty Jo Justice (Ellis) S.; m. Jeanette Martha Zett, June 19, 1971; children: Jennifer Hope, Bethany June. MusB, U. Tex., 1974; DMin, Drew U., 1991; postdoctoral, Tex. A&M U., 1996; postdoctoral fellow, U. Tex., Austin, 1996. Tchr. Manor (Tex.) Ind. Schs., 1970-73; minister Three Rivers (Tex.) Ch. of Christ, 1976-77, East Main Ch. of Christ, Holdenville, Okla., 1977-83, Sharpstown Ch. of Christ, Houston, 1983-86, Clear Lake Ch. of Christ, Houston, 1986—; intern dept. of univ. advancement and pub. rels. Rice U., Houston, 1996; intern dept. univ. advancement and pub. rels. U. Tex.-Houston Health Sci. Ctr., 1996; guest lectr. Fred-Hardeman U., Henderson, Tenn., 1992, Pepperdine U., 1996. Author: Evangelization, 1991, In the Beginning, Vol. 1, 1992, Vol. 2, 1993. Bd. dirs. Edgar A. Smith YMCA, Houston, 1987-94; mem. Mayor's Com. for Drug Prevention, Houston; active Pasadena Mcpl. Band, Pasadena Mcpl. Orch.; past pres. Summer Repertoire Theatre. Mem. Am. Acad. Ministry, Rotary (youth chair Space Ctr. chpt. 1988-89, bd. dirs. 1990, Presdl. award 1989, 90, chmn. drug awareness program, 1989, 992-93, 93-94, Paul Harris fellow 1993). Avocations: music composition and performance, drama, writing, reading. Home: 1127 Peachford Ln Houston TX 77062-2228 Office: Clear Lake Ch of Christ 938 El Dorado Blvd Houston TX 77062-4020

STEPHENS, DONALD JOSEPH, retired architect; b. Albany, N.Y., Apr. 29, 1918; s. Arthur Everett and Evangeline (Cosgrave) S.; m. Jean E. Brown Clausen, Apr. 15, 1950; children—Christian, Linda, Suzanne, Marc, Paul, Thomas. B.Arch., Rensselaer Polytechnic Inst., 1940. Archtl. engr. Watervliet Arsenal, 1941-44; assoc. architect Henry L. Blatner, Albany, 1946-56; pres. Stephens Assocs. P.C., Architects, Albany, 1956-84; mng. architect C.T. Male Assocs PC, 1985-87; mem. N.Y. State Bd. Architecture, 1976-85. Chmn. Taconic Valley Planning Assn., 1967-72; chmn. Town of Berlin (N.Y.) Planning Bd., 1960-79; pres. bd. edn. Berlin Central Sch. Dist., 1971-72. Served with USN, 1944-46, PTO. Fellow AIA (regional dir. 1974-76); mem. N.Y. State Assn. Architects (Matthew Del Gaudio award 1971). Home: PO Box 301 Berlin NY 12022-0301

STEPHENS, DONALD R(ICHARDS), banker; b. San Francisco, June 28, 1938; s. Donald Lewis and Anona Marie (O'Leary) S.; m. Christina Brinkman, Sept. 11, 1971 (div. 1996); children: Lane B., Justin H., Nicholas W., Adam H. BS, U. So. Calif., 1961; JD., Hastings Coll., 1969. Pres. Campodonico & Stephens, San Francisco, 1963-65; pres., owner Union Investment Co., San Francisco, 1966-69; assoc. Law Offices of Louis O. Kelso, 1969-72; individual practice law, San Francisco Co., 1972-77; pres. D.R. Stephens & Co., San Francisco, 1974—; chmn., CEO Bank of San Francisco Co., 1978-91, also bd. dirs.; chmn. N.Am. Trust REIT, also bd. dirs.; bd. dirs. Charles Schwab Family of Funds Inc. Bd. dirs. Bay Area Coun.; trustee St. Francis Meml. Hosp., San Francisco, 1976-82; mem. policy adv. bd. U. Calif., 1985—. Mem. Urban Land Inst., World Bus. Coun., Bohemian Club, Calif. Club. Republican. Presbyterian. Avocations: tennis, golf.

STEPHENS, DOUGLAS KIMBLE, chemical engineer; b. Monticello, Ark., June 22, 1939; s. Vardeman King and Lila Belle (McMurtery) S.; m. Mary Joan John, Dec. 4, 1957; children: Kenneth R., David B. BSChemE, U. Ark., 1962. Registered profl. engr., Tex.; cert. safety profl.; bd. cert. forensic examiner. Sr. engr., safety supt. Monsanto Co., Alvin, Tex., 1967-73, mfg. supt., 1973-78; ptnr. Robert T. Bell & Assocs., Houston, 1978-80; v.p. Tech. Inspection Svcs., Inc., Houston, 1980-84, Bell & Stephens Labs., Inc., Houston, 1980-84; pres. Stephens Engrng. Labs., Inc., Webster, Tex., 1984—; pres., CEO N.Am. Environ. Coalition, Inc., Webster, 1993—; project dir./chief engr. enviroLife enviroFoam Project, 1994—. Contbr. articles to profl. publs. Capt. U.S. Army, 1962-67, Vietnam. Decorated Bronze Star, Air medal. Mem. ASTM (mem. coms., cons.), Am. Inst. Chem. Engrs. (sect. chmn. 1976-77), Am. Soc. Safety Engrs. (cons.), Tex. Soc. Profl. Engrs. (chpt. chmn. 1991-92, pres. 1990-91, Engr. of Yr. 1992), Nat. Assn. Corrosion Engrs. (mem. com. 1978-93, cons.), Nat. Assn. Environ. Profls. Methodist. Achievements include development of ethylene cracking furnaces decoking process, waste oil recovery process, propylene storage process, depropanizer computor control process, differential thermal analysis methods for fusion bond epoxy coatings extent of cure. Home: 1116 Deats Rd Dickinson TX 77539-4426 Office: 100 E Nasa Blvd Ste 203 Webster TX 77598-5330

STEPHENS, EDWARD CARL, communications educator, writer; b. L.A., July 27, 1924; s. Carl Edward and Helen Mildred (Kerner) S.; children: Edward, Sarah, Matthew. AB, Occidental Coll., 1947; MS, Northwestern U., 1955. Advt. exec. Dancer-Fitzgerald-Sample Inc., N.Y.C., 1955-64; prof. Medill Sch. Journalism, Northwestern U., Evanston, Ill., 1964-76; prof., chmn. dept. advt. S.I. Newhouse Sch. Pub. Communications, Syracuse U., N.Y., 1976-80, dean, 1980-89; prof. comms. S.I. Newhouse Sch. Pub. Comms. Syracuse U., 1990-92, prof. emeritus, 1992—; cons. Foote, Cone & Belding Communications. Author: (novels) A Twist of Lemon, 1958, One More Summer, 1960, Blow Negative!, 1962, Roman Joy, 1965, A Turn in the Dark Wood, 1968, The Submariner, 1974, (nonfiction) Submarines, 1960. Mem. George Polk Awards Com. With USN, 1943-46, 1950-53. Capt. USNR (ret.). Decorated Purple Heart. Mem. Am. Acad. Advt. (pres. 1976-77), Assn. Edn. Journalism and Mass Communication, Authors League, Century Club of Syracuse, Alpha Tau Omega. Episcopalian.

STEPHENS, ELISA, art college president, lawyer. Pres. Acad. Art Coll., San Francisco. Office: Acad Art Coll Office of President 79 New Montgomery St San Francisco CA 94105-3410

STEPHENS, ELTON BRYSON, bank executive, service and manufacturing company executive; b. Clio, Ala., Aug. 4, 1911; s. James Nelson and Clara (Stuckey) S.; m. Alys Varian Robinson, Nov. 28, 1935; children: James Thomas, Jane Stephens Comer, Elton Bryson Jr., Dell Stephens Brooke. B.A., Birmingham-So. Coll., 1932, LLD (hon.), 1977; LL.B., U. Ala., 1936, LHD (hon.), 1990; grad., Advanced Mgmt. Program, Harvard U., 1960; LHD (hon.), Faulkner U., 1992. Bar: Ala. 1936. Regional dir. Keystone Readers Service, Birmingham, 1937-43; partner, then founder and pres. Mil. Service Co., Inc. (predecessor of EBSCO Industries, Inc.), Birmingham, 1943-58; founder EBSCO Industries, Inc., and affiliates, 1958; since pres., chmn. bd. EBSCO Industries, Inc., and affiliates, Birmingham; now chmn. bd. EBSCO Industries, Inc. and affiliates, Birmingham; bd. dirs. R.A. Brown Ins. Agy. Ltd., 1966—; chmn. EBSCO Investment Svc., Inc., 1959—, Canebsco Subscription Svc., Toronto, Ont., Can., 1972—; founder, chmn. Ala. Bancorp divsn. Highland Bank; founder EBSCO Savs. and Profit Sharing Trust, Ala. Bancorp Savs. and Profit Sharing Trust. Mem. fin. and investment com., past chmn. bd. trustees, chmn. exec. com. Birmingham-So. Coll.; trustee So. Research Inst.; former pres., chmn. bd. trustee Birmingham Met. YMCA; mem. bd., chmn. econ. pension com. Tenn.-Tombigbee Waterway Authority; founder % Clubs of Ala., founder United Art Fund/ Met. Arts Council; vice chmn., bd. dirs., hon. chmn.; vice chmn. Am. Coun. Arts, 1990-95; fundraiser Rebirth Symphony, Birmingham. Elton B. Stephens Expressway named in his honor, 1970, Elton B. Stephens Library, Clio, 1979. Mem. Birmingham C. of C. (bd. dirs.), The Club, Birmingham Press Club, Summit Club, Mountain Brook Country Club (Ala.), Rotary (pres. Homewood, Ala. 1979-80, Paul Harris fellow), Ala. Symphonic Assn. (chmn., CEI, prin. fund raiser), Ala. Acad. Honor, Alpha Tau Omega (past chmn. nat. found.), Omicron Delta Kappa, Phi Alpha Delta. Methodist. *Invest/reinvest earnings to create employment/profits for growth/expansion. Support worthwhile projects including but not limited to: education, health, religion, needy, cultural, arts, boys/girls clubs, law enforcement, conservation, nature, water resources. Share profits and protect the welfare and health of your employees with a major catastrophic medical program. These philosophies built a company I started in 1943 with capital of $5,000 and sales under $1,000,000 with under 20 employees to annual sales of over $860,000,000 and 3400 employees with adequate capital from earnings and borrowing to continue growth. EBSCO operates world wide.*

STEPHENS, GEORGE EDWARD, JR., lawyer; b. Lawrence, Kans., Mar. 26, 1936; s. George Edward and Mary Helen (Houghton) S.; m. Gretel Geiser, Dec. 31, 1965; children: Thaddeus Geiser, Edward Houghton, Mary Schoentgen. Student, U. Colo., Boulder, 1954-57, U. Colo. Sch. Medicine, Denver, 1957-59; LLB, Stanford U., 1962. Bar: Calif. 1963, U.S. Dist. Ct. (cen. dist.) Calif. 1963, U.S. Ct. Appeals (9th cir.) 1971. Law clk. to judge U.S. Dist. Ct., Los Angeles, 1962-64; assoc. ptnr. Pollock & Palmer, Los Angeles, 1964-69; ptnr. Gates, Morris, Merrill & Stephens, Los Angeles, 1969-72, Paul, Hastings, Janofsky & Walker, Los Angeles, 1972—; Mem. Coordinating Coun. on Lawyer Competence, Conf. Chief Justices, 1983-86; chmn. probate sect. L.A. County Bar Assn., 1979-80. Nat. chmn. Stanford (Calif.) U. Law Fund Quad Program, 1980-87; mem. bd. visitors Stanford Law Sch., 1982-85; founder mus. Contemporary Art, L.A., 1982; bd. dirs. Pacific Oaks Coll., 1990-94. Recipient Stanford Assocs. award, 1982. Fellow Am. Bar Found., Am. Coll. Trust and Estates Counsel, Internat. Acad. Probate and Trust Law, Fellows of Contemporary Art (bd. dirs. 1991-92); mem. ABA (chmn. standing com. specialization 1979-82, standing com. lawyer referral svcs., 1969-76, consortium delivery legal svcs. and the pub., 1979-82), Stanford Law Soc. (pres. 1972-73). Episcopalian. Clubs: Chancery (Los Angeles), Annandale Golf (Pasadena, Calif.), Valley Hunt (Pasadena). Office: Paul Hastings Janofsky & Walker 555 S Flower St Fl 23D Los Angeles CA 90071-2300

STEPHENS, JACKSON THOMAS, investment executive; b. Prattsville, Ark., Aug. 9, 1923; s. Albert Jackson and Ethel Rebecca (Pumphrey) S.; children: Jackson Thomas, Warren Amerine. Grad., Columbia Mil. Acad., Tenn., 1941; student, U. Ark., 1941-43; B.S., U.S. Naval Acad., 1946. Pres. Stephens, Inc., Little Rock, from 1957; chmn. Stephens, Inc., 1986—. Trustee U. Ark., 1948-57. Office: Stephens Inc PO Box 3507 111 Center St Little Rock AR 72201

STEPHENS, JAMES LINTON, mechanical engineer; b. Stamford, Conn., Nov. 1, 1956; s. James Regis and Beatrice Helen (Johnson) S.; m. Laura Lynn Holmes, Sept. 6, 1980; children: Mark Linton, Jaimee Lee, Matthew James. BS in Mech. Engring., BS in Biomed. Engring., Northwestern U., 1980. Registered profl. engr., Wis. Mfg. engr. Parker Hannifin Corp., Des Plaines, Ill., 1980-81, St. Mary's, Ohio, 1981-84; mfg. engr. Ohmeda divsn. BOC Group, Madison, Wis., 1984-91, sr. mfg. engr. Ohmeda divsn., 1991-95; sr. engr. Case Corp., Racine, Wis., 1995—. Mem. steering com. for engring. profl. devel. program U. Wis., Madison, 1994. Ill. State scholar, 1975. Mem. Soc. Mfg. Engrs. (treas. Madison chpt. 1984-85, 2d vice chmn. 1985-86, 1st vice chmn. 1986-87, chmn. 1987-88, certification chmn. 1988—, fundraiser 1987—, seminar and workshop leader 1987—, Chmn. plaque 1988, elected to machining tech. assn. bd. advisors 1996—). Avocations: swimming, tennis, reading science fiction. Office: Case Corp 7000 Durand Ave Racine WI 53406

STEPHENS, JAMES T., publishing executive; b. 1939; married. BA in Bus. Adminstrn., Yale U., 1961; MBA, Harvard U., 1964. With Ebsco Industries Inc., Birmingham, Ala., 1961—, asst. v.p., 1966-67, v.p., 1967-70, exec. v.p., from 1970, now pres., also bd. dirs. Office: Ebsco Industries Inc PO Box 1943 Top of Oak Mountain Hwy 280 Birmingham AL 35201

STEPHENS, JAY B., lawyer; b. Akron, Iowa, Nov. 5, 1946; s. Lyle R. and Marie (Borchers) S. BA magna cum laude, Harvard U., 1968, JD cum laude, 1973. Bar: D.C. 1973. Assoc. Wilmer, Cutler & Pickering, Washington, 1973-74; asst. spl. prosecutor Watergate Spl. Prosecution Force, Washington, 1974-75; assoc. gen. counsel Overseas Pvt. Investment Corp., Washington, 1976-77; asst. U.S. atty. Dept. Justice, Washington, 1977-81, spl. counsel to asst. atty. gen., 1981-83, dep. assoc. atty. gen., 1983-85, assoc. dep. atty. gen., 1985-86; dep. counsel to Pres. Reagan, 1986-88; U.S. atty. for D.C. Office U.S. Atty., 1988-93; ptnr. Pillsbury Madison & Sutro, Washington, 1993-97; v.p. and gen. counselengineered materials sector Allied-Signal Inc., Morristown, N.J., 1997—. Contbr. articles to profl. publs. Knox fellow Oxford, Eng., 1968-69. Mem. D.C. Bar Assn., Supreme Ct. Bar, Asst. U.S. Atty. Assn., Nat. Assn. Former U.S. Attys., Phi Beta Kappa. Republican. Presbyterian. Home: 1203 Alps Dr Mc Lean VA 22102

STEPHENS, JERRY WAYNE, librarian, library director; b. Birmingham, Ala., Sept. 10, 1949; s. William Larkin and Odell (Kerr) S.; m. Lisa Brown, June 2, 1972; children—Jeramy Wayne, Elizabeth Ashley, John Larkin. B.S. in Acctg., U. Ala.-Birmingham, 1974, M.B.A., 1976; M.L.S., U. Ala., 1977, Ph.D. in Adminstrn. Higher Edn., 1982. Svc. mgr. Hammond Organ Studios, Birmingham, 1973-74; acct. Mervyn Sterne Libr., U. Ala., Birmingham, 1974-75, asst. to dir., 1975-76, asst. dir., 1976-85, libr., dir., 1985—; interim fiscal officer Univ. Coll. U. Ala., Birmingham, 1982, interim asst. v.p. for acad. affairs, 1989-91; v.p. for acad. affairs, 1989-91; vice chmn. Network Acad. Librs., 1985-86, 95-96, chmn., 1986-88, 96; cons. Birmingham Pub. Libr., 1977—; cons. Southeastern Libr. Assn., Atlanta, 1979-80; bd. dirs. Southeastern Libr. Network, treas., 1992-93, chmn., 1993-94. Contbr. articles to profl. publs. Sponsored exec. United Way, Birmingham, 1978, sr. exec., 1982; foster parent Dept. Pensions and Securities, Birmingham, 1982-83; elder Homewood Cumberland Presbyn. Ch., Birmingham, 1982-84, 88-90. With USN, 1972-73. Named one of Outstanding Young Men Am., U.S. Jaycees, 1978, 79. Mem. ALA, SE Libr. Assn., Ala. Libr. Assn. (treas. 1977-78), Am Mgmt. Assn. Avocations: camping; softball. Home: 2621 Kemp Ct Birmingham AL 35226-1982 Office: U Ala-Birmingham Mervyn H Sterne Libr University Station Birmingham AL 35294

STEPHENS, JOE ALAN, investigative reporter; b. Mariemont, Ohio, July 26, 1959; s. Ken and Wilma (Vanover) S.; m. Dru Sefton. Student, De Pauw U., 1977-78; BA in English, Miami U., Oxford, Ohio, 1981. Editor-in-chief Clermont Sun, Batavia, Ohio, 1981-83; investigative reporter State Jour.-Register, Springfield, Ill., 1983-87; investigative and spl. projects reporter Kansas City (Mo.) Star, 1987—. Recipient George Polk award L.I. U., 1994, Fred Moen Sweepstakes award Mo. Assoc. Press Mng. Editors Assn., Columbia, 1994, Pub. Svc. award Kansas City Soc. Profl. Journalists, 1993. Mem. Investigative Reporters and Editors. Achievements include investigation of public corruption, organized crime, building safety, charity fraud and child abuse. Home: 102 E 69th Ter Kansas City MO 64113-2554 Office: Kansas City Star 1729 Grand Blvd Kansas City MO 64108-1413

STEPHENS, JOHN FRANK, association executive, researcher; b. Malone, N.Y., Nov. 9, 1949; s. J. Frank and Marjorie (Drew) S.; m. Smaroula Georgina Paras, Sept. 1, 1989; 1 child, Georgina Elizabeth. B.A., Harpur Coll., 1971; M.A., SUNY-Binghamton, 1973, Ph.D., 1977. Research assoc. Fernand Braudel Ctr., SUNY-Binghamton, 1977; asst. to provost U. Md., College Park, 1978; vis. instr. St. Mary's Coll. Md., St. Mary's City, 1978-79; dir. Alexandria Regional Preservation Office, Va., 1980-83; exec. dir. Am. Studies Assn., College Park, Md., 1983—; cons. (in field); reviewer U.S. Dept. Interior, NEH, HEW, USIA, PBS, Washington, 1983—. Author: (with Immanuel Wallerstein) Libraries and Our Civilizations, 1978, (with others) Archaeology in Urban America: A Search for Pattern Process, 1982. Exec. bd. dirs. Nat. Humanities Alliance, 1992—. Fulbright-Hays fellow, 1974-75; Spanish Govt. fellow, 1974-75. Mem. Am. Studies Assn., Fulbright Assn. Home: 4631 Bettswood Dr Olney MD 20832-2042 Office: Am Studies Assn 1120 19th St NW Ste 301 Washington DC 20036-3614

STEPHENS, LAURENCE DAVID, JR., linguist, investor, oil industry executive; b. Dallas, July 26, 1947; s. Laurence D. Sr. and Amy Belle (Schickram) S.; m. Susan Leigh Foutz, Apr. 16, 1988; 1 child, Laurence David III. MA, Stanford U., 1972, PhD, 1976. Vis. fellow Yale U., New Haven, Conn., summer 1979; rsch. fellow U. S.C., Columbia, 1980; asst. prof. U. N.C., Chapel Hill, 1982-88, assoc. prof., 1989—; CEO Stephens Family Mineral Properties and Investments, Dallas, 1994—. Co-author: Two Studies in Latin Phonology, 1977, Language and Metre, 1984, The Prosody of Greek Speech, 1994; editor ann. vol. L'Année Philologique, 1987-92; contbr. numerous articles to profl. jours. Mem. Univ. Pk. Cmty. League, Park Cities Hist. Soc., Nat. Trust for Hist. Preservation, Washington, 1989—, Dallas Opera Guild, 1992—, The Dallas Symphony Assn. Ann. Fund, Metro. Opera Guild, N.Y.C., 1992—. Recipient L'Année Philologique, NEH, 1987-89, 89-91, 91-93. Mem. Am. Inst. Archaeology, Am. Philol. Assn., Greek and Latin Linguistic Assn. (chmn. 1987-92), Linguistic Soc. Am., N.Y. Acad. Scis., Indogermanische Gesellschaft, Internat. Soc. Bibliographie Classique, Sigma Xi. Achievements include discovery of language universal regularities concerning labiovelar phonemes, laws of palatalization, the law of catathesis in Greek (pitch lowering), and grammatical and semantic constraints on discontinuous constituency; co-developer of Justeson-Stephens probability distribution for chance cognates between unrelated languages, Justeson-Stephens probability distribution of the numbers of vowels, consonants, and total phonological inventory size in the languages of the world; research on the law of the quantitative form of diachronic polysemy growth, sematic universals of aspect and modality, universals of writing systems and their evolution. Home: 3319 Greenbrier Dr Dallas TX 75225-4818 Office: Univ NC Chapel Hill Dept Classics CB # 3145 212 Murphey Hall Chapel Hill NC 27599 Address: Stephens Family Mineral Properties and Investments 4020 Colgate Ave Dallas TX 75225-5425

STEPHENS, MARJORIE JOHNSEN, lawyer; b. Dallas, Aug. 29, 1949; d. Joseph Cornelius Stephens and Marjorie Marie Johnsen; m. Andrew N. Meyercord, Dec. 27, 1971 (div. Oct. 1985); children: Andrew J., Ben, Lee. BA, Tufts U., Medford, Mass., 1971; JD, So. Meth. U., Dallas, 1974, LLM in Taxation, 1981. Bar: Tex. 1974; bd. cert. in estate planning and probate, 1981, 93. Assoc. litigation and taxation Akin Gump Strauss Hauer & Feld, Dallas, 1974-79; ptnr. estate planning and tax Meyercord, Stephens & Bartholow, Dallas, 1979-83; assoc. Copeland & Almquist, Dallas, 1984-86; head tax sect. Smith, Underwood & Hunter, Dallas, 1987-88, pvt. practice, 1988—; lectr. in field Tex. Soc. CPAs, Dallas Estate Planning Coun., Estate Planning Coun. North Tex. Contbr. articles to profl. publs. Mem. ABA, Tex. Bar Assn., Dallas Bar Assn. Office: 5956 Sherry Ln Ste 1413 Dallas TX 75225-8025

STEPHENS, MARTHA FOSTER, advertising executive; b. Lansing, Mich., Dec. 4, 1961; d. Richard Bailey and Gretchen (Meyer) Foster; m. Mark Burgis Stephens, Apr. 11, 1987; children: Emily Kaitlynn, Matthew Foster, Molly Holbrook. BA in English, Mich. State U., 1984; postgrad., Wayne State U. Mem. editorial staff Better Investing, Royal Oak, Mich., 1986-88; with communications Holtzman and Silverman, Farmington Hills, Mich., 1988-89; tech. writer, intern Unisys, Plymouth, Mich., 1989; dir. corp. svcs. and advt. Nat. Assn. Investors Corp., Royal Oak, 1989—. Mem. Nat. Investor Rels. Inst.(sec. 1991-92, v.p. mem. 1992-93, v.p. programs 1993-94, pres. 1994-95, bd. dirs. 1995—, treas. 1996-97). Avocations: computer layout and design, running. Office: Nat Assn Investors Corp PO Box 220 Royal Oak MI 48068-0220

STEPHENS, MARTHA LOCKHART, writer, researcher; b. Corpus Christi, Tex., Jan. 3, 1940; d. Hugh Rairdon and Amelia Virginia (McRee) Lockhart; m. David George Hmiel, June 10, 1961 (div. Oct. 1969); m. William Melvin Stephens Jr., June 2, 1971. BA in English Lit., Colo. Coll., 1961; MA in English Lit., U. Ariz., 1967; BFA in Drawing, U. Tex., San Antonio, 1989. Cert. tchr., Tex. English tchr. Colo., Ala., N.Y., Va. and Calif. pub. schs., 1961-68, San Antonio Ind. Sch. Dist., 1968-73; English tchr. North East Ind. Sch. Dist., San Antonio, 1973-82, level chmn. English, 1974-82, chmn. English lit. selection com., 1977, art and creative writing tchr., 1981-85, art tchr., head dept., 1986-94; presenter in field; cons., tour guide, presenter workshops San Antonio Mus. Art, 1983-86; cons., docent McNay Art Mus., San Antonio, 1987; mem. adv. bd. San Antonio Coun. Tchrs. English, 1980. One woman show Art Ctr. Gallery, 1988; two-person show Chapman Grad. Ctr., Trinity U., 1979; numerous group exhbns. including Tex. Soc. Sculptors, 1979, NOW Art Show, San Antonio, 1980, Alternate Space Gallery, San Antonio, 1983, United Bank of Austin, 1985, U. Tex., San Antonio, 1986, N.E. Ind. Sch. Dist., 1986, others; contbr. articles to profl. publs.; authorized biographer Dorothy Dehner. Sponsor/recipient Gold Crown award Columbia Sch. Press Assn., 1992, citation for excellence Scholastic Art and Writing Awards, 1992, State Champion award Tex. H.S. Press Assn., 1990, 91, 92. Mem. NEA, Tex. State Tchrs.' Assn. (pres. Tchrs. of English sect. region 10 1979), North East Tchrs.' Assn., Nat. Art Edn. Assn., Tex. Art Edn. Assn. (regional rep. 1989-93, Merit award 1986, rep. region V 1989-93, capt. region V 1991-93), San Antonio Art Edn. Assn. (pres. 1990-92, Svc. award 1993, adv. bd. 1988-93). Democrat. Episcopalian. Avocations: painting, writing, gardening, cooking, computers. Home: 10935 Whisper Valley St San Antonio TX 78230-3617

STEPHENS, MICHAEL DEAN, hospital administrator; b. Salt Lake City, May 1, 1942; married. B, Columbia U., 1966, MHA, 1970. Adminstrv. resident Mt. Sinai Med. Ctr., N.Y.C., 1969-70; asst. administr. Greenville (S.C.) Gen. Hosp., 1970-71, assoc. adminstr., 1971-72, adminstr., 1972-75; pres Hoag Meml. Hosp.-Presbyn., Newport Beach, Calif., 1975—. Mem. Am. Coll. Healthcare Execs. Home: 900 Alder Pl Newport Beach CA 92660-4121 Office: Hoag Meml Hosp Presbyn PO Box 6100 Newport Beach CA 92658-6100*

STEPHENS, NORVAL BLAIR, JR., marketing consultant; b. Chgo., Nov. 20, 1928; s. Norval Blair and Ethel Margaret (Lewis) S.; m. Diane Forst, Sept. 29, 1951; children: Jill E., John G., Sandra J. (dec.), Katherine B., James N. BA, DePauw U., 1951; MBA, U. Chgo., 1959. Asst. to v.p. ops. Walgreen Drug Co., Chgo., 1953-56; with Needham, Harper Worldwide (formerly Needham, Harper & Steers), Chgo., 1956-86; v.p. Needham, Harper Worldwide (formerly Needham, Harper & Steers), 1964-70, sr. v.p., 1970-72, exec. v.p. internat., 1972-74; exec. v.p., mng. dir. Needham, Harper Worldwide (formerly Needham, Harper & Steers), N.Y.C., 1974-75; exec. v.p. Chgo. office Needham, Harper & Steers, 1975-82, exec. v.p. internat., 1982-86; also dir.; pres. Deltacom, N.Y.C., 1971-76; pres. Norval Stephens Co., 1987—. Bd. advisors Barrington Area Arts Coun., 1985-86, bd. dirs., 1987-89; bd. dirs. N.W. Cmty. Hosp. Found., Arlington Heights, 1976-89, vice chmn., 1987-89; bd. dirs. Harper Coll. Ednl. Found., Palatine, Ill., 1977-86, pres., 1980-86; bd. dirs. Barrington Area Devel. Coun., 1978—, pres., 1994-96; bd. visitors, dir. alumni bd. DePauw U., 1979-83, pres., 1981-83, trustee, 1983—, vice chmn., 1995—. With USMCR, 1951-53. Named Young Man of Yr., Arlington Heights Jaycees, 1964; recipient Rector award DePauw U., 1976, Old Gold Goblet award for outstanding svc. DePauw U., 1994. Mem. Internat. Advt. Assn. (v.p. Midwest chpt. 1986-87), Am. Mgmt. Assn., Am. Mktg. Assn., Internat. Fedn. Advt. Agys. (exec. dir. 1988—), DePauw Alumni Assn. (pres. 1977-79), Phi Beta Kappa, Delta Tau Delta (bd. dirs. edn. found. 1987—, vice chmn. 1994-95, chmn. 1995—, 2d v.p. Arch chpt. 1988-90, 1st v.p. 1990-92, pres. 1992-94). Republican. Methodist. Home: 107 Fox Hunt Trl Barrington IL 60010-3418 Office: 1450 American Ln Ste 1400 Schaumburg IL 60173-6084 *I view my life not as a passage but a daily renewing challenge: to be better; to be a better father, husband, brother, son; to return each day an honest day's work; to bear* *witness to my beliefs and my faith; to serve my fellowman. I seek a whole life and a life of rewarding parts, each a lesson and an experience.*

STEPHENS, OLIN JAMES, II, naval architect, yacht designer; b. N.Y.C., N.Y., Apr. 13, 1908; s. Roderick and Marguerite (Dulon) S.; m. Florence Reynolds, Oct. 21, 1930; children: Olin James III, Samuel R. Student, MIT, 1926-27; MS (hon.), Stevens Inst. Tech.; MA (hon.), Brown U.; D in Arch. laurea ad honorem, U. Arch., Venice, Italy. Draftsman Henry J. Gielow, N.Y.C., 1927-28; draftsman P.L. Rhodes, N.Y.C., 1928; ptnr. Sparkman & Stephens, 1928, Inc., 1929, chief designer, 1929-78; faculty mem. Royal Designers for Ind., London. Yachts designed include Dorade, 1930, Stormy Weather, 1934, Lulu, Ranger, (with W. Starling Burgess), 1937, Baruna, Blitzen, Goose, 1938, Vim, Gesture, 1939, Llanoria, 1948, Finisterre, 1954, Columbia, 1958, Constellation, 1964, Intrepid, 1967, Charisma, Morning Cloud, 1971, Courageous, 1974, Enterprise, 1977, Freedom, 1979, others; design agt. U.S. Navy, 1939—. Recipient David Taylor medal Soc. Naval Architects & Marine Engrs., 1959, Beppe Crowe award Internat. Yacht Racing Union, 1992, Gibbs Bros. medal NAS, 1993. Fellow Soc. Naval Architects and Marine Engrs. (David W. Taylor medal 1959); mem. Nat. Acad. Engring., Am. Boat and Yacht Coun. (pres. 1959-60), N.Am. Yacht Racing Union, Offshore Racing Coun. (chmn. internat. tech. com. 1967-73, 76-79), N.Y. Yacht (tech. com. 1989—), Manhassett Bay Club (hon.), Cruising Club of Am. (tech. com. 1989—), Royal Ocean Racing Club, Royal Thames Yacht Club. Home: 80 Lyme Rd Apt 160 Kendal at Hanover Hanover NH 03755 Office: Sparkman and Stephens Inc 529 5th Ave New York NY 10017-4608

STEPHENS, PHILLIP, screenwriter, producer; b. Council Bluffs, Iowa, June 25, 1940; s. Ronald Donald and Alice Margrete (Skelton) S.; m. Elaine Jensen, July 1, 1961 (div. June 1983); children: Christopher Roland, Denise Andrea. BA in Theatre/Film, U. Denver, 1973, MA in Mass Communications, 1979. Screenwriter Mary Muphy Agy., Hollywood, Calif., 1975-78, Concept Continuum, Denver, 1978-79; prof. TV and Film Studies U. Denver, 1979—; writer, producer C-Star Internat. Entertainment, 1988-89; writer, dir., exec. producer Ravenshead Communications, Denver, 1990-92. Vol. moutain search and rescue team. Recipient Bronze medal Internat. Film and TV Festival, N.Y., 1973, 79; Phillip Stephens' Libr. Collection named in his honor U. Wyo. Mem. Author's League of Am., Dramatist's Guild, U. Film and Video Assn., Broadcast Edn. Assn., Internat. Freelance Photographers Assn., Internat. Film and Video Assn. Avocations: fly fishing, camping, photography, raising horses. Office: U Denver University Blvd Denver CO 80202

STEPHENS, RICHARD BERNARD, natural resource company executive; b. Cambridge, Mass., Dec. 24, 1934; s. Theron Walter and Emma Marie (Bernard) S.; m. Anne Monique Devant, Oct. 18, 1958; children: Ann Marie, Claire Elizabeth, Jennifer Leslie. BA in Econs., Rice U., 1956; grad. exec. program bus. adminstrn., Columbia U., 1974. Landman Tenneco Oil Co., Lafayette, La., 1960-65; v.p. La. Land and Exploration Co., New Orleans, 1965-80; pres. Freeport Oil Co., New Orleans, 1980-84, McMoRan Oil and Gas Co., New Orleans, 1984-86; sr. v.p., dep. to chmn. Freeport-McMoRan, Inc., New Orleans, 1986—, office of the chmn., 1992-93; ret.; ret. sr. advisor to chmn. Freeport, McMoran, Inc., New Orleans, 1993-96; mng. gen. ptnr. RBAS Investments, L.P. Mem. exec. bd., exec. com. New Orleans Boy Scouts Am., 1984-95; trustee Mercy Hosp. New Orleans, 1977-81, La. Nature and Sci. Ctr., New Orleans, 1985-88; pres. Dad's Club St. Martin Protestant Episc. Sch., Metairie, La., 1975-76, sch. trustee, 1976-80, bd. visitors, 1995—, chmn. ann. giving/capital funds drive, 1977; vice chmn. United Way New Orleans, 1976-77; dir. Eisenhower Ctr. U. New Orleans, 1989—, World Trade Ctr., 1992-95; mem. adv bd. So. regiona Internat. Inst. Edn., 1995—; adv. com. Malta Park, 1996—. Decorated The Sovereign Mil. Hospitaler Order of St. John of Jerusalem of Rhodes and of Malta, The Mil. and Hospitaler Order of St. Lazarus of Jerusalem. Mem. Nat. Gas Supply Assn. (steering com. 1982-86, adv. com. 1996—), Mid-Continent Oil and Gas Assn. (exec. com. 1984-88), Am. Petroleum Inst. (exec. com. 1985-88), La. Assn. Ind. Producers and Royalty Owners (dir. 1977-79), New Orleans Geol. Soc., Am. Assn. Petroleum Landmen, French-Am. C. of C., Assn. Rice Alumni (exec. bd. 1983-86, pres. 1996-97), Mil. Order World Wars, Rice Assocs., Brown Soc., Metairie Country Club, New Orleans Petroleum Club (bd. dirs. 1980-83), Commanderie Bordeaux sous Commanderie la Nouvelle Orleans, Pickwick Club, Boston Club, Lovett Soc. Republican. Roman Catholic. Avocations: wildfowl wood collecting, long distance jogging, tennis, golf. Home: 770 Gulf Shore Dr # 903 Destin FL 32541 also: 800 Rue Bourbon Metairie LA 70005-3421 Office: Freeport-McMoRan Inc 1615 Poydras St New Orleans LA 70112-1254

STEPHENS, ROBERT F., state supreme court chief justice; b. Covington, Ky., Aug. 16, 1927. Student, Ind. U.; LL.B., U. Ky., 1951. Bar: Ky. 1951. Asst. atty. Fayette County, Ky., 1964-69; judge Fayette County, 1969-75; atty. gen. Ky. Frankfort, 1976-79; justice Supreme Ct. Ky., Frankfort, 1979—, chief justice, 1982—; pres. Conf. of chief justices, 1992-93; chmn. Nat. Ctr. for State Ct., 1992-93. Staff: Ky. Law Jour. Bd. dirs. Nat. Assn. Counties, 1973-75; 1st pres. Ky. Assn. Counties; 1st chmn. Bluegrass Area Devel. Dist.; chmn. Ky. Heart Assn. Fund Drive, 1976-78. Served with USN, World War II. Named Outstanding Judge of Ky., Ky. Bar Assn., 1986, Outstanding County Judge, 1972; recipient Herbert Harley award Am. Judicature Soc., Spl. Svc. award La. Bar Assn., 1997. Mem. Warren Burger Soc., Nat. Ctr. for State Cts., Order of Coif. Democrat. Office: Ky Supreme Ct 231 Capital Bldg Rm 235 700 Capital Ave Frankfort KY 40601

STEPHENS, STEVE ARNOLD, real estate broker; b. Irby, Cheshire, Eng., May 25, 1945; came to U.S., 1983; s. Harold Dennis George and Hilda Leonora (Howell) S.; m. Lynn Williams, Apr. 14, 1983. Student, Manchester U., Eng., 1967-69. Lic. pvt. detective, Ill. From cadet to detective Cheshire (Eng.) Police, 1961-69; acting detective sgt. Merseyside (Eng.) Police, 1969-75; acting sgt. Hampshire (Eng.) Police, 1975-77; retail store owner Horsham, West Sussex, Eng., 1977-79; pvt. detective Carratu Internat., London, 1979-83, D.A.C. Stephens, Aurora, Ill., 1983-86; broker Coldwell Banker Comml.-Primus Realty, Oswego, Ill., 1986—. Bd. dirs. Aurora Crimestoppers, pres., 1995-96. Recipient Rep. Legion of Merit award, Rep. Order of Merit award. Mem. Nat. Assn. Realtors (CCIM), Comml. Investment Real Estate Inst. (cert., bd. dirs. Ill. CCIM chpt. 1992——, sec.-treas. 1994, v.p. 1995, pres. 1996), No. Ill. Comml. Assn. Realtors (dir. 1995—), Internat. Assn. Chiefs of Police, Ill. Assn. Realtors, Greater Aurora C. of C., Aurora Country Club. Avocations: travel, literature, golf. Home: 7 Saddlewood Ct Aurora IL 60506 Office: Coldwell Banker Comml Primus Realty 21 W Merchants Dr Oswego IL 60543-9456 *Work hard. Tell the truth and shame the Devil!.*

STEPHENS, THOMAS M(ARON), education educator; b. Youngstown, Ohio, June 15, 1931; s. Thomas and Mary (Hanna) S.; m. Evelyn Kleshock, July 1, 1955. BS, Youngstown Coll., 1955; MEd, Kent State U., 1957; EdD, U. Pitts., 1966. Lic. psychologist, Ohio. Tchr. Warren (Ohio) public schs., 1955-57, Niles (Ohio) public schs., 1957-58; psychologist Montgomery County, Ohio, 1958-60; dir. gifted edn. Ohio Dept. Edn., Columbus, 1960-66; assoc. prof. edn. U. Pitts., 1966-70; prof. edn. Ohio State U., 1970—, chmn. dept. exceptional children, 1972-82, chmn. dept. human services edn., 1982-87, assoc. dean Coll. Edn., 1987-92, prof., 1987-92, prof. emeritus, 1992—; clin. prof. edn. U. Dayton, Ohio, 1993—; exec. dir. Sch. Study Coun. Ohio, Columbus, 1993—; mem. Higher Edn. Consortium for Spl. Edn., chmn., 1976-77; pub., pres. Cedars Press, Inc. Author: Directive Teaching of Children with Learning and Behavioral Handicaps, 2d edit, 1976, Implementing Behavioral Approaches in Elementary and Secondary Schools, 1975, Teaching Skills to Children with Learning and Behavioral Disorders, 1977, Teaching Children Basic Skills: A Curriculum Handbook, 1978, 2d edit., 1983, Social Skills In The Classroom, 1978, 2d edit., 1991, Teaching Mainstreamed Students, 1982, 2d edit., 1988, Social Behavior Assessment Scale, 1991; dir.: Jour. Sch. Psychology, 1965-75, 80—; exec. editor: The Directive Tchr.; assoc. editor: Spl. Edn. and Tchr. Edn., Techniques, Behavioral Disorders, Spl. Edn. and Remedial Edn.; contbr. articles to profl. jours. U.S. Office of Edn. fellow, 1964-65. Mem. APA, NASP (charter), State Dirs. for Gifted (pres. 1962-63), Coun. for Exceptional Children (gov., Tchr. Educator of Yr. tchr. edn. divsn. 1985), Coun. Children with Behavioral Disorders (pres. 1972-73). Home: 551 E Cooke Rd Columbus OH 43214-2813 Office: Sch Study Coun of Ohio 665 E Granville Dublin Rd Columbus OH 43229

STEPHENS, WANDA BREWER, social services administrator, investor; b. Bolckow, Mo., Nov. 6, 1932; d. Perry Clark and Mary Carolyn (Fisher) Brewer; m. Lloyd Wesley Stephens, June 19, 1954; children: Ruth Ann, Susie Jo, John Allen, Donna Lynn. BS in home econs., U. Ark., 1954, MS, 1958. Cert. secondary edn. Home economics tchr. West Fork (Ark.) High Sch., 1954-58; pres. Devel. Child Care Assn., Fayetteville, Ark., 1971-74; pres., founding bd. Infant Devel. Ctr., Fayetteville, Ark., 1972-75, treas., 1975-81; edn. chmn., fin. com., admin. bd. Cen. United Meth. Ch., Fayetteville, Ark., 1976-79; pres. League of Women Voters, Fayetteville, Ark., 1979-83, Nat. Orgn. Women, Fayetteville, Ark., 1983-89; state legis. v.p. NOW, Fayetteville, 1985-90, 93-96; state pres. Nat. Orgn. Women Ark., Fayetteville, 1991-93; bd. sec., headstart, Econ. Opportunity Agy., Fayetteville, 1969-70; treas. Mama's Milk Investment Club, 1970-72. Co-author: Bylaws for Economic Opportunity Agy., 1969; co-editor: Washington County, Ark., 1982. Fundraiser United Fund, 1972-75; polit. organizer NOW, 1986; treas. Washington County Dem. Women, 1990-92; organizer/staff/fund Women's Libr., 1982-91; cons./organizer Ctrl. Child Care Ctr., 1977-78. Recipient Internat. 4-H Youth Exch., 1953-54, Infant Devel. Ctr. Founders Plaque Univ. Ark., 1987; named Lay Person of Yr., Ctrl. United Meth. Ch., 1977. Mem. Mental Health Assn. (Community Svc. award 1972), AAUW (pres. Fayetteville 1975-77, state treas. 1996—, Edn. Found. fellow 1984), ACLU (Susan B. Anthony award 1985), Ark. Women's Polit. Caucus (Uppity Woman award 1987, 92). Democrat. Methodist. Avocations: genealogy, reading, investing, producing cmty. access TV. Home: 1177 E Ridgeway Dr Fayetteville AR 72701-2612

STEPHENS, WILLIAM RICHARD, college president emeritus; b. Ashburn, Mo., Jan. 2, 1932; s. George Lewis and Helen S.; m. Arlene Greer, June 28, 1952; children—Richard, Kendell, Kelli. B.S., Greenville Coll., Ill., 1953; M.Ed., U. Mo., 1958; Ed.D., Washington U., St. Louis, 1964. Tchr. Sturgeon High Sch., Mo., 1955-57; asst. prof. then assoc. prof. edn. Greenville Coll., 1957-61, dir. NCATE self-study, 1960-61; spl. instr. Washington U., St. Louis, 1961-64; mem. faculty Ind. State U., 1964-70; vis. prof. Ind. U., Bloomington, 1969-70; prof. history and philosophy of edn. Ind. U., 1970-71; v.p. acad. affairs, dean of faculty Greenville Coll., 1971-77, acting pres., 1977, pres., 1977-93; pres. emeritus, 1993—; chmn., bd. dirs. Fedn. Ind. Ill. Coll. and Univs., 1991-92. Author: Social Reform and the Origins of Vocational Guidance, 1890-1925, 1970; Education of American Life (with William Van Til), 1972; also curriculum materials, reports; editor procs. ednl. meetings. Vice-chmn. Kingsbury Park Dist., Greenville, 1972-77; mem. edn. com. Bond County Mental Health Assn., 1974. Served with U.S. Army, 1953-55. Recipient Merit award Nat. Vocat. Guidance Assn., 1973; fellow Acad. Achievers, Ctrl. Coll., 1994. Mem. History of Edn. Soc. (chmn. nominating com. 1969), Midwest History of Edn. Soc. (pres. 1971-72), Philosophy of Edn. Soc., Ohio Valley Philosophy of Edn. Soc. (sec.-treas. 1967-70), Soc. Profs. Edn. (assoc. editor publs. 1968-70), Central States Faculty Colloquium (chmn. 1969—), John Dewey Soc. (pres.-elect 1978-80, pres. 1980-82, editor Insights 1973-78), North Central Assn., Assn. Free Methodist Ednl. Instns. (pres. 1980—). Home: 516 N Elm St Greenville IL 62246 Office: Greenville Coll 315 E College Ave Greenville IL 62246-1145

STEPHENS, WILLIAM THEODORE, lawyer, business executive; b. Balt., Mar. 31, 1922; s. William A. and Mildred (Griffin) S.; m. Arlene Alice Lesti, June 2, 1958; children: William Theodore Jr., Renée Adena. Grad., Balt. City Coll., 1941; student, U. Md., 1946-47; AB, JD, George Washington U., 1950, postgrad., 1951. Bar: D.C. 1951, Md. 1950, Va. 1959. Assoc. J.L. Green, Washington, 1950-51; with J.M. Cooper, Washington, 1952-54; sr. ptnr. Stephens Law Firm, Washington, 1955—; gen. counsel Exotech, Inc., Gaithersburg, Md.; bd. dirs., prin. owner BARBCO, Inc., Va., Fairfax Raquet Club; gen. counsel various nat. corps. and assns. 1st lt. AUS, 1941-45. Mem. ABA (D.C. Bar Assn. sec. taxation 1959—, sec. corps, banking and bus. law 1960—), Bar Assn. D.C. (sec. taxation 1959-68), Md. Bar Assn., Va. Bar Assn., XVI Corps Assn. (pres. 1967), Commonwealth Club, Univ. Club, Capitol Hill Club, Army-Navy Country Club, Regency Sport and Health Club, Jockey Club, LaCosta Country Club, Racquet Club Internat., Kappa Alpha (preceptor, ct. of honor, James Ward Wood Province 1988-91), Delta Theta Phi. Home: 1800 Old Meadow Rd PO Box 917 McLean VA 22102-1819 Home: 881 Ocean Dr Key Biscayne FL 33149 Home: PO Box 917 Rancho Santa Fe CA 92067 Office: 1800 Old Meadow Rd PO Box 1096 McLean VA 22101-1096

STEPHENS, WOODFORD CEFIS (WOODY STEPHENS), horse trainer, breeder; b. Stanton, Ky., Sept. 1, 1913; s. Lewis and Helen (Welch) S.; m. Lucille Elizabeth Easley, Sept. 11, 1937. Ed., Ky. Pub. Schs. Began as exercise boy, then trainer thoroughbred horses Ky., 1929—; jockey, 1931-40, profl. trainer thoroughbred horses, 1940—. Subject of biography: Guess I'm Lucky, 1985. Recipient profl. horse racing awards including: N.Y. Turf Writers Assn. Outstanding Trainer award, 1982, 83, Nat. Turf Writers Mr. Fitz award, 1982, Turf Publicists of Am. for outstanding sporting deeds benefiting horse racing, 1982, Silver Horseshoe award Ky. Derby Festival, 1983, Red Smith Good Guy award, Eclipse award for tng. of horse Swale, 1984, Gold Cup award N.Y., 1986, 87, C.V. Whitney Spl. Achievement award, 1993, 70th Ann. award N.Y. Turf Writers, 1993, Lifetime Achievement award Hialeah, 1989, others; named to Thoroughbred Racing's Hall of Fame, 1976, Horseperson of Yr. award, Fla., 1981, Legend in All Star Events, Fla., 1988, Caesars Legends of Racing, Atlantic City, 1988, Trainer of Decade AP, N.Y. Turf Writers, 1990, N.Y. Sports Mus. Hall of Fame, 1990; Ky. Col., 1963; trainer of more than 300 stake race winners, icnluding 2 Ky. Derbys, 1 Preakness, 5 Belmont Stakes; inducted into Hall of Fame, 1976, Saratoga, Hall of Fame, L.I.; Woody's Corner erected Belmont RAce Track, 1992; inducted into the Hialeah Park Classic Club, 1994; 150 silver trophies. Mem. United Thoroughbred Trainers Am., Turf and Field Club (N.Y.), Thoroughbred Club Am., Sky Island Club. Winner of 5 consecutive Belmont Stakes ranks as one of horse racings most outstanding accomplishments; life-size sculpture erected in hometown of Stanton; donated items pertinent to achievements associated with Ky. Derby and other Triple Crown races to Ky. Derby Museum, 1995. Home: 15534 Cairnryan Ct Hialeah FL 33014-2092 Office: Belmont Race Track Hempstead Elmont NY 11003 *Doing what I like best - hard work, being loyal, and I love my work, with animals.*

STEPHENSON, ALAN CLEMENTS, lawyer; b. Wilmington, N.C., Nov. 7, 1944; s. Abram Clements and Ruth (Smith) S.; m. Sherri Jean Miller, Dec. 19, 1970; children: Edward Taylor, Anne Baldwin. AB in Hist., U. N.C., 1967; JD, U. Va., 1970. Bar: N.Y. 1971. Assoc. Cravath, Swaine & Moore, N.Y.C., 1970-78, ptnr., 1978-88; mng. dir. Wasserstein, Perella and Co. Inc., N.Y.C., 1988-92; ptnr. Cravath, Swaine & Moore, N.Y.C., 1992—; bd. dirs. Victim Svcs., Inc., N.Y.C. Morehead scholar John M. Moorehead Found., 1963. Mem. N.Y. State Bar Assn., Assn. of Bar of City of N.Y., The Brook Club, The Links Club, Tuxedo Club, Union Club, Phi Beta Kappa. Home: 1107 Fifth Ave New York NY 10128-0145 Office: Cravath Swaine & Moore 825 8th Ave New York NY 10019-7416

STEPHENSON, ANN WATZ, artist; b. Fayetteville, W.Va., June 30, 1933; d. George W. and Eva J. (Weatherford) Booth; m. Roger Allen Stephenson, July 19, 1958 (div. May 1993); 1 child, David. AA, Ctrl. Acad. Art, Cin., 1955. Fashion artist Mabley & Carew, Cin., 1957-61, Shillito's Dept. Store, Cin., 1961, Gidding/Jenny, Cin., 1964; head fashion artist McAlpin's Dept. Store, Cin., 1964-77; art dir., dir. phtography Rogers Dept. Store, Grand Rapids, Mich., 1977-95; art dir., owner Ann Stephenson Designs, Charleston, W.Va., 1996—. Author, artist: Introduction to Fashion Art, 1981; fine art watercolor exhibits, 1992, 94. Recipient six Addy awards, 1975, 78. Mem. Nat. Mus. Women Arts, Rivertown Artist Guild (historian 1992). Avocations: watercolor, reading, hiking, drying flowers. Home: 1577 Lee St E Charleston WV 25311

STEPHENSON, ARTHUR EMMET, JR., investment company executive, banker; b. Bastrop, La., Aug. 29, 1945; s. Arthur Emmet and Edith Louise Stephenson; m. Toni Lyn Edwards, June 17, 1967. BS in Fin. magna cum laude, La. State U., 1967; MBA (Ralph Thomas Sayles fellow), Harvard U., 1969. Chartered fin. analyst. Adminstrv. aide to U.S. Sen. Russell Long of La., Washington, 1966; security analyst Fidelity Funds, Boston, 1968; chmn. bd., pres. Stephenson & Co., Denver, Stephenson Mcht. Banking Inc., Circle Corp.; sr. ptnr. Stephenson Ventures, Stephenson Properties; chmn. bd. dirs. StarTek, Inc., Gen. Comm., Inc., Globescope Corp.; co-founder Pub. Network, Inc.; underwriting mem. Lloyd's of London, 1978-92; founder Charter Bank and Trust, chmn., 1980-91; bd. dirs. Danaher Corp., Mountain Parks Fin. Corp.; mem. adv. bd. First Berkshire Fund, Capital Resources Ptnrs., L.P.; pub. Law Enforcement Product News, Colo. Book, Pub. Safety Product News. Mem. assocs. coun. Templeton Coll. at Oxford U., Eng.; nat. trustee Nat. Symphony Orch. at John F. Kennedy Ctr. for Performing Arts; mem. nat. steering com. Norman Rockwell Mus., Stockbridge, Mass.; past mem. Colo. small bus. coun.; del. White House Conf., 1980. Recipient Hall of Fame award Inc. mag. Mem. Harvard U. Bus. Sch. Assn. (internat. pres. 1987-88), Chief Execs. Orgn., World Pres.'s Orgn., Young Pres.'s Orgn. (Calif. Inland Empire chpt. chmn. 1992-93, area coun. mem.), Colo. Investment Advisors Assn. (treas., bd. dirs. 1975-76), Fin. Analysts Fedn., Denver Soc. Security Analysts (bd. dirs. 1975-77), Colo. Press Assn., Colo. Harvard Bus. Sch. Club (pres. 1980-81, chmn. 1981-82), Thunderbird Country Club (Rancho Mirage, Calif.), Annabel's (London), Jonathan Club (L.A.), Denver Petroleum Club, Harvard Bus. Sch. Clubs (N.Y.C., So. Calif. and Boston), Harvard Clubs (N.Y. and Boston), Omicron Delta Kappa, Phi Kappa Phi, Beta Gamma Sigma, Kappa Sigma, Delta Sigma Pi. Office: 100 Garfield St Denver CO 80206-5550

STEPHENSON, BARBERA WERTZ, lawyer; b. Bryan, Ohio, Dec. 10, 1938; d. Emerson D. and Beryl B. (Barber) Wertz; m. Gerard J. Stephenson Jr., June 22, 1960; 1 child, Thomas. Student, Smith Coll., 1956-57; BSEE, MIT, 1961; JD, U. N.Mex., 1981. Bar: N.Mex. 1981. Electronic engr. Digital Equipment Corp., Maynard, Mass., 1960-66; logic analyst Librascope, Glendale, Calif., 1966; electronic engr. Md. Dept. of Def., Ft. Meade, 1966-68; mem. tech. staff Xerox Data Systems, Rockville, Md., 1968; pvt. practice cons., Silver Spring, Md., 1969-78; pvt. practice law, Albuquerque, 1981—. Author: Financing Your Home Purchase in New Mexico, 1992; patentee analog to digital converter, kitchen calculator. Mem. N.Mex. Bar Assn. Office: 4221 Silver Ave SE Albuquerque NM 87108-2720

STEPHENSON, BETTE MILDRED, physician, former Canadian legislator; b. Aurora, Ont., Can., July 31, 1924; d. Carl Melvin and Clara Mildred (Draper) S.; grad. Earl Haig Coll. Inst.; MD, U. Toronto, 1946; m. Gordon Allan Pengelly, 1948; children: J. Stephen A., Elizabeth Anne A., C. Christopher A., J. Michael A., P. Timothy A., Mary Katharine A. Mem. med. staff Women's Coll. Hosp., 1950-90, chief dept. gen. practice, dir. outpatient dept., 1956-64; mem. med. staff N.Y. Gen. Hosp., 1967-89; elected Ont. Legislature for York Mills, 1975, 77, 81, 85; minister labor, 1975-78; minister edn., minister colls. and univs., 1978-85, treas. and dep. premier, 1985; pres. Gwillimbury Found. Post Secondary Edn.; dir. Can. Inst. Advanced Rsch., dir. edn. quality and accountability, Ontario; dir. Women's Coll. Hosp. Fellow Coll. Family Physicians Can. (chmn. nat. coordinating com. on edn. 1961-64, chmn. confs. on edn. for gen. practice 1961, 63), Acad. Med. Toronto (hon.); mem. Ont. Med. Assn. (dir. 1964-72, pres. 1970-71), Can. Med. Assn. (dir. 1968-75, pres. 1974-75), Art Gallery Ont., Royal Ont. Mus., Order of Can. (officer), Order of St. John (officer).

STEPHENSON, DONALD GRIER, JR., government studies educator; b. DeKalb County, Ga., Jan. 12, 1942; s. Donald Grier and Katherine Mason (Williams) S.; m. Ellen Claire Walker, Aug. 15, 1967; children: Todd Grier, Claire Walker. AB, Davidson Coll., N.C., 1964; MA, Princeton U., 1966, PhD, 1967. Research assoc. Nat. War Coll., Washington, 1968-70; asst. prof. govt. Franklin and Marshall Coll., Lancaster, Pa., 1970-73, assoc. prof. govt., 1973-81, prof. govt., 1981—, Charles A. Dana prof., 1989—; mem. adv. coun. to dean of the chapel Princeton U., 1974-85; Commonwealth lectr. Pa. Humanities Coun., Phila., 1987-88, 90, 92-95. Co-author: American Constitutional Development, 1977, American Government, 1992, 94, American Constitutional Law, 1996; author: The Supreme Court and the American Republic, 1981, An Essential Safeguard, 1991; contbr. articles to profl. jours. Elder, mem. session First Presbyn. Ch., Lancaster, 1973-76, 96—; judge Pa. constl. competition Dickinson Coll., 1988—. Capt. U.S. Army, 1968-70. Woodrow Wilson fellow, 1964-65, 66-67; Nat. Endowment for Humanities grantee, 1972, 85-89. Mem. Am. Polit. Sci. Assn. (Corwin award com. 1978, nominating com. Law and Courts sect. 1995), Pa. Polit. Sci. Assn. (editl. bd. Polity 1972-78), Supreme Ct. Hist. Soc. (editl. award 1990). Presbyterian. Home: 62 Oak Ln Lancaster PA 17603-4762 Office: Franklin and Marshall Coll PO Box 3003 Lancaster PA 17604-3003

STEPHENSON, DONNAN, lawyer, former state supreme court justice; b. LaHarpe, Kans., Nov. 21, 1919; s. Ralph Duane and Zoe B. (Donnan) S.; m. Patricia Marie Ledyard, May 14, 1942; children: Mark Donnan, Bruce Ledyard. B.S. in Bus. Adminstrn., U. Kans., 1941, LL.B., 1948. Bar: Kans. 1948, N. Mex. 1949. With TWA, 1948; practice law Santa Fe, 1958-70; ptrn. Bigbee & Stephenson, Santa Fe, 1949-62, Stephenson & Olmsted, 1962-66, Stephenson, Campbell & Olmsted, 1966-70; justice N. Mex. Supreme Ct., Santa Fe, 1971-76; sr. ptnr. Bigbee, Stephenson, Carpenter, Crout & Olmsted, Santa Fe, 1976-81, of counsel, 1982-88. Established and endowed Stephenson Lectures in Law and Govt. Kans. U. Law Sch. Served to lt. USNR, WWII. Decorated Bronze Star; recipient Kans. U. Law Sch. Disting. Alumnus, 1981. Fellow N.Mex. Bar Assn. Home: 1014 Bishops Lodge Rd Santa Fe NM 87501-1009

STEPHENSON, DOROTHY GRIFFITH See GRIFFITH, DOTTY

STEPHENSON, DOROTHY MAXINE, volunteer; b. Hanna, Ind., July 16, 1925; d. William John and Inez Louisa (Werner) Hunsley; m. Orville Lee Stephenson, Mar. 10, 1945 (dec. Oct. 1985). Grad. high sch., Hanna. Postal clk. U.S. Post Office, Hanna, 1943-44; bookkeeper LaPorte Co Farm Bur. Coop Assn., Hanna, 1944-45; news correspondent Hanna, Ind., 1950—; organist Wanatah (Ind.) United Meth. Ch., 1959-60, Bethel Presbyn. Ch., Union Mills, Ind., 1960—. Compiler: Werner-Wentz Connections, 1982, Inez Scribblins/Dot's Jottings, 'N Nibblins, 1986, abstractions Hanna H.S. Alumni records, 1990, record books II, III and IV for Bethel Presbyn. Ch., 1992; compiler, pub. Poetry, Music of the Soul, 1995. Publicity person Am. Heart Assn. (Ind. affiliate), LaPorte, 1982-85, LaPorte County Geneal. Soc., 1984—. Recipient Golden Poet award World of Poetry, 1988, hon. mention, 1987-88, Editor's Choice award Nat. Libr. of Poetry, Best Poems of 90's and the 1990 Nat. Anthology award, Echoes of Yesterday, 1994; Voices of America by Sparrowgrass Poetry anthologies, 1989, 90, 91, 92, Amherst Soc. anthologies, 1990, 92, Iliad Press anthologies, 1992, 93, Quill Books, 1993, Outstanding Poets of Am. anthology, 1994, Distinguished Poets of America anthology, 1993. Mem. Merry Prairie (treas. 1964—), Order Ea. Star (worthy matron 1953, 85-90). Democrat. Presbyterian. Avocations: sewing, reading, writing, photography, knitting. Home and Office: 12805 S Hunsley Rd Hanna IN 46340-9736

STEPHENSON, FRANK ALEX, environmental engineer, consultant; b. Helena, Mont., May 4, 1940; s. Alex Banning and Phyllis Jean (Smith) S.; m. Lorann Marcella Berg, July 9, 1962 (div. Aug. 1970); children: Patty Jo, Scott Alex; m. Brenda Mae Vitales, June 21, 1986; 1 child, Jennifer Jean. BS in Civil Constrn. Engring., Mont. State U., 1967; MS in Sanitary Engring., Delft U., 1973; PhD in Environ. Engring., Exeter U., 1975. Registered profl. engr., Ariz., Mont., S.D., Colo., N.Mex., Wyo., Kans. Constrn. engr. Al Johnson Co., Mpls., 1967-70; sr. engr. Stearns Roger Inc., Denver, 1975-79; ptnr. Thomas Group Inc., San Jose, Calif., 1979-85; sr. engr. CH2M Hill Inc., San Jose, Calif., 1985-87; dir. engring. western div. Dames & Moore, Phoenix, 1987-93; dir. techs. Terranext, Phoenix, 1993-97, Boeing N. Am., 1997—. Mem. Rep. Nat. Com., 1996; mem. NAFTA Com., Ariz., 1994. Recipient Ernest Cook Rsch. fellowship Royal Acad. Sci., London, 1973. Mem. AIChE, Hazardous Waste Soc. Presbyterian. Achievements include development of technology for on-line total organic carbon analysis using ultraviolet light and resistivity changes; design and installation of first reverse osmosis unit used in a nuclear (electric power) reactor. Avocations: model railroading, fishing, swimming. Home: 1702 E Aurelius Ave Phoenix AZ 85020 Office: Terranext 9230 S 51st St Phoenix AZ 85044-5681

STEPHENSON, HERMAN HOWARD, retired banker; b. Wichita, Kans., July 15, 1929; s. Herman Horace and Edith May (Wayland) S.; m. Virginia Anne Ross, Dec. 24, 1950; children: Ross Wayland, Neal Bevan, Jann Edith. BA, U. Mich., 1950; JD with distinction, U. Mo., Kansas City, 1958, LLD (hon.), 1993. Bar: Kans. 1958. With City Nat. Bank, Kansas City, Mo., 1952-54, City Bond & Mortgage Co., Kansas City, 1954-59, Bank of Hawaii, Honolulu, 1959-94; ret., 1994; chmn., exec. com., CEO, bd. dirs. Pacific Century Fin. Corp. and Bank Hawaii; bd. dirs. Bank of Hawaii Internat. Inc., Hawaiian Trust Co. Ltd.; internat. treas., dir. Pacific Basin

Econ. Coun. U.S. Mem. Com. Bd. dirs. Maunalani Found., Aloha United Way, Pacific Fleet Submarine Meml. Assn. With U.S. Army, 1950-52. Mem. Navy League of U.S., Pacific Forum/CSIS (bd. govs.), U.S.-Korea Bus. Coun., Kappa Sigma, Pi Eta Sigma, Oahu Country Club, Waialae Country Club, Rotary, Lambda Alpha Internat. Office: Bank of Hawaii PO Box 2900 Honolulu HI 96846

STEPHENSON, IRENE HAMLEN, biorhythm analyst, consultant, editor, educator; b. Chgo., Oct. 7, 1923; d. Charles Martin and Carolyn Hilda (Hilgers) Hamlin; m. Edgar B. Stephenson, Sr., Aug. 16, 1941 (div. 1946); 1 child, Edgar B. Author biorhythm compatibilities column Nat. Singles Register, Norwalk, Calif., 1979-81; instr. biorhythm Learning Tree Open U., Canoga Park, Calif., 1982-83; instr. biorhythm character analysis 1980—; instr. biorhythm compatibility, 1982—; owner, pres. matchmaking svc. Pen Pals Using Biorhythm, Chatsworth, Calif., 1979—; editor newsletter The Truth, 1979-85, Mini Examiner, Chatsworth, 1985—; researcher biorhythm character and compatibility, 1974—, biorhythm columnist Psychic Astrology Horoscope, 1989-94, True Astrology Forecast, 1989-94, Psychic Astrology Predictions, 1990-94, Con Artist Types, 1995, Pedophile (child molester) Types, 1995, Personality Types, 1996, Trouble-Addict (Suicide) Types, 1997; author: Learn Biorhythm Character Analysis, 1980, Do-It-Yourself Biorhythm Compatibilities, 1982; contbr. numerous articles to mags.; frequent guests clubs, radio, TV. Office: PO Box 3893-ww Chatsworth CA 91313 *To be happy, you have to be what is natural for you, not what someone else wants you to be.*

STEPHENSON, JAN LYNN, professional golfer; b. Sydney, Australia, Dec. 22, 1951; d. Francis John and Barbara (Green) S.; m. Eddie Vossler, 1982. Student, Australian schs. Profl. golfer, 1972—; mem. Australian Ladies Profl. Golf Assn. tour, 1972-73, U.S. Ladies Profl. Golf Assn. tour, 1974—. Winner New South Wales (Australia) Jr. Championship, 1963-69; winner Australian Jr. Championship, 1968-71, Australian Title, 1973, Sarah Coventry Championship, 1976, Birmingham Championship Ala., 1976, Women's Internat., 1978, Sun City Classic, 1980, Peter Jackson Classic, 1981, Mary Kay Classic, 1981, United Va. Bank Classic, 1981, Ladies Profl. Golf Assn. Championship, 1982, Women's Tucson Open, 1983, Women's U.S. Open, 1983, Lady Keystone Open, GNA Tournament, 1985, French Open, 1985, Santa Barbara Open, 1987, Safeco Seattle Classsic, 1987, Konica San Jose Classic, 1987, 1st LPGA Skins Game, Frisco, Tex., 1990; named Rookie of Yr., U.S. Profl. Golfers Assn., 1974; Sportsman of Yr., Sportswriters Assn., Australia, 1976. Office: care LPGA 100 International Golf Dr Daytona Beach FL 32124-1082*

STEPHENSON, MASON WILLIAMS, lawyer; b. Atlanta, May 29, 1946; s. Donald Grier and Katherine Mason (Williams) S.; m. Linda Frances Partee, June 13, 1970; children: Andrew Mason, Walter Martin. AB cum laude, Davidson Coll., 1968; JD, U. Chgo., 1971. Bar: Ga. 1971, U.S. Dist. Ct. (no. dist.) Ga. 1985. Assoc. Alston, Miller & Gaines, Atlanta, 1971-76, ptnr., 1976-77; ptnr. Trotter, Bondurant, Griffin, Miller & Hishon, Atlanta, 1977-82, Bondurant, Miller, Hishon & Stephenson, Atlanta, 1982-85, King & Spalding, Atlanta, 1985—. Mem. fin. com. Atlanta Olympic Organizing Com., 1988-90. Mem. ABA (real property, probate and trust sect.), Am. Coll. Real Estate Lawyers, State Bar Ga. (exec. com., real property law sect. 1989—), Atlanta Bar Assn. (chair real estate sect. 1981-82), Burge Hunting Club, Causeway Club, Capital City Club, Phi Delta Phi. Avocations: sailing, skiing, jogging. Office: King & Spalding 191 Peachtree St NE Atlanta GA 30303-1740

STEPHENSON, MICHELE, photographer. Dir. photography Time Mag., N.Y.C. Office: c/o Time Time & Life Bldg Time-Life Bldg Rockefeller Ctr New York NY 10020-1393

STEPHENSON, ROBERT BAIRD, energy company executive; b. Washington, Jan. 20, 1943; s. Orlando Worth and Martha Ann (Kostelak) S.; m. Sheryl Ann Fish, Jan. 10, 1967; children: Brie Danielle, Eric Baird. BS in Mech. Engring., Purdue U., 1965; MS in Nuclear Engring., U. Mich., 1970, MBA, 1972. Engr. Jersey Nuclear Co., Inc., Boston, 1972-74; engr., mgr. Exxon Nuclear Co., Inc., Richland, Wash., 1974-80; mng. dir. Exxon Nuclear GmbH, Lingen, Fed. Rep. Germany, 1980-83; mktg., sales staff Exxon Nuclear Co., Inc., Bellevue, Wash., 1983-85, v.p. adminstn., 1986; v.p. comml. div. Exxon Nuclear Co., Inc., Bellevue, 1987; pres., chief exec. officer, chmn. EPID, Inc., San Jose, Calif., 1985-86; pres., chief exec. officer Advanced Nuclear Fuels Corp., Bellevue, Wash., 1988-91; pres. CEO Siemens Nuclear Power Corp., Bellevue, 1991-92; pres., CEO, Siemens Power Corp., Milw., 1992—, also bd. dirs. Bd. regents Milw. Sch. Engring. Lt. USN, 1965-70. Mem. Am. Nuclear Soc. Avocations: sailing, boating, golf. Office: Siemens Power Corp 1040 S 70th St Milwaukee WI 53214-3164

STEPHENSON, ROBERT CLAY, real estate company executive; b. Meadville, Pa., Sept. 21, 1938; s. LeRoy Vernon and Martha Louise (Clay) S.; m. Judith Regina Trohaugh, Jan. 19, 1963; children: Robert Scott, Eric Thomas, Cynthia Lynn. BA, Allegheny Coll., 1962. Group sales rep. Conn. Gen. Life Ins., Detroit, 1962-64; salesman, broker Donovan Co., Pitts., 1964-73; v.p. Oliver Realty, Inc., Pitts., 1974-81; ptnr. Liberati/Davenport/Stephenson, Pitts., 1981, DeBartolo LDS Assocs., Pitts., 1981-85; pres. Carnegie Properties, Inc., Pitts., 1985-86; v.p. office/indsl. properties The Edward J. DeBartolo Corp., Youngstown, Ohio, 1986-94, v.p. asset mgmt., 1994-95; owner RCS Realty Co., Pitts., 1996—; pres. Strategic Investment Fund, Inc., Pitts., 1996—. Session ruling elder Bower Hill Presbyn. Ch.; twp. committeeman Rep. Party Mt. Lebanon Twp.; troop committeeman Boy Scouts Am., Bethel Park, Pa.; real estate cons. The Children's Mus., Pitts.; treas. Ducks Unltd., Washington County, Pa.; community amb. to Eng. Expt. in Internat. Living, Putney, Vt. Mem. Nat. Assn. Realtors, Pa. Assn. Realtors, Realtors Assn. Met. Pitts. (mem. vigilance/ethics com. 1967-69, mem. long range planning com. 1976-78, chmn. 1977-78, mem. R-day conf. com. 1981, mem. pub. rels. com. 1982, mem. Realtors of Yr. com. 1982—), Nat. Assn. Indsl. and Office Parks (mem. western Pa. chpt. 1978—, pres. 1981-82, bd. dirs. 1993-97, mem. nat. com. project analysis 1985), Soc. Indsl. and Office Realtors (mem. western Pa. chpt., pres. 1983, 84, 90, chmn. ann. dinner com. 1982, 89, mem. govt. rels. nat. com. 1982-83, mem. nat. com. office mktg. 1987-88), Nat. Assn. Corp. Real Estate Execs. (mem. Pitts. chpt., pres. 1982), Inst. Real Estate Mgmt., St. Clair Country Club, Bally's Scandinavian Spa, Phi Kappa Psi. Presbyterian. Avocations: fishing, snow skiing, scuba diving, golf, hunting. Home: 1895 Tilton Dr Upper St Clair PA 15241-2636 Office: Strategic Investment Fund, Inc One Oliver Plz 210 6th Ave Pittsburgh PA 15222-2602

STEPHENSON, ROSCOE BOLAR, JR., state supreme court justice; b. Covington, Va., Feb. 22, 1922. A.B., Washington and Lee U., 1943, J.D., 1947, LL.D. (hon.), 1983. Bar: Va. 1947. Ptnr. Stephenson & Stephenson, Covington, 1947-52; commonwealth's atty. Alleghany County, Va., 1952-64; ptnr. Stephenson, Kostel, Watson, Carson and Snyder, Covington, 1964-73; judge 25th Jud. Cir. Ct. Commonwealth Va., Covington, 1973-81; justice Va. Supreme Ct., Richmond, 1981—. Recipient Covington Citizen of Yr. award, 1973; recipient Outstanding Alumni award Covington High Sch., 1973. Fellow Am. Coll. Trial Lawyers; mem. Va. State Bar (council 1969-73), Va. Bar Assn., Va. Trial Lawyers Assn., Order of Coif. Home: North Ridge Hot Springs VA 24445 Office: Va Supreme Ct 100 N 9th St Richmond VA 23219-2335 also: 214 W Main St Covington VA 24426-1543

STEPHENSON, SAMUEL EDWARD, JR., physician; b. Bristol, Tenn., May 16, 1926; s. Samuel Edward and Hazel Beatrice (Walters) S.; m. Janet Sue Spotts, May 16, 1970; children: Samuel Edward III, William Douglas, Dorothea Louise, Judith Maria. BS, U. S.C., 1946; MD, Vanderbilt U., 1950. Intern Butterworth Hosp., Grand Rapids, Mich., 1950-51; instr. to asso. prof. surgery Vanderbilt U., 1955-67; prof. surgery U. Fla., 1967-95, emeritus prof. clin. surgery, 1995—; chmn. dept. surgery Univ. Hosp., Jacksonville, 1967-78. Asst. editor So. Med. Jour., 1968-88; contbr. articles to profl. jours. Co-chmn. Fla. Burn and Trauma Registry, 1974-77. Served with USNR, 1944-45. Fellow A.C.S.; mem. Am. Coll. Chest Physicians. Mason. Club: University (Jacksonville). Home: 10553 Scott Mill Rd Jacksonville FL 32257-6227 Office: 1501 San Marco Blvd Jacksonville FL 32207-2905

STEPHENSON, TONI EDWARDS, publisher, investment management executive; b. Bastrop, La., July 23, 1945; d. Sidney Crawford (dec.) and Grace Erleene Little; BS, La. State U., 1967; grad. owner/pres. mgmt. program Harvard Bus. Sch.; m. Arthur Emmet Stephenson, Jr., June 17, 1967; 1 dau., Tessa Lyn. ; pres., dir. Gen. Communications, Inc., Denver; sr. v.p., founder Stephenson & Co., Denver, 1971—; gen. ptnr. Viking Fund; ptnr. Stephenson Properties, Stephenson Ventures, Stephenson Mgmt. Co.; bd. dirs. Starpak Internat., Inc., Startek Teleservices; founder Charter Bank & Trust. Pu, Law Enforcement Product News, Pub. Safety Product News, Globescope Corp.; sec., HBS/OPM16, former dir. The Children's Hosp., St. Joseph's Hosp. Past pres. Children's Hosp. Assn. Vols., treas. Cherry Creek H.S. Parent Tchr. Conf. Orgn. Mem. Harvard Bus. Sch. Club of Colo., DAR, Delta Gamma. Clubs: Annabel's (London), Thunderbird Country, Glenmoor Country Club, Denver Petroleum.

STEPLER, RICHARD LEWIS, magazine editor; b. Norfolk, Va., Aug. 15, 1945; s. Richard Lewis and Mary Ann (Beard) S.; m. Janet Sarah Froelich, Sept. 13, 1981; children: Jesse Benjamin, Rebecca Ann. BA, NYU, 1969. From sr. editor to editor Popular Sci., N.Y.C., 1975-95; editor-in-chief Boating Mag., N.Y.C., 1996—. Mem. Nat. Assn. Sci. Writers, Am. Soc. Mag. Editors, Internat. Motor Press Assn. (v.p. 1984-91). Office: Boating Mag 1633 Broadway New York NY 10019-6708

STEPNITZ, SUSAN STEPHANIE, special education educator; b. Detroit, Mar. 1, 1948; d. N. Thomas and Dorothy (Richardson) Wagner; m. Kenneth H. Stepnitz Jr., July 25, 1970; children: Joshua, Zachary. BA in Polit. Sci., Olivet Coll., 1970; MA in Spl. Edn., Wayne State U., 1972. Tchr. Traverse Bay Area Intermed. Sch. Dist., Traverse City, Mich., 1973—; negotiator, ednl. profl. and support staff Traverse Bay Area Intermed. Sch. Dist., Travere City, Mich., 1982—; mem. spl. edn. adv. com. Mich. Bd. Edn., 1992—; mem. spl. delivery sys. edn. task force Mich. Dept. Edn., 1993-94, mem. spl. edn./gen. edn. com. Office of Spl. Edn.; mem. Comprehensive Sys. Pers. Devel. Task Force, 1996—. Dir. Handicapped Accessibility Awareness Special Kid's Day Nat. Cherry Festival , 1987—. Recipient Anne Sullivan award Mich. Edn. Assn., 1993, Friend of the Physically Impaired Assn. of Mich. award, 1994. Mem. AAUW (pres. Mich. chpt. 1987-89, Outstanding Person in Edn. award 1986, strategic planning com.), Mich. Edn. Assn. (spl. edn. tng. cadre 1990—). Home: 10729 Wood View Ter Traverse City MI 49686-9203

STEPNOSKI, MARK MATTHEW, professional football player; b. Erie, Pa., Jan. 26, 1967. Student, U. Pitts. Center Dallas Cowboys, 1989-95, Houston Oilers (now Tenn. Oilers), 1995—; player NFC Championship Game, 1992, Super Bowl XXVII, 1992, Super Bowl XXVIII, 1993. Selected to Pro Bowl Team, 1992, 93, 96. Office: Tenn Oilers Bapt Sports Park 7640 Hwy 70 S Nashville TN 37221*

STEPONAITIS, VINCAS PETRAS, archaeologist, anthropologist, educator; b. Boston, Aug. 10, 1953; s. Vincas and Elena (Povydis) S.; m. Laurie Cameron, Dec. 31, 1976; children: Elena Anne, Lillian Kazimiera. AB in Anthropology magna cum laude, Harvard U., 1974; MA in Anthropology, U. Mich., 1975, PhD in Anthropology, 1980. From lectr. to assoc. prof. dept. anthropology SUNY, Binghamton, 1979-87; assoc. prof. U. N.C., Chapel Hill, 1988-94, prof., 1995—, dir. Rsch. Labs. Anthropology, 1988—; guest worker Nat. Bur. Standards, 1979; adj. lectr. dept. anthropology SUNY, Binghamton, 1979; invited lectr. univs. U.S., Europe, 1980—. Author: Ceramics, Chronology, and Community Patterns, An Archaeological Study at Moundville, 1983; editor Southeastern Archaeology, 1984-87; regional editor Investigations in Am. Archaeology, 1987-91; mem. edit. bd. Southern Cultures, 1992—; mem. edit. adv. bd. Prehistory Press, 1990—; contbr. articles to profl. jours.; presenter papers profl. meetings, seminars; pub. book reviews; abstracts. Smithsonian Instn. fellow, 1978-79; grantee NSF, 1978-80, 83, 89-92, 94, Wenner-Gren Found., 1981, 86-88, Nat. Geographic Soc., 1987-88, Z. Smith Reynolds Found., 1992-94. Fellow Am. Anthrop. Assn.; mem. Soc. Am. Archaeology (Presdl. Recognition award 1993-94, exec. com. 1983-84, treas. 1992-94, pres. 1007), Southeastern Archaeol. Conf. (editor 1984-87, pres. 1990-92), N.C. Archaeol. Soc. (exec. sec. 1988-91, sec. 1991—), N.C. Archaeol. Coun. (exec. com. 1988-92), Archaeol. Soc., S.C., Ala. Archaeol. Soc., Miss. Archaeol. Soc., La. Archaeol. Soc., Tenn. Anthrop. Assn. Office: U NC Rsch Labs Anthropology Alumni Bldg CB 3120 Chapel Hill NC 27599-3120

STEPP, LAURA SESSIONS, journalist; b. Ft. Smith, Ark., July 27, 1951; d. Robert Paul Sessions and M. Rae Barnes; m. Carl Sessions Stepp; children: Ashli, Amber, Jeffrey. BA, Earlham Coll., 1973; MA, Columnia U., 1974. Reporter Palm Beach Times, West Palm Beach, Fla., 1974; MA Columbia U., Phila., 1975; projects editor The Charlotte (N.C.) Observer, 1979-81, asst. editorial page editor, 1981-82; Md. editor The Washington Post, 1982-86, religion editor, 1987-92, writer Style sect., 1992—. Bd. advisors U. Md. Casey Journalism Ctr. Children and Families, College Park. Recipient Nat. Reporting award Religion Writers Am., Feature Writing award AAUW, 1994. Mem. Investigative Reporters and Editors (bd. dirs. 1986-90). Office: Washington Post Co 1150 15th St NW Washington DC 20071-0001*

STEPPLER, HOWARD ALVEY, agronomist; b. Morden, Man., Can., Nov. 8, 1918; s. Alvey Morden and Sophia (Doern) S.; m. Phyllis Ivy Parsonage, May 10, 1945; 1 child, Glenn. B.S., U. Man., 1941; M.Sc., McGill U., 1948, Ph.D., 1955. Research scientist Agr. Can. Research, 1948-49; asst. prof. agronomy McGill U., 1949-57, prof., 1957-84, prof. emeritus, 1984—, chmn. agronomy dept., 1955-70, chmn. dept. plant sci., 1976-84; agrl. advisor Can. Internat. Devel. Agy., 1970-71; trustee Centro Internacional Agricultura Tropical Colombia, 1972-78, Internat. Svc. Nat. Agrl. Rsch., The Hague, 1980-84, Agrl. Devel. Coun. N.Y., 1977-85, Internat. Livestock Ctr. for Africa, Ethiopia, 1984-89; trustee Internat. Coun. Rsch. in Agroforestry, 1983-91, chmn. bd., 1984-91; interim dir. gen. Internat. Coun. for Rsch. in Agroforestry, Nairobi, 1980-81; trustee Internat. Rice Rsch. Inst., 1988-93; founding bd. dirs. So. African Ctr. Coordination in Agrl. Rsch., Botswana, 1984-85. Capt. arty. Royal Can. Arty., 1942-46. Internat. Devel. Research Centre sr. Research fellow, 1973-74. Fellow Agrl. Inst. Can. (pres. 1964-65, Internat. Agrl. Recognition award 1994); mem. Am. Soc. Agronomy, Crop Sci. Soc. Am., Can. Soc. Agronomy (pres. 1957-58, Disting. Agronomist award 1993), Rotary. Office: 21111 Lakeshore Rd, Sainte Anne de Bellevue, PQ Canada H9X 3V9

STEPTOE, MARY LOU, lawyer; b. Washington, July 15, 1949; d. Philip Pendleton and Irene (Hellen) S.; m. Peter E. Carson, Sept. 1986; children: Elizabeth Maud, Julia Grace. BA, Occidental Coll., 1971; JD, U. Va., 1974. Bar: Va., 1974, Supreme Ct., 1987, D.C. 1996. Staff atty., Bur. of Competition FTC, Washington, 1974-79, atty. advisor to commr., 1979-86, exec. asst. to chmn., 1988-89, assoc. dir., Bur. of Competition, 1989-90, dep. dir., 1990-92, acting dir., 1992-95, dep. dir., 1995-96; ptnr. Skadden Arps Slate Meagher & Flom, Washington, D.C.

STERBAN, RICHARD ANTHONY, singer; b. Camden, N.J., Apr. 24, 1943; s. Edward Joseph and Victoria Marie (Giordano) S.; children: Richard Alan, Douglas Scott, Christopher Patrick. Student, Trenton State Coll. coowner Silverline-Goldline Music Pub. Cos.; partner Nashville Sounds, Greensboro Hornets, baseball teams. Mem. gospel singing groups; mem. Stamps Quartet, bass singer, ptnr., Oak Ridge Boys, 1972—; albums include Y'All Come Back Saloon, 1977, Room Service, 1978, Oak Ridge Boys Have Arrived, 1979, Together, 1980, Greatest Hits, 1980, Fancy Free, 1981, Bobbie Sue, 1982, Oak Ridge Boys Christmas, 1982, American Made, 1983, Deliver, 1984, Greatest Hits II, 1984, Step On Out, 1985, Seasons, 1986, Christmas Again, 1986, Where The Fast Lane Ends, 1987, Heartbeat, 1987, Monongahela, 1988, Unstoppable, 1991, The Long Haul, 1992, Back to Back, 1994. Recipient with group: Grammy awards, Am. Music award for Country Group of Yr., 1982, Best Country Video award , Everday, 1985; named Best Vocal Group Acad. Country Music, 1977, 79, Best Country Group of Yr. AGVA, 1981, Number One Country Group Billboard mag., 1978, 80, Vocal Group of the Yr. Country Music Assn., 1978. Mem. Country Music Assn., AFTRA, Nat. Acad. Rec. Arts and Scis., Acad. Country Music. Office: care Oak Ridge Boys Jim Halsey Co PO Box 606498 Oklahoma City OK 73146-0648*

STERLING, DAVID MARK, graphic designer; b. Okla., Apr. 28, 1951; s. Paul J. and Roberta Myrtice (Rousseau) S. BA, Oklahoma City U., 1973; MFA, Cranbrook Acad. Art, Bloomfield Hills, Mich., 1978. Exhibit designer Omniplex, Oklahoma City, 1973-76; art dir. Indsl. Design Mag., N.Y.C., 1979-81; prin. Doublespace, N.Y.C., 1982-94; founder, prin. World Studio and World Studio Found., N.Y.C., 1992—; graphic design faculty Sch. of Visual Arts, N.Y.C., 1992—. Pub. mags. Fetish, 1979-81, Sphere, 1994—; works included in books: Graphic Style: From Victorian to Post-Modern, 1988, New American Design, 1988, Low Budget/High Quality Design, 1990, Cranbrook Design: The New Discourse, 1990, Contemporary Graphic Design, 1991, Mixing Messages: Graphic Design in Contemporary Culture, 1996; represented in permanent collections at Cranbrook Acad. Art, Libr. of Congress, Michael C. Rockefeller Arts Ctr., Cooper Hewitt Nat. Design Mus., Smithsonian Instn. Recipient Am. Inst. Graphic Arts awards for Cover Show, N.Y., 1984, for Comm. Graphics, N.Y., 1986, 90; recipient Type Dirs. Club award, 1990, 92, Best of Category award Design Rev., N.Y., 1986, Am. Assn. of Mus., 1986, 88, Am. Ctr. for Design, 1990, Indsl. Design Rev. award, 1985, 86, 88, 93, N.Y. Festival awards, Bronze Apple award Indsl. Designers Soc. Am., 1996; featured Internat. Design Mag., ID40, 1996. Democrat. Office: World Studio Ste 602 19 W 21st St Rm 602 New York NY 10010-6805

STERLING, DONALD EUGENE, retired civil engineer; b. Rootville, Pa., May 30, 1939; s. Blanche Marie (Phelps) Vanik; m. Janet Leigh Wotring, Apr. 23, 1983. A in Engring., Pa. State U., 1966; BSCE, W.Va. Inst. Tech., 1981; MS in Engring., W.Va. Coll. Grad. Studies, Charleston, 1987. Cert. engr. technician. Hwy. drafting technician W.Va. Dept. Transp., Charleston, 1965-67, hwy. engr. technician, 1967-82, design rev. engr., 1982-89, sr. rev. engr., 1989-94; civil engr. Woolpert Cons., Charleston, W.Va., 1994-96; retired, 1996. Tutor Charleston Dist. Outreach Ministries, 1981-83, counselor Camp For Under Privileged Children, 1982; treas., v.p. Kanawha City Midget Football Team, 1978. Sgt. USAF, 1959-63, with Pa. Nat. Guard, 1956-59. Recipient certs. Appreciation Kanawha City Midget Football Team, 1978, Charleston Dist. Outreach Ministries, 1981-83. Mem. ASCE (W.Va. sect. pres. 1990-91, v.p. 1989-90; pres. Charleston Br. 1988-89, sec., treas. 1987-88; corr. mem. nat. com. on employment conditions 1989-91). Democrat. Methodist. Home: 821 Scenic Dr Charleston WV 25311-1522

STERLING, DONALD JUSTUS, JR., retired newspaper editor; b. Portland, Oreg., Sept. 27, 1927; s. Donald Justus and Adelaide (Armstrong) S.; m. Julie Ann Courteol, June 7, 1963; children: Sarah, William, John. A.B., Princeton U., 1948; postgrad. (Nieman fellow), Harvard U., 1955-56. Reporter Denver Post, 1948-52; news staff mem. Oreg. Jour., Portland, 1952-82; editor Oreg. Jour., 1972-82; asst. to pub. The Oregonian, 1982-92, ret., 1992. Pres. Tri-County Community Coun., 1972-73. Recipient Izaak Walton League Golden Beaver award, 1969, Edith Knight Hill award, 1978, Jessie Laird Brodie award Planned Parenthood Assn., 1983, McCall award Women in Communications, 1987, Roger W. Williams Freedom of Info. award Oreg. Newspaper Pubs. Assn., 1989; English-Speaking Union traveling fellow, 1959. Mem. Oreg. Hist. Soc. (pres. 1977-79), Mazamas, Lang Syne Soc., City Club (Portland pres. 1973-74), Multnomah Athletic, Dial Elm Cannon (Princeton), Phi Beta Kappa. Home: 1718 SW Myrtle St Portland OR 97201-2300

STERLING, DONALD T., professional basketball team executive; b. Chgo.. Lawyer L.A. (formerly San Diego) Clippers, Nat. Basketball Assn., owner, also chmn. bd. Office: care LA Clippers LA Meml Sports Arena 3939 S Figueroa St Los Angeles CA 90037-1200*

STERLING, KEIR BROOKS, historian, educator; b. N.Y.C., Jan. 30, 1934; s. Henry Somers and Louise Noel (de Wetter) S.; BS, Columbia U., 1961, M.A., 1963, Profl. Diploma, 1965, PhD, 1973; m. Anne Cox Diller, Apr. 3, 1961; children: Duncan Diller, Warner Strong, Theodore Craig. Asst. to dean Sch. Gen. Studies, Columbia U., N.Y.C., 1959-65, rsch. grantee, Eng., 1965-66; instr. in history Pace U., N.Y.C. and Pleasantville, N.Y., 1966-71, asst. prof., 1971-74, assoc. prof., 1974-77, adj. prof., 1977—; ordnance br. historian U.S. Army Ordnance Ctr. and Sch., Aberdeen Proving Ground, Md., 1983-94, U.S. Army Combined Arms Support Command, Ft. Lee, Va., 1994—; lectr. in gen. counseling Bklyn. Coll., City U. N.Y., 1967-68; asst. acad. dean, adj. asst. prof. history, coord. Am. studies program, dir. summer session Marymount Coll., Tarrytown, N.Y., 1968-71; asst. dean Rockland C.C., SUNY, Suffern, 1971-73; vis. prof. Mercy Coll., Westchester C.C., King's Coll., Nyack Coll., U. Wis., 1971, 75, 78-80, 83, Harford (Md.) C.C., 1987-94; adj. instr. Army Logistics Mgmt. Coll., Ft. Lee, Va., 1995—; coproject dir. Am. Ornithologists Union Centennial Hist. Project, 1976-89; cons. Arno Press, Inc., 1973-78, Coun. State Colls. of N.J., 1974-75, NSF, 1983—, Am. Trust for Brit. Libr., 1986-89; active Columbia U. Seminar on History and Philosophy of Sci., 1976—; archivist, historian mem. steering com. sect. mammalogy Internat. Union Biol. Scis., 1985—. Served with U.S. Army, 1954-56. Grantee Theodore Roosevelt Meml. Fund, Am. Mus. Natural History, 1967, Nat. Geog. Soc., 1977, NSF/Am. Soc. Mammalogists, 1978, NSF, 1981-82, IREX, 1982, mem. Archives and 75th Anniversary Coms. Mem. Am. Soc. Mammalogists, Am. Ornithologists Union (cochmn. Centennial Hist. Com., mem. Archives Com., grantee, 1976, 77), Am. Soc. Environ. History (sec., mem. governing bd., editor newsletter), Rhinebeck (N.Y.) Hist. Soc. (trustee, pres. 1980-83), Harford County Com. of Md. Hist. Trust, Harford County Hist. Dist. Commn. (v.p. 1987-94), Hist. Soc. Harford County (bd. dirs. 1989-94), Assn. Bibliography of History (mem. coun. 1994—), Phi Alpha Theta, Sigma Tau Delta, Phi Delta Kappa. Democrat. Episcopalian. Author: Last of the Naturalists: The Career of C. Hart Merriam, 1974, 77; editor: Notes on the Animals of North America (B.S. Barton), 1974; assoc. editor Am. Nat. Biog., 1989—; editor, contbr.: Natural Sciences in America, 1974, 68 vols., 1974, Biologists and Their World, 1978, 77 vols.; gen. editor, contbr.: The International History of Mammalogy, 1987—; sr. editor, contbr. (with R. Harmond, G. Cevasco and L. Hammond) Biographical Dictionary of American and Canadian Naturalists and Environmentalists, 1997; editor, contbr. to numerous works in history Am. natural scis. and Am. mil. history. Home: 7104 Wheeler Rd Richmond VA 23229-6939 Office: 3901 A Ave Ste 100 Fort Lee VA 23801-1807

STERLING, RAYMOND LESLIE, civil engineering educator, researcher, consultant; b. London, Apr. 19, 1949; came to U.S., 1966; s. Richard Howard and Joan Valeria (Skinner) S.; m. Linda Lee Lundquist, Aug. 8, 1970 (div. Sept. 1982); children: Paul, Juliet, Erika; m. Janet Marie Kjera, Aug. 20, 1983; 1 child, Zoey. B in Civil and Structural Engring. with 1st class honors, U. Sheffield, Eng., 1970; MS in Geol. Engring., U. Minn., 1975, PhDCE, 1977. Registered civil engr., Minn.; chartered structural engr., Eng. Engr. trainee Met. Water Bd., London, 1968; civil engr. Egil Wefald and Assocs., Cons. Engrs., Mpls., 1969-71; structural engr. Husband and Co., Cons. Engrs., Eng., 1971-73; rsch. asst. U. Minn., Mpls., 1973-77, dir. Underground Space Ctr., 1977-95, asst. prof. dept. civil and mineral engring., 1977-83, assoc. prof., 1983-95; project. coord., structural engr. Setter, Leach and Lindstrom, Inc., Mpls., 1976-77; prin. cons. Itasca Cons. Group, Inc., Mpls., 1981-94; prof. civil engring. La. Tech. U., Ruston, 1995—, dir. Trenchless Tech. Ctr., 1995—; vice-chmn. U.S. Nat. com. on tunneling tech. NRC, NAS, 1990-91, chmn. 1992-94, mem. com. on infrastructure, 1991-93, mem. bd. infrastructure and the constructed environment, 1994-96; acting co-dir. Minn. Cold Climate Bldg. Rsch. Ctr. U. Minn., 1987-89, co-dir. Bldg. Energy Rsch. Ctr., 1986, mem. speaker's bur., active numerous other u. coms.; mem. energy adv. com. Legis. Com. on Minn. Resources, 1989-95; mem. com. on moisture control in bldgs. U.S. Bldg. Thermal Envelope Coordinating Coun., 1985-86; mem. program planning com. on bldg. founds. U.S. Dept. Energy, 1985-95; mem. adv. bd. for energy efficient residence demonstration project Nat. Assn. Home Builders, 1980; mem. Gov.'s Exxon Oil Overcharge Adv. Task Force, 1986, Mpls. Energy Future Com., 1980-81, Scientist's Inst. for Pub. Info., N.Y.; cons. U.S. Army Corps. Engrs., UN, N.Y., Opus Corp., Mpls., Dames & Moore Internat., London, City of Mpls., Larson Engring., White Bear, Minn., Pilsbury Co., Mpls., Colgate Divsn. Sch., Rochester, N.Y., many others; adv. prof. Chongqing Jianzhu U., Sichuan, People's Republic China, 1985—; vis. rschr. Nat. Inst. Pollution and Resources MITI, Japan, 1991; vis. prof. U. Mo., Rolla, 1979; Shimizu prof. civil and mineral engring., U. Minn., 1988-95; adv. prof. Tongji U., Shanghai, 1996—; mem. eminent speaker program Instn. Engrs., Australia, 1993; lectr., presenter numerous profl. meetings. Author: Earth Sheltered Housing Design: Guidelines, Examples and References, 1978, transl. into Chinese, French, Spanish and Russian, 2d. edit., 1985, (with others) Earth Sheltered Community Design: The Design of Energy-Efficient Residential Communities, 1980 (award for Best Book in Architecture and Urban Planning Profl. and Scholarly div. Assn. Am. Pubs. 1981), transl. into Spanish,

1981, Underground Building Design, 1983, translated into Japanese and Russian, others, Building Foundation Handbook, 1988, Underground Space Design, 1993, others; editor: (with others) Key Questions in Rock Mechanics: Proc. 29th U.S. Symposium on Rock Mechanics, 1988; contbr. articles to profl. jours. including Jour. Agrl. Engring., Internat. Jour. Rock Mechanics and Mining Scis., Exptl. Mechanics, many others. Recipient Young Engr. of Yr. award Minn. Fedn. Engring. Soc., 1982, Applied Rsch. award in rock mechanics NRC; elected fgn. mem. Acad. Engring. of Russian Fedn., 1993; grantee Shimizu Constrn. Co., 1987-93, Nat. Assn. Homebuilders, 1989, U.S. Dept. Energy, 1989-90, NSF, 1991, Minn. Dept. Transp., 1991, ASHRAE, 1991-92, many others. Fellow ASCE (pres. Minn. sect. 1990-91, bd. dirs. 1985-92, Young Civil Engr. of Yr. award 1982), Instn. Civil Engrs., Inst. Structural Engrs., Royal Soc. Arts, Mfrs. & Commerce; mem. NSPE, Am. Underground Constrn. Assn., Internat. Tunneling Assn. (coordinating editor jour. 1986—, co-sr. editor 1996—, vice animateur working group on costs/benefits of subsurface utilization), N.Am. Soc. Trenchless Tech. (bd. dirs. 1996—, treas. 1997—). Achievements include research in underground construction, underground space utilization, trenchless technology, rock mechanics, and energy use in buildings. Office: Trenchless Technology Ctr Louisiana Tech U PO Box 10348 Ruston LA 71272

STERLING, RICHARD LEROY, English and foreign language educator; b. Atlantic City, Feb. 18, 1941; s. Richard Leroy and Anne (Bass) S. BA, Am. U., 1968; MA, Cath. U., 1971; PhD, Howard U., 1990. Tchr. French and English, adult and continuing edn. D.C. Pub. Schs., Washington, 1969-71, 76-83; instr. French Howard U., Washington, 1973-76, grad. teaching asst., 1983-85, instr., lectr. in French, 1985-89; tchr. English Community-Based Orgns., D.C. Pub. Schs., Washington, 1989-91; asst. prof. French and English Bowie (Md.) State U., 1991-97, assoc. prof. French, 1997—; tchr. summer enrichment program for gifted children Sch. Edn., Howard U., summers 1985, 86; tchr. ESL, D.C. Pub. Schs., summer, 1989, 94; asst. coord. Humanities Immersion Program, Project Access for H.S. Students, Bowie State U., summer 1997; vice chmn. World Centennial Conf.; French, Am. and Planetary Dimensions of Saint-John Perse, U. D.C., 1987; mem. adv. coun. Northeast Conf. Teaching Fgn. Langs; humanities judge 1997 NAACP-ACT-SO Competition; presenter in field. Author: The Prose Works of Saint-John Perse: Towards an Understanding of His Poetry, 1994; author articles and book reviews. Active Assn. Democratique des Francais a L.Etranger, 1988—, Senegal friendship com. Office Cmty. and Ethnic Affairs, Prince George's County Govt., Md., 1993-94, Inst. for Haitian Cultural and Sci. Affairs, 1992-94, local arrangements com. Conf. Coll. Composition and Communication, Washington, 1995; membership com. and outreach com. St. John's Ch., Washington, 1993, ch. growth com., 1995. With U.S . Army, 1964-66. Mem. MLA, Coll. Lang. Assn., Middle Atlantic Writers Assn. (chmn. essay contest com. 1995—), Samuel Beckett Soc., Societe des Professeurs Francais et Francophones d'Amerique, Zora Neale Hurston Soc., Am. Assn. Tchrs. French (sec.-treas. Washington chpt. 1986-90), Md. Fgn. Lang. Assn. (bd. dirs.), Friends Superior Ct. Washington D.C. (bd. dirs.), Pi Delta Phi, Sigma Tau Delta. Democrat. Episcopalian. Avocations: classical music, history, travel. Home: 4235 Alton Pl NW Washington DC 20016-2017 Office: Bowie State U Dept English & Modern Langs Bowie MD 20715

STERMER, DUGALD ROBERT, designer, illustrator, writer, consultant; b. Los Angeles, Dec. 17, 1936; s. Robert Newton and Mary (Blue) S.; m. Jeanie Kortum; children: Dugald, Megan, Chris, Colin, Crystal. B.A., UCLA, 1960. Art dir., v.p. Ramparts mag., 1965-70; freelance designer, illustrator, writer, cons. San Francisco, 1970—; founder Pub. Interest Communications, San Francisco, 1974; pres. Frisco Pub Group Ltd.; commr. San Francisco Art Commn., 1997—; bd. dirs. Am. Inst. Graphic Arts; mem. San Francisco Art Commn., 1997—. Cons. editor: Communication Arts mag., 1974-90; designer: Oceans mag., 1976-82; editor: The Environment, 1972, Vanishing Creatures, 1980; author: The Art of Revolution, 1970, Vanishing Creatures, 1980, Vanishing Flora, 1994, Birds and Bees, 1994; designer 1984 Olympic medals; illustration exhbn. Calif. Acad. Scis., 1986; one-man show Jernigan Wicker Gallery, San Francisco, 1996. Mem. Grand Jury City and County San Francisco, 1989; bd. dirs. Delancey St. Found., 1990—. Recipient various medals, awards for design and illustration nat. and internat. competitions. Office: 600 The Embarcadero # 204 San Francisco CA 94107

STERN, ARTHUR PAUL, electronics company executive, electrical engineer; b. Budapest, Hungary, July 20, 1925; came to U.S., 1951, naturalized, 1956; s. Leon and Bertha (Frankfurter) S.; m. Edith M. Samuel; children: Daniel, Claude, Jacqueline. Diploma in Elec. Engring., Swiss Fed. Inst. Tech., Zurich, 1948; MSEE, Syracuse U., 1955. Mgr. electronic devices and applications lab. Gen. Electric Co., Syracuse, N.Y., 1957-61; dir. engring. Martin Marietta Corp., Balt., 1961-64; dir. ops. Bunker Ramo Corp., Canoga Park, Calif., 1964-66; v.p., gen. mgr. advanced products div. Magnavox, Torrance, Calif., 1966-79, pres. Magnavox Advanced Products and Systems Co., Torrance, 1980-90; vice chmn., bd. dirs. Magnavox Govt. and Indsl. Electronics Co., Ft. Wayne, Ind., 1987-90; pres. Ea. Beverly Hills Corp., 1991—, Calif.-Israel C. of C., 1994—; non-resident staff mem. MIT, 1956-59; instr. Gen. Elec. Bus. Mgmt., 1955-57. Chmn. engring. div. United Jewish Appeal, Syracuse, 1955-57; mem. adv. bd. dept. elec. engring. U. Calif., Santa Barbara, 1980-92; mem. Sch. Engring. Adv. and Devel. Council Calif. State U., Long Beach, 1985-90. Co-author: Transistor Circuit Engineering, 1957, Handbook of Automation, Computation and Control, 1961; also articles; U.S., fgn. patentee in field. Fellow AAAS, IEEE (pres. 1975, bd. dirs., officer 1970-77, guest editor spl. issue IEEE Trans. on Circuit Theory 1956, invited guest editor spl. issue Procs. IEEE on Integrated Electronics 1964, Centennial medal 1984, chmn. com. on U.S. competitiveness policy). Jewish.

STERN, CARL LEONARD, former news correspondent, federal official; b. N.Y.C., Aug. 7, 1937; s. Hugo and Frances (Taft) S.; m. Joy Elizabeth Nathan, Nov. 27, 1960; children: Lawrence, Theodore. A.B., Columbia U., 1958, M.S., 1959; J.D., Cleve. State U., 1966, J.D. (hon.), 1975; J.D. (hon.), New Eng. Coll. Law, 1977. Bar: Ohio 1966, D.C. 1968, U.S. Supreme Ct. 1969. Law corr. NBC News, Washington, 1967-93; dir. Office of Pub. Affairs U.S. Dept. Justice, Washington, 1993-96; Shapiro Prof. of Media and Pub. Affairs George Washington U., 1996—; lectr. Nat. Jud. Coll.; adj. prof. George Washington U., Stanford U. Editorial bd.: The Dist. Lawyer. Mem. Dept. Transp. Task Force on Assistance to Families in Aviation Disasters, 1997—. Recipient Peabody award, 1974, Emmy award, 1974, Gavel award, 1969, 74, Headliner Club award, 1991, Edmond J. Randloph award U.S. Dept. Justice. Mem. ABA (vice chmn. criminal justice sect. com. on criminal justice and the media, gov., forum com. on communications law, working group intelligence requirements and criminal code reform), AFTRA (nat. exec. bd. 1984-86, first v.p. Washington, Balt. chpt. 1985-87). Home: 2956 Davenport St NW Washington DC 20008-2165 Office: George Washington U 409C Academic Ctr 801 22nd St NW Washington DC 20052

STERN, CARL WILLIAM, JR., management consultant; b. San Francisco, Mar. 31, 1946; s. Carl William and Marjorie Aline (Gunst) S.; m. Karen Jaffe, Sept. 7, 1966 (div. Mar. 1972); 1 child, David; m. Holly Drick Hayes, Mar. 21, 1985; children: Kenneth, Matthew. BA, Harvard U., 1968; MBA, Stanford U., 1974. Cons. Boston Cons. Group, Inc., Menlo Park, Calif., 1974-77, mgr., 1977-78; mgr. Boston Cons. Group, Inc., London, 1978-80; v.p. Boston Cons. Group, Inc., Chgo., 1980-87, sr. v.p., 1987—. Lt. USNR, 1968-71. Office: Boston Consulting Group Inc 200 S Wacker Dr Chicago IL 60606

STERN, CHARLES, retired foreign trade company executive; b. Germany, Dec. 2, 1920; came to U.S., 1940, naturalized, 1943; s. Julius and Else (Br) S.; m. Eve Hamburger, Sept. 20, 1947 (dec. Apr. 1980); children—Enid S., June M. Matriculation, U. London, 1937. With J. Gerber & Co., Inc., N.Y.C., 1940—; asst. v.p. J. Gerber & Co., Inc., 1960-63, v.p., 1963-68, exec. v.p., 1968-74, pres., chief exec. officer, 1974-88, chmn., 1986-89, chmn. emeritus, 1989—, cons. Served with AUS, World War II. Mem. ASTM, Am. Inst. Imported Steel (past pres.).

STERN, CLAUDIO DANIEL, medical educator, embryological researcher; b. Montevideo, Uruguay, Feb. 9, 1954; came to U.S., 1994; s. Erico and Trude Stern. BSc with honors, U. Sussex, 1975, DPhil, 1978; MA, U. Oxford, 1985, DSc, 1994. Asst. prof. anatomy dept. Cambridge (England) U., 1984-85; assoc. prof. dept. human anatomy U. Oxford (England), 1985-93; prof., chmn. dept. genetics and devel. Coll. Physicians and Surgeons Columbia U., N.Y.C., 1994—. Contbr. articles to profl. jours.; mng. editor Mechanisms of Devel.; mem. editorial adv. bd. Devel.; mem. editorial bd. Internat. Jour. Devel. Biology. Rsch. fellow U. Coll. London, 1978-84, fellow Christ Ch. Coll., 1985-93. Office: Columbia U Dept Genetics & Devel 701 W 168th St New York NY 10032-2704

STERN, DANIEL, author, executive, educator; b. N.Y.C., Jan. 18, 1928; s. Morris and Dora (Hochman) S.; m. Gloria Shapiro, Nov. 9, 1963; 1 son, Eric Branfman. Sr. v.p., mng. dir., mem. bd. mgmt. McCann-Erickson Advt., Inc., N.Y.C., 1964-69; v.p. advt. and publicity worldwide, also dir. Warner Bros., 1969-72; v.p., dir. mktg. Longchamps, Inc., N.Y.C., 1972-73; v.p., creative dir. Lubar-Southard, Inc., N.Y.C., 1973; fellow Ctr. for Humanities, Wesleyan U., 1969, vis. prof. letters and English, 1976-79; v.p. promotion East Coast CBS Entertainment, N.Y.C., 1979-86; pres. entertainment divsn. McCaffrey & McCall, Advt., N.Y.C., 1986; prof. English and creative writing U. Houston, 1992—, Cullen disting. prof. English, 1993—; dir. Humanities, 92nd St. YMHA, 1988. Author: Girl with Glass Heart, 1953, The Guests of Fame, 1955, Miss America, 1959, Who Shall Live, Who Shall Die, 1963 (Internat. Remembrance award for fiction Bergen Belsen Assn. 1973), After the War, 1967, The Suicide Academy, 1968, The Rose Rabbi, 1971, Final Cut, 1975, An Urban Affair, 1980, Twice Told Tales, 1989 (Richard and Hinda Rosenthal Fiction award AAAL 1990), Twice Upon a Time, 1992. With U.S. Army, 1946-47. Recipint Brazos prize for best short story Tex. Inst. Letters, 1996. Mem. PEN, Nat. Book Critics Circle, Author's League.

STERN, DANIEL ALAN, business management consultant; b. Bklyn., Aug. 28, 1944; s. William Joseph and Rita (Winegarten) S.; m. Gail Lynn Eddy, June 28, 1978. BS, Cornell U., 1965, PhD, 1971; MS, U. So. Calif., 1967. Cert. coll. teaching credential, Calif. Mem. sr. staff Hughes Aircraft Co., Culver City, Calif., 1965-73; mgr. digital signal processing TRW, Redondo Beach, Calif., 1973-79; pres. Martin & stern, Inc., Manhattan Beach, Calif., 1979-83; v.p. corp. devel. ROCKCOR, Inc., Redmond, Wash., 1983-85; v.p. advanced systems Rockcor group Olin Corp., Redmond, 1985-87; v.p. advanced def. systems Olin Corp., East Alton, Ill., 1987-89, v.p. tech., 1989-90; v.p. parent co. Olin Corp., Stamford, Conn., 1990-92, chief scientist, 1991-92; ind. cons., 1992—; bd. dirs. Secure Trans., Inc., Ponoma, Calif.; cons. Mertec, 1985—, United Technologies, 1993—; mem. bd. advisors U. Conn. Advanced Materials Inst., Storrs, 1991-92; mem. tech. coun. Conf. Bd., N.Y., 1992. Councilman City of Manhattan Beach, 1990-91, mayor pro tem, 1991-92, mayor, 1992-93; bd. dirs. Congregation Tifereth Jacob. Hughes fellow Hughes Aircraft Co., 1966. Mem. IEEE, Assn. U. S. Army, Assn. Old Crows, League Calif. Cities. Republican. Jewish. Avocations: motorcycle riding, shooting. Home and Office: 473 32nd St Manhattan Beach CA 90266-3928

STERN, DAVID JOEL, basketball association executive; b. N.Y.C., Sept. 22, 1942; s. William and Anna (Bronstein) S.; m. Dianne Bock, Nov. 27, 1963; children: Andrew, Eric. B.A., Rutgers U., 1963; LL.B., Columbia U., 1966. Bar: N.Y. 1963. Assoc. Proskauer Rose Goetz & Mendelsohn, N.Y.C., 1966-74, ptnr., 1974-78; gen. counsel Nat. Basketball Assn., N.Y.C., 1978-80, exec. v.p. bus. and legal affairs, 1980-84, commr., 1984—. Trustee Beth Israel Med. Ctr., 1985—, Rutgers U. Found., 1987—, Columbia U., 1992—; mem. Martin Luther King, Jr. Fed. Holiday Commn., 1988—, White House Conf. for a Drug-Free Am., 1988; bd. dirs. NAACP, 1990-93. Mem. ABA, N.Y. State Bar Assn., Assn. Bar City N.Y. (chmn. com. on entertainment and sports 1983-86). Office: NBA Olympic Tower 645 5th Ave New York NY 10022-5910*

STERN, DIANE, broadcaster; b. Salem, Mass., May 19, 1950; d. Henderson Arthur and Marjorie Farnsworth (Green) S.; m. Neil Mark Ungerleider, Aug. 24, 1980; 1 child, Sarah Delap. BA in German Lang. & Lit., Boston U., 1972. Cert. tchr., Mass. Salesman, newscaster WMLO Radio, Danvers, Mass., 1975; news reporter, anchor WMEX (then WITS Radio), Boston, 1975-78; morning news anchor WEEI-CBS Radio, Boston, 1978-83; morning and afternoon anchor WBZ Radio & TV, Boston, 1983—. Author, rschr., narrator: (radio series) Fact or Fiction, 1979-81, Summer Jobs: The Real World Connection, 1984. Fundraiser My Bros. Table, Lynn, Mass., 1986—; telethon host, celebrity guest Children's Hosp. Telethon, Boston, 1983—. Recipient Comm. and Leadership award Toastmasters Internat., Boston, 1981, Reporting Individual Achievement award UPI, 1987; named Finalist Best Newscaster, Internat. Radio Festival N.Y., 1987. Mem. Mass. Soc. Mayflower Descendants, Mass. Audubon Soc., Trustees of the Reservations. Congregationalist. Avocations: genealogy, gardneing, improvization on piano, skiing, reading. Office: WBZ-CBS 1170 Soldiers Field Rd Boston MA 02134-1004

STERN, EDWARD ABRAHAM, physics educator; b. Detroit, Sept. 19, 1930; s. Jacob Munich and Rose (Kravitz) S.; m. Sylvia Rita Sidell, Oct. 30, 1955; children: Hilary, Shari, Miri. BS, Calif. Tech., 1951, PhD, 1955. Post-doctoral fellow Calif. Tech., Pasadena, 1955-57; asst. prof. U. Md., College Park, 1957-61, assoc. prof., 1961-64, prof., 1964-65; prof. U. Wash., Seattle, 1965—. Contbr. over 200 articles to profl. jours.; editor; three books. Recipient B. Warren award Am. Crystallography Assn., 1979; named Guggenheim fellow, Cambridge, Eng., 1963-64, NSF Sr. Post-doctoral fellow, Haifa, Israel, 1970-71, Fulbright fellow, Jerusalem, Israel, 1985-86. Fellow AAAS, Am. Physical Soc. Achievements include patent for x-ray focusing device; development of x-ray absorption fine structure techniques; research on surface plasmons, nonlinear reflection from surfaces, electronic properties of alloys, structural phase transition. Office: U Wash Dept Physics Box 351560 Seattle WA 98195-1560

STERN, FRITZ RICHARD, historian, educator; b. Breslau, Germany, Feb. 2, 1926; came to U.S., 1938, naturalized, 1947; s. Rudolf A. and Catherine (Brieger) S.; m. Margaret J. Bassett, Oct. 11, 1947 (div. 1992); children: Frederick P., Katherine Stern Brennan; m. Elisabeth Niebuhr Sifton, Jan. 1, 1996. BA, Columbia U., 1946, MA, 1948, PhD, 1953; DLitt (hon.), Oxford U., 1985; LLD (hon.), New Sch. for Social Rsch., 1997. Lectr., instr. Columbia U., 1946-51, faculty, 1953—, prof. history, 1963—, Seth Low prof. history, 1967-92, univ. prof., 1992-96, provost, 1980-83; acting asst. prof. Cornell U., 1951-53; univ. prof. emeritus Columbia U., 1997—; tchr. Free U. Berlin, 1954, Yale U., 1963; permanent vis. prof. U. Konstanz, West Germany, 1966—; sr. adviser U.S. Embassy, Bonn, 1993-94; Élie Halévy prof. U. Paris, spring 1979; Phi Beta Kappa vis. scholar, 1979-80; Tanner lectr. Yale, 1993. Author: The Politics of Cultural Despair, 1961, The Failure of Illiberalism-Essays in the Political Culture of Modern Germany, 1972, rev. edit., 1992, Gold and Iron: Bismarck, Bleichroeder and the Bldg. of the German Empire, 1977 (recipient Lionel Trilling award Columbia U.), Dreams and Delusions: The Drama of German History, 1987; editor: The Varieties of History, 1956, 71, (with L. Krieger) The Responsibility of Power, 1967; mem. editorial bd. Foreign Affairs, 1978-92; contbr. articles to profl. jours.; reviewer Fgn. Affairs, 1963-95. Trustee German Marshall Fund, 1981—, Aspen Inst. of Berlin, 1983—; senator Deutsche Nationalstiftung, 1994—; mem. Trilateral Commn., 1983-90. Decorated Officer's Cross Order of Merit Fed. Republic of Germany; fellow Center Advanced Behavioral Scis., 1957-58; fellow Social Sci. Research Council, 1960-61; fellow Am. Council Learned Socs., 1966-67; fellow Netherlands Inst. Advanced Study, 1972-73; mem. Nuffield Coll., Oxford, 1966-67, Inst. Advanced Study Princeton, 1969-70; Guggenheim fellow, 1969-70; Ford Found. grantee, 1976-77; vis. scholar Russell Sage Found., 1989, spring 1993; recipient Leopold-Lucas-prize Evang. Faculty U. Tübingen, 1984. Mem. Am. Hist. Assn., AAAS, Am. Philos. Soc., Coun. Fgn. Rels., Deutsche Akademie für Sprache und Dichtung (corr.), Berlin Brandenburgische Akademie der Wissenschaften (corr.), Orden Pour le Mérite, Germany, Phi Beta Kappa (senator-at-large 1973-78). Club: Century (N.Y.C.). Home: 15 Claremont Ave New York NY 10027-6814

STERN, GAIL FRIEDA, historical association director; b. Atlantic City, May 18, 1950; d. Herbert and Faith (Beldegreen) Stern; m. Irwin Allen Popowsky (div.); m. Shawn Paul Aubitz, Sept. 20, 1987; 1 child, Jonathan. Student, Brown U., 1972; postgrad., U. Pa., 1973. Asst. in decorative arts Phila. Mus. Art, 1972-75; asst. curator Wheaton Mus. Glass, Millville, N.J., 1973-74; assoc. dir. Pa. Humanities Coun., Phila., 1976-79; mus. curator The Balch Inst. for Ethnic Studies, Phila., 1979-83, mus. dir., 1984-93; dir. Hist. Soc. Princeton, N.J., 1993—; chair Pa. Task Force on Folk Arts and Culture, 1981-82; vice chmn. crafts panel Pa. Coun. on the Arts, Harrisburg, 1988-89; chair cultural conservation com., Pa. Heritage Affairs Commn., Harrisburg, 1990-92; participant Internat. Partnership in Mus., Singapore, 1991. Recipient pub. programming award N.J. Coun. Humanities, 1996. Mem. Mus. Coun. Phila. (v.p. 1982-83), Am. Assn. Mus./Internat. Coun. Mus. (bd. dirs.), N.J. Mus. Assn. (mem. bd. dirs.), Am. Assn. for State and Local History Awards (N.J. chair 1994-95). Home: 131 E Maple Ave Morrisville PA 19067-6235 Office: Hist Soc Princeton 158 Nassau St Princeton NJ 08542-7006

STERN, GARDNER, television writer and producer. Writer TV series, including Capital News, 1990, WIOU, 1991, Sisters, 1992; co-prodr. TV series N.Y.P.D. Blue, 1992— (Emmy award for outstanding drama series 1995). Office: care ICM 8942 Wilshire Blvd Beverly Hills CA 90211-1934*

STERN, GEOFFREY, lawyer, disciplinary counsel; b. Columbus, Ohio, Nov. 29, 1942; s. Leonard J. and Anastasia (Percin) S.; m. Barbara Shnider; children: Emily, Elizabeth; stepchildren: Courtney, Jennifer, Brian Feuer. Student, Williams Coll., 1960-63; BA cum laude, Ohio State U., 1965, JD summa cum laude, 1968. Bar: Ohio 1968. Assoc. Alexander, Ebinger, Holschuh & Fisher, Columbus, Ohio, 1968-72; ptnr. Folkerth, Calhoun, Webster & O'Brien, Columbus, Ohio, 1972-80, Arter & Hadden, Columbus, Ohio, 1980-93; disciplinary counsel Supreme Ct. of Ohio, 1993—; nat. coordinating counsel for asbestos litigation Combustion Engring. Inc. and Basic, Inc., 1985-93; lectr. on legal ethics and profl. responsibility; mem. Spl. Commn. to Review Ohio Ethics Rules, 1995—, Spl. Commn. on Legal Edn., 1995—. Sr. editor Ohio State Law Jour., 1967-68. Pres. Bexley (Ohio) City Coun., 1977-80, mem., 1973-80, mem. Bexley Civil Svc. Commn., 1983-85; v.p., trustee Creative Living, Columbus, 1981-89, Ohio Citizens Com. for Arts, Columbus, 1982-88; mem. Nat. Def. Com. on Asbestos in Bldgs. Litigation, 1986-92; pub. mem. Ohio Optical Dispensers Bd., Columbus, 1978-82. Recipient Am. Jurisprudence Evidence award Ohio State U. Coll. Law, 1967. Fellow Am. Bar Found., Columbus Bar Found., Ohio State Bar Found.; mem. Ohio State Bar Assn. (com. on legal ethics and profl. conduct, sec. 1981-90, vice chmn. 1990-92, chmn. 1992-93), Columbus Bar Assn. (profl. ethics com. 1975-86, 90-93), Order of Coif, Phi Beta Kappa, Pi Sigma Alpha. Home: 278 Crossing Creek N Columbus OH 43230-6108 Office: Disciplinary Counsel of Ohio Supreme Ct 175 S 3rd St Ste 280 Columbus OH 43215-5134

STERN, GERALD DANIEL, poet; b. Pitts., Feb. 22, 1925; s. Harry and Ida (Barach) S.; m. Patricia Miller, Sept. 12, 1952 (div.); children: Rachel, David. BA, U. Pitts., 1947; MA, Columbia U., 1949. English tchr., prin. Lake Grove (N.Y.) Sch., 1951-53; English tchr. Victoria Dr. Secondary Sch., Glasgow, Scotland, 1953-54; English instr. Temple U., Phila., 1956-63; assoc. prof. English Indiana (Pa.) U. of Pa., 1963-67; prof. English Somerset (N.J.) County Coll., 1968-82; prof. English, Writers' Workshop, U. Iowa, Iowa City, 1982—; lectr. Douglas Coll., New Brunswick, N.J., 1968; vis. poet Sarah Lawrence Coll., Bronxville, N.Y., 1978, U. Pitts., 1978; vis. prof. Columbia U., N.Y.C., 1980, Bucknell U., Lewisburg, Pa., 1988, NYU, 1989, 91, Princeton U., 1989; Fanny Hurst prof. Washington U., St. Louis, 1985; Coal chair creative writing U. Ala., Tuscaloosa, 1984. Author: (poetry) Pineys, 1971, The Naming of Beasts, 1972, Rejoicings: selected Poems 1966-72, 1973, Lucky Life, 1977 (Lamont Poetry selection 1977, Nat. Book Critics Cir. award for poetry nominee 1978), The Red Coal, 1981 (Melville Caine award Poetry Soc. Am. 1982), Paradise Poems, 1984, Lovesick, 1987, Two Long Poems, 1990, Leaving Another Kingdom: Selected Poems, 1990, Bread Without Sugar, 1992, Odd Mercy, 1995, (essays) Selected Essays, 1988. Guggenheim fellow, 1980, Am. Acad. Poets fellow, 1993; NEA grantee to be master poet for Pa. 1973-75, Creative Writing grantee, 1976, 81, 87, State of Pa. Creative Writing grantee, 1979; recipient Gov. award for excellence in arts State of Pa., 1980, Bess Hokin award Poetry, 1980, Bernard F. Connor's award Paris Rev., 1981, Am. Poetry Rev. award, 1982, Jerome J. Shestack Poetry prize Am. Poetry Rev., 1984, Ruth Lilly prize, 1996. Fellow Acad. Am. Poets. Office: U Iowa 436 EPB Iowa City IA 52242

STERN, GERALD DANIEL, lawyer; b. N.Y.C., May 16, 1933; s. Solomon Stern and Stella Schoen; m. Doris Gittelman Mar. 21, 1960 (dec. June 1996); children: Nelson M., Andrew L., Teri H. BA, NYU, 1954, LLB, 1957. Bar: N.Y. 1957, Calif. 1988, U.S. Ct. Appeals (2d cir.) 1959, U.S. Dist. Ct. (no. dist.) N.Y. 1965, U.S. Dist. Ct. D.C. 1969, U.S. Ct. Appeals (D.C. cir.) 1969, U.S. Dist. Ct. Md. 1970, U.S. Supreme Ct. 1970, U.S. Tax Ct. 1971, U.S. Ct. Appeals (9th cir.) 1987, U.S. Ct. Appeals (fed. cir.) 1987, U.S. Dist. Ct. (no. dist. Calif. 1987, so. dist. 1988). Assoc. Paul, Weiss, Rifkind, Wharton & Garrison, N.Y.C., 1957-67, ptnr., 1967-87; ptnr. Irell and Manella, Menlo Park, Calif., 1987-89, Brown & Bain, Palo Alto, Calif., 1989-91; of counsel Davis & Schroeder, Monterey, Calif., 1991-92, Law Office of Nelson M. Stern, N.Y.C. and Monterey, 1997—; adj. prof. law NYU, 1983-87. Author: The Naked First Lady — A Humorous History of Monterey Peninsula, 1992, Fog City Follies, 1995, Was it Worth Twenty-Four Dollars?, 1996, Waiting for the Tidal Wave, 1996, Giants in Gold and Grapes, 1996, Laughing at the Lawyers, 1996. Chmn. legal com., trustee Westchester Reform Temple, Scarsdale, N.Y., 1983-87. Mem. ABA, Beach Point Club, Boca West Club, Chamisol Tennis Club. Home and Office: 25493 Paseo De Cumbre Monterey CA 93940-6637 Office: 7th Fl 770 Lexington Ave Fl 7 New York NY 10021-8165

STERN, GERALD JOSEPH, advertising executive; b. Chgo., Nov. 1, 1925; s. Abraham and Mary (Spivak) S.; m. Sally R. Welham, May 28, 1950; children: Larry S., David J. B.S. in Journalism, U. Ill., 1949. Subscription sales promotion Esquire Mag., Chgo., 1949-50; v.p., creative dir. Marvin Gordon & Assos., Chgo., 1950-54; pres., chief exec. officer Stern, Walters/Earle Ludgin, Inc. (advt.), Chgo., Beverly Hills, Calif. and Ft. Lauderdale, Fla., from 1954, formerly chmn. bd., chief exec. officer, now ret.; bd. dir. Advance Leasing Corp., Ted Bates Adv. Inc.; Mem. Nat. Com. Improving Advt. Bd. dirs. Off-the-St. Club. Served with USAAF, 1943-46. Mem. Am. Assn. Advt. Agys. (treas. Chgo. div. 1973), Nat. Advt. Rev. Bd., Chgo. Advt. Club, Twin Orchard Country Club (dir., v.p.). Home: 726 Raleigh Rd Glenview IL 60025-4326

STERN, GERALD MANN, lawyer; b. Chgo., Apr. 5, 1937; s. Lloyd and Fannye (Wener) S.; m. Linda Stone, Dec. 20, 1969; children: Eric, Jesse, Maia. B.S. in Econs., U. Pa., 1958; LL.B. cum laude, Harvard, 1961. Bar: D.C. 1961, Calif. 1991, U.S. Supreme Ct. 1971. Trial atty. civil rights div. U.S. Dept. Justice, 1961-64; assoc. firm Arnold & Porter, Washington, 1964-68; ptnr. Arnold & Porter, 1969-76; founding ptnr. Rogovin, Stern & Huge, Washington, 1976-81; exec. v.p., sr. gen. counsel Occidental Petroleum Corp., Washington, 1981-82, L.A., 1982-92; spl. counsel fin. instn. fraud and health care fraud U.S. Dept. Justice, Washington, 1993-95; ind. legal cons. pvt. practice, Washington, 1995—; bd. dirs. Capital Bancorp. Author: The Buffalo Creek Disaster, 1976; co-author: Southern Justice, 1965, Narratives on Justice, 1997. Trustee Facing History and Ourselves, 1996—. Mem. ABA. Home and office: 3322 Newark St NW Washington DC 20008-3330

STERN, GUY, German language and literature educator, writer; b. Hildesheim, Germany, Jan. 14, 1922; came to U.S., 1937, naturalized, 1943; s. Julius and Hedwig (Silberberg) S.; m. Judith Owens, June 16, 1979; 1 child, Mark. B.A. in Romance Langs., Hofstra Coll., 1948; M.A. with honors in Germanic Langs., Columbia U., 1950, Ph.D. with honors, 1953. Grad. asst., then instr. Columbia U., 1948-55; asst. prof., then asso. prof. Denison U., Granville, Ohio, 1955-63; prof. German, dept. head U. Cin., 1964-73, dean univ., 1973-76; prof., chmn. Germanic and Slavic dept. U. Md., College Park, 1976-78; v.p., provost Wayne State U., Detroit, 1978-80; disting. prof. German Wayne State U., 1980—; guest prof. Goethe Inst., Freiburg U., summers 1963-66, 84, Frankfurt U., 1993, Leipzig U., 1997; adv. editor langs. and linguistics Dover Publs. Co-author: Brieflich Erzaehlt, 1956, Listen and Learn German, 1957, Say It in German, 1958, Uebung macht den Meister, 1959, An Invitation to German Poetry, 1960, Hints on Speaking German, 1961, Quick Change Pattern Drills, vol. I, 1962, vol. II, 1963, Hoer zu und Rat mit, 1964; author: Efraim Frisch: Zum Verstaendnis des Geistigen, 1964, War, Weimar and Literature, 1971, Alfred Neumann (anthology with biography), 1979, Literatur im Exil, 1989, Nazi Book Burning and the American Response, 1989,; Literarische Kultur im Exil (essay collection), 1997; editor: Konstellationen: Die besten Erzaehluhgen des Neuen Merkur, 1964; co-editor: Nelly Sachs Ausgewaehlte Gedichte, 1968; assoc. editor: Lessing Yearbook, 1970-72, edit. bd. 1972—; sr. editor, 1979-

81; contbr. articles on 18th and 20th century German lit. to profl. jours., also chpts. to books. Bd. dirs. Kurt Weill Found., sec., 1990—; bd. dirs. Leo Baeck Inst., 1967—, mem. exec. bd., 1978—; bd. dirs., chair acad. adv. com. Holocaust Meml. Mus. Greater Detroit; co-founder, pres. Lessing Soc., 1975-77; bd. dirs. Detroit Am. Jewish Com., 1988—. With AUS, 1942-45. Decorated Bronze Star; Fulbright Rsch. grantee U. Munich, 1961-63; recipient Order of Merit 1st Class, 1968, Friendship award, 1983, Germany, 1987, Grand Order of Merit, Festschrift in Honor of Guy Stern; Exile and Enlightment, 1987, Goethe medal, 1989, Presdl. award for Excellence in Teaching, 1992, Disting. Alumni award Hofstra U., 1993. Mem. Am. Assn. Tchrs. German (pres. 1970-72, Disting. Germanist of Yr. 1985, hon. mem. 1989), AAUP, Internat. PEN Club, MLA, South Atlantic MLA, Soc. for Exile Studies (v.p. 1981—). Home: 20672 Knob Woods Dr Southfield MI 48076-4033

STERN, HAROLD PETER, business executive; b. Frankfurt, Germany, Oct. 16, 1923; s. Hugo H. and Lily C. (Strauss) S.; m. Annette B. Kaplan, Nov. 28, 1958; children: Steven B., Eric K., Robert (dec.). Student, NYU, Columbia U., 1940-43. V.p., pres. Rector Internat. Corp., Mt. Vernon, N.Y., 1948—, Rector Internat. Equipment Corp., Mt. Vernon, N.Y., 1984—, Rector Mineral Trading Corp., Mt. Vernon, N.Y., 1948—; exec. sec. Cork Inst. Am., N.Y.C. Elected to Rep. State Com., Albany, N.Y.; vice chmn. Rep. Town Com., Harrison, N.Y.; mem. Nat. Coun./Small Bus. Adminstrn., Washington; commr./chmn. Westchester County Police Bd. Lt. Col. N.Y. Guard. Recipient John Egar Hoover Gold medal Am. Police Hall of Fame, Excellent Police Duty medal Nat. Assn. Chiefs of Police, Police Disting. Svc. medal Westchester County Dept. Pub. Safety, Westchester County Disting. Svc. medal Westchester County Exec. Fellow Nat. Law Enforcement Acad. (hon.). Avocations: boating, skiing, hunting, fishing. Office: Rector Internat Corp 9 W Prospect Ave Mount Vernon NY 10550-2018

STERN, HERBERT JAY, lawyer; b. N.Y.C., Nov. 8, 1936; s. Samuel and Sophie (Berkowitz) S.; children: Jason Andrew and Jordan Ezekiel (twins), Samuel Abraham, Sarah Kathrine. B.A., Hobart Coll., 1958; J.D. (Ford Found. scholar), U. Chgo., 1961; LL.D. (hon.), Seton Hall Law Sch., 1973, Hobart Coll., 1974; L.H.D. (hon.), Newark State Coll., 1973; D.C.L. (hon.), Bloomfield Coll., 1973; Litt.D. (hon.), Montclair State Coll., 1973. Bar: N.Y. 1961, N.J. 1971. Asst. dist. atty. New York County, 1962-65; trial atty. organized crime and racketeering sect. Dept. of Justice, 1965-69; chief asst. U.S. atty. Dist. of N.J., Newark, 1969-70; U.S. atty. Dist. of N.J., 1971-74, U.S. dist. judge, 1974-87; ptnr. Stern & Greenberg, Roseland, N.J., 1990—; mem. adv. com. U. Chgo. Law Sch. Author: Judgment in Berlin, 1984 (Valley Forge award Freedoms Found. 1984, Torch of Learning award Am. Friends of Hebrew U. 1987), Trying Cases to Win, Vol. I, 1991, Vol. II, 1992, Vol. III, 1993, Vol. IV, 1995. Named One of America's 10 Outstanding Young Men U.S. Jr. C. of C., 1971; Swartzer scholar U. Chgo. Law Sch., 1985; recipient Dean's Club award U. Akron Sch. Law, 1986, medal of excellence Hobart Coll., 1990. Fellow ABA, Am. Law Inst. (Clarence Darrow award), Internat. Platform Assn.; mem. ABA, N.J. Bar Assn., Fed. Bar Assn. (past pres. Newark chpt., recipient William J. Brennan, Jr. award 1987), Essex County Bar Assn., Am. Judicature Soc., Phi Alpha Delta. Subject of book Tiger in the Court, 1973. Office: 75 Livingston Ave Roseland NJ 07068-3701

STERN, HOWARD ALLAN, radio disc jockey, television show host; b. Roosevelt, N.Y., 1954; s. Ben and Ray S.; m. Alison Berns, 1978; children: Emily, Debra, Ashley Jade. BA in Comm., Boston U., 1976. Disc jockey Sta. WRNW, Briarcliff Manor, N.Y., 1976-78, Sta. WCCC, Hartford, Conn., 1978-79, Sta. WWWW, Detroit, 1979-80, Sta. WWDC, Washington, 1980-82, Sta. WNBC, N.Y.C., 1982-85, Sta. WXRK, N.Y.C., 1985—, numerous other markets, 1986—. Author: Private Parts, 1993, Miss America, 1995; TV shows include The Howard Stern Show (WOR-TV), 1990-92, The Howard Stern Interview (E!), 1992-93, The Howard Stern Show (E!), 1994—; recordings include 50 Ways To Rank Your Mother, 1982, Crucified by the FCC, 1991; pay-per-view spls./videos include: Howard Stern's Neglige and Underpants Party, U.S. Open Sores, Butt Bongo Fiesta, The Miss Howard Stern New Year's Eve Pageant. Libretarian candidate for gov. State of N.Y., 1994. Rest Stop on I-295 in N.J. named in his honor, 1995. Address: The Howard Stern Show WXRK-FM 600 Madison Ave New York NY 10022-1615 also: c/o Don Buchwald & Associates 10 E 44th St New York NY 10017-3601*

STERN, ISAAC, violinist; b. Kreminiecz, Russia, July 21, 1920; came to U.S., 1921; s. Solomon and Clara S.; m. Nora Kaye, Nov. 10, 1948; m. Vera Lindenblit, Aug. 17, 1951; children: Shira, Michael, David; m. Linda Reynolds, Nov. 3, 1996. Student, San Francisco Conservatory, 1930-37; numerous hon. degrees including, Dalhousie U., 1971, U. Hartford, 1971, Bucknell U., 1974, Hebrew U., Jerusalem, 1975, Yale U., 1975, Columbia U., 1977, Johns Hopkins U., 1979, U. Md., 1983, Tel Aviv U., 1983, NYU, 1989, U. Ill., 1992, Harvard U., 1992. Recital debut San Francisco, 1934; orchestral debut San Francisco Symphony Orch. (Pierre Monteux condr.), 1936; N.Y. debut, 1937; Carnegie Hall recital debut, 1943; N.Y. Philharm. debut (Arthur Rodzinski condr.), 1944; participated Prades Festival with Pablo Casals, 1950-52; soloist for first orchestral and recital performances at Kennedy Ctr., Washington; first Am. to perform in USSR after World War II, 1956; mem. Istomin-Rose-Stern trio, 1962-83 (Beethoven cycle w/Istomin & Rose 1970-71); performed in China at invitation of Chinese govt., 1979; performed world premieres of violin works by Bernstein, Dutilleux, Hindemith, Maxwell Davies, Penderecki, Rochberg and Schuman; has played with major orchestras, given countless recitals and performed at important festivals in the U.S., Europe, Israel, Far East, Australia and S. Am. Over 100 records, cassettes and CD's for CBS Masterworks, named Artist Laureate 1984 CBS Masterworks; made soundtrack for motion pictures Humoresque (Warner Bros.) and Fiddler on the Roof (United Artists); starred in soundtrack Tonight We Sing (20th Century Fox) and Journey to Jerusalem with Leonard Bernstein; documentary film From Mao to Mozart-Isaac Stern in China (Academy award 1981, Cannes Film Festival Special Mention), Carnegie Hall: The Grand Reopening, 1987 (Emmy award), Isaac Stern-A Life, 1991. Chmn. bd. Am.-Israel Cultural Found.; chmn. emeritus, founder Jerusalem Music Ctr.; originating mem. Nat. Endowment for the Arts; pres. Carnegie Hall, N.Y.C., 1960—. Decorated comdr. Order de la Couronne, comdr. Legion d'Honneur; comdr.'s cross (Order of Dannebrog (Denmark); recipient numerous Grammy awards, Grammy Lifetime Achievement award, 1987, Nat. medal of Honor, 1991, Presdl. medal of Freedom, 1992, numerous local city awards; named Musician of Yr. ABC/ Musical Am., 1986; Fellow of Jerusalem, 1986. Office: Carnegie Hall Corp 881 7th Ave New York NY 10019-3210*

STERN, JAMES ANDREW, investment banker; b. N.Y.C., Oct. 1, 1950; s. Arthur and Lenore (Oppenheimer) S.; m. Jane Yusem, April 13, 1975; children: Peter, David. BS, Tufts U., 1972; MBA, Harvard U., 1974. Assoc. Lehman Bros. Inc., N.Y.C., 1974-79, v.p., 1979-82, mng. dir., 1982-94; chmn. The Cypress Group, N.Y.C., 1994—; dir. K & F Industries, Inc., N.Y.C., R.P. Scherer Corp., Troy, Mich., Noel Group, Inc., N.Y.C., Lear Corp., Southfield, Mich., Cinemark U.S.A., Inc., Amtrol, Inc., West Warwick, R.I. Trustee Tufts U., Medford, Mass., 1982—. Mem. Quaker Ridge Golf Club, Beach Point Club. Clubs: Quaker Ridge Golf (Scarsdale, N.Y.), Beach Point (Mamaroneck, N.Y.). Avocations: golf, reading. Office: The Cypress Group Inc 65 E 55th St New York NY 10022-3219

STERN, JAMES COPER, sales executive; b. N.Y.C., Dec. 12, 1925; s. George Charles and Ruth (Coper) S.; m. Judith Vinson, Oct. 31, 1963 (div. Mar. 1974); children: Hillary Anne, Renee Jean; m. Ruth Nussbacker Szold, Aug. 22, 1982. BA, NYU, 1949. Trainee, exec. asst. Gardner Advt. Co., N.Y.C., 1949-50; advt. mgr. NOPCO Chem. Co., Harrison, N.J., 1950-53; account exec. Ziv TV Programs, N.Y.C., 1954-56; sales rep. United Artists Associated, N.Y.C., 1957-61; v.p., sales mgr. Allied Artists TV, N.Y.C., 1961-70; exec. v.p., gen. sales mgr. ITC Entertainment, Inc., Studio City, Calif., 1970-89; pres. JCS Syndication Svcs., L.A., 1989—. Cpl. U.S. Army, 1944-46, ETO. Mem. Internat. Radio and TV Soc., Nat. Assn. TV Program Execs., Ind. TV Program Execs. Republican. Jewish. Avocations: watercolor painting, skiing, golf, art. Home: 8455 Fountain Ave Apt 515 Los Angeles CA 90069-2543 Office: JCS Syndication Svcs 8455 Fountain Ave Apt 515 Los Angeles CA 90069-2543

STERN, JOAN NAOMI, lawyer; b. Phila., Mar. 7, 1944; d. Clarence J. and Diana D. (Goldberg) S. BA, U. Pa., 1965; JD, Temple U., 1977. Bar: Pa. 1977. Assoc. Blank, Rome, Comisky & McCauley, Phila., 1977-83, ptnr., 1983—, co-chair pub. fin. group, 1983-92, chair pub. fin. group, 1993, chair pub. fin. dept., 1994—; cons. counsel Phila. Charter Commn., 1993-94. Contbr. articles to profl. jours. Mem. Sch. Dist. Task Force on Regulatory Reform, Phila., 1987, Tax Policy and Budget Com., Phila., 1989, Phila. Mayor's Fiscal Adv. Com., 1990; chair Sch. Dist. of Phila. Task Force on Alternate Financing Strategies, 1995; bd. mgrs. Moore Coll. Art and Design, Phila., 1993—, vice chair bd. mgrs., 1995—; bd. dirs. Police Athletic League, Phila., 1994—; bd. dirs. Jewish Cmty. Ctrs. of Greater Phila., 1996—. Fellow Am. Bar Found.; mem. ABA, Nat. Assn. Bond Lawyers, Phila. Bar Assn., Phila. Bar Assn. (chmn. mcpl. govt. com. 1983—), Pa. Assn. Bond Lawyers. Office: Blank Rome Comisky & McCauley 4 Penn Center Plz Philadelphia PA 19103-2521

STERN, JOANNE THRASHER, elementary school educator; b. Norfolk, Va., Oct. 18, 1932; d. Thomas Williams and Mary Ellen (LaRue) Thrasher; m. Milford Josiah Stern, Apr. 29, 1956; children: Milford J. III, Thomas Thrasher, William Byrd. BS, James Madison U., 1952; MEd, U. Va., 1963. Cert. elem. tchr. Tchr. 5th grade City of Chesapeake, 1952-54; Tchr. Va. Beach Pub. Schs., 1957-60; tchr. Norfolk (Va.) City Pub. Schs., 1966-68, Def. Dependent Schs., Fed. Republic Germany, 1985; tchr. English Madison Middle Sch., 1987-89; tchr. ESOL 1st grade, 1988-91; prin. Marietta Mischia Toussaint Louverture Elem. Sch., 1989—, 1st grade tchr.; tchr. English Nan Ping Tchrs. Coll., summer 1993. Organist 1st Bapt. Ch. of North Miami Beach (Fla.); tchr. Holiday Bible Club, Pembrokeshire, Wales, 1996. Mem. AAUW, Women Leaders Round Table (life), Chesapeake Bay Bus. and Profl. Women, Kappa Delta Pi. Home: 920 NE 199th St Apt 309 Miami FL 33179-3085

STERN, JOSEPH SMITH, JR., former footwear manufacturing company executive; b. Cin., Mar. 31, 1918; s. Joseph S. and Miriam (Haas) S.; m. Mary Stern, June 14, 1942; children: Peter Joseph, William Frederick, Peggy Ann Graeter. AB, Harvard U., 1940, MBA, 1943; HHD (hon.), Xavier U., 1988; DSc(hon.), U. Cin., 1989. With R. H. Macy & Co., N.Y.C., 1940-41; with U.S. Shoe Corp., Cin., 1941-68; v.p. U.S. Shoe Corp., 1951-65, pres., 1965-66, chmn. bd., chief exec. officer, 1966, chmn. exec. com., 1966-68, dir., 1956-70; prof. bus. policy emeritus U. Cin. Pres. bd. trustees Cin. and Hamilton County Pub. Libr.; chmn. Cin. Bicentennial Com., Greater Cin. Tall Stacks Commn.; trustee Cin. Music Hall Assn., Cin. Hist. Soc., Children's Hosp. Med. Center, Cin. Symphony Orch., Cin Country Day Sch., 1956-72, Family Svc., Cin., 1964-82; trustee, pres. Cin. Mus. Festival Assn.; pres. bd. trustees Children's Convalescent Hosp., Cin., 1972-75; bd. overseers vis. com. univ. libr. Harvard U. Served to lt. USNR, 1943-46. Recipient Disting. Community Svc. award NCCJ, 1986, Great Living Cincinnatian award Cin. C. of C., 1989, Disting. Svc. award U. Cin. Coll. Bus., 1992. Mem. Am. Footwear Industries Assn. (life; dir.). Jewish (past pres. temple). Clubs: Literary (Cin.), Harvard (Cin.) (pres. 1965), Queen City (Cin.), Queen City Optimists, Harvard (N.Y.C.). Home: 3 Grandin Pl Cincinnati OH 45208-3402

STERN, LEO G., lawyer; b. Mpls., Apr. 10, 1945; s. Philip J. and June I. (Monasch) S.; m. Christine E. Lamb, June 29, 1968; children: Alison M., Zachary A. BA, U. Calif., Davis, 1967; JD cum laude, U. Minn., 1970. Bar: Minn. 1970, U.S. Dist. Ct. Minn. 1971, Calif. 1971, U.S. Ct. Appeals (6th, 7th and 8th cirs.) 1985, U.S. Supreme Ct. 1993; cert. mediator and arbitrator, Minn. Ptnr. Cox, King & Stern, Mpls., 1970-77, Wright, West & Diessner, Mpls., 1977-84, Fredrikson & Byron, P.A., Mpls., 1984—. Mem. Minn. Bar Assn. (governing coun. environ. and natural resources law sect. 1989-95, governing coun. litigation sect. 1995—), Am. Arbitration Assn. (arbitrator, mediator). Avocations: sailing, jogging. Home: 4331 Fremont Ave S Minneapolis MN 55409-1720 Office: Fredrikson & Byron PA 1100 International Ctr 900 2nd Ave S Minneapolis MN 55402-3314

STERN, LEONARD BERNARD, television and motion picture production company executive; b. N.Y.C., Dec. 23, 1923; s. Max and Esther (Marton) S.; m. Gloria Jane Stroock, Aug. 12, 1956; children: Michael Stroock, Kate Jennifer. Student, NYU, 1944. Dir. TV L.A., 1946-53; writer, dir., producer Jackie Gleason Show/Honeymooners, Sergeant Bilko, Steve Allen Show N.Y.C., 1953-60; founder Price-Stern-Sloan, L.A., 1959-64, v.p., 1964-69; dir. Price-Stern-Sloan, 1969—; pres. Heyday Prodns., L.A., 1962-69, 75—; v.p. Talent Assocs./Norton Simon, L.A. and N.Y.C., 1965-75. Author: (with Roger Price) Mad Libs, 1958, What Not to Name the Baby, 1960, Dear Attila the Hun, 1985; (with Roger Price and Larry Sloan) The Baby Boomer Book of Names, 1985, (with Diane L. Robison) A Martian Wouldn't Say That, 1994; writer, dir.: (motion pictures) Just You and Me, Kid, 1979, Target, 1985, Missing Pieces, 1990; creator, writer, dir. 21 TV series, including Get Smart, McMillan and Wife and He and She, 1953-89; media editor Dialogue newsletter. Mem. adv. coun. Sch. of Arts, NYU; bd. dirs. Nat. Coun. for Families and TV, Inst. for Mental Health Initiatives. Recipient Peabody award U. Ga., Writers Guild award 1956, 66, Nat. Assn. TV Arts and Scis. award 1956, 66-67, Emmy award 1956, 1966. Mem. Writers Guild Am., Dirs. Guild Am., Caucus for Producers, Writers and Dirs. (co-chmn., Mem. of Yr award 1987, Disting. Svc. award 1987), Producers Guild Am. (pres.), Bd. Motion Picture and TV Fund Found. Office: Tallfellow Prodns 1180 S Beverly Dr Ste 320 Los Angeles CA 90035-1154

STERN, LEONARD NORMAN, pet supply manufacturing company executive; b. N.Y.C., Mar. 28, 1938; s. Max and Hilda (Lowenthal) S.; m. Allison Maher; children: Emanuel Theodore, Edward Julius, Andrea Caroline. B.S. cum laude, NYU, 1956, M.B.A., 1957. Formerly pres., dir., now chmn., chief exec. officer Hartz Group, Inc., 1959—; mem. adv. bd. Chem. Bank, N.Y.C., 1970—; active real estate constrn., devel. Bd. dirs. Manhattan Day Sch., Jewish Ctr., N.Y.C.; founder Albert Einstein Coll. Medicine, 1958; mem. N.Y.C. Holocaust Meml. Commn.; founder Homes for the Homeless; trustee, chmn. fin. com. NYU. Office: Hartz Group 667 Madison Ave New York NY 10021-8029*

STERN, LOUIS WILLIAM, marketing educator, consultant; b. Boston, Sept. 19, 1935; s. Berthold Summerfield Stern and Gladys (Koch) Cohen; m. Rhona L. Grant; children: Beth Ida, Deborah Lynn. A.B., Harvard U., 1957; M.B.A. in Mktg, U. Pa., 1959; Ph.D. in Mktg, Northwestern U., 1962. Mem. staff bus. research and consumer mktg. sects. Arthur D. Little, Inc., Cambridge, Mass., 1961-63; asst. prof. bus. orgn. Ohio State U., Columbus, 1963-64; asso. prof. mktg. Ohio State U., 1966-69, prof. mktg., 1970-73; prof. mktg. Northwestern U., Evanston, Ill., 1973-75; A. Montgomery Ward prof. mktg. Northwestern U., 1975-83, chmn. dept. mktg., 1977-80, John D. Gray disting. prof. mktg., 1984—; on leave as exec. dir. Mktg. Sci. Inst., Cambridge, Mass., 1983-85; Thomas Henry Carroll Ford Found. vis. prof. Harvard U. Grad. Sch. Bus. Adminstrn., 1984-85; mem. staff Nat. Commn. on Food Mktg., Washington, 1965-66; vis. assoc. prof. bus. adminstrn. U. Calif., Berkeley, 1969-70; guest lectr. York U., U. Minn., U. Ky., UCLA, Ohio State U., U. N.C., Duke U., U. Wis., U. Pitts., U. Chgo., MIT, U. Mich., U. Pa., Cornell U., U. Mo., Norwegian Sch. Econs. and Bus. Adminstrn.; faculty assoc. Hernstein Inst., Vienna, Austria, 1976-77, Mgmt. Centre Europe, 1988-96; faculty assoc. Gemini Cons. Inc., Montvale, N.J., 1977-96, mem. midwest adv. bd., 1989-94; Xerox research prof. Northwestern U., 1981-82; cons. to FTC, 1973, 80; faculty assoc. CSC Index, 1996—. Author: Distribution Channels: Behavioral Dimensions, 1969, (with Frederick D. Sturdivant and others) Managerial Analysis in Marketing, 1970, Perspectives in Marketing Management, 1971, (with John R. Grabner, Jr.) Competition in the Marketplace, 1970, (with Adel I. El-Ansary and Anne T. Coughlan) Marketing Channels, 5th edit., 1996, (with Thomas L. Eovaldi) Legal Aspects of Marketing Strategy: Antitrust and Consumer Protection Issues, 1984; (with Adel I. El-Ansary and James R. Brown) Management in Marketing Channels, 1989; mem. editl. bd. Jour. Mktg. Rsch., 1976-82, Jour. Mktg., 1979-83, Mktg. Letters, 1988-94; contbr. articles on mktg. to profl. jours. Mem. exec. com. Northwest Area Council on Human Relations, Columbus, 1971-72. Rsch. grantee: Ohio State U., 1964-73, Mktg. Sci. Inst., 1976-77, 88-90, 92-94; recipient Harold H. Maynard award best article Jour. Mktg., 1980; named Mktg. Educator of Yr. Sales and Mktg. Execs. Internat., 1989, also Chgo. chpt. 1990, Outstanding Profl. of Yr. award, 1992, and named One of Top 6 Profs. in Kellogg Sch., Northwestern U., Grad. Mgmt. Assocs., 1984-94, (named 6 times Out-

standing Prof. Exec. Masters Program), One of Top 12 Tchrs. in U.S., Bus. Week. Mem. AAUP, Am. Mktg. Assn. (mem. program com. educators conf. 1971, chmn. com. 1978, Paul D. Converse award 1986, Richard D. Irwin Disting. Mktg. Educator of Yr. 1994), Hellenic Inst. Mktg. (hon.), Beta Gamma Sigma. Home: 724 Sheridan Rd Wilmette IL 60091-1960 Office: Northwestern U JL Kellogg Grad Sch Mgmt Dept Mktg Evanston IL 60208

STERN, MADELEINE BETTINA, rare books dealer, author; b. N.Y.C., July 1, 1912; d. Moses Roland and Lillie (Mack) S. BA, Barnard Coll., 1932; MA, Columbia U., 1934. Tchr. English N.Y.C. High Schs., 1934-43; ptnr. Leona Rostenberg Rare Books, N.Y.C., 1945—, Leona Rostenberg and Madeleine B. Stern Rare Books, N.Y.C., 1980—; lectr. history of book, feminism, pub. history, lt. Author: The Life of Margaret Fuller, 1942, Louisa May Alcott, 1950, new edit., 1996, Purple Passage: The Life of Mrs. Frank Leslie, 1953, Imprints on History: Book Publishers and American Frontiers, 1956, We the Women: Career Firsts of Nineteenth Century America, 1962, new edit., 1994, So Much in a Lifetime: The Story of Dr. Isabel Barrows, 1965, Queen of Publishers' Row: Mrs. Frank Leslie, 1966, The Pantarch: A Biography of Stephen Pearl Andrews, 1968, Heads and Headlines: The Phrenological Fowlers, 1971, Books and Book People in 19th-Century America, 1978, Antiquarian Bookselling in the United States: A History from the Origins to the 1940s, 1985, Nicholas Gouin Dufief of Philadelphia Franco-American Bookseller, 1776-1834, 1988, The Life of Margaret Fuller: A Revised Second Edition, 1991; (with Leona Rostenberg) Old and Rare: Forty Years in the Book Business, 1974, rev. edit. 1988, Between Boards: New Thoughts on Old Books, 1978, Bookman's Quintet: Five Catalogues about Books, 1980, Quest Book-Guest Book: A Biblio-Folly, 1993, Connections: Our Selves-Our Books, 1994, Old Books in the Old World: Reminiscences of Book Buying Abroad, 1996, Old Books, Rare Friends: Two Literary Sleuths and Their Shared Passion, 1997; editor: Women on the Move, 4 vols., 1972, Victoria Woodhull Reader, 1974, Louisa's Wonder Book-An Unknown Alcott Juvenile, 1975, Behind a Mask: The Unknown Thrillers of Louisa May Alcott, 1975, new edit., 1995, Plots and Counterplots: More Unknown Thrillers of Louisa May Alcott, 1976, Publishers for Mass Entertainment in 19th-Century America, 1980, A Phrenological Dictionary of 19th-Century Americans, 1982, Critical Essays on Louisa May Alcott, 1984, A Modern Mephistopheles and Taming a Tartar by Louisa May Alcott, 1987, Louisa May Alcott Unmasked: Collected Thrillers, 1995, Modern Magic: Five Stories by Louisa May Alcott, 1995, The Feminist Alcott: Stories of a Woman's Power, 1996; co-editor: Selected Letters of Louisa May Alcott, 1987, A Double Life: Newly Discovered Thrillers of Louisa May Alcott, 1988, The Journals of Louisa May Alcott, 1989, Louisa May Alcott: Selected Fiction, 1990, (co-editor) Freaks of Genius: Unknown Thrillers of Louisa May Alcott, 1991, From Jo March's Attic: Stories of Intrigue and Suspense, 1993 (Victorian Soc. award), The Lost Stories of Louisa May Alcott, 1995. Guggenheim fellow, 1943-45; recipient Medalie award Barnard Coll., 1982, Victorian Soc. award, Disting. Alumna award Barnard Coll., 1997. Mem. Antiquarian Booksellers Assn. Am. (gov. 1966-68, 78-80), Internat. League Antiquarian Booksellers, MLA, Am. Printing History Assn. (co-recipient award 1983), Authors League, Manuscript Soc. (former trustee), Phi Beta Kappa. Jewish. Home: 40 E 88th St New York NY 10128-1176 Office: Rare Books 40 E 88th St New York NY 10128-1176

STERN, MARILYN, picture editor, photographer, writer; b. Detroit, Nov. 8, 1953; d. Julian and Phyllis S. BA, Brown U., 1976. Photographer's asst. N.Y.C., 1976-82, freelance photographer, 1976—; tchr. photography pvt. practice, N.Y.C., 1980-83; freelance writer N.Y.C., 1985—; picture editor Across the Board mag., N.Y.C., 1990-96. Photographer/organizer: (book) Masked Culture: The Greenwich Village Halloween Parade, 1994; author/ photographer: Kval! Die Waldanger der Lofoten, 1990; represented in permanent collection Detroit Inst. Arts. Travel Study grantee Royal Norwegian Consulate to Norway in the U.S., 1987, Am.-Scandinavian Found., 1986. Jewish. Avocations: Go, Irish music, birding, drawing.

STERN, MARVIN, management consultant; b. Bklyn., Jan. 5, 1923; s. David and Regina (Harnik) S.; m. June Bronstein Wittlin, Mar. 24, 1945; children—Ellis Roy, Richard Keith; m. Patricia Wolberg, June 17, 1955; children—Valerie Ann, Gary Allen, Jody Amanda. B.S. in Mech. Engring., CCNY, 1943; M.S., NYU, 1947, Ph.D. in Math, 1954. Corp. staff exec. rsch. and devel. Gen. Dynamics Co., 1958-60; asst. dir. strategic weapons Office Sec. Def., Washington, 1960-61; dep. dir. def. rsch. and engring., weapons systems Office Sec. Def., 1961-62; v.p. rsch. and engring. N.Am. Aviation, Inc., El Segundo, Calif., 1962-63; mgmt. cons. L.A., 1963-64; pres. aero. systems div. Gen. Precision, Inc., Wayne, N.J., 1964-66; v.p. Rand Corp., Santa Monica, Calif., 1967-68; pres. Laird Systems, L.A., 1968-70, Marvin Stern, Inc., Santa Ynez, Calif., 1970—; sr. fellow UCLA Ctr. for Internat. and Strategic Affairs, 1990-92; cons. Office Sec. Def., Sec. Transp., Pres.'s Sci. Adv. Com., CIA; Def. Sci. Bd., Naval Res. Adv. Com. Author: (with George Gamow) Puzzle Math, 1958; editor: (with Morton Alperin) Vistas in Astronautics, 1958. Trustee Lycée Français de Los Angeles. Recipient Meritorious Civilian Service medal Sec. Def., 1962. Address: 4001 Long Valley Rd Santa Ynez CA 93460-9721

STERN, MARVIN, psychiatrist, educator; b. N.Y.C., Jan. 6, 1916; s. Jacob and Mary (Kappel) S.; m. Libby Rifkin, Jan. 18, 1942; children: Carol S., Robert M., Theodore A. B.S., CCNY, 1935; M.D., NYU, 1939. Diplomate Am. Bd. Psychiatry and Neurology. Intern in medicine and surgery Bellevue Hosp., N.Y.C., 1939-40, resident in medicine and psychiatry, 1940-42, fellow in psychiatry, 1946-47; practice medicine specializing in psychiatry N.Y.C., 1947—; asst. prof. psychiatry NYU Med. Ctr., N.Y.C., 1948-55, assoc. prof., 1955-62, prof., 1962-79, Menas S. Gregory prof. psychiatry, 1979-86, prof., 1986-95; prof. emeritus, 1995—; prof. emeritus NYU Med. Ctr., N.Y.C., 1995—, exec. chmn. dept. psychiatry, 1976-86; mem. staff NYU Hosp., Bellevue Hosp.; cons. psychiatrist VA Hosp.; cons. psychiatrist emeritus Brookdale Hosp. Served to maj. AUS, 1942-46. Fellow Am. Psychiat. Assn. (sec. dist. br. 1956-63, pres. dist. br. 1964, area chmn. 1962-63); mem. Am. Psychosomatic Assn., N.Y.C. Acad. Medicine, Harvey Soc., NYU Med. Alumni Assn. (pres. 1979-80), Phi Beta Kappa, Sigma Xi, Alpha Omega Alpha. Home: 300 E 33rd St Apt 12C New York NY 10016-9415 Office: NYU Sch Medicine 550 1st Ave New York NY 10016-6481

STERN, MICHAEL DAVID, dentist; b. Cleve., Feb. 26, 1946; s. Milton B. and Harriette (Hoffman) S.; m. Ellen Weiner, June 9, 1968; children: Gregory, Stephanie, Jeffrey. BS, Ohio State U., 1968, DDS, 1972; cert., L.I. U., N.Y.C., 1981. Cert. pain mgmt., Am. Acad. Pain Mgmt., instruction in temporomandibular joint disfunction syndrome, L.I. U. Staff dentist Office of Drs. Rhodes and Rinaldi, Cleve., 1972-73; assoc. dentist Office of William Rothkopf, DDS, Cleve., 1973-75; practice dentistry specializing in temporomandibular joint disorders Wickliffe, Ohio, 1975-93, Willoughby Hills, Ohio, 1993—; resident in cranio facial pain Coll. Dentistry U. Fla. Gainsville, 1989; media spokesperson Morning Exch., WEWS-TV, Cleve., 1981-85; cons. Richmond Hts. (Ohio) Hosp., 1983; adj. grad. lectr. Cleve. State U., 1983-84; preceptorship lectr. Case Western Res. U., Cleve., 1986-95; mem. staff Pain Ctr., Meridia South Pointe Hosp., 1991-97; TMJD and facial pain cons. Signature Sound Works, Inc. Bio-Acoustics, Athens, Ohio, 1996—. Fellow Am. Endodontic Soc., Acad. Gen. Dentistry, Internat. Coll. Craniomandibular Orthopedics; mem. ADA, Ohio Dental Assn., N.E. Ohio Dental Soc. (pub. rels. chmn. 1979-83, sec. 1996—). Avocations: cycling, automobiles, music, gardening. Office: 34950 Chardon Rd Ste 209 Willoughby OH 44094-9162

STERN, MILTON, chemical company executive; b. Boston, Apr. 20, 1927; s. Morris and Lily (Colton) S.; m. Roberta L. Navisky, July 10, 1949; children—Mark, Lawrence, Brian. B.S., Northeastern U., 1949; M.S. (Alcoa fellow), MIT, 1950; Sc.D. (Alcoa fellow), 1952. Postdoctoral fellow in metallurgy MIT, 1952-54; with Union Carbide Corp., N.Y.C., 1954-73; v.p. electronics div. Union Carbide Corp., 1968-69, exec. v.p. mining and metals div., 1969-73; v.p. exploration Kennecott Corp., N.Y.C., 1973-76; sr. v.p. Kennecott Corp. U, 1976-78, exec. v.p., 1978-82, also dir.; sr. exec. v.p. Stauffer Chem. Co., Westport, Conn., 1982-84; vice chmn. Stauffer Chem. Co., 1984—, also dir. Contbr. numerous articles in electrochemistry and metallurgy to tech. jours. Mem. vis. com. M.I.T., 1972-75; mem. corp. Northeastern U.; mem. White House Task Force on Am. Indian, 1966; bd. dirs. Assn. Am. Indian Affairs. Served with USNR, 1945-46. Recipient Nuodex award Northeastern U., 1949; Sears B. Condit award, 1949. Mem. AIME. Nat.

Assn. corrosion Engrs. (Willis R. Whitney award 1963), Am. Soc. Metals, Electrochem. Soc. (Young Authors award 1955, 58, jour. div. editor 1958-61), PGA Nat. Club, Sigma Xi, Tau Beta Pi. Patentee in field.

STERN, MITCHELL, broadcast executive. B, U. Pa., 1976; MBA, U. Chgo., 1978. With CBS TV Stas. Divsn., 1978-86; dir. planning and adminstrn. WCBS-TV CBS TV Stas. Divsn., N.Y.C.; dir. planning and adminstrn. WBBM-TV CBS TV Stas. Divsn., Chgo.; fin. analyst corp. office CBS TV Stas. Divsn.; v.p., CFO Fox TV Stas., L.A., 1986-90, v.p., sta. mgr. KTTV-Fox 11, 1989-91, sr. v.p., 1990-92, exec. v.p., COO, 1992-93, pres., COO, 1993—. Office: Fox TV Stas Inc 1999 S Bundy Dr Los Angeles CA 90025-5235

STERN, MORT(IMER) P(HILLIP), journalism and communications educator, academic administrator, consultant; b. New Haven, Feb. 20, 1926; s. Bernard and Louise Eleanor (Spiro) S.; m. Patricia Ruth Freeman, Jan. 10, 1946; children: Susan C., Margaret L. AB, U. Ark., 1947; MS, Columbia U., 1949; postgrad., Harvard U., 1954-55; PhD, U. Denver, 1969. Reporter S.W.-Am., Ft. Smith, Ark., 1946-47; night bur. mgr. UPI, Little Rock, 1947-48; reporter, polit. writer, state editor Ark. Gazette, Little Rock, 1949-51; reporter, rewrite man Denver Post, 1951-53, night city editor, 1953-54, asst. editor Rocky Mountain Empire sect., 1955-56, mng. editor, 1956-58, assoc. editor, 1958, editorial page editor, 1958-65, asst. to pub., 1965-70, editorial page editor, 1971-73; dean Sch. Pub. communication U. Ala., 1973-74; dean Sch. Journalism U. Colo., Boulder, 1974-77; lectr. journalism U. Denver, 1953-54, adj. prof., 1970, exec. dir. pub. affairs, 1977-78, exec. asst. to chancellor, 1978-84; prof., chmn. dept. journalism and mass communication U. No. Colo., Greeley, 1985-90; pres. P. Paty & Co., Georgetown, Colo., 1989—; Atwood prof. journalism U. Alaska, Anchorage, 1981-82. With USAAF, 1944-45. Elected to Georgetown, Colo. Bd. of Selectmen, Apr. 7, 1997—. Nieman fellow Harvard U., 1954-55. Mem. Assn. for Edn. in Journalism, Phi Beta Kappa, Omicron Delta Kappa, Sigma Delta Chi. Baptist. Home: PO Box 549 Georgetown CO 80444-0549

STERN, NANCY FORTGANG, mathematics and computer science, educator; b. N.Y.C., July 15, 1944; d. Murray and Selma (Karp) Fortgang; m. Robert A Stern, Sept. 3, 1964; children: Lori Anne, Melanie. AB, Barnard Coll., 1965; MS, NYU, 1968; MA, SUNY, 1974, PhD, 1978. Programmer analyst ATT, N.Y.C., 1965-67; asst. prof. Nassau Community Coll., Garden City, N.Y., 1965-68; adj. prof. Dowling Coll. SUNY, 1968-77; disting. prof. Hofstra U., Hempstead, N.Y., 1977—; rsch. cons. Am. Inst. Physics, N.Y.C., 1976-77; adv. editor John Wiley & Sons, 1977—. Author 12 textbooks on computing; asst. editor in chief Annals of the History of Computing, 1977-87; contbr. articles to profl. jours. Mem. Charles Babbage Inst., Nat. Computing Com.

STERN, PAULA, international trade advisor; b. Chgo., Mar. 31, 1945; d. Lloyd and Fan (Wener) Stern; m. Paul A. London; children: Gabriel Stern London, Genevieve Stern London. BA, Goucher Coll., 1967; MA in Middle Eastern Studies, Harvard U., 1969; MA in Internat. Affairs, Fletcher Sch. of Law and Diplomacy, 1970, MA in Law and Diplomacy, 1970, PhD, 1976; D of Comml. Sci. (hon.), Babson Coll., 1985; LLD (hon.), Goucher Coll., 1985. Legis. asst., then sr. legis. asst. U.S. Sen. Gaylord Nelson, Washington, 1972-74, 1976; guest scholar Brookings Inst., Washington, 1975-76; policy analyst Pres. Carter-V.P. Mondale Transition Team, Washington, 1977-78; internat. affairs fellow Council on Fgn. Relations, Washington, 1977-78; commr. Internat. Trade Commn., Washington, 1978-87, chairwoman, 1984-86; sr. assoc. Carnegie Endowment for Internat. Peace, Washington, 1986-88; pres. The Stern Group, 1988—; sr. fellow The Progressive Policy Inst., 1993—; bd. dirs. Westinghouse/CBS, Harcourt Gen., Avon Products, Inc., Wal-Mart Stores, Inc.; holder Howard W. Alkire chair in internat. bus. and econs. Hamline U., 1994—; mem. Pres.'s Adv. Com. for Trade Policy and Negotiations., Commn. for Econ. Devel., Overseas Devel. Coun. Author: Water's Edge--Domestic Politics and the Making of American Foreign Policy, 1979; author numerous articles and chpts. on internat. affairs. Recipient Journalism award Alicia Patterson Found., 1970-71. Mem. Coun. Fgn. Rels., Inter-Am. Found. (bd. dirs. 1980-81). Democrat. Jewish. Avocations: sculpting, tennis, ballet. Office: 3314 Ross Pl NW Washington DC 20008-3332

STERN, RALPH DAVID, lawyer; b. Longview, Tex., June 20, 1943; children: Eric, Justin. AB, Bucknell U., 1963; JD, U. Chgo., 1966. Bar: D.C. 1967, Ill. 1967, Calif. 1970, U.S. Supreme Ct. 1970. Law clk. Ill. Appellate Ct., Chgo., 1966-67; assoc. Ressman & Tishler, Chgo., 1968-70; exec. asst. Orange County Bd. Suprs., Santa Ana, Calif., 1970-71; gen. counsel San Diego City Schs., 1971-83; ptnr. Whitmore, Kay & Stevens, Palo Alto, Calif., 1983-88, Stern & Keebler, San Mateo, Calif., 1988-90; gen. counsel Schs. Legal Counsel, Hayward, Calif., 1990—; chmn. Nat. Coun. Sch. Attys., 1982-83; pres. Leagal Aid Soc. San Diego, 1976-79, Nat. Orgn. on Legal Problems of Edn., 1981-82. Editor: Law and the School Principal, 1978; contbr. articles to profl. jours. Mem. exec. bd., county membership chair Boy Scouts Am., San Diego, 1979-81; vice chmn. Laurels for Leaders, San Diego, 1980-83; mem. ednl. adminstrn. adv. com. U. San Diego, 1981-86.; mem. adv. com. West's Ednl. Law Reporter, 1981-85. Named Outstanding Young Citizen, San Diego Jaycees, 1977. Office: Schs Legal Counsel 313 W Winton Ave Rm 372 Hayward CA 94544-1136

STERN, RICHARD DAVID, investment company executive; b. New Rochelle, N.Y., Nov. 5, 1936; s. Leo and Grace Marjorie (Phillips) S.; m. Phyllis Marlene Edelstein, Nov. 20, 1966; children: Marjorie Anne, Andrew Howard. AB, Princeton U., 1958; MBA, Harvard U., 1962. CFA. First v.p. Newburger, Loeb & Co., N.Y.C., 1962-74, also dir., 1969-74; sr. investment officer Central Trust Co., Cin., 1974-76, owner bus. valuation cons. co., 1976-78; v.p. Gt. Western Bank & Trust Co. (now Norwest Bank Ariz. NA), Phoenix, 1978-84; pres. Stern, Ludke & Co. (now Stern Investment Mgmt. Co.), Phoenix, 1984—. Co-author: Air Cushion Vehicles, 1962. Trustee endowment trust Phoenix Chamber Music Soc., 1982-91; v.p., 1986-90, bd. dirs., 1982-91, 93-94; pres. Cen. Ariz. chpt. Arthritis Found., 1982-84, chmn. planned giving com., 1986-91, mem. nat. planned giving com., 1987-89; chmn. endowments and trusts com. Temple Beth Israel, Phoenix, 1980-83; dir., investment com. Endowment Found., Temple Solel, Paradise Valley, 1990—; pres. Am. Jewish Com., Phoenix, 1983-84, bd. dirs., 1980-84, adv. bd., 1985—; bd. dirs. Asian Arts Coun., Phoenix Art Mus., 1987-93, v.p., 1989-90, pres., 1990-92; trustee Ariz. Theatre Co., 1990-97, mem. regional nominating com., 1995-97, chmn., 1995-96, asst. treas., 1996-97. Mem. Phoenix Soc. Fin. Analysts (chmn. profl. conduct com. 1980-83, membership com. 1990-91, bd. dirs.), Anti-Defamation League of B'nai B'rith (dir. Ctrl. Ariz. chpt. 1986—, exec. bd. 1989—, chair nominating com. 1990-94, chair bd. devel. 1993-94, treas. 1994—), Princeton Alumni Assn. No. Ariz. (alumni schs. com. 1992—), Univ. Club (Phoenix, bd. dirs. 1990-92, fin. com. 1990-91), Harvard Bus. Sch. Club Ariz. (bd. dirs. 1991—, pres. 1993-95, treas. 1995—), Ariz. Bus. Leadership Assn. Republican. Home: 6013 E Donna Cir Paradise Vly AZ 85253-1730 Office: 2930 E Camelback Rd Ste 195 Phoenix AZ 85016-4412

STERN, RICHARD GUSTAVE, author, educator; b. N.Y.C., Feb. 25, 1928; s. Henry George and Marion (Veit) S.; m. Gay Clark, Mar. 14, 1950 (div. Feb. 1972); children: Christopher Holmes, Kate Macomber, Andrew Henry, Nicholas Clark; m. Alane Rollings, Aug. 9, 1985. B.A., U. N.C., 1947; M.A., Harvard U., 1950; Ph.D., State U. Iowa, 1954. Mem. faculty U. Chgo., 1955—, prof. English, 1965—, Helen Regenstein prof. English, 1990—. Author: Golk, 1960, Europe and Up and Down with Baggish and Schreiber, 1961, In Any Case, 1962, Teeth, Dying and Other Matters, 1964, Stitch, 1965, 1968: A Short Novel, An Urban Idyll, Five Stories and Two Trade Notes, 1970, The Books in Fred Hampton's Apartment, 1973, Other Men's Daughters, 1973, Natural Shocks, 1978, Packages, 1980, The Invention of the Real, 1982, A Father's Words, 1986, The Position of the Body, 1986, Noble Rot: Stories, 1949-88, 1989 (book of yr. award Chgo. Sun-Times 1990), Shares and Other Fictions, 1992, One Person and Another, 1993, A Sistermony, 1995 (Heartland award, nonfiction book of year); editor: Honey and Wax, 1966. Recipient Longwood Found. award, 1960, Friends of Lit. award, 1963, fiction award Nat. Inst. Arts and Letters, 1968; Nat. Coun. Arts and Humanities fellow, 1967-68, Carl Sandburg award for fiction, 1979, Arts Coun. awards, 1979, 81, Am. Acad. and Inst. of Arts and Letters medal of Merit for Novel, 1985; Rockefeller fellow, 1965, Guggenheim fellow, 1973-74. Mem. Am. Acad. Arts and Scis. Office: Dept English U Chgo Chicago IL 60637

STERN, ROBERT ARTHUR MORTON, architect, educator, writer; b. N.Y.C., May 23, 1939; s. Sidney S. and Sonya (Cohen) S.; m. Lynn G. Solinger, May 22, 1966 (div. 1977); 1 child, Nicholas S.G. BA, Columbia U., 1960; MArch, Yale U., 1965. Registered architect, Calif., Colo., Conn., Fla., Hawaii, Ill., Ind., Maine, Mass., Mich., N.H., N.J., Ohio, S.C., Tex., N.Y., D.C., Ga. Program dir. Archtl. League N.Y., 1965-66; designer Office Richard Meier, Architect, N.Y.C., 1966; cons. Small Parks Program, Dept. Parks, N.Y.C., 1966-70; urban designer, asst. to asst. adminstr. housing and devel. adminstrn. N.Y.C., 1967-70; ptnr. Robert A.M. Stern & John S. Hagmann, Architects, N.Y.C., 1969-77; prin. Robert A.M. Stern, Architects, 1977-89, prin. ptnr., 1989—; bd. dirs. Walt Disney Co.; cons. Eye on New York TV documentary, CBS-TV, 1966-67; mem. architecture com. Whitney Mus. Am. Art, 1970-76, adv. commn., archtl. sect. Venice Biennale, 1980; lectr. architecture Columbia U., 1970-72, asst. prof. 1973-77, assoc. prof., 1977-82, prof. 1982—; vis. fellow Inst. for Architecture and Urban Studies, 1974-76, trustee, 1983-85; dir. Temple Hoyne Buell Ctr. for Study Am. Architecture, 1984-88, dir. Hist. Preservation Program, 1991—; vis. lectr. Yale U., 1972, 73; vis. critic R.I. Sch. Design, 1976, U. Pa., 1977, N.C. State U., Raleigh, 1978; William Henry Bishop vis. prof. architecture Yale U., fall 1978; editorial cons. Archtl. History Found., 1979-83. Author: New Directions in American Architecture, 1969, rev. edit., 1977, George Howe: Toward a Modern American Architecture, 1975, (with Deborah Nevins) The Architect's Eye, 1979, (with John M. Massengale) The Anglo-American Suburb, 1981, (with Thomas Catalano) Raymond Hood, 1982, East Hamptons Heritage, 1982, (with John M. Massengale and Gregory Gilmartin) New York 1900, 1983, Pride of Place, 1986, (with Gregory Gilmartin and Thomas Mellims) New York 1930, 1987, (with Raymond Gastil) Modern Classicism, 1988, The House That Bob Built, 1991, The American Houses of Robert A.M. Stern, 1991, (with Thomas Mellins and David Fishman) New York 1960, 1995. Mem. N.Y.C. Mayor's Task Force on Urban Design, 1966-67, architects selection com. N.Y. Conv. Ctr., 1979; trustee Am. Fedn. Arts, 1967-79, Inst. for Architecture and Urban Studies, 1983-85; v.p. Cunningham Dance Found., 1969-73; bd. dirs. Preservation League N.Y., 1984—, Historic Landmarks Preservation Ctr., 1995—. Recipient numerous awards for archtl. works including Nat. Hon. awards of AIA, 1980, 85, 90, John Jay award Columbia Coll., 1991. Fellow AIA (bd. dirs. N.Y. chpt. 1976-78, Disting. archtl. award N.Y. chpt. 1982, 84, 85, 87, medal of honor 1984), Soc. Archtl. Historians (bd. dirs. 1975-78), Archtl. League N.Y. (pres. 1973-77, exec. com. 1977—), N.Y. State Assn. Architects (excellence in design cert. 1985), Am. Architecture Found. (bd. regents 1989-91), Skidmore, Owings and Merrill Found. (bd. dirs. 1984-90), Chgo. Inst. for Architecture and Urbanism (bd. dirs. 1990-93), Century Assn., Coffee House Club. Office: 460 W 34th St Fl 18 New York NY 10001-2320

STERN, ROBERT D., publishing executive; b. N.Y.C., Sept. 30, 1929; s. Morris and Jean (Gordon) S.; m. Natalie Greenberg, Sept. 5, 1952 (div. 1978); children: Mitchell, Bradley; m. Roslyne Paige, June 5, 1978. BA, Syracuse U., 1950; JD, NYU, 1953, LLM, 1958. Bar: N.Y. 1955, U.S. Dist. Ct. (D.C. cir.) 1953, U.S. Supreme Ct. 1967. Assoc. Fink, Weinberger, Levin & Gottschalk, N.Y.C., 1957-59, ptnr., 1959-72; chmn. Rudor Consol. Industries, N.Y.C., 1972—, Dance Mag., Inc., N.Y.C., 1985—, AGC/Sedgwick Inc., Princeton, N.J., 1990—; bd. dirs. Ctr. for Graphic Comms. Mgmt. and Tech., NYU, N.Y.C., 1979—; chmn. bd. dirs. AGC Sedgwick, Princeton, N.J., Rudor Consol. Ind. Inc.; pub. Stern's Performing Arts Directory, 1989—. Bd. dirs. YMCA, N.Y.C., 1987-90;. Mem. ABA, N.Y. State Bar Assn., Sheldrake Yacht Club (Mamaroneck, N.Y.), Birchwood Country Club (Westport, Conn.). Avocations: tennis, skiing, sailing. Home: 2 Imperial Lndg Westport CT 06880-4934 Office: 33 W 60th St New York NY 10023-7905

STERN, ROBERT MORRIS, gastrointestinal psychophysiology researcher, psychology educator; b. N.Y.C., June 18, 1937; s. Irving Dan and Nellie (Wachstetter) S.; m. Wilma Olch, June 19, 1960; children—Jessica Leigh, Alison Rachel. A.B., Franklin and Marshall Coll., 1958; M.S., Tufts U., 1960; Ph.D., Ind. U., 1963. Research assoc. dept. psychology Ind. U., 1963-65; asst. prof. psychology Pa. State U., 1965-68, assoc. prof., 1968-73, prof., 1973—, disting. prof., 1992—, head dept., 1978-87. Author: (with W.J. Ray) Biofeedback, 1977, (with W.J. Ray and C.M. Davis) Psychophysiological Recording, 1980, (with K.L. Koch) Electrogastrography, 1985; contbr. articles to profl. jours. Recipient Nat. Media award Am. Psychol. Found., 1978. Mem. Am. Psychol. Soc., Aerospace Med. Assn., Soc. Psychophysiol. Rsch., Am. Gastroent. Assn., Internat. EGG Soc., Functional Brain-Gut Rsch. Assn., Internat. Brain-Gut Soc. Home: 1360 Greenwood Cir State College PA 16803-3232 Office: Pa State U 512 Moore Bldg University Park PA 16802-3105

STERN, ROSLYNE PAIGE, magazine publisher; b. Chgo., May 26, 1926; d. Benjamin Gross and Clara (Sniderman) Roer; m. William E. Weber, May 3, 1944 (div. Mar. 1956); m. Richard S. Paige, June 28, 1958 (div. Apr. 1978); children: Sandra Weber Porr, Barbara Paige Kaplan, Elizabeth Paige (dec.); m. Robert D. Stern, June 5, 1978. Cert., U. Chgo., 1945. Profl. model, singer, 1947-53; account exec. Interstate United, Chgo., 1955-58; sales mgr. Getting To Know You Internat., Great Neck, N.Y., 1963-71, exec. v.p., 1971-78; pub. After Dark Mag., N.Y.C., 1978-82; assoc. pub. Dance Mag., N.Y.C., 1978-85, pub., 1985—, pres., pub., 1996—; bd. dirs. Rudor Consol. Industries, Inc., N.Y.C., AGC/Sedgwick, Inc., Princeton, N.J. Founding pres. Dance Mag. Found., N.Y.C., 1984-86; life mem. nat. women's com. Brandeis U., Waltham, Mass., 1958—; bd. dirs. Westport Arts Ctr.; internat. com. Dance Libr. of Israel. Mem. Pub. Relations Soc. Am., LWV, Am. Theatre Wing, Nat. Arts Club. Democrat. Jewish. Avocations: dance, theater, opera, visual arts, travel. Home: 2 Imperial Lndg Westport CT 06880-4934 Office: Dance Mag Inc 33 W 60th St 10th Fl New York NY 10023-7905

STERN, SAMUEL ALAN, lawyer; b. Phila., Jan. 21, 1929. AB, U. Pa., 1949; LLB, Harvard U., 1952. Bar: Mass. 1952, D.C. 1958. Ptnr. Wilmer, Cutler & Pickering, Washington, 1962-88, Dickstein, Shapiro & Morin, Washington, 1988-92; pvt. practice law and bus. Washington and St. Petersburg, Russia, 1992-94; counsel Rogers & Wells, Washington, N.Y.C., 1994-97; pvt. practice law and bus. Washington, 1997—; gen. counsel Global Energy Investors, LLC, Washington, 1997—; vis. prof. law Harvard U., Cambridge, Mass., 1976; dir. Internat. Law Inst., Georgetown U., 1971—, adj. prof. law, 1979-92; asst. counsel Warren Commn., 1964; cons. UN, 1974-96; bd. dirs. Ninth Moon Inc., ADEC, Inc., Stern & Co., Norandina Holdings A.V.V., Custom Software L.L.C., Megapoint Sys. Inc., Utilitrol Corp.; lectr. profl. confs. on project fin., cross-border investment, and dispute resolution. Contbr. articles to legal jours. Bd. dirs. Internat. Sci. Tech. Inst., Internat. Ctr., Washington. Mem. ABA, Am. Law Inst., Am. Soc. Internat. Law, Internat. Bar Assn., D.C. Bar Assn. Home: 2336 California St NW Washington DC 20008-1637 Office: 2445 M St NW Washington DC 20037-1435

STERN, T. NOEL, political scientist, educator; b. Pitts., July 7, 1913; s. Leon Thomas (LeFevre) and Elizabeth Gertrude (Limburg) S.; m. Katherine Frances Kirk, Dec. 28, 1940; children: S. Yolanda, Roland Craig, Ellen Cornog, Joan Thrush. B.A. with honors, Swarthmore Coll., 1934; postgrad., U. Lyons, France, 1934-35; M.A. in Polit. Sci, U. Pa., 1940, Ph.D. in Polit. Sci, 1942. Tchr. Lycée des Garçons, Roanne, France, 1934-35; prof., acting chmn. dept. govt. Boston U., 1945-53; Fulbright prof. U. Rennes, U. Strasbourg, 1952; dir. Fondation des Etats-Unis, U. Paris, France, 1953-56; acting chief UN Pub. Adminstrn. Mission to Ethiopia, 1956-57; dir. research and stats. Pa. Dept. Revenue, 1957-60; pres. West Chester State Coll., Pa., 1960-61; research prof. govt. African Studies program Boston U., 1962-63; also chief pub. adminstrn. team Boston U./US Aid, Guinea, West Africa; prof., past chmn. dept. polit. sci. U. Mass., Dartmouth, 1964-69, prof., 1969-85, prof. emeritus, 1985—, also past chmn. acad. coun.; frequent guest on radio, Boston, 1948-53, New Bedford, Fall River and Providence, 1964—. Author: Secret Family, 1988, Your Guide to Dartmouth Town Government, 1991; past mem. editl. bd. Internat. Rev. History and Polit. Sci., Revue de la Cité, Paris; contbr. to Boston U. Law Rev., Sch. and Society, New Republic, Progressive mag., Christian Sci. Monitor, Friends Jour., Quaker Life, Quaker History, Boston Globe, Providence Jour.-Bull, New Bedford Standard-Times, U. Pa. Gazette, also others; collective writings deposited in Archives of Friends Hist. Libr., Swarthmore Coll. and Libr. U. Mass., Dartmouth. Mem. permanent bd. New Eng. Yearly Mtg. of Friends; past mem. exec. com. Friends Gen. Conf., Phila.; past mem. adminstrv. bd. William Penn House, Washington; past clk. North Dartmouth Friends Mtg., past presiding clk. Sandwich Quar. Mtg. of Friends; trustee, chmn. Dartmouth Town Librs., 1995-87; bd. dirs. Cmty. Ctr. for Non-Violence, New Bedford, Mass., 1994—; mem. New England Friends Home Governing Com., Hingham, Mass., 1996—. Mem. AAUP (past pres. U. Mass.-Dartmouth chpt.), Am. Polit. Sci. Assn., LWV (acting pres. New Bedford-Fall River area 1990-91). Home: 875 Smith Neck Rd South Dartmouth MA 02748-1511

STERN, WALTER EUGENE, neurosurgeon, educator; b. Portland, Oreg., Jan. 1, 1920; s. Walter Eugene and Ida May (McCoy) S.; m. Elizabeth Naffziger, May 24, 1946; children: Geoffrey Alexander, Howard Christian, Eugenia Louise, Walter Eugene III. AB cum laude, U. Calif., MD, 1943. Diplomate: Am. Bd. Neurol. Surg. (vice chmn. 1975-80). Surg. intern, asst. resident surgery and neurol. surgery U. Calif. Hosp., 1943-46, asst. resident neurol. surgery and neuropathology, 1948; clin. clk. Nat. Hosp. Paralyzed and Epileptic, London, Eng., 1948-49; Nat. Research fellow med. sci. Johns Hopkins, 1949-50; asst. resident, resident U. Calif. Service, 1951; NIH spl. fellow univ. lab. physiology Oxford U., 1961-62; clin. instr. U. Calif., 1951; asst. prof. neurosurgery UCLA, 1952-56, assoc. prof., 1956-59, prof., 1959-87, now emeritus, chief div. neurosurgery, 1952-85, chmn. dept. surgery, 1981-87; cons. neurosurgery, Wadsworth VA Hosp. Former mem., chmn. editorial bd. Jour. Neurosurgery; contbr. articles to sci. jours., chpts. in books. Lt. to capt. M.C. AUS, 1946-48. Fellow ACS (sec.); mem. AMA, Am. Surg. Assn., Pacific Coast Surg. Assn., L.A. Surg. Soc. (pres. 1978), Am. Assn. Neurol. Surgeons (pres. 1979-80, Cushing medalist, 1992), James IV Assn. Surgeons, Western Neurosurg. Soc. (past pres.), Soc. Neurol. Surgeons (past pres.), Neurosurg. Soc. Am., Am. Neurol. Assn., Soc. Univ. Surgeons, Soc. Brit. Neurol. Surgeons (hon.), Phi Beta Kappa, Sigma Xi, Alpha Omega Alpha. Republican. Episcopalian. Home: 435 Georgina Ave Santa Monica CA 90402-1909 Office: U Calif Sch Med Rm 18-228 CHS Box 95-7039 Los Angeles CA 90095-7039

STERN, WALTER PHILLIPS, investment executive; b. N.Y.C., Sept. 26, 1928; s. Leo and Marjorie (Phillips) S.; m. Elizabeth May, Feb. 12, 1958; children: Sarah May, William May, David May. AB, Williams Coll., 1950; MBA, Harvard U., 1952. With Lazard Freres & Co., N.Y.C., 1953-54; assoc. Burnham & Co., Inc. (predecessor firm to Drexel Burnham Lambert Group, Inc.), N.Y.C., 1954-60, ptnr., 1960-71, sr. exec. v.p., 1972-73; vice chmn., mng. dir. Ea. ops. Capital Rsch. Co., 1973-95; chmn. bd. New Perspective Fund, Inc., 1973—, Fundamental Investors Inc., 1978—; chmn. Europacific Growth Fund, Inc., 1984—; chmn. bd. dirs. Emerging Markets Growth Fund, Income Fund Am., Inc., Growth Fund Am., Am. Balanced Fund, Capital Group Internat., Inc., Temple-Inland, Inc., dir.; past mem. pub. bd. Mcpl. Securities Rulemaking Bd., 1984-87; trustee Fin. Analysts Rsch. Found.; chmn. bd. trustees Hudson Inst.; instr. investment mgmt. and fin. NYU, 1956-62; dir. Birla Advantage Fund, Birla Capital Internat. AMC Ltd., Bombay, 1994—; mem. adv. bd. South African Growth Fund, 1996. Contbr. articles to profl. jours. Dir. Jewish Cmty. Rels. Coun. N.Y.; mem. Coun. Fgn. Rels.; chmn. fin. adv. com. Haddassah; trustee Am. Jewish Com., Tel Aviv U., Jaffee Inst. Strategic Studies, Tel Aviv; mem. publ. com. Commentary, 1995—; dir. Am.-Israel Friendship League, 1996—; gov. Anti-Defamation League; bd. dirs. Am. Friends of Tel Aviv U.; v.p., mem. exec. com. Washington Inst. Near East Policy; chmn. steering com. Freedom Trade with Israel. Mem. N.Y. Soc. Security Analysts (bd. dirs.), Fin. Analysts Fedn. (pres. 1971-72, bd. dirs.), Inst. Chartered Fin. Analysts (pres. 1976-77, bd. dirs.), Assn. Investment and Mgmt. Rsch. (bd. dirs., exec. com. 1990-92), Harvard Club, Econ. Club, Sunningdale Country Club, Calif. Club, Phi Beta Kappa. Jewish. Home: 450 Fort Hill Rd Scarsdale NY 10583-2413 Office: Capital Group Inc 630 5th Ave Ste 36 New York NY 10111-0100 also: Capital Group Inc 333 S Hope St Los Angeles CA 90071-1406

STERN, WILLIAM LOUIS, botanist, educator; b. Paterson, N.J., Sept. 10, 1926; s. Abram and Rose (Chrisman) S.; m. Floraet Selma Tanis, Sept. 4, 1949; children: Susan Myra, Paul Elihu. BS, Rutgers U., 1950; MS, U. Ill., 1951, PhD, 1954. Instr., then asst. prof. Yale Sch. Forestry, 1953-60; curator div. plant anatomy Smithsonian Inst., 1960-64, chmn. dept botany, 1964-67; prof. botany U. Md., College Park, 1967-79, U. Fla., Gainesville, 1979—; chmn. dept. U. Fla., 1979-85; forestry officer FAO, 1963-64; mem. sci. adv. bd. Nat. Tropical Bot. Garden, 1969-83; mem. sci. adv. com. Winterthur Mus., 1973-86 ; vis. com. Arnold Arboretum of Harvard U., 1971-77; vice chmn. Arnold Arboretum of Harvard, 1973-76; asesor cientifico U. de los Andes, Merida, Venezuela, 1975; program dir. systematic biology NSF, 1978, 79; rsch. assoc. The Kampong, 1996—. Editor: Tropical Woods, 1953-60, Plant Sci. Bull., 1962-64, Biotropica, 1968-73; asso. editor: BioSci, 1963-65, Econ. Botany, 1966-75, Phytomorphology, 1996—; mem. editorial com.: Am. Jour. Botany, 1967-69. Bd. dirs. Fairchild Tropical Garden, 1980-86; trustee Kampong Fund, 1995—. Served with USNR, 1944-46, PTO. Fellow Linnean Soc. of London; mem. Bot. Soc. Am. (pres. 1984-86), Am. Inst. Biol. Scis. (bd. dirs. 1987-89), Internat. Assn. Wood Anatomists (hon., council), Am. Soc. Plant Taxonomists (pres. 1981), Soc. Econ. Botany (treas. 1988-91), Bot. Soc. Am. (Cert. Merit 1987), Torrey Bot. Club (editor Memoirs 1971-75), Washington Bot. Soc. (pres. 1972), Internat. Soc. Tropical Foresters, Soc. Advancement Research (Philippines), Assn. for Tropical Biology, Internat. Wood Collectors Soc. (life), Phi Beta Kappa, Sigma Xi, Delta Phi Alpha, Phi Kappa Phi, Phi Sigma. Office: U Fla Dept Botany Gainesville FL 32611-8526

STERNBERG, DANIEL ARIE, musician, conductor, educator; b. Lwow, Poland, Mar. 29, 1913; came to U.S., 1939, naturalized, 1946; s. Philipp and Eva (Makowska) S.; m. Felicitas Gobineau, July 29, 1936. Baccalaureate, Realgymnasium, Vienna, 1931; student, U. Vienna, 1931-35; diploma of condr., Vienna State Acad. Music, 1935; composition study with Karl Weigl, 1931-35, conducting with Fritz Stiedry, 1935-36. Lectr., Vienna Volkshochschule, 1933-34; head piano dept. Hockaday Inst. Music, Dallas, 1940-42; dean Sch. Music, Baylor U., Waco, Tex., 1942-81; Ben H. Williams disting. prof. Sch. Music, Baylor U., 1981-82; lectr. mus. subjects. Condr. Vienna Vets. Orch., 1934-35; asst. condr. Leningrad Philharm. and Kirov Opera, 1935-36; guest condr. Leningrad and Moscow radio orchs., 1936, Dallas Symphony Orch., 1952, 65; music dir. Tbilisi (USSR) State Symphony Orch., 1936-37; mus. dir., condr. Waco Symphony Orch., 1962-87; concert accompanist. Recipient Abrams Meml. award for composition Dallas Symphony, 1948. Mem. Phi Mu Alpha, Omicron Delta Kappa. Home: 3108 Robin Rd Waco TX 76708-2275

STERNBERG, HARRY, artist; b. N.Y.C., July 19, 1904; s. Simon and Rose (Br) S.; m. Mary Elizabeth Gosney, 1939; 1 child, Leslie Louise. Student, Art Students League, N.Y.C. tchr. Art Students League, N.Y.C.; formerly head art dept. Idyllwild Sch. Music and Art, UCLA, U. So. Calif., Idyllwild (Calif.) Arts Found., 1956-63; tchr. graphics San Diego State Coll., 1967-68; artist-in-residence Palomar Coll., San Marcos, Calif.; adj. prof. painting U. Calif., Idyllwild Sch. Music and Art. Exhibited 25 Year Retrospective show, ACA and Gorezick Galleries, 1953; one-man shows ACA Gallery, N.Y.C., 9 shows 1956-82, Brigham Young U., 58, 62, 75, Gorelick Gallery, 58, Nat. Inst. Arts and Letters, 1961, Utah State U., 1962, Salt Lake Art Ctr., Salt Lake City, 1962, Heritage Gallery, L.A., 1964, Gray Gallery, Escondido, 1970, Ulrich Mus., Art Students League, N.Y.C., 1982, Galaria Palomas, San Juan, P.R., 1982-83, Deicas Gallery, La Jolla, Calif., 1983, San Diego Print Club, 1983, Mary Ryan Gallery, N.Y.C., 1984, 89, Idyllwild Sch. Art, 1985, Todd Gallery, Idyllwild, Calif., 1985-86, 89, (graphic exhbn.) Tobey Moss Gallery, L.A., 1986, Susan Teller Gallery, N.Y.C., 1989, 90, 92, Sragow Gallery, N.Y.C., 1990, graphics retrospective Art Students League, N.Y.C., 1992, Athenium, San Diego, 1992, Susan Teller Gallery, N.Y.C., 1993; woodcut exhibition Brighton Press, San Diego, 1992; traveling show Art in the Labor Movement: West Berlin, 1983, Hamburg, Fed. Republic of Germany, 1984, Stockholm, 1985, Rome, 185, England, 1985, Midtown Gallery, N.Y.C., 1991, Worcester Art Mus., 1991, Boston Mus. Fine Art, 1991, Palomar Coll. Gallery, Vista, Calif., 1993; retrospective exhbns. Walker Art Centre, Mpls., 1973, Wichita State U., 1975, Art Students League, N.Y.C., Assoc. Am. Artists, N.Y.C., Art and Design Gallery-Bonsall, 1976, Bethesda (Md.) Art Gallery, 1980, New Vistas Gallery, Vista, Calif., 1980, Libr. of Congress, 1983, Bethesda Gallery, (Md.), Midtown Gallery, N.Y.C., 1988, 89, Avonca Internat., Rancho Bernardo, Calif., 1988, Nat. Acad. Design, 1988, Associated Am. Gallery, N.Y.C., 1989, Art Students League,

N.Y.C., 1994, San Diego Mus. Art, 1994, 95; represented in permanent collections Mus. Modern Art, Met. Mus., Whitney Mus., Bklyn., Cleve., Phila. museums, Library Congress, Victoria and Albert Mus., London, Bibliothique Nationale, Paris, Syracuse U., H. de Young Meml. Mus., Wichita (Kans.) State Mus., San Francisco, Fogg Mus., Boston, Addison Gallery Am. Art, Boston, Syracuse U. Mus., Library Congress, Washington, N.Y. Pub. Library, U. Minn., Nat. Portrait Gallery, Washington, Nat. Mus., Tel Aviv, N.Z. Mus. Art, St. Lawrence U., Roberson Art Centre, Binghamton, N.Y., Cleve. Mus. Art, Ulrich Mus., Thorne Mus., Keene State Coll., Hirshorn Mus., Washington, Roanoke Mus. Fine Arts, Bklyn. Mus., 1986, La Jolla Mus. Art, San Diego, 1988, Nat. Acad. Design, 1988, Associated Am. Artists, N.Y.C., 1988, Wolfsonian Mus., Miami, Fla., San Diego Mus. Art, Susan Teller Gallery, N.Y.C., Brighton Press, Calif., U. Judaism, Santa Ysabel Gallery, Calif.; producer, dir.: motion pictures The Many Worlds of Art, 1960, Art and Reality, 1961; author: Silk Screen Color Printing, 1942, Modern Methods and Materials of Etching, 1949, Compositions, 1957, Modern Drawing, 1958, Woodcut, 1962, Short Shots and Rituals With Woodcuts, 1990, A Life, an autobiography in woodcuts, 1992. Recipient Guggenheim fellowship, 1936, 1st prize Phila. Print Club, 1942; Living Arts Found., grantee, 1960; recipient graphic prize Audubon Artists, 1955, purchase award Nat. Inst. Arts and Letters, 1972. Mem. Art Students League of N.Y.C. (hon.), Artists Equity, Artists Guild of Fine Arts Gallery (San Diego), Nat. Acad. Design, Nat. Acad. Design (N.Y.C.). Home: 2234 Hilton Head Gln Escondido CA 92026-1071 Studio: 1718 E Valley Pky Escondido CA 92027-2548

STERNBERG, PAUL, retired ophthalmologist; b. Chgo., Dec. 18, 1918; s. David M. and Sarah (Kopeka) S.; m. Dorie Betty Feitler, Dec. 24, 1949; children—Daniel P., Patricia F., Paul, Susan P., David. B.S., Northwestern U., 1938, M.D., 1940. Intern Michael Reese Hosp., Chgo., 1940-41; resident ophthalmology Michael Reese Hosp., Ill. Eye & Ear Infirmary U. Ill.; spl. fellow ophthalmology Cornell U. Med. Center, N.Y. Hosp., Wilmer Inst. Johns Hopkins, 1941-44; practice medicine, specializing in ophthalmology Chgo., from 1945; attending ophthalmologist Cook County Hosp., Michael Reese Hosp., Highland Park (Ill.) Hosp., Louis Weiss Meml. Hosp.; prof. ophthalmology Chgo. Med. Sch. Contbr. sci. articles to med. and ophthal. jours. Fellow A.C.S.; mem. Assn. for Research in Ophthalmology, Am. Assn. Ophthalmology, Am. Acad. Ophthalmology, Chgo. Ophthal. Soc., Pan-Am. Congress Ophthalmology. Clubs: Standard (Chgo.); Lake Shore Country (Glencoe, Ill.). Home: 359 Surfside Pl Glencoe IL 60022-1723 Office: 225 W Washington St Ste 2150 Chicago IL 60606-3418

STERNBERG, PAUL J., lawyer; b. Nyack, N.Y., July 14, 1933; s. Paul and Helen Louise (Butler) S.; m. Barbara Patricia Boyle, Sept. 3, 1955; children: Lucinda Abbott, Alicia Boyle, Amanda Butler (dec.). AB, Harvard U., 1954; LLB, Columbia U., 1957. Bar: N.Y. 1958, Iowa 1981. Assoc. Choate, Reynolds, Huntington & Hollister, N.Y.C., 1958-61; mng. counsel The Singer Co., N.Y.C., 1963-79; sr. v.p., gen counsel, sec. Bandag Inc., Muscatine, Iowa, 1979-86; spl. counsel Hinman, Howard, and Kattell, Binghamton and Norwich, N.Y., 1986-89; v.p., gen. counsel, sec. Raymond Corp., Greene, N.Y., 1989—; bd. dirs. G.N. Johnston Equipment Co., Ltd., Dockstocker Corp., Corp. Raymond de Mex., Legal Aid for Broome and Chenango, Inc. Capt. U.S. Army, 1961-62. Mem. ABA, Assn. of Bar of City of N.Y., N.Y. State Bar Assn., Harvard Club N.Y.C., Manursing Island Club. Office: The Raymond Corp S Canal St Greene NY 13778

STERNBERG, ROBERT JEFFREY, psychology educator; b. Newark, Dec. 8, 1949; s. Joseph Sternberg and Lilliam Myriam (Politzer) Weingast; children: Seth, Sara; m. Alejandra Campos, 1991. BA summa cum laude, Yale U., 1972; PhD, Stanford U., 1975; D honoris causa, Complutense U., 1994. Mem. faculty dept. psychology Yale U., New Haven, 1975—; prof. psychology Yale U., 1983-86, IBM prof. psychology and edn., 1986—. Editor-in-chief Ency. of Human Intelligence, Psychol. Bull., 1991-96; cons. editor Learning and Individual Differences, 1992—, Intelligence, 1977—, Devel. Rev., 1987-91, Jour. Personality and Social Psychology, 1989-91, Psychol. Rev., 1989-91; author: Intelligence, Information Processing and Analogical Reasoning, 1977, Beyond IQ, 1985, The Triarchic Mind, 1988, Metaphors of Mind, 1990, In Search of the Human Mind, 1995, (with T. Lubart) Defying the Crowd, 1995, Successful Intelligence, 1996, Pathways to Psychology, 1997. Recipient award for Excellence Mensa Edn. and Rsch. Found., 1989; Guggenheim Found. fellow, 1985-86. Fellow APA (past pres. divsns. 1 and 15, McCandless Young Scientist award divsn. devel. psychology 1982, Disting. Sci. award for early career contbn. 1981), AAAS, Am. Acad. Arts and Scis.; me. Am. Ednl. Rsch. Assn. (Rsch. Rev. award 1986, Outstanding Book award 1987, Sylvia Scribner award 1996), Soc. Multivariate Exptl. Psychology (Cattell award 1982), Nat. Assn. Gifted Children (Disting. Scholar award 1985), Phi Beta Kappa. Avocations: physical fitness, travel, reading. Home: 105 Spruce Bank Rd Hamden CT 06518-2233 Office: Yale Univ Dept Psychology PO Box 208205 New Haven CT 06520-8205

STERNBERGER, LUDWIG AMADEUS, neurologist, educator; b. Munich, Germany, May 26, 1921; s. Hugo and Emy (Welinger) S.; m. Nancy Jeanne Hoy, Dec. 13, 1961. B.A., Am. U. Beirut, 1941, M.D., 1945. Fellow Sloan Kettering Meml. Cancer Ctr., N.Y.C., 1948-50; sr. med. biochemist N.Y. State Dept. Health, Albany, 1950-54; asst. prof. medicine Northwestern U., Chgo., 1954-55; chief basic scis. div. Med. Research Labs., Edgewood Arsenal, Md., 1957-78; prof. brain research U. Rochester Med. Ctr. (N.Y.), 1978-86; prof. neurology, pathology and anatomy U. Md., Balt., 1986-92; sci. co-dir., treas. Sternberger Monoclonals, Inc., Balt., 1992—. Author: Immunocytochemistry, 1974, 3d edit, 1986; mem. editoral bd. Cell and Tissue Research, Histochemistry, Jour. Histochemistry and Cytochemistry, Jour. Neurosci. Methods, Jour. Neuroimmunology, Histochem. Jour., Electron Microscopy in Biology. Served to maj. M.C., U.S. Army, 1955-57. Recipient Paul A. Siple prize, 1972; recipient Humboldt prize for sr. U.S. scientists, 1980, Classic Author citation Inst. Sci. Info., 1983; Senator Jacob K. Javits neurosci. investigator award, 1984; 25th most frequently cited author in sci. lit. of 1984; author of one of 17 Newcomer Superstar papers among 100 most cited of all time. Mem. Histochem. Soc. (pres. 1977-78), Am. Soc. Neurochemistry (program com. 1983-84), Am. Assn. Immunologists, Endocrine Soc., Am. Acad. Allergy, Am. Assn. Neuropathologists. Lutheran. Home: 10 Burwood Ct Lutherville Timonium MD 21093-3502

STERNE, BOBBIE LYNN, city council member; b. Ohio, Nov. 27, 1919; m. Eugene Sterne (dec.); children: Lynn, Cindy. Student, Akron U., 1941-42; student, U. Cin., 1946-47. RN, Ohio. City coun. mem. City of Cin., 1971—, mayor, 1976, 79; chair human resources com., City Coun. Cin., 1987-89, cmty. devel., housing zoning and environ. com.; mem., past chair fin. and labor com.; vice chair, past chair pub. works and traffic safety com.; chair intergovtl. affairs and environ. com., 1990—; past chair urban devel. com., housing com., human resources com.; vice chair fin. com., health social and childrens svcs. com.; mem. pub. works and utilities com., law and pub. safety com., select com. on spl. projects; past mem., past chair planning commn., retirement bd.; trustee City of Cin. Retirment Sys., 1989—. Bd. dirs. YWCA Alice Paul House, Charles P. Taft Meml. fund Com., Drug and Poison Info. Ctr., Friends of the William Howard Taft Birthplace, Greater Cin. Coalition People with Disabilities, Greater Cin. and No. Ky. Women's Sports Assn., Shawn Womack Dance Project, Ohio United Way; chmn. Emergency Svcs. Coalition; exec. com. Cmty.; adv. bd. Coun. on Child Abuse, First Step Home, State Cmty. Svc., U. Cin. Long Term Care Cmty., U. Cin. Clinical Ctr. Women's Health Initiative; govt. rels. com. Cmty. Chest; mem. sch. bd. Price Hill Cmty. Recipient Coun. Jewish Women Hannah G. Solomon award 1972, Citizens Com. on Youth's Most Valuable Citizen award, Achievement award Greater Cin. Beautiful Com., 1982, Anniversary award for work with Housing for Older Ams., Inc. Better Housing League, 1982, Orchid award Tri-State Air Com., 1982, Citizen's award Ohio Assn. for the Edn. Young Children, Advocate award Women in Communications, 1983, Betty Blake Award for Tourism, 1985, Others award Salvation Army, 1986. Home: 4033 Rose Hill Ave Cincinnati OH 45229-1524

STERNE, JOSEPH ROBERT LIVINGSTON, newspaper editor, educator; b. Phila., Apr. 25, 1928; s. Robert Livingston and Edith Eisner (Heymann) S.; m. Barbara Adele Greene, Feb. 10, 1951; children—Robert Greene, Paul Livingston, Edward Joseph, Adam Heymann, Lee Winslow Greene. B.A. cum laude, Lehigh U., 1948; M.S., Columbia, 1950. Reporter Salt Lake Telegram, Salt Lake City, 1948-49, Wall Street Jour., N.Y.C., 1950-51, Dallas Morning News, 1951-53; reporter Balt. Sun, 1953-72, editorial page editor, 1972-97; sr. fellow Inst. for Policy Studies Johns Hopkins U., 1997—. Mem. Am. Soc. Newspaper Editors, Center Club, Hamilton Street Club, Phi Beta Kappa. Home: 215 Melanchton Ave Lutherville Timonium MD 21093-5321 Office: Johns Hopkins U Inst Policy Studies 3400 N Charles St Baltimore MD 21218-4167

STERNER, FRANK MAURICE, industrial executive; b. Lafayette, Ind., Nov. 26, 1935; s. Raymond E. and Maudelene M. (Scipio) S.; m. Elsa Y. Rasmusson, June 29, 1958; children: Mark, Lisa. BS, Purdue U., 1958, MS, 1959, PhD, 1962. Sr. staff specialist Gen. Motors Inst., Flint, Mich., 1962-63; dir. personnel and orgnl. research Delco Electronics, Milw., 1963-66; dir. personnel devel. and research Delco Electronics, 1966-68; partner Nourse & Sterner, Inc., Milw., 1968-69; pres., 1969-73; assoc. dean, prof. Krannert Grad. Sch. of Mgmt., Purdue U., West Lafayette, Ind., 1973-79; v.p. human resources mgmt. Johnson Controls, Inc., Milw., 1979-89; pres., chief exec. officer E.R. Wagner Mfg. Co., 1989—; pres., owner Ridgeway Devel. Inc., Milw., 1993—; bd. dirs. Wasau Homes, Inc., E.R. Wagner Mfg. Co., Children's Hosp. Health Sys. Wis., Ridgeway Devel. Inc., Am. Lung Assn. Wis., Inroads/Wis., Inc., River Edge Nature Ctr., Inc. Contbr. articles to profl. jours. Club: Reamer. Home: 1440 E Standish Pl Milwaukee WI 53217-1958 Office: ER Wagner Mfg Co 4611 N 32nd St Milwaukee WI 53209-6023

STERNER, MICHAEL EDMUND, international affairs consultant; b. N.Y.C., Dec. 26, 1928; s. Harold Walther and Leonie (Knoedler) S.; m. Courtenay Read, Mar. 30, 1957; children: Lucian, Marcellin. AB, Harvard Coll., 1951. Govt. rels. rep. Arabian-Am. Oil Co., Dhahran, Saudi Arabia, 1951-54; joined Fgn. Svc., 1956; vice consul Aden, 1957-58; polit. officer Cairo, 1960-64; desk officer Near Eastern Affairs Dept. State, 1964-70, dir. Egyptian affairs, 1970-74; amb. to United Arab Emirates Abu Dhabi, 1974-76; dep. asst. sec. state for Near East and South Asian affairs, 1977-81; mng. dir. The IRC Group, Inc., 1982—. Mem. bd. govs. Mid. East Inst. With AUS, 1954-56. Mem. Coun. Fgn. Rels. Home: 2712 36th St NW Washington DC 20007-1421 Office: 1835 K St NW Washington DC 20006

STERNFELD, MARC HOWARD, investment banker; b. N.Y.C., July 12, 1947; s. Joseph and Jeane (Richstein) S.; m. Arleen Estelle Weinreb, Aug. 25, 1968; children: Joshua, Jonathan. BA, Queens Coll., 1968; MS, NYU, 1970; MBA, Columbia U., 1971. Spacecraft programmer Grumman Aero., 1968-70; fin. analyst CBS, N.Y.C., 1971-72; rsch. asst. Nat. Bur Econ. Rsch., 1970-71; sr. analyst N.Y.C. Police Dept., 1972-75; ptnr. Arthur Andersen & Co., N.Y.C., 1975-88; prin. Morgan Stanley, N.Y.C., 1987-94; mng. dir. Salomon Bros., N.Y.C., 1994-96; pres. Trans-Form L.L.C., N.Y.C., 1995—; mng. dir. Deutsche Morgan Grenfull, Global Ops. and Tech., 1996—; mem. exec. bd. Deutsche Bank. Mem. internat. bd. dirs., exec. com. United Synagogue Conservative Judaism; chmn. Joint Commn. on Dealing with Intermarriage; past pres. Marlboro Jewish Ctr.; bd. dirs. Fedn. Monmouth County, Jewish Family and Children Svcs. of Western Monmouth County; mem. dean's coun. Tisch Sch. Arts; mem. Parents Coun., Emory U. Mem. Jazz Vt. (bd. dirs.). Avocation: piano. Home: 13 Evan Dr Morganville NJ 07751-1062

STERNHAGEN, FRANCES, actress; b. Washington, Jan. 13, 1930. Student, Vassar Coll., Perry-Mansfield Sch. of Theatre; studied with Sanford Meisner, N.Y. Tchr. Milton Acad., Mass.; actress Arena Stage, Washington, 1953-54. Debut Thieves Carnival, N.Y., 1955; plays include The Carefree Tree, The Admirable Bashville (Clarence Derwent award, Obie award), Ulysses in Night Town, Red Eye of Love, Misalliance, The Return of Herbert Bracewell, Laughing Stock, The Displaced Person, The Pinter Plays (Obie award); Broadway shows include The Skin of Our Teeth, Viva Madison Avenue, Great Day in the Morning, The Right Honorable Gentleman, The Cocktail Party, Cock-a-Doddle Dandy, Playboy of the Western World, The Sign in Sidney Brustein's Window, The Good Doctor (Tony award 1973), Equus, Angel, On Golden Pond (Drama League award), The Father, Grownups, Summer, You Can't Take It With You, Home Front, Driving Miss Daisy, Remembrance, A Perfect Ganesh, The Heiress (Tony award 1995); actress films including Up The Down Staircase, Starting Over, 1979, Outland, 1981, Independence Day, 1983, Romantic Comedy, 1983, Bright Lights, Big City, 1988, See You in the Morning, 1989, Communion, 1989, Misery, 1990, Doc Hollywood, 1991, Raising Cain, 1992; (TV series) Love of Life, The Doctors, Secret Storm, Cheers, Golden Years, Under One Roof, The Road Home; (TV movies) Who Will Save Our Children?, 1978, Prototype, 1982, Resting Place, 1986, Follow Your Heart, 1990, She Woke Up, 1992, Labor of Love: The Arlette Schweitzer Story, 1993, Reunion, 1994, Tales from the Crypt, Outer Limits, Law and Order, 1990, 96.

STERNITZKE-HOLUB, ANN, elementary school educator; b. Oklahoma City, Okla., May 5, 1952; d. James Francis and Doris Josephine (Lahr) Sternitzke; m. James Robert Holub, Apr. 4, 1987. AA, Golden West Coll., Huntington Beach, Calif., 1972; BS, Calif. State U., Fullerton, 1975, post-grad., 1976. Cert. secondary multiple subject, phys. edn. and English tchr. grades kindergarten-12, Calif.; life cert. educator Calif. Cmty. Colls. Phys. edn. and fencing instr. Fullerton Coll., 1976-82; fencing instr. Golden West Coll., Huntington Beach, 1977-83, Calif. State U., Fullerton, 1983-86; elem. phys. edn. specialist Placentia-Yorba Linda (Calif.) Unified Sch. Dist., 1989-93, elem. tchr. Bryant Ranch Sch., 1993—; puppeteer Adventure City Amusement Park, Anaheim, Calif. Mem. support staff 1984 Olympics, Long Beach, 1984; entertainer Stagelight Family Prodns., Brea, Calif., 1993—. Grantee Disneyland, 1993, 94, 95, 96, 97. Mem. AAHPERD, U.S. Fencing Assn., U.S. Olympic Soc., U.S. Fencing Coaches Assn., Calif. State U. Alumni Assn. Republican. Avocations: dance, musical theatre, puppetry, fencing, costuming. Office: Bryant Ranch Sch 24695 Paseo De Toronto Yorba Linda CA 92887-5116

STERNLICHT, SANFORD, English and theater arts educator, writer; b. N.Y.C., Sept. 20, 1931; s. Irving Stanley and Sylvia (Hilsenroth) S.; m. Dorothy Hilkert, June 4, 1950 (dec. 1977); children: David, Daniel. BS, SUNY, Oswego, 1953; MA, Colgate U., 1955; PhD, Syracuse U., 1962. Instr. SUNY, Oswego, 1959-60, asst. prof., 1960-62, prof. and dir. grad. studies in English, 1962-72, chmn. dept. theater, 1972-84; adj. prof. English Syracuse (N.Y.) U., 1984—; Leverhulme vis. prof. English U. of York, Eng., 1965-66. Author: Gull's Way, 1961, The Blue Star Commodore, 1961, Love in Pompeii, 1967, John Webster's Imagery and the Webster Canon, 1972, John Masefield, 1977, McKinley's Bulldog, 1977 (Mil. Book Club award, Saturday Evening Post Book Club award), C.S. Forester, 1981, Padraic Colum, 1985; (with E.M. Jameson) The Black Devil of the Bayous, 1971; (with E.M. Jameson) U.S.F. Constellation: Yankee Racehorse, 1981, John Galsworthy, 1986, R.F. Delderfield, 1988, Stevie Smith, 1990, Stephen Spender, 1992, Siegfried Sassoon, 1993, All Things Herriot: James Herriot and His Peaceable Kingdon, 1995, Jean Rhys, 1997; editor: The Selected Short Stories of Padraic Colum, 1985, The Selected Plays of Padraic Colum, 1986, The Selected Poems of Padraic Colum, 1988, The Selected Poems of Padraic Colum, 1988, In Search of Steview Smith, 1991, New Plays from the Abbey Theatre, 1993-1995. Lt. (j.g.) USN, 1955-59, comdr. USNR, ret. Recipient New Poets award Writer mag., 1960, Chancellor's award SUNY, 1974; fellow Poetry Soc. Am., 1964; rsch. grantee SUNY, 1963-70; named Tchr. of Yr. Syracuse U., 1986. Mem. MLA, NAACP, PEN, Shakespeare Assn. Am., Am. Conf. Irish Studies. Democrat. Jewish. Home: 128 Dorset Rd Syracuse NY 13210-3048 Office: Syracuse U Dept English Syracuse NY 13244

STERNLIEB, LAWRENCE JAY, marketing professional; b. Akron, Ohio, Aug. 19, 1951; s. Max and Mollie (Atleson) S. BA in English, Kent State U., 1974, BA in Sociology, 1974, MA in Sociology, 1977. Lic. social worker, Ohio. Social program specialist State of Ohio, Cleve., 1976-79; sr. mktg. exec. Xerox Corp., Cleve., 1979-82; nat. acct. mgr. NCR Corp., Independence, Ohio, 1983-85; sr. acct. mgr. McDonnell Douglas Corp., Independence, Ohio, 1985-87; sr. mktg. rep. Prime Computer Inc., Independence, Ohio, 1987-90; acct. exec. GE Cons. Svcs., Independence, Ohio, 1990-94; sr. sales and mktg. exec. Decarlo, Paternite and Assoc., Independence, Ohio, 1994-96; major acct. mgr. General DataComm, Inc., Cleve., 1996—; instr. Cuyahoga C.C., Cleve., 1980-81, 92. Author: Barry Storm, 1995. Mem. Cleve. Playhouse. Avocations: acting, modeling, writing, sports, physical fitness. Home: 8694 Broadview Rd Apt 228H Broadview Heights OH 44147

STERNMAN, JOEL W., lawyer; b. N.Y.C., Oct. 20, 1943; s. Abraham and Sarah (Simon) S.; children: Mark S., Cheryl A.; m. Barbara E. Shiers, March 31, 1985; children: Matthew S., Julia S. AB, Dartmouth Coll., 1965; LLB, Yale U., 1968. Bar: N.Y. 1970, U.S. Dist. Ct. (so. and ea. dists.) N.Y. 1971, U.S. Ct. Appeals (2d cir.) 1972, U.S. Supreme Ct. 1984, U.S. Ct. Appeals (6th cir.) 1985, U.S. Ct. Appeals (9th cir.) 1994, U.S. Tax Ct. 1996. Law clk. to judge U.S. Dist. Ct., New Haven, 1968-69; assoc. Rosenman Colin Freund Lewis & Cohen, N.Y.C., 1969-77; ptnr. Rosenman & Colin, N.Y.C., 1977—. Editor Yale Law Jour., New Haven, 1966-68. Mem. Phi Beta Kappa. Office: Rosenman & Colin LLP 575 Madison Ave New York NY 10022-2511

STERNS, JOEL HENRY, lawyer; b. N.Y.C., Apr. 13, 1934; s. Barney and Yvetta S.; m. Joanne Glickman, Nov. 19, 1961; children: Racel, Leslie, David. BS in Journalism, 1956; MPA, Princeton U., 1958; JD, NYU, 1967. Bar: N.J., D.C. Exec. asst. to commr., acting commr. N.J. Dept. Conservation and Econ. Devel., 1958-61; exec. asst. to adminstr. Bur. Security and Consular Affairs, U.S. Dept. State, 1961-62; regional programs coord. Alliance for Progress, 1962-64; exec. asst. to pres. Export-Import Bank U.S., 1964; dep. commr. N.J. Dept. Cmty. Affairs, 1967-68; counsel to gov. N.J., 1968-70; pres. firm Sterns, Herbert & Weinroth (P.A.), Trenton, N.J., 1970-88; mem. exec. com., compensation com. and mktg. com. Sterns, Herbert & Weinroth (merged with Hannoch-Weisman 1988), Roseland, N.J., 1988-91; pres. Hannoch-Weisman, Roseland, 1991-93, Sterns & Weinroth, Trenton, 1994—; mem. lawyers adv. com. U.S. Dist. Ct. N.J., 1995—. Mem. ABA, Am. Law Inst., Am. Judicature Soc., N.J. Bar Assn. (trustee), Mercer County Bar Assn., Assn. Princeton U. Grad. Alumni (trustee 1975-77), NYU Alumni Assn. N.J. (Disting. Alumni award 1987). Home: 1262 River Rd Titusville NJ 08560 Office: Sterns & Weinroth PO Box 1298 50 W State St Ste 1400 Trenton NJ 08607

STERNSTEIN, ALLAN J., lawyer; b. Chgo., June 7, 1948; s. Milton and Celia (Kaganove) S.; m. Miriam A. Dolgin, July 12, 1970 (div. July 1981); children—Jeffery A., Amy R.; m. Beverly A. Cook, Feb. 8, 1986; children: Cheryl L., Julia S. B.S., U. Ill., 1970; M.S., U. Mich., 1972; J.D., Loyola U., 1977. Bar: Ill. 1977, U.S. Dist. Ct. (no. dist.) Ill. 1977, U.S. Dist. Ct. (no. dist.) Ohio 1977, U.S. Dist. Ct. (ea. dist) Mich. 1986, U.S. Dist. Ct. (we. dist.) Mich. 1990, U.S. Ct. Customs and Patent Appeals 1978, U.S. Ct. Appeals (7th cir.) 1979, U.S. Ct. Appeals (Fed. cir.) 1982. Patent agent Sunbeam Corp., Oak Brook, Ill., 1972-76; ptnr. Neuman, Williams, Anderson & Olson, Chgo., 1976-84; div. patent counsel Abbott Labs., North Chgo., Ill., 1984-87; ptnr. Brinks Hofer Gilson & Lione, Chgo., 1987—; adj. prof. of law John Marshall Law Sch., 1989-90, DePaul Univ., 1990-92, Univ. Ill., 1992—. Legal advisor Legal Aid Soc., Chgo., 1974-76, Pub. Defender's Office, Chgo., 1974. Teaching fellow U. Mich., 1971-72; research grantee U. Mich., U.S. Air Force, 1971-72. Mem. ABA, Chgo. Bar Assn., Patent Law Assn. of Chgo. (com. chmn. 1982), Am. Intellectual Property Law Assn., Licensing Execs. Soc., Tau Beta Pi, Sigma Tau, Sigma Gamma Tau, Phi Eta Sigma. Jewish. Office: Brinks Hofer Gilson & Lione 455 N Cityfront Plaza Dr Chicago IL 60611-5503

STERRETT, JAMES KELLEY, II, lawyer; b. St. Louis, Nov. 26, 1946; s. James Kelley and Anastasia Mary (Holzer) S.; 1 child, Brittany. AB, San Diego State U., 1968; JD, U. Calif., Berkeley, 1971; LLM, U. Pa., 1973. Bar: Calif. 1972, U.S. Dist. Ct. (so. dist.) Calif. 1972. From assoc. to ptnr. Gray, Cary, Ames & Frye, San Diego, 1972-83; ptnr. Lillick, McHose & Charles, San Diego, 1983-90, Pillsbury, Madison & Sutro, San Diego, 1991-96, Dostart Clapp Sterrett & Coveney, LLP, 1996—. Contbr. articles to profl. jours. Bd. dirs. Holiday Bowl, San Diego, 1980—, Mus. Photog. Arts, San Diego, 1985-88, San Diego Internat. Sports Coun., 1980—, pres., 1990, chmn., 1992. Capt. USAFR, 1972. Fellow U. Pa. Ctr. Study Fin. Instns., 1971-72. Mem. ABA, Calif. Bar Assn., San Diego County Bar Assn. Republican. Episcopalian. Club: Fairbanks Ranch Country (Rancho Santa Fe) (bd. dirs. 1985-87). Avocations: golf, college football, hiking. Office: Dostart Clapp Sterrett & Coveney 4370 La Jolla Village Dr San Diego CA 92122-1253

STERRETT, JAMES MELVILLE, accountant, business consultant; b. Chicago, Dec. 25, 1949; s. James McAnlis and Antoinette (Galligan) S.; m. Joyce Mieko Motoda, Sept. 1, 1989; 1 child, Victoria Hanako. BS in Acctg., Chaminade U., Honolulu, 1988; MBA, Chaminade U., 1991. CPA, Hawaii. Cons. Profitability Cons., Honolulu, 1985-87; pres. Sterrett Cons. Group, Honolulu, 1987-88; auditor Deloitte & Touche, Honolulu, 1988-90; acct., cons. pvt. practice, Honolulu, 1990—. Mem. Nat. Soc. Pub. Accts., Nat. Assn. Tax Practitioners, Hawaii Soc. CPA's, Delta Epsilon, Sigma. Office: 1314 S King St Ste 650 Honolulu HI 96814-1941

STERRETT, SAMUEL BLACK, lawyer, former judge; b. Washington, Dec. 17, 1922; s. Henry Hatch Dent and Helen (Black) S.; m. Jeane McBride, Aug. 27, 1949; children: Samuel Black, Robin Dent, Douglas McBride. Student, St. Albans Sch., 1933-41; grad., U.S. Mcht. Marine Acad., 1945; BA, Amherst Coll., 1947; LLB, U. Va., 1950; LLM in Taxation, NYU, 1959. Bar: D.C. 1951, Va. 1950. Atty. Alvord & Alvord, Washington, 1950-56; trial atty. Office Regional Counsel, Internal Revenue Service, N.Y.C., 1956-60; ptnr. Sullivan, Shea & Kenney, Washington, 1960-68; municipal cons. to office vice pres. U.S., 1965-68; judge U.S. Tax Ct., 1968-88, chief judge, 1985-88; ptnr. Myerson, Kuhn & Sterrett, Washington, 1988-89; of counsel Vinson & Elkins, Washington, 1990—. Bd. mgrs. Chevy Chase Village, 1970-74, chmn., 1972-74; 1st v.p. bd. trustees, mem. exec. com. Washington Hosp. Center, 1969-79, chmn. bd. trustees, 1979-84; chmn. bd. trustees Washington Healthcare Corp., 1982-87; chmn. bd. trustees Medlantic Healthcare Group, 1987-89; mem. audit com. Medlantic Healthcare Group, 1990—; mem. Washington Cathedral chpt., 1973-81; mem. governing bd. St. Albans Sch., 1977-81; trustee Louise Home, 1979-89. Served with AUS, 1943; Served with U.S. Mcht. Marine, 1943-46. Fellow Am. Bar Found.; mem. ABA, Fed. Bar Assn., D.C. Bar Assn., Am. Coll. Tax Counsel, Soc. of the Cincinnati, Coun. for Future, Am. Inns. of Ct., Chevy Chase Club (bd. govs. 1979-84, pres. 1984), Met. Club, Lawyers Club, Alibi Club, Alfalfa Club, Ch. of N.Y. Club, Beta Theta Pi. Episcopalian. Office: Vinson & Elkins 1455 Pennsylvania Ave NW Washington DC 20004-1008

STERZER, FRED, research physicist; b. Vienna, Austria, Nov. 18, 1929; came to U.S., 1947, naturalized, 1952; s. Karl and Rosa (Trumer) S.; m. Betty Distel, Sept. 5, 1964 (dec.). B.S. in Physics, CCNY, 1951; M.S. in Physics, NYU, 1952, Ph.D. in Physics, 1955. With RCA, 1954-87, RCA Labs., David Sarnoff Research Center, Princeton, N.J., 1956-87; dir. microwave tech. center RCA Labs., David Sarnoff Research Center, 1972-87; dir. microwave research lab. David Sarnoff Research Ctr., 1987-88; pres. MMTC, Inc., Princeton, 1988—; Herbert J. Kayser research prof., City Coll., CUNY, 1986-87. Contbr. numerous articles to profl. publs. Fellow IEEE; mem. Am. Phys. Soc., Nat. Acad. Engring., Sigma Xi, Phi Beta Kappa. Condr. research on optical components, microwave solid-state devices and circuits, med. microwave tech. Home: 4432 Province Line Rd Princeton NJ 08540-4368 Office: MMTC Inc 12 Roszel Rd Princeton NJ 08540-6234

STETLER, C. JOSEPH, retired lawyer; b. Wapaconeta, Ohio, May 13, 1917; s. Clarence Henry and Mary Frances (Kavanaugh) S.; m. Mary Norine Delaney, Aug. 16, 1941; children: Joseph James, David John, Mary Catherine, Julia Anne, Norine Teresa and Kathleen Frances (twins). LL.B., Cath. U. Am., 1938, LL.M., 1940; postgrad., Benjamin Franklin Sch. Accounting, Washington, 1940-41; D.Sc. (hon.), Mass. Coll. Pharmacy, 1978. Bar: D.C. 1940, Ill. 1951. With various agys. U.S. Govt., 1935-51; with AMA, 1951-63; gen. counsel, dir. legal and socio-econ. div., 1951-63; exec. v.p., gen. counsel Pharm. Mfrs. Assn., Washington, 1963-65; pres. Pharm. Mfrs. Assn., 1965-79, 84-85; ptnr. Munsey, Samuel & Stetler, 1979-81, Dickstein, Shapiro & Morin, 1981-84; pvt. practice Washington, 1984-86; of counsel Royer, Shacknai & Mehle, Washington, 1986-88, Hyman, Phelps & McNamara, Washington, 1988-93; ret., 1995. Author: (with Alan Moritz) Doctor Patient and the Law, 1962, Handbook of Legal Medicine, 1964, (with Wm. Cray) Patients in Peril, The Stunning Generic Drug Scandal, 1991. Mem. staff 2d Hoover Commn., 1953-54; mem. Reagan-Bush Health Adv. Com., 1980-81, Social Security Adv. Coun., 1983. Capt. AUS, 1942-46, PTO. Mem. ABA, D.C. Bar Assn. Roman Catholic. Home: 5906 Maplewood Park Pl Bethesda MD 20814-1744

STETLER, DAVID J., lawyer; b. Washington, Sept. 6, 1949; s. C. Joseph and Norine (Delaney) S.; m. Mary Ann Ferguson, Aug. 14, 1971; children: Brian, Christopher, Jennifer. BA, Villanova U., 1971, JD, 1974. Bar: U.S. Supreme Ct. 1978, Ill. 1988, U.S. Ct. Appeals (7th cir.) 1988, U.S. Ct. Appeals (3d cir.) 1992, U.S. Dist. Ct. (ctrl. dist.) 1994, U.S. Ct. Appeals (8th cir.) 1994. Atty. IRS, Washington, 1974-79; spl. atty. tax divsn. Dept. Justice, Washington, 1975-79; asst. atty. U.S. Atty.'s Office, Chgo., 1979-88, dep. chief spl. prosecutions div., 1985-86, chief criminal receiving and appellate divsns., 1986-88; ptnr. McDermott, Will & Emery, Chgo., 1988—; lectr. Atty. Gen. Trial Advocacy Inst., Washington, 1977—. Mem. ABA (chmn. midwest subcom. White Collar Crime com. 1991-93). Office: McDermott Will & Emery 227 W Monroe St Chicago IL 60606-5016

STETLER, RUSSELL DEARNLEY, JR., private investigator; b. Phila., Jan. 15, 1945; s. Russell Dearnley and Martha Eleanor (Schultz) S. B.A. with honors in Philosophy, Haverford (Pa.) Coll., 1966; postgrad., New Sch. Social Research, 1966-67. Research asst. to Bertrand Russell, 1967; lectr. Hendon Coll., London, 1968-69; pres. Archetype, Inc., Berkeley, Calif., 1971-78; pub. Westworks, Berkeley, 1977-80; pvt. investigator, 1980-90; chief investigator Calif. Appellate Project, 1990-95; dir. of investigations N.Y. State Capital Defender Office, N.Y.C., 1995—; cons., dir. Ramparts Press, Palo Alto, 1971-80; editorial cons. Internews, Berkeley, 1973-78; faculty Caribbean Sch., Ponce, P.R., 1978-80. Author: The Battle of Bogside, 1970; co-editor: The Assassinations: Dallas and Beyond, 1976. Research grantee Atlantic Peace Found., 1969-70. Mem. Calif. Assn. Lic. Investigators, Nat. Assn. Legal Investigators, Calif. Soccer Referees Assn.-North (treas. Marin County chpt. 1982-90), Amigos de las Americas (pres. Marin chpt. 1985-88). Clubs: Mill Valley Soccer (dir. 1981), Albany-Berkeley Soccer (pres. 1977-78). Office: Capital Defender Office 80 Centre St Rm 266 New York NY 10013-4306

STETSON, DANIEL EVERETT, museum director; b. Oneida, N.Y., Jan. 3, 1956; s. Robert Everett and Barbara Elizabeth (Gray) S.; m. Catherine Marie Smith; children: Kellee, Natalie, Philip. BA in Art History, Potsdam Coll. Arts and Scis., 1978; MFA in Museology, Syracuse U., 1981. Teaching asst. fine arts dept. Potsdam (N.Y.) Coll. Arts and Scis., 1977-78; grad. asst. Syracuse (N.Y.) U. Art Collections, 1979-80; acting dir. Picker Art Gallery and Colgate U. Art Collections, Colgate U., Hamilton, N.Y., 1980-81; dir. Gallery of Art U. No. Iowa, Cedar Falls, 1981-87; dir. Davenport (Iowa) Mus. Art, 1987-91; exec. dir. Austin (Tex.) Mus. Art (formerly Laguna Gloria Art Mus.), 1991-96, founding exec. dir., 1994; exec. dir. Polk Mus. Art, Lakeland, Fla., 1996—; guest curator Joe and Emily Lowe Art Gallery, Syracuse U., 1980; mem. Inter Mus. Conservation Lab., Oberlin, 1987-91; mem. design adv. com. Iowa Capitol, Des Moines, 1989-91; panel cons. Arts Midwest/Affiliated States Art Assns. of Upper Midwest, Mpls., 1983, 88; bd. dirs. Iowa Arts Coalition, 1990-91; chair Tex. Commn. on the Arts Visual Arts Review Panel, 1994; mem. planning com. Tex. Assn. of Mus., 1994; mem. art in pub. pls. com. Austin Airport, 1995. Author/curator: (exhbn. catalog) José de Creeft (1884-1982), 1983, Contemporary Icons and Explorations, 1988, (exhbn. catalog) Philip Perlstein-Painting to Watercolors, 1983, Walter Dusenbery Classical Echoes, 1985, Jaune Quick-to-See Smith and George Longfish: Personal Symbols, 1986, Reuban Nakian: Leda and The Swan, 1983, Focus 1 Michael Boyd: Paintings, 1980, 89, Focus 2 Photo Image League, 1989, Focus 3 The Art of Haiti: A Sense of Wonder, 1989, Focus 6—Contemporary Devel. in Glass, 1990, Peter Dean: Landscapes of the Mind, 1981, Joseph Raffael, 1987, Born in Iowa-The Homecoming, 1986, Stieglitz and 40 Other Photographers—The Development of a Collection, 1991-92, New Works (Austin and Central Texas Artists), 1992, 94, Companions in Time: The Paintings of William Lester & Everett Spruce Catalogue Essay, 1993, Human Nature, Human Form Catalogue Essay, 1993, Sources and Collaborations: The Making of the Holocaust Project by Judy Chicago and Donald Woodman tour and catalog, 1994—, Bucking the Texan Myth-Scouting the Third Frontier, 1996. Bd. mem. arts coun. Cedar Arts Forum, Black Hawk County, Iowa, 1983-85; curriculum com. Leadership Investment for Tomorrow, Cedar Falls-Waterloo, Iowa, 1985-86; mem. adv. com. MBA Course of Study Styles and Strategies Non-Profit Orgns. St. Ambrose U., 1989-91, Austin BCA Arts Week Poster and Awards, 1993; mem. City of Austin Funding Process Rev. Com., 1992; Facilities Team Austin Comprehensive Arts Plan, 1991-93; mem. adv. panel Tex. Commn. Arts Visual Arts, 1993; field reviewer Inst. Mus. Svcs.-Gen. Operating Support Grant Field Reviewer, 1993; mem. arts com. Downtown Mgmt. Assn., 1995; mem. arts sub-com. Downtown Commn.; bd. dirs. Friends of the Libr., Lakeland, 1996—, Quality Improvement Coun. Harrison Arts Ctr., Lakeland, 1996—. Fellow N.E. Mus. Conf., Rochester, N.Y., 1979; grantee Iowa Arts Coun., Tex. Commn. Arts, NEA advancement program grant phase I & II, 1993-95; recipient mus. scholarship Am. Law Inst. ABA, Atlanta, Phila., 1984, 93. Mem. Am. Assn. Mus., Midwest Mus. Conf., Iowa Mus. Assn. (chair steering com. exhbn. workshop 1984-86, legis. action com. and indemnification com. 1981-90, bd. dirs. 1983-85), Tex. Assn. Mus. (program com., resources sharing com., 1992-94, Art Mus. Affinity group) Davenport Rotary (cultural affairs com. 1987-91), S.W. Mus. Conf., Fla. Art Mus. Dirs. Assn., Fla. Assn. Museums, Southeast Mus. Assn. Avocations: books, music, bike riding, visual world and media. Home: 5564 Highlands Vista Cir Lakeland FL 33813-3306 Office: Polk Mus Art Gloria 800 E Palmetto Lakeland FL 33801-5529

STETSON, EUGENE WILLIAM, III, film producer; b. Norwalk, Conn., Mar. 31, 1951; s. Eugene William Jr. and Grace Stuart (Richardson) S.; m. Jane White Watson, June 14, 1993. AB, Harvard U., 1982, postgrad. in Sch. Arts and Scis., 1986. Assoc. exec. dir. Conn. River Watershed Coun., Easthampton, Mass., 1978-81; v.p. Fairhill Oil & Gas Corp. (Fairhill Oil Ltd.-Can.), N.Y.C., Calgary, Alta., Can., 1981-84; pres. Fairhill Oil & Gas Corp. (Fairhill Oil Ltd.-Can.), N.Y.C., Calgary, 1984-92; film and TV writer and producer, 1991—; bd. dirs. Piedmont Fin. Co., Greensboro, N.C., 1978-80, Chisolm Mgmt. Corp., N.Y.C., 1983—; supr. Ottauquechee Conservation Dist., Woodstock, Vt., 1978-82; pres. Boatwright Found., N.Y.C., 1981—; exec. com. Westminster Sch., Simsbury, Conn., 1984-86; gov. Smith Richardson Found., N.Y., 1984—; trustee Proctor Acad., Andover, N.H., 1985—; co-founder River Watch Network, Montpelier, Vt., 1987—; pres. bd. dirs. Vt. Film Commn., 1996—. Mem. Vt. Gov.'s Coun. of Environ. Advisors, 1992—, Vt. Gov.'s Coun. on Bus. and the Environment, 1994—; pres. Vt. Film Commn., 1996—. Mem. Harvard-Radcliffe Club Vt. (v.p. 1994—), Harvard Club N.Y.C., Hasty Pudding Club. Home: 139 Elm St Norwich VT 05055-9445

STETSON, JOHN BATTERSON, IV, construction executive; b. Phila., Dec. 21, 1936; s. John Batterson Stetson III and Winifred (Walton) Todd; m. Solveig Weiland, Nov. 23, 1963; children: John Batterson V, Eric Weiland, Scott Walton. BA, Yale U., 1959, MArch, 1966; postgrad., U. Pa., 1969-73. Registered architect, Pa. Staff architect Bower & Fradley, Architects, Phila., 1966-68, Young & Exley, Architects, Phila., 1968-69; project architect Day & Zimmerman Assocs., Phila., 1969-71, mgr. tech. staff, 1974-76; project mgr. Schnadelbach & Braun, Phila., 1971-74; project exec. Bldg. Scis., Inc., Balt., Kinshasa, Zaire, 1976-77; project mgr. Bldg. Scis., Inc., Balt., 1977-78; sr. cons., v.p., pres. MDC Sys. unit Day and Zimmermann, Inc., Phila., 1978-95, v.p. transp. svcs. unit, 1996—. Active Haverford (Pa.) Civic Assn., 1981—. Comdr. USNR, 1959-81. Mem. Constrn. Mgmt. Assn. Am. (bd. dirs. 1986—), Am. Arbitration Assn., Constrn. Specifications Inst., Haverford Sch. Akumni Assn. Republican. Club: Merion Cricket (Haverford). Avocations: music, sailing. Home: 533 Waters Edge Newtown Square PA 19073 Office: Day & Zimmerman 1818 Market St Philadelphia PA 19103-3638

STETSON, PETER BRAILEY, astronomer; b. Middleboro, Mass., Aug. 30, 1952; s. George Robert and Estelle Marie (Ives) S.; m. Frances Eileen Bogucki, Aug. 5, 1979; children: Whitney Ann, Brailey Marie, Garrett Wilson, Leete Anthony. BA, Wesleyan U., 1974, MA, 1974; MS, Yale U., 1975, PhD, 1979. Postdoctoral astronomy dept. Yale U., New Haven, Conn., 1979-80; Carnegie fellow Mt. Wilson and Las Campanas Obs., Pasadena, Calif., 1980-83; rsch. assoc. Dominion Astrophys. Obs., Victoria, B.C., Can., 1983-84, asst. rsch. officer, 1984-86, assoc. rsch. officer, 1986-89, sr. rsch. officer, 1989—. Contbr. articles to Astrophysical Jour., Jour. of Royal Astron. Soc. Can., Annual Reviews of Astronomy and Astrophysics, Astron. Jour., Publ. Astron. Soc. of Pacific. Recipient R.M. Petrie prize lectr. Can. Astronomical Soc., 1991, Gold medal Sci. Coun. B.C., 1994. Office: Dominion Astrophys Obs, 5071 W Saanich Rd, Victoria, BC Canada V8X 4M6

STETTLER, STEPHEN F., performing company executive; b. Phila., May 1, 1952; s. Wallace Frederick and Catherine Sue (Brill) S. AB summa cum laude, Kenyon Coll., 1974; MFA in Directing, Cath. U. Am., 1982; MLitt in Theatre, Lincoln Coll., Oxford, Eng., 1983. Dir. dramatics Westminster Sch., Simsbury, Conn., 1975-80; acting coach Hartke Conservatory Cath. U., Washington, 1982; chair drama dept. St. Albans and Nat. Cathedral Schs., Washington, 1980-84; dir., instr. acting Nat. Theatre Inst. O'Neill Theater Ctr., Waterford, Conn., 1984-93; artistic dir. TNT/New Theatre Bklyn., 1985-90; producing dir. Weston (Vt.) Playhouse, 1988—; lit. asst. Arena Stage Co., Washington, 1983-84; site evaluator theatres Nat. Endowment for Arts, Washington, 1990—; panelist project grants com. Vt. Coun. Arts, Montpelier, 1993-94; mem. capital grants com. N.Y.C. Dept. Cultural Affairs, 1989; cons. various ind. schs., 1986—; guest instr. directing Teatret Vart, Norway; ednl. theatre cons., guest artist Mercersburg (Pa.) Acad., Pa. Wyoming Seminar, Pa. Dir. Who's Afraid of Virginia Woolf?, Dancing at Lughnasa, Loot, Animal Fair, Rough Crossing, Sunday Promenade, Nora, Donkeys' Years, Into the Woods, Hay Fever, Six Degrees of Separation, Spring Awakening, Mother Courage, A Midsummer Night's Dream (best play award Folger Shakespeare Libr. competition). Mem. Phi Beta Kappa. Office: Weston Playhouse PO Box 216 Weston VT 05161-0216

STETTNER, JERALD W., retail drugs stores executive; b. Miami, Fla., Mar. 31, 1952; s. Richard A. and LeJean D. (Haberman) S.; m. Linda G. Day, Dec. 22, 1978; children: Kelly R., Jarrod M., Zachary A. BS in Behavioral Mgmt., Ga. Inst. Tech., 1974. Various mgmt. positions Eckerd Drug Co., Orlando, Fla., 1974-87; regional v.p. Eckerd Corp., Clearwater, Fla., 1987—. Mem. Ga. Tech. Alumni Assn., Phi Delta Theta. Avocations: tennis, golf, skiing. Home: 3979 Arlington Dr Palm Harbor FL 34685-1069

STEUBEN, NORTON LESLIE, lawyer, educator; b. Milw., Feb. 14, 1936; s. Benjamin and Ria (Beerman) S.; m. Judith Ann Dickens, June 21, 1958; children: Sara Ann, Marc Nelson. A.B., U. Mich., 1958, J.D. with distinction, 1961. Bar: N.Y. 1962, Colo. 1975. Assoc., then ptnr. Hodgson, Russ, Andrews, Woods & Goodyear, Buffalo, 1961-68; mem. faculty U. Colo. Law Sch., Boulder, 1968—, prof. law, 1974—; of counsel Ireland, Stapleton, Pryor & Pascoe, Denver, 1980—; lectr. Law Sch., SUNY, Buffalo, 1961-68; officer Buffalo-Niagara Indsl. Devel. Corp., 1963-68, Buffalo Opportunities Devel. Corp., 1966-68; vis prof. law U. Puget Sound. Sch. Law, 1992-93; resident tax policy advisor to the govt. of Ukraine, Treas. Dept., 1997—. Author: Cases and Materials on Real Estate Planning, 1974, 3d edit., 1989; co-author: Problems in the Fundamentals of Federal Income Taxation, 1985, 3d edit. 1994, Problems in the Federal Income Taxation of Business Enterprises, 1985, 3d edit., 1996; co-editor: Bittker, Fundamentals of Federal Income Taxation, 1983; editor Jour. Affordable Housing & Cmty. Devel. Law, 1994-97; contbr. articles to profl. jours. Mem. Boulder Human Rights Commn., 1969-72, chmn., 1972-74; mem. Boulder Landlord-Tenant Com., 1973-74; trustee Boulder Open Space Bd., 1976-81, vice chmn., 1978-79, chmn., 1979-81; trustee Congregation Har Ha-Shem, Boulder, 1978-79, v.p., 1979-81, pres., 1982-84; mem. Boulder Housing Authority, 1982-89, vice chmn., 1984-85, chmn., 1985-88. Recipient S.I. Goldberg award Alpha Epsilon Pi, 1957, Disting. Svc. to Community award Buffalo Area C. of C., 1966, John W. Reed award U. Colo. Law Sch., 1970; Teaching Recognition award U. Colo.-Boulder, 1972, Teaching Excellence award, 1982; Presdl. Teaching scholar, U. Colo., 1989. Mem. ABA, N.Y. State Bar Assn., Colo. Bar Assn., Boulder County Bar Assn., Am. Law Inst., AAUP, Scribes (officer, editor Scrivener 1975-76, dir. 1979-82), Barristers Soc., Order of Coif, Tau Epsilon Rho. Democrat. Home: 845 8th St Boulder CO 80302-7408 Office: U Colo 418 Fleming Law Bldg Boulder CO 80309

STEUER, RICHARD MARC, lawyer; b. Bklyn., June 19, 1948; s. Harold and Gertrude (Vengar) S.; m. Audrey P. Forchheimer, Sept. 9, 1973; children: Hilary, Jeremy. BA, Hofstra U., 1970; JD, Columbia U., 1973. Bar: N.Y. 1974, U.S. Dist. Ct. (ea. and so. dists.) N.Y. 1974, U.S. Ct. Appeals (2d cir.) 1974, U.S. Dist. Ct. (no. dist.) N.Y. 1984, U.S. Ct. Appeals (3d cir.) 1987, U.S. Ct. Appeals (5th cir.) 1995, U.S. Supreme Ct. 1979. Ptnr. Kaye, Scholer, Fierman, Hays & Handler LLP, N.Y.C., 1973—; adj. assoc. prof. law NYU, 1985; lectr. various orgns.; neutral evaluator U.S. Dist. Ct. Ea. Dist., N.Y, 1994—. Author: A Guide to Marketing Law: Law and Business Inc., 1986; contbr. articles to profl. jours. Fellow Am. Bar Found.; mem. ABA (lectr. 1978, 85, 89, 96, editorial bd. antitrust devel. vol. 1984-86, chmn. monograph com. refusals to deal and exclusive distributorships 1983, various others, vice chmn. program com. 1988-91, chmn. spring meeting program com. 1991-92, Sherman Act sect. 1 com. 1991-93, coun. sect. antitrust law 1993-96, chmn. publs. com. 1996—), Assn. Bar City N.Y. (antitrust and trade regulation, internat. trade, lectures and CLE coms., lectr. 1983-94, chmn. antitrust and trade regulation 1995—). Office: Kaye Scholer Fierman Hays & Handler LLP 425 Park Ave New York NY 10022-3506

STEVEN, DONALD ANSTEY, dean, educator; b. Montreal, Que., Can.; s. Ivan Campbell and Margaret Jane (Anstey) S.; m. Margaret Ann MacKenzie, May 1, 1976; children: James, Denise. BMus in Composition with honors, McGill U., Montreal, 1972; MFA, Princeton (N.J.) U., 1975. Lectr. U. Western Ont., London, 1975-76; asst. prof. McGill U., Montreal, 1976-83, assoc. prof., 1983, chair dept. of performance, 1986-92, prof., 1991-92; dean of music Purchase Coll. SUNY, 1992-97, prof. Purchase Coll., 1992-97; prof., dean Coll. Performing Arts Roosevelt U., Chgo., 1997—; exec. coun. Can. League of Composers; nat. bd. dirs. Can. Music Ctr.; served on many juries. Composer: In the Land of Pure Delight, 1991, That Other Shore, 1989, Full Valleys, 1989, Orbits, 1989, Art Thou Weary, Heavy Laden, 1988, Love Where the Nights Are Long, 1987, The Breath of Many Flowers, 1986, Sapphire Song, 1986, Pages of Solitary Delights, 1985, Straight on Till Morning, 1985, Just a Few Moments Alone, 1984, Ordre Sans Ordre, 1984, Bert in Nether-Nether Land, On the Down Side, 1982, Nordring Festival Music, 1981, Wired, 1981, Night Suite, 1979, Rainy Day Afternoon, 1979, For Madmen Only, 1978, Images-Refractions of Time and Space, 1977, The Transient, 1975, Crossroads, 1974, The Gossamer Cathedral-Five Surrealistic Frescoes, 1972, Illusions, 1971, Harbinger, 1969. Advisor to vis. com. on musical instruments N.Y. Met. Mus. of Art. Recipient Gov. Gen.'s award for Chamber Music, JUNO award, Grand Prix du Disque du Canada Can. Music Coun., 1978, Broadcast Music Inc. award, 1970. Mem. N.Y. State Assn. of Coll. Music Programs (bd. dirs., sec., treas. 1992-95), Coll. Music Program, Am. Music Ctr., Can. Music Ctr. (assoc. composer). Office: Roosevelt U Coll Performing Arts 430 S Michigan Ave Chicago IL 60605-1301

STEVENS, ART, public relations executive; b. N.Y.C., July 17, 1935; m. Eva Sandberg, Mar. 19, 1972. B.A., CCNY, 1957. Pub. relations dir. Prentice Hall, Inc., Englewood Cliffs, N.J.; account exec. William L. Safire Public Relations Inc., N.Y.C., 1966-69; v.p. William L. Safire Public Relations Inc., 1967-68, pres., 1968-69; pres. Lobsenz-Stevens Inc., N.Y.C., 1970—; instr. Fairleigh Dickinson U.; weekly humor commentator WINK-TV, Ft. Myers, Fla. Author: The Persuasion Explosion, 1985, Sanibel Shell Shocked, 1992; weekly columnist Sanibel-Captiva (Fla.) Islander; contbr. articles to profl. jours. Bd. dirs. United Way of Putnam County, N.Y.; trustee Gotthelf Lupus Rsch. Inst. Mem. Publicity Club N.Y. (Disting. Service award 1969), Public Relations Soc. Am. (pub. rels. com., exec com., chmn. eligibility com., counselors acad. sect.). Club: Gipsy Trail (Carmel, N.Y., pres.). Home: 201 E 21st St New York NY 10010-6401 Office: Lobsenz-Stevens Inc 460 Park Ave S New York NY 10016-7315 *Life is not an accident. The events in one's life are not accidents either. When I look back at what I have done and the lives that have been interwined with mine, it's as though it's all been scripted by a higher power.*

STEVENS, BERTON LOUIS, JR., data processing manager; b. Chgo., Apr. 4, 1951; s. Berton Louis Sr. and Mary Cover (Kochavaris) S.; m. Janet Alene Madenberg, May 20, 1990. Student, Ill. Inst. Tech., Chgo., 1969-73. Systems and applications programmer Judge & Dolph, Ltd., Elk Grove Village, Ill., 1978-91, mgr. data processing, 1991—; instr. Adler Planetarium and Astron. Mus., Chgo., 1980-86. Editor and author newsletter Bert's Bull., 1987-90; editor newsletter No. Lights, 1990—. Recipient Regional award North Ctrl. Region Astron. League, 1989. Mem. Nat. Assn. Sys. Programmers, Internat. Occulation Timing Assn. (sec. 1975-78), Chgo. Computer Soc., Chgo. Astron. Soc. (pres. 1977, 80, 84), Racine Astron. Soc. (pres. 1979), Astron. League (exec. sec. 1993-95).

STEVENS, BRENDA JOY, educator; b. Mt. Vernon, Ohio, May 30, 1948; d. Lester Dale Wilkin and Elizabeth Irene (Ballinger) Loyd; m. LeRoy John Stevens, June 21, 1972; children: Tiffany Joy, Blake LeRoy. BS, Kent State U., 1970; MA, Mich. State U., 1979. Tchr. Mt. Vernon Pub. Schs., 1970-71, Stow (Ohio) Pub. Schs., 1971-72, Port Huron (Mich.) Area Schs., 1972—; initiator Young 5s Program, Port Huron Area Sch. Dist., 1984, mem. sci. curriculum com., 1995—, writing and literacy continuum com., 1995—; mem. 4s at Risk adv. com., Port Huron, 1988-94; mem. Port Huron Devel. Curriculum Com., 1989-93; chair Michigamme Sch. Improvement Team, Port Huron, 1990-95; chair Annual Mich. Women's history Month Essay Contest, Mich. Women's Commn. and AAUW, 1995-96. Mem. Eldercare Coalition, Lansing, 1991-93; nominations panel Mich. Women's Hall of Fame, Lansing, 1987; coach Odyssey of the Mind, Port Huron, 1987, 88, 93, 94, 95. Mem. AAUW (Mich. state pres. 1991-93, chair Edn. Found. 1988-91), Blue Water Assn. Edn. Young Children, Mus. Art and History, Univ. Women's Investment Club. Avocations: travel, beaches, reading. Home: 4520 Lakeshore Rd Fort Gratiot MI 48059-3527

STEVENS, C. GLENN, judge; b. Rockford, Ill., Oct. 29, 1941; s. Robert W. and Mary Louise (Shaughnessy) S.; m. Suzanne Ruth Corkery, July 4, 1967; children: Robert W., Angela M. BS, St. Louis U., 1964, JD, 1966. Bar: Ill. 1966, Mo. 1966, U.S. Dist. Ct. (so. dist.) Ill. 1966, U.S. Dist. Ct. (ea. dist.) Ill. 1968. Law clk. to judge U.S. Dist. Ct. (so. dist.) Ill., Springfield, Ill., 1966-67; instr. St. Louis U., 1967-68; assoc. Pope & Driemeyer, Belleville, Ill., 1967-74; ptnr. Pope & Driemeyer, Belleville, 1974-77; judge State of Ill., Belleville, 1977—. Bd. editors St. Louis U. Law Rev., 1965-66. Arbitrator Am. Arbitration Assn., St. Clair County, Ill, 1970-77. With U.S. Army, 1958-66. Mem. Mo. Bar Assn., Ill. Judges Assn., Am. Judges Assn., Ill. State Bar Assn., St. Clair County Bar Assn., East St. Louis Bar Assn., Phi Delta Phi (pres. Murphy Inn 1965-66). Democrat. Roman Catholic. Avocations: antique cars, soccer coach. Office: Saint Clair County Courthouse Public Sq Belleville IL 62220

STEVENS, CLYDE BENJAMIN, JR., property manager, retired naval officer; b. Denver, Oct. 10, 1908; s. Clyde Benjamin and Maybelle Olive (Boot) S.; m. Lucile Lillian-Louise Kip, May 5, 1933; children: Jane Stevens White, Donald Kip, Patricia Louise Stevens Schley. BS, U.S. Naval Acad., 1930; postgrad., U.S. Naval Postgrad. Sch., Annapolis, Md., 1939, U.S. Naval War Coll., Newport, R.I., 1947. Registered profl. engr. Commd. ensign USN, advanced through grades to rear adm., 1959; comdg. officer USS R-20, S-33 Plaice and Platte, 1950-52; comdr. officer USS Platte 50-52 Destroyer Squad 6, 1954-55; with torpedo prodn. and undersea weapons div. Bur. Ordnance, Washington, 1947-59; with USS Platte, 1950-52, Destroyer squad., 1955-56; program dir. Bur. Ordnance, Washington, 1952-55, 56-59; ret., 1959; product mgr. TRW, Inc., Cleve., 1959-65; rsch. engr. Boeing Co., Seattle, 1965-74, torpedo cons., 1985; apt. owner and mgr. Seattle, 1965—; torpedo cons. Goodyear Aerospace Co., Akron, Ohio, 1965. Patentee automobile generator. Decorated Navy Cross, Silver Star with oak leaf cluster. Mem. Seattle Apt. Assn. (bd. dirs. 1967-91), Army and Navy Club, Rainier Club. Republican. Episcopalian. Home and Office: 2339 Franklin Ave E Seattle WA 98102-3356

STEVENS, CONNIE, actress, singer; b. Bklyn., Aug. 8, 1938; d. Peter and Eleanore (McGinley) Ingolia; m. Maurice Elias; m. Edwin Jack Fisher (div.); children: Joely, Tricia Leigh. Grad. high sch. Show bus. debut as vocalist with, The Three Debs, Hollywood, at age 16; appeared in: Finians Rainbow for Hollywood Repertory Co.; numerous motion pictures, including Way, Way Out, Scorchy, Eighteen and Animals, Young and Dangerous, Drag Strip Riot, Rock-a-bye Baby, Parish, Susan Slade, Palm Springs Weekend, The Grissom Gang, Never Too Late, Grease II, 1983, Back to the Beach, 1987, Bring Me the Head of Dobie Gillis, 1988, Love Is All There Is, 1996; starred in TV series Wendy and Me and TV series Hawaiian Eye, 1959-62, TV films for ABC-TV Movie-of-the-Week; Call Her Mom, 1972, Playmates, Mister Jericho, Cole Porter in Paris, The Sex Symbol, 1974, Starting From Scratch, 1988; guest star on TV with, Bob Hope, Red Skelton, Englebert Humperdinck, Tom Jones, Perry Como and Laugh-In; TV appearance comedy spl. Harry's Battles; headliner at Flamingo Hotel, Las Vegas, also, Hilton Internat., Sands Hotel, Desert Inn, Aladdin, MGM, Sahara, 1969-76; stage appearances include The Wizard of Oz at Carousel Theatre in So. Calif., Any Wednesday at Melodyland, Anaheim, Calif.; made Broadway debut in Star Spangled Girl, 1967; accompanied Bob Hope around world on his Christmas tour, 1969, Persian Gulf Christmas tour, 1987. Bd. dirs. Ctr. for Plastic and Reconstructive Surgery, South Vietnam. also: The Agy 1800 Ave of the Stars Ste 400 Los Angeles CA 90067*

STEVENS, DAVID, economics educator; b. Burbank, Calif., Jan. 26, 1926; s. Frederick and Alpheus (Perkins) S.; 1 child, David Fancher. B.A., Whitman Coll., 1947; M.B.A., Stanford U., 1949; LLD (hon.), Whitman Coll., 1994. Asst. prof. Okla. State U., 1949-51; asst. prof. econs. Whitman Coll., Walla Walla, Wash., 1951-54; asso. prof. Whitman Coll., 1954-56, prof., 1956-67, Roger and David Clapp prof. of econ. thought, 1958-91, prof. emeritus, 1991—, dean adminstrn., 1954-64, chmn. faculty, 1982-85; vis. prof. Glasgow U., Scotland, 1964-66, sr. research fellow, 1980—; instr. Am. Inst. Banking. Author: Adam Smith and the Colonial Disturbances, 1976; Editor: The Wedderburn Manuscript In Adam Smith: Correspondence, 1977. Commr. Regional Planning Commn., Walla Walla County, 1960-64; chmn. Walla Walla County chpt. ARC, 1961-63, 75-77. Served to lt. J.G. U.S. Navy, 1943-46. Mem. Am. Econ. Assn., Western Econ. Assn., History of Econ. Soc. Episcopalian. Home: 602 Boyer Ave Walla Walla WA 99362-2381 Office: Whitman Coll Economics Dept Walla Walla WA 99362

STEVENS, DIANA LYNN, elementary education educator; b. Waterloo, Iowa, Dec. 12, 1950; d. Marcus Henry and Clarissa Ann (Funk) Carr; m. Paul John Stevens; 1 child, Drew Spencer. BS, Mid Am. Nazarene Coll., 1973; M in Liberal Arts, Baker U., 1989. Elem. tchr. Olathe (Kans.) Sch. Dist. #233, 1975—. Artwork appeared in traveling exhibit ARC/Nat. Art Edn. Assn., 1968. Mem. Cedarhouse Aux., Olathe, 1986—; pres. Artists' League, Olathe, 1990—. Mem. NEA, Kans. Edn. Assn., Olathe Edn. Assn. (social com.), Nat. Art Edn. Assn., Delta Kappa Gamma (profl. affairs com. mem.), Coll. Ch. of the Nazarene. Avocations: portrait art, reading biographies, power walking, exhibiting artwork. Home: 217 S Montclaire Dr Olathe KS 66061-3828

STEVENS, DONALD KING, aeronautical engineer, consultant; b. Danville, Ill., Oct. 27, 1920; s. Douglas Franklin and Ida Harriet (King) S.; BS with high honors in Ceramic Engring., U. Ill., 1942; MS in Aeros. and Guided Missiles, U. So. Calif., 1949; grad. U.S. Army Command and Gen. Staff Coll., 1957, U.S. Army War Coll., 1962; m. Adele Carman de Werff, July 11, 1942; children: Charles August, Anne Louise, Alice Jeanne Stevens Kay. Served with Ill. State Geol. Survey, 1938-40; ceramic engr. Harbison-Walker Refractories Co., Pitts., 1945-46; commd. 2d lt. U.S. Army, 1942, advanced through grades to col., 1963; with Arty. Sch., Fort Bliss, Tex., 1949-52; supr. unit tng. and Nike missile firings, N.Mex., 1953-56; mem. Weapons Systems Evaluation Group, Office Sec. of Def., Washington, 1957-61; comdr. Niagara-Buffalo (N.Y.) Def., 31st Arty. Brigade, Lockport, N.Y., 1963-65; study dir. U.S.A. ballistic missile def. studies DEPEX and X-66 for Sec. Def., 1965-66; chief Air Def. and Nuclear br. War Plans div. 1965-67, chief strategic forces div. Office Dep. Chief Staff for Mil. Ops., 1967-69; chief spl. weapons plans, J5, U.S. European Command, Fed. Republic Germany, 1969-72, ret., 1972; guest lectr. U.S. Mil. Acad. 1958-59; cons. U.S. Army Concepts Analysis Agy., Bethesda, Md., 1973-95; cons. on strategy Lulejian & Assocs., Inc., 1974-75; cons. nuclear policy and plans to Office Asst. Sec. of Def., 1975-80, 84-93; cons. Sci. Applications, Inc., 1976-78; Asst. camp dir. Piankeshaw Area coun. Boy Scouts Am., 1937; mem. chancel choir, elder First Christian Ch., Falls Church, Va., 1957-61, 65-69, 72—; elder, trustee Presbyn. Ch., 1963-65. Decorated D.S.M., Legion of Merit, Bronze Star. Mem. Am. Ceramic Soc., Assn. U.S. Army, U. Ill. Alumni Assn., U. So. Calif. Alumni Assn., Keramos, Sigma Xi, Sigma Tau, Tau Beta Pi, Phi Kappa Phi, Alpha Phi Omega. Clubs: Niagara Falls Country; Ill. (Washington); Terrapin, Rotary. Contbr. articles to engring. jours.; pioneer in tactics and deployment plans for Army surface-to-air missiles. Address: 5916 5th St N Arlington VA 22203-1010

STEVENS, DWIGHT MARLYN, educational administrator; b. Wheeler, Wis., May 13, 1933; s. Clifford and Alva Orpha (Follensbee) S.; children: Patricia Lee Stevens Vanden Heuvel, Jacqueline Ann Stevens Kreuger,

Cynthia May Stevens Manthey, Robert Louis. B.S., Eau Claire (Wis.) State U., 1957; M.S., U. Wis., 1959, Ph.D., 1972. High sch. speech tchr. Ft. Atkinson, Wis., 1957-61; high sch. prin. Oostburg, Wis., 1961-64; prin. Arrowhead High Sch., Hartland, Wis., 1964-66; dist. adminstr. Arrowhead Sch. Dist., 1966-73; dep. state supt. Wis. Dept. Pub. Instrn., Madison, 1973-81; supt. schs. Stevens Point, Wis., 1982-93; faculty U. Wis.-Whitewater, 1971, U. Wis.-Superior, 1985, U. Wis.-Stevens Point, 1988-92, 93—. Author: (with Eye, Netzer and Benson) Strategies for Instructional Management, 1980. Dir. Ford Found., Community Planning Project for Chippewa Indians, 1970-71, Nat. Validation Team, Title III, Elementary Secondary Edn. Act; cons. HEW Workshops on Innovation, Eagle River, Wis.; chmn. Wis. sch. dist. adminstrn., 1992; bd. dirs. St. Michaels Hosp., Stevens Point. Served with U.S. Army, 1953-55. Recipient Outstanding Citizenship award Waukesha County, Wis., 1974; Ford fellow John Hay Fellowship in Humanities, Williams Coll., 1963; Kettering fellow Nat. Seminar on Innovation, Honolulu, summer 1967, Outstanding Adminstrv. Practitioner award U. Wis.-Stevens Point, 1991; Disting. Alumni award U. Wis., 1980. Mem. Cen. Wis. C. of C. (pres. 1986-87), Acad. Letters and Scis. (v.p. 1987—, pres. 1988-90), Phi Delta Kappa (v.p. 1985-87), Pi Kappa Delta. Home: 3323 Echo Dells Ave Stevens Point WI 54481-5118

STEVENS, EDWARD, public relations executive; b. Cleve., Feb. 24, 1941. BA, John Carroll U., 1963. Asst. mgr., adv. constrn. dept. divsn. Warner & Swasey, 1966-69; A/E Cleve. office Dix & Eaton, 1969-71, A/E Erie office, 1971-74, v.p., gen. mgr. Erie office, 1974-79, group v.p., 1979-80, sr. v.p., gen. mgr. Erie office, 1980—, group pres., 1982; now vice chmn. Dix & Eaton, Cleveland; bd. dirs. PRSA, Cleve. Ad. Club. Recipient Erie Ad Person of the Yr. award, 1985, George Mead award, 1987. Office: Dix & Eaton/Public Rels 1301 E 9th St Ste 1300 Cleveland OH 44114-1800

STEVENS, EDWARD FRANKLIN, college president; b. Newcastle, Wyo., Sept. 7, 1940; s. Edward Downey and Esther Elizabeth (Watt) S.; m. Linda Elaine Loewenstein, June 3, 1962; children: Carla Sue, Cathy Lynne. Student, U. Denver, 1959-60; BA in Edn., Physics, Chemistry cum laude, Nebr. Wesleyan U., 1963; MA in Ednl. Psychology, Stats. and Measurement, U. Nebr., 1967; PhD in Higher Edn., Mktg., Mgmt., U. Minn., 1983; postdoctoral, Harvard U., 1991. Tchr., head basketball coach Alvo-Eagle (Nebr.) High Sch., 1963-64, Madison (Nebr.) High Sch., 1964-65; asst. basketball coach U. Nebr., Lincoln, 1965-67; head basketball coach, asst. prof. edn. Augustana Coll., Sioux Falls, S.D., 1967-71; v.p., gen. mgr. tng. Iseman divsn. U.S. Inds., Sioux Falls, 1971-74; chief devel. and instl. advancement officer Sioux Falls Coll., 1974-79, asst. prof. to prof., 1980-83; from exec. v.p. to exec. asst. pres. Kearny (Nebr.) State Coll. Found., 1979-80; pres. George Fox U., Newberg, Oreg., 1983—. Chmn. campaign Yamhill County United Way, Newberg, 1988; bd. commrs. Newberg Community Hosp., 1988-91. NDEA fellow, 1965; recipient Young Alumni Achievement award, Nebr. Wesleyan U., 1973, Leadership Fellows award, Bush Found., St. Paul, 1976. Mem. Am. Assn. Pres. Indep. Colls. and Univs., Nat. Christian Coll. Consortium (chmn. 1987-88), Nat. Assn. Intercollegiate Athletics (council pres., exec. com. 1988-92, chmn. 1992), Nat. Assn. Evangelicals (Christian higher edn. com.), Nat. Assn. Indep. Colls. and Univs., Oreg. Ind. Colls. Assn. (bd. dirs. 1983-92, chmn. 1986-87), Oreg. Ind. Colls. Found. (bd. dirs. 1983-92, vice chmn. 1993), Coun. of Ind. Colls. (bd. dirs. 1990), N.W. Assn. Schs. and Colls. (commn. on colls.), Internat. Assn. Univs. Pres., New Life 2000 (internat. com. reference), Rotary. Republican. Mem. Soc. Friends. Office: George Fox U Office of Pres 414 N Meridian St Newberg OR 97132-2625

STEVENS, EDWARD IRA, information systems educator; b. York, Pa., Oct. 13, 1937; s. Francis DeHaven and Myra Jane (Foust) S.; m. Marjorie Eleanor Bisson, Aug. 29, 1959 (div. Oct. 1978); children: Mark Edward, Whitney Lynne, Kimberly Lauren; m. Kathleen Susan Berg, May 30, 1983. AB, Davidson (N.C.) Coll., 1959; MDiv, Harvard U., 1962; PhD, Vanderbilt U., 1965. Asst. prof. psychology, then assoc. prof. Eckerd Coll. (formerly Fla. Presbyn. Coll.), St. Petersburg, 1965-69, dir. research and ednl. services, 1969-73, dir. planning, exec. asst. to pres., 1977-84, from assoc. prof. info. sys. to prof., 1984—, dir. instl. rsch. and planning, 1993—, dir. libr. svcs., 1995—, dir. info. svcs. & tech., 1996—; dean acad. affairs Northland Coll., Ashland, Wis., 1973-75, v.p., 1974-75; pres. Lyndon State Coll., Lyndonville, Vt., 1975-77; v.p. rsch. St. Clair Software Systems, Inc., Clearwater, Fla., 1985-87; cons. and lectr. in field. Contbr. articles to profl. jours. Am. Council Edn. fellow, Washington, 1969-70; Fund for Improvement Post-Secondary Edn. grantee, Washington, 1976-78. Mem. Am. Assn. Higher Edn., Acad. Mgmt., Assn. Instl. Rsch., Assn. for Computer Machinery, Phi Beta Kappa. Presbyterian. Avocations: art, antiques, photography. Home: 15501 Eastbourn Dr Odessa FL 33556-2853 Office: Eckerd Coll 4200 54th Ave S Saint Petersburg FL 33711-4744

STEVENS, ELISABETH GOSS (MRS. ROBERT SCHLEUSSNER, JR.), writer, journalist; b. Rome, N.Y., Aug. 11, 1929; d. George May and Elisabeth (Stryker) Stevens; m. Robert Schleussner, Jr., Mar. 12, 1966 (dec. 1977); 1 child, Laura Stevens. B.A., Wellesley Coll., 1951; M.A. with high honors, Columbia U., 1956. Editorial assoc. Art News Mag., 1964-65; art critic and reporter Washington Post, Washington, 1965-66; free-lance art critic and reporter Balt., 1966—; contbg. art critic Wall Street Jour., N.Y.C., 1969-72; art critic Trenton Times, N.J., 1974-77; art and architecture critic The Balt. Sun, 1978-86. Author: Elisabeth Stevens' Guide to Baltimore's Inner Harbor, 1981, Fire and Water: Six Short Stories, 1982, Children of Dust: Portraits and Preludes, 1985, Horse and Cart: Stories from the Country, 1990, The Night Lover: Art & Poetry, 1995, In Foreign Parts, 1997; contbr. articles, poetry and short stories to jours., nat. newspapers and popular mags. Recipient A.D. Emmart award for journalism, 1980, Critical Writing citation Balt.-Washington Newspaper Guild, 1980, fiction awards Md. Poetry Rev., 1992, 93, 94, 2d prize Lite Circle, 1994, 1st prize in fiction Lite Circle, 1995, 96, Balt. Writers Alliance Play Writing Contest award, 1994; art critics' fellow NEA, 1973-74, fellow MacDowell Colony, 1981, Va. Ctr. for Creative Arts, 1982-85, 88-90, 92, 93, 95, Ragdale Found., 1984, 89, Yaddo, 1991, Villa Montalvo, 1995; Work-in-Progress grantee for poetry Md. Art Coun., 1986, Creative Devel. grantee for short fiction collection Balt. Mayor's Com. on Art and Culture, 1986. Mem. Nat. Press Club Washington, Coll. Art Assn., Balt. Bibliophiles, Authors Guild, Am. Studies Assn., Poetry Soc. Am. Home: 6604 Walnutwood Cir Baltimore MD 21212-1213

STEVENS, ELLIOTT WALKER, JR., allergist, pulmonologist; b. Wilmington, N.C., Sept. 11, 1940; s. E. Walker Sr. and Margaret Ardelle (Hester) S.; m. Blanche Bonner, July 10, 1965; children: Elliott W. III, Margaret Baker. AB in French, U. N.C., 1962, MD, 1966. Diplomate Am. Bd. Internal Medicine, Am. Bd. Allergy and Immunology, Am. Bd. Pulmonery Diseases. Intern U. N.C. Hosp., Chapel Hill, N.C., 1966-67; resident Duke U., Durham, N.C., 1969-70, fellow Allergy and pulmonary diseases, 1970-72; allergist and pulmonologist Greensboro Chest Disease and Allergy Associates, Greensboro, N.C., 1972—. Capt. USAF, 1967-69. Fellow Am. Coll. Allergy and Immunology, Am. Coll. Chest Physicians. Republican. Episcopalian. Avocations: skiing, sailing. Home: 4 Round Hill Ct Greensboro NC 27408-3709 Office: Greensboro Chest Diseases & Allergy Assocs 1018 N Elm St Greensboro NC 27401-1424

STEVENS, GARY, professional jockey. Top money winner, 1991. Winner Breeder's Cup Turf Race, 1990, Breeder's Cup Juvenile, 1993, Breeder's Cup Distaff, 1994. Home: 315 S Beverly Rd # 208 Beverly Hills CA 90212*

STEVENS, GEORGE, JR., film and television producer, writer, director; b. Calif., Apr. 3, 1932; s. George Cooper and Yvonne (Shevlin) S.; m. Elizabeth Guest, July, 1965; children: Caroline, Michael, David. B.A., Occidental Coll., 1953. Asst. to George Stevens, Sr., 1951-53, motion picture prodn. asst., 1956, assoc. producer, 1957-60, TV dir., 1957-61; dir. Motion Picture Service, USIA, 1962-64, Motion Picture and TV service, USIA, 1964-67; founding dir., chief exec. Am. Film Inst., 1967-80, now co-chmn. bd.; pres. New Liberty Prodns., 1980—; founding chmn. D.C. Arts Commn., 1969; chmn. U.S. del. Internat. Film Festivals at Moscow, Cannes, Venice, Berlin, 1963-66. Motion pictures include John F. Kennedy, Years of Lightning Day of Drums, 1964, Nine From Little Rock (Acad. award), 1965, America at the Movies, 1976; creator, prodr., writer Am. Film Inst. Life Achievement Award shows, 1973-97, TV series including AFI: A Salute to James Cagney (Emmy award), The Stars Salute America's Greatest Movies, 1977, America Entertains Vice Premier Deng Tsio Peng, 1979; creator, co-prodr., writer Kennedy Ctr. Honor series, 1978-96, (6 Emmy awards, George Foster Peabody award); creator, exec. prodr. Christmas in Washington series, 1982-96; writer, prodr., dir. George Stevens: A Filmmaker's Journey, 1985 (award Nat. Bd. of Rev. of Motion Pictures, 1986, WGA award for ABC broadcast 1988); prodr., co-writer (TV miniseries) The Murder of Mary Phagan, 1988 (Emmy award, Christopher award, George Foster Peabody award), George Stevens: D-Day To Berlin (Emmy awards for writing and narration); co-exec. prodr., dir., writer (TV miniseries) Separate But Equal, 1991 (Christopher award, Emmy award). Trustee Occidental Coll., 1980-82. Served to 1st lt. USAF, 1954-56. Named to Ten Outstanding Young Men in Fed. Govt., 1963, Ten Outstanding Young Men in U.S., 1964; recipient Jury prize Chgo. Internat. Film Film Fest., 1985, Paul Selvin award Writers Guild of Am., 1991, NAACP Legal Def. Fund award. Office: Kennedy Ctr Washington DC 20566

STEVENS, GEORGE ALEXANDER, realtor; b. Loma, Mont., Nov. 10, 1923; s. Otto Oliver and Josephine (Dale) S.; m. Martha Evie Fultz, Sept. 16, 1944 (div. 1978); children: Gary, Kathleen, Arlene, Tina; m. Arleen Dorothea Largent, Nov. 14, 1978. A in Bus Admisntrn., SUNY, 1992. Prin. George Stevens Farm, Loma, Mont., 1946-93, George Stevens, Realtor, Loma, Mont., 1957-93; pres. George A. Stevens COrp., Loma, 1976-93, Gold and Silver Realty, Inc., Great Falls, Mont., 1993—. Trustee Sch. Dist. # 32, Loma, 1947-50; election judge Precinct # 7, Loma, 1953-88. With USN, 1944-46, PTO. Mem. Nat. Assn. Realtors, VFW (life), Am. Legion (life), Elks (life), Eagles Lodge. Democrat. Lutheran. Home: 810 8th Ave N Great Falls MT 59401-1036

STEVENS, GEORGE M., III, surgeon; b. Knoxville, May 29, 1934; s. George Miller and Helen Margaret (Brown) S.; m. Mary Alberta Campbell, Aug. 25, 1955; children: George IV, Julia Christine Muller, Mac Campbell. MD, U. Tenn., 1959. Diplomate Am. Bd. Orthopedic Surgery. Instr. orthopedics U. N.C., Chapel Hill, 1964-65; orthopedist Meth. Med. Ctr. Oak Ridge, Tenn., 1965—; instr. orthopedics U. Tenn. Meml. Rsch. Ctr., Knoxville, 1967-75. Fellow Internat. Coll. Surgeons, Am. Acad. Orthopedic Surgeons; mem. Am. Fracture Assn., Mid-Am. Orthopedic Assn., Tenn. Orthopedic Soc. Republican. Presbyn. Avocations: golf, flying, skeet/trap shooting, woodworking. Office: Oak Ridge Ortho Ctr 988 Oak Ridge Tpke Oak Ridge TN 37830-6930

STEVENS, GEORGE RICHARD, business consultant, public policy commentator; b. Chgo., Sept. 6, 1932; s. George and Irene (Kaczmarek) S.; m. Jeanne E. Sowden, Aug. 2, 1957; children: Stacey, Samantha, Pamela. BS with honors, Northwestern U., 1954. CPA, Ill. With Arthur Andersen & Co., 1954-78; mng. ptnr. Arthur Andersen & Co., Brussels, Belgium, 1957-71; ptnr. Arthur Andersen & Co., Chgo., 1971-78; pres. Daubert Industries, Oak Brook, Ill., 1978-80, G.R. Stevens Group, 1981—; founder, pres. Stevens Ctr. for Pub. Policy Studies, 1981—; Mem. Chgo. Com., 1979—; commr. Ill. Ednl. Facilities Authority, 1989—. Commr. Ill. State Scholarship Commn., 1981-87; vice chmn. Ill. Ind. Higher Edn. Loan Authority, 1982-88. Home and Office: 22615 N Las Lomas Ln Sun City West AZ 85375-2022

STEVENS, GERALD D., secondary education educator, consultant; b. Seattle, Apr. 9, 1941; s. James Edward and Olga Rubina (Olsen) S.; m. Michele Christine Hayek, June 16, 1973; children: Heather Corrine, Wendy Jeannette, Gerald Michael. Student, U. Wash., 1963-65; BA in Polit. Sci., Calif. State U., L.A., 1989; MA, U. So. Calif., 1995, postgrad., 1995—. Cert. tchr., Calif. Bank auditor Nat. Bank Commerce, Seattle, 1965-72; pvt. practice GEMIC L.A., 1972-86; tchr. L.A. Unified Sch. Dist., 1986-96; cons. model schs. program Fgn. Policy Assn., Washington, 1990; presenter coalition essential schs. L.A. Unified Sch. Dist., 1990-91. Author: Redistributive Econ. Justice, 1993. Vol. C.L.A.R.E. Found., Santa Monica, 1989-91. With USMC, 1960-63, PTO. Mem. So. Calif. Social Sci. Assn. (bd. dirs. 1990-94, v.p.), United Tchrs. L.A., Sierra Club. Avocations: songwriting, ceramic art. Home: Unit 2 2101 Ocean Ave Santa Monica CA 90405-2228 Office: LA Unified Sch Dist 450 N Grand Ave Los Angeles CA 90012-2123

STEVENS, GLADSTONE TAYLOR, JR., industrial engineer; b. Brockton, Mass., Dec. 16, 1930; s. Gladstone Taylor and Blanche Ruth S.; m. Jane A. Crouch, July 20, 1953; children—Robert, Bartlett. B.S.M.E., U. Okla., 1956; M.S.M.E., Case Inst. Tech., 1962; Ph.D. in Indsl. Engring, Okla. State U., 1966. Registered profl. engr., Tex., Okla. Project engr. E.I. duPont, Orange, Tex., 1956-59; research engr. Thompson-Ramo-Wooldridge, Cleve., 1960-62; asst. prof. mech. and indsl. engring. Lamar U., Beaumont, Tex., 1962-64; asst. prof. to asso. prof. indsl. engring. Okla. State U., Stillwater, 1966-75; prof., chmn. dept. indsl. engring. U. Tex., Arlington, 1975—. Author: (with J.E. Shamblin) Operations Research: A Fundamental Approach, 1974, Economic and Financial Analysis of Capital Investments, 1993; Engineering Economy, 1983. Served with AUS, 1948-52. Recipient E.L. Grant award, 1974, AMOCO Teaching award, 1979, Wellington award, 1992. Fellow Am. Inst. Indsl. Engrs.; mem. Sigma Xi, Alpha Pi Mu (nat. pres.), Tau Beta Pi, Sigma Tau, Omicron Delta Kappa. Home: 3611 Shady Park Dr Arlington TX 76013-5706 Office: U Tex Indsl Engring Arlington TX 76019

STEVENS, HENRY AUGUST, insurance agent, educator; b. Frankfurt, Main, Germany, July 21, 1921; came to U.S., 1940; m. Rosemary O'Neil, Mar. 23, 1963; children: Michael, Patrick; 1 child from previous marriage, H. Jack Fay. Student, U. Wis., 1943-44; grad., Dale Carnegie Sch., Richland, Wash., 1974. Theatre mgr. Sterling Theatres, Seattle, 1946-54, Alliance Amusement Co., Chgo., 1955-68; ins. agt. N.Y. Life Ins. Co., Richland, 1968—; regional v.p. Washington Assn. Life Underwriters, Richland, 1980; mem. adv. com. Wash. State Ins., Olympia, 1983-89. Chmn. bd. Richland YMCA, 1968; commr. Benton County Dyking Dist., Richland, 1970; chmn. Benton-Franklin Counties Bi-Centennial Commn., Tri-Cities, Wash., 1976; dist. chmn. Rep. Party, Benton County, 1980-96. Staff sgt. U.S. Army 1943-46. Recipient Nat. Quality award, Nat. Sales Achievement award. Mem. Tri-Cities Life Underwriters Assn. (pres. 1975, bd. dirs.), Tri-Cities Estate Planning Coun. (pres. 1984), Wash. State Assn. Life Underwriters (chmn. 1997), Kiwanis (pres. Chgo. club 1963, Richland club 1986-87, lt. gov. Pacific N.W. dist. 1983, chmn. dist. conv. 1971, 81, 91, sec. Pacific N.W. Found. 1994—). Avocations: stamp collecting, preparing family tree. Home: 712 Riverside Dr Richland WA 99353-5216 Office: NY Life Ins Co 8203 W Quinault St Kennewick WA 99336-7117

STEVENS, HERBERT FRANCIS, lawyer, law educator; b. Phila., Nov. 19, 1948; s. Herbert F. and Lois Marie (Kenna) S.; m. Jane Pickard, 1994; children: Sarah, Ben. SB, MIT, 1970; JD, Catholic U. Am., 1974; ML in Tax., Georgetown U., 1983. Bar: D.C. 1975, U.S. Supreme Ct. 1980. Law clk. to presiding justice Md. Ct. of Spl. Appeals, 1974-75; assoc. Morgan, Lewis & Bockius, Washington, 1975-78; ptnr. Lane & Edson, P.C., Washington, 1984-89; ptnr. Kelley Drye & Warren, Washington, 1989-93, Peabody & Brown, Washington, 1993—; adj. prof. Georgetown U. Law Ctr., 1983—; spkr. nat. confs., seminars, TV. Editor: Real Estate Aspects of the 1984 Tax Law, 1984; author: Real Estate Taxation: A Practitioner's Guide, 1986, A Developer's Guide to Low Income Housing Tax Credit, 1992, 3d edit., 1995. Bd. dirs. Ctr. for Mental Health, Inc., 1987-95, mem. exec. com.; mem. exec. com., bd. dirs. Nat. Fund for U.S. Botanic Gardens, 1992—. Mem. ABA, D.C. Bar Assn. Democrat. Methodist. Home: 8301 Hackamore Drive Potomac MD 20854 Office: Peabody & Brown 1255 23rd St NW Washington DC 20037-1125

STEVENS, JAMES HERVEY, JR., retired financial advisor; b. Balt., June 22, 1944; s. James H. and Hilda (Pearce) S.; m. Patricia Carol Donohue, Aug. 27, 1967 (div. Mar. 1983); children: James III, Carol; m. Lisa Gay Landrum, Apr. 29, 1984. BA, Duke U., 1966; MS in Fin. Scis., Am. Coll., Bryn Mawr, Pa., 1981. CLU; ChFC; CFP; registered health underwriter. Supr. New Eng. Life, Overland Park, Kans., 1969-75, agt., 1969—; v.p., treas. Creative Planning, Inc., Overland Park, 1980-95; pres. Hokanson, Lehman & Stevens, Inc., Overland Park, 1982-95; founder, chmn. Wings Over Mid-Am., Inc., 1995—; v.p. Air Care Alliance, 1997—. Contbg. editor monthly tax topics Kansas City Bus. Jour.; contbr. articles to profl. jours. Bd. dirs. Mo. div. Am. Cancer Soc., Kans. and Mo., 1982-84, Apple Valley Homes Assn., Overland Park, 1990—, pres. 1992, Cen. United Meth. Ch., Kansas City, Mo., 1990-92., North Cross United Meth., 1991—. Recipient Outstanding Young Man award, 1977; named one of Top 200 Fin. Advisors, Money Mag., 1987, Boss of Yr., Kansas City LICOMA, 1983. Mem. Kansas City Life Underwriters (pres. 1980-82, Herbert A. Hedges award 1987), Kansas City CLU & ChFC Soc. (pres. 1981-83), Mo. Life Underwriters (pres. 1984-86), Am. Soc. CLU & ChFC (vice chmn., bd. dirs.). Republican. Avocations: model railroading, collecting post-war "Lionel", comml. pilot, instrument flight instr. Home: 5200 W 98th Ter Shawnee Mission KS 66207-3221 Office: Wings Over Mid-Am Inc 115L W 103rd St # 229 Kansas City MO 64114-4737

STEVENS, JEROME HEBERT, management consultant; b. Paris, Apr. 24, 1959; came to U.S., 1991; s. Francois Hébert-Stevens and Claude Arthaud; m. Valerie Travert, Dec. 28, 1996. MD, U. Paris VII, 1987; diploma in health economics, U. Paris V, 1989; MBA, U. Pa., 1994. Attending physician Hosp. de Paris, 1987-90; COO, med. dir. Lyonnaise Santé, Paris, 1989-92; cons. mgr. APM/CSC, N.Y.C., 1994-96, mgr., 1997—. Co-author: Reengineering the Operating Room, 1996; participant med. TV series Entretiens de Bichat, 1990. Bd. dirs. GERO 92 Geriat. Assn., Paris, 1989-92. With French Army, 1985-86. Mem. Am. Coll. Physician Execs. Avocations: sailing, golf, modern art. Home: 666 5th Ave #239 New York NY 10103 Office: APM Inc 1675 Broadway New York NY 10019-5820

STEVENS, JOHN FLOURNOY, priest; b. Des Moines, June 19, 1914; s. Ralph Stoddard and Jeanne Flournoy (Thompson) S.; m. Ruth Elizabeth Brown, Jan. 19, 1945 (div. 1976); children: John Bruce, Michael Paul, James Andrew; m. Betty Louise Sinkola, June 2, 1976. BS with distinction, U.S. Naval Acad., 1938; MDiv, Va. Theol. Sem., 1948; postgrad., Johns Hopkins, 1941-42. Ordained to ministry as priest, 1949. Assoc. rector to rector Episcopal Chs., 1948-64; dir. dept. Christian social rels. Episcopal Diocese of Tex., Houston, 1964-66; mem. staff exec. coun. Episcopal Ch., 1966-74; assoc. coord. Joint Urban Prog., 1966-67, assoc. dir. gen. conv. spl. prog., 1967-69, asst. to dep. for prog., 1969-70, adminstrv. officer, also sec. exec. council, 1970-74, coord. Gen. Conv., 1972-73; bus. and circulation mgr. Episcopal Ch. Pub. Co., 1974-75, dir. Joint Strategy and Action Com., 1975-77; ret.; asst. to pastor Wheeler Ave. Bapt. Ch., Houston, 1979-80, mem clergy staff, 1980—; non-stipendiary rector Ch. of Advent, Houston, 1980-86, non-stipendiary assoc. rector Ch. of Good Shepherd, Friendswood, 1987-89, Ch. of Advent, Houston, 1991-96; chaplain Episc. Women's Caucus, 1996—; interim exec. dir. Houston Met. Mins., 1981. Author: To Tell the Story, 1963, No Place to Go, 1964. Bd. dirs. Houston Civil Liberties Union, 1963-66. Comdr. USN, 1938-46. Decorated Bronze Star medal. Fellow Episcopal Sem. of the S.W., Coll. of Preachers; mem. Episc. Soc. Cultural and Racial Unity (sec. 1964-66), Washington Fedn. Chs. (dir. 1950-53, fin. com. 1953-56), NAACP (dir. Houston chpt. 1962-66). Democrat. Episcopalian. Avocations: music, photography, golf, tennis, hiking, cooking.

STEVENS, JOHN PAUL, United States supreme court justice; b. Chgo., Apr. 20, 1920; s. Ernest James and Elizabeth (Street) S.; m. Elizabeth Jane Sheeren, June 7, 1942; children: John Joseph, Kathryn Stevens Jedlicka, Elizabeth Jane Stevens Sesemann, Susan Roberta Stevens Mullen; m. Maryan Mulholland, Dec. 1979. A.B., U. Chgo., 1941; J.D. magna cum laude, Northwestern U., 1947. Bar: Ill. 1949. Practiced in Chgo.; law clk. to U.S. Supreme Ct. Justice Wiley Rutledge, 1947-48; assoc. firm Poppenhusen, Johnston, Thompson & Raymond, 1949-52; asso. counsel sub-com. on study monopoly power, com. on judiciary U.S. Ho. of Reps., 1951; ptnr. firm Rothschild, Stevens, Barry & Myers, 1952-70; U.S. circuit judge, 1970-75; asso. justice U.S. Supreme Ct., 1975—; lectr. anti-trust law Northwestern U. Sch. Law,, 1952-54, U. Chgo. Law Sch., 1955-58; mem. Atty. Gen.'s Nat. Com. to Study Anti-Trust Laws, 1953-55. Served with USNR, 1942-45. Decorated Bronze Star. Mem. Chgo. Bar Assn. (2d v.p. 1970), Am., Ill., Fed. bar assns., Am. Law Inst., Order of Coif, Phi Beta Kappa, Psi Upsilon, Phi Delta Phi. Office: US Supreme Ct Supreme Court Bldg One 1st St NE Washington DC 20543*

STEVENS, JOHN RICHARD, architectural historian; b. Toronto, Ont., Can., Mar. 19, 1929; came to U.S., 1954; s. Walter John and Florence Rosalie (Warr) S.; m. Marion Frances Moore, May 7, 1964. Student, Columbia U., 1966-67. Comml. artist, tech. illustrator Toronto, Ont., Can. and New Haven, Conn.; asst. to curator Mystic Seaport, 1957; curator Maritime Mus. Can., Halifax, 1960-63; with dept. no. affairs Hist. Sites Divsn., 1963-66; surveyor early bldgs. Halifax, Quebec, Fredericton, Woodstock, St. John River Valley, Ea. Twps. of Quebec; lighthouses of Great Lakes, Nova Scotia, New Brunswick; with Archtl. Heritage, Inc., 1967-70; prin. John R. Stevens Assocs., Greenlawn, N.Y., 1970—; cons. hist. restoration Old Bethpage Village Restoration, 1967-94, Soc. for the Preservation L.I. Antiquities, Roslyn Preservation Corp., Smithtown Hist. Soc., Colonial Farmhouse Restoration Soc., numerous others; restorations include Van Nostrand-Starkins House, Revolutionary War "Arsenal", two c.1900 Am.-built streetcars for City of Detroit, 1976, 80, 1878 N.Y. elevated railroad car, 1983, first electric freight locomotive, 1988, c. 1880 horsecar for Rochester Mus., 1987; lectr. Dutch-Am. bldgs., street railway history. Author: Old Time Ships, 1949, H.M. Schooner Tecumseth, 1961, Ships of the North Shore, 1963, (guidebook) Ride Down Memory Lane, 1965, 2d rev. edit., 1984, Early History of Street Railways - The New Haven Area, 1982, The Derby Horse Railway and the World's First Electric Freight Locomotive, 1987; co-author/editor: Pioneers of Electric Railroading, 1991; contbr. articles on hist. bldg. tech., book revs. to profl. publs. Bd. trustees Roslyn Landmark Soc., 1980—. With U.S. Army, 1955-57. Mem. Branford Electric Rlwy. Assn. (bd. trustees 1957, 74, 80-81, 83-85, supt. equipment 1974-75, supt. bldgs. and grounds 1980-82, chmn. bd. trustees 1983, pres. 1984, 85, contbr. articles to jour.). Home and Office: 1 Sinclair Dr Greenlawn NY 11740-2607

STEVENS, JOSEPH CHARLES, psychology educator; b. Grand Rapids, Mich., Feb. 28, 1929; s. Joseph, Jr. and Anne Katheryn (Ghysels) S. A.B., Calvin Coll., Grand Rapids, 1950; M.A., Mich. State U., 1953; Ph.D., Harvard U., 1957. Instr., then asst. prof. psychology Harvard U., 1957-66; fellow John B. Pierce Found. Lab., also sr. research scientist Yale U., 1966—; cons. in field. Author: Laboratory Experiments in Psychology, 1965; co-editor: Sensation and Measurement, 1974; mem. editorial bds. profl. jours.; contbr. numerous articles to profl. jours. Grantee NSF; Grantee NIH; Grantee Air Force Office Sci. Research. Fellow AAAS, Am. Psychol. Soc., N.Y. Acad. Scis.; mem. Acoustical Soc. Am., Optical Soc. Am., Soc. Neurosci., Eastern Psychol. Assn., Gerontol. Soc. Am. Office: 290 Congress Ave New Haven CT 06519-1403

STEVENS, JOSEPH EDWARD, JR., federal judge; b. Kansas City, Mo., June 23, 1928; s. Joseph Edward and Mildred Christian (Smith) S.; m. Norma Jeanne Umlauf, Nov. 25, 1956; children: Jennifer Jeanne, Rebecca Jeanne. B.A., Yale U., 1949; J.D., U. Mich., 1952. Bar: Mo. 1952, U.S. Supreme Ct. 1973. Assoc. Lombardi, McLean, Slagle & Bernard, Kansas City, Mo., 1955-56; assoc. then ptnr. Lathrop, Koontz, Righter, Clagett & Norquist, Kansas City, Mo., 1956-81; judge U.S. Dist. Ct. (we. dist.) Mo., Kansas City, 1981—, chief judge, 1992-95; mem. adv. com. on Fed. Rules of Civil Procedure, Washington, 1987-92; bd. trustees Harry S. Truman Scholarship Found., 1995—. Bd. govs. Citizens Assn. Kansas City, 1959-70; bd. dirs., exec. com. Truman Med. Ctr., Kansas City; trustee Central United Methodist Ch., Kansas City, 1978—, Barstow Sch., Kansas City, 1978-87. Served with USNR, 1952-55. Recipient Lon O. Hocker Meml. Trial Lawyer award Mo. Bar Found., 1963, Spurgeon Smithson award, 1987, Charles E. Whittaker award Kansas City Lawyers Assn., 1996. Mem. ABA (ho. dels. 1982-88), Kansas City Met. Bar Assn., Lawyers Assn., Mo. Bar (pres. 1980-81, bd. govs. 1976-82, Pres.'s award 1995), Univ. Club, Carriage Club, Vanguard Club, Mercury Club, Beta Theta Pi, Man-of-Month Fraternity, Mo. Acad. Squires. Office: US Dist Ct 811 Grand Blvd Ste 707 Kansas City MO 64106-1909

STEVENS, JULIE ANN, peri-operative nurse; b. Normal, Ill., June 3, 1961; d. James E. and Janice J. (Richey) S. BSN with honors, Baylor U., 1984; postgrad., St. Louis U., 1997—. RN, Tex.; cert. CNOR, CNRN. Nurse intern operating rm. Parkland Meml. Hosp., Dallas, 1984-85, staff nurse, 1985-89; charter employee, staff nurse Zale Lipshy U. Hosp. at Southwestern Med. Ctr., Dallas, 1989-92, clin. coord. neurosurgery, 1992-96; staff nurse Med. City Dallas Hosp., 1996-97. Recipient Interlocking Circle of Caring award Delta Airlines, Dallas, 1986, Divisional Achievement award Zale Lipshy U. Hosp., 1994. Mem. Assn. Oper. Rm. Nurses, Am. Assn.

Neurosci. Nurses, DAR, Internat. Order of Job's Daus (past Honored Queen). Methodist. Home: 628 McBride Pointe Dr Ballwin MO 63011

STEVENS, KENNETH NOBLE, electrical engineering educator; b. Toronto, Ont., Can., Mar. 23, 1924; came to U.S., 1948, naturalized, 1962; s. Cyril George and Catherine (Noble) S.; m. Phyllis Fletcher, Jan. 19, 1957 (div. 1979); children: Rebecca, Andrea, Michael Hugh, John Noble; m. Sharon Manuel, Jan. 14, 1994. B.A.Sc., U. Toronto, 1945, M.A.Sc., 1948; Sc.D., MIT, 1952. Inst. U. Toronto, 1946-48; faculty MIT, Cambridge, 1948—; prof. elec. engring. MIT, 1963—, Clarence J. Lebel prof., 1977—; Vis. fellow Royal Inst. Tech., Stockholm, 1962-63; cons. to industry, 1952—; vis. prof. phonetics U. Coll., London, 1969-70; mem. Nat. Adv. Council on Neurol. and Communicative Disorders and Stroke NIH, 1982-86. Author: (with A.G. Bose) Introductory Network Theory; Contbr. articles to profl. jours. Trustee Buckingham Browne and Nichols Sch., 1974-80. Recipient Quintana award Voice Found., 1992, medal European Speech Comm. Assn., 1995; Guggenheim fellow, 1962. Fellow IEEE, Acoustical Soc. Am. (exec. com. 1963-66, v.p. 1971-72, pres.-elect 1975-76, pres. 1976-77, gold medal 1995), Am. Acad. Arts and Scis.; mem. NAE. Home: 51 Montrose St Somerville MA 02143-1212 Office: MIT 77 Massachusetts Ave Cambridge MA 02139-4301

STEVENS, LINDA LOUISE HALBUR, addiction counselor; b. Huron, S.D., Oct. 28, 1960; d. Alvin LeRoy and Esther Louise (Schroeder) Halbur; m. Lowell Eugene Stevens, July 26, 1980 (div. 1995); children: Lowell John, Tracie Lynn. BSW, U. N.D., 1991; MEd, N.D. State U., 1993. Lic. social worker, N.D.; lic. addiction counselor, N.D. Tracker Luth. Soc. Svcs., Hillsboro, N.D., 1990-94; addiction counselor Heartland Med. Ctr., Fargo, N.D., 1993-94, S.E. Human Svc. Ctr., Fargo, 1994—; dual diagnosis Off Main Program, Fargo, 1995; addiction counselor, SMI day treatment provider Koochiching Counseling Ctr., International Falls, Minn., 1997—. Local/state officer N.D. Women of Today, Hillsboro, 1982-87. Recipient Presdl. award of excellence N.D. women of Today, 1986, 87. Mem. NASW, Am. Counseling Assn. Avocations: golf, sewing, pets, cross country skiing. Home: 2153 County Rd 121 MNternational Falls MT 56649 Office: Koochining Counseling Ctr 1404 Highway 71 International Falls MN 56649-2154

STEVENS, LINDA TOLLESTRUP, academic director; b. Salt Lake City, Feb. 7, 1963; d. Garn Alvin and Mary Ann (Cannon) Tollestrup; 1 child, Marli Brynn. BS, U. Utah, 1984, MS, 1989. Cert. sch. counselor, Utah. Tchr. pre-sch. Adventurer's Pre-Sch., Salt Lake City, 1984; adminstr. headstart program Creative Devel. Ctr., Salt Lake City, 1984-85; vocat. evaluator Utah Divsn. Rehab. Svcs. Vocat. Evaluation, Salt Lake City, 1985-86; human resource counselor Davis Applied Tech. Ctr., Kaysville, Utah, 1986-95; advising programs coord. Pa. State U., Hazleton, 1995—; trainee Phoenix Inst., Salt Lake City, 1986, U. No. Colo., Greeley, 1986; instr. Utah State Turning Point, Salt Lake City and Provo, 1992. Mem. Golden Spike Dog Obedience Club, Ogden, Utah, 1986-90, Humane Soc. Utah, 1986—. Mem. NEA, ACA, Nat. Acad. Advising Assn., Am. Vocat. Assn., Am. Bus. Women's Assn. (v.p. 1992), Utah Vocat. Assn. (bldg. fund coord. 1989-90), Utah Fedn. Bus. and Profl. Women (Woman of Achievement award 1991), Golden Key Honor Soc., Delta Soc., Phi Eta Sigma. Mormon. Avocations: dog training, tennis, violin, piano, reading. Office: Pa State Univ Highacres Hazleton PA 18201

STEVENS, LISA GAY, minister, choral director; b. Oklahoma City, Mar. 30, 1952; d. Charles Alton and Betty Lou (Johnson) Landrum; m. Thomas Lynn Taylor, Dec. 11, 1971 (div. 1983); children: Jason Ryan, Joel Shane; m. James Hervey Stevens Jr., Apr. 29, 1984. Student, Friends U., 1970-72; BA in Music, U. Mo., Kansas City, 1983-87; MDiv with gerontology specialization, St. Paul Sch. Theology, 1987-90. Ordained deacon United Meth. Ch., 1989, elder, 1992. Adminstrv. asst./cashier McLiney and Co., Kansas City, Mo., 1978-80; choral dir. Hickman Mills Christian Community, Kansas City, 1979-82; adminstrv. asst. Hokanson, Lehman & Stevens Creative Planning, Inc., Kansas City, 1981-88; choral dir. Crossroads Reformed Ch., Shawnee Mission, Kans., 1983-84, St. Paul Sch. Theology, Kansas City, 1988-89; chaplain St. Luke's Hosp., Kingswood Manor Health Ctr., Kansas City, 1988; pastor The Belvidere United Meth. Ch., Kansas City, 1988-90, Va./Passaic United Meth. Chs., Butler, Mo., 1990-93, North Cross United Meth. Ch., Kansas City, Mo., 1993-95, Ctrl. United Meth. Ch., Kansas City, 1995-96; adj. faculty praxis team leader St. Paul Sch. Theology, 1990-93; mem. fin. and adminstrn. com. Mo. West United Meth. Conf., 1993-96, sub-com. health ins. com., 1993-95, dist. supts.' salary com., 1994-96, Kansas City north dist. supts.' com., 1994-95, conf. counseling elder, 1993-96. Solo flutist Sr. Wichita Youth Orchestra, 1969-70. Pres. Life Ins. Office Mgrs. Assn. Kansas City, 1985, chairperson pub. rels, 1984; bd. trustees Shepherd's Ctr. of Northland, 1994-95, mem. funding/fin. com., 1994-95. Mem. Butler Ministerial Alliance; Butler Chaplains Assn. (chaplain, 1991-93). Methodist. Avocations: flutist, plane enthusiast, music, artist.

STEVENS, M. ALLEN, geneticist, administrator; b. Mt. Carmel, Utah, Aug. 12, 1935; s. Joseph Merwin and Virginia (Tait) S.; m. Hermese Maw, June 6, 1960; children: Kent, Lance, Jennifer. BS, Utah State U., 1957, MS, 1961; PhD, Oreg. State U., 1967. Rsch. assoc. Campbell Soup Co., Camden, N.J., 1967-70; asst. geneticist U. Calif., Davis, 1970-74, assoc. geneticist, 1974-79, prof. geneticist, 1979; regional mgr. Campbell Soup Co., Camden, N.J., 1979-81; v.p. Campbell Inst. Agrl. Rsch., 1981-87, v.p. agrl. rsch., 1987-89; v.p. rsch. Petoseed Co., Inc., Woodland, Calif., 1989-95; sr. v.p. rsch. Seminis Vegetable Genetics, Woodland, Calif., 1996—; lectr. sci. Inst. Food Tech., 1970-73; adj. prof. U. Calif., Davis, 1979-82; vis. prof. Hebrew U., Rehovot, Israel, 1977; bd. dirs. Genetic Resources Comm. Sys., Washington, 1986-95, Am. Seed Rsch. Found., 1993—; sci. liaison officer Asian Vegetable R & D Ctr., Tainan, Taiwan, 1983-88, bd. dirs., 1990-93; mem. Nat. Plant Genetic Resources Bd., Washington, 1987-91; mem. exec. com. Internat. Food Biotech. Coun., 1987-90. Contbr. numerous articles to books and sci. jours. Mem. coord. com. Tomato Genetics Coop., 1980-90. 1st lt. U.S. Army, 1957-59. Recipient Citation of Performance U. Calif., Davis, 1992, award of Distinction, 1995; named Vol. of Yr. Coll. Agrl. and Environ. Sci. U. Calif., Davis, 1991. Fellow AAAS, Am. Soc. Horticultural Sci. (pres. 1992-93, Nat. Canners Assn. award 1968, 1977, Asgrow award 1971, 78, Campbell award 1973, Nat. Food Processors Assn. award 1980, Homer C. Thompson award 1983, Outstanding Industry Scientist 1996). Achievements include development of tomato varieties UC82, UC204. Home: 21715 County Rd 97 Woodland CA 95695 Office: Seminis Vegetable Genetics 37437 State Highway 16 Woodland CA 95695-9353

STEVENS, MARILYN RUTH, editor; b. Wooster, Ohio, May 30, 1943; d. Glenn Willard and Gretchen Elizabeth (Ihrig) Amstutz; BA, Coll. Wooster (Ohio), 1965; MAT, Harvard U., 1966; JD, Suffolk U., 1975; m. Bryan J. Stevens, Oct. 11, 1969; children: Jennifer Marie, Gretchen Anna. Bar: Mass. 1975. Tchr., Lexington (Mass.) Public Schs., 1966-69; in various editorial positions Houghton Mifflin Co., Boston, 1969—, editorial dir. sch. depts., 1978-81, editorial dir. math. and scis. Sch. Div., 1981-84, mng. editor sch. pub., 1984—. Mem. LWV, Mass. Bar Assn. Office: Houghton Mifflin 222 Berkeley St Boston MA 02116-3748

STEVENS, MARK, banker; b. Chgo., May 24, 1947; s. Joseph K. and Phoebe (Copeland) S.; m. Joyce Sue Skinner, Aug. 22, 1970; children: Mark Benjamin, Katherine Joyce. BA, W.Va. U., 1969, JD, 1972. V.p. Continental Ill. Nat. Bank & Trust Co., Chgo., 1972-79, No. Trust Co., Chgo., 1979-81; pres., CEO, No. Trust Bank Fla. N.A., Sarasota, 1981-87, chmn., pres., CEO,, 1987-96; exec. v.p. No. Trust Co. & No. Trust Corp., 1996—; pres. No. Trust Fla. Corp., Miami, 1987—; exec. v.p. No. Trust Corp. and No. Trust Co., 1996—. Trustee Ctr. Fine Arts, 1988-94, 1988-94, Miami Children's Hosp. Found., 1993-96, South Fla. Performing Arts Ctr. Found., 1993—, U. Miami, 1994, Beacon Coun., 1990—; mem. U. Miami Citizens Bd., 1988-89, Young Pres.'s Orgn., 1988—; bd. dirs. Miami Coalition and Task Force, 1988—, New World Symphony, 1991—; charter mem. Coun. of 100 Fla. Internat. Univ. Found., 1990—; hon. bd. dirs. Audubon House; mem. Orange Bowl Com., 1994. Mem. Young Pres. Orgn., Riviera Country Club, Miami Club. Office: No Trust Bank Fla 50 S LaSalle St Chicago IL 60675

STEVENS, MARTIN BRIAN, publisher; b. N.Y.C., Dec. 29, 1957; s. David Robert and Shirley (Marcus) S. Grad. high sch. Advt. artist Unitron Pubs., N.Y.C., 1977, Westchester Publs., Elmsford, N.Y., 1978; pub. Marketers Forum, Centerport, N.Y., 1981—, Swap Meet mag., Centerport, 1990—; Pub. 8 bus. directories, rep. 6 bus. book pubs.; founder Rodeo Dr. Limousine Svc., 1990-93, Mercedes-Benz Limousine Svc., 1990-93. Named Top Mail Order Dealer, Nat. Mail Dealers Counsel, 1978. Mem. Mail Order Bus. Bd. (pres. 1978-80), Better Bus. Bur., Nat. Assn. Self-Employed, Nat. Assn. Desktop Pub., L.I. Assn., Can. Direct Mail Assn. Avocations: weight training, reading. Office: Forum Pub Co 383 E Main St Centerport NY 11721-1538

STEVENS, MAY, artist; b. Boston, June 9, 1924; d. Ralph Stanley and Alice Margaret (Dick) S.; m. Rudolf Baranik, June 5, 1948; 1 child, Steven. BFA, Mass. Coll. Art, 1946; postgrad., Academie Julian, Paris, 1948-49, Art Students League, 1948. Mem. faculty Sch. Visual Arts, N.Y.C., 1964-96, Skowhegan Sch. Painting and Sculpture, 1992, Vt. Studio Ctr., 1997; lectr. Royal Coll. Art, London, 1981, U. Wis.-Racine, 1973, Coll. Art Assn., Washington, 1975. One-woman shows: Terry Dintenfass Gallery, N.Y.C., 1971, Cornell U., 1973, Douglass Coll., Rutgers U., 1974, Lerner-Heller Gallery, N.Y.C., 1975, 76, 78, 81, Clark U., 1982, Boston U. Art Gallery, 1984, Frederick S. Wight Gallery, UCLA, 1985, U. Md., College Park, 1985, Real Art Ways, Hartford, Conn., 1988, New Mus. Contemporary Art, 1988, Orchard Gallery, Derry, No. Ireland, 1988, Kenyon Coll., Gambier, Ohio, 1988, Greenville County (S.C.) Art Mus., 1991, Herter Gallery, U. Mass., Amherst, 1991, U. Colo., Boulder, 1993, U. N.Mex., Albuquerque, 1996, Mary Ryan Gallery, N.Y.C., 1996; exhibited in group shows: Inst. Contemporary Arts, London, 1980, Gemeente Mus., The Hague, 1979, Whitney Mus., 1970, Gedok, Kunsthaus, Hamburg, Germany, 1972, Everson Mus., Syracuse, N.Y., 1976, Clocktower, N.Y.C., 1986, Guerrilla Girls Exbn. at Palladium, N.Y.C., 1985, One Penn Pla., 1985, Pentonville Gallery, London, 1986, Heckscher Mus., N.Y., 1987, Univ. Art Mus., Berkeley, Calif., 1987, Mus. Modern Art, 1988, Exit Art, N.Y.C., 1988, Sao Paulo (Brazil) Mus. Modern Art, 1989, Blum Helman Gallery, N.Y.C., 1989, Univ. Art Mus., Long Beach, Calif., 1990, Angels Gate, San Pedro, Calif., 1990, Newark Mus., 1990, Städtliche Kunsthalle, Düsseldorf, Germany, 1990, DeCordova Mus., Lincoln, Mass., 1991, Exit Art, N.Y.C., 1994, Mary Delahoyd Gallery, N.Y.C., 1995, Mary Ryan Gallery, N.Y.C., 1995, Gwenda Jay Gallery, Chgo., 1995, Lizardi Harp Gallery, L.A., 1995, ACA Galleries, N.Y.C., 1996, Nassau County Mus., Roslyn, N.Y., 1997; represented in permanent collections: Metropolitan Mus. of Art, N.Y.C., Mus. Modern Art, N.Y.C., Moca, L.A., San Francisco Mus. Art, New Mus. Contemporary Art, Whitney Mus., Bklyn. Mus., Herbert F. Johnson Mus., Cornell U., Mus. Fine Arts Boston, De Cordova Mus., Lincoln, Mass.; contbr. articles to various mags. Recipient Childe Hassam Purchase awards Nat. Inst. Arts and Letters, 1968, 69, 75, N.Y. State Coun. on Arts award, 1974, Disting. Alumna award Mass. Coll. Art, 1997; MacDowell Colony fellow, 1971, 72, 74, 75, 81, 82, 84, Bunting Inst. fellow Radcliffe Coll., 1988-89; grantee NEA, 1983, Guggenheim, 1986; honoree Women's Caucus for Art, 1990. Mem. Coll. Art Assn.

STEVENS, MILTON LEWIS, JR., trombonist; b. Gt. Barrington, Mass., Nov. 10, 1942; s. Milton Lewis and Edna Laura (Coates) S.; m. Elizabeth Mruk Stevens, June 14, 1966 (dec. June 1984); m. Priscilla Storms, Dec. 28, 1985. Mus.B., Oberlin Conservatory Music, 1965; Mus.M., U. Ill., 1966; D.M.A., Boston U., 1975. Instr. Oberlin (Ohio) Conservatory Music, 1967-68; asst. prof. Boston U., 1970-73, Ohio State U., Columbus, 1973-74; prin. trombonist Denver Symphony, 1974-78, Nat. Symphony Orch., Washington, 1978—; adj. prof. Cath. U. Am., 1978—, U. Md., College Park, 1987—. Condr. Intersvc. Trombone Choir, Washington, 1991—, Washington Symphonic Brass and Percussion Ensemble, 1993—. Recipient Albert Spaulding award Berkshire Music Center, 1968. Mem. Internat. Trombone Assn. Home: 3500 Farm Hill Dr Falls Church VA 22044-1237 Office: Nat Symphony Kennedy Ctr Washington DC 20566

STEVENS, NORMAN DENNISON, retired library director; b. Nashua, N.H., Mar. 4, 1932; s. David P. and Ruth (Ackley) S.; m. Nora Bennett, Jan. 16, 1959; children: David P., Sara, Elizabeth. BA, U. N.H., 1954; MLS, Rutgers U., 1957, PhD, 1961. Acting dir. univ. librs. Howard U., Washington, 1961-63; assoc. libr. Rutgers U., New Brunswick, N.J., 1963-68; assoc. univ. libr. U. Conn., Storrs, 1968-75, univ. libr., 1975-87, dir. univ. librs., 1987-94, dir. emeritus univ. librs., 1994—, acting dir. Thomas J. Dodd Rsch. Ctr., 1995-96; exec. dir. The Molesworth Inst., Storrs, 1959—; condr. librs. N. Am. Sch. for the Artsy, White Bear Lake, Minn., 1988—; pres. The Bibliosmiles, 1993—; acting dir. Thomas J. Dodd Rsch. Ctr., 1995-96. Author: A Guide to Collecting Librariana Communications Throughout Libraries, 1983; editor: Library Humor, 1971, The Librarian, 1976, Postcards in the Library, 1995. Mem. ALA, Phi Beta Kappa, Phi Kappa Phi, Pi Sigma Alpha. Avocations: collecting library memorabilia, library humor, profl. writing. Home: 143 Hanks Hill Rd Storrs Mansfield CT 06268-2315

STEVENS, PAUL EDWARD, lawyer; b. Youngstown, Ohio, July 22, 1916; s. Raymond U. and Mary Ann (Pritchard) S.; m. Janet L. Weisert, Mar. 9, 1946; 1 son, Mark O. LL.B., Ohio State U., 1941. Bar: Ohio 1941. Practiced in Youngstown, 1941—; ptnr. Green, Schiavoni, Murphy & Stevens, 1962-71, Burdman, Stevens & Gilliland, 1971-75, Stevens & Toot, 1976-77, Paul E. Stevens Co., 1977—; prof. law Youngstown Coll. Sch. Law, 1946-60; gen. counsel Animal Charity League of Ohio, 1965—; sec.-treas. CASTLO Community Improvement Corp., 1986—. Trustee Poland Twp., Ohio, 1960-69; Republican candidate for U.S. Congress, 1959; dist. adminstrv. asst. Congressman Charles J. Carney, 19th Ohio dist., 1970-80; pres. Welsh Nat. Gymanfa Ganu Assn., 1988-90. With AUS, 1942-46. Mem. ABA, Ohio Bar Assn. (chmn. membership com. 1955), Mahoning County Bar Assn. (pres. 1953-54), Mahoning County Planning Assn. (chmn. 1990—). Unitarian. Home: 7191 N Lima Rd Youngstown OH 44514-3749 Office: 780 Boardman Canfield Rd Youngstown OH 44512-4344 *To be allowed to practice law is an honor. Therefore, an attorney must be fair and honest, but most of all, he must have respect for and love his fellow man.*

STEVENS, PAUL IRVING, manufacturing company executive; b. Lawrence, Kans., Mar. 22, 1915; s. Ira F. and Ida M. S.; m. Artie Faye Womack, Nov. 10, 1935; children: Richard Irving, Constance Irene. Student bus. adminstrn., Pasadena (Calif.) Coll., 1933-35. Indsl. engr. Consol. Aircraft Co., San Diego, 1940-49; founder, prin. stockholder, pres. United Machine Co., Ft. Worth, 1950-61; exec. v.p. Clary Corp., San Gabriel, Calif., 1962-65; pres., owner Stevens Corp., Ft. Worth, 1965-69; pres., chief exec. officer Waltham Industries, N.Y.C., 1969-71, Stevens Industries, La Jolla, Calif., 1972—, Campbell Industries, San Diego., 1976-79; chmn., pres. Stevens Air Systems, El Cajon, Calif., 1974-81; pres. Womack Motors, Inc., El Centro, Calif., 1982-90; chmn. bd. dirs., CEO Stevens Graphics Corp., Ft. Worth, 1986-95; bd. dirs. Rancho Santa Fe Nat. Bank, Calif., 1982-85, chmn. 1985-95; chmn., CEO Stevens Internat., Inc., 1995. Mem. Nat. Mgmt. Assn. (exec. com.), Presidents Assn., Civic Round Table, La Jolla Country Club, Colonial Country Club, Canyon Country Club, University Club, Ft. Worth Club, Shady Oaks Country Club. Republican. Methodist. Home: 2585 Calle Del Oro La Jolla CA 92037-2005 Office: PO Box 950 La Jolla CA 92038-0950

STEVENS, ROBERT BOCKING, lawyer, educator; b. U.K., June 8, 1933; naturalized, 1971; s. John Skevington and Enid Dorthy (Bocking) S.; m. Katherine Booth, Dec. 23, 1985; 1 child, Robin; children by previous marriage: Carey, Richard. BA, Oxford U., 1955, BCL, 1956, MA, 1959, DCL, 1984; LLM, Yale U., 1958; LLD (hon.), N.Y. Law Sch., 1984, Villanova U., 1985, U. Pa., 1987; D.Litt. (hon.), Haverford Coll., 1991. Barrister-at-law London, 1956; tutor in law Keble Coll. Oxford U., 1958-59; asst. prof. law Yale U., 1959-61, assoc. prof., 1961-65, prof., 1965-76; provost, prof. law and history Tulane U., 1976-78; pres. Haverford Coll., 1978-87; chancellor, prof. history U. Calif., Santa Cruz, 1987-91; of counsel Covington and Burling, Washington and London, 1991—; master Pembroke Coll., Oxford, 1993—; Essex Court Chambers, 1966—; vis. prof. U. Tex., 1961, U. East Africa, 1962, London Sch. Econs., 1963, Stanford U., 1966, U. Coll. London, 1991-94; cons. UN, HEW, U.S. Dept. State. Author: The Restrictive Practices Court, 1965, Lawyers and the Courts, 1967, In Search of Justice, 1968, Income Security, 1970, Welfare Medicine in America, 1974, Law and Politics, 1978, The Law School, 1983, The Independence of the Judiciary, 1993. Grantee Rockefeller Found., 1962-64, Ford Found., 1962-64, 73-74, Russell Sage Found., 1967-68, NEH, 1973-74, Nuffield Found., 1975; named Hon. fellow Keble Coll. Oxford U., 1985, Socio-Legal Ctr., 1992. Mem. Marshall Aid Meml. Commn. (chair), Rsch. com., Am. Bar Found. Home: Masters Lodgings, Pembroke Coll, Oxford OX1 1DW, England Office: Covington and Burling, Leconfield House Curzon St, London W1Y 8AS, England

STEVENS, ROBERT DAVID, librarian, educator; b. Nashua, N.H., Aug. 11, 1921; s. David Philip and Ruth (Ackley) S.; m. Helen Medora Conrad, Jan. 16, 1943; children: Ruth Wilson Robertson, Hope Conrad. A.B. magna cum laude, Syracuse U., 1942; B.S. in L.S. with honors, Columbia, 1947; M.A., Am. U., 1955, Ph.D., 1965. With Library of Congress, Washington, 1947-64; coordinator pub. law 480 programs Library of Congress, 1962-64; dir. Library East West Center, Honolulu, 1964-66; dean Grad. Sch. Library Studies U. Hawaii, Honolulu, 1966-75; chief cataloging div. Copyright Office, 1975-80, coordinator copyright collections, 1980; lectr. grad. Sch. Library Studies, U. Hawaii, 1981—; chief exec. officer Molesworth Inst. West, Inc., 1984-91, chmn., 1991-96; Fulbright lectr. U. Indonesia, 1971; U.S. del. Intergovtl. Conf. Planning Nat. Libraries Infrastructures, 1974. Author: Role of the Library of Congress in International Exchange of Government Publications, 1955, Toshokan Kyoryoku, 1970, Documents of International Organizations, 1974, Japanese and U.S. Research Libraries at the Turning Point, 1977, Short History of the School of Library and Information Studies, 1991; contbr. articles to profl. publs. Served to lt. USNR, 1943-46. Mem. Hawaii Library Assn. (pres. 1966-67), ALA (mem. council 1967-70, mem. U.S.-Japan adv. com. 1972—, chmn. 1974-76, Rlms policy and research com. 1977-81), Assocs. U. Hawaii Library (vice chmn. 1981-84), Japan Library Assn., Hui Dui, Phi Beta Kappa, Pi Sigma Alpha. Club: 15 (Honolulu). Home: 3265 Paty Dr Honolulu HI 96822-1449

STEVENS, ROBERT EDWIN, bank executive, former insurance company executive; b. Hartford, Feb. 12, 1927; s. Horace and Anna E. (Lauritzen) S.; m. Betty L. Hippler, June 30, 1951; children—Paul, Lynn, Peter. B.A., Wesleyan U., 1949. Various positions bond and common stock divs. Conn. Mut. Life Ins. Co., Hartford, 1951-71; v.p., treas. Conn. Mut. Life Ins. Co., 1972-74, sr. v.p., 1974-76, exec. v.p., 1976-89; pres. Conn. Mut. Investment Accounts, Inc., 1980-89; chmn. bd. dirs. Liberty Bank, Middletown, Conn., 1989-95; bd. dirs. Freedom Fin. Svcs. Bd. dirs. Hartford Hosp.; trustee emeritus Jacob L. and Lewis Fox Scholarship Found.; trustee emeritus Wesleyan U.; corporator Middlesex Hosp.; mem. investment com. Hartford Found. Pub. Giving. With USNR, World War II. Mem. Hartford Soc. Fin. Analysts (past pres.). Home: 46 Keighley Pond Rd PO Box 361 Cobalt CT 06414 Office: Liberty Bank Middletown CT

STEVENS, ROBERT JAY, magazine editor; b. Detroit, July 25, 1945; s. Jay Benjamin and Louise Ann (Beyreuther) S.; m. Dahlia Jean Conger, Aug. 15, 1970; children—Sandra Lee, Julie Ann. Student, Huron (S.D.) Coll., 1963-66, Wayne State U., 1968-71. Sr. staff writer Automotive News, Detroit, 1968-71; editor Excavating Contractor mag.; Cummins Pub. Co., Oak Park, Mich., 1971-78, Chevrolets, Pro Jour., Sandy Corp., Southfield, Mich., 1978-79; editor Cars and Parts mag. Amos Press, Sidney, Ohio, 1979—; truck editor Automotive Design & Devel. mag., 1971-78; lectr., speaker in field. Author articles, poems. Served with AUS, 1966-68, Vietnam. Decorated Air medal, Bronze Star, Commendation medal; recipient Alphomega Publs. award, 1965—, Robert F. Boger Meml. award for outstanding constrn. journalism, 1975, U.L.C.C. nat. editorial award Am. Pub. Works Assn., 1978. Mem. Detroit Auto Writers (past dir.), Internat. Motor Press Assn., Soc. Automotive Historians, Antique Automobile Club Am. Republican. Presbyterian. Home: 653 Ridgeway Dr Sidney OH 45365-3432 Office: PO Box 482 911 Vandemark Rd Sidney OH 45365

STEVENS, ROGER LACEY, theatrical producer; b. Detroit, Mar. 12, 1910; s. Stanley and Florence (Jackson) S.; m. Christine Gesell, Jan. 1, 1938; 1 child, Christabel. Student, Choate Sch., 1928, U. Mich., 1928-30; DHL, U. Mich., 1964; HHD (hon.), Wayne State U., 1960; DHL, Tulane U., 1960; LLD, Amherst Coll., 1968; hon. degrees, Skidmore Coll., 1969, U. Ill., 1970, Boston U., 1970, Am. U., 1979, Boston U., 1979, Miami U., 1983, Phila. Coll. Art, 1986. Former real estate broker specializing in hotels and investment properties, 1934-60; spl. asst. to the Pres. on the arts, 1964-68; chmn. Nat. Coun. on the Arts, 1965-69, Nat. Endowment for the Arts, also trustee; pres. Nat. Inst. for Music Theater; chmn. Am. Film Inst., 1969-72; chmn. adv. com. Nat. Book Award, 1970-75, 1988-89; mem. Coun. for Arts, Mass. Inst. Tech.; chmn. Fund for New Am. Plays, 1986—; mem. Pres.'s Com. on Arts and Humanities, 1982-93. Producing partner in more than 200 theatrical prodns. including Old Times, West Side Story, Cat on a Hot Tin Roof, Bus Stop, The Visit, Mary, Mary, A Man for all Seasons, The Best Man, Deathtrap, Death of a Salesman; Kennedy Ctr. prodns. include Annie, First Monday in October, On Your Toes, Mass, Jumpers, Night and Day, Wings, Texas Trilogy, Bedroom Farce, Cocktail Hour, Love Letters, Metamorphosis, A Few Good Men, Artist Descending a Staircase, Shadowlands, She Loves Me. Chmn. fin. com. Dem. Party, 1956; chmn. bd. trustees John F. Kennedy Ctr. Performing Arts, 1961-88; trustee Am. Shakespeare Theater and Acad., Choate Sch., 1982-93; bd. dirs. Met. Opera Assn., 1958—, Ballet Theatre Found., 1977—, Nat. Symphony Orch., 1981-93, Filene Ctr./Wolf Trap Farm Park for Performing Arts, 1969-92, The Washington Opera, 1988-94, Peabody Conservatory, 1979-82, Folger Libr., Acad. Am. Poets. Decorated knight comdr. Brit. Empire; Royal Order of Vasa, Sweden; grand ufficiale Order of Merit Italy; comdr.'s cross Order of Merit Fed. Republic Germany; recipient award contbn. theatre Nat. Theater Conf., 1970, , Presdl. Medal of Freedom, 1988, Nat. Medal of Arts, 1988; Kennedy Ctr. honoree, 1988. Fellow Royal Soc. Arts; mem. ANTA (exec. com.), Phi Gamma Delta. Clubs: Bohemian (San Francisco); Racquet and Tennis (N.Y.C.), Century Assn. (N.Y.C.), Pilgrims (N.Y.C.). Office: JFK Ctr Performing Arts Washington DC 20566

STEVENS, RON A., lawyer, public interest organization administrator; b. Indpls., Sept. 4, 1945; s. Granville Thomas and Charlotte May (Wheeler) S.; m. Judy Rohde, June 15, 1968; children: Samuel Thomas, Alison Elizabeth. BA, Okla. State U.; JD with honors, Ill. Inst. Tech., 1976. Bar: Ill. 1976. Staff atty. Legal Assistance Found. Chgo., 1976-79; staff atty., dir. housing agenda Bus. and Profl. People for Pub. Interest, Chgo., 1979-81; chief housing div. Office of Cook County State's Atty., Chgo., 1981-82; campaign coord. north lakefront Washington for Mayor, Chgo., 1982-83; program officer The Joyce Found., Chgo., 1983-86; pres. Citizens for a Better Environment, Chgo., 1986-89; exec. dir. United Way Santa Fe County, 1989—; adv. bd. state support ctr. on environ. hazards Nat. Ctr. for Policy Alternatives, Washington, 1987-89; chair Local Bd. EFSP, 1989—, chair Santa Fe Affordable Housing Roundtable, 1992—; bd. dirs. No. N.Mex. Grantmakers Assn. Mem. bldg. code enforcement com. Mayor's Transition Team Housing Task Force, Chgo., 1983, steering com. Chgo. Ethics Project, 1986-88; founder, chmn. Progressive Chgo. Area Network, 1981-84; bd. dirs. Uptown Recycling Sta., Chgo., 1987-89; mem. South Ctrl. Regional Coun., United Way of Am. Mem. Chgo. Coun. Lawyers (chmn. housing com. 1978-81, bd. govs. 1981-83, bd. dirs. Fund for Justice, 1986-88), Chgo. Area Runners Assn. (founder, v.p. 1977-81). Home: 739 Gregory Ln Santa Fe NM 87501-4257 Office: United Way Santa Fe County PO Box 261 Santa Fe NM 87504-0261

STEVENS, ROSEMARY A., public health and social history educator; b. Bourne, Eng.; came to U.S., 1961, naturalized, 1968; d. William Edward and Mary Agnes (Tricks) Wallace; m. Robert B. Stevens, Jan. 28, 1961 (div. 1983); children: Carey, Richard; m. Jack D. Barchas, Aug. 9, 1994. BA, Oxford (Eng.) U., 1957; Diploma in Social Adminstrn., Manchester (Eng.) U., 1959; MPH, Yale U., 1963, PhD, 1968. Various hosp. adminstrv. positions Eng., 1959-61; rsch. assoc. Med. Sch. Yale U., 1962-68, asst. prof. Med. Sch., 1968-71, assoc. prof. Med. Sch., 1971-74, prof. public health Med. Sch., 1974-76; master Jonathan Edwards Coll., 1974-75; prof. dept. health systems mgmt. and polit. sci. Tulane U., New Orleans, 1976-78; chmn. dept. health systems mgmt. Tulane U., 1977-78; prof. history and sociology of sci. U. Pa., Phila., 1979—, chmn. dept., 1980-83, 86-91, UPS Found. prof., 1990-91, dean Sch. Arts and Scis., Thomas S. Gates prof., 1991-96; vis. lectr. Johns Hopkins U., 1967-68; guest scholar Brookings Instn., Washington, 1967-68; acad. visitor London Sch. Econs., 1962-64, 1973-74. Author: Medical Practice in Modern England: The Impact of Specialization and State Medicine, 1966, American Medicine and the Public Interest, 1971, In Sickness and in Wealth: American Hospitals in the Twentieth Century, 1989, (with others) Foreign Trained Physicians and American Medicine, 1972, Welfare Medicine in America, 1974, Alien-Doctors: Foreign Medical Graduates in American Hospitals, 1978. Bd. dirs. Milbank Meml. Fund; chmn. bd. dirs. Ctr. for Advancement of Health. Fellow Am. Acad. Arts and Scis.; mem. Inst. Medicine of Nat. Acad. Sci., History of Sci. Soc., Am. Assn. for History of Medicine, Coll. Physicians of Phila., Cosmopolitan Club. Home: 1900 Rittenhouse Sq # 18 A Philadelphia PA 19103-5735 Office: U Pa History and Sociology Dept History Science 3440 Market St Philadelphia PA 19104-3325

STEVENS, ROY W., sales and marketing executive; b. Ottumwa, Iowa, Oct. 28, 1924; s. Manley O. and Ruth (Worrell) S.; m. Donna R. Borman, June 7, 1952 (dec. Jan. 1973); children: Katharine Anne Stevens Dillon, Thomas W., John M.; m. Beth A. Murphy, Apr. 20, 1974; children: Carrie Theresa, Elizabeth Mary. B.S.C., U. Iowa, 1948. With Coca-Cola Co., 1948-54, Gen. Foods Corp., 1954-67; exec. v.p. Riviana Foods, Houston, 1967-73; v.p. mktg. Hiram Walker Inc., Detroit, 1973-75; pres. Hiram Walker Inc., 1975-80, Maidstone Wine & Spirits Inc., L.A., 1980-91, Kahlua Group (Allied Domecq), 1987-91; exec. v.p. The Century Coun., Los Angeles, 1991—. Bd. dirs., past chmn. Detroit Met. YMCA; bd. dirs. L.A. Met. YMCA. Lt. (j.g.) USN, 1943-46. Mem. Sigma Alpha Epsilon, Jonathan Club, Annandale Golf Club (Pasadena, Calif.). Episcopalian. Home: 770 Huntington Cir Pasadena CA 91106 Office: The Century Coun 550 S Hope St Ste 1950 Los Angeles CA 90071-2632

STEVENS, ROY WHITE, microbiologist; b. Troy, N.Y., Sept. 4, 1934; s. Edward M. and Bernice B. (White) S.; BS, SUNY, Albany, 1956, MS, 1958; PhD, Albany (N.Y.) Med. Coll., 1965; m. Shirley A. Brehm, Aug. 4, 1956; children: Scott D., Mark G. Rsch. scientist Wadsworth Ctr., N.Y. State Dept. Health, Albany, 1967-70, assoc. rsch. scientist, 1970-73, prin. rsch. scientist, 1973—, dir. labs. for diagnostic immunology, 1979-85, retrovirology and immunology, 1985-91; adj. prof. microbiology and immunology Albany Med. Coll., 1982-92; assoc. prof. sch. pub. health SUNY, Albany, 1988—; pres. Biomed. Resource Group, Albany, 1991—; trustee Bender Hygienic Lab., Albany, 1986—. Home: 507 Acre Dr Schenectady NY 12303-5226 Office: Biomedical Resource Group PO Box 12393 Albany NY 12212-2393

STEVENS, SANDY See **STEVENSON, AMANDA**

STEVENS, SCOTT, professional hockey player; b. Kitchener, Ont., Canada, Apr. 1, 1964. Capt. St. Louis Blues, 1990-91, NJ Devils, 1992-93, 94-95. Played in NHL All-Star Game, 1985, 89, 91-94, 96; mem. Stanley Cup Championship Team, 1995; named to NHL All-Rookie Team, 1982-83, Sporting News All-Star Second Team, 1987-88, NHL All-Star First Team, 1987-88, 93-94, NHL All-Star Second Team, 1991-92, Sporting News All-Star First Team, 1993-94. Office: c/o NJ Devils PO Box 504 East Rutherford NJ 07073-0504

STEVENS, SHANE, novelist; b. N.Y.C.; s. John and Caroline (Royale) S. MA, Columbia U. mem. numerous writers confs. including Bread Loaf, Santa Barbara Writers Conf. Author: Go Down Dead, Way Uptown in Another World, Dead City, Rat Pack, By Reason of Insanity, The Anvil Chorus; (as J.W. Rider) Jersey Tomatoes (Best Novel award), Hot Tickets; contbr. articles to pubs. including N.Y. Times, Life, Washington Post; screenwriter: By Reason of Insanity, The Me Nobody Knows. Mem. Authors Guild, Writers Guild Am. *

STEVENS, SHEILA MAUREEN, teachers union administrator; b. Glendale, Calif., Nov. 1, 1942; d. Richard Chase and Sheila Mary (Beatty) Flynn; m. Jan Whitney Stevens, Sept. 12, 1964; children: Ian Whitney, Bevin Michelle. AA in Liberal Arts, Monterey Peninsula Coll., Calif., 1963; BA in Anthropology, Calif. State U., Long Beach, 1969; postgrad. studies in Edn., U. Guam, 1976-77. Tchr. U.S. Trust Territory of the Pacific, Koror, Palau Island, 1968-72, Kolonia, Ponape Island, 1972-76; tchr. Dept. Edn., Agana, Guam, 1976-79; newspaper editor Pacific Daily News (Gannett), Agana, 1979-83; comm. dir. Guam Fedn. of Tchrs., Agana, 1983-84, exec. dir., 1984-85; exec. dir. Alaska Fedn. Tchrs., Anchorage, 1985-87; labor rels. specialist N.Y. State United Tchrs., Watertown, 1987-93; regional staff dir. N.Y. State United Tchrs., Potsdam, 1993—; mem. Gov.'s Blue Ribbon Panel on Edn., Agana, Guam, 1983-85; leadership devel. coord. Am. Fedn. Tchrs., Washington, 1983—; trainer positive negotiations program Situation Mgmt. Sys., Hanover, Mass., 1988—. Author, editor: Pacific Daily News, 1981-83 (Guam Press Club awards 1981, 82, 83); contbr. articles to mag. and jours. Mem. task force on labor policy, com. on self determination, Govt. of Guam, Agana, 1984-85, Adult Basic Edn. Planning Com., 1985; mem. labor studies adv. bd., Anchorage, Alaska, 1989, regional compact coalition N.Y. State Edn. Dept., Albany, 1994. Named Friend of Edn., Carthage (N.Y.) Tchrs. Assn., 1990. Mem. NOW, ACLU, ASCD, AAUW, Am. Fedn. Tchrs. Comm. Assn. (Best Editorial award 1984), Indsl. Rels. Rsch. Assn. Democrat. Methodist. Avocations: travel, reading, free-lance writing, cross-country skiing. Office: NY State United Tchrs 12 Elm St Potsdam NY 13676-1812

STEVENS, STANLEY DAVID, local history researcher, retired librarian; b. San Francisco, Nov. 10, 1933; s. David Franklyn and Ellen Myrtle (Wixson) S.; m. Carli Ann Lewis, Sept. 3, 1960; adopted children: Alexander Lewis, Nikolas Harriman, Brooke Cayton Stevens Rich. BA, San Jose State U., 1959. Conf. officer polit. and security com. 14th Gen. Assembly, UN, N.Y.C., 1959; map libr. U. Calif., Santa Cruz, 1965-93, ret., 1993, coord. Hihn-Younger Archive, Univ. Libr., 1994—; mem. Cartographic Users Adv. Coun., 1976-86, chmn., 1982-86; presenter in field, 1971—; adj. prof. libr. sci. San Jose (Calif.) State U., 1989, 91. Author: Catalog of aerial photos by Fairchild Aerial Surveys, Inc. now in the collections of the Department of Geography, University of California at Los Angeles, 1982, Correspondence of Charles B. Younger Sr. and Charles B. Younger Jr., Santa Cruz, California Attorneys and Counsellors at Law, (vols. 1-8 of approx. 70 completed to date), 1996—, indexed edit. Santa Cruz County, California, 1997; editor, Santa Cruz County History Journal, 1994-95; also 8 others related to Hihn-Younger Archive; contbr. over 100 articles and book revs. to profl. jours. Mem. adv. com. archaeol. program Cabrillo Coll., Aptos, Calif., 1985—; bd. dirs. Santa Cruz County Hist. Soc., 1985-94, chmn. publs. com., 1985-96, mem. programs adv. coun., 1994-95; mem. Santa Cruz Orgn. for Progress and Euthenics, 1987—; bd. dirs. Friends of U. Calif.-Santa Cruz Libr., 1994—; mem. U. Calif.-Santa Cruz Emeriti Group, sec.-treas. 1996—. With U.S. Army, 1954-56; mem. collections adv. com. Santa Cruz City Mus. Natural History, 1995—. Recipient honors award geography and map div. for outstanding achievement in map librarianship Spl. Librs. Assn., 1981, cert. of commendation Santa Cruz Hist. Soc., 1986, appreciation cert. for svcs. Assn. Info. and Image Mgmt., 1989; grantee Librs. Assn. U. Calif., 1981-82, rsch. grantee Office of Pres., U. Calif., 1985-86. Mem. ALA (publs. com. Map and Geography Round Table 1986-86, editl. bd. Meridian 1989—, honors award Map and Geography Round Table 1992), Western Assn. Map Librs. (hon. life, founding pres. 1967-68, treas. 1968-89, editor Info. Bull. 1969-84, Exec. Com. award 1984), Calif. Hist. Soc., Calif. Map Soc., Pajaro Valley Hist. Assn., Santa Cruz County Geneal. Soc., Capitola Hist. Soc., El Paso de Robles Hist. Soc. (life). Democrat. Avocations: researching local history, listening to jazz and classical music. Home: 231 13th Ave Santa Cruz CA 95062-4831 Office: U Calif Map Collection Dean E McHenry Libr Santa Cruz CA 95064

STEVENS, STEPHEN EDWARD, psychiatrist; b. Phila.; s. Edward and Antonia S.; BA cum laude, LaSalle Coll., 1950; MD, Temple U., Phila., 1954; LLB, Blackstone Sch. Law, 1973; m. Isabelle Helen Gallacher, Dec. 27, 1953. Intern, Frankford Hosp., Phila., 1954-55; resident in psychiatry Phila. State Hosp., 1955-58; practice medicine specializing in psychiatry Woodland Hills, Calif., 1958-63, Santa Barbara, Calif., 1970-77; asst. supt. Camarillo (Calif.) State Hosp., 1963-70; cons. ct. psychiatrist Santa Barbara County, 1974-77; clin. dir. Kailua Mental Health Ctr., Oahu, Hawaii, 1977—. Author: Treating Mental Illness, 1961, Survival and the Fifth Dimension, 1997. Served with M.C., USAAF. Diplomate Am. Bd. Psychiatry and Neurology. Decorated Purple Heart. Fellow Am. Geriatrics Soc. (founding); mem. Am. Acad. Psychiatry and Law, AMA, Am. Psychiat. Assn., Am. Legion, DAV (Oahu chpt. 1), Caledonia Soc., Am. Hypnosis Soc., Am. Soc. Adolescent Psychiatry, Hawaiian Canoe Club, Honolulu Club, Elks (BPOE 616), Aloha String Band (founder and pres.). Home: PO Box 26413 Honolulu HI 96825-6413

STEVENS, SUZANNE DUCKWORTH, artist, educator; b. Richmond, Ind., Feb. 1, 1946; d. Delbert Raymond and Virginia (Grosvenor) Duckworth; married, 1970 (divorced 1979); 1 child, Neil D. Stevens. BA in Painting and Drawing, Fla. State U., 1968; MA in Painting and Drawing, Goddard Coll., Plainfield, Vt., 1978. Substitute counselor Crisis Intervention Home, Virginia Beach, Va., 1978-85; art instr. Contemporary Art Ctr. Va., 1979—; pvt. art instr. and artist Fine Art Studio, Virginia Beach, 1978—; artist in residence Virginia Beach Sch. Sys., 1991, 93; curator student shows Virginia Beach Ctr. for Arts, 1990—; instr. Va. Marine Sci. Mus., Virginia Beach, 1993—. One-person shows at Decker Studios, Virginia Beach, 1986, Virginia Beach Ctr. for Arts, 1987, 89, Commons Gallery, Norfolk, Va., 1990, Waterworks Visual Arts Ctr., Salisbury, N.C., 1991, Artists at Work Gallery, Virginia Beach, 1992, Ramada Plaza Resort, Virginia Beach, 1992—; exhibited in group shows at Peninsula Fine Arts Ctr., Newport News, Va., 1982, 83, 84, Virginia Beach Ctr. for Arts, 1986, 88, 94, 95, 96, Maritime Mus., Virginia Beach, 1988, Gallery 32, Virginia Beach, 1989, Seashore State Park, Virginia Beach, 1992; represented in permanent collections at Chrysler Mus., Norfolk; featured in Visions Mag. for Arts & Gallery, Virginia Beach, 1996—. Recipient Outstanding Tchr. award Gov.'s Sch. for Visual and Performing Arts, U. Richmond, Va., 1990, 93. Mem. Women in the Arts Mus., Classics Plus Dance Orgn., Tadems Dance Orgn. Democrat. Avocations: dancing, piano, tennis, reading, gardening. Home and Studio: 202 81st St Virginia Beach VA 23451

STEVENS, THEODORE FULTON, senator; b. Indpls., Nov. 18, 1923; s. George A. and Gertrude (Chancellor) S.; m. Ann Mary Cherrington, Mar. 29, 1952 (dec. 1978); children—Susan B., Elizabeth H., Walter C., Theodore Fulton, Ben A.; m. Catherine Chandler, 1980; 1 dau.; Lily Irene. B.A., U. Calif. at Los Angeles, 1947; LL.B., Harvard U., 1950. Bar: Calif., Alaska, D.C., U.S. Supreme Ct. bars. Pvt. practice Washington, 1950-52, Fairbanks, Alaska, 1953; U.S. atty. Dist. Alaska, 1953-56; legis. counsel, asst. to sec., solicitor Dept. Interior, 1956-60; pvt. practice law Anchorage, 1961-68; mem. Alaska Ho. of Reps., 1965-68, majority leader, speaker pro tem, 1967-68; U.S. senator for Alaska, 1968—, asst. Rep. leader, 1977-85; chmn. Sen. Appropriations Com. Served as 1st lt. USAAF, World War II. Mem. ABA, Alaska Bar Assn., Calif. Bar Assn., D.C. Bar Assn., Am. Legion, VFW. Lodges: Rotary, Pioneers of Alaska, Igloo #4. Home: PO Box 100879 Anchorage AK 99510-0879 Office: US Senate 522 Hart Senate Bldg Washington DC 20510

STEVENS, THOMAS CHARLES, lawyer; b. Auburn, N.Y., Oct. 17, 1949; s. Alice (Kerlin) S.; m. Christine Eleanor Brown, June 2, 1973; children: Erin, Leigh, Timothy. BA, SUNY, Albany, 1971; JD, Duke U., 1974. Bar: Ohio 1974. Mng. ptnr. Thompson, Hine & Flory, Cleve., 1991-96; with KeyCorp., Cleve., 1996—. Bd. trustees Greater Cleve. Growth Assn., 1993-96, Greater Cleve. Roundtable, 1993—; active Leadership Cleve., 1992-93. Mem. ABA, Cleve. Bar Assn., Nisi Prius. Office: KeyCorp 127 Public Sq Cleveland OH 44114-1216

STEVENS, WARREN, actor; b. Clark's Summit, Pa., Nov. 2, 1919; s. Albert Clifford and Helen Dodd (Blakeslee) S.; m. Barbara Helen Fletcher, Sept. 9, 1969; children—Adam Fletcher, Matthew Dodd; 1 son by previous marriage, Laurence Blakeslee. Student, U.S. Naval Acad., 1939-40. Appeared on: New York stage in Galileo, 1947, Sundown Beach, 1948, Smile of the World, 1949, Detective Story, 1949; appeared in numerous motion pictures, since 1950, including, Barefoot Contessa, Forbidden Planet; appeared on: numerous television shows, including Richard Boone Rep. With USN, 1937-40; with USAAF, 1942-46. Mem. Actors Studio.

STEVENS, WENDELL CLAIRE, anesthesiology educator; b. Mason City, Iowa, June 28, 1931; s. Lloyd Leroy and Amy Luella (Hodson) S.; m. Lola C. Claycomb, July 27, 1958; children: Amy P., Eric C., Mitchell L. AA, Mason City Jr. Coll., 1951; MD, U. Iowa, 1956. Diplomate Am. Bd. Anesthesiology. Intern City Hosp., Cleve., 1956-57; resident in gen. surgery U. Iowa Hosp., Iowa City, 1957-58, 60-61, resident in anesthesia, 1961-63; assoc. in anesthesia U. Iowa Coll. Medicine, Iowa City, 1963, asst. prof. anesthesia dept., 1963-67; asst. prof. U. Calif. Sch. Medicine, San Francisco, 1967-72, assoc. prof., 1972-77, prof., 1977; prof., chmn. anesthesia dept. U. Iowa Coll. Medicine, Iowa City, 1978-82; prof., chmn. anesthesia dept. Oreg. Health Scis. U., Portland, 1982-92, prof., 1992-96, prof. emeritus, 1996—. Contbr. papers and book chpts. to profl. publs. Lt. USNR, 1958-60. Recipient anesthesiology rsch. grant U. Calif., San Francisco NIH, 1969-78. Mem. Oreg. Soc. Anesthesiologists, Am. Soc. Anesthesiologists, Oreg. Med. Assn., AMA, Christian Med. Soc. Republican. Baptist. Avocations: church related activities. Office: Oreg Health Scis Ctr Dept of Anesthesiology 3181 SW Sam Jackson Park Rd Portland OR 97201-3011

STEVENS, WILBUR HUNT, accountant; b. Spencer, Ind., June 20, 1918; s. John Vosburgh and Isabelle Jane (Strawser) S.; m. Maxine Dodge Stevens, Sept. 28, 1941; children: Linda Maxine Piffero, Deborah Anne Augello. BS, U. Calif., Berkeley, 1949, MBA, 1949. CPA, Calif.; cert. fraud examiner. Staff acct. McLaren, Goode, West & Co., San Francisco, 1949-52; mng. ptnr. Wilbur H. Stevens & Co., Salinas, Calif., 1952-70; regional ptnr. Fox & Co., CPAs, Salinas, 1970-73; nat. dir. banking practice Fox & Co., CPAs, Denver, 1973-80; pres., chmn. Wilbur H. Stevens, CPA, PC, Salinas, 1980-94; chmn. Stevens, Sloan & Shah, CPAs, 1994—; adj. prof. acctg. U. Denver, 1975-78; faculty mem. Assemblies for Bank Dirs., So. Meth. U., Dallas, 1976-81, Nat. Banking Sch., U. Va., Charlottesville, 1979-87; chmn., dir. Valley Nat. Bank, 1963-71. Editor Issues in CPA Practice, 1975; contbr. articles to profl. jours. Capt. AUS, 1942-53. Decorated Bronze Star; Frank G. Drum fellow U. Calif., Berkeley, 1949. Mem. AICPA (v.p. 1971), Am. Acctg. Assn., Am. Assembly Collegiate Schs. Bus. (accreditation coun. 1975-78, 81-84), Nat. Assn. State Bds. Accountancy (pres. 1976-77), Calif. Soc. CPAs (pres. 1968-69, Disting. Svc. award 1988), Acctg. Rsch. Assn. (pres. 1973-75), Assn. Cert. Fraud Examiners, Burma Star Assn., CBI Vets. Assn., 14 AF Assn., Hump Pilots Assn., Acad. Acctg. Historians, Commonwealth Club Calif., Masons (master 1992, 97, grand lodge com. taxation), Knight Templar, 32 degree Scottish Rite, Nat. Sojourners (pres. Monterey Bay chpt. 1996), Heroes of '76 (comdr John C. Fremont chpt. 1996-97), Salinas High Twelve Club (pres. 1995), QCCC, London, Rotary (dist. gov. 1983, chmn. internat. fellowship accounts 1994-96, Paul Harris fellow 1978), Phi Beta Kappa, Beta Gamma Sigma (v.p. 1949), Beta Alpha Psi. Republican. Methodist. Home: 38 Santa Ana Dr Salinas CA 93901-4136 Office: 975 W Alisal St Ste D Salinas CA 93901-1148

STEVENS, WILLIAM DOLLARD, consulting mechanical engineer; b. Bayonne, N.J., Aug. 4, 1918; s. William B. and Beatrice (Dollard) S.; m. Mary E. King, Oct. 12, 1940; children: Sandra A. (Mrs. Jeffrey N. Melin), Barbara E. (Mrs. Dennis Gallagher), William K. B.Mech. Engring., Rensselaer Poly. Inst., 1940; postgrad., Case Inst. Tech., 1958; D.Sc. (hon.), N.J. Inst. Tech., 1986. Various engring. and mgmt. positions Babcock & Wilcox Co., N.Y.C., 1940-62; v.p. equipment div. Foster Wheeler Corp., Livingston, N.J., 1962-73, sr. v.p., 1972-74, exec. v.p., 1974-78, chmn. bd., 1978-81, dir., 1974-86, dir. emeritus, 1986-90; bd. of dir. Am. Soc. for Macro Engring., 1992—; instr. Pratt Inst., 1946-47; bd. overseers N.J. Inst. Tech., 1978-94. Contbr. articles to profl. jours.; patentee in field. Chmn. fund drive ARC, Hackensack, N.J., 1956; planning commr., Hackensack, 1955-58; trustee Bergen County Mental Health Consultation Ctr., 1955-58; bd. dirs. Metals Properties Coun.; mem. coun. Rensselaer Polytech. Inst., 1983—. Lt. USNR, 1943-45. Fellow ASME; mem. Nat. Acad. Engring., Sigma Xi, Tau Beta Pi, Phi Kappa Tau, Pi Tau Sigma. Methodist. Home and Office: 4 Stonybrook Dr N Caldwell NJ 07006-4025

STEVENS, WILLIAM JOHN, management consultant, former association executive; b. Dusseldorf, Germany, Aug. 23, 1915; arrived in U.S., 1923, naturalized, 1931; s. Peter and Margaret (Kaumanns) S.; student McCall Sch. Printing, 1933; student assn. mgmt. Northwestern U., 1947; grad. Chadwick Univ., 1993; m. Dorothy V. Santangini, Feb. 14, 1937 (dec.). With Ruttle, Shaw & Wetherill, Phila., 1931-34; partner New Era Printing Co., Phila., 1934-37; plant mgr. Marcus & Co., Phila., 1937-41; supt. Edward Stern & Co., Phila., 1941-46; exec. sec. Nat. Assn. Photo-Lithographers, N.Y.C., 1946-50, exec. v.p., 1961-64, pres., 1964-71; pres., COO NPEA Exhibits, Inc., 1971-80; owner Dorval Co., pub.; pres. Opinion-3 Graphic Arts Rsch. Agy.; exec. sec. Met. Lithographers Assn., N.Y.C., 1946-50; asst. to v.p. Miehle Co., N.Y.C., 1950-56, mgr. Phila. dist., 1956-61; cons. Sales Devel. Inst., Phila., 1960-89; mem. Am. Bd. Arbitration, 1962—; chmn. adv. commn. on graphic arts N.Y.C. Tech. Coll., 1972-95; bus. adminstr. St. Joseph's Parish, 1980-85. Named Industry Man of Yr. Nat. Assn. Photo-Lithographers, 1954, Man of Yr., N.Y. Litho Guild, 1962; recipient Presdl. Citation Office Price Adminstrn., 1946, Mktg. award North Am. Pub. Co., 1967, B'nai B'rith award, 1968, N.Y. Navigators award, 1969, N.Y. Printing Craftsman Achievement award, 1989; laureate N.Y. Printers Hall of Fame, 1980, NAPL-Soderstrom award, 1984, recipient Gold Founders medal N.Y.C. Tech. Coll., 1987. Mem. Am. Soc. Assn. Execs., Graphic Arts Assn. Execs. (pres. 1969), Nat. Assn. Litho Clubs (founder, pres. 1947, Industry award 1947, 79, sec. 1964-71), N.Y. Club Printing House Craftsmen, Gamma Epsilon Tau. Clubs: Phila. Litho (pres. 1945), N.Y. Litho (N.Y.C.). Mem. Writers Inst. Author: How To Prepare Copy for Offset Lithography, 1948, Building Construction and Floor Plans for Installing Web Offset Presses; under author: Basic Facts for Creating Effective Art/Design, Advertising, and Printing, 1996; columnist for daily press; contbr. editor articles to trade publs. Inventor Hiky-Picker, Quik-Match Color File for selection paint color samples, Stevens Foto Sizing System, Steve-O-Heat Printing Ink Dryer, "Travelr" security pocket, "Mar-Too-Nee" salad dressing. Home and Office: 4575 Barclay Cres Lake Worth FL 33463-6037

STEVENS, WILLIAM KENNETH, lawyer; b. Chgo., Apr. 19, 1917; s. Ernest James and Elizabeth (Street) S.; m. Anne Hughes, Jan. 4, 1943; children: Anne Elizabeth Stevens Fishman, William Hughes, Mary Carol Stevens Williams, Martha Street Stevens Gingrich. AB cum laude, U. Calif., Berkeley, 1938; MA, U. Chgo., 1940; JD, Harvard U., 1948. Bar: Ill. 1948, Fla. 1977. With First Nat. Bank Chgo., 1948-74, asst. v.p., 1958-61, v.p., 1961-74; ptnr. McDermott, Will & Emery, Chgo., 1974-85, Myers Krause & Stevens, Naples, Fla., 1986—. Author: Illinois Estate Administration, 1968. Chmn. Ill. Inst. Continuing Legal Edn., 1971-72; pres. Hinsdale (Ill.) Pub. Libr., 1977-79. Lt. USNR, 1941-45. Recipient Disting. Svc. award Chgo. Estate Planning Coun., 1981. Fellow Am. Coll. Trust and Estate Counsel; mem. ABA, Am. Law Inst., Chgo. Bar Assn., Ill. Bar Assn., Fla. Bar Assn. (bd. cert. estate planning and probate lawyer), Internat. Acad. Estate and Trust Law. Clubs: Mid-Day, Hinsdale Golf; Chikaming Country (Lakeside, Mich.), The Club at Pelican Bay (Naples). Home: 314 S Lincoln St Hinsdale IL 60521-4008 Office: 5811 Pelican Bay Blvd Ste 600 Naples FL 34108-2711

STEVENS, YVETTE MARIE See **KHAN, CHAKA**

STEVENSON, A. BROCKIE, artist; b. Montgomery County, Pa., Sept. 24, 1919; s. Alfred Brockie and Caroline Lansdale (Sill) S.; m. Jane Merriman Mackenzie, Dec. 23, 1978. Student, Pa. Acad. Fine Arts, 1940-41, 46-50, Barnes Found., 1946-48, Skowhegan Sch., Maine, 1950. Instr. Sch. Fine Arts, Washington U., St. Louis, 1960-62; head dept. painting and drawing Corcoran Sch. Art, 1965-81, assoc. prof. to prof. design and watercolor, 1965—. One-man shows War Paintings, London and Salisbury, Eng., 1944, Instituto Cultural Peruano-Norteamericano, Lima, Peru, 1953, Art Center, Miraflores, Lima, 1958, 60, Association Cultural Peruano-Britanica, Lima, 1959, Mickelson Gallery, Washington, 1970, Pyramid Galleries Ltd., Washington, 1973, No. Va. Community Coll., 1974, Fendrick Gallery, Washington, 1978, 84, 88; group shows include, Nat. Gallery Art, London, 1944, Pa. Acad. Fine Arts, Phila., 1948, 49, 50, 51, Sociedad Bellas Artes del, Peru, Lima, 1953, 54, 55, 56, SUNY at, Potsdam and Albany, 1971, Columbia (S.C.) Mus. Art, 1971, EXPO '74, Spokane, Wash., 1974, Corcoran Gallery, Washington, 1980; represented in permanent collections Corcoran Gallery Art, Washington, Dept. Def., Washington, Nat. Mus. Am. Art, Washington, , Phillips Collection, Washington, Fed. Res. Bank Richmond, Va., Woodward Found., Washington, Ogunquit (Maine) Mus. Art, Brown U. Libr. Milit. Coll., Providence, R.I. Served as artist corr. U.S. Army, 1941-45, ETO. Home: 6106 Yale Ave Glen Echo MD 20812-1122 Office: Corcoran Sch Art 17 and New York Ave NW Washington DC 20006

STEVENSON, ADLAI EWING, III, lawyer, former senator; b. Chgo., Oct. 10; s. Adlai Ewing and Ellen (Borden) S.; m. Nancy L. Anderson, June 25, 1955; children: Adlai Ewing IV, Lucy W., Katherine R., Warwick L. Grad., Milton Acad., 1948; A.B., Harvard U., 1952, LL.B., 1957. Bar: Ill. 1957, D.C. 1957. Assoc. Mayer, Brown & Platt, Chgo., 1958-66; ptnr. Mayer, Brown & Platt, 1966-67, 81-83, of counsel, 1983-91; treas. State of Ill., 1967-70; U.S. senator from Ill., 1970-81; chmn. SC&M Internat. Ltd., Chgo., 1991-95, pres., 1995—. Mem. Ill. Ho. of Reps., 1965-67; Dem. candidate for gov. of Ill., 1982, 86. Capt. USMCR, 1952-54. Office: 225 W Wacker Dr Chicago IL 60606-1224

STEVENSON, AMANDA (SANDY STEVENS), librettist, composer; b. Bklyn., Oct. 24, 1943; d. Haakon and Grace Svendsen; m. James W. Moseley, 1962 (div. 1965); 1 child: Elizabeth B. Moseley. Grad., Bay Ridge H.S., Bklyn., 1961. Cert. document examiner. Free lance entertainer World's Funniest Handwriting Analyst, Pitts., 1967—; interior sign designer The Sign Lady, Pitts., 1980—; adj. entertainer as Dr. Tooth. Co-author: How to Raise an Emotionally Healthy, Happy Child, 1964; composer, librettist, Nellie Bly, Victorine, (screenplay) The Last Assignment. Mem. Actors Equity Assn., Dramatists Guild, Songwriters Guild. Mem. Nat. Bur. Document Examiners. Democrat. Unitarian. Avocations: chess, art history, pen pals. Home and Office: 2305 Pleasure House Rd Virginia Beach VA 23455

STEVENSON, BEN, artistic director; b. Portsmouth, Eng., Apr. 4, 1936; came to U.S., 1968; s. Benjamin John and Florence May (Gundry) S.; m. Joan Toastivine, Jan. 6, 1968. Grad., Arts Ednl. Sch., London, 1955. Dir. Houston Ballet Acad.; mem. dance panel Tex. Commn. Arts, 1977; guest tchr. Am. Ballet Theatre, Joffrey Ballet, Royal Ballet, London, Beijing Dance Acad. Dancer Theatre Arts Ballet, London, 1952-54, Sadler's Wells Theatre Ballet, 1955-56, Royal Ballet, 1956-60, London Festival Ballet, 1960-62; appearances in Wedding in Paris, 1954-55, Music Man, London, 1962-63, Half a Sixpence, also Boys in Syracuse, London, 1964; prin. dancer, ballet master, London Festival Ballet, 1964-68; artistic dir. Harkness Ballet Youth Dancers, 1968-71, Chgo. Ballet, 1974-75, Houston Ballet, 1976—; co-dir. Nat. Ballet, Washington, 1971-74; prin. ballets choreographed include Three Faces of Eve, 1965, Cast Out, 1966, Sleeping Beauty (full length), 1967, 71, 76, 78, Fervor, 1968, Three Preludes, 1968, Forbidden, 1969, Cinderella (full length), 1969, 71, 73, 74, 76, Bartok Concerto, 1970, Nutcracker (full length), 1972, 76, Symphonetta, 1972, Courant, 1973, Swan Lake (full length), 1977, L, 1978, Britten Pas de Deux, 1979, Four Last Songs, 1979, Space City, 1980, Peer Gynt (full length), 1981, Zheng Ban Qiao, 1982, The Prince of Pagodas, 1986. Recipient 1st prize London Choreographic competitions, 1965, 66, 67, 1st prize modern ballet choreography Internat. Ballet Competition, Varna, Bulgaria, 1972, Gold medal for choreography Internat. Ballet Competition, 1982. Asso. mem. Royal Acad. Dancing (Adeline Genee Gold medal 1955). Office: Houston Ballet PO Box 130487 Houston TX 77219-0487

STEVENSON, BRYAN ALLEN, lawyer; b. Milton, Del., Nov. 14, 1959; s. Howard Carlton and Alice Gertrude (Golden) S. BA, Eastern Coll., St. Davids, Pa., 1981; MPP, Kennedy Sch. Govt., Cambridge, Mass., 1985; JD, Harvard U., 1985. Bar: Ga. 1985, Ala. 1987. Staff atty. So. Prisoners Def. Com., Atlanta, 1985—; exec. dir. Ala. Capital Representation Resource Ctr., Montgomery, 1989-95; dir. Equal Justice Initiative of Ala., Montgomery, 1995—; vis. prof. law NYU Sch. Law, 1997, U. Law Sch., 1995. Contbr. articles to publs. Recipient MacArthur Found. award, Thurgood Marshall medal of justice, Nat. Human Rights award Reebol Human Rights Found., 1989, ACLU Medal of Liberty, 1991, ABA Wisdom Award for Pub. Svc., 1991; Harvard Law Sch. Pub. Interest fellow, 1985. Avocations: music, piano and keyboards.

STEVENSON, CANDACE J., museum director. Exec. dir. N.S. Mus., Halifax, N.S., Can. Office: NS Mus, 1747 Summer St, Halifax, NS Canada B3H 3A6

STEVENSON, CAROL WELLS, secondary education educator; b. Richmond, Va., Feb. 14, 1942; d. Alfred Hatcher and Laura Dowdy (Hobson) Wells; m. James Pendleton Stevenson, June 23, 1962; children: James Brian Stevenson, Anne Pendleton Stevenson. BS in Home Econ. Edn., James Madison U., Harrisonburg, Va., 1962; MA in Adult Edn., Va. Commonwealth U., 1981. Cert. Home Econ., Collegiate Profl. Cert., Va. Home econ. tchr. Patrick Henry High Sch., Ashland, Va., 1962-66, Liberty Middle Sch., Ashland, Va., 1976—. Named Va. Home Econ. Tchr. of Yr., 1988,

Tchr. of Yr., Liberty Mid. Sch., 1983-84, 84-85, 85-86, Most Outstanding Home Econs. Tchr. in U.S., Home Baking Assn., 1994; Check Excellence regional winner State Dept. Edn., 1990. Mem. Am. Home Econs. Assn., Va. Home Econ. Assn. (Va. Home Econs. Tchr. of Yr. award 1988), Va. Home Econ. Tchr. Assn., Am. Vocat. Assn., Va. Vocat. Assn., Nat. Assn. Vocat. Home Tchrs., Future Homemakers Am. Found. Episcopalian. Home: 202 Hanover Ave Ashland VA 23005-1815 Office: Liberty Mid Sch RR 3 Box 2500 Ashland VA 23005-9225

STEVENSON, CHARLES BEMAN, business educator; b. Columbus, Ohio, Oct. 30, 1922; s. Arthur Edwin and Mary Lucille (Beman) S.; BA, George Washington U., 1960, MA, 1962; diploma U.S. Army Command and Gen. Staff Coll., 1962; postgrad. U. Pitts., 1968-74, 80-81; m. Sara DeSalles Gilroy, June 12, 1948. Enlisted in U.S. Army, 1942, commd. 2d lt., 1943, advanced through grades to lt. col., 1963, ret., 1968; prof. mil. sci. Indiana U. Pa., 1965-68, asst. prof. bus. mgmt., 1968-71, assoc. prof., 1972-89, also dir. IUP Econ. Edn. Ctr., prof. emeritus, 1991—, sec., founder IUP Coll. Bus. Adv. Coun., 1978—; founder Coll. Bus. Fgn. Student Intern. Program; v.p. Mgmt. Scis. Resources, 1988-89; pres., mgmt. cons. CBS & Assocs, 1990—; pub. policy expert Heritage Found., 1986—; founder IUP Wash. D.C. Leadership Tgn. Trips, 1987-91; lectr. in field. Mem. edn. com. Pa. C. of C. 1976-83; chmn. Indiana County ARC, 1975-76; trustee Episcopal Diocese of Pitts., 1975-78, 79-80, mem. planning commn., 1975-82; mem. vestry, sr. warden St. Peter's Episc. Ch., 1983-85; mem. Episc. Diocesan Council, 1983-85. Decorated Legion of Merit; recipient Achievement awards, honor certs. Freedoms Found. at Valley Forge, 1986, Pub. Svc. award Dept. Army, 1986; others. Mem. NRA, VFW, Ind. Personnel Assn. (pres. 1981-83) Am. Mgmt. Assn., Ret. Officers Assn., Mil. Order World Wars (comdr., founder chpt. 200), Assn. Pa. U. Bus. and Econ. Faculty (pres. 1985-88). Republican. Club: Army and Navy (Washington). Home: 1398 School St Indiana PA 15701-2567 Office: Indiana U Pa Coll Bus Indiana PA 15705

STEVENSON, DAVID JOHN, planetary scientist, educator; b. Wellington, New Zealand, Sept. 2, 1948; came to U.S., 1971; s. Ian McIvor and Gwenyth (Carroll) S. BSc, Victoria U., New Zealand, 1971; PhD, Cornell U., 1976. Rsch. fellow Australian Nat. U., Canberra, Australia, 1976-78; asst. prof. UCLA, L.A., 1978-80; assoc. prof. Calif. Inst. Tech., Pasadena, 1980-84, prof., 1984—, George van Osdol prof., 1995—; chmn. divsn. geol. & planetary scis. Calif. Inst. Tech., 1989-94. Contbr. about 100 articles to profl. jours. Named Fulbright scholar, USA, 1971-76. Fellow Am. Geophysical Union, Royal Soc. London, 1993; mem. AAAS, Am. Astron. Soc. (Urey prize 1984). Office: Calif Inst Tech 1201 E California Blvd Pasadena CA 91125-0001

STEVENSON, ELIZABETH, author, educator; b. Ancon, Panama, C.Z., June 13, 1919; d. John Thurman and Bernice (Upshaw) S. B.A. magna cum laude, PBK Agnes Scott Coll., 1941. With war time agys. U.S. Govt., Atlanta, 1942-47; order asst. Atlanta Pub. Library, 1948-56; asst. to coll. dean Emory U., Atlanta, 1960-74; from research assoc. to Candler prof. Grad. Inst. Liberal Arts, Emory U., Atlanta, 1974-87. Author: The Crooked Corridor: A Study of Henry James, 1949, Henry Adams, 1955, 97 (Bancroft prize 1956), Lafcadio Hearn, 1961, Babbitts and Bohemians, 1967, 97, Park Maker: A Life of Frederick Law Olmsted, 1977, Figures in a Western Landscape: Men and Women of the Northern Rockies, 1994; editor: A Henry Adams Reader, 1958. Guggenheim fellow, 1950-51, 58-59; grantee Rockefeller Found., 1958-59, Am. Coun. Learned Socs., 1975; recipient Faculty Rsch. Fund award Emory U., 1960s, 70s, summer stipend NEH, 1974. Mem. Authors Guild, Phi Beta Kappa. Democrat. *Whether as a product of the era or an irritant to it, the underlying assumption is that every single life is a drama worth exploring. Biography is bound by the facts, but it is also an art, a difficult art.*

STEVENSON, ERIC VAN CORTLANDT, mortgage banker, real estate executive, lawyer; b. N.Y.C., June 27, 1926; s. Harvey and Winifred (Worcester) S.; m. Judith Kittredge Herrick, Nov. 13, 1955; children: Jonathan Herrick, Michael Kirkham, Anne Kittredge, Margaret Low, Philip Eric. B.A., Yale U., 1947, LL.B., 1950. Bar: D.C. 1951, Conn. 1954. With NLRB, 1951; practice in Hartford, Conn., 1954-55, Norwich, Conn., 1957-61; with Electric Boat Co., 1956-57; rsch. assoc. Inst. Def. Analyses, 1961-63; with Labor Dept., 1963-65; rsch. dir. George Washington U., 1965-66; gen. counsel Peace Corps, 1966-68; dir. urban affairs Life Ins. Assn. Am., N.Y.C., 1969-72; mortgage banker Sonnenblick-Goldman Corp., Washington, 1973-74, Boykin Corp., 1974-82, Stevenson and Kittredge, Inc., 1978-82; sr. v.p. Mortgage Bankers Assn. Am., Washington, 1982-91; housing specialist Commn. Mental Health Svcs., Washington, 1992-95, Office Housing, HUD, Washington, 1995—; cons. Ford Found., 1963, Conn. Housing Investment Fund, 1968-69, Carnegie Corp., 1972, HUD, 1976-77, 78-80. Served with USNR, 1944-46, 51-53. Office: US Dept HUD 451 7th St SW Washington DC 20410-0001

STEVENSON, HAROLD WILLIAM, psychology educator; b. Dines, Wyo., Nov. 19, 1924; s. Merlin R. and Mildred M. (Stodick) S.; m. Nancy Guy, Aug. 23, 1950; children: Peggy, Janet, Andrew, Patricia. BA, U. Colo., 1947; MA, Stanford U., 1948, PhD, 1951; DS (hon.), U. Minn., 1996. Asst. prof. psychology Pomona Coll., 1950-53; asst. to asso. prof. psychology U. Tex., Austin, 1953-59; prof. child devel. and psychology, dir. Inst. Child Devel., U. Minn., Mpls., 1959-71; prof. psychology, fellow Center for Human Growth and Devel., U. Mich., Ann Arbor, 1971—; dir. program in child devel. and social policy U. Mich., 1978-93; adj. prof. Tohoku Fukushi Coll., Japan, 1989—, Peking U., 1990—, Inst. Psychology Chinese Acad. Scis.; mem. tng. com. Nat. Inst. Child Health and Human Devel., 1964-67; mem. personality and cognition study sect. NIMH, 1975-79; chmn. adv. com. on child devel. Nat. Acad. Scis.-NRC, 1971-73; exec. com. div. behavioral scis. NRC, 1969-72; mem. del. early childhood People's Republic of China, 1973, mem. del. psychologists, 1980; mem. vis. com. Grad. Sch. Edn., Harvard U., 1979-86; fellow Center Advanced Studies in Behavioral Scis., 1967-68, 82-83, 89-90. Recipient J.M. Cattell Fellow award in applied psychology Am. Psychol. Soc., 1994, William James Fellow award, 1995, Quest award Am. Fedn. Tchrs., 1995. Fellow Am. Acad. Arts and Scis., Nat. Acad. Edn.; mem. APA (pres. divsn. devel. psychology 1964-65, G. Stanley Hall award 1988, Bronfenbrenner award 1997), Soc. Rsch. Child Devel. (mem. governing coun. 1961-67, pres. 1969-71, chmn. long-range planning com. 1971-74, mem. social policy com. 1977-85, mem. internat. affairs com. 1991-94, Disting. Rsch. award 1993), Internat. Soc. Study Behavioral Devel. (mem. exec. com. 1977-87, pres. 1987-91), Phi Beta Kappa, Sigma Xi. Home: 1030 Spruce Dr Ann Arbor MI 48104-2847

STEVENSON, HOWARD HIGGINBOTHAM, business educator; b. Salt Lake City, June 27, 1941; s. Ralph Shields and Dorothy Dee (Higginbotham) S.; m. Fredericka O'Connell; children: William, Charles, Andrew. BS, Stanford U., 1963; MBA, Harvard U., 1965, DBA, 1969. Asst. prof. bus. Harvard U., Cambridge, Mass., 1968-72, assoc. prof., 1972-78, Sarofim Rock prof., 1982—, sr. assoc. dean for fin. adminstrn., 1991-94; v.p. Simmons Assocs., Boston, 1970-72; v.p. fin. adminstrn. Preco Corp., West Springfield, Mass., 1978-81; dir. Landmark Comms., Norfolk, Va., Camp Dresser and McKee Inc., Cambridge, Gulf States Steel, Gadsden, Ala., The Baupost Group, Inc., Cambridge, Sheffield Steel, Waltham, Mass., Quadra Capital Ptnrs., L.P., Commonwealth Capital Ptnrs., Bessemer Security Corp. Coauthor: Policy Formation and Administration, 1984, New Business Ventures and the Entrepreneur, 1985, 89, 4th edit., 1994, Entrepreneurial Ventures, 1992, Do Lunch or Be Lunc: The Power of Predictability in Creating Your Future, 1997. Trustee Rural Land Found., Lincoln, Mass., 1973-78, Boston Ballet, Suffield Land Conservancy, Conn., 1978-82; pres. Sudbury Valley Trustees. IBM Nat. Merit scholar, 1959; Ford Found. fellow, 1965. Mem. Fin. Execs. Inst., Acad. Mgmt. Club: Harvard (N.Y.C.), Longwood Cricket. Office: Baker Libr 366 Harvard U Boston MA 02163

STEVENSON, IAN, psychiatrist, educator; b. Montreal, Que., Can., Oct. 31, 1918; s. John Alexander and Ruth Cecilia (Preston); m. Octavia Reynolds, Sept. 13, 1947 (dec. Nov. 1983); m. 2d, Margaret H. Pertzoff, Nov. 29, 1985. Student, U. St. Andrews, Scotland; BS, McGill U., 1942, MD, CM, 1943. Cert. Am. Bd. Psychiatry, 1953. Asst. prof. psychiatry La. State U., New Orleans, 1949-52, assoc. prof. psychiatry, 1953-57; prof. psychiatry, chmn. U. Va. Sch. Medicine, Charlottesville, 1957-67, Carlson prof. psychiatry, head div. of personality studies, 1967—; assoc. mem. Darwin Coll., U. Cambridge, 1981—. Author: The Diagnostic Interview, 1960, Twenty Cases Suggestive of Reincarnation, 1966, Reincarnation and Biology, 1997, 10 other books; contbr. 250 articles to profl. jours. Fellow Am. Psychiat. Assn. (life); mem. AAAS, Am. Anthropol. Assn., Soc. for Psychical Rsch. London (coun. mem. and pres. 1988-89), Am. Soc. for Psychical Rsch., Soc. for Sci. Exploration (founding com.), Colonnade Club (U. Va.), United Oxford and Cambridge Univ. Club (London). Office: U of Va Health Sci Ctr Box 152 Charlottesville VA 22908

STEVENSON, JAMES D(ONALD), JR., psychologist, counselor; b. Ft. Wayne, Ind., July 6, 1943; s. James Donald Sr. and Charlotte Eileen (Starnes) S.; m. Sharon Sue Kearns, Nov. 26, 1965 (div. 1978); 1 child, E. Willow; m. Diane Kulesza, Apr. 13, 1980; 1 child, James Wesley; m. Christine Berthold, Aug. 8, 1992. BA, Whittier (Calif.) Coll., 1965; MA, Calif. State U., Northridge, 1974; PhD, Calif. Coast U., 1986. Lic. counselor, Calif. Auditor State Compensation Ins. Fund, Arcadia, Calif., 1965-66, supervising auditor, 1969-74; dir. social svcs. Buena Vista Acad., Ventura, Calif., 1974-76, benefits counselor, 1976-77; counselor Calif. Dept. of Rehab., Thousand Oaks, 1977-82; vocat. psychologist Calif. Dept. of Rehab., Pleasant Hill, 1982—; žrin. James Stevenson Pub., 1994—, Career Interest Testing Svc., Ventura and Contra Costa Counties, 1980-83; instr. Ventura Coll., 1975; cons. Ctr. for Career Evaluation, Oakland, Calif., 1986-87, St. Vincent DePaul Soc., Pittsburg, Calif., 1986—, Allied Fellowship Svcs., Oakland, 1990. Contbr. articles to profl. jours. Bd. dirs. Solano County (Calif.) Hist. Records Commn., 1995—, pres., 1997—. With U.S. Army, 1965-67, ETO. Mem. AACD, Nat. Rehab. Assn. (exec. bd. San Francisco chpt. 1986-93, pres. San Francisco East Bay divsn. 1991-92), Ventura County Mental Health Assn. (bd. dirs. 1978-81), Los Padres Rehab. Assn. (pres. Ventura chpt. 1978-79). Avocations: genealogy, hiking. Office: Calif Dept of Rehab 2285 Morello Ave Pleasant Hill CA 94523-1850

STEVENSON, JAMES LARAWAY, communications engineer, consulting; b. Detroit, Oct. 25, 1938; s. Joseph Morley and Kittie Harriet (Laraway) S.; m. Jeanie Lorraine Minkstein, Aug. 7, 1965; children: Amy Jean, Brian Morley. AAS, U.S. Armed Forces Inst., 1958; BSEE, MIT, 1960, MSEE, 1962. Cert. master radio and telecommunications engr. FCC. With USN Mercury Space Project, 1957-63; engr. Sta. WBCM-FM, Bay City, Mich., 1964-65; chief engr. Sta. WCRM, Clare, Mich., 1965-66, Sta. WSMA, Marine City, Mich., 1966; engr. Sta. WWJ-AM-FM-TV, Detroit, 1966-79; owner, mgr. Twin Oaks Comms. Engring. (name now Twin Oaks Comms. Engring. P.C.), North Branch, Mich., 1972—; charter pilot, flight & ground instr. G. B. DuPont Co., Almont Marlette Aviation Inc., 1977-82; cons. electronics engr. various cos., 1968—; expert legal witness, 1968—; mem. indsl. adv. bd. Coll. Elec. and Computer Engring., Saginaw Valley State U., 1997—. Contbr. articles to profl. jours. Sr. div. judge Detroit Met. Sci. and Engring. Fair, 1975—; search & rescue pilot, mission comdr., capt. Mich. wing CAP, 1961-81; cubmaster Pack 457 Boy Scouts Am., North Branch, 1983-85. Recipient appreciation award CAP, 1980, North Branch Area Schs., 1985, Century award Boy Scouts Am., 1984. Mem. AIAA, IEEE (sr., chmn. N.E. Mich. sect. 1987-88, 95—, bd. dirs. 1984—), NSPE, Nat. Assn. Radio Telecomm. Engrs. (sr.), Mich. Soc. Profl. Engrs. (flint chpt.), Saginaw Valley Engring. Coun. (chmn. 1990-91, sec.-treas. 1992—), Engring. Soc. Detroit (profl.), Profl. Activities Coun. Engrs. (chmn. U.S. activities bd. 1985—), Nat. Pilots Assn. (sr. pilot citation, safe pilot award 1978), Aircraft Owners and Pilots Assn., North Branch C. of C. (charter), Am. Legion, Lions (pres. North Br. club 1990-91), Radio Club Am. Avocations: amateur radio, flying. Office: Twin Oaks Comms Engring PC 2465 Johnson Mill Rd PO Box 340 North Branch MI 48461-0340

STEVENSON, JAMES RICHARD, radiologist, lawyer; b. Ft. Dodge, Iowa, May 30, 1937; s. Lester Lawrence and Esther Irene (Johnson) S.; m. Sara Jean Hayman, Sept. 4, 1958; children: Bradford Allen, Tiffany Ann, Jill Renee, Trevor Ashley. BS, U. N.Mex., 1959; MD, U. Colo., 1963; JD, U. N.Mex. 1987. Diplomate Am. Bd. Radiology, Am. Bd. Nuclear Medicine, Am. Bd. Legal Medicine, 1989; Bar: N.Mex. 1987, U.S. Dist. Ct. N.Mex. 1988. Intern U.S. Gen. Hosp., Tripler, Honolulu, 1963-64; resident in radiology U.S. Gen. Hosp., Brook and San Antonio, Tex., 1964-67; radiologist, ptnr. Van Atta Labs., Albuquerque, 1970-88, Radiology Assocs. of Albuquerque, 1988—, pres., 1994-96; radiologist, ptnr. Civerolo, Hansen & Wolf, Albuquerque, 1988-89; adj. asst. prof. radiology U. N.Mex., 1970-71; pres. med. staff AT & SF Meml. Hosp., 1979-80, chief of staff, 1980-81, trustee, 1981-83. Author: District Attorney manual, 1987. Participant breast screening, Am. Cancer Soc., Albuquerque, 1987-88; dir. profl. divsn. United Way, Albuquerque, 1975. Maj. U.S. Army 1963-70, Vietnam; col. M.C. USAR, 1988—. Decorated Bronze Star. Allergy fellow, 1960. Med.-Legal Tort Scholar award, 1987. Fellow Am. Coll. Radiology (councilor 1980-86, mem. med. legal com. 1990-96), Am. Coll. Legal Medicine, Am. Coll. Nuclear Medicine, Radiology Assn. of Albuquerque; mem. AMA (Physicians' Recognition award 1969—), Am. Soc. Law & Medicine, Am. Arbitration Assn., Albbuquerque Bar Assn., Am. Coll. Nuclear Physicians (charter), Soc. Nuclear Medicine (v.p. Rocky Mountain chpt. 1975-76), Am. Inst. Ultrasound in Medicine, N.Am. Radiol. Soc. (chmn. med. legal com. 1992-95), N.Mex. Radiol. Soc. (pres. 1978-79), N.Mex. Med. Soc. (chmn. grievance com.), Albuquerque-Bernalillo County Med. Soc. (scholar 1959), Nat. Assn. Health Lawyers, ABA (antitrust sect. 1986—), N. Mex. State Bar, Albuquerque Bar Assn., Sigma Chi. Republican. Methodist. Club: Albuquerque Country. Lodges: Elks, Masons, Shriners. Home: 3333 Santa Clara Ave SE Albuquerque NM 87106-1530 Office: Medical Arts Imaging Ctr A-6 Med Arts Sq 801 Encino Pl NE Albuquerque NM 87102-2612

STEVENSON, JOHN REESE, lawyer; b. Chgo., Oct. 24, 1921; s. John A. and Josephine R. S.; m. Patience Fullerton, Apr. 10, 1943 (dec. 1982); children: Elizabeth F., Sally H. Stevenson Fischer, John R. Jr., Patience Stevenson Scott; m. Ruth Carter Johnson, May 21, 1983. AB summa cum laude, Princeton U., 1942; LLB, Columbia U., 1949, DJS, 1952. Bar: N.Y. 1949, U.S. Supreme Ct. 1964, D.C. 1971. Assoc. Sullivan & Cromwell, N.Y.C., 1950-55, ptnr., 1956-69, 75-87, chmn., sr. ptnr., 1979-87, counsel, 1987-92; legal adv. with rank of asst. sec. U.S. Dept. State, 1969-72, chmn. adv. com. on pub. internat. law, 1986-90, mem. com. 1993—; adviser U.S. del. Gen. Assembly UN, 1969-74; chmn. U.S. del. Internat. Conf. on Air Law, The Hague, The Netherlands, 1970; mem. U.S. del. Internat. Conf. on Law of Treaties, Vienna, 1969; amb., spl. rep. of Pres. Law of the Sea conf., 1973-75; U.S. mem. Permanent Ct. of Arbitration, The Hague, 1969-79, 84-90; U.S. rep. Internat. Ct. Justice Namibia (S.W. Africa) case, 1970; spl. counsel U.S. del. Delimitation of Martime Boundary in Gulf of Maine (Can. vs. U.S.A.), 1984; mem. OAS Inter-Am. commn. on Human Rights, 1987-90; dir. Ctr. for Strategic and Internat. Studies; prin. Ctr. Excellence in Govt.; bd. dirs. Americas Soc. Author: The Chilean Popular Front, 1952; editor-in-chief Columbia Law Rev.; contbr. articles to legal and State Dept. jours. Fellow ABA (hon.); mem. Am. Soc. Internat. Law (pres. 1966-68, hon. v.p. 1968-92, 93—, hon. pres. 1992-93), N.Y. State Bar Assn. (chmn. com. on internat. law 1963-65), Internat. Law Assn., Inst. de Droit Internat. (v.p. 1987-89), Assn. of Bar of City of N.Y. (chmn. com. on internat. law 1958-61), Am. Arbitration Assn. (bd. dirs. 1984-92, exec. com., chmn. internat. sect. law com.), Coun. Fgn. Rels., Am. Law Inst., Phi Beta Kappa. Home: 1200 Broad Ave Fort Worth TX 76107 Office: Ste 800 1701 Pennsylvania Ave NW Washington DC 20006-5805

STEVENSON, KATHERINE HOLLER, federal agency administrator; b. Jan. 20, 1948; d. Jacob W. and Sheila Holler; m. Donald Stevenson, aug. 14, 1982; 2 children. BA, Skidmore Coll., 1969; MA, U. Del., 1971. Researcher Nat. portrait Gallery, Smithsonian Inst., Washington, 1971; with Nat. Park Svc., Washington, 1972-80, Denver, 1980-87, Phila., 1987-95; assoc. dir. Nat. Park Svc., Washington, 1995—. Recipient Meritorious Svc. award Dept. Interior, 1994. Office: Nat Park Svc Cultural Resource 1849 C St NW Washington DC 20240-0001

STEVENSON, KENNETH LEE, chemist, educator; b. Ft. Wayne, Ind., Aug. 1, 1939; s. Willard Henry and Luella Marie (Meyer) S.; m. Virginia Grace Lowe, Dec. 26, 1959 (dec. Mar. 1991); children: Melinda Anne, Jill Marie; m. Carmen Ramona Kmety, May 9, 1992. B.S., Purdue U., 1961, M.S., 1965; Ph.D., U. Mich., 1968. Tchr. Ladoga High Sch., 1961-63; tchr. Central High Sch., Pontiac, Mich., 1963-65; prof. chemistry Ind.-Purdue U., Ft. Wayne, 1968—, chmn. dept. chemistry, 1979-86, 87—, acting dean Sch. Sci. and Humanities, 1986-87; sabbatical visitor Solar Energy Research Inst., Golden, Colo., 1980; vis. faculty N.Mex. State U., Las Cruces, 1975-76. Author: Charge Transfer Photochemistry of Coordination Compounds, 1993, also numerous rsch. papers. Mem. Am. Chem. Soc. (chmn. Northeastern Ind. sect. 1978-79, Chemist of Yr. 1979, 93), Inter-Am. Photochem. Soc., Phi Kappa Phi, Sigma Xi. Office: Ind U-Purdue U Dept Chemistry Fort Wayne IN 46805

STEVENSON, NIKOLAI, medical association executive; b. N.Y.C., Apr. 20, 1919; s. Milivoy Stoyan Stanoyevich and Beatrice Louise Stevenson; m. Shirley Gray, Jan. 20, 1951; children: Nanette, Matthew, Julie. BA, Columbia U., 1940. Sales mgr. Nat. Sugar Refining Co., N.Y.C., 1947-54; v.p. Olavarria & Co., N.Y.C., 1954-64; founder, sr. ptnr. Stevenson, Montgomery and Clayton, N.Y.C., 1966-82; pres. Assn. for Macular Diseases, N.Y.C., 1980—; condr. ednl. seminars in field; bd. dirs. Harper's Mag. Lectr. and contbg. author Harper's Mag., Am. Heritage, Atlantic Monthly. Col. USMCR, 1940-46. Decorated Silver Star, Bronze Star. Mem. Soc. Mayflower Descendants, John Jay Assocs. of Columbia U., Sugar Club, Manhasset Bay Yacht Club, City Midday Club, Phi Gamma Delta. Episcopalian. Home: 18 Sands Ct Port Washington NY 11050 Office: Assn for Macular Diseases 210 E 64th St New York NY 10021-7480

STEVENSON, PAUL MICHAEL, physics educator, researcher; b. Denham, Eng., Oct. 10, 1954; came to U.S., 1983; s. Jeremy and Jean Helen (Jennings) S. BA, Cambridge (Eng.) U., 1976; PhD, Imperial Coll., London, 1979. Rsch. assoc. U. Wis., Madison, 1979-81, 1983-84; fellow European Orgn. for Nuclear Rsch., Geneva, 1981-83; sr. rsch. assoc. Rice U., Houston, 1984-86, asst. prof. physics, 1986-89, assoc. prof., 1989-93; prof. physics, 1993—. Contbr. articles to profl. jours. Avocation: music.

STEVENSON, PHILIP DAVIS, lawyer; b. Canton, Republic of China, Sept. 15, 1936; s. Donald Day and Lois (Davis) S.; m. Carol Rusch, June 14, 1958 (div. 1975); children: Katherine, Ross; m. Joan Ann Lukey, Oct. 8, 1976. BA, Yale U., 1958, LLB, 1961. Assoc. Robbins, Noyes & Jansen, Boston, 1961-69; assoc. Hale and Dorr, Boston, 1969-71, jr. ptnr., 1971-75, sr. ptnr., 1975—, chmn. real estate dept., 1984-90. Contbr. articles on Mass. continuing legal edn. Mem. Weston (Mass.) Planning Bd., 1968-73, chmn., 1973. Mem. ABA, Am. Coll. Real Estate Lawyers, Mass. Bar Assn., Boston Bar Assn., N.H. Bar Assn., Abstract Club. Democrat. Unitarian. Avocations: sailing, skiing. Office: Hale & Dorr 60 State St Boston MA 02109-1800

STEVENSON, ROBERT BENJAMIN, III, prosthodontist, writer; b. Topeka, Feb. 13, 1950; s. Robert Benjamin and Martha (McClelland) S.; m. Barbara Jean Sulick, June 6, 1975; children: Jody Ann, Robert Woodrow. BS, U. Miami, Coral Gables, Fla., 1972; DDS, Ohio State U., 1975, MS, MA, 1980, cert. in prosthodontics splty. tng., 1980. Practice dentistry specializing in prosthodontics Columbus, Ohio, 1981—; clin. asst. prof. Ohio State U., Columbus, 1981-87; chmn. oral cancer com. Columbus Dental Soc., 1981-85, Am. Cancer Soc., Columbus, 1985-97, Ohio divsn., 1997—; vol. dentist Provodencialis Ctr., Turks and Chicos Islands, Brit. West Indies, 1982-87. Editor: Columbus Dental Soc. Bull., 1981-87, 89-92; assoc. editor Ohio State U. Dental Alumni Quar., 1982—, Am. Med. Writer's Assn. Ohio Newsletter, 1983-86, Ohio State Journalism Alumni Assn. Newsletter, 1986-88; assoc. editor Jour. Prosthetic Dentistry, 1987-92; inventor intraoral measuring device. Vol. Am. Cancer Soc., Columbus, 1982—, Gahanna and Reynoldsburg, Ohio, 1983, 84; fundraiser Columbus council Boy Scouts of Am., 1984. Served to capt. USAF, 1975-78. Mem. ADA, Am. Coll. Prosthodontists, Ohio Dental Assn. (alt. del. 1982-89, del. 1990-92, new products editor newsletter 1988—), Carl Boucher Prosthodontic Conf. (editor 1987-92, sec. 1992—), Proscrastinator's Club Am. Avocations: playing electric organ, music, reading. Home: 1300 Southport Cir Columbus OH 43235-7642 Office: 3600 Olentangy River Rd Columbus OH 43214-3437

STEVENSON, ROBERT EVERETT, oceanography consultant; b. Fullerton, Calif., Jan. 15, 1921; m. Jeani M. Wetzel, June 20, 1988; children: Michael G., Robert K. AA, Fullerton Jr. Coll., 1941; AB, UCLA, 1946, AM, 1948; PhD, U. So. Calif., 1954. Tchg. asst. UCLA, 1946; instr. Compton (Calif.) Coll., 1947-49; lectr. U. So. Calif., L.A., 1949-51, dir. inshore rsch. Hancock Found., 1953-59, 60-61; spl. rsch. oceanographer U.S. Office Naval Rsch., London, 1959; rsch. scientist dept. oceanography and meteorology Tex. A&M U., College Station, 1961-62, dir. marine lab., prof. Grad. Sch., 1963-63; rsch. scientist Oceanographic Inst., assoc. prof. Fla. State U., Tallahassee, 1963-65; acting asst. lab. dir. Bur. Comml. Fisheries Biol. Lab., Galveston, Tex., 1965-66, asst. lab. dir., 1966-70, acting lab. dir., 1969; sci. liaison officer Office Naval Rsch., Scripps Instn. Oceanography, La Jolla, Calif., 1970-88, dep. dir. space oceanography, 1985-88; oceanography cons., Del Mar, Calif., 1988—; vis. scientist Am. Geophys. Union, 1963; disting. lectr. Am. Assn. Petroleum Geologists, 1969-72. Contbr. articles to sci. jours. With USAAF, 1942-45, ETO; capt. USAF, 1951-53. Decorated DFC, Air medal with four oak leaf clusters; recipient numerous awards Office Naval Rsch. and NASA. Fellow Geol. Soc. Am., Internat. Assn. for Phys. Scis. of Ocean (dep. sec. gen. 1985-87, sec. gen. 1987-95, emeritus sec. gen. 1995—), Marine Luftschiffer Kamradschaft (hon.), Order of Decibel, Sigma Xi. Home and Office: PO Box 689 Del Mar CA 92014-0689

STEVENSON, ROBERT MURRELL, music educator; b. Melrose, N.Mex., July 3, 1916; s. Robert Emory and Ada (Ross) S. AB, U. Tex., El Paso, 1936; grad., Juilliard Grad. Sch. Music, 1938; MusM, Yale, 1939; PhD, U. Rochester, 1942; STB cum laude, Harvard U., 1943; BLitt, Oxford (Eng.) U.; Th.M., Princeton U.; DMus honoris causa, Cath. U. Am., 1991; LHD honoris causa, Ill. Wesleyan U., 1992; LittD honoris causa, Universidade Nova de Lisboa, 1993. Instr. music U. Tex., 1941-43, 46; faculty Westminster Choir Coll., Princeton, N.J., 1946-49; faculty research lectr. UCLA, 1981, mem. faculty to prof. music, 1949—; vis. asst. prof. Columbia, 1955-56; vis. prof. Ind. U., Bloomington, 1959-60, U. Chile, 1965-66, Northwestern U., Chgo., 1976, U. Granada, 1992; cons. UNESCO, 1977; Louis Charles Elson lectr. Libr. of Congress, Washington, 1969; inaugural prf. musicology Nat. U. Mex., 1996. Author: Music in Mexico, 1952, Patterns of Protestant Church Music, 1953, La musica en la catedral de Sevilla, 1954, 85, Music Before the Classic Era, 1955, Shakespeare's Religious Frontier, 1958, The Music of Peru, 1959, Juan Bermudo, 1960, Spanish Music in the Age of Columbus, 1960, Spanish Cathedral Music in the Golden Age, 1961, La musica colonial en Colombia, 1964, Protestant Church Music in America, 1966, Music in Aztec and Inca Territory, 1968, Renaissance and Baroque Musical Sources in the Americas, 1970, Music in El Paso, 1970, Philosophies of American Music History, 1970, Written Sources for Indian Music Until 1882, 1972, Christmas Music From Baroque Mexico, 1974, Foundations of New World Opera, 1973, Seventeenth Century Villancicos, 1974, Latin American Colonial Music Anthology, 1975, Vilancicos Portugueses, 1976, Josquin in the Music of Spain and Portugal, 1977, American Musical Scholarship, Parker to Thayer, 1978, Liszt at Madrid and Lisbon, 1980, Wagner's Latin American Outreach, 1983, Spanish Musical Impact Beyond the Pyrenees, 1250-1500, 1985, La Música en las catedrales españolas del Siglo de Oro, 1993; contbg. editor: Handbook Latin Am. Studies, 1976—; editor Inter-Am. Music Rev., 1978—; contbr. to New Grove Dictionary of Music and Musicians, 17 other internat. encys. Served to capt. U.S. Army, 1943-46, 49. Decorated Army Commendation ribbon; fellow Ford Found., 1953-54, Gulbenkian Found., 1966, 81, Guggenheim Found., 1962, NEH, 1974, Comité Conjunto Hispano-Norteamericano (Madrid), 1989; recipient Fulbright rsch. awards, 1958-59, 64, 70-71, 88-89, Carnegie Found. tchg. award, 1955-56, Gabriela Mistral award OAS, 1985, Heitor Villa Lobos Jury award OAS, 1988, OAS medal, 1986, Cert. Merit Mexican Consulate San Bernardino, Calif., 1987, Silver medal Spanish Ministry Culture, 1989, Gold medal Real Conservatorio Superior, 1994, 97. Mem. Am. Musicol. Soc. (hon. life, Pacific SW chpt.), Real Academia de Bellas Artes, Hispanic Soc. Am., Am. Liszt Soc. (cons. editor), Heterofonia (cons. editor), Brazilian Musicol. Soc. (hon.), Portuguese Musicol. Soc. (hon.), Argentinian Musicol. Soc. (hon.), Orden Andrés Bello, Primera Clase, Venezuela, 1992. Avocation: playing piano. Office: UCLA Dept Music 405 Hilgard Ave Los Angeles CA 90095-9000 *American achievements are as nothing unless they are written about and remembered. My mission has been to rescue the musical past of the Americas. Present-day composers are too busy making their own music to worry about their predecessors. As a result, every new generation of composers thinks that they are the first ones to descry Mount Olympus. Not so. The past is a succession of musical and artistic glories.*

STEVENSON, THOMAS HERBERT, management consultant, writer; b. Covington, Ohio, Oct. 16, 1951; s. Robert Louis and Dolly Eileen (Minnich)

S.; m. Jackie Lowe, June 1, 1997. BA in Econs./Comm., Wright State U., 1977; cert. bank compliance officer, Bank Adminstrn. Inst., 1990. Cert. regulatory compliance mgr. Teaching asst., rsch. asst. Wright State U., Dayton, Ohio, 1975-77; teaching asst. Bowling Green (Ohio) State U., 1978; loan officer Western Ohio Nat. Bank & Trust Co., 1979-80, asst. v.p. adminstrs., 1981-82, v.p. mgmt. svcs. div., 1983-85; v.p., bank mgmt. cons. Young & Assocs., Inc., Kent, Ohio, 1985-86, exec. v.p., 1987—; legis. impact analyst Community Bankers Ohio, 1985-94, Community Bankers Ga., 1988-94; mem. exec. com. Owl Electronic Banking Network 1981-85. Author: Compliance for Community Banks, 1987, Compliance Deskbook, 1988, Internal Audit for Community Banks, 1989, Truth in Lending for the Community Bank, 1989, Bank Protection for the Community Bank, 1989, Community Reinvestment Act for the Community Bank, 1989, Executive Management Guide to an Executive Board of Directors, 1990, The Board of Directors, 1990, The Home Mortgage Disclosure Guide, 1990, A Guide to Flood Insurance, 1990, Insider Lending, 1990, A Guide to the Equal Credit Opportunity Act, 1990, Investment Management, 1990, Contingency Planning, 1990, Insider Conduct, 1990, Currency Transaction Reporting Deskbook, 1990, Property Appraisal Deskbook, 1991, Bank Protection Deskbook, 1991, Regulatory Management Deskbook, 1991, Record Retention Deskbook, 1991, Environmental Deskbook for Financial Institutions, 1992, Deposit Compliance Deskbook, 1992, Fair Housing Deskbook, 1992, Insider Lending Deskbook, 1992, CRA Deskbook, 1992, Investment Mgmt. Deskbook, 1992, Internal Audi Deskbook, 1993; contbr. articles to profl. jours. Mem. adv. bd. Upper Valley Joint Vocat. Sch. for Fin. Instns., 1981-85. Cpl. USMC, 1972-73. Recipient George Washington medal of Honor Freedom's Found., 1974. Mem. Am. Inst. Banking (adv. bd. 1982-85), Community Bankers Assn. Ohio, Community Bankers Assn. Ga., Community Bankers Assn. Ill., Bank Adminstrn. Inst., Profl. Stds. Bd., Cert. Bank Compliance Officers, Eagles Club. Republican. Mem. Ch. of Brethren. Home: 3750 Chagrin River Rd Chagrin Falls OH 44022-1130 Office: 121 E Main St Kent OH 44240-2524

STEVENSON, THOMAS RAY, plastic surgeon; b. Kansas City, Mo., Jan. 22, 1946; s. John Adolph and Helen Ray (Clarke) S.; m. Judith Ann Hunter, Aug. 17, 1968; children: Anne Hunter, Andrew Thomas. BA, U. Kans., 1968, MD. Diplomate Am. Bd. Plastic and Reconstructive Surgery, Am. Bd. Surgery. Resident in gen. surgery U. Va., Charlottesville, 1972-78; resident in plastic surgery Emory U., Atlanta, 1980-82; asst. prof. surgery U. Mich., 1982-88, assoc. prof. surgery, 1988—; chief plastic surgery Ann Arbor VA Hosp., 1982—. Served to maj. USAR, 1978-80. Fellow ACS; mem. Am. Soc. Plastic and Reconstructive Surgery. Office: UC Davis Div Plas Surg 4301 X St Ste 2430 Sacramento CA 95817-2214*

STEVENSON, WARREN HOWARD, mechanical engineering educator; b. Rock Island, Ill., Nov. 18, 1938; s. Joseph Howard and Camilla Irene (Darnall) S.; m. Judith Ann Fleener, June 7, 1959; children: Kathleen, Kevin, Kent. BSME, Purdue U., 1960, MSME, 1963, PhD, 1965. Engr. Martin Co., Denver, 1960-61; rsch. asst., instr. Purdue U., West Lafayette, Ind., 1961-65, asst. prof., 1965-68, assoc. prof., 1968-74, prof., 1974—, asst. dean engring., 1992—; guest prof. U. Karlsruhe, Germany, 1973-74; vis. prof. Ibaraki U., Hitachi, Japan, 1993; mem. tech. conf. coms. various profl. groups. Editor: Laser Velocimetry and Particle Sizing, 1979; mem. editorial bd. Jour. Laser Applications, 1988—; contbr. articles to profl. jours.; patentee in field. U.S. sr. scientist Alexander von Humboldt Found., Fed. Republic Germany, 1973. Fellow Laser Inst. Am. (bd. dirs. 1984—, pres. 1989); mem. ASME, Optical Soc. Am. Avocations: sailing, photography. Office: Purdue U Sch Mech Engring Applied Optics Lab West Lafayette IN 47907

STEVENSON, WILLIAM ALEXANDER, retired justice of Supreme Court of Canada; b. Edmonton, Alta., Can., May 7, 1934; s. Alexander Lindsy and Eileen Harriet (Burns) S.; m. Patricia Ann Stevenson; children: Catherine, Kevin, Vivian, James. BA, U. Alta., Edmonton, 1956, LLB, 1957; LLD (hon.), U. Alta., 1992. Called to Alta. bar, 1958. Ptnr. Hurlburt Reynolds Stevenson & Agrios, Edmonton, 1957-68; prof. U. Alta., 1968-70; ptnr. Reynolds Stevenson & Agrios, Edmonton, 1970-75; judge Dist. Ct. Alta., Edmonton, 1975-79; justice Ct. of Queens Bench Alta., Edmonton, 1979-80, Ct. of Appeal Alta., Edmonton, 1980-90, Supreme Ct. Can., Ottawa, Ont., 1990-92; officer Order of Can., 1997. Co-author: Civil Procedure Guide, 1995. Mem. Can. Bar Assn., Can. Inst. for Adminstrn. Justice (pres. 1983-85, hon. dir.), Nat. Jud. Inst. (hon. dir.). Home: 7 Laurier Pl, Edmonton, AB Canada T5R 5P4

STEVENSON, WILLIAM HENRI, author; b. London, June 1, 1924; s. William and Alida (Deleporte) S.; m. Glenys Rowe, July 28, 1945; children: Andrew, Jacqueline, Kevin, Sally. Student, Royal Navy Coll., 1942. Fgn. corr. Toronto (Ont., Can.) Star, 1948-58; Toronto Globe & Mail, 1958-63, Ind. TV News, London, Eng., 1964-66, CBC, 1966-77; ind. writer, broadcaster, 1977—. Author: Travels In and Around Red China, 1957, Rebels in Indonesia, 1964, Chronicles of the Israeli Air Force, 1971, A Man Called Intrepid, 1976, Ninety Minutes at Entebbe, 1976, The Ghosts of Africa, 1981; producer: TV documentaries; movie screenplays include The Bushbabies, 1970. Served as aviator Royal Navy, 1942-45. Mem. Assn. Naval Aviation U.S.A., Authors Guild, Royal Overseas League (London). Mem. Progressive Conservative Party Can. Mem. Church of England. Clubs: Royal Bermuda Yacht, Royal Hong Kong Yacht. Office: care Paul Gitlin Agy 919 3rd Ave Lbby 1 New York NY 10022-3901 Address: 25 Roxborough E, Toronto, ON Canada M4W Z2G*

STEVENTON, ROBERT WESLEY, marketing executive; b. Allentown, Pa., Nov. 2, 1948; s. Robert Wesley and Catherine May (Feineur) S; m. Deborah Damon Barrett, Aug. 29, 1977; children: Calvin Nathaniel, Alexander MacAuley. BA, Pa. State U., 1970; MA, U. Minn., 1975; Cert. Resident, Cambridge U., Eng. Mktg. specialist U.S. Bur. of Census, Washington, 1975-77; mktg. mgr. Am. Chem. Soc., Washington, 1978-83; account exec. Kreitlow & Assocs., Silver Spring, Md., 1983-84; sr. account exec. Mktg. Gen., Inc., Washington, 1984-85; v.p. Mktg. Gen., Inc., Alexandria, Va., 1985-89, sr. v.p., 1989-94; pres. Mktg. Strategies, Unltd., McLean, Va., 1994—; dir. Intelmark Corp., 1995-96; advisor Euro Broadcasting Corp., 1996—; lectr. Direct Mktg. Assn., Washington, 1988-92, Coun. Engring. and Sci. Soc. Execs., N.Y.C., 1988—; gen. chmn. Direct Mktg. Days Conv. Com., Washington, 1988. Mem. com. econ. devel. bur. Greater Washington Bd. Trade, 1989-92, bus. mktg. com., 1993-94; vol. Christ House, Alexandria, Va., 1987—. With U.S. Army, 1970-73. Recipient Capital award Nat. Leadership Coun., 1992. Mem. Am. Soc. Assn. Execs. (membership com. 1989—), Am.-European Cmty. Assn., Direct Mktg. Assn. Washington (bd. dirs. 1983-85), Soc. for Assn. Mktg. Internat. (pres. 1991-94), Assn. Svcs. Group (chmn. bd. 1996—), Order St. Etheldreda (officer 1993), Manorial Soc. Gt. Britain (life), Club at Franklin Sq., Kappa Tau Alpha. Republican. Episcopalian. Avocations: downhill skiing, bicycling, tennis. Office: Mktg Strategies Unltd 8400 Westpark Dr Ste 100 Mc Lean VA 22102-3522

STEVER, HORTON GUYFORD, aerospace scientist and engineer, educator, consultant; b. Corning, N.Y., Oct. 24, 1916; s. Ralph Raymond and Alma (Matt) S.; m. Louise Risley Floyd, June 29, 1946; children: Horton Guyford, Sarah, Margarette, Roy. A.B., Colgate U., 1938, Sc.D. (hon.), 1958; Ph.D., Calif. Inst. Tech., 1941; LL.D., Lafayette Coll., U. Pitts., 1966, Lehigh U., 1967, Allegheny Coll., 1968, Ill. Inst. Tech., 1975; D.Sc., Northwestern U., 1966, Waynesburg Coll., 1967, U. Mo., 1975, Clark U., 1976, Bates Coll., 1977; D.H., Seton Hill Coll., 1968; D.Engring., Washington and Jefferson Coll., 1969, Widener Coll., Poly. Inst. N.Y., 1972, Villanova U., 1973, U. Notre Dame, 1974; D.P.S., George Washington U., 1981. Mem. staff radiation lab. MIT, Cambridge, 1941-42; asst. prof. MIT, 1946-51, asso. prof. aero. engring., 1951-56, prof. aero. and astro., 1956-65, head depts. mech. engring., naval architecture, marine engring., 1961-65, asso. dean engring., 1956-59, exec. officer guided missiles program, 1946-48; chief scientist USAF, 1955-56; pres. Carnegie-Mellon U., Pitts., 1965-72; dir. NSF, Washington, 1972-76; sci. adviser, chmn. Fed. Council Sci. and Tech., 1973-76; dir. Office Sci. and Tech. Policy, sci. and tech. adviser to Pres., 1976-77, sci. cons., corp. trustee, 1977—; mem. secretariat guided missiles com. Joint Chiefs of Staff, 1945; sci. liaison officer London Mission, OSRD, 1942-45; mem. guided missiles tech. evaluation group Research and Devel. Bd., 1946-48; mem. sci. adv. bd. to chief of staff USAF, 1947-69, chmn., 1962-69; mem. steering com. tech. adv panel on aeros. Dept. Def., 1956-62; chmn. spl. com. space tech. NASA, chmn. research adv. com. missile and spacecraft aerodynamics, 1959-65; mem. Nat. Sci. Bd., 1970-72, mem. ex-officio, chmn. exec. com., 1972-75; mem. Def. Sci. Bd., 1962-68; mem. adv. panel U.S. Ho. Reps. Com. Sci. and Astronautics, 1959-72; mem. Pres.'s Commn. on Patent System, 1965-67; chmn. U.S.-USSR Joint Commn. Sci. and Tech. Cooperation, 1973-77, Fed. Council Arts and Humanities, 1972-76; Pres. com. Nat. Sci. medal, 1973-77. Author: Flight, 1965; Contbr. articles to profl. publs. Past trustee Colgate U., Shady Side Acad., Sarah Mellon Scaife Found., Buckingham Sch.; truste Univ. Rsch Assn., 1977—, pres., 1982-85; trustee Woods Hole Oceanographic Inst., 1980—, Univ .Corp. for Atmospheric Rsch., 1980-83; bd. dirs. Saudi Arabia Nat. Ctr. for Sci. and Tech., 1978-81; bd. govs. U.S. Israel Binat. Sci. Found., 1972-76, chmn., 1972-73; mem. Carnegie Commn. on Sci., Tech. and Govt., 1988-93. Recipient Pres.'s Cert. of Merit, 1948, Exceptional Civilian Svc. award USAF, 1956, Scott Gold medal Am. Ordinance Assn., 1960, Disting. Pub. Svc. medal Dept. Def., 1969, NASA, 1988, Nat. Medal of Sci., 1991, Vannevar Bush award NSF; comdr. Order of Merit Poland. Fellow AIAA (hon., pres. 1960-62), AAAS, Royal Aero. Soc., Am. Acad. Arts and Scis., Royal Soc. Arts, Am. Phys. Soc.; mem. NAS (chmn. assembly engring. 1979-83, chair policy divsn. 1995—), NAE (chmn. aero. and space engring. bd. 1967-69, fgn. sec. 1984-88), Acad. Engring. of Japan (fgn. mem.), Royal Acad. of Engring. of Great Britain (fgn. mem.), Cosmos Club, Bohemian, Phi Beta Kappa, Sigma Xi, Sigma Gamma Tau, Tau Beta Pi. Episcopalian. Office: 588 Russell Ave Gaithersburg MD 20877-2868

STEVES, GALE C., editor-in-chief; b. Mineola, N.Y., Dec. 20, 1942; d. William Harry and Ruth (May) S.; m. David B. Stocker, Mar. 31, 1972 (div. Apr. 1978); m. Philip L. Perrone, Aug. 14, 1983. BS, Cornell U., 1964; MA, NYU, 1966. Editorial asst. Ladies Home Jour., N.Y.C., 1966-69; seafood consumer specialist U.S. Dept. Commerce, N.Y.C., 1969-73; editor food Homelife mag., N.Y.C., 1973-74; editor food and equipment Co-Ed mag., N.Y.C., 1974-76, Am. Home mag., N.Y.C., 1976-78; editor kitchen design and equipment Woman's Day mag., N.Y.C., 1979-83; editor-in-chief Woman's Day Spls., N.Y.C., 1983-91; v.p., editor-in-chief Home Mag. Group, N.Y.C., 1991—; bd. dirs. Les Dames d'Escoffier, N.Y.C., Council of Sr. Ctrs. and Services of N.Y.C.; mem. editorial bd. Sr. Summary, N.Y.C., 1982-88. Author: Game Cookery, 1974, The International Cook, 1980, Creative Microwave Cooking, 1981, (with Lee M. Elman) Country Weekend Cooking. Chmn. alumni adv. bd. Coll. Human Ecology, Cornell U., 1993-97, mem. univ. coun., 1996—, mem. pres.;s coun. for Cornell women, 1992—. Mem. NAFE, Internat. Furnishings and Design Assn., Am. Soc. Mag. Editors, Garden Writers Assn. Am., Acad. of Women Achievers at YWCA of N.Y.C. Office: Home Magazine Group 1633 Broadway New York NY 10019-6708

STEWARD, JAMES BRIAN, lawyer, pharmacist; b. Cleve., Mar. 25, 1946; s. Louis Fred and Helen Elaine (Goodwin) S.; m. Betty Kay Krans, Dec. 14, 1968; children: Christina Lynn, Brian Michael. BS in Pharmacy, Ferris State Coll., 1969; JD, U. Mich., 1973. Bar: Mich. 1973, U.S. Dist. Ct. (we. dist.) Mich. 1979, U.S. Cir. Ct. (6th Cir.) 1980, U.S. Supreme Ct. 1986. Pharmacist Revco Pharmacies, Grand Rapids, Mich., 1969-70, Coll. Pharmacy, Ypsilanti, Mich., 1970-73; assoc. Bridges & Collins, Negaunee, Mich., 1973-80; ptnr. Steward, Peterson, Sheridan & Nancarrow, Ishpeming, Mich., 1980-94, Steward & Sheridan, Ishpeming, 1995—. Mem., chmn. Negaunee Commn. on Aging, 1974-86; mem., chmn., sec. Marquette County Commn. on Aging, 1976-82; trustee, v.p., pres. Negaunee Bd. Edn., 1984-88, 91-95; adv. bd. trustee Ishpeming Area Cmty. Fund, 1995—; mem. combined ad hoc com. Marquette County Commn. on Aging, 1996. Mem. Mich. Bar Assn., Marquette County Bar Assn. (sec.- treas., v.p., pres.), Am. Soc. for Pharmacy Law, Ishpeming Cross County Ski Club, Wawonowin Country Club, Phi Delta Chi, Rho Chi. Avocations: cross country ski racing, downhill and water skiing, running, biking, classic cars. Office: Steward & Sheridan 205 S Main St Ishpeming MI 49849-2018

STEWARD, JERRY WAYNE, air transportation executive, consultant; b. Tulia, Tex., Mar. 22, 1945; s. Joe M. and Mary Evelyn (Boggs) S.; m. Peggy L. Thomas, Nov. 18, 1978; children: Eric, Chalynda, Julie. AMT, Spartan Aeronautics, Tulsa, 1965. Designated Airworthiness Rep., U.S. FAA. Dir. quality control Braniff, Dallas, Orlando, Tex., Fla., 1966-90; dir. tech. svcs. Polaris Aircraft Leasing, San Francisco, 1990-94; cons. Roanoke, Tex., 1994—. With U.S. Army, 1966-69. Avocations: hunting, fishing, travel. Home and Office: 1820 Summer Ln Roanoke TX 76262-9129

STEWARD, LESTER HOWARD, psychiatrist, academic administrator, educator; b. Burt, Iowa, Nov. 6, 1930; s. Walter and Helen Steward; m. Patricia Byrness Roach, June 17, 1953; children: Donald Howard, Thomas Eugene, Susan Elaine, Joan Marsha. BS, Ariz. State U., 1958, MA in Sci. Edn., 1969; postgrad., Escuela Nat. U., Mex., 1971-80; PhD in Psychology, Calif. Coast U., 1974; MD, Western U. Hahnemann Coll., 1980. Rschr. drug abuse and alcoholism Western Australia U., Perth, Australia, 1970-71; intern in psychiatry Helix Hosp., San Diego, Calif., 1971-72; rschr. drug addiction North Mountain Behavioral Inst., Phoenix, 1975-77; exec. v.p., CEO James Tyler Kent Coll., 1977-80; pres., CEO Western U. Sch. Medicine, 1980-86; instr. psychology USN Westpac, Subic Bay, Philippines, 1988-91; pvt. practice preventive medicine Tecate, Baja California, Mexico, 1971-88; instr. Modern Hypnosis Instrn. Ctr., 1974—, Maricopa Tech. Community Coll., Phoenix, 1975-77; mem. Nt. Ctr. Homeopathy, Washington, Menninger Found., Wichita, Kans. Contbr. numerous papers to profl. confs. Leader Creighton Sch. dist. Boy Scouts Am., Phoenix, 1954-58. Lt. Cmdr. USN, 1949-54, 60-63, Korea. Fellow Am. Acad. Med. Adminstrs., Am. Assn. Clinic Physicians and Surgeons, Internat. Coll. Physicians and Surgeons, Am. Coll. Homeopathic Physicians, Am. Counc. Sex Therapy; mem. numerous orgns. including Nat. Psychol. Assn., Am. Psychotherapy Assn., Royal Soc. Physicians, World Med. Assn., Am. Acad. Preventive Medicine, Am. Bd. Examiners in Psychotherapy, Am. Bd. Examiners in Homeopathy, Western Homeopathic Med. Soc. (exec. dir.), Ariz. Profl. Soc. Hypnosis (founder 1974). Home: 515 W Townley Ave Phoenix AZ 85021-4566

STEWARD, OSWALD, neuroscience educator, researcher; b. Sept. 12, 1948; m. Kathy L. Pyle; children: Jessica, Oswald IV. BA in Psychology magna cum laude, U. Colo., 1970; PhD in Psychobiology, U. Calif., Irvine, 1974. Asst. prof. neurosurgery and physiology U. Va. Sch. Medicine, Charlottesville, 1974-79, assoc. prof., 1979-84, prof., 1984-86, acting chmn. neurosci. dept., 1986-88, chmn., 1988—. Author: Principles of Cellular, Molecular, and Developmental Neuroscience, 1989; contbr. about 125 articles and revs. to profl. publs. Predoctoral fellow NIMH, Bethesda, Md., 1971-74; rsch. career devel. grantee NIH, 1978-83, Jacob Javitts neurosci. grantee NIH, 1987-94. Mem. Soc. for Neurosci. (chmn. chpts. com. 1985-87). Office: U Va Sch Medicine PO Box 458 Charlottesville VA 22908*

STEWARD, WELDON CECIL, architecture educator, architect, consultant; b. Pampa, Tex., Apr. 7, 1934; s. Weldon C. and Lois (Maness) S.; m. Mary Jane Nedbalek, June 9, 1956; children: Karen A., W. Craig. Cert. in architecture and planning, Ecole des Beaux Arts, Fontainebleu, France, 1956; B.Arch., Tex. A&M U, 1957; M.S. in Architecture, Columbia U., 1961; LHD (hon.), Drury Coll., 1991. Registered architect, Tex., Nebr. Designer Perkins & Will, Architects, White Plains, N.Y., 1961-62; asst. prof. architecture Tex. A&M U., College Station, 1962-67, assoc. chmn. Sch. Architecture, 1966-69, assoc. dean, prof. Coll. Environ. Design, 1969-73; dean, prof. Coll. Architecture U. Nebr., Lincoln, 1973—; pres. Joslyn Castle Inst. Sustainable Cmtys., Omaha, 1996—; ednl. cons. People's Republic of China, 1979; project dir. Imo State U. Planning, Nigeria, 1981-88; vis. prof. Tong ji U., Shanghai, 1984; hon. prof. N.W. Inst. Architects Engrs., Xian, 1989; specialist Design USA, USSR, 1990; co-chmn. nat. coordination com. AIA Nat. Coun. Archtl. Registration Bd. Intership, Washington, 1980-81; bd. visitors Drury Coll., 1980—, Coll. Arch. U. Miami, Fla., 1993—; mem. nat. design rev. bd. GSA, Washington, 1994—; mem. founding bd. dirs. East/West Pacific Arch., U. Hawaii, 1995—; vice chmn. Design Futures Coun., Reston, Va., 1995—. Designer, Quinnipiac Elem. Sch., New Haven, Conn., 1961 (Am Assn. Sch. Adminstrs. Exhibit 1969), J.J. Buser Residence, Bryan, Tex., 1969, Steward Urban Residence, Lincoln, Nebr., 1994. Mem. Lincoln Architects, Engrs. Selection Bd., 1979-88; mem. Nat. Com. for U.S.-China Rels., N.Y.C., 1981—, Nebr. Capitol Environ. Commn., 1989—; bd. dirs. Downtown Lincoln Assn., 1996—; mem. Lincoln Planning Commn., 1996—; bd. dirs. Lincoln Children's Mus., 1996—; profl. adviser nat. design competition Wick Alumni Ctr., Lincoln, 1981; steering com. Internat. Coun. Tall Bldgs., 1992—. Grad. fellow Columbia U., 1960. Fellow AIA (pres. Brazos chpt. 1969, chmn. profl. devel. com. 1979, bd. dirs. 1979-90, dir. Cen. States 1987-90, nat. pres. 1991-92); mem. Nebr. Soc. Architects (bd. dirs. 1977—), Archtl. Found. Nebr. (bd. dirs. 1981-94, treas. 1981-94), Assn. Collegiate Schs. Architecture (bd. dirs. 1975-79), Nat. Archtl. Accrediting Bd. (bd. dirs. 1986-89, pres. 1988-89), Kazakhstan Union Architecture, Assn. Siamese Architects (hon.), Royal Inst. Canadian Architects, Fedn. Mexican Achitects, Japan Inst. Architects, Tau Sigma Delta, Phi Kappa Phi, Phi Beta Delta. Home: 125 N 11th St Lincoln NE 68508-3605 Office: U Nebr Coll Architecture Lincoln NE 68588

STEWART, ALBERT CLIFTON, college dean, marketing educator; b. Detroit, Nov. 25, 1919; s. Albert Queely and Jeanne Belle (Kaiser) S.; m. Colleen Moore Hyland, June 25, 1949. BS, U. Chgo., 1942, MS, 1948; PhD, St. Louis U., 1951. Chemist Sherwin Williams Paint Co., Chgo.; rsch. asst. dept. chemistry U. Chgo., 1947-48; instr. chemistry St. Louis U., 1949-51; exec. Union Carbide Corp., Danbury, Conn., 1951-84; prof. mktg. Western Conn. State U., Danbury, 1984—, dean Sch. of Bus., 1987-90, 94-95; cons. Ford Found., 1963-69, Union Carbide Corp., 1984-94; bd. dirs. Exec. Register, Inc., Danbury, 1985-90; assoc. Execom, Darien, Conn., 1986-90. Patentee in field. Bd. dirs. Am. Mus. Natural History, N.Y.C., 1976-85, N.Y.C. Philharm., 1975-80; arbiter Am. Arbitration Assn., N.Y.C., Danbury; active town Coun., Oak Ridge, Tenn., 1953-57. Lt. (j.g.) USNR, World War II. Recipient Cert. of Merit Soc. Chem. Professions, Cleve., 1962. Mem. Am. Mktg. Assn., Sigma Xi. Club: Rotary (Cleve., N.Y.C.). Home: 28 Hearthstone Dr Brookfield CT 06804-3006 Office: Western Conn State U 181 White St Danbury CT 06810

STEWART, ALBERT ELISHA, safety engineer, industrial hygienist; b. Urbana, Mo., Dec. 20, 1927; s. Albert E. and Maurine (Lighter) S.; m. Elizabeth O. Tice, May 31, 1958 (div.); children: Sheryl E., Mical A. BA, U. Kans., 1949; MS, U. Mo., 1958, MBA, 1970; PhD, Western States U., 1984. Registered profl. engr., Calif., cert. safety engr., cert. indsl. hygienist. Sales engr. Kaiser Aluminum and Chem. Co., Toledo, 1949-56; tchr. Kansas City (Mo.) Pub. Schs., 1959-65; indsl. hygienist Bendix Corp., Kansas City, 1960-65; safety adminstr. Gulf R&D, Merriam, Kans., 1968-71; sr. indsl. hygienist USDOL-OSHA, Kansas City, 1971-77; pres. Stewart Indsl. Hygiene, Kansas City, 1977—; adj. prof. Cen. Mo. State U. Mem. Boy Scouts Am. With U.S. Army, 1950-53. Mem. Am. Indsl. Hygiene Assn., Am. Chem. Soc., Am. Acad. Indsl. Hygiene, Am. Soc. Safety Engrs., Am. Welding Soc., Nat. Mgmt. Assn., Nat. Sci. Tchrs. Assn., Adminstrv. Govt. Soc., Am. Legion Post 596, DAV, ARC, Alpha Chi Sigma. Episcopalian. Avocations: fishing, golf, travel. Office: 8029 Brooklyn Ave Kansas City MO 64132-3516

STEWART, ALEC THOMPSON, physicist; b. Windthorst, Sask., Can., June 18, 1925; s. Arthur and Nelly Blye (Thompson) S.; m. Alta Aileen Kennedy, Aug. 4, 1960; children—A. James Kennedy, Hugh D., Duncan R. B.Sc., Dalhousie U., Halifax, N.S., Can., 1946, M.Sc., 1949, LL.D. (hon.), 1986; Ph.D., Cambridge U., Eng., 1952. Research officer Atomic Energy Can., Chalk River, Ont., Can., 1952-57; assoc. prof. Dalhousie U., Halifax, 1957-60; assoc. prof. to prof. U. N.C., Chapel Hill, 1960-68; head physics Queen's U., Kingston, Ont., 1968-74, prof. physics, 1968—; vis. prof. various univs., Can., Europe, Japan, China, Hong Kong. Author 2 books; contbr. over 100 articles to profl. jours. Recipient CAP medal for achievement in physics, 1992, Canada 125 medal, 1992. Fellow Am. Phys. Soc., Royal Soc. Can. (pres. Acad. Sci. 1984-87), Japan Soc. for Promotion Sci.; mem. Can. Assn. Physicists (pres., other offices 1970-74). Achievements include research in solid state physics, behavior of phonons, electrons, positrons and postronium in crystals and liquids, public service: nuclear reactor safety, possible hazards of power frequency electric and magnetic fields, emergency measures following a nuclear accident. Office: Queens U, Dept Physics, Kingston, ON Canada K7L 3N6

STEWART, ALEXANDER DOIG, bishop; b. Boston, Jan. 27, 1926; s. Alexander Doig and Catherine Muir (Smith) S.; m. Laurel Gale, June 5, 1953. A.B. cum laude, Harvard U., 1948, M.B.A., 1961; M.Div. cum laude, Union Theol. Sem., N.Y.C., 1951; D.D. (hon.), Gen. Theol. Sem., N.Y.C. Ordained priest Episcopal Ch., 1951; asst. (Christ Ch.), Greenwich, Conn., 1950-52; priest-in-charge (St. Margaret's Parish), Bronx, N.Y., 1952-53; rector (St. Mark's Episc. Ch.), Riverside, R.I., 1953-70; bishop Episc. Diocese Western Mass., Springfield, 1970-83; exec. for adminstrn. Episcopal Ch., N.Y.C., 1983-86, exec. v.p., mgr. pension fund, 1987-91, part-time cons., 1992—; mem. faculty Barrington Coll., 1955-70; Mem. budget and program com. Episc. Ch. U.S.A.; bd. dirs. Ch. Ins. Co., Ch. Life Ins. Co., Ch. Hymnal Corp. Author: Science and Human Nature, 1960 (Wainwright House award), The Shock of Revelation, 1967; also articles. Chmn. Urban Renewal, E. Providence, R.I., 1967-70; vice chmn. United Fund Springfield, 1972; mem. schs. and scholarship com. R.I. chpt. Harvard Coll., 1960-70; A founder, 1959-87; mem. bd. dirs., sec. corp. Health Havens, Inc., E. Providence; trustee Barrington Coll., 1971-76, Episcopal Radio-TV Found., 1980-96, Providence Country Day Sch., 1964-70, Ch. Pension Fund, N.Y.C., 1976-87; mem. corp. St. Elizabeth's Hosp., Providence, 1954-70, Springfield Hosp., 1970-84.—. Mem. Religious Research Assn., Union League (N.Y.C.), Colony Club (Springfield). Address: 75 Severn St Longmeadow MA 01106-1023

STEWART, ALLEN WARREN, lawyer; b. Manchester, N.H., Dec. 12, 1938; s. Ellwyn F. and Aelene W. (Harriman) S.; children: William, Paul, Geoffrey. BS, U.S. Naval Acad., 1961; MS, George Washington U., 1967; JD, U. Pa., 1970. Bar: Pa. 1970, U.S. Ct. Appeals (3d cir.) 1971, U.S. Supreme Ct. 1980. Morgan, Lewis & Bockius, Phila., 1970-77, ptnr., 1977-94; chmn. bd. dirs. Am. Sentinel Ins. Co., Conestoga Life Assurance Co., Tartan Mgmt. Corp. Editor: Reinsurance, 1991; contbr. articles to legal and ins. jours. Naval aviator, lt. comdr. USN, 1961-66. Mem. ABA, Pa. Bar Assn., Phila. Bar Assn. Club: Phila. Racquet. Avocations: sailing, fishing. Office: Conestoga Life Assurance Co 223 Wilmington W Chester Pike Chadds Ford PA 19317-9043

STEWART, ARLENE JEAN GOLDEN, designer, stylist; b. Chgo., Nov. 26, 1943; d. Alexander Emerald and Nettie (Rosen) Golden; m. Randall Edward Stewart, Nov. 6, 1970; 1 child, Alexis Anne. BFA, Sch. of Art Inst. Chgo., 1966; postgrad., Ox Bow Summer Sch. Painting, Saugatuck, Mich., 1966. Designer, stylist Formica Corp., Cin., 1966-68; with Armstrong World Industries, Inc., Lancaster, Pa., 1968-96, interior furnishings analyst, 1974-76, internat. staff project stylist, 1976-78, sr. stylist Corlon flooring, 1979-80, sr. exptl. project stylist, 1980-89, sr. project stylist residential DIY flooring floor divsn., 1989-96, master stylist DIY residential tile, 1992-96; creative dir. Stewart Graphics, Lancaster, Pa., 1996—. Exhibited textiles Art Inst. Chgo., 1966, Ox-Bow Gallery, Saugatuck, Mich., 1966. Home: 114 E Vine St Lancaster PA 17602-3550 Office: 114 E Vine St Lancaster PA 17602-3550

STEWART, ARTHUR IRVING, III (ART STEWART), communications executive; b. Plainfield, N.J., Aug. 1, 1958; s. Arthur Irving Jr. and Audree Claire (Rollerson) S. BS in Mass Communication, Emerson Coll., 1982. Intern Sta. KYW Newsradio/TV, Phila., 1977; news anchorman, reporter Sta. WLBR-WUFM-FM, Lebanon, Pa., 1984; ops. mgr. Sta. WMSP-FM, Harrisburg, Pa., 1984-86; sr. account exec. mktg. and sales promotion Sta. WFCC-FM, Chatham, Mass., 1987-88; account mgr. Vizwiz Film-Video, Inc., Brookline, Mass., 1989-90; pub. rels. account exec. The Interface Group, Needham, Mass., 1991-92; sr. account exec. pub. rels. Mullen Advt., 1992-93; prin. sr. counsel Reputation Mgmt., Cambridge, 1993—; dir. mktg. and pub. rels. Cape and Islands Chamber Music Festival, Cape Cod, Mass., 1988; asst. organist The United Parish, Brookline, 1982-84. Producer (radio concert broadcasts) Harrisburg Symphony Orch., 1984-86, documentary on U.S. debut tour of Westminster Cathedral Choir of London, 1985, investigative report on acid rain, 1985 (Excellence in Broadcasting award), documentary on Nat. Cathedral Washington, 1986 (Excellence in Broadcasting award). Editor OUTREACH newsletter Trinity Ch., Boston, 1990-94; mem. Bus. Social Responsibility. Recipient Excellence in Broadcasting award Pa. Assn. Broadcasters. Mem. Am. Soc. Health Care Mktg. and Planning, Nat. Law Firm Mktg. Assn., Bus. for Social Responsibility, Religious Pub. Rels. Coun., Assoc. Ch. Press, Episcopal Communicators, Am. Guild Organists (mem. comms. task force). Episcopalian. Avocations: running, bicycling, travel, the arts.

STEWART, ARTHUR VAN, dental educator, geriatric health administrator; b. Buffalo, N.Y., July 25, 1938; s. Arthur Sharpe and Doris (Simpson) S.; m. Jacqueline Fischer, June 5, 1965; children: Mark Van, Laura Kristin, Jeffrey Fischer. BS in Chemistry, U. Pitts., 1960, DMD, 1968, PhD, 1973. Clin. lic. Ky. USPHS postdoctoral fellow U. Pitts., 1968-70; chair, cmty. dentistry dept.; dean, student affairs Fairleigh Dickinson U., Teaneck, N.J., 1970-75; dean for acad. affairs U. Louisville Dental Sch., 1975-88, asst. provost, 1985-89, prof. dentistry, 1975—; dir., Ctr. on Aging U. Louisville Health Scis. Ctr., 1995—; cons. ADA, Chgo., OVAR: Geriatric Edn. Ctr., Lexington, Ky.; ednl. cons. Baylor U., Dallas; cons. Am. Assn. Dental Schs., Washington. Contbr. over 300 articles to profl. jours., chpts. to books, separately published monographs; presenter in field. Bd. mem. U. of Louisville Student Ctr., 1986-89, YMCA Camp Piomingo, Louisville, 1980-90; leader Cub Scout/Weblos, Boy Scouts of Am., Louisville, 1985-90. Recipient tchg. award Metroversity of Louisville, 1989, 90, 92; recipient over $2,000,000 in rsch. grants and awards. Mem. Ky. Dental Assn. (del. 1988—), Louisville Dental Soc. (chmn. 1994-95, Pres.'s award 1995), Ky. Assn. for Gerontology (pres. 1995-96), Quest for Excellence (dir. 1988-96), OKU Honorary Soc. (pres. 1978-79), Delphi Honorary Soc. (pres. 1980—, dir. Univ. Founder's Day Celebration 1995—). Avocations: writing, photography, philately, travel. Office: Univ of Louisville Sch of Dentistry 501 S Preston St Louisville KY 40202-1701

STEWART, BARBARA ELLEN, media specialist; b. Wilmington, Del., Oct. 20, 1939; d. William Thompson Stewart and Barbara Frances (Kelsey) Madison. BA, Alma (Mich.) Coll., 1962; MLS, Cen. Mich. U., 1980. cert. sec. tchg., Mich. English tchr. Owosso (Mich.) Pub. Schs., 1962-80, media specialist, 1981—. Mem. Am. Business Women's Assn. (at-large, head scholarship com. 1975, 79, v.p. 1978). Avocations: writing, crafts.

STEWART, BARBARA LYNNE, geriatrics nursing educator; b. Youngstown, Ohio, May 10, 1953; d. Carl Arvid and Margaret (Ashton) Swanson; m. James G. Stewart, Mar. 17, 1973; children: Trevor J., Troy C. AAS, Youngstown State U., 1973, BS, 1982. Cert. gerontol. nurse, ANCC. Asst. dist. office supr. divsn. quality assurance Bureau of Healthcare Stds. and Quality; supr., dir. nursing svcs. Peaceful Acres Nursing Home, North Lima, Ohio; nurse repondent Health Sci. Ctr. U. Colo., Denver; charge nurse Westwood Rehab. Med. Ctr., Inc., Boardman, Ohio, Park Vista Health Care Ctr., Youngstown, Ohio; dir. nursing Rolling Acres Care Ctr., North Lima, Ohio; primary instr. Alliance (Ohio) Tng. Ctr., Inc.; asst. dist. office supr. divsn. of quality assurance Bureau Healthcare Stds. and Quality, Akron, Ohio. Former instr. CPR, ARC. Mem. Tri County Dir. Nurses Assn., Nat. Gerontol. Nursing Assn. (nomination com.), Youngstown State U. Alumni Assn.

STEWART, BOBBY GENE, laboratory director; b. Jesse, W.Va., Apr. 18, 1940; s. Leonard Mart and Zeta Marie Stewart; m. Linda May Smith, Mar. 17, 1961; children: Barbara Lynn, Ramona Jean Stewart Pinkerman. Cert. in med. tech., Army Med. Svc. Sch., 1960; cert. blood banking specialist, 10th Med. Rsch. Lab., Landstuhl, Germany, 1961. Lic. nursing home adminstr., Mo.; cert. clin. lab. scientist, bioanalytical lab. mgr. Med. and x-ray technologist Oceana (W.Va.) Med. Ctr., 1962-68; clin. mgr., med. technologist Sigourney (Iowa) Med. Clinic, 1968-69; staff med. and x-ray technologist Van Buren County Hosp., Keosauqua, Iowa, 1969; dir. lab. and x-ray svcs. Scotland County Hosp., Memphis, Mo., 1969-71; dir. lab. svcs. Keller Meml. Hosp., Fayette, Mo., 1971-95, Regional Med. Assocs., Fayette, 1995—; clin. lab. mgr. Mem. city coun. City of Fayette, 1977-85, mayor pro-tem, 1980-85, chmn. parks and recreation com., 1977-80, chmn. elec. dist. com., 1981-85. With U.S. Army, 1959-62. Mem. Am. Med. Technologists (dist. councillor 1977-81, 88-93, nat. bd. dirs. 1993—, nat. treas. 1994-96, nat. v.p. 1996—, Disting. Achievement award 1976, Exceptional Merit award 1981), Mo. State Soc. of AMT (legis. chmn. 1975-90, v.p. 1973-74, 89-90, pres. 1975-76, Med. Technologist of Yr. 1977). Avocations: tennis, golf, swimming. Home: 410 Cooper St Fayette MO 65248-9630 Office: Regional Med Assocs 600 W Morrison St Fayette MO 65248-1075

STEWART, BURCH BYRON, chemist, physicist; b. Chattanooga, May 7, 1929; s. Burch Dayton and Mary Elizabeth Stewart; m. Lois Mildred Speaker, June 20, 1955 (div. Mar. 1965); children: Leslie, Alyson, Kathryn; m. Shirley Elizabeth Westervelt, June 8, 1965; children: Steven, Neal, Daryl. BS in Analytical Chemistry, U. Tenn., 1955, MS in Physical Organic Chemistry, 1957, PhD in Physical Chemistry, 1959. Sr. engr. Western Electric, Princeton, N.J., 1959-60; rsch. chemist Allied Chem., Morristown, N.J., 1960-68; mgr., asst. dir. Ciba-Geigy, Ardsley, N.Y., 1968-73; dir. Applied Rsch. Labs., Miami, Fla., 1973-86; pres. Applied Consumer Svcs., Miami, 1986—; rsch. scientist Solar Reactor Corp., Miami, 1978-79; cons. BBS Assocs., Inc., Miami, 1978-81, Worth Engring., Hialeah, Fla., 1986—, All State Engring., 1986—. Inventor and patentee in field; contbr. articles to profl. jours. and encyclopedias. Vol. Askew For Pres., Miami, 1983; pres. Miami Unitarian Soc., 1984, pres. Friends of Physics, U. Miami, 1990-92, 95-97. With USN, 1950-52. Recipient Hon. Mentionship award Westinghouse Sci. Talent Search, Knoxville, 1955; AEC grantee U. Tenn., Knoxville, 1957. Mem. Am. Chem. Soc., Am. Soc. Testing Materials, Assn. Offl. Analytical Chemists, Sigma Xi. Office: Applied Consumer Svcs 9500 NW 77th Ave Ste 5 Hialeah Gdns FL 33016-2522

STEWART, BURTON GLOYDEN, JR., banker; b. Clayton, N.C., Mar. 14, 1933; s. Burton Gloyden and Evelyn I. (Stallings) S.; m. Patricia Taylor, June 16, 1956; children: Burton Gloyden III, H. Taylor. AB, Duke U., 1955; grad. Sch. Banking of South, 1970; exec. program U. N.C., 1975. With Allstate Ins. Co., 1957-66, regional sales mgr., Charlotte, N.C., 1964-66; with Branch Banking and Trust Co., Wilson, N.C., 1966—, sr. v.p., mgr. corp. planning and mktg. div., 1972-81, mgr. corp. planning and investor rels., 1981-90; dir. investor rels., 1981—; dir. Branch Corp., 1974-82; dir. N.C. Payments System, 1980-89, v.p., 1983-86, chmn. bd. 1986-89; bd. dirs., chmn. Electronic Fin. Svcs., Inc., 1988-90. Bd. dirs. Wilson Heart Assn., 1968; bd. dirs., treas. Wilson Arts Coun., 1969-71; bd. dirs. Wilson United Way, 1974-80, 86-89, campaign chmn., 1977, pres., 1979, chmn. strategic planning com., 1986-90; mem. N.C. Gov.'s Efficiency Study Commn., 1985, N.C. Goals and Policy Bd., 1985-93. Lt. USNR, 1955-57. Mem. Nat. Investor Rels. Inst., Bank Investor Rels. Assn. (bd. dirs. 1984—, v.p. 1984-87), Am. Mgmt. Assn., N.C. Bankers Assn. (chmn. mktg. com. 1976), Wilson Country Club. Methodist. Office: 223 Nash St W Wilson NC 27893-3801

STEWART, CAMERON LEIGH, mathematics educator; b. Victoria, B.C., Can., Sept. 29, 1950; s. Ross and Greta Marie (Morris) S.; m. Ellen Papachristoforou, June 7, 1980; children: Elisa Maria, Andrew Ross. BSc, U. B.C., 1971; MSc, McGill U., Montreal, 1972; PhD, U. Cambridge, 1976. Rsch. assoc. Mathematisch Centrum, Amsterdam, 1976-77, I.H.E.S., Bures-Sur-Yvette, France, 1977-78; asst. prof. U. Waterloo, Ont., Can., 1978-82, assoc. prof., 1982-86, prof., 1986—. Contbr. articles to profl. jours. Recipient J.T. Knight prize U. Cambridge, 1974, Killam fellow Killam Estate, 1990-92. Fellow Royal Soc. Can.; mem. Can. Math. Soc., Am. Math. Soc. Avocations: golf, ice hockey. Home: 494 Heatherhill Pl, Waterloo, ON Canada N2T 1H7 Office: U Waterloo Dept Pure Math, Waterloo, ON Canada N2L 3G1

STEWART, CARL E., federal judge; b. 1950. BA magna cum laude, Dillard U., 1971; JD, Loyola U., New Orleans, 1974. Atty. Piper & Brown, Shreveport, La., 1977-78; staff atty. La. Atty. Gen. Office, Shreveport, 1978-79; asst. U.S. atty. Office U.S. Atty. (we. dist.) La., Shreveport, 1979-83; prin. Stewart & Dixon, Shreveport, 1983-85; spl. asst. dist. atty., asst. prosecutor City of Shreveport, 1983-85; judge La. Dist. Ct., 1985-91, La. Ct. Appeals (2d cir.), 1991-94, U.S. Ct. Appeals (5th cir.), 1994—; adj. instr. dept. mgmt. and mktg. La. State U., Shreveport, 1982-85. Mem. chancellor's adv. bd. La. State U., Shreveport, 1983-89, chmn., 1988-89; mem. black achievers program steering com. YMCA, 1990; active NAACP, 1988—. Capt. JAGC, 1974-77, Tex. Mem. ABA, Nat. Bar Assn., Am. Inns. of Ct. (Harry Booth chpt. Shreveport), Black Lawyers Assn. Shreveport-Bossier, La. Conf. Ct. Appeal Judges, La. State Bar Assn. (bench/bar liaison com.), Omega Psi Phi (Rho Omega chpt.). Office: US Ct Appeals 5th Cir 300 Fannin St Ste 2299 Shreveport LA 71101-3121*

STEWART, CARLETON M., banker, corporate director; b. Chgo., 1921; s. Carleton Merrill and Margaret (Lyon) S.; m. Alicia Dewar (dec.); 3 children; m. Kathryn White. Student, Stanford U., 1939-42; grad. in indsl. adminstrn., Harvard U., 1943, MBA, 1947. With Citibank, 1947-76; v.p. Citibank, N.Y.C., 1960-67, sr. v.p. in charge of Asia Pacific area, 1967-69, sr. v.p. in charge of South Asia, Middle East and Africa, 1969-73; sr. officer Citibank, London, 1973-76; dir. Grindlay's Bank Ltd., London, Banque Internat. pour L'Afrique Occidentale, Paris, 1973-76; chmn. bd., chief exec. officer Am. Security Corp. and Am. Security Bank, Washington, 1976-80; chmn. bd. Internat. Bank Miami, 1983-85; dir. Travelers Asset Mgmt. Internat. Corp., N.Y.C., 1985-87. Mayor Longboat Key, Fla., 1987-88, town commr., 1984-90, mem. ethics com., 1990—, chmn. 1992-94; mem. Planning Commn., Sarasota County, Fla., 1990-92. Capt. AUS, 1943-46.

STEWART, CHARLES EVAN, lawyer; b. N.Y.C., Mar. 4, 1952; s. Charles Thorp and Jenifer Jennings (Barbour) S.; m. Cathleen Bacich, June 26, 1982 (div. Nov. 1986); m. Patricia A. McGlothlin, Sept. 10, 1988; 1 child, Charlotte Jenifer. BA cum laude, Cornell U., 1974, JD, 1977. Bar: N.Y. 1978, U.S. Dist. Ct. (so. and ea. dists.) N.Y. 1978, U.S. Ct. Appeals (2d cir.) 1978, U.S. Ct. Appeals (D.C. and 7th cirs.) 1980, U.S. Ct. Appeals (3d, 9th and 5th cirs.) 1981, U.S. Supreme Ct. 1981, U.S. Ct. Appeals (10th cir.) 1982, U.S. Claims Ct. 1983, U.S. Ct. Appeals (6th cir.) 1986. Assoc. Donovan Leisure Newton & Irvine, N.Y.C., 1977-86; 1st v.p., assoc. gen. counsel E.F. Hutton and Co., Inc., N.Y.C., 1987-88; exec. v.p., gen. counsel Nikko Securities Co. Internat., N.Y.C., 1988—; spl. asst. dist. atty. N.Y. County, 1979-80; adj. prof. Fordham U. Law Sch., 1996—; arbitrator NYSE, NASD. Contbr. articles to legal jours. Chair Cornell U. Coun.; vice chair adv. coun. Cornell U. Coll. Arts and Scis.; mem. adv. coun. Cornell U. Law Sch.; mem. exec. com. Westminster Sch. Alumni Assn.; nat. trustee YWCA; trustee Am. Hist. Assn. Mem. Assn. of Bar of City of N.Y. (young lawyers com. 1979-83, uniform laws com. 1984-86, corp. law dept. com. 1988-91, spl. com. on Asian affairs 1989-91, securities regulation com. 1996—), Fed. Bar Coun. (com. on 2d cir. cts. 1978-93, co-chair publs. com. 1993—, trustee 1996—), Am. Soc. Internat. Law, Sec. Ind. Assn. (fed. regulation com. 1990—, chmn. 1996—, lit. com. 1994—), Downtown Athletic Club, Univ. Club, Kennebunk River Club, Arundel Beach Club, Madison Beach Club, Chevy Chase Club. Republican. Episcopalian. Home: 122 E 82nd St New York NY 10028-0822 Office: Nikko Securities Co Internat 200 Liberty St Fl 29 New York NY 10281-1003

STEWART, CHARLES LESLIE, lawyer; b. Fayetteville, Ark., Aug. 12, 1919; s. Charles Leslie and Ruth (Want) S.; m. Edalee Esther Gastrock, Aug. 30, 1941; children: William Paul, Thomas Alan, Katherine Jean, Robert Edward. A.B., U. Ill., 1940; M.A., La. State U., 1941; student, George Washington U. Law Sch., 1944-45; J.D., U. Chgo., 1947. Bar: Ill. 1948, U.S. Supreme Ct. 1954. Economist, Dept. Agr., 1941-42; adminstrv. asst. OPA, 1942-43, Bd. Econ. Warfare, 1943; exec. dir. Chgo. div. ACLU, 1946-47; practiced law Chgo., 1948-91, Glencoe, Ill., 1991—; assoc. Mayer, Brown & Platt, Chgo., 1947-55, ptnr., 1956-67, 70-71, resident ptnr. charge European office, Paris, 1967-70; v.p., gen. counsel Hart Schaffner & Marx, Chgo., 1971-73, v.p., sec., gen. counsel, 1974-83; v.p., sec., gen. counsel Hartmarx Corp., Chgo., 1983-84, v.p., sec., sr. counsel, 1984, of counsel legal dept., 1985-89; arbitrator Mandatory Arbitration Program Cir. Ct., Cook County, Ill., 1990—; mem. Am. Law Inst., 1983-90. Mem. Glencoe (Ill.) Bd. Edn., 1965-66; mem. planning com. Corp. Counsel Inst., Northwestern U. Sch. Law and Ill. Inst. Continuing Legal Edn., 1981-84, vice-chmn., 1983, chmn., 1984; mem. Glencoe Union Ch. Served with OSS, AUS, 1943-45. Mem. ABA, Ill. State Bar Assn., Chgo. Bar Assn. (com. devel. of law 1977-91, vice chmn. 1984-85, chmn. 1985-86, corp. law com. 1981-91, corp. law depts. com. 1981-83, sr. lawyers com. 1987-92), Am. Soc. Corp. Secs. (adv. com. Chgo. regional group 1978-83, vice chmn. 1979-80, chmn. 1980-81, nat. dir. 1981-84, exec. com. 1983-84, corp. practices com. 1982-87, assoc. mem. 1986-91), Skokie Country Club, Delta Phi. Avocations: genealogy, history, bridge. Home and Office: 745 Vernon Ave Glencoe IL 60022-1562

STEWART, CHRISTINE SUSAN, Canadian government official; b. Jan. 3, 1941; d. Morris Alexander Leishman and Laura Anne Doherty; m. David Ian Stewart, Aug. 24, 1963; children: Douglas Alexander, John David, Catherine Anne. Ed., Neuchatel Jr. Coll., Switzerland, U. Toronto, Ont., Can. Nurse; mem. Ho. of Commons, 1988—, mem. standing com. for external affairs and internat. trade, assoc. critic for human rights; official opposition critic Can. Internat. Devel. Agy.; sec. state L.Am. and Africa Cabinet of Prime Min. Jean Chrétien, Ottawa, 1993—. Founding exec. dir. Horizons of Friendship. Liberal. Roman Catholic. Office: Parliament Bldgs, 484 Confederation Bldg, Ottawa, ON Canada K1A 0A6 Office: Fgn Affairs & Internat Trade, 125 Sussex Dr, Ottawa, ON Canada K1A 0G2

STEWART, CINDY KATHLEEN, school social worker, educator; b. Scottsburg, Ind., June 23, 1958; d. Gordon Lee and Velva Kathleen (Henry) S. BS in Social Work, Ball State U., 1980; MS in Social Work, U. Louisville, 1981; PhD in Human Scis., Walden U., 1992. Cert. social worker, Ky., clin. social worker, Ind.; lic. sch. social worker, Ky., Ga., Fla.; diplomate Am. Bd. Examiners in Clin. Social Work. Therapist Washington County Guidance Ctr., Salem, Ind., 1981-83; psychiat. social worker Madison (Ind.) State Hosp., 1983-85; sch. social worker Bullitt County day treatment program Bullitt County Pub. Schs., Shepherdsville, Ky., 1985-92; sch. social worker Hillsborough County Schs., Tampa, Fla., 1992—; prof. social work Lindsey Wilson Coll., Shepherdsville, Ky., 1991, U. Ky., Louisville, 1988-92; psychiat. social work cons. Ind. Rehab. Svcs., Indpls., 1984-85; ; instr. adult edn. Jefferson County Pub. Schs., Louisville, 1989-92; pvt. practice Price Counseling Assocs., New Albany, Ind., 1990; workshop facilitator dropout prevention Ashland Oil Co., 1989—; mem. foster care rev. bd. Jefferson County, 1988-92. Vol. Planned Parenthood Assn., Louisville, 1988—; student sponsor ARC, Shepherdsville, 1989-92. Mem. NASW, Phi Delta Kappa, Alpha Kappa Delta. Baptist. Avocations: modeling, ceramics, acting, baking, travel.

STEWART, CLINTON EUGENE, adult education educator; b. Copperas Cove, Tex., Nov. 7, 1927; s. Albert Clyde and Marjorie Lee (Jones) Stewart. BA, Baylor U., 1950, MS in Edn., 1951, MA in Biology, 1964, EdD, 1970. Cert. profl. supr., administr., supt., elem., prin., driver edn. tchr. Prof. edn. Howard Payne U., Brownwood, Tex.; dean Howard Payne U., Tex.; supt. Kopperl Independ Sch. Dist., Tex.; assoc. prof. edn. Sul Ross State U., Alpine, Tex. Lt. TNG, 1954. Mem. Phi Delta Kappa (pres. 1987), Kappa Delta Pi, Beta Beta Beta, Alpha Epsilon Delta, Alpha Chi.

STEWART, C(ORNELIUS) VAN LEUVEN, lawyer; b. Balt., Sept. 22, 1936; s. Charles Morton and Lillie Emerson (Van Leuven) S.; m. Clare Wright Horsley, June 18, 1960; children: Clare Winston, Lillie Elliotte, Jenett Ten Eyck (dec.). BA, Yale U., 1958; LLB, U. Va., 1961. Bar: Md. 1962, D.C. Bar 1982. Assoc. in law U. Calif. Law Sch., Berkeley, 1961-62; assoc. Venable, Baetjer & Howard, Balt., 1962-69, ptnr., 1970-91; ptnr. Stewart, Plant & Blumenthal, Balt., 1991—. Bd. dirs., past pres. Irvine Natural Sci. Ctr.; bd. overseers Balt. Sch. for the Arts; past bd. dirs. Pks. and People Found., Balt. Symphony Orch. Assn., Internat. Visitors Coun. of Balt., Roland Park Country Sch., Magic Me.; past pres. Md. Ballet Co., Met. Balt. Mental Health Assn. Mem. ABA, State Bar Assn., Balt. City Bar Assn., D.C. Bar Assn., Am. Coll. Trust and Estate Counsel (Md. chpt., state chair), Internat. Acad. of Estate and Trust Law, Balt. Estate Planning Coun. (pres. 1987). Republican. Episcopalian. Office: 7 Saint Paul St Ste 910 Baltimore MD 21202-1626

STEWART, DANIEL ROBERT, retired glass company executive; b. New Kensington, Pa., July 25, 1938; s. Daniel Joseph and Sarah Madeline (Caldwell) S.; m. Marianne Colesar, Aug. 27, 1960; children—Karen Anne, Daniel John. B.S., Pa. State U., 1960, M.S., 1962, Ph.D., 1964. Research scientist Owens-Ill., Inc., Toledo, 1964-66; chief glass sci. sect. Owens-Ill., Inc., 1967-69, dir. glass and ceramic research, 1970-71, dir. corporate research labs., 1972-73, v.p. corporate staff, dir. glass and ceramic tech., 1973-83; pres. Dura Temp Corp., Holland, Ohio, 1983-94; ret., 1994; U.S. rep. steering com. Internat. Congress Glass, 1980-83. Ch. treas. Ch. of the Nazarene, 1966-83; mem. local com. Boy Scouts Am., 1975-87. PPG fellow, 1961-64. Fellow Am. Ceramic Soc. (past chmn. glass div.); mem. Nat. Inst. Ceramic Engrs. (profl. achievement in ceramic engring. award 1974), Soc. Glass Tech., Sigma Xi. Republican. Patentee in field.

STEWART, DAVID MARSHALL, librarian; b. Nashville, Aug. 1, 1916; s. David and Mary (Marshall) S.; m. Gladys Carroll, June 9, 1947; 1 son, James Marshall. B.A., Bethel Coll., 1938; B.S. in L.S, George Peabody Coll., 1939. Circulation asst. Vanderbilt U. Library, 1938-39; county librarian Ark. Library Commn., 1939-40; Tenn. supr. WPA library service projects, 1940-42; librarian Memphis State U., 1942-46; spl. asst. to chief card div. Library of Congress, Washington, 1947; librarian CIA, Washington, 1948-60; chief librarian Nashville Pub. Library, 1960-85; Instr. Peabody Library Sch., 1966-80. Bd. dirs. Council Community Agys., Nashville, Middle-East Tenn. Arthritis Found. (v.p. 1965), Friends Chamber Music Nashville, Travelers Aid Nashville. Served to lt. comdr. USNR, 1942-46. Mem. ALA, Tenn. Library Assn. (chmn. legislative com. 1961-65, v.p. 1965, pres. 1966, Honor award, 1983), Southeastern Library Assn., Pub. Library Assn. Am. (chmn. standards com. 1964-65, pres. 1966-67), Alumni Assn. Bethel Coll. (dir., Disting. Alumni award 1992). Democrat. Mem. Ch. of Christ. Clubs: Kiwanian. (Nashville), Coffee House (Nashville). Home: 6342 Torrington Rd Nashville TN 37205-3157

STEWART, DEBRA WEHRLE, university dean and official, educator; b. Petersburg, Va., May 22, 1943. BA in Philosophy and Polit. Sci., Marquette U., 1965; MA in Govt., U. Md., 1967; PhD in Polit. Sci., U. N.C., 1975. Instr. polit. sci. European divsn. U. Md., Nuremberg, Germany, 1967-69; instr. polit. sci. and pub. adminstrn. N.C. State U., Raleigh, 1974-75, asst. prof., 1975-78, assoc. prof., 1979-83, prof., 1984—, acting dir. MPA program, 1978, assoc. dean Grad. Sch., 1983-86, interim vice provost and dean Grad. Sch., 1986-88, dean Grad. Sch., 1988—, vice provost Grad. Sch., 1995—; interim chancellor U. N.C., Greensboro, 1994; mem. com. on assessment of rsch. doctorate NRC, 1992—; mem. Grad. Record Exam. Bd., 1992—, chmn.-elect, 1994-95, chmn., 1995-96; bd. dirs. Coun. Grad. Schs., 1990—, chmn.-elect, 1992-93, chmn., 1993-94; mem. Test English as Fgn. Lang. Bd., 1992-95; councilor Oak Ridge (Tenn.) Assoc. Univs., 1988-92, bd. dirs., 1993—; mem. exec. com. Coun. So. Grad. Schs., 1989-91; trustee Triangle U. Ctr. for Advanced Studies, 1989—. Author: The Women's Movement in Community Politics: The Role of Local Commissions on the Status of Women, 1980, (with G. David Garson) Organizational Behavior and Public Management, 1983, 2d edit. (with Vasu and Garson), 1990; editor: Women in Local Politics, 1980; mem. editl. bd. Rev. Pub. Pres. Adminstrn., 1981-89, Annals Pub. Adminstrn., 1982-84, Women and Politics, 1980-88, Politics and Policy, 1983-86; contbr. articles to profl. jours., chpts. to books. Recipient edn. award YWCA Acad. Women, 1988;. Mem. Nat. Assn. State Univs. and Land-Grant Colls. (bd. dirs. 1992-94, exec. com. coun. on rsch. policy and grad. edn. 1989-92, chmn. 1990-91), Am. Soc. for Pub. Adminstrn. (com. on status of women in pub. adminstrn. 1976-78, com. on profl. stds. and ethics 1980-89, chmn. com. on whistle blowing and dissent channels of profl. stds. and ethics com. 1985-86, Burchfield award 1976), So. Polit. Sci. Assn. (nominating com. 1978, coord. pub. adminstrn. sect. 1979), Women's Forum N.C., Phi Kappa Phi, Pi Sigma Alpha, Pi Alpha Alpha. Office: NC State U Grad Sch 104 Peele Hall Box 7102 Raleigh NC 27695-7102*

STEWART, DORIS MAE, biology educator; b. Sandsprings, Mont., Dec. 12, 1927; d. Virgil E. and Violet M. (Weaver) S.; m. Felix Loren Powell, Oct. 8, 1956; children: Leslie, Loren. BS, Coll. Puget Sound, 1948, MS, 1949; PhD, U. Wash., 1953. Instr. U. Mont., Missoula, 1954-56, asst. prof., 1956-57; asst. prof. U. Puget Sound, Tacoma, 1957-58; head sci. dept. Am. Kiz Lisesi, Istanbul, Turkey, 1958-62; rsch. asst. prof. U. Wash., Seattle, 1963-67, rsch. assoc. prof., 1967-68; assoc. prof. Cen. Mich. U., Mt. Pleasant, 1970-72; assoc. prof. U. Balt., 1973-81, prof., 1981-95, prof. emeritus, 1995—. Contbr. numerous articles to profl. jours. Mem. Am. Physiol. Soc., Sigma Xi. Home: 1103 Frederick Rd Baltimore MD 21228-5032

STEWART, DOROTHY K., educator, librarian; b. Bristol, Conn., Sept. 28, 1928; d. Robert and Anna Esther (Schwirtz) Konopask; m. David Benjamin Stewart, Sept. 27, 1952 (div. Nov. 1979); children: Douglas Neil, Diane Alison. BA in Romance Langs. and Lit. cum laude, Boston U., 1950; MSLS, Cath. U. Am., 1959. Children's libr. Brookline (Mass.) Pub. Libr., 1953-55, Takoma Park (Md.) Libr., 1955-57; reference libr. U.S. Geol. Survey, 1961; libr. Washington Internat. Sch., 1979-80, Office Sea Grant NOAA, Rockville, Md., 1980-82; info. specialist Life Ring, Inc., Silver Spring, Md., 1983-84; pub. svc. libr. Urban Inst., Washington, 1984-85; user svcs. coord. ERIC Clearinghouse on Tchg. and Tchr. Edn., Washington, 1985-97; ret., 1997. Active, past pres. PTA, Rockville, Md., 1973-78; chmn., mem. com. Potomac (Md.) Libr. Adv. Com., 1975-85. Mem. Spl. Librs. Assn., D.C. Libr. Assn., Capital PC User Group, French lang. clubs, Phi Beta Kappa, Beta Phi Mu. Democrat. Avocations: travel, hiking, birding, microcomputers.

STEWART, DUNCAN JAMES, lawyer; b. Amsterdam, N.Y., Apr. 24, 1939; s. William James and Maybelle Veronica (Matthews) S.; m. Susan Cobb Stewart, June 18, 1966; children: Benjamin Ross, Matthew Schuyler. AB, Cornell U., 1961, LLB, 1964. Bar: N.Y. 1964, U.S. Dist. C.t (no. dist.) N.Y. 1964. Assoc. Willkie Farr & Gallagher, N.Y.C., 1964, 67-72, ptnr., 1973—. Trustee Citizens Budget Commn., N.Y.; bd. dirs. Prospect Park Alliance, Bklyn., Network for Women's Svcs., N.Y. Mem. ABA, N.Y. State Bar Assn., Assn. of Bar of City of N.Y., Cornell Club. Democrat. Presbyterian. Home: 264 Berkeley Pl Brooklyn NY 11217-3904 Office: Willkie Farr & Gallagher 1 CitiCorp Ctr 153 E 53rd St New York NY 10022-4611

STEWART, EDGAR ALLEN, lawyer; b. Selma, Ala., Sept. 1, 1909; s. Edgar A. and Irma (Mallory) S.; m. Mamie V. Packer, Oct. 15, 1938; children: Edgar Allen III (dec.), Martha M. (Mrs. Edward B. Crosland, Jr.). B.A., U. South, 1929; LL.B., U. Ala., 1932. Bar: Ala. 1932. Since practiced Selma; sr. partner Reeves & Stewart, 1947-92; spl. agt. FBI, 1942-45; ret., 1993. Contbr. articles to profl. jours. Trustee Selma Schs., 1956-67; bd. dirs., pres. Selma YMCA, 1952-68; bd. dirs. Indsl. Devel. Bd., Selma, YMCA Blue Ridge (N.C.) Assembly, 1983-85. Fellow Am. Coll. Trial Lawyers; mem. ABA, Ala. Bar Commn. (dir. 1970-76), Am. Coll. Probate Counsel, Internat. Assn. Ins. Counsel, Nat. Assn. R.R. Counsel, Am. Counsel Assn. (bd. dirs. Presbyn. Retirement Corp. 1993), Am. Judicature Soc., Phi Beta Kappa, Phi Delta Theta, Phi Delta Phi. Home: 500 Spanish Fort Blvd Apt 356 Spanish Fort AL 36527-5012 Office: PO Box 457 Selma AL 36702-0457

STEWART, FRANK MAURICE, JR., federal agency administrator; b. Okalona, Miss., Apr. 1, 1939; s. Frank Maurice Stewart and Henryne Annette (Walker) Goode; m. Regina Diane Mosley, Dec. 26, 1964; children: Lisa Ann, Dana Joy. BA, Wesleyan U., 1961, MA in Teaching, 1963, diploma further study, 1963; postgrad., Am. U., 1982-84. Dir. urban edn. corps N.J. State Dept. Edn., Trenton, 1969-70; dir. urban teaching intern program Sch. Edn. Rutgers U., New Brunswick, N.J., 1970-71; staff asst. White House Conf. on Aging, Washington, 1971-73; chief program devel. U.S. Office of Equal Edn. Opportunity, Washington, 1973-74; chief policy analysis U.S. Adminstrn. on Aging, Washington, 1974-75; asst. exec. sec. U.S. HEW, Washington, 1975-77; dir. govt. programs U.S. Dept. Energy, Washington, 1977-80, dir. instnl. conservation programs, 1980-84, dir. state and local assistance programs, 1984-90, dep. asst. sec. for tech. and fin. assistance, 1990-93; acting asst. sec. for energy efficiency and renewable energy, 1993-94; mgr. Golden (Colo.) Field Office, U.S. Dept. Energy, 1994—; bd. dirs. Renewable Energy for African Devel., 1992-94; mem. U.S. Presdl. Del. on Sustainable Energy Devel. to South Africa, 1995, U.S. Del. to African-African-Am. Summit, Dakar, Senegal, 1995. Recipient Svc. Recognition award Assn. Phys. Plant Adminstrs., Washington, 1982, Svc. Appreciation award Nat. Assn. State Energy Officials, Washington, 1987, Midwest Rsch. Inst., 1996; named Energy Exec. of Yr. Assn. Energy Engrs., Atlanta, 1988. Mem. Sr. Execs. Assn. Episcopalian. Home: 202 S Madison St Denver CO 80206 Office: US Dept Energy Field Office 1617 Cole Blvd Golden CO 80401-3305

STEWART, GEORGE RAY, librarian; b. Birmingham, Ala., Aug. 19, 1944; s. DeWitt and Ann (McCain) S.; m. Nancy Ann Norton, June 5, 1964; children: Steven Ray, Jeffery Alan. B.A., Samford U., Birmingham, 1966, M.A., 1967; M.A., Emory U., 1971. Mem. staff Birmingham Pub. Libr., 1960—, assoc. dir., 1970-76, dir., 1976-93; system dir., 1993—; part-time instr. Grad. Sch. Libr. Svc. U. Ala.; bd. dirs. Southeastern Library Network, Inc., 1986-88. Editor: Birmingham Pub. Library Press. Bd. dirs. Red Mountain Mus., 1972-79, Literacy Coun. Ctrl. Ala., 1990-94; bd. dirs. Indsl. Health Coun., Birmingham, 1972-85, sec., 1979-81, pres. bd. dirs. 1982, 83.

Mem. ALA, Southeastern Libr. Assn. (treas. 1985-86, v.p. 1986-88, pres. 1989-90), Ala. Libr. Assn. (scholarship 1968, pres. 1976), Ala. Hist. Assn., Birmingham Hist. Assn. Office: Birmingham-Jefferson County Libr System 2100 Park Pl Birmingham AL 35203-2744

STEWART, GEORGE TAYLOR, insurance executive; b. N.Y.C., Dec. 29, 1924; s. Fargo Calvin and Berthe Adelle (Pelleton) S.; m. Bonnie Elizabeth Myers, Sept. 14, 1946; children: Diane Barbara Stewart Carrington, Susan Gail Stewart Dupuis. A.B., Wesleyan U., Conn., 1947; LHD (hon.), Lynchburg Coll., 1994. Analyst Geyer & Co., Inc., 1948-54, Shelby Cullom Davis & Co., 1954-56; v.p. Blyth & Co., Inc., N.Y.C., 1956-65; chmn., chief exec. officer 1st Colony Life Ins. Co., Lynchburg, Va., 1965-92, chmn. fin. com., 1992—; bd. dirs. Am. Mayflower Life Ins. Co., N.Y.; chmn. Greater Lyunchburg Cmty. Trust. Author: Investing in American Business, 1964. Trustee Lynchburg Coll., Jefferson's Poplar Forest, founder. Recipient Lynchburg Bi-Centennial award, 1976, Lynchburg Pro Opera Civica award, 1982, award Navy League, 1981, Outstanding Businessman award Lynchburg Coll. Bus. Sch., 1982. Mem. N.Y. Acad. Scis., Lynchburg C. of C. (pres.), Thomas Jefferson Commemoration Commn. (presdl. apptd.), N.Y. Soc. Security Analysts, Met. Club (N.Y.C.), City Midday-Drug and Chem. Club (N.Y.C.), Calif. Club (L.A.), Boonsboro Country Club of Lynchburg (bd. dirs.), Piedmont Club, Waterfront Club. Republican. Presbyterian (elder). Office: First Colony Life Ins Co PO Box 1280 Lynchburg VA 24505-1280

STEWART, GORDON CURRAN, insurance information association executive; b. Chgo., July 22, 1939; s. Henry Stewart and Evangeline (Williams) Bolton; m. Elizabeth Knorr, June 19, 1965 (div. 1968); m. Zanne Early, Dec. 20, 1995. BA, Oberlin Coll., 1960; MA, U. Chgo., 1962; student, U. Vienna, Austria, 1963; MFA, Yale U., 1967. Instr. Amherst (Mass.) Coll., 1967-68; dir. Bus. Comm. for Arts, N.Y.C., 1969-71; exec. asst. Mayor of N.Y.C., 1971-73; dir., writer N.Y.C., L.A., U.K., 1973-78; dep. chief speechwriter President of U.S., Washington, 1978-81; instr. Bus. and Govt. Acad. forums, U.S and fgn. countries, 1981-82; v.p. AMSE, N.Y.C., 1982-89; exec. v.p. Ins. Info. Inst., N.Y.C., 1989-91, pres., 1991—; cons. Am. Bus. Conf., Washington, 1982-89, Internat. Commn. for Ctrl. Am., Washington, 1986-88, Coun. on Competitiveness, Washington, 1987-88, Def. Sci. Bd., Washington, 1988-89. Writer films: The Store, 1978, Joey, 1978, Gallery, 1978; dir. (play) The Elephant Man (1st U.S. prodn.), 1977, Jesse, 1975, Cowboy Mouth, 1976, Sleep, 1977, (films) The Blazers, 1975; condr. Beggar's Opera, 1969, West Side Story, 1970. Dir. N.Y. Urban Coalition, N.Y.C., 1984-88; dir. policy Samuels for Gov., N.Y., 1974; speechwriter numerous dem. campaigns, 1974-81; mem. fin. coun. Dem. Nat. Com., 1984-88; mem. adv. coun. Dem. Leadership Coun., 1984-90. Woodrow Wilson fellow Woodrow Wilson Found., 1961. Mem. Writers Guild Am. (west), Judson Welliver Soc. of Chief Presdl. Speechwriters (sec.-treas.), Coun. Fgn. Rels., Century Assn., Yale Club. Avocations: politics, music.

STEWART, GREGORY WALLACE, physician; b. Balt., July 8, 1961; s. Don Milton and Martha (Davis) S.; married (div.); 1 child, Lauren Elizabeth; m. Bonnie Marie Johnson, June 8, 1991; children: Tess Marie, Shaid Michael. BS in Biology, Chemistry and Para-Med. Sports Therapy, Houston Baptist U., 1982; MD, U. Tex. Med. Branch Sch. of Medicine, 1986. Diplomate Am. Bd. Physical Medicine and Rehab. Resident in physical medicine and rehab. La. State U./Charity Hosp. in New Orleans, 1986-90; instr. and asst. residency Sect. Phys. Medicine and Rehab. La. State U. Sch. Medicine in New Orleans, 1990-92; clin. asst. prof. Dept. Orthopaedics Tulane U. Sch. Medicine, 1990-95; asst. prof. and residency program dir. Sect. of Phys. Medicine La. State U. Sch. Medicine in New Orleans, 1992-95; assoc. prof. orthopedics Tulane U. Sch. Medicine, 1995—, chief divsn. phys. medicine and rehab., 1995—; team physician New Orleans Night Arena Football Team, 1991-92, Tulane U., 1990—, Hahnville H.S., 1987—; physician Ballet Hysell, New Orleans; coord. sports medicine St. Charles and Plaquemines Parish Sch. Dists.; assoc. coord. sports medicine St. Bernard and Orleans Parish Sch. Dists.; mem. adv. coun. La. Sports Medicine and Safety; mem. U.S. Olympic Track and Field Trials Sports Medicine Staff, 1992; mem. sports medicine organizing com. NCAA Track and Field Championships, 1993. Contbr. numerous articles to med. jours. mem., chmn. task force on disabling violence La. Adv. Coun. on Disability Prevention, 1990-93, mem. com. on prevention of secondary disabilties; med. cons. Weiss Rehab. Ctr.; chmn. divsn. of rehab. svcs. head injury tech. assistance com. State of La.; mem. adv. com. for phys. therapy asst. program Delgado C.C.; reviewer Medicine and Sci. in Sports and Exercise Jour. of Orthopaedic and Sports Physical Therapy; abstract reviewer Nat. Head Injury Found.; grant reviewer Nat. Inst. Disability Rsch. and Rehab. Recipient Study of Personal Care Attendants for Indigent Quadriplegics grant Am. Assn. of Spinal Cord Injury Psychologists and Social Workers, 1991-93, Rehab. Long Term Tng. -Rehab. Medicine grant Rehab. Svcs. Adminstrn., 1993-95, La. Disability Prevention Program grant Sports Injury Surveillance in La., 1993-94. Fellow Am. Coll. Sports Medicine; mem. AMA, Am. Acad. Phys. Medicine and Rehab., Am. Congress Rehab. Medicine, Nat. Athletic Trainers Assn., S.E. Athletic Trainers Assn., La. State Med. Soc., La. Athletic Trainers Assn., Orleans Parish Med. Soc., La. Sports Medicine Soc. (edn. chmn. 1994—). Avocations: gardening, genealogy. Home: 4905 Clearlake Dr Metairie LA 70006-1112 Office: Dept Orthopaedics SL32 1430 Tulane Ave New Orleans LA 70112-2699

STEWART, GUY HARRY, university dean emeritus, journalism educator; b. Keyser, W.Va., Feb. 12, 1924; s. Thomas R. and Martha (Mills) S.; m. Patricia Ann Groves, Dec. 27, 1948; children: Diane, Thomas, Jeffrey. B.S.J., W.Va. U., 1948, M.A., 1949; Ph.D., U. Ill., 1957. Reporter Cumberland (Md.) Evening Times, 1941-43, Mineral Daily News-Tribune, Keyser, 1941-43; asst. editor W.Va. U., Morgantown, 1949-50, dir. grad. studies and journalism, 1960-69, dean Sch. Journalism, 1969-89; dir. pub. rels., prof. Tenn. Tech. U., Cookeville, 1950-60. Author: A Touch of Charisma, 1969. Served as ensign USNR, 1944-46, PTO. Recipient P.I. Reed Achievement award W.Va. U. Journalism ALumni Assn., 1977; named to Keyser High Sch. Legion of Honor, 1991; Guy H. Stewart Journalism Endowment Fund named in his honor. Mem. W.Va. Press Assn. (life), Assn. Edn. in Journalism and Mass Communications, Rotary (dist. gov. 1983-84), Kappa Tau Alpha (nat. pres. 1980, Top Adviser award 1987). Democrat. Methodist. Home: 525 Pocahontas Ave Morgantown WV 26505-2274

STEWART, HAROLD BROWN, biochemist; b. Chatham, Ont., Can., Mar. 9, 1921; s. John Craig and Margaret Gertrude (Brown) S.; m. Audrey Pauline Blake, Oct. 14, 1950; 1 dau., Ann Margaret. M.D., U. Toronto, 1944, Ph.D., 1950; Ph.D., Cambridge (Eng.) U., 1955. Prof. biochemistry U. Western Ont., London, 1960—; chmn. dept. biochemistry U. Western Ont., 1964-72, dean grad. studies, 1972-86, prof. emeritus, 1986—; Med. Research Council Can. vis. scientist dept. biochemistry U. Cambridge, Eng., 1971-72. Contbr. articles in biochemistry to sci. jours. Served with Royal Canadian Navy, 1945-46. Mem. Canadian, U.K. biochem. socs., Canadian Physiol. Soc., Am. Soc. Biochemistry and Molecular Biology, Coll. Physicians and Surgeons of Ont. Home: 118 Baseline Rd E, London, ON Canada N6C 2N8

STEWART, HAROLD LEROY, pathologist, educator, cancer investigator; b. Houtzdale, Pa., Aug. 6, 1899; s. Alexander and Lillie (Cox) S.; m. Cecelia Eleanor Finn, Sept. 30, 1929; children: Robert Campbell, Janet Eileen. Student, U. Pa., 1919-20, Dickinson Coll., 1921-22; M.D., Jefferson Med. Coll., 1926; grad., Army Med. Sch., Washington, 1929; research fellow, Jefferson Med. Coll., 1929-30, Harvard, 1937-39; Med. Sc.D. (hon.), Jefferson Med. Coll., 1964; D.Medicine and Surgery (hon.), U. Perugia, 1965, U. Turku, Finland, 1970; Doctor (hon.), Kagawa (Japan) Med. Sch., 1992. Diplomate Am. Bd. Pathology, Pan Am. Med. Assn. Intern Fitzimmons Gen. Hosp., Denver, 1926-27; instr. to asst. prof. pathology Jefferson Med. Coll., 1930-37; asst. pathologist Jefferson Med. Coll. Hosp., Phila. Gen. Hosp., 1929-37; pathologist Office Cancer Investigations Harvard, USPHS, 1937-39; chief lab. pathology Nat. Cancer Inst., USPHS, Bethesda, Md., 1939-69; chief pathologic anatomy dept. clin. ctr. NIH, 1954-69; organizer Registry Exptl. Cancers, 1970—, Sci. emeritus, 1976—; prin. investigator, head WHO Collaborating Centre for Rsch. on Tumors Lab. Animals, 1976-96; clin. prof. pathology Georgetown U., 1965—; Cons. FDA, 1969-71, Nat. Cancer Inst., 1970-76, Armed Forces Inst. Pathology, 1950—; cons., mem. study groups WHO, 1957-81, mem. expert adv. panel cancer, 1957-81; Mem. subcom. oncology NRC, 1947-65, mem. com. pathology, 1958-66, com. cancer diagnosis and therapy, 1951-57, mem. com. animal models and genetic stocks, 1972-75, chmn. com. histologic classification Lab. Animal Tumors, 1975-79; chmn. subcom. classification rat liver tumors NRC (Lab. Animal Tumors), 1976-79; chmn. U.S.A. Com. Internat. Coun. Socs. Pathology, 1957-62, 69-75; chmn. U.S. nat. com. Internat. Union Against Cancer, 1953-59, U.S. del., 1952-74; Mem. adv. bd. Leonard Wood Meml., 1961-66; mem. com. to advance world-wide fight against cancer Am. Cancer Soc., 1963-76; mem. med. rsch. coun. Referees, New Zealand, 1987. Mem. editoral bd. Cancer Rsch., 1941-49, A.M.A. Archives of Pathology, 1957-62, Jour. Toxicology Pathology, 1988; editorial adviser Jour. Nat. Cancer Inst, 1947-56; contbr. articles to profl. jours. Trustee Thomas Jefferson U., Phila., 1969-72. Served as pvt. USMC, 1918-19; lt. M.C. U.S. Army, 1926-29; from maj. to lt. col. M.C. AUS, 1942-46. Recipient Lucy Wortham James award James Ewing Soc., 1967, Alumni Achievement award Jefferson Med. Coll., 1966, Disting. Svc. award HEW, 1966, Honors award NIH, The Dirs. award NIH, 1988, Dean's medal Jefferson Med. Coll., 1994; Dedication Jour. Exptl. Pathology, Vol. 1, No. 2, 1987, Harold L. Stewart Fund for Exptl. Pathology and Harold L. Stewart Lectureship established at Uniformed Svcs. U. of Health Scis., Bethesda, Md., 1986; honored by dedication in two books, Harold L. Stewart Pathology award est. Jefferson Med. Coll., 1994. Mem. Soc. Clin. Pathologists (Ward Burdick award 1957), Am. Assn. Cancer Rsch. (pres. 1958-59), Am. Soc. Exptl. Pathology (hon., pres. 1995), Am. Assn. Pathologists (Gold-headed Cane award 1978), Coll. Am. Pathologists, Md. Soc. Pathologists (pres. 1950-51), Washington Soc. Pathologists (sec.-treas. 1947-51), Internat. Acad. Pathology (pres. 1953-55, F.K. Mostofi award 1976), Internat. Union Against Cancer (exec. com. 1952-70, v.p. 1962), Mass. Med. Soc., Internat. Coun. Socs. Pathology (pres. 1962), Internat. Soc. Geog. Pathology, Colegio Anatomico Brasilerio (hon.), Soc. Italiana di Cancerologia (hon.), Inst. Nat. de Cancerologia Mex. (hon.), Soc. Columbiana de Patologia (hon.), Soc. Belge d' Anatomie Pathologique (hon.), Soc. Peruana Cancerologia (hon.), Soc. Cryobiology, Soc. Toxicologic Pathologists (hon.), Japanese Cancer Soc. (hon.), Basic Found. Internat. Inst of Immanopathology Clin. Ctr. Humablt U., Berlin (hon. sci. dir.), Purdy Stout Surg. Pathology Soc. (hon.), others. Home: 119 S Adams St Rockville MD 20850-2315

STEWART, HAROLD SANFORD, real estate investment and supply executive; b. Cookeville, Tenn., Nov. 22, 1949; s. Willie Sanford and Margaret Eula (Wassom) S.; m. Diana Gail Law, May 3, 1968; children: Rhonda Gail, Scott Harold. Diploma, Nashville Vocat.-Tech. Sch., 1969. Cert. ACCA-EPIC instr., Air Conditioning Contractors of Am.; lic. real estate person, Ky. Sales and part mgr. Scotsman Supply Co., Nashville, 1967-73; salesman Brock-McVey Supply Co., Bowling Green, Ky., 1973-76; pres., gen. mgr. Eds Supply Co., Bowling Green, 1976-79, Nelsco Supply Co., Bowling Green, 1979-80; pres. Air Supply Co., Inc., Bowling Green, 1980-88; sales mgr. One Stop Supply, Inc., Bowling Green, 1988-89; pres. Bilt-Rite Constrn., Inc., Bowling Green, 1989-92; sec., treas. K&H Enterprises, Inc., Bowling Green, 1989-93; pres., gen. mgr. H.S. Properties, Bowling Green, Ky., 1989—, Stewart Supply, Inc. d/b/a/ Johnstone Supply, Bowling Green, 1993—; chmn. Ky. State Vocat. HVAC Craft Com., Frankfort, 1987, Bowling Green Vocat. HVAC Craft Com., 1980-88; nat. adv. coun. Thermaflex Mfg. Co., Kansas City, Mo., 1986-87. City clk. and trustee City of Plum Springs, Ky., 1975-79; treas. Bowling Green Civitan Club, 1973-78; trustee Jackson Grove Bapt. Ch., Bowling Green, 1975-86. Named Civitan of Yr., Bowling Green Club, 1973-75, Col., Hon. Order of Ky. Cols. Mem. Masons, Optimist. Avocations: reading, computers, tennis, jogging. Home: 536 Detour Rd Bowling Green KY 42101-6501 Office: 300 W 6th St Bowling Green KY 42101-1878

STEWART, HARRIS BATES, JR., oceanographer; b. Auburn, N.Y., Sept. 19, 1922; s. Harris B. and Mildred (Woodruff) S.; m. Elise Bennett Cunningham, Feb. 21, 1959; children: Dorothy Cunningham, Harry Hasburgh; 2d m. Louise Conant Thompson, Dec. 22, 1988. Grad., Phillips Exeter Acad., 1941; AB, Princeton, 1948; MS, Scripps Instn. Oceanography, U. Calif., 1952, PhD, 1956. Hydrographic engr. U.S. Navy Hydrographic Office expdn. to, Persian Gulf, 1948-49; instr. Hotchkiss Sch., 1949-51; research asst. Scripps Instn. Oceanography, 1951-56; diving geologist, project mgr. Geol. Diving Cons., Inc., San Diego, 1953-57; chief oceanographer U.S. Coast & Geodetic Survey, 1957-65, dept. asst. dir., 1962-65; dir. Inst. Oceanography, Environmental Sci. Services Adminstrn., U.S. Dept. Commerce, 1965-69; dir. Atlantic Oceanographic and Meteorol. Labs., NOAA, 1969-78, cons., 1978-80; prof. marine sci., dir. Center for Marine Studies, Old Dominion U., Norfolk, Va., 1980-85; adj. prof. dept. oceanography Old Dominion U., 1986—; dir. S.E. Bank of Dadeland; chmn. Fla. Commn. Marine Sci. and Tech.; mem. exec. com., earth scis. div. Nat. Acad. Scis.; chmn. adv. bd. Nat. Oceanographic Data Center, 1965-66; chmn. survey panel interagy. com. oceanography Fed. Council Sci. and Tech., 1959-67; chmn. adv. com. underseas features U.S. Bd. Geog. Names, 1964-67; mem. sci. party No. Holiday Expdn., 1951; Capricorn Expdn., 1952-53; chief scientist Explorer Oceanographic Expdn., 1960, Pioneer Indian Ocean Expdn., 1964, Discoverer Expdn., 1968, NOAA-Carib Expdn., 1972, Researcher Expdn., 1975; mem. U.S. delegation Intergovtl. Oceanographic Commn., 1961-65; mem. Gov. Calif. Adv. Commn. Marine Resources; chmn. adv. council Dept. Geol. and Geophys. Scis. Princeton; v.p. Dade Marine Inst., 1976-77, pres., 1977-79; trustee, mem. exec. com. Assoc. Marine Insts.; mem. Fisheries Mgmt. Adv. Council Va. Marine Resources Commn., 1984-85; vice chmn. adv. council Univ. Nat. Oceanographic Lab. System, 1983-85; U.S. nat. assoc. to intergovtl. oceanographic commn. UNESCO program for Caribbean, 1964-89, vice chmn., 1974. Author: The Global Sea, 1963, Deep Challenge, 1966, The Id of the Squid, 1970, Challenger Sketchbook, 1972, No Dinosaurs on the Ark, 1988, Grungy George and Sloppy Sally, 1993, Injections of Hospital Humor, 1996, Man Bites Doggerel, 1997. Bd. dirs. Vanguard Sch., Miami, 1974-76; trustee Metro Zoo, Miami, 1991—. Served as pilot USAAF, 1942-46, PTO. Decorated comendador Almirante Padilla (Colombia); recipient Meritorious award Dept. Commerce, 1960, Exceptional Service award, 1965. Fellow AAAS, Geol. Soc. Am., Nat. Tropical Bot. Gardens, Marine Tech. Soc. (v.p.); mem. Fla. Acad. Scis. (pres. 1978-79), Va. Acad. Sci., Am. Geophys. Union, Internat. Oceanographic Found. (v.p. 1974-80), Zool. Soc. Fla. (pres. 1970-73), Maine Hist. Soc., Marine Hist. Assn., Cape Ann Hist. Assn., Marine Coun. (Miami), Explorers Club (N.Y.), Prouts Neck (Maine) Yacht Club, Cosmos Club (D.C.), Club Pelican Bay (Naples, Fla.). Presbyterian. Home (summer): 11 Atlantic Dr Scarborough ME 04074-8667 Home (winter): 720 Shadow Lake Ln Naples FL 34108-8500

STEWART, HARRY A., lawyer; b. Daytona Beach, Fla., Aug. 7, 1940. BSBA, U. Fla., 1966, JD, 1973. Bar: Fla. 1974, U.S. Dist. Ct. (mid. dist.) Fla. 1974, U.S. Dist. Ct. (so. dist.) Fla. 1976, U.S. Ct. Appeals (5th cir.) 1974, U.S. Ct. Appeals (11th cir.) 1981, U.S. Supreme Ct. 1980. County atty. Broward County, Fla., 1978-84, Orange County, Fla., 1984-91; ptnr. Akerman, Senterfitt & Eidson, P.A., Orlando, Fla.; pres. Fla. Assn. County Attys., 1981-82, 89-91. Mem. ABA (natural resources law sect.), The Fla. Bar (govt. law and environ. law sects., chmn. local govt. law sect. 1981-82). Office: Akerman Senterfitt & Eidson PA PO Box 231 255 S Orange Ave Orlando FL 32801-3424

STEWART, HOMER JOSEPH, engineering educator; b. Elba, Mich., Aug. 15, 1915; s. Earl Arthur and Alta Fern (Stanley) S.; m. Frieda Klassen, June 15, 1940; children—Robert Joseph, Katherine Stanley, Barbara Ellen. Student, U. Dubuque, 1932-33; B in Aero. Engring., U. Minn., 1936; PhD, Calif. Inst. Tech., 1940. Faculty Jet Propulsion Lab. Calif. Inst. Tech., Pasadena, 1938—, prof. aeros., 1949-80, prof. emeritus, 1980—, chief research analysis sect., 1945-56, chief Liquid Propulsion Systems div., 1956-58, spl. asst. to dir., 1960-62, chief Advanced Studies Office, 1963-67, advanced studies adviser, 1967-76; dir. Sargent Industries, Inc., 1964-79, Office Program Planning and Evaluation, NASA, 1958-60; mem. tech. adv. bd. Aerojet-Gen. Corp., 1956-58, 61-70; mem. tech. evaluation group guided missile com. Research and Devel. Bd., 1948-50, chmn., 1951; mem. sci. adv. bd. USAF, 1949-56, 1959-64; mem. sci. adv. com. Ballistics Research Lab., 1959-69, 73-77. Author: Kinematics and Dynamics of Fluid Flow, sect. VI Handbook of Meteorology, 1945; Contbr. articles to tech. jours. Recipient Outstanding Achievement award U. Minn., 1954, NASA Exceptional Service medal, 1970, I.B. Laskowitz award N.Y. Acad. Scis., 1985. Fellow AIAA; mem. Am. Meteorol. Soc., Internat. Acad. Astronautics, Sigma Xi, Tau Beta Pi. Home: 2393 Tanoble Dr Altadena CA 91001-2729 Office: Aerospace Dept Calif Inst Tech Pasadena CA 91125

STEWART, ISAAC DANIEL, JR., judge; b. Salt Lake City, Nov. 21, 1932; s. Isaac Daniel and Orabelle (Iverson) S.; m. Elizabeth Bryan, Sept. 10, 1959; children: Elizabeth Ann, Shannon. BA with high honors, U. Utah, 1959, JD with high honors, 1962. Bar: Utah 1962, U.S. Dist. Ct. Utah 1962, U.S. Ct. Appeals (10th cir.) 1962, U.S. Ct. Appeals (4th cir.) 1963, U.S. Ct. Appeals (9th cir.) 1964, U.S. Ct. Appeals (8th cir.) 1965, U.S. Supreme Ct. 1965. Atty. antitrust divsn. Dept. Justice, Washington, 1962-65; asst. prof., then assoc. prof. U. Utah Coll. Law, 1965-70; ptnr. Jones, Waldo, Holbrook & McDonough, Salt Lake City, 1970-79; assoc. chief justice Utah Supreme Ct., 1979—, 1986-88, 94—; lectr. in field; mem. Utah Bd. Oil, Gas and Mining, 1976-78, chmn., 1977-78; Utah rep. Interstate Oil Compact Commn., 1977-78, exec. com. 1978-79; mem. adv. com. rules of procedure Utah Supreme Ct., 1983-87; chmn. com. on bar-press guidelines Utah Bar; mem. U. Utah search com., 1968-70; legal advisor, 1966-68. Editor-in-chief Utah Law Rev.; contbr. articles to legal jours. Chmn. subcom. on legal rights and responsibilities of youth Utah Gov's Com. on Youth, 1972; pres. Salt Lake chpt. Coun. Fgn. Rels., 1982; mem. Salt Lake City C. of C., 1974-79, mem. govtl. modernization com., 1976-78; missionary for Mormon Ch. in Fed. Republic Germany, 1953-56; bd. dirs. U. Utah Alumni Assn., 1986-89. Recipient Alumnus of Yr. award U. Utah Coll. Law, 1989. Mem. ABA, Utah Bar Assn. (com. on law and poverty 1967-69, com. on specialization 1977-78, pub. rels. com. 1968-69, chmn. com. on antitrust law 1977-78, com. on civil procedure reform 1968, mem. exec. com. bd. of appellate judges 1990—, liaison to supreme and adv. coms. evidence & profl. conduct 1986—, Appellate Judge of Yr. 1986), Salt Lake County Bar Assn., Am. Judicature Soc., Order of Coif, Phi Beta Kappa, Phi Kappa Phi, Sigma Chi (Significant Sig award 1987). Office: 332 State Capitol Building Salt Lake City UT 84114-1202*

STEWART, J. DANIEL, air force development and test center administrator; b. Savannah, Ga., June 20, 1941; s. Benjamin F. and Bessie L. (Edenfield) S.; m. Rebecca M. Smith; children: Daniel, Laura. BS in Aero. Engring., Ga. Inst. Tech., 1963, MS in Aero. Engring., 1965, PhD in Aero. Engring., 1967; M. in Mgmt. Sci., Stanford U., 1979. Mem. tech. staff applied mechanics divsn. Aerospace Corp., El Segundo, Calif., 1967-74; br. chief tech. divsn. Air Force Rocket Propulsion Lab., Edwards AFB, Calif., 1974-78, asst. for R&D mgmt., 1979-81; divsn. chief Air Force Armament Divsn., Eglin AFB, Fla., 1981-83; dir. drone control program office 3246 Test Wing, Eglin AFB, Fla., 1983-85, joint dir. US/Allied munitions program office, 1985-86; tech. dir. rsch./devel./acquisitions Air Force Armament Divsn., Eglin AFB, Fla., 1986-88; asst. to comdr. Air Force Munitions Divsn., Eglin AFB, Fla., 1988-90; tech. dir. Air Force Devel. and Test Ctr., Eglin AFB, 1990-93, exec. dir., 1993—; mem. policy coun. Scientist and Engr. Career Program, Randolph AFB, Tex., 1994—, chmn. career devel. panel, 1994-96. Bd. dirs. Internat. Found. for Telemetering, Woodland Hills, Calif., 1991-95; mem. engring. adv. bd. U. Fla., Gainesville, 1988—; mem. citizens adv. com. U. West Fla., Pensacola, 1991—; mem. civilian exec. adv. bd. Air Force Materiel Command, 1990—, also former chmn.; mem. curricular adv. com. Def. Test and Evaluation Profl. Inst., 1991—. Recipient Presdl. Meritorious Rank award Pres. of U.S., 1993. Mem. Air Force Assn. (Lewis H. Brereton award 1994), Sr. Exec. Assn., Am. Def. Preparedness Assn., Internat. Test and Evaluation Assn. (Cross medal 1994), Assn. of Old Crows, Fed. Exec. Inst. Alumni, Gulf Coast Alliance for Tech. Transfer. Avocations: tennis, golf, fishing. Office: AFDTC CD 101 W D Ave Ste 123 Eglin AFB FL 32542-5490

STEWART, JAMES BREWER, historian, author, college administrator; b. Cleve., Aug. 8, 1940; s. Richard Henry and Marion Elizabeth (Brewer) S.; m. Dorothy Ann Carlson; children: Rebecca Ann, Jennifer Lynn. BA, Dartmouth Coll., 1962; PhD, Case Western Res. U., 1968. Asst. prof. history Carrol Coll., Waukesha, Wis., 1968-69; asst. prof. history Macalester Coll., St. Paul, 1969-79, James Wallace prof. history, 1979—, provost, 1986-89; cons. Am. Coun. of Learned Socs., N.Y.C., 1988-92. Author: Joshua R. Giddings & the Tactics of Radical Politics, 1970, Holy Warriors: Abolitionists & Slavery, 1976, Liberty's Hero: Wendell Phillips, 1986 (Best Biography award, Soc. Midland Authors 1986), William Lloyd Garrison and the Challenge of Emmancipation, 1992. Rsch. fellow NEH, 1973, Am. Coun. Learned Socs., 1984. Mem. Am. Hist. Assn., Orgn. Am. Historians (nom. com. 1988-92), Soc. Historians of the Early Republic (exec. com. 1987—). Avocations: camping, gardening, furniture restoration. Home: 1924 Princeton Ave Saint Paul MN 55105-1523 Office: Macalester Coll Dept Of History Saint Paul MN 55105

STEWART, JAMES IAN, agricultural water scientist, cropping system developer, consultant; b. San Diego, Jan. 9, 1928; s. Castle Elmore and Myrtle Catherine (Hasty) S.; m. Robbie Nell Oliver, Mar. 23, 1975; children: Virginia Lane Stewart Carton, Ian Castle Stewart, Kevin Scott Overby. BSc, U. Calif., Berkeley, 1950; PhD, U. Calif., Davis, 1972. Farm advisor Agrl. Extension Svc., U. Calif., Stockton and Merced, 1950-61; extension expert Irrigation, Food and Agrl. Orgn. UN, Nicosia, Cyprus, 1962-66; assoc. rsch. water scientist U. Calif., Davis, 1966-77; supervisory soil scientist USDA/Office for Internat. Cooperation and Devel., Nairobi, Kenya, 1977-83; team leader, agrometeorologist USAID/Kenya Mission, 1977-83; founder, pres. Found. for World Hunger Alleviation Through Response Farming (WHARF), Davis, 1984—; cons., agrometeorology AID, USDA, World Bank, FAO/UNDP, 35 countries of Ams., Europe, Asia, Africa, Australia, 1965—; sci. convocations, 15 internat. countries, 1969—. Author: Response Farming in Rainfed Agriculture, 1988; creator (computer programs) Wharf, Wharfdat, 1990; contbr. numerous articles to profl. jours. Mem. Internat. Soil Sci. Soc., World Assn. Soil and Water Conservation, Internat. Com. for Irrigation and Drainage (life, U.S. com.), Indian Soc. Dryland Agr. (life), Sigma Xi, Phi Delta Theta. Achievements include pioneering research on soil water extraction by crops; crop water requirements; relations between crop yield and water evapotranspired; impacts of water deficits in different crop growth stages; relations between season rainfall behavior and season dates of onset. Developer of FAO world standard linear and weighted growth stage models for estimating crop yields from actual evapotranscription, and contributor to four-growth-period linear model for estimating crop water requirements. Developer of "response farming" methodology for design of dryland cropping systems based on historical rainfall behavior, and seasonal flexibility in their management based on realtime rainfall season date of onset, defined to meet crop establishment requirements. Home: 640 Portsmouth Ave Davis CA 95616-2738 Office: World Hunger Allev Through Response Farming PO Box 1158 Davis CA 95617-1158

STEWART, JAMES MONTGOMERY, banker; b. Detroit, May 31, 1939; s. Albert Edwin and Dagny Winter (Jensen) S.; m. Kathleen Williams, Sept. 27, 1940; children—Laura, Wendy, Kathleen. B.B.A., U. Mich., 1962, M.B.A., 1963. Asst. sec. Irving Trust Co., N.Y.C., 1966-68, asst. v.p., 1968-70, v.p., 1970-81, sr. v.p., 1981-86; regional gen. mgr. Copenhagen Handelsbank, 1986-90; gen. mgr. Den Danske Bank, N.Y.C., 1990—. Trustee Am. Scandinavian Found. Mem. Danish Am. C. of C. (bd. dirs., treas.), Anglers (v.p., bd. dirs.), Links Club (gov.), Racquet & Tennis Club, Country Club New Canaan, Beta Gamma Sigma. Republican. Avocations: trout fishing; golf; jazz; wine. Home: 130 Ramhorne Rd New Canaan CT 06840-3007 Office: Den Danske Bank 280 Park Ave New York NY 10017-1216

STEWART, JAMES PERCY, safety and risk management consultant; b. Port Credit, Ont., Can., Apr. 6, 1941; s. Clarence and Dorothy Edith (Pleasants) S.; m. Gail Jacqueline Stewart, Oct. 23, 1965; children: Colleen Ann, Heather Lynne. BJ, Carleton U., Ottawa, Ont., 1993. Aircraft accident investigator Transport Can., Hull, Que., 1981-83; chief aviation safety rsch. and analysis Transport Can., Ottawa, Ont., 1983-87, dir. aviation safety programs, 1987-91, dir. gen. sys. safety, 1991-96; pres. Stewart & Assocs., Ottawa, 1996—; pres. Meetings Internat., Ottawa, 1993—; v.p. internat. ops. The Nyden Group, Calgary, Alta., 1996—. Contbr. tech. papers to profl. publs. With Can. Armed Forces, 1961-81. Recipient UNEF II medal UN, 1974, Can. Forces decoration, 1973; named hon. cons. Oxford (Eng.) U. Aviation Study Group, 1995. Mem. Internat. Soc. Air Safety Investigators (Can. councillor 1988-94), Can. Soc. Air Safety (past pres. 1988-94).

STEWART, JANE, psychology educator; b. Ottawa, Ont., Can., Apr. 19, 1934; d. Daniel Wallace and Jessie Stewart; m. Dalbir Bindra, Aug. 5, 1959 (dec. 1981). BA with honours, Queen's U., Kingston, Ont., 1956; PhD, U. London, 1959; DSc (hon.), Queen's U., 1992. Sr. rsch. biologist Ayerst Labs., Montreal, Que., 1959-63; part-time instr. psychology Sir George,

Montreal, 1962-63; assoc. prof. psychology Williams U., Montreal, 1963-69; prof., chmn. psychology SGW Univ. (now Concordia U.), Montreal, 1969-75; prof. psychology Concordia U., Montreal, 1975—; dir. Ctr. for Studies in Behavioral Neurobiology, Concordia U., Montreal, 1990—. Fellow AAAS, APA, Can. Psychol. Assn.; mem. Soc. for Neurosci., Corp. Psychologists Province of Que., N.Y. Acad. Sci. Office: Concordia University, 1455 de Maisonneuve Blvd W, Montreal, PQ Canada H3G 1M8

STEWART, JANICE MAE, judge; b. Medford, Oreg., Feb. 13, 1951; d. Glenn Logan and Eathel Mae (Jones) S.; m. F. Gordon Allen III, Aug. 10, 1975; children—Benjamin Stewart, Rebecca Mae. AB in Econs., Stanford U., 1972; JD, U. Chgo., 1975. Bar: Ill. 1976, Oreg. 1977, U.S. Dist. Ct. Oreg. 1977, U.S. Ct. Appeals (9th cir.) 1978. Assoc. Winston & Strawn, Chgo., 1975-76, McEwen, Gisvold Rankin & Stewart, Portland, Oreg., 1976-81, ptnr., 1981-93; U.S. magistrate judge, Portland, 1993—. Mem. Multnomah County Profl. Responsibility Com., Portland, 1979-82, Oreg. Profl. Responsibility Bd., 1982-85, Oreg. State Bar Practice and Procedure Com., 1985-88, Profl. Liability Fund Def. Panel, Portland, 1985-93, Multnomah County Judicial Selection com., 1985-87, Oreg. State Bar Professionalism Com., 1989-92, Multnomah County Professionalism Com., 1995—, Coun. Ct. Procedures, 1991-93, lawyer rep. 9th Cir. Jud. Conf., 1990-93. Mem. ABA, Am. Arbitration Assn. (arbitrator 1990-93), Oreg. Bar Assn., Multnomah County Bar Assn. (dir. 1990-93), Phi Beta Kappa. Democrat. Office: 608 US Courthouse 620 SW Main St Portland OR 97205-3037

STEWART, JEFF, advertising agency executive; b. N.Y.C., May 19, 1939; s. Andrew S. and Rose (Leider) S.; m. Linda Dorr McGehee, Sept. 12, 1959; children: Charles, David, Andrea. BS, Columbia Coll., 1960. Asst. prodn. mgr. Denhard & Stewart, Inc., N.Y.C., 1960-62, art dir., 1963-66, account exec., 1966-71, pres., 1973—. Author: Trade Book Mktg., 1982. Pres. Middlesex County Young Dems., 1963-64; vol. Old Bridge Vol. Fire Dept., East Brunswick, N.J., 1963-66; scoutmaster Troop 7 Boy Scouts Am., Upper Montclair, N.J., 1970-81; elder, Presbyn. Ch., Upper Montclair, 1979-84. Mem. Commonwealth Club, Players Club. Avocations: cycling, skiing, golf, canoeing, backpacking. Home: 204 Old Beach Glen Rd Boonton NJ 07005-9525 Office: Denhard & Stewart Inc 240 Madison Ave New York NY 10016-2820

STEWART, JEFFREE ROBERT, environmental planner, artist; b. Concord, N.H., June 20, 1956; s. Robert Davison and Ruth Florence (Olney) S. BA, Evergreen State Coll., Olympia, Wash., 1983; postgrad., U. Wash., 1983-84, Inst. Creative Devel., 1989-91. River guide rafting Rio Bravo, Inc., Durango, Colo., 1981-82; forester, planner Wash. State Parks Commn., Olympia, 1983-84; fisheries biologist U. Wash., Seattle, Alaska and Aleutians, 1984-86; pub. affairs rschr. NOAA, Seattle, 1986; hazardous waste project mgr. Washington Ecology Dept., Olympia, 1987, marine waste disposal project mgr., 1988-92, interagy. liaison, facilitator policy and tech. adv. groups, 1989-90, shorelands planner, 1992—; mem. art exhbns. com. Ecology Dept., Olympia, 1994, 95; mem. adv. bd. Washington Heritage Conf., Olympia, 1992; exhbns. team coord. Arts Olympia, 1993-94, chmn. steering group, 1995-96. One man shows include Batdorf & Bronson, Olympia, 1989, 91, 93, 94, Colophon Cafe, Bellingham, Wash., 1987, 96, Dancing Goats, Olympia, 1992, Thompson Gallery, 1995; exhibited in group shows at Janet Huston Gallery, LaConner, 1991, 92, 93, Wash. State Capitol Mus., Olympia, 1991, 92, 93, Childhoods End Gallery, 1995, 96, 97, Artspace Gallery, Bay City, Oreg., 1996, 97, Lucia Douglas Gallery, Bellingham, Wash., 1996, Evergreen State Coll., 1993, Wash. Ctr. Performing Arts, 1992, 93, 94, 95, 96, 97, Valley Mus. N.W. Art, 1994, 95, 96, 97, Tacoma Art Mus., 1995, also pvt. collections. Bd. trustees Evergreen State Coll., Olympia, 1981. Recipient Competent/Able Toastmaster awards Toastmasters Internat., 1989, 91, Oil Painting award of Merit Wash. State Capitol Mus., Olympia, 1993, Wash. Pub. Employees Assn. (bd. dirs. 1992-93), Meridian Toastmasters (pres., v.p. 1989-91). Mem. Artist Trust, Arts Olympia (steering group 1994—), Profl. Geographers of Puget Sound, Mus. N.W. Art, Tacoma Art Mus., Bellevue Art Mus. Avocations: art collecting and curating, kayaking, freelance journalism, mountaineering. Home: PO Box 7397 Olympia WA 98507-7397 Office: Wash Ecology Dept PO Box 47775 Olympia WA 98504

STEWART, JEFFREY BAYRD, lawyer, commodity trading advisor; b. Chgo., Feb. 6, 1952; s. Bruce A. and Harriet B. Stewart. A.B. magna cum laude (Rufus Choate scholar), Dartmouth Coll., 1974; J.D., Emory U., 1978. Bar: Ga. 1978, U.S. Dist. Ct. (no. dist.) Ga., U.S. Ct. Appeals (5th and 11th dists.). Ptnr., chair corp. dept., Arnall Golden & Gregory, Atlanta, 1978—. Mem. editorial bd. Emory Law Jour., 1977-78. Mem. ABA, State Bar Ga. Home: 4110 Pine Heights Dr Atlanta GA 30324 Office: Arnall Golden & Gregory 1201 W Peachtree St NW Atlanta GA 30309-3400

STEWART, JOANNE, secondary school educator; b. Vancouver, Wash., Mar. 10, 1944; d. Edward Charles and Claudine Marie (Meilleur) Spencer; m. William Lemley Stewart, Sept. 2, 1966 (dec. June 1983); children: Amy Diane, Nicholas William. BS, Wash. State U., 1966, MA, 1973. Cert. tchr., Mont., Idaho, Wash., Calif. Tchr. foods Seaside High Sch., Monterey, Calif., 1966-67; tchr. home econs. Marysville (Wash.) High Sch., 1967-68, Palouse (Wash.) High Sch., 1968-73, Ennis (Mont.) High Sch., 1973-76, Genesee (Idaho) High Sch., 1976-77; instr. young family Missoula (Mont.) County High Sch., 1983-84; tchr. home econs. Woodman Sch., Lolo, Mont., 1985-86; travel cons. Travel Masters, Missoula, 1984-87; ticketing mgr. Blue Caboose Travel, Missoula, 1987-91; tchr. family and consumer scis. Victor (Mont.) High Sch., 1991—; project dir. sch.-to-work implementation Victor Sch., 1996—. Co-pres. Lolo PTO, 1980-81; v.p. Lolo Community Ctr., 1981; sec. Lolo Mosquito Control Bd., 1988—; mem. telecommunications com. Conrad Burns & Gov. Racicot; sec. state supt. edn. task force on vocat. edn., 1995-96. Marysville Edn. Assn. scholar, 1962, Future Homemakers Am. scholar, 1962. Mem. AAUW (sec. 1986, program chmn. 1987), Forestry Triangle (pres. 1981, editor cookbook 1982), Washington State Future Homemakers Am. (hon. mem.), Am. Family and Consumer Scis. Assn., Mont. Family and Consumer Scis. Assn. (bylaws chair 1994, pres. elect 1995-96, pres. 1996-97, Profl. of Yr. 1997), Mont. Vocat. Tchrs. Assn. (returning Rookie of Yr. 1992, Am. Federated Tchrs., Mont. Vocat. Family and Consumer Scis. Tchrs. (v.p. 1993-94, pres. 1994-95). Republican. Methodist. Avocations: homemaking, swimming. Home: 1200 Lakeside Dr Lolo MT 59847-9705 Office: Victor High Sch Family and Consumer Scis 425 4th Ave Victor MT 59875-9468

STEWART, JOE J., manufacturing executive; b. 1938. BSChemE, Purdue U., 1959; MA, Kansas State U., 1961; PhD, N.C. State U., 1963; DEng (hon.), Purdue U., 1994. With Aerojet-Gen. Corp., 1966-72; with Babcock & Wilcox Co., New Orleans, 1972—, v.p., 1978; pres., COO Babcock & Wilcox Co., Barberton, Ohio, 1993; now pres. Babcock & Wilcox, govt. grp., Lynchburg, VA; v.p., group exec. McDermott Marine Constrn., European Ops., 1984-87.

STEWART, JOHN EZELL, educational and business consultant; b. Sand Springs, Okla., Aug. 26, 1929; m. Elsie Louise Fonville, June 18, 1954; children: Barry, Johnetta, Rhonda, Howard. BS in Vocat. Edn., Langston (Okla.) U., 1951; MS in Gen. Supervision, Calif. State U., L.A., 1964; grad. study, U. Rich., 1980, 82. Cert. collegiate profl. tchr. Staff supr. Norfolk State U.; acct. exec., v.p. Bus. Devel.; tchr., project mgr. L.A. City Unified Sch. Dist.; edn. specialist cons. Pepperdine U., L.A.; substitute tchr. Richmond City Pub. Schs.; founder, exec. dir. Va. Adolescent Adult Rehab. Agy.; founder, prin. John Ezell Stewart Sch.; grant adminstr. Steamer Co., 1991—; faculty chmn. Mary McLeod Bethune Middle Sch.; spl. projects dir. Tchr. Human rels. Workshops; pres. Pan Hellenic Coun.; founder Motivation for Success in Life Inst., 1996. Mem. Am. Fedn. Tchrs., United Tchrs. L.A., Omega Psi Phi. Democrat. Buddhist. Avocations: self-development tapes, conducting business and training seminars.

STEWART, JOHN HARGER, music educator; b. Cleve., Mar. 31, 1940; s. Cecil Tooker and Marian (Harger) S.; m. Julia Wallace, Aug. 14, 1977; children: Barbara, Cecily Bronwen. BA, Yale U., 1962; MA, Brown U., 1972; cert., New Eng. Conservatory, 1965. With various operas including Santa Fe Opera, N.Y.C. Opera, Met. Opera, U.S. and Europe, 1965—; lectr. Mt. Holyoke Coll., South Hadley, Mass., 1988-90; dir. vocal activities Washington U., St. Louis, 1990—; dir. of voice and choral program Friends of Music, St. Louis. Office: Washington U Campus Box 1032 One Brookings Dr Saint Louis MO 63130-4899

STEWART, JOHN LINCOLN, university administrator; b. Alton, Ill., Jan. 24, 1917; s. Frederick William and Hilda (Denovan) S.; m. Joan Elsdon Guthridge, Sept. 23 1939 (div. 1964); children: Leslie Cythera Stewart Chalmers, Ann Guthridge Stewart Nutt; m. Ruth Peabody Quinn, July 11, 1964; stepchildren: Geoffrey Cornelius Quinn, Andrew Dean Quinn. AB, Denison U., 1938, ArtsD (hon.), 1964; MA, Ohio State U., 1939, PhD, 1947. Teaching asst. then instr. Ohio State U., Columbus, 1939-47; instr. UCLA, 1947-49; asst. prof. then prof. English Dartmouth Coll., Hanover, N.H., 1949-64; prof. Lit. U. Calif., San Diego, 1964-87, provost John Muir Coll., 1965-87. Author: Exposition for Science and Technical Students, 1950, The Essay, 1952, John Crowe Ransom, 1962, The Burden of Time, 1965, (with others) Horizons Circled, 1974, Ernst Krenek, 1990; contbr. articles to various publs. assoc. dir. Hopkins Ctr. for Arts, 1961-64; dir. Mandeville Ctr. for Arts, 1974-76; mem. Dartmouth Community Symphony Orch., 1949-58; trustee Kinhaven Music Sch., 1960-64, Fla. West Coast Symphony, 1958; bd. dirs. Theater and Arts Found. San Diego County, 1970; pres. La Jolla (Calif.) Friends Sch. Music, 1971-73, Friends of Music, U. Calif., San Diego. Served with Aus, 1942-45. Howard Found. fellow, 1953-54, Dartmouth Coll. fellow, 1962-63. Democrat. Avocation: performer with music ensembles. Home: 9473 La Jolla Farms Rd La Jolla CA 92037-1128 Office: U Calif San Diego Off of Provost # 0106 La Jolla CA 92093

STEWART, JOHN WRAY BLACK, college dean; b. Coleraine, Northern Ireland, Jan. 16, 1936; s. John Wray and Margaret Reid (Black) S.; m. Felicity Ann Patricia Poole, Aug. 7, 1965; children: J.W. Matthew, Hannah Louise. BSc with honors, Queen's U., Belfast, Northern Ireland, 1958, B.Agr. with honors, 1959, PhD, 1963, DSc, 1988. Registered profl. agrologist. Sci. officer chem. rsch. div. Ministry of Agr., Belfast, 1959-64; asst. prof. soil sci. dept. U. Sask., Saskatoon, Can., 1966-71, assoc. prof., 1971-76, prof., 1976-81; dir. Sask. Inst. Pedology U. Sask., 1981-89; dean Coll. Agr. U. Sask., Saskatoon, 1989—; tech. expert, cons. FAO/IAEA, U.N.D.P., Vienna, Austria, 1971, 74-75; mem. program com. Can. Global Change, 1985—; sec.-gen. Sci. Com. on Problems of Environment, Paris, 1988-92, pres., 1992-95, past pres., 1995—; cons. UNESCO, Paris, 1990; trustee Internat. Inst. Tropical Agr., Nigeria, 1991-97; mem. sci. adv. com. Inter-Am. Inst. on Global Change Rsch., 1994—. Contbr. articles to profl. publs., chpts. to books. Fellow Can. Soc. Soil Sci., Berlin Inst. Advanced Study, Am. Soc. Agronomy, Soil Sci. Soc. Am.; mem. Brit. Soc. Soil Sci., Brazilian Soc. Soil Sci., Internat. Soc. Soil Sci., Agrl. Inst. Can. Avocations: squash, racquet ball, tennis. Office: U Sask Coll Agr, 51 Campus Dr, Saskatoon, SK Canada S7N 5A8

STEWART, JONATHAN TAYLOR, psychiatrist, educator; b. Bethpage, N.Y., Mar. 15, 1956; s. Allen Theodore and Vivian (Dreiblatt) S.; m. Linda Sue Irvin, Oct. 27, 1984; children: Jacob Zachary, Aaron Joshua. BA with honors, Rollins Coll., 1976; MD, U. South Fla., 1979. Diplomate Am. Bd. Psychiatry and Neurology, Geriatric Psychiatry, Nat. Bd. Med. Examiners. Resident in psychiatry U. Fla. Coll. Medicine, Gainesville, 1979-83, assoc. prof. psychiatry, 1983-94; asst. chief psychiatry VA Med. Ctr., Gainesville, 1987-94; prof. psychiatry U So. Fla. Coll. Medicine, 1994—; chief geropsychiatry sect. Bay Pines (Fla.) VA Med. Ctr., 1994—. Contbr. articles to profl. jours., 1985—. Mem. Head Injury Adv. Council State of Fla., 1985-90, Gov.'s Alzheimer's Disease Registry Subcom., 1987—, VA Task Force on Extended Care, Washington, 1986. Fellow Am. Psychiat. Assn.; mem. Am. Geriatrics Soc., Fla. Psychiat. Soc. Jewish. Avocations: cooking, cycling, skin diving, traveling. flying. Office: VA Med Ctr Psychiatry Service 116A Bay Pines FL 33504

STEWART, JOSEPH TURNER, JR., retired pharmaceutical company executive; b. N.Y.C., Apr. 30, 1929; s. Joseph Turner and Edna (Pride) S.; m. Carol Graham, Aug. 7, 1954; children: Lisa D., Alison D. BS with honors, U.S. Mcht. Marine Acad., 1951; MBA, Harvard U., 1954. Systems analyst Warner Lambert Co., Morris Plains, N.J., 1954-56; budget dir. internat. Warner Lambert Co., 1956-60, asst. div. controller consumer products group, 1960-62, div. controller group, 1962-66; dir. adminstrn. and fin. Proprietary Drug div. Warner Lamber Co., 1966; dir. Lactona Products div. Warner Lamber Co., 1967; controller Beech-Nut subs. Squibb Corp., N.Y.C., 1968; v.p. fin. Beech-Nut subs. Squibb Corp., 1968-71, v.p. planning, corp. staff parent corp., 1971-79, v.p. fin. and planning parent co., 1979-82, sr. v.p. corporate affairs parent co., 1982-89; also bd. dirs.; cons. Johnson & Johnson, 1990—; bd. dirs. Gen. Am. Investment Corp., Liposome Co. Trustee Tax Found., 1985-89; commr. N.J. State Commn. on Income and Expenditures, 1985-88; mem. adv. com. Grad. Sch. Indsl. Adminstrn., Carnegie Mellon U., 1986-91; trustee New Sch. for Social Rsch., 1990—, U. Medicine and Dentistry of N.J. Found., 1989—; bd. dirs. Liposome Co., 1995—; vis. coun. Marine Biol. Lab., 1995—. John Hay Whitney Opportunity fellow, 1952-54. Club: Harvard (N.Y.C.). Office: Johnson & Johnson 1 Johnson And Johnson Plz New Brunswick NJ 08933-0001

STEWART, KAREN MEYER, pediatrics nurse, nursing manager; b. Bryn Mawr, Pa., June 7, 1957; d. William Stanford and Ruth May (Schrumpf) Meyer; m. James Allen Stewart, Sept. 1, 1979; children: Karrie, Matthew. BSN, U. Mich., Ann Arbor, 1979; MS, U. Minn., 1994. Grad. nurse Pediatrics Mott Children's Hosp., Ann Arbor, Mich., 1979; staff nurse, charge nurse, pediatric ICU Saint Mary's Hosp., Rochester, Minn., 1979-84; asst. head nurse pediatric ICU, 1984-89; nurse mgr., pediatric ICU, pediatric transport team Mayo Med. Ctr., Rochester, Minn., 1989—; instr. pediat. Mayo Med. Sch., Rochester, Minn., 1994—. Mem. AACN, Minn. Nurses Assn., Assn. for Care Children's Health, Minn. Orgn. Leaders in Nursing, Soc. Critical Care Medicine, Phi Kappa Phi, Sigma Theta Tau. Home: 5812 Glencroft Ln SW Rochester MN 55902-8849 Office: Mayo Eugenio Litta Children's Hosp Pediat ICU 1216 2nd St SW Rochester MN 55902-1906

STEWART, KENT KALLAM, analytical biochemistry educator; b. Omaha, Sept. 5, 1934; s. George Franklin and Grace (Sledge) S.; m. Margaret Reiber, June 10, 1956; children: Elizabeth, Cynthia, Richard, Robert. Student, U. Chgo., 1951-53; AB, U. Calif., Berkeley, 1956; PhD, Fla. State U., 1965. Guest investigator Rockefeller U., N.Y.C., 1965-67, research assoc., 1967-68, asst. prof., 1968-69; research chemist U.S. Dept. Agr., Beltsville, Md., 1970-75, lab. chief Nutrient Composition Lab., 1975-82; prof., head dept. food sci. and tech. Va. Poly. Inst. and State U., Blacksburg, 1982-85; prof. biochemistry, anaerobic microbiology, food sci./tech. Va. Poly. Inst. and State U., 1985—; sr. rsch. fellow dept. chemistry and biochemistry U. Tex., Austin, 1996—. Author articles and book chpts.; editor Jour. Food Composition and Analysis, also 2 books Patentee in field. Capt. USMCR, 1956-59. Fellow Inst. Food Technologist, AAAS; mem. Am. Chem. Soc., Assn. Ofcl. Analytical Chemists, Sigma Xi. Office: Dept Biochemistry 3900 Glengarry Dr Austin TX 78731-3812

STEWART, KIRK T., public relations executive; b. 1951. BA in polit. sci., U. So. Calif., 1973; MA in public rels./journalism, 1976. Account exec. Burson-Marsteller, 1976-79; pub. affairs dir. Info. Svcs. Dir. TRW, 1979-81; group supr. Manning Selvage & Lee, 1981-82, v.p., 1982-83, exec. v.p., 1983-84; exec. v.p., mng. dir. Manning Selvage & Lee/L.A., Calif., 1984-89; pres. Manning, Selvage & Lee Inc., N.Y.C., 1989-91, pres., CEO, 1992; chmn., CEO Manning, Selvage & Lee, Inc., N.Y.C., 1993—. Office: Manning Selvage & Lee Inc 79 Madison Ave New York NY 10016-7802*

STEWART, LYN VARN, critical care nurse; b. Charleston, S.C., July 3, 1957; d. Allen Hamilton and Merilyn (Windsor) Varn; m. James Milton Stewart Jr., May 26, 1979; children: Kevin James, Sean Allen. BA in History, Clemson U., 1979; ADN, U.S.C., 1983. Cert. BLS, ACLS. Staff RN med.-surg. units Piedmont Med. Ctr., Rock Hill, S.C., 1983-85, staff nurse progressive care unit, 1985-94, RN, asst. head nurse progressive care unit, 1991-92, preceptor coord., 1991-93, quality improvement rep. progressive care unit, 1991-92; office nurse, cardiac stress testing Carolinas Med. Group-Shiland, Rock Hill, 1995—; preceptor coord., quality improvement rep. progressive care unit Piedmont Med. Ctr., Rock Hill, 1991-92; office RN cardiac stress testing Carolinas Med. Group-Shiland, Rock Hill, 1995—. Bd. dirs. Westminster Christian Sch., Rock Hill., 1991-93, mem. yearbook staff, 1991-93, mem. PTO bd., 1992-93, coach Westminster Little Tigers soccer team, 1992-93, asst. coach Westminster Lions soccer team, 1992-93; bd. trustees Westminster Catawba Christian Sch., Rock Hill, 1993-94, mem. PTO bd., 1993-95, newsletter editor, 1992-95, co-coord. sch. soccer program, 1992—, asst. coach under-10 & under-12 soccer team, 1994-96, asst. coach jr. varsity soccer team, 1996; sec. Westminster Catawba Christian Sch. Athletic Booster Club, 1994-95; founding mem. Spirit Soccer League, Rock Hill, 1996—. Mem. S.C. Assn. Nurses Endorsing Transplantation. Avocations: creative writing, photography, children's activities. Home: 603 Greenbriar Ave Rock Hill SC 29730-3301

STEWART, MARGARET MCBRIDE, biology educator, researcher; b. Guilford County, N.C., Feb. 6, 1927; d. David Henry and Mary Ellen (Morrow) S.; m. Paul C. Lemon, June 1962 (div. 1968); m. George Edward Martin, Dec. 19, 1969. AB, U. N.C.-Greensboro, 1948; MA, U. N.C.-Chapel Hill, 1951; PhD, Cornell U., 1956; DSc (hon.), U. P.R., Mayaquez, 1996. Instr. biology Greensboro Evening Coll. U. N.C., Greensboro, 1950-51; instr. biology Catawba Coll., Salisbury, N.C., 1951-53; extension botanist Cornell U., Ithaca, N.Y., 1954-56; asst. prof. biology SUNY, Albany, 1956-59, assoc. prof., 1959-65, prof. vertebrate biology, 1965—, Disting. Teaching prof., 1977—; faculty rsch. participant Oak Ridge Assoc. Univs., 1983. Author: (with A.H. Benton) Keys to the Vertebrates of the Northeastern States, 1964, Amphibians of Malawi, 1967; contbr. numerous articles and revs. to profl. jours. Bd. dirs. E.N. Huyck Nature Preserve, Rensselaerville, N.Y., 1976-86; bd. dirs. Ea. N.Y. chpt. Nature Conservancy, 1983-88, 90-96, N.Y. State chpt., 1987-90; mem. Albany Pine Bush Commn., 1993—. Recipient Citizen Laureate award SUNY Found., 1987, Oak Leaf award Nature Conservancy, 1997; Am. Philos. Soc. rsch. grantee, 1975, 81, NSF grantee, 1978-80, Oak Ridge Assocs. Univs. grantee, 1983—. Fellow Herpetologists League (bd. dirs. 1978-80); mem. Soc. for Study of Amphibians and Reptiles (pres. 1979), Am. Soc. Ichthyologists and Herpetologists (bd. govs. 1975-80, 87-90, herpetology editor 1983-85, pres. 1996), Ecol. Soc. Am., Assn. for Tropical Biologists, Soc. Study of Evolution, III World Congress of Herpetology (mem. exec. com. 1995-97), Sigma Xi, Sigma Delta Epsilon, Phi Kappa Phi. Democrat. Presbyterian. Avocations: photography, gardening, reading, travel. Office: SUNY Dept Biol Scis 1400 Washington Ave Albany NY 12222-0100

STEWART, MARTHA KOSTYRA, editor-in-chief, lecturer, author; b. Jersey City; d. Edward and Martha (Ruszkowski) Kostyra; m. Andy Stewart, July 1, 1961 (div. 1990); 1 child, Alexis. BA in European History and Archtl. History, Barnard. Former model; former stockbroker N.Y.C.; former profl. caterer, mag. owner, editor-in-chief; mag. owner, editor-in-chief Martha Stewart Living, 1990—; lifestyle cons. for K-Mart Corp. Author: (with Elizabeth Hawes) Entertaining, 1982, Weddings, 1987; Martha Stewart Hors d'Oeurvres: The Creation and Presentation of Fabulous Finger Food, 1984, Martha Stewart's Pies and Tarts, 1985, Martha Stewart's Quick Cook Menus: Fifty-two Meals You Can Make in Under an Hour, 1988, The Wedding Planner, 1988, Martha Stewart's Gardening: Month by Month, 1991, Martha Stewart's New Old House: Restoration, Renovation, Decoration, 1992, Martha Stewart's Christmas, 1993, Martha Stewart's Menus for Entertaining, 1994, Holidays, 1994; appears in semi-monthly cooking segment on Today Show. Office: 10 Saugatuck Ave Westport CT 06880-5720 also: care Susan Magrino Agy 40 W 57th St 31st Flr New York NY 10019*

STEWART, MARY FLORENCE ELINOR, author; b. Sunderland, Durham, Eng., Sept. 17, 1916; d. Frederick A. and Mary Edith (Matthews) Rainbow; m. Frederick H. Stewart, 1945. BA, Durham U., 1938, MA, 1941. Asst. lectr. English Durham U., 1941-45, part-time lectr. English, 1948-56; part-time lectr. English St. Hild's Training Coll., 1948-56. Author: Madam, Will You Talk?, 1954, Wildfire at Midnight, 1956, Thunder on the Right, 1957, Nine Coaches Waiting, 1958, My Brother Michael, 1959 (Brit. Crime Writers Assn. award 1960), The Ivy Tree, 1961, The Moonspinners, 1962, This Rough Magic, 1964 (Mystery Writers Am. award 1964), Airs Above the Ground, 1965, The Gabriel Hounds, 1967, The Wind Off the Small Isles, 1968, The Crystal Cave, 1970 (Frederick Niven award 1971), The Little Broomstick, 1971, The Hollow Hills, 1973, Ludo and the Star Horse, 1974 (Scottish Arts Coun. award 1974), Touch Not the Cat, 1976, The Last Enchantment, 1979, A Walk in the Wolf Wood, 1980, The Wicked Day, 1983, Thornyhold, 1988, Frost on the Window and Other Poems, 1990, The Stormy Petrel, 1991, The Prince and the Pilgrim, 1996, Rose Cottage, 1997. Fellow Newnham Coll., Cambridge, 1986. Mem. P.E.N. Office: care William Morrow 1350 Avenue Of The Americas New York NY 10019-4702

STEWART, MELBOURNE GEORGE, JR., physicist, educator; b. Detroit, Sept. 30, 1927; s. Melbourne George and Ottilie (Tuholke) S.; m. Charlotte L. Ford, Jan. 23, 1954; children—Jill K., John H., Kevin G. A.B., U. Mich., 1949, M.S., 1950, Ph.D., 1955. Research assoc. dept. physics AEC, Ames Lab., Iowa State U., 1955-56, asst. prof., 1956-62, assoc. prof., 1962-63; prof. Wayne State U., Detroit, 1963-94, prof. emeritus, 1994—, chmn. dept. physics, 1963-73, assoc. provost for faculty relations, 1973-86; hon. research fellow Univ. Coll., London, 1986-87,93. Editorial bd.: Wayne State U. Press, 1969-73. Served with AUS, 1946-47. Mem. Am. Phys. Soc., AAAS, Sigma Xi, Phi Beta Kappa. Home: 415 Bournemouth Rd Grosse Pointe MI 48236-2817 Office: Dept Physics Wayne State U Detroit MI 48202

STEWART, MELVIN, Olympic athlete, swimmer. Olympic swimmer Barcelona, Spain, 1992. Recipient 200m Butterfly Gold medal Olympics, Barcelona, 1992. Office: care US Olympic Com 1750 E Boulder St Colorado Springs CO 80909-5724*

STEWART, MILTON ROY, lawyer; b. Clovis, N.Mex., Dec. 16, 1945; s. Virgil Maurice and E. Marie (Collins) S. BA, Ind. U., 1968, JD summa cum laude, 1971. Bar: Oreg. 1971, U.S. Ct. Appeals (9th cir.) 1971, U.S. Dist. Ct. (no. dist.) Oreg. 1971. Assoc. firm Davies, Biggs, et. al., Portland, Oreg., 1971-75; v.p., gen. counsel U.S. Datacorp, Portland, 1975-77; pvt. practice, Portland, 1977-86; ptnr. Davis, Wright Tremaine and predecessor firm., Portland, 1987—, mem. exec. com., mem. mgmt. com, chmn. firmwide bus. group. Chmn. emeritus Oreg. chpt. Nat. Multiple Sclerosis Soc., 1994—; mem. pres. adv. bd. Portland State U.; bd. dirs., sec. YMCA of Columbia-Willamette, Portland, 1978-81; bd. vis. Ind. U. Sch. Law. Capt. U.S. Army, 1968-78. State Farm Found. fellow, 1970; John H. Edwards fellow Ind. U. Found., 1971. Mem. Oreg. State Bar, Multnomah Athletic Club, Astoria Golf and Country Club. Office: Davis Wright Tremaine 1300 SW 5th Ave Portland OR 97201-5667

STEWART, NATHANIEL JOHNSON, emergency medicine physician; b. Savannah, Ga., Nov. 29, 1946; s. Nathaniel Johnson Sr. and Jane (Rogers) S.; m. Sarah Prescott, Aug. 3, 1975; children: Nathaniel Johnson III, Lauren Allie. BS in Biology, Armstrong State Coll., 1968; med. tech., Meml. Med. Ctr., 1969; MD, Med. Coll. Ga., 1981. Diplomate Am. Bd. Emergency Medicine. Instr. med. tech. Meml. Med. Ctr., Savannah, 1972-77; resident in emergency medicine Richland Meml. Hosp., Columbia, S.C., 1981-84, attending physician emergency medicine, 1984—, dir. for edn. and profl. svcs., 1984—, med. dir. Palmetto poison ctr., cons., 1984—, cons. hyperbarics, 1987—. Contbr. chpts. to books in field. With U.S. Army, 1969-72. Recipient award for acad. excellence Merch, Sharp & Dhome, 1981. Fellow Am. Coll. Emergency Physician; mem. AMA, S.C. Med. Assn., Am. Coll. Emergency Physicians, Columbia Med. Assn., Alpha Omega Alpha. Methodist. Avocation: computers. Office: Richland Meml Hosp Ste 350 3 Richland Medical Park Dr Columbia SC 29203-6852

STEWART, PAMELA L., lawyer; b. Bogalusa, La., Mar. 13, 1953; d. James Adrian and Patricia Lynn (Wood) Lloyd; m. Steven Bernard Stewart, Aug. 31, 1974 (div. July 1980); 1 child, Christopher. BA, U. New Orleans, 1986; JD, U. Houston, 1990. Intern La. Supreme Ct., New Orleans, 1984, Councilman Bryan Wagner, New Orleans, 1984-85; legal asst. Clann, Bell & Murphy, Houston, 1988-89, Tejas Gas Corp., Houston, 1989-90; atty. Law Offices of Pamela L. Stewart, Katy, Tex., 1991—. Bd. dirs. Alliance for Good Govt., New Orleans, 1983-84, Attention Deficit Hyperactivity Disorder Assn. Tex., 1989-90; vol. Houston Vol. Lawyers Program, Houston, 1992—. Innsbruck scholar, U. New Orleans, 1985. Fellow Inst. Politics; mem. ABA, Am. Bankruptcy Inst., Tax Freedom Inst., Nat. Assn. Consumer Bankruptcy Attys. (co-chair ethics com.), Nat. Assn. Elder Law Attys., Am. Networking Trust Planning Attys., Houston Bar Assn., Houston Bankruptcy Conf., Nat. Assn. of Chpt. 13 Trustees (assoc.), Katy Bar Assn. (3d v.p. 1997-98), Houston Assn. Debtors Attys. (pres.), Am. Acad. Estate Planning Attys. Methodist. Avocations: music, cooking, swimming, politics. Home: PO Box 61154 Houston TX 77208-1154 Office: Law Offices of Pamela L Stewart Ste 219 One West Loop South Houston TX 77027

STEWART, PATRICIA CARRY, foundation administrator; b. Bklyn., May 19, 1928; d. William J. and Eleanor (Murphy) Carry; m. Charles Thorp Stewart, May 30, 1976. Student U. Paris, 1948-49; BA, Cornell U., 1950. Fgn. corr. Irving Trust Co., N.Y.C., 1950-51; with Janeway Rsch. Co., N.Y.C., 1951-60, sec., treas., 1955-60; with Buckner & Co. and successor firms, N.Y.C., 1961-73, ptnr., 1962-70, v.p.-treas., 1970-71, pres.-treas., 1971-73; pres., treas. Knight, Carry, Bliss & Co., Inc., N.Y.C., 1971-73; pres., treas. G. Tsai & Co., Inc., 1973; v.p. Edna McConnell Clark Found. Inc., 1974-92; dir. Cmty. Found. Palm Beach and Martin Counties; bd. dirs. CVS Corp., Banker Trust Co., Bankers Trust N.Y. Corp., Trans World Airlines, 1973-85, Borden Inc., 1976-95, Continental Corp., 1976-95, Morton Norwich Inc., 1979-84; allied mem. N.Y. Stock Exch., 1962-73; past mem. nominating com. Am. Stock Exch., N.Y. Stock Exch., N.Y.C. Fin. Svcs. Corp.; dir. emeritus, past chmn. Investor Responsibility Rsch. Ctr. Trustee emerita, vice-chair Cornell U., bd. life overseers Cornell Med. Coll.; vis. com. Grad. Sch. Bus., Harvard U., 1974-80; bd. dirs. NOW Legal Def. and Edn. Fund, 1984-92, Women in Founds./Corp. Philanthropy 1980-86; v.p. fin. com. Women's Forum, 1982-90; vice chmn. CUNY, 1976-80; bd. dirs. United Way of Tri-State, 1977-81, Inst. for Edn. and Rsch. on Women and Work; voting mem. Blue Cross and Blue Shield Greater N.Y., 1975-82; trustee N.Y. State 4-H Found., 1970-76, Internat. Inst. Rural Reconstruction, 1974-79; mem. N.Y.C. panel White House Fellows, 1976-78; mem. bus. adv. coun. The Hosp. Chaplaincy. Recipient Elizabeth Cutter Morrow award YWCA, 1977, Catalyst award Women Dirs. in Corps., 1978, Trustee medal CUNY, 1983, Accomplishment award Wings Club N.Y., 1984, Women's Funding Coalition Innovators for Women$hare award, 1986, Banking Industry Achievement award Nat. Assn. Bank Women, 1987, Cert. Disting. Accomplishments Barnard Coll., 1989; named to YWCA Acad. Women Achievers. Mem. Fin. Women's Assn. N.Y., Coun. Fgn. Rels., Pi Beta Phi. Clubs: Country Club of Fla. (bd. dirs.), University (N.Y.C.); Gullane Golf (Scotland), The Glen (Scotland), North Berwick Golf (Scotland), Dunbar Golf (Scotland). Home and Office: 2613 N Ocean Blvd Delray Beach FL 33483-7367 also: Halfland Barns, North Berwick EH395PW, Scotland

STEWART, PATRICK, actor; b. Mirfield, Eng., July 13, 1940; s. Alfred and Gladys (Barraclough) S. Trained, Bristol Old Vic Theatre Sch. Performed in (theatre) Treasure Island (U.K., debut), 1959, (U.S.) A Midsummer Night's Dream (Broadway debut), 1970, A Christmas Carol, 1991, 92, 94; (TV series) Star Trek: The Next Generation, 1987-94, (mini series) I, Claudius, 1977, Tinker, Sailor, Soldier, Spy, 1979, Smiley's People, 1982, Playing Shakespeare, 1983, When the Lion Roars, 1992, (TV movies) Little Lord Fauntleroy, 1980, John Paul II, 1984, Death Train, 1993; host on Saturday Night Live, 1994; actor (films) Hennessy, 1975, Hedda, 1975, Excalibur, 1981, The Plague Dogs (voice) 1982, Dune, 1984, Lifeforce, 1985, Code Name: Emerald, 1985, Wild Geese II, 1985, The Doctor and the Devils, 1985, Lady Jane, 1986, L.A. Story, 1991, Robin Hood: Men in Tights, 1993, Gunmen, 1994, Star Trek: Generations, 1994, The Pagemaster, 1994 (voice), Jeffrey, 1995; assoc. artist with Royal Shakespeare Co., 1967—; recording: Prokofiev: Peter and the Wolf (Grammy award best spoken word album for children 1996). Office: Internat Creative Mgmt 8942 Wilshire Blvd Beverly Hills CA 90211-1934 also: Kelly Bush Pub Rels 7201 Melrose Ave Los Angeles CA 90046*

STEWART, (WILLIAM) PAYNE, professional golfer; b. Springfield, Mo., 1957; m. Tracey Stewart; children: Chelsea, Aaron. Co-champion S.W. Conf., 1979; winner Indian and Indonesian Opens, 1981, Tweed Head Classic, 1981, Magnolia Classic, 1982, Quad Cities Open, 1982, Walt Disney World Classic, 1983, Hertz Bay Hill Classic, 1987, PGA Championship, 1989, MCI Heritage Classic, 1989, 90, Byron Nelson Golf Classic, 1990, U.S. Open, 1991, Heineken Dutch Open, 1991, Morocco Open, 1992, 93, Houston Open, 1995, Skins Game Champion, 1991, 92, 93; mem. Ryder Cup U.S. team, 1987, 89, 91, 93, World Cup U.S. team, 1987, 90. Address: care PGA Tour 112 Tpc Blvd Ponte Vedra Beach FL 32082-3046*

STEWART, PETER BEAUFORT, retired beverage company executive; b. Montreal, Que., Can., Aug. 23, 1923; s. Harold Beaufort and Mary W. (Martin) S.; m. Yolande Winifred Powell, June 1955; children—Thomas B., Angus B. B.Comm., McGill U.; M.B.A., Harvard U. With Bldg. Products Ltd., Toronto, Ont., Can., 1947-62; dir., v.p. mktg. Molson Breweries Ltd., Montreal, 1962-66; pres. Molson Western Breweries Ltd., Calgary, Alta., Can., 1966-70; exec. v.p., pres. Molson Breweries Ltd., Montreal, 1970-75; exec. v.p. The Molson Cos. Ltd., Toronto, 1975-88.

STEWART, RICHARD ALFRED, business executive; b. Hartford, Conn., Nov. 2, 1945; s. Charles Alfred and Theresa (Procopio) S. BS, Valley Coll., 1967. Account exec. Bank Printing Inc., Los Angeles, 1967-70; pres. Carpet Closet Inc., Los Angeles, 1970-73; western sales mgr. Josten's, Los Angeles, 1973-84; pres. Western Internat. Premiums, Los Angeles, 1984-87; dir. corp. sales Tiffany and Co., Beverly Hills, Calif., 1987-90, dir. major program sales, 1990-92; dir. regional sales Tiffany and Co., N.Y.C., 1992-93, dir. major programs, 1992-93; v.p. sales mktg. and recognition divsn. Jostens, Memphis, 1993—; prin. The Stewart Group Sales & Mktg. Cons., 1994—; v.p. sales & mktg. Am. Gem Corp.; recognition cons. L.A. Olympic Com., 1983-84. Contbr. articles to profl. mags.; developer medals for 1984 summer Olympics. Chmn. bd. dirs. Athletes and Entertainers for Kids. Avocations: tennis, basketball, photography.

STEWART, RICHARD BURLESON, lawyer, educator; b. Cleve., Feb. 12, 1940; s. Richard Siegfreid and Ruth Dysert (Staten) S.; m. Alice Peck Fales, May 13, 1967; children: William, Paul, Elizabeth; m. Jane Laura Bloom, Sept. 20, 1992; 1 child, Emily. A.B., Yale U., 1961; M.A. (Rhodes scholar), Oxford (Eng.) U., 1963; LL.B., Harvard U., 1966; Dr. (hon.), Erasmus U., Rotterdam, 1993. Bar: D.C. 1968, U.S. Supreme Ct 1971. Law clk. to Justice Potter Stewart, U.S. Supreme Ct., 1966-67; assoc. Covington & Burling, Washington, 1967-71; asst. prof. law Harvard U., 1971-75, prof., 1975-82, Byrne prof. adminstrv. law,, 1982-89, assoc. dean, 1984-86; asst. atty. gen. environment and natural resources div. Dept. Justice, Washington, 1989-91; prof. law NYU Law Sch., 1992-94, Emily Kempin prof. law, 1994—; of counsel Sidley & Austin, 1992—; spl. counsel U.S. Senate Watergate Com., 1974; vis. prof. law U. Calif., Berkeley Law Sch., 1979-80, U. Chgo. Law Sch., 1986-87, Georgetown U., 1991-92, European U. Inst., 1995. Author: (with J. Krier) Environmental Law and Policy, 1978, (with S. Breyer) Administrative Law and Regulation, 1979, 3d edit., 1990, (with E. Rehbinder) Integration Through Law: Environmental Protection Policy, 1985, paper edit., 1987; editor: (with R. Revesz) Analyzing Superfund: Economics, Science, and Law, 1995. Fellow Am. Acad. Arts and Scis.; mem. ABA, Am. Law Inst. Office: NYU Law Sch 40 Washington Sq S New York NY 10012-1005 Address: Sidley & Austin 875 3rd Ave New York NY 10022-6225

STEWART, RICHARD DONALD, internist, educator; b. Lakeland, Fla., Dec. 26, 1926; s. LeRoy Hepburn and Zoa Irene (Hachet) S.; m. Mary Leeuw, June 14, 1952; children: R. Scot, Gregory D., Mary E. AB, U. Mich., 1951, MD, 1955, MPH, 1962; MA, U. Wis. Milw., 1979, postgrad. Diplomate Am. Bd. Internal Medicine, Am. Bd. Med. Toxicology, Acad. Toxicol. Scis. Intern Saginaw (Mich.) Gen. Hosp., 1955-56; resident U. Mich. Med. Ctr., Ann Arbor, 1959-62; dir. med. rsch. sect. Dow Chem. Co., Midland, Mich., 1962-66; staff physician Midland Hosp., 1962-66; assoc. prof., prof. Med. Coll. Wis., Milw., 1966-78, 89-91, adj. prof. Dept. Pharmacology and Toxicology, 1978—; cons. Children's Hosp. Wis., 1990-93, Internal Medicine St. Mary's Hosp., Racine, Wis., 1983-93, Dept. Emergency Medicine Milw. Regional Med. Ctr., 1993-95, sr. attending staff, 1967-90; staff Internal Medicine St. Luke's Hosp., Racine, 1983-93; dir. Poison Ctr. Ea. Wis., 1989-93; corp. med. advisor S.C. Johnson & Son, Inc., Racine, 1971-78, dir., 1978-89. Mem. adv. med. staff Milw. Fire Dept., 1975—. Cadet USAF, 1945-46. Fellow ACP, Am. Coll. Occuptl. Medicine, Am. Acad. Clin. Toxicology, Acad. Toxicological Scis.; mem. AMA, Soc. Toxicology, Wis. State Med. Soc., Racine Acad. Medicine, Rotary Internat., Phi Theta Kappa, Phi Kappa Phi, Sigma Tau Delta. Avocations: history of medicine, wilderness hiking, literature, creative writing, inventing medical devices. Home and Office: 5337 Wind Point Rd Racine WI 53402-2322

STEWART, RICHARD EDWIN, insurance consulting company executive; b. Washington, Nov. 4, 1933; s. Irvin and Florence Elsie (Dezendorf) S.; m. Barbara Lewis Dickson, Oct. 29, 1993. B.A., W.Va. U., 1955; B.A. (Rhodes scholar), Oxford (Eng.) U., 1957, M.A., 1961; J.D., Harvard, 1959. Bar: N.Y. 1960. Assoc. Royall, Koegel & Rogers, N.Y.C., 1960-63; asst. counsel to Gov. of N.Y., 1963-64, 1st asst. counsel, 1965-66; supr. ins. N.Y. State Ins. Dept., 1967-70; sr. v.p., gen. counsel First Nat. City Bank, N.Y.C., 1971-72; sr. v.p., dir. Chubb & Son Inc., N.Y.C., 1973-81; sr. v.p. Chubb Corp., N.Y.C., 1973-81, chief fin. officer, 1974-81; gov. N.Y. Ins. Exchange, N.Y.C., 1979-81; chmn. Stewart Econs., Inc., N.Y.C., 1981-90, Chapel Hill, N.C., 1990—; mem. adv. com. HUD, 1968-72; mem. Adminstrv. Conf. U.S., 1970-74; bd. dirs. Am. Arbitration Assn., 1970-80; mem. UN panel experts on Transnational Bank failure, 1991. Co-author: Automobile Insurance....For Whose Benefit?, 1970, Watergate: Implications for Responsible Government, 1974, Medical Malpractice, 1977, Managing Insurer Insolvency, 1988, Insurance Insolvency Quarantees, 1990, A Brief History of Underwriting Cycles, 1991, Niche Insurance Companies, 1997; author: Reason and Regulation, 1972, Insurance and Insurance Regulation, 1980. Trustee Coll. Ins., N.Y., 1970-78, Am. Coll. Life Underwriters, 1990-93; mem. Mayor's Com. on Taxi Regulation, 1979-82, ABA Com. to Improve Liability Ins. System, 1989; mem. panel experts on transnat. bank failure UN, 1991. Served with AUS, 1959. Mem. Nat. Acad. Pub. Adminstrn., Nat. Acad. Social Ins., Cosmos Club of Washington, Century Club of N.Y.C., Phi Beta Kappa Assn. Home and Office: 7601 Talbryn Way Chapel Hill NC 27516-7862

STEWART, ROBERT FORREST, JR., lawyer; b. Niagara Falls, N.Y., Oct. 25, 1943; s. Robert Forrest and Margaret Joanne (Mahoney) S.; m. Tara Campbell Mescal, Aug. 27, 1966; children: Jane Margaret, Laura Campbell, Rebecca Forrest. BS, Coll. Holy Cross, Worcester, Mass., 1965; JD, Georgetown U., 1968; LLM in Labor, Temple U., 1978. Bar: D.C. 1968, Del. 1969, Pa. 1976. Law clk. to presiding judge U.S. Dist. Ct. Del., Wilmington, 1968-69; judge adv. USAF, 1969-72; assoc. Morris, Nichols, Arsht & Tunnell, Wilmington, 1972-76; assoc. Obermayer, Rebmann, Maxwell & Hippel, Phila., 1976-80, ptnr., 1981-85; ptnr. Duane, Morris & Heckscher, Phila. and Wilmington, 1985-92, Dilworth, Paxson, Kalish & Kauffman, Phila. and Wilmington, 1992—. Author: At-Will Termination in Pennsylvania, 1983, Emerging Employee Rights, 1984, At-Will Termination in New Jersey, 1985, Legal Issues of Managing Difficult Employees in Delaware, 1988, Personnel and Employment Law in Pennsylvania/New Jersey/Delaware, 1990, Sexual Harassment, 1993. Chmn. Common Cause Del., Wilmington, 1974-75, 79-80, 97—; pub. mem. coun. Del. Assn. Profl. Engrs., Wilmington, 1981-90; pres. adv. bd. Cath. Charities, Diocese of Wilmington, 1976-90; bd. dirs., vice chmn. United Way Del., 1994—; mem. N.E. regional coun. United Way Am., 1993—; bd. dirs., first vice chair Assoc. United Ways, 1996-97, Del. Citizens Opposed to Death Penalty, 1993—, Bayard House, 1993—; mem. adv. bd. Seton Villa, Siena Hall and Children's Home, 1992—. Named Vol. of Yr., United Way Del., 1984; recipient United Way Del. Fellowship award, 1993. Mem. ABA ACLU (bd. dirs. Del. chpt. 1972-76, 92-95), Del. State Bar Assn., Pa. Bar Assn., Phila. Bar Assn., Del. State C. of C. (labor advisor 1980—, chmn. com. employee rels. 1987—), Rodney Sq. Club, Holy Cross Varsity Club (bd. dirs. 1981—), Coun. Engring. and Sci. Specialty Bd. (pub. mem. 1991—). Democrat. Roman Catholic. Office: Dilworth Paxson Kalish & Kauffman 3200 Mellon Bank Ctr 1735 Market St Philadelphia PA 19103-7501

STEWART, ROBERT GORDON, former museum curator; b. Balt., Mar. 5, 1931; s. Kenneth Elsworth and Ruth (Chambers) S. Student, Gilman Sch., 1946-49; B.F.A., U. Pa., 1954. Architect Ind. Nat. Hist. Park, Phila., 1954, Nat. Park Service, Phila., 1956-57; architect, curator Jefferson Barracks Hist. Park, St. Louis, 1958-61; dir. properties Nat. Trust for Historic Preservation, Washington, 1961-64; sr. curator Nat. Portrait Gallery, Smithsonian Instn., Washington, 1964-94, sr. curator emeritus, 1994—; cons. Loyalist Homestead, St. John's, N.B., Can., 1960; vis. lectr. George Washington U., 1967-70. Author: Nucleus for a National Collection, 1965, Recent Acquisitions, 1966, A Nineteenth-Century Gallery of Distinguished Americans, 1969, Henry Benbridge (1743-1812): American Portrait Painter, 1971, Robert Edge Pine, A British Artist in America 1784-1788, 1979. Dir. Landmarks of St. Louis, 1959-61; adjudicator Jamaican Nat. Art Competition, 1971; cons. The Papers of George Washington, 1990—. Served with U.S. Army, 1954-56. Mem. Md., Dorchester County, Lewes hist. socs., Walpole Soc., Assn. of Historians of Am. Art, Zeta Psi. Episcopalian.

STEWART, ROBERT HENRY, oceanographer, educator; b. York, Pa., Dec. 26, 1941; s. Robert Henry and Mildred June (Smith) S.; m. Hedvig Susan Bagdy, June 26, 1966 (div. Dec. 1976); 1 child, Alethea Ildico Stewart; m. Tracy Ann Bertolucci, July 19, 1986; children: Farrar Clee, Margaret Montgomery. BS, U. Tex., Arlington, 1963; PhD, U. Calif., San Diego, 1969. Asst. rsch. oceanographer Scripps Inst. Oceanography U. Calif., San Diego, 1969-78, assoc. rsch. oceanographer, 1978-79; assoc. rsch. oceanographer, assoc. adj. prof. Scripps Inst. Oceanography, U. Calif., San Diego, 1979-83, rsch. oceanographer, adj. prof., 1983-89; mem. tech. staff Jet Propulsion Lab., Calif. Inst. Tech., Pasadena, 1979-80, rsch. scientist, 1980-83, sr. rsch. scientist, 1983-89; prof. oceanography Tex. A&M U., College Station, 1989—; Topex/Poseidon project scientist Jet Propulsion Lab., 1980-88; mem. many NASA coms.; mem. coms. of Nat. Rsch. Coun., Nat. Acad. Scis.; mem. various internat. scientific coms.; cons. Univ. Corp. for Atmospheric Rsch. Author: Methods of Satellite Oceanography, 1985; editor: Radio Oceanography, 1978; contbr. articles to profl. jours. Trustee San Juan Capistrano Inst. Co-recipient Group Achievement award for Topex/Poseidon mission design NASA, 1993, NASA Pub. Svc. medal, 1994; U. Calif. Regents spl. fellow, 1963; NSF fellow, 1964. Mem. Am. Geophys. Union. Republican. Roman Catholic. Avocations: collect lepidoptera. Home: 8710 Appomattox Dr College Station TX 77845-5567 Office: Oceanography Dept Tex A&M U College Station TX 77843-3146

STEWART, ROBERT LEE, retired army officer, astronaut; b. Washington, Aug. 13, 1942; s. Lee Olin and Mildred Kathleen (Wann) S.; m. Mary Jane Murphy; children: Ragon Annette, Jennifer Lee. BS in Math., U. So. Miss., 1964; MS in Aerospace Engring., U. Tex., 1972; grad., U.S. Army Air Def. Sch., 1964, grad. advanced course, guided missile systems officers course, 1970. Commd. 2d lt. U.S. Army, 1964, advanced through grades to brig. gen., 1986, fire team leader armed helicopter platoon 101st Aviation Bn., instr. pilot Primary Helicopter Sch., 1967-69; bn. ops. officer, bn. exec. officer 309th Aviation Bn., U.S. Army, Seoul, Korea, 1972-73; exptl. test pilot Aviation Engring. Flight Activity U.S. Army, Edwards AFB, Calif., 1974-78; astronaut candidate NASA, 1978, mission specialist Space Shuttle Mission 41-B, 1984; mission specialist STS-51J, 1985; dep. comdr. U.S. Army Strategic Def. Command, Huntsville, Ala., 1987-89; dir. of plans U.S. Space Command, 1989-92. Decorated D.S.M., (2) Legion of Merit, (4) DFC, (2) Purple Hearts, Bronze star, Def. Superior Svc. medal, others; recipient NASA Space Flight medal, 1984, 85, Fineburg Meml. award Am. Helicopter Soc., 1984, Herman Oberth award AIAA, 1990; named Army Aviator of Yr., 1984. Mem. Soc. Exptl. Test Pilots, Assn. U.S. Army, Army Aviation Assn. Am., Assn. Space Explorers. Avocations: photography, woodworking, skiing. Home and Office: 815 Sun Valley Dr Woodland Park CO 80863-9013

STEWART, RODERICK DAVID, singer; b. North London, Eng., Jan. 10, 1945; m. Alana Collins, Apr. 6, 1979 (div. 1984); children: Alana, Sean; child with Kelly Emberg: Ruby Rachel; m. Rachel Hunter, Dec. 15, 1990, child, Renée. Singer with Jeff Beck Group, 1968-69, Faces, 1969-75; albums include (with Jeff Beck Group) Truth, 1968, Beck-Ola, 1969; (with Faces) The First Step, 1970, Long Player, 1971, A Nod Is As Good as a Wink...To a Blind Horse, 1971, Ooh La La, 1973, Coast to Coast/Overture & Beginners, 1973, Snakes and Ladders/The Best of Faces, 1976; (solo) An Old Raincoat Won't Ever Let You Down, 1969, Gasoline Alley, 1970, Every Picture Tells a Story, 1971, Never a Dull Moment, 1972, Sing it Again Rod, 1973, Smiler, 1974, Atlantic Crossing, 1975, The Best of Rod Stewart, 1976, The Best of Rod Stewart Vol. II, 1976, A Night on the Town, 1976, Foot Loose & Fancy Free, 1976, Blondes Have More Fun, 1978, Greatest Hits Vol. I, 1979, Tonight I'm Yours, 1981, Absolutely Live, 1981, Camouflage, 1984, (with Jeff Beck) Get Workin', 1985, Out of Order, 1988, Storyteller: The Complete Anthology 1964-1990, 1990, Downtown Train, 1990, Vagabond Heart, 1991, You Wear It Well, 1992, The Mercury Anthology, 1992, Once In A Blue Moon Vintage, 1993, Ridin High, The Rod Stewart Album, Unplugged...And Seated, 1993 (Grammy nomination, Best Pop Male Vocal for "Have I Told You Lately"). Named Rock Star of Year Rolling Stone mag., 1971; recipient British Rock and Pop Lifetime Achievement award, 1992; inducted into the Rock & Roll Hall of Fame, 1994. Office: Mercury Records Polygram Classics Inc 825 8th Ave New York NY 10019-7416*

STEWART, RONALD DANIEL, medical educator, government official; b. North Sydney, N.S., Can., Oct. 11, 1942; s. Donald Hugh and Edith Cavell (MacLellan) S. BA in Langs., Acadia U., Wolfville, N.S., Can., 1963, BSc in Biology and Chemistry, 1965, DSc (hon.), 1988; MD, Dalhousie U., Halifax, N.S., 1970. Diplomate Am. Bd. Emergency Medicine; license to practice medicine Province of N.S., 1989—; specialty cert. emergency medicine Provincial Med. Bd. N.S., 1989—. Resident emergency medicine L.A. County Med. Ctr., 1972-74; asst. prof. emergency medicine U. So. Calif./L.A. County Med. Ctr., 1974-76, assoc. prof. emergency medicine, 1976-78; dir. emergency medicine Presbyn. Univ. Hosp., Pitts., 1978-85; asst. prof. medicine U. Pitts. Sch. Medicine, 1978-81, prof. medicine, 1981-86; prof. anaesthesia Dalhousie U., Halifax, 1987—; dir. prehosp. care emergency svcs. U. Toronto/Sunnybrook Med. Ctr., 1987-89; prof. anaesthesia U. Toronto, 1987-90, prof. surgery, 1988-90; dir. dept. emergency medicine Sunnybrook Med. Ctr., 1987-89; vis. sabbatical scholar Faculty of Medicine, Dalhousie U., Halifax, 1989-90, vis. prof. anaesthesia, 1989-90; adj. prof. emergency medicine George Washington U., Washington, 1990—; adj. clin. prof. medicine U. Pitts., 1987—; ACLS provider Am. Heart Assn.-Calif. Chpt., 1975, ACLS instr., 1976; affiliate faculty Advanced Trauma Life Support, ACS, 1982-87; nat. faculty Am. Heart Assn., 1982-90. Contbr. articles to profl. jours. Mem. of the Legis. Assembly, Province of N.S., Halifax, 1993—, mem. exec. coun. Min. of Health, Province of N.S., Halifax, 1993—. Recipient award of merit The Can. Assn. Emergency Physicians, 1995, 25th Anniversary Recognition award Paramedic Programme of L.A., 1995, Centennial medallion City of San Francisco, 1995, The Ninth Annual Mulroy Meml. Lectureship, Northwestern U., Chgo., 1995. Fellow Am. Coll. Emergency Physicians, Royal Coll. Physicians Can.; mem. Am. Coll. Emergency Physicians (charter), N.S. Med. Soc., Can. Assn. Emergency Physicians, Can. Med. Assn., Assn. for Automotive Medicine, Nat. Assn. Emergency Med. Svcs. Physicians (mem. exec. com. 1985—), World Assn. for Emergency and Disaster Medicine (mem. exec. com. 1985—), Pitts. Emergency Medicine Found. (founder), Australian Ambulance Officers' Assn. (hon.), Australia and New Zealand Intensive Care Soc. (hon.). Mem. Liberal Party. Presbyterian. Avocations: music, canoeing. Office: PO Box 1617, Halifax, NS Canada B3J 2Y3

STEWART, ROSS, chemistry educator; b. Vancouver, B.C., Can., Mar. 16, 1924; s. David Methven and Jessie (Grant) S.; m. Greta Marie Morris, Sept. 7, 1946; children—Cameron, Ian. B.A., U. B.C., 1946, M.A., 1948; Ph.D., U. Wash., 1954. Lectr. chemistry Royal Roads Coll., Victoria, B.C., 1949-52, asst. prof., 1952-54, assoc. prof., 1954-55; asst. prof. chemistry U. B.C., Vancouver, 1955-59, assoc. prof., 1959-62, prof., 1962-89, hon. prof., 1989—. Author: Oxidation Mechanisms, 1964, Investigation of Organic Reactions, 1966, The Proton: Applications to Organic Chemistry, 1985, (with J.D. Roberts & M.C. Caserio) Organic Chemistry, Methane to Macromolecules, 1970; contbr. numerous articles to profl. jours. Fellow Royal Soc. Can., Chem. Inst. Can.; mem. B.C. Thoroughbred Breeders Soc. (pres. 1972-74), Can. Thoroughbred Horse Soc. (v.p. 1974-75). Club: Point Grey Golf (Vancouver). Avocations: breeding and racing thoroughbred horses; golf; gardening. Home: 4855 Paton St, Vancouver, BC Canada V6L 2H9 Office: U BC, Dept Chemistry, Vancouver, BC Canada V6T 1Z1

STEWART, RUTH ANN, public policy analyst, library adminstrator; b. Chgo., Apr. 4, 1942; d. Elmer Ashton and Ann (Mitchell) S.; m. David Levering Lewis; children: Allegra, Jason, Allison, Eric. Student, U. Chgo., 1960-61, Simmons Coll., 1963; BA, Wheaton Coll., Norton, Mass., 1963; MS, Columbia U., 1965; postgrad., Fisk U., 1970, Harvard U., 1976, John F. Kennedy Sch. Govt., 1987. Libr. Phillips Acad., Andover, Mass., 1963-64, Columbia U., N.Y.C., 1965-68; mktg. mgr. Macmillan Co., N.Y.C., 1968-70; asst. chief Schomburg Ctr. Research in Black Culture, N.Y.C., 1970-80; assoc. dir. for external svcs. N.Y. Pub. Libr., 1980-86; asst. Libr. of Congress for Nat. Programs, Washington, 1986-89; assoc. Dir. for Resource Devel., Congl. Rsch. Svc., Washington, 1989-95, sr. policy analyst, 1995-97; rsch. prof. Bloustein Sch. Planning and Pub. Policy Rutgers U., New Brunswick, N.J., 1997—; mem. libr. vis. com. Wheaton Coll., 1975—, trustee, sec., 1980—; mem. libr. vis. com. Harvard U., 1975-88, MIT, 1986-90; bd. dirs. Nat. Park Found., Washington, 1978-84; bd. visitors Sch. Info. Sci., U. Pitts., 1987-95; bd. dirs. Fund for Folk Culture, Santa Fe, 1991—, The Lab. Sch. of Washington, 1992-94, VOICE Internat., 1994-96, Women's Fgn. Policy Group, 1995—. Author: Portia, 1977. Fellow Internat. Coun. Mus. Mem. Coun. Fgn. Rels. Office: Rutgers U Bloustein Sch Pub Policy New Brunswick NJ

STEWART, S. JAY, chemical company executive; b. Pineville, W.Va., Sept. 18, 1938; s. Virgil Harvey and Lena Rivers (Repair) S.; m. Judith Ann Daniels, June 3, 1961; children: Julie Annette, Jennifer Amy, Steven Jay. BSChemE, U. Cin., 1961; MBA, W.Va. U., 1966. Various positions in engring., mfg., mktg. Monsanto Co., St. Louis, 1961-73; dir. mktg. Ventron Corp. subs. Thiokol, Inc., Beverly, Mass., 1973-77, gen. mgr., 1977-79; pres. Dynachem Corp. subs. Thiokol, Inc., Tustin, Calif., 1979-82; group v.p. Thiokol Corp., Newtown, Pa., 1982; group v.p. splty. chems. Morton Internat., Inc. (formerly Morton Thiokol, Inc.), Chgo., 1983-86, pres., chief oper. officer, 1986-94, also bd. dirs., 94—; chmn. bd., CEO, 1994—. Mem. Household Internat. Inc.,Northwestern U. Assocs., 1988—; trustee Rush Presbyn.-St. Luke's Med. Ctr., Chgo., 1987—; Trustee Mus. Scis. and Industry;mem. exec. comm., Soc. Chem. Industry. Recipient Disting. Alumnus award U. Cin., 1984. Mem. Am. Chem. Soc., Am. Inst. Chem. Engrs., Chmn. Mfrs. Assn. (bd. dirs. 1984-87, 94), Comml. Devel. Assn., Assn. Governing Bds. Univs. and Colls., Chem. Mktg. Assn. (bd. dirs. 1990), Comml. Club Chgo., The Chgo. Club, Econ. Club Chgo. Republican. Methodist. Office: Morton Internat Inc 100 N Riverside Plz Chicago IL 60606

STEWART, SALLY, public relations practitioner; b. Phoenix, Mar. 1, 1955; d. Biven and Nancy Sue (Spurlock) S.; children: Padraic Haines, Colin Haines. BS in Broadcast Journalism, Ariz. State U., 1977, BA in Edn., 1980. Staff writer, media rep. Salt River Project, Phoenix, 1979-81; copy editor Mesa (Ariz.) Tribune, 1981-82; mktg. adminstrv. asst. Phoenix chpt. ARC, 1983; pub. info. asst. City of Scottsdale, Ariz., 1983-84; bus. editor, asst. city editor Scottsdale Progress Tribune, 1984-86; comms. mgr. Mesa Conv. and Visitors Bur., 1986-90; mgmt. asst. Neighborhood Improvement and Housing Dept., City of Phoenix, 1990-92, Pub. Info. Office, City of Phoenix, 1992-93; comm. cons. Ariz. Pub. Svc., Phoenix, 1993—. Mem. com. Fiesta Bowl, Phoenix, 1987-89; mem. pub. rels. com. Juvenile Diabetes Found., Phoenix, 1990; mem. pub. rels. com. Children's Garden Ground Breaking, Phoenix, 1993. mem. Pub. Rels. Soc. Am. (accredited, bd. dirs. 1991-93, assembly del. 1993-95, pres. Valley of the Sun chpt. 1997). Avocations: travel, writing. Office: Ariz Pub Svc 2 Arizona Ctr 400 N 5th St Phoenix AZ 85004-3902

STEWART, SUE S., lawyer; b. Casper, Wyo., Oct. 9, 1942; d. Fraizer McVale and Carolyn Eliabeth (Hunt) Stewart; BA, Wellesley Coll., 1964; postgrad. Harvard U. Law Sch., 1964-65; JD, Georgetown U., 1967; m. Arthur L. Stern, III, July 31, 1965 (div.); children—Anne Stewart, Mark Alan; m. John A. Ciampa, Sept. 1, 1985 (div.). Admitted to N.Y. bar, 1968; clk. to Judges Juvenile Ct., Washington, 1967-68; mem. firm Nixon, Hargrave, Devans & Doyle, Rochester, N.Y., 1968-74, ptnr., 1975—; lectr. in field; trustee Found. of Monroe County (N.Y.) Bar, 1976-78. Sec., dir. United Community Chest of Greater Rochester, 1973-87, 92—; trustee, sec. Internat. Museum Photography at George Eastman House, Rochester, 1974—, Genesee Country Mus., Mumford, N.Y., 1976—; bd. dirs. Ctr. for Govtal. Research; trustee, chmn. United Neighborhood Ctr. of Greater Rochester Found., 1991—. Mem. Am. (chmn. task force on charitable giving, exempt orgns. com. tax sect. 1981—), N.Y. State (exec. com. tax sect., 1974-76, chmn. com. exempt orgns. 1975-76), Monroe County Bar Assn. (trustee 1974-75), BNA Portfolio, Pvt. Found. Distbns. Author: Charitable Giving and Solicitation. Office: Nixon Hargrave Devans & Doyle PO Box 1051 Clinton Sq Rochester NY 14603-1051

STEWART, TERESA ELIZABETH, elementary school educator; b. Cheverly, Md., Nov. 26, 1966; d. Richard Lynn and Sandra Lois (O'Neill)

S. BS in Elem. Edn. cum laude, Bowie State U., 1988, MEd in Elem. Edn., 1996. Cert. elem. tchr., Md. Asst. tchr. Tom Thumb Day Care, Bowie, Md., 1989; elem. tchr. Berwyn Bapt. Sch., College Park, Md., 1989-95, Berkshire Elem. Sch., Forestville, Md., 1995—. Dir. vacation Bible sch., youth group leader Bowie United Meth. Ch., 1988—, sec. adminstrv. coun., 1993—, chairperson pastor parish rels. com., 1996—, sec. membership com., 1993—; tchr. children's Bible class University Park Ch. of Brethren, 1990-94; instr., judge Belle-Aires Twirling Corp., Bowie, 1986—; mem. Md. Bato n Coun. Koonz, McKinney & Johnson Law Firm scholar, 1986-88. Mem. Huntington Heritage Soc., Kappa Delta Pi, Delta Kappa Gamma (chair scholarship com.). Democrat. Avocations: camping, collecting postcards and teddy bears, twirling, choral singing. Home: 14103 Bramble Ln # 104 Laurel MD 20708 Office: Berkshire Elem Sch 6201 Surrey Square Ln Forestville MD 20747-2961

STEWART, THOMAS J., wholesale distribution executive; b. 1945. CEO Svcs. Group Am. Office: Services Group of America 4025 Delridge Way SW Ste 500 Seattle WA 98106-1277 Office: 4025 Delridge Way SW Ste 500 Seattle WA 98106-1277

STEWART, THOMAS JAMES, JR., baritone; b. San Saba, Tex., Aug. 29, 1928; s. Thomas James and Gladys Naomi (Reavis) S.; m. Evelyn Lear, Jan. 8, 1955; children: Jan Lear, Bonni Lear. Mus.B., Baylor U., 1953; postgrad., Juilliard Sch. Music, 1953-54, Berlin Hochschule for Music, 1957-58. Appeared with, Met. Opera, Chgo. Opera, San Francisco Opera, Bayreuth Festival, Salzburg Festival, Vienna State Opera, Royal Opera Covent Garden, Grand Opera Paris, Deutsche Oper Berlin, La Scala, Milan, Budapest Opera, Prague Opera, 1960—, also major orchs., throughout the world. Mem. hon. coun. IVS S'hertogenbosch, The Netherlands, 1996; artistic advisor Vocal Arts Soc., Washington, 1995; mem. hon. adv. bd. George London Found. for Singers, N.Y.C., 1994. Served with USAF, 1945-49. Recipient Kammersaenger of Berlin, 1964; Richard Wagner medal, 1965; San Francisco Opera medal, 1985, Am. Artist citation N.Y. Singing Tchrs. Assn., 1995; Fulbright grantee, 1957-58.

STEWART, WARREN EARL, chemical engineer, educator; b. Whitewater, Wis., July 3, 1924; s. Earl Austin and Avis (Walker) S.; m. Jean Durham Potter, May 24, 1947; children—Marilyn, David, Douglas, Carol, Margaret, Mary Jean. B.S. in Chem. Engring, U. Wis., 1945, M.S. in Chem. Engring, 1947; Sc.D. in Chem. Engring, Mass. Inst. Tech., 1951. Project chem. engr. Sinclair Research Labs., Harvey, Ill., 1950-56; cons. Sinclair Research Labs., 1956-83; asst. prof. chem. engring. dept. U. Wis., Madison, 1956-58; assoc. prof. U. Wis., 1958-61, prof., 1961—, chmn. dept., 1973-78, McFarland-Bascom prof., 1983-96, chmn. dept., 1973-78, prof. emeritus, 1997—; cons. Engelhard Industries, Inc., Newark, 1956-58; instr. spl. courses transport phenomena Chemstrand Corp., Pensacola, Fla., 1962, Nat. U. La Plata, Argentina, 1962, Esso Rsch. & Engring. Co., 1963, 66, Phillips Petroleum Co., 1963, Am. Inst. Chem. Engrs., 1965, 68, 69, Inst. Tec. Celaya (Mex.), 1983, Univ. Autonoma de Mex., 1985; Reilly lectr. Notre Dame U., 1993. Author: (with R.B. Bird and E.N. Lightfoot) Transport Phenomena, 1960, Special Topics in Transport Phenomena, 1965, (with R.B. Bird, E.N. Lightfoot and T.W. Chapman) Lectures in Transport Phenomena, 1969; editorial advisor: Latin Am. Applied Rsch.; editorial advisor: Computers and Chem. Engring. Served to ensign USNR, 1944-46. Recipient Benjamin Smith Reynolds teaching award, 1981, Byron Bird rsch. award, 1991. Fellow Am. Inst. Chem. Engrs. (Computing in Chem. Engring. award 1985); mem. NAE, Am. Chem. Soc. (Murphree award in indsl. and engring. chemistry 1989), Am. Soc. for Engring. Edn., (Chem. Engring. Lectureship award 1983), Phi Beta Kappa, Sigma Xi, Alpha Chi Sigma (research award 1981), Phi Eta Sigma, Tau Beta Pi, Phi Lambda Upsilon, Phi Kappa Phi. Conglist. (deacon, moderator). Home: 734 Huron Hl Madison WI 53711-2955

STEWART, WILLIAM GENE, broadcast executive; b. Winfield, Kans., Dec. 10, 1923; s. Everette Dewey and Mary Lee (Nace) S.; m. Lila Jean Bohlender, June 24, 1951; 1 child: Linda Jean. BA, Denver U., 1949. Mgr. KFKA radio, Greeley, Colo., 1951-56, KGHF radio, Pueblo, Colo., 1956-58, KWRL radio, Riverton, Wyo., 1958-59; owner KLMO radio, Longmont, Colo., 1959—, partner, 1988—. Sgt. USAF, 1943-46. Recipient numerous civic awards, 1959—. Mem. Longmont Am. Legion (life), Elks Club, Moose Lodge, Rotary Club (pres. 1984-85), Fox Hills Country Club. Republican. Avocations: golf, swimming, reading. Office: KLMO-AM PO Box 799 614 Kimbark St Longmont CO 80501-4911*

STEWART-FINOCCHIARO, PENNY MORRIS, secondary school educator; b. Glendale, Calif., Sept. 30, 1949; d. C. Harold and Margaret (Nelson) Morris; m. Paul D. Finocchiaro, Apr. 9, 1996; children from previous marriage: E. Pierce III, Hailey M. BA in Speech and English, Muskingum Coll., New Concord, Ohio, 1971; MA in Edn., Nat. U., Sacramento, 1991. Cert. multiple and single subject tchr., Calif. Assoc. prod. Alhecama Players, Santa Barbara (Calif.) C.C. Dist., 1972-86; docent Santa Barbara Mus. Art, 1975-86; importer Cambridge Place Corp., Santa Barbara, 1974-86; with promotions and fund raising depts. Stewart-Bergman Assocs., Nevada City, Calif., 1986-89; travel columnist The Union, Grass Valley, Calif., 1987-90; tchr. drama and English Bear River H.S., Grass Valley, 1991—, dept. chair visual and performing arts, 1993—. Art docent coord. Deer Creek Sch., Nevada City, 1986-90, pres. Parent Tchr. Club, 1987-88. Recipient award for valuable contbn. to schs. Nevada City Sch. Dist., 1990, Dir.'s award Santa Barbara C.C., 1982. Mem. Nat. Coun. Tchrs. of English, Ednl. Theatre Assn., Calif. Ednl. Theatre Assn., No. Calif. Ednl. Theatre Assn. Avocations: art and antique collecting, rollerblading, skiing, biking, swimming, theatre. Home: 230 Fairmont Dr Grass Valley CA 95945-9709 Office: Bear River HS 11130 Magnolia Rd Grass Valley CA 95949-8366

STEWART-PÉREZ, RENICE ANN, writer; b. Milw., Jan. 2, 1947; d. Fredrick and Lucia (Stewart) Fregin; children: Jennifer Jean, Whitney Susan; m. Robert Anthony Pérez, Dec. 21, 1995. BA, U. San Diego, 1989, MA, 1991. Pres. Chubby Bumpkins, Inc., Houston, 1980-82; contracts adminstr. Gulf States Computer Svcs., Houston, 1980-82; pres. RAM Prodns., Houston, 1981-82, Pizza Internat., Inc., Houston, 1982-84; contracts adminstr. First Alliance Corp., Houston, 1982-85; freelance pub. rels. cons. San Diego, 1985-97, Plano, Tex., 1997—. Tutor U. San Diego Writing Ctr., 1987-89; founder, dir. pub. rels.-tng. Montgomery County (Tex.) Crisis Action Line, Houston, 1979-84; founder, v.p., bd. dirs. Montgomery County Rape Crisis Coalition, 1982-84, speaker, 1982-84; speaker Rape Trauma Coalition, 1982-84; mem. prodn. com. Community Women Together, Montgomery County, 1980-82; pres. Living Arts Coun., Houston, 1980-81. Named Woman of Yr. YWCA, 1981, 82. Mem. Am. Assn. Bus. Women (dir. activities Houston chpt. 1983-84), Bus. Women's Forum (bd. dir. community awareness Houston chpt. 1982-83), Assn. Women Bus. Owners, Lions (hon.), Phi Alpha Delta.

STEYER, ROY HENRY, retired lawyer; b. Bklyn., July 1, 1918; s. Herman and Augusta (Simon) S.; m. Margaret Fahr, Feb. 21, 1953; children: Hume R., James P., Thomas F. A.B. with honors in Govt. and Gen. Studies, Cornell U., 1938; LL.B. cum laude, Yale U., 1941. Bar: N.Y. 1941, various fed. cts. from 1947, U.S. Supreme Ct. 1955. Assoc. firm Sullivan & Cromwell, N.Y.C., 1941-42, 46-52, ptnr., 1953-88, ret., 1988. Trustee N.Y.C. Sch. Vol. Program, 1974-78. Served to lt. USNR, 1943-46. Mem. Am. Coll. Trial Lawyers, ABA (chmn. com. on antitrust problems in internat. trade antitrust sect. 1959-62), N.Y. State Bar Assn., Assn. of Bar of City of N.Y. (chmn. com. on trade regulation 1962-64), Order of Coif, Century Assn., Phi Beta Kappa, Phi Kappa Phi. Home: 112 E 74th St New York NY 10021-3503

STICE, JAMES EDWARD, chemical engineer, educator; b. Fayetteville, Ark., Sept. 19, 1928; s. F. Fenner and Charlotte (Anderson) S.; m. Patricia Ann Stroner, Sept. 22, 1951 (dec.); children: Susan Emily, James Clayton; m. Betty B. Gowdy, Aug. 3, 1996. BS, U. Ark., 1949; MS, Ill. Inst. Tech., 1952, PhD, 1963. Registered profl. engr., Tex., Ark. Process engr. Visking Corp., North Little Rock, Ark., 1951-53; chem. engr. Thurston Chem. Co. div. W.R. Grace & Co., Joplin, Mo., 1953-54; asst. prof. chem. engring. U. Ark., 1954-57, asso. prof., prof., 1962-68; instr. chem. engring. Ill. Inst. Tech., Chgo., 1957-62; dir. Bur. Engring. Teaching, asso. prof. chem. engring. U. Tex., Austin, 1968-73, prof. engring. edn. in chem. engring., 1973-85, T. Brockett Hudson prof. chem. engring., 1985-90, Bob R. Dorsey prof. engring., 1990-96, dir. Ctr. for Teaching Effectiveness, 1973-89; dir. Effective Teaching Inst. U. Tex. System, summer 1970; prof. emeritus, 1996—; vis. prof. U. Iberoamericana, Mexico City, summer 1977; disting. vis. prof., H.T. Person chair engring. U. Wyo., Laramie, 1996; summer cons. E.I. duPont de Nemours & Co., Inc., Savannah River Plant, Aiken, S.C., 1955, Humble Oil & Refining Co., Baytown, Tex., 1956, Universal Oil Products Co., Des Plaines, Ill., 1957, 58, Phillips Petroleum Co., Bartlesville, Okla., 1963, Ethyl Corp., Baton Rouge, 1965, U. Wis., Eau Claire, 1970—. Author: (with B.S. Swanson) Electronic Analog Computer Primer, 1965, Computadoras Analogicas Electronicas, 1971, Expansion of Keller Plan Instruction in Engineering and Selected Other Disciplines, 1975, Developing Critical Thinking and Problem-Solving Abilities, 1987. Recipient Gen. Dynamics award for excellence in tchg., 1980, Western Electric Fund award for excellence in engring. tchg., 1981, Chester F. Carlson award for innovation in engring. tchg., 1984, Outstanding Engring. Advisor award, 1993; named Outstanding Chem. Engring. Prof., 1993, Friar Soc. Tchg. Fellow, 1993-94, Outstanding Chem. Engring. Prof., 1996, Disting. Alumnus U. Ark., 1995. Fellow Am. Soc. Engring. Edn. (life mem., elected dir. 1983-85, chmn. chem. engring. div. 1988-89, bd. dirs. 1990-92, v.p. 1991-92); mem. Am. Inst. Chem. Engrs., Instrument Soc. Am. (Jour. award 1966), Scabbard and Blade, Scholia (pres. 1989-90), Sigma Xi, Delta Sigma, Sigma Chi, Phi Eta Sigma, Pi Mu Epsilon, Alpha Chi Sigma, Tau Beta Pi, Omicron Delta Kappa, Phi Lambda Upsilon, Phi Kappa Phi. Home: 4205 North Hills Dr Austin TX 78731

STICH, STEPHEN PETER, philosophy educator; b. N.Y.C., May 9, 1943; s. Samuel Joseph and Sylvia Lucille (Siegel) S.; m. Judith Ann Gagnon, Dec. 20, 1971; children: Jonathan Andrew, Rebecca Elizabeth. BA summa cum laude with distinction, U. Pa., 1964; PhD, Princeton U., 1968. Teaching asst. Princton U., 1965; asst. prof. U. Mich., 1968-73, assoc. prof., 1973-78, dir. grad. studies in philosophy, 1973-74, assoc. chmn. dept. philosophy, 1975-76; assoc. prof. U. Md., 1978-81, prof., 1981-86, dir. grad. studies in philosophy, 1982-83; prof. U. Calif., San Diego, 1986-89, dir. cognitive sci. program, 1988-89; prof. philosophy and cognitive sci. Rutgers U., New Brunswick, 1989—, acting chair dept. philosophy, 1992-93; prof. Linguistic inst., Linguistic Soc. Am., summer 1982; dir. Summer Seminar for Coll. Tchrs. NEH, 1983, 89; vis. sr. lectr. U. Sydney, 1984-85; vis. fellow Australian Nat. U., 1992; Jemison prof. humanities U. Ala., Birmingham, 1993; adj. prof. CUNY Grad. Ctr., 1994—; Erskine fellow Canterbury U., Christchurch, New Zealand, 1996; cons. Pres. Commn. for Nat. Priorities in the Eighties, Pres. Commn. on Ethics in Medicine and Biomed. and Behavioral Rsch.; mem. selection com. Mellon Fellowships in the Humanities, 1983-84; mem. Fulbright Selection Com., 1981-83, chair, 1983; vis. fellow Australian Nat. U., Rsch. Sch. Social Scis., 1992. Author: From Folk Psychology to Cognitive Science, 1983, The Fragmentation of Reason, 1990, Deconstructing the Mind, 1996; editor: Innate Ideas, 1975; (with others) The Recombinant DNA Debate, 1979, Philosophy and Connectionist Theory, 1991, Mental Representation, 1994; mem. editl. bd. Linguistics and Philosophy, 1984—, Mind and Language, 1985—, Cognitive Sci., 1990—, Minds and Machines, 1991—, Pragmatics and Cognition, 1991—, Philosophical Studies, 1992—, Philosophy of Sci., 1992—, Cognition, 1993—, Neural Network Modeling and Connectionism; mem. editl. adv. bd. Studies in Cognitive Sys.; contbr. articles to profl. jours., chpts. to books. Woodrow Wilson Nat. Fellowship Found. fellow, 1964-65, Woodrow Wilson dissertation fellow, 1967, Danforth grad. fellow, 1964-67, H.H. Ford fellow Princeton U., 1967, Coun. Philos. Studies Summer Inst. fellow, 1971, Am. Coun. Learned Socs. fellow, 1978-79, Rutgers U. competitive fellow; recipient fellowships NEH, 1974, 83-84, 96, Ctr. for Advanced Study in Behavioral Scis., Stanford, Calif., 1983; Fulbright sr. rsch. scholar, Bristol (U.K.) U., 1978-79; grantee U.S.-Israel Ednl. Found., 1979, NRC and U.S. Nat. Com. for Internat. Union of History and Philosophy of Sci., Hannover, West Germany, 1979, NSF, 1981-82. Mem. Am. Philos. Assn., Soc. for Philosophy and Psychology (pres. 1982-83, exec. com. 1980-82, 83-84, chair program com. 1979-80), Philosophy of Sci. Assn., Brit. Soc. for Philosophy of Sci., Fulbright Alumni Assn. Office: Rutgers U Philosophy Dept Davison Hall Douglass Campus New Brunswick NJ 08903

STICHT, J. PAUL, retired food products and tobacco company executive; b. Clairton, Pa., 1917. BA, Grove City Coll., 1939; postgrad., U. Pitts. With U.S. Steel Corp., 1939-44; pers. dir. Trans World Airlines, 1944-48; v.p. Campbell Soup Co., 1947-57, pres. internat., 1957-60; from exec. v.p. to pres. Federated Dept. Stores, Inc., 1960-72; chmn. exec. com., COO R.J. Reynolds Industries, Inc., Winston-Salem, N.C., 1972-73, pres., CEO, 1978-79, chmn. bd., 1979-85; chmn. RJR Nabisco, Inc., Winston-Salem, 1987-89, acting chmn., CEO, 1989. Trustee Grove City Coll.; trustee, former chmn. Caribbean/L.Am. Action; mem. bd. visitors Bowman Gray Sch. Medicine, former chmn. bd. visitors; mem. bd. visitors Fuqua Sch. Bus. Duke U. Office: Castle Springs Inc 119 Brookstown Ave Winston Salem NC 27101-5245

STICK, ALYCE CUSHING, information systems consultant; b. N.J., July 13, 1944; d. George William and Adele Margaret (Wilderotter) Cushing; m. James McAlpin Easter, July, 1970 (div. Aug. 1986); m. T. Howard F. Stick, June, 1989. AA, Colby-Sawyer Coll., 1964; student, Boston U., 1964-65, Johns Hopkins U., 1972-74; cert., Control Data Inst. and Life Office Mgmt. Assn., 1976. Claims investigator Continental Casualty Co., Phila., 1967-69; data processing coord. Chesapeake Life Ins. Co., Balt., 1970-72; sr. systems analyst Comml. Credit Computer Corp., Balt., 1972-80; v.p. Shawmut Computer Systems, Inc., Owings Mills, Md., 1980-85; pres. Computer Relevance, Inc., Gladwyne, Pa., 1985—; cons. Siani Hosp., Balt., 1982-85, AT&T, Reading, Pa., 1987-88, Dun and Bradstreet, Allentown, Pa., 1988, Arco Chem. Co., Newtown Square, Pa., 1990-91, Rohm and Haas Co., Phila., 1992-97. Designer/author: (computer software systems) Claim-Track, 1977, Property-Profiles, 1979, Stat-Model, 1989; co-designer/author: Patient-Profiles, 1983. Treas. Balt. Mus. Art, Sales and Rental Gallery, 1984. Mem. Assn. for Systems Mgmt., Data Processing Mgmt. Assn., Ind. Computer Cons. Assn., Merion Cricket Club (Haverford, Pa.). Republican. Avocations: Am. antiques, Chinese export porcelain dealer. Office: Computer Relevance Inc 1501 Monticello Dr Gladwyne PA 19035-1206

STICKEL, FREDERICK A., publisher; b. Weehawken, N.J., Nov. 18, 1921; s. Fred and Eva (Madigan) S.; m. Margaret A. Dunne, Dec. 4, 1943; children—Fred A., Patrick F., Daisy E., Geoffrey M., James E., Bridget A. Student, Georgetown U., 1939-42; BS, St. Peter's Coll., 1943. Advt. salesperson Jersey Observer daily, Hoboken, N.J., 1945-51; retail advt. salesperson Jersey Jour., Jersey City, 1951-55; advt. dir. Jersey Jour., 1955-66, publisher, 1966-67; gen. mgr. Oregonian Pub. Co., Portland, Oreg., 1967-72, pres., 1972—, publisher, 1975—. Bd. regents U. Portland; mem. adv. bd. Portland State U.; bd. dirs. Portland Rose Festival Assn., United Way Oreg.; chmn. Portland Citizens Crime Commn.; mem. adv. bd. St. Vincent's Hosp. Capt. USMC, 1942-45. Mem. Assn. for Portland Progress (dir.), Portland C. of C. (dir.), Oreg. Newspaper Pubs. Assn. (past pres.), Pacific N.W. Newspaper Assn. (pres.), Am. Newspaper Pubs. Assn., University Club, Multnomah Athletic Waverley Country Club, Arlington Club, Rotary. Office: Oregonian Pub Co 1320 SW Broadway Portland OR 97201-3411

STICKEL, PATRICK FRANCIS, publishing executive, newspaper; b. Hoboken, N.J., Apr. 17, 1950; s. Fred A. and Margaret (Dunne) S.; m. Debra Isaak, May 10, 1986. Degree in bus. mgmt., U. Portland, 1975. With advt. dept. Jersey Jour., Jersey City, 1966-67; with Oregonian Pub. Co., Portland, 1967-68, 70-75, pressman, with retail advt. dept., 1975-77, with retail & circulation depts., 1980-86, adminstrv. asst., 1987-89, gen. mgr., 1990-94, pres., 1994—; project mgr. Times Picayune, New Orleans, 1986-87. Exec. com. Oreg. Forum, Portland. 1st lt. USMC, 1977-80. Mem. Pacific N.W. Newspapers Assn. (bd. dirs.), Waverley Country Club, Univ. Club, Multnomah Athletic Club. Avocation: golf. Office: Oregonian Pub Co 1320 SW Broadway Portland OR 97201-3411

STICKLE, DAVID WALTER, microbiologist; b. Boston, Apr. 18, 1933; s. Harold Edwards and Lucille Margaret (Magee) S.; m. Mary Elizabeth DeLong, July 29, 1972. BS in Chemistry, Biology, Tufts U., 1955; MS in Pharmacy and Health, Northeastern U., Boston, 1968; MPH, U. N.C., 1969, DrPH, 1971. Bacteriologist Mass. Dept. Pub. Health, Boston, 1959-63, supr. immunology unit, 1963-68; UNC/CDC lab. dir.'s program Ctrs. for Disease Control, Atlanta, 1968-71; chief, clin. lab. improvement program Divsn. Med. Labs./Minn. Dept. Health, Mpls., 1971-82, acting dir., 1977-78, asst. dir., 1978-88; ex-officio mem. Minn. Soc. Clin. Pathologists Exec. Com., Mpls., 1977-78; mem. Proficiency Testing Com., Minn. Acad. Family Physicians, Mpls., 1977-83; adj. asst. prof. U. Minn., Mpls., 1977-88; assoc. prof. emeritus, U. Minn., 1988—. Editor: Med. Lab. Forum periodical, 1973-88. Proctor Nat. Registry of Microbiology, Mpls. Examinations for Minn., 1987-92; instr. Edina Community Edn. Programs, Minn., 1992. With U.S. Army, 1955-57. Lab. tng. grantee Ctr. for Disease Control, HEW, Atlanta, 1977-78, 1978-80, 1979-81. Mem. Am. Soc. Microbiology, Phi Sigma, Sigma Xi. Achievements include serologic tests for systemic candidiasis which were in use for many years by the Ctrs. for Disease Control, U.S. Dept. of Health and Human Svcs.

STICKLER, DANIEL LEE, health care management consultant; b. Fairmont, W.Va., Jan. 4, 1938; s. Elmer Daniel and Ruby Lee (Ball) S.; m. Donna Lou Johnson, Apr. 16, 1960; children—Dwight Lorne, Dwayne Lee, Douglas Lynn. B.S. in Civil Engring., W.Va. U., 1960; M.P.H. in Health Adminstrn., U. Pitts., 1970. Registered profl. engr., Tex. Asst. dir. Presbyn.-Univ. Hosp., Pitts., 1970-71, assoc. dir., 1971-72, adminstr., chief operating officer, 1972-76, exec. dir., chief exec. officer, 1976-83, pres., chief exec. officer, 1983-86; pres., CEO, The Cedars Med. Ctr., Miami, Fla., 1986-91; pres. DLS Assocs., Inc., Miami, 1991-95; sr. v.p. The Hunter Group, 1996—; adj. assoc. prof. Grad. Sch. Pub. Health, U. Pitts., 1976-86. Fellow Am. Coll. Hosp. Adminstrn.; mem. Palmaire Country Club. Republican. Methodist. Avocations: golf; gardening. Home and Office: 5803 Fairwoods Cir Sarasota FL 34243-3821

STICKLER, FRED CHARLES, manufacturing company executive; b. Villisca, Iowa, Dec. 11, 1931; s. Donald H. and Martha E. (Reese) S.; m. Dorothy A. Frahm, July 10, 1955; children—Mark, Lisa, Kent. B.S., Iowa State U., 1953, Ph.D., 1958; M.S., Kans. State U., 1955. Research asst. Kans. State U., 1953-55, Iowa State U., 1955-58; asst. prof., then asso. prof. agronomy Kans. State U., 1958-64; with Deere & Co., Moline, Ill., 1964-87; dir. Deere & Co. (Tech. Center), 1976-80, dir. product and market planning, 1980-87, ret., 1987—; crop and soils cons., 1988—. Bd. dirs. Upper Rock Island County YMCA, 1980-87, U.S. Fed. Grain Council, 1986-89. Mem. Am. Soc. Agronomy, Crop Sci. Soc. Am., Am. Soc. Agrl. Engrs.

STICKLER, GUNNAR BRYNOLF, pediatrician; b. Peterskirchen, Germany, June 13, 1925; came to U.S., 1951, naturalized, 1958; s. Fritz and Astrid (Wennerberg) S.; m. Duci M. Kronenbitter, Aug. 30, 1956; children: Katarina Anna, George David. M.D., U. Munich, Germany, 1949; Ph.D., U. Minn., Mpls., 1957. Diplomate Am. Bd. Pediatrics, ofcl. examiner and mem., 1965-95. Resident in clin. pathology Krankenhaus III Orden, Munich, 1950; resident in pathology U. Munich, 1950-51; intern Mountainside Hosp., Montclair, N.J., 1951-52; fellow in pediatrics Mayo Grad. Sch., Rochester, Minn., 1953-56; sr. cancer research scientist Roswell Park Meml. Inst., Buffalo, 1956-57; asst. to staff Mayo Clinic, Rochester, 1957-58; cons. in pediatrics Mayo Clinic, 1959-89, head sect. pediatrics, 1969-74; prof. pediatrics, chmn. dept. pediatrics Mayo Clinic and Mayo Med. Sch., 1974-80; mem. test com. III Nat. Bd. Med. Examiners, 1973-75; vis. prof. at various univs and instns., including U. Dusseldorf (Germany) and U. Munich, 1971, Pahlavi U., Iran, 1975, Olga Hosp., Stuttgart, Germany, 1978, Martin Luther King Hosp., Los Angeles, 1979, U. Man., 1981; mem. emeritus staff Mayo Clinic, 1989. Contbr. numerous articles to med. publs.; editorial bd. Clin. Pediatrics, 1968-76, 79—, European Jour. Pediatrics, 1976-84, Pediatrics, 1983-89. Recipient Humanitarian award Chgo. region chpt. Nat. Found. Ileitis and Colitis, 1978, award for excellence of subject matter and presentation So. Minn. Med. Assn., 1978. Mem. Am. Acad. Pediatrics, Soc. Pediatric Research, Am. Pediatric Soc., Midwest Soc. Pediatric Research (council 1967-69, pres. 1970-71, Founders award 1996), N.W. Pediatric Soc. (pres. 1973-74). Achievements include description of hereditary progressive arthropthalmopathy in 1965, now called Stickler syndrome.

STICKNEY, JESSICA, former state legislator; b. Duluth, Minn., May 16, 1929; d. Ralph Emerson and Claudia Alice (Cox) Page; m. Edwin Levi Stickney, June 17, 1951; children: Claudia, Laura, Jeffrey. BA, Macalester Coll., St. Paul, Minn., 1951; PhD (hon), Rocky Mtn. Coll., Billings, Mont., 1986. Rep. State of Mont., 1989-92; mem. Gov.'s Commn. on Post-Sec. Edn., Mont., 1973-75. Mem. Sch. Bd. Trustees, Miles City, Mont., 1968-74; mem., chmn. zoning bd., Miles City, 1975-89; mem. Govt. Study Commn., Miles City, 1974-76, United Ch. Christ Bd. Homeland Ministries, 1975-81; chmn., conf. moderator United Ch. Christ Bd. Mont.-Northern Wyo. Conf., 1980-82; chmn. Town Meeting on the Arts, Mont., 1980; mem., chmn. Miles Community Coll. Bd., 1975-89, chmn. 1978-80. Mem. Mont. Arts Coun. (chmn. 1982-85), Western States Arts Found. (vice chmn. 1984), Nat. Assembly State Arts Agys. (bd. dirs. 1982-88), AAUW (pres. 1964-66). Democrat. Avocations: writing, sewing, painting, reading.

STIDD, LINDA MARIE, rehabilitation nurse; b. Martins Ferry, Ohio, Mar. 20, 1947; d. Stephen George and Helen Jane (Cupryk) Mularcik; m. William Leroy Stidd, May 4, 1968; 1 child, Christopher Alan. Diploma, Ohio Valley Gen. Hosp., 1968; BSN, Ohio U., 1995. CRRN; RN cert. in gerontology. Staff nurse Ohio Valley Gen. Hosp., Wheeling, W.Va., 1968-69, 73-79; supr. Woodland Acres Nursing Home, St. Clairsville, Ohio, 1971-73; staff nurse Ohio Valley Med. Ctr., Wheeling, 1973-79, head nurse rehab., 1981-91; nurse mgr. OVMC Rehab. at Woodsdale, Wheeling, 1991-92; nurse mgr. for skilled care/rehab. Peterson Rehab. Hosp. and Geriatric Ctr., Wheeling, 1991-95. Mem. Assn. Rehab. Nurses, W.Va. Assn. Rehab. Nurses, W.Va. Orgn. Nurse Execs., Nat. Disting. Svc. Registry Med. and Vocat. Rehab. Democrat. Roman Catholic. Avocations: reading, travel, drawing. Office: Peterson Rehab Hosp and Geriatric Ctr Homestead Ave Wheeling WV 26003-6697

STIDHAM, SHALER, JR., operations research educator; b. Washington, Dec. 4, 1941; s. Shaler and Gladys (Ruddick) S.; m. Carolyn Jean Noble, Apr. 6, 1968; children: Christiane Wilson, Dana Claire, Ann-Elise. BA, Harvard U., 1963; MS, Case Inst. Tech., 1964; PhD, Stanford U., 1968. Asst. prof. dept. ops. rsch. Cornell U., Ithaca, N.Y., 1968-75; assoc. prof., prof. dept. indsl. engring. N.C. State U., Raleigh, 1975-86; prof. dept. ops. rsch. U. N.C., Chapel Hill, 1986—, chmn. dept. ops. rsch., 1990-95; lektor Aarhus (Denmark) U., 1971-72; guest prof. Tech. U., Denmark, Lyngby, 1976-77; vis. fellow Statis. Lab., Cambridge (Eng.) U., 1982-83; cons. Bell Telephone Labs., 1981; vis. scholar Stanford (Calif.) U., 1975, 79; invited prof. Inst. Nat. Récherche en Informatique et en Automatique, Sophia Antipolis, France, 1991-92; keynote spkr. to profl. confs., The Netherlands, Germany, Poland, France and Japan, 1977—. Bd. dirs. Friends of Coll., Raleigh, 1979-82, chmn. program com., 1981-82; bd. dirs. N.C. Symphony Found., Raleigh, 1990—, N.C. Mus. of Art Fund, Raleigh, 1996—; bd. deacons Pullen Meml. Ch., 1995—; mem. faculty coun. U. N.C., Chapel Hill, 1995—. Overseas fellow Churchill Coll., Cambridge, 1982—. Mem. Inst. for Ops. Rsch and Mgmt. Scis. (chmn. applied probability tech. sect. 1990-91, program co-chmn. internat. meeting Osaka, Japan 1989), Sigma Xi (Young Scientist Rsch. award 1978). Home: 10428 Whitestone Rd Raleigh NC 27615-1236 Office: U NC Dept Ops Rsch Cb 3180 Smith Bldg Chapel Hill NC 27599

STIEBEL, GERALD GUSTAVE, art dealer; b. N.Y.C., Sept. 28, 1944; s. Eric and Irene (Sichel) S.; m. Judith Rudner, 1965 (div. 1975); children: Catherine Lynn, Daniel James; m. Penelope Hunter, Aug. 14, 1975; 1 son, Hunter Hans. BA, C.W. Post Coll., 1965; postgrad. Study Ctr. for Fine and Decorative Arts, London, Eng., 1965-66; MA, Columbia U., 1967. With Rosenberg & Stiebel, Inc., N.Y.C., 1966—, treas., 1968—, v.p., 1971-85, pres., 1985—; mem. faculty New Sch. Social Research, 1979-84; bd. dirs. MUSE Film and TV; mem. art adv. panel IRS, 1980-83; mem. President's Cultural Property Adv. Com., 1995—. Mem. Nat. Antique and Art Dealers Assn. Am. (v.p. 1973-77, pres. 1977-79), Art Dealers Assn. Am. (dir. 1980-89), Internat. Confedn. Dealers in Works of Art (pres. 1981-84, permanent councillor 1990—), Syndicat Nat. des Antiquaires. Office: 32 E 57th St New York NY 10022-2513

STIEBER, TAMAR, journalist; b. Bklyn., Sept. 15, 1955; d. Alfred and Florence (Spector) S. Student, Rockland C.C., 1972-75, Rockland C.C., 1972-75, West London (Eng.) Coll., 1973-74; BA in Film cum laude, U. Calif., Berkeley, 1985, postgrad. in comparative lit., 1985-86; grad. police reserve academycum laude, Napa Valley Coll., 1988. Office mgr., confidential sec. AP, San Francisco, 1981-83; stringer Daily Californian, Berkeley, Calif., 1983-84; film rsch. teaching asst. U. California, Berkeley, 1984-86;

libr. and rsch. asst. Pacific Film Archive, Berkeley, 1984-86; intern San Francisco Examiner, 1984; reporter Sonoma (Calif.) Index-Tribune, 1987-88, Vallejo (Calif.) Times-Herald, 1988-89, Albuquerque Journal, 1989-94. Recipient Pulitzer prize for specialized reporting, 1990, first place pub. svc. divsn. N.Mex. Press Assn., 1990, pub. svc. award Albuquerque Press Club, 1990; first place newswriting N.Mex. Press Assn., 1991; honorable mention Assn. Press Managing Editors, 1994. Mem. AAUW, Soc. Profl. Journalists, Investigative Reporters and Editors, Internat. Platform Soc., Phi Beta Kappa. Home: PO Box 9835 Santa Fe NM 87504-9835

STIEF, LOUIS JOHN, chemist; b. Pottsville, Pa., July 26, 1933; s. Louis Norman and Dorothy Elizabeth (Bassler) S.; m. Kathleen J. Talbot, Nov. 30, 1963 (div. 1980); children—Andrew, Lorraine. B.A., La Salle Coll., 1955; Ph.D., Catholic U. Am., 1960. Nat. Acad. Scis.-NRC postdoctoral rsch. assoc. Nat. Bur. Standards, Washington, 1960-61; NATO postdoctoral fellow, ind. researcher chemistry dept. Sheffield (Eng.) U., 1961-63; sr. scientist, sr. chemist Melpar, Inc., Falls Church, Va., 1963-68; NAS-NRC sr. postdoctoral rsch. assoc. NASA/Goddard Space Flight Ctr., Greenbelt, Md., 1968-69; astrophysicist NASA/Goddard Space Flight Ctr., 1969-76, head br. astrochemistry, 1976-90, sr. scientist, 1990—; adj. prof. chemistry Cath. U. Am. Research: numerous publs., especially in Jour. Chem. Physics and Jour. Phys. Chemistry. Recipient Alumni Achievement award Cath. U. Am., 1985; NASA fellow Queen Mary Coll., U. London, 1981-82. Fellow Washington Acad. Sci.; mem. Am. Chem. Soc., Royal Soc. Chemistry, Am. Geophys. Union, Am. Astron. Soc. (div. planetary sci.), Sigma Xi. Office: NASA Goddard Space Flight Ctr Code 690 Greenbelt MD 20771

STIEFEL, ETHAN, dancer; b. Madison, Wis.; s. Alan and Mima Stiefel. Studies under Mikhail Baryshinikov, Sch. Classical Ballet, 1987; student, Fordham U., 1995—. Guest artist Nutcracker Cavalier, 1992-93; mem. Zurich Ballet, 1992. Recipient Silver medal Prix de Lausanne, 1989, emerging dance artist grant Princess Grace Found. U.S.A., 1991-92. Office: NYC Ballet NY State Theater 20 Lincoln Center Plz New York NY 10023-6913*

STIEFF, JOHN JOSEPH, legislative lawyer, educator; b. Indpls., Feb. 28, 1952; s. James Frederick and Mary Therese (Bisch) S.; m. Dusty Lee-Ann Warner, Apr. 21, 1989. BA with Distinction, Ind. U., 1973, JD, 1977. Bar: Ind. 1977. Sr. atty. Office of Bill Drafting & Rsch., Legislative Svcs. Agy., Indpls., 1977-86; dep. dir. and asst. revisor of statutes Office of Code Revision, Legislative Svcs. Agy., Indpls., 1986-92, dir. and revisor of statutes, 1992—; adj. prof. law Ind. Univ., Bloomington, 1985-86; instr. continuing legal edn. Ind. Gen. Assembly, Indpls., 1987-96; faculty mem. Nat. Conf. State Legislatures, Denver, Colo., 1988-89; assoc commr. Nat. Conf. Commrs. on Uniform State Laws, Chgo., 1993—. Editor in chief: (books) The Acts of Indiana, 1986—, The Indiana Code, 1993—; ast. editor, The Indiana Code, 1986-92. Poetry instr. Gage Inst. for Gifted Children, Indpls., 1982-86. Named Hoosier Scholar, Indiana Commn. for Higher Edn., 1970-73. Mem. Writer's Ctr. of Indpls. (founding mem.), Ind. U. Varsity Club. Avocations: travel, photgraphy, writing poetry, Am. blues music. Home: 7707 Windy Hill Way Indianapolis IN 46239 Office: Legislative Svcs Agy Office Code Revision 200 W Washington St Ste 302 Indianapolis IN 46204-2732

STIEFVATER, PAMELA JEAN, chiropractor; b. Utica, N.Y., Oct. 16, 1956; d. Kenneth Carl and Henriette Ramona (Billick) S. BS cum laude, SUNY, Oswego, 1977; D of Chiropractic cum laude, Palmer Coll., 1984. Lic. chiropractor, N.Y., Mass.; diplomate Nat. Bd. Chiropractic Examiners. Sci. tchr. Altmar, Parish, Williamstown High Sch., Parish, N.Y., 1978-80; chiropractor, owner Bayside Chiropractic, South Dennis, Mass., 1986—. Mem. Am. Chiropractic Soc., Mass. Chiropractic Soc., Cape Code Chiropractic Soc. Office: Bayside Chiropractic 430 Old Bass River Rd South Dennis MA 02660-2724

STIEHL, WILLIAM D., federal judge; b. 1925; m. Celeste M. Sullivan; children: William D., Susan M. Student, U. N.C., 1943-45; LLB, St. Louis U., 1949. Pvt. practice, 1971-78; ptnrs. Stiehl & Hess, 1978-81; ptnr. Stiehl & Stiehl, 1982-86; judge, former chief judge U.S. District Court, (so. dist.) Ill., East Saint Louis, 1986—; spl. asst. atty. gen. State of Ill., 1970-73. Mem. bd. Belleville Twp. High Sch. and Jr. Coll., 1949-50, 54-56, pres., 1956-57, Clair County, Ill., county civil atty., 1956-60. Mem. ABA, Ill. Bar Assn., St. Clair County Bar Assn. Office: US Dist Ct 750 Missouri Ave East Saint Louis IL 62201-2954*

STIEHM, JUDITH HICKS, university official, political science educator; b. Madison, Wis., Oct. 9, 1935; d. Stratton Elson and Eleanor Spencer (Kilbourn) Hicks; m. E. Richard Stiehm, July 12, 1958; children: Jamie Elizabeth, Carrie Eleanor, Meredith Ellen. Student, Oberlin Coll., 1953; BA in E. Asian Studies, U. Wis., 1957; MA in Am. History, Temple U., 1961; PhD in Polit. Theory, Columbia U., 1969. Dir. resident hons. program U. So. Calif., Los Angeles, 1970-73, asst. prof., 1970-74, assoc. prof., 1974-83, dir. program for study of women and men in soc., 1975-81, prof. polit. sci., 1983, vice provost, 1984-87; provost Fla. Internat. U., Miami, 1987-91, prof. polit. sci., 1987—; vis. prof. U. Wis., 1994, U.S. Army Peacekeeping Inst., U.S. Army War Coll., 1995-96, U.S. Army Strategic Studies Inst., U.S. Army War Coll., 1995-96; lectr. U. Wis., Madison, 1966-69, UCLA, 1969-70; vis. lectr. San Francisco State U., 1965-66; affiliate NAS Project, 1981-82; cons. UN Div. for the Advancement of Women, Calif. Elected Women, Dept. Health Edn. and Welfare, AAUW, LWV Los Angeles. Author: Nonviolent Power: Active and Passive Resistance in America, 1972, Bring Me Men and Women..., 1981, Men, Women and State Violence, 1983, Arms and the Enlisted Woman, 1989; editor: The Frontiers of Knowledge, 1976, Women and Men's Wars, 1983, Women's Views of the Political World of Men, 1984, It's Our Military, Too!, 1996; mem. editorial bd. Western Polit. Quar., 1972-75, Signs, 1981-84, Women and Politics, 1986-88. Mem. Calif. Postsecondary Edn. Commn., 1978, Calif. Adv. Coun. on Vocat. Edn., 1978-82, Def. Adv. Com. on Women in Svcs., 1979-82; bd. dirs. So. Calif. and Miami chpts. ACLU. Named Woman of Yr., Santa Monica YWCA, 1981. Mem. Am. Polit. Sci. Assn. (exec. coun. 1989), Western Polit. Sci. Assn. (pres. 1986), Women's Caucus Polit. Sci. (pres. 1996-97), Nat. Council for Research on Women (exec. council 1982), Council on Fgn. Relations, Phi Beta Kappa, Phi Kappa Phi (Army Oustanding Civilian Svc. medal, Victoria Schuck Book award). Avocations: tennis, skiing, stained glass. Home: 434 24th St Santa Monica CA 90402-3102 Office: Fla Internat U Dept Polit Sci Tamiami Trl Miami FL 33199-0001

STIER, WILLIAM FREDERICK, JR., university administrator; b. Feb. 22, 1943; m. Veronica Ann Martin, 1965; children: Mark, Missy, Michael, Patrick, Willy III. BA, St. Ambrose Coll., 1965; MA, Temple U., 1966; EdD, U. S.D., 1972; postgrad. Marquette U., 1976-77, U. Wis.-Milw. Sch. Law, summer 1977. Grad. asst. Coll. Edn., Temple U., Phila., 1965-66, various faculty positions dept. health, phys. edn. and recreation, 1968-74; pres., CEO Fla. Breeders, Inc., Largo and St. Petersburg, Fla., 1974-76, treas. Charolais of Fla., Inc., St. Petersburg and Ft. Myers, 1975-76; adminstrv. asst. to v.p., dir./coordinator satellite campus Cardinal Stritch Coll., Milw., 1976-80; chmn. dept., prof. health and phys. edn., athletic dir. Ohio No. U., Ada, 1980-83; chmn., prof. phys. edn. and sports dept. SUNY, Brockport, 1983-86, dir. intercollegiate athletics, 1983-90, grad. coord. sport mgmt., 1990—, pres. faculty senate, 1992-93, grad. coord., 1994—; pres., CEO Ednl. and Sport Mgmt. Cons., N.Y. and Ohio, 1980—; chmn. bd. dirs. Kreative Kids Learning Ctrs., Inc., 1978—; bd. dirs. Creative Children Child Care Ctrs.; cons. MacMillan Pub. Co., Inc., 1981-83, Sport Fedn., Hongkong, Singapore and Malaysia, 1987, 88, Nat. coll. Sport Coaches, Mexico City, 1990; speaker numerous confs. and convs. Author and contbr. to 25 books and compendiums in field; contbr. more than 200 articles to profl. jours.; mem. editorial bd. and reviewer profl. jours. Active ARC, 1975-90, Boy Scouts Am., 1955-59; mem. Greater Milw. Regional Day Care Adv. Com., 1979-81; adv. bd. Nat. Ctr. for Exploration Human Potential, Del Mar, Calif., 1981-84; nat. basketball coach, St. Kitts-Nevis, 1984; cons. on basketball, Mex., 1982, 90. Brockport scholar, 1984-86, 93. Mem. AAHPERD (reviewer jour. 1984—), N.Y. Assn. for Health Phys. Edn. Recreation and Dance (higher edn. sect. 1983—, pres. 1985-86, 87-88), Nat. Assn. Sport and Phys. Edn., Nat. Assn. Girls and Women's Sports, Nat. Assn. Physical Edn. in Higher Edn., Nat. Assn. of Athletic, Mktg. and Devel. Dirs., Nat. Assn. Collegiate Dirs. of Athletics, Internat. Soc. on Comparative Physical Edn. and Sports, N.Am. Soc. Sport Mgmt., Eta Sigma Gamma, Phi Epsilon Kappa, Phi Kappa Phi, Phi Epsilon Omega. Office: SUNY-Brockport Dept Phys Edn and Sport Brockport NY 14420

STIFF, ROBERT HENRY, dentist, educator; b. Pitts., Apr. 23, 1923; s. Oliver R. and Ruth A. (Goucher) S.; m. Margaret J. Raley, Oct. 18, 1945; children—Barry, Dwight, Heather. B.S., U. Pitts., 1940, D.D.S., 1945, M.Ed., 1953. Engaged in pvt. practice dentistry Pitts., 1945-59; instr. U. Pitts., 1945-50, asst. prof., 1950-53, asso. prof., 1954-65, prof., head dept. oral medicine and radiology, 1963-76, dir. clinics, 1976—; asst. dean U. Pitts. (Sch. Dental Medicine), 1979-81, assoc. dean, 1981-84; cons. U. Garyounis, Benghazi, Libya, 1978—, Pa. Dept. Health, 1964, 66, Bd. Edn., City of Pitts. (dental asst. program 1983-86). Served to capt. Dental Corps AUS, 1946-48. Fellow Am. Coll. Dentists; mem. Am. Acad. Oral Pathology, ADA (pres. 1979-80), Orgn. Tchrs. Oral Diagnosis, Pa. Dental Assn., Sigma Xi, Omicron Kappa Upsilon. Home: 4601 Doverdell Dr Pittsburgh PA 15236-1824

STIFF, ROBERT MARTIN, newspaper editor; b. Detroit, Aug. 25, 1931; s. Martin L. and Gladys (Mathews) S.; m. Cindy Rose, Aug. 30, 1980; children: David Alan, Amy Anne, Kirsten Marie. BA in Radio and Journalism, Ohio State U., 1953. Reporter, bur. chief, city editor Painesville (Ohio) Telegraph, 1953-61; deskman, asst. city editor, sports editor, city editor, day editor, state editor, asst. mng. editor St. Petersburg (Fla.) Times, 1961-67; editor St. Petersburg Evening Ind., 1967-84; dir. St. Petersburg Times Pub. Co., 1969-84; exec. editor, v.p. Tallahassee Democrat, 1985-91; pres. Bob Stiff & Assocs., Tallahassee, 1991-95; exec. editor JMT Assocs., 1991-92, 95—; mng. editor About Florida, 1991-94; editor Lexington (N.C.) Dispatch, 1995—; dir. devel. and pub. rels. Fla. Taxwatch Inc., 1992-94; bd. dir. N.C. AP News Coun., 1995—. Bd. dirs. Cancer Svcs. Davidson County. Mem. AP Assn. Fla. (pres. 1970-71), Am. Soc. Newspaper Editors (dir. 1981-87), Am. Soc. Newspaper Editors Found. (bd. dirs., treas. 1986-90), Fla. Soc. Newspaper Editors (pres. 1975-76, dir. 1971-84, 90-93), Fla. Bar Found. (bd. dirs. 1990-92), AP Mng. Editors Assn., Sigma Delta Chi (pres. West Coast chpt. 1970-710, N.C. Press Assn., Nat. Coun. Editl. Writers, Lexington Kiwanis (bd. dirs. 1996—).

STIFFLER, JACK JUSTIN, electrical engineer; b. Mitchellville, Iowa, May 22, 1934; s. John Justin and Helen Irene (Roorda) S.; m. Ardis Ann Ackerman, Aug. 21, 1955; 1 child, Julia Alise; m. Sally Voris Burns, Apr. 20, 1989. A.B. magna cum laude in Physics, Harvard U., 1956; M.S. in E.E, Calif. Inst. Tech., 1957, Ph.D., 1962; postgrad., U. Paris, 1957-58. Engr. Hughes Aircraft Corp., Culver City, Calif., 1956-57; mem. tech. staff Jet Propulsion Lab., Pasadena, Calif., 1959-67; cons. scientist Raytheon Corp., Sudbury, Mass., 1967-81; exec. v.p. Sequoia Systems, Inc., Marlborough, Mass., 1981-97; cons., 1997—; lectr. Calif. Inst. Tech., U. So. Calif., UCLA, Northeastern U. Author: Theory of Synchronous Communications, 1971; contbr. chpts. to books, articles to profl. jours. Fellow IEEE; mem. Phi Beta Kappa, Sigma Xi. Office: Sequoia Systems Inc 400 Nickerson Rd Marlborough MA 01752-4658

STIGLER, STEPHEN MACK, statistician, educator; b. Mpls., Aug. 10, 1941; s. George Joseph and Margaret (Mack) S.; m. Virginia Lee, June 27, 1964; children: Andrew, Geoffrey, Margaret, Elizabeth. BA, Carleton Coll., 1963; PhD, U. Calif., Berkeley, 1967. Asst. prof. U. Wis., Madison, 1967-71, assoc. prof., 1971-75, prof., 1975-79; prof. U. Chgo., 1979—; chmn. dept., 1986-92; Ernest DeWitt Burton Disting. Svc. prof. U. Chgo., 1992—; trustee Ctr. for Advanced Study in the Behavioral Scis., Stanford, Calif., 1986-92, 93—, chmn., 1995—. Author: The History of Statistics, 1986; contbr. articles to jours. in field. Guggenheim Found. fellow, 1976-77; Ctr. for Advanced Study in Behavioral Scis. fellow, 1978-79. Fellow AAAS, Am. Acad. Arts and Scis. (mem. coun. 1995—), Inst. Math. Stats. (Neyman lectr. 1988, pres. 1993-94), Am. Statis. Assn. (editor Jour. 1979-82, Outstanding Statistician award Chgo. chpt. 1993), Royal Statis. Soc. (Fisher lectr. 1986); mem. Internat. Statis. Inst., Bernoulli Soc., History of Sci. Soc., Brit. Soc. for History Sci., Quadrangle Club, Sigma Xi. Office: U Chgo Dept Statistics 5734 S University Ave Chicago IL 60637-1514

STIGLITZ, JOSEPH EUGENE, economist; b. Gary, Ind., Feb. 9, 1943; s. Nathaniel David and Charlotte (Fishman) S.; m. Jane Hannaway, Dec. 23, 1978; children: Siobhan, Michael, Edward, Julia. B.A., Amherst Coll., Mass, 1964; DHL (hon.), Amherst Coll., 1974; Ph.D. in Econs., MIT, 1966; M.A. (hon.), Yale U., 1970; D in Econs. (hon.), U. Leuven, 1994. Prof. econs. Cowles Found., Yale U., New Haven, 1970-74; vis. fellow St. Catherine's Coll., Oxford, Eng., 1973-74; Joan Kenney professorship Stanford U., 1974-76, 88—; Oskar Morgenstern dist. fellow Inst. Advanced Studies Math., Princeton, N.J., 1978-79; Drummond prof. polit. economy Oxford U., Eng., 1976-79; prof. econs. Princeton U., 1979-88; mem. Pres.'s Coun. Econ. Advisers, 1993-95, chmn. coun. econ. advisers, 1995-97, sr. v.p. devel. econs. and chief econs., exec. dir.; cons. World Bank, State of Alaska, Seneca Indian Nation, Bell Communications Rsch. Editor Jour. Econ. Perspectives, 1986-93; Am. editor Rev. of Econ. Studies, 1968-76; assoc. editor Am. Econ. Rev., 1968-76, Energy Econs., Managerial and Decision Econs.; mem. editl. bd. World Bank Econ. Rev. Recipient John Bates Clark award Am. Econ. Assn., 1979, Internat. prize Accademia Lincei, 1988, Union des Assurances de Paris prize, 1989; Guggenheim fellow, 1969-70. Fellow Inst. for Policy Rsch. (sr. 1991-93), Brit. Acad. (corr.); mem. Am. Econ. Assn. (exec. com. 1982-84, v.p. 1985), Am. Acad. Arts and Scis., Nat. Acad. Sci., Econometric Soc.

STIGWOOD, ROBERT COLIN, theater, movie, television and record producer; b. Adelaide, Australia, Apr. 16, 1934; came to Eng., 1956; s. Gordon and Gwendolyn (Burrows) S. Attended, Sacred Heart Coll., Adelaide. Worked as copywriter for advt. agy. Adelaide; held series of jobs, including mgr. provincial theater and halfway house for delinquents in Cambridge; opened talent agy. London, 1962; liquidated firm, 1965; became bus. mgr. for group Graham Bond Orgn.; became co-mng. dir. NEMS Enterprises, 1967; established own firm Robert Stigwood Orgn., 1967; formed RSO Records, 1973; became dir. of Polygram, 1976; co-founder (with Rupert Murdoch) R&R Films, 1979; founder Music for UNICEF. 1st ind. record producer in Eng. with release of single Johnny Remember Me; producer: films, including Jesus Christ Superstar, 1973, Bugsy Malone, Tommy, 1975, Survive, 1976, Saturday Night Fever, 1977, Grease I, 1978, Grease II, 1982, Moment By Moment, 1978, Sergeant Pepper's Lonely Hearts Club Band, The Fan, 1981, Times Square, 1980, Gallipoli, 1980, Staying Alive, 1983, Evita, 1996; stage musicals in Eng. and U.S., including, Hair, Oh! Calcutta, The Dirtiest Show in Town, Sweeney Todd, Pippin, Jesus Christ Superstar, Evita, Grease; TV producer in Eng. and U.S.; prodns. include The Entertainer (dramatic spl.); All in the Family (series), The Prime of Miss Jean Brodie (dramatic series). Bd. dirs. Police Athletic League, N.Y.C.; patron Australian Nat. Art Gallery. Recipient Tony award for best musical (Evita); named Internat. Producer of Yr. ABC Interstate Theatres, Inc., 1976, Knight of St. John of Jerusalem, Malta, 1985. Club: Royal Bermuda Yacht. Avocations: yachting, tennis. Home: Barton Manor, East Cowes, Isle of Wight England

STILES, GARY LESTER, cardiologist, molecular pharmacologist, educator; b. N.Y.C., May 22, 1949; s. Robert L. and Vivian M. (Cano) S.; m. Jane V. Black, June 7, 1971; children: Heather B., Wendy A. BS in Chemistry, St. Lawrence U., 1971; MD, Vanderbilt U., 1975. Diplomate Am. Bd. Internal Medicine, sub.-bd. Cardiovascular Medicine. Resident in internal medicine Vanderbilt U., Nashville, 1975-78; fellow in cardiology Duke U., Durham, N.C., 1978-81, asst. prof. medicine, 1981-85, assoc. prof., 1986-89, chief div. cardiology, 1989—, prof. medicine, 1990—, prof. pharmacology, 1990—; mem. sci. adv. coun. Alta. Heritage Found., Edmonton, Can., 1990—; mem. pharmacology study sect. NIH, Bethesda, Md., 1988-91. Editl. bd. Jour. Biol. Chemistry, 1990-95, Molecular Pharmacology, 1991—. Recipient Katz prize Am. Heart Assn., 1983, award Am. Fedn. Clin. Rsch., 1989; grantee Am. Heart Assn., 1987-90. Fellow Am. Coll. Cardiology (award 1993); mem. Internat. Churchill Soc., Assn. Am. Physicians, Am. Soc. Clin. Investigation. Republican. Achievements include patent in field. Office: Duke U Med Ctr Div Cardiology PO Box 3681 Durham NC 27710

STILES, MARY ANN, lawyer; b. Tampa, Fla., Nov. 16, 1944; d. Ralph A. and Bonnie (Smith) S. AA, Hills Community Coll., 1973; BS, Fla. State U., 1975; JD, Antioch Sch. Law, 1978. Bar: Fla. 1978. Legis. analyst Fla. Ho. of Reps., Tallahassee, 1973-74, 74-75; intern U.S. Senate, Washington, 1977; v.p., gen. counsel Associated Industries Fla., Tallahassee, 1978-81, gen. counsel, 1981-84, spl. counsel, 1986—; assoc. Deschler, Reed & Crichfield, Boca Raton, Fla., 1980-81; founding ptnr. Stiles, Taylor, Grace & Smith, P.A., Tampa, Fla., 1982—; shareholder, dir. Stiles, Taylor, Grace & Smith, P.A., Tampa; shareholder and dir. Six Stars Devel. Co. of Fla., Inc.; with Employers 1st Trust, Inc.; shareholder First Comml. Bank of Tampa; pres. 42nd St., The Bistro. Author: Workers' Copmensation Law Handbook, 1980-94 edit. Bd. dirs., sec. Hillsborough C.C. Found., Tampa, 1985-87, 94-96; bd. dirs. Hillsborough Area Regional Transit Authority, Tampa, 1986-89, Boys and Girls Club of Tampa, 1986—; mem. Bay Area chpt. Nat. Women's Polit. Caucus, 1993—, The Spring, 1992-93, What's My Chance, 1992-94; mem. Gov.'s Oversite Bd. on Workers' Compensation, 1989-90, Workers Comp. Rules Com., Fla. Bar, 1990-95, Workers Comp. Exec. Counsel Fla. Bar, 1990-95Jud. Nominating Commn. for Workers' Compensation Cts., 1990-93, trustee Hillsborough Cmty. Coll., 1994—, vice-chair, 1995-96, chair, 1996—. Mem. ABA, Fla. Bar Assn., Hillsborough County Bar Assn., Hillsborough Assn. Women Lawyers, Fla. Assn. Women Lawyers, Fla. Women's Alliance, Hillsborough County Seminole Boosters (past pres.). Democrat. Baptist. Club: Tiger Bay (Tampa, past pres., sec.). Avocations: boating, reading. Office: 315 S Plant Ave Tampa FL 33606-2325 also: 111 N Orange Ave Ste 850 Orlando FL 32801-2381 also: 317 N Calhoun St Tallahassee FL 32301-7605 also: 200 E Olas Blvd Ste 1730 Fort Lauderdale FL 33301-2248

STILES, PHILLIP JOHN, physicist, educator; b. Manchester, Conn., Oct. 31, 1934; married, 1956; 6 children. BS, Trinity Coll., 1956; PhD in Physics, U. Pa., 1961. Mem. rsch. staff Thomas J. Watson Rsch. Ctr. IBM, N.Y.C., 1963-70; prof. physics Brown U., 1970-89, prof. engring., 1989-93, chmn. dept. physics, 1974-80, dean Grad. Sch., dean of rsch., 1986-93; provost, vice chancellor, prof. physics N.C. State U., Raleigh, 1993—; mem. exec. com. AGS in AAU, 1990-93; mem. internat. adv. com. EP2DS; trustee NCSSM; bd. dirs. Rsch. Tri. Inst., Wake Edn. Partnership. U. Pa. fellow, 1961-62, NSF fellow, 1962-63; recipient Humboldt Sr. U.S. Sci. award, 1976, John Price Wetheral medal Franklin Inst., 1981. Mem. AAAS, Am. Physics Soc. (Oliver E. Buckley prize 1988). Office: NC State U Office Provost Vice Chancellor PO Box 7101 Raleigh NC 27695-7101

STILES, THOMAS BEVERIDGE, II, investment banking executive; b. Easton, Pa., Oct. 4, 1940; s. Ezra Martin and Vivien (de Fay) S.; m. Elaine Ann Patyk, July 2, 1966 (div. Oct. 1980); children—Thomas Beveridge III, Jonathan Ezra; m. Barbara Toll Alexander, Mar. 7, 1981. B.A., Yale U., 1963; M.B.A., Harvard U., 1968. V.p. Laird, Inc., N.Y.C., 1968-73; sr. v.p., dir. Smith Barney Harris Upham and Co., Inc., N.Y.C., 1973-82; exec. v.p., dir. E.F. Hutton & Co. Inc., N.Y.C., 1982-87; chmn., chief exec. officer Shearson Lehman Advisors Asset Mgmt. Co., N.Y.C., 1988-90; chmn., chief exec. officer Bernstein Macaulay, N.Y.C., also bd. dirs., 1988-90; CEO, chmn. Greenwich Street Advisors, N.Y.C., 1990—; also mng. dir. Smith, Barney, Inc., N.Y.C.,, 1993—; bd. dirs., treas. Cedar Lawn Cemetery, Paterson, N.J., 1973—. Served to 1st lt. M.I., U.S. Army, 1963-66. Fellow Fin. Analysts Fedn.; mem. N.Y. Soc. Security Analysts. Republican. Presbyterian. Club: Spring Lake Bath and Tennis (N.J.). Avocations: political science; tennis; swimming. Office: Greenwich St Advisors 388 Greenwich St Fl 23 New York NY 10013-2375

STILL, CHARLES NEAL, neurologist, consultant; b. Richmond, Va., Apr. 15, 1929; s. Charles Wright and Ruth (Kemp) S.; m. Dorothy Lee Varn, Dec. 27, 1958; children: Charles Herbert, Carl Nelson, Sara Alice. BS in Chemistry, Clemson U., 1949; MS in Biochemistry, Purdue U., 1951; MD, Med. U. S.C., 1959. Diplomate Am. Bd. Psychiatry and Neurology. Instr. chemistry Clemson (S.C.) U., 1951-52; rotating intern U. Chgo. Clinics, 1959-60; neurology fellow Sch. Medicine Johns Hopkins U., Balt., 1960-63; resident in neurology Johns Hopkins-Balt. City Hosp., 1960-63; NIH rsch. fellow Harvard U.-McLean Hosp., Belmont, Mass., 1963-65; chief neurology svcs. William S. Hall. Psychiat. Inst., Columbia, S.C., 1965-81, assoc. dir. gen. psychiatry and neurology, 1989-92; dir. C. M. Tucker Human Resources Ctr., Columbia, 1981-88; instr. chemistry U.S. Mil. Acad., West Point, N.Y., 1953-55; assoc. clin. prof. neurology Med. U. S.C., Charleston, 1973-92, assoc. prof. neuropsychiatry, 1976-78, prof. neuropsychiatry, 1978—; adj. prof. epidemiology Sch. Pub. Health U. S.C., Columbia, 1988-92. Author: (with others) Handbook of Clinical Neurology, 1976, Neurologic Clinics, 1984, Movement Disorders, 1986; editor The Recorder Columbia Med. Soc., 1991—; mem. editl. bd. S.C. Med. Assn., 1980—, Jour. Applied Gerontology, 1983-88; contbr. articles to profl. jours. Chmn. grants rev. bd. S.C. Dept. Mental Health, Columbia, 1973-78; mem. exec. bd. Alzheimer's Assn. Columbia, 1985-93, pres. Mid-State chpt. Alzheimer's Assn., 1991-92; med. dir. Alzheimer's Disease Registry, Columbia, 1989-92, Alzheimer's Daycare Ctr., Columbia, 1989-92; mem. Gov.'s Adv. Coun. to Alzheimer's Disease and Related Disorders Resource Coordination Ctr., 1995—. 1st lt. U.S. Army, 1952-55. Fellow Am. Acad. Neurology, Am. Geriatrics Soc., Am. Inst. Chemists (life); mem. Am. Chem. Soc., World Fedn. Neurology. Baptist. Avocations: writing, photography. Home: 2 Culpepper Cir Columbia SC 29209-2234 Office: WJB Dorn VA Med Ctr Psychiatry Svc Columbia SC 29209-1639

STILL, THOMAS WAYNE, newspaper editor, columnist; b. Alexandria, Va., July 9, 1953; s. Claude Richmond and Margaret Louise (Stratton) S.; children: Stephanie Anne, Jason Thomas, Jessica Erin. BA in Journalism, Drake U., 1973; postgrad., U. Wis., 1980-81. Copy boy The Washington Star, 1970-71; sports reporter/copy editor The Des Moines Register, 1972-73; gen. assignment reporter The Mason City (Iowa) Globe-Gazette, 1974-76; gen. assignment reporter The Wis. State Jour., Madison, 1976-77, city hall reporter, 1977-79, chief polit. reporter, 1979-85, opinion page editor, 1985-89, assoc. editor, 1989—; polit. columnist Corp. Report/Wis., Milw., 1987-95; polit. columnist/contbr. Wis. Interest, The Wis. Policy Rsch. Inst., Milw., 1992-95; syndicated columnist "Inside Wis.", 1990-95; guest presenter/lectr. Contbr. articles to newspapers. Co-founder We the People/Wis., Madison, 1992-95; vol. Black Hawk Girl Scout Coun., Madison, 1989-95; past vol. Big Bros./Big Sisters, PTO. Recipient Midwest Regional Emmy award Nat. Acad. TV Arts and Scis., 1993, 94, Pub. Svc. Journalism award Milw. Press Club, 1980, 93, Sweepstakes award AP Mng. Editors, 1976, edit. writing award Wis. Newspaper Assn., 1986-95, grant Pew Ctr. for Civic Journalism; named one of Most Influential, Madison Mag., 1987, 91, 94. Mem. Nat. Conf. Editl. Writers (conv. com. 1995). Avocations: men's senior baseball league, fast-pitch softball, city league basketball, reading, youth coaching. Home: 218 S Segoe Rd Madison WI 53705-4939 Office: Wis State Jour 1901 Fish Hatchery Rd Madison WI 53713-1248

STILLER, JENNIFER ANNE, lawyer; b. Washington, May 4, 1948; d. Ralph Sophian and Joy (Dancis) S. AB in Econs. and History, U. Mich., 1970; JD, NYU, 1973. Bar: Pa. 1973, U.S. Dist. Ct. (mid. dist.) Pa. 1977, U.S. Supreme Ct. 1978, Ill. 1979, U.S. Dist. Ct. (no. dist.) Ill. 1979, U.S. Dist. Ct. (ea. dist.) Pa. 1983, U.S. Ct. Appeals (3rd cir.) 1983, U.S. Ct. Appeals (D.C. cir.), 1996. Dep. atty. gen. Pa. Dept. Justice, Harrisburg, 1973-75, Pa. Dept. Health, Harrisburg, 1975-78; sr. staff atty. Am. Hosp. Assn., Chgo., 1978-80, mgr., dept. fed. law, 1980-81; gen. counsel Ill. Health Fin. Authority, 1981-82; sr. assoc. Berriman & Schwartz, King of Prussia, Pa., 1983-85, Wolf, Block, Schorr & Solis-Cohen, Phila., 1985-88; sr. assoc. Montgomery, McCracken, Walker & Rhoads, 1988-90, ptnr., 1990—, chair health law group, 1991—. Contbr. health law articles to profl. jours. Mem. ABA (gov. com. Health Law Forum 1994-95), Nat. Health Lawyers Assn., Am. Acad. Hosp. Attys., Forum of Exec. Women (bd. dirs. 1997—), Pa. Soc. Healthcare Attys. (pres. 1995), Phila. Bar Assn. Avocations: gardening, bicycling, hiking, music. Office: Montgomery McCracken 123 S Broad St Philadelphia PA 19109

STILLER, JERRY, actor; b. N.Y.C., June 8; s. William and Bella S.; m. Anne Meara, Sept. 14, 1954; children: Amy, Benjamin. BS in Speech and Drama, Syracuse U., 1950. Actor with nat. co. of Peter Pan, 1951, also at Henry St. Playhouse, 1941, Cherry Lane Theatre, N.Y.C., 1947, Billy Barnes Showboat, Chgo., 1950, Erie (Pa.) Playhouse, 1951, 52, Memphis Arena Theatre, 1952, Phoenix Theatre, 1954, 55, 56, Shakespeare Festival Theatre, Stratford, Conn., 1955, Compass Players, 1959, mem. Shakespeare Co. in Central Park, N.Y.C., 1957, 71, Two Gentlemen, 1971, Much Ado, 1988; Broadway appearances include The Golden Apple, 1954, The Ritz, 1975, Unexpected Guests, 1977, Hurleyburly, 1985, Three Men on a Horse, 1993, What's Wrong With This Picture?, 1994, The Three Sisters, 1997; film appearances include The Taking of Pelham 1-2-3, 1974, Airport '75, 1975, The Ritz, 1976, Those Lips, Those Eyes, 1979, Nadine, 1986, That's Adequate, 1986, Hairspray, 1986, Seize The Day, 1986, Shoeshine (Acad. award nomination, short subject 1989), A Pair of Jokers, 1990, The Pickle, 1992, Stag, 1996; Off-Broadway appearances include Bouboufoche, 1971, Passione, 1980, Prairie du Chien, 1985, (written by wife, Anne Meara) After-Play, 1995-96; mem. comedy team, Anne Meara, 1961—, Ed Sullivan Show 36 appearances; night club appearances include Compass Players, St. Louis, 1957, Happy Medium, Chgo., 1960, also Village Gate, Village Vanguard, Blue Angel, Bon Soir and, Phase Two, N.Y.C., Mr. Kelly's, Chgo., Hungry I, San Francisco, The Establishment, London, The Sands, Flamingo, Las Vegas, Harrah's, Reno and Lake Tahoe, Trump Plaza, QE II; co-star: daily TV series Take Five with Stiller and Meara, 1977-78; actor TV series Joe and Sons, 1975, Tattinger's, 1987, The Detective, The Sunset Gang, PBS, 1991, Seize the Day, 1990, The Hollow Boy, American Playhouse, 1991, Seinfeld, 1994-96; commercials: Blue Nun, United Van Lines, Amalgamed Bank, Nike, AT&T; video (co-host with Anne Meara): So You Want to be an Actor?. Recipient Disting. Alumnus award Syracuse U., 1973, Voice of Imagery award, 1975, Arents Pioneer Medal, 1979, 1st Biffy award Balt. Internat. Film Festival, Entertainment Father of Yr. award, 1977, Syracuse Walk of Stars, 1994, Syracuse U. award for Achievement in the Arts.

STILLER, SHALE DAVID, lawyer, educator; b. Rochester, N.Y., Feb. 23, 1935; s. Maurice Aaron and Dorothy (Salitan) S.; m. Ellen M. Heller; children: Lewis B., Michael J., Kenneth R.; stepchildren: William Heller, Lawrence Heller. B.A., Hamilton Coll., 1954; LL.B., Yale U., 1957; M.L.A., Johns Hopkins U., 1977. Bar: Md. 1957. Ptnr. Piper & Marbury, Balt., 1992—; lectr. U. Md. Law Sch., 1963—. Contbr. articles to profl. jours. Trustee Johns Hopkins U., Assn. Jewish Charities, Peabody Inst., Johns Hopkins Medicine, The Weinberg Found.; adv. bd. Tax Mgmt., 1972-93; chmn. Jud. Nominating Commn., Balt., 1979-83; officer, bd. dirs. Park Sch., 1973-79, pres., 1982-86; pres. Jewish Family Agy., 1972-74. Mem. ABA, Am. Law Inst., Am. Coll. Tax Counsel, Am. Coll. Trust and Estate Counsel, Order of Coif. Democrat. Jewish. Club: 14 W Hamilton St (Balt.). Home: 807 St Georges Rd Baltimore MD 21210-1408 Office: Piper & Marbury 36 S Charles St Baltimore MD 21201-3020

STILLINGER, FRANK HENRY, chemist, educator; b. Boston, Aug. 15, 1934; s. Frank Henry and Gertrude (Metcalf) S.; m. Dorothea Anne Keller, Aug. 18, 1956; children—Constance Anne, Andrew Metcalf. B.S., U. Rochester, 1955; Ph.D., Yale U., 1958. NSF postdoctoral fellow Yale U., 1958-59; with Bell Telephone Labs., Murray Hill, N.J., 1959—; head chem. physics dept. Bell Telephone Labs., 1976-79; disting. mem. tech. staff Bell Labs., 1982—; mem. evaluation panel Nat. Bur. Stds., 1975-78; mem. adv. com. for chemistry NSF, 1980-83, mem. adv. com. for advanced sci. computing, 1984-86, mem. adv. com. material and phys. sci. directorate, 1992-94; disting. lectr. chemistry U. Md., 1981; Karcher lectr. U. Okla., 1984; Trumbull lectr. Yale U., 1984; Washburn Meml. lectr. U. Nebr., 19865; Gucker lectr. Ind. U., 1987; W.A. Noyes lectr. U. Tex., 1988; Regents lectr. UCLA, 1990; Meek indsl. lectr. Ohio State U., 1990; McElvane lectr. U. Wis., 1992; Gomberg lectr. U. Mich., 1992; vis. faculty mem. Princeton U., 1996—. Assoc. editor Jour. Stat. Physics, Jour. Chem. Physics, Phys. Rev. Contbr. articles to profl. jours. Recipient Elliott Cresson medal Franklin Inst., 1978, Hildebrand award Am. Chem. Soc., 1986, Peter J. Debye award Am. Chem. Soc., 1992; Welch Found. fellow, 1974. Fellow Am. Phys. Soc. (Langmuir award 1989); mem. AAAS, Nat. Acad. Scis. Club: Early Am. Coppers Inc. Home: 216 Noe Ave Chatham NJ 07928-1548 Office: 600 Mountain Ave New Providence NJ 07974-2008

STILLINGER, JACK CLIFFORD, English educator; b. Chgo., Feb. 16, 1931; s. Clifford Benjamin and Ruth Evangeline (Hertzler) S.; m. Shirley Louise Van Wormer, Aug. 30, 1952; children: Thomas Clifford, Robert William, Susan, Mary; m. Nina Zippin Baym, May 21, 1971. BA, U. Tex., 1953; MA (Nat. Woodrow Wilson fellow), Northwestern U., 1954; PhD, Harvard U., 1958. Teaching fellow in English Harvard U., 1955-58; asst. prof. U. Ill., Urbana, 1958-61; assoc. prof. U. Ill., 1961-64, prof. English, 1964—; permanent mem. Center for Advanced Study, 1970—. Author: The Early Draft of John Stuart Mill's Autobiography, 1961, Anthony Munday's Zelauto, 1963, Wordsworth: Selected Poems and Prefaces, 1965, The Letters of Charles Armitage Brown, 1966, Twentieth Century Interpretations of Keats's Odes, 1968, Mill: Autobiography and Other Writings, 1969, The Hoodwinking of Madeline and Other Essays on Keats's Poems, 1971, The Texts of Keats's Poems, 1974, The Poems of John Keats, 1978, Mill: Autobiography and Literary Essays, 1981, John Keats: Complete Poems, 1982, Norton Anthology of English Literature, 1986, 1993, John Keats: Poetry Manuscripts at Harvard, 1990, Multiple Authorship and the Myth of Solitary Genius, 1991, Coleridge and Textual Instability, 1994; editor Jour. English and Germanic Philology, 1961-72. Guggenheim fellow, 1964-65. Fellow AAAS; mem. MLA, Keats-Shelley Assn. Am. (bd. dirs., editorial bd. Jour., Disting. Scholar award 1986), Byron Soc., Phi Beta Kappa. Home: 806 W Indiana Ave Urbana IL 61801-4838

STILLINGS, DENNIS OTTO, research association administrator, consultant; b. Valley City, N.D., Oct. 30, 1942; s. Harlow Cecil and Ruth Alice (Wolff) S. BA, U. Minn., 1965. Tchr. Henry (S.D.) Pub. Schs., 1965-66, Darby (Mont.) Pub. Schs., 1966-68; tech. rsch. libr., then mgr. hist. dept. Medtronic, Inc., Mpls., 1968-79; instr. humanities U. Minn., Mpls., 1970-72; founding dir., then curator Bakken Libr., Mpls., 1976-80; ind. antiquarian hist. cons. Mpls., 1979-81; project dir. Archaeus Project, Kamuela, Hawaii, 1981—, v.p., 1989—; exec. dir. Five Mountain Med. Cmty., 1996—, also bd. dirs.; cons. Ctr. for Sci. Anomalies Rsch., Ann Arbor, Mich., 1983—; bd. dirs. Dan Carlson Enterprises, Mpls., Hawaii Ctr. Integral Health; v.p. Waimia Coun. on Aging. Columnist Med. Progress Through Technology, 1974—; columnist Med. Instrumentation, 1973-76, guest editor, 1975; editor: Cyberphysiology: The Science of Self-Regulation, 1988, Cyberbiological Studies of the Imaginal Component in the UFO Contact Experience, 1989, The Theology of Electricity: On the Encounter and Explanation of Theology and Science in the 17th and 18th Centuries, 1990, Project 2010: On the Current Crisis in Health and Its Implications for the Hospital for the Future, 1992; founding editor: (jours.) Artifex, 1981-93, Archaeus, 1982-84, Healing Island. Bd. dirs. Hawaii Ctr. for Integral Healing. Fellow Am. Inst. Stress; mem. Assn. Sci. Study Anomalous Phenomena, Bioelectromagnetics Soc., Soc. Sci. Exploration. Avocations: Jungian psychology, golf, fishing, travel.

STILLMAN, ELINOR HADLEY, lawyer; b. Kansas City, Mo., Oct. 12, 1938; d. Hugh Gordon and Freda (Brooks) Hadley; m. Richard C. Stillman, June 25, 1965 (div. Apr. 1975). BA, U. Kans., 1960; MA, Yale U., 1961; JD, George Washington U., 1972. Bar: D.C. 1973, U.S. Ct. Appeals (10th cir.) 1975, U.S. Ct. Appeals (9th cir.) 1976, U.S. Ct. Appeals (2d cir.) 1976, U.S. Ct. Appeals (5th cir.) 1983, U.S. Ct. Appeals (4th cir.) 1985, U.S. Supreme Ct. 1976. Lectr. in English CUNY, 1963-65; asst. editor Stanford (Calif.) U. Press., 1967-69; law clk. to judge U.S. Dist. Ct. D.C., Washington, 1972-73; appellate atty. NLRB, Washington, 1973-78; asst. to solicitor gen. U.S. Dept. Justice, Washington, 1978-82; supr. appellate atty. NLRB, Washington, 1982-86, chief counsel to mem. bd., 1986-88, 94—, chief counsel to chmn. bd., 1988-94. Mem. ABA, D.C. Bar Assn., Order of Coif, Phi Beta Kappa. Democrat. Office: Nat Labor Rels Bd 1099 14th St NW Washington DC 20005-3419

STILLMAN, JOYCE L., artist, educator, writer, illustrator, consultant; b. N.Y.C., Jan. 19, 1943; d. Murray W. and Evelyn (Berger) Stillman. BA, NYU, 1964; student, Art Students League, 1965, Pratt Inst., 1972; MFA, L.I. U., 1975; postgrad., Calif. Inst. Integral Studies, 1994—. Tchr. N.Y.C. Pub. Schs., 1964-71; artist Cen. Hall Gallery, Port Washington, N.Y., 1974-76, Louis K. Meisel Gallery, N.Y.C., 1975-84, Tolarno Gallery, Melbourne, Australia, 1976—, Allan Stone Gallery, N.Y.C., 1990—; vis. assoc. prof. Towson State U., 1982; tchr. Women in Art, Tompkins Cortland C.C., 1988; lectr. Cornell U., 1990; founder Ithaca Women Artists Salon. One-person shows include Cen. Hall Gallery, Port Washington, 1975, Tolarno Gallery, Melbourne, 1976, Louis K. Meisel Gallery, N.Y.C., 1977, 80, 81, 82, Heckscher Mus., Huntington, N.Y., 1980, Holtzman Gallery, Towson (Md.) State U., 1982, Roslyn Oxley Gallery, Sydney, 1976, 82, Tomasulo Gallery, Union College, N.J., 1983, Stages, Keuka Coll., Keuka Park, N.Y., 1985, New Visions, Ithaca, N.Y., 1989, Herr-Chambliss, Hot Springs, Ark., 1990, Artist on the Lake, Hector, N.Y., 1992, Mus. Modern Art Christmas Card Collection, 1994; designer Mus. Modern Art Christmas Collection, 1978-81, 94, Time-Life Poster, 1978; exhibited in over 75 group shows, corp. and mus. collections. Recipient Flower Painting award Artist's Mag., 1986, Art Dir.'s Club 58th Annual Distinctive Merit award, 1979, N.Y. State Creative Artist's Pub. Svc. grant, 1979. Mem. AAUW, Nat. Assn. Women Artists, Allan Stone Gallery N.Y.C. Home and Studio: PO Box 662 Montour Falls NY 14865 also: 203 S Genesse St Montour Falls NY 14865

STILLMAN, M. J., physical science rsch. administrator, bioinorganic chemist; b. London, June 4, 1947; Can. citizen; BSc, U. East Anglia, 1969, MSc, 1970, PhD in Chemistry, 1973. Fellow in chemistry U. Alta., Edmonton, Can., 1973-75; from asst. prof. to assoc. prof. U. Western Ont., London, Can., 1975-86, prof. chemistry, 1986—, dir. Ctr. Chemistry and Physics, 1986—. Mem. Chem. Soc., Can. Inst. Chemistry, Am. Chem. Soc. Office: Univ Western ON Ctr Chem Phys, P&A Bldg Rm 102, London, ON Canada N6A 3K7

STILLMAN, MICHAEL ALLEN, dermatologist; b. N.Y.C., Apr. 12, 1943; s. Aaron and Anne (Turansky) S.; m. Susan Fuchs, July 8, 1973; children: Julie, Jeremy. BA, Clark U., 1963; MD, SUNY, 1967. Diplomate Am. Acad. Dermatology. Med. intern Marmonides Hosp., Bklyn., 1967-68; dermatology resident NYU Med. Ctr. and Bellevue Hosp., N.Y.C., 1970-73; pvt. practice Mt. Kisco, N.Y., 1973—; cons. in dermatology U.S. Mil. Acad., West Point, N.Y., 1973-75. Contbr. essays and articles to profl. jours. and newspapers. Bd. trustees South Salem (N.Y.) Libr., 1990—; boys varsity tennis coach John Jay H.S., Katonah, N.Y., 1996. Capt. USAF, 1968-70, Vietnam. Decorated Combat Inf. badge. Fellow Am. Soc. Dermatol. Surgeons, Am. Acad. Dermatology; mem. N.Y. State Med. Soc., Noah Worcester Dermatology Soc. Avocations: tennis, jogging, writing. Home: 33 Mead St Waccabuc NY 10597 Office: PO Box 268 Mount Kisco NY 10549-0268

STILLMAN, NINA GIDDEN, lawyer; b. N.Y.C., Apr. 3, 1948; d. Melvin and Joyce Audrey (Gidden) S. AB with distinction, Smith Coll., 1970; JD cum laude, Northwestern U., 1973. Bar: Ill. 1973, U.S. Dist. Ct. (no. dist.) Ill. 1973, U.S. Dist. Ct. (ea. dist.) Wis. 1979, U.S. Dist. Ct. (no. dist. trial bar) Ill. 1983, U.S. Ct. Appeals (7th cir.) 1974, U.S. Supreme Ct. 1981, U.S. Dist. Ct. (ctrl. dist.) Ill. 1994, U.S. Dist. Ct. (ea. dist.) Tex., 1996. Assoc. Vedder, Price, Kaufman & Kammholz, Chgo., 1973-79, ptnr., 1980—; mem. adv. bd. occupational health and safety tng. program U. Mich., Ann Arbor, 1980-83; adj. faculty Inst. Human Resources and Indsl. Rels., Loyola U., Chgo., 1983-86, mem. bd. advisors, 1986—. Author: (with others) Women, Work, and Health: Challenge to Corporate Policy, 1979, Occupational Health Law: A Guide for Industry, 1981, Employment Discrimination, 1981, Personnel Management: Labor Relations, 1981, Occupational Safety and Health Law, 1988; contbg. author: Occupational Medicine: State of the Art Reviews, 1996; contbr. articles to profl. jours. Legal advisor, v.p. Planned Parenthood Assn. Chgo., 1979-81; sec. jr. governing bd. Chgo. Symphony Orch., 1983. Recipient Svc. award Northwestern U., 1994. Mem. ABA (occupational safety and health law com. 1978—), Chgo. Bar Assn. (chmn. labor and employment law com. 1986-87), Human Resources Mgmt. Assn. Chgo. (officer, bd. dirs. 1986-88), Am. Inns of Ct. (v.p. Wigmore chpt. 1988-89), Northwestern U Sch. Law Alumni Assn. (pres. 1991-92), Coun. of 100, Smith Coll. Club Chgo. (pres. 1972), Law Club, Econ. Club Chgo., The Chgo. Com. Avocations: travel, reading, the arts, collecting art. Office: Vedder Price Kaufman & Kammholz 222 N La Salle St Chicago IL 60601-1002

STILLWELL, G(EORGE) KEITH, physician; b. Moose Jaw, Sask., Can., July 11, 1918; came to U.S., 1947, naturalized, 1964; s. George B. and Muriel (Bolster) S.; m. Mildred Ethel Cameron, Mar. 12, 1943; children: Paul, Craig. B.A., U. Sask., 1939; M.D., Queen's U., Kingston, Ont., Can., 1942; Ph.D., U. Minn., 1954. Diplomate: Am. Bd. Phys. Medicine and Rehab. Intern Gen. Hosp., Kingston, 1942-43; resident Gen. Hosp., 1945, U. Minn., Mpls., 1947-51; pvt. practice medicine specializing in phys. medicine and rehab. Mpls., 1951-54; cons. dept. phys. medicine and rehab. Mayo Clinic, Rochester, Minn., 1954-83; chmn. dept. phys. medicine and rehab. Mayo Clinic, 1973-81; instr. U. Minn., 1950-54; instr. Mayo Grad. Sch. Medicine, 1955-60, asst. prof. phys. medicine and rehab., 1960-67, asso. prof., 1967-73; prof. Mayo Med. Sch., 1973-83; vis. prof. Ohio State U., 1970. Contbr. numerous articles to med. publs. Served with M.C., Royal Can. Army, 1943-46. Mem. AMA, Am. Acad. Phys. Medicine and Rehab. (editorial Bd. Archives Phys. Medicine and Rehab. 1960-81, chmn. editorial bd. 1972-77, bd. govs. acad. 1963-70), Am. Congress Rehab. Medicine (Gold Key award 1973), Assn. Acad. Physiatrists. Unitarian. Office: Mayo Clinic Rochester MN 55905

STILLWELL, KATHLEEN ANN SWANGER, healthcare consultant; b. Glendale, Calif., Aug. 12, 1950; d. Robert Dowayne and Irene Margaret (Sawatzky) Swanger; m. Joseph Wayne Stillwell, Nov. 11, 1971; children: Shannon Kristine, Nathan Joseph. AA, Cypress Coll., 1971; AS & diploma, Golden West Coll., 1981; BA in English Lit., Long Beach State U., 1982; MPA, Health Svcs. Adminstrn., U. San Francisco, 1989. RN Calif. Staff nurse Long Beach (Calif.) Meml. Hosp., 1981-84; sr. claims analyst Caronia Corp., Tustin, Calif., 1984-87; dir. quality assurance & risk mgmt. St. Mary Med. Ctr., Long Beach, 1987-89; cons. quality assurance, risk mgmt. Am. Med. Internat., Costa Mesa, Calif., 1989-91; cons. healthcare, 1991—; adj. faculty U. San Francisco, Woodbury U., 1996; faculty Am. Soc. Healthcare Risk Mgrs. Cert. Program; v.p. Patient Care Assessment Coun., L.A., 1988-89, pres., 1989-90, bd. dirs.; pres. State Bd. Patient Care Coun., 1990-92, past pres., 1992-94; speaker in field. Vol. Calif. Health Decisions, Orange County, 1989—, PTA, Am. Cancer Soc., Patient Care Assessment Coun.; active Constnl. Rights Found.; mem. edn. com. Bus. in Soc., Bus. Leadership, 1995, World Future Soc., 1995. Mem. NLN, Am. Soc. Healthcare Risk Mgmt., Nat. Assn. Healthcare Quality (exec. fin. com. 1993-95), Am. Soc. Quality Control Profls. (sec. healthcare divsn. 1995—, chair membership 1994-95, chair-elect healthcare divsn. 1996-97, chair 1997-98), Am. Soc. Healthcare Risk Mgrs., So. Calif. Assn. Healthcare Risk Mgrs. (sec. 1989-90, mem. chmn. 1989-90), Calif. League for Nurses (bd. dirs. 1993-95), Patient Care Assessment Coun. (v.p. So. Calif. 1988, pres. So. Calif. 1989-90, state bd. pres. 1990-92, state bd. dirs. 1992-94). Democrat. Lutheran. Avocations: reading, cooking, swimming, vol. activities. Home and Office: 825 Coastline Dr Seal Beach CA 90740-5810

STILLWELL, WALTER BROOKS, III, lawyer; b. Whitehall, Wis., July 30, 1946; s. Walter Brooks Jr. and Selpha T. (Everson) S.; m. Carolyn E. Laws, Dec. 20, 1992; children: Walter, Haviland. BA cum laude, Wake Forest U., 1968; JD, U. Ga., 1971. Bar: Ga. 1971, U.S. Dist. Ct. (so. and no. dists.) Ga., U.S. Ct. Appeals (11th cir.), U.S. Supreme Ct. Assoc. Hunter, Maclean, Exley & Dunn, P.C., Savannah, Ga., 1971-74, ptnr., 1974—; adv. dir. AmeriBank, N.A., 1993—; v.p. W.E.T., Inc., 1991—, also bd. dirs. Alderman City of Savannah, 1974-92, mayor-pro-tem, 1990-92. Mem. State Bar of Ga. (real property sect., exec. com. 1986-93, chmn. 1992), Am. Coll. Real Estate Lawyers. Democrat. Baptist. Office: Hunter Maclean Exley & Dunn PC 200 E Saint Julian St Savannah GA 31401-2731

STILMAN, BORIS, computer science educator, researcher; b. Moscow, Aug. 16, 1950; came to the U.S., 1991.; s. Mikhail and Raisa (Gurevich) S.; m. Zinaida Korenblat, July 11, 1979; 1 child, Michael. MS in Math., Moscow State U., 1972; PhDs in Elec. Engring. and Computer Sci., Nat. Rsch. Inst. Elec. Engring, Moscow, 1984. Sr. engr., mathematician dept. for complex search problems The Nat. Rsch. Inst. for Elec. Engring., Moscow, 1972-75, sr. scientist dept. for complex search problems, 1975-85, sr. scientist/group leader dept. for complex search problems, 1985-88; chief dept. for software design computer tech. divsn. Nat. Rsch. Geol. Inst. for Oil Devel., Moscow, 1988-90; prin. software designer Inst. Designers Coun. The Nat. Rsch. Geol. Inst. for Oil Devel., Moscow, 1988-90; vis. prof. McGill U., Sch. Computer Sci., Montreal, 1990-91; assoc. prof. computer sci. dept. computer sci. and engring. U. Colo., Denver, 1991-94, prof. computer sci. dept. computer sci. and engring., 1994—; sci. sec. The USSR Acad. Scis. Nat. Commn., 1981-88; local divsn. chief, of. computer sci. The USSR Acad. Scis. Temporary Rsch. Group, Moscow, 1985-89; presenter in field. Author: Programming Within Structured Frame of Algorithmic Language, 1988, Theory of Linguistic Geometry in the Field of Artificial Intelligence; reviewer Annals of Math. and Artificail Intelligence, IBM Sys. Jour., Jour. of Intelligent Mfg.; contbr. 160 articles to books and articles to profl. jours.; numerous papers and presentations. Recipient The USSR Acad. Scis. and Dept. Geology Joint Rsch. grant, 1988, The USSR Acad. Scis. Rsch. grant, 1988, Sandia Nat. Labs. rsch. grantee, 1995, AFOSR Summer Faculty fellow, 1995, Chancellor's New Urban U. Lectureship awar, 1996, others. Mem. IEEE Computer Soc., Assn. for Computing Machinery, Am. Assn. for Artificial Intelligence, N.Y. Acad. Scis. Avocation: travel.

STILWELL, CHARLOTTE FINN, vocational counselor; b. San Francisco, Oct. 31, 1947; d. Frederick William and Helen Carolyn (Watson) Finn; Bobby Gene Stilwell, Dec. 17, 1937; children: Robert, Shelley, James, Joel. AA, St. Petersburg Jr. Coll., 1967; BS, Fla. State U., 1969; MA, U. South Fla., 1971; attended, U. S.C., 1972. Nat. cert. counselor; cert. sch. counselor. Dir. tutorial program Hillsborough County Schs., Tampa, Fla., 1971-72, tchr., counselor, 1972-73, h.s. counselor, 1973-77; vocat. counselor Pinellas County Schs., Clearwater, Fla., 1977—; dist. coord. Counseling for High Skills Kans. State, 1992—. Vol. Suicide & Crisis Ctrs., Tampa, St. Vincent DePaul's Soup Kitchen, St. Petersburg, Fla., 1993, Toy Shop, 1994-95, Spl. Olympics, 1996. General Electric Found. fellow. Mem. Am. Counseling Assn., Am. Sch. Counselor Assn. (Am. Sch. Counselor of Yr. 1995), Fla. Counseling Assn., Fla. Sch. Counselor Assn. (v.p. post secondary 1993-95), Phi Delta Kappa (historian 1993—), Pinellas Sch. Counselor Assn. (pres. 1991-95). Republican. Avocations: oil painting, snow skiing, sports. Office: PTEC Clearwater 6100 154th Ave N Clearwater FL 33760-2140

STILWELL, JOHN QUINCY, lawyer; b. Columbia, S.C., Sept. 20, 1933; s. James Raymond and Edna (Douglass) S.; m. Regina Besman, Apr. 18, 1965 (div. Mar. 1977); 1 child, Laura Douglass; m. Nancy O'Neil, Mar. 20, 1987; children: William S. Rogers, Richard Blake Rogers, Stephen J. Rogers, Stewart D. Rogers. AB, U. N.C., 1954; LLB, Columbia U., 1961; MA, U. Tex., Dallas, 1988, PhD, 1994. Bar: N.Y. 1962, Tex. 1990. Assoc. atty. Winthrop, Stimson, Putnam & Roberts, N.Y.C., 1961-68; v.p., gen. counsel Total Energy Leasing Corp., N.Y.C., 1968-70, pres., 1970-72; ptnr. Gibbons, Green & Rice, N.Y.C., 1972-74; chmn. Transcable Inc., N.Y.C., 1974-77, John Stilwell Assocs., Inc., Fairfield, Conn., 1977-79; sr. v.p. Kidde, Inc., Saddle Brook, N.J., 1979-85; assoc. gen. counsel Mut. of N.Y. Life, N.Y.C., 1985-87; ptnr. Akin, Gump, Strauss, Hauer & Feld, L.L.P., Dallas, 1987—. Bd. dirs., sec. Shared Housing Ctr., Inc., Dallas, 1993—; bd. dirs. Dallas County Local Workforce Devel. Bd., 1996—; trustee Consensus Found., Dallas, 1990. Served to lt. USN, 1954-58. Mem. Assn. Bar City N.Y., Dallas Bar Assn. Avocation: philosophy and communication theory. Home: 4808 Byron Ave Dallas TX 75205-3254 Office: Akin Gump Strauss 1700 Pacific Ave Ste 4100 Dallas TX 75201-4624

STILWELL, RICHARD DALE, baritone; b. St. Louis, May 6, 1942; s. Otho John Clifton and Tressie Fern (Parrish) S.; m. Elizabeth Louise Jencks, Mar. 21, 1967 (div.); m. Kerry M. McCarthy, Oct. 22, 1983. Student, Anderson Coll., 1960-62; MusB, Ind. U., 1966; MusD (hon.), Knox Coll., 1980. With Met. Opera Co., N.Y.C., 1970—. Appearances in major roles with Met. Opera, N.Y.C., Washington Opera Soc., Marseilles (France) Opera Co., Sante Fe Opera, San Francisco Opera Co., Paris Opera Co., Teatro Alla Scala, Covent Garden, Hamburg (Fed. Republic of Germany) State Opera, Glyndebourne Opera Festival, Eng., Vancouver (B.C.) Opera Co., Chgo. Opera Co., Tanglewood Festival, Israel Philharm., San Jose (Calif.) Opera, others; soloist with Nat. Symphony, Washington, Chgo. Symphony, Am. Symphony, Carnegie Hall, N.Y.C., St. Louis Symphony, Double Arts Chorale at Philharm. Hall, Met. Opera Studio at Tully Hall, N.Y.C., Boston Symphony, Los Angeles Philharm., Presl. dinner in honor of Apollo 11 astronauts, Los Angeles, 1969. Served with AUS, 1966-69. Recipient Nat. Soc. Arts and Letters award, 1963, Young Artist award St. Louis, 1963, Fisher Found. award Met. Opera Auditions, 1965. Mem. Am. Guild Musical Artists. Office: care Columbia Artists Mgmt Arbib Div 165 W 57th St New York NY 10019-2201*

STILWILL, BELLE JEAN, record company executive, printing company owner; b. Mackay, Idaho, Oct. 27, 1955; d. Allen LeRoy Stilwill and Galia Vee (Larter) Stilwill Dodd. Student, Ricks Coll., 1974-79, Def. Language Inst., 1980. Quality control Best Foods, Hermiston, Oreg., 1972-73; leader dance band Ricks Coll., Rexburg, Idaho, 1975-77; reporter Standard Jour., Rexburg, Idaho, 1976-77; news editor Chronicle-News, St. Anthony, Idaho, 1978; editor-in-chief The Scroll Ricks Coll., 1979-80; exec. asst. Rapid Printers, Monterey, Calif., 1981-82; corp. acct. Color-Ad Printers, Monterey, Calif., 1983-95; corp. acct. Bayshore Press, Scotts Valley, Calif., 1995—, v.p., 1995—; owner Stilwill & Hoover Group LLC. Author (record albums) 1st Step, 1988 (Sam Segal award 1988), Mixed Signals, 1989 (Sam Segal award 1990, Album of Month Sta. KOFE Radio Idaho), Lovin' Arms, 1990 (Sam Segal award 1991). Faculty scholar Ricks Coll., 1979-80. Mem. NAFE, NARAS, Nat. Assn. Ind. Record Distributors, Broadcast Music Industry. Home: 1199 Luxton St Seaside CA 93955-6008 Office: Bayshore Press 103 Whispering Pines Dr Ste E Santa Cruz CA 95066-4782

STIMMEL, BARRY, cardiologist, internist, educator, university dean; b. Bklyn., Oct. 8, 1939; s. Abraham and Mabel (Bovit) S.; m. Barbara Barovick, June 6, 1970; children: Alexander, Matthew. BS, Bklyn. Coll., 1960; MD, SUNY, Bklyn., 1964. Diplomate: Nat. Bd. Med. Examiners, Am. Bd. Internal Medicine. Resident Mt. Sinai Hosp., N.Y.C., 1964-65, 67-69; asst. dean admissions and student affairs Mt. Sinai Sch. Medicine, CUNY, 1970-71, assoc. dean, 1971—, asst. prof. medicine, 1972-75, assoc. prof., 1975-84, prof. medicine and med. edn., 1984—, assoc. dean acad. affairs, 1975-81, dean admissions, acad. affairs and student affairs, 1981—, assoc. attending physician, 1981-94, dean grad. med. edn., 1994—, attending physician, 1984—, acting chmn. dept. med. edn., 1980-94; mem. com. planning, priorities and evaluation N.Y. Met. Regional Med. Program, 1971-73; adv. com. Nat. Ctr. Urban Problems CUNY, 1970-71; adv. com. methadone maintenance Office of Drug Abuse Svcs. State N.Y., 1976-79; sci. adv. bd. Nat. Coun. Drug Abuse, 1978-84, N.Y. State Bd. Profl. Med. Conduct, 1983—; bd. dirs. Am. Soc. Addiction Medicine, N.Y. State Coun. on Grad. Med. Edn., Greater N.Y. Hosp. Assn. Task Force on Health Manpower. Author: Heroin Dependency: Medical Social and Economic Aspects, 1975, Cardiovascular Effects Mood Altering Drugs, 1979, Pain, Analgesia, Addiction, 1982, Ambulatory Care, 1983, The Facts about Drug Use, 1991, Drugs Abuse and Social Policy in America: The War That Must Be Won, 1996, Pain and Its Relief Without Addiction, 1997; editor Advances in Alcohol and Substance Abuse, 1980-91, Jour. Advances in Alcohol and Substance Abuse, Jour. Addictive Diseases, 1991—; assoc. editor Am. Jour. Drug and Alcohol Abuse, 1974-85; contbr. chpts. to books, articles to profl. jours. Served with M.C. USNR, 1965-67. Mem. AAUP, Am. Assn. Physicians Assts. (adv. bd. 1972-73), Am. Assn. Higher Edn., Soc. Study of Addiction to Alcohol and Other Drugs, Assn. Med. Edn. and Rsch. Substance Abuse, Inst. Study of Drug Addiction, Am., N.Y. heart assns., Am., N.Y. State socs. internal medicine, Soc. Internal Medicine County of N.Y. (dir.), Am. Coll. Cardiology, Greater N.Y. Coalition on Drug Abuse, NYS Coun. on Grad. Medical Edn., N.Y. Acad. Medicine, Nat. Coun. Alcoholism, Rsch. Soc. on Alcoholism, Am. Ednl. Research Assn., Am. Fedn. Clin. Rsch., Am. Soc. Addiction Medicine. Office: Mt Sinai Sch Med 100th St and Fifth Ave New York NY 10029

STIMPERT, MICHAEL ALAN, agricultural products company executive; b. Madisonville, La., Aug. 21, 1944; s. Warren Eugene and Louisa (Beale) S.; m. Kim Kathleen Agee, Apr. 17, 1970 (div. 1985); 1 child, Kelly Kathleen; m. Helen Marie Evans, June 27, 1987; children: Katherine Helen, Michael Adam. Student, Washburn U., 1962-64, U. Copenhagen, 1964; BA, Western Res. U., 1967; MBA, Harvard U., 1974. Asst. to group v.p. Gold Kist Inc., Atlanta, 1974, mgr. internat. div., 1975-80, dir. spl. markets and staff services, 1980-81, group v.p., 1982-86; v.p. ops. and govt. affairs Golden Peanut Co., Atlanta, 1986-89, exec. v.p., 1989-95; sr. v.p. Gold Kist Inc., Atlanta, 1996—; bd. dirs. CoBank, Denver, Agri Internat., Inc., Atlanta, G.C. Properties, Atlanta, G.K. Pecans, Atlanta, Luker Inc., Augusta, Ga., GKX Inc., Agana, Guam, chmn. Global Health Action, Atlanta; chmn. Agra Trade Financing, Inc., Atlanta. Mem. adv. bd. dirs. Internat. Svc. Assn. for Health Devel. Edn. Project, 1982-91; bd. dirs. Global Health Action. Lt. (j.g.) USN, 1967-72, Vietnam. Mem. Assn. for Corp. Growth, Japan-Am. Soc. Ga., Harvard Bus. Sch. Club Atlanta, Cherokee Town and Country Club. Democrat. Roman Catholic. Office: Gold Kist Inc 244 Perimeter Center Pkwy NE Atlanta GA 30346-2302

STIMPSON, CATHARINE ROSLYN, English language educator, writer; b. Bellingham, Wash., June 4, 1936; d. Edward Keown and Catharine

(Watts) S. A.B., Bryn Mawr Coll., 1958; B.A., Cambridge U., Eng., 1960, M.A., 1960; Ph.D., Columbia U., 1967. Mem. faculty Barnard Coll., N.Y.C., 1963-80; prof. English, dean of grad. sch., vice provost grad. edn. Rutgers U., New Brunswick, N.J., 1980-92, Univ. prof., 1991—; chmn. bd. scholars Ms. Mag., N.Y.C., 1981-92; dir. fellows program MacArthur Found., 1994—. Author: Class Notes, 1979, Where the Meanings Are, 1988; founding editor: Signs: Jour. Women in Culture and Society, 1974-81; book series Women in Culture and Society, 1981; columnist Change Mag., 1992-93. Chmn. N.Y. Council Humanities, 1984-87, Nat. Council Research on Women, 1984-89 ; bd. dirs. Stephens Coll., Columbia, Mo., 1982-85; trustee Bates Coll., 1990—. Hon. fellow Woodrow Wilson Found., 1958; Fulbright fellow, 1958-60; Nat. Humanities Inst. fellow New Haven, 1975-76; Rockefeller Humanities fellow, 1983-84. Mem. MLA (exec. coun., chmn. acad. freedom com., 1st v.p., pres. 1990), PEN, AAUP, NOW, PBS (bd. dirs. 1994—), Legal Def. and Edn. Fund (bd. dirs. 1991-96). Democrat. Home: 62 Westervelt Ave Staten Island NY 10301-1432 Office: Rutgers U 25 Bishop Pl New Brunswick NJ 08901-1178

STIMPSON, RITCHIE PLES, retired military officer; b. Black Mountain, N.C., Mar. 22, 1917; s. David Ples and Lydia Hinson Stimpson; m. Marjorie Spruce, May 3, 1942; children: Ritchie P. Jr., David Fleming. BS in Physics, Furman U., 1940. Commd. 2nd lt. USAF, 1941, advanced through grades to col., 1953; squadron comdr. 13th Tactical Reconnaissance Squadron, 1942-44; dir. ops. 24 Composite Wing, Borinquen Field, P.R., 1946-47; liaison officer Armed Forces Spl. Weapons Project to Strategic Air Commd., Offutt AFB, Nebr., 1950-52; dir. plans and negotiations Joint U.S. Asst. Adv. Group, Madrid, 1957-59; staff officer Joint Chiefs of Staff, Washington, 1960-61, Weapons Sys. Evaluation Group/Office of Sec. of Def., 1964-67; comdt. Air Force ROTC detachment Auburn (Ala.) U., 1967-71; ret. USAF, 1971; owner Ritch Stimpson Co., Inc., College Station, Tex., 1975-82; ind. writer, Dallas, 1982-93. Author: The Protestant Church and Bible Disregard the Truth, 1989, "Is It True?" Answers to Questions About the Bible, 1992. Decorated Commendation medals (2), Identification Badge, Outstanding Unit award. Mem. Air Force Assn., Greater Dallas Ret. Officers Assn., Greater Dallas Ret. Officers Assn. Investment Club, Oakridge Country Club, Furman U. Paladin Club. Republican. Methodist. Avocations: golf, travel, reading, bridge, gardening. Home: 2729 Laurel Oaks Dr Garland TX 75044-6939

STIMSON, FREDERICK SPARKS, Hispanist, educator; b. Newark, Ohio, Jan. 1, 1919; s. Fred Samuel and Leah Kate (Sparks) S. B.A., Ohio State U., 1940; postgrad., Harvard U., 1940-41; Jr. fellow in Archaeology, Princeton U., 1941-42; M.A., U. Mich., 1948, Ph.D. (Ford Found. grantee), 1952. Dir. Cultural Center for Dept. State, Medellin, Colombia, 1944-46; asst. public affairs officer Am. embassy, San Salvador, El Salvador, 1947; instr. to prof. dept. Spanish Northwestern U., Evanston, Ill., 1954-81; prof. emeritus Northwestern U., 1981—, chmn. dept., 1976-79. Author: Cuba's Romantic Poet, 1964, New Schools of Spanish American Poetry, 1970, Literatura de la América Hispánica, 3 vols, 1971-75, Los poemas más representativos de Plácido, 1976. Mem. MLA, Phi Beta Kappa. Home: 3300 S Ocean Blvd Apt 819C Highland Beach FL 33487

STINE, CATHERINE MORRIS, artist; b. Roanoke, Va., Jan. 12, 1953; d. Richard Dengler and Dorothy Geraldine (Cornog) S.; m. Norris Jewett Chumley, Oct. 22, 1983; children: Jack H.M., Nathaniel B. BFA, Mus. Sch. Fine Arts, Boston, 1975. Art dir. Ear Mag., N.Y.C., 1980-83; asst. art dir. Jacmel Jewelry, N.Y.C., 1984-88; textile designer Style Coun., N.Y.C., 1989-90, Ruvetta Designs, N.Y.C., 1990—; curator Bratton Gallery, N.Y.C., 1989. One-woman shows include Plant Factory, Boston, 1974, Sixth Sense Gallery, N.Y.C., 1986, Pinnacle Awards/Am. Women in Radio and TV, N.Y.C., 1987, Limelight Club, N.Y.C., 1987, Parker-Bratton Gallery, N.Y.C., 1987, Bratton Gallery, N.Y.C., 1988, Carol Getz Gallery, Miami, Fla., 1990, Sunnen Gallery, N.Y.C., 1993, 94, Galley B.A.I., N.Y.C., 1996; group shows include Mus. Fine Arts Gallery, Boston, 1974, Williamsburg, Bklyn., 1982, ABC No Rio, N.Y.C., 1983, 85, City Without Walls Gallery, Newark, 1984, 85, Parsons Gallery, N.Y.C., 1985, author, illustrator: The Halcyon, 1984, Hudson Valley Exhbn., Poughkeepsie, 1985, Parker-Bratton Gallery, N.Y.C., 1986, Bratton Gallery, 1989, Neo Persona, N.Y.C., 1990, Tribeca 148, N.Y.C., 1991, Helio Gallery, N.Y.C., 1991, S. Bitter Larkin, N.Y.C., 1992, Sarah Rentschler Gallery, N.Y.C., 1992, Dooley-Le Cappellaine, N.Y.C., 1993, NYU Law Sch., 1994; represented in permanent collections Art Mus. Western Va., Paramount Pictures, others. Clk. religious edn. com. Fifteenth St. Quaker Meeting, N.Y.C. Curatorial grantee Artist Space, N.Y.C., 1989. Avocations: rollerhockey, ice skating. Home: 264 E 7th St New York NY 10009-6048

STINE, GEORGE HARRY, consulting engineer, author; b. Phila., Mar. 26, 1928; s. George Haeberle and Rhea (Matilda) (O'Neill) S.; m. Barbara Ann Kauth, June 10, 1952; children: Constance Rhea, Eleanor Anne, George Willard. B.A. in Physics, Colo. Coll., 1952. Chief controls and instruments sect., propulsion br. White Sands (N.Mex.) Proving Grounds, 1952-55; chief range ops. div. U.S. Naval Ordnance Missile Test Facility at proving grounds, 1955-57; design specialist Martin Co., Denver, 1957; chief engr., pres. Model Missiles, Inc., Denver, 1957-59; design engr. Stanley Aviation Corp., Denver, 1959-60; asst. dir. research Huyck Corp., Stamford, Conn., 1960-65; sci. cons. CBS-TV, 1969, CBC, Toronto, 1969; sci. reporter Metromedia Radio News, N.Y.C., 1968; cons. Young & Rubicam Inc., N.Y.C., also Gen. Electric Co., Valley Forge, Pa., 1966-69; lectr. Franklin Inst., Phila., 1966-72; mktg. mgr. Flow Technology, Inc., Phoenix, 1973-76; cons. curator Internat. Space Hall of Fame, 1976; cons. astronautical history Nat. Air and Space Museum, Smithsonian Instn., 1965—; cons. mktg. research and surveys Talley Industries, Inc., Mesa, Ariz., 1977; cons. mktg. and comm. Flow Tech., Inc., 1976-79; cons. Sci. Applications, Inc. 1976-81, Visions of the Future, 1982-86, McDonnell Douglas Corp., 1988-90, Sci. Applications Internat. Corp., 1990, Quest Aerospace Edn., Inc., 1992—, Aero Tech., Inc., 1991; expert witness fireworks injury cases, 1984—; pres. The Enterprise Inst., Inc., 1987—; cons., writer Discover Space Computer Program, Broderbond Software, Inc., 1992-93; moderator aviation and sport rocketry conf., Bix on-line computer network, 1986—. Freelance writer, 1951—; author more than 50 books on astronautics and sci., including The Model Rocketry Manual, 1975, The Third Industrial Revolution, 2d edit., 1979, The New Model Rocketry Manual, 1977, Shuttle Into Space, 1978, The Space Enterprise, 1980, Space Power, 1981, Confrontation in Space, 1981, The Hopeful Future, 1983, The Untold Story of the Computer Revolution, 1984, The Silicon Gods, 1984, Handbook for Space Colonists, 1985, The Corporate Survivors, 1986, Thirty Years of Model Rocketry, A Safety Report, 1988, Mind Machines You Can Build, 1991, ICBM, The Making of the Weapon That Changed the World, 1991, The Handbook of Model Rocketry 6th edit., 1994, Halfway to Anywhere, 1996; author: (as Lee Correy) sci. fiction novels and stories, including Starship Through Space, 1954, Rocket Man, 1955, Contraband Rocket, 1956, Star Driver, 1980, Shuttle Down, 1981, Space Doctor, 1981, The Abode of Life, 1982, Manna, 1984, A Matter of Metalaw, 1986, (under own name) Warbots, 1988, Operation Steel Band, 1988, The Bastaard Rebellion, 1988, Sierra Madre, 1988, Operation High Dragon, 1989, The Lost Battalion, 1989, Operation Iron Fist, 1989, Force of Arms, 1990, Blood Siege, 1990, Guts and Glory, 1991, Warrior Shield, 1992, Judgement Day, 1992, Starsea Invaders # 1, First Action, 1993, Star-sea Invaders # 2, Second Contact, 1994, Star-sea Invaders # 3, Third Encounter, 1995; contbr. numerous articles to jours. Charter mem. citizen's adv. coun. Nat. Space Policy, 1981—; mem. Ariz. Space Commn., 1992—, NASA Tech. and Commercialization Adv. Com., 1995. Recipient Silver medal Assn. U.S. Army, 1967, Spl. award Hobby Industry Assn., 1969; Paul Tissandier diploma Fedn. Aeronautique Internationale, 1985, Lifetime Space Activist award Space Access Soc., 1995. Fellow AIAA (assoc.)Explorers Club, Brit. Interplanetary Soc., Am. Rocket Soc.; mem. Nat. Assn. Rocketry (hon. trustee 1978-81, founder 1957, pres. 1957-67, trustee 1978-81, Spl. Founder's award 1967, Howard Galloway Svc. award 1978, 83, 85, 87), Nat. Fire Protection Assn. (chmn. com. pyrotechnics 1974-94, Svc. award 1993, emeritus mem. 1994), N.Y. Acad. Scis., Aircraft Owners and Pilots Assn., Ariz. Pilots Assn. (dir. 1980-93, v.p. 1981-84), L-5 Soc. (v.p. 1984). Home: 2419 W Saint Moritz Ln Phoenix AZ 85023-5041 *The most interesting data are the points that fall "off the curve" because they lead to unsuspected new discoveries. I grew up on a vanishing frontier and intend to spend my life opening new frontiers—in space, because the world is no more closed than it is flat. Because of this, we do not live in a world of limits, but a limitless universe, and have a limitless future.*

STINE, ROBERT HOWARD, pediatrician; b. Nov. 1, 1929; s. Harry Raymond and Mabel Eva (Newhard) S.; m. Lois Elaine Kihlgren, Oct. 22, 1960; children: Robert E., Karen, Jonathan. BS in Biology, Moravian Coll., 1952. Diplomate Am. Bd. Pediatrics, Am. Subbd. Pediatric Allergy, Am. Allergy and Immunology. Intern St. Luke's Hosp., Bethlehem, Pa., 1960-61, resident in surgery, 1961-62; physician Jefferson Med. Coll., Phila., 1956-60; resident in pediatrics U. N.Y., Syracuse, 1962-64; resident in allergy Robert A. Cooke Inst. Allergy Roosevelt Hosp., N.Y.C., 1964-65; clin. instr. pediatrics U. Ill., Chgo., 1965-71; mem. courtesy staff Proctor Community Hosp., Peoria, Ill., 1966-77, mem. active staff, 1977—, chmn. dept. medicine, 1988—; pres. elect. med. staff, 1990-91, pres. med. staff, 1991-92; mem. teaching staff St. Francis Hosp., Peoria, 1969—; clin. instr. pediatrics Rush-Presbyn. St. Luke's Hosp., Chgo., 1971—. Lt. (j.g.), USN, 1953-56. Fellow Am. Acad. Pediatrics, Am. Acad. Allergy and Immunology, Am. Coll. Allergists, Am. Assn. Cert. Allergists; mem. Ill. Soc. Allergy and Clin. Immunology, Peoria Med. Soc. (pres.-elect 1993, pres. 1994), Christian Med. and Dental Soc. Home: 105 Hollands Grove Ln Washington IL 61571-9623 Office: 710 E Archer Ave Peoria IL 61603-2636

STINEBRING, WARREN RICHARD, microbiologist, educator; b. Niagara Falls, N.Y., July 31, 1924; s. Clifford Thomas and Signe (Arvidson) S.; m. Delores Jean Zakes, June 12, 1948; children: Dan R., Beth E., Eric. B.A., U. Buffalo, 1948; M.S., U. Pa., 1949, Ph.D., 1951. With U. Pa., Phila., 1949-55; asso. U. Pa., 1953-55; asst. prof. U. Tex. Med. Br., Galveston, 1955-57; asso. research prof. Inst. Microbiology, Rutgers U., New Brunswick, N.J., 1957-60; asst. prof. U. Pitts. Coll. Medicine, 1960-65, asso. prof., 1965-66; prof., chmn. med. microbiology U. Calif. Coll. Medicine at Irvine, 1966-68; prof. U. Vt. Coll. Medicine, Burlington, 1968-86, prof. emeritus, 1986—; chmn. med. microbiology U. Vt. Coll. Medicine, 1968-78; sabbatical leave Royal Postgrad. Med. Sch., London, 1974-75. Served with inf. AUS, 1943-45, ETO. Decorated Purple Heart.; Recipient Golden Apple award Student AMA, 1966-67, award for outstanding research and diagnosis in brucellosis eradication in Vt. Vt. Vt. Med. Assn., 1983. Mem. AAAS, Tissue Culture Assn. (ednl. com. 1970-72, chmn. 1970-72), Reticuloendothelial Soc., Am. Soc. Microbiology, Am. Soc. Mammalogy, Soc. Exptl. Biol. Medicine, Brucellosis Research Conf. (hon. patron). Research on host-parasite interactions delayed hypersensitivity, interferon stimulation by non-viral agts., brucellosis. Home: 139 N Prospect St Oberlin OH 44074-1038

STINEHART, ROGER RAY, lawyer; b. Toledo, Jan. 27, 1945; s. Forrest William and Nettie May (Twyman) S.; m. Martha Jean Goodnight, Sept. 19, 1970; children: Amanda Jean, Brian Scott. BS, Bowling Green (Ohio) State U., 1968; JD, Ohio State U., 1972. Bar: Ohio 1972. Fin. analyst Gen. Electric, Detroit, 1968-69; assoc. Gingher & Christensen, Columbus, Ohio, 1972-76, ptnr., 1976-80; sr. v.p., gen. counsel, sec. G.D. Ritzy's, Inc., Columbus, 1983-85; ptnr. Jones, Day, Reavis & Pogue, Columbus, 1980-83, 85—; adj. prof. law Capital U., Columbus, 1976-79; mem. adv. com. Ohio securities divsn. Dept. Commerce, Columbus, 1979—; fellow Columbus Bar Found., 1992—; adv. bd. The Entrepreneurship Inst., 1992-95. Contbr. Ohio State U. Coll. Law Jour., 1970-72. Gen. counsel, trustee Internat. Assn. Rsch. on Leukemia and Related Diseases, 1975—; v.p., trustee Hospice of Columbus, 1978-80; trustee Cen. Ohio chpt. Leukemia Soc. of Am., Columbus, 1983-93, v.p., 1985-87; trustee Ohio Cancer Rsch. Assocs., Columbus, 1983—, v.p., 1990—. With USMCR, 1963-68. Mem. ABA (bus. law com., franchise law com.), Ohio State Bar Assn. (corp. law com., franchise law com.), Columbus Bar Assn. (securities law com., chmn. 1981-83, bus. law com., franchise law com.), Sigma Tau Delta, Beta Gamma Sigma. Home: 2155 Waltham Rd Columbus OH 43221-4149 Office: Jones Day Reavis & Pogue 1900 Huntington Ctr Columbus OH 43215-6103

STINEMETZ, STEVEN DOUGLAS, lawyer; b. Marysville, Ohio, Nov. 23, 1957; s. Glenn Melvin and Lona Lee (Payne) S.; m. Carol Sue Bialecki, Aug. 16, 1980; children: Emily Katrina, Eric Douglas, Ellen Michelle. AB in European History, Harvard U., 1980, AM in Modern Russian History, 1983; JD, NYU, 1986. Bar: Tex. 1986, Ohio 1991, D.C. 1992. Assoc. Haynes and Boone, Dallas, 1986-90, Davis, Graham & Stubbs, Washington, 1990-92; sr. atty. Western Atlas Internat., Houston, 1992—; gen. counsel PetroAlliance Svcs. Co. Ltd., Houston, 1995—; bd. dirs. Tex. Kazakhstan Alliance, 1992—. Assoc., editor, book rev. editor NYU Jour. Internat. Law and Politics, 1984-86; contbr. articles to legal jours. Chmn. bus. com. Dallas Soviet Sister City Program, 1987-88. Harvard U. scholar, 1976-80. Mem. ABA (vice chmn. Sonreel, county coord. Azerbaijan) First Colony Com. Svc. Assn. (modification com.). Avocation: languages, games. Home: 2022 Richland Ct Sugar Land TX 77478-4414 Office: PetroAlliance Svcs Co 10011 Meadowglen Ln Houston TX 77042-3710

STINER, CARL WADE, army officer; b. LaFollette, Tenn., Sept. 7, 1936; s. Emmit Clyde and Hassie Delma (Bullard) S.; m. Carolyn Sue Reeves, Nov. 28, 1959; children: Carla, Laurie. BS, Tenn. Poly. Inst., 1958; MPA, Shippensburg (Pa.) State Coll., 1975. Commd. 2d lt. U.S. Army, 1958, advanced through grades to gen., 1990; inf. bn. officer, then brigade ops. officer 4th Inf. Div., Vietnam, 1967; comdr. 2d bn., 325 Airborne Inf. Rgt., div. ops. officer 82d Airborne Divsn., 1970; comdr. 1st Inf. Tng. Brigade, Ft. Benning, Ga., 1975; chief of staff Rapid Deployment Joint Task Force, 1980; asst. div. comdr. 82d Airborne Div.; asst. dep. dir. for politico-mil. affairs Joint Staff, Washington, until 1984; comdg. gen. Joint Spl. Ops. Command, Ft. Bragg, N.C., 1984-87, 82d Airborne Div., 1987-88, XVIII Airborne Corps, Ft. Bragg, 1988; comdr. of all forces Operation JUST CAUSE, Panama, 1989; comdr. in chief Hdqrs. U.S. Spl. Ops. Command, MacDill AFB, Fla.; ret. from active duty, 1993. Decorated D.S.M. with two oak leaf cluster, Def. D.S.M. with two oak leaf cluster, Legion of Merit with oak leaf cluster, Purple Heart, Def. Superior Svc. medal. Baptist. Avocations: golf, hunting, boating.

STINES, FRED, JR., publisher; b. Newton, Iowa, Mar. 16, 1925; s. Fred and Nella (Haun) S.; m. Dorothy G. McClanahan, Sept. 5, 1953 (dec.); children: Steven, Scott, Ann; m. Mary K. Devin, Sept. 12, 1989. B.C.S., U. Iowa, 1949. With Meredith Corp., Des Moines, 1949-90; sales promotion and mdse. mgr. Meredith Corp., 1955-63, advt. dir., 1963-66, pub., 1966-73, pub. dir. mag. div., 1973-76, v.p., gen. mgr. books and newspapers, 1976-83, sr. v.p., 1983-87, pres. book pub., 1986-90, corp. v.p. spl. projects, 1988-90; pres., prin. Concepts in Mktg., 1990—; cert. instr. Dale Carnegie courses, 1958-63. Bd. dirs. Des Moines Ballet Assn., North Am. Outdoor Group, Mpls., 1992-95; bd. dirs., v.p. Jr. Achievement of Ctrl. Iowa. Served with AUS, 1946-49. Named Farm Marketing Man of Year, 1972. Mem. Future Farmers Am. Found. (nat. chmn. 1971), Rotary Internat., Des Moines Golf and Country Club, Phi Gamma Delta (sect. chief 1983, nat. bd. dirs. 1985-89), Alpha Kappa Psi, Alpha Delta Sigma. Club: Des Moines Golf and Country (dir., pres. 1981).

STING (GORDON MATTHEW SUMNER), musician, songwriter, actor; b. Newcastle Upon Tyne, Eng., Oct. 2, 1951; s. Ernest Matthew and Audrey (Cowell) Sumner; m. Frances Eleanor Tomelty, May 1, 1976 (div. Mar. 1984); children: Joseph, Katherine; m. Trudie Styler, Aug. 22, 1992; children: Brigette, Michael, Jake, Eliot, Pauline, Giacomo. Schoolmaster Newcastle Upon Tyne, Eng., 1975-77; songwriter, singer, bass player with rock group The Police, 1977-86; mng. dir. Kaliedescope Cameras, London, from 1982. Albums recorded with The Police include Outlandos D'Amour, 1978, Reggatta De Blanc, 1979, Zenyatta Mondatta, 1980, Ghost in the Machine, 1981, Synchronicity, 1983, The Singles; Every Breath You Take, 1986; stage appearance: (Broadway) Three Penny Opera, 1989; solo albums include The Dream of the Blue Turtles, 1985, Bring On The Night, 1986, Nothing Like the Sun, 1987, The Soul Cages, 1991, Ten Summoner's Tales, 1993 (Grammy award, Best Long Form Music Video, 1994), Demolition Man (soundtrack), 1993, Mercury Falling, 1996; appeared in films Quadrophenia, 1989, The Secret Policeman's Other Ball, 1982, Brimstone and Treacle, 1982, Dune, 1984, The Bride, 1985, Plenty, 1985, Julia and Julia, 1987, Stormy Monday, 1988; rec. soundtracks for films including Brimstone and Treacle, 1982, Party, Party, 1982, The Secret Policeman's Other Ball, 1982. Recipient 12 Grammy awards with The Police and as solo artist; Downbeat mag. Readers' Poll Pop/Rock Musician of Yr. award, 1989, Downbeat mag. Readers' Poll Pop/Rock group award, 1989. Mem. Performing Rights Soc. Office: Firstars, Bugle House Noel St, London W1V 3PD, England also: Firstars 3520 Hayden Ave Culver City CA 90232-2413

STINGEL, DONALD EUGENE, management consultant; b. Pitts., Jan. 31, 1920; s. Eugene E. and Ruth I. (Liddell) S.; m. Rita Marie Sweeney, June 14, 1942; children—Donald M., Scott M., Janice L. B.S., Carnegie-Mellon U., 1941. Metall. engr. Union Carbide Corp., Alloy, W.Va., 1941; metall. engr. to works mgr. Union Carbide Corp., N.Y.C., 1946-65; pres. Alloys and Carbide div. Airco, Inc., 1965-68, Pullman Swindell, Pitts., 1969-77; chmn. Rodeway Inns Internat. and Lodging Systems, Inc., 1982-83; dir. Export-Import Bank U.S., Washington, 1977-81, Wean-United, Pitts., 1981-93. Trustee Carnegie-Mellon U. Served to maj., Ordnance Dept., AUS, 1941-46; to lt. col., Transp. Corps, U.S. Army, 1950. Mem. Country Club of N.C. Republican. Home: 1600 Morganton Rd Box X-29 Pinehurst NC 28374

STINGELIN, VALENTIN, research center director, mechanical engineer; b. Basel, Switzerland, Apr. 22, 1933; s. Paul and Hulda (Tobler) S.; m. Hedwig Wagner, Oct. 18, 1963; children: Matthias, Sibylle, Thomas. Diploma, Swiss Fed. Inst. Tech. (ETH), Zurich, 1957, Ph.D. (Silver medal 1963), 1963. Sci. co-worker Swiss Fed. Inst. Tech., 1958-63; research scientist, project leader Ingersoll Rand Corp., Princeton, N.J., 1964-67; mem. staff Battelle Research Centers, Geneva, 1967—; head engring. dept., then assoc. dir. Battelle Research Centers, 1973-75, dir. gen., 1975—; v.p. Battelle Meml. Inst., Columbus, Ohio, 1984—; v.p. indsl. bus. planning Europe and Japan Battelle Meml. Inst., 1986—; pres. Castolin & Eutectic Inst., St. Sulpice/Lausanne, Switzerland, 1986—. Mem. Swiss Soc. Physics, ASME, Swiss-Am. C. of C. (dir.). Office: Castolin & Eutectic Inst, PO Box 360, CH-1001 Lausanne Switzerland

STINI, WILLIAM ARTHUR, anthropologist, educator; b. Oshkosh, Wis., Oct. 9, 1930; s. Louis Alois and Clara (Larsen) S.; m. Mary Ruth Kalous, Feb. 11, 1950; children—Patricia Laraine, Paulette Ann, Suzanne Kay. BBA, U. Wis., 1960, MS, 1967, PhD, 1969. Planner cost acct. Kimberly-Clark Corp., Niagara Falls, N.Y., 1960-62; from asst. prof. to assoc. prof. Cornell U., Ithaca, N.Y., 1968-73; assoc. prof. U. Kans., Lawrence, 1973-76; prof. anthropology U. Ariz., Tucson, 1976-78, prof. family and cmty. medicine, 1978—; panelist anthropology program NSF, 1976-78; cons. NIH, 1974—; mem. Ariz. Cancer Ctr., 1995—; adj. prof. Nutritional Scis., 1997—; head dept. anthropology U. Ariz., 1980-89; panelist NRC/NSF Grad. Fellowship Program, 1991-95. Author: Ecology and Human Adaptation, 1975, Nature, Culture and Human History - A Biocultural Introduction to Anthropology (with Davydd J. Greenwood), 1977, Physiological and Morphological Adaptation and Evolution, 1979 (with Frank E. Poirier and Kathy B. Wreden) In Search of Ourselves: An Introduction to Physical Anthropology, 1990, 5th edit., 1994; field editor phys. anthropology The Am. Anthropologist, 1980-83; editor-in-chief Am. Jour. Phys. Anthropology, 1983-89; assoc. editor Nutrition and Cancer, 1981-95; cons. editor Collegium Antropologicum, 1985—. Mem. Gov.'s Adv. Council on Aging, State of Ariz., 1980-83. Nat. Inst. Dental Rsch. tng. grantee, 1964-68; Clark Found. grantee, Cornell U., 1973; Nat. Dairy Coun. grantee, 1985-88; Wenner-Gren Found. grantee, 1991—; fellow Linacre Coll., Oxford, 1985; vis. fellow U. London, 1991. Fellow AAAS (steering group sect. H 1987-91), Am. Anthrop. Assn., N.Y. Acad. Scis.; mem. Am. Assn. Phys. Anthropologists (exec. com. 1978-81, pres. 1989-91), Soc. for Study Human Biology, Human Biology Coun. (exec. com. 1978-81), Soc. for Study Social Biology, Am. Inst. Nutrition, Am. Soc. on Aging, Sigma Xi. Home: 6240 N Camino Miraval Tucson AZ 85718-3025 Office: U Ariz Dept Anthropology Tucson AZ 85721

STINNETT, LEE HOUSTON, newspaper association executive; b. Madisonville, Ky., Jan. 8, 1939; s. James Houston and Eolia Frances (Hutchings) S. B.A., U. Ky., 1961, M.A., 1963. Reporter Times-Picayune, New Orleans, 1963-64; med. reporter The News, Charlotte, N.C., 1965-66; devel. writer Emory U., Atlanta, 1966-67, univ. editor, 1968-69; assoc. dir. So. Newspaper Pubs. Assn. and Found., Atlanta, 1970-80; project dir. Am. Soc. Newspaper Editors, Washington, 1981-82, exec. dir., 1983—. Contbr. articles to profl. jours. Del. Arlington Civic Fedn.; active civil rights groups and polit. orgns., Washington and No. Va., Whitman-Walker Clinic, Washington; pres. Arlington Gay and Lesbian Alliance, 1989-90. Mem. Newspaper Assn. Mgrs., Four Seasons Garden (pres. 1983), ACLU of No. Va. (bd. dirs. 1992-94). Democrat. Avocations: gardening, swimming, music.

STINNETT, MARK ALLAN, lawyer; b. Jackson, Miss., Sept. 15, 1955; s. Allan J. and Joan (Mouser) S. BA in Polit. Sci., Tex. Tech U., 1977; JD, U. Tex., 1980. Bar: Tex. 1980, U.S. Dist. Ct. (no. and ea. dists.) Tex. 1981, U.S. Ct. Appeals (5th cir.) 1993. Shareholder Cowles & Thompson, Dallas, 1980—. Mem. ABA, Am. Acad. Healthcare Attys., Am. Inns of Ct., Am. Coll. Legal Medicine, Nat. Health Lawyers Assn., State Bar of Tex., Dallas Bar Assn., Tex. Assn. Def. Counsel, Dallas Assn. Def. Counsel, Def. Rsch. Inst., Am. Soc. Law, Medicine and Ethics, Nat. Fire Protection Assn., Inns Ct. (barrister Dallas chpt. 1988-91), Tex. Ctr. Legal Ethics and Professionalism, Nat. Eagle Scout Assn., Philmont Staff Assn. (pres.). Avocations: backpacking, softball, military history. Home: 9510 Hillview Dr Dallas TX 75231-1525 Office: Cowles & Thompson 901 Main St Ste 4000 Dallas TX 75202-3746

STINO, FARID K.R., biostatistician, educator, researcher, consultant; b. Cairo, Sept. 1, 1943; came to U.S., 1988; s. Kamal Ramzi and Farida (Shenouda) S.; m. Zandra Hargrove, 1968; children: Ramzi, Farida, Karim, Magdi. BSc, Cairo U., 1964; MSc, U. Ga., 1968, PhD, 1971. Instr. Cairo U., 1964-66; rsch. asst., tchg. asst. U. Ga., Athens, 1966-68, 68-71, postdoctoral fellow, 1971-72; asst. prof. Cairo U., 1972-77, assoc. prof., 1977-82, prof., 1982-88; prof. biostats. Fla. A&M U., Tallahassee, 1988—; pres. Stino Agroconsult, Giza, Egypt, 1977-88. V.p. Coptic Orthodox Ch., Tallahassee, 1990—. Mem. Am. Statis. Assn., Biometric Soc., Sigma Xi, Gamma Sigma Delta. Home: 6579 Montrose Trl Tallahassee FL 32308-1607 Office: Fla A&M U Coll Pharmacy Tallahassee FL 32307

STINSON, GEORGE ARTHUR, lawyer, former steel company executive; b. Camden, Ark., Feb. 11, 1915; s. John McCollum and Alice (Loving) S.; m. Betty Millsop, May 31, 1947; children: Thomas, Lauretta, Peter, Joel. A.B., Northwestern U., 1936; J.D., Columbia U., 1939; LL.D., U. W.Va., Bethany Coll., Theil Coll., Salem Coll. Bar: N.Y. 1939. Partner Cleary, Gottlieb, Friendly & Hamilton, N.Y.C., 1951-61; spl. asst. to atty. gen., acting asst. atty. gen. tax div. Dept. Justice, 1947-48; v.p., sec. Nat. Steel Corp. (now Nat. Intergroup, Inc.), Pitts., 1961-63; pres. Nat. Steel Corp., 1963-75, bd. dirs., 1963-86, CEO, 1966-80, chmn., 1972-81; dir. Birmingham Steel Co., Pathe Techs. Inc.; trustee emeritus Mut. Life Ins. Co. N.Y. Trustee emeritus U. Pitts.; mem. Presdl. Commn. on Internat. Trade and Investment Policy, 1970-71; chmn. U.S. Indsl. Payroll Savs. Com., 1976; trustee George C. Marshall Found. Served to lt. col. USAAF, 1941-45. Decorated Legion of Merit. Mem. Am. Iron and Steel Inst. (chmn. bd. 1969-71), Internat. Iron and Steel Inst. (bd. dirs., chmn. 1975-77), Am. Law Inst., Bus. Coun., Links Club (N.Y.C.), Duquesne Club (Pitts.), Laurel Valley Golf Club (Pitts.), Phi Beta Kappa. Home: Hunting Country Rd Tryon NC 28782

STINSON, RICHARD FLOYD, retired horticulturalist, educator; b. Cleve., Feb. 4, 1921; s. Floyd Earl and Helen M. (Schiemann) S.; children: Leigh, Laurie, Glenn, Paul, Cathy. BS, Ohio State U., 1943, MS, 1947, PhD, 1952. Instr. floriculture SUNY, Alfred, 1947-48; asst. prof. floriculture U. Conn., Storrs, 1948-55; asst. prof. horticulture Mich. State U., East Lansing, 1955-59, assoc. prof. horticulture, 1959-67; assoc. prof. agrl. edn. and horticulture Pa. State U., University Park, 1967-73, prof., 1973-79, sr. faculty mem., 1979-89, prof. emeritus, 1990—; cons. in field. Contbr. articles to profl. jours. Lt. (j.g.) USNR, 1943-46. Mem. Nat. Assn. Colls. and Tchrs. Agr. (E.B. Knight Jour. award 1992), Pa. Vocat. Agr. Tchrs. Assn., Sigma Xi, Alpha Tau Alpha, Gamma Sigma Delta, Phi Delta Kappa. Office: Pa State U 323 Agrl Adminstrn Bldg University Park PA 16802-2601

STIPANOVIC, ROBERT DOUGLAS, chemist, researcher; b. Houston, Oct. 28, 1939. BS, Loyola U., 1961; PhD, Rice U., 1966. Rsch. technician Stauffer Chem. Co., Houston, 1961; teaching asst. Rice U., Houston, 1961-62, rsch. asst., 1962-66; rsch. assoc. Stanford (Calif.) U., 1966-67; mem. grad. faculty Tex. A&M U., College Station, 1967—, asst. prof. chemistry, 1967-71; rsch. chemist Cotton Pathology Rsch. Unit USDA, College Station, 1971-87; rsch. leader USDA, College Station, 1987—; vis. rsch. scientist Agr. Can., Rsch. Ctr. London, Ont., 1985. Welch fellow Rice U., 1963-65, Grad. fellow, 1965-66. Mem. Sigma Xi. Home: 1103 Esther Blvd Bryan TX

77802-1924 Office: USDA Agrl Rsch Svc So Crops Rsch Lab 2765 F & B Rd College Station TX 77845-9593

STIPE, MICHAEL, musician; b. Decatur, Ga., 1960. Student, U. Ga. Singer R.E.M., 1980—; owner C-OO. Albums with R.E.M. include Chronic Town, 1982, Murmur, 1983 (Gold record, Rolling Stone Critics Poll Best Album of Yr. 1983), Reckoning, 1984 (Gold record), Fables of the Revolution, 1985 (Gold record), Life's Rich Pageant (Gold record), 1986, Dead Letter Office (Gold record), 1987, Document, 1987 (Platinum record), Eponymous, 1988 (Platinum record), Green, 1989 (Platinum record), Out of Time, 1991 (Platinum record, 7 Grammy nominations, Best Pop Vocals Grammy award for group 1992), Automatic for the People, 1992 (Platinum record, 4 Grammy nominations), Monster, 1994, Songs That Are Live (4 song CD), 1995, New Adventures in Hi-Fi, 1996; guest artist for following groups: 10,000 Maniacs, 1987, Indigo Girls, 1989. Recipient MTV Video Music Video of Yr. award, 1992; named Rolling Stone Critics Poll Best New Group, 1983, Rolling Stone Group Artist of Yr., 1992, Rolling Stong Male Vocalist of Yr., 1992; MTV Best Direction, Best Editing, Best Cinematography, and Breakthrough Video awards for "Everybody Hurts", 1994. Office: Warner Bros Records 3300 Warner Blvd Burbank CA 91505-4632*

STIPE, ROBERT EDWIN, design educator; b. Easton, Pa., July 18, 1928; s. J. Norwood and Ethel M. Stipe; m. Josephine Davis Weedon, 1952; children: Daniel W. Stipe, Frederick Norwood Stipe. AB in Econ., Duke U., 1950, LLB, 1953; MRP, U. N.C., 1959. Urban planning cons. City and Town Planning Assocs., Chapel Hill, N.C., 1956-57; asst. dir., prof. pub. law and govt. U. N.C. Inst. Govt., Chapel Hill, N.C., 1957-74; sr. Fulbright rsch. fellow London U., 1968-69; dir. Divsn. Archives and History N.C. Dept. Cultural Resources, Raleigh, N.C., 1974-75; vis. prof. U. N.C., Chapel Hill, 1975-77; prof. design N.C. State U., Raleigh, 1976-89; emeritus prof. design, part time prof. design N.C. State U., 1989—; lectr. Inst. Advanced Studies, Bratislava, Slovak Republic, 1992-95; bd. trustees U.S. com. Internat. Coun. on Monuments and Sites, Preservation Action, Nat. Coun. on Preservation Edn., Hist. Preservation Fund N.C., Alliance for Preservation Hist. Landscapes, Old Salem Inc., Stagville Ctr. for Preservation Tech.; trustee Nat. Trust for Hist. Preservation; bd. counsellors Conservation Trust for N.C.; mem. bd. adv. Nat. Alliance Preservation Commn. Author, editor more than 150 articles and publs. in fields of historic preservation, landscape conservation, design, urban planning, and planning law. Mem. Chapel Hill Design Review Bd.; trustee Chapel Hill Preservation Soc.; founder, bd. mem. Chapel Hill Preservation Soc. Fellow U.S. Com. Internat. Coun. on Monuments and Sites, 1986; recipient Disting. Svc. award Ruth Coltrane Cannon award, N.C. Soc. for Preservation of Antiquities, 1973, Sec. of Interior's Disting. Conservation Svc. award, 1978, Spl. award outstanding contbns. to landscape architecture Am. Soc. Landscape Archiects, N.C. chpt., 1985, Louise DuPont Crowninshield award for Superlative Lifetime Achievement in Historic Preservation, Nat. Trust for Historic Preservation, 1988, Dist. Svc. and Profl. Leadership award Nat. Coun. for Preservation Edn., 1989. Mem. Cosmos Club (Washington), Sigma Pi Kappa (First Disting. mem. 1994), Sigma Lambda Alpha (disting. mem. 1996). Home: 100 Pine Ln Chapel Hill NC 27514-4331

STIRITZ, WILLIAM P., food company executive; b. Jasper, Ark., July 1, 1934; s. Paul and Dorothy (Bradley) S.; m. Susan Ekberg, Dec. 4, 1972; children—Bradley, Charlotte, Rebecca, Nicholas. B.S., Northwestern U., 1959; M.A., St. Louis U., 1968. Mem. mktg. mgmt. staff Pillsbury Co., Mpls., 1959-62; account mgmt. staff Gardner Advt. Co., St. Louis, 1963—; with Ralston Purina Co., St. Louis, 1963—; pres., chief exec. officer, chmn. Ralston Purina Co., 1981—; bd. dirs. Angelica Corp., Ball Corp., Boatmen's Bancshares, Inc., Gen. Am. Life Ins. Co., May Dept. Stores, S.C. Johnson & Son. With USN, 1954-57. Mem. Grocery Mfrs. Assn. (dir.). Office: Ralston Purina Co Checkerboard Sq Saint Louis MO 63164*

STIRLING, JAMES PAULMAN, investment banker; b. Chgo., Mar. 30, 1941; s. Louis James and Beverly L. (Paulman) S.; m. Ellen Adair Foster, June 6, 1970; children—Elizabeth Ginevra, Diana Leslie, Alexandra Curtiss. A.B., Princeton U., 1963; M.B.A., Stanford U., 1965. Chartered fin. analyst. Vice pres. corp. fin. Kidder, Peabody & Co. (now PaineWebber), N.Y.C. and Chgo., 1965-71, 84-86; sr. v.p. corp. fin. Kidder, Peabody & Co. (now PaineWebber), 1987—; dir. internat. investments Sears Roebuck Co., Chgo. and London, 1971-75, 77-84; asst. to sec. U.S. Dept. Commerce, Washington, 1976-77; chmn. bd. Northwestern Meml. Mgmt. Corp., Chgo., 1989—; trustee Northwestern Meml. Hosp., Chgo., 1985—. Pres. jr. bd. Chgo. Symphony, 1968-70, trustee, 1970-75; trustee Tchrs. Acad. for Math. Sci., 1991—. Mem. Investment Analysts Soc., Bond Club of Chgo., Nat. Econ. Hon. Soc. Clubs: Chicago, Racquet (Chgo.); Onwentsia (Lake Forest, Ill.). Office: PaineWebber 125 S Wacker Dr Chicago IL 60606-4402

STIRLING, MICHELLE DIANNE, tax specialist, accountant; b. Buffalo, N.Y., Dec. 8, 1975; d. Ian Scott and Dianne Louise (Garland) S. BBA in Acctg., Niagara U., 1996. Acct. asst. N.Am. Adminstrs., Amherst, N.Y., 1993-96; tax preparer Michael Greenberg & Assocs., Inc., North Tonawanda, N.Y., 1996; acct. Heritage Ctrs., Buffalo, 1996—; tax preparer Vol. Income Tax Assistance, Niagara Falls, 1995. Vol. United Way, Niagara Falls, N.Y., 1987—, World Univ. Games, Niagara Falls, 1993, Niagara U. Cmty. Action Program, Niagara Falls, 1995-96, Niagara Hospice, Niagara Falls, 1995—. Scholar Niagara U., 1993-96. Mem. Inst. Mgmt. Accts., Niagara Univ. Acctg. Soc., Delta Epsilon Sigma. Avocations: bowling, crafts, working with abused animals, gardening. Home: 3801 Pine Ave Niagara Falls NY 14301

STIRRAT, WILLIAM ALBERT, electronics engineer; b. Syracuse, N.Y., Nov. 5, 1919; s. Robert William and Doris (White) S.; m. Bernice Amelia Wilson, July 13, 1958; children: Valerie Lynne, Dorothy Grace, William Ellsworth. Student, Triuna (Yaddo) Arts of the Theater Sch., 1936, Saratoga Eastman Sch Bus., 1936-37; BS in Physics, Rensselaer Poly. Inst., 1942, postgrad., 1949-50; postgrad., Rutgers U., 1951-58, Fairleigh Dickinson U., 1971. Elecs. engr. GE, Schenectady, N.Y., 1941-44; instr. physics Clarkson Coll. Tech., 1947-49; electronic engr. rsch. and devel. U.S. Army, Fort Monmouth, N.J., 1950-87; prin. engr. Eagle Tech., Inc., Eatontown, N.J., 1987-92; pres. Stirrat Arts & Scis., Freehold, N.J., 1992—. Author: (with Alex North) Unchained Melody, 1936 (Top song of Yr., Acad. award nomination 1955), Why 3? (Army award 1985); assoc. editor IEEE Transactions on Electromagnetic Compatability, 1970-76; contbr. articles to profl. jours.; patentee in field. Chmn. pub. rels. Battleground dist. Monmouth coun. Boy Scouts Am., 1970-77; mem. Rep. Congl. Leadership Coun., 1989-91; mem. Rep. Campaign Coun., 1992-93. Mem. SAR, IEEE (editor N.J. Coast sect. Scanner 1974-75), Nat. Acad. Songwriters, Internat. Songwriters Assn., Palgrave Soc., Internat. Platform Assn. Episcopalian. Achievements include development of binomial pulse. Home and Office: 218 Overbrook Dr Freehold NJ 07728-1525

STIRRATT, BETSY, artist, gallery director; b. New Orleans, Sept. 22, 1958; d. Avery and Betty Lou (Chadwick) S.; m. Jeffrey Alan Wolin, Aug. 20, 1983; children: Benjamin, Andrew. BFA, La. State U., 1980; MFA, Ind. U., 1983. Gallery dir. Fine Arts Gallery, Ind. U., Bloomington, 1987—. Exhibited works at Salon Show, Art in Gen., 1992, Meat, White, Columns, 1993, Between Mind and Body, Air Gallery, 1994, Physical Affinities, Carl Hammer Gallery, 1994, In Situ Gallery, 1995. Masters fellow Ind. Arts Commn., 1989, Arts Midwest fellow Arts Midwest, 1989, NEA fellow, 1990. Office: Fine Arts Gallery Ind Univ Bloomington IN 47405

STISKA, JOHN C., lawyer; b. Chgo., Feb. 14, 1942; s. Rudolph and Elsie Sophie (Nelson) S.; m. Janet Hazel Osuch, Aug. 8, 1964; children: Julie, Thomas, Michael, Matthew. BBA, U. Wis., 1965, JD, 1970. Bar: Wis. 1970, Calif. 1971. Assoc. ptnr. Luce, Forward, Hamilton & Scripps, San Diego, 1970-81; ptnr. Aylward, Kintz & Stiska, San Diego, 1981-86; pres., CEO Triton Group Ltd., La Jolla, Calif., 1986-87; ptnr. Brobeck, Phleger & Harrison, San Diego, 1987-90; pres., COO Intermark, Inc., La Jolla, Calif., 1990-92; pres., CEO Triton Group Ltd., 1993-94; chmn., CEO, 1994-96; sr. v.p. Qualcomm, Inc., San Diego, 1996—. 1st lt. U.S. Army, 1965-67. Mem. ABA. San Diego County Bar Assn., Calif State Bar Assn. Lutheran. Home: 5307 Soledad Rancho Ct San Diego CA 92109-1535 Office: Qualcomm Inc 6455 Lusk Blvd San Diego CA 92121-2779

STITES, C. THOMAS, journalist, publisher; b. Kansas City, Mo., July 6, 1942; s. Harold Edward and Wilma Joyce (Simmons) S.; m. Helen Marie Oakey, Sept. 9, 1967 (div. 1983), children—Mary Hannah, Harold William; m. Alexandra Mezey, May 8, 1983. Student, Williams Coll., 1960-62. Night city editor Chgo. Sun-Times, 1968-70; regional editor Phila. Inquirer, 1970-72; news editor Newsday, L.I., N.Y., 1972-79; asst. nat. editor N.Y. Times, N.Y.C., 1979-83; mng. editor Kansas City Times, Mo., 1983-85; nat. editor, assoc. mng. editor Chgo. Tribune, 1985-90; v.p. UniMedia div. Universal Press Syndicate, Kansas City, Mo., 1990—. Unitarian. Avocations: squash; music, especially jazz; reading non fiction. Office: Universal Press Syndicate 4900 Main St # 900 Kansas City MO 64112-2644

STITES, RAY DEAN, minister, college president; b. Herington, Kans., Oct. 13, 1946; s. George Darby and Edna Myrtle (Anderson) S.; m. Merelyn Kay Rich, Sept. 2, 1966; children: Ross Mitchell, Britain Darby. BA, Manhattan Christian Coll., Manhattan, Kans., 1968; MDiv, Emmanuel Sch. Religion, Johnson City, Tenn., 1974. Ordained to ministry Christian Ch., 1968. Min. Bozoo (W.Va.) Christian Ch., 1968-72; min. Cen. Christian Ch., Richardson, Tex., 1972-78, First Christian Ch., Abilene, Kans., 1979-88, Newton (Kans.) Christian Ch., 1988-91; pres. Nebr. Christian Coll., Norfolk, 1991—; instr. Ch. History, Dallas Christian Coll., 1974-76; pres. North Tex. Evangelizing Assn., 1975-77, Manhattan Christian Coll. Alumni Assn., 1983-85, Christian Evangelizing Assn. of Kans., 1987-89, 91, Kans. Christian Conv., 1989. Bd. dirs. Abilene United Way, 1981-84; mem. Dickinson County Health Dept. Adv. Bd., 1983-88, Dickinson County Coun. on Aging, 1984-88; pres. Abilene Optimist Club, 1983-84. Office: Nebr Christian Ch 1800 Syracuse Ave Norfolk NE 68701-2458

STITES, SUSAN KAY, human resources consultant; b. Colorado Springs, Colo., Sept. 20, 1952; d. William Wallace and Betty Jane (Kosley) Stites; m. Gerald Frederick Simon, Aug. 14, 1988. BA, Wichita State U., 1974; MA, Northwestern U., 1979. Benefits authorizer Social Security Adminstrn., Chgo., 1974-77; trainer Chgo. Urban Skills Inst., 1977-79; human resources mgr. Montgomery Ward, Chgo., 1979-83; mgr. tng. Lands' End, Dodgeville, Wis., 1983-87; dir. human resources Cen. Life Assurance, Madison, Wis., 1988-90; owner Mgmt. Allegories, Madison, Wis., 1987—. Author: Delegating for Results, 1992, Business Communications, 1992, Managing with a Quality Focus, 1994, Training and Orientation for the Small Business, 1994, Powerful Performance Management, 1994, Safety Management Techniques, 1995, Teaching First Aid and CPR, 1995, Alive at 25, 1995, Strategic Thinking and Planning, 1995, Teaching Alice at 25, 1996, Fundamentals of Industrial Hygiene, 1996, Recruiting, Developing and Retaining Volunteers, 1996, Creating a Credit Union University: An Administrator's Guide, 1997, Creating a Corporate University, 1997, Strategic Thinking for the Automotive Industry, 1997, Managing Sales and Service, 1997, Sales and Service Management in Credit Unions, 1997. Vol. tutor Japanese students in English, Evanston, Ill., 1977-80; reader to the blind Chgo. Coun. for the Blind, 1974-76. Named Outstanding Woman of the Yr. Wichita State U., 1974. Mem. ASTD (chpt. pres. 1988, v.p. membership 1986, region V awards chair 1992), Soc. Applied Learning Tech., Madison Area Quality Improvement Network, Assn. for Quality and Participation, Rotary (vol. fundraiser), Mendota Yacht Club (treas. 1990-94). Avocations: sailing, boardsailing, gardening, cooking, travel. Home: 3788 Highridge Rd Madison WI 53704-6206 Office: Mgmt Allegories 3788 Highridge Rd Madison WI 53718-6206

STITH-CABRANES, KATE, law educator; b. St. Louis, Mar. 16, 1951; d. Richard Taylor and Ann Carter (See) Stith; m. Jeffrey Leonard Pressman, Dec. 23, 1970 (dec. Mar. 1977); m. José Alberto Cabranes, Sept. 15, 1984; children: Alejo, Benjamin José; stepchildren: Jennifer, Amy. BA, Dartmouth Coll., 1973; MPP, J.F.K. Sch. of Govt., 1977; JD, Harvard U., 1977. Bar: D.C. 1979. Law clk. Carl McGowan/U.S. Ct. of Appeals, Washington, 1977-78, Byron White/U.S. Supreme Ct., Washington, 1978-79; staff economist Coun. of Econ. Advisers, Washington, 1979-80; spl. asst. Dept. of Justice, Washington, 1980-81; asst. U.S. atty. Dept. of Justice, N.Y.C., 1981-84; assoc. prof. Yale Law Sch., New Haven, 1985-90, prof. of law, 1990—; appt. chief justice, 1995—, mem. adv com. on federal rules of criminal procedure, 1995—; mem. Permanent Commn. on the Status of Women, State of Conn., Hartford, 1990-96. Trustee Dartmouth Coll., Hanover, N.H., 1989—, Women's Campaign Sch., 1994—. Mem. Am. Law Inst., Coun. Fgn. Rels., Conn. Bar Found. (bd. dirs. 1987—). Office: Yale Law Sch 127 Wall St New Haven CT 06511-6636

STITT, DAVID TILLMAN, judge; b. St. Louis, Apr. 9, 1943; s. David Leander and Jane Wilkinson (Dupuy) S.; m. Elizabeth Celia Santino, Apr. 30, 1981; children: Rachel Elizabeth Botkin, Samuel Thornton. AB, Davidson Coll., 1964; JD, U. Tex., 1969. Assoc. Galland, Kharasch, Calkins & Brown, Washington, 1969-71; asst. corp. counsel D.C., Washington, 1971-73, asst. U.S. atty., 1973-74; asst. county atty. Fairfax County, Va., 1975-80; county atty. Fairfax County, 1980-91; ptnr. Venable, Baetjer & Howard, McLean, Va., 1991-95; judge Cir. Ct. Fairfax County, Va., 1995—. Lt. U.S. Army, 1964-66, Vietnam. Mem. Va. State Bar Coun. (exec. com. 1991-93), Local Govt. Attys. of Va. (pres. 1983-84, Disting. Svc. award 1991), Conf. of Local Bar Assn. (chmn. 1990-91), Fairfax Bar Assn. (pres. 1986-87). Presbyterian. Home: 6503 Smoot Dr Mc Lean VA 22101-4003 Office: Fairfax County Circuit Ct 4110 Chain Bridge Rd Fairfax VA 22030-4009

STITT, DOROTHY JEWETT, journalist; b. Houston, Sept. 4, 1914; d. Harry Berkey and Gladys (Norfleet) Jewett; m. James Wilson Stitt, Feb. 14, 1939; children: James Harry, Thomas Paul. AB, Rice U., 1937; MS, Columbia U., 1938. Reporter Houston Post, 1936-38, asst. city editor, 1938; editor of publs. Jewett Family of Am., 1971-94, editor emeritus, 1994—; spl. asst. to pub. Jewett Genealogy Vols. III and IV, 1995—; Jewett family Dir.-for-Life, 1995—; gen. chmn. Jewett Family Reunion, 1996. Author, editor: The 100th Anniversary Yearbook and History of the George Taylor Chapter, DAR, 1895-1995, 1994, Easton Red Cross Fiftieth Anniversary Booklet and History—Fifty Years of Service, 1967. Mem. adv. bd. Easton Salvation Army, pub. chmn., 1956—, chmn. bd. dirs., 1964, bd. treas., 1981; bd. dirs., pub. chmn. ARC, 1952-67, vol. Lehigh Valley chpt., 1995-96; pres. Easton JC Wives, 1950-53; mem. fin. com. Little Stone House Mus. Assn., 1974-76, 80, organizing bd. dirs. sec. and pub. chmn., 1974-91; bd. dirs. Easton United Comty. Chest/United Way, 1957-60, active in publicity for 1st campaign, 1960; active East Civil Def. Comms., 1956-60; mem. bd. Montgomery County Pa. Girl Scouts USA, 1946-48, publicity chmn., initiator and editor county newsletter; den mother cub scouts Easton Boy Scouts Am., 1948-55; capt. renovation campaign area YWCA, 1956; mem. March Sch., Easton PTA, 1948-57, sec., 1952-54, v.p., 1954-56, bylaws chmn., 1953, Easton H.S., 1954-61, membership chmn., 1955-57, 59-60; bd. dirs. Easton Young Woman's Christian Assn., 1965-68, publicity chmn. Y-Teen com., 1953-68. Recipient plaques Salvation Army, 1982, 91, Jewett Family of Am., 1993, cited for Outstanding Svcs., Easton chpt. ARC, 1967, cert. for Outstanding Svc. and Support, 1997, citation Hist. and Geneal. Soc. Northampton County for outstanding svc. in restoration and pub. of Little Stone House Mus., 1993, citation United Way of Easton, 1960, Molly Pitcher gold medal of appreciation SAR, 1980. Mem. AAUW (treas. Easton br. 1950-52, newsletter initiator and editor 1951-60, rep. of br. to UN N.Y.C. conf. 1961-68, internat. rels. chmn.), UDC (Jefferson Davis chpt./Houston), DAR (George Taylor chpt. regent 1974-80, 89-95, vice regent 1980-83, historian 1971-74, 95—, pub. chmn. 1969—; Penn. state chmn. vol. svcs. 1995—), PEO (chpt. AF Houston), Easton Tavern House Soc., World Affairs Coun. Phila., Woman's Club of Easton (pres. 1961-64, bd. dirs. 1959—, pub. chmn. 1952-68, 70-82, 92—, parliamentarian 1984-92, spl. fin. chmn. 1969-78, legis. chmn. 1982-84, internat. affairs chmn. 1996—, Outstanding Woman of Yr. 1992, Gold Medal of Honor 1992), Northampton Country Club (Niners' Golf chmn. 1957-91), Women's Golf Assn. (constn. and bylaws chmn., parliamentarian 1960-92), Libr. of Congress (founding nat. mem., charter assoc.). Republican. Episcopalian. Avocations: antiques, historical research, golf, swimming, grandmothering. Home: 110 Upper Shawnee Ave Easton PA 18042-1356

STITT, FREDERICK HESSE, insurance broker; b. Chgo., Jan. 9, 1929; s. LeMoine Donaldson and Martha (Hesse) S.; m. Adena Fitzgerald, Dec. 23, 1950 (div. Nov. 1984); children: Rebecca Martha Hudecek, Mary Elizabeth Weeks, Barbara Anne Mistelle, Frederick Hesse Jr., Joyce Austin, Kathryn T.; m. Suzanne Boyce, Oct. 22, 1985; stepchildren: David Boyce Peyton, Jeffrey Buckley Peyton. PhB, U. Chgo., 1949, MBA, 1951. CLU. Group svc. rep. Travelers Ins. Co., Peoria, Ill., 1951-52, agy. svc. rep., 1952-54; agt. Travelers Ins. Co., Chgo., 1954-59; v.p. A.W. Ormiston & Co., Chgo., 1959-80, pres., 1980—; instr. ins. Roosevelt U., 1961, 62. Contbr. articles to ins. jours. Mem. Am. Soc. CLU and ChFC (chair life ins. illustration task force 1991-93, instr. Illustration questionnaire 1992-93, mem. bd. 1992-95, pres. Chgo. chpt. 1968-69, Huebner scholar 1990, Millard Graver Svc. award 1996), Assn. Advanced Life Underwriting (mem. bd. 1983-85), Chgo. Estate Planning Coun. (pres. 1976-77, Austin Fleming award 1984). Avocations: history, writing, fly fishing.

STIVEN, ALAN ERNEST, population biologist, ecologist; b. St. Stephen, N.B., Can., Nov. 12, 1935; came to U.S., 1962, naturalized, 1977; s. Alan J. and Edith G. S.; m. Julia Ann Heeb, Aug. 18, 1972; 1 son, Alan; children by previous marriage: Terry, Kim. B.S., U. N.B., 1957; M.A., U. B.C., 1959; Ph.D., Cornell U., 1962. Asst. prof. zoology U. N.C., 1962-66, asso. prof., 1966-71, chmn. biology curriculum, 1968-70, prof., 1971—, chmn. ecology curriculum, 1971-86, chmn. dept. zoology, 1967-72, acting chmn., 1979-80, assoc. chmn. dept. Biology, 1992-97; mem., chmn. NRC-NSF pre-doctoral fellowship panel, 1984-86, NRC rsch. associateship panel, 1990-93, EPA Grad. fellowship panel, 1995—; bd. chmn. Highlands Biol. Sta., 1987—. Editor: Ecology and Ecol. Monographs, 1967-73; editorial bd. Jour. Invertebrate Pathology, 1967-71; contbr. articles scholarly jours. Mem. Chapel Hill Bd. Adjustment, 1973-76. NSF rsch. grantee, 1962-82, NIH tng. grantee, 1966-70, U.S. Forest Svc. grantee, 1982-85, NC Wildlife Commn. grantee, 1988-94. Mem. Ecol. Soc. Am., Am. Soc. Naturalists, Soc. Study Evolution. Office: U NC Dept Biology Cb 3280 Coker Hall Chapel Hill NC 27599

STIVENDER, DONALD LEWIS, mechanical engineering consultant; b. Chgo., May 8, 1932; s. Paul Macon and Grace (Larsen) S.; m. Margaret Ann Lourim, Apr. 14, 1956; children—Anne, Robert, Carole. B.S. in Engring, U.S. Coast Guard Acad., 1954; M.S., U. Mich., 1959. Registered profl. engr., Mich. R & D engr. Rsch. Labs., GM Corp., Warren, Mich., 1959-92, sr. rsch. engr., 1968-92; owner, consulting engr. Stivender Engring. Assos., 1980—; cons. systems engring. disciplines. Contbr. articles tech. jours. on diesel, gas turbine and spark ignition engine combustion, emission, constrn. and electronic control aspects. Engring. officer USCG, 1950-58. Fellow Soc. Automotive Engrs. (Arch T. Colwell award 1968, 69, 79, governing bd. 1971-73); mem. NAS (naval studies bd. 1990-92), ASME, Combustion Inst., Sigma Xi. Achievements include invention of internal combustion engines and electronic control systems. Home: 1730 Hamilton Dr Bloomfield Hills MI 48302-0221

STIVER, PATRICIA ABARE, elementary education educator; b. Plattsburgh, N.Y., Nov. 17, 1941; d. Joseph LaBarge and Janet Marcella (Downs) Abare. BA, SUNY, Fredonia, 1964; MS, SUNY, Albany, 1988. Cert. elem. educator N.Y. Tchr. elem. Randolph (N.Y.) Ctrl. Sch., 1964-66; tchr. elem. Schoharie (N.Y.) Ctrl. Schs., 1966-86, asst. elem. math. coord., 1986-96, remedial math. tchr., 1986—, coord. elem. computer assisted instrn., 1986-90, math. coordinating spls., 1996—, elem. math. coordinating specialist, 1996—. Mem. ASCD, Nat. Coun. Tchrs. Math., Assn. Math. Tchrs. of N.Y. State, N.Y. State United Tchrs. and Affiliates, N.Y. State Assn. Comprehensive Edn. (U.S., Europe). Democrat. Avocations: gardening, clarinet, alto and tenor saxophone playing in bands, singing in choirs, computers, spectator sports. Home: 107 Brookside Pl PO Box 121 Schoharie NY 12157-0121 Office: Schoharie Ctrl Sch Main St Schoharie NY 12157

STIVER, WILLIAM EARL, retired government administrator; b. Madison, Ind., Mar. 30, 1921; s. John Virgil and Anna Lynne (Ryker) S.; student Hanover Coll., 1947-49; B.S., U. Calif. at Berkeley, 1951, M.B.A., 1952; m. Norma A. Cull, June 11, 1944; children—Vicki, Raymond, Gena, John. With Fed. Ser., Bur. Census, Commerce Dept., Suitland, Md., 1952-79, chief budget and finance div., 1963-73, dep. assoc. adminstr. Social and Econ. Stats. Adminstrn., 1973-75, spl. asst., assoc. dir. for adminstrn. and field ops. Bur. of Census, 1975-77, electronic data processing staff coordinator, 1977-78, ret., 1979. Served with AUS, 1942-43, 45-46. Recipient Silver medal Commerce Dept., 1969. Mem. Phi Beta Kappa, Beta Gamma Sigma. Home: 8104 Kerby Pky Ct Fort Washington MD 20744-4756

STIVERS, WILLIAM CHARLES, forest products company executive; b. Modesto, Calif., June 22, 1938; s. William P. and Helen Louise (Cummings) S.; m. Karen L. Gaspar, Aug. 6, 1961; children: William, Gregory, Michael, Kristy, Kelly, John, Jeffrey. BA, Stanford, 1960; MBA, U. So. Calif., 1963; certificate, U. Wash., 1969; grad., Advanced Mgmt. Program, Harvard U., 1977. Asst. cashier, asst. v.p., v.p. First Interstate Bank, San Francisco and Los Angeles, 1962-70; finance mgr. treas. dept. Weyerhaeuser Co., Tacoma, 1970; asst. treas. Weyerhaeuser Co., 1971, treas., 1972—, v.p., 1980-91, sr. v.p., chief fin. officer, 1991—; treas. Weyerhaeuser Real Estate Co., 1970; bd. dirs., exec. com. mem. Protection Mut. Ins. Co., Park Ridge, Ill.; bd. dirs., chmn., pres. S&S Land and Cattle Co.; nat. adv. bd. mem. Chase-Manhattan Corp. Chmn. bd. trustees Franciscan Health Sys.-West, Federal Way; bd. dirs. Pacific-Rim Fin. Ctr. Grad. Sch. Bus. Adminstrn. U. Wash.; vice chmn. fin. mgmt. com. Am. Forest and Paper Assn. Mem. Financial Execs. Inst.

STIX, THOMAS HOWARD, physicist, educator; b. St. Louis, July 12, 1924; s. Ernest William and Erma (Kingsbacher) S.; m. Hazel Rosa Sherwin, May 28, 1950; children: Susan Sherwin Fisher, Michael Sherwin. B.S., Calif. Inst. Tech., 1948; Ph.D., Princeton U., 1953. Mem. staff Plasma Physics Lab. Princeton U., 1953—, co-head exptl. div., 1961-78, asst. dir. acad. affairs, 1978-80, assoc. dir. acad. affairs, 1980-93; prof. astrophys. sci., 1962-96, assoc. chmn. dept. astrophys. sci., 1981-91; acting dir. Ctr. for Jewish Life Princeton U., 1994-95. Author: The Theory of Plasma Waves, 1962, Waves in Plasmas, 1992; mem. adv. bd. McGraw-Hill Advanced Physics Monograph Series, 1963-70; bd. editors: Physics of Fluids, 1966-68, Internat. Jour. Engring. Sci, 1969-77, Nuclear Fusion, 1975-80; assoc. editor: Phys. Rev. Letters, 1974-77. Chmn. Princeton United Jewish Appeal, 1954-55, 63-64, Princeton Hillel Found., 1972-76, pres., 1994-96. Served with AUS, 1942-45. Recipient award for disting. teaching Princeton U., 1991; NSF sr. postdoctoral fellow physics Weizmann Inst. Sci., Rehovot, Israel, 1960-61; Guggenheim Meml. Found. fellow, 1969-70. Fellow Am. Phys. Soc. (chmn. div. plasma physics 1962-63, com. internat. freedom of scientists 1983-87, chmn. 1985; James Clark Maxwell prize 1980); mem. AAUP, Sigma Xi, Tau Beta Pi. Home: 231 Brookstone Dr Princeton NJ 08540-2405

STOB, MARTIN, physiology educator; b. Chgo., Feb. 20, 1926; s. Cornelius and Theodora (Sluis) S. B.S., Purdue U., 1949, M.S., 1951, Ph.D., 1953. Mem. faculty Purdue U., Lafayette, Ind., 1953—, assoc. prof. animal scis., 1958-63, prof., 1963-92; ret., 1992—. Contbr. articles to profl. jours. Patentee prodn. of fermentation estrogen. Served with USN, 1944-46; ETO, PTO. Name Best Tchr. Sch. Agr., 1970, Best Counselor Sch. Agr., 1977, Best Counselor Purdue U., 1977. Fellow AAAS; mem. Am. Inst. Biol. Scis., Am. Soc. Animal Sci., Soc. Study of Reprodn., Soc. Study of Fertility. Episcopalian. Home: 6218 W Rd 75 N Lafayette IN 47906

STOBAUGH, ROBERT BLAIR, business educator, business executive; b. McGehee, Ark., Oct. 15, 1927; s. Robert B. and Helen (Parris) S.; m. Beverly Ann Parker, Oct. 18, 1947 (dec. 1990); children: Blair, Susan, William, Clay; m. June Gray Milton, Dec. 7, 1991. B.S. in Chem. Engring., La. State U., 1947; D. Bus. Adminstrn., Harvard Bus. Sch., 1968. Refinery engr. Exxon Corp., Baton Rouge and Venezuela, 1947-52; engring. mgr. Caltex Oil Co., N.Y., Bahrain, London, 1952-59; mgr. econ. evaluation Monsanto Co., Houston, 1959-65; lectr. Harvard Bus. Sch., Boston, 1967-70, assoc. prof., 1970-71, prof., 1972-83, Charles E. Wilson prof., 1984-96; chmn. doctoral programs Harvard Bus. Sch., 1984-89; dir. energy project Harvard Bus. Sch., Boston, 1972-83; chmn. tech. and ops. mgmt. area Harvard Bus. Sch., 1981-83; dir. Ashland Inc., Ky., 1977—, and 9 other firms, 1971-97. Co-author: Money in the Multinational Enterprise, 1973, Energy Future (best-seller list N.Y. Times and Time mag.), 1979, How To Build an Effective Small-Company Board, 1996; author: Nine Investments Abroad and Their Impact at Home, 1976, Innovation and Competition, 1988; co-editor: Technology Crossing Borders, 1984; contbr. articles on corp. governance to profl. publs., 1992-96. Mem. bd. advisors Instituto de Estudios Superiores de la Empresa, Barcelona, Spain, 1973-80; co-chmn. The Dumbarton Oaks Symposium on Energy Efficiency, Washington, 1979; bd. dirs. Alliance to Save Energy, Washington, 1979-94; chmn. Blue Ribbon Commn. on Dir.. Compensation, Nat. Assn. Corp. Dirs., 1995; expert testimony Congress; advisor to cabinet-level depts. of White House and UN; trustee French Libr. and Cultural Ctr.,

Boston, 1995—. Fellow Acad. Internat. Bus. (pres. 1979-80), Council on Fgn. Relations, Am. Econ. Assn., Nat. Assn. Corp. Dirs. (bd. dirs. 1996—, Blue Ribbon commn. on dir. professionalism 1996). Episcopalian. Clubs: Belmont Hill (Mass.); Harvard (N.Y.), Forest (Houston). Office: Harvard Bus Sch Soldiers Field Rd Boston MA 02163

STOBER, WILLIAM JOHN, II, economics educator; b. Boston, Mar. 24, 1933; s. Ralph William and Marjorie Cairncross (Duthie) S.; m. Jeannine Lynn Defries, Sept. 10, 1955. B.Sc., Washington and Lee U., 1955; M.A., Duke U., 1957, Ph.D., 1965. Instr., then asst. prof. econs. N.C. State U., Raleigh, 1959-65; asst. prof., then asso. prof. La. State U., 1965-69, acting head dept. econs., 1968-69; mem. faculty U. Ky., 1969—, prof. econs., 1974—, chmn. dept., 1979-86, 90-95, dir. grad. studies, 1979-86. Mem. Am. Econs. Assn., AAUP, So. Econ. Assn. (exec. com. 1969-71), Beta Gamma Sigma. Democrat. Home: 516 Mundys Lndg Versailles KY 40383-9468

STOBO, JOHN DAVID, physician, educator; b. Somerville, Mass., Sept. 1, 1941. BA, Dartmouth Coll., 1963; MD, SUNY, Buffalo, 1968. Intern Osler Med. Services, Johns Hopkins, Balt., 1968-69, asst. med. resident, 1969-70, chief med. resident, 1972-73; research assoc. NIH, Bethesda, 1970-72; asst. prof. Mayo Clinic and Research Found., Rochester, Minn., 1973-76; assoc. prof. Moffitt Hosp., San Francisco, 1976-82, prof., head section rheumatology, clin. immunology, 1982-85; William Osler prof. medicine, chmn. dept. medicine John Hopkins Hosp. and Univ., Balt., 1985-94, vice dean clin. sci., assoc. v.p. medicine, 1994—; v.p. Johns Hopkins Health System, Balt., 1994—; chmn., CEO Johns Hopkins Healthcare LLC, Balt. Mem. editorial bds. Jour. Immunology, 1981-86, Jour. Lab. and Clin. Investigation, 1977-82, Arthritis and Rheumatism 1980-85, Jour. Reticuleondothelial Soc., 1982-84, Jour. Clin. Investigation, 1981-86, Jour. Clin. Immunology, 1982-87, Jour. Molecular and Cellular Immunology, 1984-86, Rheumatology Internat., 1984-86, Jour. Immunology, 1985-87; contbr. numerous articles to profl. jours. Transp. and immunobiology adv. com. NIAID, 1976-81; vice chmn. research com. Arthritis Found., 1982-84, chmn., 1984-86, sr. investigator, 1974-77; bd. scientific counselors Nat. Cancer Inst., 1982—; scientific adv. bd. exec. com. Lupus Research Inst.; research adv. bd. DuPont Co., 1987-94. Recipient Merck award 1967, Maimonides Med. Soc. award 1968; SUNY fellow, 1965-66. Fellow ACP, Am. Clin. and Climatol. Assn., Balt. City Med. Soc., Interurban Clin. Club, Md. Soc. Internal Medicine; mem. AAAS, Inst. Medicine, Am. Coll. Rheumatology (pres. 1989-90), Am. Rheumatism Assn. (sec., treas., 1st v.p. 1985-89), Am. Assn. Immunologists, Am. Assn. Physicians, Am. Fedn. Clin. Rsch., Am. Soc. Clin. Investigation, Assn. Profs. Medicine (sec.-treas. 1991-92, pres. 1994-95), Alpha Omega Alpha. Office: Johns Hopkins Outpatient Ctr 601 N Caroline St Ste 2080 Baltimore MD 21205-1809

STOCK, DAVID EARL, mechanical engineering educator; b. Balt., Feb. 2, 1939; s. Walter E. and Minnie H. (Bauer) S.; m. Mary W. Wilford, Aug. 4, 1962; children: Joseph W., Katherine W. BS, Penn State U., 1961; MS, U. Conn., 1965; PhD, Oreg. State U., 1972. Test engr. Pratt & Whitney Aircraft, East Hartford, Conn., 1961-65; vol. Peace Corps, Ghana, 1965-68; prof. Wash. State U., Pullman, 1972—. Contbr. articles to profl. jours. Fellow ASME (chair multiphase flow com. 1988-90, Freeman scholar 1994). Office: Wash State U Dept Mech Materials Engr Pullman WA 99164-2920

STOCK, GREGG FRANCIS, retired association executive; b. Kansas City, Mo., Jan. 30, 1925; s. Arthur Robert and Verna Marie (Prawitz) S.; m. Sarah Ellen Smart, Nov. 8, 1947; children: Gregory Francis, Heidi Frances, Peter Huston. B.A. in Journalism; B.S. in Advt, U. Kans., 1948. Pres. Wayne-Fastock Equipment Co., Kansas City, Mo., 1953-65; dir. Kansas City Mus., 1971-82, dir. emeritus, 1982—; exec. dir. Old Santa Fe Assn., 1983-84, dir., 1984-87; exec. dir. Southwestern Assn. on Indian Affairs, Santa Fe, 1984-87, dir., 1987-90. Served to lt. (j.g.) USNR, 1943-46, PTO. Fellow Explorers Club. Home: 8345 Somerset Dr Shawnee Mission KS 66207-1843

STOCK, LEON MILO, chemist, educator; b. Detroit, Oct. 15, 1930; s. J.H. Frederick and Anna (Fischer) S.; m. Mary K. Elmblad, May 6, 1961; children: Katherine L., Ann V. BS in Chemistry, U. Mich., 1952; PhD in Chemistry, Purdue U., 1959. Instr. U. Chgo., 1958-61, asst. prof., 1961-65, assoc. prof., 1965-70, prof. dept. chemistry, 1970-96, master Phys. Scis. Collegiate div., 1970-96, prof. emeritus dept. chemistry, 1997—, assoc. dean div. Phys. Scis., 1976-81, assoc. dean, 1976-81, chmn. dept. chemistry, 1985-88; faculty assoc. Argonne (Ill.) Nat. Lab., 1984-85, joint appointment chemistry div., 1985-96, dir. chemistry div., 1988-95; exploratory rsch. assoc. Elec. Power Rsch. Inst., 1989; adv. bd. Ctr. for Applied Rsch., U. Ky., 1990-95; Brown lectr. Purdue U., 1992; Given lectr. Pa. State U., 1995; cons. Westinghouse Hanford Co., 1995-96, Phillips Petroleum Co., 1964-95, Amoco Oil Co., 1989-95, Argome Nat. Lab., 1995—. Pacific N.W. Nat. Lab., 1996—, Fluor Daniel Hanford Co., 1996—. Recipient L.J. and H.M. Quantrell prize, 1974, H.H. Storch award Am. Chem. Soc., 1987. Mem. NAS (energy engring. bd.), Am. Chem. Soc. (com. on sci. 1990-92), Coun. of Gordon Rsch. Confs. (chmn. Gordon Conf. on Fuel Sci. 1983), NRC (mem. panel on coop. rsch. in fossil energy 1984, energy engring. bd. 1984-90, mem. panel on strategic petroleum rsch. 1985, panel on rsch. needs of advanced process tech. 1992-93), Ill. Coal Bd. (program panel 1986-90, panel on prodn. techs. for transp. fuels 1990, editl. bd. Jour. Organic Chemistry 1981-86, Energy and Fuels, 1986—, mem. panel on new strategy for safety issue resolution at Hanford, 1996). Office: Argonne Nat Lab Chem Divsn Argonne IL 60439

STOCK, MAXINE, sculptor, librarian, art therapist; b. Benton Harbor, Mich., June 17, 1933; d. Laurence James and Gertrude Frances (Drake) S.; m. Allen Neil Kimmerly, Aug. 25, 1951 (div. Sept. 1976); children: Melissa, Allen Neil II, Eliza, Christopher Stock. Diploma, U. Chgo., 1951; BS in Art Edn., Andrews U., 1970; MFA, U. Notre Dame, 1975; MSLS, Atlanta U., 1986. Cert. libr., Ga.; cert. art tchr. grades K-12, Ga., Mich. Supportive svcs. art therapy Martin Luther King Elem., Benton Harbor, 1970-72; tchg. asst. studio art and history U. Notre Dame, Ind., 1973-75; exec. dir. Southeastern Sch. Creative Edn., Tifton, Ga., 1977-81; art therapist, cons., pvt. practice 6 Ga. Psychoedn. Ctrs., 1978-85; regional circulation libr. Brunswick (Ga.)-Glynn Regional Libr., 1984-93; ext. svcs. libr. Okefenokee Regional Libr. Sys., Waycross, Ga., 1993—; art therapist, bibliotherapy Artshouse, St. Simons Island, Ga., 1981—; artist-in-residence Mich. Fine Arts Coun., 1976, Ga. Coun. for the Arts, 1979; studio pottery tchr., therapist Coastal Ctr. for the Arts, St. Simons Island, 1981—. One-woman shows include St. Marys Coll., South Bend, Ind., 1974, Okefenokee Heritage Ctr., Waycross, 1994; groups shows Avery Fisher Hall, Womenart Gallery, N.Y.C., 1979. Intern Program grantee Nat. Endowment for the Arts, 1977. Mem. Am. Art Therapy Assn., Beta Phi Mu. Bahai. Office: Okefenokee Regional Libr Sys 401 Lee Ave Waycross GA 31501-3000

STOCK, PEGGY A(NN), college president, educator; b. Jan. 30, 1936; married; 5 children. BS in Psychology, St. Lawrence U., 1957; MA in Counseling, U. Ky., 1963, EdD, 1969. Lic. psychologist, Ohio. Instr., research asst. dept. psychology and spl. edn. U. Ky., Lexington, 1958-59, 63-67, staff psychologist Med. Ctr., 1964-66; dir. edn. United Cerebral Palsy of the Bluegrass, Lexington, 1959-61; exec. dir. Community Council for Physically Handicapped and Mentally Retarded, Lexington, 1962-64; dir. clin. program No. Ky. Regional Community Mental Health Ctr., Covington, 1969-71; pres. Midwest Inst. Tng. and Edn., Cin., 1971-76; assoc. prof., counseling psychologist Mont. State U., Bozeman, 1975-77, asst. dean Office of Student Affairs and Service, 1977-79; spl. asst. to pres. U. Hartford, Conn., 1979-80, assoc. prof. Coll. of Edn., 1980-85, v.p. adminstrn., 1981-86; prof., pres. Colby-Sawyer Coll., New London, N.H., 1986-95; pres. Westminster Coll. of Salt Lake City, 1995—; vis. prof. dept. sociology and edn. Thomas Moore Coll., Fort Mitchell, Ky., 1970-71; panelist Nat. Inst. Edn., 1985; cons. and lectr. in field. Contbr. chpts. to books, articles to profl. jours. Mem. coun. N.H. Coll. and Univ.; nat. bd. dirs. Med. Coll. Pa.; mem. New London Bus. Adv. Bd.; active numerous other civic orgns. Recipient Disting. Alumna award St. Lawrence U., 1989; grantee in field, most recent George I. Alden Trust, Helen Fuld Health Trust, Surdna, Cogswell, U.S. Dept. Edn., 1981-89, numerous others; fellow U. Ky., 1966-68, Am. Council Edn., 1979-80, United Jewish Com., 1981. Mem. Am. Coun. on Edn., Am. Assn. for Higher Edn., Advancement Women in Higher Edn. Avocations: breeding Arabian horses, reading, fishing. Office: Westminster Coll 1840 S 1300 E Salt Lake City UT 84105-3617

STOCK, STEPHEN MICHAEL, broadcast journalist; b. Colorado Springs, May 16, 1961; s. Ray Kesecker and Juanita Madeline (Keller) S.; m. Lynn Victoria Peithman, July 20, 1985; 1 child, Michael Stephen Ray. BA, U.N.C., 1983. From engring. tech. to gen. assignment reporter WDBJ-TV, Roanoke, Va., 1983-86; from investigative reporter to weekend anchor, producer WECT-TV, Wilmington, N.C., 1986-87; bur. chief Anderson, S.C. WYFF-TV, Greenville, S.C., 1987-91; bur. chief Ocala, Fla. WESH-TV, Orlando, 1996—; standby SE corr. NBC NewsChannel, 1995—; guest lectr. Marion County Sheriff's Office, Ocala, 1993—, U. Fla. Press Club, Gainesville, 1993—. Adv. bd. Jack Eckerd Youth Camp E-Kel-Etu, Silver Springs, Fla., 1996—; elder First Presbyn. Ch., Ocala, 1996—; founder Ocala/Marion County Town Mtg. on Violence, 1996; adv. bd. Fla. Envirothon, Ocala/Silver Springs, 1993; mem. adv. bd. Ocala Habitat for Humanity, 1996—. Named TV journalist of yr. RTNDA of Carolinas, 1989; recipient award for TV agrl. news coverage S.C. Agriculture Co., 1989. Mem. Ctrl. Fla. Press Club (best gen. news 1994, merit recognition for spot news 1995, Best Spot News award 1996, Best Investigative Report award 1996, Merit Gen. News award 1996), Soc. Profl. Journalists, Investigative Reporters and Editors Assn. Avocations: wine collecting, photography, sports, gardening, carpentry. Office: WESH-TV Bur Chief 7 E Silver Springs Blvd Ocala FL 34470-6614

STOCK, STUART CHASE, lawyer; b. St. Louis, July 19, 1946; s. Sheldon Harry and Muriel Cecile (Lovejoy) S.; m. Judith Ann Stewart, July 18, 1970; 1 child, Frederick Chase. BS with highest distinction, Purdue U., 1968; JD magna cum laude, Harvard U., 1971. Bar: Mo. 1971, Ind. 1973, D.C. 1974. Law clk. to Chief Judge Henry J. Friendly U.S. Ct. Appeals 2d cir., New York, 1971-72; law clk. to Justice Thurgood Marshall U.S. Supreme Ct., Washington, 1972-73; assoc. Covington & Burling, Washington, 1974-78, ptnr., 1978—; lectr. law U. Va., Charlottesville, 1987-90. Mem. Am. Law Inst. Office: Covington & Burling PO Box 7566 1201 Pennsylvania Ave NW Washington DC 20044

STOCKAR, HELENA MARIE MAGDALENA, artist; b. Bratislava, Czechoslovakia, Mar. 22, 1933; came to the U.S., 1968; d. Arnost J. and Helen R. (Strakova) Kubasek; m. Ivo J. Stockar, Oct. 31, 1959; children: David, Laura Bates. Diploma, Graficka Skola, Prague, 1952, Music Conservatory, Prague, 1954. Piano tchr. Music Sch., Prague, 1954-68; company pianist State Ballet/Breacrest Sch., R.I., 1968-74; piano tchr. Music Tchr. Assn., R.I., 1968-86. One-woman shows include Warwick Mus., R.I., 1986, Brown U., Providence, 1987, Westerly Art Gallery, R.I., 1987, Westerly Art Gallery/Morin-Miller, 1988, 89, Galerie Horizon, Paris, 1989, others; two-woman exhibit R.I. State Com. of Nat. Mus. of Women in the Arts, Triboro Studio, R.I., 1995; exhibited in group shows at World Congress of Czechoslovak Soc. of Art and Sci., Washington, 1988, Morin-Miller Internat., N.Y.C., 1989, Ariel Gallery, Soho, N.Y.C., 1989, Art Expo N.Y.C., 1989, R.I. State Com. Nat. Mus. Women Arts, 1995, Providence Art Club, 1996, others; represented in permanent collections around the world; featured on numerous TV shows. Recipient Second prize Nat. Competition of Children's Book Illustration, Prague, 1965; named finalist Internat. Art Competition, L.A., 1984. Mem. Nat. Mus. of Women in the Arts (R.I. state com.), Czechoslovak Soc. of Art and Sci., Music Club Providence, Chopin Club Providence, Schubert Club Providence, Chaminade Club Providence. Avocations: traveling, gardening. Office: PO Box 7282 Warwick RI 02887-7282

STOCKARD, JAMES ALFRED, lawyer; b. Lake Dallas, Tex., Aug. 4, 1935; s. Clifford Raymond and Thelma Gladys (Gotcher) S.; m. Mary Sue Hogan, Aug. 17, 1956; children—Bruce Anthony, James Alfred, Paul Andrew. BA with honors, N. Tex. State U., Denton, 1956; LLB magna cum laude, So. Methodist U., 1959. Bar: Tex. 1959. Pvt. practice Dallas, 1959-62; with Employers Casualty Co., Dallas, 1962-65; v.p. Southland Life Ins. Co., Dallas, 1965-77; sr. v.p., gen. counsel, dir. Southland Life Ins. Co., 1977-87; exec. v.p., gen. counsel, sec. Southland Fin. Corp., Dallas, 1978-87; dir. Tex. Life, Accident, Health and Hosp. Svc. Ins. Guaranty Assn., 1978-84, chmn. bd., 1980-84; ptnr. Butler & Binion, Dallas, 1987—; bd. dirs. Ins. Systems Am., Atlanta; pres., bd. dir. Dallas County Municipal Utility Dist. 1, Irving, Tex.; gen. counsel, bd. dirs. Lone Star Life Ins. Co., 1988—. Contbr. legal jours. Mem. exec. com., precinct chmn. Dallas County Dem. Com., 1971. Mem. Am., Tex., Dallas Bar Assn., Assn. Life Ins. Counsel. Methodist. Home: 3607 Asbury Dallas TX 75205-1029 Office: 750 N Saint Paul St Ste 1800 Dallas TX 75201-3255

STOCKARD, JOE LEE, public health service officer, consultant; b. Lees Summit, Mo., May 5, 1924; s. Joseph Frederick and Madge Lorraine (Jones) S.; m. Elsie Anne Chamberlain, Dec. 27, 1957. BS, Yale U., 1945; MD, U. Kans., 1948; MPH, Johns Hopkins U., 1961. Med. officer U.S. Army Med. Corps, Korea and Malaya, 1952-55; asst. prof. preventive medicine Sch. Medicine U. Md., Balt., 1955-58; dep. dir. Cholera Rsch. Lab., Dhaka, Bangladesh, 1960-63; advanced through grades to capt., epidemiologist USPHS, Washington, 1960-76, 64-67; chief preventive medicine sect. USAID, Saigon, Vietnam, 1965-68; assoc. dir. Office Internat. Health, Office of Surgeon Gen. USPHS, Washington, 1967-69; epidemiologist, med. officer Agy. for Internat. Devel., Washington, 1969-87; mem. expert adv. com. WHO, Ouagadougou, Burkina, Faso, 1987-92; mem. joint programme com. AID project officer Onchocerciasis Control Program, West Africa, 1975-87; med. officer AID Africa Bur., Washington, 1976-87; guest spkr., prof. seminar on leptospirosis, 1956; organizer plague sect. meeting 8th Internat. Congress Tropical Medicine, 1969. Author: (with others) Communicable and Infectious Diseases, 1964; contbr. articles to U.S. Armed Forces Med. Jour., N.Y. Acad. Sci. Jour. Citizens rep. on regional water quality adv. com. Low County Coun. of Govts., 1996—. Recognized for support of onchocerciasis control in West Africa by Pres. Jerry Rawlings, Rep. of Ghana, 1986. Fellow Royal Soc. Tropical Medicine and Hygiene; mem. APHA, Am. Soc. Tropical Medicine and Hygiene, Retired Officers Assn. Achievements include discovery that massive doses of benadryl will not prevent shock in Korean epidemic hemorragic fever, gangrene is not previously a recognized manifestation of bubonic plaque in S.E. Asia; co-discovery that leptospirosis can be a significant problem in troops in Malayasia. Office: 17 Angel Wing Dr Hilton Head Island SC 29926-1903

STOCKBURGER, JEAN DAWSON, lawyer; b. Scottsboro, Ala., Feb. 4, 1936; d. Joseph Mathis Scott and Mary Frances (Alley) Dawson; m. John Calvin Stockburger, Mar. 23, 1963; children: John Scott, Mary Staci, Christopher Sean. Student, Gulf Park Coll., 1954-55; BA, Auburn U., 1958; M in Social Work, Tulane U., 1962; JD, U. Ark., Little Rock, 1979. Bar: Ark. 1979, U.S. Dist. Ct. (ea. dist.) Ark. 1980. Assoc. Mitchell, Williams, Selig, Gates & Woodyard and predecessor, Little Rock, 1979-85, ptnr., 1985-94, of counsel, 1994—; bd. dirs., sec. Cen. Ark. Estate Planning Council, Little Rock, 1984-85, 2d v.p., 1985-86; pres. Cen. Ark. Estate Council, 1987-88. Assoc. editor U. Ark. Law Rev., 1978-79. Bd. dirs. Sr. Citizens Activities Today, Little Rock, 1983-88, treas., 1986-88; bd. dirs. Vol. Orgn. for Ctrl. Ark. Legal Svcs., 1986-91, sec., 1987-88, chmn., 1989-81, H.I.R.E. Inc., 1994—; sec. Little Rock Cmty. Mental Health Ctr., 1994-96, v.p., 1996—. Mem. ABA, Ark. Bar Assn. (chmn. probate and trust law sect. 1986-88), Pulaski County Bar Assn. (bd. dirs. 1994—), Am. Coll. Trust and Estate Counsel. Democrat. Methodist. Office: Mitchell Williams Selig Gates & Woodyard 320 W Capitol Ave Ste 1000 Little Rock AR 72201-3522

STOCKDALE, JAMES BOND, writer, research scholar, retired naval officer; b. Abingdon, Ill., Dec. 23, 1923; s. Vernon Beard and Mabel Edith (Bond) S.; m. Sybil Elizabeth Bailey, June 28, 1947; children: James Bond, Sidney Bailey, Stanford Baker, Taylor Burr. BS, U.S. Naval Acad., 1946; MA, Stanford U., 1962; LLD (hon.), Brown U., 1979; LHD (hon.), U. R.I., 1980; 9 other hon. degrees. Commd. ensign USN, 1946, advanced through grades to vice admiral, served as naval aviator, test pilot sch. instr., squadron comdr. of supersonic fighters, air wing comdr.; prisoner of war (sr. naval service POW) North Vietnam, 1965-73; pres. Naval War Coll., Newport, R.I., 1976-79; retired USN, 1979; pres. The Citadel, Charleston, S.C., 1979-80; sr. research fellow The Hoover Instn., Stanford U., 1981-96, emeritus, 1996; independent candidate V.P. U.S. running mate of Ross Perot, 1992. Author: A Vietnam Experience, 1985 (Freedoms Found. at Valley Forge hon. prize 1985), (with Sybil Stockdale) In Love and War, 1984, Thoughts of a Philosophical Fighter Pilot, 1995. Mem. acad. adv. bd. U.S. Naval Acad., Annapolis, 1981-94. Decorated D.F.C. (2), D.S.M. (3), Silver Star (4), Medal of Honor; inducted Carrier Aviation Hall of Fame, 1993; enshrined U.S. Naval Aviation Hall of Honor, 1996. Fellow Soc. Exptl. Test Pilots (hon.); mem. Lincoln Acad. Ill. (laureate), Congl. Medal of Honor Soc., Assn. Naval Aviation, Soc. of Cincinnati, SAR, Bohemian Club (San Francisco). Episcopalian. Home: 547 A Ave Coronado CA 92118-1917

STOCKER, ARTHUR FREDERICK, classics educator; b. Bethlehem, Pa., Jan. 24, 1914; s. Harry Emilius and Alice (Stratton) S.; m. Marian West, July 16, 1968. A.B. summa cum laude, Williams Coll., 1934; A.M., Harvard U., 1935, Ph.D., 1939. Instr. Greek Bates Coll., 1941-42; asst. prof. classics U. Va., 1946-52, assoc. prof., 1952-60, prof., 1960-84, prof. emeritus, 1984—, chmn. dept., 1955-63, 68-78, assoc. dean Grad. Sch. Arts and Scis., 1962-66; vis. asst. prof. classics U. Chgo., summer 1951. Editor: (with others) Servianorum in Vergilii Carmina Commentariorum Editio Harvardiana, Vol. II, 1946, Vol. III, 1965; assoc. editor: Classical Outlook. Served with USAAF, 1942-46; col. (ret.). Sheldon traveling fellow from Harvard, 1940-41. Mem. Va. Classical Assn. (pres. 1949-52), Mid. West and South Classical Assn. (pres. So. sect. 1960-62, pres. 1970-71), Nat. Huguenot Soc. (pres. gen. 1989-91), Am. Philol. Assn., Mediaeval Acad. Am., Poetry Soc. Va. (pres. 1966-69), S.A.R. (chpt. pres. 1972, 91), Huguenot Soc. Va. (pres. 1981-83), Raven Soc. (Raven award 1977), Phi Beta Kappa, Omicron Delta Kappa. Republican. Presbyterian (elder). Clubs: Masons, Internat. Torch, Colonnade (Charlottesville, Va.), Farmington Country (Charlottesville, Va.), Commonwealth (Richmond, Va.), Williams (N.Y.C.), Army and Navy (Washington). Home: 1434 Grove Rd Charlottesville VA 22901-3126

STOCKER, JOYCE ARLENE, retired secondary school educator; b. West Wyoming, Pa., May 13, 1931; d. Donald Arthur and Elizabeth Mae (Gardner) Saunders; m. Robert Earl Stocker, Nov. 26, 1953; children: Desiree Lee Stocker Stackhouse, Rebecca Lois Stocker Genelow, Joyce Elizabeth Stocker Scrobola. Grad. cum laude, Coll. Misericordia, Dallas, 1953; Master's equivalency diploma, Pa. Dept. Edn., 1991. Cert. tchr., Pa. Tchr. music and lang. arts West Pittston (Pa.) Sch. Dist., 1953-60; tchr. music and choral Wyoming Area Sch. Dist., Exeter, Pa., 1970-78, tchr. English composition, 1978-93, chmn. lang. arts dept., 1982-90, dir. nat. history day activities, 1982-93; state cons. Nat. History Day, 1996—. Organist, choir dir. United Meth. Ch., Wyo., 1958—; choir dir. Wyo. Centenial Choir, Wyo., 1983; mem. com., sec. Continuing Profl. Devel. Com. Pa., Exeter, 1988-93, Long Range Plan Wyo. Area Sch. Dist., Exeter, 1990-91; tutor, judge Nat. History Day; judge regional, state, and nat. events for Nat. History Day; Pa. state cons. Nat. History Day. Recipient DAR Tchr. of Yr. award, 1992-93, Wilkes U., 1990; named Outstanding Educator, Times Leader, 1993. Mem. NEA, Pa. Edn. Assn., Wyo. Edn. Assn., N.E. Pa. Writing Coun., Nat. Coun. Tchrs. English, Women Educators Internat., Orgn. Am. History, Pa. Music Educators Assn., Music Educators Nat. Coun., Nat. Coun. Social Studies, Pa. Assn. Sch. Retirees, Pa. Sch. Employees Retirement Sys. (social svcs. com.), Pa. Retired Pub. Sch. Employees Assn. (Luzerne-Wyoming counties chpt.), Pa. Coun. Social Studies, Delta Kappa Gamma (recording sec. 1991—), Phi Mu Gamma. Methodist. Avocations: reading, writing, sewing, hunting, fishing. Office: Wyoming Area Sch Dist 20 Memorial St Exeter PA 18643-2659

STOCKGLAUSNER, WILLIAM GEORGE, accountant; b. St. Louis, Dec. 25, 1950; s. William George and Mary Virginia (Lopez) S.; m. Vickie Kay Mackler, Nov. 17, 1973; children: Tyson Marshall, Jacob Cameron. BS summa cum laude, Columbia (Mo.) Coll., 1985. CPA, Mo. Staff acct. Wright-Price Inc., Jefferson City, Mo., 1974-77; staff acct. Williams-Keepers CPAs, Columbia, 1977-81, supr. acctg. svc., 1981-85, auditor, 1985-86; acct. Don Landers & Co. CPAs, Columbia, 1986-89; ptnr. Columbia, 1990—. Coach Daniel Boone Little League, Columbia, 1986-90, 94-97, Diamond Coun., 1994-97, Columbia Soccer Club, 1988-90, divsn. coord., 1991-92; campaign vol. United Way, 1991-94; mem. fin. adv. com. City of Columbia, 1996—. Mem. AICPA, Mo. Soc. CPAs (tech. standards rev. com. 1989-90), Lions (sec. Columbia club 1983-85, bd. dirs. 1986-88). Republican. Roman Catholic. Avocations: fishing, photography, running, music/guitar. Office: Don L Landers & Co 33 E Broadway Ste 190 Columbia MO 65203-4207

STOCKING, GEORGE WARD, JR., anthropology educator; b. Berlin, Dec. 8, 1928; came to U.S., 1929; s. George Ward and Dorothé Amelia (Reichhard) S.; m. Wilhelmina Davis, Aug. 19, 1949 (div. 1965); children: Susan Hallowell, Rebecca, Rachel Louise, Melissa, Thomas Shepard; m. Carol Ann Bowman, Sept. 29, 1968. BA, Harvard U., 1949; PhD, U. Pa., 1960. From instr. to assoc. prof. history U. Calif., Berkeley, 1960-68; assoc. prof. anthropology and history U. Chgo., 1968-74, prof. anthropology, 1974—, Stein-Freiler Disting. Svc. prof., 1990—, dir. Fishbein Ctr. for History Sci. and Medicine, 1981-92; vis. prof. U. Minn., Mpls., 1974, Harvard U., Cambridge, Mass., 1977, Stanford U., Palo Alto, Calif., 1983. Author: Race, Culture and Evolution, 1968, Victorian Anthropology, 1987, The Ethnographer's Magic, 1992, After Tylor, 1995; author, editor: The Shaping of American Anthropology, 1974; editor History of Anthropology, 1983-97. Fellow Ctr. for Advanced Study in Behavioral Scis., 1976-77, John Simon Guggenheim Meml. Found., 1984-85, Inst. for Advanced Study, 1992-93; Getty Ctr. for History of Art and Humanities scholar, 1988-89. Fellow Am. Anthropol. Assn., Am. Acad. Arts and Scis.; mem. Royal Anthropol. Inst. (Huxley medal 1993), History Sci. Soc. Avocations: gardening, needlepoint, bicycling. Office: Univ Chicago Dept Anthropology 1126 E 59th St Chicago IL 60637-1539

STOCKMAN, DAVID ALLEN, former federal official, congressman, financier; b. Ft. Hood, Tex., Nov. 10, 1946; s. Allen and Carol (Bartz) S. BA in Am. History cum laude, Mich. State U., East Lansing, 1968; postgrad., Harvard U. Div. Sch., 1968-70; fellow, Inst. Politics, 1974. Spl. asst. to Congressman John Anderson, 1970-72; exec. dir. Republican Conf., Ho. of Reps., 1972-75; mem. 95th Congress from 4th Dist. Mich., Interstate and Fgn. Commerce Com., Adminstrn. Com.; chmn. Rep. Econ. Policy Task Force, 1977-81; dir. Office of Mgmt. and Budget, Washington, 1981-85; mng. dir. Salomon Bros., N.Y.C., 1985-88; sr. mng. dir. The Blackstone Group, N.Y.C., 1988—; Mem. Nat. Commn. on Air Quality, 1978. Author: The Triumph of Politics: Why the Reagan Revolution Failed, 1986. Mem. Coun. on Fgn. Rels. Office: The Blackstone Group 345 Park Ave New York NY 10154-0004

STOCKMAN, JAMES ANTHONY, III, pediatrician; b. Phila., 1943. MD, Jefferson Med. Coll., 1969. Diplomate Am. Bd. Pediatrics (pres.). Intern Childrens Hosp. Pa., 1969-70, resident in pediatrics, 1970-72; fellow in pediatric hematology/oncology SUNY, Syracuse, 1972-74; now cons. prof. Duke U.; also with U. N.C., Chapel Hill. Office: Am Bd Pediatrics 111 Silver Cedar Ct Chapel Hill NC 27514-1512

STOCKMAN, STEPHEN E., former congressman; b. Bloomfield Hills, Mich., Nov. 14, 1956; m. Patti Stockman. BS in Acctg., U. Houston, 1990. Acct., tech. McKee Environ. Health, Inc., 1991-93; mem. 104th Congress from 9th Tex. dist., 1995-96; with Moody Natl. Bank, 1996—. Republican. *

STOCKMAR, TED P., lawyer; b. Denver, May 9, 1921; s. Theodore Paul and Elda Marie (Robinson) S.; m. Suzanne Louise Harl, Feb. 14, 1947; children: Stephen Harl, John Brian, Anne Baldwin Stockmar Upton. BS in Petroleum Engring., Colo. Sch. Mines, Golden, 1943; LLB, U. Denver, 1948. Bar: Colo. 1948. Ptnr. Holme Roberts & Owen Denver, 1951-91; of counsel, 1991—. Co-author: Law of Federal Oil and Gas Leases 1964, 1984; also articles. Trustee Colo. Sch. Mines, Golden, 1948-82, bd. pres., 1970-80. 1st lt. USAF, 1943-45. Mem. Denver Bar Assn., Colo. Bar Assn., Rocky Mountain Oil and Gas Assn. (dir., exec. com. 1982-93, chmn. legal com. 1986-88), Denver Country Club, Univ. Club, Law Club. Republican. Avocations: bird watching, reading, gardening. Home: 2552 E Alameda Ave Apt 8 Denver CO 80209-3324 Office: Holme Roberts & Owen LLP 1700 Lincoln St Ste 4100 Denver CO 80203-4541

STOCKMAYER, WALTER H(UGO), retired chemistry educator; b. Rutherford, N.J., Apr. 7, 1914; s. Hugo Paul and Dagmar (Bostroem) S.; m. Sylvia Kleist Bergen, Aug. 12, 1938; children—Ralph, Hugh.. S.B., MIT, 1935, Ph.D., 1940; B.Sc. (Rhodes scholar), Oxford U., 1937; D.Sc., U. Louis-Pasteur, Strasbourg, France, 1972; L.H.D., Dartmouth Coll., 1983; DSc, U. Mass., 1996. Instr. M.I.T., 1939-41, asst. prof., 1943-46, assoc. prof., 1946-52, prof., 1952-61; prof. chemistry Dartmouth, 1961-79, prof. emeritus, 1979—; instr. Columbia, 1941-43; cons. E.I. duPont de Nemours & Co., Inc., 1945—; vis. com. Nat. Bur. Standards, 1979-84. Contbr. articles on phys.

and macromolecular chemistry to sci. jours. Recipient Nat. Medal of Sci., 1987, MCA Coll. Chemistry Tchr. award 1960, ; Guggenheim fellow, 1954-55, hon. fellow Jesus Coll., Oxford, Eng., 1976, Alexander von Humboldt fellow, 1978-79. Fellow Am. Acad. Arts and Scis., Am. Phys. Soc. (Polymer Physics prize 1975); mem. NAS, Am. Chem. Soc. (assoc. editor Macromolecules 1968-74, 76-94, chmn. polymer chem. divsn. 1968, Polymer Chemistry award 1965, Peter Debye award 1974, T. W. Richards medal 1988, polymer divsn. award 1988, Oesper award 1992), Soc. Plastics Engrs. (Internat. award 1991), Soc. Polymer Sci., Japan (hon. 1991), Appalachian Mountain Club, Sigma Xi (William Procter prize 1993). Office: Dartmouth Coll Chemistry Dept Hanover NH 03755

STOCKMEYER, NORMAN OTTO, JR., law educator, consultant; b. Detroit, May 24, 1938; s. Norman O. and Lillian R. (Hitchman) S.; m. Marcia E. Rudman, Oct. 1, 1966; children: Claire, Kathleen, Mary Frances. AB, Oberlin Coll., 1960; JD, U. Mich., 1963. Bar: Mich. 1963, U.S. Ct. Appeals (6th cir.) 1964, U.S. Supreme Ct. 1974. Legis. grad. fellow Mich. State U., 1963; legal counsel Senate Judiciary Com., Mich. Legislature, 1964; law clk. Mich. Ct. Appeals, 1965, commr., 1966-68, research dir., 1969-76; assoc. prof. law Thomas M. Cooley Law Sch., 1977-78, prof., 1978—; vis. prof. Mercer U. Sch. Law, 1986, Calif. Western Sch. Law, 1993; lectr. Mich. Judicial Inst., 1995. Editor Mich. Law of Damages, 1989; contbr. numerous articles to state and nat. legal jours. Named one of 88 Greats Lansing State Jour., 1988. Fellow Am. Bar Found. (life); mem. ABA (chmn. Mich. membership 1972-73, lectr. Appellate Judges Conf. jud. seminars 1972-76, ho. del. 1988-92, editorial bd. Compleat Lawyer 1990—), Nat. Conf. Bar Founds. (trustee 1985-90, sec. 1988-89), Mich. State Bar Found. (pres. 1982-85, trustee 1971-92), State Bar Mich. (chmn. Young Lawyers sect. 1971-72, rep. assembly 1972-79, bd. commrs. 1985-93), Ingham County Bar Assn. (bd. dirs. 1981-85), Mich. Assn. Professions (bd. dirs. 1981-84, Profl. of Yr. 1988), Thomas M. Cooley Legal Authors Soc. (pres. 1982-83), Scribes (bd. dirs. 1994—), Delta Theta Phi (dean Christiancy Senate 1962; Outstanding Prof. 1984). Address: PO Box 13038 Lansing MI 48901-3038

STOCKSTILL, JAMES WILLIAM, secondary school educator; b. Springfield, Mo., Aug. 28, 1945; s. Arley Ian and Elma Jean Stockstill; m. Vicki Bell, Aug. 20, 1966 (div. 1970); 1 child, Michelle LaDawn; m. Meredith Jeanine Spencer, Dec. 26, 1974; 1 child, Danielle. BS in Edn., S.W. Mo. State U., 1969. Head football coach, phys. edn. tchr. Golden City (Mo.) High Sch., 1969-70; coach, tchr. Mountain View (Mo.) High Sch., 1970-71; journeyman bricklayer Fort Lauderdale (Fla.) BMPI Union, 1971-74; masonry contractor Waynesville, N.C., 1974-86; masonry contractor, master stone and brick masonry contractor Hillsborough, N.C., 1986—; masonry instr. Orange High Sch., Hillsborough, 1986—; owner Athenian Lady Fitness Ctr., Waynesville, 1984-86; gymnastics instr. Canton (N.C.) YMCA, 1976-80; pres. Trade and Industry Adv. Coun., Hillsborough, 1988-90; rep. VICA Skill Contest Orange High Sch., 1986-88. Author: A Collection of Poems, 1992, 93. Mem. Com. to Increase and Diversify Tax Base, Hillsborough, 1992; mem. com. to rebuild hist. monument for Town of Hillsborough, 1997. Mem. AFT. Avocations: weightlifting, karate, jogging, hiking, landscaping. Home: 2801 Canter Dr Hillsborough NC 27278-8853 Office: Orange High Sch 500 Orange High Rd Hillsborough NC 27278

STOCKTON, ANDERSON BERRIAN, electronics company executive, consultant, genealogist; b. Lithonia, Ga., Oct. 7, 1943; s. Berrian Henry and Mary Grace (Warbington) S.; m. Linda Arlene Milligan, June 9, 1963; 1 child, Christopher Lee. Cert. in cryptographic engring., USAF Acad., Wichita Falls, Tex., 1963. Supr. Western Union Telegraph Co., East Point, Ga., 1965-67; mgr. RCA Corp., Cherry Hill, N.J., 1967-72; v.p. Universal Tech., Inc., Verona, N.J., 1972-76; v.p. engring. Siemens Ag., Anaheim, Calif., 1976-84, Concorde, El Toro, Calif., 1984-85, Data Card Troy, Inc., Santa Ana, Calif., 1985-86; dir. laser engring. div. ITT, San Jose, Calif., 1986-87; v.p. S.T.A.R. Ricoh Corp., San Jose, 1988-93; v.p. mktg. QMS, Inc., Mobile, Ala., 1993-94; mng. gen. dir. IDT, Inc., Santa Clara, Calif., 1994—; cons. Hutchinson (Minn.) Tech. Corp., 1984-87, Xerox, 1993, Hewlett Packard, 1993. Author: Polled Network Communications, 1976, A Quest for the Past, 1991; patentee in field. With USAF, 1961-65. Mem. IEEE, Am. Electronics Assn. Avocations: classic car collecting, genealogical and historical research, sword, coin and stamp collecting. Home: 2086 Silence Dr San Jose CA 95148-1918 Office: IDT Inc 2972 Stender Way Santa Clara CA 95054-3213

STOCKTON, DAVID KNAPP, professional golfer; b. San Bernardino, Calif., Nov. 2, 1941; s. Gail Rufus and Audrey (Knapp) S.; m. Catherine Fay Hales, Feb. 27, 1965; children—David Bradley, Ronald Edwin. B.S. in Gen. Mgmt., U. So. Calif., 1964. Mem. Golf's All Am. Team, 1974-76. Republican. Roman Catholic. Club: Elk. Winner 11 tour tournaments including: Profl. Golf Assn., 1970, 76, Los Angeles, 1974, Hartford, 1974, Colonial, 1967, Cleve., 1968, Milw., 1968-73, Pleasant Valley, 1971, Quad Cities, 1974, Haig and Haig Open, 1968, 6 Sr. Tour tournaments, 1992 TPC Winner (sr. rookie of the yr.), 5 Sr. Tour events-Dallas Murata Reunion, Kansas City, Park City, Seattle, Transamerica at Napa; named Sr. Player of Yr. and Arnold Palmer award Dupont Cup; rep. U.S. in 2 World Cups, 1970, 76, Ryder Cup, 1971, 77; shares former record for fewest putts for 18 holes (19); U.S. Ryder Cup capt., 1991. Office: 32373 Tres Lagos St Mentone CA 92359-9611*

STOCKTON, JOHN HOUSTON, professional basketball player; b. Spokane, Wash., Mar. 26, 1962; m. Nada Stepovich, Aug. 16, 1986; 1 child, John Houston. Grad., Gonzaga U., 1984. With Utah Jazz, Salt Lake City, 1984—; mem. U.S. Olympic Basketball Team, 1992. Named to NBA All-Star team, 1989-94; holder NBA single season rec. most assists, 1991; NBA Assists leader, 1987-1992; NBA Steals leader, 1989, 92; named NBA All-Star Co-MVP, 1993, All-NBA First Team, 1994. Led NBA in most assists per gaem, 1988-93; led NBA with highest steals per game avg., 1989,1992; shares single-game playoff record for most assists, 24, 1988. Office: Utah Jazz 301 W South Temple Salt Lake City UT 84101-1216*

STOCKWELL, ERNEST FARNHAM, JR., banker; b. Boston, Dec. 18, 1923; s. Ernest Farnham and Beatrice Burr (Beach) S.; m. Fiona Munro, May 24, 1952; children: Ernest Farnham III, Diana, Elizabeth. Grad., Phillips Acad., 1941; BA, Yale U., 1945. Asst. br. mgr. First Nat. Bank Boston, 1950-55, br. mgr., 1955-56, asst. v.p., 1956-60, v.p., 1960-71; pres. Harvard Trust Co., Cambridge, Mass., 1971-77; chief exec. officer Harvard Trust Co., 1973-77; pres. Bay Banks Assos., Inc., 1977-78; v.p. First Nat. Bank Boston, 1978-80, sr. v.p., 1980-88, ret., 1988. Bd. dirs. Yale Alumni Fund, chmn., 1980; trustee Episcopal Diocesan Investment Trust, Urban Coll. Boston. Mem. Yale Club (Boston and N.Y.C.), Dedham (Mass.) Country and Polo Club. Home: 36 Dover Rd Dover MA 02030-2020

STOCKWELL, ROBERT PAUL, linguist, educator; b. Oklahoma City, June 12, 1925; s. Benjamin P. and Anna (Cunningham) S.; m. Lucy Louisa Floyd, Aug. 29, 1946; 1 child, Paul Witten. B.A., U. Va., 1946, M.A., 1949, Ph.D., 1952. Instr. English, Oklahoma City U., 1946-48; mem. linguistics staff Sch. Langs., Fgn. Service Inst., State Dept., 1952-56; mem. faculty UCLA, 1956-94, prof. English, 1962-66, prof. linguistics, 1986-94, chmn. dept., 1966-73, 80-84, prof. emeritus, 1994—; mem. com. lang. programs Am. Council Learned Socs., 1965-69. Author: (with J.D. Bowen) Patterns of Spanish Pronunciation, 1960, Sounds of English and Spanish, 1965, (with J. D. Bowen, J.W. Martin) The Grammatical Structures of English and Spanish, 1965, The Major Syntactic Structures of English, 1973, (with P.M. Schachter, B.H. Partee) Foundations of Syntactic Theory, 1977, Workbook in Syntactic Theory and Analysis, 1977; also numerous articles.; editor: (with R.S.K. Macaulay) Linguistic Change and Generative Theory, 1972, ; assoc. editor: Lang., 1973-79, Festschrift: Rhetorica, Phonologica, Syntactica: A Festschrift for Robert P. Stockwell, 1989. Served with USNR, 1943-45. Am. Council Learned Socs. fellow, 1963-64. Mem. Linguistic Soc. Am. (exec. com. 1965-68), Philol. Assn. Great Britain. Home: 4000 Hayvenhurst Ave Encino CA 91436-3850 Office: UCLA Linguistics Dept Los Angeles CA 90024

STOCKWELL, VIVIAN ANN, nursing educator; b. Hardy, Ark., Apr. 26, 1943; d. Belvin L. and Armilda L. (Langston) Cooper; m. R.D. Sneed, Mar. 16, 1963 (div. Jan. 1981); m. Homer E. Stockwell, Jan. 6, 1990; 1 child, Sherilyn. Diploma, St. Luke's Sch. Nursing, Kansas City, Mo., 1964; BS in Nursing summa cum laude, Avila Coll., Kansas City, 1987. Staff nurse operating rm. North Kansas City (Mo.) Hosp., 1972-76; pvt. scrub nurse Van M. Robinson, MD, North Kansas City, 1976-81; instr. health occupations Independence (Mo.) Pub. Schs., 1981-85; instr. Park Coll., Parkville, Mo., 1987-89, asst. to dir. dept. nursing, 1989-90. Ch. sch. tchr. Independence Blvd. Christian Ch., 1976-87, deacon, 1979-88, elder, 1988—; pres. Christian Women's Fellowship, 1994-97; mem. adult adv. bd. NCK Assembly, Internat. Order of Rainbow for Girls, 1983-94. Mem. Order Eastern Star, Sigma Theta Tau, Kappa Gamma Pi, Delta Epsilon Sigma.

STODDARD, ALEXANDRA, designer, writer, lecturer; b. Weston, Mass., Nov. 8, 1941; d. Robert Powell and Barbara Rutledge (Green) Johns; m. Brandon Stoddard (div.); children: Alexandra Brandon, Brooke Goodwin; m. Peter Megargee Brown, May 18, 1974. Diploma in design, N.Y. Sch. Interior Design, 1961. Designer McMillen, Inc., N.Y.C., 1963-77; pres., CEO Alexandra Stoddard Inc., N.Y.C., 1977—; founder, pres. Design & Art Soc., Ltd., N.Y., 1987—; bd. dirs. Fieldcrest Cannon, Inc. Author: Style for Living, A Child's Place: How to Create a Living Environment for Your Child From Birth to Adolescence, Reflections on Beauty: Lectures and Notes on Interior Design, The Postcard as Art: Bring the Museum Home (Cert. of Merit award 1986), Living a Beautiful Life: 500 Ways to Add Elegance, Order, Beauty and Joy To Every Day of Your Life, Alexandra Stoddard's Living Beautifully Together, Alexandra Stoddard's Book of Color, Gift of a Letter, Daring to be Yourself, Creating a Beautiful Home, Grace Notes, Making Choices, Alexandra Stoddard's Tea Celebrations, The Art of the Possible, Mothers: A Celebration, Gracious Living in a New World, The Decoration of Houses; contbg. editor Country Antiques and Collectibles, Decorating with Americana; contbr. articles to profl mags. and jours. Founding mem., chmn. spiritual direction com. Ch. of Heavenly Rest, 1975-77; mem. bd. regents Cathedral St. John the Divine; designated dame Am. Soc. of Order of St. John Hosp. of Jerusalem. Recipient The Burlington prize, 1975, award for design Greenwich Arts Coun., 1985, Interior Design award Brandeis U., 1986, certificate special merit Graphic Art Inst. Mem. English Speaking Union, Ch. Club, Decorators Club, Colony Club, New Eng. Soc. Republican. Episcopalian. Home: 1125 Park Ave New York NY 10128-1243 Office: Alexandra Stoddard Inc 1125 Park Ave # 6A New York NY 10128-1243

STODDARD, EDWARD JOHN, retired school superintendent; b. Monticello, N.Y., Aug. 16, 1937; s. John Harold and Anne (Driscoll) S.; m. Norma Schenke, Aug. 19, 1961; children: Paul, David, Pamela, Debra, Daniel. BS, SUNY, New Paltz, 1959, MS, 1962; profl. degree, NYU/New Paltz, 1970. Cert. social studies tchr. grades 7-12, pub. sch. adminstr., supr. N.Y. State Dept. of Edn. Social studies tchr. Monroe Woodbury Ctrl. Sch. Dist., Central Valley, N.Y., 1959-70; asst. prin. Monroe-Woodbury Jr. High Sch., Central Valley, 1970-73; supt. of schs. Chester (N.Y.) Union Free Schs., 1973-93, ret., 1993; bd. dirs. Rural Schs. Program, N.Y. state chmn. legis. com., vice-chmn.; mem. exec. coun. Orange County Interscholastic Athletic Coun., 1970-92; mem. exec. bd. and adv. coun. Mid-Hudson Sch. Study Coun., 1985-93; pres. Lucky U. Corp., Chester, 1994. Copyright BACKFIRE, 1994, trademark, 1995. Town justice Town of Chester, 1969, chmn. Narcotics Guidance Coun., 1970-73, pres. Walton Engine and Hose Co., 1986-89, lt., 1994—, past mem. town bd., past chmn., mem. village planning bd.; mem. Orange County Vol. Firemen's Assn.; mem. 1996 Orange County Leadership Class. Recipient Disting. Svc. award N.Y. State Rural Schs. Program, 1992; named Fireman of Yr., Walton Engine and Hose Co., 1970, Walton of Yr., 1984. Mem. Chester C. of C., Kiwanis Club (charter, pres. 1992-93, Disting. Kiwanian 1994).

STODDARD, ELLWYN R., sociology and anthropology educator; b. Garland, Utah, Feb. 16, 1927; s. Roscoe and Mary Lloyd (Redford) S.; m. Judith Mae DeGrieselles, May 10, 1951 (div. 1964); children: Ellwyn R. Jr., Michael Valin, Dawn D.; m. Elaine Kirby, Aug. 28, 1964; children: Jared Evan, Sunday, Summer; stepchildren: Laura Jane Packham, George H. Packham, R. Kirby Packham. BS, Utah State U., 1952; MS, Brigham Young U., 1955; PhD, Mich. State U., 1961. Instr. sociology Drake U., Des Moines, 1959-61, asst. prof., 1962-63, assoc. prof., 1964-65; assoc. prof. Tex. Western Coll., El Paso, 1965-69; prof. sociology and anthropology U. Tex., El Paso, 1970—; field researcher, dir. rsch. cons. numerous projects, Mich., Iowa, Tex., Nigeria, 1955—. Author: Mexican Americans, 1973, Maquila, 1987; sr. co-author: Patterns of Poverty along U.S.-Mexico Border, 1987; sr. editor: Borderlands Sourcebook, 1983 (SW Book award 1984); contbr. chpts. to books and over 100 articles to profl. jours. Scoutmaster troop 158, Boy Scouts Am., El Paso, 1965-68, asst. commr. Yucca coun., 1968-71. With USCG, 1944-46, PTO; 2d lt. arty. U.S. Army, 1952-53. Recipient Diamond Jubilee Disting. Achievement award in rsch. U. Tex., El Paso, 1990; numerous rsch. grants including U. Tex., El Paso, U.S. Army, Econ. Devel. Adminstrn., 1967-86, Tex. Com. for Humanities, 1979, Hoover Instn.-Stanford U., 1984. Mem. Assn. Borderlands Scholars (founder, pres. 1976-79, Outstanding Scholarship and Svc. award 1987), Phi Kappa Phi (chpt. charter, pres. U. Tex. 1982-84). Mem. LDS Ch. Office: U Tex El Paso Dept Sociology El Paso TX 79968-0558

STODDARD, GEORGE EARL, investment company financial executive; b. Perry, Oreg., Jan. 7, 1917; s. G. Earl and Elthira (Thomas) S.; m. Elma Skelton, Feb. 4, 1942; children—Evan, Jean, Robert, Patricia. A.B., Brigham Young U., 1937; M.B.A., Harvard U., 1939; LL.B., Fordham U., 1954. Investment analyst Central Hanover Bank & Trust Co., N.Y.C., 1939-42; v.p. investment ops. Equitable Life Assurance Soc. U.S., N.Y.C., 1945-79; chmn. fin. com. W. P. Carey & Co., N.Y.C., 1979—; also dir. W. P. Carey & Co. Bd. dirs. United Fund of Bronxville-Eastchester, N.Y., 1960-61; pres. Home Sch. Assn., Eastchester, 1962. Served to lt. USNR, 1942-45. Clubs: Harvard (N.Y.C.), Harvard Bus. Sch. (N.Y.C.), Univ. (N.Y.C.). Home: 11 Cedar Pl Eastchester NY 10709-1703 Office: 50 Rockefeller Plz New York NY 10020-1605

STODDARD, LAURENCE RALPH, JR., retired advertising executive; b. Mt. Kisco, N.Y., Feb. 8, 1936; s. Laurence Ralph and Alice Cary (Martin) S. BA, Colgate U., 1958; postgrad., U. Calif., Berkeley, 1958. Audience research supr. NBC, N.Y.C., 1960-66; audience measurement chief Young & Rubicam, N.Y.C., 1966-69, v.p. supr.-group supr. media planning, 1969-78, v.p dir. communications service, 1978-81, sr. v.p. communication services, group supt. media planning, 1981-86; sr. v.p., dir. media research Advt. Research Found., N.Y.C., 1986-96; ret. Served with N.G., 1960. Mem. Advt. Rsch. Found.. (chmn. mag. rsch. devel. com., mem. mag. rsch. coun. and new electronic media rsch. workshop 1994, chmn. single source symposium com.), Am. Advt. Agy. Assn. (media rsch. coun.), Advt. Computer Users Assn. (media rsch. coun.), Advt. Computer Users Assn. (bd. dirs. 1988-93, market rsch. coun. 1993—). Democrat. Episcopalian. Home: 344 W 72nd St Apt 4-E New York NY 10023-2636

STODDARD, ROGER ELIOT, librarian; b. Boston, Dec. 2, 1935; s. Merton Edgar and Helen (Bonney) S.; m. Helen Louise Heckel, May 24, 1958; children—Alison Louise, Christopher Paine. A.B., Brown U., 1957. Asst. curator Harris Coll. Am. Poetry and Plays, Brown U., Providence, R.I., 1961-63, curator, 1963-65; asst. to librarian Harvard U. Houghton Library, Cambridge, Mass., 1965-61, curator, 1965-69, assoc. librarian, 1969-85; sr. curator, 1995—; curator rare books Harvard Coll. Library, Cambridge, Mass., 1985—; lectr. English Harvard U., Cambridge, Mass., 1984-86, sr. lectr., 1986—; sec. Friends of Harvard Coll. Library, Cambridge, Mass., 1983—; faculty mem. Columbia U. Rare Book Sch., N.Y.C., 1984-85. Author: Catalogue of Books & Pamphlets Unrecorded in Wegelin's Early Am. Poetry, 1969; The Houghton Library 1942-82, 1982; Poet & Printer in Colonial & Federal America, 1983; The Parkman Dexter Howe Library, part 1: Early New England Books, 1983, Marks in Books, Illustrated and Explained, 1985 (N.E. Book Show award, 1986, Am. Library Assn. award, 1987), Put a Resolute Hart to a Steep Hill: William Gowans Antiquary and Bookseller, 1990; editor A Glance at Private Libraries, 1991; contbr. articles to profl. jours. Mem. Records and Archives Com., Concord, Mass., 1985-87; bd. dirs. Louisa May Alcott Meml. Assn., Concord, 1983—. Huntington Library fellow, San Marino, Calif., 1978; W. F. Milton fellow Harvard U. Med. Sch., Boston, 1978-80; D.W. Bryant fellow Harvard U., 1992. Mem. Bibliog. Soc. Am. (coun. mem. 1982-88, Bibliography of Am. Lit. supervisory com. chmn. 1982-91, pres. 1996—), Am. Antiquarian Soc. (coun. mem. 1989-93), Assn. Internat. de Bibliophilie, Book Club Calif., Colonial Soc. Mass. (corr. sec. 1993—), The Johnsonians, Bibliog. Soc. London (hon. sec. for Am. 1992—), Bibliog. Soc. Va., Grolier Club (N.Y.C.), Harvard Club (N.Y.C.), Odd Vols. Boston Club (exec. com. 1985-87). Home: 9 Birchwood Ln Lincoln MA 01773-4907 Office: Harvard Univ Houghton Library Harvard Yard Cambridge MA 02138

STODDARD, STEPHEN DAVIDSON, ceramic engineer, former state senator; b. Everett, Wash., Feb. 8, 1925; s. Albert and Mary Louise (Billings) S.; m. Joann Elizabeth Burt, June 18, 1949 (dec. Oct. 1993); children: Dorcas Ann, Stephanie Kay; m. Barbara L. Seitz, Feb. 18, 1995. Student, Tacoma Coll., 1944, Conn. Coll., 1946; BS, U. Ill., 1950. Asst. prodn. supr., asst. ceramic engr. Coors Porcelain Co., Golden, Colo., 1950-52; ceramics-powder metallurgy sect. leader Los Alamos (N.Mex.) Sci. Lab., U. Calif., 1952-80; pres., treas. Materials Tech. Assocs., Inc., 1978-94; cons. Ceramic Age Mag., 1958-60, Cons. Nuclear Applications for Ceramic Materials, 1958-60; Jury commr. Los Alamos County, 1969; justice of peace, 1956-62; mem. Los Alamos Sch. Adv. Council, 1966; mcpl. judge, 1976-77; chmn. Los Alamos Ordinance Rev. Com., 1958; Mem. Republican County and State Central Com., 1955—; county commr. Los Alamos, N.Mex., 1966-68; mem. Los Alamos County Planning Commn., 1962-63, N.Mex. Senate, 1981-92; bd. dirs. Mountain Cmty. Bank of Los Alamos (formerly Bank of Los Alamos), 1985—, Los Alamos Econ. Devel. Corp. Patentee in field. Bd. dirs. Sangre de Cristo coun. Girl Scouts U.S.A., 1965-71, N.Mex. chpt. Nature Conservancy, 1987—, v.p., 1993-94; bd. dris. Southwestern Assn. on Indian Affairs, Inc., 1987-91; mem. Gov.'s Commn. in Nat. and Cmty. Svc., 1993-97. With AUS, 1943-46. Decorated Bronze Star, Purple Heart, Combat Infantry Badge; recipient disting. alumni award U. Ill. Coll. Engring., 1986, Leopold Conservation award N.Mex. Nature Conservancy, 1988. Fellow Am. Inst. Chemists, Am. Ceramic Soc. (treas. 1972-74, pres. 1976-77, disting. life 1984); mem. Nat. Inst. Ceramic Engrs. (PACE award 1965, Greaves Walker award 1984), Am. Soc. Metals, Los Alamos C. of C. (citizen of yr. award 1992), Masons, Shriners (pres. 1994-95), Elks (dist. dep. grand exalted ruler 1968-69), Los Alamos Golf Assn. (dir. 1964-66), Am. Legion (nat. legis. coun. 1992-94), Sigma Xi, Alpha Tau Omega. Episcopalian. Home: 4557 Trinity Dr Los Alamos NM 87544-3528

STODDARD, WILLIAM BERT, JR., economist; b. Carbondale, Pa., Oct. 6, 1926; s. William Bert and Emily (Trautwein) S.; student Lafayette Coll., 1944-45; BS, NYU, 1950, AM, 1952; m. Carol Marie Swartz, Feb. 28, 1970; 1 child, Emily Coleman. Asst. chief acct., budget dir. Hendrick Mfg. Co., Carbondale, Pa., 1952-54, asst. dir. prodn., 1956-68, also dir.; credit corr. U.S. Gypsum Co., N.Y.C., 1954-56; investment counselor, Carbondale, 1968-73, Ridgefield, Conn., 1973—; dir. First Nat. Bank Carbondale, 1968-73; bd. dirs. Lackawanna County Mfrs. Assn., Scranton, Pa., 1960-73. Treas., trustee Aldrich Mus. Contemporary Art, Ridgefield, 1976-90; bd. dirs. Ridgefield Library and Hist. Assn., 1977-85, 87-93; trustee Ridgefield Libr. Endowment Fund Trust, 1985—. Served with U.S. Army 1946-47. Mem. Inst. Mgmt. Accts., Am. Def. Preparedness Assn., Phi Alpha Kappa, Phi Delta Theta. Republican. Methodist. Clubs: NYU (N.Y.C.), Waccabuc (N.Y.) Country, Princeton Club (N.Y.C.). Home: 59 Bridle Trl Ridgefield CT 06877-1401 Office: 23 Catoonah St Ridgefield CT 06877-4431

STODGHILL, RONALD, school system administrator; b. White Plains, N.Y., Dec. 21, 1939; s. Joseph and Marian (Wynn) Stodghill; children: Kimberly, Denise, Ronald. BS, Ea. Mich. U., 1961; MS, We. Mich. U., 1967; EdD, Wayne State U., 1981. Dir. edn. New Detroit, Detroit; deputy supt. St. Louis Pub. Schs., Mo.; supt. Wellston Pub. Schs., Mo. Mem. ASCD (sec.), Am. Assn. Advancement of Sci., Nat. Assn. Bilingual Edn. Home: 6574 Saint Louis Ave Saint Louis MO 63121-5725 Office: Wellston SD 6574 Saint Louis Ave Saint Louis MO 63121-5725

STOEBUCK, WILLIAM BREES, law educator; b. Wichita, Kans., Mar. 18, 1929; s. William Douglas and Donice Beth (Brees) S.; m. Mary Virginia Fields, Dec. 24, 1951; children: Elizabeth, Catherine, Caroline. B.A., Wichita State U., 1951; M.A., Ind. U., 1953; J.D., U. Wash., 1959; S.J.D., Harvard U., 1973. Bar: Wash. 1959, U.S. Supreme Ct. 1967. Pvt. practice, Seattle, 1959-64; asst. prof. law U. Denver, 1964-67; assoc. prof. U. Wash., Seattle, 1967-70, prof., 1970-95; Judson Falknor prof., 1995—; of counsel Karr, Tuttle, Campbell, Seattle, 1988—. Author: Washington Real Estate: Property Law, 1995, Washington Real Estate: Transactions, 1995, Basic Property Law, 1989, Law of Property, 1984, 2nd edit., 1993, Nontrespassory Takings, 1977, Contemporary Property, 1996; contbr. articles to legal jours. Bd. dirs. Cascade Symphony Orch., 1978-83, Forest Park Libr., 1975-80. Mem. Am. Coll. Real Estate Lawyers, Am. Coll. Mortgage Attys., Wash. State Bar Assn., Assn. Am. Law Schs., Order of Coif, Seattle Yacht Club. 1st lt. USAF, 1951-56. Home: 3515 NE 158th Pl Lk Forest Park WA 98155-6649 Office: U Wash Law Sch 1100 NE Campus Pkwy Seattle WA 98105-6605

STOECKER, DAVID THOMAS, banker; b. St. Louis, June 8, 1939; s. John Garth and Marie (Zahler) S.; m. Ann E. Conrad, Aug. 18, 1962; children—Lisa Ann, Susan Jane. B.S., Ind. U., 1963. Sr. v.p. comml. loans Mercantile Trust Co. N.Am., St. Louis, 1965-80; pres. Gravois-Merc. Bank, St. Louis, 1980-87; pres., chief exec. officer Bank of South County, St. Louis, 1987-95; chmn. bd., pres., CEO Ctrl. West End Bank, St. Louis, 1996—. Served to 1st lt. AUS, 1963-65. Mem. Robert Morris Assos. (pres. St. Louis 1980). Methodist. Club: Sunset Country. Office: 9100 Gravois Rd Saint Louis MO 63123-4524

STOERMER, EUGENE FILMORE, biologist, educator; b. Webb, Iowa, Mar. 7, 1934; s. Edward Filmore and Agnes Elizabeth (Ekstrand) S.; m. Barbara Purves Ryder, Aug. 13, 1960; children: Eric Filmore, Karla Jean, Peter Emil. BS, Iowa State U., 1959, PhD, 1963. Assoc. rsch. scientist, rsch. scientist U. Mich., Ann Arbor, 1965-79, assoc. prof., 1979-85, prof., 1985—; editl. advisor Jour. Paleolimonology. Contbr. over 190 articles to profl. jours. Fellow Acad. Natural Scis., Phila., 1980; recipient Darbaker prize, Bot. Soc. Am., 1993. Mem. Phycological Soc. Am. (pres. 1988-89), Internat. Assn. for Diatom Rsch. (pres. 1992-94). Home: 4392 Dexter Ave Ann Arbor MI 48103-1636 Office: U Mich Ctr for Great Lakes Ann Arbor MI 48109

STOFFLE, CARLA JOY, university library dean; b. Pueblo, Colo., June 19, 1943; d. Samuel Bernard and Virginia Irene (Berry) Hayden; m. Richard William Stoffle, June 12, 1964; children: Brent William, Kami Ann. AA, So. Colo. State Coll., Pueblo, 1963; BA, U. Colo., 1965; MLS, U. Ky., 1969; postgrad., U. Wis., 1980. Head govt. publ. dept. John G. Crabbe Library, Eastern Ky. U., Richmond, 1969-72; head. pub. services U. Wis.-Parkside Library, Kenosha, 1972-76, exec. asst. to chancellor, 1978, asst. chancellor edn. services, 1979-85; assoc. dir. U. Mich. Library, Ann Arbor, 1985-91, dep. dir., 1986-91; mem. adv. commn. Sch. Library Sci. U. Mich., Ann Arbor, 1986-92; dean librs. U. Ariz., Tucson, 1991—; vol. Peace Corps, Barbados, W.I., 1965-67; with Bowker Libr. adv. Bd., N.Y., 1985-90; UA Press Bd. of Advisors, 1995—; OCLC Rsch. Librs. Adv. Coun., 1995—. Co-author: Administration Government Documents Collection, 1974, Materials and Method for History Research, 1979, Materials and Methods for Political Science Research, 1979; assoc. editor Collection Building, 1986-91, editorial bd., 1986-95; mem. editorial bd. The Bottom Line, 1989-95; contbr. numerous articles to profl. jours. Recipient Most Outstanding Reference Quar. Article award Reference Svc. Press, 1986, Woman on the Move award Tucson Young Women's Christian Assn., 1992, Pres.'s award Ariz. Ednl. Media Assn., 1993, Student Honor Soc. Mortar Bd. award for Faculty Excellence, 1995; named Outstanding Alumnus, Coll. Libr. and Info. Sci., U. Ky., 1989. Mem. ALA (treas. 1988-92, exec. bd. dirs. 1985-92, councilor 1983-92), Assn. Coll. Rsch. Librs. (pres. 1982-83, Bibliographic Instrn. Libr. of Yr. 1991, Acad. Rsch. Libr. of Yr. 1992). Office: U Arizona Main Libr 1510 E University Tucson AZ 85721

STOHLMAN, CONNIE SUZANNE, obstetrical gynecological nurse; b. Tucson, Sept. 27, 1960; d. Irvin Wendell and Betty Jo (Stewart) Holmes; m. Bruce R. Stohlman, Sept. 14, 1991. BSN, Bishop Clarkson Coll. Nursing, 1987; BA, U. Nebr., 1982; cert. med. asst., Omaha Coll. Health Careers, 1983. Primary nurse I U. Md. Med. System, Balt., 1987-90; staff nurse St. Joseph Hosp., Omaha, 1990—; mem. quality assurance task force U. Md. Med. System, 1987-90; mem. quality assurance com. St. Joseph Hosp., 1992-96. Named to Outstanding Young Women of Am., 1986.

STOHR, DONALD J., federal judge; b. Sedalia, Mo., Mar. 9, 1934; s. Julius Leo and Margaret Elizabeth (McGaw) S.; m. Mary Ann Kuhlman, July 31,

1957 children: Elizabeth M., Anne M., Jane C., Sara M., Ellen R. BS, St. Louis U., 1956, JD, 1958. Bar: Mo. 1958, U.S. Dist. Ct. (ea. dist.) Mo. 1958, U.S. Ct. Appeals (8th cir.) 1966, U.S. Supreme Ct. 1969. Assoc. Hocker Goodwin & MacGreevy, St. Louis, 1958-63, 66-69; asst. counselor St. Louis County, 1963-65, counselor, 1965-66; U.S. atty. Ea. Dist. Mo., St. Louis, 1973-76; ptnr. Thompson & Mitchell, St. Louis, 1969-73, 76-92; judge U.S. Dist. Ct. (ea. dist.) Mo., St. Louis, 1992—. Mem. ABA, Mo. Bar Assn., Am. Judicature Soc., St. Louis Met. Bar Assn. Office: US Court & Custom House 1114 Market St Rm 813 Saint Louis MO 63101-2034

STOIBER, CARLTON RAY, government agency official; b. Vallejo, Calif., July 5, 1942; s. Raymond F. and Grace (Fairhurst) S.; m. Susanne Alexander, Sept. 10, 1966. BA summa cum laude, U. Colo., 1964, LLB, 1969; diploma cum laude, Hague Acad. Internat. Law, 1975. Bar: Colo.1969, D.C.1970, U.S. Supreme Ct. 1973. Atty. U.S. Dept. Justice, Washington, 1969-71, dir. Office of Indian Rights, 1972-74; asst. gen. counsel U.S. NRC, Washington, 1975-80, U.S. Arms Control and Disarmament Agy., Washington, 1980-81; dir. Office Nuclear Export Control U.S. Dept. State, Washington, 1981-85, dir. Office Nuclear Non-Proliferation Policy, 1988-91, dir. Office Nuclear Tech. and Safeguards, 1991-93; counselor U.S. Mission to UN Agys., Vienna, Austria, 1985-88; dir. Internat. Programs Internat. Programs USNRC, 1993—. Rhodes scholar, 1964, Norlin award for disting. achievement U. Colo., 1994. Mem. Reform Club, Am. Soc. Internat. Law, Phi Beta Kappa. Avocations: cartooning and caricaturing, mountaineering, birding. Office: US NRC 11555 Rockville Pike Rockville MD 20852-2738

STOICHEFF, BORIS PETER, physicist, educator; b. Bitol, Macedonia, June 1, 1924; s. Peter and Vasilka (Tonna) S.; m. Lillian Joan Ambridge, May 15, 1954; 1 child, Richard Peter. BSc, U. Toronto, 1947, MA, 1948, PhD, 1950, DSc (hon.), 1994; DSc (hon.), U. Skopje, Macedonia, 1981, York U., 1982, U. Windsor, 1989. McKee-Gilchrist postdoctoral fellow U. Toronto, Ont., Can., 1950-51; postdoctoral fellow NRC Can., 1951-53, sr. rsch. officer, 1954-64; vis. scientist MIT, 1963-64; prof. physics U. Toronto, 1964-89, prof., 1977-89, prof. emeritus, 1989—, chmn. engring. sci., 1972-77, H.L. Welsh lectr., 1984; sr. fellow Massey Coll., 1979—; exec. dir. Ont. Laser and Lightwave Rsch. Ctr., 1988-91; mem. NRC Can., 1977-83; govt. appointee to coun. Assn. Profl. Engrs. Ont., 1985-91; vis. sci. Stanford U., 1978; Walter E. Kaskan lectr. SUNY, Binghamton, 1980; Elizabeth Laird Meml. lectr. U. Western Ont., 1985; U.K./Can. Rutherford lectr., 1989; v.p. Internat. Union Pure and Applied Physics, 1994-96. Contbr. numerous articles to tech. jours. Decorated officer Order of Can., 1982; I.W. Killam scholar, 1977-79; Geoffrey Frew fellow Australian Acad. Sci., 1980. Fellow Royal Soc. Can. (co-fgn. sec. 1995—, Henry Marshall Tory medal 1989), Royal Soc. London, Am. Phys. Soc., Optical Soc. Am. (pres. 1976, William F. Meggers award 1981, Frederic Ives medal 1983), Indian Acad. Sci. (hon.), Macedonian Acad. Sci. and Arts (hon.), Am. Acad. Arts and Scis. (fgn. hon.); mem. Can. Assn. Physicists (pres. 1984, Gold medal for achievement in physics 1974). Achievements include development of techniques for high resolution Raman spectroscopy of gases and determination of geometrical structures many molecules; use of lasers in spectroscopic investigations including Brillouin and Raman scattering and two photon absorption; observation of stimulated Raman absorption and stimulated Brillouin scattering resulting in generation of intense hypersonic waves in solids; use of Brillouin spectra to measure elastic constants of rare gas crystals; generation of tunable coherent VUV radiation for use in atomic and molecular spectroscopy. Home: 66 Collier St Apt 6B, Toronto, ON Canada M4W 1L9 Office: U Toronto, Dept Physics, Toronto, ON Canada M5S 1A7

STOJANOWSKI, WIKTOR J., mechanical engineer; b. Filipow, Poland, June 3, 1936; arrived in Canada, 1986; s. Stanislaw and Bronislawa (Mentel) S.; m. Danuta A. Wrona, Oct. 19, 1958; children: Dorota, Anna, Robert. MS, Acad. Mining and Metallurgy, 1958, PhD in Mech. Engring., 1973. Chief engr. design Food Industry Equipment Plant, Cracow, Poland, 1958-63; sr. design engr. Chemistry Machine and Process Design, Cracow, 1963-65; tutor Acad. Mining and Metallurgy, Cracow, 1965-80, asst. prof., 1981-87; vis. lectr. U. Wis., Madison, 1980-81; project engr. Vibron Ltd., Mississauga, Ontario, Canada, 1988-90; assoc. J.E. Coulter Assocs. Engring., Willowdale, Ontario, 1991—; noise control expert Assn. Polish Mechanics Engring., Cracow, 1973-87. Co-author: Lecture of AMM #454, 1974; contbr. articles to Jour. Mech. Engring., Inter-Noise. Achievements include patent for noise eliminator of gas stream flow into atmosphere, valve for gas expansion. Home: 1 Markburn Ct, Etobicoke, ON Canada M9C 4Y6

STOKEN, JACQUELINE MARIE, physician; b. Beaver Falls, Pa., Sept. 29, 1948; d. Jack Marc and Lillian Marie Stoken; m. John F. Edge, June 2, 1990; children: Randi Elizabeth; stepchildren: Lisa Adrienne, Alexander Joseph. Nursing diploma, Presbyn.-U. Hosp. Sch. Nursing, Pitts., 1970; BS in Biology with honors, Chatham Coll., Pitts., 1986; DO, U. Osteo. Med. & Health Scis., Des Moines, 1990. RN, Pa., Iowa; cert. ACLS, BCLS. Home care staff nurse South Hills Health System, Pitts., 1976-89; intern internal medicine Des Moines Gen. Hosp., 1990-91; resident physician dept. phys. medicine and rehab. U. Minn., Mpls., 1991-94; lectr. Internat. Rehab. Med. Assn., Des Moines, 1994—; physiatrist Iowa Orthopaedic Ctr., Des Moines, 1994—; guest lectr. dept. phys. therapy U. Minn., Mpls., 1991-94, dept. occupational therapy, 1991-94, U. Osteo. Medicine and Health Sci., Des Moines, 1990-97, IOFP, 1996—; chief resident dept. phys. medicine and rehab. U. Minn., Mpls., 1992-93; mem. Iowa Gov.'s Task Force on Rural Health, 1989. Mem. AMA, Am. Acad. Phys. Medicine and Rehab., Am. Osteo. Assn. (sec. coun. student coun. pres. 1988-89), Iowa Osteo Med. Assn. (student del. ho. of dels. 1987-88, student coun. rep. 1987-88), Am. Med. Women's Assn., Am. Holistic Med. Assn., Am. Acad. Osteopathy, Cranial Acad., Sigma Sigma Phi. Avocations: knitting, yoga, water skiing, cross-country skiing, biking.

STOKER, HOWARD W., former education educator, educational administrator, consultant; b. Highland Park, Ill., July 20, 1925; s. Howard W. and Elsie S.; m. M. Annette Stoker, July 9, 1949; children: Joanne, Dianna, Patricia, Robert. EdB, Wis. State U., Whitewater, 1949; MA, State U. Iowa, 1950; PhD, Purdue U., 1957. H.S. tchr. Dixon (Ill.) Pub. Schs., 1950-55; prof. Fla. State U., Tallahassee, 1957-84; head instrnl. devel. and evaluation U. Tenn., Memphis, 1984-88; vis. prof. U. Tenn., Knoxville, 1988-89, rsch. prof. Coll. Edn., 1989-92; ednl. cons. H.W. Stoker, Inc., Knoxville, 1992—; sr. assoc. prof. Ednl. Testing Svc./So. Regional Office, Atlanta, 1979-80; test devel. cons. State of Tenn., 1989—; cons. in field. Editor Fla. Jour. Ednl. Rsch., 1974-83; contbr. chpts. to books and articles to profl. jours. With USN, 1944-46. Mem. Am. Edn. Rsch. Assn., Nat. Coun. on Measurement in Edn. (bd. mem.). Avocations: crafts, carving, swimming.

STOKER, WARREN CADY, university president; b. Union Springs, N.Y., Jan. 30, 1912; s. Ray W. and Dora Maude (Cady) S.; m. Ruth Eleanor Gabb, Aug. 30, 1934; children: Robert Warren, W. Lance, Lois Ruth. E.E., Rensselaer Poly. Inst., 1933, M.E.E., 1934, Ph.D., 1938; D Humanities, Hartford U., 1994. Instr. to asso. prof. elec. engring. Rensselaer Poly. Inst., 1934-51, prof., 1951—, head computer lab., 1952-55; dir. Hartford Grad. Center, 1955-57; dean Hartford Grad. Center (Grad. Center), 1957-70; asso. dean Rensselaer Poly. Inst. Grad Sch., 1957-69; v.p. Rensselaer Poly. Inst. Conn., 1961-74, pres., 1974-75, also trustee; pres. Hartford Grad. Center (formerly Rensselaer Poly. Inst. Conn.), 1975-76, pres. emeritus, 1976—, trustee, 1975—; trustee Mechanics Savs. Bank, Hartford, 1969-82, incorporator, 1969—. Fellow IEEE; mem. Sci. Rsch. Soc. Am., Newcomen Soc. N.Am., Am. Soc. Engring. Edn., Conn. Acad. Sci. and Engring., Sigma Xi, Tau Beta Pi, Eta Kappa Nu. Club: Hartford (Conn.). Home: 188 Main St # C Manchester CT 06040-3576 Office: 275 Windsor St Hartford CT 06120-2910

STOKES, ALLISON, pastor, researcher, religion educator; b. Bridgeport, Conn., Aug. 17, 1942; d. Hugh Vincent and Mildred Roberta (Livengood) Allison; m. Jerome Walter Stokes, June 1, 1964 (div. 1977); children: Jonathan Jerome, Anne Jennings. BA, U. N.C., 1964; MPhil, Yale U., 1976, PhD, 1981, MDiv, 1981; ThM, Harvard U., 1997. Ordained to ministry United Ch. of Christ, 1981. Acting univ. min. Wesleyan U., Middletown, Conn., 1981; assoc. pastor Orange Congl. Ch., Conn., 1981-82; chaplain, asst. prof. religion Vassar Coll., Poughkeepsie, N.Y., 1982-85; assoc. univ. chaplain Yale U., New Haven, 1985-87; pastor Congl. Ch., West Stockbridge, Mass., 1987—; rsch. assoc. Hartford (Conn.) Sem., 1987-92; founding dir. Women's Interfaith Inst. in the Berkshires, 1992—; bd. dirs. Dutchess Interfaith Coun., Poughkeepsie, 1984-85; clk., bd. dirs. Gould Farm, Monterey, Mass., 1992—. Author: Ministry after Freud, 1985, Finding Time, Finding Energy, 1996; co-author: Defecting in Place, 1994, Women Pastors, 1995; contbr. articles to profl. jours. Kanzer Fund Psychoanalysis and Humanities grantee, 1977; AAUW fellow, 1978, Merrill fellow Harvard Div. Sch., 1994. Mem. Am. Acad. Religion, Berkshire Conf. Women Historians, Kiwanis. Home: PO Box 422 Housatonic MA 01236-0422 Office: Conregational Church 45 Main St West Stockbridge MA 01266

STOKES, ARNOLD PAUL, mathematics educator; b. Bismarck, N.D., Jan. 24, 1932; s. Joel Edward and Elizabeth (Bauer) S.; m. Gaye Teresa Wims, Oct. 19, 1957; children: Michael, Jonathan, Thomas, Katherine, Christopher, Peter. Student, St. Martin's Coll., 1949-53; BS (RCA scholar), U. Notre Dame, 1955, PhD, 1959. Mathematician Research Inst. Advanced Study, Balt., 1958-60; NSF post-doctoral fellow Johns Hopkins U., 1960-61; asst. prof. Cath. U. Am., Washington, 1961-63; assoc. prof. Cath. U. Am., 1963-64; prof. Georgetown U., Washington, 1965-97, chmn. math. dept., 1967-70; Cons. NASA, Goddard Space Flight Center, Greenbelt, Md., 1962-67, NRC sr. research assoc., 1974-75; sr. mathematician Ocean Sci. divsn. Sci. Applications, Inc., McLean, Va., 1979—. Trustee Consortium D.C. Univs., 1970-75. Achievements include research on ordinary, functional differential equations, scattering theory, acoustic tomography. Home: 9916 Derbyshire Ln Bethesda MD 20817-1535 Office: Georgetown U Math Dept Washington DC 20057

STOKES, B. R., retired transportation consultant; b. Anadarko, Okla., Feb. 20, 1924; s. Robert Allan and Ethel Nan (James) S.; m. Joan Pringle, Oct. 22, 1950; children: Timothy, Leigh, Lindsey, Celia. Student, U. Okla., 1941-44; B.A., U. Calif., Berkeley, 1947. Reporter, writer Oakland (Calif.) Tribune, 1946-58; dir. info. San Francisco Bay Area Rapid Transit Dist., 1958-61, asst. gen. mgr., 1961-63, gen. mgr., 1963-74; exec. v.p. Am. Public Transit Assn., Washington, 1974-80; sr. v.p. internat. ATE Mgmt. and Service Co., Inc., 1980-95; dir. gen. Saudi Arabian Public Transport Co., 1980-81. Served with USNR, 1942-46. Recipient Salzberg medal Syracuse U., 1975; inductee Am. Pub. Transit Assn. Transit Hall of Fame, 1996; Reid Found. fellow, 1954. Office: 1911 Fort Myer Dr Arlington VA 22209-1601

STOKES, CHARLES JUNIUS, economist, educator; b. Washington, Aug. 17, 1922; s. Francis Warner and Vivienne E. (Cooke) S.; m. Anne Richardson Wood, June 13, 1946; children—Kevin Barrett, Keith Warner. A.B. with honor and distinction, Boston U., 1943, A.M., 1947, Ph.D., 1950. Mem. faculty Atlantic Union Coll., South Lancaster, Mass., 1946-60, dean coll., 1954-56; Charles A. Dana prof. econs. U. Bridgeport, Conn., 1960-94, univ. prof., 1990-94; chmn. dept. U. Bridgeport, 1960-72; prof. econs. Andrews U., Berrien Springs, Mich., 1990-94; prof. Orientador Inst. Superior de Econ. e Gestão Univ. Tecnica Lisbon, Portugal, 1992—; dir. econ. rsch., region I OPS, 1951-53; dir. Latin Am. case studies transp. Brookings Instn., 1963-64; Fulbright prof., Ecuador, 1958-59, Argentina, 1960, Peru, 1964; lectr. Inter-Am. Def. Coll., 1977-78; Staley Disting. lectr. Andrews U., 1983, founder, dir. Chan Shun Ctr. for Bus. Rsch., 1991-94; E.A. Johnson Disting. lectr., 1989; vis. prof., lectr. U. Colo., U. Conn., Clark U., Andrews U., U.S. Naval Postgrad. Sch., Yale U., Columbia U., So. Conn. State U., Atlantic Union Coll., U. Fed. de Rio Grande, 1988, U. Poona Linda, 1991, Australian Nat. U., 1992, U. Cambridge, 1991, and numerous other overseas univs.; founder, dir. Conn. Small Bus. Devel. Ctr., U. Bridgeport, 1985-90; chmn., dir. Monroe Bank & Trust Co.; cons. to industry, founds. Author: Crecimiento Economico (Economic Growth), 1964, Transportation and Economic Development in Latin America, 1968, Managerial Economics: A Case Book, 1968, Managerial Economics: A Textbook, 1969, Historic Fairfield County Churches, 1969, Urban Housing Market Performance, 1975, Economics for Managers, 1978; editor: THRUST, 1978-89; columnist Christian Sci. Monitor, Internat. Bus., 1987-92; also articles to profl. jours., columns in regional newspapers. Chmn. Lancaster (Mass.) Housing Authority, 1957-61; chmn. econ. com. Greater Bridgeport Regional Planning Agy., 1961-72; asst. dir. U.S. GAO, 1972-73; mem. Instn. for Social and Policy Studies, Yale U., 1977-85; trustee Pioneer Valley Acad., 1966-69, Andrews U., 1967-72, Atlantic Union Coll., 1968-73, Conn. Grand Opera Assn., 1980-86; mem. Conn. com. Regional Plan Assn., 1977-91; bd. dirs. Greater Bridgeport Symphony Soc., 1994, Adventist Living Ctrs., Inc., Adventist Health Sys./North, 1980-85, New Eng. Trade Adjustment Assistance Ctr., Inc.; chmn. bd. dirs., CEO Geer Meml. Hosp., 1983-89; assoc. Kellogg Ctr., U. Notre Dame, 1990-94. With AUS, 1943-46. Decorated Medal of Honor Argentina; named to College of Disting. Alumni Boston U. Coll. Liberal Arts, 1974; Sears Found. Fed. faculty fellow, 1972-73. Fellow Nat. Ctr. for Devel. Studies (Australia), New Eng. Bd. High Edn.; mem. Nat. Economists Club, Am. Econ. Assn. (pres. Conn. Valley 1966), Nat. Assn. Bus. Economists (pres. Fairfield County chpt. 1980-81), Phi Beta Kappa, Phi Kappa Phi, Phi Beta Kappa Assos., Delta Sigma Rho, Beta Gamma Sigma. Home: 264 Pepper Crossing Stepney CT 06468-1218 Office: 14 Linden Ave Bridgeport CT 06604-5725 *Success is fleeting. If only the good remains from what I have done, even that is not mine but God's.*

STOKES, DONALD GRESHAM, vehicle company executive; b. London, Mar. 22, 1914; s. Harry Potts and Marie Elizabeth (Yates) S.; m. Laura Elizabeth Courteney Lamb, May 25, 1939 (dec. Apr. 1995); 1 child, Michael Donald. Grad. mech. engring., Harris Inst. Tech., Preston, Eng., 1933; LL.D., U. Lancaster, 1967; Ph.D. in Tech, U. Loughborough, 1968; D.Sci., U. Southampton, 1969, U. Salford, 1971. Student apprentice Leyland Motors Ltd., London, 1930; export mgr. Leyland Motors Ltd., 1946-49, gen. sales and service mgr., 1949-53, dir., 1963-67; mng. dir., dep. chmn. Brit. Leyland Motor Corp. Ltd., 1967, chmn., mng. dir., 1968-73, chmn., chief exec., 1973-75; pres. Brit. Leyland Ltd., 1975-79; chmn. Brit. Arabian Adv. Co. Ltd., 1977-85; pres. Jack Barclay Ltd., 1980-90; Dutton-Forshaw Motor Group Ltd., 1980-90; v.p. Empresa Nacional de Autocamiones S.A., Spain, 1965-73; chmn. Reliant Group, 1990-94, Two Counties Radio Ltd., 1990-94. Dep. lt. for County Palatine of Lancashire; v.p. Inst. Sci. and Tech., U. Manchester, 1968-72, pres., 1972-75. Lt. col. R.E.M.E., 1939-45. Created knight, 1965, baron (life peer), 1969; decorated Territorial Decoration; officier de l'ordre de la Couronne Belgium; comdr. de l'Ordre de Leopold II. Fellow Inst. Mech. Engrs. (coun., v.p. 1971, pres. 1972), Inst. Road Transport Engrs., Inst. Civil Engrs., Royal Acad. Engring.; mem. Nat. Econ. Devel. Com. (chmn. electronics com. 1966-68), Soc. Motor Mfrs. and Traders (coun., pres. 1961-62), Worshipful Company Carmen. Home: Branksome Cliff, Westminster Rd, Poole BH13 6JW, England

STOKES, GEORGE CLIVE, healthcare administrator; b. Newport, R.I., May 22, 1947; s. Archie William and Ruth Eleanor (Barclay) S.; m. Denise Louise, May 8, 1992; children: Shelley Anne, Erin Ashley, Seth Wheeling. BA in Sociology, Wilberforce (Ohio) U., 1969; MSW, Boston Coll., 1972; exec. MBA program, Stanford U., 1993. Exec. dir. Bklyn. Plaza Med. Ctr., 1984-88; med. office adminstr. Kaiser Permanente, Farmington, Conn., 1988-91, Raleigh, N.C., 1991-92; area adminstr. Kaiser Permanente, Charlotte, N.C., 1992-95, Raleigh, 1995-96; triangle market adminstr. Kaiser Permanente, Raleigh, Durham, Chapel Hill, 1996-97; v.p., exec. dir. Kaiser Permanente triange market, Raleigh, Durham, Chapel Hill, 1997—. bd. dirs. Boy Scouts Am., Charlotte, 1993-95; mem. adv. bd. Teenage Parent Program Charlotte Mecklenburg Bd. Edn., Charlotte, 1994-95. Mem. Nat. Forum Black Adminstrs. Avocations: reading, jogging, tennis. Office: Kaiser Found Health Plan 3120 Highwoods Blvd Raleigh NC 27604-1038

STOKES, HENRY ARTHUR, journalist; b. Jacksonville, Fla., Dec. 9, 1944; s. Henry Jasper and Waneta Marian (Lord) S.; m. Carolyn Elizabeth Morley, Aug. 6, 1966; children: Elizabeth, Virginia, Katherine. AA, St. Johns River Jr. Coll., Palatka, Fla., 1966; BS in Journalism with high honors, U. Fla., 1969. Reporter Daytona Beach (Fla.) News-Jour., 1966, Palatka (Fla.) Daily News, 1966-69; reporter Fla. Times-Union, Jacksonville, 1969-71, night city editor, 1972; various editing positions Detroit News, 1972-88; asst. mng. editor Comml. Appeal, Memphis, 1988-92, mng. editor, 1992—. Mem. Memphis Literacy Coun., 1989—, chmn., 1993, 94; bd. dirs. Friends Memphis/Shelby Co. Libr., 1991—; mem. pres.' adv. coun. LeMoyne-Owen Coll., 1992—. Recipient Emig award Coll. Journalism U. Fla., 1970. Mem. AP Mng. Editors Assn., Soc. Profl. Journalists, Investigative Reporters and Editors, The Egyptians, Rotary. Mem. Unitarian-Universalist Ch. Avocations: orinthology, fly fishing. Office: Comml Appeal 495 Union Ave Memphis TN 38103-3242

STOKES, JAMES CHRISTOPHER, lawyer; b. Orange, N.J., Mar. 19, 1944; s. James Christopher and Margaret Mary (Groome) S.; m. Eileen Marie Brosnan, Sept. 7, 1968; children: Erin Margaret, Michael Colin, Courtney Dorothy. AB, Holy Cross Coll., 1966; JD, Boston Coll., 1975. Bar: Hawaii 1975, U.S. Ct. Appeals (1st and 9th cirs.) 1976, Mass. 1977, U.S. Ct. Internat. Trade 1988. Officer USMC, 1966-72; assoc. Carlsmith, Carlsmith, Wichman & Case, Honolulu, 1975-76, Bingham, Dana & Gould, Boston, 1976-82; ptnr. Bingham, Dana & Gould, London, 1980-84, Boston, 1982—. Contbr. articles to profl. jours. Active personnel bd. Town of Wellesley, Mass., 1984-89, chmn. bd., 1988-89, town moderator, 1992—. Capt. USMC, 1966-72, Vietnam. Mem. Hawaii Bar Assn., Mass. Bar Assn., Internat. Bar Assn., Boston Bar Assn., Traveller's Club (London), Union Club (Boston), Wellesley Club, German-Am. Bus. Club (Boston) (bd. dirs.). Roman Catholic. Office: Bingham Dana & Gould 150 Federal St Boston MA 02110

STOKES, JAMES SEWELL, lawyer; b. Englewood, N.J., Jan. 24, 1944; s. James Sewell III and Doris Mackey (Smith) S.; m. Esther Moger, Aug. 19, 1967; children: Jessica Neale, Elizabeth Sewell. BA, Davidson (N.C.) Coll., 1966; LLB, Yale U., 1969. Bar: Ga. 1969. Asst. to gen. counsel Office Gen. Counsel of the Army, Washington, 1969-72; assoc. Alston, Miller & Gaines, Atlanta, 1972-77; ptnr. Alston & Bird (previously Alston, Miller & Gaines), Atlanta, 1977—, lead environ. lawyer, 1978—, chmn. environ. group, 1987-96, chmn. client svcs. com., 1983-85, chmn. hiring com., 1986-87, chmn. mktg. com., 1993-94; mem. ptnr.'s com. Alston & Bird, Atlanta, 1995—; devel. com. Alston & Bird (previously Alston, Miller & Gaines), Atlanta, 1996—; speaker on environ. matters to various seminars and meetings; mem. Gov.'s Environ. Adv. Coun., 1991—, vice-chmn., 1996-97. Contbr. articles to profl. jours. Co-chmn. Spotlight on Ga. Artists V, 1986; mem. City of Atlanta Zoning Rev. Bd., 1978-85, chmn., 1984-85; bd. dirs. Brookwood Hills Civic Assn., 1975-77, pres., 1977; bd. dirs. Nexus Contemporary Arts Ctr., Atlanta, 1987-92, vice chmn. capital campaign, 1989, chmn. nominating com., 1988, chmn. fundraising com., 1987-88; bd. dirs. Butler St. YMCA N.W. br., 1973-75, Dynamo Swim Club, 1988-91, Arts Festival Atlanta, 1994—; trustee Inst. Continuing Legal Edn., Athens, 1980-81, Trinity Sch., Atlanta, 1988, 97—, Charles Loridaus Found., 1994—; mem. session Trinity Presbyn. Ch., 1986-89, 97—, clk. of session, 1988-89, chmn. cmty. concerns com., 1987-88, chmn. pers. com., 1989-90, chmn. assoc. pastor search com., 1991-92; bd. dirs. Park Pride, 1992; chmn. environ. affairs com. Ga. C. of C., Bus. Coun. Ga., 1987-92, environ. legal counsel, 1981-87; mem. spl. program Leadership Atlanta, 1979-80, Leadership Ga., 1985; mem. Ga. bd. advisors Trust for Pub. Land, 1990-95. Capt. U.S. Army, 1969-72. Decorated D.S.M.; recipient Spl. award Atlanta chpt. AIA, 1988, Mayor Andrew Young, 1985. Mem. ABA (natural resources sect.), State Bar Ga. (chmn. environ. law sect. 1979-82), Atlanta Bar Assn., City of Atlanta Hist. Preservation (policy steeering com. 1989), Atlanta C. of C. (water resources task force 1982-87, solid waste task force 1989, air quality task force 1993—), Ga. Indsl. Developers Assn. (hazardous waste com. 1983-84), Phi Beta Kappa, Omicron Delta Kappa. Avocations: swimming, bird watching, community activities. Home: 129 Palisades Rd NE Atlanta GA 30309-1532 Office: Alston & Bird One Atlantic Ctr 1201 W Peachtree St NW Atlanta GA 30309-3424

STOKES, KATHLEEN SARAH, dermatologist; b. Springfield, Mass., Oct. 18, 1954; d. John Fracis and Margaret Cecelia (MacDonnell) S.; m. William Walter Greaves, Sept. 20, 1981; children: Ian R., Spencer W., Malcolm W. BS, U. Utah, 1978, MS, 1980; MD, Med. Coll. Wis., 1987. Diplomate Am. Bd. Dermatology. Intern in internal medicine Med. Coll. Wis., Milw., 1987-88, resident in dermatology, 1988-90, chief resident, 1990-91, asst. clin. prof. dermatology, 1991—; pvt. practice, Milw., 1991—. Contbr. articles to med. jours., including Critical Care Medicine, Jour. Pediatric Dermatology. Named A Top Physician, Milw. mag., 1996. Fellow Am. Acad. Dermatology, Milw. Acad. Medicine; mem. AMA, Wis. Dermatol. Soc., Women's Dermatologic Soc., Tempo, Alpha Omega Alpha. Office: Affiliated Dermatologists 2300 N Mayfair Rd Milwaukee WI 53226-1505

STOKES, LOUIS, congressman; b. Cleveland, Ohio, Feb. 23, 1925; s. Charles and Louise (Stone) S.; m. Jeanette Frances, Aug. 21, 1960; children: Shelley, Louis C., Angela, Lorene. Student, Case Western Res. U., 1946-48; JD, Cleve. Marshall Law Sch., 1953; LLD (hon.), Wilberforce U., 1969, Shaw U., Livingstone Coll., Morehouse Coll., Meharry Coll. Medicine. Bar: Ohio 1953. Mem. 91st-105th Congresses from 21st (now 11th) Ohio dist., Washington, D.C., 1969—; ranking minority mem. appropriations subcom. on Vets. Affairs, HUD & Ind. Agys.; guest lectr., 1960—. Mem. adv. council African-Am. Inst. Internat.; mem. exec. com. Cuyahoga County Democratic Party, Ohio State Dem. Party; bd. dirs. Karamu House; trustee Martin Luther King, Jr. Center for Social Change, Forest City Hosp., Cleve. State U. Served with AUS, 1943-46. Recipient numerous awards for civic activities including Distinguished Service award Cleve. br. NAACP; Certificate of Appreciation U.S. Commn. on Civil Rights. Fellow Ohio State Bar Assn.; mem. Am., Cuyahoga County, Cleve. bar assns., Nat. Assn. Def. Lawyers Criminal Cases Fair Housing (dir.), Urban League, Citizens League, John Harlan Law Club, ACLU, Am. Legion, Kappa Alpha Psi. Clubs: Masons (Cleve.), Plus (Cleve.). Office: US Ho of Reps 2365 Rayburn House Bldg Washington DC 20515*

STOKES, MACK (MARION) BOYD, bishop; b. Wonsan, Korea, Dec. 21, 1911; came to U.S., 1929; s. Marion Boyd and Florence Pauline (Davis) S.; m. Ada Rose Yow, June 19, 1942; children: Marion Boyd III, Arch Yow, Elsie Pauline. Student, Seoul Fgn. High Sch., Korea; A.B., Asbury Coll., 1932; B.D., Duke, 1935; postgrad., Boston U. Sch. Theol., 1935-37, Harvard, 1936-37; Ph.D., Boston U., 1940; LL.D., Lambuth U., Jackson, Tenn., 1963; D.D., Millsaps Coll., 1974. Resident fellow systematic theology Boston U., 1936-38, Bowne fellow in philosophy, 1938-39; ordained to ministry Meth. Ch., deacon, 1938, elder, 1940; vis. prof. philosophy and religion Ill. Wesleyan U., 1940-41; prof. Christian doctrine Candler Sch. Theology, Emory U., 1941-56, asso. dean, Parker prof. systematic theology, 1956-72, chmn. exec. com. div. of religion of grad. sch., 1956-72; acting dean Candler Sch. Theology, Emory U. (Candler Sch.), 1968-69; bishop-in-residence Peachtree Rd. United Meth. Ch. Atlanta, 1988—; faculty mem. Inst. Theol. Studies, Oxford U., 1958; Del. Meth. Ecumenical Conf., 1947, 52, 61, 71, Holston, Gen. confs., S.E. Jurisdictional Conf., 1956, 60, 64, 68, 72; chmn. com. ministry Gen. Conf. Meth. Ch., 1960; nat. com. Nature Unity We Seek, 1956—; mem. gen. com. ecumenical affairs theol. study com. United Meth. Ch., 1968-72, com. on Cath.-Meth. relations, 1969—, bishop, 1972—. Author: Major Methodist Beliefs, 1956, rev. 15th edit., 1990, also Chinese transl., The Evangelism of Jesus, 1960, The Epic of Revelation, 1961, Our Methodist Heritage, 1963, Crencas Fundamentals Dos Methodistas, 1964, Study Guide on the Teachings of Jesus, 1970, The Bible and Modern Doubt, 1970, Major United Methodist Beliefs, 1971, Korean transl., 1977, rev. 16th edit., 1990, The Holy Spirit and Christian Experience, 1975, Korean transl., 1985, Twelve Dialogues on John's Gospel, 1975; Jesus, The Master-Evangel, 1978, Can God See the Inside of an Apple?, 1979, Questions Asked by United Methodists, Philippine transl., 1980; The Bible in the Wesleyan Heritage, 1981, Respuestas A Preguntas Que Hacen Los Metodistas Unidos, 1983, The Holy Spirit in the Wesleyan Heritage, 1985, Spanish translation, 1992, Korean translation, 1992, Scriptural Holiness for the United Methodist Christian, 1988, Talking with God: A Guide to Prayer, 1989, Theology for Preaching, 1994. Trustee Emory U., Millsaps Coll., Rust Coll., Wood Jr. Coll. Home: Peachtree House # 306 2637 Peachtree Rd NE Atlanta GA 30305 *Faith in God and basic trust in people. Knowing the direction in which to go, and moving with divine assistance toward it with persistence, resourcefulness, imagination and patience.*

STOKES, PAUL MASON, lawyer; b. Miami Beach, Fla., July 16, 1946; s. Walter Johnson and Juanita (Hemperley) S.; m. Carol Crocker, Sept. 12, 1970; children: Macon Lanford, Walter Ashley, Mary Juanita. BA, Duke U., 1968; JD, U. Chgo., 1971. Bar: Fla. 1971. Law clerk to hon. Milton Pollack U.S. Dist. Ct. (so. dist.) N.Y., N.Y.C., 1971-72; assoc. Smathers and Thompson, Miami, Fla., 1972-77, ptnr., 1977-88; ptnr. Kelley Drye & Warren, Miami, 1988—; adj. prof. law U. Miami, Coral Gables, Fla., 1987-94; pub. defender Miami Springs, Fla., 1974, City of Hialeah, Fla., 1974-75. Mem. Code Enforcement Bd. Miami Springs, 1990-92; regent Trinity Internat. U., Deerfield, Ill., 1989—. Fellow Am. Coll. Trust and Estate Coun.; mem. Dade County Bar Assn. (probate and guardianship ct. com. 1988—, bd. dirs. 1989-92, 94—), Fla. Bar (cert. wills, trusts and estates), Phi Beta

Kappa, Order of Coif. Democrat. Presbyterian. Office: Kelley Drye & Warren 201 S Biscayne Blvd Miami FL 33131-4332

STOKES, ROBERT ALLAN, science research facility executive, physicist; b. Richmond, Ky., June 25, 1942; s. Thomas Allan Stokes and Callie Mae (Ratliff) Watson; m. Elizabeth Ann Efkeman, Nov. 25, 1963 (div. 1992); m. Amy Hawthorne Carney, 1993; 1 child, Robert Curtis. BS in Physics, U. Ky., 1964; MA in Physics, Princeton U., 1966, PhD, 1968; Exec. Program, U. Mich. Bus. Sch., 1991. Asst. prof. physics U. Ky., Lexington, 1968-72, assoc. prof., 1972-76; sr. scientist Battelle, Pacific N.W. Labs., Richland, Wash., 1972-74, mgr. space scis. sect., 1974-83, assoc. mgr. geophysics rsch. and engring. dept., 1983-86, mgr. engring. physics dept., 1986-87, mgr. Applied Physics Ctr., 1987-88; dep. dir. rsch. Solar Energy Rsch. Inst., Golden, Colo., 1988-90; dep. dir. NREL, Golden, Colo., 1990-95; v.p. Midwest Rsch. Inst., Kansas City, Mo., 1990-95; mem. adv. bd. Geophysics Inst., U. Alaska, Fairbanks; v.p. So. Rsch. Inst., 1997—. Contbr. articles to profl. jours. Woodrow Wilson fellow, Princeton U., 1964, NASA fellow, 1966-68. Mem. Am. Phys. Soc., Am. Astron. Soc., Am. Geophys. Union, AAAS, Am. Solar Energy Soc., Phi Beta Kappa. Home: 24967 Foothills Dr N Golden CO 80401-8558 Office: Southern Rsch Inst PO Box 55305 Birmingham AL 35255

STOKLOS, RANDY (STOKEY STOKLOS), volleyball player; b. Pacific Palisades, Calif., Dec. 13, 1960; m. Carrie Stoklos; 1 child, Shay Leigh. Student, UCLA. Profl. volleyball tour player, 1982—; mem. U.S.A. Nat. Team, 1979-80; pres. Audio Spkrs. of Am.; model, actor. Actor: Side Out, 1990, Better Off Dead, 1985; model mag. covers. Voted AVP Most Valuable Player 1988, 89, 91; named Italian, Brazilian and Australian tour Most Valuable Player, 1991. Mem. Assn. Volleyball Profls. Won Miller Lite Chgo. Open with Brian Lewis, 1993, Nestea Open with Adam Johnson, Manhattan Beach, 1994, San Francisco, 1994; placed 2d FIVB Beach Volleyball World Championships with Sinjin Smith; ranked 1st AVP Career Earnings list and 2d on Career Open Wins; registered 100th career open, 1991, 2d player to reach that mark; won World Championships during 1st yr. on tour, 1982. Office: Assn Volleyball Profls 8th Fl Ste 600 330 Washington Blvd Marina Del Rey CA 90292-5147*

STOKSTAD, MARILYN JANE, art history educator, curator; b. Lansing, Mich., Feb. 16, 1929; d. Olaf Lawrence and Edythe Marian (Gardiner) S. BA, Carleton Coll., 1950; MA, Mich. State U., 1953; PhD, U. Mich., 1957; postgrad., U. Oslo, 1951-52. Instr. U. Mich., Ann Arbor, 1956-58; mem. faculty U. Kans., Lawrence, 1958—; assoc. prof. U. Kans., 1961-66, prof., 1966-80, Univ. Disting. prof. art history, 1980-94, Judith Harris Murphy disting. prof. art, 1994—, dir. mus. art, 1961-67, research assoc., summers 1965-66, 67, 71, 72; assoc. dean Coll. Liberal Arts and Scis., U. Kans., 1972-76; research curator Nelson-Atkins Mus. Art, Kansas City, Mo., 1969-80, consultative curator medieval art, 1980—; bd. dirs. Internat. Ctr. Medieval Art, 1972-75, 81-84, 88-96, v.p., 1990-93, pres., 1993-96, sr. advisor, 1996-97; cons., evaluator North Ctrl. Assn. Colls. and Univs., 1972—, commr.-at-large, 1984-89. Author: Santiago de Compostela, 1978, The Scottish World, 1981, Medieval Art, 1986, Art History, 1995. Recipient Disting. Service award Alumni Assn. Carleton Coll., 1983; Fulbright fellow, 1951-52; NEH grantee, 1967-68. Fellow AAUW; mem. AAUP (nat. coun. 1972-75), Archeol. Inst. Am. (pres. Kans. chpt. 1960-61), Midwest Coll. Art Conf. (pres. 1964-65), Coll. Art Assn. (bd. dirs. 1970-80, pres. 1978-80), Soc. Archtl. Historians (chpt. bd. dirs. 1971-73).

STOKVIS, JACK RAPHAEL, urban planner, entrepreneur computer consultnt and developer, government agency administrator; b. Hartford, Conn., Dec. 10, 1944; s. John and Ivette (Korda) S.; m. Evelyn Noether, May 11, 1980. A.B., Union Coll., 1967; postgrad. in bus., Boston U., 1968; M.U.P., NYU, 1973; MPhil, Columbia U., 1995. Lic. planner, N.J. Project planner Jersey City Redevel. Agy., 1970-73; sr. planner City of Jersey City, 1973-75; prin. planner City of Paterson, (N.J.), 1975-76; spl. project mgr. Gt. Falls Hist. Dist., Dept. Community Devel. City of Paterson, N.J., 1976-80; dir. Dept. Planning and Grants, East Orange, N.J., 1980-81; gen. dep. asst. sec. community planning and devel. HUD, Washington, 1981-88, asst. sec. community planning and devel., 1988-89; pres. Stokvis Assocs., Inc., Haworth, N.J., 1989—; dir. Gt. Falls Devel. Corp., Paterson, 1975-80; project dir. Revitalization of Jersey City Italian Village, 1974-79; lectr. George Washington U., Washington; adj. prof. Rutgers U. New Brunswick, N.J., Columbia U., N.Y.C., 1991—; Rep. County Committeeman; trustee Handata Libr., Coun. Excellence in Govt.; dir. Downtown N.J. Urban Land Inst., Interactive Svcs. Assn.,dir., DowntownNew Jersey. Author numerous articles in field. Founder Friends of Paterson Parks; v.p. Jersey City Preservation and Restoration Assn. Recipient Outstanding Student of Yr. award Am. Inst. Planning, NYU; recipient Environ. Quality award U.S. Dept. Environ. Protection, N.Y.C., Outstanding Grant Recognition Program award Nat. Endowment Arts, Program Implementation award Am. Planning Assn., Princeton, N.J., Secretary's award, 1989. Mem. Am. Inst. Cert. Planners, Am. Planning Assn., Nat. Trust Hist. Preservation. Office: PO Box 93 Haworth NJ 07641-0093

STOL, ISRAEL, welding engineer; b. Stockholm, Aug. 18, 1947; came to U.S., 1972; s. Haim Fima and Sara (Epstein) S.; m. Diane Reva Morron, Jan. 27, 1983; children: Hagye, Talia, Ilana. BS in Welding Engring., Ohio State U., 1976, MS in Welding Engring., 1977. Sr. welding rsch. engr. Westinghouse R & D Ctr., Pitts., 1977-85; sr. welding rsch. engr. Alcoa Tech. Ctr., Pitts., 1985-87, staff welding rsch. engr., 1987-89; mgr. assembly and joining tech. transfer Alcoa Automotive Structures Internat., Pitts., 1990-94, plant welding sys. implementation mgr., 1994-95, spl. programs mgr., cons. assembly/joining, 1995—; cons. in welding engring. Westinghouse and Alcoa, Pitts., 1977-89. Contbr. rsch. articles to profl. welding jours. Mem. Beth-El Synagogue, Pitts., 1990—. Corp. Tech. Support, 1968-69, Israel. Recipient award James Lincoln Arc Welding Found., 1986, 88. Mem. Am. Welding Soc. (A.F. Davis silver award 1990). Achievements include patents in Pressure-Differential Method for Sleeve-To-Tube Joining, Method and Apparatus for Arc Welding, Narrow Groove Welding Torch, Arc Welding Method and Electrode for Narrow Groove Welding, Corrosion Resistant Steam Generator and Method of Making the Same, High Reliability Double-Chambered Shielding System for Welding, Method and Apparatus for Controlling the Temperatures of Continuously Fed Wires, Improved Apparatus for Electrically Isolated Hot Wire Surfacing Processes, Ultrasonic Excitation of Underwater Torpedoes for Enhancing Maneuverability and others; responsibility for 140 inventions, 21 patents, and fifty corporate reports and studies in welding tech.; developed the Advanced GMA, GTA and laser welding processes; identified a new type of hydrodynamic welding instability and methods of controlling it during arc welding; developed innovative welding methods for narrow-groove GTA and GMA welding of titanium; devised new robotic GMA welding approaches. Office: Alcoa Automotive Structures Internat 100 Technical Dr Alcoa Center PA 15069-0001

STOLAR, HENRY SAMUEL, lawyer; b. St. Louis, Oct. 29, 1939; s. William Allen and Pearl Minnette (Schukar) S.; m. Mary Goldstein, Aug. 26, 1962 (dec. Nov. 1987); children: Daniel Bruce, Susan Eileen; m. Suzanne Chapman Jones, June 2, 1989. AB, Washington U., 1960; JD, Harvard U., 1963. Bar: Mo. 1963, U.S. Supreme Ct. 1972. Assoc. then ptnr. Hocker, Goodwin & MacGreevy, St. Louis, 1963-69; v.p., sec., gen. counsel LaBarge Inc., St. Louis, 1969-74; v.p., assoc. gen. counsel then sr. v.p., gen. counsel Maritz Inc., St. Louis, 1974—. Sec., bd. dirs. New City Sch. Inc., St. Louis, 1968-75; mem. St. Louis Bd. Aldermen, 1969-73, Bd. Freeholders City and County St. Louis, 1987-88; bd. dirs. Ctrl. West End Assn., 1993—; sec., bd. dirs. Forest Park Forever, Inc., 1988—. Mem. ABA, Mo. Bar, Bar Assn. Met. St. Louis, Frontenac Racquet Club, Triple A Club, Phi Beta Kappa. Home: 59 Kingsbury Pl Saint Louis MO 63112-1824 Office: Maritz Inc 1375 N Highway Dr Fenton MO 63026-1929

STOLARIK, M. MARK, history educator; b. St. Martin, Slovak Republic, Apr. 22, 1943; s. Imrich and Margita (Vavro) S.; m. Anne Helene Ivanco, June 15, 1968; children: Roman Andrej, Matthew Mark. BA, U. Ottawa, 1965, MA, 1967; PhD, U. Minn., 1974. Asst. prof. history Cleve. State U., 1972-76; hist. researcher Nat. Mus. of Man., Ottawa, Ont., Can., 1977-78; pres. Balch Inst. for Ethnic Studies, Phila., 1979-91; prof. history, chair dept. Slovak history and culture U. Ottawa, Ont., Can., 1992—; cons. Harvard Ency. Ethnic Groups, Cambridge, Mass., 1976-80; advisor State Hist. Records Bd., Harrisburg, Pa., 1982-91; cons. Ency. Canada's Ethnic Groups, 1991—. Author: film documentary Vianoce-Slovak Christmas, 1978 (2d prize 1979), Slovaks in Bethlehem, Pa., 1985, The Slovak Experience, 1870-1918, 1989. Mem. Pa. adv. com. to U.S. Commn. on Civil Rights, 1985-91. Lehigh U. fellow, 1976. Mem. 1st Cath. Slovak Union, Nat. Slovak Soc., Canadian Slovak League (pres. 1994—). Roman Catholic.

STOLBERG, IRVING J., state legislator, international consultant; b. Phila., Sept. 24, 1936; s. Ralph B.; 1 son, Robert. BA, UCLA, 1958; MA, Boston U., 1964, postgrad., 1964-66; JD (hon.), U. Hartford, 1987. Internat. campus adminstr. Nat. Student Assn., Cambridge, Mass., 1958-59; program dir. Internat. Student Ctr., Cambridge, 1959-60; Midwest dir. World Univ. Service, Chgo., 1960-63; asst. prof. So. Conn. State U., New Haven, 1966-78; mem. Conn. Gen. Assembly, 1971-93; speaker Ho. of Reps., 1983-84, 87-88, minority leader, 1985, 86, speaker-at-large, 1989, 90; prin. Internat. Solutions, 1994—; del. numerous internat. disarmament and conflict resolution confs. Del. Dem. Nat. Convs. 1968, 72, 76, 84, 88, 92; founder Caucus Conn. Dems., pres. 1995—; chmn. Caucus New Eng. State Legislatures, 1985; mem. bd. overseers Regional Lab. for Edn. in New Eng. and the Islands; bd. dirs. Dem. Nat. Com., 1986-89; appointed by Pres. to U.S. Commn. for Preservation of America's Heritage Abroad, 1995. Named Conn. Caucus Dems. Outstanding Legislator, 1974; recipient Disting. Alumni award Boston U., 1984, Presdl. medal for Community Service, So. Conn. State U., 1987. Mem. Nat. Conf. State Legislators (pres. 1987, pres. Found. 1989), Nat. Assn. Jewish Legislators (pres. 1990-91), Ctr. for Policy Alternatives (bd. dirs., CPA lifetime achievement award), Conn. Tennis Found. (bd. dirs. 1991-94). Home: 50 Roydon Rd New Haven CT 06511-2807*

STOLBERG, SHERYL GAY, journalist; b. N.Y.C., Nov. 18, 1961; d. Irving and Marcia Dawn (Papier) S. BA, U. Va., 1983. Reporter Providence Jour. Bulletin, 1983-87, L.A. Times, 1987-97, N.Y. Times, Washington. Recipient Unity award Lincoln U., 1987. Office: NY Times 1627 I St NW Washington DC 20006

STOLEN, ROGERS HALL, optics scientist; b. Madison, Wis., Sept. 18, 1937. BA, St. Olaf Coll., 1959; PhD in Physics, U. Calif., Berkeley, 1965. Fellow U. Toronto, 1964-66; mem. tech. staff solid state optics AT&T Bell Labs., Holmdel, N.J., 1966—. Recipient of R.W. Wood Prize, 1990, Optical Soc. Am. Mem. Am. Phys. Soc., Optical Soc. Am. (R. W. Wood prize 1990). Achievements include research in nonlinear properties of optical fibers, polarization preserving optical fibers, light scattering in glass. Office: AT & T Bell Labs 4B 421st Holmdel NJ 07733

STOLGITIS, WILLIAM CHARLES, professional society executive; b. Ware, Mass., Jan. 9, 1941; s. Vincent Charles and Doris (Dansereau) S.; m. Helen Elizabeth Dermody, Apr. 18, 1969. BS, U.S. Naval Acad., 1962; MS, U.S. Naval Postgrad. Sch., 1969; JD, Georgetown U., 1977. Bar: N.J. 1977, D.C. 1977. Commd. ensign USN, 1962, officer, 1962-82; exec. dir. Soc. Tech. Comm., Arlington, Va., 1982—; legal counsel Internat. Hydrofoil Assn., 1978—. Mem. ABA, D.C. Bar Assn., N.J. Bar Assn., Am. Soc. Assn. Execs., Am. Legion. Republican. Roman Catholic. Home: 3711 Military Rd Arlington VA 22207-4831 Office: Society for Tech Comm 901 N Stuart St Ste 904 Arlington VA 22203-1821

STOLL, HOWARD LESTER, JR., dermatologist; b. Buffalo, June 13, 1928; s. Howard L. and Margaret (Kahler) S.; m. Jacklyn Fay Straight, June, 1948; children—Shelley, Margaret, Amy, Howard III. A.B., Harvard U., 1948; M.D., U. Pa., 1952. Diplomate Am. Bd. Dermatology. Intern E.J. Meyer Hosp., Buffalo, 1952; resident in dermatology E.J. Meyer Hosp., 1953-55; sr. cancer research surgeon Roswell Park Meml. Inst., Buffalo, 1958-59, assoc. cancer research dermatologist, 1959-67, chief, sect. dermatology, 1984-92; mem. courtesy staff Mercy Hosp., Buffalo, 1958-70; asst. in dermatology E.J. Meyer Meml. Hosp., Buffalo, 1962-72; clin. assoc. prof. dermatology Sch. Medicine, SUNY-Buffalo, 1976-91, clin. prof., 1991—. Served to capt. U.S. Army, 1955-57. Mem. Am. Acad. Dermatology, Soc. Investigative Dermatology, Buffalo-Rochester Dermatologic Soc. Office: Roswell Park Meml Inst Elm & Carlto Sts 666 Elm St Buffalo NY 14263-0001

STOLL, JOHN ROBERT, lawyer, educator; b. Phila., Nov. 29, 1950; s. Wilhelm Friedrich and Marilyn Jane (Kremser) S.; m. Christine Larson, June 24, 1972; children: Andrew Michael, Michael Robert, Meredith Kirstin, Alison Courtney. BA magna cum laude, Haverford Coll., 1972; JD, Columbia U., 1975. Bar: Ind. 1975, U.S. Dist. Ct. (no. and so. dists.) Ind. 1975, U.S. Ct. Appeals (7th cir.) 1978, U.S. Dist. Ct. (no. dist.) Ill. 1980, (so. dist.) N.Y. 1993, Ill. 1981, N.Y. 1989. Atty. Barnes & Thornburg, South Bend, Ind., 1975-80, Mayer, Brown & Platt, Chgo., 1980—; adj. prof. law Northwestern U., Chgo., 1985—, DePaul U., Chgo., 1987; lectr. in bus. St. Mary's Coll., Notre Dame, Ind., 1977-78. Contbr. articles to profl. jours. Mem. ABA, Ind. State Bar Assn., Am. Bankruptcy Inst., Phi Beta Kappa. Office: Mayer Brown & Platt 190 S La Salle St Chicago IL 60603-3410

STOLL, LOUISE FRANKEL, federal official; b. N.Y.C., June 6, 1939; d. Abraham H. and Ruth C. (Flexo) Frankel; m. Marc H. Monheimer, Dec. 22, 1978; children: Miriam F., Malaika S., Abraham D. BA, MA in Philosophy with honors, U. Chgo., 1961; PhD, U. Calif., Berkeley, 1978. High sch. English tchr. Nairobi, Kenya, 1964-65; trustee Berkeley Unified Sch. Dist., 1971-78; mgr. govt. affairs Clean Water Program San Francisco, 1978-80, budget dir. Pub. Utilities Commn., 1980-85; sr. v.p., No. Calif. regional mgr. O'Brien-Kreitzberg and Assoc., Inc., San Francisco, 1985-93; CFO and asst. sec. budget and programs Office of Sec. Dept. Transp., Washington, 1993—; mem. Nat. Legal Affairs Com., Mid. East Com. of Anti-Defamation League of B'nai B'rith. Recipient Mayor's Fiscal Adv. award, City of San Francisco, 1984. Jewish. Avocation: bicycle riding. Office: Office of Sec Dept Transp 400 7th St SW Rm 10101 Washington DC 20590-0001

STOLL, NEAL RICHARD, lawyer; b. Phila., Nov. 7, 1948; s. Mervin Stoll and Goldie Louise (Serody) Stoll Wilf; m. Linda G. Seligman, May 25, 1972; children: Meredith Anne, Alexis Blythe. BA in History with distinction, Pa. State U., 1970; JD, Fordham U., 1973. Bar: N.Y. 1974, U.S. Dist. Ct. (ea. dist.) N.Y. 1974, U.S. Ct. Appeals (2d cir.) 1974, U.S. Ct. Appeals (11th cir.) 1982, U.S. Dist. Ct. (ea. dist.) Mich. 1983, U.S. Dist. Ct. (so. dist.) N.Y. 1974, U.S. Supreme Ct. 1986. Assoc. Skadden, Arps, Slate, Meagher & Flom, LLP, N.Y.C., 1973-81, mem., 1981—; lectr. Practicing Law-Inst., N.Y.C. Contbr. articles to profl. publs. Author: (with others) Aquisitions Under the Hart Scott Rodino Antitrust Improvements Act, 1980. Mem. Assn. Bar City of New York (mem. trade regulation com. 1983-85), ABA, N.Y. State Bar Assn. Democrat. Office: Skadden Arps Slate 919 3rd Ave New York NY 10022

STOLL, RICHARD EDMUND, retired manufacturing executive; b. Dayton, Ohio, Aug. 5, 1927; s. George Elmer and Mary Francis (Zimmerle) S.; m. Vera Mae Cohagen, Sept. 2, 1950; children: Richard Edmund, Linda Ann, Donna Gail. Student in mech. engring., MIT, 1945-47; MetE, Ohio State U., 1950. Registered profl. engr. Ill., Tex. Various staff and operating positions U.S. Steel Corp., Pitts., Chgo., Houston, 1952-78; gen. mgr. metall. services U.S. Steel Corp., Pitts., 1978-84, dir. quality mgmt. program and tech., 1984-85; corp. chief metallurgist Wheeling-Pitts. Steel Corp., Wheeling, W.Va., 1985-86, v.p., gen. mgr. flat rolled steel, 1986-87, v.p., gen. mgr., interim chief ops. officer, 1987-89, exec. v.p., 1989-91, ret., 1991; cons. McElrath & Assocs., Mpls., 1984. Contbr. articles to profl. jours.; patentee in field. Served with C.E., U.S. Army, 1950-52. Fellow Am. Soc. Metals (chmn. 1963); mem. Am. Iron and Steel Inst., Am. Inst. Mining and Metallurgy (Nat. Open Hearth award 1957, bd. dirs. 1961-68), Am. Inst. Steel Engrs., Am. Soc. Metals, Dolphin Head Golf Club. Republican. Roman Catholic. Avocation: golf. Home: 3 Kinglet Lagoon Rd Hilton Head Island SC 29926-2548

STOLL, RICHARD G(ILES), lawyer; b. Phila., Oct. 2, 1946; s. Richard Giles and Mary Margaret (Zeigler) S.; m. Susan Jane Nicewonger, June 15, 1968; children: Richard Giles III, Christian Hayes. BA magna cum laude, Westminster Coll., 1968; JD, Georgetown U., 1971. Bar: D.C. 1971, U.S. Dist. Ct. D.C. 1971, U.S. Ct. Appeals D.C. 1971, U.S. Ct. Appeals (4th cir.) 1977. Assoc. Arent, Fox, Kintner, Plotkin & Kahn, Washington, 1971-73; atty. Office of Gen. Counsel EPA, Washington, 1973-77, asst. gen. counsel, 1977-81; dep. gen. counsel Chem. Mfrs. Assn., Washington, 1981-84; ptnr. Freedman, Levy, Kroll & Simonds, Washington, 1984—; instr. environ. law and policy U. Va., Charlottesville, 1981-90. Co-author: Handbook on Environmental Law, 1987, 88, 89, 91, Practical Guide to Environment Law, 1987; contbr. articles to profl. jours.; moderator, panelist legal ednl. TV broadcasts and tapes ABA and Am. Law Inst. Elder Georgetown Presbyn. Ch.; frequent panelist and moderator on environ. law TV programs. Served to capt., USAR, 1968-76. Mem. ABA (sect. natural resources, energy and environ. law; chmn. water quality com. 1980-82, hazardous waste com. 1983-85, coun. mem. 1985-88, sect. chmn. 1990-91), Washington Golf and Country Club, McLean Racquet and Health Club. Avocations: piano, golf. Office: Freedman Levy Kroll & Simonds 1050 Connecticut Ave NW Ste 825 Washington DC 20036-5318

STOLL, ROBERT W., principal. Prin. Harrison (Ohio) Elem. Sch. Recipient Elem. Sch. Recognition award U.S. Dept. Edn., 1989-90. Office: Harrison Elem Sch 600 E Broadway St Harrison OH 45030-1323*

STOLL, WILHELM, mathematics educator; b. Freiburg, Germany, Dec. 22, 1923; came to U.S., 1960; s. Heinrich and Doris (Eberle) S.; m. Marilyn Jane Kremser, June 11, 1955; children: Robert, Dieter, Elisabeth, Rebecca. Ph.D. in Math, U. Tübingen, Fed. Republic Germany, 1953, habilitation, 1954. Asst. U. Tübingen, 1953-59, dozent, 1954-60, ausserplanmässiger prof., 1960; vis. lectr. U. Pa., 1954-55; temp. mem. Inst. Advanced Study, Princeton, 1957-59; prof. math. U. Notre Dame, 1960-88, Vincent J. Duncan and Annamarie Micus Duncan prof. math., 1988-94, prof. emeritus, 1994—, chmn. dept., 1966-68, co-dir. Ctr. for Applied Math., 1992; vis. prof. Stanford U., 1968-69, Tulane U., 1973, U. Sci. and Tech., Hefei, Anhui, People's Republic of China, summer, 1986; adviser Clark Sch., South Bend, Ind., 1963-68; Japan Soc. Promotion Sci. fellow, vis. prof. Kyoto U., summer 1983. Publs. in field. Research complex analysis several variables. Home: 54763 Merrifield Dr Mishawaka IN 46545-1519 Office: U Notre Dame Dept Math Notre Dame IN 46556

STOLLAR, BERNARD DAVID, biochemist, educator; b. Saskatoon, Sask., Can., Aug. 11, 1936; came to U.S., 1960; s. Percival and Rose (Direnfeld) S.; m. Carol A. Singer, Oct. 7, 1956; children: Lawrence, Michael, Suzanne. BA, U. Sask., 1958, MD, 1959. Intern U. Sask. Hosp., Saskatoon, 1959-60; postdoctoral fellow Brandeis U., Waltham, Mass., 1960-62; dep. chief divsn. biol. scis. USAF Office of sci. Rsch., Washington, 1962-64; asst. prof. dept. pharmacology Tufts U. Schs. Medicine and Dental Medicine, Boston, 1964-67, asst. prof. dept. biochemistry, 1967-68, assoc. prof. biochemistry/pharmacology, 1968-74, prof., 1974—, acting chmn. dept. biochemistry and pharmacology, 1984-86, chmn. dept. biochemistry, 1986—; vis. prof. internat. course in immunology and immunochemistry Mexico City, 1971; sr. fellow Weizmann Inst. Sci., Rehovot, Israel, 1971-71; vis. prof. chemistry Wellesley (Mass.) Coll., 1976, U. Tromsö, Norway, 1981; Dozor vis. prof. Ben-Gurion U. Sch. Medicine, Beer Sheva, Israel, 1986; cons. USAF Office Sci. Rsch., 1966-69, Seragen, Inc., 1983-88, Cetus, 1982-85, Gene-Trak, 1986-89, Alkermes, Inc., 1989—, Catalytic Antibodies, Inc., 1993—; mem. allergy/transplantation rsch. com. NIH/NIAID, 1990-94. Contbr. over 200 articles to profl. jours., chpts. to books; exec. editl. bd. Analytical Biochemistry, 1988—; editl. bd. Jour. Immunology, 1981-85, Molecular Immunology, 1980-95, Arthritis and Rheumatism, 1986-89, Jour. Immunological Methods, 1988—. Mem. adult edn. com. Temple Reyim, Newton, Mass. Capt. USAF, 1962-64. Recipient Copland prize U. Sask. Coll. Arts and Sci., 1958, Gold medalist, Coll. of Medicine, 1959, Medalist in Medicine, Pediatrics, Obstetrics, Gynecology, 1959; decorated Air Force Commendation medal; Weizmann Inst. Sci. sr. fellow, 1971-72; named Third Ann. Alumni Lectr., U. Sask. Coll. Medicine, 1989; rsch. grantee NSF, NIH, 1964—. Mem. AAAS, Am. Assn. Immunologists, Am. Soc. Biochemistry and Molecular Biology, Am. Coll. Rheumatology, Clin. Immunology Soc., N.Y. Acad. Sci. Office: Tufts Univ Sch Medicine Dept Biochemistry 136 Harrison Ave Boston MA 02111-1817

STOLLDORF, GENEVIEVE SCHWAGER, media specialist; b. Ames, N.Y., July 17, 1943; d. Herbert Blakely and Genevieve Agnes (Alessi) Schwager; m. John G. Stolldorf, June 25, 1972; 1 child, Nathan Schwager. AA, Auburn (N.Y.) C.C., 1963; BS, Murray State U., 1967; MA in Edn., Seton Hall U., 1975. Cert. libr. media specialist, social studies tchr. grades 7-12. Libr. So. Orangetown Schs., Orangeburg, N.Y., 1967-70; libr. media specialist Nanuet (N.Y.) Pub. Schs., 1970-78; tchr. social studies grade 9 Monroe (N.Y.)-Woodbury, 1978-80; libr. media specialist Nyack (N.Y.) Pub. Schs., 1981—. Reviewer Libr. Jour., 1981-90. Kykuit guide Hist. Hudson Valley, 1994—; active Friends of the Nyacks, Nyack. Mem. N.Y. Libr. Assn., N.Y. State United Tchrs., Sch. Libr. Media Specialists Southeastern N.Y., Nyack Tchr. Assn. (editor newsletter 1982-84), Tri-Town League Women Voters, C. of C. of the Nyacks (hon.). Avocations: travel, photography, gardening, reading. Office: Valley Cottage Elem Sch Lake Rd Valley Cottage NY 10989

STOLLER, CLAUDE, architect; b. N.Y.C., Dec. 2, 1921; s. Max and Esther (Zisblatt) S.; m. Anna Maria Oldenburg, June 5, 1946 (div. Oct. 1972); children: Jacob, Dorothea, Elizabeth; m. Rosemary Raymond Lax, Sept. 22, 1978. Student, Black Mountain Coll., N.C., 1942; M.Arch., Harvard U., 1949. Architect Architects Collaborative, Cambridge, Mass., after 1949, Shepley, Bulfinch, Richardson & Abbot, Boston, 1951; co-founder, partner firm Marquis & Stoller, San Francisco, 1956; pvt. practice architecture N.Y.C. and San Francisco, 1974-78; founder, partner Stoller/Partners, Berkeley, Calif., 1978, Stoller, Knoerr Archs., 1988-95; mem. faculty Washington U., St. Louis, 1955-56, U. Calif., Berkeley, 1957-91, prof. arch., 1968-92, acting chmn. dept., 1965-66, chair grad. studies, 1984-91; mem. Berkeley Campus Design Rev. Bd., 1985-91, chmn., 1992-93; commr. Calif. Bd. Archtl. Examiners, 1980-90, mem. exam. com., 1985-88; mem. diocesan commn. arch. Episcopal Diocese Calif., 1961—; vis. arch. Nat. Design Inst., Ahmedabad, India, 1963; planning commr. City of Mill Valley, 1961-66, Marin County Planning Commn., 1966-67; mem. pub. adv. panel archtl. svcs. GSA, 1969-71; citizens urban design adv. com. City of Oakland, Calif., 1968; vis. com. nat. archtl. accrediting bd. U. Minn. and U. Wis., Milw., 1971; coun. Harvard Grad. Sch. Design Assn., 1976—; mem. design rev. com. The Sea Ranch, Calif., 1990—. Prin. works include St. Francis Sq. Coop. Apts., San Francisco, 1961, Pub. Housing for Elderly, San Francisco, 1974, Learning Resources Bldg, U. Calif., Santa Barbara, 1975, Menorah Park Housing for Elderly, San Francisco, 1979, San Jose State U. Student Housing Project, 1984, Delta Airlines Terminal, San Francisco Internat. Airport, 1988. Served with AUS, 1943-46. Recipient numerous awards including AIA Honor awards, 1963, 64, AIA Bay Region Honor award, 1974, Concrete Reinforced Steel Inst. award, 1976, AIA award, 1976, CADA Site I Solar Housing award Sacramento, Calif., 1980, State of Calif. Affordable Housing award, 1981, PG&E Suntherm award, 1981, San Francisco Housing Authority award, 1983, Orchid award City of Oakland, 1989, Citation for achievement and svc. U. Calif., Berkeley, 1991, Design award Berkeley Design Advocates. Fellow AIA. Home: 2816 Derby St Berkeley CA 94705-1325 Office: Claude Stoller FAIA Arch 1818 Harmon St Berkeley CA 94703-2472

STOLLER, DAVID ALLEN, lawyer; b. Burlington, Iowa, Oct. 27, 1947; s. Richard L. and Marjorie E. (Thornton) S.; m. Nancy E. Leachman, July 14, 1973; children: Aaron J., Anne C., John D. BSBA, Drake U., 1970, JD, 1977. Bar: Iowa 1977, N.C., 1985, U.S. Dist. Ct. (so. dist.) Iowa 1978, U.S. Dist. Ct. (no. dist.) Iowa 1981, U.S. Ct. Appeals (8th cir.) 1981, U.S. Dist. Ct. (ea. dist.) N.C. 1997, U.S. Ct. Appeals (4th cir.) 1986; cert. mediator, N.C., 1996. Assoc. city atty. City of Des Moines, 1977-81; assoc. Connolly, O'Malley, Lillis, Hansen & Olson, Des Moines, 1981-85, Ward & Smith, New Bern, N.C., 1985-89; ptnr. Dunn, Dunn & Stoller, New Bern, 1990—. Bd. dirs. Episcopal Found. Diocese East Carolina, v.p., 1996—; bd. dirs. Thompson's Children's Home, Inc., Charlotte, N.C.; mem., pres. standing com. Episcopal Diocese of East Carolina. Eagle Scout Boy Scouts Am., 1964. Mem. ABA (torts and ins. practice, litigation, law office mgmt., dispute resolution sects.), Def. Rsch. Inst., N.C. Bar Assn. (litigation sect.), N.C. State Bar (councillor 1995—), 3rd Jud. Dist. Bar, Craven County Bar Assn., New Bern Golf and Country Club. Avocations: coaching youth soccer, basketball, T-ball. Home: 2432 Tram Rd New Bern NC 28562-7370 Office: Dunn Dunn & Stoller 3230 Country Club Rd New Bern NC 28562-7304

STOLLER, EZRA, photojournalist; b. Chgo., May 16, 1915; s. Max and Esther (Zistblatt) S.; m. Helen Rubin, Sept. 23, 1938; children: Erica, Evan, Lincoln. B.F.A., NYU, 1938. Guest lectr. U. Okla., U. Kans., U. Notre Dame, 1971, Ga. Inst. Tech., Va. Poly. Inst. and State U., 1972, Columbia Coll., 1974, 76, U. N.C., Smithsonian Instn., Harvard U., 1984-86, Harvard Grad. Sch. Design, 1985, 86, 88, U. Ariz., 1985, U. Pa., 1987, U. Orange Free State, 1995, Nat. Inst. Archtl. Edn., 1995. Exhbns. include, Max Protetch Gallery, N.Y.C., 1980, Bonafant Gallery, San Francisco, 1981, Bannenford Books, Toronto, 1981, Mpls. Art Inst., 1981, Nat. Gallery Johannesburg, 1983, Harvard GSD, 1991; author: Modern Architecture Photographs By Ezra Stoller, 1990. Recipient 1st medal for archtl. photography AIA, 1960. Mem. AIA (hon.), Am. Soc. Mag. Photographers (past pres., lifetime achievement award 1982), Archtl. League N.Y. (Gold medal 1955). Home: Kirby Ln N Rye NY 10580

STOLLER, MITCHELL ROBERT, non-profit organization administrator; b. Washington, Aug. 1, 1953; s. Sidney and Goldie (Berman) S.; m. Sheri Ann Stutsky, June 15, 1980; children: Betsy, Lauren. BS, Frostburg State Coll., 1975; postgrad., George Washington U., 1983; MA in Philanthropy and Devel., St. Mary's U. of Minn., 1997. Tchr. Charles County Bd. Edn., Waldorf, Md., 1976-81; dir. devel. Ctrl. Md. chpt. Easter Seal Soc., Balt., 1981-83, March of Dimes Birth Defects Found., Balt., 1983-86; nat. dir. spl. projects and field ops. Retinitis Pigmentosa Found., Balt., 1986-88; exec. dir. Sudden Infant Death Syndrome Assn., Landover, md., 1988-91; exec. v.p., COO Sudden Infant Death Syndrome Alliance, Columbia, md., 1991-93; pres., CEO Am. Paralysis Assn., Springfield, N.J., 1993—, bd. dirs. Bd. dirs. C.J. Found. for Sudden Infant Death Syndrome Alliance, Hackensack, N.J., 1994; fundraiser Warren (N.J.) Synagogue, 1993—; bd. dirs. Temple Har Sholom, 1997. Mem. Am. Soc. Assn. Execs. Avocations: golf, basketball league, coach children's soccer. Home: 11 Surrey Ln Basking Ridge NJ 07920-3732 Office: Am Paralysis Assn 500 Morris Ave Springfield NJ 07081-1020

STOLLER, PATRICIA SYPHER, structural engineer; b. Jackson Heights, N.Y., Dec. 16, 1947; d. Carleton Roy and Mildred Vivian (Ferron) Sypher; m. David A. Stoller Sr.; children: Stephanie Jean, Sheri Lynn. BSCE, Washington U., St. Louis, 1975; M in Mgmt., Northwestern U., 1989. R & D engr. Amcar divsn. ACF Industries, St. Charles, Mo., 1972-79; project engr. Truck Axle divsn. Rockwell Internat., Troy, Mich., 1979-81; sr. engr. ABB Impell, Norcross, Ga., 1981-83; supervising mgr., client mgr., divsn. mgr. ABB Impell, Lincolnshire, Ill., 1983—; dir. bus. devel., v.p. VECTRA (formerly ABB Impell), Lincolnshire, 1991-94; pres., CEO ASC Svcs. Co., LLC, Chgo., 1994—. Author computer program Quickpipe, 1983; patentee in field (numerous). Mem. ASCE, NAFE, Soc. Women Engrs., Am. Nuc. Soc. (mem. exec. bd. Chgo. sect. 1991-93), Comml. Real Estate Women, Young Pres. Orgn. Avocations: golf, music. Office: ASC Svcs Co LLC 300 W Washington St Ste 200 Chicago IL 60606-1720

STOLLERMAN, GENE HOWARD, physician, educator; b. N.Y.C., Dec. 6, 1920; s. Maurice William and Sarah Dorothy (Mezz) S.; m. Corynne Miller, Jan. 21, 1945; children: Lee Denise Stollerman Meyburg, Anne Barbara Stollerman DiZio, John Eliot. AB summa cum laude, Dartmouth Coll., 1941; MD, Columbia U., 1944. Diplomate Am. Bd. Internal Medicine. Clin. tng. Mt. Sinai Hosp., N.Y.C, 1944-46; chief med. resident Mt. Sinai Hosp., 1948; Dazian research fellow microbiology NYU Med. Sch., 1949-50, mem. dept. medicine, 1951-55; med. dir. Irvington House for Cardiac Children, 1951-55; prin. investigator Sackett Found. Research in Rheumatic Diseases, 1955-64; asst. prof. medicine Northwestern U., 1955-57, assoc. prof., 1957-61, prof. medicine, 1961-65; prof., chmn. dept. medicine U. Tenn., 1965-81, Goodman prof., 1977-81; physician-in-chief City of Memphis Hosps., 1965-81; prof. medicine Boston U. Sch. Medicine, 1981-95, prof. pub. health, 1991-95, prof. medicine and pub. health emeritus, 1996—; chief sect. gen. internal medicine Univ. Hosp., Boston U. Med. Ctr., 1983-86; Disting. physician VA Med. Ctr., Bedford, Mass., 1986-89; assoc. chief of staff Geriatrics and Extended Care, 1989-92; clin. dir. Bedford div. Geriatric Rsch., Ednl. and Clin. Ctr., 1989-92; dir. VA Health Svcs. Rsch. Field, 1990-93; chmn. research career program com. NIAMD-NIH, 1967-70; mem. commn. streptococcal and staphylococcal diseases U.S. Armed Forces Epidemiol. Bd., 1956-74; adv. bd. immunization practices Center for Disease Control, 1968-71; expert adv. panel cardiovascular disease WHO, 1966—; mem. Am. Bd. Internal Medicine, 1967-73, chmn. cert. exam. com., 1969-73, mem. exec. com., 1971-73; chmn. Panel on Bacterial Vaccines, FDA, 1973-80; mem. nat. adv. council Nat. Inst. Allergy and Infectious Diseases, NIH, 1978-82; mem. Dept. Health & Human Services nat. vaccine adv. com.. Editor-in-chief Advances in Internal Medicine, 1968-93, Jour. Am. Geriatric Soc., 1984-88; co-editor Hosp. Practice, 1990—; contbr. chpts. to Braunwald's Textbook of Cardiology, Harrison's Textbook of Medicine, Cecil & Loeb Textbook of Medicine, others; contbr. articles to profl. jours. Served as capt. M.C., AUS, 1946-48. Recipient Bicentennial award in internal medicine Columbia U., 1967, Disting. Alumnus award Mt. Sinai Hosp., 1989, Thewlis award Am. Geriatric Soc., 1990. Master ACP (bd. regents 1978, v.p. 1984, Bruce medal for preventive medicine 1985), Am. Coll. Rheumatology; mem. Am. Heart Assn. (mem. exec. com., pres. coun. on rheumatic fever and congenital ACP disease 1965-67), Am. Fedn. Clin. Rsch., Am. Rheumatism Assn., Am. Soc. Clin. Investigation, Cen. Soc. Clin. Rsch. (v.p. 1973-74, pres. 1974-75), Assn. Profs. Medicine (pres. 1975-76), Am. Assn. Immunologists, Assn. Am. Physicians, Infectious Disease Soc. Am. (coun. 1968-70), Phi Beta Kappa, Alpha Omega Alpha.

STOLLERY, ROBERT, construction company executive; b. Edmonton, Alta., Can., May 1, 1924; s. Willie Charles and Kate (Catlin) S.; m. Shirley Jean Hopper, June 11, 1947; children: Carol, Janet, Douglas. B.Sc. Eng., U. Alta., 1949, LL.D. (hon.), 1985; hon. LL.D., Concordia U., Montreal, Que., 1986. Field engr. Poole Constrn. Ltd., Edmonton, 1949-54, project mgr., 1954-64, v.p., 1964-69, pres., 1969-81; chmn. bd. PCL Constrn. Group Inc., Edmonton, 1979-93; chmn. PCL Constrn. HOldings, Edmonton, 1993—; bd. dirs. Melcor Devels. Ltd., Edmonton, Alta. Chmn. bus. adv. coun. U. Alta., gov. of trustees; chmn. Edmonton Community Found. Recipient Exec. of Yr. award Inst. Cert. Mgmt. Cons. of Alta., 1988, Can. Businessman of Yr. award U. Alta., 1993. Fellow Can. Acad. Engring.; mem. Assn. Profl. Engrs. (Frank Spragins Meml. award 1981), Engring. Inst. Can. (Julian C. Smith medal 1990), Conf. Bd. Can. (vice chmn. 1980-82), Constrn. Assn. Edmonton (pres. 1972, Claude Alston Meml. award), Can. Constrn. Assn. (v.p. 1970, Can. Businessman of the Yr. award 1993). Conservative. Mem. United Ch. of Canada. Club: Mayfair Golf and Country (Edmonton). Office: PCL Construction Group Inc, 5410 99 St, Edmonton, AB Canada T6E 3P4

STOLLEY, ALEXANDER, advertising executive; b. Coethen Anhalt, Germany, May 12, 1922; came to U.S., 1923, naturalized, 1929; s. Mihail and Tatiana (Rainich) Stolarevsky; m. Patricia Martin, June 26, 1944 (dec. Aug. 1970); children: Christopher, Peter, Laura Stolley Smith, Annabel Stolley Hetzer, Megan Stolley Berry; m. Bette Scott Vogt, June 15, 1973. M.E., U. Cin., 1948. With Cin. Milacron, Inc., 1941-50, dir. employee relations, 1948-50; with Northlich, Stolley, Inc., Cin., 1950-89, exec. v.p., 1959-67, pres., 1967-84; chmn. Northlich, Stolley, LaWarre, Inc. (formerly Northlich, Stolley, Inc.), Cin., 1984-89. Mem. exec. com. Cincinnatus Assn., 1968-73, sec., 1970-71, v.p., 1971-72, pres., 1972-73; mem. Cin. Council on World Affairs, 1969—; chmn. Contemporary Arts Center, Cin., 1966-67; mem. exec. com. Cin. Conv. and Visitors Bur., 1975, chmn. long range planning com., 1983; trustee Cin. Symphony Orch., 1969-75. Served to 1st lt. AUS, 1943-46. Mem. Bus., Profl. Advt. Assn., Greater Cin. C. of C. (exec. com. 1982-83). Clubs: Cincinnati Country, Cincinnati Tennis, University, Gyro., Literary, Gasparilla Beach, Lemon Bay Golf, Boca Bay Pass. Home: 4060 Main Interlochen MI 49643-9512 Home (winter): PO Box 1339 Boca Grande FL 33921-1339

STOLLEY, PAUL DAVID, medical educator, researcher; b. Pawling, N.Y., June 17, 1937; s. Herman and Rosalie (Chertock) S.; m. Jo Ann Goldenberg, June 13, 1959; children: Jonathan, Dorie, Anna. B.A., Lafayette Coll., 1957; M.D., Cornell U., 1962; M.P.H., Johns Hopkins U., 1968; M.A. hon., U. Pa., 1976. Diplomate: Am. Coll. Preventive Medicine, Am. Coll. Epidemiology. Intern U. Wis. Med. Ctr., 1962-63, resident in medicine, 1963-64; med. officer USPHS, Washington, 1964-67; asst. prof. Johns Hopkins Sch. Pub. Health, Balt., 1968-71, assoc. prof., 1971-76; Herbert C. Rorer prof. medicine U. Pa. Sch. Medicine, Phila., 1976-91; prof. and chmn. dept. epidemiology U. Md. Sch. Medicine, Balt., 1991—. Co-author: Foundations of Epidemiology, 3d edit., 1994, Epidemiology: Investigating Disease, 1995 (Am. Med. Writers Assn. award 1996); contbg. author: Case-Control Studies, 1982; mem. editl. bd. New Eng. Jour. Medicine, 1989-93, Milbank Quar., Health and Soc., 1986—; assoc. editor Clin. Pharmacology and Therapeutics, 1987-93; contbr. articles to med. jours. Mem. Physicians for Social Responsibility, 1961—. Served to lt. comdr. USPHS, 1964-67. Fellow ACP; mem. Am. Coll. Epidemiology (pres. 1987-89), Inst. Medicine of NAS, Soc. Epidemiol. Rsch. (pres. 1982-84), Am. Epidemiol. Soc. (pres. 1994—), Internat. Epidemiol. Assn. (treas. 1982-84), Johns Hopkins Soc. Scholars. Home: 6424 Brass Knob Columbia MD 21044 Office: Univ of Md Sch Medicine 660 W Redwood St Baltimore MD 21201-1541

STOLLEY, RICHARD BROCKWAY, journalist; b. Peoria, Ill., Oct. 3, 1928; s. George Brockway and Stella (Sherman) S.; m. Anne Elizabeth Shawber, Oct. 2, 1954 (div. 1981); children: Lisa Anne, Susan Hope, Melinda Ruth, Martha Brockway ; m. Lise Jane Hilboldt, 1997. B.S. in Journalism, Northwestern U., 1952, M.S., 1953; LL.D. (hon.), Villa Maria Coll., 1976. Sports editor Pekin (Ill.) Daily Times, 1944-46; reporter Chgo. Sun-Times, 1953; mem. staff weekly Life mag., 1953-73; bur. chief weekly Life mag., Los Angeles, 1961-64, Washington, 1964-68; sr. editor weekly Life mag., Europe, 1968-70; asst. mng. editor weekly Life mag., N.Y.C., 1971-73; mng. editor monthly Life mag., N.Y.C., 1982-86; founding mng. editor People mag., N.Y.C., 1974-82, Picture Week mag., N.Y.C., 1985-86; dir. spl. projects Time Inc., N.Y.C., 1987-89; editorial dir. Time Inc. Time Warner Inc., N.Y.C., 1989-93, sr. editl. adviser, 1993—. Introd. to Leigh A. Wiener, Marilyn: A Hollywood Farewell: The Death and Funeral of Marilyn Monroe, 1990; editor People Celebrates People: The Best of 20 Unforgettable Years, 1994, rev. edit., 1996; exec. prodr. (TV show) Extra, 1995-96. Bd. dirs. Dirksen Congl. Rsch. Ctr., Pekin, Ill.; chmn. Twins Found., Providence; bd. govs. Nat. Parkinson Found., Miami, Fla.; pres. Child Care Action Campaign, N.Y.C.; bd. trustees N.Y.C. Citizens Crime Commn. With USN, 1946-48. Recipient Alumni merit award Northwestern U., 1977, Alumni medal Northwestern U., 1994, Henry Johnson Fisher award for lifetime achievement in mag. pub., 1997; inducted into Am. Soc. Magazine Editors' Hall of Fame, 1996, Hall of Achievement Medill Sch. Journalism Northwestern U., 1997. Mem. Am. Soc. Mag. Editors (pres. 1982-84), Nat. Press Club, Overseas Press Club, Century Assn., Kappa Tau Alpha, Sigma Delta Chi.

STOLLMAN, ISRAEL, city planner; b. N.Y.C., Mar. 15, 1923; s. Philip and Yetta (Strelchik) S.; m. Mary Florence Callahan, Dec. 27, 1953; children—Susan Elisabeth, Katharine Rachel, Sarah Ellen. B.S. in Social Sci, CCNY, 1947; M. City Planning, MIT, 1948. Planner Cleve. Planning Commn., 1948-51; planning dir. Youngstown, Ohio, 1951-57; prof., chmn. div. city and regional planning Ohio State U., 1957-68; exec. dir. Am. Soc. Planning Ofcls., 1968-78; exec. dir. Am. Planning Assn., Washington, 1978-93, cons., 1994—; lectr. Western Res. U., 1949-51, U. Chgo., 1968-69, U. Va., 1994—; pres. Assn. Collegiate Sch. Planning, 1966-67; chmn. Charles E. Merriam Center Pub. Adminstrn., 1977-93. Trustee Alfred Bettman Found.; bd. govs. Met. Housing and Planning Council Chgo., v.p., 1969-79. Served with USAAF, 1943-45. Mem. Am. Inst. Cert. Planners (exec. dir. emeritus), Internat. Fedn. Housing and Planning (bur. mem.), Soc. for Am. City and Regional Planning History (trustee 1996—), Lambda Alpha. Avocation: stereoscopy. Home and Office: 1708 Swann St NW Washington DC 20009-5535

STOLNITZ, GEORGE JOSEPH, economist, educator, demographer; b. N.Y.C., Apr. 4, 1920; s. Isidore and Julia (Jurman) S.; m. Monique Jeanne Delley, Aug. 26, 1976; children: Cindy, Wendy, Dia. BA, CCNY, 1939; MA, Princeton U., 1942, PhD, 1952. Statistician U.S. Bur. Census, 1940-41; rsch. assoc. Princeton U. Office of Population Rsch., 1948-56; asst. prof. Princeton U., 1953-56; prof. econs. Ind. U., Bloomington, 1956-90, prof. emeritus, 1990—; dir. Ind. U. Internat. Devel. Rsch. Ctr., Bloomington, 1967-72, Ind. U. Population Inst. for Rsch. and Tng., Bloomington, 1986-91; prin. officer Population and Econ. Devel. UN, N.Y.C., 1976-78; cons. Ford Found., U.S. Congress, Rockefeller Found., UN, U.S. Dept. Commerce, U.S. Dept. Energy, U.S. Dept. HHS, U.S. Dept. State; vis. rsch. scholar Resources for the Future, 1965-67; vis. scholar Poplulation Reference Bur., 1987-88. Author books; contbr. numerous articles in population and devel. fields, testimonies on pub. utility costs of capital. Capt. USAF, 1942-46. Nat. Sci. Found. fellow, 1959-60. Mem. Population Assn. Am. (pres. 1983), Am. Econ. Assn., Am. Statis. Assn., Econometric Soc., Internat. Union Sci. Study of Population, Cosmos Club. Home: 2636 E Covenanter Ct Bloomington IN 47401-5408 Office: Ind U Population Inst Poplars # 738 Bloomington IN 47405 *Challenges are rarely more forbidding in fact than in anticipation. Early coping often pays off; faintheartedness has higher risk of loss.*

STOLOFF, NORMAN STANLEY, materials engineering educator, researcher; b. Bklyn., Oct. 16, 1934; s. William F. and Lila (Dickman) S.; m. Helen Teresa Arcuri, May 15, 1971; children: Michael E., Linda M., David M., Stephen L. BMetE, NYU, 1955; MS, Columbia U., 1956, PhD, 1961. Metall. engr. Pratt & Whitney Aircraft, East Hartford, Conn., 1956-58; prin. rsch. scientist Ford Sci. Lab., Dearborn, Mich., 1961-65; asst. prof. materials engring. Rensselaer Polytechnic Inst., Troy, N.Y., 1965-68, assoc. prof., 1968-71, prof., 1971-97; prof. emeritus Rensselaer Polytechnic Inst., Troy, 1997—; cons. Electric Boat div. Gen. Dynamics, New London, Conn., 1987-89, Martin Marietta Rsch. Labs., Balt., 1990, Rockwell Internat., Thousand Oaks, Calif., 1989, Cummins Engine Co., Columbus, Ind., 1991. Editor: (with others) High Temperature Ordered Intermetallic Alloys, 1985, Superalloys II, 1987, Physical Metallurgy and Processing of Intermetallic Compounds, 1996, others; contbr. articles to profl. jours. Recipient Fulbright Rsch. award U.S. State Dept., 1968-69, DOE Fellowship Assoc. Western U., 1995. Fellow Am. Soc. Materials Internat.; mem. The Minerals, Metals and Materials Soc., Materials Rsch. Soc. Avocations: hiking, fishing, reading. Office: Rensselaer Polytechnic Inst Materials Sci Engring Dept MRC Bldg Troy NY 12180-3590

STOLOV, JERRY FRANKLIN, healthcare executive; b. Kansas City, Mo., Jan. 31, 1946; s. I. Paul and Marion R. (Rothberg) Stolov. BA, Washington U., 1968; MPA, Roosvelt U., 1972. Adminstrv. asst. U. Ill. Chgo. Circle & Med. Sch. Campuses, Chgo., 1970-75; exec. dir. Hosp. Hill Health Svcs. Corp., Kansas City, Mo., 1976—; also bd. dirs. Hosp. Hill Health Svcs. Corp., Kansas City, 1976—; bd. dirs. Kansas City Psychoanalytic Found., treas., 1996—; adv. dir. Mchts. Bank Corp., Kansas City, 1985-92. Leadership tng. C. of C., Kansas City, 1977-78. Mem. Assn. Am. Med. Colls. (group on faculty practice), Med. Group Mgmt. Assn., Internat. City Mgrs. Assn., Am. Soc. Pub. Health Adminstrs., Acad. Polit. Sci. (contbg. mem.). Office: Hosp Hill Health Svcs Corp 800 Hospital Hill Ctr 2310 Holmes St Kansas City MO 64108-2634

STOLOV, WALTER CHARLES, physician, rehabilitation educator, physiatrist; b. N.Y.C., Jan. 6, 1928; s. Arthur and Rose F. (Gordon) S.; m. Anita Carvel Noodelman, Aug. 9, 1953; children: Nancy, Amy, Lynne. BS in Physics, CCNY, 1948; MA in Physics, U. Minn., 1951, MD, 1956. Diplomate Am. Bd. Phys. Med. and Rehab., Am. Bd. Electrodiagnostic Medicine. Physicist U.S. Naval Gun Factory, Nat. Bur. Stds., Washington, 1948-49; teaching and rsch. asst. U. Minn., Mpls., 1950-54; from instr. to assoc. prof. U. Wash., Seattle, 1960-70, prof., 1970—, also chmn., 1987—; editl. bd. Archives Phys. Medicine and Rehab., 1967-78, Muscle and Nerve, 1983-89, 92-95; cons. Social Security Adminstrn., Seattle, 1975—; sec. Am. Bd. Electrodiagnostic Medicine, 1995—. Co-editor: Handbook of Severe Disability, 1981; contbr. articles to profl. jours. Surgeon USPHS, 1956-57. Recipient Townsend Harris medal CCNY, 1990. Fellow AAAS, Am. Heart Assn.; mem. Am. Acad. Phys. Medicine & Rehab. (Disting. Clinician award 1987), Am. Congress Rehab. Medicine (Essay award 1959), Assn. Acad. Physiatrists, Am. Assn. Electrodiagnostic Medicine (pres. 1987-88), Am. Spinal Cord Injury Assn. Avocations: dancing, singing. Office: U Wash Box 356490 1959 NE Pacific St Seattle WA 98195-0004

STOLPER, EDWARD MANIN, secondary education educator; b. Boston, Dec. 16, 1952; s. Saul James and Frances A. (Liberman) S.; m. Lauren Beth Adoff, June 3, 1973; children: Jennifer Ann, Daniel Aaron. AB, Harvard U., 1974; M Philosophy, U. Edinburgh, Scotland, 1976; PhD, Harvard U., 1979. Asst. prof. geology Calif. Inst. Tech., Pasadena, 1979-82, assoc. prof. geology, 1982-83, prof. geology, 1983-90, William E. Leonhard prof. geology, 1990—, chmn. divsn. geol. and planetary sci., 1994—. Marshall scholar Marshall Aid Commemoration Commn., 1974-76, recipient Newcomb Cleve. prize AAAS, 1984, F.W. Clarke medal Geochem. Soc., 1985, Arthur Holmes medal European Union Geosci., 1997; Geochemistry fellow The Geochem. Soc. and The European Assn. for Geochemistry, 1997. Fellow Meteoritical Soc. (Nininger Meteorite award 1976), Am. Geophys. Union (James B. Macelwane award 1986), Mineral Soc. Am., Am. Acad. Arts and Scis.; mem. NAS, Geol. Soc. Am., Sigma Xi. Office: Calif Inst Tech Div Geol Planetary Sci Pasadena CA 91125

STOLPER, PINCHAS ARYEH, religious organization executive, rabbi; b. Bklyn., Oct. 22, 1931; s. David Bernard and Nettie (Rosch) S.; m. Elaine Liebman, Nov. 22, 1955; children: Akiva Psachia, Michal Hadassah Cohen, Malka Tova Kaweblum. B.A., Bklyn. Coll., 1952; M.A., New Sch. for Social Research, 1971. Rabbinical ordination Chaim Berlin-Gur Aryeh Rabbinical Acad., 1956; dir. L.I. Zionist Youth Commn., 1956-57; dir. public relations, adminstrv. dean, adviser to English-speaking students Ponevez Yeshiva, Bnai Brak, Israel, 1957-59; also prin.; instr. English and Talmud Gimnazia Bnei Akiva High Sch., 1959-77; nat. dir. youth div. Union Orthodox Jewish Congregations Am., Nat. Conf. Synagogue Youth, N.Y.C., 1959-76; founder NCSY, Torah Fund, Ben Zakai Honor Soc. Union Orthodox Jewish Congregations Am., Nat. Conf. Synagogue Youth, 1959-76; editor Jewish Youth Monthly, 1967—; exec. v.p. Union Orthodox Jewish Congregations Am., 1976-94, sr. exec., 1994—; adj. prof. Jewish studies Touro Coll., N.Y., 1975—; mem. publs., Israel, campus commns., staff mem. responsible for edn., Talmud Torah, day sch. commns. Union Orthodox Jewish Congregations Am., 1965—; del. White House Conf. on Children and Youth, 1961; cons. N. Am. Jewish Youth Conf., 1967—. Author: Tested Teen Age Activities, 1961, rev. edit., 1964, Day of Delight, 1961, Tefilah, Text and Source Book, 1963, Revelation What Happened on Sinai, 1966, Prayer, The Proven Path, 1967, The Road to Responsible Jewish Adulthood, 1967, Jewish Alternatives in Love, Dating and Marriage, 1985, The Sacred Trust, Love, Dating and Marriage, The Jewish View, 1996, Beyond Belief, Revelation for the Modern Jew, 1996; contbr. numerous articles, plays, and revs. to Jewish publs.; columnist The Jewish Press, 1994. Nat. dir. Nat. Conf. Synagogue Youth, 1995—; bd. dirs. Chaim Berlin Torah Schs.-Mesivta Rabbi Chaim Berlin-Rabbinical Acad., 1965—. Recipient Alumi Amudim award Mesivta Rabbi Chaim Berlin-Gur Aryeh Inst., 1967, award Assn. Orthodox Jewish Tchrs., 1975, citation Rabbinical Coun. Am., 1984, Jabotinsky medal, 1990, Alumnus of Yr. award Flatbush Yeshiva, 1989, Joseph K. Miller Achdut Yisrael award Shaalvim Yeshiva, 1993. Mem. Rabbinical Coun. Am. Home: 954 E 7th St Brooklyn NY 11230-2706 Office: Union Orthodox Jewish Cong of Am 333 7th Ave New York NY 10001-5004

STOLPER, WOLFGANG FRIEDRICH, retired economist, educator; b. Vienna, Austria, May 13, 1912; came to U.S., 1934, naturalized, 1940; s. Gustav and Paula (Deutsch) S.; m. Marta Voegeli, Aug. 11, 1938 (dec. July 1972); children: Thomas E., Matthew W.; m. Margot Kaufmann, 1979. M.A., Harvard U., 1935, Ph.D., 1938; Dr. honoris causa, U. Saarbrücken, Grosses Verdienstkreuz, Fed. Republic Germany, 1984. Instr. Harvard U., 1936-41; asst. prof. econs. Swarthmore Coll., 1941-48, assoc. prof., 1948-49; assoc. prof. U. Mich., 1949-53, prof., 1953-82; dir. U. Mich. (Center for Research on Econ. Devel.), 1963-70; guest prof. U. Zurich, summers, 1952, 69-79; head econ. planning unit Fed. Ministry for Econ. Devel., Lagos, Nigeria., 1960-62; cons. USAID, Ford Found., IBRD, UN; vis. prof. Inst. f. Weltwirtschaft, Kiel, 1987. Author: (with P.A. Samuelson) Protection and Real Wages, 1941, The Structure of the East German Economy, 1960, Planning Without Facts, 1966, Joseph A. Schumpeter 1883-1950. The Public Life of the Private Man, 1994; contbr. articles to profl. jours. Guggenheim fellow, 1947-48; Fulbright prof. Heidelberg, 1966; recipient Bernhard Harms medal U. Kiel, 1985. Mem. Am. Econ. Assns., Internat. Schumpeter Soc. (founding pres.). Home: 1051 Lincoln Ave Ann Arbor MI 48104-3526 Office: U Mich Dept Econs Ann Arbor MI 48109

STOLPMAN, PAUL MEINRAD, federal agency administrator. BA, St. Johns U., Minn., 1966; MBA, U. Chgo., 1969; student, London Sch. Econs., 1968-69. With EPA, Washington, 1971—, dir. office policy analysis rev., office air radiation, 1982-88, sr. adv. asst. adminstr. office air radiation, 1991-93, dir. office atmospheric programs, office air radiation, 1993—; dir. pollution control divsn. Orgn. Econ. Coop. Devel., Paris, 1988-91. Office: EPA Office Atmospheric Programs 401 M St SW Washington DC 20460-0001

STOLTIE, JAMES MERLE, academic administrator; b. Galesburg, Ill., July 10, 1937; s. Cecil James and Margaret Lucinda (Smith) S.; m. Mary Lucile Walworth, June 25, 1960; children: David, Julia, Ann. BA, Knox Coll., 1959; MMus, U. Iowa, 1960, PhD, 1962. Cert. music tchr. Ill., Iowa. Woodwind instr. Iowa City Pub. Schs., 1961-62; asst. prof. music Susquehanna U., Selinsgrove, Pa., 1962-68; from asst. prof. to prof., then dean Crane Sch. Music SUNY, Potsdam, 1968—; tchr., music dir., coord. personnel & curriculum New England Music Camp, Sidney, Maine, 1981—. Elder Presbyn. Ch. Mem. N.Y. State Assn. Coll. Music Programs (past pres.), N.Y. State Sch. Music Assn., Music Educators Nat. Conf., N.Am. Saxophone Alliance. Home: 18 Circle Dr Potsdam NY 13676 Office: The Crane Sch Music SUNY Potsdam Potsdam NY 13676

STOLTZ, ERIC, actor; b. American Samoa, 1961. Studied with Peggy Fury, William Traylor, U. So. Calif. Actor: (stage prodns.) One Flew Over the Cuckoo's Nest, 1978, Hello, Dolly!, 1979, The Seagull, 1980, The Widow Claire, 1987, Our Town, 1988 (Tony award nomination Drama Desk nomination), The American Plan, 1990, Two Shakespearean Actors, 1992, Down the Road, 1993, The Importance of Being Earnest, 1996, Three Sisters, 1997, Arms and the Man, 1997; (feature films) Fast Times at Ridgemont High, 1981, Wild Life, 1983, Mask, 1984 (Golden Globe award nomination 1985), Lionheart, 1986, Some Kind of Wonderful, 1987, Sister, Sister, Haunted Summer, Code Name Emerald, 1988, Say Anything, 1989, Manifesto, 1989, The Fly II, 1989, Memphis Belle, 1990, Singles, 1991, The Waterdance, 1991, Naked in New York, 1993, Killing Zoe, 1993, God's Army (renamed The Prophesy), 1993, Pulp Fiction, 1994, Little Women, 1994, Rob Roy, 1995, Fluke, 1995, Kicking and Screaming, 1995, Grace of My Heart, 1995, Inside, 1996, Two Days in the Valley, 1996, Anaconda, 1996, Mr. Jealousy, 1997; (TV movies) the Grass Is Greener, 1980, The Violation of Sarah McDavid, 1982, Thursday's Child, 1982, Paper Dolls, 1982, A Killer in the Family, 1983, Foreign Affairs, 1993, Roommates, 1994, Keys to Tulsa, 1997; (TV episodes) St. Elsewhere, 1983, Fallen Angels, 1994, (13 episodes) Mad About You, 1995, Partners, 1995, Homicide, 1997; actor, prodr. Bodies, at Rest and Motion, 1993, Sleep With Me, 1995, Mr. Jealousy, 1997, Highball, 1997. Office: 9830 Wilshire Blvd Beverly Hills CA 90212-1804

STOLTZFUS, VICTOR EZRA, retired university president, academic consultant; b. Martinsburg, Pa., Mar. 24, 1934; s. Ira Mark and Elsie Rebecca (Shenk) S.; m. Marie Histand Althouse, June 19, 1955; children: Kristina, Rebecca, Malinda. BA in Social Sci., Goshen Coll., 1956; BD, Goshen Bibl. Sem., 1959; MA in Sociology, Kent State U., 1964; PhD in Sociology, Pa. State U., 1970. Pastor North Lima (Ohio) Mennonite Ch., 1959-66; instr. Youngstown (Ohio) U., 1964-66, Pa. State U., University Park, 1966-70; prof. Eastern Ill. U., Charleston, 1970-81; dean Goshen (Ind.) Coll., 1981-84, pres., 1984-96. Contbr. articles to profl. jours. Mem. Am. Assn. Higher Edn. Lodge: Rotary. Avocation: raquetball. Home: 607 College Ave Goshen IN 46526-4911 Office: Goshen Coll Office of Pres Goshen IN 46526

STOLTZMAN, RICHARD LESLIE, clarinetist; b. Omaha, July 12, 1942; s. Leslie Harvey and Dorothy Marilyn (Spohn) S.; m. Lucy Jean Chapman, June 6, 1976; children: Peter John, Margaret Anne. MusB summa cum laude, Ohio State U., 1964; MusM magna cum laude, Yale U., 1967; postgrad., Columbia U. Tchrs. Coll., 1967-70. Mem. faculty Calif. Inst. Arts, 1970-75, New Eng. Conservatory, 1996; Western regional dir. Young Audiences, Inc., 1972-74, mem. nat. bd. Appeared in concerts throughout U.S., Europe, Japan, Hong Kong, Australia, 1976—; rec. artist, 1974—; debut LaScala, Milan, 1981, Carnegie Hall, N.Y.C., 1982; appeared in world premiere of Einar Englund concerto Helsinki Festival, 1991, Toro Takemitsu concerto (Fantasma/Cantos) Wales BBC, 1991, U.S. premiere of Lukas Foss concerto L.A. Philharm. Orch., 1991, Copland concert, 1993 (Emmy award for best performing arts video 1993), world premiere of Leonard Bernstein sonata for clarinet and orch. Pacific Music Festival, Sapporo, Japan, 1994.

Recipient Horatio Parker award Yale U., 1966, Avery Fisher prize, 1977, Martha Baird Rockefeller award, 1973, Grammy award, 1983, 95, Avery Fisher artist award, 1986, Disting. Alumnus award Ohio State U., 1990. Home: 6 Lincolnshire Way Winchester MA 01890-3048 Office: 201 W 54th St Apt 4C New York NY 10019-5521 *Be mindful of the breath. It gives life to the sound which sends music to the soul.*

STOLWIJK, JAN ADRIANUS JOZEF, physiologist, biophysicist; b. Amsterdam, Netherlands, Sept. 29, 1927; came to U.S., 1955, naturalized, 1962; s. Leonard and Cornelia Agnes (Van Der Bijl) S.;m. Deborah Rose, 1990. B.S., Wageningen U., Netherlands, 1948, M.S., 1951, Ph.D., 1955. Biophysicist John B. Pierce Found., New Haven, 1957-61; asso. fellow John B. Pierce Found. Lab., 1961-64, fellow, 1964, asso. dir., 1974-89; instr. dept. physiology Yale U. Sch. Medicine, New Haven, 1962-63, asst. prof., 1964-68, asst. prof. epidemiology, 1968-69, asso. prof., 1969-75, prof., 1975—, dir. grad. studies, dept. epidemiology and public health, 1992—, chmn. dept. epidemiology and pub. health, 1982-89; research fellow Harvard U., 1955-56; cons. divsn. disease prevention Conn. Health Dept., 1977—; cons. vehicle inspection program Dept. Motor Vehicles, 1979-83; mem. sci. adv. bd. EPA, 1985-93; mem. tech. adv. bd. Dept. Commerce, 1972-77. Mem. Am. Physiol. Soc., Biophys. Soc., Aerospace Med. Soc., Am. Public Health Assn., AAAS, Internat. Biometeorol. Soc., Soc. Occupational and Environ. Health, Am. Conf. Govt. Indsl. Hygienists, ASHRAE, Conn. Acad. Sci. and Engring. Club: Cosmos. Home: 165 Dromara Rd Guilford CT 06437-2391 Office: PO Box 8034 60 College St New Haven CT 06520

STOLZ, BENJAMIN ARMOND, foreign language educator; b. Lansing, Mich., Mar. 28, 1934; s. Armond John and Mabel May (Smith) S.; m. Mona Eleanor Seelig, June 16, 1962; children: Elizabeth Mona, John Benjamin. A.B., U. Mich., Ann Arbor, 1955; certificat, U. Libre de Bruxelles, Belgium, 1956; A.M., Harvard U., 1957, Ph.D., 1965. Mem. faculty U. Mich., 1964—, prof. Slavic langs. and lits., 1972—, chmn. dept., 1971-85, 89-91; cons. in field. Editor: Papers in Slavic Philology, 1977, Studies in Macedonian Language, Literature, and Culture, 1995; co-editor: Oral Literature and the Formula, 1976, Cross Currents, 1982-85, Language and Literary Theory, 1984, Mich. Slavic Publs., 1990—; co-editor, translator: (Konstantin Mihailovic): Memoirs of a Janissary, 1975; contbr. articles to profl. pubs. Served to lt. (j.g.) USNR, 1957-60. Recipient Orion E. Scott award humanities U. Mich., 1954, Fulbright scholar, 1955-56; Fgn. Area fellow Yugoslavia, 1963-64; Fulbright-Hays rsch. fellow Eng. and Yugoslavia, 1970-71; grantee Am. Coun. Learned Socs., 1968-70, 73, Internat. Rsch. and Exchs. Bd., 1985, 87, Woodrow Wilson Ctr., 1992. Mem. Am. Assn. Advancement Slavic Studies, Am. Assn. Tchrs. Slavic and East European Langs., Midwest MLA (pres. 1976), Huron Valley Tennis Club, Phi Beta Kappa, Phi Kappa Phi, Delta Upsilon. Democrat. Home: 1060 Baldwin Ave Ann Arbor MI 48104-3504 Office: Univ Mich 3040 MLB Ann Arbor MI 48109

STOLZENBERG, PEARL, fashion designer; b. N.Y.C., Oct. 9, 1946; d. Irving and Anna (Shenkman) S. Student, Fashion Inst. Tech., 1964-66. Textile stylist, designer Forum Fabrics Ltd., N.Y.C., 1966-68; freelance ceiling designer Maxwell's Plum, N.Y.C., 1968; dir. styling Beauknit Corp., N.Y.C., 1969-74; stylist, designer Mi-Bru-San Co., Inc., N.Y.C., 1983-84; gen. mgr. Laissez-Faire Inc., N.Y.C., 1984-85; merchandiser prodn. The Clothing Acad. Inc., N.Y.C., 1986-87; v.p. String of Pearls Knitwear, Inc., N.Y.C., 1988—; pres. Pearl's Cutting Ltd., N.Y.C., 1994—; cons. Tam O'Shanter Textile Ltd., Montreal, 1974-79, Mitsui, Osaka, Japan, 1976-79, Sergio Valente English Town Sportswear, N.Y.C., 1980-84; cons. merchandiser The Fashion Acad., Hollywood Crossing, Inc., N.Y.C.; owner Josu Cutting Inc., Bklyn. Mem. The Fashion Group Internat. Democrat. Jewish. Avocations: fishing, animal conservation, gourmet cooking, physical fitness. Home: 8340 Austin St Apt 1E Jamaica NY 11415-1827 Office: Pearl's Cutting Ltd 410 W 16th St New York NY 10011-5891

STOLZER, LEO WILLIAM, bank executive; b. Kansas City, Mo., Oct. 14, 1934; s. Leo Joseph and Lennie Lucille (Hopp) S.; m. Eleanor Katherine Griffith, Aug. 17, 1957; children: Joan Ellen Stolzer Bolen, Mary Kevin Stolzer Giller. BS in Acctg., Kans. State U., 1957. Teller Union Nat. Bank & Trust Co., Manhattan, Kans., 1960-62, asst. cashier, 1962-63, asst. v.p., 1963-64, v.p., 1964-69, exec. v.p., 1969-72, pres., 1972-80, chmn., CEO, 1980-95; chmn., 1995—; bd. dirs. State Mut. Life Ins. Co., Commerce Bankshares Inc., Commerce Bank-Manhattan; chmn., CEO Griffith Lumber Co.; chmn. Corp. for Am. Banking. Mem. exec. com., vice chair Kans. State U. Found.; trustee Midwest Rsch. Inst.; chmn. Riley County Savs. Bond. Capt. USAF, 1957-60. Recipient Disting. Service award Manhattan Jr. C. of C., 1968, Kans. State U. Advancement award. Mem. Am. Bankers Assn. (past treas., past exec. com., past bd. dirs.), Assn. U.S. Army (bd. dirs. Ft. Riley Ctl. Kans. chpt.), Kans. U. Alumni Assn. (devel. com.), Newcomen Soc. in N.Am. (past Kans. chmn.), KC, Beta Theta Pi. Avocation: skiing. Office: Commerce Bank 727 Poyntz Ave Manhattan KS 66502-6077

STOMMA, PETER CHRISTOPHER, lawyer; b. Milw., May 29, 1966; s. Thaddeus and Hedwig Wanda (Struszczyk) S. BSEE, Marquette U., 1988; JD, Drake U., 1991. Bar: Wis. 1991, U.S. Dist. Ct. (ea. and we. dists.) Wis. 1991, U.S. Ct. Appeals (fed. cir.) 1991, U.S. Patent and Trademark Office 1991. Sr. assoc. Andrus, Sceales, Starke and Sawall, Milw., 1991—. Vol. Discovery World, Milw., 1991-94, Lawyers' Hotline Wis., Madison, 1991—; mem. devel. com. Legal Aid Milw., 1991-93; recruiting rep. Drake U., Des Moines, Iowa, 1992-94. Mem. ABA, Am. Intellectual Property Law Assn., Wis. Intellectual Property Law Assn., St. Thomas More Lawyer's Soc., Marquette Minuteman Club, Marquette Tip Off Club. Office: Andrus Sceales Starke and Sawall 100 E Wisconsin Ave Ste 1100 Milwaukee WI 53202-4107

STOMS, DONNA SUE, librarian; b. Cin., Mar. 28, 1944; d. Richard Kirker and Rose June (Liming) Stoms; m. William Bernard Monnig, July 8, 1967 (div. 1997); children: Aaron William, Thomas Richard. BA, U. Cin., 1966; MA, Rosary Coll., 1970. Tchr. Finneytown (Ohio) H.S., 1966-69; head lit. & lang. depts. Pub. Libr. of Cin. and Hamilton County, 1970—, ref. libr., 1970-83, dept. head, 1983—, chair book selection policy com., 1993-94. Pres. Hope Cottage Guild, Covington, Ky., 1978; sec. Literacy Network of Greater Cin., 1990, mem. awards com., 1992-93. Mem. Ohioana Libr. Assn., Beta Phi Mu. Republican. Roman Catholic. Office: Pub Libr Cin & Hamilton Co Lit & Lang Depts 800 Vine St Cincinnati OH 45202-2009

STONE, ALAN, container company executive; b. Chgo., Feb. 5, 1928; s. Norman H. and Ida (Finkelstein) S.; children: Christie-Ann Stone Weiss, Joshua. B.S.E., U. Pa., 1951. Trainee, salesman Stone Container Corp., Chgo., 1951-53, dir. mktg. service, 1954-64, gen. mgr., regional mgr., 1964-72, sr. v.p. adminstrn., gen. mgr. energy div., 1972—, also dir.; pres. Atlanta St. Andrews and Bay Line R.R., 1972-94, Abbeville-Grimes R.R., 1972-94, Apache R.R., 1972-94. Pres. Jewish Vocat. Svc., Chgo., 1975-77; v.p. Sinai Temple, Chgo., 1977-84; bd. dirs. Jewish Fedn. Chgo.; vice chmn. Roycemore Sch., Evanston, Ill., 1982-87; trustee Brewster Acad., Wolfeboro, N.H.; vol. exec. for overseas needs Citizen's Democracy Corps; vol. cons. for non-profit agys., schs. and librs. Exec. Svc. Corps.; bd. dirs. Gastrointestinal Rsch. Found. Mem. Standard Club, Tavern Club, Bryn Mawr Country Club, Tamarisk Country Club, Long Boat Key Club, Beta Alpha Psi, Phi Eta Sigma, Zeta Beta Tau. Avocations: golf; sports; reading. Office: Stone Container Corp 150 N Michigan Ave Chicago IL 60601-7524

STONE, ALAN A., law and psychiatry educator, psychiatrist; b. 1929. A.B., Harvard U., 1950; M.D., Yale U., 1955. Dir. resident edn. McLean Hosp., 1962-68; lectr. Harvard U., 1966-72, asst. prof. psychiatry, 1966-69, assoc. prof., 1969-72, prof. law and psychiatry, 1972—; Touroff-Glueck prof. Law and Psychiatry, 1982—; mem. adv. com. Am. Bar Found. Project on Mentally Ill, 1967-71; mem. Mass. Gov.'s Com. for Revision Criminal Code, 1968-72; mem. com. on mentally disabled ABA, 1973-77; chmn. Mass. Com. on Psychosurgery, 1974-75; fellow Ctr. Advanced Study in Behavioral Scis., Stanford U., 1980-81; Tanner lectr. Stanford U., 1982. Served as capt. M.C., U.S. Army, 1959-61. Recipient Manfred S. Guttmacher award; Isaac Ray award, 1982. Mem. Group Advancement Psychiatry, Am. Psychiat. Assn. (trustee, v.p., pres.; chmn. com. jud. action 1974-9). Author: (with Onque) Longitudinal Studies of Child Behavior, 1961; Mental Health and Law: A System in Transition, 1975; Law, Psychiatry and Morality: Essays and Analysis, 1984; editor: (with Sue Stone) Abnormal Personality through Literature, 1966; Office: Harvard U Law Sch Cambridge MA 02138

STONE, ALAN JAY, college administrator; b. Ft. Dodge, Iowa, Oct. 15, 1942; s. Hubert H. and Bernice A. (Tilton) S.; m. Jonieta J. Smith; 1 child, Kirsten K. Stone Morlock. BA, Morningside Coll., 1964; MA, U. Iowa, 1966; MTh, U. Chgo., 1968, DMin, 1970; PhD (hon.), Kyonggi U., Korea, 1985; LLD, Stillman Coll., 1991, Sogong U., Korea, 1992. Admissions counselor Morningside Coll., Sioux City, Iowa, 1964-66; dir. admissions, asso. prof. history George Williams Coll., Downers Grove, Ill., 1969-73; v.p. coll. relations Hood Coll., Frederick, Md., 1973-75; v.p. devel. and fin. affairs W.Va. Wesleyan Coll., Buckhannon, 1975-77; dir. devel. U. Maine, 1977-78; pres. Aurora (Ill.) U., 1978-88, Alma (Mich.) Coll., 1988—; bd. dirs. Bank of Alma. Chmn. bd. Mich. Intercollegiate Athletic Assn.; bd. dirs. Mich. Coll. Found., Assn. Ind. Colls. and Univs. of Mich., Mich. Campus Compact, Korean Social Policy Inst., Seoul; chmn. United Way Gratiot County, Strategic Planning Group Gratiot County, Assn. Presbyn. Coll. Pres. Mem. Am. Assn. Higher Edn., Am. Assn. Colls., Renaissance Club, Alma Country Club. Home: 313 Maple Ave Alma MI 48801-2234 Office: Alma Coll Off of Pres Alma MI 48801

STONE, ALAN JOHN, manufacturing company executive, real estate executive; b. Dansville, N.Y., Sept. 9, 1940; s. Guthrie Boyd and Doris Irene (Wolfanger) S.; m. Sandra Barber, Aug. 22, 1964; children: Teri, Timothy, Michael. B.S. in Mech. Engring., Rochester Inst. Tech., 1963; M.B.A., U. Pitts., 1964. Engring. aide Xerox Corp., Webster, N.Y., 1960-63; gen. mgr. mech. component divsn. Stone Conveyor Co., Inc., Honeoye, N.Y., 1964-67, v.p. sales, 1968; co-founder, chief exec. officer Stone Constrn. Equipment Inc., Honeoye, 1969-86, also cons., bd. dirs., 1969—; founder, pres. Canandaigua Apts. Inc., N.Y., 1968-83; pres. Wildtrak, Inc., 1983—; founder, gen. ptnr. Stone Properties, 1986—; dir., co-founder Baker Rental Svc., Inc., 1973-75; met. adv. bd. Chase Lincoln Bank, 1981-84; co-founder, dir. Royal Lines Ltd., 1989-91; bd. dirs. Naples Biol. Rsch. Sta. Inc., v.p., 1996—; bd. dirs. Canandaigua Nat. Bank & Trust Co., chmn. 1994—. Patentee in field. Mem. Town of Richmond (N.Y.) Planning Bd., 1970-75, chmn., 1970-71; mem. Honeoye Ctrl. Sch. Bd. Edn., 1971-76, pres., 1973-74; com. chmn. pack 10 Boy Scouts Am., 1975-78; mem. Ontario County Overall Econ. Devel. Com., 1976-81; bd. dirs. F.F. Thompson Hosp., 1987-91; chmn. fin. com. United Meth. Ch., Allens Hill, 1995—. Mem. Honeoye C. of C. (chmn indsl. com. 1974-82), Constrn. Industry Mfrs. Assn. (exec. mem. new bus. challenges coun. 1980-83), Honeoye Valley Assn. (dir. 1991-95, treas. 1993-95), Griswold and Cast Iron Collectors Assn. (treas. 1994-96, fin. com. chmn. 1996—), Honeoye Area Hist. Soc. (bicentennial com. 1989), Young Pres.'s Assn., Grand Slam Club, Safari Internat., Found N.Am. Wild Sheep. Methodist. Home and Office: Box 500 5170 County Road 33 Honeoye NY 14471-0500

STONE, ALLAN DAVID, economics educator; b. Joliet, Ill., Jan. 9, 1937; s. William E. and Leona V. (Frieh) S.; m. Peggy J. Carter, Jan. 11, 1958; children: David, Richard. BA, Beloit Coll., 1961; MA, U. Okla., 1964, PhD, 1973. Asst. prof. econs. U. Tex., El Paso, 1963-65; instr. econs. Wartburg Coll., Waverly, Iowa, 1965-66; asst. prof. econs. Oklahoma City U., 1966-72; prof. econs. S.W. Mo. State U., Springfield, 1972—, dept. head, 1985-87. Served with U.S. Army, 1956-58. NSF grantee. Mem. Am. Econ. Assn., Mo. Coun. Econ. Edn. (bd. dirs. 1977-80), Phi Beta Kappa, Phi Kappa Phi. Home: 820 E Cherokee St Springfield MO 65807-2708

STONE, ANDREW GROVER, lawyer; b. L.A., Oct. 2, 1942; s. Frank B. and Meryl (Pickering) S.; divorced; 1 child, John Blair. BA, Yale U., 1965; JD, U. Mich., 1969. Bar: D.C. 1970, U.S. Dist. Ct. D.C. 1970, U.S. Ct. Appeals (D.C. cir.) 1972, Mass. 1981. Assoc. Rogers & Wells, Washington, 1969-71; atty. Bur. Competition, FTC, Washington, 1971-80; antitrust counsel Digital Equipment Corp., Maynard, Mass., 1980-83, mgr. N.E. law group, 1983-86, mgr. headquarters sales law group, 1986-88; asst. general counsel U.S. (acting), 1987, 88; corp counsel Washington, 1988-90; corp. counsel, pub. sect. mktg. Digital Equipment Corp., 1990-91; corp. counsel Thinking Machines Corp., Cambridge, Mass., 1992-95; pvt. practice Marblehead, Mass., 1995—. Corp. mem. Tenacre Country Day Sch., Wellesley, Mass., 1981-88. Mem. ABA (bus. law sect., sci. tech. sect., pub. contracts sect., vice-chmn. comml. products and svcs. com. 1983-84), Mass. Bar Assn. (internat. law steering com. 1993-94), Boston Bar Assn. (chair corp. counsel com. 1995—), Licensing Execs. Soc., Am. Arbitration Assn. (comml. arbitrator), Am. Intellectual Property Law Assn., New Eng. Corp. Counsel Assn., Assn. Ind. Gen. Counsel.

STONE, ARTHUR HAROLD, mathematics educator; b. London, Sept. 30, 1916; came to U.S., 1959; s. Aurel P. and Rosa (Schekter) S.; m. Dorothy Maharam, Apr. 12, 1942; children: David A., Ellen R. BA, Cambridge (Eng.) U., 1938, MA, 1939; PhD, Princeton U., 1941. Mem. Inst. Advanced Study, Princeton, N.J., 1941-42; instr. Purdue U., 1942-44; with Geophys. Lab., Washington, 1944-45; fellow Trinity Coll. Cambridge U., 1946-48; lectr. Manchester (Eng.) U., 1948-57, sr. lectr., 1957-61; prof. math. U. Rochester, 1961-87, prof. emeritus, 1987—; adj. prof. Northeastern U., Boston, 1988—; vis. prof. Columbia U., 1961, Yale U., 1965-66; vis. rsch. assoc. U. Calif., Berkeley, 1971-72; vis. fellow Australian Nat. U., Canberra, 1978. Mem. editorial adv. bd. Topology and Its Applications, 1971-93; mem. internat. adv. bd. Mathematica Japonica, 1991—; contbr. articles to profl. jours. Mem. AAUP, Am. Math. Soc., Math. Assn. Am., London Math. Soc. Jewish. Office: Northeastern U Dept Math Boston MA 02115

STONE, ARTHUR JOSEPH, judge; b. St. Peters, N.S., Can., 1929; s. George and Charlotte S.; m. Anna M., 1956. B.A., St. Francis Xavier U., Antigonish, N.S., 1952; LL.B., Dalhousie Law Sch., 1955; LL.M., Harvard U., 1956. Assoc., Wright & McTaggart and successor firms, 1957-83; justice Fed. Ct. Appeal, Ottawa, Ont., Can., 1983—; justice Ct. Martial Appeal Ct., Ottawa, Ont., Can., 1983—; lectr. faculty of law U. Toronto, Ont., 1971-76. Contbr. articles to profl. publs. Mem. N.S. Barristers Soc., Law Soc. of Upper Can., N.B. Barristers Soc., Law Soc. of B.C., Can. Bar Assn. (nat. exec. com. 1971-73), Can. Tax Found. (gov. 1977-79), Can. Maritime Law Assn. (pres.), Harvard U. Law Sch. Assn. Ont. (chmn. law sch. fund). Club: Toronto Marine (pres. 1977-78). Office: Fed Ct, Kent & Wellington Sts, Ottawa, ON Canada K1A 0H9

STONE, BEVERLEY, former university dean, former dean of students; b. Norfolk, Va., June 10, 1916; d. James L. and Clara (Thompson) S. B.A. in Chemistry, Randolph-Macon Woman's Coll., 1936; M.A. in Student Personnel Adminstrn, Columbia U., 1940, profl. diploma, 1956; L.H.D. (hon.), Purdue U., 1986. Tchr. Norfolk High Sch., 1936-41; instr. Tusculum Coll., 1941-43; asst. dean women U. Ark., 1946-50, assoc. dean women, 1952-54, dean women, 1954-55; asst. dean women Purdue U., 1956-67, assoc. dean women, 1967-68, dean women, 1968-74, dean students, 1974-80, ret., 1980. Author (with Barbara Cook); monograph Counseling Women, 1973. Mem. pres.'s coun. Purdue U., 1985; trustee Katherine S. Phillips Trust Fund, 1978-84; mem. lay bd. St. Elizabeth's Hosp., 1974-80, Salvation Army, Lafayette Art Mus., 1982-85, Crisis Ctr.; mem. Tippecanoe County Bd. Zoning Appeals, 1982-83, West Lafayette Cuty Coun., 1984-88; past mem. adminstrv. bd., found. bd., hon. steward 1st United Meth. Ch., West Lafayette. Lt. comdr. UNSR, 1943-46, 52-55. Recipient Outstanding Woman in Edn. award Coalition of Women's Orgns. in Greater Lafayette Area, 1978, Disting. Alumni award Purdue Pres.'s Coun., 1980, Disting. Woman award Purdue U., 1980, Woman of Achievement award Randolph-Macon Womens Coll., 1996; named Sagamore of the Wabash Gov. Ind., 1980, 85; Nat. Mortar Bd. Fellowship named in honor, 1994-95. Mem. AAUW (past pres. Fayetteville, Ark.), Nat. Assn. Women Deans and Counselors (treas., chmn. hdqs. adv. com. 1973-75, mem. 1947-85), Ind. Assn. Women Deans and Counselors, Mental Health Assn., Purdue Women's Club, Parlor Club, Randolph-Macon Women's Coll., Conway Club, Mortar Bd. Phi Beta Kappa, Kappa Delta Pi, Omicron Delta Kappa, Pi Lambda Theta, Alpha Lambda Delta (v.p. 1975-79), Zeta Tau Alpha. Home: 1807 Western Dr West Lafayette IN 47906-2239

STONE, DAVID BARNES, investment advisor; b. Brookline, Mass., Sept. 2, 1927; s. Robert Gregg and Bertha L. (Barnes) S.; m. Sara Cruikshank, June 16, 1951 (div. July 1976); children—David Stevenson, Benjamin Barnes, Peter Cruikshank, Jonathan Fitch, Andrew Hasbrouck; m. Ellen J. Desmond, Feb. 16, 1980; 1 son, Daniel Desmond. Grad., Milton (Mass.) Acad., 1945; A.B., Harvard, 1950, M.B.A., 1952; D.C.S. (hon.), Suffolk U., 1969; LL.D., Northeastern U., 1974; L.H.D., Curry Coll., 1981. Vice pres. Hayden, Stone Inc. (and predecessor), 1962-65, chmn. exec. com., 1965-67; pres. N.Am. Mgmt. Corp., 1968-78, chmn., 1978—; dir. Mass. Fin. Svcs. Group of Mut. Funds, 1989—; pres. Stonetex Oil Corp., Dallas. Pres. bd. trustees New Eng. Aquarium, 1959-70, chmn. bd. trustees, 1970-76; bd. overseers Boys Club Boston, 1956-61, treas., 1961-67; trustee Charles Hayden Found., 1966-92, Wellesley Coll., vice chmn. bd., 1992-95; chmn. Meml. Dr. Trust; mem. Woods Hole Oceanographic Instn. With U.S. Mcht. Marines, 1945-47. Mem. Investment Bankers Assn. (chmn. New Eng. group 1963, bd. govs. 1964-67). Clubs: Kittansett (Marion, Mass.); Country (Brookline, Mass). Home: Great Hill Marion MA 02738 also: 282 Beacon St Boston MA 02116-1101 Office: North American Mgmt Ten Post Office Sq Ste 300 Boston MA 02109

STONE, DAVID DEADERICK, physician, educator; b. Bristol, Va., Feb. 8, 1932; s. Albert Wallace and Margaret Clifton (Deaderick) S.; children: Margaret E., Caroline A., Jennifer R., Shannon D. BA cum laude, Vanderbilt U., 1954; MD, U. Va., 1958. Diplomate Am. Bd. Internal Medicine, Am. Bd. Gastroenterology. Intern N.Y. Hosp., 1958-59, resident, 1959-61; chief resident U. Va. Hosp., Charlottesville, 1961-62; fellow in gastroenterology Barnes Hosp., St. Louis, 1962-63; inst. in internal medicine U. Va. Sch. Medicine, Charlottesville, 1963-66, asst. prof., 1966-71, assoc. prof., 1971-76, prof., 1976-85, Disting. prof., 1985—; dir. outpatient dept. U. Va. Hosp., 1968-72, pres. clin. staff, 1971-72, dir. phys. diagnosis program, 1972-75, vice chmn. dept. internal medicine, 1979, dir. med. ICU, 1982-88, assoc. chmn. for clin. affairs, 1989. Contbr. articles to jours. in field. Recipient Robley Danglison award U. Va. Sch. Medicine, 1972, 78. Fellow ACP; mem. Am. Gastroent. Assn., Soc. Critical Care Medicine, Alpha Omega Alpha.

STONE, DAVID KENDALL, financial executive; b. Natick, Mass., Dec. 7, 1942; s. Harold Hamilton (dec.) and Mary (Perkins) S.; m. Patricia Donahue, June 12, 1965; children: Jonathan, Andrew, Timothy. AB, Franklin & Marshall Coll., 1964. CPA, N.Y. Acct. Gilfoil & McNeal, Syracuse, N.Y., 1967-69, Ernst & Whinney, Cleve., 1969-83; sr. v.p., comptroller Fiduciary Trust Co. Internat., N.Y.C., 1983-87, sr. v.p. dir. ops., 1987-92, exec. v.p., 1992—. Treas. Cerebral Palsy and Handicapped Children's Assn., Syracuse, N.Y., 1972-75. 1st lt. U.S. Army, 1964-67, Vietnam. Mem. AICPA, N.Y. State Soc. CPAs (com. on banking and savs. instns. 1983-87), Com. Banking Instns. on Taxation, N.Y. State Bankers Assn. (com. on trust ops.). Office: Fiduciary Trust Co Internat 2 World Trade Ctr New York NY 10048-0203

STONE, DAVID PHILIP, lawyer; b. N.Y.C., Sept. 11, 1944; s. Robert and Laura Stone; m. Arlene R. Stone, June 11, 1966; children: Aaron J., Rachel E. AB, Columbia U., 1967; JD, Harvard U., 1970. Bar: N.Y. 1971. Assoc. Cahill, Gordon & Reindel, N.Y.C., 1970-74, Baer & McGoldrick, N.Y.C., 1974-76; assoc. Weil, Gotshal & Manges, N.Y.C., 1976-79, ptnr., 1979—. Office: Weil Gotshal & Manges 767 5th Ave New York NY 10153-0001

STONE, DENNIS J., law educator, chief information officer, lawyer; b. Sacramento, May 25, 1948; s. Edward F. and Irene V. (Johnson) S. BA, U. Calif., Berkeley, 1970, MLS, 1971; JD, U. of Pacific, 1977. Bar: Calif. 1977. Asst. law librarian McGeorge Sch. of Law, Sacramento, 1974-77, lectr., asst. law librarian, 1977-79; law librarian, asst. prof. Gonzaga Sch. of Law, Spokane, 1979-83; law librarian, assoc. prof. law U. Conn. Sch. of Law Library, Hartford, 1983-95; v.p. Fla. Coastal Sch. Law, 1995—. Founder Can.-Am. Law Jour., 1983; founder, editor Trends in Law Library Mgmt. and Tech. Jour., 1987; contbr. articles to profl. jours. Mem. Am. Assn. Law Libraries (exec. bd. 1983-87), New Eng. Law Library Consortium (bd. dirs. 1983-85 , pres. 1986-88), Law Librarians of New Eng., So. New Eng. Law Libraries, Am. Assn. Law Libraries (spl. interest sect.). Office: Fla Coastal Sch Law 7555 Beach Blvd Jacksonville FL 32216-3003

STONE, DON CHARLES, computer science educator; b. Passaic, N.J., Sept. 5, 1942; s. Robert Porter and Catherine Cook (Lanman) S. B Engring. Physics, Cornell U., 1965; MS in Engring., U. Pa., 1967, PhD in Instnl. Systems, 1985. Asst. prof. Glassboro State Coll. (now Rowan U.), 1968-89, assoc. prof., 1989—, chair computer sci. dept., 1992—; sr. sys. analyst Intelligent Micro Sys., Inc., Narberth, Pa., 1985—. Contbr. articles to profl. jours.; patentee in field. Mem. IEEE Computer Soc., Assn. for Computing Machinery, Am. Soc. for Engring. Edn. Avocations: genealogy, graphic design, typography. Home: Apt 9B-28 2401 Pennsylvania Ave Philadelphia PA 19130-3034 Office: Rowan U Computer Sci Dept Glassboro NJ 08028

STONE, DONALD JAMES, retired retail executive; b. Cleve., Mar. 5, 1929; s. Sidney S. and Beatrice (Edelman) S.; m. Norma Fay Karchmer, Oct. 26, 1952; children—Michael, Lisa, Angela. BBA, U. Tex., Austin, 1949. With Foley's, Houston, 1949-75; v.p., gen. mdse. mgr. Foley's, 1960-75; chmn., chief exec. officer Sanger-Harris, Dallas, 1975-80; vice chmn. Federated Dept. Stores, Inc., Cin., 1980-88; bd. dirs. M Corp., Fossil, Inc., Bloom Agy., Dallas, XTEC Corp., Cin. Pres. Dallas Symphony Soc., 1980-82, 88—, chmn. Found. bd., 1989—; chmn. exec. com. Dallas Ballet, 1979; bd. dirs. Dallas Mus. Fine Art, 1979-81; mem. adv. coun. Coll. Bus. Adminstrn. U. Tex., 1981—, chmn., 1990-92; bd. dirs. Cin. Ballet, 1982-87, Cin. Symphony, 1983-88, pres., 1987; bd. Cin. overseers, chmn., 1988-92; bd. govs. Hebrew Union Coll., 1988—; bd. dirs. Aspen Inst. Humanistic Studies, 1988-94. Mem. Dallas C. of C. (chmn. cultural com. 1979-81), Assoc. Mdse. Corp. (bd. dirs., exec. com.). Democrat. Jewish. Home: 3601 Turtle Creek Blvd Dallas TX 75219-5522 Office: 3601 Turtle Creek Blvd Apt 502 Dallas TX 75219-5503

STONE, DONALD RAYMOND, lawyer; b. Madison, Wis., Mar. 6, 1938; s. Donald Meredith and June Dorothy (Graffenberger) S.; m. Dorothy Tetzlaff, June 23, 1962; children—Randall, Brian. B.S. in Physics, U. Wis., 1960, J.D., 1963. Bar: Minn. 1963, D.C. 1987, U.S. Supreme Ct. 1987. Patent atty. Honeywell, Inc., Mpls., 1963-66; patent atty. firm Burd, MacEachron, Braddock, Bartz & Schwartz, Mpls., 1966-68; with Medtronic, Inc., Mpls., 1968-87, v.p., then sr. v.p. product assurance and regulation, 1973-77, sr. v.p., sec., gen. counsel, 1977-80, sr. v.p., 1980-85, v.p., 1985-87; ptnr., mem. Burditt, Bowles & Radzius, Chartered, Washington, 1987-90; ptnr. McKenna & Cuneo, L.L.P., Washington, 1990—; condr. seminars, 1974—. Contbr. articles to profl. jours. Bd. dirs., 1st v.p. East Side Neighborhood Services, Inc., Mpls., 1976-80; bd. dirs. Guthrie Theater Found., 1979-85; mem. allocations com. United Way Mpls., 1979-86, chmn. allocations com., 1985, bd. dirs. 1985-86; mem. Citizens League of Twin Cities, 1965-86. Mem. ABA, D.C. Bar Assn., Fed. Bar Assn., Hennepin County Bar Assn., Am. Soc. Quality Control, Am. Intellectual Property Law Assn., Health Industry Mfrs. Assn. (past chmn. legal and regulatory sect., standard sect., 1975-87), Nat. Elec. Mfrs. Assn. (past chmn. med. electronics sect., 1970-76), Assn. Advancement Med. Instrumentation, Minn. State Bar Assn., Minn. Intellectual Property Law Assn. (past sec.), Minn. Corp. Counsel Assn., Regulatory Affairs. Profls. Soc., Order of Coif, Phi Delta Phi, Kappa Sigma. Episcopalian. Clubs: Mpls. Office: McKenna & Cuneo LLP 1900 K St NW Washington DC 20006-1110

STONE, EDMUND CRISPEN, III, banker; b. Charleston, W.Va., Nov. 29, 1942; s. Edmund C. and Sallie Ragland (Thornhill); S.; m. Annette Margarethe Isaksen, Nov. 26, 1965; 1 child, Kristine Margarethe. BS, U.S. Mil. Acad., 1964; MBA, U. Va., 1972. V.p. Wachovia Bank, Winston-Salem, N.C., 1972-81; exec. v.p. First Am. Corp., Nashville, from 1981; vice chmn. First Am. Nat. Bank Nashville, 1988; exec. v.p. Regions Fin. Corp. (formerly First Ala. Bancshares, Inc.), Birmingham, 1988—. Contbg. author: The International Banking Handbook, 1983. Mem. export policy task force U.S. C. of C., 1980-81. With inf. U.S. Army, 1964-70, Vietnam, Iran. Decorated Bronze Star (Valor) with oak leaf cluster, Vietnamese Cross of Gallantry, others; hon. mem. Imperial Iranian Spl. Forces, 1968. Mem. Assn. of Grads. U.S. Mil. Acad. (trustee 1992-93). Republican. Avocations: sailing; hunting; fishing. Office: Regions Fin Corp PO Box 10247 Birmingham AL 35202-0247

STONE, EDWARD CARROLL, physicist, educator; b. Knoxville, Iowa, Jan. 23, 1936; s. Edward Carroll and Ferne Elizabeth (Baber) S.; m. Alice Trabue Wickliffe, Aug. 4, 1962; children: Susan, Janet. AA, Burlington Jr. Coll., 1956; MS, U. Chgo., 1959, PhD, 1964; DSc (hon.), Washington U., Saint Louis, 1992, Harvard U., 1992, U. Chgo., 1992. Rsch. fellow in physics Calif. Inst. Tech., Pasadena, 1964-66, sr. rsch. fellow, 1967, mem.

faculty, 1967—, prof. physics, 1976-94, David Morrisroe prof. physics, 1994—, v.p. for astron. facilities, 1988-90, v.p., dir. Jet Propulsion Lab., 1991—; Voyager project scientist, 1972—; cons. Office of Space Scis., NASA, 1969-85, mem. adv. com. outer planets, 1972-73; mem. NASA Solar System Exploration Com., 1983; mem. com. on space astronomy and astrophysics Space Sci. Bd., 1979-82; mem. NASA high energy astrophysics mgmt. operating working group, 1976-84, NASA Cosmic Ray Program Working Group, 1980-82, Outer Planets Working Group, NASA Solar System Exploration Com., 1981-82, Space Sci. Bd., NRC, 1982-85, NASA Univ. Relations Study Group, 1983, steering group Space Sci. Bd. Study on Major Directions for Space Sci., 1995-2015, 1984-85; mem. exec. com. Com. on Space Research Interdisciplinary Sci. Commn., 1982-86; mem. commn. on phys. scis., math. and resources NRC, 1986-89; mem. adv. com. NASA/Jet Propulsion Labs. vis. sr. scientist program, 1986-90; mem. com. on space policy NRC, 1988-89; chmn. adv. panel for The Astronomers, KCET, 1989—. Mem. editl. bd. Space Sci. Instrumentation, 1975-81, Space Sci. Rev., 1982-85, Astrophysics and Space Sci., 1982—, Sci. mag. Bd. dirs. W.M. Keck Found. Recipient medal for exceptional sci. achievement NASA, 1980, Disting. Svc. medal, 1981, Disting. Pub. Svc. medal, 1985, Outstanding Leadership medal, 1986, 95, Am. Edn. award, 1981, Dryden award, 1983, Aviation Week and Space Tech. Aerospace Laureate, 1989, Sci. Man of Yr. award ARCS Found., 1991, Pres.'s Nat. medal of Sci., 1991, Am. Acad. Achievement Golden Plate award, 1992, COSPAR award for outstanding contbn. to space sci., 1992, LeRoy Randle Grumman medal, 1992, Disting Pub. Svc. award Aviation/Space Writers Assn., 1993, Good Scout award, 1995, Internat. von Karman Wings award, 1996; Asteroid named for Edward C. Stone, 1996; Sloan Found. fellow, 1971-73; inducted to Hall of Fame Aviation Week and Space Tech., 1997. Fellow AIAA (assoc., Space Sci. award 1984), AAAS (award 1993, Good Scout award 1995), Am. Phys. Soc. (chmn. cosmic physics divsn. 1979-80, exec. com. 1974-76), Am. Geophys. Union, Internat. Astron. Union; mem. NAS, Internat. Acad. Astronautics, Am. Astron. Soc. (divsn. planetary scis. com. 1981-84, Space Flight award 1997), Am. Assn. Physics Tchrs., Am. Philos. Soc. (Magellanic award 1992), Calif. Assn. Rsch. in Astronomy (bd. dirs., vice chmn. 1987-88, 91-94, chmn. 1988-91, 94—), Astron. Soc. Pacific (hon.), Nat. Space Club (bd. govs., Sci. award 1990), Calif. Coun. Sci. and Tech. Office: Jet Propulsion Lab 4800 Oak Grove Dr #180-904 Pasadena CA 91109-8001

STONE, EDWARD DURELL, JR., landscape architect and planner; b. Norwalk, Conn., Aug. 30, 1932; s. Edward Durell and Orlean (Vandiver) S.; m. Jacqueline Marty, Dec. 15, 1954 (div.); children: Edward D. III, Patricia Marty; m. Helen S. Eccelstone, Aug. 5, 1995. B.A. in Architecture, Yale U., 1954; M.Landscape Architecture, Harvard U., 1959. Pres. Edward D. Stone, Jr., & Assos. (P.A.), Ft. Lauderdale, Fla., 1960-89, chmn., 1989—; vis. critic, lectr. Tex. A&M U., Lawrence Inst. Tech., U. Ga., U. Mich., U. Ill., U. Va., U. Tenn.; adj. prof. landscape architecture U. Miami, Fla.; cons. First Lady's Com. More Beautiful Capital, 1965-68, Fla. Gov.'s. Conf. Environ. Quality, 1968-69; mem. Commn. Fine Arts, Washington, 1971-85; Mem. vis. com. Harvard U. Sch. Design; guest lectr. Chautaqua Inst., 1989, Golf Course Europe '89, Wiesbaden, Fed. Republic Germany, 1st Internat. Resort Conf., Tokyo, 1989, Symposium on European Recreational and Leisure Devel., Opio, France, 1989. Landscape archtl. designer: Pepsico World Hdqrs, Purchase, N.Y., 1972, Bal Harbour Shops (Fla.), 1971, El Morro Resort, Puerto La Cruz, Venezuela, 1972—, Profl. Golf Assn. Hdqrs. Master Plan, Palm Beach, Fla., 1978-79, Grand Cypress Resort, Orlando, Fla., 1983, Carambola Beach and Golf Club, St. Croix, V.I., 1988, Ft. Lauderdale (Fla.) Beach Revitalization, 1989, Onagawa, Japan, 1989, Pont Royal, Aix-en-Provence, France, 1989, Treyburn, Durham N.C., 1984, Euro Disney, Marne la Vallee, France, 1990, Riverwalk, Ft. Lauderdale, FL, 1989, El Conquistador, P.R., 1990. V.p. Landscape Architecture Found.; bd. dirs. Fla. Trust for Hist. Preservation, 1985-88. Capt. USAF, 1954-57. Recipient Profl. Landscape Architecture award HUD, 1968, awards Am. Assn. Nurserymen, 1967, 69, 70, 71, 77, 83, 88, 90, 91, Fla. Nurserymen and Growers Assn., 1982, 83, 85, 86, 88, 90, 91, 92, Am. Resort and Residential Devel. Assn., 1984, 85, 88, 89, 90, 91, 92, Interior Landscape Assn., 1984, 85. Fellow Am. Soc. Landscape Architects (13 awards 1963-88, 8 awards Fla. chpt. 1981-89, awards N.C. chpt. 1987, 88, 89, 92, medal 1994). Office: Edward D Stone Jr & Assocs 1512 E Broward Blvd Ste 110 Fort Lauderdale FL 33301-2126

STONE, EDWARD HARRIS, II, landscape architect; b. Lanesboro, Pa., Aug. 28, 1933; s. Frank Addison and Beth Lee (Brennan) S.; m. Diane Gertrude Berg, June 11, 1955; children: Randel Harris, Deborah Dee. B.S., SUNY, 1955. Landscape architect Harmon, O'Donnell & Henninger, Denver, 1955-56, U.S. Forest Service, Colo., 1958-61; regional landscape architect Alaska, 1961-64, Colo., 1964-65; chief landscape architect U.S. Forest Service, U.S. Dept. Agr., Washington, 1966-79; asst. dir. for recreation U.S. Forest Service, U.S. Dept. Agr., 1979-85; ret., 1985; with C-3 Co., Bowie, Md., 1986—. Served with AUS, 1956-57. Recipient Arthur S. Flemming award for outstanding fed. govt. service U.S. Jr. C. of C., 1969. Fellow Am. Soc. Landscape Architects (pres. 1975-76); mem. Sigma Lambda Alpha (hon.). Home and Office: 13200 Forest Dr Bowie MD 20715-4390

STONE, ELAINE MURRAY, author, composer, television producer; b. N.Y.C., Jan. 22, 1922; d. H. and Catherine (Fairbanks) Murray-Jacoby; m. F. Courtney Stone, May 30, 1944; children: Catherine Gladnick, Pamela Webb, Victoria. Student, Juilliard Sch. Music, 1939-41; BA, N.Y. Coll. Music, 1943; licentiate in organ, Trinity Coll. Music, London, 1947; student, U. Miami, 1952, Fla. Inst. Tech., 1963; PhD (hon.), World U., 1985. Organist, choir dir. St. Ingatius Episc. Ch., 1940-44; accompanist Strawbridge Ballet on Tour, N.Y.C., 1944; organist All Saints Episc. Ch., Ft. Lauderdale, 1951-54, St. John's Episc. Ch., Melbourne, Fla., 1956-59, First Christian Ch., Melbourne, 1962-63, United Ch. Christ, Melbourne, 1963-65, piano studio, Melbourne, 1955-70; editor-in-chief Cass Inc., 1970-71; dir. continuity radio Sta. WTAI, AM-FM, Melbourne, 1971-74; mem. sales staff Engle Realty Inc., Indialantic, Fla., 1975-78; v.p. pub. relations Consol. Cybertronics Inc., Cocoa Beach, Fla., 1969-70; writer, producer Countdown News, Sta. KXTX-TV, Dallas, 1978-80; assoc. producer Focus News, Dallas, 1980; host producer TV show, Focus on History, 1982-94, Epsic. Digest, 1984-90; judge Writer's Contest sponsored Brevard Cmty. Coll., 1987; v.p. Judges Fla. Space Coast Writer's Conf., 1985—, chmn., 1987. Author: The Taming of the Tongue, 1954, Love One Another, 1957, Menéndez de Avilés, 1968, Bedtime Bible Stories, Travel Fun, Sleepytime Tales, Improve Your Spelling for Better Grades, Improve Your Business Spelling, Tranquility Tapes, 1970, The Melbourne Bi-Centennial Book, 1976, Uganda: Fire and Blood, 1977, Tekla and the Lion, 1981 (1st Place award Nat. League Am. PEN Woman), Brevard County: From Cape of the Canes to Space Coast, 1988, Kizito, Boy Saint of Uganda, 1989 (2nd Place award Nat. League Am. PEN Woman 1990), Christopher Columbus: His World, His Faith., His Adventures, 1991 (1st Place award Nat. League Am. PEN Woman 1992), Elizabeth Bayley Seton: An American Saint, 1993 (3d Place award Nat. League Am. PEN Women 1994), Dimples The Dolphin, 1994 (1st Place award Fla. Space Coast Writer's Guild, 1994), Brevard at The Edge of Sea and Space, 1995, The Widow's Might, 1996 (1st place award Space Coast Writer's Contest), Carter G. Woodson Father of Black History, 1997, Maximilian Kolbe: Saint of Auschwitz, 1997; composer: Christopher Columbus Suite, 1992 (1st Place award PEN Women Music Awards 1992, 2d Place award 1993), Florida Suite for cello and piano, 1993; contbr. articles to nat. mags., newspapers including N.Y. Herald Tribune, Living Church, Christian Life; space corr. Religious News Service, Kennedy Space Ctr., 1962-78. Mem. exec. bd. Women's Assn., Brevard Symphony, 1967—; mem. heritage com. Melbourne Bicentennial Commn.; mem. Evangelism Commn. Episc. Diocese Cen. Fla., 1985-94; v.p. churchwomen group Holy Trinity Episcopal Ch., Melbourne, 1988-89, Stephen minister, 1988—, pres. churchwomen group, 1989—; bd. dirs. Fla. Space Coast Council Internat. Visitors, Fla. Space Coast Philharm., 1989—, Aid for the Arts, 1994. Recipient 1st place for piano Ashley Hall, 1935-39, S.C. State Music Contest, 1939, 1st place for piano composition Colonial Suite, Constitution Hall, Washington 1987, 88, 89, 3d place for vocal composition, 1989, honorable mention for article, 1989, 2nd place for piano composition, 1989, award lit. contest Fla. AAUW, 1989, 1st place award Fla. State PEN Women, 1990, 1st Place award Nat. Black History Essay Contest, 1990, Disting. Author of Yr. plaque Fla. Space Coast Writers Guild, 1992, 96; numerous other awards. Mem. ASCAP, Nat. League Am. PEN Women (1st place awards Tex. 1979, v.p. Dallas br. 1978-80, organizing pres. Cape Canaveral br. 1969, pres. 1988-90, 96—), Women Communications, DAR (Fla. state chmn. music 1962-63), Colonial Dames Am. (organizing pres. Melbourne chpt. 1994), Nat. Soc. DAR (organizing regent Rufus Fairbanks chpt. 1981-85, vice regent 1987—, historian 1989—), Children Am. Revolution (past N.Y. state chaplain), Am. Guild Organists (organizing warden Ft. Lauderdale), Space Pioneers, Fla. Press Episc., Aid for the Arts, Space Coast Writers Guild (past v.p.). Home: 1945 Pineapple Ave Melbourne FL 32935-7656

STONE, ELIZABETH CAECILIA, anthropology educator; b. Oxford, Eng., Feb. 4, 1949; d. Lawrence and Jeanne Cecilia (Fawtier) S.; m. Paul Edmund Zimansky, Nov. 5, 1976. BA, U. Pa., 1971; MA, Harvard U., 1973; PhD, U. Chgo., 1979. Lectr. anthropology SUNY, Stony Brook, 1977-78, asst. prof., 1978-85, assoc. prof., 1985-95, prof., 1995—; participated archaeol. in Eng., Iran, Iraq, Afghanistan; dir. archaeol. projects Ain Dara, Syria,, Tell Abu Duwari, Iraq, Ayanis Survey, Turkey. Author: Nippur Neighborhoods, 1987; co-author: (monograph) Old Babylonian Contracts from Nippur 1, 1976, Adoption in Old Babylonian Nippur and the Archive of Mannum-meshu-lissur, 1991; co-editor: The Cradle of Civilization: Recent Archaeology in Iraq-Biblical Archaeologist, 1992, Velles Paraules: Ancient Near Eastern Studies in Honor of Miguel Civil on the Occasion of His 65th Birthday, 1991; mem. editl. bd. Bull. Am. Schs. Oriental Rsch., 1993-95; contbr. articles to profl. jours. Assoc. trustee Am. Schs. of Oriental Rsch., 1983-90. Fulbright fellow, 1986-87; rsch. grantee Ford Found., 1974, Nat. Geog. Soc., 1983, 84, 88, 90, Am. Schs. of Oriental Rsch., 1987, 88, NSF, 1989-92, NEH, 1989-93. Office: SUNY Dept Anthropology Stony Brook NY 11794

STONE, ELIZABETH WENGER, retired dean; b. Dayton, Ohio, June 21, 1918; d. Ezra and Anna Bess (Markey) Wenger; m. Thomas A. Stone, Sept. 14, 1939 (dec. Feb. 1987); children: John Howard, Anne Elizabeth, James Alexander. A.B., Stanford U., 1937, M.A., 1938; M.L.S., Catholic U. Am., 1961; Ph.D., Am. U., 1968. Tchr. pub. schs. Fontana, Calif., 1938-39; asst. state statistician State of Conn., 1939-40; libr. New Haven Pub. Librs., 1940-42; dir. pub. relations, asst. to pres. U. Dubuque, Iowa, 1942-46; substitute libr. Pasadena (Calif. Pub. Libr. System), 1953-60; instr. Cath. U. Am., 1962-63, asst. prof., asst. to chmn. dept. libr. sci., 1963-67, assoc. prof., asst. to chmn., 1967-71, prof., asst. to chmn., 1971-72, prof., chmn. dept., 1972-80, dean Sch. Libr. and Info. Scis., 1981-83, prof. and dean emeritus, 1983—, lectr., 1990; libr. cons. U.S. Inst. of Peace, 1988-90; libr. Nat. Presbyn. Ch. and Ctr., Washington, 1991—, archivist, 1994—; founder, exec. dir. Continuing Libr. Edn. Network and Exchange, 1975-79; founder Nat. Rehab. Info. Ctr., 1977, project mgr., 1977-83; co-chmn. 1st World Conf. on Continuing Edn. for the Libr. and Info. Sci. Professions, 1984-85, 2nd World Conf., Barcelona, 1993. Author: Factors Related to the Professional Development of Librarians, 1969, (with James J. Kortendick) Job Dimensions and Educational Needs in Librarianship, 1971, (with R. Patrick and B. Conroy) Continuing Library and Information Science Education, 1974, Continuing Library Education as Viewed in Relation to Other Continuing Professional Movements, 1975, (with F. Peterson and M. Chobot) Motivation: A Vital Force in the Organization, 1977, American Library Development 1600-1899, 1977, (with others) Model Continuing Education Recognition System in Library and Information Science, 1979, (with M.J. Young) A Program for Quality in Continuing Education for Information, Library and Media Personnel, 1980, (with others) Continuing Education for the Library Information Professions, 1985, The Growth of Continuing Education, 1986, Library Education: Continuing Professional Education, 1993, (with others) ALA World Encyclopedia of Library and Information Science, 3d edit., 1993; author, editor: Continuing Professional Education for Library and Information Science Personnel: Papers from Seminar at Matica Slovenska, Martin Czechoslovakia, 1989; editor: D.C. Libraries, 1964-66; contbr. articles to profl. jours. Mem. Pres.'s Com. on Employment of Handicapped, 1972-88, Establishment of Elizabeth W. Stone Annual Lectureship Cath. U. Am., 1990—; pres. D.C. chpt. Am. Mothers, Inc., 1984-86, nat. v.p., 1989-91. Recipient Presdl. award Cath. U. Am., 1982, Spl. Librs. Profl. award, 1988, DCLA Ainsworth Rand Spofford Pres.'s award, 1990, Hon. Life Mem. 1994, Alumni Achievement award in libr. and info. sci. Cath. U. Am., 1990; named D.C. Mother of Yr., 1980. Mem. ALA (coun. 1976-83, v.p. 1980-81, pres. 1981-82, chmn. Nat. Libr. Week, 1983-85; founder ALA Nat. Ptnrs. for Librs. and Literacy 1984, Lippincott award 1986, Hon. Life award 1986), Assn. Libr. Info. and Sci. Edn. (pres. 1974), Am. Soc. Assn. Execs., Am. Assn. Adult and Continuing Edn., Internat. Fedn. Libr. Assns. and Instns. (chmn. Continuing Profl. Edn. Roundtable 1986-93), D.C. Libr. Assn. (hon. life, pres. 1966-67, hon. chair centennial com. 1992-94, hon. life 1994), Spl. Librs. Assn. (hon. life, pres. D.C. chpt. 1973-74), Cath. Libr. Assn. (hon. life), Continuing Profl. Edn. Libr. and Info. Sci. Pers., Soc. Am. Archivists, Cosmos Club, Phi Sigma Alpha, Beta Phi Mu, Phi Lambda Theta. Presbyterian. Home: 4000 Cathedral Ave NW # 15B Washington DC 20016-5249 Office: Cath U Am Sch Lib & Info Scis Washington DC 20064

STONE, F. L. PETER, lawyer; b. Wilmington, Del., Feb. 24, 1935; s. Linton and Lorinda (Hamlin) S.; m. Therese Louise Hannon, Apr. 7, 1969; 1 child, Lisa Judith. AB, Dartmouth Coll, 1957; LLB, Harvard U., 1960. Bar: Del. Supreme Ct. 1960, U.S. Ct. Appeals (3d cir.) 1964, U.S. Supreme Ct. 1965, U.S. Ct. Appeals (fed. cir.) 1983. Assoc. Connolly, Bove & Lodge, Wilmington, 1960-64; dep. atty. gen. State of Del., Wilmington, 1965-66; atty. Del. Gen. Assembly, Dover, 1967-68; counsel Gov. Del., Dover, 1969; U.S. atty. Dist. of Del., Wilmington, 1969-72; ptnr. Connolly, Bove, Lodge, & Hutz, Wilmington, 1972—; mem. Del. Agy. to Reduce Crime, 1969-72, Del. Organized Crime Commn., 1970-72, State Drug Abuse Coun., 1990-93, State Judicial Nominating Commn., 1991-93, State Coun. Corrections, 1992—; co-founder, adj. prof. criminal justice progra, West Chester (Pa.) U., 1975-79; chmn. Gov.'s Harness Racing Investigation Com., 1977, Del. Jai Alai Commn., 1977-78, Corrections Task Force, 1986-88. Author numerous articles. Chmn. UN Day, Del., 1989; Rep. candidate for atty. gen. Del., 1990, mem. Rep. exec. com., Wilmington region, 1991—; chmn. re-election campaign, Del. Ins. Commr., 1996; mem. Del. Gov.'s Task Force on Prison Security, 1994-95; trustee Leukemia Soc. Am., N.Y.C., 1972-74, Marywood Coll., Scranton, Pa., 1974-79, Ursuline Acad., Wilmington, 1974-80; bd. dirs. Boys & Girls Club Del., 1997—. Mem. Port of Wilmington Maritime Soc. (pres 1996—), Wilmington Country Club, Rodney Square Club, Lincoln Club Del. (pres. 1994), Wilmington Rotary (bd. dirs. 1995—), Nat. Assn. Former U.S. Attys. (bd. dirs. 1995—). Roman Catholic. Avocations: hiking/mountaineering, tennis, music. Office: Connolly Bove Lodge & Hutz PO Box 2207 1220 Market St Wilmington DE 19899 *Mu major accomplishment has been establishing and maintaining a close relationship with my family, first and foremost, regardless of what activities and accomplishments were pursued in my professional, political and community life.*

STONE, FRANZ THEODORE, retired fabricated metal products manufacturing executive; b. Columbus, Ohio, May 11, 1907; s. Julius Frederick and Edna (Andress) S.; m. Katherine Devereux Jones, Feb. 23, 1935; children: Franz Theodore, Thomas Devereux Mackay, Raymond Courtney (dec.), Catherine Devereux Diebold. AB magna cum laude, Harvard U., 1929; hon. degrees, Canisius Coll., 1975, Ohio State U., 1976. Chmn. bd. Columbus McKinnon Corp., Amherst, N.Y., 1935-86. Chmn. emeritus Arts Council in Buffalo and Erie County, 1973-86; pres. Buffalo Philharmonic Orch. Soc., 1959-61, also life dir.; chmn. emeritus Studio Arena Theatre, Buffalo, 1968-86; Nat. Conf. of Christian and Jews Brother Sisterhood citation, 1986; First Arts award Arts Council and Greater Buffalo C. of C. Recipient Gold Key award Buffalo YMCA, 1966, Red Jacket award Buffalo & Erie County Hist. Soc., 1976, Disting. Citizen award SUNY, Buffalo, 1985, Conductor's award Buffalo Philharm. Orch., 1993. Mem. Gulfstream Bath & Tennis Club, Ocean Club of Fla., Boca Raton Country Club, Pundits Club, Buffalo Country Club, Buffalo Club, Saturn Club (Buffalo), The Little Club (Gulfstream). Home: 1171 N Ocean Blvd Apt 4CS Gulf Stream FL 33483

STONE, FRED MICHAEL, lawyer; b. Bklyn., Jan. 20, 1943; s. Nathan and Rose (Silverman) S.; m. Bonnie B. Dobkin, Aug. 14, 1965; children—Jonathan, Jennifer. A.B. cum laude, Bklyn. Coll., 1964; J.D., Harvard U., 1967; LL.M., N.Y. U., 1971. Bar: N.Y. 1968. Assoc. Cadwalader, Wickersham & Taft, N.Y.C., 1967-69; asst. gen. counsel Standard & Poor's/Intercapital, Inc., N.Y.C., 1969-71; v.p., gen. counsel Neuwirth Funds, 1971-73, Mocatta Metals Corp., N.Y.C., 1973-76; sr. v.p., gen. counsel Am. Stock Exchange, Inc., N.Y.C., 1976-86; exec. v.p., gen. counsel Jamie Securities Co., Caronan Ptnrs., N.Y.C., 1986-88; sr. v.p., gen. counsel, sec. M.D. Sass Assocs., Inc., N.Y.C., 1989—; chmn. exec. com. Amex Commodities Exch., 1980-81; dir. Am. Gold Coin Exchange, Inc., 1981-85; exec. v.p., dir. Revere Copper and Brass, Inc., 1986-88; dir. Ea. Electric Motor Co., Inc., 1987-88; ofcl. adv. Drafting Com. to Revise Uniform Securities Act of Nat. conf. Uniform State Law Commrs., 1981-85; chmn. options and futures regulation subcom. of fed. regulation of securities com. ABA, 1989-91, mem. task force on Hedge Funds, 1994—; lectr. various legal seminars; sec. rules com. Investment Co. Inst., 1989-92; sec., treas. steering com. Taxable Mcpl. Bondholders Protective Com., 1990-95. Mem. Manalapan (N.J.) Twp. Zoning Bd. Adjustment, 1975-86; vice-chmn. Manalapan Dem. Com., 1988-96; Dem. candidate for Manalapan Twp. Com., 1989, 93; mem. N.J. regional exec. com. Anti-Defamation League of B'nai Brith, 1991—. Mem. ABA, Assn. of Bar of City of N.Y. (corp. law dept. comm. 1995—), Harvard U. Law Sch. Assn., Am. Stock Exch., Inc. (arbitrator 1986—), Nat. Assn. Securities Dealers Inc. (arbitrator 1986—), Nat. Futures Assn. (nominating com. 1986-88). Democrat. Jewish. Home: 15 Kingsley Dr Manalapan NJ 07726-3134

STONE, GAIL SUSAN, retired gifted, talented education educator; b. Elmhurst, Ill., Aug. 22, 1944; d. Harold Frederick Lopatka and May Anna (Lippert) Lopatka Wickham; m. Ronald Eugene Stone, Dec. 26, 1971; children: Andrew, Susanna. BA in Edn., Elmhurst Coll., 1966; M in Arts/Edn., Nat. Louis U., 1975. Cert. elem. edn. and supr. adminstrn. Tchr. first grade Shc. Dist. 89, Glen Ellyn, Ill., 1966-70; tchr. learning disability and gifted resource, kindergarten Sch. Dist. 94, North Riverside, Ill., 1972-81; gifted program coord. Sch. Dist. 102, La Grange, Ill., 1984-87, Sch. Dist. 96, Riverside, Ill., 1987-88; substitute tchr. Sch. Dist. 181, Hinsdale, Ill., 1988-92; tchr. gifted resources/spl. edn. aide Sch. Dist. 92, Broadview, Ill., 1992-93; coord. gifted program Sch. Dist. 103, Lyons, Ill., 1993-96; ret.; bd. trustees Ill. Future Problem Solving Bowl, Inc. Mem. Salt Creek Area AAUW (v.p. mem. 1986, v.p. program 1992-94), Ill. Coun. Gifted (v.p. 1979), Nat. Assn. Gifted, Children with Attention Deficit Disorder, Ill. Future Problem Solving Bowl (trustee), Alpha Xi Delta, Phi Delta Kappa. Avocations: swimming, reading, needlework. Home: 329 N Stone Ave La Grange Park IL 60526-1818

STONE, GEOFFREY RICHARD, law educator, lawyer; N.Y.C.; b. Jan. 20, 1946; s. Robert R. and Shirley (Weliky) S.; m. Nancy Spector, Oct. 8, 1977; children: Julie, Mollie. BS, U. Pa., 1968; JD, U. Chgo., 1971. Bar: N.Y. 1972. Law clk. to Hon. J. S. Kelly Wright, U.S. Ct. Appeals (D.C. cir.), 1971-72; law clk. to Hon. William J. Brennan, Jr., U.S. Supreme Ct., 1972-73; asst. prof. U. Chgo., 1973-77, assoc. prof., 1977-79, prof., 1979-84, Harry Kalven Jr. disting. svc. prof., 1984-93; dean Law Sch., 1987-93, provost, 1994—. Author: Constitutional Law, 1986, 3d edit., 1996, The Bill Of Rights In The Modern State, 1992; editor The Supreme Ct. Rev., 1991—; contbr. articles to profl. jours. Bd. dirs. Ill. div. ACLU, 1978-84; bd. advisors Pub. Svc. Challenge, 1989; bd. govs. Argonne Nat. Lab., 1994—, Nat. Opinion Rsch. Ctr., 1994—. Fellow AAAS; mem. Chgo. Coun. Lawyers (bd. govs. 1976-77), Assn. Am. Law Schs. (exec. com. 1990-93), Legal Aid Soc. (bd. dirs. 1988), Order of Coif. Office: U Chgo 5801 S Ellis Ave Chicago IL 60637-1476

STONE, HARRY H., business executive; b. Cleve., May 21, 1917; s. Jacob and Jennie (Kantor) Sapirstein; m. Lucile Tabak, Aug. 10, 1960; children: Phillip, Allan, Laurie (Mrs. Parker), James Rose, Douglas Rose. Student, Cleve. Coll., 1935-36. With Am. Greetings Corp., Cleve., 1936—, v.p., 1944-58, exec. v.p., 1958-69, vice chmn. bd., chmn. finance com., chmn audit com., 1969-78, now dir.; mem. Ofcl. U.S. Mission to India and Nepal, 1965; cons. U.S. Dept. Commerce, U.S. Dept. State; adviser U.S. del. 24th session UN Econ. Commn. for Asia and Far East, Canberra, Australia, 1968; cons. Nat. Endowment for Arts, Nat. Council on Arts. Treas. Criminal Justice Coordinating Council., 1968-82; trustee emeritus Brandeis U., also univ. fellow. Mem. Rotary (hon. pres.). Home: Suite 9D Bratenahl Pl # 2 Cleveland OH 44108-1183 Office: The Courtland Group Inc 1621 Euclid Ave #1600 Cleveland OH 44115-2107

STONE, HERBERT ALLEN, management consultant; b. Washington, Sept. 14, 1934; s. Joseph and Marion (Solomon) S.; m. Marjorie Nelke Sterling, June 14, 1964; children: Joanna, Lisa. BSc, U. Mass., 1955, MSc, 1958; PhD, U. Calif., Davis, 1962. Specialist Exptl. Sta. U. Calif., Davis, 1961-62; food scientist SRI, Menlo Park, Calif., 1962-67, dir. food and plant sci., 1967-74; pres. Tragon Corp., Redwood City, Calif., 1974—; mem. adv. bd. U. Mass. Food Sci., 1992—, Calif. Poly. U. Food Sci. and Nutrition, 1996—. Author: Sensory Evaluation Practices, 1985, 2d edit., 1993; assoc. editor Jour. Food Sci., 1977-80; contbr. sci. and tech. articles to profl. jours.; patentee in field. Fellow Inst. Food Exec. Com. (pres. S.E. divsn. 1977-78, exec. com.); mem. AAAS, Am. Soc. Enology, European Chemoreception Orgn., Ladera Oaks Club (Menlo Park, Calif.). Home: 990 San Mateo Dr Menlo Park CA 94025-5640 Office: Tragon Corp 365 Convention Way Redwood City CA 94063-1402

STONE, HERBERT MARSHALL, architect; b. N.Y.C., July 12, 1936; s. Irving and Rose (Gelb) S.; m. Linda Ann Baskind, May 30, 1960; children: Ian Howard, Matthew Lloyd. BArch, Pratt Inst., N.Y.C., 1958, postgrad., 1958-59. Registered architect, N.Y., Iowa, Kans., Ill., Wis., Minn. Designer Henry Dreyfuss Indsl. Design, N.Y.C., 1960-63; architect Max O. Urbahn Architect, N.Y.C., 1963-66; project architect Brown Healey Bock, P.C., Cedar Rapids, Iowa, 1966-73; ptnr. Brown Healey Stone & Sauer, Cedar Rapids, Iowa, 1973—, pres., 1994—; guest lectr. U.S. Inst. Theatre Tech., Seattle, 1978; speaker on design of pub. librs. ALA Nat. Conv., Miami, Fla., 1994. Prin. works include Strayer-Wood Theatre, 1978, KUNI radio sta. U. No. Iowa, 1978, Cedar Rapids Pub. Libr., 1984, Greenwood Terr. Sr. Citizen Housing, 1986, Iowa State Hist. Mus., 1988, Nat. Hot Air Balloon Mus., 1988 (Spectrum Ceramic Tile Grand award 1989), Student Ctr. Grinnell Coll., 1992, Hall of Pride, Iowa H.S. Athletic Assn., 1995. Pres. Cedar Rapids Trust for Hist. Preservation, 1981—; bd. dirs. Art in Pub. Places Com., Cedar Rapids, 1988, Cedar Rapids/Marion Arts Coun., 1988, Jane Boyd Community House, Cedar Rapids, 1988. Mem. AIA, Am. Mus. Assn., Greater Downtown Assn. Cedar Rapids. Avocations: bicycling, skiing, reading, ceramics. Home: 3730 Terrace Hill Dr NE Cedar Rapids IA 52402-2846 Office: Brown Healey Stone & Sauer PC 800 1st Ave NE Cedar Rapids IA 52402-5002

STONE, HUBERT DEAN, editor, journalist; b. Maryville, Tenn., Sept. 23, 1924; s. Archie Hubert and Annie (Cupp) S.; student Maryville Coll., 1942-43; B.A., U. Okla., 1949; m. Agnes Shirley, Sept. 12, 1953 (dec. Mar. 1973); 1 son, Neal Anson. Sunday editor Maryville-Alcoa Daily Times, 1949; mng. editor Maryville-Alcoa Times, 1949-78, editor, 1978—; v.p. Maryville-Alcoa Newspapers, Inc., 1960-90; pres. Stonecraft, 1954—. Photographer in field. Vice-chmn., chmn. Tenn. Great Smoky Mountains Park commn.; mem. State of Tenn. Hist. Commn.; co-chmn. 175th anniversary com. Maryville Coll.; mem. mayor's adv. com. City of Maryville; mem. air service adv. com. Knoxville Met. Airport Authority; bd. dirs. United Fund of Blount County, 1961-63, 74-76, vice chmn. campaign, 1971-72, chmn. campaign, 1973, v.p., 1974, pres., 1975; vice chmn. bd. dirs. Maryville Utilities Bd.; bd. dirs. Sam Houston Meml. Assn., Alcoa City Sch. Found., Blount County Hist. Trust, Nat. Hillbilly Homecoming Assn., Friendsville Acad., 1968-73, Alkiwan Crafts, Inc., 1970-73, Middle East Tenn. Regional Tourism Group; dir. Foothills Land Conservancy, Smoky Mountains Passion Play Assn., Blount County History Mus.; mem. adv. com. Blount County Alternative Center for Learning, Overlook Center, Inc., Sr. Citizens Home Assistance Svcs.; chmn. Blount County Long Range Planning for Sch. Facilities; mem. Blount County Bicentennial task force; mem. adv. bd. Harrison-Chilhowee Bapt. Acad, mem. Leadership Knoxville; co-founder, vice pres., pres. Leadership Blount County; founder, chmn. Townsend-in-the-Smokies Art Show/Sale, 1984—; mem. bd. govs. Maryville-Alcoa C.C. Orch. Soc; mem. State of Tenn. Hist. Commn.; trustee, pres. bd. trustees, deacon, chmn. evangelism, fin. & pers. coms. Bapt. Ch.; mem. Blount County Bicentennial com., State of Tenn. Hist. commn. Served from pvt. to staff sgt. AUS, 1943-45. Decorated Bronze Star; named Outstanding Sr. Man of Blount County, 1970, 77, Hon. Order Ky. Cols., Commonwealth of Ky.; recipient Pride of Tenn. award for vol. work, 1993, Outstanding Leadership award Maryville Ch. of Christ, First Tourism Pioneer award Smoky Mount. Vis. Bur. and Blount C. of C., 1994. Mem. VFW, Profl. Photographers of Am., Internat. Post Card Distbrs. Assn., Great Smoky Mountains Natural History Assn., State of Tenn. Hist. Commn., Ft. Loudoun Assn., Tenn. Jaycees (editor 1954-55, sec.-treas. 1955-56), Blount County Arts/ Crafts Guild, Jr. Chamber Internat. (senator) Maryville-Alcoa Jaycees (life mem., pres. 1953-54), Blount County (v.p. 1971, 76, pres. 1977), Townsend C. of C. (dir. 1969-71, 83-85, pres. 1983), Tenn. AP News Execs. Assn. (v.p. 1973, pres. 1974), AP Mng.

Editors Assn., Tenn. Profl. Photographers Assn., Am. Legion, Foothills Pkwy. Assn. (v.p., pres.), Chilhowee Bapt. Assn. (chmn. history com.) U. Okla. Alumni Assn. (life mem., pres. East Tenn. chpt. 1954-55), Sigma Delta Chi (life, dir. E. Tenn. chpt.), Mason, Kiwanian (pres. Alcoa 1969-70); Club: Green Meadow Country. Contbr. articles to profl. publs. Home: 1510 Scenic Dr Maryville TN 37803-5634 Office: 307 W Harper Ave Maryville TN 37801-4723

STONE, JACK, religious organization administrator. Gen. sec., hdqs. ops. officer Ch. of the Nazarene, Kansas City, Mo. Office: Ch Nazarene 6401 Paseo Blvd Kansas City MO 64131-1213*

STONE, JAMES HOWARD, management consultant; b. Chgo., Mar. 4, 1939; s. Jerome H. and Evelyn Gertrude (Teitelbaum) S.; m. Carole Marlen David, Apr. 21, 1972; children: Margaret Elisa, Emily Anne, Phoebe Jane. AB cum laude, Harvard U., 1960, MBA, 1962. Cert. mgmt. cons., CMC, 1977. Staff analyst Stone Container Corp., Chgo., 1962-64, gen. mgr., Kansas City Div., 1964-66, asst. treas., 1966-68, dir., 1969—, with exec. com., 1983—; founder, owner, CEO Stone Mgmt. Cons., 1969—; mem. strategic alliance Boston Cons. Group, 1990—, trustee, sec., exec. com. Roosevelt U., Chgo., 1983—, exec. com. edn. alliance, 1994—; co-chmn. commn. fgn. and domestic affairs Northwestern U., Evanston, Ill., 1981-85, bus. plan judge Kellogg Grad. Sch. Mgmt., 1994—; mem. vis. com. libr. U. Chgo., 1980—, The Chgo. Com., 1986—, Mid-Am. Com., Chgo., 1993—; bd. overseers IIT Stuart Sch. Bus., 1994—; bd. dirs. Fullerton Metals Corp., 1986-93, Sheridan Beverage. Mem. Chgo. Coun. Fgn. Rels., 1967, bd. dirs., 1974-78; bd. dirs., mem. exec. com. NCCJ, Chgo., 1985, presiding co-chmn., 1990—; trustee Hadley Sch. Blind, Winnetka, Ill., 1985-96, chmn. planning com., 1989—, Hadley life trustee, 1996—; vice chmn. fin. com. North Shore congregation Israel, 1995—; bd. dirs. Suzuki-Orff Sch., 1997—. Mem. Warehousing Edn. and Rsch. Coun., Inst. Mgmt. Cons. (pres. Chgo. chpt. 1981-83, regional dir. 1983-86), Coun. Logistics Mgmt. (dir. Roundtable-Chgo. 1990-94), Assn. Corp. Growth, The Exec. Club Chgo., Econs. Club, Harvard Club Chgo. (dir. 1995—), Harvard Bus. Sch. Assocs. Chgo. (dir. 1992—, pres. 1997—), Traffic Club Chgo., Standard Club, Northmoor Country Club. Avocations: family-centered activities, reading, golf, travel, coaching girls' softball. Home: 83 Woodley Rd Winnetka IL 60093-3746 Office: Stone Mgmt Corp 208 S La Salle St Chicago IL 60604

STONE, JAMES J., photographer; b. Los Angeles, Dec. 2, 1947; s. Charles S. and Sylvia S. S.B. in Arch, M.I.T., 1970; M.F.A. in Photography, R.I. Sch. Design, 1975. Mem. faculty R.I. Sch. Design, Providence, 1975-78, 93—, Boston Coll., Chestnut Hill, Mass., 1973-88. Author: A User's Guide to the View Camera, 1987, Stranger Than Fiction, 1993; editor: Darkroom Dynamics, 1979; one-man shows Anchorage Fine Arts Mus., 1977, Polaroid Gallery, Cambridge, Mass., 1978, Carl Siembab Gallery, Boston, 1979, Wesleyan U., Middletown, Conn., 1980, Visual Studies Workshop, Rochester, N.Y., 1986, San Francisco Camera Work, 1985, Robert Klein Gallery, 1987, Mitchell Mus., 1989, Huntington Mus. Art, 1990, Rice U., Houston, 1992; exhibited in group shows De Cordova Mus., Lincoln, Mass., 1972, Fogg Art Mus., Cambridge, 1974, 76, Corcoran Gallery Art, Washington, 1978-79, Mpls. Inst. Arts, 1987, Phila. Mus. Art, 1987, Nat. Mus. Am. Art, 1992; represented in permanent collection Nat. Mus. Am. Art, Washington, Corcoran Gallery Art, Fogg Art Mus., George Eastman House, Rochester, L.A. County Mus. Art, Mus. Modern Art, N.Y.C. Pres. bd. dirs. Photog. Resource Ctr., Boston. Mass. Artists Found. artists fellow, 1976, 88, New Eng. Found. for the Arts/NEA Regional Artists' fellow, 1993; artist-in-residence Alaska State Arts Coun., 1977; NEA photographic survey grantee, 1980. Office: care Robert Klein Gallery 38 Newbury St Boston MA 02116-3210

STONE, JAMES LESTER, mental health administrator; b. Syracuse, N.Y., May 31, 1940; s. Lester Herbert and Mary (Cowley) S.; BA, Syracuse U., 1962, MSW, 1964; m. Joan McDermott Borzelle, Aug. 5, 1967; children: Jeffrey Borzelle, Michael McDermott, Andrew Cowley. Dep. dir. Onondaga County detention care Syracuse, 1962-63; tchr. Fayetteville-Manlius (N.Y.) Schs., 1964-65; asst. dir. Edmond Fitzgerald Start Ctr., N.Y. State Div. Youth, Middletown, 1965-67; dir. Rochester (N.Y.) Urban Youth Home, 1967-73; asst. supt. N.Y. State Div. for Youth Tng. Sch., Industry, 1973-74, supt., 1974-78; dir. Livingston County Dept. Mental Health, Mt. Morris, N.Y., 1978-79; chief outpatient svcs. Willard Psychiat. Ctr., 1979-81; dir. community svcs. Rochester Psychiat. Ctr., 1981-82, chief treatment svc., 1982-88; dir. Monroe County Dept. Mental Health and Community Svcs., 1988-95; commr. N.Y.S. Office of Mental Health, 1995—; lectr., Rochester Inst. Tech., 1968-71; field faculty Syracuse U., 1969-74, Colgate-Rochester Div. Sch., 1983-88; cons. Disability Determination N.Y. State Dept. of Social Svcs., 1982-92; exec. bd., chmn law com. Assn. for Community Transitional Svcs.; mem. adv. com. human svcs. dept. Monroe Community Coll., 1978—; mem. adv. com. Health Assn. DayBreak Alcoholism Treatment Ctr., 1986-88; chair substance abuse com. N.Y. State Conf. Local Mental Hygiene Dirs., 1989-94; chair Conf. Local Mental Hygiene Dirs., 1994-95; mem. N.Y. State Mental Health Svcs. Coun., 1993-95. Mem. Ralph Bunche Scholarship Fund, 1992-95. With N.Y. Air N.G., 1962-68. Recipient Svc. to Youth award N.Y.S. Divsn. for Youth, 1978, John Romano award Contbns. to Community for Mental Health Mental Health Assn. of Rochester and Monroe County, 1992, Disting. Alumnus award Syracuse U. Sch. Social Work, 1995. Fellow Am. Orthopsychiat. Assn.; mem. Am. Assn. Mental Health Adminstrs., Am. Group Psychotherapy Assn., Nat. Assn. Social Workers, Acad. Cert. Social Workers. Home: 66 Yorktown Dr Webster NY 14580-2243 Office: NYS Office Mental Health 44 Holland Ave Albany NY 12229

STONE, JAMES ROBERT, surgeon; b. Greeley, Colo., Jan. 8, 1948; s. Anthony Joseph and Dolores Concetta (Pietrafeso) S.; m. Kaye Janet Friedman, May 16, 1970; children: Jeffrey, Marisa. BA, U. Colo., 1970; MD, U. Guadalajara, Mex., 1976. Diplomate Am. Bd. Surgery, Am. Bd. Surg. Critical Care. Intern Md. Gen. Hosp., Balt., 1978-79; resident in surgery St. Joseph Hosp., Denver, 1979-83; practice medicine specializing in surgery Grand Junction, Colo., 1983-87; staff surgeon, dir. critical care Va. Med. Ctr., Grand Junction, 1987-88; dir. trauma surgery and critical care, chief surgery St. Francis Hosp., Colorado Springs, Colo., 1988-91; pvt. practice Kodiak, Alaska, 1991-92; with South Denver Surg. Cons., Englewood, Colo., 1992-93, Summit Surg. Assocs., 1993-96; asst. dir. trauma Tristate Trauma System, Erie, Pa., 1996—; med. dir. LifeStar Aeromed, Erie, Pa., 1997—; asst. clin. prof. surgery U. Colo. Health Sci. Ctr., Denver, 1984—; pres. Stone Aire Cons., Grand Junction, 1988—; owner, operator Jjnka Ranch, Flourissant, Colo.; spl. advisor CAP, wing med. officer, 1992—; mem. advisor med. com. unit, 1990-92; advisor Colo. Ground Team Search and Rescue, 1994—. Contbr. articles to profl. jours.; inventor in field. Bd. dirs. Mesa County Cancer Soc., 1988-89, Colo. Trauma Inst., 1988-91. Colo. Speaks out on Health grantee, 1988; recipient Bronze medal of Valor Civil Air Patrol. Fellow Denver Acad. Surgery, Southwestern Surg. Congress, Am. Coll. Chest Physicians, Am. Coll. Surgeons (trauma com. Colo. chpt.), A:n. Coll. Critical Care; mem. Am. Coll. Physician Execs., Soc. Critical Care (task force 1988—). Roman Catholic. Avocations: horse breeding, hunting, fishing.

STONE, JEFFREY JAY, film critic, journalist, writer; b. Toronto, Ont., Can., Oct. 2, 1946; s. Philip Maurice and Mildred (Walton) S.; m. Sandra Patricia Ridob, May 2, 1970; children: Benjamin Matthew, Laura Noelle. Editor The Record-News, Smith Falls, Ont., 1972-73; reporter, columnist The Brampton (Ont.) Times, 1973-76; copy editor The Ottawa (Ont.) Citizen, 1976-80, asst. sports editor, 1980-81, asst. city editor, 1981-84, design editor, 1984-85, entertainment editor, 1985-90, entertainment columnist, 1990-94, film critic, 1994—. Patron Coun. for Arts in Ottawa, 1994. Mem. Variety Club of Can., Laurentian Jr. Music Club, Elvis Sighting Soc. Avocations: bridge, reading, chess. Office: The Ottawa Citizen, 1101 Baxter Rd, Ottawa, ON Canada K2C 3M4

STONE, JEREMY JUDAH, professional society administrator; b. N.Y.C., Nov. 23, 1935; s. I.F. and Esther (Roisman) S.; m. Betty Jane Yannet, June 16, 1957. B.S. magna cum laude, Swarthmore Coll., 1957, LL.D. (hon.), 1985; Ph.D., Stanford U., 1960. Research mathematician Stanford Research Inst., 1960-62; mem. profl. staff Hudson Inst., Croton-on-Hudson, 1962-64; research asso., arms control and disarmament Harvard Ctr. Internat. Affairs, 1964-66; asst. prof. math., lectr. polit. sci. Pomona Coll., Claremont, Calif., 1966-68; CEO Fedn. Am. Scientists, Washington, 1970—. Author: Containing the Arms Race; Some Concrete Proposals, 1966, Strategic Persuasion, 1967. Recipient award for pub. svc. Forum on Physics and Soc., Am. Phys. Soc., 1979, Fedn. of Am. Scientists Pub. Svc. award, 1994; Social Sci. Rsch. Coun. fellow in econs. Stanford U., 1968-69, Coun. Fgn. Rels. internat. affairs fellow, 1969-70. Mem. Coun. Fgn. Rels., Internat. Inst. Strategic Studies, Phi Beta Kappa. Home: 5615 Warwick Pl Bethesda MD 20815-5503 Office: Fedn Am Scientists 307 Massachusetts Ave NE Washington DC 20002-5701

STONE, JOHN FLOYD, soil physics researcher and educator; b. York, Nebr., Oct. 13, 1928; s. Harry Floyd and Anastasia (Klima) S.; m. Carol Ottilie Youngson, Aug. 2, 1953; children: Mary, Margaret, David, Jana. BS, U. Nebr., 1952; MS, Iowa State U., 1955, PhD, 1957. Lab. technician U. Nebr., 1944-53; from rsch. asst. to rsch. assoc. Iowa State U., 1953-57; from asst. to assoc. prof. Okla. State U., Stillwater, 1957-69, prof. soil physics, 1969-94; prof. emeritus, 1994—; mem. adv. agrl. panel U.S. Dept. Def., 1977-78; mem. grant evaluation panel Water Quality Grant Program, USDA, 1989, Small. Bus. Initiative Rsch. Grant Program, 1990. Editor: Plant Modification for More Efficient Water Use, 1975, Plant Production and Management under Drought Conditions, 1983; contbr. chpts. to books, rsch. articles to profl. jours.; co-patentee apparatus for measuring water content of soil; co-discoverer Nova-Cygni, 1975. Commr. Stillwater City, 1974-75; mem. Stillwater Housing Appeals Bd., 1975-79; com. mem. troop 14 Boy Scouts Am., 1976-83, merit badge counselor, 1974—; del. to jurisdictional conf. United Meth. Ch., 1968, alt. del. to gen. conf., 1968. Grantee USDA, 1980, 83, 89, 90, 91, 92, NSF, 1961, U.S. Dept. Interior, 1968, 73, 79, 89, 91, Okla. Dept. Commerce, 1988, Okla. Coun. for Applied Sci. and Tech., Energy Efficient Irrigation, 1990. Fellow Am. Soc. Agronomy (editl. bd., assoc. editor Agronomy jour. 1982-85); mem. ASCE (com. on irrigation water requirements 1979-95, chmn. task com. on calibration and use of neutron moisture meters 1990-94, State-of-the-Art of Civil Engring. award 1992), Internat. Soil Sci. Soc., Am. Geophys. Union (vis. scientist lectr. 1972), Sigma Xi, Am. Radio Relay League, Stillwater Amateur Radio Club. Democrat. Methodist. Avocations: photography, amateur astronomy, music, amateur radio.

STONE, JOHN HELMS, JR., admiralty advisor; b. Andalusia, Ala., Dec. 3, 1927; s. John Helms and Ruth May (Barker) S.;m. Mary Ham, July 24, 1950; children: Malcolm, Mary Ruth, Ronald, John T. Student Ga. Mil. Coll., U.S. Merchant Marine Sch., 1945; student, Tulane U., 1975. Master mariner, USCG. Master capt. Sea-Land Steamship, Port Newark, N.J., 1947-60; Lt. (jg) USNR, 1948-62; sr. pilot Panama Canal Co., Balboa Canal Zone, 1960-73; chief of transit op. Panama Canal Commn., Balboa Canal Zone, 1973-76; chmn. bd. local inspection Panama Canal Commn., Balboa, Republic of Panama, 1976-85; admiralty cons. John H. Stone & Assocs., Boulder, Colo., 1985—, Am. Registry Arbitrators, 1994—; admiralty advisor Phelps-Dunbar, New Orleans, 1958-79, Fowler White, Tampa, Fla., 1984, Terriberry & Assocs., New Orleans, 1992. County treas. Dem. Party, Boulder, 1989. Mem. NRA (v.p. 1970, master pistol and rifle shot), Master, Mates and Pilots Union (v.p. 1970-72). Presbyterian. Avocation: stock market. Home: 3795 Wild Plum Ct Boulder CO 80304-0460

STONE, JOHN MCWILLIAMS, JR., electronics executive; b. Chgo., Nov. 4, 1927; s. J. McWilliams and Marion (Jones) S.; m. Cheryl Johansen Cullison, Dec. 18, 1976; children: Jean Stone Savanyu, Lee Stone Nelson, John III, Michael (dec.), Shannon, Tammy. BA, Princeton U., 1950. Salesman A.B. Dick Co., Milw., 1950-51; prodn. supr. Dukane Corp., St. Charles, Ill., 1951-56, exec. v.p., 1956-62, pres., 1962-70, pres., chmn. bd., 1970—, chmn. bd., pres., CEO, 1991-97; bd. dirs. Harris Bank St. Charles. Trustee The Elgin (Ill.) Acad. (recipient Elgin medal 1984, emeritus 1985—), Phillips Exeter (N.H.) Coun., 1985—, Three Rivers Coun. Boy Scouts Am., St. Charles; mem. Delnor Cmty. Hosp. Men's Found., St. Charles. Named Exec. of Yr. Valley chpt. Profl. Secs. Internat., Aurora, 1981. Mem. Commonwealth Club of Chgo., Econ. Club of Chgo., Princeton Club of Chgo., Execs. Club of Chgo., Dunham Woods Riding Club (pres. 1967-68, 78-79, 89-90). Republican. Episcopalian. Avocation: tennis. Home: PO Box 755 Wayne IL 60184-0755 Office: Dukane Corp 2900 Dukane Dr Saint Charles IL 60174-3348

STONE, JOHN TIMOTHY, JR., writer; b. Denver, July 13, 1933; s. John Timothy and Marie Elizabeth (Briggs) S.; m. Judith Bosworth Stone, June 22, 1955; children: John Timothy III, George William. Student Amherst Coll., 1951-52, U. Mex., 1952; BA, U. Miami, 1955; postgrad., U. Miami 1955, U. Colo., 1959-60. Sales mgr. Atlas Tag, Chgo., 1955-57; br. mgr. Household Fin. Corp., Chgo., 1958-62; pres. Janeff Credit Corp., Madison, Wis., 1962-72; pres. Recreation Internat., Mpls., 1972-74; pres. Continental Royal Services, N.Y.C., 1973-74; dir. devel. The Heartlands Group/Tryon Mint, Toronto, Ont., Can., 1987-89; spl. cons. Creative Resources Internat., Madison, 1988-90, Pubs Adv. Group, 1990—; spl. cons. art and antiques Treasure Hunt Assocs., 1994—; bd. dirs. Madison Credit Bur., Wis. Lenders' Exchange. Author: Mark, 1973, Going for Broke, 1976, The Minnesota Connection, 1978, Debby Boone So Far, 1980, (with John Dallas McPherson) He Calls Himself "An Ordinary Man", 1981, Satiacum, The Chief Who's Winning Back the West, 1981, Runaways, 1983, (with Robert E. Gard) Where The Green Bird Flies, 1984, The Insiders Guide to Buying Art, 1993, Anyone's Treasure Hunt, 1995, (with Viscount Mandeville Baron Montagu, Alexander Montagu) Maverick Nobleman, 1997; syndicated columnist The Great American Treasure Hunt, 1983-87. Served with CIC, U.S. Army, 1957-59. Mem. Sigma Alpha Epsilon. Presbyterian. Clubs: Minarani, African First Shotters. Home: 1009 Starlight Dr Madison WI 53711-2724 Office: Pubs Adv Group 1009 Starlight Dr Madison WI 53711-2724

STONE, LAWRENCE, historian; b. Epsom, Surrey, Eng., Dec. 4, 1919; came to U.S., 1963, naturalized, 1970; s. Lawrence Frederick and Mabel Julia Annie (Read) S.; m. Jeanne Caecilia Fawtier, July 24, 1943; children: Elizabeth Caecilia, Robert Lawrence Fawtier. Student, U. Paris-Sorbonne, 1938; BA, MA, Christ Church, Oxford (Eng.) U., 1946; LHD, U. Chgo., 1979, U. Pa., 1986; LittD, U. Edinburgh, 1983, U. Glasgow, 1993; Oxford U., 1994; LittD, Princeton U., 1995. Bryce research student Oxford U., 1946-47; lectr. Oxford U. (Univ. Coll.), 1947-50; fellow Wadham Coll., 1950-63; mem. Inst. Advanced Study, Princeton, 1960-61; Dodge prof. history Princeton, 1963-90, chmn. dept. history, 1967-70; dir. Shelby Cullom Davis Ctr. Hist. Studies, 1968-90. Author: Sculpture in Britain: The Middle Ages, 1955, An Elizabethan: Sir Horatio Palavicino, 1956, The Crisis of the Aristocracy, 1558-1641, 1965, The Causes of the English Revolution 1529-1642, 1972, rev. edit., 1986, Family and Fortune: Studies in Aristocratic Finance in the Sixteenth and Seventeenth Centuries, 1973, Family, Sex and Marriage in England 1500-1800, 1977, The Past and the Present, 1981, An Open Elite? England 1540-1880, 1985, The Past and the Present Revisited, 1987, Road to Divorce: England 1530-1987, 1990, Uncertain Unions: Marriage in England 1660-1753, 1992, Broken Lives: Marital Separation and Divorce in England 1660-1857, 1993, also numerous articles; mem. editl. bd. Past and Present, 1959—. Served as lt. Royal Naval Vol. Res., 1940-45. Fellow Am. Acad. Arts and Scis.; Corr. mem. Brit. Acad.; mem. Am. Philos. Soc. Home: 266 Moore St Princeton NJ 08540-3476

STONE, LAWRENCE MAURICE, lawyer, educator; b. Malden, Mass., Mar. 25, 1931; s. Abraham Jacob and Pauline (Kurtz) S.; m. Anna Jane Clark, June 15, 1963; children: Abraham Dean, Ethan Goldthwaite, Katharine Elisheva. AB magna cum laude, Harvard U., 1953, JD magna cum laude, 1956. Bar: Mass. 1956, Calif. 1958. Rsch. asst. Am. Law Inst., Cambridge, Mass., 1956-57; assoc. Irell and Manella, L.A., 1957-61, ptnr., 1963, 79—; internat. tax coordinator U.S. Treasury Dept., Washington, 1961-62, tax legis. counsel, 1964-66; prof. law U. Calif., Berkeley, 1966-78; vis. prof. law Yale U., New Haven, 1969, Hebrew U. Jerusalem, 1973-74, U. So. Calif., L.A., 1984; mem. adv. group to commr. IRS, Washington, 1973-74; mem. President's Adv. Commn. on Tax Ct. Appointments, Washington, 1976-80; tax advisory bd. Little Brown Co., 1994-96. Author: (with Doernberg) Federal Income Taxation of Corporations and Partnerships, 1987, (with Klein, Bankman and Bittker) Federal Income Taxation, 1990; bd. editors Harvard Law Rev., 1955-56. Fellow Am. Coll. Tax Counsel; mem. ABA, Am. Law Inst., Internat. Fiscal Inst., Am. Arbitration Assn., L.A. County Bar Assn. (recipient Dana Latham award 1995), Phi Beta Kappa. Office: Irell & Manella 1800 Avenue Of The Stars Los Angeles CA 90067-4212

STONE, LAWRENCE MYNATT, publishing executive; b. Balt., June 24, 1945; s. David G. and Clara Ruth (Coxey) S.; m. Lois V. Smith, June 10, 1967; children: Bradley Michael, Geoffrey David. BA, U. Iowa, 1968. Prof. Northeastern Bible Coll., Essex Fells, N.J., 1968-69; missionary Africa Evangelical Fellowship, Ndola, Zambia, 1969-71; asst. to production mgr. Am. Bible Soc., N.Y.C., 1971-72; book club mgr. Iversen-Norman Assocs., N.Y.C., 1972-75; editl. v.p. Thomas Nelson Pubs., Nashville, 1976-85; pres. Rutledge Hill Press, Nashville, 1985-97, pub., chmn. bd., 1997—; book and libr. adv. com. U.S. Info. Agency, Washington, 1984-88; editor in field; ghost writer. Office: Rutledge Hill Press 211 7th Ave N Nashville TN 37219-1823

STONE, LEON, banker; b. Rockdale, Tex., Feb. 27, 1914; s. Harley J. and Ella (Strelsky) S.; m. Bess Northington, Aug. 19, 1939; children—Pebble Stone Moss, Cherry J. Stone Wallin. Student, Blinn Coll., Brenham, Tex, 1932, Sul Ross Coll., Alpine, Tex., 1934, U. Tex., 1935, Rutgers U., 1954. With Brown & Root, Houston, 1936-37; Guggenheim-Goldsmith, Austin, Tex., 1937-38; with Austin Nat. Bank, 1938—, pres., 1963-84; also dir.; bd. dirs. First State Bank, Burnet, Tex.; chmn. Southwestern Grad. Sch. Banking, So. Meth. U. Dallas. Vice chmn. Tchr. Retirement System Tex., 1956-77; bd. dirs. Presbyn. Theol. Sem., 1958—, Seton Hosp., 1966—, Mental Health and Mental Retardation Assn., 1965—. Served to lt. col. U.S. Army, ETO. Named Boss of Year, Credit Women of Austin, 1966. Mem. Am. Bankers Assn. (regional v.p. 1965—, exec. com. 1966—), Tex. Bankers Assn. (pres. 1973), Am. Inst. Banking (past pres.), Austin C. of C. (pres. 1968), Tex. Taxpayers Assn. (pres.). Clubs: Rotarian, Mason, Shriner (Jester). Office: Nations Bank PO Box 908 Austin TX 78781

STONE, LINDA CHAPMAN, physician, consultant, medical educator; b. Detroit, Apr. 20, 1943; d. Harry Walter and Kathryn Ann (Forshee) Chapman; m. Laurence B. Stone, July 10, 1965; 1 child, Robert Laurence. BA, Mich. State U., 1961-65; MA, Ohio U., 1971; MD, Ohio State U., 1979. Diplomate Am. Bd. Family Practice. Tchr. local high schs., Mich., 1965-69; instr. comms. Ohio U., 1970-71; resident physician Riverside Meth. Hosp., Columbus, Ohio, 1979-82, chief resident, 1981-82; family physician Beechwold Med. Ctr., Columbus, Ohio, 1983-93; family physician, instr. U. Mich., 1993; v.p. physician ednl. comms. U.S. Health Corp., Columbus, 1994, v.p. primary care devel., 1995-96; exec. v.p. Med. Group Ohio, 1983-97; clin. asst. prof. medicine Ohio State U., 1983-97; bd. dirs. Elizabeth Blackwell Ctr., Columbus, 1983-89, 94—, chair, 1995—; bd. dirs. Gerlach Ctr. Sr. Health, Columbus, 1995-96; cons. US Health Corp., Columbus, Ohio; mem. tchg. staff family practice resident Riverside Meth. Hosp. Healthcare adv. various women's orgns., 1983—. Fellow Am. Acad. Family Physicians; mem. AAUW, Am. Med. Women's Assn., AMA, Am. Coll. Physicians (exec.), Ohio Acad. Family Physicians (bd. dirs. 1992-96); Ctrl. Ohio Acad. Family Physicians, Ohio State Med. Assn., Soc. Tchrs. Family Medicine, Delta Gamma. Democrat. Methodist. Avocations: creative writing. Office: Med Group Ohio 300 E Wilson Bridge Rd Worthington OH 43085-2339

STONE, MARVIN JULES, physician, educator; b. Columbus, Ohio, Aug. 3, 1937; s. Roy J. and Lillian (Bedwinek) S.; m. Jill Feinstein, June 29, 1958; children: Nancy Lillian, Robert Howard. Student, Ohio State U., 1955-58; SM in Pathology, U. Chgo., 1962, MD with honors, 1963. Diplomate Am. Bd. Internal Medicine, (Hematology, Med. Oncology). Intern ward med. svc. Barnes Hosp., St. Louis, 1963-64, asst. resident, 1964-65; clin. assoc. arthritis and rheumatism br. Nat. Inst. Arthritis and Metabolic Diseases, NIH, Bethesda, Md., 1965-68; resident in medicine, ACP scholar Parkland Meml. Hosp., Dallas, 1968-69; fellow in hematology-oncology, dept. internal medicine U. Tex. Southwestern Med. Sch., Dallas, 1969-70, instr. dept. internal medicine, 1970-71, asst. prof., 1971-73, assoc. prof., 1974-76, clin. prof., 1976—, chmn. bioethics com., 1979-81; mem. faculty and steering com. immunology grad. program, Grad. Sch. Biomed. Scis., U. Tex. Health Sci. Ctr., Dallas, 1975, adj. mem., 1976—; dir. Charles A. Sammons Cancer Ctr., chief oncology, dir. immunology, co-dir. divsn. hematology-oncology, attending physician Baylor U. Med. Ctr., Dallas, 1976—; v.p. med. staff Parkland Meml. Hosp., Dallas, 1982. Contbr. chpts. to books, articles to profl. jours. Chmn. com. patient-aid Greater Dallas/Ft. Worth chpt. Leukemia Soc. Am., 1971-76, chmn. med. adv. com., 1978-80, bd. dirs., 1971-80; mem. v.p. Dallas unit Am. Cancer Soc., 1977-78, pres., 1978-80; mem. adv. bd. Baylor U. Med. Ctr. Found. With USPHS, 1965-68. Named Outstanding Full Time Faculty Mem. Dept. Internal Medicine, Baylor U. Med. Ctr., 1978, 87. Fellow ACP (gov. No. Tex. 1993-97); mem. AMA, Am. Assn. Immunologists, Am. Soc. Hematology, Internat. Soc. Hematology, Coun. Thrombosis, Am. Heart Assn. (established investigator 1970-75), Am. Soc. Clin. Oncology, Am. Osler Soc. (bd. govs. 1997—), Am. Assn. for Cancer Rsch., So. Soc. Clin. Investigation, Tex. Med. Assn., Dallas County Med. Soc., Clin. Immunology Soc., Phi Beta Kappa, Sigma Xi, Alpha Omega Alpha. Office: Baylor U Med Ctr Charles A Sammons Cancer Ctr 3500 Gaston Ave Dallas TX 75246-2017

STONE, MARVIN LAWRENCE, journalist, government official; b. Burlington, Vt., Feb. 26, 1924; s. Samuel and Anita (Abrams) S.; m. Sydell Magelaner, Nov. 20, 1949; children—Jamie Faith, Stacey Hope, Torren Magelaner. Student, Emory and Henry Coll., 1943, U. Vt., 1948; B.A., Marshall Coll., 1947; M.S., Columbia U., 1949; Litt.D., Marshall U., 1968; LL.D., Emory and Henry Coll., 1981; D.H.L., Elon Coll., 1982. Assignment reporter Huntington (W.Va.) Herald-Dispatch, 1941-43, 46-48; European corr. Internat. News Service, 1949-52, Far Eastern dir., 1952-58; Sloan Found. fellow in sci. Columbia U., 1958-59; cons. chief army research and devel., 1959-60; assoc. editor U.S. News & World Report mag., 1960-66, gen. editor, 1966-68, asso. exec. editor, 1969-70, sr. asso. exec. editor, 1971-72, exec. editor, 1973-76, v.p., editor-in-chief, 1976-85, chmn. bd., 1984-85; chmn. bd. Madana Realty Co., 1984-85; dep. dir. USIA, 1985-89; U.S. commr. gen. Seville '92' Expo, 1989-90; mem. adv. com. U.S. Patent Office, 1976-78; adj. fellow Coun. on Strategic and Internat. Studies, 1989-90; mem. adv. bd. Univ. Pubs., 1989-92, Corp. for Pub. Broadcasting program adv. bd., 1992; chmn., pres., Internat. Media Fund, 1990-95. Author: Man in Space. Trustee, v.p., bd. dirs. Washington Opera; chmn. bd. dirs. USN Meml. Found., 1981-82, vice chmn., 1983-94, bd. dirs., 1991-95; mem. nat. adv. bd. Am. U.; bd. dirs. Pub. Diplomacy Found., Am. News Women's Found., 1991. Lt. (j.g.) USNR, 1943-46. Recipient Columbia Journalism 50th Anniversary Honor award, 1963, Marshall U. Disting. Alumnus award, 1973, Nat. Disting. Alumnus award Am. Assn. State Colls. and Univs., 1977, Freedoms Found. award, 1978, 79, 80, 81, Legion of Honor Chapel of Four Chaplains, 1980, Am. Eagle award, 1983, Silver Gavel award ABA, 1983, Gold Mercury Internat. award, Rome, Nat. Communication award Boys Clubs Am., Gill Robb Wilson award U.S. Air Force Assn., Disting. Honor award USIA; named to Washington Journalists' Hall of Fame, 1990, knight Internat. Press Fellowship, Hungary, 1995, Croatia, 1996; Pulitzer traveling fellow, Columbia, Austria, 1950. Fellow Ctr. for Security and Internat. Studies (adj.); mem. White House Corrs. Assn., Am. Soc. Mag. Editors (exec. com. 1985), Nat. Press Club, Omicron Delta Kappa, Sigma Delta Chi. Clubs: Fgn. Corrs. of Japan (pres. 1956-57); Internat. (Washington), Cosmos (Washington), Caribao (Washington). Home: 6318 Crosswoods Circle Lake Barcroft Falls Church VA 22044

STONE, MERRILL BRENT, lawyer; b. Jersey City, N.J., Aug. 16, 1951; s. Leonard and Claire (Orlean) S.; m. Geri Ellen Satkin, Nov. 24, 1976; children: Jacqueline Blair, Erica Lauren. AB summa cum laude, Rutgers U., 1973; JD, Columbia U., 1976. Bar: N.J. 1976, N.Y. 1977, Fla. 1981, U.S. Dist. Ct. N.J. 1976, U.S. Dist. Ct. (so. dist.) N.Y. 1977, U.S. Dist. Ct. (so. dist.) Fla. 1983. Assoc. Kelley Drye & Warren, N.Y.C., 1976-84; resident Kelley Drye & Warren, Miami, 1983-85; ptnr. Kelley Drye & Warren, N.Y.C., 1985-92, mng. ptnr., 1992—. Editor: (comments section) Columbia Human Rights Law Rev., N.Y.C., 1975-76. Trustee Greater Miami C. of C., 1984-85. Named Harlan Fiske Stone Scholar, Columbia Law Sch., N.Y.C., 1975-76. Mem. ABA (bus. bankruptcy com. sect. on bus. law, banking law com.), Am. Soc. Corp. Secs., Fla. Bar Assn., Club 101, Weston Field Club, Phi Beta Kappa, Pi Sigma Alpha. Office: Kelley Drye & Warren LLP 101 Park Ave New York NY 10178

STONE, MINNIE STRANGE, retired automotive service company executive; b. Palatka, Fla., Mar. 10, 1919; d. James Arrious and Pansy (Thomas)

Strange; student Massey Bus. Coll., 1938-39; m. Fred Albion Stone, Nov. 30, 1939; children: Fred Albion, James Thomas, Thomas Demere. Sec., bookkeeper Sears, Roebuck & Co., Jacksonville, Fla., 1939-41; fin. sec. U.S. Army, Macon, Ga., 1941, Atlanta, 1942; sec., bookkeeper Raleigh Spring & Brake Sv., Inc. (name changed to Stone Heavy Vehicle Specialist) (N.C.), 1953-84, sec.-treas. corp., 1960-84, dir., sec. Vol. Wake County Mental Health, 1970-80; pres. YWCA, Wake County, 1973-76, bd. dirs., 1966-76; bd. dirs. Urban Ministry Ctr. Raleigh, 1983-89, mem. adv. bd., 1989—; bd. trustees Bapt. Children's Homes N.C., adv. bd., 1989-95; former mem. subcom. Gov. Coun. Older Adult Fitness. Mem. Urban Ministry Ctr., Raleigh, 1989-91; bd. trustees Bapt. Children's Homes, N.C., 1994—. Mem. N.C. Mus. of History Assocs., N.C. Art Soc., Monthly Investors Club, Coley Forest Garden Club. Republican. Baptist. Home: 920 Runnymede Rd Raleigh NC 27607-3108

STONE, OLIVER WILLIAM, screenwriter, director; b. N.Y.C., Sept. 15, 1946; s. Louis and Jacqueline (Goddet) S. Student, Yale U., 1965; B.F.A., NYU Film Sch., 1971. Tchr. Cholon, Vietnam, 1965-66; wiper U.S. Mcht. Marine, 1966; taxi driver N.Y.C., 1971. Screenwriter Midnight Express, 1978 (Acad. award for screeplay, Writers Guild Am. for screenplay); screenwriter, dir.: The Hand, 1981, (with John Milius) Conan, the Barbarian, 1982 (writer), Scarface, 1983, (writer with Michael Cimino) Year of the Dragon, 1985, (writer with David Lee Henry) 8 Million Ways to Die, 1985, dir., writer, dir. (with Richard Boyle) Salvador, 1986, Platoon, 1986 (Acad. award, Dirs. Guild award, British Acad. award); co-writer, dir.: Wall Street, 1987, Talk Radio, 1988, The Doors, 1991; screenwriter, prodr., dir.: Born on the Fourth of July, 1989 (Acad. award, 1990), Heaven & Earth, 1993; co-writer, prodr., dir.: JFK, 1991, Natural Born Killers, 1994, Nixon, 1995 (Acad. award nominee for best screenplay with Stephen J. Rivele and Christopher Wilkinson 1996); co-prodr. Reversal of Fortune, 1990; prodr.: South Central, 1992, Zebrahead, 1992, The New Age, 1993, The Joy Luck Club, 1993, (TV mini-series) Wild Palms, 1993; exec. prodr. Killer: A Journal of Murder, 1995, (HBO) Indictment: The McMartin Preschool, 1995 (Emmy award), Freeway, 1996, The People vs. Larry Flynt, 1996, Cold Around the Heart, 1996, Evita (writer), U-Turn, 1997. Served with inf. U.S. Army, 1967-68, Vietnam. Decorated Purple Heart with oak leaf cluster, Bronze Star. Mem. Writers Guild Am., Dirs. Guild Am., Acad. Motion Picture Arts and Scis. Office: Ixtlan 201 Santa Monica Blvd Fl 6 Santa Monica CA 90401-2214

STONE, PETER, playwright, scenarist; b. Los Angeles, Feb. 27, 1930; s. John and Hilda (Hess) S.; m. Mary O'Hanley, Feb. 17, 1961. BA, Bard Coll., 1951, DLitt, 1971; MFA, Yale U., 1953. Ind. stage and screen writer, 1961—. Author: (musical comedies) Kean, 1961, Skyscraper, 1965, 1776, 1969 (Tony award Best Musical Book, 1969, N.Y. Drama Critics Circle award 1969, London Plays and Players award 1969, Drama Desk award Best Musical book writer 1969), Two by Two, 1970, Sugar, 1972, Woman of the Year, 1981 (Tony award Best Musical book 1981), My One and Only, 1983, The Will Rogers Follies, 1991 (Tony award Best Musical 1991, N.Y. Drama Critics Circle award Best New Musical 1991, Grammy award 1991), Titanic, 1997, (play) Full Circle, 1973, (films) Charade, 1963 (Writers Guild award Best Comedy Film 1964, Mystery Writers Am. award Best Mystery film 1964), Father Goose, 1964 (Acad. award Best Original Screenplay 1964), Mirage, 1965, Arabesque, 1966, Secret War of Harry Frigg, 1968, Sweet Charity, 1969, Skin Game, 1971, 1776, 1972 (Christopher award for Best Film), Taking of Pelham 123, 1974, Silver Bears, 1978, Who is Killing the Great Chefs of Europe?, 1978, Why Would I Lie?, 1980, Just Cause, 1995, (TV spl.) Androcles and the Lion, 1968; (TV episodes) Studio One, 1956, Brenner, 1959, Witness, 1961, Asphalt Jungle, 1961, The Defenders, 1961-62 (Emmy award 1962), The Benefactors, 1962, Espionage, 1963, Adam's Rib, 1973-74, Ivan the Terrible, 1976, Baby on Board, 1988, Grand Larceny. Mem. Dramatists Guild (pres.), Authors League, Writers Guild Am. Home: 160 E 71st St New York NY 10021-5119 also: Stony Hill Rd Amagansett NY 11930

STONE, PETER GEORGE, lawyer, publishing company executive; b. N.Y.C., July 29, 1937; s. Leo and Anne S.; m. Rikke Linde, Dec. 26, 1974; children: Adam, Rachel. BS in Econs., U. Pa., 1959; JD, Columbia U., 1962. Bar: N.Y. 1963. Assoc. Ballon Stoll & Itzler, N.Y.C., 1963-65, Raphael, Searles & Vischi, N.Y.C., 1965-67; v.p., counsel Firedoor Corp. Am., N.Y.C., 1967-69; ptnr. Cahill, Stone & Driscoll, N.Y.C., 1969-75; v.p. fin. and law, gen. counsel Ottaway Newspapers, Inc., Campbell Hall, N.Y., 1975—; lectr., columnist on media law numerous univs. including Jud. Coll. U. Nev., Hartwick Coll., Bucknell U., U. N.C., Western Conn. State U., SUNY. Bd. dirs., trustee, treas. Daily Pennsylvanian Alumni Assn. With USAR, 1962-63. Mem. ABA (forum com. on comm. law), N.Y. State Bar Assn. (ct. and cmty., pub. events and edn., pub. info. through TV coms., com. media law), N.Y. Bar Found., N.Y. State Fair Trial Free Press Assn., Newspaper Assn. Am. (com. on employee rels., chmn. com. on legal affairs, del. 1st amendment congress, com. on pub. policy), Am. Arbitration Assn., Soc. Human Resource Mgmt., Internat. Newspaper Fin. Execs., Newspaper Pers. Rels. Assn. (chmn. legal task force, bd. dirs.), Penn Club. Office: PO Box 401 Campbell Hall NY 10916-0401

STONE, RANDOLPH NOEL, law educator; b. Milw., Nov. 26, 1946; s. Fisher and Lee Della Stone; m. Cheryl M. Bradley; children: Sokoni, Rahman, Marisa, Lee Sukari. BA, U. Wis., Milw., 1972; JD, Madison, 1975. Bar: D.C., 1975, Wis. 1975, Ill. 1977. Staff atty. Criminal Def. Consortium of Cook County, Chgo., 1976-78; clin. fellow U. Chgo. Law Sch., 1977-80; ptnr. Stone & clark, Chgo., 1980-83; staff atty., dep. dir. Pub. Defender Svc. for D.C., Washington, 1983-88; pub. defender Cook County Pub. Defender's Office, Chgo., 1988-91; lectr. U. Chgo. Law Sch., 1990, clin. prof. law, dir. Mandel Legal Aid Clinic, 1991—; adj. prof. Ill. Inst. Tech. Chgo.-Kent Coll. Law Sch., 1991, bd. overseers, 1990; lectr. law Harvard U., 1991—; mem. Ill. Bd. Admissions to the Bar, 1994—; bd. dirs. The Sentencing Project, 1986—; instr. trial advocacy workshop Harvard Law Sch., 1985-89. Adv. bd. Neighborhood Defender Svc. (Harlem), N.Y.C. Reginald Heber Smith fellow Neighborhood Legal Svcs. Program, Washington, 1975-76. Mem. ABA (sect. criminal justice coun. 1989-95, chair 1993, commn. domestic violence), Ill. State Bar Assn. (sect. criminal justice coun. 1989-92), Chgo. Bar Assn. (bd. dirs. 1990-92), Nat. Legal Aid and Defender Assn. (def. com.). Office: U Chgo Law Sch Mandel Legal Aid Clinic 6020 S University Ave Chicago IL 60637-2704

STONE, RICHARD JAMES, lawyer; b. Chgo., Apr. 30, 1945; s. Milton M. and Ruth Jean (Manaster) S.; m. Lee Lawrence, Sept. 1, 1979; children: Robert Allyn, Katherine Jenney, Grant Lawrence. B.A. in Econs., U. Chgo., 1967; J.D., UCLA, 1970. Bar: Calif. 1971, Oreg. 1994. Assoc., O'Melveny & Myers, L.A., 1971-77; dep. asst. gen. counsel U.S. Dept. Def., Washington, 1978-79; asst. to sec. U.S. Dept. Energy, Washington, 1979-80; counsel Sidley & Austin, L.A., 1981, ptnr., 1982-88; ptnr., head litigation dept. Milbank, Tweed, Hadley & McCloy, 1988-94; mng. ptnr., Zelle & Larson, LLP, L.A., 1994—; gen. counsel and staff dir. Study of L.A. Civil Disturbance for Bd. Police Commrs., 1992. Mem. Pub. Sector Task Force, Calif. State Senate Select Com. on Long Range Policy Planning, 1985-86, U.S. del. Micronesian Polit. Status Negotiations, 1978-79; mem. adv. panel Coun. Energy Resource Tribes, 1981-85; mem. vestry St. Aidan's Episcopal Ch., 1990-93, 97—; dir. Legal Aid Found., 1991—, officer 1994—, pres. 1997—. Recipient Amos Alonzo Stagg medal and Howell Murray Alumni medal U. Chgo., 1967; honoree Nat. Conf. Black Mayors, 1980; recipient spl. citation for outstanding performance Sec. Dept. Energy, 1981. Fellow Am. Bar Found.; mem. ABA, Calif. Bar Assn., Oreg. Bar Assn., L.A. County Bar Assn. (trustee 1986-88), Assn. Bus. Trial Lawyers, Phi Gamma Delta. Editor-in-chief UCLA Law Rev., 1970. Office: Zelle & Larson LLP 11601 Wilshire Blvd 6th FL Los Angeles CA 90025-1770

STONE, ROBERT ANTHONY, author; b. N.Y.C., Aug. 21, 1937; s. C. Homer and Gladys Catherine (Grant) S.; m. Janice G. Burr, Dec. 11, 1959; children: Deidre M., Ian A. Student, N.Y. U., 1958-59; Stegner fellow, Stanford, 1962. Editorial asst. N.Y. Daily News, N.Y.C., 1958-60; former actor New Orleans; former advt. copywriter N.Y.C.; writer Nat. Mirror, N.Y.C., 1965-67; novelist, 1960—; mem. faculty Johns Hopkins U., Balt., 1993-94, Yale U., 1994—; free-lance writer London, Hollywood, Calif., South Vietnam, 1967-71; writer-in-residence Princeton U., 1971-72; faculty Amherst Coll., 1972-75, 77-78, Stanford U., 1979, U. Hawaii-Manoa, 1979-80, Harvard U., 1981, U. Calif.-Irvine, 1982, NYU, 1983, U. Calif.-San Diego, 1985, Princeton U., 1985. Author: (novels) A Hall of Mirrors, 1967, Dog Soldiers, 1974 (Nat. Book award 1975), A Flag for Sunrise, 1981, Images of War, 1986, Children of Light, 1986, Outerbridge Reach, 1992, Bear and His Daughter, 1997 (screenplays) WUSA, 1970, (with Judith Rascoe) Who'll Stop the Rain, 1978; contbg. author: Best American Short-stories, 1970, 88. Served with USN, 1955-58. Recipient William Faulkner prize, 1967, John Dos Passos prize for lit., 1982; award in lit. Am. Acad. and Inst. Arts and Letters, 1982, grantee, 1988-92; Guggenheim fellow, 1971, NEH fellow, 1983. Mem. PEN (exec. bd.). Address: PO Box 967 Block Island RI 02807-0998

STONE, ROBERT EDWARD, JR., speech pathologist; b. Spokane, Wash., Feb. 20, 1937; s. Robert Edward and Merle Lucille (Beals) S.; m. Dee Ann Vick, Aug. 18, 1962; children: Kimberly, Julie, Robert. BS, Whitworth Coll., 1960; MEd, U. Oreg., 1964; PhD, U. Mich., 1971. Tchr. Lake Oswego (Oreg.) Pub. Schs., 1960-63; speech pathologist Portland (Oreg.) Pub. Schs., 1963-69; instr. U. Mich. Med. Sch., Ann Arbor, 1968-71, asst. prof., 1971-78; assoc. prof. Ind. U. Med. Sch. dept. otolaryngology, Indpls., 1978-87, Vanderbilt U. dept. otolaryngology, Nashville, Tenn., 1987—; v.p. Oreg. Speech Hearing Assn., 1964, Mich. Speech Hearing Assn. 1977; mem. sci. adv. bd. Voice Found. N.Y.C., 1973—; dir. Vanderbilt Voice Ctr., Nashville, 1992-96, dir. vocology, 1996—. Author: (book) Help Employ Laryngectomized Persons, 1983; assoc. editor Am. Jour. of Speech-Lang. Pathology,, 1993-96. Fellow Am. Speech Hearing Assn. (cert. clin. competence), Sertoma Club (sec. Indpls. 1984, v.p. 1985, pres. 1986, v.p. Nashville downtown, 1996, pres. 1997—). Office: Nashville Voice Ctr 1500 21st Ave S Ste 2700 Nashville TN 37212-3157

STONE, ROBERT RYRIE, financial executive; b. Toronto, Mar. 25, 1943; s. Frank R. and Norah I. (Varey) S.; m. Jacqueline P. Cogan, July 8, 1966; children: Charlie, Tracy. BSc, U. Toronto, 1964. Chartered acct., Can Inst. Chartered Accts. Treas., dir. fin. Gt. No. Capital Corp., Toronto, 1969-73; various positions Cominco Ltd., Vancouver, B.C., Can., 1973-78, treas., 1978-80, v.p. fin., chief fin. officer, 1980—, also bd. dirs.; bd. dirs. Highland Valley Copper, Union Bank of Switzerland; chmn. Global Stone Corp.; mem. adv. bd. Allendale Ins. Bd. dirs. Jr. Achievement Can. Mem. B.C. Inst. Chartered Accts., Fin. Execs. Inst. (pres. 1983-84). Office: Cominco Ltd, 200 Burrard St # 500, Vancouver, BC Canada V6C 3L7

STONE, ROGER DAVID, environmentalist; b. N.Y.C., Aug. 4, 1934; s. Patrick William and Kathleen Mary Stone; married; 1 child. BA in English, Yale U., 1955. Asst. to pub. Time Mag., 1959-61; corr., news bur. chief Time Mag., San Francisco, Rio, Paris, 1961-68; asst. to pres. Time Inc., N.Y.C., 1968-70; v.p. internat. dept. Chase Manhattan Bank, N.Y.C., 1970-74; pres. Ctr. for Inter-Am. Rels., N.Y.C., 1975-82; v.p. World Wildlife Fund, 1982-86, sr. fellow, 1986-90; vis. fellow, cons. on environ. issues Coun. on Fgn. Rels., 1990-92; vice chmn. ECO Inc., Washington, 1992-96; pres. Sustainable Devel. Inst., Washington, 1993—; vis. lectr. Yale Ctr. for Internat. and Area Studies, 1994-95. Author: Dreams of Amazonia, 1985, The Voyage of the Sanderling, 1990, Wildlands and Human Needs, 1991, The Nature of Development: Reports from the Rural Tropics on the Quest for Sustainable Economic Growth, 1992, Fair Tide: Sailing Toward Long Island's Future, 1996; contbr. chpts. to books; contbr. articles to Time, Life, Life en Espanol, Fgn. Affairs, N.Y. Times, Internat. Herald Tribune, Christian Sci. Monitor, Harvard Bus. Rev., USA Today Mag., Cruising World, Conservation Found. Letter, numerous others. Bd. dirs. Asian Inst. of Tech. Found., Caribbean Conservation Corp., Cintas Found., Armand G. Erpf Fund; former bd. dirs. U. Andes Found.; former bd. dirs. and exec. com. World Wildlife Fund-U.S., Ctr. for Inter-Am. Rels., Ams. Found., Accion Internat., Arts Internat., others. Lt. (j.g.) USN, 1956-59. Mem. Coun. on Fgn. Rels., Century Assn. Democrat. Episcopalian. Avocation: sailing. Home and Office: 3403 O St NW Washington DC 20007-2817

STONE, ROGER WARREN, container company executive; b. Chgo., Feb. 16, 1935; s. Marvin N. and Anita (Masover) S.; m. Susan Kesert, Dec. 24, 1955; children: Karen, Lauren, Jennifer. BS in Econs., U. Pa., 1957. With Stone Container Corp., Chgo., 1957—, dir., 1968-77, v.p., gen. mgr. container div., 1970-75, pres., chief operating officer, 1975-79, pres., chief exec. officer, 1979—, chmn. bd., chief exec. officer, 1983—; bd. dirs. Morton Internat., McDonald's Corp., Option Care, Inc. Past trustee Glenwood (Ill.) Sch. for Boys; trustee Chgo. Symphony Orch. Assn.; fellow Lake Forest (Ill.) Acad.; mem. bd. overseers Wharton Sch. Bus., U. Pa.; mem. adv. coun. Econ. Devel. Named Best or Top CEO in firm's industry Wall Street Transcript, 1981-86; recipient Top CEO award in Forest and Paper Specialty Products Industry, Fin. World Mag., 1984, Bronze award in Paper and Packaging Category, 1996. Mem. Am. Forest and Paper Assn. (chmn. bd. 1985-86, bd. dirs), Chief Execs. Orgn., Corrugated Industry Devel. Corp. (past pres.), Inst. Paper Sci. and Tech. (former trustee), The Chgo. Com., Mid-Am. Com., Chgo. Coun. Fgn. Rels., Standard Club, Tavern Club, Comml. Club, Econ. Club, Lake Shore Country Club. Republican. Office: Stone Container Corp 150 N Michigan Ave Chicago IL 60601-7524

STONE, ROSS GLUCK, orthopaedic surgeon; b. Pottsville, Pa., May 14, 1951; s. Jerome M. and Alma (Gluck) S.; m. Wendy E. Reiner, March 21, 1987; children: Melissa, Logan. BA in Philosophy, Yale U., 1973; MD, Columbia U., 1977. Diplomate Am. Bd. Orthopaedic Surgery. Intern, resident Harvard U., 1977-79; resident, vis. clin. fellow Columbia U., 1979-83; pvt. practice Atlantis, Fla., 1983—; clin. fellow in surgery Harvard Med. Sch., 1978-79; expert med. advisor Fla. Dept. Labor & Employment, 1995-97; editl. adv. bd. Am. Jour. Pain Mgmt., 1992—; chmn. surg. rev. com. Palm Beach Regional Hosp., 1995, institnl. rev. com. John F. Kennedy Med. Ctr., 1995-96, 97, divsn. ortho. surgery Columbia Hosp., 1994—. Contbr. chpt. to book and articles to profl. jours.; invented tension headache reliever device. Bd. trustees Paljms W. Hosp., Loxahatchee, Fla., 1985-88. Recipient Physician's Choice award So. Med. Assn. 88th Assembly, 1994, Scientific Poster recognition So. Med. Assn. 88th Assembly, 1994, 89th Assembly, 1995, Sr. Resident award Eastern Ortho. Assn. 14th ann. meeting, 1983, Rsch. Manuscript award Assn. for the Advancement of Med. Instrumentation, 1996. Mem. Palm Beach County (Fla.) Med. Soc. (bd. dirs. 1995—, del. Fla. Med. Assn. 1995, 96, 97, legis. com. 1995-96, 97, emergency med. svc. and disaster relief plan coms. 1994-95, health and human svcs. com. 1994-95, pub. rels. com. 1995—, chmn. pub. rels. com., 1996, 97, chmn. fin. com. 1997), Palm Beach County Med. Soc. Republican. Jewish. Avocations: weight lifting, aerobic conditioning, reading, tennis, martial arts. Office: 120 John F Kennedy Dr Ste 124 Lake Worth FL 33462-1146

STONE, RUBY ROCKER, state legislator; b. Portal, Ga., Feb. 6, 1924; d. Eddie Lee and Della (Taylor) Rocker; widowed; children: Dianne Carolyn Stone Milhollin, Raymond Edward Stone. Office mgr., dental asst. to Dr. Richard W. Collins, 1962-68; asst. to mgr. Am. Machine & Foundry Spl. Missile project Vandenberg AFB, 1959-60; sec. Idaho House State Affairs, 1970; aide to Gov. Don Samuelson, 1970-71; senate jour. clk. Idaho Ho. Reps., 1971-84, mem., 1986—, chmn. local govt. com., 1991—. Active ARC, and numerous other cmty. projects and cmty. vol. orgns. Recipient Sportsmanship award Idaho State Women's Amateur Golf Tournament, 1980, Plantation Ladies Golf Assn., Outstanding Woman award, 1993, numerous others; inducted into Idaho Sports Hall of Fame, 1993, Idaho New Agenda Hall of Fame, 1993; named Republicn Outstanding Legislator-House, 1994; 5 time golf champion Tri-Club Golf, 2 time champion Treasure Valley Ladies Golf. Mem. Nat. Orgn. Women Legislators, U.S. Golf Assn. (mem. jr. girls championship com. 1981—), Idaho Golf Assn. (bd. dirs. 1975-87, Ladies Sr. Golf champion 1982), Plantation Golf Club (13 time champion), Gowen Field Officers Club, Gowen Field Officers Wives Club, Daus. of Nile, El Korah Honored Ladies Club, Elks. Republican. Protestant. Avocations: golf, bridge, helping others. Home: 6604 Holiday Dr Boise ID 83709-2022

STONE, RUSSELL A., sociology educator; b. Medicine Hat, Alta., Can., Feb. 8, 1944; came to U.S., 1966; s. Ben and Clara G. (Gibbs) S.; m. S. Rala Stollar, Aug. 18, 1965; children: Peter H., Mira Beth. BA, McGill U., Montreal, Que., Can., 1965; PhD, Princeton U., 1971. Asst. to assoc prof. sociology SUNY, Buffalo, 1970-84, prof., 1984-91, chmn. dept. sociology, 1985-88; prof. sociology Am. U., Washington, 1991—, assoc. dean for grad. affairs, 1991-96; vis. rsch. assoc. Israel Inst. Applied Social Rsch., Jerusalem, 1977-78; vis. assoc. prof. Ben Gurion U. of the Negev, Beersheba, Israel, 1978; vis. prof. Hebrew U., Jerusalem, 1977-78. Author: Social Change in Israel: Attitudes and Events, 1982; co-author: Political Elites on Arab North Africa, 1982; editor: OPEC and the Middle East, 1977; co-editor: Change in Tunisia, 1976, Critical Essays on Israeli Social Issues and Scholarship, 1994; chmn. editorial bd. SUNY Press, 1987-90, series editor; contbr. articles to profl. jours. Mem. Am. Sociol. Assn., Middle East Studies Assn., World Future Soc., Assn. for Israel Studies (sec., treas. 1989-93). Office: Am U Dept Sociology 4400 Massachusetts Ave NW Washington DC 20016-8001

STONE, SAMUEL BECKNER, lawyer; b. Martinsville, Va., Feb. 4, 1934; s. Paul Raymond and Mildred (Beckner) S.; m. Shirley Ann Gregory, June 18, 1955; children: Paul Gregory, Daniel Taylor. BSEE, Va. Polytech. Inst. & State U., 1955; JD, George Wash. U., 1960. Bar: Md. 1960, Calif. 1963, Patent and Trademark Office. Patent examiner, 1955-58; patent adv. Naval Ordinance Lab., Silver Spring, Md., 1958-59; assoc. Thomas & Crickenberger, Washington, 1959-61, Beckman Instruments Inc., Fullerton, Calif., 1961-65; assoc. Lyon & Lyon, L.A., 1965-72, ptnr., 1972; mng. ptnr. Lyon & Lyon, Costa Mesa, Calif., 1982—; judge Disneyland Com. Svc. Awards, Anaheim, Calif., 1987. Mem. Orange County Bar Assn. (bd. dirs. 1988-91, travel seminar chair 1986-92), Orange County Patent Law Assn. (pres. 1987, bd. exec. com. 1987-90), Calif. Bar Assn. (intellectual property sect. bd. 1987-90), Am. Electronics Assn. (lawyers com. 1988—, co-chair 1996—), Orange County Venture Group (dir. 1985—, pres. 1996-97), Rams Booster Club (dir. 1984-90), Pacific Club (mem. legal adv. com., chair 1989-92). Republican. Avocations: tennis, waterskiing, music. Home: 1612 Antiqua Way Newport Beach CA 92660 Office: Lyon & Lyon 3200 Park Center Dr Ste 1200 Costa Mesa CA 92626-7108

STONE, SHARON, actress; b. Meadville, Pa., Mar. 10, 1958; d. Joe and Dorothy S; m. Michael Greenburg, 1984 (div. 1987). Student, Edinboro U. Model Eileen Ford Modeling Agy. Appeared in films Stardust Memories, 1980, Deadly Blessing, 1981, Irreconcilable Differences, 1984, King Solomon's Mines, 1985, Allan Quatermain and the Lost City of Gold, 1986, Cold Steel, 1987, Police Academy 4, 1987, Action Jackson, 1988, Above the Law, 1988, Total Recall, 1990, He Said/She Said, 1991, Scissors, 1991, Basic Instinct, 1991, Where Sleeping Dogs Lie, 1992, Sliver, 1993, Intersection, 1994, The Specialist, 1994, (also co-prodr.) The Quick and the Dead, 1995, Casino, 1995 (Golden Globe award for best actress in film 1996, Acad. award nominee for best actress 1996), Diabolique, 1996; TV appearances include Not Just Another Affair, 1982, Bay City Blues, 1983, Calendar Girl Murders, 1984, The Vegas Strip Wars, 1984, War and Remembrance, 1988, (guest) The Larry Sanders Show, 1994, Last Dance, 1996; narrator: Harlow: The Blond Bombshell, 1993. Office: CAA 9830 Wilshire Blvd Los Angeles CA 90212*

STONE, STEVEN MICHAEL, sports announcer, former baseball player; b. Cleve., July 14, 1947. BS in Edn., Kent State U. Baseball player San Francisco Giants, 1971-72, Chgo. Cubs, 1974-76, Chgo. White Sox, 1977-78, Balt. Orioles, 1979-82; baseball announcer WGN Continental Broadcasting Co., Chgo., 1982—; owner restaurant Scottsdale, Ariz. Recipient Cy Young award Am. League, 1980. Mem. Am. League All-Star Team, 1980. Office: WGN TV 2501 W Bradley Pl Chicago IL 60618-4701*

STONE, SUSAN FOSTER, mental health services professional, psychologist; b. Salem, Mass., Mar. 15, 1954; d. Bruce and Carolyn (Foster) Hoitt; m. Norman Michael Stone, May 18, 1981; children: Brittany, Forrest. Student, U. York, Eng., 1974-75; BA in Psychology, Colby Coll., 1976; MS in Clin. Psychology, Abilene Christian U., 1979; PhD in Clin. Psychology, Calif. Sch. Profl. Psychology, 1985. Lic. psychologist, Calif. Mem. emergency response team Simi (Calif.) Dept. Police, 1980-81; cons. Children's Hosp. L.A., 1984-85; postdoctoral fellow Neuropsychiat. Inst. UCLA, 1985-86; clin. dir. Santa Clarita (Calif.) Child and Family Devel. Ctr., 1987-94, dir. tng., 1994-95; cons. L.A. County Adoptions, 1985-88; expert witness L.A. Superior Ct., 1987—, State Funded Early Mental Health Initiatives, 1994; assisted in drafting congl. managed health care proposal, 1995; presenter in field. Mem. adv. coun. L.A. Foster Parent Assn., 1989-91. Office Juvenile Justice Systems grantee Spl. Children's Ctr., 1990, L.A. Regional Ctr. grantee, 1990. Mem. APA, Assn. Family and Conciliation Cts., Sierra Club, Santa Clarita C. of C. Office: 23504 Lyons Ave # 304 Newhall CA 91321

STONE, THOMAS EDWARD, defense consultant, retired rear admiral; b. Selfridge, Mich., Oct. 21, 1939; m. Lucy Lee, June 9, 1962. BS, U.S. Naval Acad., 1962; MS in Elec. Engring., Naval Postgrad. Sch., 1968; postgrad., Destroyer Dept. Head Sch., 1969. Advanced through grades to rear adm. USN, 1990, ops. officer USS Sampson, 1970; aide, flag sec. to commdr. Attack Carrier striking Force /CTF 77, 7th Fleet Vietnam, 1971-72; communications/ops. officer to comdr. in chief U.S. Naval Forces, Europe, 1972-75, exec. officer USS Mitscher, 1976-78, asst. chief of staff for communications, comdr. Naval Surface Force Atlantic, 1978-80; comdg. officer USS Preble, 1980-82; surface ops. officer, staff of comdr. Cruiser Destroyer Group 12, 1982-83; dir. Space, Command and Control Devel. Div. USN, 1984-85; comdr. U.S. Naval Communications Master Sta., Western Pacific, Guam, Marianas Island, 1985-87; comdr. Naval Telecommunications Command, 1988-90; dir. Naval Commns. info systems of Naval opers. staff, 1990-91; dir. communication programs Space & Naval Warfare Systems Command, 1991-93. Decorated Legion of Merit with three gold stars. Roman Catholic. Office: American Systems Corp 14200 Park Meadow Dr Chantilly VA 20151-2219

STONE, WILLIAM CHARLES, surgeon; b. Denver, 1935. MD, U. Oreg., 1964. Diplomate Am. Bd. Colon and Rectal Surgery, Am. Bd. Surgery. Intern Naval Hosp., Great Lakes, 1964-65; resident in gen. surgery Naval Hosp., San Diego; resident in colon and rectal surgery Lahey Clin., Boston, 1975-76; staff mem. St. Francis Hosp., Tulsa; assoc. prof. surgery U. Okla. Mem. Am. Coll. Gastroenterology, Am. Cancer Soc., Am. Soc. Gastro-Intestinal Endoscopy, Soc. Am. Gastrointestina Endoscopic Surgery. Office: 6565 S Yale Ave Ste 902 Tulsa OK 74136-8310

STONE, WILLIAM EDWARD, association executive; b. Peoria, Ill., Aug. 13, 1945; s. Dean Proctor and Katherine (Jamison) S.; m. Deborah Ann Duncan; children: Jennifer, Allison, Molly. A.B., Stanford U., 1967, M.B.A., 1969. Asst. dean Stanford U., 1969-71, asst. to pres., 1971-77; exec. dir. Stanford Alumni Assn., 1977-90, pres., chief exec. officer, 1990—; pres., dir. Alpine Chalet, Inc., Alpine Meadows, Calif., 1987—; dir. Coun. Alumni Assn. Execs., 1989-93, v.p., 1990-91, pres., 1991-92; trustee Coun. for Advancement and Support of Edn., 1988-91; bd. dirs. Univ. ProNet, Inc., chmn., 1990-92. Bd. dirs. North County YMCA, 1975-76; bd. dirs., chmn. nominating com. faculty club Stanford U., 1979-81; trustee Watkins Discretionary Fund, 1979-82; mem. community adv. bd. Resource Ctr. for Women. Recipient K.M. Cuthbertson award Stanford U., 1987, Tribute award Coun. for Advancement and Support of Edn., 1991. Mem. Stanford Hist. Soc., Stanford Assocs. Club: Stanford Faculty. Home: 1061 Cathcart Way Stanford CA 94305-1048 Office: Stanford Alumni Assn Inc 416 Santa Teresa St Stanford CA 94305-2203

STONE, WILLIAM HAROLD, geneticist, educator; b. Boston, Dec. 15, 1924; s. Robert and Rita (Scheinberg) S.; m. Elaine Morein, Nov. 24, 1947; children: Susan Joy, Debra M.; m. Carmen Maqueda, Dec. 22, 1971; 1 son, Alexander R.M. AB, Brown U., 1948; MS, U. Maine, 1949; PhD, U. Wis., 1953; ScD (hon.), U. Cordoba, Spain, 1984. Rsch. asst. Jackson Meml. Lab., Bar Harbor, Maine, 1947-48; mem. faculty dept. genetics U. Wis., Madison, 1949-83, prof., 1961-83, prof. med. genetics, 1964-83; Cowles Disting. prof. dept. biology Trinity U., San Antonio, 1983—; staff scientist S.W. Found. for Biomed. Rsch., San Antonio, 1983—; adj. prof. Cellular and Structural Biology U. Tex., San Antonio, 1983—; mem. panel blood group experts FAO, 1962-67, program dir. immunogenetics rsch., Spain, 1971-74; adj. prof. dept. cellular and structural biology, U. Tex. Health Sci. Ctr., San Antonio, 1983—; mem. Cmty. Health Svcs. Rsch. Adv. Com., 1987—, Coun. Inst. Lab. Animal Resources, NRC; mem. competitive rsch. grants panel USDA; bd. dirs. and v.p. So. Tex. Blood and Tissue Ctr., 1986—, v.p. bd., 1989-92, pres. 1995—; bd. dirs. Tex. Rsch. and Tech. Found., 1986-90, Mind Sci. Found., 1988—, Winston Sch., 1989-91, Bexar County Women's Ctr., Inst. Lab. Animal Sci., 1977-89; mem. rev. panel NSF; mem. primate study sect. Comparative Medicine Program NIH; mem. adv. com. Harvard Med. Sch. Regional Primate Rsch. Ctr.; mem. Armstrong Lab. awards com. Author: Immunogenetics, 1967; contbr. over 300 articles to profl. jours. Bd.

dirs. Bexar County Women's Ctr., Alamo Theatre Arts Coun., S. A. Libr. Assn., 1994. Recipient I.I. Ivanov medal USSR, 1974, Disting. Tex. Geneticist award, 1992; Calif. Inst. Tech. NIH fellow, 1960-61. Mem. NRC, AAAS, Am. Inst. Biol. Scis., Assembly Life Scis., Am. Soc. Immunologists, Am. Genetics Assn., Am. Aging Soc., Tex. Genetics Soc. (editor newsletter, pres.-elect 1995, pres. 1996), Am. Soc. Human Genetics, Rsch. Soc. Am., Internat. Soc. Transplant, Am. Soc. Animal Sci., Internat. Soc. Devel. Comparative Immunology, Internat. Primatological Soc., Am. Soc. Primatology, Internat. Soc. Immunology Reprodn., Fedn. Am. Soc. Exptl. Biology, Soc. Devel. and Comparative Immunology (mem. pub. affairs com.), Sigma Xi, Gamma Alpha, Beta Beta Beta. Office: Trinity U Dept Biology San Antonio TX 78212-7200 *Some things are better never than late. We need more education and less legislation. I can't believe I get paid for something I have so much fun doing. In science you don't know what the truth is until you have read what you have written. Quite often, bad luck is really good luck gone unrecognized.*

STONE, WILLIARD EVERARD, accountant, educator; b. Phila., Aug. 28, 1910; s. Theodore Williard Jr. and Blanche (Patton) S.; m. Louise Cousins Harder, May 19, 1934; children: Theodore Williard III, Donald Edwin, Richard Patton. A.B., Pa. State U., 1933; M.A., U. Pa., 1950, Ph.D., 1957. C.P.A., Pa. Auditor Pa. Liquor Control Bd., 1934-43, U.S. comptroller gen., 1943-47; partner Stone & Fisher (C.P.A.'s), Phila., 1947-50; asst. prof. accounting U. Pa. Wharton Sch. Finance and Commerce, Phila., 1951-57; assoc. prof. U. Pa. Wharton Sch. Finance and Commerce, 1957-60; prof. U. Fla., Gainesville, 1960-80; head dept. accounting U. Fla., 1960-74; bd. mgrs. U. Fla. Press, 1961-80; vis. prof. U. New South Wales, 1966; Carman G. Blough chair of acctg. U. Va., 1972-73; vis. prof. U. Port Elizabeth, 1975, Va. Poly. Inst. and State U., 1977, U. Ky., 1980-81; cons. editor Chilton Book div. Chilton Co., Phila., 1957-61, Holt, Rinehart & Winston, Inc., 1961-70; cons. to U.S. Comptr. Gen., 1963-69. Author: (with MacFarland, Ayars) Accounting Fundamentals, 1957; Co-editor: Accounting Historian's Jour.; Contbr. articles to profl. jours. Gordon Fellow Deakin U., Australia, 1981. Mem. Nat. Assn. Accountants (dir. Phila. 1954-55), Am. Inst. C.P.A.'s, Fla. Inst. C.P.A.'s, Pa. Inst. C.P.A.'s (dir. 1954-55), Am. Accounting Assn. (v.p. 1963), Acad. Accounting Historians (editor Acctg. Historians Jour. 1974-79), Beta Alpha Psi (past pres), Beta Gamma Sigma. Home: 1717 NW 23rd Ave # Pha Gainesville FL 32605-3031

STONECIPHER, HARRY CURTIS, manufacturing company executive. BS, Tenn. Polytech Inst., 1960. With GE, 1960-61, 62-86, Martin Aircraft Co., 1961-62; exec. v.p. Sundstrand Corp., 1987, pres., chief operating officer, 1987-88, pres., chief exec. officer, 1988-94, chmn., 1991-94, also past bd. dirs.; pres., CEO McDonnell-Douglas Corp., St. Louis, 1994—. Office: McDonnell-Douglas Corp McDonnell Blvd at Airport Rd Berkeley MO 63134*

STONEHILL, ERIC, lawyer; b. Rochester, N.Y., Feb. 27, 1950. BA with distinction, Northwestern U., 1970; JD, Cornell U., 1973, MBA, 1981, cert. hosp. and health svc. adminstrn., 1981. Bar: N.Y. 1974, D.C. 1981, U.S. Dist. Ct. (we. dist.) N.Y. 1974, U.S. Dist. Ct. (no. dist.) N.Y. 1976. Assoc. Harris, Beach & Wilcox, Rochester, 1973-81, ptnr., 1982—. Contbr. articles to profl. jours. Bd. dirs. Rochester Eye and Human Parts Bank, 1983-91, 92—, pres., 1987-90. Mem. Nat. Health Lawyers Assn., Am. Soc. Hosp. Attys., N.Y. State Bar Assn. (mem. health law sect.), D.C. Bar Assn., Monroe County Bar Assn., Sloan Alumni Assn., Phi Beta Kappa. Office: Harris Beach & Wilcox Granite Building 130 Main St E Rochester NY 14604-1620

STONEHILL, LLOYD HERSCHEL, gas company executive, mechanical engineer; b. South Bend, Ind., May 20, 1927; s. Charles Myers and Louise Mary (Reed) S.; m. Jean Carole Herzer, Dec. 30, 1961; children: Mark, Bill, John, Rob. BSME, Purdue U., 1949. Registered profl. engr., La. Chief engr. Rothschild Boiler & Tank Works, Shreveport, La., 1949-54; chmn. bd. dirs. Frankfort (Ind.) Bottle Gas, Inc., 1956—. Patentee in field. Founding prs. Clinton County Hosp. Authority, Frankfort, 1974; membership chmn. Clinton County Hosp. Found., Frankfort, 1982-83, 89. With U.S. Army, 1954-56. Recipient Heroism award Elks Lodge, Frankfort, 1959. Mem. Nat. Propane Gas Assn. (mktg. awards 1986, 87), Am. Legion, Purdue Alumni Assn. (Clinton County Chpt. mem. pres.' coun.), Hudson Inst., Rotary (sec. 1963-65, Paul Harris fellow), Lambda Chi Alpha (sec. 1946-47). Republican. Mem. Christian Ch. Avocations: collecting old violins, sailing, reading. Home: 1258 Forest Dr Frankfort IN 46041-3230 Office: Frankfort Bottle Gas Inc 1555 McKinley Ave Frankfort IN 46041-1805

STONEHILL, ROBERT MICHAEL, federal agency administrator; b. N.Y.C., Oct. 29, 1949; s. Frederick and Olga (Berkowitz) S.; m. Ilene Laven, June 1, 1975 (div. Nov. 1983); 1 child, David; m. Camille Recchia, Oct. 12, 1985; children: Eric, Elizabeth, Matthew. BA, CUNY, Queens, 1971; MA, U. Colo., 1973, PhD, 1976. Teaching and rsch. asst. U. Colo., Boulder, 1972-76; evaluation specialist U.S. Office Edn., Washington, 1976-83; acting dir. state and local grants div. U.S. Dept. Edn., Washington, 1984-86, dir. Ednl. Resources Info. Ctr., 1987-94, dir. state and local svcs. divsn., 1995—; del. Fed. Libr. Pre-Conf., The White House Conf. on Librs. and Info. Scis., 1990. Mem. editorial adv. bd. various jours., contbr. articles. Regents scholar, 1966-70. Mem. Am. Ednl. Rsch. Assn., Am. Soc. for Info. Sci., Nat. Coun. for Measurement in Edn. Jewish. Avocations: skiing, popular cultural history. Office: US Dept Edn ORAD/OERI State and Local Svcs Divsn 555 New Jersey Ave NW Washington DC 20208-0001*

STONEMAN, SAMUEL SIDNEY, cinema company executive; b. Boston, Dec. 18, 1911; s. David and Anne (Fleisher) S.; m. Miriam Helpern, Sept. 2, 1934; children: Jane Stein, Elizabeth Deknatel. A.B., Dartmouth Coll., 1933; J.D., Harvard U., 1936. Bar: Mass. 1936. Ptnr. Singer, Stoneman & Kirland, Boston, 1936-42; pres. Bretton Woods Co., (N.H.), 1946-56; vice chmn. bd. Gen. Cinema Corp., Chestnut Hill, Mass., 1969-84, also dir.; vice-chmn. Harcourt Gen.; dir. Shawmut Bank of Boston, N.A., Purity Supreme, Inc., Billerica, Mass., Donlevy's Inc., Boston. Vice pres., trustee Boston Symphony Orch., 1970-83; bd. overseers Hopkins Ctr. and Hood Mus., Dartmouth Coll., 1982-88; trustee Dana-Farber Cancer Inst., Boston, 1978; pres. Combined Jewish Philanthropies, 1964-66, Beth Israel Hosp., 1970-73; mem. Dartmouth Coll. Alumni Council, 1963-66; bd. dirs. Massachusetts Bay United Fund, 1966-77, Community Found. Palm Beach and Martin Counties, Fla., Kravis Performing Arts Centre, Palm Beach; mem. adv. bd. St. Mary's Hosp., Palm Beach; regional co-chmn. NCCJ, Boston, 1969-73. Served to maj. Q.M.C. AUS, 1942-46. Fellow Brandeis U., 1956—; recipient Brotherhood Human Relations citation NCCJ, 1968, Alumni award Dartmouth Coll., 1972, Disting. Grad. award Noble and Greenough Sch., 1982. Home: 200 Via Pelicano Palm Beach FL 33480-5017 Office: 1 Post Office Sq Ste 3730 Boston MA 02109-2103

STONEMAN, WILLIAM, III, physician, educator; b. Kansas City, Mo., Sept. 8, 1927; s. William and Helen Louise (Bloom) S.; m. Elizabeth Johanna Wilson, May 19, 1951; children: William Laurence, Sidney Camdon (dec.), Cecily Anne Erker, Elizabeth Wilson, John Spalding. Student, Rockhurst Coll., 1944-46; B.S., St. Louis U., 1948, M.D., 1952. Diplomate: Am. Bd. Surgery, Am. Bd. Plastic Surgery. Intern Kansas City Gen. Hosp., 1952-53; resident in surgery St. Louis U., 1953-57, resident in plastic surgery, 1957-59, mem. faculty, 1959—, assoc. prof. surgery, assoc. prof. community medicine, 1975-84, prof. surgery, community medicine, 1984-94, prof. surgery, community medicine emeritus, 1994, assoc. dean Sch. Medicine, 1973-76; exec. assoc. dean St. Louis U. (Sch. Medicine), 1976-82, dean, 1982-95, dean emeritus, 1995—, assoc. v.p. med. ctr., 1983-95; mem. adj. faculty Washington U. Sch. Medicine, St. Louis, 1968-74; chief exec. officer Bi-State Regional Med. Program, 1968-74; bd. dirs. St. Louis Office Mental Retardation/Developmentally Disabled Resources, 1980-82, Combined Health Appeal of Mo., 1990-94. Editor: Parameters, 1976-94 ; contbr. articles on plastic surgery, health care delivery planning to profl. jours. Served with US, 1946-47. Fellow ACS; mem. AMA (chmn. sect. on med. schs. 1987-, sect. alt. del. 1989-91, del. 1992-94), Mo. Med. Assn., Mem. St. Louis Met. Med. Soc., St. Louis Surg. Soc., Am. Soc. Plastic and Reconstructive Surgeons, Midwestern Assn. Plastic Surgeons. Roman Catholic. Clubs: Racquet, University. Office: St Louis U Sch Medicine 1316 Carr Lane Ave Saint Louis MO 63104-1011

STONEMAN, WILLIAM HAMBLY, III, professional baseball team executive; b. Oak Park, Ill., Apr. 7, 1944; s. William Hambly Jr. and Kathryn Jane (Hennessey) S.; m. Diane Falardeau, Dec. 6, 1969; children: Jill Helene, Jeffrey Alan. BS in Edn., U. Idaho, 1966; MEd, Okla. U., 1969. Baseball player Chgo. Cubs, 1967-68, Montreal (Que., Can.) Expos, 1969-73, Calif. Angels, 1974; mktg. mgr. Royal Trust Corp., Montreal and Toronto, Ont., Can., 1975-79, br. mgr., 1980-82; asst. to pres. Montreal Expos, 1983, v.p., 1984—; now v.p. baseball ops. Mem. All-Star Team Nat. League, 1972; no-hit games vs. Phila. Phillies, 1969, N.Y. Mets, 1972. Home: 17 Willow, PO Box 386, Hudson, PQ Canada J0P 1H0 Office: Montreal Baseball Club Inc, 4549 Pierre-de-Coubertin Ave, Montreal, PQ Canada H1V 3N7*

STONER, GARY DAVID, pathology educator; b. Bozeman, Mont., Oct. 25, 1942; married; 2 children. BS, Mont. State U., 1964; MS, U. Mich., 1968, PhD in Microbiol., 1970. Asst. rsch. scientist U. Calif., San Diego, 1970-72, assoc. rsch. scientist, 1972-75; cancer expert Nat. Cancer Inst., 1976-79; assoc. prof. pathology Med. Coll. Ohio, 1979-83; prof. pathology, 1983-92; prof. preventive medicine and pathology Ohio State U., Columbus, 1992—, assoc. dir. Ctr. for Molecular and Environ. Health, 1993—, assoc. dir. basic rsch. Comp Cancer Ctr, 1994—, prof., chmn. divsn. environ. health scis. Sch. Pub. Health, 1995—; cons. Nat. Heart Lung & Blood Inst., 1974—, EPA, 1979—, Nat. Cancer Inst., 1979—, Nat. Toxicol. Program, 1981—; lectr. W. Alton Jones Cell Sci. Ctr., 1978—; mem. study sect. NIH, 1980-88, Am. Cancer Soc., Ohio, 1982—, Am. Cancer Soc., Nat., 1995—. Grantee Nat. Cancer Inst., EPA, U.S. Army R & D Command. Mem. AAAS, Am. Assn. Cancer Rsch., Am. Tissue Culture Assn., Am. Assn. Pathologists, Am. Soc. Cell Biology. Achievements include research in carcinogenesis in human and animal model respiratory and esophagal tissues, carcinogen metabolism, mutagenesis, in vitro transformation of epithelial cells chemoprevention. Office: Ohio State U Sch Pub Health 1148 CHRI 300 W 10th Ave Columbus OH 43210-1240

STONER, GERALD LEE, neurovirologist, medical researcher; b. Elizabethtown, Pa., Feb. 8, 1943; s. Andrew Kraybill and Esther (Longenecker) S.; m. Linda Elaine Buckwalter, Aug. 1, 1964 (dec. Oct. 1994); children: Anne Marie Stoner-Eby, Andrea E. AA, Hershey (Pa.) Jr. Coll., 1963; BA in Natural Sci., Eastern Mennonite Coll., Harrisonburg, Va., 1965; PhD in Biochemistry, Columbia U., 1974. Rsch. fellow Albert Einstein Coll. Medicine, Bronx, N.Y., 1974-76; rsch. scientist Armauer Hansen Rsch. Inst., Addis Ababa, Ethiopia, 1976-81; sr. staff fellow NIH, Bethesda, Md., 1981-88; sect. chief lab. exptl. neuropathology NIH, Bethesda, 1988—; cons. WHO/IMMLEP Sci. Working Group, Geneva, 1977, 80, USPHS Hansen's Disease Rsch. Adv. Com., Carville, La., 1983-86. Mem. editl. bd. Jour. Neurovirology, 1994—; contbr. articles to profl. jours. Bd. dirs. Internat. Cmty. Sch., Addis Ababa, 1978-81, Mennonite Devel. Rehab. Bd., Addis Ababa, 1978-81, Am. Leprosy Missions, Greenville, S.C., 1987-93. Mem. AAAS, Am. Soc. Virology, Am. Soc. Microbiology, Soc. Exptl. Neuropathology (Constn. Com.), Internat. Leprosy Assn. Mennonite. Avocations: book collecting, gardening, travel. Office: NIH Bldg 36 Rm 4A-29 Bethesda MD 20892

STONER, JAMES LLOYD, retired foundation executive, clergyman; b. Point Marion, Pa., Apr. 23, 1920; s. Martin Clark and Bess (Hare) S.; m. Janice Faller Evans, Aug. 28, 1943; children: Thomas Clark, James Douglas and Geoffrey Lloyd (twins). B.S., Bethany Coll., 1941, D.D. (hon.), 1958; B.D., M.A., Yale U., 1944. Ordained to ministry Christian Ch., 1943; minister in Hamden, Conn., 1942-44; assoc. exec. sec. U. Tex., YMCA, 1944-45; dir. Student Christian Fellowship, Bowling Green State U., 1945-47, Univ. Christian Mission, Fed. Council Ch. and Nat. Council Chs., 1947-56; minister North Christian Ch., Columbus, Ind., 1956-66; asst. gen. sec. for exec. operations Nat. Council Chs., 1966-72; sr. minister Central Christian Ch., Austin, Tex., 1972-80; dep. exec. dir. Found. for Christian Living, Pawling, N.Y., 1980-83, exec. dir., 1983-87; chmn. com. recommendations Internat. Conv. Christian Chs., 1962-65; bd. mgrs. United Christian Missionary Soc., 1956-63; mem. adv. bd. Am. Bible Soc., 1966-72; life mem. coun. Christian Unity, Christian Ch.; a founder, 1st pres. LINK Award, Ridgewood, N.J., 1966-72; mem. Austin Conf. Chs., pres., 1973-75; rep. Tex. Conf. Chs., 1976-80; mem. goals com. Austin Tomorrow; mem. adv. bd. 1st Comml. Bank of Lakeway, Austin, Tex., 1990-95. Contbr. articles to profl. publs. A founder, bd. dirs. Fellowship Christian Athletes, Kansas City, Mo., 1956-68; trustee Tougaloo (Miss.) Coll., 1968-74; v.p., mem. exec. com. Ecumenical Center Continuing Edn., Yale, 1966-72; mem. exec. com. Boy Scouts Am., Austin, 1980, Dutchess County council, 1981-82; bd. mgrs. New Milford Hosp., 1983-88; bd. dirs. Holiday Hills YMCA, 1983-87; com. mem. Town of Pawling 200th Anniversary, 1985-88, Lakeway Ecumenical Ch.; co-founder Holy Week Palm Observance, Lakeway,Tex. Mem. Pawling C. of C. (exec. com. 1984-87), Fellowship of Christian Athletes (nat. adv. bd. 1994—), Masons (32 degree), Pawling Rotary Club (pres. 1983-84, dist. gov.-elect 1991-92, dist. gov. 1992-93, Paul Harris fellow), Shriners, Austin Rotary Club (spl. lifetime mem.), Lake Travis/Lakeway Rotary Club (hon.), Alpha Psi Omega, Beta Theta Pi. Home: 1134 Challenger Austin TX 78734-3802 *Fill every day with rainbow colors, and punctuate life with a positive outlook... Even the Cross of Christ is a positive sign.*

STONER, JOHN RICHARD, federal government executive; b. Ypsilanti, Mich., May 11, 1958; s. Richard P. and Marjorie G. Stoner; m. Diane Leslie Snow. BA in Govt., B in Music Edn., Lawrence U., 1981. Staff asst. Senator Robert Kasten Jr., Washington, 1981-82; staff assoc. Wis. Office Fed.-State Rels., Washington, 1982-83; intergovtl. rels. officer U.S. Dept. Transp., Washington, 1983-86, congl. rels. officer, 1989-91; dir. Office of Program and Policy Support, Rsch. and Spl. Programs Adminstrn., Dept. Transp., Washington, 1991-93; exec. dir. Republican Nat. Lawyers Assn., 1993—; rep. Primerica Fin. Svcs., 1993—; state govt. rels. mgr. Am. Trucking Assn., Inc., Alexandria, Va., 1986-88; researcher George Bush for Pres. Com., 1988; staff asst. Office of Pres.-Elect, Washington, 1988-89. Admissions contact Washington area Lawrence U., 1986-87; softball team mgr. Montgomery County Recreation League. Recipient Eagle Scout award Boy Scouts Am., 1972; Mortar Bd. scholar, 1980; Senate Rep. Policy Com. Legis. fellow, 1993—. Republican. Mem. Ch. of Christ, Scientist. Avocation: water skiing, organ. Home: 10409 Brunswick Ave Silver Spring MD 20902-4845 Office: Rep Nat Lawyers Assn 310 1st St SE Washington DC 20003-1801

STONER, PHILIP JAMES, hospital administrator; b. Brookline, Mass., Mar. 5, 1943; s. Philip and Beatrice Margaret (Murphy) S.; m. Allison Fern Leighton, Aug. 28, 1971; children: Jennifer Marie, Andrew Leighton. AS in Engring., Wentworth Inst., Boston, 1963; BS in Indsl. Engring., Millikin U., 1966; MS, Northeastern U., 1973; MBA, Western New Eng. Coll., 1980. Prodn. mgr. Goodwill Industries, Boston, 1971-72; indsl. engr. Ea. Air Lines, Boston, 1973-74; mgmt. engr. Baystate Med. Ctr., Springfield, Mass., 1974-80; v.p. for profl. svcs. Farren Meml. Hosp., Turners Falls, Mass., 1980-85; adminstr. Taylor Hosp., Bangor, Maine, 1985-87, Massena (N.Y.) Meml. Hosp., 1987-89, Falls Meml. Hosp., International Falls, Minn., 1990-93; CEO Tyrone (Pa.) Hosp., 1993—; mem. adv. bd. Rainy River Community Coll., International Falls, 1990-93. Author: (monograph) Resource Based Relative Value System, 1991. Capt. USMC, 1966-69, Vietnam. Fellow Am. Coll. Healthcare Execs.; mem. Inst. Indsl. Engrs. (sr.). Avocations: reading, jogging, making bread, boat building. Home: RR 5 Box 287A Tyrone PA 16686-9751 Office: Tyrone Hosp 1 Hospital Dr Tyrone PA 16686-1810

STONER, R(ICHARD) B(URKETT), manufacturing company executive; b. Ladoga, Ind., May 15, 1920; s. Edward Norris and Florence May (Burkett) S.; m. Virginia B. Austin, Feb. 22, 1942; children—Pamela T., Richard Burkett, Benjamin Austin, Janet Elizabeth, Rebecca Lee, Joanne Jeanena. BS, Ind. U., 1941; JD, Harvard U., 1947; LLD, Butler U., 1975, Ind. U., 1994. With Cummins Engine Co., Inc., Columbus, Ind., 1947—, various adminstrv., exec. positions, 1947-66, exec. v.p., corporate gen. mgr., 1966-69, vice. chmn. bd., 1969-88, vice chmn. emeritus, 1989—; dir. Cummins Engine Found. Dem. nat. committeeman for Ind., 1966-88; del. Dem. Nat. Conv., 1956-92; pres., bd. dirs. Irwin-Sweeney-Miller Found.; bd. dirs. Christian Found., Columbus, Ind. U. Found., 1975—; trustee Ind. U., 1971-92 (pres. bd. trustees, 1980-92). Capt. AUS, 1942-46. Mem. Ind. C. of C. (dir.). Office: Cummins Engine Co Inc Box 3005 MC-60909 Columbus IN 47202

STONESIFER, RICHARD JAMES, retired humanities and social science educator; b. Lancaster, Pa., June 21, 1922; s. Paul Tobias and Esther (Witlinger) S.; m. Nancy Jane Weaver, June 28, 1947; 1 dau., Pamela Ann. A.B., Franklin and Marshall Coll., 1946; M.A., Northwestern U., 1947; Ph.D., U. Pa., 1953. Mem. faculty Franklin and Marshall Coll., 1947-63, asso. prof. English, 1954-63, asst. to dean, 1957-60, asst. pres., 1960-63; asst. to provost, also dir. coll. gen. studies U. Pa., 1963-65; asso. prof. communications Annenberg Sch. Communications, 1963-65; dean. Coll. Liberal Arts, prof. English Drew U., Madison, N.J., 1965-71; pres. Monmouth U., West Long Branch, N.J., 1971-79; Woodrow Wilson prof. humanities and social sci. Monmouth U., 1979-82; moderator TV discussion series, 1954-60. Author: W.H. Davies: A Critical Biography, 2d edit, 1965, also articles in profl. jours.; newspaper columnist and commentator weekly; free lance journalist. Mem. Pa. Adv. Com. Ednl. Broadcasting, 1963-65; Bd. dirs. Harrisburg Area Center Higher Edn., 1963-65; trustee N.J. Cancer Inst., 1975—. Served with USAAF, 1943-46. Mem. Phi Beta Kappa. Home: PO Box 906 306 Sanders St Mullins SC 29574-4214 *My life has been devoted to higher education, and to keeping the liberal arts at the center of the enterprise, even as of necessity we put new emphases on professional and career matters. In teaching and in administration I take as fundamental guidance the teaching from ancient Greece: moderation in all things.*

STONICH, TIMOTHY WHITMAN, financial executive; b. Evanston, Ill., July 30, 1947; s. Joseph and Joyce (Whitman) S.; m. Joy Anne Harrison, June 14, 1969 (dec. Apr. 1986); m. Tamara L. Tierney, Nov. 13, 1987. B.A. in Econs., Denison U., 1969; M.B.A. in Fin., U. Chgo., 1972. Comml. banking officer Harris Bank, Chgo., 1969-74; asst. treas. Pullman Inc., Chgo., 1974-77, treas. Pullman Standard div., 1977-80; v.p. fin. Pullman Leasing Co., Chgo., 1977-80; v.p., gen. mgr. Pullman Leasing Co. Pullman Inc., 1980-83; treas. The Marmon Group, 1984-86; sr. v.p. fin. Lease Investment Corp., 1986-87; sr. v.p. fin., CFO U.S. Can Co., Oakbrook, Ill., 1987-91, exec. v.p., 1991—. Office: US Can Co 900 Commerce Dr Oak Brook IL 60523-1967

STONIER, DARYLE L., agricultural supplies company executive; married. Vice-chmn. Growmark, Inc., Bloomington, Ill., 1980—, also dir.; vice-chmn. bd. Ill. Grain Corp. Served with USN, 1953-57. Mem. Ill. Agrl. Auditing Assn. (bd. dirs.). Office: Growmark Inc 1701 N Towanda Ave Bloomington IL 61701-2090*

STONIER, TOM, theoretical biologist, educator; b. Hamburg, Germany, Apr. 29, 1927; came to U.S., 1939; BA, Drew U., 1950; MS, Yale U., 1951, PhD, 1955. Jr. rsch. assoc. Brookhaven Nat. Lab., Upton, N.Y., 1952-54; postdoctoral fellow Rockefeller U., N.Y.C., 1954-57, rsch. assoc., 1957-62; assoc. prof. biology Manhattan Coll., N.Y.C., 1962-71, prof. biology, 1971-75; dir. Pacem/in Terris Inst., N.Y.C., 1971-75; prof., head sci. and soc. U. Bradford, U.K., 1975-90, prof. emeritus, 1990—; chmn. Valiant Tech., London, 1985—. Author: Nuclear Disaster, 1964, The Wealth of Information, 1983, The Three Cs: Children, Computers and Communication, 1985, Information and the Internal Structure of the Universe, 1990, Beyond Information, 1992, Information and Meaning, 1997; contbr. numerous articles to profl. jours. Sec. Fedn. of Am. Scientists, Washington, 1967-68, mem. coun., 1965-68. With USNR, 1945-46. H.D. Hooker fellow Yale U., 1950-51, Damon Runyon Meml. fellow Rockefeller U., 1954-56, Inst. for Advanced Studies in Humanities fellow, Edinburgh U., 1989. Fellow Royal Soc. of Arts (life); mem. AAAS, N.Y. Acad. Scis., Phi Beta Kappa, Sigma Xi. Home and Office: 5 The Avenue Great Barrington MA 01230

STONNINGTON, HENRY HERBERT, physician, medical executive, educator; b. Vienna, Austria, Feb. 12, 1927; came to U.S., 1969; m. Constance Mary Leigh Hamersley, Sept. 19, 1953. MB, BS, Melbourne U., Victoria, Australia, 1950; MS, U. Minn., 1972. Diplomate Am. Bd. Phys. Medicine and Rehab., 1973. Pvt. practice Sydney, N.S.W., Australia, 1955-65; clin. tchr. U. N.S.W., Sydney, 1965-69; resident in Phys. Medicine and Rehab. Mayo Clinic, Rochester, Minn., 1969-72, mem. staff, 1972-83; assoc. prof. Mayo Med. Sch., Rochester, 1975-83; chmn. dept rehab. medicine Med. Coll. Va., Va. Commonwealth U., Richmond, 1983-88, prof. rehab. medicine, 1983-89, dir. rsch. tng. ctr., 1988-89; v.p. med. svcs. Sheltering Arms Hosp., Richmond, 1985-92; prof. and chmn. dept. phys. medicine and rehab. U. Mo., Columbia, 1992-94; med. dir. Meml. Rehab. Ctr., Savannah, Ga., 1994—; prof. rehab. medicine Emory U. Med. Sch., 1997—. Editor Brain Injury, 1987—, Pediatric Rehabilitation, 1997—; contbr. articles to profl. jours. Recipient award Rsch. Tng. Ctr. Model Sys., Nat. Inst. Disability and Rehab. Rsch., Washington, 1987, 88. Fellow Australia Coll. Rehab. Medicine, Australasia Faculty Rehab. Medicine, Royal Coll. Physicians Edinburgh (Scotland), Am. Acad. Phys. Medicine and Rehab., Am. Coun. Rehab. Medicine, Am. Assn. Acad. Physicians. Office: Meml Rehab Ctr 4750 Waters Ave Ste 307 Savannah GA 31404-6268

STOODT, BARBARA DERN, education educator, magazine editor; b. Columbus, Ohio, June 12, 1934; d. Millard Fissel and Helen Lucille (Taes) Dern; divorced; children: Linda Stoodt Neu, Susan Stoodt Price. BS in Edn., Ohio U., 1956; MA in Edn., Ohio State U., 1965; PhD, 1970; postgrad., U. Chgo., 1967. Tchr. North Charleston (S.C.) Schs., 1956-57, Cleveland Heights (Ohio) U., 1957-58, Mansfield (Ohio) Bd. Edn., 1958-59, 65-68; dir. reading, 1968; teaching assoc. Ohio State U., 1968-70; prof. edn. U. Akron, Ohio, 1970-77, U. N.C., Greensboro, 1977—; vis. prof. No. Ky. U. and U. Cin. Author: Reading Instruction, 1981, 2d edit., 1989, Teaching Language Arts, 1988; co-author: Secondary School Reading Instruction, 1987, 5th edit., 1994, Children's Literature: Discovery for a Lifetime, 1996, Riverside Reading Program. U.S. Office Edn. research grantee, 1970. Mem. Nat. Conf. on Research in English, Internat. Reading Assn. (Outstanding Dissertation award), Am. Ednl. Research Assn., Nat. Council Tchrs. English (outstanding research award 1971), Assn. for Supervision and Curriculum Devel., Assn. for Childhood Edn. Internat. Methodist. Avocations: gardening, travel, golf. Home: 7556 Pawtucket Green Cincinnati OH 45255 Office: Learning Mag 1607 Battleground Ave Greensboro NC 27408-8005

STOOKEY, GEORGE KENNETH, research institute administrator, dental educator; b. Waterloo, Ind., Nov. 6, 1935; s. Emra Gladison and Mary Catherine (Anglin) S.; m. Nola Jean Meek, Jan. 15, 1955; children—Lynda, Lisa, Laura, Kenneth. A.B. in Chemistry, Ind. U., 1957, M.S.D., 1962, Ph.D. in Preventive Dentistry, 1971. Asst. dir. Preventive Dentistry Research Inst., U. Ind., Indpls., 1968-70; assoc. dir. Oral Health Research Inst., U. Ind., 1974-81, dir., 1981—; assoc. prof. preventive dentistry Sch. of Dentistry, Ind. U., 1973-78, prof., 1978—, assoc. dean research, 1987-97, acting dean, 1996, assoc. dean acad. affairs, 1997—; cons. USAF, San Antonio, 1973—, ADA, Chgo., 1972—, Nat. Inst. Dental Rsch., Bethesda, Md., 1978-82, 91-95. Author: (with others) Introduction to Oral Biology and Preventive Dentistry, 1971, Preventive Dentistry for the Dental Assistant and Dental Hygienist, 1977, Preventive Dentistry in Action, 1972, 80 (Meritorious award 1973); contbr. articles to profl. jours. Mem. Internat. Assn. for Dental Research, European Orgn. Caries Research, Am. Assn. Lab. Animal Sci. Republican. Office: Oral Health Research Inst 415 Lansing St Indianapolis IN 46202-2855

STOOKEY, LAURENCE HULL, clergyman, theology educator; b. Belleville, Ill., Apr. 8, 1937; s. Loyd Leslie and Gladys E. (Hull) S.; m. Peggy Ann Reynolds, June 8, 1963 (div. 1990); children: Laura, Sarah. B.A., Swarthmore Coll., 1959; STB. magna cum laude, Wesley Theol. Sem., Washington, 1962; Th.D. with honors, Princeton Theol. Sem., 1971. Ordained to ministry United Meth. Ch., 1962. Pastor Peninsula-Del. Ann. Conf., United Meth. Ch., 1962-67, 71-73; instr. preaching and worship Princeton (N.J.) Theol. Sem., 1967-71; mem. faculty Wesley Theol. Sem., Washington, 1973—, Hugh Latimer Elderice prof., 1979—; guest lectr. Union Theol. Sem., Richmond, Va., McCormick Theol. Sem., Duke U. Div. Sch., Garrett-Evangel. Theol. Sem., Shenandoah (Va.) U.; vis. prof. U. Auckland, New Zealand, Melbourne Coll. Divinity; mem. Nat. Lutheran-United Meth. Bi-Lateral Theol. Dialogue, 1977-80; bd. dirs. Ctr. for Art and Religion, 1983-87, Liturgical Conf., 1983-91, 96—; officer Hymnal Revision Com. United Meth. Ch., 1984-88; cons. in field. Author: Living in a New Age: Sermons for the Season of Easter, 1978, Baptism-Christ's Act in the Church, 1982; co-author: Handbook of the Christian Year, 1986, rev. edit., 1992, Eucharist-Christ's Feast with the Church, 1993, Calendar: Christ's Time for the Church, 1996; mem. editorial bd. Homiletic, 1974-86, 96—; contbr. articles to profl. jours. Fellow Assn. Theol. Schs. in U.S. and Can., 1979-80. Fellow N. Am. Acad. Liturgy, Acad. Homiletics; mem. Fellowship United Methodists in Worship, Music and Other Arts (officer 1981-83). Home:

13500 Justice Rd Rockville MD 20853-3268 Office: 4500 Massachusetts Ave NW Washington DC 20016-5632 *The pursuit of happiness can be dangerous. To ask ourselves whether we are happy may only fasten our attention upon those demons of discontent and frustration that plague us all. The proper query is, "How best can we contribute to the welfare of others?" Individuals-and nations-do well to abandon both oppressive practices of dependency and the destructive illusion of absolute independence. True happiness comes only with the discovery that we are designed to be constructively interdependent.*

STOOKEY, NOEL PAUL, folksinger, composer; b. Balt., Dec. 30, 1937; s. George William and Dorothea (St. Aubrey) S.; m. Mary Elizabeth Bannard, Sept. 4, 1963; children: Elizabeth Drake, Katherine Darby, Anna St. Aubrey. Student, Mich. State U., 1955-58; HHD (hon.), Husson Coll., 1978. prodn. mgr. Cormac Chem. Corp., N.Y.C., 1959-60. Released album of songs Birds of Paradise, 1954; sang professionally, master ceremonies events, Mich. State U., 1955-58; profl. singer, Greenwich Village, N.Y.C., 1960-61; mem. folksinging group, Peter, Paul and Mary, 1961—; solo rec. artist for Warner Bros., 1971-74; producer folk albums for Scepter Records, Verve/Folkway Records; founder, Neworld Media, rec. studio Neworld Records, 1977-81; rec. artist: Paul And, 1971, One Night Stand, 1972, Real to Reel, 1976, Something New and Fresh, 1978, Band and Bodyworks, 1979, Wait'll You Hear This, 1982, There is Love, 1985, State of the Heart, 1985, In Love Beyond Our Lives, 1990, Peter Paul and Mommy Too, 1993, Lifelines, 1995, Lifelines Live, 1996; host Maine Pub. TV Broadcasting Series "E-Maine", 1997. Mem. AFTRA, Screen Actors Guild, ASCAP, Delta Upsilon. Club: St. Botolph's (Boston). Home: Rt 175 Blue Hill Falls ME 04615

STOOKSBURY, WILLIAM CLAUDE, minister; b. Knoxville, Tenn., June 6, 1947; s. William Claude and Vera Faye (Hudman) S.; m. Mary Jayne Moyer, Mar. 21, 1970; 1 child, William David. BS, U. Tenn., Chattanooga, 1980; MDiv, Vanderbilt U., 1987. Ordained to ministry Bapt. Ch., 1978; ordinations transfered to Unithed Meth. Ch., 1988. Min. of visitation 1st Bapt. Ch., Chattanooga, 1975-78; pastor Beacon Bapt. Ch., Rossville, Ga., 1978-80; asst. min. Ea. Pkwy. Bapt. Ch., Louisville, 1980-81; pastor 1st Bapt. Ch., Fisherville, Ky., 1981-84, Baker's Grove Bapt. Ch., Mt. Juliet, Tenn., 1984-86, Fairgarden United Meth. Ch., Sevierville, Tenn., 1988-92, Lonsdale United Meth. Ch., Knoxville, 1992—; design team urban ministry Holston Conf., Meth. Ch., Knoxville, 1992. Mem. search com. dean of human svcs. U. Tenn., Chattanooga, 1980; co-chair area II, Campbellsville Coll. Fund-raising, Ky., 1983; mem. steering com. Tenn. Alliance Strong Cmtys., Nashville, 1989—; charter mem. Ams. for Change, Washignton, 1993—; mem. nat. steering com. Clinton/Gore '96 Campaign. Named one of Outstanding Young Men of Am., Outstanding Young Assn., 1982, Dyer scholarship Vanderbilt Div., 1986. Fellow Westar Inst.; mem. ACLU, Am. Acad. Religion, Long Run Bapt. Assn. (chair asn. message com. 1984, com. to study ordination 1982, exec. bd. dirs. 1981-84), People for the Am. Way, The Interfaith Alliance, Internat. Platform Assn. Democrat. Avocation: reading. Home: 1105 Katherine Ave Knoxville TN 37921-2035 Office: Lonsdale United Meth Ch 3002 Galbraith St Knoxville TN 37921-2023

STOOPS, LOUISE, information services administrator; b. Honolulu; d. Robert Earl and Ethel Louise (Saunders) S. BA in Liberal Arts/English, U. Ariz.; MLS, Simmons Coll., 1952. Chief libr. Baker, Weeks & Co., N.Y.C., 1972-77; libr. mgr. Lehman Bros., Kuhn Loeb, N.Y.C., 1977-84; mgr. info. svcs. Bessmer Trust Co., N.Y.C., 1985—. Vol. dept. edn. Met. Mus. N.Y., 1985—. mem. Fin. Women's Assn. N.Y. (mem. internat. com. 1990-91), Spl. Librs. Assn., Chi Omega. Office: Bessmer Trust Co 630 5th Ave New York NY 10111-0100

STOORZA GILL, GAIL, corporate professional; b. Yoakum, Tex., Aug. 28, 1943; d. Roy Otto and Ruby Pauline (Ray) Blankenship; m. Larry Sttorza, Apr. 27, 1963 (div. 1968); m. Ian M. Gill, Apr. 24, 1981; 1 child, Alexandra Leigh. Student, N. Tex. State U., 1961-63, U. Tex., Arlington, 1963. Stewardess Cen. Airlines, Ft. Worth, 1963; advt. and acctg. exec. Phillips-Ramsey Advt., San Diego, 1963-68; dir. advt. Rancho Bernardo, San Diego, 1968-72; dir. corp. communications Avco Community Developers, San Diego, 1972-74; pres. Gail Stoorza Co., San Diego, 1974—, Stoorza, Ziegaus & Metzger, San Diego, 1974—; CEO Stoorza, Ziegaust, Metzger, Inc., 1993—; chmn. Stoorza/Smith, San Diego, 1984-85, Stoorza Internat., San Diego, 1984-85; CEO ADC Stoorza, San Diego, 1987—, Franklin Stoorza, San Diego, 1993—. Trustee San Diego Art Found.; bd. dirs. San Diego Found. for Performing Arts, San Diego Opera, Sunbelt Nursery Groups, Dallas. Names Small Bus. Person of Yr. Selest Com. on Small Bus., 1984, one of San Diego's Ten Outstanding Young Citizens San Diego Jaycees, 1979; recipient Woman of Achievement award Women in Communications Inc., 1985. Mem. Pubs. Soc. Am., Nat. Assn. Home Builders (residential mktg. com.), COMBO. Methodist. Clubs: Chancellors Assn. U. Calif. (San Diego), Pub. Relations, San Diego Press. Home: PO Box 490 Rancho Santa Fe CA 92067-0490 Office: Franklin Stoorza 225 Broadway Ste 1800 San Diego CA 92101-5018*

STOPHER, PETER ROBERT, civil and transportation engineering educator, consultant; b. Crowborough, Eng., Aug. 8, 1943; came to U.S., 1968; s. Harold Edward and Joan Constance (Salmon) S; m. Valerie Anne Alway, Apr. 11, 1964 (div. Feb. 1989); children: Helen Margaret Anne, Claire Elizabeth; m. Catherine Coville Jones July 7, 1990 (div. Apr. 1997). BSCE, U. Coll., London, 1964, PhD, 1967. Research officer Greater London Council, London, 1967-68; asst. prof. transp. planning, applied statistics, math. modeling Northwestern U., Evanston, Ill., 1968-70, from assoc. prof. to prof., 1973-79, vis. prof., 1980-81; asst. prof. McMaster U., Hamilton, Ontario, 1970-71; assoc. prof. Cornell U., Ithaca, N.Y., 1971-73; tech. v.p. Schimpeler Corradino Assoc., Miami, Fla., and Los Angeles, 1980-84, v.p., 1984-87; dir., CFO Evaluation and Tng. Inst., 1987-90; prin., co-founder Applied Mgmt. and Planning Group, 1988-90; prof. civil engring. La. State Univ., Baton Rouge, 1990—, dir. La. Transp. Rsch. Ctr., 1990-93; co-founder, ptnr. PlanTrans, 1994—; spl. advisor Nat. Inst. Transp. and Rd. Research, Pretoria, S. Africa, 1976-77; vis. prof. U. Syracuse, N.Y., 1971-73, U. Louvain, Belgium, 1980. Co-author Urban Transportation Planning and Modeling, 1974, Transportation Systems Evaluation, 1976, Survey Sampling and Multivariate Analysis, 1978; contbr. articles to profl. jours. Active Stephen Ministry. Recipient Fred Burgraaf prize Hwy. Research Bd., 1968, Jules Dupuit prize World Conf. on Transp. Rsch., 1992. Mem. ASCE, Am. Stats. Assn., Transp. Rsch. Bd. (com. chmn. 1970-77, 95—), Transp. Rsch. Forum (Joyce E. Yaeger Intermodel Rsch. Paper award 1994), Inst. Transp. Engrs. Democrat. Methodist. Avocations: working out, gardening, photography, reading, classical music. Home: 3533 Granada Dr Baton Rouge LA 70810-1142 Office: La State U Dept Civil and Environ Engring Baton Rouge LA 70803-6405

STOPPARD, TOM (TOMAS STRAUSSLER), playwright; b. Zlin, Czechoslovakia, July 3, 1937; s. Eugene and Martha (Stoppard) Straussler; m. Jose Ingle, 1965 (div.); m. Miriam Moore-Robinson, 1972 (div.); 4 children. MLitt (hon.), U. Bristol, Eng., 1979, Brunel U., Eng., 1979, U. Sussex, Eng., 1980. Journalist Western Daily Press, Bristol, Eng., 1954-58, Evening World, Bristol, 1958-60; free-lance reporter, 1960-63; bd. dirs. Royal Nat. Theatre, London, 1989—. Author: (plays) The Gamblers, 1965, Rosencrantz and Guildenstern Are Dead, 1966 (Plays and Players Best Play award 1967, Best Play Tony award 1968), Enter a Free Man, 1968, The Real Inspector Hound, 1968, Albert's Bridge, 1969 (Prix Italia 1968), If You're Glad I'll Be Frank, 1969, After Magritte, 1970, Dogg's Our Pet, 1971, Jumpers, 1972 (Evening Standard Best Play award 1972, Plays and Players Best Play award 1972), Travesties, 1974 (Evening Standard Best Play award 1974, Best Play Tony award 1976), Dirty Linen and New-Found-Land, 1976, Every Good Boy Deserves Favor, 1974, Night and Day, 1978 (Evening Standard Best Play award 1978), Dogg's Hamlet, Cahoot's Macbeth, 1979, The Real Thing, 1982 (Evening Standard Best Play award 1982, Best Play Tony award 1984, Best Fgn. Play Tony award 1984), Hapgood, 1988, Artist Descending a Staircase, 1988, Arcadia, 1993 (Evening Standard Best Play award 1993, Oliver award 1994), Indian Ink, 1995; (play adaptations) Tango by Slawomir Mrozek, 1966, The House of Bernarda Alba by Federico Garcia Lorca, 1973, Undiscovered Country (based on Das Weite Land by Arthur Schnitzler), 1979, On the Razzle (based on Einen Jux will er sich machen by Johann Nestroy), 1981, Rough Crossing (based on The Play's the Thing by Ferenc Molnar), 1984, Dalliance (based on Liebelei by Arthur Schnitzler), 1986; (radio plays) The Dissolution of Dominic Boot, 1964, M is for Moon Among Other Things, 1964, If You're Glad I'll Be Frank, 1966, Albert's Bridge, 1967, Where Are They Now?, 1970, Artist Descending A Staircase, 1972, The Dog It Was That Died, 1982, In the Native State, 1991, also episodes of radio serials The Dales, 1964, A Student's Diary, 1965; (screenplays) The Romantic Englishwoman, 1975, Despair, 1978, The Human Factor, 1980, (with Terry Gilliam and Charles McKeown) Brazil, 1985 (Best Screenplay Acad. award nominee 1985, Best Screenplay L.A. Critics Circle award 1985), Empire of the Sun, 1987, The Russia House, 1990; (author, dir.) Rosencrantz and Guildenstern Are Dead, 1990 (Grand prize Venice Film Festival 1990), Billy Bathgate, 1991; (teleplays) A Walk on the Water, 1963, A Separate Peace, 1966, Teeth, 1967, Another Moon Called Earth, 1967, Neutral Ground, 1968, The Engagement (based on his radio play The Dissolution of Dominic Boot), 1970, One Pair of Eyes, 1972, (with Clive Exton) Boundaries, 1975, Three Men in a Boat, 1975, Professional Foul, 1977, Squaring the Circle: Poland 1980-81, 1985; (translator) Largo Desolato by Vaclav Havel, 1987; (novel) Lord Malquist and Mr. Moon, 1966; contbr. short stories to Introduction 2, 1964. Decorated comdr. Order Brit. Empire; Ford Found. grantee, 1964; recipient John Whiting award Arts Coun. Great Britain, 1967, Evening Standard Most Promising Playwright Drama award, 1972, Shakespeare prize Hamburg, Germany, 1979. Fellow Royal Soc. Literature. Office: Peters Fraser Dunlop, The Chambers 5th Fl Lots Rd, London SW10 OXF, England

STOPPLEMOOR, CHERYL See LADD, CHERYL

STORANDT, MARTHA, psychologist; b. Little Rock, June 2, 1938; d. Farris and Floy (Montgomery) Mobbs; m. Duane Storandt, Dec. 15, 1962; 1 child, Eric. AB, Washington U., St. Louis, 1960, PhD, 1966. Lic. psychologist, Mo. Staff psychologist VA, Jefferson Barracks, Mo., 1967-68; asst. prof. to prof. Washington U., St. Louis, 1968—; mem. nat. adv. council on aging Nat. Inst. on Aging, 1984-87; editor-in-chief Jour. Gerontology, 1981-86. Author: Counseling and Therapy with Older Adults, 1983; co-author: Memory, Related Functions and Age, 1974; co-editor: The Clinical Psychology of Aging, 1978, The Adult Years: Continuity and Change, 1989, Neuropsychological Assessment of Dementia and Depression in Older Adults: A Clinician's Guide, 1994. Recipient Disting. Service award Mo. Assn. Homes for the Aging, 1984, Disting. Sci. Contbn. award Am. Psychol. Assn. div. Adult Devel. and Aging, 1988. Fellow Am. Psychol. Assn. (pres. div. 20 1979-80, council rep. 1983-84, 86-88), Gerontol. Soc. Am. Office: Washington U Dept Psychology Saint Louis MO 63130

STORARO, VITTORIO, cinematographer; b. Rome, June 24, 1940; s. Renato and Teodolinda (Laparelli) S.; m. Antonia Cafolla, Dec. 29, 1962; children: Francesca, Fabrizio, Giovanni. Student, Duca D'Aosta, Rome, 1951-56, Centro Italiano Addestramento Cinematografico, Rome, 1956-58; Degree in Cinematography, Centro Sperimentale di Cinematografia, Rome, 1958-60. Cinematographer Titanus, 1968, Paramount, 1970, 81, 87, United Artist, 1972, 76-77, 20th Century Fox, 1976, 78, Columbia, 1981, 84-86, Cronard Communications, 1982, Warner Bros., 1983, NBC, 1984-85. Cinematographer films including Youthful Youthful, 1968, The Bird With The Crystal Plummage, 1970, The Conformist, 1970, Last Tango in Paris, 1972, Nineteen Hundred, 1976, Scandalo Submission, 1977, Luna, 1978, Apocalypse Now, 1979 (Academy Award, 1979), Reds, 1981 (Acad. award 1981), One From the Heart, 1981, Wagner, 1982, Lady Hawke, 1983, Peter the Great, 1985, Ishtar, 1986, The Last Emperor, 1987 (Acad. award 1987), Tucker, 1987, New York Stories, 1988, Dick Tracy, 1990, The Sheltering Sky, 1990, Little Buddha, 1994 (Oscar nomination 1994), La Vera Vita d Antonio Hutter, 1994, L'Aguila, 1994, Flamenco, 1995, Roma Imago Urbis, 1995 (Oscar nomination 1995), Taxi, 1996. Recipient Best Cinematography award N.Y. Film Critics, 1971, Career awards Art Dir. Club Italiano, 1995, Municipality Marino, 1996, Fantafestival, 1996. Mem. Acad. Motion Picture Arts and Scis., Italian Assn. of Cinematographers (pres.). Home: Via Divino Amore 2, 00040 Rome Italy*

STORB, URSULA BEATE, molecular genetics and cell biology educator; b. Stuttgart, Germany, July 6, 1936; came to U.S., 1966; d. Walter M. Stemmer and Marianne M. (Kämmerer) Nowara. MD, U. Freiburg, Fed. Republic Germany, 1960; Germany. Asst. prof. dept. microbiology U. Wash., Seattle, 1971-75, assoc. prof., 1975-81, prof., 1981-86, head. div. immunology, 1980-86; prof. dept. molecular genetics and cell biology U. Chgo., 1986—. Mem. editl. bd. Immunity, Current Opinion in Immunology, Internat. Immunology; contbr. articles to sci. jours. Grantee NIH, NSF, Am. Cancer Soc., 1973—. Fellow Am. Acad. Arts and Scis.; mem. Assn. Women in Sci., Am. Assn. Immunology, Am. Soc. Cell Biology. Office: U Chgo 920 E 58th St Chicago IL 60637-1432

STORCH, ARTHUR, theater director; b. Bklyn., June 29, 1925; s. Sam and Bessie (Goldner) S.; children: Max Darrow, Alexander English, Bess Martin. B.A., New Sch. Social Research, 1949. Actor in Broadway prodns. End as a Man, 1953, Time Limit, 1955, Girls of Summer, 1956, Look Homeward, Angel, 1957, Night Circus, 1958, The Long Dream, 1960, The Best Man, 1961; motion pictures The Strange One, 1956, Girls of the Night, 1959, The Exorcist, 1974; dir. off-Broadway Two by Saroyan, 1961, Three by Three, 1962, Talking to You (London debut), 1962, The Typists and the Tiger, 1963, The Owl and the Pussycat, 1964, The Impossible Years, 1965, The Local Stigmatic, 1970, Under the Weather, 1965, Golden Rainbow, 1967, The Chinese and Dr. Fish, 1969, Promenade All, 1970, 42 Seconds from Broadway, 1973, Tribute, 1978, Twice Around the Park, 1982, Clarence, 1986; Of Mice and Men, 1988; dir. nat. tour The King and I, 1989; dir. Syracuse Stage Waiting for Lefty, Noon, Of Mice and Men, 1974, 75, La Ronde, The Butterfingers Angel. Mornings at Seven, Dynamo, 1975-76, A Quality of Mercy, The Seagull, 1976-77, 1976-77; dir. Love Letters on Blue Paper, End of the Beginning, 1977-78, Loved, 1978, Naked, 1979, The Comedy of Errors, 1980, The Impromptu of Outremont, 1982, The Double Bass, 1984, Arms and the Man, Handy Dandy, Cyrano de Bergerac, Romeo and Juliet, 1986, Of Mice and Men, N.Y.C., 1987, Fugue, 1988, Seven By Beckett, 1988, Look Homeward Angel, Wait Unitl Dark, Dangerous Corner, 1990, A Walk in the Woods, 1989, Finding Donis Ann, 1990, Androcles and the Lion, 1991; Lend Me a Tenor, 1992, Awake and Sing, 1993; dir., actor Love Letters, 1992; founder, producing artistic dir. Syracuse Stage; chmn. drama dept. Syracuse U., 1974-92, Arthur Storch Theatre, 1992; artistic dir. Berkshire Theatre Festival, Stockbridge, Mass., 1995—. Home: 235 W 48th St # 37C New York NY 10036 Office: Berkshire Theatre Festival Stockbridge MA 01262

STORCK, HERBERT EVAN, marketing professional; b. New Haven, Apr. 23, 1954; s. Herbert and Mary (Grove) S.; m. Susan Mary McConachie, Aug. 6, 1977; children: Christopher, Timothy, Kyle. BA, U. Bridgeport, 1976; MS, U. Wis., 1979. Asst. acct. exec. MRCA Info. Svcs., Stamford, Conn., 1980-81, acct. exec., 1981-82, group acct. mgr., 1983-84, dir. bus. devel., 1984-85, v.p. bus. devel., 1985-86, v.p., gen. mgr., 1986-90, sr. v.p., gen. mgr., 1990-92; pres., CEO Advanced Mktg. Solutions subs. NFO Rsch., Inc., Shelton, Conn., 1992—. Mem. Am. Mktg. Assn. Avocations: hiking, motorcycling, woodworking. Home: 12 Shelter Rock Rd Trumbull CT 06611-3325 Office: Advanced Mktg Solutions One Corporate Dr Ste 506 Shelton CT 06484

STOREN, THOMAS, JR. See DOHERTY, TOM

STORER, JEFFREY B., lawyer; b. 1948. AB, Harvard Coll., 1970; JD, Boston Coll., 1976. Bar: Mass. 1976. Atty. Ropes & Gray, Boston. Office: Ropes & Gray One International Pl Boston MA 02110

STORER, MARYRUTH, law librarian; b. Portland, Oreg., July 26, 1953; d. Joseph William and Carol Virginia (Pearson) Storer; m. David Bruce Bailey, Jan. 1, 1981; children: Sarah, Allison. BA in History, Portland State U., 1974; JD, U. Oreg., 1977; M in Law Librarianship, U. Wash., 1978. Bar: Oreg. 1978. Assoc. law librarian U. Tenn., Knoxville, 1978-79; law librarian O'Melveny & Myers, Los Angeles, 1979-88; dir. Orange County Law Library, Santa Ana, Calif., 1988—. Mem. Am. Assn. Law Libraries, So. Calif. Assn. Law Libraries (pres. 1986-87), Coun. Calif. County Law Librs. (sec.-treas. 1990-94, pres. 1994-96). Democrat. Episcopalian. Office: Orange County Law Library 515 N Flower St Santa Ana CA 92703-2304

STORER, NORMAN WILLIAM, sociology educator; b. Middletown, Conn., May 8, 1930; s. Norman Wyman and Mary Emily (House) S.; m. Ada Joan Van Valkenburg, Aug. 19, 1951; children: Martin Wilson, Thomas Wyman; m. Mary Ashton Pott Hiatt, Mar. 7, 1975. A.B., U. Kans., 1952, M.A., 1956; Ph.D., Cornell U., 1961. Lectr., asst. prof. Harvard U., Cambridge, Mass., 1960-66; staff assoc. Social Sci. Research Council, N.Y.C., 1966-70; prof. sociology CUNY-Baruch Coll., N.Y.C., 1970-88; prof. emeritus CUNY-Baruch Coll., 1989—; dept. chmn. CUNY-Baruch Coll., N.Y.C., 1970-85, chmn. faculty senate, 1981-84. Author: The Social System of Science, 1966, Focus on Society, 1973, 2d edit., 1980, A Leer of Limericks, 1990, (with William Flores) Domestic Violence in Suburban San Diego, 1994; editor: The Sociology of Science, 1973; column editor San Diego Writers' Monthly, 1992-94. Vol. S.D. Sheriff's Dept., 1992—. Served to sgt. AUS, 1953-55. Mem. AAAS, Phi Beta Kappa, Sigma Xi. Democrat. Home: 1417 Van Buren Ave San Diego CA 92103-2339

STORER, THOMAS PERRY, lawyer; b. Washington, July 14, 1944; s. Morris Brewster and Gretchen Geuder (Schneider) S.; m. Julia Manganip Owek, Dec. 22, 1966; children: Lingbawan Frederick, Allinnawa Elizabeth, Gessingga Nathaniel. BA in Math., Harvard U., 1965, JD, 1979; MPA, Woodrow Wilson Sch. Pub. and Internat. Affairs, 1969. Bar: Mass. 1979, U.S. Dist. Ct. Mass. 1979. Program officer U.S. Peace Corps, Kuala Lumpur, Malaysia, 1969-72; analyst, unit chief Bur. of Budget State of Ill., Springfield, 1972-74; dep. dir. Ill. Dept. Pub. Aid, Springfield, 1974-76; cons. Mass. Medicaid Program, Boston, 1976-79; assoc. Goodwin, Procter & Hoar, Boston, 1979-87, ptnr., 1987—. Vol. U.S. Peace Corps, Bontoc, Mountain Prov., Philippines, 1965-67; elder Newton (Mass.) Presbyn. Ch., Mass., 1987—. Mem. ABA, Mass. Bar Assn. Avocations: music, computers. Home: 114 Waban Hill Rd N Chestnut Hill MA 02167-1026 Office: Goodwin Procter & Hoar LLP Exchange Pl Boston MA 02109

STORETTE, RONALD FRANK, lawyer; b. N.Y.C., June 20, 1943; m. Monique Storette; 1 child, Ronald. BA summa cum laude, U. Va., 1966; JD, Harvard U., 1969; Diploma of Internat. Law, Stockholm Faculty of Law, 1970. Bar: D.C. 1973, U.S. Ct. Appeals (D.C. cir.) 1976, U.S. Supreme Ct. 1976, U.S. Dist. Ct. (so. and ea. dists.) N.Y. 1977, U.S. Dist. Ct. D.C. 1977, U.S. Ct. Appeals (2d cir.) 1978, U.S. Ct. Internat. Trade. 1978. Lectr. law Stockholm Faculty of Law, 1970-71; assoc. Jean-Pierre De Bandt, Brussels, 1971-73; chief legal counsel Textron Atlantic S.A., Brussels, 1973-75; assoc. Donovan, Leisure, Newton & Irvine, N.Y.C., 1975-79; ptnr. Fragomen, Del Rey & Bernsen, P.C., N.Y.C., 1979-88, Baker & McKenzie, N.Y.C., 1988-91, Proskauer Rose Goetz & Mendelsohn, N.Y.C., 1991—. Author: The Politics of Integrated Social Investment; An American Study of the Swedish LAMCO Project in Liberia, 1971, The Administration of Equality; An American Study of Sweden's Bilateral Development Aid, 1972; also articles. Cassal Found. fellow U. Stockholm, Sweden, 1969. Mem. ABA, N.Y. State Bar Assn., Assn. of Bar of City of N.Y., Am. Immigration Lawyers Assn., Phi Beta Kappa. Office: Proskauer Rose Goetz & Mendelsohn 1585 Broadway New York NY 10036-8200

STOREY, BOBBY EUGENE, JR., electrical engineer, engineering consultant; b. Bainbridge, Md., Jan. 26, 1958; s. Bobby E. Sr. and Rebecca J. (Seagraves) S.; m. Lynn M. Miller, May 24, 1976 (div. June 1978); 1 child, Christopher David; m. Mary H. Freeman, Feb. 14, 1992. AA in Math., Gordon Jr. Coll., 1986; BS in Applied Physics, Ga. Inst. Tech., 1988, M in Applied Physics, 1989. Engr. instrumentation and controls Va. Power Co., Mineral, 1982-85; engr. electro optics GEC Avionics, Norcross, Ga., 1988; v.p. EnerSci Inc., Norcross, 1989-94; project engr. LXE, Inc., Norcross, 1988-94; pres. E & H Enterprises, Inc., Duluth, Ga., 1994-96; mgr. engring. project office Sci. Atlanta, Inc., Norcross, Ga., 1995—. With USN, 1976-82. Mem. Internat. Orgn. Electrical and Electronic Engrs. Republican. Avocations: coins, woodworking, target shooting. Home: 2820 Bluebird Cir Duluth GA 30136-3908 Office: Sci Atlanta Inc 4386 Park Dr Norcross GA 30093-2906

STOREY, BRIT ALLAN, historian; b. Boulder, Colo., Dec. 10, 1941; s. Harold Albert and Gladys Roberta (Althouse) S.; m. Carol DeArman, Dec. 19, 1970; 1 child, Christine Roberta. AB, Adams State Coll., Alamosa, Colo., 1963; MA, U. Ky., 1965, PhD, 1968. Instr. history Auburn (Ala.) U., 1967-68, asst. prof., 1968-70; dep. state historian State Hist. Soc. Colo., Denver, 1970-71, acting state historian, 1971-72, rsch. historian, 1972-74; hist. preservation specialist Adv. Coun. on Hist. Preservation, Lakewood, Colo., 1974-88; sr. historian Bur. Reclamation, Lakewood, 1988—. Contbr. articles to profl. publs. Mem. Fed. Preservation Forum (pres. 1990-91), Nat. Coun. Pub. History (sec. 1987, pres.-elect 1990-91, pres. 1991-92), Orgn. Am. Historians (com. 1983-86, chmn. 1985-86), Victorian Soc. Am. (bd. dirs. 1977-79), Western History Assn. (chmn. com. 1982-86), Colo.-Wyo. Assn. Mus. (sec. 1974-76, pres. 1976-77), Cosmos Club (Washington). Avocation: birding. Home: 7264 W Otero Ave Littleton CO 80123-5639 Office: Bur Reclamation D 5300 Bldg 67 Denver Fed Ctr Denver CO 80225-0007

STOREY, CHARLES PORTER, lawyer; b. Austin, Tex., Dec. 4, 1922; s. Robert Gerald and Frances Hazel (Porter) S.; m. Helen Hanks Stephens, Oct. 14, 1950; children: Charles Porter, Harry Stephens, Frederick Schatz. BA, U. Tex., 1947, LLB, 1948; LLM, So. Methodist U., 1952. Bar: Tex. 1948. Pvt. practice law Dallas, 1948—; with Storey Armstrong Steger & Martin P.C. Pres. Dallas Day Nursery Assn., 1958, Greater Dallas Coun. Chs., 1970-71; chmn. Internat. Com. YMCA, 1969-71; nat. bd. dirs. U.S. YMCA, 1964-75; pres. Children's Devel. Ctr., Dallas, 1959; trustee Baylor Coll. Dentistry, 1981-90, Hillcrest Found.; trustee Southwestern Legal Found., chmn. 1980-90. 1st lt., pilot USAAF, 1943-45, ETO. Decorated Air medal. Master Dallas Inn of Ct. (pres. 1991-93); fellow Am. Coll. Trial Lawyers, Am. Bar Found., Tex. Bar Found.; mem. ABA, Tex. Bar Assn. (bd. dirs. 1976-79), Dallas Bar Assn. (pres. 1975), Philos. Soc. Tex., Dallas Country Club, Crescent Club, Idlewild Club, Phi Delta Phi, Phi Delta Theta. Mem. Christian Ch. (Disciples of Christ). Home: 4400 Rheims Pl Dallas TX 75205-3627 Office: 4600 Fountain Pl 1445 Ross Ave Dallas TX 75202-2812

STOREY, JAMES MOORFIELD, lawyer; b. Boston, Apr. 12, 1931; s. Charles Moorfield and Susan Jameson (Sweetser) S.; m. Adair Miller, Aug. 28, 1954 (div. 1973); children: Barbara Sessums Storey McGrath, Mary Sweetser Storey Meley, Susan Adair Storey Frank, Eliza Allison Tebo Storey Anderson, Alice Leovy Storey Thorpe; m. Isabelle Helene Boeschenstein, May 17, 1973. A.B., Harvard U., 1953, LL.B., 1956. Bar: Mass. 1956. Atty. SEC, Washington, 1956-57, legal asst. to chmn., 1957-59; assoc. Gaston, Snow, Motley & Holt, Boston, 1959-62; ptnr. Gaston, Snow, Motley & Holt (name changed to Gaston Snow & Ely Bartlett), Boston, 1962-87; ptnr. Dechert Price & Rhoads, Boston, 1987-94, ret., 1994, profl. trustee, corp. dir., 1994—; trustee Mt. Auburn Cemetery, Cambridge, Mass., 1980—. Mem. ABA, Boston Bar Assn., Tavern Club Boston (pres. 1985-87), City Club Corp. (pres. 1987-89), Century Assn. of N.Y. Unitarian. Home: 89A Mount Vernon St Boston MA 02108-1330 Office: Room 1239 10 Post Office Sq S 12th Fl Boston MA 02109

STOREY, KENNETH BRUCE, biology educator; b. Taber, Alta., Can., Oct. 23, 1949; s. Arthur George and Madeleine Una (Mawhinney) S.; m. Janet Margaret Collicutt, June 6, 1975; children: Jennifer, Kathryn. BSc with honors, U. Calgary, Alta., 1971; PhD, U. B.C., Vancouver, Can., 1974. Asst. prof. Duke U., Durham, N.C., 1975-79; assoc. prof. Carleton U., Ottawa, Ont., Can., 1979-85, prof., 1985—; invited lectr. at various confs., univs. Mem. editl. bd. Cryo-Letters, 1983—, Jour. Comparative Physiology, 1995—, Am. Jour. Physiology, 1994—, Experimental Biology Online, 1996—; contbr. over 300 articles to profl. jours. Recipient E.W.R. Steacie award Nat. Sci. and Engring. Rsch. Coun. Can., 1984-86, Killam sr. rsch. fellow, 1993—; Killam fellow Can. Coun., Sheffield, Eng., 1975-77. Fellow Royal Soc. Can.; mem. Am. Soc. Biol. Chemists, Can. Biochem. Soc. (Ayerst award 1989), Can. Soc. Zoology, Soc. Cryobiology. Avocations: movies, music, Renaissance art. Office: Carleton U Dept Biology, 1125 Colonel By Drive, Ottawa, ON Canada K1S 5B6

STOREY, NORMAN C., lawyer; b. Miami, Fla., Oct. 11, 1943. BA cum laude, Loyola U., L.A., 1965; JD, U. Ariz., 1968. Bar: Ariz. 1968. Law clk. to Hon. James A. Walsh U.S. Dist. Ct. Ariz.; ptnr. Squire, Sanders & Dempsey, Phoenix. Mem. ABA, State Bar Ariz., Am. Arbitration Assn.

(panelist). Office: Squire Sanders & Dempsey 40 N Central Ave Ste 2700 Phoenix AZ 85004-4424

STOREY, ROBERT DAVIS, lawyer; b. Tuskegee, Ala., Mar. 28, 1936; s. Dewitt Herald and Katie Pearl (Johnson) S.; m. Juanita Kendrick Cohen, May 9, 1959; children: Charles Kendrick, Christopher Robert Ransom, Rebecca Kate. AB, Harvard U., 1958; JD, Case Western Res. U., 1964. Bar: Ohio, 1964. Atty. East Ohio Gas Co., Cleve., 1964-66; asst. dir. Legal Aid Soc., Cleve., 1966-67; assoc. Burke, Haber & Berick, Cleve., 1967-70, ptnr., 1971-93; ptnr. Thompson, Hine & Flory, P.L.L., Cleve., 1994—; bd. dirs. GTE Corp., Stamford, Conn., Procter & Gamble Co., Cin., May Dept. Stores Co., St. Louis, Bank One, Cleve.; trustee The Kresge Found., The George Gund Found., Case Western Res. U., Spelman Coll., Univ. Sch., Great Lakes Sci. Ctr.; trustee Cleve. State U., 1971-80, chmn., 1979-80; trustee Phillips Exeter Acad., 1968-83; overseer Harvard U., 1978-84; dir. Fed. Res. Bank Cleve., 1987-90, Louisville Courier-Jour., 1984-86. Served to capt. USMC, 1958-61. Recipient Charles Flint Kellog award Assn. Episcopal Colls., 1984; named Chief Marshal, 25th Reunion, Harvard Class of 1958, 1983. Mem. Soc. Benchers, Union Club, Rowfant Club, Univ. Club, Ponce de Leon Club. Episcopalian. Home: 2385 Coventry Rd Cleveland Heights OH 44118-4074 Office: Thompson Hine & Flory LLP 3900 Key Ctr 127 Public Sq Cleveland OH 44114-1216

STORIN, MATTHEW VICTOR, newspaper editor; b. Springfield, Mass., Dec. 24, 1942; s. Harry Francis and Blanche Marie S.; m. Keiko Takita, Aug. 1, 1975; 1 child, Kenyatta; children by previous marriage: Karen, Aimee, Sean. BA, U. Notre Dame, 1964. Reporter Springfield Daily News, 1964-65, Griffin-Larrabee News Bur., Washington, 1965-69; Washington corr., city editor, Asian corr., nat. editor, asst. mng. editor, dep. mng. editor, mng. editor Boston Globe, 1969-85; dep. mng. editor U.S. News & World Report, Washington, 1985-86; editor, sr. v.p. Chgo. Sun-Times, 1986-87; editor The Maine Times, Topsham, 1988-89; mng. editor N.Y. Daily News, 1989-91, exec. editor, 1991-92; exec. editor Boston Globe, 1992-93, editor, 1993—. Recipient Disting. Polit. Reporting award Am. Assn. Polit. Sci., 1969. Home: 1501 Beacon St Brookline MA 02146-4626 Office: The Boston Globe 135 Morrissey Blvd Boston MA 02125*

STORING, PAUL EDWARD, foreign service officer; b. Ames, Iowa, Oct. 24, 1929; s. James Alvin and Edith Nora (Ryg) S.; children: Mimi Storing Harlan, Felice Storing Kite. Student, U Oslo, Norway, 1950-51; B.A., Allegheny Coll., 1952; M.A. with honors, Colgate U., 1956; postgrad., U. Wis., Madison, 1955-59. Fgn. service officer Dept. State, Washington, Mex. and Scandinavia, 1960-80; spl. asst. U.S. Sect. Internat. Boundary and Water Commn. U.S. And Mex., Washington, 1980—. Contbr. articles to profl. jours. Served to cpl. U.S. Army, 1953-55. Fellow U. Wis., 1957-58; Fulbright fellow U. Oslo, 1959-60. Mem. Am. Fgn. Svc. Assn., Fulbright Assn., Phi Beta Kappa, Delta Tau Delta (pres. 1949-50). Baptist. Avocations: swimming; tennis; travel. Office: Office of Mex Affairs Dept of State Rm 4258 Washington DC 20520-0001

STORK, DONALD ARTHUR, advertising executive; b. Walsh, Ill., June 17, 1939; s. Arthur William and Katherine Frances (Young) S.; m. Joanna Gentry, June 9, 1962; 1 child, Brian Wesley. BS, So. Ill. U., 1961; postgrad. St. Louis U., 1968-69. With Naegele Outdoor Advt., Mpls., St. Louis, 1961-63; account exec. Richard C. Lynch Advt., 1963-64; media exec. Gardner Advt. Co., 1964-69; v.p. mktg. Advanswers Media/Programming divsn. Wells Rich Greene, N.Y.C., 1975-79; pres. Advanswers divsn. WRG/BDDP, N.Y.C., 1979—. Bd. dirs. Trailblazers, Inc.; pres. Signal Hill Sch. Assn. Parents Tchrs. Recipient Journalism Alumnus of Yr. award So. Ill. U., 1971, Alumni Achievement award, 1983. Served to capt. USAFR, 1961-67. Mem. St. Louis Advt. Club, Mensa, Mo. Athletic Club, St. Clair Country Club, Alpha Delta Sigma (Aid to Advt. Edn. award 1971). Home: 27 Symonds Dr Belleville IL 62223-1905 Office: Advanswers Media/Programming 10 S Broadway Saint Louis MO 63102-1712

STORK, GILBERT, chemistry educator, investigator; b. Brussels, Belgium, Dec. 31, 1921; s. Jacques and Simone (Weil) S.; m. Winifred Stewart, June 9, 1944 (dec. May 1992); children: Diana, Linda, Janet, Philip. B.S., U. Fla., 1942; Ph.D., U. Wis., 1945; D.Sc. (hon.), Lawrence Coll., 1961, U. Paris, 1979, U. Rochester, 1982, Emory U., 1988, Columbia U., 1993, U. Wis., 1997. Sr. research chemist Lakeside Labs., 1945-46; instr. chemistry Harvard U., 1946-48, asst. prof., 1948-53; assoc. prof. Columbia U., N.Y.C., 1953-55, prof., 1955-67, Eugene Higgins prof., 1967-92, prof. emeritus, 1992—, chmn. dept., 1973-76; plenary lectr. numerous internat. symposia, named Lectureships in U.S. and abroad; cons. several cos.; chmn. Gordon Steroid Conf., 1958-59. Recipient Baekeland medal, 1961, Harrison Howe award, 1962, Edward Curtis Franklin Meml. award Stanford, 1966, Gold medal Synthetic Chems. Mfrs. Assn., 1971, Nebr. award, 1973, Roussel prize in steroid chemistry, 1978, Edgar Fahs Smith award, 1982, Willard Gibbs medal Chgo. sect. Am. Chem. Soc., 1982, Nat. Medal of Sci., 1982, Linus Pauling award, 1983, Tetrahedron prize, 1985, Remsen award, 1986, Cliff S. Hamilton award, 1986, Mony Ferst award Sigma Xi, 1987, George Kenner award, 1992, Chem. Pioneer award Am. Inst. Chemistry, 1992, Welch Found. Award in Chemistry, 1993, Allan R. Day award Phila. Chemists Club, 1994, Wolf prize, 1996; Guggenheim fellow, 1959. Fellow NAS (award in chem. sci. 1982), French Acad. Scis., Am. Acad. Arts and Scis., Am. Philos. Soc.; mem. Am. Chem. Soc. (chmn. organic chemistry divsn. 1967, award in pure chemistry 1957, award for creative work in synthetic organic chemistry 1967, Nichols medal 1980, Arthur C. Cope award 1980, Roger Adams award in organic chemistry 1991), Royal Soc. Chemistry (hon., London), Pharm. Soc. Japan (hon.), Chemists Club (hon. N.Y.). Home: 459 Next Day Hill Dr Englewood NJ 07631-1921 Office: Columbia U Dept Chemistry Chandler Hall New York NY 10027

STORKE, DWIGHT CLIFTON, JR., government official; b. Fredericksburg, Va., Sept. 6, 1939; s. Dwight Clifton and Shirley Williams (King) S.; m. Sylvia Hitch Clark, Oct. 25, 1963; children: Theresa Storke Marshall, David Wallace, John Benjamin. BS, Richmond Profl. Inst., 1962; MEd, Va. Commonwealth U., 1973; PhD with honor, Internat. Sem., Plymouth, Fla., 1990. Instr. Dept. Navy, Dahlgren, Va., 1963-71; interpreter Nat. Park Svc., Washington's Birthplace, Va., 1971-74, park ranger, 1974-87, instr., 1984-86; supt. Nat. Park Svc., Richmond, Va., 1987-89, Washington's Birthplace, 1989-94; fed. firearms instr. Nat. Park Svc., Va., 1980—; exec. dir. Mid-Atlantic Lab., King George, Va., 1994—; adj. instr. Nat. Park Svc. Tng. Acad., Grand Canyon, Ariz., 1972-75; mem. pers. mgmt. rev. bd. Nat. Park Svc., Phila., 1993—. Author: Communication Skills, 1975. Facility and program facilitator DAR, Westmoreland, Va., 1980—; capt. Va. State Guard, Fredericksburg, 1985—; dir. Shenandoah Valley Civil War Task Force, Va., 1993. Recipient Interpreter of Yr. award Mid-Atlantic region Nat. Park Svc., 1981, 82, Superior Performance award, 1986, Supt. of Yr. award Mid-Atlantic region, 1993, Meritorious Svc. award Dept. Interior, 1993. Mem. Va. Assn. Mus., No. Neck Va. Hist. Soc., Masons (master), Kappa Delta Pi. Baptist. Avocations:; history, archaeology. Office: Mid-Atlantic Lab 14294 Big Timber Rd King George VA 22485-3009

STORM, DONALD JOHN, archaeologist, historian; b. Bradford, Pa., Nov. 20, 1947; s. John Ross and Jean Lamar (Frederick) S. AA, Yuba Coll., 1967; BA, Sacramento State U., 1972; postgrad., Calif. State U., Sacramento, 1972-74, Calif. State U., Chico, 1980, U. Nev., Reno, 1988-89. Instr. Marysville (Calif.) Joint Unified Sch. Dist., 1977-78; state archaeologist Calif. Dept. Parks and Recreation, Sacramento, 1981-84; owner North Yuba Contracting, Oregon House, Calif., 1984-87; archaeologist Elko dist. Nev. Bur. Land Mgmt., Elko, 1988; asst. forest archaeologist Sierra Nat. Forest, Clovis, Calif., 1990-91; archaeol. tech. Tahoe Nat. Forest, Camptonville, Calif., summer 1980; archaeol. cons. Oregon House, 1976-81, 88-95, Davis, 1996—; instr. Yuba Coll., Marysville, Calif., 1976-78, 88-93. Activist various conservation/environ. and Native Am. groups; candidate for Yuba County Supr., 1992. With U.S. Army, 1967-70. Mem. Soc. Am. Archaeology, Soc. Hist. Archaeology, Soc. for Calif. Archaeology, Calif. Hist. Soc., Nat. Trust for Historic Preservation, So. Pacific Hist. and Tech. Soc. Avocations: stamp collecting, model railroading, history. Home and Office: 2511 Westernesse Rd Davis CA 95616

STORM, JONATHAN MORRIS, television critic; b. N.Y.C.; s. Thomas Walton and Martha Louise (Morris) S.; m. Kathleen Jo Pottick, Oct. 13, 1979. BA, Williams Coll., 1969. Reporter, city editor Rutland (Vt.) Herald, 1970-76; copy editor, assoc. editor Detroit Free Press, 1976-82; copy editor, feature editor Phila. Inquirer, 1982-89, TV critic, 1989—; radio host Sta. WPHT-AM, 1996—. Recipient Benjamin Franklin award Nat. Press Found., 1987. Mem. Hopewell Valley Golf Club (bd. govs. 1997—), Soc. Profl. Journalists (treas. Phila. chpt. 1993—). Office: Phila Inquirer 400 N Broad St Philadelphia PA 19130-4015

STORM, SANDY LAMM, secondary education educator; b. Shelbyville, Ill., Aug. 6, 1949; d. Raymond Ralph and Hazel Clara (Sands) Lamm; m. David Michael Storm, Aug. 24, 1968; children: Michael Lee, Marc David, Michelle Kimberly. BS in Edn., Eastern Ill. U., 1967-70, MSEd, 1990-91. Cert. tchr. and sch. guidance, Ill. Substitute tchr. Shelby County, Shelbyville, Ill., 1989-90; family and consumer sci. tchr. Shelbyville Sch., Shelbyville, 1990—; counselor, sports cons. Human Excellence, Shelbyville, 1991—. Mem. NEA, Internat. Assn. Neuro-Linguistical Programming (SEA welfare com.), Ill. Edn. Assn. Democrat. Avocations: counted cross stitch, reading, cooking, travel. Home and Office: PO Box 506 1102 N Long Shelbyville IL 62565

STORMDANCER, ROWAN EHLENFELDT, traditional herbalist, management consultant; b. Terre Haute, Ind., July 7, 1952; d. John Nelson and Phyllis Inez (White) Turnbloom; m. Earl J. Chidester, Jan. 18, 1971 (div. 1976) 1 child, John; m. Rollin Sakeeta Ehlenfeldt, Apr. 29, 1989; children: Brendan Lorithian, Allayne Carson. AA in English, Contra Costa Coll., 1978. Tutor English and trigonometry Contra Costa Coll., San Pablo, Calif., 1976-78; sales rep., asst. mgr. Avon, Richmond, Calif., 1977-78; sales mgr. C-Shor Sales, San Leandro, Calif., 1978-80; exec. sec. C.N. Petsas, CPA, Richmond, 1980-81; mgr., designer Jan's Attic, Bamberg, Germany, 1982-85; writing team Jovialis, Austin, Tex., 1988-89; pres., CEO Arcane Attic Ltd., Colorado Springs, Colo., 1988-95; owner Faerie Spirit, Arlington, Tex., 1989—; CEO Stormdancer Metaphys. Enterprises, Inc., Arlington, Tex., 1995—; herbal cons. North Star Gardens, Arlington, Tex., 1990—; mng. dir. Pagan Merchant Coop., Arlington, Tex., 1992—. Author: Cyclopedia Talislanta, Vol. 3, 1989, Cyclopedia Talislanta, Vol. 5, 1990. Organizer Faerie Spirit and Friends Metaphys. Faire, Colorado Springs. Mem. North Circle Circle (chairperson 1988—), Gaianauts. Avocations: herbal rsch., collecting antiques, camping, writing. Office: 8300 Calmont Ave Apt 306 Fort Worth TX 76116-3419

STORMER, HORST LUDWIG, physicist; b. Frankfurt-Main, Fed. Republic Germany, Apr. 6, 1949; came to U.S., 1977; s. Karl-Ludwig and Marie (Ihrig) S.; m. Dominique A. Parchet, 1982. Ph.D., U. Stuttgart, 1977. Mem. tech. staff AT&T Bell Labs., Murray Hill, N.J., 1977-83, head dept., 1983-91, dir. phys. rsch. lab., 1992—. Recipient Otto Klung prize Fed. Republic of Germany, 1985; Bell Labs. fellow, 1983. Fellow Am. Phys. Soc. (Buckley prize 1984), Am. Acad. Arts and Scis. Office: Lucent Technologies 700 Mountain Ave New Providence NJ 07974-1208

STORMES, JOHN MAX, instructional systems developer; b. Manila, Oct. 7, 1927; s. Max Clifford and Janet (Heldring) S.; m. Takako Sanae, July 29, 1955; children: Janet Kazuko Stormes-Pepper, Alan Osamu. BS, San Diego State U., 1950; BA, U. So. Calif., 1957, MA, 1967. Cert. secondary and community coll. tchr. Editing supr. Lockheed Propulsion Co., Redlands, Calif., 1957-61; proposals supr. Rockwell Internat., Downey, Calif., 1961-62; publs. dir. Arthur D. Little, Inc., Santa Monica, Calif., 1962-63; publs. coord. Rockwell Internat., Downey, 1963-68; project dir. Gen. Behavioral Systems, Inc., Torrance, Calif., 1969-73; tng. and comm. cons. Media Rsch. Assocs., Santa Cruz, Calif., 1973—; tng. support svc. supr. So. Calif. Gas Co., L.A., 1985—; lectr. Calif. State U., Northridge, 1991—; tng. cons. Nat. Ednl. Media, Chatsworth, Calif., 1966-81, communications cons. Opinion Rsch. Calif., Long Beach, 1974—. Co-author: TV Communications Systems For Business and Industry, 1970. Curriculum adv. bd. communications dept. Calif. State U., Fullerton, 1964-78. Sgt. U.S. Army, 1953-55, Japan. Mem. Soc. Tech. Communication (sr. mem., 2nd v.p. Orange County chpt. 1962-63), Internat. Soc. Performance and Instruction (v.p. L.A. chpt. 1989, pres. 1990). Democrat. Episcopal. Avocations: photography, sailing. Home: 9140 Brookshire Ave Apt 207 Downey CA 90240-2963 Office: So Calif Gas Co ML 15H1 Box 3249 Los Angeles CA 90051-1249

STORMONT, RICHARD MANSFIELD, hotel executive; b. Chgo., Apr. 4, 1936; s. Daniel Lytle and E. Mildred (Milligan) S.; m. Virginia Louellen Walters, Nov. 21, 1959; children: Stacy Lee Freeman, Richard Mansfield, John Frederick. B.S., Cornell U., 1958. Cert. hosp. adminstrn.; cert. hosps. industry profl. Food cost analyst, sales rep. Edgewater Beach Hotel, Chgo., 1957-58; asst. sales mgr. Marriott Hotels, Inc., Washington, 1962-64; dir. sales Marriott Hotels, Inc., Atlanta, 1964-68; resident mgr. Marriott Hotels, Inc., 1969-71; gen. mgr. Marriott Hotel, Dallas, 1971-73, Phila., 1973-74, Atlanta, 1974-79; pres. Hardin Mgmt. Co., 1979-80; v.p. Marriott Franchise div. Marriott Corp., Washington, 1981-83, v.p. ops. Courtyard by Marriott, 1981-83; pres. The Stormont Cos. Inc., Atlanta, 1984-92; chmn. bd. dirs. Stormont Trice Corp., Atlanta, 1993—; dir. Walters & Co. Cons. to Mgmt., 1975-82. Pres. Atlanta Conv. and Visitors Burs., 1975-76, chmn. bd., 1976-77, vice chmn., 1996-97; bd. trustees Young Harris Coll.; bd. dirs. Better Bus. Bur.; exec. com. Ctrl. Atlanta Progress, 1979-80; exec. coun. Boy Scouts Am.; chmn. Atlanta Conv. and Visitors Bur., 1976, chmn. elect 1996. Recipient Disting. Salesman of Yr. award Marriott, 1967, Obi T. Brewer award for Decade of Outstanding Svc., 1979. Mem. Sales and Mktg. Execs. (exec. v.p. 1969-70, pres. Atlanta 1970-71), Am. Hotel-Motel Assn. (exec. com., bd. dirs. 1993-95), Ga. Hospitality and Travel Assn. (founder, bd. dir., pres. 1989-90, chmn. bd. 1991-92, Hotelier of Yr. award 1977, Ga. Bus. and Industry Assn. (bd. dirs.), Atlanta Hotel Assn. (pres. 1976), So. Innkeepers Assn., Atlanta C. of C. (v.p. 1978-79), Gwinnett C. of C. (bd. dirs.), Cornell Soc. Hotelmen (pres. Ga. chpt. 1976, regional v.p. 1989-91). Home: 2980 Nancy Creek Rd NW Atlanta GA 30327-2000 Office: 3350 Cumberland Cir SE Ste 1800 Atlanta GA 30339-3360

STORMS, CLIFFORD BEEKMAN, lawyer; b. Mount Vernon, N.Y., July 18, 1932; s. Harold Beekman and Gene (Pertak) S.; m. Barbara H. Grave, 1955 (div. 1975); m. Valeria N. Parker, July 12, 1975; children: Catherine Storms Fischer, Clifford Beekman. BA magna cum laude, Amherst Coll., 1954; LLB, Yale U., 1957. Bar: N.Y. 1957. Assoc. Breed, Abbott & Morgan, N.Y.C., 1957-64; with CPC Internat., Inc., Englewood Cliffs, N.J., 1964—, v.p. legal affairs, 1973-75, v.p., gen. counsel, 1975-88, sr. v.p., gen. counsel, 1988—; bd. dirs. Atlantic Legal Found.; mem. N.J. Alternate Dispute Resolution panel Ctr. for Pub. Resources. Trustee Food and Drug Law Inst.; bd. dirs. CPC Ednl. Found. Mem. ABA (com. on corp. law depts.), Assn. Gen. Counsel (pres. 1992-94), Assn. Bar City N.Y. (sec., com. on corp. law depts. 1979-81), Indian Harbor Yacht Club, Sky Club, Yale Club, Phi Beta Kappa. Home: 19 Burying Hill Rd Greenwich CT 06831-2604 Office: CPC Internat Inc Box 8000 International Plz Englewood Cliffs NJ 07632-1300

STORMS, LESTER (C STORMS), retired veterinarian; b. Camas, Wash., Oct. 13, 1920; s. Roy Lester and Helen Violet (Belshe) S.; m. Marjorie Louise Hudson, Apr. 10, 1943 (div.); children: Marjorie Maureen, Terry Jo, Sandra Diane. BS in Animal Husbandry, Wash. State U., 1951, DVM, 1952. Intern Portland, 1952; gen. practice vet. medicine Camas, 1952-54; dr.'s asst. pvt. practice vet. office, Hollywood, Calif., 1954, L.A., 1954, Whittier, Calif., 1954; vet. in charge pvt. practice vet. office, Artesia, Calif., 1955-56; owner, pvt. practice vet. medicine Buena Park, Calif., 1956-86; ret., 1986; mem. adv. bd. Guide Dogs for Blind, San Rafael, Calif., 1957-58; mem. steering com. Children's Hosp., Fullerton, Calif., 1960-61. With USN, 1940-51, PTO. Decorated Air medal with 3 gold stars, DFC.; recipient Pappy Pedigoe Meml. Trophy Calif. Sports Car Racing Assn. Mem. NRA, So. Calif. Vet. Medicine Assn. (life), Am. Vet. Medicine Assn., Orange County Vet. Medicine Assn. (pres. 1958), Olde '78 Fraser's Highlanders (chief-of-staff), Explorer's Club, Adventurer's Club L.A. (sec. 1984, bd. dirs., 1980-82, 95-97), Long Beach Yacht Club, Rotary (Paul Harris fellow, pres. Buena Park chpt. 1963), Masons, Shriners (v.p., Legion of Honor). Avocations: race car driving, sailing, fishing, shooting. Home: 78th Frasers Highlanders 4316 Latona Ave Los Angeles CA 90031-1426

STORMS, MARGARET LARUE, librarian; b. Armstrong County, Pa., Mar. 11, 1938; d. Oscar Henry and Ella Margaret (Titus) Fry; m. Roger Clair Storms, Aug. 24, 1963 (dec. 1980); children: Ethel Charis, Eric Malcolm. BA in Christian Edn., Eastern Coll., 1961; MSLS, Clarion U., 1991. Organist, pianist Lee Bapt. Ch., Maine, 1965-78; tchr. sewing Beth Eden Bapt. Sch., Wheatridge, Colo., 1978-81; organist, pianist Evang. Meth. Ch., Altoona, Pa., 1984-91; libr. Manahath Sch. Theol., Hollidaysburg, Pa., 1984-90; piano tchr. Altoona, Pa., 1986-90; cataloging libr. Lancaster (Pa.) Bible Coll., 1991—; music libr. Blair Concert Chorale, Altoona, 1987-90; choir dir. Bapt. Ch., New Bethlehem, Pa., 1990-91. Nat. sec. Nat. Temperance and Prohibition Coun., 1983-89, del., sec. Prohibition Nat. Com., Denver, 1979—. Mem. Am. Theol. Libr. Assn., Harmony Club (pres. 1977), Assn. Christian Librs., Lee Lit Club (community project chmn. 1976-77). Avocations: music, needlework, sewing, knitting, reading. *The building of today is not finished. Each day influences the next. Yesterday was the foundation that set the general outline for today's framework of living—built with solid materials of learning, experiences, relationships and memories. The life materials of today include a possibility of change and involvement with others as essential to our life building. Today's building influences the interior decorating of Tomorrow and its beauty to be revealed. Thus God's blueprint will be made visible.*

STORR, ROBERT, curator painting and sculpture, artist, writer; b. Portland, Maine, Dec. 28, 1949; s. Richard J. and Virginia V. Storr; m. Rosamund Helen Morley, Sept. 1, 1979; children: Katharine, Susannah. BA, Swarthmore Coll., 1972; postgrad., Sch. Art Inst. of Chgo., 1975-78; MFA, Skowhegan (Maine) Sch. Painting and Sculpture, 1978. Assoc. dean N.Y. Studio Sch., N.Y.C., 1987-88; asst. prof. Tyler Sch. Art, Phila., 1989—; Avery prof. Bard Coll., Annandale On Hudson, N.Y., 1990-91; curator painting and sculpture Mus. Modern Art, N.Y.C., 1991—; vis. artist Cooper Union, N.Y.C., 1988-89; vis. artist, critic R.I. Sch. Design, Providence, 1988; lectr. art mus., univs. and art schs. in U.S. and abroad; coordinating curator at Moma, 1995. Author: Philip Guston, 1986; co-author: Chuck Close, 1987, (with Lars Hitue) Susan Rothenberg 15 Years a Survey, 1990, (with Kirk Varnedois) From Bauhaus to Pop: Masterworks Given By Phillip Johnson, 1996; also exhbn. catalogues; contbg. editor Art in Am.; mem. editorial bd. Art Jour.; contbr. articles to profl. jours.; exhibitions include Inst. Contemporary Art Phila., 1991, Moma, 1991, 93, 94, 95, 96. Penny McCall Found. grantee, 1988, Peter Norton Family Found. grantee, 1990. Mem. Internat. Assn. Art Critics. Office: Mus Modern Art 11 W 53rd St New York NY 10019-5401

STORRER, WILLIAM ALLIN, consultant; b. Highland Park, Mich., Mar. 22, 1936; s. Fredrick Ray and Margaret Ann (Pitts) S.; m. Carol A. Tuthill, Nov. 6, 1964 (div. June 1969); 1 child, Kirsten; m. Patricia Alice Whalley, Dec. 30, 1976. Student, Albion Coll., 1954-56; AB in Engring. Scis., Harvard U., 1959; MFA in Theatre Arts, Boston U., 1962; PhD in Comparative Arts, Ohio U., 1968. Electronics engr. Raytheon Co., Wayland, Mass., 1958-60; tech. dir. small stage Boston Arts Festival, 1961, 62; dir. dramatics Melrose (Mass.) H.S., 1962-63; dir. playhouse and repertory theatre, instr. drama-speech Hofstra U., 1963-66, instr. opera, 1965; asst. prof. theatre, dir. univ. theatre, U. Toledo, 1968-69; assoc. prof. theatre and film, dir. Southampton Coll., L.I. U., 1969-73; asst. prof. cinema studies and still photography Ithaca (N.Y.) Coll., 1973-76; assoc. prof. media arts U. S.C., Columbia, 1976-82; pres. MINDaLIVE Creative Mind Enhancement, Newark, 1980—; assoc. prof. theater and speech World Campus Afloat, Chapman Coll., 1972; edn. media specialist Newark Bd. Edn., 1990-94, Linden Bd. Edn., 1994-95, Harrison Bd. Edn., 1995=96, Rosa Parks Fine and Performing Arts H.S., Paterson, N.J., 1996. Author: The Architecture of Frank Lloyd Wright, 1974, The Frank Lloyd Wright Companion, 1993; contbr. articles to popular mags. and profl. jours. Grantee Graham Found. for Advanced Studies in Fine Arts, 1987, 94. Home and Office: 289 Highland Ave Newark NJ 07104-1301

STORRS, ALEXANDER DAVID, astronomer; b. Idaho Falls, Idaho, May 30, 1960; s. Charles Lysander and Betty Lou (Wood) S.; m. Jean Elizabeth Seitzer, Nov. 4, 1989; 1 child, Matthew. BS, MIT, 1982; MS, U. Hawaii, 1985, PhD, 1987. Postdoctoral fellow NASA/Goddard Space Flight Ctr., Greenbelt, Md., 1987-89, U. Tex., Austin, 1989-91; assoc. scientist Space Telescope Sci. Inst., Balt., 1991—. Mem. AAAS, Am. Astron. Soc. (divsn. planetary scis.), Smithsonian Air and Space Mus. Office: Space Telescope Sci Inst 3700 San Martin Dr Baltimore MD 21218-2410

STORRS, ELEANOR EMERETT, research institute consultant; b. Cheshire, Conn., May 3, 1926; d. Benjamin Porter and Alta Hyde (Moss) S.; m. Harry Phineas Burchfield, Jr., Nov. 29, 1963; children: Sarah Storrs, Benjamin Hyde. B.S. with distinction in Botany, U. Conn., 1948; M.S. in Biology, NYU, 1958; Ph.D. in Chemistry, U. Tex., 1967. Asst. biochemist Boyce Thompson Inst. for Plant Research, Yonkers, N.Y., 1948-62; research scientist Clayton Found. Biochem. Inst., U. Tex., Austin, 1962-65; biochemist Pesticides Research Lab., USPHS, Perrine, Fla., 1965-67; dir. dept. biochemistry Gulf South Research Inst., New Iberia, La., 1967-77; adj. prof. chemistry U. Southwestern La., Lafayette, 1974-77; research prof. biology, dir. comparative mammalogy lab. Fla. Inst. Tech., Melbourne, 1977-94; ret., cons. on leprosy-armadillo programs, 1975-94, mem. Faculty Senate, 1979-84; cons. in rehab. and prevention deformities leprosy Pan Am. Health Orgn., WHO, Venezuela, Argentina, Brazil, Mex., 1972-90; dep. v.p. Coll. Hansenology in Endemic Countries, 1980-85. Author: (with H.P. Burchfield) Biochemical Applications of Gas Chromatography, 1962, (with Burchfield, D.E. Johnson) Guide to the Analysis of Pesticide Residues, 2 vols, 1965; also articles, book chpts. Grantee NIH, 1968-88, CDC, 1969-73, WHO, 1973-93, Leprosy Program, 1978-93, German Leprosy Relief Assn., 1973-78, Nat. Coun. Episc. Ch., 1975-77, Brit. Leprosy Relief Assn., 1981-88; recipient plaque La. Health Dept., 1972, Disting. Alumni award U. Conn., 1975, Gold award Am. Coll. Pathologists and Am. Soc. Clin. Pathologists, 1974, Gerard B. Lambert award for spl. recognition, 1975. Fellow AAAS; mem. AAUW, Interant. Leprosy Assn., Am. Soc. Mammalogy, Am. Assn. Lab. Animal Sci. (Charles A. Griffin award 1975), East Coast Zool. Soc. (bd. dirs. 1989-92), Am. Recorder Soc., Early Music Assn., Sigma Xi. Episcopalian (vestryman). Clubs: Appalachian (Boston); Green Mountain (Bear Mountain, N.Y.); Mystik Krewe of Iberians (mem. ct. 1972, queen 1974). Pioneer devel. leprosy in exptl. animal (armadillo) reproduction. Home: 72 Riverview Ter Melbourne FL 32903-4640 *Children display interests early in their lives, and in my life, this early interest - in animals, and the beauty of nature - is one which I have never lost, but one which seems to become more important now with the passing of years. Parents can help mold a child, but should mold the child in the child's interests as my parents did, not in a mold designed by them.*

STORRY, JUNIS OLIVER, retired engineering educator; b. Astoria, S.D., Mar. 16, 1920; s. Ole Jensen and Betsey (Ruttum) S.; m. Laurel Helen Davis, June 15, 1950; children: Cheryl Ann, David Junis. B.S. in Elec. Engring., S.D. State U., 1942, M.S., 1949; Ph.D., Iowa State U., 1967. Registered profl. engr., S.D. Engr. trainee Westinghouse Electric Co., 1942; elec. engr. Bur. Ships, Navy Dept., 1942-46, Reliance Electric Co., Cleve., 1946; mem. faculty S.D. State U., Brookings, 1946-85; prof. elec. engring. S.D. State U., 1955-85, Amdahl Disting. prof. engring., 1982-85, dean engring., 1972-82, prof., dean emeritus, 1985—; mem. S.D. Elec. Bd., 1972-77. Mem. founding bd. Assn. Christian Chs. S.D., 1972-75. NSF Sci. Faculty fellow, 1964-65. Mem. IEEE (life sr. mem.), NSPE, Am. Soc. Engring. Edn., S.D. Engring. Soc. Lutheran. Home: 105 Sunnyview 3132 Sunnyview Dr Brookings SD 57006-4281

STORSTEEN, LINDA LEE, librarian; b. Pasadena, Jan. 26, 1948; d. Oliver Matthew and Susan (Smock) Storsteen. AB cum laude in History, UCLA, 1970, MA in Ancient History, 1972, MLS, 1973. Librarian, L.A. Pub. Library, 1974-79; city librarian Palmdale City Library (Calif.), 1979—. Adv. bd. So. Calif. Inter-Library Loan Network, L.A., 1979-80; mem. council South State Coop. Library System, 1981—, chmn., 1982-83, 85-86, 87-88, 89-90, 92-93; pres. So. Calif. Film Circuit, 1985-86; rec. sec. So. Antelope Valley Coordinating Council, Palmdale, 1983-84. Mem. ALA, Calif. Library Assn., Pub. Libraries Exec. Assn. So. Calif., Chinese Shar-Pei Club of Am., Rotary Internat. Home: PO Box 129 Palmdale CA 93590-9971 Office: Palmdale City Libr 700 E Palmdale Blvd Palmdale CA 93550-4742

STORVICK, CLARA AMANDA, nutrition educator emerita; b. Emmons, Minn., Oct. 31, 1906; d. Ole A. and Elise A. (Opdahl) S. AB, St. Olaf Coll., 1929; MS, Iowa State U., 1933; PhD, Cornell U., 1941. Chemistry instr. Augustana Acad., Canton, S.D., 1930-32; rsch. asst. Iowa State U., Ames, 1932-34; nutritionist Fed. Emergency Relief Adminstrn., Brainerd, Minn.,

1934-36; asst. prof. nutrition Okla. State U., Stillwater, 1936-38; rsch. asst. Cornell U., Ithaca, N.Y., 1938-41; asst. prof. nutrition U. Wash., Seattle, 1941-45; assoc. prof. nutrition to prof. Oreg. State U., Corvallis, 1945-72, prof. nutrition and head home econ. rsch., 1955-72, dir. nutrition rsch. inst., 1965-72; ret., 1972. Contbr. over 70 articles to profl. jours. Recipient Borden award Am. Home Econs. Assn., 1952, Disting. Alumni award St. Olaf Coll., 1955, Alumni Achievement award Iowa State U., Ames, 1966. Fellow AAAS, Am. Pub. Health Assn., Am. Inst. Nutrition; mem. N.Y. Acad. Scis., Am. Chem. Soc., Phi Kappa Phi, Sigma Xi., Iota Sigma Pi (nat. pres.), Omicron Nu. Republican. Lutheran. Home: 124 NW 29th St Corvallis OR 97330-5343

STORY, HUGH GOODMAN, JR., non-commissioned officer; b. New Rochelle, N.Y., Sept. 29, 1951; s. Hugh Goodman Sr. and Marilyn Joan (Mullin) S.; m. Colleen Lee McKoy, Nov. 29, 1975; children: Daniel Shawn, Michelle Ariana. BS, U.S. Naval Acad., 1974; MA, Nat. Defense U., 1995. Commd. 2d lt. USN, 1982, advanced through grades to capt. Decorated Meritorious Svc. medal (2), Commendation medal (2). Mem. Naval Helicoptor Assn., U.S. Naval Acad. Alumni Assn., ICAF Alumni Assn. Office: DUSD (ICP) 3S1082 3300 Defense Pentagon Washington DC 20301-3300

STORY, JAMES EDDLEMAN, lawyer; b. Calvert City, Ky., June 7, 1928; s. William Arthur and Estella (Harper) S.; m. Barbara Owens, Oct. 11, 1953; children: Paul, Margaret, Virginia Lee, Sara Jane, Betty Ann, James Arthur. BS, Murray State Coll., 1952; JD, U. Louisville, 1958. Bar: Ky. 1958. Tchr. Jefferson County Bd. Edn., Louisville, 1954-58; assoc. prof. U. Ky. C.C., Paducah, 1958-64; county atty. Lyon County, Eddyville, Ky., 1962-74; pub. defender Lyon County, Princeton, Ky., 1974-82; pvt. practive Eddyville, 1974—; atty. Lake Barkley Project, U.S. Army Corp Engrs., Cadiz, Ky., 1960-62. With U.S. Army, 1946-48. Mem. ATLA, Ky. Trial Lawyers Assn., Ky. Assn. Criminal Def. Lawyers, Ky. Bar Assn., Sierra Club, Wilderness Club, Kentuckians for the Commonwealth, Am. Legion, Lions. Mem. Ch. of Christ. Avocations: tennis, swimming, hunting, water skiing, boxing. Office: PO Box 216 Eddyville KY 42038-0216

STORY, MARTHA VANBEUREN, librarian; b. Morristown, N.J., Mar. 6, 1940; d. John Mohlman and Jane de Peyster vanB.; m. William Ferguson Story, Oct. 19, 1963; children: Jessica, Alexandra. BA, Wellesley Coll., 1962; MLS, U. Md., 1975. Libr. Dewberry & Davis, Fairfax, Va., 1976-77, 80-84, Ashley Hall, Charleston, S.C., 1977-80, 85-86; cataloger Norfolk (Va.) Pub. Libr., 1987-90; dir. Mathews (Va.) Meml. Libr., 1990—. Publicity chmn. Mid. Peninsula Cmty. Concert Assoc., Gloucester, Va., 1993—; mem. lay visitors com., scholarship com. Kingston Parish, Matthews, Va., 1996—. Mem. Tidewater Area Libr. Dirs. Coun., Va. Libr. Assoc. Home: Holly Cove Cricket Hill Rd PO Box 117 Hudgins VA 23076 Office: Mathews Meml Libr Main St PO Box 980 Mathews VA 23109

STORZ, JOHANNES, veterinary microbiologist, educator; b. Hardt, Germany, Apr. 29, 1931; came to U.S., 1958; s. Johannes and Theresia (Klausmann) S.; m. Hannelore Roeber, Aug. 8, 1959; children: Gisela Therese, J. Peter K., Heidi Ella. DVM, Vet. Coll., Hannover, Germany, 1958; PhD, U. Calif., Davis, 1961; Dr.honoris causae, U. Zurich, Switzerland, 1994. Diplomate Am. Coll. Vet. Microbiologists. Rsch. asst. Fed. Rsch. Ctr. Virology, Tubingen, Germany, 1957-58; lectr. U. Calif., Davis, 1958-61; asst. prof. vet. sci. Utah State U., Logan, 1961-63, assoc. prof., 1963-65; assoc. prof. vet. microbiology Colo. State U., Ft. Collins, 1965-67, prof., 1967-82; prof. and dept. head La. State U., Baton Rouge, 1982—; vis. prof. virology Justus Liebig U., Giessen, Germany, 1978-79, 90; cons. WHO, Geneva, Switzerland, 1970; pres. Workshop Human and Animal Chlamydial Infections, Buenos Aires, 1994. Author: Chlamydia and Chlamydia Ind. Disease, 1971. Mem. Internat. Rels. Commn., Baton Rouge, 1989-94; chmn. European Exhibits, Internat. Heritage Celebration, Baton Rouge, 1994. Recipient Norden Tchg. award Colo. State U., 1975, A.C. Clark Rsch. award, 1978, Rsch. award AVMA, 1983, Svc. award Gamma Sigma Delta, 1992, Alexander Von Humboldt prize, 1978. Mem. Am. Soc. Microbiology (pres. south cen. br. 1994-96), Faculty Club. Republican. Roman Catholic. Avocations: biking, swimming, mountain hiking, travel. Home: 2942 Rene Beauregard Baton Rouge LA 70820 Office: La State Univ Sch Vet Medicine S Stadium Rd Baton Rouge LA 70803

STOSKUS, JOANNA JORZYSTA, computer information systems educator; b. Newark, Feb. 10, 1947; d. Joseph B. and Anna Mary (Stopa) Jorzysta; m. Joseph Thomas Stoskus, Jr., Oct. 25, 1969; 1 child, Caryn Judith. BA in Math., Kean Coll. N.J., 1968; MA in Computer Sci., Montclair State U., 1985. Programmer, analyst Prudential Ins. Co., Newark, 1968-70, Bell Labs., Murray Hill, N.J., 1970-72; adj. instr. Middlesex County Coll., Edison, N.J., 1974-77; chairperson, prof. County Coll. of Morris, Randolph, N.J., 1977—; mem. Whippany Park's Prin.'s Adv., Whippany, N.J., 1988-90; mem. Morris Area Tech. Alliance, Morristown, 1993—, N.J. State Computer Adv., Aberden, N.J., 1993—, Sussex County Vo-Tech. Adv., Sparta, N.J., 1994—. Mem. Data Processing Mgmt. Assn., N.J. C.C. Computer Consortium, Bucknell Partents Orgn. Republican. Avocation: golf. Office: County Coll Morris 214 Center Grove Rd Randolph NJ 07869-2007

STOSSEL, JOHN, news analyst. BA in Psychology, Princeton U., 1969. Prodr., reporter Sta. KGW-TV, Portland, Oreg.; consumer editor WCBS-TV, N.Y.C., Good Morning Am.; consumer corr. 20/20, 1981—; weekly consumer reporter ABC Radio Info. Network,. Recipient 19 Emmy awards, 5 awards for Excellence in Consumer Reporting Nat. Press Club, award Nat. Environment Devel. Assn., award Retirement Rshc. Found., George Polk award Outstanding Local Radio and Television Reporting. Office: 20/20 147 Columbus Ave Fl 8 New York NY 10023-5900•

STOTHERS, JOHN B., chemistry educator; b. London, Ont., Can., Apr. 16, 1931; s. John Cannon and Florence L. (Sleigh) S.; m. Catherine Ruth Smith, June 6, 1953; children—Marta L., Margot E. B.Sc., U. Western Ont., 1953, M.Sc., 1954; Ph.D., McMaster U., 1957. Research chemist Imperial Oil Ltd., Sarnia, Ont., 1957-59; lectr. U. Western Ont., London, 1959-61, asst. prof. dept. chemistry, 1961-64, assoc. prof., 1964-67, prof., 1967-96, prof. emeritus, 1996—. Author: 13C NMR Spectroscopy, 1972; also over 200 research articles. Recipient award Merck, Sharpe & Dohme, 1971; Royal Soc. Can. fellow, 1976. Fellow Chem. Inst. Can.; mem. Sunningdale Club (London). Avocations: golf; traditional jazz. Home: 45 Mayfair Dr, London, ON Canada

STOTLER, ALICEMARIE HUBER, judge; b. Alhambra, Calif., May 29, 1942; d. James R. and Loretta M. Huber; m. James Allen Stotler, Sept. 11, 1971. BA, U. So. Calif., 1964, JD, 1967. Bar: Calif. 1967, U.S. Dist. Ct. (no. dist.) Calif. 1967, U.S. Dist. Ct. (cen. dist.) Calif. 1973, U.S. Supreme Ct., 1976; cert. criminal law specialist. Dep. Orange County Dist. Atty.'s Office, 1967-73; mem. Stotler & Stotler, Santa Ana, Calif., 1973-76, 83-84; judge Orange County Mcpl. Ct., 1976-78, Orange County Superior Ct., 1978-83, U.S. Dist. Ct. (cen. dist.) Calif., L.A., 1984—; assoc. dean Calif. Trial Judges Coll., 1982; lectr., panelist, numerous orgns.; standing com. on rules of practice and procedure U.S. Jud. Conf., 1991—, chair, 1993—; mem. exec. com. 9th Cir. Jud. Conf., 1989-93, Fed. State Jud. Conf., 1989-98, jury com., 1990-92, planning com. for Nat. Conf. on Fed.-State Judicial Relationships, Orlando, 1991-92, planning com for We. Regional Conf. on State-Fed. Judicial Relationships, Stevens, Wash., 1992-93; chair dist. ct. symposium and jury utilization Ctrl. Dist. Calif., 1985, chair atty. liason, 1989-90, chair U.S. Constitution Bicentennial com., 1986-91, chair magistrate judge com., 1992-93; mem. State Adv. Group. on Juvenile Justice and Delinquency Prevention, 1983-84, Bd. Legal Speciliazations Criminal Law Adv. Commn., 1983-84, victim/witness adv. com. Office Criminal Justice Planning, 1980-83, U. So. Calif. Bd. Councilors, 1993—; active team in tng. Leukemia Soc. Am., 1993, 95; legion lex bd. dir. U. So. Calif. Sch. Law Support Group, 1981-83. Winner Hale Moot Ct. Competition, State of Calif., 1967; named Judge of Yr., Orange County Trial Lawyers Assn., 1978, Most Outstanding Judge, Orange County Bus. Litigation Sect., 1990; recipient Franklin G. West award Orange County Bar Assn., 1985. Mem. ABA (jud. adminstrn. divsn.and litigation sect. 1984—, nat. conf. fed. trial judges com. on legis. affairs 1990-91), Am. Law Inst., Am. Judicature Soc., Fed. Judges Assn. (bd. dirs. 1989-92), Nat. Assn. Women Judges, U.S. Supreme Ct. Hist. Soc., Ninth Cir. Dist. Judges Assn., Calif. Supreme Ct. Hist. Soc., Orange County Bar Assn. (mem. numerous coms., Franklin G. West award 1984), Calif. Judges Assn. (mem. com. on judicial coll. 1978-80, com. on civil law and procedure 1980-82, Dean's coll. curriculum commn. 1981), Calif. Judges Found. Office: US Dist Ct PO Box 12339 751 W Santa Ana Blvd Santa Ana CA 92701-4509

STOTLER, EDITH ANN, grain company executive; b. Champaign, Ill., Oct. 11, 1946; d. Kenneth Wagner and Mary (Odebrecht) S. Student, Mary Baldwin Coll., 1964-66; BA, U. Ill., 1968. Asst. v.p. Harris Trust and Savs. Bank, Chgo., 1969-83; mgr. Can. Imperial Bank of Commerce, Chgo., 1983, sr. mgr., 1983-85, asst. gen. mgr. group head, 1985-88, v.p., dir. utilities, 1988-90; ptnr. Stotler Grain Co., Champaign, Ill., 1990—; pres. Homer Grain Co., 1990—; bd. dirs., mem. exec. compensation com., nominating com. Southeastern Mich. Gas Enterprises, Inc. Mem. investment com. 4th Presbyn. Ch.; past pres. liberal arts and scis. constituent bd. U. Ill., mem. pres.' coun.; mem. Friends of Libr. Bd., U. Ill. Mem. U. Ill. Found., Champaign Country Club, Art Club. Avocations: needlepoint, reading, tennis, golf, cooking. Home: 900 N Lake Shore Dr Apt 2106 Chicago IL 60611-1523

STOTT, BRIAN, software company executive; b. Eccles, Eng., Aug. 5, 1941; came to U.S., 1983; s. Harold and Mary (Stephens) S.; m. Patricia Ann Farrar, Dec. 3, 1983. BSc, Manchester U., 1962, MSc, 1963, PhD, 1971. Asst. prof. Middle East Tech. U., Ankara, Turkey, 1965-68; lectr. Inst. Sci. and Tech., U. Manchester (Eng.), 1968-74; assoc. prof. U. Waterloo (Ont., Can.), 1974-76; cons. Electric Energy Rsch. Ctr. Brazil, Rio de Janeiro, 1976-83; prof. Ariz. State U., Tempe, 1983-84; pres. Power Computer Applications Corp., Mesa, Ariz., 1984—; cons. in field. Contbr. numerous articles to rsch. publs. Fellow IEEE. Office: Power Computer Applications 1921 S Alma School Rd Ste 207 Mesa AZ 85210-3038

STOTT, GRADY BERNELL, lawyer; b. Bailey, N.C., Sept. 19, 1921; s. William Willard and Zettie Harriett (Bissette) S.; m. Mays Beal, May 9, 1952; children: Sue J., Caroline Beal. A.B., Duke U., 1947, J.D., 1952. Bar: N.C. 1952. Dist. atty. 27th Jud. Dist., Gastonia, N.C., 1957-62; partner firm Stott, Hollowell, Palmer & Windham, Gastonia, 1960—. Served with USMC, 1943-48. Fellow Am. Bar Found., Am. Coll. Trial Lawyers; mem. N.C. State Bar (pres. 1978-79), Am. Bar Assn. (del. 1980), N.C. Bar Assn., Assn. Ins. Attys. Democrat. Methodist. Club: Masons. Office: 110 W Main Ave Gastonia NC 28052-2306

STOTT, THOMAS EDWARD, JR., engineering executive; b. Beverly, Mass., May 14, 1923; s. Thomas Edward and Mildred (Ayers) S.; m. Mary Elizabeth Authelet, Feb. 26, 1944; children: Pamela, Randi, Wendy, Thomas E., Diana. BS, Tufts U., 1945. Design engr. Bethlehem Steel, Quincy, Mass., 1956-59; project engr. Bethlehem Steel, 1959-64, sr. engr. basic ship design, 1960-63, project coordinator, 1963-64; pres. Stal-Laval, Inc., Elmsford, N.Y., 1964-84, Thomas Stott & Co., Cummaquid, Mass., 1984-88; ret., 1988. Bd. dirs., treas. Friends of Prisoners, Inc.; deacon West Parish Barnstable, Mass., 1994-96, moderator, 1996—. With USNR, 1944-46. Fellow ASME (chmn. marine com., chmn. gas turbine div. exec. com., chmn. nat. nominating com., exec. sec. gas turbine div., Centennial medal 1980, R. Tom Sawyer award 1981, Dedicated Svc. award 1989), Soc. Naval Architects and Marine Engrs. Republican. Home: 51 Kates Path Yarmouth Port MA 02675-1448

STOTTER, DAVID W., marketing executive; b. Chgo., May 17, 1904; s. Max and Lena (Wolfson) S.; m. Lucille Guild, Nov. 28, 1930; 1 child, Michael David. Student, U. Chgo., 1925. Advt. writer Campbell-Ewald Co., Detroit, 1929-34; sr. writer Lord & Thomas, Chgo., 1935-42; v.p., copy dir. MacFarland, Aveyard & Co., Chgo., 1942-51; account exec. MacFarland, Aveyard & Co., 1951-62, sr. v.p., 1959-62; pres., dir. Drewrys Ltd. U.S.A., Inc., S. Bend, Ind., 1962-64; marketing dir. Campbell-Mithun, Inc., Chgo., 1964-65; v.p. Arthur Meyerhoff Assocs., Inc., Chgo., 1965—. Bd. dirs. Jewish Welfare Fund Chgo., 1954-61, Alfred Adler Inst., Chgo., 1975—; chmn. pub. relations com. Jewish United Fund, 1969. Home: 2960 N Lake Shore Dr Apt 2303 Chicago IL 60657-5661 Office: 410 N Michigan Ave Chicago IL 60611-4213

STOTTER, HARRY SHELTON, banker, lawyer; b. N.Y.C., Aug. 28, 1928; s. Jack and Adele (Sgel) S.; m. Marilyn H. Knight, Nov. 7, 1954; children: Jeffrey Craig, Cheryl dee. Student, L.I. U., 1948-49; JD, St. John's U., 1952; postgrad., N.Y. U. Law Sch., 1956-57. Bar: N.Y. 1952, N.J. 1974. Pvt. practice in N.Y.C., 1952-53, 54-56; atty. Dept. Def., 1953; with trust div. Bank of N.Y., 1956-63; exec. v.p., sr. mgmt. com. Summit Bank, Hackensack, N.J., 1963-84; div. exec. v.p. Chase Manhattan Bank, N.Y.C., 1984-94; dir., vice chmn. Chase Manhattan Trust Co. Fla., Palm Beach, Fla., 1984-87; pvt. trust and estates law practice N.J., 1974—; former mem. probate com. N.J. Supreme Ct. Jud. Conf. Mem. N.Y.C. and Bergen County estate planning couns.; former pres. bd. dirs. Bergen County coun. Girl Scouts Am.; bd. dirs., pres., chief exec. officer Bergen County United Way; treas. 2d Century Fund, Hackensack Hosp.; bd. dirs. Holy Name Hosp., Teaneck, N.J. With USN, World War II; brig. gen. Army N.G. Mem. ABA (co-chmn. nat. conf. lawyers and corp. trustees 1991-93), Am. Bankers Assn. (chmn. trust counsel com. 1991-93), N.Y. Bar Assn., N.J. Bar Assn., N.Y. County Lawyers Assn., Bergen County Bar Assn. (former trustee, former chmn. probate and estate planning com.), Fed. Bar Assn., N.Y. Militia Assn.

STOTTER, LAWRENCE HENRY, lawyer; b. Cleve., Sept. 24, 1929; s. Oscar and Bertha (Lieb) S.; m. Ruth Rapoport, June 30, 1957; children: Daniel, Jennifer, Steven. BBA, Ohio State U., 1956, LLB, 1958, JD, 1967. Bar: Calif. 1960, U.S. Supreme Ct. 1973, U.S. Tax Ct. 1976. Pvt. practice San Francisco, 1963—; ptnr. Stotter and Coats, San Francisco, 1981-97; sole practitioner, 1997—; mem. faculty Nat. Judicial Coll.; mem. Calif. Family Law Adv. Commn., 1979-80. Editor in chief: Am. Bar Family Advocate mag, 1977-82; TV appearances on Phil Donahue Show, Good Morning America. Pres. Tamalpais Conservation Club, Marin County, Calif.; U.S. State Dept. del. Hague Conf. Pvt. Internat. Law, 1979-80; legal adv. White House Conf. on Families, 1980—. Served with AUS, 1950-53. Mem. ABA (past chmn. family law sect.), Am. Acad. Matrimonial Lawyers (past nat. v.p.), Calif. State Bar (past chmn. family law sect.), San Francisco Bar Assn. (past chmn. family law sect.), Calif. Trial Lawyers Assn. (past chmn. family law sect.). Home: 2244 Vistazo St E Tiburon CA 94920-1970 Office: 1255 Columbus Ave # 200 San Francisco CA 94133-1326

STOTTLEMYER, DAVID LEE, government official; b. Waynesboro, Pa., June 1, 1935; s. Omar Samuel and Miriam (Noll) S.; m. Jane Ann Hembree, Aug. 26, 1961; children: Todd Andrew, Kristen Elizabeth, Kathryn Ann. A.B., Miami U., Oxford, Ohio, 1959; M. Pub. and Internat. Affairs (NDEA fellow), U. Pitts., 1964, also postgrad. Program and budget analyst Exec. Office of Pres., Office of Mgmt. and Budget, Washington, 1964-69; sr. mgmt. officer UN, N.Y.C., 1969-70; adviser internat. orgn. affairs U.S. Mission to UN, N.Y.C., 1971-72; counsellor internat. orgn. affairs U.S. Mission to UN, 1973-75, counsellor UN resources mgmt., 1976-77; also mem. U.S. del. 26th-31st gen. assemblies, mem. UN Com. on Contbns., 1971; mem. UN Adv. Com. on Adminstrv. and Budgetary Questions, 1973-77; dir. policy mgmt. staff Bur. Internat. Orgn. Affairs, U.S. Dept. State, Washington, 1977-80; exec. asst. to asst. sec. of state for internat. orgn. affairs Bur. Internat. Orgn. Affairs, U.S. Dept. State, 1980; mem. staff Office of Vice-Pres., Washington, 1981-83; dir. adminstrv. mgmt. service UN, N.Y.C., 1984-85; exec. asst., dir. Office of Under-Sec.-Gen. for Adminstrn. and Mgmt., UN, N.Y.C., 1986-87; pvt. practice as cons., 1987-90; dir. industry rels. NASA, Washington, 1990-91, dir. office nat. svc., 1992-93; retired, 1993; cons. pvt. practice, 1993—. Served with AUS, 1953-56. Recipient Superior Honor award State Dept., 1975. Mem. Am. Fgn. Svc. Assn. Home and Office: 5920 Sherborn Ln Springfield VA 22152-1035

STOTZKY, GUENTHER, microbiologist, educator; b. Leipzig, Germany, May 24, 1931; came to U.S., 1939; s. Moritz Stotzky and Erna (Angres) Kester; m. Kayla Baker, Mar. 17, 1958; children: Jay, Martha, Deborah. BS, Calif. Poly. State U., 1952; MS, Ohio State U., 1954, PhD, 1956. Spl. sci. employee Argonne Nat. Lab. USAEC, Lemont, Ill., 1955; rsch. assoc. Dept. Botany U. Mich., Ann Arbor, 1956-58; head soil microbiology Cen. Rsch. Labs. United Fruit Co., Norwood, Mass., 1958-63; chmn., microbiologist Kitchawan Rsch. Labs. Bklyn. Botanic Garden, Ossining, N.Y., 1963-68; assoc. prof. Dept. Biology NYU, 1967-70, prof., 1970—, chmn., 1970-77. Editor: Soil Biochemistry, 1990—; series editor Marcel Dekker, Inc., 1986-92; contbr. over 250 articles to profl. jours. and chpts. to books. With USCG, 1957. Recipient Selman A. Waksman Hon. Lecture award Theobald Smith Soc., 1989, Honored Alumnus of Yr. award Calif. Poly. State U., 1992, fellowship Japanese Soc. for Promotion of Sci., 1996; named Disting. Vis. Scientist, U.S. EPA, 1986-89. Fellow AAAS, Am. Acad. Microbiology, Am. Soc. Microbiology (Fisher Co. award for applied and environ. microbiology 1990, Excellence in Tchg. award N.Y.C. br. 1994), Am. Soc. Agronomy, Soil Sci. Soc. Am. Jewish. Avocations: fishing, reading, music. Office: NYU Dept Biology 1009 Main New York NY 10003

STOUDT, HOWARD WEBSTER, biological anthropologist, human factors specialist, consultant; b. Pitts., May 13, 1925; s. Howard Webster and Harriet Catharine (Powers) S.; m. Jean Gorey Henderson, Feb. 14, 1953; children: Katharine Webster, Roberta Henderson. AB, Harvard Coll., 1949; MA, U. Pa., 1953, PhD, 1959; SM in Hygiene, Harvard U., 1963. Rsch. asst. Harvard Sch. Pub. Health, Boston, 1952-55; rsch. specialist Air U., U.S. Air Force, Montgomery, Ala., 1955-57; rsch. assoc. Harvard Sch. Pub. Health, Boston, 1957-66, asst. prof., 1966-73; prof. community medicine Mich. State U., East Lansing, 1973-88, chmn. dept., 1973-78, prof. emeritus, 1988—; cons. Stoudt Assocs., Bath, Maine, 1988—; cons. U.S. Army, USAF, NASA, USPHS, VA, NRC, NAS, pvt. industry, 1952—. Author: Physical Anthropology of Ceylon, 1961; co-author: Human Body in Equipment Design, 1971; contbr. over 40 articles to profl. jours. Sgt. U.S. Army, 1943-46, Europe. Harrison fellow U. Pa., Phila., 1951-52, USPHS fellow, Boston, 1961-62. Fellow Human Biology Coun.; mem. AAAS, Am. Assn. Phys. Anthropologists, Am. Coll. Epidemiology, Human Factors and Ergonomics Soc. Democrat. Home and Office: 4 Schooner Ridge Rd Bath ME 04530-1639

STOUFER, RUTH HENDRIX, community volunteer; b. Pitts., June 21, 1916; d. Walter Willits and Frances (Ponbeck) Hendrix; m. William Kimball Stoufer, Sept. 8, 1937 (dec.); children: Walter Hendrix, Frances Elizabeth Stoufer Waller (dec.). BS, Iowa State U., 1937. Trustee Marcus J. Lawrence Meml. Hosp., 1989—; devel. chairperson Sedona-Verde Valley Am. Heart Assn., 1988-91; mem. adv. bd. L.A. chpt. Freedom's Found., 1965-78; mem. coord. med. adv. bd. U. Ariz., 1986—; founding chairperson Muses of the Mus. No. Ariz., 1984-85, pres., 1986-87, mem. Sinagua Soc., 1983—; bd. dirs. Nat. Charity League, L.A., 1963, Found. for Children, L.A., 1964, 65, 66; pres. Panhellenic adv. bd. U. So. Calif., 1964; key adv. U. So. Calif. chpt. Beta Alpha of Gamma Phi Beta, 1960-63. Named Woman of Yr., Inter-city Coun., Gamma Phi Beta, 1963. Avocations: Southwestern U.S. history, bridge, piano, reading. Home: 87 Doodlebug Knoll Sedona AZ 86336-6422

STOUGHTON, W. VICKERY, healthcare executive; b. Peoria, Ill., Mar. 1, 1946; s. Warner Vickery and Mary Olive (McNamara) S.; m. Christine Mary Kreder, Aug. 9, 1969; children: Zachary Benjamin, Samantha. B.S., St. Louis U., 1968; M.B.A., U. Chgo., 1973. Asst. dir. Boston Hosp. for Women, 1973-74; asst. dir. Peter Bent Brigham Hosp., Boston, 1975-77, dir., 1978-80; pres. The Toronto Hosp., Ont., Can.; asst. prof. U. Toronto, 1982-90, assoc. prof., 1991; vice chancellor health affairs, chief exec. officer Duke U. Hosp., Durham, N.C., 1991-92; pres. Smithkline Beecham Clin. Labs., Collegeville, Pa., 1992-95, Smithkline Beecham Diagnostic Systems, King of Prussia, Pa., 1996—; chmn., CEO Exigent Diagnostics Inc., King of Prussia, Pa.; bd. dirs. Sun Life Assurance Co. Bd. dirs. Toronto Symphony, 1983-86, Toronto United Way, 1988-91. Served to capt. AUS, 1969-72. Fellow Am. Coll. Hosp. Adminstrs. Home: 7 Harford Ln Radnor PA 19087-4529 Office: Exigent Diagnostics Inc POB 1539 709 Swedeland Rd King Of Prussia PA 19406

STOUP, ARTHUR HARRY, lawyer; b. Kansas City, Mo., Aug. 30, 1925; s. Isadore and Dorothy (Rankle) S.; m. Kathryn Jolliff, July 30, 1948; children—David C., Daniel P., Rebecca Ann, Deborah E. Student, Kansas City Jr. Coll., Mo. 1942-43; BA, U. Kansas City, 1950; JD, U. Mo., Kansas City, 1950. Bar: Mo. 1950, D.C. 1979. Pvt. practice law Kansas City, Mo., 1950—; prin. Arthur H. Stoup & Assocs., P.C., adr; chmn. U.S. Merit Selection Com. for Western Dist. Mo., 1981. Chmn. com. to rev. continuing edn. U. Mo., 1978-79; mem. U. Mo. Law School search com., 1994-95; trustee U. Mo.-Kansas City Law Found., 1972—, pres., 1979-82; trustee U. Kansas City, 1979—. With USNR, 1942-45. Fellow Internat. Soc. Barristers (state mem. chmn.), Am. Bar Found. (life mem.); mem. ABA (ho. dels. 1976-80), Kansas City Met. Bar Assn. (pres. 1966-67, Litigator Emeritus award 1991), Mo. Bar (bd. govs. 1967-76, v.p. 1972-73, pres. elect 1973-74, pres. 1974-75), Lawyers Assn. Kansas City Mo., Mo. Assn. Trial Attys. (sustaining), Assn. Trial Lawyers Am. (sustaining), So. Conf. Bar Pres.'s (life), Mobar Research Inc. (pres. 1978-86), Phi Alpha Delta Alumni (justice Kansas City area alumni 1955-56). Lodges: Optimists (pres. Ward Pkwy. 1961-62, lt. gov. Mo. dist. internat. 1963-64), Sertoma, B'nai B'rith. Home: 9002 Western Hills Dr Kansas City MO 64114-3566 Office: 1710 Mercantile Tower 1101 Walnut St Kansas City MO 64106-2134

STOUT, ELIZABETH WEST, foundation administrator; b. San Francisco, Mar. 4, 1917; d. Claudius Wilson and Sarah (Henderson) West; m. Bruce Churchill McDonald, Mar. 19 1944 (dec. 1952); children: Douglas, Anne; m. Charles Holt Stout, Oct. 27, 1958 (dec. 1992); stepchildren: Richard, George (dec.), Martha Stout Gilweit. Student, U. Nev., 1934-37; grad., Imperial Valley Coll., 1990. Cashier, acct. N.Y. Underwriters, San Francisco, 1937-42; sec. supply and accounts USN, San Francisco, 1942-44. Contbr. articles to profl. jours. Mem. adv. bd. Anza-Borrego Desert, Natural History Assn., 1974-84; founder Stout Paleontology Lab., Borrego Springs, Calif., 1982; found. trustee Desert Rsch. Inst., Reno, 1989—; active Black Rock Desert Project, 1989, Washoe Med. Ctr. League, 1953—, St. Mary's Hosp. Guild, 1953—. Named Disting. Nevadan U. Nev., 1993. Mem. Anza-Borrego Desert Natural History Assn. (dir. emeritus 1984), Soc. Vertebrate Paleontology, De Anza Desert Country Club, Kappa Alpha Theta. Republican. Episcopalian. Avocations: travel, writing, reading, golf.

STOUT, GLENN EMANUEL, retired science administrator; b. Fostoria, Ohio, Mar. 23, 1920. AB, Findlay U., 1942, DSc, 1973. Sci. coord. NSF, 1969-71; asst. to chief Ill. State Water Survey, Champaign, 1971-74; prof. Inst. Environ. Studies, Urbana, Ill., 1973-94, dir. task force, 1975-79; dir. Water Resources Ctr. U. Ill., Urbana, 1973-94; rsch. coord. Ill.-Ind. Sea Grant Program, 1987-94; emeritus, 1994—; Mem. Ill. Gov.'s Task Force on State Water Plan, 1980-94; bd. dirs. Univ. Coun. Water Resources, 1983-86, chmn. internat. affairs, 1989-92; mem. nomination com. for Stockholm Water Prize, 1994-96. Contbr. articles to profl. jours. Mem. Am. Water Resources Assn., Internat. Water Resources Assn. (sec. gen. 1985-91, v.p. 1992-94, exec. dir. 1984-95, pres. 1995—), Am. Meteorol. Soc., Am. Geophys. Union, N.Am. Lake Mgmt. Soc., Ill. Lake Mgmt. Assn. (bd. dirs. 1985-88), Internat. Assn. Rsch. Hydrology, Am. Water Works Assn., Kiwanis (pres. local club 1979-80, lt. gov. 1982-83), Sigma Xi (pres. U. Ill. chpt. 1985-86). Home: 920 W John St Champaign IL 61821-3907 Office: Intl Water Resource Assn 1101 W Peabody Dr Urbana IL 61801-4723

STOUT, GREGORY STANSBURY, lawyer; b. Berkeley, Calif., July 27, 1915; s. Verne A. and Ella (Moore) S.; m. Virginia Cordes, Apr. 23, 1948; 1 son, Frederick Gregory. A.B., U. Calif., 1937, LL.B., 1940. Bar: Calif. 1940. Practice law San Francisco, 1946, 52—; asst. dist. atty., 1947-52; mem. Penal Code Revision Commn. Calif.; chmn. com. State Bar Calif. Contbr. articles to profl. jours. Served to master sgt. AUS, 1942-45. Fellow Am. Coll. Trial Lawyers, Am. Bar Found.; mem. ABA, Fed. Bar Assn., Am. Bd. Trial Advocates, Nat. Assn. Criminal Def. Lawyers (sec. 1958-59, pres. 1962-63). Democrat. Episcopalian. Club: Bohemian. Home and Office: 100 Thorndale Dr Apt 359 San Rafael CA 94903-4501

STOUT, JAMES DUDLEY, lawyer; b. Lawrence County, Ill., June 22, 1947; s. Donald K. and Myrtle Irene (Pullen) S.; m. Susan A. West, Jan. 3, 1976 (div. Feb. 1985); children: Lindsey Diane, Kristi Lynn. BA, So. Ill. U., 1969; JD, U. Ill., 1974. Bar: Tex. 1974, U.S. Dist. Ct. (so. dist.) Tex. 1974, Ill. 1978, U.S. Dist. Ct. (cen. dist.) Ill. 1979, U.S. Dist. Ct. (so. dist.) Ill. 1986. Sole practice Humble, Tex., 1974-78; assoc. Law office Robert W. Dodd, Champaign, Ill., 1978-79; ptnr. Dodd, Stout, Martinkus, et al, Champaign, 1979-81, Zimmerly, Gadau, Stout, Selin & Otto, Champaign, 1981-85, Correll and Stout, Bridgeport, Ill., 1985-86; sole practice Bridgeport, 1986—. Served with U.S. Army, 1969-71. Mem. Assn. Trial Lawyers Am., Ill. Bar Assn., Tex. Bar Assn., Rotary, Lions. Lodges: Elks,

Shriners. Avocations: golf, tennis, reading. Office: 324 N Main St Bridgeport IL 62417-1524

STOUT, JUANITA KIDD, judge; b. Wewoka, Okla., Mar. 7, 1919; d. Henry Maynard and Mary Alice (Chandler) Kidd; m. Charles Otis Stout, June 23, 1942. BA, U. Iowa, 1939; JD, Ind. U., 1948, LLM, 1954; LLD (hon.), Ursinus Coll., 1965, Ind. U., 1966, Lebanon Valley Coll., 1969, Drexel U., 1972, Rockford (Ill.) Coll., 1974, U. Md., 1980, Roger Williams Coll., 1984, Morgan State U., 1985, Russell Sage Coll., 1966, Fisk U., 1988, Del. State Coll., 1990. Bar: D.C. 1950, Pa. 1954. Tchr. pub. schs. Seminole and Sand Springs, Okla., 1939-42; tchr. Fla. A&M U., Tallahassee, 1949, Tex. So. U., Houston, 1949; adminstrv. asst. to judge U.S. Ct. Appeals (3d cir.), Phila., 1950-54; pvt. practice law Turner & Stout, Phila., 1954-55; chief of appeals Dist. Atty.'s Office City of Phila., 1955-59, judge mcpl. ct., 1959-69; judge Ct. Common Pleas, Phila., 1969-88, sr. judge, 1989—; justice Supreme Ct. Pa., Phila., 1988-89; sitting as sr. judge Ct. Common Pleas. Recipient Jane Addams medal Rockford Coll., 1966, Disting. Svc. award U. Iowa, 1974, MCP/Gimbel award for humanitarianism, 1988, 89—, John Peter Zenger award John Peter Zenger Soc., 1994; named to Hall of Fame of Okla., Okla. Heritage Soc., 1981, Disting. Svc. award U. Okla. Alumni Assn. and U. Okla., 1995; Disting. Alumni svc. award Ind. U., Bloomington, 1992; named Disting. Dau. of Pa., 1988. Mem. ABA, Pa. Bar Assn., Phila. Bar Assn. (Sandra Day O'Connor award 1994), Nat. Assn. Women Judges, Nat. Assn. Women Lawyers. Democrat. Episcopalian. Home: Logan Sq E # 1803 2 Franklin Town Blvd Philadelphia PA 19103-1231

STOUT, LOWELL, lawyer; b. Tamaha, Okla., July 23, 1928; s. Charles W. and Rosetta (Easley) S.; m. Liliane Josue, Nov. 29, 1952; children: Georgianna, Mark Lowell. Student, Northeastern State Coll., Tahlequah, Okla., 1946-49, U. Okla., 1949-51; LLB, U. N.Mex., 1952. Bar: N.Mex. 1952. Ptnr. Easley, Quinn & Stout, Hobbs, N.Mex., 1954-58, Girand & Stout, Hobbs, 1958-60; pvt. practice Hobbs, 1960-80; ptnr. Stout & Stout, Hobbs, 1980—. Cpl. U.S. Army, 1952-54. Perenially listed in Best Lawyers in America. Fellow Am. Coll. Trial Lawyers; mem. Assn. Trial Lawyers Am., State Bar N.Mex., N.Mex. Trial Lawyers Assn., Lea County Bar Assn. Home: 218 W Lea St Hobbs NM 88240-5110 Office: Stout & Stout PO Box 716 Hobbs NM 88241-0716

STOUT, LYNN ANDREA, law educator; b. Albany, N.Y., Sept. 14, 1957; d. Warren White and Sally (Cowan) S. BA, Princeton (N.J.) U., 1979, MPA, 1982; JD, Yale U., 1982. Law clk. to the Hon. Gerhard A. Gesell U.S. Dist. Ct. D.C., Washington, 1982-83; assoc. Williams & Connolly, Washington, 1983-86; prof. George Washington U., Washington, 1986-90; prof. Law Ctr. Georgetown U., Washington, 1990—. Nat. Merit scholar, 1975. Mem. Phi Beta Kappa. Office: Georgetown U Law Ctr 600 New Jersey Ave NW Washington DC 20001-2075

STOUT, THOMAS MELVILLE, control systems engineer; b. Ann Arbor, Mich., Nov. 26, 1925; s. Melville B. and Laura C. (Meisel) S.; m. Marilyn J. Koebnick, Dec. 27, 1947; children: Martha, Sharon, Carol, James, William, Kathryn. BSEE, Iowa State Coll., 1946; MSE, U. Mich., 1947, PhD, 1954. Registered profl. engr., Calif. Jr. engr. Emerson Electric Co., St. Louis, 1947-48; instr., then asst. prof. U. Wash., Seattle, 1948-54; rsch. engr. Schlumberger Instrument Co., Ridgefield, Conn., 1954-56; dept. mgr. TRW/Bunker-Ramo Corp., Canoga Park, Calif., 1956-65; pres. Profimatics, Inc., Thousand Oaks, Calif., 1965-83; pvt. practice cons. Northridge, Calif., 1984—; active profl. engring. registration and certification; mem., bd. dirs. Accreditation Bd. for Engring. and Tech., 1995-98. Contbr. articles, revs., papers to profl. publs., chpts. to books. Ens. USN, 1943-46. Fellow, hon. mem. Instrument Soc. Am.; mem. IEEE (sr. mem.), NSPE, AIChE, Am. Soc. for Engring. Edn., Calif. Soc. Profl. Engrs. Achievements include four patents in computer control of industrial processes; participant in early digital computer installations for industrial process control. Home and Office: 9927 Hallack Ave Northridge CA 91324-1120

STOUT, WILLIAM JEWELL, department store executive; b. Bloomington, Ind., Dec. 14, 1914; s. Selatie Edgar and Frances M. (Blodgett) S.; m. Harriet Cracraft, June 15, 1940; children—David Bruce, Karen Louise. A.B., Ind. U., 1937. With L.S. Ayres & Co., Indpls., 1937-78, v.p., 1958-64, v.p. operation, 1964-65, exec. v.p., 1965-78; pres., dir. Citizens Gas & Coke Utility. Mem. Ind. Personnel Bd., 1952-66; dir. devel. Wabash Coll., Crawfordsville, Ind., 1978-84, cons. capital fund drives; chmn. United Fund drive, 1953; pres., bd. dirs. Flanner House; bd. dirs. St. Vincent Hosp. Found., pres., 1972-73; bd. dirs. St. Richard's Day Sch. Served to lt. comdr. USNR, 1942-46. Mem. Indpls. Personnel Assn. (past pres.), Nat. Retail Mchts. Assn., Indpls. Mchts. Assn. (pres. 1970-72), Ind., Indpls. chambers commerce. Home: 1903 Seaport Dr Indianapolis IN 46240-2832

STOUT-PIERCE, SUSAN, clinical specialist; b. Denver, June 6, 1954; d. Joseph Edward and Esther Mae (Miller) Hull; m. Jerry Lee Stout, Nov. 3, 1979 (div. Aug. 1984); m. Gary Myron Pierce, Nov. 21, 1987. AS, Denver Community Coll., 1975; BS, Met. State Coll., 1986. Cert. Radiologic Technologist, Calif., Am. Registry Radiologic Technologists. Radiologic technologist The Swedish Med. Ctr., Englewood, Colo., 1975-79, The Minor Emergency Clinic, Lakewood, Colo., 1979-80, The Children's Hosp., Denver, 1980-86, Merit Peralta Med. Ctr., Oakland, Calif., 1986-87, Am. Shared Hosp. Svcs., Oakland, 1987, HCA South Austin (Tex.) Med. Ctr., 1987-88, U. Calif., San Francisco, 1988-89; clin. imaging specialist OEC-Diasonics, Salt Lake City, 1989-92; software applications specialist Cemax, Inc., Fremont, Calif., 1992-93; mktg. specialist ADAC Healthcare Info. Systems, Houston, Tex., 1993-96; clin. specialist Elekta Instruments Inc., Atlanta, 1996—. Mem. NAFE, Am. Bus. Women's Assn. Avocations: photography, downhill skiing, bicycling. Home: 264 Rachael Pl Pleasanton CA 94566-6228

STOVALL, CARLA JO, state official, lawyer; b. Hardner, Kans., Mar. 18, 1957; d. Carl E. and Juanita Jo (Ford) S. BA, Pittsburg (Kans.) State U., 1979; JD, U. Kans., 1982. Bar: Kans. 1982, U.S. Dist. Ct. Kans. 1982. Pvt. practice, Pittsburg, 1982-85; atty. Crawford County, Pittsburg, 1984-88; gov. Kans. Parole Bd., Topeka, 1988-94; attorney general State of Kansas, Topeka, 1995—; lectr. law Pittsburg State U. 1982-84; pres. Gilston Internat. Mktg., Inc., 1988—. Bd. dirs., sec. Pittsburg Family YMCA, 1983-88. Mem. ABA, Kans. Bar Assn., Crawford County Bar Assn. (sec. 1984-85, v.p. 1985-86, pres. 1986-87), Kans. County and Dist. Attys. Assn., Nat. Coll. Dist. Attys., Pittsburg State U. Alumni Assn. (bd. dirs. 1983-88), Pittsburg Area C. of C. (bd. dirs. 1983-85, Leadership Pitts. 1984), Bus. and Profl. Women Assn. (Young Careerist 1984), Kans. Assn. Commerce and Industry (Leadership Kans. 1983), AAUW (bd. dirs. 1983-87). Republican. Methodist. Avocations: travel, photography, tennis. Home: 3561 SW Mission Ave Topeka KS 66614-3637 Office: Atty Gen Office Kansas Judicial Ctr 2nd Fl Topeka KS 66612*

STOVALL, GERALD THOMAS, religious organization administrator; b. Dallas, Mar. 4, 1940; s. James Roy and Gladys Wilton (Moore) S.; m. Marcia Louise Hearn, May 27, 1967; children: Traci Lynn, Amy Reneé, Keith Roy. BS in Edn., U. North Tex., 1964; MRE, Southwestern Bapt. Theol. Sem., 1966. Min. of music Worth St. Bapt. Ch., Dallas, 1960-64; min. music and edn. Inglewood Bapt. Ch., Grand Prairie, Tex., 1964-67, Siloam Bapt. Ch., Marion, Ala., 1967-69; min. of youth N. Dallas Bapt. Ch., 1969-71; min. of music Emmanuel Bapt. Ch., Lafayette, La., 1971-75; dir. Bapt. Student Ctr. Nicholls State U., Thibodaux, La., 1975-79, U. New Orleans, 1979—; adj. instr. New Orleans Bapt. Theol. Sem.; bd. dirs. Morality in Media, New Orleans, 1989-91, Bapt Assn. Greater New Orleans, 1990-91, Fedn. Chs., New Orleans, 1991—; workshop and conf. leader in student ministry. Mem. Am. Assn. Family Counselors, Assn. So. Bapt. Campus Ministers, La. Chaplains Assn. (bd. dirs.). Office: Bapt Student Ctr 2222 Lakeshore Dr New Orleans LA 70122-3502

STOVALL, JERRY (COLEMAN STOVALL), insurance company executive; b. Houston, July 31, 1936; s. Clifford Coleman and Maxine (Lands) S.; m. Elsie Hostetter, June 20, 1959; 1 child, Brent Allen. BBA, U. Houston, 1968. Home office adminstr. Am. Gen. Life, Houston, 1955-63, agt., agy. mgr., 1963-66, agy. mgr., regional dir. agys., regional v.p., 1969-74; sr. brokerage cons. Conn. Gen. Life, Houston, 1966-69; sr. v.p., dir. mktg. Capitol Life Ins. Co., Denver, 1974-78; v.p., dir. mktg. Integon Life Ins. Corp., Winston-Salem, N.C., 1978-81; pres. Life of Mid-Am. Ins. Co., Topeka, 1981-85; pres. Victory Life Ins. Co., Topeka, 1981-85, chmn., pres., chief exec. officer, 1981-87; pres., retired chief exec. officer Integon Life Ins. Co., Winston-Salem, N.C., 1987-91, Winston-Salem.; vice-chmn. Mktg. One Inc.; bd. dirs., vice-chmn. Ga. Internat. Life; pres., Lamar Life Ins. Co., 1992-95, ret. 1995. Bd. dirs. Winston-Salem Symphony, Jr. Acievement Miss. Inc., Andrew Jackson Coun., Boy Scouts Am.; mem. Miss. Econ. Coun.; bd. govs. Univ. Club. With U.S. Army, 1955-57. Mem. Nat. Assn. Life Cos., Nat. Assn. Life Underwriters, Am. Soc. CLUs (Gold Key Soc.), ACI Exec. Round Table (chmn. 1995). The Country Club of Jackson, Rotary Club Jackson, Rotary Internat. Home: 115 Winged Foot Cir Jackson MS 39211-2528 Office: Lamar Life Ins Co 317 E Capitol St Jackson MS 39201-3404

STOVALL, ROBERT H(ENRY), money management company executive; b. Louisville, 1926; s. Harold Samuel and Agnes C. (Hinkle) S.; m. Inger Bagger; children: Sten Torben, Harold Samuel II, Inger Benedikte, Robert Henry. B.S. in Econs., U. Pa., 1948; postgrad. in polit. economy, U. Copenhagen, 1948-49; M.B.A., N.Y. U., 1957. With E. F. Hutton & Co., 1953-67; mgr. dept. investment research E. F. Hutton & Co., N.Y.C., 1958-60, gen. partner responsible for research, 1961-67, chmn. com. investment policy, 1966-68; research dir. Nuveen Corp., N.Y.C., 1968-69; partner in mktg. and research Reynolds & Co., N.Y.C., 1969; dir. research Reynolds & Co., 1970-73; sr. v.p., dir. investment policy Dean Witter Reynolds Inc. (merger Reynolds & Co. and Dean Witter & Co., acquired by Sears, Roebuck and Co. 1981), N.Y.C., 1978-85, pub. comments on market column, 1961-85; pres. Stovall/Twenty-First Advisers, Inc., 1985—; lectr., tchr. in field; commentator Nat. Pub. Radio, 1982—; prof. fin. NYU, 1985—; regular commentator Bus. Morning, Turner Broadcasting System, 1985-88, "This Morning's Business", CBS-TV, 1988-91, "Market Wrap", Sta. CNBC/FNN-TV; governing mem. Com. on Developing Am. Capitalism, Fairfield, Conn.; bd. dirs. Trust Cos. Am., Venice, Fla. Columnist Forbes, 1968-76, Fin. World, 1979—, Sales and Mktg. Mgmt., 1995—; contbr. articles to profl. publs.; panelist: Wall St. Week, Public Broadcasting System, 1977—, Hall of Fame, 1995. Bd. overseers Grad. Sch. Bus. Adminstrn. NYU, 1984-90, U. Pa. Librs., 1992—; chmn. Security Industry Inst., 1986-88, life trustee, 1989—, trustee St. Clare's-Riverside Health Care Ctr. Found., Denville, N.J., 1980-93, Wayne County (Pa.) Meml. Hosp.; mem. found. bd. 1989—; bd. overseers Seton Hall Prep. Sch., West Orange, N.J., 1985-93; bd. sponsors Loyola Coll. in Md. Schs. Bus., 1990-95, 1991—; dir. Sarasota Opera Assn., 1993—. With U.S. Army, WWII, Italy. Mem. Inst. Chartered Fin. Analysts (CFA), N.Y. Soc. Security Analysts (past dir., vice chmn. program com.), Mensa, Sarasota Univ. Club, Union League (N.Y.C.), S.R., Kentuckians of N.Y. (pres. 1988-90), Sons of Confederate Vets., Beta Gamma Sigma. Home: 888 Blvd of Arts Sarasota FL 34236-4871 Office: Stovall/Twenty-First Advisers Inc 780 3d Ave New York NY 10017-2024

STOVER, CARL FREDERICK, foundation executive; b. Pasadena, Calif., Sept. 29, 1930; s. Carl Joseph and Margarete (Müller) S.; m. Catherine Swanson, Sept. 3, 1954; children: Matthew Joseph, Mary Margaret Stover Marker, Claire Ellen; m. Jacqueline Kast, Sept. 7, 1973. BA magna cum laude, Stanford U., 1951, MA, 1954. Instr. polit. sci. Stanford U., 1953-55; fiscal mgmt. officer Office Sec. Dept. Agr., 1955-57; asso. dir. conf. program pub. affairs Brookings Instn., 1957-59, sr. staff mem. govtl. studies, 1960; fellow Center Study Democratic Instns., Santa Barbara, Calif., 1960-62; asst. to chmn. bd. editors Ency. Brit., 1960-62; sr. polit. scientist Stanford Research Inst., 1962-64; dir. pub. affairs fellowship program Stanford U., 1962-64; pres. Nat. Inst. Pub. Affairs, Washington, 1964-70, Nat. Com. U.S.-China Relations, 1971-72; pres., dir. Federalism Seventy-Six, Washington, 1972-74; dir. cultural resources devel. Nat. Endowment Arts, 1974-78; pres., dir. Cultural Resources, Inc., Washington, 1978-85; bd. dirs. H.E.A.R. Found., 1976-86, treas., 1976-80, pres., 1980-86; bd. dirs. Ctr. for World Lit., pres., 1987-90, chmn., 1990-92; pvt. profl. cons., 1970—; scholar-in-residence Nat. Acad. Pub. Adminstrn., 1980-82; cons. to govt., 1953—. Author: The Government of Science, 1962, The Technological Order, 1963; Founding editor: Jour. Law and Edn., 1971-73; pub. Delos mag., 1987-92. Treas. Nat. Com. U.S.-China Rels., 1966-71, 82-87, 89-94, bd. dirs., 1966-74, 79-94, 95—; bd. dirs. Coord. Coun. Lit. Mags., 1966-68; trustee Inst. of Nations, 1972-76, Nat. Inst. Pub. Affairs, 1967-71, Kinesis Ltd., 1972-78; vol. Nat. Exec. Svc. Corps, 1984-89. Fellow AAAS; mem. Am. Soc. Pub. Adminstrn., Fedn. Am. Scientists, Soc. Internat. Devel., Jordan Soc. (dir. 1982-84), Nat. Acad. Pub. Adminstrn. (hon.), Md. U. Club, Internat. Soc. Panetics (pres. 1991-95, chmn. 1995—, founding mem. 1991—), Phi Beta Kappa Assocs. (hon., lectr. 1972-87), Phi Beta Kappa. Democrat. Presbyterian. Home and Office: 4109 Metzerott Rd College Park MD 20740-2082

STOVER, CAROLYN NADINE, middle school educator; b. Martinsburg, W.Va., May 30, 1950; d. Norman Robert and Garnet Agnes (Zombro) Whetzel; m. James Stenner Stover Sr., Nov. 20, 1971; children: Heather N., James S. Jr. BA in Home Econs., Shepherd Coll., 1972; cert. in advanced studies, W.Va. U., 1978; cert. in tchg. methods, Marshall U., 1973; cert. in spl. edn., Shippensburg Coll., 1972. Cert. tchr., W.Va., N.Mex.; reg. EMT. Substitute tchr. Berkeley County Schs., Martinsburg, W.Va., 1972, adult edn. instr., 1972-77, home econs. instr., 1973-83; substitute tchr. Ruidoso (N.Mex.) Mcpl. Schs., 1984-90, child find coord. Region 9 edn. coop., 1990, life skills and at-risk educator, 1991—, coord. coun., 1991-93, mem. budget com., 1993. Elder First Presbyn. Ch., Ruidoso, 1984-90, 94-96; sponsor Acad. Booster Club, Ruidoso, 1993—; instr. CPR, 1980. Named Outstanding Young Women of Am., 1981. Mem. NEA, Nat. Middle Sch. Assn., Ruidoso Edn. Assn., Rotary (youth leadership councilor 1991—). Democrat. Avocations: cross-stitching, needlework, family, sports, youth. Home: Box 7837 1007 Hull Rd Ruidoso NM 88355 Office: Ruidoso Mid Sch 100 Reese Dr Ruidoso NM 88345-6016

STOVER, DAVID FRANK, lawyer; b. Phila., May 15, 1941; s. Emory Frank and Beatrice Norah (Spinelli) S. A.B., Princeton U., 1962; J.D., U. Pa., 1965. Bar: D.C. 1966, U.S. Ct. Appeals (D.C. cir.) 1968, U.S. Ct. Appeals (9th cir.) 1969, U.S. Ct. Appeals (4th cir.) 1972. Atty. FPC, Washington, 1965-71, Tally & Tally, Washington, 1972-75; asst. gen. counsel Postal Rate Commn., Washington, 1975-79, gen. counsel, 1979-92, regulatory cons. 1992—. Author: (with Bierman, Lamont, Nelson) Geothermal Energy in the Western United States, 1978. Mem. Fed. Bar Assn. Episcopalian. Home and Office: 2970 S Columbus St # 1-B Arlington VA 22206-1450

STOVER, ELLEN SIMON, health scientist, psychologist; b. Bklyn., Nov. 21, 1950; d. Ralph and Charlotte (Tulchin) Simon; m. Alan B. Stover, June 3, 1973; children: Elena Randall Simon, Randall Alan Simon, Samantha Anne Simon. BA with honors, U. Wis., 1972; PhD, Catholic U., 1978. Cons. NIMH, Rockville, Md., 1972-74, spl. asst. to assoc. dir. extramural programs, 1976-77, chief, small grants program, 1977-79, asst., acting & chief rsch. resources br., 1980-85, dep. dir., div. basic scis., 1985-88, dir. office on AIDS, 1988—; exec. sec., drug abuse rsch. rev. com. Nat. Inst. on Drug Abuse, Rockville, 1974-76; co-chmn. AIDS rsch. behavioral coordinating com. NIH, 1993—. Recipient Superior Svc. award USPHS, 1987, 92, 93, Dir.'s award NIH, 1996. Mem. APA, Am. Psychol. Soc. Office: NIMH 5600 Fishers Ln # 10-75 Rockville MD 20857-0001

STOVER, HARRY M., corporate executive; b. 1926; married. BS, U. So. Calif., 1947. Engr. Stone & Webster Corp., 1947-48; chief engr. Raymond Internat., 1948-51, Standard Vacuum Corp., 1951-54; with A.P. Green Refracteries, 1954-76, pres., 1972-76, chief exec. officer, 1974-76, chmn., 1976; group v.p. USG Corp., 1976-79; exec. v.p. USG Corp., Chgo., 1979-88, vice chmn., 1985; chmn., chief exec. officer A.P. Green Industries Inc., Mexico, Mo., 1988-93. Served to ensign USN, 1944-46. Office: A P Green Industries Inc Green Blvd Mexico MO 65265-2980

STOVER, JAMES HOWARD, real estate executive; b. Forest Hill, W.Va., Oct. 20, 1911; s. Charles William and Zora (Goode) S.; m. May Simmons, Oct. 21, 1939 (dec.); children: Ann, Robert Bruce; m. Elizabeth J. Cobb, Dec. 27, 1977 (dec.). Student, Benjamin Franklin U., 1936-38; grad., Advanced Mgmt. Program, Harvard U., 1959, Exec. Devel. Program Ind. U., 1960, Inst. Mgmt. Northwestern U., 1960. Asst. purchasing agt. Woodward & Lothrop, Washington, 1932-35; asst. chief field supervision div., central accounts office Bur. Accounts Treasury Dept., 1935-41, asst. chief Treasury Budget sect., 1941-42, fiscal acct. Office Commr. Pub. Debt, 1946-51, chief treasury mgmt. analysis staff, 1951-63, dir. Office Mgmt. and Orgn., 1963-66, regional commr. customs Miami Region IV, 1966-72; real estate sales assoc., mgmt. cons., 1972-75; pres. Bay Realty of Fla., Inc., 1975—; Chmn. Inter-agy. Mgmt. Analysis Conf., 1958-59; mem. orgn. and mgmt. adv. com. Dept. Agr. Grad. Sch., 1956-63. Chmn. adv. coms. orgn. and procedure and legislative program Arlington (Va.) County Bd., 1958-63; pres. Tuckahoe Recreation Club, 1957; chmn. Greater Miami Fed. Exec. Coun., 1968-69; mem. exec. adv. coun. Coll. Bus. and Pub. Adminstrn., Fla. Atlantic U., 1969-80. 2d lt. to maj. AUS, 1942-46. Recipient Rockefeller Pub. Svc. award, 1959, Spl. Svc. award Treasury Dept., 1963, Exceptional Svc. award, 1965, other treasury awards, 1969, 70, 71, 72. Home: 707 Vilabella Ave Coral Gables FL 33146-1733 Office: 2335 Biscayne Blvd Miami FL 33137-4513

STOVER, JOHN FORD, railroad historian, educator; b. Manhattan, Kans., May 16, 1912; s. John William and Maud (Ford) S.; m. Marjorie Ellen Filley, Aug. 21, 1937; children: John Clyde, Robert Vernon (dec.), Charry Ellen Stover Olin. AB, U. Nebr., 1934, MA, 1937; PhD, U. Wis., 1951. Instr. social studies Arcadia (Nebr.) High Sch., 1936-37; instr. history and govt. Bergen (N.J.) Jr. Coll., 1937-41; grad. asst. history U. Wis., 1941-42, 46-47, Univ. fellow, 1946; from instr. to assoc. prof. Purdue U., Lafayette, Ind., 1947-59, prof. history, 1959-78, prof. emeritus, 1978—; Purdue Research Found. XL grantee Purdue U., summer 1957, 59, fellow in Coll.-Bus. Exchange Program, I.C. R.R.,, summer 1962; chmn. Pres.'s adv. coun. on retirement Purdue U., 1981-82. Author: The Railroads of the South, 1865-1900, 1955, American Railroads, 1961, rev. edit., 1997, A History of American Railroads, 1967, Turnpikes, Canals and Steamboats, 1969, The Life and Decline of the American Railroad, 1970, Transportation in American History, 1970, History of Illinois Central Railroad, 1975, Iron Road To The West, 1978, Sixty-Five Years of Kiwanis in Indiana, 1981, History of the Baltimore & Ohio Railroad, 1987, Seventy-Five Years of Kiwanis and Indiana, 1990; contbr. to hist. jours., books, numerous encys. and biog. works. Chmn. edn. com., mem. exec. com. Ind. Sesquicentennial Commn., 1962-67; hon. mem. Indiana Am. Revolution Bicentennial commn., 1972-82; mem. adv. council Centennial History of Ind. Gen. Assembly, 1979-83; pres. Lafayette Kiwanis Found., 1977-78. Served to capt. USAAF, 1942-46; Res., ret. George F. Hixson fellow, 1996; named Sagamore of the Wabash Gov. Ind., 1978; recipient Alumni Achievement award U. Nebr., 1985. Fellow Soc. Am. Historians; mem. Ind. Acad. Social Scis., Western History Assn., Bus. History Conf. (trustee 1973-76), Am. Hist. Assn., So. Ind. Hist. Assn. (com. on library), Nebr. Hist. Assn., Tippecanoe County Hist. Assn. (pres. 1972-74), Lexington Group (r.r. historians), AAUP, Ind. History Tchrs. Assn. (pres. 1958-59), Orgn. Am. Historians, Newcomen Soc. N.Am., Ry. and Locomotive Hist. Soc. (editorial adv. bd. for Railroad History jour., 1970-94, Sr. Achievement R.R. History award 1983), Soc. Ind. Pioneers, Civil War Round Table of Nebr., Nat. Ry. Hist. Soc., Phi Beta Kappa (hon.), Phi Alpha Theta, Delta Sigma Rho. Republican. Methodist. Club: Fortnightly, Lincoln Open Forum. Lodge: Kiwanis (local pres. 1973-74, disting. lt. gov. 1978-79, historian Ind. dist. 1980-81, 83-90. 91-92). Avocations: golf, model railroading, stamps. Home: 2114 Heritage Pines Ct Lincoln NE 68506-2866

STOVER, LEON (EUGENE), anthropology educator, writer, critic; b. Lewistown, Pa., Apr. 9, 1929; s. George Franklin and Helen Elizabeth (Haines) S.; 1 dau. by previous marriage, Laren Elizabeth; m. 2d Takeko Kawai, Oct. 12, 1956. BA, Western Md. Coll., 1950, LittD (hon.), 1980; MA, Columbia U., 1952, PhD, 1962. Instr. Am. Museum Natural History, N.Y.C., 1955-57; asst. prof. Hobart and William Smith Colls., Geneva, N.Y., 1957-63; vis. asst. prof. Tokyo U., 1963-65; assoc. prof. Ill. Inst. Tech., Chgo., 1966-74, prof. anthropology, 1974-94, prof. emeritus, 1995—; founder, 1st chmn. John W. Campbell Meml. Award, 1972; guest lectr. Brit. Film Inst., 1986; humanities cons. Champaign (Ill.) Pub. Library H.G. Wells Traveling Exhbn., 1986; commd. as Robert A. Heinlein's authorized biographer, 1988. Author: La Science Fiction Americaine, 1972, The Cultural Ecology of Chinese Civilization, 1974, China: An Anthropological Perspective, 1976, The Shaving of Karl Marx, 1982, The Prophetic Soul: A Reading of H.G. Wells's "Things to Come", 1987, Robert A. Heinlein for Twayne's United State Authors Series, 1987, Harry Harrison for Twayne's United States Authors Series, 1990, The Annotated H.G. Wells: The Time Machine, 1996, The Annotated H.G. Wells: The Island of Docotor Moreau, 1996, The Annotated H.G. Wells: The Invisible Man, 1997, The Annotated H.G. Wells: The First Men in the Moon, 1997; sr. author: Stonehenge: The Indo-European Heritage, 1979; co-author: Stonehenge: Where Atlantis Died, 1983; sr. editor: Apeman, Spaceman, 1968; co-editor: Above the Human Landscape, 1972; sci. editor: Amazing, Stories, 1967-69; cons. editor: Contemporary Authors, 1987. Recipient Chris award for best ednl. film, 1974; recipient Cine award Internat. Council Non-Theatrical Events, 1973; named Disting Faculty Lectr. Sigma Xi, 1978; honored with Stover Day Western Md. Coll., 1981. Mem. H.G. Wells Soc., Sci. Fiction Writers Am. Home: 3100 S Michigan Ave Apt 602 Chicago IL 60616-3825

STOVER, MATTHEW JOSEPH, communications executive; b. Palo Alto, Calif., May 5, 1955; s. Carl Frederick and Catherine (Swanson) S.; m. Elizabeth Biddle Richter, Apr. 27, 1985; children: Katharine Elizabeth, Madeleine Westbrook. BA, Yale U., 1976; postgrad., U. Va., 1987. Gen. mgr. K&S Assocs., Beltsville, Md., 1977-78; dir. outreach programs U.S. Office Personnel Mgmt., Washington, 1978-81; exec. asst. to chmn. Fed. Maritime Commn., Washington, 1981; exec. dir. STN Computer Services, Inc., Alexandria, Va., 1981-82; dir. corp. communications Norton Simon, Inc., N.Y.C., 1982-83; dist. mgr. corp. communications N.Y. Telephone Co., N.Y.C., 1983-86, dist. mgr. customer services, 1986-87; v.p. corp. communications Am. Express Co., N.Y.C., 1987-90, sr. v.p. communications, 1990; v.p. pub. affairs and corp. communications NYNEX Corp., White Plains, N.Y., 1990-92; pres., CEO AGS Computers, Inc., 1993-94, NYNEX Info. Resources Co., Middleton, Mass., 1994—; bd. dirs. Infoseek Corp., Nat. Assn. Mfrs., Yellow Pages Pubs. Assn., Computer and Comm. Industry Assn.; trustee Com. for Econ. Devel. Editor, pub.: (lit. mag.) Buffalo Stamps, 1971-74. Mem. Nat. Com. U.S.-China Rels. Coun. for Excellence in Govt., Yale Club. Office: NYNEX Info Resources Co 35 Village Rd Middleton MA 01949-1202

STOVER, W. ROBERT, temporary services executive; b. Phila., June 26, 1921; s. Robert William Stover and Jane Horton; m. Joan Cote; children: Stephen R., Susan J., Amy J. BS, Waynesburg Coll., 1942, LHD (hon.), 1991; postgrad., U. Ill., 1942-43, U. Pa., 1946. Founder, chief exec. officer Western Temporary Svcs., Walnut Creek, Calif., 1948—, also chmn. bd. dirs.; dir., past chmn. Presbyn. Lay Com., Phila.; mem. Latin Am. Missions Gen. Coun., Miami, Fla., Luis Palau Adv. Com., Portland, Oreg.; past chmn. Oakland Billy Graham Crusade. Former chmn. Fuller Theol. Sem., Pasadena, Calif., African Enterprise, L.A.; life mem., former nat. chmn. Young Life Campaign, Colorado Springs. Lt. USN, WWII. Office: Western Staff Svcs Inst 301 Lennon Ln Walnut Creek CA 94598-2418

STOW, GERALD LYNN, human services executive, speaker; b. Dresden, Tenn., Sept. 6, 1933; s. William Monroe and Bertha Lee (Stafford) S.; m. Barbara Kay Hassler, Sept. 5, 1954; children: Loretta Lee, Stephen Lynn, John Christopher. BS, U. Tenn., 1953, MS, 1956; BD (hon. degree), S.W. Bapt. Theological Seminary, Ft. Worth, 1964; D. Min., So. Bapt. Theological Seminary, Louisville, 1978. Pastor First Bapt. Church, Clint, Tex., 1958-60; pastor Plainview Bapt. Church, Krum, Tex., 1960-61, Sunset Heights Bapt. Church, Ft. Worth, 1961-64, So. Fulton Bapt. Church, Tenn., 1964-75, First Bapt. Church, Cookeville, Tenn., 1976-84; pres., treas. Tenn. Bapt. Chldns. Homes, Inc., Brentwood, Tenn., 1984—. Author: Life & Work Annual, 1964-82, God's Plan for the Future, 1976, Doran's Ministers Manual, 1982. Sergeant, U.S. Army, 1956-59; mem. Rotary Club, Lion's Club, Civitan Club, Cookeville, Tenn. Mem. So. Bapt. Child Care Exec., Tenn. Commission on Chldn. & Youth, Natl. Assn. of Homes & Svcs. for Chldn. Baptist. Avocations: woodworking, growing roses, reading, gardening. Office: Tenn Bapt Chldns Homes Inc 1310 Franklin Rd Brentwood TN 37027-6803

STOWE, ALEXIS MARIANI, accountant, consultant; b. Binghamton, N.Y., May 3, 1950; d. Albert Joseph and Gilda Ann (DiNardo) Mariani; m. Dennis James Stowe, June 3, 1972 (dec. Nov. 1988); children: Cort Andrew, Derek Anthony, Jilda Ann. Student, Le Moyne Coll., 1968-70; BS in Acctg., SUNY, Buffalo, 1972; MS in Acctg., SUNY, Albany, 1974; MS in Taxation, Southeastern U., 1980. CPA, N.Y., Va.; cert. fraud examiner; cert. govt. fin. mgr., cert. info. sys. auditor. In-charge acct. Ernst & Young,

CPA's, Buffalo, 1973-74; sr. corp. acct. Moog, Inc., East Aurora, N.Y., 1974-76; auditor U.S. Gen. Acctg. Office, Washington, 1976-78, 79-80; tax law specialist IRS, Washington, 1978-79; pvt. practice CPA Woodbridge, Va., 1980-87; v.p., contr. M.T. Hall, Ltd., Woodbridge, 1987-91; audit mgr. U.S. Dept. Health and Human Svcs., Washington, 1991-93; oversight mgr. Resolution Trust Corp., Washington, 1993-94; v.p., prin. Gardiner, Kamya, CPA's, Washington, 1994—; trustee pension plan M.T. Hall, Ltd., Woodbridge, 1987-90; team leader CFO task force Pres.'s Coun. on Integrity and Efficiency, Washington, 1991-93; instr. Inspector Gen. Auditor Tng. Inst., Ft. Belvoir, Va., 1992—; mem. task force on grants Govtl. Acctg. Stds. Bd., Norwalk, Conn., 1992—; mem. faculty Assn. Cert. Fraud Examiners, 1995—. Contbr. articles to profl. jours. N.Y. Regents scholar, 1968-72. Mem. AICPA, Va. Soc. CPAs, Assn. Govt. Accts. (vice chair publs. 1994—, Author's award 1991), Assn. Cert. Fraud Examiners, Info. Sys. Audit Control Assn., Cath. Daus. of Am., Chi Omega, Beta Gamma Sigma. Roman Catholic. Home: 6013 Wheeler Ln Broad Run VA 20137 Office: Gardiner Kamya & Assocs CPA 1717 K St NW Ste 601 Washington DC 20006-1501

STOWE, BRUCE BERNOT, biology educator; b. Neuilly-sur-Seine, France, Dec. 9, 1927; came to U.S., 1935; s. Leland and Ruth Florida (Bernot) S.; m. Elizabeth Louise Kwasny, June 23, 1951 (dec. June 1983); children: Mark Kwasny, Eric Bernot. BSc, Calif. Inst. Tech., 1950; MA, Harvard U., 1951, PhD, 1954; MA (hon.), Yale U., 1971. Instr. biology Harvard U., Cambridge, Mass., 1955-58, tutor biochem. scis., 1956-58, lectr. botany, 1958-59; asst. prof. Yale U., New Haven, 1959-63, assoc. prof., 1963-71, prof. biology and forestry, 1971—, dir. bot. garden, 1975-78; rsch. professor Japan Soc. Promotion Sci. U. Osaka Prefecture, 1973; vis. investigator Nat. Inst. for Basic Biology, Okazaki, Japan, 1985-86. Mem. editorial bd. Plant Physiology, Waltham, Mass., 1965-89; mem. editorial com. Ann. Rev. Plant Physiology, Palo Alto, Calif., 1968-73; cons. editor Am. Scientist, New Haven, 1985-90; contbr. sci. papers to Nature, Biochem. Jour., Analytical Biochemistry, others. With U.S. Army, 1946-47. Predoctoral fellow Atomic Energy Commn. Harvard U., 1951-53, postdoctoral fellow NSF, U. Coll. North Wales, 1954-55, fellow John Simon Guggenheim Found., 1965-66; travel grantee U. Adelaide, Waite Inst., South Australia, 1972-73. Fellow AAAS; mem. AAUP, Am. Assn. Plant Physiologists (sec. 1963-65, trustee 1970-72, 75), Bot. Soc. Am., Am. Soc. Biol. Chemistry, Phytochem. Soc., N.Am. Phytochem. Soc., French Soc. Physiol. Végétale, Conn. Acad. Arts and Scis. (chair publs. com. 1992-94). Democrat. Achievements include research in analysis and metabolism of plant hormones, lipid activation of plant hormone action, biochemistry of secondary plant products. Home: 161 Grandview Ave Hamden CT 06514-3518 Office: Yale U Dept Biology PO Box 208103 New Haven CT 06520-8103

STOWE, DAVID HENRY, arbitrator; b. New Canaan, Conn., Sept. 10, 1910; s. Ansel Roy Monroe and Marjorie (Henry) S.; m. Mildred Walker, June 7, 1932; children—David H., Richard W. Student, Washington and Lee U., 1927-30; A.B., Duke, 1931, M. Ed., 1934. Tchr. N.C., 1931-37; asst. state dir. N.C. state Employment Service, 1937-41; chief examiner Bur. Budget, Washington, 1943-47; dep. to asst. to Pres. U.S., 1947-49; adminstrv. asst. to Pres., 1949-53; arbitrator Washington, 1953-70; mem. Nat. Mediation Bd., 1970-79, chmn., 1972-75, 78; mem. atomic energy-labor mgmt. relations panel, 1962—; pub. mem. Pres.'s Missile Sites Labor Commn., 1961-67; mem. bd. Harry S. Truman Library Inst., 1981—. Recipient distinguished service award Dept. Labor, 1965. Mem. Nat. Acad. Arbitrators, Lambda Chi Alpha, Alpha Kappa Psi. Democrat. Episcopalian. Home: 717 Maiden Choice Ln Apt 417 Catonsville MD 21228-6115

STOWE, DAVID METZ, clergyman; b. Council Bluffs, Iowa, Mar. 30, 1919; s. Ernest Lewllyn and Florence May (Metz) S.; m. Virginia Ware, Nov. 25, 1943; children: Nancy F. (Mrs. Thomas S. Inui), Elizabeth Anne (Mrs. Charles Hambrick-Stowe), Priscilla B., David W. BA, UCLA, 1940; BD, Pacific Sch. Religion, 1943, ThD, 1953, DD (hon.), 1966; postgrad., Yale U., 1945-46. Ordained to ministry Congl. Ch., 1943; assoc. min. Congl. Ch., Berkeley, Calif., 1943-45, 51-53; missionary, univ. prof. Peking, China, 1947-50; chaplain, chmn. dept. religion Carleton Coll., 1953-56; ednl. sec. Am. Bd. Commnrs. and United Ch. Bd. World Ministries, 1956-62; prof. theology Beirut, 1962-63; exec. sec. div. fgn. missions Nat. Coun. Chs., 1963-64, assoc. gen. sec. overseas ministries, 1965-70; also bd. govs.; exec. v.p. United Ch. Bd. for World Ministries, 1970-85; cons. mission and religion China, 1985—; adj. prof. Andover Newton Theol. Sch., 1987—; mem. exec. coun. World Conf. on Religion and Peace, 1988-97; bd. dirs. Congl. Christian Hist. Soc.; del. 2nd, 3rd and 4th Assemblies of World Coun. of Chs.; mem. Divsn. of World Mission & Evangelism, 1963-75. Author: The Churches' Mission in the World, 1963, When Faith Meets Faith, 1963, Ecumenicity and Evangelism, 1970; also articles in religious books and periodicals. Mem. Am. Soc. Missiology (sec.-treas. Ea. fellowship 1986—), Internat. Assn. Mission Studies, Nat. Soc. Values in Higher Edn., Phi Beta Kappa, Pi Gamma Mu, Blue Key. Home: 54 Magnolia Ave Tenafly NJ 07670-2120

STOWE, MADELEINE, actress; b. L.A., Aug. 18, 1958; m. Brian Benben. Films: Stakeout, 1987, Worth Winning, 1989, Revenge, 1990, The Two Jakes, 1990, Closetland, 1991, Unlawful Entry, 1992, The Last of the Mohicans, 1992, Another Stakeout, 1993, Short Cuts, 1993, China Moon, 1993, Blink, 1994, Bad Girls, 1994, Twelve Monkies, 1995; TV movies: The Gangster Chronicles: An American Story, The Nativity, Beulah Land, Black Orchid (miniseries). Office: care UTA 9560 Wilshire Blvd Fl 5 Beverly Hills CA 90212-2401

STOWE, ROBERT ALLEN, catalytic and chemical technology consultant; b. Kalamazoo, July 26, 1924; s. Allen Byron Stowe and Doris Alfreda (Wood) Stowe Weber; m. Dorothea May Davis, Aug. 23, 1947 (div. 1973); children: Michael, Randall, Catherine, Robert; m. Marion June Smith, Oct. 20, 1973 (div. 1980). AB, Kalamazoo Coll., 1948; PhD, Brown U., 1953. Phys. chemist Dow Chem. Co., Midland, Mich., 1952-58; rsch. chemist Dow Chem. Co., Ludington, Mich., 1958-64, sr. rsch. chemist, 1964-69; sr. rsch. chemist Dow Chem. Co., Midland, 1969-72, assoc. scientist, 1972-88; ret., 1988; pres. Bobcat Techs. Ltd., Cross Village, Mich., 1988—; sr. consulting assoc. Omnitech Internat. Ltd., Midland, 1989—; bd. dirs., mem. oper. bd., chief scientist Van Tek Corp. (formerly VF Sales), 1990—; chief exec. scientist Environ. Assessments Ltd., Midland, 1990—. Contbr. articles to sci. jours.; numerous patents in U.S. and fgn. countries. Treas. Ludington Bd. Edn., 1960-63, pres., 1963-68. With USAAF, 1943-45; mem. Nat. Ski Patrol. Recipient Victor J. Azbe award Nat. Lime Assn., 1964. Fellow Am. Inst. Chemists (cert. profl. chemist); mem. Am. Chem. Soc. (program sec. divsn. indsl. and engrng. chemistry 1972-82, chmn. 1982-83, councilor 1986—, sec. gen. Catalysis Secretariat 1990, 94, Joseph P. Stewart award 1984), N.Am. Catalysis Soc., N.Am. Thermal Analysis Soc., Mich. Catalysis Soc. (sec.-treas. 1987-88, pres. 1988-89). Avocations: tennis, skiing, sailing. Home and Office: Box 173 5680 Chippewa Dr Cross Village MI 49723-0173

STOWE, ROBERT LEE, III, textile company executive; b. Charlotte, N.C., July 3, 1954; s. Robert Lee Jr. and Ruth Link (Harding) S.; m. Christine Ruth Edwards, Jan. 15, 1983; children: Christine Ruth, Lillian Rhyne. BA, Davidson (N.C.) Coll., 1976. Dir., mgmt. trainee R.L. Stowe Mills, Inc., Belmont, N.C., 1976-77, v.p., 1977-79, exec. v.p., 1979-84, chmn. bd., 1984—; bd. dirs Belmont Converting Co., Lakeview Farms, Inc., sec., treas.; pres. Robrt Lee Stowe Jr. Found., Belmont, 1978—; bd. mgrs. Wachovia Bank of N.C., Gaston County. Trustee Belmont Abbey Coll., 1987-90, Mint Mus. Art, Charlotte, 1989-92, Crossnore (N.C.) Sch., 1987, Sci. Museums, Charlotte, 1989-91, Gaston Day Sch., 1994-97, Gaston County C. of C., 1992—, Mis. of New South; trustee Daniel Jonathan Stowe Conservancy, 1990, pres., 1996; deacon, elder local Presbyn. Ch. Named one of Outstanding Young Men Am., 1979. Mem. Am. Textile Mfrs. Inst. (bd. dirs. 1989-92), Newcomen Soc. U.S., N.C. Textile Found. (bd. dirs. 1986—), Met. Club N.Y., Charlotte City Club, Charlotte Country Club, Grandfather Golf and Country Club. Republican. Avocations: golf, boating, church activities. Home: 135 N Main St PO Box 232 Belmont NC 28012 Office: RL Stowe Mills Inc 100 N Main St Belmont NC 28012-3104

STOWELL, CHRISTOPHER R., dancer; b. N.Y.C., June 8, 1966; s. Kent and Francia (Russell) S. Student, Pacific N.W. Ballet Sch., 1979-84, Sch. Am. Ballet, 1984-85. Entered corps de ballet San Francisco Ballet, 1986, promoted to soloist, 1987, prin., 1990—; guest artist Ballet Met, Ohio, Pacific N.W. Ballet, Seattle, and with Jean Charles Gil, Marseilles, France, Asami Maki Ballet, Tokyo. Created leading roles in Handel-A Celebration, Con Brio, The Sleeping Beauty, New Sleep, Connotations, Pulcinella, Meistens Mozart; other roles include Calcium Light Night, Rubies, The Sons of Horus, The Four Temperaments, Hearts, Tarantella, Flower Festival, La Fille Mal Garde, Haffner Symphony, Forgotten Land, The End, Agon, In the Middle Somewhat Elevated, Le Quattro Stagioni, Swan Lake, Job, Company B, Tchaikousky Pas de Deux, Maelstrom, Mercutio in Romeo and Juliet, The Dance House, Stars and Stripes, Ballo Della Regina, Drink to me Only With Thine Eyes, Pacific; performed in Reykjavik Arts Festival, Iceland, 1990, San Francisco Ballet at the Paris Opera Garnier, 1994. Avocations: cooking, reading, camping. Office: San Francisco Ballet 455 Franklin St San Francisco CA 94102-4438

STOWELL, JOSEPH, III, academic administrator. Head Moody Bible Inst., Chgo. Office: Moody Bible Inst 820 N La Salle Dr Chicago IL 60610-3214 Office: Sta WKES-FM PO Box 8888 Saint Petersburg FL 33738-8888*

STOWELL, KENT, ballet director; b. Rexburg, Idaho, Aug. 8, 1939; s. Harold Bowman and Maxine (Hudson) S.; m. Francia Marie Russell, Nov. 19, 1965; children: Christopher, Darren, Ethan. Student, San Francisco Ballet Sch., Sch. Am. Ballet; Lead dancer San Francisco Ballet, 1957-62, N.Y.C. Ballet, 1962-68; ballet dir., ballet master Frankfurt (Fed. Republic Germany) Opera Ballet, 1973-77; artistic dir. Pacific N.W. Ballet, Seattle, 1977—; prof. dance Ind. U., Bloomington, 1969-70; bd. dirs. Dance/USA, Washington, 1986—. Choreographer: Cinderella, Carmina Burana, Coppelia, Time & Ebb, Fauré Requiem, Hail to the Conquering Hero, Firebird, Over the Waves, Nutcracker, The Tragedy of Romeo and Juliet, Delicate Balance, Swan Lake, Time and Ebb, Through Interior Worlds, Quaternary, Orpheus. Bd. dirs. Sch. of Am. Ballet, N.Y.C., 1981—; mem. Goodwill Games Arts Com., Seattle, 1987—; chmn. dance panel NEA, 1981-85. Grantee NEA, 1980, 85; fellow NEA, 1979. Recipient Arts Service award King County Arts Commn., 1985, Outstanding Contbn. to Pacific N.W. Ballet State of Was., 1987, Best Dance Co. award The Weekly Newspaper, Seattle, 1987, Gov. Arts award, 1988, Dance Mag. award, 1996. Office: Pacific NW Ballet 301 Mercer St Seattle WA 98109-4600

STOWELL, LARRY JOSEPH, agricultural consultant; b. San Pedro, Calif., June 12, 1952; s. James E. and Dorothy L. (Geiser) S.; m. Wendy D. Gelernter, Feb. 22, 1986. BS, U. Ariz., 1977, PhD, 1982. Rsch. assoc. U. Ariz., Tucson, 1976-82; postdoctoral rschr. U. Calif., Davis, 1982-84; group leader Mycogen Corp., San Diego, 1984-88; prin. Pace Cons., San Diego, 1988—; prin., rsch. dir. Pace Turfgrass Rsch. Inst., San Diego, 1993—. Author: (with others) Microbial Products For Medicine and Agriculture, 1989, Microbial Control of Weeds, 1991, Advanced Engineered Pesticides, 1993. U. Ariz. Alumni Assn. scholar, 1978; U. Ariz. grantee, 1981. Mem. Am. Phytopath. Soc., Agronomy Soc. Am., Weed Sci. Soc. Am., Nat. Alliance Ind. Crop Cons. (bd. dirs. 1992-95), Assn. Applied Insect Ecologists (bd. dirs. 1991-95), Am. Registry Cert. Profls. in Agronomy Crops and Soils (bd. dirds. 1993—), Nat. Plant Pathology Bd. Achievements include copatents for Bioherbicide for Florida Beggarweed, Synergistic Herbicidal Compositions. Home and Office: Pace Cons 1267 Diamond St San Diego CA 92109-2645

STOWELL, ROBERT EUGENE, pathologist, retired educator; b. Cashmere, Wash., Dec. 25, 1914; s. Eugene Francis and Mary (Wilson) S.; m. Eva Mae Chambers, Dec. 1, 1945; children: Susan Jane, Robert Eugene Jr. Student, Whitman Coll., 1932-33; BA, Stanford U., 1936, MD, 1941; PhD, Washington U., 1944. Fellow in cytology Wash. U. Sch. Medicine, St. Louis, 1940-42; rsch. fellow Barnard Free Skin and Cancer Hosp., St. Louis, 1940-42, rsch. assoc., 1942-48; asst. resident in pathology Barnes, McMillan, St. Louis Children's Hosps., St. Louis, 1942-43, resident in pathology, 1943-44, asst. pathologist, 1944-48; instr. in pathology Washington U. Sch. Medicine, St. Louis, 1943-45; asst. prof. Washington U. Sch. Medicine, St. Louis, 1945-48; assoc. prof. Washington U. Sch. Medicine, St. Louis, 1948; advanced med. fellow Inst. for Cell Rsch., Stockholm, 1946-47; chmn. dept. oncology U. Kansas Med. Ctr., Kansas City, Kans., 1948-51, prof. pathology and oncology, dir. cancer rsch., 1948-59, chmn., 1951-59; sci. dir. Armed Forces Inst. Pathology, Washington, 1959-67; chmn. dept. pathology Sch. of Medicine U. Calif., Davis, 1967-69, asst. dean Sch. Medicine, 1967-72, prof. pathology Sch. Medicine, 1967-82, prof. emeritus, 1982—; dir. div. pathology Sacramento (Calif.) Med. Ctr., 1967-69; vis. prof. U. Md. Sch. Medicine, Balt., 1960-67; acting dir. Nat. Ctr. for Primate Biology, U. Calif., Davis, 1968-69, dir., 1969-71; cons. U.S. Atomic Energy commn., Los Alamos, N.Mex., 1949-54, NIH, 1949-74, Cancer Control Div. USPHS, 1949-59, others; mem. adv. med. bd. Leonard Wood Meml. found., Washington, 1965-67, numerous univs.; prin. investigator, chmn. Expert Panel on Assessment of the Practical risk to Human Health from Nitrilotriacetic Acid in Household Laundry Product, 1984-85. Contbr. 120 articles, 30 abstracts to jours. in field; editor 32 biomed. books, monographs and conf. reports, 1941-88; mem. editorial bd. Cancer Rsch., 1949-59, Lab. Investigation, 1952-71, editor, 1967-71. Recipient Meritorious Svc. award Dept. Army, 1963, Exceptional Civilian Svc. award Dept. Army, 1965, Disting. Svc. award U. Calif. Sch. Medicine, 1988; Robert E. Stowell ann. lectureship established U. Calif. Sch. Medicine, 1991 and Am. Registry of Pathology, Washington, 1991. Mem. AMA, Am. Registry of Pathology (bd. dirs. 1976-83, exec. com. 1976-82, v.p. 1976-78, pres. 1978-79, Disting. Svc. award 1995), Am. Assn. Cancer Rsch., Am. Assn. Pathologists (Gold-headed Cane award 1990), Am. Assn. Pathologists and Bacteriologists (councilor 1965-72, v.p. 1969-70, pres. 1970-71), Am. Soc. Clin. Pathologists, Am. Soc. Exptl. Pathology (councilor 1962-66, v.p. 1963-64, pres. 1964-65), Calif. Med. Soc., Calif. Soc. Pathologists, Binford-Dammin Soc. Infectious Disease Paaholo-gists, Coll. Am. Pathologists, Histochem. Soc., Internat. Acad. Pathology (councilor 1954-61, pres.-elect 1958-59, pres. 1995-60, Disting. Svc. award 1970, Diamond Jubilee award 1981, Stowell-Orbison award established 1982—), Soc. Cryobiology (bd. govs. 1968-71), Soc. Exptl. Biology and Medicine, U.S. and Can. Acad. Pathology, Yolo County Med. Soc., Assn. Mil. Surgeons U.S. (sustaining membership award 1965), Univs. Associated for Rsch. and Edn. in Path. (bd. dirs. 1975-90, sec.-treas. 1978-82, hon. dir. 1990—), Sigma Xi, Alpha Omega Alpha. Office: Univ of Calif Sch Medicine Dept of Pathology Davis CA 95616

STOWENS, DANIEL, pathologist; b. N.Y.C., Oct. 27, 1919; s. Oscar and Rose Lillian (Galkin) S.; m. Barbara Jean Hagmann, Sept. 28, 1944 (wid. May 1984); children: Daniel W., Christopher D.; m. Lamya Mary Shaheen, Mar. 20, 1985. AB, Columbia Coll., 1941; MD, Coll. Physicians and Surgeons, N.Y.C., 1943. Diplomate Am. Bd. Pediatrics, Pathology. Intern, resident Gorgas Hosp., Ancon, Canal Zone, 1944-45; instr., med. sch. Am. Univ., Beirut, 1947-48; fellow pediatrics Ochsner Clinic and Tulane Univ., New Orleans, 1948-51; resident, pathology Walter Reed Army Hosp., Washington, 1952-53; fellow, pathology Childrens Hosp., Boston, 1953-54; chief, pediatric pathology Armed Forces Inst. Pathology, Washington, 1954-58; dir. labs., assoc. prof. Childrens' Hosp./U. So. Calif. Med. Sch., L.A., 1958-60, Childrens' Hosp./U. Louisville, 1960-65; dir. labs. St. Luke's Meml. Hosp., Utica, N.Y., 1965-85; med. dir. MDS Labs, Rome, N.Y., 1985—. Author: Pediatric Pathology, 1959, 2d edit., 1965; contbr. articles to profl. jours. Maj. U.S. Army, 1945-47. Recipient 2nd prize Am. Soc. Gastroenterology, 1960. Mem. Am. Acad. Pediatrics, Am. Soc. Clin. Pathology (Gold medal 1955), N.Y. Acad. Sci., Am. Assn. Pathology, Internat. Acad. Pathology. Avocations: gardening, reading, dermatoglyphics. Home and Office: 3214 Fountain St Clinton NY 13323-3923

STOWERS, CARLTON EUGENE, writer; b. Brownwood, Tex., Apr. 14, 1942; s. Ira Milton and Fay Eloise (Stephenson) S.; m. Patricia Ann Folks, Mar. 2, 1981; children: Anson, Ashley. Student, U. Tex., Austin, 1961-63. Sportswriter Abilene (Tex.) Reporter News, 1963-64; sports editor Roswell (N.Mex.) Daily Record, 1964-65; sportswriter Lubbock (Tex.) Avalanche Jour., 1965-67; sports editor Amarillo (Tex.) Globe News, 1967-72; reporter, columnist Dallas Morning News, 1972-81; freelance writer Cedar Hill, Tex., 1981—; editor Dallas Cowboys Weekly, 1985-89. Author: (non-fiction) The Randy Matson Story, 1971, Spirit, 1973, (with E.B. Hughes) Doc, 1976, (with Trent Jones) Where the Rainbows Wait, 1978, pub. softcover as Terlingua Teacher, 1982, (with Wilbur Evans) Champions, 1978, The Overcomers, 1978, (with Roy Rogers and Dale Evans) Happy Trails, 1979 (book clubs awards, Christian Herald Family Bookshelf main selection, selected for talking book program Nat. Library Svc. for Blind and Handicapped), The Unsinkable Titanic Thompson, 1982, softcover, 1988, Journey to Triumph, 1988 (also in Spanish), (with Steve Perkins and Greg Aiello) Dallas Cowboys Bluebook III, 1982 (Spanish lang. edit. 1982), Partners in Blue: The 100-Year History of the Dallas Police Department, 1983, Friday Night Heroes, 1983, Just One Kiss Baby, 1983, (with Greg Aiello) Dallas Cowboys Bluebook IV, 1983 (Spanish lang. edit. 1983), (with Billy Olson) Reaching Higher, 1984, The Dallas Cowboys: The First 25 Years, 1984, The Cowboy Chronicles, 1984, (ghosted for Ralph Carmichael) He's Everything To Me, 1986, (ghosted for Pam Lontos) Don't Tell Me It's Impossible Until I've Already Done It., 1988, Careless Whispers, 1986 (Edgar Allen Poe award Mystery Writers Am. 1986, Oppie award S.W. Booksellers Assn. 1986, other awards and included in talking book program), The Cotton Bowl: The First 50 Years, 1986, (with Jarret Bell) Dallas Cowboys Bluebook IX, 1988, (with William C. Dear) Please...Don't Kill Me: The True Story of the Milo Murder, 1989 (Literary Guild selection), (with Larry Wansley) The FBI Undercover: The True Story of Special Agent 'Mandrake', 1989, Innocence Lost, 1990, (childrens book) A Hero Named George, 1991, (childrens book) Hard Lessons, 1994, Open Secrets, 1994, Sins of the Son, 1995; gen. editor series 8 collections sports columns Sportswriters' Eye Series, 1988, 89; writer, producer 79-week, 30 minute news feature show Countdown to '84, official show of U.S. Olympic Com., documentary African Stars '84 for African Nat. TV., football halftime feature Greatest of the Great; writer cable TV show Polaroid's Sports Camera Internat.; co-producer TV show Texas by Land: The Story of the Sesquicentennial Wagon Train; script writer syndicated radio shows Faith Made Them Great, Inside the NFL. Bd. dirs. Cedar Hill (Tex.) Libr. Assn., 1989-92; mem. adv. bd. Kevin Curnutt Found. for Brain Injury Rsch., Arlington, Tex., 1988-89. Recipient Katie awards Dallas Press Club, 1985-92, Oppie award S.W. Booksellers, 1986, Edgar Allen Poe award for best fact crime book Mystery Writers Am., 1986, Stephen Philben awards Dallas Bar Assn., 1987-92, other journalism awards Tex. Headliners Club, William Randolph Hearst Found., UPI, other; named Best Local Writer in the 1988's, reader's poll Dallas Observer. Mem. Authors Guild Am., Mystery Writers Am., Internat. Assn. Crime Writers, Profl. Football Writers Am., Tex. Sportswriters Assn. Home: 1015 Randy Rd Cedar Hill TX 75104-3035 Office: care Janet W Manus Lit Agy Inc 417 E 57th St Apt 5D New York NY 10022-3067

STOWERS, JAMES EVANS, JR., investment company executive; b. Kansas City, Mo., Jan. 10, 1924; s. James Evans Sr. and Laura (Smith) S.; m. Virginia Ann Glasscock, Feb. 4, 1954; children: Pamela, Kathleen, James Evans III, Linda. A.B., U. Mo., 1946, B.S. in Medicine, 1947. Pres. Survivors Benefit Ins. Co., Kansas City, 1956-80; chmn. bd. Am. Century Investment Mgmt. Inc., Am. Century Cos., Inc.; Am. Century Group of Mutual Funds, Kansas City, 1958—. Author: Why Waste Your Money on Life Insurance, 1967, Principles of Financial Consulting, 1971, Yes, You Can....achieve financial independence, 1992. Co-founder, pres. Stowers Inst. for Med. Rsch., Kansas City, 1995—. Capt. USAAF, 1943-45; with USAFR, 1945-57. Mem. Kansas City C. of C., Sigma Chi. Republican. Office: Am Century Svcs 4500 Main St Kansas City MO 64111-1816

STOYKO, WILLIAM NELSON, lawyer; b. Reading, Pa., Nov. 4, 1946; s. Max and Ruth Louise S.; m. Elizabeth Emily Cox, May 24, 1983; children: Greta Elizabeth, Kira Alexandra. AB in Polit. Sci., Albright Coll., 1968; JD, Georgetown U., 1973. Assoc. Miller & Murray, Reading, Pa., 1973-76, ptnr., 1976-80; assoc. legal counsel, asst. sec. Landmark Banking Corp., Ft. Lauderdale, Fla., 1980-83; sr. legal counsel, sr. v.p. Ctrl. Fidelity Banks, Inc., Richmond, Va., 1983-87, sec., 1987—, corp. exec. officer, sr. corp. counsel, 1992-96, corp. exec. v.p., 1996—; gen. counsel Ctrl. Fidelity Nat. Bank, 1996—. Bd. dirs. Berks County Heart Assn., Reading, Pa., 1978-80, Richmond (Va.) Symphony Orch., 1992—. With USAR, 1969-75. Republican. Lutheran. Avocations: reading, painting. Office: Ctrl Fidelity Banks Inc PO Box 27602 1021 E Cary St Richmond VA 23219-4000

STRAATSMA, BRADLEY RALPH, ophthalmologist, educator; b. Grand Rapids, Mich., Dec. 29, 1927; s. Clarence Ralph and Lucretia Marie (Nicholson) S.; m. Ruth Campbell, June 16, 1951; children: Cary Ewing, Derek, Greer. Student, U. Mich., 1947; MD cum laude, Yale U., 1951; DSc (hon.), Columbia U., 1984. Diplomate Am. Bd. Ophthalmology (vice chmn. 1979, chmn. 1980). Intern New Haven Hosp., Yale U., 1951-52; resident in ophthalmology Columbia U., N.Y.C., 1955-58; spl. clin. trainee Nat. Inst. Neurol. Diseases and Blindness, Bethesda, Md., 1958-59; assoc. prof. surgery/ophthalmology UCLA Sch. Medicine, 1959-63, chief div. ophthalmology, dept. surgery, 1959-68, prof. surgery/ophthalmology, 1963-68, prof. ophthalmology, 1968—, dir. Jules Stein Eye Inst., 1964-94, chmn. dept. ophthalmology, 1968-94; ophthalmologist-in-chief UCLA Med. Ctr., 1968-94; lectr. numerous univs. and profl. socs. 1971—; cons. to surgeon gen. USPHS, mem. Vision Research Tng. Com., Nat. Inst. Neurol. Diseases and Blindness, NIH, 1959-63, mem. neurol. and sensory disease program project com., 1964-68; chmn. Vision Research Program Planning Com., Nat. Adv. Eye Council, Nat. Eye Inst., NIH, 1973-75, 75-77, 85-89; mem. med. adv. bd. Internat. Eye Found., 1970-79; mem. adv. com. on basic clin. research Nat. Soc. to Prevent Blindness, 1971-87; mem. med. adv. com. Fight for Sight, 1960-83; bd. dirs. So. Calif. Soc. to Prevent Blindness, 1967-77, Ophthalmic Pub. Co., 1975—, v.p. 1990-93, Pan-Am. Ophthalmol. Found., 1985-95; chmn. sci. adv. bd. Ctr. for Partially Sighted, 1984-87; mem. nat. adv. panel Found. for Eye Research, Inc., 1984-94; mem. cons. com. Palestra Oftalmologica Panamericana, 1976-81; coord. com. Nat. Eye Health Edn. Program, 1989; mem. sci. adv. bd. Rsch. to Prevent Blindness, Inc., 1993—; mem. Internat. Coun. Opthalmology, 1993—. Editor-in-chief Am. Jour. Ophthalmology, 1993—; mem. editorial bd. UCLA Forum in Med. Scis., 1974-82, Am. Jour. Ophthalmology, 1974-91, Am. Intra-Ocular Implant Soc. Jour., 1978-79, EYE-SAT Satellite-Relayed Profl. Edn. in Ophthalmology, 1982-86; mng. editor von Graefe's Archive for Clin. and Exptl. Ophthalmology, 1976-88; contbr. over 400 articles to med. jours. Trustee John Thomas Dye Sch., Los Angeles, 1967-72. Served to lt. USNR, 1952-54. Recipient William Warren Hoppin award N.Y. Acad. Medicine, 1956, Univ. Service award UCLA Alumni Assn., 1982, Miguel Aleman Found. medal, 1992, Benjamin Boyd Humanitarian award Pan Am. Assn. Ophthalmology, 1991, Lucian Howe medal, Am. Ophthalmological Soc., 1992. Fellow Royal Australian Coll. Ophthalmologists (hon.); mem. Academia Ophthalmologica Internationales, Am. Acad. Ophthalmology (bd. councillors 1981), Found. of Am. Acad. Ophthalmology (trustee 1989, chmn. bd. trustees 1989-92), Am. Acad. Opthalmology and Otolaryngology (pres. 1977), Am. Soc. Cataract and Refractive Surgery, AMA (asst. sec. ophthalmology sect. 1962-63, sec. 1963-66, chmn. 1966-67, council 1970-74), Am. Ophthalmol. Soc. (coun. 1985-90, v.p. 1992, pres. 1993), Assn. Research in Vision and Ophthalmology (Mildred Weisenfeld award 1991), Assn. U. Profs. of Ophthalmology (trustee 1969-75, pres.-elect 1973-74, pres. 1974-75), Assn. VA Ophthalmologists, Calif. Med. Assn. (mem. ophthalmology adv. panel 1972-94, chmn. 1974-79, sci. bd. 1973-79, ho. of dels. 1974, 77, 79), Chilean Soc. Ophthalmology (hon.), Columbian Soc. Ophthalmology (hon.), Glaucoma Soc. Internat. Congress of Ophthalmology (hon.), Heed Ophthalmic Found. (chmn., bd. dirs. 1990—), Hellenic Ophthalmol. Soc. (hon.), Internat. Coun. Ophthalmology (bd. dirs. 1993—), Los Angeles County Med. Assn., Los Angeles Soc. Ophthalmology, The Macula Soc., Pacific Coast Oto-Ophthalmol. Soc., Pan-Am. Assn. Ophthalmology (council 1972—, pres. elect 1985-87, pres. 1987-89), Peruvian Soc. Ophthalmology (hon.), The Retina Soc., Barraquer Inst. (pres. 1996—), Internat. Coun. Ophthalmology. Republican. Presbyterian. Clubs: Internat., The Jules Gonin, West Coast Retina Study. Avocations: music, tennis, scuba diving. Home: 3031 Elvido Dr Los Angeles CA 90049-1107 Office: UCLA 100 Stein Plz Los Angeles CA 90095-7065

STRACHAN, DAVID E., trade association executive; b. Pitts., June 3, 1947; s. Edward Adam and Helen Joanna (Beatty) S.; m. Judith Mary Squires, Mar. 14, 1970; children: Sarah Duff, Matthew Squires. BS, W.Va. U., 1969. Cert. assn. exec. Fin. asst. SEC, Washington, 1970-71; fin. analyst Fed. Deposit Ins. Corp., Washington, 1971-72; assoc. dir. Am. Bankers Assn., Washington, 1972-78; exec. v.p. Nat. Assn. Pers. Cons., Washington, 1978-83, D.C. Assn. Realtors, Washington, 1983-89; pres. Am. Wholesale Marketers Assn., Washington, 1989—; pres. Mgmt. and Svcs. Corp., Washington, 1991—. Contbr. articles to mags. Pres. Dist. Edn. Found., Washington, 1990—. Mem. Am. Soc. Assn. Execs., Nat. Assn. Wholesale Distbrs. Republican. Presbyterian. Avocations: boat bldg., fishing. Office: Am Wholesale Marketers 1128 16th St NW Washington DC 20036-4802

STRACHAN, DONALD M., financial executive; b. Cleve., June 24, 1923; s. Harry Morris and Eva (Maffett) S.; m. Suzanne Merion, June 27, 1953; children—William, Paul. Student, St. Catherine's Coll., Cambridge (Eng.)

U., 1945; BS, U. Pa., 1947. CPA, Ohio, W.Va. With Ernst, CPA, 1947-70; staff acct. to mgr. Ernst, CPA, Cleve., 1947-63; ptnr. Ernst, CPA, Charleston, W.Va., 1964-70; v.p. fin., treas. Cleve. Electronics, Inc., 1970-74; with Barnes, Wendling & Cook, Cleve., 1974-77; treas. McGean-Rohco, Inc., Cleve., 1977-88; pvt. practice CPA Chagrin Falls, Ohio, 1988—. Mem. Orange Sch. bd., 1994—. Served with AUS, World War II. Mem. Delta Kappa Epsilon. Mem. United Ch. Christ. Clubs: Chagrin Valley Country, City. Home: 135 Millcreek Ln Chagrin Falls OH 44022-1266

STRACHAN, GRAHAM, pharmaceutical company executive; b. Dundee, Scotland, Sept. 12, 1938; arrived in Can., 1968; s. Rosalyn and Ellen Strachan. BSc, Glasgow U., 1961, MA, 1963. Registered patent and trade agt. Licensing officer Schering Inc., Switzerland, 1963-66; v.p. bus. devel. John Labatt Ltd., Can., 1967-82; pres., chief exec. officer Allelix Biopharms., Inc., Mississauga, Ont., Can., 1982—; chmn. Nat. Biotech. Adv. Com. Fellow Patent and Trademark Inst. Can.; mem. Am. Chem. Soc., Licensing Execs. Soc., Indsl. Biotech. Assn. Can. (bd. dirs.), Biotech. Indsl. Orgn. (bd. dirs. 1985—, past pres.), Can. Genetic Diseases Network (chmn.). Achievements include several patents relating to biotechnology. Home: 40 Deane Wood crescent, Etobicoke, ON Canada M9B 3B1 Office: Allelix Biopharmaceuticals Inc, 6850 Goreway Dr, Mississauga, ON Canada L4V1P1

STRACHER, ALFRED, biochemistry educator; b. Albany, N.Y., Nov. 16, 1930; s. David and Florence (Winter) S.; m. Dorothy Altman, July 4, 1954; children: Cameron, Adam, Erica. BS in Chemistry, Rensselaer Poly. Inst., 1952; MA in Chemistry, Columbia U., 1954, PhD in Chemistry, 1956. Asst. prof. SUNY Health Sci. Ctr. at Bklyn., 1959-62, assoc. prof., 1962-68, prof. biochem., 1968—, chmn. dept., 1972—, assoc. dean for research and devel., 1982-88; cons. Nat. Inst. Neurol. Communicative Disorders and Stroke NIH, 1981-84, 85-89. Editor: Muscle and Non-Muscle Motility, 1983; editorial bd. 3 jours.; editor-in-chief: Drug Targeting and Delivery; contbr. 95 articles to profl. jours. Fellow Nat. Found. for Infantile Paralysis Rockefeller Inst. for Med. Rsch., 1956-58 and Carlsberg Lab., 1958-59, Commonwealth Fund Kings Coll. U. London, 1966-67, Guggenheim Found. Oxford U., 1973-74; career scientist grantee Health Rsch. Coun. N.Y., 1962-69. Fellow AAAS; mem. Am. Soc. for Biochemistry and Molecular Biology, Harvey Soc. (treas. 1978-83), Marine Biol. Labs. (corp. 1968—). Avocations: tennis, travel. Home: 47 The Oaks Roslyn NY 11576-1704 Office: SUNY Health Sci Ctr Bklyn 450 Clarkson Ave Brooklyn NY 11203-2012

STRACK, ALISON MERWIN, neurobiologist; b. Midland, Mich., Apr. 19, 1963; d. William James and Alice (Armstrong) S. BS, U. Mich., 1985; PhD, Washington U., St. Louis, 1990. Asst. rsch. physiologist U. Calif.-San Francisco Sch. Medicine, 1990—. Contbr. articles to profl. jours. Postdoctoral grantee Am. Heart Assn., Calif. affiliate, 1993. Mem. Soc. Neurosci. Office: U Calif-San Francisco Dept Physiology 513 Parnassus Ave # 0444 San Francisco CA 94122-2722

STRACK, HAROLD ARTHUR, retired electronics company executive, retired air force officer, planner, analyst, author, musician; b. San Francisco, Mar. 29, 1923; s. Harold Arthur and Catheryn Jenny (Johnsen) S.; m. Margaret Madeline Decker, July 31, 1945; children: Carolyn, Curtis, Tamara. Student, San Francisco Coll., 1941, Sacramento Coll., 1947, Sacramento State Coll., 1948, U. Md., 1962, Indsl. Coll. Armed Forces, 1963. Commd. 2d lt. USAAF, 1943; advanced through grades to brig. gen. USAF, 1970; comdr. 1st Radar Bomb Scoring Group Carswell AFB, Ft. Worth, 1956-59; vice comdr. 90th Strategic Missile Wing SAC Warren AFB, Cheyenne, Wyo., 1964; chief, strategic nuclear br., chmn. spl. studies group Joint Chiefs of Staff, 1965-67, dep. asst. to chmn. for strategic arms negotiations, 1968; comdr. 90th Strategic Missile Wing SAC Warren AFB, Cheyenne, 1969-71; chief Studies, Analysis and Gaming Agy. Joint Chiefs Staff, Washington, 1972-74, ret., 1974; v.p., mgr. MX Program v.p. strategic planning Northrop Electronics Divsn., Hawthorne, Calif., 1974-88; ret., 1988. 1st clarinetist, Cheyenne Symphony Orch., 1969-71. Mem. Cheyenne Frontier Days Com., 1970-71. Decorated D.S.M., Legion of Merit, D.F.C., Air medal, Purple Heart; mem. Order Pour le Merite. Mem. Inst. Nav., Am. Def. Preparedness Assn., Air Force Assn., Aerospace Edn. Found., Am. Fedn. Musicians, Cheyenne Frontier Days "Heels". Home: 707 James Ln Incline Village NV 89451-9612 *The precepts which have guided me recognize the dignity of the individual and human rights. I believe that living by the Golden Rule contributes to the quality of life by making us better and more useful citizens while favorably influencing others. Integrity, ideals, and high standards reinforce one's own character. While taking pride in accomplishment, show gratitude for opportunity and humility for success. Lead by example and always do your best. Service to humanity and country is the highest calling, and the satisfaction of a job well done, approbation, respect and true friendship are one's greatest rewards.*

STRACK, STEPHEN NAYLOR, psychologist; b. Rome, N.Y., Nov. 13, 1955; s. Ralph and Grace (Naylor) S.; m. Leni Ferrero. BA, U. Calif., Berkeley, 1978; PhD, U. Miami, Fla., 1983. Psychologist L.A. County Dept. Mental Health, 1984-85; staff psychologist VA Outpatient Clinic, L.A., 1985—, dir. tng., 1992-97; clin. assoc. U. So. Calif., L.A., 1986-95; adj. prof. Calif. Sch. Profl. Psychology, L.A., 1989—; clin. prof. Fuller Grad. Sch. Psychology, Pasadena, Calif., 1986—. Author (test): Personality Adjective Check List, 1987; co-author (book): Differentiating Normal and Abnormal Personality, 1994, Death and the Quest for Meaning, 1997; cons. editor Jour. Personality Disorders, N.Y.C., 1992—, Omega, 1997—. U.S. Dept. Vets Affairs grantee, 1986-93, 96—. Fellow APA, Soc. for Personality Assessment; mem. Internat. Soc. for the Study of Personality Disorders, Calif. Psychol. Assn., European Assn. Psychol. Assessment, Soc. for Rsch. in Psychopathology, Western Psychol. Assn., Sigma Xi. Office: VA Outpatient Clinic 351 E Temple St Los Angeles CA 90012-3328

STRADER, JAMES DAVID, lawyer; b. Pitts., June 30, 1940; s. James Lowell and Tyra Fredrika (Bjorn) S.; m. Ann Wallace, Feb. 8, 1964; children: James Jacob, Robert Benjamin. BA, Mich. State U., 1962; JD, U. Pitts., 1965. Bar: Pa. 1966, U.S. Dist. Ct. (we. dist.) Pa. 1966, U.S. Dist. Ct. (ea. dist.) Pa. 1973, U.S. Dist. Ct. (mid. dist.) Pa. 1985, U.S. Ct. Appeals (4th and 5th cirs.) 1977, U.S. Ct. Appeals (3d and 11th cirs.) 1981, U.S. Supreme Ct. 1982, W.Va. 1996. Assoc. Peacock, Keller & Yohe, Washington, 1967-68; atty. U.S. Steel Corp., Pitts., 1968-77, gen. atty. workman's compensation, 1977-84; assoc. Caroselli, Spagnolli & Beachler, Pitts., 1984-87; ptnr. Dickie, McCamey & Chilcote, Pitts., 1987—. Del. Dem. Mid-Yr. Conv., 1974; mem. Dem. Nat. Platform Com., 1976; commr. Mt. Lebanon Twp., Pa., 1974-78. Served to capt. U.S. Army, 1965-67. Mem. ABA (sr. vice-chmn. worker's compensation com. 1978-94), Pa. Bar Assn. (chmn. worker's compensation law sect. 1994-95), State Bar W.Va., Allegheny County Bar Assn., Valley Brook Country Club. Democrat. Presbyterian. Office: Dickie McCamey & Chilcote 2 Ppg Pl Ste 400 Pittsburgh PA 15222-5402

STRADER, TIMOTHY RICHARDS, lawyer; b. Portland, Oreg., Jan. 17, 1956; s. Charles J. and Carol Jane (Dwyer) S.; m. Lisa M.K. Bartholomew, May 21, 1988; children: Kelly Meehan, Erin Dwyer. BBA in Mgmt., U. Notre Dame, 1978; JD, Willamette U., Salem, Oreg., 1981; LLM in Taxation, U. Fla., Gainesville, 1982. Bar: Oreg. 1981. Assoc. McEwen, Hanna, Gisvold & Rankin, Portland, 1982-85, Bullivant, Houser, Bailey, Hanna, Portland, 1985-87, Hanna, Urbigkeit, Jensen, et al., Portland, 1987-88, Hanna, Murphy, Jensen, Holloway, Portland, 1988-89; mem. Hanna, Kerns & Strader, P.C., Portland, 1989—. Mem. editorial bd. State Bar Estate Planning Newsletter, 1987—. Mem. alumni bd. Jesuit H.S., Portland, 1982-94, trustee, 1993—; bd. dirs. Valley Cath. Sch., Beaverton, 1989-95. Mem. ABA, Multnomah Bar Assn., Multnomah Athletic Club. Office: Hanna Kerns & Strader 1300 SW 6th Ave Ste 300 Portland OR 97201-3461

STRAFFON, RALPH ATWOOD, urologist; b. Croswell, Mich., Jan. 4, 1928; s. Lloyd Atwood and Verle R. (Rice) S.; m. Cary Arden Higley, Feb. 13, 1954; children: David, Daniel, Jonathan, Peter, Andrew; m. Shirley Louise Gilmore, June 20, 1987; children: Scott, Leslie. M.D., U. Mich., 1953. Diplomate: Am. Bd. Urology. Intern, then resident in surgery Univ. Hosp., Ann Arbor, 1953-56, resident in urology, 1956-59; mem. staff Cleve. Clinic, 1956—, head dept. urology, 1963-83, chmn. div. surgery, 1983-87, vice chmn. bd. govs. and chief of staff, 1987—; practice medicine specializing in urology Cleve., 1959—. Contbr. articles to med. jours. Served with AUS, 1946-48. Fellow A.C.S.; mem. Am. Assn. Genitourinary Surgeons, AMA, Am. Urol. Assn., Cleve. Acad. Medicine, Cleve. Urol. Assn., Clin. Soc. Genitourinary Surgeons, Soc. Univ. Urologists, Frederick A. Coller Surg. Soc., Am. Soc. Nephrology, Transplantation Soc., Soc. Pelvic Surgeons, Soc. Pediatric Urology, Am. Fertility Soc., Am. Assn. Clin. Urologists, Soc. Internat. d'Urologie, Am. Surg. Assn, Royal Coll. Surgeons Edinburgh (hon. fellow), Coll. Medicine South Africa (hon. fellow). Home: 19701 Shelburne Rd Cleveland OH 44118-4959 Office: 9500 Euclid Ave Cleveland OH 44195-0001

STRAHILEVITZ, MEIR, inventor, researcher, psychiatry educator; b. Beirut, July 13, 1935; s. Jacob and Chana Strahilevitz; m. Aharona Nattiv, 1958; children: Michal, Lior. MD, Hadassah Hebrew U. Med. Sch., 1963. Diplomate Am. Bd. Psychiatry and Neurology, Royal Coll. Physicians and Surgeons Can. Asst. prof. Washington U. Med. Sch., St. Louis, 1971-74; assoc. prof. So. Ill. U., Springfield, 1974-77, U. Chgo., 1977, U. Tex. Med. Br., Galveston, 1978-81; chmn. dept. psychiatry Kaplan Hosp., Rehovot, Israel, 1987-88; clin. assoc. prof. U. Wash., Seattle, 1981-88; prof. U. Tex. Med. Sch., Houston, 1988-92. Contbr. articles to profl. jours. Fellow Am. Psychiat. Assn., Royal Coll. Physicians and Surgeons Can. Achievements include patents for immunological methods for removing species from the blood circulatory system, for treatment methods for psychoactive drug dependence, for immunological methods for treating mammals; invention of use of antibodies to receptors and their fragments as drugs, of immunoadsorption treatment of hyperlipidemia, cancer, autoimmune disease and coronary artery disease, immunoassay methods for psychoactive drugs; discovery of the protective effects of Nitric Oxide (NO) on psychiatric patients. Office: PO Box 190 Hansville WA 98340-0190

STRAHM, SAMUEL EDWARD, veterinarian; b. Fairview, Kans., Feb. 9, 1936; s. Silas Tobias and Martha Mary (Beyer) S.; m. Barbara Jean Wenger, June 1, 1958; children: Gregory Lee, Bryan Scott, Andrea Marie Enloe. BS, DVM, Kansas State U., 1959. Diplomate Nat. Acad. Practice. Owner, ptnr. Osage Animal Clinic Inc., Pawhuska, Okla., 1959—, pres., 1985—; bd. 1st Nat. Bank, Pawhuska, Okla.; mem. bd. cons. Profl. Exam Svc., 1990—; mem. adv. bd. USDA Users, 1991-95; mem. adv. com. Pew Nat. Health Profession Vet. Medicine, 1991. Mem. Okla. State Sch. Bd. Assn., 1977-94, 2d v.p., 1993, 1st v.p., 1994, pres., 1996; mem. Okla. All-State Sch. Bd., 1993; mem. Pawhuska Sch. Bd., 1974—, pres., 1991-94; mem. Pawhuska Planning Commn., 1965-70; mem. Okla. State U. Centennial Commn., Stillwater, 1986-91; chmn. Am. Vet. Med. Found., 1995—; chmn. western region Nat. Sch. Bds. Assn. 1996, bd. dirs., 1996—, exec. com., 1997—. Recipient Disting. Alumni award Coll. Vet. Medicine Kans. State U., 1994, Outstanding Svc. award Nat. Sch. Bds. Assn., 1997. Mem. Am. Vet. Med. Assn. (pres. elect 1988-89, pres. 1989-90, AVMA award 1986, Coun. on Govt. Affairs, 1992—), Am. Assn. Theriogenealogy, Am. Assn. Bovine Practitioners, Am. Assn. Vet. State Bds., Am. Vet. Med. Found. (chmn. 1995—), Nat. Bd. Vet. Med. Examiners, Okla. Vet. Med. Assn. (all offices from 1959, Veterinarian of Yr. 1990), Kans. Vet. Med. Assn., Okla. Bd. Vet. Med. Examiners (pres.), Pawhuska C. of C. (pres. 1968), Pawhuska Jaycees (all offices 1959-69), Toastmasters Club. Republican. Baptist. Avocations: gardening, fishing, flying. Home: PO Box 1256 Pawhuska OK 74056-1256 Office: Osage Animal Clinic Inc PO Box 1209 Pawhuska OK 74056-1209

STRAIGHT, RICHARD COLEMAN, photobiologist; b. Rivesville, W.Va., Sept. 8, 1937. BA, U. Utah, 1961, PhD in Molecular Biology, 1967. Asst. dir. radiation biology summer inst. U. Utah, 1961-63; supervisory chemist med. svc. VA Hosp., 1965—; dir. VA Venom Rsch. Lab., 1975—; adminstrv. officer rsch. svc. VA Ctr., 1980—; dir. Dixon laser inst. U. Utah, Salt Lake City, 1985-90; pres. Western Inst. for Biomed. Rsch., Salt Lake City, 1990—; dir. Utah Ctr. for Photo Medicine, Salt Lake City, 1993—. Assoc. editor Lasers in Surgery and Medicine, 1990-95, Jour. Biomed. Optics, 1995—. Mem. AAAS, Am. Chem. Soc., Am. Soc. Photobiology, Biophysics Soc., Am. Soc. for Laser Medicine and Surgery, Utah Life Sci. Industries Assn. (charter). Achievements include research in photodynamic action on biomonomers and biopolymers, tumor immunology, effect of antigens on mammary adenocarcinoma of C3H mice, biochemical changes in aging, venom toxicology, mechanism of action of photoactive drugs, optical imaging and spectroscopy. Office: VAMC/Univ of Utah Western Inst Biomed Rsch 500 Foothill Dr Salt Lake City UT 84148-0001

STRAIN, EDWARD RICHARD, psychologist; b. Indpls., Apr. 12, 1925; s. Edward Richard and Ernestine (Kidd) S.; m. Marsha Ellen Beeler, 1972; children: Douglas MacDonald, Elizabeth Stacy, Chadwick Edward, Sarah Abigail, Zachary Richard. AB, Butler U., 1948; PhD, Duke U., 1952. Clin. psychologist Ohio State Med. Ctr., Columbus, 1952-53, Ind. U. Med. Ctr., Indpls., 1953-56; pvt. practice cons. psychology Indpls., 1956—; lectr. dept. psychology Butler U., Indpls., 1958-68; pres. Marion County (Ind.) Mental Health Assn., 1967-69. Mem. 500 Festival Assocs., Indpls., 1961—; pres. Perry Twp. (Ind.) Rep. Club, 1968-69; founder Downtown Sr. Citizens Ctr., 1961; vestryman Episcopal Ch., 1975-77, 86-88, sr. warden, 1976-77. Recipient Disting. Tech. Alumni award Arsenal Tech. H.S., 1993, Hansen H. Anderson Cmty. Svc. Merit medal Arsenal Tech. H.S., 1994. Mem. Masons, Rotary, Indpls. Club, Athletic Club, Indpls. Press Club. Office: 17 W Market St Ste 750 Indianapolis IN 46204-2929

STRAIN, JAMES ELLSWORTH, pediatrician, retired association administrator; b. Lincoln, Nebr., Apr. 23, 1923; s. Elmer Ellsworth and Tessa Elizabeth (Stevens) S.; m. Ruby Lee Shepard; children: James A., John D., Janet M. Strain McKinney, Jeffrey Lee Phillips-Strain. AB, Phillips U., Enid, Okla., 1945; MD, U. Colo., Denver, 1947. Diplomate Am. Bd. Pediatrics (examiner 1984-89, mem. 1989-93, emeritus mem. 1993—). Intern Mpls. Gen. Hosp., 1947-48; resident in pediatrics Denver Children's Hosp., 1948-50, pres. med. staff, 1964, dir. genetic unit, 1982-86; pvt. practice specializing in pediatrics, Denver, 1950-86; exec. dir. Am. Acad. Pediatrics, Elk Grove Village, Ill., 1986-93, ret., 1993; pres. med. bd. Colo. Gen. Hosp., 1969-70; clin. prof. pediatrics U. Colo. Med. Ctr., 1969-86, 93—, U. Chgo., 1987-93; mem. Colo. Med. Adv. Coun. for Title 19, 1968-75, chmn., 1968-71; mem. Task Force on Iowa Health Care Stds. Project, 1984-85; presenter numerous profl. confs. Mem. editorial bd. Pediatrics in Rev.; reviewer Jour. Pediatrics; contbr. articlest to profl. publs. Mem. Colo. Commn. on Children and Youth, 1971-75; trustee Phillips U., 1974—. Capt. U.S. Army, 1953-55. Recipient Disting. Alumnus award Phillips U., 1974, Florence Sabin award U. Colo., 1984, Excellence in Pub. Svc. award U.S. Surgeon Gen., 1988, Abraham Jacobi award AMA and Am. Acad. Pediatrics, 1994; James E. Strain Child Advocacy award established in his name Denver Children's Hosp., 1983. Fellow Am. Acad. Pediatrics (numerous offices and com. memberships at chpt., dist. and nat. level, including pres. 1982-83, Clifford Grulee award 1985); mem. APHA, AMA (mem. coun. sect. pediatrics 1971-93, chmn. coun. 1974-79, sect. del. 1978-79), Colo. Med. Soc. (mem. coun. dels. 1964-80), Denver Med. Soc. (mem. coun. dels. 1964-80), Can. Pediatric Soc., Ambulatory Pediatric Assn., Inst. Medicine, Alpha Omega Alpha. Republican. Mem. Disciples of Christ. Avocations: fishing, sports, reading.

STRAIT, ALMUTH VANDIVEER, dentist; b. Yonkers, N.Y., June 29, 1938; s. Almuth Vandiveer Strait and Hilda Louise (Brandt) Cardwell; m. Kathleen Joan Milligan, Dec. 21, 1963 (div. May 1981); m. Julia Elizabeth Roskos, Mar. 11, 1993; children: Jonathan Vandiveer, Tara Elizabeth, Tiffany Louise. BA in Bacteriology/Zoology, U. Conn., 1961; DDS, Temple U., 1965; cert. in periodontics, Ind. U., 1967. Cert. in implantology, periodontics, cosmetic dentistry. Grad. asst. bacteriology dept. U. Conn., Storrs, 1961, Temple U., Phila., 1962-64; pvt. practice assoc. R.H. Ernsting, Indpls., 1966; chief periodontics, preventive dentistry officer USN Dental Corps, Boston, 1967-68; rschr. Chelsea (Mass.) Naval Hosp., 1968; pvt. practice Old Greenwich, Conn., 1969—; mem. staff Greenwich (Conn.) Hosp. Dental Clinic, 1971—; exec. dir. Old Greenwich Dental Assocs., Inc., 1986—; dir. Dental Careers Found., Old Greenwich, 1992—. Past deacon First Congl. Ch. Lt. USN, 1962-69. Mem. Am. Soc. Periodontics, Am. Acad. Cosmetic Dentistry, Am. Analgesia Soc., Acad. Gen. Dentistry (Conn. chpt.), Fedn. Dentaire Internat., Conn. State Dental Assn., Greenwich Dental Soc. (past pres.), Western Fairfield Dental Soc., Xi Psi Phi, Beta Sigma Gamma (v.p.), Indian Harbor Yacht Club. Republican. Avocations: tennis, sailing, skiing, wood carving, chess. Office: Old Greenwich Dental Assocs 182 Sound Beach Ave Old Greenwich CT 06870-1730

STRAIT, GEORGE, country music vocalist; b. Pearsall, Tex., 1952; m. Norma. Degree in Agr., S.W. Tex. State U. Albums include Blue Clear Sky (Country Music Assn. Album of Yr. 1996), Strait Out of the Box (boxed set), Easy Come, Easy Go, Right or Wrong, Strait from the Heart, Strait Country, Does Ft. Worth Ever Cross Your Mind, 1985 (Country Music Assn. Album of Yr. 1985), Pure Country, 1986, No. 7, Something Special, 1986, Ocean Front Property, 1987, If You Aint Lovin' (You Aint Livin'), 1988, Beyond the Blue Neon, 1989, Livin' It Up, 1990, Ten Strait Hits, 1991, Chill of An Early Fall, 1991, Greatest Hits Volume I, II, Lead On, other platinum albums; #1 country hits include Fool Hearted Memory, 1982, Amarillo By Morning, 1983, You Look So Good in Love, 1984, The Chair, 1986, Baby Blue, 1989, Beyond the Blue Moon, 1989, Baby's Gotten Good At Goodbye, 1989, Love Without End, Amen, 1990, I've Come to Expect It From You, 1990, Chill of An Early Fall, 1991, If I Know Me, 1991, The Big One, 1995; (movie) Pure Country, 1992. Served with U.S. Army, until 1975. Recipient Entertainer of Yr. award Country Music Assn., 1989, 90, Entertainer of Yr. award Acad. Country Music, 1990; named Male Vocalist of Yr. Country Music Assn., 1985, 86, 96, Male Vocalist of Yr. Acad. Country Music, 1984, 85, 89, SRO Touring Artist of Yr., 1990, Top Country Vocalist Am. Music Awards, 1991.

STRAITON, ARCHIE WAUGH, electrical engineering educator; b. Arlington, Tex., Aug. 27, 1907; s. John and Jeannie (Waugh) S.; m. Esther McDonald, Dec. 28, 1932; children: Janelle (Mrs. Thomas Henry Holman), Carolyn (Mrs. John Erlinger). BSEE, U. Tex., 1929, MA, 1931, PhD, 1939. Engr. Bell Telephone Labs., N.Y.C., 1929-30; from instr. to assoc. prof. Tex. Coll. Arts and Industries, 1931-41, prof., 1941-43, head dept. engring., 1941-43; faculty U. Tex., Austin, 1943—; prof. U. Tex., 1948-63, dir. elec. engring. research lab., 1947-72, Ashbel Smith prof. elec. engring., 1963-89, Ashbel Smith prof. emeritus, 1989—, chmn. dept., 1966-71, acting v.p., grad. dean, 1972-73. Contbr. articles to profl. jours. Fellow IEEE (Thomas A. Edison medal 1990); mem. NAE, Sigma Xi, Tau Beta Pi, Eta Kappa Nu. Home: 4212 Far West Blvd Austin TX 78731-2804

STRAKA, LASZLO RICHARD, publishing consultant; b. Budapest, Hungary, June 22, 1934; came to U.S., 1950, naturalized, 1956; s. Richard J. and Elisabeth (Roeck) S.; m. Eva K. von Viczian, Jan. 20, 1962 (div. May 1981); children: Eva M., Monika E., Viktoria K. B.A. cum laude, NYU, 1959. Acct. Greatrex Ltd., N.Y.C., 1952-53; pres. Maxwell Macmillan Internat. Pub. Group, N.Y.C., 1991-92; with Pergamon Press, Inc., Elmsford, N.Y., 1954-90, v.p., 1964-68, exec. v.p., treas., 1968-74, pres., 1974-75, 80-88, chmn. bd., 1975-77, 88-90, vice chmn. bd., 1977-80, 88-89, also dir.; vice chmn. bd. Pergamon Books Ltd., Oxford, Eng., 1986-88; group v.p. Macmillan Inc., N.Y.C., 1989-91; pub. cons., 1992—; treas. Brit. Book Centre, Inc., N.Y.C., 1956-67; pres. Pergamon Holding Corp., 1981-86; chmn. bd. Microforms Internat., Inc., 1971-87. d. dirs., sec. Szechenyi Istvan Soc., N.Y.C., 1967-80, 89-93. Mem. Phi Beta Kappa. Club: K.C. Home and Office: 80 Radnor Ave Croton On Hudson NY 10520-2610

STRALEM, PIERRE, retired stockbroker; b. Chappaqua, N.Y., Oct. 17, 1909; s. Casimir Ignace and Edithe (Neustadt) S.; m. Nancy Lou D.A. Coffyn, June 11, 1936 (dec. Aug. 1995). A.B., Princeton, 1932. With Hallgarten & Co. (mems. N.Y. Stock Exchange), 1933—, partner, 1941-74; v.p., dir. Moseley Hallgarten Estabrook & Weeden Inc., 1974-79. Bd. dirs. George Jr. Republic. Mem. Court Club (Princeton, N.J.), Princeton Club (N.Y.C.). Home: 651 Bering Dr Houston TX 77057-2133

STRALEY, RUTH A. STEWART, federal agency administrator, small business owner; b. Tanner, W.Va., May 31, 1949; d. Robert Sherwood Sr. and Reta Virginia (Frymier) Stewart; m. Charles Edward Straley, Aug. 17, 1968. BS magna cum laude, U. Md., 1982. Cert. govt. fin. mgr. Budget asst. Naval Weather Svc. Command, Washington, 1972-76; budget analyst Navy Recruiting Exhibit Ctr., Washington, 1976-78, Navy Regional Data Automation Command, Washington, 1978-80; hdqrs. budget officer Naval Facilities Engring. Command, Alexandria, Va., 1980-83; fin. mgr. Naval Res. Readiness Command Region 8, Naval Air Sta., Jacksonville, Fla., 1983-93; owner, pres. Horizons Unltd. Planning Svcs., Orange Park, Fla., 1989—; comptr. Naval Pers. Support Activity Europe, Naples, Italy, 1993-94; comptroller U.S. Naval Sta., San Diego, 1994—. Treas. Eagle Bay Homeowners Assn., Orange Park, 1989-93. Named Woman of Yr., Fed. Women's Program, 1983. Mem. NAFE, Am. Soc. Mil. Comptrs. (sec. 1984-89, v.p. 1990-91, 95-96, pres. 1989-90, 91-93), Profl. Housing Mgmt. Assn., Assn. Govt. Accts. Republican. Methodist. Avocations: writing, reading, walking, gardening. Home: 432 C Ave Coronado CA 92118-1823 Office: Horizons Unltd Planning Svc PO Box 181611 Coronado CA 92178-1611

STRALING, PHILLIP FRANCIS, bishop; b. San Bernardino, Calif., Apr. 25, 1933; s. Sylvester J. and Florence E. (Robinson) S. BA, U. San Diego, 1963; MS in Child and Family Counseling, San Diego State U., 1971. Ordained priest Roman Catholic Ch., 1959, consecrated bishop, 1978. Mem. faculty St. John Acad., El Cajon, Calif., 1959-60, St. Therese Acad., San Diego, 1960-63; chaplain Newman Club, San Diego State U., 1960-72; mem. faculty St. Francis Sem., San Diego, 1972-76; pastor Holy Rosary Parish, San Bernardino, 1976-78; bishop Diocese of San Bernardino, 1978-95; pub. Inland Cath. newspaper, 1979-95; chmn. com. on lay ministry U.S. Cath. Conf./Nat. Cath. Conf. Bishops, 1993—; bishop of Reno, Nev., 1995—; bd. dirs. Calif. Assn. Cath. Campus Mins., 1960s; exec. sec. Diocesan Synod II, 1972-76; Episcopal vicar San Bernardino Deanery, 1976-78. Mem. Nat. Cath. Campus Ministries Assn. (bishop rep. 1992—). Office: PO Box 1211 Reno NV 89504-1211

STRAM, HANK LOUIS, former professional football coach, television and radio commentator; b. Chgo., Jan. 3, 1923; s. Henry L. and Nellie (Boots) S.; m. Phyllis Marie Pesha, Nov. 27, 1953; children: Henry Raymond, Dale Alan, Stuart Madison, Julia Anne, Gary Baxter, Mary Nell. Grad., Purdue U., 1948. Offensive football coach, head baseball coach Purdue U., 1948-55; offensive football coach So. Meth. U., 1956, Notre Dame U., 1958, U. Miami, 1959; head football coach Kansas City Chiefs, 1960-74, New Orleans Saints, 1976-77; color commentator CBS Sports, N.Y.C., 1978—, CBS Radio Football Broadcasts, 1978-85. Served with USAAF, 1943-46. Recipient Big 10 medal for athletes and scholarship Big 10 Conf., 1948; named Profl. Football Coach of Year Knute Rockne Club Am. and Ft. Lauderdale Touchdown Club, 1962. Office: care CBS Sports 51 W 52nd St New York NY 10019-6119*

STRANAHAN, ROBERT PAUL, JR., lawyer; b. Louisville, Oct. 29, 1929; s. Robert Paul and Anna May (Payne) S.; m. Louise Perry, May 12, 1956; children: Susan Dial, Robert Paul, Carol Payne. A.B., Princeton U., 1951; J.D., Harvard U., 1954. Bar: D.C. 1954, Md. 1964. Assoc. Wilmer & Broun, Washington, 1957-62; ptnr. Wilmer, Cutler & Pickering, Washington, 1963-94, of counsel, 1995-96; professorial lectr. Nat. Law Ctr., George Washington U., 1969-72. Served to 1st lt. USMCR, 1954-57. Mem. ABA, D.C. Bar Assn., Met. Club (Washington), Gridiron Club (Washington), Chevy Chase (Md.) Club. Home: 5316 Cardinal Ct Bethesda MD 20816-2908 Office: Wilmer Cutler & Pickering 2445 M St NW Washington DC 20037-1435

STRAND, CURT ROBERT, hotel executive; b. Vienna, Austria, Nov. 13, 1920; naturalized Am. citizen, 1943; m. Fleur Lillian Emanuel, June 14, 1946; 1 child, Karen. B.S., Cornell U., 1943. Supt. service Plaza, N.Y.C., 1947-49; asst. to v.p. Hilton Hotels Corp., 1949-53; v.p. Hilton Internat. Co., N.Y.C., 1953-64, exec. v.p., 1964-67, pres., chief exec. officer, 1967-86; chmn. Hilton Internat. Co., 1986-87; sr. v.p., dir. Trans World Air Lines, Inc.; lectr. Cornell U. Sch. Hotel Adminstrn., Ecole Superieure de Scis. Econs., Paris, NYU, Houston U.; sr. cons. Am. Express; mem. adv. panel com. Am. Hotel and Motel Assn. Mem. coun. Cornell U.; adv. bd. Aspen Found.; bd. govs. Snowmass Resort Assn., also pres.; fellow Aspen Inst. Mem. Cornell Soc. Hotelmen (Hotelier of Yr. 1986). Home: 340 E 64th St New York NY 10021-7503 Office: Am Express Tower World Fin Ctr New York NY 10285

STRAND, DEAN PAUL, disc jockey, audio engineer; b. Robbinsdale, Minn., Sept. 23, 1963; s. Gerald Everett and Sharron Elaine (Ubelhoer) S. Grad. high sch., Pine City, Minn., 1981. Lic. radio FCC. Disc jockey Skateland, Osseo, Minn., 1984-88, Glitz DJ Sound & Light Show, Mpls., 1984-89, Sta. KMOJ Radio, Mpls., 1986-88; disc jockey Today's Music Prodns., Mpls., 1989-97, Muscatine, Iowa, 1997—; audio engr., instr. Glitz

DJ Sound & Light Show, Mpls., 1986-89, Today's Music Prodns., Mpls., 1989-97, Muscatine, 1997—. Actor-dir. (cable TV music video) Tyrant Rocks the Oldies, 1984; disc jockey, audio engr. Fester's Lab, 1985—, Fester's Ravemixes, 1994—. Democrat. Mem. New Age Ch. Avocations: music, bowling, electronics, audio, dancing. Office: Today's Music Prodns 157 Sand Run Rd Muscatine IA 52761-9372

STRAND, MARION DELORES, social service administrator; b. Kansas City, Mo., Dec. 19, 1927; d. Henry Franklin and Julia Twyman (Noland) Pugh; m. Robert Carmen Scipioni, Aug. 2, 1947 (dec. 1984); children: Mark, Brian, Roberta, Laura, Steven, Mary,Angela, Julie, Victor, Robert, Lawrence; m. Donald John Strand, Sept. 1, 1985. BA, U. Kans., 1948; MS, SUNY, Brockport, 1975. Counselor N.Y. Dept. Labor, Rochester, 1971-75, 77-79; regulatory adminstr. N.Y. Dept. Social Svcs., Rochester, 1976-77, 79-81; pres. Greater Rochester Svcs., Inc. (doing bus. as Scribes & Scripts), 1982—; founder Ctr. for Law Access and Document Preparation. Columnist, local newspaper. Active polit. campaigns for women candidates, 1981—; UN envoy Unitarian Ch., Rochester, 1988-92; fin. chair William Warfield Scholarship Com., Rochester, 1988-90; chair bd. govt. affairs Genesee Valley Arthritis Found., Rochester, 1988-90; mem. parade com. 95/75 Celebration of Monroe County, 1995; mem. Lyell Av. Revitalization Com. Mem. NOW (pres. child care com. Greater Rochester sect. 1987-88, chair family issues task force), AAUW (bd. dirs., cmty. rep. Greater Rochester br., pres.-elect Greater Rochester br.), DAR (Irondequoit chpt.), Greater Rochester C. of C. (legis. com., small bus. coun. 1987—, bd. dirs. women's coun. 1981-91, pres. 1989-90), Susan B. Anthony Rep. Women's Club (program com., 1st v.p. 1994, co-chair Greater Rochester Coalition for Choice 1994-95) Golden Girls Investment Club (founder), Phi Beta Kappa, Psi Chi. Avocations: tennis, golf, art, organ playing. Home and Office: Greater Rochester Svcs Inc 105 Elmwood Ter Rochester NY 14620-3703

STRAND, NEAL ARNOLD, retired county government official; b. Canton, S.D., Mar. 25, 1924; s. Henry N. and Alma Augusta E. Strand; m. Alice E. Wolden, Aug. 19, 1979. Student, S.D. State U. County auditor Lincoln County, Canton, 1960-62; state senator S.D. State Legislature, Pierre, 1963-69; treas. State of S.D., Pierre, 1969-73; exec. dir. S.D. Assn. County Commrs., Pierre, 1973-89; county commr. County of Pennington, Rapid City, S.D., 1991-94; mem. S.D. Ho. of Reps., 1993-96, ret., 1996; mem. coun. Bur. Land Mgmt., Miles City, Mont., 1986-92; clk. sch. bd., Canton, 1966. Sgt. U.S. Army, 1945-46, PTO. Republican. Avocation: music. Home: 4822 Powderhorn Dr Rapid City SD 57702-4801 Office: Pennington County Courthouse E Saint Joe Rapid City SD 57702

STRAND, ROGER GORDON, federal judge; b. Peekskill, N.Y., Apr. 28, 1934; s. Ernest Gordon Strand and Lisabeth Laurine (Phin) Steinmetz; m. Joan Williams, Nov. 25, 1961. AB, Hamilton Coll., 1955; LLB, Cornell U., 1961; grad., Nat. Coll. State Trial Judges, 1968. Bar: Ariz. 1961, U.S. Dist. Ct. Ariz. 1961, U.S. Supreme Ct. 1980. Assoc. Fennemore, Craig, Allen & McClennen, Phoenix, 1961-67; judge Ariz. Superior Ct., Phoenix, 1967-85, U.S. Dist. Ct. Ariz., Phoenix, 1985—; assoc. presiding judge Ariz. Superior Ct., 1971-85; lectr. Nat. Jud. Coll., Reno, 1978-87. Past pres. cen. Ariz. chpt. Arthritis Found. Lt. USN, 1955-61. Mem. ABA, Ariz. Bar Assn., Maricopa County Bar Assn., Nat. Conf. Fed. Trial Judges, Phi Delta Phi, Aircraft Owners and Pilots Assn. Lodge: Rotary. Avocations: computer applications, golf, fishing. Home: 5825 N 3rd Ave Phoenix AZ 85013-1537 Office: US Dist Ct Courthouse and Fed Bldg 230 N 1st Ave Ste 3013 Phoenix AZ 85025-0002

STRANDBERG, MALCOM WOODROW PERSHING, physicist; b. Box Elder, Mont., Mar. 9, 1919; s. Malcom and Ingeborg (Riestad) S.; m. Harriet Elisabeth Bennett, Aug. 2, 1947 (dec.); children—Josiah R.W., Susan Abby, Elisabeth G., Malcom B. S.B., Harvard Coll., 1941; Ph.D., M.I.T., 1948. Research asso. M.I.T., Cambridge, 1941-48; asst. prof. physics M.I.T., 1948-53, asso. prof., 1953-60, prof., 1960-88, prof. emeritus, 1988—. Author: Microwave Spectroscopy, 1954. Fellow Am. Phys. Soc., Am. Acad. Arts and Scis., IEEE, AAAS; mem. Am. Assn. Physics Tchrs. Episcopalian. Patentee in field. Home: 82 Larchwood Dr Cambridge MA 02138-4639 Office: Mass Inst Tech 26-353 Cambridge MA 02139

STRANDBERG, REBECCA NEWMAN, lawyer; b. Ft. Smith, Ark., Apr. 22, 1951; d. Russell Lynn and Doris Jean (Lindsey) Newman; m. Jeffrey Eugene Strandberg, Nov. 23, 1979; children: Lindsey Katherine, Russell Jeffrey. BA, Tex. Christian U., 1973; JD, So. Meth. U., 1976. Bar: Tex. 1976, Md. 1981, D.C. 1983. Field atty. NLRB, New Orleans, 1976-79; legis. asst. Senator Dale Bumpers, Washington, 1979-81; pvt. practice, Montgomery County, Md., 1981-92; ptnr. Carlin & Strandberg PA, Bethesda, Md., 1992-96; prin. Rebecca Strandberg & Assocs. PA, 1996—; mem. Gov.'s Trial Ct. Nominated Commn., 1996—. Vice-pres. bd. dirs. Share-A-Ride Corp., Montgomery County, 1984; bd. mgrs. Woodside Meth. Ch., 1989-92; mem. Holy Cross Community Hosp Quality Evaluation Com., 1989—; CLE chmn. Montgomery County Bar: Am. Inns of Ct., 1990-92. Named Chmn. of Yr. Montgomery County Bar, 1992-93. Mem. ABA (litigation, labor and employment law sect. 1985—), Md. State Bar (bd. govs. 1992—, spl. com. devel. guidelines for prevention of sexual harassment 1994—, co-chair centenial pub. svc. project subcom.), Silver Spring C. of C., Montgomery County Women's Bar Assn. (chmn. membership 1982-83), Md. Women's Bar Assn., Silver Spring Bus. and Profl. Women (pres. 1984-85), SBA Women in Bus. (advocate 1982), Women's Bar D.C. Office: Rebecca Strandberg & Assocs PA 4405 E West Hwy Ste 402 Bethesda MD 20814-4535

STRANDJORD, PAUL EDPHIL, physician, educator; b. Mpls., Apr. 5, 1931; s. Edphil Nels and RuBelle Pearl (Corneliusen) S.; m. Margaret Thomas, June 27, 1953; children: Thomas Paul, Scott Nels. BA, U. Minn., 1951, MA, 1952; MD, Stanford U., 1959. Intern U. Minn., Mpls., 1959-60; resident U. Minn., 1960-63, dir. div. chemistry, dept. lab. medicine, 1963-69, asso. dir. clin. labs. dept. lab. medicine, 1967-69; asso. prof. lab. medicine U. Wash., 1969, prof., chmn. dept. lab. medicine, 1969—; prof. emeritus, 1994—; cons. VA Hosps. Author: (with E.S. Benson) Multiple Laboratory Screening, 1969, (with G. Schmer) Coagulation-Current Research and Clinical Applications, 1973. Pres. U. Wash. Physicians. With USN, 1952-55. Recipient Borden award Stanford U., 1959, Watson award U. Minn., 1962, Gerald T. Evans award Acad. Clin. Lab. Physicians and Scientists, 1976. Fellow Am. Soc. Clin. Pathologists; mem. AAAS, Acad. Clin. Lab. Physicians and Scientists (pres.), Am. Assn. Clin. Chemistry, Am. Chem. Soc., Am. Fedn. Clin. Research, Internat. Acad. Pathology, Assn. Pathology Chmn. Home: 9410 Lake Washington Blvd NE Bellevue WA 98004-5409 Office: U Wash Dept Lab Medicine SB-10 Seattle WA 98195

STRANDNESS, DONALD EUGENE, JR., surgeon; b. Bowman, N.D., Sept. 22, 1928; s. Donald Eugene and Merinda Clarine (Peterson) S.; m. Edith V., June 30, 1957; children: Erik Lee, Tracy Lynn, Jill Marie, Sandra Kay. BA, Pacific Lutheran U., 1950; MD, U. Wash., 1954. From instr. to prof. U. Wash., Seattle, 1962—; chief div. vascular surgery U. Wash., 1975-95. Served to capt. USAF, 1957-59. Recipient disting. alumnus award Pacific Lutheran U., 1980. Fellow Soc. for Vascular Surgery (pres. 1988); mem. Am. Coll. Surgeons, Am. Surg. Assn. Republican. Lutheran. Avocations: tennis, reading. Office: U Wash Dept Surgery 1959 NE Pacific St Seattle WA 98195-0004

STRANDQUIST, JOHN HERBERT, association executive; b. Menominee, Mich., June 29, 1929; s. John H. and Mary A. (Van Calligan) S.; m. Mary Gabrielle Thomas, Nov. 22, 1952; children: John H. III, Mark J., Michael T., Julie P. Headland, Bridget M. Mills, Blaise R., Skye M. Kirby, Peter S. BA, George Washington U., 1968. Cert. assn. exec., Am. Soc. Assn. Execs.; sr. profl. in human resources, Soc. Human Resource Mgmt. Enlisted USMC, 1948, advanced through ranks to lt. col., 1967, retired, 1973; asst. v.p. George Washington U., Washington, 1973-77; sr. v.p. Soc. for Human Resource Mgmt., Alexandria, Va., 1977-90; pres. Am. Assn. of Motor Vehicle Adminstrs., Arlington, Va., 1990—, also bd. dirs.; bd. dirs. AAMVAnet, Inc., IRP, Inc., Arlington. Mem. Belle Haven Country Club, Rotary (Paul Harris fellow 1992). Avocations: golf, sailing. Office: Am Assn Motor Vehicle Admns 4301 Wilson Blvd Ste 400 Arlington VA 22203-1819

STRANG, CHARLES DANIEL, marine engine manufacturing company executive; b. Bklyn., Apr. 12, 1921; s. Charles Daniel and Anna Lincoln (Endner) S. B.M.E., Poly. Inst. Bklyn., 1943. Mem. mech. engring. staff MIT, 1947-51; v.p. engring., exec. v.p. Kiekhaefer Corp. div. Brunswick Corp., Fond du Lac, Wis., 1951-64; v.p. marine engring. Outboard Marine Corp., Waukegan, Ill., 1966-68; exec. v.p. Outboard Marine Corp., 1968-74, pres., gen. mgr., 1974-80, pres., CEO, 1980-82, chmn. bd., CEO, 1982-90, chmn., 1990-93; bd. dirs., chmn. mgmt. rev. com. Outboard Marine Corp., Waukegan, 1993—. Patentee engine design and marine propulsion equipment; contbr. research papers to sci. publs. Bd. dirs. Poly. Inst. N.Y. Served with USAAF, 1944-47. Mem. Am. Power Boat Assn. (past pres.), Soc. Automotive Engrs., Union Internat. Motorboating (continental v.p. N.Am.), Sigma Xi. Home: 25679 W Florence Ave Antioch IL 60002-8734

STRANG, JAMES DENNIS, editor; b. Ashtabula, Ohio, June 23, 1945; s. Delbert Devoe and Mildred Edith (Green) S.; m. Margaret Florence Littell, Aug. 25, 1974; children: Megan Lisbeth, Amy Colleen, Benjamin Jefferson. BS in Journalism, Kent State U., 1969. Cert. firearms instr. Reporter The Star-Beacon, Ashtabula, Ohio, 1966, The Record-Courier, Kent, Ohio, 1966-69, The Cleve. Press, 1969-71; cons. Tom Rall & Assocs., Washington, 1971-72; reporter, editor The Plain Dealer, Cleve., 1973—; instr. journalism Lorain County C.C., Elyria, Ohio, 1973-74. Recipient Nat. Comdrs. award DAV, 1980, Best Editorial award AP Soc. Ohio, 1988. Mem. Nat. Conf. Editorial Writers, Soc. Profl. Journalists, Nat. Rifle Assn. (life). Unitarian-Universalist. Avocation: shooting sports. Office: The Plain Dealer 1801 Superior Ave E Cleveland OH 44114-2107

STRANG, RUTH HANCOCK, pediatric educator, pediatric cardiologist, priest; b. Bridgeport, Conn., Mar. 11, 1923; d. Robert Hallock Wright and Ruth (Hancock) S. BA, Wellesley Coll., 1944, postgrad., 1944-45; MD, N.Y. Med. Coll., 1949; MDiv, Seabury Western Theol. Sem., 1993. Diplomate Am. Bd. Pediat.; ordained deacon Episc. Ch., 1993, priest, 1994. Intern Flower and Fifth Ave. Hosp., N.Y.C., 1949-50, resident in pediatrics, 1950-52; mem. faculty N.Y. Med. Coll., N.Y.C., 1952-57; fellow cardiology Babies Hosp., N.Y.C., 1956-57, Harriet Lane Cardiac Clinic, Johns Hopkins Hosp., Balt., 1957-59, Children's Hosp., Boston, 1959-62; mem. faculty U. Mich., Univ. Hosp., Ann Arbor, 1962-89, prof. pediatrics, 1970-89, prof. emeritus, 1989—; priest-in-charge St. Johns Episcopal Ch., Howell, Mich., 1994—; dir. pediatrics Wayne County Gen. Hosp., Westland, Mich, 1965-85; mem. staff U. Mich. Hosps.; mem. med. adv. com. Wayne County chpt. Nat. Cystic Fibrosis Rsch. Found., 1966-80, chmn. med. adv. com. nat. found., Detroit, 1971-78; cons. cardiology Plymouth (Mich.) State Home and Tng. Sch., 1970-81. Author: Clinical Aspects of Operable Heart Disease, 1968; contbr. numerous articles to profl. jours. Mem. citizen's adv. coun. to Juvenile Ct., Ann Arbor, 1968-76; mem. med. adv. bd. Ann Arbor Continuing Edn. Dept., 1968-77; mem. Diocesan Com. for World Relief, Detroit, 1970-72, Am. Heart Assn. Mich. (v.p. 1989, pres. 1991); trustee Episcopal Med. Chaplaincy, Ann Arbor, 1971-96; mem. bishop's com. St. Aidan's Episc. Ch., 1966-69, sec., 1966-68, vestry, 1973-76, 78-80, 84-86, 90-91, sr. warden, 1975, 76, 78, 80, 86, 90; del. Episc. Diocesan Conv., 1980, 91; bd. dirs. Livingston Cmty. Hospice, 1995—, Emrich Conf. Ctr., 1997—; mem. Congl. Life Circle, Episcopal Diocese Mich., 1995—, mem. loans and grants com., 1995—. mem. com. on reference ann. diocesan conv., 1995-97, chmn., 1996. Mem. AMA, Am. Acad. Pediatrics, Am. Coll. Cardiology, Mich. Med. Soc., Washtenaw County Med. Soc., N.Y. Acad. Medicine, Am. Heart Assn., Women's Rsch. Club (membership sec. 1966-67), Ambulatory Pediatric Assn., Am. Assn. Child Care in Hosps., Am. Assn. Med. Colls., Assn. Faculties of Pediatric Nurse Assn./Practitioners Programs (pres. 1978-81, exec. com. 1981-84), Episc. Clergy Assn. Mich., Northside Assn. Ministries (pres. 1975, 76, 79-80). Home: 4500 E Huron River Dr Ann Arbor MI 48105-9335

STRANG, SANDRA LEE, airline official; b. Greensboro, N.C., Apr. 22, 1936; d. Charles Edward and Lobelia Mae (Squires) S.; BA in English, U. N.C., 1960; MBA, U. Dallas, 1970. With American Airlines, Inc., 1960—, mgr. career devel. for women, N.Y.C., 1972-73, dir. selection and tng., 1974-75, sr. dir. selection, tng. and affirmative action, 1975-79, sr. dir. compensation and benefits, Dallas/Ft. Worth, Tex., 1979-84, dir. passenger sales tng. and devel., 1984—; regional sales mgr. Rocky Mountain Region, Denver, 1985—; pres. The SLS Group, Inc., (DBAs) Sales Leadership Seminars, Inc., Sr. Leadership Svcs., Inc., Svc. Leadership Seminars, Inc., Speakers, Lectrs., and Seminars, Inc, 1988—. AARP, Mem. Am. Mgmt. Assn., Assn. Advancement of Women into Mgmt., Am. Soc. Tng. and Devel., Am. Compensation Assn., Internat. Platform Assn. Home: 3493 E Euclid Ave Littleton CO 80121-3663

STRANG, STEPHEN EDWARD, magazine editor, publisher; b. Springfield, Mo., Jan. 31, 1951; s. A. Edward and Amy Alice (Farley) S.; m. Joy Darlene Ferrell, Aug. 19, 1972; children: Cameron Edward, Chandler Stephen. BS in Journalism, U. Fla., Gainesville, 1973; LittD (hon.), Lee Coll., Cleve., 1995. Reporter Orlando Sentinel Star, Fla., 1973-76; editor Charisma mag. Calvary Assembly, Winter Park, Fla., 1976-81; pres. Strang Comm. Co., Lake Mary, Fla., 1981—; owner Creation House Books, 1986, Christian Retailing mag., 1986, ChrismaLife Pubs., 1990—. Founding editor Charisma mag., 1975, Ministries Today mag., 1983; founding pub. CharismaLife Learning Resources, 1990, New Man mag., 1994. Mem. steering com. N.Am. Renewal Svcs. Com., 1985—; trustee Internat. Charismatic Bible Ministries, 1986—; pres. Christian Life Missions, 1991—. Recipient First Place award Nat. Writing Championship, William Randolph Hearst Found., 1973, Alumnus of Distinction award U. Fla. Coll. of Journalism and Comm., 1994, Industry of Yr. award for Seminole County, Fla., Econ. Devel. Commn. of Mid-Fla., 1994. Mem. Internat. Pentecostal Press Assn., Christian Booksellers Assn., Fla. Mag. Assn. (pres. 1979-80), Evang. Christian Pubs. Assn., Evang. Press Assn. Republican. Mem. Assemblies of God. Avocations: racquetball, golf. Office: Strang Comm Co 600 Rinehart Rd Lake Mary FL 32746-4898

STRANG, WILLIAM GILBERT, mathematician, educator; b. Chgo., Nov. 27, 1934; s. William Dollin and Mary Catherine (Finlay) S.; m. Jillian Mary Shannon, July 26, 1958; children—David, John, Robert. S.B., MIT, 1955; B.A. (Rhodes scholar), Oxford (Eng.) U., 1957; Ph.D. (NSF fellow), UCLA, 1959. Asst. prof. mathematics MIT, 1959-63, assoc. prof., 1963-66, prof., 1966—; pres. Wellesley-Cambridge Press; hon. prof. Xian Jiaotong U., People's Republic of China, 1980. Author: An Analysis of the Finite Element Method, 1973, Linear Algebra and Its Applications, 1976, Introduction to Applied Mathematics, 1986, Calculus, 1990, Introduction to Linear Algebra, 1993, Wavelets and Filter Banks, 1996, Linear Algebra, Geodesy, and GPS, 1997. Recipient Chauvenet prize Math. Assn. Am., 1977; Sloan fellow, 1966-67; Fairchild scholar, 1981. Home: 7 Southgate Rd Wellesley MA 02181-6606 Office: MIT Math Dept Rm 2-240 Cambridge MA 02139

STRANGE, CURTIS NORTHROP, professional golfer; b. Norfolk, Va., Jan. 30, 1955; s. Thomas Wright Strange Jr. and Nancy (Ball) Neal; m. Sarah Jones; children: Thomas Wright III, David Clark. Student, Wake Forest U., 1974-76. Winner of Southeastern Amateur, 1973, NCAA, 1974, Western Amateur, 1974, Eastern Amateur, 1975, 76, North and South Amateur, 1975, 76, Va. State Amateur, 1976, World Amateur Cup, 1975, Walker Cup, 1974, Pensacola Open, 1979, Michelob-Houston Open, Mfrs. Hanover Westchester Classic, 1980, Panama Open, 1980, Sammy Davis Jr.-Greater Hartford Open, 1983, LaJet Classic, 1984, Honda Classic, Panasonic-Las Vegas Invitational, Canadian Open, 1985, Houston Open, 1986, Canadian Open, Fed. Express-St. Jude Classic, NEC World Series of Golf, 1987, Ind. Ins. Agent Open, Meml. Tournament, U.S. Open, 1988, 89, Nabisco Championships, 1988. Named to Collegiate Golf Hall of Fame, 1987, Wake Forest Hall of Fame, 1988, PGA Player-of-the-Yr., 1988; recipient Golf Writers Player-of-the-Yr. award, 1985, 87, 88, ABC Cup Japan, 1986, PGA Leading Money Winner 1985, 87-88. Avocation: hunting, fishing. Office: care IMG 1 Erieview Plz Ste 1300 Cleveland OH 44114-1715*

STRANGE, DONALD ERNEST, health care company executive; b. Ann Arbor, Mich., Aug. 13, 1944; s. Carl Britton and Donna Ernestine (Tenney) S.; m. Lyn Marie Purdy, Aug. 3, 1968; children: Laurel Lyn, Chadwick Donald. BA, Mich. State U., 1966, MBA, 1968. Asst. dir. Holland (Mich.) City Hosp., 1968-72, assoc. dir., 1972-74; exec. dir. Bascom Palmer Eye Inst./Anne Bates Leach Eye Hosp., U. Miami, Fla., 1974-77; v.p. strategic planning and rsch. Hosp. Corp. Am., Nashville, 1977-80; group v.p. Hosp. Corp. Am., Boston, 1980-82, regional v.p., 1982-87; chmn., chief exec. officer HCA Healthcare Can., 1985-87; exec. v.p. Avon Products, Inc., 1987-89; chmn. Sigecom, Ltd., 1989-94, U.S. HomeCare Corp., 1990-91; exec. v.p., COO, dir. EPIC Healthcare Group, Dallas, 1991-93; chmn, CEO TransCare Corp., Dallas, 1993-95; chmn. TheraMed Ptnrs., Bedford, N.H., 1996—; chmn., CEO First New Eng. Dental Ctrs., Inc., Boston, 1996—; bd. dirs. Access Radiology, Inc., Boston, Bon Secours Health System, Balt., Thera Med Ptnrs., Inc. Author: Hospital Corporate Planning, 1981. Mem. Harvard Club (Boston), Nat. Arts Club (N.Y.), Bay Club (Boston). Republican. Episcopalian. Office: First New Eng Dental Ctrs Inc 85 Devonshire St Boston MA 02109-3504

STRANGE, FRANCES RATHBUN, financial aid administrator, therapist; b. Wichita Falls, Tex., Aug. 14, 1949; d. Willie and Viola Gertrude (Loesby/Jarrell) Rathbun; m. Dougles William Strange, 1967 (div. Apr. 1992); children: Chad Douglas, Cameron Todd, Cooper Lane, Chance (dec.). B of Behavioral Sci., Hardin-Simmons U., 1988, MEd, 1992; M of Human Rels., U. Okla., 1990. Lic. profl. counselor. Bus. officer Hardin-Simmons U., Abilene, Tex., 1983-85; admissions office Hardin Simmons U., Abilene, Tex., 1986-88, asst. fin. aid dir., 1989-93, dir. fin. aid, 1993-96; grant coord. fin. aid Baylor U., Waco, Tex., 1985-86; social worker Dept. Human Svcs., Duncan, Okla., 1988-89; dir. fin. aid U. Sci. and Arts of Okla., Chickasha, 1996—; contract counselor Harmony Family Svcs., Abilene, 1992-96. Mem. APA, ACA, Alpha Chi. Baptist. Avocations: camping, traveling, fishing. Home: Rt 2 Box 138 Minco OK 73059

STRANGE, GARY R., medical educator; b. Mammoth Cave, Ky., Jan. 16, 1947. BS Biology and Chemistry summa cum laude, Western Ky. U., 1966, MA in Secondary Edn., 1968; postgrad. in pharmacology, Vanderbilt U., 1967-68; postgrad. in edn., U. Ky., 1968-69, MD, 1974. Diplomate Am. Bd. Emergency Medicine. Intern in ob-gyn. Letterman Army Med. Ctr., San Francisco, 1974-75; resident in emergency medicine U. So. Calif. Med. Ctr., L.A., 1977-79; attending staff emergency medicine various hosps., Calif., 1978-79, Grayson Cmty. Hosp., Leitchfield, Ky., 1979-81; dir. emergency medicine Ireland Army Cmty. Hosp., Ft. Knox, Ky., 1979-81; attending staff emergency medicine Hardin Meml. Hosp., Elizabethtown, Ky., 1980-81, various hosps., Ill., 1981—; dir. emergency medicine Mercy Hosp. and Med. Ctr., Chgo., 1981-86, assoc. dir. emergency medicine, 1986-90; chief emergency svc. U. Ill. Hosp., Chgo., 1990—; dir. U. Ill. Affiliated Hosps. Emergency Medicine Residency, Chgo., 1986-93; head dept. emergency medicine U. Ill. Coll. Medicine, 1990—, assoc. prof. emergency medicine, 1991—. Contbr. articles to profl. jours. Mem. adv. bd. on emergency med. svcs. for children Ill. Dept. Pub. Health, 1994—; mem. panels Agency for Health Care Policy/Rsch., 1994, 95; regional coord. Yr. of the Child Nat. Campaign, 1990-91; com. on pediatric emergency med. svcs. Nat. Rsch. Coun. Inst. Medicine, 1991-93. Hubbell scholar 1971-72; recipient Lange Med. Publs. award 1971-72. Fellow Am. Coll. Emergency Physicians (councillor 1987-92, coun. steering com. 1991-93, chmn. course devel. task force mktg. and diversification 1986-87, infant and childhood emergencies com. 1983—, chmn. pediatric emergencies com. 1988-90, chmn. sect. pediatric emergency medicine 1990-91, sects. task force 1992—, core content task force, Chgo., 1993); mem. AMA, Am. Bd. Emergency Medicine (bd. examiner panel 1987—), Ill. chpt. Am. Coll. Emergency Physicians (bd. dirs. 1985—, chmn. med. econs. com. 1984-87, edn. com. 1982-84, product devel. com. 1988—, various other coms.), Soc. Tchrs. Emergency Medicine (chmn. ednl. resources com. 1982-86), Soc. Acad. Emergency Medicine (chmn. edn. com. 1989-93, program com. 1989-93, task force on developing residencies in traditional med. schs. 1991-93, injury prevention com. 1991—), Ill. Med. Soc., Chgo. Heart Assn. (ACSL Affiliate Faculty 1986-91, 92—), Chgo. Med. Soc. (diagnostic and therapeutic tech. assessment panel 1991). Office: Univ Illinois Dept Emergency Medicine Univ Illinois Hospital Chicago IL 60612

STRANGE, HENRY HAZEN, judge; b. Oleary, P.E.I., Can., July 26, 1939; s. Henry Hazen and Marion Yvonne (Copp) S.; m. Heather Susan Carson, July 30, 1966; children: Elizabeth Marion, Jennifer Jody. BBA, U. N.B., Fredericton, 1961, BA, 1963, B in Civil Laws, 1964. Pvt. practice barrister, solicitor N.B., 1964-66; spl. asst. to dir. of pub. rels. Centennial Commn., Ottawa, Ont., Can., 1966-67; crown prosecutor Dept. Justice, Fredericton, N.B., 1967-71; dir. pub. prosecutions Dept. Justice, N.B., 1971-81; judge Provincial Ct., N.B., 1981—, chief judge, 1987—. Apptd. as Queen's Counsel, N.B., 1977. Mem. Can. Coun. Chief Judges (chmn. 1995). Avocations: salmon fishing, sports. Home: 664 Woodstock Rd, Fredericton, NB Canada E3B 5N7 Office: Provincial Ct, PO Box 94, Oromocto, NB Canada E2V 2G4

STRANGWAY, DAVID WILLIAM, university president, geophysicist; b. Can., June 7, 1934. BA in Physics and Geology, U. Toronto, 1956, MA in Physics, 1958, PhD, 1960; DLittS (hon.), Victoria U., U. Toronto, 1986; DSc (hon.), Meml. U. Nfld., 1986, McGill U., Montreal, Que., Can., 1989, Ritsumeikan U., Japan, 1990; D.Ag.Sc. (hon.), Tokyo U. Agr., 1991; DSc (hon.), U. Toronto, 1994. Sr. geophysicist Dominion Gulf Co. Ltd., Toronto, 1956; chief geophysicist Ventures Ltd., 1956-57, sr. geophysicist, summer 1958; research geophysicist Kennecott Copper Corp., Denver, 1960-61; asst. prof. geology U. Colo., Boulder, 1961-64; asst. prof. geophysics MIT, Cambridge, Mass., 1965-68; mem. faculty U. Toronto, 1968-85, prof. physics, 1971-85, chmn. dept. geology, 1972-80, v.p., provost, 1980-83, pres., 1983-84; pres. U. B.C., 1985—; chief geophysics br. Johnson Space Ctr., NASA, Houston, 1970-72, chief physics br., 1972-73, acting chief planetary and earth sci. divsn., 1973; vis. prof. geology U. Houston, 1971-73; interim dir. Lunar Sci. Inst., Houston, 1973; vis. com. geol. scis. Brown U., 1974-76, Meml. U. St. John's Newfoundland, 1974-79, Princeton U., 1981-86; v.p. Can. Geosci. Coun., 1977; chmn. proposal evaluation program Univs. Space Rsch. Assocs., 1977-78, Ont. Geosci. Rsch. Fund, 1978-81; Pahlavi lectr. Govt. Iran, 1978; cons. to govt. and industry, mem. numerous govt. and sci. adv. and investigative panels; hon. prof. Changchun Coll. Geology, People's Republic China, 1985, Guilin Coll. Geology, China, 1987, U. Autonoma de Guadalajara, Mex., 1996; fellow Green Coll. Oxford U., Eng.; hon. advisor Urasenke Found., Kyoto, Japan; hon. alumnus U. B.C.; bd. dirs. MacMillan Bloedel Ltd., BC Gas Ltd., Corp.-Higher Edn. Forum; chair Nat. Mus. Sci. and Tech., 1996. Author numerous papers, reports in field. Recipient Exceptional Sci. Achievement medal NASA, 1972, medal of honor Kyung Hee U., Seoul, 1996; named Kil-Sly, Haida Nation (West Coast Indians of Can.), 1993, Officer of Order of Can., 1996. Fellow Royal Astron. Soc., Royal Soc. Can., Geol. Assn. Can. (disting. fellow, pres. 1978-79, Logan Gold medal 1984); mem. AAAS, Soc. Exploration Geophysicists (Virgil Kauffman Gold medal 1974), Can. Geophys. Union (chmn. 1977-79, J. Tuzo Wilson medal 1987), Am. Geophys. Union (planetology sect. 1978-82), European Assn. Exploration Geophysicists, Soc. Geomagnetism and Geolectricity (Japan), Can. Geosci. Coun. (pres. 1980), Can. Soc. Exploration Geophysicists, Soc. Exploration Geophysics (hon.), Can.-Japan Soc. (founding dir.), Internat. House Japan, Inc.

STRASBAUGH, WAYNE RALPH, lawyer; b. Lancaster, Pa., July 20, 1948; s. Wayne Veily and Jane Irene (Marzolf) S.; m. Carol Lynne Taylor, June 8, 1974; children: Susan, Wayne T., Elizabeth. AB, Bowdoin Coll., 1970; AM, Harvard U., 1971, PhD, 1976, JD, 1979. Bar: Ohio 1979, Pa. 1983, U.S. Tax Ct. 1980, U.S. Ct. Fed. Claims 1980, U.S. Ct. Appeals (fed. cir.) 1982, U.S. Dist. Ct. (no. dist.) Ohio 1979, U.S. Dist. Ct. (ea. dist.) Pa. 1983. Assoc. Jones Day Reavis & Pogue, Cleve., 1979-82, Morgan Lewis & Bockius, Phila., 1982-84; assoc. Ballard Spahr Andrews & Ingersoll, Phila., 1984-88, ptnr., 1988—. Mem. ABA (tax sect., chair 1992-94), Phila. Bar Assn. (tax sect., chair fed. tax com. 1992, coun. mem. 1995, sec.-treas. 1996, vice chmn. 1997—). Episcopalian. Office: Ballard Spahr Andrews & Ingersoll 1735 Market St Philadelphia PA 19103-7501

STRASBURGER, JOSEPH JULIUS, retired lawyer; b. Albia, Iowa, Aug. 29, 1913; s. Joseph and Elsa (Gottlieb) S.; m. Lucile C. Lapidus, Oct. 11, 1957; 1 dau., Susan A. (dec. Jan. 1970). A.B., Knox Coll., 1934; J.D., Harvard, 1937. Bar: Ill. 1937. Assoc. firm Moses, Kennedy, Stein & Bachrach, Chgo., 1938-39; asso. gen. counsel's office Middle West Service Co., Chgo., 1939-44; ptnr. Altheimer & Gray (and predecessor firms), Chgo., 1944-87; Chmn. lawyer's handbook editorial com. Jewish Fedn. Chgo., 1968-73; mem. adv. council Ill. Inst. Continuing Legal Edn., 1970-76, exec. com., 1971-76, chmn., 1974-75; lectr. probate and tax subjects. Contbr. articles to legal jours. Mem. devel. com. Knox Coll., 1964-70, trustee, 1982-87, life trustee, 1987—; trustee Latin Sch. Chgo., 1978-84. Fellow Am. Bar Found.; mem. ABA, Ill. Bar Assn., Chgo. Bar Assn. (chmn. probate practice com.

1960-61, chmn. continuing legal edn. com. 1968-69, chmn. legal edn. com. 1972-73), Chgo. Estate Planning Council (pres. 1975-76), Phi Beta Kappa, Delta Sigma Rho, Beta Theta Pi. Jewish. Clubs: Tavern (Chgo.), Harvard (Chgo.). Home: 1335 N Astor St Chicago IL 60610-2152 Office: 10 S Wacker Dr Chicago IL 60606-7407

STRASFOGEL, IAN, stage director; b. N.Y.C., Apr. 5, 1940; s. Ignace and Alma (Lubin) S.; m. Judith Hirsch Norell, Feb. 15, 1973; children: Daniella Elizabeth, Gabrielle Sandra. BA, Harvard U., 1961. Adminstrv. asst. N.Y.C. Opera Co., 1962-64, stage dir., 1964—; tchr. music Julliard Sch. Music, N.Y.C., 1965-66, Augusta (Ga.) Coll., 1967-68; founder, previous artistic dir. Augusta Opera Co., from 1967; chmn. dept. opera New Eng. Conservatory, Boston, 1968-72; prof. opera U. Mich., Ann Arbor, 1980; stage dir. Balt. Civic Opera, Kansas City Lyric Theatre, Netherlands Opera Co., 1973—, N.Y.C. Opera, San Francisco Opera, Stuttgart Opera, Alte Oper Frankfurt, Edinburgh Festival, Aix-en-Provence Festival, Aspen Music Festival; dir. music theatre project Tanglewood Festival, Lenox, Mass., 1971-73; gen. dir. Opera Soc. Washington, 1972-75; artistic cons. Phila. Lyric Opera, 1973; dir. New Opera Theatre, Bklyn. Acad. Music, 1976-79. Author: Il Musico (music by Larry Grossman), 1990-91; editor: Ba-Ta-Clan, 1970. Served with AUS, 1966-68. Henry Russell Shaw travelling fellow, 1961-62; Ford Found. internship in performing arts, 1962-64; Internat. Inst. Edn. grantee, 1965. Mem. Phi Beta Kappa. Home: 915 W End Ave New York NY 10025-3535 Office: Sardos Artist Mgmt Corp 180 W End Ave New York NY 10023-4902*

STRASMA, JOHN DRINAN, economist, educator; b. Kankakee, Ill., Mar. 29, 1932; s. Roy and Charlotte Wilkins (Deselm) S.; m. Judith Feaster, Mar. 18, 1956 (div. 1983); children: Anne, Patricia, Susan, Kenneth, Mary; m. Anne Corry, July 21, 1984. AB, DePauw U., 1953; AM, Harvard U., 1958, PhD, 1960. Research asst. Fed. Res. Bank of Boston, 1958-59; prof. Econs. Inst., U. Chile, Santiago, 1959-72; economist UN Secretariat, 1964-65; advisor Ministry of Economy and Fin., Lima, Peru, 1970; prof. econs. and agrl. econs. U. Wis., Madison, 1972—; dir. Ctr. for Development Univ. Wis., Madison, 1996—; cons. in field; v.p., dir. Latin Am. Scholarship Program of Am. Univs., 1970-74; chmn. fin. com. Wesley Found. of Wis., 1978-87; public mem. Wis. Legis. Council Com. on Mining, 1975-90. Author: State and Local Taxation of Manufacturing Industry, 1969, Agrarian Reform in El Salvador, 1982, Agricultural Land Taxation in Developing Countries, 1987, Land Tax Reform Alternatives in Zimbabwe, 1990, Options for Redistributing Land in the New South Africa, 1993, Market-Based Land Redistribution in the New South Africa, 1993, Resolving Land Conflicts in Nicaragua, 1996, Developing Financial Markets in the Dominican Repubic, 1997. Served with U.S. Army, 1954-56. Danforth fellow, 1956-60; Recipient Outstanding Public Service award Wis. Environ. Decade, 1978. Mem. Am. Econs. Assn., Am. Agrl. Econs. Assn., Internat. Agrl. Econs. Assn., Latin Am. Studies Assn., Soc. Internat. Devel. Methodist. Office: U Wis 427 Lorch St Madison WI 53706-1513

STRASSBURGER, JOHN ROBERT, academic administrator; b. Sheboygan, Wis., Apr. 6, 1942; s. J. Robert and Elizabeth (Mathewson) S.; m. Gertrude Hunter Mackie, Aug. 24, 1968; children: Sarah Electa, Gertrude Hunter. BA, Bates, 1964; Honours degree, Cambridge (Eng.) U., 1966; PhD, Princeton U., 1976. Faculty Hiram (Ohio) Coll., 1970-82; program officer NEH, Washington, 1982-84; prof. history, exec. v.p., dean Coll., Knox Coll., Galesburg, Ill., 1984-94; pres. Ursinus Coll., Collegeville, Pa., 1995—; mem. commn. govt. rels. Am. Coun. Edn., 1997—. Contbr. articles to profl. jours. Bd. trustees Perkiomen Sch., 1997—. Mem. Am. Conf. Acad. Deans (chair 1990-91), Sunday Breakfast Club (Phila.). Office: Ursinus Coll Office of Pres Collegeville PA 19426-1000

STRASSER, GABOR, priest, management consultant; b. Budapest, Hungary, May 22, 1929; s. Rezso and Theresa (Seiler) S.; m. Linda Casselman Pemble, Aug. 16, 1958 (div. 1976); children: Claire Margaret, Andrew John; m. Joka Verhoeff, Feb. 2, 1978; children: Steven Verhoeff, Tessa Christina. BCE, City Coll. N.Y., 1954; MS, U. Buffalo, 1959; PMD, Harvard, 1968; MDiv, Va. Theol. Sem., 1992. Research engr. Bell Aircraft Co., Buffalo, 1956-61; project leader Boeing Airplane Co., Seattle, 1961-62; dept. head Mitre Corp., Bedford, Mass., Washington, 1962-68; v.p. Urban Inst., Washington, 1968-69; tech. asst. to pres.'s sci. adviser White House, 1969-71, exec. sec. pres.'s sci. and tech. policy panel, 1970-71; dir. planning Battelle Meml. Inst., Columbus, Ohio, 1971-73; pres. Strasser Assocs., Inc., Washington, 1973-92; priest Va. Diocese, 1992—. Author, editor: Science and Technology Policies-Yesterday, Today, Tomorrow, 1973; Contbr. articles to profl. jours. Served to 1st lt., C.E. USAR. Recipient 1st nat. award Gravity Research Found., 1952. Mem. Am. Inst. Aeros. and Astronautics, AAAS (chmn. indsl. sci. sect. 1974), Sigma Xi. Clubs: Cosmos (Washington), Harvard (Washington).

STRASSER, WILLIAM CARL, JR., retired college president, educator; b. Washington, Feb. 4, 1930; s. William Carl and Minnie Elizabeth (Saxton) S.; m. Jeanne Carol Peake, Sept. 17, 1954 (div.); children: Sheryl Lynn, Keith Edward, Robert Carl; m. Jane Ann Gunn, Nov. 25, 1978. BA with first honors, U. Md., 1952, MA, 1954; PhD, 1961; Carnegie postdoctoral fellow in coll. adminstrn, U. Mich., 1961-62. High sch. tchr. Cin. and Balt., 1955-57; v.p. W.C. Strasser Co., Inc., 1957-59; pub. info. specialist Balt. County (Md.) Pub. Schs., 1960-61; asst. dean, asst. prof. Sch. Edn., State U. N.Y. at Buffalo, 1962-64; rsch. asst. U.S. Office Edn., 1959-60; specialist ednl. adminstrn. U.S. Office Edn., Washington, 1964-65; asst. dir. profl. personnel Montgomery County (Md.) Pub. Schs., 1965-66; acting pres., exec. dean Montgomery Community Coll., Rockville, Md., 1966-67, pres., 1967-79, prof., 1978-86, pres. emeritus, prof. emeritus, 1986—; vis. scholar U. Calif., Berkeley, 1977-79; vice pres. Md. Council Community Coll. Presidents, 1971-72, 75-77; pres., v.p. Jr. Coll. Council Middle Atlantic States, 1969-72; founder Council Chief Exec. Adminstrs., 1973-75; mem. exec. com. Pres.'s Acad., 1975-77; mem. Gov.'s Adv. Council, Md. Higher Edn. Facilities, 1977-79; Del. UNESCO Conf. on Africa, 1961; participant 50th Anniversary Conf. Fgn. Policy Assn. U.S., 1968; mem. Congl. Internship Adv. Com., 1969-78; chmn. Montgomery County Community White Ho. Conf. on Aging, 1971; cons. Middle States Assn. Colls. and Secondary Schs., 1975—. Author: For The Community: Continuing General Education, 1979, A College For a Community, 1988; co-author: Dual Enrollment in Public and Non-Public Schools, 1965; contbr. poetry and articles to jours. Served with AUS, 1954-55. Recipient Gov. Md. Cert. Disting. Citizenship, 1979; Danforth Found. study grantee, 1972; Ford Found. grantee, 1974-75; Silver medallion for Outstanding Service, Bd. Trustees of Montgomery Coll., 1986. Mem. Am. Assn. Jr. Colls. (chmn. nat. commn. on instrn. 1969-71, mem. nat. assembly 1973, founder Pres. Acad. 1973-77), AAUP, Am. Assn. Higher Edn., Am. Mgmt. Assns., Nat. Soc. Sons. and Daus of the Pilgrims, Montgomery County C. of C. (Disting. Svc. award 1979), Rotary, Phi Kappa Phi, Omicron Delta Kappa, Pi Delta Epsilon, Phi Eta Sigma, Phi Delta Kappa. Democrat. Unitarian-Universalist. Home: 3011 Stoney Rd Shepherdstown WV 25443

STRASSMANN, W. PAUL, economics educator; b. Berlin, July 26, 1926; s. Erwin Otto and Ilse (Wens) S.; m. Elizabeth Marsh Fanck, June 27, 1952; children—Joan, Diana, Beverly. B.A. magna cum laude, U. Tex., Austin, 1949; M.A., Columbia U., 1950; Ph.D., U. Md., 1956. Econ. analyst Dept. Commerce, 1950-52; instr. U. Md., 1955; mem. faculty Mich. State U., East Lansing, 1956—, assoc. prof. econs., 1959-63, prof., 1963—; sr. research dir. ILO, Geneva, 1969-70, 73-74; cons. World Bank, AID. Author: Risk and Technological Innovation, 1959, Technological Change and Economic Development, 1968, The Transformation of Housing, 1982, (with Jill Wells) The Global Construction Industry, 1988. Served with USN, 1944-46. Mem. Am. Econ. Assn., Latin Am. Studies Assn., Phi Beta Kappa. Office: Mich State Univ Dept Econs East Lansing MI 48824

STRASSMEYER, MARY, newspaper columnist; b. Cleve., Aug. 5, 1929; d. Frederick H. and Katherine (Mullally) S. A.B., Notre Dame Coll., 1951; postgrad., Toledo U., 1952; J.D., Cleve. Marshall Coll. Law, Cleve. State U., 1981. Bar: Ohio 1983. Reporter Cleve. News, 1956-60; contbr. Cleve. Plain Dealer, 1957-60, feature writer, 1960-65, beauty editor, 1963-65, travel writer, 1963—, society editor, 1965-77, 85—; columnist, 1977—; co-creator syndicated cartoon Sneakers; co-owner Gerry's Internat. Travel Agy., Cleve., 1991—. Author: Coco: The Special Delivery Dog, 1979. Mem. Soc. Am. Social Scribes (founder, 1st pres.), Notre Dame Coll. Alumnae Assn., Women in Comm. Club: Press (Cleve.) (inducted into Hall of Fame 1994). Home: 2059 Broadview Rd Cleveland OH 44109-4145 Office: The Plain Dealer 1801 Superior Ave E Cleveland OH 44114-2107

STRATAS, NICHOLAS EMANUEL, psychiatrist; b. Toronto, Aug. 9, 1932; came to U.S., 1957; s. Emanuel Nicholas and Argero (Terezakis) S.; m. Irene Printezi, Dec. 14, 1955; children: Nicholas Andrew, Byron Aristotle, Andrew James. BA, U. Toronto, 1953, MD, 1957. Diplomate Am. Bd. Psychiatry and Neurology, Internat. Acad. Behavioral Medicine, Fedn. State Med. Bds. U.S. Rotating intern Meml. hosp., Danville, Va., 1957-58; resident in psychiatry Ea. State Hosp., Williamsburg, Va., 1958-60; chief resident in psychiatry Dorothea Dix Hosp., Raleigh, N.C., 1960-61; dir. residency tng. Dorothea Dix Hosp., Raleigh, 1961-63; dir. profl. edn. and tng. State Dept. Mental Health, N.C., 1963-66, dir. research, 1965-66, dep. commr., 1966-73; asst. clin. prof. psychiatry U. N.C. Med. Sch., 1964-69, assoc. clin. prof. psychiatry, 1969-75, clin. prof., 1984—; assoc. clin. prof. Duke U. Med. Ctr., 1980—; pvt. practice, 1960—; lectr. William & Mary U., Williamsburg, Va., 1960, U. N.C. Sch. Pub. Health, 1964-65, U. W.Va. Med. Sch., Charleston, 1968, Vanderbilt U. Sch. Med., Nashville, 1970, U. N.C. Sch. Social Work, Chapel Hill, 1973, et. al.; organizer, pres. med. staff Ea. State Hosp., Williamsburg, 1958-59; cons. pvt. orgns. 1960—, Peace Corps, 1964-69, W. Va. State Dept. Mental Health state office program devel., 1968, Nationwide Ins. Co. mgmt. devel., 1970, Drug Action of Wake County mgmt. devel., 1970-74, The Human Ecology Inst., 1973-75, U.S. Fed. Ct. of N.C. ea. dist. expert witness, 1975-76, IBM personal devel. seminars, 1978—, Finley-Dillon Realty, 1983—, The Aviation, 1986; bd. dirs. Wake County Mental Health Assn., 1964-65; staff Wake Med. Ctr., 1973—, Rex Hosp., 1973—, Raleigh Community Hosp., 1978—; founder, med. dir. Holly Hill Hosp. 1978—, Raleigh Stress & Pain Clin., 1980-84. Author: N.C. Local Mental Health Programs-A Manual, 1968, A Multi-Discipline Approach to Consultation-Edn., 1969; contbr. articles to profl. and scholarly jours. Awards dir. Boy Scouts Am., Raleigh, N.C., Webelos coord., 1968; bd. trustees Holy Trinity Greek Orthodox Ch., 1971, Sunday sch. coord., 1975-77; mem. N.C. State Art Gallery, Raleigh Cultural Ctr., 1974. Recipient Gov. N.C. awards, 1968, 70, 84, Univ. Toronto award, 1957. Fellow APHA, Am. Psychiat. Assn. (award 1970), Am. Soc. Clin. Hypnosis, Acad. Psychosomatic Medicine, Am. Coll. Forensic Psychiatry; mem. AMA, AAAS, BiofeedbackInst. Am. (cert.), Wake County Med. Assn., N.C. Med. Assn., Soc. Gen. Sys. Rsch., N.Y. Acad. Scis., Am. Orthopsychiat. Assn., Orthodox Christian Profls., Bd. Med. Examiners of N.C. (pres. 1992-93). Home: 8717 Gleneagles Dr Raleigh NC 27613 Office: Raleigh Psychiat Assocs PA 3900 Browning Pl Ste 201 Raleigh NC 27609-6508

STRATAS, TERESA (ANASTASIA STRATAKI), opera singer, soprano; b. Toronto, Ont., Can., May 26, 1938. Student, of Irene Jessner, 1956-59; grad., Faculty Music, U. Toronto, 1959; LLD (hon.), McMaster U., 1986, U. Toronto, 1994. Winner Met. Opera auditions, 1959; major roles in opera houses throughout world include: Mimi in La Bohème; Tatiana in Eugene Onegin; Susanna in The Marriage of Figaro; Nedda in Pagliacci; Marenka in The Bartered Bride; Three Heroines in Il Trittico; Violetta in La Traviata; title role in Rusalka; Jennie in Mahagonny; created title role in completed version of Lulu (Alban Berg), Paris Grand Opera, 1979; film appearances Kaiser von Atlantis, Seven Deadly Sins; Zefirelli's La Traviata, Salome, Lulu, Paganini, Zarewitsch, Eugene Oregin; Broadway debut in Rags, 1986; creator the role of Marie Antoinette Ghosts of Versailles world premiere Met. Opera, 1992; sang both female leading roles Il Tabarro, Pagliacci double bill opening Met. Opera, 1994, numerous recs. including Richard Strauss' Salomé, Songs of Kurt Weill. Decorated Order of Can.; recipient 3 Grammy awards, Emmy award, Drama Desk award, 1986, 3 Grammy nominations, Tony nomination, 1986, Tiffany award, 1994; named Performer of Yr., Can. Music Council, 1979. Office: care Met Opera Co Lincoln Center Plz New York NY 10023 also: Vincent & Farrell Associates 157 W 57th St Ste 502 New York NY 10019-2210*

STRATFORD, RAY PAUL, electrical engineer, consultant; b. Pocatello, Idaho, Feb. 26, 1925; s. Ray Percy and Olive Eudora (Jenson) S.; m. Claire Elizabeth Dennery, Sept. 2, 1949 (div. July 1969); children: Bruce Ballentyne, James Lowell, Susanne Dennery; m. Nancy Lorraine Long, Apr. 24, 1974; 1 child, Heather Lyn; stepchildren: Deborah Lorraine, David Paul. Student, Idaho State U., 1946-47; BSEE, Stanford U., 1950. Registered profl. engr., N.Y. Test engr. GE, Schenectady, N.Y., 1950-52; application GE, Schenectady, 1954-62, project mgr., 1963-73, cons. engr., 1974-85; proposal engr. GE, Phila., 1952-54, application engr., 1962-63; pvt. cons. Island Park, Idaho, 1991—; adj. prof. Rensselaer Poly. Inst., Troy, N.Y., 1988, 90. Co-author: Handbook of Industrial and Commercial Electric Power System Designs, 1995; contbr. articles to profl. jours. Missionary LDS Ch. in South Africa; mem. bldg. com. LDS Sch., Schenectady, 1962-64, coord. phys. facilities, 1980-84; mem. bldg. com. Burnt Hills Sch. Bd., Glenville, N.Y., 1963-64, YMCA, Schenectady, 1965. Fellow IEEE (life mem., chairperson static power converter com. 1972, chairperson task force standard 1973-84, co-chairperson task force standard 1984-92, contbg. author Red Book 1993, Best Paper award 1981, Outstanding achievement award 1994), Rotary International. Avocations: woodworking, family, travel. Office: PO Box 186 Island Park ID 83429-0186

STRATIGOS, WILLIAM NARGE, computer company executive; b. Huntington, N.Y., Mar. 14, 1946; s. Narge G. and Portia R. (Kleros) S.; m. Deborah Feller, Jan. 4, 1981; children: Stepahnie, Elena. BA in Biology cum laude, NYU, 1972, DDS, 1977. Lic. dentist, N.Y. Mgr. div. Med. Ctr. NYU, N.Y.C., 1966-74; mng. ptnr., dentist Stratigos Moses et al., N.Y.C., 1978-88; pres. Sigma Imaging Systems Inc., N.Y.C., 1988-95; v.p. Wang Software, N.Y., Inc., N.Y.C., 1995—; bd. dirs. Sigma Imaging Systems Inc., N.Y.C. Author: Hot Spot, 1993. Fellow NYU Acad. of Oral Rehab.; mem. Assn. for Image & Info. Mgmt. Internat. (bd. dirs., treas. exec. committee, chmn. accreditation committee), Dental Soc. of the State of N.Y., First Dist. Dental Soc., Omicron Kappa Upsilon. Greek Orthodox. Patents in field. Avocations: writing, chess, bowling. Office: Wang Software NY Inc 622 3rd Ave Fl 30 New York NY 10017-6707

STRATMAN, JOSEPH LEE, petroleum refining company executive, consultant, chemical engineer; b. Louisville, Oct. 15, 1924; s. Dominic Herman and Mary Ann (Wolf) S.; m. Elizabeth Jewell Doyle, July 1, 1950; children—Joseph Lee, Mary Elizabeth, Sharon Ann, Judith Ann. BChemE, U. Louisville, 1947. Registered profl. engr., Tex. Chem. engr. Pan Am. Refining Corp. (doing bus. as Amoco Oil Co.), Texas City, Tex., 1947-55, operating supr., 1955-61; mgr. Texas City Refining, Inc., Texas City, Tex., 1961-69, v.p., 1969-80, sr. v.p., 1980—. Bd. dirs., mem. exec. com., treas., chmn. Galveston County ARC, 1966-73; bd. dirs., mem. exec. com., chmn. Texas City Jr. Achievement, 1966-73; treas. Texas City Refining Good Govt. Fund., 1983-88. Served with USNR, 1945-46. Mem. Am. Inst. Chem. Engrs. Roman Catholic.

STRATON, JOHN CHARLES, JR., investment banker; b. Warwick, N.Y., Apr. 18, 1932; s. John Charles and Helen (Sanford) S.; m. Sally M. Strawhand (div. Mar. 1970); children: John Charles III, Sara; m. Marion S. Holder, Feb. 18, 1974 (div. Mar. 1997); 1 child, Ashley Holder Straton. B.A., U. Va., 1954. With Jas. H. Oliphant and Co., N.Y.C., 1956—; gen. ptnr. Jas. H. Oliphant and Co., 1962—, 1st v.p., 1972-75; v.p. Spencer Trask & Co., Inc., N.Y.C., 1975-77, Hornblower, Weeks, Noyes & Trask, N.Y.C., 1977-78, Loeb Rhoades, Hornblower & Co., 1978-79, Shearson Loeb Rhoades, 1979-81; v.p., fin. cons. Shearson Lehman Bros., N.Y.C., 1981-93; sr. v.p. Smith Barney, N.Y.C., 1993—; assessor Village of Tuxedo Park, 1963-70. Vestryman St. Mary's in the Tuxedo. Served to maj. AUS, 1954-56; ret. Mem. U. Va. Alumni Assn. N.Y. (pres., treas. 1973-90), Mil. Order Fgn. Wars (comdr. 1981-86, treas. 1986—), Pilgrims of U.S., Tuxedo Pk. Club, Sigma Phi Epsilon. Home: Ledge Rd Tuxedo Park NY 10987 Office: 250 Park Ave New York NY 10177-0001

STRATT, RICHARD MARK, chemistry researcher, educator; b. Phila., Feb. 21 1954; s. Stanford Lloyd and Florence Clair (Sussman) S. SB in Chemistry, MIT, 1975; PhD, U. Calif.-Berkeley, 1979. Postdoctoral rsch. assoc. U. Ill., Champaign, 1979-80, NSF postdoctoral research assoc., 1980; asst. prof. chemistry Brown U., Providence, 1981-85, assoc. prof., 1986-88, prof., 1988—, dept. chair 1996—. Contbr. articles to profl. jours. Alfred P. Sloan fellow, 1985-89; Fulbright scholar Oxford U., 1991-92. Mem. Am. Phys. Soc., Am. Chem. Soc. (vice chair theoretical chem. subdiv. 1996-97), Sigma Xi, Phi Lambda Upsilon. Office: Brown U Dept Chemistry Providence RI 02912

STRATTON, GREGORY ALEXANDER, computer specialist, administrator, mayor; b. Glendale, Calif., July 31, 1946; s. William Jaspar and Rita Phyllis (Smith) S.; m. Yolanda Margot Soler, 1967 (div. 1974); 1 child, Tiffany; m. Edith Carter, Sept. 27, 1975; stepchildren: John Henkell, Paul Henkell, D'Lorah Henkell Wismar. Student, Harvey Mudd Coll., 1964-65; BS in Physics, UCLA, 1968; MBA, Calif. Luth. U., 1977. Elec. engr. Naval Ship Weapon System Engring. Sta., Port Hueneme, Calif., 1968-73; sr. staff mem. Univac, Valencia, Calif., 1973-74; v.p. Digital Applications, Camarillo, Calif., 1974-75; cons. Grumman Aerospace, Point Mugu, Calif., 1975-76; F-14 software mgr. Pacific Missle Test Ctr., Pt. Mugu, 1976-84; software mgr. Teledyne Systems, Northridge, Calif., 1984-92, dir. engring. software dept., 1992-93; dep. dir. software engring. Teledyne Electronic Systems, Northridge, Calif., 1993-94; software mgr. Litton Guidance and Controls, Northridge, Calif., 1995—. Mem. City Coun., City of Simi Valley, Calif., 1979-86, mayor, 1986—; alt. Rep. County Cen. Com., Ventura County, 1986-88; mem. Rep. State Cen. Com., Calif., 1990—; bd. dirs. Simi Valley Hosp., 1987—. Mem. Assn. Ventura County Cities (chair 1990-91), Rotary (Paul Harris award Simi Sunrise chpt. 1989), Jaycees (pres. Simi Valley chpt. 1974-75, nat. bd. dirs. 1975-76, v.p. Calif. state 1976-77). Republican. Lutheran. Home: 254 Goldenwood Cir Simi Valley CA 93065-6771 Office: Office of Mayor 2929 Tapo Canyon Rd Simi Valley CA 93063-2117

STRATTON, JOHN CARYL, real estate executive; b. Chgo., July 11, 1920; s. John Frederick Otto and Dorothy Marjorie (Young) S.; BS cum laude, Princeton, 1949; MBA, U. New Haven, 1980; m. Lucille Waterhouse Hall, Mar. 13, 1974; children by previous marriage: Caryl Stratton Killing, John Caryl II, Susan Hall Levy, Evelyn Hall Brenton, Kenneth Hall. Chief liaison engr., Avco Mfg. Co., Stratford, Conn., 1950-55; pres. Yankee Engring. Svc., Roxbury Conn., 1955-65, Stratton Realty, Roxbury, 1965-85; dir. Auto Swage Products Inc.; lectr. U. Conn., 1968-74, Western Conn. State U., 1975-80; spl. adviser U.S. Congl. Adv. Bd. Chmn. Zoning Commn. Newtown, 1971-77; mem. Republican Nat. Com., Rep. Presdl. Task Force; corp. mem. Naples Community Hosp.; del.-at-large Rep. Party. Served with USAF, 1942-46, PTO. Decorated D.F.C., Air medal with oak leaf cluster; recipient Presdl. Achievement award, 1981. Mem. AIAA, Internat. Real Estate Fedn., Nat. Real Estate Exchange, Internat. Speakers Platform Assn., Newtown Bd. Realtors (pres. 1974, dir. 1975-79), New Milford Bd. Realtors, Conn. Assn. Realtors (v.p. 1981), Nat. Assns. Realtors, Internat. Real Estate Fedn., Realtors Nat. Mktg. Inst. (cert. real estate salesman, cert. real estate broker), Naples Bd. Realtors, Fla. Assn. Realtors Comml. Investment Realtors of Southwest Fla., Am. Assn. Individual Investors, mem. Conn. Soc of The Order of the Founders and Patriots of Am., Nat. Soc. Sons Am. Revolution, Nat. Soc. of the Order of the Founders and Patriots of America, Inc., Hump Pilots Assn., (life) Fla. Sherrif's Assn., (hon., life), Internat. Arabian Horse Assn., Arabian Horse Club Conn., Mensa, Sigma Xi. Republican. Congregationalist. Clubs: N.Y. Athletic, Princeton. Address: 10490 Regent Cir Naples FL 34109-1570

STRATTON, MARGARET MARY, art educator; b. Seattle, Nov. 12, 1953; d. Harold Wesley and Veronica Margaret (Weber) S. BA in Media Studies, Evergreen State Coll., Olympia, Wash., 1977; MA in Photography, U. N.Mex., 1983, MFA in Photography, 1985. Tchr. U. N.Mex., Albuquerque, 1983-85; artist-in-residence Wash. State Arts Commn., U. Puget Sound, Tacoma, 1985, Yakima (Wash) Elem. Sch. Dist., 1985; staff adj. faculty Evergreen State Coll., Olympia, 1985-86; asst. prof. art U. Iowa, Iowa City, 1986-92, assoc. prof., 1993—; vis. prof. Cornish Coll. Art, Seattle, 1991-92, Art Inst. Chgo., 1992-93; advisor NEA regional Intermedia Arts/Minn., Mpls., 1991; juror Women in Dirs. Chair, Chgo., 1993. Videomaker: (film festivals) Berlin Film Festival, 1995, Black Maria Film Festival (dir. award 1995); contbr.: New Feminist Photographies, 1995; one-woman shows at New Image Gallery, James Madison U., Harrisonburg, Va., 1989, Sushi Inc., San Diego, 1990, Coll. of Pacific, Stockton, Calif., 1990, Intermedia Arts Gallery, Mpls., 1991, Cornish Coll. Arts, Seattle, 1991; exhibited in group shows at Rice U., Houston, 1989, Mid-Hudson Arts and Sci. Ctr., Poughkeepsie, N.Y., 1989, Arts Ctr. Gallery, Coll. DuPage, Glen Ellyn, Ill., 1989, N.A.M.E., Gallery, Chgo., 1989, Randolph St. Gallery, Chgo., 1989, Moore Coll. Art, Phila., 1989, Union Square Gallery, N.Y.C., 1989, U. Iowa Mus. Art, Iowa City, 1990, D.C. 37 Gallery, N.Y.C., 1990, Camerawork, San Francisco, 1990, 91, 93, 94, 911 Media Arts Ctr., Seattle, 1991, Kohler Art Ctr., Wis., 1991, Rena Bransten Gallery, San Francisco, 1991, Eye Gallery, San Francisco, 1992, 93, Port Angeles (Wash.) Fine Arts Ctr., 1992, Davenport (Iowa) Art Mus., 1992, Atlanta Gallery of Photography, 1992, U. Calif., Davis, 1992, Greg Kuchera Gallery, Seattle, 1992, Henry Gallery, U. Wash., Seattle, 1992, Valparaiso (Ind.) U., 1993, Gallery N.S.W., Sydney, Australia, 1993, Allied Arts Gallery/Hanford Nuclear Complex, Richland, Wash., 1993, Mus. Contemporary Photography and State Ill. Art Gallery, Chgo., 1993, The Harvard Archive, Cambridge, Mass.,1994, Portable Works Collection, Seattle Ctr. Pavilion, 1994, Women's U. Tex., Denton, 1994, Houston Ctr. Photography, 1994, Smithsonian Instn., Washington, 1994, Nathan Cummings Found., N.Y.C., 1995, Berlin Film and Video Festival, 1995. Recipient Regional Visual Fellowship award Nat. Endowment for Arts, 1987, Interdisciplinary Arts award, Intermedia Arts Nat. Endowment for Arts/Rockefeller Found., 1988, Individual fellowship in photography Nat. Endowment fo Arts, Washington, 1990, Pub. Art awards Seattle Arts Commn., 1992, Film and Video Prodn. Regional Grant Nat. Endowment for Arts/Jerome Found., Mpls., 1993, Individual fellowship in new Genres Nat. Endowment for the Arts, Washington, 1995, fac. scholar award U. Iowa, 1996. Mem. Soc. Photographic Edn. (bd. dirs. 1991-95), Coll. Art Assn. (1st chair Gay Caucus 1990-93). Achievements include research on the effects of media on stereotypes in United States/TV/Film. Home: 1611 E Court St Iowa City IA 52245-4425 Office: U Iowa Art Dept Riverside Dr Iowa City IA 52242

STRATTON, MARIANN, retired naval nursing administrator; b. Houston, Apr. 6, 1945; d. Max Millard and Beatrice Agnes (Roemer) S.; m. Lawrence Mallory Stickney, nov. 15, 1977 (dec.). BSN, BA in English, Sacred Heart Dominican Coll., 1966; MA in Mgmt., Webster Coll., 1977; MSN, U. Va., 1981. Cert. adult nurse practitioner. Ensign USN, 1966, advanced through grades to rear adm., 1991; patient care coord. Naval Regional Med. Ctr., Charleston, S.C., 1981-83; nurse corps plans officer Naval Med. Command, Washington, 1983-86; dir. nursing svcs. U.S. Naval Hosp., Naples, Italy, 1986-89, Naval Hosp., San Diego, 1989-91; chief pers. mgmt. Bur. Medicine & Surgery, Washington, 1991-94; dir. USN Nurse Corps, Washington, 1991-94; ret. Oct. 1, 1994 USN, 1994. Decorated Disting. Svc. medal, Meritorious Svc. medal with two stars, Naval Achievement medal. mem. Interagy. Inst. of Fed. Health Car Execs.

STRATTON, RICHARD JAMES, lawyer; b. Sandwich, Ill., May 17, 1946; s. James L. and Dorothy (Olson) S.; m. Michele Disario, June 13, 1970; children: Matthew A., Laura D. AB, Harvard U., 1968, JD, 1972; MS, London Sch. of Econs., 1969. Bar: Calif. 1972, U.S. Dist. Ct. (no. dist.) Calif. 1972, U.S. Ct. Appeals (9th cir.) 1972, U.S. Dist. Ct. (cen. dist.) Calif. 1978, U.S. Dist. Ct. (so. and ea. dists.) Calif. 1979, U.S. Supreme Ct. 1979. Assoc. Bronson, Bronson & McKinnon, San Francisco, 1972-79, ptnr., 1980—; early neutral evaluator, mediator U.S. Dist. Ct. Co-author: Real Property Litigation, 1994. Trustee San Francisco Day Sch., 1987-94; bd. dirs. Legal Aid Soc. of San Francisco, 1989—. Fellow Am. Bar Found.; mem. ABA, Bar Assn. of San Francisco (bd. dirs. 1988-90), Calif. Bar Assn., Def. Rsch. Inst. (chmn. subcom. real estate brokers and agts. 1986-87), No. Calif. Assn. Def. Counsel, No. Calif. Assn. Bus. Trial Lawyers, San Francisco Barristers Club (pres. 1980), City Club, Harvard Club (San Francisco). Office: Bronson Bronson & McKinnon 505 Montgomery St San Francisco CA 94111-2552

STRATTON, ROBERT, financial company executive; b. Vienna, Austria, Aug. 14, 1928; came to U.S., 1959, naturalized, 1966; s. Kenneth Kurt and Eugenie (Schwatzer) S.; m. Elfriede Karlberger, Jan. 11, 1980; children: David Alexander, Valerie Pam. B.Sc. in Physics, Manchester U., 1949, Ph.D. in Theoretical Physics, 1952. Rsch. physicist Met. Vickers Elec. Co., Manchester, Eng., 1952-59; with Tex. Instruments, Inc., Dallas, 1959-94; dir. physics rsch. lab. Tex. Instruments, Inc., 1959-94, assoc. dir. cen. rsch. labs., 1971-72, dir. semiconductor R & D, 1972-75, dir. cen. rsch. labs., 1975-77, asst. v.p., dir. cen. rsch. labs., 1977-82, v.p. corp. staff, dir. cen. rsch. labs.,

1982-94; dir. Indsl. Outreach Elec. Materials Sci. and Tech. Ctr., U. Tex. Engring. and Tech. Inst., Austin, 1994-96; co-founder, rsch. cons. Fin. Marketplace Inc., Dallas, 1997—; dir. Indsl. Outreach Elec. Materials Sci. and Tech. Ctr., Engring. and Tech. Inst. U. Tex., Austin, 1994-96; co-founder and rsch. cons. Fin. Marketplace, Inc., 1997—. Contbr. articles to profl. jours. Bd. dirs. Indsl. Rsch. Inst., 1985-88, Coun. on Superconductivity for Am. Competitiveness, 1987-90; adv. bd. dirs. Tex. Ctr. for Superconductivity, 1989—. Fellow IEEE, Inst. Physics (U.K.), Am. Phys. Soc.; mem. NAE. Office: 12770 Coit Rd Ste 850 Dallas TX 75251-1314

STRATTON, THOMAS OLIVER, investment banker; b. Los Angeles, Feb. 14, 1930; s. Oliver Clarke and Ethel (Savage) S.; m. Carol Joyce Wilson, Feb. 21, 1953; children: Brentley Clarke, James Morris, Thomas Oliver Jr. Student, Taft Sch., 1946-48, Stanford, 1948-50; B.S., U. Calif. at Los Angeles, 1956; M.B.A., Boston U., 1960. With Security Pacific Nat. Bank, Los Angeles, 1955-56; security analyst New Eng. Mut. Life Ins. Co., Boston, 1956-60; exec. v.p., dir. Bankers Leasing Corp., Boston, 1960-64; treas. Montgomery Ward & Co., Chgo., 1964-67; pres. Investco Assoc., Inc., 1967-75, Monterey Capital, Inc., 1975—; bd. dirs. MCI Securities, Inc. Served with AUS, 1952-55. Republican. Congregationalist. Clubs: Old Capital (Monterey); Beach and Tennis (Pebble Beach); World Trade (San Francisco). Home: PO Box 3713 Carmel CA 93921-3713 Office: PO Box 7370 Carmel CA 93921-7370

STRATTON, WALTER LOVE, lawyer; b. Greenwich, Conn., Sept. 21, 1926; s. John McKee and June (Love) S.; children: John, Michael, Peter (dec.), Lucinda; m. DeAnna Weinheimer, Oct. 1, 1994. Student, Williams Coll., 1943; A.B., Yale U., 1948; LL.B., Harvard U., 1951. Bar: N.Y. 1952. Assoc. Casey, Lane & Mittendorf, N.Y.C., 1951-53; assoc. Donovan, Leisure, Newton & Irvine, N.Y.C., 1956-63; ptnr. Donovan, Leisure, Newton & Irvine, 1963-84, Gibson, Dunn & Crutcher, 1984-93; ptnr. Andrews & Kurth, N.Y.C., 1993-95, of counsel, 1996—; asst. U.S. atty. So. Dist. N.Y., N.Y.C., 1953-56; lectr. Practising Law Inst. Served with USNR, 1945-46. Fellow Am. Coll. Trial Lawyers; mem. ABA, Fed. Bar Coun., N.Y. State Bar Assn. Clubs: Indian Harbor Yacht, Colo. Arlberg, Yale (N.Y.C.). Home: 434 Round Hill Rd Greenwich CT 06831-2639 Office: Andrews & Kurth 425 Lexington Ave New York NY 10017-3903

STRATTON-CROOKE, THOMAS EDWARD, financial consultant; b. N.Y.C., June 28, 1933; s. Harold and Jeanne Mildred (Stifft); children: Karen, John Ryland; m. Suzanne Williams, Oct. 21, 1989. Student, Hunter Coll., 1951-52; BS in Marine Engring. and Transp., U.S. Maritime Acad., 1952-56; student, Washington U., St. Louis, 1961; MBA in Internat. Mktg., Banking and Fin., NYU, 1967. Commd. ensign USN, 1956, advanced through grades to lt., 1957; with Goodyear Internat. Corp., Akron, Ohio, 1960-63, Esso Internat., N.Y.C., 1958-60; dir. market info. and devel. Hotel Corp. Am., Boston, 1964-68; with Continental Grain Co., N.Y.C., 1968-72; dir. charter contracts Conoco, Stamford, Conn., 1973-75; cons. A. T. Kearney, Cleve., 1976-81; investment banker E. F. Hutton, Cleve., 1981-83, AG Edwards and Sons, Inc., Cleve., 1983-89; sr. fin. cons., registered investment adviser Merrill Lynch, Cleve., 1989-95, asst. v.p., sr. fin. cons., 1989—; chmn. Indsl. Devel. Resch. Coun., Atlanta, 1970, Indsl. Devel. Resch. Coun., Snow Mass, Colo., 1971; lectr. bus. U. R.I., Kingston, 1968-70, tchr. Bus. Coll. Internat., 1986-89. Contbr. articles to profl. jours. Mem. Findley Lake (N.Y.) Hist. Soc.; mem. Nat. Task Force Reps. for Pres. Reagan, Cleve., 1982—. Mem. Naval Res. Officers Assn., Great Lakes Hist. Soc., Soc. Naval Architects/Engrs., Navy League, U.S. Coast Guard Club (Cleve.), Univ. Club, Circumnavigators Club (life), Internat. Shipmasters Assn., Propeller Club, Army Club, Navy Club, French Creek Hist. Soc., Town Club (Jamestown, N.Y.), Masons, Shriners, Cleve. City Club, Kings Point Alumni Assn. Avocations: sailing, skiing, bird watching, gardening, sports car enthusiast. Office: Merrill Lynch 1 Cleveland Ctr 1375 E 9th St Cleveland OH 44114-1724

STRATTON-WHITCRAFT, CATHLEEN SUE, critical care, pediatrics nurse; b. Jackson, Mich., Jan. 14, 1964; d. Ronald Alfred and Shirley Anne (Wickham) Stratton; m. David R. Whitcraft, Aug. 14, 1988. BSN magna cum laude, SUNY, Brockport, 1985. Cert. critical care nurse, ACLS. Student clin. asst. Yale-New Haven Hosp., 1984; charge nurse Walter Reed Army Med. Ctr., Washington, 1990; clin. nurse, critical care med. ICU and pediatric ICU SRT-Med. Staff Agy., Springfield, Va., 1985-88; asst. head nurse Sinai Hosp., Balt., 1988-90; charge nurse surg. SICU ICU VA Med. Ctr., Balt., 1991—. 1st lt. U.S. Army Nurse Corps, 1985-88, Res., 1988-93. Recipient Cert. of Achievement, Elizabeth Dole.

STRAUB, CHESTER JOHN, lawyer; b. Bklyn., May 12, 1937; s. Chester and Ann (Majewski) S.; m. Patricia Morrissey, Aug. 22, 1959; children: Chester, Michael, Christopher, Robert. AB, St. Peter's Coll., 1958; JD, U. Va., 1961. Bar: N.Y. State 1962, U.S. Dist. Ct. (so. and ea. dists.) N.Y. 1963, U.S. Ct. Appeals (2d cir.) 1967, U.S. Supreme Ct. 1978. Assoc. Willkie Farr & Gallagher, N.Y.C., 1963-71; ptnr. Willkie Farr & Gallagher, 1971—; mem. N.Y. State Assembly, 1967-72, N.Y. State Senate, 1973-75, Dem. Nat. Com., 1976-80; mediator U.S. Dist. Ct. (so. dist.) N.Y.; neutral evaluator U.S. Dist. Ct. (ea. dist.) N.Y.; chmn. N.Y. State statewide jud. screening com., 1988-94, first dept. jud. screening com., 1983-94; mem. Senator Moynihan's jud. selection com., 1976—. Mem. Cardinal's Com. of Laity for Cath. Charities N.Y.; trustee Lenox Hill Hosp., Collins Found. With U.S. Army, 1961-63. Mem. Am. Bar Assn., N.Y. State Bar Assn., Assn. of Bar of City of N.Y.C., Kosciuszko Found., Assn. Sons of Poland. Home: 35 Prescott Ave Bronxville NY 10708-1727 Office: Willkie Farr & Gallagher 1 Citicorp Ctr 153 E 53rd St New York NY 10022-4611

STRAUB, CHESTER JOHN, JR., government official; b. Charlottesville, Va., Oct. 4, 1960; s. Chester John and Patricia (Morrisey) S.; m. Erin Mary Norton, Apr. 21, 1990. BA, Tufts U., 1982. Asst. to exec. dir. Friends of Mario M. Cuomo, Inc., N.Y.C., 1986; dep. exec. dir. N.Y. State Dem. Com., N.Y.C., 1987-89, exec. dir., 1989-90; corp. sec. Battery Park City Authority, N.Y.C., 1990-93; dep. asst. sec. Econ. Devel. Adminstrn., Washington, 1993—. Dir. campaign ops. Clinton/Gore Coordinated Campaign, N.Y.C., 1992. Democrat. Roman Catholic. Home: 716 Queen St Alexandria VA 22314 Office: Econ Devel Adminstrn Rm 7824 14th St and Constitution Washington DC 20230

STRAUB, KENNETH RICHARD, educator; b. Denver, Dec. 1, 1945; s. Eugene Curtis Sr. and Helen Margaret (Russ) S.; m. Norine Ann Forde, Dec. 18, 1971; children: Michael Anthony, Nicole Kristina. BA, Adam's State Coll., Alamosa, Colo., 1970; postgrad., Metro State Coll., Denver, 1981-83, Denver U., 1989. Cert. secondary tchr. English and social studies. Team leader, tchr. Adam's County Dist. 27J, Brighton, Colo., 1971-72; asst. mgr. Gano-Downs Men's Store, Cherry Creek, Colo., 1972-75; adminstr. Adam's County Dist 12 Alternative High Sch., Northglenn, Colo., 1975-80; educator, tchr. Adam's County Five Star Sch. System, Northglenn, 1980—; mem. alternative edn. task force Adam's County Dist. 12, Northglenn, 1990-91; pres. Colo. Options in Edn. Assn., Denver, 1976-77; cons. Adam's County Dist. 14 schs., Commerce City, Colo., 1977-78; team leader curriculum devel. Adams County Dist. 27J, Brighton, Colo., 1971-72; mem. dist. reconfiguration team Adams County 5-Star Sch. Dist. Co-chmn. author: Comprehensive District Wide Alternative Program, 1991. Recipient awards of appreciation Jr. Achievement, 1989, 90. Mem. NEA, Colo. Edn. Assn., Polit. Action Com. in Edn., Dist. 12 Tchrs. Assn. (rep. Alternative Sch. 1975-80). Roman Catholic. Avocations: reading, bowling, swimming, dancing, exercise walking. Home: 11767 Keough Dr Northglenn CO 80233-1219 Office: Adams County 5 Star Schs 11285 Highline Dr Northglenn CO 80233-3076

STRAUB, LARRY GENE, business executive; b. Great Bend, Kans., Aug. 25, 1959; s. Walter Joseph and Barbara Jane (Schartz) S.; m. Julie Ann Miller, May 25, 1985; children: Hillary Ann, Brantley Joseph. BA, Ft. Hays State U., 1988, MS, 1990; MBA, Friends U., 1995. V.p., CFO Straub Internat., Great Bend, Kans., 1983—, Celebrations Unlimited, Inc., Great Bend, Kans., 1984—; bd. dirs. First United Nat. Bank and Trust; trustee Barton County C.C., Great Bend, 1995—. Pres., bd. dirs. Kiwanis Club, Great Bend; bd. dirs. Great Bend Jaycees. Mem. Western Retailers Assn., Great Bend C. of C. (amb., pres.), Masons (32nd degree, bd. dirs.), Pi Kappa Phi (v.p. recruitment). Republican. Roman Catholic. Avocations: tennis, book collecting, skiing, history. Home: 3220 Broadway Ave Great Bend KS 67530-3716

STRAUB, PETER FRANCIS, novelist; b. Milw., Mar. 2, 1943; s. Gordon Anthony and Elvena (Nilsestuen) S.; m. Susan Bitker, Aug. 27, 1966; children: Benjamin Bitker, Emma Sydney Valli. BA, U. Wis., 1965; MA, Columbia U., 1966. English tchr. Univ. Sch., Milw., 1966-68. Author: Marriages, 1973, Julia, 1975, If You Could See Me Now, 1977, Ghost Story, 1979, Shadowland, 1980, Floating Dragon, 1983, Lesson Park and Belsize Square, 1984, Wild Animals, 1984, Blue Rose, 1985, Koko, 1988, Mystery, 1989, Houses Without Doors, 1990, Mrs. God, 1991, The Throat, 1993, The Hellfire Club, 1996; (with Stephen King) The Talisman, 1984; editor: Peter Straub's Ghosts, 1995. Recipient Brit. Fantasy award, August Derleth award, 1983, World Fantasy awards World Fantasy Conv., 1989, 93, Grand Master award World Horror Conv., 1997. Mem. PEN, Mystery Writers Am., Horror Writers Assn (award 1994). Avocations: jazz, opera, classical music.

STRAUB, PETER THORNTON, lawyer; b. St. Louis, Mar. 27, 1939; s. Ralph H. and Mary Louise (Thornton) S.; m. Wendy B. Cubbage, Dec. 29, 1964; children: Karl Thornton, Philip Hamilton, Ellen Elizabeth. A.B., Washington and Lee U., 1961, LLB, 1964. Bar: Mo. 1964, Va. 1964, U.S. Dist. Ct. (ea. dist.) Mo. 1967, U.S. Circuit Ct. Appeals (8th cir.) 1969, U.S. Supreme Ct. 1970. U.S. Circuit Ct. Appeals (D.C. cir.) 1971, Ct. Mil. Appeals 1970, U.S. Tax Ct. 1971, U.S. Bankruptcy Ct. 1991. Assoc. Evans & Dixon, St. Louis, 1966-68; asst. pub. defender St. Louis County, St. Louis, 1968-69; asst. U.S. Atty. St. Louis, 1969-71; trial atty. internal security div. Dept. Justice, Washington, 1971-72; atty.-adviser office of dep. atty. gen. Dept. Justice, 1972-73, dir. office criminal justice, spl. asst. to atty. gen., 1974; minority counsel com. on judiciary U.S. Ho. of Reps., Washington, 1973-74; gen. counsel SSS, Washington, 1974-76; sole practice Alexandria, Va., 1976—. Pres., gov. bd. Alexandria Cmty. Mental Health Ctr., 1982-95; mem. No. Va. Estate Planning Coun., 1981—; mem. pres.'s coun. Trinity Coll., Washington, 1980-87; bd. dirs. Parc East Condominium, 1990—, sec., 1992—; mem. adv. bd. Am. Heart Assn., Alexandria, 1991-92, Salvation Army, 1991—, v.p., 1994-96; chmn. Alexandria Cmty. Shelter Adv. Bd., 1995—; Va. escheat atty., City of Alexandria, 1994—. Capt. USAR, 1964-66. Recipient certificate of award Dept. Justice, 1970, certificate of appreciation Law Enforcement Assistance Adminstrn. Dept. Justice, 1974, Silver Beaver award Boy Scouts Am., Washington , 1987. Mem. ABA, Fed. Bar Assn., Va. Bar Assn., Bar Assn. Met. St. Louis, Mo. Bar Assn., Alexandria Bar Assn., Va. Trial Lawyers Assn., Nat. Eagle Scout Assn., Nat. Lawyers Club, Optimists (bd. dirs., pres. Alexandria chpt. 1984, lt. gov. Nat. Capitol Va. Dist. 1987-89), Sigma Nu. Republican. Congregationalist. Avocations: scouting, reading, bicycling. Office: 1225 Martha Custis Dr Alexandria VA 22302-2040

STRAUBER, DONALD I., lawyer; b. Bklyn., Dec. 28, 1936; s. Jacob N. and Hannah (Lebedinsky) S.; m. Rachel Leah Sklaroff, Aug. 14, 1960; 1 child, Jocelyn Emily. A.B., U. Pa., Phila., 1957; LL.B., Harvard U., 1960. Bar: N.Y. 1961, U.S. Supreme Ct. 1965. Law clk. to Judge William Herlands U.S. Dist. Ct., So. Dist. N.Y., N.Y.C., 1960-61; assoc. Cravath, Swaine & Moore, N.Y.C., 1962-70; ptnr. Chadbourne & Parke and predecessor, N.Y.C., 1971—. Mem. ABA, N.Y. State Bar Assn., Assn. of Bar of City of N.Y. Home: 1160 Park Ave New York NY 10128-1212 Office: Chadbourne & Parke 30 Rockefeller Plz New York NY 10112

STRAUCH, BARRY STUART, physician, educator; b. N.Y.C., Feb. 2, 1941; s. Leo J. and Mildred M. (Meister) S.; m. Evelyn Marion Springer, Aug. 18, 1963; children: Lara, Eric. BA, Johns Hopkins U., 1962, MD, 1965. Diplomate Am. Bd. Internal Medicine and Nephrology. Intern Yale U., New Haven, 1966-67, 69-70, resident, 1966-70, fellow, 1970-71, asst. prof., 1971-73; clin. assoc. prof. Georgetown U., Washington, 1974-94, clin. prof. medicine, 1994—; chief nephrology sect. Fairfax Hosp., Falls Church, Va., 1974—; cons. Med., Legal and Pub. Policy, Washington, 1978—; ptnr. Washington Nephrology Assocs., Bethesda, Md., 1984—, chmn., 1989—. Contbr. numerous articles to profl. jours. Bd. dirs. Helath Care Adv. Bd., Fairfax County, 1975-77; chmn. Renal Network 23, Washington, 1978-82; exec. com. Nat. Forum Network, Washington, 1978-82; bd. dirs. Mid-Atlantic Renal Coalition, Richmond, Va., 1987—. Lt. comdr. USPHS, 1967-69. Fellow ACP; mem. Am. Soc. Nephrology, Cosmos Club. Avocations: reading, exercise. Office: 8316 Arlington Blvd Fairfax VA 22031

STRAUCH, GERALD OTTO, surgeon; b. Three Rivers, Mich., July 26, 1932; s. Gerald Otto and Helen Jeanette (Zierle) S.; m. Margaret Mary Spindler, Aug. 20, 1955; children—David Mark, Susan Mary, Jean Ellen. Grad., U. Mich., M.D., 1957. Diplomate: Am. Bd. Surgery. Intern R.I. Hosp., Providence, 1957-58; resident in surgery, 1958-62; practice medicine specializing in surgery Stamford, Conn., 1964-79; chief of surgery New Britain (Conn.) Gen. Hosp., 1979-87; clin. prof. surgery N.Y. Med. Coll., 1979-80; prof. surgery U. Conn. Sch. Medicine, 1980-87; clin. prof. surgery Uniformed Svcs. Univ. Health Scis., 1984—, U. Chgo., 1988—; dir. trauma and assembly depts. Am. Coll. Surgeons, 1988—; adj. prof. surgery Northwestern U., 1988—. Contbr. numerous articles to profl. jours. Served to capt. AUS, 1962-64. Fellow ACS; mem. New Eng. Surg. Soc., Frederick A. Coller Surg. Soc., Soc. for Surgery of Alimentary Tract, Collegium Internationale Chirurgiae Digestivae, Conn. Soc. Am. Bd. Surgeons, Am. Assn. Surgery of Trauma, Ctrl. Surgery Assn., Chgo. Surg. Soc., Assn. Advancement Automotive Medicine, Shock Soc., Corr. Soc. Surgeons (editor), Sociedad de Cirujanos de Chile (hon.), Assn. Mejicana de Cirujanos Generales (hon.), Assn. Française de Chirurgie (hon.), Hellenic Surg. Soc. (hon.). Republican. Roman Catholic. Clubs: Wee Burn Country. Home: 633 Sheridan Rd Winnetka IL 60093-2323 Office: Am Coll Surgeons 55 E Erie St Chicago IL 60611-2731

STRAUCH, JOHN L., lawyer; b. Pitts., Apr. 16, 1939; s. Paul L. and Delilah M. (Madison) S.; m. Gail Lorraine Kohn, Dec. 5, 1991; children: Paul L., John M., Lisa E. BA, U. Pitts., 1960; JD magna cum laude, NYU Sch. Law, 1963. Law clk. to Judge Sterry Waterman U.S. Ct. Appeals (2d cir.), St. Johnsbury, Vt., 1963-64; assoc. Jones, Day, Reavis & Pogue, Cleve., 1964-70, ptnr., 1970—, mem. adv. com., partnership com., chmn. litigation group; mem. Statutory Com. on Selecting Bankruptcy Judges, Cleve., 1985-88; mem. lawyers com. Nat. Ctr. for State Cts. Editor-in-chief: NYU Law Rev., 1962-63. Pres., trustee Cleve. Task Force on Violent Crimes, 1985-88; trustee Legal Aid Soc., Cleve., 1978, Cleve. Greater Growth Assn., 1985-86, Citizens Mental Health Assembly, 1989-90, lawyers com. Nat. Ctr. for State Cts., 1989—. Fellow Am. Coll. Trial Lawyers (life); mem. ABA, Ohio Bar Assn., Cleve. Bar Assn. (trustee 1980-83, pres. 1985-86), Fed. Bar Assn. (trustee Cleve. chpt. 1978-79, v.p. Cleve. chpt. 1979-80), Sixth Fed. Jud. Conf. (life), Ohio Eighth Jud. Conf. (life), Order of Coif, Inns of Ct., Oakmont Country Club, Cleve. Racquet Club, 13th St. Racquet Club, The Country Club, Kiawah Island Club, Phi Beta Kappa. Home: 28149 N Woodland Rd Cleveland OH 44124-4522 Office: Jones Day Reavis & Pogue N Point 901 Lakeside Ave E Cleveland OH 44114-1116

STRAUCH, KARL, physicist, educator; b. Germany, Oct. 4, 1922; came to U.S., 1939, naturalized, 1944; s. Georg and Carola (Bock) S.; m. Maria Gerson, June 10, 1951; children—Roger A., Hans D. A.B. in Chemistry and Physics, U. Calif. at Berkeley, 1943, Ph.D. in Physics, 1950. Jr. fellow Soc. Fellows, Harvard U., 1950-53; asst. prof. Harvard U., Cambridge, Mass., 1953-57, assoc. prof., 1957-62, prof., 1962-76; dir. Cambridge Electron Accelerator, 1967-74, George Vasmer Leverett prof. physics, 1976-93, George Vasmer Leverett prof. emeritus, 1993—; researcher in high energy physics. Contbr. articles to profl. jours. Served with USNR, 1944-46. Mem. Am. Phys. Soc., Am. Assn. Physics Tchrs., Am. Acad. Arts and Scis., Phi Beta Kappa, Sigma Xi. Home: 81 Pleasant St Lexington MA 02173-6116 Office: Harvard U Dept Physics Cambridge MA 02138

STRAUGHAN, WILLIAM THOMAS, engineering educator; b. Shreveport, La., Aug. 2, 1936; s. William Eugene and Sara Chloetilde (Harrell) S.; m. Rubie Ann Barnes, Aug. 20, 1957; children: Donna Ann, Sara Arlene, Eugene Thomas. BS, MIT, 1959; MS, U. Tex., 1986; PhD, Tex. Tech. U., 1990. Registered profl. engr., Fla., Ill., Iowa, La., Tex., Wash. Project engr. Gen. Dynamics Corp., Chgo., 1959-60; chief project, design engr. Gen. Foods Corp., Kankakee, Ill., 1960-64; mgr. plant engring. Standard Brands Inc., Clinton, Iowa, 1964-66; regional mgr. Air Products & Chems., Inc., Creighton, Pa., 1966-68; gen. mgr. Skyline Corp., Harrisburg, N.C., 1968-70; cons. Charlotte, N.C., 1970-72; dir. engring. and Fla. ops. Zimmer Homes Corp., Pompano Beach, 1972-73; v.p. engring. and mfg. Nobility Homes, Inc., Ocala, Fla., 1973-78, Moduline Internat., Inc., Lacey, Wash., 1978-85; rsch. engr. U. Tex., Austin, 1985-86; lectr., rschr. Tex. Tech. U., Lubbock, 1987-90; assoc. prof. U. New Orleans, 1990-92; asst. prof. dept. civil engring. La. Tech. U., Ruston, 1992—; cons. in field, Dubach, La., 1992—; condr. workshops in field; apptd. spokesman Mfrd. Housing Industry before U.S. Congress. Contbr. articles to profl. jours. Vol. engring. svcs. Lubbock Fire Safety House, 1990; judge sci. fair Ben Franklin H.S., New Orleans, 1990. Recipient T.L. James Svc. award La. Tech. U., 1994; grantee Urban Waste Mgmt. and Rsch. Ctr., New Orleans, 1991, Shell Devel. Co., 1993, La. Edn. Quality Support Fund, Insituform Techs., Inc., Trenchless Tech. Ctr., PABCO, Inc., InLiner USA, Inc., 1995, and numerous others. Mem. ASME (life), ASCE (Student chpt. Tchr. of Yr. award 1995), NSPE, Am. Soc. Engring. Edn., Phi Kappa Phi, Sigma Xi, Chi Epsilon. Achievements include: designed, constructed and managed first plant for the prodn. of intermediate moisture pet food (Gainesburgers) in the world. Organized and directed all activities to allow Clinton, Iowa plant with a 1 mile of shoreline to continue ops. during the greatest flood of the upper Miss. River in 1965. Avocations: flying, skiing, backpacking, golf, photography. Home: 199 Sellers Rd Dubach LA 71235

STRAUMANIS, JOHN JANIS, JR., psychiatry educator; b. Riga, Latvia, Apr. 22, 1935; came to U.S., 1950; s. Janis and Ella (Fredrichson) S.; m. Carol A. Sharar, Aug. 8, 1959; children: John, Susan. BA, U. Iowa, 1957, MD, 1960, MS, 1964. Intern Georgetown U. Hosp., Washington, 1960-61; resident U. Iowa, Iowa City, 1961-64; asst. prof. Temple U., Phila., 1966-71, assoc. prof., 1971-77, prof., 1977-85; prof. psychiatry La. State U., Shreveport, 1985-92; prof. psychiatry, dir. rsch. Tulane U. Med. Sch., New Orleans, 1992—; cons. Camden County Hosp., Blackwood, N.J., 1967-85, VA Hosp., Shreveport, 1985-92, VA Hosp., New Orleans, 1992—. Contbr. articles to profl. jours. Lt. comdr. USN, 1964-65. Rsch. Career Devel. award NIMH, 1966. Fellow Am. Psychiat. Assn.; mem. ACP, Am. Psychopathol. Assn., Soc. Biol. Psychiatry, Am. EEG Assn., Phi Eta Sigma, Phi Beta Kappa, Alpha Omega Alpha. Avocations: travel, music, photography. Office: Tulane U Med Ctr Dept Psychiatry & Neurology 1430 Tulane Ave New Orleans LA 70112-2699

STRAUS, DAVID A., architectural firm executive; b. Medford, Oreg., 1943; m. Sherry Straus; 2 children. BArch, U. Oreg., 1967. Registered architect, Oreg. Founding ptnr. Skelton, Straus & Seibert, Medford, 1989—. Past bd. dirs. Medford YMCA, Rogue Valley Art Assn.; past pres. Medford Arts Commn., Arts Coun. So. Oreg.; coach Rogue Valley Soccer Assn.; leader Boy Scouts Am.; bd. dirs., past pres. Schneider Mus. Art SOSC. Ret. lt. USNR, Vietnam. Mem. AIA (past pres. So. Oreg. chpt.), Archtl. Found. Oreg. (bd. dirs.), Univ. Club Medford (past pres.), Oreg. Club So. Oreg. (past pres.), U. Oreg. Alumni Assn., Medford/Jackson County C. of C. (bd. dirs.), Rotary. Office: Skelton Straus & Seibert Arch 26 Hawthorne St Medford OR 97504-7114

STRAUS, DONALD BLUN, retired company executive; b. Middletown, N.J., June 28, 1916; s. Percy S. and Edith (Abraham) S.; m. Elizabeth Allen, Sept. 7, 1940; children: David Allen, Robert Beckwith, Sara Elizabeth. A.B., Harvard U., 1938, M.B.A., 1940. Exec. dir. labor relations panel AEC, 1954-53; v.p. Health Ins. Plan of Greater N.Y., 1953-61; pres. Am. Arbitration Assn., 1963-72, pres. research inst., 1972-81; cons. Internat. Inst. of Applied Systems Analysis, 1982-85; mem. N.Y. State Bd. Mediation, 1956-59. Chmn. bd. Planned Parenthood Fedn. Am., 1962-65; emeritus bd. dirs. Internat. Council Comml. Arbitration, Population Resources Commn., Soc. Human Ecology; emeritus trustee Carnegie Endowment for Internat. Peace, Inst. Advanced Study, Princeton, Coll. of Atlantic. Mem. Coun. Fgn. Rels. Clubs: Century Assn., Knickerbocker, Harvard of N.Y.C., Pot and Kettle (Bar Harbor, Maine). Home: PO Box 59 Mount Desert ME 04660-0059

STRAUS, ERIC L., sports association administrator; m. Adriane Straus; two children. Past exec. v.p. Walter Straus & Son, Inc., Dallas; past dir. programs and ops. Dallas Internat. Sports Comms.; asst. dir. Am. Horse Show Assn., N.Y.C., 1994-96, exec. dir., 1996—; mgr. A-rated hunter and jumper shows, combined tng. events, dressage competitions; host USCTA Area V and USDF Region 9 Championships. Mem. Tex. Hunter and Jumper Assn. (pres. four times). Office: Am Horse Show Association 220 E 42nd St Fl 409 New York NY 10017-5806

STRAUS, HELEN LORNA PUTTKAMMER, biologist, educator; b. Chgo., Feb. 15, 1933; d. Ernst Wilfred and Helen Louise (Monroe) Puttkammer; m. Francis Howe Straus II, June 11, 1955; children: Francis Howe III, Helen E., Christopher M., Michael W. AB magna cum laude, Radcliffe Coll., 1955; MS in Anatomy, U. Chgo., 1960, PhD in Anatomy, 1962. With U. Chgo., 1964—, asst. prof. anatomy, 1967-73, dean of students, 1971-82, assoc. prof., 1973-87, dean of admissions, 1975-80, prof. anatomy and biol. scis., 1987—; bd. govs. U. Chgo. Internat. House, 1987—; cons., evaluator for North Cen. Assn., 1991—. Trustee Radcliffe Coll., Cambridge, Mass., 1973-83. Recipient Quantrell Award for Excellence in teaching, U. Chgo., 1970, 87, Silver medal Case Outstanding Tchr. Program, 1987. Mem. AAAS, NCAA (acad. requirements com. 1986-92, chmn. 1990-92, rsch. com. 1996—), Nat. Sci. Tchrs. Assn., Am. Assn. Anatomists, Harvard U. Alumni Assn. (bd. dirs. 1980-83), Phi Beta Kappa (sec., treas. U. Chgo. chpt. 1984—). Avocations: gardening, crafts, travel. Home: 5642 S Kimbark Ave Chicago IL 60637-1606 Office: U Chgo 5845 S Ellis Ave Chicago IL 60637-1476

STRAUS, LEON STEPHAN, physicist; b. Takoma Park, Md., May 29, 1943; s. Sidney and Ruth Straus; m. Cheryl Sarran Straus, Apr. 4, 1970; children: Jonathan, Jennifer. BS in Physics, Antioch Coll., Yellow Springs, Ohio, 1965; M Physics, Georgetown U., 1970, PhD in Physics, 1971. Mem. rsch. staff Ctr. Naval Analyses, Alexandria, Va., 1973-75; field rep. CTF 69 Ctr. Naval Analyses, Naples, Italy, 1975-77; project mgr. Ctr. Naval Analyses, Alexandria, 1977-79; field rep. CTF 69 and CTF 66/67 Ctr. Naval Analyses, Naples, Italy, 1979-82; assoc. dep. dir. Ctr. Naval Analyses, Alexandria, 1982-85; field rep. CTF 72 Ctr. Naval Analyses, Kamiseya, Japan, 1985-87; program mgr. Ctr. Naval Analyses, Alexandria, 1987-90; field rep. COMSIXTHFLT Ctr. Naval Analyses, Gaeta, Italy, 1990-92; project mgr. Ctr. Naval Analyses, Alexandria, 1992-95, tech. dir. spl. projects, 1995—; asst. AEC, Germantown, Md., 1968-71. Contbr. articles to profl. jours. Vol. Jewish lay leader USN, Naples, 1975-77, 79-82. Recipient Fellowship Georgetown U., Washington, 1965-68. Mem. Acoustical Soc. Am., Navy Submarine League. Jewish. Achievements include planning, evaluating and documenting tests/exercises associated with U.S. Navy and joint strategy, tactics, comm. and tech. Office: Ctr Naval Analyses 4401 Ford Ave Alexandria VA 22302-1432

STRAUS, OSCAR S., II, foundation executive; b. N.Y.C., Nov. 6, 1914; s. Roger Williams and Gladys (Guggenheim) S.; m. Marion Miller Straus, 1941 (div. 1982); 1 child, Oscar S. III.; m. Joan Sutton, 1982. AB, Princeton U., 1936; postgrad., U. Dijon, summer 1936, Sch. Bus. Adminstrn. Harvard U., 1938. Pvt. sec. Internat. Labor Office, Geneva, Switzerland, 1937-38; U.S. fgn. service officer, 1940-42; divisional asst. Dept. State, 1942-43, 44-45; treas., dir., v.p., chmn. finance com. Am. Smelting & Refining Co., 1945-59; partner Guggenheim Bros., 1959-83; pres., dir. Guggenheim Exploration Co., Inc., 1963-73; gen. ptnr. Straus Minerals, 1973-88; chmn., bd. dirs. Daniel and Florence Guggenheim Found., N.Y.C.; chmn., bd. dirs. Fred L. Lavanburg Found.; bd. dirs. Mutual of Omaha, Companion Life Ins. Co., United of Omaha. Trustee emeritus Am. Mus. Natural History, Mystic Seaport, Conn.; hon. chmn. Rensselaerville (N.Y.) Inst.; trustee Congregation Emanu-El. Mem. Coun. Fgn. Rels., Cruising Club Am., River Club, Megantic Fish and Game Club, Doubles Club, Knickerbocker Club, L.I. Wyandanch Club Inc. Jewish. Home: 7 Gracie Sq New York NY 10028-8030 Office: Daniel & Florence Guggenheim Found 950 3rd Ave Fl 30 New York NY 10022-2705

STRAUS, ROBERT, behavioral sciences educator; b. New Haven, Jan. 9, 1923; s. Samuel Hirsh and Alma (Fleischner) S.; m. Ruth Elisabeth Dawson, Sept. 8, 1945; children: Robert James, Carol Martin, Margaret Dawson, John William. BA, Yale U., 1943, MA, 1945, PhD, 1947. Asst. prof. Yale U., 1948-51, research asso. applied psychology, 1951-53; acting dir. Conn.

Child Study and Treatment Home, New Haven, 1952-53; assoc. prof. preventive medicine SUNY Upstate Med. Center, 1953-56; prof. med. sociology U. Ky., Lexington, 1956-59; prof. dept. behavioral sci. Coll. Medicine, also chmn. dept. U. Ky., 1959-87; dir. for sci. devel. Med. Rsch. Inst. San Francisco, 1991-93; vis. fellow Yale U., 1968-69; vis. prof. U. Calif., Berkeley, 1978, 86; sec. Com. Med. Sociology, 1955-57; chmn. Coop. Com. Study Alcoholism, 1961-63; chmn. Nat. Adv. Com. on Alcoholism, 1966-69; mem. Nat. Adv. Coun. on Alcohol Abuse and Alcoholism, 1984-87; trustee Med. Rsch. Inst. San Francisco, 1988-93; mem. Calif. Pacific Med. Ctr. Rsch. Coun., 1993. Author: Medical Care for Seamen, 1950 (with S.D. Bacon), Drinking in College, 1953, Alcohol and Society, 1973, Escape From Custody, 1974; A Medical School is Born, 1996; co-editor: Medicine and Society, 1963; mem. editorial bd.: Jour. Studies on Alcohol. Pres., Bluegrass R.R. Mus., 1980. Mem. Inst. Medicine NAS, Am. Sociol. Assn. (chmn. med. sociology sect. 1967-68), Assn. Behavioral Scis. and Med. Edn. (pres. 1974), Am. Pub. Health Assn. (lifetime achievement award sect. on alcohol, tobacco and other drugs 1993), Acad. Behavioral Medicine Rsch., Phi Beta Kappa, Sigma Xi. Home: 656 Raintree Rd Lexington KY 40502-2874

STRAUS, R(OBERT) JAMES, lawyer; b. New Haven, Aug. 17, 1946; s. Robert and Ruth (Dawson) S.; children: Leigh Elisabeth, Amanda Craig, Emily Dawson, Robert Benjamin. B.A. cum laude, Yale U., 1968; J.D., U. Chgo., 1974. Bar: Ky. 1974, U.S. Dist. Ct. (we. dist.) Ky. 1974. Assoc., Brown, Todd & Heyburn, PLLC, Louisville, Ky., 1974-79, ptnr., 1979—. Chmn. Legal Aid Soc., Inc., Louisville, 1981-85. Served to capt. USMC, 1968-71; Vietnam. Mem. Louisville Bar Assn., Ky. Bar Assn., ABA, Jefferson Club, Louisville Boat Club. Democrat. Presbyterian. Office: 3200 Providian Ctr Louisville KY 40202-3363

STRAUS, ROGER W., JR., publishing company executive; b. N.Y.C., Jan. 3, 1917; s. Roger Williams and Gladys (Guggenheim) S.; m. Dorothea Liebmann, June 27, 1938; 1 son, Roger W. III. Student, Hamilton Coll., 1935-37; B.J., U. Mo., 1939, Litt.D. (hon.), 1976. Reporter Daily Reporter, White Plains, N.Y., 1936; feature writer Daily Reporter, 1939-40; editorial writer, reporter Columbia Missourian, 1937-39; editor, pub. Asterisk, 1939; editorial asst. Current History, 1940, assoc. editor, 1940-45; assoc. editor Forum, 1940-45; pres. Book Ideas, Inc., 1943-46; founder Farrar, Straus & Co., Inc. (now Farrar, Straus & Giroux, Inc.), 1945; pres. Farrar, Straus & Giroux, Inc., N.Y.C., 1987—; chmn. adv. bd. Partisan Rev. mag., 1959-69. Co-editor: The Sixth Column, 1941, War Letters from Britain, 1941, The New Order, 1941; Chmn. publ. bd.: Am. Judaism mag, 1955-65. Vice pres. Fred L. Lavanburg Found., 1950-80, Daniel and Florence Guggenheim Found., 1960-76; bd. dirs. Harry Frank Guggenheim Found., Manhattanville Coll., 1970-76, John Simon Guggenheim Found.; fellow N.Y. Inst. for Humanities. Served to lt. USNR, 1941-45. Mem. P.E.N., Union Am. Hebrew Congregations (pub. com. 1955-65), Sigma Delta Chi. Clubs: Lotos, Westchester Country, Players. Office: Farrar Straus & Giroux Inc 19 Union Sq W New York NY 10003-3304*

STRAUSBAUGH, SCOTT DAVID, Olympic athlete, canoeist. Olympic slalom doubles canoeist Barcelona, Spain, 1992. Recipient Gold medal canoe slalom doubles Olympics, Barcelona, 1992. Address: PO Box 163 Almond NC 28702

STRAUSER, BEVERLY ANN, education educator; b. Dunkirk, N.Y., July 19, 1956; d. Henry Frank and Agnes Frances (Bielat) Rutkowski; m. Edward Britton Strauser, Oct. 9, 1982; children: Nicholas, Douglas, Thomas. BS, Regents Coll., Albany, N.Y., 1985; MS, SUNY, Fredonia, 1990. Cert. tchr. early childhood, bus. adminstrn., N.Y. Tchr. gifted edn. and computer literacy North Collins (N.Y.) Ctrl. Sch., 1986-87; tchr. pre-sch. St. Anthony's Sch., Fredonia, 1988-91; asst. prof. edn., tchr. edn. protfolio coord. Armstrong State Coll., Savannah, Ga., 1992—; cons. Jamestown (N.Y.) Cmty. Schs., 1989-91, Jewish Ednl. Allance, Savannah, 1991-92, Meth. Daysch. of Richmond Hill, Ga., 1992-93; presenter in field. Recipient Key award Jamestown Cmty. Schs., 1990. Mem. Nat. Assn. for the Edn. of Young Children, Ga. Assn. on Young Children (bd. dirs., sr. dist. rep. 1992-94), Internat. Reading Assn., Assn. Childhood Edn. Internat. Avocations: travel, reading. Home: 264 Boyd Dr Richmond Hill GA 31324-9400 Office: Armstrong State Coll 11935 Abercorn St Savannah GA 31419-1909

STRAUSER, EDWARD B., psychologist, educator; b. Dunkirk, N.Y., June 6, 1953; s. Fredrick Edward and Lucille Ruth (Mayott) S.; m. Beverly Ann Rutkoswki; children: Nicholas, Douglas, Thomas. BS, SUNY, Fredonia, 1975; MS, Canisius Coll., 1980; EdD, SUNY, Buffalo, 1986. 4th-9th grade tchr. Pioneer Mid. Sch., Yorkshire, N.Y., 1977-82; sch. psychologist BOCES, Orchard Park, N.Y., 1982-91; asst. prof. Pembroke (N.C.) State U., 1987-88; asst. prof., then assoc. prof. Armstrong State Coll., Savannah, Ga., 1991—; cons. ACT/PEP Test Svc., Albany, N.Y., 1988, SUNY, Fredonia, 1988-89, Cleve. City Schs., 1992. Contbr. chpts. to books and articles to profl. jours. Mem. exec. bd. Erie County Spl. Olympics, Orchard Park, 1983-84; bd. dirs. N.Y. Assn. Sch. Psychologists, 1990. Recipient Citation for Contribution to field of electrothermal biofeedback research, 1986, Citation of Appreciation for Profl. Contbn., Nat. Mid. Sch. Assn., 1988, Outstanding Svc. Awd. Project Safe Place, 1995. Mem. AAUP, Am. Assn. Tchg. and Curriculum, Nat. Assn. Sch. Psychologists, N.Y. State Tchrs. of Handicapped, Ga. Mid. Level Educators, Phi Delta Kappa. Avocation: travel. Home: 264 Boyd Dr Richmond Hill GA 31324-9400 Office: Armstrong State Coll 11935 Abercorn St Savannah GA 31419-1909

STRAUSER, JEFFREY ARTHUR, public safety official; b. Dunkirk, N.Y., May 24, 1947; s. Frederick Edward and Lucille Ruth (Mayott) S.; m. Sara Rollings Ritenburg, Aug. 12, 1972; children: Deborah Ann Patz, Frederick Jeffrey. BS, SUNY, Fredonia, 1972, MS, 1987; postgrad., Columbia Pacific U., 1994—. Lt. pub. safety SUNY, Fredonia, 1972-97, instr. microbiology, 1990-91; dir. quality control NOG Inc., Dunkirk, 1978-83; instr. biology and food sci. Empire State Coll., Fredonia, 1995-97; cons. NOG Inc., 1983-97, Jamestown (N.Y.) C.C., 1997—. Bd. dirs. PPD Sewer Dist., Mayville, N.Y., 1993-97. With USNG, 1970-76. Mem. Nat. Assn. Scholars, AOAC Internat., Inst. Food Techs., Western Assn. Sanitarians, Torch Club, Chautauqua Leadership Network, Coun. for Agrl. Sci. and Tech. Avocations: enging building, auto racing, jet skiing, reading, walking. Home: 10243 Lakeside Blvd Ext Dunkirk NY 14048 Office: SUNY Dept Pub Safety Fredonia NY 14063

STRAUSER, ROBERT WAYNE, lawyer; b. Little Rock, Aug. 28, 1943; s. Christopher Columbus and Opal (Orr) S.; m. Atha Maxine Tubbs, June 26, 1971 (div. 1991); children: Robert Benjamin, Ann Kathleen. BA, Davidson (N.C.) Coll., 1965; postgrad., Vanderbilt U., Nashville, 1965-66; LLB, U. Tex., 1968. Bar: Tex. 1968, U.S. Ct. Mil. Appeals 1971. Staff atty. Tex. Legis. Coun., Austin, 1969-71; counsel Jud. Com., Tex. Ho. of Reps., Austin, 1971-73; chief counsel Jud. Com., Tex. Constl. Conv., Austin, 1974; exec. v.p. and legis. counsel Tex. Assn. Taxpayers, Austin, 1974-85; assoc. Baker & Botts, Austin, 1985-87; ptnr. Baker & Botts, 1988—. Assoc. editor Tex. Internat. Law Jour., 1968. Mem. Tex. Ho. Speakers Econ. Devel. Com., Austin, 1986-87; mem. Austin Coun. Fgn. Affairs, 1987—; dir. McDonald Obs. Bd. Visitors, 1988—; mem. adv. bd. Sch. of Social Work, U. Tex. Lyceum Assn., 1980-81, 84-88; mem. Dean's Roundtable, U. Tex. Law Sch.; elder Presbyn. Ch.; mem. exec. com. Austin Symphony Orch. Soc., 1985—, v.p., 1993-94. Capt. USNR, ret. Named Rising Star of Tex., Tex. Bus. Mag., 1983. Mem. State Bar of Tex. (coun. mem. tax sect.), Travis County Bar Assn., Headliners Club (Austin). Home: 3312 Gilbert St Austin TX 78703-2102 Office: Baker & Botts 1600 San Jacinto Blvd Austin TX 78701

STRAUSFELD, NICHOLAS JAMES, neurobiology and evolutionary biology researcher, educator; b. Claygate, England, Oct. 22, 1942. BSc in Zoology, U. Coll. London, 1965, PhD in Neurophysiology, 1968; PhD in Neurophysiology, Habilitation, Frankfurt, Germany, 1985. Prof. U. Ariz., Tucson. Author: (books) Atlas of an Insect Brain, 1976, Functional Neuroanatomy, 1983. John Simon Guggenheim fellow, 1984, MacArthur fellow, 1995; recipient award for excellence in environ. health rsch. Lovelance Inst., Albuquerque, 1995. Office: U Arizona Gould Simpson Bldg 611 PO Box 210077 Tucson AZ 85721-0077*

STRAUSS, ALBRECHT BENNO, English educator, editor; b. Berlin, May 17, 1921; came to U.S., 1940; s. Bruno and Bertha (Badt) S.; m. Nancy Grace Barron, July 30, 1978; 1 child, Rebecca Ilse; stepchildren: Carolyn, Kathryn. BA, Oberlin Coll., 1942; MA, Tulane U., 1948; PhD, Harvard U., 1956. Instr. English Brandeis U., 1951-52; teaching fellow gen. edn. Harvard U., 1952-55; instr. English Yale U., 1955-59; asst. prof. English U. Okla., Norman, 1959-60; asst. prof. English U. N.C., Chapel Hill, 1960-64, assoc. prof., 1964-70, prof., 1970-91, prof. emeritus, 1991—; lectr. Duke Inst. for Learning in Retirement, 1993—. Editor Studies in Philology, 1974-80; sec. editorial com. Yale Edit. of Works of Samuel Johnson, 1975—; mem. editorial com. Ga. edit. works of Tobias Smollett, 1973—; contbr. articles to lit. publs. Served with U.S. Army, 1942-46. Recipient Tanner Teaching award U. N.C., 1966; Fulbright fellow, Germany, 1983-84. Mem. MLA, South Atlantic MLA, Am. Soc. Eighteenth-Century Studies (pres. Southeastern group 1980-81), Coll. English Assn., Johnsonians. Republican. Jewish. Home: 396 Lakeshore Ln Chapel Hill NC 27514-1728 Office: U NC 328 Greenlaw Bldg Chapel Hill NC 27599

STRAUSS, DAVID, federal official; b. Fargo, N.D., Apr. 2, 1950. BA in Sociology, Moorhead State U., 1973, BS Polit. Sci. and Edn. magna cum laude, 1973; postgrad., Harvard U., 1992. Exec. dir. N.D. Dem. Party, 1975-76; dir. N.D. Agrl. Stblzn. and Conservation Svc., 1977-81; adminstrv. asst. Senator Quentin Burdick of N.D., 1981-88; staff dir. U.S. Senate Com. on Environment and Pub. Works, Washington, 1988-92; chief of staff U.S. Senator Jocelyn Birch Burdick of N.D., Washington, 1992, Senator John Breaux of La., Washington, 1993; dep. chief of staff Office of Vice Pres., Washington, 1993. Office: Vice Pres Old Executive Office NW Bldg Washington DC 20501

STRAUSS, DOROTHY BRANDFON, marital, family, and sex therapist; b. Bklyn.; d. Marcus and Beatrice (Wilson) Brandfon; widowed; 1 child, Josette E. MacNaughton. BA, Bklyn. Coll., 1932; MA, NYU, 1937, PhD, 1963. Diplomate Am. Bd. Sexology. Instr. Hunter Coll. CUNY, 1960-63; prof. Kean Coll., Union, N.J., 1963-77; pvt. practice and clin. supervision Bklyn. and, N.J., 1970—; clin. assoc. prof. psychiatry Downstate Med. Ctr., SUNY, Bklyn., 1974—' assoc. dir. Ctr. for Human Sexuality, 1974-82; mem. NIMH rsch. team U. Pa., 1973-82; guest lectr. Menninger Clinic, 1990. Contbr. articles on gerontology and sexual dysfunctions to profl. jours. Fellow Am. Assn. Clin. Sexologists (founding); mem. Am. Psychol. Assn., Am. Assn. for Marital and Family Therapy (clin. mem. 1971—, supr. 1981—), Am. Assn. Sex Therapists, Counselors and Educators (chairperson task force on supervision 1984-86, chairperson supr. cert. com. 1986-93, chair cert. steering com. 1992—), Soc. for Clin. and Exptl. Hypnosis, Kappa Delta Pi. Home and Office: 1401 Ocean Ave Brooklyn NY 11230-3971

STRAUSS, EDWARD ROBERT, carpet company executive; b. Jersey City, June 14, 1942; s. Abraham and Elsie Alice (Goldstein) S.; m. Martha Ann Patmore, Oct. 30, 1966; children: Jeffrey Aaron, Craig Michael. BSBA, Rutgers U., 1973. Dept. systems mgr. Port of N.Y. Authority, N.Y.C., 1961-68; account exec. Steiner Rouse & Co., N.Y.C., 1968-70; purchasing mgr. N.Y. State Urban Devel. Corp., N.Y.C., 1970-73; sales mgr. Siracco's, Staten Island, N.Y., 1973-76; carpet and TV buyer Hahnes Dept. Stores, Newark, 1976-80; sales mgr. Clodan Carpets, N.Y.C., 1980-83; regional mgr. Deans Carpets, Manchester, N.H., 1983-85; pres. Carpet Contractors Inc., N.Y.C., 1985-97; v.p. contract sales Sher Land & Farrington, N.Y.C., 1997—. Bd. dirs. Marlboro (N.J.) Little League, 1979-87, Marlboro Pop Warner Football, 1979-83. Mem. Free Sons of Israel (trustee, v.p.), Marlboro Mcpl. Swim Club (bd. dirs. 1989-91), Free and Accepted Masons (Menorah lodge # 249 1966—, master 1978). Jewish. Avocations: electric trains, sports. Office: Sher Land & Farrington 155 Avenue Of The Americas New York NY 10013-1507

STRAUSS, ELLIOTT BOWMAN, economic development consultant, retired naval officer; b. Washington, Mar. 15, 1903; s. Joseph and Mary (Sweitzer) S.; m. Beatrice Phillips, Feb. 12, 1951; children by previous marriage: Elliott MacGregor, Armar Archbold, Lydia S. (Mme. Delaunay); 1 child, Christopher Joseph. B.S., U.S. Naval Acad., 1923; student, Imperial Def. Coll., London, 1948. Commd. ensign USN, 1923, advanced through grades to rear adm., 1955; assigned ships at sea, 1923-30, 32-35; asst. naval attache London, 1935-37; staff comdr. Atlantic Squadron, 1937-40; spl. naval observer London, 1941; staff Chief Brit. Combined Ops., 1942-43; U.S. ops. officer Allied Naval Comdr.-in-Chief for Normandy Invasion, 1944; comdr. Attack Transport, Pacific, 1944-45; naval adviser 1st Gen. Assembly UN, staff Mil. Staff Com., UN, 1946; comdg. officer USS Fresno, 1946-47; staff div. strategic plans Office Chief Naval Ops., 1948-51; comdr. Destroyer Flotilla 6, 1951-52; dir. def. programs div. Office Spl. Rep. in Europe, Dept. Def. rep. econ. def., 1952-55; ret., 1955; dir. engring. Bucknell U., 1956-57; dir. U.S. ops. Mission to Tunisia, 1957-60; spl. asst. to dir. ICA, 1960; dir. AID Missions to Madagascar, 1961-63; pub. mem. Fgn. Service Inspection Corps, 1965; assoc. Laidlaw & Co., N.Y.C., 1963-66; econ. devel. cons. Gen. Electric Co., 1966-69; chmn. bd. Interplan Corp., 1969-81; rep. overseas of Interplan.; cons. Dept. State, 1970. Author profl. and newspaper articles. Bd. dirs. Am. Econ. Found.; chmn. Naval Hist. Found. Decorated Bronze Star; comdr. Order Brit. Empire; Croix de Guerre with palm France). Mem. U.S. Naval Inst., English Speaking Union (nat. bd. dirs.), Order of St. John of Jerusalem (assoc.). Mem. Ch. of England. Clubs: The Pilgrims; Army-Navy (Washington), Chevy Chase (Washington), Metropolitan (Washington); New York Yacht. Home: 2945 Garfield Ter NW Washington DC 20008-3507

STRAUSS, GARY JOSEPH, lawyer; b. N.Y.C., July 6, 1953; s. Stanley Vinson and Frieda (Fischoff) S. BA magna cum laude, City Coll. of N.Y., 1974; JD, NYU, 1977. Bar: N.Y. 1978, Fla. 1980. Assoc. Finley, Kumble, Wagner, Heine & Underberg, N.Y.C., 1977-79; ptnr. Phillips, Nizer, Benjamin, Krim & Ballon, N.Y.C., 1979-87, Gaston & Snow, N.Y.C., 1987-88; pvt. practice N.Y.C., 1988—. Mem. ABA (chmn. N.Y. com. current literature and real property law 1977), Fla. Bar Assn., N.Y. State Bar Assn. Home: 20 E 35th St Apt 8H New York NY 10016-3858 Office: 57 W 38th St Fl 9 New York NY 10018-5500

STRAUSS, HARLEE SUE, environmental consultant; b. New Brunswick, N.J., June 19, 1950; d. Robert Lemuel and Helene (Marcus) S. BA, Smith Coll., 1972; PhD, U. Wis., 1979. Postdoctoral fellow dept. biology MIT, Cambridge, 1979-81; congrl. sci. fellow U.S. House of Reps., Washington, 1981-83; spl. asst. Am. Chem. Soc., Washington, 1983-84; spl. cons. Environ. Corp., Washington, 1984-85; rsch. assoc. Ctr. for Tech., Policy and Indsl. Devel. MIT, Cambridge, 1985-86, rsch. affiliate, 1986—; sr. assoc. Gradient Corp., Cambridge, 1986-88; pres. H. Strauss Assocs., Inc., Natick, Mass., 1988—; exec. dir. Silent Spring Inst., Inc., 1994-95; adj. assoc. prof. Sch. Pub. Health, Boston U., 1990-94; lectr. Sch. Medicine, Tufts U., Boston, 1988-95; mem. steering com. Boston Risk Assessment Group, 1986-95. Co-editor, author: Risk Assessment in Genetic Engineering, 1991; author: Biotechnology Regulations, 1986; author book chpts. in field. Active Instl. Biosafety Com., Army Rsch. Lab., Natick, 1989—, Army Sci. Bd., 1994—. Mem. AAAS, Am. Chem. Soc., Am. Soc. Microbiology, Assn. for Women in Sci. (chmn. com. New England chpt. 1986-88, co-chmn. legis. com. 1985-93), Biophys. Soc. (chmn. com. 1983-84, Congl. Sci. fellow 1981-83), Soc. for Risk Analysis (pres. New England chpt. 1991-92). Jewish. Avocations: travel, hiking. Office: H Strauss Assocs Inc 21 Bay State Rd Natick MA 01760-2942

STRAUSS, HERBERT LEOPOLD, chemistry educator; b. Aachen, Germany, Mar. 26, 1936; came to U.S., 1940, naturalized, 1946; s. Charles and Joan (Goldschmidt) S.; m. Carolyn North Cooper, Apr. 24, 1960; children: Michael Abram, Rebecca Anne, Ethan Edward. A.B., Columbia U., 1957, M.A., 1958, Ph.D., 1960; postgrad, Oxford U., 1960-61. Mem. faculty U. Calif., Berkeley, 1961—, prof. chemistry, 1973—, vice chmn. dept. chemistry, 1975-81, 92-95, asst. dean. Coll. Chemistry, 1986-92, assoc. dean, 1995—; vis. prof. Indian Inst. Tech., Kanpur, 1968-69, Fudan U., Shanghai, 1982, U. Tokyo, 1982, U. Paris du Nord, 1987; chmn. IUPAC Commn. I.1, 1994—. Author: Quantum Mechanics, 1968; assoc. editor Ann. Rev. Phys. Chemistry, 1976-85, editor, 1985—. Recipient Bomen-Michaelson award Coblentz Soc., 1994, Ellis Lippincott award Optical Soc. Am., 1994; Alfred P. Sloan fellow, 1966-70. Fellow Am. Phys. Soc., AAAS; mem. Am. Chem. Soc., Sigma Xi, Phi Beta Kappa, Phi Lambda Upsilon. Achievements include research in elucidation of vibrational spectra associated with large amplitude molecular motion in gases, liquids and solids. Home: 2447 Prince St Berkeley CA 94705-2021 Office: U Calif Dept Chemistry Berkeley CA 94720-1460

STRAUSS, JEFFREY LEWIS, healthcare executive; b. Balt., Aug. 16, 1963; s. Ronald Jay and Roberta Maude (Henriques) S.; m. Melissa Marie Nieding, Sept. 2, 1990. AA in Acctg., Purdue U., Westville, Ind., 1984, BA in Acctg., 1985. Staff acct. Bon Secour Hosp., Balt., 1986-88, Helix Health Systems/Franklin Sq. Hosp. Ctr., Balt., 1988-89; budget mgr., dir. provider svcs. Rush Prudential Health Plans, Chgo., 1989-93; dir. managed care fin. ops. West Suburban Hosp. Med. Ctr., Oak Park, Ill., 1993-94; dir. West Suburban Health Providers, Inc., Oak Park, 1995-97, Info Trust, Lake Forest, Ill., 1997—. Mem. Antique Automobile Club Am. (life). Democrat. Jewish. Avocations: antique automobiles, sports, reading. Home: 497 Grosse Pointe Cir Vernon Hills IL 60061-3405 Office: Info Trust 400 Field Dr Lake Forest IL 60045

STRAUSS, JEROME FRANK, III, physician, educator; b. Chgo., May 2, 1947; s. Jerome Frank Fr. and Josephine (Newberger) S.; m. Catherine Blumlein, June 20, 1970; children: Jordan L., Elizabeth J. BA, Brown U., 1969; MD, U. Pa., 1974, PhD, 1975. Asst. prof. Sch. of Medicine U. Pa., Phila., 1976-83, assoc. prof. Sch. of Medicine, 1983-85, prof. Sch. of Medicine, 1985—, assoc. chair Sch. of Medicine, 1987—, assoc. dean Sch. of Medicine, 1990—; Luigi Mastroianni jr. prof. and dir. Ctr. Rsch. on Women's Health and Reproduction, Phila., 1990-94; prof. Inst. of Medicine NAS, Phila., 1994—; mem. Biochem. Endocrinology study sect. NIH, 1983-87; mem., chair Population Rsch. Com. Nat. Inst. Child Health and Human Devel., 1989-92. Editor; Lipoprotein and Cholesterol Metabolism in Sterodogenic Tissues, 1985, Current Topics in Membrane Research, vol. 31, 1987, Uterine and Embryonic Factors in Early Pregnancy, 1991, New Achievements in Research of Ovarian Function, 1995; (jour.) Steroids, 1993—; corr. editor Jour. Steroid Biochem. and Molecular Biology, 1990—; assoc. editor, mem. editorial bd. Jour. Lipid Rsch., 1982-90; mem. editorial bd. Endocrinology, 1986-90, 97—, Biology of Reprodn., 1986-90, Jour. of Women's Health, 1991—, Jour. Soc. Gynecologic Investigators, 1993—, Placenta, 1995—. Mem. Am. Assn. Pathologists, Am. Physiol. Soc., Soc. Gynecologic Investigation (Pres.'s Achievement award 1990), Endocrine Soc., Soc. for Study of Reprodn. (bd. dirs. 1989-91, Rsch. award 1992). Office: U Pa Dept Ob/Gyn 415 Curie Blvd Philadelphia PA 19104-4218

STRAUSS, JEROME MANFRED, lawyer, banker; b. Milw., Nov. 7, 1934; s. Emanuel and Loraine (Goetz) S.; m. Mary Beth Johnson, June, 1959 (div. Nov. 1964); 1 child, Martha Lynn; m. Susan Jean Kauffman, Dec. 30, 1967; children: Jared Lee, David Aaron. BA with honors, Ind. U., 1956; JD, NYU, 1959. Bar: Ind. 1959, Fla. 1996, U.S. Dist. Ct. (so. dist.) Ind. 1959, U.S. Tax Ct. 1965, U.S. Ct. Appeals (7th cir.) 1969. Assoc. Ice Miller Donadio & Ryan, Indpls., 1959-69, ptnr., 1969-93; sr. v.p. and regional trust mgr. Merrill Lynch Trust Co., 1993-95; with Mershon, Sawyer, Johnston, Dunwody & Cole, Miami, Palm Beach, Naples, 1995-96; of counsel Edward E. Wollman and Assocs., P.A., Naples, Fla., 1997—; established Jerome M. Strauss P.A., 1997—. Co-author: Marital Deduction Trusts, 1963, Real Estate in an Estate, 1963, Durable Powers of Attorney, 1993; contbr. articles to profl. jours., proc., others. Bd. dirs. Orton Soc., Indpls., 1970-72, Indpls., 1970-72, Indpls. Hebrew Congregation, 1979-85, Planned Giving Group of Ind., Indpls., 1988-95, Ind. Continuing Legal Edn. Forum, 1989-94; mem. Fla. Planned Giving Coun., 1995—; devel. com. COllier County, Fla. Cmty. Found., 1995—; mem. Planned Giving Com. of Lee County, Fla., 1995—. Fellow Am. Coll Trust and Estate Counsel (charitable com., estate and gift tax com. 1996—); mem. ABA (vice chmn. marital deductin com. real estate property, probate and trust sect. 1988—), Internat. Acad. Estate and Trust Law (academician 1987—), Ind. State Bar Assn. (sec. 1979-80, chmn. probate, trust and real property sect. 1970-71), Ind. Estate Planning Coun. (pres. 1970-71), Fla. State Bar Assn., Internat. Assn. of Fin. Planners of S.W. Fla., Collier County Bar Assn., Skyline Club, Columbia Club, Collier Athletic Club. Home: 1056 Diamond Lake Cir Naples FL 34114-9211 Office: 649 5th Ave S Ste 218 Naples FL 34102-6601

STRAUSS, JOHN, public relations executive; b. N.Y.C., Apr. 2, 1913; s. Nathan and Bertha Dorothy (Heineman) S.; m. Renee Valensi, Oct. 15, 1947; children: Susan Strauss Koenig, John Jay. Grad., Phillips Exeter Acad., 1931; BA, Yale U., 1935. Securities analyst Mabon & Co., N.Y.C., 1935-41; sales rep. Warner Bros. Pictures, Buffalo, 1941-45; publicist Warner Bros. Studios, Burbank, Calif., 1945-46, Columbia Studios, Hollywood, Calif., 1946-48; founder, pres. Cleary, Strauss & Irwin, 1948-64; pres. McFadden, Strauss & Irwin, Inc., 1964-75, ICPR, L.A., 1975-80, Communifax, Inc., L.A., 1980—. Trustee Oakwood Schs., 1967-70, Acad. TV Arts, 1967-70, Columbia Coll., L.A., 1979-83. Mem. Acad. Motion Picture Arts and Scis. Home and Office: 4205 Stansbury Ave Sherman Oaks CA 91423-4233

STRAUSS, JOHN STEINERT, dermatologist, educator; b. New Haven, July 15, 1926; s. Maurice Jacob and Carolyn Mina (Ullman) S.; m. Susan Thalheimer, Aug. 19, 1950; children—Joan Sue, Mary Lynn. B.S., Yale U., 1946; M.D., 1950. Intern U. Chgo., 1950-51; resident in dermatology U. Pa., Phila., 1951-52, 54-55; fellow in dermatology U. Pa., 1955-57, instr., 1956-57; mem. faculty Boston U. Med. Sch., 1958-78, prof., 1966-78; prof., head dept. dermatology U. Iowa, Iowa City, 1978—. Mem. editorial bd. Archives of Dermatology, 1970-79, Jour. Am. Acad. Dermatology, 1979-89, Jour. Investigative Dermatology, 1977-82; contbr. articles to profl. jours. Served with USNR, 1952-54. James H. Brown jr. fellow, 1947-48; USPHS fellow, 1955-57; USPHS grantee. Fellow Am. Acad. Dermatology (pres.); mem. Soc. Investigative Dermatology (sec.-treas., pres.), Dermatology Found. (pres.), Am. Bd. Dermatology (bd. dirs., pres.), Am. Dermatol. Assn. (sec., pres.), Assn. Am. Physicians, Central Soc. Clin. Rsch., Am. Fedn. Clin. Rsch., Coun. Med. Splty. Socs. (pres.), 18th World Congress Dermatology (pres.), Internat. League Dermatol. Socs. (pres. 1992-97), Internat. Com. Dermatology (pres. 1992-97), others. Research in sebaceous glands and pathogenesis of acne. Office: U Iowa Hosp & Clinics Dept of Dermatology 200 Hawkins Dr # Bt2045 1 Iowa City IA 52242-1009

STRAUSS, JON CALVERT, academic administrator; b. Chgo., Jan. 17, 1940; s. Charles E. and Alice C. (Woods) S.; m. Joan Helen Bailey, Sept. 19, 1959 (div. 1985); children: Susan, Stephanie; m. Jean Anne Sacconaghi, June 14, 1985; children: Kristoffer, Jonathon. BSEE, U. Wis., 1959; MS in Physics, U. Pitts., 1962; PhD in E.E., Carnegie Inst. Tech., 1965. Assoc. prof. computer sci., elec. engring. Carnegie Mellon U., Pitts., 1966-70; dir. computer ctr., prof. computer sci. Tech. U. Norway, Trondheim, Norway, 1970; vis. assoc. prof. elec. engring. U. Mich., Ann Arbor, 1971; assoc. prof. computer sci. Washington U., St. Louis, Mo., 1971-74, dir. computing facilities, 1971-73; dir. computing activities U. Pa., Phila., 1974-76, faculty master Stouffer Coll. House, 1978-80, prof. computer, info. scis., prof. decision sci. Wharton Sch., 1974-81, exec. dir. Univ. Budget, 1975-78, v.p. for budget, fin., 1978-81; prof. elec. engring. U. So. Calif., Los Angeles, 1981-85; sr. v.p. adminstrn. U. So. Calif., 1981-85; pres. Worcester Poly. Inst., Mass., 1985-94; v.p., chief fin. officer Howard Hughes Med. Inst., Chevy Chase, Md., 1994-97; pres. Harvey Mudd Coll., Claremont, Calif., 1997—; cons. Electronics Assocs., Inc., 1965, IBM Corp., 1960-64, Westinghouse Elec. Corp., 1959-60; bd. dirs. Wyman Gordon Co., Computervision Corp. Contbr. articles on computer systems and university mgmt. to profl. jours.; co-holder patent. Bd. dirs. Presbyn.-U. Pa. Med. Ctr., Phila., 1980-81, U. So. Calif. Kenneth Norris Jr. Cancer Hosp., L.A., 1981-85, Med. Ctr. of Ctrl. Mass., 1986-94, Worcester Acad., 1986-91, Mass. Biotech. Rsch. Inst., 1985-94. Mem. New. Eng. Assn. Schs. and Colls., Inc., Commn. on Instns. of Higher Edn., Nat. Collegiate Athletic Assn. (pres.'s commn. 1990-94). Avocations: rowing, running, sailing, swimming. Office: Harvey Mudd Coll 301 E 12th St Claremont CA 91711-5901

STRAUSS, JUDITH FEIGIN, physician; b. N.Y., Mar. 7, 1942; d. Milton M. and Blanche (Tobias) Feigin; m. Harry William Strauss, June 14, 1964; children: Cheryl, Marcy. BS, Cornell U., Ithaca, 1963; MD, SUNY, 1967. Pediatrics. Pediatric resident SUNY, N.Y.C., 1976-68, Sinai Hosp., Balt., 1968-69; fellow pediatrics and psychiatry Johns Hopkins Hosp., Balt., 1969-70; pvt. practice in pediatrics Sacramento; cons. in pediatrics Bur. of Disability Ins. Social Security, Balt., 1973-74; pediatrician East Balt. Med. Plan, 1974-76; pvt. practice in pediatrics Boston, 1980-87; dir. med. svcs. Mediqual Systems, 1988-92; pres. Strauss Healthcare Consulting, Skillman, N.J., 1992-94; v.p. med. affairs Sutter Health Bay Region, 1995; chief med. officer Calif. Advantage, Inc., Oakland, 1995—. Fellow Am. Acad. Pediatrics; mem. Am. Coll. Physicians Execs., Mass. Med. Soc., Calif. Med. Assn., Alpha Lambda Delta. Home: 45 Summit Ridge Pl Redwood City CA 94062-3935

STRAUSS, PETER, actor; b. Croton-on-Hudson, N.Y., Feb. 20, 1947; m. Nicole S.; children: Justin, Tristen. Student, Northwestern U. Performances include (films) debut in Hail Hero, 1969, Soldier Blue, 1970, The Trial of the Catonsville Nine, The Last Tycoon, 1976, Spacehunter, 1983, Nick of Time, 1995, Keys to Tulsa, 1996; (TV dramas) Rich Man, Poor Man, 1976, Rich Man, Poor Man-Book II, 1976-77, Masada, 1981, Tender is the Night, 1985, Kane and Abel, 1986; (TV spls.) The Man Without a Country, 1973, A Whale for the Killing, 1981; (TV movies) The FBI Story: The FBI Vs. the Ku Klux Klan, 1975, Attack on Terror, 1975, Young Joe, the Forgotten Kennedy, 1978, The Jericho Mile, 1979 (Emmy award), Angel on My Shoulder, 1980, Heart of Steel, 1983, Under Siege, 1986, Penalty Phase, 1986, The Proud Men, 1987, Brotherhood of the Rose, 1989, Peter Gunn, 1989, 83 Hours Till Dawn, 1990, Flight of the Black Angel, 1991, Fugitive Among Us, 1992, Trial: The Price of Passion, 1992, Men Don't Tell, 1993, The Yearling, 1994, Texas Justice, 1995, In the Lake of the Woods, 1996, (TV series) Maloney, 1996. Office: Gersh Agy 232 N Canon Dr Beverly Hills CA 90210*

STRAUSS, PETER L(ESTER), law educator; b. N.Y.C., Feb. 26, 1940; s. Simon D. and Elaine Ruth (Mandle) S.; m. Joanna Burnstine, Oct. 1, 1964; children: Benjamin, Bethany. AB magna cum laude, Harvard U., 1961; LLB magna cum laude, Yale U., 1964. Bar: D.C. 1965, U.S. Supreme Ct., 1968. Law clk. U.S. Ct. Appeals D.C. Cir., 1964-65, U.S. Supreme Ct., 1965-66; lectr. Haile Selassie U. Sch. Law, Addis Ababa, Ethiopia, 1966-68; asst. to solicitor gen. Dept. Justice, Washington, 1968-71; assoc. prof. law Columbia U., 1971-74, prof., 1974—, Betts Prof., 1985—, vice dean, 1996; gen. counsel NRC, 1975-77, Adminstrv. Conf. U.S., 1984-95; Byrne vis. prof. Sch. Law Harvard U., Cambridge, Mass., 1994. Adv. bd. Lexis Electronic Author's Press, 1995—. Recipient John Marshall prize Dept. Justice, 1970, Disting. Svc. award NRC, 1977. Editor: Administrative Law Abstracts, 1997—. Mem. ABA (chair sect. adminstrv. law and regulatory practice 1992-93, Disting. Scholarship award 1988), Am. Law Inst. Author: (with Abba Paulos, translator) Fetha Negast: The Law of the Kings, 1968; (with others) Administrative Law Cases and Comments, 1995; Introduction to Administrative Justice in the United States, 1989; (with Paul Verkuil) Administrative Law Problems, 1983; contbr. articles to law revs. Office: Columbia U Law Sch 435 W 116th St New York NY 10027-7201

STRAUSS, ROBERT DAVID, lawyer; b. Cambridge, Mass., Oct. 20, 1951; s. Walter Adolf and Lilo (Teutsch) S.; m. Deborah Mackall, Feb. 15, 1986; 1 child, Benjamin Walter. BA, Emory U., 1973, JD, 1976. Bar: Ga. 1976. Assoc. Gambrell & Russell, Atlanta, 1976-81; ptnr. Smith, Gambrell & Russell, Atlanta, 1981-89, Trotter Smith & Jacobs, Atlanta, 1989-92, Troutman Sanders, Atlanta, 1992—. Contbr. articles to profl. jours. Mem. ABA (chmn. leasing subcom. 1988-94, uniform comml. code com.), State Bar of Ga., Equipment Leasing Assn. Am. Home: 1159 Morningside Pl NE Atlanta GA 30306-3061 Office: Troutman Sanders 5200 NationsBank Plz 600 Peachtree St NE Atlanta GA 30308-2214

STRAUSS, ROBERT PHILIP, economics educator; b. Cleve., May 11, 1944; s. Harry and Carrie S.; m. Celeste G. Meade, Jan. 11, 1980; children—Sarah Elizabeth, David Anthony, Elena Nicole. A.B. in Econs., U. Mich., 1966; M.A., U. Wis., 1968, Ph.D. in Econs., 1970. Fellow Inst. Research on Poverty, 1968-69; asst. prof. econs. U. N.C., Chapel Hill, 1969-73, assoc. prof., 1973-79; econ. policy fellow Brookings Instn., Washington, 1971-72; economist U.S. Congress Joint Com. Taxation, 1975-78; prof. econs. and pub. policy Carnegie-Mellon U., Pitts., 1979—, assoc. dean Sch. Urban and Pub. Affairs, 1981-83, dir. Ctr. for Pub. Fin. Mgmt., 1984-91; dir. research Pa. Tax Commn., 1979-81; vis. prof. econs. and pub. policy U. Rochester, 1992-94. Mem. Pa. Local Tax Reform Commn., 1987; sec. faculty Carnegie-Mellon U., 1991-92. Recipient Exceptional Service award U.S. Treasury, 1972, Disting. Service award Pitts. Tax Execs. Inst., 1987; grantee NSF, U.S. Dept. Labor, U.S. Treasury, HUD, Social Security Adminstrn. Mem. Am. Econ. Assn., Econometric Soc., Am. Statis. Assn., Nat. Tax Assn., Pub. Choice Soc., Assn. for Pub. Policy and Mgmt., Am. Soc. for Pub. Adminstrn., Am. Acctg. Assn. Club: Cosmos. Home: 2307 Country Pl Export PA 15632-9059 Office: 5000 Forbes Ave Pittsburgh PA 15213-3815

STRAUSS, SIMON DAVID, manufacturing executive; b. Lima, Peru, July 24, 1911; s. Lester W. and Bertha (Miller) S.; m. Elaine Ruth Mandle, Sept. 1, 1936 (dec.); children: Peter Lester, Susan Dee (Mrs. Samuel Carson Orr); m. Janet McCloskey Robbins, Dec. 19, 1982. Student, Mackay Sch., Valparaiso, Chile, 1919-21, Townsend Harris Hall, N.Y.C., 1924-27; LL.D., U. Ariz., 1981. Asst. editor Engring. and Mining Jour., 1927-32; editor Madison Eagle, N.J., 1932-34; economist Standard Statistics Co., 1935-41; asst. to dep. adminstr. Fed. Loan Agy., 1941; asst. v.p., v.p. Metals Res. Co., 1942-45; sales dept. Asarco, Inc., 1946; sales mgr. Am. Smelting & Refining Co., 1947-71, v.p., 1949-71, exec. v.p., 1971-77, vice chmn., 1977-79, also dir., 1953-81; cons. indsl. firms, 1981—; gov. N.Y. Commodity Exchange Inc., 1947-63; dir., mem. exec. com. Zinc Inst., 1953-77, pres., 1957-59, 73-75; cons. Def. Materials Procurement Agy., 1951-52, Office Def. Moblzn., 1954-55; mem. adv. coms. Munitions Bd.; mem. adv. com. Nat. Growth Policies, 1976, vis. lectr. MIT, 1977-84, Columbia U., 1988; lectr. Pa. State U., 1978, Poly. Inst. N.Y., 1978, U. Ariz., 1979, 80, Columbia U., 1982, U. Calif., Berkeley, 1986. Author: (with L.H. Sloan) Two Cycles of Corporation Profits, 1936, (with E.H. Robie) Mineral Economics, 1959, (with W.H. Vogeley), 1976, Trouble in the Third Kingdom, 1986; contbr. articles on mining to trade jours. Trustee Manhattan Sch. Music, 1958-79, v.p., 1966-79; bd. dirs. Internat. Copper Research Assn.; mem. bd. govs. Nat. Mining Hall of Fame and Mus., Leadville, Colo., 1987—. Mem. Lead Industries Assn. (pres. 1964-66, exec. com., dir., v.p. 1967-69, pres. 1970-71), Silver Inst. (dir., pres. 1971-73, chmn. bd. 1974-76), Am. Bur. Metal Stats. (chmn. 1975-77), Copper Club (pres. 1967-68), Mining and Metall. Soc. Am. (Gold medal 1984), Am. Inst. Mining and Metall. Engrs. (hon.), Council Fgn. Relations. Clubs: Mining, Stockbridge Golf.

STRAUSS, SIMON WOLF, chemist, materials scientist; b. Bedzin, Keltz, Poland, Apr. 15, 1920; came to U.S., 1929; s. Israel Calvin and Anna (Hops) S.; m. Mary Jo Boehm, Dec. 27, 1957; children: Jack Calvin, Ruth Ann. BS in Chemistry, Polytech. Inst. of Bklyn., 1944, MS in Chemistry, 1947, PhD in Chemistry, 1950. Rsch. chemist Nat. Bur. Standards, Washington, 1951-55; from phys. chemist to head chem. metallurgy sect. Naval Rsch. Lab., Washington, 1955-63; sr. staff scientist Air Force Systems Command, Washington, 1963-80; ind. tech. cons. Washington, 1980—; mem. bd. civil svc. examiners for sci. and tech. pers. U.S. Naval Dist. of Washington, 1959-63; mem. air force panel expert tech. reviewers patents for secrecy considerations Office Air Force Judge Advocate Gen., Washington, 1965-80; co-chair com. on career planning and appraisal of sci. and engrs. Air Force Sys. Command, Washington, 1966-67; air force mem. in-house com. mgmt. rev. tech. info. program, Dept. Def., 1967; chair rsch. steering com. Air Force Dir. of Sci. Tech., Washington, 1976-80; mem., chair editorial adv. com. Washington Acad. Jour., 1983-87, chair com. on scholarly activities, 1984-88. Prin. compiler 75 Years of Scientific Thought, 1987; mem. bd. reviewers Jour. Chem. Engring. Data, 1965-66; contbr. articles to profl. jours. Judge Internat. Sci. Engring. Fair, 1970, 72, 73; nat. evaluator space shuttle student involvement program Nat. Sci. Tchrs. Assn., NASA, Washington, 1984, 85. With U.S. Army, 1944-45. Recipient Air Force Decoration for Exceptional Civilian Svc., 1980, first Disting. Career in Sci. award Wash. Acad. Scis., 1988, Disting. Svc. award, 1990. Fellow AAAS, Wash. Acad. Scis. (first Disting. Scholar-in-Residence 1984-89, pres. 1986-87, life mem. fund trustee 1988—), Am. Inst. Chemists; mem. Math. Assn. Am., Air Force Assn., Cosmos Club, Air Force Materials Lab. (hon. life mem.), Sigma Pi Sigma, Phi Lambda Upsilon, Sigma Xi. Achievements include 3 patents for electrodeposition of Cadmium on high strength steel; research and development of advanced composites technology; the development of equations for the estimation of surface tensions, viscosities and densities of liquid metals as a function of temperature. Home: 4506 Cedell Pl Temple Hills MD 20748-3805 *Living a life not just for oneself contributes not only to the elevation of humankind, but also to the enoblement and enrichment of one's own life.*

STRAUSS, STANLEY ROBERT, lawyer; b. N.Y.C., June 3, 1915; s. Maurice M. and Blanche Anna (Danciger) S.; m. Margaret Inglis Forbes, Mar. 13, 1944 (div. 1950); m. Helen Anne Cummings, Dec. 31, 1975 (dec. 1980). BA cum laude, Williams Coll., 1936; LLB, Columbia U., 1940. Bar: N.Y. 1941, D.C. 1964, U.S. Ct. Appeals (1st cir.) 1977, U.S. Ct. Appeals (3d cir.) 1986, U.S. Ct. Appeals (4th cir.) 1974, U.S. Ct. Appeals (5th cir.) 1970, U.S. Ct. Appeals (6th cir.) 1977, U.S. Ct. Appeals (8th cirs.) 1975, U.S. Supreme Ct. 1965. Assoc. Howard Henig, N.Y.C., 1940-41; atty. NLRB, Washington, 1946-52, supervising atty., 1953-59, chief counsel, 1959-63; assoc. Vedder, Price, Kaufman & Kammholz, Washington, 1963-65, ptnr., 1965-90; of counsel Ogletree, Deakins, Nash, Smoak & Stewart, Washington, 1990—. Co-author: Practice and Procedure Before the National Labor Relations Board, 3d edit., 1980, 4th edit., 1987, 5th edit., 1996. Officer U.S. Army, 1941-45, PTO. Decorated Bronze Star; Horn scholar Columbia U. Law Sch., 1937-40. Mem. ABA, Fed. Bar Assn., D.C. Bar Assn., Kenwood Country Club. Avocations: golf, tennis. Home: 4956 Sentinel Dr Bethesda MD 20816-3594 Office: Ogletree Deakins Nash 2400 N St NW Washington DC 20037-1153

STRAUSS, ULRICH PAUL, chemist, educator; b. Frankfurt, Germany, Jan. 10, 1920; s. Richard and Marianne (Seligmann) S.; m. Esther Lipetz, June 20, 1943 (dec. Sept. 1949); children—Dorothy, David; m. Elaine Greenbaum, Nov. 23, 1950; children—Elizabeth, Evelyn. A.B., Columbia U., 1941; Ph.D., Cornell U., 1944. Sterling fellow Yale U., 1946-48; faculty Rutgers U., New Brunswick, N.J., 1948—, prof. phys. chemistry, 1960-90, prof. emeritus, 1990—; also dir. Sch. Chemistry, 1965-71, chmn. dept. chemistry, 1974-80; prof. emeritus Rutgers U., 1990—. Mem. editorial bd. Macromolecules, 1990-93; contbr. articles to profl. jours. Recipient Sci. achievement award Johnson Wax Co., 1986; NSF sr. fellow Nat. Center Sci. Research, Strasbourg, France, 1961-62; Guggenheim fellow U. Oxford, Eng., 1971-72. Fellow N.Y. Acad. Scis.; mem. Am. Chem. Soc. (chmn. phys. chemistry group N.J. sect. 1956, councillor 1961-72, honored by 1-day symposium at nat. meeting N.Y.C. 1986, Excellence in Edn. award N.J. sect. 1994). Home: 227 Lawrence Ave Highland Park NJ 08904-1837 Office: Rutgers U Dept Chemistry New Brunswick NJ 08903

STRAUSS, WILLIAM VICTOR, lawyer; b. Cin., July 5, 1942; s. William Victor and Elsa (Lovitt) S.; m. Linda Leopold, Nov. 9, 1969; children: Nancy T., Katherine S. AB cum laude, Harvard U., 1964; JD, U. Pa., 1967. Bar: Ohio 1967. Pres. Strauss & Troy, Cin., 1969—; pres. Security Title and Guaranty Agy., Inc., Cin., 1982—. Trustee Cin. Psychoanalytic Inst., 1990—; dir. Suburban Fed. Savings Bank; trustee Cin. Contemporary Arts Ctr., 1997—. Mem. ABA, Nat. Assn. Office and Indsl. Parks, Ohio State Bar Assn., Cin. Bar Assn., Cin. C. of C. (mem. local govt. com. 1980—), Nat. Leased Housing Assn. Avocations: sports, jazz, world affairs. Home: 40 Walnut Ave Wyoming OH 45215-4350 Office: Strauss & Troy 201 E 5th St 2100 PNC Ctr Cincinnati OH 45202

STRAUSSLER, TOMAS See STOPPARD, TOM

STRAUSZ-HUPÉ, ROBERT, ambassador, author; b. Vienna, Austria, Mar. 25, 1903; emigrated to U.S., 1923, naturalized, 1938; s. Rudolph and Doris (Hedwig) Strausz-H.; m. Eleanor deGraff Cuyler, Apr. 26, 1938 (dec. 1976); m. Mayrose Ferreira Nugara, Aug. 22, 1979. A.M., Ph.D., U. Pa., 1944. Investment banker, 1927-37; assoc. editor Current History, 1939-41; assoc. prof. polit. sci. U. Pa., 1946-52, former prof.; spl. lectr., 1940-46; dir. Fgn. Policy Rsch. Inst., 1955-69; U.S. amb. Ceylon, 1970-72, Belgium, 1972-74, Sweden, 1974-76, NATO, 1976-77, Turkey, 1981-89; disting. fellow U.S. Inst. Peace, 1992-93. Author: The Russian-German Riddle, 1940, Axis-America, 1941, Geopolitics, 1942, The Balance of Tomorrow, 1945, International Relations, 1950, The Zone of Indifference, 1952, Power and Community, 1956, Democracy and American Foreign Policy, 1995, (with Kintner, Cottrell, Dougherty) Protracted Conflict, 1959, (with W. Kintner, Stefan Possony) A Forward Strategy for America, 1961, (with others) Building the Atlantic World, 1963, In My Time, 1967, Dilemmas Facing the Nation, 1979; editor: The Idea of Colonialism, 1958, Orbis, 1957-69. Lectr. Air War Coll., 1953. Served to lt. col. AUS. Mem. Coun. Fgn. Rels., Merion Cricket Club, Met. Club, Knickerbocker Club. Lutheran. Address: White Horse Farm 864 Grubbs Mill Rd Newtown Square PA 19073-1210

STRAVALLE-SCHMIDT, ANN ROBERTA, lawyer; b. N.Y.C., Jan. 2, 1957. Grad. cum laude, Phillips Exeter Acad., 1975; student, Occidental Coll., 1975-78, Oxford Coll., Eng., 1976-77; BS cum laude, Boston Coll., 1980; JD, Boston U., 1987. Bar: Conn. 1987, U.S. Dist. Ct. Conn. 1988, U.S. Supreme Ct. 1993. Consulting staff Arthur Andersen, Boston, 1980-82; supr. CID ops. Aetna Life & Casualty, Hartford, Conn., 1982-84; summer intern U.S. Atty.'s Office, Boston, 1985; jud. clk. Hon. Judge Thayer III N.H. Supreme Ct., 1987-88; trial lawyer Day, Berry & Howard, Hartford, 1988-91; sr. lawyer comml. litigation and appellate practice Berman & Sable, Hartford, 1991-96; asst. dir. strategic claims Traveler's Property and Casualty Corp., Hartford, 1996—; brief judge Nat. Appellate Advocacy Competition, 1996. Mem. editorial bd. Conn. Bar Jour., 1990—; contbr. articles to profl. jours. Mem. Hebron Dem. Town Com., Hebron Bd. Fin., 1995—, Hebron Sch. Bldg. Com., 1997—; justice of the peace, 1997—; apptd. mem. Hebron Bldg. Com., 1997—. Recipient Hennessey Scholar, Boston U., 1987. Mem. ABA, Conn. Bar Assn. (founder, chair appellate practice com. litigation sect. 1994-96, mem. exec. com. litigation sect.), Hartford Assn. Women Attys. Home: 51 Elizabeth Dr Hebron CT 06248 Office: Travlers/Aetna 8PB One Tower Sq Hartford CT 06183

STRAW, GARY LEE, construction company executive; b. Johnstown, Pa., May 14, 1956; s. E. Leroy and Cleda A. Straw; m. Faye L. Petrosky, Sept. 27, 1980. BA in Social Scis., Bus. and Econs., U. Pittsburgh, Johnstown, 1978. Cert. engring. technician, cert. level III engr. Nat. Inst. for Cert. in Engring. Technologies. Temperature control technician L.W. Straw & Co., Johnstown, Pa., 1977-80; design draftsman Crown Am. Corp., Johnstown, 1980; project and ops. mgr. Charles J. Merlo, Inc., Johnstown, 1980-86; v.p. Straw Constrn. Co., Inc., Johnstown, 1986—. Chmn. Richland Twp. Planning Commn., Johnstown, 1989—. Mem. Am. Concrete Inst., Am. Soc. Hwy. Engrs., Equipment Mgmt. Coun., Am. Assn. Cost Engrs. Home: 114 Timothy St Johnstown PA 15904-2438 Office: Straw Constrn 115 Sann St Johnstown PA 15904-5805

STRAWDERMAN, WILLIAM E., statistics educator; b. Westerly, R.I., Apr. 25, 1941; s. Robert Lee and Alida Browning (Dow) S.; m. Susan Linda Grube; July 20, 1985; children: Robert Lee, William Edward, Heather Lynne. BS, U. R.I., 1963; MS, Cornell U., 1965, Rutgers U., 1967; PhD, Rutgers U., 1969. Mem. tech. staff Bell Telephone Labs., Holmdel, N.J., 1965-67; prof. Stanford (Calif.) U., 1969-70; instr. Rutgers U., New Brunswick, N.J., 1967-69, prof. stats., 1970—. Contbr. over 90 articles to profl. jours. Fellow Inst. Math. Stats., Am. Statis. Assn. Office: Rutgers U Statistics Dept Hill Ctr-Busch Campus New Brunswick NJ 08903

STRAWN, FRANCES FREELAND, real estate executive; b. Waynesville, N.C., Nov. 18, 1946; d. Thomas M. and Jimmie (Smith) Freeland; m. David Updegraff Strawn, Aug. 30, 1974; children: Kirk, Trisha. AA, Brevard C.C., Cocoa, Fla., 1976; postgrad. U. Cen. Fla., 1976-77, Grad. Realtor Inst. Cert. real estate brokerage mgr., residential specialist; realtor, broker, pres. Advance Am., Inc., Orlando, 1982-89; assoc. Ann Cross, Inc., Winter Park, Fla., 1988—. Contbr. articles to Fla. Realtor, 1993, Communique, 1994. Bd. dirs. Vol. Ctr. of Cen. Fla. (rec. sec. 1989), Cen. Fla. Zool. Pk., 1989-92; co-chmn, fundraiser Black Tie Walk on the Wild Side, 1992; program chmn. Young Rep. Women, Orlando, 1983; coord. Congressman Bill Nelson's Washington Internship Program; co-ticket chmn. Art and Architecture Orlando Regional Hosp.; mem. steering com. Fla. Heritage Homecoming, Orlando, 1987; sec. Mayor's Wife's Campaign Activities, Orlando, 1986-87; vice chmn. Horizon Exec. Bd., 1987-89, chmn., 1989; recording sec. Women's Bus. Edn. Council, 1988, mem. adv. bd. , 1987, bd. dirs. 1988-90; bd. dirs. Women's Resource Ctr., 1989-90; lectr. Jr. Achievement., 1988-93; mem. steering com. scholarship dinner Crummer Bus. Coll. Rollins Coll., 1992. Mem. Creative Bus. Ownership for Women (adv. bd. 1986-88, grievance vice chmn. 1989), Nat. Assn. Realtors, Orlando Bd. Realtors (grievance com. 1985-91, profl. standards com. 1983-84, lectr. Success Series 1988—), Women's Coun. of Realtors, Women's Exec. Coun., Citrus Club (Orlando, bd. dirs 1990-95). Episcopalian. Avocations: travel, needlepoint, canoe trips, skiing. Home: 105 NW Ivanhoe Blvd Orlando FL 32804-5958 Office: Ann Cross Inc 233 W Park Ave Winter Park FL 32789-4343

STRAWN, JUDY C., public relations professional; b. Walla Walla, Wash., Oct. 8, 1950; d. Warren Clarence and Nora Melissa (Riley) S. BA in Pub. Communications, Columbia Union Coll., 1975; postgrad., UCLA, 1985—. Sec., editor Mitsubishi Bank of Calif., L.A., 1977-78; adminstrv. asst., bookkeeper Young & Rubicam West, L.A., 1978-80; advertising media coord. Thriftimart Inc (now SFI), L.A., 1980-82; dir. pub. rels. Phipps Racing Corp., Beverly Hills, Calif., 1985-86; coord. spl. projects Nat. Hot Rod Assn., Glendora, Calif., 1988-89; pvt. practice pub. rels. L.A., 1982—; legal sec. Morrison and Forester, L.A., 1989-93; legal sec. criminal def. firm Barry Tarlow, 1996—; founder and pres. Racers Who Care. Co-producer (play) Truth Be Told, 1989-90; contbr. articles to profl. jours.; author press releases. Pub. rels. and promotion for RWC Drug and Alcohol Abuse Program. Mem. Am. Auto Racing Writers and Broadcasters Assn., Amnesty Internat., Planetary Soc., Smithsonian Assocs. Democrat. Avocations: photography, writing. Office: 7095 Hollywood Blvd # 769 Los Angeles CA 90028-8903

STRAWN, SUSAN HEATHCOTE, medical administrator; b. Pasadena, Calif., Feb. 10, 1940; d. Edward McNair and Ann Heathcote (Stevens) McNair; m. Harvey G. Holtz, June 24, 1960 (div. June 1974); children: Christopher, Edward, David. AS, Butte Coll., 1973; lifetime tchg. credential, Calif. State U., Chico, 1987. Cert. respiratory therapist, 1974, cardiovascular tech., 1985. Respiratory therapist Feather River Hosp., Paradise, Calif., 1973-87; instr. respiratory therapy Butte Coll., Chico, 1982-87, instr. cardiovascular tech., 1987-95; cardiovasc. technologist Chico Cardiology, 1987-90; dir. cardiopulmonary dept. Oroville (Calif.) Hosp., 1990—; mem. adv. bd. Butte Coll., Chico, 1982—. Author 2-yr. cardiovasc. tech. program for Butte Coll., 1987. Mem. NOW, Am. Assn. Respiratory Care, Cardiovasc. Internat., Echo Soc., Calif. Soc. for Respiratory Care. Democrat. Episcopalian. Avocations: oil painting, traveling, reading, being a grandmother, raising black sheep. Home: 32 Humpyback Rd Oroville CA 95965-9104 Office: Oroville Hosp 2767 Olive Hwy Oroville CA 95966-6118

STRAYER, BARRY LEE, federal judge; b. Moose Jaw, Sask., Can., Aug. 13, 1932; s. Carl John and Nina Naomi (Carr) S.; m. Eleanor Lorraine Staton, July 2, 1955; children: Alison Lee, Jonathan Mark Staton, Colin James. BA, U. Sask., Can., 1953, LLB, 1955; BCL, Oxford U., Eng., 1957; SJD, Harvard U., 1966. Bar: Sask., 1959. Crown solicitor Gov. Sask., Regina, 1959-62; prof. law U. Sask., 1962-68; dir. constitutional rev. Gov. Can., Ottawa, 1968-72, dir. constitutional law, 1972-74, asst. dep. minister justice, 1974-83; judge Fed. Ct. Can., Ottawa, 1983—; jud. mem. Competition Tribunal Can., Ottawa, 1986-93; judge Fed. Ct. Appeal of Can., 1994—; chief justice Ct. Martial Appeal Ct. of Can., 1994—; sessional lectr. U. Ottawa, 1973-78; constitutional advisor Rep. Seychelles, Victoria, 1979; adviser Hongkong Govt. Bill of Rights, 1989. Author: Judicial Review of Legislation, 1968, Canadian Constitution and the Courts, 1983, 3d edit., 1988; contbr. articles to profl. jours. Mem. Internat. Bar Assn., Internat. Commn. Jurists, Rideau Club, Larrimac Golf Club. Office: Fed Ct, Kent & Wellington Sts, Ottawa, ON Canada K1A 0H9

STRAYHORN, RALPH NICHOLS, JR., lawyer; b. Durham, N.C., Feb. 16, 1923; Ralph Nichols and Annie Jane (Cooper) S.; m. Donleen Carol MacDonald, Sept. 10, 1949; children: Carol Strayhorn Rose, Ralph Nichols III. BS in Bus. Adminstrn., U. N.C., 1947, LLB/JD, 1950. Bar: N.C. 1950, U.S. Dist. Ct. (mid. and ea. dists.) N.C. 1950, U.S. Ct. Appeals (4th cir.) 1950. Assoc. Victor S. Bryant, Sr., Durham, 1950-55; ptnr. Bryant, Lipton, Strayhorn & Bryant, Durham, 1956-62; sr. ptnr. Newson, Graham, Strayhorn & Hedrick, Durham, 1962-78; gen. counsel Wachovia Corp., Wachovia Bank and Trust Co., N.A., Winston-Salem, N.C., 1978-88; of counsel Petree Stockton Winston-Salem, N.C., 1988—; bd. dirs. Graphics Industries, Inc., Atlanta; mem. legal adv. com. to N.Y. Stock Exch., 1986-89; adv. dir. Wachovia Bank and Trust Co., Durham, 1973-78; chmn. bd. 1st Fed. Savs. & Loan Assn., Durham, 1976-78; mem. N.C. Gen. Assembly, 1959-61; bd. of visitors U. N.C., Wake Forest U. Law Sch. Lt. comdr. USNR, 1943-46. Fellow Am. Coll. Trial Lawyers, Am. Bar Found., Internat. Assn. Def. Counsel; mem. ABA, N.C. Bar Assn. (pres. 1971-72), Newcomen Soc. of U.S., 4th Jud. Conf. Episcopalian. Clubs: Old Town Club (Winston-Salem). Office: Kilpatrick Stockton 1001 W 4th St Winston Salem NC 27101-2410

STRAYTON, ROBERT GERARD, public communications executive; b. Bklyn., Aug. 4, 1935; s. George Andrew and Kathryn Loretta (Monahan) S.; m. Patricia Cecelia Hand, Aug. 16, 1958 (div. Aug. 1972); children—Jennifer Anne, Melissa Marie, Robert Hand, Bruce Andrew; m. Jayne Helene Kramer, Mar. 4, 1983. B.A. in English, Villanova U., 1957. Accredited in pub. relations. Account exec. Carl Byoir & Assocs., Inc., N.Y.C., 1962-65; dir. pub. relations and advt. EDP div. Honeywell Inc., Wellesley, Mass., 1966-69; pres. Strayton Corp., Wellesley, Mass., 1969-84; pres., chief operating officer Gray Strayton Internat., Waltham, Mass., 1984-86; exec. v.p., vice chmn. bd. dirs. Gray and Co., Washington; exec. v.p., mng. dir. Advanced Technology div. Hill and Knowlton, Inc., 1986-89; pres. The Strayton Group Inc., 1990—. Mem. NCCJ, Boston, 1984—; trustee Bacon Free Libr., 1994—. Lt. (j.g.) USNR, 1958-61. Fellow Pub. Rels. Soc. Am. (Silver Anvil award 1968, 89, counselor, mem. exec. com. Counselors Acad. 1983-84, disting. svc. award 1984); mem. Nat. Investors Rels. Inst., Assn. Nat. Advertisers, Advt. Club Boston (trustee 1982-87), Trout Unltd. (v.p., dir. 1984-93), Atlantic Salmon Task Force (bd. dirs. 1988—), Blue Water Sailing Club (bd. govs. 1995—), Red Brook Harbor Yacht Club, Wellesley Country Club, Flycasters Club. Republican. Roman Catholic. Avocations: sailing; flyfishing; tennis; golf. Home: 18 Phillips Pond Rd Natick MA 01760-5643 Office: The Strayton Group Inc 8 Pleasant St Natick MA 01760

STRAZZELLA, JAMES ANTHONY, law educator, lawyer; b. Hanover, Pa., May 18, 1939; s. Anthony F. and Teresa Ann (D'Alonzo) S.; m. Judith A. Coppola, Oct. 9, 1965; children: Jill M., Steven A., Tracy Ann, Michael P. AB Villanova U., 1961; JD, U. Pa., 1964. Bar: Pa. 1964, U.S. Ct. Appeals (3d cir.) 1964, D.C. 1965, U.S. Dist. Ct. D.C. 1965, U.S. Ct. Appeals (D.C. cir.) 1965, U.S Dist Ct. (ea. and mid. dist.) Pa. 1969, U.S. Supreme Ct. 1969, U.S. Ct. Appeals (4th cir.) 1983. Law clk. to Hon. Samuel Roberts Pa. Supreme Ct., 1964-65; asst. U.S. atty. dept. chief appeals, spl. asst. to U.S. Atty., Washington, D.C., 1965-69; vice dean, asst. prof. law U. Pa., Phila., 1969-73; faculty Temple U., Phila., 1973—, James G. Schmidt Chair in law, 1989—, acting dean, 1987-89; chief counsel Kent State investigation Pres.'s Commn. Campus Unrest, 1970; chmn. Atty. Gen.'s Task Force on Family Violence, Pa., 1985-89; mem., chmn. justice ops. Mayor's Criminal Justice Coordinating Commn., Phila., 1983-85; Pa. Joint Council Criminal Justice, 1979-82; Com. to Study Pa.'s Unified Jud. System, 1980-82; Jud. Council Pa., 1972-82; chmn. criminal procedural rules com. Pa. Supreme Ct., 1972-85; mem. task force on prison overcrowding, 1983-85, rsch. adv. com. ,1988, Pa. Commn. on Crime and Delinquency; chmn. U.S. Magistrate Judge Merit Selection Com., 1991, mem., 1989, 90, 91; co-chair Mayor's Transition Task Force on Pub. Safety, Phila., 1992; designate D.C. Com. on Adminstrv. Justice Under Emergency Conditions, 1968. Mem. adv. bd. dirs., past pres. A Better Chance in Lower Merion; dir. Hist. Fire Mus., Phila.; dir. Neighborhood Civic Assn. Bala-Cynwyd, Pa., 1984-87. Recipient Lindback Found. award for disting. teaching, 1983, Atty. Gen.'s Advancement of Justice award, 1989, Disting. Pub. Svc. award Assn. State and County Detectives, 1989, Spl. Merit award Pa. Assn. Police Chiefs, 1989, significant contbn. to legal scholarship and edn. Beccaria award Phila. Bar Assn. and Nat. IAB Assn., 1995. Fellow Am. Bar Found.; mem. Am. Law Inst., ABA (faculty appellate judges' seminars 1977—, various coms., acad. advisor appellate judges edn. com. 1993—, reporter task force federalization criminal law 1997—), Fed. Bar Assn. (Phila. Crim. Law com. adv. bd. 1988-93, chmn. nat. criminal law com. 1991-92), Pa. Bar Assn. (commn. profl. standards 1981-84, chmn. criminal law sect., 1986-88, Spl. Merit award 1987), Phila. Bar Assn. (criminal justice sect., appellate cts. com.), del. D.C. Jud. Conf. 1985, Order of the Coif (exec. bd. U. Pa.), St. Thomas More Soc. (pres., 1985-86, past dir. Phila. area, St. Thomas More award 1996). Roman Catholic. Contbr. articles to legal jours. Home and Office: 100 Maple Ave Bala Cynwyd PA 19004-3017 Office: Temple U Law Sch 1719 N Broad St Philadelphia PA 19122-6002

STREAM, ARNOLD CRAGER, lawyer, writer; b. N.Y.C.; s. Mervyn and Sophia (Hyams) S.; m. Barbara Bloom, Oct. 1, 1967; children by previous marriages: Jane, Abigail. BA, CCNY, 1936; LLD, St. Lawrence U., 1940. Bar: N.Y. 1940, D.C. 1942. Asst. U.S. Atty. N.Y.Dist., 1940-43; ptnr. Amen, Weisman & Butler, N.Y.C., 1948-55; exec. v.p., gen. counsel C & C TV Corp., 1955-60, Hazel Bishop, Inc., 1955-60; trial lawyer, 1960-91; sr. ptnr. Monasch, Chazen & Stream, N.Y.C., 1973-82, Blum, Gersen & Stream,

N.Y.C., 1982-93; ret., 1993; former trial counsel Gulfstream Aerospace Corp., Twentieth Century-Fox Film Corp., French Embassy, N.Y.C.; spl. counsel to TV industry; vis. lectr. Tauro Coll. Law; spkr. on lit. topics for Gt. Neck Libr.; archivist Palace of the Govs. and Mus. Fine Arts, Sante Fe; tutor lit. and bus. law Santa Fe C.C. Author: (novels) The Third Bullet, Until Proven Guilty, Nemo; (short story) Sudi, others; contbr. book revs., tax series, series on constl. law, articles to profl. jours. Served to lt. col. JAGD, AUS, 1943-46. Mem. Bar of Assn. of City of N.Y. *A lawyer standing in the courtroom provides the ultimate buffer against importunate government and individual rights.*

STREAN, BERNARD M., retired naval officer; b. Big Cabin, Okla., Dec. 16, 1910; s. Ralph Lester and Maude (Hopkins) S.; m. Janet Lockey, June 12, 1935; children: Bernard M., Richard Lockey, Judy (Mrs. William S. Graves). B.S., U.S. Naval Acad., 1933; grad., Armed Forces Staff Coll., 1949, Nat. War Coll., 1958. Commd. ensign USN, 1933, advanced through grades to vice adm., 1965, designated naval aviator, 1935, assigned USS Pennsylvania, 1933-35; assigned Naval Air Sta. USN, Pensacola, Fla., 1935-36; assigned USS Saratoga USN, 1936-38, assigned San Diego Naval Sta., 1938-39; assigned Pearl Harbor Naval Air Sta. USN, Hawaii, 1939-40; assigned Naval Air Sta. USN, Jacksonville, Fla., 1940-42; comdr. Fighter Squadron 1, USS Yorktown USN, 1943-44, comdr. Air Group 98, 1944-45, comdr. Air Group 75, 1945-46, head tech. tng. program sect. Office Chief Naval Ops., 1950-51, comdg. officer Air Transp. Squadron 8, 1951-54, comdg. officer Pre-Flight Sch., 1954-56, comdg. officer USS Kenneth Whiting, 1956-57, comdg. officer USS Randolph, 1958-59, chief staff, aide to comdr. Naval Air Force, U.S. Atlantic Fleet, 1959-60, comdr. Fleet Air Whidbey, 1960-61, comdr. Patrol Force 7th Fleet, also U.S. Taiwan Patrol Force, 1961-62, asst. chief naval ops. for fleet ops., 1962-64, comdr. Carrier Div. 2, Atlantic Fleet, 1964-65, comdr. World's 1st All-Nuclear Naval Task Force, 1964, comdr. round the world cruise; dep. asst. chief for pers., Bur. Naval Pers. Dept. Navy, Washington, 1965-68; chief naval air tng. Naval Air Sta. Dept. Navy, Pensacola, Fla., 1968-71; ret., 1971; v.p. O.S.C. Franchise Devel. Corp., 1971-75; chmn. bd. Solaray Corp., 1975-80; v.p. Huet-Browning Corp., Washington. Bd. dirs. U.S. Olympic Com., 1965-68; trustee No. Va. Community Colls., 1978-82. Decorated Navy Cross, (2) D.F.C. with 2 gold stars, Air medal with 7 gold stars, Legion of Merit, D.S.M., numerous area and campaign ribbons; Disting. Svc. medal (Greece); medal of Pao-Ting (Republic of China). Mem. Mil. Order World Wars, Loyal Order Carabao, Early and Pioneer Naval Aviators Assn. (pres. 1977-79), Arlington County Tax Assn. (vice chmn. 1978-80), Md. Aviation Hist. Soc. (founder, bd. dirs. 1978-82), U.S. Naval Acad. Alumni Assn. (pres. Class 1933, 1973-88), Army Navy Club (Washington), N.Y. Yacht Club, Washington Golf and Country Club (Arlington), L.A. Country Club. Address: 1200 N Nash St Apt 846 Arlington VA 22209-3615 also: 804 N Camden Dr Beverly Hills CA 90210-3026

STREAR, JOSEPH D., public relations executive; b. N.Y.C., Nov. 5, 1933; s. Morris and Betty (Birenbaum) S. B.A., CCNY, 1955. Pres. AC&R Pub. Relations, Inc., N.Y.C., 1972-82; mng. ptnr. Kanan, Corbin, Schupak & Aronow, Inc., N.Y.C., 1982-84; pres. Strear, David & Mitchell, Inc., N.Y.C., 1984-91; now prin. Joseph Strear Pub. Rels., N.Y.C. Served to 1st lt. U.S. Army, 1955-57. Mem. Pub. Relations Soc. Am. Avocation: sports. Office: 408 W 57th St New York NY 10019-3053

STREATOR, EDWARD, diplomat; b. N.Y.C., Dec. 12, 1930; s. Edward James and Ella (Stout) S.; m. Priscilla Craig Kenney, Feb. 16, 1957; children: Edward James, III, Elinor Craig, Abigail Merrill. AB, Princeton U., 1952. Commd. fgn. service officer Dept. State, 1956; assigned ICA, 1956-58; 3d sec. embassy Addis Ababa, Ethiopia, 1958-60; 2d sec. embassy Lome Togo, 1960-62; intelligence research specialist Office Research and Analysis for Africa, Dept. State, Washington, 1962-63, staff asst. to sec. state, 1964-66, chief polit.-mil. affairs unit, 1966-67; dep. dir. polit.-mil. affairs Office Polit.-Mil. Affairs, 1967-68; dep. dir. polit. affairs U.S. Mission to NATO, 1968-69; dep. dir. Office NATO and Atlantic Polit.-Mil. Affairs, Dept. State, 1969-73; dir. office, 1973-75, dep. U.S. permanent rep. to NATO, dep. chief U.S. Mission to NATO, 1975-77; minister, dep. chief of mission Am. embassy, London, 1975-84; ambassador, U.S. rep. OECD Paris, 1984-87; bd. dirs. South Bank; chmn. New Atlantic Initiative, 1996—. U.S. dels. NATO and OECD Ministerial Meetings, 1964, 66, 69-75, 85-87; mem. 10th SEATO Coun. Min. Meeting, 1965; 2d spl. Inter-Am. Conf., 1965, Conf. Security and Coop., Europe, 1973; mem. Coun., Royal United Svcs. Inst., 1987-91, v. patron, 1991—; exec. com. The Pilgrims, Internat. Inst. Strategic Studies; gov. Ditchley Found., English Speaking Union, 1988-94; pres. Am. C. of C., U.K., 1988-94; chmn. European Coun. Am. C. of C., 1992-94; bd. dirs. Brit-Am. Arts Assn.; dir. Brit. Mus. Natural History Internat. Found.; adv. bd. Inst. U.S. Studies-U. London; mem. coun. Oxford Inst. Am. Studies; adv. com. Fulbright Commn., 1995—. Recipient Presdl. Meritorious Svc. award, 1986, Wilbur Carr award Dept. of State, 1987, Benjamin Franklin medal Royal Soc. Arts, 1992. Mem. Met. Club (Washington), Beefsteak Club, Garrick Club, White's Club (London), Mill Reef Club (Antigua). Episcopalian. Address: 80 Eaton Sq, London SW1W 9AP, England also: Chateau de St Aignan, 32480 La Romieu France

STRECK, RICHARD JAMES, medical administrator; b. Cin., June 9, 1953; s. Francis Anthony and Margaret (Banbury) S.; m. Joan Marie Garrini, Aug. 28, 1976; children Patricia Ann, Philip Anthony, Joseph John. BS, Xavier U., Cin., 1975; MD, U. Miami, 1980; MBA, Xavier U., 1991. Diplomate Am. Bd. Internal Medicine. Internal medicine resident Good Samaritan Hosp., Cin., 1980-83, emergency physician, 1983-87, medicine clerkship coord., 1988-91, assoc. dir. internal medicine residency, 1991-92, dir. internal medicine residency, 1992—, chmn. dept. medicine, 1992—; mem. med. adv. com. Prudential Ins., Cin., 1977—. Alt. del. 1st Dist. Ohio State Med. Assn., 1996—. Mem. AMA, Am. Coll. Physician Execs., Am. Coll. Physicians, Cin. Soc. Internal Meidicne, Cin. Acad. Medicine, Assn. Program Dir. Internal Medicine. Avocations: swimming, photography, gardening. Office: Good Samaritan Hosp 375 Dixmyth Ave Cincinnati OH 45220-2475

STRECKER, IGNATIUS J., archbishop; b. Spearville, Kans., Nov. 23, 1917; s. William J. and Mary B. (Knoeber) S. Student, St. Benedict's Coll., Atchison, Kans., 1931-37, Kenrick Sem., St. Louis, 1937-42, Cath. U. Am., 1944-45. Ordained priest Roman Cath. Ch., 1942; aux. chaplain USAAF, Great Bend, Kans., 1942-44; chancellor Diocese Wichita, 1948-62; bishop Diocese Springfield-Cape Girardeau, Mo., 1962-69; archbishop Archdiocese of Kansas City, Kans., 1969—; retired archbishop Archdiocese of Kansas City. Office: Chancery Office 12615 Parallel Ave Kansas City KS 66109-3718*

STRECKFUSS, JAMES ARTHUR, lawyer, historian; b. Cin., Apr. 28, 1951; s. Arthur James and Ruby Carolyn (Meyer) S.; m. Sharon Lynn Betz, Nov. 18, 1977; 1 child, Erich. BA in Polit. Sci., U. Cin., 1973; JD, Woodrow Wilson Coll. Law, 1981. Bar: Ind. Field rep. Ohio Lottery Commn., Cin., 1974-78; adminstrv. staff Powell, Goldstein, Frazer & Murphy, Atlanta, 1979-80; bailiff U.S. Ct. Appeals 11th Cir., Atlanta, 1980-81; spl. asst. Congressman Thomas Luken, Cin., 1982-84; job svc. employer com. staff State of Ohio, Cin., 1984—. Contbr.: The United States in the First World War: An Encyclopedia, 1995; mng. editor Over the Front, 1986—. Chmn. Progressive Young Dems., Cin., 1974-75. Mem. Ind. State Bar Assn., League of W.W. I Aviation Historians (pres. 1993—), Cross and Cockade Internat. Home: 3127 Penrose Pl Cincinnati OH 45211-6719

STREEB, GORDON LEE, diplomat, economist; b. Windsor, Colo., Dec. 24, 1935; s. Gerhard O. and Amelia (Martin) S.; m. Alice Junette Thomas, Aug. 11, 1962; children: Kurt, Kent, Kerry-Lynn. BSBA, U. Colo., 1959, BSChemE, 1959; PhD in Econs., U. Minn., 1978. Fgn. service officer U.S. Dept. State, Berlin, 1963-65; vice consul Am. Consulate, Guadalajara, Mex., 1965-67; instr. econs. U. Minn., 1968; examiner Bd. Examiners, 1972-73; internat. economist for trade policy Bur. Econ. and Bus. Affairs, Washington, 1973-77; econ. counselor U.S. mission European Office of the UN and other internat. orgns., Geneva, 1977-80; exec. asst. to undersec. of state on econ. affairs Washington, 1980-81; dep. asst. sec. state for econ. and social affairs Bur. Internat. Orgn. Affairs, Washington, 1981-84; dep. chief mission Am. Embassy, New Delhi, India, 1984-88; sr. inspector Dept. State, Washington, 1988-90; amb. to Zambia Am. Embassy, Lusaka, 1990-93; diplomat-in-residence The Carter Ctr., Atlanta, 1994-95; dir. Sustainable Devel. Program The Carter Ctr., 1995—. Home: 2680 Churchwell Ln Tucker GA 30084-2402 Office: The Carter Ctr One Copenhill Atlanta GA 30307

STREEP, MERYL (MARY LOUISE STREEP), actress; b. Madison, N.J., June 22, 1949; d. Harry Jr. and Mary W. Streep; m. Donald J. Gummer, 1978. BA, Vassar Coll., 1971; MFA, Yale U., 1975, DFA (hon.), 1983; DFA (hon.), Dartmouth Coll., 1981. Appeared with Green Mountain Guild, Woodstock, Vt.; Broadway debut in Trelawny of the Wells, Lincoln Center Beaumont Theater, 1975; N.Y.C. theatrical appearances include 27 Wagons Full of Cotton (Theatre World award), A Memory of Two Mondays, Henry V, Secret Service, The Taming of the Shrew, Measure for Measure, The Cherry Orchard, Happy End, Wonderland, Taken in Marriage, Alice in Concert (Obie award 1981); movie appearances include Julia, 1977, The Deer Hunter, 1978 (Best Supporting Actress award Nat. Soc. Film Critics), Manhattan, 1979, The Seduction of Joe Tynan, 1979, Kramer vs. Kramer, 1979 (N.Y. Film Critics' award, Los Angeles Film Critics' award, both for best actress, Golden Globe award, Acad. award for best supporting actress), The French Lieutenant's Woman, 1981 (Los Angeles Film Critics award for best actress, Brit. Acad. award, Golden Globe award 1981), Sophie's Choice, 1982 (Acad. award for best actress, Los Angeles Film Critics award for best actress, Golden Globe award 1982), Still of the Night, 1982, Silkwood, 1983, Falling in Love, 1984, Plenty, 1985, Out of Africa, 1985 (Los Angeles Film Critics award for best actress 1985), Heartburn, 1986, Ironweed, 1987, A Cry in the Dark, 1988 (named Best Actress N.Y. Film Critics' Circle, 1988, Best Actress Cannes Film Festival, 1989), She-Devil, 1989, Postcards From the Edge, 1990, Defending Your Life, 1991, Death Becomes Her, 1992, The House of the Spirits,1994, The River Wild, 1994, The Bridges of Madison County, 1995 (Acad. award nominee for best actress 1996), Before and After, 1996, Marvin's Room, 1997; TV film The Deadliest Season, 1977; TV miniseries Holocaust, 1978 (Emmy award); TV dramatic spls. Secret Service, 1977, Uncommon Women and Others, 1978, First Do No Harm, 1997; TV (narrator) The Velveteen Rabbit, 1985, A Vanishing Wilderness, 1990. Recipient Mademoiselle award, 1976, Woman of Yr. award B'nai Brith, 1979, Woman of Yr. award Hasty Pudding Soc., Harvard U., 1980, Best Supporting Actress award Nat. Bd. of Rev., 1979, Best Actress award Nat. Bd. of Rev., 1982, Star of Yr. award Nat. Assn. Theater Owners, 1983, People's Choice award, 1983, 85, 86, 87. Office: Creative Artists Agy 9830 Wilshire Blvd Beverly Hills CA 90212-1804

STREET, DANA MORRIS, orthopedic surgeon; b. N.Y.C., May 7, 1910; s. William Dana and Elizabeth (Clark) S.; m. Elna Alice Clare, June 18, 1940; children: Rosalyn Clare (Mrs. David R. Sprague), Dana Clark, Steven Morris, William Milo. B.S., Haverford Coll., 1932; M.D., Cornell U., 1936. Diplomate: Am. Bd. Orthopaedic Surgery. Intern pathology Duke Hosp., 1936-37, Duke Hosp. (orthopedics), 1937-38; asst. resident phys. medicine Albany (N.Y.) Hosp., 1938-39; fellow Nemour Found., 1939-40; intern orthopedics Boston City Hosp., 1940; asst. resident surgery Albany Hosp., 1940-41; intern, asst. resident orthopedics Johns Hopkins Hosp., 1941-42; fellow N.Y. Orthopaedic Hosp., 1942; chief orthopedic sect. Kennedy VA Hosp., Memphis, 1946-59; prof. surgery, chief orthopedic div. U. Ark., 1959-62; prof. surgery in residence UCLA, 1962-75; head orthopedic div. Harbor Gen. Hosp., Torrance, Calif., 1962-75, Riverside (Calif.) Gen. Hosp., 1975-77; chief orthopedic sect. Jerry L. Pettis Meml. VA Hosp., Loma Linda, Calif., 1977-80; prof. orthopedics Loma Linda U., 1975-80, emeritus, 1980—. Author: (with others) Science and Practice of Intramedullary Nailing, 1995; contbr. aricles on medullary nailing and joint replacement to med. jours.; also book chpts. Served to maj. M.C. USAAF, 1942-46. Mem. AMA, Am. Acad. Orthopaedic Surgeons, Am. Orthopaedic Assn., Calif. Med. Assn., Calif. Orthopaedic Assn., Western Orthopedic Assn., Assn. Bone and Joint Surgeons (treas. 1953-56, v.p. 1956-58, pres. 1959), Am. Fracture Assn. Presbyn. (elder, deacon, clk. sessions). Home: 44201 Village 44 Camarillo CA 93012-8935

STREET, DAVID HARGETT, investment company executive; b. Oklahoma City, Dec. 4, 1943; s. Bob Allen and Elizabeth Anne (Hargett) S.; m. Betty Ann Nichols, Oct. 1, 1966; children: Elizabeth Ann, Randall Hargett, Jeffrey David. BA in English, U. Okla., 1965; MBA in Fin., U. Pa., 1970. Vice pres. SEI Corp., 1970; v.p., prin. Street & Street, Inc., N.Y.C., 1970-74; v.p., mgr. San Francisco regional office First Nat. Bank Chicago, 1974-78; sr. v.p., CFO, treas. Bangor Punta Corp., Greenwich, Conn., 1978-84; v.p., treas. Penn Cen. Corp., Greenwich, 1984-86, v.p. fin., 1986-87; sr. v.p. fin. Penn Cen. Corp., Cin., 1987-92; exec. v.p. Gen. Cable Corp., Highland Heights, Ky., 1992-94, also bd. dirs.; pres., CEO Street Capital Group, Cin., 1994—; mem. adv. bd. Mfrs. Hanover Trust Co., 1982-88. Vice chmn. bd. dirs. Greenwich Acad. for Girls, 1984-87, chmn. bd. trustees, treas., 1987-88; trustee Cin. County Day Sch., 1990-91; mem. cmty. bd. Sta. WGUC-FM, 198-94; trustee Bethesda Hosp., Inc., 1993—; trustee Cin. Classical Pub. Radio, Inc., 1994—, Cmty. Chest Cin. Area, Inc., 1993—, treas., 1994-95; trustee John Austin Cheley Found., 1995—, Fountain Valley Sch., 1995—. 1st lt. M.I. U.S. Army, 1966-67. Mem. Greenwich Country Club. Republican. Presbyterian. Home and Office: 3425 Oyster Bay Ct Cincinnati OH 45244-2561

STREET, JOHN CHARLES, linguistics educator; b. Chgo., Apr. 3, 1930; s. Charles Larrabee and Mary Louise (Rose) S.; m. Eve Elizabeth Baker, June 4, 1975. BA, Yale, 1951, MA, 1952, PhD, 1955. Asst. prof. English Mich. State U., 1957-59; asst. prof. linguistics and Mongolian langs. Columbia, 1959-62; vis. asst. prof. linguistics U. Wash., 1962-63; assoc. prof. linguistics U. Wis., Madison, 1963-65; prof. linguistics U. Wis., 1965-92; prof. emeritus U. Wis., Madison, 1992—. Author: The Language of the Secret History of the Mongols, 1957, Khalkha Structure, 1963, The Journal of Oliver Rouse, 1983, An Ellis Family of Devon and Newfoundland, 1994. Research asso. Am. Council Learned Socs., 1959-62. Served with AUS, 1955-57.

STREET, PATRICIA LYNN, secondary education educator; b. Lillington, N.C., May 3, 1940; d. William Banks and Vandalia (McLean) S.; m. Col. Robert Gest, June 2, 1962 (div. 1985); children: Robert, Roblyn Renee. BS, Livingstone Coll., 1962; MEd, Salisbury State U., 1974; postgrad., various, 1968—. Tchr. Govt. of Guam Marianas Island, Agana, Guam, 1962-64; sec., typist USAF, Glasgow AFB, Mont., 1964-65, Syracuse (N.Y.) U. AeroSpace Engring., 1966-67; tchr. Syracuse (N.Y.) City Sch. System, 1967-69; lectr. U. of Md., Eastern Shore, Princess Anne, Md., 1970-72; tchr. Prince George's County Pub. Schs., Upper Marlboro, Md., 1973—; instr. U. Guam, Anderson AFB, 1963, U.S. Armed Forces Inst., Anderson AFB, 1963, Yorktowne Bus. Inst., Landover, Md., 1987-90, Cheseapeake Bus. Inst., Clinton, Md., 1983-89; asst. advisor student tchrs. U. Md. Ea. Shore, Princess Anne, 1972; adj. instr. Bowie State U., 1990—; conv. speaker. Mem. AAUW, NEA, ASCD, Am. Vocat. Assn., Md. Bus. Edn. Assn. (pres.-elect 1987-88, pres. 1988-89, Educator of Yr. 1989), Md. Vocat. Assn. (regional rep. 1986-89, audit chmn. 1987-89, Vocat.-Tech. Educator of Yr. 1989), Ea. Bus. Edn. Assn. (co-editor newsletter 1990-91, secondary exec. dir. 1991-94), Md. State Tchrs. Assn., D.C. Bus. Edn. Assn., Nat. Bus. Edn. Assn., Data Processing Mgmt. Assn., Internat. Soc. for Bus. Edn., Md. Bus. Edn. Com., Prince George's County Edn. Assn. Democrat. Baptist. Avocations: sewing, singing, modern creative dancing. Home: 10107 Welshire Dr Upper Marlboro MD 20772 Office: Prince George's Pub Sch Upper Marlboro MD 20772

STREET, PICABO, Olympic athlete; b. Triumph, Idaho, 1971. Silver medalist, women's downhill alpine skiing Olympic Games, Lillehammer, Norway, 1994; downhill skier U.S. Ski Team, 1994—. Named World Cup Downhill Women's Champion, 1995, 96; recipient Bronze and Gold medal World Championships, 1996. Office: US Olympic Com 1750 E Boulder St Colorado Springs CO 80909-5724

STREET, ROBERT LYNNWOOD, civil and mechanical engineer; b. Honolulu, Dec. 18, 1934; s. Evelyn Mansel and Dorothy Heather (Brook) S.; m. Norma Jeanette Ensminger, Feb. 6, 1959; children: Brian Clarke (dec.), Deborah Lynne, Kimberley Anne. Student, USN ROTC Program, 1952-57; M.S., Stanford U., 1957, Ph.D. (NSF grad. fellow 1960-62), 1963. Mem. faculty Sch. Engring. Stanford U., 1962—, prof. civil engring., assoc. chmn. dept. Sch. Engring., 1970-72, chmn. dept. Sch. Engring., 1972-80, 94-95, prof. fluid mechanics and applied math. Sch. Engring., 1972—, dir. environ. fluid mechanics lab. Sch. Engring., 1985-91, assoc. dean rsch. Sch. Engring., 1971-83, vice provost acad. computing and info. sys. Sch. Engring., 1983-85, vice provost, dean rsch. and acad. info. sys. Sch. Engring., 1985-87, v.p. for info. resources Sch. Engring., 1987-90, acting provost Sch. Engring., 1987, v.p. librs. and info. resources Sch. Engring., 1990-92, vice provost, dean of librs. and info. resources, 1992-94, William Alden and Martha Campbell prof. Sch. Engring., 1997—; vis. prof. U. Liverpool, Eng., 1970-71; vis. prof. mech. engring. James Cook U., Australia, 1995; trustee Univ. Corp. Atmospheric Rsch., 1983-94, chmn. sci. programs evaluation com., 1981, treas. corp., 1985, vice chmn. bd., 1986, chmn. bd., 1987-91; bd. dirs., sec.-treas. UCAR Found., 1987-91; bd. govs. Rsch. Libr. Group, 1990-91; chmn. Com. Preservation Rsch. Libr. Materials, Assn. Rsch. Librs., 1993; mem. higher edn. adv. bds. computer corps., 1983-94; mem. basic energy sci. adv. com. U.S. Dept. Energy, 1993-96; bd. dirs. Stanford U. Bookstore, Inc., 1993—. With C.E.C., USN, 1957-60. Sr. postdoctoral fellow Nat. Center Atmospheric Research, 1978-79; sr. Queen's fellow in marine sci., Australia, 1985; fellow N.E. Asia-U.S. Forum on Internat. Policy at Stanford U., 1985-89. Fellow AAAS; mem. ASCE (chmn. publs. com. hydraulics divsn. 1978-80, Walter Huber prize 1972), ASME (R.T. Knapp award 1986), Am. Geophys. Union, Oceanographic Soc., Am. Phys. Soc., Phi Beta Kappa, Sigma Xi, Tau Beta Pi. Office: Environ Fluid Mechs Lab Dept Civil Engring Stanford U Stanford CA 94305-4020

STREET, STEPHANIE, federal official. Dep. asst. to pres., co-dir. scheduling and advance Exec. Office of the Pres., Washington, 1995—. Office: Scheduling and Advance Exec Office of Pres 1600 Pennsylvania Ave NW Washington DC 20500-0005*

STREET, WILLIAM MAY, beverage company executive; b. Louisville, 1938. Grad., Princeton U., 1960; MBA, Harvard U., 1963. V.p. Brown-Forman Corp., Louisville, 1969, dir., mem. exec. com., 1971, sr. v.p., 1977, vice chmn., 1983—; pres., COO Brown-Forman Beverage Co. Divsn., Louisville, 1986—; pres., CEO Brown-Forman Beverages Worldwide Divsn., 1994—; vice chmn. Brown-Forman Corp., 1983—. Office: Brown-Forman Beverages Worldwide PO Box 1080 850 Dixie Hwy Louisville KY 40210-1091

STREETER, HENRY SCHOFIELD, lawyer; b. N.Y.C., May 2, 1920; s. Thomas Winthrop and Ruth (Cheney) S.; m. Mary Ann Dexter, May 16, 1959; children—Frank Sherwin, Cornelia Van Rensselaer, Natalie Thayer. B.A., Harvard U., 1942, J.D. magna cum laude, 1949. Bar: Mass. Law clk. Judge A.N. Hand, N.Y.C., 1950-51; mem. firm Ropes & Gray, Boston, 1949-94, ret., 1994. Chmn. Bd. Appeals, Wenham, Mass., 1983—; trustee, v.p. Peabody Mus. Salem, 1968—; corporator Mass. Gen. Hosp., 1976, Beverly Hosp., 1972. Served to lt. USNR, 1941-46. Mem. Mass. Hist. Soc., Am. Antiquarian Soc. (trustee 1972), Club of Odd Volumes (pres. 1995-97), Somerset Club, Myopia Hunt Club, Cruising of Am. Club, Walpole Soc., Tobique Salmon Club (pres. 1980-96), St. Andrew Lodge. Episcopalian. Avocations: sailing; shooting; fishing. Home: Old Farm Maple St Wenham MA 01984 Office: Ropes and Gray 1 International Pl Boston MA 02110-2602

STREETER, JOHN WILLIS, information systems manager; b. Topeka, Sept. 3, 1947; s. Jack and Edith Bernice (Vowels) S.; m. Nancy Ann Buck, June 15, 1968 (div. 1985); children: Sarah Beth, Timothy Paine; m. Linda Lea Wenrich Weisbender, Sept. 13, 1986; stepchildren: Michael Leon Weisbender II, Debra Ann Weisbender Johnson, Dawn Marie Weisbender. BS in Computer Sci., Kans. State U., 1973, MBA in Mgmt., 1974; postgrad., Harvard U., 1992. Computer programmer U.S.M.C., 1965-70, Kans. State U., Manhattan, 1970-74; cons., mgr., prin. Am. Mgmt. Systems, Inc., Arlington, Va., 1974-83; systems planning analyst Fed. Nat. Mortgage Assn., Washington, 1983-85; assoc. dir. computing and telecomm. Kans. State U., Manhattan, 1985-91, dir. info. systems, 1991—; mem. State of Kans. Info. Tech. Adv. Bd., 1997—. Author: Streeter Genealogy, 1985. Staff sgt. USMC, 1965-70. Recipient Navy Achievement medal in data processing Sec. Navy, 1971. Mem. IEEE, IEEE Computer Soc., Assn. for Computing Machinery, Am. Inst. Cert. Computer Profls., Cause Inc. (Kans. State U. voting mem. rep. 1987—), Streeter Family Assn. (bd. dirs. 1988—, v.p. 1990-95), Am. Legion, S.R., KC. Republican. Roman Catholic. Avocations: genealogy, history, book collecting. Home: 6765 Salzer Rd Wamego KS 66547-9636 Office: Kans State U Info Sys 2323 Anderson Ave Ste 215 Manhattan KS 66502-2912

STREETER, RICHARD BARRY, academic official; b. Albany, N.Y., Aug. 6, 1940; s. Lyle Tyler and Marion Downey S.; m. Janet Grace Marsteller, July 31, 1971; children—Jonathan Lyle, Stephanie Lyn. BA, U. Fla., 1962, MEd, 1963; EdD, U. Miami, 1972. Assoc. dir. fin. aid U. Miami, Coral Gables, Fla., 1970-73; dir. fin. aid Portland (Oreg.) State U., 1973-76, asst. dean grad. studies, dir. sponsored research, 1976-80; dir. office of research Lehigh U., Bethlehem, Pa., 1980-90; asst. v.p. rsch., dir. U. South Fla., Tampa, 1990-96; dir. USDOE/USF Tech. Deployment Ctr., 1994—; exec. dir. for econ. devel. USF, 1996—; bd. trustees Northampton County Area C.C., 1986-90; del. to Pa. Fed. of C.C. Trustees; mem. Easton area Sch. Bd. 1984-90; bd. dirs. Oak Ridge Associated Univs. Bus. mgr. Quality of Life Maintenance Orgn., 1976-80. Mem. AAAS, Nat. Coun. Univ. Rsch. Adminstrs., Soc. Rsch. Adminstrs., Coun. on Rsch. and Tech. (sch. policy com., commercialization task force), Archontes, Omega, Phi Delta Kappa. Republican. Presbyterian. Home: 507 Cliff Dr Temple Terrace FL 33617-3807 Office: U South Fla 4202 E Fowler Ave Tampa FL 33620-9900

STREETER, RICHARD EDWARD, lawyer; b. Mpls., Aug. 6, 1934; s. Donald Stivers and Beatrice Louise (Gibbs) S.; m. Charlotte Mae Tharp; children—Christopher A., Joanna G., Matthew J., Jonathan R. B.A., Yale U., 1956; LL.B., Yale Law Sch., 1959. Bar: Ohio 1960, D.C. 1964, U.S. Supreme Ct. 1964. Assoc. Thompson Hine Flory LLP, Cleve., 1960-63, 65-68, ptnr., 1968—; atty. State Dept. Legal Advisors Office, Washington, 1963, Justice Dept. Antitrust Div., Washington, 1964; asst. gen. counsel Senate Democratic Policy Com., Washington, 1964-65. Contbr. article to profl. jour. Mem. Leadership Cleve., 1981; v.p. Youth Opportunities Unltd., Cleve., 1983-96; pres. Fedn. Commty. Planning, Cleve., 1980-82, Cleve. Legal Aid Soc., 1974-76, Plan of Action for Tomorrow's Housing, Cleve., 1987-88; chmn. Ctr. for Families and Children, 1990-93; trustee City Club, Cleve., 1987-91, St. Vincent Quadrangle Inc., 1991—, Lake Erie Coll., 1993—; bd. dirs. United Way Svcs. Cleve., 1992-96. Recipient Cleve. 10 Outstanding Young Men award Jr. C. of C., 1968. Mem. ABA, Bar Assn. Greater Cleve. (trustee 1971-74, chmn. securities law sect. 1979-80, chmn. corps. banking and bus. law sect. 1983-85), Ohio State Bar Assn. (corp. law com.). Home: 472 Greenhaven Dr Chagrin Falls OH 44022-3323 Office: Thompson Hine & Flory LLP 3900 Key Ctr 127 Public Sq Cleveland OH 44114-1216

STREETER, TAL, sculptor; b. Oklahoma City, Aug. 1, 1934; s. Paul Waller and Pauline Viola (Roberts) S.; m. Dorothy Ann Romig Sheets, June 26, 1957; 1 child, Lissa. B.F.A., U. Kans., 1956, M.F.A., 1961. Prof. SUNY, Purchase, 1973—; fellow Ctr. for Advanced Visual Studies MIT, 1988—, vis. prof., 1991—; curator exhbn. The Art of the Japanese Kite, Japan Soc., N.Y.C., 1980, Ice and Air Show NEA/N.Y. Arts Coun., Lake Placid, 1983, Dayton Art Inst., 1990; Fulbright lectr., Korea, 1971; conferee Internat. Design Conf., Aspen, Colo., 1979. Exhibited in group and one-man shows N.Y. World's Fair, 1965, Whitney Mus., N.Y.C., 1965, Larry Aldrich Mus., Ridgefield, Conn., 1968, 70, Sheldon Art Mus., Lincoln, Nebr., 1970, Sculpture in Environment, Parks Dept., N.Y.C., 1970, Minami Gallery, Tokyo, 1971, Neuberger Mus., Purchase, N.Y., 1977, U. Ky. Mus., 1982, Bruckner Festival, Linz, Austria, 1982, Dayton Art Inst., 1982, AG Mus., Munich, 1983, Cleve. Art Mus., Eng., 1985, Milton Avery Mus., Bard Coll., N.Y., 1985, Citicorp Plz., Queens, N.Y., 1991, MIT Mus., 1994; represented in permanent collections Mus. Modern Art, N.Y.C., San Francisco Mus. Contemporary Art, Wadsworth Atheneum, Newark Mus., Neuberger Mus., Purchase, N.Y., Contemporary Arts Mus., Houston, Smith Coll. Mus. Art, High Mus., Atlanta, Storm King Art Center, Ark. Art Ctr., Little Rock, Milw. Art Ctr.; vis. artist-in-residence Dartmouth Coll., 1963, Bennett Coll., 1964-70, U. N.C., 1970, 72, 73, Queens Coll., N.Y.C., 1973, Penland Sch. of Crafts, 1974, 75, 76, Arcosanti Festival, Phoenix, 1978, 80, 81, Artpark, 1978, Lakefront Festival, Milw., 1981, Parsons Sch. Design, Lake Placid, 1982, Sun Valley Arts Ctr., Idaho, 1986, Walker Art Ctr., Minn., 1986; commns.: Morris Coll., N.J., 1981, N.J. State Library for Blind, 1982-84, Nat. Mus. Contemporary Art, Seoul (Republic of Korea) Olympics, 1988, Kaywon Sch. of Arts, Seoul, 1991, Total Contemporary Art Mus., Seoul, 1992, Lake Pk. Sculpture, Seoul, 1997; author: The Art of the Japanese Kite,

1974; co-editor: Art That Flies, 1991, A Kite Journey Through India, 19976; also articles; contbr. to Ency. of Japan, 1981, Grove/ Macmillan Dictionary of Art, 1996; profiled in Arts Mag., Dec., 1977, U & lc Mag., Nov., 1984, An American Portrait, CBS TV, 1986, Sky, Moon, Dragons, Kites and Smiles: Tal Streeter, An American Artist in Asia, 1994. Collaborations in Art, Sci. and Tech./N.Y. State Coun. on Arts grantee, 1978.

STREETMAN, BEN GARLAND, electrical engineering educator; b. Cooper, Tex., June 24, 1939; s. Richard E. and Bennie (Morrow) S.; m. Lenora Ann Music, Sept. 9, 1961; children: Paul, Scott. BS, U. Tex., 1961, MS, 1963, PhD, 1966. Fellow Oak Ridge Nat. Lab., 1964-66; asst. prof. elec. engring. U. Ill., 1966-70, asso. prof., 1970-74, prof., 1974-82; rsch. prof. Coordinated Sci. Lab., 1970-82; prof. elec. engring. U. Tex., Austin, 1982—, dir. Microelectronics Rsch. Ctr., 1984—, Dula D. Cockrell Centennial chair engring., 1989-96, dean Coll. Engring., 1996—; cons. in field. Author: Solid State Electronic Devices, 4th edit., 1995. Recipient Frederick Emmons Terman award Am. Soc. Engring. Edn., 1981, AT&T Found. award Am. Soc. Engring. Edn., 1987. Fellow IEEE (Edn. medal 1989), Electrochem. Soc.; mem. NAE, Tau Beta Pi, Eta Kappa Nu, Sigma Xi. Home: 3915 Glengarry Dr Austin TX 78731-3835 Office: Dean's Office Coll Engring ECJ 10.310/C2100 Austin TX 78712-1080

STREETMAN, JOHN WILLIAM, III, museum official; b. Marion, N.C., Jan. 19, 1941; s. John William, Jr. and Emily Elaine (Carver) S.; children: Katherine Drake, Leah Farrior, Burgin Eaves. BA in English and Theatre History, Western Carolina U., 1963; cert. in Shakespeare studies, Lincoln Coll., Oxford (Eng.) U., 1963. Founding dir. Jewett Creative Arts Ctr., Berwick Acad., South Berwick, Maine, 1964-70; exec. dir. Polk Mus. Art, Lakeland, Fla., 1970-75; dir. Mus. Arts and Sci., Evansville, Ind., 1975—; chmn. mus. adv. panel Ind. Arts Commn., 1977-78. Mem. Am. Assn. Museums, Assn. Ind. Museums (bd. dirs.). Episcopalian. Office: Evansville Mus Arts & Scis 411 SE Riverside Dr Evansville IN 47713-1037

STREETMAN, LEE GEORGE, sociology educator, criminology educator; b. Port Neches, Tex., Sept. 29, 1953; s. George Bernard and Roberta Valmeta (Fry) S. BA, U. Del., 1983, MA, 1985, PhD, 1995. Lectr. Ursinus Coll., Collegeville, Pa., 1990-92; asst. prof. Del. State U., Dover, Del., 1991-93; instr. Temple U., Phila., 1994; asst. prof. Cheyney (Pa.) U., 1994-96, Del. State U., Dover, 1996—; sr. rsch. analyst Admark, Inc., Horsham, Pa., 1986-88; rsch. specialist Del. Coun. Crime and Justice, Wilmington, Del., 1988-89. Author: Drugs, Delinquency, and Pregnancy, A Panel Study of Adolescent Problem Behavior, 1996, Crime Perception in Postmodern Society, 1997; contbr. articles to profl. jours. Tutor Thresholds Inmate Pre-release Program, Media, Pa., 1995. Mem. Am. Sociol. Assn., Am. Soc. Criminology, Popular Am. Culture Soc., Pa. Sociol. Soc., Soc. Study Social Problems, Alliance Prevention Adolescent Pregnancy, Sons of Confederate Vets., Cherokee Nat. Hist. Soc. Office: Dept Sociology and Criminal Justice Del State U Dover DE 19901

STREETO, JOSEPH MICHAEL, catering company official; b. New Haven, Dec. 12, 1942; s. Pasquale Joseph and Marie Veronica (Matazzaro) S. BS, Quinnipiac Coll., Mt. Caramel, Conn., 1964. Mng. dir. spl. events divsn. Culinary Enterprises, Inc., Chgo., 1986-97; project dir. Blue Plate at Symphony Ctr., Chgo., 1997—. Co-chmn. telethon Muscular Dystrophy Assn., Chgo., 1989; mem. benefit com., vol. Horizon Hospice, Chgo., 1990, 96; co-chmn. gourmet dinner Blackstone benefit DePaul U.; bd. dirs. Horizon Hospice, 1995—; active Cooks by the Books/The Chgo. Fund on Aging, 1994-96. Home: 253 E Delaware Pl Apt 10E Chicago IL 60611-1733

STREETT, WILLIAM BERNARD, university dean, engineering educator; b. Lake Village, Ark., Jan. 27, 1932; s. William Bernard and Marie Louise (Pfeffer) S.; m. Jackie Lou Heard, June 8, 1955; children—Robert Stuart, David Alexander, Kathleen Ann, Michael Richard. B.S., U.S. Mil. Acad., 1955; M.S., U. Mich., 1961, Ph.D., 1963. Commd. 2d lt. U.S. Army, 1955; founder, first dir. Sci. Research Lab. U.S. Mil. Acad., West Point, N.Y., 1968-78; asst. dean U.S. Mil. Acad., West Point, N.Y., 1968-78, ret. col., 1978; sr. research assoc. Cornell U., Ithaca, 1978-81, prof. chem. engring., 1981-95, dean engring., 1984-93; v.p. Impact-Echo Consultants, Ithaca, 1995—. Contbr. articles to profl. jours. Postdoctoral fellow NATO, 1966, Guggenheim fellow Oxford U., 1974. Mem. Am. Concrete Inst., Tau Beta Pi, Sigma Xi. Home: 105 Oak Hill Pl Ithaca NY 14850-2323 Office: Cornell U Coll Engring Hollister Hall Ithaca NY 14850

STREFF, WILLIAM ALBERT, JR., lawyer; b. Chgo., Aug. 12, 1949; s. William Albert Streff Sr. and Margaret (McKeough) Streff Fisher; m. Kathleen Myslinski, Sept. 29, 1984; children: Amanda, William III, Kimberly. BSME, Northwestern U., 1971, JD cum laude, 1974. Bar: Ill. 1974, U.S. Dist. Ct. (no. dist.) Ill. 1974, U.S. Dist. Ct. (no. dist.) N.Y. 1987, U.S. Dist. Ct. (no. dist.) Calif. 1988, U.S. Ct. Appeals (7th cir.) 1980, U.S. Ct. Appeals (9th cir.) 1988, U.S. Ct. Appeals (fed. cir.) 1982. Legal writing instr. Law Sch. Northwestern U., Chgo., 1973-74; assoc. Kirkland & Ellis, Chgo., 1974-80, ptnr., 1980—; lectr. Ill. Inst. Continuing Legal Edn., 1984; adj. prof. Northwestern U. Law Sch., 1992-94. Contbr. articles to profl. jours. Mem. adv. bd. Ill. Inst. Tech./Chgo.-Kent, 1983-86; trustee Northwestern U., Evanston, 1984-86, mem. vis. com. Law Sch., Chgo., 1988-94. Mem. ABA. Office: Kirland & Ellis 200 E Randolph St # 6100 Chicago IL 60601-6436

STREGE, TIMOTHY MELVIN, economic consultant; b. Tacoma, Wash., Sept. 6, 1952; m. Dawn Bernstein; children: Rachel, Nathan. BA, Pacific Luth. U.; MPA, Harvard U., 1986; postgrad., London Sch. Econs., 1992. Dist. adminstrv. asst. U.S. Congressman Norm Dicks, 1976-79; dir. Wash. state Kennedy for Pres. campaign, 1979-80; dep. campaign mgr. U.S. Senator Warren G. Magnuson, 1980; rsch. analyst, legis. asst. Ho. of Reps., Olympia, 1980-83; chmn. Pierce (Wash.) Transit Authority, 1978-83; dir. dist. rels. office Ho. of Reps., Olympia, 1983-84, sr. policy analyst, 1984-85; dep. mayor City of Tacoma, 1984-85; chief fin. analyst Puget Sound Water Quality Authority, Seattle, 1986-87; fin. advisor, then. exec. dir. Coun. Vocat. Tech. Insts., Renton, 1987-91; exec. v.p. Job Training Execs. of Wash., 1991-93; chmn. TAPCO Credit Union, 1991-93; exec. dir. Tacoma-Pierce County Small Bus. Incubator, 1994—; labor & natural resources economist, 1986—. Author: Employment & Job Training Impacts of Increased U.S.-Canadian Trade, 1991, Capital and Employment Relationship in an Economic Strategy, 1992, Financing Investment Capital in the Puget Sound Region, 1993. Bd. dirs. western Wash. chpt. Am. Health Edn. Consortium, 1990-92; mem. Gov.'s Adv. Coun. on Investment in Human Capital, 1990-91, Wash. State Com. on Health Occupations, 1992, Govs. Econ. Devel. Task Force, 1992—; chmn. Pierce County Law & Justice Commn., 1978-79, Community Health Care Delivery System, Pierce County, 1988-89, Fed. Res. Bank Com.: Ptnrs. Small Bus. Lending, 1996; numerous others. Recipient Disting. Svc. award Clover Park chpt. Wash. Vocat. Assn., 1988; named one of Outstanding Young Men in Am., U.S. Jaycees, 1984. Mem. Rotary. Democrat. Roman Catholic. Avocations: hiking, baseball, reading. Home: 8340 6th Ave Tacoma WA 98465-1044

STREIBEL, BRYCE, state senator; b. Fessenden, N.D., Nov. 19, 1922; s. Reinhold M. and Frieda I. (Broschat) S.; m. June P. Buckley, Mar. 23, 1947; 1 child, Kent. Attended U. N.D., Grand Forks; BS, San Francisco State Coll., 1947. Engr. U.S. Govt., Napa, Calif., 1943-46; dir. Martin Funeral Home, Stockton, Calif., 1946-55; owner Streibel Twin Oaks Farm, Fessenden, N.D., 1955—; state sen. State of N.D., Bismarck, 1981—, pres. pro tempore, 1995, state rep., 1957-75. Author: Pathways Through LIfe, 1983. Chmn. N.D. Legis. Coun., Bismarck, 1969-75; councilman Town of Fessenden, 1976-84; former pres. 20-30 Internat. Group, Sacramento, trustee, 1952-54; dir. World Coun., Sacramento, 1951-53; bd. dirs. U. N.D. Fellows, Grand Forks, 1982-86; pres. Fessenden Airport Authority, 1980—; mem. N.D. Bd. Higher Edn., 1977-81; chmn. N.D. adv. commn. U.S. Commn. on Civil Rights, 1988-93. Recipient Sioux award U. N.D. Alumni Assn., 1976, Benefactor award U. N.D. Found., 1982, William Budge award, 1983, Outstanding Svc. award Jaycees, 1988, Nat. Barn Again Farm Heritage award, 1996; named Outstanding Alumnus Theta Chi, 1987. Mem. N.D. Centennial Farm, Commodore N.D. Mythical Navy, Masons (Master), Elks, Kiwanis, Shriners, Farm Bur. Republican. Baptist. Avocations: golf, philately. Home and Office: 226 2nd St N Fessenden ND 58438-7204 Office: PO Box 467 Fessenden ND 58438-0467

STREIBICH, HAROLD CECIL, lawyer; b. Baton Rouge, June 19, 1928; s. Frederick Franklin and Margaret Rose (Foley) S.; m. Theresa Ann Grimes, Apr. 25, 1973; 1 dau. by previous marriage, Margaret Ann; stepchildren: John B. Snowden, IV, Kathryn Snowden. BA, U. Tenn., 1949; LLB, U. Va., 1953; Spl. Honors, U. Memphis, 1972. Bar: Miss. 1954, Tenn. 1960. Ptnr. Streibich & Seale and predecessor firms, Memphis, 1960—; vis. lectr. Vanderbilt U. Sch. Law, 1968-74, Brigham Young U., summer 1971, Harvard U. Law Sch., 1979, 92; prof. music, prof. entertainment law U. Memphis, 1973-91; pres. Am. Rec. Inst., 1979—. Chmn. Tenn. Athletic Commn., 1970, 74, Tenn. Civil Svc. Commn., 1996—. Served with U.S. Army, 1945-47, 50-52; ret. brig. gen. Tenn. N.G., 1980. Recipient World Boxing Assn. award as outstanding commr., 1972, various civic awards for Easter Seal, Heart Fund. Mem. ABA, NARAS (nat. v.p. 1980-81, bd. dirs., treas. 1978-79, pres. 1979-80, Gov.'s award Nashville chpt. 1972, Memphis chpt. 1976), Tenn. Bar Assn. (ho. of dels. 1978-83, v.p., bd. govs. 1983-85, chmn. copyright, entertainment and sports law sect. 1979), Miss. Bar Assn., Memphis Bar Assn. (bd. dirs. 1975-76), Am. Coll. Intellectual Property Law (pres. 1994-97), Am. Judicature Soc., Internat. Assn. Music Pubs., Summit Club, Rotary, Phi Kappa Phi, Kappa Sigma, Omega Delta Kappa, Phi Delta Phi. Home: 5475 Crescent Ln Memphis TN 38120-2449 Office: 1271 Poplar Ave Memphis TN 38104-7245

STREICHER, JAMES FRANKLIN, lawyer; b. Ashtabula, Ohio, Dec. 6, 1940; s. Carl Jacob and Helen Marie (Dugan) S.; m. Sandra JoAnn Jennings, May 22, 1940; children: Cheryl Ann, Gregory Scott, Kerry Marie. BA, Ohio State U., 1962; JD, Case Western Res. U., 1966. Bar: Ohio 1966, U.S. Dist. Ct. (no. dist.) Ohio 1966. Assoc., Calfee, Halter & Griswold, Cleve., 1966-71, ptnr., 1972—; bd. dirs. The Mariner Group Inc., Ft. Myers, Fla., Spectra-Tech Inc., Stamford, Conn., Cuyahoga Bolt & Screw, Cleve.; mem. Div. Securities Adv. Bd., State of Ohio; lectr. Case Western Res. U., Cleve. State U.; mem. pvt. sector com. John Carroll U. Trustee Achievement Ctr. for Children; mem. corp. coun. Cleve. Mus. Art. Mem. ABA, Fed. Bar Assn., Ohio State Bar Assn., Assn. for Corp. Growth, Ohio Venture Assn., Greater Cleve. Bar Assn., Ohio State U. Alumni Assn., Case Western Res. U. Alumni Assn., Newcomen Soc., Bluecoats Club (Cleve.), Mayfield Country (bd. dirs. 1985-89), Tavern Club, Union Club, Rotary, Beta Theta Pi, Phi Delta Phi. Roman Catholic. Republican. Home: 50 Windrush Dr Chagrin Falls OH 44022-6841

STREICHLER, JERRY, industrial engineer, consultant company executive; b. N.Y.C., Dec. 8, 1929; s. Samuel and Mirel (Waxman) S.; m. Rosalind Fineman, Feb. 25, 1951; children: Stuart Alan, Seth Ari, Robin Cheryl. Spl. courses cert., Newark Coll. Engring., 1951; BS magna cum laude, Kean Coll. N.J., 1956; MA, Montclair State Coll., 1958; PhD, NYU, 1963. Cons. machine designer to materials handling and auto wash cos., Montclair, N.J., 1950-67; mem. faculty dept. indsl. edn. Montclair (N.J.) State Coll., 1958-65, Trenton (N.J.) State Coll., 1965-67; prof., chmn. dept. indsl. edn. and tech. Bowling Green (Ohio) State U., 1967-78, dir. Sch. Tech., 1978-85, dean Coll. Tech., 1985-91; trustee prof., 1992, dean emeritus, trustee prof. emeritus, 1993—; pres. Tng. and Edn. Mgmt. Cons. Group, 1993—; vis. prof. S.I. Community Coll., CCNY, 1965, Rutgers U., 1967, U. Mo., 1967, U. Mich., Saginaw, 1971; cons., tchr. Newaygo Vocat. Ctr., Saginaw Career Opportunities Ctr., 1971; cons. indsl. tng., pub. schs., colls.; cons. human resource tng. and quality scis., 1984—; disting. vis. dean, spl. cons. to pres. Calif. State U., San Marcos, 1991. Asst. editor: Jour. Indsl. Tchr. Edn., 1968-70; co-editor: The Components of Teacher Education, 20th Yearbook Am. Council on Indsl. Arts Tchr. Edn.; editor: Jour. of Technology Studies; contbr. articles to profl. jours. Founding com. chmn. Ohio Coun. on Indsl. Arts Tchr. Edn., 1968-69; dir. Homeowners Assn., 1993-95. With USAF, 1951-52. Univ. honors scholar, 1963. Mem. NEA, Internat. Tech. Edn. Assn., Am. Vocat. Assn., Am. Tech. Edn. Assn., Am. Soc. Engring. Edn., Nat. Assn. Indsl. Tech., Miss. Valley Tech. Tchr. Edn. Conf., Epsilon Pi Tau, Laureate citation 1972, Disting. Svc. citation 1989), Omicron Delta Kappa, Phi Delta Kappa, Kappa Delta Pi. Office: TeMac Training & Edn Mgmt Cons PO Box 12332 La Jolla CA 92039-2332

STREICKER, JAMES RICHARD, lawyer; b. Chgo., Nov. 9, 1944; s. Seymour and De Vera (Wolfson) S.; m. Mary Stowell, Mar. 11, 1989; children: David, Sarah. AB, Miami U., 1966; JD, U. Ill., 1969. Bar: Ill. 1969, U.S. Dist. Ct. (no. dist.) Ill. 1970, U.S. Ct. Appeals (7th cir.) 1971, U.S. Supreme Ct. 1980, U.S. Dist. Ct. (ea. dist.) Wis., (no. dist.) Ind. 1986. Asst. atty. gen. State of Ill., 1970-71, asst. appellate def., 1971-75; dep. appellate def. First Dist. Ill., 1975; asst. U.S. atty. No. Dist. Ill., 1975-80; chief criminal receiving and appellate div. U.S. Attys. Office, Ill., 1979-80; ptnr. Cotsirilos, Stephenson, Tighe & Streicker, Chgo., 1980—; instr. Trial Adv. John Marshall Law Sch., 1979-80, U.S. Atty. Gens. Adv. Inst. 1978-80, Nat. Inst. for Trial Adv. 1981—; lectr. Ill. Inst. Continuing Legal Edn., Sentencing, New Techniques and Attitudes, 1986. Mem. ABA, Nat. Assn. Criminal Def. Lawyers, Am. Coll. Trial Lawyers, Am. Bd. Criminal Lawyers, Ill. State Bar Assn., Chgo. Bar Assn. Office: 33 N Dearborn St Chicago IL 60602

STREIFF, ARLYNE BASTUNAS, business owner, educator; b. Sacramento, Calif., Nov. 4; d. Peter James and Isabel (Gemnas) Bastunas; children: Peter Joshua, Joshua Gus. BS, U. Nev., 1965; postgrad., U. Calif., Davis, 1965-68, Calif. State U., Chico, 1968, 71. Cert. elem. tchr., Calif., Nev., cert. in English-specially designed lang. acad. instrn. devel. in English. Tchr. reading, lang. and kindergarten Enterprise Elem. Sch. Dist., Redding, Calif., 1965-97, tchr. kindergarten, 1988-97; owner, pres. Arlyne's Svcs., Redding, Calif., 1990-97. Author: Niko and His Friends, 1989, Niko The Black Rottweiler, 1995, Color-Talk-Spell. Mem. Rep. Women, Five County Labor Coun., Redding, 1976-93, Calif. Labor Fedn., 1974-97, AFL-CIO, 1974-97. Named Tchr. of Yr., Enterprise Sch. Dist., 1969. Mem. AAUW, Am. Fedn. Tchrs., Calif. Tchrs. Assn. (bargaining spokesperson 1968-72, exec. bd. dirs.), United Tchrs. Enterprise (pres. 1979-80, chmn. lang. com.), Calif. Reading Assn., Enterprise Fedn. Tchrs. (pres. 1974, pres.-elect 1995-97), Calif. State Fedn. Tchrs. (v.p. 1974-75, exec. bd. 1995-97), Redding C. of C., Women of Moose, Elks. Avocations: home interior design, real estate, construction, creative writing, educational advancement. Home: 1468 Benton Dr Redding CA 96003-3116 Office: Arlynes Svcs 1468 Benton Dr Redding CA 96003-3116

STREILEIN, J. WAYNE, research scientist; b. Johnstown, Pa., June 19, 1935; s. Jacob and Mina Alma (Krouse) S.; m. Joan Elaine Stein, June 15, 1957; children: Laura Anne, William Wayne, Robert Dietrich. BA in Chemistry, Gettysburg Coll., 1956; MD, U. Pa., 1960. Asst. prof., assoc. prof. genetics U. Pa. Sch. Medicine, Phila., 1965-71; prof. cell biology Southwestern Med. Sch., Dallas, 1971-84; prof., chair microbiology and immunology U. Miami, Fla., 1984-93; prof. ophthalmology and dermatology Harvard Med. Sch., Boston, 1993—; pres., dir. rsch. Schepens Eye Rsch. Inst., Boston, 1993—. Capt. USAR, 1961-67. Recipient award Alcon Rsch. Inst., 1984, Merit award Nat. Eye Inst., 1990; Markle Found. scholar, 1967. Mem. Assn. Rsch. in Vision and Ophthalmology (Procter award 1996), Am. Assn. Immunologists (chair pub. rels. 1988-93), Soc. Investigative Dermatology, Transplantation Soc. Achievements include elucidation of cellular and molecular basis of immune privilege in eye, genetic basis of effects of ultraviolet B light on cutaneous immunity, microenvironmental factor effects on tissue-restricted antigen presenting cells. Home: 44 Neptune St Beverly MA 01915 Office: Schepens Eye Rsch Inst 20 Staniford St Boston MA 02114-2508

STREISAND, BARBRA JOAN, singer, actress, director; b. Bklyn., Apr. 24, 1942; d. Emanuel and Diana (Rosen) S.; m. Elliott Gould, Mar. 1963 (div.); 1 son, Jason Emanuel. Grad. high sch., Bklyn.; student, Yeshiva of Bklyn. N.Y. theatre debut Another Evening with Harry Stoones, 1961; appeared in Broadway musicals I Can Get It for You Wholesale, 1962, Funny Girl, 1964-65; motion pictures include Funny Girl, 1968, Hello Dolly, 1969, On a Clear Day You Can See Forever, 1970, The Owl and the Pussy Cat, 1970, What's Up Doc?, 1972, Up the Sandbox, 1972, The Way We Were, 1973, For Pete's Sake, 1974, Funny Lady, 1975, The Main Event, 1979, All Night Long, 1981, Nuts, 1987; star, prodr. film A Star is Born, 1976; prodr., dir., star Yentl, 1983, The Prince of Tides, 1991; exec. prodr.: (TV movie) Serving in Silence: The Margarethe Cammermeyer Story, 1995; TV spls. include My Name is Barbra, 1965 (5 Emmy awards), Color Me Barbra, 1966; actress, prodr., dir. The Mirror Has Two Faces; rec. artist on Columbia Records; Gold record albums include People, 1965, My Name is Barbra, 1965, Color Me Barbra, 1966, Barbra Streisand: A Happening in Central Park, 1968, Barbra Streisand: One Voice, Stoney End, 1971, Barbra Joan Streisand, 1972, The Way We Were, 1974, A Star is Born, 1976, Superman, 1977, The Stars Salute Israel at 30, 1978, Wet, 1979, (with Barry Gibb) Guilty, 1980, Emotion, 1984, The Broadway Album, 1986, Til I Loved You, 1989; other albums include: A Collection: Greatest Hits, 1989, Just for the Record, 1991, Back to Broadway, 1993, Concert at the Forum, 1993, The Concert Recorded Live at Madison Square Garden, 1994, The Concert Highlights, 1995. Recipient Emmy award, CBS-TV spl. (My Name Is Barbra), 1964, Acad. award as best actress (Funny Girl), 1968, Golden Globe award (Funny Girl), 1969, co-recipient Acad. award for best song (Evergreen), 1976, Georgie award AGVA 1977, Grammy awards for best female pop vocalist, 1963, 64, 65, 77, 86, for best song writer (with Paul Williams), 1977, 2 Grammy nominations for Back to Broadway, 1994; Nat. Acad. of Recording Arts & Sciences Lifetime Achievement Award, 1994. Office: ICM 8942 Wilshire Blvd Beverly Hills CA 90211*

STREITMAN, JEFFREY BRUCE, educational administrator; b. Bronx, N.Y., Aug. 5, 1951; s. Milton and Marcia (Helfant) S.; m. Brenda Penny, July 4, 1974; 1 child, Jesse. BA cum laude, CUNY, 1974, MS, 1976; EdD, Fordham U., 1990. Guidance counselor Horizon Sch., Levitown, N.Y., 1976-80, asst. prin., 1980-84; guidance chmn. Lawrence (N.Y.) Pub. Schs., 1984-88, supr. student svcs., 1988-90; asst. supt. schs. Syosset (N.Y.) Cen. Sch. Dist., 1990-94; dep. supt. schs. Syosset Cen. Sch. Dist., 1994—. Mem. ASCD, N.Y. State Pers. Adminstrs., L.I. Pers. Adminstrs. Office: Syosset Cen Sch Dist Pell Ln Syosset NY 11791

STREITWIESER, ANDREW, JR., chemistry educator; b. Buffalo, June 23, 1927; s. Andrew and Sophie (Morlock) S.; m. Mary Ann Good, Aug. 19, 1950 (dec. May 1965); children—David Roy, Susan Ann; m. Suzanne Cope Beier, July 29, 1967. A.B., Columbia U., 1949, M.A., 1950, Ph.D., 1952; postgrad. (AEC fellow), MIT, 1951-52. Faculty U. Calif., Berkeley, 1952-92, prof. chemistry, 1963-92, prof. emeritus, 1993—, prof. grad. sch., 1995—; researcher on organic reaction mechanisms, application molecular orbital theory to organic chemistry, effect chem. structure on carbon acidities; cons. to industry, 1957—. Author: Molecular Orbital Theory for Organic Chemists, 1961, Solvolytic Displacement Reactions, 1962, (with J.I. Brauman) Supplemental Tables of Molecular Orbital Calculations, 1965, (with C.A. Coulson) Dictionary of Pi Electron Calculations, 1965, (with P.H. Owens) Orbital and Electron Density Diagrams, 1973, (with C.H. Heathcock and E.M. Kosower) Introduction to Organic Chemistry, 4th edit., 1992, A Lifetime of Synergy with Theory and Experiment, 1996; also numerous articles; co-editor: Progress in Physical Organic Chemistry, 11 vols., 1963-74. Recipient Humboldt Found. Sr. Scientist award, 1976, Humboldt medal, 1979, Berkeley citation, 1993. Fellow AAAS; mem. NAS, Am. Chem. Soc. (Calif. sect. award 1964, award in Petroleum Chemistry 1967, Norris award in phys. organic chemistry 1982, Cope scholar award 1989), Am. Acad. Arts and Scis., German Chem. Soc., Bavarian Acad. Scis. (corr.), Phi Beta Kappa, Sigma Xi. Office: U Calif Dept Chemistry Berkeley CA 94720-1460

STREKOWSKI, LUCJAN, chemistry educator; b. Grabowo, Poland, June 21, 1945; came to U.S., 1981; s. Antoni and Janina (Chrapowicz) S.; m. Alewtina Smirnova, Oct. 14, 1967; children: Rafal, Anna. BS in Polymer Chemistry with distinction, Mendeleev Inst. Chemistry, Moscow, 1967; PhD in Organic Chemistry, Polish Acad. Scis., 1972; DSc in Chemistry, Adam Mickiewicz U., Poznan, Poland, 1976. Instr. organic chemistry Adam Mickiewicz U., Poznan, 1971-72, asst. prof. dept. chemistry, 1972-78, assoc. prof. dept. chemistry, 1978-81; rsch. assoc. dept. chemistry U. Fla., Gainesville, 1981-84; asst. prof. dept. chemistry Ga. State U., Atlanta, 1984-89, assoc. prof. dept. chemistry, 1989-96, prof. dept. chem., 1996—; vis. prof. U. Fla., Gainesville, 1979-80, 81, Australian Nat. U., 1980, U. Kans., Lawrence, 1972-73. Editor: Pyridine-Metal Complexes, Vol. 14, Part 6, 1985; contbr. more than 160 articles to profl. jours.; patentee in field. Recipient award Polish Ministry Sci., 1977, Polish Chem. Soc., 1973, Polish Acad. Scis., 1972, Ga. State U., 1993; grantee Am. Chem. Soc.-Petroleum Rsch. Fund, 1985—, Solvay Pharms., 1992-93, Nat. Diagnostics, 1991-93, NIAID/NIH, 1988—, Rohm and Hass Co., 1988, Am. Cancer Soc., 1987-89, Rsch. Corp., 1985-94, Milheim Found. Cancer Rsch., 1985-86, DuPont Co., 1996-97, numerous others. Mem. Am. Chem. Soc., Internat. Soc. Heterocyclic Chemistry, Internat. Acad. Scis. of Nature and Soc. (mem. presidium). Avocation: classical music. Office: Ga State Univ Dept Chemistry Atlanta GA 30303

STRENA, ROBERT VICTOR, retired university research laboratory manager; b. Seattle, June 28, 1929; s. Robert Lafayette Peel and Mary Oliva (Holmes) S.; m. Rita Mae Brodovsky, Aug. 1957; children: Robert Victor, Adrienne Amelia. AB, Stanford U., 1952. Survey mathematician Hazen Engring., San Jose, Calif., 1952-53; field engr. Menlo Sanitary Dist., Menlo Park, Calif., 1954-55; ind. fin. reporter Los Altos, Calif., 1953-59; asst. dir. Hansen Labs. Stanford U., 1959-93, asst. dir. emeritus Ginzton Lab., 1993—; ind. fin. cons., Los Altos, 1965—; mem. Rehab. Adv. Bd., Moffett Fed. Airfield, 1994—. Active Edn. System Politics, Los Altos, 1965-80, local Boy Scouts Am., 1968-80, Maj. USAR, 1948-70. Mem. AAAS, Mus. Soc., Big X (Los Altos). Republican. Avocations: golf, sailing. Home: 735 Raymundo Ave Los Altos CA 94024-3139 Office: Ginzton Lab Stanford Univ Stanford CA 94305

STRENG, WILLIAM PAUL, lawyer, educator; b. Sterling, Ill., Oct. 17, 1937; s. William D. and Helen Marie (Conklen) S.; m. Louisa Bridge Egbert, July 8, 1967; children: Sarah, John. BA, Wartburg Coll., 1959; JD, Northwestern U., 1962. Bar: Iowa 1962, Ill. 1962, Ohio 1964, Tex. 1975. Law clk. to U.S. circuit judge Lester L. Cecil, Cin., 1963-64; asso. firm Taft, Stettinius & Hollister, Cin., 1964-70; atty.-advisor Office Sec. Tax Policy, Office Tax Legis. Counsel, Dept. Treasury, Washington, 1970-71; dep. gen. counsel Export-Import Bank U.S., Washington, 1971-73; prof. law Sch. Law, So. Methodist U., Dallas, 1973-80; vis. prof. Coll. Law Ohio State U., Columbus, 1977; partner firm Bracewell & Patterson, Houston, 1980-85; Vinson & Elkins prof. of law U. Houston Law Ctr, 1985—; vis. prof. Rice U., NYU Law Sch., 1990; disting. vis. prof. U. Hong Kong Law Faculty, 1992; Fulbright prof. U. Stockholm Law Faculty, 1993; vis. fellow law faculty Victoria U., Wellington, New Zealand, 1996; vis. law lectr. U. Leiden, The Netherlands, 1997; cons. Bracewell & Patterson, 1985—; lectr. various confs. Am. Law Inst., Practicing Law Inst., World Trade Inst., Internat. Fiscal Assn., ABA, Tex. State Bar. Author: International Business Transactions-Tax and Legal Handbook, 1978, Estate Planning, 1991, 2d edit., 1997, International Business Planning: Law and Taxation, 6 vols., 1982, 95, 96, Tax Planning for Retirement, 1989, 93, 94, 95, 96, Doing Business in China, 1990, 93, 94, 95, 96, Federal Income Taxation of Corporations and Shareholders--Forms, 1995, 96, Choice of Entity, 1994, U.S. International Estate Planning, 1996; contbr. articles to profl. jours. Served with USMC, 1962. Lutheran. Home: 1903 Dunstan Rd Houston TX 77005-1619 Office: U Houston Law Ctr Houston TX 77204-6372

STRENGTH, DANNA ELLIOTT, nursing educator; b. Texarkana, Ark., Aug. 20, 1937; d. Clyde Olin and Willie (Stephens) Elliott; m. Vernon E. Strength, Dec. 27, 1960. BSN, Tex. Christian U., 1959; MSN, Washington U., 1968; DNSc, Cath. U. of Am., 1986. Instr. The Cath. Univ. of Am., Washington; asst. prof. Georgetown Univ., Washington; assoc. prof. Tex. Christian Univ., Fort Worth; edn. leader Acad. Seminars Internat.; edn. cons. Trnascultrual Edn. Corp.; med. com. Ft. Worth Sister Cities Internat., Budapest, Hungary, and Bandung, Indonesia. Contbr. articles to profl. jours. Recipient Edn. in a Global Soc. award to study health care in Indonesia and Scandinavia, 1992-94. Mem. ANA, Tex. Nurses' Assn., Am. Assn. for History of Nursing, Lucy Harris Linn Inst., Sigma Theta Tau (Beta Alpha rsch. award). Home: 305 Birchwood Ln Fort Worth TX 76108-4601

STRENGTH, JANIS GRACE, management executive, educator; b. Ozark, Ala., Jan. 31, 1934; d. James Marion and Mary Belle (Riley) Grace; m. Robert Samuel Strength, Sept. 12, 1954; children: Stewart A., James Houston (dec.), Robert David (dec.), James Steven (dec.). BS in Home Econs. and Edn., Auburn U., 1956; MA in Edn., Washington U., St. Louis, 1978, MA in Adminstrn., 1980. Home economist Gulf Power Co., Pensacola, Fla., 1956-59; tchr. sci. Northside Jr. High Sch., Greenwood, S.C., 1961-65; tchrs. home econs. Greenwood High Sch., 1968-70; chairperson dept. sci. Parkway West Jr. High Sch., Chesterfield, Mo., 1975-82; tchr. sci. Parkway West High Sch., Chesterfield, 1982-88; v.p.-sec. Product Safety Mgmt. Inc., Gulf Breeze, Fla., 1989—; chairperson dist. Phys. Scis. Curriculum Com., 1978-85, Sci. Fair Placement Com., 1978-82, Gifted Edn., 1983-84; leader Phys. Sci. Summer Workshops, Safety Sci. Lab. Workshop; sponsor Nat. Jr. Honor Soc., Parkway West Jr. Class. Supt. youth dept. Sunday sch. Greentrails Meth. Ch., sponsor summer camp; vol. fundraiser March of Dimes, Cerebral Palsy, Multiple Schlorosis, Cancer funds; judge Parkway/Monsanto/St. Louis Post Dispatch Sci. Fairs, 1978—; mem. citizens action com. Parkway Sch. Bd., 1980-84. Mem. NEA, Nat. Sci. Tchrs. Assn., Santa Rosa Women's Club, Tiger Point Country Club (Gulf Breese), Raintree Country Club (Hillsboro, Mo.). Republican. Methodist. Office: Product Safety Mgmt Inc Gulf Breeze FL 32561

STRENGTH, ROBERT SAMUEL, manufacturing company executive; b. Tullos, La., May 14, 1929; s. Houston Orion and Gurcie Dean (Cousins) S.; BS in Indsl. Mgmt., Auburn U., 1956; m. Janis Lynette Grace, Sept. 12, 1954; children: Robert David (dec.), James Steven (dec.), Stewart Alan, James Houston (dec.). Engr., supr. plant safety Monsanto Co., 1956-74, engrng. stds. mgr. Corporate Fire Safety Center, St. Louis, 1974-78, mgr. product safety and acceptability Monsanto Polymer Products Co. (formerly Monsanto Plastics and Resins Co.), St. Louis, 1978-82, mgr. product safety, Monsanto Chem. Co., 1982-87; founder, pres. Product Safety Mgmt., Inc., 1987—. mem. com. on toxicity of materials used in rapid rail transit, NRC, 1984-87. Pres. Greenwood (S.C.) Citizens Safety Coun., 1966-68; U.S. del., tech. expert on fire safety of elec. products Internat. Electrotech. Commn. With USAF, 1948-52. Recipient S. C. Outstanding Svc. to Safety award Nat. Safety Coun., 1968; registered profl. engr., Calif.; cert. safety profl. Mem. Am. Soc. Safety Engrs., Nat. Safety Coun. (pres. textile sect. 1966), So. Bldg. Code Congress, Internat. Conf. of Bldg. Ofcls., Bldg. Ofcls. and Code Adminstrs. Internat., Nat. Fire Protection Assn. (mem. code making panel 7 nat. electrical code), ASTM Fire Test Com. (chmn. fire hazard & risk assessment sub-com., mem. exec. com. fire test com.), Nat. Inst. Bldg. Scis., Plastic Pipe and Fittings Assn. ASHRAE, Soc. Plastics Ind. (past chmn. coordinating com. on fire safety 1985-87), Nat. Acad. Scis., Cherry Hills Country Club, Raintree Plantation Golf and Country Club, Tiger Point Country Club. Republican. Methodist. Editor textile sect. newsletter Nat. Safety Coun., 1961-62. Home and Office: 3371 Edgewater Dr Gulf Breeze FL 32561-3309

STRETCH, JOHN JOSEPH, social work educator, management and evaluation consultant; b. St. Louis, Feb. 24, 1935; s. John Joseph and Theresa Carmelita (Fleming) S.; children: Paul, Leonmarie, Sylvan, Adrienne, Sharonalice; m. Barbara Ann Stewart, Mar. 16, 1985; children: Margaret, Thomas. AB, Maryknoll Coll., Glen Ellyn, Ill., 1957; MSW, Washington U., St. Louis, 1961; PhD, Tulane U., 1967; MBA, St. Louis U., 1980. Lic. clin. social worker, 1990. Instr. Tulane U., 1962-67, asst. prof., 1967-69; mem. faculty St. Louis U., 1969—, prof. social work, 1972—, asst. dean Sch. Social Service, 1976-87, dir. doctoral studies, 1976-94, dir. M.S.W. program, 1985-86; dir. rsch. Social Welfare Planning Coun. Met. New Orleans, 1962-69; cons. to United Way Met. St. Louis, Cath. Charities of Archdiocese of St. Louis, Cath. Svcs. for Children and Youth, Full Achievement, Mo. Province of S.J., Cath. Commn. on Housing, Cath. Family Svcs., Youth Emergency Svcs., Mo. State Dept. Social Svcs., U. Mo. Extension Svc., St. Joseph's Home for Boys, Marian Hall Ctr. for Adolescent Girls, Boys Town of Mo., A World of Difference, Anti Defamation League of B'nai Brith, Prog. Youth Ctr., Foster Care Coalition of Greater St. Louis; expert witness on homeless U.S. House Select Com. on Families, Children and Youth, 1987; mem. resource spl. task force on homeless Office of Sec. U.S. Dept. Housing and Urban Devel., 1989; survey design cons. U.S. Office of The Insp. Gen., 1990; methodology expert on homelessness U.S. Census Bur., 1989; expert homeless policy General Acctg. Office hearings, 1992; chair Mo. Assn. for Social Welfare Low Income Housing; mem. Comprehensive Housing Affordabiltiy Strategies (CHAS) Mo. Statewide Planning Group, Missouri Housing Devel. CHAS citizen's com., Missouri Inst. of Psychiatry, Univ. City sch. dist.; mgmt. cons. People's Issues Task Force Agricultural div. Monsanto Chemical Inc., Nat. Conf. of Christians and Jews, regional office; vis. prof. Nat. Catholic U. of Am. Sch. of Soc. Svcs., 1991, 92, U. Bristol, England, 1992, U. Calif. Sch. of Pub. Health, Berkeley, 1990; cons. Mo. Speaker of the Ho. statewide legislative task force, 1990-92; statewide grant project reviewer emergency shelter grant program Mo. Dept. of Social Svcs., 1989—; homeless svcs. grant reviewer City of St. Louis, 1996—. Editl. bd. Social Work, 1968-74, Health Progress, 1988—; manuscript referee Jour. Social Svc. Rsch., 1977—; mgmt. and evaluation content referee Wadsworth Press, Human Svcs. Press, Allyn and Bacon Press; contbr. articles profl. jours. and books. Bd. dirs. Ecumenical Housing Prodn. Corp., 1985—, pres. bd. dirs., 1993-95; pres. bd. Housing Comes First; mem. Mo. Assn. Social Welfare, 1980—, DuBourg Soc. of St. Louis U.; bd. mem. St. Louis U. Ctr. for Social Justice; mem. Salvation Army Family Haven, 1987, mem. adv. bd., 1988-92; chmn. United Way of Greater St. Louis venture grant com., 1988-91, mem. allocation com., 1985-95, mem. process and rev. com., 1991-93, inter-orgnl. priorities com., 1991-93; organizer Mo. State Nat. Coalition for the Homeless; appointee St. Louis U. Instl. Representation nat. Jesuits social Concern Group, 1993—; mem. exec. and support tng. group, St. Louis U., 1987—; mem. instnl. rev. bd. IRB St. Louis U. Med. Ctr. NIMH Career Leadership Devel. fellow, 1965-67; recipient Scholar of Yr. award Sch. Social Svc., St. Louis U., 1987; named Vol. of Yr. Ecumenical Prodn. Corp., 1990; Presdl. scholar Sch. Social Svc., 1992. Mem. AAUP (St. Louis U. chpt. exec. com. 1990—, pres. 1994—), ACLU, Acad. Cert. Social Workers (charter mem.), Nat. Assn. Social Workers, Mo. Assn. for Social Welfare (bd. dirs., Outstanding State-Wide Mem. of Yr. 1987), Coun. on Social Work Edn., Common Cause, Amnesty Internat., Nat. Com. on Vital and Health Stats. U.S. Census Bur. (subcom. on health stats. for minorities and other spl. populations of U.S. 1988—). Democrat. Roman Catholic. Home: 9100 Litzsinger Rd Saint Louis MO 63144-2214 Office: 3550 Lindell Blvd Saint Louis MO 63103-1021 *My entire professional life has been in the field of social work. My personal and professional values are derived from a dual commitment to empower the uniqueness of individuals and to enhance the development of caring communities. These goals have organized and directed my professional practice, teaching and writing. I believe that the profession of social work has a unique and singular mission in society. That mission is to advocate for and consciously bring about the social development of all people.*

STREU, RAYMOND OLIVER, financial planner, securities executive; b. Hereford, Tex., July 7, 1931; s. William Urlin and Yetta May (Hackworth) S.; m. Joan Eliz Hardwick, Nov. 24, 1953 (div. Oct. 1963); children: William Raymond, Ronald Hardwick, Russell Francis; m. Wanda Mae Daves, Sept. 2, 1964 (div. Sept. 1990); children: Rodney Jack, Randall Oliver; m. Doris Francis Wright, Mar. 6, 1993. BBA, Tex. Tech U., 1952. CFP. Co-owner Streu Hardware Co., Hereford, 1948-60; agt., broker Justice Real Estate, Hereford, 1960-62; pres. Mark IV Realtors, Hereford, 1962-73; rep., div. mgr. Waddell & Reed, Inc., Hereford, 1965-73, divsn. mgr., 1973-78; br. mgr. E.F. Hutton Fin. Svcs., Amarillo, Tex., 1978-83, Pvt. Ledger Fin. Svc., San Diego, 1983-85, Associated Planners Sec. Corp., L.A., 1985-87; pres. Asset Planning Group, Amarillo, Tex., 1983—; br. mgr. Sun Am. Securities Corp., Phoenix, 1987—. Leadership chmn. Llano Estacado coun. Boy Scouts Am., 1972-73; dir. Amarillo chpt. Am. Heart Assn., 1996—. Lt. commdr. USN, 1952-66. Mem. Internat. Assn. Fin. Planning (pres. local chpt. 1988-89), Inst. Cert. Fin. Planners, High Plains Eye Bank (life), Jaycees, Lions (pres. Amarillo chpt. 1975-76). Republican. Presbyterian. Avocations: sailing, dry fly fishing. Office: Asset Planning Group 1616 S Kentucky St Ste C-350 Amarillo TX 79102-2252

STREVEY, TRACY ELMER, JR., army officer, surgeon, physician executive; b. Shorewood, Wis., Apr. 24, 1933; s. Tracy Elmer and Margaret (Rees) S.; m. Victoria Crowley (div.); children: Virginia Ann, Tracy Elmer III, Andrew Victor; m. Elizabeth Sommers. Student, Pomona Coll., 1951-54; MD, U. So. Calif., 1958; student, Armed Forces Staff Coll., 1970-71, U.S. Army War Coll., 1977-78. Diplomate Am. Bd. Surgery, Am. Bd. Thoracic Surgery. Intern Los Angeles County Gen. Hosp., 1958-59; commd. officer U.S. Army, 1959, advanced through grades to maj. gen., 1983; resident in gen. surgery Letterman Gen. Hosp., San Francisco, 1962-66; resident in thoracic and cardiovascular surgery Walter Reed Gen. Hosp., Washington, 1968-70; comdg. officer 757 Med. Detachment OA, Ludwigsburg, Fed. Republic Germany, 1959-61; ward officer orthopaedic svc. 75th Sta. Hosp., Stuttgart, Fed. Republic Germany, 1961-62; chief profl. svc., chief surgery 85th Evacuation Hosp., Qui Nhon, Vietnam, 1967; comdg. officer 3d Surg. Hosp., Dong Tam, Vietnam, 1967-68; asst. chief thoracic and cardiovascular surgery service Fitzsimons Army Med Ctr., Denver, 1971-73, chief thoracic and cardiovascular surgery service, 1973-75; asst. dir. med. activities and dir. Profl. Edn. Gorgas Hosp., Panama Canal Zone, 1975-77; chief dept. surgery Walter Reed Army Med. Ctr., Washington, 1978-81; comdr. Brooke Army Med. Ctr., Ft. Sam Houston, Tex., 1981-83, Tripler Army Med. Ctr., Hawaii, 1983-86, U.S. Army Health Svcs. Command, San Antonio, 1986-88; ret. U.S. Army, 1988; CEO Nassau County Med. Ctr., 1988-93; pres., CEO N.Y. Hosp Med. Ctr. Queens, N.Y.C., 1993-94; v.p. N.Y. Hosp. Care Network, N.Y.C., 1994-95; v.p. for med. affairs Sisters of Mercy Health Sys., St. Louis, 1995—; asst. clin. prof. surgery U. Colo. Med. Ctr., Denver, 1973-75; prof. surgery Uniformed Services U. Health Scis., Bethesda, 1978—, vice chmn. dept. surgery, 1978-81. Contbr. articles to profl. jours. Decorated D.S.M., Legion of Merit with 2 oak leaf clusters, Meritorious Service medal with 2 oak leaf clusters, Purple Heart, Army Commendation Medal for Valor, Vietnam Cross of Gallantry with Palm; recipient Outstanding Service award U. So. Calif. Med. Alumni Assn., 1983. Fellow ACS, Am. Coll. Chest Physicians, Am. Coll. Cardiology, Am. Coll. Physician Execs. (disting.); mem. Assn. Mil. Surgeons U.S., Soc. Thoracic Surgeons, Western Thoracic Surg. Assn., Am. Assn. Thoracic Surgery, Am. Cancer Soc., Bexar County Med. Soc., ARC (bd. dirs. 1984-86), Honolulu-Pacific Fed. Exec. Bd., Masons, Rotary. Avocations: ham radio; scuba diving; golf; computer science. Home: 1509 Woodgate Dr Saint Louis MO 63131-4724 Office: 2039 N Geyer Rd Saint Louis MO 63131-3332

STREW, SUZANNE CLAFLIN, choreographer, dance educator; b. Canton, Ohio, May 31, 1935; d. William Jenney and Mildred Mae (McClellan) Claflin; m. Rudolph John Strew, Aug. 15, 1964. BS, Bowling Green (Ohio) State U., 1957; postgrad., U. Wis., summer 1962; MEd, Kent (Ohio) State U., 1964; postgrad., Ohio State U., summer 1967. Tchr. Deerfield Beach (Fla.) Pub. Sch., 1959-60; instr. dance Baldwin-Wallace Coll., Berea, Ohio, 1957-59, prof., dir., choreographer, 1961—, chmn. erson divsn., 1992—; choreographer Berea Summer Theatre, 1965—; dir. dance concert Baldwin-Wallace Coll., 1961—. Choreographer numerous prodns. including The Sound of Music, Cleve. Opers, 1992, and over 125 prodns. Advisor Laurels Hon. Soc. Recipient Cleve. Critics Circle award Cleve. Critics Circle, 1980, 81, 83, 84. Mem. AAHPERD (nat. dance sect.), OhioDance, Mortar Board, Chi Omega, Omicron De lta Kappa. Office: Baldwin-Wallace Coll Berea OH 44017

STRIBLIN, LORI ANN, critical care nurse, medicare coordinator, nursing educator; b. Valley, Ala., Sept. 23, 1962; d. James Author and Dorothy Jane (Cole) Burt; m. Thomas Edward Striblin, Oct. 26, 1984; children: Natalie Nicole, Crystal Danielle. AAS in Nursing, So. Union State Jr. Coll., Valley, Ala., 1992. RN, Ala.; cert. ACLS and BLS. Surg. staff nurse East Ala. Med. Ctr., Opelika, 1992-93, surg. charge nurse, 1993-95, critical care ICU staff nurse, 1993-95; RN case mgr. East Ala. Home Care, Opelika, 1995-96; staff devel. coord., medicare coord. Lanett (Ala.) Geriatric Ctr., 1996—; case mgr. Lanier Home Health Svcs., Valley, Ala., 1996—; med. advisor Nu Image Weight Loss Ctr., Opelika, Ala., 1996—, nurse case mgr. weight loss ctr., counselor, diet educator, 1996—; clin. instr. educator So. Union C.C., Valley, 1994—. Mem. AACN, Ala. State Nurses Assn. Baptist. Avocations: crafts, horseback riding, hiking, swimming, reading. Home: 3136 County Rd 79 Cusseta AL 36852 Office: Lanier Home Health Svcs 14 Medical Park Valley AL 36854-3665

STRICKLAND, ANITA MAURINE, retired business educator, librarian; b. Groom, Tex., Sept. 24, 1923; d. Oliver Austin and Thelma May (Slay) Pool; m. LeRoy Graham Mashburn, Aug. 12, 1945 (dec. Mar. 1977); 1 child, Ronald Gene; m. Reid Strickland, May 27, 1978. BBA, West Tex. State U., 1962, MEd, 1965; postgrad. in library sci., Tex. Women's U., 1970. Cert. tchr., Tex.; cert. librarian. Employment interviewer Douglas Aircraft Co., Oklahoma City, 1942-45; cashier, bookkeeper Southwestern Pub. Services, Groom and Panhandle, Tex., 1950-58; acct. Gen. Motors Outlet, Groom, 1958-62; tchr. bus., lang. arts Groom Pub. Schs., 1962-68; bus. tchr., librarian Amarillo (Tex.) Pub. Schs., 1968-81. Vol. Amarillo Symphony, 1980—, Amarillo Rep. Com., 1981—, Lone Star Ballet, 1981-92; docent Amarillo Mus. Art, 1987—, sec., 1987-90, 93-94; sec. Amarillo Art Alliance, 1989-90. Mem. AAUW (legis. com. 1986-88, sec. 1989-90, bd. dirs. 1989-91), Amarillo C. of C. (vol. women's divsn. 1981-86), Amarillo Christian Women's Club (asst. prayer advisor 1989-90, treas. 1995-96). Baptist. Avocations: piano, reading, swimming, tennis. Home: 6513 Roxton Dr Amarillo TX 79109-5120

STRICKLAND, ARVARH EUNICE, history educator; b. Hattiesburg, Miss., July 6, 1930; s. Eunice and Clotiel (Marshall) S.; m. Willie Pearl Elmore, June 17, 1951; children: Duane Arvarh, Bruce Elmore. BA, Tougaloo Coll., 1951; MA, U. Ill., 1953, PhD, 1962. Tchr. Hattiesburg Schs., 1951-52; instr. Tuskegee Inst., 1955-56; prin. supr. Madison County Schs., Canton, Miss., 1956-59; asst. prof. history Chgo. State U., 1962-65, assoc. prof. history, 1965-68, prof., 1968-69; prof. U. Mo., Columbia, 1969-96, prof. emeritus, 1996—, chmn. dept. history, 1980-83, interim dir. black studies program, 1994-96, sr. faculty assoc., Office of V.P. acad. affairs, 1987-88, assoc. v.p. acad. affairs, 1989-91. Author: History of the Chicago Urban League, 1966, (with Reich and Biller) Building the United States, 1971, (with Reich) The Black American Experience to 1877, 1974, The Black American Experience since 1877, 1974; editor: Working with Carter G. Woodson, (with Lorenzo J. Greene) The Father of Black History: A Diary, 1928-1930, 1989, Selling Black History for Carter G. Woodson: A Diary, 1930-33, 1996. Commr. Planning and Zoning, Columbia, Mo., 1977-80, Boone County Home Rule Charter, 1982, Mo. Peace Officers Standards and Tng. Commn., 1988-89; co-chmn. Mayors Com. to Commemorate Contbns. of Black Columbians, Columbia, 1981; mem. exec. subcom. Mayor's Ad Hoc Election '82 Com., 1982; bd. dirs. Harry S. Truman Library Inst., 1987-96. Recipient Disting. Svc. award Ill. Hist. Soc., 1957, Byler Disting. Prof. award U. Mo., 1994, St. Louis Am.'s Educator of Yr. award, 1994, Disting. Faculty award U. Mo.-Columbia Alumni Assn., 1995, Tougaloo Coll. Alumni Hall of Fame, 1995. Mem. Orgn. Am. Historians, Am. Hist. Assn., Assn. Study Afro-Am. Life and History, So. Hist. Assn., State Hist. Soc. Mo., Kiwanian, Alpha Phi Alpha, Phi Alpha Theta (internat. v.p. 1991-93, pres. 1994-95, chair adv. bd. 1996—). Democrat. Methodist. Home: 4100 Defoe Dr Columbia MO 65203-0252 Office: U Mo Dept History 101 Read Hall Columbia MO 65211

STRICKLAND, BONNIE RUTH, psychologist, educator; b. Louisville, Nov. 24, 1936; d. Roy E. and Billie P. (Whitfield) S. B.S., Ala. Coll., 1958; M.S., Ohio State U., 1960, Ph.D. (USPHS fellow), 1962. Diplomate: clin. psychology Am. Bd. Examiners in Profl. Psychology. Research psychologist Juvenile Diagnostic Center, Columbus, Ohio, 1958-60; from asst. to asso. prof. psychology Emory U., Atlanta, 1962-73; dean of women Emory U., 1964-67; prof. psychology U. Mass., Amherst, 1973—; chmn. dept. psychology U. Mass., 1976-77, 78-82, assoc. to chancellor, 1983-84; mem. adv. coun. NIMH, 1984-87; Sigma Xi nat. lectr., 1991-93. Adv. editor numerous psychology jours., acad. pub. houses; contbg. author texts personality theory.; contbr. of numerous articles on social personality and clin. psychology to profl. jours.; contbg. author of two citation classics. Recipient Outstanding Faculty award Emory U., 1968-69; Chancellor's medal disting. service U. Mass., 1983. Fellow APA (pres. divsn. clin. psychology 1983, chmn. bd. profl. affairs 1980-83, chmn. policy and planning bd. 1983-85, pres. 1987, bd. dirs. 1986-87, Outstanding Leadership award 1992), Am. Psychol. Soc. (founder 1988, bd. dirs. 1989-93), Am. Assn. Applied and Preventive Psychology (founder 1990, bd. dirs. 1990-94, pres. 1992-94), Acad. Clin. Psychology, Coun. Grad. Depts. Psychology (chmn. 1982-83). Home: 558 Federal St Belchertown MA 01007-9754 Office: U Mass Dept Psychology Amherst MA 01003-7710

STRICKLAND, GEORGE THOMAS, JR., physician, researcher, educator; b. Goldsboro, N.C., Apr. 20, 1934; s. George Thomas and Flora Ross (Bridgers) S.; m. Anne Belle Garst, Feb. 13, 1960; children: George Thomas III, Paul Garst, James Kelly. BA in History, U. N.C., 1956, MD, 1960; DCMT, London Sch. Hygiene and Tropical Medicine, Eng., 1971, PhD in Parasitology, 1974. Diplomate Am. Bd. Internal Medicine. Head dept. immunoparasitology Naval Med. Rsch. Inst., Bethesda, Md., 1972-74, program mgr. infectious diseases rsch., naval med. R&D com., 1974-76; prof., dir. rsch. and edn., dept. medicine Uniformed Svcs. U. Health Scis., Bethesda, 1976-81; staff pathologist Armed Forces Inst. Pathology, Washington, 1981-82; dir. Internat. Health Program, Sch. Medicine U. Md., Balt., 1982—, prof. microbiology, medicine, epidemiology and preventive medicine Sch. Medicine, 1982—; dir. Internat. Ctr. Med. Rsch. and Tng., Lahore, Pakistan, 1983-85; chmn., vice-chmn. Nat. Coun. Internat. Health, Washington, 1977-80; Am. co-investigator Egyptian Schistosomiasis Rsch. Project, 1990-96; prin. investigator rsch. project on Lyme disease, Md., 1993—, hepatitis C, Egypt, 1995—. Editor: Hunter's Tropical Medicine, 6th edit., 1984, 7th edit., 1991. Capt. USN, 1960-82. Fellow ACP, Infectious Diseases Soc. Am., Am. Coll. Tropical Medicine Hygiene, Royal Coll. Tropical Medicine Hygiene. Democrat. Avocations: tennis, gardening, travel, classical music. Home: 220 Hawthorn Rd Baltimore MD 21210-2504

STRICKLAND, HUGH ALFRED, lawyer; b. Rockford, Ill., May 3, 1931; s. Hugh and Marie (Elmer) S.; m. Donna E. McDonald, Aug. 11, 1956; children: Amy Alice, Karen Ann. A.B., Knox Coll., 1953; J.D., Chgo. Kent Coll. Law, 1959. Bar: Ill. 1960. Partner firm McDonald, Strickland & Clough, Carrollton, Ill., 1961—; asst. atty. gen. Ill., 1960-67, spl. asst. gen., 1967-69; pres. McDonald Title Co. Mem. Greene County Welfare Svcs. Com., 1963—, Ill. Heart Assn., 1961-65; trustee Thomas H. Boyd Meml. Hosp., 1972-95. With AUS, 1953-55. Recipient award for meritorious service Am. Heart Assn., 1964. Fellow Ill. Bar Found. (charter); mem. ABA, Ill. Bar Assn., Greene County Bar Assn. (past pres.), Southwestern Bar Assn. (past pres.), Ill. Def. Counsel, Am. Judicature Soc., Def. Rsch. Inst., Elks Club, Westlake Country Club (v.p. 1968-70, dir.), Big Sand Lake Country Club, Phi Delta Theta, Phi Delta Phi. Methodist. Home: 827 7th St Carrollton IL 62016-1421 Office: 524 N Main St Carrollton IL 62016-1027

STRICKLAND, MARSHALL HAYWARD, bishop; b. Rome, Ga., Oct. 8, 1933; s. Albert A. Strickland and Elzie Greer Strickland Morton; 1 child, Marshall H. 2d. BA, Livingstone Coll., 1951; PhD, St. Mary's Theol. Sem., Balt.; MDiv, Hood Theol. Sem., 1955, DD (hon.); DD (hon.), Allen U. Ordained deacon AME Ch. Pastor Patten Meml. AME Zion Ch., Chattanooga, David Stan AME Zion Ch., Lancaster, S.C., Hood Meml. AME Zion Ch., Bristol, Tenn., Big Zion AME Ch., Mobile, Ala., Pa. Ave. AME Zion Ch., Balt.; bishop Mid Atlantic I dist. AME Ch., Balt., sec.; bd. bishops AME Zion Ch., chmn. commn. judiciary, chmn. Am. Bible Soc., 1st vice chair brotherhood pension svc., 1st vice chair Christian edn., 2d vice chair bicentennial commn., trustee Livingstone Coll.; past mem. Ala. Consultation Ch. Union; guest pastor Gen. Conf. AME Ch., St. Paul Cathedral, others; speaker in field; guest on various radio and TV stas. Author: William E. Fine: Kennedy-The Dreamer, Church and Stae: Not Separate, Our Heritage is Our Religion, The Black Church: Black America's Salvation, The Black Church: Solving Black America's Crisis, Health Care: Preaching Prevention from the Pulpit, Rebuilding Our Cities in Partnership with the Black Church: A Master Plan; contbr. articles to profl. jours. Former chmn. bd. dirs. Mobile Community Action Authority; past mem. Commn. Organic Union; founder Zion Outreach Ctr., Balt. Recipient Humanitarian award Zion Outreach Svcs. Associated Black Charities, Econ. Devel. award HUB, Flood Relief Support award Jamaican Assn. Md. Mem. NAACP (past pres. Bristol chpt., Recognition awards Bristol and Balt. chpts.). Office: 2000 Cedar Circle Dr Baltimore MD 21228-3743*

STRICKLAND, NELLIE B., library program director; b. Belmont, Miss., Dec. 12, 1932. BS, Murray State U., 1954; MLS, George Peabody Coll., 1971. Ref. libr. Murray State Coll., Murray, Ky., 1954; asst. libr. Dept. Army, Ft. Stewart, Ga., 1955-56; field libr. U.S. Army, Japan, 1957-59; area libr. U.S. Army, Europe, 1960-66; staff libr. U.S. Army So. Command, C.Z., 1966-67; area libr. U.S. Army, Vietnam, 1967-68, staff libr., 1971-72; chief libr. U.S. Army, Ft. Benning, Ga., 1970-71; dir. library program U.S. Army Pacific, 1973-74; dir. Army libr. program Washington, 1974-94. Recipient Outstanding Performance award Ft. Benning, 1970, Armed Forces Achievement citation, 1982, 94, Order of the White Plume; Dept. of Army Tng. grantee, 1971; Dept. of Army decoration for Exceptional Civil Svc., 1994. Mem. ALA, Kappa Delta Phi, Alpha Sigma Alpha. Home: 203 S Yoakum Pky Apt 614 Alexandria VA 22304-3716

STRICKLAND, ROBERT LOUIS, business executive; b. Florence, S.C., Mar. 3, 1931; s. Franz M. and Hazel (Eaddy) S.; m. Elizabeth Ann Miller, Feb. 2, 1952; children: Cynthia Anne, Robert Edson. AB, U. N.C., 1952; MBA with distinction, Harvard U., 1957. With Lowe's Cos., Inc., North Wilkesboro, N.C., 1957—, sr. v.p., 1970-76, exec. v.p., 1976-78, chmn. bd., 1978—, chmn. exec. com., 1988—, mem. office of pres., 1970-78, also bd. dirs.; founder Sterling Advt., Ltd., 1966; v.p., mem. adminstrv. com. Lowe's Profit-Sharing Trust, 1961-87, chmn. ops. com., 1972-78; mgmt. com. Lowe's ESOP Plan, 1978—; bd. dirs. T. Rowe Price Assocs., Balt., Hannaford Bros., Portland; panelist investor rels. field, 1972—; spkr., panelist employee stock ownership, 1978—; spkr. on investor rels., London, Edinburgh, Glasgow, Paris, Zurich, Frankfurt, Milan, Vienna, Singapore, Tokyo. Author: Lowe's Cybernetwork, 1969, Lowe's Living Legend, 1970, Ten Years of Growth, 1971, The Growth Continues, 1972, 73, 74, Lowe's Scoreboard, 1978, also articles. Mem. N.C. Ho. of Reps., 1962-64, Rep. Senatorial Inner Circle, 1980-95; exec. com. N.C. Rep. Com., 1963-73; trustee U. N.C., Chapel Hill, 1987-95, chmn. bd., 1991-93; dir., dep. chmn. Fed. Res. Bank of Richmond, 1996—; com. on bus. laws and the economy N.C., 1994-97; dir. U.S. Coun. Better Bus. Burs., 1981-85; bd. dirs., v.p. Nat. Home Improvement Coun., 1972-76; bd. dirs. N.C. Sch. Arts Found., 1975-79, N.C. Bd. Natural and Econ. Resources, 1975-76; bd. dirs., govt. affairs com. Home Ctr. Inst.; trustee, sec. bd. Wilkes C.C., 1964-73; chmn., pres. bd. dirs. Do-It-Yourself Rsch. Inst., 1981-89; pres. Hardware Home Improvement Coun. City of Hope Nat. Med. Ctr., L.A., 1987-89. With USN, 1952-55, lt. Res. 1955-62. Named Wilkes County N.C. Young Man of Yr., Wilkes Jr. C. of C., 1962; recipient Bronze Oscar of Industry award Fin. World, 1969-74, 76-79, Silver Oscar of Industry award, 1970, 72-74, 76-79, Gold Oscar of Industry award as best of all industry, 1972, 87, Excellence award in corp. reporting Fin. Analysts Fedn., 1970, 72, 74, 81-82, cert. of Distinction Brand Names Found., 1970, Retailer of Yr. award, 1971, 73, Disting. Mcht. award, 1972, Spirit of Life award City of Hope, 1983, Free Enterprise Legend award Students Free Enterprise, 1994; named to Home Ctr. Hall of Fame, 1985. Mem. Nat. Assn. Over-Counter Cos. (bd. advisers 1973-77), Newcomen Soc., Employee Stock Ownership Assn. (pres. 1983-85, chmn. 1985-87), James Madison Club, Federalist Soc., Twin City Club, Forsyth Country Club, Piedmont City Club, Hound Ears Club (Blowing Rock, N.C.), Elk River Club (Banner Elk, N.C.), Roaring Gap Club (N.C.), Ponte Vedra Inn and Club (Fla.), Scabbard and Blade, Phi Beta Kappa, Pi Kappa Alpha. Home: 226 N Stratford Rd Winston Salem NC 27104 Office: Lowes Cos Inc 604 Two Piedmont Plz Winston Salem NC 27104

STRICKLAND, SANDRA JEAN HEINRICH, nursing educator; b. Tucson, Sept. 18, 1943; d. Henry and Ada (Schmidt) Heinrich; BS, U. Tex. Sch. Nursing, 1965; MS in Nursing (fellow), U. Md., 1969; DrPH, U. Tex., 1978; m. William C. Strickland, Aug. 18, 1973; children: William Henry, Angela Lee. Clin. instr. U. Tex. Sch. Nursing, Galveston, 1965-66; staff nurse Hidalgo County Health Dept., Edinburg, Tex., 1966-67; supr. nursing Tex. Dept. Health Tb Control, Austin, 1969-70; instr. St. Luke's Hosp. Sch. Nursing, Houston, 1971-72, Tex. Women's U. Sch. Nursing, Houston and Dallas, 1972-73; dir. nursing Dallas City Health Dept., 1974-80; assoc. prof. community health nursing grad. program Tex. Woman's U., Dallas, 1980-87, U. Incarnate Word, 1987—; mem. profl. adv. com. Dallas Vis. Nurse Assn., 1978-83, Santa Rosa Home Health Agy., 1991-94; mem. health adv. bd. Dallas Ind. Sch. Dist., 1976-84; chmn. nursing and health services Dallas chpt. ARC, 1984-86, bd. dirs. San Antonio chpt., 1990; Tex. Lung Assn., 1991—, bd. dirs. San Antonio Chpt., Tex. Public Health Assn. fellow, 1977. Mem. APHA, Tex. Public Health Assn., Sigma Theta Tau. Methodist. Home: 508 US Highway 90 E Castroville TX 78009-5230

STRICKLAND, TED, congressman, clergyman, psychology educator, psychologist; b. Lucasville, Ohio, Aug. 4, 1941; m. Frances Smith. BA in History, Asbury Coll.; MDiv, Asbury Seminary; PhD in Psychology, U. Ky. Clergyman, campus dir.; consulting psychologist Southern Ohio Correctional Facility; prof. psychology Shawnee State U.; mem. 103rd & 105th Congresses from 6th Ohio dist., Washington, D.C., 1993-94, 97—; mem. numerous coms. in fields of: edn. and labor, post-secondary edn. and tng., labor standards, occupational health and safety, small bus., rural enterprise, exports and environ. Democrat. Office: 336 Cannon House Office Bldg Washington DC 20515*

STRICKLAND, THOMAS JOSEPH, artist; b. Keyport, N.J., Dec. 27, 1932; s. Charles Edward and Clementine Maria (Grasso) S.; m. Ann DeBaun Browne, Apr. 28, 1992. Student, Newark Sch. Fine and Indsl. Arts, 1951-53, Am. Art Sch., 1956-59, Nat. Acad. Sch. Fine Arts with Robert Philipp, 1957-59. Judge local and nat. art shows; TV guest; instr. painting and pastels Grove House; lectr. Exhibited in one man shows at, Hollywood (Fla.) Art Mus., 1972-76, Elliott Mus., Stuart, Fla., 1974, others; exhibited in group shows at, Am. Artists Profl. League, N.Y.C., 1958, 61, Parke-Bernet Galleries, N.Y.C., 1959, 61, 64, Exposition Intercontinentale, Monaco, 1966-68, Salon Rouge du Casino Dieppe, 1967, 7e Grand Prix Internat. de Peinture de la Cote d'Azur, Cannes, 1971, Hollywood Art Mus., 1972-76, Art Guild of Boca Raton, 1973, Stagecoach Gallery, 1973, Am. Painters in Paris, 1975; represented in permanent collections, St. Vincent Coll., Elliott Mus., Martin County Hist. Soc., Salem Coll., Winston-Salem, N.C., St. Hugh Catholic Ch., Fla.; (Recipient Digby Chandler prize Knickerbocker Artists 1965, Best in Show Blue Dome Art Fellowship 1972, 1st Place, Fine Arts League, La Junta, Colo. 1973, Blue Ribbon award Cape Coral Nat. Art Show 1973, 1st prize Hollywood Art Mus. 1973, Charles Hawthorne Meml. award Nat. Arts Club Exhbn. 1977, 1st prize Miami Palette Club 1978, others.); Contbr. articles to profl. jours. and included in Best of Pastel, 1996. With AUS, 1953-55. Mem. Pastel Soc. Am., Nat. Soc. Lit. and Arts. Roman Catholic. Home: 2595 Taluga Dr Miami FL 33133-2433 *My aim in life has been to find, capture, and communicate the beauty I see in the world to others by means of painting in my Impressionistic style. To achieve this goal I have developed my talent, been dedicated to art and its disciplines. I have been uncompromising in my choice of what I paint as I paint only what I want to, preferring people and always striving to do my best.*

STRICKLAND, WILLIAM JESSE, lawyer; b. Newport News, Va., Mar. 21, 1942. BSBA, U. Richmond, 1964, JD, 1970. Bar: Va. 1969, U.S. Dist. Ct. (ea. and we. dists.) Va., U.S. Ct. Claims, U.S. Tax Ct., U.S. Ct. Appeals (4th cir.). Exec. com. coord. dept., mng. ptnr. McGuire, Woods, Battle & Boothe, Richmond, Va., 1969—; bd. dirs. Cableform Inc., Zion Crossroads, Va., Eimeldingen Corp., Indpls. Bd. dirs. Va. Found. Rsch. & Econ. Edn., Inc. Capt. USMC 1964-67, Vietnam. Mem. ABA, Va. Bar Assn., Richmond Bar Assn., Nat. Assn. Bond Lawyers, Va. Govt. Fin. Officers Assn., Local Govt. Attys. Assn., Va. Bond Club. Office: McGuire Woods Battle & Boothe 1 James River Plz Richmond VA 23219-3229

STRICKLER, HOWARD MARTIN, physician; b. New Haven, Conn., Oct. 26, 1950; s. Thomas David and Mildred Laing (Martin) S.; m. Susan Hunter, May 2, 1982; children: Hunter Gregory, Howard Martin Jr. BA, Berea Coll., 1975; MD, Univ. Louisville, 1979. Diplomate Am. Bd. Family Practice, Am. Bd. Forensic Medicine, Am. Bd. Forensic Examiners. Resident Anniston (Ala.) Family Practice Residency, 1979-82; pvt. practice Monteagle, Tenn., 1982-85; fellow in addictive diseases Willingway Hosp., Statesboro, Ga., 1985-86; faculty devel. fellow Univ. N.C., Chapel Hill, 1985-86; pvt. practice Birmingham, Ala., 1986-90; pres. Employers Drug Program Mgmt., Inc., Birmingham, 1990—; med. dir. Am. Health Svcs., Inc., 1993—; med. dir. Bradford Facilities, Birmingham, 1987-90, New Life Clinic, Bessemer, ala., Physicians Smoke Free Clinic, Birmingham, 1988-90, Am. Health Svcs., Inc., 1993—; chmn. dept. family practice and emergency medicine Bessemer Carraway Med. Ctr., 1993-95. Mem. tennis anti-doping appeals com. ATP Tour, Inc., 1997. With U.S. Army, 1969-72, Vietnam. Decorated Bronze Star, 1971, Vietnam Campaign medal, Vietnam Svc. medal 3 Stars, 1971. Fellow Am. Acad. Family Physicians, Am. Acad. Disability Evaluating Physicians; mem. Am. Soc. Addiction Medicine (cert.), Am. Coll. Occupl. and Environ. Medicine, Am. Assn. Med. Rev. Officers (cert.), Med. Assn. State of Ala., Phi Kappa Phi. Methodist. Avocations: flying, tennis, golf. Home: 868 Tulip Poplar Dr Birmingham AL 35244-1633 Office: 616 9th St S Birmingham AL 35233-1113

STRICKLER, IVAN K., dairy farmer; b. Carlyle, Kans., Oct. 23, 1921; s. Elmer E. and Edna Louise (James) S.; m. Madge Lee Marshall, Aug. 7, 1949; children—Steven Mark, Thomas Scott, Douglas Lee. B.S., Kans. State U., 1947. Owner, mgr. dairy farm Iola, Kans., 1947—; tchr. farm tng. to vets. World War II, 1947-54; judge 1st and 2d Nat. Holstein Show, Brazil, 1969-70, Internat. Holstein Show, Buenos Aires, 1972, Nat. Holstein Show, Ecuador, 1978, 10th Nat. Holstein Show, Brazil, 1980; judge Holstein Show, Australia, Mex. and Argentina, 1981, Lang Lang, 1984; judge Adelaide (Australia) Royal Show, 1987; pres Mid-America Dairymen, Inc., Springfield, MO, 1981—; appointed chmn. Nat. Dairy Bd., 1985-90; dairy leader 4-H Club, 1962-75; dir. Iola State Bank; rep. U.S. Internat. Dairy Symposium, 1994, Belo Horinzote, Brazil. Author: Wholly Cow We Did It, 1996. Trustee Allen County Community Jr. Coll.; mem. agr. edn. and rsch. com. Kans. State U., U.S. Agrl. Trade and Devel. Mission, Algeria and Tunisia, 1989. With USN, 1942-46, PTO. Recipient Silver award Holstein Friesian Assn. Brazil, 1969, Top Dairy Farm Efficiency award Ford Found., 1971, Master Farmer award Kans. State U. and Kans. Assn. Commerce and Industry, 1972, Gold award Holstein Friesian Assn. Argentina, 1972, Richard Lynng award Nat. Dairy Bd., 1990, award of merit Gamma Sigma Delta, 1987; named Man of Yr. World Dairy Exposition, 1978; portrait in Dairy Hall of Fame Kans. State U., 1974; Guest of Hon. Nat. Dairy Shrine, 1985; selected First Dairy Leader of Yr., 1996. Mem. Mid Am. Dairymen (sec. corporate bd. 1971-81, pres. 1981—), Holstein Friesian Assn. Am. (nat. dir. 1964-72), Dairy Shrine (nat. dir. 1971-81), United Dairy Industry Assn. (dir. 1971—), Nat. Holstein Assn. Am. (pres. 1979-80), Alpha Gamma Rho. Mem. Christian Ch. (elder, bd. dirs.). Club: Nat. Dairy Shrine (pres. 1978). Home: PO Box 365 Iola KS 66749-0365 Office: Mid America Dairymen Inc 3253 E Chestnut Expy Springfield MO 65802-2540

STRICKLER, JEFF, newspaper movie critic. Movie critic Mpls Star Tribune. Office: Minneapolis Star Tribune 425 Portland Ave Minneapolis MN 55415-1511*

STRICKLER, JEFFREY HAROLD, pediatrician; b. Mpls., Oct. 14, 1943; s. Jacob Harold and Helen Cecelia (Mitchell) S.; m. Karen Anne Stewart, June 18, 1966; children: Hans Stewart, Liesl Ann. BA, Carleton Coll., 1965; MD, U. Minn., 1969. Diplomate Am. Bd. Pediatrics. Resident in pediatrics Stanford (Calif.) U., 1969-73; pvt. practice Helena, Mont., 1975—; chief staff Shodair Children's Hosp., Helena, 1984-86; dir. maternal-child health Lewis and Clark County, Helena, 1978-88; chief of staff St. Peters Hosp., Helena, 1994-96; bd.dirs. Helena Health Alliance. Mem. Mont. Gov.'s Task Force on Child Abuse, 1978-79; mem. steering com. Region VIII Child Abuse Prevention, Denver, 1979-82; bd. dirs. Helena Dist. 1 Sch. Bd., 1982-88, vice chmn., 1985-87. Maj. M.C., USAF, 1973-75. Fellow Am. Acad. Pediatrics (vice chmn. Mont. chpt. 1981-84, chmn. 1984-87, mem. nat. nominating com. 1987-90, chmn. 1989-90, coun. on govt. affairs 1990-96, Wyeth award 1987); mem. Rotary (youth exchange chmn. dist. 539, 1984-88, pres. Helena 1988-89). Avocations: skiing, hiking. Office: Helena Pediatric Clinic 1122 N Montana Ave Helena MT 59601-3513

STRICKLER, MATTHEW M., lawyer; b. Bryn Mawr, Pa., June 27, 1940; s. Charles S and Mary Webster (Cornman) S.; m. Margaret Renshaw, Sept. 3, 1966; children: Matthew David, Andrew Kellogg, Timothy Webster, Edward Charles. AB, Haverford Coll., 1962; JD, Harvard U., 1965. Bar: Pa. 1965, U.S. Supreme Ct. 1975. Assoc. Ballard, Spahr, Andrews & Ingersoll, Phila., 1965-74, ptnr., 1974—; adj. prof. Temple U. Sch. Law, Phila., 1993—. Editor: Representing Health Care Facilities, 1981. Bd. dirs. Phila. chpt. Girl Scouts Am., 1978-96, v.p., 1984-90, 94-96. Mem. Union League Phila. Office: Ballard Spahr Andrews & Ingersoll 1735 Market St Ste 51 Philadelphia PA 19103-7501

STRICKLER, SCOTT MICHAEL, lawyer; b. Miami Beach, Fla., May 24, 1961; s. Lawrence Jerome and Barbara Susan (Fogelman) S.; m. Joy Ann Kohler, June 24, 1995. BS in Journalism, U. Md., 1981, JD with honors, 1985. Bar: Md. 1985, D.C. 1987, U.S. Dist. Ct. Md. 1988. Jud. law clk. 5th Jud. Cir. of Md., Annapolis, 1985-86; assoc. Stephen E. Moss, P.A., Bethesda, Md., 1986-89; ptnr., v.p. Moss, Strickler & Weaver, P.A., Bethesda, 1990-94, Moss & Strickler, P.A., Bethesda, 1994; ptnr. Moss Strickler & Sachitano, P.A., Bethesda, 1995—. Coach, dir. Bowie (Md.) Boys and Girls Club, 1976-81; dir. Bowie Basketball Sch., Inc., 1978-82; basketball coach Peninsula Athletic League, Annapolis, 1985-86, Olney (Md.) Boys and Girls Club, 1987—, I-270 Sports Club, Gaithersburg, Md., 1991—, Sports Challenge Internat., Palm Harbor, Fla., 1993—. Mem. ABA, Md. State Bar Assn., Montgomery County Bar Assn., Inst. Sports Attys., Kappa Tau Alpha. Avocations: basketball coach, participatory athletics, memorabilia collection. Home: 15117 Grey Pebble Dr Darnestown MD 20874 Office: Moss Strickler & Sachitano 4550 Montgomery Ave Ste 700 Bethesda MD 20814-3304

STRICKLIN, ALIX, publishing executive, writer, actor; b. Knoxville, Tenn., Nov. 11, 1959; d. William Joseph and Alice Carolyn (West) S.; m. Joseph Paul Chiarello, May 17, 1980 (div. May 29, 1988); 1 child, Mary Conner. BS, Rutgers U., 1987; MBA, St. Joseph's U., 1989. Fin. analyst Macmillan Pub. Co., Inc., Riverside, N.J., 1985-86; acctg. mgr. Macmillan Pub. Co., Inc., Riverside, 1986-88; bus. mgr. W.B. Saunders Co., Harcourt Brace Jovanovich, Inc., Phila., 1988-89, dir. bus. mgmt. and fin. adminstrn., 1989-91; dir. artist royalty EMI-CMG, Brentwood, Tenn., 1991-94; contr. CB of Nashville, 1994-96, Boomerang Prodns., Nashville, 1996—; pres. BackStage Studio, Nashville, 1996—; bd. dirs. PHCA, Inc.; vis. scholar Russian studies internat. program Rutgers U., 1987. Contbr. articles to profl. jours. Mem. Palmyra Twp. Planning Bd., 1991-92; com. chmn. Young Rep. Assn. South Jersey, Mt. Holly, 1989-91, officer, 1991; mem. Davidson Young Reps. Mem. DAR, Am. Fedn. Radio and TV Artists, Nashville Film/Video Assn., Mid. Tenn. Hunter Jumper Assn. (Menefee Combined Equitation award), Am. Horse Show Assn., New Eng. Women, Colonial Daus. 17th Century, Delta Zeta. Republican. Presbyterian. Avocations: classical piano, horseback riding.

STRICKON, HARVEY ALAN, lawyer; b. Bklyn., Nov. 9, 1947; s. Milton and Norma (Goodhartz) S.; m. Linda Carol Meltzer, July 2, 1972; children: Joshua Andrew, Meredith Cindy, Erica Stacey. BBA, CCNY, 1968; JD, NYU, 1971. Bar: N.Y. 1972, U.S. Dist. Ct. (so. and ea. dists.) N.Y. 1973, U.S. Ct. Appeals (2d cir.) 1973, U.S. Supreme Ct. 1975, U.S. Dist. Ct. (no. dist.) N.Y. 1980, U.S. Dist. Ct. (we. dist.) N.Y. 1981, U.S. Dist. Ct. Ariz. 1991, U.S. Dist. Ct. Conn., 1996. Law clk. U.S. Dist. Ct. (ea. dist.) N.Y., Bklyn., 1971-73; assoc. Moses & Singer, N.Y.C., 1973-80; from assoc. to ptnr. Kaye, Scholer, Fierman, Hays & Handler, N.Y.C., 1980-91; from ptnr. to counsel Paul, Hastings, Janofsky & Walker, N.Y.C., 1991—; mem. complaint mediation panel, departmental disciplinary com. appellate div., 1st dept. Supreme Ct. State N.Y. Co-author: Enforcing Judgments and Collecting Debts in New York, 1996. Mem. Nassau County Rep. Com., Great Neck, N.Y., 1982—; chmn. bd. dirs. Flushing Community Vol. Ambulance Corps. Inc., N.Y., 1981-86, vice chmn., 1987-92. Mem. ABA, N.Y. State Bar Assn., Assn. Bar City N.Y. (chmn. complaint mediation panel com. on profl. discipline), Am. Judicature Soc., Assn. Comml. Fin. Attys., N.Y. Law Inst., Bankruptcy Lawyers Bar Assn., (bd. govs. 1987-89, corr. sec. 1989—), Am. Bankruptcy Inst. Republican. Jewish. Home: 11 West Brook Rd Great Neck NY 11024-1219 Office: Paul Hastings Janofsky & Walker 399 Park Ave New York NY 10022

STRIDER, MARJORIE VIRGINIA, artist, educator; b. Guthrie, Okla.; d. Clifford R. and Marjorie E. (Schley) S. BFA, Kansas City Art Inst., 1962. Mem. faculty Sch. Visual Arts, N.Y.C., 1970—; artist-in-residence City U. Grad. Ctr. Mall, N.Y.C., 1976, Fabric Workshop, Phila., 1978, Grassi Palace, Venice, Italy, 1978. One-woman shows of sculpture, drawings and/or prints include Pace Gallery, N.Y.C., 1963-64, Nancy Hoffman Gallery, N.Y.C., 1973-74, Weather Spoon Mus., U.N.C., Chapel Hill, 1974, City U. Grad. Center Mall, 1976, Clocktower, N.Y.C., 1976, Sculpture Center, N.Y.C., 1983, Steinbaum Gallery, N.Y.C., 1983, 84, Andre Zarre Gallery, 1993, 95, Outdoor Installation, N.Y.C., 1997; one-woman travelling shows to numerous mus. across USA; exhibited in group shows The Sculpture Center, N.Y.C., 1981, Drawing Biennale, Lisbon, Portugal, 1981, Newark Mus., 1984, William Rockhill Nelson Mus., Kansas City, 1985, Danforth Mus., Framingham, Mass., 1987, Delahoyd Gallery, N.Y.C., 1992; represented in permanent collections Guggenheim Mus., N.Y.C., U. Colo., Boulder, Albright-Knox Mus., Buffalo, Des Moines Art Center, Storm King (N.Y.) Art Center, Larry Aldrich Mus., Ridgefield, Conn., City U. Grad. Center, N.Y.C., Hirschhorn Mus. and Sculpture Garden, Washington, Santa Fe (N. Mex.) Mus. of Art, also pvt. collections. Nat. Endowment for Arts grantee, 1973, 80, Longview Found. grantee, 1974, Pollock-Krasner Found. grantee, 1990, Florsheim Art Fund grantee, 1991; Va. Ctr. for Creative Arts fellow, 1974, 92, Millay Colony for Arts fellow, 1992, Yaddo Colony, 1996, 97.

STRIDSBERG, ALBERT BORDEN, advertising consultant, educator, editor; b. Wyoming, Ohio, July 22, 1929; s. Carl Alexander Herbert and Edith Vivian (Farley) S. BA with honors, Yale U., 1950; Diplome D'Etudes Franc., U. of Poitiers, Tours, France, 1951; postgrad., Am. U. Beirut, Lebanon, 1953-54; diploma, Direct Mktg. Inst., 1986. Copywriter Howard Swink Advt., Inc., Marion, Ohio, 1955-58; acct. supr. McCann-Erickson, Co., Brussels, 1958-60, J. Walter Thompson Co., Amsterdam, The Netherlands, 1960-63; asst. to internat. exec. v.p. J. Walter Thompson Co., N.Y.C., 1963-67, internat. cons. spl. projects, acquisitions and diversifications, 1969-73; cons., coord. Internat. Markets Advt. Agy., Inc., N.Y., London, 1967-69; editor-in-chief Advt. World mag., N.Y.C., 1975-77; lectr. in mktg. NYU, N.Y.C., 1978-84; lectr. in advt. Marist Coll., Poughkeepsie, N.Y., 1984-94; U.S. features editor Media Internat. Mag., London, 1984-90; assoc. prof. NYU, 1966-78; ind. cons., freelance writer on advt. and mktg. issues, N.Y.C., 1972—; seminar leader, Lagos, Nigeria, 1991. Author: Effective Advertising Self-Regulation, 1974, Progress Toward Advertising Self Regulation, 1976, Controversy Advertising, 1977, Advertising Self-Regulation, 1980. With U.S. Army, 1951-53. Fulbright fellow U. Poitiers, 1950-51, Ford. Found. fellow Beirut U., 1953-54. Mem. Internat. Advt. Assn. (cons., project coord. 1974-80), Am. Acad. advt., Yale Club N.Y.C., Elizabethan Club New Haven. Democrat. Episcopalian. Office: PO Box 1846 South Rd Sta Poughkeepsie NY 12601-0846

STRIEFSKY, LINDA A(NN), lawyer; b. Carbondale, Pa., Apr. 27, 1952; d. Leo James and Antoinette Marie (Carachilo) S.; m. James Richard Carlson, Nov. 3, 1984; children: David Carlson, Paul Carlson, Daniel Carlson. BA summa cum laude, Marywood Coll., 1974; JD, Georgetown U., 1977. Bar: Ohio 1977. Assoc., Thompson, Hine and Flory, Cleve., 1977-85, ptnr., 1985—. Loaned exec. United Way of Northeast Ohio, Cleve., 1978; trustee Cleve. Music Sch. Settlement. Mem. Am. Bar Found., ABA (mem. real estate fin. com. 1980—, vice-chair lender liability com. 1993—), Am. Coll. Real Estate Lawyers bd. govs. 1994—), Internat. Coun. of Shopping Ctrs., Nat. Assn. Office and Indsl. Parks, Urban Land Inst. (chmn. Cleve. dist. coun. 1996—), Cleve. Real Estate Women, Ohio Bar Assn. (bd. govs. real property sect. 1985—), Greater Cleve. Bar Assn. (chmn. bar applicants com. 1983-84, exec. coun. young lawyers sect. 1982-85, chmn. 1984-85, mem. exec. coun. real property sect. 1980-84, Merit Svc. award 1983, 85), Pi Gamma Mu. Democrat. Roman Catholic. Home: 2222 Delamere Dr Cleveland OH 44106-3204 Office: Thompson Hine and Flory LLP 3900 Society Ctr Key Ctr 127 Public Square Cleveland OH 44114-1216

STRIEGEL, PEGGY SIMSARIAN, advertising executive; b. Phila., July 12, 1941; d. Robert Ernest Samuel and Margaret (Miller) Thompson; m. James P. Simsarian, Sept. 4, 1965 (div. Sept. 1976); children: Catherine Ann, Sheila Thompson; m. Louis E. Striegel, Sept. 14, 1976 (div. June 1984); m. Andrew H. Schmeltz Jr., Dec. 4, 1991. BA, Sarah Lawrence Coll., 1963. Asst. editor Oxford U. Press, N.Y.C., 1963-64; picture editor Western Pub. Co., N.Y.C., 1964-66; art editor Houghton-Mifflin, Inc., Boston, 1966-68; pres. Peggy's Graphics, McLean, Va., 1968-78, Striegel Advt. and Graphics, Inc., Broken Arrow, Okla., 1978—. Lower Merion (Pa.) area coord. Shapp for Congress, Phila., 1970; area coord. and graphic designer Phillips for U.S. Congress, McLean, 1972; pres. bd. dirs. Gateway Found., Broken Arrow, 1987-89; chair, Cmty. Playhouse Broken Arrow, 1979-81; mktg. bd. chair Tulsa Philharmonic, 1985-96, exec. com., bd. dirs. 1993—; active internet radio and local TV talk show Women of the Roundtable. Recipient numerous advt. awards including several Addies and citations Tulsa Advt. Club, 1990-91, Gold Quill, 1990, cert. Merit Printing Industries Am., 1983, award of Excellence Am. Inst. Graphic Arts, 1983, Am. Corp. Identity Graphics award, 1994. Mem. Advt. Fedn. Tulsa, Bus. and Profl. Advt. Assn. (Gold Ring award 1986, 87), Women in Communications (prog. chmn. 1991), Met. Tulsa C. of C., Broken Arrow C. of C., Bus. Profl. Advt. Assn., Jr. Achievement of Tulsa (bd. dirs. 1990-94). Democrat. Presbyterian. Club: Art Directors. Avocations: tennis, swimming, sailing, jogging. Home: 6110 S 221st East Ave Broken Arrow OK 74014-2017 Office: 716 S Main St Broken Arrow OK 74012-5527

STRIER, KAREN BARBARA, anthropology educator; b. Summit, N.J., May 22, 1959; d. Murray Paul and Arlene Strier. BA, Swarthmore Coll., 1980; MA, Harvard U., 1981, PhD, 1986. Lectr. anthropology Harvard U., Cambridge, Mass., 1986-87; asst. prof. Beloit (Wis.) Coll., 1987-89; asst. prof. U. Wis., Madison, 1989-92, assoc. prof. anthropology, 1992-95, prof., 1995—; dept. chair, 1994-96; panel mem. U.S. Dept. Edn., Washington, 1989-92. Author: Faces in the Forest, 1992; mem. editorial bd. Internat. Jour. Primatology, 1990—, Primates, 1991—. Recipient Presdl. Young Investigator award NSF, 1989—. Fellow Am. Anthropol. Assn.; mem. AAAS, Am. Assn. Phys. Anthropologists, Internat. Primatological Soc., Animal Behavior Soc. Office: U Wis Dept Anthropology 5440 Social Sci Bldg 1180 Observatory Dr Madison WI 53706-1320

STRIER, MURRAY PAUL, chemist, consultant; b. N.Y.C., Oct. 19, 1923; s. Jack and Rose (Goldman) S.; m. Arlene Schimmel, Feb. 12, 1955; children: Sheri Jeanette, Karen Barbara, Robin Joy. BChemE, CCNY, 1944; MS, Emory U., 1947; PhD, U. Ky., 1952. Rsch. chemist Reaction Motors Inc. (named changed to Thiokol Co.), Denville, N.J., 1952-56; sect. head Air Reduction, Inc., Murray Hill, N.J., 1956-58; chief chemist Fulton-Irgon Corp. (now Inc. with Lithium Corp.), Lake Denmark, N.J., 1958-59; supr. Rayonier, Inc., Whippany, N.J., 1959-61; rsch. chemist McGraw Edison Co., West Orange, N.J., 1961-64; sr. rsch. scientist McDonnell Douglas Corp., Newport Beach, Calif., 1964-69; rsch. assoc. Hooker Rsch. Ctr., Grand Island, N.Y., 1969-71; phys. scientist EPA, Washington, 1972-86; cons. Rockville, Md., 1986-94, Houston, 1994—; instr. analytical chem. Upsala Coll., East Orange, N.J., 1963-64; cons. electroplating NSF, Washington, 1973-75. Contbr. articles to Jour. Am. Chem. Soc., Jour. Electrochem. Soc., Jour. Environ. Sci. & Tech. Commr. sci. and tech. commn. City of Rockville, 1985-91; vol. office consumer affairs Montgomery County, Rockville, 1989-90, dept. environ. protection, 1989-90. With USNR, 1944-46. Recipient Gold medal EPA, Washington, 1979. Fellow Am. Inst. Chemists (cert.); mem. AAAS, ASTM, Am. Chem. Soc., Electrochem. Soc. Achievements include patents on advanced solid rocket propellants, new high energy density batteries and fuel cells, improved methods for removal of toxic chemicals from water by electrochemical methods; development of less toxic dielectrics for capacitors and more facile methods for evaluation, optimal treatment methods, for removal of toxic chemicals from waters by use of chemical structure-activity approach. Home and Office: 2607 Colonial Lakes Dr Missouri City TX 77459

STRIGHT, I. LEONARD, educational consultant; b. Mercer, Pa., May 7, 1916; s. Fred L. and Martha (Dight) S.; m. Virginia Minser, July 24, 1940; children—Suzanne (Mrs. L. David York), Robert, William (dec.). B.A., Allegheny Coll., 1935, M.A., 1938, LL.D., 1978; Ph.D., Case-Western U., 1946; postgrad., U. Chgo., 1963. Math. tchr. Freedom (Pa.) High Sch., 1935-39, Indiana (Pa.) Joint High Sch., 1939-42; prof. math. Baldwin-Wallace Coll., Berea, Ohio, 1942-46, No. Mich. U., Marquette, 1946-47, Indiana (Pa.) U., 1947-57; dean Indiana (Pa.) U. (Grad. Sch.), 1957-71; acad. v.p. Ohio No. U., 1971-78; cons. in higher edn., 1978—; adj. prof. Gettysburg (Pa.) Coll., Shippensburg (Pa.) U. Contbr. articles profl. jours. Mem. Nat. Council Tchrs. Math., Am. Assn. U. Profs., N.E.A., S.A.R., Phi Delta Kappa, Phi Kappa Phi, Delta Tau Delta. Methodist. Clubs: Kiwanian (pres. 1960), Mason. Home: C-224 300 Willow Valley Lakes Dr Willow Street PA 17584

STRIKER, CECIL LEOPOLD, archaeologist, educator; b. Cin., July 15, 1932; s. Cecil and Delia (Workum) S.; m. Ute Stephan, Apr. 27, 1968. BA, Oberlin Coll., 1956; MA, NYU, 1960, PhD, 1968; MA (hon.), U. Pa., 1972. Instr., asst. prof. Vassar Coll., 1962-68; assoc. prof. U. Pa., Phila., 1968-78; prof. history of art U. Pa., 1978—, chmn. dept. history of art, 1980-87; field archaeologist Dumbarton Oaks Center for Byzantine Studies, 1966—, fellow, 1972-73; dir. survey and excavation, Myrelaion, Istanbul, 1965-66; co-dir. Kalenderhane Archaeol. Project, Istanbul, 1966-78, Aegean Dendrochronology Project, 1977-88; gen. archaeol. cons. Istanbul Metro and Bosphorus Tunnel Project, 1985-87; dir. Archtl. Dendrochronology Project, 1988—; cons. Integrated Study of Hagia Sophia Structure, 1991-95. Mem. editorial bd. Architectura: Zeitschrift für Geschichte der Architektur, 1986—. Mem. adv. bd. Ctr. for Advanced Study in the Visual Arts, 1986-88, Samuel H. Kress Found. Art History Fellowship Program, 1986-87. Served with U.S. Army, 1954-57. Fulbright grantee in Germany, 1960-62; art historian in residence Am. Acad. in Rome, 1973; NEH grantee, 1985-86. Mem. Archaeol. Inst. Am., Coll. Art Assn., Am. Research Inst. in Turkey (fellow 1965-66, pres. 1978-84), Council Am. Overseas Research Ctr. (chmn. 1980-84), Soc. of Archtl. Historians, Turkish Studies Assn., U.S. Nat. Com. for Byzantine Studies, Koldewey Gesellschaft, German Archaeol. Inst. (corr.), Oriental Club of Phila.

STRIKER, GISELA, philosophy educator; b. Gütersloh, Germany, 1943; came to the U.S., 1986; Student, Tübingen U., 1962, Hamburg U., 1962-64, Göttingen U., 1964-69, Oxford U., 1966-67; PhD, Göttingen U., 1969, Habilitation for philosophy, 1978. Asst. prof. philosophy Göttingen (Germany) U., 1971-83, prof. philosophy, 1983-86; prof. philosophy Columbia U., N.Y.C., 1986-89; prof. philosophy Harvard U., Cambridge, Mass., 1989—, George Martin Lane prof. philosophy and the classics, 1990—; Lawrence prof. of ancient philosophy U. Cambridge, 1997—; vis. asst. prof. philosophy Stanford (Calif.) U., 1974; vis. assoc. prof. philosophy Princeton (N.J.) U., 1979; Nellie-Wallace-lectr. Oxford U., 1984; vis. prof. philosophy Harvard U., 1985; Tanner lectr. Stanford U., 1987. Author: Essays on Hellenistic Epistemology and Ethics, 1996; contbr. articles to profl. jours.; pub. papers and monographs. Rsch. fellow Deutsche Forschungsgemeinschaft, 1970-71, 82-84, fellow Wissenschaftskolleg zu Berlin, 1990-91. Mem. Am. Philos. Assn., Am. Acad. Arts and Scis., N.Y. Acad. Scis. Office: Trinity Coll Dept Philosophy Cambridge MA 02138

STRIMAS, JOHN HOWARD, allergist, immunologist, pediatrician; b. Washington, Dec. 19, 1942. MD, Albany Med. Coll., 1969. Diplomate Am. Bd. Allergy and Immunology, Am. Bd. Pediat. Intern in pediat. Nassau County Med. Ctr., East Meadow, 1970-71, resident in pediat., 1971-73; fellow in allergy and immunology LSU Med. Ctr., New Orleans, 1985-88; with Bapt. Hosp., Nashville, Centennial Med. Ctr., Nashville; adj. clin. prof. Tenn. State U. Coll. Allied Health. Mem. Am. Acad. Allergy and Immunology, Am. Coll. Allergy and Immunology, Tenn. Med. Assn. Office: Idaho Med Assn Allergy Asthma Immunology Clin 1200 W Ironwood Dr Ste 202 Coeur D Alene ID 83814-2660

STRIMBU, VICTOR, JR., lawyer; b. New Philadelphia, Ohio, Nov. 25, 1932; s. Victor and Veda (Stancu) S.; m. Kathryn May Schrote, Apr. 9, 1955; children: Victor Paul, Michael, Julie, Sue. BA, Heidelberg Coll., 1954; postgrad. Western Res. U., 1956-57; JD, Columbia U., 1960. Bar: Ohio 1960, U.S. Supreme Ct. 1972. With Baker & Hostetler, Cleve., 1960—, ptnr., 1970—. Bd. dirs. North Coast Health Ministry; mem. Bay Village (Ohio) Bd. Edn., 1976-84, pres., 1978-82; mem. indsl. rels. adv. com. Cleve. State U., 1979—, chmn., 1982; mem. Bay Village Planning Commn., 1967-69; life mem. Ohio PTA; mem. Greater Cleve. Growth Assn.; bd. trustees New Cleve. Campaign, 1987—, North Coast Health Ministry, 1989—, Heidelberg Coll., 1996—. With AUS, 1955-56. Recipient Service award Cleve. State U., 1980. Mem. ABA, Ohio Bar Assn., Greater Cleve. Bar Assn., Ohio Newspaper Assn. (minority affairs com. 1987—), Ct. of Nisi Prius Club, Cleve. Athletic Club, The Club at Soc. Ctr. Republican. Presbyterian. Office: Baker & Hostetler 3200 National City Ctr 1900 E 9th St Cleveland OH 44114-3401

STRINER, HERBERT EDWARD, economics educator; b. Jersey City, Aug. 16, 1922; s. Harry and Pearl (Strynar) S.; m. Erma Steinert, Dec. 9, 1943 (div. 1970); children: Richard Alan, Deborah Jane; m. Iona V. Meredith. A.B., Rutgers U., 1947, M.A., 1948; Ph.D. (Maxwell fellow 1949-50), Syracuse U., 1951. Asst. prof. Syracuse U., 1951; economist Interior Dept., 1951-54; program dir. NSF, 1954-55, Nat. Planning Assn., 1955-57; sr. analyst Operations Research Office, Johns Hopkins, 1957-59; program dir. Brookings Inst., 1959-61, Stanford Research Inst., 1961-62; dir. Upjohn Inst., Washington, 1962-69; dean Coll. Continuing Edn. Am. U., Washington, 1969-73; dean Coll. Bus. Am. U., 1974-81, prof. econs. and mgmt., 1981-89; cons. Los Alamos Nat. Lab., 1990-91; chief planning and policy NIH, 1972-73; pres. U. Research Corp., 1973-74; assoc. faculty mem. Johns Hopkins U., 1997. Author: Toward a Fundamental Program for the Training, Employment and Economic Equality of the American Indian, 1968, Continuing Education as a National Capital Investment, 1972, Regaining The Lead: Policies for Economic Growth, 1984; co-author: Local Impact of Foreign Trade, 1960, Civil Rights, Employment and the Social Status of American Negros, 1966; Contbr. profl. jours. Mem. rev. panel Pres.'s Cabinet Com. Juv. Delinquency, 1961-63, D.C. Youth Employment Com., 1963, Pres.'s Task Force Am. Indians, 1967, White House Conf. Aging, 1971; bd. dirs. Opportunities Industrialization Ctr., NAACP, Washington. Officer inf. U.S. Army, 1943-46. Decorated Govt. China medal of merit, 1945. Home: 4979 Battery Ln Bethesda MD 20814-2634

STRINGER, DANN POLLARD, executive search firm executive; b. Syracuse, N.Y., Nov. 24, 1938; s. Sydney Walter and Helen Claire (Dann) S.; children: Jonathan, Edward, Karen; m. Shawn Carrigan, May 14, 1944: stepchildren: Brendan, Kevin, Clare. BA, St. Lawrence U., 1961. Dist. mgr. Jamesbury Corp., Worchester, Mass., 1964-68; advance man The White House, Washington, 1969-71; dep. exec. dir. White House Com. on Exec. Interchange, Washington, 1968-71; sr. assoc. Korn/Ferry Internat., L.A., 1971-74; exec. v.p. Interface Group Ltd., Washington, 1975-80; pres. Corp. Rsch. & Communications Internat., Washington, 1980-87; sr. mgr., dir. KPMG Peat Marwick Exec. Search, Washington, 1987-90; sr. mng. dir. Foster Ptnrs., Inc. (KPMG Alliance), Washington, 1990—; ptnr. Midcourt Realty, Manlius, N.Y., 1968—. Bd. dirs. Nat. Kidney Found. of Capital Area, Washington, 1990—, chmn., 1994-95; sr. advance man Reagan Campaign for Pres., 1975-76, 79-80. With U.S. Army N.G., 1960-65. Mem. Brit. Am. Bus. Assn. (bd. dirs.), Georgetown Club, Econs. Club of Washington. Republican. Avocations: yachting, skiing, tennis, fly fishing. Office: Foster Partners Inc 2001 M St NW Washington DC 20036-3310

STRINGER, HOWARD, television executive; b. Cardiff, Wales, U.K., Feb. 19, 1942; came to U.S. 1965, naturalized 1985; s. Harry and Marjorie Mary (Pook) S.; m. Jennifer Kinmond Patterson, July 29, 1978. B.A., M.A., Oxford U., 1964. Producer, dir. CBS News, N.Y.C., 1973-76, exec. producer CBS Reports, 1976-81, Evening News, 1981-84; exec. v.p., 1984-86, pres., CBS News, 1986-88, pres., CBS Broadcast Group, 1988-95; chmn., CEO Tele-TV, 1995-97; pres. Sony Corp. Am., 1997; bd. dirs. Applied Graphics Technologies. Vice-chmn American Film Inst.; trustee Presbyn. Hosp.; bd. govs. Nature Conservany, United Cerebral Palsy, Motion Picture and TV Fund Found., Ctr. for Comm. Served to sgt. U.S. Army, 1965-67, Vietnam. Recipient Emmy awards Nat. Assn. TV Arts and Scis., 1973, 79 (2), 81 (2), 83 (4); Columbia Dupont award Columbia Journalism Sch., 1979, 81; Overseas Press Club awards, 1974, 82, 79, IRTS Found. award, 1994, Pres.'s award Stage Dirs. and Choreographers Found., 1994; named to Broadcasting and Cable Hall of Fame, 1996. Presbyterian. Office: BNP Ptnrs 875 3rd Ave New York NY 10022-6225

STRINGER, JERRY RAY, magazine editor; b. Dallas, Oct. 24, 1941; s. Henry H. and Eleanor (Guess) S.; m. Chongrak Sriratanakorn, Dec. 18, 1971; children: Gary E. BS, East Tex. State U., 1964, MS, 1966. Commd. 2d lt. USAF, 1964; editl. project officer Air Univ. Rev., Maxwell AFB, Ala., 1966-69; base info. officer 631st Combat Support Group, Bangkok, Thailand, 1969-70; staff info. officer Dep. Chief of Staff for R&D, Pentagon, 1970-73; info. officer, editor Arctic Bull. mag. Office of Polar Programs, NSF, Washington, 1973-77; staff mem. air reservist mag. Air Force Res. Pub. Affairs, Bolling AFB, D.C., 1977-78; writer, editor Internal./Cmty. Rels. div. Air Force Systems Command, Bolling AFB, Washington, 1978-80; writer editor Comm. div. Office of Comptroller of Currency, Washington, 1980-82; writer, editor Air Force News Agy., Kelly AFB, Tex., 1982-83; mng. editor Airman Mag., Kelly AFB, Tex., 1983-89, exec. editor, 1989-96; editor, 1996—. Contbr. articles to profl. publs. Webelos leader Cub Scouts, San Antonio, 1984-86; asst. scoutmaster Boy Scouts Am., San Antonio, 1986-95. Col. Air Force Res., ret., 1996. Mem. Air Force Assn., Sigma Delta Chi. Avocations: hiking, camping. Home: 5615 Timberhurst San Antonio TX 78250-4148 Office: Airman Mag AFNEWS 203 Norton St Kelly A F B TX 78241-6104

STRINGER, JOHN, materials scientist; b. Liverpool, Eng., July 14, 1934; came to U.S., 1977, naturalized, 1996.; s. Gerald Hitchen and Isobel (Taylor) S.; m. Audrey Lancaster, Feb. 4, 1957; children: Helen Caroline, Rebecca Elizabeth. BS in Engring., U. Liverpool, 1955, PhD, 1958, D in Engring., 1974. Chartered engr., U.K. Lectr. Univ. Liverpool, Eng., 1957-63; fellow Battelle Columbus (Ohio) Labs., 1963-66; prof. materials sci. Univ. Liverpool, 1966-77; sr. project mgr. Electric Power Rsch. Inst., Palo Alto, Calif., 1977-81; sr. program mgr. Electric Power Rsch. Inst., Palo Alto, 1981-87, dir. tech. support, 1987-91, dir. applied rsch., 1991-95, tech. exec. Applied Sci. and Tech., 1995-96, exec. tech. fellow, 1997—; chmn. Sci. and Tech. Edn., Merseyside, Liverpool, 1971-74; pres. Corrosion and Protection Assn., London, 1972; mem. Nat. Material Adv. Bd., 1992-95, basic energy scis. adv. com., U.S. Dept. Energy, 1992—, chmn., 1996—. Editorial bd.: Oxidation of Metals Jour., 1971—; author: An Introduction to the Electron Theory of Solids, 1967; editor: (book) High Temperature Corrosion of Advanced Materials, 1989, Chlorine in Coal, 1991, Applied Chaos, 1992; contbr. over 300 articles to profl. jours. Recipient U.R. Evans award Inst. Corrosion, U.K., 1993, Campbell Meml. Lectr. of ASM Internat., 1995. Fellow AAAS, NACE Internat., AIME, Inst. Energy, Royal Soc. Arts, Instn. Corrosion (hon.); mem. ASM Internat., Materials Rsch. Soc. Office: Electric Power Rsch Inst 3412 Hillview Ave Palo Alto CA 94304-1395

STRINGER, L.E. (DEAN STRINGER), lawyer; b. Sayre, Okla., June 22, 1936; s. Rex Herman and Bessie (Morris) S.; m. Carol Ann Woodson, Aug. 31, 1963; children: Craig Woodson, Laura DeAnn. BA, Okla. State U., 1958; LLB, Harvard U., 1961. Bar: Okla. 1961, U.S. Ct. Appeals (10th cir.) 1962, U.S. Dist. Ct. (we. dist.) 1963, U.S. Supreme Ct. 1972. Assoc. Crowe, Boxley, et al (now Crowe & Dunlevy), Oklahoma City, 1961-68, mem., dir., 1968—; pres. Crowe & Dunlevy, P.C., 1979-81, chmn. litigation dept., 1987—. Pres. Okla. State U. Alumni Assn., 1972-73; bd. regents Okla. State U. and A&M Colls., Stillwater, 1986-94, vice chmn., 1989-90, chmn., 1990-91; chmn. Okla. State U. Found., Stillwater, 1982-85; dir. Okla. Heritage Assn., 1995—. Maj. Okla. N.G., 1961-71. Recipient Disting. Alumnus award Okla. State U., 1979. Fellow Am. Bar Found. (adv. rsch. com. 1996—); mem. ABA, Okla. Bar Assn., Okla. County Bar Assn., Internat. Assn. of Def. Counsel, Okla. Assn. Def. Counsel. Democrat. Methodist. Home: 325 NW 17th St Oklahoma City OK 73103-3424 Office: Crowe & Dunlevy 20 N Broadway Ave Oklahoma City OK 73102-8202

STRINGER, MARY EVELYN, art historian, educator; b. Huntsville, Mo., July 31, 1921; d. William Madison and Charity (Rogers) S. A.B., U. Mo., 1942; A.M., U. N.C., Chapel Hill, 1955; Ph.D. (Danforth scholar), Harvard U., 1973. Asst. prof. art Miss. State Coll. for Women (now Miss. U. for Women), Columbus, 1947-58; assoc. prof. Miss. State Coll. for Women (now Miss. U. for Women), 1958-73, prof., 1973-91, prof. emeritus, 1991—; regional dir. for Miss., Census of Stained Glass Windows in Am., 1840-1940. Bd. dirs. Mississippians for Ednl. Broadcasting; mem. Miss. com. Save Outdoor Sculpture, 1992-93. Fulbright scholar W.Ger., 1955-56; Harvard U. travel grantee, 1966-67; NEH summer seminar grantee, 1980. Mem. AAUW, Coll. Art Assn., Southeastern Coll. Art Conf. (dir. 1975-80, 83-89, Disting. Svc. award 1992, Miss. Hist. Soc. (award of merit, 1995), Internat. Ctr. Medieval Art, Audubon Soc., The Nature Conservancy, Sierra Club, Phi Beta Kappa, Phi Kappa Phi. Democrat. Episcopalian.

STRINGER, PATRICIA ANNE, retired secondary educator; b. Mpls., Mar. 17, 1935; d. Raphael Clarence and Marie Christine (Kwakenat) S. BS, U. Minn., 1960, MA, 1967. Cert. tchr., Minn. Tchr. Sunrise Park Jr. High Sch., White Bear Lake, Minn., 1960-72; tchr., coach Mariner High Sch., White Bear Lake, 1972-84, White Bear Lake High Sch., 1984-91; mem. adv. bd. Minn. State High Sch. League, 1973-77; cons. in phys. edn., Minn., Wis., Mont., 1978-82; dept. chair White Bear Lake Schs., 1962-91, athletic coord., 1972-82; mem. Minn. State Coaching Cert. Com., 1980. Contbr. articles to profl. jours. Named to Minn. Softball Coaches Hall of Fame, 1992, Regional Coach of Yr., 1980, 90, Minn. Softball Hall of Fame Amateur Softball Assn. Am., 1982. Mem. AAHPERD, Minn. Assn. Health, Phys. Edn., Recreation and Dance (Secondary Phys. Edn. Tchr. of Yr. 1990), Ctrl. Dist. Assn. for Health, Phys. Edn., Recreation and Dance (Secondary Phys. Edn. Tchr. of Yr. 1991), Nat. Assn. for Sports and Phys. Edn., U. Minn. Womens Physical Edn. Alumni Assn. (v.p. 1991-92, pres. 1992-97). Avocations: golf, fishing, travel. Home: 24338 Dawnridge Ct Eden Valley MN 55329-9266

STRINGER, WILLIAM JEREMY, university official; b. Oakland, Calif., Nov. 8, 1944; s. William Duane and Mildred May (Andrus) S.; BA in English, So. Meth. U., 1966; MA in English, U. Wis., 1968, PhD in Ednl. Adminstrn., 1973; m. Susan Lee Hildebrand; children: Shannon Lee, Kelly Erin, Courtney Elizabeth. Dir. men's housing Southwestern U., Georgetown, Tex., 1968-69; asst. dir. housing U. Wis., Madison, 1969-73; dir. residential life, asso. dean student life, adj. prof. Pacific Luth., Tacoma, 1973-78; dir. residential life U. So. Calif., 1978-79, asst. v.p., 1979-84, asst. prof. higher and post-secondary edn., 1980-84; v.p. student life Seattle U., 1984-89, v.p. student devel., 1989-92, assoc. provost, 1989-95, assoc. prof. edn., 1990—, chair educational leadership, 1994—. Author: How to Survive as a Single Student, 1972, The Role of the Assistant in Higher Education, 1973. Bd. dirs. N.W. area Luth. Social Services of Wash. and Idaho, pres.-elect, 1989, pres., 1990-91. Danforth Found. grantee, 1976-77. Mem. AAUP, Am. Assn. Higher Edn., Nat. Assn. Student Pers. Adminstrs. (bd. dirs. region V 1985—, mem. editl. bd. Jour. 1995—), Am. Coll. Pers. Assn., Phi Eta Sigma, Sigma Tau Delta, Phi Alpha Theta. Lutheran. Home: 4553 169th Ave SE Bellevue WA 98006-6505 Office: Seattle U Seattle WA 98122

STRINGFELLOW, GERALD B., engineering educator; b. Salt Lake City, Apr. 26, 1942; s. Paul Bennion and Jean (Barton) S.; m. Barbara Farr, June 9, 1962; children: Anne, Heather, Michael. BS, U. Utah, 1964; PhD, Stanford U., 1968. Staff scientist Hewlett Pacakrd Labs., Palo Alto, Calif., 1967-70, group mgr., 1970-80; disting. prof. elec. engring., materials sci. U. Utah, Salt Lake City, 1980—; chmn., 1994—; adj. prof. physics U. Utah, Salt Lake City, 1988—; cons. Tex. Instruments, Dallas, 1995—, AT&T-Bell Labs., Holmdel, N.J., 1986-90, Brit. Telecom., London, 1989-92; editor-in-chief Phase Diagrams for Ceramics, Vol. IX. Author: Organometallic Vapor Phase Epitaxy, 1989; editor: Metal Organic Vapor Phase Epitaxy, 1986, American Crystal Growth, 1987, Alloy Semiconductor Physics and Electronics, 1989, Phase Equilibria Diagrams-Semiconductors and Chalcogenides, 1991, High Brightness LEDs, 1997; U.S. sr. editor Jour. Crystal Growth; letters editor Jour. Electronic Materials; contbr. over 300 articles to profl. jours. Recipient U.S. Sr. Scientist award Alexander von Humboldt Soc., Bonn, Germany, 1979; guest fellow Royal Soc., London, 1990. Fellow IEEE, Japan Soc. Promotion of Sci.; mem. Am. Phys. Soc., Electronic Materials Com. (pres. 1985-87). Achievements include pioneering development of organometallic vapor phase epitaxy, development of theories of thermodynamic properties of alloy semiconductors; discovery of phenomenon of compositional latching in alloy semiconductor layers grown by epitaxial techniques. Home: 960 Donner Way Salt Lake City UT 84108-2167 Office: Dept Materials Sci Univ Utah 304 Emery St Salt Lake City UT 84104-2356

STRINGFIELD, CHARLES DAVID, hospital administrator; b. Nashville, May 11, 1939; s. Ernest Jake Stringfield and Lucille (Lovelace) Birthright; m. Ruth Dvorak, Aug. 25, 1962; children—David Fisher, John Lovelace. B.A., Vanderbilt U., 1961; cert. tchr., George Peabody Coll., 1962, M.A. in Sch. Adminstrn., 1964; M.A. in Hosp. Adminstrn., Washington U., St. Louis, 1966. Tchr. Sch. Dist. No. 11, Colorado Springs, Colo., 1962-64; adminstrv. asst., adminstrv. resident Milwaukee County Instns., Milw., 1965-66; exec. dir. Tenn. Nursing Home Assn., Nashville, 1966-67; asst. dir. Tenn. Hosp. Assn., Nashville, 1966-68; adminstrv. dir. Bapt. Hosp., Inc., Nashville, 1968-70, exec. v.p., 1970-82, exec. v.p., chief exec. officer, 1981-82, pres., chief exec. officer, 1982—; pres. dedication of C. David Springfield Bldg. to Bapt. Hosp.; mem. governing bd. Mid.-Tenn. Eye Bank Found.; bd. dirs. NationaBank/Ctrl. South, Nashville Health Care Mgmt. Found./Comprehensive Care Ctr., 1993. Author: Hospital Administrator - Physician Relationships. Recipient 1st Ann. Arthritis Found. Tribute, 1989, C. David Stringfield Dedicatory plaque Bapt. Women's Pavillion East at Mid. Tenn. Med. Ctr., Disting. Svc. award Tenn. Secondary Sch. Athletic Assn., 1993; named one of Nashville's 100 Most Influential Leaders, SOURCEBOOK, 1991, 92, one of Nashville's 100 Most Powerful People, Bus. Nashville, 1994, 95, 96, 97. Fellow Am. Coll. Hosp. Adminstrs.; mem. Am. Hosp. Assn., Am. Nursing Home Assn., Southeastern Hosp. Assn., Vol. Hosps. of Am. (bd. dirs.). Lodge: Kiwanis. Office: Bapt Hosp 2000 Church St Nashville TN 37236-0001

STRINGFIELD, HEZZ, JR., contractor, financial consultant; b. Heiskell, Tenn., Oct. 4, 1921; s. Hezz and Cecil Willie (Williams) S.; m. Helen Louise Hinton, Mar. 20, 1939; children—Carolyn Mae Joyce (Mrs. James M. Corum), Don Wayne, Gail Louise (Mrs. John D. Gamble), Debra June (Mrs. Patrick T. Cassidy). Grad. bus. adminstr., Draughon Coll., 1939; student finance and bus., U. Tenn. Fin. and bus. adminstrn. exec. Clinton Engr. Works, E.I. duPont de Nemours & Co., 1943-44; Manhattan Dist. metall. project U. Chgo., 1944-45, Monsanto Chem. Co., 1945-48; nuclear div. Union Carbide Corp., 1948-77; ind. bldg. contractor, real estate developer, 1946—, cons. gen. bus., real estate financing, 1946—; pres. FBF, Inc., 1977—; with U.S. AID Mission to Middle East; cons. with industry, govt. and edn. in developing nations, 1965; bd. dirs. Found. Mgmt. Edn., Advanced Mgmt. Council, Council for Internat. Progress in Mgmt., Inc., Found. for Internat. Progress in Mgmt.; mem. Adv. Council Univs. and Colls. Fellow Soc. Advancement Mgmt. (Profl. Mgr. citation 1963, v.p. 1958-62, exec. v.p. 1962-63, pres. 1963-64, chmn. bd. 1964-65); mem. Am. Mgmt. Assn., Am. Inst. Accountants. Baptist. Home: 921 Laurel Hill Rd Knoxville TN 37923-2024 Office: 1201 Hilton Rd Knoxville TN 37921-5902

STRINGFIELD, SHERRY, actress. BFA, SUNY, Purchase, 1989. Theater appearances include Goose and Tom Tom, Hurly Burly, Devil's Disciple, A Dream Play, Hotel Baltimore, The Kitchen, Tom Jones; appeared in (TV series) Guiding Light, 1989-92, NYPD Blue, 1993, ER, 1994— (Emmy nominee Outstanding Lead Actress in a Drama Series, 1995). Office: care Michaels Wose & Tencer 9350 Wilshire Blvd Beverly Hills CA 90212-3214 also: 9560 Wilshire Blvd Beverly Hills CA 90212

STRINGHAM, LUTHER WINTERS, economist, administrator; b. Colorado Springs, Colo., Dec. 14, 1915; s. Luther Wilson and Fern (Van Duyn) S.; m. Margret Ann Pringle, Dec. 1, 1942; 1 child, Susan Jean. B.A. summa cum laude, U. Colo., 1938, M.A. in Econs, 1939; Rockefeller fellow pub. adminstrn., U. Minn., 1939-40, Nat. Inst. Pub. Affairs, 1940-41. Economist Dept. Commerce, also OPA, 1941-43; intelligence officer Def. Dept., 1946-55; program analysis officer Office of the Sec. HEW, 1956-63, chmn. sec.'s com. mental retardation, 1961-63; exec. dir. Nat. Assn. for Retarded Children, 1963-68; intergovtl. relations officer HEW, 1968-77; planning dir. Central Va. Health Systems Agy., 1977-83. Dir. TV series Healthy Virginians, 1981-83. Mem. Pres.'s Com. Employment Handicapped, 1963-68; pres. Music for People, Inc., 1971-74; lectr. CUNY, 1971-76; mem. nat. coun. Boy Scouts Am., 1963-83; co-founder Older Virginians for Action, 1983-84; bd. dirs. Capital Area Agy. Aging, 1984-87; Midlothian Dist. rep. Keep Chesterfield Clean Corp., 1992-94; mem. Quality Coun. Greater Richmond, 1993-94. Capt. AUS, 1943-46; lt. col. USAFR, 1946-56. Mem. Am. Econ. Assn., Phi Beta Kappa, Pi Gamma Mu, Delta Sigma Rho. Home: 3101 Mount Hill Dr Midlothian VA 23113-3932

STRINGHAM, RENÉE, physician; b. Mpls., July 16, 1940; d. Clifford Leonard and Helen Pearl (Marcineak) Heinrich; children: Lars Eric, Leif Erik, Lance Devon. BS, St. Lawrence U., 1962; MD, U. Ky., 1972. Diplomate Am. Bd. Family Practice. Intern U. Fla., Gainesville, 1972-73; physician Lee County Coop. Clinic, Marianna, Ark., 1973-74; pvt. practice Coastal Health Practitioners, Lincoln City, Oreg., 1975-84; county med. officer Lincoln County Health Dept., Newport, Oreg., 1986-90; pvt. practice, 1984-90; student health Miami U., Oxford, Ohio, 1991-93; pvt. practice Macadam Clin., Portland, 1994—; cons. student health Willamette U., 1994-95; contract physician West Salem Clinic, 1995-97; med. dir. Capital Manor, 1997—; trustee Coast Home Nursing, Lincoln County, 1984-86; expert witness EPA, 1980. Facilitator Exceptional Living, 1984-86. Fellow Am. Acad. Family Practice; mem. Lincoln County Med. Soc. (pres. 1984), Oreg. Med. Assn. Avocations: spontaneous music, folk dancing, sailing.

STRIP, CAROL ANN, gifted education specialist, educator; b. Jackson, Mich., July 3, 1945; d. Harold Don and Marion Estelle (Diemer) Gillespie; m. Asriel Strip, June 15, 1978 (div. Dec. 1992); 1 child, Julie. BS, Western Mich. U., 1966, MA, 1969; PhD, Ohio State U, 1994. Cert. elem. prin., Mich.; cert. supr., ednl. specialist, Ohio. Kindergarten tchr. Kalamazoo (Mich.) Pub. Schs., 1967-74, primary tchr., 1974-75, 76-78, title 1-B adminstr., 1975-76; 4th grade tchr. Westerville (Ohio) City Schs., 1978-83; enrichment specialist Dublin (Ohio) City Schs., 1983-88, gifted edn. coord., 1988-94, gifted edn. specialist, 1988-94, gifted edn. specialist, tchr., 1994—; adv. bd. mem. Ohio Wesleyan Jr. League, Delaware, 1987—, Dublin Arts Coun., 1989—; workshop presenter in field; adj. prof. Ohio State U., Ashley U. Pub. Roeper Rev. Instr. Jour.; contbr. articles to profl. jours. Bd. dirs. Friends of the Libr., Columbus, 1978-83; com. mem. Ohio State Fair Orphans Day Com., Columbus, 1983-90. Recipient Master of Comms. award Ednl. Facilities Ctr., 1975, Golden Apple Achiever award Ashland Oil, 1993, Silver Anvil award AMA, 1972; named Ctrl. Mich. Tchr. of Yr., 1976. Fellow ASCD, Ohio Assn. Supervision Curriculum Devel., Sch. Study Coun. of Ohio, Ctrl. Ohio Coord. of Gifted, Alpha Chi Omega; mem. NEA, Ohio Ednl. Assn., Nat. Ret. Tchrs. Assn., Ohio Assn. of Gifted Children (regional rep. 1994, Outstanding Educator of Yr. 1994), Gifted Coord. of Ctrl. Ohio (pres. 1992-93), Alpha Delta Kappa. Republican. Avocations: reading, travel, music, theatre, museums. Home: 8929 Turin Hill Ct N Dublin OH 43017-9414 Office: Olentangy Elem Sch 814 Shanahan Rd Lewis Center OH 43035-9078

STRISIK, PAUL, artist; b. Bklyn., Apr. 21, 1918; s. Abraham Roger and Reine Rose (Rehbock) S.; m. Nancy Susan Samaras, Nov. 16, 1968; children: Peter, John Catherine, Ellen. Student, Art Students League, N.Y.C., 1946-48. Tchr. workshops, lectr. throughout U.S. and, Europe; tchr. Scottsdale (Ariz.) Artists Sch., Nov. 1986, 88; mng. dir. Hall Line Co., Highland Mills, N.Y., 1937-40; dir. Empire Twine & Yarn Co., N.Y.C., 1945-69. Author: The Art of Landscape Painting, 1980, Capturing Light in Oils, 1995; One-man exhbns. include, Grand Central Art Galleries, N.Y.C., 1971-84, Doll & Richards, Boston, 1965, 76, Rockport (Mass.) Art Assn., 1964-69, 75, Andover (Mass.) Gallery Fine Arts, 1969, Gordon Coll., Wenham, Mass., 1972, Johnson-Welch Gallery, Kansas City, Mo., 1978, Francesca Anderson Gallery, Boston, 1986, Dodson Gallery, Oklahoma City, 1990, So. Vt. Art Ctr., Manchester, 1994; group exhbns. include, Nat. Acad. Art, 1955-93, Allied Artists Am., N.Y.C., 1971-94, Salmagundi Club, N.Y.C., 1962-88, Knickerbocker Artists, N.Y.C., 1963-95, Am. Watercolor Soc., N.Y.C., 1963-91, Rockport Art Assn., 1956-95, North Shore Arts Assn., Gloucester, Mass., 1956-95, Am. Artists Profl. League, N.Y.C., 1960-95, Cowboy Hall of Fame, Oklahoma City, 1978-95, Artists of Am., Denver, 1981-95, NAD, 1970-93, Catto Gallery, London, 1992, Royal Watercolor Soc., London, 1992; rep. permanent collections, Parrish Mus. Art, Southampton, N.Y., Percy H. Whitney Mus., Fairhope, Ala., Mattatuck Mus., Conn., Utah State U., Peabody Mus., Salem, Mass.; appeared on NBC Today Show (TV), July, 1987. Bd. govs. Rockport Bd. Trade, 1958-60. Served with USN, 1941-45. Recipient over 170 awards, including 15 gold medals; Windsor and Newton award Knickerbocker Artists, 1965; medal of merit, 1972; FAS award Allied Artists Am., 1965; Lehrer Meml. award, 1970; Wick award Salmagundi Club, 1967; Chandler award, 1967; AWS award, 1970; Salmagundi award, 1970-73; gold medal Marsh ann. exhbn., 1967, 71; gold medal Rockport Art Assn., 1967, 72, 87, 90; Best in Show award Am. Artists Profl. League grand. nat., 1968, 72; A. Dedn award Am. Watercolor Soc., 1969; Lehman award, 1970; gold medal Hudson Valley Art Assn., 1970, Bohnert award, 1989; Ray Jones Gold medal Am. Vets. Soc. Artists, 1970; Watercolor prize Nat. Arts Club, 1970; bronze medal, 1960; Obrig prize Nat. Acad., 1972; silver medal Arts Atlantic, Mass., 1972; Gold medal Franklin Mint Gallery Am. Art, 1974; Arthur T. Hill Meml. award Salmagundi Club, 1974; Helen Gould Kennedy award Acad. Artists Ann., 1974; Claude Parsons Meml. award Am. Artists Profl. League, 1975; Grumbacher award Acad. Artists, 1975; Philip G. Shumaker award Rockport Art Assn., 1975; honored by Rockport Art Assn., 1988; Elizabeth Schlemm award, 1975; Canelli Gold Medal for oils, 1975; Isabel Steinschneider Meml. award Hudson Valley Art Assn., 1980, also Dumond award 1990; spl. tribute to Paul Strisik Hudson Valley Art Assn., 1982, 88; Silver medal Acad. Artists Assn., Springfield, Mass., 1980, Rockport Art Assn., 1993; Gold medal Academic Artists Assn., 1986, Frank Vincent Dumond Meml. award Hudson Valley Art Assn., N.Y., 1990, 94, Frank Vincent Dumond $1,000 award Hudson Valley Art Assn., N.Y., 1995; named Artist of Yr. Santa Fe, N.Mex. Rotary, 1986, over 170 awards including 15 Gold medals. Mem. NAD (academician), Nat. Acad. Western Art (gold medal 1981, 84), Oil Painters Am., Rockport Art Assn. (pres. 1968-71), Am. Watercolor Soc., Allied Artists Am., Knickerbocker Artists, Internat. Soc. Marine Painters, Am. Artists Profl. League (award 1980), Am. Acad. Taos, N. Shore Arts Assn., Santa Fe Watercolor Soc., Rockport C. of C. Club: Salmagundi. Home: 123 Marmion Way Rockport MA 01966-1928*

STRITTMATTER, PETER ALBERT, astronomer, educator; b. London, Eng., Sept. 12, 1939; came to U.S., 1970; s. Albert and Rosa S.; m. Janet Hubbard Parkhurst, Mar. 18, 1967; children—Catherine D., Robert P. B.A., Cambridge U., Eng., 1961, M.A., 1963, Ph.D., 1967. Staff scientist Inst. for Astronomy, Cambridge, Eng., 1967-70; staff scientist dept. physics U. Calif.-San Diego, La Jolla, 1970-71; assoc. prof. dept. astronomy U. Ariz., Tucson, 1971-74, prof. dept. astronomy, 1974—, Regent's prof., 1994—; dir. Steward Observatory, Tucson, 1975—; mem. staff Max Planck Inst. Radioastronomy, Bonn, W. Germany, 1981—. Contbr. articles to profl. jours. Recipient Sr. award Humboldt Found., 1979-80. Fellow Royal Astron. Soc.; mem. Am. Astron. Soc., Astronomische Gesellschaft. Office: U Ariz Steward Observatory Tucson AZ 85721

STROBEL, MARTIN JACK, motor vehicle and industrial component manufacturing and distribution company executive; b. N.Y.C., July 4, 1940; s. Nathan and Clara (Sorgen) S.; m. Hadassah Orenstein, Aug. 15, 1965; children: Gil Michael, Karen Rachel. BA, Columbia U., 1962; JD, Cleve. Marshall Law Sch., 1966; completed advanced bus. mgmt. program, Harvard U., 1977. Bar: Ohio bar 1966. Counsel def. contract adminstrn. services region Def. Supply Agy., Cleve., 1966-68; with Dana Corp., Toledo, 1968—; gen. counsel Dana Corp., 1970—, dir. govt. relations, 1970-71, asst. sec., 1971—, v.p., 1976—, sec., 1982—. Mem. ABA, Fed. Bar Assn., Machinery and Allied Products Inst., Ohio Bar Assn., Toledo Bar Assn. Office: Dana Corp PO Box 1000 Toledo OH 43697-1000

STROBER, MYRA HOFFENBERG, education educator, consultant; b. N.Y.C., Mar. 28, 1941; d. Julius William Hoffenberg and Regina Scharer; m. Samuel Strober, June 23, 1963 (div. Dec. 1983); children: Jason M., Elizabeth A.; m. Jay M. Jackman, Oct. 21, 1990. BS in Indsl. Rels., Cornell U., 1962; MA in Econs., Tufts U., 1965; PhD in Econs., MIT, 1969. Lectr., asst. prof. dept. econs. U. Md., College Park, 1967-70; lectr. U. Calif., Berkeley, 1970-72; asst. prof. grad. sch. bus. Stanford (Calif.) U., 1972-86, assoc. prof. sch. edn., 1979-90, prof., 1990—, assoc. dean acad. affairs, 1993-95, interim dean, 1994; organizer Stanford Bus. Conf. Women Mgmt., 1974; founding dir. ctr. rsch. women Stanford U., 1974-76, 79-84, dir. edn. policy inst., 1984-86, dean alumni coll., 1992, mem. policy and planning bd., 1992-93, chair program edn. adminstrn. and policy analysis, 1991-93, chair provost's com. recruitment and retention women faculty, 1992-93, chair faculty senate com. on coms., 1992-93; mem. adv. bd. State of Calif. Office Econ. Policy Planning and Rsch., 1978-80; mem. Coll. Bd. Com. Develop Advanced Placement Exam. Econs., 1987-88; faculty advisor Rutgers Women's Leadership Program, 1991-93. Author: (with others) Industrial Relations, 1972, Sex, Discrimination and the Division of Labor, 1975, Changing Roles of Men and Women, 1976, Women in the Labor Market, 1979, Educational Policy and Management: Sex Differentials, 1981, Women in the Workplace, 1982, Sex Segregation in the Workplace: Trends, Explanations, Remedies, 1984, The New Palgrave: A Dictionary of Economic Theory and Doctrine, 1987, Computer Chips and Paper Clips: Technology and Women's Employment, Vol. II, 1987, Gender in the Workplace, 1987; editor: (with Francine E. Gordon) Bringing Women Into Management, 1975, (with others) Women and Poverty, 1986, (with Sanford M. Dornbusch) Feminism, Children and the New Families, 1988; mem. bd. editors Signs: Jour. Women Culture and Soc., 1975-89, assoc. editor, 1980-85; mem. bd. editors Sage Ann. Rev. Women and Work, 1984—; mem. editorial adv. bd. U.S.-Japan Women's Jour., 1991—; assoc. editor Jour. Econ. Edn., 1991—; contbr. chpt. to book, articles to profl. jours. Mem. rsch. adv. task force YWCA, 1989—; chair exec. bd. Stanford Hillel, 1990-92; bd. dirs. Resource Ctr. Women, Palo Alto, Calif., 1983-84; pres. bd. dirs. Kaider Found., Mountain View, Calif., 1990-96. Fellow Stanford U., 1975-77, Schiff House Resident fellow, 85-87. Mem. NOW (bd. dirs. legal def. and edn. fund 1993—), Am. Econ. Assn. (mem. com. status of women in the profession 1972-75), Am. Ednl. Rsch. Assn., Indsl. Rels. Rsch. Assn., Internat. Assn. for Feminist Econs. (pres. 1997—). Office: Stanford U School of Education Stanford CA 94305

STROBER, SAMUEL, immunologist, educator; b. N.Y.C., May 8, 1940; s. Julius and Lee (Lander) S.; m. Linda Carol Higgins, July 6, 1991; children:

William, Jesse; children from previous marriage: Jason, Elizabeth. AB in Liberal Arts, Columbia U., 1961; MD magna cum laude, Harvard U., 1966. Intern Mass. Gen. Hosp., Boston, 1966-67; resident in internal medicine Stanford U. Hosp., Calif., 1970-71; rsch. fellow Peter Bent Brigham Hosp., Boston, 1962-63, 65-66, Oxford U., Eng., 1963-64; rsch. assoc. Lab. Cell Biology, Nat. Cancer Inst., NIH, Bethesda, Md., 1967-70; instr. medicine Stanford U., 1971-72, asst. prof., 1972-78, assoc. prof. medicine, 1978-82, prof. medicine, 1982—, Diane Goldstone Meml. lectr., John Putnam Merrill Meml. lectr., chief div. immunology and rheumatology, 1978—; investigator Howard Hughes Med. Inst., Miami, Fla., 1976-81. Assoc. editor Jour. Immunology, 1981-84, Transplantation, 1981-85, Internat. Jour. Immunotherapy, 1985—, Transplant Immunology, 1992—; contbr. articles to profl. jours. bd. dirs. La Jolla Inst. for Allergy and Immunology; founder Activated Cell Therapy, Inc. Served with USPHS, 1967-70. Recipient Leon Reznick Meml. Research prize Harvard U., 1966. Mem. Am. Assn. Immunology, Am. Soc. Clin. Investigation, Am. Rheumatism Assn., Transplantation Soc. (councilor 1986-89), Am. Soc. Transplantation Physicians, Western Soc. Medicine, Am. Assn. Physicians, Clin. Immunology Soc. (pres. 1996), Alpha Omega. Home: 435 Golden Oak Dr Portola Valley CA 94028-7734 Office: Stanford U Sch Medicine 300 Pasteur Dr Palo Alto CA 94304-2203

STROCK, ARTHUR VAN ZANDT, architect; b. Los Angeles, Sept. 14, 1945; s. Arthur and Eileen (Cortelyou) S.; m. Hallie vonAmmon, Mar. 22, 1969. BArch, U. Calif., Berkeley, 1971. Registered profl. architect. Asst. dean Sch. Architecture and Fine Arts U. So. Calif., Los Angeles, 1970-71; designer Allied Architects, Long Beach, Calif., 1971-73; architect Langdon and Wilson, Newport Beach, Calif., 1973-77, Lee & Strock Architects, Newport Beach, 1978-82, Strock Architects, Inc., Newport Beach, 1982-91, Pacmar Strock Group, Newport Beach, Calif., 1992—, Strock Group; guest lectr. U. Calif., Irvine; guest speaker Pacific Coast Deisgn Conf., Monterey, Calif.; mng. ptnr., head design team Shantou World Trade Ctr., Racetrack Ctr. Prin. works include I.R.W.D. Bldg., 1979 (Merit award 1982), Newport/Irvine Ctr., 1980 (Merit award 1982), Bay Corp. Ctr., 1982 (Merit award 1984), Scripps Ctr., 1985, Long Beach Airport Bus. Park, 1986, Orange County Register Hdqrs., 1986. Pres. Beacon Bay Cmty. Assn., Newport Beach, 1985-86; bd. dirs. Nat. History Found. of Orange County, 1982; bd. dirs. Bowers Mus., 1987—, pres., 1988-90, chmn., 1991-94. Fellow AIA; mem. Assn. Univ. Related Rsch. Pks., Urban Land Inst.(internat. coun.), Newport Harbor yacht Club, Sigma Chi, U.S. Sailing (sr. judge). Republican. Avocations: yachting, fishing, tennis. Home: 23 Beacon Bay Newport Beach CA 92660-7218 Office: Strock Group 23 Beacon Bay Newport Beach CA 92660-7218

STROCK, DAVID RANDOLPH, brokerage house executive; b. Salt Lake City, Jan. 31, 1944; s. Clarence Randolph and Francis (Hornibrook) S.; m. Phyllis A. Tingley, Dec. 13, 1945 (div. June 15, 1982); children: Sarah, Heidi. AA, San Mateo Coll., 1967; BS, San Jose State U., 1970. Investment exec. Paine Webber, San Jose, Calif., 1970-78; corp. trainer Paine Webber, N.Y.C., 1978-79, rsch. coord., 1979-82; br. mgr. Paine Webber, Northbrook, Ill., 1982-84, Palos Verdes, Calif., 1984-89, Napa, Calif., 1989-90; investment exec. Paine Webber, Napa, 1990—. Contbr. articles to profl. jours. Mem. San Jose Jr. C. of C. (chmn. 1977, v.p. 1978), North Napa Rotary (past pres.), Moose. Republican. Avocations: reading, Indy car racing, formula one racing, biking, whitewater rafting. Home: 3324 Homestead Ct Napa CA 94558-4275 Office: Paine Webber 703 Trancas St Napa CA 94558-3014

STROCK, GERALD E., school system administrator. Supt. Hatboro-Horsham (Pa.) Sch. Dist. State finalist Nat. Supt. Yr., 1993. Office: Hatboro-Horsham Sch Dist 229 Meetinghouse Rd Horsham PA 19044-2119

STROCK, HERBERT LEONARD, motion picture producer, director, editor, writer; b. Boston, Jan. 13, 1918; s. Maurice and Charlotte Ruth (Nesselroth) S.; m. Geraldine Polinger, Dec. 25, 1941; children: Leslie Carol, Genoa Ellen, Candice Dell. B.A., U. So. Calif., 1941, M.A., 1942. Asst. editor Metro-Goldwyn-Mayer, Culver City, Calif., 1941-42; producer IMPPRO, Culver City, 1946-51; film editor Hal Roach Studios, Culver City, 1951-53; dir., film editor Ian Tors Prodns., Culver City, 1951-58; dir. ZIV Prodns., Hollywood, Calif., 1956-61, Warner Bros., Burbank, Calif., 1958-63; ind. dir., pres. Herbert L. Strock Prodns., Hollywood, Calif., 1963—; pres., chmn. bd. Hollywood World Films Inc., lectr. U. So. Calif. Producer, dir.: I Led Three Lives, Mr. District Attorney, Favorite Story, Corliss Archer, Science Fiction Theater, Highway Patrol, Dr. Christian, Man Called X, Harbor Command, 1954; dir. Battle Taxi; assoc. producer, dir.: Tom Swift series,(TV shows) Mann of Action, Red Light and Siren Sky King; Maverick, Alaskans, Colt 45, Bronco, Cheyenne, 77 Sunset Strip, Bonanza, Hans Brinker Spl., Decisions-Decisions, (feature pictures) Perfect World of Rodney Brewster, I Was a Teenage Frankenstein, Blood of Dracula, How to Make a Monster, Rider on a Dead Horse, Strike Me Deadly, Search the Wild Wind, Magnetic Monster, Riders to the Stars, Gog - Storm Over Tibet; editor, dir.: The Crawling Hand, One Hour of Hell; editorial supr. Shark; writer, dir. Brother on the Run; editor: So Evil My Sister, Chamber-Mades; co-producer Small Miracle; editor, dir. (documentary) They Search for Survival; supervising film editor Hunger Telethon; editor (spl.) The Making of America, co-writer, film editor Hurray for Betty Boop; dir., chief prodn. coordinator for Miss World, 1976; editor (documentary) UFO Journals, UFO Syndrome, Legends, all 1979; co-dir., film editor Witches Brew, 1979; writer, film editor (TV series) Flipper, 1981. Editor post prodn. services: China--Mao to Now, Eucatastrophe, Tibet, El Papa, Night Screams, King Kung Fu; dir., editor Deadly Presence; producer, writer, dir. (med. documentary) A New Lease on Life; editor Snooze You Lose, Olympic Legacy, Water You Can Trust, Distance, Fish Outta Water; dir., editor Gramma's Gold; co-editor Infinity, Peaceful Sabbath; producer, writer, dir. (fund raising documentary) Combined Federal Campaign; co-dir., film editor Gramma's Gold; editor Detour; editor (experimental film) This Old Man..., Sidewalk Motel. Served with U.S. Army, 1940-41. Mem. Acad. Motion Picture Arts and Scis., Dirs. Guild Am., Am. Cinema Editors (dir., bd. mem. 1984-85), Motion Picture Editors Guild, Delta Kappa Alpha (pres. 1941-65), Film and Videotape Editors Guild. Democrat. Avocation: photography. Office: Herbert L Strock Prodns 6311 Romaine St Los Angeles CA 90038-2600

STROCK, JAMES MARTIN, state agency administrator, lawyer, conservationist; b. Austin, Tex., Aug. 19, 1956; s. James Martin Strock Sr. and Augusta (Tenney) Mullins. AB, Harvard U., 1977, JD, 1981; postgrad, New Coll. Oxford U., 1981-82. Bar: Colo. 1983. Tchg. asst. Harvard U., 1980-81; spl. cons. to majority leader U.S. Senate, Washington, 1982-83; spl. asst. to adminstr. EPA, Washington, 1983-85, asst. adminstr. for enforcement, 1989-91; spl. counsel U.S. Senate Com. on Environment and Pub. Works, Washington, 1985-86; environ. atty. Davis, Graham & Stubbs, Denver, 1986-88; acting dir., gen. counsel U.S. Office Pers. Mgmt., Washington, 1988-89; sec. for environ. protection State of Calif., Sacramento, 1991—; adj. prof. U. So. Calif., 1996—, mem. bd. advisors Toxics Law Reporter, 1987-89, Greenwire, 1991—; mem. Intergovtl. Policy Adv. Com., rep. U.S. Trade, 1991—. Contbr. articles to profl. jours.; moderator, producer Lay It On The Line, Sta. WDSU-TV, New Orleans, 1973-74. Bd. dirs. Youth Svc. Am., Washington, 1988-89, Environ. Law Inst., 1992—; chair Calif. United State Employees Campaign, 1996—. Capt. JAGC USAR, 1987-96. Recipient Retsie Arco Future award, 1992, Ross Essay award ABA, 1985, Environ. Leadership award Calif. Environ. Bus. Coun., 1994, Fed. Republic Germany Fellowship award, 1996; Environ. Soc. India fellow, 1997; Charles Joseph Bonaparte scholar Harvard U., 1976, Rotary Internat. scholar, 1981-82. Mem. Commonwealth Club Calif., Phi Beta Kappa. Republican. Home: 400 Spear St Ste 107 San Francisco CA 94105 Office: 555 Capitol Mall Ste 525 Sacramento CA 95814-4502

STRODE, GEORGE K., sports editor; b. Amesville, Ohio, Nov. 10, 1935; s. Mac and Edith M. (Murphey) S.; m. Jennifer Lanning (div. 1973); m. Ruth E. Wingett, July 15, 1973. BJ, Ohio U., 1958. Sports editor Zanesville (Ohio) Times Reporter, 1958, Athens (Ohio) Messenger, 1958-62; sports reporter Dayton (Ohio) Daily News, 1962-63, Columbus (Ohio) Citizen Jour., 1963-69; Ohio sports editor AP, Columbus, 1969-85; sports editor Columbus Dispatch, 1985—. Mem. Ohio AP Sports Writers Assn. (v.p. 1984—), U.S. Golf Writers Assn., U.S. Harness Writers Assn. (pres. Ohio chpt. 1968-69). Republican. Methodist. Avocations: golfing, horse racing. Office: Columbus Dispatch 34 S 3rd St Columbus OH 43215-4201

STRODE, GERALD MARVIN, physician assistant; b. Fargo, N.D., Sept. 25, 1946; s. Marvin Lloyd Strode and Ruth Elaine (Holt) Gabert; m. Cheryl Helen Ford, Sept. 25, 1982; children: Gerald John, Nicholas Daniel. Grad., U. Utah, 1975; DHL (hon.), U. Humanatic Studies, 1986. Cert. physician asst. With USNG, 1966-96; dir. rural outreach program Vets. Adminstrn., Salt Lake City, 1983-88; mem. staff physician assts. Valley Children's Hosp., Fresno, Calif., 1990-94; physician asst. Washington Orthop. and Sports Medicine, Kirkland, Wash., 1994-95; owner Physician Asst. Surg. Svcs., Kirkland, 1995—; chmn. Wash. Gov. Com. on Employment of Handicapped, Olympia, 1976-78; advisor Wash. State Bd. Med. Examiners, Olympia, 1978-82. Decorated Navy Cross. Fellow Am. Acad. Physician Assts. (del.), Wash. Acad. Physician Assts. (pres. 1979, 81), Physician Assts. Orthop. Surgery (pres.-elect 1995); mem. Ducks Unltd. (area and zone chmn. 1988—, Disting. Svc. award 1993). Republican. Lutheran. Avocations: skiing, hunting, fishing, bicycle riding, sailing. Home: 15401 206th Ave NE Woodinville WA 98072-7764 Office: Physician Asst Surg Svcs Kirkland WA 98034

STRODE, WILLIAM HALL, III, photojournalist, publisher; b. Louisville, Aug. 6, 1937; s. William Hall and Margaret (Diehl) S.; m. Elizabeth Ann Wheeler, Nov. 26, 1960 (div. 1973); children: Alissa Michelle, Erin Hall; m. Hope Powel Alexander, Nov. 12, 1977; children: Hope Ives, Charlotte Alexander. BS, Western Ky. U., 1959. News photographer Courier Jour. and Louisville Times, 1960-64, asst. dir. photography, 1968-75; photographer Courier Jour. mag., 1964-77; formed William Strode Assocs., photog. and pub. co., Louisville, 1978—, Harmony House pubs., 1984—. Author 16 books; exhbns. include Fine Arts III, 1961, Profile in Poverty, Smithsonian Instn., 1966, Documerica, in Corcoran Gallery, Washington, 1972, 73, Picture of the Year Travelling Exhibits; one man show includes Speed Mus. Active local Boy Scouts Am.; founder Nat. Press Photographers Found., 1975. Served with AUS, 1959. Recipient Headliners best photojournalism award, 1965; award for excellence for best mag. photog. reporting Overseas Press Club, 1967; co-recipient Pulitzer Prize for pub. service Courier Jour., 1967, for feature photography, 1976; Art Dirs. Gold medal, 1980, World Press Photog. Arts and Scis. award, 1985. Mem. Nat. Press Photographers Assn. (nat. ednl. chmn. 1966-68, v.p. 1973, pres. 1974, Photographer of Yr. 1966, Newspaper Mag. Picture Editor of Yr. 1968), Am. Soc. Mag. Photographers, Soc. Profl. Journalists, Sigma Chi, Kappa Alpha Mu. Methodist. Home and Office: 1008 Kent Rd Goshen KY 40026-9768

STRODEL, ROBERT CARL, lawyer; b. Evanston, Ill., Aug. 12, 1930; s. Carl Frederick and Imogene (Board) S.; m. Mary Alice Shonkwiler, June 17, 1956; children: Julie Ann, Linda Lee, Sally Payson. BS, Northwestern U., 1952; JD, U. Mich., 1955. Bar: Ill. 1955, U.S. Supreme Ct. 1970; diplomate Am. Bd. Profl. Liability Attys., Am. Bd. Forensic Examiners; cert. civil trial specialist Am. Bd. Trial Advocacy. Mem. firm Davis, Morgan & Witherell, Peoria, Ill., 1957-59; sole practice Peoria, 1959-69; prin. Strodel, Kingery & Durree Assoc., Peoria, Ill., 1969-92, Law Offices of Robert C. Strodel, Ltd., Peoria, 1992—; asst. state's atty. Peoria, 1960-61; instr. bus. law Bradley U., Peoria, 1961-62; lectr. Belli seminars, 1969-87; lectr. in trial practice; mem. U.S. Presdl. Commn. German-Am. Tricentennial, 1983. Author books and articles in med.-legal field. Gov. appointee Ill. Dangerous Drugs Advisory Council, 1970-73; gen. chmn. Peoria-Tazewell Easter Seals, 1963, Cancer Crusade, 1970; pres. Peoria Civic Ballet, 1969-70; mem. Mayor's Commn. on Human Relations, 1962-64; chmn. City of Peoria Campaign Ethics Bd., 1975; Peoria County Rep. Sec., 1970-74; campaign chmn. Gov. Richard Ogilvie, Peoria County, 1972, Sen. Ralph Smith, 1970; treas. Michel for Congress, 1977-94, campaign coord., 1982; bd. dirs. Crippled Children's Center, 1964-65, Peoria Symphony Orch., 1964-68. Served with AUS, 1956-57. Decorated Officer's Cross of Order of Merit (Fed. Republic Germany), 1984; named Outstanding Young Man Peoria Peoria Jr. C. of C., 1963. Mem. ATLA (bd. govs. 1987-96), Ill. Trial Lawyers Assn. (bd. mgrs. 1985—), ABA, Ill. Bar Assn. (Lincoln awards for legal writing 1961, 63, 65), Am. Coll. Legal Medicine, Am. Inns of Ct. (charter master of bench, Lincoln Inn-Peoria, Ill.). Club: Mason (Shriner). Home: 3908 N Pinehurst Ct Peoria IL 61614-7246 Office: Commerce Bank Bldg Ste 927 Peoria IL 61602 *The pursuit of professional excellence has been a lifetime goal, coupled with contributions to public, political and civic affairs. He who takes from his community must also contribute to it.*

STRODL, PETER, educational administrator, educator; b. Bklyn., Apr. 28, 1943; s. Chester Arthur and Evine Strodl; m. Susan Marie Strodl, May 25, 1984; children: Jonathan P. Strodl, Jennifer Lynn, Brian Smillie. BA, Concordia U., 1967; MSEd, SUNY, New Paltz, 1970; EdD, NYU, 1980, postgrad., 1989-90. Elem. tchr. Smithtown & Monroe, Woodbury, N.Y., 1966-72; unit leader East Windsor Regional Sch. Dist., Highstown, N.J., 1972-74; prin. Dunkirk (N.Y.) Pub. Schs., 1975-78; prof. de la formation de maître Commn. Scolaire Crie, Valdor, Que., Can., 1979-82; prin. Luth. Sch. of Flushing, N.Y., 1982-84; adminstrv. asst. L.I. U., Bklyn., 1986-90; asst. prof. U. Hartford, West Hartford, 1990-93; pres., asst. prof. ednl. leadership U. So. Ala., Mobile, 1993—; bd. dirs. Martin Luther H.S., Maspeth, N.Y. Author: (with others) Educational Administration, 1993; contbr. articles to profl. jours. Mem. Am. Ednl. Rsch. Assn. (pres. 1970), Ea. Ednl. Rsch. Assn. (sec. 1989-93, bd. dirs. 1986-94), Phi Delta Kappa (Rsch. award 1996). Democrat. Lutheran. Avocations: gardening, traveling, photography, writing, real estate. Home: 2211 Harrods Ct Mobile AL 36695 Office: U So Ala ILB/30 Mobile AL 36688

STROESENREUTHER, GEORGE DALE, financial executive; b. Milw., Aug. 13, 1954; s. George Dale and Alice Marie (Raisler) S.; m. Karen Lee Daniels, Aug. 29, 1981 (div. Oct. 1984); 1 child, Jason Dale; m. Lynn Louise Lloyd, Feb. 2, 1985 (div. Apr. 1995); children: Timothy George, Steven Douglas; m. LiLi Xin, Apr. 13, 1995; 1 child, George Dale III. BBA, U. Wis., 1976. CPA, Wis., N.C., Ill. Internal auditor Allis Chalmers Corp., Milw., 1977-79, sr. fin. analyst, 1979-80, mgr. cost acctg., inventory control, 1980-82; supr. cost acctg. Abbott Labs., Rocky Mount, N.C., 1982, bus. unit controller, 1982-84; sr. div. analyst Abbott Labs., North Chicago, Ill., 1984-85, plant controller, materials mgr., 1985-87; dir. internal audit Outboard Marine Corp., Waukegan, Ill., 1987-88, Asea Brown Boveri, Inc., New Berlin, Wis., 1988-90; v.p. fin., CFO ABB Process Automation, Inc., Columbus, Ohio, 1990-91, ABB Traction Inc., Elmira Heights, N.Y., 1991; fin. contr. Ams.-Pacific and Far East, Cleve., 1992-95; contr., CFO Bailey Fischer & Porter of Elsag Bailey Process Automation, Cleve., 1995; CFO US Assist Inc., Bethesda, Md., 1996—; dir. Harbor West Assn., Rocky Mount, 1983-84. Treas. Students for an Accessible Soc., Whitewater, 1976-78. Mem. AICPA, Md. Assn. CPA's. Republican. Lutheran. Avocations: fishing, golf, volleyball. Office: US Assist Inc 6903 Rockledge Dr Ste 800 Bethesda MD 20817-1859 *There is a lot of truth to the statement "The only thing constant in life is change". Those that recognize this fact and respond accordingly are best prepared to meet the challenges of the future.*

STROH, RAYMOND EUGENE, personnel executive; b. Bloomington, Ill., Aug. 13, 1942; s. Harry William and Felcie Cleo (Weaver) S.; m. Peggy Jane Whitacre, June 12, 1966; children: Rebecca Jane, David Ray. BA, So. Ill. U., 1966, U. Ill., 1977. Pers. technician Ill. Dept. Mental Health, Springfield, Ill., 1966-67; pers. officer Andrew McFarland Mental Health Ctr., Springfield, 1967-68, Manteno (Ill.) State Hosp., 1968-69; chief pers. officer Ill. Dept. Law Enforcement, Springfield, 1969-75, Ill. Dept. Revenue, Springfield, 1975-81, Ill. Dept. Mental Health, Springfield, 1981-82; pers. exec. Ill. Dept. Cen. Mgmt. Svcs., Springfield, 1982—; state govt. chmn. U.S. Savs. Bond Campaign, Springfield, 1978-82. Bd. dirs. Consumer Credit Counseling Svc., Springfield, 1988-94, sec., 1994; coun. exec. bd. Boy Scouts Am., Springfield, 1987—, v.p., 1987—, dist. commr., 1979-86, unit commr., 1970-79; bd. dirs. Ill. State Employees Credit Union, 1984-85. Recipient Patriotic Svc. awards U.S. Treasury Dept., 1979-82, Silver Beaver award Boy Scouts Am., 1987, Dist. award of merit, 1981, Area Pres. awards, 1985, 86, Scouters Key award, 1976. Mem. NRA, U. Ill. Alumni Assn., So. Ill. U. Alumni Assn., Exptl. Aircraft Assn., Aircraft Owners and Pilots Assn., Ponce De Leon Inlet Lighthouse Assn., Nat. Geog. Soc., Cornell U. Lab. of Ornithology, Abraham Lincoln Gun Club, Appalachian Trail Conf., Union County (Tenn.) Hist. Soc., Bass Anglers Sportsman Soc., Lionel Railroader Club, Wabash R.R. Hist. Soc., Theta Delta Chi. Republican. Lutheran. Avocations: aviation, hunting, fishing, bird watching, model railroading. Home: 2111 Warwick Dr Springfield IL 62704-4147 Office: Ill Dept Cen Mgmt Svcs 501 Stratton Ofc Bldg Springfield IL 62706

STROHBEHN, JOHN WALTER, engineering science educator; b. San Diego, Nov. 21, 1936; s. Walter William and Gertrude (Powell) S.; children from previous marriage: Jo, Kris, Carolyn; m. Barbara Ann Brungard, Aug. 30, 1980. BS, Stanford U., 1958, MS, 1959, PhD in Elec. Engring., 1964. Assoc. prof. engring. sci. Dartmouth Coll., Hanover, N.H., 1968-73, prof., 1973-94, assoc. dean, 1976-81, adj. prof. medicine, 1979-90, Sherman Fairchild prof., 1983-91, acting provost, 1987-89, provost, 1989-93; provost, prof. biomed. engring. Duke U., Durham, N.C., 1994—; disting. lectr. IEEE Antennas and Propagation Soc., 1979-82; vis. fellow Princeton (N.J.) U., 1993-94. Editor: Laser Propagation in the Clear Atmosphere, 1978; assoc. editor Trans. Ant and Propagation, 1969-71, Trans. Biomed. Engring., 1981-87; contbr. articles to profl. jours. Scoutmaster Boy Scouts Am., Norwich, Vt., 1971-73; bd. dirs. Norwich Recreation and Conservation Council. Fellow AAAS, IEEE, Optical Soc. Am., Am. Inst. Med. Biol. Engring. (founding); mem. Radiation Rsch. Soc., Bioelectromagnetics Soc. (bd. dirs. 1982-85), N.Am. Hyperthermia Group (pres. 1986). Avocations: jogging; hiking; skiing. Home: 3806 Chippenham Rd Durham NC 27707 Office: Duke U Provost's Office 220 Allen Box 90005 Durham NC 27708

STROHECKER, LEON HARRY, JR., orthodontist; b. Schuylkill Haven, Pa., Aug. 14, 1932; s. Leon Harry and Anna (Fabian) S.; m. Juanita Mary Puyoou, Apr. 13, 1957; children: Sandra Lee Strohecker Beckett, Leon Harry III. Student, U. Pa., 1950-53, DDS, 1957, orthodontic cert., 1960. Bd. cert. Am. Bd. Orthodontics. Pres., pvt. practice Lansdale, Pa., 1961—; dir. Face Head & Neck Pain and Trauma Ctr., Lansdale, 1987—; bd. dirs. Artman Home Retirement Ctr., Ambler; treas., bd. dirs. Valley Ctr. Mental Health Clinic, Lansdale, 1984—; guest lectr. in field. Pres. Lansdale Rotary Club, 1967-68; coun. mem. Trinity Luth. Ch., Lansdale, 1977-85, chmn. fin. com., 1980-85. Lt. (j.g.) USN, 1957-59. Mem. ADA, Internat. Acad. Head, Neck and Facial Pain, Internat. Coll. Cranio-Mandibular Orthopedics, Am. Acad. Pain Mgmt. (diplomate), Am. Assn. for Functional Orthodontics, Am. Profl. Practice Assn., Am. Soc. Dentistry for Children, Am. Acad. Oral Medicine, Am. Assn. Orthodontists, Am. Assn. Stomatologists, Am. Acad. Oral Medicine, Middle Atlantic Orthodontic Soc., Pa. Orthod ontic Soc., Phila. Orthodontic Soc., Pa. Dental Assn., Second Dist. Dental Assn., Montgomery-Bucks Dental Soc., Alpha Omega, Omicron Kappa Epsilon. Avocations: tennis, travel, bridge, water sports. Home: 1512 Cedar Hill Rd Ambler PA 19002 Office: 456 E Hancock St Lansdale PA 19446-3803

STROHM, ROBERT DEAN, publications executive; b. Chgo., Oct. 14, 1945; s. John Louis and Lillian Ann (Murphy) S.; m. Patricia Ann Quincannon, July 10, 1976; children: John Wilson, Charles Quincannon. BS, U. Ill., 1968. Assoc. editor Nat. Wildlife Fedn., Washington, 1968-73, mng. editor, 1973-81, exec. editor, 1981-88, editor-in-chief, 1989—; v.p. publs. Nat. Wildlife Fedn., 1996—. Mem. Am. Soc. Mag. Editors. Democrat. Roman Catholic. Office: Nat Wildlife Fedn 8925 Leesburg Pike Vienna VA 22182-1742

STROHMEYER, JOHN, writer, former editor; b. Cascade, Wis., June 26, 1924; s. Louis A. and Anna Rose (Saladunas) S.; m. Nancy Jordan, Aug. 20, 1949; children: Mark, John, Sarah. Student, Moravian Coll., 1941-43; A.B., Muhlenberg Coll., 1947; M.A. in Journalism, Columbia, 1948; L.H.D. (hon.), Lehigh U., 1983. With Nazareth Item, 1940-41; night reporter Bethlehem (Pa.) Globe-Times, 1941-43, 45-47; investigative reporter Providence Jour.-Bull., 1949-56; editor Bethlehem Globe-Times, 1956-84, v.p., 1961-84, dir., 1963-84; African-Am. journalism tchr. in Nairobi, Freetown, 1964; Atwood prof. journalism U. Alaska Anchorage, 1987-88, writer-in-residence, 1989—. Author: Crisis in Bethlehem: Big Steel's Struggle to Survive, 1986, Extreme Conditions: Big Oil and The Transformation of Alaska, 1993. Lt. (j.g.) USNR, 1943-45. Pulitzer Traveling fellow, 1948; Nieman fellow, 1952-53; recipient Comenius award Moravian Coll., 1971; Pulitzer prize for editorial writing, 1972; Alicia Patterson Found. fellow, 1984, 85. Mem. Am. Soc. Newspaper Editors, Pa. Soc. Newspaper Editors (pres. 1964-66), Anchorage Racquet Club. Home: 6633 Lunar Dr Anchorage AK 99504-4550

STROIK, DUNCAN GREGORY, architect, architectural design educator; b. Phila., Jan. 14, 1962; s. John Stephen and Mary Eugenia (Dorsey) S.; m. Ruth Valeira Engelhardt, Aug. 29, 1987; children: Gabrielle Marie, Raffaella Maria, Giovanni Battista. BS in Architecture, U. Va., 1984; MArch, Yale U., 1987. Registered arch., Ill. Tchg. asst. Yale U. Sch. Architecture, New Haven, Conn., 1985-87; arch. Allan Greenberg, Arch., Washington, 1987-90; assoc. prof. U. Notre Dame (Ind.) Sch. Architecture, 1990—; arch. Duncan Stroik, Arch., South Bend, Ind., 1990—; chmn. lectr. com. U. Notre Dame, Ind., 1990—, mem. undergrad. com., 1992—, com. on internat. studies, 1993-94; chmn. jury Ind. Concrete Masonry Assn., Ind., 1994. Arch., author: Building Classical, 1993; exhbns. include: U. Steubenville, 1995, N.Y. Acad. of Art, 1994, Yale U. Sch. Architecture, 1995, Chgo. Cultural Ctr., 1995, others; contbr. articles to profl. jours. With East Rock Pavilion-Design and Constrn., Yale U. Sch. Architecture, New Haven, 1985; active Habitat for Humanity, New Haven, 1987, U. Notre Dame chpt. faculty adv.; fundraiser Diocesan Bishops Appeal, Ft. Wayne/South Bend, 1993; active Carraige Hills Assn., South Bend; parish coun. mem. Cathedral St. Matthew, 1995—. Palladio and Vitruvius grantee Graham Found. for Advanced Studies, 1991, Student Rsch. grantee Promote Women and Minorities Grad. Studies, U. Notre, Dame, 1993; C.L.V. Meeks Meml. scholar Yale U., New Haven, 1987. Mem. Assn. Collegiate Schs. Architecture, Classical Architecture League, Classical Am., Nat. Trust for Hist. Preservation. Roman Catholic. Avocations: classical music, philosophy, hiking, painting. Home: 52488 Briarcliff Ln South Bend IN 46635-1104 Office: Univ Notre Dame Sch Architecture Notre Dame IN 46556

STROKE, HINKO HENRY, physicist, educator; b. Zagreb, Yugoslavia, June 16, 1927; came to U.S., 1943, naturalized, 1949; s. Elias and Edith (Mechner) S.; m. Norma Bilchick, Jan. 14, 1956; children: Ilana Lucy, Marija Tamar. BEE, N.J. Inst. Tech., 1949; MS, MIT, 1952, PhD, 1955. From rsch. asst. to rsch. assoc. Princeton (N.J.) U., 1954-57; rsch. staff lab. electronics, lectr. dept. physics MIT, 1957-63; assoc. prof. physics NYU, N.Y.C., 1963-68, prof., 1968—; dept. chmn. NYU, 1988-91; prof. associé. U. Paris, 1969-70, Ecole Normale Supérieure, 1976; vis. scientist Max Planck Inst. for Quantenoptik, Garching, U. Munich, 1977-78, 81-82, 93; cons. Atomic Instrument Co., MIT Sci. Translation Svc., Tech. Rsch. Group, Cambridge Air Force Rsch. Ctr., Am. Optical Corp., ITT Fed. Labs., NASA, others; mem. com. on line spectra on elements NAS-NRC, 1976-82; sci. assoc. CERN, Geneva, 1983—. Contbg. author: Nuclear Physics, 1963, Atomic Physics, 1969, Hyperfine Interactions in Excited Nuclei, 1971, Francis Bitter: Selected Papers, 1969, Atomic Physics 3, 1973, Nuclear Moments and Nuclear Structure, 1973, A Perspective of Physics, Vol. 1, 1977, Atomic Physics 8, 1983, Lasers in Atomic, Molecular, and Nuclear Physics, 1989; editor: Comments on Atomic and Molecular Physics, The Physical Review-The First Hundred Years. Mem. Chorus Pro Musica, Boston, 1951-54, 57-63, Münchener Bach-Chor, Munich, 1977-82, 92; Choeur pro Arte, Lausanne, 1983-92; mem. Collegiate Chorale, N.Y., 1964-94, Dessoff Choirs, 1994—. With AUS, 1946-47. Recipient Sr. U.S. Scientist award Alexander von Humboldt Found., 1977; NATO sr. fellow in sci., 1975. Fellow Am. Phys. Soc. (publs. oversight com. 1991-93), Optical Soc. Am., AAAS; mem. IEEE, European Phys. Soc., Soc. Fraçaise de Physique, Sigma Xi, Tau Beta Pi, Omicron Delta Kappa. Home: 271 Old Army Rd Scarsdale NY 10583-2619 Office: NYU Dept Physics 4 Washington Pl New York NY 10003-6603

STROLL, BEVERLY MARIE, elementary school principal; b. Akron, Ohio, Aug. 22, 1936; d. Michael Dzatko, William DeVille (stepfather) and Marie Elizabeth (Stock) Dzatko-DeVille; m. Harold E. Stroll, Aug. 22, 1959; 1 child, James. BS, Kent State, 1958, MEd, 1980, Ednl. Specialist, 1988. Cert. elem. principal, elem. supr., tchr. Elem. edn. tchr. Cleve. Pub. Schs., 1958-59; elem. edn. tchr. Akron (Ohio) Pub. Schs., 1959-80, chpt. I math tchr., 1980-85, curriculum specialist, 1985-87, program specialist, 1987-91; prin. Zion Christian Sch., Akron, 1991—; bd. mem. Zion Christian Sch., 1983—, State Supt. Adv. Bd., 1984-89. Co-chair vol. com. Nat. Inventors Hall of Fame, 1990. Named Jennings scholar Martha Holden Jennings Found., 1978-79. Mem. ASCD, Assn. Luth. Devel. Execs., Coalition Ohio Luth. Devel., Greater Clevel. Luth. Prins. Assn., Ohio Assn. Adminstrs. of State and Fed. Programs (exec. bd. 1989-91), Akron Women Adminstrs. (sec. 1988-90), Zion Lutheran Ch. (sec. 1988-96). Avocations: boating, water sports, traveling, bible study. Office: Zion Christian Sch 139 S High St Akron OH 44308-1410

STROM, BRIAN LESLIE, internist, educator; b. N.Y.C., N.Y., Dec. 8, 1949; s. Martin and Edith (Singer) S.; m. Elaine Marilyn Moskowitz, June 4, 1978; children: Shayne Lee, Jordan Blair. BS, Yale U., 1971; MD, Johns Hopkins U., 1975; MPH, U. Calif., Berkeley, 1980. Diplomate Am. Bd. Internal Medicine, Am. Bd. Epidemiology. Intern in medicine U. Calif., San Francisco, 1975-76; resident in medicine U. Calif., 1976-78, research fellow in clinical pharmacology, 1978-80; from asst. prof. to assoc. prof. medicine and pharmacology U. Pa., Phila., 1980-93, prof. medicine, 1993—, prof. biostatistics & epidemiology, 1995—; adj. asst. prof. clin. pharmacy Phila. Coll. of Pharmacy and Sci., 1981-90, adj. assoc. prof., 1990-93, adj. prof., 1993—; mem. U. Pa. Cancer Ctr., 1981—; attending staff Hosp. U. Pa., 1980—, co-dir Clin. Epidemiology Unit, 1980-91, dir., 1991—; dir. Clin. Pharmacology Cons. Svc., 1981-82; dir. Ctr. for Clin. Epidemiology and Biostats., 1993—, chair dept. biostats. and epidemiology, 1995—; lectr. in field; cons. CDC, 1981, Coun. for Internat. Orgn. of Med. Scis., Geneva, Switzerland, 1981-83, Office of Tech. Assessment, Congress of U.S., 1980-81, Aging Rev. Com., Nat. Inst. Aging, 1982, Ministry of Pub. Health, State of Kuwait, 1982, Royal Tropical Inst., Amsterdam, 1983, others. Editl. cons. Johns Hopkins U. Press, J.B. Lippincott; referee Annals of Internal Medicine, Archives of Internal Medicine, Clin. Pharmacology and Therapeutics, Digestive Diseases and Sci., Internat. Jour. Cardiology, Internat. Jour. Epidemiology, Jour. AMA, Jour. Gen. Internal Medicine, Med. Care, Primary Care Tech., Sci.; assoc. editor Jour. Gen. Internal Medicine; mem. editl. bd. 7 jours.; contbr. numerous articles to profl. jours. Nat. Acad. Scis. grantee, Rockefeller Found. grantee, NIH grantee, many others. Fellow ACP, Am. coll. Epidemiology, Am. Epidemiology Soc.; mem. Am. Fedn. Clin. Rsch., Am. Pub. Health Assn., Am. Soc. Clin. Pharmacology and Therapeutics, Am. Soc. Clin. Investigation, Internat. Soc. Pharmacoepidemiology, Internat. Epideliol. Assn., Soc. for Epidemiologic Rsch., Soc. Group Internal Medicine. Democrat. Jewish. Avocations: hiking, biking, camping, skiing. Home: 332 Hidden River Rd Narberth PA 19072-1111

STROM, CARLA CASTALDO, elementary education educator; b. Rahway, N.J., Aug. 11; d. Neil and Loretta (Gleason) Castaldo; m. George Pendleton Strom, Aug. 11, 1962; children: Karen Kimberly, Steven Karl. BS in Edn. cum laude, Syracuse U., 1961; MS in Edn. magna cum laude, U. Bridgeport, 1962; postgrad., Brown U., 1982-89, Sacred Heart U. Cert. tchr., N.Y., N.J., R.I. Tchr. Livingston Elem. Sch., Cranford, N.J., 1962-63, Sherman Sch., Cranford, 1963-65; supplementary instr. Cranford Bd. Edn., 1974-79; tutor remedial students, home instr. R.I. East Greenwich Sch. Com., 1980-83; tchr. Holy Name Sch., Providence, 1983-86, St. Thomas Regional Sch., Providence, 1986-89; tchr. sci., social studies St. Mary Sch., Bethel, Conn., 1989—; with Profl. Learning Ctr. Jupiter (Fla.) Acad., 1995-97; sci. fair coord., Danbury, Conn., 1991—; participant Here's Looking at You in the Year 2001-Drug Free America. Tchr. confraternity of Christian doctrine, 1972—, Eucharistic min. St. Mary Ch., Bethel, 1991-95; neighborhood leader East Greenwich Tanglewood Assn., 1982-84; Rep. committeewoman, Cranford, 1979-81. Recipient Drug-Free Sch. award Providence Journal, 1987. Mem. Nat. Cath. Tchrs. Assn., Nat. Sci. Tchrs. Assn., Religious Educators Am., Phi Kappa Phi, Kappa Kappa Gamma. Home: Bldg 200 Unit 301 200 Ocean Trail Way Jupiter FL 33477

STROM, J. PRESTON, JR., lawyer; b. May 21, 1959; s. Grace and J.P. Sr. S.; m. Donna Savoca, Oct. 5, 1985; 1 child, Margaret. BA, U. S.C., 1981, JD, 1984. Bar: S.C. 1984, U.S. Dist. Ct. S.C., 1984, U.S. Ct. Appeals (4th cir.) 1984. Asst. solicitor 5th Jud. Cir., S.C., 1985-86; ptnr. Leventis, Strom & Wicker, 1986-88, Harpootlian & Strom, 1988-90, Bolt, Popowski, McCulloch & Strom, 1990-93; acting U.S. atty. Office U.S. Atty., S.C., 1993, U.S. atty., 1993-96; atty. J.P. Strom Jr, P.A., Columbia, S.C., 1996—; chmn. Law Enforcement Coord. Com.; chmn. juvenile justice and child support enforcement subcom. U.S. Dept. Justice; active Atty. Gen. Adv. Com. Mem. S.C. Bar, S.C. Trial Lawyers Assn., Richland County Bar Assn. (chmn. criminal law sect.). Office: JP Strom Jr PA 1720 Main St Ste 304 Columbia SC 29201-2850

STROM, LYLE ELMER, federal judge; b. Omaha, Nebr., Jan. 6, 1925; s. Elmer T. and Eda (Hanisch) S.; m. Regina Ann Kelly, July 31, 1950; children: Mary Bess, Susan Frances, Amy Claire, Cassie A., David Kelly, Margaret Mary, Bryan Thomas. Student, U. Nebr., 1946-47; AB, Creighton U., 1950, JD cum laude, 1953. Bar: Nebr. 1953. Assoc. Fitzgerald, Brown, Leahy, Strom, Schorr & Barmettler and predecessor firm, Omaha, 1953-60, ptnr., 1960-63, gen. trial ptnr., 1963-85; judge U.S. Dist. Ct. Nebr., Omaha, 1985-87, chief judge, 1987-95, sr. judge, 1995—; adj. prof. law Creighton U., 1959-95, prof., 1996—; mem. com. pattern jury instrns. and practice and proc. Nebr. Supreme Ct., 1965-91; spl. legal counsel Omaha Charter Rev. Commn., 1973. Mem. exec. com Covered Wagon Coun. Boy Scouts Am., 1953-57, bd. trustees and exec. com. Mid-Am. Coun., 1988—; chmn. bd. trustees Marian High Sch., 1969-71; mem. pres. coun. Creighton U., 1990—. Ensign USNR and with U.S. Maritime Svc., 1943-46. Fellow Am. Coll. Trial Lawyers, Internat. Acad. Trial Lawyers; mem. ABA, Nebr. Bar Assn. (ho. of dels. 1978-81, exec. coun. 1981-87, pres. 1989-90), Omaha Bar Assn. (pres. 1980-81), Am. Judicature Soc., Midwestern Assn. Amateur Athletic Union (pres. 1976-78), Alpha Sigma Nu (pres. alumni chpt. 1970-71). Republican. Roman Catholic. Lodge: Rotary (pres. 1993-94). Office: US Dist Ct PO Box 607 Omaha NE 68101-0607

STROM, MILTON GARY, lawyer; b. Rochester, N.Y., Dec. 5, 1942; s. Harold and Dolly (Isaacson) S.; m. Barbara A. Simon, Jan. 18, 1975; children: Carolyn, Michael, Jonathan. BS in Econs., U. Pa., 1964; JD, Cornell U., 1967. Bar: N.Y. 1968, U.S. Dist. Ct. (we. dist.) N.Y. 1968, U.S. Ct. Claims 1969, U.S. Ct. Mil. Appeals 1969, U.S. Ct. Appeals ((D.C. cir.) 1970, U.S. Supreme Ct. 1972, U.S. Dist. Ct. (so. dist.) N.Y. 1975. Atty. SEC, Washington, 1968-71; assoc. Skadden, Arps, Slate, Meagher & Flom, N.Y.C., 1971-77, ptnr., 1977—. Served with USCGR, 1967-68. Mem. ABA, N.Y. State Bar Assn. (corp. law sect.), Assn. of Bar of City of N.Y. Republican. Jewish. Club: Beach Point, Marco Polo. Avocations: tennis, skiing. Office: Skadden Arps Slate Meagher & Flom 919 3rd Ave New York NY 10022

STROMBERG, ARTHUR HAROLD, retired professional services company executive; b. Los Angeles, July 17, 1928; s. Walter John and Ingfrid Christine (Olsen) S.; m. Fredna B. Copeland, Aug. 29, 1953. B.A. in Econs, U. So. Calif., 1952. Broker Francis I. duPont & Co., San Francisco, 1953-59; ptnr. Glore Forgan & Co., Chgo., San Francisco, 1959-67; v.p., dir. Eaton & Howard, San Francisco, 1967-70; chief exec. officer, chmn. bd. Thortec Internat., San Mateo, Calif., 1970-89; chmn. bd. URS Internat., Arlington, Va., 1986-91. Served with USNR, 1945-48. Mem. Bohemian Club, Burlingame Country Club. Republican.

STROMBERG, CLIFFORD DOUGLAS, lawyer; b. N.Y.C., June 1, 1949; s. George M. and Greta (Netzow) S.; m. Ava S. Feiner, June 25, 1972; children: Kimberly, Eric. BA summa cum laude, Yale U., 1971; JD, Harvard U., 1974. Bar: N.Y. 1975, D.C. 1975, U.S. Dist. Ct. (so. and ea. dists.) N.Y. 1975, U.S. Ct. Appeals (D.C. cir.) 1975, U.S. Ct. Appeals (2nd cir.) 1975, U.S. Supreme Ct. 1980. Law clk. to judge U.S. Dist. Ct. (ea. dist.) N.Y., 1974-75; assoc. Arnold & Porter, Washington, 1975-78, 80-83; dep. exec. sec. HHS, Washington, 1978-80; cons. FTC, Washington, 1980; ptnr. Dorsey & Whitney, Washington, 1983-84, Hogan & Hartson, Washington, 1984—; adj. asst. prof. emergency medicine George Washington U. Sch. Medicine, 1991—. Co-author: Mental Health and Law: A System in Transition, 1975, Alternatives to the Hospital: Ambulatory Surgery Centers and Emergicenters, 1984, Entrepreneurial Health Care: How to Structure Successful New Ventures, 1985, The Psychologist's Legal Handbook, 1988, Access to Hospital Information: Problems and Strategies: 4 Frontiers of Health Services Management 3-33, 1987, Healthcare Provider Networks: Antitrust Issues and Practical Considerations in Devels. in Antitrust Law, 1990, Healthcare Credentialing: Implications for Academic Medical Centers, 1991; mem. editl. bd. Harvard Law Rev., 1972-73; editor in chief Healthspan: The Report of Health Business and Law, 1984-87; contbr. articles to profl. jours. Bd. dirs. Nat. Children's Eye Care Found., Washington, 1985-87. Teaching fellow in govt. Harvard U., 1973-74. Fellow Am. Bar Found.; mem. ABA (chair working group health care reform 1993-96, state membership chmn. 1984, forum com. health law 1987-90, adv. com. govt. affairs 1993—, governing bd., individual rights and responsibilities sect., exec. coun., 1980-90, sec. 1984-87, chair-elect 1987-88, chair 1988-89, legal aid and indigent defendants com. 1982-87), Nat. Health Lawyers Assn., Phi Beta Kappa. Office: Hogan & Hartson 555 13th St NW Washington DC 20004-1109

STROMBERG, GREGORY, printing ink company executive; b. Milw., Feb. 10, 1948; s. Clifford Norman and Margaret Betty (Hoover) S.; m. Gail Elizabeth Steinbach, Aug. 22, 1970; children: Christopher, Brian, Ellen. BS, Marquette U., Milw., 1970. Office contact salesman Continental Can Co., Milw., 1970-78; sales rep. Sun Chem. Co., Milw., 1978-82; v.p., gen. mgr. Acme Printing Ink Co., Milw., 1982—; exec. v.p. Can. op. Acme Printing Ink Can. Ltd., 1985—, pres., 1990—; bd. dirs. Can. Ops. Acme Inks of Can.; pres. Toobee Internat., Inc., Milw., 1981—; v.p., dir. mktg. and internat. sales INX Internat. Ink Co., 1991—. Author: Toobee Air Force Flight Training Manual, 1983. Advisor Milw. Jr. Achievement, 1974; sponsor Muscular Dystrophy, 1983; asst. com. mem. Toys for Tots, Children's Hosp., Milw., 1983; active United Meth. Men. Mem. Am. Mktg. Assn., Sales and Mktg. Execs. of Milw., Am. Mgmt. Assn., Am. Soc. Quality Control Milw., Nat. Metal Decorators Assn., Nat. Assn. Printer and Lithographers, Nat. Assn. Printing Equipment and Suppliers. Home: N69w23448 Donna Dr Sussex WI 53089-3245

STROMBERG, JEAN WILBUR GLEASON, lawyer; b. St. Louis, Oct. 31, 1943; d. Ray Lyman and Martha (Bugbee) W.; m. Gerald Kermit Gleason, Aug. 28, 1966 (div. 1987); children: C. Blake, Peter Wilbur; m. Kurt Stromberg, Jan. 3, 1993; 1 child, Kristoffer Stromberg. B.A., Wellesley Coll., 1965; LL.B. cum laude, Harvard U., 1968. Bar: Calif. 1969, D.C. 1978. Assoc. Brobeck, Phleger & Harrison, San Francisco, 1969-72; spl. counsel to dir. div. corp. fin. SEC, 1972-76, assoc. dir. div. investment mgmt., 1976-78; of counsel Fulbright & Jaworski, Washington, 1978-80; ptnr. Fulbright & Jaworski, 1980-96; dir. fin. instns. and market issues U.S. Gen. Acctg. Office, Washington, 1996—; mem. adv. panel on legal issues GAO, NASD select com. on Nasdaq, 1994-96. Mem. ABA (chmn. subcom. on securities and banks, corp. laws com., bus. sect. 1982-93), D.C. Bar Assn. (chmn. steering com. bus. sect. 1982-84), Fed. Bar Assn. (chair exec. coun., securities com. 1993-95), Am. Bar Retirement Assn. (bd. dirs. 1986-90, 94-96), Phi Beta Kappa. Home: 3411 Woodley Rd NW Washington DC 20016-5030 Office: US Gen Acctg Office 441 G St NW Washington DC 20548-0001

STROMBERG, ROLAND NELSON, historian; b. Kansas City, Mo., July 5, 1916; s. Clarence Rol and Harriet (Ridgell) S.; m. Mary R. Gray, June 10, 1939; children: Eric, Juliet. AB, U. Kansas City, 1939; MA, Am. U., 1946; PhD, U. Md., 1952. With U.S. Dept. Justice, 1940-45; instr., then asst. prof., asso. prof., prof. U. Md., College Park, 1949-66; prof. So. Ill. U., Carbondale, 1966-67; prof. history U. Wis., Milw., 1967—; acting chmn. dept. art history U. Wis., 1977-78. Author: Collective Security and American Foreign Policy, 1963, An Intellectual History of Modern Europe, 1966, European Intellectual History Since 1789, 1966, 6th edit., 1994, After Everything, 1975, Religious Liberalism in Eighteenth Century England, 1954, Heritage and Challenge of History, 1971, 2d edit., 1989, Arnold J. Toynbee, 1972, Europe in the Twentieth Century, 1979, 4th edit., 1996, Redemption by War: The European Intellectuals and the 1914 War, 1982, Five Twentieth Century Thinkers, 1990, Men, Women, and History, 1994, Democracy, A Short History, 1996, others. Rockefeller Found. grantee, 1957-58; recipient Disting. Alumnus award U. Mo., Kansas City, 1966; fellow Woodrow Wilson Internat. Center for Scholars, 1974. Mem. History of Sci. Soc., Soc. Historians of Am. Fgn. Relations. Home: 7033 N Fairchild Cir Milwaukee WI 53217-3851 Office: U Wis Holton Hall Milwaukee WI 53201 *It would be more edifying to say that, as historian, I have sought an understanding of the past in order to help mankind master its future. It is probably truer to say that I have simply been fascinated by the amazing record of human actions and thoughts and by the problem of making sense of them.*

STROMBERG, ROSS ERNEST, lawyer; b. Arcata, Calif., May 5, 1940; s. Noah Anders and Anne Laura (Noyes) S.; m. Toni Nicholas, Dec. 16, 1961; m. Margaret Telonicher, Oct. 3, 1965; children: Kristin, Matthew, Gretchen, Erik. BS, Humboldt State U., 1962; JD, U. Calif., Berkeley, 1965. Bar: Calif. 1966, U.S. Dist. Ct. (no. dist.) Calif. 1966, U.S. Ct. Appeals (9th cir.) 1966. Assoc. Hanson Bridgett, San Francisco, 1965-70, ptnr., 1970-85; ptnr. Epstein Becker Stromberg & Green, San Francisco, 1985-90, Jones Day Reavis & Pogue, L.A., 1990—; chmn. Jones Day's Healthcare Specialized Industry Practice. Author: Economic Joint Venturing, 1985, Acquisition and Enhancement of Physician Practices, 1988. Pres. East Bay AHEC, Oakland, Calif., 1984-87; bd. dirs. Am. Cancer Soc., Oakland, 1984-95; bd. dirs. U.S.-China Ednl. Inst., San Francisco, 1985—, chmn., 1988—; pres. Am. Acad. Hosp. Attys. of Am. Hosp. Assn., Chgo., 1978. Mem. Health Fin. Mgmt. Assn., Nat. Health Lawyers Assn., Am. Acad. Hosp. Attys., World Trade Club, Ingomar Club. Democrat. Office: Jones Day Reavis & Pogue 555 W 5th St Ste 4600 Los Angeles CA 90013-3002

STROME, MARSHALL, otolaryngologist, educator; b. Lynn, Mass., Apr. 27, 1940; s. David and Rose (Cantor) S.; m. Deena Lazarov, Sept. 23, 1962; children: Scott Eric, Randall Alan. Degree, U. Mich., 1960, MD, 1964, MS, 1970. Resident in otolaryngology U. Mich., Ann Arbor, 1966-70; asst. prof. U. Conn., Hartford, 1971; asst. prof. Beth Israel-Harvard, Boston, 1972-77, chief otolaryngology, 1977-93; prof., chmn. otolaryngology Cleve. Clinic Found., 1993—; sr. surgeon Brigham & Women's Hosp., Boston, 1982-93; assoc. prof. harvard Med. Sch., Boston, 1989-93, Longwood ORL coord., 1982-90; mem. cons. bd. Xomed Treace Corp., Jacksonville, Fla., 1987-90; advisor SLT Laser Corp., Oaks, Pa., 1994—; dir. Great Comebacks, Gresham, Oreg.; prof. otolaryngology Cleve. Clinic Found. Health Scis. Ctr. Ohio State U., 1994; hon. guest, prin. spkr. Turkish Otolaryngol. Soc., 1997. Mem. editl. bd. Harvard Health News Letter, 1976-85; author: Differential Diagnoses in Pediatric ORL, 1975; editor: Manual of Otolaryngology, 1985, Complications of Laser Surgery of the Head and Neck, 1986. Mem. fund raising com. Belmont Hill (Mass.) Sch., 1984. Capt. U.S. Army, 1965-71. Recipient Medal, City of Paris, 1987, Sword of Saudi Arabia, 1991, Cert. of Appreciation, Ministry of Health-Singapore, 1995; named One of Best Doctors in Cleve., Cleve. Mag., 1995. Fellow ACS, Coll. Physicians and Surgeons (hon., Pakistan); mem. Am. Acad. Facial Plastic Reconstructive Surgery (Medallion of Honor 1989), Am. Acad. Otolaryngology (Honor award 1987), Am. Soc. Head and Neck Surgery; mem. Triological Soc. ((v.p. 1990-91), Cartesian Soc. (pres. 1989), U. Mich. Med. Ctr. Alumni Soc. (chair bd. govs. 1992-93, host alumni function 1994, coord. New Eng. Fund Raising 1992). Avocations: cycling, skiing, sculling, sea kyacking, tennis. Office: Cleve Clinic Found 9500 Euclid Ave Cleveland OH 44195-0001

STROME, STEPHEN, distribution company executive; b. Lynn, Mass., June 20, 1945; s. David and Rose (Cantor) S.; m. Phyllis Ruth Fields, Jan. 14, 1967; children: Michael, Rochelle. BA, Hillsdale (Mich.) Coll., 1967; MBA, Wayne State U., 1968. Trainee KMart Corp., Detroit, 1968-69; mgr. work measurement KMart Corp., Troy, Mich., 1970-73; mgr. tng., edn. Fruehauf Corp., Detroit, 1974-76, regional mgr. labor relations, 1976-78; dir. ops. Handleman Co., Clawson, Mich., 1978-80, account exec., 1980-82; v.p. computer software div. Handleman Co., Troy, 1983-85, pres. computer software/video div., 1986-87, exec. v.p., 1987-89, exec. v.p., chief oper. officer, 1990, pres., CEO, 1991—. Home: 4597 Kiftsgate Bnd Bloomfield Hills MI 48302-2331 Office: Handleman Co 500 Kirts Dr Troy MI 48084-5225

STRONACH, CAREY ELLIOTT, physicist, educator; b. Boston, Aug. 8, 1940; s. Ralph Howard and Frances Burns (Maynard) S.; m. Joan Alice Louise Venner, Aug. 20, 1966; children: John Maynard, Howard Stanley. BS, U. Richmond, Va., 1961; MS, U. Va., 1963; PhD, Coll. William and Mary, Williamsburg, Va., 1975. Instr. physics Va. State U., Petersburg, 1965-66, asst. prof., 1966-71, 72-76, assoc. prof., 1976-78, 79-80, prof., 1980—, dir. Muon Spin Rotation Rsch. Program, 1977—, dir. Solid State Physics Rsch.Inst., 1983-87, radiation safety officer, 1983-87, dir. Superconducting Materials Rsch. Program, 1988—; dir. Nanostructured Materials Research Program, 1997—; dir. Galactic Cosmic Radiation Rsch. Program, 1993—; dir. U.S.- France Joint Muon Spin Rotation Rsch. Program, 1985-91; vis. assoc. prof. U. Alta., 1978-79; guest scientist Brookhaven Nat. Lab.; mem. organizing com. Internat. Symposium on the Electronic Structure and Properties of Hydrogen in Metals, 1982, Internat. Symposium on the Physics and Chemistry of Small Clusters, 1986, From Clusters to Crystals, 1991, The Sci. and Tech. of Atomically Engineered Materials, 1995; mem. Internat. Adv. Com., Eighth Internat. Conf. on Muon Spin Rotation, mem. sci. adv. com. European Workshop on the Spectroscopy of Subatomic Species in Non-Metallic Solids, 1985, govs. com on Superconducting Supercollider, 1987; TV physics lectr., 1991-94. Contbr. 99 articles to publs. in field; playwright. Pres. Petersburg area chpt. Va. Coun. Human Rels., 1965-67; mem. Petersburg Commn. Community Rels. Affairs, 1974-77; corr. sec. Petersburg Dem. Com., 1974-77, mem., 1972-78, 79-85, vice chmn., 1981-85; mem. long-range transp. adv. com. City of Petersburg, 1994—; mem. steering com. Gilmore for Gov. '97; mem. Dramatists Guild. Fellow duPont Corp. 1961-63, NSF, 1971-72, NASA, 1976. Mem. AAAS, Am. Phys. Soc., Am. Assn. Physics Tchrs., AAUP (chpt. pres. 1968-70), Va. Acad. Sci. (sec. astronomy, math. and physics sect. 1983-84, chmn. 1984-85), Southeastern Univs. Rsch. Assn. (site selection com. 1980-81, materials sci. com. 1983-86, trustee 1983—, sci. and tech. com. 1986-88, rules com. 1988-92, edn. com. 1992-94, new projects com. 1994-95, Jefferson Lab. com. 1995—), High Speed Rail/Maglev Assn. (govt. rels. com. 1992—, Maglev Task Force, 1994—), Coun. Secular Humanism (assoc.), Los Alamos Meson Physics Facility Users' Group, Thomas Jefferson Nat. Accelerator Facility User's Group, Tri-Univ. Meson Facility Users Group, Va. Computer Networking Com., 1983-86, N.Y. Acad. Scis., Phi Beta Kappa, Sigma Xi (chpt. sec. 1977-78, chpt. pres. 1980-84, 87-88), Sigma Pi Sigma, Pi Mu Epsilon. Achievements include development (with others) of low-energy muon beam line at the AGS of Brookhaven Nat. Lab.; research in pion-nucleus interactions, heavy-ion reactions, muon spin rotation studies of high-temperature superconductors and related materials, fullerenes, heavy-fermion materials, ferromagnetic metals, metal hydrides, fatigue in metals and other materials; participation in the establishment of the Southeastern Universities Research Association and the Thomas Jefferson National Accelerator facility; discovery of formation of muonium and muonated radicals in Buckminsterfullerene; development of TV lecture series on physics. Home: 2241 Buckner St Petersburg VA 23805-2207 Office: Va State U Box 9325 Petersburg VA 23806

STRONACH, FRANK, automobile parts manufacturing executive. Chmn., dir. Magna Internat. Inc., Markham, Ont., Can., 1971—. Founder The Fair Enterprise Inst. Office: Magna Internat Inc, 36 Apple Creek Blvd, Markham, ON Canada L3R 4Y4

STRONE, MICHAEL JONATHAN, lawyer; b. N.Y.C., Feb. 26, 1953; s. Bernard William and Judith Semel (Sogg) S.; m. Andrea Nan Acker, Jan. 27, 1979; children: Noah Gregory, Joshua Samuel. BA cum laude, Colby Coll., 1974; JD, Fordham Law Sch., 1978. Bar: N.J. 1978, N.Y. 1979, U.S. Ct. Appeals (2d and 3d cirs.) 1979, U.S. Dist. Ct. (so. and ea. dists.) N.Y. 1979, U.S. Dist. Ct. N.J. 1979, Conn. 1988. Assoc. Ratheim Hoffman et al, N.Y.C., 1978-80, Botein Hays et al, N.Y.C., 1980-84; v.p., assoc. gen. counsel, asst. sec. GE Investment Corp., Stamford, Conn., 1984—; v.p., asst. sec. GE Investment Mgmt. Inc., 1988—; v.p., gen. counsel Gindoff Enterprises Inc., 1985-90. Bd. dirs. N.Y. chpt. Juvenile Diabetes Found., N.Y.C., 1981-89, vice chmn., 1981-88; mem. fin. com. Juvenile Diabetes Found. Internat., 1981-86; asst. prin. bassist Westchester Symphony Orch., Scarsdale, N.Y., 1982—, pres., 1982-87, chmn. bd., 1982-90, exec. mng. dir., 1990-93; vice-chmn. ann. dinner NCCJ, 1987; bd. dirs. Parkinson's Disease Found., 1989-96, v.p., 1991-96; active steering com. Parkinson's Disease Soc. Am., 1991-96, merger com., 1991-96; bd. dirs. Parkinson's Action Network, 1994—; trustee Jewish Cmty. Ctr. of Harrison, 1996—. Mem. ABA (chmn. pension plan investments 1989-91, chmn. asset mgmt., 1992-94, 95—, significant legis. coms. 1985-92, chmn. subcom. on joint ventures 1988-90), Am. Coll. Real Estate Lawyers, The Corp. Bar Assn., Internat. Assn. Atty's and Execs. in Corp. Real Estate, Nat. Assn. of Real Estate Investment Mgrs. (mem. sr. legal officers adv. com. 1993—), Colby Coll. Alumni Coun. (nominating com. 1994-97), Netsuke Kenkyukai Soc. Republican. Jewish. Home: 10 Genesee Trail Harrison NY 10528-1802 Office: Gen Electric Investment Corp 3003 Summer St Stamford CT 06905-4316

STRONG, CHARLES ROBERT, waste management administrator; b. Bklyn., Aug. 9, 1935; s. Charles Stanley and Ida May (Brower) S.; m. Melba Janice Cochran, July 8, 1961; children: William Charles, Colin Brower. BSME, Yale U., 1957. Registered profl. engr., Tex. Equipment engr. Remington Arms Co., Bridgeport, Conn., 1957-60; prodn. supr. Johnson & Johnson, Decatur, Ill., 1960; prodn. and maintenance dept. mgr. Johnson & Johnson, New Brunswick, N.J., 1961-66; maintenance supt. Johnson & Johnson, Chgo., 1966-70; from maintenance & engr. plant mgr. to facility engrng. mgr Johnson & Johnson, Sherman, Tex., 1970-80; cons. engr. Acurex Solar Corp., Mountainview, Calif., 1980-83; tech. v.p. Young-Montenay, Inc., Sherman, Tex., 1983-85, Metro Energy Co., Miami, 1985-86; pres. Airko Svc. Co., Miami, 1986-87; v.p., adminstr. Montenay Power Corp., Miami, 1987—. Contbr. articles to profl. jours. Dir. Greater Texoma Utility Dist., Sherman, 1982-85; pres. Texoma Valley Coun. Boy Scouts Am., Sherman, 1980-82, Salvation Army, Sherman, 1983; chmn., bd. dirs. 1st United Meth. Ch., Sherman, 1982-84; bd. dirs. United Meth. Ch., Plantation, Fla. Recipient Silver Beaver award Boy Scouts Am., 1982. Mem. ASME, N.W. Dade Hialeah, Miami Springs C. of C. (bd. dirs., trustee 1995, 96), Rotary (program chmn. 1976-85). Republican. Methodist. Avocations: watching sports, financial planning, home projects, exercising. Office: Montenay Power Corp 6990 NW 97th Ave Miami FL 33178-2500 *Whether it be athletics or in industry, I have found that hard work and developing a good team lead to success, satisfaction and self-confidence. This then will lead to the desire for continued success.*

STRONG, DAVID F., university administrator; b. Botwood, Nfld., Can., Feb. 26, 1944; m. Lynda Joan Marshall; children: Kimberley, Joanna. B.Sc., Meml. U. Nfld., 1965; M.Sc., Lehigh U., 1967; PhD, U. Edinburgh, 1970. NRC postgrad. scholar U. Edinburgh, Scotland, 1970-72; assoc. prof. teaching and rsch. Meml. U. Nfld., 1972-74, prof., acting dept. head, 1974-75, E.W.R. Steacie fellow, 1975-77, prof. dept. earth scis. univ. rsch., 1985-90, spl. adv. to pres., 1985-87, v.p. (acad.), 1987-90; W.F. James prof. pure and applied scis. St. Francis Xavier U., N.S., 1981-82; pres., vice-chancellor U. Victoria, B.C., Can., 1990—; Swiney lectr. U. Edinburgh, 1981; mem. rsch. coun. Can. Inst. Advanced Rsch., 1986—. Editor or co-editor several books; contbr. more than 200 papers to sci. lit. Recipient Atlantic Provinces Young Scientist award (Frazer medal), 1973; NRC Can. E.W.R. Steacie fellow, 1975-77; Fgn. Exch. fellow to Japan, 1976, France, 1976-77. Fellow Geol. Assn. Can. (Past Pres.'s medal 1980), Geol. Soc. Am., Royal Soc. Can.; mem. Can. Inst. Mining and Metallurgy (Disting. Svc. award 1979, Disting Llctrs. award 1983-84), Soc. Econ. Geologists. Office: U Victoria, PO Box 1700, Victoria, BC Canada V8W 2Y2

STRONG, GARY EUGENE, librarian; b. Moscow, Idaho, June 26, 1944; s. Authur Dwight and Cleora Anna (Nirk) S.; m. Carolyn Jean Roetker, Mar. 14, 1970; children: Christopher Eric, Jennifer Rebecca. BS in Edn., U. Idaho, 1966; AMLS, U. Mich., 1967. Adminstrv. and reference asst. U. Idaho, 1963-66; extension librarian Latah County Free Library, Moscow, 1966; head librarian Markeley Residence Library, U. Mich., 1966-67; library dir. Lake Oswego (Oreg.) Public Library, 1967-73, Everett (Wash.) Public Library, 1973-76; asso. dir. services Wash. State Library, Olympia, 1976-79; dep. state librarian Wash. State Library, 1979-80; state librarian Calif. State Library, Sacramento, 1980-94; dir. Queens Borough Pub. Libr., Jamaica, 1994—; dir. emeritus Calif. State Library Found., 1994—; chief exec. Calif. Libr. Svcs. Bd., 1980-94; founder, bd. dirs. Calif. State Libr. Found., 1982-94, Calif. Literary Campaign, 1984-94, Calif. Rsch. Bur., 1992; bd. dirs. No. Regional Libr. Bd., 1983-94, Queens Libr. Found., 1994—; mem. adv. bd. Ctr. for Book in Libr. of Congress, 1983-86; mem. nat. adv. com. Libr. of Congress, 1987-89; chmn. adv. bd. Calif. Libr. Constrn. and Renovation Bond Act Bd., 1989-94; vis. lectr. Marylhurst Coll., Oreg., 1968, Oreg. Divsn. Continuing Edn., 1972, San Jose State U. Sch. Libr. Svc., 1990; mem. N.Y. State Adv. Coun. Librs., 1996—; mem. chancellor's task froce ednl. tech. and librs. CUNY, 1996—; mem. N.Y. Pub. Librs. Conf. World Libr. Leaders, 1996; lectr. and cons. in field. Host, producer: cable TV Signatures Program, 1974-76, nationwide videoconfs. on illiteracy, censorship, 1985; author: On Reading-in the Year of the Reader, 1987; editor Calif. State Library Found. Bull., 1982-94 (H.W. Wilson Periodical award 1988), Western Americana in the Calif. State Library, 1986, On Reading-In the Year of the Reader, 1987, Chinatown Photographer: Louis J. Stellman, 1989, Local History Genealogical Resources, 1990, Literate America Emerging, 1991; contbr. articles to profl. jours.; editor, designer and pub. of various books. Bd. dirs., v.p. Pacific N.W. Bibliog. Ctr., 1977-80; bd. dirs. Thurston Mason County Mental Health Ctr., 1977-80, pres., 1979-80; bd. dirs. Coop. Library Agy. for Systems and Services, 1980-94, vice chmn., 1981-84; bd. dirs. Sr. Services Snohomish County, 1973-76, HISPANEX (Calif. Spanish lang. database), 1983-86; bd. govs. Snohomish County Hist. Assn., 1974-76; mem. psychiat. task force St. Peters Hosp., Olympia, 1979-80; co-founder Calif.

Ctr. for the Book, bd. dirs., 1987-94; mem. adv. bd. Calif. State PTA, 1981-86, Gov.'s Tech. Conf., 1993-94; mem. adv. com. Sch. Libr. Sci., UCLA, 1991-94, Sch. Libr. and Info. Studies, U. Calif., Berkeley, 1991-94, Libr. Sch. Queens Coll., 1996—, libr. sch. St. John's U., 1996—; mem. Oreg. Coun. Pub. Broadcasting, 1969-73, Calif. Adult Edn. Steering Com., 1988-94, N.Y. State Adv. Coun. on Librs., 1996—; chmn. collaborative coun. Calif. State Literacy Resource Ctr., 1993-94; bd. dirs. Queens coun. Boy Scouts of Am., 1994—; mem. Chancellor's Task Force on Ednl. Tech. and Librs., CUNY, 1996—; participant N.Y. Pub. Libr. Conf. of World Libr. Leaders, 1996. Oreg. Libr. scholar, 1966; recipient Disting. Alumnus award U. Mich., 1984, Disting. Svc. award Calif. Literacy Inc., 1985, Spl. Achievement award Literacy Action, 1988, Assn. Specialized and Coop. Libr. Agys. Exceptional Achievement award 1992, Gov.'s award of Achievement Govt. Tech. Conf., 1994, Advancement of Literacy award Pub. Libr. Assn., 1994, John Cotton Dana award Libr. Adminstrn. and Mgmt. Assn., 1994; named Libr. of Yr. Calif. Assn. Libr. Trustees and Commrs., 1994, Disting. Svc. award Chinese Am. Libr. Assn., 1996. Mem. ALA (legis. com. 1980-82, 95—, chair intellectual property subcom. 1995—, rep. nat. organizing com. 1996—, chmn. conf. librs. Beijing 1996, Commn. on Freedom and Equality of Access to Info. 1983-86), Am. Printing History Assn., Libr. Adminstrn. and Mgmt. Assn. (bd. dirs. 1980-88, pres. 1984-85), N.Y. Libr. Assn., Oreg. Libr. Assn. (hon. life mem., pres. 1970-71), Pacific N.W. Libr. Assn. (hon. life mem., pres. 1978-79), Calif. Libr. Assn. (govt. rels. com. 1980-94), Chief Officers of State Libr. Agys. (pres. 1984-86), Western Coun. State Librs. (pres. 1989-91), Assn. Specialized and Coop. Libr. Agys., Queens County C. of C. (bd. dirs. 1996—), Greater Jamaica Devel. Corp., Everett Area C. of C. (bd. dirs. 1974-76), METRO (bd. dirs. 1995—, treas. 1996—), Book Club of Calif., Sacramento Book Collectors Club, Roxburghe Club, The Book Collectors Club of L.A., Grolier Club, Guild of Book Workers. Office: Queens Borough Pub Libr 89-11 Merrick Blvd Jamaica NY 11432-5200

STRONG, HENRY, foundation executive; b. Rochester, N.Y., Oct. 6, 1923; s. L. Corrin and Alice (Trowbridge) S.; m. Malan Swing, June 30, 1951; children: Sigrid Anne, Barbara Kirk, Dana Elizabeth, Henry Lockwood. A.B., Williams Coll., 1949. Joined Fgn. Service, 1950; with State Dept., 1950-51; vice consul The Hague, 1951-54, Washington, 1954-55; 2d sec. U.S. Embassy, Copenhagen, 1955-58, State Dept., 1958-62, Djakarta, Indonesia, 1962-64; resigned, 1968; chmn. bd., pres. Hattie M. Strong Found., 1968—. Mem. D.C. Commn. Arts, 1968-75; mem. D.C. Bd. Higher Edn., 1973-76; vice chmn. bd. trustees J.F. Kennedy Ctr. for Performing Arts, 1975-90, hon. trustee, 1991—; bd. dirs. Nat. Symphony Orch., Pomfret Sch., Fed. City Coun., M.M. Post Found. D.C., Community Found. of Greater Washington, 1974-91, Mt. Vernon Coll., 1969-88, 91—, Nat. Capital chpt. ARC, 1994—. Republican. Episcopalian. Clubs: Chevy Chase; Metropolitan (Washington); Gibson Island (Md.). Home: 5039 Overlook Rd NW Washington DC 20016-1911 Office: Hattie M Strong Found 1620 I St NW Ste 700 Washington DC 20006-4005

STRONG, JAMES THOMPSON, management, security, human resources consultant; b. Boca Raton, Fla., Oct. 26, 1945; s. Earl William and Mary Joe (Thompson) S.; m. Lenore Jean Stager, Feb. 2, 1974; 1 child, Daria Nicole. BA in Polit. Sci., U. Calif., Riverside, 1973; MS in Strategic Intelligence, Def. Intelligence Coll., Washington, 1982. Factoring specialist. Commd. USAF, 1968, advaned through grades to maj., ret., 1990; faculty Def. Intelligence Coll., Washington, 1982-86; dir. translations USAF, 1986-88, dir. info. svcs., 1988-90; proprietary security mgr. McDonnell-Douglas Technologies, San Diego, 1990-92; owner Employment Svcs. for Bus., San Diego, 1995—; adj. prof. internat. rels. U.S. Internat. U., 1996—, internat. bus. Palomar Coll.; factor broker. Author: The Basic Industrial Counter-Espionage Cookbook, 1993, The Government Contractor's OPSEC Cookbook, 1993; co-author: The Military Intelligence Community, 1985; mem. bd. editors Internat. Jour. Intelligence and Counterintelligence, 1986—; contbr. articles to profl. jours. Recipient Disting. EEO award USAF, 1987, Def. Meritorious Svc. medal 1986, Meritorious Svc. medal, 1981, 90, Joint Svc. Commendation medal Def. Intelligence Agy./NATO, 1982, 85. Mem. Nat. Mil. Intelligence Assn. (bd. dirs. 1984—, chpt. pres. 1989, 94), Ops. Security Profls. Soc. (chpt. chair 1993, 94-96), Nat. Cargo Security Coun., San Diego Roundtable (exec. coord. 1994, 95), Assn. Former Intelligence Officers (nat. scholarship adminstr. 1994—), Am. Soc. for Indsl. Security, Air Force Assn., San Diego Soc. for Human Resource Mgmt. Republican. Avocations: bridge, golf, reading. Home and Office: Applicant Background Checks 1142 Miramonte Glen Escondido CA 92026

STRONG, JOHN DAVID, insurance company executive; b. Cortland, N.Y., Apr. 12, 1936; s. Harold A. and Helen H. S.; m. Carolyn Dimmick, Oct. 26, 1957; children: John David Jr., Suzanne. BS, Syracuse U., N.Y., 1957; postgrad, Columbia U., 1980. With Kemper Group, 1957-90, Kemper Corp., 1990-96, Empire div. sales mgr., 1972-74, exec. v.p. Fed. Kemper Ins. Co., Decatur, Ill., 1974-79, pres., bd. dirs., 1979-93, CEO, 1988-93, chmn. bd., 1989-93; vice chmn. Millikin Assocs., 1993-96, chmn., 1996—; exec. v.p., dir. Facilitators, Inc., 1995—; bd. dirs. First of Am. Bank, Decatur, 1994. Mem. adv. council Sch. Bus. Millikin U., 1975-79, 84—; bd. dirs. United Way of Decatur and Macon County, Ill., 1976-83, campaign chmn., 1978-79, pres. bd. dirs., 1979-81; pres. United Way of Ill., 1981-83; bd. dirs. DMH Commn. Svcs. Corp., 1985—, chmn., 1988-90; bd. dirs. Decatur-Macon County Econ. Devel. Found., 1983-88, DMH Health Systems, 1987-94, Richland C.C. Found., 1987-90, Symphony Ord. Guild of Decatur, 1992-96, DMH Found., 1988—; bd. dirs. Ill. Ednl. Devel. Found., 1983-90, pres., 1986-87; bd. dirs. Decatur Meml. Hosp., 1985-94, vice-chmn., 1988, chmn. 1990-92; bd. dir. Ctrl. Ill. Health Assocs., Inc., 1994, vice chmn. 1994-96; mem. steering com. Decatur Advantage, 1981-93, pres., 1988-93. Capt. USAR, 1958-69. Mem. Metro Decatur C. of C. (bd. dirs. 1977-80, 2d vice chmn. 1981-82, 1st vice chmn. 1982-83, chmn. 1983-84), Alpha Kappa Psi. Club: Decatur (bd. dirs. 1980-83, pres. 1983), Country of Decatur (bd. dirs. 1993—, pres. bd. 1995—). Office: Ste 366 First Am Ctr 250 N Water St Decatur IL 62523-1326

STRONG, JOHN SCOTT, finance educator; b. Phila., Aug. 28, 1956; s. John S. and Thelma J. (Willard) S. BS, Washington & Lee U., 1978; M of Pub. Policy, Harvard U., 1981, PhD in Bus. Econs., 1986. Rsch. fellow Harvard U., Cambridge, Mass., 1983-85, 89-90, 93, vis. asst. prof. econs., 1989-90; prof. fin. Coll. William and Mary, Williamsburg, Va., 1985—; cons. on econs. and fin. Republic of Indonesia, 1987—, MITI, Japan, 1988-89, European Bank for Reconstruction and Devel., 1993-95, Govt. of Bolivia, 1994, Govt. of Russia, 1996, Govts. of Brazil, Argentina and Uruguay, 1997. Author: Why Airplanes Crash: Aviation Safety in a Changing World, 1992, Moving to Market: Restructuring Transport in the Former Soviet Union, 1996; co-author 2 books on airline deregulation; contbr. articles to profl. jours. Fulbright scholar, 1978-79; grad. fellow NSF, 1979-82. Office: Coll William & Mary Sch Bus Williamsburg VA 23187

STRONG, JOHN WILLIAM, lawyer, educator; b. Iowa City, Aug. 18, 1935; s. Frank Ransom and Gertrude Elizabeth (Way) S.; m. Margaret Waite Cleary, June 16, 1962; children—Frank Ransom, Benjamin Waite. B.A., Yale U., 1957; J.D., U. Ill., 1962; postgrad, U. N.C., 1966-67. Bar: Ill. 1963, Oreg. 1976. Assoc. firm LeForgee, Samuels, Miller, Schroeder & Jackson, Decatur, Ill., 1963-64; asst. prof. law U. Kans., 1964-66; assoc. prof. Duke U., 1966-69; prof. U. Oreg., 1969-75; legal counsel Oreg. Task Force on Med. Malpractice, 1976; prof. U. Nebr., 1977-84, dean, 1977-81, vice chancellor for acad. affairs, 1981-84; Rosenstiel Disting. prof. law U. Ariz., 1984—; nat. sec.-treas. Order of the Coif, 1992—; cons. Nat. Judicial Coll. Author: (with others) Handbook on Evidence, 4th edit., 1992. Served with U.S. Army, 1957-59. Mem. Ill. Bar Assn., Oreg. Bar Assn., ABA, Am. Law Inst., Phi Delta Phi. Republican. Congregationalist. Home: 3220 E 3rd St Tucson AZ 85716-4233 Office: U Ariz Coll Law Tucson AZ 85721

STRONG, MARVIN E., JR., state official. Sec. Ky. Econ. Devel. Cabinet, Frankfort. Office: State of Ky Econ Devel Cabinet Capital Plz Tower 24th Fl 500 Mero St Frankfort KY 40601-1957

STRONG, ROBERT S., banker; b. N.Y.C., Jan. 27, 1949; s. Henry William and Ida Anna (Krone) S.; m. Virginia Hala, June 11, 1994; children: Lauren, Jennifer, Tracy, Emily. BA in Econs., Columbia U., 1971; MBA in Fin., NYU, 1977. Lending officer Chase Manhattan Corp., N.Y.C., 1973-77; v.p. Chase Manhattan Bank, N.Y.C., 1977-88, sr. v.p., 1988-91, sector exec., 1991—, exec. v.p., 1993—; chief credit officer Chase Manhattan Corp., N.Y.C., 1995—. Episcopalian. Office: Chase Manhattan Corp 270 Park Ave New York NY 10017-2014

STRONG, ROGER LEE, mathematics educator; b. Sturgis, Mich., May 22, 1936; s. Ronald George and Mildred (Hamacher) S.; m. Shirley Anne Knight, Apr. 20, 1958 (div. Apr. 1984); children: Rachelle, Kevin, Todd, David; m. Beverly Ann Stoops, July, 1984. BA, Eastern Mich. U., 1961; MA, U. Mich., 1964, PhD, 1975. Cert. secondary tchr., Mich. Tchr. high sch. math. Livonia (Mich.) Pub. Sch.s, 1961-88; assoc. prof. math. Francis Marion U., Florence, S.C., 1988—; adj. asst. prof. math. U. Mich., Dearborn, 1984-88; cons. Sumter (S.C.) Pub. Schs., 1990, Darlington (S.C.) Pub. Schs., 1992, Mullins (S.C.) Pub. Schs., 1997. Author: Numerical Trigonometry, 1969. With USMC, 1956-58. Named Golf Coach of Yr., Mich., 1985, Florence Educator of Yr., Optimist Club, 1993; NSF fellow, 1968-69. Mem. Math. Assn. Am., Nat. Coun. Tchrs. Math., S.C. Coun. Tchrs. Math., Country Club S.C. Episcopalian. Avocations: golf, gardening, bird watching. Home: 3728 Palmer Dr Florence SC 29506-8312 Office: Francis Marion U Dept Math Florence SC 29501

STRONG, SARA DOUGHERTY, psychologist, family and custody mediator; b. Phila., May 30, 1927; d. Augustus Joseph and Orpha Elizabeth (Dock) Dougherty; m. David Mather Strong, Dec. 21, 1954. BA in Psychology, Pa. State U., 1949; MA in Clin. Psychology, Temple U., 1960, postgrad., 1968-72; cert. in Family Therapy, Family Inst. Phila., 1978. Lic. psychologist, Pa. Med. br. psychologist Family Ct. Phila., 1960-85, asst. chief psychologist, 1985-88, chief psychologist, 1988-92; retired, 1992; pvt. practice Phila., 1992—; cons. St. Joseph's Home for Girls, Phila., 1963-84, Daughters of Charity of St. Vincent De Paul, Albany, N.Y., 1965-90. Mem. APA (assoc.), Am. Assn. Marriage and Family Therapists, Pa. Psychol. Assn., Nat. Register of Health Svc. Providers in Psychology, Family Inst. Phila. Democrat. Avocations: reading, dramatic productions, writing, Yoga.

STRONGIN, THEODORE, journalist; b. N.Y.C., Dec. 10, 1918; s. Isadore and Ida (Slevin) S.; m. Ruth Klein, Aug. 13, 1947 (dec. 1954); children: Deborah, Daniel Otto; m. Harriet Stern Rosenberg, Oct. 4, 1969 (dec. 1991). Student, Harvard, 1935-37; A.B., Bard Coll., 1941; postgrad., Juilliard Sch. Music, summers 1940, 41, fall 1946, Columbia, 1947-49. Dir. music East Woods Sch., Oyster Bay, N.Y., 1947-54; mem. music faculty Bennington (Vt.) Coll., 1954-56, Dartmouth, spring 1955; arts editor Chattanooga Times, 1957-61, Albany (N.Y.) Knickerbocker News, 1961-63; music critic, reporter, record reviewer N.Y. Times, 1963-65, music critic, reporter, recs. editor, 1965-71; columnist East Hampton (N.Y.) Star, 1972-77; Cons. Music in Our Time series, N.Y.C., 1972-73, N.Y. State Council on Arts, 1970, various art instns., 1971-77. Composer: Suite for Unaccompanied Cello, 1951, Quartet for Oboe and Strings, 1952; Author: Casals, 1966. Mem. Amagansett Village Improvement Soc., 1974-86; mem. Amagansett Residents Assn., 1975-86, bd. dirs., pres., 1975-77; dir. pub. relations Ind. Voters of East Hampton, 1971. Served to capt. AUS, 1941-46. Recipient Broude Publ. prize for piano piece, 1948. Democrat. Address: RR 1 Box 70 Brevard NC 28712-9772

STRONG-TIDMAN, VIRGINIA ADELE, marketing and advertising executive; b. Englewood, N.J., July 26, 1947; d. Alan Ballentine and Virginia Leona (Harris) Strong; m. John Fletcher Tidman, Sept. 23, 1978. BS, Albright Coll., Reading, Pa., 1969; postgrad. U. Pitts., 1970-73, U. Louisville, 1975-76. Exec. trainee Pomeroy's div. Allied Stores, Reading, 1969-70; mktg. rsch. analyst Heinz U.S.A., Pitts., 1970-74; new products mktg. mgr. Ky. Fried Chicken, Louisville, 1974-76; dir. Pitts. office M/A/R/C, 1976-79; assoc. rsch. dir. Henderson Advt., Inc., Greenville, S.C., 1979-81; sr. v.p., dir. rsch. Bozell, Jacobs, Kenyon & Eckhardt, Inc., Dallas, 1981-86, sr. v.p., dir. rsch. and strategic planning Atlanta, 1986-88; sr. v.p., dir. mktg. svcs. Bozell, Inc., Atlanta, 1988-91; sr. v.p., mng. ptnr. Henderson Adv., Inc., 1991-95; prin. Ender-Ptnr., Inc., 1995-96; v.p. mktg. Booth Rsch. Svcs., Inc., 1996—; cons. mktg. rsch. Greenville Zool. Soc., 1981; adj. prof. So. Meth. U., 1984-85. Mem. Am. Mktg. Assn. (Effie award N.Y. chpt. 1982). Republican. Episcopalian. Home: 1835 Johnson Ferry Rd Atlanta GA 30319-1922

STROOCK, DANIEL WYLER, mathematician, educator; b. N.Y.C., Mar. 20, 1940; s. Alan Maxwell and Katherine (Wyler) S.; m. Lucy Barber, Nov. 21, 1962; children: Benjamin, Abraham. AB, Harvard Coll., 1962; PhD, Rockefeller U., 1966. Vis. mem. Courant Inst., N.Y. U., 1966-69, asst. prof., 1969-72; asso. prof. math. U. Colo., Boulder, 1972-75; prof. U. Colo., 1975-84, chmn. dept. math, 1979-81; prof. math. MIT, 1984—; adj. prof. U. Colo., Beijing Normal U. Author: (with S.R.S. Varadhan) Multidimensional Diffusion Processes, 1979, (with J.D. Deutschel) Large Deviations, 1989, Probability Theory, An Analytic View, 1993; editor Math. Zeitschrift, 1992—, Ill. Jour. Math., 1976-82, Transactions of Am. Math. Soc., 1974-80, Annals of Probability, 1988-93, Advances in Math., 1995—, Jour. Functional Analysis, 1994—; contbr. articles on probability theory to profl. jours. Guggenheim fellow, 1978-79. Mem. Am. Acad. Arts and Scis., Nat. Acad. Scis. Democrat. Jewish. Home: 55 Frost St Cambridge MA 02140-2247 Office: MIT Dept Math Cambridge MA 02139

STROOCK, MARK EDWIN, II, public relations company executive; b. N.Y.C., Nov. 6, 1922; s. Irving Sylvan and Blanche (Loeb) S.; m. Hanna Marks Eiseman, June 24, 1945; children—Mark E., Carolyn E. B.A., Bard Coll., 1947. Reporter The New York Journal of Commerce, 1947-50; writer Barrons, N.Y.C., 1950-51; mng. editor Fairchild Publication, N.Y.C., 1952-53; bus. editor World Mag., N.Y.C., 1953-54; contbg. editor Time Mag., N.Y.C., 1954-56; with Young & Rubicam Inc., N.Y.C., 1956-87, sr. v.p., dir. corporate rels., cons., 1987—. Bd. trustee N.Y. Urban League, 1971-78, Alvin Ailey Dance Theatre, N.Y.C., 1977-84, Friends of the Theatre Mus. City N.Y., 1977-85; vice chmn. Covenant House, N.Y.C., 1978-90; exec. com., mktg. and communications com., assoc. nat. commr. Anti-Defamation League, 1992—. Served with U.S. Army, 1943-46. Democrat. Jewish. Home: 50 Park Ave New York NY 10016-3075 Office: Young & Rubicam Inc 285 Madison Ave New York NY 10017-6401

STROOCK, THOMAS FRANK, manufacturing company executive; b. N.Y.C., Oct. 10, 1925; s. Samuel and Dorothy (Frank) S.; m. Marta Freyre de Andrade, June 19, 1949; children: Margaret, Sandra, Elizabeth, Anne. BA in Econs., Yale U., 1948; LLB (hon.) U. Wyo., 1995. Landman Stanolind Oil & Gas Co., Tulsa, 1948-52; pres. Stroock Leasing Corp., Casper, Wyo., 1952-89, Alpha Exploration, Inc., 1980-89; ptnr. Stroock, Rogers & Dymond, Casper, 1960-82; dir. Wyo. Bancorp., Cheyenne, First Wyo. Bank, Casper; mem. Wyo. Senate, 1967-69, 71-75, 79-89, chmn. appropriations com. 1983, co-chmn. joint appropriations com., 1983-89, mem. mgmt. and audit com. P; mem. steering com. Edn. Commn. of States; amb. to Guatemala, Govt. of U.S., 1989-92; pres. Alpha Devel. Corp., 1992—; prof. pub. diplomacy U. Wyo., Casper, 1993—. Rep. precinct committeeman, 1950-68; pres. Natrona County Sch. Bd., 1960-69; pres. Wyo. State Sch. Bds. Assn., 1965-66; chmn. Casper Community Recreation, 1955-60; chmn. Natrona County United Fund, 1963-64; chmn. Wyo. State Republican Com., 1975-78, exec. com. 1954-60; delegate Rep. Nat. Convetion, 1956, 76; regional coord. campaign George Bush for pres., 1979-80, 87-88; chmn. Western States Rep. Chmn. Assn., 1977-78; chmn. Wyo. Higher Edn. Commn., 1969-71; mem. Nat. Petroleum Council, 1972-77; chmn. trustees Sierra Madre Found. for Geol. Research, New Haven; chmn. Wyo. Nat. Gas Pipeline Authority 1987-88; bd. dirs. Ucross Found., Denver; mem. Nat. Pub. Lands Adv. Council, 1981-85; chmn. Wyo. Health Reform Commn., 1993-95. Served with USMC, 1943-46. Mem. Rocky Mountain Oil and Gas Assn., Petroleum Assn. Wyo. Republican. Unitarian. Lodge: Kiwanis. Clubs: Casper Country; Casper Petroleum; Denver. Home and Office: PO Box 2875 Casper WY 82602-2875

STROPNICKY, GERARD PATRICK, theater director, consultant; b. Teaneck, N.J., Aug. 25, 1953; s. John F. and Elizabeth M. (Novotny) S.; m. Kathleen Horkay Baas, Aug. 16, 1987; children: Diane, William. BSc in Speech, Northwestern U., 1976. Founding mem. Bloomsburg (Pa.) Theatre Ensemble, 1978—, ensemble dir., 1993-96; cons. Fedapt, N.Y.C., 1984-89; cons. theatre design Bristol (Pa.) Riverside Theatre, 1986-87, F.M. Kirby Ctr., Wilkes Barre, Pa., 1988; guest dir. Fla. Shakespeare Festival, Coral Gables, 1986-87, Touchstone Theatre, Bethlehem, Pa., 1989, 91. Pa. Playwright fellow, 1991. Mem. Theatre Assn. Pa. (bd. dirs. 1991-94), Bucknell Univ. Assn. Arts (bd. dirs. 1989—). Office: Bloomsburg Theatre Ensemble 226 Center St Bloomsburg PA 17815-1752

STROSAHL, WILLIAM AUSTIN, artist, art director; b. N.Y.C., June 11, 1910; s. William August and Margaret Theresa (Peterson) S.; m. Rosemary Rachel Jordan, May 28, 1949 (dec. Dec. 1989); children: Timothy, Brian, William, Jordan, Margaret. Student, Parsons Sch. Design, 1926-27. Cub cartoonist N.Y. Evening Graphic, N.Y.C., 1927-28; art dir. Ohio Match Co., N.Y.C., 1928-29, Lindsay Assoc. Artists, N.Y.C., 1929-30; asst. art dir. J. Walter Thompson, N.Y.C., 1930-32, art dir., 1932-42; exec. art dir. William Esty Co., N.Y.C., 1942-55, creative dir., exec. v.p., 1956-69, watercolor painter, 1969—. Recipient Gold medal Allied Artist Am., 1965, 88; recipient Hallmark Audubon Artists, 1959, Gold and Silver medal Audubon Artists, 1980, Nat. Acad. Design, John Pike Meml. award, 1985, Ogden Pleisner Meml. award, 1987, William A. Paton Meml. prize, 1988, Creative Watercolor awards, 1990-91, 200 Yrs. Watercolor Painting award Met. Mus. Art, N.Y.C., 58 other awards for watercolor painting, 1946-90. Fellow Dolphin Fellowship; mem. Am. Watercolor Soc. (v.p. 1950), Am. Watercolor Soc. (hon. pres. 1983—), Nat. Art Dirs. Assn. (v.p. 1954), Nat. Acad. Design, Academician 1994—, Silvermine Guild, Allied Artists Am., Audubon Artists. Republican. Home: 301 Haviland Rd Stamford CT 06903-3324

STROSCIO, MICHAEL ANTHONY, physicist, educator; b. Winston-Salem, N.C., June 1, 1949; s. Anthony and Norma Lee (Sidbury) S.; children: Elizabeth de Clare, Charles Marshall Sidbury, Gautam Dutta. BS, U. N.C., 1970; MPhil in Physics, Yale U., 1972, PhD in Physics, 1974. Physicist Los Alamos Sci. Lab., N.Mex., 1975-78; sr. staff mem. Johns Hopkins U. Applied Physics Lab., Laurel, Md., 1978-80; prof. mgr. for electromagnetic research Air Force Office of Sci. Research, Washington, 1980-83; spl. asst. to research dir. Office of Under Sec. Def., Washington, 1982-83; policy analyst White House Office of Sci. and Tech. Policy, Washington, 1983-85; prof. dir. for microelectrons, prin. scientist U.S. Army Research Office, Research Triangle Park, N.C., 1985—; adj. prof. depts. physics and elec. and computer engring. N.C. State U., Raleigh, 1985—; adj. prof. depts. elec. engring. and physics Duke U., Durham, 1986—; vis. prof. dept. of elec. engring. U. Va., Charlottesville, 1990-95, U. Md., College Park, 1996—; mem. Congrl. Coun., 1989-91; lectr. UCLA, 1987, U. Mich., 1988; cons. U.S. Dept. Energy, Washington, 1985—; vice chmn. White House Panel on Sci. Communication, Washington, 1983-84; chmn. Dept. Def. Rsch. Instrumentation Com., Washington, 1982; assoc. mem. Adv. Group on Electron Devices, 1985-91, liaison Nat. Laser Users Facility, Rochester, N.Y., 1984; liaison Panel on Sci. Comm. and Nat. Security, NAS, 1982, Panel on Materials for High-Density Electron Packaging, 1987-90; U.S. Army liaison to JASON, 1991—; mem. U.S. Govt. coord. com. on Semiconductor Rsch. Corp., 1992—. Author: Positronium: A Review of the Theory, 1975, Onslow Families, 1977; reviewer NSF, Office of Naval Rsch., Dept. Commerce and the Natural Scis., Engring. Rsch. Coun. Can., 1981—; referee jours.; contbr. articles to profl. jours.; patentee in field. Served to capt. USAF, 1974-75. Los Alamos Sci. Lab. grantee, 1977. Fellow IEEE (exec. com. for plasma sci. 1983—), Yale Sci. and Engring. Assn. (exec. bd. dirs. 1983—); mem. Am. Phys. Soc., Phi Beta Kappa, Nat. Geneal. Soc. Home: 1921 Thorpshire Dr Raleigh NC 27615-3738 Office: US Army Research Office PO Box 12211 Durham NC 27709-2211

STROSS, JEOFFREY KNIGHT, physician, educator; b. Detroit, May 2, 1941; s. Julius Knight and Molly Ellen (Fishman) S.; m. Ellen Nora Schwartz, May 22, 1965; children: Wendy, Jonathan. BS in Pharmacy, U. Mich., 1962, MD, 1967. Diplomate Am. Bd. Internal Medicine. Intern Univ. Mich. Hosp., Ann Arbor, 1967-68, resident in internal medicine, 1971-73; instr. internal medicine U. Mich., Ann Arbor, 1973-74, asst. prof., 1974-79, assoc. prof., 1979-87, prof., 1987—; cons. Merck Sharp Dohme Co., West Point, Pa., 1982—, U.S. Dept. State, Washington, 1976—. Contbr. numerous articles to med. jours. Served to maj. USAF, 1969-71. Nat. Heart, Lung and Blood Inst. grantee, 1975—. Fellow ACP; mem. Soc. for Gen. Internal Medicine (regional chmn. 1984-86). Jewish. Home: 3541 Larchmont Dr Ann Arbor MI 48105-2853 Office: Univ of Mich Med Sch 246 Med Inn Bldg Ann Arbor MI 48109

STROTE, JOEL RICHARD, lawyer; b. N.Y.C., Apr. 19, 1939; s. Jack and Fortuna (Benezra) S.; children: Jared, Noah, Sebastian; m. Elisa Ballestas, Dec. 14, 1991. BA, U. Mich., 1960; JD, Northwestern U., 1963. Bar: N.Y. 1964, D.C. 1965, Calif. 1967, U.S. Dist. Ct. (cen. dist.) Calif. 1967, U.S. Supreme Ct. 1971. Assoc. Damman, Blank, Hirsh & Heming, N.Y.C., 1964-65, ICC, Washington, 1965-66, Capitol Records, Hollywood, Calif., 1966-67; ptnr. Strote & Whitehouse, Beverly Hills, Calif., 1967-89; of counsel Selvin, Weiner & Ruben, Beverly Hills, Calif., 1989-94; ptnr. with Cohen, Strote & Young, 1992-94; sole practice law, 1994—; judge pro tem L.A. County Mcpl. Ct., 1973—; probation monitor Calif. State Bar Ct., L.A., 1985—; pres. Liberace Found., Las Vegas, Nev., 1987—; bd. chmn. Tuesday's Child, L.A., 1989-91. Cpl. USMC, 1963-64. Mem. Calif. State Bar Assn., L.A. County Bar Assn., L.A. Copyright Soc., Beverly Hills Bar Assn., Assn. Internat. Entertainment Lawyers, Internat. Fedn. of Festival Orgns. Democrat. Jewish. Avocations: swimming, bicycling, hiking, opera, travel. Office: Joel R Strote Profl Corp 21700 Oxnard St Ste 340 Woodland Hills CA 91367-3665

STROTHER, ALLEN, biochemical pharmacologist, researcher; b. Nolan County, Tex., Feb. 20, 1928; s. Henry Allen and Minnie Etta (Taylor) S.; m. Julia Ann Gutch, Feb. 7, 1957; children: Wesley Allen, Lori Ann. BS, Tex. Tech. U., 1955; MS, U. Calif., 1957; PhD, Tex. A&M U., 1963. Rsch. asst. Tex. A&M, Coll. Sta., 1959-63; rsch. biochemist FDA, Washington, 1963-65; asst. prof. pharmacology Loma Linda (Calif.) U., 1965-70, assoc. prof., 1970-75, prof., 1975-95, retired, vol. faculty, 1995—, prof. emeritus Physiology and Pharmacology, 1997—; cons. WHO, Geneva, 1982-86. Contbr. numerous articles to profl. jours.; chpt. to WHO Bull. Pilot CAP/USAF Search and Rescue San Bernardino, Calif., 1967-75; pilot examiner CAP Air Force Aux., Norton AFB, 1970-86. Named Investigator of Yr. Walter E. McPherson Soc., Loma Linda U., 1984, Basic Sci. Fellow of Yr., 1986. Mem. Am. Soc. Pharmacology and Exptl. Therapeutics, Am. Chem. Soc., Xzenobiotic Soc. Avocations: flying, golf. Home: 74448 Nevada Cir E Palm Desert CA 92260-2269 Office: Loma Lind U Sch Medicine Loma Linda CA 92354

STROTHER, JAY D., legal editor; b. Wichita, Kans., May 31, 1967; m. Cynthia L. Mehnert, Sept. 7, 1991. BA, U. Tulsa, 1989. Editor U.S. Jr. C. of C., Tulsa, 1990-93, Assn. Legal Adminstrs., Vernon Hills, Ill., 1993—; editor-in-chief Legal Mgmt. Mag. Author: ALA News. Mem. Internat. Assn. Bus. Communicators (bd. dirs., suburban v.p. 1994—). Office: Assn Legal Adminstrs 175 E Hawthorn Pkwy Vernon Hills IL 60061-1463

STROTHER, PATRICK JOSEPH, public relations executive; b. St. Louis, Dec. 14, 1953; s. Arch Oscar Strother and Mary Margaret Boyle; m. Patricia Henning; children: Sara Ann, Ryan Joseph. BS with distinction, U. Minn., 1978; MBA, U. St. Thomas, St. Paul, 1982. V.p. investor rels. First Bank System, Mpls., 1983-90; pres. Cevette and Co. Advt. and Pub. Rels., Mpls., 1990-92; founder Strother Comms. (Rowland Worldwide affiliate), St. Paul, 1992; pres., gen. mgr. Rowland Worldwide Pub. Rels. Co.-Midwest, St. Paul, 1993-95; pres., CEO Strother Comm. Group, Mpls., 1995—; adj. prof. Coll. St. Thomas, St. Paul, 1984-86, Coll. St. Catherine, St. Paul, 1986-92. Mem. Pub. Rels. Soc. Am., Nat. Investor Rels. Inst. Avocations: 6 and 12 string guitars, studio recording, weightlifting, reading, cycling.

STROTHMAN, JAMES EDWARD, editor; b. Pitts., Mar. 27, 1939; s. Edward Charles and Harriet Hope (Jones) S.; m. Eleanor Shawfield Jacobs, Sept. 9, 1961; children—Joseph, Jill, Stuart. B.A. in Journalism, Pa. State U., 1961. Asst. city editor, city hall reporter Williamsport Grit, Pa., 1961-64; with Miami Herald, Fla., 1964-67; aerospace writer AP, Cape Kennedy, Fla., 1967-69; reporter Los Angeles bur. Electronic News, 1969-71, sr. editor computer news sect., 1971-73, mng. editor, 1973; sr. info. rep. corp. hdqrs., then program adminstr. data processing div. hdqrs. IBM Corp., 1973-77, mgr. eastern area communications data processing div., 1977-79, field communications mgr. data processing div., 1979-81, mgr. communications research div., 1981; free-lance writer and cons. Strothman Assocs., 1981-82; editor-in-chief MIS Week, N.Y.C., 1982-88; free-lance writer, cons., 1988-89; editor-in-chief Computer Pictures, Chappaqua, N.Y., 1989—; editor-in-chief

InTech Mag. Instrument Soc. Am., Research Triangle Park, N.C., 1994—. Episcopalian.

STROTHMAN, WENDY JO, book publisher; b. Pitts., July 29, 1950; d. Walter Richard and Mary Ann (Hodtum) S.; m. Mark Kavanaugh Metzger, Nov. 25, 1978; children: Andrew Richard, Margaret Ann. Student, U. Chgo., 1979-80; AB, Brown U., 1972. Copywriter, mktg. U. Chgo. Press, 1973-76, editor, 1977-80, gen. editor, 1980-83, asst. dir., 1983; dir. Beacon Press, Boston, 1983-95; v.p., pub. adult, trade and reference Houghton-Mifflin, Boston, 1995-96, exec. v.p. trade and reference divsn., 1996—; trustee Brown U., 1990-96. Edtl. adv. bd. Scholarly Pub., 1993-94; bd. editors Brown Alumni Monthly, 1983-89; chmn., 1986-89. Bd. dirs. Editorial Project for Edn., trustee, 1987-91, treas., 1988-90. Mem. Renaissance Soc. (bd. dirs. 1980-83), Assn. Am. Pubs. (Freedom to Read com.), Pubs. Lunch Club (N.Y.C.), PEN New Eng. (adv. bd.), Examiner Club, NacRe Reins. Corp. (bd. dirs.). Office: Houghton Mifflin Co 222 Berkeley St Boston MA 02116-3748

STROUD, JAMES STANLEY, lawyer; b. Wimbledon, N.D., Jan. 26, 1915; s. Herbert Montgomery and Amanda Getchell (Longfellow) S.; m. Marjorie Marsh Hovey, Sept. 11, 1940; children: Jay Stanley, Steven Hovey. AB, Jamestown Coll., 1936; JD, U. Chgo., 1939. Bar: Ill. 1939, U.S. Supreme Ct. 1945, D.C. 1972. Counsel Ill. Mcpl. Code Commn., Chgo., 1939-40; bill drafter Ill. Legis. Ref. Bur., Springfield, 1941; from assoc. to ptnr. Mayer, Brown & Platt, Chgo., 1941-71; ptnr.-in-charge Mayer, Brown & Platt, Washington, 1972-80. Bd. dirs. Chgo. Community Renewal Found., 1962-70; mem. adminstrv. bd. Nat. United Meth. Ch., Washington, 1982-84; coord. Extended Family Program, 1981-82. Capt. AUS, 1943-46. Home: Cottage 304 3300 Darby Rd Haverford PA 19041-1063

STROUD, JOE HINTON, newspaper editor; b. McGehee, Ark., June 18, 1936; s. Joseph Hilliard and Marion Rebecca (McKinney) S.; m. Janis Mizell, Aug. 21, 1957; children: Rebecca McKinney, Joseph Scott, Alexandra Jane.; m. Kathleen M. Fojtik, Nov. 1, 1981; children: Jonathan Rudolph, Anna Marion. BA, Hendrix Coll., Conway, Ark., 1957; MA, Tulane U., 1959; LLD (hon.), Eastern Mich. U., 1977, Kalamazoo Coll., 1984, Adrian Coll., 1985; D Communicating Arts (hon.), Cen. Mich. U., 1986; LittD (hon.), Mich. State U., 1987, Olivet Coll., 1995. Reporter, then editor editorial page Pine Bluff (Ark.) Comml., 1959-60; editorial writer Ark. Gazette, Little Rock, 1960-64; editorial writer then editor editorial page Winston-Salem (N.C.) Jour.-Sentinel, 1964-68; assoc. editor Detroit Free Press, 1968-73, editor, 1973—, sr. v.p., 1978—. Mem. gen. bd. publs. United Meth. Ch., 1975-76; adv. bd. Mich. Christian Advocate, 1975-79; bd. govs. Cranbrook Inst. Sci., 1978—; trustee Cranbrook Ednl. Community, 1989—; bd. dirs. S.E. Mich. chpt. ARC, 1972-88, Detroit Symphony, 1978-83; chmn. adv. com. Svc. to Mil. Families, 1974-77, chmn. program evaluation com. 1978-80; bd. assocs. Adrian Coll., 1985—; trustee Starr Commonwealth Schs., 1989—. Recipient N.C. Sch. Bell award, 1967; Mich. Sch. Bell award, 1973; William Allen White award Inland Daily Press Assn., 1973, 76, 77; citation Overseas Press Club, 1974; Paul Tobenkin award Columbia U., 1976; Disting. Service award Mich.'s Women's Commn., 1984; Laity award Detroit Ann. Conf. United Meth. Ch., 1985. Mem. Am. Soc. Newspaper Editors, Nat. Conf. Editorial Writers (program chmn. 1978, v.p. 1987-88, pres. 1988-89), Detroit Econ. Club, Detroit Com. Fgn. Relations, Sigma Delta Chi. Clubs: Detroit, Renaissance, Nat. Press. Office: Detroit Free Press 321 W Lafayette Blvd Detroit MI 48226

STROUD, JOHN FRANKLIN, engineering educator, scientist; b. Dallas, June 29, 1922; s. Edward Frank and Ethel A. Stroud; m. Dorcas Elizabeth Stroud, Feb. 4, 1944; children: Kevin, Karen, Richard. BSME, Stanford (Calif.) U., 1949, postgrad., 1949-53; cert. in fin. mgmt. for sr. execs., U. Pa., 1984. Aero. rsch. scientist NASA Ames Rsch. Lab., Moffett Field, Calif., 1949-53; thermodynamics engr. Lockheed, Burbank, Calif., 1953-55, group engr. propulsion, 1955-63, dept. engr. propulsion, 1963-70, from dept. engr. to divsn. engr. propulsion, 1970-83, chief engr. flight scis., 1983-85, divsn. engr., 1985-90, ret., 1990; cons. spl. studies in econs. and engring. sci., 1990—; mem. ad hoc adv. congrl. subcom. on high tech wind tunnels, 1985. Contbr. articles to profl. jours.; author and speaker in field. Charity fund raiser United Way, 1970-80, others. Lt., naval aviator USN, 1942-45, ETO. Decorated Battle of Atlantic. Fellow AIAA (assoc., airbreathing propulsion com. 1966-68, 80-83, chmn. many sessions 1970—); mem. Soc. Automotive Engrs. (aviation div. air transport com., propulsion com., chmn. many sessions nat. confs. 1970—, co-chmn. AIAA/SAE nat. propulsion conf. 1978). Achievements include patent for low drag external compression supersonic inlet; design and development of integrated F-104A inlet and air inductions system, integrated inlet/air induction system into the total propulsion system and airframe; management of team that developed, designed, and integrated the aeropropulsion systems on the L1011 commercial transport; devised new theory for turbulent boundary layers in adverse pressure gradients; numerous other patents pending.

STROUD, JOHN FRED, JR., state supreme court justice, judge; b. Hope, Ark., Oct. 3, 1931; s. John Fred and Clarine (Steel) S.; m. Marietta Kimball, June 1, 1958; children: John Fred III, Ann Kimball, Tracy Steel. Student, Hendrix Coll., 1949-51; BA, U. Ark., 1959, LLB, 1960. Bar: Ark. 1959, Tex. 1988, U.S. Supreme Ct. 1963. Ptnr. Stroud & McClerkin, 1959-62; city atty. City of Texarkana (Ark.), 1961; legislative asst. to U.S. Senator John L. McClellan, 1962-63; ptnr. Smith, Stroud, McClerkin, Dunn & Nutter, 1963-79, 81-95; assoc. justice Ark. Supreme Ct., Little Rock, 1980; judge Ark. Ct. Appeals, Little Rock, 1996—. Chmn. Texarkana Airport Authority, 1966-67, Texarkana United Way Campaign, 1988; pres. Caddo area coun. Boy Scouts Am., 1971-73; former trustee Ark. Nature COnservancy; former bd. dirs. Ark. Cmty. Found.; former pres. Red River Valley Assn.; former commr. Red River Compact Commn.; past vice chmn. Ark. Water Code Study Commn.; chmn. bd., chmn. coun. ministries Meth. Ch. Lt. col. USAF, 1951-56, Res. ret. Recipient award of exceptional accomplishment Ark. State C. of C., 1972, 86, Silver Beaver and Disting. Eagle awards Boy Scouts Am.; named Outstanding Young Man of Texarkana, 1966, One of Five Outstanding Young Men of Ark., 1967, Outstanding Alumnus of U. Ark. Law Sch., 1980. Fellow Am. Bar Foun.; mem. ABA, Ark. Bar Assn. (chmn. exec. coun. 1979-80, pres. 1987-88), Four States Area Estate Planning Coun. (past chmn.), State Bar Tex., Miller County Bar Assn. (past pres.), Texarkana Bar Assn. (pres. 1982-83), Ark. Bar Found. (chmn. 1974-75), Am. Coll. Trust and Estate Counsel (chmn. Ark. chpt. 1986-91), S.W. Ark. Bar Assn., Texarkana C. of C. (pres. 1969, C.E. Palmer award 1979), Texarkana Country Club (pres. 1990-92), Rotary (pres. Texarkana 1965-66). Democrat. Avocations: tennis, golf, hunting, fishing. Office: Ark Ct Appeals 625 Marshall St Little Rock AR 72201-1054

STROUD, RICHARD HAMILTON, aquatic biologist, scientist, consultant; b. Dedham, Mass., Apr. 24, 1918; s. Percy Valentine and Elizabeth Lillian (Kimpton) S.; m. Genevieve Cecelia DePol, Dec. 20, 1943; children: William DePol, Jennifer Celia Trivett. BS, Bowdoin Coll., 1939; MS, U. N.H., 1942; postgrad., Yale U., 1947-48, Boston U. Sch. Edn., 1948-49. Asst. aquatic biologist N.H. Fish and Game Dept., Concord, 1940-41; jr. aquatic biologist TVA, Norris, Tenn., 1942, asst. aquatic biologist, 1946-47; chief aquatic biologist Mass. Div. Fisheries and Game, Boston, 1948-53; asst. exec. v.p. Sport Fishing Inst., Washington, 1953-55, exec. v.p., 1955-81, editor monthly bull.; sr. scientist Aquatic Ecosystems Analysts, Fayetteville, Ark., 1983-88; founder., mng. v.p., trustee Sport Fishery Rsch. Found., Washington, 1967-88; cns. aquatic resources, 1981-89, cons. editor fish sci. publs., 1982-95; rsch. adv. bd. Sport Fishing Inst. Fund, 1988-94; Pentelow lectr. U. Liverpool, England, 1975. Author Fisheries Report for Massachusetts Lakes, Ponds, and Reservoirs, 1955; editor (ann. series) Marine Recreational Fisheries Symposia, 1982-95, Nat. Leaders of American Conservation, 1985, World Angling Resources and Challenges, 1985, Fish Culture in Fisheries Management, 1986, Multi-Jurisdictional Management of Marine Fisheries, 1986, Management of Atlantic Salmon, 1988, Planning the Future of Billfishes, Part 1, 1989, Part 2, 1990, Stemming The Tide of Coastal Fish Habitat Loss, 1991, Fisheries Management and Watershed Development, 1992, Conserving America's Fisheries, 1994; co-editor The Biological Significance of Estuaries, 1971, Black Bass Biology and Management, 1975, Predator Prey Systems in Fisheries Management, 1979; contbr. articles to various publs. Bd. dirs. Nat. Coalition Marine Conservation, 1977-96; treas. Natural Resources Coun. Am., 1961-68, chmn., 1969-71, hon. mem., 1981—. Served with U.S. Army, 1942-46. Decorated Croix de Guerre with cluster.; recipient Conservation Achievement award Nat. Wildlife Fedn., 1975, 81, SOAR award Boy Scouts Am., 1972; named to Nat. Fishing Hall of Fame, 1984. Fellow Am. Inst. Fishery Research Biologists (emeritus, Outstanding Achievement award 1981), Am. Fisheries Soc. (pres. 1979-80, hon. life mem., Outstanding Achievement award 1990); mem. Internat. Fish and Wildlife Agys., Freshwater Biol. Assn. (U.K.), Fisheries Soc. Brit. Isles, Moore County Wildlife Club (Southern Pines, N.C.), Country Club (Pinehurst, N.C.). Office: PO Box 1772 Pinehurst NC 28370-1772

STROUP, ELIZABETH FAYE, librarian; b. Tulsa, Mar. 25, 1939; d. Milton Earl and Lois (Buhl) S. BA in Philosophy, U. Wash., 1962, MLS, 1964. Intern Libr. of Congress, Washington, 1964-65; asst. dir. North Cen. Regional Libr., Wenatchee, Wash., 1966-69; reference specialist Congl. Reference div. Libr. of Congress, Washington, 1970-71, head nat. collections Div. for the Blind and Physically Handicapped, 1971-73, chief Congl. Reference div., 1973-78, dir. gen. reference, 1978-88; city libr., chief exec. officer Seattle Pub. Libr., 1988—; cons. U.S. Info. Svc., Indonesia, Feb. 1987. Mem. adv. bd. KCTS 9 Pub. TV, Seattle, 1988—; bd. visitors Sch. Librarianship, U. Wash., 1988—; bd. dirs. Wash. Literacy, 1988—. Mem. ALA (pres. reference and adult svcs. div. 1986-87, div. bd. 1985-88), Wash. Libr. Assn., D.C. Libr. Assn. (bd. dirs. 1975-76), City Club, Ranier Club. Avocations: gardening, mountain climbing, reading. Office: Seattle Pub Libr 1000 4th Ave Seattle WA 98104-1109

STROUP, KALA MAYS, state higher education commissioner. BA in Speech and Drama, U. Kans., 1959, MS in Psychology, 1964, PhD in Speech Comm. and Human Rels., 1974; EdD (hon.), Mo. Western State Coll., 1996. V.p. acad. affairs Emporia (Kans.) State U., 1978-83; pres. Murray State U., Ky., 1983-90, S.E. Mo. State U., Cape Girardeau, 1990-95; commr. higher edn. State of Mo., Jefferson City, 1995—; pres. Mo. Coun. on Pub. Higher Edn.; mem. pres.'s commn. NCAA; cons. Edn. Commn. of States Task Force on State Policy and Ind. Higher Edn.; adv. bd. NSF Directorate for Sci. Edn. Evaluation; adv. com. Dept. Health, Edn. and Welfare, chair edn. com.; citizen's adv. coun. on state of Women U. S. Dept. Labor, 1974-76. Mem. nat. exec. bd. Boy Scouts Am., nat. exploring com., former chair profl. devel. com., mem. profl. devel. com., exploring com., Young Am. awards com., 1986-87, north ctrl. region strategic planning com., bd. trustees, nat. mus. chair; mem. Gov.'s Cabinet, Gov.'s Coun. on Workforce Quality, State of Mo.; bd. dirs. Midwestern Higher Edn. Commn.; chair ACE Leadership Commn.; mem. bd. visitors Air U.; v.p. Missourians for Higher Edn.; mem. bd. St. Francis Med. Ctr. Found., 1990-95, Cape Girardeau C. of C., 1990-95, U. Kans. Alumni Assn.; pres. Forum on Excellence, Carnegie Found.; adv. bd. World Trade Ctr., St. Louis, Svc. Mems. Opty. Colls., 1997—; mem. Mo. Higher Edn. Loan Authority, 1995—, depts. econ. devel. & agrl. Mo. Global Partnership, 1995—, Mo. Tng. & Employment Coun., 1995—, Concordia U. Sys. Advancement Cabinet, State Higher Edn. Exec. Officers, 1995—, mem. com. workforce edn. and tng., 1996; bd. govs. Heartland's Alliance Minority Participation, 1995—. ACE fellow; recipient Alumni Honor Citation award U. Kans., Award Distinction Profl. Black Men's Club, S.E. Mo., 1990, Dist. Svc. to Edn. award Harris-Stowe State Coll., 1996; named to U. Kans. Womans Hall of Fame, Ohio Valley Conf. Hall of Fame, 1997. Mem. Am. Assn. State Colls. and Univs. (past bd. dirs., mem. Pres.'s Commn. on Tchr. Edn., Task Force on Labor Force Issues and Implications for the Curriculum), Mortar Board, Phi Beta Kappa, Omicron Delta Kappa, Phi Kappa Phi, Rotary (found. Ednl. awards com.). Office: Mo Dept Higher Edn 3515 Amazonas Dr Jefferson City MO 65109-6821

STROUP, RICHARD LYNDELL, economics educator, writer; b. Sunnyside, Wash., Jan. 3, 1943; s. Edgar Ivan and Inez Louise (Kellet) S.; m. Sandra Lee Price, Sept. 13, 1962 (div. Sept. 1981); children—Michael, Craig; m. Jane Bartlett Steidemann Shaw, Jan. 1, 1985; 1 child, David. Student, MIT, 1961-62; B.A., M.A., U. Wash., 1966, Ph.D. in Econs., 1970. Asst. prof. econs. Mont. State U., Bozeman, 1969-74; assoc. prof. econs. Mont. State U., 1974-78, prof. econs., 1978—; dir. Office Policy Analysis, Dept. Interior, Washington, 1982-84; vis. assoc. prof. Fla. State U., Tallahassee, 1977-78; sr. assoc. Polit. Economy Research Ctr., Bozeman, 1980—/lectr. summer univ., U. Aix (France), 1985—. Co-author: Natural Resources, 1983, Economics: Private and Public Choice, 8th edit., 1997, Basic Economics, 1993, What Everyone Should Know About Economics and Prosperity, 1993; also articles, 1972—; mem. editorial adv. bd. Regulation, 1993—. Treas., dir. Gallatin Valley Cmty. Sch. Adj. scholar Cato Inst., 1993—. Mem. Am. Econ. Assn., Western Econ. Assn., So. Econ. Assn., Mont Pelerin Soc., Phila. Soc., Pub. Choice Soc., Assn. of Pvt. Enterprise Edn. Episcopalian. Home: 9 W Arnold St Bozeman MT 59715-6127 Office: PERC 502 N 19th Ave Ste 211 Bozeman MT 59718-3124

STROUP, SHEILA TIERNEY, columnist; b. Aurora, Ill., Nov. 28, 1943; d. Lawrence Clifford and Dorothy (Vilven) Tierney; m. Merwin F. Stroup, Sept. 4, 1965; children: Keegan, Shannon, Claire. BA in Liberal Arts, U. Ill., 1965; MA in English, Southeastern La. U., 1982. Cert. secondary tchr., La. Tchr. English Great Mills (Md.) High Sch., 1966-69; feature writer St. Tammany News, Covington, La., 1974-75; grad. asst. Southeastern La. U., Hammond, 1981-82, instr. English, 1982-85; ednl. cons. Custom Computer Systems, Hammond, 1985-86; tchr. English William Pitcher Jr. High, Covington, 1987; community news writer Times-Picayune, New Orleans, 1988-90; met. page columnist New Orleans Times-Picayune, 1990—; free-lance writer, Covington, La., 1986-88; speaker and workshop leader in field. Author newspaper column Sheila Stroup, 1990 (1st Pl. award La. Press Assn. 1990); author adult and juvenile short stories included in Woman's World, Cricket, Reader's Digest, others. Recipient 1st Pl. award Deep South Writers Competition, 1979, 2d Pl. award, 1987-90; 1st Pl. award for column New Orleans Press Club, 1989, 93. Fellow AAUW (bd. dirs. 1978-88, various chairwoman positions); mem. Nat. Soc. Newspaper Columnists (v.p. 1991-93, pres. 1994—). Avocations: bike riding, reading, loves animals. Office: The Times-Picayune 1001 N Highway 190 Covington LA 70433-8962*

STROUP, STANLEY STEPHENSON, lawyer, educator; b. Los Angeles, Mar. 7, 1944; s. Francis Edwin and Marjory (Weimer) S.; m. Sylvia Douglass, June 15, 1968; children—Stacie, Stephen, Sarah. A.B., U. Ill., 1966; J.D., U. Mich., 1969. Bar: Ill. 1969, Calif. 1981, Minn. 1984. Atty. First Nat. Bank Chgo., 1969-78, asst. gen. counsel, 1978-80, v.p., 1980; sr. v.p., chief legal officer Bank of Calif., San Francisco, 1980-84; sr. v.p., gen. counsel Norwest Corp., Mpls., 1984-93, exec. v.p., gen. counsel, 1993—; mem. adj. faculty Coll. Law, William Mitchell Coll., St. Paul, 1985—; mem. Regulatory Affairs Coun., Bank Adminstrn. Inst., 1996—. Mem. ABA, Ill. Bar Assn., State Bar Calif., Minn. Bar Assn. Office: Norwest Corp 6th & Marquette Sts Minneapolis MN 55479-1026

STROUPE, HENRY SMITH, university dean; b. Alexis, N.C., June 3, 1914; s. Stephen Morris and Augie (Lineberger) S.; m. Mary Elizabeth Denham, June 2, 1942; children—Stephen Denham, David Henry. Student, Mars Hill Jr. Coll., 1931-33; B.S., Wake Forest Coll., 1935, M.A., 1937; Ph.D., Duke U., 1942. Faculty Wake Forest U., Winston-Salem, N.C., 1937—; assoc. prof. history Wake Forest U., 1949-54, prof., 1954-84, prof. emeritus, 1984—, chmn. dept. history, 1954-68, dir. evening classes, 1957-61, dir. div. grad. studies, 1961-67, dean grad. sch., 1967-84, dean emeritus, 1984—; Vis. prof. history Duke, summer 1960. Author: The Religious Press in the South Atlantic States, 1802-1865: An Annotated Bibliography with Historical Introduction and Notes, 1956; Mem. editorial bd.: N.C. Hist. Rev, 1963-69. Mem. N.C. Civil War Centennial Commn., 1959-60. Served from ensign to lt. USNR, 1943-46. Recipient Christopher Crittenden award N.C. Lit. and Hist. Assn., 1982. Mem. Am. Hist. Assn., N.C. Hist. Soc. (pres. 1965), N.C. Lit. and Hist. Assn. (pres. 1974), Phi Beta Kappa, Omicron Delta Kappa. Democrat. Baptist. Home: 2016 Faculty Dr Winston Salem NC 27106-5221

STROUTH, BARON HOWARD STEVEN, geologist, mining engineer; b. Frankfurt, Germany, Sept. 28, 1919; arrived in U.S., 1941; s. Baron Karl Siegfried and Ida (Morch) von Strauss; m. Penelope Ann Creamer-Osteen, Nov. 8, 1951. BSc, U. Sorbonne, 1939; PhD in Engring., Bretton Woods U., 1965; PhD in Engring. (hon.), Rochedale U., Can., 1970. Asst. mgr. Drexel Bros. Ltd., N.Y.C., 1941-43; pres. Std. Mining, N.Y.C., 1951-58, Stanleigh Uranium Mine, Toronto, Can., 1954-61; mng. dir. Norsul Oil and Mining Quito, Ecuador, 1961-71; dir., officer Mining and Oil Cos., various locations; founder, operator Stanleigh Uranium and Norsul Oil; sr. trustee Weingueter Baron K. S. von Strauss, Erben Trust, Vaduz, 1954—. Translator: The Cornet (Rilke), 1950; author: A Window to the Morrow, 1963, A Sonata for Frankfurt, 1987, Cities of the Break of Dawn, 1988, Beauty is Forever, 1996; patentee in mining and oil porcesses. Maj. USAR, 1943-69, ret. Recipient Conspicuous Svc. Cross, Gov. Dewey, 1947, French, Czech, Cambodian decorations. Fellow Explorers Club; mem. Can. Inst. Mining Engrs. (life), Am. Inst. Mining Engrs. (sr.), St. James Club (London), Ontario Club Toronto. Avocations: collector, antique books, pre-Colombian art, antique maps.

STROYD, ARTHUR HEISTER, lawyer; b. Pitts., Sept. 5, 1945; s. Anne (Griffiths) S.; m. Susan Fleming, July 21, 1973; 1 child, Elizabeth. AB, Kenyon Coll., 1967; JD, U. Pitts., 1972. Bar: Pa. 1972, U.S. Dist. Ct. (we. dist.) Pa. 1972, U.S. Ct. Appeals (3d cir.) 1972. Law clk. to judge U.S. Ct. Appeals (3d cir.), Phila., 1972-75; ptnr., head litigation group Reed, Smith, Shaw & McClay, Pitts., 1975—; mem. Nat. Adv. Council on Child Nutrition, U.S. Dept. Agriculture, 1984-85. Treas. Mt. Lebanon Zoning Hearing Bd., 1978-81; pres. bd. dirs. Mt. Lebanon Sch. dist., 1981-87; solicitor Allegheny County Rep. Com., 1988-95; pres. bd. dirs. Ctr. for Theatre Arts, Pitts., 1984-93; participant Leadership Pitts., 1991-92; chair bd. dirs. Mt. Lebanon Hosp. Authority, 1993—; coun. U. Pitts. Cancer Inst., 1993—; mem. alumni coun. Kenyon Coll., 1996—. Lt. USNR, 1969-71. Mem. Pa. Bar Assn., Allegheny County Bar Assn., Acad. Trial Lawyers (bd. govs.), Duquesne Club. Episcopalian. Avocations: skiing. Home: 17 Saint Clair Dr Pittsburgh PA 15228-1830 Office: Reed Smith Shaw & McClay 435 6th Ave Pittsburgh PA 15219-1809

STRUBBE, THOMAS R., diagnostic testing industry executive; b. Ft. Wayne, Ind., Mar. 30, 1940; s. Rudolph C. and Maverne E. (Wagoner) S.; children: Tracy Lynn, Patrick Thomas, Christina Lee. B.S., Ind. U., 1962; J.D., Tulane U., 1965. Bar: Ind. 1965, Ill. 1969. Atty. Lincoln Nat. Life Ins. Co., Ft. Wayne, 1965-66; asst. counsel Lincoln Nat. Life Ins. Co., 1967-68; with Washington Nat. Corp., Evanston, Ill., 1968-90; gen. counsel Washington Nat. Corp., 1973-79, sec., 1970-84, v.p., 1975-79, sr. v.p., 1979-83, exec. v.p., 1983-84, pres., 1984-90, also bd. dirs., mem. exec. com.; pres., chief exec. officer Osborn Labs. Inc., Olathe, Kans., 1990—, also bd. dirs. Trustee Glencoe (Ill.) Union Ch., 1984-87; v.p., bd. dirs., exec. com. Chgo. chpt. Epilepsy Found. Am., 1975-79; bd. dirs. Assn. Retarded Citizens Ill., 1985-89, Northlight Theater, 1984-89. Lt. USNR, 1965-71. Lincoln Found. grantee, 1964. Mem. ABA, Assn. Life Ins. Counsel, Nat. Investor Rels. Inst., Am. Soc. Corp. Secs., Home Office Life Underwriters Assn., Ind. Bar Assn., Ill. Bar Assn., Skokie Country Club (Ill.), Shadow Glen Golf Club (Kans.), Hideaway Beach Club (Fla.). Office: Osborn Labs Inc PO Box 2920 Shawnee Mission KS 66201-1320

STRUBEL, ELLA DOYLE, advertising executive; b. Chgo., Mar. 14, 1940; d. George Floyd and Myrtle (McKnight) D.; m. Richard Craig G'sell, Apr. 26, 1969 (div. 1973); m. Richard Perry Strubel, Oct. 23, 1976; stepchildren: Douglas Arthur, Craig Tollerton. BA magna cum laude, Memphis State U., 1962; MA, U. Ill., 1963. Staff asst. Corinthian Broadcasting Co., N.Y.C., 1963-65; dir. advt.& pub. rels. WANE-TV, Ft. Wayne, Ind., 1965-66; asst. dir. advt. WBBM-TV, Chgo., 1966-67, mgr. sales promotion, 1967-69, dir. advt. sales promotion & info. svcs., 1969-70; dir. pub. rels. Walthaw Watch Co., Chgo., 1973-74; mgr. advt. promotion & pub. rels. WMAQ-TV, Chgo., 1974-76; v.p. corp. rels. Kraft, Inc., Glenview, Ill., 1985-87; sr. v.p. corp. affairs Leo Burnett Co., Inc., Chgo., 1987-92, exec. v.p., 1992—. Bd. dirs. Rehab. Inst. Chgo., Chgo. Pub. Libr. Found., Leadership Greater Chgo., Family Focus; pres. Women's Bd. Rehab. Inst., 1982-84; chair Chgo. Network, 1994-95. Named Outstanding Woman in Comms. in Chgo., YWCA, 1995, one of 100 Most Influential Women in Chgo., Crain's Chgo. Bus., 1996. Mem. Northwestern U. Assocs., Casino Club. Democrat. Presbyterian. Home: 55 W Goethe St Chicago IL 60610-2233 Office: Leo Burnett Co Inc 35 W Wacker Dr Chicago IL 60601-1614

STRUBEL, RICHARD PERRY, manufacturing company executive; b. Evanston, Ill., Aug. 10, 1939; s. Arthur Raymond and Martha (Smith) S.; m. Linda Jane Freeman, Aug. 25, 1961 (div. 1974); children: Douglas Arthur, Craig Tollerton; m. Ella Doyle G'sell, Oct. 23, 1976. B.A., Williams Coll., 1962; M.B.A., Harvard U., 1964. Assoc. Fry Cons., Chgo., 1964-66, mng. prin., 1966-68; with N.W. Industries, Inc., Chgo., 1968-83, v.p. corp. devel., 1969-73, group v.p., 1973-79, exec. v.p., 1979-83, pres., 1983; chmn. bd., pres. Buckingham Corp., N.Y.C., 1972-73; pres., chief exec. officer Microdot Inc., Chgo., 1983-94; mng. ptnr. Tandem Ptnrs. Inc., Chgo., 1990—; trustee Benchmark Funds of The No. Trust Co., Chgo., and various mutual funds of Goldman Sachs Asset Mgmt., N.Y.C.; bd. dirs. Kaynar Technologies Inc., Orange, Calif. Trustee U. Chgo.; bd. dirs. Children's Meml. Hosp., Children's Meml. Med. Ctr.; chair vis. com. Divinity Sch., U. Chgo. Presbyterian. Clubs: Casino, Chicago, Comml., Racquet of Chgo., Commonwealth (Chgo.). Office: Tandem Ptnrs Inc 70 W Madison St Ste 1400 Chicago IL 60602-4267

STRUDLER, ROBERT JACOB, real estate development executive; b. N.Y.C., Sept. 22, 1942; m. Ruth Honigman, Aug. 29, 1965; children: Seth, Keith, Craig. BS in Indsl. and Labor Relations, Cornell U., 1964; LLB, Columbia U., 1967. Bar: N.Y. 1967, Fla. 1973. Assoc. firms in N.Y.C., 1967-71; v.p., chmn. operating com. U.S. Home Corp., Clearwater, Fla., 1972-76, v.p. legal affairs, 1976-77, v.p. ops., 1977-79; sr. v.p. ops. U.S. Home Corp., Houston, 1979-81, sr. v.p. acquisitions, 1981-84, pres., chief operating officer, 1984-86, co-chmn., chief exec. officer, 1986—. Pres., trustee Sch. for Young Children; mem. pres.' adv. coun. U. St. Thomas. Co-recipient Builder of Yr. award Profl. Builder Mag., 1994, Bronze award Wall Street, 1995. Mem. ABA, N.Y. State Bar Assn., Fla. Bar Assn., Cornell Real Estate Coun., Nat. Assn. Homebuilders (chmn. high prodn. coun. 1991-93). Home: 11110 Greenbay St Houston TX 77024-6729 Office: US Home Corp 1800 West Loop S Houston TX 77027-3210

STRUELENS, MICHEL MAURICE JOSEPH GEORGES, political science educator, foreign affairs consultant; b. Brussels, Belgium, Mar. 10, 1928; m. Godelieve de Wilde, Aug. 2, 1949; children: Alain, Patricia, Brigitte, Bernard, Jean Paul (dec.). B.A., Coll. St. Pierre, Brussels, 1944; M.A., Antwerp U., Belgium, 1949; Ph.D., Am. U., Washington, 1968. Insp. econ. affairs Congo Govt., Leopoldville, 1950-54, chief insp. econ. affairs, 1954-55, dep. commr. transp., 1955-57; dir. Info. and Public Relations Office for Congo, Brussels, 1957-58, Congo Tourism Pavillion, Internat. World's Fair, Brussels, 1958-59; dir. gen. Belgian Congo and Ruanda Urundi Tourist Office, Congo, 1959; chmn. African Commn. Internat. Union Ofcl. Travel Orgns., Geneva, 1959-60; ofcl. Katanga rep. in U.S., N.Y.C., 1960-63; dir. gen. Internat. Inst. for African Affairs in Can., 1963-64; spl. asst. to prime minister Democratic Republic Congo; fgn. affairs minister, adviser to Congo UN del., adviser Congo embassy Democratic Republic Congo, Washington, N.Y.C., 1964-66; dir. Eurafrica, Consultants on Fgn. Affairs, Washington, 1966—; prof. polit. sci., French, internat. bus. Am. U., 1968-93; prof. emeritus, 1993; dir. Ctr. Rsch and Documentation on European Community Am. U., 1971—, chmn. faculty rels. com., 1986-87, chmn. grad. studies com., SIS, 1989-90; dir. E.C. Inst. in Europe, 1978-93, U. Antwerp Exchange Program, 1979-83; dir. EPSCI/ESSEC (France) Exchange Program, 1980-84, chmn. internat. bus. dept., 1980-84; dir. exchange program Bus. Sch. of Poly., U. Madrid, 1981-84; investment adviser, 1977—; adminstr. French Parish, , 1974-75, Ctr. Studies on Internat. Relations, 1987-96, Econs. and Bus., La Rochelle, France, 1987-96; exec. v.p. Eglise St. Louis Corp., French-Speaking Union, Washington, 1974-75; mgr. by agreement with European Communities, European Documentation Ctr. (CERDEC), accessing by satellite EC Data Banks, 1985— and providing through WCL Libr. of Am. U., On Line Pub. Access Cataloging, 1991—. Author: (with Inforcongo) Congo Belge et Ruanda-Urundi, 1958; monograph Le Canada à l'Heure de l'Afrique, 1964; The United Nations in the Congo - or ONUC and International Politics, 1976. Recipient Internat. Union Ofcl. Travel Orgns. Poster award Brussels, 1958, Etoile de Service en Argent King of Belgium, 1956; chevalier de l'Ordre Royal du Lion, 1957; Faculty award for outstanding contbn. to acad. program devel. Coll. Bus. Adminstrn., Am. U., 1979; Faculty award for outstanding teaching, 1980, 82, 84; Faculty award for outstanding service to Am. U., 1981. Mem. Golden Key, Phi Sigma Alpha. Clubs: Cosmos (Washington); Bukavu Royal Sports (founder 1950, pres. 1951-54, hon. pres. 1957) (Congo). Lodge: Rotary. Home: 1374 Woodside Dr Mc Lean VA 22102-1536 *"Ad Augusta per Angusta". Using Latin, French writer Victor Hugo said it all! Nothing comes easy and "success," a very personal percep-*

tion indeed, requires a great deal of luck, perseverance and hard work. True success, though, is directly related to the pursuit of happiness, which in turn is a state of mind. If and when I reach eternity, I'll then be able to tell how successful I was during my passage on earth.

STRUEVER, STUART MCKEE, archaeologist; b. Peru, Ill., Aug. 4, 1931; s. Carl Chester and Martha McKee (Scobee) S.; m. Alice Russell Melcher, Aug. 21, 1956 (div. June 1983); children: Nathan Chester, Hanna Russell; m. Martha Lee Hopkins, Nov. 12, 1988. AB, Dartmouth Coll., 1953; MA, Northwestern U., 1960; PhD, U. Chgo., 1968. Instr. U. Chgo., 1964-65; from asst. prof. to prof. Northwestern U., Evanston, Ill., 1965-84; pres. Ctr. Am. Archaeology, Evanston, Ill., 1964-84, Crow Canyon Archaeological Ctr., Denver, 1985-92; chair Crow Canyon Ctr., Denver, 1993-96; bd. archaeological cons. Tenn. Valley Authority. Knoxville, 1975-88. Author: Koster: Americans in Search of Their Past, 1979; editor: (book series) Studies in Archaeology Series, 1977-92. Recipient Alumni Achievement award U. Chgo., 1976; medal Hist. Preservation Garden Club Am., N.Y.C., 1994; Humanities fellow Ill. Humanities Coun., 1984. Mem. Soc. Am. Archaeology (pres. 1975-76, Disting. Svc. award, 1995), Soc. Profl. Archaeologists (bd. dirs. 1976), Phi Beta Kappa. Office: Crow Canyon Ctr 1777 S Harrison St PH # 1 Denver CO 80210-3925

STRUGGLES, JOHN EDWARD, management consultant; b. Wilmette, Ill., Nov. 29, 1913; s. William George and Sarah Adell (Chambers) S.; m. Dorothy Eloise Goetz, Oct. 23, 1937; 1 child, John Kirk. Student, Miami U., Oxford, Ohio, 1932-34. Supt. Consol. Biscuit Co., Chgo., 1934-37; sales rep. Pillsbury Mills, Chgo., 1937-41; various personnel and operating positions Montgomery Ward & Co., Chgo., Kansas City, Denver, 1941-50; v.p. personnel Montgomery Ward & Co., 1950-53; co-founder, co-chmn. Heidrick & Struggles, Inc., Chgo., 1953—. With USNR, World War II. Republican. Home: 505 Sheridan Rd Winnetka IL 60093-2639 Office: Heidrick Struggles Inc 233 S Wacker Dr Chicago IL 60606-6306

STRUL, GENE M., communications executive, former television news director; b. Bklyn., Mar. 25, 1927; s. Joseph and Sally (Chartoff) S.; student journalism U. Miami (Fla.), 1945-47; m. Shirley Dolly Silber, Aug. 7, 1949 (dec.); children: Ricky, Gary, Eileen. News dir. Sta. WIOD AM-FM, Miami, 1947-56; assignment editor, producer Sta. WCKT-TV, Miami, 1956-57, news dir., 1957-79; dir. broadcast news Miami News, 1957; free-lance writer newspapers and mags.; cons. dept. comm. U. Miami, 1979, dir. public relations, 1979-80; v.p. Hernstadt Broadcasting Corp., 1980-81; dir. corp. comm. Burnup & Sims, 1981-90; dir. comm. Printing Industry of South Fla., 1990-92, Printing Assn. Fla., 1992—. Comm. dir. United Way of Dade County, 1981. Served with AUS, 1945. Recipient Peabody award, 1975; Preceptor award Broadcast Industry conf., San Francisco State U.; Abe Lincoln awards (2) So. Baptist Radio-TV Conf.; Nat. Headliners awards (5); led Sta. WSVN (formerly WCKT) to more than 200 awards for news, including 3 Peabody awards, Emmy award. Mem. Nat. Acad. Television Arts and Scis. (past gov. Miami chpt.), Radio-TV News Dirs. Assn., Fla. AP Broadcasters (past pres.), Greater Miami C. of C., Nat. Broadcast Editorial Assn., Sigma Delta Chi (2 nat. awards). Home: 145 SW 49th Ave Miami FL 33134-1228

STRULL, GENE, technology consultant, retired electrical manufacturing company executive; b. Chgo., May 15, 1929; s. Albert and Helen (Wolf) S.; m. Joyce Landsbaum, July 6, 1952; children—David Jay, Brian Lee. B.S.E.E., Purdue U., 1951; M.S., Northwestern U., 1952, Ph.D. in Elec. Engring, 1954. With Westinghouse Electric Corp., 1954-93; supervisory engr., adv. engr., mgr. solid state tech.-aerospace Westinghouse Electric Corp., Balt., 1958-68; mgr. sci. and tech. systems devel. div., mgr. advanced tech. labs. Westinghouse Electric Corp., 1968-78, dep. gen. mgr. systems devel. div., 1979-81, gen. mgr. advanced tech. div., 1981-93, exec. dir. tech., 1987-93; cons. Army Sci. Bd., 1979-83, NRC-NAS, 1980-82, Def. Sci. Bd., 1981-83, NSF, 1992-97; cons. NASA, 1967-87, com. chmn., 1976-78; adv. com. panel USNR, 1989. Contbg. author: Integrated Electronic Systems, 1970, Integrated Circuit Technology, 1967; contbr. articles to profl. jours.; patentee in field. Gene Strull Tech. Ctr. at Westinghouse Electric Corp. Advanced Tech. Labs. named in his honor, Balt., 1993; named Outstanding Elec. Engr. award Purdue U., 1994. Fellow IEEE (life, Govt. Industry Svc. award 1987, Frederik Philips award 1991); mem. Md. Acad. Scis. (chmn. 1978-80). Home: One Gristmill Ct # 606 Baltimore MD 21208

STRUM, BRIAN J., real estate executive; b. Bklyn., Nov. 27, 1939; s. Max J. and Beatrix (Galitzky) S.; m. Mickey Weiss, Nov. 19, 1966; children: Ira, Howard, Beth. BA, Bklyn. Coll., 1960; LLB, NYU, 1963. Bar: N.Y. 1964, N.J. 1969; CLU; counselor of real estate. Atty. Gilbert, Segall and Young, N.Y.C., 1963-65; assoc. res. atty. Prudential Ins. Co. Am., N.Y.C., 1965-67, various positions, law dept., 1967-75, v.p. real estate investments, 1975-86; chmn. Prudential Property Co., Newark, 1986-92; CEO Prudential Realty Group, Newark, 1992-94; Silverstein chair of real estate devel. NYU, 1995—; pres., trustee Prudential Realty Trust, 1985-94; mem. adv. bd. Chgo. Title & Trust Co., N.Y.C., 1982-96. Editor: Financing Real Estate in the Inflationary Eighties, 1981; contbr. articles to profl. jours. With USAR, 1963-69. Recipient Disting. Cmty. Svc. award Brandeis U., 1983, Urban Leadership award NYU, 1990, Good Scout award N.Y.C. coun. Boy Scouts Am., 1991, Nat. Achievement awrd D.A.R.E. Am., 1993. Fellow Anglo Am. Real Property Inst. (charter); mem. ABA (chmn. real property, probate and trust law sects. 1984-85), N.Y. State Bar Assn. (chmn. real property sect. 1975-76), Urban Land Inst. (coun. mem.), Am. Coll. Real Estate Lawyers (charter), Am. Soc. Real Estate Counselors. Office: NYU Real Estate Inst Rm 509 11 W 42d St New York NY 10036-8002

STRUM, JAY GERSON, lawyer; b. N.Y.C., July 6, 1938; s. John and Dorothy (Chaikind) S.; m. Patricia Ann Burtis, Jan. 25, 1969; children: Daniel, Jennifer. BA in polit. sci. magna cum laude, CCNY, 1959; LLB, Harvard U., 1962. Bar: N.Y. 1963, U.S. Dist. Ct. (so. and ea. dists.) N.Y. 1963, U.S. Ct. Appeals (2d cir.) 1965, U.S. Supreme Ct. 1979. Trial atty. SEC, N.Y.C., 1963-65; ptnr. Coon, Dubow, Kleinberg & Strum, N.Y.C., 1965-67; assoc. Kaye, Scholer, Fierman, Hays & Handler, N.Y.C., 1967-70, ptnr., 1971—. Mem. ABA, Assn. of Bar of City of N.Y., Phi Beta Kappa. Club: Harvard (N.Y.C.). Office: Kaye Scholer Fierman Hays & Handler 425 Park Ave New York NY 10022-3506

STRUNK, BETSY ANN WHITENIGHT, education educator; b. Bloomsburg, Pa., May 28, 1942; d. Mathias Clarence and Marianna (Naunas) Whitenight; children: Robert J. Jr., Geoffrey M. BS in Edn., Bloomsburg U., 1964; MEd, West Chester U., 1969; cert. mentally/physically handicapped, Pa. State U., 1981; postgrad., Wilkes U., St. Joseph's U., Drexel U., Western Md. Coll. Cert. elem. edn., spl. edn.; cert. single engine pvt. pilot. Tchr. Faust Sch., Bensalem (Pa.) Twp., 1964, Eddystone (Pa.) Elem. Sch., 1964-66, Lima Elem. Sch., Rose Tree Media Sch. Dist., 1966-69, Rose Tree Media (Pa.) Sch. Dist., 1977—; adj. prof. Wilkes Coll., Wilkes-Barre, Pa., 1981-86; instr. Delaware C.C., Media, 1986; instr., dir. ground sch. edn. Brandywine Airport, West Chester, Pa., 1986-88; instr. Drexel U., Phila., 1989—, Performance Learning Systems, Inc., Emerson, N.J. and Nevada City, Calif., 1981—; rep. FAA, Phila., 1986-88; owner, ptnr. Whitenight Homestead Family Partnership, Bloomsburg, Pa.; spl. edn. resource rm. specialist, tchr. cons. Media Elem. Sch., Rose Tree Media Sch. Dist., spl. edn. supervisory selection com.; curriculum designer pvt. pilot ground sch.; instr. and course designer introduction to flying and pilot companion course; chairperson profl. devel. com. Rose Tree Media Sch. Dist., 1992; mem. Insvc. Coun. of Delaware County, 1992—; mem. educator's adv. com. Phila. Franklin Inst., 1990-92, 95—; cons. ednl. programs, 1988—; owner, designer Betsy's Belts, Del., N.J., Pa., 1970-74; mem. gov. bd. Southeastern Tchr. Leadership Ctr. West Chester (Pa.) U.; learning support specialist Glenwood Elem. Sch., Media, Pa., 1994—, educator liason between sr. citizens and learning support students Lima Estates Retirement Home and Glenwood Elem. Sch., 1994—; presenter State of Pa. Lead Tchr. Conf., 1994, Ind. Sch. Tchrs. Assn., 1995; project dir. video documentary Performance Learning Sys., Calif., 1994. Program dir. video documentaries including Learning Through Live Events and Teaching Skills for the 21st Century, 1995; contbr. articles to profl. jours. Mem. Middletown Free Libr. Bd., 1977-79; officer Riddlewood Aux. to Riddle Meml. Hosp., Media, 1973-78; chairperson Lima (Pa.) Christian Nursery Sch., 1973, March of Dimes, Middletown, 1973; pres. Roosevelt PTG (Elem. Sch.), Media, 1982; com. person, v.p. Middletown Twp. Dem. Com., 1974; capt. March of Dimes, Media, 1987-91, Diabetes Assn., Media, 1989-91; mem. Vietnamese refugee com. Media Presbyn. Ch., 1975, mem., 1967—; vol. Tyler Arboretum, Middletown Twp., 1980-82. Recipient 1st Pl. Color Divsn. Photography award Pa. Colonial Plantation, 1st pl. Color Divsn. in Photography Bloomsburg State Fair, 1994; Fine Arts in Spl. Edn. grantee Pa. Dept. Edn., 1993-94. Mem. NEA, ASCD, Pa. ASCD, Rose Tree Media Edn. Assn. (profl. devel. com. chairperson 1992-93, profl. devel. com. rep. 1990-93, Exceptional Svc. award), Pa. State Edn. Assn., Nat. Staff Devel. Coun., Aircraft Owners and Pilots Assn., Tyler Arboretum, Media Soc. Performing Arts, Phila. Zoo, Chester County Hist. Soc., Longwood Gardens. Democrat. Avocations: reading, writing, interior decorating, nature walking, gardening. Home: 203 Cohasset Ln West Chester PA 19380-6507 Office: Rose Tree Media Sch Dist Glenwood Elem Sch Pennell Rd Media PA 19063

STRUNK, ORLO CHRISTOPHER, JR., psychology educator; b. Pen Argyl, Pa., Apr. 14, 1925; s. Orlo Christopher and Katherine Elizabeth (Glasser) S.; m. Mary Louise Reynolds, July 3, 1947; children: Laura Louise, John Christopher. Certificate, Churchman Bus. Coll., Easton, Pa., 1948; A.B., W. Va. Wesleyan Coll., Buckhannon, 1953; S.T.B., Boston U., 1955, Ph.D., 1957. Exec. sec. Inst. Pastoral Care, Mass. Gen. Hosp., 1955-57; grad. asst. Boston U., 1955-57, instr. psychology of religion, 1956; instr. Boston U. (Sch. Theology), 1957-58, 62; assoc. prof. psychology W. Va. Wesleyan Coll., 1957-60, dean, prof. psychology, 1959-69; prof. psychology of religion Boston U., 1969-86; also faculty counselor, supr. Albert V. Danielsen Inst.; part-time faculty Webster U., 1994—; pastoral psychotherapist The Coastal Samaritan Ctr., Myrtle Beach, S.C., 1986—; assoc. dir., staff psychologist Ecumenical Counseling Svc., Inc., Melrose, Mass.; rsch. cons. Religion in Edn. Found., Calif. Author: Readings in the Psychology of Religion, 1959, Religion: A Psychological Interpretaton, 1962, Mature Religion: A Psychological Study, 1965, The Choice Called Atheism, 1969, The Psychology of Religion, 1971, Dynamic Interpersonalism for Ministry, 1973, The Secret Self, 1976, Privacy: Experience, Understanding, Expression, 1983; mng. editor: Jour. Pastoral Care. Served with USAAF, 1943-46. Decorated Air medal with five oak leaf clusters. Fellow Am. Psychol. Assn.; mem. W.Va. Assn. Acad. Deans (pres.). Methodist (elder). Home: 1068 Harbor Dr SW Calabash NC 28467-2300 *It is my conviction that life is a mystery to be lived more than it is a problem to be solved. As such, I have tried to develop a style of life which permits me to be open to a wide range of experiences guided by a simple principle which requires me to do battle with all those conditions which disrupt my and others freedom to live an authentic life of openness and continuous growth. The central principle guiding the openness to life is found in the spirit of Jesus Christ which includes love of Self, others, and my God. The task of working out these abstractions in a concrete manner is difficult and mysterious - but never, never dull.*

STRUNK, ROBERT CHARLES, physician; b. Evanston, Ill., May 29, 1942; s. Norman Wesley and Marion Mildred (Ree) S.; m. Alison Leigh Gans, Apr. 3, 1971; children: Christopher Robert, Alix Elizabeth. BA in Chemistry, Northwestern U., 1964, MS in Biochemistry, 1968, MD, 1968. Lic. MD, Ariz., Colo., Mass., Mo. Resident in pediatrics Cin. Children's Hosp., 1968-70; pediatrician Newport (R.I.) Naval Hosp., 1970-72; rsch. fellow in pediatrics Harvard Med. Sch., Boston, 1972-74; asst. prof. pediatrics U. Ariz. Health Sci. Ctr., Tucson, 1974-78; dir. clin. svcs. Nat. Jewish Ctr. for Immunology and Respiratory Med., Denver, 1978-87; sabbatical leave Boston Children's Hosp., 1984-85; dir. divsn. allergy and pulmonary medicine Children's Hosp., St. Louis, 1987--; pediatrician Barnes and Allied Hosp., St. Louis, 1987--; prof. pediatrics Sch. Medicine Washington U., St. Louis, 1987--. Recipient Allergic Disease Acad. award Nat. Inst. Allergy and Infectious Disease of NIH. Mem. Am. Acad. Allergy and Immunology, Am. Thoracic Soc. Office: Washington U Sch Med Dept Pediatrics 400 S Kingshighway Blvd Saint Louis MO 63110-1014

STRUNZ, KIM CAROL, military officer; b. Caro, Mich., May 3, 1954; d. Herbert James and Geraldine (Elliott) S. AAS with honors, Delta Coll., 1974; BS with honors, Alma Coll., 1980; postgrad., Ctrl. Mich. U., 1978-80; MPA, U. Okla., 1989. Diplomate Am. Coll. Healthcare Execs. Commd. 2d lt. U.S. Army, 1980, advanced through grades to maj.; telecomms. ctr. specialist 178th signal co. U.S. Army, Heidelberg, Germany, 1974-77; chief plans, ops., tng. and security med. dept. activity U.S. Army, Bremerhaven, Germany, 1980-82; ambulance platoon leader Co. C 47th med. bn. U.S. Army, Furth, Germany, 1982-83; exec. officer dental activity U.S. Army, Ft. Lee, Va., 1983-85; adjutant Kenner Army Comty. Hosp. U.S. Army, Ft. Lee, 1985; comdr. med. co. 47th Field Hosp. U.S. Army, Ft. Sill, Okla., 1986-88; chief pers. svcs. divsn. 121st Evac. Hosp. 18th med. command U.S. Army, Seoul, Korea, 1988-89; chief mil. pers. br. William Beaumont Army Med. Ctr., El Paso, Tex., 1990-92, comdr. troop command, 1992-93; career planning officer U.S. Total Army Personnel Command, Alexandria, Va., 1993-95; pers. policy analyst Office of the Army Surgeon Gen., Falls Church, Va., 1995—. Contbr. rsch. articles to profl. jours. Vol. Therapeutic Horsemanship Assn., El Paso, Alexandria Hosp.; mem. Highland Presbyn. Ch. Softball Team, El Paso. Mem. Am. Soc. Pub. Adminstrn., Assn. U.S. Army, Army Women's Profl. Assn. Presbyterian. Avocations: horseback riding, fishing, skiing, hiking. Home: 801 N Howard St Apt 306 Alexandria VA 22304-5460

STRUPP, HANS HERMANN, psychologist, educator; b. Frankfurt am Main, Germany, Aug. 25, 1921; came to U.S., 1939, naturalized, 1945; s. Josef and Anna (Metzger) S.; m. Lottie Metzger, Aug. 19, 1951; children: Karen, Barbara, John. AB with distinction, George Washington U., 1945, AM, 1947, PhD, 1954; MD (hon.), U. Ulm, Fed. Republic of Germany, 1986. Diplomate in clin. psychology Am. Bd. Profl. Psychology; lic. clin. psychologist, Tenn. Research psychologist Human Factors Ops. Research Labs., Dept. Air Force, Washington, 1949-54; supervisory research psychologist, personnel research br. Adj. Gen.'s Office, Dept. of Army, Washington, 1954-55; dir. psychotherapy research project Sch. Medicine, George Washington U., Washington, 1955-57; dir. psychol. services, dept. psychiatry U. N.C. Sch. Medicine, Chapel Hill, 1957-64; asso. prof. psychology U. N.C. Sch. Medicine, 1957-62, prof., 1962-66; prof. dept. psychology Vanderbilt U., Nashville, 1966-76, dir. clin. tng., dept. psychology, 1967-76, disting. prof., 1976-94, Harvie Branscomb disting. prof., 1985-86; disting. prof. emeritus, 1994—. Mem. editorial adv. bd. Psychotherapy: Theory, Research and Practice, 1963—, Jour. Cons. and Clin. Psychology, 1964—, Jour. Nervous and Mental Disease, 1965—, Jour. Am. Acad. Psychoanalysis, 1972—, Jour. Contemporary Psychotherapy, 1972-86, Psychiatry Research, 1979-86, Jour. Profl. Psychology, 1976-89; founding editor Psychotherapy Rsch., 1990-95; others; contbr. chpts. to books, articles and revs. to profl. jours. Recipient Helen Sargent meml. prize Menninger Found., 1963; Alumni Achievement award George Washington U., 1972; Disting. Profl. Achievement award Am. Bd. Profl. Psychology, 1976, Disting. Profl. Contbns. to Knowledge award Am. Psychol. Assn., 1987; others. Fellow Am. Psychol. Assn. (mem. exec. council 1964, exec. bd. 1969-72, council of reps. 1970-73, chmn. com. on fellows div. psychotherapy 1970-74, pres. div. clin. psychology 1974-75, recipient Disting. Profl. Psychologist award 1973, Disting. Scientist award 1979), Tenn. Psychol. Assn., AAAS; mem. Eastern Psychol. Assn., Southeastern Psychol. Assn., Am. Psychopathol. Assn., Soc. for Psychotherapy Research (pres. 1972-73, Career Contbr. award 1986), Psychologists Interested in Advancement of Psychoanalysis, Phi Beta Kappa, Sigma Xi. Home: 4117 Dorman Dr Nashville TN 37215-2404 Office: Vanderbilt U Wilson Hall Dept Psychology Nashville TN 37240 *Scientific and professional work is a very personal endeavor. It is the pursuit of meaning and the search for answers to the existential questions that have occupied mankind through the ages. Thus, the motivation to do one's best within one's limited powers is nothing altruistic although it counts as a great reward to kindle a spark in others. As a refugee from Nazi Germany, I remain deeply grateful for the opportunities my adopted country has provided me.*

STRUPP, JACQUELINE VIRGINIA, small business specialist, insurance professional; b. Montevideo, Uruguay, July 24, 1963; d. Gunther and Silvia (Klemens) S.; children: Matias, Mercedes. BA with hons. cum laude, NYU, 1986. Customer svc. mgr. Games Mag./Mail Order, N.Y.C., 1984-86; treas., property mgr., asst. to chief exec. officer Hudson Properties, Lyndhurst, N.J., 1986-90; sales assoc. Bloomingdale's, Palm Beach Gardens, Fla., 1990-91, staff tng. supr. and pers. asst., 1991-92; legal asst., bookkeeper Gov.'s Bank and Bruce W. Keihner, Palm Beach, Fla., 1993; assoc. Ideas & Things, 1994—; freelance bus. mgr., 1993—, personal and bus. coach, 1993—; ind. ins. agt. specializing in health ins. for self-employed bus. owners.

STRUPP, JOHN ALLEN, oncologist; b. Chapel Hill, N.C., Dec. 13, 1958; s. Hans Hermann and Lottie (Metzger) S.; m. Dana Morris, Oct. 20, 1984; children: Emily, Joshua, Suzanne. BA, U. N.C., 1980; MD, U. Tenn., 1985. Diplomate Nat. Bd. Med. Examiners. Intern, resident in internal medicine U. Pitts. Hosp., 1985-88; fellow in med. oncology Vanderbilt U., Nashville, 1988-90; med. oncologist St. Thomas Med. Group, Nashville, 1990—; chief divsn. hematology/oncology St. Thomas Hosp., Nashville, 1994—; med. dir. Response Oncology, Inc., 1991—; asst. clin. prof. dept. medicine Vanderbilt U. Sch. Medicine, 1993—; bd. dirs. Alive Hospice, Inc., chmn. quality improvement com., 1997; med. adv. bd. Coram Healthcare, Inc., 1994—. Campaign chmn. physician's divsn. Nashville Jewish Fedn., 1994-95, 95-96; bd. dirs. Nashville chpt. Am. Jewish Com., 1994-96; parents com. Univ. Sch. Nashville Capital Campaign, 1996. Mem. Am. Coll. Physicians, Am. Soc. Clin. Oncology, Tenn. Med. Assn. (alt. del.), Nashville Oncology Soc., Nashville Acad. Medicine, Phi Beta Kappa. Home: 30 Old Club Ct Nashville TN 37215 Office: 4230 Harding Rd Ste 400 Nashville TN 37205-2013

STRUTHERS, MARGO S., lawyer. BA, Carleton Coll., 1972; JD cum laude, U. Minn., 1976. Atty., shareholder Moss & Barnett, P.A. and predecessor firms, Mpls., 1976-93; ptnr. Oppenheimer Wolff & Donnelly, Mpls., 1993—. Mem. Am. Acad. Healthcare Attys., Nat. Health Lawyers Assn., Minn. State Bar Assn. (bus. law sect., chairperson nonprofit com., former chairperson and governing coun. mem. health law sect.), Minn. Soc. Healthcare Attys. (former pres.). Office: Oppenheimer Wolff & Donnelly Plaza VII 45 S 7th St Ste 3400 Minneapolis MN 55402-1632

STRUTIN, KENNARD REGAN, lawyer, educator, law librarian; b. Bklyn., Dec. 1, 1961; s. Fred and Estelle (Brodzansky) S. BA summa cum laude, St. John's U., Jamaica, N.Y., 1981; JD, Temple U. Sch. Law, Phila., 1984; MLS, St. John's U., 1994. Bar: N.Y. 1986, U.S. Dist. Ct. (ea. and so. dists.) N.Y. 1990, U.S. Dist. Ct. (no. and we. dists.) N.Y. 1991, U.S. Ct. Appeals (2d cir.) 1990, U.S. Ct. Appeals (fed. cir.) 1991, U.S. Tax Ct. 1991, U.S. Ct. Mil. Appeals 1991, U.S. Supreme Ct. 1990. Atty. pvt. practice, West Hempstead, N.Y., 1986; trial atty. Nassau County Legal Aid Soc., Hempstead, N.Y., 1987-88, Orange County Legal Aid Soc., Goshen, N.Y., 1988-90; atty. pvt. practice, West Hempstead, N.Y., 1990-91; staff atty. N.Y. State Defenders Assn., Albany, N.Y., 1991-93; adj. asst. prof. St. John's U., Jamaica, N.Y., 1993-96; small claims tax assessment hearing officer Supreme Ct., Nassau, Suffolk, N.Y., 1993-96; law libr. Syracuse U. Coll. of Law, 1996—; spkr. lawyer in classroom Nassau County Bar Assn., Mineola, N.Y., 1987-94; spkr. pre-release program Correctional Facilities, Lower Hudson Valley, N.Y., 1989-94. Contbr. articles to profl. jours. Recipient Gold Key in History award, 1981, Cert. Achievement in History award, 1980, Cert. Acad. Excellence, St. John's U., 1994, Orange County Exec. Recognition award, 1990, 93. Mem. Am. Assn. Law Librs., Beta Phi Mu. Office: Syracuse U Coll of Law H Douglas Barclay Law Libr Syracuse NY 13244-1030

STRUTTON, LARRY D., newspaper executive; b. Colorado Springs, Colo., Sept. 12, 1940; s. Merril and Gladys (Sheldon) S.; m. Carolyn Ann Croak, Dec. 3, 1960; children—Gregory L., Kristen. A.A. in Electronics Engring., Emily Griffith Electronics Sch., 1968; B.S. in Bus. Mgmt. and Systems Mgmt., Met. State Coll., 1971; diploma in Advanced Mgmt. Program, Harvard U., 1988. Printer Gazette Telegraph, Colorado Springs, Colo., 1961-64; prodn. dir. Rocky Mountain News, Denver, 1964-80, pres., 1990, pres. and CEO, 1991—; exec. v.p. ops. and advt. Detroit Free Press, 1981-83; v.p. ops. Los Angeles Times, 1983-85, exec. v.p. ops., 1986-90. Mem. adv. com. Rochester Inst. Tech., 1984—. Mem. Am. Newspaper Pubs. Assn. (chmn. 1987, chmn. TEC com. 1985-86), R&E Council (research and engring. council of the Graphic Arts Industry Inc.). Club: Lakeside Golf (Los Angeles). Home: 50 Glenmoor Cir Englewood CO 80110-7121 also: Rocky Mountain News 400 W Colfax Ave Denver CO 80204*

STRUTZ, WILLIAM A., lawyer; b. Bismarck, N.D., May 13, 1934; s. Alvin C. and Ina Vee (Minor) S.; m. Marilyn Seagly, Aug. 31, 1957; children: Heidi Jane Mitchell, Colin Christopher, Nathaniel Paul. Student, Drake U., 1952-53; BA, North Ctrl. Coll., 1956; postgrad., Washington and Lee U., 1956-57; JD, U. N.D., 1959. Bar: N.D. 1959, U.S. Dist. Ct. N.D. 1959, U.S. Ct. Appeals (8th cir.) 1961. Atty., pres. Fleck, Mather & Strutz, Ltd., Bismarck, N.D., 1959—; mem. grievance com. N.D. Supreme Ct., Bismarck, 1974-77, chmn. supreme ct. svcs. com., 1979—. Bd. dirs. Vets. Meml. Pub. Libr., Bismarck, Shiloh Christian Sch., Bismarck, 1978—; pres. student body North Ctrl. Coll., 1956. Recipient Herbert Harley award Am. Judicature Soc., 1991. Mem. ABA, Am. Bd. Trial Advs. (adv.), Lions Club. Methodist. Avocations: reading, rare book collecting, music, sports. Home: 1238 W Highland Acres Rd Bismarck ND 58501-1259 Office: Fleck Mather Strutz Ltd 400 E Broadway Ave Bismarck ND 58501-4038

STRUVE, GUY MILLER, lawyer; b. Wilmington, Del., Jan. 5, 1943; s. William Scott and Elizabeth Bliss (Miller) S.; m. Marcia Mayo Hill, Sept. 20, 1986; children: Andrew Hardenbrook, Catherine Tolstoy, Frank Leroy Hill, Guy Miller, Beverly Marcia Wise Hill (dec.), Elena Wise Struve-Hill. A.B. summa cum laude, Yale U., 1963; LL.B. magna cum laude, Harvard U., 1966. Bar: N.Y. 1967, D.C. 1986, U.S. Dist. Ct. (so. dist.) N.Y. 1970, U.S. Dist. Ct. (ea. dist.) N.Y. 1973, U.S. Dist. Ct. (no. dist.) Calif. 1979, U.S. Dist. Ct. D.C. 1987, U.S. Ct. Appeals (2d cir.) 1969, U.S. Ct. Appeals (D.C. cir.) 1973, U.S. Ct. Appeals (8th cir.) 1976, U.S. Ct. Appeals (9th cir.) 1979, U.S. Supreme Ct. 1971, U.S. Dist. Ct. (we. dist.) N.Y. 1991. Law clk. Hon. J. Edward Lumbard, Chief Judge United States Ct. Appeals for 2d Circuit, 1966-67; assoc. firm Davis Polk & Wardwell, 1967-72, ptnr., 1973—; ptnr. Ind. Counsel's Office, 1987-94. Mem. ABA, N.Y. State Bar Assn., Assn. of Bar of City of N.Y. (chmn. com. antitrust and trade regulation, 1983-86), Am. Law Inst. Home: 116 E 63rd St New York NY 10021-7303 Office: Davis Polk & Wardwell 450 Lexington Ave New York NY 10017-3911

STRUYK, ROBERT JOHN, lawyer; b. Sanborn, Iowa, May 17, 1932; s. Arie Peter and Adriana (VerHoef) S.; m. Barbara Damon, Sept. 7, 1963; children: Arie Franklin, Damon Nicholas, Elizabeth Snow. BA, Hope Coll., 1954; MA, Columbia U., 1957; LLB, U. Minn., 1961. Bar: Minn., U.S. Dist. Ct. Minn. Secondary tchr. Indianola (Iowa) Pub. Schs., 1957-58; assoc., then ptnr. Dorsey & Whitney, Mpls., 1961—. Episcopalian. Clubs: Mpls., Minikahda. Office: Dorsey & Whitney 220 S 6th St Minneapolis MN 55402-4502

STRYKER, JAMES WILLIAM, automotive executive, former military officer; b. Grand Rapids, Mich., Apr. 20, 1940; s. John Alvin and Marian (Anderson) S.; m. Eleanor Marie Finger, Sept. 26, 1964; children: James William II, Marian Marie, Kathryn Alison Greenbauer. BS, U.S. Mil. Acad., 1963; MA, U. Mich., 1972; postgrad., U.S. Army Command and Gen. Staff Coll., 1978. Commd. 2d lt. U.S. Army, 1963; battery exec. officer 6th/20th field arty. U.S. Army, Ft. Carson, Colo., 1964-65; advisor U.S. Army, Vietnam, 1965-66; battery comdr. 4th/3d field arty. U.S. Army, Ft. Hood, Tex., 1967-68; advisor U.S. Army, Thailand, 1969-70; S-3 ops. officer 1st/7th F.A., Ft. Riley, Kans., 1972-73; assoc. prof. history U.S. Mil. Acad., West Point, N.Y., 1973-77; chief nuclear ops. Ctrl. Army Group NATO, Heidelberg, Germany, 1978-81; dir., project mgr. tank-automotive command U.S. Army, Warren, Mich., 1981-86; ret. U.S. Army, 1986; program mgr. military vehicles operation GMC Truck, Pontiac, Mich., 1987-95; cross brand portfolio mgr. Pontiac-GMC Divsn. GM Corp., Pontiac, Mich., 1996—. Author: (with others) Encyclopedia of Southern History, 1977; co-author: Early American Wars, 1978. Decorated Legion of Merit, Bronze Star medal, Def. Meritorious Svc. medal, Meritorious Svc. medal with oakleaf cluster, Army Commendation medal with oakleaf cluster, U.S. Army/Vietnamese Cross of Gallantry with palm and gold star. Mem. NRA (life), Am. Def. Preparedness Assn. (dir. Detroit chpt. 1991-92, 94—, 2d v.p. 1995, 1st v.p. 1995-96, pres. 1996—), Assn. U.S. Army (dir. Detroit chpt. 1990-95), Gordon Setter Club Am., Nodrog Setter Club Mich. Avocations: hunting, skeet shooting, trout fishing, field training English and Gordon Setters. Home: 168 First St Romeo MI 48065-5000 Office: Pontiac-GMC Divsn MC 482-A29-B25 31 E Judson St Pontiac MI 48342-2206

STRYKER, SHELDON, sociologist, educator; b. St. Paul, May 26, 1924; s. Max and Rose (Moskevitz) S.; m. Alyce Shirley Agranoff, Sept. 7, 1947; children: Robin Sue, Jeffrey, David, Michael, Mark. B.A. summa cum laude, U. Minn., 1948, M.A., 1950, Ph.D., 1955. Mem. faculty Ind. U., 1951—, prof. sociology, 1964—, disting. prof. sociology, 1985—; dir. Inst.

Social Research, 1965-70, 89-94, chmn. dept. sociology, 1969-75; co-dir. Ctr. for Social Rsch., 1989-94; cons. in field; mem. social scis. research rev. com. NIMH, 1974-79, chmn., 1976-79, mem. research scientist devel. award com., 1981-85. Editor: Sociometry, 1966-69, Rose Monograph Series of Am. Sociol. Assn., 1971-73, Am. Sociol. Rev., 1982-85; assoc. editor: Social Problems, 1957-59; author books, monographs, articles, chpts. in books. Served with AUS, 1943-46. Fellow Social Sci. Research Council, 1959-60, Ctr. Advanced Behavioral Scis., 1986-87; Fulbright research scholar Italy, 1966-67. Mem. Am. Sociol. Assn. (nat. coun. 1965-67, 80-81, chmn. social psychology sect. 1978-79, chmn. publs. com. 1991-93, Cooley-Mead award), Ohio Valley Sociol. Soc. (coun. 1965-67), North Ctrl. Sociol. Assn. (pres. 1978-79), Sociol. Rsch. Assn. (coun. 1978-84, pres. 1983-84), Phi Beta Kappa. Home: 3710 Saint Remy Dr Bloomington IN 47401-2418

STRYKER, STEVEN CHARLES, lawyer; b. Omaha, Oct. 26, 1944; s. James M. and Jean G. (Grannis) S.; m. Bryna Dee Litwin, Oct. 20, 1972; children: Ryan, Kevin, Gerrit, Courtney. BS, U. Iowa, 1967, JD with distinction, 1969; postgrad., Northwestern Grad. Sch. Bus., 1969-70, DePaul U., 1971. Bar: Iowa 1969, Tex. 1986; CPA, Ill., Iowa. Sr. tax acct. Arthur Young & Co., Chgo., 1969-72; fed. tax mgr. Massey Ferguson, Des Moines, 1972-74; fed./state tax mgr FMC Corp., Chgo., 1974-78; gen. tax atty. Shell Oil Co., Houston, 1978-81, asst. gen. tax counsel, 1981-83, gen. mgr., 1983-86, v.p., gen. tax counsel, 1986—. Mem. ABA, Texas Bar Assn., Iowa Bar Assn., Am. Inst. CPA's, Ill. Soc. CPA's, Iowa Soc. CPA's., Tax Execs. Inst., Am. Petroleum Inst. Republican. Home: 10819 Everwood Ln Houston TX 77024-5416 Office: Shell Oil Co 1 Shell Plz Ste 4570 Houston TX 77001

STUART, ANNE ELIZABETH, journalist, freelance writer, educator; b. Lansing, Mich., Nov. 5, 1956. BA in English and Journalism with honors, Mich. State U., 1979; MS in Journalism, Columbia U., N.Y.C., 1986. Reporter, editor Star-Gazette/Sunday Telegram, Elmira, N.Y., 1980-83; reporter Knickerbocker News, Albany, N.Y., 1983-85; intern Newsday, Long Island, N.Y., 1985; freelance writer N.Y.C. and Boston, 1985-87; reporter The Patriot Ledger, Quincy, Mass., 1987-90, AP, Boston, 1990-94; mng. editor CIO, WebMaster Mags., Framingham, Mass., 1994—; instr. adult edn. programs, Boston, Brookline, Mass., Cambridge, Mass.; instr. Northeastern U., 1990-91, Emerson Coll., 1989. Contbr. chpts. to health and travel books; contbr. articles to Boston mag., L.A. Times, Washington Post, Chgo. Tribune, Mass. Health Care, Boston Herald, Newsday, Seventeen, Northeastern Mag., and other publs.; mng. editor Mich. State U. newspaper The State News, 1978-79, other State News reporting and eidting, 1975-78. Knight Found. for Specialized Journalism fellow, 1988; Brookdale Inst. scholar, Scripps-Howard Found. Jacqueline Radin Newsday scholar, 1985-86, recipient nat. 1st pl. in-depth reporting Sigma Delta Chi Mark of Excellence Competition, 1986, 1st pl. in-depth reporting and feature writing, 1986, statewide 3d pl. N.Y. State Assn. Press Competition Am. Acad. Family Physicians, 1983, Nat. Well-Done award Gannett Co., 1982, statewide 2d pl. in news Detroit Press 1979, La Nacion Press award, 1990. Office: CIO Communications 492 Old Conn Path Framingham MA 01701

STUART, CAROLE, publishing executive; b. N.Y.C., Feb. 22, 1941; d. Frank and Sally (Stern) Rose: m. Lyle Stuart, Feb. 4, 1982; 1 child, Jennifer Susan Livingston. Student, Bklyn. Coll. Pub. Lyle Stuart Inc., Secaucus, N.J.; assoc. pub. Carol Pub. Group, N.Y.C.; pub. Barricade Books, Inc., N.Y.C. Author: Why Was I Adopted?, To Turn You On, 39 Sex Fantasies for Women, (with Claire Ciliotta), Why Am I Going to the Hospital?, I'll Never Be Fat Again, How To Lose 5 Pounds Fast, The Affair. Mem. Authors Guild, Women's Media Group, Wine and Food Soc. N.Y., Emily's List. Home: 1530 Palisade Ave Ste 6L Fort Lee NJ 07024-5470 Office: Barricade Books 150 5th Ave New York NY 10011-4311

STUART, CHARLES EDWARD, electrical engineer, oceanographer; b. Durham, N.C., Feb. 9, 1942; s. Charles Edward and Wilma Kelly Stuart; m. Margaret Ann Robinson, Jan. 9, 1982; children: Marjorie Kelly, Heather Alison. BSEE, Duke U., 1963. Engr. Westinghouse Electric Corp., Balt., 1963-65; sr. engr. Booz Allen Hamilton, Chevy Chase, Md., 1966-68; rsch. dir. B-K Dynamics Inc., Huntsville, Ala., 1969-78; oceanographer Office of Naval Rsch., Arlington, Va., 1979-84; dir. maritime system office Advanced Rsch. Projects Agy., Arlington, 1985—. Contbr. 12 papers on ocean acoustics to profl. jours. Recipient Am. Def. Preparedness Assn. award, Bushnell award for career contbns. to undersea warfare, 1996. Mem. IEEE (sr., ad. com. 1991-93), Assn. Unmanned Vehicle Systems (trustee 1989-93). Methodist. Achievements include leading work in development of unmanned undersea vehicle technology. Home: 4718 17th St N Arlington VA 22207-2031 Office: Advanced Rsch Projects Agy 3701 Fairfax Dr Arlington VA 22203-1700

STUART, DAVID EDWARD, anthropologist, author, educator; b. Calhoun County, Ala., Jan. 9, 1945; s. Edward George and Avis Elsie (Densmore) S.; B.A. (Wesleyan Merit scholar 1965-66), W.VA. Wesleyan Coll., 1967; M.A. in Anthropology, U. N.Mex., 1970, Ph.D., 1972, postdoctoral student, 1975-76; m. Cynthia K. Morgan, June 14, 1971. Research assoc. Andean Center, Quito, Ecuador, 1970; continuing edn. instr. anthropology U. N.Mex., 1971-72, research archeologist Office Contract Archeology, 1974, research coordinator, 1974-77, asst. prof. anthropology, 1975-77, assoc. prof. anthropology, 1984—, asst. v.p. acad. affairs, 1987-95, assoc. v.p. academic affairs, 1995—; asst. prof. Eckerd Coll., St. Petersburg, Fla., 1972-74; cons. archeologist right-of-way div. Pub. Service Co. N.Mex., Albuquerque, 1977-78; cons. anthropologist Bur. Indian Affairs, Albuquerque, 1978, Historic Preservation Bur. N.Mex., Santa Fe, 1978-81, Nat. Park Service, 1980, Albuquerque Mus., 1981; sr. research assoc. Human Systems Research, Inc., 1981-83, Quivira Research Center, Albuquerque, 1984-86; bd. dirs. Table Ind. Scholars, 1979-83, pres., bd. dirs. Rio Grande Heritage Found., Albuquerque and Las Cruces, 1985-87; advisor Human Systems Research, Inc., Tularosa, N.Mex., 1978-80, Albuquerque Commn. on Hist. Preservation, 1984-86. Grantee Eckerd Coll., 1973, Historic Preservation Bur., 1978-80. Essayist award N.Mex. Humanities Council, 1986. Mem. Am. Anthrop. Assn., Royal Anthrop. Inst. Gt. Britain, N.Mex. Archeol. Council, Albuquerque Archeol. Soc. (pres. 1986-88), Descs. Signers Declaration Independence, Sigma Xi, Phi Kappa Phi. Presbyterian. Co-author: Archeological Survey: 4 Corners to Ambrosia, N.Mex., 1976, A Proposed Project Design for the Timber Management Archeological Surveys, 1978, Ethnoarcheological Investigations of Shepherding in the Pueblo of Laguna, 1983; Author: Prehistoric New Mexico, 1981, 2d edit., 1984, 3d edit., 1988, Glimpses of the Ancient Southwest, 1985, The Magic of Bandelier National Monument, 1989, Power and Efficiency in Eastern Anasazi Architecture, 1994, others; columnist New Mexico's Heritage, 1983-87, others. Editor: Archeological Reports, No. 1, 1975, No. 2, 1981. Office: U NMex Rm 263 Student Svcs Ctr Albuquerque NM 87131 *Personal philosophy: In academics, as in life, reliability, integrity and compassion are far more precious than mere intellectual brilliance.*

STUART, FRANK ADELL, county official; b. Tahoka, Tex., Dec. 18, 1928; s. John Franklin and Mary Elizabeth (Reed) S.; m. Mary Louise Wheat Crelia, Feb. 2, 1962; children: Rita, Donna, Franklin, Burce, Susan, Mary, Chris. BBA, Tex. Tech U., 1979. Asst. cashier Am. State Bank, Lubbock, Tex., 1949-52, Citizen Nat. Bank, Lubbock, 1953-59; acct. in pvt. practice Lubbock, 1960-63; asst. mgr. Gibson Discount Ctr., Lubbock, 1964-77; tax. assessor and collector Lubbock County, Lubbock, 1979-94, ret., 1994. Served to col. Tex. State Guard, 1988—. Mem. Tax Assessor-Collectors Assn. Tex., Lubbock C. of C., Masons, YorkRite, Scottish Rite, Shriners, Yellow House Lodge, Daylight Lodge. Baptist. Home: 2704 57th St Lubbock TX 79413-5605

STUART, GARY MILLER, railroad executive; b. Normal, Ill., May 8, 1940; s. Henry Woodward and Ruth Amy (Miller) S.; m. Sylvia Georgeades, Oct. 10, 1965; children: David, Peter, Paul, Michael. BS, MIT, 1962; MA, Harvard U., 1965. With Ford Motor Co., Dearborn, Mich., 1965-74, Gen. Foods Corp., White Plains, N.Y., 1974-81; dir. operational rsch. Union Pacific Corp., Bethlehem, Pa., 1981-83, asst. treas., 1983-87, treas., 1987-89, v.p., treas., 1990—; bd. dirs. ACE Ltd., Hamilton, Bermuda, 1988—, Union Pacific Resources Group, Ft. Worth, 1995-96. Bd. govs. Lehigh Valley Cmty. Found., 1992—; bd. dirs. Sta. WLVT-TV/Lehigh Valley Pub. TV, 1992-94. NSF fellow, 1962-65, Hon. Woodrow Wilson fellow, 1962. Mem. Fin. Execs. Inst., Assn. Am. Railroads (chmn. treas. div. 1992-93). Office: Union Pacific Corp 8th & Eaton Aves Bethlehem PA 18018

STUART, GERARD WILLIAM, JR., investment company executive, city official; b. Yuba City, Calif., July 28, 1939; s. Gerard William and Geneva Bernice (Stuke) S.; student Yuba Jr. Coll., 1957-59, Chico State Coll., 1959-60; A.B., U. Calif., Davis, 1962; M.L.S., U. Calif., Berkeley, 1963; m. Lenore Frances Loroña, 1981. Rare book librarian Cornell U., 1964-68; bibliographer of scholarly collections Huntington Library, San Marino, Calif., 1968-73, head acquisitions librarian, 1973-75; sec.-treas., dir. Ravenstree Corp., 1969-80, pres., chmn. bd., 1980—; pres., chmn. bd. William Penn Ltd., 1981—. Councilman City of Yuma, 1992-96, also dep. mayor, 1995; bd. dirs. Ariz. Humanities Coun., 1993—. Lilly fellow Ind. U., 1963-64. Mem. Bibliog. Soc. Am., Phi Beta Kappa, Alpha Gamma Sigma, Phi Kappa Phi. Clubs: Rolls-Royce Owners; Grolier (N.Y.C.); Zamorano (Los Angeles). Office: 204 S Madison Ave Yuma AZ 85364-1421

STUART, HAROLD CUTLIFF, lawyer, business executive; b. Oklahoma City, July 4, 1912; s. Royal Cutliff and Alice (Bramlitt) S.; m. Joan Skelly, June 6, 1938 (dec. 1994); children: Randi Stuart Wightman, Jon Rolf; m. Frances Langford, Nov. 18, 1994. J.D., U. Va., 1936. Bar: Okla. 1936, D.C. 1952. Ptnr. Stuart, Biolchini, Turner & Givran, Tulsa; judge Common Pleas Ct., 1941-42; asst. sec. air force, 1949-51; chmn. bd. 1st Stuart Corp., radio, oil, real estate and investments, Tulsa; dir. Lowrance Electronics, Inc., Tulsa; spl. cons. to sec. Air Force, 1961-63; mem. Okla. Hwy. Commn., 1959-63; bd. dirs. Great Empire Broadcasting Inc., Wichita, Kans. Trustee emeritus Lovelace Found., Albuquerque; trustee N.Am. Wildlife Fedn; mem. Nat. Eagle Scout Coun. Boy Scouts Am., Disting. Eagle Scout; past pres. Air Force Acad. Found., chmn. bd. Served from 1st lt. to col. USAAF, 1942-46, ETO. Decorated Bronze Star (U.S.); comdr. Order of St. Olav; King Haakon 7th Victory medal; medal of Liberation (Norway); Croix de Guerre (Luxembourg); named to Okla. Aviation and Space Hall of Fame, Okla. Hall of Fame. Mem. Am., Okla., D.C. bar assns., Air Force Assn. (dir., nat. pres., chmn. bd. 1951-52), Tulsa C. of C., Tulsa Headliner, Falcon Found. (vice chmn.), Ducks Unltd. (trustee), Delta Kappa Epsilon. Democrat. Clubs: Southern Hills Country, The Boston (Tulsa); Burning Tree (Washington), Willoughby Golf, The Amb. (Stuart, Fla.). Home: PO Box 96 Jensen Beach FL 34958-0096 also: 4590 E 29th St Tulsa OK 74114-6208

STUART, JAMES, banker, broadcaster; b. Lincoln, Nebr., Apr. 11, 1917; s. Charles and Marie (Talbot) S.; m. Helen Catherine Davis, July 24, 1940; children: Catherine, James, William Scott. BA, BS, U. Nebr., 1940, HHD (hon.), 1990; HHD (hon.), U. Nebr., 1990, DHL (hon.), 1990. Chmn. bd. Stuart Mgmt. Co.; mng. ptnr. Stuart Enterprises; chmn. exec. com., bd. dirs. Nat. Bank Commerce, Lincoln; pres. Stuart Found. Founder, trustee Nebr. Human Resources Rsch. Found., 1948—; trustee Bryan Meml. Hosp., 1952-58, U. Nebr. Found., 1956—, Nebr. U. Endowment Fund for Disting. Tchrs.; mem. Lincoln Found., 1955—, Lincoln Sch. Bd., 1961-64, pres., 1964; chmn. bd. trustees 1st Plymouth Ch., Lincoln, 1956; pres. Lincoln Community Chest, 1960. With AUS, 1942-45. Recipient Disting. Svc. award U. Nebr., 1961, Alumni Achievement award, 1980; named Nebraskan of Yr., Lincoln Rotary Club, 1997. Mem. U. Nebr. Alumni Assn. (past pres.), Lincoln U. Club, Country Club of Lincoln, Gitchigami Club (Duluth, Minn.), Sunrise Country Club (Rancho Mirage, Calif.), Thunderbird Country Club. Home: 2801 Bonacum Dr Lincoln NE 68502-5723 Office: 852 Nbc Ctr Lincoln NE 68508

STUART, JAMES FORTIER, musician, artistic director; b. Baton Rouge, Dec. 22, 1928; s. Evander Morgan and Jeanne (Fortier) S. Mus.B., La. State U., 1950, B.Music Edn., 1950, Mus.M., 1954; Mus.D., U. Rochester, 1968. Asst. prof. voice, dir. opera Boston U.; also Boston Conservatory, 1964-68; prof. music, dir. opera Kent (Ohio) State U., 1968—; founder, artistic dir. Kent Light Opera Co., 1969—, Nat. Light Opera Co., 1977—; artistic dir. Ohio Light Opera Co., Wooster, 1979—; pres. Stuart Prodns., Ltd., Cleve., 1974—; mus. cons. Internat. Hospitality Mgmt., Inc., Cleve., 1974. Tenor soloist maj. opera cos. and symphonies, N.Y.C., Boston, Phila., Atlanta and New Orleans, 1950-70; leader tenor Am. Savoyards, 1956-60, Martyn Green Gilbert and Sullivan Co., 1961-67; translator into English from original French text: Auber's Fra Diavolo, 1988, Lecocq's Fille de Madame Angot, 1989, Ciboulette (Reynaldo Hahn), 1990, Offenbach's M. Choufleuri, 1996, Millöcker's Der Bettelstudent, 1996. Recipient Significant Sig Outstanding Achievement in Lyric Theatre award Sigma Chi, 1995; inducted Coll. of Fellows of Am. Theatre, 1996. Office: Ohio Light Opera Wooster Coll Wooster OH 44691 *A man's greatest contribution to society is developing himself to the fullest. Only after he has accomplished this can he be of service to his fellow human beings.*

STUART, JOHN MCHUGH, JR., public relations consultant, retired foreign service officer; b. Albany, N.Y., Apr. 21, 1916; s. John McHugh and Marie (Fitzgerald) S.; m. Ruth Sherman, June 24, 1944 (dec. May 1977). Student, U. Santa Clara, 1934-35; B.A., Georgetown U., 1939; M.A., George Washington U., 1966; grad., Air War Coll., 1966. Reporter, editor, 1938-44; fgn. service officer Office Mil. Govt. U.S., Germany, 1945-50, USIA, 1954-71; press attache Am. embassy, New Delhi, 1962-65; pub. affairs officer U.S. Mission in Geneva, 1956-61; fgn. corr. Voice of Am., Korea and Germany, 1950-56; press counselor Am. embassy, Saigon, 1966-67; sr. adviser pub. affairs U.S. Mission to UN, N.Y.C., 1967-71; spl. adviser U.S. del. 26th UN Gen. Assembly, 1971; spokesman U.S. del. conf. on human environment, Stockholm, 1972; adviser 31st Gen. Assembly, 1976, 3d UN Law of Sea Conf., N.Y., 1977, VIth and Xth Spl. Gen. Assemblies on Disarmament, 1978, 82; now cons. internat. pub. affairs N.Y.C., also Washington; adviser European Security Conf., USIA, 1973, Agri-Energy Roundtable, Geneva, 1981. Served with SHAEF, World War II. Mem. Nat. Press Club. Home and Office: 180 West End Ave Apt 27L New York NY 10023-4919

STUART, JOSEPH MARTIN, art museum administrator; b. Seminole, Okla., Nov. 9, 1932; s. Arch William and Lillian (Lindsey) S.; BFA in Art, U. N.Mex., 1959, MA in Art, 1962; m. Signe Margaret Nelson, June 18, 1960; 1 dau., Lise Nelson Stuart. Dir., Roswell (N.Mex.) Museum and Art Center, 1960-62; curator U. Oreg. Mus. Art, 1962-63; dir. Boise (Idaho) Gallery Art, 1964-68, Salt Lake (City) Art Ctr., 1968-71, S.D. Art Mus., Brookings, 1971-93; prof. art S.D. State U., 1971-93; represented in permanent collections: Civic Fine Arts Ctr., Sioux Falls, S.D., Coll. Idaho, Eureka Coll., Salt Lake Art Ctr., Sioux City (Iowa) Art Ctr., U. N.Mex. Art Mus., West Tex. State U.. With USN, 1951-55. Mem. Phi Kappa Phi. Unitarian. Author: Index of South Dakota Artists, 1974; Art of South Dakota, 1974, Harvey Dunn: Son of the Middle border, 1984, Art for a New Century, 1989; The Legacy of South Dakota Art, 1990; author numerous exhbn. catalogs.

STUART, LILLIAN MARY, writer; b. Chgo., Nov. 7, 1914; d. Ira and Katherine (Tries) Daugherty; m. Robert Graham Stuart, Aug. 7, 1936 (dec. Sept. 1969); 1 child, Mary Leone. Asst. to pres. Weisberger Bros., South Bend, 1933-42; head TWX distbn. Davis-Monthan AFB, Tucson, 1946-48; artist and music tchr., 1945-55; interviewer-counselor Ariz. State Employment Commn., Tucson, 1955-70; residence dir. YWCA, Tucson, 1970-71; tax preparer Tucson, 1971-72; U.S. census taker U.S. Govt., N.Mex., 1976, 80; mng. Luna County Rep. Party, Deming, 1976; tchr. YWCA, Tucson, 1969, El Paso Coll. Bus., 1972; tutor math, English, 1981; travel lectr. various civic groups and clubs; radio reader Lighthouse for the Blind, El Paso, 1983-89; spkr. Internat. Women's Day Celebration, 1996. Contbr. stories to The Quarterly; author: (series of biographies) Lighthouse for the Blind; actress Studebaker Players, South Bend, 1936-42, South Bend Theatre, 1936-42, (film) Extreme Prejudice, 1986; writer Centennial Mus. at U. Tex., El Paso, 1992-95. Counselor, vol. Crisis Ctr., Deming, 1975-77. Recipient plaques and prizes for various pieces of writing. Mem. Mensa, Rosicrucians, Sisters in Crime. Episcopalian. Avocations: travel, art. Address: 2710 W Ashby Pl Apt 323 San Antonio TX 78201-5380

STUART, LORI AMES, public relations executive; b. Hempstead, N.Y., Oct. 23, 1957; d. Henry Aschner and Janet (Hackel) Goldman; m. John Robert Ames, Jan. 30, 1982 (div. July 1990); 1 child, Robert Walter Ames; m. Robert John Stuart, July 27, 1991. BA, Hofstra U., 1979. Publicist Jane Wesman Pub. Rels., N.Y.C., 1980-84, v.p., 1991—; publicist, publicity mgr. William Morrow & Co., N.Y.C., 1984-89, publicity dir., 1989-90; lectr., mentor NYU, 1994. Jewish. Avocations: fishing, travel, reading, writing. Office: Jane Wesman Pub Rels 928 Broadway Ste 903 New York NY 10010-6008

STUART, LYLE, publishing company executive; b. N.Y.C., Aug. 11, 1922; s. Alfred and Theresa (Cohen) L.; m. Mary Louise Strawn, Sept. 26, 1946; children: Sandra Lee, Rory John.; m. Carole Livingston, Feb. 4, 1982; 1 dau., Jenni. Student pub. schs., N.Y.C.; PhD (hon.), State of Calif. Reporter Internat. News Service, 1945, Variety, 1945-46; script writer Dept. State, Voice of Am., 1946; editor Music Bus. mag., 1946-48; founder Expose, 1951; pub. The Independent, 1951-75; bus. mgr. MAD mag., 1952-54; pres. Citadel Press, 1970-89; founder Lyle Stuart, Inc., 1956; pres. University Books, Inc., 1983—, Hot News, 1983, Barricade Books, 1990—; Founder North Bergen (N.J.) Pub. Library. Prodr. Chinese Festival of Music, 1952-62; author: God Wears A Bowtie, 1949, The Secret Life of Walter Winchell, 1953, Mary Louise, 1970, Casino Gambling for the Winner, 1978, Lyle Stuart on Baccarat, 1983, 2d edit., 1995, Map of Life, 1996, Winning at Casino Gambling, 1995. Served with AUS, 1942-44. Mem. Am. Booksellers Assn., Silurians, Nat. Acad. TV Arts. and Scis., N.Y. Zool. Soc., Soc. Ky. Cols. Home: 1530 Palisade Ave Ste 6L Fort Lee NJ 07024-5470 Office: Barricade Books Inc 150 5th Ave New York NY 10011-4311

STUART, MARIE JEAN, physician, hematologist, researcher; b. Bangalore, India, Sept. 11, 1943; came to U.S., 1967; d. Norman and Dorothy (Dias) S. BS, Madras (India) U., MB. Asst. prof. pediatrics SUNY Health Sci. Ctr., Syracuse, 1972-76, assoc. prof., 1976-81, prof. pediatrics, 1981-87; prof. chief hematology and oncology div. St. Christophers Hosp. for Children and Temple U., Phila., 1987—; prof. thrombosis rsch. Temple U., 1987—; mem. nat. child health com. Nat. Inst. Child Health and Human Devel., Bethesda, Md., 1982-86; mem. nat. heart, lung and blood rsch. tng. com., NIH, Bethesda, 1993—. Contbr. articles to profl. jours.; contbr. book chpts. Recipient Rsch. award Temple U., 1997. Mem. Am. Fedn. Clin. Research. Am. Pediatric Soc., Soc. for Pediatric Research. Mem. Christian Ch. Avocations: music, art. Home: 10B W Society Hill Towers Philadelphia PA 19106 Office: St Christophers Hosp Children Div Hematolog Philadelphia PA 19134

STUART, MARTY, country music singer, musician, songwriter; b. Philadelphia, Miss., Sept. 30, 1958; m. Cindy Cash (div.). With The Sullivan Family, 1970, Lester Flatt & the Nashville Grass, 1972-79, Johnny Cash, 1980-86; studio musician on albums with Willie Nelson, Emmylou Harris, Neil Young, Billy Joel, Bob Dylan, George Jones others; co-prodr. album A Joyful Noise, 1991; albums include Marty, With A Little Help From My Friends, 1977, Busy Bee Cafe, 1982, Marty Stuart, 1986, Hillbilly Rock, 1989, Tempted, 1991, This One's Gonna Hurt You, 1992, Let There Be Country, 1992, Love & Luck, 1994, Marty Party Hit Park, 1995, Honky Tonkin's What I Do Best, 1996. Recipient (with Travis Tritt) Grammy award for The Whiskey Ain't Workin', 1993, Country Music Assn. Vocal Event of Yr. (with Travis Tritt), with Asleep at the Wheel 1994 Grammy for Instrumental Performance "Red Wing." Office: 119 17th Ave S Nashville TN 37203-2707

STUART, MARY, actress; b. Miami, Fla., July ; d. Guy M. and Mary (Stuart) Houchins; m. Richard Krolik, Aug. 1, 1951 (div.); children: Cynthia, Jeffrey M.; m. Wolfgang Neumann, 1986. Student pub. schs., Tulsa. Appears in leading role: Search For Tomorrow, NBC-TV, N.Y.C., 1951-86; songwriter, singer, Columbia Records, 1956, Bell Records, 1973; Author: (autobiography) Both of Me, 1980 (Lit. Guild selection). Mem. Actors Equity Assn., AFTRA, Screen Actors Guild, ASCAP. Episcopalian.

STUART, RAYMOND WALLACE, lawyer; b. Chattanooga, Feb. 13, 1941; s. Raymond Newton and Mary Vance (Wallace) S.; m. Peggy Woodward, Dec. 19, 1965; children: Raymond Warren, Laura Wallace Hopkins. BS in Physics, U. Cin., 1963, JD, 1972. Bar: Ohio 1972. Pvt. practice Cin., 1972-74; atty. USIA, Washington, 1975-89, dep. gen. counsel, 1989—. Exec. editor Univ. Cin. Law Review, 1971-72. Capt. U.S. Army Spl. Forces, 1963-69. Avocations: hunting, fishing, reading. Home: 9894 Becket Ct Fairfax VA 22032-2412 Office: USIA Office of Gen Counsel 301 4th St SW Washington DC 20547-0009

STUART, ROBERT, container manufacturing executive; b. Oak Park, Ill., Aug. 3, 1921; s. Robert S. and Marie (Vavra) Solinsky; m. Lillian C. Kondelik, Dec. 5, 1962 (dec. May 1978); m. Lila Winterhoff Peters, May 21, 1982. BS, U. Ill., 1943; LLD, U. Ill., Chgo., 1982. Sec.-treas., gen. mgr. Warren Metal Decorating Co., 1947-49; asst. to gen. mgr. Cans, Inc., 1950-52; asst. to v.p., then v.p. Nat. Can Corp., Chgo., 1953-59, exec. v.p., 1959-63, pres., 1963-69, chief exec., 1966-69, chmn. bd., chief exec. officer, 1969-73, chmn. bd., 1973-83, chmn. fin. com., 1983, mem. corp. devel. com., until 1986, chmn. emeritus, 1986—; past pres., bd. dirs. Corp. Responsibility Group of Greater Chgo. Past pres., bd. dirs. Chgo. Crime Commn.; dir. Nat. Crime Prevention Coun.; founding chmn. Nat. Minority Supplier Devel. Coun., 1972-73, Lloyd Morey Scholarship Fund: Freedoms Found. at Valley Forge, trustee; bd. assocs. Chgo. Theol. Sem.; trustee Ill. Masonic Med. Ctr.; mem. adv. bd. Salvation Army, Broader Urban Involvement and Leadership Devel.; chmn. emeritus World Federalist Assn.; past pres., past trustee, chmn. Cen. Ch. Chgo. Congregationalist; chmn. Assn. to Unite the Democracies; numerous other civic activities. Capt. AUS, 1943-46. Mem. Pres.'s Assn. of Ill. (founding chmn. 1972-73), Naples Yacht Club, Capitol Hill Club (Washington), Chgo. Club, Econ. Club, Comml. Club, Yacht Club, Met. Club, Little Ship Club (London), Mason (32 degree), Rotary (past pres. Chgo. club, past dist. gov.), Alpha Kappa Lambda (past nat. pres.). Home: 400 E Randolph St Apt 3810 Chicago IL 60601-7304 Office: 400 E Randolph St Fl 6B Chicago IL 60601-7363

STUART, ROBERT CRAMPTON, economics educator; b. Chemainus, B.C., Can., Oct. 22, 1938; s. Alexander Graham Robert and Olive C. (Chalk) S.; m. Beverly Joy, June 12, 1964; children: Craig Robert, Andrea Joy. B of Commerce in Econs., U. B.C., Vancouver, 1961; MSc in Econs., U. Wis., 1961, cert. in Russian studies, 1965, PhD in Econs., 1969. Vis. prof. econs. Princeton U., 1978-93; prof. econs. Rutgers U., 1976—; dir. grad. studies, 1985-86; chmn. dept. Rutgers U., 1986-89; vice chair dept., 1995—. Mem. Assn. Comp. Econ. Studies (editor), Mid Atlantic Slavic Conf. (pres.), Am. Assn. Advancement of Slavic Studies, Miata Club of Am., Photographic Soc. Am. Democrat. Avocations: antique auto collecting, photography. Home: 34 Sturwood Dr Belle Mead NJ 08502-3124 Office: Rutgers U Dept Of Econs New Brunswick NJ 08403

STUART, SANDRA KAPLAN, federal official; b. Greensboro, N.C.; d. Leon and Renee (Myers) Kaplan; children: Jay Jr., Timothy; m. D. Michael Murray. BA, U. N.C., Greensboro; JD, Monterey Coll. Law. Chief legis. asst. Rep. Robert Matsui, Washington, 1979-81; legis. dir., assoc. staff Ho. of Appropriations and Budget Coms., Washington, 1981-87; adminstrv. asst. Rep. Vic Fazio, Washington, 1987-89, chief of staff, 1990-93; asst. sec. def. legis. affairs Dept. Def., The Pentagon, Washington, 1993—. Office: Office Legis Affairs Dept Def The Pentagon Washington DC 20301-1300

STUART, WALKER DABNEY, III, poet, author, English language educator; b. Richmond, Va., Nov. 4, 1937; s. Walker Dabney Jr. and Martha (vonSchilling) S.; m. Sandra Westcott, Jan. 20, 1983; children—Martha, Nathan vonSchilling, Darren Wynne. A.B., Davidson Coll., 1960; A.M., Harvard U., 1962. Instr. Coll. William and Mary, Williamsburg, Va., 1961-65; prof. English Washington and Lee U., Lexington, Va., 1965—, S. Blount Mason Jr. prof. English, 1991—; vis. prof. Middlebury (Vt.) Coll., 1968-69, Ohio U., Athens, 1975, U. Va., Charlottesville, 1981-83. Author: The Diving Bell, 1966, A Particular Place, 1969, The Other Hand, 1974, Friends of Yours, Friends of Mine, 1974, Round and Round, 1976, Nabokov: The Dimensions of Parody, 1978, Rockbridge Poems, 1981, Common Ground, 1982, Don't Look Back, 1987, Narcissus Dreaming, 1990, Sweet Lucy Wine, 1992, Light Years: New and Selected Poems, 1994, Second Sight: Poems for Paintings by Carroll Cloar, 1996, Long Gone, 1996. Recipient Dylan Thomas prize Poetry Soc. Am., 1965, Gov.'s award State of Va., 1979, Individual Artist fellowship Va. Commn. for Arts, 1995; Nat. Endowment for Arts lit. fellow, 1975, 82; Guggenheim fellow, 1987-88. Mem. Authors Guild Am. Avocations: food, travel. Home: 30 Edmondson Ave Lexington VA 24450-1904 Office: Washington and Lee U Dept English Lexington VA 24450

STUART, WALTER BYNUM, III, banker; b. Baton Rouge, Oct. 5, 1922; s. Walter Bynum and Rosa (Gauthreaux) S.; m. Rita Kleinpeter, May 20, 1944; children—Walter Bynum IV, Robert, Douglas, Ronald, Scott. B.S., La.

State U., 1943. Adminstrv. mgr. Kaiser Aluminum & Chem. Corp., 1946-63; v.p. First Nat. Bank Commerce, New Orleans, 1963-65, sr. v.p., 1965, exec. v.p., 1965-73; vice chmn. bd., dir. 1st Nat. Bank Commerce, New Orleans, 1973-78; exec. v.p. 1st Commerce Corp., New Orleans, 1972-73, pres., 1973-75, vice-chmn. bd., 1975-78, dir., 1973-78; pres. Am. Bank & Trust Co., Lafayette, La., 1978-86, cons.; assoc. dir., mem. faculty Sch. Banking La. State U., 1973-75, dir., 1975-78; mem. Faculty Assemblies for Bank Dirs. Campaign group chmn. industry com., mem. United Fund for Greater New Orleans Area, 1974; mem. research com. Pub. Affairs Research Council La., 1973-76, v.p., trustee, 1973-76; bd. dirs. Bur. Govtl. Research, 1973-77, Council Better La., 1975—; pres. New Orleans Indsl. Devel. Bd., 1973-75. Served to lt. (j.g.) USNR, 1943-46. Mem. C. of C. of Greater New Orleans Area (v.p. 1973-75, bd. dirs.), Am. Bankers Assn., La. Bankers Assn. (pres. 1977), Am. Mgmt. Assn., Kappa Alpha, Delta Sigma Pi, Beta Gamma Sigma. Democrat. Roman Catholic. Office: Jefferson at Lee Lafayette LA 70501 *Recognizing that life is the experiencing of reality, and that reality is simply a continuing series of problems, I long ago decided that I would treat a problem as an opportunity. Every incident of difficulty has always invited my intense interest as a challenge, and my thoughts have been immediately marshalled for positive effort. My life has been most rewarding because I believe that "a problem is an opportunity!".*

STUART, WALTER BYNUM, IV, lawyer; b. Grosse Tete, La., Nov. 23, 1946; s. Walter Bynum III and Rita (Kleinpeter) S.; m. Lettice Lee Binnings May 18, 1968; children: Courtney Lyon, Walter Burke V. Student Fordham U., 1964-65; BA, Tulane U., 1968, JD, 1973. Bar: La. 1973, U.S. Dist. Ct. (ea. and we. dists.) La. 1974, U.S. Tax Ct. 1974, U.S. Supreme Ct. 1981, U.S. Dist Ct. (so. dist.) Colo. 1987, U.S. Dist. Ct. (so. dist.) Tex. 1989. Ptnr. Stone, Pigman, Walther, Wittman and Hutchinson, New Orleans, 1973-78, Singer Hutner Levine Seeman and Stuart, New Orleans, 1978-81, Gordon, Arata, McCollam and Stuart, New Orleans, 1981-88, Vinson & Elkins, Houston, 1988—; instr. Tulane U. Law Sch., 1978-82; mem. faculty Banking Sch. of the South; bd. dirs. Inst. Politics; mem. adv. bd. City Atty.'s Office, New Orleans, 1978-79. Bd. dirs., gen. counsel Houston Grand Opera, 1992—. Mem. ABA, La. Bar Assn., Tex. Assn. Bank Counsel (pres. 1994-95), La. Bankers Assn. (chmn. bank counsel com.). Office: Vinson & Elkins 2500 First City Tower 1001 Fannin St Houston TX 77002-6706

STUART, WILLIAM CORWIN, federal judge; b. Knoxville, Iowa, Apr. 28, 1920; s. George Corwin and Edith (Abram) S.; m. Mary Elgin Cleaver, Oct. 20, 1946; children: William Corwin II, Robert Cullen, Melanie Rae, Valerie Jo. BA, State U. Iowa, 1941, JD, 1942. Bar: Iowa 1942. Pvt. practice Chariton, 1946-62, city atty., 1947-49; mem. Iowa Senate from, Lucas-Wayne Counties, 1951-61; justice Supreme Ct. Iowa, 1962-71; judge U.S. Dist. Ct., So. Dist. of Iowa, Des Moines, 1971-86, sr. judge, 1986—. With USNR, 1943-45. Recipient Outstanding Svc. award Iowa Acad. Trial lawyer, 1987, Iowa Trial Lawyers Assn., 1988, Spl. award Iowa State Bar Assn., 1987, Disting. Alumni, U. Iowa Coll. Law, 1987. Mem. ABA, Iowa Bar Assn., Am. Legion, All For Iowa, Order of Coif, Omicron Delta Kappa, Phi Kappa Psi, Phi Delta Phi. Presbyterian. Club: Mason (Shriner). Home: 216 S Grand St Chariton IA 50049-2139

STUBBERUD, ALLEN ROGER, electrical engineering educator; b. Glendive, Mont., Aug. 14, 1934; s. Oscar Adolph and Alice Marie (LeBlanc) S.; m. May B. Tragus, Nov. 19, 1961; children: Peter A., Stephen C. B.S. in Elec. Engring, U. Idaho, 1956; M.S. in Engring, UCLA, 1958, Ph.D., 1962. From asst. prof. to assoc. prof. engring. UCLA, 1962-69; prof. elec. engring. U. Calif., Irvine, 1969—; assoc. dean engring. U. Calif., 1972-78, dean engring., 1978-83, chair elec. and computer engring., 1993—, interim dean engring., 1994-96; chief scientist U.S. Air Force, 1983-85; dir. Elec. Communications and Systems Engring. divsn. NSF, 1987-88. Author: Analysis and Synthesis of Linear Time Variable Systems, 1964, (with others) Feedback and Control Systems, 2d edit., 1990, (with others) Digital Control System Design, 2d edit., 1994; contbr. articles to profl. jours. Recipient Exceptional Civilian Svc. medal USAF, 1985, 90. Fellow IEEE (Centennial medal 1984), AIAA, AAAS; mem. INFORMS, Sigma Xi, Sigma Tau, Tau Beta Pi, Eta Kappa Nu. Office: U Calif Dept ECE Irvine CA 92697

STUBBINS, HUGH A(SHER), JR., architect; b. Birmingham, Ala., Jan. 11, 1912; s. Hugh Asher and Lucile (Matthews) S.; m. Diana Hamilton Moore, Mar. 3, 1938 (div. 1960); children: Patricia, Peter, Hugh Asher III, Michael; m. Colette Fadeuilhe, Sept. 1960 (dec. 1992); m. June M. Kootz, 1994. BS in Architecture, Ga. Inst. Tech., 1933; MArch, Harvard U., 1935. Pvt. practice Boston, 1935-38, 41—; formed partnership, 1938-40; pvt. practice Birmingham, 1940; assoc. prof. Grad. Sch. Design Harvard U., 1946-52, chmn. dept. architecture, 1953, mem. vis. com. Grad. Sch. Design, 1958-72; pres. Hugh Stubbins & Assocs., Inc., 1957-83, also chmn. bd. dirs., 1983-92; vis. critic-in-residence, Yale U., 1948-49, U. Oreg., 1950; sec. Rotch traveling Scholarship, 1971-80; Thomas Jefferson prof. architecture U. Va., 1979; mem. adv. coun. Sch. Architecture, Princeton U., 1962-65; mem. Harleston Parker Medal Com., 1973. Designer Berlin Congress Hall, 1957, Countway Libr. Medicine, Harvard U., Fed. Res. Bank, Boston, U. Va. Law Sch., Citicorp Ctr., N.Y.C., St. Peter's Ch., N.Y.C., Fifth Ave. Pl., Pitts., 1988, Bank One, Indpls., 1989, Landmark Tower, Minoto-Mirai 21, Yokohama, Japan, 1989, Ronald Reagan Presdl. Libr., 1990, numerous other bldgs.; exec. architect Phila. Stadium. Hon. mem. Boston Archtl. Ctr.; chmn. design adv. com. Boston Redevel. Authority, 1964-76; mem. design rev. panel Worcester Redevel. Authority, 1966-70; mem. adv. com. Office Fgn. Bldgs. Ops., U.S. Dept. State, 1979-82; bd. dirs. Benjamin Franklin Found.; mem. arts and archtl. com. Kennedy Meml. Libr.; mem. Fgn. Bus. Coun., Commonwealth of Mass., 1978-79; mem. nat. adv. bd. Ga. Inst. Tech., 1978-81; trustee Tabor Acad., 1974-78; mem. adv. bd. Whitney Libr. Design, 1976-78. Recipient Alpha Rho Chi medal, 1933, 3d prize at competition Nat. Smithsonian Gallery of Art, 1939, Progressive Architecture 1st Design award, 1954, Arcadia Achievement award, 1957, Rodgers and Hammerstein award, 1961, award Am. Inst. Steel Constrn., 1970, award Archtl. Record, 1971, award Prestressed Concrete Inst., 1971, award of merit Inst. So. Affairs and So. Acad. Letters, Arts and Scis., 1973, citation Am. Assn. Sch. Adminstrs., 1974, award for environ. design, 1975, award of merit Libr. Bldgs. award for Nathan Marsh Pusey Libr., Harvard U./AIA/ALA, 1976, Spl. Energy award for Shiraz Tech. Inst., Am. Assn. Sch. Adminstrs./AIA, N.E. Regional Coun. award Fed. Res. Bank, 1979, Thomas Jefferson Meml. medal U. Va., 1979, R.S. Reynolds Meml. award Citicorp, 1981, numerous other awards. Fellow AIA (v.p. 1964-65, jury fellows 1974-75, chmn. Nat. Honor award com. 1966, 79, 80, award of merit 1970, honor award 1979, firm award 1967), Mexican Soc. Archs. (hon.), AAAS; mem. NAD (academician), Mass. Assn. Archs., Boston Soc. Archs. (;res. 1969-70, award of honor 1988), Archl. League N.Y. (silver medal 1958), Harvard Club, Laurel Brook Club, Malapan Yacht Club, The Little Club (Gulf Stream, Fla.), Century Club (N.Y.C.), Soc. Four Arts (Palm Beach), Beta Theta Pi, Omicron Delta Kappa. Home: 6110 N Ocean Blvd Boynton Beach FL 33435 Home (summer): 199 Brattle St Cambridge MA 02138-3345

STUBBLEFIELD, DANA WILLIAM, professional football player; b. Cleve., Nov. 14, 1970. Student, U. Kans. Defensive tackle San Francisco 49'ers, 1993—. Selected to Pro Bowl, 1994, 95. Achievements include member San Francisco 49'ers Super Bowl XXIX Champions, 1994. Office: San Francisco 49'ers 4949 Centennial Blvd Santa Clara CA 95054-1229*

STUBBLEFIELD, PAGE KINDRED, banker; b. Bloomington, Tex., Aug. 28, 1914; s. Edwin Page and Vinnye L. (Kindred) S.; m. Dorothea Mock, July 7, 1940; children—Edwin Mark, Bob Lynn. Student, Southwestern U., Georgetown, Tex., 1931; B.B.A., U. Tex., Austin, 1936. Mgr. Page Stubblefield Gen. Mdse., 1936-42; owner-operation P.K. Stubblefield Ins. Agy., 1946-51; asst. v.p. pub. relations Victoria (Tex.) Bank & Trust Co., 1951-52, v.p., 1952-58, sr. v.p., 1958-69, pres., 1969-81, chmn. bd., from 1977, chmn. bd. dirs., 1984-88; pres. Victoria Bankshares, Inc., 1974-84; cmty. adv. dir. Norwest Bank Tex., South Ctrl., Victoria; past chmn. bd. dirs. Victoria Bankshares, Inc.; past chmn. bd. dirs. Victoria Bank and Trust Co. Hon. mem. U. Tex. Centennial Commn. With fin. dept. USAAF, 1942-45. Mem. Plaza Club, Victoria Country Club. Home: 2402 N De Leon St Victoria TX 77901-4814 Office: 120 S Main St Ste 414 Victoria TX 77901-8144

STUBBLEFIELD, THOMAS MASON, agricultural economist, educator; b. Taxhoma, Okla., Apr. 16, 1922; s. Temple Roscoe and Martha Lacy (Acree) S.; BS, N.Mex. State Coll., 1948; MS, A. and M. Coll. Tex., 1951, PhD, 1956; postgrad. U. Ariz., 1954; m. Martha Lee Miller, Mar. 7, 1943; children: Ellen (Mrs. Richard Damron), Paula (Mrs. James T. Culbertson), Thommye (Mrs. Gary D. Zingsheim). Specialist cotton mktg. N.Mex. State Coll., 1948; extension economist, then asst. agrl. economist U. Ariz., Tucson, 1951-58, from assoc. prof. to prof., 1958-64, prof. and agrl. economist, 1964-83, emeritus prof., 1983—, acting asst. dir. agrl. expt. sta., 1966-68, asst. to dir. sta., 1973-74, chief party Brazil contract, 1968-70. Mem. Pima Council Aging, 1974-77, 80-90; chmn. adv. com. Ret. Sr. Vol. Program, Pima County, 1974-77, 80-90, mem. 1974-97. Chmn. bd. Saguaro Home Found., 1980-85. With AUS, 1942-45. Author bulls. in field. Adv. bd. Unified Cmty., 1994—. Home: 810 W Calle Milu Tucson AZ 85706-3925

STUBBS, DAVID H., vascular surgeon; b. Cape Girardeau, Mo., Jan. 25, 1946; s. Thad Lee and E. Elizabeth (Dorton) S.; m. Gail Ann Heinemann, Mar. 20, 1982; children: Thadeus, Courtney, Zachary, Rebecca. BA, Westminster Coll., 1968; MD, U. Mo., 1972. Diplomate Am. Bd. Surgery (cert. in vascular surgery, gen. surgery and surg. critical care). Vascular surgery fellow U. Mo. Med. Ctr., Columbia, 1977-79, asst. prof. surgery, 1979-80; vascular surgeon Iowa Clinic, Des Moines, 1980—; chmn. dept. gen. surgery Iowa Meth. Med. Ctr., Des Moines, 1990-95, chmn. dept. surgery, 1995—; bd. dirs. Iowa Clinic. Contbr. author: Griffith's 5 Minute Clinical Consult, 1995, 3d edit., 1997. Asst. scoutmaster, Boy Scouts Am., 1995—. Maj. Med. Corps USAR, 1972-80. Mem. Midwestern Vascular Soc., Peripheral Vascular Soc., Soc. Critical Care Medicine, Iowa Vascular Surgery Soc. (pres. 1990-92), Soc. for Clin. Vascular Surgery, Midwest Surg. Assn. Avocations: gardening, hunting, fishing. Office: Iowa Clinic 1440 Pleasant St Ste 100 Des Moines IA 50314-1728

STUBBS, DONALD CLARK, secondary education educator; b. Providence, Mar. 6, 1935; s. Edward J. and Margaret Eleanor (Clark) S.; m. Lorraine Alice Thivierge, Apr. 3, 1969 (dec. Jan. 1986); 1 child, Derek C.; m. Jean Elizabeth Stubbs. AB, Cath. U. Am., Washington, 1959, MS, 1966; postgrad., St. John's U., N.Y.C., 1960. Tchr. Bishop Loughlin Meml. High Sch., Bklyn., 1959-61, Bishop Bradley High Sch., Manchester, N.H., 1961-66; tchr., sci. dept. chair LaSalle Mil. Acad., Oakdale, N.Y., 1966-69, Ponaganset Regional High Sch., Glocester, R.I., 1969—. Home: 51 Woodland Ave Smithfield RI 02917-4117 Office: Ponaganset High Sch Anan Wade Rd North Scituate RI 02857

STUBBS, GERALD, biochemist, educator; b. Hobart, Australia, May 9, 1947; came to the U.S., 1976; m. Rebecca Lynn Harris; children: Andrew, Tamsin, Anneliese, Rachel. BSc, Australian Nat. U., 1968; DPhil, Oxford U., 1972. Sci. asst. Max Planck Inst., Heidelberg, Fed. Republic of Germany, 1973-76; rsch. assoc. Brandeis U., Waltham, Mass., 1976-83; asst. prof. Vanderbilt U., Nashville, 1983-87, assoc. prof., 1987-90, prof., 1990—. Contbr. articles to profl. jours. Achievements include determination of molecular structure of tobacco mosaic virus. Office: Vanderbilt U Dept Molecular Biology PO Box 1820 Nashville TN 37235-1820

STUBBS, JAMES CARLTON, retired hospital administrator; b. MaGee, Miss., Jan. 26, 1924; s. James Sylvester and Katie Lucille (Grayson) S.; m. Essie Geraldine Shows, June 17, 1949; 1 child, James Hilton. Mgr. R. & A. Appliance store, MaGee, Miss., 1950; field insp. Miss. Mental Instn. Bd., Jackson, 1950-52; dir. Miss. Eleemosynary Bd., Jackson, 1952-75, Miss. State Hosp., Whitfield, 1975-88. Chmn. Miss. Reimbursement Commn., 1965-85; pres. Jackson-Vicksburg Hosp. Coun., 1977-79, 79—; mem. Miss. Coun. on Aging; chmn. Miss. Mental Health Planning Coun., 1988—, chmn., 1988-89; bd. dirs. Goodwill Industries, 1989—; chmn. bd. dirs., 1993, elected vice chmn. Cmty. Mental Health/Mental Retardation Commn., 1995, chmn., 1996-97; mem. exec. com., 1991—; mem. Friends of Miss. State Hosp., 1986—, bd. dirs., 1988—, pres., 1995-96; deacon Broadnoor Bapt. Ch., 1990; torchbearer Olympic Torch Relay, Jackson, Miss., 1996. Charter mem. Sports Hall of Fame U. S. Miss. Mem. Nat. Assn. Reimbursement Officers, Miss. Mental Health/MentalRetardation Coun., Epilepsy Found., Miss. Mental Health Assn., Miss. Pub. Health Assn., Hinds County Mental Health Assn. (apptd. commr. to mental health commn. 1993—), Assn. Mental Health Adminstrs., Am. Coll. Hosp. Adminstrs., Am. Acad. Health Adminstrn., Miss. Hosp. Assn. (fin. com., dir., bd. govs. 1979-82, 85-87, chmn. 1986-87, speaker ho. of dels. 1987-88), Capital Area Mental Health Assn. (bd. dirs. 1988-90, life bd. dirs. emeritus 1994—, v.p. 1997—), Colonial Country Club (bd. dirs.), Quarter Century Club, M Club, Big Gold Club, Hardwood Club (U. So. Miss.). Home: 5430 Pine Lane Dr Jackson MS 39211-4016

STUBBS, JAN DIDRA, retired travel industry executive, travel writer; b. Waseca, Minn., June 19, 1937; d. Gordon Everett and Bertha Margaret (Bertsch) Didra; m. James Stewart Stubbs, Nov. 24, 1962; children: Jeffrey Stewart, Jacqueline Didra. BA in Speech/English, U. Minn., 1961; cert. travel counselor, Inst. Cert. Travel Agts., 1988. Sales agt. United Airlines, Mpls., 1961-64; interior decorator Lloyd and Assocs., St. Paul, 1964-66; v.p. Stubbs and Assocs., Textiles, St. Paul, 1966-83; account exec. Twin Cities Mag., Mpls., 1983-85; account exec. Internat. Travel Arrangers, St. Paul, 1985-86, asst. dir. sales, 1986-88; mgr. Dayton's Group Holidays, Mpls., 1988-96, ret., 1996; sr. acct. exec. Dayton's Corp. Travel, Mpls., 1996—; writer for Mgmt. Assistance Project; acct. exec. Dayton's Corp. Travel; travel coord. Mpls. Inst. Art. V.p. Jr. Women's Assn. of Minn. Symphony Orch.; chairperson 60th anniversary Jr. League of St. Paul, sec., 1967—, sustaining mem.; deacon Ho. of Hope Presbyn. Ch., St. Paul, 1970; mem. Unied Way adv. bd. corporate giving Dayton Hudson Corp. Named Outstanding Alumni, Coll. Liberal Arts, U. Minn., 1995, Women of Yr. 1995-96 Minn. Exec. Women in Tourism. Mem. AAUW, Inst. Cert. Travel Agts., Am. Soc. Travel Agts., Minn. Exec. Women in Tourism (publicity com. 1987-88, by-laws chmn. 1989-90, sec. 1988-89, 90, fedn. dir. 1990—, v.p., 1993, pres. 1993-94), Internat. Fedn. Women in Travel (alt. gov. Mid-Am. region, standing com. dir. historian, gov. mid-Ams. area I 1994, 95), Jr. Assistance League, St. Paul Pool and Yacht Club, Alpha Omicron Pi (pres. 1958-59, alumni pres. 1962), Whitefish Chain Yacht Club (sec.), U. Minn. Alumni Assn. Republican. Avocations: reading, water sports, travel, photography, cooking, skiing, classical music, writing. Home: 1575 Boardwalk Ct Saint Paul MN 55118-2747 Office: Dayton's Corp Travel 700 on the Mall Mail Stop 750 Minneapolis MN 55402

STUBBS, KENDON LEE, librarian; b. Washington, Apr. 6, 1938; s. Donald Harrison and Rosalee Adelia (Brown) S.; m. Patricia Townsend, June 3, 1961; children—Christopher, Peter, Timothy. B.A., St. John's Coll., Annapolis, Md., 1960; M.A., U. Va., 1964; M.S., Columbia U., 1965. Sr. asst. in manuscripts U. Va. Library, Charlottesville, 1965, reference librarian, 1966-76, acting acquisitions librarian, 1967-68, assoc. univ. librarian, 1976-87, assoc. univ. libr. for pub. svcs., 1987-92; acting univ. libr., 1993, assoc. univ. libr., 1994—; cons. U.S. Dept. Edn., Washington, 1982-84. Author: Quantitative Criteria for Academic Research Libraries, 1984; editor: Cumulated Assn. Research Libraries Statistics, 1981, Rsch. Libr. Statistics, 1990, ARL Statistics, 1992-95, Japanese Text Initiative on World Wide Web, 1995—; contbr. articles on library stats., rsch. to profl. publs., Internet. Mem. Am. Stats. Assn., Assn. of Rsch. Librs. (mem. stats. com., vis. program officer 1995-97), Bibliog. Soc. U. Va. (pres. 1975-78, v.p. 1978—). Office: Alderman Libr U Va Charlottesville VA 22903

STUBBS, MARILYN KAY, education administrator; b. Great Bend, Kans., Mar. 21, 1950; d. John Calvin and Roseanna (Edler) Rapp; m. Stephen Richard Stubbs, Apr. 4, 1970; children: Adam Richard, Anna Elizabeth. BA in English, Kans. State U., 1972. Asst. instr. Kans. State U., Manhattan, 1972; educator All Saints Sch., Kansas City, Kans., 1973-74, Archdiocese of Kansas City, Mo., 1975-78; adminstrv. asst. Sherwood Ctr. for the Exceptional Child, Kansas City, Mo., 1979-89; assoc. dir. Sherwood Ctr. for the Exceptional Child, Kansas City, 1989—; cons., trainer N.W. Mo. Autism Consortium, Kansas City, 1993—, Mo. State Team on Positive Behavior Support, Kansas City, 1994—, Autism Team Tng. Project, Kansas City, 1995-96; trainer Jackson County (Mo.) Bd. Svcs., Kansas City, 1995-96. Writer (newsletter) Sherwood Chronicle, 1980-86; editor (newsletters) Sherwood Chronicle, 1986—, Families Addressing Auditory Integration Training, 1993-95. Mem. spkrs. bur. United Way, Kansas City, Mo., 1982—; mem. Assn. United Way Execs., 1989—; advocacy com. mem. Met. Coun. on Devel. Disabilities, 1990-94. Named Parent of Yr., Sherwood Parents Assn., Kansas City, Mo., 1985. Mem. Autism Soc. Am. (sec. Western Mo. chpt. 1993), Assn. for Severly Handicapped, Am. Assn. on Mental Retardation, Astron. Soc. Kansas City, Divers Alert Network. Avocations: horseback riding, astronomy, scubadiving, skiing, hunting. Office: Sherwood Center 7938 Chestnut Ave Kansas City MO 64132-3606

STUBBS, SUSAN CONKLIN, statistician; b. Washington, July 26, 1935; d. Maxwell Robertson and Marcia (Nye) Conklin; m. LeRoy Carter Hostetter, May 20, 1975 (div. 1988); m. Joel Richard Stubbs, Sept. 20, 1992. BA, Pa. State U., 1957. Economist Bur. of Census, Suitland, Md., 1973-74; economist Bur. of Labor Statistics, Washington, 1974-78, supervisory economist, 1978-84; statistician IRS, Washington, 1984-95, chief rschr. stats. of income divsn., 1989-92, coord. for indsl. classification, 1994-95; ret., 1995; cons. joint com. on taxation, IRS, 1992-94; DPM legis. fellow, 1988. Contbr. articles to profl. jours. Leader, del., com. mem., chmn., v.p., bd. dirs., nominating com. Girl Scout Coun. Nation's Capital, Washington, 1968-97; sec., treas. Middlesex Beach Assn., Bethany, Del., 1991-94; jobs editor Caucus for Women in Statistics, Washington, 1992-95; mentor Mentors Inc., Washington, 1992-94. Mem. Am. Statis. Assn., Tax Economist Forum, Woman's Club Northumberland County (pres. 1996-97). Avocations: sailing, swimming, gardening, reading. Home: Rt 3 Box 65EA Heathsville VA 22473

STUBBS, THOMAS HUBERT, company executive; b. Americus, Ga., Aug. 16, 1944; s. Hubert F. and Elizabeth (Askew) S.; m. Mary Louise Quarles, Mar. 19, 1965; children: Thomas C., Chad P. BS, Auburn U., 1966. CPA, Ala., Ga., Miss. Sr. acct. Peat, Marwick, Mithcell and Co., Birmingham, Ala., 1966-72; supr. L. Paul Kassauf and Co., CPA's, Birmingham, 1972-73; staff mem. Snow, Stewart and Bradford, Birmingham, 1973-75; v.p. Cen. Computer Svcs., Inc., Birmingham, 1975-79, Cen. Bancshares of the South, Birmingham, 1979-81; ptnr. Bradford and Co., CPA's, Gulf Shore, Ala., 1981-82; v.p., trust officer Deposit Guaranty Nat. Bank, Jackson, Miss., 1983; treas. Data Supplies, Inc., Norcross, Ga., 1983-88; treas. Stevens Graphics, Inc., Atlanta, 1988-89, v.p., 1989-90, pres. bus. products div., 1990-93, v.p., CFO, 1994—. Served with USNG, 1966-72. Mem. Am. Inst. CPA's, Ala. Soc. CPA's, Ga. Soc. CPA's, Miss. Soc. CPA's. Republican. Presbyterian. Avocations: tennis, jogging, golf. Home: 2875 Towne Village Dr Duluth GA 30155-7616 Office: 713 RD Abernathy Blvd SW Atlanta GA 30310

STUBER, CHARLES WILLIAM, genetics educator, researcher; b. St. Michael, Nebr., Sept. 19, 1931; s. Harvey John and Minnie Augusta (Wilks) S.; m. Marilyn Martha Cook, May 28, 1953; 1 child, Charles William Jr. BS, U. Nebr., 1952, MS, 1961; PhD, N.C. State U., 1965. Vet., agrl. instr. Broken Bow (Nebr.) H. S., 1956-59; research asst. U. Nebr., Lincoln, 1959-61; research geneticist Agrl. Rsch. Svc., USDA, Raleigh, N.C., 1962-75, supervisory research geneticist, research leader, 1975—; prof. genetics & crop sci. N.C. State U., Raleigh, 1975—. Assoc. editor Crop Sci. Jour., 1979-82, tech. editor, 1984-86, editor, 1987-89; contbr. over 190 articles to profl. jours., chpts. to books. Chmn. coun. on ministries and numerous offices Highland United Meth Ch., Raleigh. Lt. USN, 1952-56. Named Outstanding Scientist of Yr., USDA-ARS, 1989; recipient Genetics and Plant Breeding award Nat. Coun. Comml. Plant Breeders, 1995. Fellow Am. Soc. Agronomy, Crop Sci. Soc. Am. (editor-in-chief 1987-91, pres. 1992-93, Crop Sci. Rsch. award 1995); mem. AAAS, Genetics Soc. Am., Am. Genetic Assn. (sec. 1984-86), Sigma Xi, Phi Kappa Phi. Avocations: windsurfing, water skiing, sailing. Home: 1800 Manuel St Raleigh NC 27612-5510 Office: USDA-ARS NC State U Dept Genetics PO Box 7614 Raleigh NC 27695

STUBER, IRENE ZELINSKY, writer, researcher; b. Cleve., Nov. 1, 1928; d. Joseph Frank and Marian (Kulchar) Zelinsky; m. Joseph Francis Stuber, Apr. 9, 1948 (div. Aug. 1954); children: Catherine, Geraldine, William. Student, Cleve. Coll., 1946-48. Editor Cleve. Kegler, 1954-60; publs. dir. Miami (Fla.)-Dade C. of C., 1963-65; staff writer Hollywood (Fla.) Sun-Tattler, 1966-67; urban affairs writer Ft. Lauderdale (Fla.) News, 1967-74; tech. editor Bell Aerospace, New Orleans, 1977-78; owner Kulchar's Jewelry, New Orleans, 1974-83, Hot Springs, Ark., 1983-90; freelance writer. Author: Undelete: Women of Achievement, 1997; rschr., writer (Internet newsletter) Women of Achievement and Herstory, 1994-97; writer (Internet newsletter) Catt's Claws, 1995-97; freelance writer on women's history. Mem. ctrl. com. Broward County (Fla.) Dem. Party, 1974, mem. com. Garland County (Ark.) Dem. Party, 1993, 96—; newsletter editor, corr. sec. Va. Clinton Kelley Dem. Women's Club, Hot Springs, 1995-96. Recipient Pub. Svc. award City of Hollywood, 1967, Journalistic Excellence award AP, 1967, Recognition of Svcs. award Fla. Bar Assn., 1968. Mem. NOW (Ark. chpt. pres. 1993-94, Hot Springs chpt. pres. 1992-96). Avocation: "missionary" to introduce women to Internet and women's history to Internet. Home: PO Box 6185 Hot Springs National Park AR 71902

STUCHINS, CAROL MAYBERRY, nursing executive; b. Melrose, Mass., May 19, 1946; d. Robert Morton and Marion Evelyn (Fairchild) Mayberry; m. Robert Frederick Stuchins, Nov. 9, 1986. BS in Nursing, Boston U., 1969, MS, 1975. RN, Fla., Mass.; cert. rehab. RN. Staff nurse Univ. Hosp., Boston, 1969-70, head nurse, 1970-74, 76-79, nursing supr., 1974-75, nurse mgr., 1979-81; clin. coord. Mt. Auburn Hosp., Cambridge, Mass., 1975-76; dir. nursing Meml. Hosp. Santa Barbara, Calif., 1981-84; v.p. nursing Bon Secours Hosp., North Miami, Fla., 1984-92; nurse mgr. Mercy Hosp., Miami, Fla., 1992—; mem. Commn. for Future Nursing in Fla., 1987-90. Author: Coping with Neurologic Problems Proficiently, 1979. Mem. Assn. Nurse Execs., Assn. Rehab. Nurses, Dade County Assn. Rehab. Nurses (pres. 1988-90), Sigma Theta Tau. Office: Mercy Hosp 3663 S Miami Ave Miami FL 33133-4253

STUCK, WANDA MARIE, special education educator; b. Schoolcraft, Mich., Oct. 25, 1934; d. Glen Robert and Luella Esther (Porter) Shearer; m. Paul Revere Stuck, June 15, 1958; children: Pamela Joyce, Lauri Linn, Jeffrey Paul. BS, Western Mich. U., 1968, MA, 1978. Tchr. spl. edn. Vicksburg, Mich., 1968-90; tchr. adult edn. sewing Cunningham Fabrics, Vicksburg, Mich., 1982-88; tchr. adult edn. computers Edwardsburg (Mich.) Sch., 1994—, tchr. spl. edn., home econs., 1991—; prof. seamstress, Schoolcrest, Mich., 1953—; clk. Fields Fabric, Kalamazoo, Mich., 1991—. mem. bd. dirs. Meth. Ch., Schoolcraft, 1994—; mem. Ladies Libr., Schoolcraft, 1969—. Mem. AAUW, Coun. Exceptional Children, Learning Disabilities Assn. Mich., Order of Ea. Star, Order of Eagles. Methodist. Avocations: sewing, reading, quilting. Home: 16101 S 2nd St Schoolcraft MI 49087-9728 Office: Edwardsville Mid Sch 69410 Section St Edwardsburg MI 49112-9655

STUCKEMAN, HERMAN CAMPBELL, architectural engineer; b. Pitts., Aug. 7, 1914; s. Herman Sydney and Alma (Campbell) S.; m. Margaret Eleanor Rockwell, Aug. 28, 1940; children: Ellen Campbell, Alan Rockwell, Joyce Thayer. B.S. in Architecture, Sch. Engring. Pa. State U., 1937. Architect Edward B. Lee, Pitts., 1938-39, Gen. State Authority, Harrisburg, Pa., 1940-41, Prack & Prack, Texarkana, Tex. and Pitts., 1941-42; ptnr. Delta Mfg. Co., Milw., 1942-45; gen. mgr. Delta Mfg. Co., 1945-50; v.p. Rockwell Mfg. Co., Pitts., 1950-73; dir. real estate Rockwell Internat. Corp. (merger Rockwell Mfg. Co. and N.Am. Rockwell), 1973-75; chmn. Precise Corp., 1975—. Clubs: Duquesne, Pittsburgh Athletic, Longue Vue (Pitts.). Lodge: Rotary. Home: 300 Fox Chapel Rd Pittsburgh PA 15238-2331 *Be fair with those with whom you work and associate. At all times, be honest and truthful. Give credit for work well done. Develop enthusiasm in the organization and set the goals high. Set an example by working hard. Get the work done on time.*

STUCKEY, HELENJEAN LAUTERBACH, counselor educator; b. Bushnell, Ill., May 17, 1929; d. Edward George and Frances Helen (Simpson) Lauterbach; m. James Dale Stuckey, Sept. 30, 1951; children: Randy Lee, Charles Edward, Beth Ellen. BFA, Ill. Wesleyan U., 1951; MEd, U. Ill., 1969. Cert. art tchr., guidance, psychology instr.; lic. clin. profl. counselor, Ill. Display designer Saks Fifth Ave., Chgo., 1951; interior designer Piper City, Ill., 1953-63; art tchr. Forrest (Ill.)-Strawn-Wing Schs., 1967-68; tchr., counselor Piper City Schs., 1969-74; counselor, art tchr. Ford Cen. Schs., Piper City, 1974-85; psychiatric counselor Community Resource Counseling Ctr., Ford County, Ill., 1985-87; history tchr., counselor Iroquois West High Sch., Gilman, Ill., 1987-88; spl. needs coord. Livingston County Vocat., Pontiac, Ill., 1988-93; ret., 1993; clin. profl. counselor, pvt. practice Piper City, 1995—. Job skills coord. Livingston Area Edn. for Employment, 1994. Mem. AACD, Ill. Counseling Assn., Ill. Mental Health Counselors Assn., Ill. Ret. Tchrs., Delta Kappa Gamma (v.p., sec., program chmn., pres.). Presbyterian. Avocations: skiing, reading, travel, sewing, playing flute.

STUCKEY, SUSAN JANE, perioperative nurse, consultant. Diploma in nursing, The Polyclinic Med. Ctr., 1971; BBA in Health Care Adminstrn., Pa. State U., 1985; cert., Del. County C.C., Media, Pa., 1988; MBA, Kutztown U., 1995. RN, Pa.; cert. operating rm. nurse; cert. RN first asst. Charge nurse Nightingale Nursing Home, Camp Hill, Pa., 1971-72; clin. educator oper. rm. svcs., staff nurse Harrisburg (Pa.) Hosp., 1972-80; adminstr., nursing coord. Hillcrest Women's Med. Ctr., Harrisburg, 1978-81; office mgr., pvt. scrub nurse Office Dr. Henry Train, Harrisburg, 1979-82; with Kimberly Nurses Med Temps, Cleve., 1982-84; sr. splty. nurse oper. rm. Harrisburg Hosp., Harrisburg, 1984-86, splty. supr. surg. svcs. dept., 1986-90; 1st asst. laser/abdominal endoscopy Women's Med. Assocs. P.C., Harrisburg, 1990-96; 1st asst., cons., propreitor Peri Operative Care Assocs., Harrisburg, 1996—; first asst., cons. C.B. Laser Assocs. Inc., Camp Hill, Pa., 1990-96; faculty mem. Pa. Jr. Coll. Med. Arts. Contbr. articles to profl. jours. Mem. Assn. Oper. Rm. Nurses, Am. Assn. Gynecol. Laparoscopists, Am. Soc. for Laser Medicine and Surgery. Home: 68 Fairfax Village Harrisburg PA 17112-9556 Office: Peri Operative Care Assocs 68 Fairfax Vlg Harrisburg PA 17112-9556

STUCKWISCH, CLARENCE GEORGE, retired university administrator; b. Seymour, Ind., Oct. 13, 1916; s. William Henry and Clara Sophia (Benter) S.; m. Esther Elizabeth Ebert, Dec. 19, 1942; children: William, Stephen, David, Deborah, Stephanie. B.A. magna cum laude, Ind. U., 1939; Ph.D., Iowa State U., 1943. Mem. faculty U. Wichita, Kans., 1943-60; prof. chemistry U. Wichita, 1958-60; prof., chmn. dept. N.Mex. Highlands U., Las Vegas, 1960-64; prof., exec. officer dept. chemistry SUNY, Buffalo, 1964-68; prof., chmn. dept. U. Miami, Coral Gables, Fla., 1968-72; asso. v.p. advanced studies and research, dean Grad. Sch. U. Miami, 1972-81, exec. v.p., provost, 1981-82; ret.; mem. council Oak Ridge Assn. Univs. Contbr. articles to profl. jours. Mem. AAAS, Am. Chem. Soc., Lions, Phi Beta Kappa, Sigma Xi, Phi Kappa Phi. Democrat. Lutheran. Patentee in chem. intermediates and pharms.

STUCKY, KEN, clergy member, church organization administrator, foundation executive. Dir. stewardship Missionary Church, Inc., Fort Wayne, Ind., exec. dir. investment found.; editor Priority. Office: The Missionary Ch PO Box 9127 3811 Vanguard Dr Fort Wayne IN 46899-9127

STUCKY, SCOTT WALLACE, lawyer; b. Hutchinson, Kans., Jan. 11, 1948; s. Joe Edward and Emma Clara (Graber) S.; m. Jean Elsie Seibert, Aug. 18, 1973; children: Mary-Clare, Joseph. BA summa cum laude, Wichita State U., 1970; JD, Harvard U., 1973; MA, Trinity U., 1980; LLM with highest honors, George Washington U., 1983; postgrad. Nat. War Coll., 1993. Bar: Kans. 1973, U.S. Dist. Ct. Kans. 1973, U.S. Ct. Appeals (10th cir.) 1973, U.S. Ct. Mil. Appeals 1974, U.S. Supreme Ct. 1976, D.C. 1979, U.S. Ct. Appeals (D.C. cir.) 1979. Assoc. Ginsburg, Feldman & Bress, Washington, 1978-82; chief docketing and service br. Nuclear Regulatory Commn., Washington, 1982-83; legis. counsel U.S. Air Force, Washington, 1983-96, gen. counsel sen. com. on armed svcs., 1996—; lectr. bus. law Maria Regina Coll., Syracuse, N.Y., 1977; congressional fellow Office Senator John Warner, 1986; res. judge adv. U.S. Air Force Res., Washington, 1982—; col. Appellate Mil. Judge, USAF Ct. Criminal Appeals, 1991-95; sr. reservist USAF Judiciary, 1995—. Served to capt. USAF, 1973-78. Decorated Air Force Meritorious Svc. medal with two oak leaf clusters, Commendation medal with oak leaf cluster. Mem. Fed. Bar Assn., Judge Advs. Assn. (bd. dirs. 1984-88), Res. Officers Assn., Wichita State U. Alumni Assn. (pres. chpt. 1981-86, nat. bd. dirs. 1986-92), Phi Delta Phi, Phi Alpha Theta, Phi Kappa Phi, Omicron Delta Kappa, Sigma Phi Epsilon. Republican. Episcopalian. Club: Army and Navy (Washington). Lodge: Mil. Order of Loyal Legion of U.S. (state comdr. and recorder 1984-92, nat. treas. 1987-89, nat. vice comdr. 1989-93, nat. comdr.-in-chief 1993-95), Sons of Union Vets. of Civil War (chpt. vice comdr. 1986-88). Contbr. articles to profl. jours. Home: 4404 Burlington Pl NW Washington DC 20016-4422 Office: Sen Armed Svcs Com 228 Russell Senate Office Bldg Washington DC 20510-6050

STUCKY, STEVEN (EDWARD), composer; b. Hutchinson, Kans., Nov. 7, 1949; s. Victor Eugene and Louise Doris (Trautwein) S.; m. Melissa Jane Whitehead, Aug. 22, 1970; children: Maura Catharine, Matthew Steven. MusB, Baylor U., 1971; MFA, Cornell U., 1973, DMA, 1978. Vis. asst. prof. Lawrence U., Appleton, Wis., 1978-80; prof. Cornell U., Ithaca, N.Y., 1980—, chmn. dept. music, 1992-97; composer-in-residence L.A. Philharm. Orch., 1988—. Author: Lutoslawski and His Music, 1981 (Deems Taylor award ASCAP 1982); composer: Voyages, 1984, Boston Fancies, 1985, Dreamwaltzes, 1986, Concerto for orch., 1987, Son et Lumière, 1988, Angelus, 1990, Impromptus, 1991, Four Poems of A.R. Ammons, 1992, Ancora, 1994, Double Flute Co., 1994, Fanfares and Arias, 1994, Pinturas de Tamayo, 1995, Music for Saxophones and Strings, 1996; received commn. from Nat. Endowment for Arts, 1982, Koussevitzky Found., 1991, Meet the Composer, 1995. Bd. advisors Barlow Endowment, 1993-97; bd. dirs. MacDowell Colony, 1993-95. Fellow Guggenheim Found., Nat. Endowment for the Arts. Avocation: gardening. Office: Theodore Presser Co care One Presser Pl Bryn Mawr PA 19010

STUDDS, GERRY EASTMAN, former congressman; b. Mineola, N.Y., May 12, 1937; s. Eastman and Beatrice (Murphy) S. B.A., Yale U., 1959, M.A.T., 1961. Fgn. service officer State Dept., Washington, 1961-63; exec. asst. to presdl. cons. for a nat. service corps White House, 1963; legis. asst. to Sen. Harrison Williams U.S. Senate, 1964; tchr. St. Paul's Sch., Concord, N.H., 1965-69; mem. 93d-97th Congresses from 12th Mass. dist., 1973-83, 98th-103rd Congresses from 10th Mass. dist., 1983-96; chmn. com. Merchant Marine and Fisheries, 1993; mem. commerce com., resources com., ranking minority of Fisheries, Wildlife and Oceans subcomm. Candidate for U.S. Congress from 12th Dist. Mass., 1970; del. Democratic Nat. Conv., 1968. Office: US House of Reps 237 Cannon Bldg Ofc Bureau Washington DC 20515-0528*

STUDE, EVERETT WILSON, JR., rehabilitation counselor, educator; b. Fresno, Calif., Dec. 27, 1939; s. Everett Wilson and Vera Mae (Williams) S.; m. Mary-Ann Meadows, June 11, 1960; children: Susan, Sandra. B.A., Pasadena (Calif.) Coll., 1961; M.S., Calif. State U., Los Angeles, 1963; cert. psychiat. intern, U. Oreg. Med. Sch., 1965; Ed.D., U. So. Calif., 1972. Counseling psychol. trainee VA Hosp., Long Beach Calif., 1963; rehab. counselor Calif. Dept. Rehab., Pasadena, 1963-66; asst. to regional adminstr. Calif. Dept. Rehab., Los Angeles, 1966-67; vocat. rehab. coordinator, dir. tng. Rehab Research and Tng. Center, U. So. Calif. Sch. Medicine, 1967-71, instr., fieldwork coordinator Sch. Edn. rehab. counseling masters degree program, 1967-71; mem. faculty Calif. State U., Fresno, 1971—; prof. rehab. counseling Calif. State U., 1976, program coordinator, 1980-92; vocat. expert, social security disability ins. program Bur. Hearing and Appeals, 1972—; contract rehab. counselor VA, 1981-85; vocat. econ. analyst Vocat. Econs., Inc., 1990—. Author: Ethics and the Counselor, 1975; also articles. Chmn. Pasadena Jaycees Jr. Golf Tournament, 1964; bd. dirs. Day Care Center, Friends Community Ch., Fresno, 1976-77, mem. ministry and cousel, 1977-80, chmn., 1980. Recipient numerous grants; selected to give First Ann. Andrew F. Marrin Meml. lecture, 1978. Mem. Am. Coun. Assn. (senator 1975-78, chmn., treas. Western Region br. assembly, 1979-81, bd. dirs. 1981-84, mem. Ethical Stds. and Practice Com. 1985-88), Nat. Rehab. Assn. (exec. bd. So. Calif. 1969-71, pres. San Joaquin Valley chpt. 1978-79), Calif. Rehab. Counselors Assn. (pres. 1971-72, 1985-86, newsletter editor 1975-77, 1986-93, Outstanding Contbn. to Profession award 1977, Citation Merit 1978), Calif. Assn. for Coun. and Devel. (pres. 1973-74, mem. Profl. Stds. and Ethical Practices com. 1987-92, mem. editorial bd. 1990-94), Nat. Coun. on Rehab. Edn. (mem. editorial bd. 1987—, 2d v.p. 1989-90, 1st v.p. 1990-91, pres. 1991-92, past pres. 1992-93). Address: 2727 W Bluff Ave Apt 117 Fresno CA 93711-7014

STUDEBAKER, IRVING GLEN, mining engineering consultant; b. Ellensburg, Wash., July 22, 1931; s. Clement Glen and Ruth (Krause) S.; (widowed); children: Ruth, Betty, Raymond, Karl, Donna. BS in Geol. Engring., U. Ariz., 1957, MS in Geology, 1959, PhD in Geol. Engring., 1977. Registered profl. engr., Wash., Nev., Ariz., Colo., Mont. Geophys. engr. Mobil, 1959-61; civil engr. City of Yakima, Wash., 1964-66; instr. Yakima Valley Coll., 1962-67; sr. rsch. geologist Roan Selection Trust, Kalulushi, Zambia, 1967-72; sr. mining engr. Occidental Oil Shale, Grand Junction, Colo., 1974-81; prof. Mont. Coll. Mining Sch., Butte, 1982-96; prof. emeritus, 1996—; cons. in field. Sgt. U.S. Army, 1951-54, Korea. Mem. N.W. Mining Assn., Geol. Soc. Am., Soc. for Mining and Metall. Engring., Soc. Econ. Geologists, Mont. Mining Assn., Sigma Xi (pres. Mont. tech. chpt. 1990-91). Avocations: golf, travel. Home and Office: 165 S 340th St #A Federal Way WA 98003-6623

STUDEBAKER, JOHN MILTON, utilities engineer, consultant, educator; b. Springfield, Ohio, Mar. 31, 1935; s. Frank Milton and Monaruth (Beatty) S.; m. Virginia Ann Van Pelt, Mar. 12, 1960; 1 child, Jacqueline Ann Allcorn. BS in Law, LaSalle U., Chgo., 1969; MS and PhD in Indsl. Engring., Columbia Pacific U., San Rafael, Calif., 1984. Cert. plant engr. Am. Inst. Plant Engrs., profl. cons. Acad. Profl. Cons. & Advisors. Indsl engr. Internat. Harvest Co., 1957-60, supr. indsl. engring., 1960-66, gen. supr. body assembly, 1967-68, mgr. indsl. engring., 1968-70; mgr. manufacturing engring. Lamb Electric Co., 1970-72, Cascade Corp., 1972-78; engring. mgr. Bundy Tubing Corp., Winchester and Cynthia, Ky., 1978-84; chmn. The Studebaker Group, Inc., Alexandria, Va., 1989—; instr. numerous univs. including Boston U., Clemson U., Cornell U., Harvard U., Duquesne U., U. Ala., U. Ill., U. Wis., Ga. State U., James Madison U., Tex. Tech. U., U. Calif., Calif. State U., Columbia U., Fairleigh Dickinson U., San Francisco State U.; instr. Am. Mgmt. Assn., Rochester Inst. Tech., Ctr. for Profl. Advancement. Author: Slashing Utility Costs Handbook, 1992, Natural Gas Purchasing Handbook, 1994, Electricity Retail Wheeling Handbook, 1995, Electricity Purchasing Handbook, 1996, Utility Negotiation Handbook, 1997. Mem. NSPE, Am. Inst. Plant Engrs. (cert.), Assn. Energy Engrs. (instr.), Doctorate Assn. N.Y. Educators. Republican. Office: Studebaker Group Inc 5285 Shawnee Rd Ste 106 Alexandria VA 22312-2328

STUDER, PATRICIA S., psychologist; b. Ft. Scott, Kans., Sept. 3, 1942; d. Herb E. Studer and Mary Edith (McElroy) Cook; children: Mary Paige, Catherine Ann. BS, Cen. Mo. State U., Warrensburg, 1964; MS, Pittsburg (Kans.) State U., 1975. Lic. psychologist, Mo.; cert. elem. tchr., Mo. Supervisory tchr. Cen. Mo. State U., 1966; tchr. Consolidated Sch. Dist. 1, Hickman Mills, Mo., 1964-68; clin. psychologist Nevada (Mo.) State Hosp., 1977-80, chief unit psychologist, 1980-83; dir. psychology dept., staff psychologist Raphael Ctr. Hosp., Nevada, 1982-83; dir., psychologist Nevada Counseling Ctr., 1983-91; adj. med. staff Nevada Regional Med. Ctr., 1983—; dir. Ctr. for Human Devel., Nevada, Mo., 1992—; guest lectr. Cottey Coll., Nevada, 1983-91; practicum supr. Pittsburg State U., 1980—; clin. supr. Cmty. Counseling Cons., Cinton, Mo., 1987-88; cons. psychologist Barton County Meml. Hosp., 1993—, Heartland Hosp., Nevada, 1995—; mem. Com. for Drug Free Schs., Nevada, 1988—, cons. psychologist, 1988-90; cons. psychotherapist Nevada Child Abuse Coun., 1981-82. Mem. The Nelson-Adkins Mus. Art; mem. Mo. Regional Adv. Coun. on Alcohol and Drug Abuse, 1985-94, v.p., 1988, 92; bd. dirs. Mental Health Adv. Bd., 1993—, Sch. Health Adv. Com., 1994—. Mem. APA (assoc.), Mo. Psychol. Assn., Soroptimist Internat. of Nevada (pres. 1992-93), Rotary Internat., Nevada Vernon County C. of C. Avocations: tennis, remodeling, environmental issues. Office: Ctr for Human Devel PO Box 472 Nevada MO 64772-0472

STUDER, WILLIAM ALLEN, county official; b. Chgo., July 27, 1939; s. William Gotlieb and Annette Elizabeth (Bruzek) S.; m. Donna Barnes Bray, Dec. 26, 1961; children: Scott, Shannon. BS in Indsl. Mgmt., Ga. Inst. Tech., 1961; MS in Guidance and Counseling, Troy State U., 1975, MS in Mgmt., 1978; student, Air War Coll., Maxwell AFB, Ala., 1980-81. Commd. 2d lt. USAF, 1961, advanced through grades to maj. gen., 1989; legis. liaison U.S. Senate, Washington, 1981-83; dir. fighter ops./tng. USAF Hdqrs. Europe, Ramstein AB, Fed. Republic Germany, 1983-84; vice comdr. 10th Tactical Reconnaissance Wing RAF USAF, Alconbury, Eng., 1984-85, comdr. 10th Tactical Reconnaissance Wing RAF, 1985-86; cmdr. 81st Tactical Fighter Wing RAF USAF, Bentwaters, Eng., 1986-87; comdr. 316th Air Div/Kaiserslautern USAF, Ramstein AB, Fed. Republic Germany, 1987-88; vice comdr. 12th Air Force/U.S. So. Command USAF, Bergstrom AFB, Tex., 1988-90; comdr. 13th Air Force USAF, Clark AFB, The Philippines, 1990-91; dir. ops. CENTCOM/J-3, MacDill AFB, Fla., 1992-94; ret. USAF, 1994; dir. pub. safety dept. Hillsborough County, Tampa, Fla., 1994—. Decorated D.S.M., Legion of Merit with oak leaf cluster, DFC with three oak leaf clusters, Bronze Star, Air medal with 35 oak leaf clusters; Legion of Honor, Bronze Cross medal (The Philippines). Mem. Daedalians, Quiet Birdmen, Rotary. Avocations: golf, reading. Home: 5312 W Crescent Dr Tampa FL 33611-4126 Office: Hillsborough County Pub Safety Dept Tampa FL 33601

STUDER, WILLIAM JOSEPH, library director; b. Whiting, Ind., Oct. 1, 1936; s. Victor E. and Sarah G. (Hammersley) S.; m. Rosemary Lippie, Aug. 31, 1957; children: Joshua E., Rachel Marie. B.A., Ind. U., 1958, M.A., 1960, Ph.D. (Univ. fellow), 1968. Grad. asst. div. Library Sci., Ind. U., 1959-60, reference asst., 1960-61; spl. intern Library of Congress, 1961-62, reference librarian, sr. bibliographer, 1962-65; dir. regional campus libraries Ind. U., Bloomington, 1968-73; assoc. dean univ. libraries Ind. U., 1973-77; dir. libraries Ohio State U., Columbus, 1977—; mem. Library Services and Constrn. Act Adv. Com. of Ind., 1971-76, Adv. Coun.on Fed. Library Programs in Ohio, 1977-85, chmn., 1980-81; mem. ARL Office Mgmt. Studies Adv. Com., 1977-81, ARL Task Force on Nat. Library Network Devel., 1978-83, chmn., 1981-83, com. on preservation, 1985-88, vice-chmn., 1989-90, chmn., 1991-92, task force on scholarly communication, 1983-87, bd. dirs., 1981-84, com. stats. and measurement, 1993—; mem. network adv. com. Library of Congress, 1981-88; mem. library study com. Ohio Bd. Regents, 1986-87; mem. steering com. Ohio Library and Info. Network (Ohio Link), 1987-90; bd. dirs. Ctr. Rsch. Librs., 1989-96, vice-chmn., 1993-94, chmn., 1994-95, sec., chmn. membership com., 1990-93; mem. adv. coun. Ohio Link Libr., 1990—, chmn., 1991-92, policy adv. coun., governing bd., 1991-92. Contbr. articles to profl. jours. Trustee On Line Computer Libr. Ctr. Inc., 1977-78; del. On Line Computer Libr. Ctr. Users Coun., 1983-91; mem. rsch. librs. adv. com. OnLine Computer Libr. Ctr., 1989-95, vice chair, chair-elect, 1993-94, chair, 1994-95; bd. dirs. Ohio Network of Librs. Ohionet, 1977-87, chmn., 1980-82, 86-87, treas., 1983-86; mem. Columbia U. Sch. Library Svc. Conservation Programs, vis. com., 1987-90; mem. nat. adv. coun. to commn. on preservation and access, 1989-92; treas. Monroe County (Ind.) Mental Health Assn., 1968-76; active Mental Health Social Club, 1971-73; budget rev. com. United Way, 1975-77; bd. dirs. Mental Health Assn. Recipient citation for participation MARC Insts., 1968-69; Louise Maxwell award Ind. U., 1978. Mem. ALA, Ohio Libr. Assn. (bd. dirs. 1980-83), Assn. Coll. and Rsch. LIbrs. (bd. dirs. 1977-81, com. on activities model for 1990, 1981-82, chmn. libr. sch. curriculum task force 1988-89), Acad. Libr. Assn. Ohio, Torch Club (pres. 1993-94), Phi Kappa Phi (pub. rels. officer 1982-83, sec. 1983-85), Phi Eta Sigma, Alpha Epsilon Delta., Beta Phi Mu. Home: 724 Olde Settler Pl Columbus OH 43214-2924 Office: Ohio State U William Oxley Thompson Meml Libr 1858 Neil Ave Columbus OH 43210-1225

STUDIN, JAN, publishing executive. Pub. Woman's Day Machette Filipacchi Mags., Inc., N.Y.C. Office: Machette Filipacchi Mags Inc 1633 Broadway New York NY 10019*

STUDLEY, JAMIENNE SHAYNE, lawyer; b. N.Y.C., Apr. 30, 1951; d. Jack Hill and Joy (Cosor) S.; m. Gary J. Smith, July 14, 1984. BA magna cum laude, Barnard Coll., 1972; JD, Harvard U., 1975. Bar: D.C. 1975, U.S. Dist. Ct. D.C. 1978. Assoc. Bergson, Borkland, Margolis & Adler, Washington, 1976-80; spl. asst., sec. U.S. HHS, 1980-81; assoc. Weil, Gotshal & Manges, Washington, 1981-83; assoc. dean law sch. Yale U., New Haven, 1983-87; lectr. law, 1984-87; syndicated columnist Am. Lawyer Media, 1990-91; exec. dir. Nat. Assn. for Law Placement, Washington, 1987-90, Calif. Abortion Rights Action League, 1992-93; dep. gen. counsel U.S. Dept. Edn., 1993—; vis. scholar adj. faculty U. Calif., Berkeley, 1990-93. Pres. Conn. Women's Ednl. and Legal Fund, Hartford, 1986-87; mem. bd. advisors Nat. Assn. Pub. Interest Law Pub. Svc. Challenge; founder, bd. dirs. Washington Area Women's Fedn., 1997—. Mem. ABA (commn. on women in the profession 1991-94, chair edit. bd. Perspectives, chair coord. coun. legal edn. 1996-97), D.C. Bar Assn., Bar Assn. San Francisco, Women's Bar Assn., Assn. Alumnae Barnard Coll. (bd. dirs. 1978-81), Barnard in Washington (pres. 1977-78), Phi Beta Kappa. Home: 5349 MacArthur Blvd Washington DC 20016 Office: Office of the Gen Coun Dept of Edn 600 Independence Ave SW Washington DC 20202-0004

STUEART, ROBERT D., university information services director, educator. B.A., So. Ark. U., 1956; cert. Russian lang., 1958; M.S.L., La. State U., 1962; library sci. advanced cert., U. Pitts., 1969, Ph.D., 1971. Library asst. in reference and cataloging So. State Coll., Magnolia, Ark., 1953-56; librarian, tchr. Desha County (Ark.) Public Schs., 1956-57; library asst. microforms room, serials and Russian cataloging La. State U. Library, 1960-62; with U. Colo. Libraries, 1962-66, head circulation dept., 1964-65, instr., adminstrv. asst. to dir. libraries, 1965-66; asso. prof. library sci., asst. dir. libraries for systems and processes Pa. State U., 1966-68; vis. lectr. U. Pitts. Grad. Sch. Library and Info. Scis., 1968-71, Coll. Librarianship Wales, 1971-72; asso. prof., asst. dean U. Denver Grad. Sch. Librarianship, 1972-74; dean, prof. library and info. sci. Simmons Coll. Grad. Sch. Library and Info. Sci., Boston, 1974-94; prof., exec. dir. CLAIR Asian Inst. Tech., Bangkok, 1994—; cons., speaker in field. Author: The Area Specialist Bibliographer: An Inquiry Into His Role, 1972, (with John T. Eastlick) Library Management, 1975, 3d edit, 1987, (with Barbara Moran) Library and Information Center Management, 4th edit., 1993, Michelle My Chelle, 1987, (with Maureen Sullivan) Performance Appraisal and Evaluation, 1991; editor: (with George Miller) Collection Development, 1980, (with Richard Johnson) New Horizons for Academic Libraries, 1979; Academic Librarianship, 1982, Information Needs of the 80s, 1982; gen. editor Founds. of Library and Info. Sci., 1979-87; contbr. articles and revs. to profl. publs. Mem. Mass. Gov.'s Planning Com. for White Ho. Conf. on Librs., 1976-79, Mass. Br. Libr. Commrs., 1989—, chair, 1993-94; mem. ALA Internat. Rels. Roundtable, China Programs com., United Bd. for Christian Higher Edn. in China; chair U.S.-USSR Commn. on Libr. Cooperation, 1987-92, US-CIS/BALTIC Com. on Archives and Librs. Recipient Melville Dewey medal, 1980, Blackwell NA award, 1980, Disting. Alumni award So. Ark. U., 1984, Disting. Grad. award U. Pitts., 1985, ALISE Svc. award 1987, Beta Phi Mu award, 1990, Outstanding Alumni award La. State U., 1991; John F. Kennedy Found. fellow, 1991-92, Humphrey OCLC Forrest Press Internat. award, 1994. Mem. ALA (coun. 1978-81, 84-91, exec. bd. 1987-91, chmn. pub. com. 1983-84, chmn. internat. rels. com. 1991-92), Assn. Libr. and Info. Sci. Edn. (pres. 1983-84, Assn. Coll. and Rsch. Librs. (editl. bd. Coll. and Rsch. librs. 1973-74), Libr. Adminstrn. and Mgmt. Assn. (chmn. stats. com. for libr. edn. 1978-81, Libr. Edn. Divsn. pres. 1977-78), Rsch. Roundtable, Am. Soc. Info. Scis., Spl. Librs. Assn., New Eng. Libr. Assn., Mass. Libr. Assn. (Libr. Advocate award 1994), Internat. Fedn. Libr. Assns. (standing com. on libr. edn. 1986-90, mem. exec. bd. 1991—), New Eng. Hist. Geneal. Soc. (bd. dirs.). Office: Asian Inst Tech, PO Box 4, Keong Luang Pathum Thani 12120, Thailand

STUEBNER, JAMES CLOYD, real estate developer, contractor; b. Phila., Dec. 15, 1931; s. Erwin A. and Frances (Quinn) S.; children: Kathleen, Stephen, James, Susan, Elizabeth; m. Susan Rae Peterson, June 16, 1990. BA, Dartmouth Coll., 1953. Sales engr. Rohm & Haas Co., Phila., 1956-69; pres. Structural Plastics Corp., Mpls., 1961-69; pres., gen. ptnr. Stuebner Properties, Mpls., 1969—; pres. Northland Inn and Exec. Conf. Ctr., 1988—; CEO Five Star Realty and Devel. Co., Mpls., 1992—. Mem. Minn. Conv. Ctr. Commn., St. Paul, 1988; commr. Minn. Econ. Devel. Commn., St. Paul, 1985; bd. dirs. Bach Soc. of Minn., Mpls., 1986—, Minn. Orchestral Assn., Mpls., 1988-91. Sgt. U.S. Army, 1953-55. Mem. Nat. Assn. Office and Indsl. Parks (bd. dirs. Minn. chpt. 1976-85, 81-90, pres. 1978-80, 92-93, nat. pres. 1983-84, v.p. 1981-81, Developer of Yr. award 1987, Minn. Bus. Person of Yr. award 1990, vice chmn. indsl. devel. forum 1996, chmn. 1997). Avocations: sailing, running, singing. Office: Five Star Realty and Devel Co 7000 Northland Dr N Minneapolis MN 55428-1502

STUECK, WILLIAM NOBLE, small business owner; b. Elmhurst, Ill., May 20, 1939; s. Otto Theodore and Anna Elizabeth (Noble) S.; m. Martha Lee Hemphill Stueck, June 2, 1963; children: Matthew Noble, Erika Lee. BS, U. Kans., 1963. Owner, pres. Suburban Lawn & Garden, Inc., Overland Park, Kans., 1953—; chmn. bd. Mark Twain Bank South, Kansas City., Mo., 1984—. Bd. dirs. Ronald McDonald House, Kansas City; ambassador Am. Royal, Kansas City, 1983. Mem. Am. Assn. Nurserymen, Mission Valley Hunt Club (master 1986—), Leavenworth Hunt Club, Saddle & Sirloin Club. Home: 6701 W 167th St Stilwell KS 66085-9235 Office: Suburban Lawn & Garden Inc 13635 Wyandotte St Kansas City MO 64145-1516

STUEHRENBERG, PAUL FREDERICK, librarian; b. Breckenridge, Minn., Mar. 14, 1947; s. Henry Ernest Frederick and Marian Violet (Sandberg) S.; m. Suzanne Elaine Draper, June 14, 1969 (div. Apr. 1982); m. Carole Lee DeVore, Aug. 1, 1983. BA, Concordia Sr. Coll., 1968; MDiv, Concordia Sem., 1972; STM, Christ Sem., 1974; MA, U. Minn., 1978, PhD, 1988. Asst. libr. U. Minn., Mpls., 1974-82; monographs libr. Yale Divinity Libr., New Haven, 1982-91, div. libr., 1991—; adj. assoc. prof. in theol. lit. Yale Divinity Sch., New Haven, 1993—; asst. pastor Christ Meml. Luth. Ch., Plymouth, Minn., 1974-82; adj. pastor Bethesda Luth. Ch., New Haven, 1984—; sec. Luth. Student Found., Mpls., 1978-81. Contbr. articles to profl. jours. Sec. North Haven (Conn.) Libr. Bd., 1989—. Mem. Am. Theol. Libr. Assn., Soc. Bibl. Lit., Am. Acad. Religion, North Haven Meml. Libr. Assn. Home: 280 Bayard Ave North Haven CT 06473-4307 Office: Yale U Div Sch Libr 409 Prospect St New Haven CT 06511-2167

STUELAND, DEAN THEODORE, emergency physician; b. Viroqua, Wis., June 24, 1950; s. Theodore Andrew and Hazel Thelma (Oftedahl) S.; m. Marlene Ann McClurg, Dec. 30, 1972; children: Jeffrey, Michael, Nancy, Kevin. BSEE, U. Wis., 1972, MSEE, 1973, MD, 1977. Diplomate Am. Bd. Internal Medicine, Am. Bd. Geriatric Medicine, Am. Bd. Emergency Medicine; cert. in addictions medicine, cert. med. rev. officer. Resident Marshfield (Wis.) Clinic, 1977-80, emergency physician, dir. emergency svc., 1981-93; emergency physician Riverview Hosp., Wisconsin Rapids, Wis., 1980-81; med. dir. Nat. Farm Medicine Ctr., Marshfield, 1986—, alcohol and other drug abuse unit St. Joseph's Hosp., Marshfield, 1988—; exec. com. Marshfield Clinic, 1989-91, 93-95, treas., 1993-95, v.p., 1997—, ACLS state affiliate faculty Am. Heart Assn., 1984—, nat. faculty, 1992-97; mem. emergency med. svcs. adv. bd. State of Wis., 1994-97. Contbr. articles to profl. jours. Charter mem., pres. Hewitt (Wis.) Jaycees, 1984; bd. dirs. Northwood County chpt. ARC, 1988-95, Wood County Partnership Coun., 1993—. Fellow ACP, Am. Coll. Emergency Physicians (bd. dirs. Wis. chpt. 1984-90, v.p. 1990-91, pres. 1991-92, counselor 1993—), Am. Coll. Preventive Medicine; mem. Biomed. Engring. Soc. (sr. mem.), Am. Soc. Addictions Medicine. Mem. Missionary Alliance Ch. (bd. govs., treas. 1991-97). Office: Marshfield Clinic 1000 N Oak Ave Marshfield WI 54449-5703

STUFANO, THOMAS JOSEPH, investigative firm executive; b. Newport, R.I., July 23, 1955; s. Thomas and Zoe Anne (Halsey) S.; m. Sheila Murphy Stufano, May 22, 1978 (div. July 1988); 1 child, Christine Anne; m. Rene Ellen Goldfarb, Nov. 10, 1994. BSc in Criminal Justice, Pacific Western U., 1988, MBA, 1990; PhD in Criminal Justice, Clayton U., 1992; disting. grad., U.S. Air U., 1992; DSc in Mil. Scis., Eurotechnical Rsch. U., 1997. Legis. rschr. Rhode Island Ho. of Reps., Providence, R.I., 1978-79; sub com. investigator U.S. Ho. of Reps., Washington, 1979-81; law enforcement staff rschr. State of Fla., 1981-88; intelligence officer U.S. Govt., Washington, 1988-96, 96—; COO, Starlink Technologies, Colorado Springs, Colo.; cons. crime commn. State of Fla., 1986-87, U.S. Govt., Washington, 1990-92, State of R.I., Providence, 1979-80; pres. Commn. on Aviation Terrorism, 1990. Contbr. articles to profl. jours. Mem. Rep. Senatorial Inner Circle, Washington, 1992—; instr. ARC, Fla., 1994—; mem. adv. bd. Nat. Civil Def., Washington, 1988—; pres. Round Table. Recipient 3 Presdl. Commendation Pres. of U.S., 1988, 91, 94, Commendation U.S. Ho. of Reps. and Senate, 1982, 91, commendation Prime Minister Lady Margaret Thatcher, 1991, Citation R.I. Ho. of Reps., 1980, Gov. of Mass., 1980, Tenn., Fla., Ky., 1990. Mem. Air Force Assn., Res. Officers Assn., World Assn. of Investigators, Civil Air Patrol, Aircraft Owners and Pilots Assn., Profl. Assn. of Diving Instrs. (instr., Platnuim Diving award 1989), Am. Kempo Karate Assn. (5th degree blackbelt), Order of Ky. Cols. Roman Catholic. Avocations: scuba diving, airplane pilot, parachuting, bicycling. Home: PO Box 852 131 Aspen Dr Woodland Park CO 80863

STUFFLEBEAM, DANIEL LEROY, education educator; b. Waverly, Iowa, Sept. 19, 1936; s. LeRoy and Melva Stufflebeam; m. Carolyn T. Joseph; children: Kevin D., Tracy Smith, Joseph. BA, State U. Iowa, 1958;

MS, Purdue U., 1962, PhD, 1964; postgrad., U. Wis., 1965. Prof., dir. Ohio State U. Evaluation Ctr., Columbus, 1963-73; prof. edn., dir. Western Mich. U. Evaluation Ctr., Kalamazoo, 1973—. Author monographs and 15 books; contbr. chpts. to books, articles to profl. jours. Served with U.S. Army, 1960. Recipient Paul Lazersfeld award Evaluation Rsch. Soc., 1985. Mem. Am. Ednl. Rsch. Assn., Nat. Coun. on Measurement in Edn., Am. Evaluation Assn. Baptist. Office: Western Michigan Univ The Evaluation Ctr Kalamazoo MI 49008-5178

STUHAN, RICHARD GEORGE, lawyer; b. Braddock, Pa., July 1, 1951; s. George and Pauline Madeline (Pavlocik) S.; m. Mary Ann Cipriano, Aug. 23, 1975; children: Brendan George, Sara Katherine, Brian Christopher, Caitlin Emily. BA summa cum laude, Duquesne U., 1973; JD, U. Va., 1976. Bar: Va. 1976, D.C. 1977, U.S. Ct. Appeals (D.C. cir.) 1977, U.S. Ct. Appeals (4th cir.) 1977, U.S. Claims Ct. 1979, U.S. Supreme Ct. 1980, U.S. Ct. Appeals (3d cir.) 1981, U.S. Ct. Appeals (11th cir.) 1982, U.S. Dist. Ct. (no. dist.) Ohio 1985, Ohio 1986. Assoc. Arnold & Porter, Washington, 1976-84; of counsel Jones, Day, Reavis & Pogue, Cleve., 1984-86, ptnr., 1987—. Mem. Va. Law Review, 1974-76. Recipient Gold Medal for Gen. Excellence, Duquesne U., 1973,. Mem. Order of Coif. Democrat. Roman Catholic. Avocations: tennis, swimming, basketball, home repair. Home: 2865 Falmouth Rd Shaker Heights OH 44122-2838 Office: Jones Day Reavis & Pogue 901 Lakeside Ave Cleveland OH 44114-1116

STUHL, OSKAR PAUL, scientific and regulatory consultant; b. Wilhelmshaven, Fed. Republic Germany, Dec. 23, 1949; s. Johannes Alexander and Johanna Wilhelmine (Hoelling) S. Dipl. Chem., U. Duesseldorf, 1976, Dr.rer.nat., 1978. Tutor, Inst. Organische Chemie, U. Dusseldorf, 1975-76, sci. assoc., 1976-79; mgr. product devel. Drugofa GmbH, Cologne, Fed. Republic Germany, 1980; mgr. sci. rels. RJRN, Cologne, 1981-88, mgr. sci. svcs., 1989-94; co-founder, co-owner WRK Internat., 1996—; cons. in field, 1995—; Mem. editl. bd. Beitraege zur Tabakforschung Internat.,1986-96. Mem. Dusseldorf Museums Verein, Verein der Freunde des Hetjens-Museums, Verein der Freunde des Stadtmuseums Dusseldorf, Met. Mus. Art (N.Y.C.), Friends Royal Acad. Arts, London, Art Soc. of Rheinlande and Westfalen, Gesellschaft der Freunde der Kunstammlung NRW; Gesellschaft der Freunde und Foerderer der Univ. Dusseldorf; Zuercher Kunstgesellschaft; Freundeskreis Theatermuseum, Dusseldorf; Foerderverein NRW-Stiftung; Forum fuer Film (Duesseldorf); Deutsch- Japanische- Gesellschaft. Mem. Gesellschaft Deutscher Chemiker, Gesellschaft Deutscher Naturforscher und Aerzte, Max-Planck-Gesellschaft, Deutsche Gesellschaft fuer Arbeits hygiene, Am. Chem. Soc. (including various divs.), Chem. Soc. Japan, N.Y. Acad. of Scis., Royal Soc. Chemistry, Am. Pharm. Assn., Acad. Pharm. Rsch. and Sci., AAAS, Internat. Union Pure and Applied Chemistry, Am. Soc. Pharmacognosy, Fedn. Internat. Pharmaceutic, Christlich Demokratische Union, CDU-Mittelstands und Wirtschaftsvereinigung. Roman Catholic. Clubs: Vereinigung AC Dusseldorf; PCL (London); KDStV Burgundia-Leipzig (Zu Dusseldorf) im CV, Golf Club Velbert. Contbr. articles to profl. jours.; patentee in field. Office: PO Box 140544, D-40075 Dusseldorf Germany

STUHLINGER, ERNST, physicist; b. Niederrimbach, Germany, Dec. 19, 1913; came to U.S., 1946, naturalized, 1955.; s. Ernst and Pauline (Werner) S.; m. Irmgard Lotze, Aug. 1, 1950; children: Susanne, Tilman, Hans Christoph. PhD, U. Tuebingen, Germany, 1936. Asst. prof. Technische Hochschule, Berlin, Germany, 1936-41; guidance and control equipment rocket Devel. Center, Peenemunde, Germany, 1943-45; with Guided Missile Devel. Office, Ft. Bliss, Tex., 1946-50; physicist Ordnance Missile Labs., Huntsville, Ala., 1950-56, Army Ballistic Missile Agy., 1956-60; dir. Space Scis. Lab., George C. Marshall Space Flight Center, NASA, Huntsville, Ala., 1960-68; assoc. dir. for sci. George C. Marshall Space Flight Center, NASA, 1968-76; sr. research scientist, adj. prof. U. Ala. at Huntsville, 1976-84; sr. research assoc. Teledyne Brown Engring. Corp., Huntsville, 1984-88; cons. aerospace cos.; vis. scientist Tech. U. Munich, W. Germany, 1978, Max Planck Inst. Nuclear Physics, Heidelberg, 1983-85; cons. Teledyne-Brown Engring., 1984-90. Author: Ion Propulsion for Space Flight, 1964; co-author: Skylab, A Guidebook, 1973, Project Viking, 1976, Aufbruch in Den Weltraum, 1992, Wernher von Braun, Crusader for Space, 1994. Served with German Army, 1941-43, Russian Campaign. Recipient Humboldt prize Tech. U. Munich, 1978. Fellow Am. Astronautical Soc., Am. Rocket Soc. (dir.), AIAA (tech. dir.), Brit. Interplanetary Soc.; mem. Internat. Acad. Astronautics, Von Braun Astron. Soc. (dir.), Austrian Astron. Soc. (hon.), Am. Optical Soc., Deutsche Roentgengesellschaft (hon.), Deutsche Physikalische Gesellschaft, Deutsche Gesellschaft Fuer Luft und Raumfahrt (hon.), Hermann Oberth Gesellschaft (hon.), Sigma Xi. Rsch. cosmic rays, nuclear physics, 1934-41, electric space propulsion, 1947—, studies on manned missions to Mars, 1954—. Home: 3106 Rowe Dr SE Huntsville AL 35801-6151

STUHR, DAVID PAUL, business educator, consultant; b. Ridgewood, N.J., Oct. 10, 1938; s. Edward Philip and Theresa Alma (Cherny) S. B Engring., Yale U., 1960; MS, Rensselaer Poly. Inst., 1962; PhD, NYU, 1972. Research fellow Fed. Res. Bank of N.Y., N.Y.C., 1968-69, cons. economist, 1969-92; assoc. in bus. Columbia U. Grad. Sch. Bus. Adminstrn., N.Y.C., 1969-72, asst. prof. fin., 1972-73; assoc. prof. fin. Rutgers U. Grad. Sch. Bus. Adminstrn., Newark, N.J., 1973-77; assoc. prof. fin. Fordham U., Faculty of Bus., N.Y.C., 1977—, acting dean faculty, 1984-85; assoc. dean Fordham U. Coll. Bus. Adminstrn., Bronx, N.Y., 1980-83, dean, 1983-87; pres. faculty senate Fordham U., Bronx, N.Y., 1994-95, assoc. v.p. for acad. affairs, 1995—; mem. bus. faculty com. Regents Coll. degrees SUNY, Albany, 1987—. Contbr. articles to profl. jours. Mem. Exec. bd. Bergen coun. Boy Scouts Am., 1979-95; mcpl. chmn. Ho-Ho-Kus (N.J.) Rep. Com., 1968—; chair fin. com. St. Gabriel the Archangel Ch., Saddle River, N.J., 1986—. Mem. Am. Econ. Assn. (life), Am. Fin. Assn. (life), Fin. Mgmt. Assn., Phila. Soc. (founding mem., trustee 1977-80, treas. 1979—). Republican. Roman Catholic. Avocations: backpacking, camping, skiing. Office: Fordham Univ Dept Fin Bronx NY 10458

STUHR, ELAINE RUTH, state legislator; b. Polk County, Nebr., June 19, 1936; m. Boyd E. Stuhr, 1956; children: Cynthia (Stuhr) Hendricks, Teresa (Stuhr) Robbins, Boyd E., Jr. Student, U. Nebr. Tchr. jr. and sr. vocat. h.s. Lincoln (Nebr.) Schs.; senator Nebr. State Senate, Lincoln, 1994—; farmer Bradshaw, Nebr.; former asst. instr. U. Nebr., Lincoln; participant farmer to farmer assignment to Russia with Winrock, Internat., 1993, to Lithuania with Vol., 1993; former pres. Agrl. Womens Leadership Network; former mem. bd. dirs. Feed Grains Coun., Nebr. Corn Bd.; agrl. adv. com. for Congressman Doug Bereuter. Past pres., bd. dirs. Found. for Agrl. Edn. and Devel.; former mem. exec. com. and bd. dirs. Agrl. Coun. Am.; leader 4H Club; mem. adv. com. Nebr. Extension Svc.; bd. dirs. Nebr. Family Comty. Leadership Program; chmn. Nebr. Agrl. Leadership Coun. Office: Nebr State Capitol Dist # 24 Lincoln NE 68509

STUIVER, MINZE, geological sciences educator; b. Vlagtwedde, Groningen, The Netherlands, Oct. 25, 1929; came to U.S., 1959; s. Albert and Griet (Welles) S.; m. Annie Hubbelmeyer, July 12, 1956; children: Ingrid, Yolande. D.Sc. in Physics, U. Groningen, 1953, Ph.D. in Biophysics, 1958. Research assoc. Yale U., New Haven, 1959-62; sr. research assoc., dir. Radiocarbon Lab. Yale U., 1962-69; prof. geol. sci. and zoology U. Wash. Seattle, 1969-82, prof. geol. sci. and quaternary scis., 1982—, dir. Quaternary Isotope Lab, 1972—. Editor: Radiocarbon, 1976-88; mem. editorial bd.: Quaternary Research, 1974—, Isotope Geoscience, 1983—. Named Alexander von Humboldt sr. scientist Fed. Republic Germany, 1983. Mem. Geol. Soc. Am., Am. Quaternary Assn. Office: U Wash Box 351360 Seattle WA 98195-1360

STUKEL, JAMES JOSEPH, academic administrator, mechanical engineering educator; b. Joliet, Ill., Mar. 30, 1937; s. Philip and Julia (Mattivi) S.; m. Mary Joan Helpling, Nov. 27, 1958; children: Catherine, James, David, Paul. B.S. in Mech. Engring, Purdue U., 1959; M.S., U. Ill., Champaign-Urbana, 1963, Ph.D., 1968. Research engr. W.Va. Pulp and Paper Co., Covington, Va., 1959-61; mem. faculty U. Ill., 1968—, prof. mech. engring., 1975—, dir. Office Coal Research and Utilization, 1974-76, dir. Office Energy Research, 1976-81, dir. pub. policy program Coll. Engring., 1981-84, assoc. dean Coll. Engring. and dir. Expt. Sta., 1984-85; dean Grad. Coll., vice chancellor for research U. Ill. at Chgo., 1985-86, exec. vice chancellor, vice chancellor academic affairs, 1986-91, interim chancellor, 1990-91, chancellor, 1991-95, pres., 1995—; v.p. Chgo. Tech. Park Corp., 1985-88. pres., 1990-91; exec. sec. midwest Consortium Air Pollution, 1972-73, chmn. bd. dirs., 1973-75; mem. adv. bd. regional studies program Argonne (Ill.) Nat. Lab., 1975-76; adv. com. Energy Resources Commn., 1976; chmn. panel on dispersed electric generating techs. Office Tech. Assessment, U.S. Congress, 1980-81; chmn. rev. adv. bd. tech. rev. dist. heating and combined heat and power systems Internat. Energy Agy, OECD, Paris, 1982-83; cons. in field. Contbr. articles to profl. jours. Pres. parish council Holy Cross Roman Cath. Ch., Urbana, 1967-68. Mem. ASCE (State-of-the-Art of Civil Engring. award 1975), ASME, AAAS, Sigma Xi, Phi Kappa Phi, Pi Tau Sigma. Home: 2650 N Lakeview Ave Apt 1610 Chicago IL 60614-1819 Office: PO Box 4348 2833 Univ Hall M/C 105 Chicago IL 60680-4348

STULC, JAROSLAV PETER, surgeon, educator; b. Teplitz, Czechoslovakia, Sept. 14, 1947; came to U.S., 1948; s. Jaroslav Pavel and Emilie Vanca Stulc; m. Diana Susan Minassian, Dec. 27, 189; children: Alexan Christopher, Evan Thomas. BA, Cornell Coll., Mt. Vernon, Iowa, 1969; MD, U. Iowa, 1973; student, Naval War Coll., 1997. Diplomate Am. Bd. Surgery. Intern SUNY, Syracuse, 1973-75; resident in surgery Georgetown U., Washington, 1975-80, instr. surgery, 1979-80; instr. surgery, fellow transplant surgery Loyola U., Chgo., 1980-83; fellow surg. oncology Roswell Park Cancer Inst., Buffalo, 1983-85, attending surgeon, 1985-90; asst. prof. surgery SUNY, Buffalo, 1988-91; chief surgery VA Hosp., Buffalo, 1990-91; attending surgeon Trover Clinic Found., Madisonville, Ky., 1991—; clin. faculty U. Louisville, 1991—; co-dir. Mahr Cancer Ctr., Madisonville, 1992—. Editor Ky. Med. Jour., Physician Focus; contbr. articles and abstracts to publs. Vis. lectr. outreach program Am. Cancer Soc., bd. dirs. Ky. chpt., 1993—. Capt. USNR, 1987—. Fellow ACS (cert. advanced trauma life support), Internat. Coll. Surgeons; mem. AMA, AAAS, Am. Soc. Gastrointestinal Endoscopy, Am. Soc. Abdominal Surgeons, Am. Soc. Clin. Oncology, Soc. Am. Gastrointestinal Surgeons, Nat. Surg. Adjuvant Breast and Bowel Protocl, Ea. Coop. Oncology Group, Iowa Jr. Acad. Sci., Chgo. Assn. Immunologists, Roswell Park Surg. Soc., Buffalo Surg. Soc., Acad. Surg. Rsch., Assn. Acad. Surgery, Adrian Kantrowitz Surg. Rsch. Soc., VFW, Tri Beta. Presbyterian. Home: 1200 College Dr Madisonville KY 42431-9182 Office: Trover Clinic Found 435 N Kentucky Ave Madisonville KY 42431-1768

STULCE, MIKE, Olympic athlete, track and field. Olympic track and field participant Barcelona, Spain, 1992. Recipient Shotput Gold medal Olympics, Barcelona, 1992. Office: care US Olympic Com 1750 E Boulder St Colorado Springs CO 80909-5724*

STULL, DANIEL RICHARD, retired research thermochemist, educator, consultant; b. Columbus, Ohio, May 28, 1911; s. Lucius Walter and Irene Mabel (Haldeman) S.; m. Ruth Louise Keck, Sept. 26, 1936 (dec. 1982); children: Louise Irene Stull Hassman, Richard Walter; m. Mary Morton Lowe, Apr. 28, 1984. BS in Chemistry, Math., Baldwin-Wallace Coll., 1933; PhD in Chemistry, Johns Hopkins U., 1937. Asst. prof. chemistry East Carolina U., Greenville, N.C., 1937-40; rsch. crew leader Dow Chem. Co., Midland, Mich., 1940-50, rsch. tech. expert, 1950-60, dir. thermal lab., 1960-69, rsch. scientist, 1969-76, cons., 1976-77; ret., 1976; rsch. adv. com. Mfg. Chemists Assn., Washington, 1958-65, NRC rev. bd. Nat. Bur. Stds., Washington, 1959-70; rsch. mem., commr. Internat. Union Pure and Applied Chemistry, 1963-72; printer Hobby Print Shop, Alembic Press, 1954-92; plenary spkr. 50th Calorimetry Conf., Washington, 1995. Author: Fundamentals of Fire and Explosion, 1976; author, editor books Joint Army Navy Airforce Rocket Propulsion Group, 1958-76; co-author: Chemical Thermodynamics of Organic Compounds, 1948-69; contbr. to more than 70 sci. rsch. publs. Fin. chmn. 1st United Meth. Ch., Midland, 1948-58; mem. Cosmos Club, Washington, 1967-72; mem. ch. choir various cmtys., 1928-97. Recipient Hugh Huffman Meml. award Calorimetry Conf., Ames, Iowa, 1965, Alumni Merit award Baldwin-Wallace Coll., Berea, Ohio, 1968, Book award Rsch. Soc. Am., 1969. Fellow Am. Inst. Chemists; mem. AAAS, Am. Chem. Soc. (local sect. award 1980), Sigma Xi, Phi Beta Kappa, Phi Lambda Upsilon. Achievements include extensive compilation of vapor pressure data, development of automatic strip chart recorder for platinum resistance thermometry, 1st automatic recording low temperature calorimeter, computer program to calculate thermodynamic functions, thermal equilibria. Home: 1113 W Park Dr Midland MI 48640-4277

STULL, DONALD LEROY, architect; b. Springfield, Ohio, May 16, 1937; s. Robert Stull and Ruth Branson; m. Patricia Ann Ryder, Dec. 29, 1959 (div. Dec. 1985); children: Cydney Lynn, Robert Branson, Gia Virginia. BArch, Ohio State U., 1961; MArch, Harvard U., 1962. Registered arch., Calif., Conn., Fla., Ky., Maine, Md., Mass., Mich., Mo., N.H., N.J., N.Y., Pa., R.I., Tenn., Tex., Va., D.C. Pres. Stull Assocs., Inc., Boston, 1966-83; pres. Stull and Lee, Inc., Boston, 1983—; mem. Loeb fellowship com. Harvard Grad. Sch. Design, Cambridge, 1969-80; mem. adv. bd. Boston Archtl. Ctr., 1972-80, Mus. Nat. Ctr. of Afro-Am. Artists, Boston, 1978—, Ohio State U. Sch. Architecture, 1980—; design prof. Harvard Grad. Sch. Design, 1974-81; mem. vis. design studio, Rice University, Houston, Tex., spring 1993; mem. vis. com. Yale Sch. Art and Architecture, New Haven, Conn., 1972-76, William Henry Bishop chair Yale Sch. Architecture, 1975; mem. nat. presdl. design award jury Nat. Endowment for Arts, 1984, 88; bd. overseers The Inst. of Contemporary Art, Boston, 1996-97. Trustee Shaw U., 1973-75, Boston Found. for Architecture, 1992—; mem. design adv. panel, Balt., 1976-80; chmn. Mass Art Commn., Boston, 1978-80; commr. Boston Art Commn., 1980-92; mem. Design Adv. Group, Cambridge, 1980-90, 94—; commr. Boston Civic Design Commn., 1987—; adv. com. Suffolk Sch. Bus. Mgmt., 1989-95; bd. dirs Historic Boston, 1990—, Mus. of Afro-Am. History, Boston, 1979—; trustee Mass. Coll. Art, 1995—. Recipient Presdl. Design award Nat. Endowment for Arts, 1988; named one of Outstanding Young Men Boston, 1969, Outstanding Young Men Am., 1970, Centennial Yr. Outstanding Alumnus Ohio State U., 1970. Fellow AIA (nat. design com. 1972-84); mem. Boston Soc. ARchitects (bd. dirs. 1969, AIA Regional Design award 1975, 80, 89), Mass. Soc. Architects (bd. trustees Mass. 1995). Office: Stull and Lee Inc 38 Chauncy St Ste 1100 Boston MA 02111-2301

STULL, FRANK WALTER, elementary school educator; b. Easton, Pa., June 4, 1935; s. George Washington and Minnie Elizabeth S.; m. Darlene Joy Hunsicker, Aug. 2, 1958; children: James, Ronald, Wendy. BS, East Stroudsburg State Coll., 1956; MEd, Lehigh U., 1966. Cert. tchr., N.J. Tchr. Korea Heung-Up Bank, Seoul, Korea, 1957-58, Howell Twp. Elem. Sch., Freehold, N.J., 1958-59, Holland Twp. Elem. Sch., Milford, N.J., 1959-91; lectr. Friends of U.S. Navy, 1992—. Bd. dirs., sec., treas., mgr. Hunterdon County Sch. Employees Fed. Credit Union, Phillipsburg, N.J., 1969-87, mem.adv. com., 1995; merit badge counselor Boy Scouts Am., 1970-84, cubmaster, 1971-72; active Friends of USN, 1992—; treas., mem. Hist. Preservation Commn. Holland Twp., 1993—; bd. govs. Riegel Ridge Cmty. Ctr., 1997—. Recipient Meritorious Svc. award N.J. Credit Union League, 1988, Tchr. Recognition award State N.J. Gov., 1987, Disting. Achievement award for rsch. and preservation of history of Holland Twp. and surrounding areas; named Outstanding Elem. Tchr. Am., 1972; Experienced Tchr. in Geography fellow Pa. State U., 1967. Mem. NEA, Holland Twp. Edn. Assn., Hunterdon County Edn. Assn., N.J. Edn. Assn., Phi Delta Kappa (chartered mem. Zeta Gamma chpt.). Avocations: photography, travel. Home and Office: 806 Rugby Rd Phillipsburg NJ 08865-2033

STULTS, WALTER BLACK, management consultant, former trade organization executive; b. Hightstown, N.J., Oct. 25, 1921; s. C. Stanley and Nettie M. (Black) S.; m. Ann D. Haynes, June 28, 1947; children: Andrew Haynes, Thomas Stanley. BA, Williams Coll., 1943; MA (Woodrow Wilson fellow), Princeton U., 1949. Teaching asst. Princeton (N.J.) U., 1946-49; legis. asst. to U.S. Senator Robert Hendrickson, Washington, 1949-50; staff dir. U.S. Senate Small Bus. Com., Washington, 1950-61; pres. Nat. Assn. Small Bus. Investment Cos., Washington, 1961-86; prin. W.B. Stults, Cons., Chapel Hill, N.C., 1979—; dir. Pardee & Curtin Lumber Co., Pardee Resources Co., Phila.; chmn. Coun. Small and Ind. Bus. Assns., 1976-81. Pres. Carol Woods Residents Assn.; dir. Carol Woods Retirement Comty., 1995-97. With USAAF, 1943-46. Mem. Am. Soc. Assn. Execs. Republican. Congregationalist. Clubs: The Exchequer, Masons, Chapel Hill Country.

STULTZ, NEWELL MAYNARD, political science educator; b. Boston, June 13, 1933; s. Irving Washburn and Marjorie May (MacEachern) S.; m. Elizabeth Petronella Olckers, Apr. 6, 1958; children: Elliot Andries, Amy Elizabeth. A.B., Dartmouth Coll., 1955; M.A., Boston U., 1960, Ph.D., 1965; M.A. hon., Brown U., 1968. Fulbright exchange scholar U. Pretoria, South Africa, 1955-56; asst. prof. polit. sci. Northwestern U., Evanston, Ill., 1964-65; asst. prof. to prof. polit. sci. Brown U., Providence, 1965—, assoc. grad. dean, 1970-74, assoc. dean of faculty, 1993—; vis. fellow Yale U.-South African Research Program, 1977; vis. prof. U. South Africa, Pretoria, 1980; James Gathings lectr. Bucknell U., Lewisburg, Pa., 1980. Author: Afrikaner Politics in South Africa, 1974, Who Goes to Parliament?, 1975, Transkei's Half Loaf, 1979, (bibliography) South Africa, 1989, 2d edit., 1993; co-author: South Africa's Transkei, 1967; co-editor: Governing in Black Africa, 1970, 2d edit., 1986. V.p. World Affairs Council R.I., 1983. Served as lt. (j.g.) USN, 1956-59. Fulbright fellow, 1955-56; NDEA grantee, 1959-62; Ford Found. fellow, 1962-64; Rockefeller Found. fellow, 1976-77. Unitarian. Home: 371 New Meadow Rd Barrington RI 02806-3729 Office: Brown U Dept Polit Sci PO Box 1844 Providence RI 02912-1844

STULTZ, THOMAS JOSEPH, newspaper executive; b. Ironton, Ohio, July 28, 1951; s. Riley Frederick and Mary (Leslie) S.; m. Patricia Ann Conley, Dec. 18, 1971; children: Leslie Faye, Jessica Kristin. Student, Ohio U., 1969-71, Marshall U., 1971, U. N.C., Chapel Hill. Reporter Ashland (Ky.) Daily Ind., 1970-73, Orlando (Fla.) Sentinel, 1973; owner/pub. Greenup County Sentinel, Greenup, Ky., 1973-80; editor, writer Bob Jones U., Greenville, S.C., 1980; advt. dir. Daily Adv., Greenville, 1980-81; dir. cmty. publs. Anderson (S.C.) Ind. Mail, 1981-84; v.p., gen. mgr. Leader Newspapers, Inc., Charlotte, N.C., 1984-86; mktg. dir. Suburban Newspapers Greater St. Louis, 1986-88; v.p. Multimedia Newspaper Co., Greenville, 1988-96; pres. pub. divsn. Gray Comms. Sys., Inc., Albany, Ga., 1996—; pres., owner Internat. Employment Gazette, Greenville, 1989—. Deacon, tchr. Temple Bapt. Ch., Flatwoods, Ky., 1978-80. Republican. Avocations: golf, travel, reading, church and missions activities. Home: 6 Titleist Ct Taylors SC 29687-6651 Office: Gray Comms Sys Inc PO Box 48 Albany GA 31701

STUMBO, JANET L., justice; b. Prestonsburg, Ky.; d. Charles and Doris Stanley S.; m. Ned Pillersdorf; children: Sarah, Nancee, Samantha. BA, Morehead State U., 1976; JD, U. Ky., 1980. Bar: Ky. 1980, W. Va. 1982. Staff atty. to Judge Harris S. Howard Ky. Ct. Appeals, 1980-82; asst. county atty. Floyd County, 1982-85; pvt. practice Turner, Hall & Stumbo, P.S.C., 1982-88; prosecutor Floyd Dist. Ct. and Juvenile Ct.; ptnr. Stumbo, DeRossett & Pillersdorf, 1989; judge Ct. Appeals, Ky., 1989-93, Supreme Ct. of Ky., 1993—. Named to Morehead State U. Alumni Assn. Hall of Fame, 1990; recipient Justice award Ky. Women Advocates, 1991, Outstanding Just award Ky. Women Advocates, 1995, Bull's Eye award Women in State Govt. Network, 1995. Office: Ky Supreme Ct Capital Bldg Rm 226 700 Capital Ave Frankfort KY 40601 also: 169 N Arnold Ave Ste 502 Prestonsburg KY 41653

STUMP, BOB, congressman; b. Phoenix, Apr. 4, 1927; s. Jesse Patrick and Floy Bethany (Fields) S.; children: Karen, Bob, Bruce. B.S. in Agronomy, Ariz. State U., 1951. Mem. Ariz. Ho. of Reps., 1957-67; mem. Ariz. Senate, 1967-76, pres., 1975-76; mem. 95th-105th Congresses from 3rd Dist.Ariz., 1976—; mem. Nat. Security Com. With USN, 1943-46. Mem. Am. Legion, Ariz. Farm Bur. Republican. Seventh-day Adventist. Office: 211 Canon House of Representatives Washington DC 20515-0303 also: 230 N 1st Ave Rm 5001 Phoenix AZ 85025-0230*

STUMP, JOHN EDWARD, veterinary anatomy educator, ethologist; b. Galion, Ohio, June 3, 1934; s. Clarence Willard and Mabel Katherine (Pfeifer) S.; m. Patricia Anne Auer, Aug. 7, 1955; children—Karen, James. D.V.M. summa cum laude (Borden award for acad. excellence 1958), Ohio State U., 1958; Ph.D., Purdue U., 1966. Pvt. practice vet. medicine Bucyrus, Ohio, 1958-61; mem. faculty Purdue U., West Lafayette, Ind., 1961-91; prof. vet. anatomy Purdue U., 1976-91, prof. emeritus vet. anatomy, 1991; vis. prof. dept. physiol. scis. Sch. Vet. Medicine, U. Calif.-Davis, fall 1980; vis. prof. Coll. Vet. Medicine, Tex. A&M U., spring 1981. Recipient Autotutorial Excellence award Student AVMA, 1974, Amoco Found. Purdue undergrad. teaching award, 1979, Norden Disting. Tchr. award Purdue U., 1977, Outstanding Tchr. award Purdue U. Alumni Found., 1978; named Outstanding Tchr. Freshman Vet. Students, Purdue U., 1987. Mem. AVMA, Ind. Vet. Med. Assn., World Assn. Vet. Anatomists, Am. Assn. Vet. Anatomists (pres. 1977-78), Am. Assn. Anatomists, Am. Vet. Soc. Animal Behavior, Ind. Acad. Sci., Sigma Xi, Phi Zeta, Gamma Sigma Delta. Republican. Presbyterian. Club: Tecumseh Kiwanis (pres. 1973).

STUMP, JOHN SUTTON, lawyer; b. Clarksburg, W.Va., Aug. 7, 1929; s. John Sutton and Helen (Mannix) S.; m. Elaine Claire Scammahorn, Sept. 14, 1968; children—John Sutton IV, James Felix. Student, Washington and Lee U., 1946-47, LL.B., 1957; B.S. in Commerce, U. N.C., 1951. Bar: W.Va. 1957, Va. 1957, D.C. 1983. Assoc. Jackson, Kelly, Holt & O'Farrell, Charleston, W.Va., 1957-58, Boothe, Dudley, Koontz & Boothe, Alexandria, Va., 1958-61, Boothe, Dudley, Koontz & Blankingship, Fairfax and Alexandria, Va., 1962-63; ptnr. Boothe, Dudley, Koontz, Blankingship & Stump, Fairfax and Alexandria, 1963-71, Boothe, Prichard & Dudley, 1971-87, McGuire, Woods, Battle & Boothe, 1987—. Served to lt. comdr. USNR, 1951-54, 61-62. Fellow Am. Coll. Trial Lawyers; mem. Am. Law Inst. Home: 8329 Weller Ave Mc Lean VA 22102-1717 Office: 8280 Greensboro Dr Mc Lean VA 22102-3807

STUMPE, WARREN ROBERT, scientific, engineering and technical services company executive; b. Bronx, N.Y., July 15, 1925; s. William A. and Emma J. (Mann) S.; children: Jeffrey, Kathy, William. B.S., U.S. Mil. Acad., 1945; M.S., Cornell U., 1949; M.S. in Indsl. Engring, N.Y. U., 1965; grad., Command and Gen. Staff Coll., 1972, Army War Coll., 1976; Ph.D. (hon.), Milw. Sch. Engring., 1982. Registered profl. engr., N.Y., Fla., Wis. Commd. 2d lt., C.E. U.S. Army, 1945, advanced through grades to capt., 1954; with (65th Engr. Bn.), 1945-48; asst. prof. mechanics U.S. Mil. Acad., 1951-54; resigned, 1954; from capt. to col. Res., 1958-79; dep. gen. mgr., gen. engring. div. AMF, Stamford, Conn., 1954-63; exec. v.p. Dortech, Inc., Stamford, 1963-69; dir. systems mgmt. group Mathews Conveyor div. REX, Darien, Conn., 1969-71; dir. research and devel. Rexnord, Inc., Milw., 1971-73, v.p. corp. research and tech., from 1973, v.p. bus. devel. sector, 1981-83, v.p., chief tech. officer, 1983-86; pres. Rexnord Techs., Milw., 1986-87; v.p. Radian Corp., Milw., 1987-90; civilian aide to sec. army for State of Wis., 1981-85; mem. adv. bd. technology transfer program U. Wis.-Whitewater. Contbr. articles to profl. jours. Founder, pres. No. Little League, Stamford, 1965-69; pres. Turn of River Jr. High Sh. PTA, 1967-68; vice chmn. for Wis. Dept. Def., Nat. Com. Employer Support Guard and Res.; bd. regents Milw. Sch. Engring.; mem. liaison coun. Coll. Engring., U. Wis., also mem. indsl. adv. coun.; mem. adv. coun. Marquette U.; mem. Wis. Gov.'s Task Force on Energy, Coun. Great Lakes Govs.' Regional Econ. Devel. Commn., 1987-88; bd. dirs. MRA-Inst. Mgmt., Inc. Mem. Am. Water Pollution Control Fedn., Indsl. Rsch. Inst. (pres., dir.), Wis. Assn. Rsch. Mgrs. (founder), West Point Soc. Wis., Tau Beta Pi, Phi Kappa Phi. Clubs: Wis., Ozaukee Country.

STUMPF, BERNHARD JOSEF, physicist; b. Neustadt der Weinstrasse, Rhineland, Germany, Sept. 21, 1948; came to U.S., 1981; s. Josef and Katharina (Cervinka) S. Diploma physics, Saarland U., Saarbrucken, West Germany, 1975, Dr.rer.nat., 1981. Rsch. asst. physics dept. Saarland U., Saarbrucken, 1976-81; rsch. assoc. Joint Inst. Lab. Astrophysics, U. Colo., Boulder, 1981-84; instr. physics, physics dept. NYU, N.Y.C., 1984-86, asst. rsch. scientist Atomic Beams Lab., 1984-85, assoc. rsch. scientist Atomic Beams Lab., 1985-86; vis. assoc. prof. physics dept. U Windsor (Ont., Can.), 1986-88; assoc. prof. physics dept. U. Idaho, Moscow, 1988—; chmn. Conf. on Atomic and Molecular Collisions in Excited States, Moscow, 1990. Contbr. articles to profl. jours. German Sci. Found. postdoctoral fellow U. Colo., 1981-83. Mem. AAUP, German Phys. Soc., Am. Phys. Soc. Home: 825 W C St Moscow ID 83843-2108 Office: U Idaho Dept Physics Moscow ID 83844-0903

STUMPF, DAVID ALLEN, pediatrician and neurologist; b. L.A., May 8, 1945; s. Herman A. and Dorothy F. (Davis) S.; children: Jennifer F., Kaitrin E.; m. Elizabeth Dusenbery, Feb. 2, 1989; stepchildren: Todd Coleman, Shilo Walker. BA, Lewis and Clark Coll., 1966; MD cum laude, U. Colo., 1972, PhD, 1972. Pediatric intern Strong Meml. Hosp., Rochester, N.Y., 1972-73, resident, 1973-74; neurology resident Harvard Med. Sch., Boston, 1974-77;

dir. pediatric neurology U. Colo. Health Sci. Ctr., Denver, 1977-85; chief neurology Children's Meml. Hosp., Chgo., 1985-89; chmn. neurology, Benjamin and Virginia T. Boshes Prof. Northwestern U., 1989—; mem. sci. adv. co. Muscular Dystrophy Assn., 1981-87. Editorial bd. Neurology, 1982-87; contbr. articles to sci. jours. NIH grantee, 1979-84; Muscular Dystrophy Assn. grantee, 1977-89; March of Dimes grantee, 1983-85; recipient Lewis and Clark Coll. Disting. Alumni award, 1991. Fellow Am. Acad. Neurology; mem. Child Neurology Soc. (counsellor 1982-84, pres. 1985-87), Am. Neurol. Assn., Am. Pediatric Soc., Soc. Pediatric Rsch. Presbyterian. Home: 540 Judson Ave Evanston IL 60202-3084 Office: 645 N Michigan Ave Ste 1058 Chicago IL 60611-2814

STUMPF, HARRY CHARLES, lawyer; b. New Orleans, May 1, 1944; s. John Frederick and Amy Ruth (Lynch) S.; m. Mary Frances Henricks, Aug. 27, 1966 (div. Dec. 3, 1992); children: Ashley Frances Stumpf Borges, Piper Lynch, Harry Charles Jr.; m. Cynthia Anne Torgersen, Dec. 14, 1996. BBA, Tulane U., 1967, JD, 1968. Bar: La. 1968, U.S. Dist. Ct. (ea. dist.) La. 1968, U.S. Ct. Appeals (5th cir.) 1968, U.S. Supreme Ct. 1995. Assoc./of counsel Knight, D'Angelo & Knight, Gretna, La., 1968-83; ptnr. Stumpf, Dugas, LeBlanc, Papale & Ripp, Gretna, La., 1983—. Lector/commentator St. Anthony Ch., Gretna, 1970—; trustee La. Cystic Fibrosis, New Orleans, 1975-78. Recipient Outstanding Svc. award West Jefferson Levee Dist., 1994. Fellow La. Bar Found.; mem. Jefferson Bar Assn., Westbank Rotary (dir. 1970—), Semreh Club. Avocations: golf, boating, skiing, computers. Office: Stumpf Dugas LeBlanc Papale & Ripp 901 Derbigny St Ste 200 Gretna LA 70053-6205

STUMPF, MARK HOWARD, lawyer; b. Chgo., Jan. 25, 1947; s. Samuel Enoch and Jean (Goodman) S.; m. Elizabeth Bruce, Nov. 18, 1972; children: Nicholas, Anna, Lawrence, Gillian. AB, Harvard U., 1969, JD, 1972. Bar: N.Y. 1973, D.C. 1977, U.S. Dist. Ct. (so. and ea. dists.) N.Y. 1973. Assoc. Paul, Weiss, Rifkind, Wharton & Garrison, N.Y.C., 1972-76; assoc. Arnold & Porter, Washington, 1976-80, ptnr., 1981-92, sr. ptnr., 1993—; bd. dirs. Martha's Table, Washington. Co-author: Shark Repellents and Golden Parachutes; author: (with others) Latin American Sovereign Debt Management, 1990. Decorated Order of Generalísimo Francisco de Miranda, 1st Class (Republic of Venezuela) 1991. Mem. ABA, Harvard Club N.Y.C. Democrat. Episcopalian. Home: 3820 Jocelyn St NW Washington DC 20015-1920 Office: Arnold & Porter 555 12th St NW Washington DC 20004-1200

STUMPF, PAUL KARL, biochemistry educator emeritus; b. N.Y.C., N.Y., Feb. 23, 1919; s. Karl and Annette (Schreyer) S.; married, June 1947; children: Ann Carol, Kathryn Lee, Margaret Ruth, David Karl, Richard Frederic. AB, Harvard Coll., 1941; PhD, Columbia U., 1945. Instr. pub. health U. Mich., Ann Arbor, 1946-48; faculty U. Calif., Berkeley, 1948-58, prof., 1956-58; prof. U. Calif., Davis, 1958-84, prof. emeritus, 1984—; chief scientist Competitive Rsch. Grants Office USDA, Washington, 1988-91; cons. Palm Oil Rsch. Inst., Kuala Lumpur, Malaysia, 1982-92; mem. sci. adv. bd. Calgene, Inc., Davis, 1990-93; mem. sci. adv. panel Md. Biotech. Inst., 1990-92; Inaugural lectr. Tan Sri Dato'Seri B. Bek-Nielsen Found., Kuala Lumpur, 1996. Co-author: Outlines of Enzyme Chemistry, 1955, Outlines of Biochemistry, 5th edit., 1987; co-editor-in-chief Biochemistry of Plants, 1980; exec. editor Archives of Biochemistry/Biophysics, 1965-88; contbr. over 250 articles to profl. jours. Mem. planning commn. City of Davis, 1966-68. Guggenheim fellow, 1962, 69; recipient Lipid Chemistry award Am. Oil Chemists Soc., 1974, Sr. Scientist award Alexander von Humboldt Found., 1976, Superior Svc. Group award USDA, 1992, Award of Excellence, Calif. Aggie Alumni Found., 1996. Fellow AAAS; mem. NAS, Royal Danish Acad. Scis., Am. Soc. Plant Physiologists (pres. 1979-80, chmn. bd. trustees 1986-90, Stephen Hales award 1974, Charles Reid Barnes Life Membership award 1992), Yolo Fliers Country Club (Woodland, Calif.). Avocation: golf. Home: 764 Elmwood Dr Davis CA 95616-3517 Office: Univ of Calif Molecular/Cellular Biology Davis CA 95616

STUMPF, SAMUEL ENOCH, philosophy educator; b. Cleve., Feb. 3, 1918; s. Rev. Louis and Elizabeth (Jergens) S.; m. Jean Goodman, July 3, 1943; children—Paul Jergens, Mark Howard, Samuel Enoch. B.S., U. Calif. at Los Angeles, 1940; B.D., Andover Newton Theol. Sch., 1943; postgrad., Columbia, 1946; Ph.D., U. Chgo., 1948. Asst. prof. ethics Vanderbilt U., 1948-49, asso. prof., 1949-52, prof. philosophy, chmn. dept., 1952-67, prof. philosophy emeritus, 1984—; vis. prof. med. ethics Vanderbilt U. (Med. Sch.), 1973-74; research prof. jurisprudence Vanderbilt U. (Law Sch.), 1974-77; research prof. med. philosophy Vanderbilt U. (Med. Sch.), 1974—, prof. law, 1977-84, prof. law emeritus, 1984—, also asst. to chancellor, 1966-67; pres. Cornell Coll., Mt. Vernon, Iowa, 1967-74; Gates lectr. Grinnell Coll., 1951; Keese lectr. U. Chattanooga, 1962; Decell lectr. Millsaps Coll., 1963; Louttit-George lectr. Washington Coll., 1967; Willson lectr. Southwestern U., 1970. Author: Philosophical Problems; Elements of Philosophy, A Democratic Manifesto, Socrates to Sartre, Morality and the Law, Philosophy: History and Problems; Contbr. articles to profl. jours. Trustee Food Safety Coun., 1976-80, Food and Drug Law Inst., 1978—. Lt. USNR, 1943-46. Carnegie research grantee, 1949; Ford fellow Harvard, 1955-56; Rockefeller fellow Oxford (Eng.) U., 1958-59. Mem. Am. Council on Legal and Polit. Philosophy, Am. Philos. Assn., Phi Beta Kappa. Home: 424 Page Rd Nashville TN 37205-4244

STUMPF, WALTER ERICH, cell biology educator, researcher; b. Oelsnitz, Sachsen, Germany, Jan. 10, 1927; came to U.S., 1963; m. Ursula Emily Schwinge, May 20, 1961; children: Andrea, Martin, Carolin, Silva. MD summa cum laude, Humboldt U., Berlin, 1952; PhD, U. Chgo., 1967; D in Biol. Humanities (hon.), U. Ulm, Germany, 1987. Resident in neurology and psychiatry Humboldt U., Berlin, 1954-57; resident in neurology and psychiatry U. Marburg, 1957-61, resident in radiobiology, 1961-62; rsch. assoc. U. Chgo., 1963-67, asst. prof., 1967-70; assoc. prof. U. N.C., Chapel Hill, 1970-73, prof., 1973-95, mem. labs. for reproductive biology and neurobiology program, mem. Cancer Rsch. Ctr., Carolina Population Ctr., mem. curriculum in toxicology; vis. psychiatrist Maudsley Hosp., London, 1959; vis. prof. Max-Planck Inst. for Cell Biology, Wilhelmshaven, Germany, 1975, U. Ulm, 1981; rsch. advisor Chugai Pharm. Co., Ltd., Tokyo, 1992-95; cons. Harris Mfg. Co., North Billerica, Mass., Rsch. Triangle Inst., Chemistry and Life Scis. Divsn., Rsch. Triangle Park, N.C., Merck Sharp and Dome, Westpoint, Pa.; exec. com. NRC, Inst. of Lab. Animal Resources, Nat. Acad. Scis., 1979-81, coun. Inst. of Lab. Animal Res., 1978-81, com. Soc. for Exptl. Biology and Medicine, 1987-92, founder Internat. Inst. Drug Distbn. Cytopharmacology and Cytoxicology, Chapel Hill, N.C., 1995—. Editor: Autoradiography of Diffusible Substances, 1969, Anatomical Neuroendocrinology, 1975, Autoradiography and Correlative Imaging, 1995; mem. editl. bd. Neuroendocrinology Letters, 1979-87, Exptl. Aging Rsch., 1975-85, Jour. Histochemistry and Cytochemistry, 1982-90, Cell and Tissue Rsch., 1982-88, Molecular and Cellular Neurosci., 1989-94, Biomed. Rsch., 1991-94, Histochemistry, 1992-96; contbr. numerous articles to profl. jours. Recipient Humboldt Found. award, 1989. Mem. AAAS, Am. Assn. Anatomists, N.Y. Acad. Scis., Soc. for Exptl. Biology and Medicine, Soc. for Neurosci., Endocrine Soc., Internat. Brain Rsch. Orgn., Am. Soc. Zoologists, Histochem. Soc. (coun. 1977-81), Histochem. Gesellschaft (Feulgen lectureship 1982), Internat. Soc. Xenobiotics (charter), Internat. Inst. Drug Distbn. Cytopharmacology and Cytotoxicology (founder). Home: U NC Sch Medicine 2612 Damascus Church Rd Chapel Hill NC 27516 Office: Internat Inst Drug Distribution Cytopharmacology & Cytotoxicology Chapel Hill NC 27516

STUMPFF, ROBERT THOMAS, academic administrator; b. Lewistown, Pa., June 25, 1945; s. Harry Clarence and Marjorie Louise (Bossinger) S.; m. Sylvia Simmons, Apr. 22, 1972; children: Robert Dale, Cherie Lynn Stumpff Zimmer. BS, U. Md., 1968; cert., U. Ky., 1978. Adminstrv. asst. to dir. athletics U. Md., College Park, 1968-69, asst. dir. Md. student union, 1969-72, assoc. dir. Md. student union, 1973-80, acting dir. Md. student union, 1974-75, bus. mgr. athletics, 1980-81, asst. athletic dir., 1982-88, mgr. gen. svcs. phys. plant, 1988—; cons. U.S. Naval Acad. Athletic Assn., Annapolis, Md., 1984; assisting minister St. Paul's Luth. Ch., Fulton, Md., 1996—. Author, editor: Maryland Wrestling, 1964-65, 68-69 (Nation's Best award); asst. editor: Maryland Football Guide, 1965-69, Maryland Basketball, 1964-65, 68-69. Mem. ch. coun. Abiding Savior Lutheran Ch., Columbia, Md., 1986-87; mem. Lutheran campus ministry bd. U. Md., 1995—. Mem. Am. Pub. Works Assn., Solid Waste Assn. Am. (cert. mcpl. solid waste mgr., bd. dirs. Mid-Atlantic chpt. 1992-94), Nat. Solid Wastes Mgmt. Assn. Md.-Del. Solid Waste Assn., Md. Recyclers Coalition, Nat. Recycling Coalition, Coll. and U. Recycling Coun., Assn. Phys. Plant Adminstrs., U. Md. Alumni Assn. (life), U. Md. Terrapin Club, U. Md. M Club Found. (life, bd. dirs. 1970—, past pres.), Omicron Delta Kappa (Sigma Chpt. faculty sec.-treas. 1972-76, faculty adviser 1976-91, faculty coord. 1991—). Avocations: reading, sight-seeing. Home: 8206 Bubbling Spring Laurel MD 20723-1079 Office: Univ Md Phys Plant Svc Bldg College Park MD 20742-6055

STUNDZA, THOMAS JOHN, journalist; b. Lawrence, Mass., Mar. 4, 1948; s. John Anthony and Matilda (Stanulonis) S. BA, Merrimack Coll., 1970; MA, Valparaiso U., 1975. Reporter Eagle-Tribune, Lawrence, 1968-70, Post-Tribune, Gary, Ind., 1970-73; bus. editor Post-Tribune, Gary, 1974-78; steel editor Am. Metal Market, Pitts., 1978-80; news editor Am. Metal Market, N.Y.C., 1981-83; sr. editor Purchasing mag., Boston, 1984-94, exec. editor, 1995—; editor Purchasing's Buying Strategy Forecast newsletter, Boston, 1988—; editor audiotape news programming Purchasing's Metal-sWatch!, 1994—; instr. journalism Valparaiso (Ind.) U., 1976, U. Pitts., 1980. Pres. Porter County (Ind.) Youth Svc. Bur., 1976-78. Recipient Honor Roll award U.S. Izaak Walton League, 1973, Paul Tobenkin award Columbia U., 1974; Pub. Affairs Reporting award Am. Polit. Sci. Assn., 1971, Ind. Reporting award AP Mng. Editors, 1976, Newswriting awards Ind. Pub. Health Assn., 1972-74, Amos Tuck Media award Dartmouth Coll., 1977. Mem. Soc. Am. Bus. and Econ. Writers, Soc. Profl. Journalists. Home: 144 Shore Dr Winthrop MA 02152-1286 Office: 275 Washington St Newton MA 02158-1646

STUNDZA, WILLIAM ANTHONY, mental health and retardation nurse; b. Lawrence, Mass., June 1, 1952; s. John A. and Matilda J. (Stanulonis) S. BA, Merrimack Coll., North Andover, Mass., 1974; postgrad., N.E. Broadcasting, Boston, 1977; cert. nursing asst., No. Essex C.C., Haverhill, Mass., 1985; Lic. Practical Nurse, Essex Agr. and Tech. Inst., Hathorne, Mass., 1989; AS in Nurse Edn., Northshore C.C., Danvers, Mass., 1993; BSN, Salem (Mass.) State Coll., 1997. Nurse Greater Lynn (Mass.) Mental Health/Mental Retardation Assn., 1989-91; lic. practical nurse community residents' program Walter E. Fernald State Sch., Waltham, Mass., 1991-93; staff nurse geri-psych unit speciality Winthrop Hosp., Winthrop, Mass., 1993-94; charge nurse Correctional Med. Sys. of Mo., Concord, Mass., 1994; staff nurse Ctr. for Behavioral Medicine Holy Family Hosp., Methuen, Mass., 1994-96; psychiat. nurse On-Duty Med. Mass., Inc., Arlington, Mass., 1996-97, Mass. DMH Tewksbury Hosp., 1996, Home Health VNA Found., Haverhill, Mass., 1997—.

STUNKARD, ALBERT JAMES, psychiatrist, educator; b. N.Y.C., Feb. 7, 1922; s. Horace Wesley and Frances (Klank) S. BS, Yale U., 1943; MD, Columbia U., 1945; MD (hon.), U. Edinburgh, 1992. Intern in medicine Mass. Gen. Hosp., Boston, 1945-46; resident physician psychiatry Johns Hopkins Hosp., 1948-51, rsch. fellow psychiatry, 1951-52; rsch. fellow medicine Columbia U. Svc., Goldwater Meml. Hosp., N.Y.C., 1952-53; Commonwealth rsch. fellow, then asst. prof. medicine Cornell U. Med. Coll., 1953-57; mem. faculty U. Pa., 1957-73, 76—, prof. psychiatry, 1962-73, 76—, Kenneth Appel prof. psychiatry, 1968-73, chmn. dept., 1962-73; prof. psychiatry Med. Sch., Stanford U., 1973-76. Contbr. articles on psychol., physiol., sociol. and genetic aspects of obesity to profl. jours. Capt. M.C., AUS, 1946-48. Ctr. for Advanced Study in Behavioral Scis. fellow, 1971-72, Dist. Service award Am. Psychiatric Association, 1994. Mem. Inst. Medicine of NAS, Am. Assn. of Chmn. of Depts. of Psychiatry (past pres.), Acad. Behavioral Medicine Rsch. (past pres.), Am. Psychosomatic Soc. (past pres.), Assn. Rsch. in Nervous and Mental Diseases (past pres.), Soc. Behavioral Medicine (past pres.). Achievements include contributions to the behavioral and pharmacological treatment of obesity and to understanding of sociological, physiological, psychological and genetic contributions to the disorder. Office: U Pa Sch Medicine Dept Psychiatry 3600 Market St Ste 734 Philadelphia PA 19104-2641

STUNTEBECK, CLINTON A., lawyer; b. Hibbing, Minn., May 25, 1938; s. Robert F. and S. Mary (Conti) S.; m. Mary Joan Carmody, Nov. 23, 1963; children: Robin, M. Alison, Susan, John, William. BA in Psychology, U. Minn., 1960; LLB, U. Maine, 1968. Bar: Pa. 1969, U.S. Dist. Ct. (ea. dist.) Pa. 1969. Ptnr., chmn. corp. fin. and securities Schnader, Harrison, Segal & Lewis, Phila., 1968—; bd. dirs. Markel Corp., Greater Phila. First Partnership for Econ. Devel.; lectr. corp. and securities law. Contbr. articles to profl. jours. Pres. Radnor (Pa.) Twp. Bd. Commn., 1981-83, 92—; bd. visitors U. Maine Sch. Law; trustee Cabrini Coll. dir. Am. Heart Assn.; bd. dirs. Am. Heart Assn. Capt. USAF, 1960-65. Mem. ABA, Am. Law Inst., Pa. Bar Assn., Phila. Bar Assn., Securities Industry Assn. (law and compliance com.), U. Maine Law Alumni Assn. (pres. 1974-76), Union League Phila., Phila. Country Club, Sunday Breakfast Club, Corinthian Yacht Club. Avocations: sailing, skiing, golf, tennis. Home: 371 Rose Glen Dr Wayne PA 19087-4410 Office: Schnader Harrison Segal 1600 Market St Ste 3600 Philadelphia PA 19103-7286

STUPAK, BART T., congressman, lawyer; b. Feb. 29, 1952; m. Laurie Ann Olsen; children: Ken, Bart Jr. AA in Criminal Justice, Northwestern Mich. C.C., Traverse City, 1972; BS in Criminal Justice, Saginaw Valley State Coll., 1977; JD, Thomas M. Cooley Law Sch., 1981. Patrolman Escanaba City Police Dept., 1972-73; state trooper Mich. Dept. State Police, 1973-84; instr. State Police Tng. Acad., 1980-82; atty., 1981-84, Hansley, Neiman, Peterson, Beauchamp, Stupak, Bergman P.C., 1984-85; ptnr. Stupak, Bergman, Stupak P.C., 1985-88; mem. Mich. Ho. of Reps., 1989-90; prin. Bart T. Stupak P.C., 1991—; mem. 103rd-105th Congresses from 1st Mich. dist., 1993—; mem. commerce subcom. on health & environment. Nat. committeeman Boy Scouts Am., coach Menominee Youth Baseball Assn., Little League; active Wildlife Unltd., Menominee Woods and Streams Assn., Menominee County Hist. Soc.; adv. com. Bay Pines Juv. Detection Ctr. Mem. Nat. Rifle Assn., Sons of the Am. Legion, Knights of Columbus, Elks Club, State Employees Retirees Assn., fin. com. Holy Spirit Catholic Ch. Democrat. Office: US Ho of Reps 1410 Longworth Washington DC 20515*

STUPPI, CRAIG, lawyer; b. San Francisco, Mar. 4, 1946. BA with honors, U. Calif., Santa Barbara, 1968; JD, Stanford U., 1971. Bar: Calif. 1972, U.S. Dist. Ct. (no., ctrl. and ea. dists.) Calif. 1972, U.S. Ct. Appeals (9th cir.) 1972, U.S. Supreme Ct. 1975. Mem. Bronson, Bronson & McKinnon LLP, San Francisco. Mem. Am. Bankruptcy Inst., State Bar Calif., Bar Assn. San Francisco, Bar Area Bankruptcy Forum. Office: Bronson Bronson & McKinnon LLP 505 Montgomery St San Francisco CA 94111-2552

STURDEVANT, CHARLES OLIVER, physician, neuropsychiatrist; b. Atkinson, Nebr., Aug. 8, 1907; s. John Newton and Clara Katherine (Zimmerman) S.; m. Helen Henricks; children: William, Charles, John; m. Nancy Elizabeth Quick, May 8, 1945; 1 child, Richard Anthony. BSc, U. Nebr., 1929, MD, 1932. Diplomate Am. Bd. Psychiatry and Neurology. Student asst. in neuropsychiatry U. Nebr., 1930-32; rotating intern Emmanuel Hosp., Portland, Oreg., 1932-33; fellow in psychiatry Columbia U., N.Y.C., 1933-35; assoc. in neurology and psychiatry U. Oreg. Med. Sch., 1935-42; assoc. clin. prof. UCLA, 1951-74; mem. hon. staff St. John's Hosp., Santa Monica, Calif., 1976—, Santa Monica Hosp., 1946—, Hoag Hosp. Presbyn., Newport Beach, Calif., 1994—; chief of psychiatry St. John's Hosp., Santa Monica, 1954-76; med. dir. Capistrano by the Sea Hosp., Dana Point, Calif., 1976-90; clin. prof. psychiatry U. Irvine, Calif., 1981—. Author: (with others) Psychiatric Emergencies, 1964; contbr. articles to profl. jours. Mem. counter propaganda com. State of Oreg., 1941-42; bd. dirs. Travelers Aid Soc., Portland, 1939-42, Multiple Sclerosis Soc., L.A., 1949-50; mem. Social Svc. Com., L.A., 1949-50. Maj. U.S. Army, 1942-46. Fellow AMA, Am. Psychiat. Assn. (life), North Pacific Soc. Neurology and Psychiatry (life); mem. Orange County Psychiat. Soc., Calif. Med. Soc., Med. Rsch. and Edn. Soc. (founder), Newport Harbor Yacht Club, Skunk Point Yacht Club, Sigma Xi. Avocations: sailing, NHYC, gardening. Home: 26 Pienza Laguna Niguel CA 92677-8623

STURDEVANT, WAYNE ALAN, computer-based training development administrator; b. Portland, Oreg., Apr. 3, 1946; s. Hervey Sturdevant and Georgia (Rawls) Bright; m. Helen F. Radbury, Sept. 24, 1976; children: Wayne Jr., Stephen, John, Brian, Daniel. BS in Edn., So. Ill. U., 1980. With USAF, 1964-85; supt. USAF On-Job-Tng. Adv. Svc., 1978-82; chief USAF On-Job-Program Mgmt., 1982-85; ret., 1985; lead engr. instl. tech. McDonnell Douglas Corp., St. Louis, 1985-88; mgr., instr. sys. design Southeastern Computer Cons., Inc., Austin, 1988—; developed advanced concepts in occupational edn. and computer-based tng. design, innovations in support of ISO 9000. Contbr. articles on mgmt. and tng. innovations in the work place to profl. jours. Mem. Bishop LDS Ch., 1983-84, mem. stake presidency, 1990-96; mem. exec. bd. Boy Scouts Am., 1986—. Recognized for leadership in multi-nat. programs; recipient Citation of Honor Air Force Assn., 1980, Award of Merit Boy Scouts Am., 1996; named Internat. Man of Yr., Internat. Biog. Ctr., Cambridge, Eng., 1992. Republican. Avocations: reading, camping. Home: 9214 Independence Loop Austin TX 78748-6312

STURGE, KARL, surgeon; b. Bklyn., June 24, 1935; s. Percy and Dora (Leonard) S.; m. Edna Clark, June 10, 1961; children: Karl E., Mark W., Edna Lynn, Clarke S. BS, U. Miami, 1957; MD, Seton Hall U., 1961. Diplomate Am. Bd. Urology. Chief surgery Columbia-Deering Hosp., Miami, Fla., 1989—, chief of staff, chmn. med. bd. Lt. col. USAF, 1962-72. Mem. Am. Lithotrypsy Soc., Fla. Med. Assn., Fla. Urol. Soc., Dade County Med. Assn., Greater Miami Urology Soc. Republican. Episcopalian. Office: 9299 Coral Reef Dr Ste 205 Miami FL 33157-1776

STURGE, MICHAEL DUDLEY, physicist; b. Bristol, Eng., May 25, 1931; came to U.S., 1961, naturalized 1991; s. Paul Dudley and Rachel (Graham) S.; m. Mary Balk, Aug. 21, 1956; children: David Mark, Thomas Graham, Peter Daniel, Benedict Paul. BA in Engring. and Physics, Gonville and Caius Coll., Cambridge, Eng., 1952; PhD in Physics, Cambridge U., 1957. Staff Mullard Rsch. Lab. (now Philips), Redhill, Eng., 1956-58; sr. rsch. fellow Royal Radar Establishment, Malvern, Eng., 1958-61; tech. staff Bell Labs., Murray Hill, N.J., 1961-83, Bellcore, Red Bank, N.J., 1984-86; prof. dept. physics Dartmouth Coll., Hanover, N.H., 1986—; rsch. assoc. Stanford U., 1965, U. B.C., Vancouver, Can., 1969; vis. prof. Technion, Haifa, Israel, 1972, 76, 81, 85, Williams Coll., Williamstown, Mass., 1982, 84, Trinity Coll., Dublin, 1989, 93, 96, U. Fourier, Grenoble, France, 1989, 91; exch. scientist Philips Rsch. Lab., Eindhoven, The Netherlands, 1973-74; vis. scholar U. Sheffield, Eng., 1996. Contbr. over 130 papers in solid state physics to profl. publs.; co-editor: Excitons, 1982; editor Jour. of Luminescence, 1984-90. Fellow Am. Phys. Soc.; mem. Am. Assn. Physics Tchrs. Office: Dartmouth Coll Dept Physics Wilder Lab Hanover NH 03755-3528

STURGEN, WINSTON, photographer, printmaker, artist; b. Harrisburg, Pa., Aug. 27, 1938; s. George Winston and Gladys Erma (Lenker) S.; m. Nancy Kathryn Otto, Jan. 23, 1959 (div. 1981); 1 child, Bruce Eugene Sturgen; m. Jessica Sheldon, Mar. 15, 1988. BS in Forestry, Pa. State U., 1960; postgrad., U. N.H., 1961-62; M of Forestry, Pa. State U., 1964; postgrad., U. Oreg., 1966-68. Cert. profl. photographer. Devel. engr. Weyerhaeuser Co., Longview, Wash., 1964-66; mgr. Wickes Lumber Co., Elkhorn, Wis., 1968-70; dir. ops. Wickes Wanderland, Inc., Delavan, Wis., 1970-72; owner, mgr. Sturgen's Cleaners, Delavan, 1972-80, Images by Sturgen, Delavan, 1980-84; instr. photography continuing edn. dept. Western N.Mex. U., 1988-90; juror numerous orgns., 1982—. One-man shows include Artesia (N.Mex.) Mus. and Art Ctr., 1992, Delavan Art Mus., 1984, Donnell Libr., N.Y.C., 1992; exhibited in group shows at Carlsbad (N.Mex.) Mus., 1992, Sister Kenny Inst., 1992, (3rd Pl.), 93 (1st Pl.), 94, Deming Ctr. for the Arts, N.Mex., 1991, Shellfish Collection, Silver City, N.Mex., 1989, 90, 91, 92, 93, Thompson Gallery, U. N.Mex., 1989, Profl. Photographers Assn. of N.Mex., 1985, 86, 87, 88 (awards), Union Gallery, U. N.Mex., 1987, Gallery Sigala, Taos, N.Mex., 1986, World Trade Ctr., N.Y.C., 1992, 93, 94, Internat. Exposition of Photography, 1983, 84, 85, 87, Beyond Photography Touring Exhibit, 1991-92, An Am. Collection Touring Exhibit, San Francisco, Washington, Brussels, Tokyo, 1993-95, Sapporo (Japan) Internat. Print Biennial, 1993, Very Spl. Arts/N.Mex. Touring Exhibit, 1993-94, Ctr. Contemporary Art, St. Louis, 1994 (Purchase award), many others; donation of all personal work Southwestern Regional Med. Ctr., N.Mex., 1996; pub. poetry, numerous articles in field. Founder, chmn. Winter Arts Festival, Silver City, N.Mex., 1988-90; com. mem. Taos Fall Arts Festival, 1985; com. chair Oktoberfest, Delavan, 1976-80; donated personal work to Southwestern Regional Med. Ctr., N.Mex., 1996. Residency grant Wurlitzer Found., 1987, 89. Mem. Very Spl. Artists N.Mex., Very Spl. Artists Washington, Enabled Artists United, Fuller Lodge Art Ctr. Avocations: painting, printmaking, photography. Home: 3357 Cerrillos Rd # 111 Santa Fe NM 87505

STURGEON, CHARLES EDWIN, management consultant; b. Cherryvale, Kans., May 30, 1928; s. William Charles and Lucile Myrtle (Gill) S.; children by previous marriage: Carol Ann, John Randolph, Richard Steven; m. Karen B. Riggan, May 21, 1988. A.A., Independence Jr. Coll., 1948; B.S., U. Kans., 1951; postgrad., U. Tulsa Grad. Sch., 1953-56; grad., Advanced Mgmt. Program, Harvard Bus. Sch., 1977. Research engr. Stanoline Oil and Gas, Tulsa, 1953-56; production supr. Vulcan Materials Co., Wichita, Kans., 1956-62; maintenance supt. Vulcan Materials Co., 1962-64, mgr. tech. services, 1964-69; plant mgr. Vulcan Materials Co., Newark, N.J., 1970-71; gen. mktg. mgr., v.p. mktg. Vulcan Materials Co., Wichita, 1971-73; v.p. mfg. Vulcan Materials Co., Birmingham, Ala., 1974-77, pres. chem. div., 1977-87, pres., sr. v.p., 1987-90; prin. CESCO Cons. Co., Birmingham, 1990-96, Sturgeon Energy Co., Birmingham, 1996—. Adv. U. Kans. Sch. Chem. Engring. Served with U.S. Army, 1951-53. Mem. Am. Inst. Chem. Engrs., Nat. Mgmt. Assn., Chlorine Inst. (bd. dirs.), Chem. Mfg. Assn., Soc. Chem. Industries, Soc. of Materials, The Club Inc., Tau Theta Pi, Tau Beta Pi, Sigma Tau. Republican. Presbyterian.

STURGES, HOLLISTER, III, museum director; b. Kingston, N.Y., July 1, 1939; s. Hollister Jr. and Elizabeth (Betz) S.; m. Caroline Berg (div.); children: Kimberly, William Steele.; m. Judith Layson; 1 child, Elizabeth Layson. BA in Comparative Lit., Cornell U., 1962; MA in Art History, U. Calif., Berkeley, 1969, MPh in Art History, 1972. Cert. tchr., Calif. Tchr. English Placer High Sch., Auburn, Calif., 1963-66; instr. U. Mo., Kansas City, 1972-80; curator European art Joslyn Art Mus., Omaha, 1980-84; chief curator Indpls. Mus. Arts, 1984-87; dir. Springfield (Mass.) Mus. Fine Arts, 1988-95, George Walter Vincent Smith Art Mus., 1988-95; exec. dir. Bruce Mus., Greenwich, Conn., 1995—; Panelist NEA, 1982, 86, 90; organizer art exhbns. Love Isolation and Darkness & the Art of Edward Munch, 1996. Author: (exhbn. catalogue) Angels and Urchins: Images of Children at the Joslyn, 1980, (exhbn. catalogue) Jules Breton and the French Rural Tradition, 1982, (exhbn. catalogue) New Art from Puerto Rico, 1990; co-author: (exhbn. catalogue) Art of the Fantastic: Latin America, 1920-87, 1987; author, editor: The Rural Vision: France and Americans in the late Nineteenth Century, 1987; author, co-editor: (mus. catalogue) Joslyn Art Museum Paintings and Sculptures from the Permanent Collections, 1987, (mus. handbook) Indianapolis Museum of Art: collections handbook, 1988. Bd. dirs. World Affairs Coun., 1989-95. Kress Found. fellow, 1974. Mem. Coll. Art Assn., Am. Assn. Mus., New Eng. Mus. Assn. Avocations: squash, canoeing, chess. Office: Bruce Museum 1 Museum Dr Greenwich CT 06830-7157

STURGES, JOHN SIEBRAND, management consultant; b. Greenwich, Conn., Feb. 12, 1939; s. Harry Wilton and Elizabeth Helen (Niewenhous) S.; AB, Harvard U., 1960; MBA, U. So. Calif., 1965; cert. EDP, NYU, 1972; cert. exec. program. Grad. Sch. Bus., U. Mich., 1982. Cert. profl. mgmt. cons., sr. profl. in human resources, cert. mgmt. cons.; m. Anastasia Daphne Bakalis, May 6, 1967; children: Christina Aurora, Elizabeth Athena. With Equitable Life Assurance Soc. U.S., N.Y.C., 1965-79, mgr. systems devel., 1965-70, dir. compensation and benefits, 1971-75, v.p., personnel and adminstrv. svcs., 1975-79; sr. v.p. personnel Nat. Westminster Bank U.S.A., N.Y.C., 1979-82; corp. sr. v.p. adminstrn. and human resources Willis-Corroon Corp., N.Y.C., 1982-84; mng. dir. human resources Marine Midland Bank, N.Y.C., 1984-87; mng. dir. Siebrand-Wilton Assocs., N.Y.C., 1986-87, pres., 1987—. Lay reader St. Peters Episcopal Ch., Freehold, N.J., 1972—. Lt. USNR, 1960-65. Mem. Internat. Found. Employee Benefit Plans, Commerce Assocs., Soc. for Human Resource Mgmt. (dir. 1979—), Am. Compensation Assn., Human Resources Planning Soc., Inst. Mgmt. Cons. (bd. dirs. 1992—), Cons. Bur., Monmouth-Ocean Devel. Coun. (dir. 1989-95), Beta Gamma Sigma (dir. N.Y. 1978—), Phi Kappa Phi. Republican. Clubs: India House, Harvard (N.Y.C., Boston, Princeton, N.J., dir. 1991-97), Nassau Club. Office: Siebrand-Wilton Assocs Inc PO Box 2498 New York NY 10008-2498

STURGESS, GEOFFREY J., aeronautical research engineer. Aero. and mech. rsch. engr. Innovative Scientific Solutions, Inc., Beavercreek, Ohio. Recipient Energy Systems award AIAA, 1994. Home: 1747 Lesourd Dr Beavercreek OH 45432-2478

STURGIS, ROBERT SHAW, architect; b. Boston, July 8, 1922; s. George and Rosamond Thomas (Bennett) S.; m. Chiquita Mitchell, Dec. 20, 1947; children: Susanna Jordan, Roger Bennett, John Hanson, Ellen Shaw. Grad., St. Mark's Sch., Southboro, Mass., 1939; AB, Harvard, 1947, MArch, 1951. Architect Kilham, Hopkins, Greeley & Brodie, Boston, 1952-55, Shepley, Bulfinch, Richardson & Abbott, Boston, 1955-64, Robert S. Sturgis, Boston, 1964-68; ptnr. Feloney & Sturgis (architects), Cambridge, 1969-75, Robert Sturgis, FAIA, 1975—; head critic Boston Archtl. Ctr., 1955-66, instr., 1988—, chair edn. com., 1989-95; dir., 1971-93, 95—; vis. lectr. Va. Poly. Inst., Blacksburg, 1970, Boston U., Yale U., 1975; urban design cons. Haverhill, Lynn and Cambridge, Mass., also, Atlanta.; mem. overseers' vis. com. Sch. Design Harvard, 1965-70; chmn. Gov.'s Task Force Arts and Cultural Facilities, 1972; chmn. bd., lectr. Boston Archtl. Center, 1981-85; cons. Maine State Capitol com., 1989-90. Prin. works include Cotting House, Harvard Bus. Sch., 1968, Architects' Plan for Boston, 1961, AIA Urban Design Assistance Team Program, 1967; urban designs for, Atlanta, Haverhill, Kendall Sq., Cambridge; contbr. articles to profl. jours. Served with USAAF, 1942-45. Fellow AIA (chmn. urban planning and design com. 1970, mem. planned growth task group 1988-92, Presdl. citation 1988); mem. Boston Soc. Architects (pres. 1972, chmn. civic design com. 1959-67, chmn. regional design com. 1988—, mem. joint regional transp. com. 1994—). Home and Office: 5 Doublet Hill Rd Weston MA 02193-2304

STURLEY, MICHAEL F., law educator; b. Syracuse, N.Y., Feb. 14, 1955; s. Richard Avern and Helen Elizabeth (Fisher) S.; m. Michele Y. Deitch, July 2, 1989; 1 child, Jennifer Diane Sturley. BA, Yale U., 1977, JD, 1981; BA in Jurisprudence, Oxford U., 1980, MA, 1985. Bar: N.Y. 1984, U.S. Dist. Ct. (so. and ea. dists.) N.Y. 1984, U.S. Supreme Ct. 1987. Law clk. to Judge Amalya L. Kearse, U.S. Ct. Appeals for 2d Cir., N.Y.C., 1981-82; law clk. to Justice Lewis F. Powell, Jr. U.S. Supreme Ct., Washington, 1982-83; assoc. Sullivan & Cromwell, N.Y.C., 1983-84; asst. prof. law U. Tex. Law Sch., Austin, 1984-88, prof., 1988—; vis. prof. Queen Mary and Westfield Coll., U. London, 1990, advisor Restatement (3d) of Property (servitudes), 1989—. Compiler, editor: The Legislative History of the Carriage of Goods by Sea Act and the Travaux Préparatoires of The Hague Rules, 3 vols., 1990; mem. editl. bd. Jour. Maritime Law and Commerce, 1989—, book rev. editor, 1993—; contbg. author: Benedict on Admiralty, 1990—; contbr. articles to legal jours. Mem. Am. Law Inst., Maritime Law Assn. (proctor). Office: U Tex Sch Law 727 E 26th St Austin TX 78705-3224

STURMAN, LAWRENCE STUART, health research administrator; b. Detroit, Mar. 13, 1938; married, 1959; 4 children. BS, Northwestern U., 1957, MS, MD, 1960; PhD in Virology, Rockefeller U., 1968. Intern Hosp. Univ. Pa., 1960-61; staff assoc. virology Nat. Inst. Allergy and Infectious Disease, 1968-70; rsch. physician virology Wadsworth Ctr. N.Y. State Dept. Health, 1970-92, dir. divsn. clin. sci., 1989-92, dir., 1992—; asst. prof. microbiology and immunology Albany Med. Coll., 1979-93; chmn., prof. dept. biomed. sci. Sch. Pub. Health N.Y. State U., Albany, 1985-95, prof., 1995—. Mem. AAAS, Am. Soc. Microbiology, Am. Soc. Virology, N.Y. Acad. Sci., Sigma Xi. Achievements include research in viral pathogenesis; public health, scientific basis of public health practice; biomedical research and public policy; laboratory regulation/quality assurance; graduate education in biomedical sciences; viral disease. Office: NY State Dept Health Wadsworth Ctr Albany NY 12201

STURROCK, THOMAS TRACY, botany educator, horticulturist; b. Havana, Cuba, Dec. 9, 1921; s. David and Ruth Esther (Earle) S. (parents U.S. citizens); m. Jeanne Norquist, June 30, 1948; children—Nancy Elizabeth, John David, Barbara Jeanne Sturrock Morris, Catherine Ann Sturrock Hilliard, Robert Charles. B.S. in Agr. with honors, U. Fla., Gainesville, 1943, M.S. in Agr, 1943, Ph.D., 1961. Ptnr. Sturrock Tropical Fruit Nursery, 1946-56; insp. Fla. State Plant Bd., 1956-57; tchr. Palm Beach (Fla.) High Sch., 1957-58; research asst. U. Fla., 1958-60; instr. Palm Beach Jr. Coll., 1960-64; asst. prof. botany Fla. Atlantic U., 1964-68, assoc. prof., 1968-74, prof., 1974-89, prof. emeritus, 1989—, asst. dean Coll. Sci., 1971-89. Pres. West Palm Beach Jaycees, 1951-52; scoutmaster Gulf Stream council Boy Scouts Am., 1946-55, cubmaster, 1960-62, dist. chmn., 1961-63, exec. bd., 1961—, v.p., 1969-70, 80—. Served with USAAF, 1943-46. Recipient Silver Beaver award, 1951, Disting. Eagle Scout award Boy Scouts Am., 1989. Mem. Fla. Hort. Soc., Fla. Acad. Scis., Sigma Xi. Presbyterian. Home: 1010 Caribbean Rd West Palm Beach FL 33405-2408

STURTEVANT, BRERETON, retired lawyer, former government official; b. Washington, Nov. 24, 1921; d. Charles Lyon and Grace (Brereton) S. B.A., Wellesley Coll., 1942; J.D., Temple U., 1949; postgrad., U. Del., 1969-71. Bar: D.C. 1949, Del. 1950. Research chemist E.I. duPont DeNemours & Co., 1942-50; law clk. Del. Supreme Ct., 1950; gen. practice law Wilmington, Del., 1950-57; partner Connolly, Bove & Lodge, Wilmington, 1957-71; examiner-in-chief U.S. Patent and Trademark Office Bd. Appeals, Washington, 1971-88; Adj. prof. law Georgetown U., 1974-79. Trustee Holton-Arms Sch., Bethesda, Md., 1977-96, chmn. or mem. all coms., trustee emerita, 1997—. Mem. Am., Del. bar assns., Exec. Women in Govt. (charter mem., chmn. 1978-79). Episcopalian. Clubs: Wellesley College, Washington-Wellesley (pres. 1982-84). Home: 1227 Morningside Ln Alexandria VA 22308-1042

STURTEVANT, JULIAN MUNSON, biophysical chemist, educator; b. Edgewater, N.J., Aug. 9, 1908; s. Edgar Howard and Bessie Fitch (Skinner) S.; m. Elizabeth Reihl, June 8, 1929; children: Ann Sturtevant Ormsby, Bradford. AB, Columbia U., 1927; PhD, Yale U., 1931; ScD (hon.), Ill. Coll., 1962; Sc.D. (hon.), Regensburg U., 1978. Instr. chemistry Yale U., New Haven, 1931-39, asst. prof., 1939-46, assoc. prof., 1946-51, prof., 1951-77, sr. research scientist, 1977—; staff mem. Radiation Lab., MIT, Cambridge, 1943-46; vis. prof. U. Calif.-San Diego, 1966-67, 69-70; vis. fellow Battelle Seattle Research Ctr. and U. Wash., 1972-73, Stanford U., 1976-77. Contbr. numerous articles to profl. jours. Recipient Huffman award Calorimetry Conf. U.S.A., 1964; William DeVane award Yale U., 1978; Innovator in Biochemistry award Med. Coll. Va., 1984, Wilbur Cross medal Yale U., 1987; Guggenheim fellow Cambridge U., 1955-56; Fulbright scholar U. Adelaide, Australia, 1962-63; vis. scholar, Stanford U., 1975-76; Alexander von Humboldt sr. scientist award, 1978-79. Fellow AAAS, Am. Acad. Arts and Scis.; mem. Nat. Acad. Sci., Am. Chem. Soc., Am. Soc. Biol. Chemists, Conn. Acad. Sci. and Tech.

STURTEVANT, PETER MANN, JR., television news executive; b. Northampton, Mass., Feb. 27, 1943; s. Peter Mann and Katharine Bryan (Hobson) S.; m. Anne Elizabeth Fitzpatrick, July 12, 1969 (div. Dec. 1984); 1 child, Amanda Hadden; m. Toni E. Siegel, Apr. 14, 1985; 1 child, Gillian Lee. BA, Wilmington Coll., 1965; MA, U. Iowa, 1967. Assoc. prodr. CBS News, Washington, 1967-71; bur. chief Viet Nam CBS News, Saigon, 1971-73; nat. news editor CBS News, N.Y.C., 1974-80, asst. v.p. spl. events, 1981-83, producer 60 Minutes, 1984-85; exec. news editor CNN, N.Y.C., 1985-86; prodr. Today's Bus. Buena Vista TV, N.Y.C., 1987; dir. news coverage CNBC, Fort Lee, N.J., 1988-90; v.p., mng. editor CNBC, Ft. Lee, N.J., 1991-94; sr. v.p. Internat. Bus. News NBC, 1994—. Named Disting. Alumnus, Wilmington Coll., 1975; named to Journalism Hall of Fame, U. Iowa Sch. Journalism, 1988. Mem. Nat. Acad. Cable Programming (nominated ACE award 1992, 93, 94), Soc. Profl. Journalists, Deadline Club N.Y., The Asia Soc., Overseas Press Club (bd. dirs.). Episcopalian. Avocations: racquet sports, landscaping, travelling, philately, parenting. Home: 90 Riverside Dr New York NY 10024-5306 Office: NBC 30 Rockefeller Plz New York NY 10112

STURTEVANT, RUTHANN PATTERSON, anatomy educator; b. Rockford, Ill., Feb. 7, 1927; d. Joseph Heylmun and Virginia (Wharton) P.; m. Frank Milton Sturtevant Jr., Mar. 18, 1950; children: Barbara (dec.), Jill Sturtevant Rovanl, Jan Sturtevant Cassidy. BS, Northwestern U., 1949, MS, 1950; PhD, U. Ark., 1972. Instr. life scis. Ind. State U., Evansville, Ind., 1965-72; asst. prof. Ind. State U., 1972-74; asst. prof. anatomy Ind. U. Sch. Medicine, Evansville, 1972-74, U. Evansville, 1972-74; lectr. anatomy Northwestern U., Chgo., 1974-75; asst. prof. anatomy and surgery Loyola U., Maywood, 1975-81; assoc. prof. Loyola U. Sch. Medicine, Maywood, 1981-88; prof. Loyola U. Sch. Medicine, 1988-90, prof. emerita, 1990—. Contbr. articles to profl. jours.; editorial bd. Chronobiology Internat., 1988-90; reviewer numerous profl. jours. Mem. Mayor's Task Force on High Tech. Devel., Chgo., 1983-85; exec. bd. Anatomical Gifts Assn. Ill., Chgo., 1978-89. Grantee, Pott's Found., NIH, others, 1978-88. Mem. Am. Assn. Anatomists, So. Soc. Anatomists (councillor 1978-80), Internat. Soc. Chronobiologists, Am. Soc. Pharmacology and Exptl. Therapeutics, Soc. for Exptl. Biology and Medicine, Am. Assn. Clin. Anatomists, League of Underwater Photographers, Chgo. Area Camera Assn., Sarasota Scuba Club, Sigma Xi. Avocations: underwater photography, scuba diving. Address: 5760 Midnight Pass Rd Unit 610-D Sarasota FL 34242

STURTEVANT, WILLIAM T., fundraising executive, consultant; b. Balt., Feb. 2, 1947; s. Charles N. and Mary Jane (Thomson) S.; m. Teresa L. Woollen Sturtevant, Apr. 8, 1988; children: Stephanie A., Robert E., Melissa N. BBA, Western Mich. U., Kalamazoo, 1969; MBA, Wayne State U., Detroit, 1971. Cert. Fin. Planner. Devel. officer WTVS, Detroit, 1969-71; legis. aide Mich. House of Reps., Detroit, 1971-73; pres. Portage Rubber Co., Kalamazoo, Mich., 1973-76; sr. devel. officer Western Mich. U., Kalamazoo, Mich., 1976-79; v.p. devel. Lake Erie Coll., Painesville, Ohio, 1979-80; dir. planned giving U. Ill. Found., Urbana, 1980—; bd. dirs. Warren and Clara Cole Found., Chgo., 1989—, Jagdish N. Sheth Found., Urbana, Ill., 1991—, The Lauritsen Family Found., Urbana, 1994—; cons. pvt. practice, Mahomet, Ill., 1990—; pres. Inst. for Charitable Giving, Chgo., 1990—. Mem. Union League Club, Chgo., 1990—. Named Planned Giving Prof. of Yr., Planned Giving Today, 1995. Mem. Nat. Soc. Fundraising Execs., Coun. for Advancement and Support of Edn. Avocations: reading, tennis, travel. Home: 702 S Mahomet Rd Mahomet IL 61853 Office: U Ill Found Harker Hall MC-386 1305 W Green St Urbana IL 61801-2945

STURTZ, DONALD LEE, physician, naval officer; b. Coshocton, Ohio, Apr. 18, 1933; s. Walter Raymond and Helene Josephine (Kubic) S.; m. Alice Marie McGuire, June 11, 1955; children: Jimalee, Janel. BS, U.S. Naval Acad., Annapolis, Md., 1955; MD, U. Pa., 1965; diploma med. care catastrophe, London, 1996. Diplomate Am. Bd. Surgery. Surg. resident USN, Phila., 1965-70; ship's surgeon USN, 1970-71; staff surgeon Bethesda Naval Hosp., USN, 1971-80; chief of surgery San Diego Naval Hosp., USN, 1980-84; exec. officer Oakland (Calif.) Naval Hosp., USN, 1984-85; prof. clin. surgery USN, Bethesda, Md., 1985-87; commd. Naval Med. Command USN, 1987-88; fleet surgeon USN, Norfolk, Va., 1989-91; surgeon USUHS, Bethesda, Md., 1991—. Contbr. articles to profl. jours. Recipient B.D. Larrey award for Surgical Excecellence, Surgical Dept. USUHS, Bethesda, 1988. Fellow ACS (gov. 1985-88); mem. Am. Assn. for Surgery of Trauma, Assn. Mil. Surgeons, USN Inst. Republican. Methodist. Avocations: travel, antiquing, music, reading. Office: USUHS Dept Surgery 4301 Jones Bridge Rd Bethesda MD 20814-4712

STUTZMAN, THOMAS CHASE, SR., lawyer; b. Portland, Oreg., Aug. 1, 1950; s. Leon H. and Mary L. (Chase) S.; BA with high honors, U. Calif., Santa Barbara, 1972; JD cum laude, Santa Clara U., 1975; m. Wendy Jeanne Craig, June 6, 1976; children: Sarah Ann, Thomas ChaseJr. Bar: Calif. 1976; cert. family law specialist. Pvt. practice, San Jose, Calif., 1976-79; pres., sec., CFO Thomas Chase Stutzman, P.C., San Jose, 1979—; legal counsel, asst. sec. Ctrl. Valley Cirs., Inc., Cypress Human Resources, Inc., DMJ Pro Care, Inc., Sparacino's Foods, Tax Firm, Inc., United Charities, Marina Assocs. Inc., Midnight Fraction Mine Inc., Forbord Enterprises, D.A.M. Good Engring./Mfg., Inc., E.M.I. Oil Filtration Systems, Inc., China Villa, Inc., Creative Pacifica, Inc., Am. West Furniture Mfg., Inc., Cody Electronics, Inc., Advanfab Corp., Am. First Tech., Analog Engring., Inc., Excel-Law Video, Inc., First Am. Real Estate Financing Co., Hoffman Industries, Inc., Info. Scan Tech., Inc., PRD Construction Mgmt. Svcs., Unifed Homes, Inc., Marine Biogenic Pharm. USA, Inc., Miller Networks, Mi Pueblo Mt. View, Inc., others; instr. San Jose State U., 1977-78. Bd. dirs. Santa Cruz Campfire, 1978-80, Happy Hollow Park, 1978-80, 83-86, Pacific Neighbors, pres., 1991-92. Mem. Calif. Bar Assn., Santa Clara County Bar Assn. (chmn. environ. law com. 1976-78, exec. com. family law, exec. com. fee arbitration com.), Assn. Cert. Law Specialist, San Jose Jaycees (Dir. of the Year 1976-77), Almaden Valley Rotary Club, Lions (dir. 1979-81, 2d v.p. 1982-83, 1st v.p. 1983-84, pres. 1984-85), Masons, Phi Beta Kappa. Congregationalist Office: 1625 The Alameda Ste 626 San Jose CA 95126-2224

STUTZMAN, WARREN LEE, electrical engineer, educator; b. Elgin, Ill., Oct. 22, 1941; s. James Earl and Christina Louise (Steidinger) S.; m. Claudia Janeanne Morris, Dec. 20, 1964; children: Darren Morris, Dana Lynn. BEE, U.Ill., 1964, AB in Math., 1964; MEE, Ohio State U., 1965, PhD in Elec. Engring., 1969. Asst. prof. Va. Poly. Inst. and State U., Blacksburg, 1969-74, assoc. prof., 1974-79, prof., 1979—, Thomas Phillips prof. engring., 1992—. Author: (with G. Thiele) Antenna Theory and Design, 1981, Polarization in Electromagnetic Systems, 1993. Fellow IEEE. Office: Va Poly Inst & State U Elec Engring Dept Blacksburg VA 24061-0111

STUTZMANN, NATHALIE, classical vocalist; b. Paris. Student piano, bassoon and chamber music, Ecole de l'Opéra de Paris. Performer: (operatic prodns.) Debussy's Pelleas et Mélisande, Florence and Bonn, Mussorgsky's Boris Godunov at the Liceu, Barcelona, Bordeaux, Gounod's Romeo et Juliette, Zurich, Mozart's Die Zauberflöte, Opéra de Paris Bastille, Aix-en-Provence Festival; appearances in recitals include London Wigmore Hall, Amsterdam Concertgebouw, Salle Gaveau, St. Denis Festival, Alte Oper, N.Y., Lincoln Ctr., Berkeley, Calif., P.R.; vocal performances include: Mahler Third Symphony, Weisbaden, (with Gary Bertini) Knaben Wunderhorn, Stuttgart, Kindertotenlieder, Paris, Lugano, (with Nicolas Harnoncourt) Bach's St. Matthew's Passion, (with Maestro Wolfgang Sawallisch) Bach's St. John's Passion, Italy, Ombra Felice, London Symphony Orch., Mahler 2d Symphony, Cleve. Orch., L'enfant et les Sertilegis (Ravel), Boston Symphony, Mozart Requiem, Mostly Mozart Festival, N.Y.C.; participated in numerous audio and video recordings. Recipient Deutsche Schallplattenkritik prize for Schumann recording, 1993. Office: care Herbert H Breslin Inc 119 W 57th St Ste 1505 New York NY 10019-2401

STUVER, FRANCIS EDWARD, former railway car company executive; b. Greenville, Pa., Aug. 22, 1912; s. Willard Seeley and Anna Katherine (Henry) S.; m. Jessie Lucile Bright, Jan. 26, 1938; children: Robert Edward, Nancy (Mrs. Randolph Patrick Mutdosch). Grad. high sch. With Greenville Steel Car Co. (subsidiary Pitts. Forgings Co.), 1937—, chief accountant, 1944-46, asst. treas., 1946-54, asst. sec., 1948-56, treas., 1956-61, v.p., 1956-61, exec. v.p., 1961-75, ret., 1975; pres. Greenville Savs. & Loan Assn., 1977-83, dir., 1949-83; dir. Greenville Steel Car Co., 1961-74, Pitts. Forgings Co., 1975-80. Bd. dirs. Municipal Authority Borough Greenville, 1946-74, treas., 1946-73; bd. dirs., mem. exec. com. Mercer County br. Pa. Economy League, 1949-64; bd. dirs., treas., chmn. finance com. Greenville Hosp., 1953-59. Mem. Am. Ry. Car Inst. (dir. 1964-75). Clubs: Masons, Elks, Moose, KP, Greenville Country. Home: 46 Chambers Ave Greenville PA 16125-1856 Office: Greenville Steel Car Co Foot of Union St Greenville PA 16125

STUX, IVAN ERNEST, financial executive; b. Temesvar, Romania, July 27, 1945; came to U.S., 1965; s. George Stux. PhD in Math., Courant Inst., 1973; MBA, Columbia U., 1977. Asst. prof. math. dept. Columbia U., N.Y.C., 1973-77, assoc. prof. Sch. Bus., 1977-79; mgmt. cons. McKinsey & Co., N.Y.C., 1979-84; prin. Morgan Stanley & Co., Inc., N.Y.C., 1984—. Home: 27 W 69th St New York NY 10023-4740 Office: Morgan Stanley & Co Inc 1585 Broadway Frnt 6 New York NY 10036-8200

STWALLEY, WILLIAM CALVIN, physics and chemistry educator; b. Glendale, Calif., Oct. 7, 1942; s. Calvin Murdoch and Diette Clarice (Hanson) S.; m. Mauricette Lucille Frisius, June 14, 1963; children: Kenneth William, Steven Edward. BS, Calif. Inst. Tech., 1964; PhD, Harvard U., 1968. Asst. prof. U. Iowa, Iowa City, 1968-72, assoc. prof., 1972-75, prof. dept. chemistry, 1975-93, prof. dept. physics and astronomy, 1977-93, dir. Iowa Laser Facility, 1979-93, dir. Ctr. for Laser Sci. and Engring., 1987-89, George Glockler prof. physical scis., 1988-93; program dir. NSF, Washington, 1975-76 (leave of absence); prof. and head dept. physics, prof. chemistry U. Conn., Storrs, 1993—; program chmn. Internat. Laser Sci. Conf., 1985, co-chmn., 1986, chmn., 1987; lectr. Chinese Acad. Scis., 1986. Editor books in field; contbr. more than 240 articles to profl. publs. Japan Soc. for Promotion of Sci. fellow, 1982; Sloan fellow, 1970-72; numerous grants in field, 1970—. Fellow Am. Phys. Soc. (sec.-treas. divsn. chem. physics 1984-90, vice chair/chair/past chair Topical Group on Laser Sci. 1989-92), Optical Soc. Am.; mem. AAAS, Am. Chem. Soc. Democrat. Avocations: comic books and cartoons, philately. Home: 21 Britony Dr Mansfield Center CT 06250-1647 Office: Dept Physics U-46 U Conn Storrs CT 06269-3046

STYAN, JOHN LOUIS, English literature and theater educator; b. London, July 6, 1923; came to U.S., 1965; s. Louis and Constance Mary (Armstrong) S.; m. Constance W. M. Roberts, Nov. 17, 1945; children: Leigh, Day Campbell, Kim, Valentina Ebner. B.A., Cambridge (Eng.) U., 1947, M.A., 1948. Staff tutor lit., drama U. Hull, Eng., 1950-63; sr. staff tutor U. Hull, 1963-65; prof. English U. Mich., Ann Arbor, 1965-74, chmn. dept. English, 1973-74; Andrew Mellon prof. English U. Pitts., 1974-77; Franklyn Bliss Snyder prof. English lit. Northwestern U., 1977-87, prof. emeritus, 1987—, prof. theater, 1984-87, prof. theater emeritus, 1987—; chmn. acad. coun. Shakespeare Globe Theatre Ctr. (N.A.), 1981-87. Author: The Elements of Drama, 1960, The Dark Comedy, 1962, The Dramatic Experience, 1965, Shakespeare's Stagecraft, 1967, Chekhov in Performance, 1971, The Challenge of the Theatre, 1972, Drama Stage and Audience, 1975, The Shakespeare Revolution, 1977, Modern Drama in Theory and Practice, 3 vols, 1981, Max Reinhardt, 1982, All's Well That Ends Well, Shakespeare in Performance series, 1984, The State of Drama Study, 1984, Restoration Comedy in Performance, 1986, The English Stage: A History of Drama and Performance, 1996. Served to lt. Royal Arty., 1941-45, Eng. Recipient Robert Lewis medal for lifetime achievement in theatre rsch. Kent State U., 1995; sr. rsch. fellow NEH, 1978-79, Guggenheim Found. fellow, 1983. Mem. Guild Drama Adjudicators, Brit. Drama League, MLA, Internat. Shakespeare Assn., Royal Over-Seas League. Home: Oak Apple Cottage, Barnes Ln, Milford on Sea Hampshire S041 0RP, England

STYCOS, JOSEPH MAYONE, demographer, educator; b. Saugerties, N.Y., Mar. 27, 1927; s. Stravos and Clotilda (Mayone) S.; m. Maria Nowakowska, Nov. 25, 1964; children: Steven Andrew, Christina Mayone (by previous marriage), Marek. AB, Princeton U., 1947; PhD, Columbia U., 1954. WithBur. Applied Social Rsch. Columbia U., 1948-50, lectr. sociology, 1951-52; project co-dir. U. P.R., 1952-53; postgrad. PC fellow U. N.C., 1954-55; assoc. prof. sociology St. Lawrence U., 1955-57; faculty Cornell U., Ithaca, N.Y., 1957—, prof. sociology, 1963—, chmn. dept., 1966-70, dir. Latin Am. program, 1962-66, dir. internat. population program, 1962-88, prof. rural sociology, 1987—, dir. population and devel. program, 1988-92; Fulbright-Hayes Disting. prof. U. Warsaw, Poland, 1979; external examiner U. Ife, Nigeria, 1973; Cons. AID, 1962-64; sr. cons. Population Council, 1963-74, 77-79; cons. Airlie Found., 1972-73, Inst. for Research in Social Behavior, 1974, Clapp & Mayne, Inc., 1974, Ford-Rockefeller Population Program, 1977, Nat. U. Costa Rica, 1979, U. P.R., 1979; trustee Population Reference Bur., 1964-68, cons., 1968-74; mem. exec. com. Internat. Planned Parenthood Fedn., West Hemmis, 1965-71, cons., 1971-77; adv. com. population and devel. OAS, 1968-70; mem. bd. Population Assn. Am., 1968-71, editorial cons. demography, 1965-69; adv. panel population Nat. Inst. Child Health and Human Devel., Dept. Health, Edn. and Welfare, 1969; co-chmn. population task force U.S. Nat. Commn. for UNESCO, 1972-73; adv. council, interdisciplinary communications program Smithsonian Instn., 1974-76; cons. Pan Am. Health Orgn., WHO, 1975; cons. steering com., acceptability task force WHO, 1978-85; cons. UNESCO, 1978-79, UN Fund for Population Activities, 1979-82, WHO, 1987-90; co-dir. Spanish family life project U. Complutense de Madrid, 1978-80; internat. adv. coun. Internat. Ctr. Photography, 1979—; Fulbright-Hays prof. Nat. U. Costa Rica, spring 1986; chmn. U.S. Census Adv. Com. on Population Stats., 1983-84; mem. Fulbright-Hays program Nat. Screening Com. Cen. Am., 1989-92; population rsch. team Environ. & Natural Resources Policy & Tng. Project, 1992-96; planning com. Global Omnibus Environ. Survey (GOES) Human Dimensions of Global Environ. Change Program, 1993—, chair, 1996—. Author: (with Hussein Abdel Aziz Sayed, Roger Avery and Samuel Firdman) Community Development and Family Planning: An Egyptian Experiment, 1988; mem. editl. bd. Human Orgn., 1962-64; editor: Demography as an Interdiscipline, 1989. Mem. council Cornell U., 1969-70. Mem. Rural Sociological Soc., Am. Sociological Assn., Population Assn. of Am., Internat. Union for the Scientific Study of Population. Home: 28 Twin Glens Rd Ithaca NY 14850-1041 Office: Cornell U Population & Devel Program Warren Hall Ithaca NY 14853-7801

STYER, ANTOINETTE CARDWELL, middle school counselor; b. Martinsville, Va.; d. John E. Cardwell and I. Lois Cardwell Shelton; children: Yvette D., Christopher P. BA in Liberal Arts, Temple U., 1975; MEd in Elem./Secondary Sch. Counseling, Antioch U., Phila., 1980. cert. sec. prin., 1994. Sec. Edward S. Cooper, M.D., Phila., 1960-66; rsch. asst. Temple U., Phila., 1971-73; confidential sec. Sch. Dist. Phila., 1967-71, sec., 1974-76, social worker Child Care Ctr., 1976-86, sch. counselor elem. edn., 1986-89; secondary edn. counselor Sch. Dist. Phila. Roosevelt Mid. Sch., Phila., 1989—; sch. evaluator Mid. States Assn. of Colls. and Schs.; co-organizer Project Exposure: Bus.; chaperone student visit to colls., Atlanta; interviewee Nat. Opinion Rsch. Ctr., Phila., 1971-72; mgmt. trainee GSA divsn. U.S. Govt., Phila., 1987; del. leader People to People Student Amb. Programs, Australia, 1993, Russia and the Baltic States, 1994, U.K. and Ireland, 1995, South Africa, 1996. Past chair 75th anniversary com. Pinn Meml. Bapt. Ch., scholarship com., new mem. com., aides to first lady and women's support group; mem. bd. dirs. Day Care Com.; ann. vol. United Negro Coll. Fund Telethon, mem. small bus. fundraising com. Mem. Nat. Coun. Negro Women, Pa. Sch. Counselors Assn., Mid. States Assn. Colls. and Schs., Delta Sigma Theta (life, chpt. journalist, chair May Week, del. to regional conv., mem. scholarship com.), Phi Delta Kappa. Home: 925 E Roumfort Rd Philadelphia PA 19150-3215 Office: Sch Dist Phila Roosevelt Mid Sch Washington Ln Musgrave St Philadelphia PA 19144

STYLES, BEVERLY, entertainer; b. Richmond, Va., June 6, 1923; d. John Harry Kenealy and Juanita Russell (Robins) Carpenter; m. Wilbur Cox, Mar. 14, 1942 (div.); m. Robert Marascia, Oct. 5, 1951 (div. Apr. 1964). Studies with Ike Carpenter, Hollywood, Calif., 1965—; student, Am. Nat. Theatre Acad., 1968-69; studies with Paula Raymond, Hollywood, 1969-70; diploma, Masterplan Inst., Anaheim, Calif., 1970. Freelance performer, musician, 1947-81; owner Beverly Styles Music, Joshua Tree, Calif., 1971—; v.p. spl. programs Lawrence Program of Calif., Yucca Valley, Calif.; talent coord., co-founder Quiet Place Studio, Yucca Valley, 1994; mem. exec. bd., awards dir. Am. chpt. Diogenes Process Group, 1996—. Composer: Joshua Tree, 1975, I'm Thankful, 1978, Wow, Wow, Wow, 1986, Music for The Whispering, 1994, World of Dreams, 1996, Thank You God, 1996; piano arrangements include Colour Chords and Moods, 1995, Desert Nocturne, 1996; records include The Perpetual Styles of Beverly, 1978; albums include The Primitive Styles of Beverly, 1977; author: A Special Plan to Think Upon, The Truth as Seen by a Composer, 1978, A Special Prayer to Think Upon, 1983. Mem. ASCAP (Gold Pin award), Profl. Musicians Local 47 (life), Internat. Platform Assn. Republican. Avocation: creating abstract art. Office: PO Box 615 Joshua Tree CA 92252-0615

STYLES, RICHARD GEOFFREY PENTLAND, retired banker; b. Regina, Sask., Can., Dec. 3, 1930; s. Alfred G. and C. Ila (Pentland) S.; m. Jacqueline Joyce Frith, Oct. 31, 1959; children: Leslie Diane, David Patrick. B. in Commerce, U. Sask., 1951; Program for Mgmt. Devel., Harvard U., 1964. With Royal Bank Can., 1951-87, various domestic and internat. positions; vice chmn. Royal Bank Can., Toronto, Ont., until 1987; ret., 1987; formerly involved with Orion Royal Bank and bank's internat. subs., London, 1961-64; chmn., bd. dirs. Grosvenor Internat. Holdings Ltd.; bd. dirs. Echo Bay Mines Ltd., Fairwater Capital Corp., The Geon Co., Onex Corp., ProSource Distbn. Svcs., The Royal Trust Co., Scott's Restaurants Inc., Working Ventures Can. Fund Inc. Bd. dirs. Toronto Symphony Found.; bd. govs. Mt. Sinai Hosp. Mem. Toronto Club, Rosedale Golf Club. Office: Royal Bank Plz Ste 3115, Toronto, ON Canada M5J 2J5

STYLES, TERESA JO, producer, educator; b. Atlanta, Oct. 19, 1950; d. Julian English and Jennie Marine (Sims) S. BA, Spelman Coll., 1972; MA, Northwestern U., 1973. Researcher CBS News, N.Y.C., 1975-80, producer, 1980-85; instr. mass communications, English Savannah (Ga.) State Coll., 1985-89, asst. prof. English, 1990; asst. prof. mass comm. and women studies dir. Bennett Coll., Greensboro, N.C., 1990-93; asst. prof. mass comm. N.C.

A&T State Univ., Greensboro, 1993—. Researcher documentary CBS Reports: Teddy, 1979 (Emmy cert.); assoc. producer documentaries for CBS Reports: Blacks: America, 1979 (Columbia Dupont cert. 1979), What Shall We Do About Mother?, 1980 (Emmy cert.), The Defense of the U.S., 1980 (Columbia Dupont cert.). Adv. bd. Greensboro Hist. Mus., Eastern Music Festival, Women's Short Film Project. Mem. Writers Guild Am. (bd. dirs. east), Dirs. Guild Am. (bd. dirs. east), African Am. Atelier (Greensboro, N.C. bd. dirs.), Eastern Music Festival (bd. dirs.). Avocation: swimming. Home: 4400 Suffolk Trail Greensboro NC 27407

STYNE, DENNIS MICHAEL, physician; b. Chgo., July 31, 1947; s. Irving and Bernice (Coopersmith) S.; m. Donna Petre, Sept. 5, 1971; children: Rachel, Jonathan, Juliana, Aaron. BS, Northwestern U., 1969, MD, 1971. Diplomate Am. Bd. Pediats. Intern in pediatrics U. Calif., San Diego, 1971-72, resident in pediatrics, 1972-73; resident in pediatrics Yale U., New Haven, 1973-74; fellow in pediatric endocrinology U. Calif., San Francisco, 1974-77, asst. prof. pediatrics, 1977-83; assoc. prof. U. Calif., Davis, 1983-90; prof., 1990—, chair pediatrics, 1989—. Author numerous book chpts., contbr. articles to profl. jours. Mem. Endocrine Soc., Soc. Pediat. Rsch., Am. Pediat. Soc., Am. Acad. Pediats., Lawson Wilkins Soc. for Pediat. Endocrinology. Avocations: sailing, music. Office: UC Davis Med Ctr Dept Pediatrics 2516 Stockton Blvd Fl 2 Sacramento CA 95817-2208*

STYNES, STANLEY KENNETH, retired chemical engineer, educator; b. Detroit, Jan. 18, 1932; s. Stanley Kenneth and Bessie Myrtle (Casey) S.; m. Marcia Ann Meyers, Aug. 27, 1955; children: Peter Casey, Pamela Kay, Suzanne Elizabeth. B.S., Wayne State U., 1955, M.S., 1958; Ph.D., Purdue U., 1963. Lab. asst. U. Chgo., 1951; instr. Purdue U., 1960-63; asst. prof. chem. engring. Wayne State U., Detroit, 1963-64, assoc. prof., 1964-71, prof., 1971-92, dean engring., 1972-85, prof. emeritus, 1992—; dir. Energy Conversion Devices, Inc., Troy, Mich.; cons. Schwayder Chem. Metallurgy Co., 1965; chemistry dept. Wayne State U., 1965-66, Claude B. Schneible Co., Holly, Mich., 1968. Contbr. engring. articles to profl. jours. Mem. coun. on environ. strategy S.E. Mich. Coun. Govts., 1976-81; bd. dirs. Program for Minorities in S.E. Mich.; sec.-treas. Mich. Ednl. Rsch. Info. Triad; bd. dirs. Sci. and Engring. Fair of Met. Detroit, pres., 1983; bd. dirs. Midwest Program for Minorities in Engring., Sci. Ctr. Met. Detroit. Ford Found. fellow, 1959-63; DuPont fellow, 1962-63; Wayne State U. faculty research fellow, 1964-65. Fellow AIChE (past chmn. Detroit sect.), Engring. Soc. Detroit (past bd. dirs.), Mich. Soc. Profl. Engrs. (pres. 1987-88); mem. AAAS, Am. Chem. Soc., Engring. Sci. Devel. Found. (pres. 1992-94), Argonne Univs. Assn. (del.), Adult Learning Inst. (bd. dirs. 1994—), Sigma Xi, Tau Beta Pi, Omicron Delta Kappa, Phi Lambda Upsilon. Presbyterian. Home: 20161 Stamford Dr Livonia MI 48152-1246 Office: Coll Engring Wayne State U Detroit MI 48202

STYRON, WILLIAM, writer; b. Newport News, Va., June 11, 1925; s. William Clark and Pauline Margaret (Abraham) S.; m. Rose Burgunder, May 4, 1953; children: Susanna Margaret, Paola Clark, Thomas, Claire Alexandra. Student, Christchurch Sch., Davidson Coll.; Litt.D., Davidson Coll., 1986; A.B., Duke U., 1947, Litt.D., 1968. Fellow Am. Acad. Arts and Letters at Am. Acad. in Rome, 1953; fellow Silliman Coll., Yale, 1964—; jury pres. Cannes Film Festival, 1983. Author: novels Lie Down in Darkness, 1951, The Long March, 1953, Set This House on Fire, 1960, The Confessions of Nat Turner, 1967 (Pulitzer prize 1968, Howells medal Am. Acad. Arts and Letters 1970), Sophie's Choice, 1979 (Am. Book award 1980), In the Clap Shack (play), 1972, This Quiet Dust, 1982, Darkness Visible, 1990, A Tidewater Morning, 1993; also articles, essays, revs.; editor: Best Stories from the Paris Rev., 1959; adv. editor: Paris Rev., 1953—; mem. editorial bd. The Am. Scholar, 1970-76. Decorated Commandeur de l'Ordre des Arts et des Lettres, Commandeur Legion d'Honneur (France); recipient Duke U. Disting. Alumni award, 1984, Conn. Arts award, 1984, Prix Mondial del Duca, 1985, Elmer Holmes Bobst award for fiction, 1989, Edward MacDowell medal for excellence in the arts, 1988, Nat. Mag. award, 1990, Nat. medal of Arts, 1993, Medal of Honor, Nat. Arts Club, 1995, Common Wealth award, 1995. Mem. Am. Acad. Arts and Scis., Am. Acad. Arts and Letters, Soc. Am. Historians, Signet Soc., Harvard, Académie Goncourt, Phi Beta Kappa. Democrat.

STYSLINGER, LEE JOSEPH, JR., manufacturing company executive; b. Birmingham, Ala., June 28, 1933; s. Lee Joseph and Margaret Mary (McFarl) S.; m. Catherine Patricia Smith, Apr. 30, 1960; children—Lee Joseph III, Jon Cecil, Mark Joseph. Student, U. Ala., 1952. Pres., chief exec. officer Altec Industries, Inc. and predecessors, truck equipment mfrs., Birmingham, 1956-89, chief exec. officer, chmn. bd., 1989-92, chmn., 1992—; bd. dirs. Regions Fin., Mead Corp., So. Rsch. Tech., Inc., Jemison Investment Co., Birmingham, Ala., Children's Harbor, Electronic Healthcare Systems, So. Rsch. Inst. Pres. cabinet U. Ala., Tuscaloosa; bd. dirs. St. Vincent's Hosp. Mem. Nat. Assn. Mfrs., Newcomen Soc., Operation New Birmingham, U.S. C. of C., Birmingham C. of C., Bus. Coun. Ala., Country Club Birmingham, Mountain Brook Club, Shoal Creek Club, Willow Point Golf and Country Club, Rotary. Roman Catholic. Home: 3260 E Briarcliff Rd Birmingham AL 35223-1305 Office: 210 Inverness Center Dr Birmingham AL 35242-4808

STYVE, ORLOFF WENDELL, JR., electrical engineer; b. Winnebago, Minn., Feb. 1, 1936; s. Orloff Wendell and Katharine (Drake) S.; m. Jane Carol Meister, Feb. 25, 1961 (div. 1981); children: Elizabeth Anne, David John, Robert Peter, Susan Katharine. BEE, U. Minn., 1959. Registered profl. engr., Wis. Dist. distbn. engr. Wis. Electric Power Co., Menomonee Falls, 1959-69; div. distbn. engr., then svc. ctr. engring. supr. Wis. Electric Power Co., West Bend, 1969-73; planning engr. Wis. Electric Power Co., Milw., 1973-76, sr. underground dist. engr., 1976-84, elec. engr. underground dist., 1984-94; cons. elect. distbn. engr. Slinger (Wis.) Utilities, 1995-96, utility mgr., 1996; dir. WPPI, 1996, sr. engr., cons. engring., 1996—; mem. elec. bd., West Bend, 1972-94. Mem. IEEE (voting mem. 1993, insulated conductors com. 1991—), Assn. of Edison Illuminating Cos. (cable engring. sect. 1991-94), Am. Nat. Stds. Inst. (distbn. transformer stds. com. 1985-88), Masons (dir. local #2 UAOTW 1974-85, bd. dirs. 1983-85), Scottish Rite (chmn. stage properties & elec. effects com. 1986—, Wis. Player's award Valley of Wis. 1989, Svc. award 1991), Shriners (potentate's aide emeritus Tripoli Shrine 1986), Nat. Honor Soc. Avocations: amateur theater, camping. Office: Cons Engring 644 Fair St West Bend WI 53095-2504

SU, HELEN CHIEN-FAN, research chemist; b. Nanping, Fujian, China, Dec. 26, 1922; came to U.S. 1949; d. Ru-chen and Sieu-Hsien (Wong) Su. BA, Hwa Nan Coll., China, 1944; MS, U. Nebr., Lincoln, 1951; PhD, U. Nebr., 1953. Cert. profl. chemist. Asst. instr. in chemistry Hwa Nan Coll., Fuzhou, Fujian, China, 1944-49; prof. chemistry Lambuth Coll., Jackson, Tenn., 1953-55; rsch. asst. Auburn Rsch. Found., Auburn, Ala., 1955-57; sr. chemist, project ldr. Borden Chem. Co., Phila., 1957-63; scientist Lockheed-Ga. Rsch. Lab., Marietta, Ga., 1963-67; rsch. chemist Agrl. Rsch. Svc., USDA, Savannah, Ga., 1968-90. Contbr. numerous articles to profl. jours., chpts. in books; patentee in field. Recipient IR-100 award, Indsl. Research Mag., 1966. Fellow Am. Inst. Chemists, Ga. Inst. Chemists; mem. ACS, AAAS, N.Y. Acad. Sci., Entomol. Soc. Am., Ga. Entomol. Soc., Sigma Xi, Sigma Delta Epsilon. Methodist. Avocations: reading, gardening. Home: 5978 Robin Hood Ln Norcross GA 30093-3804 Office: USDA-ARS 3401 Edwin Ave Savannah GA 31405-1607

SU, JUDY YA HWA LIN, pharmacologist; b. Hsinchu, Taiwan, Nov. 20, 1938; came to U.S., 1962; d. Ferng Nian and Chiu-Chin (Cheng) Lin; m. Michael W. Su; 1 child, Marvin. BS, Nat. Taiwan U., 1961; MS, U. Kans., 1964; PhD, U. Wash., 1968. Asst. prof. dept. biology U. Ala., Huntsville, 1972-73; rsch. assoc. dept. anesthesiology U. Wash., Seattle, 1976-77, acting asst. prof. dept. anesthesia, 1977-78, rsch. asst. prof., 1978-81, rsch. assoc. prof., 1981-89, rsch. prof., 1989—; mem. surg. anesthesiology & trauma study sect. NIH, 1987-91; vis. scientist Max-Planck Inst. Med. Rsch., Heidelberg, West Germany, 1982-83; vis. prof. dept. anesthesiology Mayo Clinic, Rochester, Minn., Med. Coll. Wis., 1988; editorial bd. cons. Jour. Molecular & Cellular Cardiology, London, 1987—, European Jour. Physiology, Berlin, Germany, Muscle & Nerve, Kyoto, Japan, 1989—, Anesthesiology, Phila., 1987—, Molecular Pharmacology, 1988—, Jour. Biol. Chemistry, 1989—, Am. Jour. Physiology, 1990—; mem. rsch. study com. Am. Heart Assn., 1992-95. Contbr. articles to profl. jours. Grantee Wash. Heart Assn., 1976-77, 1985-87, Pharm. Mfrs. Assn. Found., Inc., 1977, Lilly Rsch. Labs, 1986-88, Anaquest, 1987—, NIH, 1978—; recipient Rsch. Career Devel. award NIH, 1982-87; rsch. fellowship San Diego Heart Assn., 1970-72, Max-Planck Inst., 1982-83. Mem. AAAS, Biophys. Soc., Am. Soc. for Pharmacology and Exptl. Therapeutics, Am. Physiol. Soc., Am. Soc. Anesthesiologists. Home: 13110 NE 33rd St Bellevue WA 98005-1318 Office: U Wash Dept Anesthesiology Box 356540 Seattle WA 98195-6540

SU, KENDALL LING-CHIAO, engineering educator; b. Fujian, China, July 10, 1926; came to U.S., 1948; s. Ru-chen and Sui-hsiong (Wang) S.; m. Jennifer Gee-tsone Chang, Sept. 10, 1960; children: Adrienne, Jonathan. BEE, Xiamen U., Peoples Republic China, 1947; MEE, Ga. Inst. Tech, 1949; PhD, Ga. Inst. Tech., 1954. Jr. engr. Taiwan Power Co., Taipei, Republic China, 1947-48; asst. prof. Ga. Inst. Tech., Atlanta, 1954-59, assoc. prof., 1959-65, prof., 1965-70, Regents prof., 1970-94, Regents' prof. emeritus, 1994—; mem. tech. staff Bell Labs., Murray Hill, N.J., 1957. Author: Active Network Synthesis, 1965, Time-Domain Synthesis of Linear Networks, 1969, Fundamentals of Circuits, Electronics, and Signal Analysis, 1978, Handbook of Tables for Elliptic-Function Filters, 1990, Fundamentals of Circuit Analysis, 1993, Analog Filters, 1996; mem. sci. adv. com. Newton Graphic Sci. mag., 1987—. Fellow IEEE (life); mem. Sigma Xi (pres. Ga. Inst. Tech. chpt. 1968-69, 72-73, Faculty Rsch. award 1957), Phi Kappa Phi, Eta Kappa Nu. Methodist. Office: Ga Inst Tech Sch Elec & Comp Engring Atlanta GA 30332-0250

SU, SHIAW-DER, nuclear engineer; b. Tainan, Republic of China, Jan. 20, 1945; came to U.S., 1969; s. Hsin-Chun and King-New (Chen) S.; m. Shi-Ju Wang, June 30, 1968; children: Eastor Y., Wesley Y. BS, Nat. Tsing Hua U., Republic of China, 1968; MS, Purdue U., 1971. Registered profl. nuclear engr., Calif. Engr. Burns & Roe Inc., Oradell, N.J., 1971-72; prin. Gen. Atomics, San Diego, Calif., 1972-95; pres. China Nuclear Corp., Taiwan, 1990-91, Peak Engring., San Diego, Calif., 1995-96, Morrison Kundsen Corp., Las Vegas, Nev., 1996—. Mem. Am. Nuclear Soc., Chinese Inst. Engrs. (life). Avocations: tennis, swimming, ping-pong, bridge. Home: 2028 Scarlet Rose Dr Las Vegas NV 89134-6638 Office: Morrison Knudsen Corp MS423 1180 Town Center Dr # Ms423 Las Vegas NV 89134-6363

SUAREZ, LOUIS A., cardiothoracic surgeon; b. Havana, Cuba, Dec. 30, 1947; came to U.S., 1962; s. Louis A. and Irma C. (Abate-Daga) S.; m. Denise Marie Boland, June 2, 1973; children: Louis A. III, Megan, Michael. BS, Loyola U., Chgo., 1970; MD, U. Ill., Chgo., 1974. Diplomate Am. Bd. Surgery, Am. Bd. Thoracic Surgery, Am. Bd. Surg. Critical Care. Intern U. Wis. Hosp., Madison, 1974-75, resident in surgery, 1977-81, resident in cardiothoracic surgery, 1981-83; staff surgeon Appleton (Wis.) Med. Ctr., 1983—; chief cardiac surgery Appleton Heart Inst., 1993—; staff surgeon Theda Clark Med. Ctr., 1992—; chief surgery Unified Med. Staff, Appleton, 1994-96. Lt. comdr. USNR, 1975-77. Fellow ACS, Am. Coll. Cardiology, Am. Coll. Chest Physicians, Soc. for Thoracic Surgery, Wis. Surg. Soc. (coun. 1990-96), Wis. Surg. Travelling Club. Roman Catholic. Home: 2011 N Nicholas St Appleton WI 54914-2211 Office: Appleton Heart Surgeons 820 E Grant St Appleton WI 54911

SUAREZ, XAVIER LOUIS, lawyer, former mayor; b. Las Villas, Cuba, May 21, 1949; m. Rita Suarez; 4 children. BE, Villanova U., 1971, hon. degree, 1988; M of Pub. Policy, JD, Harvard U., 1975. Bar: Fla. 1975. Instr. bus. law Biscayne Coll., 1977-78; mayor City of Miami, 1985-93; ptnr. Jorden, Schulte & Burchette, Miami, 1988-93, Shutts & Bowen, Miami, 1993—; mem. criminal justice coun. Dade County, Miami, Fla., 1980. Chmn. Miami Affirmative Action Bd., 1981, Downtown Devel. Authority, 1985—; chmn. bd. regents Cath. Univ., 1988-89; bd. advisors Harvard U. Kennedy Sch. Govt. Inst. Politics, Cambridge, Mass., St. Thomas U. Sch. Law. Mem. Fla. Bar Assn., Cuban Bar Assn. Office: Shutts and Bowen 1500 Miami Ctr 201 S Biscayne Blvd Miami FL 33131-4332

SUAREZ-MURIAS, MARGUERITE C., retired language and literature educator; b. Havana, Cuba, Mar. 23, 1921; came to U.S., 1935, naturalized, 1959; d. Eduardo R. and Marguerite (Vendel) S.-M. AB, Bryn Mawr Coll., 1942; MA, Columbia U., 1953, PhD, 1957. Lectr. in Spanish Columbia U., 1954-56; pub. rels. officer med. divsn. Johns Hopkins U., 1957-58; asst. prof. Spanish and French Sweet Briar Coll., 1958-59, Hood Coll., 1960-61; lectr. Cath. U., 1960-63, asst. prof., summers 1960-62, assoc. prof., summers 1964-66; asst. prof. dept. langs. and linguistics Am. U., 1961-63, assoc. prof., 1963-66; prof. dept. classical and modern langs. Marquette U., Milw., 1966-68; prof. Spanish and Portuguese U. Wis., Milw., 1968-83, chmn., 1972-75; guest prof. U. South Africa, Pretoria, 1980. Author: La Novela Romántica en Hispanoamérica, 1963, Antología Estilística de la Prosa Moderna Española, 1968, Essays on Hispanic Literature/Ensayos de Literatura Hispana, 1982; contbr. articles to profl. jours.; editor: Gironella's Los Cipreses Creen en Dios, 1969; designed built homes, 1987-93. Mem. Nat. Trust for Historic Preservation. Roman Catholic. Home: 1315 Cold Bottom Rd Sparks MD 21152-9518

SUAREZ RIVERA, ADOLFO ANTONIO, archbishop; b. San Cristobal de las Casas, Mexico, Jan. 9, 1927. Ordained priest Roman Cath. Ch., 1952; bishop of Tepic, 1971-80, Tlalnepantla, 1980-83; archbishop of Monterrey, 1984—. Office: Porfirio Barba Jacob No 906, Col Anahuac, CP 66450 San Nicolas de Garza Nuevo Leon, Mexico also: Zuazua # 10o Sur con Ocampo, Apartado Postal 7, CP 64000 Monterrey Nuero Leon, Mexico*

SUBA, ANTONIO RONQUILLO, retired surgeon; b. Philippines, Apr. 25, 1927; came to U.S., 1952, naturalized, 1961; s. Antonio Mesina and Valentina Cabais (Ronquillo) S.; m. Sylvia Marie Karl, June 16, 1956; children—Steven Antonio, Eric John, Laurinda Ann, Gregory Karl, Timothy Mark, Sylvia Kathleen. M.D., U. St. Thomas, Philippines, 1952. Diplomate: Am. Bd. Surgery. Intern St. Anthony's Hosp., St. Louis, 1952-53; resident St. Louis County Hosp., St. Louis, 1953-57; trainee Nat. Cancer Inst., Ellis Fischel State Cancer Hosp., Columbia, Mo., 1957-59; chief surg. services U.S. Army, Bremerhaven, Germany, 1959-61; practice medicine specializing in gen. and hand surgery St. Louis, 1961-89; ret., 1989; pres., prin. ARS (P.C.), 1971-84. Contbr. feature articles to Philippine publs., 1946-51, articles to med. jours. Fellow A.C.S.; mem. AMA, Pan-Pacific, Mo. surg. assns., St. Louis Surg. Soc., Am. Assn. Hand Surgery. Club: K.C. Home: 12085 Heatherdane Dr Saint Louis MO 63131-3119

SUBAK, JOHN THOMAS, lawyer; b. Trebic, Czechoslovakia, Apr. 19, 1929; came to U.S., 1941, naturalized, 1946; s. William John and Gerda Maria (Subakova) S.; m. Mary Corcoran, June 4, 1955; children—Jane Kennedy, Kate, Thomas, Michael. BA summa cum laude, Yale U., 1950, LLB, 1956. Bar: Pa. 1956. From assoc. to ptnr. Dechert, Price & Rhoads, Phila., 1956-76, v.p., gen. counsel, dir., 1976-77; group v.p., gen. counsel, dir. Rohm and Haas Co., Phila., 1977-93; counsel Dechert Price & Rhoads, Phila., 1994—; bd. dirs. Newport Corp. Editor: The Bus. Lawyer, 1982-83. Bd. dirs. Am. Cancer Soc., 1982-95; trustee Smith Coll. Lt. (j.g.) USN, 1950-53. Mem. ABA (chmn. corp. and bus. law sect. 1984-85), Am. Law Inst. (coun. mem.), Defender Assn. of Phila. (v.p., bd. dirs. 1982-95), Merion Cricket Club, Lemon Bay Club. Democrat. Roman Catholic. Office: Dechert Price & Rhoads 1717 Arch St Philadelphia PA 19103-2713

SUBAK-SHARPE, GERALD EMIL, electrical engineer, educator; b. Vienna, Austria, June 15, 1925; came to U.S., 1959, naturalized, 1967; s. Robert and Nelly (Brull) S.; m. Genell Jackson, Nov. 23, 1963; children: David, Sarah and Hope (twins). BS with 1st class honors, Univ. Coll., London, 1951; PhD, U. London, 1965; ScD, Columbia U., 1969. Rsch. engr. Brit. Telecommunications Rsch., Taplow, Eng., 1951-58; mem. tech. staff Bell Labs., Murray Hill, N.J., 1959-64, cons., 1977-78; assoc. prof. elec. engring. Manhattan Coll., Bronx, N.Y., 1966-68; prof. elec. engring. CCNY, N.Y.C., 1968—; v.p. G.S. Sharpe Communications Inc., 1981—. Author: (with A.B. Glaser) Integrated Circuit Engineering, 1978; contbr. articles on network structure and semicondr. theory to profl. jours. Served as lt. Royal Warwickshire Regt., 1944-47. Recipient Prof. of Yr. award Eta Kappa Nu/CCNY, 1985-86. Fellow Instn. Elec. Engrs. (London); mem. IEEE (sr.), N.Y. Acad. Scis. Nat. Trust for Historic Preservation. Home: 606 W 116th St Apt 71 New York NY 10027-7024 Office: CCNY Dept Elec Engring Convent Ave New York NY 10027 also: Knollcroft New Concord NY 12060

SUBER, ROBIN HALL, former medical and surgical nurse; b. Bethlehem, Pa., Mar. 14, 1952; d. Arthur Albert and Sarah Virginia (Smith) Hall; m. David A. Suber, July 28, 1979; 1 child, Benjamin A. BSN, Ohio State U., 1974. RN, Ariz., Ohio. Formerly staff nurse Desert Samaritan Hosp., Mesa, Ariz. Lt. USN, 1974-80. Mem. ANA, Sigma Theta Tau.

SUBLER, EDWARD PIERRE, advertising executive; b. Shelby, Ohio, Mar. 24, 1927; s. Leo John and Dorotha (Armstrong) S.; m. Alice Ellen Carpenter, Sept. 8, 1956; children: Leo, Scott, Dorotha. B.A., Denison U., 1950; grad. advanced mgmt. course, Emory U. Mgr. product advt. Westinghouse Electric Co., Mansfield, Ohio, 1950-65; mgr. advt. and sales promotion Bell & Howell Co., Chgo., 1965-69; v.p. mdsg. Westinghouse Consumer Products Co., 1969-76; sr. v.p. Ketchum Advt., Pitts., 1976-92, ret., 1992. Served with USN, 1945-46. Mem. Am. Mktg. Assn., Am. Assn. Advt. Agencies (regional chmn.), Catawba Island Club, Bus./Profl. Adv. Assn. (Pitts. Advt. Exec. of Yr. 1988), U.S. Power Squadron. Presbyterian. Home: 2881 N Firelands Blvd Port Clinton OH 43452-3028

SUBLETT, CARL CECIL, artist; b. Johnson County, Ky., Feb. 4, 1919; s. Tandy and Beulah (Fitzpatrick) S.; m. Helen C. Davis, Aug. 20, 1942; children: Carol, Eric. Student, Western Ky. U., 1938-40, Univ. Center, Florence, Italy, 1945, U. Tenn., 1955-56. Indsl. engr., draftsman Enterprise Wheel & Car Corp., Bristol, Va., 1946-49; staff artist Bristol, Va.-Tennesean & Herald Courier, 1950-52; artist, asst. mgr. Bristol Art Engravers, 1952-54; art dir. Advt., Knoxville, Tenn., 1954-65; prof. art U. Tenn., Knoxville, 1966-82; juror Watercolor Soc. Ala., Birmingham, 1979, Jacksonville U. Ann., 1980; juror Bristol Art Guild 8th ann. juried exhbn., 1993. Artist prize-winning watercolors, 1964, drawing Soc. Nat. Exhbn., 1965, Artists U.S.A., 1971-72, 73-74, 74-75; one-man shows in oil and watercolors, 1995—; numerous exhbns. art in embassies program, 1964—; numerous exhbns. featured in publs. Taipei Fine Arts Inst. including Allied Publs. Inc.; numerous exhbns. in catalogs Tenn. State Mus., Nashville, Artist U.S.A., others; retrospective exhbn. Knoxville Mus. Art, 1991; invitational show Hampton III Gallery, Ltd., Taylors, S.C., 1992, Union U., Jackson, Tenn., 1991, Collector's Gallery, Nashville, 1960, 93, 96, Bennett Galleries, Knoxville, 1992-93, 95. Hon. mem. Oak Ridge Tenn.Community Art Ctr. Served with U.S. Army, 1943-45. Recipient Purchase Mead Corp. Painting of Yr., Atlanta, 1963, Grumbacher Washington Watercolor Club, 1964, Rudolph Leach Am. Watercolor Soc., N.Y.C., 1972, Purchase Watercolor U.S.A., Springfield, Mo., 1975, Lifetime Achievement award Knoxville Arts Coun. and Knoxville Mus. of Art, 1994. Mem. NAD (Alfred Easton poor prize 1995), Bristol Art Guild (treas. 1951-54), Tenn. Watercolor Soc. (gold medal 1973, award of merit 1974, 75, 77, 78, 81, 84, 85), Knoxville Watercolor Soc., Port Clyde (Maine) Arts and Crafts Soc., Watercolor USA Soc., Knoxville Mus. Art. Methodist. Home and Studio: 2104 Lake Ave Knoxville TN 37916-2802 *We are creatures of history; credit your helpers, share your successes, and the future will reward your time.*

SUBLETTE, JULIA WRIGHT, music educator, performer, adjudicator; b. Natural Bridge, Va., Sept. 13, 1929; d. Paul Thomas and Annie Belle (Watkins) Wright; m. Richard Ashmore Sublette, Oct. 18, 1952; children: C. Mark, Carey P., Sylvia S. Bennett, Wright D. BA in Music, Furman U., 1951; MusM, Cin. Conservatory, 1954; postgrad., Chautauqua Inst., N.Y., 1951-52; PhD, Fla. State U., 1993. Ind. piano tchr., 1953—; instr. music and humanities Okaloosa-Walton C.C., Niceville, Fla., 1978—; panelist Music Tchr. Nat. Conv., Milw., 1992; instr. art humanities Troy State U., Ala. Editor Fla. Music Tchr., 1991—; contbr. articles to profl. music jours. Mem. AAUW, Music Tchrs. Nat. Assn. (cert., chmn. so. divsn. jr. high sch. piano/instrumental contests 1986-88), Fla. State Music Tchrs. Assn., So. Assn. Women Historians, Southeastern Hist. Keyboard Soc., Friday Morning Music Club, Colonial Dames of 17th Century Am., Pi Kappa Lambda. Avocations: reading, travel, folk music, herb gardening. Home: 217 Country Club Rd Shalimar FL 32579-2203

SUBOTNICK, STUART, food service executive; b. 1942. JD, Bklyn. Law Sch., N.Y., 1968; LLM, NYU, 1974. With Medromedia, Inc., 1967-82, sr. v.p. fin., 1982-86, bd. dirs., exec. v.p., 1986; gen. ptnr., exec. v.p. Metromedia Co., 1986—; vice chmn. bd. Metromedia Steakhouses, Inc., Vandalia, Ohio, 1988—; bd. dirs. Metromedia Steakhouses, Inc.; investor, operator N.Y./N.J. Metro Stars, Seacaucus, N.J., 1995—. Office: 1 Meadowlands Plz East Rutherford NJ 07073*

SUCHECKI, LUCY ANNE, elementary education educator; b. East Cleveland, Ohio, May 3, 1945; d. Ben and Adelaide V. (Maneri) Urban; m. Robert K. Suchecki, Aug. 19, 1972. BS, Bowling Green State U., 1967; MA, Oakland U., 1981. Cert. elem. tchr., Mich. Elem. tchr. L'Anse Creuse Pub. Schs., Mt. Clemens, Mich., 1967—; grade cons. (book) Michigan, 1991. Active Immaculate Conception Ch., 1969—, Anchor Bay Women's Pool League, 1972—. Mem. NEA, MEA, MEA-NEA (local 1), L'Anse Creuse Ednl. Assn. (sec. 1968—), New Baltimore Hist. Soc. Roman Catholic. Avocations: boating, swimming, pool. Home: 8504 Anchor Bay Dr Clay MI 48001-3507 Office: Marie C Graham Elem Sch 25555 Crocker Blvd Harrison Township MI 48045-3443

SUCHENEK, MAREK ANDRZEJ, computer science educator; b. Warsaw, Poland, May 2, 1949; came to U.S., 1986; s. Tadeusz Aleksander and Barbara Krystyna (Zych) S.; m. Ewa Aleksandra Czerny, July 30, 1974 (div. 1991). MSc in Math. Engring., Warsaw Tech. U., 1973, PhD in Tech. Scis. with distinction, 1979. Instr. Warsaw (Poland) Tech. U., 1973-79, asst. prof., 1979-88; vis. asst. prof. Wichita (Kans.) State U., 1986-88; assoc. Nat. Inst. for Aviation Rsch., Wichita, 1987-90; assoc. prof. Wichita (Kans.) State U., 1988-89, assoc. prof., chair, 1989-90; prof. Calif. State U.-Dominguez Hills, Carson, 1990-96, prof., co-chair, 1996, prof., chair, 1997—; mem. organizing com. Internat. Symposium on Methodologies for Intelligent Sys., 1989-90; program com. Ann. Ulam Math. Conf., 1990-91, Internat. Conf. on Computing and Info., 1992—; referee NSF, 1990-92, Annals of Math. and Artificial Intelligence, 1992-93, Jour. Logic Programming, 1992-94; presenter in field. Author: (with Jan Bielecki) ANS FORTRAN, 1980, (with Jan Bielecki) FORTRAN for Advanced Programmers, 1981, 2d edit., 83, 3d edit., 88 (Minister of Sci. Higher Edn. and Techs. prize 1982); reviewer Zentralblatt fur Mathematik, 1980-89, Math. Reviews, 1989-91; mem. editorial bd.: Ulam Quarterly, 1990—; contbr. articles to profl. jours. Recipient rsch. grants Polish Govt., 1974-76, 85-86, FAA, 1988-90. Mem. AAUP, The Assn. for Logic Programming, Computer Soc. IEEE, Assn. Symbolic Logic, Sigma Xi (chpt. pres.). Avocations: cats, collectibles, swimming, target shooting. Home: 830 N Juanita Ave Unit 4 Redondo Beach CA 90277-2270 Office: Calif State Univ Dominguez Hills 1000 E Victoria St Carson CA 90747-0001

SUCHKOV, ANATOLY, astronomer; b. Kalai-Khumb, USSR, May 14, 1944; came to the U.S., 1991; s. Alexander and Anna (Nazarenko) S.; m. Galina (Sidorenko) Soutchkova, Jan. 4, 1965; children: Svetlana, Vera. Candidate of sci., Tajik State U., 1970; DSc, Moscow State U., 1980. Scientist Inst. Astrophysics, Dushanbe, Tajikistan, 1965-69, sr. scientist, 1969-72; prof. astrophysics Rostov (USSR) State U., 1972-80, head dept. astrophysics, 1980-93; planning scientist Space Telescope Sci. Inst., Balt., 1993-94, assoc. scientist, 1994—; vis. scientist Space Telescope Sci. Inst., 1991-93; head space rsch. and astronomy divsn. North Caucasus Sci. Ctr., Rostov-on-Don, USSR, 1980-91. Author: The Milky Way Galaxy, 1995, Galaxies: Familiar and Puzzling, 1988, The Galaxy, 1984; contbr. articles to profl. jours. Mem. Am. Astron. Soc. Achievements include discovery of the discreteness of the metallicity distribution of the stellar populations of the galaxy; formulation of the theory of active phases of the evolution of the galaxy; determination of the parameters of the spiral structure of the galaxy; revealing of the two-dimensional age-metallicity relation for the nearby stars; discovery of the absence of a dependence of the main sequence of F stars on heavy element abundance. Home: 8 Deaven Ct Baltimore MD 21209 Office: Space Telescope Sci Inst 3700 San Martin Dr Baltimore MD 21218-2410

SUCHODOLSKI, RONALD EUGENE, publishing company executive; b. Bklyn., May 17, 1946; s. John Florence Burke; m. Carolyn Cortese, Dec. 4, 1977; children: Keith, Craig. BA, CUNY, 1973, MA, 1975. Dir. product mktg. Holt, Rinehart & Winston, N.Y.C., 1973-80; dir. product devel. Instructo/McGraw-Hill, Malvern, Pa., 1980-83; dir. sch. div. Childcraft, Edison, N.J., 1984-89; pres. Judy/Instructo div. Paramount Publs. Inc., Eden Prairie, Minn., 1989-93; sr. v.p. mktg. sales Paramount Supplemental

Educ., Morristown, N.J., 1993-95; pres. Childcraft Edn. Corp., 1995—. Sgt. U.S. Army, 1966-67, Vietnam. Mem. Nat. Sch. Supply and Equipment Assn., Ednl. Dealers and Suppliers Assn. Home: 15 Lance Rd Lebanon NJ 08833-5007

SUCHY, SUSANNE N., nursing educator; b. Windsor, Ont., Can., Sept. 20, 1945; d. Hartley Joseph and Helen Viola (Derrick) King; m. Richard Andrew Suchy, June 24, 1967; children: Helen Marie, Hartley Andrew, Michael Derrick. Diploma, St. Joseph Sch. Nursing, Flint, Mich., 1966; BSN, Wayne State U., 1969, MSN, 1971. RN, Mich. Afternoon supr., staff nurse oper. and recovery rm. St. John Hosp., Detroit, 1966-70; nursing instr. Henry Ford Community Coll., Dearborn, Mich., 1972—, on leave 1988-90; CNS/case mgr. surg. nursing Harper Hosp., Detroit, 1988-89; CNS case mgr. oncology, 1989—; mem. Detroit Demonstration Site Team for defining and differentiating ADN/BSN competencies, 1983-87. Contbr. articles to profl. jours. Past bd. dirs., pres. St. Pius Sch. Mem. ANA, AACH, N.Am. Nursing Diagnosis Assn. (by-law com. chmn. 1992—), Mich. Nursing Diagnosis Assn. (pres. 1987-90, elected by-law chmn. 1991-92, treas. 1993—), NLN, Mich. Nurses Assn. (cabinet nursing practice 1996—, conv. com. 1996—), Detroit Dist. Nurses Assn. (past chmn. nominating com., legis. com., sec. 1994-96), Oncology Nursing Soc. (gov. rels. chmn. 1992—, presenter abstract conf. 1991, 95, poster presentations ann. conf. 1991-93, 95, 96), Daus. of Isabella (internat. dir. 1992-96, local auditor 1995—, state vice regent 1997—, cir. auditor 1995-97), Wayne State U. Alumni Assn., Sigma Theta Tau (nominating com. 1991-93). Roman Catholic. Home: 12666 Irene St Southgate MI 48195-1765 Office: Henry Ford CC 5101 Evergreen Rd Dearborn MI 48128-2407

SUCKIEL, ELLEN KAPPY, philosophy educator; b. Bklyn., June 15, 1943; d. Jack and Lilyan (Banchefsky) Kappy; m. Joseph Suckiel, June 22, 1973. A.B., Douglass Coll., 1965; M.A. in Philosophy, U. Wis., 1969, Ph.D. in Philosophy, 1972. Lectr. philosophy U. Wis., Madison, 1969-71; asst. prof. philosophy Fla. State U., Tallahassee, 1972-73; asst. prof. philosophy U. Calif., Santa Cruz, 1973-80, assoc. prof., 1980-95, prof., 1995—, provost Kresge Coll., 1983-89. Author: The Pragmatic Philosophy of William James, 1982, Heaven's Champion: William James's Philosophy of Religion, 1996, also articles, book introductions and chpts. Mem. Am. Philos. Assn., Soc. for Advancement Am. Philosophy. Office: U Calif Cowell Coll Santa Cruz CA 95064

SUDAK, HOWARD STANLEY, physician, psychiatry educator; b. Cleve., Nov. 13, 1932; s. Sol and Leona (Simms) S.; m. Diane M. Ressler, Dec. 25, 1955 (dec.); children: Ellen, Nancy, Janet, David; m. Donna M. Miller, Mar. 25, 1995. AB in Chemistry magna cum laude, Case Western Res. U., 1954, MD, 1958. Diplomate Am. Bd. Psychiatry and Neurology (sr. examiner 1991—). Intern in medicine Univ. Hosps. Cleve., 1958-59, resident in psychiatry, 1959-62; clin. assoc. NIMH, Bethesda, Md., 1962-64; chief psychiatry Cleve. VA Med. Ctr., 1964-84; asst. prof. psychiatry Case Western Res. U., Cleve., 1964-74, assoc. prof., 1974-82, prof., 1982—, vice dean Med. Sch., 1985-92; chmn. dept. psychiatry The Pa. Hosp., Phila., 1992—; psychiatrist-in-chief Inst. of Pa. Hosp., Phila., 1992—; clin. prof. psychiatry U. Pa. Sch. Medicine, 1993-94; prof. psychiatry, vice chmn. psychiatry/human behavior Thomas Jefferson U., Phila., 1994—; mem. profl. adv. coun. Youth Suicide Nat. Ctr., Washington, 1986—; com. mem. Ctrs. for Disease Control, Atlanta, 1990-91. Editor: Suicide in the Young, 1984, Clinical Psychiatry, 1985; cons. editor Suicide and Life Threatening Behavior, 1988—; contbr. numerous articles to profl. jours., chpt. to books. Dir. Inst. for Urban Health, Cleve., 1990-92. Grantee NIMH, 1972-73, 83-86. Fellow Am. Psychiat. Assn., Am. Coll. Psychiatrists, Am. Coll. Psychoanalysts; mem. Am. Assn. Suicidology (trustee 1988-90), Am. Suicide Found. (trustee 1987—, pres. 1989-91), Phi Beta Kappa, Alpha Omega Alpha. Avocations: biking, sailing, reading, tennis, jazz and classical music. Home: 321 S Lawrence Ct Philadelphia PA 19106 Office: Inst of Pa Hosp 111 N 49th St Philadelphia PA 19139-2718

SUDAN, RAVINDRA NATH, electrical engineer, physicist, educator; b. Chineni, Kashmir, India, June 8, 1931; came to U.S., 1958, naturalized, 1971; s. Brahm Nath and Shanti Devi (Mehta) S.; m. Dipali Ray, July 3, 1959; children: Rajani, Ranjeet. B.A. with first class honors, U. Punjab, 1948; diploma, Indian Inst. Sci., 1952, Imperial Coll., London, 1953; Ph.D., U. London, 1955. Engr., Brit. Thomson-Houston Co., Rugby, Eng, 1955-57; Engr. Imperial Chem. Industries, Calcutta, India, 1957-58; research assoc. Cornell U., Ithaca, N.Y., 1958-59; asst. prof. elec. engring. Cornell U., 1959-63, assoc. prof., 1963-68, prof., 1968-75, IBM prof. engring., 1975—, dir. Lab. Plasma Studies, 1975-85, dep. dir. Cornell Theory Ctr., 1985-87; cons. Lawrence Livermore Lab., Los Alamos Sci. Lab., Sci. Applications Inc., Physics Internat. Co.; vis. research asso. Stanford U., summer 1963; cons. U.K. Atomic Energy Authority, Culham Lab., summer 1965; vis. scientist Internat. Center Theoretical Physics, Trieste, Italy, 1965-66, summers 1970, 73, Plasma Physics Lab. Princeton U., 1966-67, spring 1989, Inst. for Advanced Study, Princeton, N.J., spring 1975; head theoretical plasma physics group U.S. Naval Research Lab., 1970-71, sci. adviser to dir., 1974-75; chmn. Ann. Conf. on Theoretical Aspects of Controlled Fusion, 1975, 2d Internat. Conf. on High Power Electron and Ion Beam Research and Tech., 1977. Mem. editl. bd. Physics of Fluids, 1973-76, Comments on Plasma Physics, 1973, Nuclear Fusion, 1976-84, Physics Reports, 1990—; co-editor Handbook of Plasma Physics; contbr. over 220 articles to sci. jours. Recipient Gold medal Acad. Scis. of the Czech Republic, 1993. Fellow IEEE, AAAS, Am. Phys. Soc. (Maxwell prize 1989), Nat. Rsch. Coun. (chmn. Plasma Sci. com. 1993—). Achievements include patents (with S. Humphries, Jr) intense ion beam generator. Office: Cornell Univ 369 Upson Hall Ithaca NY 14853-7501

SUDARKASA, MICHAEL ERIC MABOGUNJE, lawyer, consultant; b. N.Y.C., Aug. 5, 1964; s. Akinlowan Mabougunje and Niara Gloria (Marshall) S.; m. Joyce Ann Johnson, Nov. 22, 1990; children: Jasmine Ayana Yetunde, Jonathan Michael, Maya Elisabeth, Marielle Imar. Student, Howard U., 1983; BA in History with honors, U. Mich., 1985; JD, Harvard U., 1988; postgrad., U. San Diego, Paris, 1990. Bar: Fla. 1989, U.S. Ct. Appeals (D.C.) 1990. Tech. asst. African Devel. Bank, Abidjan, Ivory Coast, 1988-89; founder, counsel 21st Century Africa, Inc., Lincoln University, Pa., 1989; assoc. Steel Hector & Davis, Miami, Fla., 1990; pres. 21st Century Africa, Inc., Washington, 1990-97; dir. Internat. Trade & Investment Promotion Svcs. Labat-Anderson, McLean, Va., 1997—; bd. dirs. Africa News Svc. Online. Author: The African Business Handbook: A Practical Guide to Business Resources for U.S./Africa Trade and Investment, 1991-92, 93-94, 96-97. Named One of 30 Leaders of Future, Ebony mag., 1991; recipient Muhammad Kenyatta Young Alumni award Harvard Black Law Students Assn., 1992. Mem. ABA (chmn. African law com. 1995—), Internat. Bar Assn., Nat. Bar Assn., Soc. for Internat. Devel. (bd. dirs. D.C. chpt.), Coun. on Fgn. Rels. Avocations: sports, reading, travel. Office: Labat-Anderson Internat Trade & Investment Promotion Svcs 8000 Westport Dr Ste 400 McLean VA 22102

SUDARSKY, JERRY M., industrialist; b. Russia, June 12, 1918; s. Selig and Sara (Ars) S.; m. Mildred Axelrod, Aug. 31, 1947; children: Deborah, Donna. Student, U. Iowa, 1936-39; BS, Poly. U. Bklyn., 1942; DSc (hon.), Poly. U. N.Y., 1976. Fonder, CEO Bioferm Corp., Wasco, Calif., 1946-66; cons. to Govt. of Israel, 1966-67; founder, chmn. Israel Chems., Ltd., Tel Aviv, 1967-72; chmn. I.C. Internat. Cons., Tel Aviv, 1971-73; vice chmn., bd. dirs. Daylin, Inc., L.A., 1972-76; pres., chmn. J.M.S. Assocs., L.A., 1976-82; vice chmn. bd. dirs. Jacobs Engring. Group Inc., Pasadena, Calif., 1982-94; chmn. Alexandria Real Estate Equities Inc., Pasadena, 1997—. Patentee in field of indsl. microbiology. Bd. govs. Hebrew U., Jerusalem; trustee Polytechnic U. N.Y., 1976—; bd. dirs. Arthritis Found., L.A., 1989-94, Mgmt. Edn. Assn., UCLA, 1990—. Served with USNR, 1943-46. Mem. AAAS, Am. Chem. Soc., Brentwood Country Club (L.A.), Sigma Xi. Office: Alexandria Real Est Equ Inc 251 S Lake Ave Ste 700 Pasadena CA 91101-3003

SUDBRINK, JANE MARIE, sales and marketing executive; b. Sandusky, Ohio, Jan. 14, 1942; niece of Arthur and Lydia Sudbrink. BS, Bowling Green State U., 1964; postgrad. in cytogenetics Kinderspital-Zurich, Switzerland, 1965. Field rep. Random House and Alfred A. Knopf Inc., Mpls., 1969-72, Ann Arbor, Mich., 1973, regional mgr., Midwest and Can., 1974-79, Can. rep., mgr., 1980-81; psychology and ednl. psychology adminstrv. editor Charles E. Merrill Pub. Co. div. Bell & Howell Corp., Columbus, Ohio, 1982-84; sales and mktg. mgr. trade products Wilson Learning Corp., Eden Prairie, Minn., 1984-85; fin. cons. Merrill Lynch Pierce Fenner & Smith, Edina, 1986-88; sr. editor Gorsuch Scarisbrick Pubs., Scottsdale, Ariz., 1988-89; regional mgr. Worth Publs., Inc. - von Holtzbrinck Pub. Grp., N.Y.C., 1988—. Lutheran. Home and Office: 3801 Mission Hills Rd Northbrook IL 60062-5729

SUDBURY, JOHN DEAN, religious foundation executive, petroleum chemist; b. Natchitoches, La., July 29, 1925; s. Herbert J. and Mary Flora S.; m. Jean Elizabeth Jung, July 18, 1947; children: John Byron, James Vernon (dec.), Linda Gail. BS, U. Tex., Austin, 1943, MA, 1947, PhD, 1949. Registered profl. engr., Okla. With Conoco Inc., various locations, 1949-83; asst. to v.p. tech. Conoco Inc., N.Y.C., 1970-72; v.p. coal research Conoco Coal Devel. Co. subs. Conoco Inc., Pitts., 1972-83; pres. Ea. European Mission & Bible Found., Houston, 1983—. Author: Oil Well Corrosion, 1956; contbr. articles to profl. jours. Mem. Ponca City (Okla.) Sch. Bd., 1965-67; trustee Okla. Christian Coll., 1968—. Served with USN, 1943-45. Recipient Frank Newman Speller award Nat. Assn. Corrosion Engrs., 1967. Mem. Am. Chem. Soc., N.Y. Acad. Scis., AAAS, Sigma Xi. Republican. Mem. Ch. of Christ. Club: Woodlands Country (Tex.). Patentee in energy field. Home: 42 Cascade Springs Pl Spring TX 77381-3101 Office: PO Box 90755 Houston TX 77290-0755

SUDDICK, PATRICK JOSEPH, defense systems company executive; b. London, Ont., Can., Sept. 27, 1923; s. Percy Edward and Eva Isobel (Jones) S.; m. Mary Agnes Walsh, July 7, 1951; children: Paul, Peter, Michael Jane Suddick Reynolds, Mark. BA in Sci., U. Toronto, 1949. With Honeywell Ltd., 1953-84; project mgr. comml. div. Honeywell Ltd., Scarborough, Ont., Can., 1953-57, asst. mgr. mil. products, 1957-58, market mgr. EDP div., 1958-65, gen. mgr. EDP div., 1965-68; v.p. EDP div. Honeywell Ltd., Willowdale, Ont., Can., 1968-70, v.p. and dir., 1970-84. Served with Can. Arty., 1942-46. Mem. Assn. Profl. Engrs. Ont., NATO Indsl. Adv. Group. Roman Catholic.

SUDHIVORASETH, NIPHON, pediatrician, allergist, immunologist; b. Bangkok, Thailand, 1940. MD, Chulalongkorn Hosp. U., Bangkok, 1966. Diplomate Am. Bd. Pediatrics, Am. Bd. Allergy and Immunology. Intern Ch. Home Hosp., Balt., 1967-68; resident in pediatrics St. Lukes Hosp., N.Y.C., 1968-69, Beth Israel Hosp., N.Y.C., 1969-70; fellow in allergy Metro Hosp., N.Y. Med. Coll., N.Y.C., 1970-72; staff Marshall Meml. Hosp., Tex., 1978—; pvt. practice. Mem. AMA, Am. Acad. Allergy, Asthma, and Immunology, Am. Acad. Pediats., Am. Coll. Allergy and Immunology. Office: PO Box 2087 705 S Grove St Marshall TX 75670-5220

SUDOR, CYNTHIA ANN, marketing and corporate sponsorship consultant; b. Hershey, Pa., June 11, 1952; d. Milan and Mary (Strahosky) Sudor. BS in Design, Drexel U., 1974. Various mktg. positions in advt., promotion and publicity Hersheypark, Hershey, Pa., 1975-85, dir. sales and mktg., 1985-90; dir. destination mktg. Hershey Entertainment and Resort Co., 1990-91, dir. corp. sponsorship, 1991; owner Cynthia A. Sudor Enterprises, Grantville, Pa., 1992—, mktg.. corp. sponsorship consulting, 1992—; freelance writer, spkr., seminar presenter. Contbr. to Apprise Mag., Harrisburg, Pa., 1994—, Funworld Mag., Alexandria, Va., 1987-90. Bd. dirs., mktg. chair Profiles In Excellence, Inc., Harrisburg, 1993—. Recipient Best Seminar award Internat. Assn. Amusement Parks and Attractions (IAAPA), Dallas, 1988. Mem. Women in Comms. Inc. Avocations: travel, writing, Ukrainian egg decorating, reading, horseback riding. Office: Cynthia A Sudor Enterprises 1205 Ridge Rd Grantville PA 17028-9135

SUDOW, THOMAS NISAN, marketing services company executive, broadcaster; b. Stevens Point, Wis., Nov. 7, 1952; s. Noah and Gertrude (Fein) S.; m. Michele Ross, Aug. 8, 1976; children: Erin, Noah, Nathaniel. Student, U. Wis., 1971, Jerusalem Inst., Israel, 1972; BA, Kent State U., 1976; MSW, Yeshiva U., N.Y.C., 1980. Tchr. Akron (Ohio) Hebrew High Sch., 1976-78; sr. assoc. Jewish Cmty. Fed. of Cleve., 1978-85; exec. dir. Am. Friends of Hebrew U., Beachwood, Ohio, 1986-88; v.p. Cleve. Coll. of Jewish Studies, Beachwood, 1988-93, Solid Sound Rec. Studio, Chgo., 1980—; pres. T.N.S. and Assocs., 1993—; exec. producer, host Sports Talk for Kids Radio Network, Cleve., 1993—; instr. Kent (Ohio) State U., 1976-78; radio host Cleve. Hockey Jour. on the Air, Tonight in Baseball, Play by Play, H.S. Hockey Game of the Week. Columnist Family Recreation mag., The Cleve. Hockey Jour. Exec. bd. dirs. Kent Sunday Sch., 1976-78; bd. dirs. Park Synagogue, Cleveland Heights, Ohio, 1986—, pres. Men's Club, 1989-91; bd. dirs. Cleve. Pops Orch.; regional program chair FJMC Conv., v.p. Gt. Lake region, 1992—, pres. cabinet, 1995—, chmn. Cleve. region, 1995-97, internat. exec. com., 1997—; founding dir. Congregation Cmty. Inst. Adult Jewish Studies, 1988-93; hon. dir. Bejing Ctr. for Jewish Studies, 1993—; mem. bd. trustees Beachwood C. of C., 1993—, v.p., 1995—. Recipient Young Leadership award, United Jewish Appeal, N.Y.C., 1976, No. Ohio Live award of Achievement Media, 1996; named Man of the Yr. Park Synagogue, Cleveland Heights, 1986; Sherman fellow Brandeis U., Waltham, Mass., 1986. Mem. NASW, Conf. Jewish Communal Svc. Workers (chmn. 1986-93), Assn. Jewish Communal Orgn. Profs. (regional chmn. 1981-85), Conf. Alternatives in Jewish Edn., Glass Inst. (chmn. 1986-87), Wahoo Club (pres.), Cleve. Indians Heavy Hitters, Nat. Soc. Fundraising Exec., Ohio Fundraising Exec. Coun., Cleve. Cavs Rebouders (bd. dirs.), Sports Media and Mktg. Assn. Ohio, Crohn's and Colts Found. of No. Ohio (bd. dirs.). Avocations: sports, photography, family, humor. Office: TNS and Assocs 3665 Tolland Rd Cleveland OH 44122-5140

SUE, ALAN KWAI KEONG, dentist; b. Honolulu, Apr. 26, 1946; s. Henry Tin Yee and Chiyoko (Ohata) S.; m. Ginger Kazue Fukushima, Mar. 19, 1972; 1 child, Dawn Marie. BS in Chemistry with honors, U. Hawaii, 1968; BS, U. Calif., San Francisco, 1972, DDS, 1972. Film editor, photographer Sta. KHVH-TV ABC, Honolulu, 1964-71; staff dentist Strong-Carter Dental Clinic, Honolulu, 1972-73; dentist Waianae Dental Clinic, Honolulu, 1972-73; pvt. practice Pearl City, Hawaii, 1973—; chief exec. officer Dental Image Specialists, Pearl City, 1975—; dental dir. Hawaii Dental Health Plan, Honolulu, 1987—; dental cons. Calif. Dental Health Plan, Tustin, 1987—, Pacific Group Med. Assn., The Queen's Health Care Plan, Honolulu, 1993—; dental cons. Pacific Group Med. Assn., 1994—; cons. Hawaii Mgmt. Alliance Assn., 1996—; bd. dirs. Kula Bay Tropical Clothing Co., Hawaiian Ind. Dental Alliance; mem. exec. bd. St. Francis Hosp., Honolulu, 1976-78, chief dept. dentistry, 1976-78; mem. expert med. panel Am. Internat. Claim Svc., 1995—. Mem. adv. bd. Health Svcs. for Sr. Citizens, 1976—; mem. West Honolulu Sub-Area Health Planning Coun., 1981-84; mem. dental task force Hawaii Statewide Health Coordinating Coun., 1980, mem. plan devel. com., 1981-84; vol. oral cancer screening program Am. Cancer Soc.; v.p. Pearl City Shopping Ctr. Merchants Assn., 1975-84, 92-93, pres., 1994—. Regents' scholar U. Calif., San Francisco, 1968-72. Fellow Pierre Fauchard Acad., Acad. Gen. Dentistry; mem. ADA, Acad. Implants and Transplants, Am. Acad. Implant Dentistry, Hawaii Dental Assn. (trustee 1978-80), Honolulu County Dental Soc. (pres. 1982), Am. Acad. and Bd. Head, Facial, Neck Pain and TMJ Orthopedics, Intertel, Internat. Platform Assn., Mensa, Porsche Club, Pantera Owners Club, Mercedes Benz Club. Democrat. Avocations: cars, tennis, photography, gardening. Office: Dental Image Specialists 850 Kam Hwy Ste 116 Pearl City HI 96782-2603

SUEDFELD, PETER, psychologist, educator; b. Budapest, Hungary, Aug. 30, 1935; emigrated to U.S., 1948, naturalized, 1952; s. Leslie John and Jolan (Eichenbaum) Field; m. Gabrielle Debra Guterman, June 11, 1961 (div. 1980); children: Michael Thomas, Joanne Ruth, David Lee; m. Phyllis Jean Johnson, Oct. 19, 1991. Student, U. Philippines, 1956-57; B.A., Queens Coll., 1960; M.A., Princeton U., 1962, Ph.D., 1963. Research assoc. Princeton U.; lectr. Trenton State Coll., 1963-64; vis. asst. prof. psychology U. Ill., 1964-65; asst. prof. psychology Univ. Coll. Rutgers U., 1965-67, assoc. prof., 1967-71, prof., 1971-72, chmn. dept., 1967-72; prof. psychology U. B.C., Vancouver, 1972—; head dept. U. B.C., 1972-84, dean faculty grad. studies, 1984-90; cons. in field; chmn. Can. Antarctic Rsch. Program. Author: Restricted Environmental Stimulation: Research and Clinical Applications, 1980; editor: Attitude Change: The Competing Views, 1971, Personality Theory and Information Processing, 1971, The Behavioral Basis of Design, 1976, Psychology and Torture, 1990, Restricted Environmental Stimulation: Theoretical and Empirical Developments in Flotation REST, 1990, Psychology and Social Policy, 1991; editor Jour. Applied Social Psychology, 1975-82; assoc. editor Environment and Behavior, 1992—; contbr. articles to profl. jours. Served with U.S. Army, 1955-58. Recipient Antarctica svc. medal, 1994, Donald O. Hebb award, 1996; grantee NIMH, 1970-72, Can. Coun., 1973—, Soc. Sci. Rsch. Coun. Can., 1973—, Nat. Rsch. Coun. Can., 1973-90, NIH, 1980-84. Fellow Royal Soc. Can., Can. Psychol. Assn. (pres.-elect 1997), Am. Psychol. Assn., Am. Psychol. Soc., Acad. Behavioral Medicine Research, Soc. Behavioral Medicine, N.Y. Acad. Scis.; mem. Soc. Exptl. Social Psychology, Phi Beta Kappa, Sigma Xi. Office: U BC, Dept Psychology, Vancouver, BC Canada V6T 1Z4

SUELTENFUSS, SISTER ELIZABETH ANNE, academic administrator; b. San Antonio, Apr. 14, 1921; d. Edward L. and Elizabeth (Amrein) S. BA in Botany and Zoology, Our Lady of Lake Coll., San Antonio, 1944; MS in Biology, U. Notre Dame, 1961, PhD, 1963. Joined Sisters of Divine Providence, Roman Cath. Ch., 1939; tchr. high schs. Okla. and La., 1942-49; mem. summer faculty Our Lady of Lake U. (formerly coll.), San Antonio, 1941-49, mem. full-time faculty, 1949-59, chmn. biology dept., 1963-73, pres., 1978-97; mem. adminstrv. staff to superior gen. Congregation Divine Providence, 1973-77. Author articles in field. Bd. dirs. Am. Cancer Soc., San Antonio chpt. ARC, Mind Sci. Found., YWCA, Alamo Pub. Telecom. Bd., S.W. Rsch. Found., I Have a Dream Found., Inst. Ednl. Leadership, Trim and Swim, San Antonio Edn. Partnership; bd. dirs., past chairperson San Antonio Pub. Libr. Recipient Achievement and Leadership awards U. Notre Dame, 1979, Svc. to Community award, 1991, Headliner award Women in Comms., 1980, Good Neighbor award NCCJ, 1982, Brotherhood award, 1992, Today's Woman award San Antonio Light, 1982, Outstanding Women award San Antonio Express-News, 1983, Spirit of Am. Woman award J.C. Penney, 1992, Lifetime Achievement award, 1993, Svc. to Edn. awrd Ford Found., 1993; named to San Antonio Women's Hall of Fame, 1985. Mem. AAUP, AAUW, San Antonio 100 Tex. Women's Forum, San Antonio Women's C. of C., Hispanic Assn. Colls. and Univs., Greater San Antonio C. of C. (past vice chmn.), San Antonio Coun. Pres. (past pres.), San Antonio Women's Hall of Fame (past pres.). Home and Office: Our Lady of the Lake U Office of Pres 411 SW 24th St San Antonio TX 78207-4689

SUEN, CHING YEE, computer scientist and educator, researcher; b. Chung Shan, Kwang Tung, China, Oct. 14, 1942; s. Stephen and Sin (Kan) S; m. Sheung Ling Chan, May 12, 1970; children: Karwa, Karnon. BSc in Engring., U. Hong Kong, 1966, MSc in Engring., 1968; M.A.Sc., U. B.C., 1970, PhD, 1972. Asst. prof. computer sci. Concordia U., Montreal, Can., 1972-76, assoc. prof., 1976-79, prof., 1979, chmn., 1980-84, dir. Centre for Pattern Recognition and Machine Intelligence, 1988—, assoc. dean faculty engring. and computer sci., 1993—; vis. scientist Rsch. Lab. of Electronics, MIT, Cambridge, 1975, 76, 78-79; invited prof. Ecole Polytechnique Fédérale de Lausanne, Switzerland, 1979, Institut de Recherche d'Informatique et d'Automatique, Rocquencourt, France, 1976, 78, 79; co-founder, co-chmn. Internat. Conf. on Document Analysis and Recognition, St.-Malo, France, 1991, Tsukuba Sci. City, Japan, 1993, chmn., Montreal, Can., 1995; founder, chmn. Internat. Workshop on Frontiers in Handwriting Recognition, Montreal, 1990; organizer numerous confs. Author: Computational Analysis of Mandarin, 1979, Computational Studies of the Most Frequent Chinese Words and Sounds, 1986, (with Z.C. Li, T.D. Bui, Y.Y. Tang) Computer Transformation of Digital Images and Patterns, 1989; editor: (with R. De Mori) Computer Analysis and Perception Vol. 1, Visual Signals, 1982, Computer Analysis and Perception Vol. 2, Auditory Signals, 1982, (with R. De Mori) New Systems and Architectures for Automatic Speech Recognition and Synthesis, 1985, Computational Studies of the Most Frequent Chinese Words and Sounds, 1986, (with R. Plamondon and M.L. Simner) Computer Recognition and Human Production of Handwriting, 1989, Frontiers in Handwriting Recognition, 1990, Operating Expert System Applications in Canada, 1992, (with P.S.P. Wang) Thinning Methodologies for Pattern Recognition, 1994; assoc. editor Signal Processing, 1979—, Pattern Recognition Letters, 1982—, Pattern Recognition, 1983—, IEEE Transactions on Pattern Analysis and Machine Intelligence, 1986-89, Internat. Jour. Pattern Recognition and Artificial Intelligence, 1986—; founder, editor-in-chief Computer Processing of Chinese and Oriental Langs., 1982-93; adviser IEEE Transactions on Pattern Analysis and Machine Intelligence, 1989—; author more than 300 publs.; patentee in field. Recipient award Fedn. Chinese Can. Profls., 1988; Swire scholar U. Hong Kong, 1967, ITAC/NSERC award Info. Tech. Assn. Can. and Natural Scis. and Engring. Rsch. Coun. Can., 1992. Fellow IEEE (advisor Computer Soc.), Royal Soc. Can., Internat. Assn. for Pattern Recognition (gov.); mem. Chinese Lang. Computer Soc. (v.p. 1987-90, pres. 1990-93, award 1988), Can. Image Processing and Pattern Recognition Soc. (pres. 1984-90, award 1997). Office: Concordia U Dept Computer Sci, 1455 Maisonneuve W Ste GM-606, Montreal, PQ Canada H3G 1M8

SUEN, JAMES YEE, otolaryngologist, educator; b. Dermott, Ark., Oct. 9, 1940; s. Yee Gow and Mary (Chaing) S.; m. Karen Hannahs; children: Brent, Tiffany, Bradley, Brennan. BA in Zoology, U. Tex., 1962; BS, MD, U. Ark., 1966. Diplomate Am. Bd. Otolaryngology. Rotating intern San Francisco Gen. Hosp., 1966-67; resident in gen. surgery U. Ark. Med. Ctr., Little Rock, 1969-70, resident in otolaryngology, 1970-73; advanced sr. fellow M.D. Anderson Hosp. and Tumor Inst., Houston, 1973-74, faculty assoc., 1974; asst. prof. U. Ark. Coll. Medicine, Little Rock, 1974-76, assoc. prof., 1976-78, prof. otolaryngology, 1978—, chief div. otolaryngology, 1974-78, chmn. dept. otolaryngology and head and neck surgery, 1978—. Author, editor: Cancer of the Head and Neck, 1981, 3d edit., 1996, Emergencies in Otolaryngology, 1986. Capt. USAF, 1967-69. Recipient Disting. Alumnus award U. Tex., M.D. Anderson Cancer Ctr., 1995; named Chinese Man of Yr., Chinese Soc. Ark., 1983, Disting. Citizen of Yr. Gov. Ark., 1991. Fellow ACS, Am. Acad. Otolaryngology and Head and Neck Surgery, Am. Soc. Head and Neck Surgery (pres. 1993-94, coun. 1988-92); mem. Soc. Univ. Otolaryngologists. Methodist. Avocation: sculpturing. Office: U Ark Coll Medicine 4301 W Markham St Little Rock AR 72205-7101

SUER, MARVIN DAVID, architecture, consultant; b. Phila., Apr. 4, 1923; m. Gertrude Litvin, 1947; children: Marsha Suer Clark, Sharon, Deborah Suer Berman. BArch, U. Pa., 1950. Registered architect, N.J., Pa. Ptnr. Suer & Livingston, 1961-62, Suer, Livingston & Demas, 1962-69; dir. tech. prodn. Eshbach, Pullinger, Stevens & Bruder, Phila., 1969-74; assoc. Ballinger, Phila., 1974-79, Bartley Long Mirenda, Phila., 1979-85, S.T. Hudson Internat., Phila., 1986-95; archtl. cons., 1996—. Archtl. works include State Hosp. for Crippled Children addition, 1964, Huey Elem. Sch., Phila., 1964, Dist. No. 4 Health Ctr., Phila., 1967, Stephen Smith Towers, 1969, Foxchase Br. Libr., 1969. Chmn. bd. trustees Phila. Found. for Architecture, 1980-81. With C.E., AUS, 1943-46. Fellow AIA (pres. Phila. chpt. 1968, 125th Yr. citation 1982); mem. Tau Sigma Delta. Home: 305 Overlook Ave Willow Grove PA 19090-2806

SUESS, JAMES FRANCIS, clinical psychologist; b. Evanston, Ill., Aug. 8, 1950; s. James Francis and Rae Love (Miller) S.; m. Linda Grace Powell, July 31, 1976; 1 child, Misty Lynne. BS, U. So. Miss., 1974, MS, 1978, PhD, 1982. Lic. psychologist, N.Y., Ala.; diplomate Am. Bd. Profl. Psychology, Am. Bd. Med. Psychotherapists, Profl. Assn. Custody Evaluators, Am. Coll. Forensic Examiners, Am. Bd. Forensic Medicine. Assoc. psychologist State of Miss., Ellisville, 1978-80; clin. psychologist SUNY Med. Sch./Erie County Med. Ctr., Buffalo, 1982-84, supervisiong clin. psychologist, 1984-87, assoc. dir., 1987—; dir. practica SUNY Med. Sch., 1982-90, faculty counsel, 1988—; cons. Buffalo Dept. Social Svcs., 1985—; mem. spkrs. bur. Erie Alliance for Mentally Ill, 1986—; vis. prof. U. Guadalajara Sch. Medicine, 1985—; clin. dir. Stickney Adolescent Ctr. Mobile Met. Hosp. Ctr., 1993-97; chmn., dir. Physicians' Psychiat. Clinic, 1997—. Author: Annotated Bibliography of Sex Roles, 1972, Personality Disorder and Self Psychology, 1991; contbr. articles to refereed jours. including Perceptual and Motor Skills, Jour. Clin. and Consulting Psychology, Am. Annals of Deaf. With USAR, 1969-76. Fellow Am. Orthopsychiat. Assn., Soc. Personality Assessment; mem. Am. Psychol. Assn. Home: 407 Stillwood Ln Mobile AL 36608-5847 Office: Physicians Psychiat Clinic 10 N Mobile St Mobile AL 36607-3121

SUESS, JAMES FRANCIS, retired psychiatry educator; b. Rock Island, Ill., Nov. 27, 1919; s. Joseph John and Elizabeth Ida (Dalton) S.; m. Rae Love Miller, Mar. 24, 1946; children: Rae Anne, James Francis, John Randall. B Med. Sci., Northwestern U., 1950, MD, 1952; postgrad., Coll.

Physicians and Surgeons, Columbia U. and N.Y. Psychiat. Inst., 1958. Diplomate Am. Bd. Psychiatry and Neurology (examiner various times). Intern USPHS Hosp., New Orleans, 1952-53; resident in psychiatry Warren (Pa.) State Hosp., 1953-56, clin. dir., 1956-62; asst. prof. psychiatry U. Miss. Med. Sch., Jackson, 1962-65, assoc. prof., 1965-69, prof., 1969-82; prof. emeritus, 1982—, chmn. dept., 1967-69, 73-75, asst. dean, 1978-82; assoc. chief staff for edn. VA Med. Ctr., Jackson, 1978-82; vis. prof. Inst. Psychiatry, London, 1977, 83; referee editl. bd. Am. Jour. Psychiatry, Washington. Contbr. articles to med. jours., including Am. Jour. Psychiatry, Jour. Med. Edn., chpts. to books. Capt. U.S. Army, 1941-45. Fellow Am. Psychiat. Assn., So. Psychiat. Assn. (edn. com. 1973-77), Miss. Psychiat. Assn. (pres. 1968-69); mem. Am. Assn. Dirs. Psychiat. Tng. (a founder, exec. bd. 1969-71). Avocations: piano, organ, golf, duplicate bridge. Home: 1415 Radcliffe St Jackson MS 39211-4824

SUFLAS, STEVEN WILLIAM, lawyer; b. Camden, N.J., Oct. 7, 1951; s. William V. and Dorothy (Stafre) S.; m. Rochelle B. Volin, Apr. 15, 1978; children: Allison, Rebecca, Whitney. BA, Davidson Coll., 1973; JD with honors, U. N.C., 1976. Bar: N.J. 1976, Pa. 1978, U.S. Dist. Ct. N.J., U.S. Ct. Appeals (3d cir.). Field atty. NLRB, Phila., 1976-80; assoc. Archer & Greiner P.C., Haddonfield, N.J., 1980-86, ptnr., 1986—. Mem. ABA, Pa. Bar Assn., Phila. Bar Assn., N.J. Bar Assn. (exec. com. labor and employment law sect. 1985—, officer 1993—), Order of Coif, Omicron Delta Kappa. Office: Archer & Greiner PC 1 Centennial Sq Haddonfield NJ 08033-2328

SUGAR, PETER FRIGYES, historian; b. Budapest, Hungary, Jan. 5, 1919; s. Peter S. and Margit (Pongor) S.; m. Sally Bortz, June 18, 1955; children: Steven P., Klari A., Karen L. B.A., CCNY, 1954; M.A., Princeton, U., 1956, Ph.D., 1959. Instr. history Princeton U., 1957-59; asst. prof. history U. Wash., Seattle, 1959-63; assoc. prof. U. Wash., 1963-69, prof., 1969-89, now prof. history emeritus; assoc. dir. U. Wash. (Inst. Comparative and Foreign Area Studies.). Author: The Industrilization of Bosnia-Hercegovina, 1878-1919, 1963, Southeastern Europe under Ottoman Rule, 1354-1804, 1977, A History of Hungary, 1990, Eastern European Nationalism in the Twentieth Century, 1995, Nationality and Society in the Ottoman and Habsburg Europe, 1997, and others. Guggenheim Found. fellow, 1964-65; Woodrow Wilson fellow, 1954-55; Fulbright fellow, 1984. Mem. Am. Hist. Assn., Am. Assn. Advancement of Slavic Studies, Western Slavic Assn., Am. Assn. Study of Hungarian History. Home: 11737 12th Ave NE Seattle WA 98125-5007 Office: U Wash Dept History Seattle WA 98195

SUGAR, SANDRA LEE, art consultant; b. Balt., May 18, 1942; d. Harry S. and Edith Sarah (Levin) Pomerantz; children: Gary Lee, Terry Lynn. BS in Edn. and English, Towson State U., 1965; MS in Edn. and Applied Behavioral Scis., Johns Hopkins U., 1986. Chairperson arts exhibit Balt. Arts Festival, 1979; med. interviewer Johns Hopkins Sch. of Hygiene, Balt., 1980-82; copy writer Concepts & Communications, Balt., 1984; instr. art history and world cultures Catonsville Community Coll., Balt., 1981-85; instr. English Community Coll. of Balt., 1981-85; instr. English and math. Info. Processing Tng. Ctr., Balt., 1985; info. specialist Info. of Md. New Directions for Women, Balt., 1986; trainer, job developer Working Solutions, Balt., 1987-88; art gallery dir. Renaissance Fine Arts Gallery, Bethesda, Md., 1988-93; art cons. Bethesda, 1994—; judge nat. high sch. sci. fiction contests. One-woman show, Bethesda, Md., 1997; exhibited in group shows, 1979, 80; author poetry collection; editor mus. guides' newsletter Guidelines, 1978; arts editor poetry jour., 1997; represented by Georgetown Art Gallery, 1997. Docent Balt. Mus. of Art, 1973-86; festival coordinator Internat. Brass Quintet Festival, Balt., 1986; chairperson spl. events Balt. PTA, 1978-82; bd. dirs. Citizens Planning and Housing Assn., Balt., 1980-82; mem. women's com., ctr. stage hand Balt. Ballet, 1979-84, Balt. Symphony, 1979-80. Recipient F.J. Bamberger scholarship, Johns Hopkins U., 1985, Mayoral Vol. of Yr. award Balt. Mus. Art, 1979.

SUGARBAKER, EVAN R., nuclear science research administrator; b. Mineola, N.Y., Nov. 17, 1949; married, 1985; 1 child. BA, Kalamazoo Coll., 1971; PhD in Physics, U. Mich., 1976. Rsch. assoc. nuclear structural rsch. lab. U. Rochester (N.Y.), 1976-78; vis. asst. prof. physics U. Colo., 1978-80; asst. prof. physics Ohio State U., Columbus, 1981-86, assoc. prof. physics, 1986-94, prof. physics, 1994—; co-prin. investigator NSF grant, 1981-88, 95—, prin. investigator, 1988-95; bd. dirs. Los Alamos Meson Physics Facility Users Group, Inc., 1990-92; cons. Los Alamos Nat. Lab., 1991-94. Mem. AAAS, Am. Phys. Soc., Am. Assn. Physics Tchrs. Office: Dept Physics Ohio State U 174 W 18th Ave Columbus OH 43210-1106

SUGARMAN, ALAN WILLIAM, educational administrator; b. Boston, Sept. 26, 1924; s. Henry and Dorothy (Adams) S.; m. Alice Mulhall, 1974; children: Michael, Susan, Ellen, William, Jane, James. BS, Boston U., 1948; MA, Columbia U., 1949, EdD, 1967; postgrad., SUNY, Albany, 1954-56. Entrance examiner Boston U., 1947-48; tchr. Public Schs. Hudson, N.Y., 1950-54; prin. jr. high sch. Public Schs. Hudson, 1954-56, prin. sr. high sch., 1956-61; prin. Spring Valley (N.Y.) Sr. High Sch., 1961-67; dir. secondary edn. Ramapo Central Sch. Dist. No. 2, Spring Valley, 1967-69; asst. supt. instrn. Ramapo Central Sch. Dist. No. 2, 1969-73; prin. Ramapo Sr. High Sch., Spring Valley, 1969; supt. schs. Connetquot Central Sch. Dist. Islip, Bohemia, N.Y., 1973-80, Ft. Lee (N.J.) Sch. Dist., 1980—; adj. prof. N.Y. U., N.Y.C., U. P.R., Rio Piedras, Hofstra U., 1967—; prof. Fordham U., N.Y.C., 1969. Athletic dir. East River Day Camp, N.Y.C., summer 1949; group worker St. John's Guild, summer 1950; asst. dir. Tenn. Work Camp, Unitarian Service Com., summer 1951; dir. spl. activities Hudson Youth Bur., Hudson, N.Y., summer 1952; exec. dir. Jewish Community Center, Hudson, 1953-56; chmn. vis. coms. Middle States Commn. Colls. and Secondary Schs., 1958-76; chmn. county leadership tng. com., mem. Rockland County exec. council Boy Scouts Am., 1956; bd. dirs. Bergen County Red Cross; corr. sec. Rockland County Negro Scholarship Fund, Inc.; pres. Spring Valley Youth Activities Com., 1956-58; bd. dirs., past campaign co-chmn. Greater Hudson Community Chest; bd. dirs., 2d v.p. Hudson Youth Recreation Center, 1958-61; bd. dirs. Rockland County br. Am. Cancer Soc., 1958-61, Columbia Meml. Hosp., 1959-61; chmn. Town of Islip Health Usage Com., 1973; bd. dirs. Am. Heart Assn. N.J. affiliate, 1993—. Served with AUS, 1944-46, ETO. Recipient Disting. Svc. award Hudson Jr. C. of C., 1960, Ft. Lee Citizen of Yr. award VFW, Bergen County Citizen of Yr. award VFW, 1989, N.J. State Elks Alcohol and Drug Prevention award, 1989, St. Michael's award, 1992, PBA Silver Life Card award, 1993, EIA award Greek Orthodox Archdiocese, 1993; named Adminstr. of Yr., Fordham U., 1990, B'nai Brith Man of Yr., 1995. Mem. Nat. Honor Soc. Secondary Schs. (hon.), Nat. PTA (hon. life), Am. Assn. Sch. Adminstrs., Assn. Supervision and Curriculum Devel., Nat. Sch. Public Relations Assn., Assn. Sch. Bus. Ofcls., Nat. Soc. Study Edn., DAV, VFW, Jewish War Vets., Rotary (bd. dirs.), Phi Delta Kappa (Adminstr. of Yr. award 1990), Kappa Delta Pi, Pi Gamma Mu. Jewish (bd. edn.). Home: Shelter Bay Club 1225 River Rd Apt 7B Edgewater NJ 07020-1461 Office: 255 Whiteman St Fort Lee NJ 07024-5629

SUGARMAN, IRWIN J., lawyer; b. Dayton, Ohio, June 17, 1943; s. Nathan and Esther (Goldstein) S.; 1 child, Alexander David Sugarman. BA, Rutgers U., New Brunswick, N.J., 1965; JD, Rutgers U., Newark, 1968. Bar: N.Y. 1968. Law clk. to Judge Edmund Palmieri U.S. Dist. Ct. for So. Dist. N.Y., N.Y.C., 1968-69; assoc. Debevoise Plimpton Lyons & Gates, N.Y.C., 1969-79; ptnr. Schulte Roth & Zabel, N.Y.C., 1979—. Bd. dirs. Santa Fe Opera, 1989-94. Office: Schulte Roth & Zabel 900 3rd Ave New York NY 10022-4728

SUGARMAN, JULE M., children's services consultant, former public administrator; b. Cin., Sept. 23, 1927; s. Melville Harty and Rachel Wolf (Meyer) S.; m. Sheila Mary Shanley, May 20, 1956 (dec.); children: Christopher, Maryanne, Jason, James; m. Candace Sullivan, Apr. 2, 1989. Student, Western Res. U., 1945-46; A.B. with highest distinction, Am. U., 1951. Dir. Head Start, 1965-69; adminstr. Human Resources Adminstrn., N.Y.C., 1970-73; chief adminstrv. officer City of Atlanta, 1974-76; vice chmn. CSC, Washington, 1977-78; dep. dir. Office Personnel Mgmt., 1979-81; mng. dir. Human Service Info. Ctr., 1981-83; v.p. Hahnemann U., 1983-86; sec. Wash. State Dept. Social and Health Services, 1986-89; exec. dir. Spl. Olympics Internat., Washington, 1989-91; chmn. Ctr. on Effective Svcs. for Children, Washington, 1991—. Served with U.S. Army, 1946-48. Recipient Meritorious Service award Dept. State, 1963, Alumni Service award Am. U., 1977, Disting. Pub. Svc. award Nat. Acad. Pub. Adminstrn., 1988. Home: 2555 Pennsylvania Ave NW Washington DC 20037-1613 Office: PO Box 27412 Washington DC 20038-7412

SUGARMAN, MATTHEW S., historic site adminstrator. Park ranger trainee Golden Gate Area Calif. State Parks, 1972, patrol resource ranger Montane Area, 1972-76, supervising ranger campground ops. Pt. Mugu Area, 1976-77, from tng. supervisor to supervising ranger Santa Monica Mtn., 1977-81, supervising ranger vis. svcs. Klamath Dist. South Sector, 1981-85; park supt. Gold Rush Dist. Marshall Gold Discovery, State Hist. Park, 1985—. Mem. El Dorado County Sesquicentennial Commn. Mem. El Dorado County Recreation Profls., El Dorado County Law Enforcement Adminstrs., El Dorado County C. of C. (bd. dirs.). Office: Marshall Gold Discovery State Hist Pk PO Box 265 Coloma CA 95613-0265 also: care Marshall Gold Discovery PO Box 265 Coloma CA 95613-0265

SUGARMAN, MICHAEL, physician, rheumatologist; b. Galveston, Tex., May 26, 1945; s. Harold and Amelia (Hirsch) S.; m. Hilda Roberta Krug, Aug. 26, 1967; children: Jason, Steven. BS, U. Calif., Berkeley, 1966; MD, U. Calif., San Francisco, 1970. Diplomate Am. Coll. Physicians, Am. Coll. Rheumatology. Rheumatologist Fullerton Internal Medicine Ctr., Fullerton, Calif., 1976—. Fellow Am. Coll. Rheumatology, Orange County Rheumatism Soc.; mem. AMA, Orange County Med. Assn. Office: St Jude Heritage Med Group 433 W Bastanchury Rd Fullerton CA 92835-3404

SUGARMAN, MYRON GEORGE, lawyer; b. San Francisco, Nov. 7, 1942; s. Irving Carden and Jane Hortense (Weingarten) S.; m. Cheryl Ann Struble, June 8, 1968 (div. 1993); children: Andrew, Amy, Adam; m. Cynthia Wilson Woods, Apr. 16, 1994. BS, U. Calif., Berkeley, 1964, JD, 1967. Assoc. Cooley, Godward LLP, San Francisco, 1972-77, ptnr., 1977—. Served to capt. U.S. Army, 1968-71. Fellow Am. Coll. Trust and Estate Counsel, Am. Coll. Tax Counsel, Am. Bar Found.; mem. U. Calif. Alumni Assn. (bd. dirs. 1985-88), San Francisco Tax Club (pres. 1990), San Francisco Grid Club. Avocations: skiing, tennis. Office: Cooley Godward LLP 1 Maritime Plz San Francisco CA 94111-3404

SUGARMAN, PAUL RONALD, lawyer, educator, academic administrator; b. Boston, Dec. 14, 1931; m. Susan J. Sugarman; children: Amy J., Ellen J. AA, Boston U., 1951, JD cum laude (Law Week award 1954, asso. editor law rev. 1952-54), 1954; LLD (hon.), Suffolk U., 1989. Bar: Mass. 1954, U.S. Supreme Ct. 1965. Ptnr. Sugarman & Sugarman, Boston, 1967-90, 94—; prof. law, dean Suffolk U. Law Sch., Boston, 1990-94; mem. Atty. Gen. Mass. Hwy. Law Study Commn., 1965, Mass. Gov.'s Select Com. on Jud. Needs, 1976; bd. bar overseers Supreme Jud. Ct., 1984-88, chmn., 1985-88; advocate Am. Bd. Trial Advocates; spl. master, commr. Boston Mcpl. Ct. Report Supreme Jud. Ct. of Mass., 1990. Trustee Mass. Bar Found., 1980-81. Served as officer AUS, 1955-58. Recipient Courageous Adv. award, Mass. Acad. Trial Attys., 1984, William O. Douglas First Amendment Freedom award, Anti-Defamation League, 1986, Silver Shingle award for svc. to legal profession Boston U. Sch. Law, 1989, Jurisprudence award Am. Orgn. for Rehab. through Tng. Fedn., 1991, Civil Justice award Am. Bd. trial Adv., 1993. Fellow Am. Coll. Trial Lawyers, Am. Bar Found., Mass. Bar Found., Internat. Soc. Barristers; mem. Am. Bar Assn., Mass. Bar Assn. (pres. 1976-77, chmn. com. on recall of ret. judges 1982-86, Gold Medal award 1991), Am. Trial Lawyers Assn. (gov. 1966-68, pres. Mass. chpt. 1968-70), Boston Bar Assn., Boston U. Sch. Law Alumni Assn. (pres. 1979-80). Office: Sugarman and Sugarman PC One Beacon St Boston MA 02108

SUGARMAN, ROBERT GARY, lawyer; b. Bronx, N.Y., Sept. 3, 1939; s. Eugene Leonard and Frances (Solomon) S.; m. Brenda Harrison, Sept. 8, 1963 (div. 1984); children: Dana, Alison; m. Surie Rudoff, June 16, 1985; children: Amanda, Jason. BA, Yale U., 1960, LLB, 1963. Bar: N.Y. 1963, Fla. 1963, U.S. Supreme Ct. 1971, U.S. Dist. Ct. (so. dist.) N.Y. 1966, U.S. Dist. Ct. (ea. dist.) N.Y. 1982, U.S. Ct. Appeals (2d cir.) 1970, U.S. Ct. Appeals (10th cir.) 1971. Assoc. Sugarman, Kuttner & Fuss, N.Y.C., 1966, Sullivan & Cromwell, N.Y.C., 1966-72; assoc. Weil, Gotshal & Manges, N.Y.C., 1972-75, ptnr., 1975—. Author: (with others) Litigation Strategy and Tactics , 1979, Deposition Strategy Law and Forms, 1980, Masters of Trial Practice, 1988; contbr. articles on intellectual property law to profl. jours. Assoc. counsel N.Y. State Constl. Conv., Albany, N.Y., 1967; pres. Hillel of N.Y., 1986-88. Served to capt. U.S. Army, 1963-65. Fellow Am. Coll. Trial Lawyers; mem. Assn. of Bar of City of N.Y. (chmn. comm. and media law com. 1989-92, mem. copyright com. 1996—), B'nai Brith (internat. bd. govs. 1975-85), Anti-Defamation League (nat. commn. 1981—, nat. exec. com. 1988—, vice-chmn. 1990-92, chmn. intergroup rels. com. 1992-94, chmn. civil rights com. 1994—). Democrat. Jewish. Office: Weil Gotshal & Manges 767 5th Ave New York NY 10153-0001

SUGARMAN, SAMUEL LOUIS, retired oil transportation and trading company executive, horse breeder; b. Montague, Mass., Apr. 18, 1927; s. Julius William and Minnie S.; m. Marlene Rodenz, Mar. 3, 1958; children—Jord Ann, Shawn, Jay Scott, Robin. B.S., U.S. Merchant Marine Acad., 1947; postgrad., N.Y. State Sch. Indsl. and Labor Relations, Cornell U., 1950; M.B.A. with distinction, Harvard U., 1953. Dir. market research and spl. projects Gulf Oil U.S., Houston, 1968-70; mgr. new venture investments Gulf Oil Corp., Pitts., 1972-74; exec. v.p. Gulf Trading & Transp. Co., Pitts., 1974-86; sr. v.p. Gulf Exploration and Prodn. Co., Houston; pres. Gulf Overseas Commodities Ltd. Served with USNR, 1953-55.

SUGERMAN, ABRAHAM ARTHUR, psychiatrist; b. Dublin, Ireland, Jan. 20, 1929; came to U.S., 1958, naturalized, 1963; s. Hyman and Anne (Goldstone) S.; m. Ruth Nerissa Alexander, June 5, 1960; children: Jeremy, Michael, Adam, Rebecca. BA, Trinity Coll., Dublin, 1950, MB, BChir, BA in Obstetrics, 1952; DSc, SUNY, Bklyn., 1962. Diplomate Am. Bd. Psychiatry and Neurology. House officer Meath Hosp., Dublin, 1952-53, St. Nicholas Hosp., London, 1953-54; sr. house physician Brook Gen. Hosp., London, 1954; registrar in psychiatry Kingsway Hosp. Derby and Kings Coll. Med. Sch., Newcastle, Eng., 1955-58; clin. psychiatrist Trenton (N.J.) Psychiat. Hosp., 1958-59; cons. psychiatry, 1964-80; rsch. fellow Downstate Med. Ctr., Bklyn., 1959-61; chief investigative psychiatry sect. N.J. Bur. Rsch., Princeton, 1961-73; cons. rsch., assoc. psychiatrist Carrier Clinic, Belle Mead, N.J., 1968-72, 78-90, dir. outpatient svcs., 1972-74, 77-78, med. dir., 1974-77; dir. rsch. Carrier Found., Belle Mead, N.J., 1972-79; med. dir. addiction recovery svcs. Cmty. Mental Health Ctr., U. Medicine and Dentistry of N.J., Piscataway, 1990-93; cons. psychiatry Med. Ctr., Princeton, N.J., 1972—; clin. assoc. prof. psychiatry Rutgers Med. Sch. (now Robert Wood Johnson Med. Sch.), New Brunswick, N.J., 1972-78, clin. prof., 1978—; vis. prof. Rutgers Ctr. for Alcohol Studies, 1977-83, Hahnemann Med. Coll., Phila., 1978-93; contbg. faculty Grad. Sch. Applied and Profl. Psychology, Rutgers U., 1974-78. Editor: (with Ralph E. Tarter) Alcoholism: Interdisciplinary Approaches to an Enduring Problem, 1976, Expanding Dimensions of Consciousness, 1978; contbr. articles to profl. jours. Bd. dirs. N.J. Mental Health R & D Fund, Princeton, 1968-74; v.p. Jewish Family Svc., Trenton, 1972-78; 1st v.p. Trenton Hebrew Acad., 1972-75. Fellow AAAS, Am. Psychiat. Assn., Am. Coll. Neuropsychopharmacology, Am. Coll. Clin. Pharmacology, Am. Coll. Psychiatrists, Royal Coll. Psychiatrists; mem. AMA, Soc. Biol. Psychiatry, Assn. Rsch. Nervous and Mental Diseases, Ea. Psychol. Assn., Am. Soc. Addiction Medicine. Office: 100 Herrontown Rd Princeton NJ 08540-2927

SUGG, JOHN LOGAN (JACK SUGG), advertising executive; b. Hillsboro, Ill., June 2, 1914; s. Norman J. and Clythera (McDavid) S.; m. Jean Ellen Morrison, Feb. 7, 1942; children: Michael L., Patrick M., Terry Jean. B.A., Lake Forest Coll., 1938. Engaged in newspaper work, 1938-41; with Cole & Weber, Inc., 1946—, pres., 1968-72, chmn. bd., 1972-76, chmn. exec. com., 1976-80; ret., 1981; pres. Assoc. Oreg. Industries, 1968-69. Bd. dirs. Emanuel Med. Center Found.; chmn. bd. dirs. Portland Better Bus. Bur., 1975—. Served to lt. comdr. USN, 1941-45. Named Oreg. Advt. Man of Year, 1965. Mem. Portland C. of C. (dir.), Am. Assn. Advt. Agys. (chmn. Western region 1970-71). Clubs: Arlington (pres. 1975—), Multnomah Athletic, Portland Golf. Home: 2415 SW Timberline Dr Portland OR 97225-4129 *When young people seek my advice concerning careers in the advertising agency field, this is what I tell them: "Advertising can be rich and rewarding for one who has an understanding of human motivation, basic skills in communication, capacity for plain hard work and the ability to shrug off disappointment. But if you're not confident that you can achieve management status by age 40, go into another field. Advertising's daily firing-line is for the young and venturesome.".*

SUGG, ROBERT PERKINS, former state supreme court justice; b. Eupora, Miss., Feb. 21, 1916; s. Amos Watson and Virgie Christian (Cooper) S.; m. Elizabeth Lorraine Carroll, June 23, 1940; children: Robert Perkins, Charles William, John David. Student, Wood Jr. Coll., 1933-34, Miss. State U., 1935-37, Jackson Sch. Law, 1939-40. Bar: Miss. Practice law, 1940-51, chancery judge, 1951-71; asso. justice Miss. Supreme Ct., 1971-83; county pros. atty. Webster County, Miss., 1949-50; spl. chancery judge Hinds, Scott and Jasper counties, Miss., 1989, sr. judge, 1990—; mem. adv. council Nat. Ctr. for State Cts., 1973-79. Bd. govs. Miss. Jud. Coll., 1973-80; literacy missions assoc. Home Mission Bd. of So. Bapt. Conv., 1983—. Served with USAAF, 1942-43. Named Outstanding Citizen, Eupora Jr. C. of C., 1970, Alumnus of Year, Wood Jr. Coll., 1973; recipient Service to Humanity award Miss. Coll., 1976, Literacy Missions Svc. award Home Mission Bd. of So. Bapt. Conv., 1995. Mem. Miss. State Bar, Am. Judicature Soc., CAP (Miss. Wing, squadron comdr. 1974-76), Am. Legion (post comdr. 1950). Democrat. Baptist (chmn. bd. deacons 1964). Home: 1067 Meadow Heights Dr Jackson MS 39206-6021

SUGGARS, CANDICE LOUISE, special education educator; b. Pitts., Jan. 16, 1949; d. Albert Abraham and Patricia Louise (Stepp) S. BS in Elem. Edn., W.Va. U., 1972; MS in Spl. Edn., Johns Hopkins U., 1979, Cert. Advanced Studies, 1986. Clin. supr./head tchr. The Kennedy Krieger Inst., Balt., 1974-80, inpatient coord., 1980-83, ednl. evaluator, 1980-85, spl. educator/pediatric rehab. team, 1985-86; spl. edn. cons. Charleston County (S.C.) Sch. Dist., 1986-90, spl. edn. pre-sch. tchr., 1990-95; pvt. tutor children with spl. needs and disabilities, Charleston, 1995—; spl. needs cons. U. S.C., 1996—; mem. adv. bd. S.C. Accelerated Schs. Project, Charleston, 1994-95. Contbg. author: Disadvantaged Pre-School Child, 1979, Leisure Education for the Handicapped Curriculum, 1984. Exhibitor ann. conv. S.C. State Sch. Bd. Assn., 1994. Mem. Coun. for Exceptional Children (hospitality chair 1987-89, publicity chair 1989-90), Nat. Assn. for Edn. of Young Children. Avocations: singing, reading, travel, tennis. Home: 29 Savage St Apt B Charleston SC 29401-2409

SUGGS, JOSEPHINE GREENWAY, controller; b. Lula, Ga., Dec. 19, 1946; d. Marvin W. and Lucille (Echols) Greenway; m. Ray M. Suggs, May 31, 1969; children: Jeffrey Ray, Martin Ryan. Cert. in computer programming, Lanier Tech. Inst., 1979; AA, Am. Inst. Profl. Bookkeepers, 1989. Contr. Hilb, Rogal & Hamilton Co., Gainesville, Ga., 1988—. Vol. ARC, 1979—, N.E. Ga. Med. Aux., 1993—. Mem. NAFE, Am. Bus. Women, Am. Inst. Profl. Bookkeepers, Nat. Assn. Ins. Women, Ins. Women Gainesville. Baptist. Avocation: community involvement. Home: 5906 Homer Hwy PO Box 364 Lula GA 30554

SUGGS, MARION JACK, minister, college dean; b. Electra, Tex., June 5, 1924; s. Claude Frank and Lottie Maye (Gibson) S.; m. Ruth Barge, Nov. 13, 1943; children: Adena Ruth Suggs Beck, James Robert, David Nathan. BA, U. Tex., 1946; BD, Tex. Christian U., 1949; PhD, Duke U., 1954. Ordained to ministry Christian Ch. (Disciples of Christ), 1948. Min. First Christian Ch., Gladewater, Tex., 1948-50, Wendell Christian Ch., N.C., 1950-52; asst. prof. Brite Div. Sch. Tex. Christian U., Ft. Worth, 1952-54, assoc. prof., 1954-56, prof., 1956-89, dean Brite Div. Sch., 1977-89; emeritus dean and prof. Tex. Christian U., Fort Worth, 1989—; mem. com. on ministry Christian Ch. in S.W., 1976-89; chmn. coun. on theol. edn. Div. Higher Edn., 1987-88, mem. ch. fin. coun., 1985-89, bd. dirs.; mem. gen. bd. Christian Ch. (Disciples of Christ), 1986-87; lectr. min.'s week Tex. Christian U., 1961, Lexington Theol. Sem., 1966, S.W. Mo. State U., 1977; mem. Disciples-Roman Cath. Internat. Bilateral Conv., 1978-87. Author: The Layman Reads His Bible, 1957, The Gospel Story, 1960 (Adult Book of Yr. Christian Lit. Com. 1960), Wisdom, Christology and Law in Matthew's Gospel, 1970 (Christian Rsch. Found. award 1967); also articles ; co-editor: Studies in the History and Text of the New Testament, 1967, New English Bible: Oxford Study Edition, 1976 (Religious Book award 1977), The Oxford Study Bible, Revised English Bible, 1992. Bd. dirs. Granville T. Walker Found. G.H. Kearns fellow, 1951, Am. Coun. Learned Socs. fellow, 1963-64, Assn. Theol. Schs. fellow, 1963-64; recipient Disting. Alumnus award Tex. Christian U., 1973, Brite Divinity Sch., 1997. Mem. Soc. Bibl. Lit., Studiorum Novi Testamenti Societas, Internat. Greek N.T. Project, Phi Beta Kappa, Alpha Kappa Delta, Pi Gamma Mu, Theta Phi. Democrat. Home: 5605 Winifred Dr Fort Worth TX 76133-2501

SUGGS, MICHAEL EDWARD, lawyer; b. Conway, S.C., Nov. 9, 1962; s. Edward and Rebecca S. BSBA, U. S.C., 1985, JD, 1992. Bar: S.C. 1992, U.S. Dist. Ct., S.C., 1995. Asst. pub. defender Def. Corp. Horry County, Conway, S.C., 1993—. Troop 847 com. Boy Scouts Am., Loris, S.C., 1985—; coun. City of Loris, 1994—. Recipient Eagle Scout award Boy Scouts Am., 1976. Mem. ABA, S.C. Assn. Criminal Def. Lawyers, Horry County Bar Assn., Loris C. of C. Methodist. Home: 4932 Circle Dr Loris SC 29569-3146 Office: Def Corp Horry County PO Box 1666 114 Laurel St Conway SC 29526

SUGIHARA, KENZI, publishing executive; b. Kearny, N.J., Oct. 4, 1940; s. Kyuichi and Shinobuko (Yamaguchi) S.; m. Roslyn Forbes, Dec. 1966 (div. Mar. 1981); children: Kenichi, Takeo, Akira, Fumio; m. Nancy Elizabeth Kirsh, June 8, 1981; 1 child, Toshiro. BA, NYU, 1963. Supr. McGraw Hill, Inc., N.Y.C., 1965-67; assoc. dir. coll. product dept. Harcourt Brace Jovanovich Inc., N.Y.C., 1978-82, dir. electronic pub., 1982-83; v.p., pub. Bantam Electronic Pub. div., pub. Bantam Reference Books, Bantam Profl. Books, Bantam Doubleday Dell, N.Y.C., 1983-93; v.p., pub. Random House Reference & Electronic Pub. (Random House Inc.), 1993-95; pres. Sugihara and Rose, 1995—. Democrat. Presbyterian. Home: 585 W End Ave # 15D New York NY 10024-1715

SUGIKI, SHIGEMI, ophthalmologist, educator; b. Wailuku, Hawaii, May 12, 1936; s. Sentaro and Kameno (Matoba) S.; AB, Washington U., St. Louis, 1957, M.D., 1961; m. Bernice T. Murakami, Dec. 28, 1958; children: Kevin S., Boyd R. Intern St. Luke's Hosp., St. Louis, 1961-62, resident ophthalmology, Washington U., St. Louis, 1962-65; chmn. dept. ophthalmology Straub Clinic, Honolulu, 1965-70, Queen's Med. Ctr., Honolulu, 1970-73, 80-83, 88-90, 93—; assoc. clin. prof. ophthalmology Sch. Medicine, U. Hawaii, 1973—. Served to maj. M.C., AUS, 1968-70. Decorated Hawaiian NG Commendation medal, 1968. Fellow ACS; mem. Am., Hawaii med. assns., Honolulu County Med. Soc., Am. Acad. Ophthalmology, Contact Lens Assn. Opthalmologists, Pacific Coast Oto-Ophthal. Soc., Pan-Pacific Surg. Assn., Am. Soc. Cataract and Refractive Surgery, Am. Glaucoma Soc., Internat. Assn. Ocular Surgeons, Am. Soc. Contemporary Ophthalmology, Washington U. Eye Alumni Assn., Hawaii Ophthal. Soc., Rsch. To Prevent Blindness. Home: 2398 Aina Lani Pl Honolulu HI 96822-2024 Office: 1380 Lusitana St Ste 714 Honolulu HI 96813-2443

SUGINTAS, NORA MARIA, veterinarian, scientist, medical company executive, performing arts dancer; b. Evergreen Park, Ill., Mar. 12, 1956; d. George and Mary (Navickas) S. BS in Biol. Scis. with highest distinction, U. Ill., Chgo., 1978; DVM, U. Ill., 1982. Lic. veterinarian, Ill. Profl. hosp. specialist Abbott Labs., Detroit, 1983-87; anes./crit. care patient monitoring equipment acct. exec. Shiley, Inc., Detroit, 1987-91; anesthesia and critical care monitoring equipment sales exec. and cons. Ohmeda, Detroit, 1991-94; regional mgr. Criticare Systems, Detroit, 1994-95, nat. acct. dir., 1995-96; dir. corp. accounts Isolyser Health Care, 1996—. Journalist The Lithuanian World-Wide Daily Newspaper, 1975; author: The Production of S-Adenosylmethionine by Saccharomyces cerevisiae and Candida utilis. Troop leader Girl Scouts Lithuanian, Chgo., 1972-77, camp dir., 1977. Recipient Louis Pasteur award for Academic Excellence in the Biol. Scis. and Ind. Rsch. U. Ill., 1978. Mem. NAFE, Econ. Club Detroit, Phi Beta Kappa. Republican. Avocations: hiking, nature preservation, photography, internat. politics. Office: 6284 Aspen Ridge West Bloomfield MI 48322-4433

SUGIOKA, KENNETH, anesthesiologist educator; b. Hollister, Calif., Apr. 19, 1920; s. Seigiro and Kameno (Takeda) S.; m. Mary Trabue Hinternhoff, June 18, 1966; children—Stephanie, Colin, Kimi (by previous marriage), Nathan, Brian. B.S., U. Denver, 1945; M.D., Washington U., St. Louis, 1949. Intern, resident U. Iowa, 1949-52, instr. anesthesiology, 1952; asst.

prof. surgery N.C. Meml. Hosp., Chapel Hill, 1954-62, assoc. prof. surgery, 1962-64; prof. surgery, chmn. div. anesthesiology U. N.C., 1964-69, prof., chmn. dept. anesthesiology, 1969-83; prof. anesthesiology and physiology Duke U., 1985—; vis. prof. Physiol. Inst., U. Göttingen, Fed. Republic of Germany, 1963, Kings Coll. Med. Sch., London, Max-Planck Inst. Physiology, Dortmund, Fed. Republic of Germany, 1976-77; vis. prof. Royal Coll. Surgeons, Eng., 1983-84; dir. Morgan Creek Land Co.; mem. adv. com. on anesthetic and life support drugs FDA; bd. alumni U. Denver. Author textbook of clin. anesthesiology; contbr. articles to profl. jours. Pres. Triangle Opera Theater. Served to capt., M.C. USAF, 1952-54. Recipient spl. research fellowship NIH, 1961-62. Fellow Faculty Anaesthesiologists Royal Coll. Surgeons (Eng.) (hon.); mem. Soc. Acad. Anesthesia Chairmen (past pres.). Home: 319 Bayberry Dr Chapel Hill NC 27514-9116

SUGIYAMA, KAZUNORI, music producer; b. Tokyo, Aug. 18, 1950; came to U.S., 1976; s. Hiroshi and Michiko (Maeda) S.; m. Emi Fukui, Aug. 11, 1981. BS, Waseda U., 1974, postgrad., 1974-75; MA, Boston U., 1977. Jr. adminstrv. officer Japanese Mission to UN, N.Y.C., 1978-88; rep. N.Y. Toshiba EMI Records, Jazz Div., Tokyo, 1990-93; rep. U.S., exec. producer DIW/Avant Records, Tokyo, 1991—; exec. producer Tzadik Records, N.Y.C., 1995—; corr. Jazz Life, Tokyo, 1980-88; columnist OCS News, N.Y.C., 1982-90. Rec. engr. (album) Bud and Bird/Gil Evans, 1988 (Grammy); prodr. V/Ralph Peterson, 1990 (Jazz Album of Yr.); co-prodr. The Nurturer/Geri Allen, 1991 (2d pl. Jazz Album of Yr.), Big Band & Quartet/David Murray, 1992 (Best Prodn. Jazz Album of Yr.), Picasso/David Murray, 1993 (3d pl. Jazz Album of Yr.); translator Autobiography of Miles Davis, 1989. Mem. NARAS, USTA. Avocations: tennis, travel. Office: 93 Mercer St Apt 3W New York NY 10012-4452

SUH, DAE-SOOK, political science educator; b. Hoeryong, Korea, Nov. 22, 1931; came to U.S., 1952; s. Chang-Hee and Chong-Hee (Paek) S.; m. Yun-Ok Park, Oct. 29, 1960; children: Maurice, Kevin. BA, Tex. Christian U., 1956; MA, Ind. U., 1958; PhD, Columbia U., 1964. Asst. prof. U. Houston, 1965-67, assoc. prof., 1968-71; prof. polit. sci., dir. Ctr. for Korean Studies, U. Hawaii, Honolulu, 1972-95; prof. policy studies Korea Found., 1994—. Author: The Korean Communist Movement, 1967, Documents of Korean Communism, 1970, Korean Communism, 1980, Kim Il Sung, 1988. Mem. Conv. Ctr. Authority, Honolulu, 1989-94. Grantee Social Sci. Rsch. Coun.-Am. Coun. Learned Socs., 1963, East-/West Ctr., Columbia U., 1971, The Wilson Ctr. for Scholars, 1985, Fulbright, 1988. Mem. Am. Polit. Sci. Assn. (life), Assn. for Asian Studies. Avocations: tennis, golf. Home: 7122 Niumalu Loop Honolulu HI 96825-1635 Office: U Hawaii at Manoa Dept Political Sci 2424 Maile Way Honolulu HI 96822-2223

SUHL, HARRY, physics educator; b. Leipzig, Fed. Republic Germany, Oct. 18, 1922; s. Bernhard and Klara (Bergwerk) S.; widowed. BSc, U. Wales, 1943; PhD, U. Oxford, 1948, DSc (hon.), 1970. Temp. exptl. officer British Admiralty, England, 1943-46; mem. tech. staff Bell Labs., Murray Hill, N.J., 1948-60; prof. physics U. Calif.-San Diego, La Jolla, 1961—. Editor (with others) book series: Magnetism, 1961-74. Guggenheim fellow, 1968-69, NSF fellow, 1971. Fellow Am. Phys. Soc., Am. Acad. Arts and Scis.; mem. NAS. Office: U Calif Dept Physics 9500 Gilman Dr La Jolla CA 92093-5003

SUHR, GERALDINE M., medical/surgical nurse; b. Sumner, Iowa, Mar. 16, 1960; d. Marvin Edward and Peggy Marie (Reiser) S. Diploma, Allen Meml. Luth. Sch. Nursing, Waterloo, Iowa, 1982; student, U. No. Iowa, Cedar Falls, 1979, U. Tenn., 1995. Sr. ship's nurse Carnival Cruise Lines, Miami, Fla.; emergency room and ICU/CCU nurse New Hampton (Iowa) Community Hosp.; charge nurse Trav Corps, Malden, Mass., Flying Nurses, Dallas, Hosp. Staffing Inc., Fla.; charge nurse, critical care nurse So. Hills Hosp., Nashville.

SUHR, J. NICHOLAS, lawyer; b. N.Y.C., Nov. 14, 1942; s. Heinrich P. and Anna H. (Isenschmid) S.; m. Anne Aylett Stone, July 6, 1965; children: John Nicholas Jr., Erika Christl. BA, U. Va., 1964; JD, Am. U., 1967. Bar: N.Y. 1967, N.J. 1969, U.S. Supreme Ct. 1989. Assoc., ptnr. Topken & Farley, N.Y.C., 1967-73, Conboy, Hewitt, O'Brien & Boardman, N.Y.C., 1973-86; counsel Hunton & Williams, N.Y.C., 1986-87, Quinn, Cohen, Shields & Bock, N.Y.C., 1987-88; ptnr. Quinn & Suhr, White Plains, N.Y., 1988-95, Herzfeld & Rubin, P.C., N.Y.C., 1995—, Chase, Kurshan, Suhr, Herzfeld & Rubin, Newark, 1996—; arbitrator U.S. Dist. Ct. N.J., Trenton, 1985—, Am. Arbitration Assn., N.Y.C., 1976—. Contbr. articles to profl. jours.; commentator Ct. TV network. Mem. ABA, N.Y. State Bar Assn., N.J. State Bar Assn., U.S. Supreme Ct. Bar, Internat. Law Soc., Consular Law Soc., Def. Rsch. Inst., German Soc. of N.Y.C. (v.p., sec., trustee 1976—), German-Am. Sch. Assn. (v.p., trustee 1986—), German Seamen's Mission N.Y. (pres., dir. 1972—). Lutheran. Avocations: fishing, woodworking. Office: Herzfeld & Rubin PC 40 Wall St New York NY 10005-2301

SUHR, PAUL AUGUSTINE, lawyer; b. Sonwunri, Chonbuk, Korea, Jan. 20, 1940; came to U.S. 1966; s. Chong-ju and Oksuk (Pang) So; m. Angeline M. Kang Suhr; 1 child, Christopher. BA, Campbell Coll., Buies Creek, N.C., 1968; MA, U. N.C., Greensboro, 1970; MS, U. N.C., Chapel Hill, 1975; JD, N.C. Cen. U., 1988. Bar: N.C. 1989, U.S. Dist. Ct. (ea. and mid. dist.) N.C. 1989, U.S. Ct. Appeals D.C. 1990, U.S. Ct. Appeals (4th cir.) 1992. Bibliographer N.C. Div. of State Libr., Raleigh, 1975-78; dir. Pender County Pub. Libr., Burgaw, N.C., 1978-80; libr. Tob. Lit. Svc., N.C. State U., Raleigh, 1980-85; pvt. practice law Law Office of Paul A. Suhr, Raleigh & Fayetteville, 1989—. Author short stories and novelettes various lit. mags., jours. and revs. Mem. Human Resources and Human Rels. Adv. Commn., City of Raleigh, 1990-95, chmn., 1994-95. N.C. Humanities Com. grantee, 1979-80; recipient Presdl. award President of Korea, 1992. Mem. ABA, ATLA, N.C. Bar Assn., N.C. Trial Lawyers Assn., Wake County Bar Assn. (bd. dirs.), D.C. Bar Assn. Democrat. Roman Catholic. Avocations: gardening, fishing, writing. Office: 1110 Navaho Dr Ste 605 Raleigh NC 27609-7322

SUHRE, WALTER ANTHONY, JR., retired lawyer and brewery executive; b. Cin., Jan. 17, 1933; s. Walter A. and Elizabeth V. (Heimbuch) S. B.S. in Bus. Adminstrn., Northwestern U., 1956; LL.B. with honors, U. Cin., 1962. Bar: Ohio 1962, Mo. 1982. Assoc. Taft, Stettinius & Hollister, Cin., 1962-65; with Eagle-Picher Industries, Inc., Cin., 1965-82, v.p., gen. counsel, 1970-82; v.p., gen. counsel Anheuser-Busch Cos., Inc., St. Louis, 1982-94; ret., 1993. Served with USMC, 1956-59. Mem. Old Warson Country Club. Republican. Presbyterian. Home: 48 Woodcliffe Rd Saint Louis MO 63124-1336

SUHRHEINRICH, RICHARD FRED, federal judge; b. 1936. BS, Wayne State U., 1960; JD cum laude, Detroit Coll. Law, 1963, LLM, 1992; LLM, U. Va., 1990. Bar: Mich. Assoc. Moll, Desenberg, Purdy, Glover & Bayer, 1963-67; asst. prosecutor Macomb County, 1967; ptnr. Rogensues, Richard & Suhrheinrich, 1967; assoc. Moll, Desenberg, Purdy, Glover & Bayer, 1967-68; ptnr. Kitch, Suhrheinrich, Saurbier & Drutchas, 1968-84; judge U.S. Dist. Ct. (ea. dist.) Mich., Detroit, 1984-90, U.S. Ct. Appeals (6th Cir.), Detroit, 1990—. Mem. State Bar Mich., Ingham County Bar Assn. Office: US Ct Appeals 6th Cir Rm 241 USPO & Fed Bldg 315 W Allegan St Lansing MI 48933-1514*

SUHRSTEDT, TIM, cinematographer. Films include: Forbidden World, 1982, Android, 1982, The House on Sorority Row, 1983, Suburbia, 1984, Teen Wolf, 1985, City Limits, 1985, Space Rage, 1985, Stand Alone, 1985, Mannequin, 1986, Critters, 1986, Feds, 1988, Mystic Pizza, 1988, Split Decisions, 1988, Doin' Time on Planet Earth, 1988, Bill and Ted's Excellent Adventure, 1989, Men at Work, 1990, Noises Off, 1992, Don't Tell Mom the Babysitter's Dead, 1992, Traces of Red, 1992, Getting Even with Dad, 1993; TV films include: The Ratings Game, 1984, And the Children Shall Lead, 1985, Dead Solid Perfect, 1988, She Knows Too Much, 1989, The Cover Girl and the Cop, 1989, Man Against the Mob: The Chinatown Murders, 1990, Pair of Aces, 1990; (TV series) Chicago Hope (Emmy award for Outstanding Individual Achievement in Cinematography for a Series 1995). Office: care Dattner & Assocs 10635 Santa Monica Blvd Ste 165 Los Angeles CA 90025-4997*

SUINN, RICHARD MICHAEL, psychologist; b. Honolulu, May 8, 1933; s. Maurice and Edith (Wong) S.; m. Grace D. Toy, July 26, 1958; children: Susan, Randall, Staci, Bradley. Student, U. Hawaii, 1951-53; B.A. summa cum laude, Ohio State U., 1955; MA in Clin. Psychology, Stanford U., 1957, PhD in Clin. Psychology, 1959. Lic. psychologist, Colo.; diplomate Am. Bd. Profl. Psychology (trustee 1996—). Counselor Stanford (Calif.) U., 1958-59, rsch. assoc. Med. Sch., 1964-66; asst. prof. psychology Whitman Coll., Walla Walla, Wash., 1959-64; assoc. prof. U. Hawaii, Honolulu, 1966-68; prof. Colo. State U., Ft. Collins, 1968—, head dept. psychology, 1972-93; cons. in field; psychologist U.S. Ski Teams, 1976, Olympic Games, U.S. Women's Track and Field, 1980 Olympic Games, U.S. Ski Jumping Team, 1988, U.S. Shooting Team, 1994; mem. sports psychology adv. com. U.S. Olympic Com., 1983-89; reviewer NIMH, 1977-80, 94—. Author: The Predictive Validity of Projective Measures, 1969, Fundamentals of Behavior Pathology, 1970, The Innovative Psychological Therapies, 1975, The Innovative Medical-Psychiatric Therapies, 1976, Psychology in Sport: Methods and Applications, 1980, Fundamentals of Abnormal Psychology, 1984, 88, Seven Steps to Peak Performance, 1986, Anxiety Management Training, 1990; editorial bd.: Jour. Cons. and Clin. Psychology, 1973-86, Jour. Counseling Psychology, 1974-91, Behavior Therapy, 1977-80, Behavior Modification, 1977-78, Jour. Behavioral Medicine, 1978-83, Behavior Counseling Quar., 1979-83, Jour. Sports Psychology, 1980—, Clin. Psychology: Science and Practice, 1994—, Professional Psychology, 1994—; author: tests Math. Anxiety Rating Scale, Suinn Test Anxiety Behavior Scale, Suinn-Lew Asian Self-identity Acculturation Scale. Mem. City Council, Ft. Collins, 1975-79, mayor, 1978-79; mem. Gov.'s Mental Health Adv. Council, 1983, Colo. Bd. Psychologist Examiners, 1983-86. Recipient cert. merit U.S. Ski Team, 1976, APA Career Contbn. to Edn. award, 1995; NIMH grantee, 1963-64; Office Edn. grantee, 1970-71. Fellow APA (chmn. bd. ethnic minority affairs 1982-83, chmn. edn. and tng. bd. 1986-87, policy and planning bd. 1987-89, publs. bd. 1993—, bd. dirs. 1990-93), Behavior Therapy and Rsch. Soc. (charter); mem. Assn. for Advancement Psychology (trustee 1983-86), Assn. for Advancement Behavior Therapy (sec.-treas. 1986-89, pres. 1992-93), Asian Am. Psychol. Assn. (bd. dirs. 1983-88), Am. Bd. Behavior Therapy (bd. dirs. 1987—), Phi Beta Kappa, Sigma Xi. Home: 808 Cheyenne Dr Fort Collins CO 80525-1560 Office: Colo State U Dept Psychology Fort Collins CO 80523

SUITER, JOHN WILLIAM, industrial engineering consultant; b. Pasadena, Calif., Feb. 16, 1926; s. John Walter and Ethel May (Acton) S.; BS in Aero. Sci., Embry Riddle U., 1964; m. Joyce England, Dec. 3, 1952; children: Steven A., Carol A. Cons. indsl. engr., Boynton Beach, Fla., 1955—. Instr. U. S.C. Tech. Edn. Ctr., Charleston, 1967-69. Pilot USAF, 1944-46. Registered profl. engr., Fla. Mem. Am. Inst. Indsl. Engrs., Soc. Mfg. Engrs. (sr.), Computer and Automated Sys. Assn., Methods-Time Measurement Assn. (assoc.), Soc. Quality Control. Home: PO Box 5262 Grove City FL 34224-0262

SUITS, BERNARD HERBERT, philosophy educator; b. Detroit, Nov. 25, 1925; s. Herbert Arthur and Helen Dorothy (Carlin) S.; m. Nancy Ruth Berr, July 3, 1952; children—Mark, Constance. B.A., U. Chgo., 1944, M.A., 1950; Ph.D., U. Ill., 1958. Investigator venereal disease USPHS, 1950-51; personnel officer Detroit Civil Service Commn., 1952-54; instr. philosophy U. Ill., Urbana, 1958-59; asst. prof. Purdue U., 1959-66; asso. prof. U. Waterloo, Ont., 1966-72; prof. philosophy, chmn. dept. U. Waterloo, 1972—, asso. dean arts for grad. affairs, 1981—; vis. prof. U. Lethbridge, Alta., Can., 1980, U. Bristol, Eng., 1980, disting. prof. emeritus U. Waterloo, 1995. Author: The Grasshopper: Games, Life, and Utopia, 1978, paper, 1990; Contbr. to profl. jours. and books. Served with USNR, 1944-46. Mem. Canadian, Am. philos. assns., Philos. Soc. for Study of Sport (pres. 1975—). Office: U Waterloo, Dept Philosophy, Waterloo, ON Canada

SUITS, DANIEL BURBIDGE, economist; b. St. Louis, June 27, 1918; s. Hollis Emerson and Dorothy Dandridge (Halyburton) S.; m. Adelaide Evens Boehm, Feb. 14, 1942; children—Evan Halyburton, Holly Boehm Suits Kazarinoff. A.B. in Philosophy, U. Mich., 1940, M.A. in Econs, 1942, Ph.D. in Econs, 1948. Asst. prof. econs. dept. U. Mich., 1950-55, assoc. prof., 1955-59, prof., dir. research seminar in quantitative econs., 1959-69; dir. Am. Studies Ctr., Kyoto, Japan, 1958; prof. econs. U. Calif., Santa Cruz, 1969-74; prof. econs. Mich. State U., East Lansing, 1974-86, prof. emeritus, 1986—; vis. prof. People's U., Beijing, 1985, Fudan U., Shanghai, 1987, Swarthmore Coll., 1988; disting. vis. prof. Kalamazoo Coll., 1989; cons. to various state and fed. agys.; rsch. assoc. Ctr. Econ. Rsch., Athens, Greece, 1962-63. Author: Statistics: An Introduction to Quantitative Economic Research, 1963, Theory and Application of Econometric Models, 1963, Principles of Economics, 1970, rev. edit., 1973; originator Suits Index tax progressivity; contbr. articles to tech. jours. Served alt. mil. duty 1942-46. Recipient Disting. Faculty award Mich. State U., 1980; sr. fellow East-West Population Inst., 1978—. Fellow Econometric Soc., Am. Statis. Assn.; mem. Am. Econ. Assn. Mem. Soc. of Friends. Home: 1446 Karlin Ct East Lansing MI 48823-2333 Office: Mich State U Econs Dept East Lansing MI 48824

SUJANSKY, EVA BORSKA, physician, educator; b. Bratislava, Slovak Republic, Feb. 14, 1936; d. Stefan and Terezia (Kaiserova) Borsky; m. Eduard Sujansky, Apr. 2, 1960 (dec. 1979); children: Paul, Walter. MD, Comenius U., Bratislava, Czechoslovakia, 1959. Diplomate Am. Bd. Pediats., Am. Bd. Med. Genetics. Resident in pediats. U. Iowa, Iowa City, 1971-73; fellow in human genetics Mt. Sinai Sch. Medicine, N.Y.C., 1973-74; clin. genetist Beth Israel Hosp., N.Y.C., 1973-74; dir. clin. genetics Sch. Medicine, U. Colo., Denver, 1974-90, assoc. prof. pediats., biochemistry, biophysics and genetics, 1981—; co-dir. divsn. genetic svcs. The Children's Hosp., U. Colo., Denver, 1990—. Contbr. articles to profl. jours. Fellow Am. Acad. Pediats., Am. Soc. Human Genetics, Am. Coll. Med. Genetics (founding fellow). Avocations: fine arts, reading, travel. Office: U Colo Med Ctr 1056 E 19th Ave Denver CO 80218-1007

SUKO, LONNY RAY, judge; b. Spokane, Wash., Oct. 12, 1943; s. Ray R. and Leila B. (Snyder) S.; m. Marcia A. Michaelsen, Aug. 26, 1967; children: Jolynn R., David M. BA, Wash. State U., 1965; JD, U. Idaho, 1968. Bar: Wash. 1968, U.S. Dist. Ct. (ea. dist.) Wash. 1969, U.S. Dist. Ct. (we. dist.) Wash. 1978, U.S. Ct. Appeals (9th cir.) 1978. Law clk. U.S. Dist. Ct. Ea. Dist. Wash., 1968-69; assoc. Lyon, Beaulaurier & Aaron, Yakima, Wash., 1969-72; ptnr. Lyon, Beaulaurier, Weigand, Suko & Gustafson, Yakima, 1972-91, Lyon, Weigand, Suko & Gustafson, P.S., 1991-95; U.S. magistrate judge, Yakima, 1971-91, 95—. Mem. Phi Beta Kappa, Phi Kappa Phi. Office: PO Box 2726 Yakima WA 98907-2726

SULC, DWIGHT GEORGE, investment advisor; b. Oklahoma City, May 25, 1948; s. George Bennett and Hedvika (Kyzivat) S. BA, U. Tex., 1971; JD, Tuebingen U., Germany, 1979, LLD, 1983. Cert. securities and exch. commn., Paris, U.S. Investment advisor Paris, Berlin, London, 1974-83, Oklahoma City, 1984—; strategic planning advisor cmty. orgns., Oklahoma City, 1989. Author: A National Neighborhood Association System for America, 1991, Building A Volunteer Neighborhood Watch Patrol, A Civic Leadership Training Manual of the Council of Confederated Neighborhoods of America, 1996, Czechoslovak Society of Arts and Sciences World Congress, Brno: Strategic Management Design for the International Society of Arts Management and the Arts, 1996. Chmn. strategic planning com. Federally Employed Women Assn., Tinker AFB, 1990; founder The Coun. of Confederated Neighborhoods of Am. Inc., Oklahoma City, 1991, The Internat. Soc. for the Arts Management and the Arts, Praha, Czechoslovakia/London/Oklahoma City, 1994; pres. Mil. Park chpt. Coun. Confederated Neighborhoods of Am., 1992. Rsch. grantee Fulbright, Berlin, 1980, Brusselles, 1981. Mem. Nat. Assn. Parliamentarians (pres. 1994). Presbyterian. Avocation: music. Home: 3321 N Virginia Ave Oklahoma City OK 73118-3044

SULC, JEAN LUENA (JEAN L. MESTRES), lobbyist, consultant; b. Worcester, Mass., Mar. 17, 1939; d. Emilio Beija and Julia Luena; m. Lee Gwynne Mestres, Oct. 9, 1965 (div. Dec. 1973); m. Lawrence Bradley Sulc, Nov. 4, 1983. BS in Psychology, Tufts U., 1961; M in Urban and Regional Planning, U. Colo., 1976. Lic. real estate, Va.; lic. pvt. pilot. Mem. staff U.S. fgn. svc. Dept. State, Washington, 1962-65; intern Adams County Planning Dept., Brighton, Colo., 1974-75; cons. office policy analysis City and County of Denver, 1976; program dir. Coun. Internat. Urban Liaison, Washington, 1976-79; asst., dir. internat. Cities Svc. Oil & Gas Corp., Washington, 1980-81; govt. affairs rep. Cities Svc., OXY USA Inc., Washington, 1982-89; mgr. fed. rels. OXY USA Inc., Washington, 1990-95; pres. EdgeSystem.XXI, Washington, 1996—; chmn. govt. affairs com. L.P. Gas Clean Fuel Coalition, Irvine, Calif., 1990-92. Author, editor: (newsletter) Dayton Climate Project, 1979-80; contbr. articles to newsletters. Vol. Reagan/Bush and Bush/Quayle Presdl. Campaigns and Inaugural Coms., Washington, 1984-89; pres. Hale Found., Nathan Hale Inst., Washington, 1984-85; mem. nat. panel consumer arbitrators Better Bus. Burs., Va., 1991—. Recipient Presdl. citation Nat. Propane Gas Assn., 1992; Minority Intern grantee Denver Regional Coun. Govts., 1974-76. Mem. ASTD, ABA (assoc., arbitration sect.), Am. League Lobbyists (chmn. energy sect., bd. dirs. 1994—, sec. 1996—), Women in Govt. Rels., Assn. Image Cons. Internat., Psi Chi. Episcopalian. Avocations: skiing, fitness, dancing, sports shooting, gourmet cooking. Office: EdgeSystemXII 927 15th St NW Ste 1000 Washington DC 20005-2304

SULCER, FREDERICK DURHAM, advertising executive; b. Chgo., Aug. 28, 1932; s. Henry Durham and Charlotte (Thearle) S.; m. Dorothy Wright, May 2, 1953; children—Thomas W., Ginna M., David T. BA, U. Chgo., 1949, MBA, 1963. Reporter UP Assn., Chgo., 1945-46; reporter AP, 1947; with Needham, Harper & Steers Advt., Chgo., 1947-78, dir., 1965-78, sr. account dir., 1965-66, mem. exec. com., 1966-78, exec. v.p., 1967, dir. N.Y. div., 1967-78; pres. N.Y. div. Needham, Harper & Steers Advt., 1974-75; chmn. bd. NH & S Internat., 1975-76; pres. Sulcer Communication Co., Inc., 1977-78; group exec., dir. Benton & Bowles (advt.), 1978-85; dir. bus. devel. D'Arcy Masius Benton & Bowles, advt., N.Y.C., 1985-90; vice-chmn. bd. dirs. DDB Needham Worldwide, N.Y.C., 1990-95; founder, prin. The Persuasion Group, N.Y.C., 1995—; Schering-Plough disting. vis. prof. corp. comm. Fairleigh Dickinson U., Madison, N.J., 1993-96. Served to capt. C.E. AUS, 1950-53. Mem. Am. Assn. Advt. Agys. (bd. govs. N.Y. chpt.), Internat. Advertisers Assn., Alpha Delta Phi. Home and Office: The Persuasion Group 350 W 50th St Ste PH 1-D New York NY 10019-6664

SULEYMANIAN, MIRIK, biophysicist; b. Chartar, Karabagh, Armenia, Jan. 20, 1948; came to U.S., 1992; s. Avanes and Gohar (Hakopian) S.; m. Nelia Agababian, Mar. 24, 1973; children: Hovanes, Gagik. Diploma, Yerevan (Armenia) State U., 1973; PhD, Inst. Exptl. Biology, Yerevan, 1981, DS, 1990. Rsch. worker Acad. Scis. Armenia, Yerevan, 1975-81, sr. rsch. worker, 1981-88, leading rsch. worker, 1988-92; rsch. assoc. dept. physiology Va. Commonwealth U., Richmond, 1992—. Contbr. over 50 articles to profl. jours. Fellow U. Bristol, Gt. Britain, 1978, rsch. fellow Limnological Inst., Tihany, Hungary, 1979, 83, dept. muscle physiology Ruhr U. Bochum, Germany, 1987-88. Mem. Biophys. Soc. U.S.A., Internat. Soc. Heart Rsch. Achievments include research in cell volume regulation, the relationship between electrogenic sodium pump activity and cell volume and membrane surface area changes, the effect of the latter on the number of functioning protein molecules in the membrane having enzymatic, receptor and carrier properties, water flow through the neuronal membrane and its effect on the kinetics and amplitude of ionic currents, membrane water channels and their role in osmotic water transport in cardiac myocytes. Office: Va Commonwealth U Sanger Hall 1101 E Marshall St Richmond VA 23298-5008

SULG, MADIS, corporation executive; b. Tallinn, Estonia, May 25, 1943; came to U.S., 1950; s. Hand Eduard and Erika (Turk) S.; m. Mary Diane Detellis, Dec. 30, 1967; children: Danielle Marie, Michaella Erika. SB in Indsl. Mgmt., MIT, 1965, SM in Mgmt., 1967. Cons. Barss, Reitzel & Assocs., Cambridge, Mass., 1970-71; mgr. planning and research Converse Rubber Co., Wilmington, Mass., 1971-75; dir. bus. planning and devel. AMF, Inc., Stamford, Conn., 1975-79; sr. v.p. planning and devel. Bandag, Inc., Muscatine, Iowa, 1978-88; pres. Prime Investments, 1988—, Muscatine Natural Resources Corp., 1981-88; chmn., chief exec. officer Sieg Auto Parts, Davenport, Iowa, 1989-93; COO Hammer's Plastic Recycling, Iowa Falls, Iowa, 1994, Purethane, Inc., West Branch, Iowa, 1994—. With U.S. Army, 1968-70. Presbyterian. Avocations: bridge; jogging; swimming. Home: 260 West Side Dr Iowa City IA 52246-4342 Office: Purethane Inc One Purethane Pl West Branch IA 52358

SULGER, FRANCIS XAVIER, lawyer; b. N.Y.C., Sept. 3, 1942; s. John J. and Regina (Slawkowska) S.; m. Helga Nelsen, July 23, 1968; children: Derek N., Justin D. BA, Fordham U., 1964; JD, Harvard U., 1967. Bar: N.Y. 1970, U.S. Dist. Ct. (so. dist.) N.Y. 1979. Atty. F.I. duPont & Co., N.Y.C., 1968-70; assoc. Townsend & Lewis, N.Y.C., 1970-73, Thacher Proffitt & Wood, N.Y.C., 1973-78; ptnr. Thacher Proffitt & Wood, 1978—. Trustee Wildcliff Mus., New Rochelle, N.Y., 1970-74; mem. U.S. Olympic Rowing Com., Colorado Springs, Colo., 1980-84. Mem. U.S. Rowing Assn. (bd. dirs. 1979-84), N.Y. Athletic Club (rowing chmn. 1979-95), Larchmont (N.Y.) Yacht Club. Avocations: rowing, collecting antiques, computers. Home: 10 Meadow Ln Greenwich CT 06831-3709 Office: Thacher Proffitt & Wood 2 World Trade Ctr New York NY 10048-0203

SULIK, DORIE, realtor, marketing professional; b. Cleve., Apr. 11, 1942; d. Howard Anthony and Henrietta (Schulhauser) Nieberding; divorced; children: Jodie Frydl, Rob. Grad. high sch., Euclid, Ohio. Realtor Hilltop Realty, Cleve., 1977-82, residential sales agt., 1982-90; from adminstr. mktg. and sales to dir. devel. mktg. HGM-Hilltop Condominium Assocs., Cleve.; from mktg. mgr. to dir. sales and mktg. new homes dept. Realty One, Cleve.; dir. builder mktg. Smythe Cramer Co., Cleve., 1990—. Mem. Cleve. Bldg. Industry Assn. (chmn. assoc. adv. coun. 1994, chmn. sales and mktg. coun. 1990, Assoc. of Yr. 1991, 94, Outstanding Mktg. Person of Yr. 1993), Builder Mktg. Soc. (trustee 1992-94), Nat. Sales and Mktg. Coun. of Nat. Assn. Home Builders (trustee 1992-94), Inst. Residential Mktg. (trustee 1996—). Roman Catholic. Avocations: boating, skiing, reading, walking, golf. Home: 8501 Waterside Dr Sagamore Hls OH 44067-3214 Office: Smythe Cramer Co 5800 Lombardo Ctr Ste 200 Cleveland OH 44131-2550

SULIK, EDWIN (PETE SULIK), health care administrator; b. Bryan, Tex., Feb. 1, 1957; s. Edwin Peter and Bonny Jo (Robertson) S.; m. Kolleen Marie Stevens, Aug. 8, 1981; 1 child, Laine Sheridan. Student, Blinn Jr. Coll., 1977-78, U. Tex., 1977, Tex. A&M U., 1977-83; BBA, Ky. Western. U., 1990; MBA, Ky. Western U., 1994. Lic. long term care adminstr.; cert. preceptor. Sr. v.p. ops. Sherwood Health Care, Inc., Bryan, 1976-90, pres., 1990—; sec.-treas. Sherwood Health Care, Inc., Lubbock, Tex., 1987-89; pres. Sherwood Health Care, Inc., Bryan, 1990, Lubbock, 1990; pres., owner Brazos Mgmt. Health Care, Inc., Bryan, 1991; owner Sherwood Forest Children's Ctr., 1991; pres. Sherwood Gardens Adult Day Health Care, 1996. Mem. Lt. Gov. Bullock's Nursing Home Work Group, 1991-92; participant state debate with Lt. Gov. Hobby, Austin, Tex., 1987; mem. Legis. Oversight Com.; active St. Joseph Sch. Bd. Fellow Am. Coll. Health Care Adminstrs., Am. Health Care Assn., Tex. Health Care Assn. (bd. dirs. 1987-90, chair, chpt. pres. 1987-88, facility stds. com. 1987—, payment for svcs. com. 1987—, Medicare com. 1989—, Omnibus Budget Reconciliation Act of 1987 com. 1987—, patient admission screening and resident rev. com. 1989—, legis. com. 1987-89, co-chair budget and fin. com. 1990-91, automation com. 1990-91, pilot project site NHIC automation 1990-91, nursing home quality and case mix demonstration pilot project 1995—), Bryan Coll. C. of C. Inner Cir., Am. Assn. Ret. Persons (Medicare/Medicaid steering com.), Tex. A&M U. Century Club, KC, Elks. Republican. Roman Catholic. Avocations: racquetball, golf, bowling, bow fishing, water skiing. Home: PO Box 3553 Bryan TX 77805-3553 Office: Sherwood Health Care Inc 1401 Memorial Dr Bryan TX 77802-5218

SULIMIRSKI, WITOLD STANISLAW, banker; b. Lwow, Poland, May 18, 1933; came to U.S., 1957; s. Tadeusz and Olga (Lepkowska) S.; m. Teresa Maria Boniecka, Dec. 28, 1957; children: Elizabeth Sulimirski Blakeslee, Adam, Edward. BA with honors, Cambridge U., 1953, MA, 1957. With Irving Trust Co., N.Y.C., 1957-89, exec. v.p., 1986-89; pres. Servus Assocs., Inc., N.Y.C., 1989-95; chmn. exec. com. Intercap Investments, Inc., N.Y.C., 1989—; chmn. Am. Bank in Poland, Warsaw, 1989-91, LBS Bank N.Y., 1990—; exec. dir. Am. Investment Initiative in Poland, Warsaw, 1992-94; bd. dirs. Bank Pekao SA, Warsaw, 1993-95, 12th Nat. Investment Fund, Warsaw, 1994—, Bank Gdanski, Gdansk, 1995—, Bicentennial Publs., N.Y.C., 1996—. Treas. Polish Inst. Arts and Scis., Inc., N.Y.C., 1976—; vice chmn. Kosciuszko Found., Inc., N.Y.C., 1983—; chmn. Polish Assistance, Inc., N.Y.C., 1984-92; bd. dirs. Middle East Policy Coun., Washington, 1984—, Nat. U.S.-Arab C. of C., Washington, 1987-93. Mem.

Bronxville Field Club, Knights of Malta. Roman Catholic. Office: Intercap Investments Inc 430 Park Ave Fl 10 New York NY 10022-3505

SULKIN, HOWARD ALLEN, college president; b. Detroit, Aug. 19, 1941; s. Lewis and Vivian P. (Mandel) S.; m. Constance Annette Adler, Aug. 4, 1963; children—Seth R., Randall K. PhB, Wayne State U., 1963; MBA, U. Chgo., 1965, PhD, 1969; LHD (hon.), De Paul U., 1990. Dir. program rsch., indsl. rels. ctr. U. Chgo., 1964-72; dean Sch. for New Learning, De Paul U., Chgo., 1972-77; v.p. De Paul U., Chgo., 1977-84; pres. Spertus Inst. Jewish Studies, Chgo., 1984—; St. Paul's vis. prof. Rikkyo U., Tokyo, 1970—; cons., evaluator North Central Assn., Chgo., 1975—. Contbr. articles to profl. jours. Sec.-treas. Grant Park Cultural and Ednl. Cmty., Chgo., 1984—; bd. dirs. Chgo. Sinai Congregation, 1972—, pres., 1980-83; bd. dirs. S.E. Chgo. Commn., 1980—, United Way, 1984—, Crusade of Mercy United Way, 1990—; bd. dirs., chmn. Parliament of World's Religions, 1989—. Mem. Adult Edn. Assn. U.S.A., Acad. Internat. Bus., Cliff Dwellers (Chgo.), The Standard Club. Office: Spertus Inst of Jewish Studies 618 S Michigan Ave Chicago IL 60605-1900

SULLENBERGER, ARA BROOCKS, mathematics educator; b. Amarillo, Tex., Jan. 3, 1933; d. Carl Clarence and Ara Frances (Broocks) Cox; m. Hal Joseph Sullenberger, Nov. 2, 1952; children: Hal Joseph Jr., Ara Broocks Sullenberger Switzer. Student, Randolph-Macon Woman's Coll., 1951-52, So. Meth. U., 1952, U. Tex., Arlington, 1953, Amarillo Coll., 1953-54; BA in Math., Tex. Tech. U., 1955, MA, 1958; postgrad., Tex. Christian U., 1963-67, U. N. Tex., 1969-80, Tarrant Jr. Coll., Fort Worth, Tex., 1972-83. Cert. tchr., Tex. Math. tchr Tom S. Lubbock (Tex.) High Sch., 1955-56; instr. math. Tex. Tech U., Lubbock, 1956-63; teaching fellow math. Tex. Christian U., Ft. Worth, 1963-64; chmn. dept. math. Ft. Worth Country Day Sch., 1964-67; instr. math. Tarrant County Jr. Coll.-South, Ft. Worth, 1967-70, asst. prof. math., 1970-74, assoc. prof. math., 1974-95; prof. emeritus, 1995—, ret., 1995; cons. Project Change, Ft. Worth, 1967-68; math. scis. advisor Coll. Bd., Princeton, N.J., 1979-83; math. book reviewer for various pub. cos. including Prentice-Hall, McGraw Hill, D.C. Heath, Prindle, Weber & Schmidt, MacMillan, Harcourt, Brace Jovanovich, West Worth, Saunders, Wadsworth. Contbr. article, book revs. to profl. publs.; author book supplement to Intermediate Algebra, 1990. Active mem. Jr. League of Ft. Worth, 1954-73, sustaining mem., 1973—; editor newsletter Crestwood Assn., Ft. Worth, 1984, 86, 91, membership sec., 1985, 90, 91, 95, pres., 1988-89, crime patrol capt., 1993, v.p., 1993, treas., 1987, 96, sec., 1997-98. Recipient award for excellence in teaching Gen. Dynamics, 1968. Mem. Math. Assn. Am. (life), Nat. Coun. Tchrs. Math. (life), Am. Math. Assn. Two-Yr. Colls. (life), Tex. Math. Assn. Two-Yr. Colls. (charter, v.p. 1997-99), Tex. Jr. Coll. Tchrs. Assn., Pi Beta Phi. Republican. Episcopalian. Avocations: grandchildren, reading, pets, walking, writing. Home: 600 Eastwood Ave Fort Worth TX 76107-1020

SULLENBERGER, DONALD SHIELDS, air force officer, business executive; b. Knoxville, Tenn., Sept. 30, 1940; s. Archibald Jack and Rebecca Pauline (Myers) S.; m. Karen Sue Long, June 10, 1961; children: Douglas, Robert, Erik. BA magna cum laude, U. Nebr., Omaha, 1966; MBA, U. Mont., Missoula, 1979; MS, Golden Gate U., 1990, Marymount U., 1995. Lic. comml. airline pilot. Commd. 2d lt. USAF, 1962, advanced through grades to col., 1984; dir. tng. and evaluation USAF, Da Nang AFB, Vietnam, 1971-73; dir. ICBM ops./tng. USAF, Great Falls, Mont., 1973-76; several posts USAF, Madrid, 1976-79; comdr. USAF, Moody AFB, Ga., 1979-84; dep. comdr. for maintenance USAF, Myrtle Beach AFB, S.C., 1984-85; base comdr. USAF, Homestead AFB, Fla., 1985-87; div. and gen. mgr. Holloman Support div. Dyncorp, Alamogordo, N.Mex., 1987-91; corp. v.p. Dyncorp, Reston, Va., 1991-95; pres. Apogee Cons. Enterprises, Knoxville, Tenn., 1995—; ind. cons., Washington, 1995—. Bd. dirs. United Way, Alamogordo, 1989-91; bd. dirs. Vision 2000 of Homestead City Coun., 1985-87; mem. Reston Quality Roundtable, 1991-94. Decorated Legion of Merit, DFC, Bronze Star, Air medal (10), Meritorious Svc. medal (4), Joint Svc. Commendation medal. Mem. VFW, Am. Soc. Quality Control, Quality Productivity and Mgmt. Assn., Am. Mgmt. Assn., Am. Legion. Avocations: running, conditioning, flying. Home: 5212 Hickory Hollow Rd Knoxville TN 37919 Office: Apogee Cons Enterprises 5212 Hickory Hollow Rd Knoxville TN 37919-9315

SULLIVAN, ADÈLE WOODHOUSE, organization official; b. Trenton, N.J.; d. William and Adaline Dearth (Fox) Woodhouse; m. Harold E. Erb, May 27, 1929 (dec. Nov. 1957); m. William H. Sullivan, Jr., Mar. 17, 1960 (dec. Dec. 1985); 1 child, Nancy Elizabeth (Mrs. Joseph P. Thorne). Student, Rider Coll., 1925-27; LHD, Lincoln Meml. U., 1968. Mem. DAR, 1931—; state regent DAR, N.Y., 1953-56, hon. state regent for life, 1956—, nat. rec. sec. gen., 1956-59, 1st v.p. gen., 1959-62, nat. pres. gen., 1965-68, hon. pres. gen. for life, 1968—, organizing chmn. Centennial Jubilee, 1983-89; founder, pres. Nat. DAR Exec. Club, 1962-64; pres. Nat. DAR Officers Club, 1978-80; past trustee DAR Schs. Kate Duncan Smith, Grant, Ala., Tamassee, S.C., Crossnore, N.C.; sec. Air Corps office Keystone Aircraft Corp., 1927-29; sec., treas. Power Machinery Corp., N.Y.C., 1961-65. Pres. Woodhull Day Sch. PTA, Hollis, N.Y., 1942-44; chmn. student loan fund women's aux. ASME, 1946-48; v.p. N.Y. colony New Eng. Women, 1963-65; mem. Women's Nat. Adv. Commn. for Nixon, 1968; chmn. N.Y. Women for Buckley, 1970, Women's Nat. Rep. Campaign Com., 1972; mem. nat. adv. bd. Am. Security Coun.; vis. U.S. Troops, Vietnam, Jan., 1968; bd. dirs. Nat. Symphony Orch. Assn., 1965-68, Friends of Historic St. George's Ch., Hempstead, L.I., 1960-67; bd. dirs., exec. v.p. nat. affairs Cultural Laureat Found., Inc., 1973-77 ; mem. awards jury Freedoms Found., 1966-67; mem. nat. honors com. Women's Hall of Fame, Inc.; program chmn. Women's Soc., Scarsdale Community Bapt. Ch., 1977-80, trustee, 1980-86. Recipient commendation award U.S. Navy for work with DAR, World War II. award for outstanding svc. to nation Am. Coalition Patriotic Socs., 1967, Freedom Found. medal of honor, 1967, Gold medal Nat. Soc. New Eng. Women, 1969, Nat. Capital USO Disting. Svc. cert., 1968. Mem. Am. Friends of Lafayette (exec. coun.), Hon. Soc. Ky. Cols., Ams. for Patriotism, Inc. (organizing past pres.). Home and Office: 41 Tanners Dr Wilton CT 06897 *To aid in promoting a sense of responsible citizenship through education. To do each task undertaken to the best of my ability. To endeavor to do unto others as I would have them do unto me. To have the satisfaction of having a young woman say she had been favorably influenced by me.*

SULLIVAN, ALFRED DEWITT, academic administrator; b. New Orleans, Feb. 2, 1942; s. Dewitt Walter and Natalie (Alford) S.; m. Marilyn Janie Hewitt, Sept. 1, 1962 (div. May 1989); children: Alan, Sean; m. Dorothy Madeleine Hess, Apr. 1993. BS, La. State U., 1964, MS, 1966; PhD, U. Ga., 1969. Asst. prof. Va. Poly. Inst. and State U., Blacksburg, 1969-73; assoc. prof., then prof. Miss. State U., Starkville, 1973-88; dir. Sch. Forest Resources Pa. State U., University Park, 1988-93; dean coll. natural resources U. Minn., St. Paul, 1993—. Contbr. articles to profl. jours. Fellow Am. Coun. on Edn., 1987-88, NDEA fellow U. Ga., 1966-69; assoc. Danforth Found., 1981. Mem. Soc. Am. Foresters. Office: U Minn 235 Natural Resources Adminstrn Bldg 2003 Upper Buford Cir Saint Paul MN 55108-6146*

SULLIVAN, ALLEN TROUSDALE, securities company executive; b. Nashville, Dec. 16, 1927; s. William Albert and Eleanor (Allen) S.; m. Barbara Oman, Nov. 12, 1955; children: Merida, Louise. Mgr. Ralph Nichols Co., Nashville, 1949-56; ptnr. J.C. Bradford & Co., Nashville, 1956—. Bd. dirs. Loves & Fishes; pres. bd. Monroe Harding Children's Home. With USN, 1943-46. Mem. Nashville Security Dealers Assn. (pres. 1989). Clubs: Belle Meade (Nashville), Nashville City (Nashville). Home: 7 Valley Frg Nashville TN 37205-4725 Office: JC Bradford & Co 330 Commerce St Nashville TN 37201-1805

SULLIVAN, ANNE DOROTHY HEVNER, artist; b. Boston, Mar. 17, 1929; m. James Leo Sullivan, Jan. 20, 1951; children: Maura, Mark, Lianne, Christopher. Student, Northeastern U., 1973-75; BA, U. Mass., Lowell, 1977; postgrad., De Cordova Mus., Lincoln, Mass., 1978-81. Art dir., instr. Whistler House Mus., Lowell, Mass., 1971-73, 96; art instr., dir. alternatives for individual devel. program U. Mass., Lowell, 1976-84; incorporator Depot Square Artists Gallery, Lexington, Mass., 1981-84; dir., art cons. Abbey Art Gallery, Boston, 1987-88; juried artist Emerson Umbrella Ctr. for Arts, Concord, Mass., 1989-92; juried artist Brush with History Gallery, Lowell, Mass., 1992-96, instr., 1996; juror, lectr., demonstrator, tchr. to art groups and assns., 1971—. Exhibited in nat. juried group shows at Fed. Res. Gallery, Boston, 1990, 92, 94, 96, Brush With History Gallery, 1990-96, Lowell Urban Nat. Pk., 1996, Midwest Mus. of Am. Art, Elkhardt, Ind., 1991, Cahoon Mus., Cotuit, Mass., 1991, Sumner Mus., Washington, 1992, Whistler Mus., 1992, 95, 96, Duxbury Mus., 1992, Attleboro (Mass.) Mus., 1992, C.L. Wolfe Art Club, N.Y.C., 1992, 96, N.E. Ctr.-U. N.H., 1992, Emerson Umbrella at Fed. Res. Boston, 1993, Bentley Coll., Walham, Mass., 1993, Fitchburg (Mass.) Mus., 1994, U. Mass. Med. Sch., Worcester, 1994, Whistler Mus. Invitational Exhibit of Paintings, Lowell, 1995, Fuller Mus.-Printmakers' Monotype Exhibit, Brockton, Mass., 1995, Nat. Assn. Women Artists 107th Ann., N.Y.C., 1996, N.Am. Open Competition, Boston, 1996; represented in permanent collections at Neil Sulier Art Collection, Lexington, Ky., The New Eng. Bank, Shawmut Bank, Bay Banks, Concord Nat. Bank, Amoskeag Banks, N.H., 1st Capital Bank of Concord, N.H., Sheraton Corp., Boston, Calif., New Orleans, Women's Caucus for the Arts, Sarasota, Fla., 1997 (Best of Show); artist: watermedia series/abstracts; author: Abstracts in Watercolor, 1996. Bd. dirs. Human Svcs. Corp., Lowell, 1971-72; v.p. Whistler Mus. Art, 1972-73; chmn. Lowell Arts Coun., 1980-81; mem. Mass. Arts Advocacy Coun., Boston, 1982. Recipient M.M. Rines award for outstanding contemporary painting N.Am. Open Competition, Fed. Res. Gallery, Boston, 1994, Catharine Lorillard Wolfe Art Club, Inc. award, 1992, Catharine L. Wolfe Art Club, N.Y., 1996, Am. Artist Mag., 1996, hon. mention All New Eng. Competition, 1989, Fitchburg Mus. 59th Ann., 1994, 2d prize Cahoon Mus., 1991, M. Hoarty & C. Grimm award, No. Am. Open Competition, award Am. Artist Mag., 1996. Mem. Nat. Assn. women Artists (Martha Reed Meml. award 1988, Leila Sawyer Meml. award 1994), New Eng. Watercolor Soc. (bd. dirs. 1984-92), Monotype Guild New Eng. (pres. 1992-93), Nat. League Am. Penwomen (award of excellence 1990), Copley Soc. (Copley Artist award). Home: 28 Rindo Park Dr Lowell MA 01851-3413

SULLIVAN, AUSTIN PADRAIC, JR., diversified food company executive; b. Washington, June 26, 1940; s. Austin P. Sullivan and Janet Lay (Patterson); m. Judith Ann Raab, June 8, 1968; children: Austin P. III, Amanda, Alexander. AB cum laude, Princeton U., 1964. Spl. asst. to dep. dir. N.J. Office Econ. Opportunity, Trenton, 1965-66; prof. staff mem. Com. on Edn. and Labor, U.S. Ho. of Reps., Washington, 1967-71, legis. dir., 1971-76; dir. govt. relations Gen. Mills, Inc., Mpls., 1976-78, v.p., corp. dir. govt. relations, 1978-79, v.p. pub. affairs, 1979-93, v.p. corp. comms. and pub. affairs, 1993-94, sr. v.p. corp. rels., 1994—; lectr. fed. labor market policies Harvard U., 1972-76, Boston U., 1972-76. Bd. dirs., exec. com. Guthrie Theatre, Mpls., 1978-84, Minn. Citizens for the Arts, 1980-83, Mpls. Cmty. Bus. Employment Alliance, 1982-84, Urban Coalition Mpls., 1978-80; chmn. Pub. Affairs Coun., 1993-94; chmn. Mpls. Pvt. Industry Coun.,1983-87; mem. Nat. Commn. on Employment and Tng., 1979-81; chmn. Gov.'s Coun. on Employment and Tng., 1976-82; co-chmn. Gov's Comn. on Dislocated Workers, 1988-89; mem. steering com. Minn. Meeting, 1982-94; bd. advisors Dem. Leadership Coun., 1986—; Minn. C. of C., bd. dirs. 1993—; prin. the Coun. for Excellence in Govt., 1988-95; With USMC, 1957-59. Eleanor Roosevelt fellow in interracial relations, 1964-65. Mem. Conf. Bd., Coun. of Pub. Affairs Execs. (chmn. 1989-90), Grocery Mfrs. Assn. (chmn. state govt. rels. task force 1989-90, govt. affairs coun. 1991—), Greater Mpls. C. of C. (bd. dirs., exec. com. 1980-86, 90-93), Bus. Roundtable (pub. info. com. 1987—). Home: 17830 County Rd 6 Minneapolis MN 55447-2905 Office: Gen Mills Inc One Gen Mills Blvd Minneapolis MN 55426

SULLIVAN, BARBARA, publishing company executive. Pres. Reed Info. Svcs., New Providence, N.J., v.p. EMI. Office: Reed Elsevier New Providence 121 Chanlon Rd New Providence NJ 07974-1541 also: Cahners 245 W 17th St New York NY 10011*

SULLIVAN, BARBARA BOYLE, management consultant; b. Scranton, Pa., Apr. 12, 1937; d. Edmund F. and Mary R. (O'Connell) Boyle; m. John L. Sullivan Jr. BS in Bus. Adminstrn., Drexel U., 1958; PhD (hon.), Newton Coll., 1975, Gwynedd Mercy Coll., 1975. With IBM, 1959-72; systems engring. mgr. Ea. and Cen. Europe IBM, Vienna, Austria, 1967-70; mgmt. devel. mgr. IBM, 1970, mgr. spl. programs, 1970-71, sales mgr., asst. br. mgr., 1971-72; pres. Boyle/Kirkman Assocs., N.Y.C., 1972-88; mng. ptnr. Innovation Assocs., Framingham, Mass., 1988-92; bd. dirs. Equitable Resources, Inc., 1974-96, chair compensation com., 1989-92, audit com., 1991, mem. audit, pension trust, and compensation com.; cons. major corps. on human resource devl. programs, organizational change programs, changing work force; condr. exec. leadership and visionary and strategic planning awareness seminars Harvard Bus. Sch., Internat. Mgmt. Conf. Trustee Drexel U.; mem. Pres.'s adv. com. Gwynedd Mercy Coll., adv. com. Drexel U. Coll. Bus. Adminstrn.; vice chmn. bd. trustee Marymount Manhattan Coll., N.Y., bd. regents Mt. St. Mary's Coll., L.A., 1982-88. Featured in numerous mags., books, radio and TV programs, including CBS 60 Minutes; named Bus. Person of Yr. St. Johns U., 1973, One of 50 Leaders for Future, Time mag., 1979. Mem. AAUW, Women's Forum, Weston Womens' League, Boston Club. Home: 264 St Andrews St Simons Island GA 31522

SULLIVAN, BARRY, lawyer, educator; b. Newburyport, Mass., Jan. 11, 1949; s. George Arnold and Dorothy Bennett (Furbush) S.; m. Winnifred Mary Fallers, June 14, 1975; children: George Arnold, Lloyd Ashton. AB cum laude, Middlebury Coll., 1970; JD, U. Chgo., 1974. Bar: Mass. 1975, Ill. 1975, Va. 1995, U.S. Dist. Ct. (no. dist.) Ill. 1976, U.S. Ct. Appeals (7th cir.) 1976, U.S. Ct. Appeals (10th cir.) 1977, U.s. Supreme Ct. 1978, U.S. Ct. Appeals (11th cir.) 1986, U.S. Ct. Appeals (5th and 9th cirs.) 1987, U.S. Ct. Appeals (fed. cir.) 1993, U.S. Ct. Appeals (D.C. cir.) 1994. Law clk. to judge John Minor Wisdom U.S. Ct. Appeals (5th cir.), New Orleans, 1974-75; assoc. Jenner & Block, Chgo., 1975-80; asst. to solicitor gen. of U.S. U.S. Dept. of Justice, Washington, 1980-81; ptnr. Jenner & Block, Chgo., 1981-94; dean, prof. law Washington and Lee U., Lexington, Va., 1994—; spl. asst. atty. gen. State of Ill., 1989-90; lectr. in law Loyola U., Chgo., 1978-79; adj. prof. law Northwestern U., Chgo., 1990-92, 93-94, vis. prof., 1992-93; Jessica Swift Meml. lectr. in constnl. law Middlebury Coll., 1991. Assoc. editor U. Chgo. Law Rev., 1973-74; contbr. articles to profl. jours. Trustee Cath. Theol. Union at Chgo., 1993—; mem. vis. com. U. Chgo. Divinity Sch., 1987—. Yeats Soc. scholar, 1968; Woodrow Wilson fellow, Woodrow Wilson Found., 1970. Mem. ABA (chmn. coord. com. on AIDS 1988-94, mem. standing com. on amicus curiae briefs 1990—, mem. coun. of sect. of individual rights and responsibilities 1993—, mem. council of legal edn. com. on law sch. adminstrn. 1994—), Va. Bar Assn., Bar Assn. 7th Fed. Cir. (vice chmn. adminstrv. justice com. 1985-86), Am. Law Inst., Law Club Chgo., Phi Beta Kappa. Democrat. Roman Catholic. Home: 201 Jackson Ave Lexington VA 24450-2007 Office: Washington and Lee U Sch Law Sydney Lewis Hall Lexington VA 24450

SULLIVAN, BEN FRANK, JR., real estate broker; b. Brookesmith, Tex., Aug. 10, 1919; s. Ben Frank and Vera Scott (Hennigan) S.; m. Frances Louise Levisay, Dec. 28, 1946; children: Thomas James, Ben Charles, Harold Lyndon. Student, Tarleton State U., 1937-39; BS, Tex. A&M U., 1941. Commd. 2d lt. U.S. Army, 1942, advanced through grades to capt., 1943-46; capt. U.S. Army Res., 1946-53, ret., 1953; sales/mktg. Armour & Co., Ft. Worth, 1946; owner Grocery Bus., Bangs, Tex., 1946-48; postmaster U.S. Postal Svc., Bangs, 1947-66, rural mail carrier, 1966-75; owner/broker Sullivan Real Estate, Bangs, 1963—; owner Sullivan Ranch, Bangs, 1962—; owner oper. Oil & Gas Prodn. on Ranch, Bangs, 1974—; owner, mgr. Home Bldg. & Sales, Bangs, 1965-94. Sunday sch. tchr., ch. supt., chmn. ofcl. bd. Bangs United Meth. Ch.; trustee Brownwood Dist. Ctrl. Tex. Conf. United Meth. Ch., 1983—, also chmn. bd.; committeeman Meth. Home, Waco, 1982-83; mem. steering com. to form Brookesmith Water Corp., Brown County, Tex., 1971, bd. dirs., 1971-73. With U.S. Army, 1941-46. Decorated 2 bronze stars, WWII victory medal. Mem. Brown County C. of C. (bd. dirs. 1993-95), Am. Legion (comdr. post # 308 1949), Masons, Order of Ea. Star, Shriners, Lions (pres. 1963-64). Methodist. Avocations: hunting, fishing, boating, sports, travel, reading.

SULLIVAN, BERNARD JAMES, accountant; b. Chgo., June 25, 1927; s. Bernard Hugh and Therese Sarah (Condon) S.; m. Joan Lois Costello, June 9, 1951; children: Therese Lynn Scanlan, Bernard J., Geralyn M. Snyder. BSC, Loyola U., Chgo., 1950. CPA, Ill. Staff Bansley and Kiener, Chgo., 1950-66, ptnr., 1966-82, mng. ptnr., 1982—; bd. dirs. Associated Acctg. Firms, Internat.; exec. com. Moore Stephens and Co., U.S.A., 1984—, Arbitrator Nat. Assn. Security Dealers. Served with USN, 1945-46. Mem. Am. Inst. CPA's, Ill. Soc. CPA's, Govt. Fin. Officer Assn., Internat. Found. Employee Benefit Plans, Delta Sigma Pi. Clubs: Beverly Country (Chgo.), Metropolitan (Chgo.). Lodges: Elks, K.C. Avocations: golf, sports, travel. Home: 9636 S Kolmar Ave Oak Lawn IL 60453-3214 Office: Bansley & Kiener 125 S Wacker Dr Chicago IL 60606-4402

SULLIVAN, BILL, church administrator. Dir. Church Growth Division of the Church of the Nazarene, Kansas City, Mo. Office: Church of Nazarene 6401 Paseo Blvd Kansas City MO 64131-1213*

SULLIVAN, BRENDAN V., JR., lawyer; b. Providence, Mar. 11, 1942. AB, Georgetown U., 1964, JD, 1967. Bar: R.I. 1967, D.C. 1970, U.S. Dist. Ct. D.C. 1970, U.S. Ct. Appeals (D.C. cir.) 1970, U.S. Supreme Ct. 1972, U.S. Dist. Ct. Md. 1974, U.S. Ct. Appeals (4th cir.) 1981, U.S. Ct. Appeals (3d cir.) 1979, U.S. Ct. Appeals (6th cir.) 1991, U.S. Ct. Appeals (9th cir.) 1996. Mem. Williams & Connolly, Washington; lectr. Practicing Law Inst., 1981—, Md. Inst. for Continuing Profl. Edn. of Lawyers, Inc., 1979—, D.C. Criminal Practice Inst., 1975-81. Author: Grand Jury Proceedings, 1981, Techniques for Dealing with Pending Criminal Charges or Criminal Investigations, 1983, White Collar Criminal Practice Grand Jury, 1985. Fellow Am. Coll. Trial Lawyers; mem. ABA, R.I. Bar Assn., D.C. Bar. Office: Williams & Connolly 725 12th St NW Washington DC 20005-3901

SULLIVAN, CATHERINE MARY, home health care agency administrator; b. Winter Park, Fla., Apr. 23, 1962; d. Andrew Edward and Jean Frances (DeSalvo) McCaw; m. Cornelius Francis Sullivan, Nov. 19, 1960. BA in Biology, Belmont (N.C.) Abbey Coll., 1985. With microbiology dept. Orlando (Fla.) Regional Med. Ctr., 1985-86; mktg. sec. MetLife Healthcare Network Fla., Inc., HMO, 1986-87; dir. client svcs. Alan Health Care Svcs., Freehold, N.J., 1987—. Roman Catholic. Avocations: tennis, travel, reading.

SULLIVAN, CHARLES, university dean, educator, author; b. Boston, May 27, 1933; s. Charles Thomas and Marion Veronica (Donahue) S.; divorced; children: Charles Fulford, John Driscoll, Catherine Page. BA in English, Swarthmore Coll., 1955; MA, NYU, 1968, PhD in Social Psychology, 1973; MPA, Pa. State U., 1978. Predoctoral fellow NYU, 1964-68; postdoctoral fellow Ednl. Testing Svc., Princeton, N.J., 1973-74; asst. prof. psychology Ursinus Coll., Collegeville, Pa., 1973-78; mgmt. cons., 1978-86; adj. prof. Pa. State U., Radnor, Pa., 1978-80; prof., head dept. pub. adminstrn., dir. student svcs. Southeastern U., Washington, 1986-89; asst. dean Grad. Sch. Arts and Scis. Georgetown U., Washington, 1989-92, assoc. dean Grad. Sch. Arts and Scis., 1992—, professorial lectr., dept. psychology, 1994-95; exec. dir. Doylestown Found., Doylestown, Pa., 1958-73; adj. prof. social and behavioral scis. U. Md., 1984-96; lectr., spkr. on lit. and art Cooper-Hewitt Mus., N.Y.C., Nat. Soc. Arts and Letters, Washington, Martin Luther King Jr. Libr., Washington, Met. Mus. Art, N.Y.C., Smithsonian Instn., Washington, Children's Book Fair, N.Y.C., Nat. Mus. Women in Arts, Lombardi Cancer Rsch. Ctr., Georgetown U., Arts Club of Washington, Phillips Collection, Corcoran Gallery of Art. Author: Alphabet Animals, 1991, The Lover in Winter, 1991, Numbers at Play, 1992, Circus, 1992, Cowboys, 1993, A Woman of A Certain Age, 1994. Out of Love, 1996; editor: America in Poetry, 1988, 2d edit., 1992, 3d edit., 1996, Imaginary Gardens, 1989, Ireland in Poetry, 1990, Children of Promise, 1991, Loving, 1992, American Beauties, 1993, Here Is My Kingdom, 1994, Fathers and Children, 1995, Imaginary Animals, 1996. Mem. bd. trustees Folger Poetry Bd., 1988-92; Nat. Soc. Arts and Letters, 1992-94, Am. Acad. Liberal Edn., 1995—; pres. Am. Found. Arts, 1995—. Mem. Am. Poetry Soc., Acad. Am. Poets, Cosmos Club. Office: Georgetown U Grad Sch 302 Intercultural Ctr Washington DC 20057

SULLIVAN, CLAIRE FERGUSON, marketing educator; b. Pittsburg, Tex., Sept. 28, 1937; d. Almon Lafayette and Mabel Clara (Williams) Potter; m. Richard Wayne Ferguson, Jan. 31, 1959 (div. Jan. 1980); 1 child, Mark Jeffrey Ferguson; m. David Edward Sullivan, Nov. 2, 1984. BBA, U. Tex., 1958, MBA, 1961; PhD, U. North Tex., 1973; grad., Harvard Inst. Ednl. Mgmt., 1991. Instr. So. Meth. U., Dallas, 1965-70; asst. prof. U. Utah, Salt Lake City, 1972-74; assoc. prof. U. Ark., Little Rock, 1974-77, U. Tex., Arlington, 1977-80, Ill. State U., Normal, 1980-84; prof., chmn. mktg. Bentley Coll., Waltham, Mass., 1984-89; dean sch. bus. Met. State Coll. Denver, 1989-92, prof. mktg., 1992—; cons. Denver Partnership, 1989-90, Gen. Tel. Co., Irving, Tex., 1983, McKnight Pub. Co., Bloomington, Ill., 1983, dental practitioner, Bloomington, 1982-83, Olympic Fed., Berwyn, Ill., 1982, Denver Partnership Econ. Devel. Adv. Coun., 1989-91; mem. African-Am. Leadership Inst. Gov. Bd. Contbr. mktg. articles to profl. jours. Direct Mktg. Inst. fellow, 1981; Ill. State U. rsch. grantee, 1981-83. Mem. Am. Mktg. Assn. (faculty fellow 1984-85), Beta Gamma Sigma. Republican. Methodist. Home: 408 E 10th Ave Salt Lake City UT 84103 Office: Met State Coll Dept Mktg MSCD Box 79 PO Box 173362 Denver CO 80217-3362

SULLIVAN, COLLEEN ANNE, physician, educator; b. Lucknow, India, Feb. 11, 1937; came to U.S., 1961; d. Douglas George and Nancy Irene (MacLeod) S.; m. Alexander Walter Gotta, July 17, 1965; 1 child, Nancy Colleen. MB ChB, U. St. Andrews, Scotland, 1961. Diplomate Am. Bd. Anesthesiology, Am. Coll. Anesthesiologists. Rotating intern Nassau Hosp., Mineola, N.Y., 1961-62; clin. instr. Cornell U., N.Y.C., 1962-64; resident in anesthesiology N.Y. Hosp./Cornell U., 1962-64; fellow in anesthesiology Meml. Sloan-Kettering Cancer Ctr., N.Y.C., 1964-67, asst. prof. Cornell U. Med. Coll., 1978-79; assoc. dir. anesthesia St. Mary's Hosp.-Cath. Med. Ctr., Bklyn., 1968-78; clin. assoc. prof. SUNY, Bklyn., 1979-90, clin. prof. anesthesiology, 1990—, clin. dir. anesthesia, 1990-93; clin. dir. anesthesia Kings County Hosp., Bklyn., 1983-90, med. dir. ambulatory surg. unit, 1993—. Author numerous chpt. in anesthesiology textbooks; contbr. articles to profl. jours. Mem. N.Y. State Soc. Anesthesiologists (ho. of dels. 1983—, asst. editor Sphere 1990-95, com. sci. program 1990—). Republican. Roman Catholic. Avocations: reading, cooking. Office: Kings County Hosp Dept Anesthesia 450 Clarkson Ave Brooklyn NY 11203-2012

SULLIVAN, CONNIE CASTLEBERRY, artist, photographer; b. Cin., Jan. 8, 1934; d. John Porter and Constance (Alf) Castleberry; m. John J. Sullivan, June 6, 1959; children: Deirdre Kelly, Margaret Graham. BA, Manhattanville Coll., 1957. spl. lectr. Cin. Contemporary Art Ctr., 1984, Toledo Friends of Photography, 1991, U. Ky. Art Mus., 1993, Dennison U. Sch. Art, 1993, El Instituto de Estudios Norte Americanos, Barcelona, 1994, Ctr. for Photography, Bombay, India, 1997. One-woman shows include Contemporary Art Ctr. Cleve., 1982, Cin. Contemporary Arts Ctr., 1983, Fogg Art Mus., Cambridge, Mass., 1983, 90, Neikrug Gallery, N.Y.C., 1984, Camden Arts Ctr., London, 1987, Evanston Art Ctr., Chgo., 1987, Silver Image Gallery Ohio State U., Columbus, 1988, Jean-Pierre Lambert Galerie, Paris, 1988, 96, David Winton Bell Gallery, Brown U., Providence, 1989, Toni Burckhead Gallery, Cin., 1989, Rochester Inst. Tech., 1991, Fotomus. im Münchner Stadtmus., Munich, 1992, U. Ky. Art Mus., Lexington, 1993, Internat. Photography Hall, Kirkpatrick Mus. complex, Oklahoma City, 1993, Institut d'Estudios Fotografics de Catalunya, Barcelona, Spain, 1994, Cheekwood Art Mus., Nashville, 1994, Museo Damy di Fotografia Contemporanea, Brescia, Italy, 1995, Photography Gallery U. Notre Dame, Ind., 1995, Louisville Visual Art Assoc., Watertower, Louisville, KY, 1995, Museo Damy, Milan, 1997, Ctr. for Photography, Bombay, India, 1997; exhibited in numerous group shows including Robert Klein Gallery, Boston, 1981, Cin. Art Mus., 1981, 84, 85, 93, Witkin Gallery, N.Y.C., 1984, Milw. Art Mus., 1986, Dayton (Ohio) Art Inst., 1987, J.B. Speed Art Mus., Louisville, 1988, Trisolini Gallery Ohio U., 1989, Ohio U., Athens, 1989, Centre Nat. Photographie, Paris, 1989, Cleve. Ctr. for Contemporary Art, 1991, Tampa Mus. Art, 1991, 93, Images Gallery, 1991, Dayton Art Inst./Mus. Contemporary Art Wright State U., Dayton, 1992, Bowling Green State U. Sch Art, 1992, Carnegie Arts Ctr., Covington, Ky., 1993, POLK Mus. Art, Lakeland, Fla., 1993, Tampa (Fla.) Mus. Art, 1993, Adams Landing Fine Art Ctr., Cin., 1995, Checkwood Mus. Art, Nashville, 1995, Photo Forum Gallery, 1995, 96, Jean-Pierre Galerie, 1996, Soros Ctr. Contemporary Art, Kiev, Ukraine, 1996, Dom Khudozhnikiv, Kharkiv, Ukraine, 1996, Wolf Photographic Galleries, Cin., 1996, Columbus Mus. Art, 1996, Louisville Visual Art Assn., Water Tower, 1997; represented in numerous permanent collections Tampa Mus. of Art, Münchner Stadt Mus., Munich, Germany, Museo Damy, Brescia, Italy, Ctr. Creative Photography, Tucson, Detroit Inst. Arts, Biblioteque National, Paris, Internat. Photography Hall of Fame and Mus., Kirkpatrick Ctr. Mus. Complex, Okla. City, Nelson Gallery-Atkins Mus., Kansas City, Ctr. for Photography, Bombay, Milw. Art Mus., Mus. Photography Arts, San Diego, Musee Nat. D'Art Modern, Centre Georges Pompidou, Paris, Denver Art Mus., Boston Mus. Fine Arts, Stanford U. Mus. Art, Palo Alto, Indpls. Art Mus., New Orleans Mus. Art, Fogg Mus., Cambridge, Mass., numerous others; also pvt. collections; author: Petroglyphs of the Heart, Photographs by Connie Sullivan, 1983; work represented in numerous publs. Trustee Images Ctr. for Fine Photography, Cin., 1986-94. Arts Midwest fellow NEA, 1989-90; recipient award Toledo Friends Photography Juried Show, 1986, Best of Show award, 1988, Images Gallery, 1986, Pres.'s Coun. for Arts award Manhattanville Coll., 1991, Treasure of the Month award Mus. Fine Arts St. Petersburg, Fla., 1995; Aid to Individual Artists grantee Summerfair, 1987, travel grantee Ohio Arts Coun., 1995, 97; named Hyde Park Living Person of Yr., 1996. Mem. McDowell Soc. Avocations: travel, reading, gardening, music. Home and Studio: 9 Garden Pl Cincinnati OH 45208-1056

SULLIVAN, CORNELIUS WAYNE, marine biology educator, research foundation administrator, government agency administrator; b. Pitts., June 11, 1943; s. John Wayne and Hilda Sullivan; m. Jill Hajjar, Oct. 28, 1966; children: Shane, Preston, Chelsea. BS in Biochemistry, Pa. State U., 1965, MS in Microbiology, 1967; PhD in Marine Biology, U. Calif., San Diego, 1971. Postdoctoral fellow Scripps Inst. Oceanography, La Jolla, Calif., 1971-74; asst. prof. marine biology U. So. Calif., L.A., 1974-80, assoc. prof., 1980-85, prof., 1985—, dir. marine biology sect., 1982-91; dir. Hancock Inst. Marine Studies, L.A., 1991-93; dir. Office of Polar Programs Nat. Sci. Found., Washington, 1993—; dir. U.S. Antarctic Program, 1993—; vis. prof. U. Colo., Boulder, 1981-82, MIT, Cambridge, 1981-82, U.S. Army Cold Regions Rsch. & Engring. Lab., Hanover, 1989, Goddard Space Flight Ctr., Greenbelt, Md., 1990; field team leader Sea Ice Microbial Communities Studies, McMurdo Sound, Antarctica, 1980-86; chief scientist/cruise coord. Antarctic Marine Ecosystem Rsch. at the Ice Edge Zone Project, Weddell Sea, 1983, 86, 88; mem. BIOMASS Working Party on Pack-Ice Zone Studies, 1983-86, ecol. rsch. rev. bd. Dept. Navy, 1982-85; So. Ocean Ecology Group Specialist Sci. Com. on Antarctic Rsch.; chmn. SCOR working group 86 "Sea Ice Ecology" sci. com. on oceanic rsch.; mem. polar rsch. bd. NAS, 1983-86; chmn. com. to evaluate polar rsch. platforms Nat. Rsch. Coun., 1985—; mem. dir. policy group NSF, 1993—. Patent in Heat Sensitive Bacterial Alkaline Phosphatase; mem. editl. bd. Jour. Microbiol. Methods, 1982-85, Polar Biology, 1987—; contbr. over 100 articles to profl. jours. Head of delegation Com. Mgrs. of Nat. Antarctic Programs, New Zealand, Italy, U.K., 1993—; mem. U.S. Delegation Antarctic Treaty, 1993—; consultative meetings; With USPHS, 1969-71. Fellow USPHS, 1969-71; recipient Antarctic Svc. medal of U.S., NSF, 1981. Fellow AAAS. Office: NSF 4201 Wilson Blvd Ste 755 Arlington VA 22230-0001

SULLIVAN, DANIEL J., artistic director; b. Wray, Colo., June 11, 1940; s. John Martin and Mary Catherine (Hutton) S.; children: Megan, John, Rachel M. BA, San Francisco State U. Actor, Actor's Workshop, San Francisco, 1963-65; actor, dir. Lincoln Center Repertory, N.Y.C., 1965-73; dir. (broadway) I'm Not Rappaport, also numerous regional theatres, 1973-79; resident dir. Seattle Repertory Theater, 1979-81, artistic dir., 1981-97. Recipient Drama Desk award N.Y. Theatre Critics, 1972. Mem. Nat. Endowment for Arts. Democrat. Office: Seattle Repertory Theatre 155 Mercer St Seattle WA 98109-4639*

SULLIVAN, DANIEL JOSEPH, journalist; b. Worcester, Mass., Oct. 22, 1935; s. John Daniel and Irene Ann (Flagg) S.; m. Helen Faith Scheid, 1965; children: Margaret Ann, Benjamin, Kathleen. AB, Holy Cross Coll., 1957; postgrad., U. Minn., 1957-59, U. So. Calif., 1964-65, Stanford U., 1978-79. Reporter Worcester Telegram, Mass., 1957, Red Wing Republican Eagle, Minn., 1959, St. Paul Pioneer Press, 1959-61; music and theater critic Mpls. Tribune, 1962-64; comedy writer Dudley Riggs' Brave New Workshop, 1961-64; music writer/theater reviewer N.Y. Times, 1965-68; theater critic L.A. Times, 1969-90; dramaturge Eugene O'Neill Theatre Ctr., Waterford, Conn., 1972-73, 93-95; instr. Nat. Critics Inst., Waterford, 1977-92, assoc. dir., 1993—; adj. prof. U. Minn., Mpls., 1990-94; juror theater panel Nat. Endowment for Arts, 1983; juror Pulitzer Prize for Drama, 1985, 89, 92; pres. L.A. Drama Critics Circle, 1970-71, Ctr. for Arts Criticism, St. Paul, 1992-95. Mem. Am. Theater Critics Assn. (founding).

SULLIVAN, DANIEL THOMAS, electrical engineer, consultant; b. Aurora, Ill., Feb. 2, 1961; s. Audie Kyle and Eloise (Fischer) S. BSEE, U. Ill., Champaign, 1984; MSEE, Naval Postgrad. Sch., Monterey, Calif., 1992. Combat info. ctr. officer USN-USS Niagara Falls, Guam, 1985-88; ship's navigator USN-USS Sample, Pearl Harbor, Hawaii, 1988; main propulsion asst. USN-USS Sterett, Phillipines, 1989-90; dep. dir., automated data processing dept. Navy Occupational Devel. & Analysis Ctr., Washington, D.C., 1993-94; sr. systems engr. for the Joint Recruiting Info. Support System Lockheed Martin Tech. Svcs., Falls Church, Va., 1994-95; lead systems analyst to EPA's integrated database for enforcement analysis Lockheed Martin Tech. Svcs., Washington, D.C., 1995-97; lead sys. analyst Lockheed Martin Tech. Svcs., New Orleans, 1997—; cons. Defense Info. Systems Agy., Falls CH., 1994—. Contbr. articles to profl. jours. Tutor Thomas Jefferson Jr. H.S., Washington D.C., 1994. Lt. USN, 1984-94. Recipient Navy Achievement medal USN, 1987, 88, Navy Commendation medal, 1994, Performance Excellent award Pres. Lockheed Martin Svcs., Falls Church, 1995. Mem. IEEE, Eta Kappa Nu Nat. Engring. Honor Soc. Republican. Avocations: computers, running, personal growth. Home: 13310 Cleveland Ln Fort Washington MD 20744

SULLIVAN, DANNY, professional race car driver; b. Mar. 9, 1950; m. Brenda Sullivan; 1 child, Driscoll. Winner Indpls. 500, 1985; Indy Car champion winning 17 Indy Car races, 1988. Office: 434 E Cooper St Ste 201 Aspen CO 81611-1859

SULLIVAN, DENNIS JAMES, JR., public relations executive; b. Jersey City, Feb. 23, 1932; s. Dennis James and Mary Theresa (Coyle) S.; m. Constance Rosemary Shields, Jan. 31, 1953; children: Denise Sullivan Morrison, Mary Agnes Sullivan Wilderotter, Colleen Sullivan Bastkowski, Andrea Sullivan Doelling. AB, St. Peters Coll., 1953; postgrad., U. Md., 1955; MBA, U. Pa., 1973. Various line and staff positions N.J. Bell, 1955-61, N.Y. Telephone Co., 1961-64, 67-68; various line and staff positions AT&T, N.Y.C., 1964-67, 68-76, dir. mktg., 1972-74, asst. v.p., 1974-76; v.p. mktg. Ohio Bell Telephone Co., Cleve., 1976-78; v.p. consumer info. services AT&T-Am. Bell, Parsippany, N.J., 1978-83; exec. v.p. Cin. Bell Telephone Co., 1983-84, pres., 1984-87, also bd. dirs.; exec. v.p., chief fin. officer Cin. Bell Inc., 1987-93; ret., 1993; bd. dirs. Fifth Third Bancorp & Bank, Anthem Ins. Co., Access Corp. Author: Videotex, IEE Nat. Conf., 1981. Bd. dirs. Boy Scouts, Cin. Bd. Edn., 1993—; gen. chmn. United Way, 1990—. Lt. (j.g.) USN, 1953-55, ret. comdr. USNR, 1976. Mem. Fin. Exec. Inst., Commonwealth Club, Cin. Country Club, Queen City Club, Bankers Club, Met. Club. Roman Catholic. Office: DP Pub Relsc Hist Cable House 2245 Gilbert Ave Cincinnati OH 45206-3000

SULLIVAN, EDWARD, periodical editor; b. Sharon, Pa., 1956. BA in Journalism, Johns Hopkins U., 1979. From news editor to mgr. publs. Am. Soc. Quality Control, 1979-87; acquisitions editor Panel Publishers, 1987-89; mng. editor Bldg. Operating Mgmt., Milw., 1989—. Office: Bldg Operating Mgmt 2100 W Florist Ave Milwaukee WI 53209-3721

SULLIVAN, EDWARD JOSEPH, lawyer, educator; b. Bklyn., Apr. 24, 1945; s. Edward Joseph and Bridget (Duffy) S.; m. Patte Hancock, Aug. 7, 1982; children: Amy Brase, Molly Elsasser, Mary Christine. MA, St. John's U., 1973; JD, Willamette U., 1969; MA, cert. Urban Studies, Portland State U., 1974, Cert. in Urban Studies, 1974; LLM, Univ. Coll., London, 1978; diploma in law, Univ. Coll., Oxford, 1984. Bar: Oreg. 1969, D.C. 1978, U.S. Dist. Ct. Oreg. 1970, U.S. Ct. Appeals (9th cir.) 1970, U.S. Supreme Ct. 1972. Counsel Washington County, Hillsboro, Oreg., 1969-75; legal counsel Gov. of Oreg., Salem, 1975-77; ptnr. O'Donnell, Sullivan & Ramis, Portland, Oreg., 1978-84, Sullivan, Josselson, Roberts, Johnson & Kloos, Portland, Salem and Eugene, Oreg., 1984-86, Mitchell, Lang & Smith, Portland, 1986-90, Preston Gates & Ellis, Portland, 1990—; bd. dirs., pres. Oreg. Law Inst. Contbr. numerous articles to profl. jours. Chmn. Capitol Planning Commn., Salem, 1975-77, 78-81. Mem. ABA (local govt. sect., com. on planning and zoning, adminstrv. law sect.) Oreg. State Bar Assn., D.C. Bar Assn., Am. Judicature Soc., Am. Polit. Sci. Assn. Democrat. Roman Catholic. Office: Preston Gates & Ellis 111 SW 5th Ave Ste 3200 Portland OR 97204-3635

SULLIVAN, EMMET G., judge; b. Washington, June 4, 1947; s. Emmet A. and Eileen G. Sullivan; m. Nan Sullivan; children, Emmet, Erik. BA in Polit. Sci., Howard U., 1968, JD, 1971. Law clk. to Hon. James A. Washington, Jr. Superior Ct. D.C.; from assoc. to ptnr. Houston and Gardner, 1973-80; ptnr. Houston, Sullivan & Gardner, 1980-84; judge Superior Ct. D.C., 1984-92; assoc. judge U.S. Ct. Appeals (D.C. cir.), 1992—. Reginald Heber Smith fellow. Office: US Courthouse 333 Constitution Ave NW Washington DC 20001-2802*

SULLIVAN, EUGENE JOHN JOSEPH, manufacturing company executive; b. N.Y.C., Nov. 28, 1920; s. Cornelius and Margaret (Smith) S.; m. Gloria Roesch, Aug. 25, 1943; children: Eugene John Joseph, Edward J., Robert C., Elizabeth Ann Hansler. B.S., St. John's U., 1942, D.Commerce, 1973; M.B.A., N.Y. U., 1948. With chem. div. Borden, Inc., N.Y.C., 1946—; beginning as salesman, successively asst. sales Borden, Inc., 1957-58, exec. v.p., 1958-64; pres. Borden Chem. Co. div. Borden, Inc.; v.p. Borden, Inc., 1964-67, exec. v.p., 1967-73, pres., chief operating officer, 1973-79, chmn., pres., chief exec. officer, 1979-86; former adj. prof., now prof. St. John's U., 1987—; bd. dirs. W.R. Grace & Co.; chmn. bd. dirs. Hamilton Fund; trustee Atlantic Mut. Ins. Co. Trustee, vice chmn., past sec. St. John's U.; trustee N.Y. Med. Coll., Cath. Health Assn.; chmn. Commn. on Cath. Health Care. Served as lt. USNR, 1942-46; lt. Res. Mem. Coun. Fgn. Rels., Knights of Malta, Knights of Holy Sepulchre, Knights of St. Gregory, Univ. Club, Plandome Country Club, Westhampton Country Club. Office: Borden Inc 277 Park Ave New York NY 10172

SULLIVAN, EUGENE JOSEPH, food service company executive; b. Phila., Sept. 30, 1943; s. Eugene Joseph and Helen Patricia (Gartland) S.; m. Judith Ann Heller, June 12, 1965; children: Christine, Kimberly, Gregg. BS in Acctg., U. Scranton, 1965. Mgr. Swift & Co., 1965-72; with Dobbs Houses, Inc., Memphis, 1972-85, v.p., gen. mgr., 1977-82, sr. v.p., 1982-84, pres., 1984-85; pres. CKG Enterprises, Inc., Memphis, 1986—. Office: CKG Enterprises Inc 1642 E Shelby Dr Memphis TN 38116-7228

SULLIVAN, EUGENE RAYMOND, federal judge; b. St. Louis, Aug. 2, 1941; s. Raymond Vincent and Rosemary (Kiely) S.; m. Lis Urup Johansen, June 18, 1966; children—Kim, Eugene II. BS, U.S. Mil. Acad., 1964; JD, Georgetown U., 1971. Bar: Mo. 1972, D.C. 1972. Law clk. to judge U.S. Ct. Appeals (8th cir.), St. Louis, 1971-72; assoc. Patton Boggs & Blow, Washington, 1972-74; asst. spl. counsel The White House, Washington, 1974; trial counsel U.S. Dept. of Justice, Washington, 1974-82; dep. gen. counsel U.S. Air Force, Washington, 1982-84; gen. counsel U.S. Air Force, 1984-86; gov. Wake Island, 1984-86; judge U.S. Ct. Appeals (Armed Forces), Washington, 1986-90, 95—, chief judge, 1990-95; mem. Fed. Commn. To Study Honor Code at West Point, 1989-90. Trustee U.S. Mil. Acad., 1989—. With US Army, 1964-69. Decorated Bronze Star, Air medal, airborne badge, ranger badge, others. Republican. Roman Catholic. Home: 6307 Massachusetts Ave Bethesda MD 20816-1139 Office: US Ct Appeals (Armed Forces) 450 E St NW Washington DC 20442-0001

SULLIVAN, FRANK, JR., state supreme court justice; b. Mar. 21, 1950; s. Frank E. and Colette (Cleary) S.; m. Cheryl Gibson, June 14, 1972; children: Denis M., Douglas S., Thomas R. AB cum laude, Dartmouth Coll., 1972; JD magna cum laude, Ind. U., 1982. Bar: Ind. 1982. Mem. staff Office of U.S. Rep. John Brademas, 1974-79, dir. staff, 1975-78; with Barnes & Thornburg, Indpls., 1982-89; budget dir. State of Ind., 1989-92; exec. asst. Office of Gov. Evan Bayh, 1993; assoc. justice Ind. Supreme Ct., 1993—. Mem. ABA, Ind. State Bar Assn., Indpls. Bar Assn. Home: 6153 N Olney St Indianapolis IN 46220-5166 Office: State House Rm 321 Indianapolis IN 46204-2728

SULLIVAN, F(RANK) VICTOR, university administrator, retired educator; b. Wichita, Kans., Mar. 5, 1931; s. Frank Townsend and Olive Mae (Kinseley) S.; m. Mary-Kate Larson, June 2, 1956; children: Mark Kenneth, Olive Louise. BS, Friends U., 1953; MA, U. No. Colo., 1957; EdD, U. Ill., 1964. Tchr. indsl. arts Minneha Pub. Schs., Wichita, 1953-56; instr. indsl. arts Friends U., Wichita, 1956-60; instr. U. Ill. H.S., 1960-63; rsch. assoc. Illini Blind Project, U. Ill., 1963-64; asst. prof. Sch. Tech., Pittsburgh (Kans.) State U., 1964-66, assoc. prof., 1966-68, prof., 1968-96, chair dept. tech. studies, 1978-85, interim dean Sch. Tech. and Applied Sci.,, 1980-82, dean Sch. Tech. and Applied Sci., 1985-96, prof. and dean emeritus, 1996—, exec. dir. Bus. & Tech. Inst., 1997—; bd. dirs. Am. Inst. Design and Drafting, Bartlesville, Okla., Kans. Tech. Enterprise Corp., Topeka.$Dir. Business & Technology Inst. & Ctr. for Design, Develop. & Production, Pittsburgh State U., 1997—. Mem. ESEA (dir./author secondary exploration of tech. Title II project 1971-74, dir. curriculum from contemporary industry summer 1967), Am. Soc. for Engring. Edn. Home: 510 Thomas St Pittsburg KS 66762-6526 Office: Pittsburg State Univ Wilkerson Alumni Ctr Pittsburg KS 66762

SULLIVAN, G. CRAIG, household products executive; b. 1940. BS, Boston Coll., 1964. With Procter & Gamble Co., 1964-69, Am. Express Co., 1969-70; regional sales mgr. Clorox Co., Oakland, Calif., 1971-76, v.p. mktg., 1976-78, mgr. food svc. sales devel., mgr. bus. devel., 1978-79, gen. mgr. food svc. products divsn., 1979-81, v.p. food svc. products divsn., 1981, v.p. household products, 1981-89, group v.p. household products, 1989-92, chmn. bd., pres., CEO, 1992—. Office: The Clorox Co PO Box 24305 Oakland CA 94623-1305

SULLIVAN, GEORGE ANERSON, orthodontist; b. Bon Aqua, Tenn.; s. Joe Marble and Ruby Christine (Luther) S.; m. Edie M. Timmons, May 11, 1957; children: Scott Patrick, Shawn Michael. AS, Henry Ford Community Coll., Dearborn, Mich., 1957; student, Eastern Mich. U., 1958-59; DDS, U. Mich., 1963, MS, 1966. Diplomate Am. Bd. Diplomates. Pvt. practice specializing in orthodontics Phoenix, 1966—; pres. Ammons Meml. Dental Clinic, Phoenix, 1979-80. Chmn. Phoenix Meml. Hosp., 1977-80. Served with USNR, 1955-63. Mem. Am. Assn. Orthodontics, Cen. Ariz. Dental Soc., Ariz. State Dental Assn., ADA, Ariz. Orthodontic Soc., Pacific Coast Soc. Orthodontics, Optimist Club (pres. Phoenix chpt. 1967-68), Lions (pres. 1972-73), Elks. Republican. Avocations: motorhome travel, fishing. Office: 4805 W Thomas Rd Ste D Phoenix AZ 85031-4005 also: 10752 89th St Ste 111 Scottsdale AZ 85260

SULLIVAN, GEORGE EDMUND, editorial and marketing company executive; b. N.Y.C., Feb. 3, 1932; s. Timothy Daniel and Helen Veronica (Danaher) S.; m. Carole Ann Hartz, Sept. 4; 1954; children—Patricia Lynn, George Edmund, Michael Frank. B.A., Iona Coll., 1957; M.Ed., Rutgers U., 1961; Ph.D., Walden U., 1980. Tchr. English Holmdel Twp. and Keyport (N.J.) Pub. Schs., 1957-62; field mgr. regional mktg. Harcourt, Brace & World, Inc., N.Y.C., 1962-69; v.p. sales Noble & Noble, Publishers, Inc., 1969-72, sr. v.p., chief exec. officer, 1972-78; pres. Sullivan Ednl. Assos., Inc., Scottsdale, Ariz., 1978—; cons. to pub. and pvt. schs. on improving writing instrn. and scholastic aptitude test scores; instr. English and advanced placement/honors program Bayonne (N.J.) H.S., 1988-94; adj. St. Peter's Coll. Writing Program, 1990-94. Author numerous books on English lang., writing and map reading skills. Served with USAF, 1950-52. Mem. Assn. Am. Publishers (ofcl. rep. 1972-82), Keyport Edn. Assn. (pres. 1960-62), Am. Mgmt. Assn. Home: 7714 E 1st Ave Scottsdale AZ 85251-4602 *The world is full of people who don't really care. Any person who chooses a worthy activity and really cares about doing it the right way, the best way, the most perfect way despite all adversity, will succeed. Really caring is the fuel that generates miracles.*

SULLIVAN, GEORGE EDWARD, author; b. Lowell, Mass., Aug. 11, 1927; s. Timothy Joseph and Cecilia Mary (Shea) S.; m. Muriel Agnes Moran, May 24, 1952; 1 son, Timothy. B.S., Fordham U., 1952. Pub. relations mgr. Popular Library, N.Y.C., 1952-55; pub. relations dir. AMF, N.Y.C., 1955-63; adj. prof. Fordham U. Author: numerous books including: The Supercarriers, 1981 (Jr. Lit. Guild selection), The Gold Hunter's Handbook, 1981 (Outdoor Life book club and Popular Sci. book club selections), The Art of Base Stealing, 1982 (Jr. Lit. Guild selection), Great Imposters, 1982, Quarterback, 1982, Inside Nuclear Submarines, 1982, Anwar el-Sadat: The Man Who Changed Mid-East History, 1982, Pope John Paul: The People's Pope, 1984, Mr. President, 1984, Work When You Want to Work, 1985, The Thunderbirds, 1986, Work Smart, Not Hard, 1987, How the White House Really Works, 1988, Mikhail Gorbachev, 1988, The Day Man Walked on the Moon, 1989, All About Basketball, 1990, The Day They Bombed Pearl Harbor, 1991, Racing Indy Cars, 1992, Mathew Brady, His Life and Photographs, 1993, The Day Women Got the Vote, 1994, Black Artists in Photography, 1995, Alamo!, 1996, Not Guilty, 1997, Great Civil War Photographs, 1997. Served with USN, 1945-48. Mem. PEN, Authors Guild, Am. Soc. Journalists and Authors. Roman Catholic.

SULLIVAN, GEORGE MURRAY, transportation consultant, former mayor; b. Portland, Oreg., Mar. 31, 1922; s. Harvey Patrick and Viola (Murray) S.; m. Margaret Eagan, Dec. 30, 1947; children: Timothy M., Harvey P. (dec. July 1996), Daniel A., Kevin Shane, Colleen Marie, George Murray, Michael J., Shannon Margaret, Casey Eagan. Student pub. schs.; D.P.A. (hon.), U. Alaska, 1981. Line driver Alaska Freight Lines, Inc., Valdez-Fairbanks, 1942-44; U.S. dep. marshal Alaska Dist., Nenana, 1946-52; mgr. Alaska Freight Lines, 1952-56; Alaska gen. mgr. Consol. Freightways Corp. of Del., Anchorage, 1956-67; mayor of Anchorage, 1967-82; exec. mgr. Alaska Bus. Council, 1968; sr. cons. to pres. Western Air Lines Inc., 1982-87; former legis. liaison for Gov. of Alaska; now cons.; past mem. Nat. Adv. Com. on Oceans and Atmosphere, Joint Fed.-State Land Use Planning Commn.; past chmn. 4-state region 10 adv. com. OEO; mem. Fairbanks City Council, 1955-59, Anchorage City Council, 1965-67, Greater Anchorage Borough Assembly, 1965-67, Alaska Ho. of Reps., 1964-65. Trustee U. Alaska Found.; chmn. Anchorage Conv. and Visitors Bur.; bd. dirs. Western council Boy Scouts Am., 1958-59. Served with U.S. Army, 1944-46. Mem. Nat. Def. Transp. Assn. (life mem., pres. 1962-63), Nat. League Cities (dir.), Pioneers of Alaska, Alaska Mcpl. League (past pres.), Anchorage C. of C. (exec. com. 1963-65, treas. 1965-66, dir.), Alaska Carriers Assn. (exec. com.), Alaska Transp. Conf. (chmn.), U.S. Conf. Mayors (exec. com.), VFW (comdr. Alaska 1952). Club: Elks. Home and Office: George M Sullivan Co 1345 W 12th Ave Anchorage AK 99501-4252 *America is truly the land of opportunity, and I feel that the success with which God has blessed my life attests to this fact. I have been blessed four times. Not only was I born in America, but I have lived my life in Alaska. My other two blessings are my wonderful and supportive wife and our eight healthy children.*

SULLIVAN, GREGORY PAUL, secondary education educator; b. Buffalo, June 13, 1957; s. Jerome Patrick and Gloria Mae (Struble) S.; m. Sarah Davis Houston, May 17, 1986; children: Patrick Benjamin, Ryan Christopher. BS in Indsl. Edn., State U. Coll., Oswego, N.Y., 1979; MA in Indsl. Edn., Ball State U., 1983. postgrad. collegiate profl. teaching cert. Grad. asst. mfg. lab. Ball State U., Muncie, Ind., 1982-83; tchr. tech. edn. John Rolfe Mid. Sch., Richmond, Va., 1979-86, Horton Mid. Sch., Pittsboro, N.C., 1986-88, Dunbar Mid. Sch., Lynchburg, Va., 1988-93; supr. career-tech. programs Lynchburg City Schs., 1993—; coord./judge regional and nat. mfg. contest Tech. Edn. and Collegiate Assn., 1988—; coord. Eisenhower Grant, 1991-92. Asst. dir. Camp Minnehaha, Minnehaha Springs, W.Va., 1979-88. Named Va. Tchr. of Yr., Va. Dept. Edn., 1993. Mem. Soc. Mfg. Engrs. (internat. edn. com. career guidance 1984, 91), Internat. Tech. Edn. Assn. (mem. editl. rev. bd. The Tech. Tchr., delphi com. critical issues and concerns tech. edn. 1992), Coun. Tech. Tchr. Edn. (student svcs. com. 1991), Va. Tech. Edn. Assn. (v.p. 1997), Va. Coun. Tech. Edn. Suprs. (pres. 1997), Phi Delta Kappa, Epsilon Pi Tau, Kappa Delta Pi. Avocations: intramural sports, golf, tennis, running. Home: 724 Sanhill Dr Lynchburg VA 24502-4924 Office: Lynchburg City Schs 10th and Court Sts PO Box 1599 Lynchburg VA 24505-1599

SULLIVAN, JAMES, consultant; s. James E. and Kathern (Bilms) S.; m. Iris Rodriguez, June 11, 1965. BS in Indsl. Tech., Tenn. Tech. U., 1967; AS in Engring. Tech., Gratham Sch. Engring., 1976; MS in Prodn. Mgmt., Clayton U., 1977; BPS in Mfg. Engring., Elizabethtown Coll., 1977; MA in Bus. Mgmt., Ctrl. Mich. U., 1978; BS in Elec. Tech., Empire State Coll., 1980; MA in Indsl. Mgmt., Cen. Mich. U., 1980, MA in Personal Mgmt., 1982; BSBA, Thomas A. Edison State Coll., 1982; BS in Logistics and CIM, Empire State Coll., 1991; PhD in Adminstrn., Inst. Profl. Studies, 1992. Apprentice machinist, 1955-59, mgr. svc., 1959-63, asst. coord. maintenance, 1967, methods engr., 1967-68, plant engr., sr. indsl. engr., 1968-75, sr. indsl. engr., 1975-84, indsl. mfg. engr., lead engr. III, 1984-86, mgr. ops., 1986-87, sr. cons., 1988—. Author: A Church in Error, 1971; contbr. articles to profl. jours. Mem. Am. Inst. Plant Engring., Svc. Engring. Soc., Soc. Mfg. Engring (cert.), ASHREA, ALOA, Sigma Iota Epsilon. Home: 240 Jean Wells Dr Goose Creek SC 29445-3521

SULLIVAN, JAMES F., physicist, educator; b. Cin., Mar. 7, 1943; s. James E. and Alma L. (Lienesch) S.; m. Sylvia J. Kasselmann, Aug. 16, 1969; 1 child, Robert L. BS, Xavier U., 1965, MS, 1969. Instr. physics Brebeuf Prep. Sch., Indpls., 1965-67; instr. physics OMI Coll. Applied Sci., U. Cin., 1968-71, asst. prof. physics, 1971-77, assoc. prof. physics, 1977-88, prof. physics, 1988—; summer faculty researcher Solar Energy Rsch. Inst., Golden, Colo., 1980; mem. high sch. evaluation team N. Ctrl. Assn., Cin., 1983, 84, 85. Author: Technical Physics, 1988; Co-author: Laboratory Manual for General Physics, 1973, 83, 90, 92, Physics for Technology Laboratory Manual, 1995. Organizer of events St. Xavier H.S. Alumni, Cin., 1983—; vol. examiner Am. Radio Relay League for U.S. Fed. Comm. Commn., Newington, Conn., 1984—; judge physics category Ohio State Sci. Fair, Delaware, Ohio, 1986—; chief negotiator faculty and librs. U. Cin., 1995. Named Faculty Mem. of Yr., Gamma Alpha chpt. Tau Alpha Phi, 1983. Mem. AAUP (v.p. U. Cin. chpt. 1994-96), Internat. Platform Assn., Am. Assn. Physics Tchrs. (founder, past pres., assoc. sec. So. Ohio sect. 1993—, com. on instrnl. media 1994—, chief organizer and presenter Fundamentals of Radio workshop Toronto, Ont., Can. 1985, Columbus, Ohio 1986, Bozeman, Mont. 1987, Orono, Maine 1992, Boise, Idaho 1993, South Bend, Ind. 1994, College Park, Md. 1996), Ohio Valley Amateur Radio Assn. (pres. 1997—), Am. Soc. Engring. Edn., Ohio Acad. Sci., Internat. Platform Assn., Ohio Valley Amateur Radio Assn. (pres. 1997—). Achievements include supervising successful attempt of OMI Coll. Applied Sci. contact of shuttle Challenger during STS-51F mission, 1985. Office: Univ Cin 2220 Victory Pkwy Cincinnati OH 45206-2822

SULLIVAN, JAMES FRANCIS, university administrator; b. Pitts., Sept. 15, 1930; s. Francis P. and Leona C. (Patterson) S.; m. Carol Rea, Sept. 10, 1955; children—Leslie Ann, Daniel Paul. B.A., Dartmouth Coll., 1953; M.S., U. Colo., 1956; Ph.D., U. Pitts., 1965. Asst. city mgr. Monterey, Calif., 1957-60; city mgr. Ojai, Calif., 1960-62; asst. prof. U. Pitts., 1965-66; vice-chancellor U. Calif. at Riverside, 1969-74; assoc. prof. Grad. Sch. Adminstrn., 1974-78; assoc. dir. Dry Lands Rsch. Inst., 1974-78; vice chancellor U. Calif., Davis, 1978-91, dean univ. extention, 1980-91; vice chancellor U. Calif., Santa Cruz, 1995-96, asst. v.p. systemwide Office of Pres., 1996—. Served with USAF, 1954-55. Home: 1005 Rodeo Rd Pebble Beach CA 93953-2720

SULLIVAN, JAMES GERALD, business owner, postal letter carrier; b. Bad Axe, Mich., Sept. 13, 1935; s. John Thomas and Frances Eugena (O'Henley) S.; m. Florence Marie Tack, Sept. 12, 1959; children: Kevin Michael, Kathleen Marie. Student, U. Detroit, 1957-58, Highland Park Coll., 1959-60. Owner Jerry's Barber Shop, Kinde, Bad Axe, Mich., 1963-66, 79—; purchasing agt. Thumb Elec. Coop., Ubly, Mich., 1966-79, Walbro Corp., Cass City, Mich., 1979-80; sales rep. Thumb Blanket, Bad Axe, Mich., 1980-81, Sta. WLEW, Bad Axe, 1981-82; sr. regional mgr. Pri Am. Fin. Svcs., Bad Axe, 1985—; treas. Colfax Twp., Bad Axe, 1979-90; rural letter carrier PO, Bad Axe, 1982—; loss clk., Toplis & Harding Wagner & Gliddon, Detroit, 1959-61; inventory control clk., Carrick Products Co., Royal Oak, Mich., 1957-59. pres., Huron County (Mich.) Twp. Assn., 1988-90; leader Boy Scouts Am., Bad Axe,1975-77. Served in U.S. Army, 1954-56. Mem. Huron County Rural Letter Carriers Assn. (pres. 1990—), Armed Forces Vets. Club of the Nat. Rural Letter Carriers Assn. (Mich. divsn.), Am. Legion, 4-H Club (pres. 1948-50), Lions (pres. 1979-80), Cmty. Club (pres. 1976-77), KC (mem. coun. #1546), Ushers Club Sacred Heart Ch. Republican. Roman Catholic. Avocations: gardening, golf, swimming, snowmobiling, fishing. Home: 122 W Richardson Rd Bad Axe MI 48413-9108

SULLIVAN, JAMES KIRK, forest products company executive; b. Greenwood, S.C., Aug. 25, 1935; s. Daniel Jones and Addie (Brown) S.; m. Elizabeth Miller, June 18, 1960; children: Hal N., Kim J. BS in Chemistry, Clemson U., 1957, MS, 1964, PhD, 1966; postgrad. program for sr. execs., MIT, 1975; DSc (hon.), U. Idaho, 1990. Prodn. supr. FMC Corp., South Charleston, W.Va., 1957-62; tech. supt. FMC Corp., Pocatello, Idaho, 1966-69; mktg. mgr. FMC Corp., N.Y.C., 1969-70; v.p. govtl. and environ. affairs Boise (Idaho) Cascade Corp., 1971-97, mem. new dist. bd., 1997—; chmn. trust and investment com. Key Bank Idaho, 1983-90, exec. com., 1983-97; bd. dirs., chmn. audit com. Key Trust Co. of the West; chmn. adv. bd. U. Idaho Coll. Engring., 1966-70, 80-87, centennial campaign, 1987-89, rsch. found., 1980-82; mem. Accreditation Bd. Engring. and Tech., Inc., 1994—; bd. dirs. Pub. Employees Retirement Sys. of Idaho. Contbr. articles to profl. jours.; patentee in field. Mem. Coll. of Forest and Recreation Resources com. Clemson U., Idaho Found. for Pvt. Enterprise and Econ. Edn., Idaho Rsch. Found., Inc., Idaho Task Force on Higher Edn.; bd. dirs. Idaho Found. for Excellence in Higher Edn., Exptl. Program to Stimulate Competitive Rsch. NSF, N.W. Nazarene Coll., 1988-90, Boise Philharm., 1996—, Pub. Employees Retirement Sys. of Idaho, 1996—; mem. Len B. Jordan Pub Affairs Symposium; trustee Idaho Children's Emergency Fund, 1984—; trustee Bishop Kelly H.S., 1987-89; chmn. Bishop Kelly Found., 1972-79, 85-89; chmn. adv. bd. U. Idaho Coll. Engring., Am. Forest and Paper Assn., Govtl. Affairs Com., Environ. Com., Future Options Group; bd. dirs. Boise Master Chorale, 1995—. 1st lt. U.S. Army, 1958-59. Recipient Presdl. Citation U. Idaho, 1990. Mem. AIChE, Am. Chem. Soc., Bus. Week Found. (chmn. Bus. Week 1980), Am. Forest and Paper Assn. (environ. and health coun., product and tech. com., solid waste task force), Bus. Roundtable (environ. com.), Idaho Assn. Commerce and Industry (past chmn. bd. dirs.), C. of C. of U.S. (pub. affairs com.). Republican. Home: 5206 Sorrento Cir Boise ID 83704-2347 Office: Boise Cascade Corp 1111 W Jefferson St PO Box 50 Boise ID 83728

SULLIVAN, JAMES LENOX, clergyman; b. Silver Creek, Miss., Mar. 12, 1910; s. James Washington and Mary Ellen (Dampeer) S.; m. Velma Scott, Oct. 22, 1935; children: Mary Beth (Mrs. Bob R. Taylor), Martha Lynn (Mrs. James M. Porch, Jr.), James David. B.A., Miss. Coll., 1932, D.D., 1948; Th.M., So. Bapt. Theol. Sem., 1935. Ordained to ministry of Baptist Ch., 1930; pastor Baptist Ch., Boston, Ky., 1932-33, Beaver Dam, Ky., 1933-38, Ripley, Tenn., 1938-40, Clinton, Miss., 1940-42; pastor First Bapt. Ch., Brookhaven, Miss., 1942-46, Belmont Heights, Nashville, 1946-50, Abilene, Tex., 1950-53; exec. sec., treas. Bapt. Sunday Sch. Bd., Nashville, 1953-73; pres. Bapt. Sunday Sch. Bd., 1973-75; exec. sec. Broadman Press, 1953-75, Convention Press, 1955-75; pres. So. Bapt. Conv., 1977. Author: Your Life and Your Church, 1950, John's Witness of Jesus, Memos for Christian Living, Reach Out, Rope of Sand with Strength of Steel, God Is My Record, Baptist Polity As I See It, Southern Baptist Polity at Work in a Church; also articles and manuals. Trustee Union U., Cumberland U., So. Bapt. Theol. Sem., Hardin-Simmons U., Midstate (Tenn.) Bapt. Hosp., Hendrick Meml. Hosp., Tex. Recipient E.Y. Mullins Denominational Service award, 1973; named Miss. Bapt. Clergyman of Century. Mem. Baptist World Alliance (exec. com. 1953-80, v.p. 1970-75). Clubs: Rotary (Ripley, Tenn.); Lions (Brookhaven, Miss.); Kiwanis (Abilene, Tex.).

SULLIVAN, JAMES LEO, organization executive; b. Somerville, Mass., Dec. 11, 1925; s. James Christopher and Anna Agnes (Kilmartin) S.; m. Anne Dorothy Hevner, Jan. 20, 1951; children: Maura, Mark, Lianne, Christopher. BS in History and Govt. cum laude, Boston Coll., 1950, MEd in Adminstrn. and Fin., 1958; DCS (hon.), Suffolk U., 1990. Asst. town mgr. Arlington, Mass., 1957-62; town mgr. Watertown, Conn., 1962-65; chief adminstrv. officer Town of Milton, Mass., 1965-68; city mgr. Cambridge, Mass., 1968-70, 74-81, Lowell, Mass., 1970-74; sr. research asst. MIT, 1970-71; pres. Greater Boston C. of C., 1981-91, H.M.S. Mktg., Boston, 1991—; chmn. Mass. Gov.'s Local Govt. Adv. Com., 1978; del. to Orgn. Econ. and Cooperative Devel., Paris, 1979; chmn. New Eng.-Can. Bus. Coun., 1983; pres. Careers for Later YEars, 1983; bd. dirs. Input-Output Computer Svcs., Imagen Inc., Mass. Bus. Devel. Corp. Trustee Emerson Coll., 1984-88, mem. fin. and investment com., 1985-88; bd. dirs. Bunker Hill Community Coll. Found., 1988—; mem. Adv. Com. on Reorgn. of Mass. Ct. System, 1991—, chmn. budget subcom. 1991—; bd. overseers Univ. Hosp. Boston. With USN, 1943-46. Mem. Mass. League of Cities and Towns (pres. 1978), Mass. Mayors Assn., Internat. City Mgmt. Assn., Nat. League Cities, Am. C. of C. Execs. (bd. dirs. 1988—). Club: World Trade (bd. govs. 1986—). Office: HMS Mktg 65 Franklin St Boston MA 02110-1303

SULLIVAN, JAMES N., fuel company executive; b. San Francisco, 1937. Student, U. Notre Dame, 1959. Formerly v.p. Chevron Corp., until 1988, now vice chmn., dir., 1988—. Office: Chevron Corp 575 Market St San Francisco CA 94105-2823*

SULLIVAN, JAMES STEPHEN, bishop; b. Kalamazoo, July 23, 1929; s. Stephen James and Dorothy Marie (Bernier) S. Student, St. Joseph Sem.; BA, Sacred Heart Sem.; postgrad., St. John Provincial Sem. Ordained priest, Roman Cath. Ch., 1955, consecrated bishop, 1972. Assoc. pastor St. Luke Ch., Flint, Mich., 1955-58; assoc. pastor St. Mary Cathedral, Lansing, Mich., 1958-60, sec. to bishop, 1960-61; assoc. pastor St. Joseph (Mich.) Ch., 1961-65, sec. to bishop, 1965-69; assoc. pastor Lansing, 1965, vice chancellor, 1969-72; aux. bishop, vicar gen. Diocese of Lansing, 1972-85, diocesan consultor, 1971-85; bishop Fargo, N.D., 1985—. Mem. Nat. Conf. Cath. Bishops (bishop's liturgical commn.). Office: Chancery Office PO Box 1750 1310 Broadway Fargo ND 58107-4419*

SULLIVAN, JAY MICHAEL, medical educator; b. Brockton, Mass., Aug. 3, 1936; s. William Dennis and Wanda Nancy (Kelpsh) S.; m. Mary Suzanne Baxter, Dec. 30, 1964; children: Elizabeth, Suzanne, Christopher. B.S. cum laude, Georgetown U., 1958, M.D. magna cum laude, 1962. Diplomate Nat. Bd. Med. Examiners, Am. Bd. Internal Medicine. Med. intern Peter Bent Brigham Hosp., Boston, 1962-63; resident Peter Bent Brigham Hosp., 1963-64, 66-67, chief resident, 1969-70, fellow in cardiology, 1964-66, dir. hypertension unit, 1970-74; Nat. Heart Inst. fellow, 1964, Med. Found. research fellow, 1967; preceptorship in biol. chemistry Harvard U. Med. Sch., Boston, 1967-69; asst. prof. medicine Harvard U. Med. Sch., 1970-74; dir. med. services Boston Hosp. for Women, 1973-74; prof. medicine, chief div. cardiovascular diseases U. Tenn. Coll. Medicine, Memphis, 1974—; vice-chmn. dept. medicine U. Tenn. Coll. Medicine, 1982-85; mem. staff Regional Med. Ctr., Memphis, VA, Bapt. Meml. hosps., U. Tenn. Medical Center-Wm. F. Bowld Hosp., Le Bonheur Children's Hosp., Saint Jude Children's Rsch. Hosp.; fellow Council for High Blood Pressure Research; cons. Nat. Heart, Lung and Blood Inst., 1974—, VA, 1983—. Contbr. articles to sci. jours. Served with M.C., U.S. Army, 1963-70. Fellow ACP, Am. Coll. Cardiology (bd. govs., pres. Tenn. chpt.); mem. AAAS, Am. Heart Assn. (fellow coun. on circulation, chpt. pres. 1982-83, affiliate pres. 1994-95), Assn. Univ. Cardiologists, Assn. Profs. Cardiology, Internat. Soc. Hypertension, Am. Fedn. Clin. Rsch., Racquet Club Memphis, Sigma Xi, Alpha Omega Alpha, Alpha Sigma Nu. Roman Catholic. Home: 517 Magnolia Mound Dr Memphis TN 38103 Office: Univ TN Divsn Cardiovascular Diseases 951 Court Ave Rm 353D Memphis TN 38103-2813

SULLIVAN, BROTHER JEREMIAH STEPHEN, former college president; b. Boston, June 25, 1920; s. John Joseph and Bridget Claire (Quirke) S. BA, Cath. U. Am., 1943, STL, 1957, STD, 1959; MA in Classics, Manhattan Coll., 1950; MA in Philosophy, Boston Coll., 1955; LLD (hon.), La Salle U., 1979; LHD (hon.), Coll. Mt. St. Vincent, 1987. Tchr. St. Peters High Sch., S.I., N.Y., 1943-48, St. Marys High Sch., Waltham, Mass., 1948-53; instr. theology and classics De La Salle Coll., Washington, 1953-59; asst. prof. theology Manhattan Coll., N.Y.C., 1959-63, assoc. prof., 1963, acad. v.p., 1963-70, exec. v.p., provost, 1970-75, pres., 1975-87; La Salle provincialate, dir. devel. programs Christian Bros. Acad., Lincroft, N.J., 1988—. Contbr. articles to profl. jours. Chmn. N.Y.C. com. on Ind. Colls. and Univs., 1978-79; chmn. com. on Sci. and Tech., 1981; trustee African Med. Rsch., LaSalle U.; bd. dirs., chmn., FSC Found. Mem. Coll. Theology Soc. (dir., nat. treas. 1960-71), Cath. Theol. Soc. Am., Cath. Bibl. Assn., Nat. Cath. Ednl. Assn., Nat. Cath. Devel. Coun., AAUP, Phi Beta Kappa, Delta Mu Delta. Address: Christian Bros Acad Lincroft NJ 07738

SULLIVAN, JIM, artist; b. Providence, Apr. 1, 1939; s. James Henry, Jr. and Frances Winifred (Welch) S.; m. Marie-Louise Paulson. B.F.A., R.I. Sch. Design, 1961; postgrad., Stanford, 1962-63. Prof. emeritus art Bard Coll., Annandale-on-Hudson, N.Y., 1966-95, prof. emeritus, 1995—. One-man shows Paley and Lowe Gallery, N.Y.C., 1971, 73, Henri Gallery, Washington, 1974, Fischback Gallery, N.Y.C., 1974, Willard Gallery, N.Y.C., 1978, Nancy Hoffman Gallery, N.Y.C., 1980, 82, 84, 86, 88, Foker Skulima Gallery, Berlin, Germany, Anne Jaffe Gallery Bay Harbor Islands, Fla. 1990; exhibited in group shows including, Whitney Mus., Mus. Modern Art, Columbus Gallery Fine Arts, Worcester Art Mus., Corcoran Gallery Art, Washington; pub. collections including Met. Mus., Whitney Mus., Albany State Mus., Wadsworth Atheneum, Philip Morris INc., Owens Corning Coll., Amerada Hess. Recipient Hinda and Richard Rosenthal award Am. Acad. Arts and Letters, 1973; Stanford grantee, 1962-63; R.I. Sch. Design European Honors program Rome, 1960-61; Fulbright fellow, Paris; Fulbright fellow, 1961-62; Guggenheim fellow, 1972-73; grantee Nat. Endowment for Arts, 1982. Home: 59 Wooster St New York NY 10012-4349 Office: Bard Coll Dept Art Annandale On Hudson NY 12504

SULLIVAN, JOHN FOX, publisher; b. Phila., Oct. 19, 1943; s. Neil Joseph S. and Mary (Fox) Cullumbine; m. Beverly Knight Lilley, June 10, 1978; stepchildren: Buchanan, Brooke, Whitman, Justin Lilley. BA, Yale U., 1966; MBA, Columbia U., 1968. Staff econ. analyst U.S. Dept. Def., Washington, 1968-69; asst. to pub. Newsweek Internat., N.Y.C., 1970-73, asst. mng. dir., 1974-75; pres., pub. Nat. Jour. Inc., Washington, 1975—. Mem. editl. adv. bd. Who's Who. Bd. dirs. Arena Stage, Times Mirror Found., Nat. Gallery Cartoon Art; trustee Monterey Inst. Internat. Studies. Episcopalian. Clubs: 1925 F Street; Yale (N.Y.C.). Home: 1412 28th St NW Washington DC 20007-3145 Office: Nat Jour 1501 M St NW Ste 300 Washington DC 20005-1700*

SULLIVAN, JOHN LOUIS, JR., retired search company executive; b. Macon, Ga., Aug. 27, 1928; s. John Louis and Elizabeth (Macken) S.; m. Barbara Boyle, Aug. 17, 1974; children: John, Katherine, Betsy, Ted. A.B. in Econs., Duke U., 1950; M.B.A., U. Pa., 1957; postgrad. Advance Mgmt. Program, Harvard U., 1975. Br. mgr. IBM, Phila., 1962-63; mgr. edn. IBM, Endicott, N.Y., 1963-64; asst. to pres. Data Processing Div. IBM, White Plains, N.Y., 1965-67; dist. mgr. Data Processing Div. IBM, Washington, 1967-69; mgr. eastern and fed. regions Memorex Corp., 1969-71; v.p. mktg. Infonet div. Computer Sci. Corp., El Segundo, Calif., 1971-75; exec. v.p. Fin. Service Group-ADP Inc., Clifton, N.J., 1975-77; sr. v.p. Heidrick & Struggles Inc., San Francisco and Los Angeles, 1977-82, dir., 1977-82, office mgr., 1979-82; v.p., mng. dir. Korn-Ferry Internat., Los Angeles, 1982-87; v.p., mng. ptnr. Korn-Ferry Internat., Boston, 1987-94; ret., 1994. Bd. dirs., mem. exec. com. March of Dimes, Los Angeles County; bd. regents Mount St. Mary's Coll., Los Angeles. Served to lt. (j.g.) USN, 1950-53. Mem. Harvard U. Bus. Sch. Alumni Assn. (dir.). Democrat. Clubs: Regency (Los Angeles), Bankers (San Francisco), Atheneum (Pasadena), Mission Hills (Rancho Mirage), Calif. Yacht (Los Angeles), Harvard (Boston). Office: Korn Ferry Internat 101 Federal St Boston MA 02110-1817 also: Korn Ferry Internat 1800 Century Park E Los Angeles CA 90067-1501

SULLIVAN, JOHN MAGRUDER, II, government affairs administrator; b. Hattiesburg, Miss., Sept. 23, 1959; s. Camillus Caruthers and Elizabeth Josephine (McLeod) S.; m. Stacy Lynn Robinson; children: John Magruder III, Caitlyn Caruthers. BS, U. So. Miss., 1983. Cert. Am. Planners. Corp. liaison Chevron, Hattiesburg, Miss., 1983-88; dir. Best Leasing, Jackson, Miss., 1988-89; state dir. Muscular Dystrophy Assn., Jackson, Miss., 1989-90; adminstr. govt. affairs Tri State Brick and Tile Co. Inc./Medlin & Assocs., Jackson, 1990-95; planner for bus. devel. divsn. City of Jackson, 1995-96; planner and developer, Theo Costas Properties, Exec. Office Devel., Jackson, 1996; owner Red Brick Farm Inc.; cons. in field. Author: Hattiesburg Statistical Summary, 1983. Disaster relief vol. ARC; ind. lobbyist health care, ins., tourism; mem. Miss. Battlefield Commn. Mem. Nat. Assn. Equipment Lessors, Nat. Assn. Planners, Miss. Assn. Planners, First Families of Miss., Civil War Roundtable, Masons, Pi Kappa Alpha. Republican. Episcopalian. Avocations: horses, golf. Home: 1955 Douglas Dr Jackson MS 39211-6604 Office: 415 Yazoo St Jackson MS 39201-1900

SULLIVAN, JOSEPH B., retired judge; b. Detroit, May 30, 1922; s. Joseph A. and Winifred R. (Bruin) S.; m. Mary Sullivan, June 6, 1946; children: Kathleen (Mrs. Thomas Lewand), Timothy. PhB, U. Detroit, 1947, JD, 1957. Bar: Mich. 1958. Mem. firm Sullivan, Sullivan, Ranger & Ward, Detroit, after 1958; head criminal div. Atty. Gen.'s Office State of Mich., 1963-64; exec. sec. to mayor City of Detroit, 1962, commr. purchasing, 1967-69; clk. Wayne County, 1970-74; judge Wayne County Cir. Ct., 1975-86, Mich. Ct. Appeals, 1986-93; ret., 1993. Mem. Detroit Charter Revision Com., 1970-73, past bd. dirs. Mercy Coll., Detroit. With AUS, 1943-46. Mem. Soc. Irish-Am. Lawyers, Mich. Bar Assn., U. Detroit Alumni Assn., Cath. Lawyers Assn. Democrat. Home: 842 Park Ln Grosse Pointe MI 48230-1853 Office: 900 First Federal Bldg Detroit MI 48226

SULLIVAN, JOSEPH M., bishop; b. Bklyn., Mar. 23, 1930. Ed. Immaculate Conception Sem., Huntington, N.Y., also, Fordham U. Ordained priest Roman Catholic Ch., 1956; consecrated titular bishop of Suliana and aux. bishop of Bklyn., 1980—. Office: Diocese of Bklyn Chancery Office 75 Greene Ave # C Brooklyn NY 11238-1003*

SULLIVAN, JOSEPH PETER, risk and insurance management consultant; b. Boston, Sept. 8, 1939; s. Joseph Francis and Mary Anna S.; m. Rachael Anne Cullen, Dec. 22, 1974; children: Philip, Sandra, Susan, Frederick. B Gen. Studies, U. Nebr., 1968; MA, U. No. Colo., 1973, Cen. Mich. U., 1976. Sr. acct. exec. Arkwright Ins., Greenwich, Conn., 1977-83; v.p. Frenkel & Co., N.Y.C., 1983-84; sr. account exec. Republic Hogg Robinson, N.Y.C., 1984-85; v.p. Alexander & Alexander, N.Y.C., 1985-92, Hugh Wood Inc., N.Y.C., 1992-93, Crawford-THG, N.Y.C., 1993—; assoc. Miller-Heiman Internat., 1986-92; instr. Dale Carnegie and Assocs., 1980-87; ajd. prof. ins. The Coll. of Ins., N.Y.C., 1991—. Mem. membership com. Met. Rep. Club; bd. advisors The Salvation Army. With U.S. Army, 1956-77, ETO, Korea and Vietnam. Decorated Bronze Star. Mem. Soc. Human Resource Mgmt., Assn. Former Intelligence Officers (life), Ret. Officers Assn. (bd. dirs. Knickerbocker chpt.), Soc. CPCU's, Am. Soc. CLU's, Nat. Assn. Health Underwriters, Profl. Liability Underwriting Soc., N.Y. Soc. Security Analysts, Soc. Competitive Intelligence Profls., Advt. Club N.Y., Toastmasters, N.Y. Athletic Club, Rotary, Masons, Shriners. Republican. Roman Catholic. Avocations: American history, photography, collecting old photographic prints and antique photographic equipment. Home: 105 Oldfield Rd Fairfield CT 06430-6660 Office: Crawford-THG 17 State St New York NY 10004 *Four decades of risk management consulting experience with private and military entities. Expertise is in assessing, controlling and financing the risks of lossto client assets. Advises commercial clients on all forms of insurance and associated risk and loss assessment and mitigation programs to effectively protect enterprise and reduce total cost of risk. Licensed as an insurance broker, consultant, general adjuster and private investigator, and holds many professional designations from societies in the commercial insurance and risk management field.*

SULLIVAN, KAREN LAU, real estate company executive, campaign consultant, federal commissioner; b. Honolulu, Jan. 21, 1948; d. Ralph Karn Yee and Beatrice (Loo) Lau; m. Paul Dennis Sullivan, Apr. 24, 1976. BA, Whittier Coll., 1970; MA, U. Hawaii, 1987. Staff asst. to Congresswoman Patsy Mink U.S. Ho. Reps., Washington, 1974, staff asst. subcom. mines and mining, 1975-77, legis. asst. to Congressman Cec Heftel, 1977-79; spl. asst. to asst. to Pres. for policy and women's affairs The White House, Washington, 1979; spl. asst. office of sec. of transp. U.S. Dept. Transp., Washington, 1979-81; regional dir. mid-Atlantic states Mondale-Ferraro Presdl. Campaign, Washington, 1984; dep. nat. field dir. Paul Simon Presdl. Campaign, Washington, 1987-88; Ill. dir. forum inst. Martin & Glantz Polit. Cons., San Francisco, 1988; regional dir. western states Clinton-Gore Presdl. Campaign, Little Rock, 1992; dep. dir. for pub. outreach Office of Pres.-Elect Bill Clinton, Little Rock/Washington, 1992-93; v.p. Hoaloha Ventures, Inc., Honolulu, 1981—. U.S. alt. rep. South Pacific Commn., 1995-97. Mem. Carter/Mondale Alumni Fund, The Carter Ctr. Avocations: downhill skiing, auto racing. Home and Office: 810-K N Kalaheo Ave Kailua HI 96734

SULLIVAN, KENNETH JOSEPH, strategic and intelligence programs analyst; b. N.Y.C., Sept. 19, 1949; s. John Joseph Sullivan and Eileen Teresa (Hannaway) Klein; m. Nan Nivin, May 22, 1971; 1 child, Brian Patrick. BE in Chem. Engring., Stevens Inst. Tech., 1971; MS in Systems Mgmt., U. Southern Calif., 1978. Commd. 2d lt. U.S. Air Force, 1971; advanced through grades to lt. col., 1988; navigator 374th Tactical Airlift Wing, Clark Air Force Base, Philippines, 1973-74; navigator, tng. flight instr. 509th Bomb Wing, Pease Air Force Base, N.H., 1974-78, chief of plans br., mission dir. tanker task force, 1978-80; chief instr., navigator upgrade tng. 55th Strategic Reconnaissance Wing, Offutt Air Force Base, Nebr., 1980-83, chief airborne battle staff, 1983-84, chief, command and control tng., 1984-85; chief, combat ops. plans divsn. Strategic Air Command Hdqs., Offutt Air Force Base, Nebr., 1985-89; nuclear command and control system studies mgr. U.S. Nuclear Command Control System Support Staff, Falls Church, Va., 1989-90, chief, assessments br., 1990-94; ret., 1994; sr. analyst JAYCOR, McLean, Va., 1994—. Exec. sec. Homeowner's Assn. Papillion, Nebr., 1982; asst. cub master Boy Scouts Am., Nebr., 1985-86; soccer coach Youth Soccer League, Nebr., 1985-87; adv. bd. Woodridge PTA, Va., 1989-94. Decorated Air medal. Mem. Armed Forces Comm. and Electronics Assn. (office rep. 1990-93), Air Force Assn., Ret. Officers Assn., Stevens Inst. Tech. Alumni Assn. (class fund agt. 1982-94), Sigma Nu. Avocations: computing, camping, hiking. Home: 12595 Cricket Ln Woodbridge VA 22192-5239 Office: JAYCOR 1410 Spring Hill Rd Mc Lean VA 22102-3008

SULLIVAN, LAURA PATRICIA, lawyer, insurance company executive; b. Des Moines, Oct. 16, 1947; d. William and Patricia S. BA, Cornell Coll., Iowa, 1971; JD, Drake U., 1972. Bar: Iowa 1972. Various positions Ins. Dept. Iowa, Des Moines, 1972-75; various legal positions State Farm Mut. Auto Ins. Co., Bloomington, Ill., 1975-81, sec. and counsel, 1981-88, v.p., counsel and sec., 1988—; v.p., sec., dir. State Farm Cos. Found., 1985—; sec. State Farm Lloyd's, Inc., 1987—; v.p., counsel and sec. State Farm Fire and Casualty Co., 1988—; v.p., counsel and sec. State Farm Gen. Ins. Co., 1988—, also bd. dirs.; v.p. counsel, sec., dir. State Farm Life and Accident Assurance Co.; v.p. counsel, sec. State Farm Annuity and Life Assurance Co., State Farm Life Ins. Co.; dir. State Farm Indemnity Co., Bloomington, Ill., 1995—; bd. dirs. Ins. Inst. for Hwy. Safety, Nat. Conf. Ins. Guaranty Funds, chmn., 1995-97. Trustee John M. Scott Indsl. Sch. Trust, Bloomington, 1983-86; bd. dirs. Scott Ctr., 1983-86, Bloomington-Normal Symphony, 1980-85, YWCA of McLean County, 1993-95; chmn. Ins. Inst. for Hwy. Safety, 1987-88. Mem. ABA, Iowa State Bar Assn., Am. Corp. Counsel Assn., Am. Soc. Corp. Secs. Office: State Farm Mut Automobile Ins Co 1 State Farm Plz Bloomington IL 61710-0001

SULLIVAN, LEON HOWARD, clergyman; b. Charleston, W.Va., Oct. 16, 1922; m. Grace Banks, Aug. 1945; children—Howard, Julie, Hope. B.A., W.Va. State U., 1943, H.H.D. (hon.), 1956; student, Union Theol. Sem., N.Y.C., 1943-45; M.A. in Religion, Columbia U., 1947; D.D. (hon.), Va. Union U., 1956, Dartmouth Coll., 1968, Princeton U., 1969, Yale U., 1971; D.H.L. (hon.), Del. State Coll., 1966; D.Social Scis. (hon.), Villanova U., 1968; LL.D. (hon.), Beaver Coll., 1967, Swarthmore Coll., 1968, Bowdoin Coll., 1968, Denison U., 1968, Gannon Coll., 1969, Temple U., 1969; Ed.D. (hon.), Judson Coll., 1967. Ordained to ministry Bapt. Ch., 1941. Pastor Zion Bapt. Ch., Phila., 1950-88, now pastor emeritus; founder, chmn. bd. Zion Home for Ret., 1960—, Opportunities Industrialization Ctrs. Am., 1964—, Zion Investment Assocs., Inc., Progress Aerospace Inc.; dir. Girard Bank Phila., Gen. Motors Corp. Pres. Internat. Found. for Edn. and Self-Help, 1984—. Named One of Ten Outstanding Young Men Am., U.S. Jr. C. of C., 1955; One of 100 Outstanding Young Men Am., Life mag., 1963; recipient Freedom Found. award, 1960; Russwurm award Nat. Pubs. Assn., 1963; Edwin T. Dalhberg award Am. Bapt. Conv., 1968; Am. Exemplar medal, 1969; Phila. Book award; Phila. Fellowship Commn. award; Presdl. Medal of Freedom, 1991; Disting. Svc. award Pres. Cote d'Ivoire, 1991. *

SULLIVAN, LOUIS WADE, former secretary health and human services, physician; b. Atlanta, Nov. 3, 1933; s. Walter Wade and Lubirda Elizabeth (Priester) S.; m. Eve Williamson, Sept. 30, 1955; children: Paul, Shanta, Halsted. B.S. magna cum laude, Morehouse Coll., Atlanta, 1954; M.D. cum laude, Boston U., 1958. Diplomate: Am. Bd. Internal Medicine. Intern N.Y. Hosp.-Cornell Med. Ctr., N.Y.C., 1958-59, resident in internal medicine, 1959-60; fellow in pathology Mass. Gen. Hosp., Boston, 1960-61; rsch. fellow Thorndike Meml. Lab. Harvard Med. Sch., Boston, 1961-63; instr. medicine Harvard Med. Sch., 1963-64; asst. prof. medicine N.J. Coll. Medicine, 1964-66; co-dir. hematology Boston U. Med. Ctr., 1966; assoc. prof. medicine Boston U., 1968-74; dir. hematology Boston City Hosp., 1973-75; also prof. medicine and physiology Boston U., 1974-75; dean Sch. Medicine, Morehouse Coll., Atlanta, 1975-89, pres., until 1989, 1993—; sec. Dept. of Health and Human Svcs., Washington, 1989-93; non-exec. dir. GM, 1993—; mem. sickle cell anemia adv. com. NIH, 1974-75; ad hoc panel on blood diseases Nat. Heart, Lung Blood Disease Bur., 1973, Nat. Adv. Rsch. Coun., 1977; mem. med. adv. bd. Nat. Leukemia Assn., 1968-70, chmn., 1970; researcher suppression of hematopoiesis by ethanol, pernicious anemia in childhood, folates in human nutrition. John Hay Whitney Found. Opportunity fellow, 1960-61; recipient Honor medal Am. Cancer Soc., 1991. Mem. Am. Soc. Hematology, Am. Soc. Clin. Investigation, Inst. Medicine, Phi Beta Kappa, Alpha Omega Alpha. Episcopalian. Office: Morehouse Sch Medicine Office of the Pres 720 Westview Dr SW Atlanta GA 30310-1458

SULLIVAN, MARCIA WAITE, lawyer; b. Chgo., Nov. 30, 1950; d. Robert Macke and Jacqueline (Northrop) S.; m. Steven Donald Jansen, Dec. 20, 1975; children: Eric Spurlock, Laura Macke, Brian Northrop. BA, DePauw U., 1972; JD, Ind. U., 1975. Assoc. Arnstein, Gluck, Weitzenfeld & Minow, Chgo., 1975-76; ptnr. Greenberger and Kaufmann, Chgo., 1976-86, Katten Muchin & Zavis, Chgo., 1986—; adj. prof. Kent Coll. Law, Ill. Inst. Tech., Chgo., 1991-94; pres. Chgo. Real Estate Edn. Initiative, 1996-97. Mem. ABA, Ill. Bar Assn., Chgo. Bar Assn., Am. Land Title Assn. (mem. lender's coun.). Avocations: bicycling, cross country skiing, gardening, camping. Office: Katten Muchin & Zavis 525 W Monroe St Ste 1600 Chicago IL 60661-3629

SULLIVAN, MARTIN EDWARD, museum director; b. Troy, N.Y., Feb. 9, 1944; s. John Francis and Helen Edna (Lynch) S.; m. Katherine Mary Hostetter, May 9, 1981; children: Abigail, Bethany. BA in History, Siena Coll., 1965; MA in History, U. Notre Dame, 1970, PhD in History, 1974. Exec. dir. Ind. Commn. for Humanities, Indpls., 1972-75; dir. pub. programs NEH, Washington, 1976-81; pres. Inst. on Man and Sci., Rensselaerville, N.Y., 1981-83; dir. N.Y. State Mus., State Edn. Dept., Albany, N.Y., 1983-90, The Heard Mus., Phoenix, 1990—; trustee Am. Indian Ritual Object Repatriation Found., N.Y.C., 1992—; chair U.S. Govt. Cultural Property Adv. Com., 1995—. Author: Museums, Adults and the Humanities, 1981, Inventing the Southwest: The Fred Harvey Company and Native American Art, 1996; contbr. articles to profl. jours. Trustee Phoenix Cmty. Alliance, 1991—, Am. Fedn. Arts, 1994—; mem. Native Am. Repatriation Act Adv. Com., 1992—. Served in U.S. Army, 1966-68. Mem. Am. Assn. Mus. (v.p. 1990-93, mem. exec. com. internat. com. 1992—). Democrat. Home: 4601 E Solano Dr Phoenix AZ 85018-1280 Office: The Heard Mus 22 E Monte Vista Rd Phoenix AZ 85004-1433

SULLIVAN, MARY JANE, elementary school educator; b. Mason City, Iowa, Nov. 23, 1947; d. Lawrence Wesly and Elizabeth Barbara (Steinbach) Kohler; m. Mark Jay Sullivan, June 26, 1993. BS, Mankato (Minn.) State U., 1970; MS, Iowa State U., 1982. Cert. tchr. K-9, coach K-12, Iowa. Tchr. 5th grade Keokuk (Iowa) Cmty. Sch., 1970-77, West Bend (Iowa) Cmty. Sch., 1977-80; tchr. 6th grade North Mahaska Cmty. Sch., New Sharon, Iowa, 1980—. Author: (poetry teaching book) Poetry Pals, 1982. Mem. Regional telecomms. Coun., Des Moines, 1994—; treas. New Sharon Activities Com., 1988—; mem. Iowa Pub. TV, Des Moines, Iowa Heritage Assn., Des Moines. Named County Sci. Tchr. of Yr., Mahaska County Conservation Bd., Oskaloosa, Iowa, 1992; sci. grantee Ctrl. Coll., Iowa Dept. Edn. Mem. NEA, ASCD, Iowa State Edn. Assn. (exec. bd. negotiations), Nat. Staff Devel. Coun. (mem. 1st acad.), Kappa Delta Pi, Phi Delta Kappa (v.p. 1990-91). Roman Catholic. Avocations: reading, cross stitch, walking, gardening. Office: N Mahaska Elem Sch 204 W Maple New Sharon IA 50207

SULLIVAN, MARY JEAN, elementary school educator; b. Cambridge, Mass., May 13, 1956; d. Joseph Leo and Jean Marie (Isaac) S. BA, Flagler

Coll., 1978; postgrad., U. No. Fla., 1980—, Fla. State U., 1992, Okla. State U., 1992. Cert. elem. educator, Fla. Tchr. grade 2 St. Agnes Sch., St. Augustine, Fla., 1978-79; tchr. grades 1 through 5 Evelyn Hamblen Elem. Sch., St. Augustine, 1979-91; tchr. grade 5 Osceola Elem. Sch., St. Augustine, 1991—, chair math./ sci.; adv. Sci. Club; chairperson, St. John's County Tchr. Edn. Coun., 1985—, SACS Evaluation Team, Duval County Schs., 1988, 89, 90; rep. tchr. edn. coun.; sch. improvement co-chair, 1994-95; trainer coll. intern students; mem. St. John's County Accomplished Practices Acad., 1995, 96. Developer tchr. edn. coun. tng. handbook for State of Fla. Active PTO, past pres., Cub Scouts Am., past asst. program dir., Cathedral-Basilica Ch., United Child Care After Sch. Program, 1988-89; coord. summer recreation Evelyn Hamblen Sch., St. Augustine, 1987-90; dir. tournament Pam Driskell Meml. Paddle Tennis Scholarship Fund, 1986, 87, 88, 89; vol. United Way Olympic Torch Run, summer 1996. Grantee Fla. Coun. Elem. Edn., 1981-82, Summer Enhancement, 1988-89, Fla. Inst. Oceanography, 1994, St. John's County Horizon award mini-grantee, 1994, 96, Fla. Assn. for Computer Edn., 1994, Fla. Humanities Coun., 1995; recipient Human Rels. award State of Fla., 1992, NEWEST award, 1992, award Geography Summer Inst., 1992; named Kiwanis Tchr. of Month, 1993. Mem. NEA, Nat. Sci. Tchrs. Assn., Fla. Tchg. Profession, Fla. Assn. Staff Devel. (planning com.), Fla. Geographic Alliance, Fla. Assn. Computer Edn., St. John's Educator Assn., Fla. Assn. for Sci. Tchrs., ASCD. Office: Osceola Elem Sch 1605 Osceola Elem Sch Rd Saint Augustine FL 32095

SULLIVAN, MARY ROSE, English language educator; b. Boston, May 13, 1931; d. John Joseph and Elinor Mary (Crotty) Sullivan. BA, Emmanuel Coll., Boston, 1952; MA, Cath. U. Am., 1957; PhD, Boston U., 1964. Tchr. Woburn Pub. Schs., Mass., 1957-60; faculty Emmanuel Coll., Boston, 1960-66; prof. English U. Colo., Denver, 1966-96; mem. book reviewing staff San Diego Mag., 1980-90. Author: Browning's Voices in the Ring and the Book, 1969; co-editor: (3 vols.) letters of E.B. Browning to M.R. Mitford, 1836-54, 1983, Women of Letters: Selected Letters of E.B. Browning to M.R. Mitford, 1987, Crime Classics, 1990, Elizabeth Barrett Browning: Selected Poetry and Prose, 1993; editl. bd. English Lang. Notes, 1970-96. Served to capt. USNR, 1952-83. Am. Council Learned Socs. fellow, 1973. Mem. Browning Inst., Boston Browning Soc., Mystery Writers of Am.

SULLIVAN, MICHAEL DAVID, state supreme court justice; b. Hattiesburg, Miss., Dec. 2, 1938; s. Curran W. and Mittie (Chambers) S.; m. Catherine Ainsworth Carter; children: David Paul, Rachel Michel, Margaret Elizabeth, Sarah Catherine. BS, U. So. Miss., 1960; JD, Tulane U., 1966; LLM in Jud. Process, U. Va., 1988. Atty. Hattiesburg, Miss., 1967-75; chancellor Miss. Chancery Ct. Dist. 10, 1975-84; justice Miss. Supreme Ct., Jackson, 1984—. Office: Miss Supreme Ct PO Box 117 Jackson MS 39205-0117*

SULLIVAN, MICHAEL FRANCIS, III, executive; b. DuBois, Pa., Mar. 11, 1948; s. Michael F. and Mary Jane (Borger) S.; m. Janice Marie Calame, May 30, 1969 (dec.); children: Courtney, Shannon, Michael IV. BS in English & Speech, Bowling Green State U., 1969; MEd in Curriculum Devel., Wright State U., 1971; EdD in Instructional Technology, Va. Polytech Inst. & State U., 1976. Specialist in instructional design Md. State Dept. Edn., Balt., 1974-80, asst. state supt. in instructional technology, 1980-86; sr. edn. cons. UNISYS Corp., Bluebell, Pa., 1986-87, product mktg. mgr., 1987-88, dir. strategic planning and devel., 1988-90; exec. dir. Agy. for Instructional Technology, Bloomington, Ind., 1990—. Contbr. articles to profl. jours. Office: Agency for Instructional Tech Box A Bloomington IN 47402

SULLIVAN, MICHAEL JOACHIM, financial executive; b. Offenbach, Germany, Apr. 30, 1954; s. Donald and Eleanor (Denver) S.; m. Marianne Murphy, July 7, 1990. BA, LeMoyne Coll., 1976; MS, Syracuse U., 1980, MBA, 1993. Counselor County of Onondaga, Syracuse, N.Y., 1976-79, rsch. tech. 1, 1979, rsch. tech. 2, 1980-81, adminstrv. planning and funding coord., 1982-85, budget analyst 3, 1985, budget analyst 4, 1985-86, dep. dir. mgmt. and budget, 1986-87, dir. mgmt. and budget, 1988-92, commr. of fin., CFO, 1992-95; chief fiscal officer Loretto, Inc., N.Y., 1995—. Bd. dirs. Lourdes Camp, Inc., Syracuse, 1980—, Syracuse Opera, 1994—; mem. fin. com. Interreligious Coun., Syracuse, 1993—; mem. Thursday morning roundtable Univ. Coll., Syracuse, 1991—; mem. adminstrv. com. Immaculate Conception Cathedral Ch. Mem. N.Y. State Govt. Fin. Officers Assn. (chmn. ctrl. region 1993-95, bd. dirs. 1993-95), Govt. Fin. Officers Assn. (Disting. Budget award 1988-92), Beta Gamma Sigma. Roman Catholic. Avocations: gardening, reading, culture. Home: 4644 Bloomsbury Dr Syracuse NY 13215-2326 Office: Loretto Inc 710 E Brighton Ave Syracuse NY 13205-2208

SULLIVAN, MICHAEL PATRICK, marine officer; b. L.A, Aug. 22, 1933; s. Charles Gardner and Ann (May) S.; m. Nicole Marie St. Germaine; children: Steven, John, Byron. BA, San Diego State U., 1971; MS, Coll. Naval Warfare, 1976. Commd. 2d lt. USMC, 1956, advanced through grades to maj. gen.; comdg. officer VMFA-323 and MAWTU USMC, El Toro, Calif., 1973-75, comdg. officer Marine Aircraft Group II, 1980-83; with Group 3A 1st Marine Aircraft Wing USMC, Okinawa, Japan, 1976-77; AVN evaluator Combat Readiness Evaluation System USMC, Washington, 1977-80; comdg. officer Marine Aircraft Group-41, Dallas, 1983-85; comdg. gen., asst. wing comdr. 2d Marine Aircraft Wing MCAS, Cherry Point, N.C., 1985-88; dep. comdr. War Fighting Ctr. Marine Corps Combat Devel. Command Devel. Command, Quantico, Va., 1988-90; dep. comdr. Fleet Marine Force, Atlantic Norfolk, Va., 1990-91; asst. v.p. First Citizens Bank, N.C. Mem. Marine Corps Aviation Assn. (A.A. Cunninghamaward, Aviator of Yr. 1974, Silver Hawk award 1990), Marine Corps. Assn., Marine Corps Mustang Assn., Golden Eagles.

SULLIVAN, MICHAEL PATRICK, food service executive; b. Mpls., Dec. 5, 1934; s. Michael Francis and Susan Ellen (Doran) S.; m. Marilyn Emmer, June 27, 1964; children: Katherine, Michael, Maureen, Bridget, Daniel, Thomas. BS, Marquette U., 1956; JD, U. Minn., 1962. Bar: Minn. 1962, U.S. Dist. Ct. Minn. 1962, U.S. Supreme Ct. 1975, U.S. Ct. Appeals (8th cir.) 1978. Assoc., Gray, Plant, Mooty, Mooty & Bennett, Mpls., 1962-67, ptnr., 1968-67, mng. ptnr., 1976-87; pres., chief exec. officer Internat. Dairy Queen, Inc., 1987—; bd. dirs. The Valspar Corp., Allianz Life Ins. Co. N.Am., Opus U.S. Corp.; instr. U. Minn. Law Sch., 1962-67; lectr. continuing legal edn.; spl. counsel to atty. gen. Minn., 1971-79, 82-84. Contbr. articles to profl. jours. Bd. dirs. Legal Aid Soc. Mpls.; bd. trustees Fairview Hosps., St. Paul Sem; bd. govs. Children's Miracle Network; bd. dirs. Met. Mpls.YMCA; pres. Uniform Law Commn., 1987-89. Served with USN, 1956-59. Mem. ABA (ho. of dels., 1984-89), Minn. Bar Assn. (gov. 1974-86), Hennepin County Bar Assn. (pres. 1978-79), Am. Bar Found., Am. Law Inst., Order of Coif. Roman Catholic. Office: Internat Dairy Queen 7505 Metro Blvd Minneapolis MN 55439-3020

SULLIVAN, MORTIMER ALLEN, JR., lawyer; b. Buffalo, Sept. 19, 1930; s. Mortimer Allen Sr. and Gertrude (Hinkley) S.; m. Maryanne Calella, Nov. 20, 1965; children: Mark Allen, Michael John. BA, U. Buffalo, 1954. Bar: N.Y. 1964, U.S. Dist. Ct. (we. dist.) N.Y. 1966, U.S. Dist. Ct. (no. dist.) N.Y. 1967, U.S. Supreme Ct. 1970. Counsel liability claims Interstate Motor Freight System, Grand Rapids, Mich., 1964-82; v.p. J.P.M. Sullivan, Inc., Elmira, N.Y., 1959-67; govt. appeal agt. U.S. Selective Service System, 1967-71; dep. sci. div. Erie County (N.Y.) Sheriff's Office, 1971—, lt., 1986—. Inventor (with others) in field; creator, dir. video depiction JudiVision, 1969; composer High Flight, 1983. Chmn. com. on Constn. and Canons Episcopal Diocese of Western N.Y., 1975-96; bd. dirs. Erie County Sheriff's Found., Inc., 1987—; bd. dirs. Orchard Park (N.Y.) Symphony Orch., 1975-97, v.p., 1977-79, 91-94. With USAF, 1954-57; spl. agt. Air Force Office of Spl. Investigations, 1972-87, col. res. ret. Decorated Legion of Merit. Mem. Erie County Bar Assn. (chmn. law and tech. com., 1970-81), Transp. Lawyers Assn., Kappa Alpha Soc. Republican. Clubs: Saturn (Buffalo); Wanakah (N.Y.) Country. Avocation: aviation. Home: 19 Knob Hill Rd Orchard Park NY 14127 Office: 88 S Davis St PO Box 1003 Orchard Park NY 14127-1003

SULLIVAN, NEIL MAXWELL, oil and gas company executive; b. McKeesport, Pa., May 25, 1942; s. Thomas James and Jane Mason (Ginn) S.; m. Holly Abolt; children: Margaret Blair, Mason Pedrick. BS, Dickinson Coll., 1970; MS, Tulane U., 1994; postgrad., U. S.C., 1992—. Exploration geologist Bass Enterprises, Midland, Tex., 1976-77; dist. geologist ATAPCO, Midland, 1977-78, Anadarko Prodn. Co., Midland, 1978-79, chief geologist, 1979-80, v.p. exploration, regional mgr., Houston, 1980-82; exploration ops. mgr. Valero Producing Co., San Antonio, 1982-85, v.p. exploration, New Orleans, 1985-87; pres. Bluebonnet Petroleum Co., New Orleans, Eastover, S.C., 1987—; mem. Dept. Interior Outer Continental Shelf Com. adv. bd., 1985-87. Editor: Petroleum Exploration in Thrust Belts and Their Adjacent Forelands, 1976, Ancient Carbonate Reservoirs and Their Modern Analogs, 1977, Guadalupian Delaware Mountain Group of West Texas and Southeast New Mexico, 1979, Deep Water Sands in the Gulf Coast Region, 1988 , Offshore Louisiana Geology: An Onshore Exploration Model, 1988, Risk: Evaluation and Management, 1989, Volga-Ural Basin Analysis, 1993, Northern Marginal Zone of the Pricaspian Basin, 1996. Bd. dirs. Permian Basin Grad. Ctr., Midland, 1979; com. chmn. Mus. of S.W., Midland, 1978. Served with USAF, 1964-68. Mem. Geol. Soc. Am., Am. Assn. Petroleum Geologists (cert. petroleum geologist), New Orleans Geol. Soc. (chmn. continuing edn. com. 1987-89), South Tex. Geol. Soc. (nominating com. chmn. 1985), Soc. Econ. Paleontologists and Mineralogists (pres. Permian Basin sect. 1979), Am. Inst. Profl. Geologists (cert. profl. geologist). Lodge: Elks. Home: 10240 Garners Ferry Rd Eastover SC 29044

SULLIVAN, NEIL SAMUEL, physicist, researcher, educator; b. Wanganui, Wellington, N.Z., Jan. 18, 1942; came to U.S., 1983; s. Reynold Richard and Edna Mary (Alger) S.; m. Robyn Annette Dawson, Aug. 28, 1965; children: Raoul Samuel, Robert Alexander and David Charles (twins). BSc with 1st class honors, U. Otago, N.Z., 1964, MSc in Physics, 1965; PhD in Physics, Harvard U., 1972. Postdoctoral rsch. Centre d'Etudes Nucleaires, Saclay, France, 1972-74, rsch. physicist, 1974-82; prof. physics U. Fla., Gainesville, 1982—, chair physics dept., 1989—; co-prin. US Nat. High Magnetic Field Lab., 1991. Contbr. numerous articles on quantum solids and nuclear magnetism to profl. jours., 1971—. Recipient prix Saintour, College de France, Paris, 1978, prix LaCaze, Academie des Sciences, Paris, 1982; Fulbright exch. grantee, 1965; Frank Knox Meml. fellow Harvard U., Cambridge, Mass., 1965-67. Mem. AAAS, Am. Assn. Physics Tchrs., Inst. Physics, Societe Francaise de Physique, European Phys. Soc., Am. Phys. Soc., Groupement Ampere. Current work: Investigation of fundamental properties of solid hydrogen and solid helium at very low temperatures; studies of molecular motions using nuclear magnetic resonance; orientational disorder in molecular crystals, cryogenic detectors for dark matter particles and other cosmological relics of big bang theory; discovery of quadrupole glass phase of solid hydrogen, anomalous nuclear spin-lattice relaxation of solid 3He at interfaces; development of NMR techniques to study molecular dynamics at very low temperatures, quantum diffusion in solid hydrogen; design of ultra-sensitive low-noise cryogenic UHF detectors. Subspecialties: Condensed matter physics; Low temperature physics; High magnetic fields. Home: 4244 NW 76th Ter Gainesville FL 32606-4132

SULLIVAN, NICHOLAS G., science educator, speleologist; b. Phila., Dec. 20, 1927; s. Edward James and Florence (Delaney) S. BS, Cath. U. Am., 1950; MSc, U. Pitts., 1954; PhD, U. Notre Dame, 1961. Asst. prof. U. Notre Dame (Ind.), 1961-63; asst. prof., assoc. prof., prof. La Salle Coll., Phila., 1963-78, asst. to pres., 1972-74; prof. sci. Manhattan Coll., Riverdale, N.Y., 1979—; vis. prof. U. Alaska, Anchorage, 1961, U. NSW, Sydney, Australia, 1963; chmn. U.S. Deep Caving Team. Author: Speleology, the Study of Caves, 1962; contbr. over 200 articles on speleology to profl. jours. Trustee Gwynedd (Pa.) Mercy Coll., 1963-75, Nat. Speleological Found., Washington, 1978-84, Charles Lindbergh Found., 1989—. Fellow Nat. Speleological Soc. (hon. life, trustee 1955-79, pres. 1957-63), Royal Geog. Soc., AAAS, N.Y. Acad. Scis., Explorers Club (pres. 1989-92, trustee 1968—, Explorer's medal Phila. chpt. 1978, Sweeney medal 1979); mem. Sydney Speleological Soc. (hon. life), South African Speleological Soc. (hon. life), Rittenhouse Club, Bankstown Sports Club (Sydney).

SULLIVAN, PATRICIA A., academic administrator; b. S.I.; m. Charles Sullivan. Grad., St. John's U.; MS in Biology, NYU, PhD in Biology. Tchg. fellow, NIH pre-doctoral fellow NYU; post-doctoral fellow in cell biology Upstate Med. Ctr., Syracuse, N.Y.; vis. fellow Cornell U., 1976; tchr. Wells Coll., N.Y.; dir. biology honors program Tex. Woman's U., 1979-81; dean Salem Coll., Winston-Salem, 1981-87; v.p. acad. affairs Tex. Woman's U., 1987-94, interim pres., 1993-94; chancellor U. N.C., Greensboro, 1995—; pres. Assn. Tex. Colls. and Univs. Acad. Affairs Officers, Assn. So. Colls. for Women, N.C. Assn. Chief Acad. Officers; active numerous coms. Tex. Higher Edn. Coordinating Bd.; lectr. in field. Contbr. articles to profl. jours. Office: U NC 303 Mossman Bldg Greensboro NC 27412-5001

SULLIVAN, PATRICIA G., maternal, child and women's health nursing educator; b. Denver, June 26, 1948; d. Dale F. and Wilma (Fritz) Greb; m. Michael T. Sullivan, Sept. 10, 1971; children: Nicholas O., Matthew Alexander, Adam Michael. BS, Loretto Heights Coll., 1971; MS, U. Colo., 1976. Cert. bereavement svcs. counselor. Clin. instr. Loretto Hts. Coll., 1977-81; instr. pathophysiology U. Denver, summers 1983, 84; coord. women's health edn. Swedish Med. Ctr., Englewood, Colo., 1985-86; coord. childbirth edn. Med. Ctr. Hosp., Odessa, Tex., 1986-88; instr. nursing Midland (Tex.) Coll., 1990—; cons. Mosby's Med. Nursing & Allied Health Dictionary. Reviewer: Basic Nursing and Practice 3rd edit. 1995. Counselor RTS Bereavement Svcs., 1996. Mem. AWHONN, Tex. Nurses Assn., Tex. Jr. Coll. Tchrs. Assn., Assn. Reproductive Health Profls., Sigma Theta Tau. Home: 2803 Douglas Ave Midland TX 79701-3831 Office: Midland Coll 3600 N Garfield St # 213 Midland TX 79705-6329

SULLIVAN, PAUL WILLIAM, communications specialist; b. Brockton, Mass., Dec. 7, 1939; s. Augustus Henry and Pearl Irene (Chisholm) S.; children: Todd Andrew, Geoffrey Scott, Dustin Raymond; m. Frances Tina Brown, Jan. 23, 1989. BA cum laude, Yale U., 1961; MA, U. Fla., 1971; PhD, So. Ill. U., 1977. Gen. mgr. Chronicle Pub. Co., Stoughton, Mass., 1962-67; editor Easton Bull., N. Easton, Mass., 1963-70; pub., editor Associated Weekly Newspapers, Stoughton, 1967-70; instr. dept. mass comm. Moorhead (Minn.) State U., 1971-73; assoc. prof., chmn. dept. comm. U. Evansville, Ind., 1973-78; prof., chmn. dept. journalism Temple U., Phila., 1978-87; pvt. practice comm. cons., sales tng. cons. Indian Rocks Beach, Fla., 1986-92; pvt. practice comm. and fin. cons. Sullivan Comms., Indian Rocks Beach, 1992—; mng. gen. ptnr. Atlantis Adventure Ltd. Partnership, Largo, Fla., 1996—; mem. rev. panel Harry S Truman Scholarship Found., 1981-86. Author: The Modern Free Press Fair Trial Precedent, 1987, monograph News Piracy, 1978; co-author, editor: The Teaching of Graphic Arts, 1977, The Art of Consulting, 1989; contbr. articles to profl. jours. Mem. Gov.'s Commn. for Pa. Lottery, 1981. Mem. Assn. for Edn. in Journalism and Mass Communications, Soc. Profl. Journalists, Pa. Soc. Newspaper Editors (bd. dirs. 1980-87), Phila. Bar Assn. (media rels. com. 1982-87), ACLU. Avocations: photographer, landscape gardening. Office: PO Box 1049 Indian Rocks Beach FL 33785-1049 *Never underestimate the power of a liberal education to keep opening doors into the future. That education coupled with what I learned from my father and keep learning from my wife has made all the difference.*

SULLIVAN, PEGGY (ANNE), librarian; b. Kansas City, Mo., Aug. 12, 1929; d. Michael C. and Ella (O'Donnell) S. A.B., Clarke Coll., 1950; M.S. in L.S, Cath. U. Am., 1953; Ph.D. (Tangley Oaks fellow, Higher Edn. Act Title II fellow), U. Chgo., 1972. Children's public librarian Mo., Md., Va., 1952-61; sch. library specialist Montgomery County (Md.) public schs., 1961-63; dir. Knapp Sch. Libraries Project, ALA, 1963-68, Jr. Coll. Library Info. Ctr., 1968-69; asst. prof. U. Pitts., 1971-73; dir. Office for Library Personnel Resources, ALA, Chgo., 1973-74; dean of students, assoc. prof. Grad. Library Sch., U. Chgo., 1974-77; asst. commr. for extension services Chgo. Public Library, 1977-81; dean Coll. Profl. Studies, No. Ill. U., DeKalb, 1981-90; dir. univ. librs. No. Ill. U., 1990-92; exec. dir. ALA, 1992-94; assoc. Tuft & Assocs., 1995—; dean Grad. Sch. Libr. and Info. Sci. Rosary Coll., 1995—; instr. several grad. libr. edn. programs, 1958-73, UNESCO cons. on sch. librs., Australia, 1970; trustee Clarke Coll., 1969-72; sr. ptnr. Able Cons., 1987-92. Author: The O'Donnells, 1956, Impact: The School Library and the Instructional Program, 1966, Many Names for Eileen, 1969, Problems in School Media Management, 1971, Carl H. Milam and the American Library Association, 1976, Opportunities in Library and Information Science, 1977, Realization: The Final Report of the Knapp School Libraries Project, 1968; (with others) Public Libraries: Smart Practices in Personnel, 1982. Mem. ALA, Cath. Libr. Assn. Roman Catholic. Home: 2800 N Lake Shore Dr Apt 816 Chicago IL 60657-6202 Office: Rosary Coll Grad Sch Libr and Info Sci 7900 Division St River Forest IL 60305-1066 *Opportunities to use my abilities in a variety of public services have enriched my life, as I hope the results have enriched and empowered others.*

SULLIVAN, PETER MEREDITH, lawyer; b. Santa Monica, Calif., Nov. 9, 1952; s. Charles H. and Mary Jane (Menzel) S.; m. Mary T. Krueger, May 25, 1978. AB, Columbia Coll., 1974; JD, Fordham U., 1977. Assoc. atty. Kaye, Scholer, N.Y., 1977-81, Gibson Dunn & Crutcher, L.A., CA, 1981-86. Contbr. articles to profl. jours. Mem. ABA, N.Y. State Bar Assn., Calif. State Bar Assn. Roman Catholic. Office: Gibson Dunn & Crutcher 200 Park Ave New York NY 10166-0005

SULLIVAN, RICHARD LEO, brokerage house executive; b. Cin., Nov. 16, 1953; s. Robert John and Joanne Patricia (Lusby) S.; m. Nancy Carol Pulliam, Sept. 30 , 1978; children: Katherine Cain, Richard Walker. BBA, Drexel U., 1976. CPA, N.C. Acct. Ernst & Young, Winston-Salem, N.C., 1976-79; controller Summit Communications, Inc., Winston-Salem, 1979-80, dir. adminstrn., 1981-82; v.p. portfolio mgr. Smith Barney, Inc., Winston-Salem, 1982—. Mem. AICPA (mem. France forum), N.C. Assn. CPA's. Home: 787 Oaklawn Ave Winston Salem NC 27104-2223 Office: Smith Barney Harris Upham 110 S Stratford Rd Winston Salem NC 27104-4244

SULLIVAN, ROBERT EDWARD, lawyer; b. San Francisco, May 18, 1936; s. Edward C. S. and Mary Jane (Sullivan); m. Maureen Lois Miles, June 14, 1958 (dec. 1972); children: Teresa Ann, Andrew Edward, Edward Braddock. BS, U. San Francisco, 1958; LLB, U. Calif-Berkeley, 1961. Bar: Calif. 1962. Assoc. Pillsbury, Madison & Sutro, San Francisco, 1963-70, ptnr., 1971—; lectr. bus. law Calif. Continuing Edn. Bar and Practicing Law Inst.; v.p., treas., dir. MPC Ins., Ltd., 1986-93. Contbr. articles to profl. jours. Bd. dirs., exec. com. mem., sec. San Francisco Opera Assn., 1993—. 1st lt. U.S. Army, 1961-63. Mem. ABA, State Bar Calif. (com. corps. 1979-82, chmn. 1981-82, mem. exec. com. bus. law sect. 1982-85, vice chmn. 1983-84, chmn. 1984-85, advisor 1985-86, mem. partnership com. 1990-92, chmn. ltd. liability co. drafting com. 1992-93), San Francisco Bar Assn., Bankers Club San Francisco (bd. dirs.). Democrat. Roman Catholic. Office: Pillsbury Madison & Sutro LLP 235 Montgomery St San Francisco CA 94104-2902

SULLIVAN, ROBERT JOSEPH, lawyer; b. Ashville, N.C., Oct. 8, 1940; s. Daniel Joseph and Anne (McKann) S.; m. Paula Van Buskirk, Feb. 6, 1965; children: Robert Joseph Jr., Andrew Paul, Emily Elizabeth. AB, Stanford U., 1963; JD, UCLA, 1966. Bar: Calif. 1967, U.S. Dist. Ct. (ea. dist.) Calif. 1967, U.S. Ct. Appeals (9th cir.) 1967. Deputy atty. gen. Office Atty. Gen., Sacramento, Calif., 1967-71; staff, sr. counsel, chief counsel Calif. State Employees Assn., Sacramento, 1971-73; prin. Turner & Sullivan, Sacramento, 1973-91; ptnr. Nossaman, Gunther, Knox & Elliott, Sacramento, 1991—. Contbg. author: California Public Agency PRactice, 1988, California Adminstrative Mandamus, 1989. Bd. trustees Stanford Settlement, Sacramento, 1989; pro tem judge Sacramento Superior Ct., 1988—, arbitrator, 1980-88. Calif. Soc. Healthcare Attys. (bd. dirs. 1988—), Sacramento County Bar Assn. (chmn. healthcare law sect. 1990). Office: Nossaman Gunther Knox & Elliott 915 L St Ste 1000 Sacramento CA 95814-3705

SULLIVAN, ROBERT MARTIN, educational fundraiser; b. Holyoke, Mass., Feb. 12, 1953; s. James John and Emily Mae (Belzarini) S. AB, St. Anselm Coll., 1975; EdM, Harvard U., 1986. Fundraiser Nat. Multiple Sclerosis Soc., N.Y.C., 1976-77; asst. to v.p. devel. St. Anselm Coll., Manchester, N.H., 1977-81, dir. ann. fund, 1981-85, asst. to pres., 1985-91; dir. of devel. St. Anselm Coll., Manchester, 1991—. Mem. Agy. Rels. and Allocations Com., Greater Manchester United Way, 1988—; mem. Common Cause, 1989—; campaign vol. N.H. Cath. Charities, Manchester, 1989-90. Mem. Nat. Soc. Fund Raising Execs., N.H. Coun. on Fund Raising, Am. Assn. Higher Edn., Coun. Advancement and Support of Edn., Rotary. Democrat. Roman Catholic. Office: St Anselm Coll 100 Saint Anselms Dr Manchester NH 03102-1310

SULLIVAN, ROBERT SCOTT, architect; b. Alexandria, La., Sept. 8, 1955; s. Robert Wallace and Harriette Henri (Fedric) S. BA cum laude, Tulane U., 1979, BArch, 1979. Registered architect, N.Y., Calif., La.; cert. Nat. Coun. of Archtl. Registrations Bds. Staff architect Cavitt, McKnight, Weymouth, Inc., Houston, 1979-81, Hardy, Holzman, Pfeiffer Assocs., N.Y.C., 1981-83; ptnr. Sullivan, Briggs Assocs., N.Y.C., 1983-86; cons. Butler, Rogers, Baskett, N.Y.C., 1985-86; prin. R. Scott Sullivan AIA, Berkeley, Calif., 1986-89; ptnr. Talbott Sullivan Archs., Albany, Calif., 1989-94, Scott Sullivan, Arch., Berkeley, 1994—; cons. Neometry Graphics, N.Y.C., 1983-86, dir, 1986—; bd. dirs. Middleton/Sullivan Inc., Alexandria, 1981—. Works include specific design projects at N.Y. Hist. Soc. exhibit Grand Cen. Terminal, N.Y.C., 1982, The Houston Sch. of Performing Visual Arts, 1980, The Pingry Sch., Bernards Twp., N.J., 1982, Arts Ctr. at Oak Knoll Sch., Summit, N.J., 1986. Vestry St. Mark's Episc. Ch., Berkeley, 1988-89, 97—; bd. dirs. The Parsonage, Episcopal Diocese Calif., 1992-94; cons. Commn. Accessibility, Episcopal Diocese Calif., 1991-93, 95-96. Mem. AIA, Calif. Council Architects, Archtl. League N.Y.C., Nat. Trust for Hist. Preservation, Royal Archtl. Inst. of Can. (assoc.), Tau Sigma Delta. Democrat. Episcopalian.

SULLIVAN, RUTH ANNE, librarian; b. Portland, Maine, Jan. 15, 1955; d. Lawrence P. and Mary Louise (Gilman) S.; m. Charles H. Sullivan, May 1, 1982; children: Nora J., Ian J. BA, Wheaton Coll., 1979; MLS, U. Ariz., 1980. Serials ref. Mass. Bay Community Coll., Wellesley, 1980-81; asst. dir. Bristol Community Coll., Fall River, Mass., 1981-86, chief libr., 1986—. Office: Bristol Community Coll 777 Elsbree St Fall River MA 02720-7307

SULLIVAN, SELBY WILLIAM, lawyer, business executive; b. Houston, Oct. 8, 1934; s. John Francis and Lois Blanch (Selby) S.; m. Diane Pace; children: Selby William, Tricia, Lisa, Terry, Jack. B.A., Rice U., 1956; postgrad., Stanford U., 1956-57; LL.B. with honors, U. Tex., 1963. Bar: Tex. 1963, Fla. 1971. Ptnr. Andrews, Kurth, Campbell & Jones, Houston, 1963-72; pres. Fla. Gas Co., 1973-79, chief exec. officer, 1974-79, chmn. bd., 1977-79; exec. v.p., chief fin. and adminstrv. officer, dir., mem. exec. office Continental Group Inc., N.Y.C., 1979-80; ptnr. Maguire Vooris & Wells, Orlando, Fla., 1982-83; owner, chmn., chief exec. officer Hubbard Constrn. Co., 1984-89; chmn. bd. Orange Paving and Constrn. Co., 1984-89, Orlando Paving Co., 1984-89; owner, chmn., pres. Diamond S. Ranch, Inc., Meridian Homes, 1989—; chmn., pres. Summit Land Co., 1989—, Sullivan Investments, 1989—; dir. Sun Banks of Fla., Electric Fuels Corp., Fla. Progress Corp. Bd. dirs. Orange Bowl Com., Rice U., Fla. Bus. Forum, 1974-80; chmn. Rollins Coll. Sch. Bus., 1985-88; vice chmn. bd. dirs. Fla. Coun. 100. Mem. ABA, Fla. Bar Assn., Tex. Bar Assn., Interstate Natural Gas Assn. Am. (dir. 1975-79), Am. Natural Gas Assn. (bd. dirs. 1978-79), So. Gas Assn. (bd. dirs. 1976-79), Fla. C. of C., Interlachen Country Club (chmn., pres., bd. dirs. 1984—), Blind Brook Club, River Club, Country club of the Rockies (bd. dirs.), Eldorado Country Club (bd. dirs.), Eagle Springs Golf Club, Plantation Country Club. Home: PO Box 1740 Eagle CO 81631-1740

SULLIVAN, SHAUN S., lawyer; b. Albany, N.Y., Dec. 25, 1940; s. Charles Patrick and Dorothy Beatrice (Stuart) S.; divorced; children: Sara Stuart, Jennifer Landon. AB with honors, Fairfield U., 1962; LLB, Fordham U., 1966. Bar: N.Y., Conn., U.S. Dist. Ct. (so. dist.) N.Y., U.S. Dist. Ct. Conn., U.S. Ct. Appeals (2d cir.), U.S. Supreme Ct. Assoc. Cahill, Gordon, N.Y.C., 1966-69, Wiggin & Dana, New Haven, 1969—. Fellow Am. Coll. Trial Lawyers (Best Lawyers 1987-97, chair ADR Comm.), Conn. Bar Found., Am. Bar Found.; memt. Internat. Bar Assn. Home: 40 Cliff St New Haven CT 06511-1344 Office: Wiggin & Dana One Century Tower New Haven CT 06508-1832

SULLIVAN, STEVE JOSEPH, editor, journalist; b. St. Louis, Nov. 9, 1954; s. Donald R. and Ruth (Maiers) S. BA, George Mason U., 1978. Legis. asst. Congressman Moris Udall, Washington, 1975-76; freelance writer Network News, Inc., Washington, 1979-82; researcher, writer Record Rsch., Inc., Washington, 1982-85; reporter Land Devel. Inst., Washington, 1985-87; mng. editor Land Devel., Inc., Washington, 1987—. Author: Pop Memories: The History of American Popular Music, 1890-1954, 1985, A Practical Guide to FIRREA, 1989, VaVaVoom, 1995; co-author: The New Work Out Game, 1991; contbr. articles to mags.; editor Glamour Girls, Then and Now,

1994—. Avocations: popular culture research, music. Office: PO Box 34501 Washington DC 20043-4501

SULLIVAN, STUART FRANCIS, anesthesiologist, educator; b. Buffalo, July 15, 1928; s. Charles S. and Kathryn (Duggan) S.; m. Dorothy Elizabeth Faytol, Apr. 18, 1959; children: John, Irene, Paul, Kathryn. BS, Canisius Coll., 1950; MD, SUNY, Syracuse, 1955. Diplomate Am. Bd. Anesthesiology. Intern Ohio State Univ. Hosp., Columbus, 1955-56; resident Columbia Presbyn. Med. Ctr., 1958-60; instr. anesthesiology Columbia U. Coll. Physicians and Surgeons, N.Y.C., 1961-62, assoc., 1962-64, asst. prof., 1964-69, assoc. prof., 1969-73; prof. dept. anesthesiology UCLA, 1973-91, vice chair anesthesiology, 1974-77, exec. vice chair, 1977-90, acting chmn., 1983-84, 87-88, 90-91, prof. emeritus, 1991—. Served to capt. M.C., USAR, 1956-58. Fellow NIH, 1960-61; recipient research career devel. award NIH, 1966-69. Mem. Assn. Univ. Anesthetists, Am. Physiol. Soc., Am. Soc. Anesthesiologists. Home: 101 Foxtail Dr Santa Monica CA 90402-2047 Office: UCLA Sch Medicine Dept Anesthesiology Los Angeles CA 90024

SULLIVAN, TERESA ANN, law and sociology educator, academic administrator; b. Kewanee, Ill., July 9, 1949; d. Gordon Hager and Mary Elizabeth (Finnegan) S.; m. H. Douglas Laycock, June 14, 1971; children: Joseph Peter, John Patrick. BA, Mich. State U., 1970; MA, U. Chgo., 1972, PhD, 1975. Asst. prof. sociology U. Tex., Austin, 1975-76, assoc. prof. sociology, 1981-87, dir. women's studies, 1985-87, prof. sociology, 1987—, prof. law, 1988—, assoc. dean grad. sch., 1989-90, 1992-95, chair dept. sociology, 1990-92, vice provost, 1994-95, v.p., grad. dean, 1995—; asst. prof. sociology U. Chgo., 1977-81; pres. Southwestern Sociol. Assn., 1988-89; mem. faculty adv. bd. Hogg Found. Mental Health, 1989-92; mem. sociology panel NSF, 1983-85. Author: Marginal Workers Marginal Jobs, 1978; co-author: As We Forgive Our Debtors, 1989 (Silver Gavel 1990), Social Organization of Work, 1990, 2d edit. 1995; contbr. articles and chpts. to profl. jours. Bd. dirs. Calvert Found., Chgo., 1978, CARA, Inc., Washington, 1985; mem. U.S. Census Bur. Adv. Com., 1989-95, chmn., 1991-92; mem. sociology panel NSF, 1983-85; trustee St. Michael's Acad., 1996—. Leadership Tex. 1994. Fellow AAAS (liaison to Population Assn. Am. 1989-91, chair sect. K 1996), Sociol. Rsch. Assn., Am. Sociol. Assn. (sec. 1995—, editor Rose Monograph Series 1988-92), Soc. Study of Social Problems (chair fin. com. 1986-87), Population Assn. Am. (bd. dirs. 1989-91, chair fin. com. 1990-91). Roman Catholic. Avocations: volkssporting, sci. fiction. Office: U Tex Office Grad Studies Main Bldg 101 Austin TX 78712

SULLIVAN, TERRY BRIAN, semiconductor plant executive; b. Cheyenne, Wyo., May 13, 1946; s. Clifford T. and Mabel I. (Thompson) S.; m. Kathleen C. O'Keefe, Dec. 16, 1967; children: Joyce, Michelle, Karen, Jennifer. BA in Psychology, Santa Clara U., 1968, MBA, 1978. Corp. stores mgr. Signetics Corp., Sunnyvale, Calif., 1973-76, corp. materials mgr., 1977-82, corp. fin. goods/materials mgr., 1983-88, corp. purchasing mgr., 1988-92; v.p. quality and strategic ops. Dyna-Craft, Inc., Santa Clara, Calif., 1992-93; site ops. and foundry mgr. Philips Semiconductors, Albuquerque, 1994—; instr. N.Am. Philips Mgr. Mgmt. Program, N.Y.C., 1990—, Internat. Purchasing Mgrs. Seminar, Eindhoven, The Netherlands; chair Corp. Cycle Time Reduction Program, 1992. Patentee sporting goods equipment. Bd. dirs. Credit Union 1 of Kans., Topeka, 1972-73; mem. coun. N.Mex. Disting. Pub. Svc. Awards, Santa Fe, 1996-97; trustee Anderson/Abruzzo Internat. Balloon Mus., Albuquerque. Capt. USAF, 1969-73. Mem. Am. Prodn. and Inventory Control Soc., Nat. Purchasing Mgrs. Assn., Soc. Am. Inventors, Assn. Techs. Industry N.Mex. (co-founder, bd. dirs. 1996—), Assn. Commerce and Industry (bd. dirs. 1995—), Albuquerque Econ. Forum, N.Am. Purchasing Coun., Tanoan Country Club. Roman Catholic. Avocations: golf, skiing. Office: Philips Semiconductors Mail Stop 02 9201 Pan American Fwy NE Albuquerque NM 87113-2129

SULLIVAN, TERRY T., newspaper publishing executive; b. Cedar Rapids, Iowa; married; 5 children. BS in Bus., Skidmore Coll. With Gannett Co. Inc., Arlington, Va., 1980-83; human resources dir. Gannett West, Reno, Nev., 1983-85; divsn. v.p. USA Today, Arlington, 1985—. Past bd. mem. United Way, Arlington County, Va., Vol. Clearinghouse Washington, Skidmore Coll. Alumi Assn.; past mem. Employer's Com. Pres.'s Com. Employment People with Disabilities. Mem. Newspaper Pers. Rels. Assn. (past pres., Catalyst award 1991), Human Resources Planning Soc., Soc. Human Resource Mgmt., Sr. Pers. Execs. Forum (Washington), Washington Human Resources Forum. Office: USA Today 1000 Wilson Blvd Arlington VA 22209-3901*

SULLIVAN, THOMAS CHRISTOPHER, coatings company executive; b. Cleve., July 8, 1937; s. Frank Charles and Margaret Mary (Wilhelmy) S.; m. Sandra Simmons, Mar. 12, 1960; children: Frank, Sean, Tommy, Danny, Kathleen, Julie. B.S., Miami U., Oxford, Ohio, 1959. Div. sales mgr. Republic Powdered Metals, Cleve., 1961-65; exec. v.p. Republic Powdered Metals, 1965-70; pres., chmn. bd. RPM, Inc., Medina, Ohio, 1971-78; chmn. bd. RPM, Inc., 1978—; bd. dirs. Pioneer Standard Electronics, Inc., Cleve., Nat. City Bank, Cleve., Cleve. Clinic Found., Huffy Corp., Dayton, Ohio. Trustee Culver (Ind.) Ednl. Found., Cleve. Tomorrow; bd. dirs. Urban Community Sch., Cleve., Malachi House, Cleve., bd. dirs., adv. com. May Dugan Ctr. Cleve. Lt. (j.g.) USNR, 1959-60. Mem. Nat. Paint and Coatings Assn. (bd. dirs., exec. com.), Nat. Assn. Securities Dealers (bd. govs. 1986-88, long-range strategic planning com.). Roman Catholic. Office: RPM Inc 2628 Pearl Rd Medina OH 44256-7623

SULLIVAN, THOMAS PATRICK, academic administrator; b. Detroit, July 8, 1947; s. Walter James and Helen Rose (Polosky) S.; m. Barbara Jean Fournier, Aug. 9, 1968; children: Colleen, Brendan. BA in English, U. Dayton, 1969; M. Edn. and Adminstrn., Kent State U., 1971; postgrad., U. Mich., 1988. Tchr. Resurection Elem. Sch., Dayton, Ohio, 1968-69; administr. residence hall Kent (Ohio) State U., 1969-71; program mgr. residence hall Ea. Mich. U., Ypsilanti, 1971-73, adminstrv. assoc., 1973-76, dir. housing, 1976-83; assoc. provost Wayne County Community Coll., Belleville, Mich., 1983-84; dir. budget and mgmt. devel. Wayne County Community Coll., Detroit, 1984-85, sr. v.p. acad. affairs, acting provost, 1985-86; acting exec. dean Wayne County Community Coll., Belleville, 1986-88; dir. budget and mgmt. devel. Wayne County Community Coll., Detroit, 1988-89; pres. Cleary Coll., Ypsilanti, 1989—; part-time instr. English and math. Schoolcraft Coll., Livonia, Mich., 1980-90. Home: 44954 Patrick Dr Canton MI 48187-2551 Office: Cleary Coll 2170 Washtenaw Rd Ypsilanti MI 48197-1744

SULLIVAN, THOMAS PATRICK, lawyer; b. Evanston, Ill., Mar. 23, 1930; s. Clarence M. and Pauline (DeHaye) S.; divorced; children: Margaret Mary, Timothy Joseph, Elizabeth Ann; m. Anne Landau. Student, Loras Coll., Dubuque, Iowa, 1947-49; LL.B. cum laude, Loyola U., Chgo., 1952. Bar: Ill. 1952, Calif. 1982. Asso. firm Jenner & Block, Chgo., 1954-62; partner Jenner & Block, 1963-77, 81—; U.S. atty. for No. Dist. Ill., Chgo., 1977-81. Contbr. articles to profl. jours. Served with U.S. Army, 1952-54. Decorated Bronze Star.; Recipient medal of excellence Loyola U. Law Sch., 1965; Ill. Pub. Defender Assn. award, 1972. Fellow Am. Coll. Trial Lawyers; mem. Am., Ill., Fed. Seventh Circuit, Chgo. bar assns., Fed. Bar Assn., Am. Law Inst., Am. Judicature Soc., Chgo. Council Lawyers. Office: Jenner & Block 1 E Ibm Plz Chicago IL 60611-3586

SULLIVAN, TIMOTHY, lawyer; b. Detroit, May 16, 1948; s. Paul Gilmary and Virginia (Rosier) S.; m. Marsha Rosenberg Sullivan, June 19, 1971; children: Eileen A., Hugh V. BA Journalism, U. Mich., 1970; JD, Georgetown U., 1975. Bar: Va. 1975, D.C. 1976. Contract negotiator CIA, Washington, 1973-75; assoc. Fried, Frank, Harris, Shriver & Kampelman, Washington, 1975-78; ptnr. Capell, Howard, Knabe & Cobbs P.A., Washington, 1978-83, Dykema Gossett, Washington, 1983-95; lectr. in field. Narrator (audio cassette) How to Negotiate Government Contracts, 1986. Citizen mem. Alexandria Commn. Persons with Disabilities, Va., 1992—. Sgt. U.S. Army, 1970-73. Mem. ABA, Nat. Contract Mgmt. Assn., Univ. Club Washington (bd. admissions), Congl. Country Club (bd. govs.). Roman Catholic. Avocations: reading, sports. Office: Adduci Mastriani & Schaumberg LLP Ste 250 1140 Connecticut Ave NW Washington DC 20036

SULLIVAN, TIMOTHY J., journalist; b. White Plains, N.Y., Sept. 8, 1952; s. Timothy John and Henrietta Mary (Hasey) S.; m. Margaret Pierpont, Aug. 30, 1980. BA in English, Windham Coll., Putney, Vt., 1974. Mng. editor Gannett Westchester Newspapers, White Plains, 1978-86; asst. metro editor So. Conn. Newspapers, Stamford, Conn., 1987; editor Am. Lawyer Media, N.Y.C., 1987-91; corr. Courtroom TV Network, N.Y.C., 1992—; corr., sr. reporter, script writer The System, weekly documentary series, 1994—. Author: Unequal Verdicts: The Central Park Jogger Trials, 1992. Mem. Mystery Writers of Am. Avocations: bicycling, backbacking. Office: Court TV 600 3rd Ave New York NY 10016

SULLIVAN, TIMOTHY JACKSON, law educator, academic administrator; b. Ravenna, Ohio, Apr. 15, 1944; s. Ernest Tulio and Margaret Elizabeth (Caris) S.; m. Anne Doubet Klare, Jan. 21, 1973. AB, Coll. William and Mary, 1966; JD, Harvard U., 1969; LLD (hon.), U. Aberdeen, Scotland, 1993. Asst. prof. law Coll. William and Mary, Williamsburg, Va., 1972-75, assoc. prof., 1975-78, prof., 1978-85, Bryan prof. law, dean, 1985-92, pres., 1992—; exec. asst. for policy Office of Gov. Charles S. Robb, Richmond, Va., 1982-85; atty. Freeman, Drapers' Co., London, 1992; vis. prof. law U. Va., Charlottesville, 1981; exec. dir. Gov.'s Commn. on Va.'s Future, Richmond, 1982-84; vice-chmn. Gov.'s Commn. on Fed. Spending, Richmond, 1986; mem. Gov.'s Fellows Selection Com., 1985-90, Gov.'s Commn. on Sexual Assault and Substance Abuse on the Coll. Campus (chmn. enforcement subcom.), 1991-92; counsel Commn. on Future of Va.'s Jud. System, 1987-89. Mem. Va. State Bd. Edn., Richmond, 1987-92; chair Gov.'s Task Force on Intercollegiate Athletics, 1992-93. Decorated Bronze Star. Fellow Am. Bar Fedn., Va. Bar Fedn.; mem. ABA, Va. State Bar, Va. Bar Assn., Bull and Bear Club, Phi Beta Kappa, Omicron Delta Kappa, Univ. Club (N.Y.C., Washington). Democrat. Avocations: wine, swimming, reading. Home: Pres House Williamsburg VA 23185 Office: Coll William & Mary PO Box 8795 Williamsburg VA 23187-8795

SULLIVAN, WALTER FRANCIS, bishop; b. Washington, June 10, 1928; s. Walter Francis and Catherine Jeanette (Vanderloo) S. B.A., St. Mary's Sem. U., Balt., 1947; S.T.L., St. Mary's Sem. U., 1953; J.C.L., Catholic U. Am., 1960. Ordained priest Roman Catholic Ch., 1953; asst. pastor St. Andrews Ch., Roanoke St. Mary's, Star of Sea, Ft. Monroe, 1956-58; sec. Diocesan Tribunal, 1960-65; chancellor Diocese of Richmond, Va., from 1965; rector Sacred Heart Cathedral, Richmond, from 1967; ordained aux. bishop of Richmond, 1970, bishop of Richmond, 1974—. Office: Chancery Office 811 Cathedral Pl Ste B Richmond VA 23220-4801*

SULLIVAN, WALTER LAURENCE, writer, educator; b. Nashville, Jan. 4, 1924; s. Walter Laurence and Aline (Armstrong) S.; m. Jane Harrison, Aug. 30, 1947; children: Pamela Sullivan Chenery, Walter Laurence, John Harrison. BA, Vanderbilt U., 1947; MFA, U. Iowa, 1949; Litt.D., Episc. Theol. Sem., Lexington, Ky., 1973. Instr. dept. English Vanderbilt U., Nashville, 1949-52, asst. prof., 1952-57, assoc. prof., 1957-63, prof., 1963—; lectr. on pub. TV. Author: Sojourn of a Stranger, 1957, The Long, Long Love, 1959, Death by Melancholy: Essays on Modern Southern Fiction, 1972, A Requiem for the Renascence: The State of Fiction in the Modern South, 1976, In Praise of Blood Sports and Other Essays, 1990, Allen Tate: A Recollection, 1988, A Time to Dance, 1995, The War the Women Lived, 1995; co-author: Southern Fiction Today: Renascence and Beyond, 1969, Southern Literary Study: Problems and Possibilities, 1975, Writing From the Inside, 1983; writer, narrator film for pub. TV; contbr. articles to pubs. 1st lt. USMC, 1943-46. Ford Found. fiction fellow, 1951-52; Rockefeller Found. fiction fellow, 1957-58. Mem. Fellowship of So. Writers. (vice chancellor 1997—). Roman Catholic. Home: 6104 Chickering Ct Nashville TN 37215-5002 Office: Vanderbilt U Dept English Nashville TN 37235

SULLIVAN, WILLIAM COURTNEY, retired communications executive; b. Webster Groves, Mo., Aug. 26, 1928; s. William J. and Corinne (Courtney) S.; m. Valerie Blaes, June 20, 1953; children: William C. Jr., Kathleen M., Margaret M. Stonecipher. Student, St. Louis U., 1946-49, J.D. cum laude, 1952. Atty. Southwestern Bell Telephone Co., St. Louis, 1956-58, atty. Mo.-Ill. area, 1958-64, gen. atty. Kans. area, 1964-70, gen. atty. Mo.-Ill., 1970-74, gen. solicitor Mo.-Ill., 1974-75, gen. solicitor gen. headquarters, 1975-84, v.p., assoc. gen. counsel, 1984-91;, 1991. Bd. dirs. Sea & Sky Found., Miami, 1985—, Town and Country Police Commn., Mo., 1986-91, Corp. Disputes Resolution, Inc., 1990-94. Capt. USAF, 1952-55. Mem. ABA, Mo. Bar Assn., Kans. Bar Assn., St. Louis Bar Assn., Bellerive Country Club, The Club, Pelican Bay Country Club. Roman Catholic. Avocations: golf, tennis, reading, sailing, travel.

SULLIVAN, WILLIAM FRANCIS, lawyer; b. San Francisco, May 6, 1952; s. Francis Michael and Jane Frances (Walsh) S.; m. Joanne Mary Nebeling; children: Matthew, Meghan, Kathleen. AB, U. Calif., Berkeley, 1974; JD, UCLA, 1977. Bar: Calif. 1977, U.S. Dist. Ct. (no. dist.) Calif. 1977, U.S. Ct. Appeals (9th cir.) 1977, U.S. Dist. Ct. (ea. dist.) Calif. 1978, U.S. Ct. Appeals (D.C. cir.) 1979, U.S. Ct. Appeals (fed. cir.) 1985, U.S. Dist. Ct. (so. dist.) Calif. 1986, U.S. Dist. Ct. (cen. dist.) Calif. 1990, U.S. Supreme Ct. 1986. Assoc. Chickering & Gregory, San Francisco and Washington, 1977-81; assoc. Brobeck, Phleger & Harrison, San Diego and San Francisco, 1981-84, ptnr., 1984—; mng. ptnr. Brobeck, Phleger & Harrison, San Diego, 1992-96; firmwide mng. ptnr. Brobeck, Phleger & Harrison, 1996—; panelist Calif. Continuing Edn. Bar; instr. Fed. Practice Program, U.S. No. Dist., chair Litigation sect., 1992, U.S. Dist. Ct. (no. dist.) Calif., 1980; instr. Coll. of Advocacy, Hastings Law Sch.; adv. bd. AMICUS Info. Svcs. Mem. ABA, Assn. Bus. Trial Lawyers (bd. govs. San Diego chpt. 1993-95), Calif. Bar Assn. (litigation sect.), San Francisco Bar Assn., San Diego Bar Assn., Barristers Club San Francisco (bd. dirs. 1984-86, pres. 1985), Calif. Young Lawyers Assn. (bd. dirs. 1986-89, sec. 1987-99, 1st v.p. 1988-89). Democrat. Roman Catholic. Office: Brobeck Phleger & Harrison 550 W C St Ste 1300 San Diego CA 92101-3532

SULLOWAY, FRANK JONES, historian; b. Concord, N.H., Feb. 2, 1947; s. Alvah Woodbury and Alison (Green) S.; 1 child, Ryan. AB summa cum laude, Harvard U., 1969, AM in History of Sci., 1971, PhD History of Sci., 1978. Jr. fellow Harvard U. Soc. Fellows, 1974-77; mem. Sch. Social Sci. Inst. for Advanced Study, Princeton, N.J., 1977-78; rsch. fellow Miller Inst. for Basic Rsch. in Sci., U. Calif., Berkeley, 1978-80; rsch. fellow MIT, Cambridge, 1980-81, vis. scholar, 1989—; postdoctoral fellow Harvard U., Cambridge, 1981-82, vis. scholar, 1984-89; rsch. fellow Univ. Coll., London, 1982-84; Vernon prof. biography Dartmouth Coll., Hanover, N.H., 1986. Author: Freud, Biologist of the Mind, 1979 (Pfizer award History Sci. Soc. 1980), Born to Rebel, 1996; contbr. numerous articles on Charles Darwin and Sigmund Freud to profl. jours. Fellow NEH, 1980-81, NSF, 1981-82, John Simon Guggenheim Meml. Found., 1982-83, MacArthur Found., 1984-89; recipient golden plate award Am. Acad. Achievement, 1997. Fellow AAAS (mem. electorate nominating com. sect. L 1988-91, 94-97); mem. Am. Psychol. Soc., Human Behavior and Evolution Soc., History of Sci. Soc. (fin. com. 1987-92, com. on devel. 1988-92). Home: 18 Traymore St Cambridge MA 02140-2214 Office: MIT Bldg E51-093 Cambridge MA 02139

SULTAN, TERRIE FRANCES, curator; b. Asheville, N.C., Oct. 28, 1952; d. Norman and Phyllis Ellen (Galumbeck) Sultan; m. Christopher French, June, 1988. BFA, Syracuse U., 1973; MA, John F. Kennedy U., 1985. Exhbn. dir. Source Gallery, San Francisco, 1982-83; adj. curator Oakland (Calif.) Mus., 1984-85; dir. pub. affairs and pub. programs New Mus. Contemporary Art, N.Y.C., 1986-88; curator contemporary art Corcoran Gallery of Art, Washington, 1988—. Author: Representation and Text in the Work of Robert Morris, 1990, Redefining The Terms of Engagement: The Art of Louise Bourgeois, 1994, Neik Kemps: Behind the Facade of Analytical Order (a Series of Propositions), 1995, Painting Outside Painting, 1995, Petah Coyne: black/white/black, 1996; also exhbn. catalogues. Mem. Am. Assn. Museums, Coll. Art Assn., ArTable. Democrat. Office: The Corcoran Gallery Art 17th St New York Ave NW Washington DC 20006

SULTANA, NAJMA, psychiatrist; b. Nirmal, Andhra, India; July 22, 1948; came to U.S. 1973; d. Khaja Moinuddin and Mujib (Unnisa) Begum; m. Khaja Mohiuddin, July 8, 1971 (div. 1978); m. M. Rashid Chaudhry, Oct. 16, 1981 (div. 1991). M.B.B.S. Gandhi Med. Coll., Hyderaba, India, 1973. Resident in psychiatry SUNY/Kings County Hosp. Ctr., Bklyn., 1976-78, fellow child psychiatry, 1978-80; asst. clin. physician S. Beach Psychiat. Ctr., S.I., N.Y., 1980-81; asst. clin. prof. SUNY Downstate Med. Ctr., N.Y.C., 1981-94; attending psychiatrist King's County Hosp., Bklyn., 1981-94, Creedmore Psychiatric Ctr., 1994—. Exec. bd. mem. Balkan Rape Response Team; co-pres. Coalition for Intervention Against Genocide in Bosnia; past pres. Am. Fedn. of Muslims from India, nat. chairperson. Womem's Welfare Com., Am. Fedn. of Muslim from India; founding mem. G.O.P.I.O.; bd. dirs. T.O.U.C.H. Recipient Non-Resident Indian Internat. Women's award, 1992. Mem. Am. Psychiat. Assn. Democrat. Muslim.

SULTANIK, KALMAN, professional society administrator; b. Miechow, Poland, Apr. 12, 1916; came to U.S., 1952, naturalized, 1966; s. Samuel and Gitla (Wechadlowski) S.; m. Broniz Burganski, Jan. 28, 1947; children: Aaron, Samuel. Student, Sch. Econs., Tel aviv, 1949-51, columbia U., 1954-57; LL.B., Columbia U., 1976. Leader Hanoar Hatzioni, Poland, 1935-39; co-founder Ichud Movement, Postwar Poland; active Aliyah Bet, 1946-48; del. 22d Zionist Congress, Basel, Switzerland, 1946; mem. Central Com. Liberated Jews, Munich, Germany, 1947; with World Confedn. United Zionists, N.Y.C., 1948—, exec. co-pres., 1972—; chmn. Thedor Herzl Found., 1975—; sponsor monthly lit. publ. Midstream and Herzl Press, 1974—. Author: The World Confederation of General Zionists: Its Aims, Program and Achievements, 1974; editor: The Zionist Movement in the New Era, 1955, Zionism for Our Day, 1960; contbr. articles to profl. jours. V.p. World Jewish Congress, 1977—; bd. dirs. United Israel Appeal, 1973; mem. U.S. Holocaust Meml. Council, 1980—; sec.-gen. Gen. Zionist Constructive Fund, 1948—; head orgn. dept. World Zionist Orgn., 1981. Home: 120 E 81st St New York NY 10028-1428 Office: 110 E 59th St New York NY 10022-1304*

SULTZER, BARNET MARTIN, microbiology and immunology researcher; b. Union City, N.J., Mar. 24, 1929; s. Moses Joseph and Florence Gertrude (Fischer) S.; m. Judith Ray Moreinis, Aug. 26, 1956; 1 child, Steven Bennett. BS, Rutgers U., 1950; MS, Mich. State U., 1951, PhD, 1958. Rsch. assoc. Princeton (N.J.) Labs., Inc., 1958-64; from asst. prof. to prof. microbiology SUNY, Bklyn., 1964-94, prof. emeritus, 1994—, interim chmn. dept. microbiology, 1980-82; vis. scientist Karolinska Inst., Stockholm, 1971-72; vis. prof. Pasteur Inst., Paris, 1979-80; adj. prof. Fels Inst. of Cancer Rsch. and Molecular Biology, Temple U., Phila., 1995—; v.p. rsch. Stem Cell Therapeutics, King of Prussia, Pa. Assoc. editor Jour. of Immunology, 1983-86; contbr. book chpts. and over 60 articles to profl. jours. on microbiology and immunology; mem. editl. bd. Infection and Immunity, 1980-94. Pres. Tenants Assn. Gateway Plz., Manhattan, N.Y., 1990-92; mem. Cmty. Bd. #1, Manhattan, 1989-94. 1st lt. USMC, 1952-55. Pres.'s fellow Am. Soc. Microbiology, 1957; grantee USPHS, NIH, Office of Naval Rsch., 1967-94. Mem. AAAS, Am. Soc. Microbiology, Am. Assn. Immunologists, N.Y. Acad. Sci., Harvey Soc., Internat. Endotoxin Soc., Reticuloendothelial Soc., Sigma Xi. Achievements include patent for chemical detoxification of endotoxins and discovery of the genetic basis for mammalian responses to endotoxins including immunological and pathophysiological effects; co-discoverer of a mammalian gene controlling cellular response to lipopolysaccharide endotoxin; developed first commercial immunological pregnancy test. Office: SUNY Health Sci Ctr 450 Clarkson Ave Brooklyn NY 11203-2012

SULYK, STEPHEN, archbishop; b. Balnycia, Western Ukraine, Oct. 2, 1924; s. Michael and Mary (Denys) S. Student, Ukrainian Cath. Sem. of Holy Spirit, Fed. Republic Germany, 1945-48, St. Josaphat's Sem., 1948-52; Licentia in Sacred Theology, Cath. U. Am., 1952. Ordained priest Ukrainian Cath. Ch., 1952. Assoc. pastor Omaha, 1952; assoc. pastor Bklyn., 1953, Minersville, Pa., 1954, Youngstown, Ohio, 1955; pastor Ch. Sts. Peter and Paul, Phoenixville, Pa., 1955, St. Michael's Ch., Frackville, Pa., 1957-61, Assumption of Blessed Virgin Mary Ch., Perth Amboy, N.J., 1962-81; sec. Archeparchy Chancery, 1956-57; adminstr. St. Nicholas, Phila., 1961; archbishop Met. of Ukraine-Rite Catholics of Archeparchy, Phila., 1981—; vice chmn. Priests Senate, 1977-78; bd. dirs. Diocesan Adminstrn., 1972-79; pres. Ascension Manor, Inc.; archbishop Ukranian Rite Caths. Archeparchy Phila., Met. Ukranian-Rite Caths. U.S.A.; chmn. Priest's Senate; chmn. ad-hoc inter-rite com. Nat. Cath. Conf. Bishops/U.S. Cath. Conf., 1991. Mem. Providence Assn. Am. (Supreme Protector), Coll. Bishops of Roman Cath. Ch., Presidium of Synod of Ukranian Cath. Bishops (treas.). Office: Archdiocese of Philadelphia 827 N Franklin St Philadelphia PA 19123-2004*

SULZBERGER, ARTHUR OCHS, newspaper executive; b. N.Y.C., Feb. 5, 1926; s. Arthur Hays and Iphigene (Ochs) S.; m. Barbara Grant, July 2, 1948 (div. 1956); children: Arthur Ochs, Karen Alden; m. Carol Fox, Dec. 19, 1956 (dec. Aug. 1995); 1 child, Cynthia Fox; 1 adopted child, Cathy; m. Allison Stacey Cowles, Mar. 9, 1996. B.A., Columbia, 1951; LL.D., Dartmouth, 1964, Bard Coll., 1967; L.H.D., Montclair State Coll., 1972, Tufts U.; LLD (hon.), U. Scranton; L.H.D., Columbia U., 1992. With N.Y. Times, N.Y.C., 1951—; asst. treas. N.Y. Times, 1958-63, pres., 1963-79, pub., 1963-92, chmn., chief exec. officer, 1963—, also bd. dirs.; dir. Times Printing Co., Chattanooga. Trustee emeritus Columbia U.; trustee Met. Mus. Art, chmn. bd. trustees, 1987—. Served to capt. USMCR, World War II. Mem. SAR, Overseas Press Club, Explorers Club, Met. Club (Washington). Office: NY Times Co 229 W 43rd St New York NY 10036-3913

SULZBERGER, ARTHUR OCHS, JR., newspaper publisher; b. Mt. Kisco, N.Y., Sept. 22, 1951; s. Arthur Ochs Sulzberger and Barbara Winslow Grant; m. Gail Gregg, May 24, 1975; children: Arthur Gregg, Ann Alden. BA, Tufts U., 1974; postgrad., Harvard U. Bus. Sch., 1985. Reporter The Raleigh (N.C.) Times, 1974-76; corr. AP, London, 1976-78; Washington corr. N.Y. Times, 1978-81, city hall reporter, 1981, asst. metro editor, 1981-82, group mgr. advt. dept., 1983-84, sr. analyst corp. planning, 1985, prodn. coordinator, 1985-87, asst. pub., 1987-88, dep. pub., 1988-92, pub., 1992—; bd. dirs. Times Square Business Improvement Dist. Bd. dirs. N.Y.C. Outward Bound Ctr., N.Y.C., 1988, chmn. 1992. Mem. Newspaper Assn. of Am. Office: The NY Times 229 W 43rd St New York NY 10036-3913*

SUMANTH, DAVID JONNAKOTY, industrial engineer, educator; b. Machilipatnam, India, Jan. 28, 1946; came to U.S., 1972; s. John Devraj and Nancy (David) Jonnakoty; m. Chaya J. Victor, June 26, 1974; children: John J., Paul J. BME, Osmania U., India, 1967, MME, 1969; MS in Indsl. Engring., Ill. Inst. Tech., 1974, PhD in Indsl. Engring., 1979. Tchg./rsch. asst. Ill. Inst. Tech., Chgo., 1973-78, instr., 1979; asst. prof. indsl. engring. U. Miami, Coral Gables, Fla., 1979-83, founding dir. productivity research group, 1979—, dir. grad. studies, 1980-83, assoc. prof. indsl. engring., 1983-88, Coll. Engring. coordinator MBA/MSIE, 1984-93; prof. indsl. engring. U. Miami, Coral Gables, 1988—; chmn. 1st and 2d Internat. Conf. on Productivity Rsch., 3d, 4th, 5th Internat. Conf. on Productivity and Quality Rsch. Author: Productivity Engineering and Management, 1984, internat. student edit., 1985, Spanish edit., 1990, Indian edit., 1990, coll. custom series edit., 1994, also instrs. manual, (script) Total Productivity Management, 1985; editor: Productivity Management Frontiers-I, 1987, II, 1989, Productivity and Quality Management Frontiers III, 1991, IV, 1993, V, 1995, VI, 1997. Recipient over 60 honors, awards and recognitions including YMCA Edn. Gold medal, 1969, Freedoms Found., 1987; fellow U. Miami Eaton Honors Coll., 1986, fellow World Acad. Productivity Sci., 1989; gov.'s appointee as sr. judge Fla. Sterling award, 1992-93, judge, 1993-97. Mem. Am. Inst. Indsl. Engrs. (sr. mem., pres. Miami chpt. 1982-83, bd. dirs. 1983-84, nat. asst. dir. productivity mgmt. 1984—, chairperson rsch. com. 1987, Outstanding Indsl. Engr. of Yr. Miami chpt. 1983, 84); Productivity Ctr. (trustee 1985-89), Internat. Soc. for Productivity and Quality Rsch. (founder 1993, founding pres. 1993-95, chmn. 1995—). Republican. Baptist. Avocations: reading, writing, people. Office: U Miami Productivity Rsch Group Coral Gables FL 33124

SUMAYA, CIRO VALENT, pediatrician, educator; b. Brownsville, Tex., Aug. 1, 1941; s. Jorge Longoria and Irene (Valent) S.; m. Carmen Gonzalez, Apr. 8, 1967; children: Ciro II, Jaimes Andres. BA, U. Tex., Austin, 1962; MD, U. Tex., Galveston, 1966; MPH, M in Tropical Medicine, Tulane U., 1973. Specialist in pediatrics and infectious diseases. Clinic physician health dept. Tb Control, New Orleans, 1972-73; asst. prof. sch. medicine U. Calif., Los Angeles, 1973-74; asst. prof. pediatrics and pathology U. Tex. Health Sci. Ctr., San Antonio, 1976-77, prof., 1983-94, assoc. dean affiliated programs, continuing med. edn., 1986—; dir. South Tex. Health Research Ctr., 1989—; program dir. Area Health Edn. Ctr. for South Tex., 1990—; adminstr. health resources and svcs. adminstrn. PHS HHS, 1994—; mem. Presdl. Task Force Health Care Reform, 1994. Contbr. articles to profl. jours. Med. liaison Juvenile Diabetes, San Antonio, 1980-82; bd. dirs. San Antonio Library Found., 1985-89. Capt. USAF, 1967-69. Mem. Infectious

Disease Soc. of Am., Soc. for Pediatric Research, Soc. of Med. Dirs. of Continuing Med. Edn., Am. Acad. Pediatrics, Am. Soc. for Virology, Mex.-Am. Physicians Assn. of S. Tex. (v.p. 1986-87), San Antonio Pediatric Soc. (sec.-treas. 1985, v.p. 1986, pres.), Phi Beta Kappa, Alpha Omega Alpha. Roman Catholic. Avocations: classical piano, gardening. Office: Health Res & Svc Admin 5600 Fishers Ln Rockville MD 20857-0001

SUMBERG, ALFRED DONALD, professional association executive; b. Utica, N.Y., Nov. 22, 1928; s. Samuel M. and Rachel Frances (Silverstein) S.; m. Dolly Primakow, June 26, 1955; children: Susan Diane Beldon, Laurie Darlene Sumberg. Student, Utica Coll., 1946-48, Hebrew Union Coll., 1948-50; AB, U. Cin., 1950, MA, 1951; PhD, U. Wis., 1960; LHD (hon.), U. Cin., 1994. Exec. dir., founding dir. Am. Jewish Tercentenary Com. Wis. Wis. Jewish Archives, 1954-55; instr. history U. Wis., Parkside, 1955-56; prof. history and econs. East Stroudsburg (Pa.) U., 1956-67; vis. prof. history U. Cin., Cin., 1954, 58, 67; assoc. gen. sec., dir. govt. rels. AAUP, Washington, 1967-94; founding pres. N.E. Pa. Sch. Employees Fed. Credit Union, 1960-67; mem. exec. com. educator's ad hoc com. on copyright law, 1976-94, co-chair ad hoc com. for the creation of a cabinet-level dept. of edn., 1978-80, com. for edn. funding v.p.-treas., 1980-82, pres., 1982; bd. dirs. The Tuition Exch., 1988-96. Contbr. articles to profl. jours., chpts. to books. Bd. dirs., chair edn. com. The Hist. Found. of Pa., 1961-67; pres. The Hist. Assn. Northeastern Pa., 1963-67, Monroe County (Pa.) Hist. Soc., 1965-67; edn. coord. Mondale-Ferraro campaign, 1984; vol. Nat. Exec. Svc. Corps, 1994—. Mem. AAUP, Am. Hist. Assn., Nat. Trust for Hist. Preservation, U.S. Capitol Hist. Soc., Am. Econs. Assn., Nat. Economists Club, Nat. Dem. Club, Libr. of Congress Assocs., U. Cin. Alumni Assn. (life, pres. Washington chpt. 1972-74), U. Wis. Alumni Assn. (life, pres. Washington chpt. 1978-80), Phi Alpha Theta, Kappa Delta Pi, Utica Coll. Alumni Assn. Democrat. Jewish. Home and Office: 1309 Fallsmead Way Rockville MD 20854

SUMERS, ANNE RICKS, ophthalmologist, museum director; b. Beverly, Mass., May 8, 1957; d. David Frank and Anne Russell (Russell) Ricks; m. Elliott H. Sumers, May 31, 1983; children: Ben, Ted. BA in English Lit. with honors, U. Mich., 1979; MD, U. Cin., 1983. Diplomate Am. Bd. Ophthalmology. Intern in internal medicine Mt. Auburn Hosp., Cambridge, Mass., 1984; resident in ophthalmology NYU/Bellevue Hosp., 1984-87; ptnr. Ridgewood (N.J.) Ophthalmology, PC, 1990—; dir. N.J. Childrens Mus., Paramus, N.J., 1992—; co-owner Saddle River (N.J.) Market, 1995—; team ophthalmologist N.Y. Giants Football Team, 1994—; state coord. N.J. Turn Off Your TV Week, 1994, 95, 96; spkr. in field. Author: The Offical M.D. Handbook, 1983; writer, host Channel 11/WPIX Wonder Zone, 1993; interviewed on Good Morning Am., Am.'s Talking, NJN Discover N.J., Comcast Cablevision, Cablevision, Fox Channel 5 Good Day N.Y., 1992-95, numerous radio shows. Named one of 10 N.J. Women of Yr., N.J. Woman Mag., 1993; profiled in AMA News, Med. Econs., The N.Y. Times, Star Ledger, Argus and other newspapers and mags. Fellow Am. Acad. Ophthalmology (media spokesperson, media info. com.); mem. AMA, Assn. Youth Museums, N.J. Acad. Ophtholmology (bd. govs. 1997), Alpha Omega Alpha. Office: Ridgewood Ophthalmology PC 1200 E Ridgewood Ave Ridgewood NJ 07450-3937

SUMICHRAST, JOZEF, illustrator, designer; b. Hobart, Ind., July 26, 1948; s. Joseph Steven and Stella Sumichrast; m. Susan Ann Snyder, June 22, 1972; children—Kristin Ann, Lindsey Ann. Student, Am. Acad. Art, Chgo. Illustrator Stevens Gross, Chgo., 1971-72; illustrator Eaton & Iwen, Chgo., 1972-73, Graphique, Chgo., 1973-74; pres. Jozef Sumichrast, Deerfield, Ill., 1975—. Author, illustrator: Onomatopoeia, Q is For Crazy; exhbns. include: 200 Years of Am. Illustration, N.Y. Hist. Soc. Mus., Chgo. Hist. Soc., Finland Lath Mus., Library of Congress, Los Angeles County Mus. Art, Md. Inst. Graphic Art, State Colo. Community Coll., Tokyo Designers Gakiun Coll.; represented in permanent collections: Soc. Illustrators, Chgo. Hist. Soc., Milw. Art Dirs. Club, Phoenix Art Dirs. Club, Columbia Coll., U. Tex., contbr. numerous articles to profl. periodicals. Recipient award for children's book Chgo. Book Clinic, 1978; Gold medal Internat. Exhibition of Graphic Arts, Brazil, 1981; Gold medal Chgo. Artist Guild, 1980, 81; Silver medal N.Y. Art Dirs. Club, 1983; numerous others. Mem. Soc. Illustrators.

SUMMERALL, PAT (GEORGE ALLAN SUMMERALL), sportscaster; b. Lake City, Fla., May 10, 1931; m. Katherine Summerall; children: Susan, Jay, Kyle. Degree in Education, U. Ark., M. in Russain History. Football player Detroit Lions, 1952-53, Chgo. Cardinals, 1953-57, N.Y. Giants, 1958-61; played briefly in St. Louis Cardinals baseball orgn.; with CBS Sports, 1962-94; dir. sports Sta. WCBS-Radio, N.Y.C., 1964-71; host morning program Sta. WCBS-TV, 1966-67; sportscaster early news Sta. WCBS-TV, N.Y.C.; with CBS Radio Network; sportscaster Sports Time, Predictions, Profiles; host CBS Sports Spectacular.; lead play-by-play announcer NFL Football coverage CBS Sports, anchor golf and tennis coverage; sports commentator, football analyst Fox Network, 1994—. Named Sportscaster of Yr., 1977. Office: care FOX Network 1211 Ave of Amer New York NY 10036*

SUMMERFIELD, JOHN ROBERT, textile curator; b. St. Paul, Feb. 21, 1917; s. Isaac and Irene (Longini) S.; m. Anne Benson, July 14, 1945. S.B. in Mech. Engring., MIT, 1938; M.B.A., U. Calif.-Berkeley, 1947, Ph.D. in Econs., 1954. Asst. prof. Sloan Sch. Mgmtg., MIT, 1952-54; br. chief CIA, Washington, 1954-56; project leader The Rand Corp., Santa Monica, Calif., 1956-62; corp. economist Douglas Aircraft Co., Santa Monica, 1962-66; v.p. econ. planning Western Airlines, Los Angeles, 1966-70; staff v.p. econ. planning Pan Am. Airways, N.Y.C., 1970-71; pres. Summerfield Assocs., Pacific Palisades, Calif., 1972-92; vis. curator Fowler Mus. Cultural History, UCLA, 1993—. Co-curator exhbns. of antique Minangkabau ceremonial textiles from West Sumatra, Textile Mus., Washington, 1990-91, Santa Barbara (Calif.) Mus. Art, 1991, Bellevue (Wash.) Art Mus., 1992, Utah Mus. Fine Art, 1992. Served to lt. USNR, 1942-45.

SUMMERFORD, BEN LONG, retired artist, educator; b. Montgomery, Ala., Feb. 3, 1924; s. Ben Long and Ollie Jo (Gilchrist) S.; m. Christene Morris, Jan. 30, 1951; children: Jeffrey(dec.), Rebecca, James. Student, Birmingham-Southern Coll., 1942-43; B.A., Am. U., 1948, M.A., 1954; student, Ecole des Beaux Arts., Paris., 1949-50. Staff art dept. Am. U., 1950-88, chmn. dept., 1957-66, 70-86, prof., 1960-88; prof. emeritus, 1988—; artist in residence Dartmouth Coll., 1993. One-man shows include, Balt. Mus. Art, Goucher Coll., Franz Bader Gallery, Washington, Jefferson Place Gallery, Washington; one-man show include Phillips Collection, Washington; represented in permanent collection, Watkins Gallery, Phillips Gallery Art, Corcoran Gallery Art, all Washington, numerous group shows of paintings. Served to ensign USNR, 1943-46. Fulbright fellow, France, 1949-50; J. Paul Getty scholar, Phillips Collection, 1990-91. Home: PO Box 2086 Shepherdstown WV 25443-2086 Office: Am U Dept Art Washington DC 20016

SUMMERLIN, GLENN WOOD, advertising executive; b. Dallas, Ga., Apr. 1, 1934; s. Glenn Wood and Flora (Barrett) S.; student Ga. Inst. Tech., 1951-52; BBA, Ga. State U., 1956, MBA, 1967; m. Anne Valley, Oct. 16, 1971; 1 child, Wade Hampton; children by previous marriage: Glenn Wood III, Edward Lee. Prodn. mgr. Fred Worrill Advt., Atlanta, 1956-65; v.p. sales Grizzard, Atlanta, 1965-74, pres., 1974-94, vice chmn., 1994—. Vice chmn. Polaris dist. Boy Scouts Am., 1967. Vice chmn. Ga. State U. Found., 1974; chmn. distributive edn. adv. com. DeKalb Coll., 1974-76; bd. founders Geo. M. Sparks Scholarship Fund; bd. dirs. Atlanta Humane Soc., 1971—, treas., 1973, 81-82, 84-86, asst. treas. for capital devel., 1987—; mem. steering com. to Honor Hank Aaron, 1982; lay rep. animal care com. Emory U., 1984-85; mem. adv. bd. Families in Action, 1985-86, Soc. Nonprofit Orgns.; bd. dirs. Travelers Aid Metro. Atlanta, 1989-90; mem. Atlanta Sr. Marketers Coun. 100; chmn.'s coun., mem. mktg. adv. com. Crow Canyon Archeol. Ctr., 1993-95. Recipient C.S. Bolen award So. Council Indsl. Editors, 1967; named Outstanding Young Man in DeKalb County, DeKalb Jaycees, 1967, Alumnus of Year, Ga. State U., 1973; recipient Direct Mail Spokesman award Direct Mktg. Assn., 1973. Mem. Mail Advt. Svc. Assn. (pres. N.Ga. chpt. 1959-60), Ga. Assn. Bus. Communicators (pres. 1966-67), Am. Mktg. Assn. (pres. Atlanta chpt. 1973-74), Ga. State U. Alumni Assn. (pres. 1971-72, dir. 1966-78), Sales and Mktg. Execs. Atlanta (dir. 1969-71), Ga. Bus. and Industry Assn. (bd. govs. 1974-76), Assoc. Mail Advt. Agys. (pres. 1975-77), Nat. Soc. Fund Raising Execs. (bd. dirs. Ga. chpt. 1984, cert. 1983), Ga. Arms Collectors Assn. (dir. 1974-76, Pres.'s award 1973), Southeastern Antique Arms Collectors (charter; bd. dirs. 1978—), Assn. Am. Sword Collectors (charter), Mid-Am. Antique Arms Soc. (charter), Mensa, Soc. Animal Welfare Adminstrs., Travelers Aid of Atlanta (bd. dirs. 1989-90), Am. Humane Assn., Omicron Delta Kappa. Home: 1133 Ragley Hall Rd NE Atlanta GA 30319-2511 Office: Grizzard 1144 Mailing Ave SE Atlanta GA 30315-2508

SUMMERLIN, WILLIAM TALLEY, allergist, immunologist, dermatologist; b. Anderson, S.C., 1938. MD, Emory U., 1964. Diplomate Am. Bd. Allergy and Immunology, Am. Bd. Dermatology, Am. Bd. Dermatopathology. Intern U. Tex. Med. Br., 1964-65; resident in dermatopathology Stanford, Palo Alto, 1967-70; resident in immunology U. Minn., Mpls., 1971-73, fellow in immunology, 1971-73; staff mem. St. Mary's Hosp., Rogers, Ark.; pvt. practice Regional Dermatology and Allergy Ctr. Mem. AMA, Am. Acad. Dermatology, Am. Coll. Allergy and Immunology, Am. Acad. of Cosmetic Surgery, Am. Soc. for Mohs Surgery, Am. Subspecialty Bd. of Dermatopathology. Office: Derm Allergy Clin NW Ark PA 1105 W Chestnut St Rogers AR 72756-3529

SUMMERS, ANDY (ANDREW JAMES SOMERS), popular musician; b. Poulton-Fylde, England, Dec. 31, 1942; m. Kate Unter (div.); 1 child, Layla. Attended, UCLA, 1969-73. Performed with Zoot Money's Big Roll Band, Dantalion's Chariot, The Soft Machine, The Animals; worked in bands led by Neil Sedaka, Kevin Coyne, Kevin Ayers, Strontium 90; lead guitarist The Police, 1977-84; solo artist, 1984—; albums: (with The Police) Outlandos D'Amour, 1978, Reggatta De Blanc, 1979, Zenyatta Mondatta, 1980, Ghost in the Machine, 1981, Synchronicity, 1983, The Singles; Every Breathe You Take, 1986; (with Robert Fripp) I Advance Masked, 1982, Bewitched, 1984; (solo) XYZ, 1987, Mysterious Barricades, 1988, The Golden Wire, 1989, Charming Snakes, 1990, World Gone Strange, 1991, Synaesthesia, 1995; film soundtracks: Down & Out in Beverly Hills, 1986, Out of Time, 1988, End of the Line, 1988, Weekend at Bernies, 1989. Office: Private Music 9014 Melrose Ave Los Angeles CA 90069*

SUMMERS, ANITA ARROW, public policy and management educator; b. N.Y.C., Sept. 9, 1925; d. Harry I. and Lillian (Greenberg) Arrow; m. Robert Summers, Mar. 29, 1953; children: Lawrence H., Richard F., John S. BA, Hunter Coll., 1945, DHL (hon.), 1995; MA, U. Chgo., 1947. Sr. econ. analyst Standard Oil Co. N.J., N.Y.C., 1947-54; asst. in econs. Yale U., New Haven, Conn., 1956-59; lectr. dept. econs. Swarthmore (Pa.) Coll., 1965-71; sr. economist Fed. Res. Bank Phila., 1971-75, research officer, 1975-79; adj. prof. pub. policy U. Pa., Phila., 1979-82, prof. pub. policy and mgmt., 1982—, dept. chair, 1983-88, co-dir Wharton Urban Decentralization Project, 1987—, sr. scholar Nat. Ctr. on the Edn. Quality of the Workforce, 1991—; expert witness schs. fin. Md., Mass., Va., 1980-85, Md., Va., 1996, bd. dirs. William Penn Found., Phila.; chair bd. dirs. Mathematica Policy Rsch., Inc., Princeton, N.J. Author: Economic Report on the Philadelphia Metropolitan Area, 1985, Economic Development within the Philadelphia Metropolitan Area, 1986, Local Fiscal Issues in the Philadelphia Metropolitan Area, 1987; editor: Urban Change in the United States and Western Europe, 1992; contbr. articles to profl. jours. Chair econ. subcom. Pa. Three Mile Island Commn., Harrisburg, 1979; pres. Lower Merion (Pa.) LWV, 1963-65; mem. Mayor's Econ. Roundtable, Phila., 1984-88; mem. rsch. policy coun., 1992-94, Com. for Econ. Devel. Rockefeller Found. resident scholar, Bellagio, Italy, 1986. Mem. Am. Econ. Assn., Assn. for Pub. Policy and Mgmt. (policy coun. 1986), Phi Beta Kappa. Avocations: needlepoint, cooking. Home: 641 Revere Rd Merion Station PA 19066-1007 Office: U Pa Wharton Sch Dept Pub Policy and Mgmt Philadelphia PA 19104

SUMMERS, CAROL, artist; b. Kingston, N.Y., Dec. 26, 1925; s. Ivan Franklin and Theresa (Jones) S.; m. Elaine Smithers, Oct. 2, 1954 (div. Aug. 1967); 1 son, Kyle; m. Joan Ward, May 6, 1974. B.A., Bard Coll., 1951, D.F.A. (hon.), 1974. Tchr. Hunter Coll., Sch. Visual Arts, Haystack Mountain Sch. Crafts, Bklyn. Mus. Art Sch., Pratt Graphic Art Ctr., Chelterham Twp. Art Ctr., Valley Stream Community Art Ctr., U. Pa., Columbia Coll., U. Calif., Santa Cruz, San Francisco Art Inst., U. Utah, Logan, Art Study Abroad, Paris, Casa de Espiritus Allegres Marfil, Mex., USIS workshop tour, India, 1974, 79. Represented in permanent collections at, Mus. Modern Art, Bklyn. Mus., N.Y. Pub. Libr., Libr. of Congress, Nat. Gallery, Victoria and Albert Mus., London, Bibliotheque Nationale, Paris, Kinstmuseum, Basil, Lugan (Switzerland) Art Mus. Grenchen (Switzerland) Art Mus., Malmo (Sweden) Mus., Los Angeles County Mus., Phila. Mus., Balt. Mus., Seattle Mus., Boston Mus., Art Inst. Chgo., Am. embassies in Russia, Can., India, Thailand, Fed. Republic Germany and Eng.; traveling exhibit, Mus. Modern Art, 1964-66; retrospective exhbn. Brooklyn Mus., 1977, Nassau County Mus. Art, 1990, Belles Artes, San Miquel de Allende, Mex., 1992, Miami U. Art Mus., Oxford, Ohio, 1995. Served with USMCR, 1944-48, PTO. Italian govt. study grantee, 1954-55; Louis Comfort Tiffany Found. fellow, 1955, 60; John Simon Guggenheim Found. fellow, 1959; Fulbright fellow, Italy, 1961; Coun. for Internat. Exch. Scholars rsch. grantee, India, 1993-94. Mem. NAD, Calif. Soc. Printmakers. Address: 2817 Smith Grade Santa Cruz CA 95060-9764

SUMMERS, CLYDE WILSON, law educator; b. Grass Range, Mont., Nov. 21, 1918; s. Carl Douglas and Anna Lois (Yontz) S.; m. Evelyn Marie Wahlgren, Aug. 30, 1947; children: Mark, Erica, Craig, Lisa. B.S., U. Ill., 1939, J.D., 1942; LL.M., Columbia, 1946, J.S.D., 1952; LL.D., U. Leuven, Belgium, 1967, U. Stockholm, 1978. Bar: N.Y. 1951. Mem. law faculty U. Toledo, 1942-49, U. Buffalo, 1949-56; prof. law Yale U., 1956-66, Garver prof. law, 1966-75; Jefferson B. Fordham prof. law U. Pa., 1975-90; prof. emeritus, 1990—; Hearing examiner Conn. Commn. on Civil Rights, 1963-71. Co-author: Labor Cases and Material, 1968, 2d edit., 1982, Rights of Union Members, 1979, Legal Protection for the Individual Employee, 1989, 2d edit., 1995; co-editor: Labor Relations and the Law, 1953, Employment Relations and the Law, 1959, Comparative Labor Law Jour., 1984—. Chmn. Gov.'s Com. on Improper Union Mgmt. Practices N.Y. State, 1957-58; chmn. Conn. Adv. Council on Unemployment Ins. and Employment Service, 1960-72; mem. Conn. Labor Relations Bd., 1966-70, Conn. Bd. Mediation and Arbitration, 1964-72. Guggenheim fellow, 1955-56; Ford fellow, 1963-64; German-Marshall fellow, 1977-78; NEH fellow, 1977-78, Fullbright fellow, 1984-85. Mem. Nat. Acad. Arbitrators, Am. Arbitration Assn. (nat. chmn.), Internat. Soc. Labor Law and Social Legislation. Congregationalist. Home: 753 N 26th St Philadelphia PA 19130-2429 Office: U Pa Sch Law 3400 Chestnut St Philadelphia PA 19104-6204

SUMMERS, FRANK WILLIAM, librarian; b. Jacksonville, Fla., Feb. 8, 1933; s. Frank Wesley and Kathleen (Gilreath) S.; 1 son, William Wesley. B.A., Fla. State U., 1955; M.A., Rutgers U., 1959, Ph.D., 1973. Libr. Jacksonville Pub. Libr., 1955, 57; sr. libr. Linden (N.J.) Pub. Libr., 1958-59; dir. Cocoa (Fla.) Pub. Libr., 1959-61; assoc. libr. Providence Pub. Libr., 1961-65; libr. Fla. State Libr., 1965-69; research fellow Rutgers U., New Brunswick, N.J., 1969-70; asst. dean, prof. Coll. Librarianship, U. S.C., 1971-76, dean, 1976-85; dean Sch. Libr. and Info. Studies Fla. State U., Tallahassee, 1985-94, prof., 1994—; lectr. Libr. Sch. U. R.I., 1964-95; libr. surveys in Fla., Ohio, N.Y., S.C., N.C., Ky., Tex. Contbr. profl. jours. Mem. R.I. Bd. Library Commrs., 1964-65. Served to lt. (j.g.) USNR, 1955-57. Mem. ALA (exec. bd., v.p., pres.-elect 1987-88, pres. 1988-89, Joseph W. Lippincot award 1996), R.I. Libr. Assn. (pres.), S.C. Libr. Assn. (pres.), Assn. Am. Libr. Schs. (pres.), Beta Phi Mu (exec. sec. 1996—). Home: 505 Live Oak Plantation Rd Tallahassee FL 32312-2335 Office: Fla State Univ Sch Info Studies Tallahassee FL 32306-2048

SUMMERS, HARDY, state supreme court vice chiefjustice; b. Muskogee, Okla., July 15, 1933; s. Cleon A. and Fern H. Summers; m. Marilyn, Mar. 16, 1963; children: Julia Clare, Andrew Murray. BA, U. Okla., 1955, LLB, 1957. Asst. county atty. Muskogee County, 1960-62; pvt. practice law Muskogee, 1962-76; dist. judge 15th dist. Okla. Dist. Ct., 1976-85; justice Okla. Supreme Ct., Oklahoma City, 1985—. Sec. Muskogee County Election Bd., 1965-72. Capt. JAGC, USAF, 1957-62. Mem. ABA, Okla. Bar Assn., Okla. Jud. Conf. (pres. 1984). Avocations: fishing, hunting, classical music. Office: Okla Supreme Ct 242 State Capital Bldg Oklahoma City OK 73105

SUMMERS, JAMES IRVIN, retired advertising executive; b. Lexington, Mo., July 10, 1921; s. William E. and Elizabeth (Hoeflicker) S.; m. Priscilla Barstow West, Jan. 15, 1948 (div. 1985); children: Susanne Cornelia, Elizabeth Barstow, James Irvin, Daniel Edward; m. Jane Browning Beckwith, Oct. 4, 1986 (div. Feb. 1996). With Harold Cabot & Co. Inc., Boston, 1946-86, exec. v.p., 1960-77, pres., chief exec. officer, dir., chmn. exec. com., 1977-86; mem. editorial bd. Sta. WEEI, Boston, 1985-90, also bd. dirs. Mem. exec. com., bd. dirs., v.p., chmn. Pub. Info. Com., Mass. Bay United Way, 1979-84; chmn. Swampscott Rep. Fin. Com., 1964-75; trustee, bd. mgrs., exec. com. Mass. Eye & Ear Infirmary; trustee Family Svc. Assn. Greater Boston, 1952-62; bd. dirs. Mass. Taxpayers Com., 1984-87; pres. Lit. Vols. Mass., 1987-88; pub. rels. bd. USS Constn. Mus., 1988-91. With USAAF, 1941-45. Decorated Bronze Star. Mem. Greater Boston Advt. Club (bd. dirs. 1984-86), Internat. Fedn. Advt. Agys. (bd. dirs. 1985-86), Am. Assn. Advt. Agys. (bd. dirs., treas. 1985-86), New. Eng. Broadcasters Assn. (bd. dirs. 1985-86), Bay Club, Madison Square Garden Club, Tedesco Country Club, Boca Raton Resort and Club. Home: Boca Highlands 4748 S Ocean Blvd PH 3 Highland Beach FL 33487

SUMMERS, JOSEPH FRANK, author, publisher; b. Newnan, Ga., June 26, 1914; s. John Dawson and Anne (Blalock) S.; BA in Math., U. Houston, 1942; profl. cert. meteorology, UCLA, 1943, U. Chgo., 1943; postgrad., U. P.R., 1943-44; MA in Math., U. Tex. at Austin, 1947; postgrad. Rice U., 1947-49; m. Evie Margaret Mott, July 8, 1939 (dec. May 1989); children: John Randolph, Thomas Franklin, James Mott. With Texaco Inc., Houston, 1933-42, 49-79, mgr. data processing, 1957-67, asst. gen. mgr. computer svcs. dept., 1967-79, automation cons., 1979-83; pres. Word Lab Inc., Houston, 1983—; instr. math. AAC, Ellington Field, Tex., 1941-42, U. Tex. at Austin, 1946-47. Pres. Houston Esperanto Assn., 1934-39; vol. tutor Thousand Points of Light, 1991—. Capt. AAC, 1942-46. Rice U. fellow, 1947-49. Mem. Assn. Computing Machinery (pres. 1956-58), Nat. Assn. Accts. (past bd. dir.), Am. Petroleum Inst. (mem. data processing and computing com. 1955-59), Rice U. Hist. Soc., Rice U. Assocs., Esperanto League N.Am., Universal Esperanto Assn. Author: Mathematics for Bombadiers and Navigators, 1942, Wholly Holey Holy, An Adult American Spelling Book, 1984. Contbg. author: American Petroleum Institute Drilling and Production Practices.

SUMMERS, LAWRENCE, deputy secretary treasury department; b. New Haven, 1954; m. Victoria Summers; 2 daughters (twins), 1 son. SB, MIT, 1975; PhD, Harvard U., 1982. Faculty MIT, 1979-82; domestic policy economist Pres'. Coun. Econ. Advisors, 1982-83; Nathaniel Ropes prof. Harvard U., Cambridge, Mass., 1983-93; v.p. devel. econs., chief economist World Bank, 1991-93; under sec. for internat. affairs dept. U.S. Dept. Treasury, Washington, 1993-95, dep. se., 1995—. Author Understanding Unemployment; co-author Reform in Eastern Europe; editor series Tax Policy and the Economy; contbr. numerous articles to profl. jours. Recipient John Bates Clark medal, 1993, Alan Waterman award NSF. Fellow Econometric Soc., Am. Acad. Arts and Scis. Office: US Dept Treasury Office of Dep Sec 1500 Pennsylvania Ave NW Washington DC 20220-0001

SUMMERS, LORRAINE DEY SCHAEFFER, librarian; b. Phila., Dec. 14, 1946; d. Joseph William and Hilda Lorraine (Ritchey) Dey; m. F. William Summers, Jan. 28, 1984. B.A., Fla. State U., 1968, M.S., 1969. Extension dir. Santa Fe Regional Library, Gainesville, 1969-71; pub. library cons. State Library of Fla., Tallahassee, 1971-78, asst. state librarian, 1978-84; dir. adminstrv. services Nat. Assn. for Campus Activities, Columbia, S.C., 1984-85; asst. state librarian State Library of Fla., Tallahassee, 1985—; cons. in field. Contbr. articles to profl. jours. Del. Pres.'s Com. on Mental Retardation Regional Forum, Atlanta. 1975; del. Fla. Gov.'s Conf. on Library and Info. Services, 1978, 90. Mem. ALA (orgn. com. 1979-83, council 1982-84, 93-97, resoluti ons com. 1983-85, mem. legislation com. 1993-95, nominating com. 1996), Assn. Specialized and Coop. Library Agys. (dir. 1976-82, chmn. planning and orgn. com. 1976-80, chmn. nominating com., 1980-81, chmn. by laws com. 1985-86, exec. bd. state library agy sect. 1983-86, pres. 1987-88, chmn. standards rev. com. 1990-92), Southeastern Library Assn. (exec. bd. 1976-80, v.p., pres.-elect 1994-96, pres. 1996—), Fla. Library Assn. (sec. 1978-79, dir., 1976-80 nominating com., 1995-96), Zonta (dir. 1992-95). Democrat. Methodist. Office: State Library Fla Ra Gray Bldg Tallahassee FL 32399

SUMMERS, MAX (DUANNE), entomologist, scientist, educator; b. Wilmington, Ohio, June 5, 1938; s. John Williams Summers and Helen Jane (Rolfe) Summers Kantner; children, Mark William, Keith Dwayne; m. Sharon Braunagel, Dec. 28, 1991. AB magna cum laude, Wilmington Coll., 1962; PhD, Purdue U., 1968. Asst. prof. U. Tex., Austin, 1969-73, assoc. prof., 1973-75; prof. entomology Tex. A&M U., College Station, 1977-83, Disting. prof., 1983—, chair agrl. biotech., chair agrl. biotech., dir. Ctr. Advanced Invert. Molec. Sci., 1988—; vis. prof. U. Calif., Berkeley, 1976. Editor Virology Jour., 1983—; exec. editor Protein Expression and Purification; contbr. more than 200 articles to profl. jours.; co-inventor Baculovinas Expression Vector System. Recipient J.V. Osmun Profl. Achievement award, 1988, President's award of honor Tex. A&M U., 1988, Alumni award Wilmington Coll., 1988; Alumni award Purdue U., 1989, Disting. Alumni award, 1992. Fellow AAAS, Am. Acad. Microbiology; mem. NAS, Am. Soc. for Virology (councilor 1982-85, pres. 1991-92), Am. Soc. Microbiology (lectr. Found. for Microbiology 1986-87), Soc. for Invertebrate Pathology, Genetics Soc. Am., Internat. Com. on Taxonomy of Viruses (exec. com., chair invertebrate virus subcom. 1988-93), Am. Soc. for Biochemistry and Molecular Biology, Entomol. Soc. of Am., Am. Acad. Microbiology, Sigma Xi. Home: 1908 Streamside Way Bryan TX 77807-2715 Office: Tex A&M U Dept Entomology 324 Minnie Belle Heep College Station TX 77843-2475

SUMMERS, ROBERT, economics educator; b. Gary, Ind., June 20, 1922; s. Frank and Ella (Lipton) Samuelson; m. Anita Arrow, Mar. 29, 1953; children: Lawrence Henry, Richard Fredric, John Steven. B.S., U. Chgo., 1943; Ph.D., Stanford, 1956; postgrad. (Social Sci. Research Council fellow), King's Coll., U. Cambridge, Eng., 1951-52. Instr. Stanford, 1949-50; mem. faculty Yale, 1952-59, asst. prof., 1956-59; staff mem. Cowles Found., 1955-59; economist RAND Corp., Santa Monica, Calif., 1959-60; cons. RAND Corp., 1960-80; mem. faculty U. Pa. Wharton Sch., 1959—, prof., 1967—, chmn. grad. group in econs., 1967-70, 73-76. Author: (with Lawrence R. Klein) The Wharton Index of Capacity Utilization, 1966, (with others) Strategies for Research and Development, 1967, (with others) A System of International Comparisons of Gross Product and Purchasing Power, 1975, International Comparisons of Real Product and Purchasing Power, 1978, (with others) World Product and Income, 1982; contbr. articles to profl. jours. Served with AUS, 1944-46. Ford Found. faculty rsch. fellow London Sch. Econs., 1966-67; NSF grantee 1957-59, 63-66, 80-82, 86-90, 92-94, 95-97, 97—; resident scholar Rockefeller Found. Study Ctr., 1986. Fellow Econometric Soc.; mem. AAUP, Am. Econs. Assn., Am. Statis. Assn. Home: 641 Revere Rd Merion Station PA 19066-1007 Office: U Pa Dept Econ Philadelphia PA 19104-6297

SUMMERS, ROBERT SAMUEL, lawyer, author, educator; b. Halfway, Oreg., Sept. 19, 1933; s. Orson William and Estella Bell (Robertson) S.; m. Dorothy Millicent Kopp, June 14, 1955; children: Brent, William, Thomas, Elizabeth, Robert. BS in Polit. Sci., U. Oreg., 1955; postgrad. (Fulbright scholar), U. Southampton, Eng., 1955-56; LLB, Harvard U., 1959; postgrad. rsch., Oxford U., 1964-65, 74-75, 81-82, 88-89; LLD (hon.), U. Helsinki, Finland, 1990, U. Göttingen, Germany, 1994. Bar: Oreg. 1959, N.Y. 1974. Asso. King, Miller, Anderson, Nash and Yerke, Portland, Oreg., 1959-60; asst. prof. law U. Oreg., 1960-63, asso. prof., 1964-68; vis. asso. prof. law Stanford U., 1963-64; prof. U. Oreg., 1968-69; prof. Cornell U., 1969-76, McRoberts prof. law, 1976—; summer vis. prof. Ind. U., 1969, U. Mich., 1974, U. Warwick, Eng., 1975, Australia Nat. U., U. Sydney, Australia, 1977; vis. Fulbright prof. U. Vienna, Austria, 1985; Goodhart vis. prof. Cambridge U., Eng., 1991-92; H. Hurst Eminent vis. scholar U. Fla., 1995; rsch. fellow Merton Coll., oxford U., 1981-82, Exeter Coll., Oxford U., 1988-89; cons. Cornell Law Project in pub. schs., N.Y., 1969-74, Law in Am. Soc. project Chgo. Bd. Edn., 1968-69; instr. Nat. Acad. Jud. Edn., 1976—; mem. faculty Salzburg Seminar in Am. Studies, 1990; ofcl. advisor Drafting commn. on New Civil Code for Russian Fedn., 1994-96. Author: Law, Its Nature, Functions and Limits, 1986; (with Hubbard and Campbell) Justice and Order Through Law, 1973; (with Bozzone and Campbell) The American Legal System, 1973; (with Speidel and White) Teaching Materials on Commercial Transactions, 1987, Collective Bargaining and Public Benefit Conferral-A Jurisprudential Critique, 1976, The Uniform Commercial Code, 1988, 4th edit., 1995; (with White) Het Pramatisch Instrumentalisme, 1981, Instrumentalism and American Legal Theory, 1982, Lon L. Fuller-Life and

Work, 1984; (with Atiyah) Form and Substance in Anglo-American Law, 1987; (with Hillman) Contract and Related Obligation, 1987; (with MacCormick and others) Interpreting Statutes-A Comparative Study, 1991, Nature of Law and Legal Reasoning, 1993; contbr. book revs. and articles to profl. jours.; editor: Essays in Legal Philosophy, vol. 1, 1968, vol. 2, 1971. Social Sci. Research Council fellow, 1964-65. Mem. Am. Law Inst., Assn. Am. Law Schs. (chmn. sect. jurisprudence 1972-73), Am. Soc. Polit. and Legal Philosophy (v.p. 1976-78), Internat. Acad. Comp. Law, Internat. Assn. of Legal and Social Philosophy Am. Soc. (pres. 1989-91), Austrian Acad. of Scis., Phi Beta Kappa. Republican. Congregationalist. Office: Cornell U Sch Law Myron Taylor Hall Ithaca NY 14853

SUMMERS, THOMAS CAREY, lawyer; b. Frederick, Md., Feb. 9, 1956; s. Harold Thomas and Doris Jean (Culler) S.; m. Robin Ann Stalnaker, May 12, 1990; children: Kristin, Heather, Lindsay. BA, Dickinson Coll., 1978; JD, U. Balt., 1981. Bar: Md. 1981, U.S. Dist. Ct. Md. 1981, D.C. 1986. Assoc. Ellin & Baker, Balt., 1979-89, Peter G. Angelos, Balt., Md., 1989—. Mem. ABA, Md. State Bar Assn., Md. Trial Lawyers Assn. Democrat. Lutheran. Avocation: golf. Office: Law Offices of P G Angelos One Charles Ctr Baltimore MD 21201

SUMMERS, TRACY YVONNE, assistant principal; b. Raymond, Miss., Aug. 12, 1961; d. Neil and Bessie (Christian) S.; divorced, Feb. 1982; 1 child, Shundria Anntawnette. BS in Bus. Edn., Jackson State U., 1985, M in Bus. and Math. Edn., 1988, specialist in sch. adminstrn., 1990; postgrad., U. Miss., 1990-91, Miss. State U., 1993—. Cert. tchr., secondary supr., secondary prin., vocat. dir., Miss. Clk. dept. pers. City of Jackson, Miss., 1978-85; tchr. math. Brinkley Jr. High Sch., Jackson Pub. Sch. Dist., 1985-91; asst. prin. Brinkley Mid. Sch., Jackson Pub. Sch. Dist., 1991-94, Hardy Middle Sch., 1994-95; cheerleading sponsor Brinkley Jr. High Sch., 1986-90. Dir. singles ministry College Hill Bapt. Ch. Edn. Found. Trust co-grantee, 1990-91, 91-92, 92-93; Entergy Corp. grantee, 1990-91. Mem. ASCD, South Ednl. Rsch. Assn., Phi Delta Kappa. Home: 5334 Sheronn St Jackson MS 39209-3721 Office: Hardy Middle School 545 Ellis Ave Jackson MS 39209-6202

SUMMERS, WILLIAM COFIELD, science educator; b. Janesville, Wis., Apr. 17, 1939; s. Crosby Hungerford and Rebecca Delores (Cofield) S.; m. Wilma Jean Poos, July 24, 1965; 1 child, Emily Alexandra. BS, U. Wis., 1961, MS, 1963, Phd, MD, 1967; MA, Yale U., 1977. Post-doctoral fellow MIT, Cambridge, Mass., 1967-68; asst. prof. Yale U., New Haven, 1968-70, assoc. prof., 1970-77, prof., 1977—; cons. NIH, Bethesda, Md., 1976—. Editor Nucleic Acids Research Jour., 1977-79, Gene jour., 1984-91; contbr. articles to profl. jours. Cons. Anna Fuller Fund, New Haven, 1973-88, Searle Scholars Program, Chgo., 1980-84; trustee Leukemia Soc. Am., N.Y.C., 1981-85, Yale-China Assn., New Haven, 1982-88, 94—. Mem. Am. Soc. Biochemistry and Molecular Biology, Am. Soc. for Microbiology, History Sci. Soc., Am. Assn. Hist. Medicine. Office: Yale U Sch Medicine 333 Cedar St New Haven CT 06510-3206

SUMMERS, WILLIAM KOOPMANS, neuropsychiatrist, researcher; b. Jefferson City, Mo., Apr. 14, 1944; s. Joseph S. and Amy Lydia (Koopmans) S.; m. Angela Forbes McGonigle, Oct. 2, 1972(div. Apr. 1985); children: Elisabeth Stuart, Wilhelmina Derek. Student, Westminster Coll., Fulton, Mo., 1962-64; BS, U. Mo., 1966; MD, Washington U., St. Louis, 1971. Internal medicine intern Barnes Hosp-Washington U., St. Louis, 1971-72; resident in internal medicine Jewish Hosp., St. Louis, 1972-73; resident in psychiatry Rsch. Hosp., St. Louis, 1973-76; asst. prof. U. Pitts., 1976-78, U. So. Calif., L.A., 1978-82; asst. clin. prof. rsch. UCLA, 1982-88; rschr. Arcadia, Calif., 1988-92, Albuquerque, 1992—. Patentee in field. Mem. AMA, ACP, Am. Psychiat. Assn., Soc. Neurosci., N.Y. Acad. Scis., Am. Fedn. Clin. Rsch. Episcopalian. Avocation: gardening. Office: 201 Cedar St SE Ste 404 Albuquerque NM 87106-4924

SUMMERSELL, FRANCES SHARPLEY, organization worker; b. Birmingham, Ala.; d. Arthur Croft and Thomas O. (Stone) Sharpley; m. Charles Grayson Summersell, Nov. 10, 1934. Student U. Montevallo, Peabody Coll.; LHD (hon.) U. Ala., 1996. Ptnr., artist, writer Assoc. Educators, 1959—. Vice chmn. Ft. Morgan Hist. Commn., 1959-63; active DAR, Magna Charta Dames, U. Women's Club (pres. 1957-58), Daus. Am. Colonists (organizing regent Tuscaloosa 1956-63). Recipient Algernon Sidney Sullivan award U. Ala., 1994. Mem. Tuscaloosa County Preservation Soc. (trustee 1965-78, svc. award 1975), Birmingham-Jefferson Hist. Soc., Ala. Hist. Assn. (exec. bd. Ala. Review 1991—), XXXI Women's Hon. Soc., Omicron Delta Kappa, Iota Circle, Anderson Soc. Clubs: University (Tuscaloosa). Co-author: Alabama History Filmstrips, 1961; Florida History Filmstrips, 1963; Texas History Filmstrips, 1965-66; Ohio History Filmstrips, 1967 (Merit award Am. Assn. State and Local History 1968); California History Filmstrips, 1968; Illinois History Filmstrips, 1970. Home: 1411 Caplewood Dr Tuscaloosa AL 35401-1131

SUMMERTREE, KATONAH See WINDSOR, PATRICIA

SUMMERVILLE, RICHARD M., mathematician, retired academic administrator. Provost Christopher Newport Univ., prof. emeritus math. Office: Christopher Newport U Dept Math 50 Shoe Ln Newport News VA 23606-2998

SUMMITT, PATRICIA HEAD, college basketball coach; b. Henrietta, Tenn., June 14, 1952; d. Richard and Hazel Head; m. R.B. Summitt; 1 child, Ross Tyler. BS in Phys. Edn., U. Tenn., Martin, 1974; MS in Phys. Edn., U. Tenn., Knoxville, 1975. Head women's basketball coach U. Tenn., Knoxville, 1974—; head coach 1st U.S. Jr. Nat. team, 1977 (2 gold medals in internat. play), U.S. Nat. team William R. Jones Cup Games, 1979, World Championships, 1979, Pan Am. Games, 1979 (2 gold medals, 1 silver medal); asst. coach U.S. Women's Olympic Basketball team, 1980-84, head coach, 1984 (gold medal); assoc. athletics dir., U. Tenn.; past v.p. USA BASKETBALL; past Olympic rep. adv. com. to USA BASKETBALL; bd. trustees Basketball Hall of Fame; bd. dirs. Women's Basketball Hall of Fame. Active Big Bros./Big Sisters; hon. chair Tenn. Easter Seal Soc., 1985, 87, 88, 89; Tenn. chair Am. Heart Assn., 1994. Recipient Silver medal as co-capt. U.S. Olympic Women's Basketball team, 1976, Gold medal, Pan Am. Games team, 1975, Silver medal U.S. World Univ. Games team, 1973; named Naismith Coll. Coach of Yr., 1987, 89, 94, WBCA/Converse Coach of Yr., 1983-95. Mem. Chi Omega. Office: Univ Tenn Lady Vols 1600 Stadium Dr Rm 207 Knoxville TN 37996-4610

SUMMITT, (WILLIAM) ROBERT, chemist, educator; b. Flint, Mich., Dec. 6, 1935; s. William Fletcher and Jessie Louise (Tilson) S.; m. Nancy Jo Holland, Apr. 2, 1956; children: Elizabeth Louise, David Stanley. A.S., Flint Jr. Coll., 1955; B.S. in Chemistry, U. Mich., 1957; Ph.D., Purdue U., 1961. Research asso., instr. chemistry Mich. State U., 1961-62, asst. prof. metallurgy, mechs. and materials, 1965-68, asso. prof., 1968-73, chmn. dept. metallurgy mechs. and materials sci., 1972-78, prof., 1973-92, prof. emeritus, 1992; research chemist Corning Glass Works, 1962-65; cons. in field. NRC Sr. Research asso. Air Force Materials Lab., Fairborn, Ohio, 1974-75. Research, publs. in corrosion, failure analysis, optical properties of materials, spectroscopy, and color sci. Mem. ASTM, Am. Chem. Soc., Am. Phys. Soc., Am. Soc. Metals, Nat. Assn. Corrosion Engrs., Sigma Xi. Home: 8535 Clough Dr Grayling MI 49738-8438 Office: Dept Materials Sci & Mechs Michigan State Univ East Lansing MI 48824

SUMMITT, ROBERT LAYMAN, pediatrician, educator; b. Knoxville, Tenn., Dec. 23, 1932; s. Robert Luther and Mary Ruth (Layman) S.; m. Joyce Ann Sharp, Dec. 23, 1955; children: Robert Layman Jr., Susan Kelly Summitt Pridgen, John Blair. Student, Davidson Coll., 1950-51; MD, U. Tenn., 1955, MS in Pediatrics, 1962. Diplomate Am. Bd. Pediatrics, recert. in pediatrics, 1983, 92, Am. Bd. Med. Genetics (bd. dirs. 1985-89). Rotating intern U. Tenn. Meml. Research Ctr. and Hosp., Knoxville, 1956; asst. resident in pediatrics U. Tenn. Coll. Medicine and City of Memphis Hosp., 1959-60, chief resident, 1960-61; USPHS fellow in pediatric endocrinology U. Tenn. Coll. Medicine, Memphis, 1961-62; fellow in med. genetics U. Wis.-Madison, 1963; asst. prof. pediatrics, child devel. U. Tenn., Memphis, 1964-68, assoc. prof., 1968-71, prof. pediatrics and anatomy, 1971—, dean Coll. Medicine, 1981—, provost, 1988-91; cons. President's Commn. on Mental Retardation, 1979-80; CEO U. Tenn. Med. Group, 1983-93, chmn., 1983—; mem. Coun. on Grad. Med. Edn., 1990-96. Lt. M.C., USN, 1957-59, rear admiral USNR, ret. 1992. NIH grantee, 1965—; recipient Alumni Pub. Service award U. Tenn. Alumni Assn., 1980-81, U. Tenn. Coll. Medicine Student Body Disting. Tchr. award, 1981-82, 82-83, 83-84, 84-85, 85-86, Outstanding Alumnus award U. Tenn. Coll. of Medicine, 1984, Etteldorf Pediatric Alumni award U. Tenn., Memphis, 1996. Fellow Am. Coll. Med. Genetics, Am. Acad. Pediatrics (Tenn. Pediatrician of Yr. Tenn. chpt. 1996); mem. AMA (rep. to accreditation coun. on grad. med. edn. 1995—), Tenn. Med. Assn., Memphis-Shelby County Med. Soc. (bd. dirs. 1994—, v.p. West Tenn. 1997—, Disting. Svc. award 1997), Am. Soc. Human Genetics, Soc. Pediatric Rsch., Coun. Deans of AAMC, Jour. Rev. Club (Memphis), Tenn. Pediatric Soc. (Tenn. Pediatrician of Yr. 1996). Office: U Tenn Coll Medicine 800 Madison Ave Memphis TN 38103-3400

SUMMITT, ROBERT MURRAY, circuit judge; b. Sweetwater, Tenn., Jan. 14, 1924; s. Murray Dyer and Vina Mae (Brakebill) S.; m. Florence Varnell, May 14, 1955; children: Virginia Anne Sharber, Robert M. Jr., Laura Stephens, Martin Dyer. JD, U. Tenn., 1949; postgrad., Nat. Jud. Coll., 1972, 79, 82, Am. Acad. Jud. Edn., 1974, 75, 76, 77, U. Tenn., 1978. Bar: Tenn. 1949, U.S. Supreme Ct. 1956. Pvt. practice Chattanooga, 1949-68; cir. judge Tenn. Jud. 1st Div. 11th Jud. Dist. Ct., Tenn., 1968—; served on Tenn. Supreme Ct., 1990; pres. Tenn. Jud. Conf., 1980, ec., v.p., exec. com. mem., 1980-84, past chmn. nominating com., continuintg edn. com., past chmn.; mem. Tenn. Ct. of the Judiciary; past chmn. ad hoc fed. diversity com. National Conf. State Trial Judges, past chmn. task force on jud. support, past chairman State Jud. Assn., chmn. fin. and budget com., Tenn. rep. to nat. conf. Author: (with others) Tenn. Trial Judges Benchbook; contbr. articles to profl. jours. State chmn., nat. rep., Inner City com. chmn., Boy Scouts Am. (Silver Beaver award 1976); bd. dirs. Salvation Army; mem. Freedom's Found.; bd. dirs., trustee, past Sunday Sch. tchr. First Centenary United Meth. Ch. Decorated Red Cross of Constantine; recipient Nat. Heritage award Downtown Sertoma Club, 1984; named Young Man of Yr., Jaycees, 1959. Mem. ABA (past chmn. Nat. Conf. State Trial Judges 1991-92, mem. judicial adminstrn. divsn. coun., judicial coun. House of Dels.), Tenn. Bar Assn., Chattanooga Bar Assn. (bd. govs.), Am. Judicature Soc., Am. Judges Assn., Internat. Acad. Trial Judges, Silver Falcon Assn., Air Force Assn., Res. Officers Assn., Retired Res. Officers Assn., U. Tenn. Alumni Assn. Century Club, Order of the Arrow, City Farmers Club, Half-Century Club, SAR (chancellor), Mason, Royal Order Jesters, Royal Order Scotland, Eastern Star, Alhambra Temple, Rotary, Phi Delta Phi, Sigma Alpha Epsilon. Avocations: gardening, beekeeping, hunting. Home: 957 Ravine Rd Signal Mountain TN 37377-3054 Office: 11th Jud Dist Hamilton County Courthouse Chattanooga TN 37402-1401*

SUMNER, DANIEL ALAN, economist, educator; b. Fairfield, Calif., Dec. 5, 1950. B.S. in Agrl. Mgmt., Calif. State Poly. U., 1971; M.A. in Econs., Mich. State U., 1973; M.A. in Econs., U. Chgo., 1977, Ph.D., 1978. Post-doctoral fellow, labor and population group, econ. dept. Rand Corp., Santa Monica, Calif., 1977-78; asst. prof. N.C. State U., Raleigh, 1978-83, assoc. prof., 1983-87, prof. 1987-92; resident fellow, Resources for the Future, Washington, 1986-87; sr. economist Pres.'s Council of Econ. Advisers, 1987-88; dep. asst. sec. for econs. USDA, 1990-91, asst. sec. for econs., 1992-93. Frank H. Buck Jr. prof. dept. agrl. econs. U. Calif., Davis, 1993—, dir. Calif. Agril. Issues Ctr., 1997—. Author and editor books and monographs; contbr. chpts. to books, articles in profl. jours. Named Alumnus of Yr., Calif. State Poly. U., 1991; recipient Quality of Rsch. Contribution award Am. Agrl. Econ. Assn., 1996. Mem. Am. Econ. Assn., Econometric Soc., Am. Agrl. Econs. Assn., Internat. Assn. Agrl. Economists. Office: U Calif Davis Dept Agrl Econ Davis CA 95616

SUMNER, DAVID GEORGE, association executive; b. Norwich, Conn., Apr. 22, 1949; s. Raymond W. and Ruth M. (Crooks) S.; m. Linda Ann Churma, June 27, 1980; 1 child, Deryn Anne. MA in Polit. Sci., Mich. State U., 1970; MBA, U. Conn., 1979. Corr. Travelers Ins. Co., Hartford, Conn., 1971-72; asst. sec. Am. Radio Relay League, Newington, Conn., 1972-76, asst. gen. mgr., 1976-82, gen. mgr., 1982-85, exec. v.p., 1985—. Bd. dirs. Windham Regional Planning Agy., Willimantic, Conn., 1991—; mem. Coventry Dem. Town Com., 1995—; mem. spectrum planning and policy adv. com. U.S. Dept. Commerce, 1994—. Recipient Calcutta Key, Radio Soc. Gt. Britain, 1989, Region I award Internat. Amateur Radio Union, 1989; Radio Club Am. fellow, 1991. Mem. Newington C. of C. (bd. dirs. 1988-90). Democrat. Congregationalist. Avocation: amateur radio. Office: Am Radio Relay League 225 Main St Newington CT 06111-1400

SUMNER, DAVID SPURGEON, surgery educator; b. Asheboro, N.C., Feb. 20, 1933; s. George Herbert and Velna Elizabeth (Welborn) S.; m. Martha Eileen Sypher, July 25, 1959; children: David Vance, Mary Elizabeth, John Franklin. BA, U. N.C., 1954; MD, Johns Hopkins U., 1958. Diplomate Am. Bd. Surgery; cert. spl. qualification gen. vascular surgery, 1983, 93. Intern in surgery Johns Hopkins Hosp., Balt., 1958-59, resident in gen. surgery, 1960-61; resident in gen. surgery U. Wash. Sch. Medicine, Seattle, 1961-66; clin. investigator in vascular surgery VA Hosp., Seattle, 1967, 70-73; asst. surgery U. Wash. Sch. Medicine, Seattle, 1961-66, instr. surgery, 1966-70, asst. prof. surgery, 1970-72, assoc. prof. surgery, 1972-75; prof. surgery, chief sect. peripheral vascular surgery So. Ill. U. Sch. Medicine., Springfield, 1975-84, Disting. prof. surgery, chief sect. peripheral vascular surgery, 1984—; staff surgeon Seattle VA Hosp., 1973-75, Univ. Hosp., Seattle, 1973-75, St. John's Hosp., Springfield, 1975—, Meml. Med. Ctr., Springfield, 1975—; mem. VA Merit Review Bd. Surgery, 1975-78; mem. vascular surgery rsch. award com. The Liebig Found., 1990-95, chmn., 1994; bd. dirs. Am. Venous Forum Found., 1993-95; vis. prof. Cook County Hosp., Chgo., 1971, Washington U., St. Louis, 1976, U. Tex., San Antonio, 1978, Wayne State U., Detroit, 1978, U. Ind., Indpls., 1979, Ea. Va. Med. Sch., Norfolk, 1979, Case-Western Res. U., Cleve., 1980, U. Chgo., 1981, U. Manitoba, Winnipeg, Can., 1983, and others to present; dist. lectr. Yale U., 1982; guest examiner Am. Bd. Surgery, St. Louis, 1982, assoc. examiner, 1989, certifying examination gen. vascular surgery, 1993, 94; lectr. in field. Author: (with D.E. Strandness Jr.) Ultrasonic Techniques in Angiology, 1975, Hemodynamics for Surgeons, 1975, (with R.B. Rutherford, V. Bernhard, F. Maddison, W.S. Moore, M.O. Perry) Vascular Surgery, 1977, (with J.B. Russell) Ultrasonic Arteriography, 1980, (with F.B. Hershey, R.W. Barnes) Noninvasive Diagnosis of Vascular Disease, 1984, (with R.B. Rutherford, G. Johnson Jr., R.F. Kempczinski, W.S. Moore, M.O. Perry, G.W. Smith) Vascular Surgery, 3d edit., 1989, (with A.N. Nicolaides) Investigation of Patients With Deep Vein Thrombosis and Chronic Venous Insufficiency, 1991, (with R.B. Rutherford, G. Johnson, K.W. Johnston, R.F. Kempczinski, W.C. Krupski, W.S. Moore, M.O. Perry, A.J. Comerota, R.H. Dean, P. Gloviczki, K.H. Johansen, T.S. Riles, L.M. Taylor Jr.) Vascular Surgery, 4th edit., 1995; author 150 chpts. to books; mem. editl. adv. bd. Vascular Diagnosis and Therapy, 1980-84; mem. editl. bd. advisors Appleton Davies, Inc., 1983—; mem. editl. review bd. Jour. Soc. of Non-Invasive Vascular Tech., 1987—; mem. editl. bd. Jour. Vascular Surgery, 1987—; series editor Introduction to Vascular Tech., 1990—; mem. exec. editl. com. Phlebology, 1987-91; mem. Internat. Editl. Adv. Bd., 1991; mem. editl. com. Internat. Angiology, 1992—; contbr. over 140 articles to profl. jours. Lt. col. U.S. Army, 1967-70. Recipient fellowship in surg. rsch. Johns Hopkins U. Sch. Medicine, 1959-60, fellowship Am. Cancer Soc., Inc., 1965-66, Appleton-Century Crofts Scholarship award, 1956, Mosby Scholarship award, 1958. Fellow Am. Coll. Surgeons (Wash. chpt. 1971-75, Ill. chpt. counselor 1981-83), Cyprus Vascular Soc. (hon.); mem. AMA, Soc. Univ. Surgeons, Soc. Vascular Surgery (constn. and by-laws com. 1983, Wiley Fellowship com. 1990), Internat. Soc. Cardiovascular Surgery (N.Am. chpt. program com. 1985-88), Am. Surg. Assn., Am. Heart Assn. (stroke coun., cardiovascular surgery coun. 1978), Soc. Noninvasive Vascular Tech. (hon.), Vascular Surgery Biology Club, Am. Venous Forum (organizing com. 1987, founding mem. 1988, chmn. membership com. 1988-91, treas. 1992-95), Cardiovascular Sys. Dynamics Soc., Internat. Soc. Surgery, Vascular Soc. So. Africa (hon.), North Pacific Surg. Assn., Ctrl. Surg. Assn., Midwestern Vascular Surg. Soc. (counselor 1977-79, pres.-elect 1980-81, pres. 1981-82), So. Assn. for Vascular Surgery, Ill. Heart Assn., Ill. Med. Soc., Ill. Surg. Soc., Chgo. Surg. Soc., Seattle Surg. Soc., Sangamon County Med. Soc., Henry N. Harkins Surg. Soc., Harbinger Soc., Phi Eta Sigma, Phi Beta Kappa, Sigma Xi, Alpha Omega Alpha. Presbyterian. Achievements include research in surgical hemodynamics and noninvasive methods for diagnosing peripheral vascular disease. Avocations: painting, sailing, history, computers. Home: 2324 W Lake Shore Dr Springfield IL 62707-9521 Office: So Ill U Sch Medicine Dept Surgery 800 N Rutledge St Springfield IL 62702-4911

SUMNER, GORDON, JR., retired military officer; b. Albuquerque, July 23, 1924; s. Gordon and Esstella (Berry) S.; m. Frances Fernandes, May, 1991; children: Ward T., Holly Rose. AS, N.Mex. Mil. Inst., 1943; BA, La. State U., 1955; MA, U. Md., 1963. Commd. 2d. lt. U.S. Army, 1944, advanced through grades to lt. gen., 1975, ret., 1978; founder, chmn. Cypress Internat., 1978-96; chmn. La Mancha Co., Inc., 1981-89, Sumner Assoc.; cons. U.S. Depts. State and Def; amabassador at large for Latin Am.; spl. advisor U.S. Dept. State; nat. security advisor Pres.' Bi-Partisan Commn. Cen. Am.; vis. staff mem. Los Alamos Nat. Lab. Contbr. articles to profl. jours. Decorated D.S.M., Silver Star, Legion of Merit with three oak leaf clusters, Disting. Flying Cross with 13 oak leaf clusters, Bronze Star, Army Commendation medal with oak leaf cluster, Purple Heart. Mem. Phi Kappa Phi, Pi Sigma Alpha. Office: La Mancha Co 100 Cienega St Ste D Santa Fe NM 87501-2003

SUMNER, GORDON MATTHEW See STING

SUMNER, JAMES DUPRE, JR., lawyer, educator; b. Spartanburg, S.C., Nov. 30, 1919; s. James DuPre and Frances Grace (Harris) S.; m. Evvie Lucille Beach, Apr. 1, 1945 (dec.); children: Chery Erline (Mrs. Horacek), James DuPre III; m. Doris Kaiser Malloy, Oct. 20, 1972; children: John L. Malloy III, Mary Margaret Malloy, Kenneth S. Malloy, James M. Malloy. AB, Wofford Coll., 1941; LLB, U. Va., 1949; LLM, Yale U., 1952, JSD, 1955. Bar: Va. 1948, Calif. 1957. Practice law Los Angeles, 1957—; instr. law U. S.C., 1949-52; assoc. prof. UCLA, 1952-55, prof., 1955—; distinguished vis. prof. Instituto Luigi Sturzo, Rome, 1959; vis. prof. U. Tex., 1962, U. So. Calif., 1971; lectr. Calif. Bar Rev. Co-author: An Anatomy of Legal Education; contbr. articles to profl. jours. Lt. col. inf. AUS, 1941-46, ETO. Decorated Silver Star, Purple Heart with oak leaf cluster. Mem. Calif. Bar Assn., Va. Bar Assn., Westwood Village Bar Assn. (pres.), Rotary (pres. Westwood Village chpt.), L.A. Country Club, Braemar Country Club, Bel Air Assn. (bd. dirs.), Westwood Village Sertoma Club (pres.), Marrakesh Golf Club, Sertoma (pres.). Republican. Methodist. Home: 10513 Rocca Pl Los Angeles CA 90077-2904

SUMNER, MALCOM EDWARD, agronomist, educator; b. June 7, 1933. BSc in Agriculture, Chemistry and Soil Sci., U. Natal, South Africa, 1954, MSc in Agriculture, Soil Physics cum laude, 1958; PhD in Soil Chemistry, U. Oxford, Eng., 1961. Sr. lectr. dept. soil sci. U. Natal, 1955-57, assoc. prof. dept. soil sci., 1961-71, prof., head dept. soil sci. and agrometeorology, 1971-77; prof. dept. agronomy U. Ga., Athens, 1977-91, regents' prof., coord. environ. soil sci. program dept. crop and soil scis., 1991—; hon. prof. dept. agrl. and environ. sci. U. Newcastle-Upon-Tyne, Eng., 1989—; cons. Brit. Commonwealth Devel. Corp., 1967-82, South African Chamber of Mines, 1969-76, FAO-UNDP Program, India, 1986-87, Food and Fertilizer Tech. Ctr., ASPAC, Taiwan, 1986, Combustion Chems. Corp., 1987-90, Masstock Inc., 1988, AGRILAB, 1987-93, Standard Fruit Co., Honduras, 1992, Australian Ctr. Internat. Agrl. Rsch., 1992. Author: (with B. Ulrich) Soil Acidity, 1991, (with B.A. Stewart) Soil Crusting: Physical and Chemical Processes, 1992; author: (with others) Interactions at the Soil Colloid-Soil Solution Interface, 1989, Ecological Indicators, 1992, Sustainable Land Management in the Tropics: What Role for Soil Science?, 1993, Innovative Management of Subsoil Problems, 1993, MacMillan Encyclopedia of Chemistry, 1993; contbr. 184 articles to profl. jours. Recipient Excellence in Rsch. award Ag Alumni, 1989, Sr. Frederick McMaster fellowship, 1992, Agronomic Rsch. award American Soc. of Agronomy, 1995. Fellow Soil Sci. Soc. Am. (Rsch. award 1991), Am. Soc. Agronomy (Werner L. Nelson award 1991, Soil Sci. award 1991). Office: U Ga Dept Crop & Soil Scis Athens GA 30602

SUMNER, WILLIAM MARVIN, anthropology and archaeology educator; b. Detroit, Sept. 8, 1928; s. William Pulford Jr. and Virginia Friel (Umberger) S.; m. Frances Wilson Morton, June 21, 1952 (div. 1975): children: Jane DeVault, William Morton; m. Kathleen A. MacLean, Apr. 7, 1989. Student, Va. Mil. Inst., 1947-48; B.S., U.S. Naval Acad., 1952; Ph.D., U. Pa., 1972. Dir. Am. Inst. Iranian Studies, Tehran, Iran, 1969-71; asst. prof. Ohio State U., Columbus, 1971-73, assoc. prof., 1974-80, prof. anthropology, 1981-89, prof. emeritus, 1989—; dir. Oriental Inst., prof. Near Eastern langs. and civilizations U. Chgo., 1989—; dir. excavations at Tal-e Malyan (site of Elamite Anshan) sponsored by Univ. Mus., U. Pa., 1971—; v.p. Am. Inst. Iranian Studies, 1983-86. Contbr. chpts. to books, articles and essays to profl. jours. Served to lt. comdr. USN, 1952-64. Grantee NSF, 1975, 76, 79, NEH, 1988. Office: Univ Chgo Oriental Inst 1155 E 58th St Chicago IL 60637-1540

SUMPTER, DENNIS RAY, lawyer, construction company executive; b. Lake Charles, La., Apr. 26, 1948; s. Griffin Ray and Winnie Marie (Vincent) S.; m. Brenda Sue Waite, June 8, 1968; children: Leslie, Stephanie. JD, La. State U., 1975; BA in Government, McNeese U., 1981. U.S. Dist. Ct. (we. dist.) La., U.S. Ct. Appeals (5th cir.). Atty. Sumpter Law Offices, Sumpter, La., 1976—; mayor City of Sulphur, La., 1978-90; judge ad hoc Sulphur City Ct., 1980; mem. La. Commn. for Law Enforcement, Baton Rouge, 1985-86; constrn. co. exec., 1988-94. Pres. La. Mcpl. Assn., State of La., 1985-86; vice chmn. bd. dirs. West Calcasieu Airport, Sulphur, 1986-92. SSgt. USAF, 1967-71, Vietnam. Mem. La. Bar Assn., La. Trial Lawyers, S.W. La. Bar Assn. (ethics com., 1978), S.W. La. Trial Lawyers, Nat. Coll. Advocacy Trial Advocate, La. High Sch. Rodeo Assn. (v.p., pres.). Office: 1003 S Huntington St Sulphur LA 70663-4837

SUMPTER, SONJA KAY, elementary school educator; b. Weston, W.Va., Aug. 12, 1948; d. Glen A. and Sarah R. (White) Wade; m. Charles Fredrick Sumpter, Mar. 25, 1967; children: Lisa Marie Sumpter Pethtel, Charles Fredrick II. BS in Elem. Edn., Glenville (W.Va.) State Coll., 1984; MS in Edn., W.Va. Wesleyan Coll., 1993; postgrad., W.Va. U., 1994. Cert. tchr. elem. edn. 1-6, math. 5-8. Tchr. Weston (W.Va.) Jr. H.S., 1984-92; tchr. Robert Bland Mid. Sch., Weston, 1992—, team leader, 1992-94. Mem. Nat. Coun. Tchrs. Math., Order Ea. Star. Republican. Baptist. Avocations: singing, walking, macrame. Home: RR 4 Box 297 Weston WV 26452-9517 Office: Robert Bland Middle School 358 Court Ave Weston WV 26452-2008

SUMRALL, HARRY, journalist; b. Palestine, Tex., Oct. 15, 1950; s. Harry Glenn and Sherea Sue (Selden) S.; m. Leslie Leizear, Dec. 19, 1954; 1 child, Samuel Harry. BA, George Mason U., 1974. Writer, critic The Washington Post, 1978-81; contbg. writer The New Republic, Washington, 1979; assoc. editor Rock Concert Mag., Washington, 1979; music writer San Jose (Calif.) Mercury News/Knight Ridder News Svc., 1982—; advisor New Music Am., Washington, 1983; lectr., guest San Francisco State U., 1991; guest critic Sta. KGO, San Francisco, 1991—. Author: Pioneers of Rock and Roll, 1994, Giants of Country Music, 1995; contbg. author: New Grove Dictionary of American Music, 1983; broadcaster: (radio program) Rockology, 1989. Paneslist Chatauquas for Congress, Washington, 1979. Fellow New Music Am., 1980. Office: San Jose Mercury News 750 Ridder Park Dr San Jose CA 95131-2432*

SUMRALL, KENNETH IRVIN, religious organization administrator; b. Ellisville, Miss., Dec. 24, 1926; s. Irvin Earnest and Amber Beatrice (Bynum) S.; m. Wanda Ruth Till, Oct. 17, 1947; children: John, Elizabeth, Stanley, Marlene. BA, William Carey Coll., 1957; MS in Speech, U. So. Miss., 1959; M in Religious Edn., New Orleans Bapt. Theol. Sem., 1962; LLD (hon.), Internat. Theol. Sem., 1986. Agt. Penisular Life Ins. Co., Pensacola, Fla., 1949-51; pastor So. Bapt. Conv., Pensacola, 1954-64; pres., founder Liberty Ministries, Pensacola, 1964-90, Ch. Foundational Network, Pensacola, 1995—; pres., founder Globe Missionary Evangelism, Pensacola, 1971-90, Liberty Fellowships of Min. and Chs., Pensacola, 1975-94, Nat. Leadership Confs., Pensacola, 1978-88, The Secret Place, Pensacola, 1994-96. Author: Manifestation of the Sons of God, 1969, What's Your Question?, 1968, New Wine Bottles, 1975, From Glory to Glory, 1979, Organized Flexibility, 1984, Confidence: The Key to Overwhelming Victory, 1994; editor: Chit-Chat, 1992-96. With U.S. Army, 1945-47. Mem. Scenic Hills Golf Club. Republican. Avocations: golf, hunting, landscaping. Home and Office: 4900 Forest Creek Dr Pace FL 32571

SUMRELL, GENE, research chemist; b. Apache, Ariz., Oct. 7, 1919; s. Joe B. and Dixie (Hughes) S. BA, Eastern N.Mex. U., 1942; BS, U. N.Mex., 1947, MS, 1948; PhD, U. Calif., Berkeley, 1951. Asst. prof. chemistry Eastern N.Mex. U., 1951-53; sr. rsch. chemist J. T. Baker Chem. Co., Phillipsburg, N.J., 1953-58; sr. organic chemist Southwest Rsch. Inst., San Antonio, 1958-59; project leader Food Machinery & Chem. Corp., Balt., 1959-61; rsch. sect. leader El Paso Natural Gas Products Co. (Tex.), 1961-64; project leader So. utilization research and devel. div. U.S. Dept. Agr., New Orleans, 1964-67, investigations head, 1967-73, rsch. leader Oil Seed and Food Lab., So. Regional Rsch. Ctr., 1973-84, collaborator, 1984— . Contbr. numerous papers to profl. jours. Served from pvt. to staff sgt. AUS, 1942-46. Mem. AAAS, Am. Chem. Soc., N.Y. Acad. Scis., Am. Inst. Chemists, Am. Oil Chemists Soc., Am. Assn. Textile Chemists and Colorists, Rsch. Soc. Am., Phi Kappa Phi, Sigma Xi. Achievements include patents in field. Home: PO Box 24037 New Orleans LA 70184-4037 Office: 1100 Robert E Lee Blvd New Orleans LA 70124-4305

SUN, HUN H., electrical engineering and biomedical engineering educator; b. Shanghai, China, Mar. 27, 1925; s. Yu F.and Tuk F. Sun; m. Nancy Liu, Jan. 30, 1951; 1 child, Elizabeth A. BSEE, Chiao-Tung U., Shanghai, 1946; MSEE, U. Wash., 1950; PhD, Cornell U., 1955. Asst. prof. elect. engring. Drexel U., Phila., 1953-56, assoc. prof., 1956-59, prof., 1959—, dir. Biomed. Engring. and Scis. Inst., 1964-74, chmn. elec. engring. dept., 1973-78, E.O. Lange prof., 1978-95, prof. Emeritus, 1995—; NIH spl. fellow MIT, Cambridge, Mass., 1963-64; cons. Wright-Patterson AFB, Dayton, Ohio, 1963-65; mem. study com. NIH, Bethesda, Md., 1981-85; mem. adv. com. NSF, Washington, 1985-88; adj. prof. Temple U. Dept. Physiology, 1971-91. Author: Synthesis of R. C. Networks, 1967; editor in chief Annals of Biomed. Engring., 1984-94; mem. editl. bd. Automatica (London), 1974-90, Critical Rev. in Bioengring, 1978-81; cons. editor Elec. Engring. Monograph Series, 1964-67; contbr. chpts. to books, articles to profl. jours. Mem. Com. on Art and Sci. Franklin Inst., 1969-82. Recipient 1st Rsch. Achievement award Drexel U., 1973. Fellow IEEE (editor in chief Trans. Biomed. Engring. 1972-78); mem. Biomed. Engring. Soc. (founding), Sigma Xi (life). Home: 939 Hedgerow Ct Blue Bell PA 19422-2408 Office: Drexel Univ Dept Elec Engring Philadelphia PA 19104

SUNAMI, JOHN SOICHI, designer; b. N.Y.C., June 10, 1949; s. Soichi and Suyeko (Matsushima) S.; m. Marialyce Norman, Apr. 21, 1973; children: Christopher Andrew-Solchi, Jennifer Kiyoko. BA, CCNY, 1969. Cert. Gemological Inst. Am. Vol. Peace Corps, Jamaica, W.I., 1969-71; jeweler N.Y.C. and Columbus, Ohio, 1971-82; dir. mktg. Knight's Inn/Cardinal Industries, Columbus, 1982; founder, exec. designer Nimbus, Columbus, 1983—. Designer/sculptor pub. artwork IntroCenter, 1990; designer logo identities for various cos.; exhibited paintings and sculpture; author poems and essays. Bd. dirs. William H. Thomas Gallery, Columbus, 1992-93; v.p., bd. dirs. South Side Settlement House, Columbus, 1982-93; mem. cultural diversity outreach com. United Way of Franklin County, 1993—. Recipient 1st prize Macworld Gallery/Macworld Mag., 1985. Mem. Columbus C. of C., Columbus Art League. Avocations: music, travel. Home: 419 Fairwood Ave Columbus OH 43205-2202 Office: Nimbus 413 Fairwood Ave Columbus OH 43205-2202

SUND, JEFFREY OWEN, publishing company executive; b. Bklyn., June 19, 1940; children: Catherine, Meredith. BA, Dartmouth Coll., 1962. Sales rep. Prentice-Hall, Englewood Cliffs, N.J., 1967-73; sales rep. Houghton Mifflin, Boston, 1973-74, coll. div. editor, 1974-77, editor-in-chief, 1977-86, v.p., editorial dir., 1986-89; pres., chief exec. officer Richard D. Irwin, Burr Ridge, Ill., 1989-96; pres. McGraw-Hill Higher Edn., Burr Ridge, 1996—. Lt. USN, 1962-66. Office: McGraw Hill Higher Edn 1333 Burr Ridge Pkwy Burr Ridge IL 60521-6423

SUND, KELLY G., public health science administrator; b. Northridge, Calif., Oct. 22, 1966; d. Donald C. and Evelyn M. (Miller) S. BS in Biol. Scis., Stanford U., 1988, MS in Biol. Scis., 1989. Rsch. assoc. Health & Environ. Scis. Group, Ltd., Washington, 1990-92, assoc. dir. rsch., 1992-95, dir. GLP-Lab., 1994-95, dir. rsch., 1995-97; sci. outreach coord. Wireless Tech. Rsch., Washington, 1994-95, ongoing surveillance coord., 1996-97; occpl., environ. health tchr. George Washington U., Washington, 1995—; presenter in field. Contbr. articles to profl. jours. Big sister Big Bros./Big Sisters, Palo Alto, Calif., 1985-89; counselor D.C. AIDS Info. Line, Washington, 1990-97; spkr. AIDS Edn. Spkrs. Bur., Washington, 1991. Recipient U.S. Achievement Acad. Nat. award. Mem. Soc. for Risk Analysis (comm. working group leader 1992-93), Met. Washington Mensa (spl. interest group leader 1990-96, area coord. 1993, scrivener 1993-94, testing coord. 1994—, proctor 1995—). Avocations: dancing, languages.

SUNDARESAN, MOSUR KALYANARAMAN, physics educator; b. Madras, India, Sept. 2, 1929; parents Mosur Ramanathan and Kanakavalli Kalyanaraman; m. Bharathy Sundaresan, June 7, 1957; children: Sudhir, Sujata. BSc with honors, Delhi U., 1947, MSc, 1949; PhD, Cornell U., 1955. With Atomic Energy Establishment, Bombay, 1955-57; postdoctoral fellow NRC, Can., 1957-59; reader in physics Punjab U., Chandigarh, India, 1959-61; prof. physics Carleton U., Ottawa, Can., Can., 1961-95; hon. disting. rsch. prof. physics Carleton U., Ottawa, 1995—. Mem. Can. Assn. Physicists, Am. Phys. Soc., Am. Assn. Physics Tchrs., Inst. Particle Physics Can.

SUNDBERG, ALAN CARL, former state supreme court justice, lawyer; b. Jacksonville, Fla., June 23, 1933; s. Robert Carl and Gertrude Harriet (Rudd) S.; children: Allison, Angela, Laura, Alan, William. BS, Fla. State U., 1955; LLB, Harvard U., 1958; LLD (hon.), Stetson U., 1977. Bar: Fla. 1958. Practiced in St. Petersburg, 1958-75; justice Supreme Ct. Fla., 1975-82, chief justice, 1980-82; sr. atty. Carlton, Fields, Ward, Emmanuel, Smith & Cutler, P.A., Tallahassee, 1982—; gen. counsel, spl. counsel to pres. Fla. State U., Tallahassee, 1997—; com. mem. on rules of practice and procedure of Judicial Conf. of U.S. Author: Process and Appearance, Civil Practice Before Trial, 1963. Mem. Salvation Army Adv. Bd.; chmn. bd. trustees Canterbury Sch. Fla., Inc.; bd. dirs. Fla. Gulf Coast Symphony, St. Petersburg Symphony; trustee Pinellas County Law Library; mem. Fla. Sentencing Guidelines Commn., 1982-89; chmn. Fla. Bench Bar Commn. Mem. ABA, Fla. Bar Found. (past 2d v.p.), St. Petersburg Bar Assn., Fla. Bar Assn. (spl. commn. referall contingency fees), Pinellas Trial Lawyers Assn., Internat. Acad. Trial Lawyers, Am. Coll. Trial Lawyers, Best Lawyers in Am., Phi Beta Kappa, Phi Kappa Phi, Omicron Delta Kappa, Phi Delta Phi, Dragon, Suncoasters. Democrat. Episcopalian. Office: Carlton Fields Ward Emmanuel Smith & Cutler PC Fla State U PO Box 190 Tallahassee FL 32302-0190

SUNDBERG, CARL-ERIK WILHELM, telecommunications executive, researcher; b. Karlskrona, Sweden, July 7, 1943; came to U.S., 1984; s. Erik Wilhelm and Martha Maria (Snaar) S. MEE, U. Lund, Sweden, 1966, PhD, 1975. Tchr., rsch. asst., lectr. U. Lund, 1966-75, rsch. prof. (docent), 1977-84; rsch. fellow European Space Agy., Nordwijk, The Netherlands, 1975-76; disting. mem. tech. staff AT&T Bell Labs., Murray Hill, N.J., 1984-96, Lucent Technologies, Bell Labs., 1997—; cons. L.M. Ericsson, Gothenburg, Sweden, 1976-77, Bell Labs., Crawford Hill, N.J., 1981-82; instr. Carl Cranz Gesellschaft, Oberpfaffenhofen, Fed. Republic Germany, 1990-93. Co-author: Digital Phase Modulation, 1986, Source-Matched Mobile Communications, 1995; contbr. articles to profl. jours.; patentee in field. Served in Swedish Navy, 1968. Fellow IEEE (Best Paper award 1986, guest editor Jour. on Selected Areas in Comm. 1988-89), IEE Marconi Premium (Best Paper award 1989); mem. Swedish Union Radio-Scientifique Internationale, Svenska Electric Engrs., Riksförening (Sweden), CF Civil Engrs. förbundet (Sweden). Lutheran. Avocations: travel, history, photography. Home: 25 Hickory Pl Apt A11 Chatham NJ 07928-1465 Office: Lucent Technologies Bell Labs RM 2C-480 600 Mountain Ave New Providence NJ 07974-2008

SUNDBERG, MARSHALL DAVID, biology educator; b. Apr. 18, 1949; m. Sara Jane Brooks, Aug. 1, 1977; children: Marshall Isaac, Adam, Emma. BA in Biology, Carleton Coll., 1971; MA in Botany, U. Minn., 1973, PhD in Botany, 1978. Lab. technician Carleton Coll., Minn., 1973-74; teaching asst. U. Minn., Mpls., 1974-76, rsch. asst., 1976-77; adj. asst. prof. Biology U. Wis., Eau Claire, 1978-85, mem. faculty summer sci. inst., 1982-85; instr. La. State U., Baton Rouge, 1985-88, asst. prof. Biology, 1988-91, coord. dept. Biology, 1988-93, assoc. prof. Biology, 1991-97; prof., chair divsn. biol. scis. Emporia State U., 1997—. Author: General Botany Laboratory Workbook, 5th revision, 1984, General Botany 1001 Laboratory Manual, 1986, General Botany 1002 Laboratory Manual, 1987, Biology 1002 Correspondence Study Guide, 1987, Boty 1202: General Botany Laboratory Manual, 1988, Biol 1208: Biology for Science Majors Laboratory Manual, 1988, 2d edit., 1989, Instructor's Manual for J. Mauseth, Introductory Botany, 1991; contbr. articles to profl. jours. Judge sci. fairs, La. schs., 1985—; coach Baton Rouge Soccer Assn., 1991-96; asst. scoutmaster, Boy Scouts Am. Troop 5, 1991—. Brand fellow U. Minn., 1976-77, Faculty Grants scholar U. Wis., 1984-85. Fellow Linnaean Soc. London; mem. NSTA, AAAS, Am. Inst. Biol. Scis. (coun. mem. at large 1992-95), Assn. Biology Lab. Edn., Bot. Soc. Am. (chmn. teaching sect. 1985-86, workshop com. teaching sect. 1983-84, slide exchange/lab. exchange teaching sect. 1980-89, edn. com. 1991, 92, Charles H. Bessey award 1992), Internat. Soc. Plant Morphologists, Nat. Assn. Biology Tchrs., Soc. Econ. Botany, The Nature Conservancy, Sigma Xi (sec. 1982-84, v.p. 1984-85). Home: 1912 Briarcliff Emporia KS 66801 Office: Emporia State U Divsn Biol Scis 1200 Commercial St Emporia KS 66801-5057

SUNDBERG, R. DOROTHY, physician, educator; b. Chgo., July 29, 1915; d. Carl William and Ruth (Chalbeck) S.; m. Robert H. Reiff, Dec. 24, 1941 (div. 1945). Student, U. Chgo., 1932-34; B.S., U. Minn., 1937, M.A., 1939, Ph.D., 1943, M.D., 1953. Diplomate: Am. Bd. Pathology. Instr., asst. prof. anatomy U. Minn., 1939-53, asso. prof., 1953-60, prof., 1960-63, prof. of lab. medicine and anatomy, 1963-73, prof. lab. medicine, pathology and anatomy, 1973-84, emeritus prof., 1984—; hematologist, dir. Hematology Labs., 1945-74, hematologist, co. dir., 1974-84. Editorial bd.: Soc. Exptl. Biology and Medicine, until 1975; mem. editorial bd.: Blood, 1960-67; assoc. editor, 1967-69. Recipient Lucretia Wilder award for research in anatomy, 1943. Mem. Am. Assn. Anatomists, Internat., European Soc. Hematology, Sigma Xi. Home: 1255 Shenandoah Ct Marco Island FL 34145-5023 also: 2618 158th Ave NE Ham Lake MN 55304-5834

SUNDBERG, RICHARD JAY, chemistry educator; b. Sioux Rapids, Iowa, Jan. 6, 1938; s. Ernest Julius and Rosa Paulina Christina (Christensen) S.; m. Lorna Swift, 1962 children—Kelly, Jennifer. B.S., U. Iowa, 1959; Ph.D., U. Minn., 1962. Mem. faculty dept. chemistry U. Va., Charlottesville, 1964—, prof., 1974—. Author monograph: Chemistry of Indoles, 1970; author (with F. A. Carey) Advanced Organic Chemistry, 1990. Served to 1st lt. U.S. Army, 1962-64. Mem. Am. Chem. Soc., Internat. Soc. Heterocyclic Chemistry. Lutheran. Home: 2001 Greenbrier Dr Charlottesville VA 22901-2916 Office: U Va Dept Chemistry Mccormick Rd Charlottesville VA 22904

SUNDBY, SCOTT EDWIN, law educator; b. Aurora, Ill., Oct. 24, 1958; s. Elmer Arthur and Marilyn Edruth (Koeller) S.; m. Katie Louise Rees, June 15, 1980; children: Russell Taylor, Christopher Scott, Kelsey Kathleen. BA, Vanderbilt U., 1980; JD, Cornell U., 1983. Bar: Calif. 1985, U.S. Dist. Ct. (no. dist.) Calif. 1985. Law clk. to judge U.S. Ct. Appeals for 11th Cir., Savannah, Ga., 1983-84; prof. law U. Calif. Hastings Coll. Law, San Francisco, 1984-92; prof. Washington and Lee U., Lexington, Va., 1992—; spl. asst. U.S. Atty. (so. dist.), Fla., 1994-95. Editor-in-chief Cornell Law Rev., 1982-83. Mem. Order of Coif, Phi Beta Kappa. Office: Washington and Lee Univ Sch Law Lexington VA 24450

SUNDE, MILTON LESTER, retired poultry science educator; b. Volga, S.D., Jan. 7, 1921; s. Andrew Carl and Clara Josephine (Mehl) S.; m. Genevieve C. Larson, Dec. 29, 1946; children: Roger, Scott, Robert. BS in Poultry Sci., S.D. State Coll., 1947; MS in Biochemistry, U. Wis., 1949, PhD in Nutrition, 1950. Instr. in poultry sci. U. Wis., Madison, 1949-51, asst. prof., 1951-55, assoc. prof., 1955-57, prof., 1957-64, 66-71, prof., chmn. dept. poultry sci., 1964-66, 71-85, prof. emeritus, 1987—; mem. nutrition adv. bd. Nat. Rsch. Coun., Washington, 1970-78; cons. Min. of Agriculture Govt. of Venezuela, 1964, FAO, India, 1977; poultry scientist Rockefeller Found., 1960. Patentee Vitamin D compounds; assoc. editor: Poultry Sci. Jour., 1964-72, 77-83; contbr. articles to profl. jours. and chpts. to books. Inducted into Am. Poultry Hall of Fame, 1992; recipient Award Am. Poultry Hist. Soc., 1996. Fellow Poultry Sci. Assn. (pres. 1967-68, v.p. 1965-67, Hist. award 1996), World Poultry Sci. Assn. (coun. 1970—, chmn. nutrition program com. 1974, chmn. scientific papers 1981-84, v.p. U.S. br. 1979-84, pres. 1984-89, v.p. 1988-96). Lutheran. Avocations: consulting with Cage Bird people. Office: U Wis Poultry Sci Dept Madison WI 53706

SUNDEL, MARTIN, social work educator, psychologist; b. Bronx, N.Y., Sept. 22, 1940; s. Louis and Pauline (Brotman) S.; m. Sandra Stone, Aug. 22, 1971; children: Adam Daniel, Jenny Rebecca, Ariel Pauline. B.A. cum laude, St. Mary's U., 1961; M.S.W., Worden Sch. Social Service, 1963; M.A., U. Mich., 1968, Ph.D., 1968. Social group work supr. Valley Cities Jewish Community Ctr., Van Nuys, Calif., 1963-65; asst. prof. U. Mich. Sch. Social Work, Ann Arbor, 1968-71; postdoctoral fellow Harvard U. Lab. Community Psychiatry, Boston, 1971-72; dir. research and evaluation River Region Mental Health-Mental Retardation Bd., Louisville, 1972-77; adj. prof. Kent. Sch. Social Work-U Louisville, 1972-77, assoc. clin. prof. dept. psychiatry and behavioral scis., 1974-77, assoc. in psychology, 1975-77; sr. research assoc. The Urban Inst., Washington, 1977-80; pvt. practice psychology Dallas; Dulak Disting. prof. U. Tex., Arlington, 1980-89, prof., 1980-95; prof. Fla. Internat. U., North Miami, Fla., 1995—; mental health cons. UN High Commn. for Refugees in Cyprus, 1993-95; mem. profl. adv. coun. Dallas Geriatric Rsch. Inst., 1980-89; mem. long-range planning com. Dallas Jewish Coalition for the Homeless, 1986-95; mem. coordinating com. Arlington Human Svcs. Project, 1981-90, Mayor's Forum on Human Svc. Needs Assessment, Ft. Worth, 1983-86; vis. prof. U. So. Calif. Sch. Social Work, spring 1985. Author: (with Sandra Stone Sundel) Behavior Modification in the Human Services, 1975, 3d edit., 1993; Be Assertive, 1980; co-editor: Assessing Health and Human Service Needs, 1983, Individual Change Through Small Groups, 2d edit., 1985, Midlife Myths, 1989; mem. editorial bds. and cons. to profl. jours. Mem. APA, NASW (mem. futures commn. 1979-85, mem. steering com. Dallas 1986-90), Behavior Therapy and Rsch. Soc. (charter clin. fellow), Acad. Cert. Social Workers, Coun. Social Work Edn., Internat. Soc. for the Sys. Scis. Home: 3804 Barbados Ave Cooper City FL 33026 Office: Fla Internat U Sch Social Work North Miami Campus ACI-234 Miami FL 33181

SUNDELIUS, HAROLD W., geology educator; b. Escanaba, Mich., July 6, 1930; s. Herbert A. and Caroline (Johnson) S.; m. Charlene P. Swanson, May 21, 1955; children: Karin, Kristine. AB, Augustana Coll., Rock Island, Ill., 1952; MS, U. Wis., 1957, PhD, 1959. Geologist U.S. Geol. Survey, Washington, 1959-65; asst. prof. geology Wittenberg U., Springfield, Ohio, 1965-67, assoc. prof., 1967-74, prof., 1974-75, assoc. dean Coll., 1971-75; v.p., dean Coll., Augustana Coll., 1975-88, prof. geology, 1988-95, ret., 1995; cons. Dow Chem. Co., Midland, Mich., 1957, minerals dept. Exxon, Houston, 1968-75. Contbr. articles to geol. jours., chpt. to book. Bd. dirs. Luth. Hosp., Moline, Ill., 1984-89, Swenson Swedish Immigration Rsch. Ctr., Rock Island, 1984—. With U.S. Army, 1953-55, Korea. Fulbright fellow, Oslo, 1952-53, C.K. Leith fellow, 1955-57, Univ. fellow, 1957-58. Fellow Soc. Econ. Geologists, Geol. Soc. Am.; mem. Nat. Assn. Geology Tchrs., Rock Island C. of C. (bd. dirs.), Rotary (bd. dirs. Rock Island chpt.), Phi Beta Kappa, Sigma Xi. Lutheran. Home: 4310 26th Ave Rock Island IL 61201-5723 Office: Augustana College 600 38th St Rock Island IL 61201

SUNDELOF, JON GRENVILLE, microbiologist; b. Washington, Nov. 28, 1944; s. Herbert G. W. and Mabel Doris (Ferger) S.; m. Joan Elizabeth Ely, Sept. 13, 1967; children: Deborah Jean, Jeffrey Eric. BA, Rutgers U., 1976. LPN, N.J. Lab. technician Gulton Industries, Metuchen, N.J., 1963-64; technician Merck & Co. Inc., Rahway, N.J., 1964-67, jr. scientist, 1971-85, sr. scientist, 1985—. County committeeman Middlesex Rep. Party, 1988-94. With U.S. Army 1967-71. Decorated Bronze star. Mem. AAAS, VFW, Am. Soc. for Microbiology, Am. Legion. Avocations: golf, bowling, private pilot. Home: 517 Willow Ave Piscataway NJ 08854-4532 Office: Merck & Co Inc (R80T-100) PO Box 2000 Rahway NJ 07065

SUNDERLAND, RAY, JR., retired insurance company executive; b. N.Y.C., Nov. 12, 1913; s. Ray and Rose (Goehl) S.; m. Melva Joyce Mace, June 13, 1943; 1 son, Joel Wayne. Grad., Sch. Profl. Accountancy Practice, Pace Coll., 1948, Sch. Bus. Adminstrn., Columbia U., 1968. CPA, N.Y. With comptroller's dept. Brown Bros. Harriman & Co., N.Y.C., 1934-40; sr. auditor Price Waterhouse & Co., N.Y.C., 1940-50; with N.Y. Life Ins. Co., N.Y.C., 1950-79; gen. auditor N.Y. Life Ins. Co., 1969-71, comptroller, 1971-79, v.p., 1971-75, sr. v.p., 1975-79; comptroller N.Y. Life Fund, Inc., 1972-79. Author and publisher: The Descendants of William Sunderland and Allied Families, 1988. Pres. community scholarship fund local sch. dist., Locust Valley, N.Y., 1958-62, pres. parents club, 1958-62; bd. dirs. Vis. Nurse Assn. L.I., N.Y., 1982-93, Vis. Nurse Assn. of Oyster Bay-Glen Cove, N.Y., 1982-92; mem. Locust Valley Libr. (long range planning com. 1992, nominating com. for bd. trustee mems. 1992-93); historian Inc. Village of Lattingtown, N.Y. Fellow Am. Coll. Genealogists (v.p. N.Y. area 1990—); mem. NRA (life), SAR (Huntington, N.Y. chpt.), Am. Coun. Life Ins. (fin. reporting principles com. 1977-78), Nat. Geneal. Soc., Geneal. Soc. Southwestern Pa., Locust Valley Hist. Soc. (N.Y.). Home: 3 Wood Ln Locust Valley NY 11560-1628

SUNDERLAND, ROBERT, cement company executive; b. Omaha, Dec. 21, 1921; s. Paul and Avis Marie (Peters) S.; m. Terri Reed, Nov. 21, 1959; children—Sharon Marie, Lori Diane. B.S. in Bus. Adminstrn, Washington U., St. Louis, 1947; LL.D. (hon.), Bethany Coll., Lindsborg, Kans., 1980. With Ash Grove Cement Co., Overland Park, Kans., 1947—; sec., asst. treas. Ash Grove Cement Co., 1953-57, treas., 1957-61, v.p., treas., 1961-67, chmn. bd., 1967-91, hon. chmn., 1992—. Trustee The Sunderland Found., Kansas City. Served with USAAF, 1942-46, Philippines. Mem. Kansas City Club, Shadow Glen Golf Club, Sigma Chi. Republican. Presbyterian. Office: Ash Grove Cement Co 8900 Indian Creek Pky Ste 600 Shawnee Mission KS 66210-1513

SUNDERMAN, DUANE NEUMAN, chemist, research institute executive; b. Wadsworth, Ohio, July 14, 1928; s. Richard Benjamin and Carolyn (Neuman) S.; m. Joan Catherine Hoffman, Jan. 31, 1953; children: David, Christine, Richard. BA, U. Mich., 1949, MS, 1954, PhD in Chemistry, 1956. Researcher Battelle Meml. Inst., Columbus, Ohio, 1956-59; mgr. Battelle Meml. Inst., Columbus, 1959-69, assoc. dir., 1969-79, dir. internat. programs, 1979-84; sr. v.p. Midwest Rsch. Inst., Kansas City, Mo., 1984-90, exec. v.p., 1990-94; exec. v.p. Midwest Rsch. Inst., Golden, Colo., 1990-94; dir. Nat. Renewable Energy Lab., Golden, Colo., 1990-94, dir. emeritus, 1994—. Contbr. numerous articles to profl. jours. Bd. dirs. Mid-Ohio chpt. ARC, 1982-83, U. Kansas City, 1985-90, Mo. Corp. for Sci. and Tech., Jefferson City, 1986-90. Mem. AAAS, Am. Chem. Soc. Republican. Presbyterian. Avocation: computers.

SUNDERMAN, FREDERICK WILLIAM, physician, educator, author, musician; b. Altoona, Pa., Oct. 23, 1898; s. William August and Elizabeth Catherine (Lehr) S.; m. Clara Louise Baily, June 2, 1925 (dec. 1972); children: Louise (dec.), F. William, Joel B. (dec.); m. Martha-Lee Taggart, May 3, 1980. BS, Gettysburg Coll., 1919, ScD (hon.), 1952; MD, U. Pa., 1923, MS, 1927, PhD, 1929. Diplomate Am. Bd. Internal Medicine, Am. Bd. Pathology (v.p. 1944-50 life trustee 1950—), Nat. Bd. Med. Examiners. Intern, then resident Pa. Hosp., 1923-25; assoc. rsch. med. U. Pa., Phila., 1925-48; assoc. in chem. divsn. William Pepper Lab. U. Pa. Hosp., Phila., 1929-48; physician U. Pa. Hosp., 1929-48; med. dir. Office of Sci. R & D, 1943-46; physician, hon. pathologist Pa. Hosp., 1988—; mem. faculty U. Pa. Sch. Medicine, Phila., 1925-47; assoc. prof. research medicine, also lectr. U. Pa. Sch. Medicine; acting head med. dept. Brookhaven Nat. Lab., Upton, N.Y., 1947-48; chief chem. div. William Pepper Lab. Clin. Medicine, U. Pa. Med. Sch., 1933-47; prof. clin. pathology, dir. Temple U. Lab. Clin. Medicine, 1947-48; med. dir. govt. explosives lab. Carnegie Inst. Tech. and Bur. Mines, 1943-46; head dept. clin. pathology Cleve. Clinic Found., 1948-49; dir. clin. research M.D. Anderson Hosp. Cancer Research, Houston, 1949-50; dir. clin. labs. Grady Meml. Hosp., Atlanta, 1949-51; prof. clin. medicine Emory U. Sch. Medicine, 1949-51; chief clin. pathology Communicable Disease Center, USPHS, 1950-51; med. adviser Rohm & Haas Co., 1947-71; med. cons. Redstone Arsenal, U.S. Army Ordnance Dept., Huntsville, Ala., 1947-49; cons. clin. pathology St. Joseph's Hosp., Tampa, Fla., 1965-66; attending physician Jefferson Hosp., Phila., 1951—, dir. div. metabolic research, clin. prof. medicine, 1951-67, clin. prof. medicine, 1951-74, hon. clin. prof. medicine, 1975—; dir. Inst. Clin. Sci., 1965—; prof. pathology Hahnemann U. Med. Coll., 1970—, co-chmn. dept. lab. medicine, 1970-75, prof. emeritus, 1989; med. adviser and cons. bus. and industry, 1947—; dir. internat. seminars on clin. chemistry and pathology, 1947—; guest lectr. Beijing (People's Republic of China) Med. U., 1989. Author, editor 36 books on clin. chemistry and pathology; author: Our Madeira Heritage, 1979, Musical Notes of a Physician, 1982, Painting with Light, 1993; editor-in-chief Annals Clin. Lab. Sci., 1970—; mem. editl. bd. Am. Jour. Clin. Pathology, 1939-87, Am. Jour. Indsl. Medicine, 1979-85; cons. editor Am. Jour. Occupl. Medicine, 1979-85; also over 350 articles. Trustee Gettysburg Coll., 1967-89, chmn. bd. trustees, 1972-74, hon. life trustee, 1986—; bd. dirs. Mus. Fund Soc. Phila., 1938—, hon. life bd. dirs., 1993—; bd. dirs. Dwight D. Eisenhower Soc., 1984—, German Soc. Pa., 1986—, Geog. Soc. Phila., 1995; violin soloist Chautauqua Summer Series, Ea. U.S., 1919-20; guest soloist Concerto Soloists Pa., 1979, 83, 84, Pa. String Tchrs. Assn., Gettysburg, 1959, Westchester, 1962, 63, 67, 68, Trenton (N.J.) Tchrs. Coll. Orch., 1965; Internat. String Conf. soloist World Congress on Arts and Medicine, Carnegie Hall, N.Y.C., 1992. Recipient Naval Ordnance Devel. award, 1946, cert. appreciation War Dept., 1947, Honor medal Armed Forces Inst. Pathology, 1964; recipient Meritorious Svc. award, 1979, Honor award Latin Am. Assn. Clin. Biochemistry, 1976, Disting. Svc. award Am. Soc. Clin. Pathology-Coll. Am. Pathologists, 1988, Life-time Achievement award in clin. chemistry Joint Congresses of IX Congresso Nacional de la Sociedad Espanola de Quimica Clin., 2d Internat. Congress Therapeutic Drug Monitoring and Toxicology, and 4th Internat. Congress on Automation and New Tech., Spain, 1990, John Gunther Reinhold award Phila. Sect. Am. Assn. for Clin. Chemistry, 1991, Jacob Ehrenzeller award Res. Assn. Pa. Hosp., 1993; named Disting. Alumnus Gettysburg Coll., 1963; Sunderman Seminar Rm. dedicated at Bermuda Biol. Sta. for Rsch., 1992; 1st ann. F. William Sunderman award for Disting. Community Svc. and Excellence in a Chosen Field of Endeavor established by Rho Deuteron chpt. Phi Sigma Kappa, Gettysburg Coll; recipient Nat. Phi Sigma Kappa Disting. Alumnus award, 1995. Fellow ACP (life), Royal Soc. Medicine (hon., life), Royal Soc. Health Great Britain (life); mem. Am. Assn. History Medicine, Am. Diabetes Assn., AMA, Am. Soc. Clin. Investigation, Royal Soc. Health, AAUP, Endocrine Soc., Am. Assn. Biol. Chemistry, AAAS, Am. Chem. Soc., Internat. Union Pure and Applied Chemistry (nickel subcom. Commn. on Toxicology), Inst. Occupational Health (Finland), Outokumpu Oy (Finland), Am. Assn. Clin. Chemists (award for outstanding efforts in edn. and tng. 1981, John Gunther Reinhold award 1991), Coll. Am. Pathologists (founding gov., Pathologist of Yr. award 1962, Pres.'s Honor award 1984), Am. Soc. Clin. Pathology (pres. 1951, archives com. 1977—, intersoc. pathology coun. 1976—, interpathology soc. coun. 1976—, Ward Burdick award 1975, Continuing Edn. Distinguished Service award 1976), Assn. Clin. Scientists (pres. 1957-59, dir. edn. 1959—, diploma honor 1960, ann. goblet award 1964, Gold-headed cane 1974), Coll. Physicians of Phila. (sec. 1946-48, hon. pres. arts medicine sect. 1995, Disting. Service award 1980, 85, 90, 95), Knight of Order of St. Vincent of Portugal (Disting. Svc. cross, Order of merit, (das Verdienstkreuz), Bundesrepublik Deutschland, 1989), Am. Indsl. Hygiene Assn., Am. Occupational Medicine Assn., Med. Soc. Pa., Nat. Soc. Med. Research, Nat. Acad. Clin. Biochemistry, Pan Am. Med. Assn., Pa. Assn. Clin. Pathology, Philadelphia County Med. Soc., Mus. Fund Soc. Phila. (hon. life), Soc. Toxicology, Brit. Assn. Clin. Biochemists (hon.), Soc. Pharm. and Environ. Pathologists (hon.), Internat. Union Pure and Applied Chemistry, Inst. Occupational Health Finland (nickel subcom. commn. toxicology), Phi Beta Kappa, Pa. Assn. Pathologists (Recognition award more than 50 yrs. contbns. to medicine and practice of pathology), Sigma Xi, Alpha Omega Alpha, Phi Sigma Kappa (1st annual F. William Sunderman award for Cmty. Svc Rho Deuteron chpt. Gettysburg Coll. 1995, Nat. Disting. Alumnus award grand chpt. 1995). Lutheran. Spl. symposium given in honor for lifetime achievement, Internat. Union Pure and Applied Chemistry, Finland, 1988. Home: 1833 Delancey Pl Philadelphia PA 19103-6606 Office: Pa Hosp Inst for Clin Sci 301 S 8th St Duncan Bldg 3A Philadelphia PA 19106-4014

SUNDERMEYER, MICHAEL S., lawyer; b. Kansas City, Mo., Feb. 8, 1951; s. Edgar W. and Ruth (Shobe) S.; m. Susan Talarico; children: Kim Marie, Mark Shobe. BA, U. Kans., 1973; JD, U. Va., 1976. Bar: D.C., Md., Va., U.S. Dist. Ct. D.C., U.S. Dist. Ct. Md., U.S. Dist. Ct. (ea. dist.) Va., U.S. Ct. Appeals (D.C. cir.), U.S. Ct. Appeals (4th cir.), U.S. Ct. Appeals (5th cir.). Law clk. to Hon. John Minor Wisdom U.S. Ct. Appeals (5th cir.), New Orleans, 1976-77; law clk. to Hon. Harry A. Blackmun U.S. Supreme Ct., Washington, 1977-78; assoc. Williams & Connolly, Washington, 1978-84, ptnr., 1985—. Editor-in-chief Va. Law Rev., 1975-76.

Mem. ABA. Office: Williams & Connolly 725 12th St NW Washington DC 20005-3901

SUNDIN, MATS JOHAN, professional hockey player; b. Sollentuna, Sweden, Feb. 13, 1971. Selected 1st round NHL entry draft Que. Nordiques, 1989; traded Toronto Maple Leafs, 1994, right wing, 1994—; played in Europe during 1994-95 NHL lockout; named to Swedish League All-Star Team 1990-91, 91-92; selected NHL All-Star Game, 1996. Office: care Toronto Maple Leafs, 60 Carlton St, Toronto, ON Canada M5B 1L1

SUNDLUN, BRUCE, former governor; b. Providence, R.I., Jan. 19, 1920; s. Walter I. and Jane Z. (Colitz) S.; m. Marjorie G. Lee, Dec. 15, 1985; children by previous marriage: Tracy, Stuart, Peter, Mark Santelia, Kimberly Gerrie, Kara Hewes. BA, Williams Coll., 1942; LLB, Harvard U., 1949; student, Air Command and Staff Sch., 1948; DSBA (hon.), Bryant Coll., 1980; DBA (hon.), Roger Williams Coll., 1980; LLD (hon.), Johnson and Wales U., 1993, Williams Coll., 1993. Bar: R.I. and D.C. 1949. Asst. U.S. atty., Washington, 1949-51; spl. asst. to U.S. atty. gen., Washington, 1951-54; pvt. practice Washington and Providence, R.I., 1954-76; v.p., gen. counsel, dir. Outlet Co., Providence, 1960-76, pres., CEO, 1976-84, chmn. bd., CEO, 1984-88; gov. of R.I., 1990-92, 92-95; pres. Exec. Jet Aviation, Inc., Columbus, Ohio, 1970-76, chmn. bd., 1976-84; incorporator, bd. dirs. Communications Satellite Corp., 1962-92; chmn. Round Hill Devel. Ltd., 1989-90. Mem. adv. group Nat. Aviation Goals, 1961; chmn. Inaugural Medal Com., Washington, 1961, 65; vice chmn. Inaugural Parade Com., 1961; bd. visitors USAF Acad., 1978-80; mem. R.I. Capital Center Commn., 1980, R.I. Legis. Pay Commn., 1980; vice chmn. Providence Rev. Com., 1981, chmn., 1982-85; mem. Providence Sch. Bd., 1985-90; mem. Providence Housing Authority, 1987, chmn. 1987-90; del. Dem. Nat. Conv. 1964, 68, 80, 88, 92, R.I. Constl. Conv., 1985; Dem. candidate for gov. R.I., 1986, 88, 90, 92; mem. exec. com. Dem. Gov. Assn., 1990-94; vice chmn. CONEG, 1992-94, chmn., 1994, chmn., vice chmn. Com. on Economy Nat. Gov. Assn., 1992-94, chmn. N.E. Gov. Assn., 1994; pres. Washington Internat. Horse Show, 1970-75, trustee, 1975-90; pres. Providence Performing Arts Ctr., 1978-90; bd. dirs. Touro Synagogue, Newport, R.I., 1979—, Miriam Hosp., 1985-90; bd. dirs. Temple Beth El, Providence, 1979-84, v.p., 1984-88, pres., 1988-91; bd. dirs. Trinity Repertory Theater, 1980-89, chmn., 1984-89; trustee R.I. Philharm. Orch., 1981-90; trustee Providence Preservation Soc., 1981-90, v.p., 1987-90; trustee Newport Art Mus., 1985, pres., 1987-91; pres. Providence Found., 1985-86; pres. R.I. C. of C. Fedn., 1981-84, bd. dirs., 1977-81; pres. Greater Providence C. of C., 1978-81, bd. dirs. 1976-85; bd. dirs. New Eng. Coun., 1978, vice chmn., 1980-81, chmn., 1981-83; trustee Bryant Coll., 1989—. Capt. USAAF, 1942-45; col. USAFR, ret., 1980. Decorated D.F.C., Air medal with oak leaf cluster, Purple Heart; chevalier Legion d'Honneur (France); Prime Minister's medal (Israel). Mem. Hope Club, Univ. Club, Spouting Rock Beach Assn., Clambake Club, Ida Lewis Club, Yacht Club (R.I.), 1925 F Street Club (Washington), Delta Upsilon. Home: Seaward Cliff Ave Newport RI 02840*

SUNDQUIST, DONALD, governor, former congressman, sales corporation executive; b. Moline, Ill., Mar. 15, 1936; s. Kenneth M. and Louise (Rohren) S.; m. Martha Swanson, Oct. 3, 1959; children: Tania, Andrea, Donald Kenneth. BA, Augustana Coll., 1957. Div. mgr. Josten's, Inc., 1961-72; exec. v.p. Graphic Sales of Am., Memphis, 1972, pres., 1973-82; mem. 98th-103rd Congresses from 7th Tenn. dist., Washington, 1983-94; gov. State of Tenn., Nashville, 1995—; vice chmn. bd. Bank of Germantown, Tenn. Past mem. White House Commn. Presdl. Scholars; past chmn. Jobs for High Sch. Grads. of Memphis; chmn. Congl. Steering Com. George Bush for Pres., 1988, 92; nat. campaign mgr. Howard Baker for Pres., 1979; dir. com. ops., alt. del. Republican Nat. Conv., 1980; chmn. Shelby County Rep. Party, 1975-77; alt. del. Rep. Nat. Conv., 1976; exec. com. Rep. Nat. Com., 1971-73; nat. chmn. Young Rep. Nat. Fedn., 1971-73; sec. Bedford County Election Commn., 1968-70; chmn. Tenn. Young Rep. Fedn., 1969-70; dir. Mid-South Coliseum, Am. Council Young Polit. Leaders, 1972-74, U.S. Youth Council, 1972-75; bd. govs. Charles Edison Meml. Youth Fund; nat. adv. bd. Distributive Edn. Clubs Am.; mem. U.S. del. study tour, People's Republic of China, 1978, study tour, USSR, 1975. Served with USN, 1957-59. Lutheran. Lodge: Kiwanis. Office: Office of Gov State Capitol Bldg Nashville TN 37243-0001

SUNDQUIST, ERIC JOHN, American studies educator; b. McPherson, Kans., Aug. 21, 1952; s. Laurence A. and Frances J. (Halene) S.; m. Tatiana Kreinine, Aug. 14, 1982; children: Alexandra, Joanna, Ariane. BA, U. Kans., 1974; MA, Johns Hopkins U., 1976, PhD, 1978. Asst. prof. English Johns Hopkins U., Balt., 1978-80; asst. prof. English U. Calif., Berkeley, 1980-82, assoc. prof., 1982-86, prof. English, 1986-89; prof. English UCLA, 1989-97, chair dept. English, 1994-97; dean Coll. Arts and Scis. Northwestern U., Evanston, Ill., 1997—; vis. scholar U. Kans., 1985, dir. Holmes grad. seminar, 1993; dir. NEH Summer Seminar for Coll. Tchrs., U. Calif., Berkeley, 1986, 90, UCLA, 1994; cons. Calif. Coun. for Humanities, 1986-87; prof. Bread Loaf Sch. English, Middlebury (Vt.) Coll., 1987, 89, Sante Fe, 95; mem. fellowship com. Newberry Libr., 1987, 88, 92; dir. NEH Summer Seminar for Secondary Sch. Tchrs., Berkeley, 1988; vis. prof. UCLA, 1988; Andrew Hilen vis. prof. U. Wash., 1990; Lamar Meml. lectr. in so. states Mercer U., 1991; Gertrude Conaway Vanderbilt prof. English Vanderbilt U., Nashville, 1992-93; mem. fellowship cons. Nat. Humanities Ctr., 1992, 93; acad. specialist in Am. studies Tel Aviv U., 1994; mem. adv. bd. Colloquium for the Study of Am. Culture, Claremont (Calif.) Grad. Sch. & Huntington Libr., 1994—. Author: Home as Found: Authority and Genealogy in Nineteenth-Century American Literature, 1979 (Gustave Arlt award Coun. Grad. Schs. in U.S. 1980), Faulkner: The House Divided, 1983, The Hammers of Creation: Folk Culture in Modern African-American Fiction, 1992, To Take the Nations: Race in the Making of American Literature, 1993 (Christian Gauss award Phi Beta Kappa 1993, James Russell Lowell award MLA 1993, Choice Outstanding Acad. Book 1994); co-author: Cambridge History of American Literature, Vol. II, 1995; editor: American Realism: New Essays, 1982, New Essays on Uncle Tom's Cabin, 1986, Frederick Douglass: New Literary and Historical Essays, 1990, Mark Twain: A Collection of Critical Essays, 1994, Cultural Contexts for Ralph Ellison's Invisible Man, 1995, Oxford W.E.B. DuBois Reader, 1996; mem. adv. bd. Studies in Am. Lit. and Culture, 1987-90, gen. editor, 1991-97; mem. editl. bd. Am. Lit. History, 1987—, Ariz. Quar., 1987—; assoc. editor Am. Nat. Biography, 1990—; cons. The Libr. of Am., 1992—; consulting reader African-Am. Rev., 1992—; contbr. articles to profl. jours. Am. Coun. Learned Socs. fellow, 1981, NEH fellow, 1989-90, Guggenheim fellow, 1993-94 (declined). Mem. MLA (chair adv. coun. Am. lit. sect. 1994, mem. exec. com. divsn. 19th Century Am. lit. 1994-97), Am. Studies Assn. (chair John Hope Franklin Prize com. 1993, mem. nat. coun. 1994-97, mem. fin. com. 1995-97, and other coms.), Am. Lit. Assn., Orgn. Am. Historians, So. Hist. Assn., So. Am. Studies Assn. (mem. exec. com. 1993-97), Phi Beta Kappa. Office: Northwestern U Coll Arts and Scis 1918 Sheridan Rd Evanston IL 60208-0847

SUNDQUIST, JAMES LLOYD, political scientist; b. West Point, Utah, Oct. 16, 1915; s. Frank Victor and Freda (Carlson) S.; m. Beth Ritchie, Dec. 25, 1937 (dec. 1982); children: Erik L., Mark L., James K.; m. Geraldine Coote, Dec. 3, 1983. Student, Weber Coll., 1932-34, HHD (hon.), 1990; student, Northwestern U., 1934-35; BS, U. Utah, 1939; MS in Pub. Adminstrn, Syracuse U., 1941; DDS (hon.), Carthage Coll., 1987. Reporter Salt Lake Tribune, 1935-39; adminstrv. analyst U.S. Bur. Budget, 1941-47, 49-51; reports and statistics officer Office Def. Moblzn., 1951-53; dir. mgmt. control European Command, U.S. Army, Berlin, 1947-49; asst. to chmn. Democratic Nat. Com., 1953-54; asst. sec. to gov. N.Y. State, 1955-56; asst. to U.S. Senator Clark, 1957-62; dep. under sec. agr., 1963-65; sr. fellow Brookings Instn., 1965-85, emeritus, 1985—, dir. govtl. studies, 1976-78; adj. prof. Smith Coll., 1975-78; Sec. platform com. Dem. Nat. Conv., 1960, 68. Author: Politics and Policy: The Eisenhower, Kennnedy and Johnson Years, 1968, Making Federalism Work, 1969 (Louis Brownlow award for best pub. adminstrn. book), Dynamics of the Party System, 1973 2d edit., 1983, Dispersing Population: What America Can Learn form Europe, 1975, The Decline and Resurgence of Congress, 1981 (Hardeman prize for best book on Congress), Constitutional Reform and Effective Government, 1986, 2d edit., 1992; editor Internat. Rev. Adminstrv. Scis., 1980-89, Beyond Gridlock?, 1993, Back to Gridlock?, 1995. Mem. Gov.'s Commn. on Va.'s Future, 1983-84. Recipient Exceptional Civilian Service award War Dept., 1945, Lifetime Achievement award Maxwell Sch. (Syracuse U.) Alumni Assn., 1994; sr. Research fellow U. Glasgow, Scotland, 1972-73. Mem. Nat. Acad. Pub. Adminstrn., Am. Soc. Pub. Adminstrn., Am. Polit. Sci. Assn. (treas. 1980, Charles E. Merriam award 1985), Am. Acad. Arts and Scis. Home: 3016 N Florida St Arlington VA 22207-1808 Office: 1775 Massachusetts Ave NW Washington DC 20036-2188

SUNDQUIST, JOHN A., religious organization executive. Exec. dir. Internat. Ministries Am. Bapt. Chs., Valley Forge, Pa.; chair internat. mission secs. Gen. Coun. of Bapt. World Alliance. Trustee No. Bapt. Sem., Lombard, Ill., Internat. Bapt. Sem., Prague. Office: Am Bapt Chs Internat Ministries PO Box 851 Valley Forge PA 19482-0851

SUNDQUIST, MARIA ALEXANDRA, diplomat; b. Buenos Aires, Argentina, Feb. 4, 1943; came to U.S., 1962; d. Alberto Oscar and Filomena (Cacciavillani) Garcia; m. Ralph H. Gunther, Oct. 10, 1964 (div. 1970); m. Erik Lindon Sundquist, Mar. 1, 1975; 1 child, Karin Alexandra. BA, Smith Coll., 1964; MA in Econs., NYU, 1969. Economist Chase Manhattan Bank, N.Y.C., Chem. Bank, N.Y.C.; asst. comml. attache Am. Embassy, Jeddah, Saudi Arabia, 1980-82; 1st sec. Am. Embassy, Paris, 1982-86; econ. officer U.S. Dept. of State, Washington, 1986-90; legis. asst. U.S. Senate, Washington, 1990-91; consul gen. U.S. Dept. of State, Bordeaux, France, 1991-94; econ. counselor Am. Embassy, Rabat, Morocco, 1995—. Pearson fellow, 1990-91. Avocations: history, mysteries, opera, gastronomy. Office: Am Embassy, PSC 74 Box 19, Rabat APO AE 09718, Morocco

SUNDSTROM, HAROLD WALTER, public relations executive; b. Chgo., Jan. 26, 1929; s. Elmer A. and Rosalind Lillian (Busse) S.; m. Mary Olin, Oct. 1, 1955; children: Geoffrey Lee, Lori Lynn, Deborah Barron. AA, Wright Jr. Coll., 1949; BA, Mich. State U., 1952, MA, 1954. Fgn. svc. info. officer USIA, Tokyo, Jakarta, Seoul, 1955-61; sr. pub. rels. assoc. Eli Lilly and Co., Indpls., 1962-66; v.p., dir. pub. rels. Eisenhower People to People Program, Kansas City, Mo., and Copenhagen, 1966-68; govt. and pub. affairs rep. North Ctrl. States Automobile Mfrs. Assn., Kansas City, 1968-69; speechwriter, pub. rels. cons. Commdr.-in-Chief U.S. Pacific Forces, Aiea, 1969-75; pres. No. Ariz. Comm., Inc., Flagstaff, 1975-79; asst. sec., dir. pub. affairs U.S. Internat. Trade Commn., Washington, 1977-87; v.p. pub. affairs and publs. Export-Import Bank U.S., Washington, 1987-89; pres. Halamar, Inc., Manassas, Va. and Easley, S.C., 1983—; freelance writer and poet. Author: The American West, 1956, Garuda, Introducing Indonesia, 1957, Politics and Nationalism in Indonesia, 1962, Faces of Asia: Korea, 1965, The Northern Arizona Scene, 1976, American Collie Champions, Vol. I, 1979, Vol. II, 1980, Vol. III, 1987, Collies - A Complete Pet Owners Manual, 1994; editor, pub. Hawaiian Dog Rev., 1972-76, Collie Cues, The Alaska Cir., The Arizona Cir., Internat. Lhasa Apso Rev., Sandwich Isles Dog Gazette, Travel Writer, Honolulu Sun Press, 1972-76. With U.S. Army, 1947-48, 52-53, Tokyo. Recipient People to People Disting. Svc. award, 1967, George Washington Honor medal Freedam Found., 1968, Silver Beaver award, Aloha coun. Boy Scouts Am., 1975. Fellow Japan Soc. N.Y.; mem. Pub. Rels. Soc. Am. (past pres. Hawaii chpt., Silver Anvil award 1973), Dog Writers Assn. Am. (pres. 1984-92, Disting. Svc. award 1993), Dog Writers Ednl. Trust (vice chmn.), Collie Club Am. (pres. 1984-86), Collie Club Am. Found. (pres. 1990-92), Am. Kennel Club (del. 1986—), Pi Sigma Alpha, Phi Kappa Sigma. Republican. Avocations: pure-bred dog breeding and showing, power boating, travel, photography. Home and Office: 401 Watson Rd Easley SC 29642-8357

SUNDT, HARRY WILSON, construction company executive; b. Woodbury, N.J., July 5, 1932; s. Thoralf Mauritz and Elinor (Stout) S.; m. Dorothy Van Gilder, June 26, 1954; children: Thomas D., Perri Lee Sundt Touche, Gerald W. BS in Bus. Adminstrn., U. Ariz., 1954, postgrad., 1957-59. Salesman ins. VanGilder Agys., Denver, 1956-57; apprentice carpenter M.M. Sundt Constrn. Co., Tucson, 1957-58, estimator, 1958-59; adminstrv. asst. M.M. Sundt Constrn. Co., Vandenberg AFB, 1959-62; sr. estimator M.M. Sundt Constrn. Co., Tucson, 1962-64, div. mgr., 1964-65, exec. v.p., gen. mgr., 1965-75, pres., chmn., 1975-79; pres., chmn. Sundt Corp., Tucson, 1980-83, chmn., chief exec. officer, 1983—; bd. dirs. Tucson Electric Power Co., Nations Energy Co. Pres. Tucson Airport Authority, 1982; bd. dirs. U. Ariz. Found. 1981. 1st lt. U.S. Army, 1954-56. Recipient Disting. Citizen award U. Ariz., 1982, Centennial Medallion award, 1989. Mem. Tucson Country Club. Republican. Episcopalian. Avocation: tennis. Home: 6002 E San Leandro Tucson AZ 85715-3014 Office: Sundt Corp PO Box 26685 4101 E Irvington Rd Tucson AZ 85714-2118

SUNDY, GEORGE JOSEPH, JR., engineering executive; b. Nanticoke, Pa., Apr. 22, 1936; s. George Joseph Sr. and Stella Mary (Bodurka) S.; m. Stella Pauline Miechur, May 21, 1966; children: Sharon Ann, George Joseph III. BS, Pa. State U., 1958. Rsch. engr. Bethlehem (Pa.) Steel Corp., 1959-85; reliability engr. Flo-Con Systems, Inc. (name now Vesuvius USA), Champaign, Ill., 1985-90; reliability mgr., 1990-96, slide gate product line specialist, 1996—. Patentee in field. Mem. Am. Soc. Materials, Am. Ceramics Soc., Iron and Steel Soc. AIME, Keramos, Sigma Tau. Democrat. Roman Catholic. Home: 604 E South Mahomet Rd Mahomet IL 61853-3602 Office: Vesuvius USA 1404 Newton Dr Champaign IL 61821-1069

SUNELL, ROBERT JOHN, retired army officer; b. Astoria, Oreg., June 5, 1929; s. Ernest and Grace L. S.; m. JoAnn L. Toikka, Dec. 29, 1951; children—Perry Sunell Peterson, Patti Sunell Sigl, Robert P. Student, U. Oreg., 1949-53; B.E., U. Nebr., 1963; M.S., Shippensburg State Coll., 1973. Commd. U.S. Army, 1953, advanced through grades to maj. gen., 1983, ret., 1987; exec. officer 1st Brigade, 4th Inf. div. U.S. Army, Vietnam, 1966-67, comdr. 2d Bn., 8th Inf., 4th Inf. div., 1969-70; chief Bn. and Brigade Tactical Ops. div. Armor Sch. U.S. Army, Ft. Knox, Ky., 1973-74, dep. dir. Armored Reconnaissance Scout Vehicle Task Force, 1974-76; dep. program mgr. XM1 Tank Systems U.S. Army, Warren, Mich., 1976-78; comdr. 11th Armored Cav. Regt. U.S. Army, Germany, 1978-79; comdr. Army Tng. Support Ctr. U.S. Army, Ft. Eustis, Va, 1980-83; program mgr. Tank Systems U.S. Army, Warren, Mich., 1983-86; dir. Armored Family of Vehicles Task Force, Fort Eustis, Va., 1986-87; apptd. adv. bd. dirs. Land Combat Com., Assn. of U.S. Army, 1995; cons. U.S. Army Sci. Bd.; founder Suonperra, Inc., 1987. Decorated Silver Star, Legion of Merit, Bronze Star, Meritorious Service award, Disting. Service medal. Mem. U.S. Army Assn., Armor Assn. Republican.

SUNG, KUO-LI PAUL, bioengineering educator. MA in Biology, Coll. William and Mary, 1975; MS in Physiology, Columbia U., 1977; PhD in Physiology, Rutgers-Columbia U., 1982; PhD in Bioengring. (hon.), Chongqing U., China, 1993. Teaching asst. dept. biology Taiwan U., 1970-72; rsch. asst. dept. biology Coll. Willam and Mary, 1972-74; rsch. asst. dept. physiology Coll. Physicians and Surgeons, Columbia U., 1974-77, rsch. worker dept. physiology, 1977-81, staff assoc. sci. dept. physiology and cellular biophysics, 1982; lectr. divsn. of circulatory physiology and biophysics dept. of physiology and cellular biophysics, Coll. Physicians and Surgeons Columbia U., 1986, 87; lectr. Inst. Biomedical Sci. Academia Sinica, 1987; assoc. rsch sci. dept. physiology and cellular biophysics Coll. Physicians and Surgeons, Columbia U., 1982-88; organizer and instr. Cell Biophysics Workshop Academia Sinica and Nat. Sci. Coun., Taiwan, China, 1987; assoc. rsch. bioengineer III, lectr. dept. applied mechanics and engring. scis.-bioengineering U. Calif.-San Diego, La Jolla, 1988-92, assoc. prof. of orthopaedic dept., Sch. Medicine, 1992-95, prof. orthopaedics and bioengring. depts., 1992—; lectr. bioengineering ctr. Chongqing U., China, 1993; full mem. cancer ctr. U. Calif., San Diego, 1991, Inst. for Biomedical Engring., 1991—; organizer Cellular Adhesion: Signaling and Molecular Regulation Am. Physiol. Soc., 1994, main speaker Cell Biophysics Workshop Academia Sinica and Nat. Sci. Coun., China, 1987, Cellular Adhesion Workshop, West China of Med. Scis., China, 1993. Author various publs. Recipient New Investigator Rsch. award NIH, 1984-87, Best Jour. Paper award ASME, 1989, Chancellor award U. Calif., San Diego, 1988-89, The Whitaker Found. award, 1990, Melville medal ASME, 1990, Lamport award Biomedical Engring. Soc., 1992; Dr. Yat-Sen Sun Fellow Taiwan, China, 1967; Walter Russell Scholar, 1980-82. Mem. AAAS, Am. Physiol. Soc., N.Am. Soc. of Biorheology, Internat. Soc. of Biorheology, Biomedical Engring. Soc., Microcirculatory Soc., Sigma Xi. Achievements include research in influence of tumor suppressor genes on tumor cell metastasis, biophysical properties and molecular organization of cell membranes, healing mechanism of human ligament cells, adhesion between osteoblast and biomaterials, biophysical properties of blood cells and endothelial cells in inflammatory reponse, energy balance and molecular mechanisms of cell-cell interactions in immune response, intracellular ions, intracellular transmition and cell activation. Office: Univ Calif San Diego Bioengineering Orthopaedics 0412 La Jolla CA 92093

SUNG, NAK-HO, science educator; b. Seoul, Republic of Korea, Sept. 30, 1940; s. K.Y. and B.S. (Lee) S.; m. Chong Sook Paik, May 13, 1972; 1 child, Andrew J. BS, Seoul Nat. U., 1964; MS, U. Chgo., 1967; ScD, MIT, 1972. Process engr. Hanil Nylon Industry, Republic of Korea, 1963-66; tchg. asst. U. Chgo., 1966-67; rsch. asst. MIT, Cambridge, Mass., 1967-72, rsch. assoc., 1972-74, asst. prof., 1974-78; asst. prof. Tufts U., Medford, Mass., 1978-80, assoc. prof., 1980-85, prof., 1985—, dir. Lab. for Materials Interfaces, 1989—; vis. prof. Chengdu (China) U. Sci. and Tech., 1985, U. Conn., Storrs, 1985; bd. dirs. JNG Internat. Inc., 2C Optics, Inc., Korean Lang. Sch., Lexington, Mass.; cons. Sunkyong Group, Seoul, 1976—, U.S. Army Material and Mech. Rsch. Ctr., Watertown, Mass., Johnson and Johnson, W.R. Grace Corp.; pres. N.E. chpt. Korean Scientists and Engrs. Assn. in Am., Boston, 1977-78. Editor: Science and Technology of Polymer Processing, 1979; also over 80 publs. and one patent. Mem. Am. Chem. Soc., Am. Phys. Soc., Soc. Plastic Engrs., Adhesion Soc., Am. Inst. Chem. Engrs., Korean Am. Soc. New Eng. (bd. dirs.). Office: Tufts Univ Lab for Materials Interfaces Dept Chem Engring Medford MA 02155

SUNIA, TAUSESE, governor. Formerly lt. gov. Ter. of Am. Samoa, Pago Pago, now gov. Office: Office of the Gov Am Samoa Govt Pago Pago AS 96799*

SUNLEY, EMIL MCKEE, economist; b. Morgantown, W.Va., July 30, 1942; s. Emil McKee and Nelle Berniece (Traer) S.; m. Judith Evelyn Steere, Dec. 23, 1966; children: Rachel Anne, Gillian Traer, Neil Steere. B.A., Amherst Coll., 1964; M.A., U. Mich., 1965, Ph.D., 1968. Economist office tax analysis Dept. Treasury, Washington, 1968-73; assoc. dir. office tax analysis Dept. Treasury, 1973-75, dep. asst. sec. for tax policy, 1977-81; sr. fellow Brookings Instn., Washington, 1975-77; dir. tax analysis Deloitte & Touche, Washington, 1981-92; asst. dir. fiscal affairs dept. Internat. Monetary Fund, 1992—. Mem. editl. bd. Nat. Tax Jour., 1992-95. Mem. Commn. on RR Retirement Reform, 1987-90. Mem. Am. Econ. Assn., Nat. Tax Assn. (pres. 1995-96), Tax Analysts (bd. dirs. 1982-93). Episcopalian. Office: Internat Monetary Fund Rm IS3-210 Fiscal Affairs Dept Washington DC 20431

SUNSHINE, EUGENE SAMUEL, university and public administrator; b. N.Y.C., Jan. 22, 1950; s. Simon and Elsie (Kopstein) S.; m. Hollis Adrienne Leach, Mar. 25, 1973; children: Bradley Randall, Emily Jeanne. B.A., Northwestern U., 1971; M.P.A., Syracuse U., 1972. Project asst. urban devel. corp. State of N.Y., Elmira and N.Y.C., 1972-75; sr. budget examiner div. of budget State of N.Y., Albany, 1975-77, dir. energy conservation, 1977-82, state treas., dep. commr. Dept. Taxation and Fin., 1982-85, deputy commr. tax policy analysis Dept. Taxation and Fin., 1986-87; treas. Johns Hopkins U., Balt., 1987-88, sr. v.p. adminstrn., treas., 1988-89; sr. v.p. adminstrn. Johns Hopkins U., 1989—. Contbr. articles to profl. jours. Mem. exec. com. Cerebral Palsy Ctr. for Disabled, Albany, 1983-87, co-chmn. telethon, 1985-87. Recipient Disting. Service award N.Y. State Energy Office, 1981, Alfred E. Smith award Am. Soc. for Pub. Adminstrn., 1982. Office: Johns Hopkins U Garland Hall Baltimore MD 21218

SUNUNU, JOHN E., congressman; m. Kitty Sununu; children: John Hayes, Grace. B in Mech. Engring., Mass. Inst. Tech., M in Mech. Engring.; MBA, Harvard Grad. Sch. Bus. Mem. 105th Congress from 10th N.H. dist.; designengr. Remec, Inc., 1987-90; mgr., ops. specialist Pittiglio, Rabin, Todd & McGrath, 1990-92; chief fin. officer, dir. ops. Teletrol Sys. Inc.; cons. JHS Assocs., Ltd.; mem. house budget com., natural resources working group, house govt. reform and oversight com., house small bus. com.; vice-chmn. Nat. Econ. Growth, Natural Resources and Regulatory Affairs sub-com.; mem. Rep. Policy com. Active N.H. C. of C., N.H. Bus. and Industry Assn., N.H. High Tech Coun. Roman Catholic.

SUOJANEN, WAINO W., management educator; b. Maynard, Mass., Jan. 12, 1920; s. Waino I. and Milma (Lindroos) S.; m. Doris G. Stinson, Dec. 24, 1948; children—Wayne William, James Norman. BS, U. Vt., 1942; MBA, Harvard U., 1946; PhD, U. Calif. at Berkeley, 1955. Chief acct. UARCO Inc., Oakland, Calif., 1947-49; div. acct. Chris-Craft Corp., Salem, Oreg., 1949-50; Asst. prof. Sch. Bus. Adminstrn., U. Calif. at Berkeley, 1950-59; assoc. prof. U.S. Naval Postgrad. Sch., Monterey, Calif., 1959-61; dir. research and devel. mgmt. program Air Proving Ground Center, Eglin AFB, Fla., 1961-64; prof., chmn. dept. mgmt. U. Miami, Fla., 1964-70; prof. mgmt. Ga. State U., Atlanta, 1970-90, prof. emeritus, 1990—; adv. editor Chandler Pub. Co., 1965-71; mem. mgmt. adv. panel NASA, 1968-71; cons. U.S. Army Mgmt. Engring. Tng. Activity, 1954-89, U.S. Office Pers. Mgmt., 1964-84; fin. mgmt. cons. to comptr. Office Asst. Sec. Def., 1957-61; cons. in logistics mgmt. tng. Office Assn. Sec. Def. for Installations and Logistics, 1964-66; cons. in mgmt. edn. and tng. Office Asst. Sec. Def. for Manpower, 1966-67; lectr. mgmt. Royal Victorian Chamber Mfrs., Melbourne, Australia, summer 1968; bd. dirs. Russian-Am. Tech. Alliance, 1992—. Author: The Dynamics of Management, 1966, (with others) The Operating Manager-An Integrative Approach, 1974, Perspectives in Job Enrichment and Productivity, 1975, Management and the Brain: An Integrative Approach to Organizational Behavior, 1983. Treas. Alameda County Mental Health Assn., 1953-56; bd. dirs. Vol. Atlanta, 1971-76. With Vt. Nat. Guard, 1937-40; capt. AUS, 1942-46; lt. col. USAF, ret., 1980. Recipient McKinsey Found. Book award, 1966. Mem. Acad. Mgmt, AAAS, Phi Beta Kappa, Alpha Kappa Psi, Beta Alpha Psi, Beta Gamma Sigma, Pi Gamma Mu, Sigma Iota Epsilon. Home: 1270 Mayflower Ave Melbourne FL 32940-6722

SUOMI, PAUL NEIL, alumni association director; b. Ishpeming, Mich., July 15, 1937; s. Niilo John and Florine Blanche (LaCombe) S.; m. Martha Jean Banaglio, July 18, 1964; children: Michael Paul, Mark Joseph, Matthew John. Student, William & Mary Coll., Norfolk, Va., 1957-58; BA, No. Mich. U., 1962, MA in Ednl. Adminstrn., 1972. Asst. to v.p. adminstrv. affairs No. Mich. U., Marquette, 1969-72, asst. to asst. to pres. of univ. rels., 1972-76, news bur. chief, 1976-82, dir. comm., acting dir. alumni rels., 1982-84, dir. alumni rels., 1984—; panelist The Coun. for the Advancement & Support of Edn., 1973, 75, 79, 83, 88, 91, 94; panelist, cons. Midwest Labor Press Assn., 1975. Editor: (book) Coaching Better Basketball, 1964; co-publ., contbg. writer: (quarterly newspaper) Horizons, 1984—. Trustee Am. Lung Assn., 1981-89, pres., 1986-88; trustee Upper Mich. Lion's Eye Bank, 1983-85; bd. dirs. K.I. Sawyer AFB Heritage Mus., 1994—. With USN, 1955-58. Recipient Exceptional Achievement award Coun. Advancement & Support Edn., 1976, 83, Vol. of Yr. award Am. Lung Assn., 1985. Mem. Air Force Assn. (bd. dirs. Northland chpt. 1992—), Econ. Club of Marquette County (bd. dirs. 1986—, pres. 1995-96). Roman Catholic. Avocations: jogging, reading, popular music. Home: 44 Elder Dr Marquette MI 49855-1630 Office: No Mich U Alumni Assn Presque Isle Ave Marquette MI 49855

SUPAN, RICHARD MATTHEW, health facility administrator; b. Palo Alto, Calif., June 22, 1953; s. James Arthur and Nancy Ann (Rhein) S.; m. Bernadette Joan Bayer, Sept. 8, 1979; children: Raymond, Valerie, Joanna. AA, Foothill Coll., 1973; BSC, Santa Clara U., 1975, MBA, 1979. Cost acctg. supr. Electron Devices div. Litton Industries, San Carlos, Calif., 1975-78; cost acctg. mgr. Microwave Tube div. Varian Assocs., Palo Alto, Calif., 1978-81, ops. controller, 1981-84; dir. acctg. Varian Assocs., Palo Alto, Calif., 1984-85; controller Electron Device & Systems Group, Varian Assocs., Palo Alto, Calif., 1985-89, Oncology Systems, Varian Assocs., Palo Alto, Calif., 1989-95; v.p. ops. & fin. Intraop Med., Inc., Santa Clara, Calif., 1995—. Mem. Beta Gamma Sigma (hon.). Avocation: coach, league official youth sports. Home: 5915 Amapola Dr San Jose CA 95129-3058

SUPERNEAU, DUANE WILLIAM, geneticist, physician; b. Ogden, Utah, Dec. 31, 1950; s. Richard Edwin and Mary Ellen Superneau; m. Connie A. Saltalamacchia, Apr. 21, 1978; children: Adam, Ashley, Allison. BA, Carroll Coll., 1973; MD, U. Wash., 1977. Asst. prof. dept. med. genetics U. So. Ala., Mobile, 1982-87, assoc. prof. dept. med. genetics, 1987-91; chief divsn. med. genetics Ochsner Clinic, New Orleans, 1991—; clin. asst. prof. dept. biometry and genetics La. State U., New Orleans, 1992—, clin. asst. prof. dept. pediatrics, 1994—. Bd. dirs. Assn. Retarded Citizens, 1991—, pres. 1994-96; bd. dirs. Jefferson Parish Human Svcs. Authority, Jefferson Parish,

La., 1992—. Roman Catholic. Office: Ochsner Clin Dept Pediat Pathology Ob-Gyn 1514 Jefferson Hwy New Orleans LA 70121-2429

SUPINO, ANTHONY MARTIN, lawyer; b. Weehawken, N.J., Oct. 1, 1962; s. Anthony Edward and Gloria (DeBari) S.; m. Lori Ann Michaud, May 27, 1989. BA, Rutgers U., 1984, postgrad., 1984-85, JD, 1988. Bar: N.J. 1988, U.S. Dist. Ct. N.J. 1988, N.Y. 1989, U.S. Dist. Ct. (so. dist.) N.Y. 1990, U.S. Ct. Appeals (3d cir.) 1991. Law sec. to the Hon. Marie L. Garibaldi Supreme Ct. of N.J., Jersey City, 1988-89; litigation assoc. Cravath, Swaine & Moore, N.Y.C., 1989-92; spl. litigation assoc. Chadbourne & Parke, N.Y.C., 1992-93; ptnr. Arkin, Schaffer & Supino, N.Y.C., 1994-96, Supino & Michaud, N.Y.C., West Orange, N.J., 1996—. Community organizer Human Serve Fund, New Brunswick, N.J., 1984. Democrat. Avocations: coin collecting, sports, weightlifting. Home: 91 Maple St Millburn NJ 07041-2113 Office: Supino & Michaud 747 3rd Ave Fl 14 New York NY 10017-2803

SUPPES, PATRICK, statistics, education, philosophy and psychology educator; b. Tulsa, Mar. 17, 1922; s. George Biddle and Ann (Costello) S.; m. Joan Farmer, Apr. 16, 1946 (div. 1970); children: Patricia, Deborah, John Biddle; m. Joan Sieber, Mar. 29, 1970 (div. 1973); m. Christine Johnson, May 26, 1979; children: Alexandra Christine, Michael Patrick. BS, U. Chgo., 1943; PhD (Wendell T. Bush fellow), Columbia U., 1950; LLD, U. Nijmegen, Netherlands, 1979; Dr. honoris causa, Académie de Paris, U. Paris V, 1982. Instr., Stanford U., 1950-52, asst. prof., 1952-55, assoc. prof., 1955-59, prof. philosophy, statistics, edn. and psychology, 1959-92, prof. emeritus; founder, chief exec. officer Computer Curriculum Corp., 1967-90. Author: Introduction to Logic, 1957, Axiomatic Set Theory, 1960, Sets and Numbers, books 1-6, 1966, Studies in the Methodology and Foundations of Science, 1969, A Probabilistic Theory of Causality, 1970, Logique du Probable, 1981, Probabilistic Metaphysics, 1984, Estudios de Filosofia y Metodologi de la Ciencia, 1988, Language for Humans and Robots, 1991, Models and Methods in the Philosophy of Science, 1993; (with Davidson and Siegel) Decision Making, 1957, (with Richard C. Atkinson) Markov Learning Models for Multiperson Interactions, 1960, (with Shirley Hill) First Course in Mathematical Logic, 1964, (with Edward J. Crothers) Experiments on Second-Language Learning, 1967, (with Max Jerman and Dow Brian) Computer-assisted Instruction, 1965-66, Stanford Arithmetic Program, 1968, (with D. Krantz, R.D. Luce and A. Tversky) Foundations of Measurement, Vol. 1, 1971, (with M. Morningstar) Computer-Assisted Instruction at Stanford, 1966-68, 1972, (with B. Searle and J. Friend) The Radio Mathematics Project: Nicaragua, 1974-75, 1976 (with D. Krantz, R.D. Luce and A. Tversky) Foundations of Measurement, Vol. 2, 1989, Vol. 3, 1990, (with Colleen Crangle) Language and Learning for Robots, 1994, (with Mario Zanotti) Foundations of Probability with Applications, 1996. Served to capt. USAAF, 1942-46. Recipient Nicholas Murray Butler Silver medal Columbia, 1965, Disting. Sci. Contbr. award Am. Psychol. Assn., 1972, Tchrs. Coll. medal for disting. service, 1978, Nat. medal Sci. NSF, 1990; Center for Advanced Study Behavioral Scis. fellow, 1955-56; NSF fellow, 1957-58. Fellow AAAS, Am. Psychol. Assn., Am. Acad. Arts and Scis., Assn. Computing Machinery; mem. NAS, Math. Assn. Am., Psychometric Soc., Am. Philos. Assn., Am. Philos. Soc., Assn. Symbolic Logic, Am. Math Soc., Académie Internationale de Philosophie des Scis. (titular), Nat. Acad. Edn. (pres. 1973-77), Am. Psychol. Assn., Internat. Inst. Philosophy, Finnish Acad. Sci. and Letters, Internat. Union History and Philosophy of Sci. (div. logic, methodology and philosophy of sci., pres. 1975-79), Am. Ednl. Research Assn. (pres. 1973-74), Croatian Acad. Scis. (corr.), Russian Acad. Edn. (fgn.), Norwegian Acad. Sci. and Letters (fgn.), European Acad. Scis. and Arts, Chilean Acad. Scis., Sigma Xi.

SUPPLE, JEROME H., academic administrator; b. Boston, Apr. 27, 1936; m. Catherine Evans; 3 children. BS in Chemistry, Boston Coll., 1957, MS in Organic Chemistry, 1959; PhD in Organic Chemistry, U. New Hampshire, 1963. Asst. prof. chemistry SUNY Coll., Fredonia, 1964-69, assoc. prof., 1969-76, prof., 1976-78, acting dept. chair, 1975-76, assoc. dean for arts and scis., 1972-73, assoc. v.p. for acad. affairs, 1973-78, acting v.p. for acad. affairs, 1977, dean for gen. and spl. studies, 1977-78; assoc. provost for undergrad. edn. SUNY Cen. Adminstrn., 1974-75; prof. chemistry, v.p. for acad. affairs SUNY Coll., Plattsburgh, acting pres., 1978-89, on leave 1988-89; acting provost, v.p. for acad. affairs SUNY Coll., Postsdam, 1988-89; prof. chemistry, pres. S.W. Tex. State U., San Marcos, 1989—; Faculty fellow NSF, vis. rsch. faculty U. East Anglia, Norwich, Eng., 1970-71. Author books; contbr. numerous articles to profl. jours. Mem. Tex. Gov.'s total quality mgmt. steering com. Eastman Kodak rsch. fellow. Mem. AAAS, Am. Chem. Soc., Am. Assn. Higher Edn., Am. Assn. State Colls. and Univs., Am. Coun. on Edn. (mem. commn. on govtl. rels.), So. Assn. Colls. and Schs. Commn. on Colls., Tex. Coun. on Econ. Edn. (bd. dirs.), Tex. Coun. Pub. Univ. Pres. and Chancellors (state affairs and exec. com.), Tex. Assn. Coll. Tchrs., Tex. Higher Edn. Master Plan Adv. Com., San Marcos C. of C. Econ. Devel. Coun., San Marcos Rotary, Golden Key, Sigma Xi (past pres. Fredonia club), Phi Eta Sigma (hon.), Omicron Delta Kappa (hon.). Office: SW Tex State U Office of Pres 1020 J C Kellam Bldg San Marcos TX 78666

SUPUT, RAY RADOSLAV, librarian; b. Columbus, Ohio, May 13, 1922; s. Elias and Darinka (Balac) S.; m. Mary Grace Hansen, May 23, 1953 (dec. Nov. 1980); children: David Ray, Dorothy Mary; m. Milana Preradov, July 12, 1986. B.A., Ohio State U., 1950; M.S.L.S., Case Western Res. U., 1951, Ph.D., 1972; M.A., U. Chgo., 1955. Librarian Northwestern U., Evanston, Ill., 1951-52; reference and circulation librarian Law Library, U. Chgo., 1952-54, cataloger, 1954-57; asso. librarian Garrett-Evang. Theol. Sem., Evanston, 1957-58; head librarian Garrett-Evang. Theol. Sem., 1958-64; asst. dir. libraries and adj. lectr. dept. Slavic and E. European langs. Sch. Library Sci. Case Western Res. U., Cleve., 1964-67; acting dir. libraries Case Western Res. U., 1967-68; adj. instr. Case Western Res. U. (Sch. Library Sci.), 1965-69; librarian Case Western Res. U. (Freiberger Library), 1968-69; dir. univ. library, head dept. and prof. library sci. Ball State U., Muncie, Ind., 1969-78; univ. librarian, head dept. and prof. library service Ball State U., 1978-81, prof. library service, also adj. prof. library sci., 1981-82, chmn. dept. library and info. sci., prof. library sci., 1982-87, prof. library sci., info. sci. emeritus, 1987—. Contbr. articles to profl. jours. Nat. Endowment for Humanities and Council on Library Resources Inc. grantee. Mem. ALA, AAUP, African Violet Soc. Am., Am. Theol. Libr. Assn., Serb Nat. Fedn., Ohio Hist. Soc. Eastern Orthodox.

SURACI, CHARLES XAVIER, JR., retired federal agency administrator, aerospace education consultant; b. Washington, Feb. 10, 1933; s. Charles Xavier and June Celcia (Hunter) S.; m. Florence Patricia De Mino, May 23, 1970. Cadet, Penn Mil. Coll. (now Widener U.), 1951-53; grad., Nat. Acad. Broadcasting Sch., Washington, 1959; student, Columbia Union Coll., 1962-63, 72, Catholic U., 1969; grad. extension course, CAP Staff Coll., 1974; BA, Calif. Christian Coll., 1977, HHD (hon.), 1977; grad., USAF Inspectors Gen. Sch., Eglin AFB, Fla., 1982; also grad. numerous other govt. schs. and courses. Served with USAF, 1953-57; enlisted CAP, 1957, commd. 1st lt., 1961; advanced through ranks to Col. CAP USAF Aux, 1974; co-founder Wheaton-Silver Spring Cadet Squadron; comdr. Nat. Capital Wing, 1973-76; dep. chief of staff cadet activities Middle East region, 1977-79, dir. cadet tng., 1979-82, insp. gen., 1982—; with Harry Diamond Lab., U.S. Army, Adelphi, Md., 1963—, material publs. asst., 1963-68, later asst. to motor transp. officer, now supply specialist, logistics sect. Mem. youth com. YMCA, Silver Spring, Md., 1962-69, mem. bd. mgmt., 1967—; bd. dirs. Am. Youth Com.; mem. Commn. on Children and Youth Bd. Montgomery County, Md.; mem. Montgomery County Juvenile Ct. Com., 1978-86; choir mem. Blessed Sacrament Cath. Ch., Washington; co-chmn. Right to Life Com. K.C.-Rosensteel Coun.; mem. bd. dirs. Pregnancy Aid Ctr., College Park, Md. Recipient Leader and Svc. award Silver Spring YMCA, 1968, 69, CAP Meritorious Svc. award Dept. Def., 1969, 1977, cert. of commendation from Pres. Richard Nixon, 1970, CAP Exceptional Service award Congressman Lester Wolff of N.Y., 1972, award Montgomery County C. of C., 1973, commendation Gov. of Tenn., 1975, letter of commendation Washington Mayor Walter Washington, 1977, Dept. Outstanding Patriotic Civilian Service award, 1977, Md. Vol. Cmty. honor award Montgomery County, 1981, Vol. Activist award, 1984, George Washington Honor medal Valley Forge Freedom Found., 1995, Patrick Henry medal for patriotic achievement Military Order of the World Wars, 1995; named Air Man of Month USAF, 1956; grand marshall Rockville, Md., Meml. Day parade, 1971; honored by Md. Ho. Dels., 1974, D.C. Govt., 1977; recipient numerous AF and CAP ribbons and medals, Dept. of Army Spl. Act or Svc. award, Dept.of the Army Superior Performance award, 1987, Pres.'s Vol. Action award nomination Pres. of the U.S., 1988, 1991, Cmty. Svc. award Wheaton-Kensington News, Bethesda Chevy Chase Current, Montgomery County Press Assn., 1990, Outstanding support Aviation Career Day Tuskegee Airmen and Commdg. Gen. of D.C. Air Nat. Guard, 1992, spl. award State of Md. for training over 1000 youth cadets in the CAP in 31 yrs., 1986, plaque name displayed at U.S. Army-Harry Diamond Lab, Adelphi, Md., Pro-Life award Knights of Columbus-Rosensteel Coun., 1992, Frank G. Brewer Meml. Aerospace award-CAP Middle East Region HQ, 1984, 1991, 1992, CAP-U.S. Air Force Auxiliary Meritorious Svc. award Middle East Region HQ, 1993, Man of the Year award State of Md. Air Force Assn., 1993, Cert. Appreciation Md. Air Force Assn. Aerospace Edn., 1993-95, Exceptional Svc. award U.S. Air Force Auxiliary, 1994-95. Mem. Air Force Assn. (bd. dirs., v.p. aerospace edn. Thomas W. Anthony chpt. Andrews AFB, Md. 1996—, medal of Merit 1990, Exceptional svc. award 1991, 94, Commd. Officer of Yr. 1995, Spl. cert. appreciation 1996, Disting. Svc. as Inspector Gen. 1991), Nat. Aerospace Assn., Navy League, Army Aviation Assn., Fed. Ret. Employees Assn., Tuskegee Airmen Inc., Mil. Order of World Wars (jr. vice comdr. Bethesda chpt. 1996—), Nat. Officers Assn., Md. Press Assn. Montgomery County, Md. Private Industry Coun. (bd. dirs. Opportunity Skyway program), Knights of Columbus (chmn. Pro-Life Father Rosensteel coun., Outstanding Leadership Pro-Life activities 1990-91, Outstanding Svc. award 1993-94, Honored Guest of Yr. 1996-97), Alumni Assn. Widener U. Democrat. Club: Andrews AFB Officers (Md.). Lodge: KC. 2 plaques in his name displayed at Columbia Union Coll., Takoma Park, Md., Widener U. (formerly Pa. Mil. Coll.), Chester. Home: Rock Creek Hills 9817 La Duke Dr Kensington MD 20895-3156 Office: USAF Aux CAP Mid East Region Hdqrs Office of Insp Gen 9817 La Duke Dr Kensington MD 20895-3156

SURACI, PATRICK JOSEPH, clinical psychologist; b. Rochester, N.Y., May 31, 1936; s. Frank and Josephine Rosalie (Marino) S. PhD in Psychology, New. Sch. for Social Rsch., N.Y.C., 1981. Cert. clin. psychologist, N.Y. Intern in clin. psychology Morrisania Neighborhood Family Care Ctr., Montefiore Hosp., N.Y.C., 1979-80; staff psychologist N.Y. Police Dept., 1981-83; pvt. practice N.Y.C., 1982—; adj. lectr. N.Y. Inst. Tech., N.Y.C., 1975-78, John Jay Coll. Criminal Justice, CUNY, 1973-81; adj. asst. prof. Baruch Coll. Psychology Dept., CUNY, 1983-92; vol. Manhattan Ctr. for Living, 1994-96. Author: Male Sexual Armor. Erotic Fantasies and Sexual Realities of the Cop on the Beat and the Man in the Street, 1992. Mem. The Nat. Arts Club. With U.S. Army, 1959-62. Mem. APA, N.Y. State Psychol. Assn. (task force on AIDS), Actors Equity, Screen Actors Guild. Office: 8 Gramercy Park S New York NY 10003-1718

SURBECK, LEIGHTON HOMER, retired lawyer; b. Jasper, Minn., Oct. 8, 1902; s. James S. and Kathryn (Kilpatrick) S.; m. Margaret H. Packard, 1926. B.S., S.D. State Sch. Mines, 1924; J.D. magna cum laude, Yale, 1927; L.H.D., S.D. Sch. Mines and Tech., 1957; LL.D., Central Coll., 1973; D.Humanitarian Services, Northwestern Coll., Iowa, 1980; LL.D., Hope Coll., 1986; DHL (hon.), Judson Coll., Elgin, Ill., 1995. Bar: N.Y. 1929. Law sec. to Chief Justice Taft, 1927-28; assoc. Hughes, Schurman & Dwight, N.Y.C., 1928-34; mem. firm Hughes, Schurman & Dwight, 1934-37; mem. firm Hughes, Hubbard & Reed, N.Y.C., 1937-70, counsel, 1970—. Author: Success on the Job, 1957, The Success Formula that Really Works, 1986. Trustee Pacific Sch. Religion, Berkeley, Calif., 1962-80, Golden Gate U., San Francisco, 1979-91, Central Coll., Pella, Iowa, 1966-78, Collegiate Boy's Sch., N.Y.C., 1975-78; chmn. Yale Law Sch. Fund, 1971-75. Served as col. AUS, 1942-45; chief econ. br. M.I. 1944-45. Recipient Yale medal Yale Alumni, 1975, Distinguished Service award Yale Law Sch., 1976; Horatio Alger award, 1977; named Centennial Alumnus State of S.D., 1989. Mem. ABA, N.Y. State Bar Assn., N.Y. County Bar Assn., Assn. of Bar of City of N.Y., Siwanoy Country Club, Univ. Club (N.Y.C.), Menlo Country Club (Woodside, Calif.), Masons, Order of Coif, Sigma Tau., Delta Theta Phi. Mem. Marble Collegiate Ch. (elder 1962-78). Home: 88 Faxon Rd Atherton CA 94027-4046 *Every honest, best effort prayerfully and with enthusiasm toward noble purposes useful beyond self always pays off handsomely, often at the most unexpected time, in the most unexpected ways and from the most unexpected sources.*

SURBER, DAVID FRANCIS, public affairs consultant, syndicated TV producer, journalist; b. Covington, Ky.; s. Elbert and Dorothy Kathryn (Mills) S.; BA in Physics, Thomas More Coll., 1960; LLD (h.c.), London Inst. Applied Research, 1973. Owner, The P.R. Co., pub. affairs counseling, Covington, 1960—. Spl. corr. Am. newspapers to Vatican II, Rome, Italy, 1965. Mem. Bd. Adjustment (Zoning Appeals), Covington, 1964-84, chmn., 1971-84; chmn. Covington Environ. Commn., 1971-72, Commn. Strip Mining, 1967-68; mem. pub. interest adv. com. Ohio River Valley Water Sanitation Commn., 1976-82; mem. water quality adv. com. Ohio-Ky.-Ind. Regional Council Govts., 1975-82; mem. environ. adv. council City of Cin., 1981-84; apptd. by Sec. of Energy to Nat. Coal Coun., 1992, 1994, 1996—. Mem. rehab. com. Community Chest Greater Cin., 1972-78, mem. agy. admissions com., 1972-78, mem. priorities com., 1972-78. Pres. bd. dirs. Cathedral Found., 1968-70; trustee Montessori Learning Center, 1973-75, Bklyn. Spanish Youth Choir; founding mem. Mayor's Task Force on the Environment, Cin., 1972-73; Dem. candidate for U.S. Ho. Reps., 1972; mem. Ky. Nature Preserves Commn., 1976-79. Recipient Community Service award Thomas More Coll., 1975. Mem. AFTRA, Tri-State Air Com. (chmn. 1973-74), Izaak Walton League (pres. Ky. 1973, dir. Ky.; nat. dir.), ACLU, Mousquetaires d'Armagnac, Nat. Inst. Urban Wildlife (bd. dirs. 1987-96). Producer: (syndicated weekly T.V. series) Make Peace with Nature, WKRC-TV, Cin., 1973—, Strip Mining: Two Views, 1972; Energy: Where Will It Come From; How Much Will It Cost, 1975; Atomic Power for Ohio, 1976; A Conversation With The Vice President, 1976; The Bad Water, 1977, The Trans-Alaska Pipeline: A Closeup Report, 1977, Acid Rain: A World View, 1986-89, Energy Independence in the U.K., 1992, Unhappy Prospects: Acid Rain & Global Climate Change, 1995. Office: PO Box 15555 Covington KY 41015-0555

SURBER, EUGENE LYNN, architect; b. Hagerstown, Md., May 15, 1938; s. Eugene Wicker and Kathryn Gertrude (Hunt) S.; m. Margaret Ann Sparks, May 7, 1983; 1 child, James Eugene. BArch, Ga. Inst. Tech., 1964. Registered architect, Ga. Intern architect Edwards & Portman Architects, Atlanta, 1964-65, J. Robert Carlton & Assocs., Richmond, Va., 1965-66; assoc. architect Jova/Daniels/Busby Architects, Atlanta, 1966-71; prin. Surber Barber Choate & Hertlein Architects, Inc., Atlanta, 1971—; mem. bldg com. Cath. Archdiocese Atlanta, 1990-95, chmn., 1994-95. Prin. works include N.E.-Intown YWCA (Ga. Trust award 1992), Newman Presbyn. Ch. (Ga. Trust award 1992), The Buggyworks (Fulton City Devel. award 1987), The Castle (Atlanta Urban Design award 1991), Wade Hampton Clubhouse and Cottages (So. Home awards 1990), Hillcrest Chapel (Ga. Trust award 1991), Byron Depot (Ga. Trust award 1991), Upson House (Ga. Trust award 1980), Franklin House (Ga. Trust award 1986), Acad. of Medicine (Ga. Assn. AIA award 1983, Ga. Trust award 1985). Past chmn. Ga. Nat. Register Rev. Bd., 1990; trustee Ga. Trust for Historic Preservation, 1989-95, chmn. restoration com. Lt. USN, 1961-64. Fellow AIA (sec. Atlanta chpt. 1989-90, v.p. 1990-91, Hist. Preservation award 1986, Ivan Allen Sr. award 1992, Silver medal Atlanta chpt. 1993, Bronze medal 1974), Ga. Assn. AIA (state preservation coord. 1986—, Bronze medal 1993). Avocation: gardening. Office: Surber Barber Choate & Hertlein Archs Inc 1389 Peachtree St NE Ste 350 Atlanta GA 30309-3038

SURBONE, ANTONELLA, medical oncologist, bioethics researcher; b. Turin, Italy, Aug. 11, 1957; d. Walter and Anita (Pugno) S. MD, U. Turin, 1982; postgrad., U. Milan, Italy, 1987, 92. Fellow Nat. Cancer Inst., Milan, 1983-84, asst., 1988-91; vis. assoc. Nat. Cancer Inst., Bethesda, Md., 1985-87; attending Meml. Sloan-Kettering Cancer Ctr., N.Y.C., 1990-91; vice chmn. dept. oncology Santa Chiara Hosp., Pisa, Italy, 1991-94; attending, mem. Meml. Sloan-Kettering Cancer Ctr., 1994—; prof. Oncology and Ethics Italy, U.S., 1992—; investigator Nat. Cancer Inst., Bethesda, 1987—. Editor, author: Annals of the New York Acad. Scis., 1993, 97; contbr. articles to profl. jours. Mem. UNICEF, Italy and U.S., 1985—. Fellow ACP; mem. AAAS, AMA, Italian Assn. for Med. Oncology (coord. 1993—), Am. Soc. Clin. Oncology, N.Y. Acad. Scis., Am. Assn. for Cancer Rsch., Multinat. Assn. for Supportive Care in Cancer, Internat. Soc. for Psychooncology, European Soc. for Med. Oncology, Amnesty Internat. Avocations: ballet dancing, philosophy.

SURDAM, ROBERT MCCLELLAN, retired banker; b. Albany, N.Y., Oct. 28, 1917; s. Burke and LeMoyne (McClellan) S.; m. Mary Caroline Buhl, July 8, 1946; children—Peter Buhl, Robert McClellan, Mary Caroline. B.A. cum laude, Williams Coll., 1939. With Nat. Bank Detroit, 1947-88, exec. v.p., 1964-66, pres., 1966-72, chmn. bd., 1972-82, also bd. dirs., 1966-88. Served to lt. comdr. USNR, 1941-46. Mem. Detroit Club, Country Club of Detroit, Yondotega Club, Jupiter Island Club (Hobe Sound, Fla.), Little Traverse Yacht Club (Harbor Springs, Mich.), Rolling Rock Club (Ligonier, Pa.), Hobe Sound Yacht Club, Little Harbor Club (Harbor Springs, Mich.). Home: 396 Provencal Rd Grosse Pointe MI 48236-2959

SURDOVAL, DONALD JAMES, accounting and management consulting company executive; b. N.Y.C., Aug. 26, 1932; s. Donald J. and Catherine A. (Slevin) S.; m. Patricia Fitzpatrick, May 28, 1955; children: Donald, Lisa, John, Catherine, Brian. B.B.A., Manhattan Coll., 1954. C.P.A., N.Y., N.J. Mgr. Touche Ross & Co., 1956-63; treas. Mohican Corp., 1963-65; asst. controller, then v.p., controller Litton Industries, 1965-68; v.p., controller Norton Simon Inc., N.Y.C., 1968-81; owner Donald J. Surdoval, C.P.A. and Mgmt. Cons. Co., Waldwick, N.J., 1982—; dir. Fuller O'Brien Paint Co. Bd. dirs. Calvary Hosp., N.Y.C., Our Lady of Mercy Hosp. Served to 1st lt. USMCR, 1954-56. Mem. Fin. Execs. Inst., Hackensack Golf Club, Saddle River Valley Lions (treas.). Home: 12 Warewoods Rd Saddle River NJ 07458-2713 Office: 20 Franklin Tpke Waldwick NJ 07463-1749

SURGENT, SUSAN PEARL, human resources specialist; b. Binghamton, N.Y., Jan. 6, 1963; d. Victor J. and Joan A. (Linville) Courtney; m. David M. Surgent, Sept. 7, 1985. AAS in Bus., Broome C.C., Binghamton, 1982; BS in Applied Social Sci magna cum laude, Binghamton U., 1993. Notary pub., N.Y. Mktg. asst. Johnson Camping, Inc., Binghamton, 1982-84; employment asst. CAE-Link Corp., Binghamton, 1984-85, adminstr. facility benefits, 1985-90, adminstr. corp. benefits, 1990-94; regional sales mgr. Prepaid Health Plan, Binghamton, N.Y., 1994-97; human resources specialist Lourdes Hosp, Binghamton, 1997—. Vol. educator Sch. and Bus. Alliance, Broome and Tioga counties, 1992—. Mem. Internat. Soc. Employee Benefit Profls., Golden Key, Phi Theta Kappa. Democrat. Episcopalian. Avocations: travel, collectibles, antiques. Home: 93 Albany Ave Johnson City NY 13790-1503 Office: Lourdes Hosp 169 Riverside Dr Binghamton NY 13905-4126

SURH, YOUNG-JOON, medical educator; b. Seoul, Korea, Sept. 26, 1957; came to the U.S., 1985; s. Jung-Chun and Kyung-Ok (Yoon) S.; m. Young-Kyu Lee, Jan. 10, 1983; 1 child, Jee-Hyuk. BS, Seoul (Korea) Nat. U., 1981, MS, 1983; PhD, U. Wis., 1990. Tchg. staff Seoul (Korea) Nat. U., 1983-85; rsch. asst. U. Wis., Madison, 1985-90, tchg. asst., 1988; rsch. assoc. Harvard Med. Sch., Boston, 1990; postdoctoral assoc. MIT, Cambridge, Mass., 1991-92; asst. prof. Yale Sch. Medicine, New Haven, 1992-96; adv. bd. Soc. Biomed. Rsch., Rockville, Md., 1994—; editl. bd. mem. Mutation Rsch. (Elsevier Sci.), 1997—. Author: Adv. Exp. Medicine Biol., 1991, Advances in Pharmacology, 1994, Handbook Exp. Pharmacol., 1994. 2d lt., 1983-84, Korea. Recipient Best Paper award U. Ill., Urbana, 1989, Spl. Interest Rsch. award Am. Cancer Soc., 1992. Mem. Internat. Soc. for the Study Xenobiotics, Am. Assn. for Cancer Rsch. (assoc.), N.Y. Acad. Scis. (acting), Sigma Xi. Achievements include first demonstration of formation of a covalently bound adduct between vitamin C and an ultimate electrophilic and carcinogenic metabolite; first demonstration of DNA adduct formation in vivo from electrophilic sulfate esters. Avocation: hiking. Home: 604 Eagle Hts Apt E Madison WI 53705-1518 Office: Seoul Nat U Coll Pharmacy, Shinlimdong Kwanak-gu, Seoul 151-742, Republic of Korea

SURJAATMADJA, JIM BASUKI, research engineer; b. Malang, Indonesia, Apr. 17, 1945; came to U.S., 1971; s. Rudolph and Gwat Nio (Oei) S.; m. Agnes Irmawati Said, Aug. 26, 1971; children: Sylvia Michelle, Amy Lynn. MS, Inst. Technol. Bandung, Bandung, Indonesia, 1970, Okla. State U., 1972; PhD, Okla. State U., 1976. Registered profl. engr., Okla. System engr. IBM, Jakarta, Indonesia, 1970-71; rsch. asst. Okla. State U., Stillwater, 1972-76; project engr. Fluid Power Rsch., Stillwater, 1972-76; from engr. to prin. engr. Halliburton Energy Svcs., Duncan, Okla., 1976—. Author: Introduction to Fluid Logic, 1976; contbr. more than 36 articles to profl. jours. and confs. Recipient Young Engrs. award S.W. region Okla. Soc. Profl. Engrs., 1979, Okla. Soc. Profl. Engrs., 1980. Fellow ASME; mem. Soc. Petroleum Engrs. (chmn.), U.S. Water Jet Tech. Assn. Achievements include 29 patents in area of fluid systems, automated systems, artificial intelligence, laboratory instruments, oil well-related tools, and industrial cleaning tools. Home: 1105 Timbercreek Dr Duncan OK 73533-1143 Office: Halliburton Energy Svcs 2600 S 2nd Duncan OK 73536

SURKIN, ELLIOT MARK, lawyer; b. Phila., Apr. 22, 1942; s. Hersh M. and Minnie (Shore) S.; m. Carol E. Foley, May 26, 1973; 1 child, Jennifer Dykema. A.B., Princeton U., 1964; LL.B., Harvard U., 1967. Bar: Mass. 1967. Assoc. Hill & Barlow, Profl. Corp., Boston, 1967-73; mem. Hill & Barlow, Profl. Corp., 1973—, chmn. mgmt. com., 1988-92, chmn. real estate dept., 1996—; lectr. law Harvard U., 1975-96; vis. lectr. MIT, Ctr. for Real Estate, 1996—. Chmn. bd. Boston Ctr. Arts, 1972-81, dir., mem. exec. com., 1981-83, hon. dir., 1983—; trustee, mem. fin. com. and exec. com., vice chmn. bd., clk. Wang Ctr. for Performing Arts, Boston, 1980—; mem. New Eng. com. Legal Def. Fund NAACP, 1976-93; mem. Chappaquiddick local com. Trustees of Reservations, 1982—, chmn. local com. 1986—, trustee 1985—, mem. adv. coun. 1988-94, mem. standing com. 1994—, mem. exec. com. 1996—, chmn. standing com., 1997—; dir. Sheriff's Meadow Found., 1994-97. Mem. ABA, Am. Law Inst., Am. Coll. Real Estate Lawyers, Mass. Bar Assn., Boston Bar Assn., St. Botolph Club, Harvard Club of Boston, Edgartown Yacht Club, Country Club of Brookline, Mass. Home: 1784 Beacon St Newton MA 02168-1434 Office: Hill & Barlow PC One International Place Boston MA 02110-2607

SURKS, MARTIN I., medical educator, endocrinologist; b. N.Y.C., May 21, 1934. A.B., Columbia U., 1956; M.D., NYU, 1960. Diplomate Nat. Bd. Med. Examiners, Am. Bd. Internal Medicine, Am. Bd. Endocrinology and Metabolism; lic. physician, N.Y. State. Intern Montefiore Hosp., N.Y.C., 1960-61, jr. asst. resident in medicine, 1961-62; sr. asst. resident VA Hosp., Bronx, 1962-63; postdoctoral research fellow Nat. Inst. Arthritis and Metabolic Diseases, 1963-64; assoc. in medicine Albert Einstein Coll. Medicine, Bronx, 1967-69, asst. prof. medicine, 1969-72, assoc. prof., 1972-78, prof., 1978—, assoc. prof. lab. medicine, 1978-85, prof., 1985—, prof. pathology, 1994—; co-dir. endocrine rsch. lab. Montefiore Hosp., Bronx, 1969-76, head div. endocrinology and metabolism, 1976-96, attending, 1981—; attending N. Cen. Bronx Hosp., 1976—; program dir. divsn. endocrinology, diabetes and metabolism Albert Einstein Coll. Medicine; Van Meter lectr. Am. Thyroid Assn., Seattle, 1973; mem. merit rev. bd. VA, 1976-79; mem. endocrine study sect. NIH, 1981-85. Editorial bd. Endocrinology, 1974-78, Endocrine Research Communications, 1974—, Am. Jour. Physiology: Endocrinology and Metabolism, 1982-85, Jour. Clinical Endocrinal Metabolism, 1991-95; assoc. editor Endocrinology, 1986-87. Contbr. articles to profl. jours. Served to capt. M.C., U.S. Army, 1964-66. Grantee U.S. Army, Am. Cancer Soc., USPHS, Nat. Cancer Inst.; Schering fellow, 1968. Fellow ACP; mem. Am. Thyroid Assn. (Van Meter prize, 1973; program com. 1975-77, 3d v.p. 1976-77, chair membership com. 1977-78, 80-81, dir. 1982-83, 87-90, nominating com. 1982-85, chair awards and prizes com. 1983-84, dir. 1988-92, sec. 1993—), Endocrine Soc. (manpower liaison com. 1983-86, fin. com. 1995—, internat. endocrine congress com. 1995—), N.Y. Zool. Soc., Am. Fedn. Clin. Rsch., Am. Bd. of Internal Medicine (sect. of endocrinology and metabolism 1987-95, chmn. 1991-95, bd. dirs. 1991-95), Harvey Soc., Am. Physiology Soc., AAAS, Am. Soc. Clin. Investigation, European Thyroid Assn. (corr.), Assn. Am. Physicians, Am. Soc. Cell Biology, Assn. Program Dirs. Endocrinology, Diabetes, and Metabolism (coun. 1995-97, pres. 1997), Interurban Clin. Club (councillor 1987-89), Phi Beta Kappa, Alpha Omega Alpha. Office: Montefiore Med Ctr 111 E 210th St Bronx NY 10467-2401

SURLES, CAROL D., university president; b. Pensacola, Fla., Oct. 7, 1946; d. Elza Allen and Versy Lee Smith; divorced; children: Lisa Surles, Philip Surles. BA, Fisk U., 1968; MA, Chapman Coll., 1971; PhD, U. Mich., 1978. Personnel rep. U. Mich., Ann Arbor, 1973-78; vice chancellor-adminstrn. U. Mich., Flint, 1987-89; exec. asst. to pres., assoc. v.p. for human resources U. Cen. Fla., Orlando, 1978-87; v.p. acad. affairs Jackson State U., Miss., 1989-92; v.p. adminstrn. and bus. Calif. State U., Hayward,

1992-94; pres. Tex. Woman's U., Denton, Dallas, Houston, 1994—. Trustee Pub. Broadcasting Ch. 24, Orlando, 1985-87; bd. dirs. First State Bank, Denton, Tex., Tex.-N.Mex. Power Co., TNP-Enterprise. Recipient Outstanding Scholar's award Delta Tau Kappa, 1983. Mem. AAUW, Am. Assn. Colls. and Univs., Golden Key Honor Soc., Mortar Bd. Soc., Dallas Citizens' Coun., Dallas Women's Found., Coun. of Pres. (Austin, Tex.), Phi Kappa Phi, Alpha Kappa Alpha. Methodist. Avocation: playing piano and oboe.

SURLES, RICHARD HURLBUT, JR., law librarian; b. Norfolk, Va., Mar. 28, 1943; s. Richard H. and Elda Florine (Belvin) S.; m. Judith Louise Coffin, May 29, 1964; children—Stephanie Anne, Richard H. B.A., Tex. A&M U., 1963; J.D., U.Houston, 1967; M.L.L., U.Wash., 1969. Bar: Colo. 1971. Asst. to law librarian U. Houston, 1966-68; asst. to law librarian King county Law Library, Seattle, 1968-69; dir. of law library, prof. law U. Denver, 1969-71, U. Tenn., Knoxville, 1971-76, U. Oreg., Eugene, 1976-81; dir. of law library, prof. law U. Ill., Champaign, 1981—, prof. libr. adminstrn., 1991. Author: Legal Periodical Management Data, 1977. Mem. Am. Assn. Law Libraries. Republican. Office: Ill Coll of Law 504 E Pennsylvania Ave Champaign IL 61820-6909

SURLS, JAMES, sculptor; b. Terrell, Tex., 1943. BS, Sam Houston State Coll., 1965; MFA, Cranbrook Acad. Art, 1969. instr. sculpture So. Meth. U., Dallas, 1970-75; assoc. prof. U. Houston, 1975-83. Commd. works include Pine Flower Buford TV Inc., Tyler, Tex., 1979, The Brazos Flower Brazos Ctr. and Arena/Pavilion Complex, Bryan, Tex., 1986, There Used to be a Lake (with Robert Creeley), Poets Walk, Citicorp Plz., L.A., 1988, Points of View Market Sq. Park Project, Houston, 1991, To the Point GTE Telephone Operators World Hdqrs. Hidden Ridge, Irving, Tex., 1991; exhibited in group shows at San Francisco Mus. Modern Art, 1975, 82, Solomon R. Guggenheim Mus., N.Y., 1977, Whitney Mus. Am. Art, 1979, 83, 84, 85, Fine Art for Fed. Bldgs., 1972-79, Smithsonian Instn., Washington, 1980, Mus. Fine Arts Houston, 1983, Art Inst. Chgo., 1986, Albright-Knox Art Gallery, Buffalo, N.Y., 1987; one-man shows include Arthur Roger Gallery, New Orleans, 1989, Barry Whistler Gallery, Dallas, 1989, 92, Hiram Butler Gallery, Houston, 1989, 92, Jan Weiner Gallery, Kansas City, Mo., 1990, 92, Contemporary Mus. Honolulu, 1991, Marlborough Gallery, N.Y.C., 1988, Gerald Peters Gallery, Dallas, 1988, Dallas Art Mus., 1991, Braustein/Quay Gallery, San Francisco, 1992, Allen Ctr. Gallery, Houston, 1992. Fellow Nat. Endowment Arts, 1979; named Tex. Artist of Yr. Houston Area Art League, 1991. also: care Marlborough Gallery 40 W 57th St New York NY 10019*

SURMA, JANE ANN, secondary education educator; b. Chgo., Dec. 11, 1947; d. John James and Genevieve (Buettner) S. BS, Barry U., Miami, Fla., 1969; MST, U. Ill., 1974. Tchr. phys. edn. Little Flower H.S., Chgo., 1969-72; tchr. English, phys. edn. and health, coach Oak Lawn (Ill.) Cmty. H.S., 1974—. Named Coach of Yr. Southtown Economist, 1992, Boy's Volleyball Ill. State Championship Coach, 1994, Fred Parks Coach of Yr., 1995. Mem. AAHPERD, Ill. H.S. Coaches Assn., Ill. H.S. Assn., Nat. Coun. Tchrs. English. Roman Catholic. Office: Oak Lawn Cmty HS Oak Lawn IL 60453

SUROVELL, EDWARD DAVID, real estate company executive; b. Washington, Mar. 20, 1940; s. Samuel and Florence Deborah (Starfield) S.; m. Barbara Ann Bartelmes, Apr. 26, 1958 (div. Jan. 1974); children: David Alexander, Claire Katherine. BA, Columbia U., 1962; postgrad., U. Mich., 1968-71. Lic. real estate broker, Mich. Copy editor Harcourt, Brace & World, Inc., N.Y.C., 1963-65; editor Princeton (N.J.) U. Press, 1965-67, Scott, Foresman Co., Glenview, Ill., 1967-68, U. Mich., Ann Arbor, 1970-73; real estate agt. Fletcher & Klein, Inc., Ann Arbor, 1973-75; sales mgr. Charles Reinhart Co., Ann Arbor, 1975-82; pres. Edward Surovell Co., Realtors, Ann Arbor, 1982—. Chmn. Ann Arbor City Planning Commn., 1988-91, sec., 1995—; active Downtown Devel. Authority, Ann Arbor, 1991-95, vice chair, 1994-95; trustee, sec. Ann Arbor Dist. Libr., 1996—. Mem. Nat. Assn. Realtors, Mich. Bd. Profl. Cmty. Planners, Hist. Soc. Mich. (trustee 1992—, v.p. 1996—), Ann Arbor Area Bd. Realtors (v.p. 1984, pres. 1985, Realtor of Yr. 1990), Univ. Mus. Soc. (bd. dirs. 1992—). Avocations: book collecting, arts philanthropy. Home: 2024 Vinewood Blvd Ann Arbor MI 48104-3614 Office: Edward Surovell Co/Realtors 1886 W Stadium Blvd Ann Arbor MI 48103-7007

SURREY, MILT, artist; b. N.Y.C., Mar. 18, 1922; s. Leopold and Pauline Schleifer; m. Eleanor Gallant, Sept. 15, 1946; children—Elaine, Robert, David. Student, Coll. City N.Y., 1939-42. Represented in permanent collections, Allentown (Pa.) Art Mus., Butler Inst. Am. Art, Youngstown, Ohio, Cin. Art Mus., Coll. Mus., Hampton (Va.) Inst., Columbia (S.C.) Mus. Art, Davenport (Iowa) Mus., Detroit Inst. Arts, Evansville (Ind.) Mus. Art, Hickory (N.C.) Mus. Art, Jacksonville (Fla.) Art Mus., Lowe Art Center, Syracuse (N.Y.) U., Massillon (Ohio) Mus., Miami (Fla.) Mus. Modern Art, Springfield (Mo.) Art Mus., Telfair Acad. Arts and Scis., Savannah, Ga., Holyoke (Mass.) Mus. Natural History, Theodore Lyman Wright Art Center, Beloit (Wis.) Coll., Treat Gallery, Bates Coll., Lewiston, Maine. Served with AUS, 1942-45. Mem. Am. Fedn. Arts. Home: 425 E 58th St New York NY 10022-2300

SURRIDGE, STEPHEN ZEHRING, lawyer, writer; b. N.Y.C., Dec. 12, 1940; s. Robert George and Florence Elizabeth (Zehring) S.; m. Helen Frances McKenna, Mar. 15, 1969; children: Christopher S., Jonathan R., Matthew W., Martha H. BA magna cum laude, Yale U., 1962; MBA, JD, U. Mich., 1969. Bar: Wis. 1969, Mich. 1969. Assoc. Quarles & Brady, Milw., 1969-76, ptnr., 1977-89; freelance writer, 1990—. Author: (monograph) Seven Thunders of Revelation, 1985, Revelation Revisited, 1995. 1st lt. U.S. Army, 1963-65. Mem. Phi Beta Kappa. Mem. Christian Ch. Home: 4480 N Ardmore Ave Shorewood WI 53211-1418

SURSA, CHARLES DAVID, banker; b. Muncie, Ind., Nov. 5, 1925; s. Charles Vaught and Ethel Fay (Schukraft) S; m. Mary Jane Palmer, Feb. 2, 1947; children: Ann Elizabeth, Janet Lynne, Charles Vaught, Laura Jane. BSChemE, Purdue U., 1946; MBA, Harvard, 1948. Executive NBD Bank N.A. (formerly Summit Bank, Indsl. Trust & Savings), Muncie, Ind., 1946-51, pres., 1951-80; chmn. bd., pres. NBD Bank N.A. (formerly Summit Bank, Indsl. Trust & Savings), Muncie, 1980-88, chmn. bd., CEO, 1988-90, chmn. bd., 1990-94, chmn. emeritus, 1994—; bd. dirs. Old Rep. Life Ins. Co., Chgo., Home Owners Life Ins. Co., Chgo., Old Rep. Internat. Corp., Chgo., Ball Meml. Hosp., Inc., Old Rep. Ins. Co., Greensburg, Pa., Old Rep. Life Ins. Co. N.Y.C., Am. Bus. & Merc. Ins. Group, Chgo., Am. Bus. & Merc. Reassurance Co., Chgo., bd. dirs., pres. Com. Svcs. Coun. of Del. County, 1973-74. Treas. Muncie Symphony Assn., 1949-62, pres., 1962-72, 2d v.p., 1978-80, dir., 1991—; bd. dirs., pres. The Cmty. Found. of Muncie and Del. County, Inc., 1985-97. Recipient Outstanding Young Man award Ind. Jr. C. of C., 1956, Hon. Jaycees award, 1974. Mem. Ind. Banker's Assn., Ind. Pres.'s Orgn. (treas. 1980-86), Ind. Soc. of Chgo., Internat. Wine and Food Soc., Delaware County C. of C., Ind. State C. of C., Muncie C. of C. (pres. 1959-60), Rotary (pres. 1964-65), Delaware Country Club (pres., bd. dirs. 1964), Elks, Phi Gamma Delta. Republican. Presbyterian. Home: 3410 W University Ave Muncie IN 47304-3970 Office: NBD Bank NA 220 Walnut Plz Muncie IN 47305-2804

SURWIT, RICHARD SAMUEL, psychology educator; b. Bklyn., Oct. 7, 1946; s. David and Ethel (Turetsky) S.; m. Sandra E. Cummings, May 23, 1982; children: Daniel Alan, Sarah Jeanne. AB, Earlham Coll., 1968; PhD, McGill U., Montreal, Que., Can., 1972; postgrad., Harvard U., Boston. Postdoctoral fellow Harvard Med. Sch., 1972-74, instr., 1974-76, asst. prof., 1976-77; assoc. prof. psychiatry Duke U. Med. Ctr., Durham, N.C., 1977-83, prof., 1980, 83—, vice chmn., 1993—; prof. psychology Duke U., 1991-96; CEO Healthware Corp., Chapel Hill, N.C., 1983—; pres., CEO Healthware Corp. Author: Fear and Learning To Cope, 1978, Behavioral Approaches to Cardiovascular Diseases, 1982; co-discoverer uncoupling protein-2. Recipient rsch. devel. award NIMH, 1980, rsch. scientist award NIMH, 1993. Fellow APA, Soc. Behavioral Medicine (pres. 1994), Acad. Behavioral Medicine. Achievements include; discovery in 1997, of CO-UCP2, a novel gene related to obesity and diabetes. Home: 3804 Sweeten Creek Rd Chapel Hill NC 27514-9706 Office: Duke U Med Ctr PO Box 3842 Durham NC 27710

SURYANARAYANAN, RAJ GOPALAN, researcher, consultant, educator; b. Cuddalore, Tamil Nadu, India, Apr. 19, 1955; came to U.S., 1985; s. Natesan and Pushpa (Subramanian) Rajagopalan; m. Shanti Venkateswaran, Nov. 24, 1985; children: Priya Mallika Sury, Meera Sindu Sury. B in Pharmacy, Banaras Hindu U., Varanasi, India, 1976, M in Pharmacy, 1978; MS, U. BC, Vancouver, Can., 1981, PhD, 1985. Mgmt. trainee Indian Drugs and Pharms. Lts., Rishikesh, India, 1978; supr. Roche Products, Bombay, India, 1979; teaching asst. U. BC, Vancouver, BC, Can., 1979, 82-83; asst. prof. pharmaceutics U. Minn., Mpls., 1985-92, assoc. prof., 1992—; dir. grad. studies, 1994—; cons. numerous pharm. cos. in U.S., 1987—. Contbr. articles to profl. jours.; patentee quantitative analysis of intact tablets. Recipient numerous grants for rsch., U.S., 1985—. Mem. Am. Assn. Pharm. Scientists, Am. Assn. Colls. Pharmacy. Hindu. Avocations: Tamil literature, sports. Home: 1861 Moore St Saint Paul MN 55113-5530 Office: U Minn Coll of Pharmacy 308 Harvard St SE Minneapolis MN 55455-0353

SUSANKA, SARAH HILLS, architect; b. Bromley, Kent, England, Mar. 21, 1957; d. Brian and Margaret (Hampson) Hills; m. Lawrence A. Susanka, July 4, 1980 (div. May 1984); m. James Robert Larson, Sept. 4, 1988. BArch, U. Oreg., 1978; MArch, U. Minn., 1983. Registered architect. Prin. Mulfinger, Susanka, Mahady & Ptnrs., Mpls., 1983—; Contbr. articles to profl. jours. Mem. AIA Minn. Avocation: writing. Home: 70 Upper Afton Ter Saint Paul MN 55106-6849 Office: Mulfinger Susanka Mahady & Ptnrs 43 Main St SE Minneapolis MN 55414-1029

SUSCHITZKY, PETER, cinematagrapher. Cinematographer: (films) It Happened Here, 1962, The War Game, 1966, Privilege, 1967, A Midsummer Night's Dream, 1968, Charlie Bubbles, 1968, Leo the Last, 1970, Melody/Swalk, 1971, The Pied Piper, 1972, Henry VIII and His Six Wives, 1972, That'll Be the Day, 1974, All Creatures Great and Small, 1975, Lisztomania, 1975, The Rocky Horror Picture Show, 1976, Valentino, 1977, The Empire Strikes Back, 1980, Krull, 1983, Falling in Love, 1984, Dead Ringers, 1988, Where the Heart Is, 1990, Naked Lunch, 1992, The Public Eye, 1992, The Vanishing, 1993, M. Butterfly, 1993, Immortal Beloved, 1994. Office: Sandra Marsh Mgt 9150 Wilshire Blvd Ste 220 Beverly Hills CA 90212-3429*

SUSKIND, DENNIS A., investment banker; b. Staten Island, N.Y., Dec. 13, 1942; s. Morris and Ida (Levine) S.; m. Cynthia Ann Leverenz, Sept. 14, 1968; children—Brian, John Paul, Pamela Claire, Audrey Elizabeth. Student, Pace Coll., N.Y.C. Vice pres. J. Aron & Co., N.Y.C., 1962-81; ptnr. Goldman Sachs & Co., N.Y.C., 1981—; bd. dirs. Merc. Exchange, 1972-80, Gold Inst., Washington, 1980-90; bd. dirs. Commodity Exchange, Inc., N.Y.C., 1980-87, 1st vice chmn., 1989-91; lectr. Fin. Times Conf., 1983, 84, 86—. Bd. dirs. East End chpt. Nature Conservancy, Arthur Ashe Inst. for Urban Health, pres.; trustee Collegiate Sch., N.Y.C. Mem. AIME, Silver Inst., Futures Industry Assn., Southampton Golf Club, Atlantic Golf Club (Bridgehampton, N.Y.). Home: 136 E 79th St New York NY 10021-0328 Office: Goldman Sachs & Co 85 Broad St New York NY 10004-2434

SUSKIND, RAYMOND ROBERT, physician, educator; b. N.Y.C., Nov. 29, 1913; s. Alexander and Anna (Abramson) S.; m. Ida Blanche Richardson, Dec. 27, 1944; children: Raymond Robert, Stephen Alexander. AB, Columbia U., 1934; student medicine, Edinburgh, Scotland, 1938-39; MD, SUNY, Bklyn., 1943. Intern Cin. Gen. Hosp., 1944, resident in dermatology, 1944-46, 48-49; research fellow in indsl. health U. Cin., 1948-50; research asst. bacteriology N.Y. U., 1934-36; research asst. pharmacology, 1936-37; practice medicine specializing in dermatology Cin., 1949-62; mem. faculty U. Cin., 1948-62, asso. prof. dermatology, 1952-62, dir. dermatol. research program Kettering Lab., 1948-62, Jacob G. Schmidlapp prof., chmn. dept. environ. health, dir. Kettering Lab., 1969-85, Jacob G. Schmidlapp prof. emeritus Inst. Environ. Health, 1985—, prof. medicine and dermatology, 1969-85, prof. emeritus medicine and dermatology, 1985—; attending physician U. Hosps., Cin., 1969—; dir. environ. and occupational dermatology program Ctr. for Occupational Health, U. Cin. Hosp., Cin., 1985—; prof., head divsn. environ. medicine, prof. dermatology U. Oreg. Med. Sch., 1962-69; chmn. stds. adv. com. on cutaneous and eye hazards OSHA, 1978; Gehrmann lectr. Am. Acad. Occupl. Medicine, 1977; founding mem. certifying bd. Am. Bd. Toxicology, 1978-83; mem. nat. air quality adv. com. EPA, 1970-73; mem. com. on health related effects of herbicides VA, 1979-83; cons. on Agt. Orange studies; mem. panel on human health effects of stratospheric change NAS, 1977-85; trustee Dermatology Found., 1975-80; master, trustee Fernald Settlement Fund Program, Long Term Health Effects of Ionizing Radiation Exposure from Nuclear Fuel Processing Plant, 1989—; cons. Accreditation Coun. for Grad. Med. Edn.; advisor Sch. of Pub. Health, Mahidol U., Bangkok; vis. prof. dermatology Columbia U., 1996. Contbg. editor Am. Jour. Indsl. Medicine, 1979-89, now reviewer; mem. editorial bd. Annals Internal Medicine, 1983-86, Chemosphere, 1987-96; reviewer Archives Internal Medicine, Jour. AMA, Am. Jour. Pub. Health; contbr. articles to profl. jours., chpts. to books. Mem. Cin. Air Pollution Bd., 1972-76, chmn., 1974-75; bd. dirs. Cin. Chamber Music Soc., 1987-92. Served to capt. M.C. AUS, 1946-48. Recipient award Project Hope, 1984, Robert A. Kehoe award of merit Am. Acad. Occupational Medicine, 1987, Presdl. citation for outstanding contbns. to occupational medicine Am. Acad. Dermatology, 1988, Daniel Drake medal U. Cin., 1985, Disting. Alumni Achievement award SUNY Coll. Medicine, 1993; fellow U. Cin. Grad. Sch., 1971—. Fellow A.C.P.; mem AMA (adv. panel on toxicology council sci. affairs 1980-85), Am. Occupational Med. Assn. (chmn. dermatology com. and policy group 1958-66, dir. 1969-75, Health Achievement in Industry award 1977), Soc. Investigative Dermatology (dir., v.p., hon. mem. 1984—), Am. Acad. Dermatology (chmn. edn. com.), N.Y. Acad. Scis., Am. Indsl. Hygiene Assn., Soc. for Occupational and Environ. Health (councillor), AAAS, Am. Dermatol. Assn., Japanese Dermatol. Assn. (hon.), Chilean Dermatol. Soc. (hon.), Sigma Xi, Alpha Omega Alpha. Achievements include first description of inhibiting effect of ultraviolet radiation on allergic skin reactions; research on cutaneous toxicology, on effects of exposure to chlorinated dioxins, on effects of ionizing radiation on populations living in the vicinity of nuclear fuel processing plants. Office: Dept Environ Health U Cin Coll Medicine 3223 Eden Ave Cincinnati OH 45267-0001

SUSKIND, RONALD STEVEN, journalist; b. Kingston, N.Y., Nov. 20, 1959; s. Walter Burton and Shirley Lila (Berman) S.; m. Cornelia Kennedy, May 4, 1986; children: Walter Kennedy, Harry Owen. BA in Govt. and Fgn. Affairs, U. Va., 1981; MS in Journalism, Columbia U., 1983. No. Va. field coord. Charles Robb for Gov., Alexandria, Va., 1981; campaign mgr. John Downey for U.S. Senate, New Haven, 1982; news asst., interim reporter The New York Times, 1983-85; city/state reporter The St. Petersburg (Fla.) Times, 1985-86; sr. editor Boston Bus. Mag., 1987-88, editor, 1988-90; staff reporter The Wall Street Jour., Boston, 1990-93; sr. nat. affairs writer The Wall Street Jour., Washington, 1993—; instr. advanced journalism Harvard U., Cambridge, Mass., 1987-93; mag. cons. Big Ideas, Inc., Boston, 1988-90; commentator Sta. WBUR, Boston, 1989-93. Recipient Pulitzer prize for feature writing, 1995, Benjamin Fine award Nat. Assn. Secondary Sch. Prins., 1995, Nat. Writing award Ball State U., 1995. Office: The Wall Street Jour 1025 Connecticut Ave NW Washington DC 20036

SUSKIND, SIGMUND RICHARD, microbiology educator; b. N.Y.C., June 19, 1926; s. Seymour and Nina Phillips S.; m. Ann Parker, July 1, 1951; children: Richard, Mark, Steven. A.B., NYU, 1948; Ph.D., Yale U., 1954. Research asst. biology div. Oak Ridge Nat. Lab., 1948-50; USPHS fellow NYU Med. Sch., N.Y.C., 1954-56; mem. faculty Johns Hopkins U., Balt., 1956—, prof. biology, 1965-96, prof. emeritus, 1996—, Univ. ombudsman, 1988-91, dean grad. and undergrad. studies, 1971-78, dean Sch. Arts and Scis., 1978-83; head molecular biology sect. NSF, 1970-71; cons. NIH, 1966-70, Coun. Grad. Schs., Mid States Assn. Colls. and Secondary Schs., 1973—, NSF, 1986; vis. scientist Weizmann Inst. of Sci., Israel, 1985; trustee Balt. Hebrew U., 1985-93; mem. adv. bd. La. Geriatric Ctr., 1990—. Author: (with P.E. Hartman) Gene Action, 1964, 69, (with P.E. Hartman and T. Wright) Principles of Genetics Laboratory Manual, 1965; editor: (with P.E. Hartman) Foundations of Modern Genetics series, 1964, 69; mem. sci. editorial bd. Johns Hopkins U. Press, 1973-76, 88-91. With USNR, 1944-46. NIH grantee, 1957-76. Fellow AAAS; mem. Am. Soc. Microbiology, Genetics Soc. Am., Am. Assn. Immunology, Am. Soc. Biol. Chemistry and Molecular Biology, Coun. Grad Schs., Assn. Grad. Schs., Northeastern Assn. Grad. Schs. (exec. com. 1975-76, pres. 1977-78). Research in microbial biochemical genetics and immunogenetics. Office: Johns Hopkins U Dept Biology and McCollum-Pratt Inst 34th and Charles Sts Baltimore MD 21218

SUSKO, CAROL LYNNE, lawyer, accountant; b. Washington, Dec. 5, 1955; d. Frank and Helen Louise (Davis) S. BS in Econs. and Acctg., George Mason U., 1979; JD, Cath. U., 1982; LLM in Taxation, Georgetown U., 1992. Bar: Pa. 1989, D.C. 1990; CPA, Va., Md. Tax acct. Reznick Fedder & Silverman, P.C., Bethesda, Md., 1984-85; sr. tax acct. Pannell Kerr Forster, Alexandria, Va., 1985; tax specialist Coopers & Lybrand, Washington, 1985-87; supervisory tax sr. Frank & Co., McLean, Va., 1987-88; editorial staff Tax Notes Mag., Arlington, Va., 1989-90; adj. faculty Am. U., Washington, 1989—; tax atty. Marriott Corp., Washington, 1993-94; tax mgr. Host Marriott Inc., Washington, 1994—. Mem. ABA, AICPAs, Va. Soc. CPAs, D.C. Soc. CPAs, D.C. Bar Assn., Women's Bar Assn. of D.C., Am. Assn. Atty.-CPAs. Office: Host Marriott Dept 910 10400 Fernwood Rd Washington DC 20058

SUSLICK, KENNETH SANDERS, chemistry educator; b. Chgo., Sept. 16, 1952; s. Alvin and Edith (Paul) S.; m. Adele Mazurek; 1 child, Benjamin Adam. BS with honors, Calif. Inst. Tech., 1974; PhD, Stanford U., 1978. Rsch., teaching asst. Stanford (Calif.) U., 1974-78; chemist Lawrence Livermore (Calif.) Lab., 1974-75; asst. prof. U. Ill., Urbana, 1978-84, assoc. prof., 1984-88, prof. of chemistry, 1988—, Alumni Rsch. Scholar prof., 1995—; prof. Beckman Inst. for Advanced Sci. and Tech., Urbana, 1989-92; prof. of materials sci. and engring. U. Ill., Urbana, 1993—; vis. fellow Balliol Coll., Inorganic Chemistry Lab., Oxford U., Eng., 1986; bd. dirs. Ney Ultrasonics, Inc., 1993—; sci. bd. dirs. VivoRx, Inc., 1994—; cons. in field. Editor: High Energy Processes in Organometallic Chemistry, 1987, Ultrasound: Its Chemical, Physical and Biological Effects, 1988, Comprehensive Supramolecular Chemistry, vol. 5, 1996; editl. bd. Ultrasonics, 1992-96; patentee isotope separation by photochromatography, protein microspheres, drug delivery, blood substitutes; contbr. articles to profl. jours. Fellow DuPont Found., 1979-80, Sloan Found., 1985-87; recipient Rsch. Career Devel. award NIH, 1985-90, NSF Spl. Creativity award 1992-94, Material Rsch. Soc. medal, 1994. Fellow AAAS, Am. Acoustical Soc. Royal Soc. Arts, Mfrs. and Commerce (Silver medal 1974); mem. Am. Chem. Soc. (chmn. sect. 1987-89, Nobel Laureate Signature award 1994). Avocations: sculpting, folk music. Office: U Ill Dept Chemistry 505 S Mathews Ave Urbana IL 61801-3617

SUSMAN, MILLARD, geneticist, educator; b. St. Louis, Sept. 1, 1934; s. Albert and Patsy Ruth S.; m. Barbara Beth Fretwell, Aug. 18, 1957; children: Michael K., David L. A.B., Washington U., St. Louis, 1956; Ph.D., Calif. Inst. Tech., 1962. With microbial genetics research unit Hammersmith Hosp., London, 1961-62; asst. prof. genetics U. Wis., Madison, 1962-66, assoc. prof., 1966-72, prof., 1972—, chmn. lab. genetics, 1971-75, 77-86, assoc. dean med. sch., 1986-95, acting dean Sch. Allied Health Professions, 1988-90, vice dean med. sch., 1994-95; spl. advisor to the dean med. sch. U. Wis., 1995; dir. Ctr. for Biology Edn., Madison, 1996—; phage course instr., Cold Spring Harbor, N.Y., 1965. Co-author: Life on Earth, 2d edit., 1978, Human Chromosomes: Structure, Behavior, Effects, 3d edit., 1992; contbr. articles to sci. jours. Mem Genetics Soc. Am., AAAS, Sigma Xi, Phi Beta Kappa, Phi Eta Sigma, Omicron Delta Kapp. Home: 2707 Colgate Rd Madison WI 53705-2234 Office: 507 Genetics Blvd Madison WI 53706

SUSMAN, MORTON LEE, lawyer; b. Detroit, Aug. 6, 1934; s. Harry and Alma (Koslow) S.; m. Nina Meyers, May 1, 1958; 1 child, Mark Lee. BBA, So. Meth. U., 1956, JD, 1958. Bar: Tex. 1958, U.S. Dist. Ct. (so. dist.) Tex. 1961, U.S. Ct. Appeals (5th cir.) 1961, U.S. Supreme Ct. 1961, U.S. Ct. Appeals (11th cir.) 1981, D.C. 1988, U.S. Ct. Appeals (D.C. cir.) 1988, N.Y. 1990, Colo. 1996. Asst. U.S. atty., Houston, 1961-64, 1st asst. U.S. atty., 1965-66, U.S. atty., 1966-69; ptnr. Weil, Gotshal & Manges and predecessor firm Susman & Kessler, Houston, 1969—. Lt. USNR, 1958-61. Fellow Am. Coll. Trial Lawyers, Tex. Bar Found.; mem. ABA, Fed. Bar Assn. (dir., Younger Fed. Lawyer award 1968), Tex. Bar Assn., Skyline Country Club (Tucson). Democrat. Jewish. Home: 3238 Ella Lee Ln Houston TX 77019-5924 Office: Weil Gotshal & Manges 700 Louisiana St Ste 1600 Houston TX 77002-2722

SUSMAN, STEPHEN DAILY, lawyer; b. Houston, Jan. 20, 1941; s. Harry and Helene Gladys (Daily) S.; m. Karen Lee Hyman, Dec. 26, 1965; children: Stacy Margraeta, Harry Paul. B.A. magna cum laude, Yale U., 1962; LL.B. summa cum laude, U. Tex. Austin, 1965. Bar: Tex. 1965, U.S. Supreme Ct 1960. Law clk. U.S. Ct. Appeals (5th cir.), New Orleans, 1965-66, U.S.Supreme Ct., Washington, 1966-67; ptnr. Fulbright & Jaworski, 1966-75; spl. counsel to atty. gen. Austin, Tex., 1975; sr. ptnr. Susman Godfrey, Houston, 1980—; vis. prof. law U. Tex., Austin, 1975; chmn. adv. com. on discovery Tex. Supreme Ct. Bd. dirs. Contemporary Arts Mus., Assn. Yale Alumni, Yale Devel. Fund, Southwest Legal Found., Inns of Ct. Recipient ADL Jurisprudence award, 1995; named one of Best Trial Lawyers in Am., Nat. Law Jour., 1989; named Best Litigator in World, Comml. Litigation. Mem. ABA (antitrust sect., mem. coun. litigation sect., chmn. task force on fast track litigation), State Bar Tex., Am. Law Inst., Assn. Trial Lawyers Am., Houston Bar Assn., Yale Club (Houston, N.Y.C.), Houston Trial Lawyers Assn., Tex. Assn. Civil Trial Specialists, Houston Club, Houstonian Club, Petroleum Club (Dallas), Quinnipiac Club (New Haven). Avocations: jogging, hiking. Office: 1st Interstate Bank 1000 Louisiana St Ste 5100 Houston TX 77002-5013

SUSSE, SANDRA SLONE, lawyer; b. Medford, Ma., June 1, 1943; d. James Robert and Georgie Coffin (Bradshaw) Slone; m. Peter Susse, May 10, 1969 (div. May 1993); 1 child, Toby. BA, U. Mass., 1981; JD, Vt. Law Sch., 1986. Bar: Mass. 1986, U.S. Dist. Ct. Mass. 1988, U.S. Ct. Appeals (1st cir.) 1995. Staff atty. Western Mass. Legal Svcs., Springfield, 1986—. Mem. ABA, Mass. Bar Assn., Women's Bar Assn. Mass. Avocations: hiking, German literature, films, skating. Office: Western Mass Legal Svcs 145 State St Springfield MA 01103-1927

SUSSENGUTH, EDWARD HENRY, computer company executive, computer network designer; b. Holyoke, Mass., Oct. 10, 1932; s. Edward Henry and Mary Frances (Murphy) S.; m. Ann Paula Coughlin, Jan. 31, 1959; children—Edward Henry III, John Andrew. A.B., Harvard U., 1954, Ph.D., 1964; M.S., MIT, 1959. Researcher IBM Corp., Poughkeepsie, N.Y., 1959-64; mem. research and devel. staff IBM Corp., Menlo Park, Calif., 1964-70; mgr. IBM Corp., Raleigh, N.C., 1970-77; div. dir. IBM Corp., White Plains, N.Y., 1977-80; fellow IBM Corp., Raleigh, 1980-91; pres. IBM Acad. Tech., 1989-91; cons., 1991—. Contbr. articles to profl. jours.; patentee in field. Bd. dirs. Wake County Hosp. System, Raleigh, 1985-96. Served to lt. USN, 1954-57. Recipient Interface award Data Communications, 1988. Fellow IEEE (Simon Ramo medal, 1989); mem. NAE, Assn. Computing Machinery, Sigma Xi. Club: MacGregor Downs Country (Cary, N.C.) (gov. 1980-85), Amelia Island. Avocations: golf; photography. Home and Office: 411 Rutherglen Dr Cary NC 27511-6436

SUSSER, MERVYN WILFRED, epidemiologist, educator; b. Johannesburg, South Africa, Sept. 26, 1921; came to U.S., 1965; s. Solomon and Ida Rose (Son) S.; m. Zena Athene Stein, Mar. 28, 1949; children: Ida, Ezra, Ruth. MB, BChir, U. Witwatersrand, Union of South Africa, 1950; diploma pub. health, London Conjoint Bd., 1960; DMS (hon.), U. Witwatersrand, 1993. Med. officer, then supt. Alexandra Health Centre and Univ. Clinic, Johannesburg, 1952-55; successively lectr., sr. lectr., reader, head dept. social and preventive medicine Manchester (Eng.) U., 1957-65; also med. officer div. mental health Salford, Eng.; prof., chmn. div. epidemiology Sch. Pub. Health, Columbia U., N.Y.C., 1966-78, Gertrude H. Sergievsky prof. epidemiology, dir. Sergievsky Ctr., 1977-91; Sergievsky prof. emeritus, spl. lectr., 1992—; cons. WHO, 1962, 66-72, 79, 90, NIH, NAS. Author: (with W. Watson) Sociology in Medicine, 1962, 2d edit., 1971, (with W. Watson and K. Hopper), 3d edit., 1985, Community Psychiatry: Epidemiologic and Social Themes, 1968, Causal Thinking in the Health Sciences: Concepts and Strategies of Epidemiology, 1973, (with others) Famine and Human Development: Studies of the Dutch Hungerwinter 1944-45, 1975, (with D. Rush and Z. Stein) Diet in Pregnancy: A Randomized Controlled Trial of Nutritional Supplements, 1980, Epidemiology, Health and Society: Selected Essays, 1987, (with Jennie Kline and Zena Stein) Conception to Birth:

Epidemiology of Prenatal Development, 1989; editor Am. Jour. Pub. Health, 1992—. With South African Defence Force, 1940-45. Belding scholar Assn. Aid Crippled Children, 1965-66; Guggenheim fellow, 1972; Disting. Svc. award Coll. Physicians and Surgeons, Columbia U., 1994. Fellow Royal Coll. Physicians (Edinburgh), Am. Pub. Health Assn. (John Snow award 1994), Am. Epidemiol. Soc., Am. Coll. Epidemiol., N.Y. Acad. Medicine; mem. Internat. Epidemiol. Assn., World Psychiat. Assn., Soc. Epidemiol. Rsch., Soc. Pediatric Epidemiol. Rsch., Physicians Forum. Home: 100 Pinecrest Dr Hastings Hdsn NY 10706-3702 Office: 630 W 168th St New York NY 10032-3702

SUSSEX, JAMES NEIL, psychiatrist, educator; b. Northcote, Minn., Oct. 2, 1917; s. Rollo and Florence (Bartholomew) S.; m. Margaret Ann Garty, Apr. 25, 1943; children: Margaret Eileen, Mary Patricia, Barbara Lorraine, Teresa Virginia. AB, U. Kans., 1939, MD, 1942. Diplomate: Am. Bd. Psychiatry and Neurology (dir. for child psychiatry 1966-70, dir. 1975-83, pres. 1982). Commd. lt. (j.g.), M.C. U.S. Navy, 1943, advanced through grades to comdr., 1955; intern (Naval Hosp.), Chelsea, Mass., 1942-43; resident psychiatry (Naval Hosp.), Vallejo, Calif., 1946-49; fellow child psychiatry Phila. Guild Guidance Clinic, 1949-51; asst. chief neuropsychiatry Naval Hosp., Bethesda, Md., 1951-55; resigned, 1955; mem. faculty Med. Coll. Ala., 1955-68, prof. psychiatry, chmn. dept., 1959-68; psychiatrist-in-chief U. Ala. Hosps. and Clinics, 1959-68; faculty U. Miami Sch. Medicine, Fla., 1968—; prof. psychiatry U. Miami Sch. Medicine, 1970—, chmn. dept., 1970-83, chmn. emeritus, 1983—, spl. asst. to v.p. for med. affairs for geriatric medicine program, 1983-86; mem. adv. bd. Nat. Psychiat. Residency Selection Plan, 1965—; mem. Med. Adv. Bd. Ednl. Film Prodn., 1966—; cons. Bur. Rsch., U.S. office Edn., 1966-72; dir. Ala. Planning for Mental Retardation, 1964—; mem. psychiatry tng. rev. com. NIMH; mem. exec. com. Am. Bd. Med. Spltys., 1980-83. Editor: Jour. Ala. Soc. Med. History, 1957-63; editorial bd.: Jour. Am. Acad. Child Psychiatry, 1966-70. Mem. Am. Assn. Psychiat. Svcs. for Children (coun. 1966—, pres. 1972-74), Coun. Med. Specialty Socs. (pres. 1988-89), Accreditation Coun. for Grad. Med. Edn. (exec. com. 1989-94, chmn. 1992-93), Phi Beta Kappa, Nu Sigma Nu. Home: 6950 SW 134th St Miami FL 33156-6975

SUSSKIND, CHARLES, engineering educator, author, publishing executive; b. Prague, Czech Republic; came to U.S., 1945, naturalized, 1946; s. Bruno Bronislav and Gertruda (Seger) S.; m. Teresa Gabriel, May 1, 1945; children: Pamela Susskind Pettler, Peter Gabriel, Amanda Frances. Student, City U., London, 1939-40; B.S., Calif. Inst. Tech., 1948; M.Engring., Yale U., 1949, Ph.D., 1951. Research asst. Yale U., 1949-51; research assoc. Stanford U., 1951-55, lectr., asst. dir. Microwave Lab., 1953-55; mem. faculty U. Calif., Berkeley, 1955—; prof. U. Calif., 1964-91; prof. emeritus U. Calif., Berkeley, 1991—; asst. dean Coll. Engring. U. Calif., 1964-68, also statewide adminstr., 1969-74; vis. prof. U. London, 1961-62, U. Geneva, Switzerland, 1968-69; cons. EPA Sci. Adv. Bd., 1982-92; cons. electronics industry, govt., publishers; dir. San Francisco Press, Inc. Author: (with M. Chodorow) Fundamentals of Microwave Electronics, 1964, (with L. Schell) Exporting Technical Education, 1968, Understanding Technology, 1973, 74, 85 (transl. into Dutch, French, Italian, Korean, Spanish, Indian edit. in English), Twenty-Five Engineers and Inventors, 1976, (with F. Kurylo) Ferdinand Braun, 1981, (with M.E. Rowbottom) Electricity and Medicine: History of their Interaction, 1984, Janáček and Brod, 1985, Heinrich Hertz: A Short Life, 1995; editor: (with M. Hertz) Heinrich Hertz: Memoirs, Letters, Diaries, bilingual edit., 1977; editor-in-chief Ency. Electronics, 1962. Served with USAAF, 1942-45. Named to Hon. Order Ky. Cols. Fellow IEEE; mem. AAAS, Histor of Sci. Soc., Soc. for History of Tech., Instn. Elec. Engrs. (London), Faculty Club of Berkeley (bd. dirs. 1972-73), Sigma Xi (pres. Berkeley chpt. 1972-73), Tau Beta Pi. Office: U Calif Coll Engring Berkeley CA 94720-1770

SUSSKIND, HERBERT, biomedical engineer, educator; b. Ratibor, Germany, Mar. 23, 1929; came to U.S., 1938; s. Alex and Hertha (Loewy) S.; m. E. Suzanne Lieberman, June 18, 1961; children: Helen J., Alex M., David A. BChE cum laude, CCNY, 1950; MChE, NYU, 1961. Engr., sect. supr. Brookhaven Nat. Lab., Upton, N.Y., 1950-77, biomed. engr., 1977-94, asst. to chmn. med. dept., 1989-94, rsch. collaborator, 1994—; assoc. prof. medicine SUNY, Stony Brook, 1979—. Co-inventor 3 patents in field. Co-founder, 1st pres. Huntington Twp. Jewish Forum, Huntington, N.Y., 1970-73; trustee Huntington Hebrew Congregation, 1970-78. Mem. Biomed. Engring. Soc., Soc. Nuclear Medicine, Am. Thoracic Soc., Am. Nuclear Soc. (exec. com., treas. L.I. Sect., 1978-83), Am. Inst. Chem. Engrs., CCNY Alumni Assn. (pres. 1982-84), CCNY Engring. & Architecture Alumni Assn., N.Y.C. (pres. 1963-65). Office: Brookhaven Nat Lab Box 5000 Bldg 490 Upton NY 11973-5000

SUSSKIND, LAWRENCE ELLIOTT, urban and environmental planner, educator, mediator; b. N.Y.C., Jan. 12, 1947; s. David J. and Marjorie H. (Friedman) S.; m. Miriam Mason, June 8, 1968 (div. Dec. 1982); m. Leslie Webster Tuttle, Dec. 12, 1982; children: Noah Gates, Lily Webster. A.B. in Sociology, Columbia U., 1968; M.C.P., MIT, 1970, Ph.D. in Urban Planning, 1973. Asst. prof. urban and environ. planning MIT, Cambridge, 1971-74, assoc. prof., 1974-82, prof., 1982-95, Ford prof., 1995—, head dept., 1978-82, dir. MIT-Harvard Pub. Disputes Program, 1980—; exec. dir. program on negotiation Harvard U. Law Sch., Cambridge, 1984-87; sr. fellow program on negotiation, 1988—; pres. Consensus Bldg. Inst. Author: Paternalism, Conflict and Co-Production, 1983, Proposition 1 1/2; Its Impact on Massachusetts, 1983, Resolving Environmental Regulatory Disputes, 1983, Breaking the Impasse, 1987, Environmental Diplomacy, 1994, Reinventing Congress for the 21st Century, 1995, Dealing With an Angry Public, 1996; sr. editor, founder Environ. Impact Assessment Rev., 1980-96; editl. policy bd. Negotiation Jour., 1984—. Mem. Am. Inst. Cert. Planners, Soc. for Profls. in Dispute Resolution. Jewish. Home: 32 Jericho Hill Rd Southborough MA 01772-1007 Office: MIT 3-411 Cambridge MA 02139

SUSSKIND, TERESA GABRIEL, publisher; b. Watford, Eng., came to U.S., 1945, naturalized, 1948; d. Aaron and Betty (Fox) Gabriel; m. Charles Susskind, May 1, 1945; children: Pamela Pettler, Peter Gabriel, Amanda. Ed. U. London, 1938-40. Profl. libr. Calif. Inst. Tech., Pasadena, 1946-48, Yale U., New Haven, Conn., 1948-51, Stanford U., Calif., 1951-52, SRI Internat., Menlo Park, Calif., 1953; founder, pres. San Francisco Press, Inc., 1959—. With Women's Royal Naval Svc., 1943-45. Author: A Room of One's Own Revisited, 1977. Active in cultural affairs; bd. govs. San Francisco Symphony, 1986-89. Mem. Town and Gown Club (Berkeley, Calif., pres. 1984-85). Office: PO Box 426800 San Francisco CA 94142-6800

SUSSMAN, ALEXANDER RALPH, lawyer; b. Bronx, N.Y., Sept. 24, 1946; s. Herman R. and Claire (Blumenson) S.; m. Edna Rubin, Mar. 24, 1973; children: Jason, Carl, Matthew, Eric. AB cum laude, Princeton U., 1968; JD, Yale U., 1972. Bar: N.Y. 1973, U.S. Dist. Ct. (so. and ea. dists) N.Y. 1974, U.S. Ct. Appeals (2d, 3d, 5th, 6th, 8th and 10th cirs.) 1983, U.S. Supreme Ct. Law clk. to justice U.S. Dist. Ct., N.Y.C., 1972-73; assoc. Cravath, Swaine & Moore, N.Y.C., 1974-76; assoc. Fried, Frank, Harris, Shriver & Jacobson, N.Y.C., 1977-79, ptnr., 1979—. Author: (with A. Fleischer, Jr.) Responses to Takeover Bids, 1997, Takeover Defense, 2 vols., 1997; editor Yale Law Jour., 1971-72. Vice pres. litigation, exec. com., bd. dirs. N.Y. Lawyers for Pub. Interest, 1983—; bd. dirs., mem. exec. com. Legal Aid Soc., 1987-93. Fulbright scholar U. Bordeaux, 1969. Mem. ABA, Am. Law Inst., N.Y. State Bar Assn., Assn. of Bar of City of N.Y. (fed. cts. com. 1984-87, jud. com. 1987-90, chmn. legal assistance com. 1988-91, Marden lectr. com. 1991-94, chmn. mergers and acquisitions com. 1995—). Home: 20 Oak Ln Scarsdale NY 10583-1627 Office: Fried Frank Harris Shriver & Jacobson 1 New York Plz New York NY 10004

SUSSMAN, ARTHUR MELVIN, law educator; b. Bklyn., Nov. 17, 1942; m. Rita Padnick; children: Eric, Johanna. BS, Cornell U., 1963; LLB magna cum laude, Harvard U., 1966. Bar: N.Y. 1967, Ill. 1970. Assoc. atty. Cahill, Gordon, Reindel & Ohl, N.Y.C., 1966-67; from assoc. atty. to ptnr. Jenner & Block, Chgo., 1970-77; legal counsel So. Ill. U., Carbondale, 1977-79; gen. counsel, v.p. legal affairs and govt. rels. U. Chgo., 1979-84, gen. counsel, v.p. adminstrn., 1984-88, lectr. law Grad. Sch. Bus., 1986—, master Broadview Hall, 1986-87, resident master Woodward Ct., 1987—, bd. dirs. Lab. Schs., 1985; gen. counsel, v.p. adminstrn. Argonne (Ill.) Nat. Lab., 1988—; exec. dir. Borman Commn., U.S. Mil. Acad., 1976; chmn., bd. dirs. Ency. Birt., Inc., 1995-96; presenter in field. Contr. articles to profl. jours. Mem. Ill. Sec. of State's Com. on Not-for-Profit Corp. Act, 1984-85; chair regional selection panel Harry S. Truman Scholarship Found.; bd. dirs. Chapin Hall for Children, 1986—. Capt. JAGC, U.S. Army, 1967-70. Fulbright fellow, London, 1987. Mem. Nat. Assn. Coll. and Univ. Attys., Am. Coun. Edn. Office: U Chgo Office of Legal Counsel Office of Legal Counsel 5801 S Ellis Ave Rm 503 Chicago IL 60637-1476

SUSSMAN, BARRY, author, public opinion analyst and pollster, journalist; b. N.Y.C., July 10, 1934; s. Samuel and Esther (Rosen) S.; m. Peggy Earhart, Jan. 20, 1962; children: Seena, Shari. BA, Bklyn. Coll., 1956. Reporter Herald Courier, Bristol, Va., 1960-62, mng. editor, 1962-65; editor Washington Post, 1965-69, city editor, 1970-73, spl. Watergate editor, 1972-74, pollster, pub. opinion analyst, 1975-87; co-founder, co-dir. Washington Post-ABC News poll, 1981-87; columnist Washington Post Nat. Weekly, 1983-87; mng. editor nat. affairs UPI, Washington, 1987; ind. pub. opinion analyst and pollster, 1988—. Author: The Great Coverup: Nixon and the Scandal of Watergate, 1974, What Americans Really Think, 1988, (with Lowell P. Weicker, Jr.) Maverick, 1995. Recipient Drew Pearson award for Nat. Reporting, 1972, 1st Prize award Washington Newspaper Guild, 1973, Editor of Yr. award Washington Newspaper Guild, 1973. Mem. Am. Assn. for Pub. Opinion Rsch. (exec. coun. 1985-87). Jewish. Avocation: chess.

SUSSMAN, BRIAN JAY, meteorologist, weather broadcaster; b. L.A., Apr. 3, 1956; s. Alan E. and Beverly A. (Carlson) S.; m. Sue Ann Rittenhouse, June 18, 1978; chilren: Elisa, Samuel, Benjamin. BS, U. Mo., 1978. Reporter, anchor Sta. KCBJ-TV, Columbia, Mo., 1977-80; weather anchor Sta. KOLO-TV, Reno, 1980-83; on-air meteorologist Sta. KNTV-TV, San Jose, Calif., 1983-87, Sta. KDKA-TV, Pitts., 1987-89; substitute weatherman CBS This Morning, N.Y.C., 1988-93; on-air meteorologist Sta. KPIX-TV, San Francisco, 1989—. Co-author: (textbook) For Spacious Skies, 1987, rev. edit., 1989. Recipient Best Weathercast award Radio-TV News Dirs. Assn., 1987, 90-95, AP, 1989, 90-96, Advancement of Learning Through Broadcasting award NEA, 1989. Mem. Am. Meteorol. Soc. (Seal of Approval cert.). Avocations: pub. speaking, adult ice-hockey. Office: Sta KPIX-TV 855 Battery St San Francisco CA 94111-1503

SUSSMAN, DAVID WILLIAM, lawyer; b. N.Y.C., Aug. 7, 1954; s. Leonard Richard and Frances Grace (Rukeyser) S.; m. Ruth Ellen Levine, Mar. 16, 1985; children: Jane, Rebecca. BA, U. Pa., 1976, MA, 1976; JD, Columbia U., 1980. Bar: N.Y. 1981, U.S. Dist. Ct. (so. and ea. dist.) N.Y. 1981, U.S. Ct. Appeals (2d cir.) 1989, U.S. Supreme Ct. 1987. Assoc. Marshall, Bratter, Greene, Allison & Tucker, N.Y.C., 1980-81; law clk. to judge David N. Edelstein U.S. Dist. Ct. (so. dist.) N.Y., 1981-83; assoc. Simpson Thacher & Bartlett, N.Y.C., 1983-87, Cole & Deitz, N.Y.C., 1987-89; gen. counsel N.Y. Yankees, Bronx, 1989-92, exec. v.p., gen. counsel, 1992-94; bd. dirs., gen. counsel Historic Dists. Coun., N.Y.C., 1988-93. Mem. Community Bd. #2, N.Y.C., 1988-90; bd. dirs. N.Y. Urban League, 1996—. Mem. ABA, Assn. of the Bar of the City of N.Y., Phi Beta Kappa. Office: NY Yankees Yankee Stadium E 161st St & River Ave Bronx NY 10451

SUSSMAN, GERALD, publishing company executive; b. Balt., Feb. 21, 1934; s. Hyman Jacob and Sylvia (Applebaum) S.; m. Arla Ilene Ellison, Aug. 25, 1963; children: Daniel Leonard, Andrew Louis. B.A., U. Md., 1956. Co-founder, prin. Investors Service of Md., Balt., 1956-60; coll. traveller Oxford U. Press, Inc., N.Y.C., 1961-62; coll. sales mgr. Oxford U. Press, Inc., 1962-69, gen. advt. mgr., 1970-73, v.p., dir. mktg., 1974-79, sr. v.p., dir. mktg., 1979-83, sr. v.p., dir. adminstrn. and planning, 1983—. Mem. Assn. Am. Pubs. (chmn. mktg. com.), Assn. Am. Univ. Presses (chmn. mktg. com. 1980-81), Pubs. Advt. Club, Phi Alpha Theta. Democrat. Jewish. Home: 8 Opatut Ct Edison NJ 08817-2923 Office: Oxford U Press Inc 198 Madison Ave New York NY 10016-4308

SUSSMAN, JEFFREY BRUCE, public relations and marketing executive; b. N.Y.C., Mar. 15, 1943; m. Suzy Hirschland-Prudden, 1964 (div. 1981); 1 child, Robert; m. Barbara Ramsay, 1984. BA in English, NYU, 1969. Pres. Suzy Prudden Studios, N.Y.C., 1975-81; v.p. Zachary and Front, N.Y.C., 1981-88; pres. Jeffrey Sussman, Inc., N.Y.C., 1988—; instr. The New Sch., N.Y.C. Author: Creative Fitness for Baby and Child, 1972, Suzy Prudden's Family Fitness Book, 1975, Fit for Life, 1977, See How They Run, 1978, Suzy Prudden's Spot Reducing Program, 1979, Suzy Prudden's Pregnancy and Back-To-Shape Exercise Program, 1980, I Can Exercise Anywhere, 1981, How to Sleep Without Drugs, 1986, Power Promoting: How to Market Your Business to the Top!, 1997; book rev. editor The Manhattan Tribune, 1969-75; contbr. book revs. to N.Y. Times Book Rev., 1974; bi-monthly columnist Weight Watchers Mag., 1977-79; contbr. articles to profl. jours. Press sec. N.Y.C. Coun.-Henry Stern, 1981. Avocations: photography, writing, music, painting, drawing. Home and Office: 249 E 48 St New York NY 10017

SUSSMAN, LEONARD RICHARD, foundation executive; b. N.Y.C., Nov. 26, 1920; s. Jacob and Carrie (Marks) S.; m. Frances Rukeyser, May 9, 1942 (div. 1958); m. Marianne Rita Gutmann, May 28, 1958; children: Lynne, David William, Mark Jacob. A.B., NYU, 1940; M.S. in Journalism, Columbia U., 1941. Copy editor N.Y. Morning Telegraph, news editor radio sta. WQXR, 1941; cable editor San Juan (P.R.) World Jour., also corr. Business Week mag., 1941-42; editor fgn. broadcast intelligence svc. FCC, 1942; press sec. to Gov. of P.R., 1942-43; dir. info. in N.Y. for Govt. of P.R., 1946-49; regional dir., then nat. exec. dir. Am. Coun. Judaism, 1949-66; cons. pub. affairs cons. Nationwide Ins. Cos. (and indsl. subs.), 1955-57; mem. editorial com. Coun. Liberal Chs., 1956-59; exec. dir. Freedom House, 1967-88, 96, sr. scholar in internat. communications, 1988—; evaluator Fulbright Program Bd. Fgn. Scholarships, 1990-92; exec. dir. Willkie Meml., 1970-88; adj. prof. journalsim and mass communication NYU, N.Y.C., 1990—; organizer, dir. Freedom House/Books USA, 1968-85; editor Freedom at Issue, bimonthly, 1970-81; mem. U.S. Dels. to Conf. World Communicaiton Yr./83, 1982-83; organizer acad. confs.; participant Internat. Conf. on Press Freedom, Venice, Italy, 1976, 77, Cairo, 1978, Talloires, 1981, 83, San Jose, Costa Rica, Johannnesburg, and Santiago Chile, 1987, also others; mem. panel competition in space Congl. Office Tech. Assessment, 1982-83. Author: American Press-Under Siege?, 1973, Mass News Media and The Third World Challenge, 1977, Glossary for International Communications: Warning of a Bloodless Dialect, 1983, Spanish version, 1987, Power, The Press and the Technology of Freedom: The Coming of Age of ISDN, 1990, The Culture of Freedom: The Small World of Fulbirght Scholars, 1992, Good News Bad News, 1994, Can A Free Press Be Responsible? To Whom?, 1995, The Press: Pressed and Oppressed, 1995, The Journalist as Pariah: Press Freedom, 1996, The Global Airscape, 1996, Democracy, Yes; Press Freedom, Maybe, 1997, Press Law Epidemic: Press Freedom, 1997; editor: Three Years at the East-West Divide, 1983, Today's American: How Free?, 1986; contbr. sects. to books, articles to profl. jours. and newspapers; project dir.: Big Story-How the American Press and Television Reported and Interpreted the Crisis of Tet-1968 in Vietnam and Washington, 1977; eidtor: textbook series, also quar. mag. Issues, 1953-66; editl. bd. Polit. Comm. and Persuasion. Trustee Internat. Coun. on Future of Univ., 1973-84; bd. dirs. World Press Freedom Com., 1977—; chmn. Friends of Survey Mag. Charitable Trust, London, 1978-92; mem. U.S. Nat. Commn. for UNESCO, 1979-85, vice-chmn., 1983-85; mem. U.S. dels. to internat. conf. on space, African Aid, UNESCO, London Info. Forum. Decorated Legion of Merit; recipient Ann. First Amendment award N.Y. br. Soc. Profl. Journalists, 1988. Mem. Internat. Inst. Comm., Internat. Press Inst., Internat. Assn. Mass Comm. Rsch., Century Club. Home: 215 E 73rd St New York NY 10021-3653 Office: 120 Wall St Fl 26 New York NY 10005-4001

SUSSMAN, MARTIN VICTOR, chemical engineering educator, inventor, consultant; b. N.Y.C.; s. Samuel and Selma (Bagno) S.; m. Jeanne Fowler, Aug. 22, 1953; children: M. Ann Edmunds, Eve Leslie, David Fowler. B.S., CCNY; M.S., Columbia U., Ph.D., 1958. Registered profl. engr. Mass.; lic. marine engr. Instr., research assoc. chem. dept. Fordham U., N.Y.C., 1949-50; research fellow chem. engring. dept. Columbia U., 1951-53; sr. engr., research engr. Pioneering Lab., DuPont, Del., 1953-58; co-founder, 1st dept. chem. engring in Turkey Robert Coll., Istanbul, Turkey, 1958-61; prof. chem. engring. dept. Tufts U., Medford, Mass., 1961—; dept. chmn., established PhD and MS programs Tufts U., 1961-71; cons. engring. edn. US AID, Brazil and Uruguay, 1963, Ethiopia, 1965; cons. engring. edn. Ford Found., India, 1971, 72, 73, 74, 79; coord. engring. edn. NSF, New Delhi, 1967-68; vis. prof. MIT, 1976, U. Capetown, Republic South Africa, 1990; Disting. vis. scholar Va. Poly. Inst., 1980; vis. scholar chem. engring. dept. U. Cambridge, Eng., 1996-97; hon. rsch. fellow U. Exeter, 1990; introduced grad. chem. engring program Tufts U.; co-founder chem. engring. dept. Robert Coll., Turkey. Author: Elementary General Thermodynamics, 1972, 89, Availability (Exergy) Analysis, 1980; patentee in field. Mem. Town Meeting, Lexington, Mass., 1971-78. Served with U.S. Maritime Service, 1945-47, U.S. Coast Guard. NIH Spl. Research fellow, 1968; AEC fellow, 1951; Fulbright Hays lectr., 1977; Erskine fellow U. Canterbury (N.Z.), 1983; Meyerhoff fellow Weizman Inst. Sci., 1984-85. Fellow Am. Inst. Chem. Engrs., Am. Inst. Chemists; mem. Am. Chem. Soc., Sigma Xi, Tau Beta Pi (eminent engr. 1974). Achievements include invention of "Incremental Draw Process" for synthetic fiber manufacture now in use by industry, "Fibra-Cel" tissue culture matrix, establishment of first modern chemical engineering department in a Turkish university, introduced graduate degree in chem. engring. program at Tufts U. Office: Tufts U Dept Chem Engring Medford MA 02155

SUSSMAN, MONICA HILTON, lawyer; b. N.Y.C., Apr. 2, 1952. BA cum laude, Syracuse U., 1973; JD, Hofstra U., 1977. Bar: Va. 1977, D.C. 1978. Legis. coun. N.Y. State Gov's. Office, Washington, 1977-79; spl. asst. to under sec. U.S. Dept. HUD, Washington, 1979-80, br. chief office State Agy. and Bond Fin. programs, 1980-82, office gen. counsel, 1982-83, also bd. dirs., 1988-95, v.p., 1989-93, treas. Nat. Housing Conf., 1990-93, also programs and regulations dep. gen. counsel; ptnr. McDermott, Will & Emery, Washington; now ptnr. Peabody & Brown, Washington, 1996; bd. dirs. Nat. Leased Housing Assn. Mem. ABA, Mortgage Bankers Assn. (insured project subcom.), D.C. Bar, Va. State Bar. Office: Peabody & Brown 1255 23rd St NW Ste 800 Washington DC 20037-1125

SUSSNA, EDWARD, economist, educator; b. Phila., Nov. 26, 1926; s. Louis and Manya (Prytzycka) S.; m. Sylvia Fishman, Mar. 8, 1953; children: Audrey Francine, Ellen Sondra. B.A., Bklyn. Coll., 1950; M.A., U. Ill., 1952, Ph.D., 1954. Instr. U. Ill., 1952-54; asst. prof. Lehigh U., 1956-57; prof. bus. adminstrn. and econs. U. Pitts., 1957—; dir. ctr. for exec. edn. Grad. Sch. Bus. U. Pitts., 1983-89; dir. mgmt. program for execs. Center for Econ. Edn., Grad. Sch. Bus., acad. dir. study program in Hong Kong and Peoples Republic China, spring 1989, 95; inaugural prof. MBA program Bratislava Sch. Econs., Slovakia, 1996; vis. Fulbright prof. U. Tehran, Iran, adviser, 1972-73; cons. Bur. of Budget, Dept. HEW, Dept. Transp., UN Indsl. Devel. Orgn., Bell Telephone Co., Alcoa, Westinghouse Corp., NSF, Pitts. Nat. Bank, Japanese Regional Bankers Assn., others; vis. prof. UCLA, 1970, Ecole Superieure des Scis. Economiques et Commerciales, Paris, 1976-77, U. East Asia, Hong Kong and Macau, winter 1986; vis. scholar Internat. Inst. Mgmt., Berlin, spring 1982. Contbr. articles to profl. jours. Served with U.S. Mcht. Marine, 1944-47; Served with AUS, 1954-56. Vis. prof. under Ford Found. fellowship Harvard, 1960-61; guest scholar under Ford Found. fellowship Brookings Instn., Washington, 1962-63. Mem. Am. Econ. Assn., Am. Fin. Assn., Strategic Mgmt. Inst., Beta Gamma Sigma, Omicron Delta. Home: 1538 S Negley Ave Pittsburgh PA 15217-1420

SUSTAR, T. DAVID, college president. Pres. East Coast Bible Coll., Ch. of God, Charlotte, N.C., 1996—. Office: East Coast Bible Coll 6900 Wilkinson Blvd Charlotte NC 28214-3100

SUSTENDAL, DIANE, editor, consultant; b. New Orleans, Aug. 30, 1944; d. George and Mary (Anderson) S. Student, La. State U., 1963-64; cert., John McCrady Sch. Fine Arts, 1966. Asst. art critic Times-Picayune, New Orleans, 1966-68, fashion and beauty editor, 1970-82; asst. mng. editor spl. studies div. Frederick A. Praeger, N.Y.C., 1969; assoc. editor M & Men's Wear mags., Fairchild Publs., N.Y.C., 1982-83; pres. Diane Sustendal & Assocs., Editorial & Creative Svcs., N.Y.C.; cons. Men's Fashions of the Times, N.Y. Times, N.Y.C., 1983-86; fashion and interior design editor N.Y. Daily News, 1990-91; freelance writer, editor. Bd. dirs. New Orleans Ballet, 1971-73. Recipient award La. Press Anns., 1972, Aldo award Men's Fashion Assn. Am., 1985. Mem. Fashion Group N.Y. Republican. Home: 181 E 73rd St Apt 4G New York NY 10021-3514

SUTCLIFFE, ERIC, lawyer; b. Calif., Jan. 10, 1909; s. Thomas and Annie (Beare) S.; m. Joan Basché, Aug. 7, 1937; children: Victoria, Marcia, Thomas; m. Marie C. Paige, Nov. 1, 1975. AB, U. Calif., Berkeley, 1929, LLB, 1932. Bar: Calif. 1932. Mem. firm Orrick, Herrington & Sutcliffe, San Francisco, 1943-85, mng. ptnr., 1947-78. Trustee, treas., v.p. San Francisco Law Libr., 1974-88; founding fellow The Oakland Mus. of Calif.; bd. dirs. Merritt Peralta Found., 1988; past bd. dirs. Hong Kong Bank of Calif., Friends of U. Calif. Bot. Garden, sec. Fellow Am. Bar Found (life); mem. ABA (chmn state regulation securities com. 1960-65), San Francisco Bar Assn. (chmn. corp. law com., 1964-65), San Francisco C. of C. (past treas., dir.), State Bar Calif., Pacific Union Club, Bohemian Club, Phi Gamma Delta, Phi Delta Phi, Order of Coif. Home: 260 King Ave Oakland CA 94610-1231 Office: Old Fed Reserve Bank Bldg 400 Sansome St San Francisco CA 94111-3304

SUTCLIFFE, MARION SHEA, writer; b. Washington, July 29, 1918; d. James William and Ida (Hewitt) Shea; m. James Montgomery Sutcliffe, Aug. 23, 1941; 1 child, Jill Marion. BMus, Boston Conservatory Music, 1956-60; EdM, Boston State Coll., 1969. Cert. music, English, psychology and reading tchr., Mass. Tchr. Milford (Mass.) Pub. Schs., 1966-70; tchr. music Worcester (Mass.) Pub. Schs., 1970-71; reading tchr. Natick and Newton (Mass.) Pub. Schs., 1971-73; real estate developer Sutcliffe Family Trust, South Dennis, Mass., 1969—; developer Delray Beach Club, Dennisport, Mass.; mfr. A&A Assocs., South Dennis, 1989—; dir., sec. bd. mgrs. The Soundings Resort, Dennisport, Mass., 1990—. Songwriter Diablo, 1954. Founder, mgr. Boston Women's Symphony, 1962-66. Fuller grantee New England Conservatory, 1957, grantee State Mass., 1957. Mem. AAUW, DAR, Nat. Am. Theatre Organ Soc., Ea. Mass. Am. Theatre Organ Soc. (bd. dirs. 1989-92), Organ-Aires (v.p. 1991—), West Dennis Garden Club, Amateur Organists Assn. Internat. Episcopalian. Avocations: painting, playing the organ, swimming, gardening, walking. Home: 145 Cove Rd South Dennis MA 02660-3515 Office: 60 Macarthur Rd Natick MA 01760-2938

ŠUTEJ, VJEKOSLAV, conductor; b. Rijeka, Croatia, July 31, 1951; s. Josip and Alemka (Stefanini) Š.; m. Linela Malici; 1 child Alemka. Degree, Music Acad., Zagreb, Croatia, 1975. Music dir. Opera Split, Split, Croatia, 1985-90, La Fenice, Venice, Italy, 1990-93, Orquesta Simfonica de Sevilla, Seville, Spain, 1991—, Houston Grand Opera, Houston, Tex., 1994—. Home: 510 Preston HGO Houston TX 77002-1954 Office: Houston Grand Opera 510 Preston St Houston TX 77002-1504

SUTER, ALBERT EDWARD, manufacturing company executive; b. East Orange, N.J., Sept. 18, 1935; s. Joseph Vincent and Catherine (Clay) S.; m. Michaela Sams Suter, May 28, 1966; children: Christian C., Bradley J., Allison A. BME, Cornell U., 1957, MBA, 1959. Pres., chief exec. officer L.B. Knight & Assocs., Chgo., 1959-79; v.p. internat. Emerson Electric Co., St. Louis, 1979-80, pres. motor div., 1980-87, group v.p., 1981-83, exec. v.p., 1983-87, vice chmn., 1987; pres., chief operating officer, dir. Firestone Tire & Rubber Co., Akron, Ohio, 1987-88; pres., chief operating officer Whirlpool Corp., Benton Harbor, Mich., from 1988; exec. v.p. Emerson Electric Co., St. Louis, until 1990, pres., COO, 1990-92, sr. vice chmn., COO, 1992—; bd. dirs. NationsBank Corp. (formerly Boatmen's Bancshares, Inc.). Bd. dirs. Jr. Achievement Nat. Bd., Colorado Springs, Colo., Jr. Achievement Miss. Valley, St. Louis Sci. Ctr. Bd.; chmn. Torch div. St. Louis chpt. United Way, 1982-86. Mem. Glenview (Ill.) Country Club, St. Louis Club, Old Warson Country Club , Log Cabin Club. Republican. Episcopalian. Office: Emerson Electric Co PO Box 4100 Saint Louis MO 63136-8506

SUTER, JON MICHAEL, academic library director, educator; b. Holdenville, Okla., Oct. 30, 1941; s. Franklin Hyatt and Erma (Abee) S. BA cum laude, East Cen. State Coll., 1963; MLS, U. Okla., 1964; PhD, Ind. U., 1973. Asst. libr. East Cen. State Coll., Ada, Okla., 1964-76; assoc. libr. East Cen. U., Ada, Okla., 1976-84; dir. libr. Houston Bapt. U., 1984—; chmn. Libr. Edn. Div. Okla. Libr. Assn., 1981, Coll. Rsch. Libr. Div., Okla., 1982. Contbr. articles to profl. jours. Pres. Ada Camp Gideons Internat., 1980-82. Higher Edn. Act fellow Ind. U., 1969-71. Mem. Popular Culture Assn., Richard III Socl., Med. Acad., Renaissance Soc., Patristics Soc. Republican. Baptist. Avocations: comic books, medieval history. Home: 8271 Wednesbury Ln Houston TX 77074-2918 Office: Houston Bapt U - Moody Libr 7502 Fondren Rd Houston TX 77074-3204

SUTER, WILLIAM KENT, federal court administrator, former army officer, lawyer; b. Portsmouth, Ohio, Aug. 24, 1937; s. William Chauncey Suter and Ruth Margaret Fritz; m. Margaret Jean Bogart, May 23, 1959; children: William B., Charles W. BA in Social Scis., Trinity U., San Antonio, 1959; LLB, Tulane U., 1962. Bar: La. 1962, U.S. Supreme Ct. 1967, D.C. 1988. Commd. 1st lt. U.S. Army, 1962, advanced through grades to maj. gen., 1985; comdt. JAG Sch., Charlottesville, Va., 1981-84; chief judge Legal Svcs. Agy., Falls Church, Va., 1984-85; asst. JAG Dept. Army, Washington, 1985-89, JAG, 1989-91; ret. U.S. Army, 1991; clk. U.S. Supreme Ct., Washington, 1991—. Mem. ABA, Fed. Bar Assn., Federalist Soc. Presbyterian. Home: 5917 Reservoir Heights Ave Alexandria VA 22311-1017 Office: US Supreme Ct 1 First St NE Washington DC 20543

SUTERA, SALVATORE PHILIP, mechanical engineering educator; b. Balt., Jan. 12, 1933; s. Philip and Ann (D'Amico) S.; m. Celia Ann Fielden, June 21, 1958; children: Marie-Anne, Annette Nicole, Michelle Cecile. B.S. in Mech. Engring, Johns Hopkins, 1954; postgrad., U. Paris, 1955-56; M.S., Calif. Inst. Tech., 1955; Ph.D., Cal. Inst. Tech., 1960; M.A. (hon.), Brown U., 1965. Asst. prof. mech. engring. Brown U., Providence, 1960-65; asso. prof. Brown U., 1965-68, exec. officer div. engring., 1966-68; prof. dept. mech. engring. Washington U., St. Louis, 1968-97, chmn. dept., 1968-82, 86-97, Spencer T. Olin prof. engring. and applied sci., 1997—; vis. prof. U. Paris VI, 1973. Assoc. editor: Jour. Biochem. Engring.; mem. editorial bd. Circulation Rsch., 1975-82. Fulbright fellow Paris, 1955. Fellow ASME, Am. Inst. of Med and Biol. Engring. (founding); mem. ASHRAE, Biomed. Engring. Soc., Am. Acad. Mechanics, Internat. Soc. Biorheology, N.Am. Soc. Biorheology (pres.-elect 1986-89, pres. 1989-90), Am. Soc. Artificial Internal Organs, Am. Soc. Engring. Edn., AAAS, AIAA (Lindbergh award St. Louis sect. 1988), Tau Beta Pi, Pi Tau Sigma. Republican. Roman Catholic. Research in fluid mechanics, heat transfer, blood flow, rheology of suspensions. Home: 830 S Meramec Ave Saint Louis MO 63105-2539

SUTHERLAND, ALAN ROY, foundation administrator; b. N.Y.C., Jan. 15, 1944; s. Arthur Abbott and Margaret Louise (Schweitzer) S. BFA, Pratt Inst., Bklyn., 1964; MPA, NYU, 1969, PhD, 1984. Personnel dir. Manhattan Psychiat. Ctr., N.Y.C., 1966-72; dep. dir. Rockland Children's Psychiat. Ctr., Orangeburg, N.Y., 1972-74; dep. dir. L.I. Devel. Ctr., Melville, N.Y., 1974-78, dir., 1978-80; personnel dir. Kiamesha (N.Y.) Concord, Inc., 1982-83; program dir. Vols. Am., N.Y.C., 1983-86; sr. staff officer Nat. Acad. Scis., Washington, 1986-88; dep. dir. U.S. Interagy. Coun. on Homeless, Washington, 1988-89; exec. dir. Travelers Aid Internat., Washington, 1989-91, AIDS Ctr. of Queens County, Rego Park, N.Y., 1992-96; exec. v.p. Am. Immigration Law Found., Washington, 1997—. Editor: Homlessness, Health and Human Service Needs. Recipient citation N.Y.C. Coun., 1986. Mem. ASPA, World Futurist Soc. Lutheran. Avocation: weightlifting. Home: 1617 15th St NW Washington DC 20009-3801 Office: 1400 Eye St NW Fl 12 Washington DC 20005-2208

SUTHERLAND, BRUCE, composer, pianist; b. Daytona Beach, Fla.; s. Kenneth Francis and Norma (Williams) S.; Mus.B. cum laude, U. So. Calif., 1957, Mus.M., 1959; studies with Halsey Stevens, Ellis Kohs, Ethel Leginska, Amparo Iturbi. Harpsichord soloist with Telemann Trio in concert tour, 1969-70; tchr. master class for pianists U. Tex., Austin, 1971; dir. Bach festivals Music Tchrs. Assn. Calif., 1972-73, dir. Artists of Tomorrow Music Festivals Music Tchrs. Assn. Calif., 1984-88, compositions performed in numerous contemporary music festivals in U.S., 1957—; piano faculty Calif. State U. at Northridge, 1977—; tchr. master class for pianists UCLA, 1995—, adjudicator music competitions and auditions Nat. Guild Piano Tchrs. U. So. Calif., 1996, others; dir. Brentwood-Westwood Symphony ann. competition for young artists, 1981-88; composer: Allegro Fanfara for Orch., world premiere conducted by José Iturbi with Bridgeport Symphony Orch., 1970; Saxophone Quartet, 1971; Quintet for Flute, Strings, Piano, 1972; Notturno for Flute and Guitar, 1973; also string trio, piano and vocal works. Recipient grand prize Internat. Competition Louis Moreau Gottschalk, 1970; Stairway of Stars award Music Arts Soc., Santa Monica, 1973; named one of Los Angeles' Finest Piano Tchrs., New West Mag., 1977; honored as Dist. Tchr. of Anders Martinson, presdl. scholar in arts, 1991, Disting. Tchr. White House Commn. on Presidential Scholars, 1991; honored by Nat. Found. Advancement Arts 1989, 91, 93. Mem. Nat. Assn. Am. Composers and Condrs., Music Tchrs. Nat. Assn., Music Tchrs. Assn., Calif. Assn. Profl. Music Tchrs., Pi Kappa Lambda.

SUTHERLAND, DENISE JACKSON (DENISE SUZANNE JACKSON), ballerina; b. N.Y.C., Oct. 19, 1951; d. John Henry and Audrey Kepple J.; m. Donald James Sutherland, July 22, 1985; 1 child, Conor. Grad., Profl. Children's Sch., 1969; student, Am. Ballet Ctr.; studied with, Robert Joffrey, Maggie Black, David Howard. Joined Joffrey Ballet, 1969, leading ballerina; ret., 1986; chmn., bd. trustees Profl. Children's Sch., 1987—;cons. to dance program Nat. Endowment for Arts, 1991—; trustee Joffrey Ballet, 1986-90, bd. of Vistors N.C. Sch. Arts, 1993—. Featured in three Dance in Am. programs PBS; video dictionary of Classical Ballet, guest artist with N.Y.C. Opera, Detroit Symphony, numerous regional ballet cos., in fundraising galas Met. Opera House. Trustee Dance Notation Bur., 1985-87. Home: PO Box 154 Glen Head NY 11545-0154

SUTHERLAND, DONALD, actor; b. St. John, N.B., Can., July 17, 1935; m. Lois Hardwick; m. 2d, Shirley Douglas; children: Kiefer, Rachel; m. 3d, Francine Racette; children: Roeg, Rossif, Angus. Grad., U. Toronto, 1958. Actor: London Acad. Music and Dramatic Art, Perth Repertory Theatre, Scotland, also Nottingham, Chesterfield, Bronley, Sheffield, (plays) The Spoon River Anthology, The Male Animal, The Tempest, August for People (London debut), On a Clear Day You Can See Canterbury, The Shewing Up a Blanco Posnet, (films) The World Ten Times Over, 1963, The Castle of the Living Dead, 1964, Dr. Terror's House of Horrors, 1965, Fanatic, 1965, The Bedford Incident, 1965, Promise Her Anything, 1966, The Dirty Dozen, 1967, Sebastian, 1968, Oedipus the King, 1968, Interlude, 1968, Joanna, 1968, The Split, 1968, Start the Revolution Without Me, 1969, The Act of the Heart, 1970, M*A*S*H, 1970, Kelly's Heroes, 1970, Little Murders, 1970, Alex in Wonderland, 1971, Klute, 1971, Johnny Got His Gun, 1971, Steelyard Blues, 1972, Lady Ice, 1972, Alien Thunder, 1973, Don't Look Now, 1973, S*P*Y*S, 1974, The Day of the Locust, 1975, End of the Game, 1976, Casanova, 1976, 1900, 1976, The Eagle Has Landed, 1977, Animal House, 1978, Invasion of the Body Snatchers, 1978, The Great Train Robbery, 1979, The Kentucky Fried Movie, 1978, Murder by Decree, 1979, Bear Island, 1979, A Man, A Woman and a Bank, 1980, Nothing Personal, 1980, Ordinary People, 1980, Eye of the Needle, 1981, Gas, 1981, The Disappearance, Blood Relative, Threshold, 1983, Max Dugan Returns, 1983, Crackers, 1984, Heaven Help Us, 1985, Revolution, 1985, The Trouble with Spies, 1987, The Wolf at the Door, 1987, Apprentice to Murder, 1988, The Rosary Murders, 1988, Lock Up, 1989, Lost Angels, 1989, A Dry White Season, 1989, Backdraft, 1991, JFK, 1991, Eminent Domain, 1991, Buffy the Vampire Slayer, 1992, Younger and Younger, 1993, Shadow of the Wolf, 1993, Six Degrees of Separation, 1993, The Puppet Masters, 1994, Quicksand, Disclosure, 1994, Outbreak, 1995, Bethune: The Making of a Hero, FTA; TV shows and movies include Marching to the Sea, The Death of Bessie Smith, Hamlet at Elsinore, The Saint, The Avengers, Gideon's Way, The Champions, The Winter of Our Discontent, 1984, Ordeal By Innocence, 1985, Buster's Bedroom, Citizen X, 1995 (Emmy award). Decorated officier dans l'Ordre des Artes et des Lettres (France); officer Order of Can. Office: PMK care Katherine Olin 955 Carrillo Dr Los Angeles CA 90048-5400 also: 760 N La Cienega Blvd Los Angeles CA 90069-5231

SUTHERLAND, DONALD GRAY, lawyer; b. Houston, Jan. 19, 1929; s. Robert Gray and Elizabeth (Cunningham) S.; m. Mary Reynolds Moodey, July 23, 1955; children: Stuart Gray, Elizabeth Dana. BS, Purdue U., 1954; LLB, Ind. U., Bloomington, 1954. Bar: Ind. 1954, U.S. Dist. Ct. (so. dist.) Ind. 1954, U.S. Tax Ct. 1956, U.S. Ct. Claims 1957, U.S. Ct. Appeals (7th cir.) 1981, U.S. Ct. Appeals (3d cir.) 1984, U.S. Ct. Internat. Trade 1987, U.S. Supreme Ct. 1987. Assoc. Ice Miller Donadio & Ryan, Indpls., 1954-64, ptnr., 1965—; practitioner in residence Ind. U. Sch. of Law, Bloomington, 1987; trustee, pres. Pegasus Funds, Detroit; trustee, chmn. bd. dirs., pres. Bison Money Market Fund., Indpls., 1982-92. Contbr. articles to numerous profl. jours. Bd. dirs., v.p. Japan-Am. Soc. of Ind., Inc., Indpls., 1988—; bd. dirs. Conner Prairie Inc., Fishers, Ind., 1988—, v.p., 1989-90, chmn. bd., 1990-93; tennis ceremonies 10th Pan-Am. Games, Indpls., 1987; bd. dirs. The Children's Bur. Indpls., 1962-73, v.p., 1968-70, pres., 1970-72; bd. dirs. Orchard Country Day Sch., Indpls., 1970-73, Episc. Cmty. Svcs., Indpls., 1965-73, v.p., 1968, pres., 1969; trustee United Episc. Charities, Indpls., 1970-71, pres., 1971. Cpl. USMC, 1946-48. Mem. ABA, Internat. Bar Assn., Ind. State Bar Assn., Indpls. Bar Assn., Woodstock Club, Econ. Club (bd. dirs. Ind. chpt. 1988-94). Republican. Avocations: tennis, opera. Office: Ice Miller Donadio & Ryan 1 American Sq Box 82001 Indianapolis IN 46282-0002

SUTHERLAND, DONALD JAMES, investment company executive; b. Teaneck, N.J., Jan. 2, 1931; s. Conrad James and LaVinia Marie (Peters) S.; m. Denise Jackson, July 22, 1985; children: Paige, Donald, Shelley, Julie, Conor. A.B., Princeton U., 1953; M.B.A., Harvard U., 1958; LH.D (hon.), St..Michael's Coll., 1981. Regional sales mgr. Dahlstrom Corp., Jamestown, 1958-60; assoc. McKinsey & Co., N.Y.C., 1961-64; v.p. Laird, Inc., N.Y.C., 1965-67, New Court Securities Corp., N.Y.C., 1968-70; pres. Quincy Assocs., Inc., N.Y.C., 1970-75; pres., corp. gen. ptnr. Quincy Ptnrs., Glen Head, N.Y., 1975—; chmn. bd. Crane Hoist Engring. Corp., 1975-79, Am. Spring & Wire Splty. co., Inc., 1977-82, Muehlhausen Bros. Spring & Mfg. Co., Inc., 1977-82, Lewis Spring & Mfg. Co., Inc., 1979-82, Ohio Locomotive Crane Co., Inc., 1981-86, Water Products Co., 1988-89, Publix Shirt Co., L.P., 1979-91, Quincy Packaging Group, L.P., 1984-91, Will & Baumer, Inc., 1984-94, Quincy Spring Group, Inc., 1986-94, Quincy Techs., Inc., 1987—, PCI Group, Inc., 1987-93, Perfection Forms Corp., 1990-94, Tectron Tube Corp., 1991-95, The Lion Brewery Inc., 1993—, Cavert Wire Co., Inc., 1994—; chmn. bd., pres. Ala. Metal Products Co. Inc., 1976-77. Contbr. articles to profl. jours. Trustee Sheltering Arms Children's Svc., 1973-75, St. Michael's Coll., 1972—, Cancer Rsch. Inst., 1984—, Joffrey Ballet, 1982-91, pres. 1985-87, Barry Goldwater Scholarship and Excellence in Edn. Found., 1991—, Hofstra U., 1992—; mem. vis. com. Fordham Bus. Sch., 1987—, Villa I Tatti Coun., 1991—, The New Sch., 1992—, Muhlenberg Coll., 1992—, steering com. Human Rights Watch, Helsinki, 1996—; adv. bd. World Policy Inst., 1996—; Nassau County (N.Y.) Planning Commn., 1965-68, Internat. Coun. of World Monuments Fund, 1991—. Lt. (j.g.) USN, 1953-56. Mem. The Creek (gov. 1987—, treas. 1991-93), Cap and Gown (trustee 1981—), The Links, Beaver Dam Winter Sports Club, Econ. Club of N.Y.C. Democrat. Roman Catholic. Office: PO Box 154 Glen Head NY 11545-0154

SUTHERLAND, DONALD WOOD, cardiologist; b. Kansas City, Mo., July 29, 1932; s. Donald Redeker and Mary Frances (Wood) S.; m. Margaret Sutherland, Sept. 11, 1954 (div. 1994); children: Kathleen Massar, Ellen Baltus, Richard, Ann, Julia McMurchie; m. Roslyn Ruggiero Elms, Mar. 31, 1995. BA, Amherst Coll., 1953; MD, Harvard U., 1957. Intern, resident Mass. Gen. Hosp., Boston, 1957-60; fellow in cardiology U. Oreg., Portland, 1961-63; pvt. practice Portland, 1963—; assoc. clin. prof. medicine Oreg. Health Sci. U., Portland, 1967—; chief of staff St. Vincent Hosp. and Med. Ctr., Portland, 1971-72. Contbr. articles to profl. jours. Fellow Am. Heart Assn., Am. Coll. Cardiology (pres. Oreg. chpt. 1972); mem. Multnomah Athletic Club, North Pacific Soc. Internal Medicine (pres. 1985), Pacific Interurban Clin. Club. Avocations: flying private planes, scuba diving. Home: 4405 SW Council Crest Dr Portland OR 97201-1534 Office: Columbia Cardiology Ltd 9155 SW Barnes Rd Ste 233 Portland OR 97225-6629

SUTHERLAND, FRANK, publishing executive, editor; b. Mount Juliet, Tenn., May 31, 1945; s. Ernest Franklin Sr. and Fontelle (Moore) S.; m. Natilee Duning; children: Kate, Daniel. BA, Vanderbilt U., 1970. Reporter The Tennessean, Nashville, Tenn., 1963-77, zone editor, 1977-78, city editor, 1978-82, v.p., news editor, 1989—; editor The Shreveport (La.) Times, 1988-89; mng. editor The Hattiesburg (Miss.) Am., 1982-86; exec. editor The Jackson (Tenn.) Sun, 1986-88. Mem. Soc. Profl. Journalists (middle Tenn. chpt. pres. 1974-81, nat. bd. dirs. 1974, nat. treas. 1981, sec. 1982, pres.-elect 1983, pres. 1984-85), Am. Soc. Newspaper Editors (mem. steering com., reporters com. for freedom of press 1979-82). Office: The Tennessean 1100 Broadway Nashville TN 37203-3116

SUTHERLAND, GAIL RUSSELL, retired industrial equipment manufacturing company executive; b. Rush Lake, Wis., Dec. 20, 1923; s. Gail Marion and Edith (Grueb) S.; m. Leone Marie Witkowski, Mar. 10, 1945; children: Keith Allan, Glenn Elliott. BS in Agr., U. Wis., Madison, 1947, BSME, 1948, MS in Agrl. Engring., 1949. Div. engr. Deere & Co., Ottumwa, Iowa, 1949-63; mgr. product engring. Deere & Co., Des Moines, 1963-77; dir. product planning Deere & Co., Moline, Ill., 1977-80, dir. product engring. planning, 1980-83, dir. product engring., 1983-84, v.p. engring., 1984-86, v.p. engring. and tech., 1986-87. Mem. editorial adv. bd. Mfg. Engring. Mag., 1987; inventor: cotton harvester blower discharge, combine soybean header, beet harvester flail feeder, pasture renovator cutter. Served as ensign USN, 1943-46. Mem. Nat. Acad. Engring., Am. Soc. Agrl. Engrs. (Engr. of Yr. 1980, Disting. Engr. of Yr. 1983), Soc. Automotive Engrs., Am. Nat. Standards Inst. (bd. dirs. 1984-86). Republican. Home and Office: 16 Mason Ln Bella Vista AR 72715-5548

SUTHERLAND, GEORGE LESLIE, retired chemical company executive; b. Dallas, Aug. 13, 1922; s. Leslie and Madge Alice (Henderson) S.; m. Mary Gail Hamilton, Sept. 9, 1961 (dec. Mar. 1984); children: Janet Leslie, Gail Irene, Elizabeth Hamilton; m. Carol Brenda Kaplan, Feb. 19, 1986. BA, U. Tex., Austin, 1943, MA, 1947, PhD, 1950. With Am. Cyanamid Co., various locations, 1951-87; asst. dir. research and devel. Princeton, N.J., 1969-70, dir. research and devel., agr. div., 1970-73; v.p. med. research and devel. Pearl River, N.Y., 1973-86, dir. med. research div., 1978-86, dir. chem. research div., 1980-81; v.p. corp. research tech. Pearl River, 1986-87. Served with USN, 1944-46. Mem. Assn. Research Dirs. (pres. 1975-76), AAAS, Am. Chem. Soc. Home: 42 Sky Meadow Rd Suffern NY 10901-2519

SUTHERLAND, DAME JOAN, retired soprano; b. Sydney, Australia, Nov. 7, 1926; d. McDonald S.; m. Richard Bonynge, 1954; 1 son. Student, Royal Coll. Music, London, 1951. Appeared concert and oratorio performances, Australia; appeared in: opera Judith, Syndey Conservatory of Music; debut Covent Garden in Magic Flute, 1952; Italian debut in Handel's Alcina, Teatro la Fenice, Venice, 1960, Bellini's Puritani, Glyndebourne Festival, Sussex, Eng., 1960, Bellini's Beatrice di Tenda, La Scala, 1961, Rossini's Semiramide, La Scala, 1962, Meyerbeer's Les Huguenots, La Scala, 1962, N.Y. debut, Carnegie Hall, 1961; Opera debut Lucia, 1961; opened Sutherland-Williamson Opera Co. tour, Australia, 1965; appeared: Handel's Julius Caesar, Hamburg Opera, 1969, Bellini's Norma, Met Opera, 1970, opened, Lyric Opera Chgo. with, Semiramide, 1971, San Francisco Opera with, Norma, 1972, San Francisco Opera with, Trovatore, 1975, Met. Opera with, I Puritani, 1976, Vancouver Opera with, Le Roi de Lahore, 1977; premiered new prodn., Met. Opera in, Tales of Hoffmann, 1973; 1st prodn. in Am. in 80 years Esclarmonde, Massenet, San Fancisco Opera, 1974; author: (with Richard Bonynge) The Joan Sutherland Album, 1986. Decorated Order of Merit, comdr. and dame comdr. Order Brit. Empire, 1991; Companion, Order Australia, 1991; recipient Grammy award for best classical vocal soloist, 1981. Fellow Royal Coll. Music. Office: care Ingpen & Williams, 26 Wadham Rd, London SW15 2LR, England also: care Colbert Artist Mgmt 111 W 57th St New York NY 10019-2211

SUTHERLAND, KIEFER, actor; b. London, Eng., Dec. 21, 1966; s. Donald and Shirley Douglas S.; m. Camelia Kath, Sept. 12, 1986 (div.); children: Michelle Kath, Sarah. Appearances include (theater) debut in Throne of Straw, 1977, (films) Max Dugan Returns, 1983, The Bay Boy, 1984 (Genie award nominee 1984), At Close Range, 1986, Crazy Moon, 1986, Stand By Me, 1986, The Lost Boys, 1987, The Killing Time, 1987, Promised Land, 1987, 1969, 1988, Bright Lights, Big City, 1988, Young Guns, 1988, Renegades, 1989, Chicago Joe and the Showgirl, 1990, Flashback, 1990, Flatliners, 1990, The Nutcracker Prince (voice), 1990, Young Guns II, 1990, Article 99, 1991, Twin Peaks: Fire Walk With Me, 1992, A Few Good Men, 1992, The Vanishing, 1993, The Three Musketeers, 1993, The Cowboy Way, 1994, Eye for an Eye, 1995, A Time to Kill, 1996, The Last Days of Frankie the Fly, 1996, Freeway, 1996, Truth or Consequences N.M, 1997, Dark City, 1997; (TV movies) Trapped in Silence, 1986, Brotherhood of Justice, 1986, Last Light, 1993. Office: Internat Creative Mgmt 8942 Wilshire Blvd Beverly Hills CA 90211*

SUTHERLAND, MALCOLM READ, JR., clergyman, educator; b. Detroit, Nov. 11, 1916; s. Malcolm Read and Edith Ione (Osborne) S.; m. Mary Anne Beaumont, Dec. 23, 1943; children: Malcolm Read III, Maryanne B. AB, Miami (Ohio) U., 1938; MS, Western Res. U., 1941; BD, Fed. Theol. Faculty U. Chgo., 1945; LLD, Emerson Coll., 1963; LHD, Meadville-Lombard Theol. Sch., 1975. Ordained to ministry Unitarian Universalist Assn., 1945. Dir. boys work Goodrich Social Settlement, Cleve., 1938-40; housing mgr. Cleve. Met. Housing Authority, 1940-41; regional housing supr. Farm Security Adminstrn., 1941-42; housing mgmt. supr. FPHA, 1942-43; pastor in Ill., Va., Mass., 1944-60; exec. v.p. Am. Unitarian Assn., 1959-61; Robert Collier prof. ch. and soc., pres., dean faculty Meadville Theol. Sch. of Lombard Coll., Chgo., 1960-75; minister Harvard (Mass.) Unitarian Ch., 1975-94, min. emeritus, 1994—; minister emeritus Thomas Jefferson Meml. Ch., Charlottesville, Va., 1985—; adj. prof. dept. ministry Andover Newton Theol. Sch., 1992—; exec. dir. U.S. Com. World Conf. on Religion and Peace, N.Y.C., 1980-83, internat. coun., 1984—, also v.p. U.S. exec. coun.; bd. dirs. Unitarian Universalist Svc. Com., Beacon Press; chmn. editl. adv. com. bd. Christian Register, 1955-60; field rep. Unitarian Svc. Com., Mex., 1950-51; mem. sr. secretariat World Conf. Religion and Peace, Kyoto, 1970 and del. to Louvain, 1974, Princeton, 1979, Nairobi, 1984, Melbourne, Australia, 1989, Reva del Garda, Italy, 1994, hon. pres., 1994—; cons. Niwano Peace Found., Tokyo, 1982-96; lectr., del. Japan-U.S. consultation on peace Internat. Assn. for Religious Freedom, 1970; trustee Dana McLean Greeley Found. for Peace and Justice, 1986-94, trustee emeritus, 1994—; Thomas Minns lectr., Boston, 1955, Charlottesville, Va., 1978, Berry St., lectr., Boston, 1956; Harvard chair lectr. Warner Free Lectrs., 1985, 93; chmn. common. coun. Chgo. Cluster of Theol. Schs., inc., 1970-74; pres. Inst. on Religion in an Age of Sci., 1969, 75-77, hon. v.p., 1980—, acad. fellow, 1988; bd. dirs., sec. Ctr. for Advanced Study Religion and Sci., Chgo., 1965—. Author: Personal Faith, 1955, Creators of the Dawn, 1979, Star Light, Star Bright, 1993; co-chmn. publs. bd. jour. religion and sci. Zygon, 1964—; also articles. Bd. govs. Harris Manchester Coll., Oxford U., 1968—, hon. fellow, 1974—. Recipient Disting. Svc. award Charlottesville (Va.) Jr. C. of C., 1949, Disting. Svc. award Internat. Assn. Religious Freedom, 1975, Disting. Svc.award Konko Kyo Chs. Am., 1975. Mem. Unitarian Universalist Ministers Assn., Phi Delta Theta, Phi Mu Alpha, Alpha Kappa Delta, Omicron Delta Kappa. Club: Bucks Harbor Yacht (Maine) (commodore 1979-81). Home: 21 Woodside Rd Harvard MA 01451-1616

SUTHERLAND, MICHAEL CRUISE, librarian; b. Morgantown, W.Va., Aug. 29, 1938; s. Charles Fish and Mildred (Haymond) S. BA in English, San Fernando Valley State U., 1967, postgrad., 1968-69; postgrad., UCLA, 1967, MLS, 1970. Office asst., clk. Lindsay & Hall, L.A., 1959-60; libr. asst. I, bindery clk. Biomed. Libr. UCLA, 1961-65; jr. adminstrv. asst. Dept. Pub. Works City of L.A., 1967; intermediate clk. typist San Fernando Valley State U., Northridge, Calif., 1967-69; libr. I, tchg. asst. Grad. Sch. Libr. and Info. Sci. UCLA, 1970; spl. collections libr. Occidental Coll., L.A., 1970—; attendee numerous workshops and seminars; organizer Western Books Exhbn. at various librs. throughout the Western U.S., 1992, 96; judging organizer, 1993. Author numerous exhbn. catalog booklets; author: (with others) Encyclopedia of Library and Information Sciences, 1979, Western Books Exhibition Catalog, 1986, Striking Research Gold: Distinguished Collections in California Independent Academic Libraries, 1988; contbr. articles to profl. jours. Active Neighborhood Watch, AIDS Quilt Program. Mem. ALA (rare books and manuscripts divsn.), Assn. Coll. and Rsch. Librs., Rounce and Coffin Club (sec., treas.), Robinson Jeffers Assn., Tor House Found., Zamorano Club. Office: Occidental Coll Mary Clapp Libr 1600 Campus Rd Los Angeles CA 90041-3314

SUTHERLAND, RAYMOND CARTER, clergyman, English educator emeritus; b. Horse Cave, Ky., Nov. 5, 1917; s. Raymond Carter and Nellie Ruth (Veluzat) S. A.B., U. Ky., 1939, M.A., 1950, Ph.D., 1953; grad., Gen. Theol. Sem., N.Y.C., 1942; postgrad., St. John's Theol. Sem., Camarillo, Calif., 1948, Gen. Theol. Sem., N.Y.C., 1979. Ordained priest Episcopal Ch., 1942, reactivated, 1985; curate St. Luke's Ch., Anchorage, Louisville, 1942-44; prof. English U. Tenn., Knoxville, 1953-57; mem. faculty Ga. State U., Atlanta, 1957-84; prof. English Ga. State U., 1965-84, dir. English grad. studies, 1978-84, prof. emeritus, 1985—; lectr. Oriental ceramics, events in nature as prototypes for classical myths, China's dragon in Pensee; spkr., panel Ga. State U. Author: Medieval English Conceptions of Hell as Derived from Biblical, Patristic and Native Germanic Sources, 1953, The Religious Background of Swift's Tale of a Tub, 1958, The Mechanics of Verification, 1963, 64-72; author of Japanese haiku, 1960-65; contbr. articles to profl. jours. Served as chaplain AUS, 1944-47. Omicron Delta Kappa disting. prof., 1979-80. Mem. Alumni Assn. Gen. Theol. Sem., Am. Assn. Advancement Humanities, Medieval Acad. Am., MLA, New Chaucer Soc., Heraldry Soc. Eng., Oriental Ceramics Soc. Eng., Ky. Hist. Soc., Hart County Hist. Soc., Phi Kappa Phi, Omicron Delta Kappa. Office: care Episcopal Diocese of Atlanta 2744 Peachtree Rd NW Atlanta GA 30305-2937

SUTHERLAND, ROBERT L., engineering company executive, educator; b. Fellsmere, Fla., May 15, 1916; s. John Alexander and Georgia Myrtle (Legg) S.; m. Mary-Alice Reed, May 18, 1945; children: Rober Hynes (dec.), Wayne Muzzy, Connie Anne, Nancy Lee, John Gary. B.S., U. Ill., 1939, M.S., 1948. Registered profl. engr., Ill., Iowa, Wyo. Devel. engr. Firestone Tire & Rubber Co., Akron, Ohio, 1939-41; research engr. Borg & Beck div. Borg-Warner Corp., Chgo, 1941; test engr. Buick Motor Div. Gen. Motors Corp., Melrose Park, Ill., 1942-43; sr. engr. research dept. Aeronca Aircraft Corp., Middletown, Ohio, 1943-45; research asso. Coll. Engring., U. Ill., 1945-48; asst., then asso. prof. mech. engring. State U. Iowa, Iowa City, 1948-58; city engr. Coralville, Iowa, 1950-53; prof. mech. engring. U. Wyo., Laramie, 1958-80; prof. emeritus U. Wyo., 1980—, head dept., 1960-70, rsch. assoc., 1989-92; pres. Skyline Engring. Co. Inc., Laramie, 1972—; research engr. Collins Radio Co., Cedar Rapids, Iowa, summer 1954, cons. engr., 1950-56; staff engr. Environ. Test Lab., Martin Co., Denver, summer 1960; dir. Hunter Mfg. Co., Iowa City, 1955-58, sec. bd., 1956-58. Author: Engineering Systems Analysis, 1958, History of the University of Wyoming College of Engineering 1893-1993, 1993; contbr. articles to profl. jours. Bus. adviser mfg. group Jr. Achievement, Middletown, 1943-44; mem. Iowa City Sch. Study Coun., 1956-58; mem. Civil Air Patrol, Chgo., 1941-43, Laramie, Wyo., 1995—; legis. fellow to Nat. Conf. State Legislatures, 1982-84. Co-recipient Richard L. Templin award ASTM, 1952. Fellow ASME (life, regional v.p. 1965-67); mem. Soc. Automotive Engrs., Sigma Xi, Sigma Tau, Pi Tau Sigma, Tau Beta Pi. Methodist (steward, chmn. ofcl. bd. 1964-65, trustee 1966-69, pres. bd. 1967-69, lay leader 1969-72, chmn. council ministries 1973-75, chmn. finance com. 1975-79). Club: Kiwanian (dir. Laramie chpt. 1963-65, 79-82, pres. 1966, div. lt. gov. 1970-71, life mem. 1978). Home: 1420 Sanders Dr Laramie WY 82070-4710

SUTHERLAND, WILLIAM OWEN SHEPPARD, English language educator; b. Wilmington, N.C., Jan. 19, 1921; s. William Owen Sheppard and Mary Owen (Green) S.; m. Madeline Ethel Cooley, Sept. 12, 1947; children: Madeline, William, John, Thomas. A.B. in English with honors, U. N.C., 1942, M.A., 1947, Ph.D., 1950. Instr. English U. N.C., Chapel Hill, 1950-51; instr. Northwestern U., Chgo., 1951-54; asst. prof. U. Tex., Austin, 1954-58, assoc. prof., 1958-65, prof., 1965—, chmn. dept., 1983-90, faculty humanist rep. Deans of Humanities of Southwest Conf., 1980; cons. Ednl. Testing Svc. and Coll. Bd., Princeton, N.J., 1965-72, NEH, Washington, 1978—. Author: Art of the Satirist, 1965; co-editor: The Reader, 1960, Six Contemporary Novels, 1961; index An Index to 18th Century Periodicals, 1800, 1956. Served to capt. C.E. U.S. Army, 1942-45. Recipient Scarborough Excellence in Tchg. award U. Tex. Austin, 1959, Liberal Arts Pro Bene Meritis award, 1996, Pres. Assocs. Tchg. award, 1982; NEH grantee, 1978-79. Mem. MLA, South Central MLA (exec. com. 1967-69), AAUP (state v.p. 1970-71), Nat. Council Tchrs. English (dir. 1974-78). Democrat. Episcopalian. Home: 3610 Highland View Dr Austin TX 78731-4033 Office: U Tex Dept English Austin TX 78712

SUTHERLUND, DAVID ARVID, lawyer; b. Stevens Point, Wis., July 20, 1929; s. Arvid E. and Georgia M. (Stickney) S. BA, U. Portland, 1952; JD, U. N.Mex., 1957; postgrad., U. Wis., 1957. Bar: D.C. 1957, U.S. Supreme Ct. 1961. Atty. ICC, Washington, 1957-58; counsel Am. Trucking Assn., Washington, 1958-62; assoc. and ptnr. Morgan, Lewis & Bockius, Washington and Phila., 1962-72; ptnr. Fulbright & Jaworski, Washington and Houston, 1975-83; sr. ptnr. Zwerling, Mark & Sutherlund, Washington and

Alexandria, Va., 1987-91; spl. counsel LaRoe, Winn, Moerman & Donovan, Washington, 1983—; prin. Sutherlund & Assocs., Washington, 1989—; bd. dirs., gen. counsel Nat. Film Svc., 1962-75; mem. family div. panel Pub. Defender Svc. for D.C., 1972-76. Founder, chmn. bd. govs. Transp. Law Jour, 1969-74. Vice chmn. Nat. Capitol Area coun. Boy Scouts Am., 1975-78; mem. bd. regents U. Portland, 1985-91. Spl. agt. CIC, U.S. Army, 1952-54. Mem. ABA, Fed. Bar Assn., D.C. Bar Assn., Transp. Lawyers Assn., Am. Arbitration Assn. (nat. panel arbitrators 1970—), Am. Judicature Soc., Internat. Club (Washington), Primsoll Club (New Orleans), Balboa Bay Club (Newport Beach, Calif.). Office: 2600 Virginia Ave NW Ste 1000 Washington DC 20037-1905

SUTIN, NORMAN, chemistry educator, scientist; b. Ceres, Republic of South Africa; came to U.S., 1956; s. Louis and Clara (Goldberg) S.; m. Bonita Sakowski, June 29, 1958; children: Lewis Anthony, Cara Ruth. B.Sc., U. Cape Town (S. Africa), 1948, M.Sc., 1950; Ph.D., Cambridge U. (Eng.), 1953. Research fellow Durham U. (Eng.), 1954-55; research assoc. Brookhaven Nat. Lab., Upton, N.Y., 1956-57, assoc. chemist, 1958-61; chemist Brookhaven Nat. Lab., 1961-66, sr. chemist, 1966—, dept. chmn., 1988-95; affiliate Rockefeller U., N.Y.C., 1958-62; vis. fellow Weizmann Inst., Rehovoth, Israel, 1965; vis. prof. SUNY-Stony Brook, 1968, Columbia U., N.Y.C., 1968-69, Tel Aviv U., Israel, 1973-74, U. Calif.-Irvine, 1977, U. Tex. Austin, 1979. Editor: Comments on Inorganic Chemistry Jour., 1980-87; mem. editorial bd. Jour. Am. Chem. Soc., 1985-89, Inorganic Chem., 1986-89, Jour. Phys. Chem., 1987-92; contbr. articles to profl. jours. Mem. NAS, Am. Acad. Arts and Scis., Am. Chem. Soc. (recipient award for disting. svc. in advancement of inorganic chemistry 1983). Office: Brookhaven Nat Lab Dept of Chemistry Upton NY 11973

SUTMAN, FRANCIS XAVIER, university dean; b. Newark, Dec. 20, 1927; s. Joseph L. and Ella (Joyce) S.; m. Mabel Ranagan, Apr. 1, 1956; children—Frank J., Catherine J., Elizabeth A. AB, Montclair State U., 1949, MA, 1952; EdD, Columbia U., 1956. Instr. pub. secondary schs. N.J., 1949-55; instr. chemistry Upsala Coll., 1953-55; asst. prof. Wm. Paterson Coll., 1955-57; chmn., assoc. prof. natural scis. Inter-Am. U. P.R., 1957-58; prof. gen. edn., chmn. SUNY at Buffalo, 1958-62; prof. sci. edn., chmn. dept. secondary edn., dir. Merit Bilingual Center Temple U., 1962-82; dean Coll. Edn., Fairleigh Dickinson U., 1982-87; tech. rsch. staff Exxon Engring. & Rsch. Lab., Linden, N.J., 1955; vis. lectr. Rutgers U.; cons. India AID Project; vis. prof., scientist Hebrew U., Israel; sr. scholar Temple U., 1988—; vis. sci. educator, program dir. edn. and human resources NSF, 1989-93; exec. dir. curriculum devel. coun., Rowan U., N.J., 1993—; del. OAS Coun. Sci. Edn. and Culture, 1971; co-dir. Environ. Edn. Conf. Environ. Protection Svc., Jerusalem, 1975; cons. fed., state, local sch. dists.; dir. spl. tech. project Huazhong U., China, 1980-87; co-dir. chem. edn. conf. Tianjin Normal U., 1984. Author: Concepts in Chemistry, 1962, 2d edit., 1968, What Kind of Environment Will Our Children Have?, 1971, Educating Personnel for Bilingual Settings: Today and Beyond, 1979, Teaching English Through Science, 1985, Improving Learning in Science and Basic Skills Among Diverse Student Populations, 1995. Active Haddonfield (N.J.) Bd. Edn., 1976-79; v.p. alumni bd. Montclair State Coll., 1988. Recipient N.J. Gov.'s Edn. award, 1987, award Hispanic Congress of Pa., 1980, Alumni Citation Montclair State Coll., 1988. Fellow AAAS; mem. NSTA, Am. Chem. Soc., Am. Assn. Colls. Tchr. Edn. (chief instnl. rep. 1968-87), Nat. Assn. Rsch. Sci. Tchg. (pres.), N.J. Gov.'s Acad., Phi Delta Kappa (5 rsch. awards). Home: 128 Stratton Ln Mount Laurel NJ 08054-3301 Office: Temple U 454 Ritter Hall Philadelphia PA 19122 also: Rowan Univ Curriculum Devel Coun Glassboro NJ 08028 *Professional success comes after one accepts the paradoxes of life: willing to accept conflict and criticism, and willing to give of one's self for a cause. But even then timing must be right.*

SUTNICK, ALTON IVAN, dean, educator, researcher, physician; b. Trenton, N.J., July 6, 1928; s. Michael and Rose (Horwitz) S.; m. Mona Reidenberg, Aug. 17, 1958; children: Amy Sutnick Plotch, Gary Benjamin Sutnick. A.B., U. Pa., 1950, M.D., 1954; postgrad. studies in biomed. math., Drexel Inst. Tech., 1961-62; postgrad. studies in biometrics, Temple U., 1969-70. Diplomate Am. Bd. Internal Medicine. Rotating intern Hosp. U. Pa., 1954-55, resident in anesthesiology, 1955-56, resident in medicine, 1956, USPHS postdoctoral research fellow, 1956-57; asst. instr. anesthesiology, then asst. instr. medicine U. Pa. Sch. Medicine, 1955-57; resident in medicine Wishard Meml. Hosp., Indpls., 1957-58; chief resident in medicine Wishard Meml. Hosp., 1960-61; resident instr. medicine Ind. U. Sch. Medicine, Indpls., 1957-58; USPHS postdoctoral research fellow Temple U. Hosp., 1961-63; instr., then assoc. in medicine Temple U. Sch. Medicine, 1962-65; mem. faculty U. Pa. Sch. Medicine, 1965-75, assoc. prof. medicine, 1971-75; clin. asst. physician Pa. Hosp., 1966-71; research physician, then assoc. dir. Inst. Cancer Research, Phila., 1965-75; vis. prof. medicine Med. Coll. Pa., Phila., 1971-74; prof. medicine Med. Coll. Pa., 1975—; dean Allegheny U. of the Health Scis. (formerly Med. Coll. Pa.), 1975-89, sr. v.p., 1976-89; v.p. Ednl. Commn. Fgn. Med. Grads, 1989-95; dir. clin. devel. Am. Oncologic Hosp., Phila., 1973-75; attending physician Phila. VA Hosp., 1967-89, Allegheny U. Hosps., 1971—; cons. in field; mem. U.S. nat. com. Internat. Union Against Cancer, 1969-72; mem. Nat. Conf. Cancer Prevention and Detection, 1973, Nat. Cancer Control Planning Conf., 1973; vice chmn. Gov. Pa. Task Force Cancer Control, 1974-76, chmn. com. cancer detection, 1974-76; mem. health rsch. adv. bd. State of Pa., 1976-78; mem. diagnostic rsch. adv. group Nat. Cancer Inst., 1974-78; chmn. coord. com., comprehensive cancer ctr. program Fox Chase Cancer Ctr., U. Pa. Cancer Ctr., 1975; cons. WHO, Govt. of India, 1979, Govt. of Indonesia, 1980, entire S.E. Asia region, 1981, U. Zimbabwe, 1989, Minister of Health of Poland, 1992, Israel Sci. Coun., 1992, U. Autonoma de Guadalajara, Mex., 1993, Generalitat de Catalunya, Spain, 1993, Ministry of Health Russian Fedn., 1993; mem. Inst. de Pos-Graduacae Medica Carlos Chagas, 1993, Fondazione Smith Kline, Italy, 1995, Assn. Med. Schs. Europe, 1995, U. Jordan, 1995, U.S.-China Ednl. Inst., 1996, Georgian Postgrad. Med. Found., 1996, Instituto Universitario de Ciencias Biomedicas, Argentina, 1996, faculyt of medicine, U. Saarland, Germany, 1996, Ctr. for Med. Edn., Ben Gurion U., Israel, 1996, Hungarian Nat. Health Ins. Fund, 1996, Carelift Internat., 1997, Netherlands and Russian med. schs.; rep. for internat. med. and health scis. edn. Allegheny U. of the Health Scis., 1996—; dir. internat. med. edn. Carelift Internat., 1997—. Author numerous articles in field.; Asst. editor: Annals Internal Medicine, 1972-75; editorial bd. other med. jours. Bd. dirs. Phila. Coun. Internat. Visitors, 1972-77, Israel Cancer Rsch. Fund, 1975-95; nat. bd. dirs. Am. Assocs. Ben Gurion U., 1991—, Phila. divsn., 1986—, assoc. chair, 1993-95; bd. Internat. med. Scholar Program, 1988-89, Sight Savers Internat., 1988-91; trustee Ednl. Commn. Fgn. Med. Grads., 1987-89; adv. commn. Internat. Participation Phila. '76, 1973-76. Capt. M.C. AUS, 1958-60. Recipient Arnold and Marie Schwartz award in medicine AMA, 1976, Torch of Learning award Am. Friends of Hebrew U., 1981, medal Ben Gurion U. of Negev, Israel, 1985, medal U. Cath. de Lille, France, 1987, medal U. Belgrade, Yogoslavia, 1988, Founder's award and medal Med. Coll. Pa., 1989, St. Thomas Aquinas award Santo Tomas U. Med. Alumni Assn., The Philippines, 1989, medal Kiev Med. Inst., Ukraine, 1991, Benjamin Albagli medal Inst. de Pos-Graduacao Medica Carlos Chagas, Brazil, 1993, shield Coll. Physicians and Surgeons, Pakistan, 1993, medal Ukrainian State Med. U., 1994, medal Universidad de Cantabria, Spain, 1994. Fellow ACP, Coll. Physicians Phila. (censor 1977-86 , councillor 1977-86); mem. AMA, AAAS, Am. Fedn. Clin. Research (pres. Temple U. chpt. 1964-65), Am. Assn. Cancer Research, Am. Soc. Clin. Oncology, Am. Dermatoglyphics Assn., Assn. Am. Cancer Insts., Assn. Am. Med. Colls., Northeast Consortium on Med. Edn. (treas. 1983-89, chmn. 1986-87), Council of Deans of Pvt. Free-Standing Med. Schs. (co-founder, nat. chmn. 1983-85), Pa. Council Deans (chmn. 1987-89), Am. Cancer Soc. (vice chmn. service com. Phila. div. 1974-76, bd. dirs. 1974-80, chmn. awards com. 1976), Am. Lung Assn., Am. Heart Assn., NAFSA-Assn. Internat. Educators, Pan Am. Med. Assn., Phila. Coop. Cancer Assn., N.Y. Acad. Scis., Pa. Heart Assn., Heart Assn. Southeastern Pa., Pa. Med. Soc., Phila. County Med. Soc. (chmn. com. internat. med. affairs 1964-72), Pa. Lung Assn., Phila. Assn. for Clin. Trials (bd. dirs. 1980-81), Health Systems Agy. Southeastern Pa. (gov. bd., exec. com. 1983-87, sec. 1985-87), Am. Assn. Ben Gurion U. (bd. dirs. 1986—), Soc. des Medecins Militaires Français, Assn. Med. Edn. in Europe, Soc. Española de Educacion Medica, Internat. Med. Sch. Affiliates Consortium (co-founder, vice chmn. 1985-87), Phi Beta Kappa, Sigma Xi, Alpha Omega Alpha (councillor 1963-65). Discovered assn. of hepatitis B surface antigen with hepatitis; performed 1st studies of pulmonary surfactant in adult human lung disease; developed cancer screening system based on risk status; pioneer in describing non-A non-B hepatitis, pioneer in showing relationship of body iron stores to cancer susceptibility and life expectancy; organized first symposium on problems of foreign medical graduates; coined word "ergasteric" for lab.-contracted disease; responsible for advances in assessment of clinical competence. Office: Sutnick Assocs 2135 Saint James St Philadelphia PA 19103-4804

SUTOWSKI, THOR BRIAN, choreographer; b. Trenton, N.J., Jan. 27, 1945; s. Walter X. and Kathryn (Tang) S.; m. Sonia Arova, Mar. 11, 1965; 1 dau., Ariane. Student San Diego Ballet, 1958-63, San Francisco Ballet, 1963-64, Nat. Ballet, 1964. Cert. solotanzer (solo dancer), Genossenschaft Deutscher Buhnen-Angehorigen, West Germany. Soloist, Norwegian State Opera, Oslo, 1965-70; 1st soloist Hamburgische Staatsoper, Hamburg, Ger., 1970-71; dir. San Diego Ballet, 1971-76, Ballet Ala., Birmingham, 1978-81; dir. State of Ala. Ballet, Birmingham, 1982-83; chmn. Ala. Sch. Fine Arts, Birmingham, 1976-96; assoc. dir. Calif. Ballet Co., San Diego, 1996—; artistic advisor, choreographer Asami Maki Ballet, Toyko, 1976-79; choreographer Atlanta Ballet, 1980-87, resident choreographer Atlanta Ballet Co., 1987-93; dance advisor Ala. State Arts Council, Montgomery, 1977-78; advisor Tenn. Ballet Co.; dance advisor Miss. Arts Council; choreographer Ballet South and State of Ala. Ballet; mem. City of Atlanta Mayor's Review Fellowship panel, 1987; adj. prof. choreography U. Ala., Tuscaloosa, 1988—; commd. choreograher Bavarian State Ballet-State Opera, Munich, 1994. Recipient Pub. TV Emmy award, 1976; Obelisk award for Choreography, 1977, 78, 79, 80; grantee Ford Found., 1964, Nat. Endowment Arts, 1973-74. Mem. Am. Guild Mus. Artists. Republican. Lutheran. Office: Calif Ballet Co 8276 Ronson Rd San Diego CA 92111-2015

SUTPHEN, HAROLD AMERMAN, JR., retired paper company executive; b. Verona, N.J., Feb. 13, 1926; s. Harold Amerman and Marion Esther (Mason) S.; m. Greta May Peterson, June 24, 1950; children—Judith Amerman, Peter Lehmann, Pamela Torrance. Grad., Phillips Exeter Acad., 1944; B.S. in Mech. Engring, Princeton, 1950. With Universal Oil Products Co., Chgo., 1950-51, Texaco, Inc., 1951-52; bus. research analyst Arthur D. Little, Inc., 1952-56; asst. div. mgr. adminstrn., fine papers div. W.Va. Pulp and Paper Co. (name now changed to Westvaco Corp.), 1956-60, v.p., 1967-80, sr. v.p., 1980-88, mgr. fine papers div., 1974-88, dir., 1975-88; v.p., treas. U.S. Envelope Co., Springfield, Mass., 1960-62, pres., CEO, 1962-67, chmn. bd., 1967-74; bd. dirs. Assessment Appeals, Fairfield, Conn., 1993—, chmn. Served with AUS, 1944-46. Mem. Holland Soc. N.Y., Phi Beta Kappa. Clubs: Country of Fairfield (Conn.); Weston (Conn.) Gun. Home: 33 Hill Brook Ln Fairfield CT 06430-7169

SUTTER, BRENT COLIN, hockey player; b. Viking, Alta., Can., June 10, 1962. Hockey player N.Y. Islanders Nat. Hockey League, 1982-92, hockey player Chgo. Blackhawks, 1992—; played in All-Star Game, 1985; mem. Stanley Cup championship team, 1982, 85; capt. N.Y. Islanders, 1987-92. Office: Chgo Blackhawks 1901 W Madison St Chicago IL 60612-2459

SUTTER, ELEANOR BLY, diplomat; b. N.Y.C., Oct. 21, 1945; d. Samuel M. and Sylvia Gertrude Bly; children: Deborah, Willis. BA, Swarthmore Coll., 1966; MA, Am. U., 1978; postgrad., U.S. Army War Coll., 1997. Instr. English Thammasat U., Bangkok and Udornthani Tchr. Tng. Coll., 1967-71, Lomonosov State U., Moscow, 1973-74; rschr. Kennan Inst. for Advanced Russian Studies, 1977-79; fgn. svc. officer Office Soviet Internal Affairs, Dept. of State, 1979-80; fgn. svc. officer U.S. Embassy, Kinshasa, 1980-82, London, 1982-85; fgn. svc. officer Office of Strategic Nuclear Policy, Dept. of State, 1986-88, Office of Soviet Union Affairs, Dept. of State, 1988-90, U.S. Embassy, Moscow, 1990-92; charge d'affaires ad interim U.S. Embassy, Bratislava, 1993, dep. prin. officer, 1993-95, dep. chief of mission, 1995-96; office dir. Dept. of State, Washington, 1997—; exec. dir., exec. sec., advisor U.S. Del. to Nuclear and Space Talks, Geneva, 1987-91; teaching fellow Russian lit. The Am. U., 1976-77; escort interpreter and translator Dept. of State, 1976. Co-author: Final Report of the Kennan Institute's Soviet Research Institutes Project, 1981. Founder Camp Wocsom, Moscow, 1974. Mem. Am. Fgn. Svc. Assn. Avocations: music, folk dance. Office: Dept of State c/o Fgn Svc Lounge Washington DC 20520

SUTTER, JOHN RICHARD, manufacturer, investor; b. St. Louis, Jan. 18, 1937; s. Richard Anthony and Elizabeth Ann (Henby) S.; m. Mary Etta Trexler, Apr. 4, 1964 (div. Nov. 1983); children: John Henby, Mary Elizabeth, Sarah Katherine; m. Madeline Ann Traugott Stribling, June 5, 1984; 1 stepchild, William Stribling. BA, Princeton U., 1958; MBA, Columbia U., 1964. CPA, N.Y., Mo. Mgr. Price Waterhouse, N.Y.C., 1964-71; pres. John Sutter and Co., Inc., St. Louis, 1972-86, Handlan-Buck Co., St. Louis, 1975-88; investor, 1988—; pres. Pamlico Jack Group, Oriental, N.C., 1989—; pres. Sutter Mgmt. Corp., St. Louis, 1972-79. Mem. Chpt. Christ Ch. Cathedral, 1987-88. Mem. AICPAs, Mo. Soc. CPAs, Neuse Sailing Assn., Cape Lookout Power Squadron, Sailing Club of Oriental. Episcopalian. Clubs: Princeton, Oriental Dinghy. Avocations: painting, sailboat racing, ocean cruising. Home and Office: 410 Whittaker Point Rd PO Box 481 Oriental NC 28571-0481

SUTTER, JOSEPH F., aeronautical engineer, consultant, retired aircraft company executive; b. Seattle, Wash., Mar. 21, 1921; m. Nancy Ann French, June 14, 1943. B.A., U. Wash., 1943. Various engring. positions Boeing Comml. Airplane Co., Seattle, 1946-65, dir. engring. for Boeing 747, 1965-71, v.p., gen. mgr. 747 div., 1971-74, v.p. program ops., 1974-76, v.p. ops. and product devel., 1976-81, exec. v.p., 1981-86, cons., 1986-87; cons. Boeing Comml. Airplane Co., 1987—; chmn. aerospace safety adv. panel NASA, 1986; mem. Challenger Accident Commn., 1986. Served to lt. j.g. USN, 1943-45. Recipient Master Design award Product Engring. mag., 1965, Franklin W. Kolk Air Transp. Progress award Soc. Aero. Aerospace Coun., 1980, Elmer A. Sperry award, 1980, Nuts & Bolts award Transport Assn., 1983, Nat. Medal Tech., U.S. Pres. Reagan, 1985, Sir Kingsford Smith award Royal Aero. Soc. in Sydney, 1980, Wright Bros. Meml. Trophy, 1986; Joseph F. Sutter professorship established in his honor at U. Wash., Boeing Co., 1992. Fellow Royal Aero Soc. (hon.), AIAA (Daniel Guggenheim award 1990); mem. Internat. Fedn. Airworthiness (pres. 1989). Office: Boeing Comml Airplane Co PO Box 3707 Mail Stop 13-43 Seattle WA 98124

SUTTER, LAURENCE BRENER, lawyer; b. N.Y.C., Feb. 5, 1944; s. Meyer and Beatrice Sutter; m. Betty A. Satterwhite, June 9, 1979. AB, Columbia Coll., 1965; JD, N.Y.U., 1976. Bar: N.Y. 1977, U.S. Dist. Ct. (so. and ea. dists.) N.Y. 1977. Assoc. Shea & Gould, N.Y.C., 1976-80, Meyer, Suozzi, English & Klein P.C., Mineola, N.Y., 1980-82; assoc. counsel publs. Gen. Media Internat., Inc., N.Y.C., 1982-96, sr. v.p., gen. counsel, 1997—. With N.Y. Army N.G., 1966-72. Mem. ABA, Assn. of Bar of City of N.Y. (mem. com. on civil rights 1986-89, mem. com. on comm. and media law 1989-92, mem. com. on copyright and lit. property 1994—). Democrat. Jewish. Avocation: music. Office: Gen Media Internat Inc 277 Park Ave Fl 4 New York NY 10172-0499

SUTTER, LINDA DIANE, health services administrator; b. Queens, N.Y., Oct. 6, 1948; d. Robert Henry Sutter and Mary Lillian (Knapp) Lavers; m. Steven Thomas Centore, Aug. 16, 1975. BA in Psychology, SUNY Binghamton, 1970; MEd in Counseling, Ohio U., 1973; MBA, U. Lowell, 1989; MPA, Harvard U., 1997. Lic. mental health counselor, lic. nursing home adminstr.; lic. cert. social worker; EMT. Asst. dean women, counselor Curry Coll., Milton, Mass., 1973-75; cons. self-employed Milton, Mass., 1975-80; dir. emergency and cmty. support svcs. Solomon Mental Health Ctr., Lowell, Mass., 1980-90; dir. cmty. svcs. Merrimack Valley Area Office/Dept. Mental Health, Lowell, Mass., 1990-92; asst. supt. for program and ops. Solomon Mental Health Ctr., Lowell, Mass., 1992-93, supt., 1993-96. Mem. Am. Coll. Health Care Execs. (assoc.), Women in Health Care Mgmt. (steering com. 1994-96), Greater Boston EMT Assn. (bd. dirs. 1991—). Democrat. Roman Catholic. Avocations: theater, ballet. Home: 735 Varnum Ave Lowell MA 01854-2029

SUTTER, MORLEY CARMAN, medical scientist; b. Redvers, Sask., Can., May 18, 1933; s. Christian Benjamin and Amelia (Duke) S.; m. Virginia Frances Mary Laidlaw, June 29, 1957; children—Gregory Robert, F. Michelle, Brent Morley. M.D., U. Man., 1957, B.Sc., 1957, Ph.D., 1963. Intern Winnipeg (Man.) Gen. Hosp., 1956-57, resident, 1958-59; teaching fellow pharmacology U. Man., 1959-63; supr. Downing Coll., Cambridge U., 1963-65; asst. prof. pharmacology U. Toronto, 1965-66; asst. prof. pharmacology U. B.C., 1966-68, asso. prof., 1968-71, prof., 1971—, head dept. pharmacology, 1971-87; mem. staff Vancouver (B.C.) Hosp. & Health Sci. Ctr., St. Paul's Hosp.; mem. Minister of Health's Adv. Com. on Drugs, Province of B.C., 1971-87. Contbr. articles to sci. jours. Recipient Gov. Gen. medal, 1950; Med. Research Council of Can. fellow, 1959-63; Wellcome Found. Travelling fellow, 1963; Imperial Chem. Industries fellow, 1963-65; Med. Research Council scholar, 1966-71. Mem. Pharmacol. Soc. Can. (treas. 1969-72, sec. 1986-89), British Pharmacol. Soc., Am. Soc. Pharmacology and Exptl. Therapeutics, Can. Med. Assn., N.Y. Acad. of Scis. Office: U BC Faculty Medicine Therapeutics, 2176 Health Scis Mall/Dept Pharmacology, Vancouver, BC Canada V6T 1Z3

SUTTER, RICHARD ANTHONY, physician; b. St. Louis, July 20, 1909; s. John Henry and Molly Louisa (Schuchman) S.; m. Elizabeth Henby, June 15, 1935; children—John Richard, Jane Elizabeth; Judith Sutter Hinrichs. AB, Washington U., St. Louis, 1931, MD, 1935. Diplomate Am. Bd. of Preventive Medicine, Am. Bd. of Occupational Medicine. Intern St. Louis City Hosp., 1935-36; asst. to Otto Sutter, M.D., 1937; founder, med. dir. Sutter Clinic, St. Louis, 1947-84; mem. faculty Washington U. Sch. Medicine; apptd. physician mem. nat. adv. com. on occupational safety and health OSHA, 1971-75; med. dir. St. Louis Internat. Airport, 1964-84, emeritus med. dir., 1988—; mem. Mo. Gov.'s Council on Occupational Health and Safety, Gov's Adv. Com. on Worker's Compensation, Com. on Vocat. Rehab.; cons. Barnes/Sutter Health Care, 1984-91; hon. cons. St. Mary's Hosp. East St. Louis, Ill., 1991—; mem. emeritus staff Barnes, Lutheran, Deaconess hosps.; dir. Blue Cross/Blue Shield. Contbr. articles to med. publs. Bd. dirs. Downtown St. Louis, Inc. (hon. chmn. membership com., Leadership award 1994); past dir. Blue Cross/Blue Shield; mem. St. Louis Merc. Libr. Assn., Jefferson Nat. Expansion Commn., Commn. on Future of Washington U., mem. aviation com. Regional Commerce and Growth Assn. Served to lt. col. M.C., U.S. Army, 1941-46, ETO. Decorated Bronze Star; recipient Man of Yr. award St. Louis chpt. Beta Theta Pi, 1974; Alumni Achievement award Washington U. Med. Sch., 1985; Richard A. and Elizabeth H. Sutter chair Occupational, Indsl. and Environ. Medicine named in honor, Washington U. Sch. Medicine, 1993; Am. Lung Assn. honoree, 1997. Fellow APHA, Am. Coll. Occupational and Environ. Medicine (Health Achievement in Industry award 1978), Am. Coll. Preventive Medicine, Am. Indsl. Hygiene Assn. (emeritus, mem. Internat. com. occupational health); mem. AMA (coun. on occupational health, coun. on aviation and space medicine), Mo. Med. Assn. (del.), St. Louis Met. Med. Soc. (hon., pres. 1947, Dr. Robert Schlueter award for Leadership 1994), Am. Assn. Ry. Surgeons (past pres.), Cen. States Soc. Ind. Medicine and Surgery (past pres.), Univ. Club, Old Warson Country Club, Washington U. Faculty Club, Eliot Soc. (founder, life), Yachting Club Am. (founder), Bradenton Country Club. Avocations: aviation, hunting, golf, fishing, estate management. Home and Office: 7215 Greenway Ave Saint Louis MO 63130-4126 also: Condo 321 6701 Gulf Of Mexico Dr Apt 321 Longboat Key FL 34228-1323

SUTTER, WILLIAM PAUL, lawyer; b. Chgo., Jan. 15, 1924; s. Harry Blair and Elsie (Paul) S.; m. Helen Yvonne Stebbins, Nov. 13, 1954; children: William Paul, Helen Blair Sutter Doppelheuer. A.B., Yale U., 1947; J.D., U. Mich., 1950. Bar: Ill. 1950, Fla. 1977, U.S. Supreme Ct. 1981. Assoc. Hopkins & Sutter (and predecessors), Chgo., 1950-57; ptnr. Hopkins & Sutter (and predecessors), 1957-89, of counsel, 1989—; mem. Ill. Supreme Ct. Atty. Registration Commn., 1975-81. Contbr. articles on estate planning and taxation to profl. jours. Chmn. Winnetka Caucus Com., 1966-67; pres., trustee Lucille P. Markey Charitable Trust, 1983-97 ; precinct capt. New Trier Twp. (Ill.) Rep. party, 1960-68; asst. area chmn. New Trier Rep. Orgn., 1968-72; trustee Gads Hill Center, pres., 1962-70, chmn., 1971-80; trustee Northwestern Meml. Hosp., 1983—; bd. dirs. Chgo. Hort. Soc., 1982—; mem. dean's coun. Sch. Medicine, Yale U., 1991—. Served to 1st lt. AUS, 1943-46. Fellow Am. Bar Found., Am. Coll. Trust and Estate Counsel (bd. regents 1977-83, exec. com. 1981-83); mem. ABA (ho. dels. 1972-81, chmn. com. on income estates and trusts, taxation sect. 1973-75), Ill. Bar Assn. (bd. govs. 1964-75, pres. 1973-74), Chgo. Bar Assn. (chmn. probate practice com. 1963-64), Am. Law Inst., Internat. Acad. Estate and Trust Law, Am. Judicature Soc., Ill. LAWPAC (pres. 1977-83), Order of Coif, Phi Beta Kappa, Phi Delta Phi, Chi Psi, Tavern Club, Mid-Day Club, Indian Hill Club, Law Club, Legal Club, Gulf Stream Golf Club, Country Club Fla., Ocean Club (Fla.) (bd. govs. 1993—, sec. 1993-97, pres. 1997—). Episcopalian. Home: 96 Woodley Rd Winnetka IL 60093-3746 also: 6110 N Ocean Blvd Ocean Ridge FL 33435 Office: Hopkins & Sutter 3 First National Pla Chicago IL 60602

SUTTERFIELD, DEBORAH KAY, special education educator; b. Amarillo, Tex., Apr. 22, 1956; d. Gail DeWayne and Esther Jane (Rogge) Quine; m. Thomas Wayne Sutterfield, Dec. 6, 1980; 1 child, Tristan Thomas. AD, Amarillo Jr. Coll., 1976; BS, Tex. Woman's U., 1978. Cert. in spl. edn., elem. edn. Jr. high resource tchr. Dumas (Tex.) Ind. Schs., 1978-80; substitute tchr. Amarillo Ind. Schs., 1980-81, secondary multiple handicapped tchr., 1981-95, functional living instr., 1995—; pvt. tutor, Amarillo, 1988-94. Vol. Vol. Action Ctr., Amarillo, 1991-94; active Boy Scouts Am., 1989—; bd. dirs. Amarillo Civic Chorus. Mem. Coun. for Exceptional Children, Assn. Tex. Profl. Educators, Tex. Learning Disabilities Assn., Tex. Soc. Augmentative and Alternate Comm. Methodist. Avocations: counted cross-stitch, reading, table games. Home: 1909 Beech St Amarillo TX 79106-4505

SUTTERLIN, JAMES S., political science educator, researcher; b. Frankfort, Ky., Mar. 15, 1922; s. Frederick J. and Agnes (Douglas) S.; m. Betty C. Berven, June 24, 1950 (dec. Jan. 1989); children: Rose E., Sabrina, Jamie Ann, James E. BA, Haverford Coll., 1943; postgrad., Harvard U., 1949, 67; hon. degree in jurisprudence, Kyung Hee U., Seoul, Korea, 1973. Vice-consul U.S. Fgn. Svc., Berlin, 1946-48; polit. officer U.S. Mission, Berlin, 1951-54; 1st sec. U.S. Embassy, Tel Aviv, 1954-56; desk officer U.S. State Dept., Washington, 1956-60; 1st sec. U.S. Embassy, Tokyo, 1960-63; counselor U.S. Embassy, Bonn, 1963-68; dir. U.S. Dept. State, Washington, 1969-72, insp.-gen., 1972-74; dir. UN, N.Y.C., 1974-87; dir. rsch. L.I. U., Bklyn., 1985-87, adj. prof., 1985—; fellow/lectr. Yale U., New Haven, 1988—. Author: Berlin—Symbol of Confrontation, 1989, UN and the Maintenance of Security, 1995. Elder Presbyn. Ch., Rye, N.Y., 1976—; chmn. Samaritan House, White Plains, N.Y., 1990-95; pres. Wainwright House, Rye, 1995-96; chmn. acad. coun. on the UN Brown U., 1995—. 1st lt. U.S. Army, 1945-46. Recipient Grosse Verdienstkreuz, Fed. Republic of Germany, 1974. Mem. UN Assn. of U.S.A., Am. Coun. on Germany, Coun. Fgn. Rels., Phi Beta Kappa. Avocation: gardening. Home: 17 N Chatsworth Ave Apt 6KL Larchmont NY 10538 Office: Yale U 34 Hillhouse Ave New Haven CT 06511-3704

SUTTLE, DORWIN WALLACE, federal judge; b. Knox County, Ind., July 16, 1906; s. William Sherman and Nancy Cordelia (Hungate) S.; m. Anne Elizabeth Barrett, Feb. 1, 1939 (dec.); children: Stephen Hungate, Nancy Joanna Suttle Walker (dec.); m. Lucile Cram Whitecotton, Aug. 21, 1956; stepchildren: Fred and Frank Whitecotton. JD, U. Tex., 1928. Bar: Tex., U.S. Supreme Ct. 1960. Practiced law Uvalde, Tex., 1928-64; U.S. dist. judge Western Dist. Tex., 1964—; now sr. judge. Democrat. Methodist. Office: US District Court 655 E Durango Blvd San Antonio TX 78206-1102*

SUTTLES, WILLIAM MAURRELLE, university administrator, clergyman; b. Ben Hill, Ga., July 25, 1920; s. Wiley Maurrelle and Eddie Lou (Campbell) S.; m. Julia Lanette Lovern, Jan. 28, 1950. B Comml. Studies, Ga. State U., 1942; M Religious Edn., Emory U., 1953, ThM, 1947; MDiv, Yale U., 1946; EdD, Auburn U., 1958; DD, Mercer U., 1972; D Humanities, Tift Coll., 1978; LLD, Atlanta Law Sch., 1978. Ordained to ministry Baptist Ch., 1938. Asst. registrar Ga. State U., 1942-44, asst. prof. English and speech, 1946-55, assoc. prof. speech, 1955-57, prof., 1957—, prof. ednl. adminstrn. and higher edn., 1970—, also chmn. dept. speech, 1955-62, dean students, 1956-62, v.p. acad. affairs, 1964-69, exec. v.p., provost, 1970—, acting pres., exec. v.p., provost, 1987—; pres. emeritus, 1989; exec. asst. to Gov. Joe Frank Harris Ga., 1989-91; pastor Haralson (Ga.) Bapt. Ch., 1950—, Luthersville (Ga.) Bapt. Ch., 1951-62; v.p., pers. dir. Rich's, Inc., Atlanta, 1962-64; dir. Ga. Fed. Bank; adv. dir. First Union Nat. Bank of Ga. (ret.). Chmn. Joint Citizens Adv. Com. to Study Atlanta/Fulton County Govts., 1967-69, State Adv. Com. on Consol. Edn. Progs., 1983-90, Christmas Seal Tribute Dinner, Am. Lung Assn., 1985; mem. S.E. regional manpower adv. com. U.S. Dept. Labor, 1972-74, Ga. Adv. Coun.

Edn., 1985-87; trustee John and Mary Franklin Found., Ga. State U. Found., George M. Sparks Scholarship Fund, Ga. Coun. Moral/Civic Concerns, 1981—, Christian Coun. Met. Atlanta, Ga. Bapt. Homes; dir. John Mercer Found., Ga. Bapt. Children's Homes & Families Ministries,1996—. With USN, 1944-46. Recipient medal of St. Paul, Greek Orthodox Archdiocese N. and S.Am., 1976, Community Svc. award Christian Coun. Met. Atlanta, 1985, Christmas Seal Tribute Am. Lung Assn., 1988, Gold medal award Religious Heritage Am., 1989, Medal of Honor DAR, 1990, Nat. Edn. award Am. Legion, 1992; co-recipient Abe Goldstein human rels. award Anti Defamation League B'nai Brith, 1984; named Rural Min. of Yr. for Ga., Progressive Farmer mag. and Emory U., 1959, Clergyman of Yr. for Ga., Ga. region NCCJ, 1971, One of 300 Who Have Shaped Atlanta, Atlanta mag., 1976, Ga. State U. Disting. Alumnus, 1989; selected as Exemplary Disting. Bivocational Minister in Town and Country area Nat. Coun. Bivocational Ministries, 1988. Mem. Atlanta C. of C., Ga. State U. Athletic Assn. (trustee 1982-89), Ga. State U. Alumni Assn. (pres. 1967, bd. dirs. 1963-74), Masons (33 degree, grand chaplain of grand masonic lodge of Ga. 1994-95), Shriners, Kiwanis (pres. 1966), Commerce Club, Blue Key, Mortar Bd., Phi Kappa Phi, Beta Gamma Sigma, Phi Eta Sigma, Omicron Delta Kappa, Alpha Kappa Psi, Kappa Phi Kappa, Phi Delta Kappa, Kappa Delta Pi, Sigma Pi Alpha, Sigma Tau Delta, Sigma Nu (grand chaplain 1979-82, 86-92, 94—, vice regent 1992-96, Hall of Honor, 1996), Alpha Lambda Delta. Home: 2734 Piney Wood Dr East Point GA 30344-1956 Office: Ga State U Univ Plaza Atlanta GA 30303

SUTTON, BARRETT BOULWARE, former insurance company executive; b. Forsyth, Ga., July 6, 1927; s. James Phinazee and Katherine Woodward (Boulware) S.; m. Mary Terecia Wade, Sept. 1, 1948; children: Katherine (Mrs. John P. Apel), Barrett Boulware, Wade. AB, Vanderbilt U., 1949, LLB, 1950. Bar: Tenn. 1950. With Life and Casualty Ins. Co. Tenn., Nashville, 1950-85; gen. counsel Life and Casualty Ins. Co. Tenn., 1970-83, sr. v.p., 1972-85, also dir. Pres. Nashville Council Community Services, 1968-70, Nashville Travelers Aid Soc., 1970-72; chmn. Nashville U.S.O. Com., 1960-62; treas. Nashville Sr. Citizens, 1980; bd. dirs., sec. Oak Hill Sch., 1983-88, chmn., 1988-90; bd. dirs., treas. Exchange Club Charities, Inc., 1984-87. With USNR, 1945-46. Mem. Assn. Life Ins. Counsel, Order of Coif, Phi Beta Kappa. Presbyterian (elder). Clubs: Belle Meade Country, Nashville Exchange. Home: 750 Greeley Dr Nashville TN 37205-2634

SUTTON, BERRIEN DANIEL, beverage company executive; b. Axson, Ga., Jan. 24, 1926; s. Frank and Commie (Brooker) S.; m. Verda Lee Adams, June 6, 1953; 1 child, Kathryn. B.B.A., U. Ga., 1948. From traveling auditor to St. Louis dist. mgr. Coca-Cola Co., 1948-62; from v.p. sales to pres., gen. mgr. Coca-Cola Bottling Co., St. Louis, 1962-66; pres. Assoc. Coca-Cola Bottling Co., Inc., Daytona Beach, Fla., 1966-82; past mem. pres.'s adv. coun. Coca-Cola Co.; past pres., bd. govs. Coca-Cola Bottlers Assn. Past gen. campaign chmn., v.p., dir., mem. exec. com. United Fund East Volusia County; past mem. exec. com. Civic League Halifax Area; past trustee Bethune Cookman Coll.; past mem. bd. dirs. Daytona Beach Symphony Soc. Served with USNR, 1944-46. Mem. 49ers, Young Pres. Orgn., Rotary (past bd. dirs., treas., pres. Daytona Beach club). Methodist. Home: 20 Habersham Park NW Atlanta GA 30305-2856

SUTTON, CHARLES RICHARD, architect, designer; b. Sand Springs, Okla., June 25, 1927; s. Charles A. and Violet L. Sutton; m. Jean Rector, Dec. 18, 1949; children: John Isaac, Adam Franklin. BArch, Okla. State U., 1950; MArch, Cranbrook Acad. Art, Bloomfield Hills, Mich., 1954. Draftsman Parr & Aderhold, Oklahoma City, 1950-53; draftsman/designer Coston, Frankfurt & Short, Oklahoma City, 1954-55; designer I.M. Pei & Assocs., N.Y.C., 1957-62; designer/office dir. John Carl Warnecke & Assocs., Washington, Honolulu, 1962-68; pres. Charles R. Sutton & Asscs. Inc., Honolulu, 1968-85; ptnr. Sutton Candia Ptnrs., Honolulu, 1985-94; pres. Sutton Candia Inc., 1995—; lectr. in design Columbia U., 1958-62; cons. Honolulu Waterfront Master Plan, 1984; mem. design rev. bd. Kaanapali Resort, Maui, Hawaii, 1985, Kapolei New Town, Oahu, Hawaii, 1991; lectr. in urban design sch. arch. U. Hawaii, 1994-96; authority engr. Hawaii Conv. Ctr., 1995-96. Archtl. designer East West Ctr., 1961, Hawaii State Capitol, 1962-68; planner designer Honolulu Capitol Dist., 1965-68; architect Aloha Tower Pla,1974-78. Founding mem., v.p. Hist. Hawaii Found.; bd. dirs. Kakaako Improvement Assn., Hawaii, 1990—. Recipient 1st prize Kalakaua Comml. Area Competition (Bishop Estate), 1971, Vladimir Ossipoff FAIA award to honor design excellence in the profession of arch. U. Hawaii Sch. Arch., 1997; Lloyd Warren fellow Nat. Inst. for Archtl. Edn., N.Y., Paris, 1955-56. Fellow AIA (pres. Hawaii sect. 1973, fellowship 1980); mem. Waikiki Yacht Club (commodore 1984). Mem. Christian Ref. Ch. Avocations: sailing, painting, photography. Home: 3077 Wailani Rd Honolulu HI 96813-1005

SUTTON, DANA FERRIN, classics educator; b. White Plains, N.Y., Oct. 10, 1942; s. Joseph Guy Jr. and Eleanor Sutton; m. Kathryn A. Sinkovich, Aug. 16, 1975. BA, The New Sch. for Social Rsch., N.Y.C., 1965; MA, U. Wis., 1966, PhD, 1970. Lectr. Herbert Lehman Coll., CUNY, 1969-72; postdoctoral rsch. Darwin Coll., Cambridge, Eng., 1972-74, U. Auckland, New Zealand, 1974-75; asst. prof. U. Ill., Urbana, 1975-79; prof. U. Calif., Irvine, 1979—, dept. chair., 1986-94; assoc. dir. Thesaurus Linguae Graecae Project, Irvine, 1991—. Author: The Greek Satyr Play, 1975, numerous other books and monographs; editor: William Gager: The Complete Works, 1994, The Complete Works of Thomas Watson (1556-1592), 1995; contbr. articles to profl. jours. John Guggenheim fellow, 1975-76. Mem. Am. Philol. Assn., Calif. Classical Assn. Office: U Calif Dept of Classics 156 Humanities Hall Irvine CA 92697-5025

SUTTON, DOLORES, actress, writer; b. N.Y.C.. BA in Philosophy, NYU. Appeared in plays including Man With the Golden Arm, 1956, Career, 1958, Machinal, 1960, Rhinoceros, Liliom, She Stoops to Conquer, Hedda Gabler, Anna Karenina, Eccentricities of a Nightingale, Brecht on Brecht, Young Gifted and Black, Luv, The Friends, The Web and the Rock, The Seagull, Saturday, Sunday, Monday, The Little Foxes, What's Wrong With This Picture, The Cocktail Hour, My Fair Lady (Broadway revival), 1994, My Fair Lady (nat. tour), 1993-94; films include The Trouble With Angels, Where Angels Go, Trouble Follows, Crossing Delancey, Crimes and Misdeameanors, Tales of the Darkside: TV appearances include Studio One, Hallmark Hall of Fame Prodn. An Wilderness, Theatre Guild of the Air: Danger, Suspense, Gunsmoke, Valiant Lady, General Hospital, From These Roots, As the World Turns, Edge of Night, F. Scott Fitzgerald in Hollywood, Patty Hearst Story, All in the Family, Bob Newhart Show, All My Children, others; TV writer Lady Doc, The Secret Storm, Loving; playwright: Down at the Old Bull and Bush, The Web and the Rock, Company Comin', Born Yesterday, 1995, A Perfect Ganesh, 1995, Detail of a Larger Work, 1995, The Front Page, 1996, The Exact Center of the Universe, 1997, A Drop in the Bucket, 1997. Mem. League of Profl. Theatre Women (bd. dirs.), Ensemble Studio Theatre (bd. dirs.).

SUTTON, DOUGLAS HOYT, nurse; b. McHenry, Ill., Oct. 27, 1962; s. Hoyt Douglas Sutton and Barbara (Sutton) Hensley. Cert. in emergency med. tech., Polk Community Coll., Winter Haven, Fla., 1985; ADN, SUNY, Albany, 1990, BS in Nursing, 1991, BS in Psychology, 1993; MSN, U. Fla., 1995; MPA, Troy State U., 1997. Cert. adv. nursing adminstrn., rehab. reg. nurse. Nurse adminstr. Bartow (Fla.) Meml. Hosp., 1991-94; paramedic Polk County Emergency Med. Svcs., Bartow, Fla., 1984-88; edn. cons. Moore Pubs., 1990-94; mgr. orthopedics and skilled care programs Columbia Healthcare, Inc., Gainesville, 1995—. Mem. Am. Assn. Rehab. Nurses, Am. Coll. Healthcare Adminstrs., Sigma Theta Tau. Home: 7200 SW 8th Ave S-121 Gainesville FL 32607

SUTTON, FRANCIS XAVIER, social scientist, consultant; b. Oneida, Pa., July 7, 1917; s. Frank James and Rose Marie (Burns) S.; m. Ruth Jacqueline Young, Aug. 24, 1948; children: Peter, Sean, Philip, Elizabeth. BS, Temple U., 1938; MA, Princeton U., 1940, Harvard U., 1941; PhD, Harvard U., 1950. Jr. fellow, Soc. Fellows Harvard U., Cambridge, Mass., 1946-49, asst. prof., lectr., 1949-54; program officer, overseas rep. Ford Found., N.Y.C., 1954-67, dep. v.p., acting v.p., 1968-83; cons. Ford Found. and Harvard U., 1983-85; acting pres. Social Sci. Rsch. Coun., N.Y.C., 1985-86, also bd. dirs., chmn., 1985-92; cons. Rockefeller Found, U.S. Agy. for Internat. Devel. and World Bank, N.Y.C. and Washington, 1987-92; acting dir. Rockefeller Study and Conf. Ctr., Bellagio, Italy, 1990-92; cons. Aga Khan U., 1992—. Author: The American Business Creed, 1956; editor: A World to Make/Development in Perspective, 1989; contbr. articles to profl. jours. and chpts. to books. Pres. Am. Found. for Intellectual Coop. with Europe, N.Y.C., 1987-93; mem. bd. fgn. scholarships Dept. State, Washington, 1961-63; bd. dirs. Nat. Ctr. on Adult Literacy, U. Pa., Phila., 1990—; mem. adv. bd. Ctr. on Philanthropy, City Univ., N.Y.C., 1988—; mem. Coun. Internat. Partnerships in Sci. and Tech., N.Y. Acad. Scis., 1995—. Capt. U.S. Army Air Corps, 1941-45. Fellow AAAS; mem. Council on Fgn. Relations, Assn. for Asian Studies (Disting. Service award 1984). Democrat. Club: Century Assn. (N.Y.C.). Avocations: piano playing, dancing, snorkeling. Home: 80 Bellair Dr Dobbs Ferry NY 10522-3504

SUTTON, GEORGE WALTER, research laboratory executive, mechanical engineer; b. Bklyn., Aug. 3, 1927; s. Jack and Pauline (Aaron) S.; m. Evelyn D. Kunnes, Dec. 25, 1952; children—James E., Charles S., Richard E., Stewart A. B. Mech. Engrng. with honors, Cornell U., 1952; M.S., Calif. Inst. Tech., 1953, Ph.D. magna cum laude, 1955. Rsch. scientist Lockheed Missile Co., 1955; rsch. engr. Space Sci. Lab. GE, 1955-61, mgr. magnetohydrodynamic power generation, 1962-63; vis. Ford prof. MIT, 1961-62; sci. adviser Hdqrs. USAF, 1963-65; with Avco Rsch. Lab., 1965-83, dir. laser devel., 1971-82, v.p., 1972-82, v.p., tech. dir. Helionetics Laser div., 1983-85; v.p. JAYCOR, San Diego, 1985-90; dir. E-O rsch. Kaman Aerospace Corp., Tucson, 1990-92; chief scientist Aero Thermal Tech., Inc., Arlington, Va., 1993-96; prin. engr. ANSER, Arlington, Va., 1996—; cons. Energy Agy., 1977-79, Arms Control Agy., 1986; lectr. magnetohydrodynamics U. Pa., 1960-63, Stanford, 1964; developer of ablation heat protection for ICBM and high energy lasers, pioneer aero-optics, missile interceptor tech. Author: (with A. Sherman) Engineering Magnetohydrodynamics, 1965, Direct Energy Conversion, 1966; editor-in-chief Jour. AIAA, 1967-96; editor-in-chief emeritus, 1997—; editor various procs.; contbr. some 93 articles to profl. jours. Served with USAAF, 1945-47. Recipient Arthur Flemming award for outstanding govt. service, 1965. Fellow AIAA (chmn. plasmadynamics tech. com., Thermophysics award 1980, Disting. Svc. award 1988), ASME, AAAS, Nat. Acad. Engrng. Avocations: tennis, travel, sailing. Office: Ste 800 1215 Jefferson Davis Hwy Arlington VA 22202 *I have been blessed with certain abilities and I strain to utilize and sharpen them to the maximum. But I do the right thing - always. Love of my family and my desire to do best for them have led to situations wher my values could have been compromised. I still did the right thing. It has usually worked out best for my family and myself, and preserved my sense of honor and integrity.*

SUTTON, GREGORY PAUL, obstetrician, gynecologist; b. Tokyo, Dec. 12, 1948; (parents Am. citizens); s. Vernon S. And Vonna Lou (Streeter) S.; m. Judith Craigie Holt, June 26, 1977; children: Anne Craigie, James Streeter. BS in Chemistry with honors, Ind. U., 1970; MD, U. Mich., 1976. Diplomate Am. Bd. of Ob/Gyn. Assoc. prof., chief divsn. gynecologic oncology Ind. U. Sch. Medicine, Indpls., 1986—. Cancer Clin. fellow Am. Cancer Soc., Phila., 1981-83; recipient Career Devel. award Am. Cancer Soc., 1986-89. Fellow Am. Coll. Obstetrics and Gynecology; mem. Gynecologic Oncology Group (cert. Spl. Competence in Gynecologic Oncology 1985), Marion County Med. Soc., Ind. State Med. Soc., Bayard Carter Soc., Soc. of Gynecologic Oncologists, Gynecologic Oncology Group, Hoosier Oncology Group. Avocations: swimming, cycling, woodworking. Office: Ind U Cancer Ctr 535 Barnhill Rd Indianapolis IN 46202-5203*

SUTTON, HARRY ELDON, geneticist, educator; b. Cameron, Tex., Mar. 5, 1927; s. Grant Edwin and Myrtle Dovie (Fowler) S.; m. Beverly Earlene Jewell, July 7, 1962; children: Susan Elaine, Caroline Virginia. B.S. in Chemistry, U. Tex., Austin, 1948, M.A., 1949; Ph.D. in Biochemistry, U. Tex., 1953. Biologist U. Mich., 1952-56, instr., 1956-57, asst. prof. human genetics, 1957-60; asso. prof. zoology U. Tex., Austin, 1960-64; prof. U. Tex., 1964—, chmn. dept. zoology, 1970-73, asso. dean Grad. Sch., 1967-70, 73-75, v.p. for research, 1975-79; mem. adv. council Nat. Inst. Environ. Health Scis., 1968-72, council sci. advs., 1972-76; mem. various coms. Nat. Acad. Scis.-NRC; cons. in field; bd. dirs. Associated Univs. for Research in Astronomy, 1975-79, Argonne Univs. Assn., 1975-79, Univ. Corp. for Atmospheric Research, 1975-79, Associated Western Univs., 1978-79. Author: Genes, Enzymes, and Inherited Disease, 1961, An Introduction to Human Genetics, 1988, Genetics: A Human Concern, 1985; editor: First Macy Conference on Genetics, 1960, Mutagenic Effects of Environmental Contaminants, 1972, Am. Jour. Human Genetics, 1964-69. Trustee S.W. Tex. Corp. Public Broadcasting, 1977-80, sec., 1979-80; bd. dirs. Ballet Austin, 1978-84; mem. Austin Arts Commn., 1991-95. Served with U.S. Army, 1945-46. Mem. AAAS, Am. Soc. Human Genetics (dir. 1961-69, pres. 1979), Genetics Soc. Am., Am. Soc. Biochem. and Molecular Biology, Am. Chem. Soc., Tex. Genetics Soc. (pres. 1979), Am. Genetic Assn., Headliners Club (Austin), Town and Gown Club. Achievements include research and publications in human genetics. Home: 1103 Gaston Ave Austin TX 78703-2507 Office: Dept Zoology Univ Tex Austin TX 78712

SUTTON, JAMES ANDREW, diversified utility company executive; b. Gary, Ind., June 29, 1934; s. Winfield Alexander and Margaret (Aulwurm) S.; m. Beverly Joan McCorkle, Aug. 27, 1955; children—James II, Susan, Stephen, Scot. BSChemE, Purdue U., 1957. V.P., gen. mgr./gas products Linde div. Union Carbide Corp., Danbury, Conn., 1978-82; sr. v.p. compressed gases UGI Corp., Valley Forge, Pa., 1982-84, exec. v.p., COO, 1984-85, pres., COO, 1985-86, pres., CEO, 1986-88, chmn., pres., CEO, 1989-94; chmn., CEO UGI Corp., Valley Forge, 1994-95, chmn., 1995-96; bd. dirs. Gilbert Assocs., Inc., Reading, Pa.; former mem. Mellon PSFS Bd., Phila.; former mem. bd. trustees Thomas Jefferson U. Chmn. United Way Chester/Montgomery Counties Region, 1991; former mem., bd. dirs., mem. exec. com. Reading is Fundamental, Washington. Lt. U.S. Army, 1958. Mem. Phila. Country Club, Oyster Reef Country Club.

SUTTON, JOHN EWING, judge; b. San Angelo, Tex., Oct. 7, 1950; s. John F. Jr. and Nancy (Ewing) S.; m. Jean Ann Schofield, July 2, 1977; 1 son, Joshua Ewing; 1 stepson, Michael Brandon Ducote. BBA, U. Tex., 1973, JD, 1976. Bar: Tex. 1976, U.S. Tax Ct. 1977, U.S. Ct. Claims, 1977, U.S. Dist. Ct. (no. dist.) Tex. 1977, U.S. Ct. Appeals (5th cir.) 1978, U.S. Dist. Ct. (we. dist.) Tex. 1979, U.S. Supreme Ct. 1980; CPA, Tex. With Daugherty, Kuperman & Golden, Austin, 1975-76; tax specialist Peat, Marwick, Mitchell & Co., CPAs, Dallas, 1976-77; ptnr. Shannon, Porter, Johnson, Sutton, and Greendyke Attys. at Law, San Angelo, Tex., 1977-87; judge 119th Dist. Ct. of Tex., 1987—. Treas. Good Shepherd Episcopal Ch., San Angelo, 1979-81; co-chmn. profl. div. United Way, San Angelo, 1980-82; trustee Angelo State U. Found., 1987—, pres., 1988-91, 95—, v.p., 1992-94, sec.-treas., 1991-92. Mem. ABA, Tex. Bar Assn., Tom Green County Bar Assn. (sec.-treas. young lawyers 1977-78), AICPAs, Tex. Soc. CPAs (bd. dir. 1980-87, pres. San Angelo chpt. 1980-81, mem. state exec. com. 1981-82, 86-87, state sec. 1986-87, chmn. profl. ethics com. 1985-86, Young CPA of Yr. 1984-85), Concho Valley Estate Planning Council (v.p. 1979-80, also dir.). Office: Tom Green County Courthouse San Angelo TX 76903

SUTTON, JOHN F., JR., law educator, university dean, lawyer; b. Alpine, Tex., Jan. 26, 1918; s. John F. and Pauline Irene (Elam) S.; m. Nancy Ewing, June 1, 1940; children: Joan Sutton Parr, John Ewing. J.D., U. Tex., 1941. Bar: Tex. 1941, U.S. Dist. Ct. (we. dist.) Tex. 1947, U.S. Ct. Appeals (5th cir.) 1951, U.S. Supreme Ct. 1960. Assoc. Brooks, Napier, Brown & Matthews, San Antonio, 1941-42; spl. agt. FBI, Washington, 1942-45; assoc. Matthews, Nowlin, Macfarlane & Barrett, San Antonio, 1945-48; ptnr. Kerr, Gayer & Sutton, San Angelo, Tex., 1948-50, Sutton, Steib & Barr, San Angelo, 1951-57; prof. U. Tex.-Austin, 1957-65, William Stamps Farish prof., 1965-84, A.W. Walker centennial chair, 1984—, dean Sch. Law, 1979-84. Editor: (with Wellborn) Materials on Evidence, 8th edit., 1996, (with Dzienkowski) Cases and Materials on Professional Responsibility of Lawyers, 1989, (with Schuwerk) Guideline to the Texas Disciplinary Rules of Professional Conduct, 1990; contbr. articles to profl. jours. Served to 1st lt. JAGC USAR, 1948-54. Fellow Am. Bar Found. (life), Tex. Bar Found. (life); mem. ABA (com. on ethics 1970-76), State Bar Tex. (com. on rules of profl. conduct, com. adminstrn. rules of evidence), Inter-Am. Bar Assn., Fed. Bar Assn., Philos. Soc. Tex., Order of Coif, Phi Delta Phi, San Angelo Country Club, River Club of San Angelo,. North Austin Rotary (pres. 1969). Presbyterian. Home: 3830 Sunset Dr San Angelo TX 76904-5956 Office: U Tex Sch Law 727 E 26th St Austin TX 78705-3224

SUTTON, JOHN PAUL, lawyer; b. Youngstown, Ohio, July 24, 1934; m. Jane Williamson, Aug. 20, 1958; children—Julia, Susan, Elizabeth. B.A., U. Va., 1956; J.D., George Washington U., 1963. Bar: Calif. 1965. Patent examiner U.S. Patent Office, Washington, 1956, 59-62; law clk. U.S. Ct. Customs and Patent Appeals, Washington, 1962-64; assoc. Flehr, Hohbach, Test, Albritton & Herbert, San Francisco, 1964-68; ptnr. Limbach, Limbach & Sutton, San Francisco, 1969-91; spl. counsel Heller, Ehrman, White & McAuliffe, San Francisco, 1992-95; of counsel Medlin & Carroll, San Francisco, 1995, Bryan, Hinshaw, Cohen & Barnet, San Francisco, 1996—; adj. instr. Practicing Law Inst., 1968-69; continuing edn. program Calif. State Bar, 1972, 75, U. Calif. Law Sch., Berkeley, 1975, 84. Contbr. articles to legal jours. Served with USNR, 1956-59. Mem. Calif. Patent Law Assn. (pres. 1975), San Francisco Patent Law Assn. (pres. 1976), State Bar Calif. (exec. com. patent sect. 1975-77), Am. Chem. Soc. Democrat. Episcopalian. Home: 2421 Pierce St San Francisco CA 94115-1131 Office: Bryan Hinshaw et al 425 California St San Francisco CA 94104-2102

SUTTON, JULIA SUMBERG, musicologist, dance historian; b. Toronto, Ont., Can., July 20, 1928; d. Samuel L. and Anne R. (Rubin) Sumberg. AB summa cum laude, Cornell U., 1949; MA, Colo. Coll., 1952; PhD, U. Rochester, 1962. Instr. music history New Sch. for Social Research, 1962-63; instr. music Queens Coll., CUNY, 1963-66; chmn. dept. music history and musicology New Eng. Conservatory Music, 1971-90, chmn. faculty senate, 1971-73; prof. emerita New England Conservatory Music, 1992; vis. asst. prof. George Peabody Coll. for Tchrs., 1966-67; instr. NYU, summers 1963, 64; pvt. tchr. piano, 1949-65; lectr., rsch. dir. in musicology, music as related to the dance; presenter numerous workshops and summer insts. on Renaissance dance. Dance dir. N.Y. Pro Musica prodn. An Entertainment for Elizabeth, Caramoor, N.Y., Saratoga, N.Y., U. Ariz., Stanford U., UCLA, 1969, ann. nationwide tours, 1970-1973; dance dir. Descent of Rhythm and Harmony, Colorado Springs, Colo., 1970, Renaissance Revisited, Phila., 1972, An Evening of Renaissance Music and Dance, York U., Toronto, 1974; author: Jean Baptiste Besard's Novus Partus 1617, 1962; editor: Thoinot Arbeau: Orchesography 1588, 1967; translator, editor: Fabritio Caroso: Nobiltà di dame 1600, 1986, rev. 1995; producer, co-dir. (tng. video) Il Ballarino, 1991; contbr. numerous articles to profl. jours. and Internat. Ency. of Dance. Mem. Am. Musicological Soc., Soc. of Dance History Scholars, Phi Beta Kappa.

SUTTON, LEONARD VON BIBRA, lawyer; b. Colorado Springs, Colo., Dec. 21, 1914; s. Benjamin Edmund and Anne (von Bibra) S.; B.A., Colo. Coll., 1937; fellow Nat. Inst. Pub. Affairs, 1937-38; J.D., U. Denver, 1941; grad. Inf. Officers Sch., Ft. Benning, Ga., 1942; LLD (hon.) Colo. Coll., 1987, U. Denver, 1989, U. Colo., 1990. Bar: Colo. 1941, U.S. Supreme Ct., U.S. Tax Ct., U.S. Ct. Claims, U.S. Ct. Internat. Trade (former Customs Ct.), U.S. Ct. Mil. Appeals. Practiced law, Colorado Springs, 1941-42, 46-56; justice Colo. Supreme Ct., 1956-68, chief justice, 1960, 66; chmn. Fgn. Claims Settlement Commn. U.S., 1968-69; pvt. practice law, Denver, 1969—. Chmn. Colo. Statute Revision Com., 1964-67; participant Fgn. Trade Seminar, 1935, Germany; del. various nat. and internat. bar assn. confs.; lectr.; past vice chmn. com. internat. cts. World Peace Through Law Commn.; past chmn. Colo. World Peace Through Law Com., World Habeas Corpus Com., Colo.; hon. mem. N.J. World Trade Com., 1976—; mem. Colo. Democratic Cen. Com., 1948-56, mem. exec. com., 1948-58, chmn. rules com., 1955-56; del. Dem. Nat. Conv., 1952; past pres. Garden of the Gods Rotary Club. Former trustee Inst. Internat. Edn., N.Y.C.; regent Dana Coll., Blair, Nebr., 1976-78; chmn. bd. govs. U. Denver, 1985-90, mem., 1991—; chmn. Pioneer Soc. U. Denver, 1989, mem., 1990—. Capt., AUS, World War II. Recipient Grand Order of Merit Fed. Republic Germany, 1987. Mem. Colo. (Jr. Bar past chmn.), Internat., Inter-Am. (council), Am. (past chmn. com. on internat. cts., former mem. council sect. internat. law), Colo. Bar Assn., Denver Bar Assn., D.C. Bar Assn., Mexican Acad. Internat. Law, Buenos Aires Bar Assn. (hon.), Washington Fgn. Law Soc. (pres. 1970-71, now hon. mem.), Consular Law Soc. N.Y. (hon.), Phi Delta Phi. Episcopalian. Clubs: Wyoming One Shot Antelope Past Shooter's (pres. 1985-86); Colo. Harvard Bus. Sch. (assoc.); Mason (33 degree), Shriners; Garden of Gods, Kissing Camels (Colorado Springs); Cosmos (Washington). Author: Constitution of Mexico, 1973. Contbr. articles on law, jud. adminstrn. and internat. relations to jours. Home: Unit 1908 3131 E Alameda Ave Denver CO 80209-3409

SUTTON, LYNN SORENSEN, librarian; b. Detroit, July 31, 1953; d. Leonard Arthur Edward and Dorothy Ann (Steele) Sorensen; m. Richard Dale Sutton, May 2, 1981 (div. Sept. 1992); children: Elizabeth, Alexander, Derek. AB, U. Mich., 1975, MLS, 1976. Dir. Med. Libr. South Chgo. Cmty. Hosp., 1976-77; corp. dirs. librs. Detroit-Macomb Hosp. Corp., Detroit, 1977-86; dir. librs. Harper Hosp., Detroit, 1987-88; dir. Sci. and Engring. Libr. Wayne State U., Detroit, 1989-95, dir. undergrad. libr., 1996—; cons. Catherine McAuley Health Sys., Ann Arbor, Mich., 1993. Contbr. articles to profl. jours. Mem. ALA, Assn. Coll. and Rsch. Librs. (budget and fin. com. 1995—), Mich. Health Scis. Librs. Assn. (pres. 1987-88), Met. Detroit Med. Libr. Group (pres. 1983-84), Phi Beta Kappa, Beta Phi Mu. Lutheran. Office: Wayne State U Undergrad Libr Detroit MI 48202-3918

SUTTON, PAT LIPSKY, artist, educator; b. N.Y.C., Sept. 21, 1941; d. Bernard G. and Bernice D. (Brown) S.; children: David Lipsky, Jonathan Lipsky. BFA, Cornell U., 1963; attended, Bklyn. Mus. Art Sch., 1960, 61; postgrad., Art Student's League, 1963; MA, Hunter Coll., 1968. Mem. faculty Fairleigh Dickinson U., 1968-69, Hunter Coll., 1972, San Francisco Art Inst., 1974; assoc. prof. U. Hartford, 1983—; guest lectr. Hirshhorn Mus., 1975, Va. Commonwealth U., Bennington Coll., 1977, U. Pitts., 1974, NYU, 1983, SACI, Florence, 1986, Springfield Mus., 1987, 88, U. Miami, 1992, Pollock-Krasner House and Study Ctr., East Hampton, L.I., N.Y., 1995; guest lectr. Parsons Sch. Design, 1990, lectr., 1982-83, 90; guest lectr. Am. U., 1997; instr. SUNY, Purchase, 1980-81; mem. adv. coun. Cornell U. Coll. Art and Architecture, 1988—. One-woman shows include Andre Emmerich Gallery, N.Y.C., 1970, 72, 74, 75, Deichter O'Reilly Gallery, 1976, Medici-Berenson Gallery, 1976, Everson Mus., 1970, Gloria Luria Gallery, Miami, 1988, Slater-Price Gallery, N.Y.C., 1986, Hartell Gallery Cornell U., 1989, Andre Zarre Gallery, 1991, Virginia Miller Gallery, Coral Gables, Fla., 1994; exhibited in group shows at Whitney Mus. Am. Art, 1971, Hirshhorn Mus. and Sculture Garden, 1975, Promenade Gallery, Hartford, 1984, U. Mass. Art Gallery, Amherst, 1987, Gloria Luria Gallery, 1988, 92, Andre Zarre Gallery, 1990, 95, Denise Renè Gallery, Paris, 1993, Gallery One, Toronto, Can., 1996, Snyder Fine Art, N.Y.C., 1996, Lori Bookstein/Fine Arts, 1997; represented in permanent collections Herbert Johnson Mus., Itaca, N.Y., Witney Mus., Hisrhhorn Mus., Walker Art Ctr., Hunter Coll., Fogg Art Mus., Harvard U., San Francisco Mus. Art, Bklyn. Mus., Wadsworth Atheneum, Hartford; stage designer (play) Custody, Westbeth Theatre, N.Y.C., 1991. Grantee N.Y. State Coun., 1972, N.Y. Found. Arts, 1992, sponsorship from Winsor and Newton Paint Co., 1992; fellow Va. Ctr. for Creative Arts, 1986, 93, Tyrone Guthurie Centre, Co., Moneghan, Ireland, 1996. Home: 11 Riverside Dr New York NY 10023-2504

SUTTON, PETER ALFRED, archbishop; b. Chandler, Que., Can., Oct. 18, 1934. BA, U. Ottawa, 1960; MA in Religious Edn, Loyola U., Chgo., 1969. Ordained priest Roman Catholic Ch., 1960, bishop, 1974; oblate of Mary Immaculate; high sch. tchr. St. Patricks, Ottawa, Ont., 1961-63, London (Ont.) Cath. Cen. Sch., 1963-74; bishop of Labrador-Schefferville, Que., Can., 1974—; archbishop Missionary Diocese of Keewatin-Le Pas, Man., 1986, apptd. coadjustor archbishop, 1986—, archbishop, 1986—; mem. Can. Conf. Cath. Bishops, mem. social affairs commn.; mem. Western Cath. Conf. of No. Bishops, Man. Bishops; accompanying Bishop L'Arch Internat. (homes for mentally handicapped), 1983—. Contbr. religious articles to newspapers. Address: PO Box 270, 108 1st St W, The Pas, MB Canada R9A 1K4

SUTTON, RICHARD LAUDER, lawyer; b. Dover, Del., July 4, 1935; s. Richard and Anna Kimber (Massey) S.; m. Violette Witwer, June 25, 1960; children: Jane Valentine, Richard Mohler. A.B. with distinction, U. Del., 1957; LL.B., Yale U., 1960. Bar: Del. 1961. Law clk. to Judge Edwin D. Steel, U.S. Dist. Ct., Wilmington, Del., 1960-61; assoc. firm Morris Nichols Arsht & Tunnell, Wilmington, 1961-65; ptnr. Morris Nichols Arsht & Tunnell, 1966—; v.p., sec. Prodair Corp.; mem. antitrust and trade regulation com. U.S. C. of C., 1976-80, mem. council on governance, 1980-82. Chmn.

Del. Gov.'s Higher Edn. Commn., 1976; treas., bd. dirs., mem. exec. com. Greater Wilmington Devel. Coun., 1970-82; trustee Wilmington Pub. Libr., 1974-96; bd. dirs. Grand Opera House, Inc., 1976-92, Am. Judicature Soc., U. Del. Libr. Assocs.; chmn. William H. Heald Scholarship Fund. Mem. ABA, Am. Law Inst., Del. Bar Assn., Confrererie des Chevaliers du Tastevin, Soc. Colonial Wars, The Brook, Wilmington Club, Wilmington Country Club, Pine Valley Golf Club, Vicmead Hunt Club, The Seminole, U.S. Srs. Golf Assn., Royal and Ancient Golf Club, Phi Beta Kappa, Phi Kappa Phi, Omicron Delta Kappa, Phi Delta Phi. Home: 10 Barley Mill Dr Wilmington DE 19807-2218 Office: PO Box 1347 Wilmington DE 19899-1347

SUTTON, RONNIE NEAL, state legislator, lawyer; b. Pembroke, N.C., June 17, 1941; s. Willie French and Vergie Mae (Oxendine) S.; m. Genny Chavis, June 19, 1967; children: Ronette, Fonda Lynn. BA, U. West Fla., 1970; MS, Naval War Coll., 1977; MA, Ctrl. Mich. U., 1979; JD, U. N.C., 1985. Commd. ensign USN, 1958, advanced through grades to comdr., ret., 1982; atty. Sutton Law Office, Pembroke, 1985-97; rep. N.C. Ho. of Reps., Raleigh, 1993—; bd. dirs. Lumber River Legal Svcs., Pembroke, N.C. Cancer Inst., Lumberton; bd. found. dir. U. N.C., Pembroke, 1992—. Chmn. Robeson County Dem. Party, Lumberton, 1991-92. Mem. Pembroke Kiwanis Club (pres. 1991-92, Kiwanian of Yr. 1992). Democrat. Home: RR 1 Box 154 Pembroke NC 28372-9721 Office: NC Ho of Reps Jones St Raleigh NC 27601

SUTTON, ROYAL KEITH, marketing professional; b. Tomah, Wis., Feb. 18, 1932; s. Rollin E. Sutton and Anna M. (Doebel) S.; m. Kathryn E. Bennett, April 7, 1957; children: Patricia Petite, Gregg Bennett, Margaret Mary. Student, Omaha U., 1958-59, Luzerne Community Coll. Lic. ins. salesperson, real estate salesperson. Photographer Rinehart-Marsden Studio, Omaha, 1953-72; salesperson N.Y. Life Ins. Co., Scranton, Pa., 1972-75, Educators Mut. Life Ins. Co., Scranton, 1975-83; mgr. time-share resort Ski Side Village, Tannersville, Pa., 1983-84; dir. mktg. Coachman's Beach Club, Cape May, N.J., 1984-86; owner 1898 Mktg., Dallas, Pa., 1987—; mgmt. cons. Coachman's Motor Inn, Cape May. Author: Faces of Courage, 1972. Served with USAF, 1951-55. Republican. Methodist. Avocation: travel. Office: 1898 Marketing 62 Dallas s/c #303 Dallas PA 18612

SUTTON, SAMUEL J., lawyer, educator, engineer; b. Chgo., July 21, 1941; s. Samuel J. and Elaine (Blossom) S.; m. Anne V. Sutton, Aug. 28, 1965; children: Paige, Jean, Leah, Jepson. BA in History and Philosophy, U. Ariz., 1964, BSEE, 1967; JD, George Washington U., 1969. Bar: Ariz. 1969, D.C. 1970, U.S. Ct. Appeals (fed. cir.) 1983. Patent atty. Gen. Electric Co., Washington, Phoenix, 1967-70; ptnr. Cahill, Sutton & Thomas, Phoenix, 1970—; prof. law Ariz. State U., Tempe, 1975—; expert witness Fed. Dist. Cts., 1983—; trial cons. to numerous lawyers, 1972—; v.p. engring. Shintech, Inc., 1991—; arbitrator Am. Arbitration Assn., Phoenix, 1971—. Author: Patent Preparation, 1976, Intellectual Property, 1978, Art Law, 1988, Law, Science and Technology, 1991, Licensing Intangible Property, 1994, Commercial Torts, 1995; exhibited in group shows at Tanner Sq., Phoenix, Tucson Art Inst., Mobil Corp., Mesa, Ariz., Cox Devel. Co., Tempe, Ariz., Downtown Phoenix, Desert Bot. Garden, Phoenix, Gateway Ctr., Phoenix, Sedona Sculpture Garden, Construct Gallery, Phoenix. Chmn. air pollution hearing bd. City of Phoenix, Maracopa County, 1970-85. Recipient Patent prize Patent Resources Group, 1979, Publ. award IEEE, 1967, Genematus award U. Ariz., 1964, Disting. Achievement award Ariz. State U., 1980, Construct Sculpture prize, 1989. Avocation: large scale steel sculpture. Office: Cahill Sutton & Thomas 2141 E Highland Ave Ste 155 Phoenix AZ 85016-4737

SUTTON, WALTER, English educator; b. Milw., Jan. 25, 1916; s. Walter Evender and Maud (Farrington) S.; m. Vivian Irene Ryan, Dec. 22, 1941; 1 dau., Catherine S. Penner. B.A., Heidelberg Coll., 1937; M.A., Ohio State U., 1938, Ph.D., 1946. Instr. English U. Rochester, 1946-47; successively asst. prof., asso. prof., prof. English, dir. grad. studies, chmn. dept. English Syracuse (N.Y.) U., 1948—, now distinguished prof. humanities, 1971—; Vis. prof. U. Minn., summer 1960; vis. prof., sr. vis. fellow Council Humanities Princeton, 1960-61; vis. prof. U. Wash., summer 1966, Colgate U., 1967, U. Hawaii, summer 1968; Mem. com. examiners advanced lit. test Grad. Record Exam., 1962-72. Author: The Western Book Trade, 1961, Modern American Criticism, 1963, American Free Verse: The Modern Revolution in Poetry, 1973; Editor: Ezra Pound: A Collection of Critical Essays, 1963, (with Richard Foster) Modern Criticism: Theory and Practice, 1963, (with Vivian Sutton) Plato to Alexander Pope: Backgrounds of Modern Criticism, 1966, (with others) American Literature: Tradition and Innovation, 1969-74, Pound, Thayer, Watson and The Dial: A Story in Letters, 1994; editorial bd.: (with others) Am. Lit., 1973-76. Served with USCGR, 1942-45. Recipient Ohioana Book award, 1963; Howald fellow Ohio State U., 1947-48. Mem. AAUP, Am. Soc. Aesthetics, Am. Studies Assn., Modern Lang. Assn. Am. Office: Dept English 401 HL Syracuse U Syracuse NY 13244

SUTTON, WILLIAM BLAYLOCK, pastor; b. Little Rock, Aug. 10, 1942; s. Richard Otto and Bettye (Blaylock) S.; m. Martha Davis, Apr. 19, 1968; children: Blake, Bryan, Stephen. BBA, Baylor U., 1964; BD, Southwestern Bapt. Theol. Sem., Ft. Worth, 1967; ThM, Internat. Theol. Sem., Orlando, Fla., 1982, DD, 1984. Ordained to ministry So. Bapt. Conv., 1965. Pastor North Hopkins Bapt. Ch., Sulphur Springs, Tex., 1965-67, 1st Bapt. Ch. Pine Hills, Orlando, 1969-77, Windsor Park Bapt. Ch., Ft. Smith, Ark., 1977-86; assoc. pastor Dauphin Way Bapt. Ch., Mobile, Ala., 1968-69; pastor 1st Bapt. Ch., McAllen, Tex., 1986—; v.p. Fla. Bapt. Pastors Conf., Orlando, 1973; pres. Ark. Bapt. Pastors Conf., Ft. Smith, 1983; trustee fgn. mission bd. So. Bapt. Conv., Richmond, Va., 1990—. Bd. visitors Criswell Coll., Dallas, 1991. Office: 1st Bapt Ch 1200 Beech Ave Mcallen TX 78501-4606

SUTTON, WILLIS ANDERSON, JR., sociology educator; b. Atlanta, July 18, 1917; s. Willis Anderson and Louneal (Walton) S.; m. Dorothy Rebecca Drake, Dec. 22, 1941; children: Willis Anderson III, Franklin Drake, Sarah Sutton Haggard. Student, Young Harris Jr. Coll., 1934-36; B.A., U. N.C., 1939, M.A., 1941, Ph.D., 1952. Project dir. WPA, Ga., 1940-41; instr. Emory U., Atlanta, 1948-52; asst. prof. U. Ky., Lexington, 1952-58; asso. prof. U. Ky., 1959-68, prof. sociology, 1968-82, chmn. dept., 1976-82. Author: Village Level Workers and Their Work, 1962. Served to 2d lt. U.S. Army, 1941-45. Ford Found. fellow India, 1959-60. Mem. Am. Sociol. Assn., Soc. Study Social Problems, Soc. Study Symbolic Interaction, So. Sociol. Soc., North Central Sociol. Soc. Democrat. Presbyterian.

SUTTON-STRAUS, JOAN M., journalist; b. Mimico, Ont., Can., Nov. 30, 1932; d. Frederick Edward and Anna May (Taylor) Treble; m. Walter J. Sutton, Feb. 1955 (div. 1979); children: Walter John, Deborah Anne.; m. Oscar S. Straus, Mar. 1982. Fashion editor Toronto Telegram, 1972; lifestyle editor, daily columnist Sutton's Place, Toronto Sun, 1972-79; daily commentator Sta. CFRB, Toronto, 1974-77; columnist Toronto Star, 1979; agt. gen. to U.S. Ont., 1990-91; columnist Toronto, Calgary, Edmonton and Ottawa Sun. Fin. Post, 1992-94. Author: Lovers and Others, 1974, Once More with Love, 1975, Clothing and Culture, 1975, Lovelines, 1979, All Men are not Alike, 1980, A Legacy of Caring, 1996. Former mem. adv. bd. Peggy Guggenheim Mus.; former trustee Am. Acad. Dramatic Arts; nat. gov. The Shaw Festival; trustee Am. Friends of Can., The Banff Ctr.; dir. Citizens Com. for N.Y.C., Soc. Meml. Sloan-Kettering Cancer Ctr. Recipient Judy award Garment Salesmen Ont., 1964, Canada medal, 1993; named Can. Woman of Yr., N.Y.C., 1990; honored with Freedom of City of London. Home: 7 Gracie Sq New York NY 10028

SUUBERG, ERIC MICHAEL, chemical engineering educator; b. N.Y.C., Nov. 23, 1951; s. Michael and Aino (Berg) S.; m. Ina Inara Vatvars, Apr. 26, 1987; 1 child, Alessandra Anna. BSChemE, MIT, 1974, MSChemE, 1974, BS in Bus. Mgmt., 1974, MS in Bus. Mgmt., 1976, ScD in Chem. Engring., 1978. Asst. prof. chem. engring. Carnegie-Mellon U., Pitts., 1977-81; asst. prof. engring. Brown U., Providence, 1981-84, assoc. prof. engring., 1984-90, prof. engring., 1990—, rep. exec. com. fluids, thermal and chem. processes group, 1991—; vis. scientist Centre National de la Recherche Scientifique, Mulhouse, France, 1988; invited lectr. Ministry Edn., Monbusho, Japan, 1991, 93. Mem. internat. editorial bd. Fuel, 1988—; mem. editorial adv. bd. Energy and Fuels, 1990-93; contbr. over 75 articles to profl. jours. Elected mem. Estonian Am. Nat. Coun., N.Y.C., 1984—, v.p. 1996—. Vice Chancellor's Rsch. Best Practice fellow U. Newcastle, Australia, 1995. Mem. AIChE, Combustion Inst., Am. Chem. Soc. (chmn. divsn. fuel chemistry 1991, bd. dirs.-at-large 1995-97). Office: Brown Univ Divsn Engring Box D Providence RI 02912

SUWYN, MARK A., building products executive; b. Denver, Aug. 12, 1942. BS in Chemistry, Hope Coll., Holland, Mich., 1964; PhD in Inorganic Chemistry, Wash. State U., 1967. From R&D to gen. mgmt. positions DuPont Co., 1967-91, sr. v.p. imaging and med. products, 1989-91; exec. v.p. Internat. Paper, Purchase, N.Y., 1991-95; CEO Louisianna Pacific Corp., Portland, 1995—. Office: Louisianna Pacific Corp 111 SW 5th Ave Portland OR 97204-3604

SUYCOTT, MARK LELAND, naval flight officer; b. Riverside, Calif., Oct. 3, 1956; s. Morgan L. Suycott and Dixie L. (Drury) Bobbitt; m. Lisa Lyn Brammer, Oct. 1, 1983. BSCE, U. Mo., 1979; MS in Aero. Engring., Naval Postgrad. Sch., Monterey, Calif., 1987; test flight officer, U.S. Naval Test Pilot Sch., Patuxent River, Md., 1987; student, Def. Sys. Mgmt. Coll., Ft. Belvoir, Va., 1994. Commd. ensign USN, 1979, advanced through grades to comdr., 1995; aviation armament divsn. officer Fighter Squadron Thirty Three, Virginia Beach, Va., 1981-84; flight test project officer Pacific Missile Test Ctr., Point Mugu, Calif., 1987-89; air ops. officer Comdr. U.S. 7th Fleet, Yokosuka, Japan, 1989-91; ops./maintenance officer Fighter Squadron 11, San Diego, 1992-93; dep. asst. program mgr. Naval Air Sys. Command, Arlington, Va., 1994-97; instr. Def. System Mgmt. Coll., Fort Belvoir, Va., 1997—. Decorated Meritorious Svc. medal, Navy Commendation medal (2), Navy Achievement medal; named Outstanding Grad. U.S. Naval Test Pilot Sch. Mem. AIAA (sr.), Soc. Flight Test Engrs., Assn. Naval Aviation, NAt. Eagle Scout Assn., Masons (master mason), Omicron Delta Kappa, Tau Beta Pi, Chi Epsilon, Alpha Phi Omega (life). Avocations: running, sailing, skiing. Office: Def Systems Mgmt Coll 9820 Belvoir Rd Fort Belvoir VA 22060-5565

SUYDAM, PETER R., clinical engineer, consultant; b. Jersey City, Apr. 1, 1945; s. Stedman Mills and Winifred M. (Murphy) S.; m. Patricia Cunniff, Feb. 2, 1970 (dec. 1976); m. Jaimy Slifka, Feb. 11, 1978; children—Ryckren Stedman, Stephen Michael. Student in engring. Rensselaer Poly. Inst.; student in pre-medicine, psychology, U. Rochester; B.S. in Bio-Engring., U. Ill.-Chgo., 1975. Cert. clin. engr.; cert. health care safety profl. Dir. clin. engring. Rush-Presbyn.-St. Luke's Med. Ctr., Chgo., 1975-81; pres. Syzygy, Inc., Chgo., 1978-81; lead auditor quality assurance Callaway Nuclear Power Plant, Union Elec. Co., St. Louis, 1981-84; sr. cons. Ellerbe Assocs., Inc., Mpls., 1984-86; div. mgr. CH Health Technologies, Inc., St. Louis, 1986—; project mgr. Landmark Contract Mgmt., Inc., 1988-89; dir. healthcare tech. planning The Cannon Corp., 1989-91; tech. advisor New V.I.P. Hosp., Riyadh, Saudi Arabia, 1991-92; dir. mid. east ops. E.C.R.I., 1992—; staff cons. Joint Commn. on Accreditation for Hosps., Chgo., 1978-81; mem. tech. com. Safe Use of Electricity in Patient Care Areas of Health Care Facilities; mem. Bd. Examiners for Clin. Engring. Cert., 1980-85; com. mem. Midwest Med. Group Standards, Chgo. Hosp. Council, 1976-81. Contbr. articles to profl. jours. Served with USN, 1967-73. Mem. Assn. Advancement Med. Instrumentation (elec. safety com. 1980—), AAAS, IEEE (chpt. chmn. group on engring. in medicine and biology), Instrument Soc. Am., Am. Nat. Standards Inst., Am. Hosp. Assn., Nat. Fire Protection Assn. (health care, elec. and engring. sects.), Am. Soc. Hosp. Engrs., Am. Soc. Quality Control. Current work: Biotechnology applications in medicine and industry; quality assurance-all fields. Subspecialties: Biomedical engineering; Clinical engineering. Office: 5200 Butler Pike Plymouth Meeting PA 19462-1241

SUZIEDELIS, VYTAUTAS A., engineering corporation executive; b. Kaunas, Lithuania, June 22, 1930; s. Simas and Antanina S. B.S., Northeastern U., 1954; M.S., N.Y. U., 1955. With Stone & Webster Engring. Corp., Boston, 1956-90, chief power engr., 1972-74, v.p., 1974-76, sr. v.p., 1976-79, exec. v.p., 1979-87, dir., 1975-87, cons., 1987-90; pres. Vasair Corp., Brockton, Mass., 1977-91. Mem. ASME, Aircraft Owners and Pilots Assn., Pi Tau Sigma (hon.). Republican. Roman Catholic. Home: 6849 Grenadier Blvd PH-05 Naples FL 34108

SUZUKI, BOB H., university president. Formerly v.p. acad. affairs Calif. State Univ., Northridge; pres. Calif. State Poly. Univ., Pomona, 1991—. Office: Calif State Polytech Univ Office of Pres 3801 W Temple Ave Pomona CA 91768-2557*

SUZUKI, HIDETARO, violinist; b. Tokyo, June 1, 1937; came to U.S., 1956; s. Hidezo and Humi (Sakai) S.; m. Zeyda Ruga, May 16, 1962; children: Kenneth Hideo, Nantel Hiroshi, Elina Humi. Diploma, Toho Sch. Music, Tokyo, 1956, Curtis Inst. Music, 1963. Prof. violin Conservatory Province Que., Quebec, 1963-79, Laval U., Quebec, 1971-77, Butler U., Indpls., 1979—. Concertmaster Que. Symphony Orch., 1963-78, Indpls. Symphony Orch., 1978—; performed as concert violinist Can., U.S., Ea. and Western Europe, Cuba, Japan, S.E. Asia, 1951—, formerly performed in USSR; guest condr. orchs. in numerous concerts, broadcasts, 1968—; mem. jury Mont. Internat. Competition, 1979, Internat. Violin Competition, 1979, Internat. Violin Competition of Indpls., 1982, 86, 90, 94; artistic dir. Suzuki and Friends chamber music series, 1980—; rec. artist. Office: Indpls Symphony Orch 45 Monument Cir Indianapolis IN 46204-2907

SUZUKI, HOWARD KAZURO, retired anatomist, educator; b. Ketchikan, Alaska, Apr. 3, 1927; s. Goerge K. and Tsuya S.; m. Tetsuko Fujita, Sept. 12, 1952; children: Georganne, Joan, James, Stanley. BS, Marquette U., 1949, MS, 1951; PhD, Tulane U., 1955. Instr. anatomy Yale U. Sch. Medicine, 1955-58; asst. prof. anatomy U. Ark. Med. Center, Little Rock, 1958-62; asso. prof. U. Ark. Med. Center, 1962-67, prof., 1967-70; prof. anatomy, asso. dean health related professions U. Fla., Gainesville, 1970-71; prof. anatomy U. Fla. (Coll. Medicine), 1970-71; dean U. Fla. (Coll. Health Related Professions), 1971-79; prof. anatomy U. Fla. (Coll. Medicine and Health Related Professions), 1979-90, ret., 1990; cons. NIH, VA, NASA; vis. research prof. U. Utah Sch. Medicine, 1962. Contbr. articles to profl. jours. Bd. dirs. Civitan Regional Blood Bank, 1977—; regional v.p. Fla. Retarded Citizens Assn., 1974-76; mem. Fla. Adv. Council on Voc. Edn., 1978-86, chmn., 1981; active United Way. Fellow AAAS; mem. Soc. Exptl. Biol. Medicine, Am Assn. Anatomists, Am. Soc. Allied Health Professions, Am. Soc. Marine Artists, Sigma Xi. Episcopalian. Home: 4331 NW 20th Pl Gainesville FL 32605-3436

SUZUKI, ISAMU, microbiology educator, researcher; b. Tokyo, Aug. 4, 1930; emigrated to Can., 1962; s. Jisaku and Michie (Baba) S.; m. Yumiko Kanehira, May 16, 1962; children: Kenji, Miyo, Kohji. B.Sc.Agr., U. Tokyo, 1953; Ph.D., Iowa State U., 1958. NIH postdoctoral fellow Western Res. U., 1958-60; instr. Inst. Applied Microbiology, U. Toyko, 1960-62; asst. prof. mcirobiology U. Man., Winnipeg, Can., 1964-66, assoc. prof., 1966-69, prof., 1969—, head. dept., 1972-85. Contbr. articles on sulfur-oxidizing bacteria, chemoautotrophic bacteria, mechanism of inorganic oxidation to sci. jours. NRC of Can. postdoctoral fellow, 1962-64. Mem. AAAS, Can. Soc. Microbiologists, Can. Biochem. Soc., Am. Soc. Microbiology, Sigma Xi. Office: U Manitoba Dept Microbiology, Winnipeg, MB Canada R3T 2N2

SUZUKI, JON BYRON, dean, periodontist, educator; b. San Antonio, July 22, 1947; s. George K. and Ruby (Kanaya) S. BA in Biology, Ill. Wesleyan U., 1968; PhD magna cum laude in Microbiology, Ill. Inst. Tech., 1971; DDS magna cum laude, Loyola U., 1978. Med. technologist Ill. Masonic Hosp. and Med. Ctr., Chgo., 1966-67; instr. lab. in histology and parasitology Ill. Wesleyan U., Bloomington, 1967-68; med. technologist Augustana Hosp., Chgo., 1968-69; rsch. assoc., instr. microbiology Ill. Inst. Tech., Chgo., 1968-71; clin. rsch. assoc. U. Chgo. Hosps., 1970-71; clin. microbiologist St. Luke's Hosp. Ctr., Columbia Coll., Physicians and Surgeons, N.Y.C., 1971-73; assoc. med. dir. Paramed. Tng. and Registry, Vancouver, B.C., Can., 1973-74; dir. clin. labs. Registry of Hawaii, 1973-74; chmn. clin. labs. edn. Kapiolani Community Coll., U. Hawaii, Honolulu, 1974; lectr. periodontics, oral pathology Loyola U. Med. Ctr., Maywood, Ill., 1974-90; lectr. stomatology Northwestern U. Dental Sch., Chgo., 1982-90; NIH rsch. fellow depts. pathology and periodontics Ctr. for Rsch. in Oral Biology, U. Wash.-Seattle, 1978-80; prof. dept. periodontics and microbiology U. Md. Coll. Dental Surgery, Balt., 1980-90; mem. attending faculty divsn. dentistry and oral and maxillofacial surgery The Johns Hopkins Med. Inst., Balt., 1985—; practice dentistry specializing in periodontics Balt., Pitts.; dean Sch. Dental Medicine, U. Pitts., 1989—; cons. Dentsply Internat., York, Pa., U.S. Army, Walter Reed Med. Ctr., Washington, U.S. Army, Ft. Gordon, Ga., USN, Nat. Naval Med. Command, Bethesda, The NutraSweet Co., Deerfield, Ill.; cons. Food and Drug Adminstrn., Rockville, Md.; mem. Oral Biology/medicine study sect. NIH, Bethesda, 1985-90; mem. nat. adv. dental rsch. coun. NIH/NIDR, Bethesda, 1994—; vis. scientist to Moscow State U., USSR, 1972, NASA, Houston, 1976-92; lectr. Internat. Congress Allergology, Tokyo, 1973; lab. dir. Hawaii Dept. Health. Author: Clinical Laboratory Methods for the Medical Assistant, 1974; mem. editorial bd. Am. Health Mag.; contbr. articles on research in microbiology, immunology and dentistry to sci. jours. Instr. water safety ARC, Honolulu, 1973-90. Recipient Pres.'s medallion Loyola U., Chgo., 1977; named Alumnus of Yr., Ill. Wesleyan U., 1977. Fellow Acad. Dentistry Internat., Am Coll. Dentists, Internat. Coll. Dentists, Am. Coll. Stomatognathic Surgeons; mem. AAAS, ADA (vice chair coun. sci. affairs), AAUP, Am. Acad. Periodontology (diplomate), Am. Inst. Biol. Scis., Internat. Soc. Biophysics, Internat. Soc. Endocrinologists, Ill. Acad. Sci. , Am. Internat. Assn. Dental Rsch. (pres. Md. chpt.), Am. Acad. Microbiology (diplomate), Am. Acad. Microbiology (diplomate, examiner), N.Y. Acad. Scis., Sigma XI, Omicron Kappa Upsilon (past nat. pres., exec. sec.), Beta, Beta, Beta Hon. Soc. Home: 3501 Terrace St Pittsburgh PA 15213-2523 Office: U Pitts Sch Dental Medicine Dean's Office Pittsburgh PA 15261

SUZUKI, KUNIHIKO, biomedical educator, researcher; b. Tokyo, Japan, Feb. 5, 1932; came to U.S., 1960; s. Nobuo and Teiko (Suzuki) S.; m. Kinuko Ikeda, Dec. 20, 1960; 1 child, Jun. BA in History and Philosophy of Sci., Tokyo U., 1955, MD, 1959; MA (hon.), U. Pa., 1971. Diplomate Nat. Bd. Med. Licensure Japan. Rotating intern USAF Hosp. Tachikawa, Tokyo, Japan, 1959-60; asst. resident in neurology Bronx (N.Y.) Mcpl. Hosp. Ctr.-Albert Einstein Coll. Medicine, 1960-61, resident in neurology, 1961-62, clin. fellow in neurology, 1962-64; instr. in neurology Albert Einstein Coll. Medicine, Bronx, 1964, asst. prof., 1965-68; assoc. prof. U. Pa. Sch. Medicine, Phila., 1969-71, prof. neurology and pediatrics, 1971-72; prof. neurology Albert Einstein Coll. Medicine, 1972-86, prof. neurosci., 1974-86; prof. neurology and psychiatry, faculty curriculum in neurobiology U. N.C. Sch. Medicine, Chapel Hill, 1986—; dir. UNC Neurosci. Ctr., Chapel Hill, 1986—; staff dept. neuropsychiatry Tokyo U. Faculty Medicine, 1960, U. Pa. Inst. Neurol. Scis., 1969-72; attending physician Bronx Mcpl. Hosp. Ctr., 1976-86, Hosp. Albert Einstein Coll. Medicine, 1977-86; vis. prof. fellowship Japan Soc. for Promotion Sci., 1980, Yamada Sci. Found., 1981; mem. neurology B study sect. NIH, 1971-75, guest scientist, 1984-85, program com. mental retardation and devel. disabilities, 1989-92; mem. basic neurosci. task force Nat. Inst. Neurol. and Communicative Disorders and Stroke, 1978, adv. panel directions and opportunities for future research, 1983, bd. sci. counselors, NIH, 1980-84; mem. adv. com. on fellowships Nat. Multiple Sclerosis Soc., 1974-77; jury St. Vincent Internat. award for Med. Sci., 1979; mem. adv. com. Eunice Kennedy Shriver Ctr., Waltham, Mass., 1974-84; med. adv. bd. Children's Assn. for Research on Mucolipidosis Type IV, 1983—; mem. U.S. Nat. Com. for Internat. Brain Research Orgn., 1985-89. Editor: Ganglioside Structure and Function, 1984; chief editor Jour. Neurochemistry, 1977-82, dep. chief editor, 1975-77; mem. editl. bd. Jour. Neuropathology and Exptl. Neurology, 1981-83, Neurosci., 1975—, Molecular Chem. Neuropathology, 1983—, Neurochem. Rsch., 1985-89, Metabolic Brain Disease, 1985-87, Molecular Brain Rsch., 1985—, Jour. Molecular Neurosci., 1987—, Developmental Neurosci., 1987—, Jour. Neurosci. Rsch., 1993-97; contbr. articles to profl. jours. Mem. Nat. Adv. Commn. on Multiple Sclerosis, 1973-74; mem. med. adv. bd. United Leukodystrophy Found., 1982-86, Nat. Tay-Sachs and Allied Diseases Assn., 1971—, Canavan Found., 1992—. Recipient A. Weil award Am. Assn. Neuropathologists, 1970, Saul R. Korey Lectureship, 1993, M. Moore award, 1975; Jacob K. Javits Neurosci. Investigator award NIH, 1985, 92, Humboldt Sr. Rsch. award Humboldt Found., 1990, Eminent Scientist award Inst. Phys. Chem. Rsch., Japan, 1995. Mem. NAS, AAAS, Am. Soc. for Neurochemistry (prs. 1985-87, coun. 1973-77, 87-91, Basic Neurochemistry Lectureship 1995), Internat. Soc. for Neurochemistry (coun. 1987-89, treas. 1989-93, pres. 1993-95), Soc. for Neurosci., Am. Soc. Biochemistry and Molecular Biology, Am. Acad. Neurology, Japanese Med. Soc. Am. (Disting. Scientist award 1985), Japanese Neurochem. Soc., Internat. Brain Rsch. Orgn., Am. Soc. Human Genetics, Japan Soc. Inherited Metabolic Disease (hon.). Avocations: piano, photography, bird watching, skiing. Office: U N C Chapel Hill Neurosci Ctr Campus Box 7250 Chapel Hill NC 27599-7250

SUZUKI, MICHIO, mathematics educator; b. Chiba, Japan, Oct. 2, 1926; came to U.S., 1952; s. Kyosuke and Taka (Saito); m. Naoko Akizuki, Nov. 11, 1952; 1 child, Kazuko. B.S., U. Tokyo, 1945-48, Ph.D., 1952; hon. degree, U. Kiel, Fed. Republic Germany, 1991. Asst. prof. math. U. Ill.-Urbana, 1955-57, assoc. prof., 1958, prof., 1959—, prof. Center Advanced Study, 1968—; research assoc. Harvard U., 1956; vis. prof. U. Chgo., 1960; mem. Inst. Advanced Study, Princeton, N.J., 1962, 68, 81. Recipient Acad. prize Japan Acad., 1974; Guggenheim fellow, 1962. Mem. Am. Math. Soc. (council 1962-71), Math. Soc. Japan. Home: 2406 Melrose Dr Champaign IL 61820-7607 Office: Dept Math U Ill 1409 W Green St Urbana IL 61801-2943

SUZUKI, NOBUTAKA, chemistry educator; b. Nishio, Aichi, Japan, Nov. 8, 1942; s. Kihachiro and Masayo (Miwa) S.; m. Fumiko Sato, Mar. 21, 1971; children: Mina, Kumi. B of Chemistry, Nagoya U., Japan, 1966, D of Chemistry, 1972. Asst. prof. dept. chemistry Mie U., Tsu, Japan, 1971-88, assoc. prof., 1988; sr. rschr. Biophoton project JRDC, Sendai, Japan, 1988-90; assoc. prof. Shimonoseki (Japan) Nat. U. Fisheries, 1990-92, prof., 1993—; postdoctoral staff Johns Hopkins U., Balt., 1977-79. Author: Natural Products Chemistry, 1975, 2d rev. edit., 1983, Bioluminescence of Chemiluminescence, Current Status, 1991, Oxygen Radicals, 1992, Chemistry of Functional Dyes, vol. 2, 1993, Bioluminescence and Chemiluminescence, status report, 1993, Bioluminescence and Chemiluminescence: Fundamentals and Applied Aspects, 1994, Maillard Reactions in Chem., Food, and Health, 1994, Food Factors: Chemistry and Cancer Prevention, 1997, Bioluminescence and Chemiluminescence, Molecular Reporting and Photons, 1997, Food Factors: Chemistry and Cancer Prevention, 1997; editor: (book) The Roles of Oxygen in Chemistry and Biochemistry, 1988, (book/tape) Scientific English in Fisheries, 1992, English for Science and Technological Experiments, 1994, English for Pharmacy and Medical Science, 1995, English for International Conference, 1995. Recipient Internat. Tech. Exch. Soc. award, 1995, Rsch. award Internat. Battery Material Assn., 1997; grantee Naito Meml. Found., 1977, Tokai Sci. Rsch. Found., 1986, Agrl. Biol. Chemistry Japan, 1990, Kiei-Kai Sci. Rsch. Found., 1991-96, Skylark Rsch. Found., 1992, The Sci. and Tech. Agy., Japan, 1994-96, Internat. Tech. Exch. K-Found., 1996-97, Internat. Battery Material Assn. Mem. Am. Chem. Soc., Am. Soc. for Photobiology, Agrl. Biol. Soc. Japan, Chem. Soc. Japan, Japan Soc. Sci. Fisheries, Internat. Tech. Exch. Soc. (bd. dirs. 1995—). Office: Nat U Fisheries, Yoshimi, Shimonoseki Yamaguchi 75965, Japan

SUZUKI, TSUNEO, molecular immunologist; b. Nagoya, Aichi, Japan, Nov. 23, 1931; s. Morichika and Toshiko (Kita) S.; widowed; children: Riichiro, Aijiro, Yozo. BS, U. Tokyo, 1953, MD, 1957; PhD, U. Hokkaido, 1967. Asst. prof. U. Kans. Med. Ctr., Kansas City, 1970-79, assoc. prof., 1979-83, prof., 1983—, interim chair, 1994—; mem. NIH Study Sect., Washington, 1983-87. Contbr. articles to profl. jours. Postdoctoral fellows U. Wis., 1963-66, 69-70, U. Lausanne, Switzerland, 1966-67, U Toronto, 1969; recipient Fulbright Travel award, 1962, Sr. Investigator award, U. Kans. Med. Ctr., 1990. Mem. Am. Assn. Immunologists, Am. Soc. Biological Chemists (Travel award 1988). Home: 3620 W 73rd St Prairie Village KS 66208-2903 Office: U Kans Med Ctr Dept Microbiology 3901 Rainbow Blvd Kansas City KS 66160-0001

SVADLENAK, JEAN HAYDEN, museum administrator, consultant; b. Wilmington, Del., Mar. 4, 1955; d. Marion M. and Ida Jean (Calcagni) Hayden; m. Steven R. Svadlenak, May 26, 1979. BS in Textiles and Clothing, U. Del., 1977; MA in History Mus. Studies, SUNY, Oneonta, 1982; postgrad., U. Calif., Berkeley, 1982. Curatorial asst. The Hagley Mus., Wilmington, 1976-77; curator of costumes and textiles The Kansas City (Mo.) Mus., 1978-82, chief curator, 1982-84, assoc. exec. dir. for collection and exhibits mgmt., 1984-86, interim pres., 1986-87, pres., 1987-89; researcher, guest curator N.Y. State Hist. Assn., Cooperstown, 1980; grant reviewer Inst. for Mus. Svcs., 1985-89; ad hoc faculty U. Kans., 1991—, U. Mo., Kansas City, 1992—. Mem. Am. Assn. Mus. (surveyor mus. assessment program 1985-89, mem. accreditation vis. com. 1990—), Am. Assn.

State and Local History, Costume Soc. Am., Heritage League Kansas City (bd. dirs. 1987-89), Midwest Mus. Conf. (coun. 1992-94), Mo. Mus. Assocs. (pres. 1992-94, com. on mus. profl. tng. 1993—, 2d v.p. 1994-96). Avocations: music, sports, photography, cooking. Home: 624 Romany Rd Kansas City MO 64113-2037

SVAGER, THYRSA ANNE FRAZIER, university administrator, retired educator; b. Wilberforce, Ohio, July 16; d. G. Thurston and E. Anne Frazier; m. Aleksandar Svager. AB, Antioch Coll., Yellow Springs, Ohio, 1951; MA, Ohio State U., 1952, PhD, 1965. Statist. analyst Wright Patterson AFB (Ohio), 1952-53; instr. Tex. So. U., Houston, 1953-54; from asst. to assoc. prof. Ctrl. State U., Wilberforce, 1954-66, prof., chmn., 1966-85, v.p. acad. affairs, 1985-89, exec. v.p., provost, 1989—; adj. faculty Antioch Coll., 1964; vis. prof. Nat. Sci. Found. Inst., 1966-67; vis. faculty MIT, 1969; cons. in field. Author: Essential Mathematics, 1976, rev. edit., 1983, Compact Facts-Calculus, 1980, (workbook) Modern Elementary Algebra, 1969. NSF grantee, 1969-71, 76-79; recipient Svc. award Jack and Jill Am., 1985, Edn. award Green County Women's Hall of Fame, 1986, Edn. award Top Ladies of Distinction Wilberforce chpt., 1985, Svc. award Challenge 95 Human Needs Task Force, 1992. Mem. NAACP, Nat. Urban League, Math. Assn. Am., Nat. Assn. Math., Nat. Coun. Tchrs. of Math., Assn. Computing Machinery, Assn. Study Afro-Am. Life and History, Phi Mu Epsilon, Beta Kappa Chi, Alpha Kappa Mu, Alpha Kappa Alpha (life). Avocations: travel, tournament bridge, antique glass. Office: Ctrl State U PO Box 174 Wilberforce OH 45384-0174

SVAHN, JOHN ALFRED, government official; b. New London, Conn., May 13, 1943; s. Albert Russell and Esther Marilu (Caffero) S.; m. Jill Weber, July 12, 1977; children: Kirsten Marie, John Alfred III. B.A. in Polit. Sci, U. Wash., 1966; postgrad., U. Pacific, 1970-73, Georgetown U., 1973-74. Spl. asst. to dir. Calif. Dept. Public Works, 1966-70; chief dep. dir. Calif. Dept. Social Welfare, 1971-73, dir., 1973; acting commr. Community Services Adminstrn., HEW, Washington, 1973-74; commr. Assistance Payments Adminstrn., 1973-76; dep. adminstr. Social and Rehab. Service, 1974-75; adminstr. Social and Rehab. Svcs., 1975-76; mgr. Haskins and Sells, 1976-79; pres. John A. Svahn, Inc., Annapolis, Md., 1979-81; U.S. commr. social security Balt., 1981-83; undersec. HHS, Washington, 1983-84; assst. to Pres. for policy devel. Washington, 1984-86; chmn. Maximus Inc., Washington, 1988-94; U.S. commr. Commn. for Study of Alternatives for Panama Canal, 1987-92; exec. v.p. The Wexler Group, Washington, 1995—. Mem. Nat. Devel. Disability Adv. Council, 1975-76, Pres.'s Transition Team, 1980-81, Calif. Health Care Commn., 1972, pub. affairs com. United Way Am., 1987—; chmn. Govs. Commn. on Corrections Health Care, Md., 1990—; assoc. mem. Calif. Republican State Cen. Com., 1970-72; bd. dirs. Nat. Aquarium, Balt.; bd. dirs. Health Care Svcs. NAS Inst. Medicine, 1987-92; mem. Gov.'s Privatization Coun., 1992—. Served to lt. USAF, 1966-68. Named Outstanding Young Man in HEW, 1974; recipient Sec.'s citation, 1975, Adminstr.'s spl. citation, 1975. Mem. Phi Delta Phi, Zeta Psi. Republican. Clubs: Annapolis Yacht, Sailing of the Chesapeake. Office: 1356 Beverly Rd Mc Lean VA 22101-3625

SVANBORG, ALVAR, geriatrics educator, researcher; b. Umea, Sweden, Nov. 15, 1921; s. Arvid and Althea (Lindstrom) S.; m. Marianne Lindh, Dec. 11, 1948; children: Catharina, Elisabeth, Anna, Arvid. MD, Karolinska Inst., Stockholm, 1948, Phd, 1951. With U. Goteborg, Gothenburg, Sweden, 1954—, prof. geriatric and long term med. care, 1976-88, prof. emeritus geriatric and long term med. care, 1988—; prof. medicine U. Ill. Chgo., 1988-96, Beth Fowler Vitoux and George E. Vitoux Disting. prof. geriatric medicine, 1994-96, prof. emeritius, 1996—; sci. advisor Swedish Nat. Bd. Health & Welfare, Stockholm, 1968-88; advisor, cons. WHO, Geneva, 1970—; chmn. Fedn. Gerontology Nordic Countries, 1977-88; advisor US Govtl. Orgn., NIH, U.S. Senate and The White House. Mem. editorial bd. Jour. Clin. Exptl. Gerontology, 1977, Archives of Gerontology & Geriatrics, 1977, Comprehensive Gerontology, 1986-89, Aging, Clin. and Exptl. Rsch., 1989, Drugs & Aging, 1992, Encyclopedia of Gerontology, 1996. Expert Supreme Nat. Swedish Ins. Ct., Stockholm, 1969-88; Swedish del. UN, 1982; mem. expert adv. panel to dir. gen. WHO, 1984—; program dir. AMVETS Reactivation Ctr., Edward Hines, Jr. VA Hosp., Chgo. Recipient Thureus prize U. Uppsala, Sweden, 1980, Gothenburg City Gold medal, 1983, Brookdale Fgn. award Brookdale Found., 1985, Sandoz prize Internat. Assn. Gerontology, 1987. Mem. Royal Soc. Art and Scis. of Sweden, Ill. Geriatric Soc., Am. Geriatric Soc., Gerontol. Soc. Am., Alpha Omega Alpha. Home: 175 No Harbor Dr Apt 1011 Chicago IL 60601 also: 13 Herrgaardsgatan, S-412 74 Goeteborg Sweden Office: U Ill 840 S Wood St Chicago IL 60612-7317

SVEC, HARRY JOHN, chemist, educator; b. Cleve., June 24, 1918; s. Ralph Joseph and Lilian Josephine (Pekarek) S.; m. Edna Mary Bruno, Oct. 27, 1943; children—Mary, Peter, Katherine, Jan, Thomas, Jean, Benjamin, Daniel, Lillian. BS, John Carroll U., 1941; PhD in Phys. Chemistry, Iowa State U., 1949. Asst. chemist Iowa State U., 1941-43; research asso. Inst. Atomic Research, 1946-50, asst. prof. chemistry, 1950-55, assoc. prof., 1955-60, prof., 1960-83, emeritus prof., 1983—, Disting. prof. in scis. and humanities, 1978—; asso. chemist Ames Lab., 1950-55; chemist Ames Lab., Dept. Energy, 1955-60, sr. chemist, 1960-85, program dir., 1974-85, assoc. scientist, 1983—; jr. chemist Manhattan Project, 1943-46; cons., lectr. in field. Author lab. manual in phys. chemistry; contbr. numerous articles to profl. publs.; founding editor: Internat. Jour. Mass Spectrometry and Ion Processes, 1968-86. NSF grantee, 1972-82; EPA grantee, 1974-81; AEC grantee, 1950-74; ERDA grantee, 1974-77; Dept. Energy grantee, 1977-87; Am. Water Works Assn. grantee, 1977-79. Fellow AAAS, The Chem. Soc., Am. Chem. Soc.; mem. ASTM, Geochem. Soc., Am. Soc. Mass Spectroscopy (charter, v.p. 1972-74, pres. 1974-76), Sigma Xi, Alpha Sigma Nu, Phi Lambda Upsilon, Alpha Chi Sigma (cons. 1985—). Roman Catholic. Home: 2427 Hamilton Dr Ames IA 50014-8203 Office: Iowa State U 1605 Gilman Hall Ames IA 50014-8203 *Success in anything we choose to do requires a commitment. The degree of one's success depends directly on the kind of commitment that is made.*

SVEDA, MICHAEL, management and research consultant; b. West Ashford, Conn., Feb. 3, 1912; s. Michael and Dorothy (Druppa) S.; m. Martha Augusta Gaeth, Aug. 23, 1936; children—Sally Anne, Michael Max. B.S., U. Toledo, 1934; Ph.D. (Eli Lilly research fellow), U. Ill., 1939. Tchr. chemistry U. Toledo, 1932-35, U. Ill., 1935-37; research, sales and product mgmt. positions E.I. du Pont de Nemours & Co., Inc., 1939-54; mgmt. counsel Wilmington, Del., 1955-59; dir. acad. sci. projects NSF, 1960-61; corp. assoc. dir. research FMC Corp., 1962-64; mgmt. and research counsel to academia, industry and govt., 1965—; lectr. univs., 1961—, fed. govt., groups, 1965—; mem. adv. com. on creativity in scientists and engrs. Rensselaer Poly. Inst., 1965—. Numerous appearances on pub. and comml. TV and radio. Named Outstanding Alumnus U. Toledo, 1954. Fellow AAAS (life); mem. Am. Chem. Soc., Sigma Xi, Phi Kappa Phi, Alpha Chi Sigma, Phi Lambda Upsilon. Patentee chems. and processes in polymers, pesticides, chem. intermediates; synthesizer, discoverer cyclamates, sweetening agts., 1937; deviser new concepts and patentee 3 dimensional models complex orgns., selection key personnel; new approach to diets, taking off human fat; new use Boolean algebra, theory of sets in people problems; active drive to have cyclamate sweeteners reinstated, 1973—. Address: Revonah Woods 228 West Ln Stamford CT 06905-3959 *Basic capacity for intelligence is given to us through inheritance. Knowledge—and stupidity—we acquire or develop. My objective has been to minimize my acquisition of, or contribution to, stupidity, while developing as much new knowledge as possible for mankind.*

SVEINSSON, JOHANNES, former city and county government official, building material sales engineer; b. Winnipeg, Man., Can., Nov. 30, 1912; m. M. Eleanor Lundstedt, 1938; children: Joleen Sveinsson Kinney, Kenneth J., Johannes. Student, Fresno State Coll., 1935, U. Calif.-Berkeley, 1940. With Pacific Rock & Gravel & Paving Co., Los Angeles, 1935-41; counselor Calif. Dept. Corrections, 1941-76. Bd. dirs. Anti Poverty, Monterey County, 1965-75, Monterey County Med. Assn., 1977, Sr. Citizens, Monterey County, 1982-88; v.p. Monterey Bay Govts., Monterey, Santa Cruz and San Benito Counties, 1960-83; mem. Gonzales City Council Calif., 1960-83; pres. Calif. League of Cities, Monterey Bay Div., 1976-77; mayor Gonzales, 1981-83; mem. Monterey County Grand Jury, Salinas, Calif., 1983—; mem. Monterey County Grand Jury, 1991. Served with USAAF, 1942-45. Mem. Calif. League Cities (bd. dirs. pub. safety com. 1962-74), Icelandic Assn. No. Calif. (pres. 1966), Am. Scandanavians of Calif. (pres. 1975). Democrat. Home: Apt 103 211 N 40th Ave Yakima WA 98908

SVENDSBYE, LLOYD AUGUST, college president, clergyman, educator; b. Hamlet, N.D., May 26, 1930; s. Anders A. and Gudrun J. (Birkelo) S.; m. Annelotte Frieda Erika Moertelmeyer, Dec. 20, 1958. BA, Concordia Coll., Moorhead, Minn., 1951, DD (hon.), 1983; BTh, Luther Theol.Sem., 1954; postgrad, U. Erlangen, Germany, 1954-55, Columbia U., 1959-60; ThD, Union Theol. Sem., 1966; LLD (hon.), Gettysburg Coll., 1977; LHD (hon.), Kilian C.C., 1992. Ordained to ministry, 1955; asst. pastor Our Saviours Luth. Ch., Mpls., 1955-56; adminstrv. asst. to dir. 3d Assembly Luth. World Fedn., 1956-57; asst. prof. religion Concordia Coll., 1957-59; asst. pastor Trinity Lutheran Ch., Bklyn., 1959-61; chmn. dept. religion Concordia Coll., 1962-66; editor in chief Augsburg Publ. House, Mpls., 1966-71; v.p., dean St. Olaf Coll., 1971-74; pres., prof. ch. history Luther Theol. Sem., St. Paul, 1974-82; pres. Northwestern Luth. Theol. Sem., 1976-82; pres. Luther Northwestern Theol. Sem., 1982-87, prof. ch. history, 1982-87; pres. Augustana Coll., Sioux Falls, S.D., 1987-92; v.p. Am. Luth. Ch., 1981-87; Mem. Am. Luth. Ch.-Luth. Ch. Am. coop. com., 1974-78; Luth. World Fedn. Com. on Info. Services, 1971-76; mem. Com. on Luth. Unity, 1978-82, Commn. To Form a New Luth. Ch., 1982-86. Chmn. senate dist. 49A, Dem. Farm Labor Com., 1970-71; bd. dirs. Luth. Brotherhood, 1970-95, Luth. Gen. and Health Care Sys., Park Ridge, Ill., 1981-87; trustee Luth. Deaconess Hosp., Mpls., 1970-71, Fairview-Southdale Hosp., 1975-87, Fairview Cmty. Hosps., 1979-87. Recipient Alumni Achievement award Concordia Coll., 1974. Home: 2500 Quentin Ct Saint Louis Park MN 55416-1900

SVENGALIS, KENDALL FRAYNE, law librarian; b. Gary, Ind., May 16, 1947; s. Frank Anthony and Alvida Linnea (Matheus) S.; m. Deborah Kay Andrews, May 23, 1970; children: Hillary Linnea, Andrew Kendall. BA, Purdue U., 1970, MA, 1973; MLS, U. R.I., 1975. Reference librarian Roger Williams Coll., Bristol, R.I., 1975, Providence (R.I.) Coll., 1975-77; asst. law librarian R.I. State Law Library, Providence, 1976-82, state law librarian, 1982—; adj. prof. libr. and info. studies U. R.I., 1987—. Author: The Legal Information Buyer's Guide and Reference Manual, 1996—; editor: The Criv Sheet, 1988-94; contbr. articles to profl. jours. Chmn. jud. branch United Way Com. R.I., 1980. Mem. Am. Assn Law Librs. (state, ct. and county libr. spl. interest sect., recipient Connie E. Bolden significant publ. award 1993, bd. dirs. 1986-88, 96—), Law Librs. New Eng. (treas. 1983-85, v.p. 1985-86, pres. 1986-87), Com. on Rels. with Info. Vendors (editor 1988-94), New Eng. Law Libr. Consortium (v.p. 1990-92, pres. 1992-94). Republican. Lutheran. Home: 17 Mosher Dr Barrington RI 02806-1909 Office: RI State Law Libr Frank Licht Jud Complex 250 Benefit St Providence RI 02903-2719

SVENSON, CHARLES OSCAR, investment banker; b. Worcester, Mass., June 28, 1939; s. Sven Oscar and Edahjane (Castner) S.; m. Sara Ellen Simpson, Nov. 15, 1968; children: Alicia Lindall, Tait Oscar. A.B., Hamilton Coll., 1961; LL.B., Harvard U., 1964; LL.M., Bklyn. Law Sch., 1965. Bar: N.Y. 1965, U.S. Dist. Ct. (so. dist.) N.Y. 1965, U.S. Ct. Appeals (2d. cir.) 1965. Atty. Dewey, Ballantine, Bushby, Palmer & Wood, N.Y.C., 1964-68; v.p. Goldman Sachs & Co., N.Y.C., 1968-75; sr. v.p. Donaldson, Lufkin & Jenrette, N.Y.C, 1975-89; mng. dir., 1989—. Trustee Kirkland Coll., Clinton, N.Y., 1976-78; trustee Hamilton Coll., Clinton, 1979-83, 90—. Mem. ABA, N.Y. State Bar Assn., Assn. of Bar of City of N.Y. Clubs: Tuxedo (Tuxedo Park, N.Y.); Harvard (N.Y.C.). Home: 1185 Park Ave New York NY 10128-1308 Office: Donaldson Lufkin & Jenrette Securities Corp 277 Park Ave New York NY 10172

SVENSSON, LARS GEORG, cardiovascular and thoracic surgeon; b. Barbeton, Republic South Africa, Aug. 11, 1955; came to U.S., 1986; s. Karl-Georg and Marianne S.; m. Marion Frances Robinson, June 14, 1986. MB, BCh, U. Witwatersrand, Johannesburg, South Africa, 1978, MSc (Med.), 1983, PhD, 1986. Diplomate Gen., Vascular and Cardiothoracic Surgery. Resident in surgery Johannesburg Hosp., 1981-86; fellow cardiovascular surgery Cleve. Clinic Found., 1986-87; fellow cardiovascular surgery Baylor Coll. of Medicine, Houston, 1987-89, resident cardiothoracic surgery, 1989-91; attending surgeon Meth. Hosp., VA Med. Ctr., Houston, 1991-92; attending surgeon Lahey Clinic, Burlington, Mass., 1993—, dir. Aortic Surgery Ctr. and Marfan Syndrome Clinic, 1993—; spkr. in field. Contbr. numerous articles to profl. jours. including Jour. Vascular Surgery, Chest, Ann. Thoracic Surgery, Jour. Thoracic, Cardiovascular Surgery and Anesthesia. Recipient Good Fellowship award Treverton Coll., 1970, Cert. of Merit South African Sugar Assn., 1972, Robert Niven award 1974-76, DeBakey Heart Fund Rsch. award 1988, 89, 90, 91, V.A. Rag Rsch. Fund award 1992; Dana Fund Rsch. fellowship, 1994, David Lurie Rsch. fellowship 1985; Davis and Geck Surg. Rsch. scholarship, 1985. Fellow Am. Coll. Surgeons, Royal Coll. Surgeons, Coll. Surgeons and Physicians of South Africa, Royal Coll. Surgeons in Can. in Vascular and Cardiothoracic Surgery, Am. Coll. Cardiology; mem. AMA, Soc. Thoracic Surgeons. Achievements include animal research to find methods of intraoperatively locating the spinal cord blood supply and methods to prevent paraplegia after aortic surgery; investigation of methods to protect the brain, spinal cord and kidneys; study of hydrogren injection to localize spinal cord supply in humans, study of intrathecal papaveine in patients undergoing aortic surgery, minimizing use of homologous blood for major aortic surgery, particularly of the ascending and aortic arch; novel operations for ascending and aortic arch surgery; first reported replacement of the entire aorta from the heart to the aortic bifurcation during a single operation; pioneered a technique for doing minimal access "keyhole" heart surgery; (with E. Stanley Crawford) wrote the first definitive textbook on the aorta entitled Cardiovascular and Vascular Disease of the Aorta; devel. an approach for minimal access to the heart for heart operations.

SVETLOVA, MARINA, ballerina, choreographer, educator; b. Paris, May 3, 1922; came to U.S. from Australia, 1940; d. Max and Tamara (Andreieff) Hartman. Studies with Vera Trefilova, Paris, 1930-36, studies with L. Egorova and M. Kschessinska, 1936-39; studies with A. Vilzak, N.Y.C., 1940-57; D honoris causa, Fedn. Francaise de Danse, 1988. Ballet dir. So. Vt. Art Ctr., 1959-64; dir. Svetlova Dance Ctr., Dorset, Vt., 1965—; prof. ballet dept. Ind. U., Bloomington, 1969-92, prof. emeritus, 1992—, chmn. dept., 1969-78; choreographer Dallas Civic Opera, 1964-67, Ft. Worth Opera, 1967-83, San Antonio Opera, 1983, Seattle Opera, Houston Opera, Kansas City Performing Arts Found. Ballerina original Ballet Russe de Monte Carlo, 1939-41; guest ballerina Ballet Theatre, 1942, London's Festival Ballet, Teatro dell Opera, Rome, Nat. Opera, Stockholm, Sweden, Suomi Opera, Helsinki, Finland, Het Nederland Ballet, Holland, Cork Irish Ballet, Paris Opera Comique, London Palladium, Teatro Colon, Buenos Aires, others; prima ballerina Met. Opera, 1943-50, N.Y.C. Opera, 1950-52; choreographer: (ballet sequences) The Fairy Queen, 1966, L'Histoire du Soldat, 1968; tours in Far East, Middle East, Europe, S.Am., U.S.; performer various classical ballets Graduation Ball; contbr. articles to Debut, Paris Opera. Mem. Am. Guild Mus. Artists (bd. dirs.), Conf. on Ballet in Higher Edn., Nat. Soc. Arts and Letters (nat. dance chmn.). Office: 2100 E Maxwell Ln Bloomington IN 47401-6119 also: 25 W 54th St New York NY 10019-5404

SVINKELSTIN, ABRAHAM JOSHUA, information technology executive; b. Stuttgart, Germany, Nov. 14, 1948; came to U.S., 1950; s. Emanuel and Sabina (Lederman) S.; m. Janet Mostel, Nov. 7, 1976; children: Jeremy David, Rachel Sabina, Ilana Michelle. BS in Aerospace Engring., Poly. U. N.Y., 1970; MS in Ops. Rsch. and Engring. Math., Columbia U., N.Y.C., 1971; MS in Computer Sci., SUNY, Stony Brook, 1972. Programmer/analyst Bank Leumi, Tel Aviv, Israel, 1973-74; assoc., cons. Monchik Weber Assocs., N.Y.C., 1974-79; ptnr., cons. Computer Programming Assocs., N.Y.C., 1979-84; project leader Shearson Lehman Bros., N.Y.C., 1984-87; asst. v.p. Warner Ins. Svcs., Fair Lawn, N.J., 1988-92; v.p. software devel. Everlink Corp., N.Y.C., 1992-94; project mgr. Am. Internat. Group, N.Y.C., 1994—. Pres. Seminole Condominiums, Forest Hills, N.Y., 1979-86; Cub Scout den leader Boy Scouts Am. Mem. Data Processing Mgmt. Assn., MIS Network Assocs. (v.p. adminstrn./fin. 1992-94), Sigma Gamma Tau. Libertarian. Jewish. Home: 13-61 Finn Ter Fair Lawn NJ 07410 Office: Am Internat Group 160 Water St Fl 10 New York NY 10038-4922

SWACKHAMER, GENE L., bank executive; b. Frankfort, Ind., 1938. BS, Purdue U., 1960; MS, Cornell U., 1963; PhD, Purdue U., 1966. Pres. emeritus Farm Credit Bank Balt., Sparks, Md.; agrl. economist Kansas City Federal Reserve Bank, 1966-69; dep. gov. U.S. Govt. Farm Credit Adminstrn., 1970-76. Mem. editl. bd. Choices Mag. Trustee, treas. Nat. 4-H Coun. Lt. USN, 1962. Named Disting. Alumnus, Purdue U., 1994. Mem. World Pres. Orgn., Nat. Policy Assn., Alpha Gamma Rho (dir.). Office: Farm Credit Bank Balt 16429 Yeoho Rd Sparks Glencoe MD 21152-9553

SWADOS, ELIZABETH A., composer, director, writer; b. Buffalo, Feb. 5, 1951; d. Robert O. and Sylvia (Maisel) S. B.A., Bennington Coll., 1972. Composer, mus. dir. Peter Brook's Internat. Theatre Group, Paris,, Africa, U.S., 1972-73; composer-in-residence La Mama Exptl. Theater Club, N.Y.C., 1977—; mem. faculty Carnegie-Mellon U., 1974, Bard Coll., 1976-77, Sarah Lawrence Coll., 1976-77. Author: The Girl With the Incredible Feeling, 1976, Runaways, 1979, Lullaby, 1980, Sky Dance, 1980, Listening Out Loud: Becoming a Composer, 1988, The Four of Us, 1991, The Myth Man, 1994; composer theatrical scores: Medea, 1969 (Obie award 1972), Elektra, 1970, Fragments of Trilogy, 1974, The Trojan Women, 1974, The Good Women of Setzuan, 1975, The Cherry Orchard, 1977, As You Like It, 1979, The Sea Gull, 1980, Alice in Concert, 1980, (with Garry Trudeau) Doonesbury, 1983, Jacques and His Master, 1984, Don Juan of Seville, 1989, The Tower of Evil, 1990, The Mermaid Wakes, 1991; composer, dir., adapter, mem. cast: Nightclub Cantata, 1977 (Obie award 1977); composer, adapter (with Andrei Serban) Agamemnon, 1976, The Incredible Feeling Show, 1979, Lullaby and Goodnight, 1980; composer, dir., adapter: Wonderland in Concert, N.Y. Shakespeare Festival, 1978, Dispatches, 1979, Haggadah, 1980, The Beautiful Lady, 1984-86, Swing, 1987, Esther: A Vaudeville Megillah, 1988, The Red Sneaks, 1989, Jonah, 1990; author, composer, dir.: Runaways, 1978 (Tony award nominee for best musical, best musical score, best musical book 1978); adapter: Works of Yehuda Amichi, Book of Jeremiah; composer music for films: Step by Step, 1978, Sky Dance, 1979, Too Far to Go, 1979, OHMS, 1980, Four Friends, 1982, Seize the Day, 1986, A Year in the Life, 1986, Family Sins, 1987; composer music CBS Camera Three shows, 1973-74, PBS short stories, 1979, CBS-TV and NBC-TV spls.; composer: Rap Master Ronnie, 1986; composer, dir. Swing, Bklyn. Acad. Music, 1987; performer: Mark Taper Forum, Los Angeles, 1985, Jerusalem Oratorio, Rome, 1985. Recipient Outer Critics Circle award, 1977; Creative Artists Service Program grantee, 1976; N.Y. State Arts Council playwriting grantee, 1977—; Guggenheim fellow. Mem. Broadcast Music Inc., Actors Equity. Jewish. Home: 112 Waverly Pl New York NY 10011-9109*

SWAGGART, JIMMY LEE, evangelist, gospel singer; b. Ferriday, La., Mar. 15, 1935; s. W. L. and Minnie Bell S.; married; 1 child. Began preaching on street corners Mangham, La., 1955; traveled throughout U.S. preaching at revival meetings, recording and marketing gospel songs, 1960's, preacher on TV and radio broadcasts; min., pastor Jimmy Swaggart Ministries, Baton Rouge. Gospel albums include This Is Just What Heaven Means To Me, 1971, There Is A River, 1972; author: (with Robert Paul Lamb) To Cross A River, 1977. Office: PO Box 262550 Baton Rouge LA 70826-2550*

SWAILS, NORMAN E., church officer; b. St. Joseph, Mo.; m. Darleen Craven; children: Tom, Jan Shannon, John. AA, Graceland Coll., 1950; BA, Mo. Valley Coll., 1952. CFP. Exec. Boy Scouts Am., 1954-78, asst. chief scout exec., nat. dir. fin., 1978-85; mem. highest fin. coun. Reorganized Ch. of Jesus Christ of Latter Day Saints, 1985-88; presiding bishop, 1988—; Reorganized Ch. of Jesus Christ of Latter Day Saints. Active Hope House. Mem. Rotary, Independence C. of C. Office: Reorganized Ch of Jesus Christ of Latter Day Saints PO Box 1059 Independence MO 64051*

SWAIM, CHARLES HALL, lawyer; b. Delta, Colo., Dec. 31, 1939; s. H. Albert and Janet (Hall) S.; m. Patricia Fahey, Oct. 9,, 1976; children: Caitlin Fahey, Bryan Hall. Grad. Geophys. Engr., Colo. Sch. Mines, 1961; JD, NYU, 1964. Asst. counsel Tex. Instruments Inc., Dallas, 1964-71; assoc. Hale & Dorr, Boston, 1971-74, ptnr., 1974—. Served to capt. U.S. Army, 1965-67, Vietnam. Mem. ABA, Mass. Bar Assn., Boston Bar Assn., Comml. Law League Am. Office: Hale & Dorr 60 State St Boston MA 02109-1800

SWAIM, DAVID DEE, diversified company financial executive; b. Ft. Wayne, Ind., Aug. 12, 1947; s. Carl Edwin and Pauline E. (Johnson) S.; m. Barbara Lynn Strock, June 21, 1969; children: Emily Anne, Benjamin Dee, Thomas Ryan. BS in Acctg., Ind. U., 1969. Sr. auditor Price Waterhouse & Co., Indpls., 1970-76; controller VideoInd., Inc., Indpls., 1976-77; treas., chief fin. officer Bindley Western Industries, Inc., Indpls., 1977-90, v.p., 1979-90, sr. v.p., 1986-90; v.p., treas., bd. dirs. Bennett Mktg. Svcs., Indpls., 1990-91; pres. Ironwood Corp., 1991—; bd. dirs., officer all subs. of Bindley Western Industries, Inc. Mem. Am. Inst. CPAs, Ind. CPA Soc., Fin. Execs. Inst. Republican. Methodist. Lodge: Masons.

SWAIM, JOSEPH CARTER, JR., lawyer; b. S.I., N.Y., Jan. 15, 1934; s. J. Carter and Charlotte (Klein) S.; m. Elizabeth Lenora Owen, Aug. 2, 1958; children: Laura, Charles. BA, Oberlin Coll., 1955; JD, Columbia U., 1958. Bar: U.S. Dist. Ct. (we. dist.) Pa. 1960, Pa. 1961, U.S. Ct. Appeals (3rd cir.) 1964. Assoc. Kirkpatrick & Lockhart, Pitts., 1961-68, ptnr., 1968—. Bd. dirs. Davis and Elkins (W.Va.) Coll., 1976-82; bd. pensions Presbyn. Ch. U.S.A., Phila., 1982-89; trustee, bd. sec. The Alban Inst., Inc., Bethesda, Md., 1991-94; trustee, sec.-treas. Henry C. Frick Edn. Com., Pitts., 1978-94; bd. dirs., former pres. Family Resources, Pitts., 1975—; bd. dirs., Sec. Desert Ministries, Inc., Palm Beach, Fla.; chmn. permanent jud. commn. Pitts. Presbytery, 1994—; mem. adv. com. Henry L. Frick Ednl. Fund Buhl Found., Pitts., 1994—. With U.S. Army, 1959-61. Mem. ABA, Pa. Bar Assn., Allegheny County Bar Assn. Republican. Clubs: Duquesne, Allegheny (bd. dirs., sec. 1976—) (Pitts.). Avocations: tennis, reading. Home: 740 Scrubgrass Rd Pittsburgh PA 15243-1124 Office: Kirkpatrick & Lockhart 1500 Oliver Building Bldg Pittsburgh PA 15222-2312

SWAIM, MARK WENDELL, molecular biologist, gastroenterologist; b. Winston-Salem, N.C., Dec. 4, 1960; s. Donnie Lee and Bernice Earline (Brown) S. BA summa cum laude, U. N.C., 1983; MD, Duke U., 1990, PhD with honors, 1990. Diplomate Am. Bd of Internal Medicine, Am. Bd. Forensic Medicine, Am. Bd. Forensic Examiners. Resident Dept. of Med. Duke U. Med. Ctr., Durham, N.C., 1990-93; fellow gastroenterology Duke U. Med. Ctr., 1993—, clin. med. instr.; instr. clin. medicine Duke U. Sch. Medicine; vis. med. resident Nat. Taiwan U., Taipei, 1991, 92; book rev. panelist The Pharos of Alpha. Contbr. articles to profl. jours, Encyclopedia Britannica Great Ideas Today, 1996. Recipient Med. Sci. Training Program fellow Nat. Inst. of Health, 1983-90, numerous acad. scholarships. Mem. ACP, Am. Coll. Gastroenterology, Am. Soc. for Gastrointestinal Endoscopy, Am. Assn. for Study Liver Diseases, Reticuloendothelial Soc., Am. Coll. Forensic Examiners, Alpha Omega Alpha (pres. Duke chpt. 1989), Phi Beta Kappa, Sigma Xi, Phi Lambda Upsilon, Sigma Pi Sigma. Avocations: photography, traveling, chamber music. Home: 231-A Bridgefield Pl Durham NC 27705 Office: Duke Univ Medical Ctr PO Box 3913 Durham NC 27710

SWAIM, RUTH CAROLYN, secondary education educator; b. Oklahoma City, May 3, 1940; d. G. Dale and Helen H. (Meister) Arbuckle; children: Stanley Kent, Sharon Gay. BS in Edn., U. Okla., 1963. Cert. secondary edn. tchr., Calif., Okla. Math. substitute tchr. USN Mil. Dependent, Sangley Pt., Philippines, 1961-63; math. tchr. Norman (Okla.) Pub. Schs., 1963, Bartlesville (Okla.) Pub. Schs., 1963-65, Dewey (Okla.) Pub. Schs., 1965-67; math. lab. instr. L.A. City Schs., 1975-83, math. tchr., 1984—; chair All Sch. Tutorial Program Taft High Sch. Instr. first Aid ARC, 1961-67; trustee Woodland Hills Community Ch., 1989—. Recipient Cert. Merit ARC, 1965, hon. svc. award PTA, 1980; named Outstanding Math. Tchr. Tandy, 1989-90. Mem. Nat. Coun. Tchrs. Math., NEA, Calif. Tchrs. Assn., Kappa Delta Pi. Home: 4555 San Feliciano Dr Woodland Hills CA 91364-5037 Office: Taft High Sch 5461 Winnetka Ave Woodland Hills CA 91364-2548

SWAIMAN, KENNETH FRED, pediatric neurologist, educator; b. St. Paul, Nov. 19, 1931; s. Lester J. and Shirley (Ryan) S.; m. Phyllis Kammerman Sher, Oct. 1985; children: Lisa, Jerrold, Barbara, Dana. BA magna cum laude, U. Minn., 1952, BS, 1953, MD, 1955; postgrad., 1956-58. Diplomate Am. Bd. Psychiatry and Neurology, Am. Bd. Pediatrics, Am. Bd. Psychiatry and Neurology with Spl. Competence in Child Neurology. Intern Mpls. Gen. Hosp., 1955-56; resident in pediatrics, fellow in pediatrics to chief resident U. Minn. Hosp., 1956-58, spl. fellow in pediatric neurology, 1960-63, dir. pediatric neurology tng. program, 1968-94, various to interim head dept. neurology, 1994—; chief pediatrics U.S. Army Hosp., Ft. McPherson, Ga., 1958-60; asst. prof. pediatrics, neurology U. Minn. Med. Sch., Mpls., 1963-66; prof., dir. pediatric neurology U. Minn. Med. Sch., 1969—, mem. internship adv. coun. exec. faculty, 1966-70, interim head dept. neurology, 1994-96; postgrad. fellow pediatric neurology Nat. Inst. Neurologic Diseases and Blindness, 1960-63, assoc. prof., 1966-69; cons. pediatric neurology Hennepin County Gen. Hosp., 1963—, Mpls., St. Paul-Ramsey Hosp., St. Paul Children's Hosp., Mpls. Children's Hosp.; vis. prof. numerous univs. including Loyola U., 1982, U. N.Mex., 1982, U. Ind. Med. Sch., 1983, U. Kyushu, Shiga, Nagoya, Tokyo, 1985, Driscoll Children's Hosp., Corpus Christi, Tex., 1986, Inst. Nacional de Pediatria, Mexico City, 1986, U. de Concepion, Chile, 1989, Beijing U. Med. Sch., 1989, Xian Med. U., China, 1989, Children's Hosp. of Mich., Detroit, 1990, Hong Kong Child Neurology Soc., 1995, others; lectr. in field; guest worker NIH, NICHD, Bethesda, Md., 1978-79, 79-81. Author: (with Francis S. Wright) Neuromuscular Diseases in Infancy and Childhood, 1969, Pediatric Neuromuscular Diseases, 1979, (with Stephen Ashwal) Pediatric Neurology Case Studies, 1978, 2d edit., 1984, Pediatric Neurology: Practice and Principles, 1989; editor: (with John A. Anderson) Phenylketonuria and Allied Metabolic Diseases, 1966, (with Francis S. Wright) Practice Pediatric Neurology, 1975, 2d edit., 1982; mem. editorial bd.: Annals of Neurology, 1977-83, Neurology Update, 1977-82, Pediatric Update, 1977-85, Brain and Devel. (Jour. Japanese Soc. Child Neurology), 1980—, Neuropediatrics (Stuttgart), 1982-92; editor-in-chief: Pediatric Neurology, 1984—; contbr. articles to sci. jours. Chmn. Minn. Gov.'s Bd. for Handicapped, Exceptional and Gifted Children, 1972-76; mem. human devel. study sect. NIH, 1976-79, guest worker, 1978-81. Served to capt. M.C. U.S. Army, 1958-60. Fellow Am. Acad. Pediatrics, Am. Acad. Neurology (rep. to nat. coun. Nat. Soc. Med. Rsch.); mem. Soc. Pediatric Rsch., Ctrl. Soc. Clin. Rsch., Ctrl. Soc. Neurol. Rsch., Internat. Soc. Neurochemistry, Am. Neurol. Assn., Minn. Neurol. Soc., AAAS, Midwest Pediatric Soc., Am. Soc. Neurochemistry, Child Neurology Soc. (1st pres. 1972-73, Hower award 1981, Founder's award 1996, chmn. internat. affairs com., 1991—, mem. long range planning com. 1991—), Internat. Assn. Child Neurologists (exec. com. 1975-79), Profs. of Child Neurology (1st pres. 1978-80, mem. nominating com. 1986—), Japanese Child Neurology Soc. (Segawa award 1986, mem. nominating com. 1986—, chair internat. affairs com. 1991—, mem. long range planning com. 1991—), Soc. de Psiquiatria y Neurologia de la Infancia y Adolescencia, Phi Beta Kappa, Sigma Xi. Office: U Minn Med Sch Dept Pediatric Neurology 1821 University Ave W Saint Paul MN 55104-2801 also: UMHC Box 30 420 Delaware St SE Minneapolis MN 55455-0374

SWAIN, DONALD CHRISTIE, retired university president, history educator; b. Des Moines, Oct. 14, 1931; s. G. Christie and Irene L. (Alsop) S.; m. Lavinia Kathryn Lesh, Mar. 5, 1955; children: Alan Christie, Cynthia Catherine. BA, U. Dubuque, 1953; MA in History, U. Calif., Berkeley, 1958, PhD, 1961; D (hon.), U. Louisville, 1995, Bellarmine Coll., 1995. Asst. rsch. historian U. Calif., Berkeley, 1961-63; mem. faculty U. Calif., Davis, 1963-81, prof. history, 1970-81, acad. asst. to chancellor, 1967-68, asst. vice chancellor acad. affairs, 1971, vice chancellor acad. affairs, 1972-75; acad. v.p. U. Calif. System, Berkeley, 1975-81; pres. U. Louisville, 1981-95, pres. emeritus, 1995—, prof. history, 1981-95; ret., 1995; bd. dirs. LGE Energy. Author: Federal Conservation Policy, 1921-33, 1963, Wilderness Defender: Horace M. Albright and Conservation, 1970; co-editor: The Politics of American Science 1939 to the Present, 1965. Mem. bd. govs. J.B. Speed Art Mus.; mem. exec. com. Ky. Hist. Soc. Lt. (j.g.) USNR, 1953-56. Recipient William B. Hellestine award Wis. State Hist. Soc., 1967, Disting. Tchg. award U. Calif., Davis, 1972, Wilson Wyatt award U. Louisville Alumni Assn., 1995; named Louisvillian of Yr., 1995. Democrat. Presbyterian. Home: 2506 Belknap Beach Rd Prospect KY 40059-9050 Office: U Louisville Alumni Ctr Louisville KY 40292

SWAIN, MELINDA SUSAN, elementary education educator; b. Sacramento, Oct. 30, 1944; d. William A. and Maxine (Wickberg) S. BA, Aurora U., 1967; MA, U. N.Mex., 1981. Cert. early adolescence/generalist Nat. Bd. Profl. Tchg. Standards, 1995. Tchr. 1st grade Crownpoint (N.Mex.) Elem. Sch., 1968-69, tchr. English as second lang., 1969-71; tchr. English as second lang. Church Rock (N.Mex.) Elem. Sch., 1971-72; tchr. kindergarten Sky City Elem. Sch., Gallup, N.Mex., 1972-73; program specialist Gallup-McKinley County Schs., 1973-82; tchr. 5th grade Lincoln Elem. Sch., Gallup, 1982-96; office for civil rights program compliance officer Gallup-McKinley County Schs., 1996—; mem. Dist. Task Force, Gallup, 1989—. Columnist N.Mex. Jour. Reading, 1991-97. Recipient N.Mex. World Class Tchrs. Project award, 1994-95. Mem. N.Mex. Coun. Internat. Reading Assn. (pres. 1984, state coord. 1991-97), Gallup Reading Coun. of Internat. Reading Assn. (pres., membership dir. 1977—). Avocations: mountain biking, reading, computers, RV-ing. Home: 1000 Country Club Dr Gallup NM 87301 Office: Gallup-McKinley County Schs PO Box 1318 Gallup NM 87305-1318

SWAIN, ROBERT, artist; b. Austin, Tex., Dec. 7, 1940; s. Robert O. and Beth (Brower) S.; m. Annette Carol Leibel, Oct. 4, 1969. B.A., Am.U., 1964. Prof. fine arts Hunter Coll.; vis. artist to various schs., univs., including Bklyn. Mus. Art Sch., 1975, 77, 78; dept. architecture Harvard U. Grad. Sch. Design, 1977. One-man shows, Thenan Gallery, N.Y.C., 1965, Fischbach Gallery, N.Y.C., 1968-69, Everson Art Museum, N.Y.C., 1974, Susan Galdwell Gallery, N.Y.C., 1974, 75, 78, Tex. Gallery, Houston, 1975, Columbus (Ohio) Gallery Fine Arts, 1976, Nina Freundenhein Gallery, Buffalo, 1978, group shows include, Mus. Modern Art, N.Y.C., 1968, Grand Palais, Paris, 1968, Kunsthaus, Zurich, Switzerland, 1969, Tate Gallery, London, 1969, Corcoran Gallery Art, Washington, 1969, Whitney Mus. Am. Art, N.Y.C., 1971, Albright-Knox Gallery, Buffalo, 1971, Mus. Modern Art Internat. Circulating Exhbn.-Latin Am., 1974-75; represented in permanent collections, Corcoran Gallery Art, Walker Art Center, Mpls., Va. Mus. Fine Arts, Richmond, Everson Art Mus., Columbus Gallery Fine Arts, Detroit Inst. Art, Albright-Knox Mus., works include archtl. installations, Am. Republic Ins. Co., Des Moines, 1969, N.K. Winston Corp., N.Y.C., 1969, Schering Labs., Bloomfield, N.J., 1970, Skidmore, Owings and Merrill, N.Y.C., 1970, Kahn & Mallis Assos., N.Y.C., 1972, Harris Bank, Chgo., 1977, Powell/Kleinschmidt Chgo., 1977, Travenol Labs., Deerfield, Ill., 1977, Skidmore, Owings and Merrill, Chgo., 1977. John Simon Guggenheim Meml. Found. fellow, 1969; Nat Endowment for Arts grantee, 1976. Home and Office: 57 Leonard St 4th Fl New York NY 10013

SWAIN, WILLIAM GRANT, landscape architect; b. Covington, Ky., Sept. 5, 1923; s. George Wellington and Emma Grant (Holmes) S.; m. Sybil Yvonne Harris, Mar. 30, 1946 (div. 1954); 1 son, Grant Marc; m. Marjorie Page Reno, Dec. 21, 1957; children: Margaret Page, Jill Holmes. B.Arch., Carnegie-Mellon U., 1952. Registered landscape architect, Pa. Ptnr. Griswold, Winters, Swain & Mullin, Pitts., 1957-75; pres. GWSM Inc., Pitts., 1975-83; chmn. bd. GWSM Inc., 1983—; chmn. Interprofl. Council on Environ. Design, Washington, 1974. Author: (with Ralph E. Griswold) Opportunities in Landscape Architecture, 1978. Mem. Mayor's Com. on Community Improvement, Monroeville, Pa., 1965; bd. dirs. W. Pa. Conservancy, Pitts., 1970—, Rachel Carson Homestead Assn., Springdale, Pa., 1976—; mem. Pa. State Art Commn., Harrisburg, 1977-84, chmn., 1981-84. Served as 1st lt. U.S. Army, 1943-46, ETO. Decorated Purple Heart; recipient Service award Carnegie-Mellon U. Alumni Fedn., 1963. Fellow Am. Soc. Landscape Architects (pres. 1973-74 recipient medals), Phi Kappa Phi. Republican. Episcopalian. Club: University (dir.) (1976-82). Home: 413 Harper Dr Monroeville PA 15146-1235 Office: GWSM Landscape Architects 1101 Greenfield Ave Pittsburgh PA 15217-2930 *The central thread of my life is a sense of loyalty to those for whom I have worked or served in professional capacities. I have been motivated to do my best for all who depend on me. It remains my belief that volunteer service to one's community is an obligation.*

SWAISGOOD, HAROLD EVERETT, biochemist, educator; b. Ashland, Ohio, Jan. 19, 1936; s. Ray Weaver and Jennie (Morr) S.; m. Janet Cromwell, Sept. 15, 1956; children—Mark Harold, Ronald Ray. B.S., Ohio State U., 1958; Ph.D. in Chemistry (NIH fellow), Mich. State U., 1963. Reserach asst. Mich. State U., 1958-63; postdoctoral research asso. NIH, 1963-64; asst. prof. food sci. and biochemistry N.C. State U., 1964-67, asso. prof., 1967-72, prof., 1972-84, William Neal Reynolds prof., 1984—; vis. prof. U. Lund, Sweden, 1974, chmn. biotech. program. Editor for Ams., Comments on Agr. and Food Chemistry; assoc. editor Jour. Food Biochemistry, 1983—; mem. editorial bd. Jour. Dairy Sci, 1975—, Jour. Food Sci, 1978—, Nahrung-Food, 1995—; contbr. articles, chpts. to profl. publs. USPHS fellow, 1963-64. Fellow Am. Chem. Soc. (agriculture food chem. divsn., award advancement of application of agrl. and food chemistry sponsored by IFF 1994); mem. Am. Inst. Nutrition, Am. Soc. Biochemists and Molecular Biologists, AAAS, Am. Dairy Sci. Assn. (Borden awardee 1987), Inst. Food Technologists, Sigma Xi, Phi Kappa Phi, Gamma Sigma Delta. Democrat. Methodist. Achievements include research in protein structure, interactions, and functionality; characteristics and applications of immobilized enzymes; patents in field. Office: NC State U Dept Food Sci Raleigh NC 27695

SWALIN, RICHARD ARTHUR, scientist, company executive; b. Mpls., Mar. 18, 1929; s. Arthur and Mae (Hurley) S.; m. Helen Marguerite Van Wagenen, June 28, 1952; children: Karen, Kent, Kristin. B.S. with distinction, U. Minn., 1951, Ph.D., 1954. Rsch. assoc. GE, 1954-56; mem. faculty U. Minn., Mpls., 1956-77, prof., head Sch. Mineral and Metall Engring., 1962-68, assoc. dean Inst. Tech., 1968-71, dean Inst. Tech., 1971-77; acting dir. Space Sci. Center, 1965; v.p. tech. Eltra Corp., N.Y.C., 1977-80; v.p. R & D Allied-Signal Corp., Morristown, N.J., 1980-84; dean Coll. Engring. and Mines U. Ariz., Tucson, 1984-87, prof., 1984-94; pres. Ariz. Tech. Devel. Corp., Tucson, 1987; prof. emeritus U. Ariz., Tucson, 1995—; guest scientist Max Planck Inst. für Phys. Chemie, Göttingen, Fed. Republic Germany, 1963, Lawrence Radiation Lab., Livermore, Calif., 1967; cons. to govt. and industry; bd. dirs. Medtronic Corp., BMC Industries; corp. adv. bd. AMP Inc., 1990-93. Author: Thermodynamics of Solids, 2d edit, 1972; Contbr. articles to profl. jours. Dir. div. indsl. coop. U. Ariz. Found., 1985-86; trustee Midwest Research Inst., 1975-78, Sci. Mus. Minn., 1973-77, Nat. Tech. U., 1983-90. Recipient Disting. Teaching award Inst. Tech., U. Minn., 1967, Leadership award U. Minn. Alumni, 1993; NATO sr. fellow in sci., 1971. Mem. Sigma Xi, Tau Beta Pi, Phi Delta Theta, Gamma Alpha. Home: 171 Condon Ln Port Ludlow WA 98365 Office: U Ariz Ariz Materials Lab 4715 E Fort Lowell Rd Tucson AZ 85712-1201

SWALLING, JOHN CHRISTIAN, accountant, president; b. Anchorage, Sept. 13, 1949; s. Albert Christian and Minnie H. (Dooley) S.; m. Mary Ann Campbell, May 29, 1972; children: Kate, Matthew, Paul, Ryann. BBA, Notre Dame U., 1971. CPA, Alaska. Various staff and mgmt. positions Arthur Young & Co., Anchorage, San Francisco, 1971-83; ptnr. Arthur Young & Co., Anchorage, 1983-87, Ernst & Whitney & Co., Anchorage, 1987-89, Ernst & Young & Co., Anchorage, 1989-91; pres. Swalling & Assocs. CPAs, Anchorage, 1991—; mng. ptnr. Profl. Travel Svc., 1978—; v.p. Innovative Cooking Enterprises Inc., 1994—. Active Providence Hosp., Anchorage, 1986—, Anchorage Conv. and Visitors Bur., 1986—, Cath. Social Svcs., 1991—, Anchorage Mus. Found., 1992—, Multiple Sclerosis Soc., 1982-92; mem. Anchorage organizing com. Winter Olympic Games, chmn., 1990-97, bd. dirs., 1984-97, treas., 1984-89. Mem. AICPA (pub. svc. award 1990), Alaska State Bd. Pub. Accountancy (bd. dirs. 1991-95), Alaska Soc. CPAs (bd. dirs. 1979-85, sec. 1981, pres. 1983, pub. svc. award 1990), Anchorage Rotary (bd. dirs. 1992-93). Office: Swalling & Assocs CPAs 3301 C St Ste 520 Anchorage AK 99503-3956

SWALM, THOMAS STERLING, aerospace executive, retired military officer; b. San Diego, Sept. 28, 1931; s. Calvin D. and Margaret A. (Rynning) S.; m. Charlene La Vern Garner, June 26, 1954; children: Edward Steven, Lori Ann. BS, U. Oreg., 1954; MS in Pub. Adminstrn., George Washington U., 1964; grad., Air Command and Staff Coll., 1964, Nat. War Coll., 1974. Commd. USAF, 1954, advanced through grades to maj. gen., 1982; instr. fighter-interceptor weapons sch. USAF, Tyndall AFB, Fla., 1956; pilot 434th Fighter-Day Squadron USAF, George AFB, Calif., 1957-58; engring. test pilot and flight examiner 50th Tactical Fighter Wing, 10th Tactical Fighter Squadron USAF, Toul-Rosieres AFB, France, and Hahn AFB, Fed. Republic Germany, 1958-61; hdqrs. 12th USAF, Waco, Tex., 1961-64; instr. pilot, flight examiner 4453d Combat Crew Tng. Wing USAF, Davis-Monthan AFB, Ariz., 1965-66; flight comdr. 12th Tactical Fighter Wing USAF, Cam Ranh Bay AFB, Republic Vietnam, 1966-67; comdr. air-to-air flight, instr. and chief R&D/OT&E sect. Fighter Weapons Sch., Nellis AFB, Nev., 1967-70; comdr., leader Thunderbirds USAF, 1970-73; chief fighter attack directorate USAF, Kirtland AFB, N.Mex., 1974-75, dep. dir. test and evaluation, 1975-76; from vice comdr. to comdr. 8th Tactical Fighter Wing USAF, Kunsan AFB, Republic of Korea, 1976-78; comdr. 3d Tactical Fighter Wing USAF, Clark AFB, Philippines, 1978-79; comdr. 57th Fighter Weapons Wing, comdr. fighter weapons sch. USAF, Nellis AFB, Nev., 1979-80; comdr. 833d air div. USAF, Holloman AFB, N.Mex., 1980-81; comdr. tactical air warfare ctr. USAF, Eglin AFB, Fla., 1981-86; ret. USAF, 1986; pres. T. Swalm and Assocs., Ft. Walton Beach, Fla., 1986-91; v.p. Melbourne Systems Div. Grumman Corp., 1991-95; pres. T. Swaim and Assocs., Melbourne, Fla., 1995—; v.p. Applications Group Internat., Inc., Atlanta, 1986-89; scientific adv. bd. USAF, 1994—. Mem. editorial bd. Jour. Electronic Def., 1983-86; contbr. articles to profl. jours. Hon. chmn. Heart Assn., Las Vegas, Nev., 1972; exec. dir. Boy Scouts Am., Las Vegas and Alamagordo, N.Mex., 1970-81; chmn. AFA Scholarship Found., 1989-91; active Fla. Govs. Coun. for TQM, 1992-94; bd. dirs. Jr. Achievement, Ctrl. Fla., 1992-94; mem. USAF scientific adv. bd., 1994-98. Decorated D.S.M., Legion of Merit with two oak leaf clusters, DFC, Air medal with 14 oak leaf clusters, Vietnam Service medal with three service stars, Republic Vietnam Campaign medal; recipient R.V. Jones Trophy Electronic Security Command, 1984. Mem. Air Force Assn. (exec. advisor, Jerome Waterman award 1985, Jimmy Doolittle fellow 1986), Thunderbirds Pilots Assn., Old Mission Beach Athletic Club (founder), Assn. Old Crows (editl. bd. R.V. Jones trophy 1984), Order of Daedalians (flight capt.), Melbourne C of C. (trustee 1993-95), Sigma Nu. Republican. Presbyterian. Avocations: golf, tennis, sailing.

SWAN, BARBARA, artist; b. Newton, Mass., June 23, 1922; d. Carl Lilja and Clara May (Knowlton) S.; m. Alan D. Fink, June 28, 1952; children: Aaron, Joanna. B.A., Wellesley Coll., 1943; B.F.A., Boston Mus. Sch., 1948. Faculty mem. Wellesley Coll., 1947-48, Milton (Mass.) Acad., 1952-55, Boston U., 1961-64. Exhibited one-woman shows Boston Pub. Libr., 1994, Alpha Gallery, Boston, 1970, 73, 76, 80, 83, 87, 92, Addison Gallery Am. Art, Andover, Mass., 1973; group shows Inst. Contemporary Art, Boston, 1960, Boston Mus. Fine Arts, 1976, Nat. Inst. Arts and Letters, N.Y.C., 1976, Danforth Mus., Framingham, Mass., 1981; represented permanent collections Boston Mus. Fine Arts, Phila. Mus. Art, Worcester Mus., Nat Portrait Gallery. MacDowell Colony grantee Peterborough, N.H., 1947-48; Albert Whittin traveling fellow Boston Mus. Sch., Europe, 1949-51, Bunting fellow Radcliffe Coll., 1961-63; recipient Wellesley Coll. Alumnae Lifetime Achievement award, 1996. Democrat. Address: 808 Washington St Brookline MA 02146-2122

SWAN, BETH ANN, nursing administrator; b. Phila., Nov. 11, 1958; d. John H. and Elizabeth A. Jenkins; m. Eric J. Swan, Apr. 11, 1987. BSN, Holy Family Coll., Phila., 1980; MSN, U. Pa., 1983, PhD in Nursing, 1996. RN, Pa.; cert. adult nurse practitioner ANCC. Nursing dir. admission evaluation ctr. Hosp. of U. Pa., Phila., 1980—. Mem. ANA, Assn. Health Svcs. Rsch., Pa. Nurses Assn., Am. Acad. Nurse Practitioners, Am. Acad. Ambulatory Nursing Care, Sigma Theta Tau.

SWAN, GEORGE STEVEN, law educator; b. St. Louis. BA, Ohio State U., 1970; JD, U. Notre Dame, 1974; LLM, U. Toronto, 1976, SJD, 1983. Bar: Ohio 1974, U.S. Dist. Ct. (so. dist.) Ohio 1975, U.S. Supreme Ct. 1987, U.S. Ct. Appeals (6th and 11th cirs.) 1993, U.S. Ct. Appeals (10th cir.) 1994, Ga. 1997; ChFC, CLU, CFP; registered investment advisor, Sec. of State, N.C., 1990. Asst. atty. gen. state of Ohio, Columbus, 1974-75; jud. clk. Supreme Ct. Ohio, Columbus, 1976-78; asst. prof. Del. Law Sch., Wilmington, 1980-83, assoc. prof., 1983-84; prof. law St. Thomas U. Law Sch., Miami, Fla., 1984-88; jud. clk. U.S. Ct. Appeals 7th cir., Chgo., 1988-89; assoc. prof. N.C. Agrl. & Tech. State U., Greensboro, 1989-96; vis. prof. John Marshall Law Sch., Atlanta, 1996—. Contbr. articles to law jours. Mem. Ohio State Bar Assn., Internat. Assn. for Fin. Planning, Am. Polit. Sci. Assn., Inst. CFP's. Office: John Marshall Law Sch 1422 W Peachtree St NW Atlanta GA 30309-2947

SWAN, HENRY, retired surgeon; b. Denver, May 27, 1913; s. Henry and Carla (Denison) S.; m. Mary Fletcher Wardwell, June 25, 1937 (div. Jan. 25, 1964); children: Edith, Henry, Gretchen; m. Geraldine Morris Fairchild, Mar. 21, 1964. AB magna cum laude, Williams Coll., 1935, DSc (hon.), 1958; MD cum laude, Harvard U., 1939. Diplomate Nat. Bd. Med. Examiners, Am. Bd. Surgery. Pathology fellow Colo. Gen. Hosp., Denver, 1939-40; intern surgery Peter Bent Brigham Children's Hosp., Boston, 1940-42; pathology fellow Children's Hosp., Boston, 1942-43; asst. in surgery Harvard Med. Sch., Boston, 1942-43; from asst. to assoc. prof. surgery U. Colo. Med. Sch., 1946-50, prof. surgery, head dept. surgery, 1950-61, prof. surgery, rsch., 1963-82, prof. emeritus, 1985—. Author: Thermoregulation and Bioenergetics, 1974; assoc. editor Jour. Cardiovasc. Surgery, 1956-70, AMA Archives Surgery, 1956-66; contbr. articles to profl. jours. With AUS, 1943-45, ETO. Mem. ACS, AMA (Gold medal for original rsch. 1955), AAAS, Acad. Surg. Rsch. (medallion for exptl. surgery 1996), Am. Surg. Assn., Am. Assn. Thoracic Surgery, Soc. for Cryobiology, Soc. Univ. Surgeons, Soc. Vascular Surgery, Halsted Soc., Surgery Biology Club, Ctrl. Surg. Assn., Western Surg. Assn., Internat. Cardiovasc. Soc., Internat. Soc. Surgery, Assn. Surgery Costa Rica, Soc. Surgeons Chile, Soc. Cardiology Chile, Soc. Pediat. Mex., Denver Acad. Surgery, Denver Clin. and Path. Soc., Phi Beta Kappa, Alpha Omega Alpha. Republican. Episcopalian. Avocations: sailing, tennis, fly fishing, duck hunting, golf. Home: 6700 W Lakeridge Rd Lakewood CO 80227

SWAN, HENRY, forester, consultant; b. Barre, Mass., Jan. 15, 1935; m. Freda Theopold, June 26, 1960. BS in Forestry, U. Maine, Orono, 1957; MBA, Harvard U., 1963. Registered profl. forester. Asst. dist. ranger U.S. Forest Svc., Laconia, N.H., 1957-61; investment officer John Hancock Ins. Co., Boston, 1963-68; v.p. Keystone Funds Inc., Boston, 1968-76, Legg Mason & Co., Washington, 1976-77; pres. Wagner Woodlands, Inc., Lyme, N.H., 1977-96; chmn. Wagner Forest Investments, Inc., Lyme, 1981—; gen. ptnr. Wagner Woodlands & Co., Lyme, 1981—; chmn., pres. Wagner Forest Mgmt. Ltd., Lyme, 1992—; chmn. adv. com. White Mountain Nat. Forest, Laconia, 1989—; bd. dirs. W.J. Cowee, Inc., Berlin, N.Y. Commr. Conn. River Valley Resource Com., Charlestown, N.H., 1988—; mem. bd. visitors dept. natural resources U. N.H., Durham 1988—; advisor Lake Baikal Watershed Program, Ulan Ude, Buryat, 1991-92, No. Forest Lands, Concord, N.H., 1989-91. Recipient Outstanding Mgmt. of Natural Resources award Northeastern Loggers Assn., 1986. Mem. Am. Forestry Assn., Soc. Am. Foresters (Outstanding Svc. award N.Y. chpt. 1991), Soc. for Protection of N.H. Forests (chmn. 1986-88, chmn. emeritus 1988—, trustee emeritus), Upper Valley Land Trust, Trout Unltd., Harvard Club N.Y., Harvard Club Boston. Republican. Episcopalian. Avocations: skiing, sailing, fly fishing, woodworking. Home: 133 Breck Hill Rd Lyme NH 03768 Office: Forest Mgmt Ltd 150 Oxford Rd PO Box 160 Lyme NH 03768

SWAN, KENNETH CARL, surgeon; b. Kansas City, Mo., Jan. 1, 1912; s. Carl E. and Blanche (Peters) S.; m. Virginia Grone, Feb. 5, 1938; children: Steven Carl, Kenneth, Susan. A.B., U. Oreg., 1933, M.D., 1936. Diplomate: Am. Bd. Ophthalmology (chmn. 1960-61). Intern U. Wis., 1936-37; resident in ophthalmology State U. Iowa, 1937-40; practice medicine specializing in ophthalmology Portland, Oreg., 1945—; staff Good Samaritan Hosp.; asst. prof. ophthalmology State U. Iowa, Iowa City, 1941-44; asso. prof. U. Oreg. Med. Sch., Portland, 1944-45, prof. and head dept. ophthalmology, 1945-78; Chmn. sensory diseases study sect. NIH; mem. adv. council Nat. Eye Inst.; also adv. council Nat. Inst. Neurol. Diseases and Blindness. Contbr. articles on ophthalmic subjects to med. publs. Recipient Proctor Rsch. medal, 1953, Disting. Svc. award U. Oreg., 1963, Meritorious Achievement award U. Oreg. Med. Sch., 1968, Howe Ophthalmology medal, 1977, Aubrey Watzek Pioneer award Lewis and Clark Coll., 1979, Disting. Alumnus award Oreg. Health Scis. U. Alumni Assn., 1988, Disting. Svc. award, 1988, Mentor award Oreg. Health Scis. Found., 1996; named Oreg. Scientist of Yr. Oreg. Mus. Sci. and Industry, 1959. Mem. Assn. Research in Ophthalmology, Am. Acad. Ophthalmology (v.p. 1978, historian), Soc. Exptl. Biology and Medicine, AAAS, AMA, Am. Ophthal. Soc. (Howe medal for distinguished service 1977), Oreg. Med. Soc., Sigma Xi, Sigma Chi (Significant Sig award 1977). Home: 4645 SW Fairview Blvd Portland OR 97221-2624 Office: Ophthalmology Dept Oreg Health Scis U Portland OR 97201

SWAN, PEER ALDEN, scientific company executive, bank director; b. Beverly, Mass., June 16, 1944; s. E.M. and Stella (Alden) S.; m. Nancy Carol Mosier, Jan. 24, 1969; children: Michael, Ashley. AA, Orange Coast Coll., Costa Mesa, Calif., 1966; BA, Calif. State U., Fullerton, 1973. Fin. analyst Brunswich, Costa Mesa, 1974-76; asst. treas. Pacific Sci. Co., Newport Beach, Calif., 1977-84, treas., 1984—; dir. SC Bancorp, Downey, Calif., 1992—. Dir. Irvine (Calif.) Ranch Water Dist., 1979—, County Sanitation Dist. Orange County, Fountain Valley, Calif., 1985—, So. Calif. Water Com., Irvine, 1984-92, Nat. Water Rsch. Inst., Fountain Valley, 1991—. Capt. U.S. Army, 1966-71, Vietnam. Avocations: sailing, hiking. Home: 7 Terraza Dr Newport Beach CA 92657-1510 Office: Pacific Sci Co 620 Newport Center Dr Ste 700 Newport Beach CA 92660-8007

SWAN, RICHARD GORDON, retired mathematics educator; b. N.Y.C., Dec. 21, 1933; s. A. Gordon and Rose (Nespor) S.; m. Erdmuthe J.D.B. Plesch-Ritz, Mar. 18, 1963; children—Adrian Alexander, Irit Alexandra. AB, Princeton U., N.J., 1954, PhD, 1957. From instr. to prof. U. Chgo., 1958-96, ret., 1996. Author: Theory of Sheaves, 1964, Algebraic K-Theory, 1968, K-Theory of Finite Groups and Orders, 1970; editor Am. Jour. Math., 1977-83, Jour. Algebra, 1981-95; contbr. articles to profl. jours. Alfred P. Sloan fellow, 1961-65; recipient Cole prize in Algebra Am. Math. Soc., 1970. Fellow AAAS; mem. Nat. Acad. Scis., Am. Math. Soc., Math. Assn. Am., Sigma Xi. Avocation: music. Home: 700 Melrose Ave Apt M3 Winter Park FL 32789-5610

SWAN, WILLIAM, actor; b. Buffalo, N.Y., Feb. 6, 1932; s. Earl B. and Irene (Hall) S. Student, Geller Workshop, L.A. Appeared in films including Lady in a Cage, Hotel, The Parallax View, Bombers B-52; more than 200 TV guest appearances including Streets of San Francisco, Quincy, Perry Mason, Felony Squad, Twilight Zone, Have Gun Will Travel, Cannon, Barnaby Jones; appeared in off-Broadway plays, including Anne of a Thousand Days, Night Fishing in Beverly Hills; appeared in regional theatres including A Delicate Balance, The Rehearsal, The Cocktail Hour, California Suite, The Middle Ages, Stained Glass, What the Butler Saw, The Price, Golf with Alan Shepard, and others; appeared in TV day-time drama, All My Children, 1982—. Trustee Berkshire Theatre Festival, Stockbridge, Mass., 1984—. Sgt. U.S. Army, 1948-49, ETO. Mem. Acad. TV Arts and Scis., The Players. Democrat. Avocation: tennis. Home: 141 E 55th St Apt 12B New York NY 10022-4036 Home: Barberry Close Monterey MA 01245

SWANBERG, EDMUND RAYMOND, investment counselor; b. Newton, Mass., Oct. 18, 1921; s. Raymond C. and Olga (Clement) S.; m. Ruth P. Mattson, May 24, 1943; children: Linda Ruth, Charles Howard, Peter Bush. BS, MIT, 1943; MBA, NYU, 1951. Chartered Investment Counselor. Assoc. Scudder, Stevens & Clark, Boston, 1946-48; assoc. Scudder, Stevens & Clark, N.Y.C., 1948-61, ptnr., sr. v.p., 1961-85, mng. dir., 1985-86, adv. mng. dir., 1987-97; pres., dir. Scudder Devel. Fund, 1970-86, Scudder Capital Growth, 1982-86, Scudder Internat. Fund, 1975-86. Capt. AUS, 1943-46. Mem. Assn. for Investment Mgmt. and Rsch., N.Y. Soc. Security Analysts, Internat. Soc. Fin. Analysts, Racquet and Tennis Club (N.Y.C.), Somerset Club (Boston), Country Club of New Canaan (Conn.), Blind Brook Club (N.Y.), Mill Reef Club (Antigua), Wharf Rat Club (Nantucket), Union Club (N.Y.C.), Ekwanok Club (Vt.). Republican. Presbyterian.

SWANEY, THOMAS EDWARD, lawyer; b. Detroit, Apr. 25, 1942; s. Robert Ernest and Mary Alice (Slinger) S.; m. Patricia Louise Nash, Sept. 9, 1967; children: Julia Bay, Mary Elizabeth, David Paul. AB, U. Mich., 1963, JD, 1967; postdoctoral, London Sch. Econs., 1967-68. Bar: Ill. 1968. From assoc. to ptnr. Sidley & Austin, Chgo., 1968—; bd. dirs. Corey Steel Co., Cicero, Ill., Gertrude B. Nielsen Child Care & Learning Ctr., Northbrook, Ill., Ward C. Rogers Found., Chgo. Trustee H. Earl Hoover Found., Glencoe, Ill., 1986—, RF Found., Chgo., 1992—; trustee, bd. pres. 1st Presbyn. Ch., Evanston, Ill., 1984-87, 96—; bd. dirs. Lakeland Conservancy, Minocqua, Wis., 1987—. Mem. ABA, Ill. State Bar Assn., Chgo. Bar Assn., Legal Club Chgo. Office: Sidley & Austin 1 First Natl Plz Chicago IL 60603-2003

SWANGER, STERLING ORVILLE, appliance manufacturing company executive; b. Battle Creek, Iowa, Jan. 5, 1922; s. Orville M. and Alma Louise (Messing) S.; m. Maxine O. Hindman, July 2, 1950; 1 son, Eric. B.S., Iowa State U., 1947; student U. Va., 1965. Registered profl. engr., Iowa. Indsl. engr. Maytag Co., Newton, Iowa, 1947-52, methods engr., 1952-54, asst. chief methods engr., 1954-57, chief methods engr., 1957-68, mgr. prodn. engring., 1968-71, mgr. engring., 1971-74, asst. v.p. mfg., 1974-75, v.p. mfg., 1975-86, sr. v.p. and chief mfg. officer, 1986-87, also dir., cons., 1987—. Mem., Newton Planning and Zoning Commn., 1966-70; trustee Newton Skiff Hosp., 1970-85, chmn., 1982-85, Progress Industries, 1987-90; chmn. Progress Industries, 1991. Served with AUS 1943-46. Mem. Nat. Soc. Profl. Engrs., Iowa Engring. Soc., Nat. Mgmt. Assn., Am. Mgmt. Assn., Am. Ordnance Assn. Republican. Presbyterian. Clubs: Newton Country, Elks.

SWANK, ANNETTE MARIE, software designer; b. Lynn, Mass., Nov. 9, 1953; d. Roland Paterson and Rita Mary (Edwards) S. BSEE and Computer Sci., Vanderbilt U., 1975; postgrad., Pa. State U., 1992—. Lead programmer GE, Phila., 1975-80; system analyst SEI Corp., Wayne, Pa., 1980-82; mgr., designer Premier Systems, Inc., Wayne, Pa., 1982-85, dir., 1985-88, tech. advisor, 1988-90, tech. architect, 1990-92; tech. architect Funds Assocs. Ltd., Wayne, 1992—. Designer: (programming lang. and data dictionary) Vision, 1985. Treas. Master Singers, Plymouth Meeting, Pa., 1987-88. Mem. Assn. for Computing Machinery, Gamma Phi Beta (com. chmn. alumna Phila. 1986-87). Avocations: singing, dancing, bowling, bridge, wine tasting. Home: 136 Pinecrest Ln King Of Prussia PA 19406-2368 Office: Funds Assocs Ltd 100 Berwyn Pk Berwyn PA 19312

SWANK, EMORY COBLENTZ, world affairs consultant, lecturer; b. Frederick, Md., Jan. 29, 1922; s. George Phillip and Mary Ruth (Coblentz) S.; m. Margaret Katherine Whiting, May 12, 1949. A.B., Franklin and Marshall Coll., 1942; A.M., Harvard, 1943. With U.S. Dept. State, 1946-75; vice consul U.S. Dept. State, Shanghai, China, 1946-48, Tsingtao, China, 1948-49; 2d sec. Am. Embassy, consul U.S. Dept. State, Djakarta, Indonesia, 1950-51, Moscow, U.S.S.R., 1953-55; polit. analyst, fgn. service officer U.S. Dept. State, Washington, 1956-57; consellor of legation U.S. Dept. State, Bucharest, 1958-60; spl. asst. to sec. of state U.S. Dept. State, 1961-63; assigned Nat. War Coll., Ft. L.J. McNair, Washington, 1963-64; counselor of embassy, dep. chief of mission Am. Embassy, Vientiane, Laos, 1964-67; minister Am. Embassy, Moscow, USSR, 1967-67; dep. asst. sec. state for European affairs Am. Embassy, 1969-70; ambassador to Cambodia, 1970-73; polit. adviser to CINC, Atlantic, and Supreme Allied Comdr., NATO Atlantic Forces, 1973-75; pres., chief exec. officer Cleve. Council on World Affairs, 1977-87, hon. trustee, 1987—. Served with AUS, 1943-46. Decorated Bronze Star medal; recipient Superior Honor award Dept. of State, 1973; Alumni Citation award Franklin and Marshall Coll., 1973. Mem. Phi Beta Kappa. Address: 65 Kendal Dr Oberlin OH 44074-1903

SWANK, ROY LAVER, physician, educator, inventor; b. Camas, Wash., Mar. 5, 1909; s. Wilmer and Hannah Jane (Laver) S.; m. Eulalia F. Shively, Sept. 14, 1936 (dec.); children: Robert L., Susan Jane (Mrs. Joel Keizer) Stephen (dec.); m. Betty Harris, May 23, 1987. Student, U. Wash., 1926-30; M.D., Northwestern U., 1935; Ph.D., 1935. House officer, resident Peter Bent Brigham Hosp., Boston, 1936-39; fellow pathology Harvard Med. Sch., 1938-39; mem. staff neurol. unit Boston City Hosp., 1945-48; asst. prof. neurology Montreal Neurol. Inst., McGill U., 1948-54; prof. medicine and neurology, head divsn. neurology Oreg. Med. Sch., 1954-75, prof. emeritus, 1975—; dir. Swank Multiple Sclerosis Clinic, Beaverton, Oreg., 1994—; prof. neurology, head divsn. neurology Oreg. Med. Sch., 1954-75; pres. Pioneer Filters, 1970-78. Served to maj. M.C. AUS, 1942-46. Recipient Oreg. Gov.'s award for research in multiple sclerosis, 1966. Mem. Am. Physiol. Soc., Am. Neurol. Assn., European Microcirculation Soc., Sigma Xi. Achievements include invention of micro embolic filler; research of physical chemical changes in blood after fat meals and during surgical shock, platelet-leukocyte aggregation in stored blood in hypotensive shock; low-fat diet in multiple sclerosis; research of physical chemical changes in multiple sclerosis (plasma proteins); importance of plasma proteins in multiple sclerosis; investigation of breakdown of blood-brain barrier by infused micro embli, and by in vitro produced micro emboli due to aggregated red blood cells. Home: 789 SW Summit View Dr Portland OR 97225-6185 Office: Swank Multiple Sclerosis Clin 13655 SW Jenkins Rd Beaverton OR 97005-1139

SWANKIN, DAVID ARNOLD, lawyer, consumer advocate; b. Boston, Jan. 18, 1934; s. Max and Anne (Rotefsky) S.; m. Jeanne Phyllis Herrick; 1 dau., Sheryl. A.B., Brandeis U., 1954; M.S., U. Wis., 1957; J.D., George Washington U., 1962. Mgmt. intern U.S. Dept. Labor, Washington, 1957-60; spl. asst. to asst. sec. labor U.S. Dept. Labor, 1961-63, dep. asst. sec. labor, 1967; dir. Bur. Labor Standards, 1967-68; exec. sec. Pres.'s Consumer Adv. Council, Washington, 1964; exec, dir. Pres's Com. on Consumer Interests, Washington, 1965-66; Washington rep. Consumer's Union, 1969-71; exec. dir. Consumer Interests Found., 1971-73; sr. partner Swankin & Turner, 1973—; pres. Regulatory Alternatives Devel. Corp., 1985—; pres. Citizen Advocacy Ctr. 1994—; cons. U.S. Dept. Labor; pres. Citizen Advocacy Ctr., 1994—. Mem. Pres.'s Council, Brandeis U., 1968-69. Served with AUS., 1954-56. Recipient Jump award U.S. Govt., 1969. Mem. Am. Bar Assn., Ombudsman Com. Home: 300 N Cherry St Falls Church VA 22046-3522 Office: 1424 16th St NW Washington DC 20036-2211

SWANN, BRIAN, writer, humanities educator; b. Wallsend, Northumberland, Eng., Aug. 13, 1940; came to U.S., 1963, naturalized, 1980; s. Stanley Frank and Lilyan Mary (Booth) S.; m. Roberta Metz. B.A., Queens' Coll., Cambridge U., 1962. M.A., 1965; Ph.D., Princeton U., 1970. Instr. Princeton U., 1964-65; lectr., 1968-70, asst. prof., 1970-72; instr. Rutgers U., 1965-66; asst. prof. humanities Cooper Union for Advancement Sci. and Art, N.Y.C., 1972-75, assoc. prof., 1975-80, prof., 1980—, acting dean, 1990-91; dir. Bennington Writing Workshops, 1988-91. Author: (poetry) The Middle of the Journey, 1982, Song of The Sky: Versions of Native American Song-Poems, 1993, Wearing the Morning Star: Native American Song-Poems, 1996, also many other books of fiction, translations, children's books; The Plot of the Mice, 1984, A Basket Full of White Eggs, 1988; editor: Smoothing The Ground: Essays of Native American Oral Literature, 1983; (with Arnold Krupat) Recovering the Word, 1987, I Tell You Now: Autobiographical Essays by Native American Writers, 1987, Coming to Light: Contemporary Translations of the Native Literatures of North America, 1995; Essays on the Translation of Native American Literatures, 1992; editor The Smithsonian Series of Essays on Native American Literatures, 1990—. NEA fellow, 1981; Creative Arts in Pub. Service grantee, 1982. Office: Cooper Union Adv Sci & Art Faculty Humanities & Social Sci Cooper Sq New York NY 10003

SWANN, ERIC JERROD, professional football player; b. Pinehurst, N.C., Aug. 16, 1970. Student, Wake Tech. Coll. Defensive tackle Ariz. Cardinals, Phoenix, 1991—. Selected to Pro Bowl, 1995. Office: Arizona Cardinals PO Box 888 Phoenix AZ 85001-0888*

SWANN, JERRE BAILEY, lawyer; b. Gadsden, Ala., May 12, 1939; s. Julius Seth and Alma Nell (McCartney) S.; m. Jane Goodwillie, June 26, 1965 (div. Jan. 1977); children: Jerre B. Jr., Eliza W.; m. Cynthia Pangia, Sept. 17, 1977. BA, Williams Coll., 1961; postgrad., U. St. Andrews, Scotland, 1961-62; LLB, Harvard U., 1965. Bar: N.Y. 1966, Ga. 1968, U.S. Dist. Ct. (no. and mid. dists.) Ga., U.S. Dist. Ct. (ea. dist.) Tex., U.S. Ct. Appeals (1st, 4th, 5th, 8th, 11th cirs.). Law clk. U.S. Dist. Ct. (so. dist.) N.Y., N.Y.C., 1965-67; assoc. Kilpatrick & Cody, Atlanta, 1967-72, ptnr., 1972—. Contbr. numerous articles to profl. jours. Mem. ABA, Ga. Bar Assn., Internat. Trademark Assn. (bd. dirs. 1989-91, editor-in-chief Trademark Reporter 1988-90), Cherokee Town and Country Club, Phi Beta Kappa. Democrat. Avocation: woodworking. Home: 9905 Huntcliff Trce Atlanta GA 30350-2715 Office: Kilpatrick & Cody 1100 Peachtree St Atlanta GA 30309

SWANN, LYNN CURTIS, sportscaster, former professional football player; b. Alcoa, Tenn., Mar. 7, 1952; s. Willie and Mildred (McGarity) S. B.A., U. So. Calif., 1974. Wide receiver Pitts. Steelers Profl. Football Team, 1974-83, leading receiver in team history, 1981; commentator ABC Sports, 1976—. Entertainment and media apppearances as dancer with Twyla Tharp and Peter Martines Omnibus TV Spl., 1980, guest star Night of 100 Stars I, 1982, 100 Stars II, 1985; host and narrator Britten's Young Person's Guide to Orchestra, Wheeling Symphony Orch., 1982; host of 13 part art edn. spl. Arts Alive, PBS, 1984; major character in episodes Paper Chase, 1984, Hotel, 1984, Love American Style, 1985; other appearances on various TV shows including 20/20, Good Morning America, Merv Griffin, Hollywood Squares, others; intermittent host daily talk show Pittsburgh 2Day, 1985—. Spokesman for Big Bros./Big Sisters Assn.; trustee Pitts. Ballet Theatre, creator youth scholarship program; bd. dirs. Scott Newman Juvenile Drug and Alcohol Prevention Found.; bd. dirs. U. So. Calif. Sch. Journalism Alumni Assn. Named All Pro, 1976 77, 78, Most Valuable Player in Super Bowl X, 1976, Pitts. Multiple Sclerosis Athlete of Yr., 1980, NFL Man of Yr., 1981; holder 4 Super Bowl records, 2d in 2 categories; mem. Pitts. Steelers All-Time Team, 50th Anniv.; named to NFL Hall of Fame Team of Decade/1970's, AP, UPI, Kodak All Am. Teams, Pop Warner Hall of Fame; recipient Image award NAACP, 1979, Ebonics Soc. award, Outstanding Alumni award U. So. Calif., 1984, Oleg Cassini Competitors Fashion award, 1985. Mem. Screen Actors Guild, AFTRA. Office: Swann Inc 600 Grant St Ste 4870 Pittsburgh PA 15219-2801*

SWANN, RANDE NORTOF, public relations executive; b. Louisville, July 14, 1952; d. Thomas Joseph and Garrith Louise (Hines) Nortof; m. William Donald Swann, Nov. 20, 1977; children: Nicole, Amy. BA, Hollins Coll. For Women, Roanoke, Va., 1974; MS, U. Louisville, 1980. Various positions Hollins Coll. For Women, Roanoke, 1971-74; exec. dir. USO-Louisville (Ky.) Svc. Club, Inc., 1974-81; asst. campaign dir. Metro United Way, Louisville, 1981-82; pub. affairs dir. Jefferson County Pub. Schs., Louisville, 1983-89; pub. rels. dir. Regional Airport Authority of Louisville & Jefferson County, 1989—; speaker workshops and confs. in field, including Internat. Quality and Productivity Ctr., Nat. Seminar, Atlanta, 1995, ACI-NA Aviation Edn. Tour Guide Conf., St. Louis, 1995, Mtkg./Comms. Conf., Tex., 1995, Ann. Conf., Toronto, 1994, numerous others. Patron Actors Theatre Louisville; mem. pub. rels. adv. com. Metro United Way, 1987-88. Recipient numerous profl. advt. awards, including grand prize comm. contest Airport Coun. Internat.-N.Am., 1994, award Ad. Club Louisville, 1995, nat. summit awards for creativity, 1995. Mem. Internat. Assn. Bus. Communicators (Silver Quill award of excellence, award of merit, Landmarks of Excellence award 1984-88, 95), Pub. Rels. Soc. Am. (dist. award of excellence, regional award 1983-88, Landmarks of Excellence award 1995), Nat. Sch. Pub. Rels. Assn. (4 Golden Achievement awards, 2 sch. publs.-comm. awards, Nat. Award of Honor 1984-88), Airport Coun. Internat. (vice chmn. mktg. and comm. group), Ky. Assn. Govt. Communicators (Blue Pencil awards), Hollins Coll. Alumnae Club, also others. Democrat. Presbyterian. Avocations: reading, traveling. Office: Regional Airport Authority PO Box 9129 Louisville KY 40209-0129

SWANSBURG, RUSSELL CHESTER, medical administrator educator; b. Cambridge, Mass., Aug. 6, 1928; s. William W. and Mary A. (Pierce) S.; m. Laurel Swansburg, Sept. 1951; children: Philip Wayne, Michael Gary, Richard Jeffrey. Diploma, N.S. Hosp. Sch. Nursing, 1950; BSN, Western Res. U., 1952; MA in Nursing Edn., Columbia U., 1961; PhD, U. Miss., 1984. CNAA. Asst. adminstr. U. of S. Ala. Med. Ctr., Mobile; v.p. U. South Ala., Mobile; prof. Auburn U., Montgomery, Ala., Med. Coll. of Ga., Augusta; mil. cons. USAF Surgeon Gen., 1972; sr. med. svc. cons., 1973-76; nurse cons. VA Med. Ctr., Tuskegee, Ala., 1987-88; mem. editl. adv. bd. Nursing Adminstrn. Manual. Author: Team Nursing: A Programmed Learning Experience, 1968, Inservice Education, 1968, The Measurement of Vital Signs, 1970, The Team Plan, 1971, Management of Patient Care Services, 1976, Strategic Career Planning and Development, 1984, The Nurse Manager's Guide to Financial Management, 1988, Management and Leadership for Nurse Managers, 1990, 2d edit. 1996, Introductory Management and Leadership for Clinical Nurses, 1993, Staff Development: A Component of Human Resource Development, 1994, Budgeting and Financial Management for Nurse Managers, 1997, (audiovisual course) Nurses & Patients: An Introduction to Nursing Management, 1980; contbr. articles to profl. publs. Bd. dirs. Air Force Village Found., Alzheimer's Care and Research Found. Col. USAF, 1956-76. Decorated Legion of Merit; recipient award for outstanding work in hosp. adminstrn. Ala. State Nurses' Assn., 1985. Fellow AONE, Ala. Orgn. Nurse Exec's. (past state pres.); mem. Council Grad. Edn. Adminstrn. in Nursing (sec.), Ala. Acad. Sci., Sigma Xi, Phi Kappa Phi, Sigma Theta Tau. Home and Office: 4917 Ravenswood Dr Apt 1711 San Antonio TX 78227-4356

SWANSEN, DONNA MALONEY, landscape designer, consultant; b. Green Bay, Wis., July 8, 1931; d. Arthur Anthony and Ella Marie Rose (Warner) Maloney; m. Samuel Theodore Swansen, June 27, 1959; children: Jessica Swansen Bonelli, Theodor Arthur Swansen, Christopher Currie Swansen. AS in Integrated Liberal Studies, U. Wis., 1956; AS in Landscape Design, Temple U., 1982. Bridal cons. Richard W. Burnham's, Green Bay, 1951-54, 57-58; asst. buyer Shreve Crump & Low, Boston, 1958-59; buyer Harry S. Manchester, Madison, Wis., 1959-62; ptnr. Corson Borie & Swansen, Ambler, Pa., 1976, Swansen & Borie, Ambler, 1977-82; owner, operator Donna Swansen/Design, Ambler, 1983—; v.p. Energy Islands Internat. Inc., East Troy, Wis., 1963-94. Editor: Internat. Directory Landscape Designers, 1993. Mem. search com. for chair dept. landscape architecture and horticulture Temple U., 1987, curriculum rev. com., 1993; mem. Gwynedd (Pa.) Monthly Meeting of Friends (Quakers), 1974—; Dem. candidate for judge elections, 1988; co-founder Friends of Rising Sun, Ambler, Ambler Area Arts Alliance, 1975-76; founder, 1st pres. Plant Ambler, 1973-83; mem. adv. com. Green Bay Bot. Garden, 1993—; chair Temple U. Exhibit, Do It, Dig It (entry named Best in Show Pa. Hort. Soc., Phila., 1987). Recipient Key to the Borough, Borough of Ambler, 1972; winner urban beautification project Roadside Coun. Am., Ambler, 1975, award of Distinction Assn. Profl. Landscape Designers, 1996, Athena award Wissahickon Valley C. of C., 1996. Mem. Assn. Profl. Landscape Designers (cert., co-founder, 1st pres. 1989-91, bd. dirs. 1989-95, 1st pres. Landscape Design Network Phila. 1978-85), Sigma Lambda Alpha. Democrat. Avocations: putting people and plants together, encouraging women, travel, gardening. Home and Office: 221 Morris Rd Ambler PA 19002

SWANSEN, SAMUEL THEODORE, lawyer; b. Milw., June 6, 1937; s. Theodore Lawrence and Clarinda Dingwall (Crittenden) S.; m. Donna Rae Elizabeth Maloney, June 27, 1959; children: Jessica Swansen Bonelli, Theodor Arthur, Christopher Currie. AB, Dartmouth Coll., 1959; LLB, U. Wis., 1962. Bar: Wis. 1962, Pa. 1964, U.S. Supreme Ct. 1969. Law clk. to presiding justice Wis. Supreme Ct., Madison, 1962-63; assoc. Dechert, Price & Rhoads, Phila., 1963-68, 70-73, ptnr., 1973-93; asst. dist. atty. City of Phila. Dist. Atty.'s Office, 1968-70, chief frauds div., 1969; pvt. practice Phila., 1963—, Blue Bell, Pa., 1994—; adj. prof. law Temple U., Phila., 1970-80; lectr. Pa. Bar Inst., Nat. Bus. Inst., Ctr. Profl. Edn., 1985—. Editor, author U. Wis. Law Rev., 1960-62. Violinist, trombonist North Penn Symphony Orch., 1977—; mem. Gwynedd Monthly Meeting of Friends, 1974—; bd. dirs. Friends Rehab. Program, Inc., Phila., 1966-73, 85—, Franklin Found., Phila., 1969—; v.p., sec., bd. dirs. Foulkeways at Gwynedd, 1979—, pres., 1986-97; chmn. bd. dirs. Friends Life Care at Home, Inc., 1990—, bd. dirs., 1985—; bd. dirs. Friends Retirement Concepts, Inc., Gwynedd, Pa., sec. bd. dirs., 1985-96; hon. bd. dirs. Friends Neighborhood Guild, Greater Phila. Fedn. Settlements; corp. mem. Anna T. Jeanes Found., Fox Chase, Phila., 1985-93, Associated Svcs. for Blind, Phila, 1974-91, Bach Festival of Phila., 1989—, pres. 1993—; dir., sec. Energy Islands Internat., Inc., 1963—; mem. Nat. Network of Estate Planning Attys., 1993—, accredited estate planner Nat. Assn. of Estate Planners & Couns., 1995—. Fellow Esperti Peterson Inst. Wealth Strategies Planning, 1996—. Mem. ABA, Pa. Bar Assn., Phila. Bar Assn., Dartmouth Club Phila., Delta Upsilon, Phi Delta Phi. Republican. Mem. Soc. of Friends. Home: 221 Morris Rd Ambler PA 19002 Office: 640 Sentry Pky Ste 104 Blue Bell PA 19422-2317

SWANSON, AUGUST GEORGE, physician, retired association executive; b. Kearney, Nebr., Aug. 25, 1925; s. Oscar Valderman and Elnora Wilhelmina Emma (Block) S.; m. Ellyn Constance Weinel, June 28, 1947; children: Eric, Rebecca, Margaret, Emilie, Jennifer, August. BA, Westminster Coll., Fulton, Mo., 1951; MD, Harvard U., 1949; DSc (hon.), U. Nebr., 1979. Intern King County Hosp., Seattle, 1949-50; resident internal medicine U. Wash. Affiliated Hosp., 1953-55, neurology, 1955-57; resident neurology Boston City Hosp., 1958; dir. pediatric neurology, then dir. div. neurology U. Wash. Med. Sch., Seattle, 1958-67; assoc. dean acad. affairs U. Wash. Med. Sch., 1967-71; v.p. acad. affairs Assn. Am. Med. Colls., Washington, 1971-89, v.p. grad. med. edn., exec. dir. Nat. Resident Matching Program, 1989-91, ret., 1991; vis. fellow physiology Oxford (Eng.) U., 1963-64; cons. in field. Author articles brain function, physician edn., med. manpower. With USNR, 1943-46, 50-53. Markle scholar medicine, 1959-64; recipient Abraham Flexner awd. for Distinguished Service to Medical Education, Assn. of Am. Medical Coll., 1992. Mem. Inst. Medicine, Nat., Acad. Sci., Am. Neurol. Assn. Home: 3146 Portage Bay Pl E # H Seattle WA 98102-3878

SWANSON, AUSTIN DELAIN, educational administration educator; b. Jamestown, N.Y., June 11, 1930; s. Manley Moris and Beulah Marjorie (Waite) S.; m. Marilyn Jean Peterson, Mar. 31, 1956; children: Paul Delain, Karin Lorine Swanson Daun. BS, Allegheny Coll., 1952; MS, Columbia U., 1955, EdD, 1960. Tchr. Ramapo Cen. High Sch., Suffern, N.Y., 1955-58; rsch. assoc. Tchrs. Coll. Columbia U., N.Y.C., 1958-63; prof. ednl. adminstrn. SUNY, Buffalo, 1963—, chair dept. ednl. orgn. adminstrn. and policy, 1991-97; vis. scholar Inst. Edn. U. London, 1979, 93, Zold Inst., Israel, 1988. Author: Modernizing the Little Red School House, 1979, School Finance: Its Economics and Politics, 1991, 2d edit., 1996, Fundamental Concepts of Educational Leadership, 1995; contbr. articles to profl. jours. WiTh U.S. Army, 1952-54. Fellow Stanford U., 1969-70; Fulbright scholar U. Melbourne, Australia, 1986. Mem. Am. Ednl. Rsch. Assn., Am. Edn. Fin. Assn., Politics of Edn. Assn., Phi Delta Kappa. Republican. Lutheran. Office: SUNY Grad Sch Edn Buffalo NY 14260

SWANSON, BERNET STEVEN, consulting engineer, former educator; b. Chgo., Nov. 20, 1921; s. Bernet Stephanie and Emma (Conrad) S.; m. Lucile A. Clapham, June 12, 1948; children—Brian Bernet, David Herbert. BS, Armour Inst. Tech., 1942; MS, Ill. Inst. Tech., 1944, PhD, 1950. Mem. faculty Ill. Inst. Tech., Chgo., 1950-85; prof. chem. engring. Ill. Inst. Tech., 1960-85, head dept., 1967-85; cons. engr., 1944—. Author: Electronic Analog Computer, 1965. Mem. Am. Inst. Chem. Engrs., Instrument Soc. Am., Am. Soc. Engring. Edn., Sigma Xi, Alpha Chi Sigma, Phi Lambda Upsilon. Home: 2n151 Swift Rd Lombard IL 60148-1185 Office: 3300 S Federal St Chicago IL 60616-3732

SWANSON, CHARLES ANDREW, mathematics educator; b. Bellingham, Wash., July 11, 1929; s. Clarence Otto and Esther (Hougen) S.; m. Carolyn Marie Dennis, Aug. 5, 1957; children—Laird Randall, Denise Claire. BA, U. B.C., 1951, MA, 1953; PhD, Cal. Inst. Tech., 1957. Prof. U. B.C., Vancouver, 1957-94, prof. emeritus math., 1994—. Author: An Introduction to Differential Calculus, 1962, Comparison and Oscillation Theory of Linear Differential Equations, 1968; Contbr. articles to tech., profl. jours. Office: U British Columbia, Dept Math, Vancouver, BC Canada V6T 1Z2

SWANSON, CHERYL ANN, small business owner, nurse; b. L.A., Feb. 17, 1967; d. Donald Herbert Cox and Mary Rosalie (Bowlds) Hook; m. Timothy Howard Swanson, Feb. 28, 1982 (div. Sept. 1987); 1 child, Christopher Michael. BSN magna cum laude, U. Ariz., 1995. RN, Ariz.; CCRN. Sales mgr. Double M Gem, Pocatello, Idaho, 1987-89, Desert Gem, Tucson, 1990-93; owner, mgr. AAA Loan & Jewelry, Tucson, 1993—; critical care nurse St. Joseph's Hosp., 1995. Scholar Idaho State U., 1988-89, M.B. and C.J. O'Connel scholar U. Ariz., 1995. Mem. ANA, Nat. League for Nursing, Golden Key, Sigma Theta Tau, Phi Kappa Phi. Democrat. Roman Catholic. Avocations: travel, writing, reading. Office: AAA Loan & Jewelry 1902 S Craycroft Rd Tucson AZ 85711-6621

SWANSON, DANE CRAIG, naval officer, pilot; b. Guam, Feb. 13, 1955; s. George Clair and Norma Francis (Brown) S.; m. Marla S.; children: Bryce, Brittany. BS in Naval Architecture, U.S Naval Acad., 1977; MA, Webster U., 1980; grad., USAF Test Pilot Sch., 1985. Commd. ensign USN, 1977, advanced through grades to comdr., 1992; flight instr. USN, Kingsville, Tex., 1978-80; asst. ops. officer USS Eisenhower VF-142 USN, 1981-84; test pilot Air Test and Evaluation Air Test and Evaluation Squadron Four USN, Point Mugu, Calif., 1985-88; ops. officer USS Saratoga VF-103 USN, 1988-91; anti-air appraisal officer Naval Air System Command USN, Washington, 1991—. Decorated 4 Air medals, 2 Battle E awards, CNO Safety S, CINLANFLT golden anchor, Meritorious Service medal, Navy Commendation medal with Combat V, Nat. Defense medal, numerous Unit awards. Mem. Soc. Exptl. Test Pilots, U.S. Naval Inst., Officers Christian Fellowship. Republican. Baptist. Avocations: backpacking, golf, fishing, hunting.

SWANSON, DAVID HEATH, agricultural company executive; b. Aurora, Ill., Nov. 3, 1942; s. Neil H. and Helen J. (McKendry) S.; children: Benjamin Heath, Matthew Banford. B.A., Harvard U., 1964; M.A., U. Chgo., 1969. Account exec. 1st Nat. Bank Chgo., 1967-69; dep. mgr. Brown Bros. Harriman & Co., N.Y.C., 1969-72; asst. treas. Borden, Inc., N.Y.C., 1972-75; v.p., treas. Continental Grain Co., N.Y.C., 1975-77, v.p., CFO, 1977-79, gen. mgr. European div., 1979-81, exec. v.p. and gen. mgr. World Grain div., 1981-83, corp. sr. v.p., chief fin. and adminstrv. officer, 1983-86, group pres., 1985-86; pres., CEO Cen. Soya, Ft. Wayne, Ind., 1986-93; chmn. Premiere Agri Tech., Inc., Ft. Wayne, 1994—; chmn., CEO Explorer Nutrition Group, N.Y.C., 1995-96; pres., CEO, Countrymark Coop., Inc., Indpls., 1996—; mem. adv. bd. U.S. Export-Import Bank, 1985-86; mem. Gov.'s Agrl. Bd. Ind.; bd. dirs. Fiduciary Trust Internat., Conrail. Mem. Internat. Policy Coun. on Agr. and Trade; mem. adv. bd. Purdue U. Agr. Sch.; mem. Gov.'s Econ. Devel. Ind. Bd.; bd. govs. Exec. Coun. on Fgn. Diplomats and U.S. Agr. Libr.; gov. Found. for U.S. Constn. Mem. Coun. Fgn. Rels., Nat. Assn. Mfrs. (bd. dirs.), Ind. C. of C. (bd. dirs.), Am. Alpine Club (bd. dirs.), Links Club, Racquet and Tennis Club, Explorers Club (bd. dirs., sec., pres.). Republican. Congregationalist. Office: Countrymark Coop Inc 950 N Meridian St Indianapolis IN 46204-1077

SWANSON, DAVID H(ENRY), economist, educator; b. Anoka, Minn., Nov. 1, 1930; s. Henry Otto and Louise Isabell (Holiday) S.; m. Suzanne Nash, Jan. 19, 1952 (dec. Sept. 1990); children: Matthew David, Christopher James; m. Joanne Perkins, Feb. 1, 1991. BA, St. Cloud State U., 1953; MA, U. Minn., 1955, PhD, Iowa State U., 1987. CPCU. Economist area devel. dept. No. States Power Co., Mpls., 1955-56, staff asst., v.p. sales, 1956-57, economist indsl. devel. dept., 1957-63; dir. area devel. dept. Iowa So. Utilities Co., Centerville, 1963-67, dir. econ. R & D, 1967-70; dir. New Orleans Econ. Devel. Coun., 1970-72; div. mgr. Kaiser Aetna Texas, New Orleans, 1972-73; dir. corp. rsch. United Svcs. Automobile Assn., San Antonio, 1973-76; pres. Lantern Corp., 1974-79; adminstr. bus. devel. State of Wis., Madison, 1976-78; dir. Ctr. Indsl. Rsch. and Svc., Iowa State U., Ames, 1978-89, mem. mktg. faculty Coll. Bus. Adminstrn., 1979-85, principal rsch. assoc., econ. devel. Insts., Ga., Insts. Tech, 1996—; dir. Iowa Devel. Commn., 1982-83; mem. adv. bd. Iowa Venture Capital Fund, 1985-88; dir. Applied Strategies Internat. Ltd., 1983-88; dir. econ. devel. lab. Ga. Inst. Tech., Atlanta, 1989-93; adv. bd. Nat. Tech. Transfer Ctr., 1992-96; exec. on loan Nat. Inst. of Stds. and Tech., 1993-96; chmn. Iowa Curriculum Assistance System, 1984-85. Mem. Iowa Airport Planning Coun., 1968-70; mem. adv. coun. office Comprehensive Health Planning, 1967-70; mem. adv. coun. Ctr. Indsl. Rsch. and Svc., 1967-70, New Orleans Met. Area Com., 1972-73; mem. Iowa Dist. Export Coun., 1978-88; mem. Atlanta Dist. Export Coun., 1989-96; mem. region 7 adv. coun. SBA, 1978-88; dir. Mid-Continent R&D Council, 1980-84; chmn. Iowa del. White House Conf. on Small Bus., 1980; chmn. Gov.'s Task Force on High Tech., 1982-83; chmn. Iowa High Tech. Coun., 1983-86; adv. com. U. New Orleans, 1971-73; county fin. chmn. Rep. Party, 1966-67; bd. dirs. Greater New Orleans Urban League, 1970-73, Indsl. Policy Coun., 1984-88; mem. Iowa Gov.'s Export Coun., 1984-89; v.p. Iowa Sister State Friendship Com., 1985-87, pres. 1988; chmn. nat. adv. coun. Fed. lab. Consortium, 1985—, chair 1993-96, mem. 1985, Ga. Tech. Faculty Assembly, 1990-92; pres. Chattahoochee Run Homeowners Assn., 1997—; mem. planning com. Internat. Tech. Teamster Conf., 1997; mem. adv. com. Georgia Ogethorpe Quality Award, 1997, Georgians Mfg., 1997. Served with USAF, 1951-52. Mem. Am. Indsl. Ext. Alliance (pres. 1992-96), Nat. Assn. Mgmt. Tech. Assistance Ctrs. (pres. 1985, bd. dirs. 1982-86), Tech. Transfer Soc. (bd. dirs. 1984-94, v.p. 1987-90, pres.-elect 1991-92, pres. 1992-93), Oak Ridge Associated Univs. (tech. transfer adv. coun. 1992-95), Ga. Fin. Developers Assn., Ga. 2000, Profl. Developers Assn., Nat. Univ. Continuing Edn. Assn., Internat. Coun. Small Bus., Rotary (bd. dirs. 1986-88), Toastmasters (past pres.). Episcopalian. Home: 1415 Chattahoochee Run Dr Suwanee GA 30174 Office: Econ Devel Inst Ga Insts of Tech 224 O'Keefe Bldg Atlanta GA 30332

SWANSON, DON RICHARD, university dean; b. L.A., Oct. 10, 1924; s. Harry Windfield and Grace Clara (Sandstrom) S.; m. Patricia Elizabeth

Klick, Aug. 22, 1976; children—Douglas Alan, Richard Brian, Judith Ann. BS, Calif. Inst. Tech., 1945; MA, Rice U., 1947; PhD, U. Calif., Berkeley, 1952. Physicist U. Calif. Radiation Lab., Berkeley, 1947-52, Hughes Research and devel. Labs., Culver City, Calif., 1952-55; research scientist TRW, Inc., Canoga Park, Calif., 1955-63; prof. Grad. Library Sch., U. Chgo., 1963—, dean, 1963-72, 77-79, 86-90; mem. Sci. Info. Council, NSF, 1960-65; mem. toxicology info. panel Pres.'s Sci. Advisory Com., 1964-66; mem. library vis. com. Mass. Inst. Tech., 1966-71; mem. com. on sci. and tech. communication Nat. Acad. Scis., 1966-69. Editor: The Intellectual Founds. of Library Education, 1965, The Role of Libraries in the Growth of Knowledge, 1980; co-editor: Operations Research: Implications for Libraries, 1972, Management Education: Implications for Libraries and Library Schools, 1974; mem. editorial bd.: Library Quarterly, 1963—; Contbr.: chpt. to Ency. Brit, 1968—; sci. articles to profl. jours. Trustee Nat. Opinion Research Center, 1964-73; Research fellow Chgo. Inst. for Psychoanalysis, 1972-76. Served with USNR, 1943-46. Mem. Am. Soc. for Info. Sci. Home: 5825 S Dorchester Ave Apt 14E Chicago IL 60637-1733 Office: U Chgo Divsn Humanities 1010 E 59th St Chicago IL 60637-1512

SWANSON, DONALD ALAN, geologist; b. Tacoma, July 25, 1938; s. Leonard Walter and Edith Christine (Bowers) S.; m. Barbara Joan White, May 25, 1974. BS in Geology, Wash. State U., 1960; PhD in Geology, Johns Hopkins U., 1964. Geologist U.S. Geol. Survey, Menlo Park, Calif., 1965-68, 71-80, Hawaii National Park, 1968-71; sr. geologist Cascades Volcano Obs. U.S. Geol. Survey, Vancouver, Wash., 1980-90, rsch. scientist-in-charge, 1986-89; sr. geologist U.S. Geol. Survey, Seattle, 1990-96; assoc. dir. Volcano Systems Ctr. U. Wash., 1993-96; scientist-in-charge Hawaiian Volcano Obs., 1997—; affiliate prof. U. Wash., 1992—; cons. U.S. Dept. Energy, Richland, Wash., 1979-83; volcanologist New Zealand Geol. Survey, Taupo, 1984; advisor Colombian Volcano Obs., Manizales, 1986. Assoc. editor Jour. Volcanology and Geothermal Rsch., 1976—, Jour. Geophys. Rsch., 1992-94; editor Bull. of Volcanology, 1985-90, exec. editor, 1995—; contbr. numerous articles to profl. jours. Recipient Superior Service award U.S. Geol. Survey, 1980, Meritorious Service award U.S. Dept. Interior, 1985; postdoctoral fellow NATO, 1964-65. Fellow Geol. Soc. Am.; mem. AAAS, Am. Geophys. Union, Sigma Xi. Avocation: hiking. Home: 417 Linaka St Hilo HI 96720 Office: US Geol Survey Hawaiian Volcano Obs PO Box 51 Hawaii National Park HI 96718

SWANSON, DONALD FREDERICK, retired food company executive; b. Mpls., Aug. 6, 1927; s. Clayton A. and Irma (Baiocchi) S.; m. Virginia Clare Hannah, Dec. 17, 1948; children—Donald Frederick, Cynthia Hannah Lindgren, Janet Clare Webster. B.A., U. Minn., 1948. With Gen. Mills, Inc., 1949-85, div. v.p., dir. marketing flour, dessert and baking mixes, 1964-65, v.p., gen. mgr. grocery products div., 1965-68, v.p., corporate adminstrn. officer consumer foods group, fashion div., transp. and purchasing depts., advt. and marketing services, 1969, exec. v.p. craft, game and toy group, fashion group, direct marketing group, travel group, dir., 1968-76, sr. exec. v.p. consumer non-foods, 1976-85, chief financial officer, 1977-79, sr. exec. v.p. restaurants and consumer non-foods, 1980-81, vice chmn. restaurants and consumer non-foods, 1981-85; ret. chmn. bd. Soo Line Corp. Served with AUS, 1946-47. Mem. Lafayette Club, Mpls. Club, Wayzata Country Club, Royal Poinciana Golf Club, Phi Kappa Psi. Home: 2171 Gulf Shore Blvd N Apt 504 Naples FL 34102-4685 Office: 641 Lake St E Wayzata MN 55391-1760

SWANSON, EMILY, state legislator; b. Oak Park, Ill., Jan. 12, 1947; m. Tim Swanson; 2 children. BA, Bennington Coll.; MA, U. Calif., Berkeley. Mem. Mont. Ho. of Reps. Home: 15042 Kelly Canyon Rd Bozeman MT 59715-9625 Office: Mont Ho of Reps State Capitol Helena MT 59620*

SWANSON, FRED A., communications designer, borough councilman; b. Pitts., July 22, 1946; s. Earl F. and Irene F. (McQuaide) S.; m. Leticia Garcia; children: Thomas R., Melissa A., Todd A. Student, Robert Morris Coll., 1964-65, 75-78. Laborer Equitable Gas Co., Pitts., 1965; technician AT&T Long Lines, Pitts., 1970-78; tech. designer AT&T, Pitts., 1978—. Baseball coach Brentwood (Pa.) Athletic Assn.; football coach Brentwood Dukes; founding mem. The Am. Air Mus. Staff sgt. USAF, 1965-70. Mem. Libr. of Congress (assoc.), Am. Mus. Natural History, Smithsonian Assocs., Non-Commd. Officers Assn., Am. Legion (past vice comdr.). Democrat. Roman Catholic. Avocations: golf, coaching football. Home: 4023 Lawnview Ave Brentwood PA 15227

SWANSON, GILLIAN LEE, law librarian; b. Bozeman, Mont., Sept. 13, 1961; d. Garry Arthur and Betty Ellen (McIelwain) S.; m. Thomas Darryl Fox, June 23, 1990. BA in Philosophy, U. Calgary, Alta., Can., 1985; LLB, U. Western Ont., London, Ontario, Can., 1988. Bar: Ont. 1991. Student-at-law Daniel, Wilson (formerly Harris, Barr), St. Catharine's, Ont., 1989-90; law libr. Banc One Corp., Columbus, Ohio, 1993—. Vol. tutor ESL Adult program, Columbus Public Schs., 1991—. Mem. Law Soc. Upper Can. Avocations: legal reference for banking and commercial issues, and for Canadian and American immigration and refugee legal and social issues. Home: 100 E Henderson Rd Columbus OH 43214-2717 Office: Banc One Corp 100 E Broad St Columbus OH 43215-3607

SWANSON, JACK, broadcast executive; b. Oak Park, Ill., Oct. 19, 1946; s. Milton and Emily (Yonco) S.; m. Melanie R. Morgan, Feb. 18, 1989; children: Greg, Christopher. BS, Boston U., 1968; JD, Chgo.-Kent U., 1979. Announcer WXHR-FM, Cambridge, Mass., 1966-67; anchor, reporter WEEI Newsradio, Boston, 1967-68, WLS Radio, Chgo., 1973-79; news dir. WTSO Radio, Madison, Wis., 1970-73; news dir. KGO Newstalk 810, San Francisco, 1979-82, ops. dir., 1982-90; gen. mgr. King Newstalk 1090/ Classic KING FM, Seattle, 1990-92, v.p., gen. mgr., 1992-94; ops. dir. KGO Radio, San Francisco, 1994—. With U.S. Army, 1968-70. Office: KGO Radio 900 Front St San Francisco CA 94111-1427

SWANSON, KARIN, hospital administrator, consultant; b. New Britain, Conn., Dec. 8, 1942; d. Oake F. and Ingrid Lauren Swanson; m. B. William Dorsey, June 26, 1965 (div. 1974); children: Matthew W., Julie I., Alison K.; m. Sanford H. Low, Oct. 14, 1989. BA in Biology, Middlebury Coll., 1964; MPH, Yale U., 1981. Biology tchr. Kents Hill (Maine) Sch., 1964-66; laboratory instr. Bates Coll., Lewiston, Maine, 1974-78; asst. to gen. dir. Mass. Eye and Ear Infirmary, Boston, 1979-80; v.p. profl. services Portsmouth (N.H.) Hosp., 1981-83; v.p. Health Strategy Assn. Ltd., Chestnut Hill, Mass., 1983-85; v.p. med. affairs Cen. Maine Med. Ctr., Lewiston, 1986-89; health care mgmt. cons. Cambridge, Mass., 1989-91; CEO Hahnemann Hosp., Brighton, Mass., 1991-94; adminstr. Vencor Hosp., Boston, 1994-95; pres., CEO The Laser Inst. New Eng., Newton, Mass., 1996—. Mem. Phi Beta Kappa. Avocations: reading, gardening, walking. Home: 198 Glen St Natick MA 01760-5606

SWANSON, LLOYD OSCAR, former savings and loan association executive; b. Mpls., June 26, 1913; s. Carl G. and Ellen (Peterson) S.; m. Eileen E. Hedlof, Mar. 29, 1958; children: Marcia L. (Mrs. Joseph Mascee), Paul L., J. Bradley, Craig R. Student, U. Minn., 1930-31; B.A., Gustavus Adolphus Coll., 1935, L.H.D. (hon.), 1968. Dir. admissions and pub. relations Gustavus Adolphus Coll., 1935-37; spl. agt. John Hancock Life Ins. Co., Mpls., 1937-42; gen. agt. Nat. Life Ins. Co., Mpls., 1942-62; pres. First Fed. Savs. and Loan Assn., Mpls., 1962-77; chmn. bd. First Fed. Savs. and Loan Assn., 1967-84; chmn. bd. dirs. The Security Corp., 1967-84; dir. Soderberg Optical Co., St. Paul. Former trustee, chmn. bd. trustees Gustavus Adolphus Coll., St. Peter, Minn.; trustee Greater Gustavus Fund, 1952—; former chmn. bd. pensions Luth. Ch. in Am.; former chmn. bd. trustees Fairview Cmty. Hosps. Mem. Savs. League Minn. (dir., pres. 1970), Swedish Coun. Am. (mem. bd.), Athletic Club, Interlachen Country Club (past mem. bd. govs.), Royal Poinciana Golf Club (Naples, Fla.). Home: 2171 Gulf Shore Blvd N Naples FL 34102-4694 Office: 4900 IDS Tower Minneapolis MN 55402

SWANSON, LORNA ELLEN, physical therapist, athletic trainer, researcher; b. Bridgeport, Conn., July 22, 1954; d. Harold Carl and Marna Ellyn (French) S.; m. James M. Kelley, Oct. 16, 1993; 1 child, Ellen Elizabeth Kelley. BFA in Dance, So. Meth. U., 1975, MFA in Dance, 1978; BS in Phys. Therapy, U. Tex., Dallas, 1984; PhD in Exercise Sci., U. Tenn., 1994. Lic. phys. therapist, Tenn. Mem. faculty Brookhaven Coll., Dallas, 1982-84; staff therapist St. Mary's Med. Ctr., Knoxville, Tenn., 1984-85, Ft. Sanders Regional Med. Ctr., Knoxville, 1985-86, Knoxville Sports Therapy, 1991-92; program dir., mem. faculty Roane State C.C., Harriman, Tenn., 1987-92; clin. specialist Ft. Sanders Ctr. for Sports Medicine, Knoxville, 1992-93, mgr., 1994-96; clin. specialist Ft. Sanders Therapy Ctr. West, Knoxville, 1996-96; ballet Instr. East Tenn. Acad. performing Arts, 1996—; grad. asst. athletic dept. U. Tenn., Knoxville, 1989-91; reviewer Jour. Orthopedic and Sports Phys. Therapy, 1993, 94; adj. faculty Pellissippi State Tech. C.C., 1994.; instr. East Tenn. Acad. Performing Arts, 1995-96; speaker at state and nat. profl. confs. Contbr. chpt. to book and articles to profl. jours. Ballet mistress Victoria Bolen Dance Theatre, Knoxville, 1986-88; mem. bd. of trust Appalachian Ballet Co., 1995—. Helen B. Watson dissertation rsch. awardee U. Tenn. Mem. Am. Phys. Therapy Assn. (bd. content experts 1990-93), Tenn. Phys. Therapy Assn., Nat. Athletic Tng. Assn. (cert. athletic trainer), Tenn. Athletic Tng. Assn., Nat. Strength and Conditioning Assn. (cert. specialist), Neurodevel. Treatment Assn. (nominating com. 1987-89). Democrat. Lutheran. Avocations: music, sports, reading, dance, choreography. Office: Ft Sanders Therapy Ctr West Ste 204 200 Fort Sanders West Blvd Knoxville TN 37922-3357

SWANSON, MICHAEL ALAN, sales and marketing executive; b. Ticonderoga, N.Y., Aug. 26, 1958; s. Vernon George and Evelyn Marie (Vigliotti) S.; m. Lynette Ann Vagush, Apr. 14, 1993; children: Connor Michael, Alex William, Taylor Ann. A in Bus. Mgmt., Hudson Valley C. C., Troy, N.Y., 1978; BA in Bus. Mgmt., SUNY, Utica, 1981. City dispatcher Roadway Express, Tonawanda, N.Y., 1983-84, sales rep., 1984-86; acct. exec. Ryder Truck Rental, Albany, 1986-87; acct. rep. Roadway Package Sys., Albany, 1987-89; N.J. geographic nat. acct. exec. Roadway Package Sys., Trenton, 1989-92, pharmaceutical specialist, nat. acct. exec., 1992-95; v.p. sales and mktg. Caliber Logistics Health Care (formerly Mediquik Express), Chapel Hill, N.C., 1995—, Caliber Systems Co. (formerly Roadway Svcs.), Chapel Hill, 1995—. Mem. Am. Mktg. Assn., Nat. Assn. Chain Drug Stores, Coun. Logistics Mgmt., Health and Personal Care Conf. Republican. Episcopalian. Avocations: tennis, golf, drums, racquetball. Home: 1104 Colehurst Crescent Apex NC 27502 Office: Caliber Logistics Health Care Inc 1717 Legion Rd Chapel Hill NC 27514-2396

SWANSON, NORMA FRANCES, federal agency administrator; b. Blue Island, Ill., Oct. 24, 1923; d. Arnold Raymond and Bessie Oween (Bewley) Brown; m. George Clair Swanson, Mar. 18, 1948; 1 child, Dane Craig. AB, Asbury Coll., 1946; BS cum laude, Eastern Nazarene Coll., Wollaston, Mass., 1970; MA cum laude, Ind. Christian U., 1986. Confidential asst. dep. undersec. interagy. intergovt. affairs U.S. Dept. Edn., Washington, 1981—; pres. Window to the World, Inc., Schroon Lake, N.Y., 1985—; asst. dir. edn. Commn. Bicentennial U.S. Constn., Washington, 1987—; dir. Horizons Plus Values Program Hampton Roads Va. Detention Homes; dir. Project Fresh Start Washington D.C. Pub. Sch., 1993-96; cons. Conf. Industrialized Nations, Williamsburg, Va., 1982, Nellie Thomas Inst. Learning, Monterey, Calif., 1981-82. Author: Dear Teenager, A Teen's Guide to Correct Social Behavior, 1987, A Constitution is Born, A Teacher's Guide to Resource Materials, 1987, Sunlights and More, Bright Beginnings, 1993, Vol. II, 1996, The Ones that Count and Other Stories with Values to Live By, 1994, A Think and Write Journal Sunlights and More Vol. II, 1996, (story album) The Ones that Count and Other Stories with Virtues to Live By, 1996; editor: (anthology) Horizons Plus; developer ednl. materials; theorem artist Early Life mag., 1974. Bd. regents Ind. Christian U., 1986—; program dir. Tidewater (Va.) Outreach, 1992; dir. project Fresh Start, Washington Pub. Sch., 1993-94; dir. youth outreach with values program U.S. Dept. Juvenile Justice, 1992-93. Recipient J.C. Penney award for volunteerism, 1993, Precision Tune awrd for svc. tto Washington Inner-City Schs. Republican. Baptist. Avocation: theorem painting. Address: 11 Cross Manor Rd #D Saint Inigoes MD 20684-3003

SWANSON, PATRICIA K., university official; b. St. Louis, May 8, 1940; d. Emil Louis and Patricia (McNair) Klick; 1 child, Ivan Clatanoff. BS in Edn., U. Mo., 1962; postgrad., Cornell U., 1963; MLS, Simmons Coll., 1967. Reference librarian Simmons Coll., Boston, 1967-68; reference librarian U. Chgo., 1970-79, sr. lectr. Grad. Library Sch., 1974-83, 86-88, head reference service, 1979-83, asst. dir. for sci. libraries, 1983-93, acting asst. dir. for tech. svcs., 1987-88, assoc. provost, 1993—; project dir. Office Mgmt. Svcs., Assn. Rsch. Librs., 1982-83; speaker in field; cons. on libr. mgmt., planning and space. Author: Great is the Gift that Bringeth Knowledge: Highlights from the History of the John Crerar Library, 1989; contbr. articles to profl. jours. Office: U of Chicago Office of the Provost 5801 S Ellis Ave Rm 501 Chicago IL 60637-1476

SWANSON, PAUL RUBERT, minister; b. Bakersfield, Calif., May 13, 1943; s. Roland Hilding and Myrtle Isabelle (Magnuson) S.; m. Mary Elizabeth Greene, June 18, 1967; children: Kristen Ann, Karlynn Marie, Jonathan Paul. BA, Pacific Luth. U., 1966; MDiv, Luth. Sch. Theology, 1970. Ordained minister, Luth. Ch. Pastor 1st Luth. Ch., Anaconda, Mont., 1970-76, King of Kings Luth. Ch., Milwaukie, Oreg., 1976-84; asst. to bishop Pacific N.W. Synod-Luth. Ch. in Am., Portland, Oreg., 1984-87; bishop Oreg. Synod-Evang. Luth. Ch. Am., Portland, 1987—; bd. dirs. Legacy Health System, Portland. Regent Pacific Luth. U., Tacoma, 1987—; bd. dirs. Emanuel Hosp., Portland, 1987; chmn. bd. dirs. Hearthstone, Inc., Anaconda, 1973-76; bd. dirs. Ecumenical Ministries Oreg., Portland, 1984—. Recipient Disting. Svc. award Pacific Luth. U., 1993. Avocation: golf.

SWANSON, PEGGY EUBANKS, finance educator; b. Ivanhoe, Tex., Dec. 29, 1936; d. Leslie Samuel and Mary Lee (Reid) Eubanks; m. B. Marc Sommers, Nov. 10, 1993. BBA, U. North Tex., 1957, M. Bus. Edn., 1965; MA in Econs., So. Meth. U., 1967, PhD in Econs., 1978. Instr. El Centro Coll., Dallas, 1967-69, 71-78, bus. div. chmn., 1969-71; asst. prof. econs. U. Tex., Arlington, 1978-79, asst. prof. fin., 1979-84, assoc. prof., 1984-86, chmn. dept. fin. and real estate, 1986-88, prof. fin., 1987—; expert witness various law firms, primarily Tex. and Calif., 1978—; cons. Internat. Edn. Program, 1992—; curriculum cons. U. Monterrey, Mexico, 1995. Contbr. articles to profl. jours. Vol. Am. Cancer Soc., Dallas, Arlington, 1981—, Meals on Wheels, Arlington, 1989—; mem. adv. bd. Ryan/Reilly Ctr. for Urban Land Utilization, Arlington, 1986-88. Mem. Fin. Exec. Inst. (chmn. acad. rels. 1987-88), Internat. Bus. Steering Com. (chmn. 1989-91), Am. Fin. Assn., Am. Econ. Assn., Fin. Mgmt. Assn. (hon. faculty mem. Nat. Honor Soc. 1985-86), Southwestern Fin. Assn. (program com. 1987-88, 96), Acad. of Internat. Bus. (program com. 1992-95), Phi Beta Delta (membership com. 1987-89). Republican. Episcopalian. Avocations: tennis, gardening. Home: 4921 Bridgewater Dr Arlington TX 76017-2729 Office: U Tex at Arlington UTA Box 19449 Arlington TX 76019

SWANSON, PHILLIP DEAN, neurologist; b. Seattle, Oct. 1, 1932; s. William Dean and Kathryn C. (Peterson) S.; m. Sheila N. Joardar, Apr. 20, 1957; children: Stephen, Jennifer, Kathryn, Rebecca, Sara. B.S., Yale U., 1954; student, U. Heidelberg, 1952-53; M.D., Johns Hopkins U., 1958; Ph.D. in Biochemistry, U. London, 1964. Intern Harvard med. svc. Boston City Hosp., 1958-59; resident in neurology Johns Hopkins Hosp., Balt. City Hosp., 1959-62; asst. prof. U. Wash. Sch. Medicine, Seattle, 1964-68; assoc. prof. U. Wash. Sch. Medicine, 1968-73, prof., 1973—, head divsn. neurology, 1967-95; mem. med. adv. bd. Puget Sound chpt. Nat. Multiple Sclerosis Soc., 1967—, chmn., 1970-74; mem. com. to combat Huntington's Disease Nat. Sci. Council, 1975-84. Author: (with others) Introduction to Clinical Neurology, 1976; editor: Signs and Symptoms in Neurology, 1984; contbr. articles to profl. jours. NIH spl. fellow, 1962-64; NIH grantee. Fellow Am. Acad. Neurology; mem. Am. Neurol. Assn., Assn. Univ. Profs. Neurology (pres. 1975-76), Am. Heart Assn., Am. Soc. Neurochemistry, Internat. Soc. Neurochemistry, Biochem. Soc. (London), Am. Soc. Clin. Investigation (emeritus). Home: 6537 29th Ave NE Seattle WA 98115-7234 Office: U Wash Sch Medicine Dept Neurology Seattle WA 98195

SWANSON, RALPH WILLIAM, aerospace executive, consultant, engineer; b. Mpls.; m. Virginia May Peoples (dec.); children: John W., Timothy R.; m. Patricia Anne Smith. BS in Aero. Engring., U. Minn., 1947; MS in Nuclear Engring., N.C. State U., 1954; PhD in Engring., Kennedy-Western U., 1989. Design engr. Los Alamos (N.Mex.) Sci. Lab., 1948-52; asst. prof. physics Air Force Inst. Tech., Wright Patterson AFB, Ohio, 1954-56; chief radiation div. armed forces spl. weapons project Pentagon, Washington, 1957-61; dep. chief staff plans and programs Air Force Eastern Test Range, Patrick AFB, Fla., 1961-64; dep. for programs and requirements Air Force Nat. Range Div., Patrick AFB, Fla., 1964-65; mgr. advanced programs IBM Corp., Kennedy Space Center, Fla., 1965-75; chief engr. Planning Rsch. Corp., Kennedy Space Center, 1975-79, dep. project mgr., gen. mgr., 1979-87; project mgr. Bamsi, Inc., Kennedy Space Center, 1987-93; freelance cons., Cocoa Beach, Fla., 1987—; pres. Profl. Mgmt. Group, Inc., Cocoa Beach. Bd. dirs. Brevard Achievement Ctr., Rockledge, Fla., 1977—. Col. USAF, 1941-65, ETO and Korea, ret. Mem. Air Force Assn., Assn. AFIT Grads., MacIntosh Computer User Group, Masons, Shriners, Sigma Xi, Sigma Pi Sigma. Republican. Avocations: scuba diving, under water photography, jogging.

SWANSON, RICHARD WILLIAM, statistician; b. Rockford, Ill., July 26, 1934; s. Richard and Erma Marie (Herman) S.; m. Laura Yoko Arai, Dec. 30, 1970. BS, Iowa State U., 1958, MS, 1964. Ops. analyst Stanford Rsch. Inst., Monterey, Calif., 1958-62; statistician ARINC Rsch. Corp., Washington, 1964-65; sr. scientist Booz-Allen Applied Rsch., Vietnam, 1965-67, L.A., 1967-68; sr. ops. analyst Control Data Corp., Honolulu, 1968-70; mgmt. cons., Honolulu, 1970-73; exec. v.p. SEQUEL Corp., Honolulu, 1973-75; bus. cons. Hawaii Dept. Planning and Econ. Devel., Honolulu, 1975-77, tax rsch. and planning officer Dept. Taxation, 1977-82; ops. rsch. analyst U.S. Govt., 1982-89; shipyard statisician U.S. Govt., 1989—. Served with AUS, 1954-56. Mem. Hawaiian Acad. Sci., Sigma Xi. Home: 583 Kamoku St Apt 3505 Honolulu HI 96826-5240 Office: Pearl Harbor Naval Shipyard PO Box 400 Honolulu HI 96809-0400

SWANSON, ROBERT DRAPER, college president; b. Sioux City, Iowa, Aug. 6, 1915; s. Alfred and Tida Ruth (Draper) S.; m. Roberta B. Clements, May 5, 1941 (dec. Oct. 1975); children: Sara Louise, Mark Robert; m. Dorothy B. Howe, Aug. 4, 1979. A.B., Park Coll., 1937; student, U. Iowa, 1937; B.D., McCormick Theol. Sem., 1941; D.D., James Millikin U., 1950; L.H.D., Tusculum Coll., 1966, Olivet Coll., 1971, Central Mich. U., 1979, Alma Coll., 1981; LL.D., Hillsdale Coll., 1968, Hope Coll., 1981. Dir. athletics, phys. edn. Park Coll., 1937-38; ordained to ministry Presbyn. Ch., 1941; pastor Second Presbyn. Ch., Tulsa, 1941-45; dean of students McCormick Sem., 1946-47, v.p., prof. preaching, 1948-56; pres. Alma Coll., 1956-80, pres. emeritus, 1980—; dir. Gen. Telephone Co. Mich. Served as lt. (j.g.), Chaplain's Corps USNR, 1945-46. Recipient Disting. Alumni award Park Coll., 1971, Disting. Alumnus award McCormick Theol. Sem., 1981. Mem. Phi Beta Kappa. Club: Rotary (Alma). Home: 4105 Riverview Dr Alma MI 48801-9563

SWANSON, ROBERT KILLEN, management consultant; b. Deadwood, S.D., Aug. 11, 1932; s. Robert Claude and Marie Elizabeth (Kersten) S.; m. Nancy Anne Oyaas, July 19, 1958; children: Cathryn Lynn, Robert Stuart, Bart Killen. BA, U. S.D., 1954; postgrad., U. Melbourne, Australia, 1955. With Gen. Mills, Inc., Mpls., 1955-58, 71-79, v.p., 1971-73, group v.p., 1973-77, exec. v.p., 1977-79; with Marathon Oil Co., Findlay, Ohio, 1958-60; sr. v.p., dir. Needham, Harper & Steers, Inc., Chgo., 1961-69; joint mng. dir. S. H. Benson (Holdings) Ltd., Eng., 1969-71; pres., chief operating officer Greyhound Corp., Phoenix, 1980; chmn., chief exec. officer Del E. Webb Corp., Phoenix, 1981-87; chmn. RKS Inc., Phoenix, 1987—; bd. dirs. Am. S.W. Concepts Inc., Ariz. Desert Seguaro; chmn. Grossman's Inc., Boston, 1994—. 2d lt. U.S. Army, 1955. Fulbright scholar, 1954-55; Woodrow Wilson scholar. Mem. U.S. Coun. Fgn. Rels., U.K. Dirs. Inst., U.S. Internat. Scholars Assn., English Speaking Union. Episcopalian. Office: RKS Inc 5600 N Palo Cristi Rd Paradise Vly AZ 85253-7543

SWANSON, ROBERT LAWRENCE, oceanographer, academic program administrator; b. Balt., Oct. 11, 1938; s. Lawrence Wilbur and Hazel Ruth S.; BS in Civil Engring., Lehigh U., 1960; MS in Oceanography, Oreg. State U., 1965, PhD in Oceanography, 1971; cer. Hydrographer.; m. Dana Lamont, Sept. 12, 1963; children: Lawrence Daniel, Michael Nathan. Commd. ensign U.S. Coast and Geodetic Survey (now NOAA), 1960, advanced through grades to capt., 1978, ops. officer U.S. Pathfinder, 1965, comdg. officer U.S. Marmer, 1966, chief oceanographic div. Nat. Ocean Survey, NOAA, Rockville, Md., 1969-72, mgr. Marine Ecosystems Analysis, N.Y. Bight Project, Stony Brook, 1973-78, dir. Office of Marine Pollution Assessment, NOAA, Rockville, 1978-83; research assoc. Sea Grant, NOAA, Stony Brook, 1983-84, comdg. officer, U.S. Researcher, Miami, 1984-86; chief internat. activities group NOAA, Rockville, 1986; exec. dir. Office Oceanic and Atmospheric Research NOAA, Rockville, 1986-87; dir. Waste Mgmt. Inst. SUNY, Stony Brook, 1987—; adj. prof. Marine Scis. Research Center, SUNY, Stony Brook, 1976—; mem. Suffolk County Coun. Environ. Quality, 1988—, N.Y. State Oversight Com. on Brookhaven Nat. Lab., 1996—; chmn. Coastal Mgmt. Commn. Vills. Head of the Harbor and Nissequogue, 1994—; trustee Three Village Hist. Soc., 1994—; cons. in field; co-chair L.I. Environ. Econ. Roundtable, 1995—. Recipient Karo award Am. Soc. Mil. Engrs., 1972; Silver medal U.S. Dept. Commerce, 1973; Program and Adminstrn. Mgmt. award NOAA, 1975, Unit citation, 1981; sr. exec. fellow John F. Kennedy Sch. Govt., Harvard U., 1983., Spl. Achievement award, 1987, NOAA Corps. Commendations, 1987. Mem. Am. Mil. Engrs., N.Y. Acad. Scis., ASCE (chmn. hydrography and oceanography com. 1972-74), AAAS, Am. Geophys. Union, Marine Tech. Soc. (chmn. marine pollution com. 1982-92), Sigma Xi. Presbyterian. Club: Cosmos. Co-author and co-editor: Oxygen Depletion and Associated Benthic Mortalities in N.Y. Bight, 1979; co-editor: Floatable Wastes and the Region's Beaches; mem. editorial bd. N.Y. Bight Monograph Series, 1973-81; co-pub. Waste Mgmt. Rsch. Report, 1988-95; mem. editl. bd. Chemistry and Ecology, 1995—; mem. adv. bd. L.I. Hist. Jour., 1995—. Home: 46 Harbor Hill Rd Saint James NY 11780 Office: SUNY Waste Reduction and Mgmt Inst Stony Brook NY 11794-5000

SWANSON, ROBERT LEE, lawyer; b. Fond du Lac, Wis., July 15, 1942; s. Walfred S. and Edna F. (Kamp) S.; m. Mary Ruth Francis, Aug. 19, 1967; children: Leigh Alexandra, Mitchell Pearson. BS, U. Wis., 1964; JD, Valparaiso U., 1970; LLM, Boston U., 1979. Bar: Wis. 1970, U.S. Dist. Ct. (ea. dist.) Wis. 1970, U.S. Dist. Ct. (we. dist.) Wis. 1974, U.S. Tax Ct. 1981, U.S. Dist. Ct. (cen.) Ill. 1988. Atty. Kasdorf, Dahl, Lewis & Swietlik, Milw., 1970-73; atty., ptnr. Wartman, Wartman & Swanson, Ashland, Wis., 1973-80; city atty. City of Ashland, Wis., 1976-80; atty., ptnr. DeMark, Kolbe & Brodek, Racine, Wis., 1980-95; ptnr. Hartig, Bjelajac, Swanson & Koenen, Racine, 1995—; lectr. civil rights and discrimination laws, 1980—; lectr. bus. law Cardinal Strich U., 1996—. Columnist (legal) Burlington Std. Press, 1991—, Wis. Restaurant Assn. Mag., 1986. Vice comdr. USCG Aux. Bayfield (Wis.) Flotilla, 1975-81; v.p., bd. dirs. Meml. Med. Ctr., Ashland, 1975-80; chmn. Ashland County Rep. Party, 1976-79; vol. atty. ACLU Wis., 1975—. 1st lt. U.S. Army, 1964-66. Named one of Outstanding Young Men of Am., Jaycees, 1978; recipient Disting. Achievement in Art and Sci. of Advocacy award Internat. Acad. Trial Lawyers, 1970. Mem. Racine County Bar Assn. (bd. dirs. 1986-89), Wis. Acad. Trial Lawyers, Def. Rsch. Inst., Am. Hockey Assn. U.S. (coach, referee 1983—), Am. Legion, The Federalist Soc. Avocations: softball, volleyball, hockey. Home: 333 Hollow Creek Rd Racine WI 53402-2637 Office: Hartig Bjelajac Swanson & Koenen 601 Lake Ave Racine WI 53401-0038

SWANSON, ROBERT MCLEAN, retired business educator; b. Union City, Pa., Aug. 11, 1920; s. Peter Leonard and Mary Edna (McLean) S.; m. Marie Manda, May 25, 1946; children: Catherine, Robert Jr., Mary Ann, Christina. BS in Edn., Ind. U. of Pa., 1942; MA, Columbia U., 1949, EdD, 1953. Bus. tchr. Darlington (Pa.) Joint Schs., 1946-48; prof. bus. Thiel Coll., Greenville, Pa., 1948-52; vis. prof. Teachers Coll. Columbia U., N.Y.C., 1953; prof. bus. Ball State U., Muncie, Ind., 1954-85, head dept. bus. edn., 1961-67, prof. emeritus, 1985—. Author: (with others) Century 21 Accounting, 1967, 72, 77, 82, 87, 92, 95; (software) Interactive Accounting, 1997. Charter bd. dirs. Muncie Hosp. Hospitality House, 1983-86. Maj. U.S. Army, 1942-46, ETO. Mem. Nat. Bus. Edn. Assn., Ind. Bus. Edn. Assn., Delta Pi Epsilon. Roman Catholic. Avocations: home computer, traveling. Home: 1719 E Wexley Rd Bloomington IN 47401-4357

SWANSON, ROY ARTHUR, classicist, educator; b. St. Paul, Apr. 7, 1925; s. Roy Benjamin and Gertrude (Larson) S.; m. Vivian May Vitous, Mar. 30, 1946; children: Lynn Marie (Mrs. Gerald A. Snider), Robin Lillian, Robert Roy (dec.), Dyack Tyler, Dana Miriam (Mrs. Jon Butts). B.A., U. Minn., 1948, B.S., 1949, M.A., 1951; Ph.D., U. Ill., 1954. Prin. Maplewood Elementary Sch., St. Paul, 1949-51; instr. U. Ill., 1952-53, Ind. U., 1954-57; asst. prof. U. Minn., Mpls., 1957-61; assoc. prof. U. Minn., 1961-64, acting chmn. classics, 1963-64, prof. classics, chmn. comparative lit., 1964-65; prof. English Macalester Coll., St. Paul, 1965-67; coord. humanities program, 1966-67; prof. comparative lit. and classics U. Wis.-Milw., 1967—, prof. English, 1990—, chmn. classics dept., 1967-70, 86-89, chmn. comparative lit., 1970-73, 76-83, coord. Scandinavian studies program, 1982-96; cons. St. Paul Tchrs. Sr. High Sch. English, 1964. Author: Odi et Amo: The Complete Poetry of Catullus, 1959, Heart of Reason: Introductory Essays in Modern-World Humanities, 1963, Pindar's Odes, 1974, Greek and Latin Word Elements, 1981, The Love Songs of the Carmina Burana, 1987, Pär Lagerkvist: Five Early Works, 1989; editor Minn. Rev., 1963-67; Classical Jour., 1966-72; contbr. articles to profl. jours. With AUS, 1944-46. Decorated Bronze Star; recipient Disting. Teaching award U. Minn., 1962, Disting. Teaching award U. Wis.-Milw., 1974, 91. Mem. Am. Philol. Assn., Am. Comparative Lit. Assn., Modern Lang. Assn., Soc. for Advancement Scandinavian Study, Phi Beta Kappa (pres. chpt. 1975-76). Home: 11618 N Bobolink Ln Mequon WI 53092-2804 Office: U Wis Dept Classics & Comp Lit PO Box 413 Milwaukee WI 53201-0413

SWANSON, RUNE E., financial executive; b. Chgo., Aug. 9, 1919; s. John E. and Emma C. (Carlson) S.; m. Lenore Reed, Mar. 18, 1944; children: Deborah, Cynthia, Patricia. B.S. in Commerce (Univ. scholar), Northwestern U., 1943. Asst. contr. U.S. Gypsum Co., Chgo., 1946-56; contr. Internat. Minerals & Chem. Corp., Chgo., 1956-60, Mobil Chem. Co., N.Y.C., 1960-66; v.p. fin. Nat. Gypsum Co., Dallas, 1966-84; assoc. Swearingen Co., 1985-86; pres. Swanson Assocs., Dallas, 1986—; instr. Northwestern U. Served as lt. USNR, 1943-46, PTO. Mem. Fin. Execs. Inst., Northwood Country Club, Dallas Knife and Fork Club, Rotary, Masons, Scottish Rite, Shriners. Republican.

SWANSON, SHIRLEY JUNE, registered nurse, adult education educator; b. Dade City, Fla., Feb. 26, 1942; d. Alan John and Ollie Mae (Jackson) S.; m. James A. Whatley, 1960 (div. 1962); 1 child, Marsha L. Glunt; m. Jerald Ward Steen, Sr., June 7, 1963; children: Linda A. Stanley, Jerald Ward, Jr., Jerald Wagner. AA, Hillsborough C.C., 1974; BA, U. South Fla., 1975; AS, Gupton-Jones Coll., 1992, No. Maine Tech. Coll., 1996; postgrad., Calif. Coll. Health Scis. RN; cert. in elem. and adult edn. scis., Maine; cert. mortician. Personal life underwriter Home Ins. Co., N.Y.C., 1979-82; with L.L. Bean, Freeport, Maine, 1988-90; tchr. biology Caribou (Maine) Adult Edn., 1994-96; owner Alan's Dau.'s Place, 1988—, Angel Quilts, 1996—; spkr. in field. Author, editor Coffee Break, 1963-64; editor: Osiris Yearbook, 1991-92. Ofcl. spinner Fla. State Fair, Tampa, 1984-85; spinner East Animal Farm/Westshore Mall, Tampa, 1984-85; guest spinner Town of Westfield (Maine) Jubilee Days, 1995; hospice vol. Vis. Nurses of Aroostook County, Caribou, 1995—. Billerica, Mass. O.E.S. scholar, 1975, Am. Bd. Funeral Svc. Edn. scholar, 1992, Caribou Adult Edn. Sys. scholar, 1995. Mem. Phi Theta Kappa, Pi Sigma Eta. Roman Catholic. Avocations: wool spinning, commision quilting, tutoring, weaving, travel. Home: PO Box 3314 Portland ME 04104-3314 Office: Caribou Adult Edn Ctr Sweden St Caribou ME 04736

SWANSON, WALLACE MARTIN, lawyer; b. Fergus Falls, Minn., Aug. 22, 1941; s. Marvin Walter and Mary Louise (Lindsey) S.; m. Susan W. Swanson; children: Kristen Lindsey, Eric Munger. B.A. with honors, U. Minn., 1962; LL.B. with honors, So. Methodist U., 1965. Bar: Tex. 1965. Since practiced in Dallas; assoc. Coke & Coke, Dallas, 1965-70; ptnr. firm Johnson & Swanson, Dallas, 1970-88; prin. Wallace M. Swanson, P.C., Dallas, 1988—; chmn., CEO Ace Cash Express Inc., Irving, Tex., 1987-88, State St. Capital Corp., 1990—. Served with USNR, 1960-65. Mem. ABA, Tex. Bar Found., State Bar Tex. (securities com. 1972-86, chmn. 1978-80, coun. bus. law sect. 1980-86), Dallas Bar Assn., Crescent Club. Methodist. Address: 3816 Miramar Ave Dallas TX 75205-3126

SWANSON-SCHONES, KRIS MARGIT, developmental adapted physical education educator; b. Mpls., Mar. 22, 1950; d. Donald Theodore Swanson and Alice Alida (Swanson) Suhl; m. Gary Wallace Suhl, Apr. 6, 1974 (div. Aug. 1985); m. Gregory Edward Schones, Dec. 30, 1989. BA, Augsburg Coll., 1972. Cert. devel. adapted phys. edn. tchr., phys. edn. tchr., health tchr., coach/corrective therapist. Devel. adapted phys. edn. tchr. St. Paul Schs., 1972—, adapted athletic dir., 1989—; mem. adapted athletics adv. bd. Minn. State H.S. League, 1992—. Author: On the Move, 1979. Chmn. hospitality Tanbark Club, Lakeville, Minn., 1992—, mem. show cmty., 1991—; mem. outreach com. Spl. Olympics, Minn., 1989-94. Recipient Nutrition Edn. grant Fed. Govt., 1978-79, Christmas Album grant Spl. Olympics, 1989, Internat. Spl. Olympics Coach award Minn. Spl. Olympics, 1991. Mem. NEA, AAHPERD, Minn. Edn. Assn., Minn. Assn. Adapted Athletics (exec. bd. 1989—, sec. exec. bd. 1990—). Avocations: showing horses and dogs, gardening, fishing. Home: 16280 Webster Ct Prior Lake MN 55372-9772 Office: Humboldt Jr High Sch 440 Humboldt Ave Saint Paul MN 55107-2806

SWANSTROM, THOMAS EVAN, economist; b. Green Bay, Wis., May 17, 1939; s. Alfred Enoch and Elizabeth Nan (Thomas) S.; m. Nancy Anne Roche; children: Amy, Scott. Student, U. Notre Dame, 1957-59; B.A., U. Wis., 1962, M.A., 1963; postgrad., Am. U., 1963-66. Economist, U.S. Bur. Labor Statistics, Washington, 1963-66; dir. research Population Ref. Bur., Washington, 1966-68; economist Sears, Roebuck & Co., Chgo., 1968-70, market analyst, 1970-72, mgr. catalog research, 1972-75, asst. mgr. econ. research, 1974-80, chief economist, 1980-90; pres. Consumer Econs., Chgo., 1991—; mem. bus. research adv. council Bur. Labor Stats. Contbr. articles to industry publs. Mem. Nat. Assn. Bus. Economists, Conf. Bus. Economists.

SWANTON, SUSAN IRENE, library director; b. Rochester, N.Y., Nov. 29, 1941; d. Walter Frederick and Irene Wray S.; m. Wayne Holman, Apr. 12, 1969 (div. June 1973); 1 child, Michael; life ptnr. James Donald Lathrop; children: Kathryn, Kristin. AB, Harvard U., 1963; MLS, Columbia U., 1965. Libr. dir. Warsaw (N.Y.) Pub. Libr., 1963-64, Gates Pub. Libr., Rochester, N.Y., 1965—. Pres. Drug and Alcohol Coun., Rochester, 1985-91, mem. adv. coun., 1992-94; bd. dirs., co-chairperson info. svcs. Rochester Freenet, 1995—. Mem. Gates-Chili Coun. Rochester Met. C. of C. (pres. 1982, sec. 1990-94, Citizen of Yr. 1995), Harvard Club of Rochester (mem. adv. bd.). Office: Gates Pub Libr 1605 Buffalo Rd Rochester NY 14624-1637

SWANTON, VIRGINIA LEE, author, publisher, bookseller; b. Oak Park, Ill., Feb. 6, 1933; d. Milton Wesley and Eleanor Louise (Linnell) S. BA, Lake Forest (Ill.) Coll., 1954; MA in English Lit., Northwestern U., 1955; cert. in acctg., Coll. of Lake County, Ill., 1984. Editorial asst. Publs. Office, Northwestern U., Evanston, Ill., 1955-58; reporter Lake Forester, Lake Forest, 1959; editor Scott, Foresman & Co., Glenview, Ill., 1959-84; copy editor, travel coord. McDougal Littell/Houghton Mifflin, Evanston, 1985-94; sr. bookseller B. Dalton Bookseller, Lake Forest, Ill., 1985—; author, pub. Gold Star Publ. Svcs., Lake Forest, 1994—. Contbr. articles to profl. jours. Mem. bd. deacons First Presbyn. Ch. of Lake Forest; mem., sec. bd. dirs., newsletter editor Career Resource Ctr., Inc., Lake Forest; corr. sec. Presbyn. Women, First Presbyn. Ch. at Lake Forest; current events discusssion vol. Lake Forest/Lake Bluff Sr. Ctr. Mem. Internat. Reading Assn., Deerpath Art League, Chgo. Women in Pub. Presbyterian. Avocation: gardening. Office: Gold Star Publ Svcs PO Box 125 Lake Forest IL 60045

SWANZEY, ROBERT JOSEPH, data processing executive; b. Bklyn., Feb. 4, 1935; s. Robert and Olivia (MacIntosh) S.; m. Marie Shannon, Nov. 23, 1957; children: Barbara Ann, Stephen. BA, Pace Coll., 1962. Teller Mfrs. Hanover Trust, N.Y.C., 1953-56; programmer N.Y. Cen. R.R., N.Y.C., 1956-64; systems analyst Schenley Industries, N.Y.C., 1964-70; v.p. systems and programming Raam Info. Services, Inc., N.Y.C., 1970-75; sr. v.p. ops. Century Bus. Credit Corp. (formerly Century Factors, Inc.), N.Y.C., 1975—. Treas. St. Patrick's Sports Programs, Bklyn., 1984-88; dir. basketball St. Patrick's Cath. Youth Orgnl. Program, Bklyn., 1976-84. Co-recipient Adult of Yr. award St. Patrick's Cath. Youth Orgn., 1983. Mem. Factors-Controllers Assn. (treas. 1983-84). Avocations: golf, music. Office: Century Bus Credit Corp 119 W 40th St New York NY 10018-2500

SWAP, WALTER CHARLES, academic dean, psychology educator; b. Seattle, Jan. 23, 1943; s. Clifford Lloyd and Edna Frances (Hastings) S.; m. Susan Webster McAllister, June 25, 1966 (dec.); m. Dorothy André Leonard, May 3, 1997; children: Clifford John, Alison Frances. BA, Harvard U., 1965; PhD, U. Mich., 1970. Prof. psychology Tufts U., Medford, Mass., 1971-95, chmn. psychology dept., 1983-89, dean undergrad. edn., 1990-94; dean colls., 1994—. Editor, author: Group Decision Making: 1984; contbr. articles to scholarly jours. Mem. Am. Psychol. Soc., Soc. for Exptl. Social Psychology. Democrat. Unitarian-Universalist. Avocations: competitive road running, musical performing, organic gardening. Home: 9 Harrison St Winchester MA 01890-2416 Office: Tufts U Ballou Hall Medford MA 02155

SWART, BONNIE BLOUNT, artist; b. Shreveport, La., May 19, 1939; d. Jonathan Prescott and Alice Florence (Crawford) Blount; m. Carter Eaton Swart; children: Kathleen Anne Nelson, Nancy Laurie Michel, Sherry Colleen Swart. Student, U. Calif., Davis, Ventura Coll., 1997. Exhibited in group exhibitions at Am. Acad. Equine Art, 1989, 92, 93, 94, 96, 97, Nat. Mus. of the Horse, Lexington, Ky., Pastel Soc. of the West Coast, Sacramento, 1995, 96, 97, Annual Exhbn. on Animals in Art, La. State U., Baton Rouge, 1995, 96, Art At the Dog Show, Wichita, Kans., 1995, Harness Tracks of Am., Lexington, 1994, 96, Am. Acad. of Equine Art, Louisville, 1992, 93, 96, Arabian Jockey Club Art Auction, Delaware Park, Del., 1991, Equine Rsch. Benefit, Morvin Park, Leesburg, 1991, Arabian Horse Trust Art Auction, Scottsdale, 1990, Women Artist's of the West, Louisville, 1989, 97, Internat. Arabian Horse Assn., Ky. Horse Park, Louisville, 1989, Arabian Horse Trust Mus. Exhibit, Westminster, Colo., 1987-89, Oil Painters of Am., Taos, N.Mex., 1997; represented in pvt. collections. Mem. Am. Acad. Equine Art (assoc.), Knickerbocker Artists (signature mem.), Pastel Soc. West Coast (signature mem.). Home: 191 Church Tree Rd Crescent City CA 95531-9331

SWARTLING, DANIEL JOSEPH, chemistry educator, researcher; b. Black Falls, Wis., Sept. 3, 1960; s. Ronald James Swartling and Jean Marie (Welda) Trester. BS, Winona State U., 1985; PhD, U. N.D., 1989. Rsch. asst. Purdue U., West Lafayette, Ind., 1989-90; rsch. assoc. U. Chgo., 1990-92; teaching fellow S. Meth. U., Dallas, 1992-94; asst. prof. chemistry Tenn. Tech. U., Cookeville, 1994—; cons. ARCH Rsch. Corp., Chgo., 1992—. Contbr. chpt. to book; contbr. articles to prof. jours. Mem. Am. Chem. Soc., Am. Scientific Glassblowers Soc., Am. Orchid Soc., Sigma Xi. Avocations: radio, gardening, cycling, sports, music. Office: Tenn Tech U P O Box 5055 Cookeville TN 38505

SWARTWOUT, JOSEPH RODOLPH, obstetrics and gynecology educator, administrator; b. Pascagoula, Miss., June 17, 1925; s. Thomas Roswell and Marshall (Coleman) S.; m. Brandon C. Leftwich, Jan. 23, 1989. Student, Miss. Coll., 1943-44; MD, Tulane U., 1951. Intern Touro Infirmary, New Orleans, 1951-52; asst. in obstetrics and medicine Tulane U., 1952-53, instr., 1955-60; Nat. Found. fellow Harvard U., 1953-55; asst. in medicine Peter Bent Brigham Hosp., Boston, 1953-55; assoc. in obstetric rsch. Boston Lying-In-Hosp., 1953-55; asst. prof. U. Pitts., 1960-61; assoc. prof. Emory U., Atlanta, 1961-66; assoc. prof. ob-gyn. U. Chgo., 1967-80; chief ob-gyn. at Prime Health, also clin. assoc. prof. U. Kans. Sch. Medicine, 1978-80; prof. dept. ob-gyn. Mercer U. Sch. Medicine, Macon, Ga., 1980-95, prof. emeritus, 1995; dist. health dir. Dist. 5-2, Macon, Ga., 1996—; dist. dir. Ga. Divsn. Pub. Health, Macon, 1996—. Fellow Am. Coll. Obstetricians and Gynecologists, Am. Heart Assn. (coun. clin. cardiology), Am. Acad. Reproductive Medicine; mem. AAAS, AMA, APHA, Population Assn. Am., Med. Assn. Ga., Bibb County Med. Soc. Home: 1622 Peach Pkwy Fort Valley GA 31030

SWARTZ, B(ENJAMIN) K(INSELL), JR., archaeologist, educator; b. L.A., June 23, 1931; s. Benjamin Kinsell and Maxine Marietta (Pearce) S.; m. Cyrilla Casillas, Oct. 23, 1966; children: Benjamin Kinsell III, Frank Casillas. AA summa cum laude, L.A. City Coll., 1952; BA, UCLA, 1954, MA, 1958; PhD, U. Ariz., 1964. Curator Klamath County Mus., Oreg., 1959-61, rsch. assoc., 1961-62; asst. prof. anthropology Ball State U., Muncie, Ind., 1964-68, assoc. prof., 1968-72, prof., 1972—; vis. sr. lectr. U. Ghana, 1970-71; exch. prof. U. Yaounde, Cameroon, 1984-85; field rschr. N.Am. and West Africa; mem. exec. bd., pres. Am. Com. to Advance the Study of Petroglyphs and Pictographs, Soc. for Am. Archaeology Rock Art Interest Group and rep. to Internat. Fedn. Rock Art Orgns.; bd. dirs., sec.-treas. Cou n. Conservation Ind. Archaeology; mem. adv. bd. Am. Com. for Preservation of Archaeol. Collections. Editor: Archaeological Reports; contbr. revs. and articles to profl. jours.; author books, monographs in field, including: West African Culture Dynamics, 1980, Indiana's Prehistoric Past, 1981, Rock Art and Posterity, 1991, Proceedings of Ist Internat. South African Rock Art Assn. Conf., 1991. Klamath County chmn. Oreg. Statehood Centennial, 1959. With USN, 1954-56. Fellow AAAS, Ind. Acad. Sci.; mem. Current Anthropology (assoc.), Soc. Am. Archaeology, Soc. African Archaeologists, Internat. Com. Rock Art, Ind. Fedn. Tchrs. (higher edn. trustee, exec. bd.), Sigma Xi, Lambda Alpha (nat. coun., exec. sec.). Home: 3600 W Brook Dr Muncie IN 47304-2923 Office: Ball State U Dept Anthropology Muncie IN 47306-0435

SWARTZ, CHRISTOPHER JOHN, musician, instrument designer/builder; b. El Paso, Tex., Dec. 25, 1951; s. Grant Leroy and Mildred Charlotte (Zass) S. AA, Trident Tech., 1980. Co-owner Perimeter Records, Atlanta, 1986-96, Outer Loop Prodns., Atlanta, 1996—; recorded numerous audio cassettes, 1983—; played numerous live concerts, 1970—; lectr. in field. Albums include ISO, 1986, Music for Home Built Instruments, 1987, 11 X 2, 1988; video cassettes include Solo/Live at Klang, 1991, The Music of Stockhausen, 1993; author: Percussion, String and Wind Instruments, 1990. Office: Outer Loop Prodns PO Box 451376 Atlanta GA 31145

SWARTZ, DONALD EVERETT, television executive; b. Mpls., Mar. 7, 1916; s. Albert L. and Sara (Shore) S.; m. Helen Gordon, Mar. 24, 1940; children: Stuart, Lawrence, Gary. Grad. high sch. Owner Ind. Film Distbrs., 1940-53, Tele-Film Assocs., 1953-57; pres., gen. mgr. KMSP-TV, Mpls., 1957-79; pres. United TV, Inc. (subs. 20th Century Fox Film Corp. until 1981); operating KMSP-TV, KTV4, Salt Lake City, KBHK-TV, San Francisco KMOL-TV, San Antonio; CEO United Television, Inc., Mpls., 1979-85; cons. KMOL-TV, 1985—; founder Tele-Video Assocs., 1985—, Tele-Video Entertainment, 1985—; owner/mgr. Donald Investment Co., 1989—. Vice pres. Twin City Broadcast Skills Bank (scholarship program), St. Paul Arts and Sci. Inst.; pres. U. Minn. Heart Hosp.; mem. Gov.'s Commn. Bicentennial; bd. dirs. Mpls. United Jewish Fund and Council; Mem. Mpls. Inst. Arts, Mpls., St. Paul chambers commerce, Minn. Orch. Assn., Citizens League, U. Minn. Alumni Assn. Elected Minn. Pioneer Broadcaster of Yr., 1992. Mem. Press Club (Mpls.), Advt. Standard Club (Mpls.), Hillcrest Country Club (St. Paul), Variety Club, Mission Hills Country Club (Rancho Mirage, Calif.), Oak Ridge Country Club (Mpls.), B'nai B'rith. Jewish (pres. temple). Home: 2221 Youngman Ave Saint Paul MN 55116-3055 Office: 15 S 5th St Minneapolis MN 55402

SWARTZ, DONALD PERCY, physician; b. Preston, Ont., Can., Sept. 12, 1921; s. Simon Wingham and Lydia (Ethell) S.; m. Norma Mae Woolner, June 24, 1944 (dec. May 1980); children: Ian Donald, Rhonda Swartz Peterson; m. Isabelle Liz Dales, Apr. 21, 1984. B.A., U. Western Ont., 1951, M.D. cum laude, 1951, M.S. cum laude, 1953. Intern Victoria Hosp., London, Ont., 1951-52; asst. resident Westminster Hosp., London, 1953-54; resident Johns Hopkins U., Balt., 1954-58; asst. prof. ob-gyn. U. Western Ont., London, 1958-62; prof. Columbia U., N.Y.C., 1962-72; dir. ob-gyn. Harlem Hosp.; prof. dept. ob-gyn. Albany (N.Y.) Med. Coll., 1972—, chmn., 1972-79, chief sect. gen. gynecology, 1982-88, head. div. gen. gynecology, 1988—, acting chmn., 1992; vis. prof. ob-Gyn. U. Rochester, N.Y., 1981. Assoc. editor: Advances in Planned Parenthood. Vice pres., pres. Assn. Planned Parenthood Physicians, 1972-74. Served with RCAF, 1942-45. NRC Can. fellow, 1952-53; Am. Cancer Soc. fellow, 1956-57; Markle scholar, 1958-63. Fellow Royal Coll. Surgeons Can., Am. Coll. Obstetricians and Gynecologists, Am. Gynecologic Soc., Am. Gyn-Ob Soc., Am. Fertility Soc., Royal Soc. Health, Soc. Gynecologic Surgeons. Home: 24 Devon Rd Delmar NY 12054-3534 Office: Albany Med Coll 47 New Scotland Ave Albany NY 12208-3412 *It has been a privilege and a challenge to participate in the forefront of the revolutionary changes in the health care of women during the past four decades. Acceptance, initiation and implementation of positive change have been guidelines for gratifying action.*

SWARTZ, JACK, chamber of commerce executive b. Dodge City, Kans., Nov. 24, 1932; s. John Ralph and Fern (Cave) S.; m. Nadine Ann Langlois, Aug. 4, 1956; children: Dana, Shawn, Tim, Jay. A.A., Dodge City Community Coll., 1953; student St. Mary of Plains Coll., 1953-55, 58; B.A. in Econs., Washburn U., 1974, B.B.A., 1973. Vice pres. D.C. Terminal Elevator Co., Dodge City, Kans., 1957-65; exec. v.p. Kans. Jaycees, Hutchinson, 1965-68, Kans. C. of C. and Industry, Topeka, 1968-82; pres. Nebr. C. of C. and Industry, Lincoln, 1982—. Past chmn., bd. regents U.S. C. of C. Inst. U. Colo. Served with U.S. Army, 1955-57. Named Outstanding Local Pres. in State, Kans. Jaycees, 1961, Outstanding Young Man of Yr., Dodge City Jaycees, 1961; Outstanding State Vice Pres., U.S. Jaycees, 1962, Outstanding Nat. Dir., 1963. Mem. Am. Soc. Assn. Execs. (cert.), Am. Chamber Commerce Execs. (bd. dirs., cert.), Nebr. Chamber Commerce Execs. (sec.-treas.), Nebr. Soc. Assn. Execs. (past pres.), Nebr. Fedn. Bus. Assns. (pres. 1986-88), Washburn U. Alum. (bd. dirs.). Republican. Roman Catholic. Lodge: Rotary. Home: 2744 Laurel St Lincoln NE 68502-5142 Office: Nebr C of C and Industry 1320 Lincoln Mall PO Box 95128 Lincoln NE 68509

SWARTZ, JAMES EUGENE, international business educator, army officer; b. Chgo., Aug. 16, 1946; s. James Arthur and Margaret Jean (Conroy) S.; m. Zaijun Liang, June 29, 1996. BJ, U. Mo., 1969, MA, 1971; M in Mil. Art and Sci., U.S. Army Command & Gen. Staff, Ft. Leavenworth, Kans., 1980; PhD, U. Iowa, 1985. Reporter Washington Star, 1971-72; mng. editor Sports Digest Mag., Miami, Fla., 1973-74; Eisenhower fellow Smithsonian Instn., Washington, 1978-79; chair advt. So. Meth. U., Dallas, 1981-86; commd. capt. U.S. Army, 1978, advanced through grades to col., 1993; comdr. 1st Bn, 185th Armor U.S. Army, San Bernardino, Calif., 1988-89; comdr. 2d brigade, 91st divsn. U.S. Army, Norco, Calif., 1995-96; historian Office of Chmn. Joint Chiefs of Staff, Washington, 1996-97; prof. internat. bus. Calif. State Poly. U., Pomona, 1987—; sr. svc. coll. fellow Inst. Advanced Tech., U. Tex., Austin, 1996-97; strategist Office of Joint Chiefs of Staff, Washington, 1997—. Contbr. articles to profl. jours. Project dir. Boys Republic, Chino, Calif., 1996. Decorated Army Achievement medals (2), Army Commendation medal, Meritorious Svc. medals (2); named Outstanding Young Man of Am., 1983. Mem. Internat. Bus. Assn., Am. Acad. Advt., Sr. Army Res. Comdrs. Assn., Assn. of U.S. Army, Res. Officers Assn., Nat. Guard Assn. U.S. Avocations: swimming, reading. Home: 3801 W Temple Ave Pomona CA 91768

SWARTZ, JON DAVID, psychologist, educator; b. Houston, Dec. 28, 1934; s. Orville Elmo and Nina June (Baker) S.; m. Carol Joseph Hampton, Oct. 20, 1966; children: Eric Jason McFarland, Sally Katherine Baker, Edward Joseph Bryson. BA, U. Tex., Austin, 1956, MA, 1961, PhD, 1969, postgrad. (fellow), 1973-74. Research and teaching asst. dept. psychology U. Tex., 1956-62, asst. prof. dept. ednl. psychology, 1969-72; assoc. prof. psychology, chmn. U. Tex.-Permian Basin, 1974-78, chmn. anthropology and sociology, 1975-78, field dir., 1962-65; asst. dir. Austin Longitudinal Research project, 1965-69, co-dir., 1969-74; research scientist Hogg Found. for Mental Health, 1972-74; prof. edn. and psychology Southwestern U., Georgetown, Tex., 1978-90, vis. prof. psychology, 1991; dir. testing and guidance Southwestern U., 1978-81, holder Brown vis. chair, 1978-82, assoc. dean for libraries and learning resources, 1981-90; coord., adminstrv. head Killeen office Cen. Counties Ctr. for MHMR Svcs., Temple, Tex., 1990-91; chief psychol. svcs. Temple, Tex., 1991—; lectr. Nat. U., Mexico, 1962. Author: (with W.H. Holtzman) Inkblot Perception and Personality, 1961, (with C.C. Cleland) Mental Retardation: Approaches to Institutional Change, 1969, Administrative Issues in Institutions for the Mentally Retarded, 1972, Exceptionalities Through the Lifespan: An Introduction, 1982, Multihandicapped Mentally Retarded, 1973, (with W.H. Holtzman, R. Diaz-Guerrero) Personality Development in Two Cultures, 1975; editor: (with C.C. Cleland, L.W. Talkington) Profoundly Mentally Retarded, 1976, (with R.K. Eyman, C.C. Cleland) Research with the Profoundly Retarded, 1978, Holtzman Inkblot Technique: An Annotated Bibliography (supplement), 1988, (with R.C. Reinehr, W.H. Holtzman) Holtzman Inkblot Technique: An Annotated Bibliography 1956-1982, 1983, SW U. Bibliographic Series, 1986-90, (with R.C. Reinehr) Handbook of Old-Time Radio, 1993; contbr.: Handbook of Texas, 1996; editorial assoc.: Current Anthropology, 1971-77; assoc. editor: Am. Corrective Therapy Jour, 1971-81, Exceptional Children, 1982-84; mem. editorial bd.: Texas Psychologist, 1979-83 , Phi Kappa Phi Jour./Nat. Forum, 1976-80; editorial cons.: Mental Retardation, 1972-77; book rev. editor: Jour. Biol. Psychology, 1972-80; book rev. editor for English lang. publs.: Revista Interamericana de Psicologia, 1983-89; cons. editor Jour. Personality Assessment, 1981-90; contbr. over 400 articles to profl. jours. Mem. Mayor's Drug Abuse Panel, Odessa, Tex., 1975-78; chmn. adv. bd. Human Potentials Center, Permian Basin Community Centers for Mental Health and Mental Retardation, Odessa and Midland, Tex., 1975-78; bd. govs. Mood-Heritage Mus., 1984-90. U.S. Office Edn. fellow, 1964-66; recipient Franklin Gilliam prize Humanities Research Center U. Tex., 1965; Spencer Research award Nat. Acad. Edn., 1972; Faculty Fellowship award Southwestern U., 1981. Fellow AAAS, Am. Psychol. Soc., Soc. Personality Assessment; mem. Western Rsch. Conf. on Mental Retardation, Am. Acad. Mental Retardation, Southwestern Psychol. Assn., Bell County Psychol. Assn., Sigma Xi, Psi Chi, Mu Alpha Nu, Delta Tau Kappa, Phi Kappa Phi, Phi Delta Kappa. Office: Cen Counties Ctr for MHMR Svcs 304 S 22nd St Temple TX 76501-4726 *All my life I have had teachers, in school and out, who challenged me to do more than I thought I was capable of doing. Any success I have achieved, I owe to them and their efforts in my behalf.*

SWARTZ, MORTON NORMAN, medical educator; b. Boston, Nov. 11, 1923; s. Jacob H. and Janet (Heller) W.; m. Cesia Rosenberg, Sept. 18, 1956; children: Mark David, Caroline Joan. BA, Harvard Coll., 1945; MD, Harvard U., 1947; MD (hon.), U. Geneva, Switzerland, 1988. Diplomate Am. Bd. Internal Medicine (subsplty. exam. com. 1971-76, bd. govs. 1979-85). Med. intern and resident Mass. Gen. Hosp., Boston, 1947-50, chief resident in medicine, 1953-54; USPHS postdoctoral rsch. fellow Johns Hopkins U., McCollum-Pratt Inst. Enzymology, Balt., 1954-56; chief infectious disease unit Mass. Gen. Hosp., Boston, 1956-90, chief James Jackson Firm, med. svcs., 1990—; assoc. prof. medicine Harvard Med. Sch., Boston, 1967-73, prof., 1973—; vis. assoc. prof. biochemistry, Stanford Med. Sch., Palo Alto, Calif., 1969-70. Author: (with others) Osteomyelitis, 1971; editor: Current Clinical Topics in Infectious Diseases, 1980—; assoc. editor New Eng. Jour. Medicine, 1981—; contbr. articles to profl. jours. 1st lt. U.S. Army, 1950-52. Sir MacFarlane Burnett lectr. Australasian Soc. Infectious Disease, 1981. Fellow ACP (master 1988, Disting. Tchr. award 1989); mem. Am. Soc. Biochemistry and Molecular Biology, Am. Soc. for Clin. Investigation, Assn. Am. Physicians, Infectious Diseases Soc. Am. (Bristol award 1984, Feldman award 1989), Inst. Medicine, Nat. Inst. Child Health and Devel. (bd. sci. counselors 1992—, chmn. 1995—). Jewish. Avocations: biology, bird watching. Home: 54 Shaw Rd Chestnut Hill MA 02167-3122 Office: Mass Gen Hosp Dept Medicine Gray Bigelow Bldg #840 Boston MA 02114-2620*

SWARTZ, ROSLYN HOLT, real estate investment executive; b. Los Angeles, Dec. 9, 1940; d. Abe Jack and Helen (Canter) Holt; m. Allan Joel Swartz, June 2, 1963. AA, Santa Monica (Calif.) Coll., 1970; BA summa cum laude, UCLA, 1975; MA, Pepperdine U., 1976. Cert. community coll. instr., student-personnel worker, Calif. Mgr. pub. relations Leader Holdings, Inc., L.A., 1968-75, pres., 1991—; sec., treas. Leader Holdings, Inc., North Hollywood, Calif., 1975-81, pres., 1981-91; chief exec. officer Beverly Stanley Investments, L.A., 1979—; pres. Leader Properties, Inc., The Leader Fairfax, Inc., Leader 358, Inc., Leader 359, Inc., Leader Ventura, Inc., 1996—. Condr. An Oral History of the Elderly Jewish Community of Venice, Calif. at Los Angeles County Planning Dept. Library, 1974. Founder L.A. County Mus. Art, Music Ctr. L.A. County, West Alumni Ctr., UCLA; mem. Hadassah (life), Friends of the Hollywood Bowl; bd. dirs. Am. Friends of Haifa Med. Ctr. L.A., West L.A. Symphony; capital patron Simon Wiesenthal Ctr. Fellow Phi Beta Kappa (bicentennial); mem. NAFE, AAUW, Am. Soc. Profl. and Exec. Women, Nat. Women's Hall of Fame, Am. Pub. Health Assn., Am. Pharm. Assn., Comml. Real Estate Women, L.A. World Affairs Coun., Town Hall (life), Century City C. of C., UCLA Alumni Assn. (life), UCLA Founders Circle, Women's Coun. Women's Guild Cedars-Sinai Med. Ctr., UCLA Prytanean Alumnae Assn., Santa Monica Coll. Alumni Assn. (life), Phrateres Internat., Order of Eastern Star, Phi Alpha Theta. Alpha Gamma Sigma, Alpha Kappa Delta, Phi Delta Kappa, Pi Gamma Mu. Avocation: horticulture. Office: PO Box 241784 Los Angeles CA 90024-9584

SWARTZ, STEPHEN ARTHUR, banker, lawyer; b. Boston, Oct. 7, 1941; s. Norman and Frances S.; m. Karen M. McLoughlin, Aug. 18, 1992; children: Marti Anne, Nanci Beth, Lori Ellen, Stephen Arthur, Jr., Kerry Anne. BA in Polit. Sci., U. Mass., 1963; LLB, Boston U., 1966; postgrad. in fin. and mgmt, Boston Coll., 1968-70. Bar: Mass. 1967, N.Y. 1971. Asst. counsel Fed. Res. Bank Boston., 1968-70, Irving Trust Co., N.Y.C., 1970-74; counsel, asst. sec. Charter N.Y. Corp., N.Y.C., 1974-77; v.p., asst. dir. investor communications Charter N.Y. Corp., 1977-79; v.p., dir. investor communications Irving Bank Corp., N.Y.C., 1979-86; v.p. investor relations Seamen's Corp., N.Y.C., 1986-88, sr. v.p., corp. sec., 1990; sr. v.p. investor rels. H.F. Ahmanson & Co., L.A., 1990—. Served to capt. AUS, 1966-68, Vietnam. Decorated Bronze Star (2), Army Commendation medal (2), Air medal (2); Vietnamese Honor medal 1st class. Mem. ABA, Mass. Bar Assn., N.Y. State Bar Assn., Nat. Investor Rels. Inst. (former bd. dirs., treas. L.A. chpt.), Bank Investor Rels. Assn. (founder, former pres., bd. dirs., dir.), Bedford Riding Lns. Assn. Home: 2084 Liliano Dr Sierra Madre CA 91024-1557 Office: HF Ahmanson & Co 4900 Rivergrade Rd Baldwin Park CA 91706-1404

SWARTZ, THOMAS R., economist, educator; b. Phila., Aug. 31, 1937; s. Henry Jr. and Elizabeth (Thomas) S.; m. Jeanne Marie Jourdan, Aug. 12, 1961; children: Mary Butler, Karen Miller, Jennifer, Anne, Rebecca. BA, LaSalle U., 1960; MA, Ohio U., 1962; PhD, Ind. U., 1965. Asst. prof. U. Notre Dame, Ind., 1965-70, assoc. dept. chair, 1968-70, assoc. prof., 1970-78, acting dir. grad. studies, 1977-78, prof. econs., 1978—, dir. program econ. policy, 1982-85; resident dir. U. Notre Dame London Program, 1990-91, U. Notre Dame Austrualia Program, Fremantle, 1996; vis. prof. U. Notre Dame London Program 1982, 85; fiscal cons. Ind. Commn. State Tax, Indpls., 1965-68, also spl. tax cons., 1971-81, City of South Bend, Ind., 1972-75. Co-editor: The Supply Side, 1983, Changing Face of Fiscal Federalism, 1990, Urban Finance Under Siege, 1993, Taking Sides, 7th edit., 1995, America's Working Poor, 1995; contbr. articles to profl. jours. Bd. dirs. Forever Learning Inst., South Bend, Ind., 1988-93; mem. steering com. Mayor's Housing Forum, South Bend, 1989—; chair Com. Svcs. Block Grant, South Bend, 1985-90, Econ. Devel. Task Force, South Bend, 1985. Rsch. fellow Nat. Ctr. Urban Ethnic Affairs, 1979-85; recipient Danforth Assoc. award Danforth Found., 1972-86, Tchg. award Kanzajian Found., 1974. Democrat. Roman Catholic. Avocation: racquetball. Home: 402 Marquette Ave South Bend IN 46617-1157 Office: U Notre Dame Dept Econs 414 Decio Hall Notre Dame IN 46556-5644

SWARTZ, WILLIAM JOHN, transportation resources company executive/retired; b. Hutchinson, Kans., Nov. 6, 1934; s. George Glen and Helen Mae (Prather) S.; m. Dorothy Jean Parshall, June 5, 1956; children: John Christopher, Jeffrey Michael. BSME, Duke U., 1956; JD, George Washington U., 1961; MS in Mgmt. (Alfred P. Sloan fellow), MIT, 1967. With AT & SF Ry., 1961-78, 79—, asst. v.p. exec. dept., 1973-77, v.p. adminstrn., 1977-78, exec. v.p., 1979-83; exec. v.p. Santa Fe Industries, Chgo., 1978-79, pres., 1983-90; vice chmn. Santa Fe So. Pacific, 1983-90; pres. AT & SF Ry., 1986-89. Past bd. dirs. Chgo. Mus. Sci. and Industry; mem. Dean's Coun. Duke U. Sch. Engring; mem. regent's cir. Mus. N.Mex., 1996—. With USMC, 1956-59. Mem. Assn. Am. R.R. (past bd. dirs.). Republican. Methodist. Home: 1201 Ojo Verde Santa Fe NM 87501

SWARTZ, WILLIAM JOHN, managed care company executive; b. Detroit, Nov. 11, 1939; s. Harry August Swartz and Genevieve Ilene (O'Donnell) Ammon; m. Mary Katherine Ragan, May 20, 1962 (div. May 1983); children: Laura M., William R., John T.; m. Susan Theresa Cook, Nov. 18, 1983; children: David Elliott, Philip Andrew. BA in Math. and Philosophy, U. Detroit, 1964; postgrad., Purdue U., 1969-70, U. Chgo., 1970-71. Lic. life-health agt., Mich. Dir., mgr. provider rels. Blue Cross Blue Shield Mich., Detroit, 1966-84; dir. mktg. and health svcs. Preferred Health Plan, subs. Henry Ford Health Sys., Detroit, 1984-86; dir. western region Sr. Mercy Health Plans, Farmington Hills, Mich., 1986-87; dir. network mgmt. Aetna Health Plans, Southfield, Mich., 1987-96; sr. mgr. network mgmt. Aetna U.S. Healthcare, Southfield, Mich., 1996—. Vol. PTO, Howell Pub. Schs.; past sec. Highland Twp. Rd. Commn.; past treas. Highland Twp. Bldg. Authority. Mem. Am. Acad. Med. Adminstrs., Mich. Health and Hosp. Assn. (legis. panel), Greater Detroit Area Health Coun. (data mgmt. forum), Nat. Health Lawyers Assn. Office: Aetna Health Plans 26957 Northwestern Hwy Ste 140 Southfield MI 48034-8456

SWARTZ, WILLIAM RICK, school psychologist; b. Buffalo, Dec. 27, 1951; s. William Wallace and Ruth Mae (Williams) S.; m. Saundra Kay Hess, June 21, 1980. BS in Edn., Bucknell U., Lewisburg, Pa., 1974; MS in Edn., Bucknell U., 1976; MEd, Shippensburg (Pa.) State U., 1982. Sch. psychologist Waynesboro (Pa.) Area Sch. Dist., 1976—; ednl. cons. Mont Alto Campus, Pa. State U., 1990-93. Mem. Assn. of Sch. Psychologists of Pa., Coun. for Exceptional Children. Avocations: theater, music, art. Office: Waynesboro Area Sch Dist 210 Clayton Ave # 72 Waynesboro PA 17268-2014

SWARTZBAUGH, MARC L., lawyer; b. Urbana, Ohio, Jan. 3, 1937; s. Merrill L. and Lillian K. (Hill) S.; m. Marjory Anne Emhardt, Aug. 16, 1958; children: Marc Charles, Kathleen Marie, Laura Kay. BA magna cum laude, Wittenberg Coll., 1958; LLB magna cum laude, U. Pa., 1961. Bar: Ohio 1961, U.S. Dist. Ct. (no. dist.) Ohio 1962, U.S. Claims Ct. 1991, U.S. Ct. Appeals (6th cir.) 1970, U.S. Ct. Appeals (3d cir.) 1985, U.S. Ct. Appeals (Fed. cir.) 1995, U.S. Supreme Ct. 1973. Law clk. to judge U.S. Ct. Appeals (3d cir.), Phila., 1961-62; assoc. Jones, Day, Reavis & Pogue, Cleve., 1962-69, ptnr., 1970—. Note editor U. Pa. Law Rev., 1960-61. Co-chmn. Suburban Citizens for Open Housing, Shaker Heights, Ohio, 1966; v.p. Lomond Assn., Shaker Heights, 1965-68; trustee The Dance Ctr., Cleve., 1980-83; amb. People to People Internat., 1986; chmn. legal divsn. Cleve. campaign United Negro Coll. Fund, 1989-96. Mem. ABA (litigation sect.), Fed. Bar Assn., Ohio Bar Assn., Cleve. Bar Assn., Order of Coif, Beta Theta Pi. Democrat. Club: 13th St Racquet (Cleve.). Avocations: poetry, painting, music, skiing, squash, photography. Office: Jones Day Reavis & Pogue N Point 901 Lakeside Ave E Cleveland OH 44114-1116

SWARTZENDRUBER, DALE, soil physicist, educator; b. Parnell, Iowa, July 6, 1925; s. Urie and Norma (Kinsinger) S.; m. Kathleen Jeanette Yoder, June 26, 1949; children: Karl Grant, Myra Mae, John Keith, David Mark. BS, Iowa State U., 1950, MS, 1952, PhD, 1954. Instr. sci. Goshen (Ind.) Coll., 1953-54; asst. soil scientist U. Calif., Los Angeles, 1955-56; assoc. prof. soil physics Purdue U., West Lafayette, Ind., 1956-63; prof. Purdue U., 1963-77; prof. soil physics U. Nebr., Lincoln, 1977—; vis. prof. Iowa State U., 1959, Ga. Inst. Tech., 1968, Hebrew U. Jerusalem at Rehovot, 1971, Griffith U., Brisbane, Australia, 1989-90, Centre for Environ. Mechanics, CSIRO, Canberra, Australia, 1990; vis. scholar Cambridge (Eng.) U., 1971. Contbr. articles on soil physics to profl. jours.; assoc. editor: Soil Sci. Soc. Am. Proc., 1965-70; mem. editorial bd. Geoderma (Amsterdam), 1975-93; editor: Soil Sci., 1976—. Fellow Soil Sci. Soc. Am. (Soil Sci. award 1975, Editors' citation for excellence in manuscript rev. 1993), Am. Soc. Agronomy; mem. AAAS, Am. Geophys. Union, Internat. Soc. Soil Sci., Am. Sci. Affiliation, Sigma Xi. Mennonite. Achievements include research in water infiltration into soil, validity of Darcy's equation for water flow in soils, measurement of water and solid content in soils, mathematical solutions to problems of water flow in saturated and unsaturated soils. Home: 1400 N 37th St Lincoln NE 68503-2016 Office: U Nebr E Campus Dept Agronomy 133 Keim Hall Lincoln NE 68583 *Along with complete dedication and honesty in spirit and action, bring to each task a new thought, or ask the implications, should the customary or conventional wisdom not hold.*

SWARTZLANDER, EARL EUGENE, JR., engineering educator, former electronics company executive; b. San Antonio, Feb. 1, 1945; s. Earl Eugene and Jane (Nicholas) S.; m. Joan Vickery, June 9, 1968. BSEE, Purdue U., 1967; MSEE, U. Colo., 1969; PhD, U. So. Calif., 1972. Registered profl. engr., Ala., Calif., Colo., Tex. Devel. engr. Ball Bros. Rsch. Corp., Boulder, Colo., 1967-69; Hughes fellow, mem. tech. staff Hughes Aircraft Co., Culver City, Calif., 1969-73; mem. rsch. staff Tech. Svc. Co., Santa Monica, Calif., 1973-74; chief engr. Geophys. Systems Corp., Pasadena, Calif., 1974-75, staff engr. to sr. staff engr., 1975-79, project mgr., 1979-84, lab. mgr., 1985-87; dir. ind. R&D TRW Inc., Redondo Beach, Calif., 1987-90; Schlumberger Centennial prof. engring. dept. elec. and computer engring. U. Tex., Austin, 1990—; gen. chmn. Internat. Conf. Wafer Scale Integration, 1989, 11th Internat. Symposium on Computer Arithmetic, 1992, 31st Ann. Asilomar Conf. on Signals, Sys., and Computers, 1997, others; gen. chmn. Internat. Conf. Application Specific Array Processors, 1990, co-gen. chmn., 1994; chmn. 3d Internat. Conf. Parallel and Distributed Sys., Taiwan, 1993. Author: VLSI Signal Processing Systems, 1986; editor: Computer Design Development, 1976, Systolic Signal Processing Systems, 1987, Wafer Scale Integration, 1989, Computer Arithmetic Vol. 1 and 2, 1990, Application Specific Processors, 1996; editor-in-chief Jour. of VLSI Signal Processing, 1989-95, IEEE Transactions on Computers, 1991-94, IEEE Transactions on Signal Processing, 1995; editor: IEEE Transactions on Computers, 1982-86, IEEE Transactions on Parallel and Distributed Systems, 1989-90; hardware area editor ACM Computing Revs., 1985—; assoc. editor: IEEE Jour. Solid-State Circuits, 1984-88; contbr. more than 150 articles to profl. jours. and tech. conf. procs. Bd. dirs. Casiano Estates Homeowners Assn., Bel Air, Calif., 1976-78, pres., 1978-80; bd. dirs. Benedict Hills Estates Homeowners Assn., Beverly Hills, Calif., 1984—, pres., 1990-95. Recipient Disting. Engring. Alumnus award Purdue U., 1989, U. Colo., 1997, Outstanding Elec. Engr. award Purdue U., 1992, knight Imperial Russian Order St. John of Jerusalem (Knights of Malta), 1993. Fellow IEEE; mem. IEEE Computer Soc. (bd. govs. 1987-91, Golden Core mem. 1996), IEEE Signal Proc. Soc. (bd. govs. 1992-94), IEEE Solid-State Cirs. Coun. (sec. 1992-93, treas. 1994—), Eta Kappa Nu, Sigma Tau, Omicron Delta Kappa. Office: U Tex Austin Dept Elec Computer Engring Austin TX 78712

SWARZ, JEFFREY ROBERT, securities analyst, neuroscientist; b. Newark, Nov. 9, 1949; s. Irvin Brad and Blanche S. (Marcus) S.; m. Kathy Helen Kafer, June 20, 1976. B.S. with honors, U. Calif.-Irvine, 1971; Ph.D. (NIMH trainee 1971-74, NIH fellow 1975-76), U. Rochester, 1976. Postdoctoral fellow in neurovirology Johns Hopkins U. Sch. Medicine, 1976-79; staff fellow Infectious Disease br. NIH, Bethesda, Md., 1979-80; dir. biotech. group Teknekron Research Inc., McLean, Va., 1980-81; pres. AgroBiotics, Inc., Balt., 1981-82, Urbana, Ill., 1981-82; sr. scientist Pall Corp., Glen Cove, N.Y., 1982-83, sr. mktg. mgr. biotech., 1983-85; dir. mktg. and sales, 1985-86; biotech./health care analyst Goldman Sachs & Co., 1986-92; dir. CS First Boston, N.Y.C., 1992—; cons. U.S. Senate Subcom. on Sci., Tech. and Space, 1979-80. Author: (with others) Genetic Engineering: Issues and Trends, 1982; contbr. numerous articles to profl. jours. Recipient Undergrad. Research award Bank of Am., 1970-71, Nat. Research Service award, 1976-79. Mem. Univ. Club, N.Y. Athletic Club, Neptune Boat Club. Democrat. Jewish. Office: CS First Boston 11 Madison Ave New York NY 10010-3629

SWARZ, SAHL, sculptor; b. N.Y.C., May 4, 1912; s. Samuel and Ida (Fass) S.; m. Naoco Kumasaka, May 1978. Student, Clay Club, N.Y.C., 1928-34, Art Students League, N.Y.C., 1930-31. Asso. Dir. Clay Club (and successor, Sculpture Center), 1938-54; creative sculpture in Italy, 1951-63; residence Am. Acad. in, Rome, 1955-57; lectr. sculpture Columbia U., N.Y.C., 1966-68, asst. prof., 1969-78; instr. Pratt Inst., Bklyn., 1964; instr. New Sch. for Social Rsch., 1965, 66; vis. lectr. art U. Wis., 1966; trustee Mus. Contemporary Sculpture, Tokyo; lectr. art dept. Nippon U., Tokyo, 1997. Author, illustrator: Blueprint for the Future of American Sculpture, 1943, also monograph.; one man exhbns. Sculpture Ctr., 1954, 57, 60, 62, 66, 71, 74, 78, Art Alliance, Phila., 1958, Fairweather-Hardin Gallery, Chgo., 1963, Brandeis U., Waltham, Mass., 1964, (retrospective exhbn.) Fair Lawn (N.J.) Pub. Library, 1977, Saikaya Gallery, Fujisawa, Japan, 1983, Mus. Contemporary Sculpture, Tokyo, 1985, Shonan Gallery, Fujisawa, Japan, 1985, 90, 93, (retrospective exhbn.) Toni de Rossi Gallery, Verona, Italy, 1983, 87, 91, Takashimaya Gallery, Yokohama, Japan, 1984, Atagoyama Gallery, Tokyo, 1988, 91, 94, 1st exhibition of painting Toni de Rossi Gallery, Verona, Italy, 1992, 96, Move Gallery Chigasaki, Japan, 1993; group shows include Fairmount Park Internat., Phila., 1948, Whitney Mus. Am. Art, 1948, 58, 60, 62, 64, Pa. Acad., 1948, 52, 54, 57, 60, 62, 66, Bklyn Mus., 1935, Detroit Inst. Fine Arts, 1957, San Francisco Mus., 1955, U. Ill., 1960, 62, others; represented in permanent collections Norfolk (Va.) Mus., Whitney Mus. Am. Art, Ball State Tchrs. Coll., Williams Coll. Mus., Ford Found., Mpls. Inst. Fine Arts, Va. Mus. Fine Arts, Richmond, Newark Mus., N.J. State Mus. at Trenton, Vatican Mus. Collection Modern Religious Art, Rose Art Mus., Brandeis U., Stamford (Conn.) Mus., Columbia U., others; bronze group The Guardian at Brookgreen (S.C.), Gardens Mus.; terra cotta wall sculpture, Linden, (N.J.), Post Office, sculptural designs, Fed. Courthouse, Statesville, N.C.; equestrian monument Gen. Bidwell, Buffalo; fountain commn., Spruce Run State Park, N.J.; mall sculpture, Pittsfield, Mass.; monument to Demeter in stainless steel, Fujisawa, Japan; subject of biography: Fifty Years of Sculpture by Sahl Swarz. Chmn. sculpture panel N.J. Coun. on Arts. With AUS, 1941-45. Grantee Am. Acad. Arts and Letters, 1955; Guggenheim fellow, 1955, 58. Address: Kumasaka-Swarz, 11-9 2 Chome Ishigami, Kugenuma, Fujisawa, Kanagawa 251, Japan *The essence of creativity is in the searching after the form. Search leads to revelation, understanding, knowledge. Realization of one's ignorance is the first step to the attainment of wisdom. A wise man makes a work of art out of life itself.*

SWATEK, FRANK EDWARD, microbiology educator; b. Oklahoma City, June 4, 1929; s. Clarence Michael and Bessie (Doubek) S.; m. Mary Frances Over, Jan. 28, 1951; children: Frank Edward, Lorraine Beth Butcher, Martha Lynn Bradshaw, Susan Ann Denny, Cheryl Lee. B.S. in Zoology, San Diego State Coll., 1951; M.A. in Microbiology, UCLA, 1955, Ph.D., 1956. Mem. faculty Calif. State U. at Long Beach, 1956-92, prof. microbiology, 1962-82, chmn. dept., 1960-82; cons. to industry, 1953—; cons. dept. dermatology Long Beach VA Hosp., 1956—; lectr. postgrad. medicine U. So. Calif., 1958—; adj. prof. clin. med. U. Calif., Irvine, 1980—; mem. fuel sect. Coordinating Research Council, 1961—. Author: Textbook of Microbiology, 1967, Laboratory Manual and Workbook for General Microbiology, 1969; also articles. Fellow Royal Soc. Health, Am. Acad. Microbiology; mem. Am. Soc. Microbiology (chmn. bd. edn. and tng. 1980-85, Carski Found. Disting. Teaching award 1974), Internat. Platform Assn., Sigma Xi, Lambda Xi Alpha, Phi Kappa Phi. Club: Long Beach Aquatic (pres. 1963-65). Research on med. mycology. Home: 812 Stevely Ave Long Beach CA 90815-5022

SWATSKY, BEN, church administrator. Exec. dir. Evangelical Free Church Mission, Minneapolis, Minn. Office: The Evang Free Ch Am 901 E 78th St Minneapolis MN 55420-1334

SWATT, STEPHEN BENTON, communications executive, consultant; b. L.A., June 26, 1944; s. Maurice I. and Lucille E. (Sternberger) S.; m. Susan Ruth Edelstein, Sept. 7, 1968; 1 child, Jeffrey Michael. BSBA, U. Calif., 1966, M in Journalism, 1967. Writer San Francisco Examiner, 1967; reporter United Press Internat., L.A., 1968-69; producer news Sta. KCRA-TV, Sacramento, Calif., 1969-70, reporter news, 1970-79, chief polit. and capitol corres., 1979-92; exec. v.p. Nelson-Lucas Communications, Sacramento, 1992—; guest lectr. Calif. State U., Sacramento. Contbr. articles to profl. jours. With USCG, 1966. Recipient No. Calif. Emmy NATAS, 1976-77, Pub. Svc. award Calif. State Bar, 1977, Exceptional Achievement Coun. advancement and Support of Edn., 1976, Nat. Health Journalism award Am. Chiropractic Assn., 1978. Mem. Soc. Profl. Journalists (8 awards), Capitol Corres. Assn., U. Calif. Alumni Assn., Sacramento Press Club. Avocations: hiking, jogging, fishing. Office: Nelson Comms Group 1029 J St Ste 400 Sacramento CA 95814-2825

SWAYNE, DAVID EUGENE, avian pathologist, researcher; b. Yellville, Ark., Sept. 22, 1958; s. Dallas Eugene and Mary Sue (Shipman) S.; m. Anita Jane Walker, July 4, 1981; children: Rachel Miranda, Tyler Dallas, Kyle David. BSA, U. Ark., 1980; DVM, MSc in Vet. Pathology, U. Mo., 1984; PhD in Vet. Pathology, U. Ga., 1987. Diplomate Am. Coll. Vet. Pathologists, Am. Coll. Poultry Veterinarians. Asst. prof., assoc. prof. Ohio State U., Columbus, 1987-94; supervisory vet. med. officer, lab. dir. S.E. Poultry Rsch. Lab., USDA Agr. Rsch. Svc., Athens, Ga., 1994—; adj. assoc. prof. U. Ga., Athens, 1994—. Mem. editl. bd. Avian Diseases; contbr. articles to Avian Diseases, Vet. Pathology, Infection and Immunity, Avian Pathology. Grantee USDA, 1991. Mem. AVMA, Am. Assn. Avian Pathologists (New Investigator award 1992), World Vet. Poultry Assn., Poultry Sci. Assn. Mem. Ch. of Christ. Achievements include research in avian influenza and intestinal spirochetosis. Office: USDA/ARS/SEPRL 934 College Station Rd Athens GA 30605-2720

SWAZEY, JUDITH POUND, institute president, sociomedical science educator; b. Bronxville, N.Y., Apr. 21, 1939; d. Robert Earl and Louise Titus (Hanson) Pound; m. Peter Woodman Swazey, Nov. 28, 1964; children: Elizabeth, Peter. AB, Wellesley Coll., 1961; PhD, Harvard U., 1966. Rsch. assoc. Harvard U., 1966-71, lectr., 1969-71, rsch. fellow, 1971-72; cons. com. brain scis. NRC, 1971-73; staff scientist neuroscis. rsch. program MIT, Cambridge, 1973-74; assoc. prof. dept. socio-med. scis. and community medicine Boston U., 1974-77, prof., 1977-80, adj. prof. Schs. Medicine and Pub. Health, 1980—; exec. dir. Medicine in the Pub. Interest, Inc., Boston and Washington, 1979-82, 89-93; pres. Coll. of the Atlantic, Bar Harbor, Maine, 1982-84, Acadia Inst., Bar Harbor, 1984—; mem. Army Sci. Bd., 1987-92. Author: Reflexes and Motor Integration, the Development of Sherrington's Integrative Action Concept, 1969, (with others) Human Aspects of Biomedical Innovation, 1971, (with R. C. Fox) The Courage to Fail, a Social View of Organ Transplants and Hemodialysis, 1975, rev. edit., 1978 (hon. mention Am. Med. Writers Assn., C. Wright Mills award Am. Sociol. Assn.), Chlorpromazine in Psychiatry, a Study of Therapeutic Innovation, 1974, (with K. Reeds) Today's Medicine, Tomorrow's Science, Essays on Paths of Discovery in the Biomedical Sciences, 1978; editor: (with C. Wong) Dilemmas of Dying, Policies and Procedures for Decisions Not to Treat, 1981, (with F. Worden and G. Adelman) The Neurosciences: Paths of Discovery, 1975, (with R. C. Fox) Spare Parts, Organ Replacement in American Society, 1992; assoc. editor IRB: A Jour. of Human Subjects Rsch., 1979—; mem. editl. bd. Sci. and Engring. Ethics, 1994—; contbr. articles to profl. jours. Mem. Maine Dept. Human Svcs. Bioethics Adv. Com. (chair 1991-94); mem. Commn. on Rsch. Integrity, 1994-95; bd. dirs. Maine Bioethics Network, 1994—. Wellesley Coll. scholar, 1961; Wellesley Coll. Alumnae fellow Harvard U., 1966, NIH predoctoral fellow, 1966, Radcliffe Coll. Coll. grad. fellow, 1966. Mem. AAAS (sci. freedom and responsibility com. 1986-89), Inst. Medicine NAS (mem. health scis. policy bd. 1986-89), Grad. Record Exam. (bd. dirs. 1987-91), Sherrington Soc., Phi Beta Kappa, Sigma Xi. Office: Acadia Inst PO Box 43 Bar Harbor ME 04609

SWEARER, DONALD KEENEY, Asian religions educator, writer; b. Wichita, Kans., Aug. 2, 1934; s. Edward Mays and Eloise Catherine (Keeney) S.; m. Nancy Chester; children: Susan Marie, Stephen Edward. AB cum laude, Princeton U., 1956, MA, 1965, PhD, 1967; BD, Yale U., 1962, STM, 1963. Instr. English dept. Bangkok Christian Coll., 1957-60; adminstrv. asst. Edward W. Hazen Found., New Haven, 1961-63; instr., then asst. prof. Oberlin (Ohio) Coll., 1965-70; assoc. prof. Swarthmore (Pa.) Coll., 1970-75, prof. Asian religions, 1975—, Eugene M. Lang Rsch. prof., 1987-92, Charles and Harriet Cox McDowell prof., 1993—, chair dept. religion, 1986-91; Numata prof. Buddhist studies U. Hawaii, 1993; adj. prof. U. Pa., Phila., 1979—, Temple U., Phila., 1991—; film. cons. ABC, 1972, BBC, 1977, WGBH, 1991-93; lectr. Smithsonian Instn., 1982—, Asia Soc. N.Y., 1982—; bd. dirs. Soc. Buddhist-Christian Studies, 1994—. Author: Wat Haripunjaya, 1976, Dialogue. The Key to Understanding Other Religions, 1977, Buddhism and Society in Southeast Asia, 1981; co-author: For the Sake of the World. The Spirit of Buddhist and Christian Monasticism, 1989; co-editor: Ethics, Wealth and Salvation. A Study in Buddhist Social Ethics, 1989, Me-and-Mine, Selected Essays of Bhikkhu Buddhadasa, 1989, The Buddhist World of Southeast Asia, 1995; mem. editl. bd. Jour. Religious Ethics, 1978-93, Jour. Ecumenical Studies, 1983—; asst. editor Jour. Asian Studies, 1978-80; book rev. editor S.E. Asia Religious Studies Rev., 1985-93; contbr. articles to various publs. Adult edn. Swarthmore Presbyn. Ch., 1985-87, 92-93. Asian religious study fellow Soc. Religion in Higher Edn., Sri Lanka, Thailand, Japan, 1967-68, NEH sr. fellow Thailand, 1972-73, Rockefeller Found. humanities fellow, Thailand, 1985-86, Guggenheim fellow, 1994, Fulbright fellow Dept. Edn., 1994; sr. rsch. scholar Fulbright Found., 1989-90, 94; NEH transl. grantee, 1990-91. Mem. AAUP, Assn. Asian Studies (bd. dirs. 1977-80), Am. Acad. Religion (v.p. mid-Atlantic region 1971-72), Am. Soc. Study of Religion, Soc. Buddhist-Christian Studies (bd. dirs. 1995—), Phi Beta Kappa. Democrat. Home: 109 Columbia Ave Swarthmore PA 19081-1615 Office: Swarthmore Coll Dept Religion 500 College Ave Swarthmore PA 19081-1306

SWEARER, WILLIAM BROOKS, lawyer; b. Hays, Kans.. Grad., Princeton U., 1951; law degree, U. Kans., 1955. Bar: Kans. 1955. Pvt. practice Hutchinson, Kans., 1955—; ptnr. Martindell, Swearer & Shaffer, Hutchinson, 1955—; mem. Kans. Bd. Discipline for Attys., 1979-92, chmn., 1987-92. With U.S. Army, 1952-53, Korea. Mem. ABA, Kans. Bar Assn. (pres. 1992-93, various offices, mem. coms.), Kans. Assn. Sch. Attys. (pres. 1989-90), Reno County Bar Assn. Office: PO Box 1907 Hutchinson KS 67504-1907

SWEARINGEN, DAVID CLARKE, physician, musician; b. Shreveport, La., Apr. 23, 1942; s. David C. and Alverne (Walker) S.; m. Marion Joan Adams; children: David, Joy. BS, Centenary Coll., 1963; MD, La. State U., 1967. Intern Confederate Meml. Med. Ctr., Shreveport, 1967-68, resident in ophthalmology, 1968-71; staff ophthalmologist U.S. Naval Hosp., Memphis, 1971-73; pvt. practice in ophthalmology Shreveport, 1973-78; jr. officer of deck USS Halsey CG23, 1979; comdr. med. corps, head dept. ophthalmology, chmn. utilization rev. com. ophthalmology, family practice resident instr. opthalmology U.S. Naval Hosp., Jacksonville, Fla., 1981-84; med. dir. Bio Blood Components, Shreveport, 1985-88; dir. phys. health support svcs. Ctrl. La. State Hosp., Pineville, La., 1991—, exec. hosp. and med. exec. com., chmn. infection control and pharmacy, therapeutics com.; chmn. infection control com., pharmacy and therapeutics com.; pres. Shreveport Eye and Ear Soc., 1973-74; med. cons. Cenla Chem. Dependency Coun., Pineville, 1989—, Work Tng. Facility, Pineville, 1989—. Prin. bassoonist Cenla Symphonic Band, Pineville, 1988—; mem. Jacksonville Fla. Concert Choral, 1978-81; vestry mem. St. Michaels Ch., Pineville; active Am. Mus. Natural History Assocs. Recipient AMA Physician Recognition award for Continuing Med. Edn. Mem. Internat. Platform Assn., So. Med. Assn., Nat. Parks and Conservation Assn., N.Y. Acad. Scis., La. Wildlife Fedn., Wilderness Soc., Nature Conservancy, Smithsonian Assocs., Cousteau Soc., Soc. Hist. Preservation, Environ. Def. Fund, Planetary Soc., Nat. Audubon Soc., Am. Legion, Alpha Epsilon Delta, Gamma Beta Gamma, Nu Sigma Nu. Republican. Episcopalian. Avocations: organ and bassoon music, collectibles, breeding exotic birds, shipmodel building. Home: 10 Azalea Rd Pineville LA 71360-8004 Office: Ctrl La State Hosp PO Box 5031 242 W Shamrock Ave Pineville LA 71360-6439

SWEASY, JOYCE ELIZABETH, government official, military reserve officer; b. Key West, Fla., Apr. 25, 1948; d. James Alfred and Josephine Mary (Fassel) Messick. BFA, Phila. Coll. Art, 1971; A in Bus. Adminstrn., Howard County Community Coll., 1985; grad., Army Command and Gen. Staff Co, 1988. Commd. 1st lt. U.S. Army, 1978, advanced through grades to lt. col., 1996; contract specialist U.S. Army, Adelphi, 1978-84, analyst procurement Lab. Command,, 1984-85; appointed command competition adv. Sec. of the Army, Adelphi, 1985-91; dep. chief of staff procurement, 1991-92, div. chief small bus. adminstrn., 1992-94; chief constrn. and arch. engring. contracting NIH, Bethesda, Md., 1994—; owner, operator Hand Made 'N Ellicott City, Md., 1983—; owner, gen. mgr. Data Solutions. Contbr. numerous articles to profl. jours. Mem. Font Hill Citizens Orgn., Ellicott City, 1987—. Mem. U.S. Army Res. Officers Assn, Nat. Contract Mgrs. Assn., Am. Def. Preparedness Assn. Republican. Roman Catholic. Avocations: skiing, private pilot/flying, backpacking, skydiving, writing short stories. Home: 4008 Arjay Cir Ellicott City MD 21042-5608 Office: NIH Bethesda MD 20892

SWEDBERG, ROBERT MITCHELL, opera company director; b. Glendale, Calif., Feb. 7, 1950; s. William Miller and Marion (Mitchell) S.; m. Melissa Ellen Libby, Aug. 4, 1954; children: Olivia Lauren, Erik Andrew. BA, BM, Calif. State U., Northridge, 1975. Dir. edn. and spl. projects, production stage mgr. Seattle Opera, 1978-82; mgr., artistic dir. N.C. Operas (now called Opera Carolina), Charlotte, 1982-87; gen. dir. Syracuse (N.Y.) Opera, 1987-90; dir. opera program Syracuse U., 1989-90; gen. dir. Orlando (Fla.) Opera, 1990—; stage dir. Anchorage Opera, 1979-81, San Francisco Opera, 1982, Greater Buffalo Opera, 1988; judge auditions Met. Opera, 1986—; cons. Nat. Endowment for Arts, 1991—; dir. opera studies program U. Cen. Fla., 1996—. Host: Opera Hour Sta. WMFE, Orlando. Bd. dirs. arts svcs. coun. World Cup Spl. Events Com., Italian Cultural Soc., Downtown Orlando partnership; mem. Leadership Orlando, 1995, Leadership Ctrl. Fla., 1996. Recipient Tiffany award Civic Morning Mus., 1989, Jaycees award, 1990. Avocations: camping, fishing. Home: 9437 Lake Douglas Pl Orlando FL 32817-2603 Office: Orlando Opera Co 1111 N Orange Ave Orlando FL 32804-6407

SWEED, PHYLLIS, publishing executive; b. N.Y.C., Dec. 6, 1931; d. Paul and Frances (Spitzer) S.; m. Leonard Bogdanoff (dec. Oct. 1975); children: Patricia Romano (dec. June 1994), James Alan. BA, NYU, 1950. Asst. buyer Nat. Bellas Hess, N.Y.C., 1950; assoc. editor Fox-Shulman Pub., N.Y.C., 1951-57; products editor McGraw-Hill Pub., N.Y.C., 1957-61; mng. editor Haire Pub., N.Y.C., 1962-66; editor Gifts & Decorative Accessories Mag., 1966-78; sr. v.p. Geyer-McAllister Pub., N.Y.C., 1978—, editor, co-pub., 1978-95, editor-in-chief, co-pub., 1995—. Bd. dirs. Frances Hook Scholarship Fund, 1989-96. Recipient Editorial Excellence award Indsl. Mktg., 1964, Nat. Assn. Ltd. Edit. Dealers award, 1993, 96, MagWek Excellence award, 1992, Dallas Mkt. Ctr. award, 1969, 80, 82. Mem. Nat. Assn. Ltd. Ed. Dealers (assoc.), Internat. Furnishings and Design Assn. Avocations: gardening, collecting antique Belleek. Home: 505 Laguardia Pl New York NY 10012-2001 Office: Geyer-McAllister Publs 51 Madison Ave New York NY 10010-1603

SWEEDLER, BARRY MARTIN, federal agency administrator; b. Bklyn., Mar. 11, 1937; s. Louis and Sadie (Bloch) S.; m. Kathryn Grace Stewart, June 26, 1988; children by previous marriage: Ian, Elizabeth. BME, CCNY, 1960; MBA, Baruch Sch., CUNY, 1966. Registered profl. engr., N.Y. Asst. and jr. engr. N.Y. State Pub. Svc. Commn., N.Y.C., 1960-66, sr. gas engr., 1966-69; chief pipeline safety div. Nat. Transp. Safety Bd., Washington, 1969-74, dep. dir. Bur. Surface Transp. Safety, 1974-76, dep. dir., acting dir. Bur. Plans and Programs, 1976-79, dep. dir. Bur. Tech., 1979-82, dir. Bur. Safety Programs, 1982-90; dir. Office of Safety Recommendations Nat. Transp. Safety Bd., 1990—; guest lectr. Inst. Gas Tech., 1973, U. Md., 1974, U. Calif., San Diego, 1986, 88-89, U. N.Mex., 1987, U. Calgary, 1988; participant Internat. Workshop on High Alcohol Consumers and Traffic, Paris, 1988; presented policy and tech. papers on alcohol and drug abuse in transp. at numerous internat. symposiums and congresses including 34th Internat. Congress on Alcoholism and Drug Dependencies, Calgary, Atla., Can., 1985, 10th Internat. Conf. on Alcohol, Drugs & Traffic Safety, Amsterdam, The Netherlands, 1986, and Internat. Symposium on Young Drivers Alcohol and Drug Impairment, Amsterdam, 1986; co-editor proc., chmn. alcohol, drugs and traffic safety program 35th Internat. Congress on Alcoholism and Drug Dependencies, Oslo, Norway, 1988, the 12th Internat. Conf. on Alcohol, Drugs and Traffic Safety, Cologne, 1992, 36th Internat. Inst. on Prevention and Treatment of Alcoholism, Stockholm, 1991, 12th World Congress of Internat. Assn. Accident and Traffic Medicine, 1992, 13th Internat. Conf. on Alcohol, Drugs and Traffic Safety, Adelaide, Australia, 1995. Author (with others) Gas Engineers Handbook, 1985, Alcohol - Minimizing the Harm, 1997; contbr. numerous articles on transp. safety to jours.; mem. editorial bd. Jour. Traffic Medicine, 1989—; numerous TV and print media interviews. Bd. dirs. Great Falls (Va.) Citizens Assn., 1980-85, Tysons Manor Home Owners Assn., Vienna, Va., 1973-77; mem. Fairfax County (Va.) oversight com. on drinking and driving, 1984—, chmn., 1986-88. Recipient Presdl. Rank of Meritorious Exec., 1987. Mem. ASME, Transp. Rsch. Bd. NAS (chmn. com. on alcohol, other drugs and transp. 1991-97, com. on transp. of hazardous materials 1972-78, com. on highway/R.R. grade crossing safety 1977-86, com. on utilities 1972-79), Internat. Coun. Alcohol and Addictions (co-chmn. sect. on traffic safety 1988—), Internat. Coun. Alcohol, Drugs and Traffic Safety (sec. 1992—, co-editor coun. newsletter ICADTS Reporter 1990—), Am. Acad. Forensic Scis. (adv. mem. drugs and driving com. 1988—), Operation Lifesaver (program devel. coun. 1987—), Nat. Safety Coun. (motor vehicle occupant protection com. 1983—), Am. Pub. Works Assn. (exec. com. utility location and coordination coun. 1980-87, hon. life mem.), Internat. Transp. Safety Assn. (editor assn. newsletter ITSA Report 1994—). Jewish. Avocations: tennis, hiking, bicycling. Office: Nat Transp Safety Bd Office of Safety Recommendations 490 L'enfant Plz SW Washington DC 20594-0001

SWEEN, JOYCE ANN, sociologist, psychologist, educator; b. N.Y.C.; d. Sigfried Joseph Ellmer and Julie (Hollins) Ellmer Hutchins; children: Terri Lynn, James Michael. B.S. in Math., Antioch Coll., 1960; M.S. in Exptl. Psychology, Northwestern U., 1965, Ph.D. in Social Psychology/Evaluation Research, 1971; Univ. fellow Northwestern U., Evanston, Ill., 1960-63, dir. computer ops. Inst. Met. Studies, Northwestern U., 1965-70; asst. prof. sociology DePaul U., Chgo., 1971-74, assoc. prof., 1974-80, prof., 1980-83, prof. sociology and pub. service, 1983—; cons. Nat. Commn. on Violence, 1968; evaluator Office Adolescent Pregnancy Programs, 1988-92, Office of Substance Abuse Prevention, 1988-93, Office of Treament Improvement, 1988-93, dropout prevention program Aspira of Ill., 1984-88, Dept. of Edn., 1989-95, AIDS edn. program, Ctrs. for Disease Ctrl., 1992, Chgo. Dept. Health, 1993-95, Ctr. For Substance Abuse Treatment, 1995—; cons. in field. NIH grantee, 1971-75, 78-81; NSF grantee, 1979-82; AMA grantee, 1991. Mem. Internat. Sociol. Assn., Am. Sociol. Assn., Am. Psychol. Assn., Am. Evaluation Assn., Midwest Sociol. Soc., AAAS, Sigma Xi. Rsch., publs. on fertility, African polygyny, childlessness, teen pregancy, urbanization, social effects of assassination, evaluation methodology, exptl. regression designs, sch. dropout prevention, AIDS edn., bilingual education, violence. Office: DePaul U Dept Sociology 2323 N Seminary Ave Chicago IL 60614-3211

SWEENEY, ARTHUR HAMILTON, JR., metal manufacturing executive, retired army officer; b. Charleston, W.Va., Nov. 9, 1920; s. Arthur Hamilton and Neva Pauline (Davies) S.; m. Veronica Frances Donovan, Dec. 27, 1952. S.B., MIT, 1942; M.B.A., Harvard, 1947. Commd. officer U.S. Army, advanced through grades to maj. gen.; comdg. officer U.S. Army Springfield (Mass.) Armory, 1965-67, U.S. Army Watervliet (N.Y.) Arsenal, 1967-68; dep. comdg. gen. U.S. Army Weapons Command, Rock Island, Ill., 1968-70; comdg. gen. Quinhon Support Command, Vietnam, 1970, DaNang Support Command, Vietnam, 1970-72, White Sands Missile Range, N.Mex., 1972-74, U.S. Army Materiel Mgmt. Agy., Europe, 1974-76; dep. chief of staff for logistics U.S. Army Forces Command, 1976-78; ret., 1978; corporate dir., v.p. corp. devel. Reynolds Metals Internat., Richmond, Va., 1978-91; exec. cons. Bd. of Def. Enterprise Fund, 1994. Decorated D.S.M. with oak leaf cluster, Legion of Merit with oak leaf cluster, Joint Services Commendation medal, Army Commendation medal. Home: 2956 Hathaway Rd Richmond VA 23225-1728

SWEENEY, ASHER WILLIAM, state supreme court justice; b. Canfield, Ohio, Dec. 11, 1920; s. Walter William and Jessie Joan (Kidd) S.; m. Bertha M. Englert, May 21, 1945; children: Randall W., Ronald R., Garland A., Karen M. Student, Youngstown U., 1939-42; LL.B., Duke U., 1948. Bar: Ohio 1949. Practiced law Youngstown, Ohio, 1949-51; judge adv. gen. Dept. Def., Washington, 1951-65; chief Fed. Contracting Agy., Cin., 1965-68; corp. law, 1968-77; justice Ohio Supreme Ct., Columbus, 1977—. Democratic candidate for Sec. of State Ohio, 1958. Served with U.S. Army, 1942-46; col. Res. 1951-68. Decorated Legion of Merit, Bronze Star; named to Army Hall of Fame Ft. Benning, Ga., 1981. Mem. Ohio Bar Assn., Phi Delta Phi. Democrat. Home: 6690 Drake Rd Cincinnati OH 45243-2706 Office: Ohio Supreme Ct 30 E Broad St Fl 3D Columbus OH 43215-3414

SWEENEY, CLAYTON ANTHONY, lawyer, business executive; b. Pitts., Oct. 20, 1931; s. Denis Regis and Grace Frances (Roche) S.; m. Sally Dimond, Oct. 4, 1958; children—Sharon, Lorrie, Maureen, Clayton Anthony, Tara, Megan. B.S., Duquesne U., 1957, LL.B., 1962. Bar: Pa. 1962, U.S. Supreme Ct. 1968. Supr. transp. claims H.J. Heinz Co., Pitts., 1955-57; mgr. market research Murray Corp. Am., Pitts., 1957-62; ptnr. Buchanan, Ingersoll, Rodewald, Kyle and Buerger, Pitts., 1962-78; sr. v.p. Allegheny Ludlum Industries, Inc., Pitts., 1978-81; exec. v.p., chief adminstrv. officer Allegheny Internat., Inc., Pitts., 1981-84, vice chmn., 1984-85; ptnr., mng. dir. Dickie, McCamey & Chilcote, Pitts., 1986—, also bd. dirs.; bd. dirs. Wilkinson Sword Group Ltd., U.K., Landmark Savs. and Loan Assn., Liquid Air N.Am., Halbouty Energy Co., Koppers Holding Corp., Koppers Industries, Inc., Schaefer Mfg., Inc., Schaefer Marine, Inc., Schaefer Equipment, Inc.; adj. prof. Duquesne U. Sch. Law; lectr. Pa. Bar Inst. Bd. dirs. Met. Pitts. Pub. Broadcasting, Inc., Diocesan Sch. Bd., Roman Cath. Diocese Pitts., Toner Inst., Christian Assocs. of Southwestern Pa., Wesley Inst., Inc., Jr. Achievement S.W. Pa., YMCA Western Pa.; chmn. Seton Hill Coll.; mem. St. Thomas More Sch. Bd., Bethel Park, Pa.; chmn. St. Francis Med. Ctr., St. Francis Health System; chmn. bd. DePaul Inst. With U.S. Army, 1953-55. Named one of 100 Most Disting. Living Alumni Duquesne U. Century Club, 1978. Mem. Acad. Trial Lawyers Allegheny County, ABA, Pa. Bar Assn., St. Thomas More Soc. Home: 232 Thornberry Cir Pittsburgh PA 15234 Office: Dickie McCamey & Chilcote Ste 400 2 PPG Pl Pittsburgh PA 15222-5402

SWEENEY, D.B., actor. Appeared in films Power, 1986, Fire With Fire, 1986, Gardens of Stone, 1987, No Man's Land, 1987, Eight Men Out, 1988, Memphis Belle, 1990, The Cutting Edge, 1992, Fire In the Sky, 1993, Roommates, 1995, Spawn, 1997. Office: Internat Creative Mgmt 8942 Wilshire Blvd Beverly Hills CA 90211*

SWEENEY, DANIEL THOMAS, cable television company executive; b. N.Y.C., Sept. 25, 1929; s. Daniel Thomas and Rose Marie (Delorenzo) S.; m. Anita Geraldine Madeo, Feb. 14, 1953; children: John, William, Robert, Ellen, Daniel, David. BS, N.Y. State Maritime Coll., 1952; LLB, Fordham U., 1957; LLM, NYU, 1962. Bar: N.Y. Assoc. Kirlin, Campbell and Keating, N.Y.C., 1957-62; dep. county atty. Nassau County, Garden City, N.Y., 1962-65, undersheriff, 1965-66, dep. county exec., 1966-69; chmn., chief exec. officer Mitchel Field Devel. Corp., Garden City, 1969-71; pres. Sweeney/Edman Enterprises Inc., Hempstead, N.Y., 1971-72; exec. v.p., chief oper. officer HBO, N.Y.C., 1972-73; dir. Cablevision Systems Corp., Woodbury, N.Y., 1973—; pres. Channel 21, Sta. WLIW-TV, Garden City, N.Y., 1970-74. Chmn. L.I. State Pk. and Recreation Com., Babylon, N.Y., 1976-83, Jones Beach State Pkwy. Authority, Babylon, N.Y., 1976-79; mem. L.I. Power Auth., 1996-97. Lt. comdr. USN, 1952-54, Korea. Democrat. Roman Catholic. Home: 94 Glenlawn Ave Sea Cliff NY 11579-2038 Office: Cablevision Systems Corp 1 Media Crossways Woodbury NY 11797-2062

SWEENEY, DAVID BRIAN, lawyer; b. Seattle, June 23, 1941; s. Hubert Lee and Ann Louise (Harmon) S.; m. Janice Kay Goins, June 18, 1983; children: Stuart, Jennifer, Ann, Katharine. B.A. magna cum laude, Yale U., 1963; LL.B., Harvard U., 1967. Bar: Wash. 1968, U.S. Dist. Ct. (we. dist.) Wash., 1968, U.S. Ct. Appeals (9th cir.) 1968. Assoc. Roberts, Shefelman, Lawrence, Gay and Moch, Seattle, 1968-75; ptnr. Roberts, Shefelman, Lawrence, Gay & Moch, later Roberts & Shefelman, then Foster, Pepper and Shefelman, 1976—. Mem. Seattle-King County Bar Assn., Wash. State Bar Assn., ABA, Estate Planning Council of Seattle. Republican. Presbyterian. Clubs: College, Harbor. Home: 17506 SE 46th St Bellevue WA 98006 Office: Foster Pepper & Shefelman 1111 3rd Ave Fl 34 Seattle WA 98101-3207

SWEENEY, DEIDRE ANN, lawyer; b. Hackensack, N.J., Mar. 17, 1953; d. Thomas Joseph and Robin (Thwaites) S. AB cum laude, Mt. Holyoke Coll., 1975; JD, Fordham U., 1978. Assoc. Curtis, Mallet-Prevost, Colt & Mosle, N.Y.C., 1978-84, Eaton & Van Winkle, N.Y.C., 1984-86; ptnr. Jacobs, Persinger & Parker, N.Y.C., 1986—; adj. instr. Adelphi U., N.Y.C., 1982-86. Class agt. Mt. Holyoke Coll. Alumni Fund, South Hadley, Mass., 1975-80; chmn. nominating com. Mt. Holyoke Class of 1975, 1990-94; mem. Archdiocese N.Y. Bequests and Planned Gifts Com., 1988—. Mem. Assn. of Bar of City of N.Y. (uniform state laws com. 1982-85). Democrat. Roman Catholic.

SWEENEY, FRANCIS E., state supreme court justice; b. Jan. 26, 1934; married; 4 children. BSBA, Xavier U., 1956; JD, Cleve.-Marshall Law Sch., 1963. Profl. football player Ottawa Rough Riders, Ont., Can., 1956-58; mem. legal dept. Allstate Ins. Co., Cleve., 1958-63; asst. prosecuting atty. Cuyahoga County, Cleve., 1963-70; judge Cuyahoga County Ct. of Common Pleas, Cleve., 1970-88; judge (8th cir.) U.S. Ct. Appeals, Cleve., 1988-92; justice Ohio Supreme Ct., Columbus, 1992—. With U.S. Army, 1957-58. Recipient Legion of Honor award Xavier U., 1956, Outstanding Jud. Svc. award Ohio Supreme Ct., 1972-85, Alumnus of Yr. award Xavier U., 1977. Office: Ohio Supreme Ct 30 E Broad St Fl 3 Columbus OH 43215-3414*

SWEENEY, JAMES LEE, engineering and economic systems educator, consultant; b. Waterbury, Conn., Mar. 22, 1944; s. James Wallace and Aletha B. Sweeney; m. Susan L. Van Every, Aug. 21, 1971; children: Erin, Ryan, Regan. BSEE, M.I.T., 1966; PhD in Engring.-Econ. Systems, Stanford U., 1971. Dir. office energy systems, modeling and forecasting U.S. Fed. Energy Adminstrn. Washington, 1974-76; with Stanford U. 1967—, prof. engring.-econ. systems, 1971—, chmn. dept. engring.-econ. systems, 1991-96, chmn. dept. engring.-econ. systems and ops. rsch., 1996—; dir. Energy Modeling Forum, 1978-85, chmn. Inst. Energy Studies, 1981-84, cons. faculty Sch. of Law, 1980-82, mem. steering com. Ctr. Econ. policy Rsch., 1982—, dir., 1984-86; cons. U.S. Dept. Energy, NRC, Exxon, Charles River Assocs. Recipient Disting. Service award Fed. Energy Adminstrn., 1975. Mem. Am. Econ. Assn., Internat. Assn. Energy Econs. (past v.p. for publs.), Eta Kappa Nu, Tau Beta Pi, Rotary (past pres.), Menlo Circus Club. Co-author: Macroeconomics Impacts of Energy Shocks, 1987, Fuels to Drive Our Future, 1990; editor: Handbook of Natural Resources and Energy Economics, 1985, 93; contbr. numerous publs. in field to profl. jours. Home: 445 El Escarpado Stanford CA 94305-8431 Office: Stanford U Dept Engring-Econ Systems and Ops Rsch Terman Engring Ctr Rm 312 Stanford CA 94305-4023

SWEENEY, JAMES RAYMOND, lawyer; b. Chgo., Feb. 19, 1928; s. John Francis and Mae J. (McDonald) S.; m. Rhoda W. Davis, May 15, 1987; children from previous marriage: Margaret Elizabeth, John Francis, Thomas Edward. B.S., U. Notre Dame, 1950; J.D., Northwestern U., 1956. Bar: Ill. 1956. With firm Schroeder, Hofgren, Brady & Wegner, Chgo., 1956-61; ptnr. Hofgren, Wegner, Allen, Stellman & McCord, Chgo., 1962-71, Coffee, Wetzel, Sweeney, Chgo., 1971-72, Coffee & Sweeney, 1972-76, Mason, Kolehmainen, Rathburn & Wyss, Chgo., 1976-82, McWilliams, Mann, Zummer & Sweeney, 1983-86, Mann, McWilliams, Zummer, & Sweeney, 1986-89, Lee, Mann, Smith, McWilliams & Sweeney, 1989-91, Lee, Mann, Smith, McWilliams, Sweeney & Ohlson, 1991—; commr. for disbarment matters Ill. Supreme Ct., 1963-73; mem. hearing div. Atty. Registration and Discipline Comm., 1974-77, chmn. commn. 1983-90. Bd. dirs., sec. Highland Park (Ill.) Hosp., 1972-79. Served as lt. (j.g.) USN, 1950-53; lt. comdr. Res. ret. Mem. ABA (coun. patent, trademark and copyright sect., sec. 1978-82), Ill. State Bar (assembly 1990-96), Chgo. Bar Assn. (sec. 1977-79), Bar Assn. 7th Cir., Intellectual Property Law Assn. Chgo., Patent Law Assn. Chgo. (pres. 1974), The Law Club Skokie (Ill.), Country Club, Union League Club. Home: 505 N Lake Shore Dr Chicago IL 60611-3427 Office: Lee Mann Smith McWilliams Sweeney & Ohlson 209 S La Salle St Ste 410 Chicago IL 60604-1203

SWEENEY, JOHN JOSEPH, labor union administrator; b. N.Y.C., May 5, 1934; s. John and Patricia Sweeney; m. Maureen Power; children: John, Patricia. B in Econs., Iona Coll., 1956. With Internat. Ladies Garment Workers (now UNITE); contract dir., Local 32B Svc. Employees Internat. Union, N.Y.C., 1960-76, exec. bd., 1972-80, pres., Local 32B, 1980-95; v.p. AFL-CIO, Washington, 1981-95; pres. AFL-CIO, N.Y.C., 1995—; trustee Am. Ctr. Internat. Labor Solidarity, George Meany Ctr. Labor Studies; served with Nat. Com. on Employment Policy, 1985; U.S. worker del. Internat. Labor Orgn., Geneva, 1984, 85, 91; adv. coun. Fed. Mediation & Conciliation Svc. Author: America Needs A Raise, 1996; co-author: Solutions for the New York Force, 1989; co-editor: Family andWork: Bridging the Gap, 1987. Trustee Asian-Am. Labor Studies Ctr., Iona Coll.; bd. dirs. Cath. Youth Orgn., Citizen-Labor Energy Coalition, ARC; served with adv. council Fed. Mediation and Conciliation Svc.; del. Nat. Dem. Convention, 1992, 96. Recipient David L. Clendenin award Workers Def. League N.Y., 1981, Quirk award 8th Ann. John H. Fanning Conf. on Labor-Mgmt. Rels., 1983. Mem. Am. Arbitration Assn. (bd. dirs.). Democrat. Office: AFL-CIO 815 16th St NW Washington DC 20006

SWEENEY, JOHN LAWRENCE, lawyer; b. Staten Island, N.Y., Jan. 5, 1962; s. Lawrence Patrick and Lauretta (Kronen) S.; m. Karen Anne Hrenak, Aug. 26, 1988; children: Conor, Lauren, Devin, Pearse. BA, Yale U., 1984; JD magna cum laude, Seton Hall U., 1990; LLM in Taxation, NYU, 1993. Bar: N.J. 1990, U.S. Dist. Ct. N.J. 1990, N.Y. 1991, U.S. Tax Ct. 1995. Assoc. Connell, Foley & Geiser, Roseland, N.J., 1990-92, Lampf, Lipkind, Prupis & Pettegrew, West Orange, N.J., 1992-93; atty. pvt. practice, Morristown, N.J., 1993—. Interview supr. Yale Alumni Schs. Com., 1991—; charter mem. Seton Hall Prep Hall of Fame Com., 1984-94. Mem. N.J. Bar Assn., N.Y. Bar Assn., Morris County Bar Assn., Yale Club Ctrl. N.J. (trustee 1991-94). Home: 102 Runnymede Pkwy New Providence NJ 07974-1440 Office: 51 Dumont Pl Morristown NJ 07960-4125

SWEENEY, JOHN W., III, newspaper executive; b. Jersey City, N.J., July 11, 1946; s. John William Jr. and Rita Constance (Dillon) S.; m. Jo Ellen Cooley, Nov. 7, 1970; children: John W. IV, Jessica Elizabeth. BA in English, King's Coll., Wilkes Barre, Pa., 1968. Dealer sales Humble Oil/Exxon, Washington, 1968-69; nat. automotive mgr. Washington Post, 1969-74; advt. dir. Trenton (N.J.) Times, 1974-78, Boston Herald, 1978-80; advt. dir. Houston Chronicle, 1980-83, sales & mktg. dir., 1983-86, v.p. sales & mktg., 1986-91, v.p., gen. mgr., 1991—. Chmn. mktg. com. United Way Tex. Gulf Coast, Houston, 1985-86, 90-91; bd. dirs. Jr. Achievement, Houston, 1991—, Better Bus. Bur., Houston, 1991—; mem. adv. bd. Houston Ballet, 1988-92. Mem. Newspaper Assn. Am. (bd. govs. 1993—, mem. mktg. ops. com. 1993—). Avocations: golf, coaching youth sports. Office: Houston Chronicle 801 Texas St Houston TX 77002-2906*

SWEENEY, LUCY GRAHAM, psychologist; b. Davenport, Iowa, Nov. 14, 1946; d. B. Graham and Dorothy (Lawson) S.; m. Richard N. Tiedemann, Dec. 2, 1978 (div. 1989); 1 child, Susan Lee. AA, William Woods Coll., 1966; BA with honors, U. Denver, 1968; MA in Devel. Psychology, Columbia U., 1977; PsyD, Rutgers U., 1990. Cert. family therapist. Profl. actress, 1968-73; dir. therapeutic play and recreation program St. Luke's Med. Ctr., N.Y.C., 1973-78; child life coord. St. Francis Hosp., Hartford, Conn., 1978-80; clinician Resolve Community Counseling Ctr., Scotch Plains, N.J., 1981-84; staff psychologist women's inpatient unit Lyons (N.J.) VA Med. Ctr., 1990; psychologist women's treatment program Fair Oaks Hosp., Summit, N.J., 1990-92; cons. Kessler Inst. for Rehab., East Orange, N.J., 1992-94, Resolve Community Counseling Ctr., Scotch Plains, N.J., 1992—; pvt. practice Westfield, N.J., 1993—. Contbr. articles to profl. jours. Recipient John Weyandt award for Outstanding Student in Theatre U. Denver, 1968. Mem. APA, N.J. Psychol. Assn., Phi Theta Kappa. Home: 21 Harwich Ct Scotch Plains NJ 07076-3165

SWEENEY, MARK OWEN, publisher; b. Cherryvale, Kans., Dec. 27, 1942; s. Paul Eldon and Clelia Eugenia (Bosette) S.; m. Janet Lynn Turner, July 24, 1964; children—Douglas, Jonathan. Grad., Moody Bible Inst., 1963; B.A., Pacific Coll., 1965; M.A., Wheaton Coll., Ill., 1967. Instr. history Cascade Coll., Portland, Oreg., 1967-70; editor Moody Bible Inst., Chgo., 1970-72; exec. producer Moody Corr. Sch., Moody Bible Inst. (Radio div.), 1972-74; dir. public relations Moody Bible Inst. (dir. Moody Lit. Ministries), 1974-77, mgr. publ. div., 1977-81; dir. Victor Books, Scripture Press Publs., 1981-83, v.p., 1983-90; pubr., COO Victor Books, Scripture Press Publs., Wheaton, Ill., 1990-94; corp. v.p., pub. Scripture Press Publs., Inc. and Victor Books, Wheaton, 1994-95; C.O.O. Killion McCabe and Assocs., Dallas, 1995—. Mem. Christian Booksellers Assn., Evang. Christian Pubs. Assn. (past chmn. bd.), Nat. Assn. Evangelicals. Home: 5939 Deseret Trail Dallas TX 75252 Office: Killion McCabe and Assocs 900 Coit Central Tower 12001 N Central Expy Dallas TX 75243-3700

SWEENEY, MICHAEL ANDREW, newspaper editor; b. York, Pa., Nov. 27, 1948; s. Felix William and Deuris C. (Ehehalt) S.; m. Linda Carol Gillam, Nov. 20, 1976; children: Barbara Catherine, Matthew Allan. BA in Communication Art, Seton Hall U., 1972; MA in Polit. Sci., Rutgers U., 1981. Reporter The Courier-News, Bridgwater, N.J., 1972-75, asst. night editor, 1975-77, night editor, 1977-78, nat. editor, 1978-79, asst. news editor, 1980-81; news editor The Advocate Southern Conn. Newspapers Inc., Stamford, Conn., 1981-83, exec. news editor, 1983-85, asst. mng. editor, 1985-88; editorial page editor Greenwich Time/So. Conn. Newspapers, Inc., 1988—, columnist, 1991—. Contbr. articles to profl. jours. Roman Catholic. Avocations: gardening, computers. Office: Greenwich Time 20 E Elm St Greenwich CT 06830-6529*

SWEENEY, RICHARD JAMES, economics educator; b. San Diego, Jan. 13, 1944; s. John Joseph and Catherine Scott (Spahr) S.; m. Joan Long, June 19, 1965; children: Robin Scott, Erin Michaela. BA, UCLA, 1965; PhD, Princeton U., 1972. Acting asst. prof. econs. UCLA, 1968-71; asst. prof. Tex. A&M U., College Station, 1971-73; dep. dir. office of internat. monetary research U.S. Dept. Treasury, Washington, 1973-77; Charles M. Stone prof. econs. and fin. Claremont (Calif.) McKenna Coll., 1977-89, chmn. dept. econs., 1987-89; Sullivan/Dean prof. internat. fin. Georgetown U., Washington, 1989—; vis. assoc. prof. econs. U. Va., Charlottesville, 1975; vis. prof. bus. adminstrn. Dartmouth Coll., Hanover, N.H., 1979; vis. prof. fin. Gothenburg (Sweden) Sch. Econs., 1991, 92, 93, 94, 95, 96. Author: A Macro Theory with Micro Foundations, 1974, Principles of Microeconomics, Macroeconomics, 1980, Wealth Effects and Monetary Theory, 1988, Profit-Making Speculation in Foreign Exchange Markets, 1992; author, editor: Exchange Rates, Trade and the U.S. Economy, 1985; contbr. articles to profl. jours. Fellow NSF 1966-68, Woodrow Wilson Found. 1965; grantee Gen. Electric Found., 1980, Mid.-Am. Found., 1987, Earhart Found., 1988. Mem. Western Econ. Assn. (editor Econ. Inquiry jour. 1984-96), Am. Econ. Assn., Am. Fin. Assn., Western Fin. Assn., Phi Beta Kappa. Democrat. Avocations: writing, weightlifting, walking, aerobics. Office: Sch Bus Adminstrn Georgetown U Washington DC 20057

SWEENEY, ROSEMARIE, medical association administrator; b. Fall River, Mass., Sept. 2, 1950; d. John Francis and Phyllis (Field) S.; m. Edmund Burke Rice, Feb. 24, 1978; 1 child, Jonathan Field Rice. Student, Hillsdale Coll., 1968-69; BA, Am. U., 1972, MPA, 1978. Profl. staff mem. Office of Rep. Margaret Heckler, Washington, 1972-74; staff assoc. fed. agy. affairs Am. Osteo. Assn., Washington, 1974-78, govt. affairs rep., 1978-79; dir. Washington office Am. Acad. Family Physicians, Washington, 1979-82; v.p. socioeconomic affairs and policy analysis, 1992—; mem. family practice adv. com. George Washington U., Washington, 1990—. Vol. Montgomery County Sexual Assault Svc., Rockville, Md., 1984-93; mem. Glen Echo Fire Dept., Bethesda, Md., 1986-92, Victim Svcs. Adv. Bd., Md., 1987-93; chmn. victim svc. adv. bd. Montgomery County, Md., 1991-93; bd. dirs. Westmoreland Children's Ctr., Bethesda. Recipient Outstanding Svc. award Montgomery County Crisis Ctr., Md., 1986, Outstanding Performance award Montgomery County Sexual Assault Svc., Md., 1987, Recognition award Soc. Tchrs. Family Medicine, Kansas City, Mo., 1990, Govs.' Sixth Annual Victim Assistance award, Balt., 1991. Mem. Women in Govt. Rels. Avocations: running, volunteer work, reading. Office: Am Acad Family Physicians 2021 Massachusetts Ave NW Washington DC 20036-1011

SWEENEY, THOMAS JOSEPH, JR., lawyer; b. N.Y.C., Oct. 29, 1923; s. Thomas Joseph and Johanna M. (Flynn) S.; m. Robin Virginia Thwaites, May 30, 1947; children: Thomas Joseph, III, Deidre Ann. BA, N.Y. U., 1947; JD, Columbia U., 1949. Bar: N.Y. 1949. Assoc. in law Columbia U. Law Sch., 1949-50; assoc. Cravath, Swaine & Moore, N.Y.C., 1950-62; with Morgan Guaranty Trust Co. N.Y., 1962-89, v.p., 1965-76, sr. v.p., sr. trust officer, 1976-89, chmn. instl. trust and investment com., 1989—; ptnr. Decker, Hubbard, Welden & Sweeney, N.Y.C.; bd. dirs. W.R. Kenan Fund. Trustee Pinkerton Found., Jean and Louis Dreyfus Found. 2d lt. USAAF, 1943-45. Mem. N.Y. State Bar Assn. Democrat. Roman Catholic. Home: 525 Teaneck Rd Ridgefield Park NJ 07660-1100 Office: Decker Hubbard 30 Rockefeller Plz New York NY 10112

SWEENEY, VONNY HILTON, promotion company executive; b. Brownsville, Pa., Aug. 24, 1947; d. James and Ann Hilton; divorced; 1 child, Howard Hilton Sweeney. AA, Am. River Coll., 1971; BA, Calif. State U., Sacramento, 1974. Nat. promotion coord. Sussex Records, L.A., 1974; adminstr. asst. promotion and pub. rels. Playboy, L.A., 1974-76; mgr. Polydor rec. artists Alton McClain & Destiny, L.A., 1976-80; mgr. Polygram rec. artists Lace Wing, L.A., 1985-90; pres. James Brown West, Inc., Hollywood, Calif., 1990—; cons., publicist James Brown Prodns., Augusta, Ga., 1974—; founder, chair Annual Pre-Grammy Gala, L.A., 1980—. Asst. producer Ebony Music Awards, L.A., 1975. Fundraiser various politicians, L.A. and Sacramento, 1974—; mem. com. Miss Black L.A., 1990. Mem. Nat. Acad. Recording Arts and Scis., Am. Film Inst. Office: PO Box 691354 West Hollywood CA 90069-9354

SWEET, CHARLES G., paralegal school administrator, dean; b. Lewiston, Maine, Aug. 5, 1918; s. Alfred H. and Gladys (Greenleaf) S.; m. Margaret Gibson, July 29, 1948 (div. 1966); children: David W., Barbara G.; m. Martha Gossard, Nov. 10, 1966. AB, Pa. State U., 1939; LLB, Harvard U., 1946. Bar: Pa. 1947, D.C. 1947. Practiced in Washington, Pa., 1947-64; pres. judge Washington County Ct. Common Pleas, Washington, 1964-84; pres., dean Paralegal Careers Inc., Tampa, Fla., 1985-93; pres. Pa. Conf. State Trial Judges, 1979-80; judge adv. Dale Mabry Post, Am. Legion, Tampa. Contbr. articles to profl. jours. Del. Dem. Nat. Conv., Chgo., 1952; regional dir. Pa. Young Dems., 1954-55; former mem. Pa. Commn. on Police and Corrections; past pres. Ctrl. Washington County United Fund, bd. dirs. Pa. United Fund, 1974-82, Fla. United Fund, Tampa, 1984-86. With USMC, 1941-46; lt. col. Res. ret. Recipient Robert Steward award Domestic Rels. Assn. Pa., 1980, Man of Yr. award Washington C. of C., 1983, award Coun. on Alcohol and Drug Abuse, 1983, law enforcement commendation medal SAR, 1983, cert. of svc. United Way Tampa, 1988. Mem. Am. Arbitration Assn. (panel arbitrators), Washington County Bar Assn. (pres. 1960-61), Am. Legion (dist. officer Fla. & Pa. 1954-93, nat. law enforcement com.). Episcopalian. Avocations: foreign travel, Civil War. Home: 3501 Bayshore Blvd #1501 Tampa FL 33629-8901 Office: 10913 N Dale Mabry Hwy Tampa FL 33618-4112

SWEET, CHARLES WHEELER, executive recruiter; b. Chgo., June 11, 1943; s. Charles Wheeler and Alice Nomi (Grush) S.; m. Joy Ann Weidenmiller, Mar. 23, 1968; children: Charles III, Kimberly Ann, Rebecca Townsend. AB, Hamilton Coll., Clinton, N.Y., 1965; MBA, U. Chgo., 1968. Salesman Procter & Gamble, Chgo., 1965-67; with pers. Ford, Dearborn, Mich., 1968-69, R.R. Donnelley, Chgo., 1969-72; exec. recruiter A.T. Kearney Inc. Exec. Search, Chgo., 1972—, pres., 1988—; bd. dirs. Gt. Bank of Algonquin. Trustee Village Barrington Hills, Ill., 1985—; chmn. bd., exec. advisor No. Ill. U., 1979-88; bd. dirs. Rehab. Inst. Chgo., 1987—. Mem. AESC, Barrington Hills Country Club (bd. dirs. 1993-96). Avocations: tennis, bridge. Home: 92 Meadow Hill Rd Barrington IL 60010-9601 Office: A T Kearney Inc 222 W Adams St Chicago IL 60606-5307

SWEET, CYNTHIA KAY, business administrator; b. Highland, Kans., Feb. 21, 1949; d. Jack Wendull and Ruthanna (Dittemore) Hedrick; m. Roger Keith Alexander, 1968; children: Karen Joyce, Melinda Ruth Anne; m. Erich Christian Sweet, Oct. 31, 1990. Student, U. Kans., 1968, North Peralta Coll., 1973-74, U. Colo., 1976-79; BS in Bus. Tech., Empire State Coll., 1984. Computer operator Computer Ctr. U. Colo., Boulder, 1977-79; subscription coord. Inst. Arctic & Alpine Rsch., Boulder, 1979; computer operator Computer Ctr. Rensselaer Poly. Inst., Troy, N.Y., 1979-80, dir. devel. info. svcs., 1982-85; rsch. analyst N.Y. State Mus., Albany, 1979-80, project mgr., 1980-82; product mgr. Info. Assocs., Rochester, N.Y., 1985-89, sr. program mgr., 1990-92; applications mgr. Claris Corp., Santa Clara, Calif., 1989-90; custom programming mgr. Datatel, Fairfax, Va., 1992-94; exec. dir. advancement solutions TRG, Phoenix, 1994-96; dir. profl. svcs. USA Group Info. Solutions, 1996—; freelance fundraising cons., Albany and Rochester, 1984-89. Contbr. articles to profl. jours. Activity coord. Info. Assocs./ United Way, Rochester, 1985-89, 91-92; mem. festival staff meml. Art Gallery, Rochester, 1987-89; bd. dirs. Draper Dance Theatre, Rochester, 1988-92. Mem. NSFE, Coun. for Advancement and Support of Edn., Project Mgmt. Inst., Am. Mus. Assn. Avocations: camping, hiking, gardening, gourmet cooking, reading. Office: USA Group Info Solutions 4343 E Camelback Rd Phoenix AZ 85018

SWEET, JAMES BROOKS, oral and maxillofacial surgeon; b. Darlington, Pa., Mar. 28, 1934; s. Lufay Anderson and Margaret Jean (Brooks) S.; m. N. Gayle Laird, Oct. 11, 1958; children: James Brooks II, Laird Anderson, Bradley Stephen. BA, Lafayette Coll., 1956; DDS, U. Pitts., 1964, DMD, 1974; MS in Dentistry, NYU, 1975. Aviation flight officer USNR, 1957; advanced through grades to dir. USPHS; rotating intern USPHS Hosp., Staten Island, N.Y., 1964-65, resident oral and maxillofacial surgery, 1970-73; chief dept. dentistry Fed. Correctional Inst. Hosp., Ashland, Ky., 1965-67, Terminal Island, Calif., 1967-70; chief oral and maxillofacial surgery Clin. Ctr. NIH, Bethesda, Md., 1973-80; chief dept. dentistry and oral and maxillofacial surgery USPHS Hosp., Nassau Bay, Tex., 1980-81; ret. USPHS, 1981; assoc. prof. dept. oral and maxillofacial surgery Health Sci. Ctr. U. Tex., Houston, 1981-84; prof., 1984—; asst. clin. prof. med. br. U. Tex., Galveston, 1980-; assoc. attending physicianBen Taub Gen. Hosp., Houston, 1984-; cons. oral and maxillofacial surgery self study guides, Stoma Press, Seattle, 1983-; cons. VA Hosp., Houston, 1986-. Contbr. articles to profl. jours.; editorial reviewer: Annals of Internal Medicine, 1977-. Coach basketball Olney (Md.) Boys Club, 1975-80; mem. aim rev. Tex. area USCG, 1981-82. Lt. USNR, 1957-64. Fellow Am. Assn. Oral and Maxillofacial Surgeons; mem. Tex. Soc. Oral and Maxillofacial Surgeons, Houston Soc. Oral and Maxillofacial Surgeons, Am. Assn. Dental Schs., USPHS Profl. Assn., NIH Sailing Club, Omicron Kappa Upslion (pres. Mu Mu chpt. 1993-94). Presbyterian. Avocations: sailing, swimming, real estate, travelling. Office: U Tex Health Sci Ctr 6516 John Freeman St Houston TX 77030-3402

SWEET, LOWELL ELWIN, lawyer; b. Flint, Mich., Aug. 10, 1931; s. Leslie E. and Donna Mabel (Latta) S.; m. Mary Ellen Ebben, Aug. 29, 1953; children: Lawrence Edward, Diane Marie, Sara Anne. BA in Psychology, Wayne State U., 1953, LLB, U. Wis., 1955. Bar: Wis. 1955, U.S. dist. ct. (ea. dist.) Wis. 1955, U.S. dist. ct. (no. dist.) Ill. 1958. Ptnr., Morrissy, Morrissy, Sweet & Race and predecessors, Elkhorn, Wis., 1957-70; shareholder, pres. Sweet & Reddy, S.C., Elkhorn, 1970—; instr. gen. practice sect. U. Wis. Law Sch. 1978, 79, 86, 90; lectr. real estate law Wis. Bar, Gateway Tech. Carthage Coll. Inst., 1974—. Author Phased Condominiums for Matthew Bender, 1992; co-editor: Condominium Law Handbook, 1981, 93; mem. editorial bd. Workbook for Wis. Estate Planners, 1990. Mem. Walworth County Republican Com.; sect. Wis. Joint Survey Commn. on Debt Mgmt. Served with CIC, U.S. Army, 1955-57. Named Outstanding Young Man, Elkhorn Jaycees, 1966; recipient citation for service in drafting Wis. Condominium Law, Wis. Legislature, 1978. Fellow ABA; mem. Wis. Bar Assn. (gov. 1972-75, 91-93), Walworth County Bar Assn., Am. Judicature Soc., Assn. Trial Lawyers Am., The Best Lawyers in Am., Am. Coll. Real Estate Lawyers, Kiwanis, Lions, Moose, KC. Home: 411 W Marshall St Elkhorn WI 53121-1624 Office: Sweet & Reddy SC 114 N Church St Elkhorn WI 53121-1202

SWEET, LYNN D., journalist; b. Chgo., May 15, 1951; d. Jason and Ione Dover S. AB, U. Calif., Berkeley, 1973; MS in Journalism, Northwestern U., Evanston, Ill., 1975. Reporter Independent-Register, Libertyville, Ill., 1975-76; reporter Chgo. Sun-Times, 1976-93, polit. writer, bur. chief Washington bur., 1993—. Bd. dirs. Northwestern Univ.'s Medill Sch. of Journalism Alumni Bd., 1990-93. Office: 1206 National Press Building Washington DC 20045-2200*

SWEET, PHILIP W. K., JR., former banker; b. Mt. Vernon, N.Y., Dec. 31, 1927; s. Philip W.K. and Katherine (Buhl) S.; m. Nancy Frederick, July 23, 1950; children—Sandra H., Philip W.K. III, David A.F. AB, Harvard U., 1950; MBA, U. Chgo., 1957. Pres., dir. The No. Trust Co., Chgo., 1975-81; chmn., chief exec. officer No. Trust Corp., 1981-84. Alderman City of Lake Forest, Ill., 1972-74; adv. com. United Negro Coll. Fund; vis. com. U. Chgo. Grad. Sch. Bus.; trustee Chgo. Zool. Soc., past chmn. 1988-93; life trustee Rush-Presbyn.-St. Luke's Med. Ctr.; vestryman Episc. Ch., 1971-74, 86-89. Mem. Soc. Colonial Wars (gov. Ill. chpt. 1978-80), Chgo. Sunday Evening Club (trustee, chmn.), Econ. Club, Comml. Club, Chgo. Club, Commonwealth Club (past pres.), Old Elm Club (Highwood, Ill.), Onwentsia Club (v.p., gov.), Shoreacres Club (past pres. Lake Bluff).

SWEET, ROBERT WORKMAN, federal judge; b. Yonkers, N.Y., Oct. 15, 1922; s. James Allen and Delia (Workman) S.; m. Adele Hall, May 12, 1973; children by previous marriage—Robert, Deborah, Ames, Eliza. B.A., Yale U., 1944, LL.B., 1948. Bar: N.Y. 1949. Asso. firm Simpson, Thacher & Bartlett, 1948-53; asst. U.S. atty. So. Dist. N.Y., 1953-55; asso. firm Casey, Lane & Mittendorf, 1955-65, partner, 1957-65; counsel Interdepartmental Task Force on Youth and Juvenile Delinquency, 1958-78; dep. mayor City of N.Y., 1966-69; partner firm Skadden, Arps, Slate, Meagher & Flom, N.Y.C., 1970-77; mem. hearing office N.Y.C. Transit Authority, 1975-77; U.S. dist. judge So. Dist. N.Y., N.Y.C., 1978—; participant USIA Rule of Law Program in Albania, 1991; observer Albanian elections, 1992. Pres. Community Service Soc., 1961-78; trustee Sch. Mgmt. Urban Policy, 1970—, Taft Sch.; vestryman St. Georges Epis. Ch., 1958-63. Served to lt. (j.g.) USNR, 1943-46. Recipient Alumni citation of merit Taft Sch., 1985, various other awards, citations for service as dept mayor N.Y.C. Mem. ABA, Assn. of Bar of City of N.Y., N.Y. Law Inst., N.Y. County Lawyers Assn., State Bar Assn., Am. Legion (comdr. Willard Straight Post). Clubs: Quaker Hill Country, Century Assn., Merchants, Indian Harbor Yacht, Mid City Rep.

SWEET, WILLIAM HERBERT, neurosurgeon; b. Kerriston, Wash., Feb. 13, 1910; m. Paul Williams and Daisy Eleanor (Pool) S.; m. Elizabeth Jane Dutton, July 29, 1978; children: David Rowland, Gwendolyn Sweet Fletcher, Paula Sweet Carroll. SB, U. Wash., 1930; BSc, Oxford U., 1934, DSc, 1957; MD, Harvard U., 1936; DHC (hon.), Université Scientifique et Médicale de Grenoble, France, 1979; DSc (hon.), Ohio State U., 1993. Diplomate Am. Bd. Psychiatry and Neurology, Am. Bd. Neurol. Surgery. Rhodes rsch.scs fellow Nat. Hosp. for Nervous Disease, London, 1939; asst. in neurosurgery Mass. Gen. Hosp., Boston, 1945-47; asst. neurosurgeon Mass. Gen. Hosp., 1947-48, assoc. vis. neurosurgeon, 1948-57, vis. neurosurgeon, 1957-61, chief neurol. svc., 1961-77, sr. neurosurgeon, 1977-96; asst. in surgery Harvard U. Med. Sch., Boston, 1945-46; instr. surgery Harvard U. Med. Sch., 1946-47, assoc. in surgery, 1947-48, asst. prof. surgery, 1948-54, assoc. clin. prof., 1954-58, assoc. prof., 1958-65, prof., 1965-76, prof. emeritus, 1976—; hon. surgeon Mass. Gen. Hosp., 1996—; cons., lectr. in field; trustee Neuro-Rsch. Found. Inc., 1951—, pres., 1971—; trustee Neurosci. Rsch. Found. Inc., 1961—, pres., 1961-76. Author: (with J.C. White) Pain: Its Mechanisms and Neurosurgical Control, 1955, Pain and the Neurosurgeon: A Forty Year Experience, 1969; editor books in field; contbr. articles to profl. jours., chpts. to books, monographs in medicine. Sci. trustee Assoc. Univs. Inc. (AUI), rep. Harvard U., 1958-82, hon. trustee, 1982—. Served with AUS, 1941-45. Rhodes scholar, 1932-34; Arthur Tracy Cabot fellow Harvard U. Med. Sch., 1935-36; Commonwealth Fund fellow, 1940-41, Royal Coll. Surgeons of Edinburgh hon. fellow, 1986. Mem. Am. Acad. Arts and Scis., Am. Pain Soc., AAAS, Am. Acad. Surgery, Am. Acad. Neurology, ACS, Am. Assn. Neurol. Surgeons, Am. Neurol. Assn., Am. Physiol. Assn., Am. Surg. Assn., Assn. de chirgiens Suisses (corr.), Assn. for Research in Nervous and Mental Diseases, Congress Neurol. Surgeons (hon.), Electroencephalographic Soc., Halsted Soc., Internat. Assn. for Study Pain, Internat. Brain Research Orgn., Internat. Soc. Psychiat. Surgery, Internat. Soc. Surgery, Italian Neurosurg. Soc. (corr.), New Eng. Neurosurg. Soc., Research Soc. Neurol. Surgeons, Royal Soc. Medicine, Scandinavian Neurosurg. Soc. (corr.), Societe de Neuro-Chirurgie de Langue Francaise (hon.), Soc. Brit. Neurol. Surgeons, Soc. for Neurosci., Spanish-Portuguese Neurosurg. Soc. (hon.), Soc. Neurol. Surgeons, Egyptian Soc. Neurol. Surgeons (hon.). Office: 309 Goddard Ave Brookline MA 02146-7425

SWEETEN, GARY RAY, religious counseling educator; b. Ina, Ill., May 5, 1938; s. Thomas Jefferson and Leota Leone (Taylor) S.; m. Karen J. Sweeten, Nov. 21, 1961; children: Julia Rae, Timothy Andrew. AA, Rend Lake Coll., 1960; BS, So. Ill. U., 1965, MS, 1967; EdD, U. Cin., 1975. Tchr., coach pub. schs. Ina, Bellerive and Mt. Vernon, Ill., 1960-65; asst. dean U. Cin., 1967-69, asst. to univ. provost, 1969-73; minister of Christian edn. Coll. Hill Presbyn. Ch., Cin., 1973-76, minister of counseling and growth, 1973-89; chief exec. officer, pres. Lifeway Counseling Ctr., Cin., 1989—; founder, chairperson Equipping Mins. Internat., Cin., 1978—; cons., founder Sweeten Creative Cons., Cin., 1970—; founder, pres. Christian Info. Com., Cin., 1978—; pres., bd dirs. Presbyn. Renewal Ministry, Oklahoma City, 1980-85; founder Lifeway Inst. for Continuing Edn., Lifeway Internat., Telgios Moscow Counseling Ctr. Author: Listening: For Heaven's Sake, 1993; author numerous articles, monographs, tng. manuals. Bd. dirs. Citizens Against Substance Abuse. Named Outstanding Alumni Rend Lake Coll., Ina, 1986. Mem. Ohio Assn. Counselor Devel., Christian Assn. Psychol. Studies. Avocation: travel. Home: 11863 Tennyson Dr Cincinnati OH 45241-2195 Office: Lifeway Counseling Ctr 4015 Executive Park Dr Cincinnati OH 45241-4017

SWEETING, LINDA MARIE, chemist; b. Toronto, Ont., Can., Dec. 11, 1941; came to U.S., 1965, naturalized, 1979; d. Stanley H. and Mary (Robertson) S. BSc, U. Toronto, 1964, MA, 1965; PhD, UCLA, 1969. Asst. prof. chemistry Occidental Coll., L.A., 1969-70; asst. prof. chemistry Towson (Md.) State U., 1970-75, assoc. prof., 1975-85, prof., 1985—; guest worker NIH, 1976-77; program dir. chem. instrumentation NSF, 1981-82; vis. scholar Harvard U., 1984-85; contractor U.S. Army MRICD, 1991-93. Bd. dirs. Chamber Music Soc. Balt., 1985-91. Exec. com. Exptl. NMR. Conf. 1985-87, local arr. chair 1986. Mem. Md. Acad. Scis. (mem. sci. council 1975-83, 89-94), Assn. for Women in Sci. (treas. 1977-78, Woman of Yr. 1989), Am. Chem. Soc. (mem. women chemists Com. 1983-89), AAAS, Nature Conservancy, Sierra Club, Phi Lambda Upsilon, Sigma Xi (sec. TSU Club 1979-81, Towson chpt. pres. 1987-88, 91-92, sec. 1995—, mid-Atlantic nominating com. 1987-90, regional dir. 1988-89, nat. nominating com. 1991-94). Office: Towson State U Dept Chemistry Baltimore MD 21252-7079

SWEETLAND, ANNETTE FLORENCE (ANNIE SWEETLAND), special education educator; b. Dallas; d. George R. and Odessa (Donnhue) S.; children: George William Davison, James Erron Davison; m. Ralph J. Guinn. BS in Edn., U. Okla., 1988, MS in Edn., 1992. Tchr. multi-handicapped students Noble (Okla.) Pub. Sch., 1988-90; child-find S.E.A.R.C.H. coord. and preschool handicap tchr. Shawnee (Okla.) Pub. Sch., 1989-93; regional coord. Sooner Start Okla. Dept. Edn., Norman, 1993-94; case mgr. II Developmental Disabilities Scv. Divsn./DHS, State of Okla., Oklahoma City, 1994-95; spl. educator Okla. Youth Ctr., 1995-96; tchr. El Reno Pub. Schs., Oklahoma City, 1996—; mgr. group home Able Group Homes, Norman, Okla., 1989-90; dir. returning adult program St. Gregory's Coll., Shawnee, 1990-91. Mem. ARC, ACA, Coun. for Exceptional Children, Okla. Edn. Assn.

SWEETLAND, LORAINE FERN, librarian, educator; b. Morristown Corners, Vt., Aug. 13, 1933; d. William Eric and Sylbil Bedina (Bailey) Bloomfield; m. Ronald David Sweetland, July 1, 1950; children: Kathy L. (dec.), Dale J. Bettis. BS in Elem. Edn., Columbia Union Coll., 1968; MS in Library Sci., Syracuse U., 1973. Tchr. 1st and 2d grade Beltsville (Md.) Seventh-Day Adventist Sch., 1960-67; asst. libr., cataloger Vt. Tech. Coll., Randolph Ctr., 1968-69; middle sch. libr. Barre (Vt.) City Schs., 1970-74; tchg. prin. Cen. Vt. Seventh-Day Adventist Sch., Barre, 1974-76, Brooklawn Seventh-Day Adventist Sch., Bridgeport, Conn., 1976-81; med. libr. Washington Adventist Hosp., Takoma Park, Md., 1981-85; dir. libr. svcs. Seventh-Day Adventists World Hdqs., Silver Spring, Md., 1985-95; med. libr. cons., Balt., 1983-85; pres. Oasis, 1993-94; tchr. Home Study Internat., Silver Spring, Md., 1995—, IPS-Info. Problem Solvers, Laurel, 1995—. Book reviewer Libr. Jour., 1990—. Trustee Randolph (Vt.) Pub. Library, 1970-71; sec. Nat. Area Hosp. Council, Washington, 1985. Mem. Assn. Seventh-Day Adventist Librarians, Laurel Rotary Club (bulletin editor 1990-94). Republican. Avocations: gardening, photography, knitting, sewing, crocheting. Home and Office: 10182 High Ridge Rd Laurel MD 20723-1782

SWEETMAN, BEVERLY YARROLL, physical therapist; b. Phila., Apr. 8, 1939; d. Albert Henry and Theresa (Payne) Yarroll; m. Denman John Sweetman, Apr. 1, 1961; children: Denman Eric, John Albert. BA in Biology, Hood Coll., 1961; cert. phys. therapist, Hahnemann U., 1983. Rsch. technician Mass. Gen. Hosp., Boston, 1961-62, Princeton (N.J.) U., 1965-66; part owner, phys. therapist Pain & Stress Control Ctr., Allentown, Pa., 1983-85; pvt. practice Body Ease Phys. Therapy Ctr., Grants Pass, Oreg., 1985; pvt. practice, pres. Body Ease Phys. Therapy Ctr., Staunton and Charlottesville, Va., 1986—; developer and co-presenter Total Body Concept Seminars; lectr. in field; v.p. VMG Med., Staunton, 1988—; cons., co-presenter seminars Lossing Orthopedic, Mpls., 1985—. Fellow Am. Back Soc.; mem. Am. Phys. Therapy Assn. Office: Body Ease Phys Therapy Ctr 409 Walnut Hills Rd Staunton VA 24401-9467

SWEETS, HENRY HAYES, III, museum director; b. Lexington, Ky., May 8, 1949; s. Henry Hayes Jr. and Elizabeth (Keith) S.; m. Nancy Riley, Jan. 28, 1984; children: Amy Louisa, Henry Hayes IV. BS in Chemistry, U. Ill., 1971, MEd., 1973; MA in History, U. Del., 1978. Tchr. Scotch Plains (N.J.)-Fanwood High Sch., 1972-74, Byron (Ill.) High Sch., 1974-76; mus. dir. Mark Twain Mus., Hannibal, Mo., 1978—. Author: A Sesquicentennial History of the Hannibal, Missouri Presbyterian Church; editor The Fence Painter. Bd. dirs. Becky Thatcher coun. Girl Scouts U.S., 1984-88; mem. bd. edn. Hannibal, Mo. Pub. Schs., 1991—. Mem. Nat. Trust for Hist. Preservation. Methodist. Office: Mark Twain Home and Mus 208 Hill St Hannibal MO 63401-3316

SWEETSER, GENE GILLMAN, quality assurance professional, state legislator; b. Burlington, Vt., Apr. 24, 1948; s. Archelaus William and Stella Ruth (Brink) S.; m. Elizabeth Ann Hannett, Apr., 1967 (div. May 1972); 1 child, Analei; m. Susan Williams, Aug. 27, 1978 (div. Feb. 1995); 1 child, Virginia Lucretia. BA Polit. Sci. and Environ. Sci., Johnson State Coll., Vt., 1978; MS in Adminstrn., St. Michael's Coll., Vt., 1993. Maintenance machinist Avdel Internat., Inc., Parsippany, N.J., 1982-84; machine shop supr. Mitec Systems, Inc., Williston, Vt., 1984-84; maintenance supr. Fonda, Inc., Albans, Vt., 1985-88; asst. quality control mgr. Chatham Precision, Hinesburg, Vt., 1988-91; state representative Vt. State Ho. of Reps., 1990—; prodn. control IBM, Essex, Vt., 1992—; mem. Bd. Civil Authority, Essex, Vt., 1988—, Justice of the Peace, 1988—; mem. com. ways and means Vt. State Ho. of Reps., 1994—. Founder, bd. dirs. paper recycling program Worcester Vol. Fire Dept., 1978-82; founder, bd. dirs. Worcester Film Soc., 1978-82, Worcester Views Newsletter, 1978-82; vice chmn. Ctrl. Ct. Regional Planning Commn., 1980-82; vol. The Holiday Project, 1987-89; coach Essex Youth Soccer, 1988, 89; player agt. for minor league Essex Little League Assn., 1990; v.p. Survivors of Crime, Inc. With USMC, 1969-72, Vt. Army nat. Guard, 1978—. Address: 28 Foster Rd Essex Junction VT 05452-3316

SWEEZY, JOHN WILLIAM, political party official; b. Indpls., Nov. 14, 1932; s. William Charles and Zuma Frances (McNew) S.; BS in Mech. Engring., Purdue U., 1956; MBA, Ind. U., 1958; student Butler U., 1953-54, U. Ga., 1954-55, Ind. Cen. Coll., 1959; m. Carole Suzanne Harman, July 14, 1956; children: John William, Bradley E. Design, test engr. Allison div. GM, Indpls., 1953-57; power sales engr. Indpls. Power & Light Co., 1958-69; dir. pub. works City of Indpls., 1970-72; chmn. Marion County Rep. Cen. Com., 1972—; bd. dirs. Lorco Engring., Indpls., Indpls. Industrial Products, Acme Screw & Mfg., Inc., Telnet, Inc., Landmarks Ltd., Innovative Investment Co. Bd. dirs. Indpls. Humane Soc.; chmn. 11th Dist. Rep. Com., 1970, 73—; chmn. Nat. Assn. Urban Rep. County Chmn.; alt. del. Rep. Nat. Conv., 1968, del., 1972, 76, 80, 84, 88, 92, del., mem. credentials com., 1984, 88; mem. credentials com., 1980; mem. Rep. Nat. Com., 1984—, exec. com., 1984—; mem. Warren Schs. Citizens Screening Com., 1958-72; bd. dirs. Warren Devel. Com. With AUS, 1953-55. Mem. AMA, Mensa, Sigma Iota Epsilon. Home: 2089 S German Church Rd Indianapolis IN 46239-9620 Office: 12 N Delaware St Indianapolis IN 46204-3205

SWEEZY, PAUL MARLOR, editor, publisher; b. N.Y.C., Apr. 10, 1910; s. Everett Benjamin and Caroline (Wilson) S.; m. Zirel Dowd, June 17, 1961; children by previous marriage: Samuel Everett, Elizabeth MacDougall, Martha Adams. BA, Harvard U., 1931, PhD, 1937; LittD (honoris causa), Jawaharlal Nehru U., 1983. With econs. dept. Harvard U., 1934-42; editor Monthly Rev., 1949—; vis. prof. Cornell U., Stanford U., New Sch. Social Research, U. Calif., Davis, Yale U., Hosei U., Tokyo, U. Manchester, Eng.; lectr. Cambridge (Eng.) U., 1971; pres. Monthly Rev. Found., Inc. Author or editor: Monopoly and Competion in the English Coal Trade, 1950-1850, 1938, The Theory of Capitalist Development, 1942, Socialism, 1949, The Present as History, 1953; co-author: (with Leo Huberman) Cuba: Anatomy of a Revolution, 1960, (with Paul Baran) Monopoly Capital, 1966, (with Leo Huberman) Socialism in Cuba, 1969, (with Charles Bettelheim) On the Transition to Socialism, 1971, (with Harry Magdoff) The Dynamics of U.S. Capitalism, 1972, Modern Capitalism and Other Essays, 1972, (with Harry Magdoff) The End of Prosperity, 1977, Post Revolutionary Society, 1981, (with Harry Magdoff) The Deepening Crisis of U.S. Capitalism, 1981, Four Lectures on Marxism, 1981, (with Harry Magdoff) Stagnation and Financial Explosion, 1987, (with Harry Magdoff) The Irreversible Crisis, 1988. Served with AUS, 1942-46. Decorated Bronze Star; recipient David A. Wells prize, 1938. Home: 2 Lindsley Dr Larchmont NY 10538-3808 Office: 122 W 27th St Fl 10 New York NY 10001-6227*

SWENKA, ARTHUR JOHN, food products executive; b. Lone Tree, Iowa, Oct. 21, 1937; s. Samuel Joseph and Verdis Mary (Weed) S.; m. Elizabeth Simms, July 1956 (div. 1976); children: Lee Arthur, Timothy John; m. Dixie Jo Meade, Feb. 1982. Gen. equivalency diploma, U.S. Army, 1957. Truck driver U.S. Mail, Oelwein, Iowa, 1958-59, Stiles Supermarket, Oelwein, 1959-60; salesman Hoxie Inst. Wholesale Co., Waterloo, Iowa, 1960-68, slaes mgr., 1968-69, br. mgr., 1969-70; br. mgr. Hoxie Inst. Wholesale Co., Waterloo and Mason City, Iowa, 1970-72, Nobel Inc., Albuquerque, 1972-81; pres. Nobel/Sysco Food Svcs. Co., Albuquerque, 1981-84, Denver, 1985-95; sr. v.p. ops. Sysco Corp., Houston, 1995—; mem. Dirs. Coun., Houston, 1985—. Treas., bd. dirs. Albuquerque Conv. and Visitors Bur., 1975-80; v.p., bd. dirs. Albuquerque Internat. Balloon Festival, 1975-82; bd. dirs. New Day Home for Runaway Children, Albuquerque, 1980-89, Found. St. Joseph's Hosp., Kodak Internat. Balloon Fiesta, Albuquerque. Republican. Roman Catholic. Avocation: hot air ballooning. Home: 7112-32 Pan American Fwy Albuquerque NM 87109 Office: Nobel/Sysco Food Svcs Co 601 Comanche NE Albuquerque NM 87125

SWENSEN, CLIFFORD HENRIK, JR., psychologist, educator; b. Welch, W.Va., Nov. 25, 1926; s. Clifford Henrik and Cora Edith (Clovis) S.; m. Doris Ann Gaines, June 6, 1948; children—Betsy, Susan, Lisa, Timothy, Barbara. B.S., U. Pitts., 1949, M.S., 1950, Ph.D., 1952. Diplomate Am. Bd. Profl. Psychology. Instr. U. Pitts., 1951-52; clin. psychologist VA, 1952-54; from asst. prof. to assoc. prof. U. Tenn., Knoxville, 1954-62; assoc. prof. psychology Purdue U., West Lafayette, Ind., 1962-65, prof., 1965—; dir. clin. tng. Purdue U., 1975-85; vice chair U. Senate, 1994-95; vis. prof. U. Fla., 1968-69, U. Bergen, Norway, 1976-77, 83-84; cons. VA, 1981 White House Conf. on Aging, others; Am. Psychol. Assn.-NSF Disting. Sci. lectr., 1968-69; Fulbright-Hays lectr., Norway, 1976-77. Author: An Approach to Case Conceptualization, 1968; Introduction to Interpersonal Relations, 1973; contbr. chpts. to books, articles to profl. jours. Served with USN, 1944-46. Recipient Gordon A. Barrows Meml. award for disting. contributions to psychology, 1990. Fellow APA (pres divsn. cons. psychology 1976-77), Am. Psychol. Soc., Soc. Personality Assessment, Am. Assn. Applied and Preventive Psychology, Acad. of Clin. Psychology; mem. Midwestern Psychol. Assn., Southeastern Psychol. Assn., Ind. Psychol. Assn., Gerontol. Soc., Sigma Xi, Psi Chi. Republican. Mem. Ch. of Christ. Home: 611 Hillcrest Rd West Lafayette IN 47906-2349 Office: Purdue U Dept Psychol Scis West Lafayette IN 47907

SWENSEN, LAIRD S., orthopedic surgeon; b. Provo, Utah, Oct. 5, 1944; s. Russel Brown and Beulah (Strickler) S.; m. Gloria Elaine Matoza, Sept. 23, 1973; children: Lara Ann, Christine, Russel, Tracy, Laird. BA in Chemistry, Brigham Young U., 1968; MD, George Washington U., 1972. Diplomate Am. Bd. Orthopedic Surgery; cert. added qualifications in surgery of hand, 1992. Intern San Francisco Gen. Hosp., 1972-73; resident in orthopedics U. Calif., San Francisco, 1973-77; pvt. practice orthopedic surgery Salt Lake City, 1978—; fellow in hand and microvascular surgery Jack Tupper, 1978; vice chmn. dept. surgery LDS Hosp.; chmn. divsn. orthopedics LDS Hosp., 1991-92; assoc. clin. prof. dept. orthop. surgery U. Utah, 1979, asst. clin. prof., 1990—; vol. surgeon Orthopedics Overseas, Nepal, 1988, 90, Bhutan, 1992; med. advisor Tibetan Resettlement Project, Salt Lake City. Active 4th St. Homeless Clinic, 1995. Fellow Am. Acad. Orthopedic Surgery; mem. Western Orthopedic Assn. (pres. Utah chpt. 1991), Am. Soc. Surgery of Hand, Utah State Med. Assn. Avocation: mountaineering. Office: 324 10th Ave Salt Lake City UT 84103-2853

SWENSEN, MARY JEAN HAMILTON, graphic artist; b. Laurens, S.C., June 25, 1910; d. Elvin A. and Della (Brown) Hamilton; m. Oliver Severn Swensen, Mar. 3, 1943 (dec.). BS, Columbia U., 1956, MA, 1960; Cert. Notable, U. Madrid, Spain; postgrad., Ariz. State U., 1974-80. mem. 1st USSA sr. internat. cross-country skiing team. One person shows at Colo. Fed. Savs. and Loan Assn., Denver, 1978, Panoras Gallery, N.Y.C., 1963; exhibited in group shows at Soc. Western Artist, M.H. de Young Mus., San Francisco, 1964, Nat. Art Roundup, Las Vegas, 1965, Fine Arts Bldg., Colo. State Fair, Pueblo, 1965, Duncan Gallery, Paris, 1974, Colo. Fed. Savs. & Loan Assn., Denver, 1978; graphics arts in pub. collections at Met. Mus. Art, N.Y.C., Nat. Graphic Arts Collection, Smithsonian Inst., Laurens (S.C.) Pub. Libr., N.Y.C. Pub. Libr. Assoc. Libr. of Congress, Archael. Inst. Am., Smithsonian Instn., Johns Hopkins. Recipient Duncan Gallery Prix de Paris, 1974, Notable award M.H. de Young Mus., 1964, YWCA of U.S.A. Gold Medal as most admired athlete of yr., 1977, USSA Nat. Vets. X-Country Racing Team Gold, Silver and Bronze medals for downhill, giant slalom, slalom, and cross-country sr. citizen and vet. races, 1963-79. Mem. Internat. Platform Assn., Am. Mensa, Columbia Club N.Y., Delta Phi Delta. Home (winter): Exec Towers Assn Condo 19A 207 W Clarendon Ave Phoenix AZ 85013-3443

SWENSON, CHRISTINE ERICA, microbiologist; b. N.Y., Apr. 27, 1953; d. Oscar Adolf and Marjorie Claire (Wareing) S.; m. James Yasinski, Sept. 6, 1980; children: Jeffrey, Emma. BA, Middlebury Coll., 1975; PhD, Cornell U., 1980. Postdoctoral fellow Rockefeller U., N.Y., 1980-82, U. Calif., San Francisco, 1982-84; scientist The Liposome Co., Inc., Princeton, N.J., 1984-

88, dir., 1988—. Office: The Lipsome Co Inc One Research Way Princeton NJ 08540

SWENSON, COURTLAND SEVANDER, musician; b. Akron, Iowa, July 2, 1936; s. Clifford Sevander and Selma Lillian (Swanson) S.; m. Bonnie Jan Hull, Aug. 23, 1966; children: Callan Sevander, Corey McAllister. BFA, U. S.D., 1958, MusM, 1962; postgrad., U. Ill., 1968-69, U. Würzburg, Fed. Republic Germany, 1976. Tchr. music Sibley (Iowa) Public Schs., 1958-60; mem. faculty U. S.D., Vermillion, 1960-94; prof. music U. S.D., 1973-94; ret., 1994; instr., chmn. fine arts Ramey AFB, P.R., 1971-72; musical dir. Black Hills Playhouse, Custer Park, S.D., 1963-78; cons. music, Guatemala, 1977; prin. percussionist Sioux City (Iowa) Symphony, 1964-71; prin. timpanist Sioux Falls (S.D.) Symphony, 1973-76; bd. dirs. Arnie B. Larson Shrine to Music of Antique Instruments, 1970-87. Mem. S.D. Arts Coun., 1987-90. Named Best Tchr. U. S.D., 1967, 83; recipient Burlington No. Found. award for excellence in teaching, 1987. Mem. Percussive Arts Soc. Address: 3386 Laurel Grv S Jacksonville FL 32223-7816

SWENSON, ERIC DAVID, town official, lawyer; b. Glen Cove, N.Y., Oct. 27, 1954; s. Robert Fritz and Florence Betty (Bullard) S.; m. Deborah Catherine Johnston, Aug. 31, 1991. BA, SUNY, New Paltz, 1976; JD, St. John's Sch. Law, 1986; grad. cert. in waste mgmt., SUNY, Stony Brook, 1993. Bar: N.Y., D.C. Canvas field mgr. N.Y. Pub. Interest Rsch. Group, N.Y.C., 1978-79, project coord., 1979-81; legal file clerk Jessel Rothman, P.C., Mineola, N.Y., 1981-82; environ. control specialist trainee Town of Oyster Bay, Syosset, N.Y., 1982-83, environ. control specialist, 1983-88, supt. environ. control, 1988—; mem. Nat. Environ. Leadership Coun., Washington, 1990—; bd. dirs. Support for People with Oral, Head and Neck Cancer, Inc., Locust Valley. Contbr. articles to profl. jours. 2d v.p. Locust Valley (N.Y.) Rep. Club, 1991-92; active Village of Sea Cliff (N.Y.) Recycling Task Force, 1991—; regional coord. Earth Day '80, Western N.Y., 1980. Mem. N.Y. State Assn. for Solid Wast Mgmt. (pres. 1993-95, sec./treas. 1995—), N.Y. State Bar Assn., Kiwanis (North Shore Club). Avocations: outdoors, home brewing, cooking. Home: 31 Bay Ave Sea Cliff NY 11579-1039 Office: Town of Oyster Bay 150 Miller Pl Syosset NY 11791-5603

SWENSON, ERIC PIERSON, publishing company executive; b. South Orange, N.J., Sept. 21, 1918; s. Svante Magnus and Dorothy Wharton (Mendelson) S.; m. Patricia Morgan, Sept. 14, 1945 (div. June 1965); children: Juliet Morgan Swenson Carter (dec.), Karen Rosamond Swenson McCollom, Dana Graham Swenson Seberg, Hilary Lloyd SwensonMoody; m. Ann Brooke Kirkland, Aug. 5, 1965; 1 child, Alexandra Brooke. Grad. magna cum laude, St. Paul's Sch., Concord, N.H., 1937; B.A. with high orations, Yale, 1941. Publicity asst., editor Pocket Books, Inc., N.Y.C., 1945-47; publicity, editor William Sloane Assos., N.Y.C., 1947-51; sr. editor, vice chmn., dir. W.W. Norton & Co., N.Y.C., 1951-91, editor emeritus, hon. bd. dirs., 1991—; bd. dirs. SMS Ranch Co., Stamford, Tex., Ctr. for Marine Conservation, Washington, Trafalger Sq. Pub. Co. Inc., North Pomfret, Vt. Author: The South Sea Shilling, 1952. With USN, 1941-45, PTO. Clubs: New York Yacht, Cruising of Am., Royal Yacht Squadron, Indian Harbor Yacht, Yale, Storm Trysail, Royal Ocean Racing, Coun. on Fgn. Rels. Home: 99 Eleven O'Clock Rd Weston CT 06883 Office: 500 5th Ave New York NY 10110

SWENSON, FAYE LORENE, executive and management development firm administrator; b. Springfield, Minn., Sept. 19, 1964; d. Charles Kenneth and Faith Lorene (Seymour) Pederson; m. Timothy Dennis Swenson, June 6, 1987 (div. June 1997). BA magna cum laude, Luther Coll., Decorah, Iowa, 1987. Psychometrist Personnel Decisions Internat., Mpls., 1987-88, assoc. cons., 1988-89, client rels. cons., 1989-94, sales trainer, 1991-94, acct. mgr., 1995-97, account exec., 1997—. Mem. Sales and Mktg. Execs., Phi Beta Kappa. Avocations: golf, skiing, gardening, reading, ice fishing. Home: 1117 Marquette Ave #1202 Minneapolis MN 55403 Office: Pers Decisions Internat 45 S 7th St Minneapolis MN 55402-1614

SWENSON, GEORGE WARNER, JR., electronics engineer, radio astronomer, educator; b. Mpls., Sept. 22, 1922; s. George Warner and Vernie (Larson) S.; m. Virginia Laura Savard, June 26, 1943 (div. 1970); children: George Warner III, Vernie Laura, Julie Loretta, Donna Joan; m. Joy Janice Locke, July 2, 1971. BS, Mich. Coll. Mining and Tech., 1944, E.E., 1950; MS, MIT, 1948; PhD, U. Wis., 1951. Asso. prof. elec. engring. Washington U., St. Louis, 1952-53; prof. U. Alaska, 1953-54; asso. prof. Mich. State U., 1954-56; faculty U. Ill., Urbana, 1956—, prof. elec. engring. and astronomy, 1958-88, prof. emeritus, 1988—; acting head dept. astronomy U. Ill., 1970-72, head dept. elec. and computer engring., 1979-85; dir. Vermilion River Obs., 1968-81; vis. scientist Nat. Radio Astronomy Obs., 1964-68; cons. to govt. agys. and other sci. bodies; sr. rsch. assoc. U.S. Army Constrn. Engring. Rsch. Lab., 1988-95; adj. prof. elec. engring. Mich. Technol. U., 1996—. Author: Principles of Modern Acoustics, 1953, An Amateur Radio Telescope, 1980; co-author: Interferometry and Synthesis in Radio Astronomy, 1986; contbr. articles to profl. jours. 1st lt. USASG, WWII. Recipient citation for disting. service to engring. U. Wis., 1984; Guggenheim fellow, 1984-85. Fellow IEEE, AAAS; mem. NAE, Am. Astron. Soc., Internat. Sci. Radio Union (U.S. nat. com. 1965-67, 80-82), Internat. Astron. Union, Inst. Noise Control Engring. (cert.), Sigma Xi, Eta Kappa Nu, Tau Beta Pi, Phi Kappa Phi. Achievements include chairing conceptual design group which produced the concept/proposal for the Very Large Array of National Radio Astronomy Observatory; designed and built two large innovative radio telescopes for the University of Illinois. Home: 1107 Kenwood Rd Champaign IL 61821-4718 Office: U Ill 328 CSRL 1308 W Main St Urbana IL 61801-2307

SWENSON, HAROLD FRANCIS, crisis management consultant; b. N.Y.C., Apr. 28, 1915; s. Charles Henry and Ethel Marie (Igoe) S.; AB, Manhattan Coll., 1938; student Fordham U. Law Sch., 1938-41; m. Mildred Chandler, Dec. 31, 1943; 1 dau., Sally. Mem. law firm Root, Clark, Buckner & Ballantine, N.Y.C., 1938-41; spl. agt. FBI, 1941-47; indsl. relations exec. Gulf Oil, San Tome, Venezuela, 1947-52; employee relations and security exec. Sears, Roebuck & Co., Chgo., 1953-54; with State Dept., Washington, 1955-65, Def. Dept., Washington, 1965-68; pres., chief exec. officer, dir. Bishop's Service Inc., N.Y.C., 1969-73; v.p. surveys, mktg. and fgn. ops. Intertel Inc., Washington, 1974-78; with law dept., security exec. Chesebrough-Pond's Inc., Greenwich, Conn., 1978-86, crisis mgmt. cons. exec., 1986—. Polit. attache U.S. Embassy, Buenos Aires, Argentina, 1956-62. Served with USMC, 1944-46, PTO. Mem. Soc. Former FBI Agts., Internat. Assn. Chiefs of Police, Capital Marines, Mil. Order Carabao, U.S. Naval Inst., Mil. Order Fgn. Wars, Marine Corps. Hist. Soc., Bad Ems Golf Alumni, Air Crew Assn. of London, FBI-Marine Corps Assn. (N.Y.), Epsilon Sigma Pi, Beta Sigma. Clubs: Chantilly Golf and Country (Centerville, Va.); Pathfinders (London); American (Buenos Aires). Home: 3873 Tusico Pl Fairfax VA 22030-3925 also: 7337 Oak Moss Dr Sarasota FL 34241-6222

SWENSON, KAREN, poet, journalist; b. N.Y.C., July 29, 1936; d. Howard William and Dorothy (Trautman) S.; m. Michael Shuter, 1958 (div. 1971); 1 son, Michael. B.A., Barnard Coll., 1959; M.A., NYU, 1971. Free lance journalist; preliminary judge CAPS grants, 1975; judge Walt Whitman Award, Acad. Am. Poets, 1976, 88. Author: An Attic of Ideals, 1974, East-West, 1980, A Sense of Direction, 1989, The Landlady in Bangkok, 1994. Runner up Arvon Poetry award, Ann Stanford Poetry award, 1988; winner Nat. Poetry Series, 1993; Yaddo fellow, 1987, 89, Albee Found fellow, 1990-91. Mem. Century Assn. Home: 25 W 54th St New York NY 10019

SWENSON, MARY ANN, bishop. Bishop Rocky Mountain Conf., Denver. Office: Rocky Mountain Conference 2200 S University Blvd Denver CO 80210-4708

SWENSON, ORVAR, surgeon; b. Halsingborg, Sweden, Feb. 7, 1909; s. Carl Albert and Amanda (Johnson) S.; m. Melva Criley, Sept. 11, 1941; children: Melva, Elsa, Wenda. AB, William Jewell Coll., 1933, DSc (hon.), 1993; M.D., Harvard U., 1937; Dr hc, U. Aix, Marseilles, France, 1975. Diplomate Am. Bd. Surgery. Intern Peter Bent Brigham and Children's hosps., Boston, 1939-41; chief resident in surgery Peter Bent Brigham Hosp., 1944-45; Arthur Tracy Cabot fellow Harvard Med. Sch., 1941-44; surgeon Peter Bent Brigham Hosp., 1945-50, Children's Hosp., Boston, 1947-50; surgeon-in-chief Boston Floating Hosp. Infants and Children, 1950-60; asso. surgery Harvard Med. Sch., 1947-50; prof. pediatric surgery Tufts U. Med. Sch., 1957-60; surgeon-in-chief Children's Meml. Hosp., Chgo., 1960-73; prof. surgery Northwestern U. Med. Sch., 1960-73, U. Miami, Fla., 1973-78; chmn. sect. surgery Am. Acad. Pediatrics, 1954-57; lectr. Alex Simpson Smith Lecture Inst. of Child Health, U. London, 1954, Blackfan Lecture Harvard Med. Sch., Boston Children's Hosp., 1958; spl. guest lectr. 16th Gen. Assembly, Japan Med. Congress, 1963; Felton Bequest vis. prof. surgery Univs. Sidney and Melbourne, 1959; vis. prof. U. Bombay, 1980. Author: Pediatric Surgery, 1958; mem. editorial bd. Pediatrics, 1962-68. Recipient Mead Johnson award, 1952, Ladd award Surg. sect. Am. Acad. Pediatrics, 1969, Achievement award Modern Medicine mag., 1971, Frank Billings award AMA, 1949; Swenson Vis. Professorship established in his honor Tufts U. Sch. Medicine, 1987, Swenson Chair in Pediatric Surgery established in 1990. Hon. fellow Royal Coll. Surgeons (Dublin, Ireland), Royal Coll. Physicians and Surgeons Can., Brit. Assn. Pediatric Surgeons (hon., Denis Brown medal 1979); mem. A.C.S., Am. Surg. Assn., Soc. Univ. Surgeons, Am. Pediatric Surg. Assn. (pres. 1973). Discovered cause and cure of Hirschsprung's Disease, 1948. Home: PO Box 41 Rockport ME 04856-0041 also: 172 Cabo de Lagos Fort Pierce FL 34951

SWENSSON, EARL SIMCOX, architect; b. Nashville, July 28, 1930; s. Earl Ebenezer and Viola Lazelle (Simcox) S.; m. Suzanne Dickenson, June 6, 1953; children: Krista, Lin, Kurt. BS in Bldg. Design, Va. Poly. Inst. and State U., 1952, MSArch, 1953; MSArch, U. Ill., 1955. Registered architect 28 states. Founder, prin. Earl Swensson Assocs., Inc., Nashville 1961—; adj. prof. Va. Poly. Inst., Blacksburg, 1971-72, Auburn U., 1976-83; lectr. in field. Contbr. articles to profl. jours. patentee systamodule for pharmacies. Author: (with Richard L. Miller and Earl S. Swensson) New Directions in Hospital and Healthcare Facility Design, 1995. Bd. dirs. Metro Arts Commn., 1979-86, Middle Tenn. Health Systems Aug. 1973-78, Leadership Nashville Alumni Groups, 1984—; mem. bd. advisers U. Tenn. Sch. Architecture, 1982, chmn., 1985-88; mem. architecture program adv. coun. Auburn U., 1990-94. Recipient Jefferson award Am. Inst. Public Service, Nashville chpt., 1985; named Outstanding Nashvillian of Yr. Downtown Kiwanis Club, 1992. Fellow AIA. Presbyterian. Office: Earl Swensson Assocs 2100 W End Ave Ste 1200 Nashville TN 37203-5225

SWERDLOFF, MARK HARRIS, lawyer; b. Buffalo, Sept. 7, 1945; s. John and Joan (Harris) S.; m. Ileen Pollock, Dec. 24, 1967; 1 child, Jonathan Edward. BA, SUNY, Buffalo, 1967; JD, U. Conn., 1975. Bar: Conn. 1975, U.S. Dist. Ct. Conn. 1975, U.S. Ct. Appeals (2d cir.) 1983, U.S. Supreme Ct. 1985, Fla. 1977. Assoc. Wilson, Asbel & Channin, Hartford, Conn., 1975-78; ptnr. Swerdloff & Swerdloff, West Hartford, Conn., 1978—; pres. Arpus Enterprises, Old Saybrook Conn., 1993—; trial fact finder Superior Ct., Hartford, 1990—; arbitrator Dispute Resolution Inst., Hartford, 1990—. Mem. ABA, Conn. Bar Assn., Conn. Trial Lawyers Assn. Democrat. Jewish. Avocations: photography, travel, cooking. Home: 9 Beacon Heath Farmington CT 06032 Office: Swerdloff & Swerdloff 433 S Main St West Hartford CT 06110-1670

SWERDLOW, AMY, historian, educator, writer; b. N.Y.C., Jan. 20, 1923; d. Joseph and Esther (Rodner) Galstuck; m. Stanley H. Swerdlow, Nov. 27, 1949 (dec. Sept. 1991); children: Joan Swerdlow-Brandt, Ezra, Lisa Thomas. BA, NYU, 1963; MA, Sarah Lawrence Coll., 1973; PhD, Rutgers U., 1984. Prof. emerita Sarah Lawrence Coll., Bronxville, N.Y., 1981-95, dir. grad. studies in women's history, 1983-95, dir. women's studies program, 1983—; mem. adv. bd. Feminist Press, 1973—. Editor, co-author: Families in Flux, 1980, reprint, 1989; author: Women Strike for Peace; Traditional Motherhood and Radical Politics in the 1960s, 1993; editor Feminist Perspective on Homework and Childcare, 1978; co-editor: Class, Race and Sex: The Dynamics of Control, 1983, Rethinking Women's Peace Studies, 1995; contbr. Sights on the Sixties; Reflections on a Critical Time, Women and Militarism: Essays in History, Politics and Social Theory, Give Peace a Chance, The Abolitionist Sisterhood: Women's Political Culture in Antebellum America, 1994, American History as Women's History, 1994. Mem. nat. bd. and non-governmental orgn. rep. Peace History Soc. conf. Rutgers U. fellow, 1977-81, Woodrow Wilson Dissertation fellow, 1980. Mem. Orgn, Am. Historians, Berkshire Conf. in Women's History. Home: 150 Claremont Ave Apt 4C New York NY 10027-4679

SWERDLOW, MARTIN ABRAHAM, physician, pathologist, educator; b. Chgo., July 7, 1923; s. Sol Hyman and Rose (Lasky) S.; m. Marion Levin, May 19, 1945; children—Steven Howard, Gary Bruce. Student, Herzl Jr. Coll., 1941-42; BS, U. Ill., 1945; MD, U. Ill., Chgo., 1947. Diplomate: Am. Bd. Pathology. Intern Michael Reese Hosp. and Med. Center, Chgo., 1947-48; resident Michael Reese Hosp. and Med. Center, 1948-50, 51-52, mem. staff, 1974—, chmn. dept. pathology, v.p. acad. affairs, 1974-90; pathologist Menorah Med. Ctr., Kansas City, Mo., 1954-57; asst. prof., pathologist U. Ill. Coll. Medicine, Chgo., 1957-59, assoc. prof., 1959-60, clin. assoc. prof., 1960-64, clin. prof., 1964-66, prof., pathologist, 1966-72, assoc. dean, prof. pathology, 1970-72; prof. pathology, chmn. U. Mo., Kansas City, 1972-74; prof. pathology U. Chgo., 1975-89, Geever prof., head pathology U. Ill., 1989-93, Geever prof., head pathology emeritus, 1993—; mem. com. standards Chgo. Health Systems Agy., 1976—. Served with M.C. U.S. Army, 1944-45, 50-54. Recipient Alumnus of Yr. award U. Ill. Coll. Medicine, 1973; Instructorship award U. Ill., 1960, 65, 68, 71, 72. Mem. Chgo. Pathology Soc. (pres. 1980—), Am. Soc. Clin. Pathologists, Coll. Am. Pathologists, Internat. Acad. Pathology, Am. Acad. Dermatology, Am. Soc. Dermatopathology, Inst. Medicine, AMA. Jewish. Office: U Ill Coll Medicine Dept Pathology 1819 W Polk St Chicago IL 60612-7331 *My credo these years has been to care about patients, students, colleagues, employees, my institution and the many publics I serve. Honesty and thoroughness has been a basic life style, irrespective of the cost. With all, competence is a necessity and ongoing. Continuous responsibility for my education and learning is my way of living.*

SWERN, FREDERIC LEE, engineering educator; b. N.Y.C., Sept. 9, 1947; s. Reuben Swern and Anne Lillian Goldberg; m. Gayle Regina Unger, Dec. 25, 1969; children: Lauren, Michael. BEE, City Coll., N.Y.C., 1969; MSEE, Newark Coll. Engr., 1974; PhD Engr. Sci., N.J. Inst. Tech., 1981. Registered profl. engr., N.J. Engr. Navigation and Control divsn. Bendix, Teterboro, N.J., 1969-72, UNIVAC, divsn. Sperry Rand, Morris Plains, N.J., 1972-73; sr. systems analyst Chubb & Son Inc., Short Hills, N.J., 1973-78; sr. engr. Flight Systems divsn. Bendix, Teterboro, N.J., 1978-84; cons. Swerlin Assoc., 1981—; assoc. prof. engring Stevens Inst. Tech., Hoboken, N.J., 1984—; researcher, cons., Westinghouse Elevator, Morristown, N.J., 1987, NASA Langley Rsch. Center, Hampton, Va., 1979-82, 1985-90, Hyatt Clark Industries, Clark, N.J., 1984-85, U.S. Army Armament Rsch. and Devel. Ctr., 1985-92, Gen. Motors Corp., Warren, Mich., 1983-84; reviewer Prentice-Hall, Englewood Cliffs, N.J.; cons. Gov. Commn. on Sci. and Tech., 1985-86. Contbr. to profl. jours. Mem. Inst. Elec. Electronic Engrs., Am. Soc. Mech. Engrs., Assn. Computing Machinery, Am. Inst. Aeronautics and Astronautics, Sigma Xi, Pi Tau Sigma. Achievements include Automatic Flight Control System Patent using instrument landing system information and including inertial filtering means for reduced ILS noise; Aircraft Control System Patent using inertial signals; Improved Flare Control Patent for transport aircraft. Home: 53 Village Rd Florham Park NJ 07932-2412 Office: Stevens Institute of Technology Mechanical Engring Lab Castle Point Hoboken NJ 07030

SWETLIK, WILLIAM PHILIP, orthodontist; b. Manitowoc, Wis., Jan. 31, 1950; s. Leonard Alvin and Lillian Julia (Knipp) S.; m. Cheryl Jean Klein, June 30, 1973 (div.); children: Alison Elizabeth, Lindsey Ann, Adam William; m. Joyce M. Caris, Mar. 10, 1995. Student, Luther Coll., Decorah, Iowa, 1968-70; DDS, Marquette U., 1974; MS in Dentistry, St. Louis U., 1977. Diplomate Am. Bd. Orthodontics. Resident in gen. dentistry USPHS, Norfolk, Va., 1974-75; practice dentistry specializing in orthodontics Green Bay, Wis., 1977—; instr. oral pathology NE Wis. Tech. Coll., Green Bay, 1979-86. Author: (with others) Orthodontic Headgear, 1977. Mem. Prevention Walking Club, Family Crisis Ctr. of Green Bay. Served as lt. USPHS, 1974-75. Fellow Coll. Diplomates Am. Bd. Orthodontics; mem. ADA, Am. Assn. Orthodontists, Wis. Dental Assn. (Continuing Edn. award 1986), Wis. Soc. Orthodontists, Orthodontic Edn. and Research Found., Brown Door Kewaunee Dental Soc. (program chmn. 1985-86, sec., treas. 1986-87, v.p. 1987-88, pres. 1988-89), St. Louis U. Orthodontic Alumni Assn. (pres. 1988-89), Acad. Gen. Dentistry, Violet Club of Am. Roman Catholic. Avocations: racquetball, skiing, jogging, raising violets, recording equipment. Home: 2160 Greenleaf Rd DePere WI 54115-8621 Office: 2654 S Oneida St Green Bay WI 54304-5302

SWETMAN, GLENN ROBERT, English language educator, poet; b. Biloxi, Miss., May 20, 1936; s. Glenn Lyle and June (Read) S. BS, U. So. Miss., 1957, MA, 1959; PhD, Tulane U., 1966; m. Margarita Ortiz, Feb. 8, 1964 (div. 1979); children: Margarita June, Glenn Lyle Maximilian, Glenda Louise. Instr., U. So. Miss., 1957-58, asst. prof., 1964-66; instr. Ark. State U., 1958-59, McNeese U., 1959-61; instr. English, Univ. Coll. Tulane U., 1961-64, spl. asst. dept. elec. engring., 1961-64; assoc. prof. La. Inst. Tech., 1966-67; prof., head dept. langs. Nicholls State Coll., Thibodaux, La., 1967-69, head dept. English, 1969-71, prof., 1971-91, prof. emeritus, William Carey Coll., Gulfport, Miss., 1991—; writer in residence, prof. English William Carey Coll., Gulfport, Miss., 1991—. Ptnr., Breeland Pl., Biloxi, Miss., 1960—; stringer corr. Shreveport (La.) Times, 1966—; ptnr. Ormuba, Inc., 1975—; cons. tech. writing Union Carbide Corp., Am. Fedn. Tchrs. State v.p. Nat. Com. to Resist Attacks on Tenure, 1974—. Subdiv. coord. Rep. Party, Hattiesburg, Miss., 1964. With AUS, 1957. Recipient Poetry awards KQUE Haiku contest, 1964, Coll. Arts contest, L.A., 1966, Black Ship Festival, Yoqosuka, Japan, 1967; Green World Brief Forms award Green World Poetry Editors, 1965. Mem. MLA, S. Cen. MLA, So. Literary Festival Assn. (v.p. 1975-76, 82-83, pres. 1984-85), Coll. Writers Soc. La. (pres. 1971-72, exec. dir. 1983—), IEEE, Am. Assn. Engring. Edn., La. Poetry Soc. (pres. 1971-74, 1986—), Internat. Boswellian Inst., Nat. Fedn. State Poetry Socs. (2d v.p., nat. membership chmn. 1972-74, pres. 1976-77), Nat. Soc. Scholars and Educators (bd. dirs. 1982—, sec. exec. bd. 1986—, sec. bd. dirs. 1968—, sec. soc. 1989—), Am. Fedn. Tchrs. (chpt. pres. 1973-78), Nat. Fedn. State Poetry Socs. (1st v.p. 1975-76, exec. bd. 1972—), Phi Eta Sigma, Omicron Delta Kappa. Book reviewer Jackson (Miss.) State Times, 1961. Poems pub. in various publs. including Poet, Prairie Schooner, Trace, Ball State U. Forum, Film Quar., Poetry Australia, numerous others worldwide; (books of poems) Tunel de Amor, 1973, Deka #1, 1973, Deka #2, 1979, Shards, 1979, Concerning Carpenters, 1980, Son of Igor, 1980; A Range of Sonnets, 1981, Christmas, 1982, Poems of the Fantastic, 1990; contbr. articles (147) to encys.; cons. editor (poetry) Paon Press, 1974—, Scott-Foresman, 1975; editorial bd. Scholar and Educator, 1980—. Home: PO Box 146 Biloxi MS 39533-0146 Office: Nicholls State U Thibodaux LA 70310 also: William Carey Coll 1856 Beach Dr Gulfport MS 39507-1508

SWETNAM, DANIEL RICHARD, lawyer; b. Columbus, Ohio, Dec. 22, 1957; s. Joseph Neri and Audrey Marguerite (Mason) S.; m. Jeannette Deanna Dean, June 7, 1980; children: Jeremiah Daniel, Laura Janelle, Andrew Michael. BA, Ohio State U., 1979; JD, U. Cin., 1982. Bar: Ohio 1982, U.S. Dist. Ct. (so. dist.) Ohio 1982, U.S. Ct. Appeals (6th cir.) 1986, U.S. Supreme Ct. 1986. Assoc. Schwartz, Warren & Ramirez, Columbus, 1982-88, ptnr., 1989-96; mem. Schottenstein, Zox & Dunn, Columbus, 1997—. Deacon Grace Brethren Ch., Worthington, Ohio, 1989—; mem. Grace Brethren Christian Schs. Commn., 1993—. Mem. ABA, Ohio State Bar Assn., Columbus Bar Assn., Comml. Law League Am., Order of Coif. Republican. Avocations: golf, tennis. Home: 2178 Stowmont Ct Dublin OH 43016-9563 Office: Schottenstein Zox & Dunn 41 S High St Columbus OH 43215-6101

SWETNAM, MONTE NEWTON, petroleum exploration executive; b. Alexandria, La., Oct. 9, 1936; s. Montreville Morris and Margaret Elizabeth (Cullison) S.; m. Elaine Adelia Taylor, Dec. 21, 1957; children: Scott David, Robert Troy. Student, Johns Hopkins, 1955-58; B.S. in Geology, U. Wyo., 1960, M.S. in Geology, 1961; M.B.A. in Bus. Adminstrn, Pepperdine U., 1978. Registered geologist, Calif. Exploration geologist Amerada Petroleum Corp., Durango, Colo., 1961-63; exploration geologist Tenneco Oil Co., Durango, 1963-65; dist. project geologist Tenneco Oil Co., Bakersfield, Calif., 1965-69; div. staff geologist Tenneco Oil Co., Bakersfield, 1969; partner Argonaut Oil & Gas Cons., Denver, 1969-71; internat. exploration mgr. Tesoro Petroleum Corp., San Antonio, 1971-73; v.p. internat. exploration Tesoro Petroleum Corp., 1973-74, sr. v.p. exploration, 1974-82; pres. Tesoro-Bolivia Petroleum Co., 1975-82, Tesoro-Algeria Petroleum Co., 1975-82; sr. v.p. exploration Natural Resource Mgmt. Corp./NRM, Dallas, 1983-86; sr. v.p. exploration and prodn. Harken Energy Corp., 1987-89, exec. v.p., 1991-93; pres. Harken Exploration Co., 1988-91, Harken Bahrain Oil Co., 1989-93; exec. v.p., chief oper. officer Giant Exploration and Prodn. Co., Farmington, N.Mex., 1994-96; v.p. refining ops. Giant Industries, Inc., Scottsdale, Ariz., 1996—; pres. Canyon Marinas, Inc., San Antonio. Contbr. articles to profl. jours. Mem. Am. Assn. Petroleum Geologists, Geol. Soc. Am., Sigma Xi. Republican. Clubs: Alamo Yacht, Lake Canyon Yacht. Home: 30600 N Pima Rd # 49 Scottsdale AZ 85262 Office: 23733 N Scottsdale Rd Scottsdale AZ 85255-3465

SWETS, JOHN ARTHUR, psychologist, researcher; b. Grand Rapids, Mich., June 19, 1928; s. John A. and Sara Henrietta (Heyns) S.; m. Maxine Ruth Crawford, July 16, 1949; children—Stephen Arthur, Joel Brian. B.A., U. Mich., Ann Arbor, 1950, M.A., 1953, Ph.D., 1954. Instr. psychology U. Mich., Ann Arbor, 1954-56; asst. prof. psychology M.I.T., Cambridge, 1956-60, assoc. prof. psychology, 1960-63; v.p. Bolt Beranek & Newman Inc., Cambridge, 1964-69, sr. v.p., 1969-74, gen. mgr. research, devel. and cons., dir., 1971-74; chief scientist BBN Labs., Cambridge, 1975—; lectr. dept. clin. epidemiology Harvard Med. Sch., 1985-88, dept. health care policy, 1988—; mem. corp. Edn. Devel. Ctr., Newton, Mass., 1971-75; vis. rsch. fellow Philips Labs., The Netherlands, 1958; Regents' prof. U. Calif., 1969; advisor vision com., com. on hearing and bioacoustics NAS-NRC, 1960-96; mem. Commn. on Behavioral Social Scis. and Edn., NRC, 1988-92, vice chair, 1992-93, chmn., 1993-96; sci. advisor, cons., lectr. numerous govtl. and profl. orgns. Author: Signal Detection Theory and ROC Analysis in Psychology and Diagnostics, 1996; co-author: (with D.M. Green) Signal Detection Theory and Psychophysics, 1966, (with R.M. Pickett) Evaluation of Diagnostic Systems: Methods From Signal Detection Theory, 1982; editor: Signal Detection and Recognition by Human Observers, 1964, (with L.L. Elliott) Psychology and the Handicapped Child, 1974, (with D. Druckman) Enhancing Human Performance, 1988; mem. editl. bd. Med. Decision Making, 1980-85, Psychol. Sci., 1989-94, Psychol. Rev., 1995-97, Jour. Exptl. Psychology: Applied, 1995-97; contbr. articles to profl. jours. Past mem. numerous civic orgns.; mem. corp. Winchester Hosp., Mass., 1981-84. Fellow AAAS (coun. 1986-89), APA (Disting. Sci. Contbn. award 1990), Am. Acad. Arts and Scis., Acoustical Soc. Am. (exec. coun. 1968-71), Soc. Exptl. Psychologists (chmn. 1986, exec. com. 1986-89, Howard Crosby Warren medal 1985), Am. Psychol. Soc.; mem. NAS (Troland award com. 1991, chmn. 1992), Psychonomic Soc., Psychometric Soc., Soc. Math. Psychology, Sigma Xi, Sigma Alpha Epsilon, Winchester Country Club. Congregationalist (moderator). Office: BBN Corp 10 Moulton St Cambridge MA 02138-1119

SWETT, ALBERT HERSEY, retired lawyer, business executive, consultant; b. Medina, N.Y., Feb. 18, 1923; s. Raymond Fuller and Marion (Hersey) S.; m. Mary Stewart, Oct. 10, 1944; children: Marion Hersey Swett Robinson, Margaret Stewart Swett Haskell, Albert Louis. Grad., The Hill Sch., 1941; B.Engring., Yale U., 1944; LL.B., Harvard U., 1949. Bar: N.Y. 1949. Assoc. Harris, Beach & Wilcox, Rochester, N.Y., 1949-56, ptnr., 1957-66; v.p., gen. counsel Xerox Corp., Stamford, Conn., 1966-75; v.p., gen. counsel Coca-Cola Co., Atlanta, 1975-78, v.p., counsel to chmn., 1978-80; ind. cons., 1980—. Trustee Practising Law Inst., 1977-83. Served with USNR, 1942-46. Mem. Assn. Gen. Counsel (emeritus), Tau Beta Pi. Republican. Methodist. Lodge: Masons. Home: PO Box 30319 River Ranch FL 33867-0319

SWETT, STEPHEN FREDERICK, JR., principal, educator; b. Englewood, N.J., Sept. 14, 1935; s. Stephen Frederick and Frances (Gulotta) S.; B.A., Montclair State Coll., 1959, M.A., 1965; Ed.D. in Ednl. Adminstrn., Rutgers U., 1976, graduate North Light Art School, 1995; m. Annette Palazzolo, Nov. 18, 1961; children—Susan, Kimberly Ann, Stephen Laurence. Tchr., Long Branch (N.J.) High Sch., 1961-62, Roselle Park (N.J.) High Sch., 1962-73; research asst. Rutgers U., New Brunswick, N.J., 1973-74; instructional supr. Elmwood Park (N.J.) Schs., 1974-76, Morris Hills Regional Schs., Denville, N.J., 1976-77; asst. prin. Lawrence High Sch., Lawrenceville, N.J., 1977-79; prin. Stafford Intermediate Sch., Manahawkin, N.J., 1979-94, recreation and art cons., 1994—. participant NSF Inst. in physics, chemistry and math. Seton Hall U., 1964, Newark Coll. Engring., 1965, Stevens Inst. Tech., summers 1966-68. Served with AUS, 1959-61. Mem. Roselle Park

Edn. Assn. (pres. 1971-73). Nat. Soc. Study Edn., Am. Assn. Physics Tchrs., Am. Inst. Physics, Am., N.J. assns. sch. adminstrs., Nat. Assn. Elementary and Middle Sch. Adminstrs., N.J. Assn. Elementary and Middle Sch. Adminstrs., Nat. Assn. Secondary Sch. Prins., Phi Delta Kappa (sec. Rutgers chpt. 1977-80, v.p. 1980-82, pres. 1983-84). Research on sch. fin. Home: 12 Louis St Old Bridge NJ 08857-2235

SWEZEY, CHARLES MASON, Christian ethics educator, administrator; b. Charlottesville, Va., May 16, 1935; s. Fenton Hendy and Catherine Jane (Mason) S.; m. Mary Evelyn Knight, June 16, 1960; children: Christopher Stephen, Margaret Fenton, Mary Mason. BA, Washington and Lee U., 1957; BD, Union Theol. Sem., 1961; STM, Yale U., 1962; MA, Phd, Vanderbilt U., 1974, 78. Ordained to ministry, Presbyterian Ch., 1962. Asst. minister Lexington (Va.) Presbyn. Ch., 1962-70; stated clk. Lexington Presbytery, 1967-68; vis. lectr. Mary Baldwin Coll., Staunton, Va., 1966-67, 68; asst. prof. Union Theol. Sem., Richmond, Va., 1974-80, assoc. prof., 1980-83, prof. Christian ethics, 1983—, dean of faculty, 1990-95; mem. coop. com. on examination for candidates, Presbyn. Ch. U.S.A., 1978-88. Editorial bd. Interpretation, Richmond, 1981-92; co-editor: James Gustafson's Theocentric Ethics, 1988; contbr. articles to theol. publs. Bd. dirs. Va. Blood Svcs., 1987-95; mem. Human Fetal Tissue Transplantation panel NIH, Bethesda, Md., 1988. Grantee Danforth Found., 1968-69; Woodrow Wilson Found. fellow, 1970-71. Mem. Soc. Christian Ethics. Office: Union Theol Sem 3401 Brook Rd Richmond VA 23227-4514

SWHIER, CLAUDIA VERSFELT, lawyer; b. Mineola, N.Y., Jan. 15, 1950; d. William Holly and Ruth (Gerland) Versfelt; ; children: James Robert, Jeffrey William. BA in Philosophy magna cum laude, Yale U., 1972; JD cum laude, Harvard U., 1975. Bar: Ind. 1975. Assoc. Barnes & Thornburg, Indpls., 1975-82, ptnr., 1982—. Mem. editorial bd. Harvard Law Rev., 1973-75; editor Thrift Law in Rev., Banking Law in Rev., 1989—. Mem. ABA, Ind. Bar Assn., Indpls. Bar Assn. Republican. Presbyterian. Avocations: skiing, swimming, aerobics. Office: Barnes & Thornburg 1313 Mchts Bank Bldg Indianapolis IN 46204

SWIBEL, HOWARD JAY, lawyer, investment advisor; b. Chgo., July 9, 1950; s. Charles Robert and Seena (Minkus) S.; m. Sheryl Siegel, June 19, 1973; children: Matthew, Brian, Justin, Alison. BA, Harvard U., 1972, JD, 1975. Bar: Ill. 1975, U.S. Dist. Ct. (no. dist.) Ill. 1975, U.S. Ct. Appeals (7th cir.) 1977. Ptnr. Kirkland & Ellis, Chgo., 1975-83, Arnstein & Lehr, Chgo., 1983-; mem. Nat. Conf. Commrs. on Uniform State Laws, Chgo., 1976—; mem. Midwest Regional Bd. Anti-Defamation League. Mem. instl. rev. bd. Ill. Cancer Council, Chgo., 1986—; pres. Cmty. Found. Jewish Edn. Met. Chgo., 1986-. Mem. ABA, Ill. Bar Assn., Chgo. Bar Assn., Harvard Club (bd. dirs. Chgo. 1975-85). Jewish. Avocations: investments, tennis, skiing, travel. Office: Arnstein & Lehr 120 S Riverside Plz Ste 1200 Chicago IL 60606-3910

SWIBEL, STEVEN WARREN, lawyer; b. Chgo., July 18, 1946; s. Morris Howard and Gloria S.; m. Leslie Cohen; children: Deborah, Laura. BS, MIT, 1968; JD, Harvard U., 1971. Bar: Ill. 1971, U.S. Dist. Ct. (no. dist.) Ill. 1971, U.S. Tax Ct. 1973, U.S. Ct. Appeals (7th cir.) 1981. Assoc. Sonnenschein Carlin Nath & Rosenthal, Chgo., 1971-78, ptnr., 1978-84; ptnr. Rudnick & Wolfe, 1984-93; ptnr. Schwartz, Cooper, Greenberger, Krauss Chartered, 1993—; adj. prof. taxation Ill. Inst. Tech. Kent Coll. Law, Chgo., 1989—; lectr. in field. Contbr. articles to profl. jours. Ednl. counselor MIT, 1979—; bd. dirs. MIT Alumni Fund, 1992-95, Ragdale Found., 1987—, treas. 1987-92. Recipient Lobdell Disting. Svc. award MIT Alumni Assn., 1989. Mem. ABA (com. partnerships sect. taxation), Ill. Bar Assn., Chgo. Bar Assn. (fed. taxation com., exec. subcom. 1984—, chmn. subcom. on real estate, partnerships and tax sheltered investments 1986-87, vice chmn. 1988-89, chmn. 1989-90), Met. Club, MIT Club (dir. Chgo. chpt. 1980-91, 96—, sec. 1980-87, pres. 1987-89), Sigma Xi, Tau Beta Pi, Eta Kappa Nu. Office: Schwartz Cooper Greenberger & Krauss Chartered 180 N La Salle St Ste 2700 Chicago IL 60601-2709

SWICK, HERBERT MORRIS, medical educator, neurologist; b. Baton Rouge, Nov. 22, 1941; s. Edgar Haight and Mary Ellen (Morris) S.; m. Mary Lynne McCluggage, June 29, 1963; children: Kristin Ann, Elizabeth May, Diane Marie. BA with honors, Johns Hopkins U., 1963, MD, 1966. Cert. Am. Bd. Psychiatry and Neurology, Am. Bd. Pediatrics. Resident in pediat. Johns Hopkins U., Balt., 1966-69; resident in neurology U. Ky., Lexington, 1971-74, asst. prof. neurology and pediat., 1974-75; from asst. to prof. neurology and pediat. Med. Coll. Wis., Milw., 1975-94, asst. dean med. edn., interm chmn. dept. neurology, 1987-88, from assoc. to sr. assoc. dean acad. affairs, 1988-93, sr. assoc. dean for acad. programs, 1993-94; prof. neurology, sr. assoc. dean acad. affairs U. Kans. Sch. Medicine, Kansas City, 1994—; acting chmn. dept. history and philosophy of medicine Sch. Medicine U. Kans., Kansas City, 1995; interim exec. dean U. Kans. Sch. Medicine, Kansas City, 1995-97; chief dept. neurology Children's Hosp. Wis., Milw., 1981-87, acting chmn. dept. neurology, 1987-88; vis. prof. neurol. edn. Mayo Clinic and Found., Rochester, Minn., 1985. Contbr. numerous articles to profl. jours. Bd. dirs. Milw. Chamber Music Soc., 1982-88, pres. 1986-88. Served to lt. commdr., USN, 1969-71. Fulbright sr. scholar, 1978. Fellow Am. Acad. Neurology (edn. com., undergrad. edn. subcom. 1985-89); mem. Am. Assn. History Medicine, Child Neurology Soc. (archives and history com. 1981-88, exec. com. 1982-86, sci. selection com. 1983, 84), Columbia History of Medicine Club, Internat. Child Neurology Assn., Milw. Acad. Medicine (coun. 1993-94), Profs. of Child Neurology, Wis. Neurol. Soc. (sec.-treas. 1981-82, pres.-elect 1982-84, pres. 1984-85), Assn. Univ. Profs. in Neurology (undergrad. edn. com. 1979-86), Assn. Am. Med. Colls. (coun. deans 1995—).

SWID, STEPHEN CLAAR, business executive; b. N.Y.C., Oct. 26, 1940; s. David and Selma (Claar) S.; m. Nan Goldman, Mar. 1, 1963; children: Robin, Scott, Jill. BS, Ohio State U., 1962. Mgmt. trainee Alside Aluminum Co., Akron, Ohio, 1962-63; securities analyst Dreyfus Fund, N.Y.C., 1963-66; sr. investment officer Oppenheimer Fund, N.Y.C., 1966-67; gen. ptnr. City Assocs., 1967-69, Swid Investors, N.Y.C., 1970-78; co-chmn. bd. Gen. Felt Industries Inc., Saddle Brook, N.J., 1974-86, Knoll Internat., 1977-86; chmn. bd., CEO SBK Entertainment World, Inc., N.Y.C., 1986-89; chmn., chief exec. officer SCS Comm., N.Y.C., 1989—; chmn. strategy com., dir. Inst. for East-West Studies; dir. Rexene Corp.; gen. ptnr. Swid Ptnrs. Trustee Solomon Guggenheim Mus.; mem. vis. com. 20th century art Met. Mus. Art; past trustee Horace Mann Sch., N.Y.C.; former exec. vp. bd. dirs. Lenox Sch. N.Y.; chmn. Mcpl. Art Soc. Office: SCS Communications 152 W 57th St New York NY 10019-3301

SWIDEN, LADELL RAY, travel company executive; b. Sioux Falls, S.D., June 17, 1938; s. Alick and Mildred Elizabeth (Larson) S.; m. Phyllis Lorriane Enga, Sept. 10, 1961; children: David, Daniel, Shari. BSEE, S.D. State U., 1961; MBA, U. S.D., 1982. Registered profl. engr., S.D., Minn. Instrument engr. Honeywell, Mpls., 1962-67; v.p. sales Swiden Appliance and Furniture, Sioux Falls, 1967-68; engring. mgr. Raven Industries, Inc., Sioux Falls, 1968-84; v.p. engring. Beta Raven Inc., St. Louis, 1984-85; pres. Delta Systems, Inc., St. Louis, 1985-86; acting dir. Engring. and Environ. Rsch. Ctr. S.D. State U., Brookings, 1986-94, dir. univ./industry tech. svc., 1986-94; v.p. Village Travel Inc., Brookings, 1994—; bd. dirs. Brookings Econ. Devel. Ctr.; mem. Carlson Wagonlit Travel Assoc. Adv. Bd. Patentee in field. Chmn. Indsl. Devel. Com., Brookings, 1989-90, vice-chair, 1988-89; chmn. bldg. com. Ascension Luth. Ch., 1988-90. Mem. NSPE, Nat. Assn. of Mgmt. and Tech. Assistance Ctrs. (bd. dirs.), Instrument Soc. Am., Aircraft Owners and Pilots Assn., Exptl. Aircraft Assn., Am. Bonanza Soc., S.D. Engring. Soc. (pres. N.E. chpt. 1991-92), Rotary, Elks. Avocations: flying, travel. Home: 105 Heather Ln Brookings SD 57006-4123 Office: Village Travel Inc 1715 6th St Brookings SD 57006-1677

SWIDLER, JOSEPH CHARLES, lawyer; b. Chgo., Jan. 28, 1907; s. Abraham and Dora (Cromer) S.; m. Gertrude Tyrna, 1944; children: Ann, Mark. Student, U. Ill., U. Fla.; Ph.B., U. Chgo., 1929, J.D., 1930. Pvt. law practice Chgo., 1930-33; asst. solicitor U.S. Dept. Interior, 1933; mem. legal dept. TVA, 1933-57; gen. counsel, sec., chmn. bd. TVA Retirement System, 1945-57; counsel Alien Property Bur., Dept. Justice, 1941, Power Div., War Prodn. Bd., 1942; pvt. practice law Knoxville and Nashville, 1957-61; chmn. FPC, 1961-65; mem. Water Resources Council, 1964-65, Swidler & Belnap, Washington, 1966-70; chmn. N.Y. State Pub. Service Commn., Albany, 1970-74; dir. Inst. Pub. Policy Alternatives, SUNY, Albany, 1974-75; ptnr. Leva, Hawes, Symington, Martin & Oppenheimer, Washington, 1975-82; counsel Swidler & Berlin, Washington, 1982—; bd. dirs. Nat. Regulatory Rsch. Inst.; mem. adv. coun. Electric Power Rsch. Inst., 1973-80, Gas Rsch. Inst. Served with USNR, 1943-45. Fellow Nat. Acad. Pub. Adminstrn. Home: 8100 Connecticut Ave Apt 1608 Bethesda MD 20815 Office: 3000 K St NW Washington DC 20007-5109

SWIECICKI, MARTIN, neurosurgeon; b. Camden, N.J., June 29, 1934; s. Martin E. and Annetta Swiecicki; m. Gloria J. Whelpley; children: Diane, Annette, Karen, Sheryl, Martin C. BA, Colgate U., 1956; MD, Hahnemann Med. Sch., 1960. Diplomate Am. Bd. Neurol. Surgery. Intern West Jersey Hosp., Camden, 1960-61; resident in neurological surgery Jefferson U., Phila., 1961-65; mem. staff in neurol. surgery West Jersey Hosp., Camden, Berlin, N.J., 1967—, chief Neurol. Surgery, 1967-89; clin. assoc prof. Neurol. Surgery Hahnemann Med. Coll., Phila., 1977—. Contbr. articles to profl. jours. Recipient N.J. Gov.'s award for Outstanding Svcs., 1970, 71, 72, 73, Award for Support and Svc. Boy Scouts Am., 1992. Fellow ACS; mem. AMA, Camden County Med. Soc. (v.p.1993, pres. 1995), West Jersey Med. Soc., N.J. State Med. Soc., N.J. Neurosurg. Soc.(sec.-treas. 978-79, pres. 1981, chmn. peer rev. com. 1983-89, mem. peer rev. com. 1977—), Camden County Med. Soc. (exec. com. 1977—, v.p. 1993, pres.- elect 1994, pres. 1995), Soc. Air Force Clin. Surgeons, Am. Assn. Neurol. Surgeons. Office: Neurosurg Assocs NJ 2301 E Evesham Rd Ste 406 Voorhees NJ 08043-4505

SWIENER, RITA ROCHELLE, psychologist, educator; b. Pitts., July 31, 1941; d. Julius D. and Rose (Sheinbein) Swiener; 1 child, Samuel L. Schuff. BA, U. Mo., St. Louis, 1970; MA in Psychology, So. Ill. U., Edwardsville, 1973. Prof. Psychology State Cmty. Coll., East St. Louis, Ill., 1972-96; pvt. practice St. Louis, 1972—; adj. faculty St. Louis C.C., Meramac, 1993—; pres. Ill. C.C. Faculty Assn., 1979-80; trustee State Univs. Retirement Sys., 1990; pres. local 3912 IFT-AFT, East St. Louis, 1983-92; chairperson social and behavior panel Ill. C.C. Bd. and Bd. of Higher Edn. Articulation Initiative, 1992-96. Pres. Call-for-Help, Inc., Edgemont, Ill., 1990-92, 94-97; pres. and founder Santa's Helpers, Inc., St. Louis, 1966—; mem., founder Joy E. Whitener scholarship com. U. Mo. at St. Louis, 1990—. Recipient Outstanding C.C. Faculty Mem. award Ill. C.C. Trustees Assn., 1985, David Erikson award for Outstanding Leadership Ill. C.C. Faculty Assn., 1988, Hometown Hero award KPLR-TV, Suburban Jour., Hardees, St. Louis, 1994, Christmas Spirit award KSD-TV, John Pertzborn, St. Louis, 1990. Mem. APA, U. Mo. St. Louis Psychology Alumni Assn. (treas. 1989-91, Disting. Alumni award 1992), St. Louis Women Psychologist, Mo. Psychol. Assn. Jewish. Avocations: boating, travel, reading. Home: 7832 Balson Ave Saint Louis MO 63130-3624

SWIFT, CALVIN THOMAS, electrical and computer engineering educator; b. Quantico, Va., Feb. 6, 1937; s. Thomas and Elsie (Hill) S.; m. Joanne Taylor, Sept. 5, 1959; children: Pamela, Janet. B.S., MIT, 1959; M.S., Va. Poly. Inst., 1965; Ph.D., William and Mary Coll., 1969. Research engr. N. Am. Aviation Co., Downey, Calif., 1959-62; aerospace technologist NASA, Hampton, Va., 1962-81; prof. elec. and computer engring. U. Mass., Amherst, 1981—; cons. engring., Amherst, 1981—. Editor: Transactions on Geoscience and Remote Sensing, 1980-84; assoc. editor: Jour. Oceanic Engring., 1980-84. F.L. Thompson fellow NASA, 1977. Fellow IEEE; mem. Internat. Union Radio Sci. (chmn. Commn. F 1988-91), Antennas and Propagation Soc. (adminstrv. com. 1974-77, 80-85), Geosci. and Remote Sensing Soc. (adminstrv. com. 1978-86, pres. 1985, Disting. Achievement award 1994). Office: U Mass Dept Elec & Computer Engring Amherst MA 01003

SWIFT, EDWARD FOSTER, III, investment banker; b. Chgo., Nov. 1, 1923; s. Theodore Philip I and Elizabeth (Hoyt) S.; m. Joan McKelvy, July 2, 1947; children: Theodore Philip II, Edward McKelvy, Lockhart McKelvy, Elizabeth Hoyt; m. Carol Coffey Whipple, June 21, 1968. Grad., Hotchkiss Sch., 1941; BA, Yale U., 1945. With Esmark, Inc. (formerly Swift & Co.), 1947-75, asst. to v.p. charge meat packing plants, 1958, asst. v.p., 1958-59, v.p. for provisions, fgn., casings and storage, 1959-64, exec. v.p., 1964-75; vice-chmn. Chgo. Corp., 1975-79; vice chmn. Bacon, Whipple & Co., Chgo., 1980-84; mng. dir. A.G. Becker Paribas Inc., Chgo., 1984-85; with E.F. Hutton and Co., Chgo., 1985-87; mng. dir. Shearson Lehman Hutton Inc, Chgo., 1987-92; bd. dirs. Santa Fe Pacific Pipelines, Inc. Chmn. So. Ind. chpt. United Negro Coll. Fund, 1956; trustee Northwestern U., Evanston, Ill.; bd. dirs. Northwestern Meml. Hosp., Chgo. Served to capt. U.S. Army, 1942-46. Mem. Chgo. Assn. Commerce and Industry (bd. dirs.), Scroll and Key, Chgo. Club, Racquet Club, Econ. Club, Valley Club, Comml. Club, Onwentsia Club, Old Elm ClubBirnam Wood Golf Club, Aurelian Honor Soc. Home: 1500 N Astor St Chicago IL 60610-1640 Office: 70 W Madison St Ste 1400 Chicago IL 60602-4267

SWIFT, FRANK MEADOR, lawyer; b. N.Y.C., Dec. 27, 1911; s. Frank Meador and Alberta (Rankin) S.; m. Harriet Elizabeth Simpson, May 30, 1944; children: Frank Meador, Thomas Lamar. Student, Emory U., 1930-32; LL.B., U. Ga., 1935. Bar: Ga. 1935. Partner Swift, Currie, McGhee & Hiers, Atlanta, 1965-82; of counsel Swift, Currie, McGhee & Hiers, 1982—. Served to comdr. USNR, 1942-46. Mem. Am., Ga. bar assns., Lawyers Club Atlanta, Am. Judicature Soc. Republican. Presbyn. Clubs: Piedmont Driving. Home: 3150 Palisades Ct Marietta GA 30067-5130 Office: Swift Currie McGhee & Hiers 1355 Peachtree St NE Atlanta GA 30309-3269

SWIFT, HUMPHREY HATHAWAY, manufacturing executive; b. Phila., Apr. 18, 1915; s. Robert Wesselhoeft and Edith (Steel) S.; m. Dorothea Banks, Apr. 8, 1943 (dec. 1951); children: Edith S., Alexandra Swift Bigelow; m. Pamela Ann Whitney, June 6, 1953; children: Pamela Swift Tarnower, Hope S. Baker, Alison Clarke. AB, U. N.C., 1939. Salesman Swift & Anderson Inc., 1946-50; mgr. sales Standard Thermometer Inc., Boston, 1951-55, pres., 1960-70; exec. v.p. Swift Instruments Inc., Boston, 1959-68, pres., 1968—; v.p. Swift Instruments Internat. S.A., Boston, 1959-68, pres., 1968—. Mem. Hingham (Mass.) Adv. Com., 1965-66, Hingham Town Com., 1955-60; trustee Manomet Obs., 1994—, New Eng. Deaconess Hosp., 1954-73; overseer U.S. Constitution Mus., 1995—, Childrens Hosp., 1990-95, hon. overseer, 1995—. Mem. World Trade Ctr., Photog. Mktg., Nat. Sporting Good Assn., St. Anthony Club, New Bedford Yacht Club, Hingham Yacht Club, Corinthians. Republican. Episcopalian. Avocations: sailing, skiing. Office: Swift Instruments Inc 952 Dorchester Ave Boston MA 02125-1219

SWIFT, JANE MARIA, former state senator; b. North Adams, Mass., Feb. 24, 1965; d. John Maynard and Jean Mary (Kent) S.; m. Charles T. Hunt III, Feb. 19, 1994. BA in Am. Studies, Trinity Coll., Hartford, Conn., 1987. Exec. mgmt. trainee G. Fox & Co., Hartford, 1987-88; adminstrv. aide Sen. Peter C. Webber, Boston, 1988-90; mem. Mass. State Senate, Boston, 1991-96; coord. strategic devel. of regional airports Mass. Port Authority, Boston, 1997—; 3d asst. minority leader, 1993—. Republican. Roman Catholic. Office: Massport 10 Park Plz Boston MA 02116 also: Jane Swift for Congress PO Box 551 5 North St Pittsfield MA 01202*

SWIFT, JILL ANNE, industrial engineer, educator; b. Memphis, Nov. 12, 1959; d. Gary Green and Sharon (Willoughby) Brown; m. Fredrick Wallace Swift, June 12, 1987; children: Andrew, Samantha. BS, Memphis State U., 1981, MS, 1982; PhD, Okla. State U., 1987. Registered profl. engr., Fla.; cert. quality engr. Design engr. DuPont Co., Glasgow, Del., 1982-83; head dept. physics Coll. Boca Raton, Fla., 1983-87; asst. prof. indsl. engring. U. Miami, Coral Gables, Fla., 1987-96; quality cons., 1996—; vis. scholar Air Force Inst. Tech., Wright-Patterson AFB, Ohio, 1988; cons. A.T. Kearney, Amman, Jordan, 1990; quality liaison U. Miami Inst. Study of Quality in Mfg. and Svc., 1988—; cons., spkr. in field. Author: Introduction to Modern Statistical Quality Control and Management, 1995, Principles of Total Quality Control, 1996; co-author: Principles of Total Quality, 1997; contbr. articles to profl. publs. Mem. IIE (chpt. dir. 1988-90, Christmas toy dr. coord. 1989, 90), Am. Soc. Engring. Edn., Am. Soc. Quality Control, Phi Kappa Phi, Alpha Pi Mu (faculty adviser 1988-96), Tau Beta Pi. Republican. Avocations: racquetball, water skiing, cross-stitch, reading, roller blading.

SWIFT, JOHN FRANCIS, health care advertising company executive; b. N.Y.C., June 15, 1935; s. John F. and Mary Veronica (Kehoe) S.; m. Eleanor H. Cunniff, Oct. 10, 1964; children—John Francis, Sharon Ann. B.S. in Bus. Adminstrn, Seton Hall U., 1960, postgrad., 1960-61. Mktg. research mgr. Lederle Labs. div. Cyanamid Internat., 1960-63; account exec. Robert A. Becker Advt. Agy., N.Y.C., 1963-66; mgr. new products Chesebrough Ponds Co., N.Y.C., 1966-68; v.p. Frohlich Intercon Co., N.Y.C., 1968-72; pres., chief exec. officer Lavey/Wolff/Swift, Inc., N.Y.C., 1972-91, chmn., chief exec. officer, 1991-94; pres., chief exec. officer BBDO Health & Med. Comms. Inc., 1977-91; chmn., chief exec. officer Health & Med. Comms. Inc., 1991—; vice chmn. Lyons Lavey Nickel Swift, Inc., 1995—. Bd. govs. Cathedral Healthcare Systems, 1991—; chmn. Cathedral Healthcare Found., 1994—. Served with USN, 1955-57. Mem. Pharm. Advt. Coun. (pres. 1979), Bio-Med. Mktg. Assn., Canoe Brook (Summit, N.J.), Skytop Club (Pa.), Boca Raton (Fla.) Country Club, N.Y. Athletic Club. Home: 32 Peppermill Rd Chatham Twp NJ 07928-1312 also: 600 S Ocean Blvd Boca Raton FL 33432 also: 76 Bay Point Harbour Pt Pleasant NJ 08742-5509 Office: Health and Medical Communications Inc 488 Madison Ave New York NY 10022-5702

SWIFT, JONATHAN, educator, tenor; b. Glasgow, Scotland, Apr. 26, 1932; came to U.S., 1948, naturalized, 1954; s. John Francis and Catherine Little (McGowan) S.; M.A., Wayne State U., 1957; postgrad. Ecole Normale Superieure de St. Cloud, Paris, 1954-55; cert. Conservatoire Nat. de Musique (France), 1955; postgrad. U. Mich., 1959, Cambridge U., 1981; PhD, Mich. State U., 1983, studied with Georges Jouatte, Paris Opera. On-camera tchr. French, Sta. WTVS, Detroit, 1955-56, Am. lit., 1960-62; instr. French, Wayne State U., Detroit, 1955-60; tchr. English, French and social studies Detroit Pub. Schs., 1957-64; tchr. English and history Glasgow Corp. Schs., 1967; tchr. English and French, Livonia (Mich.) Pub. Schs., 1967; chmn. English dept. Stevenson High Sch., Livonia, 1970-78, dir. Sch. Global Edn., 1978—; sr. lectr. Mich. State U. Debut in opera as Alfredo in La Traviata, 1961; host PBS TV and cmty. t.v. series Global Connections, Time Out for Opera; leading tenor with Detroit Piccolo Opera Co., 1961-86, Detroit Grand Opera Assn., 1965, Mich. Opera Co., 1961-64; concert soloist with major symphonies in U.S., Can., Europe, Australia, 1961-81; appeared as tenor soloist in various radio and TV programs, 1961-81; rec. artist with Scotia and Andis (U.K.). Recipient French Govt. medal, 1954; tribute Mich. State Legislature, 1984, NEA Applegate-Dorros award, 1987, MEA Siddall Internat. award, 1987, Philo Farnsworth award Alliance Cmty. Media, 1990, 94, 95, Hometown award Nat. Fedn. Local Cable Programmers, 1994, Nat. TV award Nat. Assn. Telecomm. Officers and Advs., 1995; Fulbright scholar, 1954-55. Mem. Soc. Friends of St. George, Descs. of Knights of Garter. Roman Catholic. Contbr. articles and poems to profl. and lit. jours. Office: 33500 6 Mile Rd Livonia MI 48152-3156

SWIFT, RICHARD G(ENE), composer, educator; b. Middlepoint, Ohio, Sept. 24, 1927; s. Lisle Russell and Josephine (Ladd) S.; m. Dorothy Zackrisson, Feb. 10, 1951; children: Jeremy, John, Joel. MA, U. Chgo., 1956. Assoc. prof. music U. Calif., Davis, 1956-67, prof., 1967-91, prof. emeritus, 1991—, chmn. dept., 1963-71; vis. prof. Princeton U., 1977; faculty research lectr. U. Calif., 1983-84. Composer: A Coronal, 1954, String Quartet I, 1956, II, 1958, III, 1964, Sonata for Clarinet and Piano, 1957, Sonata for Solo Violin, 1958, Eve, 1959, Stravaganza III for Clarinet, Violin and Piano, 1960, Concerto for Piano and Chamber Ensemble, 1961, Extravaganza for Orchestra, 1962, Domains, I, II, III, 1963, Bucolics, 1964, Concerto for Violin and Chamber Ensemble, 1967, Music for A While, 1969, Thanatopsis, 1971, Prime, 1973, Quartet IV, 1973, Specimen Days, 1976, Mein blaues Klavier, 1979, Concerto II for piano and chamber ensemble, 1980, Quartet V, 1982, Things of August, 1985, Roses Only, 1991, In Arcadia, 1994; consulting editor: 19th Century Music. Served with AUS, 1950-52. Recipient award Rockefeller Found., 1956, 68; award Fromm Found.; Composers String Quartet award, 1973; award Nat. Endowment for Arts, 1976; Inst. award Am. Acad. and Inst. Arts and Letters, 1978; Disting. Teaching award U. Calif., 1980. Fellow Inst. Creative Arts; mem. Am. Music Ctr., ASCAP, Soc. for Music Theory, The Soc. of Composers. Home: 568 S Campus Way Davis CA 95616-3523

SWIFT, RICHARD J., engineering company executive; b. 1944. BS, U.S. Mil. Acad., 1966; MS, Purdue U., 1972; MBA, Fairleigh Dickinson U., 1972. With TVA, 1970-72; with Foster Wheeler Corp., Clinton, N.J., 1972-76, from various mgmt. positions to pres., COO, 1977-94, chmn. bd., pres., CEO, 1994—; with Union Carbide Corp., 1976-77. Served U.S. Army, 1966-70. Office: Foster Wheeler Corp Perryville Corp Pk Clinton NJ 08809*

SWIFT, ROBERT FREDERIC, music educator; b. Ilion, N.Y., July 7, 1940; s. Frederic Fay and Ruth Eleanor (Ainslie) S.; m. Margot Sue Werme, Nov. 24, 1962; children: Jeffrey Robert, Jennifer Sue. BS, Hartwick Coll., 1962, MA, 1968; PhD, Eastman Sch. Music, Rochester, N.Y., 1970. Music instr. West Winfield (N.Y.) Cen. Sch., 1962-67, N.Y. State Music Camp, Oneonta, 1962—, Brighton High Sch., Rochester, 1970-71; asst. prof. music Eastman Sch. Music, Rochester, 1971-76; assoc. prof. music Memphis State U., 1976-79; prof. music, dept. chmn. Plymouth State Coll. of U. N.H., Plymouth, 1979—; choral conductor USA, United Kingdom, Australia, New Zealand, South America, Can. Author: Music from the Mountains: The New York State Music Camp, 1947-96; compuser numerous musical compositions. Ch. musician Christian Sci., Presbyn., Bapt. chs. Nat. Def. Edn. Act Title IV fellow U. Rochester, 1967-70; recipient Disting. Teaching award Memphis State U., 1979, Disting. Teaching award Coll. for Lifelong Learning of U. System of N.H., 1987. Mem. N.H. Music Edn. Assn., Music Educators Nat. Conf., Am. Choral Dirs. Assn., Coll. Music Soc., Royal Sch. Ch. Music, Phi Mu Alpha Sinfonia, Kappa Delta Pi. Republican. Mem. Christian Science Ch. Home: PO Box 125 Plymouth NH 03264-0125 Office: Plymouth State Coll Dept Music And Theatre Plymouth NH 03264

SWIFT, STEPHEN JENSEN, federal judge; b. Salt Lake City, Sept. 7, 1943; s. Edward A. and Maurine (Jensen) S.; m. Lorraine Burnell Facer, Aug. 4, 1972; children: Carter, Stephanie, Spencer, Meredith, Hunter. BS, Brigham Young U., 1967; JD, George Washington U., 1970. Trial atty. U.S. Dept. Justice, Washington, D.C., 1970-74; asst. U.S. atty. U.S. Atty.'s Office, San Francisco, 1974-77; v.p., sr. tax counsel Bank Am. N.T. & S.A., San Francisco, 1977-83; judge U.S. Tax Ct., Washington, 1983—; adj. prof. Golden Gate U., San Francisco, 1978-83, U. Balt., 1987—. Mem. ABA, Calif. Bar Assn., D.C. Bar Assn. Office: US Tax Ct 400 2nd St NW Washington DC 20217-0001

SWIFT, STEVEN EDWARD, gynecologist, educator; b. Washington, Nov. 22, 1961; s. Hallock Freeman and Carol Ann (Nutter) S.; m. Alisa Marian Josef, Aug. 11, 1984; children: J. Dylan, W. Brooks. BA in Zoology cum laude, Miami U., Oxford, Ohio, 1983; MD, Ohio State U., 1987. lic., S.C. Fellow in urogynecology U. Calif., Irvine, 1991-93; resident in ob-gyn Med. U. S.C., 1987-91, asst. prof. ob-gyn, 1993—; v.p. Landacre Rsch. Soc., Columbus, 1986-87; presenter in field. Contbr. chpts. to books: Urogynecology and Urodynamics, 1996, Gynecologic Surgery, 1995, Ambulatory Gynecology, 1995; contbr. articles to profl. jours. including Obstetrics/Gynecology, Internat. Urogynecology Jour. Core mem. Young Adult Catholics, Charleston, S.C., 1995; active Circle K Svc. Orgn., Oxford, Ohio, 1982. Fellow Am. Coll. Obstetricians-Gynecologists; mem. AMA, Am. Urogynecological Soc., Assn. Profs. Ob-Gyn, Donald Ostergard Gynecologic Soc. Home: 539 Flambeau Mount Pleasant SC 29464 Office: Med. U. S.C. Dept Ob-Gyn 171 Ashley Ave Charleston SC 29425-0001

SWIFT, WILLIAM CHARLES, professional baseball player, Olympic athlete; b. Portland, Maine, Oct. 27, 1961. Student, Maine. Mem. U.S. Olympic Baseball Team, 1984; with Seattle Mariners, 1984-91; pitcher San Francisco Giants, 1991-94, Colo. Rockies, 1994—. Nat. League Earned Run Average leader, 1992. Office: Colo Rockies 2001 Blake St Denver CO 80205-2008*

SWIG, ROSELYNE CHROMAN, art advisor; b. Chgo., June 8, 1930; m. Richard Swig, Feb. 5, 1950; children—Richard, Jr., Susan, Marjorie, Carol. Student, U. Calif.-Berkeley, UCLA; DFA (hon.), San Francisco Art Inst., 1988. Pres. Roselyne C. Swig Artsource, San Francisco, 1977-94; apptd. by President Clinton as Dir. Art in Embassies program U.S. Dept. of State, 1994—. Trustee San Francisco Mus. Modern Art, U. Art Mus., Berkeley, Calif.; past bd. trustees Mills Coll., Oakland, Calif., United Jewish Appeal; ex officio bd. mem. Jewish Mus. San Francisco; bd. dirs. Am. Jewish Joint Distbn. Com.; vice chair fine art adv. panel Fed. Res. Sys.; past past pres., bd. dirs. Jewish Cmty. Fedn. San Francisco, the Peninsula, Marin and Sonoma Counties; past commr. San Francisco Pub. Libr.; past bd. dirs. San Francisco Opera, Am. Coun. for Arts, KQED Broadcasting Sys.; past. pres. Calif. State Summer Sch. Arts, past chair bd. trustees San Francisco Art Inst.; past pres. San Francisco Arts Commn.; past nat. v.p. Am./Israel Pub. Affairs Com.; past chair bd. trustees U. Art mus. Avocations: skiing; boating; tennis.

SWIGER, ELINOR PORTER, lawyer; b. Cleve., Aug. 1, 1927; d. Louie Charles and Mary Isabelle (Shank) Porter; m. Quentin Gilbert Swiger, Feb. 5, 1955; children: Andrew Porter, Calvin Gilbert, Charles Robinson. BA, Ohio State U., 1949, JD, 1951. Bar: Ohio 1951, Ill. 1979. Sr. assoc. Robbins, Schwartz, Nicholas, Lifton & Taylor, Ltd., Chgo., 1979—. Author: Mexico for Kids, 1971, Europe for Young Travelers, 1972, The Law and You, 1973 (Literary Guild award), Careers in the Legal Professions, 1978, Women Lawyers at Work, 1978, Law in Everday Life, 1977. Mem. Northfield Twp. (Ill.) Bd. Edn., 1976-83; mem. Glenview (Ill.) Fire and Police Commn., 1976-86; chmn. Glenview Zoning Bd. Appeals, 1987—. Mem. ABA (chmn. pub. edn. com. urban, state and local govt. sect. 1982-85), Ill. Bar Assn. (chmn. local govt. sect. 1986-87, chmn. legal edn. sect. 1991-92), Ill. Coun. Sch. Attys. (chmn.), Women Bar Assn. Ill., Chgo. Bar Assn. (chmn. legis. exec. com. 1990-92), Soc. Midland Authors. Republican. Home: 1933 Burr Oak Dr Glenview IL 60025 Office: Robbins Schwartz Nicholas Lifton & Taylor 29 S La Salle St Ste 860 Chicago IL 60603-1505

SWIGER, ELIZABETH DAVIS, chemistry educator; b. Morgantown, W.Va., June 27, 1926; d. Hannibal Albert and Tyreeca Elizabeth (Stemple) Davis; m. William Eugene Swiger, June 2, 1948; children: Susan Elizabeth Swiger Knotts, Wayne William. BS in Chemistry, W.Va. U., 1948, MS in Chemistry, 1952, PhD in Chemistry, 1964. Instr. math. Fairmont (W.Va.) State Coll., 1948-49, instr. math. and phys. sci., 1956-57, instr. chemistry, 1957-60, asst. prof. chemistry, 1960-63, assoc. prof. chemistry, 1964-66, prof. chemistry, 1966—, chmn., div. sci., math. and health careers, 1991-92; NSF fellow rsch. W.Va. U., Morgantown, 1963-64; prof. emeritus, 1992; advisor Am. Chem. Soc. student affiliates, 1965-88. Author: Morton Family History, 1984-94, Davis-Winters Family History, 1994, Civil War Letters and Diary of Joshua Winters, 1991; contbr. articles to profl. jours. Bd. dirs. Prickett's Fort Meml. Found., Fairmont, 1988—, chmn. elect, 1990-92, chair., 1992—, Blacks Chapel Meml. Found., 1993—, rep. adv. coun. to Bd. Regents, Fairmont State Coll., Charleston, 1977-78, rep. instl. bd. advisors, Fairmont, 1990-92. NSF grantee, 1963; named Outstanding Prof. W.Va. Legislature, Charleston, 1990. Mem. Am. Chem. Soc. (sec. chmn. North W. Va. 1975, 83), W.Va. Acad. Sci. (pres. 1978-79, exec. com. edn. chmn. 1990-93), The Nature Conservancy (bd. dirs. W.Va. chpt. 1970-86, chmn. 1980-82), AAUW. Republican. Methodist. Avocations: local history, genealogy, gardening, computers. Home: 1599 Hillcrest Rd Fairmont WV 26554-4807 also: 382 Laird Dr Freeport FL 32439

SWIGER, L. A., agricultural studies educator. Diploma in animal husbandry, Ohio State U., 1954, MS, 1957, PhD, 1960. Geneticist USDA, Lincoln, Neb., 1959, assoc. prof. animal sci., experiment sta. statistician; prof. animal genetics, grad. chmn/ Ohio State U.; prof. animal sci., dept. head Va. Tech, Blacksburg, 1980-86, assoc. dean rsch. Coll. Agrl. and Life Scis., 1986-92, interim dean, 1992-93, dean, 1993—. Recipient Rockefeller Prentice Meml. award Am. Soc. Animal Sci., 1984. Office: Va Tech Coll Agrl and Life Sci Blacksburg VA 24061-0402

SWIGERT, JAMES MACK, lawyer; b. Carthage, Ill., Sept. 25, 1907; s. James Ross and Pearl (Mack) S.; m. Alice Francis Titcomb Harrower, July 7, 1931 (dec. 1990); children: Oliver, David Ladd, Sally Harper (Mrs. Hamilton). Student, Grinnell Coll., 1925-27; SB, Harvard U., 1930, LLB, 1935. Bar: Ill. 1935, Ohio 1937. With Campbell, Clithero & Fischer, Chgo., 1935-36, Taft, Stettinius & Hollister, Cin., 1936—; ptnr. Taft, Stettinius & Hollister, 1948-79, sr. ptnr. and chmn. exec. com., 1979-85, of counsel, 1985—; dir., mem. exec. com. Union Cen. Life Ins. Co., 1963-79; dir., chmn. audit com. Philips Industries, 1975-82. Author articles on labor rels. and labor law. Bd. dirs. Cin. Symphony Orch., 1976-78; trustee, chmn. exec. com. Am. Music Scholarship Assn., 1987-92. Republican. Presbyterian. Clubs: Queen City (past dir.), Cincinnati Country (past v.p., dir.), Queen City Optimists (past pres.), Tennis (past pres.), Recess (past pres.), Harvard Law (past pres.) (Cin.). Home: 2121 Alpine Pl Cincinnati OH 45206-2690 Office: 1800 Star Bank Ctr Cincinnati OH 45202

SWIGGART, CAROLYN CLAY, lawyer; b. Bloomington, Ill., Sept. 19, 1958. AB, Wellesley Coll., 1980; JD, U. Conn., 1983. Bar: Mass. 1983, Conn. 1985, U.S. Dist. Ct. Mass. 1985, U.S. Dist. Ct. Conn. 1986, U.S. Supreme Ct. 1989. With firm Millar & Ambrette, Darien, Conn. Dist. rep. Representative Town Meeting, Darien, Conn., 1990-94. Mem. Conn. Bar Assn. (co-chmn. Basic Practice Manual 1991-94, editor Basic Practice Manual 1986-91), Stamford Regional Bar Assn., Mass. Bar Assn., Tokeneke Club. Avocations: sailing, tennis. Office: Millar & Ambrette 23 Old Kings Hwy S Darien CT 06820-4538

SWIGGER, KEITH, dean; b. Hutchinson, Kans., Feb. 3, 1943; s. Paul Clarke and Loneta (Miller) S.; children: Jessica, Nathaniel. BA, U. Chgo., 1965, MA, 1975; MA, Ind. U., 1967; PhD, U. Iowa, 1973. Sketchwriter Marquis Who's Who, Chgo., 1963-67; teaching asst. Ind. U., Bloomington, 1967; teaching asst. U. Iowa, Iowa City, 1968-73, lectr., 1973-74, libr., 1976-77; asst. prof. East Tex. State U., Commerce, 1977-81; asst. prof. libr. scis. Tex. Woman's U., Denton, 1981-85, assoc. prof., 1985-89, prof., 1989—, interim dean Sch. Libr. Sci., 1991-92, dean Sch. Libr. and Info. Studies, 1992—, dir. Ctr. for Consulting and Planning, 1997—. Contbr. numerous articles to profl. jours. Bd. dirs. ACLU, Denton, 1990-92, Emily Fowler Pub. Libr., Denton, 1995—, vice chair, 1997. Rsch. grantee OCLC, Inc., 1990-91, Career Tng. grantee U.S. Office Edn., 1990-97; postdoctoral fellow Coun. on Libr. Resources U. Chgo., 1974-75. Mem. ALA, Tex. Libr. Assn., Young Adult Libr. Svcs. Assn., Pub. Libr. Assn., Libr. and Info. Tech. Assn., Tex. Faculty Assn., Assn. Libr. Info. Sci. Edn. Office: Tex Womans Univ Sch Libr and Info Studies PO Box 425438 Denton TX 76204-5438

SWIGGETT, HAROLD E. (HAL), writer, photographer; b. Moline, Kans., July 22, 1921; s. Otho Benjamin and Mildred (Spray) S.; ed. high sch.; m. Wilma Caroline Turner, Mar. 1, 1942; children: Gerald, Vernon. Staff photographer San Antonio Express-News, 1946-67, head dept., 1955-67; freelance writer/photographer San Antonio, 1947—, full-time, 1967—; ordained minister So. Baptist Ch. Served with USAAC, World War II. Recipient 10th ann. Outstanding Am. Handgunner award, 1982, Lifetime Cicero award, 1991, St. Gabriel Possenti medal, 1991; named to Am. Handgunner Hall of Fame, 1987, Anschutz/PSI Gun Writer of Yr., 1990, Handgun Hunter Hall of Fame, 1991. Mem. NRA (life), Wildlife Unltd. (pres. chpt. 1955-58), Outdoor writers Assn. Am. (dir. 1969-72), Tex. Outdoor Writers Assn. (pres. 1967-68), Ducks Unltd., Tex. Rifle Assn. (life), Internat. Handgun Metallic Silhouette Assn. (life), Game Conservation Internat. Republican. Contbg. author books game hunting, gun-oriented paperbacks; author: Hal Swiggett on North American Deer, 1980; sr. editor Harris Publs., Guns/Hunting, Tex. Fish & Game; editor: Handguns 95; contbg. editor Gun Digest, North Am. Hunter. Home: 539 Roslyn Ave San Antonio TX 78204-2456

SWIHART, H. GREGG, real estate company executive; b. San Francisco, Sept. 25, 1938; s. Lawson Benjamin and Violet Mary (Watters) S.; B.A., U. Ariz., 1958; postgrad. U. Heidelberg (W.Ger.), 1958-59, Harvard U., 1959-60; M.A., Boston U., 1961; postgrad. U. Freiburg (West Germany), 1961-65; m. Ilse Paula Rambacher, Dec. 24, 1958; children—Tatjana Etta, Brett Marc, Natascha Theda. Stock broker Walston & Co., Tucson, 1966-71; with Solot Co., Tucson, 1971-74; pres. Cienega Properties, Inc., property mgmt. and investment, Tucson, 1975-77; pres. GT Realty Assocs., Ltd., Tucson, 1977—. Mem. Tucson Com. Fgn. Relations, 1973—; pres. Forum for Greater Outdoors, 1977-79; bd. dirs. Tucson Mus. Art, 1968-74, pres. 1969-70; pres. and trustee Canelo Hills Sch., 1977-79. Cert. property mgr. Mem. Tucson Bd. Realtors, Inst. Real Estate Mgmt. (pres. Tucson-So. Ariz. chpt. 1982, mem. nat. governing council 1985-87), Inst. Real Estate Mgmt. (governing council 1985-87, Property Mgr. of Yr. award So. Ariz. chpt. 1988), Realtors Nat. Mktg. Inst. Clubs: Harvard (pres. 1973-74), Active 20-30 (pres. 1969), Downtown Tucson. Home: Tunnel Springs Ranch PO Box 555 Sonoita AZ 85637 Office: 4003 E Speedway Blvd Ste 110 Tucson AZ 85712-4555

SWIHART, JAMES W., JR., diplomat; b. Washington, DC, July 25, 1946; s. James Wilbur and Ruth (Inge) S.; m. Ellen Jane Cendo Mar. 30, 1968; children: Jennifer Anne, Christopher John. BA, Columbia Coll., 1968. Vice consul Am. Embassy, Belize, Brit. Honduras, 1970-72; 2nd sec., polit. officer Am. Embassy, Belgrade, Yugoslavia, 1972-74; ops. officer ops. ctr. Dept. State, Washington, 1974-75, country officer for Italy and the Vatican, 1975-78; polit./mil. officer for U.S. Mission Berlin Dept. State, 1978-82; officer C.S.C.E. Bur. European Affairs Dept. State, Washington, 1982-83, officer for Fed. Republic of Germany, 1983-84; consul gen., prin. officer U.S. Consulate Gen., Zagreb, Yugoslavia, 1984-1988; mem. sr. seminar Dept. State, Washington, 1988-89, dir. Bur. for Ea. European and Yugoslavia Affairs, 1989-1991; min. counselor, deputy chief of mission Am. Embassy, Vienna, Austria, 1991-94, Chargé d'Affaires ad interim, 1993; amb. to Lithuania Am. Embassy, Vilnius, 1994-97; sr. fellow Inst. for Strategic Studies/Nat. Def. U., Washington, 1997—. Avocations: piano, harpsichord, jogging, classical music appreciation. Home and Office: American Embassy Vilnius Dept of State Washington DC 20521-4510 Office: Am Embassy Vilnius Psc 78 # V APO AE 09723-9998

SWIHART, JOHN MARION, retired aircraft manufacturing company executive; b. New Winchester, Ohio, Dec. 27, 1923; s. Harry Miron and Fay I. (Cress) S.; m. Gail G. Carter, Nov. 8, 1986; children from previous marriages: Vicki Ann, John Richard, Thomas Marion, Mark Andrew, Karen Lee, Laurie Christine, Stacey Anne. BS in Physics, Bowling Green State U., 1947; BS in Aero. Engring., Ga. Inst. Tech., 1949, postgrad., 1951-53; postgrad., U. Va., 1951-53. Asst. group leader propulsion group NASA, 1956-58, group leader spl. projects, 1958-59, head advanced configurations group aircraft, 1959-62, chief large supersonic tunnels br., 1962; with Boeing Co., 1962-89; dep. dir. internat. sales Boeing Co., Renton, Wash., 1974-75; v.p. Japan Boeing Internat. Corp. Boeing Co., Tokyo, 1973-74; program mgr. 7X7 Boeing Co., Kent, Wash., 1975-76; dir. new airplane product devel., sales, mktg. Boeing Co., Seattle, 1976-78; dir. product devel., sales mktg. Boeing Co., 1978-79, v.p. U.S., Can. sales, 1979-83, v.p. govt. tech. liaison, 1983-85, corp. v.p. airplane market analysis, 1985; corp. v.p. internat. affairs Boeing Co., Seattle, 1985-89; ret., 1989. Contbr. over 100 articles to profl. jours. 1st lt. USAAF, 1943-45. Decorated D.F.C., Air medal with 3 oak leaf clusters; recipient Wright Bros. Meml. Lectureship award, 1987, Maurice Roy medal for internat. cooperation Internat. Coun. Aeronautical Scie., 1992. Fellow AIAA (hon., chmn. airdraft design com. Pacific N.W. sect. 1969-70, gen. chmn. aircraft sys. and design meeting 1977, pres. 1990-91), Royal Aero. Soc., Internat. Soc. for Air-Breating Engines (pres. 1993—); mem. Japan-Am. Soc. (pres. 1978-79), Wash. State China Rels. Coun. (past pres.).

SWILLER, RANDOLPH JACOB, internist; b. N.Y.C., Jan. 21, 1946; s. Abraham Irving and Helen (Emmer) S.; m. Florence Tena Davis, Sept. 3, 1967; children: Jeremy Adam, Rebecca Susan, Steven Eric. BA in Biology cum laude, Hofstra U., 1968; MD, Chgo. Med. Sch., 1972. Diplomate Am. Bd. Psychiatry and Neurology, Am. Bd. Med. Examiners. Intern Long Island Jewish-Hillside Med. Ctr., New Hyde Park, N.Y., 1972-73; psychiatric resident SUNY Downstate Med. Ctr., Bklyn., 1973-76; asst. attending psychiatrist Maimonides Med. Ctr., Bklyn., 1976-78; medical resident, mem. med. ethics com. Jewish Hosp. Med. Ctr. of Bklyn., 1978-80; fellow in hematology North Shore U. Hosp., Manhasset, N.Y., 1980-81; attending physician in internal medicine Fla. Med. Ctr., Lauderdale Lakes, 1982—, mem. med. utilization rev. com., 1986—, mem. credentials and qualifications com., 1990—; attending physician in internal medicine Coral Springs (Fla.) Med. Ctr., 1987—, mem. med. utilization rev. com., 1987-89. Mem. ACP, AMA, Am. Soc. Internal Medicine, Fla. Med. Assn., Broward County Med. Assn., Am. Psychiat. Assn. Democrat. Jewish. Achievements include research in disseminated intravascular coagulation in obstetrical practice, angioimmunoblatic lymphadenopathy syndrome. Avocation: piano. Office: 7710 NW 71st Ct Ste 304 Fort Lauderdale FL 33321-2932

SWILLING, PAT, professional football player; b. Toccoa, Ga., Oct. 25, 1964. Student, Ga. Tech. U. With New Orleans Saints, 1986-92, Detroit Lions, 1993-95, Oakland (Calif.) Raiders, 1995—. Named to Pro Bowl Team, 1990-93; named outside linebacker Sporting News NFL All-Pro Team, 1991, 92; led league in sacks, 1991. Office: Oakland Raiders 1220 Harbor Bay Pky Alameda CA 94502*

SWINBURN, CHARLES, lawyer; b. Bowness on Windermere, Cumbria, Eng., Apr. 11, 1942; came to U.S., 1949; s. Joseph and Myra (Sullivan) S.; m. Carol Ann Ditzler, Dec. 16, 1972; children: Ann Elizabeth, Catherine Knowles. BA in Psychology, Princeton U., 1963; MBA, Harvard U., 1971; JD, U. Pa., 1993. Industry analyst U.S. Dept. Transp., Washington, 1971-73, chief Industry Analysis Div., 1973-76, dep. asst. sec., 1979-83; assoc. adminstr. fed. assistance Fed. R.R. Adminstrn., Washington, 1976-79; v.p. FS Rollins Environ. Svcs. Inc., Wilmington, Del., 1983-90; assoc. Morgan, Lewis & Bockius, Washington, 1993—; mem., bd. dirs. RailAmerica, Inc. Capt. USMC, 1963-69; major USMCR, 1970-75. Decorated DFC (2), Air medal (35); recipient Presdl. Disting. Exec. award, 1980, Dept. Transp. Meritorious Achievement award, 1976, 78, 81. Home: 1713 Maple Hill Pl Alexandria VA 22302-3927

SWINBURN, JOHN S., professional association executive. BA in Social Scis. and English, U. Tex., 1975; postgrad., Sam Houston State U., 1975-76. Rsch. intern Tex. Dept. Corrections, Huntsville, 1976-77; mgr. spl. projects Birkman & Assocs., Inc., Birkman-Mefferd Rsch. Found., Houston, 1977-79; asst. tech. activities dir. Nat. Assn. Corrosion Engrs. Internat., Houston, 1979-80, tech. activities dir., 1980-82, assoc. exec. dir., 1982-85; sr. mgmt. exec. Humes & Assocs., Inc., Chgo., 1985-86; pres. Anthem Group, Inc., Chgo., 1986-88; dir. corp. comm. Bostrom Corp., Chgo., 1988-89; exec.dir. Internat. Assn. Assembly (formerly Auditorium) Mgrs., Irving, Tex., 1989—. Mem. Am. Soc. Assn. Execs. (cert., mem. internat. com. 1995—), Tex. Soc. Assn. Execs. (chmn. exhbn. com. 1994-95), Dallas/Ft. Worth Soc. Assn. Execs. (program chmn. Assn. Day in North Tex. 1991, treas. 1993-94, v.p. 1994-95, pres.-elect 1996-97, instr. cert. assn. exec. study course 1990—). Office: Internat Assn Assembly Mgrs 4425 W Airport Fwy Ste 590 Irving TX 75062-5831

SWINDELL, ARCHIE CALHOUN, JR., research biochemist, statistician; b. Greenville, Tex., Sept. 26, 1936; s. Archie Calhoun and Louise Evelyn (Ellis) S.; m. Dolores Dyer Holland, Dec. 28, 1962; children: Randy Zidick, Matthew Earle. BS in Chemistry, So. Methodist U., 1958; M. Nutritional Sci., Cornell U., 1965, PhD in Biochemistry, 1968. NIH postdoctoral fellow Duke U. Med. Ctr., Durham, N.C., 1968-70; rsch. sci. positions in biochemistry, pharmacology, statis. Pfizer, Inc., Groton, Conn., 1970-95; statis. cons., 1995—. Contbr. articles on cholesterol metabolism, hormone action, cell culture, actions of drugs, data analysis, stats. to profl. jours., 1968-93. Patentee trimazosin, doxazosin as anti-atherosclerosis agt. ; mem. Town Coun., Groton, Conn., 1991—. Served with U.S. Army, 1958-61. NIH fellow Cornell U., Ithaca, N.Y., 1967. Mem. AAAS, Am. Stat. Assn., Am. Heart Assn., Am. Assn. Artificial Intelligence, Sigma Xi. Club: Shennecossett Yacht (Groton). Avocations: astronomy, woodworking. Home: 192 Monument St Groton CT 06340-3915 Office: Pfizer Inc Cen Rsch Eastern Point Rd Groton CT 06340-4947

SWINDELLS, WILLIAM, JR., lumber and paper company executive; b. Oakland, CA, 1930; married. B.S., Stanford U., 1953. With Willamette Industries, Inc., Portland, Oreg., 1953—; sr. v.p. prodn., mktg. bldg. materials Willamette Industries, Inc., until 1978, exec. v.p., 1978-80, pres. forest products div., 1980-82, pres., chief exec. officer, 1982-96, also dir., chmn., 1984—; dir. Oreg. Bank, Portland. Office: Willamette Industries 1300 SW 5th Ave Portland OR 97201-5667*

SWINDLER, DARIS RAY, physical anthropologist, forensic anthropologist; b. Morgantown, W.Va., Aug. 13, 1925; s. George Raymond and Minnie Mildred (McElroy) S.; m. Kathryn Pardo, Nov. 10, 1977; children: Gary, Darece, Linda, Dana, Bruce, Geoffry, Jason. AB, W.Va. U., 1950; MA, U. Pa., 1952, PhD, 1959. Instr. Cornell Med. Sch., N.Y.C., 1956-57, W.Va. Med. Sch., Morgantown, 1957-59; asst. prof. Med. Coll. S.C., Charleston, 1959-64; assoc. prof. Mich. State U., East Lansing, 1964-68; prof. phys. anthropology, comparative primate anatomy, dental anthropology U. Wash., Seattle, 1968-91, prof. emeritus anthropology, 1991—; emeritus curator comparative primate anatomy Burke Mus., Seattle, 1991—; cons. King County Med. Examiner, Seattle, 1968—; vis. sr. scientist U. Frankfurt, Germany, 1982-83, Com. on Scholarly Commns. with Peoples Republic of China, 1987-88; vis. prof. U. Zurich, 1992; field participant Valley of Kings Expdn., Egypt., 1990-93; vis. prof. U. Padua, Italy, 1994. Author: A Racial Study of the West Nakani of New Britain, 1962, Dentition of Living Primates, 1976, Systematics, Evolution and Anatomy, Comparative Primate Biology; (with C.D. Wood) Atlas of Primate Gross Anatomy, 1973 (Gov's. award 1973), (with J. Sirianni) Growth and Development of Pigtailed Macaque, 1985, (with A. Drusini) Paleontologia Umana, 1997. Served with USN, 1943-46. Recipient Alexander von Humboldt Sr. U.S. Scientist awrd, Germany, 1981. Fellow AAAS, Explorer's Club; mem. Am. Assn. Phys. Anthropologists (v.p. 1976-78), Dental Anthropology Assn. (pres. 1990-92), Internat. Primatology Soc., N.Y. Acad. Sci., Italian Primatol. Assn., Sigma Xi.

SWINERTON, WILLIAM ARTHUR, retired construction company executive; b. San Francisco, Dec. 12, 1917; s. Alfred Bingham and Jane Thomas (Hotaling) S.; m. Mary Nichols Clark, June 5, 1943; children: Leslie Engelbrecht, Susan McBaine, James B., Sarah Blake. B.S., Yale, 1939; postgrad., Stanford, 1940. With Swinerton & Walberg Co., San Francisco, 1940-88, ret. Served with USMCR., 1940-46. Decorated Bronze Star. Clubs: Pacific Union, Burlingame Country. Home: PO Box 620265 Redwood City CA 94062-0265

SWING, JOHN TEMPLE, association executive, lawyer; b. London, Eng., June 7, 1929; s. Raymond Gram and Betty (Gram) S.; m. Devereux Loy Powell, June 19, 1976; children by previous marriage: Jennifer Anne, John Mead. A.B. cum laude, Harvard Coll., 1950; LL.B., Yale U., 1953. Bar: N.Y. 1955, Conn. 1956. Asso. firm Becket and Wagner, Lakeville, Conn., 1955-60; partner Becket and Wagner, 1960-61; partner firm Rorabeck and Swing, Canaan, Conn., 1961-63; dir. adminstrn. Council on Fgn. Relations, N.Y.C., 1963-67; assoc. exec. dir. Coun. on Fgn. Rels., 1967-72; v.p., sec. Council on Fgn. Relations, 1972-85, acting pres., 1985-86, exec. v.p., 1986-93; of counsel Coun. on Fgn. Rels., 1993—; pres., CEO Fgn. Policy Assn., N.Y.C., 1993-95, pres. emeritus, 1995—; mem. adv. com. on law of the sea NSC, 1974-81; mem. U.S. del. to 3d UN Conf. on Law of the Sea, 1974-81, spl. adv. to del., 1977-78, alt. rep., 1978-81; expert cons. Dept. State, 1977-81; mem. adv. bd. Center for Oceans Law and Policy, U. Va. Sch. Law, 1975—; bd. dirs. Council on Ocean Law, 1980—. Contbr. articles to profl. jours. Selectman Town of Salisbury, Conn., 1959-61, 61-63; vice chmn. Salisbury Democratic Town Com., 1959-63; Dem. candidate State Senate, Conn., 1962; trustee Putney Sch. (Vt.), 1983-89, 96—, chmn., 1986-89; bd. dirs. Non-Profit Coordinating Com. of N.Y., 1984—, chmn. 1984-89, designated founding chmn., 1989. Mem. Am. Soc. Internat. Law, Internat. Law Assn., Bar Assn. of City of N.Y. (chmn. com. on lawyer's role in search for peace 1980-82, coun. on internal affairs 1987-96), Fgn. Policy Assn. (bd. dirs. 1993—), Nat. Coun. World Affairs Orgn. (bd. dirs. 1993-96), Coun. Fgn. Rels., Century Club (sec. 1984-86, chair com. on disting. visitors 1992-96), Fishers Island Yacht Club. Home: 61 E 86th St Apt 51 New York NY 10028-1037 Office: 470 Park Ave S Fl 2 New York NY 10016-6819

SWING, WILLIAM EDWIN, bishop; b. Huntington, W.Va., Aug. 26, 1936; s. William Lee and Elsie Bell (Holliday) S.; M. Mary Willis Taylor, Oct. 7, 1961; children—Alice Marshall, William Edwin. B.A., Kenyon Coll., Ohio, 1954-58; D.Div. (hon.), Kenyon Coll., 1980; M.A., Va. Theol. Sem., 1958-61, D.Div., 1980. Ordained priest Episcopal Ch. Asst. St. Matthews Ch., Wheeling, W.Va., 1961-63; vicar St. Matthews Ch., Chester, W.Va., 1963-69, St. Thomas Ch., Weirton, W.Va., 1963-69; rector St. Columba's Episcopal Ch., Washington, 1969-79; bishop Episcopal Ch. Calif., San Francisco, 1980—; chmn. bd. Ch. Div. Sch. of the Pacific, 1983-84; founder, chmn. Episcopal Found. for Drama, 1976—. Republican. Home: 2006 Lyon St San Francisco CA 94115-1610 Office: Episcopal Ch Diocesan Office 1055 Taylor St San Francisco CA 94108-2209*

SWING, WILLIAM LACY, ambassador; b. Lexington, N.C., Sept. 11, 1934; s. Baxter Dermot and Mary Frances (Barbee) S.; AB, Catawba Coll., 1956, LLD (hon.), 1980; BD, Yale U., 1960; postgrad. Oxford U., U. Tuebingen (Germany), 1961, Hofstra U.; LLD (hon.), 1994; m. Yuen Fong Cheong; children: Brian Curtis, Gabrielle. Vice consul Am. Consulate, Port Elizabeth, Republic of South Africa, 1963-66; internat. economist Bur. Econ. Affairs, Dept. State, 1966-68; consul, chief consular sect. Am. Consulate Gen., Hamburg, Germany, 1968-72; internat. rels. officer, desk officer for Federal Republic of Germany, Dept. State, Washington, 1972-74; dep. chief of mission, counselor Am. Embassy, Bangui, Central African Republic, 1974-76; fellow Center for Internat. Affairs, Harvard U., 1976-77; dep. dir. Office of Cen. African Affairs, 1977-79; ambassador to People's Republic of Congo, 1979-81; amb. to Republic of Liberia, Monrovia, 1981-85; amb. to South Africa, 1989-92; amb. to Fed. Republic of Nigeria, 1992-93; amb. to Haiti, 1993—; dir. Fgn. Svc. Career Devel. and Assignments, 1985, 87; sr. dep. asst. sec. state for pers., 1987-89. Recipient Meritorious Honor award USIA, 1971, Superior Honor award Dept. State, 1985, Presdl. Disting. Svc. award, 1985, Presdl. Meritorious Svc. award, 1987, 90, 94, Equal Employment Opportunity award Dept. State, 1988, Disting. Honor award, 1994, Valor award, 1995, Disting. Svc. award, 1996. Mem. Am. Fgn. Svc. Assn., Army and Navy Club (Washington), Yale Club (Washington and N.Y.C.), Harvard Club (Washington), Internat. Club (Washington), Lions. Co-editor: Education for Decision, 1963. Office: Am Embassy Port-Au-Prince State Dept Washington DC 20521-3400

SWINGLE, HOMER DALE, horticulturist, educator; b. Hixson, Tenn., Nov. 5, 1916; s. Edward Everett and Sarah Elizabeth (Rogers) S.; m. Gladys F. Wells, Dec. 21, 1942 (dec. June 1961); 1 child, Janet Faye Swingle Sciscioli; m. Ella Margaret Porterfield, Dec. 19, 1962. BS, U. Tenn., 1939; MS, Ohio State U., 1948; PhD, La. State U., 1966. Tchr. vocat. agr. Spring City (Tenn.) High Sch., 1939-46; hort. specialist U. Tenn., Crossville, 1946-47; from asst. prof. to prof. horticulture U. Tenn., Knoxville, 1948-79, prof. emeritus non-credit program, 1979—; cons. in plant and water rels. Oak Ridge (Tenn.) Nat. Lab., 1971-75; chmn. collaborators Vegetable Breeding Lab. USDA, Charleston, S.C., 1975. Cons. editor: Growing Vegetables and Herbs, 1984; contbr. 49 articles to sci. jours. Fellow Am. Soc. Hort. Sci. (chmn. so. sect. 1970-71); mem. Lions (life), Gamma Sigma Delta (pres. U. Tenn. chpt. 1977, teaching award of merit 1978-79). Republican. Methodist. Home: 3831 Maloney Rd Knoxville TN 37920-2823

SWINNEY, HARRY LEONARD, physics educator; b. Opelousas, La., Apr. 10, 1939; s. Leonard Robert and Ethel Ruth (Bertheaud) S.; m. Gloria Luyas, Oct. 21, 1967; 1 child, Brent Luyas (dec.). BS in Physics, Rhodes Coll., 1961; PhD in Physics, Johns Hopkins U., 1968. Vis. asst. prof. Johns Hopkins U., 1970-71; asst. prof. physics NYU, 1971-73; assoc. prof. CCNY, 1973-77, prof., 1978; prof. physics U. Tex., Austin, 1978—, Trull Centennial prof., 1984-90, Sid Richardson Found. regents chair, 1990—, dir. Ctr. Nonlinear Dynamics, 1985—; Morris Loeb lectr. Harvard U., 1982. Editor: Hydrodynamic Instabilities and the Transition to Turbulence, 1985; contbr. articles to profl. jours. Regents chair Sid Richardson Found., 1990—. Grantee NSF, Dept. Energy, NASA, Office Naval Rsch., Welch, others; Guggenheim fellow, 1982-83. Fellow Am. Phys. Soc. (exec. bd. 1992-94, Fluid Dynamics prize 1996); mem. NAS, Am. Acad. Arts and Scis., Am. Assn. Physics Tchrs. Democrat. Methodist. Office: U Tex Dept Physics Ctr Nonlinear Dynamics Austin TX 78712

SWINSON, ANGELA ANTHONY, physician; b. Washington, Nov. 5, 1960; d. Edgar and Phosia Lee (Hanna) Anthony; m. Kevin Lamont Swinson, June 28, 1986; 1 child, Erik Alan. BA, Johns Hopkins U., 1983, MPH, 1991; MD, Georgetown U., 1987. Diplomate Am. Bd. Forensic Examiners, Am. Bd. Forensic Medicine. Phlebotomist Georgetown U. Hosp., Washington, 1984; med. resident Homewood Hosp. Ctr., Balt., 1987-88; clinic physician Ea. Chest Clinic, Balt., 1990-91; resident in preventive medicine Johns Hopkins Sch. Hygiene and Pub. Health, Balt., 1990-92; asst. med. dir. Occupl. Med. Svc., NIH, Bethesda, Md., 1992—; mem. workgroup Prince George's County, Cheverly, Md., 1991-92. Contbr. articles to profl. jours. Sr. leader Girl Scouts Cen. Md., Balt., 1981-83; mem. inspirational choir Faith African Meth. Episcopal Ch., Laurel, Md., 1993—, mem. mass choir, 1993—, mem. scholarship com., 1995—, instr. vacation Bible sch.,

1995; bd. dirs. Nat. Consortium for African Am. Children, Inc., 1995—. Grantee Nat. Med. Fellowships, 1983-85. Mem. APHA, Am. Coll. Occupl. and Environ. Medicine, Am. Coll. Forensic Examiners, Delta Sigma Theta (Golden Life, co-chair phys. & mental health com., Columbia, Md. alumnae chpt. treas., Mu.Psi chpt. 1980-82, pres. Mu Psi chpt. 1982-83, Minerva award 1981, chpt. award 1983). Avocations: music, art, aerobic exercise, religious activities. Office: NIH Occupl Med Svc Bldg 10 Rm 6C-306 10 Center Dr Bethesda MD 20892

SWINSON, SUE WHITLOW, secondary education educator; b. Rocky Mount, Va., Apr. 14, 1939; d. Homer P. and Etholene R. (Ramsey) Whitlow; m. Arthur Pitt Burgess, 1961 (div. 1975); 1 child, Robert A.; m. William Edward Swinson, Jr., Sept. 7, 1979. AB, Coll. of William & Mary, 1961; MEd, Ga. State U., 1978. Cert. lifetime profl. DT-5. Tchr. Latin Chesterfield (Va.) County Bd. Edn., 1961-62; Army tchr. USAF I, Augsburg, Germany, 1962-64; tchr. Latin Henrico County Bd. Edn., Richmond, Va., 1965-68; tchr. Latin, English, history DeKalb County Bd. Edn., Decatur, Ga., 1974-92; tchr. Latin and English Randolph County Bd. Edn., Cuthbert, Ga., 1992—; book selection com. DeKalb County Bd. Edn., Decatur, 1983-84. Co-author, editor quar. bull. The Georgia Classicist, 1985-86; co-author: (resource guide) Ga. Advanced Latin State Dept. Resource, 1992-93; co-author: (curriculum guide) Latin Curriculum Guides. Named Ga. Latin Tchr. of Yr., Ga. Classical Assn., 1986, 92, recipient Student-Tchr. Achievement Recognition award, 1991-92, 96-97. Mem. Am. Classical League, Ga. Classical Assn. (co-editor state paper 1985-86), Fgn. Lang. Assn. of Ga., Profl. Assn. Ga. Educators. Republican. Methodist. Avocations: reading, golf, fishing, gardening, bridge. Home: RR 2 Box 254-d Georgetown GA 31754-9579 Office: Randolph-Clay HS Rte 4 Box 279 Cuthbert GA 31740

SWIRE, EDITH WYPLER, music educator, musician, violist, violinist; b. Boston, Feb. 16, 1943; d. Alfred R. Jr. and Frances Glenn (Emery) Wypler; m. James Bennett Swire, June 11, 1965; 1 child, Elizabeth Swire-Falker. BA, Wellesley (Mass.) Coll., 1965; MFA, Sarah Lawrence Coll., Bronxville, N.Y., 1983; postgrad., Coll. of New Rochelle, 1984-85. Tchr. instrumental music, viola, violin The Windsor Sch., Boston, 1965-66; tchr., dir. The Lenox Sch., N.Y.C., 1967-76; music curriculum devel. The Nightingale-Bamford Sch., N.Y.C., 1968-69; head of fine arts dept. The Lenox Sch., N.Y.C., 1976-78, head of instrumental music, 1978-80; founder, dir., tchr. of string sch. Serpentine String Sch., Larchmont, N.Y., 1981—; mem. founding com. Inter Sch. Orch., N.Y.C., 1972, trustee, 1976—; panelist Nat. Assn. Ind. Sch. Conf., N.Y.C., 1977. Mem. music and worship com., Larchmont Ave. Ch., 1978-82, 88. Mem. Westchester Musicians Guild, N.Y. State Music Tchrs. Assn., Music Tchrs. Nat. Assn., Music Tchrs. Coun. Westchester (program com.), Violin Soc. Am., Wellesley in Westchester, Am. String Tchrs. Assn., The Viola Soc. of N.Y. Avocations: study of Alexander technique, chamber music, encouraging music in schools. Home and Office: 11 Serpentine Trl Larchmont NY 10538-2618

SWIST, MARIAN IRENE, emergency nurse; b. Pottsville, Pa., Oct. 26, 1941; d. Thomas Francis and Marian C. (Munster) Moran; m. John J. Swist, Aug. 3, 1963 (dec.); children: Christine M. Swist Mullen, Robert J. Diploma in nursing, Reading (Pa.) Hosp., 1962. RN, Pa.; cert. emergency nursing pediatric course. Staff nurse Reading Hosp. Med. Ctr., 1962-65; staff nurse emergency dept. Pottstown Meml. Med. Ctr., 1971—. Mem. Alumni Assn. Reading Hosp. Sch. Nursing.

SWIT, LORETTA, actress; b. N.J., Nov. 4, 1939. Student, Am. Acad. Dramatic Arts, Gene Frankel Repertoire Theatre, N.Y.C. Broadway appearances include Same Time Next Year, Any Wednesday, Mame, The Mystery of Edwin Drood, Shirley Valentine, Chgo. (winner Sarah Siddons award 1990); films include Stand Up and Be Counted, 1972, Freebie and the Bean, 1974, Race with the Devil, 1975, S.O.B, 1980, Beer, 1985, Whoops, 1987, Apocalypse (U.K.), 1987; star TV series M*A*S*H, 1972-83 (Emmy awards for Outstanding Supporting Actress in a Comedy series 1979-81); TV movies include Shirts/Skins, 1973, The Last Day, 1975, Mirror, Mirror, 1979, Valentine, 1979, Friendships, Secrets and Lies, 1979, Cagney and Lacey, 1981, Games Mother Never Taught You, 1982, First Affair, 1983, The Execution, 1985, Dreams of Gold: The Mel Fisher Story, 1986, My Dad Can't Be Crazy, Can He?, Hell Hath No Fury, 1992, A Killer Among Friends, 1993; star on major dramatic shows and musical variety shows, including Bob Hope Christmas Special, Perry Como, The Muppets. Mem. AFTRA, Screen Actors Guild, Actors Equity. Address: The Artists Group 10100 Santa Monica Blvd Ste 305 Los Angeles CA 90067*

SWITZER, BARRY, professional football coach, former university athletic coach; b. Crossett, Ark., Oct. 5, 1937; s. Frank and Louise Switzer; m. Kay Switzer, 1963 (div. 1983); children: Greg, Kathy, Dove. BA, U. Ark., 1960. Asst. football coach U. Ark., 1960-65; asst. football coach U. Okla., 1966-72, head coach, 1973-89; head coach Dallas Cowboys, 1994—. author: Bootlegger's Boy, 1990. Served with U.S. Army. Named Coach of Year, 1973, AP/UPI Nat. Champions (shared with U. So. Calif.), 1974, consensus champions, 1975, 85. Coach winning Orange Bowl team, 1976, 79-81, 86-87, winning Super Bowl team (Super Bowl XXX), 1995. Office: Dallas Cowboys 1 Cowboys Pky Irving TX 75063-4945*

SWITZER, MAURICE HAROLD, publisher; b. Toronto, Ont., Can., Mar. 28, 1945; s. Harold Switzer and Ruby (Marsden) Hicks; m. Mary Helene Pavlik; children: Andrea Zimperi, Adin, Lisa Doracka. Student, Trent U., Peterborough, Ont., 1964-65. Journalist Belleville (Ont.) Intelligencer, 1965-67, sports editor, 1967-72, mng. editor, 1972-79; mng. editor Oshawa (Ont.) Times, 1979-81; pub. Timmins (Ont.) Daily Press, 1981-86, Sudbury (Ont.) Star, 1986-92, Winnipeg (Man.) Free Press, 1992-94; ret.; owner Media Help Svcs., 1994—; dir. program devel. aboriginal medicine First Nations Tech. Inst., 1996—. Author: Bruno Cavallo a Conversation, 1991. Mem. elders coun. Mississaugas of Rice Lake First Nation.

SWITZER, PAUL, statistics educator; b. St. Boniface, Man., Can., Mar. 4, 1939. B.A. with honors, U. Man., 1961; A.M., Harvard U., 1963, Ph.D., 1965. Mem. faculty Stanford (Calif.) U., 1965—, now prof. stats. and earth scis., chmn. dept. stats., 1979-82. Fellow Internat. Statis. Inst., Am. Statis. Assn. (editor jour. 1986-88), Inst. Math. Stats. Office: Stanford U Dept Stats Stanford CA 94305-4065

SWITZER, ROBERT LEE, biochemistry educator; b. Clinton, Iowa, Aug. 26, 1940; s. Stephen and Elva Delila (Allison) S.; m. Bonnie George, June 13, 1965; children: Brian, Stephanie. BS, U. Ill., 1961; PhD, U. Calif., Berkeley, 1966. Research fellow Lab. Biochemistry, Nat. Heart Inst., Bethesda, Md., 1966-68; asst. prof. biochemistry U. Ill., Urbana, 1968-73; assoc. prof. U. Ill., 1973-78, prof. biochemistry and basic med. scis., 1978—, dept. head, 1988-93; mem. biochemistry study sect. NIH, 1985-89, chmn., 1987-89; guest prof. U. Copenhagen, 1995. Author: (with John M. Clark) Experimental Biochemistry, 1977; mem. bd. editors Jour. Bacteriology, 1977-82, 85—, Archives Biochemistry and Biophysics, 1977—, Jour. Biol. Chemistry, 1980-85; contbr. articles to profl. jours. NSF predoctoral fellow, 1961-66; NIH postdoctoral fellow, 1966-68; Guggenheim fellow, 1975. Mem. Am. Soc. for Biochemistry and Molecular Biology, Am. Soc. Microbiology, Am. Chem. Soc., AAAS, Sigma Xi. Home: 404 W Michigan Ave Urbana IL 61801-4948 Office: U Ill Dept Biochemistry 600 S Mathews Ave Urbana IL 61801-3602

SWITZER, SAMUEL THOMAS, non-profit administrator; b. Cowgill, Mo., Feb. 5, 1951; s. William Thomas and Lova Nadine (Hayden) S.; m. Carolyn Beth Stephens, Aug. 7, 1971; children: Samuel Andrew, Jennifer Elaine. BSBA summa cum laude, William Jewell Coll., 1973; cert. mgmt. program, Rockhurst Coll., 1978. CPA, Mo. Asst. bank examiner Fed. Res. Bank St. Louis, 1973-74; cashier, asst. contr. Kansas City (Mo.) Life Ins. Co., 1974-77; contr., asst. treas. Belsaw Machinery Co., Kansas City, Mo., 1977-80; coord. spl. projects Kansas City Power and Light Co., 1980-81; dir., sec.-treas. Scudder Communications Assocs., Inc., Gladstone, Mo., 1982-87; treas. Midwestern Sem. Housing Corp., Kansas City, Mo., 1981-93; v.p. Midwestern Bapt. Theol. Sem., Kansas City, 1981-93; CFO, dir. Open Options, Inc., 1993—; chmn. So. Bapt. Sems. Bus. Officers Coun., 1986, 91; notary pub., State of Mo., 1982—. Bd. govs. William Jewell Coll. Alumni Assn., Liberty, Mo., 1973—; bd. dirs. Kearney (Mo.) Devel. Corp., 1977-80; ordained deacon 1st Bapt. Ch., Kearney, 1977, chair fin. com., pers. com., tchr. Sunday sch.; league treas., dir. of ofcls., coach Kearney Holt Youth Soccer Club, 1982-93; league coord., coach Kearney Holt Recreation Assn., 1985-91; mem. religious life com. William Jewell Coll., 1989—, chair 1989-92; bd. dirs. Kearney R-1 Sch. Bd., 1991-94, liaison mem. strategic planning com., 1992; mem. Sr. Link Adv. Bd., 1994—; pres. William Jewell Coll. Soccer Booster Club, 1995—; pianist Tryst Falls (Mo.) Bapt. Ch., 1996—. Mem. Kansas City C. of C., Clay County Devel. Commn. (gold crown mem.), Phi Beta Kappa, Phi Mu Alpha. Republican. Avocations: hunting, skiing, boating, farm management, conservation. Home: 17009 NE 134th Ter Kearney MO 64060-8910 Office: Open Options Inc 3217 Broadway St Ste 100 Kansas City MO 64111-2414

SWOAP, DAVID BRUCE, children's relief official, art gallery director; b. Kalamazoo, Aug. 12, 1937; s. Orlo Frederick and Aileen Esther (Hempy) S. B.A. in Govt. with honors, Denison U., 1959; M.A. in Govt, Claremont Grad. Sch., 1961; D.Sci. (hon.), U. Osteo. Medicine and Health Scis., Des Moines, 1981. Asst. sec. Calif. State Pers. Bd., Sacramento, 1972-73; chief dep. dir., acting dir. Calif. State Dept. Social Welfare, Sacramento, 1973; dir. Calif. State Dept. Social Welfare, 1973-74, Calif. State Dept. Benefit Payments, 1974-75; sr. rsch. asso. Rep. Study Com., U.S. Ho. of Reps., Washington, 1975-76; profl. staff mem. U.S. Senate Com. on Fin., Washington, 1976-79; legis. dir. U.S. Senator William L. Armstrong, Washington, 1979-81; dep. sec. HHS, Washington, 1981-83; sec. health and welfare State of Calif., Sacramento, 1983-85; ptnr. Franchetti & Swoap, San Francisco, 1985-90; vice chmn. Sacramento Advs., 1991—; chmn. bd. dirs. Hope Unltd. Internat., San Diego, 1991-96, chmn. bd. internat. advisors, 1996—; owner The David Bruce Gallery, Carlsbad, Calif., 1995—; owner Mana Olana Farms, Hakalau, Hawaii. Elder Presbyn. Ch.; bd. dirs. Friends of SOS Children's Villages, 1989-91; mem. bd. regents John F. Kennedy U., 1990-93. Rotary Club Found. fellow, 1961-62. Mem. Wycliffe Assocs., Phi Beta Kappa, Delta Upsilon. Republican. Office: 300 Carlsbad Village Dr Ste 207 Carlsbad CA 92008-2991

SWOBODA, LARY JOSEPH, state legislator; b. Luxemburg, Wis., May 28, 1939; s. Joseph Francis and Catherine Magdalene (Daul) S.; m. Janice Marie Hendricks, Nov. 16, 1968. BS in Speech and Edn., U. Wis., Milw., 1963, MS in Polit. Sci., 1965, EdS, 1988; postgrad., U. Wis., Madison, 1988—. Cert. ednl. specialist. Speech and English tchr. So. High Sch., Brussels, Wis., 1963-67; tchr. Luxemburg Schs., 1967-70; mem. Wis. State Legislature, Madison, 1970—; chair adminstrv. rules com. Wis. State Assembly, Madison, 1993—; exec. dir. Wis. Nat. and Cmty. Svc. Bd., Madison. Active Dem. County Unit. Mem. K.C., Luxemburg C. of C., Lions, Phi Eta Sigma, Kappa Delta Pi, Phi Kappa Phi, Phi Delta Kappa. Roman Catholic. Avocations: reading, attending concerts, drama. Home: 1835 Broadway Dr Sun Prairie WI 53590-1758 Office: Wis Nat and Cmty Svc Bd 101 W Wilson St Madison WI 53703-3213

SWOFFORD, DONALD ANTHONY, architect; b. Houston, Apr. 14, 1947; s. Harry and Henrian (Engbrock) S.; m. Virginia M. Bauler, May 23, 1985; 1 child, James McShea. B.Arch., Tex. A&M U., 1969; M.Arch., U. Va., 1976. Registered architect, Va., Tex., D.C., Nat. Council Archtl. Registration Bds., lic. instrument pilot. Architect, urban designer City of Dallas, 1970-72; Office Milton L. Grigg, FAIA, Architects, 1972-78; prin., owner Wood, Swofford Assocs., Charlottesville, Va., 1978—; pres. Traditional Am. Concepts Ltd., 1983—. Author Dallas Hist. Landmark Program, 1972. Prin. works include Joseph Jarvis residence, 1978, Shrinemont Conf. Ctr., Episcopal Diocese of Va., Orkney Springs, 1981, United Coal/Martha Washington Inn, Bristol, Va., 1985, office and studio WVIR TV, 1985, restoration Farley, Culpeper, Va., 1987, restoration St. Francis Assisi Cath. Ch., Stanton, Va., 1988, restoration and additions Goochland County (Va.) Courthouse, 1989, Montpelier, home of James Madison, 1986, George M. McMath residence, Locustville, Va., 1991, restoration of Higlands, home of James Monro, Charlottesville, 1991, Holy Name of Mary, Bedford, Va., 1994, restoration of Clover Hill Tavern, Appomattox, Va., 1994, hist. rehab. of Danville Rail Passenger Sta., restoration of Gen. George C. Marshall Home, Leesburg, Va., 1994, Danville City Courthouse, Danville, Va., 1995. Cub Master, Pack 119, Stonewall Jackson Coun. Recipient Tex.-AIA Design award, 1969-70, Loudon County award for Jarvis Residence, 1985; Jefferson fellow, 1972-73. Mem. AIA (mem. hist. resources com., mem. steering com., James River chpt. Design award for Farley 1991, Nat. Trust for Hist. Preservation Great Am. Homes award for Farley 1992, James River chpt. Design award for Danville Rail Passenger Sta. 1995), Va. Soc. Architects, Albemarle County Hist. Soc., Nat. Trust Historic Preservation, Soc. Archtl. Historians, Assn. Preservation Tech. Office: Wood Swofford Assocs Archs 812 E High St Charlottesville VA 22902-5126

SWOFFORD, ROBERT LEE, newspaper editor, journalist; b. Berryville, Ark., Aug. 22, 1949; s. Andrew Madison and Verna Mae (England) S.; m. Karen King, Jan. 24, 1969 (div. 1977); children: Teri, Toby; m. Sandra Dunn, 1978 (div. 1979); m. B. Joanna Rongren, Feb. 14, 1981; 1 child, Tyler. AA, Coll. of the Sequoias, 1969; student, Calif. State U., 1969-71. Photographer, reporter, news editor The Advance-Register, Tulare, Calif., 1965-78; city editor The Record Searchlight, Redding, Calif., 1978-81; suburban editor, Neighbors editor The Sacramento Bee, 1981-86; assoc. metro. editor, cmty. editor The Orange County Register, Santa Ana, Calif., 1986-89; exec. news editor The Press Democrat, Santa Rosa, Calif., 1989-90, mng. editor, 1990—. Mem. Assoc. Press Mng. Editors, Calif. Soc. of Newspaper Editors (bd. dirs.). Office: The Press Democrat 427 Mendocino Ave Santa Rosa CA 95401-6313

SWOPE, CHARLES EVANS, banker, lawyer; b. West Chester, Pa., June 16, 1930; s. Charles S. and Edna (McAllister) S.; m. Stephanie Swope; 1 son, Charles E. BS, Bucknell U., 1953; JD, Washington and Lee U., U. Va., 1959; MS, Ind. Coll., 1966; attended Naval War Coll., Judge Adv. Gen. Sch., 1957, Command and Staff Coll., 1969; D of Pub. Svc. (hon.), West Chester U., 1994. Assoc. firm Gawthrop & Greenwood, Attys., West Chester, Pa., 1960; pres., chmn. bd., sr. trust officer 1st Nat. Bank, West Chester, 1965—, also chmn. bd. dirs.; pres. Eachus Dairy Co., 1970-84; pres., bd. dirs. West Chester Corp.; bd. dirs. Madison Co., Penjerdel, Penn Mut. Ins. Co., dir.1st Nat. Bank West Chester; pres. Automobile Assn. Chester County; lectr. corp. law. Pres., West Chester Civic Assn., 1964; co-chmn. Chester County Heart Assn. Drive, West Chester Community Center Bldg. Drive, 1970-90, 175th Anniversary West Chester; mem. Nat. Football Found. and Hall of Fame; dir. Chester County council Boy Scouts Am., 1961-97; bd. dirs. Chester County Service, pres. Swope Found. Trust; bd. dirs., v.p. West Chester U. Found.; pres. West Chester Found.; mem. Marine Corps. Scholarship Found.; chmn. Bus. and Indsl. Council of Chester County, pres., 1981; chmn. Easter Seal Soc. Chester County; mem. Com. to Restore Tun Tavern; trustee, West Chester U., 1962-72, pres. bd. trustees, 1966-72; trustee Chester County Devel. Fund, Dr. Charles S. Swope Scholarship Fund, Hatfield Home; YMCA trustee Chester County Hosp. Corp. Served to maj. USMC, 1952-58, col. Res. Decorated Legion of Merit, Nat. Def. medal, Navy Commendation medal, Meritorious Service medal; recipient Coll. Football Centennial award, 1970; Congressional Medal of Merit, 1981; Disting. Eagle Scout award Boy Scouts Am., 1983. Mem. ABA, VFW (life), Pa. Bankers Assn. (chmn. Legis. com. 1965, 70), U.S. Naval Inst., Assn. Univ. Trustees Pa., Am. Soc. Internat. Law, Chester County Bar Found. (v.p.), Greater West Chester C. of C. (pres. 1963), Marine Corps League Chester County (vice comdr. 1960-72), Freedoms Found., Am. Legion (life mem.), Chester County Hist. Soc. (founders award), Marine Corps Res. Officer Assn. (nat. pres. 1982-83, vice chmn. bd. dirs.), Marine Corps Assn., Marine Corps League, Pa. C. of C., Navy League U.S., Washington and Lee Law Sch. Assn., Bucknell, West Chester U. alumni assns., Pa. Economy League, Brandywine Valley Assn., Maxwell Football Club, Phi Alpha Delta, Phi Kappa Psi. Republican. Methodist (ofcl. bd.). Clubs: West Chester (Pa.) Golf and Country; Union League (Phila.) Italian Social; Sky Top; Great Oaks Yacht and Country, Masons, Rotary (pres. West Chester, Pa., 1968-69, Paul Harris fellow), Elks. Home: 200 W Ashbridge St West Chester PA 19380-2371 Office: First Nat Bank 9 N High St West Chester PA 19380-3002

SWOPE, DONALD DOWNEY, retired banker; b. Martinsville, Ill., Feb. 26, 1926; s. Roy V. and Dorothy Irene (Downey) S.; m. Earla Long, Aug. 16, 1960. BS, Ind. State U., 1950. With Ill. Savs. and Loan Commn., Springfield, Ill., 1950-77, chief dept. commr., 1971-77; exec. v.p. Bank for Savs. & Loan Assn., Chgo., 1977-81, pres., 1981-90, dir. Dir., treas. Country Fair White Elephant, Green Valley, Ariz. With USNR, 1944-63. Mem. VFW (life), Nat. Assn. State Savs. and Loan Suprs. (pres. 1972-73), Am. Legion (life), C. C. Green Valley, Kiwanis (pres. Crete, Ill. 1977-78, treas. Green Valley, Ariz. 1994, 95), Elks (treas.).

SWOPE, JEFFREY PEYTON, lawyer; b. Evanston, Ill., June 11, 1945; s. Oliver P. and Elspeth E. (Cahill) S.; m. Linda Lee, Aug. 26, 1967; children: Matthew, Gregory, Timothy. AB, Harvard U., 1967, JD, 1970. Bar: Mass. 1970, U.S. Dist. Ct. Mass. 1971, U.S. Ct. Appeals (1st cir.) 1973, U.S. Ct. Claims 1974, U.S. Supreme Ct. 1979. Assoc. Palmer & Dodge, Boston, 1970-76, ptnr., 1977—; treas. Social Law Libr., Boston, 1984—. Treas. Ella Lyman Cabot Trust, Holliston, Mass., 1979—. Mem. Mass. Audubon Soc. (bd. dirs. 1985—). Home: 54 Hyde St Newton Highlands MA 02161-1206 Office: Palmer & Dodge 1 Beacon St Boston MA 02108-3107

SWOPE, RICHARD T., federal agency administrator; married Jane Swope; children: Patricia, Shannon. BA in Bus. Adminstrn., Grove City (Pa.) Coll., 1964; grad., Squadron Officer Sch., Maxwell AFB, Atlanta, 1970, Armed Forces Staff Coll., Norfolk, Va., 1976, Indsl. Coll. Armed Forces, Ft. Lesley J. McNair, Washington, 1976; MBA, U. Utah, 1977; grad., Air War Coll., Maxwell AFB, 1985. Commd. 2d lt. USAF, 1964, advanced through grades to lt. gen., 1996; F-4 fighter pilot USAF, Bitburg Air Base, Ariz., 1966, Holloman AFB, W. Germany, 1966-70; weapons officer USAF, Udorn Royal Thai Air Base, Thailand, 1971-72; weapons officer Royal Air Force USAF, Lakeheath, Eng., 1971-72; weapons instr. Europe Tatics Sch. USAF, Zaragoza Air Base, Spain; chief fighter assignments Air Force Mil. Pers. Ctr. USAF, Randolph (Tex.) AFB, 1976-79; ops. officer, squadron comdr. USAF, Kunsan Air Base, S. Korea, 1979-80; comdr. USAF, Clark AFB, The Philippines, 1980-81; asst. dep. fighter ops. Hdqs. Pacific Air Forces USAF, Hickam AFB, Hawaii, 1981-83; chief flying US. Air Force Weapons Sch. USAF, Nellis AFB, Nev., 1983-84; vice comdr. USAF, Luke AFB, Ariz., 1985-87; chief of staff Hdqs. Pacific Air Forces USAF, Hickam AFB, Hawaii, 1987; comdr. USAF, Yokota Air Base, Japan, 1988-89; insp. gen. Hdqs. Pacific Air Forces USAF, Hickam AFB, Hawaii, 1989-90; comdr. USAF, Ramstein Air Base, Germany, 1992-94; asst. chief staff ops. and logistics Allied Forces Ctrl. Europe USAF, Brunssum, The Netherlands, 1992-94; comdr. USAF, Andersen AFB, Guam, 1994-96; insp. gen. office sec. air force Dept. Air Force, Washington, 1996—. Decorated D.S.M., Def. Superior Svc. medal, Legion of Merit with 2 oak leaf clusters, Air medal with 14 oak leaf clusters, Air Force Outstanding Unit award with 2 oak leaf clusters. Office: SAF/IG 1140 Air Force Pentagon Washington DC 20330-1140*

SWORD, CHRISTOPHER PATRICK, microbiologist, university dean; b. San Fernando, Calif., Sept. 9, 1928; s. Christopher Patrick and Mary (Ross) S.; m. Mary Rose Gerhardt, June 18, 1959; children—Mary Anne, Carolyn, Jacqueline, Christopher. B.S. in Biology, Loyola U., Los Angeles, 1951; Ph.D. in Microbiology, UCLA, 1959. Research asso. in microbiology U. Kans., 1958-59, from asst. prof. to prof., 1959-70; research asso. Argonne (Ill.) Nat. Lab., 1961; prof. life scis., chmn. dept. Ind. State U., Terre Haute, 1970-76; prof. microbiology Center Med. Edn., 1971-76; prof. microbiology, dir. research, grad. dean S.D. State U., Brookings, 1976—; cons., evaluator for N. Cen. Assn. Colls. and Schs. Author numerous articles in field. Grantee USPHS, grantee Am. Heart Assn. Mem. AAAS, AAUP, Am. Soc. Microbiology, Nat. Coun. U. Rsch. Adminstrs., Coun. Grad. Schs., Midwestern Assn. Grad. Schs., Sigma Xi, Phi Kappa Phi. Home: 1500 Buffalo Trl Brookings SD 57006-3608 Office: SD State U Grad Sch Brookings SD 57007

SWORT, ARLOWAYNE, retired nursing educator and administrator; b. Bartlesville, Okla., Dec. 9, 1922; d. Arlington L. and Clara E. (Church) S. Diploma, St. Luke's Hosp. Sch. Nursing, Kansas City, Mo., 1944; BSN, U. Colo., 1958; MS in Nursing, Cath. U. Am., 1961; EdD, Columbia U., 1973. Dean, prof. Sch. Nursing U. Tex. Health Scis. Ctr., Houston, 1977-83, prof. nursing, 1983-85; prof., assoc. in adminstrn. Johns Hopkins U. Sch. Nursing, Balt., 1985-87; prof., assoc. dean for adminstrn. and grad. acad. affairs Johns Hopkins U. Sch. Nursing, Balt., 1987-89, sr. assoc. dean, 1990-91. Recipient numerous rsrch. grants. Mem. ANA, NLN, APHA, AAUW, Am. Assn. for History of Nursing Inc., Am. Assn. Univ. Adminstrs., Am. Assn. for Higher Edn., Am. Nurses Found.-Century Club, Am. Assn. Nurse Execs., Nat. Gerontol. Nurses Assn., Found. for Nursing of Md., Inc., Sigma Theta Tau, Kappa Delta Pi. Home: 1317 Kollman Dr Hondo TX 78861-1014

SWYMER, STEPHEN, principal. Prin. Gen. Wayne Mid. Sch., Malvern, Pa. Recipient Blue Ribbon award U.S. Dept. Edn., 1990-91. Office: Gen Wayne Mid Sch 20 Devon Rd Malvern PA 19355-3071*

SYDNOR, EDGAR STARKE, lawyer; b. Lynchburg, Va., Nov. 30, 1943; s. Charles Raine and Louise Allen (Starke) S.; m. Rita Frances Johnson, Dec. 28, 1965; children: Edgar Starke Jr., Elizabeth Sydnor Norris, Carlton Allen. BA in English, Washington & Lee, 1966, JD, 1973. Bar: Va. 1973. Assoc. Edmunds, Williams, Robertson, Sackett, Baldwin & Graves, Lynchburg, 1973-75, ptnr., 1975-81; atty. Vulcan Materials Co., Birmingham, Ala., 1981-84; gen. atty. Vulcan Materials Co., Birmingham, 1984-88, asst. gen. counsel, dir. pub. affairs, 1988-95, elected officer of co., 1992—, asst. gen. counsel chems. and environ., 1995—. Mem., bd. dirs. Pub. Affairs Rsch. Coun. of Ala., Birmingham, 1988—, Birmingham Summerfest, 1988—, Cornerstone Schs. Ala., Birmingham, 1995—. Capt. USAF, 1966-71. Presbyterian. Avocations: reading, walking, computers. Office: Vulcan Materials Co 1 Metroplex Dr Birmingham AL 35209-6805

SYDNOR, ROBERT HADLEY, state government geologist; b. Whittier, Calif., July 1, 1947; s. Thurston Edward and Mary Edith (Thompson) S.; divorced; 1 child, Christopher. BA, Whittier Coll., 1969; MS, U. Calif.-Riverside, 1975. Registered geologist, Calif., Alaska, Ariz.; cert. engring. geologist, Calif.; cert. hydrogeologist, Calif. Asst. petroleum geologist Mobil Oil Corp., Anchorage, 1970-71; staff engring. geologist Leighton & Assocs., Irvine, Calif., 1973-77; assoc. engring. geologist Orange County, Laguna Niguel, Calif., 1977-79; sr. engring. geologist VTN Corp., Irvine, 1979; chief engring. geologist R&M Cons., Inc., Irvine, 1979-82; supervising geologist Calif. Div. Mines and Geology, San Francisco, 1982-90, sr. engr. geologist, Sacramento, 1990—; mem. exam. com. Calif. State Bd. of Registration for Geologists and Geophysicists, Sacramento, 1977—, chmn., 1978. Co-author (CDMG spl. bubl. 117) Guidelines for Evaluating and Mitigating Seismic Hazards in Calif., 1997; co-editor CDMG spl. publ. on the 1989 Loma Prieta earthquake, 1992 Cape Mendocino earthquake, 1992 Landers earthquake, 1994 Northridge earthquake; contbr. many cons. reports on landslides and seismicity. Mem. alumni scholarship com. U. Calif.-Riverside, 1978-86; mem. City of Los Angeles Grading Appeals Bd., 1979-84; alt. mem. County of Orange Grading Appeals Bd., 1980-84. Donnel Foster Hewett fellow U. Calif., 1972. Mem. Calif. Acad. Sci. (life), Assn. Engring. Geologists (assoc. editor Bull. 1979-86, chmn. So. Calif. sect. 1979-80), Geol. Soc. Am., Seismol. Soc. Am. (life), Am. Assn. Petroleum Geologists, Am. Inst. Profl. Geologists, Nat. Assn. Geology Tchrs., Am. Quarternary Assn., Arctic Inst. N.Am. (life), ASTM, Am. Geophys. Union (life), Sigma Gamma Epsilon (life). Republican. Presbyterian. Home: 4930 Huntridge Ln Fair Oaks CA 95628-4823 Office: Calif Divsn Mines and Geology 801 K St Ste 12 31 Sacramento CA 95814-3518

SYED, MOINUDDIN, electrical engineer; b. Jaipur, Rajhastan, India, Feb. 1, 1947; came to U.S., 1969; s. Masihuddin and Aisha Bibi (Ali) S.; m. Nasim Afroz Mustfai, Jan. 7, 1972; children: Mohsin, Ahson, Mona, Hasan. BEE, U. Karachi, Pakistan, 1968; MSEE, Tulane U., 1971. Registered profl. engr., Ont., Can. Sci. staff mem. Bell No. Rsch., Ottawa, Can., 1973-79; staff engr. Ont. region Bell Can., Toronto, 1979-80; sr. planning engr. Contel Calif., Victorville, 1980-82, supervising engr., 1982-85, 88-96; staff engr. Contel Corp., Bakersfield, Calif., 1985-88; sect. mgr. GTE Calif., Victorville, 1996—; mem. ICEP com. Bell No. Rsch., Ottawa, 1973-80, Bell Can., Toronto, 1985-86; quality task force Contel Corp., Bakersfield, 1985-86; project mgr. Contel Calif., Victorville, 1988-89, chmn. spl. task force on fiber to home project, 1993-96; featured speaker USTA Conv., Portland, Oreg., 1977; participant continuing edn. programs Chapman Coll., Golden Gate U., Victor Valley Coll.; teaching and rsch. asst. Tulane U., 1969-73. Co-author: Characterization of Electrical Environment, 1976; contbr. articles to jours. Scholar Fauji Found., 1962-64, Ministry Edn., 1964-68. Mem. IEEE. Achievements include rsch. in elec. protection of telecom network, telecom protection for power stations, and use of fiber optics technology in telecommunications. Office: GTE Calif 13911 Park Ave Ste 200 Victorville CA 92392-2407

SYKES, ALSTON LEROY, analytical chemist, musician; b. Chgo., Sept. 1, 1948; s. Leslie McKoy and Perline Alphonsine (Holden) S.; m. Elizabeth White, Feb. 10, 1973; children: Brian A., Kevin M. BS in Chemistry, Campbell U., 1972. Cert. profl. chemist. Intern in chemistry N.C. State Bur. of Invest, Raleigh, 1970-72; chemist N.C. Dept. Natural Resources, Raleigh, 1972-77, Rsch. Triangle Inst., Research Triangle Park, N.C., 1977-80; sr. scientist TRW/Radian Corp., Research Triangle Park, N.C., 1980-88; corp. quality assurance mgr., lab. dir. Acurex Environ., Research Triangle Park, N.C., 1988-93; prin. scientist, mgr. Quanterra Environ. Svcs., Raleigh, 1994—; pres. RTP Labs., Inc., 1993—. Author (computer database) NIOSH Analytical Methods, 1986; contbr. articles to profl. jours. Mem. Am. Chem. Soc., Air and Waste Mgmt. Assn. Achievements include research in air sampling and analysis methods; developed new methods for testing indoor air, ambient air, recycling, and pollutant sources; contractor U.S. EPA rsch. labs, 1977—. Office: RTP Labs Inc 8100A Brownleigh Dr Raleigh NC 27612

SYKES, BRIAN DOUGLAS, biochemistry educator, researcher; b. Montreal, Que., Aug. 30, 1943; s. Douglas Lehman and Mary (Anber) S.; m. Nancy Lynne Sengelaub, May 25, 1968; children: David, Michael. B.Sc., U. Alta., 1965; Ph.D., Stanford U., 1969. Asst. prof. chemistry Harvard U., Cambridge, Mass., 1969-74; assoc. prof. Harvard U., 1974-75; assoc. prof. biochemistry U. Alta. (Can.), Edmonton, 1975-80, prof., 1980—, McCalla rsch. prof., 1994-95. Assoc. editor Biochemistry and Cell Biology, 1983-93; mem. editl. bd. Bull. Magnetic Resonance, 1983—, Magnetic Resonance in Chemistry, 1983-95; assoc. editor Jour. Biomolecular NMR 1991—. Recipient Steacie prize Nat. Sci. Engring. Rsch. Coun., 1982, Kaplan Rsch. award, 1992; Woodrow Wilson fellow, 1965, Alfred P. Sloan fellow, 1971. Fellow Royal Soc. of Can.; mem. Can. Biochem. Soc. (pres., Ayerst award 1982), Biophys. Soc. (councillor 1989-92), Am. Chem. Soc., Protein Soc. Home: 11312 37th Ave, Edmonton, AB Canada T6J 0H5

SYKES, GRESHAM M'CREADY, sociologist, educator, artist; b. Plainfield, N.J., May 26, 1922; s. M'Cready and Beatrice (Evans) S.; m. Carla Adelt, July 13, 1946. A.B. summa cum laude, Princeton U., 1950; Ph.D. (Woodrow Wilson fellow 1950-51, Univ. fellow 1951-52), Northwestern U., 1953; M.A. (hon.), Dartmouth Coll., 1961. Instr. sociology Princeton U., 1952-54, asst. prof., bicentennial preceptor, 1954-58; assoc. prof. Northwestern U., Evanston, Ill., 1958-60; prof. sociology Dartmouth Coll., Hanover, N.H., 1960-63; chmn. dept. Dartmouth Coll., 1961-63; exec. officer Am. Sociol. Assn., 1963-65; research prof. law and sociology, dir. adminstrn. of justice program U. Denver, 1965-72; chmn. dept. sociology U. Houston, 1973; prof. sociology U. Va., Charlottesville, 1974-88, chmn. dept., 1978-81, emeritus prof., 1988—; chmn. Salzburg (Austria) Seminar in Am. Studies, summer 1965; working as artist, with frequent group and one-man exhbns., 1988—. Author: Crime and Society, rev. edit., 1967, The Society of Captives, 1958, Law and the Lawless, 1969, Social Problems in America, 1971, Criminology, 1978, rev. edit., 1992, The Future of Crime, 1980; criminology editor Jour. Criminal Law, Criminology and Police Sci., 1959-64; assoc. editor Rev. Am. Sociol. Assn., 1960-62, Contemporary Sociology, 1977-80, Criminology, 1980-84; contbr. articles and revs. to Ency. Britannica, profl. jours. Served to capt., C.E. AUS, 1942-46, ETO. Recipient Edwin H. Sutherland award Am. Soc. Criminology, 1980. Home: 311 2nd St NW # B Charlottesville VA 22902-5011

SYKES, JOLENE, publishing executive. Pub. Fortune Time, Inc., N.Y.C. Office: Time Inc Time Life Bldg Rockefeller Ctr New York NY 10020-1393*

SYKES, LYNN RAY, geologist, educator; b. Pitts., Apr. 16, 1937; s. Lloyd Ascutney and Margaret (Woodburn) S. BS, MS, MIT, 1960; PhD in Geology, Columbia U., 1964. Phys. sci. aide geophys. lab. U.S. Geol. Survey, Silver Spring, Md., summer 1956; participant summer coop. program Geophys. Svc. Inc., Dallas, 1958; Summer Rsch. fellow Woods Hole (Mass.) Oceanographic Inst., 1959; rsch. asst. Lamont-Doherty Earth Obs.-Columbia U., 1961-64, rsch. assoc. in seismology, 1964-66, adj. asst. prof. geology, 1966-68, asst. prof., 1968-69, assoc. prof., 1969-73, prof., 1973-78, Higgins prof. earth and environ. scis., 1978—, mem. univ. com. on acad. priorities, 1977-79; research geophysicist earth scis. labs. U.S. Dept. Commerce, 1966-68; Mem. panel polar geophysics Nat. Acad. Scis., 1968; adv. com. to ESSA Rsch. Labs., 1968-69; mem. subcom. geodesy and cartography applications steering com. NASA, 1968-70; mem. com. on world-wide standardized network Nat. Acad. Scis./NRC, 1969, com. seismology, 1972-73, panel earthquake prediction, 1973-75; organizing sec. Internat. Symposium Mech. Properties and Processes of Mantle of Internat. Upper Mantle Com., 1970; mem. panel on deep crustal drilling in marine areas JOIDES, 1970-71; advisor N.Y. State Geol. Survey and N.Y. State Environ. Protection Agy., 1970-80; mem. U.S. Geodynamics Panel on Mid-Atlantic Ridge, 1971-72; mem. working group U.S./USSR Joint Program for Earthquake Prediction, 1973-77; mem. U.S. Del. on Earthquake Prediction to USSR, fall, 1973; mem. adv. com. on proposals for earthquake prediction U.S. Geol. Survey, 1974, adv. panel earthquake hazards program, 1977-82; mem. U.S. Tech. Del. for talks on treaty on Threshold Limitations Underground Nuclear Explosions, Moscow, USSR, summer, 1974; mem. rev. panel earth scis. NSF, 1974-77; mem. study groups on plate interiors and Cocos and Caribbean plates U.S. Geodynamics Com.; mem. U.S. Seismology Group to People's Republic of China, fall, 1974; vis. prof. Earthquake Rsch. Inst. of Tokyo (Japan) U., fall 1974; Fairchild vis. scholar Calif. Inst. Tech., 1981; vis. fellow Clare Hall, Cambridge U., 1982; chmn. nat. earthquake prediction evaluation coun., U.S. Geol. Survey, 1984-88; mem. com. acad. priorities Columbia U., 1977-78, Columbia U. Arms Control Seminar, 1984-93, mem. external rev. com. Nat. Earthquake Hazards Reduction Program, 1987-88; mem. com. on verification of nuclear testing, treaties, Office Tech. Assessment, U.S. Congress, 1986-87; participant Belmont (Md.) Conf. on Nuclear Test Ban Policy, 1988; U.S. com. for decade of natural hazards reduction NRC, 1989-90; participant on TV show NOVA. Contbg. author: History of the Earth's Crust, 1968, Geodynamics of Iceland and the North Atlantic Area, 1974, Encounter with the Earth, 1975; Assoc. editor: Jour. Geophys. Research, 1968-70; Contbr. numerous articles to profl. jours. Pres. Far West 77th St. Block Assn., N.Y.C., 1973-74. Recipient H. O. Wood award in seismology Carnegie Instn. of Washington, 1967-70, Edward John Noble Leadership award during first three years grad. study, Pub. Service award Fedn. Am. Scientists, 1986, John Wesley Powell award U.S. Geol. Survey, 1991; Sloan fellow, 1969-71; grantee NSF, AEC, Air Force Office Sci. Rsch., NASA, N.Y. State Sci. and Tech. Found., N.Y. State Atomic and Space Devel. Authority, U.S. Geol. Survey, Sloan Found., John D. and Catherine T. MacArthur Found., Carnegie Corp., 1988-89; Guggenheim fellow, 1988-89; Proctor & Gamble scholar. Fellow Am. Geophys. Union (Macelwave award to Outstanding Young Geophysicist for 1970, Walter H. Bucher medal for original contbns. to basic knowledge of Earth's crust 1975, pres. sect. tectonophysics 1972-74, pres. sect. on seismology 1982-84), Seismol. Soc. Am., Geol. Soc. Am., Geol. Soc. London; mem. Nat. Acad. Scis., Am. Acad. Arts and Scis., Royal Astron. Soc., N.Y. Acad. Scis. (pres. geol. sect. 1970-71). Research includes maj. contbns. on plate tectonics, earthquake prediction and discrimination of underground nuclear explosions from earthquakes, arms control. Home: 100 Washington Springs Rd Palisades NY 10964-1624 Office: Columbia U Lamont-Doherty Earth Obs Palisades NY 10964

SYKES, MELVIN JULIUS, lawyer; b. Balt., Jan. 9, 1924; s. Philip Louis and Sara (Klein) S.; m. Judith Janet Konowitz, Sept.24, 1950; children: David K., Rachel A., Daniel E., Israel J. Grad., Balt. City Coll., 1940, Balt. Hebrew Coll., 1941; AB with honors, Johns Hopkins U., 1943; LLB magna cum laude, Harvard U., 1948. Bar. Md. 1949, U.S. Ct. Appeals (4th cir.) 1949, U.S. Dist. Ct. Md. 1950, U.S. Supreme Ct. 1955. Law clk. to Judge Morris A. Soper U.S. Ct. Appeals (4th cir.), 1948-49; pvt. practice Balt., 1949—; draftsman Md. Dept. Legis. Reference, 1949-50; rsch. cons. Md. Commn. Adminstrv. Orgn., 1951-52; reporter Md. commns. to study judiciary, 1953, to revise laws relating to pub. svc. commn., 1953-55; mem. standing com. on rules of practice, procedure Md. Ct. Appeals, 1954-72, 78—; mem. legis. coun. Commn. on Revision Condemnation Laws, 1961-63, Balt. Charter Revision Commn., 1962-63; pres. Bar Libr. of Balt., 1962-63; mem. Md. Constl. Conv. Commn., 1966-67; cons. Gov. Md. Commn. to Revise Testamentary Laws, 1967-69; mem. Gov. Md. commns. to study state aid to nonpub. edn., 1969-71, on annotated code Md., 1970-78. Co-author: West's Maryland Procedural Forms, 1964; co-translator Elon, Jewish Law—History, Principles, Sources, 1994. Mem. governing coun. Am. Assn. Jewish Edn., 1968-81; v.p. Balt. Jewish Coun., 1970-72; bd. dirs. Balt. chpt. Am. Jewish Com., Balt. Neighborhoods, Inc.; mem., former chmn. bd. trustees Balt. Hebrew Coll. With USAF, 1943-45. Fellow Am. Coll. Trial Lawyers, Am. Coll. Trust and Estate Counsel, Am. Bar Found., Md. Bar Found. (chmn. 1981-83); mem. ABA, Am. Law Inst., Md. Bar Assn., Balt. City Bar Assn. (lectr. continuing edn. programs), Am. Jewish Congress, Zionist Orgn. Am., B'nai B'rith, Phi Beta Kappa Fellows. Democrat. Home: 3811 Fords Ln Baltimore MD 21215 Office: 310 Maryland Bar Ctr 520 W Fayette St Baltimore MD 21201-1781

SYKES, RICHARD BROOK, microbiologist; b. Eng., Aug. 7, 1942; married; 2 children. BS, Paddington Coll., 1965; MS, London U., 1968; PhD, Bristol U., 1972; PharmD (hon.), U. Madrid. Head antibiotics rsch. unit Glaxo Rsch. Labs., 1972-77; asst. dir. dept. microbiology Squibb Inst. Med. Rsch., 1977-79, dir. microbiol., 1979-83, v..p. infectious diseases, 1983-86; dep. chief exec. Glaxo Group Rsch., Ltd., 1986; dir. group R & D Glaxo Holdings, p.l.c., 1987-93; chmn., chief exec. Glaxo Group Rsch., Ltd., 1987-93; dep. chmn., chief exec. Glaxo Holdings, p.l.c., 1993—, now pres. R&D; vis. prof. King's Coll., London, Bristol U.; chmn., chief exec. Glaxo Group Rsch. Ltd.; pres. Glaxo Inc. Rsch. Inst. Mem. Brit. Lung Found. Bus. Leader Group (chmn.), Coun. Sci Tech., Ctr. Exploitation Sci Tech. Office: Glaxo Research Inst 5 Moore Pl Durham NC 27701-4613

SYKES, STEPHANIE LYNN, library director, archivist, museum director; b. Hamilton, Ont., Can., Sept. 14, 1948; d. Harold Joseph John and Ida Fern (Merritt) S. BA with honors, U. Western Ont., London, Ont., 1971; MA in History, U. Western Ont., 1978, MLS, 1984; cert. edn., Althouse Coll., Ont., 1972. Archival asst. D.B. Weldon Libr., London, Ont., Can., 1974-77; govt. pubs. libr. D.B. Weldon Libr., London, Ont., 1977-80; tech. svcs. libr. Bell Canada Hist. Svcs., Montréal, Québec, Can., 1980-81, sect. mgr. archives, 1981-83, dir. archives, libraries, and museum, 1983—; dir. Bell Can. Inst. for Profl. Devel., 1995—. Editor: (catalogue) Regional Collection D.B. Weldon Library, 1977. Mem. Soc. Quebec Mus., Assn. Can. Archivists, Soc. Am. Archivists. Office: Bell Inst for Profl Devel, 700 De La Gauchetiere W, Montreal, PQ Canada H3B 4L1

SYKES, TRACY ALLAN, lawyer; b. Waukesha, Wis., Apr. 27, 1961; s. George and Florence May (Fowler) S. BA in Econs. magna cum laude, U. Wis., Eau Claire, 1983; JD, Boston U., 1986. Bar: Mass. 1986, U.S. Ct. Appeals (1st cir.) 1986, U.S. Dist. Ct. Mass. 1986, Minn. 1988, U.S. Ct. Appeals (8th cir.) 1988, U.S. Dist. Ct. (ea. dist.) Wis. 1989, U.S. Dist. Ct. Minn. 1990, D.C. 1992. Assoc. Rubin & Rudman, Boston, 1986-88, Doherty, Rumble & Butler, Mpls., 1988-90, Robins, Kaplan, Miller & Ciresi, Mpls., 1990-92; ptnr. Robins, Kaplan, Miller & Ciresi, Mpls. and Boston, 1992—; mediator Crime and Justice Found., Boston, 1987-88. Author: Hiring, Firing and Managing, 1992, ADA...Employers' Perspective, 1993. Mem. ABA, ATLA, Minn. Bar Assn., Boston Bar Assn., D.C. Bar Assn. Avocations: golf, scuba diving, photography. Office: Robins Kaplan Miller Ciresi 222 Berkeley St Boston MA 02116-3748

SYKORA, BARBARA ZWACH, state legislator; b. Tracy, Minn., Mar. 5, 1941; d. John M. and Agnes (Schueller) Zwach; m. Robert G. Sykora, 1965; children: Mona, John, Kara, Mary. BA, St. Catherine Coll., 1963. Tchr. Springfield (Mass.) Sch., 1963-64, Roseville (Minn.) Sch., 1964-66; mem. Minn. Ho. of Reps., St. Paul, 1994—. Vice chmn. 2d Congl. Dist. Rep. Com., Minn., 1978-82; chmn. 6th Congl. Dist. Rep. Com., 1982-86, 2d congl. dist. Senator Durenberger Campaign, 1980-82, Senator Pillsbury Campaign, Wayzata, Minn., 1980, Ind. Rep. State Com., Minn., 1987-93; dist. dir. Office Congressman Rod Grams, 1993-94; bd. mem. Animal Humane Soc. Hennepin County, Minn. Acad. Excellence Found. Mem. Twin West C. of C., Napkins/Minnetonka Rotary.

SYKORA, HAROLD JAMES, military officer; b. Tripp, S.D., Mar. 10, 1939; s. James J. and Mary (Tucek) S.; m. Patricia Ann Friedrich, Dec. 26, 1962; children: Montgomery James, Gina Marie. BS, U. S.D., 1961, MA in Math., 1965; postgrad., U. Wis., 1971-72, Indsl. Coll. Armed Forces, Ft. McNair, Washington, 1987-88. Math. tchr. Mitchell (S.D.) Sr. High Sch., 1961-64, 65-71, 72-74; commd. U.S. Army; advanced through grades to maj. gen.; with U.S. Army Command and Gen. Staff Coll., Ft. Leavenworth, Kans., 1974-75; exec. officer hdqs. 147th F.A. S.D. N.G., Pierre, 1975-80; tng. officer hdqrs. S.D. N.G., Rapid City, 1980-83, chief of staff, 1983-87, adj. gen., 1988—. Alumni Achievement award U. S.D., 1996. Mem. N.G. Assn. U.S., N.G. Assn. U.S. (pres. 1979-80), Am. Legion, Assn. U.S. Army, Adjutant's Gen. Assn. U.S. (sec. 1991-97, Army res. forces policy com. 1992-97, chmn. Army res. forces policy com. 1995-97), Kiwanis. Republican. Roman Catholic. Home: 5204 Pinedale Hts Rapid City SD 57702-2079 Office: SD NG 2823 W Main St Rapid City SD 57702-8170

SYLBERT, PAUL, production designer, art director; b. N.Y.C., Apr. 16, 1928. Art dir.: (films) The Wrong Man, 1956, (with Rolland M. Brooks and Howard Hollander) Teenage Millionaire, 1961; prodn. designer: (films) (with Richard Sylbert) Baby Doll, 1956, (with R. Sylbert) A Face in the Crowd, 1957, The Tiger Makes Out, 1967, The Drowning Pool, 1975, One Flew Over the Cuckoo's Nest, 1975, Mikey and Nicky, 1976, Hardcore, 1979, Kramer vs. Kramer, 1979, Wolfen, 1979, Resurrection, 1980, Blow Out, 1981, Gorky Park, 1983, Without a Trace, 1983, Firstborn, 1984, The Pope of Greenwich Village, 1984, The Journey of Natty Gann, 1985, Ishtar, 1987, Nadine, 1987, The Pick-Up Artist, 1987, Biloxi Blues, 1988, Fresh Horses, 1988, Career Opportunities, 1991, (with W. Steven Graham) The Prince of Tides, 1991 (Academy award nomination best art direction 1991), Rush, 1992, Sliver, 1993, Milk Money, 1994; prodn. designer, art dir.: (films) Riot, 1969, (with Edwin O'Donovan) Heaven Can Wait, 1978 (Academy award best art direction 1978); screenwriter: The Steagle, 1971, (with David Shaber) Night Hawks, 1981. Address: 52 E 64th St Ste 3 New York NY 10021-7356 Office: IATSE Local 876 11365 Ventura Blvd Ste 315 Studio City CA 91604-3148*

SYLBERT, RICHARD, production designer, art director; b. N.Y.C., Apr. 16, 1928. V.p. prodn. Paramount Pictures, 1975-78. Art dir.: (films) Patterns, 1956, Wind Across the Everglades, 1958, The Fugitive Kind, 1960, Mad Dog Coll, 1961, Splendor in the Grass, 1961, Walk on the Wild Side, 1962, Lilith, 1964, The Pawnbroker, 1965, The Heartbreak Kid, 1972, (TV series) Inner Sanctum, 1951-53; prodn. designer: (films) Crowded Paradise, 1956, (with Paul Sylbert) Baby Doll, 1956, Edge of the City, 1957, (with P. Sylbert) A Face in the Crowd, 1957, Murder, Inc., 1960, The Young Doctors, 1961, The Connection, 1962, How to Murder Your Wife, 1965, Who's Afraid of Virginia Woolf?, 1966 (Academy award best art direction 1966), Grand Prix, 1966, The Graduate, 1967, Rosemary's Baby, 1968, The April Fools, 1969, Catch-22, 1970, Carnal Knowledge, 1971, Fat City, 1972, The Day of the Dolphin, 1973, Chinatown, 1974 (Academy award nomination best art direction 1974), The Fortune, 1975, Shampoo, 1975 (Academy award nomination best art direction 1975), Players, 1979, Reds, 1981 (Academy award nomination best art direction 1981), Frances, 1982, Partners, 1982, Breathless, 1983, The Cotton Club, 1984 (Academy award nomination best art direction 1984), Under the Cherry Moon, 1986, Shoot to Kill, 1988, Tequila Sunrise, 1988, Bonfire of the Vanities, 1990, Mobsters, 1991, Carlito's Way, 1993; prodn. designer, art dir.: (films) Long Day's Journey into Night, 1962, (with Phil Jeffries) The Manchurian Candidate, 1962, All the Way Home, 1963, Dick Tracy, 1990 (Academy award best art direction 1990), (TV movie) Last Hours Before Midnight, 1975; assoc. prodr.: (films) What's New Pussycat?, 1965; visual arts cons.: (films) The Illustrated Man, 1969; set designer: (theatre) The Prisoner of Second Avenue, 1971-74, A Big Killing in Little Saigon, 1996. office: c/o Art Directors 11365 Venture Blvd # 315 Studio City CA 91604*

SYLK, LEONARD ALLEN, housing company executive, real estate developer; b. Phila., Feb. 25, 1941; s. Harry S. and Gertrude (Bardy) S.; m. Barbara Ann Lovenduski, Dec. 1, 1975; children: Tristan, Tyler, Galen. BS in Econs., U. Pa., 1963; MBA, Columbia U., 1965. Cert. comml. property builder. Founder, chmn. bd., chief exec. officer Shelter Systems Corp., Hainesport, N.J., 1965—; bd. dirs. Home Owners Warranty Corp., N.J., v.p., 1988—; bd. dirs. Am. Arbitration Assn., Internat. Housing Com., Nat. Comml. Builders Coun., 1986—; vice chmn. USA Bancshares, Inc.; chmn., bd. govs. Mid. East Forum; trustee Nat. Bldg. Sys. Coun., 1986—; pressdl. advisor on housing trade with Soviet Union, 1990. Contbr. articles to industry publs. Chmn. ann. awards dinner Jewish Nat. Fund, Phila., 1987, v.p., bd. dirs.; bd. dirs. Phila. Orch. Assn., 1990—; bd. dirs. Pa. Ballet, 1994—, exec. com., 1996—; bd. dirs. Resources for Childrens' Health, 1993—, Acad. Music, Phila., 1990—, Jewish Nat. Fund, 1987—, Rock Sch. of Pa. Ballet, 1995—; N.J. chmn. Builders for Bush, 1988; trustee Hahnemann U. and Hosp., 1991—, St. Christopher's Hosp. for Children, Phila., 1994—, St. Peter's Sch., Phila., 1995—. Named Man of Yr., 1988; recipient Tree of Life award presented by Rt. Hon. Margaret Thatcher, 1995. Mem. Nat. Assn. Homebuilders (com. chmn., nat. bd. dirs. 1984—, mem. exec. com. 1990, 97, fundraising chmn. 1991, Man of Yr. in Industrialized Housing 1990), Wood Truss Coun. Am. (bd. dirs. 1983—, pres. 1987, named to Hall of Fame 1990), Builders League South Jersey (v.p., bd. dirs. 1984—), N.J. Builders Assn. (bd. dirs., com. chmn., exec. com. 1990—), Le Club (N.Y.C.), Atlantic City Country Club, Vesper Club, Union League, Capitol Club (Washington), Masons. Republican. Home: 500 Delancey St Philadelphia PA 19106-4106 Office: Shelter Systems Corp Park Ave Hainesport NJ 08036

SYLKE, LORETTA CLARA, artist; b. Parkston, S.D., Nov. 4, 1926; d. Jacob and Maria Magdelin (Frey) Sprecher; m. Arthur C. Sylke, Apr. 26, 1961; children: Michael Arthur, Patricia, Constance, Sharon, Catherine, Charles (dec.). Grad. H.S., Chgo. Works have appeared at N.Mex. Art League, Albuquerque, 1991, El Dorado Gallery, Colorado Springs, Mont. Miniature Show, Billings, The New Eng. Fine Art Inst., The N.E. Trade Ctr., Woburn, Mass., 1993, El Dorado Gallery, Colorado Springs, 1993, 20th Annual Am. Nat. Miniature Show, Laramie, Wyo., Art in the Park, Lenexa, Kans., Gov.'s office, Madison, Wis., Custer County Art Ctr., Miles City, Mont., 1995, Laramie (Wyo.) Miniature Show, 1995; juried exhbns., Beloit, Wis., Miniature Show: Custer County Art Ctr., Miles City, Mont., 1995, 96, Miniature Exhbn., Carson City, Nev., 1996; represented in pvt. collections. Recipient Masco award Madison Art Supply, 1982. Mem. Nat. Mus. Women in the Arts, Wis. Women in the Arts, Catherine Lorillarr Wolfe Art Club (N.Y.C.). Avocations: sewing, gardening. Home: N4392 Wicks Landing Princeton WI 54968-8508 Office: 1714 Studio Princeton WI 54968

SYLLA, RICHARD EUGENE, economics educator; b. Harvey, Ill., Jan. 16, 1940; s. Benedict Andrew and Mary Gladys (Curran) S.; m. Edith Anne Dudley, June 22, 1963; children: Anne Curran, Margaret Dudley. BA, Harvard U., 1962, MA, 1965, PhD, 1969. Prof. econs. and bus. N.C. State U., Raleigh, 1968-90; Henry Kaufman prof. history fin. insts. and markets NYU, N.Y.C., 1990—, prof. econs., 1990—; cons. Citibank NA, N.Y.C., 1979-82, Chase Manhattan Bank, N.Y.C., 1983-85; vis. prof. U. Pa., Phila., 1983, U. N.C., Chapel Hill, 1988. Author: The American Capital Market, 1975; co-author: Evolution of the American Economy, 1980, 2d edit., 1993, A History of Interest Rates, 1991, rev. edit., 1996; co-editor: Patterns of European Industrialization, 1991, Anglo-American Financial Systems, 1995; editor Jour. Econ. History, 1978-84. Study fellow NEH, 2975-76; Rsch. grantee NSF, 1985-94, Rsch. grantee Sloan Found., 1995-97. Mem. Am. Econs. Assn., Econ. History Assn. (v.p. 1987-88, trustee 1977-88, Arthur H. Cole prize 1970), Bus. History Conf. (trustee 1991-94), So. Econ. Assn. (v.p. 1981-82), Cliometrics Soc. (trustee 1997—). Avocations: golf, hiking, fishing, stamp collecting, arts. Home: 110 Bleecker St Apt 23D New York NY 10012-2106 Office: NYU 44 W 4th St New York NY 10012-1106

SYLVESTER, GEORGE HOWARD, retired air force officer; b. Riverside, N.J., Aug. 10, 1927; s. Ralph Davis and Dorothy Clarisse (Mealley) S.; m. Elaine Ruth Winderling, June 7, 1949; children—Wendy, Susan, David. B.S., U.S. Mil. Acad., 1949; M.A., Georgetown U., 1956. Commd. 2d lt. U.S. Air Force, 1949, advanced through grades to lt. gen., 1976; pilot, 1949-54; asst. prof. social scis. U.S. Mil. Acad., 1956-60; long-range planner Hdqrs. U.S. Air Force, 1961-64; mil. asst. to sec. def., 1964-66; squadron comdr. F-4 squadron Vietnam, 1966; comdr. Danang Air Base, Vietnam, 1967; dir. test Eglin AFB, Fla., 1968-70; asst. dir. tactical systems test and evaluation Office Sec. Def., 1970-73; dep. for systems ASD, Wright-Patterson AFB, Ohio, 1973-74; vice comdr. ASD, 1974-76, comdr., 1976-79; vice comdr. AF Systems Command, Andrews AFB, Md., 1979-81; ret., 1981, ind. aerospace cons., 1981—. Decorated D.S.M. with 1 oak leaf cluster, Legion of Merit with 2 oak leaf clusters, D.F.C., Air medal with 7 oak leaf clusters, Air Force Commendation medal with 2 oak leaf clusters. Lutheran. Home: 4839 Conicville Rd Mount Jackson VA 22842-2800

SYLVESTER, JOHN EDWARD, social worker; b. N.Y.C., Apr. 13, 1949; s. John and Esther (Larkin) S.; m. Dolores Alcantara, July 2, 1974. BA in Psychology, CUNY, 1975; cert. in social work, Fordham U., 1977. Program coord. Mid. Bronx (N.Y.) Sr. Citizen's Coun., 1980-82; assoc. editor N.Y.C. Self-Help Clearing House, 1978-80; case worker Cath. Guardian Soc., N.Y.C., 1982-83, Assn. for Advancement of the Blind, Queens, N.Y., 1984-86; probation officer N.Y.C. Dept. of Probation, Bronx, 1987-88; parole officer N.Y. State Div. of Parole, N.Y.C., 1988-92; program dir. Ehrlich Supported Housing Program for Homeless Univ. Consultation and Treatment Ctr. for Mental Hygiene, Bronx, 1992-95; tenant organizer N.W. Bronx Cmty. and Clergy Coalition, 1997—. Mem. Am. Servicemen's Union, N.Y.C., 1968; vol. ARC, N.Y.C., 1973. With USMC, 1967-70, Vietnam. Named one of Outstanding Young Men in Am., U.S. Jaycees, 1982. Mem. Assn. Black Social Workers, Amnesty Internat. Home: 2116 Clinton Ave Bronx NY 10457-3628

SYLVESTER, MICHAEL LANE, vocalist; b. Noblesville, Ind., Aug. 21, 1951; s. Charles Jr. and Judith Ann (Pickett) S.; m. Sandra Michele Weed, Aug. 3, 1973 (div. Oct. 1979); 1 child, Steven David; m. Michele Ann Kidd, May 15, 1981; 1 child, Griffin Parker. MB, Westminster Choir Coll., 1974; MusM, Ind. U., 1978. Assoc. prof. voice Ind. U., Bloomington, 1974-78; asst. prof. voice Ind. Ctrl. U., Indpls., 1976-78; prof. voice Cameron U., Lawton, Okla., 1978-79. Appeared in maj. opera houses throughout world; leading roles at The Met. Opera, N.Y., The Royal Opera at Covent Garden, London, The Vienna State Opera, Milan's Teatro alla Scala, San Francisco Opera, The Chgo. Lyric, Berlin State Opera, Paris' Opera Bastille. Recipient Alumni Merit award Westminster Choir Coll., 1993, 1st place Met. Opera Auditions, Met. Opera Nat. Coun., N.Y.C., 1986, MacAllister Voice Competition, Indpls., 1986, San Francisco Opera Merola, 1982. Mem. Am. Guild Musical Artists. Republican. Avocations: writing, computer programming.

SYLVESTER, RONALD CHARLES, newspaper writer; b. Springfield, Mo., Feb. 10, 1959; s. Edgar Donald and Barbara Jean (Hedgecock) S.; 1 child, Christian Alexander. Sports writer Springfield (Mo.) News-Leader, 1976-88, entertainment writer, 1988-96, gen. assignment news reporter, 1996—; mem. media panel Leadership Music, Nashville, 1993. Author: Branson: On Stage in the Ozarks, 1994; contbr. articles to New Country Music, Gannett News Svc., Colliers Ency. Bd. dirs. Entertainers Guild of Branson, Mo., 1993-94. Mem. Country Music Assn. Mem. Christian Ch. (Disciples of Christ). Avocations: music, reading, outdoor recreation. Office: Springfield News-Leader 651 N Boonville Ave Springfield MO 65806-1005

SYLVESTRE, JEAN GUY, former national librarian; b. Sorel, Que., Can., May 17, 1918; s. Maxime Arthur and Yvonne Marie (Lapierre) S.; m. Francoise Poitevin, Feb. 27, 1943; children: Marie, Jean, Paul. B.A., U. Ottawa, 1939, B.Ph., 1940, M.A., 1942, D.L.S. (hon.), 1969, D.Litt. (hon.), 1970, LL.D. (hon.), 1974, 75, 82. Translator Dept. Can. Sec. of State, 1942-44; editor Wartime Info. Bd., 1944-45; asst. pvt. sec. to minister of justice, 1945-47, pvt. sec. to sec. of state for external affairs, 1947-48, pvt. sec. to prime minister, 1948-50; adminstrv. officer Dept. Resources and Devel., 1950-53; asst. librarian Library of Parliament, Ottawa, Ont., 1953-56; asso. parliamentary librarian Library of Parliament, 1956-68, nat. librarian, 1968-83; pres., chmn. bd. Can. Inst. for Hist. Microprodns., 1983-86; chmn. Ottawa Valley Book Festival, 1988-92; hon. chmn., 1993—. Author: Louis Francoeur, journaliste, 1941, Situation de la poésie canadienne, 1941, Anthologie de la poésie canadienne-française, 1943, 58, 64, 66, 68, 74, Poétes catholiques de la France contemporaine, 1944, Sondages, 1945, Impressions de théâtre, 1950, Amours, délices et orgues, 1953, Panorama des lettres canadiennes-francaises, 1964, Canadian Writers, 1964, Literature in French Canada, 1967, A Century of Canadian Literature, 1967, The Future of the National Library of Canada, 1980, Guidelines for National Libraries, 1987 French, Spanish and Arabic edits., 1988; also articles in profl. jours., encys.;

editor: A Canadian Errant (J.P. Manion), 1960; editor: Canadian Universities Today, 1961, Structures sociales du Canada francais, 1967. Chmn. Gov. Gen.'s Lit. Awards, 1960-62; organizer, chmn. World Poetry Conf., Expo 1967; chmn. Can. Council Com. on Aid-to-Publs., 1960-68; lectr. U. Ottawa Library Sch., 1954-71; v.p. Can. Library Week Council, 1965-67; Bd. dirs. Can. Writers Found., pres., 1960-61. Decorated comdr. Ordre International du Bien Public, officer Order of Can.; comdr. Order of Merit of Poland; recipient Centennial medal., Outstanding Pub. Service award, Internat. Fedn. Libr. Assn. medal. Fellow Royal Soc. Can. (hon. sec. 1959-62, pres. sect. I 1963-64, hon. libr. 1969-91, pres. 1973-74); mem. Soc. Ecrivains Canadiens, Can. Libr. Assn. (life), Ont. Libr. Assn. (hon. life), Can. Assn. Info. Sci. (pres. 1971-72), Assn. Scis. et Techniques (life). Home: 2286 Bowman Rd, Ottawa, ON Canada K1H 6V6

SYMANSKI, ROBERT ANTHONY, treasurer; b. Mineola, N.Y., June 17, 1946; s. Anthony John and Mary (Jozef) S.; m. Eileen Margaret Eardley; children: Susan, Robert, Patti. AAS, SUNY, Delhi, 1966; BBA, Pace U., 1972; MBA, Fairleigh Dickinson U., 1984. Sr. credit rep. Union Carbide Corp., N.Y.C., 1967-71; credit mgr. GAF Corp., N.Y.C., 1971-73; dir. cash mgmt. GAF Corp., Wayne, N.J., 1973-77; mgr. corp. cash Coca-Cola Bottling Co. N.Y., Hackensack, N.J., 1977-81; asst. treas. The BOC Group Inc., Montvale, N.J., 1981-86; treas. The BOC Group Inc., Murray Hill, N.J., 1986—. Sgt. USAF, 1967-69. Mem. Nat. Assn. Corp. Treas., Treasury Mgmt. Assn., Fin. Execs. Insts. Roman Catholic. Home: 16 Susan Dr Chatham NJ 07928-1049 Office: The BOC Group Inc 575 Mountain Ave New Providence NJ 07974-2097

SYMCHOWICZ, SAMSON, biochemist; b. Krakow, Poland, Mar. 20, 1923; came to U.S., 1954; s. Chiel and Esther M. S.; m. Sarah R. Nussbaum, May 24, 1953; children: Esther, Beatrice, Caren. Chem. engr., Poly. Inst. Prague, Czechoslovakia, 1950; MS in Chemistry, Bklyn. Poly. Inst., 1956; PhD in Biochemistry, Rutgers U., 1960. Asst. biochemist McGill U., Montreal, Que., Can., 1951-54, SUNY, 1954-56; biochemist Schering-Plough Corp., Bloomfield, N.J., 1956-73, assoc. dir. biol. rsch., 1973-80, dir. drug metabolism, 1980-92. Editorial bd. Drug Metabolism and Disposition; contbr. over 90 sci. papers to profl. publs. Mem. Am. Soc. Microbiology, Am. Chem. Soc., N.Y. Acad. Sci., Soc. Pharmacology and Exptl. Therapeutics.

SYME, SHERMAN LEONARD, epidemiology educator; b. Dauphin, Man., Can., July 4, 1932; came to U.S., 1950; s. Robert and Rose (Bay) S.; m. Marilyn Elaine Egenes, July 28, 1932; children: Karen, David, Janet. BA, UCLA, 1953, MA, 1955; PhD, Yale U., 1957. Commd. USPHS, Washington, 1957-68; advanced through grades to chief Tng. Sta. USPHS, San Francisco, 1962-68; sociologist USPHS, Washington, 1957-60; exec. sec. NIH, Bethesda, Md., 1960-62; prof. emeritus epidemiology U. Calif., Berkeley, 1968—; chmn. Dept. Epidemiology, U. Calif., 1975-80; vis. prof. Teikyo U., Tokyo, 1977, York (Eng.) U., 1975, St. Thomas Sch. Medicine, London, 1980, U. London, 1989; expert adv. panels WHO, Geneva, 1975—. Co-editor Social Stress and Heart Disease, 1967, Social Support and Health, 1985; contbr. 115 articles to profl. jours. Fellow Am. Heart Assn., Soc. Epidemiol. Research; mem. Inst. Medicine, Am. Epidemiol. Soc. Office: U Calif Sch Pub Health Pub Health Biology & Epidemiology 140 Warren Hall Berkeley CA 94720-7361

SYMENS, MAXINE BRINKERT TANNER, restaurant owner; b. Primghar, Iowa, June 12, 1930; d. George Herman and Irene Marie (Dahnke) Brinkert; m. Jack Frederiksen Tanner, Dec. 28, 1950 (dec. Oct. 1976); m. Delbert Glenn Symens, Sept. 26, 1981. BS magna cum laude, Westmar Coll., 1970. Cert. tchr., Iowa. Elem. tchr. Rural Sch. O'Brien Co., Primghar, 1949-54, Gaza (Iowa) Com. Sch., 1954-60; secondary tchr. Primghar Com. Sch., 1960-81; fitness salon owner Slim 'N' Trim, George, Rock Rapids, Iowa, 1982-87; restaurant owner George Cafe, 1985-90, Pizza Ranch, 1988-96; with network mktg. divsn. Espial and STS, Global Prosperity & Family of Eagles, 1996—; advt. sales cons. for Internet advt. Pres. Primghar Edn. Assn., 1970-71. Mem. George C. of C., George Kiwanis Club (sec. 1991-95), Delta Kappa Gamma. Lutheran. Home: 307 Dell St NE George IA 51237-1030

SYMINGTON, J. FIFE, III, governor; b. N.Y.C., Aug. 12, 1945; s. John Fife Jr. and Martha (Frick) S.; m. Leslie Marion Barker, June 1, 1968 (div. Jan. 1973); childen: Fife IV, Scott; m. Ann Pritzlaff, Feb. 7, 1976; children: Whitney, Richard, Tom. Student, Harvard U., 1968. Ptnr. Lincoln Property Co., Phoenix, 1972-76; chmn. of the bd. The Symington Co., Phoenix, 1976-89; gov. State of Ariz., 1991—. Precinct committeeman Ariz.'s Legis. Dist. 24, Paradise Valley; fin. chmn. State Republican Party, Phoenix, 1982-84; campaign advisor Rep. John Rhodes, Sen. John McCain, Ariz.; chmn. Phoenix Citizens Police Protection Bond Com., 1988; v.p. bd. trustees Heard Mus.; mem. Men's Art Coun., Environ. Quality Commn., 1971-73, Ariz. Children's Found.; dep. sheriff Maricopa County Air Posse; exec. bd. Phoenix Community Alliance. Capt. USAF, 1968-71. Mem. Western Govs.' Assn. (chmn. 1992—). Episcopalian. Office: Govs Office 1700 W Washington St Phoenix AZ 85007-2812*

SYMMERS, WILLIAM GARTH, international maritime lawyer; b. Bronxville, N.Y., Nov. 30, 1910; s. James Keith and Agnes Louise (Shuey) S.; m. Marina Baruch, Apr. 25, 1936; children: Benjamin Keith, Ann St. Clair (Mrs. Edward L. Reed); m. Anne H. Ellis, Mar. 20, 1946; children: Barbara (Mrs. Thomas M. Bancroft, Jr.), Susan (Mrs. Peter Amory Bradford), Deborah. Grad., Lawrenceville (N.J.) Sch., 1929; AB, U. Va., 1933, JD, 1935. Bar: N.Y. 1937, U.S. Supreme Ct. 1940, D.C. 1953. Assoc. Bigham, Englar, Jones & Houston, N.Y.C., 1935-37; mem. Dow and Symmers, N.Y.C., 1940-56; founding ptnr. Symmers, Fish & Warner, N.Y.C., 1956-91; ret.; admiralty counsel U.S. Maritime Commn., 1937-41; spl. counsel to naval affairs com. U.S. Ho. of Reps.; active investigation loss of SS Normandie, 1942; counsel War Shipping Adminstrn. Vessel Oper. Agts., 1942-45, admiralty and shipping litigation; U.S. del., v.p. Antwerp Conf., Comité Maritime Internat., 1947; also del. Maritime Law Assn. U.S. to succeeding confs., Amsterdam, 1949, Brighton, 1952, Madrid, 1955, N.Y.C., 1966, Tokyo, 1968, Rio de Janeiro, 1977, Montreal, 1981; titular mem. Comité Maritime Internat., 1955—; mem. U.S. Supreme Ct. adv. com. on admiralty rules, 1960-72. Contbr. articles to maritime publs. Mem. ABA, Assn. Bar City of N.Y. (chmn. admiralty com. 1953-56), Am. Soc. Internat. Law, Maritime Law Assn. U.S. (chmn. com. revision U.S. Supreme Ct. admiralty rules 1952-56, mem. exec. com. 1958-61, 1st v.p. 1964-66), Internat. Maritime Arbitration Orgn. (U.S. rep. 1978-81), St. Andrew's Soc. N.Y., English-Speaking Union U.S., Down Town Assn., N.Y. Yacht Club, Indian Harbor Yacht Club (Greenwich, Conn.), Phi Delta Phi, Phi Delta Theta. Address: 444 E 52nd St New York NY 10022-6446

SYMMES, WILLIAM DANIEL, lawyer; b. Spokane, Wash., Sept. 10, 1938; s. William John and Sheila (Deacon) S.; m. Jayne Peters, June 20, 1959; children: Ashley, William. AB cum laude, Georgetown U., 1960; MBA, Columbia U., 1962; LLB, Stanford U., 1965. Bar: Calif. 1966, U.S. Ct. Appeals (9th cir.) 1966, Wash., 1968, U.S. Supreme Ct. 1982. Assoc. Burris & Lagerlof, L.A., 1965-68, Witherspoon, Kelley, Davenport & Toole, Spokane, 1968—; adj. prof. Gonzaga U., Spokane, 1971-77; part owner, officer, dir. Pacific Coast League AAA Spokane Indians, 1978-82, Las Vegas Stars, 1983-85. Bd. dirs. Greater Spokane Sports Assn., 1984—, Spokane Youth Sports Assn., 1985—, also others. Named Outstanding Young Man Yr. Spokane Jr. C. of C., 1969. Fellow Am. Coll. Trial Lawyers; mem. ABA, Am. Bd. Trial Advocates, Wash. State Bar Assn., Calif. Bar Assn., Spokane County Bar Assn. (chmn. jud. liaison com. 1982-84), Def. Rsch. Inst., Wash. Def. Lawyers Assn., Spokane C. of C., Empire Club, Spokane Club, Manito Golf and Country Club. Home: 3606 S Eastgate Ct Spokane WA 99203-1411 Office: Witherspoon Kelley Davenport & Toole 1100 Nat Bank Bldg Spokane WA 99201

SYMMONDS, RICHARD EARL, gynecologist; b. Greensburg, Mo., Mar. 19, 1922; s. Emmett E. S. A.B., Central Coll., Fayette, Mo., 1943; M.D., Duke U., 1946; M.S. in Ob-Gyn, U. Minn., 1953. Intern Los Angeles County Hosp., 1946, resident in Ob-Gyn, 1950-53, resident in gen. surgery, 1954-56; practice medicine specializing in gen. surgery Rochester, Minn., 1958—; mem. faculty Mayo Clinic, Rochester, 1953—, prof. gynecologic surgery, 1960—, chmn. dept., 1970-92, chmn. emeritus, 1992—. Contbr. articles to profl. jours. Served with USN, 1947-49. Fellow A.C.S.; mem. Am. Gynecol. Soc., Am. Assn. Obstetricians and Gynecologists, Soc. Pelvic Surgeons, Soc. Gynecologic Oncologists, Am. Coll. Obstetricians and Gynecologists. Office: 200 1st St SW Rochester MN 55902-3008

SYMON, LINDSAY, retired neurological educator; b. Aberdeen, Scotland, Nov. 4, 1929; s. William Lindsay and Isabel (Shaw) S.; m. Pauline Barbara Rowland, Aug. 14, 1953; children: Lindsay Fraser, Barbara Rosemary, Fiona Margaret. MB, ChB with honors, Aberdeen U., Scotland, 1951; Diplomate, Royal Coll. Surgeons, Edinburgh, 1957, Royal Coll. Surgeons, London, 1959. Jr. specialist, house surgeon Royal Infirmary, Aberdeen, Scotland, 1952-3; surgical registrar Royal Infirmary, Aberdeen, 1956-58; clin. rsch. fellow med. rsch. coun. neurosurgical registrar Middlesex & Maida Vale Hosp., London, 1958-61, sr. registrar in Neurosurgery, 1962-65; Rockefeller travelling fellow in medicine Wayne U., Detroit, 1961-62; cons. neurosurgeon Nat. Hosp. for Nervous Diseases, London, 1965-78; cons. St. Thomas Hosp., London, 1970-78, hon. cons., 1978-95; prof. Neurol. Surgery Inst. Neurology U. London Nat. Hosp. Queens Sq., London, 1978-95; cons. (hon.) Hammersmith Hosp., London, Royal Ear, Nose and Throat Hosp., London; civilian advisor in Neurol. Surgery, The Royal Navy. Contbr. articles to profl. jours.; mem. many editorial bds. med. jours. Vol. Mobile Neurosurg. Unit, Territorial Army, Keogh Barracks, Mytchett, 1975-81. Maj. Royal Army Med. Corps, 1953-55. Decorated with Territorial decoration, The Queen, 1968, Comdr. of British Empire, Queen's Birthday, 1994. Fellow ACS (hon.), Royal Coll. Surgeons (Edinborough), Royal Coll. Surgeons (London), Royal Soc. Medicine (hon.); mem. Soc. Brit. Neurol. Surgeons, World Fedn. Neurosurg. Socs. (pres. 1989-93), Caledonian Slub, St. andrews Royal and Ancient Golf Club, others. Avocations: golf, medieval history. Home: Maple Lodge Rivar Rd, Wiltshire Shalbourne Marlborough SN8 3QE, England

SYMONDS, NORMAN LESLIE, computer programming specialist; b. Hawthorne, Calif., July 10, 1953; s. Malcolm F. and Nancy J. (Raab) S.; m. Catherine Anne Meades, Jan. 1, 1994. BA in Math., U. Calif., Berkeley, 1978; MBA in Mgmt. Sci., U. So. Calif., 1981. Programmer Burroughs Corp. (Unisys), Pasadena, Calif., 1978-81; sr. systems analyst Sungard Fin. Systems, Canoga Park, Calif., 1981-89; programming project leader Dames & Moore, L.A., 1989—. Avocations: chess, martial arts, tennis, hiking, fine dining. Home: 24120 Mariano St Woodland Hills CA 91367-5822 Office: Dames & Moore 911 Wilshire Blvd Ste 700 Los Angeles CA 90017-3436

SYMONDS, PAUL SOUTHWORTH, mechanical engineering educator, researcher; b. Manila, Aug. 20, 1916; came to U.S., 1917; s. George R.B. and Claire Louise (Southworth) S.; m. Ilese Powell, Jan. 23, 1943; children: Alan Powell, Robin Peter. BS, Rensselaer Poly. Inst., 1938; MS, Cornell U., 1941, PhD, 1943; Docteur en Sciences Appliquées (hon.), Faculté Polytechnique de Mons, Belgium, 1988. Instr. mechanics Cornell U., Ithaca, N.Y., 1941-43; physicist Naval Research Lab., Washington, 1943-47; asst. prof. engring. Brown U., Providence, 1947-51, assoc. prof., 1951-54, prof., 1954-83, prof. engring. rsch. emeritus, 1983—, chmn. div. engring., 1959-62. Editl. bd. Quar. Applied Math., 1965—; mem. adv. bd. Internat. Jour. Mech. Sci., 1978—; mem. editl. adv. bd. Internat. Jour. Impact Engring., 1983—, Computer Methods in Applied Mechanics and Engring., 1983—; also numerous papers in tech. jours. Recipient Fulbright award 1949-50, 57-58; fellow Imperial Chem. Industries, Cambridge, U.K., 1950-51; Guggenheim fellow Swansea, Wales, 1957-58; NSF sr. postdoctoral fellow Oxford, Eng., 1964-65. Fellow ASME, ASCE, Am. Acad. Mechanics; mem. Internat. Assn. Bridge and Structual Engring. Home: 229 Medway St Apt 110 Providence RI 02906-5300 Office: Brown U Divsn Enging Providence RI 02912

SYMON-GUTIERREZ, PATRICIA PAULETTE, dietitian; b. Orange, N.J., Jan. 21, 1948; d. Michael and Aneilia (Jablonski) Symon; m. Alfonso Pelayo Gutierrez, Jan. 20, 1990. Dietetic cert., N.Y. Inst. Dietetics, 1967; BS in Dietetics, Ga. Coll., 1978; MS in Nutrition and Dietetics, Finch U. Health Scis., Chgo., 1996. Lic. dietitian, Fla. Staff dietitian Landmark Learning Ctr., Opa-Loka, Fla., 1982-86; food svc. dir., dietitian Palm Ct. Nursing and Rehab. Ctr., Wilton Manors, Fla., 1986-87; food svc. dir. Canteen Co.-Dade County Juvenile Ctr., Miami, Fla., 1987-88; food svc. dir., dietitian Manor Care-Boca Raton, Fla., 1988-90, Manor Care-Plantation, Fla., 1990-92; dir. dietary svcs., dietitian Menorah House, Boca Raton, 1992-96; dir. nutritional svcs. PersonaCare of Pompano, Pompano Beach, Fla., 1996—; pvt. practice Nutrionally Yours, 1997—. Mem. Am. Dietetic Assn., Phi Sigma, Phi Upsilon Omicron. Episcopalian. Avocations: arts and crafts, reading, swimming, cooking. Home: 8991 Sunset Strip Sunrise FL 33322-3737

SYMONS, EDWARD LEONARD, JR., lawyer, educator, investment advisor; b. Pitts., Dec. 21, 1941; s. Edward Leonard and Lillian Mae (Daniel) S.; m. Louise Quinn, July 18, 1970; children: Amy, Colin. B.A., Cornell U., 1963; J.D. summa cum laude, U. Pitts., 1969. Assoc., ptnr. Reding, Blackstone, Rea & Sell, Pitts., 1969-72; asst. atty. gen., chief counsel Pa. Dept. Banking, Harrisburg, 1972-74; prof. law U. Pitts. Sch. Law, 1974—; tax cons., Wash. State, 1987, Del., 1995; pres. Dollins Symons Mgmt., Inc., 1983—; exec. v.p. investments Smithfield Trust Co., 1996—; mem. adv. coun. Conflict Resolution Ctr. Internat., 1994—; mem. bd. internat. scholars Ctr. for Comml. Law Studies, Queen Mary and Westfield Coll., U. London, 1993—. Co-author: Pennsylvania Professional Corporations, 1974, Banking Law Teaching Materials, 1st edit., 1976, 3d edit., 1991, Regulation of Financial Institutions, 1997; contbr. articles to profl. jours. Commr. Mt. Lebanon, Pa., 1976-80; bd. dirs. Performing Arts for Children, Pitts., 1980-84, Mt. Lebanon Hosp. Authority, 1993—, St. Clair Hosp. Found., Pitts., 1994—, St. Clair Hosp Bd., 1995—. 1st lt. arty. AUS, 1964-66, Korea. Mem. ABA (banking law com., consumer fin. svcs. com., devel. in investment svcs. com.), Order of Coif. Office: U Pitts Sch Law 3900 Forbes Ave Pittsburgh PA 15213

SYMONS, J. KEITH, bishop; b. Champion, Mich., Oct. 14, 1932. Student, St. Thomas Sem., Bloomfield, Conn., St. Mary Sem., Balt. Ordained priest Roman Catholic Ch., 1958, consecrated bishop, 1981. Titular bishop of Siguritanus and aux. bishop of St. Petersburg Fla., 1981-83, bishop of Pensacola-Tallahassee, 1983-90, bishop of Palm Beach, 1990—. Office: PO Box 109650 Palm Beach Gardens FL 33410

SYMONS, JAMES MARTIN, theater and dance educator; b. Jacksonville, Ill., May 7, 1937; s. James and Pauline (Barton) S.; m. Judith White, Nov. 14, 1959; children: Tracy, Kelly, Carrie. BA, Ill. Coll., 1959; MA, So. Ill. U., 1964; PhD, Cornell U., 1970. Asst. prof. Yankton (S.D.) Coll., 1964-67; assoc. prof. Coll. St. Catherine, St. Paul, 1970-74, SUNY, Albany, 1974-77; prof., chair Trinity U., San Antonio, 1977-84; prof., chair theatre and dance dept. U. Colo., Boulder, 1984—; actor Off-Broadway, N.Y.C., 1959, Mo. Repertory Theatre, Kansas City, 1984; dir., actor Colo. Shakespeare Festival, Boulder, 1985—, producing artistic dir., 1994-95; leader People-to-People Del. of Theater Educators, USSR and Czechoslovakia, 1991. Author: Meyerhold's Theatre of the Grotesque, 1971 (Freedley Meml. award Theatre Libr. Assn. 1971); contbr. articles to scholarly jours. Lt. (j.g.) USN, 1960-63. Mem. Assn. for Theatre in Higher Edn. (pres. 1989-91), Assn. for Communication Adminstrn. (pres. 1990). Democrat. Methodist. Office: U of Colorado Dept Theatre And Dance Boulder CO 80309

SYMONS, JAMES MARTIN, environmental engineer, educator; b. Champaign, Ill., Nov. 24, 1931; s. George Edgar and Virginia (Thompson) S.; m. Joan Mildred Kinsman, June 29, 1958; children: Andrew James, Linda Joan, Julie Ann. BCE, Cornell U., 1954; SM in San. Engring., MIT, 1955, ScD in San. Engring., 1957. Registered engr., Tex.; diplomate Am. Acad. Environ. Engrs. Asst. prof. san. engring. MIT, 1957-62; rsch. engr. USPHS, Cin., 1962-1970; supr. rsch. engr. U.S. EPA, Cin., 1970-82; prof. civil engring. U Houston, 1982-95; Cullen disting. prof. civil engring. U. Houston, 1995—. Contbr. articles to profl. jours. Fellow ASCE; mem. Am. Water Works Assn. (hon., life, chmn. water quality div. 1980-81), Water Environment Fedn., Nat. Acad. Engring. Methodist. Avocations: photography, golf. Office: U of Houston Dept Civil Environ Eng Houston TX 77204-4791

SYMONS, ROBERT SPENCER, electronic engineer; b. San Francisco, July 3, 1925; s. Spencer W. and Avesia (Atkins) S.; m. Alice Faye Smith, Dec. 21, 1960; children: Julia Ann, Robert Spencer Jr. BS, Stanford U., 1946, MS, 1948. Engr. Eitel-McCullough, Inc., San Bruno, Calif., 1947, Heinz & Kaufman, South San Francisco, 1948, Pacific Electronics Co., Los Gatos, Calif., 1949; sr. engring. mgr. Varian Assocs., Palo Alto, Calif., 1950-83; tech. dir. Litton Industries, San Carlos, Calif., 1983—. Recipient Charles B. Thornton award for Advanced Technology Achievement, 1991. Patentee in field. Served to 1st lt. AUS, 1950-53. Fellow IEEE (assoc. editor Transactions on Electron Devices jour. 1980-83); mem. Phi Beta Kappa, Tau Beta Pi. Club: Commonwealth of Calif. Home: 290 Surrey Pl Los Altos CA 94022-2146 Office: Litton Industries 960 Industrial Rd San Carlos CA 94070-4116

SYMONS, TIMOTHY JAMES MCNEIL, physicist; b. Southborough, Kent, Eng., Aug. 4, 1951; came to U.S., 1977; s. Henry McNeil and Catherine Muriel (Rees) S.; m. S.B. Master, Mar. 1, 1987; children: Henry Benjamin, Daniel Robert. BA, Oxford (Eng.) U., 1972, MA, DPhil, 1976. Rsch. fellow Sci. Rsch. Coun., Eng., 1976-77; postdoctoral fellow Lawrence Berkeley (Calif.) Lab., 1977-79, div. fellow, 1979-84, sr. physicist, 1984—, dir. nuclear sci. div., 1985-95; vis. scientist Max-Planck Inst., Heidelberg, Germany, 1980-81; mem. U.S. nuclear physics del. to USSR, 1986; mem. program adv. coms. Gesellschaft fur schwerionen forschung, 1987-88, Continuous Electron Beam Accelerator Facility, 1989-92, Brookhaven Nat. Lab., 1991-92; mem. policy com. Relativstic Heavy Ion Collider, 1988—; mem. nuclear scis. adv. com. NSF, 1997—. Contbr. over 70 articles to sci. jours. Fellow Am. Phys. Soc. (chmn. Bonner prize com. 1990). Avocations: music, gardening, travel. Office: Lawrence Berkeley Lab Nuclear Sci Divsn 1 Cyclotron Rd 70A-3307 Berkeley CA 94720

SYMOSEK, PETER FRANK, research scientist; b. Lawrence, Mass., Sept. 22, 1953; s. Frank John and Theresa Alice (McTiernan) S. BS, Merrimack Coll., North Andover, Mass., 1978; ScM, Brown U., 1980, PhD, 1985. Sr. prin. rsch. scientist Honeywell, Inc., Mpls., 1985—. Contbr. articles to IEEE Jour., Computer Graphics Image Processing. Mem. IEEE, Soc. Photo-optical Instrumentation Engrs., Toastmasters. Avocations: golfing, scuba diving, swimming, bicycling, reading. Office: Honeywell Tech Ctr MN65-2500 3660 Technology Dr # Mn65-250 Minneapolis MN 55418-1006

SYNAN, EDWARD ALOYSIUS, JR., clergyman, former institute president; b. Fall River, Mass., Apr. 13, 1918; s. Edward Aloysius and Mary F. (McDermott) S. AB, Seton Hall Coll., 1938; student, U. Louvain, Belgium, 1938-40, Immaculate Conception Sem., Darlington, N.J., 1940-41; STL, Cath. U. Am., 1942; LMS, Pontifical Inst. Medieval Studies, Toronto, 1951; MA, PhD, U. Toronto, 1952. Ordained priest Roman Cath. Ch., 1942. Curate Immaculate Conception Ch., Montclair, N.J., 1942-44; prof. philosophy, chmn. dept. Seton Hall U., South Orange, N.J., 1952-59; prof. history of mediaeval philosophy Pontifical Inst. Mediaeval Studies, U. Toronto, 1959, pres., 1973-79, acting pres., 1989-90. Author: The Popes and The Jews in the Middle Ages, 1965, The Works of Richard of Campsall, Vol. I, 1968, Vol. II, 1982; assoc. editor, contbr.: The Bridge, Yearbook of Judaeo-Christian Studies, 1955-62; adv. bd.: Speculum, 1971-74; contbr. chpts. to books, articles and revs. to publs. Served as capt. (chaplain) USAAF/.USAF, 1944-48. Fellow Royal Soc. Can.; mem. Am. Cath. Philos. Assn. (Aquinas medal 1991), Mediaeval Acad. Am., Renaissance Soc. Am., Am. Soc. Polit. and Legal Philosophy. Address: 59 Queen's Park, Toronto, ON Canada M5S 2C4

SYNNOTT, MARCIA GRAHAM, history educator; b. Camden, N.J., July 4, 1939; d. Thomas Whitney and Beatrice Adelaide (Colby) S.; m. William Edwin Sharp, June 16, 1979; children: Willard William Sharp, Laurel Beth Sharp. AB, Radcliffe Coll., 1961; MA, Brown U., 1964; PhD, U. Mass., 1974. History tchr. MacDuffie Sch., Springfield, Mass., 1963-68; instr. U. S.C., Columbia, 1972-74, asst. prof., 1974-79, assoc. prof. history, 1979-97, dir. grad. studies history dept., 1990-92, prof. history, 1997—. Author: The Half-Opened Door, 1979; contbr. essays to books. Fulbright scholar, 1988; Am. Coun. Learned Socs. grantee, 1981. Mem. Am. Hist. Assn., So. Hist. Assn., Orgn. Am. Historians (membership com. 1990-93), S.C. Hist. Assn. (pres. 1994-95), History of Edn. Soc. (mem. editl. bd. 1996—). Avocations: historic sites and museums, snow skiing, walking. Office: U SC Dept History Columbia SC 29208

SYNNOTT, WILLIAM RAYMOND, retired management consultant; b. Fall River, Mass., Dec. 29, 1929; s. William Joseph and Marie Aurore (Labrie) S.; m. Suzanne Pauline Moseley, Oct. 21, 1967; children—Dianne, Mark, Amy. Grad. cert., Rutgers U. Stonier Grad. Sch. Banking, 1958; B.S. summa cum laude, Boston U., 1973; grad. advanced mgmt. program, Harvard U., 1973. Sr. v.p. Bank of Boston, 1967-87; sr. dir. The Yankee Group, Boston, 1987-88; dir. Nolan Norton & Co., Lexington, Mass., 1988-91; pres. W.R. Synnott Assocs., Wellesley Hills, Mass., 1990-94; lectr., seminar leader on info. technology worldwide. Author: The Information Weapon, 1987; co-author: Information Resource Management, 1981. Served as sgt. U.S. Army, 1951-53, Korea. Avocations: skiing; tennis; golf. Home: Green Hill Rd Jackson NH 03846

SYNODINOS, JOHN ANTHONY, academic administrator; b. Balt., Sept. 6, 1934; s. Anthony John and Jean (Asimakes) S.; m. Glenda J. Davis, Sept. 5, 1959; children: Jean Louise Ganias, Victoria Lynn Gertenbach. BS, Loyola Coll., Balt., 1959; EdM, Temple U., 1977; DHL, Lebanon Valley Coll., 1996. Control buyer Montgomery Ward, Balt., 1959-60; asst. dir. admissions Johns Hopkins U., Balt., 1960-63, dir. spl. events, 1963-65, assoc. dir. pub. rels., 1965-67, asst. dir. Ctr. for Study Social Orgn. Schs., 1960-68; assoc. dir. devel. Franklin & Marshall Coll., Lancaster, Pa., 1968-70, asst. to pres., 1970-71, v.p. advancement, 1971-84; ptnr. John A. Synodinos & Assocs., Lancaster, 1984-88; pres. Lebanon Valley Coll., Annville, Pa., 1988-96, pres. emeritus, 1996—; prin. Franklin Cons. Group, 1997—; bd. dirs. Econ. Devel. Corp. Lebanon County, Pa. Bd. dirs. United Way Lebanon County, 1989-93, Children's Sch., 1996—; trustee Children and Family Svcs., 1996—. Cpl. U.S. Army, 1952-55. Mem. Coun. Advancement & Support of Edn., Fortnightly Club (Lancaster) (pres. 1980). Greek Orthodox. Avocation: acting. Home: 25 Cart Way Lebanon PA 17042-9469 Office: Lebanon Valley Coll Dept History Annville PA 17003-0501

SYPHERD, PAUL STARR, microbiologist; b. Akron, Ohio, Nov. 16, 1936; s. Pearle Clinton and Mary Mildred (Flanick) S.; m. Linda J. Burden, Mar. 19, 1983; children: David Paul, Mary Denise, Gregory Dean, Cynthia Jean, Sean Michael Watkins, Scott Christopher Watkins. BS, Ariz. State U., 1959; MS, U. Ariz., 1960; PhD, Yale U., 1963. NIH postdoctoral fellow U. Calif., San Diego, 1962-64; asst. prof. U. Ill., Urbana, 1964-68, assoc. prof., 1968-70; assoc. prof. microbiology U. Calif. Coll. Medicine, Irvine, 1970-72, prof., 1972-93, chmn. dept., 1974-87, vice chancellor rsch., 1989-93, dean grad. studies, 1989-93; sr. v.p., provost U. Ariz, Tucson, 1993—; mem. NIH study sect., 1977-80, 87-91, chmn., 1990-91; mem. microbiology test com. Nat. Bd. Med. Examiners, 1980-84; mem. panel on basic biomed. scis. Nat. Rsch. Coun., 1981-86. Editor Jour. Bacteriology, 1979-83, mem. editorial bd., 1969-74; editor Molecular and Cellular Biology, 1980-87; contbr. articles to profl. jours. Sr. fellow NSF, 1970. Mem. AAAS, Am. Soc. Microbiology, Am. Soc. for Biochemistry and Molecular Biology, Am. Acad. for Microbiology. Office: U Ariz 512 Administration Tucson AZ 85721

SYROPOULOS, MIKE, school system director; b. Kato Hora, Navpactos, Greece, Jan. 18, 1934; came to U.S., 1951; s. Polykarpos Dimitri and Constantoula P. (Konstantinopoulos) S.; m. Sandra Francis Flick, Jan. 3, 1942; children: Pericles, Connie, Tina. BS, Wayne State U., 1960, MEd, 1965, EdD, 1971. Cert. secondary tchr., Mich. Tchr. Detroit Pub. Schs., 1960-66, dept. head, 1966-67, acting supr., 1967-69, rsch. asst., 1969-74, program assoc., 1976—; asst. dir. Wayne (Mich.) County Intermediate Dist., 1974-76. Contbr. articles to reports. V.p. St. John Greek Orthodox Ch., Sterling Heights, Mich., 1987, pres., 1988. With U.S. Army, 1956-58. Mem. ASCD, Am. Edn. Rsch. Assn., Am. Hellenic Edn. Progressive Assn. (athletic dir. 1992, treas. 1994, sec. 1995, lt. gov. 1996, gov. 1997), Mich. Assn. Supervision Curriculum (bd. dirs. 1994-95, 95-96), Mich. Edn. Rsch. Assn. Greek Orthodox. Avocation: golfing. Home: 46602 Red River Dr Macomb MI 48044-5442 Office: Detroit Pub Schs 5035 Woodward Ave Detroit MI 48202-4015

SYTSMA, FREDRIC A., lawyer; b. Grand Rapids, Mich., Jan. 12, 1944. BA, Mich. State U., 1964; JD, U. Mich., 1968. Bar: Mich. 1968. Mem. Varnum, Riddering, Schmidt & Howlett, Grand Rapids. Fellow Am. Coll. Trust and Estate Counsel; mem. ABA, State Bar Mich. (mem. coun. probate and estate planning sect. 1977—, chmn. 1986-87), Grand Rapids Bar

Assn. Office: Varnum Riddering Schmidt & Howlett PO Box 352 333 Bridge St NW Grand Rapids MI 49501-0352

SYVERTSON, CLARENCE ALFRED, engineering and research management consultant; b. Mpls., Jan. 12, 1926; s. Alfred and Esther Louise (Goertemiller) S.; m. Helen Hammond Gonnella, May 4, 1953 (dec. May 1981); 1 child, Marguerite Louise.; m. JoAnn Mary Caruso, May 8, 1982. B. Aero. Engring., U. Minn., 1946, M.S., 1948; postgrad., Stanford U., 1950-57; grad., Advanced Mgmt. Program, Harvard U., 1977. Research scientist Ames Aero. Lab., NACA, Moffett Field, Calif., 1948-58; exec. dir. Joint Dept. Transp./NASA Civil Aviation Research and Devel. Policy Study, 1970-71; with Ames Research Center, NASA, Moffett Field, 1958-84; dep. dir. Ames Research Center, NASA, 1969-78, dir., 1978-84; mem. adv. bd. Coll. Engring., U. Calif., Berkeley, 1980-85; cons. prof. Stanford U., 1985-88. Served with U.S. Army, 1946-47. Recipient invention and contbn. award NASA, 1964, Exceptional Service medal, 1971, Disting. Service medal, 1984, Outstanding Achievement award U. Minn., 1982, Commanders award for civilian service U.S. Army, 1984. Fellow AIAA (Lawrence Sperry award 1957), Am. Astronautical Soc.; mem. Nat. Acad. Engring. Home: 14666 Springer Ave Saratoga CA 95070-5748

SZABAD, GEORGE MICHAEL, lawyer, former mayor; b. Nizhni Novgorod, Russia, Feb. 21, 1917; s. Michael and Nita (Szereszewski) S.; m. Shirley Meyers, Nov. 8, 1938 (dec. Dec. 1992); children: Peter James, Ellen Jo Szabad Ljung; m. Janet Fulton, Dec. 16, 1995. B.S., Columbia U., 1937, LL.B., 1939. Bar: N.Y. 1940. Participated reorgn. Asso. Gas & Electric System, 1940-42; with Dept. Labor, 1942-47, chief appellate sect., 1944-47; with Dept. State, 1945-46; with firm Blum, Haimoff, Gersen, Lipson, Slavin & Szabad, N.Y.C., 1947—, ptnr., 1949-80; former mayor Village of Scarsdale, N.Y.; v.p. Burndy Corp., 1956-76, sr. v.p., 1976-82. Served with USCG, 1943; Served with OSS, U.S. Army, 1945. Mem. Am. Arbitration Assn. (panel), Assn. Bar City N.Y., Am., Fed. bar assns. Club: Scarsdale Town. Home: 3300 Darby Rd Haverford PA 19041-1061 *Apart from personal relationships and professional and corporate career, my greatest fulfillment comes from the work in the field of human and intergroup relations to preserve and strengthen the American pluralist miracle, based on the balance of unity and diversity.*

SZABAN, MARILYN C., small business owner; b. Palmer, Mass., Dec. 24, 1942; d. Joseph J. and Sophie V. (Duda) Martowski; m. Richard J. Szaban, June 9, 1962 (dec. 1993); children: Gregory John, Deborah Ann, Michael John. BFA summa cum laude, U. So. Maine, 1986; student, Notre Dame Coll., 1983. Owner, pres. Automotive Parts and Supply Co., Inc., Ramsdell & Van Dyke, Worcester, Mass., 1977—; co-owner, pres. Plymouth (N.H.) Auto Supply, Inc., 1980—; owner, pres. Transfigurations, Worcester, 1996—; bd. dirs. APSCO, Worcester, PASCO, Plymouth; art tchr. Jewish Comm. Ctr., Worcester, 1991, 92. Designer for Transfigurations, 1996; artist Portland Rev. of the Arts, 1986. Bd. dirs., art tchr. gallery com., Art Guild of Farmington, Conn., 1988-90. Recipient hon. mention Manchester Inst. Arts & Scis., 1981, 82, recognition award, 1983, Nat. Competition Juried Art Shows, Northeast and Mid-Atlantic States, 1981—. Mem. Plymouth C. of C. Avocations: fine arts, competition in juried art shows. Home: 30 Olde Colony Dr Shrewsbury MA 01545-1637 Office: Transfigurations 100 W Boylston St Worcester MA 01606-2824 also: Automotive Parts & Supply Co Inc Ramsdell & Van Dyke Inc 98 W Boylston St Worcester MA 01606-2824

SZABLYA, HELEN MARY, author, language professional, lecturer; b. Budapest, Hungary, Sept. 6, 1934; came to U.S., 1963; d. Louis and Helen (Bartha) Kovacs; m. John Francis Szablya, June 12, 1951; children: Helen, Janos, Louis, Stephen, Alexandra, Rita, Dominique-Mary. Diploma in Sales, Mktg., U.B.C., 1962; BA in Fgn. Lang., Lit., Wash. State U., 1976. Freelance writer, translator, 1967—; columnist Cath. News, Trinidad, W.I., 1980-91; adult educator TELOS Bellevue (Wash.) C.C., 1987-89; adult educator Pullman-Spokane (Wash.) C.C., 1976-80; faculty Christian Writers' Conf., Seattle, 1983-88, Pacific N.W. Writers' Conf., Seattle, Tacoma, 1987—; hon. consul for Wash., Oreg., Idaho Republic of Hungary, 1993—; lectr. Washington Commn. for Humanities, 1987-89. Author: (with others) Hungary Remembered, 1986 (Guardian of Liberty award, 1986, George Washington Honor medal, Freedoms Found. award 1988), 56-os Cserkészcsapat, 1986, (with others) The Fall of the Red Star, 1996 (1st prize Wash. Press Assn., 1st prize Nat. Fedn. Press Women); pub., editor Hungary Internat. newsletter, 1990-93; columnist Hungarian Bus. Weekly, 1994-95; translator: Emlékezünk, 1986, Mind Twisters, 1987. Recipient Nat. 1st place editl. Nat. Fedn. Press Women, 1987, Senator Tom Martin Meml. award Pacific N.W. Writers Conf., 1979; grantee Hungarian Am. Assn. Wash., 1986, Wash. Com. for Humanities, 1986; named Cmty. Woman of Yr., Am. Bus. Women Assn., 1990. Mem. AAUW, Wash. Press Assn. (pres. 1987-88, 1st and 2nd place awards, several editorial and profile awards 1983, 87, 89, 90, 91, 92, Communicator of Achievement award 1987), Nat. Fedn. Press Women (Affiliate Pres.' award 1988, bd. dirs. edn. fund N.W. quadrant, mem. 21st century planning com.), Authors Guild, Am. Translators Assn., Arpad Acad. (Gold medal 1987), Nat. Writers Club, Internat. P.E.N. Club, Sigma Delta Chi (editl. award 1989). Avocations: children, reading, dancing, swimming, traveling. Home and Office: 4416 134th Pl SE Bellevue WA 98006-2104

SZABLYA, JOHN FRANCIS, electrical engineer, consultant; b. Budapest, Hungary, June 25, 1924; arrived in Can., 1957, naturalized, 1962; came to U.S., 1963, naturalized, 1979; s. John and Alexandra (Huszar) S.; m. Helen M. Bartha-Kovacs, June 12, 1951; children—Helen A., Janos L., Louis J., Stephen J.P., Alexandra H.R., Rita H.C., Dominique-Mary H. Diploma edn., Jozsef Nador U., Budapest, 1948, diploma engring., 1947, Dr. Econs., 1948. Registered profl. engr., Wash., Mont., Alaska, Wyo., Oreg., Colo., Idaho, B.C. and Ont., Can. Design engr. Ganz Elec. Works, Budapest, 1947-56; assoc. prof. Tech. U. Budapest, 1951-56; assoc. prof. U. B.C., Vancouver, 1957-63; prof. elec. engring. Wash. State U., 1963-82, now prof. emeritus; vis. prof. Technische Universitat Braunschweig, 1973-74, U. W.I., 1983—, U. Wash., 1985—, Seattle U., 1987; mgr. electrical, instrumentation and control engring. EBASCO Services Inc., 1981-90; ret., 1990; cons. engr., v.p. Szablya Cons., Inc., 1990—. Contbr. numerous articles to profl. jours., publ. over 150 articles. Recipient Zipernowszky medal Hungarian Inst. Elec. Engrs., 1954, Academia Gold medal ARPAD, 1991. Fellow IEEE, Instn. Elec. Engrs. (London); mem. Osterreichischer Verband der Elekrotechnik, European Register Higher Tech. Professions, Sigma Xi. Roman Catholic. Home: 4416 134th Pl SE Bellevue WA 98006-2104

SZABO, ALBERT, architect, educator; b. N.Y.C., Nov. 7, 1925; s. Benjamin and Jane (Margolies) S.; m. Brenda Dyer, Dec. 26, 1951; children: Ellen Szabo Laughlin, Stephen, Rebecca Szabo Salvadori, Jeannette. Student, Bklyn. Coll., 1942-47, Inst. Design, Chgo., 1947-48; MArch, Harvard U., 1952. Apprentice Marcel Breuer Architect, 1947-48; instr. Inst. Design, Chgo., 1951-53; prof. architecture Grad. Sch. Design Harvard U., Cambridge, Mass., 1954-96; prof. emeritus, 1996—; chmn. dept. archtl. scis. Harvard U., Cambridge, Mass., 1964-68, assoc. chmn., head tutor dept. visual and environ. studies, 1968-70, prof. visual and environ. studies, chmn. dept. visual and environ. studies, 1970-72, sec. faculty design, 1964-74, prof. visual and environ. studies, 1970-91; archtl. design practice with Brenda Dyer Szabo, Chgo. and Cambridge, 1953—; ptnr. Soltan/Szabo Assocs., Inc., Cambridge, 1967-71; vis. prof. Rensselaer Poly. Inst., 1967-68; Fulbright cons. to municipality of Tehran, Iran; Fulbright Hayes lectr. in architecture, Tehran, 1972, Kabul U. Afghanistan, 1974-76; cons. U.S. AID, Afghanistan, 1974-76, Govt. Afghanistan, 1974-76; acting curator Loeb Fellowship in Advanced Environ. Studies, 1974, cons. King Faisal U. Coll. Architecture and Planning, 1983; mem. edn. com. Boston Archtl. Ctr. Sch. Architecture, 1981-90; Osgood Hooker prof. visual art Faculty of Arts and Scis., 1991-96, prof. emeritus, 1996—. Author: (with others) The Shape of Our Cities, 1957; editor: (with others) Housing generated by User Needs, 1972, (with B.D. Szabo) Preliminary Notes on Indigenous Architecture of Afghanistan, 1978, (with T.J. Barfield) Afghanistan: An Atlas of Indigenous Domestic Architecture, 1991 (Outstanding Acad. Book award ALA 1992). Served with USAAF, 1944-45. Recipient Alpha Rho Chi medal Harvard U., 1952; Wheelwright travelling fellow Harvard U., 1963, Nat. Endowment for Arts fellow, 1980; Tozier Fund rsch. grantee Harvard U., 1963, Milton Fund rsch. grantee, 1966, 72, 77, 84, 87, Faculty rsch. grantee, 1978, The Aga Khan Program Islamic Architecture grantee, 1988. Mem. Boston Soc. Architects (assoc.), AIA, Assn. Collegiate Schs. Architecture (N.E. regional dir. 1969-70), Mass. Assn. Architects. Office: Harvard U Carpenter Ctr 19 Prescott St Cambridge MA 02138-3902

SZABO, BARNA ALADAR, mechanical engineering educator, mining engineer; b. Martonvasar, Hungary, Sept. 21, 1935; came to U.S., 1967, naturalized, 1974; s. Jozsef and Gizella (Ivanyi) S.; m. Magdalin Gerstmayer, July 23, 1960; children: Mark, Nicholas. B.A.Sc., U. Toronto, Ont., Can., 1962; M.S., SUNY, Buffalo, 1966, Ph.D., 1969. Registered profl. engr., Mo. Mining engr. Internat. Nickel Co. Can., 1960-62; engr. Acres Cons. Services Ltd., Niagara Falls, Can., 1962-66; instr. SUNY, Buffalo, 1966-68; mem. faculty Washington U., St. Louis, 1968—, prof. mech. engring., 1974—, Albert P. and Blanche Y. Greensfelder prof., 1975—, dir. Ctr. Computational Mechanics, 1977-92; chmn. engring. software Rsch. and Devel., Inc., St. Louis, 1989—. Author: (with Ivo Babuska) Finite Element Analysis, 1991; contbr. articles to profl. jours. Fellow U.S. Assn. Computational Mechanics (founding mem.); mem. ASME, Hungarian Acad. Sci., Soc. Engring. Sci. Club: St. Louis Soaring Assn. Home: 48 Crestwood Dr Clayton MO 63105-3033 Office: Washington U Campus Box 1129 Saint Louis MO 63130-4899

SZABO, DANIEL, government official; b. Budapest, Hungary, Mar. 23, 1933; came to U.S., 1950, naturalized, 1954; s. Alexander and Maria (Berger) S.; m. Corinne Holiber, July 3, 1955; children—Nancy Beth, Peter Stuart. B.A., CCNY, 1957; M.A., Johns Hopkins U., 1959. Internat. economist U.S. Tariff Commn., 1959-60; desk officer for Vietnam, Cambodia and Laos U.S. Dept. Commerce, 1960-63; spl. asst. to U.S. Senator Jacob K. Javits, 1963-69; dep. asst. sec. state for Inter-Am. Affairs, Washington, 1969-74; sr. adviser Inter-Am. Devel. Bank, Washington, 1974-95; cons Rockville, Md., 1995—; mem. nat. adv. coun. Am. Jewish Com. Mem. exec. coun. Washington area chpt. Am. Jewish Com. Served with U.S. Army, 1954-56. Home: 11600 Danville Dr Rockville MD 20852-3716 *In approaching life I want my work to represent a service to our society. I am attracted to new ideas and new ways of solving old problems.*

SZABO, DENIS, criminologist, educator; b. Budapest, Hungary, June 4, 1929; s. Jenö and Catherine (Zsiga) S.; m. Sylvie Grotard; children—Catherine, Marianne. Doctorate in Social and Polit. Scis., U. Louvain, Belgium, 1956; diploma in criminology, Sorbonne U., Paris, 1958; hon. doctorate, U. Sienna, Italy, 1984, U. Budapest, Hungary, 1985, U. Aix-Marseille, 1992, Pateios U., 1996. Asst. in sociology U. Louvain, 1951-56; lectr. sociology Cath. Univs., Paris, Lyon, 1956-58; mem. research group Centre Nat. de la Recherche Scientifique, Paris, 1954-58; asst. prof. sociology U. Montreal, 1958, assoc. prof., 1959-66, founder, dir. dept. criminology, 1960-70, prof., 1966—; founder, dir. Internat. Center for Comparative Criminology, 1969-84; prof. emeritus, 1995—; emeritus prof. law U. Ecuador, Quito, 1984. Author, editor: Canadian Criminal Justice System, 1977, Criminologie et Politique Criminelle, 1978, La Criminologie Empirique au Quebec, 1985, Science et Crime, 1986, De L'Anthropologie a la criminologie comparee, 1993, Le Traite di criminologie Empirique, 1993. Decorated officer Order Can.; recipient Beccaria award German Society Criminology, 1970; named prof. emeritus Law Faculty, Central U. Ecuador, Quito, 1984; named Comdr. Nat. Order Merite Hungarian Republic, 1996, Chevalier Des Arts et des Lettres, France, 1996. Fellow Royal Soc. Can., Am. Sociol. Soc., Am. Soc. Criminology (exec. coun., Sutherland award 1968); mem. Internat. Soc. Criminology (pres. 1978-85, hon. pres.), Can. Soc. Criminology (v.p. 1962-64), Soc. de Criminology (v.p. 1962-64), Soc. de Criminologie du Que. (sec.-gen. 1960-70), Internat. Assn. Sociology, Nat. Order of Merit (comdr. Ivory coast 1987), Hungarian Acad. Scis. (elected). Roman Catholic. Home: PO Box 26, Georgeville, PQ Canada J0B 1T0 Office: 3150 Jean Brillant, Montreal, PQ Canada H3C 3J7

SZABO, JOSEPH CLARK, labor lobbyist; b. Evergreen Park, Ill., Dec. 26, 1957; s. Joseph Frank and Shirley Jean (Clark) S. AAS, South Suburban Coll., 1984; BA, Governors State U., 1990. Train condr. Metra/ICG, Chgo., 1976-96; state dir. Ill. legis. bd. United Transp. Union, 1996—; mem. labor/mgmt. com. Metra, Chgo., 1988—. Chmn. Riverdale (Ill.) Zoning Bd./Plan Commn., 1981-86; commr. Ivanhoe Park Bd., Riverdale, 1982-87; trustee Village of Riverdale, 1987-97, mayor 1997—. Mem. United Transp. Union (sec.-treas. local 1290 1984-90, legis. rep. 1987-96, vice chmn. state legis. bd. 1992-96), Calumet Region Enterprise Zone (bd. dirs. 1989—), Calumet Region Indsl. Assn. (bd. dirs. 1990-92, 95—), Dolton Riverdale Jaycees (treas. 1979-80, v.p. 1980-81, pres. 1981-82, Jaycee of Yr. 1980, 81, Disting. Svc. award 1981, Outstanding Loca. Pres. 1982, Outstanding Jaycee 1990), Elks. Methodist. Home: 14211 S Tracy Ave Riverdale IL 60627-2341

SZABO, PETER JOHN, investment company executive, financial planner, mining engineer, lawyer; b. Bklyn., Nov. 22, 1946; s. Paul Simon and Marita Ellen (Coughlin) S.; m. Dorothy Anne Steward, Nov. 14, 1970; children: Peter, David, John Paul Steward. BS in Mining Engring., Columbia U., 1968; LLB, LaSalle Law Sch., 1975; MS in Fin. Planning, Coll. Fin. PLanning, 1994. registered profl. engr., CFP. Mining engr. Halecrest Co., Mt. Hope, N.J., 1973-74; mgr. solid fuels & minerals Ford, Bacon & Davis, N.Y.C., 1974-75; asst. v.p. Mfrs. Hanover Trust Co., N.Y.C., 1975-77, Irving Trust Co., N.Y.C., 1977; v.p. Republic Nat. Bank of Dallas, 1977-80; mgr. bus. devel. AMOCO Minerals, Denver, 1980-84; investment broker B.J. Leonard, Denver, 1984-85; investment exec. Wedbush Nobel Cook, Denver, 1985; regional sr. v.p. Alliance Fund Distbrs., N.Y.C., 1985-92, sr. v.p., 1992—; mining engr. U.S. Bur. Mines, Dallas, 1971-72, IRS, Washington, 1972-73. Treas. Columbia Sch. Engring., 1968—. Lt. USMC, 1969-71, Vietnam, capt. Res. Mem. VFW (post sr. vice comdr. 1993-94, post comdr. 1994-95, all state team post comdrs. 1995, 16th dist. jr. vice comdr. 1995—, 16th dist. sr. vice comdr. 1996—, nat. aide-de-camp 1995-96), Mil. Order of the Cootie (sr. vice comdr. 1994-95). Republican. Roman Catholic. Avocations: sailing, golf, tennis, jogging, scripophily. Home and Office: Alliance Fund Distbrs 810 Oxford Way Benicia CA 94510-3646*

SZABO, ZOLTAN, medical science educator, medical institute director; b. Szeged, Hungary, Oct. 5, 1943; came to U.S., 1967; s. Imre and Maria (Szikora) S.; m. Wanda Toy, Dec. 5, 1976; children: Eva, Maria. Student, U. Med. Sch., Szeged, 1962-65; PhD, Columbia Pacific U., 1983. Tech. dir. microsurgery lab. R.K. Davies Med. Ctr., San Francisco, 1972-80; dir. Microsurgery and Operative Endoscopy Tng. (MOET) Inst., San Francisco, 1980—; assoc. dir. advanced laparoscopic surgery tng. ctr. Sch. Medicine U. Calif., San Francisco, 1992-96; rsch. assoc. oral and maxillofacial surgery U. of Pacific, San Francisco, 1980-83, adj. asst. prof., 1983—. Author: Microsurgery Techniques, vol. 1, 1974, vol. 2, 1984 (1st Place award for excellence in med. writing 1982); co-author: Tissue Approximation in Endoscopic Surgery, 1995; editor-in-chief Surgical Technology Internationa, Vol. 3, 1994, Vol. 4, 1995, Vol. 5, 1996; contbr. chpt. books, articles to profl. jours. With U.S. Army, 1969-71. Recipient cert. of Merit, AMA, 1978, commendation Accreditation Coun. for Continuing Med. Edn., 1984, 90, 94, Spl. Recognition award Sch. Medicine Cen. U. Venezuela, 1988, Sci. Poste Sessions Hon. Mention award Am. Urol. Assn., 1992, 1st prize Roundtable for New Techs. and Innovations we. sect., 1992, James Barrett Brown award Am. Assn. Plastic Surgeons, 1993. Fellow Internat. Coll. Surgeons (Disting. Svc. award 1994); mem. Hungarian Gynecol. Soc. (hon.), Medico-Dental Study Guild Calif., Internat. Microsurg. Soc., Soc. Am. Gastrointestinal Endoscopic Surgeons (hon., 1st prize Residents and Fellows Rsch. and Sci. Presentation 1992), Am. Fertility Soc., Am. Soc. Reconstructive Microsurgery (assoc.), Am. Soc. for Peripheral Nerve. Avocations: gardening, landscaping, oil painting, travel, competitive air pistol target shooting. Office: Microsurgery Operative Endoscopy Tng Inst 153 States St San Francisco CA 94114-1403

SZALKOWSKI, CHARLES CONRAD, lawyer; b. Amarillo, Tex., Apr. 14, 1948; s. Chester Casimer and Virginia Lee (Hess) S.; m. Jane Howe, Dec. 28, 1971; children: Jennifer Lee, Stephen Claude. BA, BS in Acctg., Rice U., 1971; MBA, JD, Harvard U., 1975. Bar: Tex. 1975. Assoc. Baker & Botts, L.L.P., Houston, 1975-82, ptnr., 1983—; speaker in field. Chmn. ann. fund campaign Rice U., Houston, 1991-93, chmn. fund coun., 1995-96; chmn. adminstrv. bd. St. Luke's United Meth. Ch., Houston, 1994; bd. dirs., DePelchin Children's Ctr., Houston, 1996—; adv. bd. Meth. Home, Waco, MIT Enterprise Forum of Tex., Houston, The Entrepreneurship Inst., Houston. Mem. ABA (fed. regulation of securities com.), Am. Law Inst., State Bar Tex. (chmn., vice chmn. bus. law sect. 1990-92), Houston Bar Assn. (chmn., vice chmn., corp. counsel sect. 1988-90), Harvard Law Sch. Assn. Tex. (pres. 1983-84), Tex. Bus. Law Found. (bd. dirs., exec. com. 1988—, vice chmn. 1995—), Assn. Rice U. Alumni (chmn. various coms. 1981-86), Assn. for Corp. Growth (adv. bd. Houston chpt.), Lincoln's Inn Soc., Houston Philos. Soc. Office: Baker & Botts LLP 1 Shell Plz 910 Louisiana St Houston TX 77002-4916

SZALLER, JAMES FRANCIS, lawyer; b. Cleve., Jan. 22, 1945; s. Frank Paul and Ellen Grace (O'Malley) S.; m. Roberta Mae Curtin, Oct. 23, 1967 (div. Aug. 1975); m. Charlene Nancy Smith, Apr. 28, 1984. AA, Cuyahoga Community Coll., 1967; BA, Cleve. State U., 1970, JD cum laude, 1975. Bar: Ohio 1975, U.S. Dist. Ct. (no. dist.) Ohio 1975, U.S. Supreme Ct. 1982, U.S. Ct. Appeals (6th cir.) 1983, U.S. Ct. Appeals (4th cir.) 1986. Assoc. Metzenbaum, Gaines & Stern (now Gaines & Stern Co. L.P.A.), Cleve., 1975-79; sr. ptnr. Brown & Szaller Co., L.P.A., Cleve., 1979—; lectr. law Cleve. State U., 1978-81. Mem. editorial bd. Cleve. State U. Law Rev., 1973-75.; contbr. articles to profl. jours. Mem. ABA, Fed. Bar Assn., Ohio State Bar Assn., Greater Cleve. Bar Assn., Cleve. Acad. Trial Lawyers, Ohio Acad. Trial Lawyers, Assn. Trial Lawyers Am., Nat. Coll. Advocacy (advocate). Democrat. Roman Catholic. Avocations: gourmet cooking, automobile racing. Office: Brown & Szaller Co LPA 14222 Madison Ave Cleveland OH 44107-4510

SZAMEK, PIERRE ERVIN, anthropologist, researcher; b. Budapest, Hungary; s. Eugene Jeno and Olga S. Grad., The Pingry Sch., Elizabeth, N.J.; B.A., Upsala Coll., 1942; M.A., Columbia U., 1944; A.M., fellow, Princeton U., 1946, Ph.D., 1947. Corr. Cen. European Press Service, 1939; etymol. asst. in linguistic anthropology to Dr. Harold H. Bender, etymol. editor The Webster Dictionary, 1947-48; vis. post-doctoral research fellow Princeton U., 1947-48; ednl. broadcasting CBS, N.Y.C., 1948-65; research anthropologist Newark, 1950—; exec. dir. Internat. Ctr. Ednl. Advancement, 1984—, chancellor, 1989; vis. prof. anthropology Drew U., 1966-67, N.J. State Coll., 1968-71; Disting. vis. prof. Seton Hall U., 1980; lectr. New Sch. for Social Research, 1980; dir. Am. Sci. Research and Mktg.; mem. radio program Invitation to Learning, CBS Network, 1948-63; permanent chmn., moderator Invitation to Ideas, Nat. Pub. Broadcasting Series, 1981—; anthrop. cons. CBS-TV, 1950-65; chmn. bd. The Logos Scientific Rsch. Ctr., 1989; special anthrop. cons. Nat. Com. for Habitat in affiliation with UNCHS, sr. vice chmn. for Hungarian devel., the Hungarian Nat. Com. for Habitat; sr. rsch. scientist, anthrop. cons. XEL Advanced Techs. Internat. Ltd. (XELAT); chancellor Gen. Conv. Planetary Preservation; founder (with Eugene Paul Wigner and Daniel J.G. Peabody-Smidt) Millennium Three SuperProject. Author, contbg. critic: Invitation to Learning, 1966; contbg. editor Green Earth; contbr. numerous articles, broadcasts in Am. jours. and fgn. press; inventor multi-gyro ball-bearing, dual stage radio communications synthesizer; patentee. Served with USCGR, 1942-43. Decorated victory medal, knight Order of Star (Italy); knight officer Gold Cross of Royal Order of Phoenix (Greece); Order of St. Agatha (San Marino); chevalier de l'Ordre des Palmes Académiques, chevalier de la Legion d'Honneur (France); officer Order St. John (Eng.); N.J. Com. for Humanities fellow; NEH Match Fund grantee, 1947. Fellow Royal Anthrop. Inst. Gt. Britain and Ireland; mem. AAUP, Am. Oriental Soc., Am. Acad. Polit. Sci., N.J. Acad. Sci. Office: care Law Offices PO Box 255 Glen Ridge NJ 07028-0255

SZANTAI, LINDA MARIE, speech and language therapist; b. Phila., Dec. 21, 1957; d. Richard George Reckeweg and Eileen Theresa (Wrenn) Renders; m. Paul Matthew Vidunas, July 22, 1978 (div. Dec. 1987); m. Stephen Michael Szantai, Sept. 16, 1989. BS, Trenton State Coll., 1986. Cert. in speech correction, N.J. Speech/lang. therapist Dept. Corrections, State of N.J., Skillman, 1986-89, Ventnor (N.J.) Sch. Dist., 1989—, Port Republic (N.J.) Sch., 1989-92, Estell Manor (N.J.) Sch. Dist., 1995—. Mem. Kappa Delta Pi (pres. Greater Trenton chpt. 1985-86, recognition award 1986), Phi Kappa Phi (Outstanding Freshman Achievement award 1983).

SZAREK, STANISLAW JERZY, mathematics educator; b. Ladek Zdroj, Poland, Nov. 13, 1953; came to U.S., 1980, naturalized, 1994; s. Mieczyslaw and Bronislawa (Brzezinska) S.; m. Malgorzata Chwascinska, June 22, 1980; children: Martina, Natalia; 1 stepchild, Olga. M in Math., Warsaw (Poland) U., 1976; PhD in Math. Scis., Polish Acad. Scis., Warsaw, 1979. Rsch. asst. Math. Inst. Polish Acad. Scis., Warsaw, 1976-79, rsch. fellow, 1979-83; asst. prof. Case Western Res. U., Cleve., 1983-87, prof., 1987—, chair math. dept., 1994-96; prof. U. Paris, 1996—; vis. positions U. Ill., Urbana, 1980, Ohio State U., Columbus, 1981, U. Tex., Austin, 1981-83, Inst. des Hautes Etudes Scientifiques, Bures-Sur-Yvette, France, 1986-89, U. Paris, 1990, 92, 95, Math. Scis. Rsch. Inst., Berkeley, Calif., 1996. Contbr. articles to profl. jours. Recipient Prize of Sci. Sec., Polish Acad. Scis., 1979; rsch. grantee NSF, 1983—, U.S.-Israel Binat. Sci. Found., 1993—; Sloan fellow Alfred P. Sloan Found., 1986-88. Mem. Am. Math. Soc. Avocations: skiing, sailing, diving, bridge, travel. Office: Case Western Res U Dept of Math Cleveland OH 44106

SZAREK, WALTER ANTHONY, chemist, educator; b. St. Catharines, Ont., Can., Apr. 19, 1938; s. Anthony and Sophia (Kania) S. BSc, McMaster U., 1960, MSc, 1962; PhD, Queen's U., 1964. Postdoctoral fellow in chemistry Ohio State U., Columbus, 1964-65; asst. prof. biochemistry Rutgers U., New Brunswick, N.J., 1965-67; asst. prof. chemistry Queen's U., Kingston, Ont., 1967-71, assoc. prof., 1971-76, prof., 1976—, dir. Carbohydrate Research Inst., 1976-85; founding mem., prin. investigator Neurochem, Inc., 1993—; cons. to govt. and industry; mem. Premier's Coun. Tech. Fund. Mem. editorial adv. bd. Carbohydrate Rsch. jour., 1973—, Jour. of Carbohydrate Chemistry, 1994—; contbr. articles on chemistry of carbohydrates to profl. jours. Recipient Teaching Excellence award Queen's U. Arts and Sci. Undergrad. Soc., 1988-89. Fellow Chem. Inst. Can.; mem. AAAS, Am. Chem. Soc. (chmn. divsn. carbohydrate chemistry 1982-83, Claude S. Hudson award in carbohydrate chemistry 1989, Melville L. Wolfrom award 1992), Inst. Theol. encounter with Sci. and Tech., Royal Soc. Chemistry, N.Y. Acad. Scis., Soc. Glycobiology. Roman Catholic. Office: Queen's U, Dept Chemistry, Kingston, ON Canada K7L 3N6

SZARKA, LASLO JOSEPH, pharmaceutical company executive; b. Hungary, Sept. 6, 1935; naturalized; s. Geza and Ilona (Woditsch) S.; m. Violet Varkonyi; children: Monica, Lawrence. MS, U. Budapest, Hungary, 1961, PhD, 1967. Rsch. assoc. Chinoin, Budapest, 1963-64; sect. head Drug Rsch. Inst., Budapest, 1964-71; rsch. investigator E.R. Squibb & Sons, New Brunswick, N.J., 1974-81; asst. dir. E.R. Squibb & Sons, New Brunswick, 1981-86; dir. Bristol-Myers-Squibb, New Brunswick, 1986—. Patentee 25 patents in Biotech.; contbr. articles to profl. jours. Mem. AAAS, AIChE, N.Y. Acad. Sci., Am. Chem. Soc. Avocations: travel, tennis, hiking, music. Office: Bristol Myers Squibb PO Box 191 New Brunswick NJ 08903-0191

SZARWARK, ERNEST JOHN, lawyer; b. South Bend, Ind., May 11, 1951; s. Stanley I. and Genevieve (Zalejski) S.; m. Mary Christy Smith, June 3, 1978; children: Mary Cresap, Catherine Case. BS with highest honors, U. Notre Dame, 1973, JD with highest honors, 1976. Bar: Ind. 1976, U.S. Claims Ct. 1977, U.S. Tax Ct. 1977, U.S. Ct. Appeals (7th cir.) 1980, Fla. 1982, U.S. Ct. Appeals (6th cir.) 1986. Atty. advisor to Hon. Richard C. Wilbur U.S. Tax Ct., Washington, 1976-78; assoc. Barnes & Thornburg, South Bend, 1978-85, ptnr., 1985—. Bd. dirs. South Bend Art Ctr., 1985-88; mem. fin. com. Stanley Clark Sch. Fellow Ind. Bar Found.; mem. Ind. Bar Assn. (bd. dirs. taxation sect. 1985-93, chmn. taxation sect. 1992-93), Ind. Soc. of Chgo., Polish Nat. Alliance, Michiana Arts and Scis. Council, South Bend Country Club. Roman Catholic. Avocations: golf, cross country skiing, numismatics, reading. Office: Waller Lansden Dortch & Davis Nashville City Ctr 511 Union St Ste 2100 Nashville TN 37219-1752

SZASZ, THOMAS STEPHEN, psychiatrist, educator, writer; b. Budapest, Hungary, Apr. 15, 1920; came to U.S., 1938, naturalized, 1944; s. Julius and Lily (Wellisch) S.; m. Rosine Loshkajian, Oct. 19, 1951 (div. 1970); children: Margot Szasz Peters, Susan Marie Szasz Palmer. AB, U. Cin., 1941, MD, 1944; DSc (hon.), Allegheny Coll., 1975, U. Francisco Marroquin, Guatemala, 1979. Diplomate: Nat. Bd. Med. Examiners, Am. Bd. Psychiatry and Neurology. Intern 4th Med. Service Harvard, Boston City Hosp., 1944-45; asst. resident medicine Cin. Gen. Hosp., 1945-46, asst. clinician internal medicine div. out-patient dispensary, 1946; asst. resident psychiatry U. Chgo. Clinics, 1946-47; tng. research fellow Inst. Psychoanalysis, Chgo., 1947-48; rsch. asst. Inst. Psychoanalysis, 1949-50, staff mem., 1951-56; practice medicine, specializing in psychiatry, psychoanalysis Chgo., 1949-54,

Bethesda, Md., 1954-56, Syracuse, N.Y., 1956—; prof. psychiatry SUNY Health Sci. Ctr., Syracuse, 1956-90, prof. psychiatry emeritus, 1990—; vis. prof. dept. psychiatry U. Wis., Madison, 1962, Marquette U. Sch. Medicine, Milw., 1968, U. N.Mex., 1981; holder numerous lectureships, including C.P. Snow lectr. Ithaca Coll., 1970; E.S. Meyer Meml. lectr. U. Queensland Med. Sch.; Lambie-Dew orator Sydney U., 1977; Mem. nat. adv. com. bd. Tort and Med. Yearbook; cons. com. mental hygiene N.Y. State Bar Assn.; mem. research adv. panel Inst. Study Drug Addiction; adv. bd. Corp. Econ. Edn., 1977—. Author: Pain and Pleasure, 1957, The Myth of Mental Illness, 1961, Law, Liberty and Psychiatry, 1963, Psychiatric Justice, 1965, The Ethics of Psychoanalysis, 1965, Ideology and Insanity, 1970, The Manufacture of Madness, 1970, The Second Sin, 1973, Ceremonial Chemistry, 1974, Heresies, 1976, Karl Kraus and the Soul-Doctors, 1976, Schizophrenia: The Sacred Symbol of Psychiatry, 1976, Psychiatric Slavery, 1977, The Theology of Medicine, 1977, The Myth of Psychotherapy, 1978, Sex by Prescription, 1980, The Therapeutic State, 1984, Insanity: The Idea and its Consequences, 1987, The Untamed Tongue: A Dissenting Dictionary, 1990, Our Right to Drugs: The Case for a Free Market, 1992, A Lexicon of Lunacy, 1993, Cruel Compassion, 1994, The Meaning of Mind, 1996; editor: The Age of Madness, 1973; cons. editor of psychiatry and psychology: Stedman's Medical Dictionary, 22d edit, 1973; contbg. editor: Reason, 1974—, Libertarian Rev., 1986—; mem. editorial bd. Psychoanalytic Rev, 1965—, Jour. Contemporary Psychotherapy, 1968—, Law and Human Behavior, 1977—, Jour. Libertarian Studies, 1977—, Children and Youth Services Rev, 1978—, Am. Jour. Forensic Psychiatry, 1980—, Free Inquiry, 1980—. Comdr. M.C., USNR, 1954-56. Recipient Stella Feiss Hofheimer award U. Cin., 1944, Holmes-Munsterberg award Internat. Acad. Forensic Psychology, 1969; Wisdom award honor, 1970; Acad. prize Institutum atque Academia Auctorum Internationalis, Andorra, 1972; Distinguished Service award Am. Inst. Pub. Service, 1974; Martin Buber award Midway Counseling Center, 1974, Thomas S. Szasz award Ctr. Ind. Thought , 1990, Alfred R. Lindesmith award for achievement in field of scholarship and writing Drug Policy Found., 1991; others; named Humanist of Year Am. Humanist Assn., 1973; Hon. fellow Postgrad. Center for Mental Health, 1961, Mencken award, 1981, Humanist Laureate, 1984, Statue of Liberty-Ellis Island Found. Archives Roster, 1986. Fellow Am. Psychiat. Assn. (life), Am. Psychoanalytic Assn., Internat. Psychoanalytic Soc., Western N.Y. Psychoanalytic Soc. Home: 4739 Limberlost Ln Manlius NY 13104-1405 Office: 750 E Adams St Syracuse NY 13210-2306

SZAZ, ZOLTAN MICHAEL, association executive; b. Budapest, Hungary, Jan. 3, 1930; came to U.S., 1950; s. Geza and Magda (Nagy) S.; m. Jayne Anne Davis, Sept. 7, 1957 (div. Nov. 1995); children: Claire Anne, Anna Maria, Mary Carol, Christopher Michael; m. Elizabeth Susan Almassy, Nov. 11, 1995. BA cum laude, St. John's U., Collegeville, Minn., 1951; MA in History, Cath. U. Am., 1953, PhD in Polit. Sci., 1956. Instr, asst. prof. history St. John's U., Jamaica, N.Y., 1960-64; assoc. prof. polit. sci. Seton Hall U., South Orange, N.J., 1965-68, Troy (Ala.) State U., 1971-72; exec. v.p. Am. Fgn. Policy Inst., Washington, 1968—; immigration cons. Washington, 1987—; exec. v.p. Nat. Confedn. Am. Ethnic Groups, Washington, 1979-90, nat. sec., 1990—. Author: Germany's Eastern Frontiers, 1960, Die deutsche Ostgrenze, 1961, Southeast Asia, 1984, Erdely Vedelmeben (In Defense of Transylvania), 1996. Speechwriter on ethnic issues 1960 Nixon Campaign; founding mem. Rep. Nat. Heritage Group Coun., Washington, 1970; sec. Internat. Rels. Am. Hungarian Fedn., 1965-90; founding pres. U. Profs. for Acad. Order, 1970-71. Recipient Ellis Island Medal of Honor, N.Y. State Bicentennial Commn., 1986, Medal of Honor, Transylvanian World Fedn., São Paulo, Brazil, 1983. Roman Catholic. Home: 4201 Massachusetts Ave NW Washington DC 20016-4701 Office: Nat Confedn Am Ethnic Group 4720 Massachusetts Ave NW Washington DC 20016-2346

SZCZARBA, ROBERT HENRY, mathematics educator, mathematician; b. Dearborn, Mich., Nov. 27, 1932; s. Michael and Julie (Hanas) S.; m. Arlene Lee Roschild, June 18, 1955; children: Garrett Lee, Cheryl Anne. BS, U. Mich., 1955; MA, U. Chgo., 1957, PhD, 1960. Instr. DePaul U., 1959-60; ONR rsch. assoc. Yale U., New Haven, 1960-61, asst. prof. math., 1961-65, assoc. prof., 1965-74, prof., 1974—; chmn. dept. Yale U., 1980-83; acting chmn. dept. Yale U., New Haven, fall 1995, dep. provost phys. scis. and engring., 1989-95; vis. mem. Inst. Advanced Study, Princeton, N.J., 1964-65, 72. Author: Calculus in Vector Spaces, 1979, Multivariable Calculus, 1982. Mem. Bethany Bd. Fin., Conn., 1971-77; treas. Bethany Democratic Com., 1980-83. NSF postdoctoral fellow, 1964-65. Mem. Am. Math. Soc., Conn. Acad. Arts and Scis. Office: Yale U Dept Math PO Box 208283 New Haven CT 06520-8283

SZCZEPANSKI, SLAWOMIR ZBIGNIEW STEVEN, lawyer; b. Lodz, Poland, Mar. 9, 1948; s. Wladyslaw and Janina Szczepanski; m. Cynthia Ellen Weagley, Sept. 30, 1972; children: Christine, Diana. BS in Chem. Engring., Rensselaer Poly. Inst., 1971; MS in Chem. Engring., Rennselaer Poly. Inst., 1972; JD, Union U., Albany, N.Y., 1975. Bar: N.Y. 1976, D.C. 1976, Ill. 1977, U.S. Dist. Ct. (no. dist.) Ill. 1977, U.S. Ct. Appeals (fed. cir.) 1988. Atty. Philips Petroleum Co., Washington, 1975-77; from assoc. to ptnr. Willian, Brinks, Hofer, Gilson & Lione, Chgo., 1977-95; of counsel Arnold White and Durkee, Chgo., 1996—. Author: Licensing in Foreign and Domestic Operations, 1985—; editor (legal periodical) Licensing Law and Business Report, 1986—; contbr. articles to profl. jours. Mem. ABA, Am. Intellectual Property Law Assn., Internat. Assn. Protection Indsl. Property, Assn. Trial Lawyers of Am., Nat. Advocates Soc., Licensing Execs. Soc., Intellectual Property Law Assn. of Chgo., Univ. Club. Avocations: tennis, sailing. Home: 641 W Willow St Apt 107 Chicago IL 60614-5176 Office: Arnold White & Durkee 800 Quaker Tower 321 N Clark St Chicago IL 60610

SZCZERBA, VICTOR BOGDAN, electrical engineer, sales engineer; b. Chgo., Oct. 21, 1966; s. Bogdan and Zosia (Mika) S. BSEE, Marquette U., 1989; postgrad., U. Calif., Berkeley, 1996—. Sales engr. New Vision Computers, Milw., 1988-89; mktg. engr. Cypress Semicondr., San Jose, Calif., 1989-91; regional sales mgr. AMD/NEXGEN, Milpitas, Calif., 1991-96; sr. acct. mgr. Sun Micro Sys., Mountain View, Calif., 1996—; sales engr. Trinity Tech., Mountainview, Calif., 1991-92; cons. S3, Santa Clara, 1991-92; tutor Project Read. Mem. Knights of St. Patrick (pres. 1988-89), Sigma Phi Delta (v.p. 1987-88). Republican. Roman Catholic. Avocations: skiing, investing. Home: 827 University Ave Palo Alto CA 94301-2132

SZEBEHELY, VICTOR G., aeronautical engineer; b. Budapest, Hungary, Aug. 10, 1921; s. Victor and Vilma (Stockl) S.; m. Jo Betsy Lewallen, May 21, 1970; 1 dau., Julia. M.E., U. Budapest, 1943, Ph.D. in Engring, 1945; Dr. (hon.), Eotvos U. Budapest, 1991. Asst. prof. U. Budapest, 1945-47; research asso. State U. Pa., 1947-48; asso. prof. Va. Poly. Inst., 1948-53; research asso. Model Basin, U.S. Navy, 1953-57; research mgr. Gen. Electric Co., 1957-62; asso. prof. astronomy Yale U., 1962-68; prof. aerospace engring. U. Tex., Austin, 1968—; chmn. dept. U. Tex., 1977-81, R.B. Curran Centennial chair in engring., 1983—; cons. NASA-Johnson Space Center, U.S. Air Force Space Command, Lawrence Berkeley Lab., U. Calif. Author 18 books; contbr. over 200 articles on space research, celestial mechanics and ship dynamics to profl. jours. Knighted by Queen Juliana of Netherlands, 1956. Fellow AIAA, AAAS; mem. Am. Astron. Soc. (Brouwer award div. dynamical astronomy 1977), Internat. Astron. Union (pres. commn. on celestial mechanics), NAE, European Acad. Arts, Scis., Lit. Home: 2501 Jarratt Ave Austin TX 78703 Office: U Tex Dept Aerospace Engring & Engring Mechs Austin TX 78712

SZEFLER, STANLEY JAMES, pediatrics and pharmacology educator; b. Buffalo, Aug. 24, 1948; s. Stanley and Bernice Laura (Platt) S.; m. Christine M. Drezek, Dec. 26, 1970; children: David, Paul. BS, SUNY, Buffalo, 1971, MD, 1975. Resident pediatrics Children's Hosp. Buffalo, 1975-77; postdoctoral fellow in clin. pharmacology and allergy immunology SUNY, Buffalo, 1977-79, asst. prof. pediatrics and pharmacology, 1979-82; assoc. prof. pediatrics and pharmacology U. Colo., Denver, 1982-90, prof. pediatrics, pharmacology, 1990—; dir. clin. pharmacology Children's Hosp., Buffalo, 1979-82, Nat. Jewish Ctr. for Immunology and Respiratory Medicine, Denver, 1982—. Contbr. articles to profl. jours. Mem. steering com. asthma camp for children Am. Lung Assn., Denver, 1987—. Maj. USAR, 1979-88. NIH grantee, 1980-84, 90—, FDA grantee, Denver, 1988-91. Fellow Am. Acad. Allergy, Asthma and Immunology (chmn. asthma, rhinitis and respiratory disease interest sect.), Am.Acad. Pediats. (liaison mem. com. drugs). Avocations: baseball, soccer. Office: Nat Jewish Ctr Dept Immunology/Respiratory Med 1400 Jackson St Denver CO 80206-2761

SZEGO, CLARA MARIAN, cell biologist, educator; b. Budapest, Hungary, Mar. 23, 1916; came to U.S., 1921, naturalized, 1927; d. Paul S. and Helen (Elek) S.; m. Sidney Roberts, Sept. 14, 1943. A.B., Hunter Coll., 1937; M.S. (Garvan fellow), U. Minn., 1939, Ph.D., 1942. Instr. physiology U. Minn., 1942-43; Minn. Cancer Research Inst. fellow, 1943-44; rsch. assoc. OSRD, Nat. Bur. Standards, 1944-45, Worcester Found. Exptl. Biology, 1945-47; rsch. instr. physiol. chemistry Yale U. Sch. Medicine, 1947-48; mem. faculty UCLA, 1948—, prof. biology, 1960—. Named Woman of Year in Sci. Los Angeles Times, 1957-58; Guggenheim fellow, 1956; named to Hunter Coll. Hall of Fame, 1987. Fellow AAAS; mem. Am. Physiol. Soc., Am. Soc. Cell Biology, Endocrine Soc. (CIBA award 1953), Soc. for Endocrinology (Gt. Britain), Biochem. Soc. (Gt. Britain), Internat. Soc. Rsch. Reprodn., Phi Beta Kappa (pres. UCLA chpt. 1973-74), Sigma Xi (pres. UCLA chpt. 1976-77). Achievements include rsch. and numerous publs. on steroid protein interactions, mechanisms of hormone action and lysosome participation in normal cell function. Home: 1371 Marinette Rd Pacific Palisades CA 90272-2627 Office: U Calif Dept Molecular Cell & Devel Biology Los Angeles CA 90095-1606

SZELENYI, IVAN, educator; b. Budapest, Apr. 17, 1938; came to the U.S., 1981; s. Gusztav and Julianna (Csapo) S.; m. Kataline Varady, Jan. 31, 1960; children: Szonja, Lilla, Balazs. PhD, Hungarian Acad. Scis., Budapest, 1973, DSc, 1990; hon. doctorate, Budapest U. Econs., 1992. Rsch. fellow Hungarian Acad. Scis., Budapest, 1963-75; found. prof. Flinders U., Adelaide, Australia, 1975-80; prof. U. Wis., Madison, 1981-86; disting. prof. CUNY Grad. Ctr., 1986-88; prof. UCLA, L.A., 1988—. Author: Urban Inequalities under State Socialism, 1983, Socialist Entrepreneurs, 1988 (C. Wright Mills award 1989); co-author: Intellectuals on the Road to Class Power, 1979. Mem. Hungarian Acad. Scis. *

SZENBERG, MICHAEL, economics educator, editor, consultant; b. Sosnowiec, Poland, Apr. 8, 1934; came to U.S., 1961, naturalized, 1966; s. Henry and Sara (Rosensaft) S.; m. Miriam Silverstein, Sept. 2, 1962; children: Naomi, Avi. Student, Bar Ilan U., Israel, 1959-61; BA summa cum laude, L.I. U., 1963; PhD, CUNY, 1970. Faculty L.I. U., Bklyn. Center, 1965—, prof. econs., 1974-83; prof. econs. Lubin Grad. Sch. Bus. Pace U., 1983—; dir. Ctr. Applied Rsch., 1994—; adj. prof. Hunter Coll., 1970-76, Pace U., 1975-83; founder, dir. Lecture Bur. Econs., 1973; chmn. 1st Met. Grad. Conf. Econs., 1973; assoc. mem. Ctr. Tech. Assessment, Newark Coll. Engring., 1973; vis. prof. econs. NYU, summers 1977, 78, 79; cons. in field. Author: Economics of the Israeli Diamond Industry, 1973, The Welfare Effects of Trade Restrictions: A Case Study of the United States Footwear Industry, 1977, The Economics of the American Footwear Industry, 2d edit., 1984; editor: Essays in Economics, The John Commons Memorial Lectures, 1986, Eminent Economists: Their Life Philosophies, 1992; assoc. editor: Am. Economist, 1973-75, editor-in-chief, 1975—; econs. co-editor: Cambridge Univ. Press Encyclopedia; contbr. articles to profl. jours. and chpts. to books. Served with Israeli Air Force, 1956-59. Recipient Dean Hudson award L.I. U., 1962, Am. Coll. Abroad award, 1962, Dean Abelson award CUNY, 1963; fellow econs. CUNY, 1963; grantee Israel Diamond Inst., 1970; recipient Irving Fisher Monograph award, 1971; fellow Internat. Honor Soc. in Econs., 1972; grantee Dept. Labor, 1975; recipient Kenan award for teaching excellence Pace U., 1983, Schalkenbach Found. Research award, 1987, First Prize Recognition award for scholarly productivity, 1989, Tchr. of the Year Pace U., 1992, Teaching Excellence award Acad. Bus. Admin., 1993, Achievement award CUNY, 1993, Outstanding Publication award Pace U., 1993, 94, 95, Outstanding Svc. award Pace U., 1996, scholarly rsch. awards for basic and applied rsch. Pace U., 1996. Mem. Atlantic Econ. Soc., Internat. Trade and Fin. Assn., Internat. Fedn. Sci. Editors, Ea. Econ. Assn., Am. Econ. Assn., Assn. Cultural Econs., Internat. Honor Soc. Econs. (exec. bd. 1975—, regional dir. 1971-74), Optimates Soc. (pres. 1972-80). Home: 1442 E 9th St Brooklyn NY 11230-6405

SZEP, PAUL MICHAEL, editorial cartoonist; b. Hamilton, Ont., Can., July 29, 1941; came to U.S., 1966; s. Paul Joseph and Helen (Langhorne) S.; m. Angela Diane Garton, Feb. 27, 1965 (div. 1976); children: Amy, Jason. A.O.C.A., Ont. Coll. Art, 1964; A.O.C.A. hon. degree, 1975, Framingham State Coll., 1975, Worcester State Coll., 1980, William Penn Coll., 1981. Sports cartoonist Hamilton Spectator, 1958-61; graphics designer Financial Post, Toronto, Ont., 1965-66; editorial cartoonist Boston Globe, 1966—; vis. fellow Harvard U., 1981; lectr. various univs. Author: In Search of Sacred Cows, 1967, Keep Your Left Hand High, 1969, At This Point in Time, 1973, The Harder They Fall, 1975, Unvote for a New America, 1976, Them Damned Pictures, 1977, Warts and All, 1979, To a Different Drummer, 1983, The Gang of Eight, 1985, The Next Szep Book, 1985, Often in Error, Never in Doubt, 1987, And Then Jack Said to Arnie, 1991, And Then Arnie Told Chi Chi And Then Chi Chi Said to Fuzzy, 1993, And Then Fuzzy Told Seve, 1996, Not Just Another Szep Book, 1997, And Then Seve Told Freddy, 1997; editl. cartoonist Sta. WNEV-TV, Boston; contbr. Golf Digest. Served with F.A. Royal Canadian Army, 1957-58. Recipient Pulitzer prize, 1974, 77, award Sigma Delta Chi, 1974, 77, Toyl award Boston Jaycees, 1976, Headliners award, 1977, Reuben award for best editorial cartoonist Nat. Cartoonist Soc., 1979, Thomas Nast award; Internat. Cartoonist award, Best Sports Cartoonist award Nat. Cartoonists Soc., 1988. Mem. Soc. Illustrators, Kittansett Club, Harvard Club, Weston Golf Club. Home: 7 Stetson St Brookline MA 02146-3406 Office: Boston Globe Boston MA 02107

SZER, WLODZIMIERZ, biochemist, educator; b. Warsaw, Poland, June 3, 1924; came to U.S., 1968; s. Max and Chaia (Szapiro) S.; m. Felicja Kirsz, Oct. 1, 1946; children: Caroline, Ilona. M.S. in Chemistry, U. Lodz (Poland), 1950; Ph.D. in Biochemistry, Inst. Biochemistry and Biophysics, Polish Acad. Scis., 1959. Dozent Inst. Biochemistry and Biophysics, Warsaw, 1963-68; asst. prof., then assoc. prof. biochemistry Sch. Medicine, NYU, N.Y.C., 1968-73, prof., 1973—. Contbr. articles and revs. to profl. jours. Recipient Jacob K. Parnas Polish Biochem. Soc., 1964; recipient Faculty Am. Cancer Soc., 1973; USPHS grantee, 1971—. Mem. Am. Soc. Biol. Chemists, Harvey Soc. Office: NYU Sch Medicine Dept Biochemistry 550 1st Ave New York NY 10016-6481

SZERI, ANDRAS Z., engineering educator; b. Nagyvarad, Hungary, June 6, 1934; came to U.S., 1967; s. Andras F. and Julie (Farkas) S.; m. Mary J. Parkinson, Apr. 25, 1962; children: Andrew J., Elizabeth C., Maria J. B.S. with 1st class honors, U. Leeds, Eng., 1959, Ph.D., 1962. Research engr. English Electric Co., Stafford, Eng., 1962-64; prof. Universidad Santa Maria, Valparaiso, Chile, 1964-66; asst. prof. U. Pitts., 1967-70, assoc. prof., 1970-76, prof. math., 1977-93, prof. mech. engring., 1977-94, chmn. dept. mech. engring., 1984-87, William Kepler Whiteford prof. engring., 1990-94; Robert Lyle Spencer prof. mech. engring., chmn. U. Del., Newark, 1994—; cons. Westinghouse Electric Co., Pitts., 1967-82; external examiner U. W.I., 1989—. Editor: Tribology, 1980. Fellow ASME (assoc. editor Jour. Tribology 1978-87, tech. editor 1987-93); mem. Am. Acad. Mechanics, The Soc. Rheology, Soc. Engring. Sci., Soc. Natural Philosophy. Office: U Del Dept Mech Engring Newark DE 19716

SZEWCZYK, ALBIN ANTHONY, engineering educator; b. Chgo., Feb. 26, 1935; s. Andrew Aloysius and Jean Cecelia (Wojcik) S.; m. Barbara Valerie Gale, June 16, 1956; children: Karen Marie Knop, Lisa Anne, Andrea Jean Simpson, Terese Helen Sinka. BS, U. Notre Dame, 1956, MS, 1958; PhD, U. Md., 1961. Staff engr. Northrop Aircraft Corp., Hawthorne, Calif., 1956-57; grad. asst. U. Notre Dame, Ind., 1957-58, asst. prof. engring., 1962-65, assoc. prof., 1965-67, prof., 1967—, chmn. dept., 1978-88; research asst. U. Md., College Park, 1958-61, postdoctoral researcher, 1961-62; mem. tech. staff Aerospace Corp., El Segundo, Calif., 1962; cons. Argonne (Ill.) Nat. Lab., 1968-80, Miles Lab., Elkhart, Ind., 1983-88, Chung Shan Inst. Sci. and Tech., Taiwan, 1987-89; vis. prof. Imperial Coll., London, 1989, Kernforschungzentrum, Karlsruhe, Germany, 1990. Editor: Development in Mechanics, 1971. Fellow ASME, AIAA (assoc.); mem. AAAS, Am. Phys. Soc., Am. Soc. Engring. Edn., N.Y. Acad. Sci., Sigma Xi, Pi Tau Sigma, Sigma Gamma Tau. Roman Catholic. Club: South Bend Country (bd. dirs. 1982-89, pres. 1986-88). Avocations: golfing, model railroading. Home: 17331 Willowbrook Dr South Bend IN 46635-1750 Office: Dept Aero & Mech Engring U Notre Dame Notre Dame IN 46556

SZIGETI, MICHELLE MARIE, critical care nurse; b. South Bend, Ind., Mar. 21, 1954; d. Eugene Peter and Patricia Joyce (May) S. RN, Meml. Hosp., South Bend, 1976; BS, St. Francis Coll., Joliet, Ill., 1990. Cert. critical care nurse. Charge nurse cardiac intermediate care Meml. Hosp., South Bend, 1976-83, charge nurse cardio vascular intensive care, 1983—; tchr. cardiovasular intensive care Meml. Hosp. of South Bend, 1991—. Mem. AACN. Home: 112 S Mccombs St South Bend IN 46637-3330

SZILAGYI, D(ESIDERIUS) EMERICK, surgeon, researcher, educator; b. Nagykaroly, Hungary, June 20, 1910; came to U.S.,, naturalized, 1931; m. Martha Evelyn Fowlkes Harper (dec.); children: Martha, Christine; m. Sally Bolton, 1989. Diploma, Calvinist Coll., Klausenburg, Hungary, 1928; exam., U. Paris-Sorbonne; student, U. Debrecen; MD, U. Mich., 1935, MS, 1940; MD (hon.), Semmelweis Med. U., Budapest, Hungary, 1988. Diplomate Am. Bd. Surgery. Intern U. Mich. Hosp., Ann Arbor, 1935-36, asst. resident in surgery, 1936-37, instr. pathology, 1937-39; asst. resident in surgery Henry Ford Hosp., Detroit, 1939-42, chief resident, 1945, asst. surgeon, 1945-46, assoc. surgeon, 1946-49, chief div. II gen. surgery, 1949-66, chmn. dept. surgery, 1966-75, cons. vascular surgery, 1975—, chief of staff, 1968-71; emeritus clin. prof. surgery U. Mich. Med. Sch., Ann Arbor; dir. med. dept. Ford Rubber Plantations, Para, Brazil, 1942-45; Edwin A. Jarecki Meml. lectr. Albert Einstein Med. Ctr., Phila., 1964; David W. Yandell lectr. U. Louisville Med. Sch., 1973; William Mayo lectr. U. Mich., 1978; Matas Meml. lectr. XV Internat. Congress of Internat. Cardiovascular Soc., Athens, Greece, 1981. Editor Jour. Vascular Surgery, 1983—; contbr. articles to profl. jours. Mem. ACS, AMA, Am. Fedn. Clin. Rsch., Am. Surg. Assns., Am. Thyroid Assn., Ctrl. Surg. Assn. (past pres.), Internat. Soc. Cardiovascular Surgery (past chpt. pres.), Internat. Soc. Surgery, Midwestern Vascular Surg. Soc. (past pres.), Soc. Vascular Surgery (past pres.), Western Surg. Assn. (past v.p., pres.), Detroit Acad. Surgery, Detroit Surg. Assn., Mich. Med. Soc., Wayne County Med. Soc.; hon. mem. Sociedad Argentina de Angiologia, Sociedad Columbiana de Angiologia, Royal Australasian Coll. Surgeons, Deutsche Gesellschaft für Gefässchirurgie, Hungarian Soc. of Angiology. Home: 1008 Stratford Pl Bloomfield Hills MI 48304-2934 Office: Henry Ford Hosp 2799 W Grand Blvd Detroit MI 48202-2608 *I regard it as an accidental stroke of good fortune that the beginning of my career as a surgeon coincided with the birth of a new branch of the surgical art: the surgery of the arterial system. Thus, I had the rare opportunity of making and publishing observations that were original and useful not because of their brilliance but because of their newness. The contribution for which I may perhaps take personal credit was a firm determination to describe my observations objectively and draw my conclusions honestly.*

SZILAGYI, SHERRY ANN, psychotherapist, lawyer; b. Cheverly, Md.; d. John Alex and Mary Ann (Mazzola) S. BA in Edn.-Social Work Psychology magna cum laude, U. Md., Catonsville, 1989; MSW summa cum laude, U. Md., Balt., 1990, JD cum laude, 1995. Lic. cert. social worker, clin.; cert. health ins. analyst; lic. child rights advocate, daycare provider, Md. Dir. Teen and Community Ctr., Crofton, Md., 1987-89; social worker Dept. Social Svcs. and Child Protection, Hyattsville, Md., 1988-89; clin. therapist Mental Health Ctr., Annapolis, Md., 1989-90; pvt. practice, Columbia, 1990—; clin. therapist Sexual Assault Crisis Ctr., Annapolis, Md., 1990—; tutor, rschr. U.Md., College Park, 1989—; comty. chair Balt. Domestic Violence Advocacy Project, 1994—. State of Md. scholar, 1988, Acad. Law scholar, 1995. Mem. ABA, APA, AACD, NASW, NOW, Women's Bar Assn., Psi Chi, Phi Kappa Phi. Avocations: skiing, retreats, computers, research, massage. Office: ACPC 6535 Huntshire Dr Ste B Elkridge MD 21075-6165

SZILASSY, SANDOR, retired lawyer, library director, educator; b. Magyarbarnag, Hungary, Apr. 9, 1921; came to U.S., 1957; s. Sandor Sr. and Jolan (Fenyves) S.; m. Clara Ida Varkonyi, July 21, 1951; children: Peter S., Thomas S., Paul A. D. LLD, U. Budapest, Hungary, 1944, Lawyer-Judge Dipl., 1949; MA, Ind. U., 1959. Practicing atty., pres. law firm Veszprém, Hungary, 1944-56; asst. libr. Anderson (Ind.) Coll. Libr., 1959-61; head div. sci. and tech. Auburn (Ala.) U. Libr., 1961-68; head libr., assoc. prof. Ind. State U., Evansville, 1968-69; dir. libr., prof. U. Tampa, Fla., 1969-72; dir. librs. Rowan Coll. of N.J., 1972-94; v.p. Ala. Acad. Sci., 1963-68; pres. Coun. N.J. Coll. and Univ. Librs., 1978-79, 89-90, Librs. Unltd., N.J., 1981-82, 88-89; cons. numerous orgns; radio commentator, Sta. WTEL, Phila., 1987-91. Author: Revolutionary Hungary, 1971 (Arpad Acad. Gold medal 1972), Ein Amerikanischer Diplomat uber Ungarn, 1974, Hungary's Road to Trianon, 1988, numerous others; author book chpts.; mem. editorial bd. Ency. Hungarica, 1989—; contbr. essays, studies, articles to profl. jours., newspapers, mags. Bd. elders Presbyn. Ch., Lakeland, Fla., 1970-72; 1st Hungarian United Ch. of Christ, Miami, 1996—. Recipient Legion of Honor award Chapel of Three Chaplains, 1981. Mem. N.J. Acad. Libr. Network (exec. bd. 1988—), Tri-State Coll. Libr. Coop. (pres. 1975-76, 88-89, Johanniter Order Knights (Germany), Arpad Acad. (sect. pres. 1979—), Phi Alpha Theta. Mem. Reformed Ch. Avocations: research, writing, reading, swimming, hiking. Home: 133 N Pompano Beach Blvd Pompano Beach FL 33062-5725

SZKODY, PAULA, astronomy educator, researcher; b. Detroit, July 17, 1948; d. Julian and Pauline (Wolski) S.; m. Donald E. Brownlee, Mar. 19, 1976; children: Allison, Carson. BS in Astrophysics, Mich. State U., 1970; MS in Astronomy, U. Wash., 1972, PhD in Astronomy, 1975. Rsch. asst. Observatoire de Geneve, 1969, Kitt Peak Nat. Obs., 1970; rsch., teaching asst. U. Wash., Seattle, 1970-75, rsch. assoc., lectr., 1975-82, sr. rsch. assoc., 1982-83, rsch. assoc. prof., 1983-91, rsch. prof., 1991-93, prof., 1993—; part-time mem. faculty Seattle U., 1974-75, 82, Bellevue Coll., 1975-77; vis. scientist Kitt Peak Nat. Obs., 1976; vis. instr. UCLA, 1977, adj. asst. prof., 1980, 81; vis. asst. prof. U. Hawaii, 1978; vis. assoc. prof. Calif. Inst. Tech., 1978-79, 80, mem. XTE users com., 1996—; mem. users com. Internat. Ultraviolet Explorer, 1983-85, 93-97; mem. A.J. Cannon adv. com. AAUW, 1986-91, chmn. 1988-90; mem. mgmt. ops. working group on Ultraviolet/Visual/Relativity, NASA, 1988-91. Contbr. numerous articles to profl. jours. Recipient Annie J. Cannon award, 1978. Fellow AAAS (mem. nominating com. 1990-93, chairperson 1993, mem.-at-large 1995—); mem. Am. Assn. Variable Star Observers, Am. Astron. Soc. (councilor 1996—), Internat. Astron. Union (v.p. 1997—); mem. commn. 42 organizing com. 1991—), Astron. Soc. Pacific (bd. dirs. 1988-92), Phi Beta Kappa. Office: U Wash Dept Astronomy Box 351580 Seattle WA 98195

SZMANDA, LUCILLE MARIE, retired vocational school educator; b. Mishicot, Wis., Apr. 27, 1924; d. Walter Jacob and Clara Mary (Heinzen) Dirkmann; m. Robert Louis Szmanda, June 5, 1943; children: Robert Louis, William, Donald, Jeffery, Mary Clare, Timothy, Thomas, Margaret Ann. Student, Waukesha County Tech. Coll., 1967, LaSalle U., Chgo., 1970. Owner Park Upholstery & Decorating, East Troy, Wis., 1966-77; instr. upholstery program Gateway Tech. Coll., Kenosha, Wis., 1970-77, Waukesha Tech. Coll., Pewaukee, Wis., 1973-77; instr. upholstery diploma program Milw. Area Tech. Coll., 1977-95; ret., 1995; advisor Vocat. Indsl. Clubs Am., Milw., 1978-84; chair subcom. Task Force for Diversity, Milw., 1989-95. Mem. Milw. Vocat. Assn. (mem. award com. 1992-95, named Tchr. of Yr. 1990). Roman Catholic. Avocations: antique furniture, sewing, historical sites. Home: Unit 112 5253 N Lovers Lane Rd Milwaukee WI 53225-3039

SZMIT, FREDERICK ANDREW, paper manufacturing company executive; b. Lowell, Mass., May 26, 1938; s. Andrew and Jane (Dziekiewicz) S.; m. Frances Slavin, May 20, 1960; children: Kathleen Anne, Andrew Michael. BS, Lowell U., 1959; postgrad. program for mgmt. devel., Harvard U., 1981. Chemist Geigy Chem. Co., Ardsley, N.Y., 1960-61; mill mgr. Spaulding Fibre Co., North Rochester, N.H., 1961-71; mill mgr. Boise-Cascade Splty. Div., Brattleboro, Vt., 1971-78, mfg. mgr., 1978-83, gen. mgr., 1983-85; dir. Old Forge Pulp & Paper, Lyons Falls, N.Y., 1986—; pres., chief exec. officer, bd. dirs. Lyons Falls (N.Y.) Pulp & Paper, Inc., 1985—, Lyons Falls Hydroelectric, Inc., 1986—; bd. dirs. Am. Paper Inst., N.Y.C., 1976-85, Associated Industries of Vt., Montpelier, 1977-85, Bank of Vt. Adv. Bd., Brattleboro, 1980-85; del. Vt. Gov.'s Conf. Forest Industries, Montpelier, 1985. Pres. Southern Vt. Health Services Corp., Brattleboro, 1984-87; pres. Brattleboro Meml. Hosp., 1981-84; chmn. United Fund of

Brattleboro, 1979. Mem. Am. Paper Inst. (bd. dirs.), Paper Industry Mgmt. Assn., Associated Industries of N.Y., Tech. Assn. Pulp and Paper. Home: 54 S Shore Rd Spofford NH 03462-4016

SZOKA, EDMUND CASIMIR CARDINAL, archbishop; b. Grand Rapids, Mich., Sept. 14, 1927; s. Casimir and Mary (Wolgat) S. B.A., Sacred Heart Sem., 1950; J.C.B., Pontifical Lateran U., 1958, J.C.L., 1959. Ordained priest Roman Catholic Ch., 1954; asst. pastor St. Francis Parish, Manistique, Mich., 1954-55; sec. to bishop Marquette, Mich., 1955-57, 59-62; chaplain St. Mary's Hosp., Marquette, 1955-57; tribunal, notary, defender of bond Marquette, 1960-71; asst. chancellor Diocese of Marquette, 1962-69, chancellor, 1970-71; pastor St. Pius X Ch., Ishpeming, Mich., 1962-63, St. Christopher Ch., Marquette, 1963-71; bishop Diocese of Gaylord, Mich., 1971-81; archbishop of Detroit, 1981-90; elevated to cardinal, 1988; sec.-treas. Mich. Cath. Conf., Lansing, 1972-77; chmn. region VI Nat. Conf. Cath. Bishops, 1972-77; treas., mem. adminstrv. bd. and adminstrv. com., budget and fin. com. Nat. Conf. Cath. Bishops/U.S. Cath. Conf., 1981-84; trustee, mem. exec. com., chmn. com. for univ. relations Cath. U. Am., 1981-90; trustee Nat. Shrine of the Immaculate Conception, Washington, 1981-90; chmn. bd. trustees Cath. Telecommunications Network Am., 1984-90; pres. Prefecture for Econ. Affairs of the Holy See, 1990; mem. Secretariat of State, 2d sect. Coun. for Rels. with States. Mem. Congregation for Insts. Consecrated Life and Socs. Apostolic Life, Congregation for Causes of Saints, Congregation for Bishops, Congregation for Evangelization of Peoples, Congregation for Clergy. Address: Prefecture for Econ Affairs, 00120 Vatican City Vatican City

SZOVERFFY, JOSEPH, educator, medieval scholar; b. Clausenbourgh, Transylvania, June 19, 1920. MA, State Coll. H.S. Tchrs., Budapest, 1944; PhD, Budapest U., 1943; PhD, U. Fribourg, 1950. Prof. fgn. lang. Glenstall Coll. (Ireland), 1950-52; archivist Irish Folklore Commn., Dublin, 1952-57; spl. prof. classics and medieval Latin U. Ottawa, 1957-58, asst. prof., 1958-59; from asst. prof. to assoc. prof. German philology U. Alta., 1959-62; assoc. prof. mediaeval German lit. Yale U., 1962-65; prof. German, medieval lit. Boston Coll., 1965-70, acting chmn. German studies, dir. grad. studies, 1968-70; prof. comparative lit. SUNY-Albany, 1970-77, chmn. dept., 1972-75; vis. prof. Byzantine studies Dumbarton Oaks Ctr. Byzantine Studies, Washington, 1977-78; prof. medieval lit. Sch. Hist. Studies, Inst. Advanced Study, 1978-79; Richard Merton vis. prof. Inst. Medieval Studies Freie U., Berlin (W.Ger.), 1980—; hon. rsch. assoc. Harvard Ukrainian Research Inst., Harvard U., 1975—; with Inst. Advanced Studies, Berlin, 1983-84; vis. prof. Medieval Studies U. Vienna, Austria, 1984-85, 87-88. Author: Der hl Christophorus und sein Kult, 1942; Irisches Erzahlgut im Abendland, 1957; Annalen der lateinischen Hymnendichtung I-II, 1964-65; Weltliche Dichtungen des lateinischen Mittelaters, 1970; Peter Abelard's Hymnarius Paraclitensis Vol I-II, 1975; Bermanistische Abhandlugen, 1977; A Guide to Byzantine Hymnography, Vol I-II, 1979-80; Repertorium Novum Hymnorum Medii Aevi, Vol I-IV, 1982, Religious Lyrics of the Middle Ages, 1983, A Concise History of the Medieval Latin Hymnody, 1985, Typology of Latin Hymns, 1988, Turnhout Across the Centuries...Harvard Lectures, 1988, Secular Latin Lyrics, Vol. I-IV, 1992-95, Memoirs, 1996. Recipient Chgo. Folklore prize U. Chgo., 1954; fellow Guggenheim Found. 1961, 69-70, Am. Philos. Soc., 1965, 72, Ctr. Medieval and Early Renaissance Studies, SUNY, 1973—, NEH, 1978-79; grantee Guggenheim Found. 1963, 71, 75. Mem. Mediaeval Acad. Am., MLA, Am. Comparative Lit. Assn., Conn. Acad., West Berlin Acad.

SZUCH, CLYDE ANDREW, lawyer; b. Bluefield, W.Va., Nov. 22, 1930; s. Nicholas and Aranka (Rubin) S.; m. Rosalie Hirschman Wulfson, Sept. 5, 1954; children: Peter Alan, Richard Coleman. BA, Rutgers, 1952; LLB, Harvard U., 1955. Bar: N.J. 1955, U.S. Dist. Ct. N.J. 1955, U.S. Ct. Appeals (3rd cir.) 1958, U.S. Supreme Ct. 1962. Law clk. to assoc. justice William J. Brennan Jr. U.S. Supreme Ct., Washington, 1956-57; asst. U.S. atty. U.S. Attys. Office, Newark, 1957-58; assoc. Pitney, Hardin & Kipp, Newark, 1958-62; ptnr. Pitney, Hardin, Kipp & Szuch, Morristown, N.J., 1962—; mem. panel Ctr. for Pub. Resources, N.J.; bd. dirs. Vt. Rlwy. Inc., Clarendon & Pittsford R.R. Co., Burlington, Vt., Brennan Ctr. for Justice; panelist AAA Large Complex Cases. Gov. N.J. region Nat. Conf. Christians & Jews. Fellow Am. Bar Found.; mem. ABA, Am. Law Inst., N.J. State Bar Assn., Morris County Bar Assn., Essex County Bar Assn., Fed. Bar Assn. (N.J. chpt.), Ctr. Pub. Resources Panel, Nat. Legal Aid Defender Assn., Hist. Soc. U.S. Ct. Appeals for 3d Cir., Park Ave. Club. Office: Pitney Hardin Kipp & Szuch PO Box 1945 Morristown NJ 07962-1945

SZUCS, ANDREW ERIC, training manager; b. Cleve., Apr. 25, 1946; s. Andrew Elmer and Katherine (Krizsak) S.; m. Laura Jean Nyhan, June 4, 1971; children: Andrew Edward, Eric Stephen. BA, U. Dayton, 1968; Diploma, Cleve. Inst. Electronics, 1972; MBA, Wright State U., 1984. Pub. affairs specialist USAF, Laughlin AFB, Tex., 1968-70; exhibit rschr., writer USAF Orientation Group, Wright-Patterson AFB, Ohio, 1970-73; cmty. rels. dir. Wright-Patterson AFB, 1973-77; publ. mgr. Air Force Logistics Command, Wright-Patterson AFB, 1977-85, chief pub. officer, 1985-90; civilian command tng. mgr./admisntrn. Air Force Materiel Command, Wright-Patterson AFB, 1990—. Contbr. articles to profl. jours. (AWA Jour. award 1986). Staff sgt. USAF, 1968-73. Named Disting. Alumnus, St. Ignatius High Sch., Cleve., 1994. Mem. Soc. Aerospace Communicators, Nat. Press Club, Am. Radio Relay League, Amateur Satellite Corp., U.S. Soccer Fedn. (referee), Ohio High Sch. Athletic Assn. (referee), Wright State U. Bus. Alumni Assn. (rec. sec. 1985-89), Nat. Assn. Sports Ofcls. Roman Catholic. Avocations: ham radio operator, creative writing, trainer for pvt. soccer team. Home: 1135 Mint Springs Dr Fairborn OH 45324-5728 Office: Edn and Tng Divsn HQ AFMC/DPER Wright Patterson AFB OH 45433

SZUHAJ, BERNARD FRANCIS, food research director; b. Lilly, Pa., Nov. 27, 1942; s. Theodore and Rose Dorothy (Karmen) S.; m. Carole Ann Brady, Dec. 26, 1964; children: Matthew, Timothy, Bernard. BS, Pa. State U., 1964, MS, 1966, PhD, 1969. Grad. asst. Pa. State U., Univ. Park, Pa., 1964-66; research asst. Pa. State U., Univ. Park, 1966-68; scientist Cen. Soya Co., Inc., Fort Wayne, Ind., 1968-73; research dir. Cen. Soya Co., Inc., Fort Wayne, 1973-84, dir. food research, 1984—; v.p. Am. Oil Chemists'Soc. Found., Ill., 1988—; bd. dirs. POS Pilot Plant Corp., Saskatoon, Canada, 1987—. Patentee in field; co-editor Lecithins, 1985; editor: (lecithins) Sources Manufacture & Uses, 1989. Mem. Am. Oil Chemists' Soc. (bd. dirs. 1989—), Am. Chem. Soc., Inst. Food Technologists, Inst. Shortening & Edible Oils, Sigma Xi. Democrat. Roman Catholic. Office: Cen Soya Co Inc PO Box 1400 Fort Wayne IN 46801-1400

SZULC, TAD, journalist, commentator; b. Warsaw, Poland, July 25, 1926; came to U.S., 1947, naturalized, 1954; s. Seweryn and Janina (Baruch) S.; m. Marianne Carr, July 8, 1948; children: Nicole, Anthony. Student, U. Brazil, 1943-45; LHD (hon.), Am. Coll. Switzerland, 1987. Reporter AP, Rio de Janeiro, 1945-46; corr. at UN for UPI, 1949-53; mem. staff N.Y. Times, after 1953; corr. N.Y. Times, Latin Am., 1955-61; with Washington bur. N.Y. Times, 1961-65, 69-72, corr. to Spain and Portugal, 1965-68, corr. to Eastern Europe, 1968-69, commentator fgn. policy, 1972—. Author: Twilight of the Tyrants, 1959, The Cuban Invasion, 1962, The Winds of Revolution, 1963, Dominican Diary, 1965, Latin America, 1966, Bombs of Palomares, 1967, United States and the Caribbean, 1971, Czechoslovakia since World War II, 1971, Portrait of Spain, 1972, Compulsive Spy: The Strnage Career of E. Howard Hunt, 1974, The Energy Crisis, 1974, Innocents at Home, 1974, The Illusion of Peace, 1978, Diplomatic Immunity, 1981, Fidel: A Critical Portrait, 1986, Then and Now: The World Since WW II, 1990, The Secret Alliance, 1991, Pope John Paul II: The Biography, 1995. Decorated Cross of Chevalier of Legion d'Honneur France, Order of Duarte, Sánchez, Meliá Dominican Republic; recipient Maria Moors Cabot gold medal Columbia U., Medal of Honor, World Bus. Coun., 1987. Mem. Overseas Press Club (award for best mag. interpretation fgn. affairs 1976, citations 1966, 74-75, 77-78, award for best book on fgn. affairs 1979, 86, 91), Cosmos Club. Address: 4515 29th St NW Washington DC 20008-2144

ZWARC, MICHAEL, polymer scientist; b. Poland, June 9, 1909; came to S., 1952; s. Maier and Regina (Prager) S.; m. Marja Frenkel, Aug. 6, 1933; ildren: Raphael, Myra, Rina. Ch.E., Warsaw Poly. Inst., Poland, 1932; hD in Organic Chemistry, Hebrew U., Jerusalem, 1945; PhD in Phys. Chemistry, Manchester (Eng.) U., 1947, DSc (hon.), 1949; D (hon.), U. Leuven, Belgium, 1974; D.Sc. (hon), Uppsala U., Sweden, 1975, Louis Pasteur U., Strasbourg, France, 1978. Researcher Hebrew U., Jerusalem, 1935-45; researcher Manchester U., Eng., 1946-52, univ. fellow, lectr. phys. chemistry, 1949-52; mem. faculty SUNY-Syracuse Coll. Environ. Scis., 1952-79; disting. prof. chemistry SUNY-Syracuse Coll. Forestry, 1964-80, dir. polymer ctr., 1966-80, prof. emeritus, 1980—. Author: Carbanions, Living Polymers and Electron Transfer Processes, 1968, Ionic Polymerization and Living Polymers, 1993; editor: Ions and Ion Pairs in Organic Chemistry, Vol. I, 1972, Vol. II, 1974, Ionic Polymerization Fundamentals, 1996. Recipient Polymer Chemistry award Am. Chem. Soc., 1970, Herman Mark award, 1989; Gold medal Internat. Soc. Plastics Engrs., 1972, Benjamin Franklin Soc., 1978, Kyoto prize for advanced tech., 1991. Fellow Royal Soc. (London); mem. Polish Acad. Scis. (fgn.), Soc. Polymer Sci. (Japan). Office: Univ So Calif Hydrocarbon Rsch Insti Los Angeles CA 90089

SZWED, BERYL J., school system administrator, mathematics educator; b. Bklyn., Mar. 21, 1948; d. Jules and Bertha (Dlugash) Cooper; m. Joseph Szwed, May 28, 1970; children: Nissa, Rory, Joshua. BS in Elem. Edn., SUNY, Cortland, 1970; MS in Guidance, Counseling, Tex. A and I U., 1973; postgrad, SUNY, Oswego; postgrad., U. N.H. Cert. elem. tchr. K-6 perm., Math. secondary 7-12. Guidance counselor, test dist. coord. Cato-Meridian Sch. Dist., N.Y.; test adminstr. Fed. Correctional Inst., Raybrook, N.Y.; remedial Math. specialist, cons. Lake Placid (N.Y.) Schs.; adj. instr. math. North Country C.C., Saranac Lake, N.Y.; math. cons.; coordinating mentor N.Y. State Elem. Math. Mentors, 1993—; mem. Mid. Sch. MATHLINE, 1994—; master tchr. Internat. Tchr. Tng. Inst., Montreal, 1997. Editor (newsletter to parents); creator Pamper Your Child With Math program; contbr. rsch. to profl. jours.; presenter workshops in field. Area staff devel. com., vice chmn. Instructional TV Sch. Svc. com. WCFE, Plattsburgh, N.Y.; coord., chmn. scholarship com. Adirondack Festival Am. Music; sec., grant writer Adirondack Singers; chair Messiah Sing-In; sec. Town Hall Players; co-chair Saranac Lake Winter Carnival Skating Race, sports chair; treas. Saranac Lake (N.Y.) High Sch. Parent, Teacher, Student Assn. 1994—. Grantee Adirondack Tchr. Ctr., 1988, 89, 96, NYSACE, 1989, 95, Mathematics in the 21st Century, 1990, NSF Leadership Network, 1991-93. Mem. ASCD (assoc.), Nat. Coun. Tchrs. Math., N.Y. State Assn. Math. Suprs., Assn. Math. tchrs. N.Y. State (Essex County chmn., Hamilton County chmn., Warren County chmn., elem. rep. exec. bd., rec. sec. to exec. bd., external affairs com. chmn., presenter), N.Y. State Assn. Compensatory Educators, Delta Kappa Gamma (chpt. treas.). Home: 64 Riverside Dr Saranac Lake NY 12983-2319

SZYBALSKI, WACLAW, molecular geneticist, educator; b. Lwów, Poland, Sept. 9, 1921; came to U.S., 1950, naturalized, 1957; s. Stefan and Michalina (Rakowska) S.; m. Elizabeth Hunter, Feb. 5, 1955; children: Barbara A. Szybalski Sandor, Stefan H. BSChemE, Poly. Inst. Lwów, 1943; DSc, Inst. Tech., Gdańsk, Poland, 1949; Ph.D. (hon.), U. Marie Curie, Lublin, Poland, 1980, U. Gdańsk (Poland), 1989. Asst. prof. Inst. Tech., Gdańsk, 1946-50; mem. staff Cold Spring Harbor (N.Y.) Biol. Labs., 1951-55; asst. prof. Inst. Microbiology, Rutgers U., New Brunswick, N.J., 1955-60; prof. oncology McArdle Lab., U. Wis.-Madison, 1960—; mem. recombinant DNA adv. com. (RAC) NIH, 1974-78; Wendel H. Griffith meml. lectr. St. Louis U., 1975. Author numerous papers, revs., abstracts and books in field; editor-in-chief: Gene, 1976-96, hon. and founding editor-in-chief, 1996—; mem. editorial bd. other jours. Recipient Karl A. Forster lecture award U. Mainz, 1970, A. Jurzykowski Found. award in biology, 1988, Hilldale award in biology U. Wis., 1994, Gold G.J. Mendel Hon. medal for merit in biol. scis. Acad. Scis. of Czech Republic, 1995; Cogene lectr. Internat. Union Biochem., Nairobi, 1987, Cairo, 1988, Harare, Zimbabwe, 1989. Mem. AAAS, Am. Soc. Biochemists, Genetic Soc. Am., Am. Soc. Microbiologists (chmn. virology divsn. 1972-74, chmn. divsn. IV 1974-75), European Molecular Biology Orgns. (lectr. 1971, 76), Polish Soc. Microbiologists (hon.), Italian Soc. Exptl. Biology (hon.), Polish Med. Alliance (hon.), Polish Acad. Scis. (fgn. mem.). Home: 1124 Merrill Springs Rd Madison WI 53705-1317 Office: U Wis McArdle Lab Madison WI 53706 *The profession should also be the hobby and a constant source of enjoyment and satisfaction.*

SZYGENDA, STEPHEN A., electrical and computer engineering educator, researcher; b. McKeesport, Pa., Oct. 5, 1938; s. Stephen A. Sr. and Elizabeth B. (Zolczer) S.; m. Marie A. Deli, Apr. 2, 1960; children: Stepahnie Livingston, Diana, Mark. BS, Fairleigh Dickinson U., 1965; MS, Northwestern U., 1967, PhD, 1968. Registered profl. engr., Tex. Engr. Comprehensive Design, N.J., 1959-62; mem. tech. staff Bell Telephone Labs., N.J., Ill., 1962-68; assoc. prof. elec. engring. and computer engring. U. Mo., Rolla, 1968-70; prof. elec. engring. and computer engring. So. Meth. U., Dallas, 1970-73; prof. elec. engring. and computer engring. U. Tex., Austin, 1973-86, dir. Ctr. for Tech. Tran., 1986-89, Clint Murchison Sr. Chair of Free Enterprise prof., 1986-96, chmn. elec. and computer engring. dept., 1993-96; dean sch. engring. U. Ala., Birmingham, 1996—; pres. CCSS, Austin, 1972-81, Comsat Gen. Int. Sys., Austin, 1981-83, SBI, Inc., Austin, 1985—; pres., CEO Rubicon Group, Austin. 1983-85; active Tex. Gov. Coun. for Sci. and Tech., 1984-87. Contbr. articles to profl. jours. Dir. Laguna Gloria Mus., Austin, 1981-83; pres. bd. Austin Ballet, 1983. With USN, 1956-59. Fellow IEEE (bd. dirs. 1973-75 Svc. awards 197, 79, 83, 87, 96), SDPS; mem. Assn. Computing Machinery (Svc. award 1975, 79, 87, 88, Disting. lectr. 1991-95). Roman Catholic. Achievements include pioneering in CAD, simulation, fault tolerant computing, telecommunications, entrepreneurship, and software engineering. Home: 3620 Shandwick Pl Birmingham AL 35242 Office: U Ala Dean Sch Engring Birmingham AL 35294-4461

SZYMANSKI, EDNA MORA, rehabilitation psychology and special education educator; b. Caracas, Venezuela, Mar. 19, 1952; came to U.S., 1952; d. José Angel and Helen Adele (McHugh) Mora; m. Michael Bernard, Mar. 30, 1973. BS, Rensselaer Poly. Inst., 1972; MS, U. Scranton, 1974; PhD, U. Tex., 1988. Cert. rehab. counselor. Vocat. evaluator Mohawk Valley Workshop, Utica, N.Y., 1974-75; vocat. rehab. counselor N.Y. State Office Vocat. Rehab., Utica, N.Y., 1975-80; sr. vocat. rehab. counselor N.Y. State Office Vocat. Rehab., Utica, 1980-87; rsch. assoc. U. Tex., Austin, 1988-89; asst. prof. U. Wis., Madison, 1989-91, assoc. prof., 1991-93, assoc. dean sch. edn., 1993-97, dir. rehab. rsch. and tng. ctr., 1993-96, prof. rehab. psychology and spl. edn., 1993—, chair dept. rehab. psychology and spl. edn., 1997—, fellow tchg. acad., 1997—; cons. Rsch. Assocs. Syracuse, N.Y., 1988-90. Co-author various book chpts.; co-editor: Rehabilitation Counseling Basics and Beyond, 1992; co-editor Work and Disability, 1996, Rehabilitation Counseling Bull., 1994—; contbr. articles to profl. jours. Mem. Pres.'s Com. on Employment of People with Disabilities, Washington, 1987-97. Recipient Rsch. award Am. Assn. Counselor Edn. and Supr., 1991. Mem. ACA (chair rsch. com. 1992-94, Rsch. awards 1990, 93, 95), Am. Rehab. Counseling Assn. (pres. 1985-86, rsch. award 1989, 94, Disting. Profl. award 1997), Coun. Rehab. Edn. (chair rsch. com. 1990-95, v.p. 1993-95), Nat. Coun. Rehab. Edn. (chair rsch. com. 1992—, Rehab. Edn. Rschr. of Yr. 1993, New Career in Rehab. Edn. award 1990). Office: U Wis Dept Rehab Psychology and Spl Edn 432 N Murray St Madison WI 53706-1407

SZYMCZAK, EDWARD JOSEPH, mechanical engineer; b. Anderson, Tex., Sept. 28, 1938; s. Harold and Verna (Walkoviak) S.; m. Lorena Jane Sharp, Sept. 26, 1964; children: Denise, Lisa, Brian. Student, U. St. Thomas, 1958; BSME, Tex. A&M, 1961; MBA, U. Houston, 1970. Registered profl. engr., Tex. Engr. trainee to engring. mgr. Cameron Iron Works, Houston, 1961-90; dir. engring. ea. hemisphere Cooper Oil Tool Div./Cooper Industries, London, 1990-91; dir. engring. Cooper Oil Tool Div./Cooper Industries, Houston, 1991-95, Cameron div. Cooper Cameron Corp., Houston, 1995—; chmn. indsl. adv. bd. U. Southwestern La., Lafayette; councilor Tex. A&M U. Rsch. Found., College Station, 1994—; mem. mech. engring. adv. bd. U. Tenn., Knoxville, 1996—. Patentee (8) on oil tool equipment. Mem. ASME, Tex. A&M Former Students Assn., Tex. A&M 12th Man Found., Tex. A&M Mech. Engring. Acad. Disting. Grads., Soc. Petroleum Engrs., Nat. Assn. Corrosion Engrs., Tau Beta Pi. Republican. Roman Catholic. Avocations: ranching, farming, mechanic, investing, technical and personnel recruiting. Home: 4002 Cypress Hill Spring TX 77388

SZYMONIAK, ELAINE EISFELDER, state senator; b. Boscobel, Wis., May 24, 1920; d. Hugo Adolph and Pauline (Vig) Eisfelder; Casimir Donald Szymoniak, Dec. 7, 1943; children: Kathryn, Peter, John, Mary, Thomas. BS, U. Wis., 1941; MS, Iowa State U., 1977. Speech clinician Waukesha (Wis.) Pub. Sch., 1941-43, Rochester (N.Y.) Pub. Sch., 1943-44; rehab. aide U.S. Army, Chickasha, Okla., 1944-46; audiologist U. Wis., Madison, 1946-48; speech clinician Buffalo Pub. Sch., 1948-49, Sch. for Handicapped, Salina, Kans., 1951-52; speech pathologist, audiologist, counselor, resource mgr. Vocat. Rehab. State Iowa, Des Moines, 1956-85; mem. Iowa Senate, Des Moines, 1989—. Mem. Des Moines City coun., 1978-88; bd. dirs. Nat. League Cities, Wahsington, 1982-84, Civic Ctr., House of Mercy, Westminster House, Iowa Leadership Consortium, Coun. on Internat. Understanding, Iowa Commn. on Status of Women, Young Women's Christian Assn.; chairperson Greater Des Moines Coun. for Internat. Understanding, United Way, 1987-88, Urban Dreams, Iowa Maternal and Child Health com. Named Woman of Achievement YWCA, 1982, Visionary Woman, Young Women's Resource Ctr. Mem. Am. Speech Lang. and Hearing Assn., Iowa Speech Lang. and Hearing Assn. (pres. 1977-78), Nat. Coun. State Legislators (fed. state com. on health, adv. com. on child protection), Women's Polit. Caucus, Nexus (pres. 1981-82, mem. Supreme Ct. Select Com.). Avocations: reading, traveling, swimming. Home: 2116 44th St Des Moines IA 50310-3011 Office: State Senate State Capitol Des Moines IA 50319

TA, TAI VAN, lawyer, researcher; b. Ninh Binh, Vietnam, Apr. 16, 1938; came to U.S., 1975; s. Duong Van and Loan thi (Pham) T.; m. Lien-Nhu Tran, Oct. 26, 1967; children: Becky, John, Khuong Virginia, Dora. LLB, U. Saigon, Vietnam, 1960; MA, U. Va., 1964, PhD, 1965; LLM, Harvard U., 1985. Bar: Mass. 1986, U.S. Dist. Ct. Mass. 1987. Prof. U. Saigon Law Sch., 1965-75, Nat. Sch. Adminstrn., 1965-75; ptnr. Tang thi Thanh Trai & Ta Van Tai, 1968-75; legal researcher Reed Smith Shaw & McClay, Pitts., 1975; rsch. assoc. Harvard U. Law Sch., Cambridge, Mass., 1975—; pvt. practice, Brookline, Mass., 1986—; rsch. scholar NYU Law Sch., N.Y.C., 1990-94; cons. Milbank Tweed Hadley & McCloy, N.Y.C., 1979, Shearman & Sterling, N.Y.C., 1979, Paul Weiss Rifkind Wharton and Garrison, N.Y.C., 1989, 90. Co-author: The Laws of Southeast Asia, 1986, The Le Code: Law in Traditional Vietnam, 1987, Investment Law in Vietnam, 1990; author: Vietnamese Tradition of Human Rights, 1988; contbr. articles to profl. jours. V.p. Vietnamese Refugees Assn., Mass., 1976-79; advisor to Vietnamese community, Mass., 1989—. Fulbright scholar 1960-62; grantee Asia Found., 1972, Ford Found., 1975-76, Aspen Inst. 1993. Avocations: piano, swimming, foreign languages. Home: 145 Naples Rd Brookline MA 02146-2548 Office: Harvard U Law Sch Pound 423 1563 Massachusetts Ave Cambridge MA 02138-2903

TAAFFE, EDWARD JAMES, geography educator; b. Chgo., Dec. 11, 1921; s. Edward James and Julia Loretta (Murphy) T.; m. Marialyce Dunne, Sept. 7, 1948; children: Maura Joan, Edward James Jr., Michael Robert, Julianne, Susan Deirdre, Brian Thomas, Karen Elizabeth, David Matthew. BS in Meteorology, NYU, 1944; BS in Journalism, U. Ill., 1945; SM in Geography, U. Chgo., 1949, PhD in Geography, 1952. Istr. U. Ill., Chgo., 1948-51; from instr. to asst. prof. econs. dept. Loyola U., Chgo., 1951-56; from asst. to assoc. prof. geography dept. Northwestern U., Evanston, Ill., 1956-63; prof. Geography dept. Ohio State U., Columbus, 1963—, chmn. geography dept., 1963-75; mem. editorial bd. cons. World Book Atlas, Chgo., 1963-69; cons. editor McGraw-Hill Pub. Co., 1969-79; adv. bd. geography coun. Ontario U., Toronto, Can., 1972-73. Author: (books) Air Pass Hinterland of Chicago, 1952, The Peripheral Journey-To-Work, 1963, Geography of Transportation, 1996; editor: (book) Geography, 1973. 1st lt. USAAF, 1943-46, West Europe. Mem. Assn. Am. Geographers (counselor 1966-69, v.p. 1970-71, pres. 1971-72, Honors award 1982, Edward Ullman award 1990), Nat. Coun. Geog. Edn. (Master Tchr. award 1983), Soc. Sci. Rsch. Coun. (dir.-at-large 1970-74). Roman Catholic. Home: 4314 Olentangy Blvd Columbus OH 43214-3036 Office: Ohio State U Dept Geography 154 N Oval Mall Columbus OH 43210-1330

TAAFFE, JAMES GRIFFITH, university administrator, educator; b. Cin., Sept. 15, 1932; s. Griffith C. and Mary (Ropp) T.; m. Donna Click, June 8, 1955 (dec. 1986); children: Lauren Kathleen, Patrick Michael; m. Allison S. Blair, Nov. 7, 1987; 1 child, Michael Sean. AB, Columbia U., 1954; MA, Ind. U., 1956, PhD, 1960. Instr. English Williams Coll., Williamstown, Mass., 1959-62; asst. prof. English Vassar Coll., 1962-64; from asst. prof. to prof. English Case Western Res. U., Cleve., 1964—, chmn. advanced placement in English, 1968-73, chmn. dept., 1969-72, asst. to pres., 1971-72, dean grad. studies, 1972-74, v.p. undergrad. and grad. studies, 1974-81, univ. v.p. acad. affairs, 1981-86, acting chair dept. theatre arts, 1989-90; v.p. for acad. affairs U. Ala., Tuscaloosa, 1990-91, prof. English, 1990—, provost, v.p. for acad. affairs, 1991-96; mem. Joint Council, East Cleve. Sch. Dist., 1970. Co-author: A Milton Handbook, 1970; editor: Abraham Cowley, 1970; co-editor: Poems on Poetry, 1965, Reading English Poetry, 1971. Newberry Libr. fellow, 1964; Am. Philos. Soc. fellow, 1967, 69; NEH fellow, 1971. Mem. MLA, Milton Soc., Dante Soc. Home: 9201 Enterprise Ave NE Tuscaloosa AL 35406-1005

TAAM, RONALD EVERETT, physics and astronomy educator; b. N.Y.C., Apr. 24, 1948; s. Lawrence and Julia (Louie) T.; m. Rosa Wen Mei Yang, Oct. 19, 1974; children: Jonathan, Alexander. BS, Poly. Inst., N.Y.C., 1969; MA, Columbia U., 1971, PhD, 1973. Postdoctoral fellow U. Calif., Santa Cruz, 1973-76; vis. faculty U. Calif., Berkeley, 1976-78; asst. prof. Northwestern U., Evanston, Ill., 1978-83, assoc. prof., 1984-86, prof. physics and astronomy, 1986—, chmn. physics and astronomy, 1995—. Fellow Am. Phys. Soc.; mem. Am. Astron. Soc., Royal Astron. Soc., Internat. Astron. Union. Office: Dept Physics and Astronomy Northwestern U 2145 Sheridan Rd Evanston IL 60208-0834

TABACHNICK, NORMAN DONALD, psychiatrist, educator; b. Toronto, Ont., Can., Feb. 21, 1927. BS, U. Ill., 1947, MD, 1949; PhD in Psychoanalysis, So. Calif. Psychoanalytic Inst., 1977. Diplomate Am. Bd. Med. Examiners, Am. Bd. Psychiatry and Neurology. Intern Michael Reese Hosp., 1949-50; resident in psychiatry U.S. VA Hosp., Bedford, Mass., 1950-51, U.S. AFB, Biloxi, Miss., 1951-52, L.A. County Gen. Hosp., 1953-54; staff psychiatrist Sepulveda VA Hosp., 1976-78; pvt. practice L.A.; mem. staff Resthaven Sanitarium, U. So. Calif. Med. Ctr., L.A. County, Westwood Hosp., Edgemont Hosp., Cedars-Sinai Med. Ctr.; mem. staff Neuropsychiatric Inst. UCLA; clin. prof. psychiatry U. So. Calif., L.A., 1970-75, UCLA, 1975—; hon. mem. med. staf. Resthaven Cmty. Med. Health Ctr., 1973; guest lectr. Cedars-Sinai Med. Ctr., 1985; mem. adv. bd. divsn. psychoanalysis Nassau County Med. Ctr.; mem. faculty Calif. Sch. Profl. Psychology, L.A. Ctr. Group Psychotherapy, Grad. Ctr. Child Devel. and Psychotherapy; cons. L.A. County Coroner's Office, 1963-70, Bur. Vocat. Rehab., Jewish Family Svc., profl. adv. bd. Resthaven Sanitarium, Marianne Frostig Sch. Ednl. Therapy, W. Valley Ctr. Edl. Therapy. Author: Accident or Suicide?, 1973; mem. edtl. bd. Jour. Acad. Psychoanalysis, book rev. editor, 1978; mem. edtl. bd. Internat. Jour. Psycho-analytic Psychotherapy, 1979-83; reviewer Am. Jour. Psychiatry, 1983—, Jour. Neuropsychiatry and Clin. Neuro Scis., 1988-90; contbr. articles to profl. jours.; cons. (film) Suicide Prevention: The Physician's Role, 1967, Highlights of the 1964 American Psychiatric Association; cons., participant The Thin Edge--Guilt., 1975. Assoc. chief psychiatrist L.A. Suicide Prevention Ctr., 1968-76, prin. investigator; mem. adv. com. Walter Briehl Human Rights Found., 1984; v.p., bd. dirs. Suicide Prevention Ctr., Inc.; bd. dirs. Inst. Suicide Prevention, L.A., 1996, chmn. funding a crisis line com., 1997. Rsch. grantee Founds. Fund Rsch. Psychiatry, 1963, NIMH, 1970. Fellow Am. Psychiatric Assn. (life), Am. Acad. Psychoanalysis (pres. 1974, chmn. nominating com. 1975, trustee, chmn. com. on rsch., mem. edtl. bd. The Acad., presdl. citation 1975); mem. Internat. Psychoanalytic Assn., Internat. Assn. Suicide Prevention, Am. Psychoanalytic Assn. (cert. 1977, mem. com. liason with AAAS 1977-80), Am. Assn. Suicidology, (founder, mem. edtl. bd. Life-Threatening Behavior, cert. recognition 1996) Inst. Contemporary Psychoanalysis (founding mem., trustee 1990-93), So. Calif. Psychoanalytic Inst. (pres., tng. and supervising analyst, mem. selection rsch. clin. assocs. com.), So. Calif. Psychoanalytic Soc. (dir. rsch. divsn. 1970-81, chief investigator 1976-88, chmn. com. rsch. award stds. 1979, pres.-elect 1980, 86, pres. 1981, 87-90), Med. Rsch. Assn. So. Calif., So. Calif. Psychiat. Soc. (mem. consultation and violence panel), L.A. County Med. Assn. Office: 505 N Bonhill Rd Los Angeles CA 90049-2325

TABACKMAN, STEVEN CARL, lawyer; b. Balt., Apr. 2, 1950; s. Nathan and Evelyn (Caplan) T.; m. Leslie Adele Stout, Dec. 27, 1986; children: Alexa, Robert, Julia, Lia. BA with distinction, U. Va., 1971, JD, 1976. Bar: Va. Supreme Ct. 1976, D.C. Ct. Appeals 1977, U.S. Dist. Ct. D.C. 1978, U.S. Dist. Ct. Md. 1990, U.S. Dist. Ct. (ea. dist.) Va. 1992, U.S. Ct. Appeals

(D.C. cir.) 1978. Law clk. to Hon. Leonard Braman D.C. Superior Ct., Washington, 1976-77; law clk. to Hon. Theodore R. Newman, Jr. D.C. Ct. Appeals, Washington, 1977-78; asst. U.S. atty. U.S. Atty.'s Office D.C., Washington, 1978-88; assoc., ptnr. Perkins Coie, Washington, 1988-94; ptnr. Tigue, Patton, Tabackman & Babbin, Washington, 1994—. Mem. editorial bd. Money Laundering Law Reporter, 1990—; contbr. articles to profl. jours. Gen. counsel Duke Ellington Fund, Washington, 1988—. Fellow Am. Bd. Criminal Lawyers; mem. ABA, Nat. Assn. Criminal Def. Lawyers. Home: 1458 Highwood Dr McLean VA 22101 Office: Tigue Patton Tabackman & Bobbon 1747 Pennsylvania Ave NW Washington DC 20006

TABATZNIK, BERNARD, physician, educator; b. Mir, Poland, Jan. 8, 1927; came to U.S., 1959, naturalized, 1966; s. Max and Fay (Ginsberg) T.; m. Marjorie Turner, Jan. 8, 1956; children: Darron Mark, Keith Donald, Ilana Wendy; m. Charline Edwards Harmon, Aug. 7, 1992. B.Sc., U. Witwatersrand, South Africa, 1945; M.B., B.Ch., 1949. Intern Baragwanath Hosp., Johannesburg, South Africa, 1950-51, Hillingdon Hosp., Ashford Hosp., also research unit Canadian Red Cross Meml. Hosp., Taplow, Eng., 1951-54; med. registrar Ashford Hosp., 1954-56, Johannesburg Gen. Hosp., 1956-58; physician Baragwanath Hosp., 1958-59; fellow medicine Johns Hopkins Sch. Medicine, 1959-60, fellow cardiology, 1960-61, asst. prof. medicine, 1966—; head cardiopulmonary div. Sinai Hosp., Balt., 1961-72; asso. chief medicine Sinai Hosp., 1964-72; chief cardiology dept. North Charles Gen. Hosp., Balt., 1972; also dir. med. edn., dir. Postgrad. Inst., coordinator ambulatory services; med. dir. Nurse Practitioner-Physician Asst. Program, Ch. Hosp., Balt., 1987-90. Contbr. articles to profl. jours. Recipient Save-A-Heart Humanitarian award, 1977, Maimonides award, 1983, Shaarei Zion Humanitarian award, 1987. Fellow Royal Coll. Physicians (London); mem. South African Cardiac Soc., Am. Heart Assn., Md. Heart Assn. (chmn. health careers 1964-66), Laennec Cardiovascular Sound Group. Home: HC 3 Box 180 Monterey VA 24465-9313 Office: 8417 Bellona Ln Baltimore MD 21204-2014

TABBERNEE, WILLIAM, academic administrator, theology educator; b. Rotterdam, The Netherlands, Apr. 21, 1944; came to U.S., 1991; s. Adrianus and Neeltje Jannetje (Koonings) T.; m. Sandra Violet Parker, Jan. 15, 1966; children: Nicole, Jason, Michelle. Primary tchr. cert., Coburg Tchr. Coll., 1965; diploma in religious edn., Melbourne Coll. Divinity, 1968, lic. in theology, 1968; diploma with honors, Churches of Christ Theol. Coll, 1970; BA with honors, U. Melbourne, 1972; STM, Yale U., 1973; PhD, U. Melbourne, 1979. Ordained to ministry Churches of Christ in Australia, 1970. Headmaster Swan Reach Primary Sch., Victoria, Australia, 1966; tchr. Newlands H.S., Melbourne, Australia, 1967-68; min. The Patch Church of Christ, Victoria, Australia, 1971-72; lectr. Coll. of the Bible, Melbourne, 1973-76; lectr. Coll. of the Bible, 1977-80, chair dept. Christian thought and systematic theology, 1977-80; dean Evang. Theol. Assn., Melbourne, 1979-80; prin. Coll. of the Bible, 1981-91; pres., prof. Christian thought and history Phillips Theol. Sem., Enid and Tulsa, Okla., 1991—; part-time lectr. Coll. of the Bible, 1971-72. Editor, author (with others): Marriage in Australian Churches, 1982, Initiation in Australian Churches, 1984, Australian Churches' Response to Baptism, Eucharist and Ministry, 1986, Ministry in Australian Churches, 1987, Montanist Inscriptions and Testimonia, 1997; contbr. numerous articles to profl. jours. Mem. Am. Acad. Religion, Assn. Disciples Theol. Discussion, N. Am. Patristics Soc., Australian and New Zealand Soc. Theol. Studies, Internat. Bilateral Commn. Dialogue Between Disciples Ecumenical Consultative Counc. and Pontifical Counc. Promotion Christian Unity, Internat. Bilateral Commn. Dialogue Between Disciples Ecumenical Counc. and World Alliance Reformed Chs. Office: Phillips Theological Sem PO Box 2335 Enid OK 73702

TABELL, ANTHONY, financial analyst; b. Bklyn., Aug. 5, 1931; s. Edmund Weber and Margaret (Suydam) T.; m. Ellen Margaret Molwitz, May 23, 1953; children—Margaret Ellen, Roberta Jane, Sarah Elizabeth. Grad., St. Luke's Sch., New Canaan, Conn., 1948; A.B., Colgate U., 1952; student, N.Y. U., 1957-65. With Walston & Co. Inc., N.Y.C., 1954-70, v.p., 1961-65, sr. v.p., dir., 1965-70; asso. Delafield, Harvey, Tabell div. Janney, Montgomery Scott, Inc., Princeton, N.J., 1970-83, v.p. parent co., 1971-83; mng. dir. Delafield, Harvey, Tabell Inc., Princeton, 1983-92; sr. v.p. U.S. Trust Co. of N.J., Princeton, 1992-93. Served with AUS, 1952-54. Mem. N.Y. Soc. Security Analysts, Market Technicians Assn. (pres. 1975-76), Nassau Club. Episcopalian. Home: 76 Crooked Tree Ln Princeton NJ 08540-2950

TABER, EDWARD ALBERT, III, investment executive; b. Jacksonville, Fla., Aug. 25, 1943; s. Edward Albert, Jr. and Janet Gladys (Bickford) T.; m. Teresa Marie Scheidle, Nov. 13, 1982; children: Linley Marie, Laura Elizabeth, Lisa Kimberly. AB, Dartmouth Coll., 1965; MBA, Harvard Coll., 1971. V.p., treas. Fed. Home Loan Bank, Boston, 1971-73; v.p. T. Rowe Price Assocs., Inc., Balt., 1975-92, also bd. dirs.; sr. exec. v.p. Legg Mason, Inc., 1992—. Capt. USMC, 1965-69, Vietnam. Decorated Silver Star, Purple Heart. Republican. Episcopalian.

TABER, MARGARET RUTH, electrical engineering technology educator, electrical engineer; b. St. Louis, Apr. 29, 1935; d. Wynn Orr and Margaret Ruth (Feldman) Gould Stevens; m. William James Taber, Sept. 6, 1958. B.Engring. Sci., Cleve. State U., 1958, B.E.E., 1958; M.S. in Engring., U. Akron, 1967; Ed.D., Nova U., 1976; postgrad., Western Res. U., 1959-64. Registered profl. engr., Ohio; cert. engring. technologist. Engring. trainee Ohio Crankshaft Co., Cleve., 1954-57, devel. engr., 1958-64, tng. dir., 1963-64; instr. elec.-electronic engring. tech. Cuyahoga Community Coll., Cleve., 1964-67, asst. prof., 1967-69, assoc. prof., 1969-72, prof., 1972-79, chmn. engring. tech., 1977-79; assoc. prof. elec. engring. tech. Purdue U., West Lafayette, Ind., 1979-83, prof., 1983—; lectr. Cleve. State U., 1963-64; mem. acad. adv. bd. Cleve. Inst. Electronics, 1981—, ednl. cons., author, 1979—. Author: (with Frank P. Tedeschi) Solid State Electronics, 1976, (with Eugene M. Silgalis) Electric Circuit Analysis, 1980, (with Jerry L. Casebeer) Registers, (with Kenneth Rosenow) Arithmetic Logic Units, Timing and Control, Memory Units, 1980, 6809 Architecture and Operation, 1984, Programming I: Straight Line, 1984; contbr. articles to profl. jours. Bd. dirs. West Blvd. Christian Ch., deaconess, 1974-77, elder, 1977-79; deacon Federated Ch., 1981-84, 86-89, Stephen Leader, 1988—; mem. Cancer Support Group; co-chair svc. and rehab. com. Am. Cancer Soc., 1992—; vol. CanSurmount, 1993—; vol. Lafayette Reading Acad., 1992—; ednl. resource vol., vol. tchr. Sunburst Farm Rainbow Acres, Inc., Ariz., 1988—. Recipient Helen B. Schleman Gold Medallion award Purdue U., 1991, The Greater Lafayette Community Survivorship award, 1994, Outstanding Alumni award U. Akron Coll. Engring., 1994; Margaret R. Taber Microcomputer Lab. named in her honor Purdue U., 1991; NSF grantee, 1970-73, 78. Fellow Soc. Women Engrs. (counselor Purdue chpt. 1983—, Disting. Engring. Educator award 1987); mem. IEEE (sr.), Am. Bus. Women's Assn. (ednl. chmn. 1964-66), Am. Soc. Engring. Edn., Am. Tech. Edn. Assn., Tau Beta Pi (hon.), Phi Kappa Phi. Avocations: robotics; camping; housekeeping. Home: 3036 State Rd 26 W West Lafayette IN 47906-4743 Office: Purdue U Elec Engring Tech Dept Knoy Hall Tech West Lafayette IN 47907

TABER, PATRICK E., computer programmer; b. Lawrence, Kans., June 4, 1972; s. Patrick E. and Shirley M. (Pruske) T. BS, Trinity U., San Antnonio, Tex., 1994. Tech. support/programmer Southwest Software, Austin, 1995—. Home: 7201 Hart Lne # 2071 Austin TX 78731

TABER, ROBERT CLINTON, retired army officer; b. Ithaca, N.Y., Oct. 11, 1917; s. Laurence Sebring and Ethel (Lanning) T.; m. Jane Feeter, July 20, 1940 (dec. 1982); 1 child, John Robert; m. Lynn Parker, June 12, 1992. B.S., Cornell U., 1938; grad., Army War Coll., 1958. Commd. 2d lt. U.S. Army, 1940; advanced through grades to lt. gen.; comdg. gen. Joint U.S. Mil. Adv. Group Cambodia, 1963; asst. div. comdr. 82d Airborne Div., 1964-65; asst. comdt. U.S. Army Command and Gen. Staff Coll. Leavenworth, Kans., 1965-66; chief of staff U.S. Army Vietnam, 1967-68; dir. doctrine and systems Dept. Army, 1968-69; comdg. gen. 3d Inf. Div. Germany, 1970-71; prin. dep. asst sec. def. manpower and res. affairs, 1971-74. Decorated DSM with 2 oak leaf clusters, Legion of Merit with 3 oak leaf clusters, Soldiers medal, Bronze Star, Purple Heart, Joint Commendation medal, Army Commendation medal with 2 oak leaf clusters, Air medal with 2 oak leaf clusters. Mem. U.S. Naval Acad. Sailing Sqdn. Clubs: Cruising of Am, Ocean Cruising, Internat. Aerobatic. Home: 2109 Fox Ridge Rd Tuscaloosa AL 35406-3057

TABIN, JULIUS, patent lawyer, physicist; b. Chgo., Nov. 8, 1919; s. Sol and Lillian (Klingman) T.; m. Johanna Krout, Sept. 7, 1952; children: Clifford James, Geoffrey Craig. B.S., U. Chgo., 1940, Ph.D. in Physics, 1946; LL.B., Harvard U., 1949. Bar: Calif., D.C. 1949, Ill. 1950. Jr. physicist metall. lab. U. Chgo., 1943-44; physicist Los Alamos Sci. Lab. (U. Calif.), N.Mex., 1944-45, Argonne Nat. Lab., AEC, Chgo., 1946; staff mem., group supr. Inst. Nuclear Studies, Mass. Inst. Tech., 1946-49; patent examiner U.S. Patent Office, Washington, 1949-50; asso. firm Fitch, Even, Tabin & Flannery, Chgo., 1950-52; mem. firm Fich, Even, Tabin & Flannery, 1952—; lectr. U. Chgo., 1959. Mem. Am., D.C., Calif., Ill., Chgo. bar assns., Sigma Xi. Home: 162 Park Ave Glencoe IL 60022-1352 Office: 135 S La Salle St Chicago IL 60603-4105

TABLER, BRYAN G., lawyer; b. Louisville, Jan. 12, 1943; s. Norman Gardner and Sarah Marie (Grant) T.; m. Susan Y. Beidler, Dec. 28, 1968 (div. June 1987); children: Justin Elizabeth, Gillian Gardner; m. Karen Sue Strome, July 24, 1987. AB, Princeton U., 1969; JD, Yale U., 1972. Bar: Ind. 1972, U.S. Dist. Ct. (so. dist.) Ind. 1972, U.S. Dist. Ct. (no. dist.) Ind. 1976, U.S. Ct. Appeals (7th cir.) 1976, U.S. Supreme Ct. 1976. Assoc. Barnes & Thornburg, Indpls., 1972-79, ptnr., chmn. environ. law dept., 1979-94; v.p., gen. counsel, sec. IPALCO Enterprises, Inc., 1994—; sr. v.p., gen. coun., sec. Indpls. Power & Light Co., 1994—; mem. exec. com. Environ. Quality Control, Inc., Indpls., 1985—. Mem. Indpls. Mus. of Art, 1972—; bd. dirs. Indpls. Symphony Orch. 1st lt. U.S. Army, 1964-68, Vietnam. Mem. Ind. C. of C. (chmn. air com.), Indpls. C. of C. (govt. affairs coun. 1986-94), ABA, Ind. Bar Assn., Bar Assn. of the 7th Cir., Indpls. Bar Assn. Avocations: trap and skeet shooting, reading, golf. Home: 8932 Wickham Rd Indianapolis IN 46260-1644 Office: Indpls Power & Light Co One Monument PO Box 1595 Indianapolis IN 46206

TABLER, NORMAN GARDNER, JR., lawyer; b. Louisville, Oct. 15, 1944; s. Norman Gardner and Marie (Grant) T.; m. Dawn Carla Martin, May 6, 1989; 1 child, Rachel Ann Ayres-Tabler. BA, Princeton U., 1966; MA, Yale U., 1968; JD, Columbia U., 1971. Bar: Ind. 1971, U.S. Dist. Ct. (so. dist.) Ind. 1971. Assoc. Baker & Daniels, Indpls., 1971-77, ptnr., 1978-96; sr. v.p. corp. affairs, gen. counsel Clarian Health Ptnrs., Inc., Indpls., 1996—; adj. prof. Ind. U. Law Sch., Indpls., 1984-88; mem. adv. com. Ctr. for Law and Health, Ind. U., Indpls., 1987-91; mem. antitrust task force Ind. Dept. Health, 1993-94; lectr. Ind. U. Law Sch., 1992-96. Bd. dirs. Ind. Repertory Theatre, Inc., Indpls., 1984—, Indpls. Art Ctr., 1988-93, Indpls. Pub. Broadcasting, 1992—, Indpls. 500 Festival, 1992—, Brickyard 400 Festival, 1993—, Found. of Indy Festivals, 1995—, Indy Festivals, 1995—; mem. Ind. Sec. of State's Com. on Revision of Ind. Nonprofit Corp. Act, 1989-92; mem. Ind. Ednl. Fin. Authority, 1989-93; mem. Ind. Recreational Devel. Commn., 1993—; mem. Medicaid Task Force Ind. Commn. Health Policy, 1990-92; mem. nat. bd. law reps. PBS. Mem. ABA (health care com. sect. antitrust law, forum com. on health law, health care com. of sect. bus. law), Ind. Bar Assn. (health law sect.), Indpls. Bar Assn. (health law sect.), Am. Acad. Healthcare Attys. (com. on managed care and integrated delivery sys., com. on environ. law and OSHA, com. on antitrust, acad. med. ctrs. com.), Nat. Health Lawyers Assn., U.S. Squash Racquets Assn., Princeton Alumni Assn. Ind. (pres. 1988-97), Indpls. Athletic Club (bd. dirs. 1994—), Skyline Club (bd. govs. 1992—), Princeton Club N.Y., Indpls. Press Club. Avocations: reading biographies, squash. Office: Clarian Health Ptnrs Inc Office Corp Affairs Box 1367 Indianapolis IN 46206-1367

TABLER, WILLIAM BENJAMIN, architect; b. Momence, Ill., Oct. 28, 1914; s. Clyde Lyeth and Frances Beatrice (Ridley) T.; m. Phyllis May Baker, June 12, 1937; children: William, Judith. B.S. cum laude, Harvard U., 1936, B.Arch., 1939, M.Arch., 1939. Architect specializing in hotels; prin. works include Hilton hotels in N.Y.C., Dallas, Pitts., San Francisco, Toronto, Rye Town, N.Y., Long Branch and Woodcliff Lake, N.J., Washington and Izmir, Turkey; Conrad Internat. Istanbul, Turkey; Intercontinental hotels in Lahore, Rawapindi, Jamaica, Ras Al Khaimah, Jeddah, Nairobi, Lusaka, Dacca, Amman, Karachi and Jerusalem; Marriott Bklyn. and Phila., Sheraton Universal City, New Orleans, Brussels and Sheraton Centre, Toronto; Meridien hotels in Colombo, Sri Lanka, Cairo and Heliopolis, Egypt and Jakarta, Indonesia, Othon Palace in Rio and Bahia; Registry in Bloomington and Scottsdale; Grand Kempinski, Dallas; Hosts of Houston and Tampa; Sonesta Bermuda; Radisson Duluth, Lough Key, Ireland; New Otani L.A., Chosen, Korea; Stouffers, Chgo. and St. Louis; Bonaventure Montreal; Hanover, Woodstock and Princeton Inns; 15 Hospitality Motor Inns; also Harper and Stony Brook Coll. Dormitories; many others; mem. bldg. constrn. adv. council N.Y.C. Bldg. Dept., 1967—. Bd. dirs. Manhattan Eye, Ear and Throat Hosp., Community Hosp., Glen Cove. Served as lt. USNR, 1943-46, PTO. Recipient Horatio Alger award Am. Schs. and Colls. Assn., 1958; 1st prize for excellence in design Internat. Hotel, Queens C. of C., N.Y., 1958; Producers Council award, 1967. Fellow AIA (nat. chmn. bldg. codes com., pres. N.Y. chpt. 1967-68), ASCE; mem. Royal Inst. Brit. Architects, Bldg. Research Inst., N.Y. Bldg. Congress, NYU Hotel and Restaurant Soc., Am. Nat. Standards Inst. (exec. com. constrn. standards bd.), Nat. Fire Protection Assn. (chmn. sect. com. on residential occupancies, com. on safety to life), Ave. of Americas Assn. (bd. dirs.). Club: Harvard (bd. mgrs., exec. com., chmn. house com. N.Y.C.). Home: 44 Wolver Hollow Rd Glen Head NY 11545-2808 Office: 333 7th Ave New York NY 10001-5004

TABNER, MARY FRANCES, secondary school educator; b. Rochester, N.Y., Dec. 11, 1918; d. William Herman and Mary Frances (Willenbacher) Arndt; m. James Gordon Tabner, June 27, 1942; 1 child, Barbara Jean. BA, SUNY, Albany, 1940, MA, 1959; postgrad., U. Rochester, N.Y., 1944, 45, Northwestern U. (John Hay fellow), 1963-64, U. Manchester (Eng.), 1971-72. Tchr. history pub. schs. Mattituck, N.Y., 1940-43, Gorham, N.Y., 1943-46; tchr. pub. schs. Waterford, N.Y., 1949-55; tchr. social studies Shaker High Sch., Latham, N.Y., 1959-83, also dir., 1959-83, ret., 1983; tchr. ch. history Our Lady of Assumption Ch., Latham; dir. seminar in Russian Studies; tchr. Shaker Heritage. Author bibliographies on Russian history, Am. studies. Mem. Citizens Exch. Coun. N.Y. State Regents independent study grantee, 1966. Mem. AAUW, Nat. Coun. Social Studies, N.Y. State United Tchrs. Assn., Advancement Slavic Studies, SUNY Albany Alumni Assn., Albany Inst. History and Art, Capital Dist. Coun. Social Studies, Shaker Heritage Soc. (trustee, guide, tchr.), Nat. Trust Historic Preservation, English Speaking Union, Am. Assn. Retired Persons. Republican. Roman Catholic. Home: 557 Columbia St Cohoes NY 12047-3807

TABOR, BEVERLY ANN, elementary school educator; b. Dallas, Feb. 12, 1943; m. Charles W. Tabor, Aug. 22, 1964; children: Shawn, Josh. BS in Edn., U. N. Tex., 1964, MEd in Guidance, Counseling, 1970. Cert. tchr. elem. art, guidance and counseling, supr., Tex. Elem. tchr. Ft. Davis (Tex.) Ind. Sch. Dist., 1964-65, Mesquite (Tex.) Ind. Sch. Dist., 1965-69, 71-97; counselor Amarillo (Tex.) Ind. Sch. Dist., 1970-71; mem. ins. adv. com. Tchr. Retirement Sys. of Tex., Austin, 1986-97; chmn. site based mgmt. com. Tosch Elem. Sch., Mesquite, 1992-94, mentor for new tchrs., student tchrs., H.S. students considering the tchg. profession. Life mem. Tosch Elem. PTA, 1985—. Named to Apple Corps, 1995. Mem. Tex. State Tchrs. Assn. (life), Mesquite Edn. Assn., Alpha Delta Kappa (past pres. Mesquite). Avocations: arts and crafts. Home: 5321 Meadowside Dr Garland TX 75043-2733 Office: Tosch Elem Sch 2424 Larchmont Dr Mesquite TX 75150-5233

TABOR, CURTIS HAROLD, JR., library director; b. Atlanta, July 3, 1936; s. Curtis Harold and Gertrude Olive (Casey) T.; m. Dorothy May Corbin, June 30, 1957 (dec. June 1996); children: Timothy M., John M. AA, Fla. Coll., Temple Terrace, 1957; BA, Harding Coll., 1960; MA, Butler U., 1967; MDiv, Bapt. Missionary Assn. Theol. Sem., Jacksonville, Tex., 1974; MLS, Tex. Woman's U., 1977. Min. Ch. of Christ, Bowling Green, Ky., 1960-61, Hamilton, Ont., Can., 1961-64, Indpls., 1964-67, Nacogdoches, Tex., 1967-75, Dallas, 1976-77, Columbus, Miss., 1977-79, Tampa, Fla., 1993—; tchr. Gt. Lakes Christian Coll., Beamville, Ont., Can., 1961-64; bible chair Stephen F. Austin State U., Nacogdoches, 1967-75; prof., libr. Fla. Coll., Temple Terrace, 1979-85, libr. dir., 1985—; participated archaeol. excavations, Tell Gezer, Israel, 1969, Tell Lachish, Israel, 1980. Author: (with others) Resurrection, 1973, Biblical Authority, 1974, The Lord of Glory, 1980, Making a Difference: Florida College, the First Fifty Years, 1996. Cub master Cub Scouts Am., Nacogdoches, 1970-75; pres. Nacogdoches Baseball Assn., 1974-75. Recipient scouters key Cub Scouts Am., 1975. Mem. ALA, Fla. Libr. Assn., Tampa Bay Libr. Consortium (treas. 1986-89), Eta Beta Rho, Beta Phi Mu. Republican. Mem. Ch. of Christ. Avocation: Am. radio operator-KC4XS-Locksmith. Home: 12316 Kelly Ln Thonotosassa FL 33592-2754 Office: Fla Coll Libr 119 N Glen Arven Ave Tampa FL 33617-5527

TABOR, EDWARD, physician, researcher; b. Washington, Apr. 30, 1947; married; 4 children. BA, Harvard U., 1969; MD, Columbia U., 1973. Intern and resident Columbia-Presbyn. Med. Ctr., N.Y.C., 1973-75; rsch. investigator Bur. Biologics, Bethesda, Md., 1975-83; dir. divsn. anti-infective drug products FDA, Rockville, Md., 1983-88; assoc. dir. for biol. carcinogenesis Nat. Cancer Inst./NIH, Bethesda, 1988-95; dir. divsn. transfusion transmitted diseases FDA, Bethesda and Rockville, Md., 1995—. Contbr. articles to more than 200 publs. Capt. USPHS, 1975—. Achievements include research in hepatitis viruses, hepatocellular carcinoma. Office: FDA/CBER HFM-310 1401 Rockville Pike Rockville MD 20852-1428

TABOR, JOHN KAYE, retired lawyer; b. Uniontown, Pa., Apr. 19, 1921; s. Edward Otto and Marguerite B. (Kaye) T.; m. Kate Hill Williams, Dec. 13, 1952; children: John Kaye, William H. BA, Yale U., 1943; BA (Henry fellow), Corpus Christi Coll., Cambridge, Eng., 1947, MA, 1950; LLB, Harvard U., 1950; DHL, Alliance Coll., 1974. Bar: N.Y. 1950, Pa. 1953, D.C. 1976. Assoc. Winthrop, Stimpson, Putnam & Roberts, N.Y.C., 1950-53; assoc. Kirkpatrick, Pomeroy, Lockhart & Johnson, Pitts., 1953-58, ptnr., 1958-63; ptnr. Kirkpatrick, Lockhart, Johnson & Hutchison, Pitts., 1970-73, Purcell & Nelson, Washington, 1976-80, Reavis & McGrath, Washington, 1980-85; adj. prof. law George Mason U., Arlington, Va., 1986-87; pvt. practice Washington, 1985-90; sec. commerce State of Pa., 1963-67, sec. internal affairs, 1967-68, sec. labor and industry, 1968-69; chmn. Pa. Indsl. Devel. Authority, 1963-67; sec. Pa. Gen. State Authority, 1967-69; under sec. U.S. Dept. Commerce, Washington, 1973-75; chmn. housing task force and housing strike force Allegheny County Health and Welfare Assn., 1970-73. Trustee Masaryk Publs. Trust; bd. dirs. Citizens Assn. of Georgetown, 1985-89, 91; vestryman St. John's Ch., Georgetown. Lt. USNR, 1943-46, PTO. Mem. ABA (ad hoc criminal code and civil RICO coms.), Met. Club (Washington), Phi Beta Kappa. Home: 1616 34th St NW Washington DC 20007-2710

TABOR, MARY LEEBA, literary magazine editor, author; b. Balt., Mar. 3, 1946; d. Gerson and Freda (Roseman) T.; m. Ardell Louis Persinger, Sept. 16, 1984; children: Benjamin George Hammerschlag, Sarah Esther Hammerschlag. BA with high honors, U. Md., 1966; MA in Teaching, Oberlin Coll., 1967; postgrad., U. Chgo., 1988, Ohio State U., 1996—. Tchr. Towson (Md.) High Sch., 1967-70; employment profl. Ctr. for Naval Analyses, Alexandria, Va., 1970-71; tchr. adult edn. Montgomery County (Md.) Bd. Edn., 1975-80; editor pub. affairs Am. Petroleum Inst., Washington, 1980-83, writer, editor-in-chief, 1983-86, mgr. environ., health and pub. affairs, 1986-89, dir. pub. affairs writing, 1989-96; assoc. fiction editor The Jour., lit. mag. Ohio State U., Columbus, 1996—; advisor on high sch. sci. curriculum reform NSTA, Washington, 1991-96. Debate judge Nat. Cath. Forensic High Sch. League, Bethesda (Md.)-Chevy Chase High Sch., 1991-93; bd. dirs. Bethesda Jewish Congregation, 1993—. Mem. Nat. Press Club, Phi Beta Kappa, Phi Kappa Phi, Alpha Lambda Delta. Office: The Jour Ohio State U Dept English 164 W 17th Ave Columbus OH 43210-1326

TABOR, SANDRA LAVONNE, legal association administrator; b. Devils Lake, N.D., Dec. 19, 1954; d. Allen Thomas and LaVonne (Everson) T. BS in Edn., U. N.D., 1977, JD, 1981. Bar: N.D. 1981, U.S. Dist. Ct. N.D. 1982, U.S. Ct. Appeals (8th cir.) 1983. Corp. counsel Knife River Coal Mining Co., Bismarck, N.D., 1981-85, corp. counsel, asst. sec., 1985-87; asst. v.p. corp. communications MDU Resources Group, Inc., Bismarck, 1987-88, v.p., 1988-89; compliance project mgr. Engring. Sci., Inc., La Jolla, Calif., 1989-92; exec. dir. State Bar Assn. of N.D., Bismarck, N.D., 1992—; spl. asst. atty. gen. State of N.D., Bismarck, 1984-89. Contbr. articles to profl. jours. Bd. dirs. N.D. Spl. Olympics, Grand Forks, 1987—; bd. dirs. City Ctr. Partnership, 1994—; mem. adv. panel Met. Transp. Coun., 1994—; mem. Commn. on Gender Fairness in the Cts., 1994—; mem. N.D. Crime Victims Coun., 1994—; sec.-treas. N.D. Commn. for CLE, 1992—; sec. Jud. Nominating Com., 1994—. Decorated Army Commendation medal with 1 oak leaf cluster. Mem. N.D. State Bar Assn., N.D. Bar Found. (sec.-treas. 1992—), N.D. Women's Golf Assn. (pres. 1997—), N.D. Jr. Golf Club (bd. dirs. 1995—), Riverwood Golf Assn. (pres. 1986-87). Lutheran. Avocations: golf, tennis, water and snow skiing, bridge. Office: State Bar Assn ND PO Box 2136 Bismarck ND 58502-2136

TABORN, JEANNETTE ANN, real estate investor; b. Cleve., June 9, 1926; d. Ralph Mason and Catherine MArie (Mitchell) Tyler; m. Albert Lorenzo Taborn, Oct. 4, 1947 (dec. 1994); children: Wesley Orren, Annette Loren, KAren Faye, Albert Lorenzo II, Thomas Tyler. Student, Ohio State U., 1944-47. Real estate agt. and investor Cleve., 1947-61; tech. proofreader Sass-Widder Tech Writers, Port Hueneme, Calif., 1961-66, Upjohn Co., Kalamazoo, Mich., 1966-84; mktg. rep. pvt. practice, Kalamazoo, Mich., 1984—; facilitator Healing Racism Series. Pres. Kalamazoo County Parent Tchr. Student Assn., 1975; active YWCA, 1981, NAACP, 1983; Kalamazoo Pub. Sch. bd., 1978; Greater Kalamazoo Arts Coun., 1979, Mich. sch. bd. vocat./Edn., Liberty com. C. of Com.; pres. Loy Norrix Trustee Fund, 1983; trustee Kalamazoo Intermediate Sch.; regional mgr. Al Williams. Recipient Cmty. Medal of Arts. Mem. So. West Mich. Alzheimer's Assn. (bd. mem.), Delta Sigma Theta (Mary McLeod Bethune award). Mem. Bahai Faith. Office: PO Box 50853 Kalamazoo MI 49005-0853

TACAL, JOSE VEGA, JR., public health official, veterinarian; b. Ilocos Sur, Philippines, Sept. 5, 1933; came to U.S., 1969; s. Jose Sr. and Cristina (Vega) T.; m. Lilia Caccam, 1959; children: Joyce, Jasmin, Jose III. DVM, U. Philippines, Quezon City, 1956; diploma, U. Toronto, 1964. Diplomate Am. Coll. Vet. Preventive Medicine; lic. vet., Calif. Provincial veterinarian Philippine Bur. Animal Industry, Manila, 1956-57; instr. vet. medicine U. Philippines, Quezon City, 1957-64, asst. prof., chmn. dept. vet. microbiology, pathology and pub. health, 1965-69; pub. health veterinarian San Bernardino (Calif.) County Dept. Pub. Health, 1970-83, sr. pub. health veterinarian, program mgr., sect. chief, 1984—; zoonotic diseases lectr. Calif. State U., San Bernardino, spring 1984; lectr. U. Calif. Extension, Riverside, spring, 1985; vis. prof. vet. pub. health U. Philippines at Los Banos, Laguna, 1988; participant 1st Internat. Conf. on Emerging Zoonoses, Jerusalem, 1996; presenter in field, including 4th Internat. Symposium on Ectoparasites of Pets, U. Calif., Riverside, 1997, program presenter, 1997. Columnist L.A. Free Press, 1991, Pilipinas Times, 1993, Mabuhay Times, 1994-95; contbr. more than 50 articles to profl. jours. Pres. Filipino Assn. of San Bernardino County, Highland, Calif., 1979; charter mem. Greater Inland Empire Filipino Assn., Highland, 1986—; del. First Filipino Media Conf. N.Am., L.A., 1993; mem. San Bernardino County Africanized Honey Bee Task Force, 1993—; participant 1st Internat. Conf. on Emerging Zoonoses, Jerusalem, 1996; mem. San Bernardino County Africanized Honey Bey Task Force, 1993—. Recipient Donald T. Fraser Meml. medal U. Toronto, 1964, Cert. of Merit, Philippine Vet. Med. Assn., 1965, Cert. of Appreciation Calif. State Bd. Examiners in Vet. Medicine, 1979, 84, Cert. of Recognition, Congressman George E. Brown Jr., 42d Congl. Dist. Calif., 1994, Assemblyman Joe Baca, 62d Assembly Dist., Calif. State Legis., 1994, Colombo Plan Study fellow Can./Philippine Govts., 1963-64. Mem. AAAS, AVMA, Orange Belt Vet. Med. Assn., Western Poultry Disease Conf., Soc. for Advancement of Rsch., Nat. Trust for Historic Preservation, N.Y. Acad. Scis., Phi Kappa Phi, Phi Sigma. Office: San Bernardino County Dept Pub Health 351 N Mountain View Ave San Bernardino CA 92401-1609

TACHA, ATHENA, sculptor, educator; b. Larissa, Greece, Apr. 23, 1936; came to U.S., 1963; MA, Nat. Acad. Fine Arts, Athens, Greece, 1959; MA in Art History, Oberlin Coll., 1961; PHD, U. Paris, 1963. Curator modern art Allen Art Mus., Oberlin, Ohio, 1963-73; prof. art Oberlin Coll., 1973—. One-woman shows include Zabriskie Gallery, N.Y., 1979, 81, Max Hutchinson Gallery, N.Y., 1984, High Mus. Art, Atlanta, 1989, Franklin Furnace, N.Y., 1994, and many other exhibits throughout the world, 1966—; prin. pub. commns. include sculptures at Dept. Environ. Protection, Trenton, N.J., Case-Western Res. U., Cleve., U. South Fla., Ft. Myers, Low Water Dam Riverfront Pk., Tulsa, Dept. of Transp., Hartford, Conn., City of Sarasota, Fla., Ecology Dept. U. Minn., St. Paul; collections include Hirshhorn Mus., Washington, Mus. Fine Arts, Houston, Nat. Coll. Fine Arts, Washington, Cleve. Mus. Art, Allen Art Mus., Oberlin; author: (as A. T.

Spear) Rodin Sculpture in the Cleveland Museum of Art, 1967, Brancusi's Birds, 1969; contbr. articles to profl. jours. Recipient 1st prize May Show, Cleve. Mus. Art, 1968, 71, 79; NEA grantee, 1975. Home: 291 Forest St Oberlin OH 44074-1509

TACHA, DEANELL REECE, federal judge; b. Jan. 26, 1946. BA, U. Kans., 1968; JD, U. Mich., 1971. Spl. asst. to U.S. Sec. of Labor, Washington, 1971-72; assoc. Hogan & Hartson, Washington, 1973, Thomas J. Pitner, Concordia, Kans., 1973-74; dir. Douglas County Legal Aid Clinic, Lawrence, Kans., 1974-77; assoc. prof. law U. Kans., Lawrence, 1974-77, prof., 1977-85, assoc. dean, 1977-79, assoc. vice chancellor, 1979-81, vice chancellor, 1981-85; judge U.S. Ct. Appeals (10th cir.), Denver, 1985—; U.S. sentencing commr., 1994—. Office: US Ct Appeals 10th Cir 4830 W 15th St Ste 100 Lawrence KS 66049-3885

TACHIWAKI, TOKUMATSU, chemistry educator; b. Kyoto, Japan, Oct. 27, 1938; s. Sensuke and Yasu (Kishimoto) T.; m. Teruko Otsubo, May 25, 1965; children: Kenji, Yasushi, Yuuko. B. Tech., Doshisha U., Kyoto, 1961, M. Tech., 1963; D Tech., Osaka (Japan) U., 1992. Asst. prof. dept. chem. engring. Doshisha U., Kyoto, 1963-83, lectr. prof. dept. chem. engring., 1983-88, assoc. prof. dept. chem. engring., 1988-94, prof., 1994—. Contbr. articles to profl. jours. Mem. Am. Inst. Chem. Engrs. Avocations: golf, gardening, fishing. Home: 11-41 Tenjinyama Miyamaki, Kyotanabe City, Kyoto 610-03, Japan Office: Doshisha U Dept Chem Engring & Material Sci, 1-3 Miyakotani Tatara, Kyotanabe City 610-03 Kyoto Japan

TACHMINDJI, ALEXANDER JOHN, systems engineering consultant; b. Athens, Greece, Feb. 16, 1928; came to U.S., 1950, naturalized, 1958; s. John and Athina (Andreades) T.; m. Diane E. Primeau, Dec. 4, 1965. B.Sc. with distinction, King's Coll., U. Durham, England, 1949; B.Sc. with honors, King's Coll., U. Durham, 1950; M.S., MIT, 1951; postgrad., U. Md., 1951-54. Head research and propeller br. David Taylor Model Basin, Washington, 1951-59; head tactical warfare group Inst. for Def. Analyses, Washington, 1959-64; asst. dir., dept. dir. sci. and tech. div. Inst. for Def. Analyses, 1964-69, dir. systems evaluation div., 1969-72; dir. tactical tech. office Def. Advanced Research Projects Agy., Washington,, 1972-73; dep. dir. Def. Advanced Research Projects Agy., 1973-75; chief scientist The MITRE Corp., McLean, Va., 1975-76, v.p., 1976-79, v.p. and gen. mgr. Washington ops., 1979-84; sr. v.p. and gen. mgr. C3I divsn. The MITRE Corp., Bedford, Mass., 1984-85, sr. v.p., 1985-89; cons., 1989—. Editor: Jour. Def. Rsch., 1969-91; patentee in field. Recipient Meritorious Civilian Svc. award USN, 1956, Sec. of Def. Meritorious Civilian Svc. medal, 1975. Fellow AAAS, AIAA (pubs. com. 1976-91, fin. com. 1990—), Royal Inst. Naval Architects; mem. Ops. Rsch. Soc. Am., Soc. Naval Architects and Marine Engrs. (chmn. hydroelasticity panel, 1967-73, hydrodynamics com. 1967-86), Sigma Xi. Club: Cosmos (Washington).

TACK, THERESA ROSE, women's health nurse; b. Lunenburg, Vt., Nov. 10, 1940; d. Gustave L. and Blanche Rose Fournier; m. Dennis M. Tack, Sept. 2, 1961; children: Lynelle Scullard, Karyn Terry, LeAnn Gomez. Diploma, Cen. Maine Gen. Hosp., 1961. Cert. ACLS, neonatal resuscitation Am. Heart Assn. Staff nurse neurosurgery unit Hillcrest Med. Ctr., Tulsa, 1961-62; staff nurse cardiovascular unit Meth. Hosp., Houston, 1962-65; staff nurse St. John's Hosp., Red Wing, Minn., 1979-85, Wasatch County Hosp., Heber City, Utah, 1985—. columnist, Nurses Notes in Wasatch Wave, Heber City, Utah, 1990—.

TACKER, WILLIS ARNOLD, JR., academic administrator, medical educator, researcher; b. Tyler, Tex., May 24, 1942; s. Willis Arnold and Willie Mae (Massey) T.; m. Martha J. McClelland, Mar. 18, 1967; children: Sarah Mae, Betsy Jane, Katherine Ann. BS, Baylor U., 1964, MD, PhD, 1970. Lic. physician, Ind., Alaska, Tex. Intern Mayo Grad. Sch. Medicine Mayo Clinic, Rochester, Minn., 1970-71; pvt. practice Prudhoe Bay, Alaska, 1971; instr. dept. physiology Baylor Coll. Medicine, Houston, 1971-73, asst. prof. dept. physiology, 1973-74; clin. prof. family medicine Ind. U. Sch. Medicine, West Lafayette, Ind., 1981—; vis. asst. prof. Biomed. Engring. Ctr., Purdue U., West Lafayette, 1974-76, assoc. prof. Sch. Vet. Medicine, 1976-79; assoc. dir. William A. Hillenbrand Biomed. Engring. Ctr., Purdue U., West Lafayette, 1980-93, prof. Sch. Vet. Medicine, 1979—, acting dir., 1991-93; exec. dir. Hillenbrand Biomed. Engring. Ctr., 1993-95; vis. rsch. fellow Sch. Aerospace Medicine, Brooks AFB, San Antonio, 1982; with Corp. Sci. and Tech., State of Ind., 1985-88; presenter, cons. in field. Author: Some Advice on Getting Grants, 1991; co-author: Electrical Defibrillation, 1980; author: (with others) Handbook of Engineering and Medicine and Biology, 1980, Implantable Sensors for Closed-Loop Prosthetic Systems, 1985, Encyclopedia of Medical Devices and Instrumentation, 1988; contbr. numerous articles to profl. jours. Chmn. bd. dirs. Assn. Advancemnt Med. Instrumentation Found., Arlington, Va., 1987-95. Mem. Am. Heart Assn. (bd. dirs. Ind. affiliate 1975-81, med. edn. com. 1975-81, pub. health edn. com. 1975-81, chmn. ad hoc com. CPR tng. for physicians 1976-77, rsch. review com. 1988-90), Am. Physiol. Soc., Ind. State Med. Assn., Tippecanoe County Med. Soc., Assn. Advancement Med. Instrumentation (chmn. various coms., bd. dirs. 1981-84, pres. 1985-86), Am. Men and Women Sci., Alpha Epsilon Delta, Beta Beta Beta, Soc. Sigma Xi. Achievements include research in biomedical engineering, cardiovascular physiology, medical education, emergency cardiovascular care, motor evoked potentials, skeletal muscle ventricle; patents for an apparatus and method for measurement and control of blood pressure, electrode system and method for implantable defibrillators, pressure mapping system with capacitive measuring pad. Office: Purdue U 1293 A A Potter Bldg 204 West Lafayette IN 47907

TACKETT, STEPHEN DOUGLAS, education services specialist; b. Waverly, Ohio, Apr. 27, 1939; s. James Elbert and Zelma Iola (Manahan) T.; m. Magdalena Schneider, Jan. 4, 1958; children: Doris, Janice, Jerry, Suzanne. AA, El Paso C.C., 1974; BS, SUNY, Albany, 1976; MA, Ball State U., 1979. Nat. cert. counselor; lic. profl. clin. counselor. Enlisted U.S. Army, 1955, advanced through grades to Command Sgt. Maj., 1973, retired, 1982; instr. Mt. Wachusett C.C., Gardner, Mass., 1979-81; asst. dir. Evaluation U.S. Army Sgts. Maj. Acad., Ft. Bliss, Tex., 1981-82; dir. substance abuse treatment Sun Valley Hosp., El Paso, Tex., 1982-84; from guidance counselor to ednl. svcs. officer U.S. Army, Germany, 1984-86, 88-90; edn. advisor U.S. Army Sgts. Maj. Acad., Fort Bliss, 1990-92; edn. svcs. specialist Mil. Entrance Processing Sta., El Paso, 1992—; mem. adv. bd. for Counselor Edn. U. Tex., El Paso, 1983. Cubmaster Boy Scouts Am., Ft. Leonard Wood, Mo., 1970-71, com. mem., Frankfurt, Germany, 1972-73, asst. scoutmaster, Kaiserslautern, Germany, 1976-79. Mem. ACA, Am. Vocat. Assn., Nat. Assn. Secondary Sch. Prins., N.Mex. Sch. Counselors Assn., Tex. Assn. Secondary Sch. Prins., Tex. Counseling Assn. Office: Mil Entrance Processing Sta 700 E San Antonio Ave Fl 5 El Paso TX 79901-7020

TACKETT, WILLIAM EDWARD, school system administrator; b. Salem, N.J., Aug. 26, 1957; s. Bill and Beverly Ruth (Appleby) T. B in Religious Edn., Valley Forge Christian Coll., 1976; MEd, Temple U., 1984; MA, Glassboro State U., 1992; postgrad., LaSalle U., Phila. Tchr. Pennsville (N.J.) Christian Acad., 1980-82; prin. Cumberland Christian Sch., Vineland, N.J., 1982-86; tchr., asst. prin. Elsonboro (N.J.) Twp. Sch., 1986-92; prin. Salem (N.J.) County Spl. Svcs., 1992-93; adminstrv. pool Brandywine Sch. Dist., Wilmington, Del., 1993-94; asst. prin. Alloway (N.J.) Twp. Sch., 1994—; dir. Pennsville Day Camp, 1980-86; asst. pastor Pennsville Assembly of God, 1980-84, 1986-88; assoc. pastor First Assembly of God, Carney's Point, N.J., 1990—. Mem. adv. bd. Drug Awareness, Pennsville, N.J., 1990, Big Brother, Big Sister bd., Salem County, N.J., 1991. Named Tchr. of Yr., N.J. Dept. Edn., Elsinboro, N.J., 1988. Avocations: canoeing, sailing, hiking, camping, bicycling. Home: 19 Glen Dr Pennsville NJ 08070-2525 Office: Alloway Twp Sch Cedar St Alloway NJ 08001

TACKMAN, ARTHUR LESTER, newspaper publisher, management consultant; b. Chgo., July 28, 1916; s. Arthur Lester and Lucy Louise (Gutekunst) T.; m. Mary Lillian Connor, Mar. 31, 1939; children: Arthur Lester III, Laurence Connor, Alan Rhead. BA, Ohio State U., 1938, MPA, 1939. With various depts. U.S. Govt., Washington, 1938-49; staff asst., mem. pers. policy bd. Dept. Def., Washington, 1949; asst. mgr. Savannah river plant AEC, Aiken, S.C., 1950-55; asst. dir. inspection AEC, Washington, 1955-59, dir. pers., 1959-65; dir. pers. HUD, Washington, 1965-70; mgmt. cons. Glenwood, N.Mex., 1970-78; owner, operator Deep Creek Ranch, Inc., Glenwood, 1972—; publisher Catron Co. Pub. Co., Inc., Reserve, N.Mex., 1986-91. Pres. Gila Nat. Forest Permittees, Reserve, 1978-86; mem., treas. N.Mex. Pub. Lands Coun., Albuquerque, 1967-87; coun. mem. Boy Scouts Am., S.C., Washington, 1950-65. Lt. USN, 1943-46. Recipient Man Yr. Award Aiken County C. of C., 1953, Citation for Meritorious Svc. United Def. Fund, 1957. Mem. N.Mex. Press Assn. Democrat. Unitarian. Home: Deep Creek Ranch Glenwood NM 88039

TACKOWIAK, BRUCE JOSEPH, lawyer; b. Milw., July 10, 1956; s. Eugene Charles and Bernadine (Van Engle) T.; m. Deborah A. Moore, Dec. 11, 1994. BA in History and Polit. Sci., U. Wis., 1979; cert. emergency med. technician, Madison Area Tech. Coll., 1981; Diploma in Internat. and Comparative Law, Magdalen Coll., U. Oxford, Eng., 1986; JD, U. San Diego, 1988. Bar: Calif. 1990, Ill. 1991, U.S. Dist. Ct. (ctrl. and so. dists.) Calif. 1990, U.S. Ct. Appeals (4th cir.) 1990. Atty. LaFollette, Johnson, De Haas, Fesler & Ames, L.A., 1990-92, Hillsinger & Costanzo, L.A., 1992-93, Roxborough, Pomerance & Gallegos, LLP, L.A., 1993—; assoc. Am. Inns of Ct., 1992—. Sr./mng. editor U. San Diego Jour. Contemporary Legal Issues, 1987-88. Mem. ABA, ATLA, Calif. Bar Assn., Los Angeles County Bar Assn., Ill. Bar Assn., Chgo. Bar Assn., World Futurist Soc. (profl.). Avocations: team sports, running, tennis. Office: Roxborough, Pomerance & Gallegos LLP 10866 Wilshire Blvd Ste 1200 Los Angeles CA 90024-4336

TACKWELL, ELIZABETH MILLER, social worker; b. Caney, Kans., Mar. 14, 1923; d. Jesse Winfield and Mattie (Shuler) Miller; m. Joseph J. Tackwell, Dec. 13, 1946 (dec. Mar. 1988); children: Steven, Tiana Tackwell David, Christy Tackwell. BA cum laude, U. Okla., 1953, MSW, 1962. Bd. cert. diplomate Am. Bd. Examiners in Clin. Social Work; lic. social worker, Okla. Social worker Dept. Pub. Welfare, Tulsa/Cleve./Okla. County, Okla., 1958-59; med. social analyst Dept. Pub. Welfare, Okla., 1960-61; assoc. John Massey M.D. Clinic, Oklahoma City, 1964-69; clin. asst. prof. Okla. U. Sch. Social Work, Oklahoma City, 1964—; asst. prof., clin. instr. dept. psychiatry/behavioral scis. Okla. U. Health Scis. Ctr., Oklahoma City, 1963—; psychiat. social worker VA Med. Ctr., Oklahoma City, 1961-97, chief mental health sect., 1976-97, adminstrv. dir. day treatment ctr., 1993-97; pvt. practice Oklahoma City, 1971—; psychiat. surveyor Health Care Fin. Adminstrn., Dept. Human Svcs., Washington, 1985—. Recipient Svc. Commendation award DAV, 1980, Chi Omega Scholastic award, Awards Am. Ex-Prisoners of War, 1994, 95, 96. Mem. NASW (diplomate in clin. social work, pres. Okla. chpt. 1971-73, Social Worker of the Yr. Western Okla. chpt. 1975, Lifetime Achievement award Okla. chpt. 1997), Acad. Cert. Social Workers, Okla. Health and Welfare Assn. (conf. chmn. 1975—), Pi Gamma Mu (Chi Omega award for scholastic achievement). Home and Office: 1328 Tarman Cir Norman OK 73071-4846

TADDEO, DOMINIC, transportation executive; b. Montreal, Que., Can., Mar. 21, 1939; s. Donat and Loretta (DiGiovanni) T.; m. Angela Nucci; children: Anthony, Mark. B.Commerce, Loyola Coll., 1959. Internal auditor Torne, Riddell & Co.; sr. internal auditor, chief acct. Pratt & Whitney Aircraft of Can. Ltd.; dir. fin. Montreal Port Corp., dir. fin. and adminstrn., dir. ops., dep. gen. mgr., CEO, gen. mgr., CEO, pres., CEO, 1991—. Chmn. bd. Electronic Data Interchange for Commerce, Montreal, 1990; mem. Round Table on Devel. and Promotion of Ea. Montreal, 1989—, Montreal Maritime Industry Round Table; co-pres. fund raising campaign Montreal Symphony Orch., 1996; v.p. corp. campaign Heart and Stroke Found. of Que.; former dir. St. Mary's Hosp. Found., chmn. ball, 1991; co-chmn. ann. collection Ch. of Montreal, 1992, 93; past mem. bd. dirs. Cedars Cancer Fund of Royal Victoria Hosp.; past v.p. La Commission Scolaire Baldwin-Cartier. Named Transport Personality of the Yr., Province of Que., 1989; recipient Award of Distinction Faculty of Commerce and Adminstrn. of Concordia U., 1989, Personality of Yr. award Can.-Italian Bus. and Profl. Assn., Inc., 1989, Transfreight Gov., 1994, Dimensions 1995 award Order of Chartered Adminstrs. of Que., 1995. Mem. Can. Port and Harbour Assn. (pres. 1983), Am. Assn. Port Authorities (chmn. 1989-90), Internat. Assn. Ports and Harbors (2d v.p. 1995, dir. 1985—, exec. com. 1986—). Office: Montreal Port Corp, Wing #1 Cite du Havre Port Montreal Bldg, Montreal, PQ Canada H3C 3R5

TADE, GEORGE THOMAS, university dean; b. Casey, Ill., Dec. 17, 1923; s. Thomas Clement and Lena (Myers) T.; m. Wilma Jean Daily, July 7, 1946; children—Mitzi Jean Tade Mills, Terry Nan Tade Helmick. B.S., Ind. State U., 1945, M.S., 1946; Ph.D., U. Ill., 1955. Ordained to ministry Disciples of Christ Ch., 1946. Asst. prof., then assoc. prof. speech Greenville (Ill.) Coll., 1946-53, dean coll., prof. speech, 1953-59; dean Chapman (Calif.) U., 1959-62; prof. speech, chmn. dept., chmn. div. humanities Tex. Christian U., Ft. Worth, 1962-72, acting dean Sch. Fine Arts, 1972-73, dean Sch. Fine Arts, 1973-87, dean Coll. Fine Arts and Communication, 1987-89, emeritus dean, 1989—; interim headmaster Ft. Worth Acad., 1989-90; cons. communication to pvt. and govt. agy.; coord. liberal arts study N. Central Assn. Colls., 1959. Contbr. numerous articles to profl. jours. Councilman-at-large, Greenville, Ill., 1956-59; bd. dirs. Ft. Worth Acad., Van Cliburn Internat. Piano Competition; mem. exec. bd. Arts Council, Ft. Worth and Tarrant County. Mem. Speech Communication Assn., So. Speech Assn. (exec. council 1972-75), Western Coll. Deans Assn. (sec. 1960-62), Internat. Council Fine Arts Deans, Nat. Conf. Acad. Deans (vice chmn. 1984, chmn. 1985), Tex. Council on Arts in Edn. (v.p. 1975-77, pres. 1978-80), Tex. Speech Communication Assn. (pres. 1973-74), Pi Kappa Delta, Gamma Theta Upsilon, Sigma Alpha Eta. Mem. Univ. Christian Ch. (chmn. gen. bd., trustee 1973-75). Home: 3705 Arborlawn Dr Fort Worth TX 76109-3304

TADIAN, LUANNE F. B., financial analyst, consultant, researcher; b. Colorado Springs, Colo., Mar. 29, 1965; d. Carlos Solomon and Josie Dolores (Vigil) C'DeBaca; m. Nishan Thaddeus Tadian, Dec. 30, 1985; children: Joshua Abel, Zachary Solomon. BS in Psychology and Biology, U.N.Mex., 1988; MBA, Calif. State U., L.A., 199. Lic. in real estate law, series 6 and 63, Nat. Assn. Securities Dealers. Jr. v.p. prodn. Sentry Mortgage, Albuquerque, 1988-89; rsch. cons., L.A., 1991-93; account mgr. Beverly Hills Group Fin. Mgmt. Specialists, L.A., 1993-96; mgr. customer support Daylight Transport/DayWest Express, 1996—. Bd. dirs., chmn. vol. recognition, mem. pub. rels. and resource devel. coms. Calif. Litracy, San Gabriel, 1993—; del. Rep. Planning Com. Mem. NAFE, Nat. Assn. Women Bus. Owners, Nat. Assn. Life Underwriters, Beta Gamma Sigma. Republican. Roman Catholic. Home: House C 269 S Walnut Grove Ave San Gabriel CA 91776-1711

TADIKONDA, SIVAKUMARA SARMA KEDARA, mechanical and aerospace engineer; b. Guntur, India, Aug. 11, 1960; s. Nagamallaiah and Rajeswari Tadikonda; m. Mallika Tadikonda; children: Naga Virinchi, Mahathi. B of Tech., Indian Inst. Tech., Madras, 1983; MS, Rutgers U., 1986, PhD, 1989. Project engr. Dynacs Engring. Co. Inc., Palm Harbor, Fla., 1990-92; sr. flight systems engr. Grumman Space Sta. Integration Div., Reston, Va., 1992-93; sr. prin. egnr. McDonnell Douglas Aerospace, Seabrook, Md., 1993—; vis. prof. Rutgers U., New Brunswick, N.J., 1989-90; adj. assoc. prof. Cath. U. Am., Washington, 1995—. Contbr. articles to profl. jours. Mem. ASME, AIAA. Avocations: music, tennis, chess. Office: McDonnell Douglas Aerospace 7404 Executive Pl Lanham Seabrook MD 20706-2268

TAECKENS, PAMELA WEBB, bank executive; b. Oklahoma City, June 2, 1959; d. L. Gregory and Carolyn S. (Pace) Webb; m. Douglas R. Taeckens, Sept. 29, 1984. BS, U. Ariz., 1980; postgrad., Northwestern U., Evanston, Ill., 1989, 91. Audit analyst NBD Bank, Flint, Mich., 1985-88, trust adminstr., 1988-90, trust officer, 1990-92, asst. v.p., 1993—; Active membership com. YWCA of Greater Flint, 1990-94, fin. com., 1994—. Mem. Fin. Women Internat. Republican. Methodist. Avocations: skiing, stitching, reading. Office: NBD Bank G-2413 S Linden Rd Ste 7 Flint MI 48532

TAFEL, EDGAR, architect; b. N.Y.C., Mar. 4, 1912; s. Samuel and Rose (Chary) T. Student, NYU, 1930-32. Sr. fellow Frank Lloyd Wright's Taliesin Fellowship, Spring Green, Wis., 1932-41; practice architecture N.Y.C., 1946—; lectr. USIS, Eng., Israel, India, Netherlands, 1972-73, New Sch. for Social Rsch., N.Y.C., 1974; faculty Smithsonian Instn., 1978; co-producer, actor (video) The Frank Lloyd Wright Way. Author: Years with Frank Lloyd Wright, About Wright, 1993; contbr. articles to profl. jours.; Prin. works include: Protestant Chapel at Kennedy Airport, 1964, First Presbyn. Ch. Addition, 1959, De Witt Ch., all N.Y.C., Fine Arts Bldg., State U. N.Y. at Geneseo, 1967, Fulton-Montgomery Community Coll, Johnstown, N.Y., 1969, Grace Ch, White Plains, 1970, Allentown (Pa.) Art Mus. addition, 1975, Columbia-Greene Community Coll, Hudson, N.Y., 1974, Salvation Army Corps Community Centers; master plans for: State Coll. at Geneseo, York Coll., N.Y.C., Cadet Corps Hdqrs., Bronx, N.Y.; designed over 100 residences. Bd. dirs. N.Y.C. Mission Soc. Served with AUS, World War II, CBI. Recipient award of merit for Presbyn. Ch. Fifth Ave. Assn., N.Y.C., service citation State U. N.Y. Coll. at Geneseo, 1970. Fellow AIA; mem. Nat. Acad. Arts (assoc.), Taliesin Fellowship (coun.), Fallingwater (adv. com.). Home and Office: 14 E 11th St New York NY 10003-4402

TAFLOVE, ALLEN, electrical engineer, educator, researcher, consultant; b. Chgo., June 14, 1949; s. Harry and Leah (Natovich) T.; m. Sylvia Hinda Friedman, Nov. 6, 1977; children: Michael Lee, Nathan Brent. BS with highest distinction, Northwestern U., 1971, MS, 1972, PhD, 1975. Assoc. engr. IIT Rsch. Inst., Chgo., 1975-78, rsch. engr., 1978-81, sr. engr., 1981-84; assoc. prof. Northwestern U., Evanston, Ill., 1984-88, prof., 1988—; originator 6-yr. BS/PhD degree program in engring. Northwestern U., 1988—; cons. Electric Power Rsch. Inst., Palo Alto, Calif., 1985-86, Lawrence Livermore Nat. Lab., 1985-87, Lockheed Missiles and Space Co., Sunnyvale, Calif., 1985-88, MRJ Inc., Oakton, Va., 1987-90, U.S. Naval Rsch. Lab., Washington, 1988-95, Cray Rsch., Inc., Eagan, Minn., 1991—, Village of Wilmette, Ill., 1991-93, City of Wheaton, Ill., 1991-92, B.C. Hydro, Vancouver, Can., 1991-92, Commonwealth Edison, Chgo., 1992—, MIT Lincoln Lab., 1992-93, The Intec Group, 1995—. Co-author: Computational Electromagnetics: Integral Equation Approach, 1993; author: Computational Electrodynamics: The Finite-Difference Time-Domain Method, 1995; contbr. 10 book chpts. and over 60 articles to profl. jours.; patentee in field. Keynote spkr. Salishan Conf. on High-Performance Computing, 1994, Instn. Elec. Engrs. Internat. Conf. on Antennas and Propagation, 1995. Recipient Adviser of Yr. award Northwestern U., 1991; Cabell fellow, 1975; rsch. grantee USAF, Electric Power Rsch. Inst., Lawrence Livermore Nat. Lab., NSF, Office Naval Rsch., Gen. Dynamics Corp., Northrop Corp., Lockheed Corp., Sci. Applications, Inc., Cray Rsch., Inc., Northwestern Meml. Hosp., NASA Ames Ctr., NASA Lewis Ctr., 1977—. Fellow IEEE (Best Paper award 1983); mem. AAAS, IEEE Antennas and Propagation Soc. (Disting. nat. lectr. 1990-91, chmn. tech. program com. Internat. Symposium 1992), Electromagnetics Acad., Internat. Union Radio Sci. (commn. B, D and K), N.Y. Acad. Scis., Sigma Xi, Eta Kappa Nu, Tau Beta Pi. Achievements include pioneer of finite-difference time-domain method in computational electromagnetics. Office: Northwestern U Dept Elec and Comp Engring 2145 Sheridan Rd Evanston IL 60208-0834

TAFOYA, ARTHUR N., bishop; b. Alameda, N.Mex., Mar. 2, 1933; s. Nicholas and Rosita Tafoya. Ed., St. Thomas Sem., Denver, Conception (Mo.) Sem. Ordained priest Roman Cath. Ch., 1962. Asst. pastor Holy Rosary Parish, Albuquerque, 1962-65; pastor Northern N.Mex., from 1965, San Jose Parish, Albuquerque; rector Immaculate Heart of Mary Sem., Santa Fe; ordained bishop of Pueblo Colo., 1980—. Office: 1001 N Grand Ave Pueblo CO 81003-2915*

TAFT, BOB, state official; b. Jan. 8, 1942; m. Hope Taft; 1 child, Anna. BA, Yale U., 1963; MA, Princeton U., 1967; JD, U. Cin., 1976. Pvt. practice; rep. Ohio Ho. Reps., 1976-80; commr. Hamilton County, Ohio, 1981-90; sec. of state Ohio, 1990—. Office: 30 E Broad St Fl 14 Columbus OH 43215-3463

TAFT, DAVID DAKIN, chemical executive; b. Cleve., Mar. 27, 1938; s. Kingsley A. and Louise D. T.; m. Sararose Leonard, July 8, 1961; children: Amy Rose, Kingsley Leonard, Elisabeth Kirkland. AB, Kenyon Coll., 1960; PhD in Chemistry, Mich. State U., 1963. Sr. rsch. chemist Archer-Daniels Midland, 1964-67; mgr. polymer rsch. Ashland Chem., 1967-72; dir. comml. devel. Gen. Mills Chems., 1972-74; v.p., dir. R&D, Henkel Corp., 1973-78, group v.p. consumer and splty. products, 1978-81, exec. v.p. chem. products div., 1981-82, also dir.; gen. mgr. materials div. Raychem Corp., Menlo Park, Calif., 1983-84; gen. mgr. Telecom group, 1983-86; v.p. Raychem Corp., 1984-93, v.p. manufacturing, 1986-93; COO Landec Corp., Menlo Park, Calif., 1993—. Author: Fundamentals of Powder Coatings; bd. editors Research Mgmt. Jour. Trustee Mpls. Soc. Fine Arts, 1981-83, Kenyon Coll., 1990—. Mem. Comml. Devel. Assn., Indsl. Research Inst., Am. Chem. Soc., Kenyon Alumni Assn. (pres. 1978). Republican. Presbyterian. 24 patents in field. Office: Landec Corp 3603 Haven Ave Menlo Park CA 94025-1010

TAFT, RICHARD GEORGE, lawyer; b. Ann Arbor, Mich., Mar. 13, 1913; s. George J. and Wilhemina (Voigt) T.; m. Pauline Joyner, Sept. 1942 (dec.); 1 child, Richard George (dec.); m. Margaret Gessner, Sept. 1946 (div. Aug. 1949); m. Louise Hutto, 1953 (div. Feb. 1960); m. Louise Holmberg, Dec. 30, 1960; 1 stepdau., Jamy Coulson. B.S., U. Okla., 1935, LL.B., 1940. Bar: Okla. 1940; C.P.A., Okla. With FCA, 1935-37; since practiced in Oklahoma City; assoc. firm Campbell, Randolph, Mahin & Mosteller, 1940-41, Mosteller & McElroy, 1946-48, Billups, Wood & Champlin C.P.A.s, 1948-51; mem. McAfee & Taft P.C., and predecessors, 1951—. Mem. Norman Planning Commn., 1966-69; pres. Okla. Bd. Corrections, 1967-69; trustee, chmn. fin. com. Presbyn. Health Found.; trustee Oklahoma County Med. Soc. Community Found.; mem. dean's council U. Okla. Law Center. Served to lt. col. USAAF, 1941-45. Mem. ABA, Okla. Bar Assn., Am. Judicature Soc., Phi Delta Phi, Phi Gamma Delta. Republican. Home: 603 Okmulgee St Norman OK 73071-4626 Office: McAfee & Taft PC Two Leadership Sq Oklahoma City OK 73102

TAFT, SETH CHASE, retired lawyer; b. Cin., Dec. 31, 1922; s. Charles Phelps and Eleanor K. (Chase) T.; m. Frances Prindle, June 19, 1943; children: Frederick, Thomas, Cynthia, Tucker. B.A., Yale U., 1943, LL.B., 1948. Bar: Ohio 1948. Assoc. Jones, Day, Reavis & Pogue, Cleve., 1948-59, ptnr., 1959-88. Mem. Cuyahoga County (Ohio) Bd. Commrs., 1971-78, pres., 1977-78; mem. Cuyahoga County Charter Commn., 1958-59; Rep. candidate for mayor of Cleve., 1967, for gov. of Ohio, 1982; pres. Fedn. for Community Planning, Cleve., 1986-89, Cleve. Internat. Program, 1990-94; chmn. Substance Abuse Initiative Greater Cleve., 1989—. With USNR, 1943-46. Home: 6 Pepper Ridge Rd Cleveland OH 44124-4904 Office: Jones Day Reavis & Pogue 901 Lakeside Ave E Cleveland OH 44114-1116

TAFT, SHELDON ASHLEY, lawyer; b. Cleve., Mar. 2, 1937; s. Kingsley Arter and Louise Parsons (Dakin) T.; m. Rebecca Sue Rinehart, Dec. 26, 1962; children: Mariner R., Ashley A., Curtis N. BA, Amherst Coll., 1959; LLB, Harvard U., 1962. Bar: Ohio 1962. Assoc. Vorys, Sater, Seymour & Pease, Columbus, Ohio, 1965-69, 71-73, ptnr., 1974—; chief legal counsel Pub. Utilities Commn. Ohio, Columbus, 1969-71; Ohio bd. advisors Chgo. Title Ins. Co., 1967—. Rep. candidate for justice Ohio Supreme Ct., 1974; trustee Opera Columbus, 1989—, pres., 1991-93, life trustee, 1995—. 1st lt. USAF, 1963-65. Mem. ABA (pub. utilities sect.), Ohio State Bar Assn. (pres. pub. utilities com. 1984-87), Columbus Bar Assn. (pub. utilities com.), Ohio Camera Collectors Soc. (pres. 1985-87), Rocky Fork Hunt and Country Club, Capital Club, 41 Club. Congregationalist. Avocations: camera collecting, sailing. Home: 27 Sessions Dr Columbus OH 43209-1440 Office: Vorys Sater Seymour & Pease PO Box 1008 52 E Gay St Columbus OH 43216-1008

TAFT, WILLIAM HOWARD, journalism educator; b. Mexico, Mo., Oct. 24, 1915; s. Raymond E. and Ferrie (Dains) T.; m. Myrtle Marie Adams, Jan. 18, 1941; children: Marie, William Howard, Alice. AB, Westminster Coll., 1937; B in Journalism, U. Mo., 1938, MA, 1939; PhD, Western Res. U., 1951. Dir. pub. rels. Hiram (Ohio) Coll., 1939-40, 47-48; asst. prof. journalism Youngstown (Ohio) Coll., 1946-48; prof. Defiance (Ohio) Coll., 1948-50; assoc. prof. Memphis State Coll., 1950-56; prof. U. Mo., Columbia, 1956-81, assoc. dean grad. programs, 1980-81; yearbook cons., 1957—. Author: Let's Publish That Top-Rated Yearbook, 1961, (with others) Modern Journalism, 1962, Missouri Newspapers, 1964, Missouri Newspapers, When and Where, 1808-1962, 1964, American Journalism History, 1968, rev. edit., 1977, Newspapers as Tools for Historians, 1970, (with others) Mass Media and the National Experience, 1971, Donrey Media; A Low Profile Group, 1976, Magazines for the Eighties, 1981, Encyclopedia of 20th Century Journalists, 1986, Missouri Newspapers and the Missouri Press Association, 125 Years of Service, 1867-1992, 1992, Wit and Wisdom of Country Editors, 1996; contbr. articles to profl. jours. and encys. With USAAF, 1941-45. Recipient Faculty-Alumni citation U. Mo., 1979, Alumni

Achievement award Westminster Coll., 1987; rsch. fellow Washington Journalism Ctr., 1967. Mem. Assn. Edn. Journalism and Mass. Comm. (Presdl. award 1991), Boone County Hist. Soc. (past pres.), Kiwanis (past pres., Churchman of Yr. 1987, Kiwanian of Yr. 1993, life), Delta Tau Delta (life), Pi Delta Epsilon, Kappa Tau Alpha (nat. treas., exec. dir. 1962-91). Republican. Methodist. Home: 107 Sondra Ave Columbia MO 65202-1416

TAGATZ, GEORGE ELMO, obstetrician, gynecologist, educator; b. Milw., Sept. 21, 1935; s. George Herman and Beth Elinore (Blain) T.; m. Susan Trunnell, Oct. 28, 1967; children: Jennifer Lynn, Kirsten Susan, Kathryn Elizabeth. A.B., Oberlin Coll., 1957; M.D., U. Chgo., 1961. Diplomate Am. Bd. Obstetricians and Gynecologists, Am. Bd. Reproductive Endocrinology (examiner, bd. reproductive endocrinology 1976-79). Rotating intern Univ. Hosps. of Cleve., 1961-62, resident in internal medicine, 1962-63; resident in ob-gyn U. Iowa, 1965-68; sr. research fellow in endocrinology U. Wash. dept. obstetrics and gynecology, 1968-70; asst. prof. ob-gyn U. Minn. Med. Sch., 1970-73, asso. prof., 1973-76, prof., 1976—, asst. prof. internal medicine, 1970-73, dir. div. reproductive endocrinology, 1974-92; mem. fertility and maternal health adv. com. FDA, USPHS, HHS, 1982-86; cons. in field, 1986-87. Ad hoc editor: Am. Jour. Ob-Gyn, Fertility and Sterility; contbr. articles to profl. publs. Served with M.C. U.S. Army, 1963-65. Mem. AMA, Minn., Hennepin County med. socs., Minn. Obstet. and Gynecol. Soc., Am. Coll. Ob-Gyn (subcom. on reproductive endocrinology 1979-82), Endocrine Soc., Am. Fertility Soc., Central Assn. Obstetricians and Gynecologists, U. Iowa Ob-Gyn Alumni Soc. Home: 5828 Long Brake Trl Minneapolis MN 55439-2622 Office: U Minn Hosps & Clinic PO Box 395 Minneapolis MN 55455

TAGER, JACK, historian, educator; b. Bklyn., Oct. 18, 1936; s. Alexander and Mildred T.; children: David, Miriam. B.A., Bklyn. Coll., 1958; M.A., U. Calif.-Berkeley, 1959; Ph.D., U. Rochester, N.Y., 1965. Asst. prof. Ohio State U., Columbus, 1964-67; prof. history U. Mass., Amherst, 1967—; dir. univ. honors program U. Mass., 1978-82. Author: The Intellectual as Urban Reformer: Brand Whitlock and the Progressive Movement, 1968, The Historical Atlas of Massachusetts, 1991, also articles; editor: Urban Vision, 1970, Massachusetts in the Gilded Age, 1985. Served with U.S. Army, 1959, 61-62. Mem. Orgn. Am. Historians, Am. Hist. Assn. Home: PO Box 2417 Amherst MA 01004-2417 Office: U Mass History Dept Amherst MA 01003

TAGGART, G. BRUCE, government program executive; b. Phila., Apr. 8, 1942; s. Robert Henry Taggart and Rachael Elizabeth Burtt. BS in Physics, Coll. William and Mary, 1964; postgrad. in engineering mechanics, U. Pa., 1964-65; PhD in Physics, Temple U., 1971. Instr. dept. physics Drexel U., Phila., 1970; asst. prof. dept. physics Va. Commonwealth U., Richmond, 1971-77, assoc. prof., 1977-82, prof., 1982-83; from mgr. materials sci. tech. to prin. staff mem., phys. scis. tech. divsn. BDM Internat., McLean, Va., 1983-90; program dir. materials theory, divsn. materials rsch. NSF, Washington, 1990—; vis. asst. prof. dept. physics Temple U., Phila., 1970-71; rsch. assoc. with theory group Oak Ridge (Tenn.) Nat. Lab., 1974; vis. prof. dept. theoretical physics Oxford (Eng.) U., 1978, Fed. U. Pernambuco, Recife, Brazil, 1980; vis. assoc. prof. dept. physics U. Ill., Urbana, 1978-79; guest worker with statis. physics group thermophysics divsn. Nat. Inst. Standards and Tech., Gaithersburg, Md., 1978-88; lectr. dept. physics and astronomy U. Md., College Park, 1989-90; vis. scientist divsn. materials rsch. on leave from BDM Internat., NSF, 1989-90; presenter in field. Referee: Phys. Rev., Physics Letters, Jour. of the Physics and Chemistry of Solids, Acad. Press, DARPA, NSF; contbr. numerous articles to profl. jours. Scholar Coll. William and Mary, 1964; Ford fellow U. Pa., 1964-65; NSF summer fellow and Univ. fellow Temple U., 1971. Mem. AAAS, Am. Phys. Soc. (condensed matter physics divsn., materials physics divsn., high polymer physics divsn.), Materials Rsch. Soc., Sigma Pi Sigma. Achievements include research in condensed matter physics, materials science and statistical mechanics. Office: Nat Sci Found Divsn Materials Rsch 4201 Wilson Blvd Arlington VA 22230-0001

TAGGART, GANSON POWERS, management consultant; b. Albany, N.Y., Aug. 16, 1918; s. Ralph Cone and Ruth Harriett (Townsend) T.; m. Paulett Long, June 30, 1945; children: H.Tee, Paulett Long, Cornelia V.C. BS. in Chem. Engring., U. Mich., 1940, M.S. in Chem. Engring., 1941; postgrad., Northeastern Sch. Advanced Mgmt., 1964. Registered engr., Mass. Mng. dir. Badger N.V., The Hague, Netherlands, 1965-70; v.p. world sales Badger Co., Cambridge, Mass., 1970-71; sr. v.p., dir. Badger Co. Inc., Cambridge, 1978-82; mgmt. cons. Devel. Scis. Inc., Sandwich, Mass., 1972-77; chmn. bd. Serapis Energy Inc., Boston, 1982-85, dir.; pres. Mgmt. Systems Inc., 1984—; chmn. bd. William K. Stout Pub. Co., 1995—. Contbr. articles to mags. Oil mem. Energy Facilities Siting Coun. Mass., Boston, 1979-82; mem. Winchester (Mass.) Planning Bd., 1971-77, Winchester Town Meeting, 1960-64; mem. exec. com. Internat. Sch. The Hague, 1965-70; trustee Ledges Condominium Assn., USS Constn. Mus., 1989-95, treas. 1991-92; moderator Winchester Unitarian Soc., 1983-93; active Mus. Sci., Boston, Found. Global Cmty. Lt. (j.g.) USNR, 1944-48. Mem. AIChE (chmn. Boston sect. 1955, Order of Xiphias), Soc. Chem. Industry (London), Conservation Law Found., Am. Chem. Soc., World Bus. Acad., Inst. Noetic Scis., Chemists Club (N.Y.C.), Annisquam Yacht Club (Gloucester, Mass.), Downtown Club (Boston). Office: PO Box 516 7 Church St Winchester MA 01890-0716 *Hard work and flexibility in doing and thinking pays big dividends, as long as you are honest with yourself and others. I have always tried to see things from the other person's point of view, to give them the benefit of the doubt. I strive always to do the best I can and I do not spend a lot of time analyzing or criticizing what is wrong with others. And most important is a wonderful wife who accepts constructively life as it is dealt to you.*

TAGGART, LINDA DIANE, women's health nurse; b. Balt., June 14, 1940; d. Louis and Annie Helena (Heertje) Glick; divorced; 1 child, Keri Anne. AS in Nursing, Pensacola Jr. Coll., 1967; BA, U. West Fla., 1970; postgrad., St. Joseph's Coll., 1976-78. RN, Fla., Ala. Staff nurse Bapt. Hosp., Pensacola, Fla., 1967-70, head nurse, 1970-72; dir. in-svc. edn. Baycrest, Inc. Extended Care Facility, Pensacola, 1973, DON, 1973-74; DON Medica Media, Pensacola, 1974; clinical adminstr. Cmty. Healthcare Ctr. (formerly Medica Media), Pensacola, 1974—; dir. sex and health edn. Cmty. Healthcare Ctr., Pensacola, 1974—; regional dir. Medica Media, ea. U.S., 1990; testified before Jud. com. U.S. Ho. of Reps., 1994 appeared on network Tv programs Dateline, 48 Hours, Turning Point, Nightline. Contbr.: The Gideon Project, 1993; contbr. articles to popular mags.; appeared on network TV programs including Dateline NBC, 48 Hours, Nightline, Turning Point, ABC, CNN. Bd. dirs. Rape Crisis Ctr., Pensacola, 1976-91, chair, 1980, 84, 89 (Addie Brooks award 1984); mem. exec. com. Lakeview Community Mental Health Ctr., Pensacola, 1989 (Expression of Appreciation award 1980-91). Recipient Pioneer/Heroe award Fla. Abortion Coun., 1989, Woman of Yr. award NOW, 1995, Women's Equity Day award 1986. Mem. Am. Assn. Sex Educators, Counselors and Therapists (cert. sex educator), Religious Coalition for Reproductive Choice, People for Am. Way, Internat. Platform Assn. Democrat. Presbyterian. Avocations: skiing, jewelry design, cross-stitch, reading, ballroom dancing. Office: Cmty Healthcare Ctr 6770 N 9th Ave Pensacola FL 32504-7346

TAGGART, THOMAS MICHAEL, lawyer; b. Sioux City, Iowa, Feb. 22, 1937; s. Palmer Robert and Lois Allette (Sedgwick) T.; m. Dolores Cecilia Baroway Renfro, Jan. 4, 1963; children: Thomas Michael Jr., Theodore Christopher; m. Mary Ann Gribben, Feb. 7, 1976. BA, Dartmouth Coll., 1959; JD, Harvard U., 1965. Bar: Ohio 1965, U.S. Dist. Ct. (so. dist.) Ohio 1967, U.S. Dist. Ct. (no. dist.) Ohio 1981. Ptnr. Vorys, Sater, Seymour & Pease, Columbus, Ohio, 1965—; lectr. Ohio Legal Ctr. Inst., Ohio Mfrs. Assn., Capital U. Ctr. for Spl. and Continuing Legal Edn. Served to capt. USMC, 1959-63. Mem. ABA, Ohio Bar Assn. (bd. govs. 1991-97, liability ins. com. 1996-97, pres. 1997-98, trustee Found. 1996-97), Columbus Bar Assn. (mem. bd. govs., pres. 1989-90), Ohio Assn. Civil Trial Attys., Am. Arbitration Assn., Columbus Area C. of C., Univ. Columbus Club. Methodist. Home: 145 Stanbery Ave Columbus OH 43209-1465 Office: Vorys Sater Seymour & Pease 52 E Gay St Columbus OH 43215-3108

TAGGE, ANNE KATHERINE, not-for-profit organization administrator; b. Waltham, Mass., Oct. 20, 1954; d. Raymond and Anne (Weller) T. BA, Wellesley Coll., 1977. Pres., founder Susan Lee Campbell Inst., Wellesley, Mass., 1986—; spkr. Contbr. to newspapers, mags., jours., books. Recipient U.S./UNEP Achievement award, honoree Rolex awards for Enterprise; Town of Wellesley scholar, Fulbright scholar; Salzburg Seminar fellow; French Ministry Fgn. Affairs grantee. Mem. Explorers Club. Home: Moshup Trail Martha's Vineyard MA 02535 Office: 37 Avon Rd Wellesley MA 02181-4618

TAGIURI, CONSUELO KELLER, child psychiatrist, educator; b. San Francisco; d. Cornelius H. and Adela (Rios) Keller; m. Renato Tagiuri; children: Robert, Peter, John. BA, U. Calif.-Berkeley; MD, U. Calif.-San Francisco. Diplomate Am. Bd. Psychiatry and Neurology. Resident psychiatry Mass. Gen. Hosp., Boston; staff psychiatrist Children's Hosp., Boston, 1951-59; med. dir. Gifford Sch., Weston, Mass., 1965-85; chief psychiatrist Cambridge (Mass.) Guidance Ctr., 1961-84; mem. faculty dept. psychiatry Harvard Med. Sch., Cambridge, 1965—; cons. early childhood program Children's Hosp., 1985—. Contbr. articles in field to books. Fellow Am. Orth. psychiat. Assn., Mass. Med. Soc., New Eng. Council Child Psychiatry.

TAGLIABUE, PAUL JOHN, national football league commissioner; b. Jersey City, Nov. 24, 1940; s. Charles and Mary T.; m. Chandler M. Minter, Aug. 28, 1965; children: Drew, Emily. BA, Georgetown U., 1962; JD, NYU, 1965. Bar: N.J 1965, D.C. 1969. Atty. to sec. def. Dept. Def., Washington, 1966-69; assoc. Covington & Burling, Washington, 1969-74, ptnr., 1969-89; commissioner NFL, N.Y.C., 1989—. Contbr. articles to profl. jours. Mem. ABA (chmn. sports and entertainment industry com. antitrust sect. 1986), D.C. Bar Assn. Office: NFL Commr's Office 280 Park Ave New York NY 10017-1216*

TAGLIAFERRI, LEE GENE, investment banker; b. Mahanoy City, Pa., Aug. 14, 1931; s. Charles and Adele (Cirilli) T.; B.S., U. Pa., 1957; M.B.A., U. Chgo., 1958; m. Maryellen Stanton, Apr. 29, 1962; children—Mark, John, Maryann. Div. comptroller Campbell Soup Co., Camden, N.J., 1958-60; securities analyst Merrill, Lynch, Pierce, Fenner & Smith, Inc., N.Y.C., 1960-62; asst. v.p. U.S. Trust Co. of N.Y., 1962-71; v.p. corporate finance div. Laidlaw & Co., Inc., N.Y.C., 1972-73; pres. Everest Corp., N.Y.C., 1973—; dir. Fairfield Communities Inc., UEC, Inc., LRA, Inc., Industrialized Bldg. Systems, Inc. Past pres. West Windsor Community Assn. Trustee Schuyler Hall, Columbia, Madison Sq. Boys Club. Served with AUS, 1953-55. K.C. Clubs: University of Pa., Princeton (N.Y.C.). Home: 77 Lillie St Princeton Junction NJ 08550-1307 Office: 1 Penn Plz New York NY 10119

TAGLIATTINI, MAURIZIO, construction executive, research historian, writer; b. Messina, Italy, June 2, 1933; came to U.S., 1959, naturalized, 1970; s. Giovanni and Vittoria (Federighi) T.; m. Marsha Croce, Nov. 4, 1973 (div. 1979). Diploma of Geometra, Inst. Tech. per Geometri, Modena, Italy. Founder, past pres. Tagliattini Marble Co., N.Y.C. Author: The Discovery of North America by European Navigators (with a critical study on the origin of Christopher Columbus), 1992. With NATO Air Force, 1957-58. Roman Catholic.

TAGUCHI, YOSHITAKA, architect; b. Urawa, Japan, Feb. 12, 1933; s. Washio and Masa Taguchi; m. Yukiko Misuda, Apr. 21, 1968; children: Naeko, Morihiko. B in Architecture, Tokyo Inst. Tech., 1955. Dir. design div. Ministry Posts and Telecom., Tokyo, 1979-84; dir. gen. bldg. dept. Ministry Post and Telecommunication, Tokyo, 1984-87; prin. Taguchi Yoshitaka Architect Office, Tokyo, 1987-89; pres. Marunouchi Architects & Engrs., Tokyo, 1989—. Prin. works include Mielbarque Matsuyama, Mielbarque Okayama, Casa de Kampo Urayasu, Fukuoka Ctrl. Post Office, Nagoya Sorting Office, Sapparo Ctrl. Post Office, Miyazaki Ctrl. Post Office., KDD Kobe, Kampo Hotel Ohme, Internat. Telecom Japan. Mem. Japan Inst. Architects. Home: Naruse 5092-3-803, Machidashi, Tokyo 194, Japan Office: Yurakucho 1-8-1-419, Chiyodaku, Tokyo 100, Japan

TAGUE, CHARLES FRANCIS, retired engineering, construction and real estate development company executive; b. N.Y.C., Aug. 16, 1924; s. Charles and Isabelle (Carey) T.; m. Alicia Patricia Murtha, Aug. 6, 1949; children: Patrick, Charles, Thomas, Mary Alicia Haberman, James, Beth Anne Giuliano. B.S., Fordham U., 1952. Auditor Scovell, Wellington & Co., N.Y.C., 1951-57; comptroller Chem. Constrn. Corp., N.Y.C., 1957-75; controller Burns and Roe, Inc., Oradell, N.J., 1975-81; fin. dir. Alfred Sanzari Enterprises, Hasbrouck Heights, N.J., 1981-84; v.p. fin. Alexander Summer Co., 1984-93; ret., 1993; domestic and fgn. tax cons. Mem. Colts Neck (N.J.) Sports Found.; active Boy scouts Am.; mem. Lacawac Sanctuary Steering Com.; pres. parish coun. Ch. of Presentation; mem. pastoral coun. St. Thomas More Cath. Ch. Served with USNR, 1943-46, PTO, ETO, NATOUSA. Mem. Controllers Inst., Nat. Contract Mgmt. Assn., Assn. Govt. Accountants. Democrat. Roman Catholic. Address: PO Box 401 Lake Ariel PA 18436-0401

TAI, CHEN-TO, electrical engineering educator; b. Soochow, China, Dec. 30, 1915; came to U.S., 1943; m. Chia Ming Shen, Apr. 28, 1941; children: Arthur, Bing, Julie, David, James. BSc, Tsing Hua U., Beijing, 1937; DSc, Harvard U., 1947. Rsch. fellow Harvard U., Cambridge, Mass., 1947-49; sr. rsch. scientist Stanford Rsch. Inst., Palo Alto, Calif., 1949-54; assoc. prof. Ohio State U., Columbus, 1954-56, prof., 1960-64; prof. Tech. Inst. Electronics, Brazil, 1956-60; prof. U. Mich., Ann Arbor, 1964-86, prof. emeritus, 1986—. Author: Dyadic Green's Functions, 1971, 2d edit., 1994, Generalized Vector and Dyadic Analysis, 1991, 2d edit., 1997; contbr. numerous articles to profl. jours. Fellow IEEE (life, Centennial award 1985); mem. U.S. Nat. Acad. Engring. Home: 1155 Arlington Blvd Ann Arbor MI 48104-4023 Office: Univ of Mich Dept EECS Ann Arbor MI 48109

TAI, FRANK, aerospace engineering consultant; b. Omaha, Apr. 10, 1955; s. Shou Nan and May (Chuang) T.; m. Lorraine Mae Fesq, May 14, 1988. BSME, U. Calif., Berkeley, 1977; MS in Automatic Controls Engring., MIT, 1979. Design engr. satellite attitude control systems Ball Aerospace, Boulder, Colo., 1979-84; engr. satellite attitude control systems TRW, Redondo Beach, Calif., 1984-88; mgr. engring. Microcosm, Inc., Torrance, Calif., 1988-89; pres., engring. cons., founder Tech. Advancements, Inc., Playa del Rey, Calif., 1989—. Contbr. articles to profl. jours. Mem. AIAA, Am. Astronautical Soc., Sigma Xi, Tau Beta Pi, Pi Tau Sigma. Office: Tech Advancements Inc 6738 Esplanade St # 300 Playa Del Rey CA 90293-7525

TAI, JULIA CHOW, chemistry educator; b. Shanghai, China, Dec. 15, 1935; came to U.S., 1957; d. Fei-chen and Jean-tson (Liao) Chow; m. Hung-Chao Tai, Aug. 14, 1960; children: Eve, Helen, Michael. BS in Chemistry, Nat. Taiwan U., 1957; MS in Chemistry, U. Okla., 1959; PhD in Chemistry, U. Ill., 1963. Rsch. assoc. Wayne State U., Detroit, 1963-66, 67-68; vis. assoc. prof. Nat. Taiwan U., Taipei, Republic of China, 1968-69; asst. prof. U. Mich., Dearborn, 1969-73, assoc. prof., 1973-79, prof. chemistry, 1979—. Contbr. articles to sci. jours. Mem. Am. Chem. Soc., Quantum Chemistry Program Exch., Mich. Coll. Chemistry Tchrs. Assn. Avocations: music, reading. Office: Univ Mich Dearborn 4901 Evergreen Rd Dearborn MI 48128-2406

TAICHMAN, NORTON STANLEY, pathology educator; b. Can., May 27, 1936; s. Louis and Frances (Kline) T.; m. Louise Sheffer, June 1, 1958; children: Russell, Susan, Darren, Leslie, Audrey. DDS, U. Toronto, 1961; Diploma in Periodontics, Harvard U., 1964; PhD, U. Toronto, 1967; MSc (hon.), U. Pa., 1972. Asst. prof. U. Toronto, 1967-69, assoc. prof., 1969-72; prof. pathology dept. sch. dental medicine U. Pa., Phila., 1972—, chmn. dept. pathology, 1972-95; assoc. dean acad. affairs, 1990-95. Recipient Birnberg award Columbia U., 1987, Disting. Alumnus award Harvard U., 1988. Mem. Internat. Assn. Dental Rsch. (Rsch. Basic Sci. award 1985), Am. Soc. Microbiology, Soc. for Leukocyte Biology. Office: U Pa Dept Dental Pathology 4010 Locust St Philadelphia PA 19104-6002

TAIGANIDES, E. PAUL, agricultural and environmental engineer, consultant; b. Polymylos, Macedonia, Greece, Oct. 6, 1934; s. Pavlos Theodorou and Sophia ((Elezidou) T.; m. Maro Taiganides, Dec. 25, 1961; children: Paul Anthony, Tasos E., Katerina. BS in Agri. Engring., U. Maine, 1957; MS in Soil and Water Engring., Iowa State U., 1961, D of Environ. Engring., 1963. Cert. engr., Iowa, Colo. Rsch. assoc., asst. prof. Iowa State U., Ames, 1957-65; prof. Ohio State U., Columbus, 1965-75; mgr., chief tech. adviser UN, FAO, Singapore, Singapore, 1975-84, mgr., chief engr., 1984-85; mgr., chief tech. adviser UN, FAO, Kuala Lumpur, Malaysia, 1985-87; mgr., owner EPT Cons., Columbus, 1987—; cons. EPD/Hong Kong, 1988-92, WHO, UN, Denmark, Poland, Czechoslovakia, 1972-75, Internat. Devel. Rsch. Ctr., Can., China, Asian, 1984-89, NAE, Thailand, 1990, FAO, Malaysia, Foxley & Co., Nu-Tek Foods; environ. advisor to Bertam Devel. Corp., Kuala Lampur, Malaysia, 1992—; waste cons. to U.S. Feed Grains Coun., Taiwan, Malaysia, 1992, Venezuela, 1993; pres. Fan Engring., (US) Inc., 1991—, Red Hill Farms, Ohio, 1992—. Author: (video) Waste Resources Recycle, 1985, Pig Waste Treatment and Recycle, 1992; editor: Animal Wastes, 1977; coeditor Agricultural Wastes/ Biological Wastes, 1979; contbr. articles to profl. jours. Bd. govs., v.p. Singapore Am. Sch., Singapore, 1978-83; clergy-laity congress Greek Orthodox Ch., Houston, 1974. Recipient rsch. awards EPA, 1971-75, Water Resources Inst., 1968-73; rsch. grantee UNDP, FAO, IDRC, GTZ, Asean, 1975-88. Fellow Am. Soc. Agrl. Engrs. (chmn. dept., A.W. Farral award 1974), Am. Assn. Environ. Engrs. (diplomate); mem. Am. Soc. Engring. Edn. (div. chmn.), Singapore Lawn Tennis Assn. (v.p. 1980-84), Am. Club (mgmt. com. 1980-85), Sigma Xi. Greek Orthodox. Avocations: tennis, classical music, folk dancing. Home and Office: 1800 Willow Forge Dr Columbus OH 43220-4414

TAIMUTY, SAMUEL ISAAC, physicist; b. West Newton, Pa., Dec. 20, 1917; s. Elias and Samia (Hawatt) T.; BS, Carnegie Inst. Tech., 1940; PhD, U. So. Calif., 1951; m. Betty Jo Travis, Sept. 12, 1953 (dec.); children: Matthew, Martha; m. Rosalie Richards, Apr. 3, 1976. Physicist, U.S. Naval Shipyard, Phila. and Long Beach, Calif., 1942-46; rsch. asst. U. So. Calif., 1947-51; sr. physicist U.S. Naval Radiol. Def. Lab., 1950-52, SRI Internat., Menlo Park, Calif., 1952-72; sr. staff engr. Lockheed Missiles & Space Co., Sunnyvale, Calif., 1972-89; cons. physicist, 1971—. Mem. Am. Phys. Soc., Sigma Xi. Episcopalian. Contbr. articles to sci. publs. Patentee in field. Home: 3346 Kenneth Dr Palo Alto CA 94303-4217

TAISHOFF, LAWRENCE BRUCE, publishing company executive; b. Washington, Aug. 30, 1933; s. Sol Joseph and Betty (Tash) T.; m. Nancy Lee Stuckey, Sept. 17, 1962 (div. 1979); children: Robert Paul, Randall Lawrence, Jonathan Bradford. AB, Duke U., 1955. Asst. dir. Sta. WTOP-TV, Washington, 1955-56; with Broadcasting Publs., Inc., Washington, 1958—, pres., pub., 1971-91, chmn., 1991—, also dir.; adviser Cahners Consumer/Entertainment Pub. div. Cahners Pub. Co., 1991—; v.p. Jolar Corp., Washington, 1952-72, dir., 1958-72; gen. ptnr. Jolar Assocs., Washington, 1972—; chmn. bd., pres. Graphictype, Inc., 1976-86, also dir.; chmn., pres. Solar Corp., 1982-86; chmn. Broadcasting-Taishoff Found., 1982—; chmn., CEO Chuckie Broadcasting, Ardmore, Okla., 1993—, Trustco, Washington, 1988—; trustee Washington Journalism Ctr., 1982-93, Nat. Press. Found., 1993—, mem. adv. bd., 1993—; bd. dirs. Nat. Press Found., 1982—, mem. exec. com., 1990-94; mem. journalism and communications exec. com. Capital Campaign for Arts and Sci., Duke U., 1984—; bd. advisors Am. Journalism Ctr., Budapest, 1991-95; bd. dir. Ardissone, Naples, Fla., 1994—; mem. White House Press Corps, 1983—; mem. Met. Washington Bd. Trade, 1970—. Co-author radio and TV segment Britannica Book of the Year, 1983—. Team capt. pubs. div. United Givers Fund drive, 1965; mem. admissions adv. com. Duke Alumni Assn., 1968-70; mem. U.S. Senate and Ho. of Reps. Periodical Press Gallery, 1958—; trustee Broadcast Pioneers Ednl. Fund Inc., 1985; judge VFW Voice of Democracy contest, 1978—; mem. bd. judges Peabody awards, 1985-91; mem. Am. U. Sch. Communications Disting. Adv. Commn., 1985—; mem. Founders Soc. Duke U., 1985—, The Mus. of TV and Radio Roundtable, 1988-89; bd. dirs. Ardissone, Naples, Fla., 1994—; chmn., trustee Taishoff Family Found.; cons. High Point Gen. Contracting Inc., Naples, Fla.; ptnr. L & D Ventures, LLC, Naples, Fla. With AUS, 1956-58. Mem. IEEE (sr.), Internat. Radio & TV Soc., Broadcast Pioneers (life, bd. dirs., exec. com. Broadcast Pioneers Library), Am. Sportscasters Assn. (exec. com. 1990—), White House Corrs. Assn., Naples Area C. of C., Nat. Press Club, Woodmont Country Club (Rockville, Md.), Bryce Resort Club (Basye, Va.), Cosmos Club (Washington), Sigma Delta Chi, Zeta Beta Tau. Jewish. Office: 4420 Mercantile Ave Naples FL 34104-3348

TAIT, ELAINE, restaurant critic. Restaurant critic The Phila. Inquirer, Phila., Pa. Office: The Philadelphia Inquirer 400 N Broad St Philadelphia PA 19130-4015

TAIT, JOHN CHARLES, Canadian government official; b. Montreal, Que., Can., Dec. 4, 1945; s. John Watterson and Eleanor (Raymond) T.; m. Sonia Plourde. BA, Princeton U., 1967, Oxford (Eng.) U., Eng., 1969; MA, Oxford (Eng.) U., 1995; BCL, McGill U., Montreal, 1972. Bar: Que. 1974. Asst. sec. Cabinet Privy Coun. Office, Can., 1978-81; asst. dep. minister Can. Dept. Indian Affairs, 1981-83; asst. dep. minister Can. Dept. Justice, 1983-86, dep. solicitor gen., 1986-88; dep. minister of justice Can. Dept. Justice, Ottawa, Ont., Can., 1988-94; sr. advisor Privy Coun. Office, Ottawa, 1994—; Skelton-Clark fellow Queen's U., 1994-95. Sr. fellow Can. Ctr. for Mgmt. Devel., 1994-96; coord. of Security and Intelligence, Privy Coun. Office, 1996—; Rhodes scholar, Eng., 1967. Mem. Can. Bar Assn. Avocation: sports. Office: Privy Council Office, 80 Wellington St, Ottawa, ON Canada K1A 0A3

TAIT, JOHN REID, lawyer; b. Toledo, Apr. 7, 1946; s. Paul Reid and Lucy Richardson (Ruddew) T.; m. Christina Ruth Bjornstad, Mar. 12, 1972; children: Gretchen, Mary. BA, Columbia Coll., 1968; JD, Vanderbilt U., 1974. Bar: Idaho 1974, U.S. Dist. Ct. Idaho 1974, U.S. Ct. Appeals (9th cir.), U.S. Supreme Ct., Nez Perce Tribal Ct. Assoc. Keeton & Tait, Lewiston, Idaho, 1974-76, ptnr., 1976-86, 89—, Keeton, Tait & Petrie, 1986-88, Keeton & Tait, 1989—. Chmn. bd. No. Rockies Action Group, Helena, Mont., 1985-86, bd. dirs. 1981-88, Lewiston Hist. Preservation Commn., Idaho, 1975-94, chmn., 1988-94; bd. dirs. Idaho Legal Aid Svcs., Boise, 1975—, Idaho Housing Agy., Boise, 1984-91, St. Joseph Regional Med. Ctr. Found., Inc., 1989-94, Lewiston Ind. Found. for Edn., Inc., 1996—; vestry Episcopal Ch. of the Nativity, 1996—; Dem. precinct committeeman, 1976-86, state committeeman, 1977-94; co-chmn. Idaho state re-election com. John V. Evans, 1978; Idaho del. Nat. Dem. Conv., N.Y., 1980, mem. standing com. on credentials, N.Y., 1980, San Francisco, 1984; regional dir. Idaho State Dem. Party, 1996—; treas. Larry LaRocco for Congress, 1990, 92; vestryman Episcopal Ch. of Nativity, 1996—. With U.S. Army, 1968-71. Recipient Pro Bono Svc. award Idaho State Bar 1988, Community Recognition award Lewiston Intergovtl. Coun., 1992, Spl. Recognition award Idaho Legal Aid Svcs., Inc., 1993. Mem. ABA, ATLA, NACDL, Idaho Trial Lawyers Assn. (regional dir. 1976-77, 86-88, 96—), Clearwater Bar Assn. (sec. 1974-76, pres. 1984-86), Consumer Attys. Calif. Democrat. Office: Keeton & Tait 312 Miller St Ste E Lewiston ID 83501-1944

TAIT, PATRICIA ANN, secondary education educator; b. Sacramento, Calif., Nov. 26, 1942; d. Frank Scott and Anna Mae (Chubbey) Smith; m. Arthur Fitzwilliam Tait, Jr., Dec. 27, 1968; children: Arthur Fitzwilliam III, Lauryn Kristine. BS in Edn., Tex. Western Coll., 1965; BA in English, U. Tex., El Paso, 1966, MA in English, 1974. Cert. secondary educator, English, ESOL, Fla., Tex. Tchr. English Cheyenne Mountain High Sch., Colorado Springs, 1966-69; tchr. English, dept. chairperson Christ the King Internat. Sch., Okinawa, Japan, 1970-71; pres. Accurate Secretarial and Typing Svc., 1971—; tchr. English Forest High Sch., Ocala, Fla., 1979—, co-chair Eng. dept., 1990—; cons. Fla. Writing Project, Gainesville, 1984—; presenter Marion County Tchrs. English, Ocala, 1985—. Author: Joseph Conrad: The Development of Character in the Jungle, 1974. Named Master Tchr., State of Fla., 1983-84, 84-85. Mem. NEA, Nat. Coun. Tchrs. English, Fla. Coun. Tchrs. English, Marion County Tchrs. English, Marion County Edn. Assn., Fla. Tchrs. Profl. Edn. Assn. Democrat. Episcopalian. Avocations: equine activities. Home: 5109 SE 4th St Ocala FL 34471-3304 Office: Forest High Sch 1614 SE Fort King St Ocala FL 34471-2535

TAIT, ROBERT E., lawyer; b. Lima, Ohio, Sept. 3, 1946; s. Robert and Helen (Smith) T.; m. Donna G. Dome, June 22, 1968; children: Heather, Jennifer, Robert. BA, Kenyon Coll., 1968; JD, U. Mich., 1973. Bar: Ohio 1973, U.S. Dist. Ct. (so. dist.) Ohio. 1976, U.S. Dist. Ct. (no. dist.) Ohio 1976, U.S. Dist. Ct. Md. 1980, U.S. Ct. Appeals (6th cir.) 1981, U.S. Supreme Ct. 1982. Ptnr. Vorys, Sater, Seymour & Pease, Columbus, Ohio, 1973—. Staff counsel Govs. Select Com. on Prevention Indsl. Accidents, Columbus, 1977-78. Served with U.S. Army, 1969-70. Fellow Columbus Bar Found.; mem. ABA (litigation sect., products liability com.), Ohio Bar Assn. (worker's compensation com.), Columbus Bar Assn. (workers compensation and professionalism coms.), Def. Rsch. Inst. (workers compensation com.), Columbus Def. Assn., Assn. Def. Trial Attys. (exec. com. 1991-94). Clubs: Capital, Columbus Country. Home: 2045 Wickford Rd Columbus OH 43221-4223 Office: Vorys Sater Seymour & Pease PO Box 1008 52 E Gay St Columbus OH 43215-3161

TAJIMA, GEORGE KAZUO, electronics company executive; b. L.A., June 27, 1921; s. Masumi and Tamayo (Takagi) T.; m. Taz Uragami, Sept. 17, 1943; children: Robert George, David Masumi, Carol R. Jergenson. BSEE, U. Calif., Berkeley, 1942, MSEE, 1948. Rsch. engr. Wheelco Instruments Inc., Chgo., 1943-45; lectr. U. Calif., Berkeley, 1948-53; engring. mgr. TRW, Inc., L.A., 1953-61; v.p., gen. mgr. San Diego divsn. Plessey Co., 1961-72; pres., CEO Technetics Inc., El Cajon, Calif., 1972—; dir. Hytech Corp., San Diego, 1960-61. Mem. East County Econ. Devel. Coun., La Mesa, Calif., 1995—. Lt. U.S. Army, 1943-45. Mem. IEEE (life, gen. chmn. internat. conf. on engring. in ocean environment 1971), Armed Forces Comms. and Electronics Assn., Computer and Electronics Mktg. Assn. Republican. Methodist. Avocations: winter sports, windsurfing, licensed pilot. Home: 6307 La Pintura Dr La Jolla CA 92037

TAJON, ENCARNACION FONTECHA (CONNIE TAJON), retired educator, association executive; b. San Narciso, Zambales, Philippines, Mar. 25, 1920; came to U.S., 1948; d. Espiridion Maggay and Gregoria (Labrador) Fontecha; m. Felix B. Tajon, Nov. 17, 1948; children: Ruth F., Edward F. Teacher's cert., Philippine Normal Coll., 1941; BEd, Far Eastern U., Manila, 1947; MEd, Seattle Pacific U., 1976. Cert. tchr., Philippines. Tchr. pub. schs. San Narciso and Manila, 1941-47; coll. educator Union Coll. Manila, 1947-48; tchr. Auburn (Wash.) Sch. Dist., 1956-58, Renton (Wash.) Sch. Dist., 1958-78; owner, operator Manila-Zambales Internat. Grill, Seattle, 1980-81, Connie's Lumpia House Internat. Restaurant, Seattle, 1981-84; founder, pres. Tajon-Fontecha, Inc., Renton, 1980—, United Friends of Filipinos in Am. Found., Renton, 1985—; founder Labrador Fontecha and Baldovi-Tajon Permanent Scholarship Fund of The Philippine Normal U., 1990; co-founder The United Filipino-Am. Coll. Fund for the USA and the Philippines, 1995; bd. mem. World Div. of the Gen. Bd. of Global Ministries of the United Meth. Ch., 1982-84, Ch. Women United Seattle Chapt.; mem. advisory bd Univ. Wash. Burke Mus., 1991—; mem. King TV Asian Am. Adv. Forum, 1993. Editor bull. Renton 1st United Meth. Ch., 1994. Bd. dirs. women's divsn. Gen. Bd. Global Ministries United Meth. Ch., 1982-84, Renton Area Youth Svcs., 1980-85, Girl's Club Puget Sound, Ethnic Heritage Coun. Pacific N.W., 1989—; mem. Mcpl. Arts Commn., Renton, 1980—; chairperson fundraising steering com. Washington State Women's Polit. Caucus, 1985-89; governing mem. nat. steering com. state coun. Nat. Women's Polit. Caucus, 1990—; mem. vol. action, 1990 Goodwill Games, Seattle; vol. worker Native Am. Urban Ministries, 1990—; mem. adv. bd. Renton Cmty. Housing Devel.; mem. cmty. adv. bd. U. Wash. Thomas Burke Meml. Mus., 1990—; mem. program com. UN, 1992—; mem. Asian Pacific task force Ch. Coun. Greater Seattle, 1993—; mem. Renton-Rainier area planning com. World Day of Prayer, 1997; coord. establishment and devel. Seattle-Renton area United Filipino-Am. Coll. Fund, 1995, coord. internat. buffet dinner United Filipino-Am. Coll. Fund for U. Wash., Filipino Youth Empowerment Project and Mentor's Child Sponsoring Program; emeritus bd. mem. Ethnic Heritage Coun. Pacific N.W., 1993—; co-chmn. Ann. Filipino and Filipino Am. youth Activities Pres.'s Day Spelling Bee Greater Seattle and Vicinity, 1990-96; coord. Ecumenical World Cmty. Day celebration luncheon Greater Seattle unit Ch. Women United, 1994. Recipient spl. cert. of award Project Hope, 1976, U.S. Bicentennial Commn., 1976, UNICEF, 1977, Spirit of Liberty award Ethnic Heritage Coun. Pacific Northwest, 1991; named Parent of Yr. Filipino Community of Seattle, Inc., 1984, One of 500 Seattle Pacific U. Centennial "Alumni of a Growing Vision", 1991. Mem. NEA, Wash. State Edn. Assn. (bd. dirs. 1990-92), Am. Assn. Ret. Persons, Nat. Ret. Tchrs. Assn., Renton Ret. Tchrs. Assn., U. Wash. Alumni Assn. (life), U. Wash. Filipino Alumni Assn. (pres. Wash. state chpt. 1985-87), Renton Hist. Mus. (life), Internat. Platform Assn., United Meth. Women, Pres.'s Forum, Alpha Sigma, Delta Kappa Gamma. Democrat. Avocations: reading, bowling, crocheting, cooking, walking. Home and Office: 2033 Harrington Pl NE Renton WA 98056-2303 *The values learned in school and taught by my beloved parents such as hard steady work, optimism, enthusiasm, individualism, creativity, getting along with people, listenability, trusting, flexibility, integrity, respectability, faithfulness, thankfulness, givingfulness, forgivingfulness, lovingfulness, prayerfulness, and selfhelpfulness helped me to live a full rounded well balanced life even at retirement.*

TAKAHASHI, JOSEPH S., neuroscientist; b. Tokyo, Dec. 16, 1951; s. Shigeharu and Hiroko (Hara) T.; m. Barbara Pillsbury Snook, June 28, 1985; children: Erika S., Matthew N. BA, Swarthmore (Pa.) Coll., 1974; PhD, U. Oreg., 1981. Pharmacology rsch. assoc. NIMH, NIGMS, Bethesda, Md., 1981-83; asst. prof. Northwestern U., Evanston, Ill., 1983-87; assoc. chmn. Neurobiology and Physiology Northwestern U., Evanston, Ill., 1988—, assoc. prof., 1987-91, prof., 1991-96; Walter and Mary Elizabeth Glass prof. life scis. Northwestern U., Evanston, Ill., 1996—; acting assoc. dir. Inst. for Neuroscience Northwestern U., Evanston, 1988-95; active NIMH Psychobiology and Behavior Rev. Com., 1988-92; mem. Nat. Mental Health Adv. Coun., 1997—. Assoc. editor Neuron; mem. adv. bd. Jour. Biol. Rhythms, 1984—; contbr. more than 95 articles to profl. jours. Grantee Bristol-Myers Squibb, 1995—; recipient Alfred P. Sloan award A.P. Sloan Found., 1983-85, Searl Scholars award Chgo. Cmty. Trust, 1985-88, Merit award NIMH, 1987, Honma prize in Biol. Rhythms Honma Found., 1986, Presdl. Young Investigator award NSF, 1985-90, 6th C.U. Ariens Kappers award Netherlands Soc. for Advancement Nat. Scis., Medicine and Surgery, 1995. Mem. AAAS, Soc. Neurosci., Assn. for Rsch. in Vision and Ophthalmology, Soc. for Rsch. on Biol. Rhythms (mem. adv. bd. 1986—), Mammalian Genome Soc. Achievements include discovery of the expression of circadian oscillations in cells from vertebrates; and identification of first circadian clock gene in mice. Office: Northwestern U Neurobiology 2153 North Campus Dr Evanston IL 60208-3520

TAKAHASHI, KEIICHI, zoology educator; b. Yokkaichi, Japan, May 31, 1931; s. Shozo and Toshi (Imamura) T.; m. Mihoko Terada, Sept. 26, 1957; children: Michiko, Yoshiki. BSc, U. Tokyo, 1953, MSc, 1955, PhD, 1960. Instr. U. Tokyo, 1956-68, assoc. prof., 1968-73, prof., 1973-92, emeritus prof., 1992—; prof. Internat. Christian U., Tokyo, 1992—; rsch. fellow Bedford Coll., U. London, 1960-62; dir. Misaki Marine Biol. Sta., U. Tokyo, 1988-92. Contbr. numerous articles to profl. jours. Mem. Japanese Soc. for Comparative Physiology and Biochemistry (pres. 1990-93), Japan Soc. for Biol. Scis. in Space (v.p. 1987-92), Japan Soc. for Biol. Scis. Edn. (v.p. 1984-95), Japan Soc. for Cell Biology (councillor 1983), Zool. Soc. Japan (councilor), Japan Soc. for Sci. Edn. (bd. dirs.), Inst. of Biology of U.K., Sci. Coun. of Japan. Mem. Christian Ch. Avocations: music, arts. Home: 14-31 Yochomachi, Shinjuku-Ku, Tokyo 162, Japan Office: Internat Christian U Dept Biology, 3-10-2 Osawa, Mitaka, Tokyo 181, Japan

TAKANISHI, LILLIAN K., elementary school educator; b. Koloa, Hawaii, May 19, 1935; d. Saburo and Ayano (Ishida) Kunioka; m. Kenso Takanishi, July 11, 1959; children: Kendra Shizuyo, Kendace Tami. BS in Edn., N.E. Mo. State Tchrs. Coll., 1956; postgrad., U. Hawaii. Cert. profl. edn. Tchr. grade 4 Eleele (Hawaii) Sch., ret., 1990, site coord. After Sch. Plus Program, 1990—; facilitator parent community network ctr., Eleele Sch., 199-97; asst. dir. Eleele/Kamehameha Summer Sch., 1991, 92, 93; tchr. Waimea/Kamehameha Summer Sch., 1994. Adv. jr. Girl Scouts of the U.S., sr. 4H Club, jr. Y-Teens, Civil Air Patrol. Recipient Kauai Dist.'s Dept. of Edn. Sustained Superior Performance and Employee of Yr. award, 1992-93. Mem. Hawaii State Tchrs. Assn. (v.p., sec., treas. Kauai chpt.), Parent Teacher Student Assn. (treas., grade level chmn.), Kau Ele Pepe Safety Action Team, Nana's House (bd. dirs. 1997—), Ho'o Lokahi, Delta Kappa Gamma (2d v.p. Eta chpt., sec.). Home: PO Box 396 Eleele HI 96705-0396

TAKANO, MASAHARU, physical chemist; b. Tainan, Taiwan, Jan. 20, 1935; s. Shuzo and Misao (Rengakuji) T.; m. Hiroko Takenoshita, Aug. 28, 1965; children: Kentaro, Jojiro, Miwako. B.S., Hokkaido U., 1957; M.S., U. Tokyo, 1959, D.Sc., 1963. Postdoctoral fellow McGill U, Montreal, 1963-67; with Monsanto Co., St. Louis, 1967-90; pres. Takano Internat., St. Louis, 1991—; cons. on bus., travel, tech. Sr. contbr. articles on phys. chemistry to profl. jours. Fellow Am. Inst. Chemists; mem. AAAS, Am. Chem. Soc., Am. Phys. Soc., Japan Am. Soc., Japanese Am. Citizens League, Nat. Geog. Soc., World Affairs Coun., Japan Soc., Mo. Sheriffs Assn. (hon.). Buddhist. Home: 13146 Roundstone Ct Saint Louis MO 63146-3642 Office: 425 N New Ballas Rd Ste 280 Saint Louis MO 63141-6848 *This country has everything which other countries envy: a vast land, rich environment, natural resources and opportunities. We can work for all human beings if we want, and there are a million things to do.*

TAKASAKI, ETSUJI, urology educator; b. Tokyo, Apr. 24, 1929; s. Kuranosuke and Fumi Takasaki; m. Sachiko Shinkai, Nov. 1, 1960; children: Satoshi, Masumi, Hiromi. MD, U. Tokyo, 1955, D. Med. Sci., 1960. Instr. urology U. Tokyo, 1960-62, asst. prof., 1962-67; chief. urol. svc. Musashino Red Cross Hosp., Tokyo, 1967-69, Komagome Met. Hosp., Tokyo, 1969-74; prof. urology Dokkyo U. Sch. Medicine, Tochigi, Japan, 1974-95, emeritus prof., 1995—; lectr. U. Tokyo, 1969-74. Author: Urolithiasis, 1978; contbr. articles to Japanese Jour. Urology, 1960, Jour. Urology, 1986, Urologia Internat., 1989, 95, British Jour. Urology, 1994, Internat. Jour. Urology, 1996. Mem. Japanese Urol. Assn. (bd. dirs. 1963—), Japanese Soc. Andrology (bd. dirs. 1982—), Japanese Soc. Endourology and ESWL (bd. dirs. 1988—), Internat. Soc. Urology (Paris). Avocation: Kendo (Japanese fencing).

TAKASUGI, NAO, state official, business developer; b. Oxnard, Calif., Apr. 5, 1922; s. Shingoro and Yasuye (Hayashi) T.; m. Judith Shigeko Mayeda, Mar. 23, 1952; children—Scott, Russell, Ronald, Tricia, Lea. B.S., Temple U., 1945; M.B.A., U. Pa. Wharton Sch., 1946. Mem. city council City of Oxnard, Calif., 1976-82, mayor, 1982-92; mem. Calif. State Assembly, 1992—, chmn. revenue and taxation com.; bus. developer, cons. Mem. Oxnard Planning Commn., 1974-76; pres. World Trade Ctr. Assn., Oxnard; apptd. (by Calif. gov.) chmn. UN Anniversary; assemblyman Calif. State Assembly 37th Dist. Decorated Order of Sacred Treasure with Gold Rayette medal Japanese Gov., 1992. Mem. Ventura County Japanese Am. Citizens League, World Trade Ctr. Assn. (pres. Oxnard chpt.), U.S. Conf. Mayors (mem. nat. adv. bd.), Nat. League of Cities (nat. bd. dirs.), Ventura County Transp. Com., League Calif. Cities (bd. dirs.), South Coast Area Bd. Dirs. (chmn. transp. com.), Assn. Ventura County Cities, Oxnard Housing Authority (chmn.), Oxnard Redevel. Agy. (chmn.), Optimists Club (Oxnard). Republican. Methodist. Home: 1221 El Portal Way Oxnard CA 93035-2511 Office: State Capitol Rm 5158 Sacramento CA 95814-4906 also: 221 Daily Dr Ste 7 Camarillo CA 93010-5833

TAKASUGI, ROBERT MITSUHIRO, federal judge; b. Tacoma, Sept. 12, 1930; s. Hidesaburo and Kayo (Otsuki) T.; m. Dorothy O. Takasugi; children: Jon Robert, Lesli Mari. BS, UCLA, Los Angeles, 1953; LLB, JD, U. So. Calif., 1959. Bar: Calif. bar 1960. Practiced law Los Angeles, 1960-73; judge East Los Angeles Municipal Ct., 1973-75, adminstrv. judge, 1974, presiding judge, 1975; judge Superior Ct., County of Los Angeles, 1975-76; U.S. dist. judge U.S. Dist. Ct. (cen. dist.) Calif., 1976—; nat. legal counsel Japanese Am. Citizens League; guest lectr. law seminars Harvard U. Law Sch. Careers Symposium; commencement spkr.; mem. Legion Lex U. So. Calif. Law Ctr.; chmn. Pub. Defs. Indigent Def. & Psychiat. Panel Com.; mem. Affirmative Action Com., Habeas Corpus-Death Penalty Com., Exec. Com., Jury Com., Settlement Rule Com., Adv. Com. on Codes of Conduct of the Jud. Conf. of the U.S., 1988-92, Code of Conduct of Judges. Mem. editorial bd. U. So. Calif. Law Rev., 1959; contbr. articles to profl. jours. Mem. Calif. adv. com. Western Regional Office, U.S. Commn. on Civil Rights; chmn. blue ribbon com. for selection of chancellor L.A. C.C. With U.S. Army, 1953-55. Harry J. Bauer scholar, 1959; recipient U.S. Mil. Man of Yr. award for Far East Theater U.S. Army, 1954, Jud. Excellence award Criminal Cts. Bar Assn., cert. of merit Japanese-Am. Bar Assn., Disting. Svc. award Asian Pacific Ctr. and Pacific Clinics, 1994, Freedom award Sertoma, 1995, Pub. Svc. award Asian Pacific Am. Legal Ctr. So. Calif., 1995, Trailblazer award So. Calif. region NAPABA, 1995, Spl. award Mex. Am. Bar Assn., 1996; named Judge of Yr. Century City Bar Assn., 1995. Mem. U. So. Calif. Law Alumni Assn. (dir.). Office: US Dist Ct 312 N Spring St Los Angeles CA 90012-4701

TAKEI, TOSHIHISA, otolaryngologist; b. L.A., Apr. 19, 1931; s. Taketomi and Mitsue (Hagihara) T.; m. Emiko Kubota, Jan. 25, 1955; children: H. Thomas, T. Robert. BA, UCLA, 1954; MD, Boston U., 1962. Diplomate, Am. Bd. Otolaryngology. Intern L.A. County Harbor Gen. Hosp., 1962-63; resident in otolaryngology L.A. County/U. So. Calif. Med. Ctr., 1963-67; staff physician Covina (Calif.) Ear, Nose & Throat Med. Group, 1968—; asst. prof. Sch. Medicine, U. So. Calif., L.A., 1968—. 1st lt. U.S. Army, 1955-56, Korea. Fellow Am. Acad. Otolaryngology, Royal Soc. Medicine. Republican. Buddhist. Office: Covina ENT Med Group Inc 236 W College St Covina CA 91723-1902

TAKEMOTO, CORY NOBORU, mathematics educator; b. Honolulu, June 29, 1962; s. Nobuo and Ritsuko Takemoto; m. Karen Noriko Hara, Aug. 25, 1990. BS, U. Hawaii, 1985, profl. diploma, 1986, MA, 1990. Tchr. Kailua (Hawaii) High Sch., 1986-87; substitute tchr. Punahou Sch., Honolulu, 1990-91; lectr. math. Honolulu C.C., 1991-92, instr. math., 1993-94; instr. math. Leeward C.C., Pearl City, Hawaii, 1994—. Mem. Math. Assn. Am. Avocations: singing, bicycling. Office: Leeward CC 46-045 Ala Ike Pearl City HI 96782

TAKETOMI, SUSAMU, physicist, researcher; b. Chiba City, Japan, Sept. 25, 1950; s. Manjiro and Kimie (Kida) T. B of Engring., U. Tokyo, 1975; DSc, Keio U., Yokohama, Japan, 1989. Rschr. Ctrl. Rsch. Lab. Fuji Elec. Co. Ltd., Yokosuka City, Japan, 1975-85; rschr. Matsumotoyushi Seiyaku Co. Ltd., Yao City, Japan, 1985—; vis. rschr. Keio U., Yokohama, Japan, 1985-89, Seikei U., Tokyo, 1990-95, U. Ctrl. Fla., 1995-96, U. Wash., Seattle, 1996—; lectr. in field. Author: (book) Magnetic Fluids: Principle and Application, 1988, Magnetic Fluid Handbook, 1995. Mem. Am. Phys. Soc., Japan Phys. Soc., Japan Applied Phys. Soc. Avocation: playing violin. Home: 14321 32d Ave NE #307 Seattle WA 98125 Office: U Wash Dept Material Sci/Engring Seattle WA 98195

TAKUMI, ROY MITSUO, state representative; b. Honolulu, Oct. 13, 1952; m. Wanda A. Kutaka; children: Aisha, Jaron. BA, Friends World Coll., 1991; MPA, U. Hawaii, 1993. Cmty. organizer Osaka, Japan, 1977-83; program dir. Am. Friends Svc. Com., Honolulu, 1984-90; polit. coord. Hawaii State AFL-CIO, Honolulu, 1990-92; rep. Ho. of Reps., Honolulu, 1992—. Office: State Ho of Reps State Capitol Honolulu HI 96813

TALALAY, PAUL, pharmacologist, physician; b. Berlin, Mar. 31, 1923; came to U.S., 1940, naturalized, 1946; s. Joseph Anton and Sophie (Brosterman) T.; m. Pamela Judith Samuels, Jan. 11, 1953; children—Antony, Susan, Rachel, Sarah. S.B., Mass. Inst. Tech., 1944; student, U. Chgo. Sch. Medicine, 1944-46; M.D., Yale U., 1948; D.Sc. (hon.), Acadia U., 1974. House officer, asst. resident surg. services Mass. Gen. Hosp., Boston, 1948-50; asst. prof. surgery U. Chgo., 1950-51, asst. prof. biochemistry, 1955-57, asso. prof., then prof., 1957-63; asst. prof. Ben May Lab. Cancer Research, 1951-57, asso. prof., then prof., 1957-63; John Jacob Abel prof., dir. dept., pharmacology and exptl. therapeutics Johns Hopkins Sch. Medicine, 1963-75, John Jacob Abel Distinguished Service prof., 1975—, Am. Cancer Soc. prof., 1958-63, 77—; sr. asst. surgeon USPHS, 1951-53; vis. prof. Guy's Hosp. Med. Sch., London, 1970, 74-76; nat. adv. cancer council USPHS, 1967-71; vis. com. dept. biology Mass. Inst. Tech., 1964-67; bd. sci. advisers Jane Coffin Childs Meml. Fund for Cancer Research, 1971-80; bd. sci. consultants Sloan-Kettering Inst. Cancer Research, 1971-81. Hon. editorial adv. bd.: Biochem. Pharmacology, 1963-68; editorial bd.: Jour. Biol. Chemistry, 1961-66, Molecular Pharmacology, 1965-68, 71-80; editor-in-chief, 1968-71. Recipient Premio Internationale La Madonnina Milan, 1978; Med. Alumni Disting. Service award U. Chgo., 1978; Am. Cancer Soc. scholar, 1954-58; Guggenheim Meml. fellow, 1973-74. Fellow Am. Acad. Arts and Scis.; mem. AAAS (Theobald Smith award med. scis. 1957), Nat. Acad. Scis., Am. Philosophical Soc., Am. Soc. Biol. Chemists, Am. Soc. Clin. Investigation, Biochem. Soc., Am. Chem. Soc., Am. Soc. Pharm. and Exptl. Therapeutics, Phi Beta Kappa, Sigma Xi, Alpha Omega Alpha. Home: 5512 Boxhill Ln Baltimore MD 21210-2039 Office: Johns Hopkins U Sch Medicine Baltimore MD 21205

TALAMANTES, ROBERTO, developmental pediatrician; b. Juarez, Chihuahua, Mex., June 19, 1952; came to U.S., 1955; s. Cruz and Viviana (Monarez) T.; m. Blanca Yolanda Chavez, Aug. 19, 1972; children: Christian, Steven. BS in Biology, U. Colo., 1972; MD, U. Autonoma Ciudad Juarez, 1979. Rotating intern Baylor Coll. Medicine, Houston, 1980-81, pediat. resident, 1981-84, devel. pediat. fellow, 1984-86; pvt. practice Gen. Devel. Pediatrics, Las Cruces, N.Mex., 1986—; pres. IPA N.Mex., 1993-96; dir. Cimarron HMO, 1993-96; pres. elect med. staff Meml. Med. Ctr., Las Cruces, 1993-94, pres., 1994-95, sec., 1992-94. With U.S. Army, 1972-74. Fellow Am. Acad. of Pediatrics, Soc. of Devel. Pediatrics; mem. N.Mex. Podiatric Soc., N.Mex. Med. Soc. Republican. Avocations: chess, guitar. Office: Hillside Circle Las Cruces NM 88011

TALBERT, BOB, newspaper columnist. Columnist Detroit Free Press. Office: Detroit Free Press Inc 321 W Lafayette Blvd Detroit MI 48226*

TALBERT, JAMES LEWIS, pediatric surgeon, educator; b. Cassville, Mo., Sept. 26, 1931; s. William David and Frances (Lewis) T.; m. Alice Quintavell, July 25, 1958; children: William David, Alison Whitney. B.A., Vanderbilt U., 1953, M.D., 1956. Diplomate: Am. Bd. Surgery (with cert. of spl. competence in pediatric surgery), Am. Bd. Thoracic Surgery. Intern, then resident in surgery Johns Hopkins Hosp., 1956-64, resident in pediatric surgery, 1964-65, Harvey Cushing fellow, 1958-59; instr. surgery, Garrett scholar pediatric surgery Johns Hopkins U. Med. Sch., 1965-66, asst. prof., 1966-67; mem. faculty U. Fla. Med. Sch., Gainesville, 1967—; prof. pediatric surgery, chmn. div., chief children's surgery U. Fla. Med. Sch., 1970—; mem. affiliated faculty VA Hosp., Gainesville; med. dir. Fla. Regional Med. Program for Diagnosis and Treatment Cancer in Children, 1970-73, N. Referral Center Children's Med. Service Program Fla., 1970-80; chmn. Alachua County Emergency Med. Services Adv. Council, 1973-75; chmn. emergency med. services com. N. Central Fla. Health Planning Council, 1972-73; mem. Fla. Emergency Med. Services Adv. Council, 1973-75, 76-79. Author numerous articles in field; contbr. 16 chpts. to books. Served with USPHS, 1960-62. Recipient Founders medal, Roche award Vanderbilt U. Med. Sch., 1956. Fellow ACS (chmn. Fla. trauma com. 1969-77, gov.-at-large 1979-85, sec. bd. govs. 1982-85, rep. to Coun. of Med. Spl. Socs. 1988-89), Am. Acad. Pediatrics (exec. com. sect. oncology and hematology 1978-85); mem. AMA, Am. Pediatric Surg. Assn. (founding mem., chmn. trauma com. 1976-79), Pediatric Oncology Group (chmn. group retreat 1980), Am. Fedn. Clin. Rsch., Assn. Acad. Surgery, Soc. U. Surgeons, Soc. Pediatric Rsch., Am. Coll. Emergency Physicians, Am. Surg. Assn., Halsted Soc., Am. Assn. Surgery Trauma, Am. Burn Assn., Am. Pediatric Soc., Brit. Assn. Pediatric Surgeons, Soc. Internat. Chirurgie, So. Soc. Pediatric Rsch., So. Surg. Assn., Fla. Med. Assn., Fla. Heart Assn. (chmn. cardio-pulmonary resuscitation com. 1972-76), Fla. Assn. Pediatric Surgeons (pres. 1976-78), Fla. Assn. Pediatric Tumor Programs (pres. 1973—), Alachua County Med. Soc. (chmn. emergency med. svcs. adv. com. 1973-75), Phi Beta Kappa, Alpha Omega Alpha, Phi Eta Sigma. Office: J Hillis Miller Health Ctr PO Box 100286 Gainesville FL 32610-0286

TALBERT, MELVIN GEORGE, bishop; b. Clinton, La., June 14, 1934; s. Nettles and Florence (George) T.; m. Ethlelou Douglas, June 3, 1961; 1 child, Evangeline. BA, So. U., 1959; MDiv, Interdenominational Theol. Ctr., Gammon Theol. Sem., Atlanta, 1962; DD hon., Huston Tillotson Coll., Austin, 1972; LLD (hon.), U. Puget Sound, Tacoma, 1987. Ordained deacon, Meth. Ch., 1960 , elder, 1962, elected to episcopacy, United Meth. Ch., 1980. Pastor Boyd Chapel, Jefferson City, Tenn., 1960-61, Rising Sun, Sunrise, Tenn., 1960-61, St. John's Ch., L.A., 1961-62, Wesley Ch., L.A., 1962-64, Hamilton Ch., L.A., 1964-67; mem. staff So. Calif.-Ariz. Conf. United Meth. Ch., L.A., 1967-68; dist. supr. Long Beach dist. So. Calif.-Ariz. Conf. United Meth. Ch., 1968-73; gen. sec. Gen. Bd. Discipleship, Nashville, 1973-80; resident bishop Seattle area Pacific N.W. conf. United Meth. Ch., 1980-88, resident bishop San Francisco area Calif.-Nev. Conf., 1988—, sec. coun. bishops, 1988—; mem. exec. com. World Meth. Coun., 1976-81, 84—; mem. governing bd. Nat. Coun. Chs., 1980—; v.p., chmn. funding com. Gen. Commn. on Religion and Race, 1980-84, pres., 1984-88; chmn. Missional Priority Coordinating com. Gen. Coun. Ministries, 1980-84; mem. Gen. Commn. on Christian Unity and Interreligious Concerns, 1984—, African Ch. Growth and Devel. Com., 1981-84; pres. elect Nat. Coun. Ch. Christ in the U.S.A., pres. Mem. steering com. Student Non-Violent Coordinating com. Atlanta U. Ctr., 1960-61; trustee Gammon Theol. Sem., Atlanta, 1976—, U. Puget Sound, Tacoma, 1980-88 , Sch. Theology at Claremont, Calif., 1981-88, Pacific Sch. Religion, 1988—; bd. dirs. Glide Found., 1988—. Recipient award of merit for outstanding svc. in Christian edn. Gen. Bd. Edn., 1971; recipient Spl. achievement award Nat. Assn. Black Bus. Women, 1971; Nat. Meth. scholar, 1960; Crusade scholar, 1961. Mem. Theta Phi. Democrat. Home: 8735 W Camden Dr Elk Grove CA 95624-3037*

TALBERT, ROY, JR., history educator; b. Cheraw, S.C., Aug. 1, 1943; s. Roy and Betty Jean (Harper) T.; BA (Furman Scholar), Furman U., 1965; MA (NDEA fellow), Vanderbilt U., 1967, PhD, 1971; grad. Inst. Ednl. Mgmt., Harvard U., 1981; grad. Computer Literacy Inst., Pepperdine U., 1983; Jane Boyd Holbert, Oct. 24, 1986; children: Matthew, Rebecca Anne, Drew, Elizabeth. Sr. teaching fellow Vanderbilt U., Nashville, 1967-70; asst. prof. history Ferrum (Va.) Coll., 1974-76, dir. curriculum and programs, 1976-79; vice chancellor for acad. affairs Coastal Carolina U., Conway, 1979-84, assoc. prof. history, 1979-89, prof., 1989—, chmn. 1991—; producer, host The Public Eye, TV show, 1978-79; host Waccamaw Mag., TV show, 1983; project dir. numerous film, TV and pub. programming projects for community and civic groups, 1975-79. Served to capt. U.S. Army, 1970-72. Mem. So. Hist. Assn., Orgn. Am. Historians. Methodist. Author: FDR's Utopian: Arthur Morgan of the TVA, 1987, Negative Intelligence: The Army and the American Left, 1917-41, 1991, No Greater Legacy: The Centennial History of Willcox, McLeod, Buyck and Williams, 1995. Home: 106 Wofford Ln Conway SC 29526-8823 Office: Coastal Carolina Univ History Dept Conway SC 29526

TALBOT, ARDITH ANN, editor; b. Superior, Nebr., Mar. 11, 1933; d. Charles Howard and Dollie Eunice (Ryan) Snell; m. Richard Charles Talbot, Oct. 17, 1954; children: Richard Daryl, Robert Charles. BA in Edn., U. Nebr., 1956. Recorded Friends min., 1993. Tchr. high sch. Pub. Schs., Juniata, Nebr., 1957-59, Hudson, Iowa, 1962-68, New Providence, Iowa, 1968-71; owner Retail Bookstore, Sutherland, Iowa, 1971-72, Marshalltown, Iowa, 1972-74, Mason City, Iowa, 1974-89; mgr. book store Friends United Mktg., Richmond, Ind., 1986-89; mgr., editor Friends United Press, Richmond, Ind., 1989—. Republican. Avocations: antiques, public speaking. Home: PO Box 343 Lynn IN 47355-0343 Office: Friends United Meeting 101 Quaker Hill Dr Richmond IN 47374-1926

TALBOT, BERNARD, government medical research facility official, physician; b. N.Y.C., Oct. 6, 1937; s. Harry and Gertrude (Salkin) T.; m. Ane Katrine Larsen, June 2, 1963; children: Akia, Kamilla. B.A., Columbia U., 1958, M.D., 1962; Ph.D, MIT, 1967. NIH postdoctoral fellow MIT, 1962-69; NSF postdoctoral fellow U. Rome, 1969-70; commd. USPHS, 1975—, advanced through grades to med. dir.; med. officer Nat. Cancer Inst., Bethesda, Md., 1971-75; spl. asst. intramural affairs NIH, Bethesda, 1975-78; spl. asst. to dir. NIH, 1978-81; dep. dir. Nat. Inst. Allergy and Infectious Diseases, Bethesda, 1981-87, med. officer nat. ctr. for rsch. resources, 1987—. Contbr. articles on protein chemistry to profl. jours., chpts. on recombinant DNA guidelines to books. Recipient Commendation medal USPHS, 1977, Meritorious Service medal, 1984. Mem. Phi Beta Kappa. Office: NIH 9000 Rockville Pike Bethesda MD 20814-1436

TALBOT, DONALD ROY, consulting services executive; b. Bridgeport, Conn., Jan. 23, 1931; s. Grant Edward and Elvera (Gilbert) T.; m. Beverly Rinebold, Aug. 15, 1953; children: Donna, Randall, Theodore, Timothy, Thomas. B in Marine Engring., N.Y. State Maritime Coll. Project engr. atomic power equipment div. GE, San Jose, Calif., 1952-58; mgr. nuclear labs., nuclear div. Martin Marietta Corp., Balt., 1958-62, project dir. nuclear div., 1962-67; dir. spl. studies Martin Marietta Corp., Friendship, Md., 1967-71; project dir. environ. programs Martin Marietta Corp., Balt., 1971-74; dir. environ. tech. ctr. Martin Marietta Corp., Relay, Md., 1974-83; gen. mgr. environ. systems div. Martin Marietta Corp., Columbia, Md., 1984-87; corp. v.p. Versar, Inc., Springfield, Va., 1987-89; pres. R.E. Mgmt. Svc., Inc., Towson, Md., 1989—. Recipient Antarctica Svc. medal Civil Engrs. Corps USN, 1965, Cert. of Appreciation Sec. Dept. Commerce, 1975. Avocation: outdoor activities. Home: 712 Hickory Lot Rd Baltimore MD 21286-1427 Office: R E Mgmt Svcs Inc PO Box 10614 Baltimore MD 21285-0614

TALBOT, EARL ARMOUR, lawyer; b. Chgo., Jan. 23, 1939; s. George A. and Ollie (Tadd) T.; m. Lydia A. Hildreth, June 20, 1964; children: Elizabeth, Earl A. Jr. AB, Wabash Coll., 1961; JD, U. Ill., 1964. Bar: Ill. 1964. Title examiner, trust adminstr. Chgo. Title & Trust Cofd., 1964-67; ptnr. Kirkland & Ellis, Chgo., 1967-85, Hoogendoorn, Talbot, Davids, Godfrey & Milligan, Chgo., 1985—. Contbr. to legal jours. Pres. Ill. conf. United Ch. of Christ, 1991-92. Mem. ABA, Ill. Bar Assn., Chgo. Bar Assn., Am. Coll. Real Estate Lawyers, Univ. Club, Plaza Club, Lambda Alpha. Mem. United Ch. of Christ. Office: Hoogendoorn Talbot Davids Godfrey & Milligan 122 S Michigan Ave Chicago IL 60603-6107

TALBOT, EMILE JOSEPH, French language educator; b. Brunswick, Maine, Apr. 12, 1941; s. Joseph Emile and Flora (Schinck) T.; m. Elizabeth Mullen, Aug. 6, 1966; children: Marc, Paul. BA, St. Francis Coll., Biddeford, Maine, 1963; MA, Brown U., 1965, PhD, 1968. Instr. French U. Ill., Urbana, 1967-68, asst. prof., 1968-73, assoc. prof., 1973-86, prof., 1986—, head dept. French, 1988-94. Author: Stendhal and Romantic Esthetics, 1985, Stendhal Revisited, 1993; editor: La Critique stendhalienne, 1979; assoc. editor: Quebec Studies, 1993-96; rev. editor: The French Review, 1979-82, Quebec Studies, 1988-93; mem. editl. bd.: Nineteenth-Century French Studies, 1986—, La Revue Francophone, 1990-96, Etudes Francophones, 1996—. Fellow Ctr. for Advanced Study U. Ill., 1973, assoc., 1988; NEH fellow, 1973-74; Camargo Found. fellow, France, 1976. Mem. MLA, Am. Comparative Lit. Assn., Am. Assn. Tchrs. French, Assn. for Can. Studies in U.S., Am. Coun. for Quebec Studies (v.p. 1995—). Roman Catholic. Office: U Illinois Dept French 707 S Mathews Ave Urbana IL 61801-3625

TALBOT, HOWARD CHASE, JR., retired museum administrator; b. New Berlin, N.Y., Oct. 6, 1925; s. Howard Chase and Gladys (Jacobs) T.; m. Alice Caroline Losee, Sept. 11, 1948; children—Julia Anna, Judith Ann, James Clayton. Student, Utica (N.Y.) Sch. Commerce, 1946-47. Acct. Leatherstocking Corp., Cooperstown, N.Y., 1947-51; asst. dir., then asst. treas. Nat. Baseball Hall of Fame and Mus., Cooperstown, 1951-78; dir. Nat. Baseball Hall of Fame and Mus., 1978-93; ret., 1993; dir. N.Y. Central Mut. Fire Ins. Co., Edmeston. Trustee Village of Cooperstown, 1957-62, mayor, 1962-63; bd. dirs. Little League Mus., Williamsport, Pa. Served with AUS, 1942-46. Mem. Am. Legion. Republican. Clubs: Cooperstown Rotary (past pres.), Masons.

TALBOT, JOHN DUDLEY, college administrator; b. Summit, N.J., Jan. 12, 1953; s. Jacques and Harriet Talbot; m. Marie Antionette Kehl, Dec. 15, 1975; children: James, Trisha. Student, Ripon Coll., 1985-88. Controls engr. Ripon (Wis.) Coll., 1976-81, asst. dir. phys. plant, 1981-91, dir. phys. plant, 1991-97; systems engr. Johnson Controls, Appleton, Wis., 1997—. With USN, 1971-75. Mem. IEEE, ASHRAE, Assn. Energy Engrs., Assn. of Phys. Plant Adminstrs., Acoustical Signal Processing Soc., Math. Assn. Am., Wis. Assn. Phys. Plant Adminstrs., Madison Area Safety Coun., Constrn. Specifications Inst. Republican. Avocation: digital signal processing. Home: N7583 Radio Rd Ripon WI 54971-9231 Office: Johnson Controls Am Dr Neenah WI 54912

TALBOT, LEE MERRIAM, ecologist, educator, association executive; b. New Bedford, Mass., Aug. 2, 1930; s. Murrell Williams and Zenaida (Merriam) T.; m. Martha Walcott Hayne, May 16, 1959; children: Lawrence Hayne, Russell Merriam. B.A., U. Calif., Berkeley, 1953, M.A., 1963, Ph.D., 1963. Biologist Arctic Research Lab., Point Barrow, Alaska, 1951; staff ecologist Internat. Union for Conservation, Brussels, 1954-56; ecologist, dir. East African ecol. research project Nat. Acad. Scis., Govts. of Kenya and Tanzania, 1959-63; wildlife advisor UN Spl. Fund, Africa, 1963-64; dir. S.E. Asia project Internat. Union for Conservation, 1964-65; resident ecologist, field rep. for internat. affairs Smithsonian Instn., Washington, 1966-70; sr. scientist, dir. internat. activities Pres.'s Council on Environ. Quality, Washington, 1970-78; sr. sci. advisor Internat. Council Sci. Unions, Paris, 1978-83; dir. conservation, spl. sci. advisor World Wildlife Fund Internat., Switzerland, 1978-80; dir. gen. Internat. Union for Conservation of Nature and Natural Resources, Gland, Switzerland, 1980-83; research fellow Environ. and Policy Inst., East West Ctr., 1983-87; vis. fellow World Resources Inst., Washington, 1984-89; sr. environ. advisor World Bank, 1984—; pres. Lee Talbot Assocs. Internat., 1991—; sr. prof. environ. scis., internat. affairs and pub. policy George Mason U., Va., 1994—; cons. UNESCO, World Bank, Asian Devel. Bank, Nat. Geog. Soc., Inter-Am. Devel. Bank, The Nature Conservancy, U.S. Govt., U. Calif., UN Spl. Fund, WHO, UN Environment Program, UN Univ., UN Devel. Programme Govts. Laos, People's Republic China; conservation coord. Internat. Biol. Program, 1965-70; v.p. Fauna and Flora Internat., London; bd. dirs., chmn. bd. Ecologically Sustainable Devel., Inc., Inst. Ecosys. Studies. Author 14 books and monographs; contbr. articles to profl. jours. Active Boy Scouts Am., Geneva, 1980-82, Washington, 1987—. With USMC, 1953-54. Decorated officer Order of Lion (Senegal); recipient Fgn. Field Rsch. award Nat. Acad. Scis., 1959, CINE Golden Eagle award, 1969, Albert Schweitzer medal, 1975, Regents Lectureship award U. Calif.-Santa Barbara, 1986, Pierre Chaleur prize for lit. French Acad. Scis., 1993; finalist Univ.-Wide Tchg. Excellence award George Mason U., 1997. Fellow Royal Geog. Soc., Royal Soc. Arts, AAAS, N.Y. Zool. Soc.; mem. Am. Inst. Biol. Scis. (Disting. Svc. award 1979), Acad. Medicine, World Conservation Union (hon.), Am. Assn. for Club of Rome, Am. Soc. Mammalogists, Ecol. Soc., Wildlife Soc. (Outstanding Publ. award 1963), Soc. for Conservation Biology, Internat. Soc. for Ecol. Econs., Boone and Crockett Club (N.Y.C.), Explorers Club (N.Y.C.), Cosmos Club (Washington), Sigma Xi, Phi Kappa Sigma. Achievements include incorporation of ecological principles in international development; development of new principles for management of wild resources; biodiversity conservation; definition of ecosystem dynamics of tropical savannahs including role of fire, feeding habits and migrations of wild herbivores; development and negotiation of international agreements for environmental protection. Home: 6656 Chilton Ct Mc Lean VA 22101-4422 *My career is based on two premises: first, that our most important challenges are environmental issues which determine the earth's carrying capacity for human life and, equally important, the quality of that life; and second, that it is important to obtain direct experience in as much of the world as possible (over 125 countries so far) to understand the human ecological setting as a basis for action to improve it.*

TALBOT, MATTHEW J., oil company executive, rancher; b. Sept. 4, 1937; s. Matthew J. and Margaret A. (Green) T.; m. Maureen Donlan, June 3, 1958; children: Maureen A., Matthew J., Kathleen M. BBA in Acctg., Iona Coll., 1963. Acct. S.D. Leidesdorf (now Ernst & Young), N.Y.C., 1961-67; sr. analyst Gen. Foods Corp., White Plains, N.Y., 1967-68; asst. to comptroller Tosco Corp., Los Angeles, 1968-70, comptroller, 1970-83, v.p., 1972-76, sr. v.p., 1976-78, exec. v.p., 1978-83; pres. Tosco Corp., Santa Monica, Calif., 1983-87, Talbot Ranch, 1987—; s.r. consultant Edward White & Co., Woodland Hills, 1987—. Treas., bd. dirs. Ctr. Theatre Group, Los Angeles; trustee Craft and Folk Art Mus., Los Angeles. Mem. Am. Inst. CPA's, Fin. Execs. Inst., Sunkist Growers. Roman Catholic. Office: Edward White & Co 21700 Oxnard StSte 400 Woodland Hills CA 91367-3642

TALBOT, PAMELA, public relations executive; b. Chgo., Aug. 10, 1946. BA in English, Vassar Coll., 1968. Reporter Worcester, Mass. Telegram and Gazette, 1970-72; account exec. Daniel J. Edelman, Inc., Chgo., 1972-74, account supr., 1974-76, v.p., 1976-78, sr. v.p., 1978-84, exec. v.p., gen. mgr., 1984-90; pres. Edelman West, Chgo., 1990—; Consumer Worldwide, 1995. Office: Edelman Pub Rels 200 E Randolph Dr Fl 63 Chicago IL 60601-6705*

TALBOT, PHILLIPS, Asian affairs specialist; b. Pitts., June 7, 1915; s. Kenneth Hammet and Gertrude (Phillips) T.; m. Mildred Aleen Fisher, Aug. 18, 1943; children: Susan Talbot Jacox, Nancy, Bruce Kenneth. BA, U. Ill., 1936, BS in Journalism, 1936; student, London Sch. Oriental Studies, 1938-39, Aligarh Muslim U., India, 1939-40; Ph.D., U. Chgo., 1954; LL.D. (hon.), Mills Coll., 1963. Reporter, Chgo. Daily News, 1936-38; corr. Chgo. Daily News, India and Pakistan, 1946-48, 49-50; assoc. Inst. Current World Affairs, Eng. and India, 1938-41; part-time Inst. Current World Affairs, 1946-51; instr. U. Chgo., 1948-50; instr. Columbia U., N.Y.C., 1951; exec. dir. Am. Univs. Field Staff, 1951-61; asst. sec. Near Eastern and S. Asian affairs Dept. State, 1961-65; U.S. ambassador to Greece, 1965-69; pres. Asia Soc., N.Y.C., 1970-81; emeritus Asia Soc., 1981—; Phi Beta Kappa vis. scholar, 1973-74. Author: (with S.L. Poplai) India and America, 1958, India in the 1980s, 1983; editor: South Asia in the World Today, 1950. Trustee emeritus Aspen Inst., U.S.-Japan Found.; counselor United Bd. for Christian Higher Edn. in Asia; elder Presbyn. Ch. 2d lt. cav. Officers Res. Corps, 1936; 1st lt. N.G., 1937-38; lt. comdr. USNR, 1941-46. Mem. Am. Acad. Diplomacy, Coun. Am. Ambs., Assn. Asian Studies, Coun. Fgn. Rels., Century Assn., Cosmos Club. Address: 200 E 66th St New York NY 10021-6728

TALBOT, PRUE, biology educator. BA, Wilson Coll., 1966; MA, Wellesley Coll., 1968; PhD, U. Houston, 1972. Postdoctoral fellow U. Houston; from asst. prof. to assoc. prof. U. Calif., Riverside, 1977-85, prof., 1986—. Assoc. editor several profl. jours.; contbr. articles to profl. jours. Mem. Am. Soc. Cell Biology, AAAS, Crustacean Soc., Sigma Xi. Office: U Calif Riverside Dept Biology Riverside CA 92521

TALBOT-KOEHL, LINDA ANN, dancer, ballet studio owner; b. Fremont, Ohio, July 22, 1956; d. Donald Ray and Doris Ann (Opperman) Talbot; m. James G. Koehl, July 30, 1983. Student, U. Akron, 1974-76; BA in Psychology, Heidelberg Coll., 1984. Owner, instr. BalleTiffin, Inc., Tiffin, Ohio, 1987—; choreographer Heidelberg Summer Theater, Tiffin, 1986, Singing Collegians, 1993; choreographer Calvert H.S. Theater, Tiffin, 1986-88, Swing Choir, 1987-89, 91-92. Appeared (ednl. film) Rights on the Job, State of Ohio Dept. Edn., 1986. Mem. Dance Masters Am., Nat. Multiple Sclerosis Soc., The Ritz Players (choreographer 1985, 88-89, 96, make-up designer, advisor 1989-92, sound booth operator 1993—). Avocations: reading, photography, music, community theater, travel. Home and Office: BalleTiffin Inc 449 Melmore St Tiffin OH 44883-3628

TALBOTT, BEN JOHNSON, JR., lawyer; b. Louisville, May 2, 1940; s. Ben Johnson and Elizabeth (Farnsley) T.; m. Sandra Riehl, Oct. 19, 1963; children: Elizabeth, Betty, John, Ben, Sandra. AB magna cum laude, Xavier U., Cin., 1961; LLB, Harvard U., 1964. Bar: Ky. 1965, U.S. Ct. Appeals (6th cir.) 1967. Law clk. to presiding justice U.S. Dist. Ct. Ky., Louisville, 1964-65; assoc. Middleton, Reutlinger & Baird, Louisville, 1965-68, ptnr., 1968-80; ptnr. Westfall, Talbott & Woods, Louisville, 1980—; atty. Stitzel-Weller Distillery, 1970-72, Louisville Gen. Hosp., 1974-83, Louisville and Jefferson County Bd. Health, 1974-80, U. Louisville, Louisville, 1980—. Mem. adv. bd. Louisville 15, Sta. WKPC-TV, Bd. dirs., 1972-74, pres. 1974; past bd. dirs. U. Louisville Found., U. Louisville Med. Sch. Fund Orgn.; bd. dirs. Louisville Theatrical Assn., 1971—, pres., 1975-76, chmn., 1977-78; bd. dirs. Def. Enterprise Fund, 1994—; bd. dirs. Macauley Theatre, 1975, TARC Adv. Com., 1971, Jefferson County Capital Constrn. Com., 1971, Louisville Orch., 1976-86, pres., 1979-81; bd. trustees, trustee U. Louisville, 1970-79, sec., 1974, vice chmn., 1975, chmn. fin. com., 1976; bd. dirs. Ky. Ctr. for the Arts, 1983—, Louisville Lung Assn., 1974-75, treas., 1975; bd. dirs. Historic Homes Found., 1972-78, v.p. 1978, advisor, atty. 1978—. Named Outstanding Young Man of Louisville, Louisville Jaycees, 1976. Mem. ABA, Ky. Bar Assn. (chmn. 1989, Gen. Practice Session of the CLE), Louisville Bar Assn. (past mem. exec. com.), The Def. Rsch. and Trial Lawyers Assn., Harvard Law Sch. Assn. of Ky. (sec. 1965, pres. 1989—), Phi Kappa Phi. Avocations: golf, tennis, skiing. Home: 566 Blankenbaker Ln Louisville KY 40207-1167 Office: Westfall Talbott & Woods 501 S 2nd St Louisville KY 40202-1864

TALBOTT, FRANK, III, lawyer; b. Danville, Va., Mar. 26, 1929; s. Frank and Margaret (Jordan) T.; m. Mary Beverley Chewning, July 11, 1952; children: Beverley, Frank IV. BA, U. Va., 1951, LLB, 1953. Bar: Va. 1952. Gen. practice law Danville, 1956-66; with Dan River Inc., 1966-76, v.p., gen. counsel, 1968-76; partner firm Clement, Wheatley, Winston, Talbott & Majors, Danville, 1977-78; individual practice law Danville, 1979-92; gen. counsel Va. Mfrs. Assn. Inc., 1983-92; of counsel Woods, Rogers & Hazlegrove, Danville, Va., 1992—; chmn. adv. bd. NationsBank, Danville, 1984-94. Vice-chmn. Danville Sch. Bd., 1964-70; trustee Va. Student Aid Found., 1963-68; bd. dirs. United Fund Danville, 1959-63, Meml. Hosp., Danville, 1977-90. Served with AUS, 1953-56. Decorated Commendation medal. Fellow Am. Bar Found. (life); mem. Va. Bar Assn. (v.p. 1965-66, exec. com. 1967-70), Danville Bar Assn. (pres. 1965-66), Am. Judicature Soc., Newcomen Soc., U. Va. Alumni Assn. (bd. mgrs.), Danville Golf Club, German Club, Farmington Country Club, Country Club Va., Delta Psi, Phi Alpha Delta. Methodist. Home: 420 Maple Ln Danville VA 24541-3532 Office: PO Box 560 Danville VA 24543-0560

TALBOTT, RICHARD DAVID, retired physician; b. Jackson, Mich., Dec. 31, 1930; s. James Ernest and Ellen (McGowan) T.; m. Katherine Marie Bonney, June 18, 1983; children: James M., William J., Judith M. AB, Yale U., 1952; MD, Northwestern U., 1956. Diplomate Am. Bd. Orthopaedic Surgery. Intern Denver Gen. Hosp., 1956-57; resident St. Luke's Hosp., Denver, 1957-58, Lahey Clinic, Boston, 1958-59, Shriners Hosp. for Crippled Children, Springfield, Mass., 1959-60, Boston City Hosp., 1960-61; pvt. practice Orthopaedic Assocs., P.C., Denver, 1961-86; dir. dept. orthopaedic surgery Denver Gen. Hosp., 1987-95; prtnr. InMed Evaluations, Denver, 1995-97, ret., 1997. Avocations: boating, fishing, tennis, golf. Home: Four Polo Field Ln Denver CO 80209 Office: InMed Evaluations 135 W 10th Ave Denver CO 80204-4013

TALBOTT, STROBE, journalist; b. Dayton, Ohio, Apr. 25, 1946; s. Nelson S. and Josephine (Large) T.; m. Brooke Lloyd Shearer, Nov. 14, 1971; children: Devin Lloyd, Adrian Nelson. BA, Yale U., 1968, MA (hon.), 1976; MLitt, Oxford U., Eng., 1971. East european corr. Time Mag., 1971-73, U.S. state dept. corr., 1973-75, white house corr., 1975-77, diplomatic corr., 1977-84, chief Washington bur., 1984-89; editor at large, 1989-94; deputy sec. Dept. State, 1994—. editor, translator: Khrushchev Remembers, 1970, Khrushchev Remembers: Last Testament, 1974; author: Endgame: Inside Story of SALT II, 1979, Deadly Gambits: Reagan Administration & Arms Controls, 1984, The Russians and Reagan, 1984, Reagan and Gorbachev, 1987, Master of the Game, 1988. Trustee Yale U. 1976-82, Hotchkiss Sch., 1982-87; bd. dirs. Carnegie Endowment Internat. Peace; Council on Fgn. Relations. Recipient Edward Weintal Prize for Disting. Diplomatic Reporting Georgetown U., Overseas Press Club award, Stanley Hillman award. Office: Deputy Sec Dept of State 2201 C St NW Washington DC 20520*

TALENT, JAMES M., congressman, lawyer; b. St. Louis, Mo., Oct. 18, 1956; m. Brenda Lyons, 1984; children: Michael, Kathleen Marie. BA in Polit. Sci., Washington U., 1978; JD, U. Chgo. Law Sch., 1981. Law clk. 7th Ct. Appeals, 1981-82; adj. prof. law, 1982-84; mem. Mo. State Ho. Reps., 1984-93; minority leader, 1989-93; mem. 103rd-105th Congresses from 2nd Mo. Dist., 1993—, mem. econ. & ednl. opportunity com., nat. security com., chmn. small bus. subcom. on regulation and paperwork. Legislative Achievement award Mo. Hosp. Assn., 1989. Mem. Mo. Bar Assn. (Award for significant contbns. to adminstrv. justice 1989), Mo. C. of C. (Spirit of Enterprise award 1990), Order of the Coif. Republican. Office: US Ho Reps 1022 Longworth Office House Members Washington DC 20515-2502*

TALESE, GAY, writer; b. Ocean City, N.J., Feb. 7, 1932; s. Joseph Francis and Catherine (DiPaola) T.; m. Nan Ahearn, June 10, 1959; children—Pamela, Catherine. B.A. in Journalism, U. Ala., 1953. Staff writer N.Y. Times, N.Y.C., 1955-65; writer Esquire mag., N.Y.C., 1960. Author: New York - A Serendipiter's Journey, 1961, The Bridge, 1964, The Overreachers, 1965, The Kingdom and the Power, 1969, Fame and Obscurity, 1970, Honor Thy Father, 1971, Thy Neighbor's Wife, 1980, Unto the Sons, 1992; co-author: (with Barbara Lounsberry) The Literature of Reality, 1995; contbr. articles to Esquire mag., others. Served to 1st lt. AUS, 1954-56. Mem. P.E.N. (v.p. 1984-87, bd. dirs. 1980—), Phi Sigma Kappa. Home: 109 E 61st St New York NY 10021-8101 also: 154 E Atlantic Blvd Ocean City NJ 08226-4511

TALESE, NAN AHEARN, publishing company executive; b. N.Y.C., Dec. 19, 1933; d. Thomas James and Suzanne Sherman (Russell) Ahearn; m. Gay Talese, June 10, 1959; children: Pamela Frances, Catherine Gay. B.A., Manhattanville Coll. of Sacred Heart, 1955. Fgn. exchange student 1st Nat. City Bank, London and Paris, 1956; editorial asst. Am. Eugenics Soc., N.Y.C., 1957-58, Vogue mag., N.Y.C., 1958-59; copy editor Random House Pub., N.Y.C., 1959-64; assoc. editor Random House Pub., 1964-67, sr. editor, 1967-73; sr. editor Simon & Schuster Pubs., N.Y.C., 1974-81; v.p. Simon & Schuster Pubs., 1979-81; exec. editor, v.p. Houghton Mifflin Co., N.Y.C., 1981-83, v.p., editor-in-chief, 1984-86, v.p., pub., editor-in-chief, 1986-88; sr. v.p. Doubleday & Co., N.Y.C., 1988-90; pres., pub., editorial dir. Nan A. Talese Books, 1990—. Home: 109 E 61st St New York NY 10021-8101

TALIAFERRO, NANCY ELLEN TAYLOR, artist; b. Richmond, Va., Feb. 16, 1937; d. Samuel Beryl and Nancy Loomis (Brinton) Taylor; m. Charles Mitchell Taliaferro, July 3, 1958; children: Chester Parsons, Nancy Brinton. BFA, Va. Commonwealth U., 1959. Comml. artist, illustrator, 1959-63, drawings, pastel portraits, 1963—, oil paintings, 1978—. Exhbns. include Women's Resource Ctr., U. Richmond, 1985, Jacob Javits Fed. Bldg., N.Y.C., 1986, Va. Gen. Assembly and State Capitol Bldgs., 1989, 91, 93, The Art Gallery, Ashland Va., 1992-97, Uptown Gallery, Richmond, 1992-97, Du Pont Art Gallery, Washington and Lee U., Lexington, Va., 1993, The Chrysler Mus., Norfolk, Va., 1994, nat. Assn. Women ARtists Traveling Exhibit, 1996—, Peninsula Fine Arts Ctr., Newport News, Va., 1997. Recipient award The Artists Mag., 1992. Mem. Nat. Assn. Women Artists (Medal of Honor 1995, Audrey Hope Shirk Meml. award 1995), Uptown Gallery (charter mem.), James River Art League, U. Painters. Republican. Methodist. Home: 6724 Forest Hill Ave Richmond VA 23225-1802 Studio: 8413 Forest Hill Ave Richmond VA 23235-3125

TALIMCIOGLU, NAZMI METE, civil and environmental engineer, educator; b. Bolu, Turkey, Dec. 9, 1961; came to U.S., 1983; s. Kemal Selcuk and Perihan (Kip) T.; m. Nurhan Toguc, Aug. 17, 1987. BS, Istanbul Tech. U., 1982; ME, Stevens Inst. Tech., 1985, PhD, 1991. Computer cons. computer ctr. Stevens Inst. Tech., Hoboken, N.J., 1986-88, rsch. asst. civil/environ. engring. dept., 1989-91, rsch. asst., prof. ctr. for environ. engring., 1991—. Contbr. articles to profl. jours. V.p. Stevens Turkish Students Assn., Hoboken, 1989. Recipient scholarship Turkish Govt., 1983-86; named Outstanding Young Man of Am., Outstanding Young Men of Am., 1989, 92. Mem. ASCE, N.Y. Acad. Sci., Turkish Archtl. and Engring. Soc., Nat. Groundwater Assn., Am. Geophys. Union, Sigma Xi. Achievements include development of a state-of-the-art computer model for evaluation of the impact of contaminated soils on groundwater quality. Office: Stevens Tech CEE Edwin E Stevens Bldg Rm 320 Hoboken NJ 07030

TALINGDAN, ARSENIO PREZA, health science administrator; b. Dolores, Abra, The Philippines, Mar. 30, 1930; came to U.S., 1973; s. Mariano T. and Candida (Tordil) Preza; m. Josefa Fernandez Biason. Apr. 21, 1954; children: Melda, Arsenio Jr., Jocelyn Almerick, Mario, Abe. AA, U. Philippines, 1951, AB, MPA, 1955; MAPA, The Am. U., 1956; BS, La Salle Extention U., Chgo., 1977; MBA, Century U., 1983, PhD, 1985. Cert. nursing home adminstr., life, health and securities underwriter. Job analyst, orgn. analyst, budget examiner Kroeger & Assocs. Project, Philippine Budget Commn., Manila, 1954-55; scholar, tech. asst., participant USA-ICA-NEC Program, 1955-56; supr. mgmt. analyst Philippine Budget Commn., Manila, 1957-59; asst. budget dir., IBM coordinator U. Philippines, Quezon City, 1959-65, mgmt. specialist, chief of studies, 1969-70; asst. v.p. for budget and mgmt. Sarmiento Enterprises, Inc., Makati, Rizal, Philippines, 1965-69; adminstr. Philippine Gen. Hosp., Manila, 1970-73; budget and facilities mgr. Hunter Coll., CUNY, N.Y.C., 1973-76; acctg. systems editor J.C. Penney Co., N.Y.C., 1977; regional med. care adminstr. N.Y. State Dept. Health, Office Health Systems Mgmt., N.Y.C., 1977-78; assoc. med. care adminstr., Medicaid mgmt. info. systems Dept. Health State of N.Y., N.Y.C., 1978—; with dental Medicaid program Dept. Health State of N.Y., 1978-82, with med. ops. br., 1982-84, with dental ops. br., 1984-91, with patient care investigations, long term care program, 1991—; asst. prof., chmn. social scis. dept. U.P. Coll., Manila, 1969-73; 1st Philippine tech. assistance fellow on orgn. and mgmt. U.S. Agy. for Internat. Devel., Washington, 1955-56; professorial lectr. U. Philippines, Manila, 1960-69. Co-author: Accounting, Auditing and Internal Auditing, 1964; author: Public Administration and Management, 1966, Management and Supervision, 1966, Work Simlification Handbook, 1957 and others; contbr. articles to profl. jours. Pres. Abra Varsitarians, Quezon City, 1949-53; founder, Dolores Young Men and Women's Assn., Manila, Abra, 1949-71; founder, pres. Philippine Execs. and Profls. Golf Assn., Quezon City, 1965-69, others. Maj. Res. Officer, Philippine Army, 1960-73. Recipient Hall of Nations award Am. U., 1956, Pub. Health Sci. award Del. Valley Assn. Philippines, 1980, Profl. award in Pub. Adminstrn. U. Philippines Alumni Assn. Am., 1991. Mem. Pub. Employees Fedn., U. of the Philippines Alumni Assn. in N.J. (founder, 1st pres. 1979-83), U. of the Philippines Alumni Assn. in Am. (founder, 1st pres. 1980-83), Filipino Am. Soc. of Teaneck (pres. 1983-84). Republican. Avocation: writing.

TALKE, FRANK EBERHARD, education educator; b. Dresden, Germany, Sept. 16, 1939; came to U.S., 1965; s. Artur and Louise T.; m. Kathryn Ann Talke; children: Stefan, Kristen, Kurt. Diploma Engring., U. Stuttgart, Germany, 1965; MS, U. Calif., Berkeley, 1966, PhD, 1968. Mgr. IBM, San Jose, Calif., 1969-86; prof. U. Calif. San Diego, 1986—, chair AMES dept., 1993-95; vis. prof. U. Calif. Berkeley, 1984. Author numerous tech. papers; patentee in field. Mem. ASME, IEEE (chair local sect. 1990-92). Office: Univ Calif San Diego 9500 Gilman Dr La Jolla CA 92093-5003

TALKINGTON, ROBERT VAN, state senator; b. near Patrick, Tex., Aug. 23, 1929; s. William Henry and Nannie J. (Patrick) T.; m. Donna Jill Schmaus, Mar. 25, 1951; children—Jill Talkington McCaskill, Jacki Talkington Chase, James, Thomas, Lisa. A.A., Tyler Jr. Coll., 1949; B.S., U. Kans., 1951, LL.B., 1954, J.D., 1971. Bar: Kans. 1954. County atty. Allen County, Kans., 1957-63; city atty. Moran, Kans., 1968—; mem. Kans. Ho. of Reps. from 10th Dist., 1969-73; mem. Kans. Senate from 12th Dist., 1973-89, v.p., 1977-81, majority leader, 1981-85, pres., 1985-89; mem. State Bd. of Regents, 1995—; chmn. Republican Party, Allen County, 1964-68, state treas., 1964-66; mem. Kans. Turnpike Authority, 1977-85, 89-93. Trustee Iola Pub. Libr., 1962-70; mem. adv. bd. Greater Univ. Fund, U. Kans., 1967-72. With U.S. Army Counter Intelligence Corp, 1954-56. Mem. Am. Legion, Sigma Alpha Epsilon, Phi Delta Phi. Clubs: Masons, Shriners, Elks. Home: 20 W Buchanan St Iola KS 66749-1823 Office: 20 N Washington St Iola KS 66749-2836

TALL, FRANKLIN DAVID, mathematics educator; b. N.Y.C., Apr. 21, 1944; s. Martin and Faye T. AB, Harvard U., 1964; PhD, U. Wis., 1969. Asst. prof U. Toronto, Ont., Can., 1969-74; assoc. prof. U. Toronto, 1974-80, prof. math., 1980—. Author: (monograph) Set Theoretic Consistency Results and Topological Theorems Concerning the Normal Moore Space Conjecture and Related Problems, 1977, The Work of Mary Ellen Rudin, 1993. Nat. Scis. and Engring. Research Council Can. grantee, 1973—. Mem. Am. Math. Soc., Can. Math. Soc., Assn. Symbolic Logic, Japan-Can. Soc., Internat. Assn. Neurolinguistic Programming. Office: U Toronto, Dept Math, Toronto, ON Canada M5S 1A1

TALLCHIEF, MARIA, ballerina; b. Fairfax, Okla., Jan. 24, 1925; d. Alexander Joseph and Ruth Mary (Porter) T.; m. Henry Paschen, Jr., June 3, 1956; 1 child, Elise. DFA (hon.), Lake Forest (Ill.) Coll., Colby Coll., Waterville, Maine, 1968, Ripon Coll., 1973, Boston Coll., Smith Coll., 1981, Northwestern U., Evanston, Ill., 1982, Yale U., 1984, St. Mary-of-the-Woods (Ind.) Coll., 1984, Dartmouth Coll., 1985, St. Xavier Coll., 1989. Ballerina Ballet Russe de Monte Carlo, 1942-47; with N.Y.C. Ballet Co., 1947-65, prima ballerina, 1947-60; founder Chgo. City Ballet, 1979; now artistic dir. Lyric Opera Ballet; prima ballerina Am. Ballet Theatre, 1960; founder Sch. Chgo. Ballet. Guest star, Paris Opera, 1947, Royal Danish Ballet, 1961; created roles in Danses Concertantes, 1944, Night Shadow, 1946, Four Temperaments, 1946, Orpheus, 1948, The Firebird, 1949, Bourée Fantastique, 1949, Capriccio Brillante, 1951, À la Françaix, 1951, Swan Lake, 1951, Caracole, 1952, Scotch Symphony, 1952, The Nutcracker, 1954, Allegro Brillante, 1956, The Gounod Symphony, 1958; appeared in films Presenting Lily Mais, 1943, Million Dollar Mermaid, 1953. Named Hon. Princess Osage Indian Tribe, 1953; recipient Disting. Service award U. Okla., 1972, award Dance mag., 1960, Jane Addams Humanitarian award Rockford Coll., 1973, Bravo award Rosary Coll., 1983, award Dance Educators Am., 1956, Achievement award Women's Nat. Press Club, 1953, Capezio award, 1965, Leadership for Freedom award Roosevelt U. Scholarship Assn., 1986. Mem. Nat. Soc. Arts and Letters. Office: Lyric Opera Ballet 20 N Wacker Dr Ste 860 Chicago IL 60606-2805*

TALLENT, ROBERT GLENN, chemical and environmental engineer, entrepreneur; b. Nashville, July 4, 1954; s. Glenn Oliver and Virginia Jo (Bell)

T.; m. Sandra Marie McKenzie, Aug. 2, 1986; 1 child, Emily Suzanne (dec.). BE, Vanderbilt U., 1976; MS, George Washington U., 1996. Cert. Scuba diving instr. trainer, emergency med. technician. Dir. tng. Am. Watersports Co., Oxon Hill, Md., 1980-83; chem. engr. Naval Sea Systems Command, Washington, 1980-87; pres. Caribbean Ventures, Alexandria, Va., 1984-88; dist. course dir. Profl. Assn. Diving Instrs., Va., Md., Del., Washington, 1984—; staff Am. Systems Corp., Chantilly, Va., 1988-89; account exec. Data Link Info. Solutions, Inc., Falls Church, Va., 1989-90; pres. Internat. Diving Inst., 1988-91, Nut'N But Nuts, Stafford, Va., 1990-91, Earthworks Internat., Stafford, 1991—; engr. Info. Spectrum, Inc., 1994-96, SEMCOR, 1996—; pres. The Triton Found., 1997—; pres. Triton Found., Inc., 1997—. Author: Caribbean Ventures Dive Travel Notebook, 1986. Dist. commr. Boy Scouts Am., Stafford, Va., 1988-97; pres. The Triton Found., Inc., 1997—. Lt. (j.g.) USN, 1976-80. Recipient Wood Badge Boy Scouts Am., 1994, Eagle Scout, 1969, Internat. Cmty. Svc. award PADI, 1994. Mem. Nat. Eagle Scout Assn. (life mem.), Just Clowning Around No. Va., Undersea Med. Soc., Clowns of Am. Internat. Republican. Methodist. Avocations: squash, Chinese culture, music, clowning, scuba diving. Home: 30 Larkwood Ct Stafford VA 22554-1585

TALLENT, STEPHEN EDISON, lawyer; b. Columbus, Nebr., Aug. 10, 1937; s. William E. and Helen T.; m. Martha Sutcliffe, Apr. 6, 1971; 1 child, Jennifer Diane. BA, Stanford U.; JD, U. Chgo., LLD (hon.), Lincoln U. Bar: Calif. 1963, U.S. Dist. Ct. (so. and cen. dists.) Calif. 1965, U.S. Dist. Ct. (so. and ea. dists.) N.Y., 1989, U.S. Ct. Appeals (D.C. cir.) 1981, U.S. Ct. Appeals (2d cir.) 1987, U.S. Ct. Appeals (3d cir.) 1980, U.S. Ct. Appeals (4th cir.) 1982, U.S. Ct. Appeals (6th cir.) 1986, U.S. Ct. Appeals (9th cir.) 1968, U.S. Ct. Mil. Appeals 1965, U.S. Supreme Ct. 1973. Ptnr. Gibson, Dunn & Crutcher, L.A., 1962-96; pvt. practice, Washington, 1997—; former adj. prof. Loyola Law Sch., L.A.; mem. vis. com. U. Chgo. Law Sch. Former mem. Calif. Atty. Gen.'s adv. com. for Evaluation of Anti-Organized Crime Programs; mem. L.A. Town Hall, L.A. World Affairs Council; mem. bd. visitors Stanford Law Sch.; founding dir. Am. Employment Law Coun., 1993—. Fellow Coll. Labor and Employment Lawyers (founding, pres. 1995—); mem. ABA (chair elect labor and employment law sect.), Calif. Bar Assn., D.C. Bar Assn., N.Y. Bar, Los Angeles County Bar Assn., Indsl. Rels. Rsch. Assn. Home: 7020 Glenbrook Rd Bethesda MD 20814-1223 Office: Gibson Dunn & Crutcher 1050 Connecticut Ave NW Ste 900 Washington DC 20036-5320 also: 333 S Grand Ave Los Angeles CA 90071-1504

TALLENT, WILLIAM HUGH, chemist, research administrator; b. Akron, Ohio, May 28, 1928; s. Charles Othar and Agnes Annette (Johnson) T.; m. Joy Anne Redfield, Aug.23, 1952; children: Elizabeth Ann, Cinda Marie, Raymond Charles. BS, U. Tenn., 1949, MS, 1950; PhD, U. Ill., 1953. Chemist Nat. Heart Inst., Bethesda, Md., 1953-57, G.D. Searle & Co., Skokie, Ill., 1957-64; head new crops evaluation investigations Agr. Rsch. Svc., USDA, Peoria, Ill., 1964-69, chief indsl. crops lab., 1969-74, asst. dir., 1974-75, ctr. dir. No. Regional Rsch. Ctr., 1975-83, regional adminstr. N.E. region, 1983-84; asst. adminstr. Agr. Rsch. Svc., USDA, Washington, 1984-94; tech. transfer advisor Agr. Rsch. Svc., USDA, Beltsville, Md., 1994—. Recipient Merit award Gamma Sigma Delta, 1979, Presdl. Rank award for Sr. Execs., 1988, NASA Tech. 2002 award for lifetime achievement in tech. transfer, 1992. Mem. AAAS, Am. Chem. Soc., Soc. Econ. Botany. Home: Apt 4L 6100 Westchester Park Dr College Park MD 20740-2852 Office: USDA Agr Rsch Svc Bldg 005 BARC-W Beltsville MD 20705-2350

TALLET, MARGARET ANNE, theatre executive; b. Binghamton, N.Y., Feb. 14, 1953; d. George Francis and Wilma Ann (Wagner) T.; m. Peter A. Myks, July 6, 1991. BA, St. Mary's Coll., 1975; MBA, SUNY, 1979. Asst. dir. Parrish Art Mus., Southampton, N.Y., 1979-81; assoc. dir. devel. Detroit Inst. Arts Founders Soc., 1981-92; v.p. Franco Pub. Rels. Group, Detroit, 1992-96; pres. Music Hall Ctr. for the Performing Arts, 1996—. Bd. dirs. Aid for AIDS Rsch., 1987-92, Detroiters at Heart, 1992—; mktg. com. Mich. Career Found., Detroit, 1992—. Mem. Pub. Rels. Soc. Am. Roman Catholic. Office: Music Hall Ctr for Performing Arts 350 Madison St Detroit MI 48226-2255

TALLETT, ELIZABETH EDITH, biopharmaceutical company executive; b. London, Apr. 2, 1949; d. Edward and Edith May (Vickers) Symons; m. James Edward Wavle Jr.; children: James Edward Tallett, Alexander Martin Tallett, Christopher Andrew Wavle. BS with honors, U. Nottingham (Eng.), 1970. Ops. rsch. analyst So. Gas Bd., 1970-73; mgmt. svcs. mgr. Warner-Lamber (UK), Eastleigh, Eng., 1973-77, strategic planning mgr., 1977-81; internat. dir. strategic planning Warner-Lambert, Morris Plains, N.J., 1981-82, corp. dir. strategic planning, 1982-84; dir. mktg. ops. Parke-Davis, Morris Plains, 1984-87; exec. v.p. therapeutic products Centocor, Malvern, Pa., 1987-89, pres. pharms. div., 1989-92; pres., CEO Transcell Techs., Inc., Monmouth Junction, N.J., 1992-96, Dioscor, Inc., Stockton, N.J., 1996—; bd. dirs. Prin. Mut. Life Ins. Co., Varian Assoc., Inc.; dir. Biotech. Coun. N.J., Prosperity N.J., Inc. Contbr. articles to profl. jours. Apptd. by Gov. Christine Todd Whitman to Prosperity N.J. Commn., 1995—. Mem. Ch. of Eng. Avocations: acting, badminton, travel, skiing.

TALLEY, BRIAN CHANDLER, broadcasting executive; b. Litchfield, Ill., May 27, 1955; s. Hayward Leroy and Emma Mae (Chandler) T.; m. Lea Ann Edwards; 1 child, Chandler Paul. BS in Radio-TV Communications, Murray State U., 1977. V.p. engrng. ops. Talley Broadcasting Corp., Litchfield, 1977—. Mem. Soc. Broadcast Engrs. (chpt. sec.-treas. 1991-92), Macoupin County Amateur Radio Club. Avocations: amateur radio, photography, boating, motorcycling. Office: WSMI Radio RR 16 Litchfield IL 62056

TALLEY, CAROL LEE, newspaper editor; b. Bklyn., Sept. 10, 1937; d. George Joseph and Viola (Kovash) T.; children—Sherry, Jill, Scott. Student, U. Ky., 1955-57, Ohio U., 1957-58. Reporter Easton (Pa.) Daily Express, 1958-60; reporter N.J. Herald, 1962-64, edn. editor, 1964-66; reporter Daily Advance, Dover, N.J., 1966-68, polit. editor, investigative reporter, from 1969, mng. editor, 1974-81; editor Evening Sentinel, Carlisle, Pa., 1982—; Mem. A.P. Task Force N.J., 1970, Pa. Associated Press Mng. Editor's Bd. Dirs. Past bd. dirs. Helen Stevens Cmty. Mental Health Ctr. (chair), Carlisle; past pres. bd. dirs. Stevens Mental Health Ctr., Carlisle. Recipient pub. service awards Nat. Headliners, 1971, Sigma Delta Chi, 1971, George Polk Meml. award for local reporting, 1974, Dew Meml. award Pa. Newspaper Pub.'s Assn., 1985. Mem. Pa. Newspaper Editors Soc., Kiwanis Club. Office: 457 E North St Carlisle PA 17013-2620

TALLEY, CHARLES RICHMOND, commercial banking executive; b. Richmond, Va., Dec. 23, 1925; s. Charles Edward and Marie (Throckmorton) T.; m. Anne Marie Smith, June 4, 1948; children: Laurie Anne, Charles Richmond Jr. B.A. in Econs, U. Richmond, 1949; postgrad., Sch. Banking Rutgers U., 1959-61, Sch. Fin. Pub. Relations, Northwestern U., 1954-55; grad. exec. program, U. Va., 1974. Asst. cashier 1st & Mchts. Nat. Bank, Richmond, 1955-57; asst. v.p. 1st & Mchts Nat. Bank, 1957-63, v.p., 1963-69, sr. v.p., 1969-73, exec. v.p., 1973-84; corp. exec. officer Sovran Bank N.A., 1984-86, ret., 1986; ret., 1986; bd. dirs. Security Atlantic Life Ins. Co., Richmond; v.p., bd. dirs. Security Atlantic Ins. Agy., Richmond; bd. dirs. Sovran Properties, Inc.; vice chmn. bd. dirs. Va. Edn. Loan Authority, 1983-87, chmn., 1988-91. Pres. Richmond Jr. C. of C., 1960-61; pres. Bapt. Extension Bd. Va., 1973-75, bd. dirs., 1985-95; treas. Richmond chpt. Nat. Found., 1956—; v.p., mem. exec. com. Richmond Eye and Ear Hosp., pres. 1988-91; bd. dirs. Commonwealth Eye and Ear Inst., 1986-89; bd. dirs. Richmond Symphony Orch., Richmond Better Bus. Bur. With USNR, 1944-46. Mem. Richmond Met. C. of C. (bd. dirs. 1979-89), Richmond Clearing House Assn. (pres. 1977), Willow Oaks Country Club Richmond (pres. 1971), Bull and Bear Club, Farmington Country Club (Charlottesville, Va.), Rotary (bd. dirs. Richmond 1981-83), Tides Lodge Golf and Country Club (Irvington, Va.). Home: 4301 Stratford Rd Richmond VA 23225-1060

TALLEY, DARRYL VICTOR, professional football player; b. Cleveland, July 10, 1960. Degree in Physical Edn., U. W.Va., 1983. Linebacker Buffalo Bills, 1983-95, Minn. Vikings, 1995—. Named linebacker The Sporting News Coll. All-Am. Team, 1982, outside linebacker The Sporting News NFL All-Pro Team, 1990, 93. Played in Pro Bowl, 1990, 91. Office: Minn Vikings 9520 Viking Dr Eden Prairie MN 55344*

TALLEY, JANE, artist, educator; b. Spur, Tex., Oct. 17, 1929; d. Marshall Herff and Louise (Winfield) Applewhite; m. Oran Kent Talley, Feb. 28, 1948; children: Carleen Dolan, Linda Oldham. Attended, U. Tex., 1946-48. Gallery artist Top of the Line Gallery, Ft. Worth, 1980-89, Morales Gallery, Nags Head, N.C., 1985-91, Artenegies Gallery, Ft. Worth, 1988—, Tarbox Gallery, San Diego, 1990-92, Riuer Gallery, Reno, Nev., 1992-94; Castleberry Gallery, Arlington, Tex., 1992—; gallery artist Richelle Gallery, Bedford, Tex., 1993-94; art tchr. Imagination Celebration, Ft. Worth, 1993; demonstrator various workshops. Recipient Merit award Nat. Watercolor Okla., 1987, Citation award Tex. Fine Arts Assn., 1988. Mem. Soc. Watercolor Artists (bd. dirs., Pres. award 1994), Tex. Watercolor Soc. (Merit award 1982), Southwestern Watercolor Soc. Avocations: bird watching, beach combing, photography. Home: 8255 Carrick Fort Worth TX 76116

TALLEY, KEVIN DAVID, public relations executive; b. Williamsport, Pa., May 26, 1951; s. James Andrew and Joan (Lindauer Miller) T.; m. Frances Clare McEntee, 1974; children: Jason Roth, Kevin Patrick. BA, Cath. U., 1974; MA with honors, Am. U., 1976. Press sec. to Senate Rep. Leader Hugh Scott, 1971-76, press sec., chief of staff to U.S. Rep. Bill Goodling, 1976-81; campaign mgr. George Bush for Pres. Campaign, Pa., 1980; dir. ops. Reagan/Bush Campaign, Pa., 1980; chief of staff to U.S. Senator John Heinz, 1981-85; campaign mgr. Heinz Senate Campaign, 1982; dep. to chmn. Nat. Rep. Senatorial Com., 1985-87; fundraising & campaign consul Bill Goodling for Congress Com., Washington, 1992—; pres. People for John Heinz, Inc., 1982-91, 94—; real estate developer, 1988-91; v.p. govt. rels. Dutko & Assoc., 1992-94; COO DCS Group, 1995-97; founder, pres. Synergy Ptnrs., Inc., Washington, 1997—. Named one of Outstanding Young Men of Am., 1980. Mem. Phi Kappa Theta (Man of Yr. 1973). Roman Catholic. Office: Synergy Ptnrs Inc 1206 Walter St SE Washington DC 20003-1448

TALLEY, LINDA JEAN, food scientist, dietitian; b. Hearne, Tex., July 15, 1948; d. Roy Wesley and Dorothy Louise (Allen) Dugger; m. Thomas James Talley, May 15, 1970; children: John Paul, Jo Ann. BS in Food Tech., Tex. A & M U., 1969, MS in Food Sci. and Tech., 1979, PhD in Food Sci. and Tech., 1981. Registered dietitian Am. Dietetic Assn.; registered sanitarian; lic. dietitian, Tex. Technician I soil and crop scis. dept. Tex. A & M U., College Station, 1969-72; technician I in horticulture scis. Tex. A&M U., College Station, 1977-78, grad. asst., 1978-81; quality assurance mgr. food products divsn. Southland Corp., Ft. Worth, 1972-73; pub. health inspector Ft. Worth Pub. Health Dept., 1973-74; dir. quality assurance plant sanitation and product devel. Kimbell Foods, Inc., Mfg. Divsn., Ft. Worth, 1974-75; profl. cons. Ft. Worth, 1975-76; v.p., cons. TALCO, Dallas, 1981-91; sr. food scientist Enersyst Devel. Ctr., Inc., Dallas, 1990—; presenter in field. Contbr. articles to profl. jours. Mem. Inst. Food Techs., Sigma Xi, Phi Tau Sigma. Avocations: gardening, reading, needlework. Home: 911 Ridgecrest Denton TX 76205-5415 Office: Enersyst Devel Ctr 2051 Valley View Ln Dallas TX 75234-8920

TALLEY, ROBERT BOYD, physician; b. Scottsbluff, Nebr., Jan. 21, 1931; s. Richard Bedelle and Eloise Earline (Taylor) T.; m. Louise Carroll Settle, Dec. 28, 1954; children—Robert Boyd, Edwin T. Student, Northwestern U., 1949-52; M.D., U. Colo., 1956. Diplomate Am. Bd. Internal Medicine. Intern Wayne County Gen. Hosp., Eloise, Mich., 1956-57; resident State U. Iowa, Iowa City, 1959-62, instr. dept. internal medicine, 1962-63, postdoctoral fellow dept. internal medicine, 1962-63; practice medicine specializing in internal medicine and gastroenterology Stockton, Calif.; clin. instr. medicine U. Calif.-San Francisco, 1965-70; chief staff St. Joseph's Hosp., chief of medicine, 1975-77, trustee, 1974—; cons. Calif. HCSA Data Com.; mem. adv. com. on nat. health ins. Ways and Means Com., U.S. Congress, 1978-80 dir. Delta IPA, 1980—; v.p. statewide Calif. PPO, United Preferred Provider Orgn., 1982; mem. exec. com., sec. United Founds. for Med. Care, 1978-79, treas., 1980-82, v.p. 1982-84, pres., 1984—; pres. San Joaquin Found. for Med. Care, 1973-79. Served with USN, 1957-59. Packard undergrad. scholar in surgery, 1956. Fellow ACP (community service com. 1971-81, trustee Commn. on Profl. and Hosp. Activities 1973-82, pres., chmn. bd. 1979-81); mem. HMO's Group Health Assn. of Am. (tech. adv. com. 1982-84), Inst. Medicine of Nat. Acad. Scis., AMCRA (bd. dirs. 1984—), Calif. Acad. Medicine, San Joaquin Med. Soc., Calif. Med. Assn., Sigma Nu. Office: 1805 N California St Ste 201A Stockton CA 95204-6032

TALLEY, ROBERT MORRELL, aerospace company executive; b. Erwin, Tenn., Mar. 13, 1924; s. Robert Taylor and Anna Laura (Morrell) T.; m. Mary Sue Williams, June 5, 1948; children: David, Carol. Student, East Tenn. State Coll., 1942-43, U. Va., 1943-44; B.S. U. S.C., 1945; M.S., U. Tenn., 1948, Ph.D., 1950. Chief infrared br., chief solid state div. U.S. Naval Ordnance Lab., White Oak, Md., 1951-58; mgr. lab. Santa Barbara Rsch. Ctr. subs. Hughes Aircraft, Calif., 1958-69, v.p., 1969-76, pres., 1976-89, ret.; chair engring. com. U. Calif.-Santa Barbara Found. Contbr. articles to profl. jours.; patentee in field. Trustee U. Calif.-Santa Barbara Found.; bd. dirs. Industry Edn. Coun., Santa Barbara. With USN, 1943-46. Fellow Am. Phys. Soc.; mem. Optical Soc. Am., LaCumbre Club, Sigma Xi.

TALLEY, TRUMAN MACDONALD, publisher; b. N.Y.C., Feb. 3, 1925; s. Truman Hughes and Helen Nicholson (Macdonald) T.; m. Madelon DeVoe, Oct. 17, 1953; children: Melanie, Macdonald, Marina. Student, Buckley Sch., Deerfield Acad., Sorbonne, 1945-46; grad. cum laude, Princeton U., 1949. Assoc. editor New Am. Libr. of World Lit., N.Y.C., 1949-59; editorial v.p. New Am. Libr. of World Lit., 1959-64; pres., editl. dir. Weybright & Talley, N.Y.C., 1966-78; pub. Truman Talley Books with Times Books, 1978-82; with E.P. Dutton, 1983—; mem. grad. bd. Princeton Tiger, 1950—. Trustee Clinton Hall Assn. Merc. Libr., N.Y.C. With AUS, 1943-46, ETO. Decorated Purple Heart. Mem. P.E.N. Clubs: Anglers, Brook, Maidstone, Southampton Beach. Office: Truman Talley Books/Dutton Penguin USA 375 Hudson St New York NY 10014-3658

TALLEY, WILLIAM GILES, JR., manufacturing company executive; b. Adel, Ga., Sept. 25, 1939; s. William Giles and Mary (McGlamry) T.; BSBA, U. S.C., 1961; m. Jacqueline Vickery, Apr. 14, 1962; children: William Giles, John Lindsey, Bronwyn Ashley. Mgmt. trainee Talley Veneer & Crate Co., Inc., Adel, 1961-62, plant mgr., salesman, Waynesboro, Ga., 1965-67; with Talley's Box Co., Leesburg, Fla., 1962-69, plant mgr., partner, 1967-69; gen. mgr. Growers Container Coop., Inc., Leesburg, 1969-96; pres. Talley Acres, Inc., 1979—, pres. Talley Classic Woods, Inc., 1992—; bd. dirs. Sun Trust Bank Ctrl. Fla., N.A., Orlando, Fla. Past chmn. and bd. dirs. Leesburg Hosp. Assn. Served with USAAF, 1961. Mem. Leesburg C. of C. (dir.), Fla. Forestry Assn. (dir. 1977-96), Elks, Kiwanis, Sigma Alpha Epsilon. Republican. Methodist. Home: 2206 Talley Court Rd Leesburg FL 34748-3177 Office: PO Box 490817 Leesburg FL 34749-0817

TALLICHET, LEON EDGAR, retired publishing executive, financial administrator; b. Tupelo, Miss., Jan. 10, 1925; s. Leon Edgar and Irene Elizabeth (Reid) T.; m. Betty Jean Baumann, May 31, 1947; children: Judie Elizabeth, Kathryn Louise. BME, U. Louisville, 1946; MBA, Harvard U., 1949. Office mgr. Brown-Forman Distillers Corp., Louisville, 1949-58; from asst. sec.-treas. to sr. v.p., treas. Courier-Jour. and Louisville Times Co., Std. Gravure Corp., and WHAS/Inc., Louisville, 1958-86, dir., 1975-86; fin. adminstr. Barry Bingham, Sr., Louisville, 1987-88, Mary C. Bingham, 1987-95; pres. chpt. Fin. Exec. Inst., 1969-70. Bd. dirs. Met. United Way Louisville, 1972-74; chmn. investment com. Ky. Ctr. for Arts Endowment Fund, 1991-96; fin. com. Louisville Cmty. Found., 1988—; commr., treas. City of Ten Broeck, Ky., 1988—. With USNR, 1943-46, lt. USNR, 1950-52.

TALLMAN, CLIFFORD WAYNE, school system administrator, consultant; b. Columbus, Ohio, June 13, 1932; s. Frank Albert and Ella Louise (Ott) T.; m. Ruth Anne Fletcher, Apr. 6, 1958; children: Martin, David, Kathryn Haines. BS in Edn., Capital U., 1954; MA, Ohio State U., 1960; EdS, Bowling Green U., 1965. Cert. supt., Ohio, Ill., Mich., Ky., Pa., N.Y. Tchr. Southwestern City Schs., Grove City, Ohio, 1954-60; supt. Republic (Ohio) Local Schs., 1960-63, Columbus Grove Schs., Grove City, 1963-65, Jackson Local Schs., Massillon, Ohio, 1965-73, Brecksville (Ohio) City Schs., 1973-78, Kent County Schs., Independence, Ky., 1978-80, Otsego Local Schs., Tontogany, Ohio, 1980-86; prof. Bowling Green (Ohio) U., 1980-86; supt. Coloma (Mich.) Community Schs., 1986-93; pres. Tallman Ednl. Cons., 1993—; prof. Southwestern C.C., 1996—; ednl. cons. AMA, Chgo., 1963; commr. Right to Read, Washington, 1973; cons. Am. Arbitratioin Assn., Tech. Adv. Svcs. for Attys.; speaker at local, state and nat. edn. profl. orgns. Contbr. articles to profl. jours. Active Berrien County Hist. Assn., Coloma, Selective Svc. Bd., Washington; newsletter editor Rotary Club, Coloma, 1986-90. With USNR, 1951-54, USA, 1954-56. I/D/E/A scholar, 1969; Found. for Econ. Edn. scholar, 1971; named to Honorable Order Ky. Cols. Mem. Ohio Edn. Assn., Mich. Assn. Sch. Bds., Berrien Assn. Sch. Adminstrs., Am. Assn. Sch. Adminstrs., Mich. Assn. Sch. Adminstrs., Buckeye Assn. Sch. Adminstrs., Coloma C. of C., Bowling Green U. Alumni Assn., Rotary, Lions, Phi Delta Kappa. Lutheran. Avocations: gardening, computers, organ music, chess, traveling. Home: 5540 Red Arrow Hwy Coloma MI 49038-9730 Office: PO Box 550 Coloma MI 49038-0550

TALLMAN, RICHARD C., lawyer; b. Oakland, Calif., Mar. 3, 1953; s. Kenneth A. and Jean M. (Kemppe) T.; m. Cynthia Ostolaza, Nov. 14, 1981. BSC, U. Santa Clara, 1975; JD, Northwestern U., 1978. Bar: Calif. 1978, Wash. 1979, U.S. Dist. Ct. (no. dist.) Calif. 1979, U.S. Dist. Ct. (we. dist.) Wash. 1979, U.S. Ct. Appeals (9th cir.) 1979, U.S. Dist. Ct. Hawaii 1986. Law clk to Hon. Morrell E. Sharp U.S. Dist. Ct. (we. dist.) Wash., Seattle, 1978-79; trial atty. U.S. Dept. Justice, Washington, 1979-80; asst. U.S. atty. U.S. Dist. Ct. (we. dist.) Wash., Seattle, 1980-83; ptnr. Schweppe, Krug & Tausend, PS, Seattle, 1983-89; mem. Bogle & Gates, PLLC, Seattle, 1990—; chmn. western dist. Wash. Lawyer Reps. to Ninth Cir. Jud. Conf., 1996-97. Instr. Nat. Park Svc. Seasonal Ranger Acad., Everett and Mt. Vernon, Wash., 1983-93; chmn. Edmonds C.C. Found., Lynnwood, Wash., 1990-92; gen. counsel Seattle-King County Crime Stoppers, 1987—; mem. exec. bd., chief Seattle Coun. Boy Scouts Am., 1997—. Mem. ABA, FBA (trustee 1992-93, v.p. 1994, pres. 1995), Seattle-King County Bar Assn., Rainier Club, Wash. Athletic Club. Avocations: hunting, hiking, fishing. Office: Bogle & Gates Two Union Sq 601 Union St Seattle WA 98101-2327

TALLMAN, ROBERT HALL, investment company executive; b. Creston, Iowa, Aug. 10, 1915; s. Ralph H. and Hazel Verne (Hall) T.; m. Elizabeth Childs, Sept. 19, 1938; children: Susan, Mary, Timothy. BS, U. Nebr., 1937. Trainee to dist. mgr. Firestone Tire & Rubber Co., Akron, Ohio, 1937-50; pres. Tallman Oil Co., Fargo, N.D., 1950-80; chmn. bd. State Bank of Hawley, Minn., 1966-70, 1st Nat. Bank of Barnesville, Minn., 1965-88; pres. Tallman Investment Ent., Fargo, 1980—; pres., dir. Dak Tech. Inc.; dir. Bell Farms. Past pres. Fargo Bd. Edn., N.D. Petroleum Coun.; past pres. St. Lukes Hosp. Assn.; past chmn. trustees 1st Congl. Ch. of Fargo. Mem. Fargo C. of C. (past pres.), Am. Assn. Ret. Persons, Nat. Rifle Assn., N.D. State U. Teammakers Club (past pres.), Fargo Country Club, Kiwanis (past pres.), Masons, Shriners, Elks. Republican. Congregationalist. Avocations: golf, hunting, fishing, travel, photography. Home: 3201 16th Ave S Fargo ND 58103-4517 Office: Box 9723 2108 S University Dr Fargo ND 58103-5348

TALLMER, MARGOT SALLOP, psychologist, psychoanalyst, gerontologist; b. N.Y.C., Sept. 8, 1925; d. Harry and Mildred (Schifrin) Sallop; m. Jonathan Tallmer, Apr. 12, 1949 (dec.); children—Mary, Megan, Jill, Andrew. M.S., N.Y. U., 1948; M.A., Yeshiva U., 1962, Ph.D., 1967. Mem. faculty dept. ednl. founds. Hunter Coll., N.Y.C., 1969—, assoc. prof., 1976-79, prof., 1979-94, prof. emeritus; staff psychologist Mt. Sinai Hosp., 1967-68; postgrad. Center for Mental Health, 1968-69; pvt. practice psychoanalysis N.Y.C., 1967—; faculty, trustee, bd. dirs. Nat. Psychol. Assn. for Psychoanalysis; faculty N.Y. Ctr. for Psychoanalytic Tng. Editor: Sex and Life Threatening Illness, HIV Testing Positive, The Child and Death, also books on aging and loss; editorial bd. Current Issues in Psychoanalysis, Psychoanalytic Rev.; contbr. chpts. to textbooks, articles to profl jours. Mem. APA, Boston Soc. Gerontologic Psychiatry, N.Y. State Psychol. Assn. (pres. divsn. adult devel. and aging). Address: 26 E 81st St New York NY 10028-0246

TALLY, LURA SELF, state legislator; b. Statesville, N.C., Dec. 9, 1921; d. Robert Ottis and Sara (Cowles) Self; A.B., Duke U., 1942; M.A., N.C. State U., Raleigh, 1970; m. J.O. Tally, Jr., Jan. 30, 1943 (div. 1970); children: Robert Taylor, John Cowles. Tchr., former guidance counselor Fayetteville (N.C.) city schs.; mem. N.C. Ho. of Reps. from 20th Dist., 1971-83, chmn. com. higher edn., from 1975, also 1980-83, vice chmn. com. appropriations for edn., 1973-86; state senator from 12th Dist. N.C., 1983-95; chmn. N.C. Senate Com. of Natural Resources, Community Devel. and Wildlife, 1987, Environment and Natural Resources, 1989-94. Past pres. Cumberland County Mental Health Assn., N.C. Historic Preservation Soc.; trustee Fayetteville Tech. Inst., 1981-94; mem. Legis. Research com. Mem. Am. Personnel and Guidance Assn., Fayetteville Bus. and Profl. Women's Club, Kappa Delta, Delta Kappa Gamma. Methodist. Club: Fayetteville Woman's (past pres.). Office: W Jones St Raleigh NC 27601

TALLY, TED, screenwriter; b. Winston-Salem, N.C., Apr. 9, 1952; s. David K. and Dorothy E. (Spears) T.; m. Melinda Kahn, Dec. 11, 1977. BA, Yale U., 1974, MFA, 1977. Scripts include (plays) Terra Nova, 1977 (Kazan award Yale U. 1977, Theron Rockwell Field prize Yale U. 1977, Obie award 1984), Hooters, 1978, Coming Attractions, 1980 (John Gassner Playwriting award N.Y. Outer Critics Cir. 1981), Silver Linings, 1983, Little Footsteps, 1986, (with others) Urban Blight, 1988, The Gettysburg Sound Bite, 1989, (screenplays) White Palace, 1990, The Silence of the Lambs, 1991 (Acad. award best adapted screenplay 1991, Writers Guild award), Before and After, 1995, The Juror, 1995, (TV) Hooters, 1983, Terra Nova, 1984, The Father Clements Story, 1987 (Christopher award 1988). Columbia Broadcasting Sys. Found. Playwriting fellow Yale U., 1977, Guggenheim fellow, 1985-86; N.Y. State Creative Artists Pub. Svc. grantee, 1980, NEA Playwriting grantee, 1983-84. Office: ICM 8942 Wilshire Blvd Beverly Hills CA 90211-1934*

TALMADGE, JOHN BARNES, science foundation administrator; b. Needham, Mass., Mar. 30, 1936; s. Nelson Alcorn and Mildred Francis (Barnes) T.; m. Elinor Beth Dunsmore, Nov. 27, 1965 (div. Nov. 1976); children: Leslie Jean, Alison Elinor; m. Patricia Russell, Apr. 24, 1993. BA, Williams Coll., 1958. Pub. info. officer NASA Ames Rsch. Ctr., Moffett Field, Calif., 1962-64; adminstrv. asst. to pres. Reed Coll., Portland, Oreg., 1964-66; adminstrv. asst. to Congressman John Dellenback, U.S. Ho. of Reps., Washington, 1967; fed. rels. assoc. Assn. Am. Colls., Washington, 1968-70; various positions NSF, Washington, 1970, now head Polar coordination, 1986—. Staff asst. Lodge for Senate, Mass., 1962, McCall for Sec. State, Oreg., 1964; campaign mgr. Dellenback for Congress, Eugene, Oreg., 1966. Capt. USMCR, 1958-61. Episcopalian. Avocations: hiking, canoeing, ecotourism. Home: 3000 Catheral Ave NW#412A Washington DC 20016 Office: Geosciences 4201 Wilson Blvd Arlington VA 22203-1859

TALMAGE, DAVID WILSON, microbiology and medical educator, physician, former university administrator; b. Kwangju, Korea, Sept. 15, 1919; s. John Van Neste and Eliza (Emerson) T.; m. LaVeryn Marie Hunicke, June 23, 1944; children: Janet, Marilyn, David, Mark, Carol. Student, Maryville (Tenn.) Coll., 1937-38; BS, Davidson (N.C.) Coll., 1941; MD, Washington U., St. Louis, 1944. Intern Ga. Baptist Hosp., 1944-45; resident medicine Barnes Hosp., St. Louis, 1948-50; fellow medicine Barnes Hosp., 1950-51; asst. prof. pathology U. Pitts., 1951-52; asst. prof., then assoc. prof. medicine U. Chgo., 1952-59; prof. medicine U. Colo., 1959—, prof. microbiology, 1960-86, disting. prof., 1986—, chmn. dept., 1963-65, assoc. dean, 1966-68, dean, 1969-71; dir. Webb-Waring Lung Inst., 1973-83, assoc. dean for research, 1983-86; mem. nat. council Nat. Inst. Allergy and Infectious Diseases, NIH, 1963-66, 73-77. Author: (with John Cann) Chemistry of Immunity in Health and Disease; editor: Jour. Allergy, 1963-67, (with M. Samter) Immunological Diseases. Served with M.C. AUS, 1945-48. Markle scholar, 1955-60. Mem. NAS, Inst. Medicine, Am. Acad. Allergy (pres.), Am. Assn. Immunologists (pres.), Phi Beta Kappa, Alpha Omega Alpha. Office: U Colo Sch Med Box C321 Denver CO 80262

TALMAGE, LANCE ALLEN, obstetrician/gynecologist, career military officer; b. Vandergrift, Pa., Feb. 23, 1938; s. Guy Wesley and Martha Lois (Bradstock) T.; m. Diana Elizabeth Heywood, June 23, 1962; children: Tamara, Lance, Tenley. BS in Chem. Engring., U. Toledo, 1960; MD, U. Mich., 1964. Flight surgeon 24th Infantry Divsn. U.S. Army, Europe, 1966-69; resident U. Mich. Med. Ctr., Ann Arbor, 1969-73; clin. prof. Med. Coll. Ohio, Toledo, 1987—; adminstrv. dir. Ctr. for Women's Health, Toledo, 1987—; brigadier gen. 112th Med. Brigage Ohio Army Nat. Guard,

Columbus, 1995—; pres. med. staff Toledo Hosp., 1989-91, chair dept. Ob-gyn., 1979-86; pres. Toledo Lucas County Acad. Medicine, 1994-95. Cabinet mem. United Way, Toledo, 1994-96; hon. chmn. March of Dimes Mothers, Toledo, 1989; pres. Ottawa Hills (Ohio) Athletic Boosters, 1986-88, team physician, 1983—. Fellow Am. Coll. Surgeons, Am. Coll. Obstetricians & Gynecologists (dist. chair 1996—); mem. AMA, Ohio State Med. Assn., Kiwanis, Pi Kappa Phi Alumni Assn., U. Toledo Alumni Assn. Republican. Lutheran. Office: The Toledo Ob-Gyn Assocs 2109 Hughes Dr Ste 200 Toledo OH 43606-5100

TALMI, YOAV, conductor, composer; b. Kibbutz Merhavia, Israel, Apr. 28, 1943; diploma Rubin Acad. Music, Tel Aviv; postgrad. diploma Juilliard Sch. Music; m. Erella Gottesmann; 2 children. Assoc. condr. Louisville Orch., 1968-70; co-condr. Israel Chamber Orch., 1970-72; artistic dir., condr. Gelders Symphony Orch., Arnhem, 1974-80; prin. guest condr. Munich Philharm. Orch., 1979-80; artistic dir., condr. Israel Chamber Orch., 1984-88; music dir. New Israeli Opera, 1985-89, San Diego Symphony Orch., 1990-96, Waterloo Festival, N.J., 1994-95 ret., 1996; guest condr. Berlin Philharm., Munich Philharm., London Philharm., Philharmonia, Royal Philharm., Concertgebouw, Rotterdam Philharm., Israel Philharm., Tokyo Symphony, New Japan Philharm., Vienna Symphony, St. Petersburg Philharm., Pitts. Symphony, Detroit Symphony, St. Louis Symphony, Houston Symphony, Dallas Symphony, N.Y. Chamber Symphony, L.A. Chamber Orch., Oslo Philharm., Tonhalle Orch. Zurich, others. Composer: Dreams for choir a capella, Music for Flute and Strings; Overture on Mexican Themes (recorded), 3 Monologues for Flute Solo (pub.), Inauguration Fanfare; recs. include: Bruckner 9th Symphony (Oslo Philharm.), Glière 3rd Symphony, Brahms Sextet/4 Serious Songs, Rachmaninov's Isle of the Dead, Berlioz Overtures, Berlioz Romeo et Juliette, Berlioz Harold in Italy (San Diego Symphony), Tchaikowsky/Schoenberg, Bloch/Barber/Grieg/Puccini (Israel Chamber Orch.); (with Erella Talmi) works for flute and piano. Recipient Boskovitch prize for composition, Israel, 1965; Koussevitzky Meml. Conducting prize, Tanglewood, 1969; award Ruppert Found. Condr. competition, London, 1973. Home: PO Box 1384, Kfar Saba 44113, Israel Office: ICM Artists 40 W 57th St New York NY 10019-4001

TALTON, CHESTER LOVELLE, bishop; b. El Dorado, Ark., Sept. 22, 1941; s. Chester Talton and Mae Ola (Shells) Henry; m. Karen Louise Warren, Aug. 25, 1963; children: Kathy Louise, Linda Karen, Frederick Douglass, Benjamin Albert. BS, Calif. State U., Hayward, 1967; MDiv, Ch. Divinity Sch. of Pacific, 1970. Ordained to ministry Episcopal Ch., as deacon, 1970, as priest, 1971, as bishop, 1991. Vicar Good Shepherd Episc. Ch., Berkeley, Calif., 1970-71, St. Mathias Mission, Seaside, Calif., 1971-73, Ch. of the Holy Cross, Chgo., 1973-76; curate All Sts. Episc. Ch., Carmel, Calif., 1971-73; rector St. Philips Episc. Ch., St. Paul, 1976-81, St. Philips Ch., N.Y.C., 1985-90; mission officer Parish of Trinity Ch., N.Y.C., 1981-85; suffragan bishop Diocese of L.A., Episc. Ch., 1990—. Pres. Community Svc. Coun. Greater Harlem, N.Y.C., 1985-90, Upper Manhattan Child Devel. Ctr., N.Y.C., 1985-90, Peter Williams Jr. Housing Corp., N.Y.C., 1988-90. Mem. Union of Black Episcopalians. Home: 3350 Raymond Ave Altadena CA 91001-4431 Office: Episc Diocese LA PO Box 2164 1220 W 4th St Los Angeles CA 90051*

TALUCCI, SAMUEL JAMES, retired chemical company executive; b. Newark, Del., Feb. 13, 1929; s. Anthony and Josephine (Valocchi) T.; m. Charlotte Sisofo, Sept. 22, 1951 (dec. Oct. 1985); children: Samuel J., Charlene, Anthony, Catherine, Christina, Louisa; m. Louise Coulter, Oct. 1987. BS, U. Del., 1951. Resident mgr. Italian Subs. Rohm & Haas Co., Milan, 1956-58; gen. mgr. Italian Subs. Rohm & Haas Co., 1958-66; mng. dir. Brit. Subs. Rohm & Haas Co., London, 1966-68; dir. European ops. Rohm & Haas Co., Phila., 1968; asst. gen. mgr. Internat. div. Rohm & Haas Co., 1971, v.p. gen. mgr. Plastics div., 1974, v.p. corporate bus., group dir. agrl. and indsl. chems. Plastics div., 1975-83, regional dir. N.Am. region, 1983-89, ret., 1989. Bd. dirs. Rosemont Coll. Mem. Nat. Agrl. Chems. Assn. (bd. dirs.), Pa. Chamber Bus. & Industry (bd dirs.), Middle States Assn. Colls. and Secondary Schs. (mem. commn. on secondary schs.). Address: 140 Golf House Rd Haverford PA 19041-1060

TALVI, ILKKA ILARI, violinist; b. Kuusankoski, Finland, Oct. 22, 1948; came to U.S., 1977; s. Veikko Tuomo and Irja Margareta (Saajos) T.; m. Judith Frances Aller, Sept. 4, 1969 (div. Aug. 1982); children: Silja Joanna, Sonja Louisa; m. Marjorie Jill Kransberg, Aug. 29, 1984; children: Anna Mirjam, Sarah Lilian. Diploma in violin, Sibelius Acad., Helsinki, Finland, 1966; student Heifetz master class, U. So. Calif., 1967-68; student, Curtis Inst., Phila., 1968-69; pvt. studies, Bouillon, Odnoposoff, Paris, Vienna, 1965-67. Lectr. Sibelius Acad., Helsinki, 1969-75, Porin Musiikkiopisto, Pori, Finland, 1970-76; concertmaster Malmö (Sweden) Symphony, 1976-77; prin. Los Angeles Chamber Orch., Pasadena, Calif., 1979-85; concertmaster Seattle Symphony, 1985—, Seattle Opera, 1985—, Waterloo Festival, N.J., 1988—; guest concertmaster Seattle Symphony, 1983-85; freelance violinist, film, TV, and recording industries, Los Angeles, 1977-85. Performed as soloist and in recital in Europe, U.S., 1965—; appeared in Finland, U.S., 1972—; played Klami Violin Concerto, Albert "In Concordian," Diamond 2, violin concerto and numerous other recordings. Recipient Kuusankoski (Finland) award, 1967, numerous grants, Finland, 1965-75. Lutheran. Avocations: dogs, computers, science. Home: 3456 10th Ave W Seattle WA 98119-1413 Office: Seattle Symphony Seattle Center House 305 Harrison St Fl 4 Seattle WA 98109-4623*

TALWANI, MANIK, geophysicist, educator; b. Patiala, India, Aug. 22, 1933; came to U.S., 1954; s. Bir Sain and Saraswati (Khosla) T.; m. Anni Fittler, Apr. 3, 1958; children: Rajeev Manik, Indira, Sanjay. BSc with honors, Delhi U., India, 1951, MSc, 1953; PhD, Columbia U., 1959; PhD (hon.), Oslo U., 1981. From rsch. scientist to assoc. prof. Lamont-Doherty Geol. Obs., Columbia U., N.Y.C., 1959-70, dir. obs., 1972-81; prof. Columbia U., N.Y.C., 1970-82; dir. Ctr. for Crustal Studies Gulf R & D Co., Pitts., 1981-83; chief scientist exploration div. Gulf R & D Co., Houston, 1983-85; Schlumberger prof. geophysics Rice U., Houston, 1985—; cons. Govt. of Iceland, 1982—; dir. Geotech. Rsch. Inst., Houston Advanced Rsch. Ctr., Woodlands, 1985—; co-chmn. exec. com. Energy Rsch. Clearing House; Sackler disting. lectr. U. Tel Aviv, 1987; mem. adv. coun. Indian Oil and Gas Corp.; prin. investigator Apollo 17 first gravity measurements on moon. Co-author: Geophysical Atlas of the Norwegian Sea; editor 7 books on earth sci., Maurice Ewing Meml. Symposium; co-editor: Geophysical Atlases of Indian, Atlantic and Pacific Oceans; contbr. over 100 papers to profl. jours. Recipient Krishnan award Indian Geophys. Union, 1964, Exceptional Sci. Achievement award NASA, 1973, Guggenheim award, 1974, Alfred Wegener medal European Union Geoscis., 1993; Fulbright-Hays fellow, 1974. Fellow AAAS, Am. Geophys. Union (James B. Macelwane award 1964, Maurice Ewing award 1981), Geol. Soc. Am. (George P. Woollard award 1984); mem. Soc. Exptl. Geophysicists, Am. Assn. Petroleum Geologists, Norwegian Acad. Scis., Petroleum Club, Acad. Nat. Scis. Russian Fedn., Houston Geophys. Soc. (hon. mem. 1993), Houston Philos. Soc, Sigma Xi. Home: 1111 Hermann Dr Apt 10 D Houston TX 77004-6929 Office: Rice U PO Box 1892 Houston TX 77251-1892

TAMAN, LARRY, Canadian provincial official. Law clk. to Mr. Justice Laskin Supreme Ct. Can., 1971; tchr. law, assoc. dean Osgoode Hall Law Sch., 1971-80; with firm McMillan, Binch, Toronto, 1980-89; litigation ptnr. Tory Tory DesLauriers & Binnington, 1989-94; dep. atty. gen. Province of Ont., Toronto, 1994—; asst. atty. gen. for constl. law and policy, 1987-89. Office: Office of Dep Atty Gen Ont, 720 Bay St 11th Fl, Toronto, ON Canada M5G 2K1

TAMARELLI, ALAN WAYNE, chemical company executive; b. Wilkinsburg, Pa., Aug. 13, 1941; s. John Adam Tammarelli and Florence Eleanor (Heacock) T.; m. Carol Ann Crawford, Aug. 3, 1963; children: Robin Carol, Alan Wayne. BS, Carnegie Mellon U., 1963, MS, 1965, PhD, 1966; MBA, NYU, 1972. Engr. Exxon Corp., Linden, N.J., 1966, project leader, 1968-70; corp. planner Engelhard Minerals & Chem. Corp., Newark, 1970-71, asst. to exec. v.p., 1971-74, gen. mgr., 1974-77, v.p., 1977-79, group v.p., 1979-81; sr. v.p. Engelhard Corp., Iselin, N.J., 1981-83; chmn., chief exec. officer Dock Resins Corp, Linden, NJ, 1983—. Mem. exec. com. nat. adv. coun. for environ. policy and tech. U.S. Dept. Environment Protection, Gov's. Econ. Task Force, N.J.; mem. exec. com. Alliance for Union County. Capt. U.S. Army, 1966-68. NSF fellow, 1963-66. Mem. Synthetic Organic Chems. Mfrs. Assn. (chmn., vice chmn., bd. govs.), Am. Chem. Soc., N.Y. Paint and Coatings Assn. (chmn., pres., v.p., sec., treas., bd. dirs.), Chem. Industry Coun. (chmn., bd. dirs., exec. com.), N.J. Energy Rsch. Inst. (founding trustee), Am. Mgmt. Assn., N.Y. Acad. Scis., Scabbard and Blade, Rotary (pres., v.p., sec. Linden Club), Linden Indsl. Assn. (pres.), Sigma Xi, Tau Beta Pi, Phi Kappa Phi, Omicron Delta Kappa. Home: 49 Wexford Way Basking Ridge NJ 07920-2432 Office: Dock Resins Corp 1512 W Elizabeth Ave Linden NJ 07036-6323

TAMAREN, MICHELE CAROL, special education educator; b. Hartford, Conn., Aug. 2, 1947; d. Herman Harold and Betty (Leavitt) Liss; m. David Stephen Tamaren, June 8, 1968; 1 child, Scott. BS in Elem. Edn., U. Conn., 1969; MA in Spl. Edn., St. Joseph Coll., West Hartford, Conn., 1976. Cert. elem. and spl. edn. tchr., Conn., Mass. Tchr. N.Y. Inst. for Spl. Edn., Bronx, 1971-74; ednl. cons. Renbrook Sch., West Hartford, 1975-78; grad. instr. St. Joseph Coll., 1978; elem. tchr. Acton (Mass.) Pub. Schs., 1969-70, tchr. spl. edn., 1978-94; learning specialist and writer Educators Pub. Svc., Cambridge, Mass., 1994-96; inclusion and behavioral specialist Acton (Mass.) Pub. Schs., 1996—; ednl. cons. to schs., parents, orgns., pubs., 1980—; internat. and nat. lectr. on bldg. self-esteem in classroom, 1988—. Author: I Make a Difference!, 1992; also articles. Bd. dirs. United Way of Acton-Boxborough. Horace Mann grantee Mass. Dept. Edn., 1987, 88, Mass. Gov.'s Alliance Against Drugs, 1992. Mem. Coun. for Exceptional Children, Learning Disabilities Assn., Orton Dyslexia Soc., Nat. Ctr. Learning Disabilities, Nat. Coun. for Self-Esteem, Internat. Platform Assn., Phi Kappa Phi, Kappa Delta Pi. Avocations: travel, writing, reading, distance walking. Home: 15 Willis Holden Dr Acton MA 01720-3208

TAMARO, GEORGE JOHN, consulting engineer; b. Weehawken, N.J., Mar. 16, 1937; s. Giorgio Angelo and Giacomina (Chiesa) T.; m. Rosemary Ann Volta, June 24, 1961; children: Peter Louis, Jean Marie, Paul Anthony, Mark Joseph. B of Civil Engring., Manhattan Coll., 1959; M of Civil Engring., Lehigh U., 1961; M of Archtl. Tech., Columbia U., 1969. Profl. engr., N.Y., N.J., D.C., Md., Pa., Calif., Ill., Tex., La., Wis., Wash., R.I., Ark., Mo., Miss.; structural engr., Ill., Mass.; geotech. engr., Calif.; chartered engr., U.K.; registered European engr. Staff engr. Port Authority of N.Y. & N.J., N.Y.C., 1961-71; v.p., chief engr. ICOS Corp. Am., N.Y.C., 1971-80; ptnr. Mueser Rutledge Cons. Engrs., N.Y.C., 1980—. Patentee in field; author tech. papers. Chmn. Bergen County Planning Bd., N.J., 1978-82; vice-chair Leonia (N.J.) Planning Bd., 1971-89; mem. Bd. Adjustment, Leonia, 1974-76; councilman Borough Governing Body, Leonia, 1972. Fellow ASCE (Martin S. Kapp Found. Engr. award 1987), Instn. Civil Engrs. U.K., Instn. Structural Engrs. U.K.; mem. Nat. Acad. Engring., Internat. Soc. Soil Mechs. and Found. Engrs., Post-Tensioning Inst. (com. on rock and soil anchors), Deep Found. Inst. (slurry wall com.), The Moles (trustee), Coun. on Tall Bldgs. and Urban Habitat, Am. Inst. Steel Constrn., Chi Epsilon (hon. mem. award 1990), Tau Beta Pi. Avocations: sailing, photography.

TAMASANIS, DOUGLAS THOMAS, physicist; b. Brighton, Mass., Oct. 26, 1960; s. Thomas Paul and Beverly Claire (Greeley) T.; m. Deborah Kaye Liston, July 10, 1987; 1 child, Stephen Douglas. BS in Radiol. Health Physics, U. Lowell, 1982, MS in Radiation Physics, 1985, MS in Sys. Engring., 1986. From instr. Math. dept. to sr. rsch. fellow Rsch. Found. U. Lowell, Mass., 1981-84; scientist Porter Cons., Ardemore, Pa., 1984-85; sr. scientist, ptnr. Arcon Corp., Waltham, Mass., 1985-94; dir. sys. engring. Arcon Sys., Waltham, 1994-96; IT mgr. Video Guide, Bedford, Mass., 1996—. Sr. tech. editor Byte Mag., Peterborough, N.H., 1994-95; contbr. articles to profl. jours. Mem. IEEE (sr.), Am. Geophys. Union, Sigma Xi. Achievements include computationally efficient algorithm to calculate propagation loss of electromagnetic waves in vegetation media, statistical description and electromagnetic scattering from rough surfaces radar signal simulation programs; design and implementation of several corporate computor networks including security, remote access and Internet access, algorithm to determine airborne radionuclide concentration from high range detector response, radar signal simulation models. Office: Arcon Corp 260 Bear Hill Rd Waltham MA 02154-1018

TAMBARO, MARIE GRACE, health specialist, nursing educator; b. N.Y.C., June 28, 1946; d. Louis Vincent and Jeanette (Motto) Nunziato; m. Arthur Michael Tambaro, Sept. 20, 1964; children: Celeste, Joseph, Arthur Michael Jr., Louis Derek. BSN with honors, CUNY, 1981; postgrad., Seton Hall U., 1985. CCRN, ACLS. Critical care staff nurse Richmond Meml. Hosp., S.I., N.Y., 1980-83; nursing insgr. Brookdale C.C., Lincroft, N.J., 1983—; health specialist Holmdel (N.J.) Bd. Edn., 1990—. Apptd. to Holmdel Twp. Bd. of Health, 1989—, Holmdel Bd. of Edn. Dist. Instrnl. Coun., 1994; chair Holmdel Drug and Alcohol Commn., 1986-88; rep. to N.J. State Drug and Alcohol Commn., 1987. Mem. AAUW. Republican. Roman Catholic. Avocations: reading, gourmet cooking, fitness. Home: 15 Seven Oaks Dr Holmdel NJ 07733-1924 Office: Holmdel Twp Bd Edn 4 Crawfords Corner Rd Holmdel NJ 07733-1908

TAMBIAH, STANLEY JEYARAJAH, anthropologist; b. Sri Lanka, Jan. 16, 1929; came to U.S., 1973; s. Charles Rajakone and Eliza Chellamma (Moothathamby) T.; m. Mary Wynne Huber, Mar. 15, 1969; children: Jonathan Anand, Matthew Arjun. BA, U. Ceylon, Peradeniya, 1951; PhD, Cornell U., 1954; DLitt (hon.), Jaffna U., Sri Lanka, 1981; LHD (hon.), U. Chgo., 1991; LittD (hon.), U. Peradeniya, Sri Lanka, 1991. Lectr. U. Ceylon, 1955-60; UNESCO tech. assistance expert Thailand, 1960-63; Smuts fellow U. Cambridge (Eng.) and Commonwealth fellow St. John's Coll., U. Cambridge, 1963-64; lectr. U. Cambridge, 1964-72; fellow Clare Hall, 1965-70; fellow, tutor grad. students, dir. studies in social anthropology King's Coll., 1970-72; fellow Center for Advanced Study in Behavioral Scis., Palo Alto, Calif., 1968-69; prof. anthropology U. Chgo., 1973-76; prof., curator South Asian ethnology Peabody Museum, Harvard U., 1976—; chmn. dept. anthrop. Harvard U., 1984-87; Malinowski meml. lectr. London Sch. Econs., 1968; Radcliffe-Brown meml. lectr. Brit. Acad., 1979; Radhakrishnan meml. lectr. Oxford U., 1982; Kingsley Martin meml. lectr. Cambridge U., 1982, Lewis Henry Morgan meml. lectr., Rochester U., 1984, Am. Ethnol. Soc. disting. lectr., 1988, Daryll Forde meml. lectr. U. Coll., London, 1991, Hilldale lectr. U. Wis., 1996, Japanese Assn. Ethnology disting. lectr., 1997. Author: Buddhism and the Spirit Cults in Northeast Thailand, 1970, (with Jack Goody) Bridewealth and Dowry, 1973, World Conqueror and World Renouncer, A Study of Religion and Polity in Thailand against a Historical Background, 1976, The Buddhist Saints of the Forest and the Cult of Amulets, 1984, Culture, Thought and Social Action, 1986, Sri Lanka: Ethnic Fratricide and the Dismantling of Democracy, 1986, Magic, Science, Religion, and the Scope of Rationality, 1990, Buddhism Betrayed? Religion, Politics and Violence in Sri Lanka, 1992, Leveling Crowds: Ethnonationalist Conflicts and Collective Violence in South Asia, 1996. Social Sci. Rsch. Coun. Gt. Britain grantee, 1971; NSF grantee, 1978; Guggenheim fellow, 1982; vis. scholar Phi Beta Kappa, 1990-91; vis. scholar in residence Dumbarton Oaks, Washington, 1995. Fellow Am. Acad. Arts and Scis., Royal Anthrop. Inst. (Curl Bequest prize 1964, Rivers Meml. medal 1973), Am. Anthrop. Assn.; mem. Assn. Asian Studies (pres. 1989-90, presdl. address 1990), Nat. Acad. of Scis. of U.S. Office: Harvard U Dept Anthropology Cambridge MA 02138

TAMBORLANE, WILLIAM V., JR., physician, biomedical researcher, pediatrics educator; b. N.Y.C., Aug. 25, 1946; s. William and Eleanor (Bernabo) T.; m. Kathleen Mary Blinn, Dec. 27, 1969; children: Melissa, Amy, James. BS, Georgetown U., 1968, MD, 1972. Diplomate Am. Bd. Pediatrics, Am. Bd. Pediatric Endocrinology. Attending physician Yale New Haven Hosp., 1977—; asst. prof. pediatrics Yale U., New Haven, 1977-81, dir. Children's Diabetes Ctr., 1977—; assoc. prof. pediatrics Sch. Medicine, New Haven, 1981-86; acting chief Pediatric Endocrinology, New Haven, 1982-83; chief pediatric endocrinology and diabetes Yale Sch. Medicine, 1985—, prof. prdiatrics, 1986—; program dir. Yale Children's Clin. Rsch. Ctr., N.H., Conn., 1986—; chmn. Lawson Wilkens Diabetes Com., 1988-89. Editor: Yale Guide to Children's Nutrition, 1997. Recipient Jonathan May award, Charles Best award Am. Diabetes Assn., 1979, Clin. Investigator award NIH, 1979-82. Mem. Am. Fedn. Clin. Rsch., Am. Soc. Clin. Investigation, Endocrine Soc., Soc. Pediatric Rsch., Phi Beta Kappa. Office: Yale U Sch Med Children's Clin Rsch Ctr 333 Cedar St New Haven CT 06510-3206

TAMBS, LEWIS ARTHUR, diplomat, historian, educator; b. San Diego, July 7, 1927; s. Fred B. and Marguerite Johanna (Tambs) Jones; m. Phyllis Ann Greer, 1982; children: Kari, Kristin, Jennifer, Heidi, Greer, Michael, Alexa. B.S., U. Calif.-Berkeley, Berkeley, 1953; M.A., U. Calif.-Santa Barbara, 1962, Ph.D., 1967. Plant engr. Standard Brands, San Francisco, 1953-54; pipeline engr. Creole Petroleum Co., Caracas, Maracaibo, Venezuela, 1954-57; gen. mgr. Cacyp, Maracaibo, 1957-59; instr. Creighton U., 1965-67, asst. prof., 1967-69; prof. history Ariz. State U., Tempe, 1969-82, 87—, dir. Center Latin Am. Studies, 1972-76; cons. Nat. Security Council, 1982-83; U.S. ambassador to Colombia, 1983-85, U.S. ambassador to Costa Rica, 1985-87. Author: East European and Soviet Economic Affairs, 1975, Historiography, Method and History Teaching, 1975, (with others) Hitler's Spanish Legion, 1979; editor: United States Policy Toward Latin America, 1976, Inter-American Policy for the 80's; co-author periodical guides; contbr. articles to profl. jours. Bd. dirs. Ariz.-Mex. Commn., 1974-82, Coun. Inter-Am. Security, 1979-90. With U.S. Army, 1945-47, 50-51. Faculty grantee Ariz. State U., 1970, 71, 74, 78, 79. Roman Catholic. Office: Ariz State U Dept History Tempe AZ 85287-2501

TAMBURRO, GIOVANNA M., artist; b. Corona, N.Y., Nov. 6; d. Carlo and Grace (Emanuela) Parente; m. americo M. Tamburro; children: Luana, Robert, Lisa. Assoc. in Fine Arts, Nassau C.C., 1977; postgrad., N.Y. Tech. Inst., 1982-83. Chiropractic asst. Office of Dr. Robert Tamburro, Hicksville, N.Y., 1985—; art tchr. to deaf children, Westbury and Hicksville, N.Y., 1974; health and wellbeing contbr. low fat diet Nassau County Med. Ctr., N.Y. State Coll. Human Ecology, Cornell U., Ithaca, N.Y. Exhibited in shows at Firehouse Gallery, 1973 (1st prize in graphics), Stix-Port Washington Libr., Stix-L.I. Black Artist Assn., 1977, N.Y. Tech. Inst., 1982-83, Huntington Art League (award 1990), East Islip Art League, 1990 (award), Jean Paris/Blossom Show (award), Graphic Eye Gallery, Port Washington, 1992, L.I. Librs., Lynn Kottler Galleries; contbr. poems to Nat. Libr. Poetry, The Poet Band Co. Va., Kent Publs., Nat. Soc. Poets. Recipient award Internat. Soc. Poets, 1994. Mem. Trustees of Nat. Mus. of Women in ARts (assoc.).

TAMBURRO, PETER JAMES, JR., social studies secondary school educator; b. Hoboken, N.J., Jan. 20, 1947; s. Peter James and Rose Catherine (Verta) T.; m. Andrea Everitt Huber, Aug. 21, 1976; children: Peter James III, Christopher Harding, Matthew Everitt. BA in Polit. Sci, Dickinson Coll., 1969; MAT in Social Studies, Trenton State Coll., 1973. Cert. secondary sch. tchr., social studies, N.J. Tchr. Morris Sch. Dist., Morristown, N.J., 1973-76, Hanover Park Regional High Sch. Dist., East Hanover, 1976—; cross country, volleyball coach Hanover Park H.S., East Hanover, 1990—; judge Bicentennial Com., N.J.; asst. basketball coach Caldwell (N.J.) Coll., 1989-93; cons. Hist. Commn., East Hanover, N.J., 1989-92; cons. for developing AP history programs; asst. basketball coach Hanover Park H.S., 1994-97; mem. hist. comm. Washington Twp., 1994—; curriculum adv. com. Washinton Twp., 1996-97. Author: Gateway to Morris, 1993; editor: (with Dale Brandreth) The Chess Diary of Rudolph Spielmann, 1995; editor Atlantic Chess News, 1973-76; contbr. articles to chess mags.; nationally syndicated columnist for U.S. Chess Fedn., 1994-95 (National Chmn., Historical Committee, U.S. Chess Fedn. 1994-97), Chess Journalists of Am. (v.p. 1996-97). Rep. County Committeeman, Hanover Twp., N.J., 1984-88; legis. aide to Assemblyman Robert Martin, Trenton, N.J., 1985-89; mem. Hist. Commn., Washington Twp., N.J., 1994-96; scoutmaster Boy Scouts Am., 1994-97. With U.S. Army, 1969-71. Recipient Taft fellowship Taft Inst. on Two Party Govt., Fairleigh Dickinson U., 1984, Woodrow Wilson fellowship Woodrow Wilson Found., 1991, National fellowship Coun. for Basic Edn., Washington, 1993, Chess Journalists of Am. award, 1995, 96; named N.J.'s Outstanding Tchr. of History, DAR, 1990 ; grantee NSF, 1978, Dodge Found., Madison, N.J., 1987. Mem. Nat. Coun. for Social Studies, Morris County Hist. Soc., Hanover Park Regional Ednl. Assn. (v.p. 1994-95, pres. 1995—), N.J. Edn. Assn. Avocations: rare books, chess. Home: 3 Powder Mill Rd Long Valley NJ 07853-3034 Office: Hanover Park High Sch 63 Mount Pleasant Ave East Hanover NJ 07936-2601

TAMEN, HARRIET, lawyer; b. Yonkers, N.Y., May 17, 1947; d. Saul and Lily (Balglau) T. A.B., Bryn Mawr Coll., 1969; J.D., George Washington U., Washington, 1973. Bar: N.Y. 1974, U.S. Dist. Ct. (so. dist.) N.Y. 1975. Atty., W.T. Grant, N.Y.C., 1974-76; atty. City of N.Y. Office Econ. Devel., Div. Real Property, N.Y.C., 1977-81; atty. Credit Lyonnais Bank, N.Y.C., 1981-86, Chase Manhattan Bank, 1986-89; v.p., counsel internat. corp. fin. Citibank, 1989-92, partner, Claugus Tamen & Orenstein, 1992-93; pvt. practice, N.Y.C., 1994—. Bd. dirs. Dromenon Theatre, N.Y., 1980-86, Nat. Dance Inst., N.Y., 1982, chmn. bd. dirs., 1984-87; chmn. bd. dirs. Theatre & Dance Alliance, 1989-90; del. exch. program Women in Law, South Am., 1987—; mem. campaign staff Ed Koch for Mayor, N.Y.C., 1977, steering com. Soviet Am. Banking Law Working Group, 1991—; guest lectr. Moscow Conf. on Banking, 1992, Ulaan Baatar, Mongolia, 1993-94, 96, Harriman Inst. of Columbia U., 1994; co-chair N.Y. Lawyers Com. for Clinton-Gore. Mem. ABA, Assn. Bar City N.Y.

TAMIN, AZAIBI, molecular virologist, researcher; b. Muar, Johor, Malaysia, Mar. 9, 1959; came to U.S., 1984; s. Hj Tamin Sahandan and Kamisah Hassan; m. Zabedah Ismail, Sept. 1, 1984; children: Adam Zulfaqar Azaibi, Afiq Zulfaiz Azaibi. BS in Microbiology with honors, U. Leeds, Eng., 1983; PhD in Microbiology, Oregon State U., 1989. Tutor in microbiology Nat. U. Malaysia, 1983-84; teaching asst. Oreg. State U., Corvallis, 1985-86; rsch. asst. Oregon State U., Corvallis, 1986-88; rsch. fellow U.S. NRC & Ctrs. for Disease Control & Prevention, Atlanta, 1989-91; rsch. scientist Ctrs for Disease Control & Prevention measles sect., Atlanta, 1991—; pres. A2Z Cons. Contbr. articles to profl. jours. Capt. Outward Bound Sch., Malaysia (Merit award), 1978; boy-sgt. Royal Military Coll., Malaysia, 1978; pres. Malaysian Student Union, U. Leeds, Eng., 1983. Recipient scholarship Ministry of Edn., Malaysia, 1978-83, scholarship Dept. Pub. Svc., 1984-89, N.L. Tartar fellowship, 1989, postdoctoral fellowship U.S. NRC, CDC, 1989-91. Mem. AAAS, Am. Soc. Virology, Am. Soc. Microbiology, N.Y. Acad. Scis. Islamic. Achievements include first to report a mutation in the cis-acting element in a gene responsible for both temperature sensitivity and drug resistant phenotypes; first to report an optimal in vitro neutralization activity of wildtype measles virus in the presence of both anti-fusion protein and anti-hemagglutinin protein antibodies; research in molecular pathobiology and evolution studies of continental U.S. orthopuxviruses; research in poxvirus and baculovirus expression system, immune response and antigenic studies of measles virus and molecular biology of equine morbillivirus. Office: Ctrs Disease Control & Prevention Measles Sect MS C22 Atlanta GA 30333

TAMIR, THEODOR, electrophysics researcher, educator; b. Bucharest, Roumania, Sept. 17, 1927; came to U.S., 1958, naturalized, 1968; s. Martin and Helena (Hart) Berman; m. Hadassah Cohen, Oct. 5, 1949; children: Jonathan, Yael. B.S. Technion, Israel Inst. Tech., 1953, Dipl. Ingenieur, 1954, M.S., 1958; Ph.D., Poly. Inst. Bklyn., 1962. Instr. Technion Israel Inst. Tech., Haifa, 1956-58; mem. rsch. staff Poly. Inst., Bklyn., 1958-62; mem. faculty Poly. Univ., Bklyn., N.Y., 1962—; prof. electrophysics Poly. Inst. N.Y., 1969-92, Univ. prof., 1992—, head dept. elec. engring., 1974-79; sci. and engring. cons. to indsl. and govtl. labs. Editor, author: Integrated Optics, 1975 (transl. into Russian and Chinese), Guided Wave Optoelectronics, 1988 (transl. into Russian); co-editor: Springer Series in Optical Sciences, 1979—; contbr. chpts. to books, articles to profl. jours. Served with Israeli Army, 1947-49. Awarded Instn. Premium, 1964, Electronics Premium, 1967, Instn. Elec. Engrs., London; citation for disting. research Polytechnic chpt. Sigma Xi, 1978. Fellow IEEE, Instn. Elec. Engrs. (London), Optical Soc. Am.; mem. Internat. Union Radio Sci., Sigma Xi. Home: 981 E Lawn Dr Teaneck NJ 07666-6604

TAMKIN, S. JEROME, business executive, consultant; b. L.A., Apr. 19, 1926; s. William W. and Thelma (Brandel) T.; m. Judith Deborah, Mar. 23, 1963; children: Windy Lynn, Gary William, Sherry Dawn. B.S., U. So. Calif., 1950; M.A., Fremont Coll., 1951, Ph.D., 1952; LL.D., St. Andrews U., London, 1954. Mem. rsch. staff chemistry dept. U. Calif. at Los Angeles, 1943; rsch. chemist, analyst supr. synthetic rubber div. U.S. Rubber Co., 1943-44; pres., gen. mgr. Majicolor, Inc., Los Angeles, 1947-49; rsch. engr. Coll. Engring., U. So. Calif., 1946-48; gen. mgr. Pan Pacific Oil Co., Long Beach, Calif., 1948-55; plant mgr. indsl. sales and mfg., 1953-55; v.p., sales mgr. Wilco Co., Los Angeles, 1948-55; v.p. charge indsl. sales and mfg.

Wilco Co., 1953-55; v.p., sales mgr. Unit Chem. Corp., Los Angeles, 1955-56; pres. Phillips Mfg. Co. (merger Instl. Food Equipment Corp.), Los Angeles, 1957-62, Waste King Corp. (subs. Instl. Food Equipment Corp.), 1962-67; also dir.; v.p., dir. Dyna Mfg. Co., Los Angeles, 1962-68; pres., dir. Profl. Rsch. Inc., Los Angeles, 1965-73; exec. v.p. Am. Med. Internat., Inc., Beverly Hills, Calif., 1966-71; dir. Am. Med. Internat., Inc., 1966-89; sec., dir. Rodger Young, Inc., L.A., 1971-77; pres., chmn. bd. TGT Petroleum Corp., Wichita, 1972—; pres., dir. Tamkin Cons. Corp., 1978—; owner, operator Tamkin Securities Co., 1979-86; vice chair bd., dir. Integrated Voice Solutions Inc., Chattanooga, 1991-96; bd. dirs. CAPP Care Inc., Newport Beach, Calif., 1991—; tech. cons. Daylin Inc., Beverly Hills, 1973-75; bd. dirs. Healthcare Decisions, Inc., Newport Beach, Calif., 1996—. Contbr. articles to profl. jours. Cmty. warden W. Adams-Baldwin Hills Cmty. CD, 1950-52; bd. govs. We. Los Angeles County coun. Boy Scouts Am.; dep. sheriff Los Angeles County, 1949; bd. dirs. Sunair Home Asthmatic Children; city commr. L.A. Bd. Environ. Quality, 1972-73; bd. dirs. Recovery Found., Fund for Higher Edn.; mem. exec. com. adv. coun. crime prevention L.A. Police, 1985—; U. Calif. at Irvine trustee Calif. Coll. Medicine, 1989-94; bd. visitors UCLA Sch. Medicine, 1990—; trustee Morehouse Sch. Medicine, 1995—, Scripps Found. for Medicine and Sci., 1996—. Served as officer USNR, 1944-46. Mem. AIM, Am. Mgmt. Assn., Inst. Aero. Scis., Am. Soc. Naval Engrs., Soc. Am. Mil. Engrs., Am. Chem. Soc., IEEE, Soc. Motion Picture and TV Engrs., Am. Inst. Chem. Engrs., Soc. Advancement Mgmt., U.S. Naval Inst., Calif. Scholarship Fedn. (life), Nat. Eagle Scout Assn., Sunrise Country Club, The Springs Country Club, Malibu Riding and Tennis Club, Alpha Eta Rho. Patentee electronic gas detector, circuits for automatic control hazardous vapors. Home: Pacific Palisades CA Office: 2100 Sawtelle Blvd Ste 201 Los Angeles CA 90025-6237

TAMMEN, JAMES F., plant pathologist, educator; b. Sacramento, Calif., Feb. 27, 1925; m. Marilyn L. McDonald, Aug. 17, 1947; children: Jeanne M. Arnold, Janice E. Menoher. Student, Sacramento Coll., 1945-46; BS in Plant Sci. with honors, U. Calif., Davis and Berkeley, 1949; PhD in Plant Pathology, U. Calif., Berkeley, 1954. Jr. plant pathologist Calif. Bureau Plant Pathology, Riverside, Calif., 1949-50; jr. plant pathologist dept. plant pathology U. Calif., Berkeley, 1953-54; plant pathologist, chief plant pathology lab. State Plant Bd. Fla., Gainesville, 1954-56; asst. prof. dept. botany and plant pathology Pa. State U., University Park, 1956-61, assoc. prof. dept. botany and plant pathology, 1961-65, prof. dept. plant pathology, 1965-76, acting head dept. plant pathology, 1963-65; head dept. plant pathology Pa. State U., University Pk., 1965-76, rsch. scientist advance hort. systems, adj. prof. dept. plant pathology, 1989—; prof., dean coll. agriculture, dir. internat. programs in agriculture Inst. Agr., Forestry and Home Econs. U. Minn., Mpls., 1976-81; pres. Oglevee Assocs. Inc., 1981-86; rsch. scientist, dir. tech. transfer. Inst. Food and Agrl. Sci. U. Fla., Gainesville and Alachua, 1986-89; mem. univ. senate Pa. State U., 1959-62, 66-71, coll. agriculture rep. univ. senate coun., 1968-71, univ. senate com., 1968-71, grad. sch. policy com., 1967-70, chmn. grad. sch. governance com., 1969-71, pres. task force on univ. governance, 1970-71, chmn. grad. sch. com. on teaching and researching traineeships, 1972-73, chmn. univ. hearing bd., 1973-74, pres.'s com. for selection univ. provost, 1975-76, chmn. com. for major in plant protection coll. agriculture, 1972-74, chmn. selections com. for dept. head. coll. agriculture, 1974; mem. univ. com. for assessment undergrad. and grad. instrn. costs U. Minn., 1977-81, univ. com. for devel. budget alternatives, 1978-79, search and screening com., acad. v.p., 1979, univ. task force for exch. program with People's Rep. China, 1979-81, univ. task force for exch. program with Cuba, 1978-81, univ. bd. for internat. food. and agrl. devel, 1978-81; mem. agrl. futures fund. Inst. Agriculture, Forestry and Home Econs., 1979-81; chmn. pro tempore Intersociety Consortium for Plant Protection, 1975, chmn., 1976; mem. task force U.S. Nat. Programs Rsch. for Agriculture, 1968; mem. NRC divsn. biology and agriculture agriculture bd. com. on genetic vulnerabability major crops NAS, 1971-72; mem. com. to evaluate acad. progress Cornell U., 1970, U. N.H., 1971, Oreg. State U., 1975, U. Fla., 1975, 86, USDA, ARS, 1982, Pa. State U., 1984; mem. policy, organizing and program coms., chmn., hon. v.p. 11th Internat. Congress Plant Protection, 1975-79; organizer, chmn. symposium profl. concepts, chmn. resolution com. 3rd Internat. Congress Plant Pathology, Munich, 1978; mem. Minn. Coun. for Coord. Edn. in Agriculture, 1976-78, recorder, 1978-79, vice-chmn., 1979-80, chmn., 1980-81; mem. Am. Florists's Endowment/USDA New Crops com. Soc. Am. Florists, 1985-86; cons., invited lectr. and speaker in field. Mem. editorial bd. Annual Revs. Phytopathology, 1976-77; contbr. 5 chpts. to books., 39 articles to profl. jours. With U.S. Army Corps, 1943-45, ETO. Recipient Rsch. award Am. Carnation Soc., Distinction award Internat. Geranium Conf. Award of Distinction, Am. Phytopathological Soc., 1993. Fellow Am. Phytopath. Soc. (chmn. com. for epidemiology and meteorology 1968-70, sustaining assoc. com. 1969-70, N.E. divsn. councillor 1968-70, councillor and sr. councillor-at-large 1970-72, v.p. 1972-73, pres.-elect 1973-74, pres. 1974-75, chmn. program com. 1973-74, com. for long-range planning 1975-77, organizer com. for pub. responsibilities 1975-76, chmn. 1976-79, organizer past pres. com. 1975-76, spl. com. plant dr. degree 1983-86, editl. bd., assoc. editor Plant Disease 1982-86, spl. com. endowment fund 1985-86, chmn. bd. dirs. endowment fund 1986-93, Disting. Svc. award 1993), Am. Soc. Hort. Sci., Coun. Agrl. Sci. and Tech., Phi Alpha Xi, Sigma Xi (sec. Pa. state chpt. 1968-70, v.p. 1971, pres. 1972), Gamma Sigma Delta. Achievements include patent in field. Office: Pennsylvania State U Dept Plant Pathology University Park PA 16802

TAMMEUS, WILLIAM DAVID, journalist, columnist; b. Woodstock, Ill., Jan. 18, 1945; s. W. H. and Bertha H. (Helander) T.; m. Marcia Bibens, Nov. 29, 1996; children: Lisen, Kate; stepchildren: Christopher L. Johnston, Daniel Bednarczyk, Kathryn Bednarczyk, David Bednarczyk. BJ, U. Mo., Columbia, 1967; postgrad., U. Rochester, 1967-69. Reporter Rochester (N.Y.) Times-Union, 1967-70; reporter Kansas City (Mo.) Star, 1970-77, Starbeams columnist, 1977—; syndicated columnist N.Y. Times News Svc., 1989—. Editor-at-large Presbyn. Outlook, 1993; contbg. editor Mo. Life mag., 1980-81; commentator Sta. KCPT-TV, 1979-90. Co-recipient Pulitzer prize for gen. local reporting of Hyatt Regency Hotel disaster, 1982, recipient 1st pl. opinion-editl. divsn. Heart of Am. award Kansas City Press Club, 1991, 1st pl. opinion-analysis divsn. Heart of Am. award Kansas City Press Club, 1993, 1st pl. column divsn., 1994. Mem. Nat. Soc. Newspaper Columnists (v.p. 1990-92, pres. 1992-94, 1st pl. items divsn. Writing award 1992), Soc. Profl. Journalists. Presbyterian. Office: 1729 Grand Blvd Kansas City MO 64108-1413

TAMMINGA, CAROL ANN, neuroscientist; b. Grand Rapids, Mich., Jan. 26, 1946; d. Samuel William and Freda (Hekman) T.; children: Cristan Fredericka, Bonnie Michael. BS, Calvin Coll., 1966; student, U. Tubingen, Fed. Republic of Germany, 1966-67; MD, Vanderbilt U., 1971. Lic. physician, Ill., Md. Vivian Allen fellow Vanderbilt Med. Sch., 1968-71; intern in medicine Blodgett Meml. Hosp., Grand Rapids, Mich., 1971-72; resident in psychiatry U. Chgo., 1972-74, chief resident in psychiatry, 1974-75, instr. dept. psychiatry, 1975-77, asst. prof. psychiatry, 1978-79; assoc. prof. psychiatry U. Md., Balt., 1979-85, chief inpatient rsch. program, 1979—, prof. psychiatry, 1985—; chief clin. investigator Manteno (Ill.) State Hosp., 1975-79; chief clin. biochemsitry unit Nat. Inst. Neurologic & Communicative Diseases & Stroke NIH, Bethesda, Md., 1979-85; mem. treatment devel. and assessment rsch. rev. com. NIMH, 1981-85, 90-94, 96—; mem. FDA Psychopharm Adv. Com., 1990-92, 97, chair, 1991-92; cons. in field. Author: Schizophrenia: Scientific Progress, 1988, Schizophrenia Research, 1989; editorial bd. Am. Jour. Psychiatry, Biol. Psychiatry, Jour. Nervous and Mental Diseases, Schizophrenia Bull., Schizophrenia Rsch., Functional Neurology, Progress in Neuroendocrinimmunology, Progress in Neuro-Psychopharmacology and Biol. Psychiatry; contbr. articles to Archive Gen. Psychiatry Sci., Am. Jour. Psychiatry, Jour. Neural Transmission, Lancet, Physiol. Behavior, and other. Recipient McAlpin award Nat. Assn. Mental Health, 1979, Dean award, 1995; Beauchamp scholar, 1971; Found. for Rsch. in Psychiatry fellow, 1975-76, NIMH fellow, 1978-79. Mem. AAAS, Am. Psychiatric Assn., Am. Coll. Neuropharmacology, Internat. Psychoneuroendocrine Soc., Soc. Neurosci., Biol. Psychiatry. Achievements include research in schizophrenia. Office: U Md PO Box 21247 Baltimore MD 21228-0747

TAMORI, DAVID ISAMU, secondary education educator; b. Oakland, Calif., Sept. 20, 1949; s. Shoji Masaharu and Shizu (Akiyama) T.; m. Carolee Jean Zoff, Feb. 14; children: Tina Maria Tamori Riggs, Leanna Gean, Mesha Lynn. AA, Diablo Valley Coll., 1969; BA, Chico State Coll., 1970, secondary teaching credential, 1971. Art tchr., chmn. dept. visual and performing arts Oroville (Calif.) High Sch., 1973—, head coach wrestling, 1973—; staff mem. Calif. Art Project, Calif. State U., Humboldt, Walker Creek and Chico, 1989—; art panelist Calif. Commn. Tchr. Credentialling, Sacramento, 1990-92; art panelist Ednl. Testing Svc., Princeton, N.J., 1990—; mem. Nat. Bd. for Profl. Teaching Stds./Far West Lab. for Ednl. R&D Art Assessment, 1994—; mem. bias rev. commn. Nat. Evaluation Sys., Inc., 1994—. Devel. team mgr. Sensei Concord/Oroville Judo Club, 1973—, yodan 4 degree black belt. Mem. Calif. Arts Edn. Assn. (North Area pres., Secondary Art Educator of Yr. 1992-93), Calif. Tchrs. Assn., Oroville Secondary Tchrs. Assn., Calif. Arts Project. Avocations: Middle-east drumming, ceramics, jewelry design, computer videographics. Home: 111 Putnam Dr Oroville CA 95966-9457

TAMRES, MILTON, chemistry educator; b. Warsaw, Poland, Mar. 12, 1922; s. Morris and Lillian (Solberg) T.; m. Francoise Raymonde Lucot, Aug. 16, 1960; children—Louise R., Marc P. B.A. in Sci., Bklyn. Coll., 1943; Ph.D., Northwestern U., 1949. Control chemist Celanese Corp., Cumberland, Md., 1943-44; research and teaching fellow Northwestern U., Evanston, Ill., 1944-48; instr. chemistry U. Ill., Champaign-Urbana, 1948-51, asst. prof., 1951-53; asst. prof. chemistry U. Mich., Ann Arbor, 1953-57, assoc. prof., 1957-63, prof., 1963-87, prof. emeritus, 1987—; vis. scholar U. Tokyo, 1974. Contbr. articles to profl. jours. Guggenheim fellow, 1959-60; Am. Chem. Soc.-Petroleum Research Fund Internat. fellow, 1966-67. Fellow AAAS, Am. Inst. Chemists; mem. Am. Chem. Soc., Sigma Xi, Phi Lambda Upsilon (past nat. pres.), Alpha Chi Sigma. Home: 1307 Brooks St Ann Arbor MI 48103-3171 Office: Univ Mich 3533 Chemistry Ann Arbor MI 48109

TAMURA, CARY KAORU, fundraiser; b. Honolulu, Jan. 9, 1944; s. Akira and Harue (Otake) T.; m. Denise Jeanne Mitts, Oct. 17, 1987; children from previous marriage: Jennifer Joy, Matthew D. Student, U. Hawaii, 1961-63; BA in Philosophy, Nyack Coll., 1966; MA in Theology, Fuller Sem., 1986. Cert. fund-raising exec. Dir. svc. tng. ops. Fin. Adv. Clinic of Hawaii, Honolulu, 1972-76; dir. planned giving The Salvation Army, Honolulu, 1976-78; planned giving cons. InterVarsity Christian Fellowship, Portland, Oreg., 1978-80; account exec. Am. Income Life, Portland, Oreg., 1980-81; dir. planned giving The Salvation Army, Portland, Oreg., 1981-84, L.A., 1984-85; dir. devel., planned giving U. So. Calif., 1985-90; dir. gift planning UniHealth America, Burbank, Calif., 1990-94; pvt. gift planning cons. Brea, Calif., 1995—; bd. dirs. Nat. Com. on Planned Giving, Indpls., 1991-93, sec. exec. com., 1993; mem. adv. com., adj. faculty UCLA Extension; lectr. in field. Bd. dirs. Japanese Evang. Missionary Soc., 1990-95, v.p., 1993; bd. deacons Evang. Free Ch., 1992-95. With U.S. Army, 1969-72. Mem. Planned Giving Round Table So. Calif. (pres. 1989-91, Pres.'s award 1992), Nat. Soc. Fund Raising Execs., (bd. dirs. Greater L.A. chpt. 1990—, v.p. 1993, 95, chmn. Fund Raising Day 1994, treas. 1996-97, Profl. Fund Raiser of Yr. award 1995), So. Calif. Assn. Hosp. Developers, Asian Pacific Legal Soc. (exec. adv. bd. 1995—). Republican. Avocations: photography, golf, travel. Home and Office: 1413 Robert Ct Brea CA 92821-2165

TAN, AMY RUTH, writer; b. Oakland, Calif., Feb. 19, 1952; d. John Yueh-han and Daisy Ching (Tu) T.; m. Louis M. DeMattei, Apr. 6, 1974. BA in Linguistics and English, San Jose (Calif.) State U., 1973, MA in Linguistics, 1974; LHD (hon.), Dominican Coll. San Rafael, 1991. Specialist lang. devel. Alameda County Assn. for Mentally Retarded, Oakland, 1976-80; project dir. M.O.R.E. Project, San Francisco, 1980-81; free-lance writer, 1981-88. Author: The Joy Luck Club, 1989 (Nat. Book Critics Circle award for best novel nomination 1989, L.A. Times Book award nomination 1989, Gold award for fiction Commonwealth Club 1990, Bay Area Book Reviewers award for best fiction 1990), The Kitchen God's Wife, 1991, The Moon Lady, 1992, The Chinese Siamese Cat, 1994, The Hundred Secret Senses, 1995; also numerous short stories and essays; screenwriter, prodr.: (film) The Joy Luck Club, 1993. Recipient Best Am. Essays award, 1991. *

TAN, BOEN HIE, analytical biochemist, biomedical scientist; b. Padangan, Java, Indonesia, Dec. 14, 1926; s. King Hoo and Bwan Nio (Oei) T. BS, U. Leyden, Holland, 1952, MS, 1955, ScD, 1962. Profl. nuclear medicine specialist. Fellow, asst. prof. U. Leyden, Holland, 1953-55, 62-64; fellow, rsch. assoc. Max Planck Inst., Gottingen, Germany, 1961-62, U. Minn., Mpls., 1955-61, 64-68, 1972-73; rsch. assoc. N.Y. Hosp., Cornell Med. Ctr., N.Y.C., 1968-72; rsch. assoc., prof. U. Groningen, Maastricht, Holland, 1973-81; rsch. assoc. U. South Ala., Mobile, 1982-92; analytical biochemist Ala. Dept. Environ. Mgmt., Montgomery, 1992—. Contbr. over 55 articles to profl. jours. Treas. "Aesculapius" Leyden U. Pharm. Student Assn., 1952-53. Mem. Nederlandse Vereniging voor Nucleaire Geneeskunde, Am. Assn. for Clin. Chemistry, FASEB, AAAS, Am. Chem. Soc. Achievements include research on sulfhydryl, disulfide groups in denatured, renatured proteins; purification, analysis, pharmacokinetic, pharmacological activities of new drugs; alpha-1-antitrypsin, plasma proteins, enzymes, inhibitors, fibrin formation lysis; vanadate-sulfhydryl complexes and PDE activities, DNA damage and repair; diabetes and the heart. Home: PO Box 230451 Montgomery AL 36123-0451 Office: Ala Dept Environ Mgmt 1890 Dickinson Dr # A Montgomery AL 36109

TAN, COLLEEN WOO, communications educator; b. San Francisco, May 6, 1923; d. Mr. and Mrs. S.H. Nq Quinn; m. Lawrence K.J. Tan; children: Lawrence L., Lance C. BA in English/Am. Lit., Ind. U., 1950, MA in English, 1952; MA in Speech Arts, Whittier Coll., 1972; postgrad., U. Calif. Berkeley, 1952-53. Cert. secondary edn. tchr., K-12, community coll., Calif. Tchng. aide English U. Calif., Berkeley, 1952-53; tchr. English and Social Studies Whittier (Calif.) High Sch., 1957-60; prof. speech comms. Mt. San Antonio Coll., Walnut, Calif., 1960-94; dir. forensics, 1969-80; sen. acad. senate Mt. San Antonio Coll., Walnut, Calif., 1982-90, faculty rep., 1990—; mem. numerous collegiate coms., campus advisor to Chinese Club and Asian Students Assn. Recipient Woman of Achievement Edn. award San Gabriel Valley, Calif. YWCA, 1995; named Outstanding Prof. Emeritus, Mt. San Antonio Coll. Found., 1994. Mem. AAUW (pres. Whittier Br. 1982, cultural interests chair Calif. state divsn. 1985-87, Fellowship award 1973-74, Las Distinguidas award 1992), Calif. Asian-Am. Faculty Assn., Delta Kappa Gamma, Phi Beta Kappa (Outstanding Educator of Am. award 1972). Roman Catholic. Avocations: creative writing, reading fiction, attending theater, music, dance. Home: 13724 Sunrise Dr Whittier CA 90602-2547 Office: Mt San Antonio 1100 N Grand Ave Walnut CA 91789-1341

TAN, ENG MENG, immunologist, biomedical scientist; b. Seremban, Malaysia, Aug. 26, 1926; came to U.S., 1950; s. Ming Kee and Chooi Eng (Ang) T.; m. Liselotte Filippi, June 30, 1962; children: Philip, Peter. B.A., Johns Hopkins U., 1952, M.D., 1956. Rsch. assoc. Rockefeller U., N.Y.C., 1962-65; asst. prof. Washington U. Sch. Medicine, St. Louis, 1965-67; assoc. mem. Scripps Rsch. Inst., LaJolla, Calif., 1967-70, mem., 1970-77, dir. Autoimmune Disease Ctr., 1982—; prof. U. Colo. Sch. Medicine, Denver, 1977-82; chmn. allergy and immunology rsch. com. NIH, Bethesda, Md., 1982-84; mem. nat. arthritis adv. bd. HHS, Washington, 1981-85. Contbr. chpts. to books, articles to profl. jours. Named to Nat. Lupus Hall Fame, 1984; recipient U.S. Sr. Scientist award Humboldt Found., Fed. Republic Germany, 1986, award Ciba-Geigy-Internat. League Against Rheumatism, 1989, Carol Nachman award Wiesbaden, Fed. Republic Germany, 1989, Paul Klemperer award and medal N.Y. Acad. Medicine, 1993, City of Medicine award, Durham, N.C., 1996. Fellow AAAS; mem. Arthri tis Found. (Lee Howley Sr. award 1989), Am. Coll. Rheumatology (pres. 1984-85, Disting. Investigator award 1991), Assn. Am. Physicians, Am. Soc. Clin. Investigation, Western Assn. Physicians (v.p. 1980-81), Am. Assn. Immunologists, Brazilian Soc. Rheumatology (hon.), Australian Rheumatism Assn. (hon.), Brit. Soc. Rheumatology (hon.). Rsch. on characterization of autoantibodies in autoimmune diseases, systemic lupus erythematosus, scleroderma, Sjogren's syndrome, myositis and mixed connective tissue disease; relationship of autoantibodies to pathogenesis. Home: 8303 Sugarman Dr La Jolla CA 92037-2224 Office: Scripps Rsch Inst 10550 N Torrey Pines Rd La Jolla CA 92037-1000

TAN, HUI QIAN, computer science and civil engineering educator; b. Tsingtao, China, June 12, 1948; s. Dumen Tan and Ruifan Rao; m. Ren Zhong, June 16, 1994; children: William W., Danny D. BA, Oberlin Coll., 1982; MS, Kent State U., 1984, PhD, 1986. Asst. prof. computer sci. and civil engrng. U. Akron, Ohio, 1986-89, assoc., 1990—; rsch. prof. Kent (Ohio) State U., 1987. Contbr. articles to profl. jours. Grantee NASA, 1987—, 91—, NSF, 1988-92. Mem. IEEE Computer Soc., Assn. for Computing Machinery, SIGSAM Assn. for Computing Machinery, Phi Beta Kappa. Avocations: classical music, history, literature, swimming, cycling.

TAN, JAMES, physician; b. Aug. 3, 1938; married. AA, U. Philippines, 1960, MD, 1965. Diplomate in internal medicine and infectious diseases Am. Bd. Internal Medicine; cert. physician, Ohio. Intern Philippine Gen. Hosp., Manila, 1964-65, resident in internal medicine, 1965-67; tng. Bangkok, 1967-68; fellow in infectious diseases U. Cin. Coll. Medicine, 1968-71; mem. staff U. Cinn. Med. Ctr., other Cin. hosps., 1971-74, Akron (Ohio) Gen. Med. Ctr., 1975—; active staff Summa Health System, 1975—; prof. medicine Northeastern Ohio Univs. Coll. Medicine, Rootstown, 1979—, vice chmn. dept. internal medicine, 1993—, chmn. infectious disease sect., 1977—. Contbr. articles to profl. jours.; reviewer for jours. Fellow ACP (gov. Ohio chpt. 1995—), Am. Coll. Chest Physicians, Infectious Disease Soc. Am. (Ohio sec. 1994—); mem. Am. Soc. for Microbiology, Am. Soc. Internal Medicine, Ohio State Med. Soc., Soc. for Hosp. Epidemiologists, Assn. Program Dirs. in Internal Medicine, Alpha Omega Alpha. Office: Akron City Hosp 525 E Market St Akron OH 44304-1619

TAN, LI-SU LIN, accountant, insurance executive; b. Keelung, Taiwan, Republic of China, Mar. 7, 1956; came to U.S. 1985; d. I-Chang and Sung-Mei (Chen) Lin; m. Bert T. Tan, Aug. 19, 1985; children: Patricia Tan, Peter Puwen Tan, Lotus Tan. BBA, Nat. Taiwan U., 1978; MBA, Ill. Inst. Tech., 1991. CPA, Ill., Taiwan; lic. ins. agt., Ill. Asst. mgr. Arthur Anderson, Taipei, 1978-85; practitioner Li-Su Lin, CPA, Taipei, 1981-85, Li-Su Lin Tan, CPA, Naperville, Ill., 1988-90; pres. Lisu L. Tan & Co., Ltd., CPAs, Naperville, Ill., 1990—; agt. Mut. of Omaha Co., Lombard, Ill., 1991-94, Met. Life and Affiliated Cos., Bloomingdale, Ill., 1993—. Chair family Naperville Chinese Assn., 1990. Mem. AICPA (tax divsn., quality control program), Ill. Soc. CPAs, Taipei First Girls High Alumni Assn. (treas. 1990-94), Greater Chgo. Area Taiwanese Am. C. of C. (bd. dirs. 1995—). Buddhist. Avocations: travel, art collecting, photography. Office: Lisu L Tan & Co Ltd CPAs 620 Bakewell Ln Naperville IL 60565-1641

TAN, SENG C., research scientist, materials research executive; b. Kluang, Johore, Malaysia, June 4, 1955; came to U.S., 1980; s. Kim L. and Chen (Lee) T.; m. Ming Yung Chen, Aug. 3, 1985; children: Anthony Wenwei, Max Bowen, James Seemin. BS in Mech. Engring., Nat. Taiwan U., 1978; PhD, U. Utah, 1983. Teaching asst. Nat. Taiwan U., Taipei, 1978-79; rsch. asst. U. Utah, Salt Lake City, 1980-83; rsch. assoc. NRC, Washington, 1984-86; sr. rsch. scientist AdTech Sys. Rsch. Inc., Dayton, Ohio, 1986-90; rsch. fellow, rsch. assoc. prof. Northwestern U., Evanston, Ill., 1991-92; pres., CEO Wright Materials Rsch. Co., Beavercreek, Ohio, 1990—. Author: Stress Concentration in Laminated Composites, 1994; contbr. more than 40 articles to profl. jours. Recipient fellowships, contracts, and grants. Mem. ASTM, ASME, Am. Soc. for Composites (founder-mem.), SAMPE, Soc. Mfg. Engrs. Avocations: jogging, ballroom dancing, music, badminton. Home and Office: 3591 Apple Grove Dr Beavercreek OH 45430-1480 also: Lab 1948 Woodman Center Dr Dayton OH 45420-1165

TAN, TJIAUW-LING, psychiatrist, educator; b. Pemalang, Java, Indonesia, June 2, 1935; came to U.S., 1967; naturalized, 1972; s. Ping-Hoey and Liep-Nio (Liem) T.; m. Esther Joyce Kho, June 2, 1961; children: Paul Budiman, Robert Yuling, Alice Ayling. BS, U. Indonesia Faculty Medicine, 1957, MD, 1961; postgrad. U. Indonesia, Jakarta, 1961-65, U. Calif. at L.A., 1967-71, Pa. State U., 1971-72. Diplomate Am. Bd. Psychiatry and Neurology, Am. Bd. Gen. Psychiatry, Am. Bd. Geriatric Psychiatry. Lectr. psychiatry U. Indonesia, Jakarta, 1965-67; psychiat. cons. Central Gen. Hosp., Jakarta, 1965-67; postdoctoral fellow U. Calif. at L.A. Brain Rsch. Inst., 1967-69; asst. rsch. psychiatrist, dept. psychiatry Neuropsychiat. Inst. U. Calif., L.A., 1969-70; asst. prof. psychiatry Pa. State U., 1972-87; assoc. prof. psychiatry Pa. State U., 1987—; chief inpatient psychiatry Univ. Hosp. Milton S. Hershey Med. Ctr., 1972—, dir. Behavioral Medicine Clinic, co-dir. Biofeedback Lab., 1975—; cons. psychiatry Family and Children's Svc. Lebanon County, Lebanon, Pa., 1971-79, Bd. dirs. Retarded Children's Assn. Dauphin County, Inc., 1971-73. Fellow Am. Psychiat. Assn.; mem. Pa. Psychiat. Soc., Central Pa. Psychiat. Soc., Assn. Advancement Behavior Therapy, Assn. Applied Psychophysiology and Biofeedback, Soc. Behavioral Medicine, Assn. Psychophysiol. Study of Sleep, Am. Acad. Sleep Disorder Medicine, Am. Assn. for Geriatric Psychiatry, Am. Geriatric Soc. Contbr. articles to profl. jours. Home: 1478 Bradley Ave Hummelstown PA 17036-9143 Office: Pa State U Coll Medicine Dept Psychiatry 500 University Dr Hershey PA 17033-2360

TAN, VERONICA Y., psychiatrist; b. Manila, The Philippines, Oct. 8, 1944; came to U.S., 1970; children: Terrence, Kristine. MD, U. St. Thomas, Manila, 1969. Diplomate Am. Bd. Psychiatry and Neurology. Intern U. Ill. Hosp., Chgo., 1970-71; resident Lafayette Clinic and Children's Hosp., Detroit, 1971-75; child and adolescent psychiatrist Bon Secours Hosp., Grosse Pointe, Mich., 1993—; med. dir. Children's Ctr. Wayne County, Mich. Author: The Gifted Child, 1970.

TAN, WILLIAM LEW, lawyer; b. West Hollywood, Calif., July 25, 1949; s. James Tan Lew and Choon Guey Louie; m. Shelly Mieko Ushio. BA, U. Pa., 1971; JD, U. Calif. Hastings Coll. Law, San Francisco, 1974. Bar: Calif. 1975, U.S. Dist. Ct. (cen. dist.) Calif. 1975, U.S. Ct. Appeals (9th cir.) 1975, U.S. Supreme Ct. 1979. Assoc. Hiram W. Kwan, Los Angeles, 1974-79; ptnr. Mock & Tan, Los Angeles, 1979-80; sole practice Los Angeles, 1980-81; ptnr. Tan & Sakiyama, L.A., 1981-86, 88—, Tan & Sakiyama, P.C., L.A., 1986-88; bd. dirs. Am. Bus. Network, L.A.; pres., bd. dirs. Asian Rsch. Cons., L.A., 1983-85; mem. adv. bd. Cathay Bank, 1990-91; bd. dirs. Asian Pacific Am. Legal Ctr. Co-founder Asian Pacific Am. Roundtable, L.A., 1981; chmn. bd. dirs. Leadership Edn. for Asian-Pacifics, L.A., 1984-87; alt. del. Dem. Nat. Conv., San Francisco, 1984; mem. Calif. State Bd. Pharmacy, Sacramento, 1984-92, v.p., 1988-91, pres., 1991-92; mem. L.A. City and County Crime Crisis Task Force, 1981, L.A. Asian Pacific Heritage Week Com., 1980-85, Asian Pacific Women's Network, L.A., 1981, L.A. City Atty.'s Blue Ribbon Com. of Advisors, 1981, cmty. adv. bd. to Mayor of L.A., 1984, allocations vol. liaison team health and therapy divsn. United Way, L.A., 1986, mem. nominating com. bd. dirs. 1994—; bd. dirs. Chinatown Svc. Ctr., L.A., 1983; conf. advisor U.S.-Asia, L.A., 1981-83; mem. L.A. city atty. Housing Adv. Com.; mem. Pacific Bell Consumer Product Adv. Panel, 1986-90; vice chair cmty. adv. bd. Sta. KCET-TV, PBA, 1993-94; mem. adv. commn. State of Calif. Com. on State Procurement Practices, 1989-90; mem. L.A. City Attys. Citizens' Task Force on Pvt. Club Discrimination, 1989-90; mem. Calif. Med. Summit, 1993; mem. Mayor's Commn. Children, Youth and Families, 1993-96; mem. pub. access subcom. Mayor's Spl. adv. Com. on Tech. Implementation, 1994-96. Named one of Outstanding Young Men of Am., 1979. Mem. ABA (mem. numerous coms.), ATLA, Calif. State Bar Assn. (vice chmn. com. ethnic minority rels. 1983-85, chmn. pub. affairs com. 1981-82, mem. others), L.A. County Bar Assn. (trustee 1984-86, vice chair human rights com. 1980-82, mem. numerous coms.), So. Calif. Chinese Lawyers Assn. (pres. 1980-81, chmn. 1987-88, mem. various coms.), Minority Bar Assn. (chmn. 1981-82, sec. 1980-81, chmn. adv. bd. 1982-83), Asian Pacific Bar of Calif., Nat. Asian Pacific Am. Bar, Japanese Am. Bar Assn., Bench and Bar Media Coun., Consumer Attys. of Calif., Soc. Intercultural Edn. (conf. coord., advisor panelist tng. and rsch. com. 1983). Avocations: gourmet cooking, bicycling, swimming, tennis, water color painting. Office: 300 S Grand Ave Ste 2750 Los Angeles CA 90071-3137

TANAKA, HARUMI, linguist, educator; b. Tokyo, Kanto, Sept. 16, 1930; s. Suehiro and Aiko (Sugiura) T. BA in English, Rikkyo U., Tokyo, 1952; BA in Linguistics, Tokyo U. Edn., 1954, MA in Linguistics, 1956; PhD in Linguistics, Brown U., 1971. Lic. English tchr. Instr. Rikkyo U., Tokyo, 1960-63, assoc. prof., 1963-68; assoc. prof. Tokyo U. Edn., 1968-76; prof. Nanzan U., Nagoya, Japan, 1976—; vis. rschr. East-West Ctr., Honolulu, 1974-76. Author: An Introduction to Linguistics, 1975, Invitation to Linguistics, 1978, Seminar in Linguistics, 1982, Seibido's Dictionary of Linguistics, 1988. Pianist Ensemble Eucalyptus, Nagoya, 1980—. Mem. Japan Assn. Coll. English Tchrs. (trustee 1973-94, 96—), Inst. for Rsch. in Lang. Tchg. (trustee 1971—), English Linguistic Soc. Japan (trustee 1988-95). Avocations: playing piano, listening to music, collecting stamps, traveling. Office: Nanzan U, 18 Yamazato-cho Showa-ku, Nagoya 466, Japan

TANAKA, KAY, genetics educator; b. Osaka, Japan, Mar. 2, 1929; came to U.S., 1969; d. Kumaji and Fusa (Nakamae) T.; m. Tomoko Hasegawa, Nov. 5, 1954; children: Atau, Elly Margaret. MD, U. Tokyo, 1956, Dr. Med. Sci., 1961; MA (hon.) Yale U., 1983. Asst. prof. medicine Harvard Med. Sch., Boston, 1969-73; sr. research scientist Yale U., New Haven, Conn., 1973-82, prof. genetics, 1983-94, prof. emeritus, 1995—; mem. biochemistry study sect. NIH, Bethesda, Md., 1983-84. Contbr. numerous articles to sci. jours., chpts. to books. Grantee NIH, 1971-95, March of Dimes, 1974-92. Mem. Am. Soc. Biol. Chemistry, Am. Soc. Human Genetics, Soc. Inborn Metabolic Disorders. Office: Yale U Dept Genetics 333 Cedar St New Haven CT 06510-3206

TANAKA, KOUICHI ROBERT, physician, educator; b. Fresno, Calif., Dec. 15, 1926; s. Kenjiro and Teru (Arai) T.; m. Grace Mutsuko Sakaguchi, Oct. 23, 1965; children—Anne M., Nancy K., David K. B.S., Wayne State U., 1949, M.D., 1952. Intern Los Angeles County Gen. Hosp., 1952-53; resident, fellow Detroit Receiving Hosp., 1953-57; instr. Sch. Medicine, UCLA, 1957-59, asst. prof. medicine, 1959-61, asso. prof. medicine, 1961-68, prof., 1968—; asso. chmn., chief hematology, dept. medicine Harbor-UCLA Med. Center, Torrance, Calif., 1961—. Served with AUS, 1946-48. Fellow ACP (gov. so. Calif. region I 1993-97); mem. Am. Fedn. Med. Rsch., Western Soc. Clin. Investigation, L.A. Soc. Internal Medicine (pres. 1971), Am. Soc. Hematology, Internat. Soc. Hematology, Western Assn. Physicians, Am. Soc. Clin. Investigation, Assn. Am. Physicians, Sigma Xi, Alpha Omega Alpha. Research red cell metabolism. Home: 4 Cayuse Ln Rancho Palos Verdes CA 90275-5172 Office: Harbor UCLA Med Ctr PO Box 2910 Torrance CA 90509-2910

TANAKA, PATRICE AIKO, public relations executive. BA, U. Hawaii, 1974. Editor Hawaii Press Newspapers, 1974-77; dir. pub. rels. Hotel Inter-Continental Maui, 1977-79; from acct. exec. to sr. v.p. and creative dir. Jessica Dee Comm., N.Y.C., 1979-87, exec. v.p., gen. mgr., 1987-90; CEO, creative dir. PT&Co., N.Y.C., 1990—. Bd. dirs. Girl Scout Coun. Greater N.Y., 1996—. Recipient Mothering That Works award Working Mother mag., 1994; named one of nation's 500 Most Influential Asian Ams. Avenue mag., 1996; featured in books Dive Right in The Sharks Won't Bite—The Entrepreneurial Woman's Guide to Success, 1995, American Dreamers, Visionaries and Entrepreneurs, 1995. Mem. UNICEF (bd. dirs.), Asian Pacific Am. Women's Leadership Inst. (founding bd. dirs.), N.Y. Women in Comm. (Matrix award for Pub. Rels. 1996), Women Execs. in Pub. Rels., U. Hawaii Alumni Assn. (bd. dirs. N.Y. chpt.). Home: 225 E 36th St #4D New York NY 10016 Office: Patrice Tanaka & Co Inc (PT&Co) 320 W 13th St Fl 7 New York NY 10014-1200

TANAKA, RICHARD I., computer products company executive; b. Sacramento, Dec. 17, 1928; s. G. and Kei Tanaka; m. Edith M. Arita, Aug. 18, 1951; children: Steven Richard, Jean Elizabeth, John Richard, Anne Mariko. BS with highest honors, U. Calif., Berkeley, 1950, MS, 1951; PhD, Calif. Inst. Tech., 1958. Sr. rsch. engr. N.Am. Aviation, Inc., 1951-54; mem. tech. staff Hughes Aircraft Co., 1954-57; dept. mgr., sr. mem. comuter rsch. Lockheed Missiles & Space Co., Palo Alto, Calif., 1957-65; sr. v.p. Cal Comp (Calif. Computer Products, Inc.), Anaheim, 1966-77; pres. Internat. Tech. Resources Co., Tustin, Calif., 1977-80; pres., CEO Systonetics, Inc., Fullerton, Calif., 1980-86; pres. Lundy Electroincs & Sys., Inc., Glen Head, N.Y., 1986-89; chmn., CEO, pres. Scan-Optics, Inc., Manchester, Conn., 1989-97; vis. prof. U. Calif., Berkeley, 1962. Author: Residue Arithmetic and Its Applications to Computer Technology, 1967. Hughes fellow Calif. Inst. Tech., 1955-57. Fellow IEEE (pres. computer soc. 1965-66, centennial medal, Golden Core award 1996); mem. Internat. Fedn. Info. Processing (pres. 1974-77, hon. life mem., U.S. del.), Am. Fedn. Info. Processing Socs. (pres. 1969-71, disting. service award 1983), Phi Beta Kappa, Tau Beta Pi, Eta Kappa Nu. Home: 10321 Shadyridge Dr Santa Ana CA 92705 Office: Scan-Optics Inc 169 Progress Dr Manchester CT 06040-2294

TANAKA, RICHARD KOICHI, JR., architect, planner; b. San Jose, Calif., Oct. 16, 1931; s. Richard Inoru and Mae Yoshiko (Koga) T.; m. Barbara Hisako Kumagai, Oct. 7, 1961; children: Craig, Todd, Sandra, Trent. BArch, U. Mich., 1954; M in Urban Planning, Calif. State U., San Jose, 1978. Exec. v.p. Steinberg Group, San Jose, L.A., 1954—; bd. dirs. Happi House Restaurants, Inc., 1972—. Author: American on Trial, 1988. Dir. Human Rels. Com., San Jose, 1969-73; dir., pres. Bicentennial Com., San Jose, 1974-77; bd. dirs. Santa Clara County Sch. Bd. Assn., 1980—; pres. Internment of Local Japanese Ams., San Jose, 1984—; past pres., trustee East Side H.S. Dist., San Jose, 1971-92, Japanese Am. Citizens League, San Jose; mem. bd. govs. Boy Scouts Am., San Jose, 1978—, NCCJ, San Jose, 1976—; past pres. Tapestry and Talent, 1976-80; trustee San Jose/ Evergreen C.C., 1992—, pres., 1993-94, 97—; bd. dirs., first v.p. Calif. C.C. Trustees, 1997—. Mem. AIA, Am. Planning Inst., Constrn. Specification Inst., Rotary. Avocations: golf, painting. Home: 14811 Whipple Ct San Jose CA 95127-2570 Office: 60 Pierce Ave San Jose CA 95110-2819

TANAKA, RON S., hotel executive. Sr. v.p. design, constrn., devel. Canadian Pacific Hotels & Resorts, Toronto, Ont., Canada. Office: Canadian Pacific Hotels & Resorts, 1 University Ave #1400, Toronto, ON Canada M5J 2P1

TANCREDI, JAMES J., lawyer; b. Hartford, Conn., Apr. 1, 1954; s. Joseph I. and Angelina C. (Lanza) T.; children: Lauren, Jamie, Brian. BA in Urban Studies and Polit. Sci., Coll. Holy Cross, 1976; JD, U. Conn., 1979. Bar: Conn. 1979, U.S. Dist. Ct. Conn. 1979, U.S. Ct. Appeals (2d cir.) 1982, U.S. Dist. (so. dist.) N.Y. 1988, U.S. Supreme Ct., 1991. Assoc. Day, Berry & Howard, Hartford, 1979-86, ptnr., 1986—, chmn. bankruptcy dept., 1996—. Bd. dirs., treas. Conn. Mental Health Assn., Hartford, 1986-89. Mem. ABA (bus. sect.), Am. Bankruptcy Inst., Conn. Bar Assn. (exec. com. mem. bankruptcy section). Congregationalist. Office: Day Berry & Howard CityPlace I Hartford CT 06103

TANCREDI, LAURENCE RICHARD, med. staff appt. Brookhaven Nat. Labs. Clin. Ctr., 1966—; v.p. Internat. Acad. Law and Mental Health, 1987-95; pvt. practice, N.Y.C., mem. tech. bd. dirs. Milbank Meml. Fund, N.Y.C., 1981-84; mem. adv. com. on transplantations Health Care Fin. Adminstrn., Dept. Health and Human Svcs., 1981-84; nat. adv. bd. NIMH Ctr. for the Study of Pub. Mental Health N.Y. State Office Mental Health, 1994—; mem. cmty. svcs. bd. Dept. Mental Health, Mental Retardation and Alcohol Svcs., City of N.Y., 1995—; mem. sci. adv. com. Am. Suicide Found., 1995—; cons. Commn. on Med. Profl. Liability, co-prin. investigator study ABA, 1978-80; cons. in field. Office: 129B E 71st St New York NY 10021-4201

TANDON, RAJIV, psychiatrist, educator; b. Kanpur, India, Aug. 3, 1956; came to U.S., 1984; s. Bhagwan Sarup and Usha (Mehrotra) T.; m. Chanchal Nammi Vohra; children: Neeraj, Anisha, Gitanjali. Student, St. Xavier's Coll., Bombay, India, 1974; BS, All India Inst., New Delhi, 1980; MD, Nat. Inst. of MH, India, 1983. Sr. resident Mental Health and Neuro-Scis., India, 1983-84; resident U. Mich. Hosps., Ann Arbor, 1984-87, attending psychiatrist, 1987—; dir. schizophrenia program U. Mich., Ann Arbor, 1987—, assoc. prof., 1993—; cons. Lenawee County Community Mental Health, Adrian, Mich., 1985—. Author: Biochemical Parameters of Mixed Affective States; Negative Schizophrenic Symptoms: Pathophysiology and Clinical Implications; contbr. more than 120 articles to profl. jours. Recipient Young Scientist's award Biennial Winter workshop on Schizophrenia, 1990, 92, Travel award Am. Coll. Neuropsychopharmacology/Mead, 1990, Rsch. Excellence award Am. Assn. Psychiatrists from India, 1993, Sci. award, Best Drs. in Am. award, 1994-95, Gerald Klerman award for outstanding rsch. by a Nat. Alliance for Rsch. in Schizophrenia and Depression young investigator, 1995. Mem. Am. Psychiat. Assn. (Wisneiwski Young Psychiatrist Rschr. award 1993), World Fedn. Mental Health, Soc. for Neurosci., N.Y. Acad. Scis., Soc. Biol. Psychiatry, Mich. Psychiat. Soc. Democrat. Hindu. Office: U Mich Med Ctr Dept Psychiatry 1500 E Medical Center Dr # 9C Ann Arbor MI 48109-0005

TANE, SUSAN JAFFE, retired manufacturing company executive; b. N.Y.C.; d. Irving and Beatrice (Albert) J.; m. Irwin R. Tane; children by previous marriage: Robert Wayne, Stephen Mark. BS, Boston U., 1964; postgrad., Hofstra U., C.W. Post U. Elem. sch. tchr. Long Beach, N.Y., 1964-67; pres. Fashions by Appointment, Glen Cove, N.Y., 1967-71; adminstrv. asst. Peerless Sales Corp., Elmont, N.Y., 1967-71; sales mgr., then mktg. dir. United Utensils Co., Inc., Port Washington, N.Y., 1973-78; v.p. ops. and control United Molded Products div. United Utensils Co., Inc., Port Washington, 1978-80; v.p. mktg. Utensco, Port Washington, 1980-88; bd. dirs. Peerless Aerospace Corp. Co-inventor plastic container and handling assembly. Trustee, sr. v.p. Am. Jewish Congress; mem. Dirs. Circle, Folger Shakespeare Libr.; life mem. Hadassah, Ronald McDonald House; mem. Friends of the Arts-L.I. U., Inner Circle-Nassau County Mus. Art; friend N.Y. Pub. Libr.; bd. dir. Poe Found.; pres. Susan Jaffe Tane Found. Mem. Boston U. Alumni Assn. Home: 249 12th Ave Sea Cliff NY 11579-1021 Office: PO Box 735 Glenwood Landing NY 11547-0735

TANENBAUM, BASIL SAMUEL, engineering educator; b. Providence, R.I., Dec. 1, 1934; s. Harry Milton and Rena Ada (Herr) T.; m. Carol Binder, Aug. 26, 1956; children: Laurie, Stephen, David. B.S. summa cum laude, Brown U., 1956; M.S. (NSF fellow, 1956-60), Yale U., 1957, Ph.D. in Physics, 1960. Staff physicist Raytheon Co., Waltham, Mass., 1960-63; prof. engrng. Case Western Res. U., Cleve., 1963-75; dean of faculty Harvey Mudd Coll., Claremont, Calif., 1975-93, prof. engrng., 1975—; Norman F. Sprague, Jr. prof. of life scis. Harvey Mudd Coll., Claremont, 1996—; vis. scientist Cornell U., Arecibo (P.R.) Obs., 1968-69; vis. assoc. prof. Northwestern U., Evanston, Ill., 1970; vis. scholar U. Calif. Irvine Beckman Laser Inst., 1993-94; mem. sci. adv. com. Nat. Astronomy and Ionosphere Ctr., 1972-77, Calif. Poly. Inst., Pomona, 1976-87; mem. engrng. and sci. adv. com. Calif. State U., Fullerton, 1976-87; mem. nat. adv. com. Rowan Coll., Glassboro, N.J., 1993—, chmn. curriculum subcom.; mem. Eisenhower adv. com. Calif. Postsecondary Edn. Com., 1993—; dir. Minority Engrs. Indsl. Opportunity Program, 1973-75; dir. summer sci. program Thacher Sch., Ojai, Calif., 1977-82; cons. various corps., univ. labs., govt. agys. Author: Plasma Physics, 1967. Woods Hole Oceanog. Inst. fellow, 1959; sr. Sterling fellow Yale U., 1959; recipient Case Western Res. U. Wittke teaching award, 1974, Henry T. Mudd prize Harvey Mudd Coll., 1996. Mem. AAAS, Am. Phys. Soc., Am. Soc. for Engrng. Edn., IEEE, AAUP, Sigma Xi (research award 1969). Home: 611 W Delaware Dr Claremont CA 91711-3458 Office: Harvey Mudd Coll 301 E 12th St Claremont CA 91711-5901

TANENBAUM, BERNARD JEROME, JR., corporate executive; b. Little Rock, Nov. 26, 1934; s. Bernard Jerome and Naomi (Dante) T.; m. Patricia Wise, June 9, 1955; children: Bernard Jerome III, Albert Wise. B.B.A., Tulane U., 1956; D.Pub. Service, Ark. Bapt. Coll., 1974. Salesman Dantan Co., Dumas, Ark., 1955; buyer Dantes Stores, Dumas, 1956-61; exec. v.p. Dante and Tanenbaum, Dumas, 1961; pres. UDS Inc. (formerly United Dollar Stores, Inc.), Dumas, 1967—; pres. Pudata Inc.; chmn. JAT II, Inc., vice chmn. Ark. Tax Revision Commn. County chmn. ARC, 1957-60; v.p., dir. Desota coun. Boy Scouts Am.; pres. Henry S. Jacobs Camp, S.W. region Union Am. Hebrew Congregations, also vice chmn. bd. trustees, mem. exec. com., mem. nat. com. camps and instns., rep. S.W. region to long-range planning com.; chmn. N.Am. bd. World Union Progressive Judiasm, 1995, mem. exec. governing body, 1989; pres., dir. Camp Assn. So. Temples; mem. bd. govs. Hebrew Union Coll.-Jewish Inst. of Religion; trustee adv. bd. Tulane U.; trustee Leo N. Levi Hosp., 1994; bd. dirs. Dante & Tanenbaum Found., Ark. dept. NCCJ, Ark. chpt. Arthritis Found., Hot Springs Music Festival, 1995, "50 for the Future", Hot Springs, 1995; bd. dirs. Hot Spring Documentary Film Inst., 1994, chmn., 1996. Recipient Ark. Ten Outstanding Young Men award, 1971, Outstanding Service award Sickle Cell Anemia Found., 1973, Distinguished Arkansan award, 1974. Mem. Ark. Retail Mchts. Assn. (dir.), Dumas Mchts. Assn. (past chmn.), Dumas Jr. C. of C. (past pres.), Ark. Jr. C. of C. (past internat. dir.), Dumas C. of C., Zeta Beta Tau.; mem. B'nai B'rith (past dir.). Jewish religion (past pres., trustee temple). Club: Mason (32). Home: 130 S Lakeland Pt Hot Springs National Park AR 71913-7608 Office: 1401 Malvern Ave Ste 160 Hot Springs National Park AR 71901-6370

TANENBAUM, JAY HARVEY, lawyer; b. N.Y.C., Nov. 17, 1933; s. Leo Aaron and Regina (Stein) T.; m. Linda Goldman, May 28, 1961; children: Susan Hillary, Steven Eric. BA, Hobart and William Smith Colls., 1954; LLB, Union U., 1957, JD, 1961. Bar: N.Y. 1957, U.S. Dist. Ct. (so. dist.) N.Y. 1961, U.S. Supreme Ct. 1967. Internat. trader Associated Metals and Minerals Corp., N.Y.C., 1960-64; pvt. practice, N.Y.C., 1964—; corp. counsel Internat. Gate Corp., Gen. Gate Corp. Mem. N.Y. State Bar Assn., N.Y. Trial Lawyers Assn., Bronx County Bar Assn. Jewish. Club: St. James (London), Le Club (N.Y.).

TANG, CHAO, physicist; b. Nanchang, China, Oct. 2, 1958; came to U.S., 1981; s. Danlin Tang and Yansheng Cheng; m. Laurel Q. Peng, Apr. 10, 1994; 1 child, Daniel. BS, U. Sci. Tech. China, 1981; PhD, U. Chgo., 1986. Rsch. assoc. Brookhaven Nat. Lab., Upton, N.Y., 1986-88, Inst. Theoretical Physics, Santa Barbara, Calif., 1988-91; rsch. scientist NEC Rsch. Inst., Princeton, N.J., 1991—. Contbr. articles to profl. jours.; referee Phys. Rev. and Phys. Rev. Letters, 1987—, Europhysics Letters, Jou. de Physique, 1992—, Jour. Statis. Physics, 1992—, Sci., 1996—, Chem. Phys. Letters, 1996—. Recipient Telegdi prize, U. Chgo., 1982. Mem. Am. Phys. Soc., Overseas Chinese Physics Assn. Achievements include discovery of self-organized criticality and contributions in areas of statistical physics, non-linear dynamical systems, condensed matter physics, and protein folding. Home: 4 Dannys Way Cranbury NJ 08512-2943 Office: NEC Rsch Inst 4 Independence Way Princeton NJ 08540-6634

TANG, ESTHER DON, development consultant, retired social worker; b. Tucson, Mar. 5, 1917; d. Don Wah and Yut (Gnan) Fok; m. David W. Tang, June 14, 1942; children: Patricia Karen Tang Crowley, Diana Cherly Tang Simones, David. Jr., Elizabeth Carol. Student, Draughn's Bus. Sch., San Antonio, 1936, U. Ariz., 1938-41; DHL (hon.), U. Ariz., 1992, LHD (hon.), 1992. Owner, operator supermarket, Tucson, 1940-66; exec. dir. Pio Decinio Ctr. Cath. Diocese, Tucson, 1966-85; cons., ptnr., vice chmn. bd. Netwest Devel. Corp., Tucson, 1985—. Mem. Tucson Airport Authority, 1975—; chmn. Tucson-Taichung Sister Cities, 1979-91; chmn. Tucson Sister Cities Steering Com., 1984—, Sister Cities Assn. Tucson, 1990, Ariz. Pers. Bd.; chmn. bd. dirs. Pima Community Coll., 1975-85; pres. bd. dirs. Pima Coun. on Aging, 1986-90; coord. U.S. Bicentennial, Tucson; mem. adv. bd. Ariz. Dept. Econ. Security. Named Woman of Yr., City of Tucson, 1955, Woman of Yr. in Adminstrn., 1968, Lady Comdr. the Holy Sepluchre Jerusalem; recipient Disting. Friend of the Humanities award Nat. Adv. Bd., 1989, Jefferson award Ariz. Daily Star, 1987, Svc. award Pima Coun. on Aging, 1987-89, Disting. Svc. award U. Pima C.C. Found., 1988, Roots and Wings Comty. award, 1988, Rosie award So. Ariz. Ctr. Against Sexual Assault, 1990, Lifetime Achievement award YWCA, 1992, 93. Mem. Soroptimist (hon.). Roman Catholic. Avocations: travel, cooking, golf. Home: 701 E Camino De Los Padres Tucson AZ 85718-1921 Office: Netwest Devel Corp 2221 E Broadway Blvd Ste 211 Tucson AZ 85719-6032

TANG, GEORGE CHICKCHEE, investment executive; b. Hong Kong, Nov. 8, 1964; came to U.S., 1984; s. George and Margaret Tang. BS, Case Western Res. U., 1987; MS, Northwestern U., 1989. Registered securities rep., commodity rep., ins. agt., Ill.; chartered fin. analyst; cert. investment mgr. cons. With AT&T Bell Labs., Naperville, Ill., 1989-92; fin. cons. Smith Barney, Oakbrook, Ill., 1992—; spkr., lectr. in field. Contbr. fin. columns to Chgo. Chinese Daily News, 1993—, Chinese Am. News, 1993—, China Jour., 1994—. Writer ARC, Cleve., 1985-86; spkr. on environ. protection City Coun. Hong Kong, 1982. Recipient Champion of Wildlife Conservation award Hong Kong Std., 1982. Mem. Inst. CFA's (chartered), Assn. for Investment and Rsch., Inst. for Investment Mgmt. Cons. (cert.), Orgn. Chinese Ams. (internal v.p. Chgo. chpt. 1994-95, pres. 1995—). Avocations: tennis, swimming, bridge, golf, art. Office: Smith Barney 1 Tower Ln Villa Park IL 60181-4671

TANG, IRVING CHE-HONG, mathematician, educator; b. Macau, China, Dec. 29, 1931; came to U.S., 1948; s. Man-yan and Susie Wei-chun (Chung) T. BS, U. Calif., Berkeley, 1952; MS, U. Ill., 1953; DS, Washington U., St. Louis, 1965. Chartered engr., Brit. Engrng. Coun. Design engr. Friden Calculators, San Leandro, Calif., 1955-56; staff engr. IBM Corp., San Jose, Calif., 1956-66; postdoctoral fellow U. Oslo, 1966-68; head math. dept. NSW Inst. Tech., Sydney, Australia, 1969-76, Hong Kong Poly., 1977-89; prof. math. Phillips U., Enid, Okla., 1989-91, Oklahoma City C.C., Rose State Coll., 1991-94, Okla. State U., Oklahoma City, 1994—. Contbr. articles to profl. jours. Fellow Brit. Computer Soc.; mem. Math. Assn. Am., Hong Kong Math. Soc. (pres. 1977-81), Sigma Xi, Tau Beta Pi, Eta Kappa Nu. Office: Okla State U Dept Math Dept Math 900 N Portland Ave Oklahoma City OK 73107-6120

TANG, PAUL CHI LUNG, philosophy educator; b. Vancouver, B.C., Can., Jan. 23, 1944; came to U.S., 1971; s. Pei-Sung and Violet (Wong) T. BSc with high distinction, U. B.C., 1966; MA in Edn., Simon Fraser U., Vancouver, 1971; MA, Washington U., St. Louis, 1975, PhD, 1982; cert. in ethics, Kennedy Inst. Ethics, 1983; diploma in piano, U. Toronto, 1962. Teaching asst. philosophy of edn. Simon Fraser U., 1969-71; instr. philosophy St. Louis C.C. at Meramec, Kirkwood, Mo., 1975-82; instr., lectr. philosophy Washington U., 1972-76; adj. asst. prof. Harris-Stowe State Coll., St. Louis, 1980-82; asst. prof. philosophy Grinnell (Iowa) Coll., 1982-85; asst. prof. to assoc. prof. to prof. dept. philosophy Calif. State U., Long Beach, 1985—, chmn. dept. philosophy, 1988-94; vis. lectr. philosophy So. Ill. U., Edwardsville, 1978-79. Contbr. numerous articles and revs. to profl. publs.; editor Philosophy of Sci. Assn. Newsletter, 1985-90; asst. editor Philosophy of Sci. acad. jour., 1972-75. Senator Internat. Parliament for Safety and Peace, Palermo, Italy. Decorated knight Templar Order of Jerusalem, knight Order Holy Cross of Jerusalem, knight comdr. Lofsenic Ursinius Orer, chevalier Grand Crois de Milice du St. Sepulcre; recipient cert. of merit Student Philosophy Assn., 1988-90, 93-94, spl. award, 1992; named faculty advisor of yr. Assoc. Students, 1987, 90, 91, 95, Highland Lord of Camster, Scotland, 1995; Paul Tang prize in philosophy named in his honor, 1996—; fellow Washington U., 1971, summer rsch. fellow Calif. State U., 1988, NEH fellow Harvard U., 1988, NEH Summer Seminar fellow, 1968; internat. scholar Phi Beta Delta, interdisciplinary scholar Phi Kappa Phi, 1993; grantee vis. philosophers program Coun. for Philos. Studies, 1987, 91, 92; Disting. Vis. Scholars and Artists Fund, Calif. State U., 1988, 89, rsch. grantee, summer 1996. Fellow World Lit. Acad.; mem. Am. Philos. Assn. (Excellence in Tchg. award 1995, 97), Philosophy of Sci. Assn., History of Sci. Soc., Kennedy Inst. Ethics, Hastings Ctr., Iowa Philos. Soc. (pres. 1985-86), Internat. Platform Assn., Brit. Soc. Philosophy of Sci., Soc. Philosophy and Psychology, Maison Internat. des Intellectuels de l'Acad. Francaise, Internat. Order Merit (Eng.), Golden Key (hon., Internat. Man of Yr. 1995-96), Order Internat. Fellowship (Eng.), numerous others. Avocations: hiking, tennis, chess, music, travel. Home: 5050 E Garford St Apt 228 Long Beach CA 90815-2859 Office: Calif State U Dept Philosophy 1250 N Bellflower Blvd Long Beach CA 90840-0006

TANG, WILSON HON-CHUNG, engineering educator; b. Hong Kong, Aug. 16, 1943; came to U.S., 1962, naturalized, 1979; s. Shu-Chun and Shui-Kuen Chan T.; m. Bernadette Yim, July 29, 1969; children: Tze-John, Joyce Wing-Yi. BS, MIT, 1966, MS, 1967; CE, PhD, Stanford U., 1969. Asst. prof. civil engring. U. Ill., Urbana-Champaign, 1969-74, assoc. prof., 1974-79, prof., 1979—, assoc. head dept. civil engring., 1989-91; prof., head dept. Hong Kong U. Sci. and Tech., 1996—; Guggenheim fellow Norwegian Seotech. Inst., Oslo, Imperial Coll., London, 1976-77; vis. prof. Nat. U. Singapore, U. Hong Kong, 1983, prin. Wilson Tang and Assocs., 1986—; cons. to indsl. firms and govtl. agys. on reliability evaluation of structure and geotech. performances; mem. rev. panel Fulbright awards. Author: (with A. H-S. Ang.) Probability Concepts in Engineering Planning and Design, Vol. I, 1975, Vol. II, 1984; mem. editorial bd. Internat. Jour. Structural Safety, 1989—. Guggenheim fellow, 1976; NSF research grantee, 1972—; recipient Campus teaching award, 1991. Fellow ASCE (scholar 1965, Outstanding Tchr. award 1980, chmn. com. on reliability of offshore structures 1984-87, State of the Art Paper award 1990, co-chmn. com. on geotech. safety and reliability, 1993—); mem. Geotech. Bd. of Nat. Rsch. Coun. (chmn. com. on workshop on Reliability Methods for Risk Mitigation in Geotech. Engring. 1992-95), Am. Soc. Engring. Edn., Internat. Geostatis. Assn., Internat. Assn. for Structural Safety and Reliability, Internat. Assn. for Civil Engring. Reliability and Risk Analysis, Internat. Soc. Soil Mechanics and Found. Engring., Chinese-Am. Asssn. Natural Disaster Mitigation Rsch. (bd. dirs. 1989-91). Home: 310 E Willard St Urbana IL 61801-6653 Office: Hong Kong U Sci & Tech, CSE Dept, Clear Water Bay Kowloon, Hong Kong

TANGOREN, GULEN F., retired anesthesiologist, pain management specialist; b. Istanbul, Turkey, July 7, 1934; came to U.S., 1959; d. Ahmet Hamdi Iyigun and Hasene Kant; married; 5 children. MD, U. Istanbul, 1957. Diplomate Am. Bd. Pain Mgmt. Pvt. practice; sec., treas. dept. anesthesia Sibley Meml. Hosp.; ret. Founding mem. Muslim Community Ctr.; active Simon Viescutul Ctr. Fellow Am. Coll. Anesthesiologists; mem. AMA, Am. Soc. Anesthesiologists, Md., D.C. Soc. Anesthesia, Internat. Anesthesia Soc. Republican. Muslim. Home: 6456 Windermere Cir Rockville MD 20852-3539

TANGUAY, NORBERT ARTHUR, retired municipal police training officer; b. Winchendon, Mass., May 22, 1933; s. Arthur T. and Yvonne (Brunette) T.; (div.); children: MIchael N., Theresa Y., Mark T.; m. Sherrie Ann Miller, Aug. 17, 1983; 1 child, William Arthur. Comml. pilot cert., East Coast Aero Tech., Lexington, Mass., 1957; AS, Manchester (Conn.) C.C., 1974. Lic. comml. pilot. Ins. cons. Met. Life Ins. Co., Manchester, Conn., 1966-70; lt. U. Conn. Police Dept., Storrs, 1970-75; tng. officer Mcpl. Police Tng. Acad., Meriden, Conn., 1975-94; owner Tanguay Pubs., Centennial State Investigations; rangemaster Mcpl. Police Tng. Acad., 1977—; lectr. on child abuse, Conn., 1977—. Author: Dispatcher's Guide to Crimes/ Incidents in Progress, 1988, Police Officers Response Guide to Crimes/ Incidents in Progress, 1991; inventor: handgun muscle trainer, 1993. With U.S. Navy, 1951-55, Korea. Mem. NRA, VFW, Narcotic Enforcement Officers Assn., Nat. Assn. Fed. Lic. Firearms Dealers, Internat. Assn. Law Enforcement Firearms Instrs. Democrat. Roman Catholic. Avocations: golf, gardening, swimming, chess.

TANHAM, GEORGE KILPATRICK, retired research company executive; b. Englewood, N.J., Feb. 23, 1922; s. Francis Thomas and Irene (Kilpatrick) T.; m. Mary Finch, 1958 (div. 1962); m. Barbara Hunt, May 27, 1966 (div. 1989); children: George K., Gerald Francis, Helen Tanham Woods, Barbara Tanham Stampora, Maedi Carney, Ruth Tanham Marshall, Ramsey; m. Kathleen Van Wyck, Oct. 27, 1989. BA, Princeton U., 1943; MA, Stanford U., 1947, PhD, 1951. Assoc. prof., master student houses Calif. Inst. Tech., Pasadena, 1947-55; research staff Rand Corp., Santa Monica, Calif., 1955-58; dep. to v.p. Rand Corp., Washington, 1958-64, 65-68, v.p., trustee, 1971-82, sr. researcher, 1982-87, cons., 1987—; assoc. dir. AID, Saigon, Vietnam, 1964-65; minister counsellor U.S. Embassy, Bangkok, Thailand, 1968-70; cons. ESL, Sunnyvale, Calif.; lectr. in field. Author: Communist Revolutionary Warfare: The Vietminh in Indochina, 1961, 67, 85, War Without Guns: American Civilians in Rural Vietnam, 1966, Contribution a l'Histoire de la Resistance Belge, 1971, Trial in Thailand, 1974; co-author: (with Douglas S. Blaufarb) Who Will Win a Key: An Answer to the Puzzle of Revolutionary War, 1989, (with Marcy Agmon) The Indian Air Force: Trends and Prospects, 1996, (with K. Bhapal and A. Mattoo) Securing Indian, (with Ralph Salmi and Cesar Majul) Conflict Resolution in Islam, 1997. Bd. visitors Patterson Sch. of Diplomacy and Internat. Commerce, U. Ky., 1985-95, U. Pitts., 1982-92; bd. dirs. Ethics and Pub. Policy Ctr., 1988—; adv. trustee Rand Corp., 1988—. Served with U.S. Army, World War II. Decorated Purple Heart, Silver Star with oak leaf cluster, Air medal; Croix de Guerre avec etoile d'argent (Republic of France); Most Exalted Order of White Elephant (Thailand); Belgian-Am. Edn. Found. grantee, 1950; Ford Found. fellow, 1952-53; Social Scis. Research Council grantee, 1955-57; grantee U.S. Inst. Peace and Rockefeller Found., 1989-91, Alton Jones Found. 1996-98; Rajiv Gandhi Found. vis. fellow, New Delhi, 1995. Mem. Coun. Fgn. Rels., Internat. Inst. Strategic Studies, Cosmos Club, Spl. Forces Club (London), India Internat. Ctr. (New Delhi). Avocations: music, travel, gardening, sports. Home: PO Box 373 Strasburg VA 22657-0373 Office: Rand 1333 H St NW Washington DC 20005-4707

TANICK, MARSHALL HOWARD, lawyer, law educator; b. Mpls., May 9, 1947; s. Jack and Esther (Kohn) T.; m. Cathy E. Gorlin, Feb. 20, 1982; children: Lauren, Ross. BA, U. Minn., 1969; JD, Stanford U., 1973. Bar: Calif. 1973, Minn. 1974. Law clk. to presiding justice U.S. Dist. Ct., Mpls., 1973-74; assoc. Robins, Davis & Lyons, Mpls., 1974-76; ptnr. Tanick & Heins, P.A., Mpls., 1976-89, Mansfield & Tanick, Mpls., 1989—; prof. constrn., real estate and media law U. Minn., Mpls., 1983—, Hamline U., St. Paul, 1982—; prof. constl. law William Mitchell Coll. Law, 1994. Editor: Hennepin Lawyer, Bench, Bar and Litigation mag.; contbr. articles to mags.

Avocation: writing. Home: 1230 Angelo Dr Minneapolis MN 55422-4710 Office: Mansfield & Tanick 900 2nd Ave S Minneapolis MN 55402-3314

TANIGUCHI, TOKUSO, surgeon; b. Eleele, Kauai, Hawaii, June 26, 1915; s. Tokuichi and Sana (Omaye) T.; BA, U. Hawaii, 1941; MD, Tulane U., 1946; 1 son, Jan Tokuichi. Intern Knoxville (Tenn.) Gen. Hosp., 1946-47; resident in surgery St. Joseph Hosp., also Marquette Med. Sch., Milw., 1947-52; practice medicine, specializing in surgery, Hilo, Hawaii, 1955—; chief surgery Hilo Hosp.; teaching fellow Marquette Med. Sch., 1947-49; v.p., dir. Hawaii Hardware Co., Ltd. Capt. M.C., AUS, 1952-55. Diplomate Am. Bd. Surgery. Fellow Internat., Am. colls. surgeons; mem. Am., Hawaii med. assns., Hawaii County Med. Soc., Pan-Pacific Surg. Assn., Phi Kappa Phi. Contbr. articles in field to profl. jours. Patentee automated catheter. Home: 277 Kaiulani St Hilo HI 96720-2530

TANIS, JAMES ROBERT, library director, history educator, clergyman; b. Phillipsburg, N.J., June 26, 1928; s. John Christian and Bertha Marie (Tobiasson) T.; m. Florence Borgmann, June 26, 1963; children—Marjorie Martha, James Tobiasson. B.A., Yale, 1951; B.D., Union Theol. Sem., N.Y.C., 1954; Dr. Theol., U. Utrecht, Netherlands, 1967; LittD (hon.), Dickinson Coll., Carlisle, Pa., 1994. Ordained to ministry Presbyn. Ch., 1954. Co-pastor Greystone Presbyn. Ch., Elizabeth, N.J., 1954-55; librarian, mem. faculty Harvard Div. Sch., 1956-65; univ. librarian Yale U., 1965-68; mem. faculty Yale Div. Sch., 1968-69; dir. libraries, prof. history Bryn Mawr (Pa.) Coll., 1969—. Author: Calvinistic Pietism in the Middle Colonies, 1967; co-author: Bookbinding in America, 1983, Images of Discord/De Tweedracht Verbeeld, 1993, Fantasy and Fashion, 1996. Knighted as Officer in Order of Orange-Nassau, The Netherlands, 1993. Home: 105 Burnside Rd Villanova PA 19085-1315 Office: Bryn Mawr Coll Canaday Libr 101 N Merion Ave Bryn Mawr PA 19010-2859

TANIS, NORMAN EARL, retired university dean, library expert; b. Grand Rapids, Mich., Aug. 15, 1929; s. Aaron Orrie and Gertrude (Medendorp) T.; m. Terese R. Tiernan; children: Kathryn, Laura. AB, Calvin Coll., 1951; AM in Libr. Sci., U. Mich., 1952, MA in History, 1956, MA in Edn., 1961; DHL (hon.), U. San Fernando, 1973; LLD (hon.), Mid-Valley Coll. Law, 1976. Cataloger Strauss Meml. Libr., U. Mich., 1951-52; statis. clk. polio vaccine evaluation ctr. U. Mich., Ann Arbor, 1955; libr. Henry Ford Community Coll., Dearborn, Mich., 1956-63, head libr., 1963-66; dir. librs. Kans. State U., Pittsburg, 1966-69; dean librs. Calif. State U., Northridge, 1969-91, ret., 1991, librarian emeritus; team mgr./planner robotically controlled book storage unit Leviathian II, Calif. State U., 1986-91, chmn. editl. adv. bd. for univ. history, 1988-91; trustee San Fernando Valley Coll. Law, 1977-79; mem. adv. coun. Libr. Sch., UCLA, 1970-77; mem. adv. com. Libr. Sch., U. So. Calif., 1971-74; disting. alumnus-in-residence Sch. Info. and Libr. Svc., U. Mich., 1989; part-time libr. Our Lady Queen of the Angels Sem., 1993-94; assoc. Libr. Congress. Co-author: Three Hundred Million Books, 1974, Problems in Developing Academic Library Collections, 1974, Native Americans of North America, 1975, Lynton R. Kistler: Printer-Lithographer, 1976, Cost Analysis of Library Functions: A Total System Approach, 1978, China in Books, 1979, India and its People, A Bibliography, 1980, The Twilight of Orthodoxy in New England, 1987; contbr. articles to profl. publs.; editor: Northridge Facsimilie Series, 1974-91; exec. editor Santa Susana Press, 1975-91. Mem., lectr., extraordinary eucharistic min. and catechist for prison ministries St. John Eudes Roman Cath. Ch., Chatsworth, Calif.; postulant Oblates of Monastery of Risen Christ, San Luis Obispo, Calif., 1991—; with Knights of the Imaculata Militia. With USMCR, 1948-50; with U.S. Army, 1952-54. Named knight comdr. Supreme Order and Mil. of Temple of Jerusalem, 1990—, knight of Order of St. Constantine, 1991—, mil. and hospitaller knight of Order of St. Lazarus of Jerusalem, 1992—. Mem. ALA, Nat. Librs. Assn. (pres. 1980), Bibliog. Soc. Calif. State U.-Northridge, Acad. and Rsch. Librs. (pres. 1983-84), ALA divsn. Cath. Libr. Assn., Order of St. Lawrence-Malta (duke), Marine Meml. Club (San Francisco), Rounce and Coffin Club, Phi Beta Phi, Phi Beta Mu. Home: 10009 Jovita Ave Chatsworth CA 91311-3938 Office: Calif State U Libr Rm 202 1811 Nordhoff St Northridge CA 91324

TANIUCHI, KIYOSHI, retired mechanical engineering educator; b. Kahoku-choo, Kami-gun, Kōchi-ken, Japan, Aug. 8, 1926; s. Takeshi and Toshi (Yoshimoto) T.; m. Teiko Wakamatsu, Jan. 7, 1960; 1 child, Satoshi. Student, Kanto Gakuin Tech. Coll., Yokohama, Japan, 1946; BEng, Meiji U., Tokyo, 1952, DEng (hon.), 1980. Asst. Meiji U. Sch. Sci. and Tech., Kawasaki-shi, Japan, 1957-81, lectr. mech. engring., 1981-91, assoc. prof., 1991-95; ret. Meiji U. Sch. Sci. and Tech., 1995; instr. engring. Shibaura Inst. Tech., Ohmiya-shi, Saitama-ken, Japan, 1974-90. Co-author 3 books on mech. engring.; also papers. Mem. ASTM, Internat. Soc. Optical Engring., Soc. Exptl. Mechanics, Japanese Soc. Mech. Engrs. Avocations: photography, art appreciation. Home: 5-10-12 Wakamatsu, Sagamihara 229, Japan

TANKIN, RICHARD SAMUEL, fluid dynamics engineer, educator; b. Balt., July 14, 1924; s. Harry Jacob and Bertha (Haberer) T.; m. Anne Raudelunas, Dec. 2, 1956; children: Roberta, David, John. B.A., Johns Hopkins U., 1948, B.S., 1950; M.S., Mass. Inst. Tech., 1954; Ph.D., Harvard U., 1960. Asst. prof. U. Del., 1960-61; mem. faculty Northwestern U., 1961—, prof. fluid dynamics, 1968—, chmn. dept. mech. engring. and astronautical scis., 1973-78. Served with AUS, 1943-44; Served with USNR, 1944-45. Mem. ASME, Am. Inst. Aeros. and Astronautics, Am. Geophys. Union, Tau Beta Pi. Home: 820 Ridge Ter Evanston IL 60201-2430

TANKOOS, SANDRA MAXINE, court reporting services executive; b. Bklyn., Nov. 12, 1936; d. Samuel J. and Ethel (Seltzer) Rich; m. Kenneth Robert Tankoos, Mar. 17, 1957; children: Robert Ian, Gary Russell, Jenine Sheryl. AA, Stenotype Inst., 1957; BA, Queens Coll., 1969; MA, C.W. Post Coll., 1973. Cert. stenotype reporter, 1959. Ct. reporter free lance, N.Y.C., 1957-70; tchr. Spanish, various high schs., L.I., 1970-76; pres. Tankoos Reporting, N.Y.C., 1976—, Ar-Ti Recording, Mineola, N.Y., 1977—. Contbr. articles to profl. jours. Past pres., bd. dirs. Temple Sinai, Roslyn Hts., N.Y., 1989-91, Am. Jewish Acad., West Hempstead, 1984-91, LWV, Roslyn, 1969-75, NOW, Nassau County, 1975-77; bd. dirs. Religious Action Ctr., Washington. ARZA, 1997—. Avocations: writing, piano. Home: 77 Shepherd Ln Roslyn Heights NY 11577-2508 Office: Ar-Ti Recording Inc 142 Willis Ave Mineola NY 11501-2613 also: Tankoos Reporting Co 11 John St New York NY 10038-4009

TANNEHILL, DARCY ANITA BARTINS, academic administrator; b. Pitts., May 14, 1958; d. Joseph Paul Bartins and Ileane Anita (Roy) Bartins Yerman; m. Gary Edward Mack, Oct. 28, 1979 (div. Apr. 1989); 1 child, Courtney Anita; m. Norman Bruce Tannehill Jr., Feb. 14, 1991; stepchildren: Andrea, Bruce. BA, Duquesne U., 1978, MSEd, 1986; postgrad., U. Pitts. Rsch. asst. U. Pitts., 1979-81; adult edn. tchr. Allegheny Intermediate Unit, Pitts., 1985-86, counselor, statistician, 1986-90; coord. evening programs Robert Morris Coll., Coraopolis, Pa., 1990-92; asst. dir. academic svcs. Robert Morris Coll., Coraoplis, Pa., 1992-93; assoc. dir. academic svcs. Robert Morris Coll., Corapolis, Pa., 1993-94, assoc. dean admissions, 1994-96, assoc. dean of enrollment mgmt. adult and cont. edn., 1996—. Mem. AAHE, NAWE, Pa. Am. coun. on Edn., Nat. Identification Program. Republican. Presbyterian. Avocations: reading, music. Home: 4482 Battleridge Rd McDonald PA 15057 Office: Robert Morris Coll Narrows Run Rd Coraopolis PA 15108 also: 600 Fifth Ave Pittsburgh PA 15219

TANNEHILL, JOHN C., aerospace engineer, educator; b. Salem, Ill., Oct. 14, 1943; s. John Bell and Pearl Hanna (Trulin) T.; m. Marcia Kay George, Jan. 28, 1967; children: Michelle, Johnny. BS, Iowa State U., 1965, MS, 1967, PhD, 1969. Aerospace engr. NASA Flight Rsch. Ctr., Edwards, Calif., 1965; mem. tech. staff Aerospace Cor., El Segundo, Calif., 1967; NASA-ASEE fellow NASA Ames Rsch. Ctr., Moffett Field, Calif., 1970-71; asst. prof. aerospace engring. Iowa State U., Ames, 1969-74, assoc. prof., 1974-79, prof., 1979—, mgr. Computational Fluid Dynamics Ctr., 1984—; chmn. bd. Engring. Analysis, Inc., Ames, 1976—. Co-author: Computational Fluid Mechanics and Heat Transfer, 1984, 2d edit., 1997, Handbook of Numerical Heat Transfer, 1988; contbr. articles to profl. jours. NSF trainee, 1965-68; Iowa State U. Rsch. Found. fellow, 1968-69; NASA fellow, 1970-71. Fellow AIAA (chmn. Iowa sect. 1989-91); mem. Am. Soc. Engring. Edn., Sigma Xi, Sigma Gamma Tau, Tau Beta Pi. Home: 3214 Greenwood Cir Ames IA 50014-4570 Office: Aerospace Engring & Engring Mechanics Dept Aerospace & Mechs Engring Ames IA 50011

TANNEHILL, NORMAN BRUCE, JR., consultant, educator; b. Pitts., Aug. 22, 1950; s. Norman B. and Maxine (Hart) T.; m. Marianne Witt, Sept. 22, 1979 (div. July 1990); children: Andrea, Norman Bruce III; m. Darcy Anita Bartins, Feb. 14, 1991; 1 child, Courtney. BSBA, Robert Morris Coll., Coraopolis, Pa., 1975, MS, 1989. Cert. cons. to mgmt. Owner, CEO Tannehill Info. Sys. Ltd., Coraopolis, 1989—; adj. faculty Robert Morris Coll., 1989-97, C.C. of Allegheny County, Pitts., 1991—, C.C. of Beaver County, Monaca, Pa., 1994—. Mem. IEEE Computer Soc., Assn. for Computing Machinery, Assn. for Ednl. Comms. Tech., Mensa. Home: 4482 Battleridge Rd Mc Donald PA 15057-2587

TANNEN, DEBORAH FRANCES, writer, linguist; b. Bklyn., June 7, 1945; d. Eli S. and Dorothy (Rosen) T. BA, SUNY, Binghamton, 1966; MA, Wayne State U., 1970, U. Calif., Berkeley, 1976; PhD, U. Calif., 1979. English instr. Mercer County C.C., Trenton, N.J., 1970-71; lectr. in acad. skills CUNY, Bronx, N.Y., 1971-74; asst. prof. Georgetown U., Washington, 1979-85, assoc. prof. linguistics, 1985-90, prof. linguistics, 1989-91, univ. prof., 1991—; McGraw disting. lectr. in writing Coun. for Humanities and dept. anthropology Princeton U., fall 1991; visitor Inst. for Advanced Study, Princeton, spring 1992; fellow Ctr. for Advanced Study in Behavioral Scis., Stanford, Calif., 1992-93. Author: Lilika Nakos, 1983, Conversational Style: Analyzing Talk Among Friends, 1984, That's Not What I Meant!: How Conversational Style Makes or Breaks Your Relations With Others, 1986, Talking Voices: Repetition, Dialogue and Imagery in Conversational Discourse, 1989, You Just Don't Understand: Women and Men in the Workplace: Analysis, Sex. and Power, 1990, Gender and Discourse, 1994, Talking From 9 to 5: Women andMen's Conversational Styles Affect Who Gets Heard, Who Gets Credit, and What Gets Done at Work, 1994; editor: Analyzing Discourse: Text and Talk, 1982, Spoken and Written Language: Exploring Orality and Literacy, 1982, Coherence in Spoken and Written Discourse, 1984, Perspectives on Silence, 1985, Linguistics in Context: Connecting Observation and Understanding, 1988, Gender and Conversational Interaction, 1993, Framing In Discourse, 1993, (play) An Act of Devotion, 1994. Rockefeller Humanities fellow, 1982-83; grantee NEH, 1980, 85, 86; recipient Elizabeth Mills Crothers prize U. Calif., 1976, Dorothy Rosenberg Meml. prize U. Calif., 1977, Joan Lee Yang Meml. Poetry prize U. Calif., 1977, Shrout Short Story prize, 1978, Emily Chamberlain Cook prize, 1978. Office: Georgetown U Linguistics Dept Washington DC 20057

TANNENBAUM, BERNICE SALPETER, association executive; b. N.Y.C.; d. Isidore and May Franklin; BA, Bklyn. Coll.; 1 child, Richard Salpeter. chmn. Commn. on the Status of Women of the World Jewish Congress; mem. exec. bd. Am. sect. World Jewish Congress, chmn. internat. affairs com.; mem. Zionist Gen. Council; active Exec. World Zionist Orgn.; bd. govs., mem. gen. assembly Jewish Agy.; bd. dirs., v.p. United Israel Appeal; mem. exec. com. Am. Zionist Mvmt.; mem. Conf. of Pres. of Maj. Jewish Orgns.; nat. pres. Hadassah, N.Y.C., 1976-80; nat. chmn. Hadassah Internat., 1984-95; v.p. Jewish Telegraphic Agy.; bd. govs. Hebrew U. Office: Hadassah 50 W 58th St New York NY 10019-2505

TANNENBAUM, STEVEN ROBERT, toxicologist, chemist; b. N.Y.C., Feb. 23, 1937; m. Carol Eigen, Sept. 6, 1959; children: Lisa, Mark. BS in Food Tech, MIT, 1958, PhD in Food Sci. and Tech, 1962. Asst. prof. MIT, Cambridge, 1964-69, assoc. prof., 1969-74, prof. chemistry and toxicology divsn. toxicology, registration and admissions officer, 1981-95, dir. divsn., 1996—; vis. prof. Hebrew U. of Jerusalem, 1973-74; BASF vis. prof. U. Kaiserslautern, 1994; mem. adv. com. on biochemistry and chem. carcinogenesis Am. Cancer Soc., 1977-81; bd. sci. advisors divsn. cancer etiology, NCI, 1994-95, Frederick Cancer Sch. Facility, 1995—, Nat. Cancer Inst., 1989-93; mem. cancer spl. program adv. com., 1979-82; mem. peer rev. com. Nat. Toxicology Program, 1983-85; founder, bd. dirs. Vicam, Ltd., Partnership; mem. sci. adv. bd. Xenometrix, Inc., Transcend Pharmaceutics. Editor: (with R.I. Mateles) Single-Cell Protein, 1968, (with D.I.C. Wang) Single-Cell Protein II, 1975, (with others) The Economics, Marketing and Technology of Fish Protein Concentrate, 1974, (with J.R. Whitaker) Food Proteins, 1977, Nutritional Safety Aspects of Food Processing, 1979, (with others) Gastrointestinal Cancer: Endogenous Factors, 1981, (with R.A. Scanlan) N-Nitroso Compounds, 1981; mem. editl. bd. Japanese Jour. Cancer Rsch., 1986—, Chem. Rsch. Toxicology, 1988-91, 95—, Cancer Epidemiology, Prevention and Biomarkers, 1990—, Cancer Rsch., 1993—; contbr. over 300 articles to profl. jours. Mem. AAAS, NAS (Inst. Medicine), Am. Chem. Soc., Inst. Food Technologists (sect. councillor N.E. chpt. 1966-69, Samuel Cate Prescott Rsch. award 1970, Babcock Hart award 1980), editorial bd. sci. jour. 1970-73, Am. Inst. Nutrition, Am. Assn. Cancer Rsch., Sigma Xi. Achievements include 7 U.S. patents. Office: MIT Dept Chemistry Toxicology Bldg 16 Rm 822a 77 Massachusetts Ave Cambridge MA 02139-4301 *Motto: Crisis equals danger plus opportunity.*

TANNENBERG, DIETER E. A., retired manufacturing company executive; b. Chevy Chase, Md., Nov. 24, 1932; s. E.A. Wilhelm and Margarete Elizabeth (Mundhenk) T.; m. Ruth Hansen, Feb. 6, 1956; 1 child, Diana Tannenberg Collingsworth Cann Marlinski. BSME, Northwestern U., 1959. Registered profl. engr., N.Y., Conn., Ohio, Ill., Ind., Wis., N.J. Supervising engr. Flexonics div. Calumet & Hecla, Inc., Chgo., 1959-61, chief engr., 1961-63, program mgr. advanced space systems, 1963-65, dir. mfg. services, 1965-67; dir. mfg. engring. SCM Corp., Cortland, N.Y., 1967-69; tech. dir. internat. Singer Co., N.Y.C., 1969-71; v.p. ops. internat. div. Addressograph-Multigraph Corp., Cleve., 1971-74; mng. dir. Addressograph Multigraph GmbH, Frankfurt/Main, W. Ger., 1974-78; v.p., gen. mgr. Europe, Middle East, Africa AM Internat. Inc., Chgo., 1978-79; pres. AM Bruning div., 1979-82, AM Multigraphics Div., Mt. Prospect, Ill., 1982-86; corp. v.p. AM Internat., Inc., 1981-83, corp. sr. v.p., 1983-86; chmn. bd. dirs., pres., chief exec. officer Sargent-Welch Sci. Co., Skokie, Ill., 1986-89; pres., CEO Exhib-itGroup, Inc., Elk Grove Village, Ill., 1990-91, Bell & Howell Document Mgmt. Products Co., Chgo., 1991-94, Bell & Howell Postal Sys. Inc., Chgo., 1994-97; corp. v.p. Bell & Howell Co., Skokie, Ill., 1991-97; chmn. AM Internat. GmbH, Frankfurt, 1977-86; bd. dirs. Gerard Daniel & Co., GDC Internat., Inc. Contbr. chpts. to handbooks, articles to tech., trade mags.; patentee in machinery field. Served with M.I., U.S. Army, 1953-56. Named Man of Yr. Quick Print Mag., 1985. Mem. NSPE, ASME, ASCE, Assn. Reprodn. Materials Mfrs. (bd. dirs. 1979-82, v.p. 1980-82), Nat. Assn. Quick Printers (bd. dirs. 1982-84), Nat. Printing Equipment and Supplies Mfg. Assn. (bd. dirs. 1983-86, chmn. govt. affairs com. 1985-86), Computer and Bus. Equipment Mfg. Assn. (bd. dirs. 1983-86, 91-93), Soc. Am. Value Engrs. (hon. v.p. 1985—), Value Found. (trustee 1985—), Barrington Hills Country Club, Club, Pi Tau Sigma.

TANNENWALD, PETER, lawyer; b. Washington, Apr. 8, 1943; s. Judge Theodore and Selma (Peterfreund) T.; m. Carol B. Baum, May 25, 1969; 1 child, Jonathan Mark. AB, Brown U., 1964; LLB, Harvard Coll., 1967. Bar: U.S. Dist. Ct. D.C. 1968, U.S. Ct. Appeals (D.C. cir.) 1968, U.S. Supreme Ct. 1972. Assoc. Arent, Fox, Kintner, Plotkin & Kahn, Washington, 1967-74, ptnr., 1975-94; ptnr. Irwin, Campbell & Tannenwald, P.C., Washington, 1994—. Columnist The LPTV Report, 1988-92. Mem. cmty. coun. Sta. WAMU-FM, Washington, 1986-93, 94—; dir. Brown Broadcasting Svc., Inc., Providence, 1970—; chmn. maj. law firms divsn. Nat. Capital Area affiliate United Way, 1977-79. Mem. Harvard Law Sch. Assn. D.C. (pres. 1979-80), Harvard Law Sch. Assn. (sec. 1982-84). Avocations: electronics, photography. Office: Irwin Campbell Tannenwald 1730 Rhode Island Ave NW Washington DC 20036-3120

TANNENWALD, THEODORE, JR., federal judge; b. Valatie, N.Y., July 28, 1916; s. Theodore and Myra (Barnet) T.; m. Selma Peterfreund, Aug. 3, 1940; children: Peter, Robert. A.B. summa cum laude, Brown U., 1936; LL.B. magna cum laude, Harvard U., 1939; D.L.L., U. Cin., 1976; D.H.L., Hebrew Union Coll., 1976. Bar: N.Y. 1939, D.C. 1946. Assoc. Weil, Gotshal & Manges, N.Y.C., 1939-42; ptnr. Weil, Gotshal & Manges, 1947-65; judge U.S. Tax Ct., Washington, 1965-81; chief judge U.S. Tax Ct., 1981-83, sr. judge, 1983—; prin. legal cons. Lend Lease Adminstrn., 1942; acting asst. chief, fgn. funds control Dept. State, 1942-43; spl. cons. sec. war, 1943-45, cons. sec. def., 1947-49, coun. to spl. asst. to pres., 1950-51; asst. dir., chief of staff to dir. for mut. security Exec. Office pres., 1951-53; spl. counsel to Moreland Commn., 1955-58; N.Y. mem. Tri-State Tax Commn., 1958-59; mem. Pres.'s Task Force on Fgn. Aid, spl. asst. to sec. state, 1961; professorial lectr. George Washington U. Sch. Law, 1968-76; lectr. Sch. Law U. Miami, 1976-85; disting. adj. prof. Sch. Law U. San Diego, 1985-90; adj. prof. Sch. Law U. Miami, 1996—. Hon. chmn., hon. mem. bd. govs. Hebrew Union Coll.-Jewish Inst. Religion; mem. nat. exec. coun. Am. Jewish Com. Mem. ABA, Fed. Bar Assn., D.C. Bar Assn., Am. Law Inst., Coun. Fgn. Rels., Cosmos Club (D.C.), Phi Beta Kappa. Office: US Tax Ct 400 2nd St NW Washington DC 20217-0001

TANNER, DANIEL, curriculum theory educator; b. N.Y.C., Sept. 22, 1926; s. Jack and Lillian (Jupiter) T.; m. Laurel Nan Jacobson, July 11, 1948 (div. 1988). BS with honors, Mich. State U., 1949, MS, 1952; Ph.D. (Univ. Scholar), Ohio State U., 1955. Asst. prof. edn. San Francisco State Coll., 1955-60; assoc. prof. edn., coord. Midwest program on airborne TV instrn. Purdue U., 1960-62; assoc. prof. edn., assoc. dir. internat. program for edn. leaders Northwestern U., 1962-64; assoc. prof. rsch. divsn. tchr. edn. City U. N.Y., 1964-66; prof. edn., dir. Ctr. for Urban Edn., U. Wis.-Milw. Sch. Edn., 1966-67; prof. edn., dir. grad. programs in curriculum theory and devel. Grad. Sch. Edn., Rutgers U., New Brunswick, N.J., 1967—; chmn. dept. curriculum and instrn. Grad. Sch. Edn., Rutgers U., 1969-72, faculty rsch. fellow, 1974-75, 88-89; vis. lectr. U. Kansas City, summer 1956, Tchrs. Coll. Columbia, summer 1966; vis. prof. Emory U., summer 1968, SUNY, Binghamton, winter 1968, U. London, 1975, King Abdulaziz U., Saudi Arabia, winter 1992, U. Iowa, summer 1996; disting. lectr. ASCD, 1985, 86, Dewey Meml. lectr., 1984, Raths Meml. lectr., SUNY, 1984; Leadership Inst. lectr. U. Del., summer 1990; disting. lectr. Rider U., 1996; vis. scholar U. London Inst. Edn., 1974-75; mem. rev. bd. coll. work-study program U.S. Office Edn., 1965; mem. symposium on comparative curriculum history Inst. Sci. Edn. Kiel U., Fed. Republic Germany, 1989; del. leader Citizen Amb. Program, People-to-People Internat., Republic of South Africa, 1996; cons. U. Tex. Med. Ctr., 1961-62, Chgo. Sch. Survey, 1964-65, ctr. Urban Edn., N.Y.C., 1964-65, West Chgo. Sch. Survey, 1963-64, Nat. Ednl. TV Ctr., N.Y.C., 1963, Campbell County (Va.) Sch. Survey, 1970, Memphis Schs., 1977-78, ASCD Commn. on Gen. Edn., 1980-81, West Orange, N.J., Curriculum Study, 1984, ASCD Commn. on Secondary Sch. Practices, 1985, ASCD Ednl. Policy Task Force, 1985, NASSP Curric Coun., 1985-95; SUNY Buffalo External Evaluation, 1988; dir. Nat. Curriculum Inst., 1987, Perth Amboy (N.J.) Schs., 1996-97; delivered founder's day address Delaware Valley Coll., 1985. Author: Schools for Youth: Change and Challenge in Secondary Education, 1965, Secondary Curriculum: Theory and Development, 1971, Secondary Education: Perspectives and Prospects, 1972, Using Behavioral Objectives in the Classroom, 1972, Curriculum Development: Theory into Practice, 3rd edit., 1995, Supervision in Education, 1987, History of the School Curriculum, 1990, Crusade for Democracy: Progressive Education at the Crossroads, 1991; cons. editor, contbg. author: Ann. Review of Rsch. for Sch. Leaders, 1996, Curriculum Issues, 87th Yearbook NSSE, 1988, Ency. of Ednl. Rsch., 5th edit., 1982, Readings in Education Psychology, 1965, Yearbook of the Association for Student Teaching, 1962, The Great Debate, Our Schools in Crisis, 1959, Educational Issues in a Changing Society, 1964, Programs, Teachers and Machines, 1964, View on American Schooling, 1964, The Training of America's Teachers, 1975, Curriculum and Instruction, 1981; co-author: Teen Talk: Curriculum Materials in Communications, 1971; co-editor: Improving the School Curriculum, 1988, Restructuring for an Interdisciplinary Curriculum, 1992, Curriculum Issues and the New Century, 1995; contbg. editor: Ednl. Leadership, 1969-74; mem. editorial bd.: Tex. Tech. Jour. Edn., 1984-89, Teaching Edn., 1986-90, Jour. Curriculum Supervision; editorial cons.: Ency. of Ednl. Rsch., 5th edit., Jour. Ednl. Psychology, Ann. Rev. of Rsch. for Sch. Leaders; contbr. Atlantic Monthly Bull. of Atomic Scientists and other nat. mags., ednl. jours. Trustee Delaware Valley Coll., Doylestown, Pa., 1981-95; bd. dirs. Ohio State Alumni Assn. N.J., 1990-96. Recipient Excellence award Edn. Press Am., 1989, Distinguished Educator award Rider U., 1996. Fellow AAAS, John Dewey Soc. (bd. dirs. 1985-88, archivist 1989—); mem. AAUP, Am. Ednl. Rsch. Assn., N.Y. Acad. Sci., Am. Polit. Sci. Assn., Am. Ednl. Studies Assn., Nat. Soc. Study Edn., Phi Kappa Phi, Phi Delta Kappa (Svc. award 1957). Home: Highwood Rd Somerset NJ 08873 Office: Grad Sch Edn Rutgers U New Brunswick NJ 08903 *The essential quality of education and life is growth. Hence problems must be seen as opportunities and not as limitations if solutions are to be found and progress is to be made.*

TANNER, DAVID HAROLD, professional roof consultant; b. Union City, Pa., Nov. 20, 1945; s. Harold Oliver and Doris Louise (Wright) T.; m. Janet Patterson, Aug. 24, 1968; children: Jonathan David, Daniel James. BS in Edn., Calif. Univ. of Pa., 1967; MS in Edn., SUNY, Oswego, 1968; grad., USAF Air Commd. & Staff Coll., 1995. Cert. U.S. Naval aviator, 1969, USAF sr. pilot, 1979; FAA cert. comml. pilot; cert. tchr., Pa., N.Y. Structural steel layout Erie (Pa.) City Iron Works, 1968; navy P-3 pilot USN Atlantic Fleet, Jacksonville, Fla., 1968-72; indsl. edn. tchr. Carlisle (Pa.) Area Sch. Dist., 1972, So. Middleton Sch. Dist., Boiling Springs, Pa., 1972-73, Cumberland Valley Sch. Dist., New Cumberland, Pa., 1973-74; mgr. engring. svcs. Carlisle Syntec Systems, 1974-79; v.p. Carroll-Tanner Assocs., Corning, N.Y., 1980-81; tech. dir. C.F. Evans Roofing & Sheet Metal, Elmira, N.Y., 1982-86; roofing dir. HCFF Architects, Elmira, N.Y., 1986-96; pres. Tanner Roof Cons., Horseheads, N.Y., 1996—; asbestos bldg. inspector N.Y. State Dept. Health, Albany, N.Y., 1989—; dir. intelligence 914 Airlift Wing, Air Force Res., Niagara Falls, N.Y., 1988—. Author: Owner's Manual of Roof Inspection, Maintenance and Repair, 1992. Sunday sch. tchr. Maranatha Christian & Missionary Alliance Ch., Horseheads, N.Y., 1981—. Lt. USN, 1968-72, Atlantic and Europe; vet. Operation Desert Shield/Storm, 1990-91, Persian Gulf, Asst. Wing Intelligence Officer, Maj. USAF. Recipient Full Grad. Sch. fellowship Title V, U.S. Dept. Edn., SUNY, Oswego, 1967; named Disting. Naval grad., 1969, Disting. grad. USAF Intelligence Command, 1989. Mem. Constrn. Specifications Inst., Roof Cons. Inst., Res. Officer Assn., Classic Chevy Club, Am. Legion, Nat. Trust for Hist. Preservation, Epsilon Pi Tau, Phi Sigma Pi, Phi Delta Kappa. Mem. Christian and Missionary Alliance Church. Avocations: farming, hunting, historical restoration, cabinetmaking, antique autos, motorcycling. Office: Tanner Roof Cons 183 Sing Sing Rd Horseheads NY 14845-1073

TANNER, DEE BOSHARD, retired lawyer; b. Provo, Utah, Jan. 16, 1913; s. Myron Clark and Marie (Boshard) T.; m. Jane Barwick, Dec. 26, 1936 (div. Aug. 1962); children: Barry, Diane McDowell; m. Reeta Walker, Dec. 6, 1981. BA, U. Utah, 1935; LLB, Pacific Coast U., 1940; postgrad., Harvard U., 1936, Loyola U., L.A., 1937. Bar: Calif. 1943, U.S. Dist. Ct. (so. dist.) Calif. 1944, U.S. Ct. Appeals (9th cir.) 1947, ICC 1964, U.S. Dist. Ct. (ea. dist.) Calif. 1969, U.S. Supreme Ct. 1971. Assoc. Spray, Davis & Gould, L.A., 1943-44; pvt. practice L.A., 1944; assoc. Tanner and Sievers, L.A., 1944-47, Tanner and Thornton, L.A., 1947-54, Tanner, Hanson, Meyers, L.A., 1954-64; ptnr. Tanner and Van Dyke, L.A., 1964-65, Gallagher and Tanner, L.A., 1965-70; pvt. practice Pasadena, Calif., 1970-95; retired, 1995. Mem. L.A. Bar Assn., World Affairs Assn., Harvard Law Sch. Assn., Lawyers' Club L.A. Home and Office: 1720 Lombardy Rd Pasadena CA 91106-4127

TANNER, DOUGLAS ALAN, lawyer; b. Palo Alto, Calif., Aug. 30, 1953; s. Bernard R. and Caroline (Orris) T.; m. Carol Scilacci, May 28, 1977; children: Lauren Elizabeth, Wynn Ann, Leigh Caroline. AB in History, Stanford U., 1974, MBA, 1978, JD, 1978. Bar: Calif. 1978, U.S. Dist. Ct. (no. dist.) Calif. 1978, U.S. Ct. Appeals (9th cir.) 1979, N.Y. 1987. Law clk. to judge U.S. Ct. Appeals (9th cir.), San Francisco, 1978-79; assoc. Orrick, Herrington & Sutcliffe, San Francisco, 1979-83; ptnr. Orrick, Herrington & Sutcliffe, San Jose, Calif., 1984-86, N.Y.C., 1986-89; ptnr. Milbank, Tweed, Hadley & McCloy, 1989-92, Hong Kong, 1992—. Mem. San Francisco Barristers (chmn. corps. com. 1981-82), Order of Coif, Phi Beta Kappa. Republican. Episcopalian. Home: C-9 Stanley Knoll, 42 Stanley Village Rd, Stanley Hong Kong Office: Milbank Tweed Hadley & McCloy, 3007 Alexandra Hs/16 Chater Rd, Hong Kong Hong Kong

TANNER, HAROLD, investment banker; b. N.Y.C., May 7, 1932; s. Irving and Pauline (Steinlauf) T.; m. Estelle Newman, July 6, 1957; children: David, James, Karen. B.S., Cornell U., 1952; M.B.A., Harvard U., 1956. V.p., dir. Blyth & Co. Inc., N.Y.C., 1956-69; exec. v.p. New Court Securities Corp., N.Y.C., 1969-76, Blyth Eastman Dillon & Co., Inc., N.Y.C., 1977-80; ptnr. Salomon Bros. Inc., 1980-81, mng. dir., 1981-87; pres. Tanner & Co., Inc., N.Y.C., 1987—; co-founder Vol. Urban Cons. Group; dir. TIG Holdings, Inc. Chmn. bd. trustees Cornell U., Russell Sage Found. Lt. (j.g.) USNR, 1952-54. Mem. Coun. on Fgn. Rels., Century Country Club, Harmonie

Club. Home: 18 Kensington Rd Scarsdale NY 10583-2217 Office: 650 Madison Ave New York NY 10022-1029

TANNER, HELEN HORNBECK, historian; b. Northfield, Minn., July 5, 1916; d. John Wesley and Frances Cornelia (Wolfe) Hornbeck; m. Wilson P. Tanner, Jr., Nov. 22, 1940 (dec. 1977); children: Frances, Margaret Tanner Tewson, Wilson P., Robert (dec. 1983). AB with honors, Swarthmore Coll., 1937; MA, U. Fla., 1949; PhD, U. Mich., 1961. Asst. to dir. pub. rels. Kalamazoo Pub. Schs., 1937-39; with sales dept. Am. Airlines Inc., N.Y.C., 1940-43; teaching fellow, then teaching asst. U. Mich., Ann Arbor, 1949-53, 57-60, lectr. extension svc., 1961-74, asst. dir. Ctr. Continuing Edn. for Women, 1964-68; project dir. Newberry Libr., Chgo., 1976-81, rsch. assoc., 1981-95, sr. rsch. fellow, 1995—; dir. D'Arcy McNickle Ctr. for Indian History, 1984-85; cons., expert witness Indian treaties; mem. Mich. Commn. Indian Affairs, 1966-70. Author: Zespedes in East Florida 1784-1790, 1963, 89, General Green Visits St. Augustine, 1964, The Greeneville Treaty, 1974, The Territory of the Caddo Tribe of Oklahoma, 1974, The Ojibwas, 1992; editor: Atlas of Great Lakes Indian History, 1987, The Settling of North America: An Atlas, 1995. NEH grantee, 1976, fellow, 1989; ACLS grantee, 1990. Mem. Am. Soc. Ethnohistory (pres. 1982-83), Am. Hist. Assn., Conf. L.Am. History, Soc. History Discoveries, Chgo. Map Soc., Fla. Hist. Soc., Hist. Soc. Mich. Home: 5178 Crystal Dr Beulah MI 49617-9618 Office: The Newberry Libr 60 W Walton St Chicago IL 60610-3305

TANNER, JACK EDWARD, federal judge; b. 1919; m. Glenda M. Martin; children: Maryetta J. Greaves, Donnetta M. Gillum. Sole practice Tacoma, 1955-78; judge U.S. Dist. Ct. (we. dist.) Wash., Tacoma, 1978—, now sr. judge. Mem. Nat. Bar Assn. Office: US Dist Ct 1717 Pacific Ave Rm 3144 Tacoma WA 98402-3234*

TANNER, JIMMIE EUGENE, college dean; b. Hartford, Ark., Sept. 27, 1933; s. Alford C. and Hazel Ame (Anthony) T.; m. Carole Joy Yant, Aug. 28, 1958; children—Leslie Allison, Kevin Don. BA, Okla. Baptist U., 1955; MA, U. Okla., 1957, PhD, 1964. Assoc. prof. English, Franklin Coll., Ind., 1964-65; prof. English, Okla. Bapt. U., Shawnee, 1958-64, 65-72; v.p. acad. affairs Hardin-Simmons U., Abilene, Tex., 1972-78, La. Coll., Pineville, 1978-80; dean William Jewell Coll., Liberty, Mo., 1980—, interim pres., 1993-94. Contbr.: The Annotated Bibliography of D.H. Lawrence, Vol. 1, 1982, Vol. 2, 1985. Mem. Shawnee Sch. Bd., 1966-72; mem. edn. commn. So. Bapt. Conv., 1967-72. So. Fellowships Fund fellow, 1960-61; Danforth fellow, 1962-63. Mem. AAUP, Am. Assn. for Higher Edn. Democrat. Baptist. Avocations: tennis; photography. Home: 609 Lancelot Dr Liberty MO 64068-1023 Office: William Jewell Coll Office Provost Liberty MO 64068 *As I reflect on my life, the thought that presses on me is my incredible luck at having been born in America in the 20th century, my good fortune in having the opportunity for education, for a satisfying career, for supportive family, friends, mentors at every stage of my life. I must recognize any accomplishment as communal as well as individual.*

TANNER, JOHN S., congressman, lawyer; b. Dyersburg, Tenn., Sept. 22, 1944; s. E.B. and Edith (Summers) T.; m. Betty Ann Portis, Sept. 2, 1967; children: Elizabeth Tanner Atkins, John Portis. BS, U. Tenn., 1966, JD, 1968. Bar: Tenn., 1968. Mem. Tenn. Ho. of Reps., 1976-88, 101st-104th Congresses from 8th Tenn. dist., Washington, 1988—; mem. Ways and Means; co-chmn. Cong. Sportsmen's Caucas. Active Obion County Cancer Soc.; bd. visitors USAF Acad.; founding mem., co-chmn. The Blue Dog Coalition; former mem. bd. visitors U.S. Mil. Acad. Lt. USN, 1968-72; col. Tenn. Army N.G., 1974—. Mem. Obion County C. of C., Obion County Bar Assn., Rotary. Democrat. Disciples of Christ. Avocations: golf, hunting. Office: US House of Reps 1127 Longworth Bldg Washington DC 20515-4208

TANNER, JUDITH ANN, retired speech-language pathologist; b. Muncie, Ind., Nov. 1, 1934; d. Joseph C. and Anna (Hamming) Silvers; m. John E. Tanner, June 9, 1957; children: Jill A. Tanner Kamman, John Joseph. BS, Ball State U., 1956, MS, 1972. Cert. tchr., Ind. Speech pathologist Howard County Schs., Kokomo, Ind., 1956-57; tchr. hard of hearing Indpls. Schs., 1957-61; speech pathologist Randolph Ctrl. Schs., Winchester, Ind., 1965-92, ret., 1992. Bd. dirs. Community Concert, Randolph County, 1987—. Mem. Ind. Speech, Lang. and Hearing Assn. (sch. svcs. com. 1990—), Speech and Hearing Area Educators (honors and awards com. 1987—), Ind. Lawyers Aux. (chmn. laaw related edn. 1993-94, treas. 1994-95, pres.-elect 1995-96, pres. 1996-97). Republican. Methodist. Home: 400 Westwood Dr Winchester IN 47394-1933

TANNER, LAUREL NAN, education educator; b. Detroit, Feb. 16, 1929; d. Howard Nicholas and Celia (Solvich) Jacobson; m. Daniel Tanner, July 11, 1948; m. Kenneth J. Rehage, Nov. 25, 1989. BS in Social Sci, Mich. State U., 1949, MA in Edn., 1953; EdD, Columbia U., 1967. Pub. sch. tchr., 1950-64; instr. tchr. edn. Hunter Coll., 1964-66, asst. prof., 1967-69; supr. Milw. Pub. Schs., 1966-67; mem. faculty Temple U., Phila., 1969—, prof. edn., 1974-89, prof. emerita, 1993—; prof. edn. U. Houston, 1989-96; vis. professorial scholar U. London Inst. Edn., 1974-75; vis. scholar Stanford U., 1984-85, U. Chgo., 1988-89; curriculum cons., 1969—; disting. vis. prof. San Francisco State U., 1987. Author: Classroom Discipline for Effective Teaching and Learning, 1978, La Disciplina en la enseñanza y el Aprendizaje, 1980, Dewey's Laboratory School: Lessons for Today, 1997; co-author: Classroom Teaching and Learning, 1971, Curriculum Development: Theory into Practice, 1975, 3d edit., 1995, Supervision in Education: Problems and Practices, 1987, (with Daniel Tanner) History of the School Curriculum, 1990; editor Nat. Soc. Study Edn. Critical Issues in Curriculum, 87th yearbook, part 1, 1988. Faculty rsch. fellow Temple U., 1970, 80, 81; recipient John Dewey Rsch. award, 1981-82, Rsch. Excellence award U. Houston, 1992; Spencer Found. rsch. grantee, 1992. Mem. ASCD (dir. 1982-84), Soc. Study Curriculum History (founder, 1st pres. 1978-79), Am. Edn. Rsch. Assn. (com. on role and status of women in edn. R & D 1994-97), Profs. Curriculum Assn. (Factotum 1983-84, chair membership com. 1994-95), Am. Ednl. Studies Assn., John Dewey Soc. (bd. dirs. 1989-91), Alumni Coun. Tchrs. Coll. Columbia U. *In my view, America has progressed over the years, and the best days are still to come. We have the single necessary resource to solve our most urgent problems and achieve our deepest moral values —human intelligence.*

TANNER, MARTIN ABBA, statistics and human oncology educator; b. Highland Park, Ill., Oct. 19, 1957; s. Meir and Esther Rose (Bauer) T.; m. Anat Talitman, Aug. 14, 1984; 1 child, Noam Ben. B.A., U. Chgo., 1978, Ph.D., 1982. Asst. prof. stats. and human oncology U. Wis., Madison, 1982-87, assoc. prof., 1987-90, dir. lab., prof. and dept. chair dept. Biostatistics U. Rochester, 1990-94; prof. dept. of statistics Northwestern U., 1994—; cons. Kirkland & Ellis, 1980-82; mem. Nat. Inst. Allergy and Infectious diseases study sect., 1994—; reviewer NIH, NSF, VA. Assoc. editor Jour. Am. Stat. Assn., 1987—; contbr. articles to profl. jours. Recipient New Investigator Research award NIH, 1984, Mortimer Spiegelman award Am. Pub. Health Assn., 1993; NSF grantee, 1983, 95, NIH grantee, 1986—. Fellow Royal Statis. Soc., Am. Statis. Assn.; mem. AAAS, Mensa, Sigma Xi. Avocations: classical guitar; medieval poetry. Office: Northwestern U 2006 Sheridan Rd Evanston IL 60208-0852

TANNER, PATRICIA RUTH, gerontology nurse; b. Trego, Mont., July 30, 1935; d. Elmer E. and Jennie M. (Dukeshire) Pomeroy; children: Michael F. Ehart, Crystal Y. Blair, Karen Alexander. AS, Walla Walla (Wash.) C.C., 1973. Dir. nursing edn. Desert Palms Convalescent Hosp., Indio, Calif.; dir. nursing svc. Leisure Lodge, Mountain Home, Ark.; day charge nurse Hill Brook Nursing Home, Clancy, Mont.; charge and staff relief nurse Nursing Profls. Inc. Nursing Agy., Yakima, Wash., 1989-92; charge nurse Selah (Wash.) Convalescent Facility, 1991-92; med. and treatment on-call nurse Yakima Convalescent, 1993-94, med. and treatment nurse, 1995—; part-time and on-call nurse, resident care coord. Chinook Convalescent Ctr., 1994—, p.m. charge nurse, 1995—; resident care coord., staff devel., infection control nurse Selah Convalescent, 1995; p.m. medication nurse Yakima (Wash.) Convalescent, 1995—. Mem. Wash. State Nurse's Assn., Nightingale Soc. (pres.). Home: 1411 Naches Heights Rd Yakima WA 98908-8849

TANNER, R. MARSHALL, lawyer; b. Santa Monica, Calif., Dec. 4, 1946; s. Stanley Robert and Kathryn (Lau) Tanner; m. Colleen Bonner, Sept. 3, 1969; children: David, Brent, Julie, Glenn, Scott, Holly. BA, Brigham Young U., 1970; JD, UCLA, 1977. Ptnr. Lawler, Felix & Hall, L.A., 1977-86, Pettit & Martin, Newport Beach, Calif., 1986-95, Sheppard, Mullin, Richter & Hampton, 1995—. Lt. USNR, 1970-74. Mem. Calif. State Bar Assn., Orange County Bar Assn. Mem. LDS Ch. Office: Sheppard Mullin Richter & Hampton 650 Town Center Dr 4th Fl Costa Mesa CA 92626-1882

TANNER, ROBERT HUGH, engineer, consultant; b. London, July 22, 1915; s. George John and Evelyn (Stratton) T.; m. Joan Margaret Garnham, July 6, 1940; children: Christopher John, Rosemary June, Peter Pinckney, David Stephen. BS in Engring., U. London, 1936, MS in Engring., 1962; LLD, Concordia U., 1989. Registered profl. engr., Eng., Fla. From TV to rsch. engr. BBC, London, 1936-47; from engr. to dir. info. No. Electric Co., Ltd., Ottawa, Can., Ont., 1947-70; dir. info. Bell-No. Rsch., Ottawa, Can., Ont., 1970-72; pres. IEEE, N.Y.C., 1972; dir. indsl. rsch. Can. Dept. Comm., Ottawa, 1973-75; pvt. practice cons. engr. Naples, Fla., 1975—; cons. in field. Inventor various patents. Maj. Brit. Army, 1939-45, ETO. Fellow IEEE (pres. 1972, McNaughton Gold medal 1974, Pratt award 1981, Award for Engring Professionalism, 1993), Acoustical Soc. Am., Engring. Inst. Can., Instn. of Elec. Engrs.; mem. Nat. Coun. Acoustical Cons. (bd. dirs. 1982-88). Episcopalian. Office: PO Box 655 Naples FL 34106-0655

TANNER, W(ALTER) RHETT, lawyer; b. Athens, Ga., May 16, 1938; s. John Bryson and Walterette (Arwood) T.; m. Carolyn Laverne Watson, Nov. 11, 1967; 1 child, Walter Rhett (dec. 1989). AB cum laude, U. Ga., 1960, JD cum laude, 1962. Bar: Ga. 1961. Assoc. Hansell, Post, Bandon & Dorsey, Atlanta, 1963-66; ptnr. Hansell, Post, Bandon & Dorsey, 1966-89; ptnr. Jones, Day, Reavis & Pogue, Atlanta, 1989-95, of counsel, 1995—. Bd. dirs. Atlanta Symphony Orch., 1975-95, mem. exec. com., 1977-86, v.p., 1978, chmn. maj. gifts campaign, 1980, bd. counsellors, 1996—; mem. Leadership Atlanta, 1980, Leadership Ga., 1982; mem. bd. visitors Grady Meml. Hosp., 1983-92; bd. dirs. Econ. Opportunity Atlanta, 1986-87; trustee Ga. Legal History Found., 1986—, acting pres., 1996—. Lt. comdr. USNR, 1964-72. Mem. ABA, Atlanta Bar Assn. (bd. dirs. 1982-87, exec. com. 1983-87), State Bar Ga. (vice chmn. bar and media com. 1979-82), Atlanta Bar Found. (trustee 1985-91), U. Ga. Alumni (pres. chpt. 1973-74, chmn. Atlanta/Met. coun. 1975, mem. state bd. mgrs., v.p. 1976-78), Atlanta Lawyers Club, Gridiron, Capital City Club, Phi Beta Kappa, Omicron Delta Kappa, Phi Kappa Phi, Phi Delta Phi, Delta Tau Delta. Office: Jones Day Reavis & Pogue 3500 One Peachtree Ctr 303 Peachtree St NE Atlanta GA 30308-3201

TANOUS, PETER JOSEPH, banker; b. N.Y.C., May 21, 1938; s. Joseph Carrington and Rose Marie (Mokarzel) T.; BA in Econs., Georgetown U., 1960; m. Barbara Ann MacConnell, Aug. 18, 1962; children: Christopher, Helene, William. With Smith, Barney & Co., Inc. (now Smith Barney, Inc.), N.Y.C., 1963-78, 2d v.p., mgr. Paris office, 1967, v.p., 1968-78, resident European sales mgr., Paris, 1969-71, internat. sales mgr., N.Y.C., 1971-78, 1st v.p., 1975-78; chmn. bd. Petra Capital Corp., N.Y.C., 1978-81, dir.; pres. Lynx Investment Advisory Inc., Washington, 1992—; exec. v.p., Bank Audi (USA), N.Y.C., 1984-92; del. U.S.-Saudi Arabian Joint Econ. Commn. Bus. Dialogue; trustee Browning Sch., N.Y.C., 1987-93; bd. dirs. Cedars Bank, L.A., Interstate Resources, Inc., Rosslyn, Va. Chmn. Am. Task Force for Lebanon, Washington, 1988-91; bd. advisors Coll. Arts and Scis. Georgetown U., 1986-95. 1st lt. AUS, 1961-63. Recipient Medal of Honor Ellis Island, 1994. Mem. Am. Geographical Soc. (councillor), Georgetown U. Alumni Assn. (gov. 1968-71), Georgetown Club France (pres. 1968-71). Roman Catholic. Clubs: Met. (N.Y.C.), University (Washington); Automobile de France (Paris). Author: The Earhart Mission, 1979, Investment Gurus, 1997; co-author: The Petrodollar Takeover, 1975, The Wheat Killing, 1979. Earhart Mission, 1979. Office: 1100 Connecticut Ave NW Washington DC 20036

TANPHAICHITR, KONGSAK, rheumatologist, allergist, immunologist, internist; b. Bangkok, Feb. 22, 1946; came to U.S., 1971; s. Boonchoo and Hong (Nayakovit) T.; m. Sirirat Tareesung, June 17, 1973; children: Saksiri Marc, Marisa. Student, Mahidol U., Bangkok, Thailand, 1964-66, MD cum laude, 1970. Diplomate Am. Bd. Internal Medicine, Am. Bd. Rheumatology, Am. Bd. Allergy and Immunology; cert. Rheumatologist Royal Coll. Physicians Can. Straight med. intern Detroit Gen. Hosp.-Wayne State U., 1971-72; resident Barnes Hosp.-Washington U., St. Louis, 1972-74, fellow in rheumatology and immunology, 1974-76; instr. in medicine Washington U., St. Louis, 1976-77, asst. prof. medicine, 1977—; attending physician Barnes Hosp., St. Louis, 1976—, Jewish Hosp. of St. Louis, 1981—; dir. Allergy, Rheumatology & Immunology Specialists, St. Louis; cons. rheumatology Washington U., St. Louis, 1976—. Author: Amyloid Fibrils in Joint Fluid, 1976, Studies of Tolerance in NZB/NZW Mice, 1977, Vasculitis and Multiple Sclerosis, 1980, Buddhism and Science, 1987, Buddhism: Answers to Common Questions, 1990, Buddhism Answers Life, 1995. Dharma tchr., bd. dirs., sec. Wat Phrasriratanaram Buddhist Temple, St. Louis, 1983—; co-dir. Buddhist Coun., St. Louis, 1985-90. Fellow ACP, Am. Acad. Allergy and Immunology, Am. Coll. Rheumatology, Royal Coll. Physicians Can.; mem. Thai Physicians Assn. Am. (nat. treas. 1997—, treas. Midwest chpt. 1994, sec. 1997), Thai Assn. Greater St. Louis (pres.), Thai Temple Karate Shorinryu Club (Black Belt). Avocations: karate, karaoke, insight meditation, swimming. Home: 12413 Ladue Rd Saint Louis MO 63141-8100 Office: Allergy Rheum & Immun Specs 11115 New Halls Ferry Rd Florissant MO 63033-7613

TANQUARY, OLIVER LEO, minister; b. Springfield, Ill., Nov. 18, 1918; s. Lawrence Henry and Minnie (Potter) T.; m. Winifred Lillian Keen, June 24, 1939; children: Sylvia June, Lowell Emerson. BA, U. Pacific, 1933; MA, Boston U., 1940, STB, 1941; EdD, Fla. State Christian Coll., 1972; postgrad., Walden U., 1977-79. Ordained to ministry United Meth. Ch., 1941; cert. tchr., pub. sch. adminstr., Calif. Min. Hughes Meml. Meth. Ch., Edmonds, Wash., 1941-44; dir. guidance and rsch. County of Humboldt, Calif., 1948-52; min. Union Congl. Ch., Braintree, Mass., 1952-58, Paradise Hills Congl. Ch., San Diego, 1958-62; dir. guidance and counseling Paso Robles (Calif.) City Schs., 1962-68; dir. guidance and vocat. counseling County of Inyo, Calif., 1968-72; min. 1st Congl. Ch., Big Timber, Mont., 1972-77, 1st Meth. Ch., Big Pine, Calif., 1979-84, United Ch. of Christ, Quartz Hill, Calif., 1984-91; chaplain Mayflower Gardens Retirement Cmty., Quartz Hill, 1986-91; dir. vocat. counseling YMCA, San Diego, 1958-68; del. So. Calif. Conf., United Ch. of Christ, Pasadena, Calif., 1984-91, moderator Kern Assn., Calif., 1990; pres. Big Timber Ministerial Assn., 1967. Author: Choosing My Vocation, 1968, Foundations to Fulfillment, 1991, Our Rewarding Responses, 1997, (booklets) At Home in the Universe, 1944, Providential Guidance, 1954; contbr. articles to denominational publs. Mem. Inter-County Libr. Bd. So. Calif., 1982, Inyo County Schs. Adv. Bd., 1982-83, Inyo County Grand Jury, 1983-84. 1st lt., chaplain USAAF, 1944-48. Recipient svc. award Kiwanis Club, Paso Robles, Calif., 1965. Mem. Masons.

TANSELLE, GEORGE THOMAS, English language educator, foundation executive; b. Lebanon, Ind., Jan. 29, 1934; s. K. Edwin and Madge R. (Miller) T. BA magna cum laude, Yale U., 1955; MA, Northwestern U., 1956, PhD, 1959. Instr. Chgo. City Jr. Coll., 1958-60; instr. U. Wis., Madison, 1960-61, asst. prof., 1961-63, assoc. prof., 1963-68, prof. English, 1968-78; v.p. John Simon Guggenheim Meml. Found., 1978—; adj. prof. English and comparative lit. Columbia U., 1980—; mem. Planning Inst. Commn. on English, 1961; mem. exec. com. Ctr. for Edits. Am. Authors, 1970-73; mem. adv. com. for drama for bicentennial Kennedy Ctr., 1974-76; mem. Soviet-Am. symposium on editing Ind. U., 1976; mem. adv. com. Howells Meml., Kittery Point, 1976-78; exec. com. Ctr. for Scholarly Edits., 1976-81; mem. nat. adv. bd. Ctr. for Book, Libr. of Congress, 1978—; mem. adv. bd. Burton's Anatomy of Melancholy, 1978—, Pub. and Printing History, A Guide to Manuscript Resources in the U.S., 1980—; bd. dirs. Lit. Classics of U.S., Inc., 1979—, chmn. editl. standards com., 1979—, corp. sec., 1989—; mem. adv. com. N.Am. imprints program, 1980-92; Hanes lectr. U. N.C., 1981; mem. adv. coun. Rosenbach Mus. and Libr., 1980—; mem. adv. coun. Ind. U. Inst. Adv. Study, 1983—; mem. faculty Summer Rare Book Sch., Columbia U., 1984—; mem. adv. bd. Ctr. for Am. Culture Studies, Columbia U., 1985-94; mem. adv. coun. Am. Trust for the Brit. Libr., 1987—; Rosenbach lectr. U. Pa., 1987; mem. adv. coun. Am. Literary Manuscripts project, 1988—; bd. dirs. 18th Century Short-Title Catalogue/N.Am., Inc., 1988—, chmn., 1994—, Mark Twain Edition Project, 1991—; mem. vis. com. Lilly Libr., 1988-92; mem. adv. bd. Ctr. for Renaissance and Baroque Studies, U. Md., 1990—; mem. adv. com. Writings of J.F. Cooper, 1990—. Author: Royall Tyler, 1967, Guide to the Study of United States Imprints, 1971, A Checklist of Editions of Moby-Dick, 1976, Selected Studies in Bibliography, 1979, The History of Books as a Field of Study, 1981, Textual Criticism since Greg, 1987, A Rationale of Textual Criticism, 1989, Parkman Dexter Howe Library, Hawthorne and Melville, 1989, Textual Criticism and Scholarly Editing, 1990, Libraries, Museums, and Reading, 1991, A Description of Descriptive Bibliography, 1992, The Life and Work of Fredson Bowers, 1993; co-editor: The Writings of Herman Melville, 1968—, Samuel Johnson's Translation of Sallust, 1993; editor: Library of Am. Melville, 1982-83, Books as a Way of Life: Essays by Gordon N. Ray, 1988; mem. editorial bd. Contemporary Literature, 1962-91, Abstracts of English Studies, 1964-78, Papers of Bibliog. Soc. Am, 1968-80, Resources for American Literary Study, 1971—, Analytical and Enumerative Bibliography, 1977—, Review, 1978—, Am. Literature, 1979-82, Literary Research, 1986-90, Common Knowledge, 1991—, Book History, 1996—; contbr. articles to books and profl. jours. Mem. coun. Friends of Columbia U. Librs., 1990-94; bd. dirs. Friends of Lilly Libr., 1990-92. Recipient Kiekhofer Teaching award U. Wis., 1963, Jenkins award for bibliography, 1973; Guggenheim fellow, 1969-70; Am. Council Learned Socs. fellow, 1973-74; Nat. Endowment for the Humanities fellow, 1977-78, Laureate award Am. Printing History Assn., 1987. Mem. MLA (mem. exec. com. bibliog. evidence group 1974-75, methods of lit. rsch. div. 1979-83, chmn. 1982, mem. Hubbell award Com. Am. lit. sect. 1978-82, chmn. 1982, mem. com. on prize for ind. scholars 1983-87, chmn. 1985-87, chmn. ad hoc com. on future of print record 1993-95), Modern Humanities Rsch. Assn., Bibliog. Soc. London (pres. Am. Friends 1992—), Bibliog. Soc. Australia, Bibliog. Soc. Am. (mem. council 1970-94, vice chmn. publs. com. 1974-76, chmn. 1981-84, sec. 1976-78, chmn. com. on regional groups, 1978-80, 2d v.p. 1978-80, 1st v.p. 1980-82, pres. 1984-88), Bibliog. Soc. U. Va. (pres. 1992—), Oxford, Cambridge, Edinburgh, Birmingham, No. Ill., Can. bibliog. socs. (mem. coun.), Soc. for Bibliography of Natural History, Printing Hist. Soc. (Am. corr. 1970-84), Am. Printing Hist. Assn. (trustee N.Y. chpt. 1979-85), Pvt. Librs. Assn., Ind. Research Libraries Assn. (com. on standards for rare book cataloging in machine-readable form 1978-79), Fellows Morgan Libr., Manuscript Soc. (bd. dirs. 1974-79), Am. Pub. Libr. Film Project (bd. advisors 1993—), Am. Antiquarian Soc. (mem. publs. com. 1972-81, chmn. com. 1978-81, mem. council 1974-92, hon. councillor, 1992—, del. to Am. Coun. Learned Socs. 1978-93, exec. com. dels., 1987-89, chmn. exec. com. program on book in Am. culture 1983-89, com. on edn., 1982-85, chmn., 1983-85, chmn. com. on libr. 1988-91), Soc. Textual Scholarship (adv. bd. 1979—, pres. 1981-83), The Johnsonians (chmn. 1993), Melville Soc. (pres. 1982), Book Club Calif., Typophiles, Guild Book Workers, Wis. Acad. Scis., Arts and Letters, Renaissance Soc. Am., Am. Soc. 18th-Century Studies, Renaissance English Text Soc., Assn. Documentary Editing (chmn. Julian Boyd award com. 1986, Boydston award com. 1995), Soc. Scholarly Pub., Assn. internationale de bibliophilie, Soc. History of Authorship, Reading and Publishing (bd. dirs. 1993—), Phi Beta Kappa. Clubs: Century, Yale, Caxton, Grolier (publs. com. 1979-82, 83-87, 97—, council 1980—, small exhbns. com. 1979-87, chmn. 1980-82, sec. 1982-86, chmn. library com. 1985-86, pres. 1986-90), Odd Volumes. Office: John Simon Guggenheim Meml Found 90 Park Ave New York NY 10016

TANSEY, ROBERT PAUL, SR., pharmaceutical chemist; b. Newark, Apr. 27, 1914; s. William Austin and Charlotte E. (Endler) T.; m. Natalie C. McMahon, Feb.22, 1941; children—Barbara, Carol, Robert, David. B.S., Rutgers U., 1938, M.S. in Pharm. Organic Chemistry, 1950. Sect. head Schering Corp., Bloomfield, N.J., 1953-58; mgr. research Strong Cobb Arner, Inc., Cleve., 1958-63; tech. dir., v.p. Vet. Labs., Inc., Lenexa, Kans., 1963-84, cons., 1984—. Registered pharmacist, N.J., Mo., Ohio. Contbr. articles to profl. jours. Patentee in field (5). Mem. Am. Pharm. Assn., Rho Chi, Kappa Psi. Club: Toastmasters (cert.). Home: 11141 Glen Arbor Rd Kansas City MO 64114-5118

TANSILL, FREDERICK JOSEPH, lawyer; b. Washington, Feb. 27, 1948; s. Frederick Riker and Mary Eileen (Loftus) T.; m. Joan Louise Trefsgar, July 10, 1971; children: Brendan Frederick, Brooke Charlotte, Charlotte Trefsgar. BA with honors, Brown U., 1970; JD, Georgetown U., 1974, LLM in Taxation, 1982. Bar: D.C. 1974, U.S. Tax Ct. 1976, Va. 1983. Assoc. Cross, Murphy & Smith, Washington, 1974-77; ptnr. Bird & Tansill, Washington, 1977-79; assoc. Ober, Grimes & Shriver, Washington, 1979-81; ptnr. Lewis, Mitchell & Moore, Vienna, Va., 1981-86; counsel Boothe, Prichard & Dudley, McLean, Va., 1986-87; ptnr. McGuire, Woods, Battle & Boothe, McLean, 1987-90; shareholder Verner, Liipfert, Bernhard, McPherson & Hand, Chartered, McLean, 1990—; bd. dirs. Atlantic Trust Co. Fellow Am. Coll. Trust and Estate Counsel; mem. ABA, Va. Bar Assn. (coun. taxation sect. 1989-92, coun. and legis. com. wills sect. 1993—, trusts and estates sect. 1983—, bd. govs. 1988-96, chmn. bd. govs. 1991-92, co-chmn. spl. task force lawyers as fiduciaries 1993-95), D.C. Bar Assn. (steering com. estates, trusts and probate law sects. 1995—, co-chair 1997—), Fairfax County Bar Assn. (chmn. will sect. 1986, chmn. tax sect. 1987-88, CLE com. 1988-89), No. Va. Estate Planning Coun. (exec. com. 1987-92, pres. 1990-91), Tower Club (bd. dirs. 1988—). Office: Verner Liipfert Bernhard McPherson & Hand 8280 Greensboro Dr Ste 601 Mc Lean VA 22102-3807

TANSILL, FREDERICK RIKER, retired judge; b. Washington, July 12, 1914; s. Frederick Guida and Elizabeth Estele (Riker) T.; m. Mary Eileen Loftus, Dec. 31, 1940; children: Claire Tansill Hermann, Constance Tansill Gelfuso, Fred, Celine Tansill Kramer, Eileen Tansill Suddath. BSS, Georgetown U., 1936, JD, 1941; postgrad., Benjamin Franklin U., 1951-53. Bar: D.C. 1940. Credit reporter Dun & Bradstreet, Washington, 1938; instr. R.O.T.C., Georgetown U., 1940-42; spl. atty. IRS, N.Y.C., 1945-48; ptnr. Goodwin, Rosenbaum & Meacham, Washington, 1948-68, Cox, Langford & Brown, Washington, 1968-69, McInnis, Wilson, Munson & Woods, Washington, 1969-72, Bird & Tansill, Washington, 1972-79, Ober, Grimes & Shriver, Balt. and Washington, 1979-80; spl. trial judge U.S. Tax Ct., 1980-86; sole practice Washington, 1986—; instr. tax Ben Franklin U., 1956-57, instr. econs., 1967; appointed hearing examiner of two cases Legal Svcs. Corp., 1987, 89. Acting gen. counsel Children to Children, Inc., Washington, 1975-79; bd. dirs. Woodley Park Community Assn., Washington, 1968-76, v.p., 1975-76; pres. parish council Roman Cath. ch., 1973-76, 78-79. Served with AUS, 1940-45. Mem. ABA, Fed. Bar Assn., D.C. Bar Assn., Bar Assn. D.C., Delta Theta Phi. Republican. Home: 3001 Veazey Ter NW Apt 516 Washington DC 20008-5401

TANSOR, ROBERT HENRY, investor; b. Chgo., Apr. 1, 1935; s. John S. and Leora Caroline (Buhmann) T.; m. Stephanie Trainor, Sept. 10, 1977; children: John Frederick, Adam Robert. BS, Northwestern U., 1957. CPA, Ill., N.J. Sr. acct. Arthur Young & Co., Chgo., 1961-65; mem. corp. staff Litton Industries, 1965-67; v.p. fin., controller Royal Typewriter Co., Conn., 1968-72, Sweda Internat. div. Litton Industries, Pinebrook, N.J., 1973-75; v.p. fin., adminstrn. Paramount Pictures Corp., N.Y.C., 1975-77, Otis Elevator Corp., Farmington, Conn., 1977-83; v.p. fin., chief fin. officer Gulton Industries Inc., Princeton, N.J., 1983-86; sr. v.p., treas., chief fin. officer The Polymer Corp., Reading, Pa., 1986-89; pvt. investor, 1989—. Served to lt. (j.g.) USN, 1957-61; ret. comdr. USNR, 1980. Mem. AICPA, Ill. CPA Soc., Fin. Execs. Inst., Navy League U.S. Republican. Roman Catholic. Avocations: golf, swimming, theater, music.

TANUR, JUDITH MARK, sociologist, educator; b. Jersey City, Aug. 12, 1935; d. Edward Mark and Libbie (Berman) Mark; m. Michael Isaac Tanur, June 2, 1957; children: Rachel Dorothy, Marcia Valerie. BS, Columbia U., 1957, MA, 1963; PhD, SUNY, Stony Brook, 1972. Analyst Biometrics Rsch., N.Y.C., 1955-67; lectr. SUNY, Stony Brook, 1967-71, from asst. prof. to prof. sociology, 1971-94, disting. teaching prof., 1994—; cons. NBC, N.Y.C., 1976-89, Lang. of Data Project, Los Altos, Calif., 1980-89, Inst. for Rsch. on Learning, 1994-95; mem. Com. on Nat. Stats. of NAS, 1980-87; trustee NORC, U. Chgo., 1987—. Editor: Statistics: A Guide to the Unknown, 1972, Internat. Encyclopedia of Statistics, 1978, Cognitive Aspects of Survey Methodology, 1984, Questions About Questions, 1991; editor Internat. Ency. of Social Scis., N.Y.C., 1963-67; contbr. articles to sci., statis. and social sci. jours. Bd. dirs. Vis. Nurse Svc., Great Neck, N.Y., 1970—; bd. govs. Gen. Soc. Survey, Chgo., 1989-92. Sr. rsch. fellow, Am. Statis. Assn./NSF/Bur. Labor Statistics, 1988-89. Fellow, AAAS, Am. Statis. Assn.; mem. Internat. Statis. Inst., Phi Beta Kappa. Home: 17 Longview Pl

Great Neck NY 11021-2508 Office: SUNY Dept Sociology Stony Brook NY 11794

TANZER, LESTER, editor; b. N.Y.C., Aug. 3, 1929; s. Charles and Clara (Ente) T.; m. Marlene June Luckton, June 29, 1949; children—Stephen Drew, Jeffrey Marc, Andrew Wayne, M. David. A.B., Columbia U., 1951, M.S., Sch. Journalism, 1952. Reporter, Washington bur. Wall St. Jour., 1952-59; assoc. editor Changing Times mag., Washington, 1959-64; assoc. editor U.S. News & World Report, Washington, 1964-76, mng. editor, 1976-85; editor Cosmos Jour., 1990-93. Author: (with Stefan Ilok) Brotherhood of Silence, 1962; editor: The Kennedy Circle, 1961. Mem. Nat. Symphony Assn. Club: Cosmos. Home: 4859 30th St N Arlington VA 22207-2715

TANZI, CAROL ANNE, interior designer; b. San Francisco, Apr. 9, 1942; d. Raymond Edward and Anne Marie Giorgi. BA, U. San Jose, Calif., 1966. Teaching credential, Calif.; cert. interior designer, Calif. Home furnishings coord. R.H. Macy's, San Francisco, 1966-72; owner, pres. Carol A. Tanzi & Assocs., Burlingame, Calif., 1972—; instr. interior design Recreational Ctrs., Burlingame/Foster City, Calif., 1972-85; design cons. Am. Cancer Soc., San Mateo, Calif., 1994-95; mem. adv. com. for interior design students Coll. San Mateo, 1984-87; head designer San Mateo Battered Women's Shelter Pro Bono, 1993. Interior designer mags. Sunset, 1982, House Beautiful, 1992, 1001 Home Ideas, 1983; monthly cable TV program Interior Design by Tanzi, 1994—. Pres. Aux. to Mission Hospice, Burlingame, 1988-89, Hist. Soc. Burlingame, 1992-93; pres. Cmty. for Edn., Burlingame, 1996; mem. adv. com. Breast Ctr./Mills Peninsula Hosp., 1994—; mem. Oaks Hist. Adv. Bd., 1993-94; commr., pres. San Mateo County Commn. on Status of Women, 1990-95. Recipient Recogniton of Outstanding Performance Rotary Club of Burlingame, 1988—, Congl. Recognition U.S.A., Burlingame, 1994, Commendation Bd. Suprs., County of San Mateo, 1994, Recognition Calif. Legis. Assembly, Burlingame, 1994; named Superior Interior Designer Bay Area San Francisco Examiner, 1991, Woman of Distinction Soroptimist International, Burlingame/San Mateo, 1994. Mem. Am. Soc. Interior Designers (v.p. 1988, Presdl. Citation for disting. svc. 1986, 87, 88, Calif. Peninsula Chpt. Design award 1995), Burlingame C. of C. Women's Forum (chair 1986-95), Rotary Club of Burlingame (sec. 1988—). Avocations: miniatures, reading, exercising, basketball. Home: 1528 Columbus Ave Burlingame CA 94010-5512 Office: Carol A Tanzi & Assocs PO Box 117281 Burlingame CA 94011-7281

TANZMAN-BOCK, MAXINE M., psychotherapist, hypnotherapist, consultant; b. New Brunswick, N.J., Mar. 30, 1957. BA is Sociology, Rutgers U., 1980; MSW, Fordham U., 1984. Lic. clin. social worker. Therapist Van Ost Inst. for Family Living, Englewood, N.J.; pvt. practice Wayne, N.J., 1986—; cons. Union City Schs., N.J., Physicians Weight Loss Ctr., Wayne; psychotherapist Cath. Cmty. Svcs., Paramus, N.J.; with Family Svcs. Gergen County, N.J.; vol. probation counselor, residence counselor Svc. Ctrs., N.J.; social worker St. Lawrence Rehab. Ctr., N.J.; designer and presenter workshops. Featured cable TV 1990; host weekly call in therapy show on radio, 1991-92. Mem. NASW, Acad. Cert. Social Workers, Am. Assn. Behavioral Therapists, Am. Assn. Profl. Hypnotherapists. Office: 25 Packanack Lake Rd Wayne NJ 07470-5809

TANZMANN, VIRGINIA WARD, architect; b. Tuxedo, N.Y., July 6, 1945; d. John A. Ward and Helen Pfund. BA in Architecture, Syracuse U., 1968, BArch, 1969. Registered architect, Calif., Nev., NCARB. Intern architect Burke Kober Nicolais Archuleta, Los Angeles, 1969-72; project architect Daniel L. Dworsky & Assocs., Los Angeles, 1972-74, SUA, Inc., Los Angeles, 1974-75; staff architect So. Calif. Rapid Transit Dist., L.A., 1975-78; prin. The Tanzmann Assocs., L.A., 1978—. Prin. works, clients, include transp. facilities, housing, retail stores, comml. and office facilities 8 railroad stations, L.A. MTA Red and Blue Lines, L.A. Metro North Hollywood Sta., Conv. Ctr. Expansion Team, Renovation of Hollywood Bowl, Petroleum Lab. Chevron USA, Inc., El Segundo, Calif., Hyperion Treatment Plant, UCLA Med. Ctr., L.A. Unified Sch. Dist., L.A. Mission, So. Calif. Gas Co. Valencia, Gas Co. Computer Ctr., L.A. Dept. Water and Power, Oxnard Housing Authority, L.A. Housing Authority, Rehab 8 SRO hotels. Work exhibited: Monterey Design Conf., Calif., 1981, 87, 100/100 Exhibit, PDC, 1995. Pres. YWCA of L.A., 1984-87. founder, Kay Bixby Libr. on Volunteerism, 1992; mem. exec. com. United Way of L.A., 1992-93, bd. dirs. 1992-93; pres. Vol. Ctr. L.A., 1990-91, mem., 1973-94; exec. com. Dorland Mountain Arts Colony, 1990-91; mem. Mus. Contemporary Art, L.A. Conservancy; founder Women's Transp. Coalition, 1993, pres. 1993, 94, 95, 96, 97; bd. dirs. Info Line, 1995, 96, 97. Recipient Vesta award, 1991, Architect of Yr. award Women Construction Owners and Execs., 1994. Fellow AIA (AIACC bd., 1989-91, 92-94, L.A. pres. 1994); mem. Assn. Women in Architecture (pres. 1977-78, 87-88), Archtl. Guild (treas. 1987-88, v.p. 1988-89, pres. 1990), Calif. Women in Environ. Design (founder), Architects Designers and Planners for Social Responsibility, L'Union Internationale des Femmes Architectes. Office: The Tanzmann Assocs 820 E 3rd St Los Angeles CA 90013-1820

TAO, CHIA-LIN PAO, humanities educator; b. Soochow, Kiangsu, China, July 7, 1939; came to U.S., 1961; d. Tsung-han and Hoi-chin Pao; m. Jing-shen Tao, Aug. 22, 1964; children: Rosalind, Jeanne, Sandy. BA, Nat. Taiwan U., Taipei, 1961; MA, Ind. U., 1963, PhD, 1971. Assoc. prof. Nat. Taiwan U., Taipei, 1969-76, 78-79; vis. assoc. prof. U. Ariz., Tucson, 1976-78, 79-85, assoc. prof., 1989—; v.p. Hist. Soc. for 20th Century China in N.Am., 1992-93, pres., 1993-94. Editor, author: Studies in Chinese Women's History 4 vols., 1979-95. Mem. Tucson-Taichung Sister-City Com., Tucson, 1984—; sec. Ariz. Asian Am. Assn., 1989, dir., 1989-93. Rsch. grantee Nat. Sci. Coun., Taipei, 1971-72, 73-74, Harvard-Yenching Inst., Cambridge, Mass., 1972-74, Pacific Cultural Found., Taipei, 1984-85. Mem. Assn. for Asian Studies (pres. Western conf. 1994), Tucson Chinese Am. Profl. Soc. (pres. 1996), Tucson Chinese Assn. (bd. dirs.). Democrat. Office: Dept East Asian Studies Univ Ariz Tucson AZ 85721

TAO, RONGJIA, physicist, educator; b. Shanghai, China, Jan. 28, 1947; came to U.S., 1979; s. Yun Tao and Xiao-Mei Zou; m. Weiying Duanmu, Dec. 22, 1976; children: Han, Jing. MA, Columbia U., 1980, PhD, 1982. Rsch. assoc. U. Wash., Seattle, 1982-84; rsch. fellow U. Cambridge, Eng., 1984; rsch. asst. prof. U. So. Calif., L.A., 1984-85; asst. prof. physics Northeastern U., Boston, 1985-89; asst. prof. physics So. Ill. U., Carbondale, 1989-91, assoc. prof. physics, 1991-92, prof. physics, 1993—, chmn. dept. physics, 1994—; cons. UN Developing Program, N.Y. and China, 1992—; chair Internat. Conf. on Electrorheological Fluids, Carbondale, 1991, Feldkirch, Austria, 1993. Editor, author: Electrorheological Fluids, 1992, Electrorheological Fluids, Mechanism, Properties, Materials and Applications, 1994; contbr. articles to profl. publs. Office of Naval Rsch. grantee, 1990, 92, NSF grantee, 1996; recipient award Omni mag., 1987. Mem. Am. Phys. Soc. Achievements include discovery that electric-field induced solidification is the physical mechanism of electrorheological fluids, the crystalline structure of electrorheological fluids is a body-centered tetragonal lattice. Office: So Ill U Dept Physics Carbondale IL 62901

TAPE, GERALD FREDERICK, former association executive; b. Ann Arbor, Mich., May 29, 1915; s. Henry A. and Flora (Simmons) T.; m. Josephine Waffen, June 18, 1939; children: Walter Richard, James William, Thomas Gerald. A.B., Eastern Mich. U., 1935, Sc.D. (hon.), 1964; M.S., U. Mich., 1936, Ph.D., 1940. Asst. physics Eastern Mich. U., 1933-35, U. Mich., 1936-39; instr. physics Cornell U., 1939-42; staff mem. radiation lab. Mass. Inst. Tech., 1942-46; asst., then assoc. prof. physics U. Ill., 1946-50; asst. to dir., then dep. dir. Brookhaven Nat. Lab., 1950-62; v.p., then pres. Associated Univs., Inc., 1962-63, pres., 1969-80, spl. asst. to pres., 1980-82; commr. AEC, 1963-69; U.S. rep. to IAEA with rank of amb., 1973-77; former pres., cons. Associated Univs., Inc.; dir. Sci. Service Inc., 1971—, Atomic Indsl. Forum, 1970-73; mem. Pres.'s Sci. Adv. Com., 1969-73, Def. Sci. Bd., 1970-73, chmn., 1970-72; mem. sci. adv. com. IAEA, 1972-73; mem. gen. adv. com. ERDA, 1975-77; mem. adv. council Electric Power Rsch. Inst., 1978-85; mem. U. Chgo. bd. govs. for Argonne Nat. Lab., 1982-85; cons. Def. Nuclear Facilities Safety Bd., 1991—. Author: (with L.J. Haworth) Relay Radar Chapter of MIT Radiation Laboratory Technical Series, 1947; also papers, reports. Recipient Army-Navy Certificate of Appreciation, 1947, Meritorious Civilian Service medal Sec. Def., 1969, Dept. State Tribute Appreciation, 1969, Dept. Def. medal for pub. service, 1973; Henry DeWolf Smyth Nuclear Statesman award Atomic Indsl. Forum/Am. Nuclear Soc., 1978; Disting. Pub. Service award NSF, 1980; Disting. Assoc. award Dept. Energy, 1980; Enrico Fermi award U.S. Energy Dept., 1987; decorated comdr. Order Leopold II, Belgium. Fellow Am. Phys. Soc., Am. Nuclear Soc., AAAS; mem. Nat. Acad. Engring., Am. Astron. Soc., Phi Beta Kappa, Sigma Xi, Phi Kappa Phi, Kappa Delta Pi. Home: Apt 502 4970 Sentinel Dr Bethesda MD 20816-3569

TAPELLA, GARY LOUIS, manufacturing company executive; b. Antioch, Calif., Sept. 1, 1943; s. Anthony M. and Mary (Lopez) T.; m. Karen Kent, June 24, 1967; children: Robert, Michael. BA in Internat. Rels., San Francisco State U., 1969. Staff asst. Rheem Mfg. Co., N.Y.C., 1969-71; plant mgr. Rheem Can., Vancouver, 1971-73; mktg. mgr. Rheem Can., Toronto, 1973-79; regional sales mgr. Rheem Mfg. Co., New Orleans, 1979-80; mng. dir. Rheem Far East, Singapore, 1980-85; gen. mgr. Rheem Can., Toronto, 1985-89; corp. v.p. internat. Rheem Mfg. Co., N.Y.C., 1989-90, chief oper. officer, 1990-91, pres., chief exec. officer, 1991—; dir. various Rheem Cos. With USN, 1961-63. Avocation: scuba diving. Office: Rheem Mfg Co 405 Lexington Ave Fl 22 New York NY 10174-2299

TÀPIES, ANTONI, painter, sculptor; b. Barcelona, Spain, Dec. 13, 1923. Attended, Royal Coll. Art, London; ArtsD (hon.), U. Barcelona, 1988, U. Glasgow, Scotland, 1990. One man shows include Palacio Mudejar, Seville, Spain, 1992, Mus. Modern Art, N.Y.C., 1992-93, Detroit Inst. Arts, 1992-93, Mus. de Arte Contemporaneo, Caracas, Venezuela, 1993, Galerie Adriana Schmidt, Stuttgart, Germany, 1993, Galerie Lelong, Paris, 1994, Lunds Konsthall, Lund, Sweden, 1994, Galerie Nat. du Jeu de Paume, Paris, 1994, Guggenheim Mus., N.Y.C., 1995; sculpture include Waddington Galleries, London, 1992, Antoni Tàpies & Eduardo Chillida, Schirn Kunsthalle, Frankfurt, Germany, 1993, Magic Blue, Galerie Beyeler, Basel, Switzerland, 1994, Nitsch, Baselitz, Poliakoff, Kirkeby; commn. Monument to Picasso, City of Barcelona, 1983, large mosaic, Plaza Cataluña, Santa Boi, Barcelona, 1983, sculpture Núvol i Cadira, Fundació Antoni Tàpies, Barcelona, 1990, mural, Catalan pavilion, 1992, mural, Internat. Olympics pavilion, 1992; author: Memoria Personal, 1978. Recipient Guggenheim Found. award, 1964, Peace prize Spanish Assn. for UN, 1984, Picasso medal UNESCO, 1993. Mem. Royal Acad. Arts (Stockholm), Gesellschaft Bildener Kustler Österreichs (hon.), Kunstlerhaus (hon.), Royal Acad. Arts London (hon.), Am. Acad. Arts and Scis. (hon.). Home: Saragossa 57, Barcelona 6 Spain Office: Pace Gallery 142 Greene St New York NY 10012-3236 Address: 32 E 57 St New York NY 10022*

TAPLETT, LLOYD MELVIN, human resources management consultant; b. Tyndall, S.D., July 25, 1924; s. Herman Leopold and Emiley (Nedvidek) T.; B.A., Augustana Coll., 1949; M.A., U. Nebr., 1958; postgrad. S.D. State U., U. S.D., U. Iowa, Colo. State U.; m. Patricia Ann Sweeney, Aug. 21, 1958; children: Virginia Ann, Sharon Lorraine, Carla Jo, Carolyn Patricia, Catherine Marie, Colleen Elizabeth. Accredited pers. mgr. Profl. Human Resources. Tchr., Sioux Falls (S.D.) public schs., 1952-69; with All-Am. Transport Co., Sioux Falls, 1969-78, Am. Freight System, Inc., Overland Park, Kans., 1978-79; dir. human resources and public relations, corp. affirmative action compliance ofcl. Chippewa Motor Freight Inc., Sioux Falls, 1979-80; human resource and mgmt. cons., 1980-81; mgr. Sioux Falls Job Svcs. 1981-85, Pioneer Enterprises, Inc., 1985-86; ops. mgr. ATE Environ., Inc., 1986-88, cons. Royal River Casino, 1988-90; acad. dean Huron U., Sioux Falls, 1990-92, instr. econs. Coll. Bus., 1992—; chmn. Chippewa Credit Union; mem. adv. bd. dirs. Nelson Labs., Sioux Falls 1981-82; evening mgmt. instr Nat. Coll., Sioux Falls, 1981-90, chmn. adv. com., 1984—, Huron U., 1990—, S.F. Washington High Sch. Sports Heritage 1899-1989. Past bd. dirs. Jr. Achievement, United Way, Sioux Vocat. Sch. for Handicapped; past mem. Gov.'s Adv. Bd. for Community Adult Manpower Planning; chmn. bus. edn. adv. com. Sioux Falls Public Schs., 1982-85; chmn. adv. com. South East Area Vocat. Sch., 1982-85 ; mem. alumnae bd. Augustana Coll., 1985-88. Capt. USMC, 1943-46, 50-52, Korea. Recipient V.F.W. Commendation award, 1990, Liberty Bell award S.D. Bar Assn., 1967; Sch. Bd. award NEA/Thom McAn Shoe Corp., 1966, S.D. Unsung Heroes Edn. Recognition award 1992; named Boss of Yr., Sioux Falls, 1977; cert. tchr. and counselor, S.D. Mem. Am. Soc. for Personnel Adminstrn. (accredited personnel mgr. life, S.D. dist. dir. 1980-84), Am. Trucking Assn. (mem. pub. rels. coun.), NEA (life mem., Pacemaker award), S.D. Edn. Assn. (life), Sioux Falls Personnel Assn. (past pres.), Sales and Mktg. Club Sioux Falls, Sioux Falls Traffic Club, VFW (life, Nat. Polit. Action Recognition award 1990), Am. Legion. Republican. Roman Catholic. Clubs: Toastmasters (past gov. dist. 41, Disting. Toastmaster award, Outstanding Toastmaster award dist. 41, Hall of Fame 1977), Elks. Contbr. articles to nat. mags. Office: Huron U PO Box 90003 Sioux Falls SD 57105-9060

TAPLEY, BYRON DEAN, aerospace engineer, educator; b. Charleston, Miss., Jan. 16, 1933; s. Ebbie Byron and Myrtle (Myers) T.; m. Sophia Philen, Aug. 28, 1959; children: Mark Byron, Craig Philen. B.S., U. Tex., 1956, M.S., 1958, Ph.D., 1960. Registered profl. engr., Tex. Engr. Structural Mechanics Research Lab. U. Tex., Austin, 1954-58, instr. mech. engring., 1958, prof. aerospace engring. and engring. mechanics, 1960—, chmn. dept. aerospace engring. and engring. mechanics, 1966-77, Woolrich prof. engring., 1974-80, dir. Ctr. Space Research, 1983—; dir. Tex. Space Grant Consortium, 1990—; Clare Cockrell Williams chair in aerospace engring. U. Tex., Austin, 1984—; mem. adv. com. on guidance control and nav. NASA, 1966-67, com. on space rsch., panel I, 1974-76, chmn. region IV, engring. coun. on profl. devel., 1974-76; chmn. geodesy com. NRC, 1981-84, mem. aeros. and space engring. bd., 1984-86, mem. space sci. bd., chmn. com. on earth studies, 1988-91; bd. dirs. Tex. Space Grant Consortium. Editor: Celestial Mech. Jour, 1976-79; assoc. editor: Jour. Guidance and Control, 1978-79; assoc. editor: Geophys. Revs, 1979-81. Dir. Tex. Space Grant Consortium, 1990—. Recipient NASA Exceptional Sci. Achievement medal, 1983, NASA Pub. Svc. medal, 1994. Fellow AAAS (pres. engring. sect.), AIAA (chmn. com. on astrodynamics 1976-78, mech. and control of flight award 1989), Am. Geophys. Union (pres. geodesy sect. 1984-86); mem. ASME, IEEE, NAE, Am. Acad. Mechanics, Am. Astronautical Soc. (pres. divsn. dynamic astronomy 1988-89, Dirk Brouwer award 1995), Soc. Engring. Sci., Internat. Astron. Union, Sigma Xi, Pi Tau Sigma, Sigma Gamma Tau, Phi Kappa Phi, Tau Beta Pi. Home: 3100 Perry Ln Austin TX 78731-5327

TAPLEY, DONALD FRASER, university official, physician, educator; b. Woodstock, N.B., Can., May 19, 1927; s. Roy Donald and Velma (Fraser) T.; m. Caroline Southall, Sept. 14, 1957; children—Katherine, Elizabeth, Sarah Tapley Bangs. B.S., Acadia U., 1948; M.D., U. Chgo., 1952. Intern Presbyn. Hosp., N.Y.C., 1952-53; asst. resident, 1953-54, asst. attending physician, 1957-64, assoc. attending physician, 1964-72, attending physician, 1972—; Life Ins. Research fund fellow dept. physiol. chemistry Johns Hopkins U., Balt., 1954-56; Jane Coffin Childs fellow dept. physiol. chemistry Oxford U., Eng., 1956-57; asst. prof. medicine Columbia U., 1956-64, assoc. prof., 1964-72, prof., 1972—, assoc. dean for faculty affairs Coll. Physicians and Surgeons, 1970-73, acting dean, 1973-74, dean, 1974-84, alumni prof., sr. dep. v.p., 1984—. Trustee Morris Jumel Mansion, The Riverkeeper, The Mary Imogene Bassett Hosp., Cooperstown, N.Y. Contbr. numerous articles to profl. publs. Assoc. editor Endocrinology Mag., 1963-68. Mem. Am. Soc. Clin. Investigation, Endocrine Soc., Am. Thyroid Assn., Harvey Soc., N.Y. Med. and Surg. Soc. Office: Columbia U Coll Physicians & Surgeons 630 W 168th St New York NY 10032-3702

TAPLEY, JAMES LEROY, retired lawyer, railway corporation executive; b. Greenville, Miss., July 10, 1923; s. Lester Leroy and Lillian (Clark) T.; m. Priscilla Moore, Sept. 9, 1950. AB, U. N.C., 1947, JD with hons., 1950. Bar: N.C. 1951, D.C. 1962. With So. Ry. Co., Washington, 1953-83; gen. solicitor So. Ry. Co., 1967-74, asst. v.p. law, 1974-75, v.p. law, 1975-83; v.p. Washington counsel Norfolk So. Corp., Washington, 1983-87. Mem. Phi Beta Kappa, Kappa Sigma. Clubs: Chevy Chase.

TAPLEY, PHILIP ALLEN, English language and literature educator; b. Blackwell, Okla., June 11, 1938; s. Robert G. Sr. and Valena M. (Simmons) T.; m. Mary Stringer, Aug. 10, 1974; children: Mary Margaret, Laura Katherine. BA, U. North Tex., 1960, MA, 1962; PhD, La. State U., 1974. Cert. secondary tchr., Tex. Teaching asst. U. North Tex., Denton, 1960-61; teaching asst. La. State U., Baton Rouge, 1961-65, 68-69, instr., 1965-68; asst. prof. La. Coll., Pineville, 1969-74, assoc. prof., 1974-80, acting chmn. dept. English, journalism and langs., 1980, prof. dept. English, journalism and langs., 1980—; maj. scholar, presenter La. Endowment for the Humanities, Alexandria, 1977—; vis. cons. Ctrl. La. Electric Co., Pineville, 1989-95. Author: A History of First United Methodist, 1976, 2d edit., 1989, (with others) Proceedings of the Red River Symposium, 1987, 2d edit., 1991, Issues and Indentities in Literature, 1997; contbr. articles to profl. jours. Pres., Friends of Rapides Libr., Alexandria, 1985-86, 97, bd. dirs., 1996—; bd. dirs. Arna Bontemps Mus., 1995—. Mellon Found. fellow, 1982, 88, Ford Found. fellow, 1989. Mem. AAUP, South Ctrl. MLA (program chair so. lit. 1979), La. Folklore Soc. (pres. 1978-79), Hist. Assn. Ctrl. La. (pres. 1978-80, bd. dirs. 1978—), Phi Kappa Phi, Alpha Chi, Sigma Tau Delta, Omicron Delta Kappa, Sigma Delta Chi. Democrat. Episcopalian. Avocations: reading, music, historic preservation, folklore collecting. Home: 1721 Polk St Alexandria LA 71301-6334 Office: La Coll English Dept 1140 College Dr Pineville LA 71359-0001

TAPLIN, FRANK E., JR., trustee education and arts institutions and associations; b. Cleve., June 22, 1915; s. Frank Elijah and Edith R. (Smith) T.; m. Ngaio I. Thornton, Sept. 3, 1943 (div. Mar. 1951); children: Caroline I. Taplin Ruschell, Jennifer Taplin Jerome, David F.; m. Margaret A. Eaton, Apr. 27, 1953; stepchildren: Jennifer A. Sichel Dickerman, Martha D. Sichel Kelly, Susan Sichel Panella. BA in History, Princeton U., 1937; MA in Jurisprudence (Rhodes scholar), Oxford U., 1939; JD, Yale U., 1941; MusD (hon.), Cleve. Inst. Music, 1981; DHL (hon.), Fordham U., 1984; Dr. Mus. Arts (hon.), Manhattan Sch. Music, 1984; LLD (hon.), Rider Coll., 1988. Bar: Ohio 1946. With firm Jones, Day Cockley & Reavis, Cleve., 1946-50; asst. to Sen. Taft in Ohio senatorial campaign, 1950; pvt. bus. investments Cleve., 1951-57; asst. to pres. Princeton U., 1957-59; chmn. bd. Scurry-Rainbow Oil, Ltd., 1954-74; trustee Inst. for Advanced Study, Princeton U., 1972-88, trustee emeritus, 1988—; dir. NACCO Industries, Inc., trustee Environ. Def. Fund., 1990—; pres. Cleve. Inst. Music, 1952-56; trustee Cleve. Orch., 1946-57, pres., 1955-57; pres. Nat. Council Met. Opera, 1961-64; dir. Met. Opera Assn., 1961-91, hon. dir., 1991—, pres., chief exec. officer, 1977-84; hon. trustee Bradford (Mass.) Coll.; trustee Princeton (N.J.) Day Sch., 1966-72, Princeton Area United Community Fund, 1963-76; mem. Princeton U. Music Dept. Adv. Council, 1960-85, hon. mem., 1987—, chmn., 1965-71; trustee Sarah Lawrence Coll., 1969-77, chmn., 1973-77, hon. trustee, 1977—; trustee Lincoln Center for Performing Arts, 1972-88, trustee emeritus, 1988—, vice chmn., 1981-84; trustee, founding pres. Lincoln Center Chamber Music Soc., 1969-73; fellow Morgan Library; mem. council Friends Princeton Library; chmn. bd. Marlboro Sch. Music, 1964-70; now trustee; trustee Woodrow Wilson Nat. Fellowship Found., 1972—, Am. Schs. Oriental Research, 1970-75, Western Res. Hist. Soc., Cleve.; internat. bd. dirs. United World Colls., London, 1973-76; also chmn. United World Colls. (U.S. com.), 1973-75; bd. dirs. Am. Friends of Covent Garden and Royal Ballet, Friends of Aldeburgh Festival.; mem. vestry Trinity Ch., Princeton, 1984-87. Vice chmn. council of fellows Morgan Library, 1987-90. Served from ensign to lt. comdr. USNR, 1941-46. Decorated hon. mem. (mil. div.) Order Brit. Empire.; recipient Gold Medal award Nat. Inst. Social Scis., 1983, Disting. Service award Third St. Music Sch. Settlement, 1983. Mem. ABA, Assn. Am. Rhodes Scholars, Am. Philos. Soc., Am.-Scandinavian Found. (exec. trustee), Univ. Club (N.Y.C.), Century Assn. (N.Y.C., bd.mgmt. 1981-84), Springdale Golf Club, Nassau Club (Princeton), Pretty Brook Club (Princeton), Tavern Club (Cleve.).

TAPLIN, WINN LOWELL, historian, retired senior intelligence operations officer; b. Saint Albans, Vt., Oct. 3, 1925; s. Winn Lowell and Elinor (Cunningham) T.; m. Ellajean Allard, July 16, 1949; children: Leslie Taplin Baumann, Mark Allard. BSCE, U. Mich., 1946, AB, 1948, AM, 1950, PhD, 1956. Oper. officer CIA, Washington, 1955-81; cons. Stowe, Vt., 1981-94, Sarasota, Fla., 1994—. Author: Secret New England: Spies of the American Revolution, 1991, We Vermonters, 1992. Pres. Vt. Hist. Soc., 1989-93, trustee; pres. Mansfield View Water Corp., Stowe, 1989-92. 1st lt. USMC, 1943-46, U.S., 1950-52, Korea. Decorated Bronze Star, Intelligence Medal of Merit. Mem. Central Intelligence Retirees Assn., Assn. Former Intelligence Officers (dir. New England chpt.), First Day Cover Soc., Am. Philatelic Assn., Am. Legion, Disabled Am. Vets., U. Mich. Club Sarasota (dir. 1994—), Sigma Chi. Avocations: historical research, genealogy, classical music, stamp collecting. Home (summer): 903 Worcester Loop Stowe VT 05672-4326 Home: 7641 Sandalwood Way Sarasota FL 34231-5333

TAPP, MAMIE PEARL, educational association administration; b. Aiken, S.C., July 20, 1955; d. Willie Lee and Nancy (Madison) Garrett; m. Anthony Karl Tapp, Aug. 13, 1983; children: Anthony K. II, Barry Garrett, Myles Jarvis. BA, CUNY, 1977; MA, New Sch. for Social Rsch., 1984; postgrad., Nova Southeastern U., 1994—. Flight attendant Capitol Airlines, Jamaica, N.Y., 1976-81; pers. assoc. Cmty. Svc. Soc., N.Y.C., 1982-83; pers. specialist Marriott Hotel, Tampa, Fla., 1983-84; dir. placement Tampa Coll., 1984-86, facility coord., 1986-87, compliance officer, 1987-88; career counselor Alpha House, Tampa, 1988-91; career specialist U. Tampa, 1991-96, adj. prof., 1992-93; career specialist Jr. Achievement Greater Tampa, Inc., Tampa, 1996—; tchr. asst. program adv. com. mem, Jr. Achievement Greater Tampa, Inc., 1996—; tchr. asst. program adv. com. Hillsborough H.S., 1996—. Author: Resumes, 1992, Cover Letters, 1991, Thank You Letters, 1992. Bd. dirs. Children's Mus. Tampa, 1992-94; com. mem. United Way, Tampa, 1994-95; mem. bd. St. Peter Claver Cath. Sch., Tampa, 1995—, exec. com. Glee Club, 1995. Recipient Outstanding Bus. Woman award Am. Bus. Women's Assn., Tampa, 1987, Cmty. Svc. award Tampa Connections, 1993. Mem. AAUW, Am. Vocat. Assn., Fla. Assn. Women in Edn. Roman Catholic. Avocations: reading, sewing. Office: Jr Achievement Greater Tampa 5118 N 56th St Ste 123 Tampa FL 33610-5481

TAPPÉ, ALBERT ANTHONY, architect; b. Pitts., Aug. 12, 1928; s. Albert Anthony and Martha Ann (McKee) T.; m. Jean Bates, June 27, 1963; children: Eliza Bruce, Albert Anthony III. Student, William and Mary Coll., 1947-48, Fontainebleau Fine Art and Music Sch., 1951; B.S., U. Va., 1952; M.Arch., MIT, 1958, M.City Planning. Designer, McLeod & Ferrara (Architects), Washington, 1954-55; planner Boston City Planning Bd., 1957-58; architect and planner Architects Collaborative, Cambridge, Mass., 1958-61; partner Huygens & Tappé, Inc. (architects and planners), Boston, 1962-80; pres. A. Anthony Tappé & Assocs., Inc., Boston, 1980—; instr. dept. city planning MIT, 1959-60; cons. architect Mass. Bur. Library Extension, 1965-76; chmn. bldg. commn., Brookline, Mass., 1977, mem. bd. examiners, Brookline; v.p. Guild Religious Architecture; mem. Back Bay Archtl. Commn.; bd. dirs. Boston Archtl. Center, 1980; vis. architect Am. Acad. in Rome, 1997. Author: Guide to Planning a Library Building, 1967; important works include: Longy Concert Hall, Cambridge, Mass., Campus N.H. Coll., Franklin Park Zoo, Boston, Lynn Inst. for Savs., Interfaith Religious Ctr., Columbia, Md., student housing W.Va. Wesleyan Coll., Hotel, Costa Smeralda, Sardinia, Newton Pub. Libr., Beverly Pub. Libr., Am. Coll., Athens, Greece; also residences in U.S., France, Switzerland, housing projects in New Eng. Served with AUS, 1946-47, 52-54. Recipient Progressive Architecture Design award, 1966, 1st place single family category Plywood Design Awards Program, 1973, award of Merit, 1974. Fellow AIA (mem. nat. urban planning and design com. 1975, citation, hon. mentions 1969, 1st honor award 1970, honor award New Eng. Regional Council 1976); mem. Mass. Assn. Architects (exec. com.), Boston Soc. Architects (dir., v.p. 1981-82, pres. 1982-83), Am. Inst. Planners, Am. Planning Assn., Am. Inst. Cons. Planners. Clubs: Union Boat (Boston); Eastern Point Yacht (Gloucester, Mass.). Home: 58 Euston St Brookline MA 02146-4045 Office: 132 Lincoln St Boston MA 02111-2526

TAPPER, DAVID, pediatric surgeon; b. Balt., Aug. 26, 1945; s. Herman A. and Sylvia Phyllis (Golomb) T.; m. Susan Irene Wagner, June 25, 1968; children: Joellen, Erica, Jacalyn, Aaron. BS, U. Md., College Park, 1966; MD, U. Md., Balt., 1970. Surg. intern and resident U. Calif. San Francisco Med. Ctr., 1970-73; pediatric surg. rsch. fellow Boston Children's Hosp., 1973-75; sr. and chief surg. resident U. Calif., San Francisco, 1975-77; sr. and chief pediatric surg. fellow Children's Hosp., Boston, 1977-79; asst. prof. surgery Harvard Med. Sch., Boston, 1979-83; surgeon-in-chief Children's Hosp. Med. Ctr., Seattle, 1983—; prof. surgery and pediatrics U. Wash., Seattle, 1983—, vice chmn. dept. surgery, 1986—; bd. dirs. Am. Bd. Surgery, Phila., 1991—. Served to maj. USAR, 1971-82. Fellow ACS; mem. Am. Surg Assn., Am. Pediatric Surgery Assn. (bd. govs. 1993-96), Soc. Univ. Surgeons, Pacific Coast Surg. Soc., Halsted Surg. Soc. Republican. Jewish. Office: Children's Hosp Med Ctr 4800 Sand Point Way NE Seattle WA 98105-3901

TAPPER, JOAN JUDITH, magazine editor; b. Chgo., June 12, 1947; d. Samuel Jack and Anna (Swoiskin) T.; m. Steven Richard Siegel, Oct. 15, 1971. BA, U. Chgo., 1968; MA, Harvard U., 1969. Editor manuscripts Chelsea House, N.Y.C., 1969-71, Scribners, N.Y.C., 1971; editor books Nat. Acad. Scis., Washington, 1972-73; assoc. editor Praeger Pubs., Washington, 1973-74; editor New Rep. Books, Washington, 1974-79; mng. editor spl. pubs. Nat. Geog. Soc., Washington, 1979-83; editor Nat. Geog. Traveler, Washington, 1984-88; editor-in-chief Islands, internat. mag., Santa Barbara, Calif., 1989—; editl. dir. Islands Pub. Co., Santa Barbara, 1996—. Recipient Pacific Asia Travel Assn. Journalist of the Yr. award, 1995. Mem. Am. Soc. Mag. Editors, Soc. Am. Travel Writers (editors' coun.), Channel City Club. Democrat. Jewish. Avocations: travel, reading, tennis. Home: 603 Island View Dr Santa Barbara CA 93109-1508 Office: Islands Mag 3886 State St Santa Barbara CA 93105-3112

TAQQU, MURAD SALMAN, mathematics educator; b. Mar. 21, 1942. Diploma in physics, Inst. Tech., Lausanne, Switzerland, 1965; licence in math., U. Lausanne, 1966; MA, Columbia U., 1969, PhD, 1972. Lectr. math. Hebrew U., Jerusalem, 1972-73; postdoctorate rsch. fellow Weizmann Inst., Rehovot, Israel, 1973-74; asst. prof. Cornell U., Ithaca, N.Y., 1974-81, assoc. prof., 1981-85, prof., 1985-86; prof. Boston U., 1985—; vis. assoc. prof. Stanford (Calif.) U., 1981-82; vis. rsch. scientist Courant Inst., NYU, N.Y.C., 1985; vis. scholar Harvard Coll., Cambridge, Mass., 1987-88; organizer profl. confs.; cons. sci. reviewer. Author: Stable Non-Gaussian Random Processes: Stochastic Models with Infinite Variance, 1994; editor: Dependence in Probability and Statistics, 1986; assoc. editor Stochastic Processes and their Applications, 1989—; contbr. articles to profl. publs. Recipient William J. Bennett award IEEE Comms. Soc., 1995, W.R.G. Baker prize award IEEE, 1996; John Simon Guggenheim fellow, 1987. Fellow Inst. Math. Stats., Am. Math. Soc., Internat. Statis. Inst., Ops. Rsch. Soc. Am., Bernoulli Soc. Office: Boston U Dept Math 111 Cummington St Boston MA 02215-2411

TAQUEY, CHARLES HENRI, writer, consultant; b. Paris; came to U.S., 1937, naturalized, 1942; s. Henri and Marguerite (Normand) T.; m. Ruth McVitty, Feb. 1, 1947 (dec. May 1994); children: Antony, Chantal Sanders. B.S., U. Paris, 1929; Lauréat, Ecole Libre des Sciences Politiques, 1933; Licencié and Lauréat, D.E.S, Paris Law Sch., 1934. French Treasury rep. Paris, London, Berlin, N.Y.C., 1934-39; local currencies mgr. ECA, 1948-51; staff officer Exec. Office of Pres., 1952-57; fgn. service econ. officer Am. embassies Phnom-Penh, Cambodia, Tunis, Tunisia, Kingston, Jamaica; also detailed to Dept. Commerce as dep. dir. fgn. activities mgmt., 1957-70; mgmt. cons., ecol. economist (internat. trade and resources recovery), 1970—; expert witness Internat. Trade Commn., Ways and Means Com. U.S. Ho. of Reps., GAO, fgn. govts. Author: German Financial Crisis, 1931, Richard Cobden, 1938, Trusts and Patents, 1946, Obstacles to Development in Indonesia, 1952, Fisheries in Cambodia, 1959, Against Full Employment, 1973, Democracy and Socialism, 1976, Transnational Corporations and the State, 1979, Beyond Free Trade, 1983, Free Trade, Morality of Nations, 1987. Served as lt., arty. French Army, 1940; lt., arty. AUS, 1942-46; capt. 1952. Mem. Consumers for World Trade. Address: 1681 31st St NW Washington DC 20007-2968 also: Les Quatre Vents, 84580 Oppède France

TARAN, LEONARDO, classicist, educator; b. Galarza, Argentina, Feb. 22, 1933; came to U.S., 1958, naturalized, 1976; s. Miguel and Liuba (Etlis) T.; m. Judit Sofia Lida, Dec. 10, 1971; 1 child, Gabriel Andrew. Legal degree, U. Buenos Aires, 1958; Ph.D. in Classics, Princeton U., 1962. Jr. fellow Inst. Research in Humanities, U. Wis., 1962-63, Center Hellenic Studies, Washington, 1963-64; asst. prof. classics U. Calif., Los Angeles, 1964-67; mem. faculty Columbia U., 1967—, prof. Greek and Latin, 1971—, Jay prof. Greek and Latin, 1987—, chmn. dept., 1976-79; mem. Inst. Advanced Study, Princeton, N.J., 1966-67, 78-79; trustee Assn. Mems. Inst. Advanced Study, 1974-79; mem. mng. com. Am. Sch. Classical Studies, 1976—. Author: Parmenides, 1965, Asclepius of Tralles, Commentary to Nicomachus' Introduction to Arithmetic, 1969, Plato, Philip of Opus and the Pseudo-Platonic Epinomis, 1975, Anonymous Commentary on Aristotle's De Interpretatione, 1978, Speusippus of Athens, 1981; co-author: Eraclito: Testimonianze e imitazioni, 1972; Editorial bd.: Columbia Studies in the Classical Tradition, 1976-80. Am. Coun. Learned Socs. fellow, 1966-67, 71-72, Guggenheim Found. fellow, 1975, NEH fellow, 1986-87; grantee Am. Philos. Soc., 1963, 71, 75, Am. Coun. Learned Socs., 1968, 72, NEH, 1985-87, 88-89. Mem. Am. Philol. Assn., Classical Assn. Atlantic States, Soc. Ancient Greek Philosophy, Assn. Guillaume Budé. Home: 39 Claremont Ave New York NY 10027-6824 Office: Columbia U 615 Hamilton Hall New York NY 10027

TARANIK, JAMES VLADIMIR, geologist, educator; b. Los Angeles, Apr. 23, 1940; s. Vladimir James and Jeanette Downing (Smith) T.; m. Colleen Sue Glessner, Dec. 4, 1971; children: Debra Lynn, Danny Lee. B.Sc. in Geology, Stanford U., 1964; Ph.D., Colo. Sch. Mines, 1974. Chief remote sensing Iowa Geol. Survey, Iowa City, 1971-74; prin. remote sensing scientist Earth Resources Observation Systems Data Ctr., U.S. Geol. Survey, Sioux Falls, S.D., 1975-79; chief non-renewable resources br., resource observation div. Office of Space and Terrestrial Applications, NASA Hdqrs., Washington, 1979-82; dean mines Mackay Sch. Mines U. Nev., Reno, 1982-87, prof. of geology and geophysics, 1982—, Arthur Brant chair of geology and geophysics, 1996—; pres. Desert Research Inst., Univ. and Community Coll. System Nev., 1987—; adj. prof. geology U. Iowa, 1971-79; vis. prof. civil engring. Iowa State U., 1972-74; adj. prof. earth sci. U. S.D., 1976-79; program scientist for space shuttle large format camera expt. for heat capacity mapping mission, liaison Geol. Scis. Bd., Nat. Acad. Scis., 1981-82; dir. NOAA Coop. Inst. Aerospace Sci. & Terrestrial Applications, 1986-94; program dir. NASA Space Grant consortium Univ. and Community Coll. System Nev., Reno, 1991—; team mem. Shuttle Imaging Radar-B Sci. Team NASA, 1983-88, mem. space applications adv. com., 1986-88; chmn. remote sensing subcom. SAAC, 1986-88; chmn. working group on civil space commercialization Dept. Commerce, 1982-84, mem. civil operational remote sensing satellite com., 1983-84; bd. dirs. Newmont Gold Co., 1986—; mem. adv. com. NASA Space Sci. and Applications Com., 1988-90, Nat. Def. Exec. Res., 1986—, AF studies bd., com. on strategic relocatable targets, 1989-91; mem. pre-launch rev. bd., NASA, Space Radar Lab., 1993-94; mem. fed. lab. rev. task force, NASA, 1994—; prin. investigator Japanese Earth Resources Satellite, 1991-94; mem. environ. task force MEDEA, Mitre Corp., McLean, Va., 1993—; cons. Jet Propulsion Lab. Calif., Hughes Aircraft Corp., Lockheed-Marietta Corp., Mitre Corp., TRW; developer remote sensing program and remote sensing lab. for State of Iowa, ednl. program in remote sensing for Iowa univs. and U. Nev., Reno; program scientist for 2d space shuttle flight Office Space and Terrestrial Applications Program; mem. terrestrial geol. applications program NASA, 1981—; co-investigator Can. Radarsat Program, 1995—. Contbr. to profl. jours. Served with C.E. U.S. Army, 1965-67; mil. intellegence officer Res. Decorated Bronze Star medal; recipient Spl. Achievement award U.S. Geol. Survey, 1978, Exceptional Sci. Achievement medal NASA, 1982, NASA Group Achievement award Shuttle imaging radar, 1990, NASA Johnson Space Ctr. Group Achievement award for large format camera, 1985; NASA prin. investigator, 1973, 83-88, prin. investigator French Spot-1 Program to Evaluate Spot 1986-88; NDEA fellow, 1968-71. Fellow AAAS, Geol. Soc. Am., Explorers Club, Am. Soc. Photogrammetry Remote Sensing; mem. IEEE, AIAA (sr.), Am. Astron. Soc. (sr.), Internat. Acad. Astronautics, Soc. Exploration Geophysicists, Am. Geophys. Union, Am. Assn. Petroleum Geologists, Soc. Mining Engrs. Am. Inst. Metallurgical Engrs., Soc. Econ. Geologists, Bohemian Club San Francisco. Home: PO Box 7175 Reno NV 89510-7175 also: 2108 Calle De Espana Las Vegas NV 89102-4013 Office: Univ & Community Coll Sys Desert Rsch Inst Pres Reno NV 89512 *I have always been in awe of the universe in which we live and the little time we have on earth to perceive and understand it.*

TARANOW, GERDA, English language educator, researcher, author; b. N.Y.C.; d. Samuel and Sabina (Ostro) T. B.A., NYU, 1952, M.A., 1955; Ph.D., Yale U., 1961, postdoctoral studies, 1962-63. Instr. English, U. Ky., Lexington, 1963-65, asst. prof., 1965-66, Syracuse U., N.Y., 1966-67; asst. prof. Conn. Coll., New London, 1967-70, assoc. prof., 1970-76, prof., 1976—; referee NEH, Washington, 1972—. Author: Sarah Bernhardt: The Art Within the Legend, 1972, The Bernhardt Hamlet: Culture and Context, 1997. Yale U. fellow, 1962-63, NEH fellow, 1980-81. Mem. MLA, Am. Soc. Theatre Research, Soc. for Theatre Research (England), Internat. Fedn. for Theatre Research, Société d'Histoire du Théâtre (France). Avocations: opera; theatre; ballet. Office: Conn Coll PO Box 5567 New London CT 06320

TARANTINO, DOMINIC A., accounting firm executive; b. San Francisco, Aug. 1, 1932; m. Leona Lazzareschi, July 24, 1954; children: John Robert, Stephen, Leanne. BS, U. San Francisco, 1954. With Price Waterhouse, 1957—, mem. policy bd. and mgmt. com., 1979-93, vice chmn. tax svcs., 1982-88, co-chmn. bd., mng. ptnr., 1988-93; chmn. Price Waterhouse World Firm, 1995—; mem. IRS Commr.'s Adv. Group, 1978. Recipient Delta Sigma Pi Career Achievement award, 1997. Mem. AICPA (mem. bd. dirs. 1988-95, vice chair 1992-3, chmn. 1993-94, Dixon Meml. award 1990). Office: Price Waterhouse 1251 Ave Of The Americas New York NY 10020-1104

TARANTINO, QUENTIN, film director, screenwriter; b. Knoxville, Tenn., Mar. 27, 1963; s. Tony and Connie T. Screenwriter, dir., actor: Reservoir Dogs, 1992, Pulp Fiction, 1994 (Palme d'Or,Cannes Internat. Film Festival, 1994, Academy award best original screenplay 1994); screenwriter: True Romance, 1993; story: Natural Born Killers, 1994; producer: Killing Zoe, 1994; film appearances include Sleep With Me, 1994, Destiny Turns On the Radio, 1995; TV appearances include The Golden Girls, All-American Girl; actor: Desperado, 1995, Girl 6, 1996, From Dusk Till Dawn, 1996, Full Tilt Boogie, 1997; producer: Red Rain, 1995, Four Rooms, 1995, From Dusk Till Dawn, 1996, Curdled, 1996; dir., writer, prodr. Jackie Brown, 1997; dir. (TV series) ER, 1994. Office: A Band Apart Production Capra Bldg 112 10202 Washington Blvd Culver City CA 90232-3119 also: 6201 W Sunset Blvd Ste 35 Los Angeles CA 90028-8704 also: WMA 151 El Camino Dr Beverly Hills CA 90212*

TARAR, AFZAL MUHAMMAD, management consultant; b. Gujranwala, Punjab, Pakistan, Apr. 1, 1962; came to the U.S., 1989; s. Abdul Wahid and Ghulam Sugra Tarar.$D. Saiko Mori, Sept. 8, 1988. BE in Computer Engring., Tsinghua U., 1988; MS in Computer Sci., Case Western Res. U., 1991. Systems specialist EG&G, Inc., Beijing, 1986-89; cons. Cap Gemini Am., Cleve., 1990-91; officer, project mgr. KeyCorp./Key Svcs. Corp., Cleve., 1991-95; mgr. Deloitte & Touche Consulting Group, N.Y.C., 1995—. Mem. Am. Mgmt. Assn., Internat. Assn. Knowledge Engrs., Soc. for Mgmt. Applied Intelligent and Relevant Techs. in Fin. Svcs., Japan Soc. Cleve. (trustee 1992-94), Strategic Leadership Forum.

TARAS, PAUL, physicist, educator; b. Tunis, Tunisia, May 12, 1941; emigrated to Can., 1957, naturalized, 1962; s. Wladimir and Benita (Koort) T.; m. Marja-Leena Malinen, Aug. 3, 1963; children—Lisa Helene, Michele Anne. B.A.Sc., U. Toronto, 1962, M.A., 1963, Ph.D., 1965. Asst. prof. physics U. Montreal, Que., Can., 1965-70; assoc. prof. U. Montreal, 1970-76, prof., 1976—; spokesman U. Montreal in rsch. projects. Helios, SDC, Babar. Rsch. on nuclear and particle physics; co-managed conception and constrn. of 8pi Spectrometer, Chalk River Nuclear Labs, 1984-86; contbr. articles to profl. jours.; presenter papers to profl. confs. U. Toronto, Province of Ont., U.K. Atomic Energy Authority fellowships; France-Que., NRC, Natural Scis. and Engring. Research Council Can. grantee. Mem. Am. Phys. Soc., Can. Assn. Physicists. Home: 1639 Norway Rd, Montreal, PQ Canada H4P 1Y3 Office: Univ de Montreal, Lab Physique Nucleaire, Montreal, PQ Canada H3C 3J7

TARASI, LOUIS MICHAEL, JR., lawyer; b. Cheswick, Pa., Sept. 9, 1931; s. Louis Michael and Ruth Elizabeth (Records) T.; m. Patricia Ruth Finley, June 19, 1954; children: Susan, Louis Michael III, Elizabeth, Brian, Patricia, Matthew. BA, Miami U., Ohio, 1954; JD, U. Pa., 1959. Bar: Pa. 1960, U.S. Dist. Ct. (we. dist.) Pa. 1960, U.S. Ct. Appeals (3d cir.) 1964, U.S. Supreme Ct. 1969, U.S. Dist. Ct. (we. dist.) Tex. 1988, U.S. Ct. appeals (4th cir.) 1994. Assoc., owner Burgwin, Ruffin, Perry & Pohl, Pitts., 1960-68; ptnr. Conte, Courtney & Tarasi, Beaver County, Pa., 1968-78, Tarasi & Tighe, Pitts., 1978-82, Tarasi & Johnson, P.C., Pitts., 1982-95, Tarasi & Assocs. P.C., Pitts., 1995—. Mem. parish coun. St. James Ch., Sewickley, Pa.; mem. Sewickley Borough Allegheny Coun. With U.S. Army, 1954-56. Fellow Internat. Soc. Barristers; mem. Assn. Trial Lawyers Am. (gov., rep.), Pa. Trial Lawyers Assn. (pres. 1979-80), Acad. Trial Lawyers Allegheny County, Allegheny County Bar Assn., Pa. Bar Assn., West Pa. Trial Lawyers Assn. (pres. 1975), St. Thomas More Soc. (award 1991), Melvin Belli Soc. Democrat. Roman Catholic. Avocations: reading, golf, lecturing. Home: 1 Way Hollow Rd Sewickley PA 15143-1192 Office: The Tarasi Law Firm PC 510 3rd Ave Pittsburgh PA 15219-2107

TARBELL, DAVID S., federal agency administrator; married. BS in Mgmt., Rensselaer Poly. Inst.; M in Pub. Policy Analysis, U. Pa. Presdl. mgmt. intern U.S. Govt., 1979-81; asst. for energy security policy Office of Under Sec. Def. for Policy, U.S. Dept. Def., 1981-83, dep. dir. internat. econ. and energy affairs, 1983-85, dir., 1985-94, dir. Def. Tech. Security Adminstrn., 1994—; mgr. responsibility-sharing effort during Desert Shield/Desert Storm; past mem. staff NSC, dir. internat. econ. affairs, 1987. Office: Dept of Defense DTSA 400 Army Drive Ste 3 Arlington VA 22202-2803*

TARBELL, DEAN STANLEY, chemistry educator; b. Hancock, N.H., Oct. 19, 1913; s. Sanford and Ethel (Millikan) T.; m. Ann Hoar Tracy, Aug. 15, 1942; children: William Sanford, Linda Tracy, Theodore Dean. A.B., Harvard U., 1934, M.A., 1935, Ph.D., 1937. Postdoctoral fellow U. Ill., 1937; mem. faculty U. Rochester, 1938—, successively instr., asst. prof., asso. prof., 1938-48, prof. chemistry, 1948-62, Charles Frederick Houghton prof. chemistry, 1960—, chmn. dept., 1964—; Disting. prof. chemistry Vanderbilt U., 1967—, Branscom disting. prof., 1975-76, disting. prof. emeritus, 1981—; Guggenheim fellow and vis. lectr. chemistry Stanford U., 1961-62; Fuson lectr., 1972; cons. USPHS, Army Q.M.C.; mem. various sci. adv. bds. to govt. agencies. Author: Autobiography, 1996, (with Ann T. Tarbell) Roger Adams, Scientist and Statesman, 1981, Essays on the History of Organic Chemistry in the United States, 1875-1955, 1986 , also papers on history of chemistry. Recipient Herty award Ga. Sect. Am. Chem. Soc., 1973 Dexter award Div. History of Chemistry Am. Chem. Soc., 1989; Guggenheim fellow, 1946-47. Mem. Nat. Acad. Sci., Am. Chem. Soc. (chmn. div. history of chemistry 1980-81), Chem. Soc. London, Am. Acad. Arts and Scis., History of Sci. Soc. Home: 6033 Sherwood Dr Nashville TN 37215-5734

TARBI, WILLIAM RHEINLANDER, secondary education educator, curriculum consultant, educational technology researcher; b. San Bernardino, Calif., Feb. 23, 1949; s. William Metro and Sue (Rheinlander) T.; m. Jenny Workman, Apr. 10, 1980 (div. 1985); m. Michele Hastings, July 4, 1990; children: Amy, Melissa. AA, Santa Barbara City Coll., 1969; BA in History, U. Calif., Santa Barbara, 1976; MA, U. Redlands, 1992. Cert. secondary edn. social studies tchr., Calif. Reporter AP, Santa Barbara, Calif., 1976-80, UPI, Seattle, 1980-85, Golden West Radio Network, Seattle, 1980-85; tchr. Redlands (Calif.) Unified Sch. Dist., 1988—; cons. IMCOM, Redlands, 1985—. Mrm. E Clampus Vitus, Phi Delta Kappa. Avocations: painting, photography, writing, gardening, fencing.

TARBOX, GURDON LUCIUS, JR., retired museum executive; b. Plainfield, N.J., Dec. 25, 1927; s. Gurdon Lucius and Lillie (Hodgson) T.; BS, Mich. State U., 1952; MS, Purdue U., 1954, D Pub. Svc. U. S.C., 1993; m. Milver Ann Johnson, Sept. 25, 1952; children—Janet Ellen LeGrand, Joyce Elaine Schumacher, Paul Edward, Lucia Ann. Asst. dir. Brookgreen Gardens, Murrells Inlet, S.C., 1954-59, trustee, 1959—, dir., 1963-94, pres., 1990—. Chmn. Georgetown County Mental Health Commn., 1964-66; mem. exec. council Confedn. S.C. Local Hist. Socs., 1976—; trustee S.C. Hall Fame, 1976—, S.C. Heritage Trust, 1981-86, S.C. Mansion Commn., 1986—. Served with AUS, 1946-48. Recipient Francis K. Hutchinson medal for svc. to conservation The Garden Club of Am., 1995. Mem. Soc. Am. Foresters, Am. Assn. Bot. Gardens and Arboreta (dir. 1971-74, sec.-treas. 1982, v.p. 1983, pres. 1985-86), Georgetown County Hist. Soc. (pres. 1970-74), Am., Royal hort. socs., Am. Assn. Mus. (council 1983), Southeastern Mus. Conf. (dir. 1977-80), S.C. Fedn. Museums (pres. 1974-76), Am. Assn. State and Local History, S.C. Confedn. Local Hist. Socs. Episcopalian. Lodge: Rotary (pres. 1979-80). Home: 641 Crooked Oak Dr Pawleys Island SC 29585

TARBUTTON, LLOYD TILGHMAN, motel executive, franchise consultant; b. Easton, Md., Jan. 3, 1932; s. William Lloyd and Ethel Ford T.; m. Virginia Rachael Johnson, Nov. 1, 1952 (div. 1977); children: Gregory Alan, Kenton Lyle.; m. Layne E. Johnson, Apr. 15, 1981; 1 stepchild, C. Todd Woolston. Dr Comml. Sci. in Mktg., Pacific Western U. Grad. Realtors Inst.; cert. franchise exec., La. State U., cert. hotel adminstr. Divsn. sales mgr. Reuben H. Donnelley Corp. (advt. agy.), Norfolk, Va., 1953-58; owner, operator Tie Centre Stores, Norfolk, 1958-60; gen. mgr. Hembree Realty Co., Norfolk, 1960-62; chmn. bd., dir. Tarbutton Assocs., Inc., comml. real estate, real estate tax assessment Contesting, hotel-motel mgmt., and franchise cons., Norfolk, 1962—; co-founder, dir., pres., chmn. bd. Econo Lodges of Am. (formerly Econ-Travel Motor Hotel Corp.), Norfolk, 1967-83, chmn. bd. emeritus, 1983—; co-founder, chief judge Franchising Hall of Fame, Washington, 1979-82; co-founder, chmn. Coun. Franchise Suppliers, Washington, 1986-88. Author: Franchising--The How To Book, 1986. Trustee Edn. Found. Old Dominion U., 1979-86, chmn. bd. trustees Ctr. Econ. Edn., Old Dominion U., 1983-84. Hon. editor Hotel and Motel Mgmt. Mag., 1974-83; hon. mem. Motel Day's Com. Internat. Hotel and Motel Ednl. Exposition, 1974-83; recipient Hon. Tchr. award Maury High Sch., Norfolk, 1959. Mem. Internat. Franchise Assn. (hon. life, chmn. bd. dirs., chmn. 1st Asian Symposium on Franchising, Tokyo 1978, 1st European Symposium on Franchising, Amsterdam 1978, 1st Indonesian Symposium on Franchising, Jakarta 1991), Internat. Council Hotel/Motel Mgmt., Va. Hotel and Motel Assn., Realtor's Inst. Norfolk (chmn. 1965), Nat. Assn. Realtors, Nat. Assn. Real Estate Brokers, Norfolk Bd. Realtors (dir., v.p.), Internat. Sales Execs. Club (dir., v.p., Distinguished Sales award 1957), Norfolk C. of C., Internat. Platform Assn., Airplane Owners and Pilots Assn. Presbyterian. Clubs: Cove Point Yacht (commodore), Cavalier Golf and Yacht, Town Point, Registry Resort Tennis. Office: Birdneck Pla Bldg 700 Oriole Dr Virginia Beach VA 23451-4950 *I believe the greatest assist to my progress in business and personal life came when I became more aware of the "value of self" and thus others.*

TARDE, GERARD, magazine editor. Editor Golf Digest, Trumbull, Conn. Office: Golf Digest 5520 Park Ave Trumbull CT 06611-3426

TARDIF, JEAN, federal agency administrator; b. Courcelles, Quebec, Canada, Aug. 4, 1939; s. Antonio and Marie-Louise (Labrecque) T.; m. Ginette Lague, Aug. 21, 1965; 1 child, Violaine. BA, U. Laval, 1961; BSc, U. Montreal, 1964, MA, 1965. With Ecole Nat. Adminstrn., Leopoldville, Congo, 1965-67; prof. U. Congo, Lubumbashi, Zaire, 1966-67; dir. Min. Edn., Quebec, 1968-75; cabinet dir. Agy. Coop. Culture & Technology, Paris, 1975-78; dir. Min. Internat. Rels., Quebec, 1978-80; reps. Del. Affaires Francophones, Paris, 1980-84; del. Del. du Quebec BXL, Brussels, Belgium, 1984-86; dir. gen. Min. Internat. Affairs, Quebec, 1988—. Avocations: harpsichord, organ, tennis. Office: Min Internat Rels, 525 Blvd Rene-Levesque East, Quebec, PQ Canada G1R 5R9

TARDIO, THOMAS A., public relations executive; b. Pa., Jan. 26, 1952. V.p. strategic planning and other positions Columbia Pictures Industries, 1979-88; CFO, v.p. adminstrn. Rogers & Cowan, Inc., L.A., 1988-89, exec. v.p. entertainment sect., 1989-91, pres., CEO, 1991-95; co-chmn. mng. dir., 1996—. Mem. So. Calif. chmn. U.S. Olympic Com. Mem. Pub. Rels. Soc. Am., Nat. Acad. Recording Arts and Scis., Acad. Motion Picture Arts and Scis. Office: Rogers & Cowan Inc Ste 500 1888 Century Park E Los Angeles CA 90067-1702

TARDOS, ANNE, artist, composer, writer; b. Cannes, France, Dec. 1, 1943; d. Tibor and Berthe (Steinmetz) T.; m. Oded Halahmy, Nov. 6, 1976 (div. Dec. 1979); m. Jackson Mac Low, Jan. 20, 1990; step-children: Mordecai-Mark Mac Low, Clarinda Mac Low. Attended, Akademie für Musik und Darstellende Kunst, Vienna, Austria, 1961-63, Art Students League of N.Y., 1963-69. guest tchr. Sch. Visual Arts, N.Y.C., 1974, 87, SUNY, Albany, 1986, U. Calif., San Diego, 1990, Schule für Dichtung in Wien, Vienna, Austria, 1992-94. Author: (book) Cat Licked the Garlic, 1992, Mayg-shem Fish, 1995; composer: (CD) Chance Operation: Tribute to John Cage, 1993, Open Secrets, 1993, Museum Inside the Telephone Network, 1991, (cassette) Gatherings, 1980, Songs and Simultaneities, 1985; exhbns. include Jack Tilton Gallery, N.Y.C., 1989, Mus. of Modern Art, Bolzano, Italy, 1989, Venice Biennale, Venice, Italy, 1990, Galerie 1900-2000, Paris, 1990, Mus. of Modern Art, N.Y.C., 1993; (radio plays) Stimmen, 1986, Among Men, 1996, (with Jackson Mac Low) Phoneme Dance for John Cage, 1986.

TARDY, MEDNEY EUGENE, JR., otolaryngologist, facial plastic surgeon; b. Scottsburg, Ind., Dec. 3, 1934. MD, Ind. U., 1960. Diplomate Am. Bd. Otolaryngology (v.p. 1993, pres. 1994). Intern Tampa Gen. Hosp., 1960-61; resident in otolaryngology U. Ill. Hosp., 1963-67, fellow head, neck and plastic surgery, 1967-68; otolaryngologist St. Joseph Hosp., Chgo.; prof. clin. otolaryngology U. Ill.; pvt. practice Chgo.; dir. divsn. facial plastic and reconstructive surgery U. Ill.; prof. clin. otolaryngology Ind. U. Med. Ctr., Indpls. Pres. Am. Bd. Otolaryngology; bd. govs., Chgo. Symphony Orch., Hubbard St. Dance Co., Chgo. Mem. ACS, Am. Acad. Facial Plastic and Reconstructive Surgery, Am. Acad. Otolaryngology, Am. Laryngological Soc., Am. Rhinological Soc. Office: 2913 N Commonwealth Ave Ste 430 Chicago IL 60657-6211

TAREN, JAMES ARTHUR, neurosurgeon, educator; b. Toledo, Nov. 10, 1924; s. Joseph Clarence and Mary Frances (Walker) T. BS, U. Toledo, 1948; MD, U. Mich., 1952. Diplomate Am. Bd. Neurosurgery. Intern U. Mich. Hosp., Ann Arbor, 1952-53, resident in surgery, 1953-54, resident neurosurgery, 1955-57; clin. instr. U. Mich. Med. Sch., Ann Arbor, 1955-57, instr. neurosurgery, 1957-58, asst. prof., 1958-63, assoc. prof., 1963-67, prof. neurosurgery, 1967—, dir. neurobehavioral sci. program, 1975-78, assoc. dean acad. programs, 1978-87, dir. Brain Tumor Lab., 1985-88; dir. Integrated Acad. Info. Mgmt., 1988-89; dir. neuromodulation program U. Mich. Med. Sch., Ann Arbor, 1994—; neurosurgeon Wayne County Gen. Hosp., Eloise, Mich., 1957-71, VA Hosp., Ann Arbor, 1957-73, U.S.S. Hope (Project Hope), Peru, 1962, Ecuador, 1963, Guinea, 1965; vis. prof. Hosp. Foch, Paris, 1966-67, St. Anne Hosp., Paris, 1981, Karolinski Inst., Stockholm, 1981, Haukland Sykehus, Bergen, Norway, 1984, Gumma U., Japan, 1989, Nihon U. Sch. Medicine, Tokyo, 1990. Author, co-editor: Correlative Neurosurgery, 1969, 3rd edit., 1982; contbr. articles to profl. jours. Dep. med. examiner Washtenaw County Dept. Health, Ann Arbor, 1962—. Served with USMC, 1943-46, PTO. Fellow NIH, 1953; rsch. fellow in neurosurgery Boston Children's Hosp., Peter Bent Brigham Hosp., Boston, 1955. Fellow ACS; mem. AMA, Congress of Neuro. Surgeons, Am. Assn. Neuro. Surgery, Am. Assn. Med. Colls., Am. Soc. for Stereotactic and Functional Neurosurgery, Am. Neuromodulation Soc. (treas. 1994—), Royal Soc. Medicine (affiliate), Brit. Med. Soc., Internat. Assn. Study of Pain, Ferrari Club Am. Office: U Mich Hosps Sect Neurosurgery Box 0338 2124 Taubman Ann Arbor MI 48109

TARGAN, DONALD GILMORE, lawyer; b. Apr. 7, 1933; s. Solomon and Mollie (Simons) T.; m. Pamela Targan. BA, Juanita Coll.; JD, Am. U., 1961. Bar: N.J. 1961. Assoc. Arcus & Cooper, Atlantic City, N.J., 1961-65; atty. U.S. Atty.'s Office, Camden, N.J., 1966-69; ptnr. Targan & Kievit, Atlantic City, 1969—. Book rev. editor Am. U. Law Jour., 1960, editor-in-chief, 1961; contbr. articles to legal jours. With U.S. Army, 1954-56. Burton Smith scholar, 1961. Mem. ATLA, Assn. Trial Lawyers N.J. (bd. dirs. 1983), Am. Bd. Trial Advocates (cert. civil trial atty.), N.J. State Bar Assn. Home: 1706 Shore Rd Northfield NJ 08225-2218 Office: Targan & Kievit 1 S New York Ave Atlantic City NJ 08401-8012

TARGOVNIK, SELMA E. KAPLAN, physician; b. N.Y.C., Apr. 22, 1936; d. Harry A. and Helen (Goodstein) Kaplan; m. Jerome H. Targovnik, Dec. 2, 1961; children: Nina Rebecca, Labe Eric (dec.), Diane Michelle. BA, NYU, 1957; MD, Albert Einstein Coll. Medicine, 1961. Diplomate Am. Bd. Dermatology. Intern Kaiser Found. Hosp., San Francisco, 1961-62; resident in internal medicine Bellevue Hosp., NYU Med. Ctr., 1962-63, U. Colo. Med. Ctr., Denver, 1963-64; rsch. fellow, resident in dermatology Boston U. Med. Ctr., 1964-66, mem. staff, 1968-69; mem. staff NYU Med. Ctr., 1966-68; practice medicine specializing in dermatology, Phoenix, 1969—; mem. staff St. Joseph's Hosp., Phoenix, St. Luke's Hosp., Phoenix, Columbia Hosp., Phoenix; mem. staff Good Samaritan Hosp., Phoenix, chief divsn. dermatology, 1985-90. Bd. dirs. ACLU, Ari z., 1973-78, 83-94, Congregation Beth El, Phoenix, 1971-75, Flagstaff Festival of the Arts, 1984-86; active Jewish Nat. Fund. Fellow Am. Acad. Dermatology, Assocs. for the Weizmann Inst. of Sci., Assocs. for the Technion Inst.; mem. Am. Technion Soc. (bd. dirs. 1988—, pres. Ariz. divsn. 1990-92), Dermatology Found.,

Sonoran Dermatologic Soc. Southwestern Dermatologic Soc., Pacific Dermatologic Soc., Noah Worcester Dermatologic Soc., Phi Beta Kappa, Mu Chi Sigma, Pi Delta Phi, Beta Lambda Sigma. Democrat. Jewish. Home: 3706 E Rancho Dr Paradise Valley AZ 85253-5023 Office: 1300 N 12th St Ste 503 Phoenix AZ 85006-2849

TARINO, GARY EDWARD, lawyer; b. Jersey City, Oct. 3, 1951; s. Edward G. and Veronica (Scimeca) T.; m. Maureen Fitzpatrick, May 9, 1987. BA summa cum laude, Rutgers U., 1973, JD, 1976. Bar: N.J. 1976, U.S. Dist. Ct. N.J. 1976, D.C. Ct. Appeals 1978, U.S. Supreme Ct. 1980, N.Y. 1982, U.S. Dist. Ct. (so. dist.) N.Y. 1988, U.S. Dist. Ct. (ea. dist.) N.Y. 1990. Assoc. Winne, Banta, Rizzi & Harrington, Hackensack, N.J., 1976-79; asst. pros. Bergen County Pros. Office, Hackensack, 1979-83, chief organized crime squad, 1981-83; atty. Automatic Data Processing, Inc., Roseland, N.J., 1983—; assoc. gen. counsel, staff v.p. Automatic Data Processing, Inc., Roseland, 1994—; pub. defender Borough of Maywood, N.J., 1978; bd. dirs. N.J. Coun. Econ. Edn., 1990—; master Sidney Reitman Employment Law Am. Inn Ct., 1995—. Bd. dirs. Am. Heart Assn., N.J., 1976-81, Middlesex County (N.J.) chpt., 1973-81; trustee Integrity, Inc., 1991-97; grad. Leadership N.J., 1989. Recipient cert. of appreciation U.S. Treasury Dept., 1983, letter of commendation PBA, 1983, Alumni Vol. Leadership award 1st Ann. Leadership N.J., 1991. Office: Automatic Data Processing 1 A D P Blvd Roseland NJ 07068-1728

TARITAS, KAREN JOYCE, telemarketing executive; b. Ft. Wayne, Ind., June 5, 1957; d. George and Patricia Louise (Smith) T. BS, Purdue U., 1988; AAS, Ind. U., 1980. Billing rep., experience analyst Lincoln Nat. Life Ins. Co., Ft. Wayne, 1974-82; customer svc. rep., underwriting asst. K&K Ins. Co., Ft. Wayne, 1984-86; telemarketing mgr. Stanley Steemer Carpet Cleaner, Ft. Wayne, 1990—. Mem. Am. Mus. Nat. History, Smithsonian Instn., Libr. Congress, Purdue U. Alumni Club, Ind. U. Alumni Club, Delta Sigma Pi. Avocations: collecting music boxes, cross stitch/needlepoint. Home: 4414 Hanna St Fort Wayne IN 46806-4744 Office: 5109 Industrial Rd Fort Wayne IN 46825-5215

TARJAN, ROBERT WEGG, retired information services executive; b. Evanston, Ill., July 28, 1943; s. Robert David and Constance Rita (Wegg) T.; m. Elizabeth Lindner; children: Robert J., Anne Marie, Katie, Michael, Eileen. BS in Math., Loyola U., Chgo., 1965. Programmer Kemper Nat. Ins. Cos., Long Grove, Ill., 1965-67, supr., 1967-79, teleprocessing mgr., 1969-78, tech. systems mgr., 1978-81, ops. and system support mgr., 1981-85, asst. mgr. info. svcs., 1985-86, v.p. info. svcs., 1986-97; bd. dirs. Acord, Pearl River, N.Y. Roman Catholic. Avocation: golf.

TARKOFF, MICHAEL HARRIS, lawyer; b. Phila., Oct. 3, 1946. BA, U. Miami, 1968, JD, 1971. Bar: Fla. 1973, U.S. Supreme Ct. 1976, N.Y. 1983, U.S. Tax Ct. 1984. Asst. pub. defender Miami Pub. Defender's Office, Fla., 1973-77; guest lectr. U. Miami Sch. Law, 1977; ptnr. Flynn, Rubio & Tarkoff, Miami, 1977-83; ptnr. Flynn and Tarkoff, Miami, 1983-90; pvt. practice, 1990—; mem. substantial asst. in trafficking cases com. criminal law sect. Fla. Bar. Mem. Dade County Dem. Exec. Com., 1970-72, Tiger Bay; legal counsel Dade County Dem. Com., 1978. Sponsor, South Fla. coun. Boy Scouts Am.; USTA sectional umpire, Fla. sec. dist. 8, dir.; with FTA Jr. Tournament Com., del., FTA Dist. Dir. Officials. Mem. ABA, Fla. Bar Assn. (narcotics practice, legis. com. criminal law sect., crim. law sect., fed. practice com., criminal procedure rules subcom. 1989-95), Nat. Inst. Trial Advocacy (mem. faculty), Nat. Assn. Criminal Def. Lawyers (membership com., NORML legal com.), Fla. Criminal Def. Lawyers Assn. Office: 100 SE 2nd St Fl 35 Miami FL 33131-2100

TARLETON, LARRY WILSON, newspaper editor; b. Wadesboro, N.C., July 19, 1943; s. Harold Wilson and Martha (Roberson) T.; m. Judith Elaine Huntley, Sept. 8, 1963; children: Laurie Leigh, Larry Huntley. BA in Journalism, U. N.C., 1965. Reporter The Charlotte (N.C.) Observer, 1965-73; sporte writer The Miami (Fla.) Herold, 1973-74; sports editor The Charlotte Observer, 1974-76; exec. sports editor, mng. editor, exec. editor The Dallas Times Herald, 1976-88; exec. editor The Post and Courier, Charleston, S.C., 1988—. Mem. Am. Soc. Newspaper Editors, S.C. Press Assn., Dallas Press Club (pres. 1988). AP Mng. editors, AP Sports Editors. Avocations: golf, travel. Home: 27 New St Charleston SC 29401-2405 Office: The Post and Courier 134 Columbus St Charleston SC 29403-4809*

TARLETON, ROBERT STEPHEN, producer and distributor fine arts videos; b. N.Y.C., Feb. 27, 1946; s. Rollin and Helen (Boyle) Tarleton. BA, Wesleyan U., Middletown, Conn, 1968; postgrad. studies, U. Pa., Columbia, N.Y.U. V.p., exec. dir. Intercollegiate Broadcasting System, Vails Gate, N.Y., 1973-74; adjudicator U.S. VA, N.Y.C., 1974-88; prin. Applause Prodns., Inc., Port Washington, N.Y., 1989&. Author: (book) The Spirit of Kappa Alpha, 1994; (booklet) Always...Everywhere. Mem. operating com. John Philip Sousa Band Shell, Port Washington, 1985—. Staff sgt. U.S. Air Force, 1969-73. Recipient several svc.-wide awards for journalism while in air force. Mem. Broadcast Found. of Coll., Univ. Students (bd. dirs. 1977), Omega Gamma Delta (nat. pres. 1970-82, 96—, nat. sec. 1989—), Kappa Alpha Soc. (internat. sec. 1993—). Avocations: amateur radio, philately. Home and Office: 89 Longview Rd Port Washington NY 11050

TARLOV, ALVIN RICHARD, former philanthropic foundation administrator, physician, educator, researcher; b. Norwalk, Conn., July 11, 1929; s. Charles and Mae (Shelinsky) T.; m. Joan Hylton, June 12, 1956 (div. 1976); children: Richard, Elizabeth, Jane, Suzanne, David. BA, Dartmouth Coll., 1951; MD, U. Chgo., 1956. Intern Phila. Gen. Hosp., 1956-57; resident in medicine U. Chgo. Hosps., 1957-58, 62-63, research assoc., 1958-61; asst. prof. medicine U. Chgo., 1963-68, assoc. prof., 1968-70, prof., 1970-84, chmn. dept. medicine, 1969-81; chmn. grad. med. edn. nat. adv. com. HHS, Washington, 1980; pres. Henry J. Kaiser Family Found., Menlo Park, Calif., 1984-90; sr. scientist New Eng. Med. Ctr., Boston, 1990—, exec. dir. The Health Inst., 1995—; prof. of Pub. Health Harvard U., Boston, 1990—; prof. of medicine Tufts U., 1990—. Pres. Med. Outcomes Trust, Inc., 1993—; chmn. bd., pres. Mass. Health Data Consortium, 1994—. Served to capt. U.S. Army, 1958-61. Recipient Research Career Devel. award NIH, 1962-67; John and Mary Markle Found. scholar, 1966-71. Mem. ACP (master), Inst. Medicine of Nat. Acad. Scis. Office: The Health Inst New Eng Med Ctr 750 Washington St # 345 Boston MA 02111-1526

TARN, NATHANIEL, poet, translator, educator; b. Paris, June 30, 1928; s. Marcel and Yvonne (Suchar) T.; children : Andrea, Marc. BA with honors, Cambridge (Eng.) U., 1948, MA, 1952; postgrad., U. Sorbonne, U. Paris, 1949-51; MA, U. Chgo., 1952, PhD, 1957; postgrad., London Sch. Econs., 1953-58. Anthropologist Guatemala, Burma, Alaska, and other locations, 1952—; prof. comparative lit. Rutgers U., 1970-85, prof. emeritus modern poetry, comparative lit, anthropology, 1985; vis. prof. SUNY, Buffalo and Princeton, 1969-70. Author: Old Savage/Young City, 1964, Where Babylon Ends, 1968, The Beautiful Contradictions, 1969, October, 1969, A Nowhere for Vallejo, 1971, Lyrics for the Bride of God: Section: The Artemision, 1972, The Persephones, 1974, Lyrics for the Bride of God, 1975, The House of Leaves, 1976, Birdscapes, with Seaside, 1978, The Desert Mothers, 1985, At the Western Gates, 1985, Palenque, 1986, Seeing America First, 1989, Flying the Body, 1993, Multitude of One, 1995, Scandals in the House of Birds, 1997, Views from the Weaving Mountain: Selected Essays in Poetics and Anthropology, 1991, Scandals in the House of Birds: Shamans & Priests on Lake Atitlan, 1997; co-author: (with Janet Rodney) The Forest, 1978, Atitlan/Alashka, 1979, The Ground of Our Great Admiration of Nature, 1978; contbg. author: Penguin Modern Poets No. Seven: Richard Murphy, Jon Silkin, Nathaniel Tarn, 1965, A.P.E.N. Anthology of Contemporary Poetry, 1966, The Penguin Book of Modern Verse Translation, 1966, Poems Addressed to Hugh MacDiarmid, 1967, Music and Sweet Poetry: A Verse Anthology, 1968, Frontier of Going: Anthology of Space Poetry, 1969, Shaking the Pumpkin, 1972, America: A Prophecy, 1973, Open Poetry, 1973, Active Anthology, 1974, Symposium of the Whole, 1983, Random House Book of Twentieth Century French Poetry, 1983, Beneath a Single Moon: Buddhism in American Poetry, 1991, American Poetry since 1950: Innovators and Outsiders, 1993; translator: The Heights of Macchu Picchu (Pablo Neruda), 1966, Stelae (Victor Segalen), 1969, Zapotec Struggles, 1993; editor, co-translator: Con Cuba: An Anthology of Cuban Poetry of the Last Sixty Years, 1969, Selected Poems (Pablo Neruda), 1970; editor Cape Edits. and founder-dir. Cape Goliard Press, J. Cape Ltd., 1967-69. Recipient Guinness prize for poetry, 1963. Office: PO Box 8187 Santa Fe NM 87504-8187

TARNOFF, PETER, governmental official; b. N.Y.C., Apr. 19, 1937; s. Norman Tarnoff and Henrietta (Goldfarb) Laing; m. Daniele Oudinot, Jan. 13, 1962 (div. Oct. 1981); children: Nicholas, Alexander; m. Mathea Falco, Dec. 24, 1981; 1 child, Benjamin. Student, U. Paris, 1956-57, postgrad., 60-61; BA, Colgate U., 1958; postgrad., U. Chgo., 1958-60. Joined Fgn. Svc., Dept. State, 1961; spl. asst. to amb. Am. Embassy, Bonn, Fed. Republic Germany, 1969; trainee Nat. Sch. Adminstrn., Paris, 1970; prin. officer Am. Consulate Gen., Lyon, France, 1971-73; dep. chief of mission Am. Embassy, Luxembourg, 1973-75; dir. Office Rsch. and Analysis for Western Europe Dept. State, Washington, 1975-76, exec. sec. Dept. State, 1977-81; fgn. affairs fellow Dept. State, San Francisco, 1981-82; exec. dir. World Affairs Coun. No. Calif., San Francisco, 1983-86; pres., dir. Coun. on Fgn. Rels., N.Y.C., 1986-93; under sec. state for polit. affairs Dept. State, Washington, 1993—. Office: Dept State 2201 C St NW Washington DC 20520-0001

TARNOPOL, MICHAEL LAZAR, bank executive; b. 1936; s. Irving and Charlotte (Weber) T.; m. Lynne Lichtenstein, June 29, 1958; children: Lisa Silverman, Lori Moore. Gen. ptnr., sr. mng. dir., also bd. dirs. Lehman Bros. Inc., 1959-75; with Bear Stearns Cos. Inc., 1975—, vice-chmn., bd. dirs.; chmn. investment banking divsn., bd. dirs. Bear Stearns Internat.; bd. dirs. Leslie Fay Cos. Bd. dirs. U.S. Equestrian Team, Cap Cure Found., U.S. Polo Assn., U.S. Polo Tng. Found., Robert Steel Found., Inc.; pres.'s coun. Solomon R. Guggenheim Found.; trustee U. Pa., bd. overseers Wharton Sch. Mem. Palm Beach Polo Club, Palm Beach Country Club, Harmonie Club, East Hampton Tennis Club, Greenwich Polo Club (bd. dirs.). Office: 245 Park Ave New York NY 10167-0002

TARNOW, MALVA MAY WESCOE, post-anesthesia care nurse; b. Allentown, Pa., July 27, 1942; d. Frederick H. and Malva M. (Tharp) Wescoe; m. Donald F. Tarnow, Aug. 5, 1967; children: Dean, Elizabeth. Diploma, Bellevue Sch. Nursing, N.Y.C., 1963; BS in Hosp. Mgmt., Pacific Christian Coll., 1978. Cert. peri anesthesia nurse. Staff nurse recovery rm. Bellevue Hosp., N.Y.C., 1963-66; charge nurse recovery rm. Los Angles County Gen. Hosp., L.A., 1966-68; staff nurse post anesthesia care unit Los Robles Regional Med. Ctr., Thousand Oaks, Calif., 1968-70, 73-93; staff nurse ICU and CCU Ventura County Gen. Hosp., Ventura, Calif., 1970; charge nurse peri anesthesia care unit Granada Hills (Calif.) Community Hosp., 1989—. Mem. Am. Soc. Peri Anesthesia Nurses (Calif. alt. dir. 1990-93), Peri Anesthesia Nurses Assn. Calif. (dist. bd. dirs. 1980-84, 89-90, treas. 1984-86, pres. 1987-88). Home: 2769 Redondo Cir Camarillo CA 93012-8229

TARONJI, JAIME, JR., lawyer; b. N.Y.C., Nov. 20, 1944; s. Jaime and Ruth (Vazquez) T.; m. Mary Pineda, May 16, 1970; children: Ian A., Mark N., Nicole V. BA, George Washington U., 1972; JD, Georgetown U., 1976. Bar: Va. 1977, U.S. Ct. Appeals (4th and D.C. cirs.) 1977, D.C. 1978, U.S. Dist. Ct. D.C. 1978. Congl. intern U.S. Ho. of Reps., Washington, 1971; asst. to dep. staff dir. U.S. Commn. on Civil Rights, Washington, 1972-76; trial atty. FTC, Washington, 1976-79; antitrust counsel Westinghouse Electric Corp., Pitts., 1979-81; group legal counsel Dana Corp., Toledo, 1982-88; v.p., gen. counsel, asst. sec. Packaging Corp. Am. subs. Tenneco, Evanston, Ill., 1988-95; corp. law cons., 1995-96; law v.p. NCR Corp., Dayton, 1996—. Author: The 1970 Census Undercount of Spanish Speaking Persons, 1974. Editor: Puerto Ricans in the U.S., 1976. Bd. dirs. Puerto Rican Legal Def. and Edn. Fund. Served to capt. M.I., U.S. Army, 1965-70, Vietnam. Recipient spl. achievement award U.S. Commn. on Civil Rights, 1976; award for meritorious service FTC, 1979. Mem. ABA (antitrust and litigation sects.), Am. Corp. Counsel Assn., Fibre Box Assn. (chmn. legal adv. com.), Am. Forest and Paper Assn. (paper industry gen. counsel group). Democrat. Roman Catholic. Home: 1146 Furlong Dr Libertyville IL 60048-3701 Office: R/JB Morton Internat Bldg 1603 Orrington Ave Evanston IL 60201-3841

TARPLEY, BRENDA MAE See LEE, BRENDA

TARPY, ELEANOR KATHLEEN, social worker; b. Pawtucket, R.I.; d. Stephen and Mary F. (Nolan) T. AB, Brown U., 1937; MS in Social Work, Boston U., 1947. Lic. social worker, Mass. Social worker R.I. Child Welfare, Providence, 1937-47, supr., 1947-49; supr. VA Regional Office, Providence, 1949-54, VA Med. Ctr., Brockton, Mass., 1954-90; ret., 1990. Contbg. author: Current Psychiatric Therapies, vol. 4, 1964. Mem. Nat. Assn. Social Work, (past com. chair). Home: 929 Armistice Blvd Pawtucket RI 02861-3321

TARPY, THOMAS MICHAEL, lawyer; b. Columbus, Ohio, Jan. 4, 1945; s. Thomas Michael and Catherine G. (Sharshal) T.; m. Mary Patricia Canna, Sept. 9, 1967; children: Joshua Michael, Megan Patricia, Thomas Canna, John Patrick. A.B., John Carroll U., 1966; J.D., Ohio State U., 1969. Bar: Ohio 1969, U.S. Dist. Ct. (so. dist.) Ohio 1972, U.S. Dist. Ct. (no. dist.) Ohio 1974, U.S. Ct. Appeals (6th cir.) 1982. Assoc. Vorys, Sater, Seymour & Pease, Columbus, 1969-76, ptnr., 1977-85; v.p., chief adminstrv. officer Liebert Corp, Columbus, 1985-87; ptnr. Vorys, Sater, Seymour & Pease, Columbus, 1987—. Chmn. Columbus Graphics Commn., 1980; mem. Columbus Area Leadership Program, 1975. Served with U.S. Army, 1969-75. Mem. ABA, Ohio State Bar Assn., Columbus Bar Assn. Office: Vorys Sater Seymour & Pease PO Box 1008 52 E Gay St Columbus OH 43215-3161

TARR, CHARLES EDWIN, physicist, educator; b. Johnstown, Pa., Jan. 14, 1940; s. Charles Larned and Mary Katherine (Wright) T.; m. Bex Suzanne Harrell, Sept. 4, 1964 (div. Feb. 1977); m. Gudrun Kiefer, Nov. 18, 1977. B.S. in Physics (Morehead scholar 1957-61), U. N.C., Chapel Hill, 1961, Ph.D., 1966. Research assoc. U. N.C., Chapel Hill, 1966, U. Pitts., 1966-68; mem. faculty U. Maine, Orono, 1968—; assoc. prof. physics U. Maine, 1973-78, prof., 1978—, chmn. dept., 1977-79, assoc. dean Coll. Arts and Scis., 1979-81, acting dean Grad. Sch., 1981-87, acting v.p. research, 1984-87, dean Grad. Sch., 1987—; past docent U. Groningen, Netherlands, 1975-76; dir. Maine Toxicology Inst., 1992—, co-chair, 1993, chair, 1994; mem. exec. com. Coun. Rsch. Policy and Grad. Edn. of Nat. Assn. State Colls. and Land Grant Univs., 1993—; cons. in field. Contbr. articles to profl. jours. NASA grantee, 1970-72; NSF grantee, 1972—. Mem. IEEE, Am. Phys. Soc., Assn. Computing Machinery, Northeastern Assn. Grad. Schs. (mem. at large 1988—, pres. elect 1990-91, pres. 1991—), Sigma Xi. Quaker. Home: 519 College Ave Orono ME 04473-1211 Office: Univ Maine Off Dean Grad Sch Orono ME 04469

TARR, CURTIS W., business executive; b. Stockton, Calif., Sept. 18, 1924; s. F.W. and Esther (Reed) T.; m. Elizabeth May Myers, 1955 (div. 1978); children: Pamela Elizabeth, Cynthia Leigh; m. Marilyn Van Stralen, 1979 (div. 1991); m. Mary Katherine Stegmiller, 1992. B.A., Stanford U., 1948, Ph.D., 1962; M.B.A., Harvard U., 1950; L.H.D., Ripon Coll., 1965, Grinnell Coll., 1969, Lincoln Coll., 1980; LL.D., Lawrence U., 1974, Ill. Wesleyan U., 1980. Rsch. asst., instr. Harvard U., 1950-52; v.p. Sierra Tractor & Equipment Co., Chico, Calif., 1952-58; staff mem. 2d Hoover Commn., 1954-55; asst. dir. summer session Stanford U., 1961-62, dir., 1962-63, asst. dean humanities and scis., 1962-63, lectr. bus. sch., 1962-63; pres. Lawrence U., Appleton, Wis., 1963-69; asst. sec. for manpower and res. affairs Air Force, 1969-70; dir. SSS, Washington, 1970-72; under sec. state for security assistance, 1972-73, acting dep. under sec. state for mgmt., 1973; v.p. overseas devel. Deere & Co., Moline, Ill., 1973; v.p. parts distbn. and materials mgmt. Deere & Co., 1973-81, v.p. mgmt. devel., 1981-83; dean and prof. Johnson Sch. Mgmt., Cornell U., 1984-89, prof. mgmt., 1989-90, dean emeritus, 1990—; vice chmn. Intermet Corp., 1992-95; bd. dirs. Intermet Corp., Atlanta, State Farm Mut. Ins. Co., Bloomington, Ill., Phyton Corp., Ithaca, N.Y., State Farm Life Ins. Co.; mem. Internat. Rsch. Coun. Ctr. for Strategic and Internat. Studies, Washington, 1989-92; adj. prof. mgmt. Emory U., 1991-93. Author: Private Soldier, 1976, By the Numbers, 1981, Youth, 1994. trustee Inst. Paper Chemistry, 1963-69, Morehouse Sch. Medicine, Atlanta, 1994—; chmn. Task Force on Govt. Orgn., Fin. and Tax Distbn. for State Wis., 1967-69; chmn. Def. Manpower Commn., 1974-76, Ill. State Scholarship Commn., 1978-79, Quad Cities Grad. Study Ctr., 1982-84, Rep. candidate for Congress 2d Dist., Calif., 1958; trustee Am. Coll., Bryn Mawr, Pa., 1989-92. Served with AUS, 1943-46, ETO. Recipient Exceptional Civilian Service medal Air Force Dept., 1970; Distinguished Service award SSS, 1975. Mem. University Club (Chgo., N.Y.C.), Cosmos (Washington). Methodist.

TARR, DAVID WILLIAM, political scientist, educator; b. Melrose, Mass., July 25, 1931; s. Charles Howard and Pauline (Bryant) T.; children: Susan, Bryant. B.A., U. Mass., 1953; M.A., U. Chgo., 1956, Ph.D., 1961. Instr. Amherst and Mt. Holyoke colls., 1958-59; nat. def. analyst Legis. Reference Service, Library of Congress, 1959-62; research assoc. Washington Center Fgn. Policy, 1962-63; mem. faculty U. Wis.-Madison, 1963—, prof. polit. sci., 1969—, dir. nat. security studies group, 1966-69, chmn. dept., 1972-75, fellow Inter-univ. Seminar on armed Forces and Soc., 1975—, dir. Ctr. for Internat. Cooperation and Security Studies, 1988—; rsch. assoc. Ctr. Sci. and Internat. Affairs Harvard U., 1977. Author: American Strategy in the Nuclear Age, 1966, Nuclear Deterrence and International Security: Alternative Nuclear Regimes, 1991; co-editor: Modules in Security Studies, 1974; contbr. articles to profl. jours. Chmn. U. Wis. Athletic Bd., 1979-86. Served to 1st lt. AUS, 1953-55. Rockefeller grantee, 1962-63; fellow, 1977. Mem. Internat. Studies Assn., Am. Polit. Sci. Assn. Unitarian.

TARR, DELBERT HOWARD, JR., seminary president, clergyman; b. Aitkin, Minn., June 14, 1934; s. Delbert Howard and Catherine Elizabeth (Boomer) T.; m. Dorothy D. Hill, June 12, 1954; children: Cindy Sharon, Terry Mark, Randel Ray. B.A. in Bible, North Central Bible Coll., 1956; postgrad. Ecole Lemania, Switzerland, 1959-60; M.A. in Comm., U. Minn., 1969; Ph.D. in Comm., 1979. Ordained to ministry Assemblies of God Ch., 1957; pastor Assemblies of God Ch., Hopkins, Minn., 1956-58; apptd. fgn. missionary Burkina Faso (formerly Upper Volta), West Africa, 1960-63; dir. Mossiland Bible Sch., 1964-67; co-founder, dean West African Advanced Sch. Theology, Lome, Togo, 1970-73; prof., coordinator cross-cultural comm. studies Assemblies of God Theol. Sem. (formerly Assemblies of God Grad. Sch.), Springfield, Mo., 1973-77, dean missions div., 1977-80, chmn. missions dept., 1980-82; pres. Calif. Theol. Sem., Fresno, 1983-90, Assemblies of God Theol. Sem., 1990—; guest lectr. Far East Advanced Sch. Theology, Manila, Philippines, 1983. Author: Double Image, 1994. Research grantee African speech mannerisms, 1976-77. Mem. Am. Soc. Missiology, Acad. Evangelism, Soc. Pentecostal Studies, Greenleaf Servant Leadership. Office: Assemblies of God Theol Sem 1445 N Boonville Ave Springfield MO 65802-1894

TARR, JOEL ARTHUR, history and public policy educator; b. Jersey City, May 8, 1934; s. Max Alfred and Florence (Levin) Tartalsky; m. Arlene Green, Sept. 2, 1956 (div. June 1969); children: Michael Jay, Joanna Sue; m. Tova Brafman, Aug. 11, 1978; children: Maya Leah, Ilana Ariel. BS, Rutgers U., 1956, MA, 1957; PhD, Northwestern U., 1963. Asst. prof. Calif. State U., Long Beach, 1961-66; vis. prof. U. Calif., Santa Barbara, 1966-67; asst. prof. Carnegie Mellon U., Pitts., 1967-70, assoc. prof., 1969-72, prof. history and pub. policy, 1973-90, Richard S. Caliguiri prof. urban and environ. history and policy, 1990—, dir. program in tech. and soc., 1975-87, co-dir. program in applied history and social sci., 1978-86, acting dean Sch. Urban and Pub. Affairs, 1986, assoc. dean Coll. Humanities and Social Sci., 1988-91, acting dean Coll. Humanities and Social Sci., 1991-92, acting head dept. history, 1992-93. Author: A Study in Boss Politics, 1971; editor: Patterns of City Growth, 1974, Retrospective Technology Assessment, 1977, Transportation Innovation and Spatial Change in Pittsburgh, 1850-1934, 1978, Pittsburgh-Sheffield: Sister Cities, 1986, Technology and the Rise of the Networked City in Europe and America, 1988, The Search for the Ultimate Sink: Urban Pollution in Historic Perspective, 1996. Bd. dirs. Action Housing, Pitts., 1983; trustee Hist. Soc. Western Pa., 1993—. NEH fellow, 1969-70; grantee NSF, 1975-79, 78-80, 83-85, NOAA, 1982-84; recipient Robert Doherty Prize for contbns. to excellence in edn., 1992. Mem. AAAS, Pub. Works Hist. Soc. (pres. 1982-83, Abel Wolman prize 1989), Orgn. Am. Historians, Pub. History Assn. (nat. council), Am. Soc. Environ. History, Soc. for the History of Tech. Democrat. Jewish. Home: 5418 Normlee Pl Pittsburgh PA 15217-1116 Office: Carnegie-Mellon U Schenley Pk Pittsburgh PA 15213

TARR, RALPH WILLIAM, lawyer, former federal government official; b. Bakersfield, Calif., Sept. 29, 1948. BA, Dartmouth Coll., 1970; MPA, Calif. State U., 1973; JD, U. Calif., Hastings, 1976. Extern to assoc. justice Calif. Supreme Ct., 1976; rsch. atty. to presiding justice Ct. Appeal (5th dist.) Calif., 1976-77; assoc. Baker, Manock & Jensen, Fresno, Calif., 1977-81, dir., mem. exec. com., 1981-82; mem. adminstrv. com. Fed. Register, Washington, 1982-85; dep. asst. atty. gen. U.S. Dept. Justice, Washington, 1982-84, acting asst. atty. gen., 1984-85; solicitor U.S. Dept. Interior, Washington, 1985-89, counselor to the solicitor, 1989-90; pvt. practice L.A., 1990—. Home: 24011 Alder Pl Calabasas CA 91302-2394 Office: Andrews & Kurth LLP 601 S Figueroa St Fl 4200 Los Angeles CA 90017-5747

TARR, ROBERT JOSEPH, JR., publishing executive, retail executive; b. Freeport, N.Y., Dec. 7, 1943; s. Robert Joseph and Janet Christman (Laughton) T.; m. Molly Worthington Upton, Feb. 28, 1970; children: William Upton, Robert Joseph, III, David Worthington. BS, U.S. Naval Acad., 1966; MBA, Harvard U., 1973; MA, Fletcher Sch. Law & Diplomacy, 1976. Asst. v.p. corp. fin. Paine Webber Jackson Curtis, Boston, 1973-75; dir. corp. planning, then v.p., treas. Gen. Cinema Corp., Chestnut Hill, Mass., 1976-78, sr. v.p., 1978-83, exec. v.p., COO, 1983-85, pres., COO, 1985-91; pres., CEO, COO Harcourt Gen., Inc. (Gen. Cinema Corp., 1993), Chestnut Hill, Mass., 1991-97; pres., COO The Neiman Marcus Group, Inc., 1987-91, pres., bd. dirs., CEO, COO, 1991-97; bd. dirs. John Hancock Mutual Life Ins. Co. Trustee Tenacre Country Day Sch. Lt. USN, 1966-71. Mem. Univ. Club (Boston), Comml. Club Boston, Quissett Yacht Club, Brae Burn Country Club. Home: 40 White Oak Rd Wellesley MA 02181-1435

TARRANCE, VERNON LANCE, JR., public opinion research executive; b. Harlingen, Tex., Dec. 4, 1940; s. Vernon Lance Sr. and Mary Gilmore (Rea) T.; m. Eugenia Aline McCuistion, July 2, 1966; children: Vernon Lance III, Haloway McCuistion, Kyle Rea. BA, Washington & Lee U., 1962; postgrad., U. Mich., 1971; MA, Am. U., 1973; postgrad., Harvard U., 1973-74. Dir. research Tex. Rep. Party, Austin, 1964-67, Rep. Nat. Com., Washington, 1969-70; spl. asst. to dir. U.S. Census Bur., Washington, 1970-73; v.p. Decision Making Info. Inc., Santa Ana, Calif., 1974-77; pres., founder Tarrance, Hill, Newport & Ryan, Houston, 1977-92; bd. dirs. Gallup Orgn., 1987-92; pres., mng. dir. Gallup China Ltd., Beijing, 1993-95; vis. prof. polit. sci. Tex. A&M U., 1995-96; scholar in residence Washington and Lee U., 1996; cons. Gallup Internat. Rsch. Ctr., Lincoln, Nebr.; co-chmn. adv. adjustment panel U.S. Census. Co-author: A New Force in American Politics, 1972, The Ticket Splitter, 1990; editor: Texas Precinct Votes '66, '68, '70. Fellow John F. Kennedy Inst. Politics Harvard U., 1973-74; named one of 150 People Who Influence Fed. Govt. Nat. Jour. Mag., 1986. Mem. Asia Soc., Houston World Affairs Coun., Coun. on Fgn. Rels. (Houston com.), Kappa Sigma. Avocations: mountain trekking, golf, aviculture, travel.

TARRANT, R(ICHARD) J(OHN), classicist, educator; b. Bklyn., Apr. 4, 1945; s. John Joseph and Bertha (Slaney) T.; m. Jacqueline Brown, Sept. 14, 1968. B.A., Fordham U., 1966; D.Phil., Oxford U., 1972; A.M. hon., Harvard U., 1982. P.S. Allen jr. research fellow Corpus Christi Coll., Oxford, Eng., 1968-70; lectr. Univ. Coll., Toronto, Ont., Can., 1970-71, asst. prof., 1971-74, assoc. prof., 1974-79; prof. U. Toronto, 1979-82; prof. Greek and Latin Harvard U., Cambridge, Mass., 1982-87, Carl A. Pescosolido prof. Roman civilization, 1987-93, Pope prof. Latin language and Literature, 1993—, chmn. dept., 1988-94; acting dean Grad. Sch. Arts and Scis., 1995-96; vis. Mellon prof. Inst. for Advanced Study, Princeton, 1991-92; vis. fellow Corpus Christi Coll. U. Oxford, 1992. Author: Greek and Latin Lyric Poetry in Translation: A Bibliographical Survey, 1972, Seneca, Agamemnon, 1976, (with others) Texts and Transmission: A Survey of the Latin Classics, 1983, Seneca's Thyestes, 1985; editor Phoenix: Jour. Classical Assn. Can., 1978-82, Harvard Studies in Classical Philology, 1985-88, 93-94; editorial bd. Toronto Medieval Latin Texts, 1977—, Cambridge Classical Texts and Commentaries, 1992—; advisory bd. Text: Transactions of the Soc. for Textual Scholarship, 1994—; contbr. articles to profl. jours. Cabot fellow, 1993-94; Marshall scholar, 1966-69. Mem. Am. Philol. Assn. (bd. dirs. 1987-89, v.p. publs. 1992-95), Cambridge Philol. Assn., Classical Assn. Can., Classical Assn. New Eng., Phi Beta Kappa. Office: Harvard U Dept. Classics 319 Boylston Hall Cambridge MA 02138

TARRANT, ROBERT FRANK, soil science educator, researcher; b. Portland, Oreg., Mar. 11, 1918; s. Frank A. and Vera Leona (Tibbils) T.; m. Jean Inez Horton, Sept. 20, 1941; children: Christopher R., Susan J., Brian H., Stephanie A. Tarrant Martin. BS, Oreg. State U., 1941. Soil scientist USDA Pacific N.W. Forest Research Sta., Portland, 1946-71, asst. dir., 1971-74, dep. dir., 1975, dir., 1975-79; prof. forest scis. Oreg. State U., Corvallis, 1979—. Co-editor: The Biology of Alder, 1968, From the Forest to the Sea, 1988, Biology and Management of Red Alder, 1994; contbr. articles, reports to profl. jours. Bd. dirs. Oreg. Easter Seal Soc., Portland, 1969-75, pres., 1971-73. Served to lt. comdr. USN, 1942-45, ETO, PTO, also 1950-52. Recipient Superior Svc. award USDA, Washington, 1971, Tarrant Rsch. fellowship Oreg. State U., 1993—. Mem. N.W. Sci. Assn. (hon. life), Oreg. Hardwoods Commn., Sigma Xi Rsch. Soc. Episcopalian. Home: 2660 SW Fairmont Dr Corvallis OR 97333-1424

TARRANTS, WILLIAM EUGENE, government official; b. Liberty, Mo., Dec. 9, 1927; s. Joseph Eugene and Mildred Jane (Wright) T.; m. Mary Jo Edman, Jan. 19, 1952 (div. 1981); children: James Timothy, Jennifer Lynn; m. Lorna D. Lundberg, Sept. 24, 1988; stepchildren: David Murphy, Christine Walls, Janelle McCrea. B in Indsl. Engring., Ohio State U., 1951; MS in Indsl. Engring., 1959; PhD, NYU, 1963. Registered profl. engr., Calif., Ohio, N.Mex. Instr. indsl. engring. Ohio State U., Columbus, 1958-59; asst. prof., research asso. N.Y. U., 1959-64; chief accident research div. Bur. Labor Stats., Dept. Labor, Washington, 1964-67; dir. manpower devel. div. Nat. Hwy. Traffic Safety Adminstrn., Dept. Transp., 1967-80; chief scientist Office of Program and Demonstration Evaluation, 1980-84; program analyst Office of Occupant Protection, 1984-87, program analyst evaluation staff, 1987-90, also chmn. sci. and tech. info. adv. bd., 1984-91; instr. Johns Hopkins U., 1984-91, U. Md., 1991-92; planning and adminstrn. transp. safety mem. Transp. Rsch. Bd., NAS; cons. on safety program evaluation Indsl. Commn. Ohio, 1959; exec. com. Related Accreditation Commn., 1994—; accreditation bd. Engring. and Tech., Inc., 1994—. Contbr.: chpt. to Selected Readings in Safety, 1973, Readings in Industrial Accident Prevention, 1980; Author: chpt. to A Selected Bibliography of Reference Materials in Safety Engineering and Related Fields, 1967, Dictionary of Terms Used in the Safety Profession, 1971, Measurement of Safety Performance, 1980, Handbook of Occupational Safety and Health, 1987, also manuals and articles in field; mem. editorial bd.: Jour. Safety Research, Accident Analysis and Prevention, An Internat. Jour.; editor-in-chief: Traffic Safety Evaluation Research Rev. Trustee, ch. chmn. Evang. Covent Ch., 1976-80, 84-88, region 8 rep. to bd. trustees East Coast Conf., 1986-92. Capt. USAF, 1951-57. Recipient Founder's Day award NYU, 1963, 1st pl. Nat. Tech. Paper awards, 1961, 63, 67, cert. for outstanding performance Nat. Hwy. Traffic Safety Adminstrn., 1973, 86, Disting. Svc. to Safety award Nat. Safety Coun., 1989, Disting. Career Svc. award U.S. Dept. Transp., 1990; inducted into Safety and Health Hall of Fame Internat., 1990. Fellow Am. Soc. Safety Engrs. (dir., v.p. rsch. and tech. devel., pres. 1977-78, chmn. acad. accreditation coun. 1978—, fellow rev. bd. 1980-88, Pres.'s award 1996); mem. AAAS, Am. Soc. Safety Rsch. (trustee), Am. Inst. Indsl. Engrs., Human Factors Soc., System Safety Soc., Evaluation Rsch. Soc., Vets. of Safety, Am. Nat. Stds. Inst. (stds. com.), Soc. for Risk Analysis, Nat. Safety Coun. (chmn. rsch. projects com. 1973-78, exec. com. indsl. conf. 1977-78, Disting. Svc. award 1989), Alpha Pi Mu, Kappa Delta Pi. Mem. Evangelical Covent Ch. (trustee, ch. chmn. 1976-80, 84-88). Home: 606 Woodsmans Way Crownsville MD 21032-2317 Office: 400 7th St SW Washington DC 20590-0001 *We often look with awe at the successful person, much as we admire a well designed structure or a beautiful painting. Behind the finished product usually lies exhaustive effort, frustration, disappointment, and even failure which is obscured by the glow of accomplishment. Success is achieved by some ability, lots of hard work, perserverance, courage of convictions, help and support from others, a desire to reach a goal, self-discipline, and considerable personal sacrifice as we make choices concerning the use of our limited resources. The ability to bounce back from adversity is crucial. Most important of all is the strength and insight gained through prayer and the willingness to permit your life to be guided by Christian faith.*

TARRO, GIULIO, virologist; b. Messina, Italy, July 9, 1938; s. Emanuele and Emanuela (Iannello) T. MD, U. Naples, 1962, postgrad. in nervous diseases, 1968, PhD in Virology, 1971; postgrad. in med. and biol. scis., Roman Acad., 1979; hon. degree, U. Pro Deo, Albany, N.Y., 1989, St. Theodora Acad., N.Y., 1991, Constantinian U., Cranston, R.I., 1996. Asst. in med. pathology Naples U., Italy, 1964-66; rsch. assoc. divsn. virology and cancer rsch. Children's Hosp., Cin., 1965-68; asst. prof. rsch. pediat. U. Cin. Coll. Medicine, 1968-69; rsch. fellow Nat. Rsch. Coun., Naples, 1966-74, rsch. chief, 1974; prof. oncologic virology Coll. Medicine U. Naples, 1971-85, prof. microbiology and immunology Sch. Specialization, 1972—; chief divsn. virology D. Cotugno Hosp. for Infectious Diseases, Naples, 1973—; dean faculty natural and phys. scis. Nobile Accademia di Santa Teodora Imperatrice, Capua, Italy, 1993—; sr. scientist Nat. Cancer Inst. Frederick (Md.) Ctr., 1973; project dir. Nat. cancer Inst., Bethesda, Md., 1971-75; edn. min. rep. Zool. Sta., Naples, 1975-79; cons. Italian Pharmacotherpic Inst., Rome, 1980—; pres. De Beaumont Bonelli Found. for Cancer Rsch., Naples, 1978—, nat. com. on bioethics, 1995—. Author: Virologia Oncologica, 1979 (award 1985), Patologia dell'AIDS, 1991, Con il Cancro si Può Vivere, 1992, AIDS Cosa Possiamo Fare Cosa Dobbiamo Sapere, 1994; contbr. over 300 sci. papers to profl. publs.; patentee in field. Pres. Sci. Cultural Com., Torre Annunziata, Italy, 1984, Tumor Prevention Assn., Rome, 1984; mem. acad. senate Constantinian U., Providence, 1990, U. Pro Deo, N.Y., 1994. Maj. Italian Navy, 1982-84, lt. col., 1993-95. Decorated Comdr. Nat. Order of Merit, 1991, Star of Europe, 1980; recipient Internat. Lenghi award Lincei Acad., 1969, Gold Microscope award Italian Health Min., 1973, Knights of Humanity award Internat. Register of Chivalry, Malta, 1978, gold medal of Culture, Pres. of Italian Republic, 1975, Culture award, 1985, 1st prize in Biomed. Rsch., Italian Acad. Arts and Scis., 1987, Castello di Pietrarossa award, Italy, 1991, gold Cesare award Padova, 1991, 20th Century award in Medicine, 1994, Knight of Grand Cross Sovereign Constantinian order of St George, 1993, Gold Little Horse, Transnat. European Federation, Rome 1996. Fellow AAAS; mem. Am. Soc. Microbiology, Am. Assn. for Cancer Rsch., Internat. Assn. for Leukemias, Internat. League Drs. for Abolition of Vivisection (pres. 1992—), Italian Soc. Immuno-Oncology (v.p. 1975—, pres. 1990—), Italian Assn. for Viral Study and Rsch. (pres. 1995—), Assn. Res. Prevention of Cancer (mem. sci. com. 1995), Nat. Order Journalists, N.Y. Acad. Scis., Lions (pres. Pompei chpt. 1987-89, vice gov. dist. 108y 1991-92, pres. to fight cancer 1992-94, pres. com. sci. and life 1994-95, pres. com. to fight drug addiction and AIDS 1995-97, Melvin Jones fellow 1993). Roman Catholic. Achievements include discovery of RSV virus in infant deaths in Naples. Home: 286 Posillipo, 80123 Naples Italy Office: D Cotugno Hosp USL 41, 54 Quagliariello, 80131 Naples Italy

TARR-WHELAN, LINDA, policy center executive; b. Springfield, Mass., May 24, 1940; d. Albert and Jane Zack; m. Keith Tarr-Whelan; children: Scott, Melinda. BSN, Johns Hopkins U., 1963; MS, U. Md., 1967. Program dir. AFSCME AFL-CIO, Washington, 1968-74, union area dir., 1974-76; adminstrn. dir. N.Y. State Labor Dept., Albany, N.Y., 1976-79; dep. asst. to pres. Carter White House, Washington, 1979-80; dir. govt. rels. NEA, Washington, 1980-86; CEO, pres. Ctr. for Policy Alternatives, Washington, 1986—, bd. dirs., 1985—; apptd. U.S. rep. UN Commn. on Status of Women, 1996—. Bd. dirs. Benton Found., Adv. Inst., Ind. Sector; pres. State Issues Forum; mem. Freddie Mac Affordable Housing Adv. Bd. Recipient Disting. Grad. award Johns Hopkins U., 1981, Breaking the Glass Ceiling award, 1996; leadership fellow Japan Soc., 1987-88. Democrat. Avocations: walking, travel. Home: 3466 Roberts Ln Arlington VA 22207-5335 Office: Ctr for Policy Alternatives 1875 Connecticut Ave NW Washington DC 20009-5728

TARSKY, EUGENE STANLEY, accountant, management and systems consultant; b. Meriden, Conn., Mar. 10, 1935; s. Joseph and Fannie (Apkin) T.; m. Irene M. Goldstein, Sept. 22, 1957; children: Julie B., Jeffrey A. Grad., U. Mass., 1957; M of Sci. in Taxation, Bentley Coll., 1978. CPA, Mass. Salesman, mgr. Margene Supply Co., Springfield, Mass., 1951-57; entry level acct. Coopers & Lybrand, Boston, 1957-58, auditor, system designer, 1961-64; CPA Martin Braver & Co., Chestnut Hill, Mass., 1964-65; pvt. practice Boston, 1965-70; ptnr. Orlando C. Moyer & Co. CPAs, Boston, 1970-72; pvt. practice Newton, Mass., 1972-82; pres. Eugene S. Tarsky CPA, Inc., Needham, Mass., 1982—; guest lectr. Continuing Edn. Program, Northeastern U., Boston, 1980, Boston U., 1982; presenter in field. Bd. dirs., asst. treas. Hospice of the Good Shepherd, Newton, 1982-85; bd. dirs., treas. Newton Boys and Girls Club, 1988-96. With USAF, 1958-61. Recipient Benefactor of Youth award West Suburban YMCA, 1986, 89. Mem. AICPA, Mass. Soc. CPA's (speaker's bur. 1976—, discussion leader continuing edn. program 1983-90, mgmt. of acctg. practice com. 1984-89, Disting. Speaker award 1985), Route 128 Practitioners Forum (guest lectr. 1990, 93), Newton-Needham C. of C. (bd. dirs. 1975-76, 81-90, treas. 1986-87, pres. 1987-88, Outstanding Leadership award 1989, 10-Yr. Loyal Svc. award 1990), Kiwanis (bd. dirs. Newton 1989-94). Avocations: swimming, golf, bridge, travel, family. Home: 280 Boylston St Chestnut Hill MA 02167 Office: 56 Pickering St Needham MA 02192-3156

TARSON, HERBERT HARVEY, university administrator emeritus; b. N.Y.C., Aug. 28, 1910; s. Harry and Elizabeth (Miller) T.; m. Lynne Barnett, June 27, 1941; 1 son, Stephen. Grad., Army Command Gen. Staff Coll., 1942, Armed Forces Staff Coll., 1951, Adavnced Mgmt. Sch. Sr. Air Force Comdrs., George Washington U., 1954; B.A., U. Calif., Los Angeles, 1949; Ph.D., U.S. Internat. U., 1972. Entered U.S. Army as pvt., 1933, advanced through grades to maj., 1942; transfered to U.S. Air Force, 1947, advanced through grades to lt. col., 1949; adj. exec. officer Ft. Snelling, Minn., 1940-42; asst. adj. gen. 91st Inf. Div., 1942-43; chief of personnel, advance sec. Comd. Zone, ETO, 1944-45; dir. personnel services 8th Air Force, 1946-47; dep. dir. dept. info. and edn. Armed Forces Info. Sch., 1949-51; dir. personnel services Japan Air Def. Force, 1951-53, Continental Air Command, 1953-62; dir. adminstrv. services, spl. asst. to Comdr. 6th Air Force Res. Region, 1962-64; ret., 1964; asst. to chancellor L.I. U., Brookville, 1964-69; dean admissions Tex. State Tech. Inst., San Diego Indsl. Center, 1970-72; v.p. acad. affairs Nat. U., San Diego, 1972-75, sr. v.p., 1975-88, founding sr. v.p. emeritus, 1988—. Decorated Bronze Star medal with oak leaf cluster, Air Force Commendation medal with 2 oak leaf clusters. Fellow Bio-Med Research Inst.; mem. Doctoral Soc. U.S. Internat. U., Am. Soc. Tng., Devel., World Affairs Council, Air Force Assn., Navy League U.S., Pres.'s Assos. of Nat. U. (presidential life). Home: 4611 Denwood Rd La Mesa CA 91941-4803 *The greatest motivating force in my life is to explore the challenging frontiers of the future. Nothing can be compared to it.*

TARTER, CURTIS BRUCE, physicist, science administrator; b. Louisville, Sept. 26, 1939; s. Curtis B. and Marian Turner (Cundiff) T.; m. Jill Cornell, June 6, 1964 (div. 1975); 1 child, Shana Lee; m. Marcia Cyrog Linn, Sept. 6, 1987. BS, MIT, 1961; PhD, Cornell U., 1967. Tchg. asst. Cornell U., Ithaca, N.Y., 1961-63, rsch. asst., 1964-67; physicist Lawrence Radiation Lab., Livermore, Calif., summers 1962, 63; staff mem. theoretical physics divsn. U. Calif., Lawrence Livermore Nat. Lab., 1967-69, group leader macroscopic properties of matter, 1969-71, assoc. divsn. leader, 1971-74, group leader opacities, 1972-78, divsn. leader, 1974-84; dep. assoc. dir. for physics Lawrence Livermore Nat. Lab., 1984-88, assoc. dir. for physics, 1988-94, dep. dir., 1994; dir., 1994—; sr. scientist Applied Rsch. Labs. Aeronutronic divsn. Philco-Ford Corp., 1967; lectr., grad. student advisor dept. applied sci., U. Calif., Davis/Livermore, 1970—; cons. Hertz Found., 1970—, field com. study on astronomy in the 80's, NRC, 1980; mem. Army Sci. Bd., Washington, 1989-96; mem. Calif. Coun. on Sci. and Tech., 1996—. Contbr. numerous articles to profl. jours. Mem. AAAS, Am. Phys. Soc., Am. Astron. Soc., Internat. Astron. Union. Republican. Avocations: golf, squash, bridge. Home: 676 Old Jonas Hill Rd Lafayette CA 94549-5214 Office: Lawrence Livermore Nat Lab PO Box 808 Livermore CA 94551-0808

TARTER, FRED BARRY, advertising executive; b. Bklyn., Aug. 16, 1943; s. Irving and Edna (Kupferberg) T.; children: Scott Andrew, Heather Michelle, Megan Elizabeth. BS, CCNY, 1966. Pres. Jamie Publs. Hootenanny Enterprises, Inc., 1962-65; mdse. dir. Longines Symphonette Soc., 1965-67; with Universal Communications, Inc., N.Y.C., 1967—, pres., CEO, 1969-74; exec. v.p. Deerfield Communications, Inc., N.Y.C., 1974-87, pres., CEO, 1977-88; pres. Deerfield Books, Inc., N.Y.C., 1988-89; pub. S.E.W. mag., N.Y.C., 1977-88; pres. The Rainbow Group Ltd., N.Y.C., 1988—; bd. dirs. Caribbean Internat. News Corp., Screenvision, Inc., Lakeside Group, Inc., Boardwalk Entertainment, Ltd.; chmn. The Pharmacy Fund, Inc.; vice chmn. Affinity Comm., Inc.; exec. prodr. Joanne Carson's VIP's Miss Am. Teenager Pageant, 1972-73; pres. The Programme Exch., U.K. Ltd.; prodr. Spenser Judas Goat, 1995, Ceremony, 1996, Wounded Heart, 1996, Lover's Leap, 1996, Hearts Adrift, 1995, Marriage Counselor, 1994, Spenser: Pale Kings & Princes, 1995, Spenser: A Savage Place, 1995, Reasons of the Heart, 1996. Mem. Friars Club, The Reform Club (London), Met. Club (N.Y.). Home: 300 E 59th St New York NY 10022-2058 Office: The Pharmacy Fund Inc 680 Fifth Ave New York NY 10019 *An integral part of success is the capacity for failure. Persistence, combined with responsibility, has proven to be the winning combination time and again.*

TARTER, MICHAEL ERNEST, biostatistician, educator; b. Bronx, N.Y., Dec. 20, 1938; s. William Tarter and Frieda Browdy; m. Orna Benzenburg, Aug. 30, 1975; children: Douglas, Robin. BA in Math., UCLA, 1959, MA in Math., 1961, PhD in Biostats., 1963. Asst. prof. U. Mich., Ann Arbor, 1964-66, assoc. prof., 1967; assoc. prof. U. Calif., Irvine, 1968-70; assoc. prof. U. Calif., Berkeley, 1970-76, prof., 1977—. Author books and articles; editor: Jour. Am. Statis. Assn. (screening editor for applications 1971-80). Fellow Am. Statis. Assn. (chmn. com. resources biometrics sect. 1981—, editorial bds. computational stats. and data analysis 1983-86, biometrics 1976-84, communications in stats. 1977—). Office: U Calif Sch Pub Health Dept Biomed Environ Health Scis 140 Warren Hall Berkeley CA 94720-7361

TARTIKOFF, BRANDON, broadcast executive; b. L.I., N.Y., Jan. 13, 1949; m. Lilly Samuels, 1982; children: Calla Lianne, Elizabeth Justine. B.A. with honors, Yale U., 1970. With promotion dept. ABC TV, New Haven, Conn., 1971-73; program exec. dramatic programming Sta. WLS-TV (ABC), Chgo., 1973-76; mgr. dramatic devel. ABC TV, N.Y.C., 1976-77; writer, producer Graffiti; dir. comedy programs NBC Entertainment, Burbank, Calif., 1977-78, v.p. programs, 1978-80, pres., 1980-90; chmn. NBC Entertainment Group, 1989-91, Paramount Pictures, 1991-92, New World Entertainment, Ltd., 1994—. Co-author: The Last Great Ride, 1992. Named 1 of 10 Outstanding Young Men Am. U.S. Jaycees, 1981; recipient Tree of Life award Jewish Nat. Found., 1986. Office: H Beale Co 11755 Wilshire Blvd Ste 2200 Los Angeles CA 90025-1543*

TARUN, ROBERT WALTER, lawyer; b. Lake Forest, Ill., Sept. 1, 1949; s. Donald Walter and Bonnie Jean (Cruickshank) T.; m. Helen J. McSweeney, May 1, 1987; children: Abigail Esch, Tyler Vincent, Parker Donald, Aimée Dakota. AB, Stanford U., 1971; JD, DePaul U., 1974; MBA, U. Chgo., 1982. Bar: Ill. 1974, Calif. 1975, U.S. Dist. Ct. (no. dist.) Ill. 1974, U.S. Dist. Ct. (we. dist.) Ark. 1986, U.S. Dist. Ct. (so. dist.) Ind. 1995, U.S. Dist. Ct. (no. dist.) Calif. 1995, U.S. Dist. Ct. (ea. dist.) Mich. 1996, U.S. Ct. Appeals (7th cir.) 1975, U.S. Ct. Appeals (5th cir.) 1992, U.S. Ct. Appeals (3d cir.) 1993, U.S. Ct. Appeals (Fed. cir.) 1995, U.S. Ct. Appeals (9th and 11th cirs.) 1996, U.S. Supreme Ct. 1978. Asst. atty. gen. State of Ill., Chgo., 1974-76; asst. U.S. atty. U.S. Dept. Justice, Chgo., 1976-79, dep. chief criminal div., 1979-82, exec. asst. U.S. atty. no. dist. Ill., 1982-85; ptnr. Reuben & Proctor, Chgo., 1985-86, Isham, Lincoln & Beale, Chgo., 1986-88, Winston & Strawn, Chgo., 1988—; lectr. criminal law practice Northwestern U. Sch. Law, 1986; instr. Atty. Gen.'s Advocacy Inst., Washington, 1980-85, Nat. Inst. Trial Adv., 1990. Author: (with Dan K. Webb) Corporate Internal Investigations, 1993. Bd. dirs. Chgo. Ctrl. Area Com., 1994—. Fellow Am. Coll. Trial Lawyers (mem. fed. criminal procedure com. 1993—); mem. ABA, Bar Assn. San Francisco, Chgo. Bar Assn., Nat. Assn. Criminal Def. Lawyers, U. Chgo. Grad. Sch. Bus. Alumni Assn. (bd. dirs. 1986), Racquet Club, Wong Sun Soc. (San Francisco), Kenilworth Club, Chgo. Stanford Assn. Presbyterian. Avocations: screenplays, architecture, 20th Century Louisiana politics, forensic science. Office: Winston & Strawn 35 W Wacker Dr Ste 4700 Chicago IL 60601-1614

TARVER, JACKSON WILLIAMS, newspaper executive; b. Savannah, Ga., Mar. 2, 1917; s. Otis Merritt and DeLuth (Williams) T.; m. Margaret Birch Taylor, Mar. 24, 1940; children: Jack Williams, Margaret (Mrs. Peter Jason). Student, U. Ga., 1936; A.B., Mercer U., 1938, LL.D., 1965. Reporter Vidalia (Ga.) Advance, 1938; editor Toombs County (Ga.) Democrat, 1939-40, Macon (Ga.) News, 1940-43; asso. editor Atlanta Constn., 1943-49; asst. to pres. Atlanta Newspapers, Inc. (pub. Atlanta Jour., Atlanta Constn.), 1950-53, gen. mgr., 1953-58, v.p., 1956-58, pub., 1958—, also dir.; chmn. Fed. Res. Bank of Atlanta, 1962-68; chmn., dir. Theaters Service Co.; vice chmn. Cox Enterprises, Inc.; dir. So. Bell Telephone Co., Am. Motors Corp., Maccabees Mut. Ins. Co.; chmn. A.P., 1977-82. Mem. Ga. Bd. Edn., 1942-43; trustee Mercer U. Reid Found. fellow to S.A., 1949; recipient Humanitarian of Yr. award Inst. Human Relations, 1979. Mem. Am. Newspaper Pubs. Assn. (chmn. bur. advt. 1962-64), So. Newspaper Pubs. Assn. (pres. 1976-77), Am. Soc. Newspaper Editors, Sigma Delta Chi, Sigma Alpha Epsilon. Clubs: Capital City (Atlanta), Piedmont Driving (Atlanta), Commerce (Atlanta), Stadium (Atlanta). Office: 72 Marietta St NW Atlanta GA 30303-2804

TARVER, MICHAEL KEITH, lawyer; b. Monroe, La., Oct. 12, 1941; s. Mike Davis and Bernadine (Kilcrease) T. Student, U. Paris Inst. Polit. Studies, 1962; BA, Tulane U., 1963, LLB, 1966; LLM, NYU, 1967. Bar: La. 1966, N.Y. 1987. Assoc. Jones, Walker, Waechter, Poitevent, Carrere & Denegre, New Orleans, 1967-72, ptnr., 1972-95, ret., 1995. Asst. editor Tulane Law Rev., 1961-63. Mem. Am. Coll. Real Estate Lawyers, Phi Beta Kappa. Roman Catholic. Home: 828 Burgundy St New Orleans LA 70116-3062

TARVIN, ALBERT LEON, writer; b. Atlanta, Nov. 27, 1929; s. Wilter Cicel and Sara Alice (Westbrooks) T.; children: Valerie Susan Tarvin-Kibler, William Clay, William Walter; m. Christle Jean Holzman, July 6, 1991. BS, Utah State U., 1966; MS in Secondary Edn., U. So. Calif., 1969; MS in Pers. Mgmt., Troy State U., Montgomery, Ala., 1980; MS in Nat. Studies, Air War Coll., Montgomery, 1974. Enlisted USAF, 1948, advanced through grades to col.; comdr. 1956th Comm. Group USAF, Yokota AB, Japan, 1974-78; retired USAF, 1978; headmaster Lowndes Acad., Hanyeville, Ala., 1978-80; field engr. Westinghouse Electric Corp., Balt., 1980-90; instr. Bauder Coll., Ft. Lauderdale, Fla., 1984-91; tax cons. Gulf Breeze, Fla., 1988—; author, freelance writer, Gulf Breeze, 1984—. Author: Chelsea, Chelsea, 1994, 2nd printing 1996, Chelsea, The Final Chapter, 1995, Twenty-One Divorcees, 1995, Run, Chelsea, Run, 1996, Till Death Do Us Part, 1996; writer Santa Rosa Sun, 1993-94. Decorated Legion of Merit. Mem. West Fla. Literary Fedn. Inc. (treas. 1992-94). Republican. Lutheran. Avocations: physical tng., golf, camping. Home and Office: 6064 Mayberry Ln Milton FL 32570-8875

TASA, KENDALL SHERWOOD, chemistry educator; b. Greenville, Tex., Apr. 29, 1947; s. Kenneth A. and Juanita (Holley) T.; m. Patricia Ann Langford, Mar. 28, 1969; children: Laura Ann, Heather Denise. BS, East Tex. State U., 1967, MS, 1969, EdD, 1973. Tchr. Lone Oak (Tex.) High Sch., 1969-72; prof. chemistry Brazosport Coll., Lake Jackson, Tex., 1973—, pres. faculty assembly, 1990-91, chmn. div. Math. and Sci., 1991—. Contbr. articles to sci. jours. Chmn. adminstrv. bd. 1st United Meth. Ch., Angleton, Tex., 1991-93. Mem. Tex. Jr. Coll. Tchrs. Assn. (campus rep., resolutions com. 1993-94). Republican. Avocations: golf, upland bird hunting, astronomy, tennis. Office: Brazosport Coll 500 College Dr Lake Jackson TX 77566-3136

TASAKA, SHUJI, engineering educator; b. Imabari, Japan, Mar. 6, 1949; s. Masaaki and Atsuko (Tasaka) T.; m. Mari Tamura, Oct. 8, 1977; children: Misato, Keisuke. BE, Nagoya (Japan) Inst. Tech., 1971; ME, U. Tokyo, 1973, PhD in Electronic Engring., 1976. Rsch. assoc. Nagoya Inst. Tech., 1976, lectr., 1976-78, assoc. prof., 1978-92, prof. dept. elec. and computer engring., 1992—, dept. head, 1996-97. Author: Performance Analysis of Multiple Access Protocols, 1986. Mem. IEEE, Inst. Electronics, Info. and Comm. Engrs. (sec. tech. com. on info. networks 1987-89, assoc. editor IEICE Transactions on Comm.), Info. Processing Soc. Japan, Assn. for Computing Machinery. Avocations: reading, music, movies. Home: Hanami-dori 1-94-4 Showa-ku, Nagoya 466, Japan Office: Nagoya Inst Tech/Elec & Comp Eng, Gokiso-cho Showa-ku, Nagoya 466, Japan

TASH, MARTIN ELIAS, publishing company executive; b. N.Y.C., Jan. 24, 1941; s. David and Esther (Milch) T.; m. Arlene Sue Klein, June 23, 1962; children: Nathan, Faye, Jill. B.B.A., Baruch Sch. City Coll. N.Y., 1962. C.P.A. Staff accountant S.D. Leidesdorf & Co. (C.P.A.'s), N.Y.C., 1962-66; v.p. fin., dir. LMC Data Inc., N.Y.C., 1966-71; with Plenum Pub. Corp., N.Y.C., 1971—, chmn. bd., pres., 1977—; chmn. bd. Gradco Systems, Inc., 1990—. Office: Plenum Pub Corp 233 Spring St New York NY 10013-1522

TASH, PAUL C., editor-in-chief; b. South Bend, Ind., July 17, 1954; s. Robert N. and Barbara R. (Eller) T.; m. Karyn E. Krayer, Aug. 19, 1983; children: Kaley Marie, Kendyl Barbara. BA, Ind. U., 1976; LLB, Edinburgh (Scotland) U., 1978. Reporter Times Pub. Co., 1978-83, city editor, 1983-86, metro editor, 1986-90, editor, pub. Fla. Trend Mag., 1990-91, Washington Bur. chief, 1991-92; exec. editor, v.p. St. Petersburg Times, 1992—; Bd. dirs. Times Pub. Co., Fla. Trend Mag. Scholar Marshall Aid Commemoration Commn., 1976-78. Mem. Phi Beta Kappa. Home: 111 Bay Point Dr NE Saint Petersburg FL 33704-3805 Office: St Petersburg Times 490 1st Ave S Saint Petersburg FL 33701-4204

TASHIMA, ATSUSHI WALLACE, federal judge; b. Santa Maria, Calif., June 24, 1934; s. Yasutaro and Aya (Sasaki) T.; m. Nora Kiyo Inadomi, Jan. 27, 1957; children: Catherine Y., Christopher I., Jonathan I. AB in Polit. Sci., UCLA, 1958; LLB, Harvard U., 1961. Bar: Calif. 1962. Dep. atty. gen. State of Calif., 1962-67; atty. Spreckels Sugar divsn. Amstar Corp., 1968-72, v.p., gen. atty., 1972-77; ptnr. Morrison & Foerster, L.A., 1977-80; judge U.S. Dist. Ct. (ctrl. dist.) Calif., L.A., 1980-96, U.S. Ct. Appeals (9th cir.), Pasadena, Calif., 1996—; mem. Calif. Com. Bar Examiners, 1978-80. With USMC, 1953-55. Mem. ABA, State Bar Calif., Los Angeles County Bar Assn. Democrat. Office: US Ct Appeals PO Box 91510 125 S Grand Ave Pasadena CA 91105-1621*

TASKER, JOHN BAKER, veterinary medical educator, college dean; b. Concord, N.H., Aug. 28, 1933; s. John Baker and Catherine Mabel (Baker) T.; m. Grace Ellen Elliott, June 17, 1961; children—Sybil Alice, Sarah Catherine, Sophia Ethel. DVM, Cornell U., 1957, PhD, 1963. Instr. Cornell U., Ithaca, N.Y., 1960-61; from assoc. prof. to prof. Cornell U., 1967-78; from asst. prof. to assoc. prof. Colo. State U., Fort Collins, 1963-67; prof. vet. clinical pathology, assoc. dean La. State U., 1978-84; dean Coll. Vet. Medicine Mich. State U., East Lansing, 1984-94; prof. vet. pathology Coll. Vet. Medicine/Mich. State U., East Lansing, 1984-95; dean, prof. emeritus Mich. State U., East Lansing, 1995; cons. Ralston-Purina Co., St. Louis, 1978, Universidad Nacional P. Urena, Dominican Republic, 1980, U. Nebr., Lincoln, 1982-83. Editor: Veterinary Clinics of North America, 1976. Served to 1st lt. U.S. Army, 1958-60. Recipient Outstanding Instr. award Colo. State U. Vet. Coll., 1967; Norden Teaching award Cornell U. Vet. Coll., 1977. Mem. AVMA, Del. Vet. Med. Assn., Am. Coll. Vet. Pathologists (diplomate; examiner 1972-74), Am. Soc. Vet. Clin. Pathology (pres. 1971-72), Assn. Am. Vet. Med. Colls. (exec. com. 1986-91, pres. 1989-90). Avocations: reading; traveling. Home: RR 2 Box 238C Delmar DE 19940

TASKER, STEVEN JAY, professional football player; b. Leoti, Kans., May 19, 1962. Student, Dodge City C.C.; B in Communication Studies, Northwestern, 1985. With Houston Oilers, 1985-86; wide receiver Buffalo Bills, 1986—. Played in Pro Bowl 1987, 90-93. Office: Buffalo Bills 1 Bills Dr Orchard Park NY 14127-2237*

TASMAN, ALLAN, psychiatry educator; b. Louisville, Ky., Feb. 8, 1947; s. Goodman and Zelda Tasman; m. Cathy Faye Goldstein, May 24, 1970. BA in Chemistry, Franklin and Marshall Coll., 1969; MD, U. Ky., 1973. Diplomate Am. Bd. Psychiatry and Neurology. Resident in psychiatry U. Ky. Med. Sch., Lexington, 1973-74, U. Cin. Med. Ctr., 1974-76; asst. prof. psychiatry U. Conn. Med. Sch., Farmington, 1976-82, assoc. prof. psychiatry, 1982-88, prof. psychiatry, 1988-91; prof. psychiatry and behavioral scis., tenure and chmn. U. Louisville Sch. Medicine, 1991—. Editor: Annual Review of Psychiatry, Vol. ll, 1992, Clinical Challenges in Psychiatry, 1993, Less Time to Do More, 1993, Textbook of Psychiatry, 1996 (sr. editor); dep. editor Jour. of Psychotherapy Practice and Rsch. Fellow Am. Psychiat. Assn. (v.p. 1996—, Nancy Roeske award for excellence in med. student edn. 1991); mem. Am. Assn. Dirs. of Psychiat. Residency Tng. (pres. 1993-94), Assn. Acad. Psychiatry (pres. 1993-94), Am. Assn. of Chmn. of Depts. of Psychiatry (pres. 1996-97). Office: U Louisville Sch Medicine Dept Psychiatry & Behavioral Scis Louisville KY 40292

TASMAN, WILLIAM SAMUEL, ophthalmologist, medical association executive; b. Phila., 1929. MD, Temple U., 1955. Intern Phila. Gen. Hosp., 1955-56; resident in ophthalmology Wills Eye Hosp., Phila., 1959-61; fellow Mass. Eye and Ear Infirmary, Boston, 1961-62; prof., chmn. dept. ophthalmology Jefferson Med. Coll., Phila., 1985—; attending surgeon Wills Eye Hosp., Phila., 1974—, ophthalmologist-in-chief, 1985—. Mem. AMA, Am. Acad. Ophthalmologists (sec. ann. meeting 1992—), Pa. Acad. Ophthalmologists, Am. Ophthal. Soc. Office: Wills Eye Hosp 900 Walnut St Philadelphia PA 19107-5509

TASSÉ, ROGER, lawyer, former Canadian government official; b. Montreal, Que., Can., 1931. BA, Coll. St. Marie, Montreal, 1952; Lic. in Law, U. Montreal, 1955; diploma d'Etudes Superieures, U. Ottawa, Ont., Can., 1957. Bar: Que. 1956, Ont. 1986; called to Queens Counsel 1971. Joined Dept. Justice, 1956, civil law counsel for Can. govt., from 1957, supt. bankruptcy, 1965-68, asst. dep. min. consumer and corp. affairs, 1968-72; dep. min. Dept. of Solicitor Gen., 1972-77; dep. min. of justice, atty. gen. of Can., 1977-85; ptnr. Land Michener Lash Johnston, Toronto and Ottawa, Noel Décary Aubry & Assocs., Hull, Que., 1985-88; exec. v.p. legal and environ. affairs Bell Can., 1988-91; of counsel Fraser & Beatty, Toronto, 1992-95, Gowling, Strathy & Henderson, Ottawa, 1995—; prin. constl. advisor to Spl. Joint Com. of the Senate and the House of Commons on a Renewed Can., 1991-92. Mem. Citizens' Forum on Canada's Future, 1990; co-chair task force Can. Mags., 1993; mem. DTH Panel, 1995. Decorated officer Order of Can. Avocations: skiing, tennis. Office: Gowling Strathy & Henderson, 160 Elgin St Ste 2600, Ottawa, ON Canada K1P 1C3

TASSINARI, MELISSA SHERMAN, toxicologist; b. Lawrence, Mass., Sept. 26, 1953; m. R. Peter Tassinari (dec.); children: Michael, Emily, Sara. AB, Mt. Holyoke Coll., 1975; postgrad., U. St. Andrews, Scotland, 1973-74; PhD, Med. Coll. Wis., 1979. Diplomate Am. Bd. Toxicology. Rsch. asst. in orthopedic surgery., Lab. Human Biochemistry Children's Hosp. Med. Ctr., Boston, 1981-83; rsch. affiliate in toxicology Toxicology Dept. Forsyth Dental Ctr., Boston, 1983-86, staff assoc., 1986-89; asst. prof. cell biology U. Mass. Med. Ctr., Worcester, 1989-91; mgr. reproductive and developmental toxicology Pfizer Ctrl. Rsch., Groton, Conn., 1991—; rsch. fellow oral biology Harvard Sch. Dental Medicine, Boston, 1978-81, instr. oral biology and pathophysiology, 1981-83; asst. prof. biol. scis. Wellesley Coll., Mass., 1983-86, cons. teratology Arthur D. Little, Inc., Cambridge, Mass., 1985-91; asst. prof. biology Simmons Coll., Boston, 1986-87. Contbr. abstracts, articles to profl. jours. Mem. Teratology Soc., Neurobehavioral Teratology Soc., Mid Atlantic Reproduction and Teratology Assn. (steering com. 1994), Soc. Toxicology. Office: Pfizer Central Research Eastern Point Rd Groton CT 06340

TASSONE, GELSOMINA (GESSIE TASSONE), metal processing executive; b. N.Y.C., July 8, 1944; d. Enrico and A. Cira (Petriccione) Gargiulo; children: Ann Marie, Margaret, Theresa, Christine; m. Armando Tassone, Mar. 20, 1978. Student, Orange County Community Coll., 1975-79, Iona Coll., 1980—. Head bookkeeper Gargiulo Bros. Builders, N.Y.C., 1968-72; pres., owner A&T Iron Works, Inc., New Rochelle, N.Y., 1973—. Recipient Profl. Image award Contractors Coun. Greater N.Y.C., 1986; named Businesswoman of Yr., Contractors Coun. Greater N.Y.C., 1985, N.Y. State Small Bus. Person of Yr., 1988, Entrepreneur of Yr. Inc. mag., 1990; company named a Successful Small Bus. Co. Westchester County C. of C./BSBA, 1986-88. Mem. Nat. Ornamental and Miscellaneous Metal Assn., Builders Inst. Westchester and Putnam County, Westchester Assn. Women Bus. Owners, Profl. Women in Constrn., Westchester C. of C. Office: A&T Iron Works Inc 25 Cliff St New Rochelle NY 10801-6803

TATA, GIOVANNI, publishing executive; b. Taranto, Italy, Apr. 26, 1954; came to U.S., 1974, naturalized, 1982; s. Vito and Angela (Colucci) T.; m. Brenda Susan Smith, Feb. 14, 1978; children: Elizabeth Ariana, Katherine Allison, Margaret Anne, Michael Anthony. BS cum laude (scholar), Brigham Young U., 1977, MA, 1980; grad. cert. area studies U. Utah, 1980; PhD, 1986; postgrad. U. Turin (Italy), 1980-81. Archaeologist, Utah State Hist. Soc., Salt Lake City, 1979; instr. dept. langs. U. Utah, Salt Lake City, 1983-85; Mediterranean specialist Soc. Early Hist. Archaeology, Provo, Utah, 1978-91; mus. curator Pioneer Trail State Park, Salt Lake City, 1982-83; instr. dept. art Brigham Young U., Provo, 1982-84; research fellow Direzione Generale per la Cooperazione Scientifica Culturale e Technica, Rome, 1980-81; research curator Utah Mus. Fine Arts, Salt Lake City, 1985-87; chmn. 35th Ann. Symposium on the Archaeology of the Scriptures, 1986; pres. Transoft Internat., Inc., 1988—, Mus. Info. Systems, 1987-93; chmn. Taras Devel. Corp., 1994—. Chmn. MuseuMedia, Inc., 1995—. Republican. Mem. Ch. Jesus Christ of Latter-day Saints. Mem. Am. Assn. Museums, Internat. Coun. Museums, Utah State Hist. Soc. Home: PO Box 2194 Provo UT 84603-2194 Office: Taras Devel Corp 117 #250 W Center St Provo UT 84603

TATARSKII, VALERIAN IL'ICH, physics researcher; b. Kharkov, USSR, Oct. 13, 1929; s. Il'ya A. and Elizabeth A. (Lapis) T.; m. Maia S. Granovskaia, Dec. 22, 1955; 1 child, Viatcheslav V. MS, Moscow State U., 1952; PhD, Acoustical Inst. Acad. Scis., 1957; DSc, Gorky State U., 1962. Scientific rschr. Geophys. Inst. Acad. Sci. USSR, Moscow, 1953-56; scientific rschr. Inst. Atmospheric Physics, Acad. Sci. USSR, Moscow, 1956-59, sr. scientific rschr., 1959-78, head lab., 1978-90; head dept. Lebedev. Phys. Inst. Acad. Sci., Moscow, 1990-91; sr. rsch. assoc. U. Colo. Coop. Inst. for Rsch. in Environ. Sci., Boulder, 1991—, NOAA/ERL Environ. Tech. Lab., Boulder. Author: Wave Propagation in a Turbulent Medium, 1961, 67, The Effect of the Turbulent Atmosphere on Wave Propagation, 1971, Principles of Statistical Radiophysics, 1989; contbr. articles to profl. jours. Recipient of Max Born award, 1994, Optical Soc. of Am., USSR State prize, 1990. Fellow Optical Soc. Am. (Max Born award 1994); mem. Russian Acad. Sci., U.S.A. Nat. Acad. Engring. (fgn. assoc.), N.Y. Acad. Sci. Avocations: classical music, kayaking. Office: NOAA ERL ETL 325 Broadway St Boulder CO 80303-3337

TATE, BARBARA MARIE, art director; b. Canton, Ohio, Jan. 13, 1958; d. John Lawrence and Dolores Magaret (Hill) T.; m. Charles Allan Kerecz, May 25, 1985. Student, Kent State U., 1975-79, Sch. Visual Arts, N.Y.C., 1979-80. Assoc. art dir. All in Style Mag., N.Y.C., 1975-81; art dir. Macy's, N.Y.C., 1981-83, Direct Mktg. Group, N.Y.C., 1983, Avon, N.Y.C., 1983-84; design dir. Tateworks, N.Y.C., 1984—. Avocations: interior design, art photography, Alpine skiing, golf, filmmaking. Office: 24 W 30th St Fl 6 New York NY 10001-4443

TATE, CURTIS E., management educator; b. Trezvant, Tenn., July 5, 1920; s. Curtis E. and Mary Kathryn (Haskins) T.; m. Evelyn Ruth Mann, Apr. 12, 1945 (div. May, 1969); m. Mary Jim Combs, Aug. 28, 1977; children: Curtis Emory, Milton Oglesby. Student, N. Ga. Coll., 1943-44, U. Ga., 1945-46; AB, Bethel Coll., 1946; MS, U. Tenn., 1952. Clk. Family Gen. Grocery, Trezevant, Tenn., 1938-42; clk. purchasing dept. P&G Defense Corp., Milan, Twnn., 1942; plant mgr. Keathley Pie Co., Memphis, 1946-50; instr. Furman U., Greenville, S.C., 1952-53; bus. mgr. Lander Coll., Greenwood, S.C., 1953-56; from asst. to assoc. prof. Coll. of Bus. Adminstrn. U. Ga., Athens, 1956-92; prof. emeritus Terry Coll. of Bus. U. Ga., Athens, 1991—; bd. dirs. Flexible Products, Inc., Marietta, Ga., 1968-76, Case Pub. Corp.; asst. dean fund raising, 1991—. Co-author: Successful Small Business Management, 1975, latest rev. edit., 1985, Complete Guide to Your Own Business, 1977, Dow-Jones-Irwin Business Papers, 1977, Bus. Policy: Administrative, Strategic and Constitigency Issues, 1983, 92, Managing for Profits, 1984, Small Business Management and Entrepreneurship, 1992; mem. adv. bd. Am. Jour. Case Rsch. With U.S. Army, 1942-45, ETO. Fellow N. Am. Case Rsch. Assn. (sec., v.p., bd. dirs., pres. so. casewriters, Outstandinc Case Contbr. 1992), Acad. Mgmt., Kiwanis, Sigma Iota Epsilon, Beta Gamma Sigma. Home and Office: 1640 Broadlands Dr Watkinsville GA 30677-2148

TATE, HAROLD SIMMONS, JR., lawyer; b. Taylors, S.C., Sept. 19, 1930; s. Harold Simmons and Cleone (Clayton) T.; m. Elizabeth Anne Coker, Dec. 22, 1952; children—Mary Elizabeth Anne, Martha Coker, Virginia Clayton. Grad. cum laude, Harvard U., 1951, JD, 1956, postgrad., 1954. Bar: S.C. 1956. Ptnr. firm Sinkler and Boyd, P.A. (formerly Boyd, Knowlton, Tate & Finlay), Columbia, S.C., 1962—; chmn. U.S. Dist. Ct. (S.C.) Adv. Com., 1984—; lectr. Am. Law Inst.-ABA seminars; mem. adv. com. on rules and procedures U.S. Ct. Appeals (4th cir.), 1990-95. Co-author: South Carolina Appellate Practice, 1985; bd. editors Federal Litigation Guide Reporter, 1985—; contbr. articles and book revs. to profl. jours. Chmn. Richland County Mental Health Ctr., 1965-66; co-chmn. Columbia Hearing and Speech Ctr., 1962-64; mem. admission and scholarship com. Harvard U., 1961—; chmn. subcom. on legislation, legislation and fin. study commn. Gov.'s Adv. Group on Mental Health Planning, 1963-65; chmn. Columbia Bd. Supervisory of Registration, 1961-70; pres. Columbia Philharm. Orch., 1966-67, Town Theatre, 1967-70; trustee Richland County Pub. Libr., 1973-78, Hist. Columbia Found., 1971-75, Caroliniana soc., 1978—, Bostick Charitable Trust, 1968—; bd. mgrs. S.C. Hist. Soc., 1993—; commr. S.C. Commn. of Archives and History, 1995—. Capt. U.S. Army, 1951-53. Mem. ABA, Am. Law Inst., Am. Judicature Soc., S.C. Bar Assn., Assn. Bar City N.Y., Richland County Bar Assn., Harvard Law Sch. Assn. S.C. (sec.-treas. 1968-70, pres. 1988—), Forest Lake Country Club, Columbia Drama Club (pres. 1963-64), Palmetto Club (sec. 1963-70, pres. 1973-76), The Forum Club, Harvard Club (N.Y.C.), Harvard Club S.C. Episcopalian. Home: 15 Gibbes Ct Columbia SC 29201-3923 Office: Sinkler & Boyd 1426 Main St Columbia SC 29201-2834

TATE, JAMES VINCENT, poet, English educator; b. Kansas City, Mo., Dec. 8, 1943; s. Samuel Vincent Appleby and Betty Jean Whitsitt. BA, Kans. State Coll., 1965; MFA, U. Iowa, 1967. Instr. U. Iowa, Iowa City, 1966-67; vis. lectr. U. Calif., Berkeley, 1967-68; asst. prof. English Columbia U., N.Y.C., 1969-71; from assoc. prof. to dist. univ. prof. English U. Mass., Amherst, 1971—; poet-in-residence Emerson Coll., 1970-71; cons. Coord. Coun. Literary Mags., 1971-74, Ky. Arts Commn., 1979; mem. Bollingen Prize Com., 1974-75; poetry editor Dickinson Rev., 1967-76; trustee, assoc. editor Pym-Randall Pr., 1968-80; assoc. editor Barn Dream Pr. Author: (poems) Cages, 1966, The Destination, 1967, The Lost Pilot, 1967 (Yale Younger Poets award 1966), Notes of Woe, 1968, Camping in the Valley, 1968, Mystics in Chicago, 1968, The Torches, 1968, Row with Your Hair, 1969, Is There Anything?, 1969, Shepherds of the Mist, 1969, Amnesia People, 1970, Are You Ready Mary Baker Eddy, 1970, Deaf Girl Playing, 1970, The Oblivion Ha-Ha, 1970, Wrong Songs, 1970, Hints to Pilgrims, 1971, Nobody Goes to Visit the Insane Anymore, 1971, Absences, 1972, Apology for Eating Geoffrey Movius' Hyacinth, 1972, A Dime Found in the Snow, 1973, Hottentot Ossuary, 1974, Marfa, 1974, Suffering Bastards, 1975, Who Gets the Bitterroot?, 1976, Viper Jazz, 1976, Riven Doggeries, 1979, The Rustling of Foliage, the Memory of Caresses, 1979, If It Would All Please Hurray, 1980, Land of Little Sticks, 1981, Constant Defender, 1983, Just Shades, 1985, Reckoner, 1986, Distance from Loved Ones, 1990, Selected Poems, 1991 (Pulitzer Prize for poetry 1992), Worshipful Company of Fletchers, 1993 (Nat. Book Award for Poetry 1994); (novel) Lucky Darryl, 1977. Named Poet of Yr. by Phi Beta Kappa, 1972; recipient Nat. Inst. Arts and Letters award for poetry, 1974; Mass. Arts and Humanities fellow, 1975, Guggenheim fellow, 1976, Nat. Endowment for the Arts fellow, 1980. Office: U Mass Dept English Amherst MA 01002*

TATE, RANDALL J. (RANDY TATE), former congressman; b. Puyallup, Wash., Nov. 23, 1965; m. Julie; 1 child. AA, Tacoma C. C., Wash.; BA in Econs. and Polit. Sci., We. Wash. U. Mem. Wash. Ho. of Reps., 1988-94, 104th Congress from 9th Wash. dist., 1994-96; former mem. com. rules, com. fin. instns. and ins., judiciary com., Wash. Ho. Reps.; mem. Congrl. com. transp. and infrastructure, com. govt. reform. Home: 13011 Meridian E # 301 Puyallup WA 98373 Address: 5616 99th St Ct E Puyallup WA 98374*

TATE, SHEILA BURKE, public relations executive; b. Washington, Mar. 3, 1942; d. Eugene L. and Mary J. (Doherty) Burke; m. William J. Tate, May 2, 1981; children: Hager Burke Patton, Courtney Paige Patton. BA in Journalism, Duquesne U., 1964; postgrad. in mass communications, U. Denver, 1975-76. former chairperson bd. dirs. Corp. for Pub. Broadcasting. Rsch. asst. Westinghouse Air Brake Co.; asst. account exec. Falhgren and Assos.; copywriter Ketchum, MacLeod and Grove, 1964-66; account exec. Burson-Marsteller Assocs., Pitts., 1967; sr. v.p. Burson-Marsteller Assocs., Washington, 1985-87; public rels. mgr. Colo. Nat. Bank, Denver, 1967-70; account exec. Hill and Knowlton, Inc., Houston, 1977-78; v.p. Hill and Knowlton, Inc., Washington, 1978-81; dep. to the chmn. Hill and Knowlton Inc., Washington, 1987-88; press sec. to First Lady White House, Washington, 1981-85; press sec. George Bush for Pres. Campaign, 1988; press sec. to Pres.-elect George Bush, 1988-89; vice chmn. Cassidy and Assocs. Pub. Affairs, Washington, 1989-91; pres. Powell Tate, Washington, 1991—; bd. dirs. Corp. for Pub. Broadcasting (former mem.), vice chmn., 1990-92, chmn., 1992-94. Mem. civilian pub. affairs adv. bd. U.S. Mil. Acad.; mem. adv. bd. Ronald Reagan Inst. Emergency Medicine, George Washington U. Hosp., Washington; bd. dirs. Arlington (Va.) Health Found. Mem. Nat. Press Club, Nat. Press Found. (bd. dirs.). Clubs: Duquesne U. Century, F Street, Washington Golf and Country, Farmington Country Club. Office: Powell Tate 700 13th St NW Ste 1000 Washington DC 20005-3960

TATE, STONEWALL SHEPHERD, lawyer; b. Memphis, Dec. 19, 1917; m. Janet Graf; children: Adele Shepherd, Shepherd Davis, Janet Reid Walker. BA, Southwestern at Memphis (now Rhodes Coll.), 1939; JD, U. Va., 1942; LLD (hon.), Samford U., 1979, Suffolk U., 1982, Capital U., 1989, Rhodes Coll., 1993. Bar: Va. 1941, Tenn. 1942. Mem. Martin, Tate, Morrow & Marston, P.C. (and predecessor firms), Memphis, 1947—; chmn. pres.'s coun. Rhodes Coll., 1995-96, bd. trustees, 1967-77, 80-84. Pres. Episcopal Churchmen of Tenn., 1961-62; sec. standing com. Episcopal Diocese of Tenn., 1969-71; pres. Chickasaw Coun. Boy Scouts Am., 1967-78. With USNR, 1942-46; comdr. USNR; ret. Decorated Order of Cloud Banner (China); recipient Silver Beaver award Boy Scouts Am., 1963, Disting. Eagle Scout award, 1980, Disting. Svc. medal Rhodes Coll., 1978, Disting. Alumni award, 1991, Lawyers' Lawyer award Memphis Bar Assn., 1990; Memphis Rotary Club Civic Recognition award, 1983; Paul Harris fellow, 1985. Fellow Am. Bar Found., Am. Coll. Trust and Estate Counsel, Internat. Acad. Estate and Trust Law, Coll. Law Practice Mgmt. (hon.), Tenn. Bar Found., Memphis and Shelby County Bar Found.; mem. ABA (chmn. standing com. on profl. discipline 1973-76, chmn. standing com. on scope and correlation of work 1977, chmn. task force on lawyer advt. 1977, pres. ABA 1978-79, chmn. standing com. on lawyer competence 1986-92), Am. Judicature Soc. (past bd. dirs.), Am. Law Inst., Am. Arbitration Assn. (large complex case panel 1993—), Lawyer-Pilots Bar Assn., Tenn. Bar Assn. (pres. 1963-64), Memphis and Shelby County Bar Assn. (pres. 1959-60), Nat. Conf. Bar Pres. (pres. 1972-73), U.S. 6th Cir. Jud. Conf. (life), U. Va. Law Sch. Alumni Assn. (mem. exec. coun. 1974-77), Rhodes Coll. Alumni Assn. (pres. 1951-53), Order of Coif, Raven Soc., Rotary (pres. 1982-83, bd. dirs. 1974, 80-84, 89-90), Phi Beta Kappa, Omicron Delta Kappa, Phi Delta Phi, Sigma Alpha Epsilon (highest effort award N.Y.C. Alumni Assn. 1979). Office: Martin Tate Morrow & Marston PC Falls Bldg 22 N Front St Ste 1100 Memphis TN 38103-2109

TATE, THADDEUS W(ILBUR), JR. (THAD TATE), history educator, historical institute executive, historian; b. Winston-Salem, N.C., May 27, 1924; s. Thaddeus Wilbur and Elizabeth Kent (Llewellyn) T. A.B., U. N.C., 1947, M.A., 1948; Ph.D., Brown U., 1960. Historian U.S. Nat. Park Service, 1948-54; research assoc. Colonial Williamsburg Found., (Va.), 1954-57, asst. dir. research, 1957-61; book rev. editor William and Mary Quar., Williamsburg, 1961-66, editor, 1966-72; asst. prof. history Coll. William and Mary, 1961-64, assoc. prof., 1964-69; prof. Coll. William and Mary, 1969-90; Murden prof. humanities Coll. William and Mary, 1990-92, emeritus, 1992—; dir. Inst. Early Am. History and Culture, Williamsburg, 1972-89, Commonwealth Ctr. for Study of Am. Culture, Williamsburg, 1988-92. Author: Negro in Eighteenth-Century Williamsburg, 1966; co-author: Colonial Virginia: A History, 1986, The College of William and Mary: A History, 1993; co-editor, contbg. author: Chesapeake in the Seventeenth Century, 1979; co-editor: Saints and Revolutionaries, 1984, An Uncivil War: The Southern Backcountry in the American Revolution, 1985; mem. adv. bd.: Environ. Rev., 1976-85; chair editorial adv. bd.: Papers of John Marshall. Mem. Williamsburg Wetlands Bd., 1980-93; chair bd. dirs. Va. Found. for Humanities and Pub. Policy, 1989-95; mem. tercentary commn. Coll. William and Mary, 1988-93. With USNR, 1943-46. Recipient Grad. Alumni citation Brown U., 1985; Thomas Jefferson award Coll. William and Mary, 1986; Brown U. fellow, 1949-51; NEH fellow, 1982-83; fellow Am. Council Learned Socs., 1970-71. Mem. Orgn. Am. Historians, Am. Hist. Assn., So. Hist. Assn., Va. Hist. Soc. (hon.), Am Soc. Legal History, Mass. Hist. Soc., Am. Soc. Environ. History, Assocs. John Carter Brown Library, Am. Antiquarian Soc., Library Co. Phila., Hist. Soc. Episcopal Ch. (1st v.p. 1996—), Phi Beta Kappa, Phi Alpha Theta. Democrat. Episcopalian. Home: 313 Half Burns Lane Williamsburg VA 23185-3908

TATEL, DAVID STEPHEN, federal judge; b. Washington, Mar. 16, 1942; s. Howard Edwin and Molly (Abramowitz) T.; m. Edith Sara Bassichis, Aug. 29, 1965; children: Rebecca, Stephanie, Joshua, Emily. BA, U. Mich., 1963; JD, U. Chgo., 1966. Bar: Ill 1966, U.S. Dist. Ct. (no. dist.) Ill. 1966, U.S. Dist. Ct. D.C. 1970, U.S. Ct. Appeals (7th and D.C. cirs.) 1970, U.S. Supreme Ct. 1971, U.S. Ct. Appeals (5th cir.) 1976, U.S. Ct. Appeals (11th and 4th cirs.) 1986. Instr. U. Mich., Ann Arbor, 1966-67; assoc. Sidley & Austin, Chgo. and Washington, 1967-69, 70-72; dir. Chgo. Lawyer's Com., 1969-70, Nat. Lawyers Commn. for Civil Rights Under Law, Washington, 1972-74; dir. Office for Civil Rights HEW, Washington, 1977-79; ptnr. Hogan & Hartson, Washington, 1979-94; cir. judge U.S. Ct. Appeals (D.C. cir.), Washington, 1994—; lectr. Stanford U. Law Sch., 1991-92; co-chmn. Nat. Lawyers Com. for Civil Rights Under Law, Washington, 1989-91; chmn., bd. dirs. Spencer Found., Chgo., 1990—. Mem. vis. com. to law sch. U. Chgo., 1986-89; spl. master U.S. Dist. Ct. D.C., Washington, 1988-89; mem. Montgomery County Bd. Edn. Com. on Excellence in Tchg., Rockville, Md., 1985-87; mem. adv. com. on the governance of edn. Carnegie Found. for Advancement in Tchg., Princeton, N.J., 1980-82; acting gen. counsel Legal Svcs. Corp., Washington, 1975-76; bd. dirs. Refugee Policy Group, Washington, 1985-90; mem. Pew Forum on Edn. Reform, 1992-96. Mem. D.C. Bar Assn. (bd. govs. 1980-81), Chgo. Coun. Lawyers (bd. govs. 1969-70). Office: 333 Constitution Ave NW Washington DC 20001-2802*

TATERA, JAMES FRANK, chemist, process analysis specialist; b. Milw., June 27, 1946; s. Harry Frank and Agnes Rose (Szymanowski) T.; m. Kaaren Marie Piekarski, Sept. 9, 1972; children: Patrick, Monica, David. BS in Chemistry, Math., U. Wis., Oshkosh, 1968; postgrad., U. Minn., 1968, 71-73; MBA, Cen. Mich. U., 1982. Cert. specialist in analytical tech. Teaching rsch. assoc. chemistry dept. U. Minn., Mpls., 1968, 71-73; analytical chemist Dow Corning Corp., Midland, Mich., 1973-76, scale up engr. new products commercialization, 1976-78, prodn. bldg. supt. prodn. dept., 1978-80; analytical systems specialist project and plant engring. Dow Corning Ltd., Barry, Wales, 1981-84; analytical systems supr. plant engring. & maintenance Dow Corning Corp., Carrollton, Ky., 1984-85, analytical systems specialist plant engring. and maintenance, 1985-87, sr. analytical and control specialist project engring., 1988-90, sr. analytical systems specialist strategic change program, 1991—; session developer, panelist, presenter in field; U.S. nat. com. Internat. Electrotech. Commn., Paris, 1993, Milan, 1994, Montreal, 1996, U.S. nat. com. tech. advisor subcom. 65D, 1993—. Contbr. articles to profl. jours., chpts. to books. 1st lt. arty. U.S. Army, 1969-71. Decorated Bronze Star, Bronze Star with oak leaf cluster. Mem. Am. Chem. Soc. (rep. Vol. in Pub. Outreach program, sect. careers program and nat. chemistry week com.), Instrument Soc. Am. (dir.-elect, sec. and treas. analysis divsn. 1994-96, dir. analysis divsn. 1996—, chmn. SP 76 stds. com. 1991-96, pres. N.E. Mich. sect. 1979-80, various sect. offices 1976-79), Air and Waste Mgmt. Assn. (optical sensing divsn. indsl. issues and applications com. on enhanced monitoring), Elks, Am. Legion, VFW, KC, Delta Sigma Phi, Phi Lambda Upsilon, Sigma Iota Epsilon. Roman Catholic. Home: 2038 Ridgewood Dr Madison IN 47250-2729 Office: Dow Corning Corp 4770 Hwy 42 E Mail Stop 32 Carrollton KY 41008

TATGENHORST, (CHARLES) ROBERT, lawyer; b. Cin., Apr. 21, 1918; s. Charles and Clara (Strebel) T.; m. Louise Thompson, Sept. 6, 1951; children: David, John, James, Richard. A.B., Dartmouth Coll., 1940; LL.B., U. Cin., 1947. Bar: Ohio 1947. Asst. atty. gen. State of Ohio, 1947-49; asso. firm Taft, Stettinius & Hollister, Cin., 1951-58; ptnr. firm Tatgenhorst & Tatgenhorst, Cin., 1958-61; prin. firm Robert Tatgenhorst & Assocs., Cin., 1961-85; ptnr. Tatgenhorst & Bruestle, Cin., 1986—, 1986-95; adj. prof. law Chase Coll. Law, No. Ky. U., 1962-86. Pres. Westwood Civic Assn., Cin., 1959, Meth. Union, 1960; chmn. dist. Boy Scouts Am., 1970; trustee Twin Towers Retirement Ctr., 1968-93, Westwood United Meth. Ch., bd. trustees 1985-88, pres., 1990-92, trustee, 1992. With CIC U.S. Army, 1942-46. Mem. Ohio State Bar Assn., Cin. Bar Assn. (sec. 1973-75), Ryland Lakes Country Club, Optimists (pres. Cin. club 1962), Dartmouth of Cin. Club (pres. 1965), Masons (33 deg.), Sigma Alpha Epsilon, Phi Alpha Delta (pres. 1946). Republican.

TATHAM, DAVID FREDERIC, art historian, educator; b. Wellesley, Mass., Nov. 29, 1932; s. Richard Merton and Florence Elizabeth (Mallette) T.; m. Cleota Reed, Dec. 12, 1979. A.B., U. Mass., 1954; M.A., Syracuse U., 1960, Ph.D., 1970. Dean students Syracuse (N.Y.) U., 1966-71, assoc. prof. fine arts, 1972-78, prof., 1978—, chmn. dept. fine arts, 1980-86. Author: The Lure of the Striped Pig, 1973, Prints and Printmakers of New York State, 1986, Winslow Homer and the Art of the Book, 1990, Winslow Homer and the Illustrated Book, 1992, Fishing in the North Woods, 1995, Winslow Homer in the Adirondacks, 1996, (exhbn. catalogs) Winslow Homer Drawings, 1979, Art, Artists and Museums, 1980, Bolton Brown, 1981, Abraham Tuthill, 1983; contbr. articles to profl. jours. Served with U.S. Army, 1956. Daniels research fellow, 1974; Am. Philos. Soc. grantee, 1980, 86; Am. Art Jour. award for outstanding scholarship, 1984; NEH grantee, 1987-88. Mem. Am. Antiquarian Soc. (rec. sec. 1988-93), Coll. Art Assn., Fellow Athenaeum of Phila. Home: 329 Westcott St Syracuse NY 13210-2107 Office: Syracuse U Dept Fine Arts Bowne Hall Syracuse NY 13244

TATHAM, JULIE CAMPBELL, writer; b. N.Y.C., June 1, 1908; d. Archibald and Julia deFres (Sample) Campbell; student pvt. schs., N.Y.C.; m. Charles Tatham, Mar. 30, 1933; children—Charles III, Campbell. Author more than 30 juvenile books including: The Mongrel of Merryway Farm, 1952; The World Book of Dogs, 1953; To Nick from Jan, 1957; author Trixie Belden series, 1946—, Ginny Gordon series, 1946—; co-author Cherry Ames and Vicki Barr series, 1947—; author: The Old Testament Made Easy, 1985; many series books transl. into fgn. langs.; contbr. numerous mag. stories and articles to popular publs., 1935—; free-lance writer, 1935—; contbr. numerous articles to Christian Sci. publs., including Christian Sci. Monitor, 1960—. Address: 1202 S Washington St Apt 814 Alexandria VA 22314-4446

TATNALL, GEORGE JACOB, aeronautical engineer; b. Cin., Aug. 9, 1923; s. George Henry and Ida Mae (Hazelbaker) T.; m. G. Virginia Morgan, Feb. 5, 1949; children: Robert, William, Jeffrey, Thomas, Jane. BSME in Aeronautics, U. Pitts., 1949. Devel. engr. Naval Air Devel. Ctr., Warminster, Pa., 1949-57; supr. electro-mech. design br., supr. radome antenna sect. Naval Air Devel. Ctr., Warminster, 1957-62, 63-78; engring. group leader Corning (N.Y.) Glass Works, 1962-63; cons. Semcor, Inc., Warminster, 1979-81; cons. pvt. practice Warminster, 1982-84; cons. Rome Rsch. Corp., New Hartford, N.Y., 1993-95; Tech. advisor Seventh Fleet USN, S.E. Asia, during Vietnam War, 1971. Contbr. to sci. papers presented at confs. (many also pub. in proceedings); author: (with others) chpt. in book Environmental Simulation and Test Data; author: manuals and documentation aircraft equipment. With US Army AF, 1943-45, China. Mem. AIAA (pres. U. Pitts. chpt. 1948), VFW, Flying Tiger U.S. 14th Air Force Assn. Achievements include patents for Speed Brake Retarding Mechanism for an Air Dropped Store, Air Dropped Minature Sonobuoy, Rotatable and Tiltable Radome with ind. scan and tilt antenna; developed low noise coupling through laminar boundary layer for acoustic homing missile, test facilities for supersonic rain erosion of aircraft materials. Home: 551 Walter Rd Warminster PA 18974-5553

TATUM, JOAN GLENNALYN JOHN, secondary school educator; b. Scottsbluff, Nebr., Jan. 5, 1934; d. Glenn Edwin and Blanche Constance (Dundon) John; m. William Earl Tatum, Apr. 6, 1954 (div. Apr. 1988); children: Cherie Elizabeth Tatum Love, Michele Tatum Brackett, John William, Amy Denise Tatum Stanton. AA, U. Fla., 1954; BA, U. South Fla., 1969, MA, 1971. Cert. tchr., Fla. Substitute tchr. Pub. Sch. Dist., Sarasota, Fla., 1966-67; bus., vocat. edn. tchr. Riverview High Sch., Sarasota, 1969-96, Sarasota Tech. Inst., 1969—; curriculum coord. bus.-vocat. edn. dept. Riverview H.S., 1990—, instructional tech. facilitator, 1996—; adj. prof. St. Francis Coll., Joliet, Ill., 1988, 91, 93, 94; state and dist. textbook evaluation teams Fla. Dept. Edn., Sarasota, sch. to dist. tech. rep., 1985—; chmn. Riverview Tech. Com., 1987—; assoc. master tchr. State Fla. Bd. Edn., 1984-87; coun. chair Dist. Sch. Based Mgmt., Sarasota, 1991-93; chmn. Riverview Sch. Based Mgmt., 1991-93; project coord. Riverview Sr. Acad. Integrated Studies, 1991-95; dance tchr. various studios, Sarasota, 1949-67; sec. and office staff various govtl., cmty. and dance studios, Sarasota, 1951-59. Supervisory com. Sarasota Coastal Credit Union, 1985—. Senate Edn. scholar Sarasota High/Fla. Legislature, 1951; named Tchr. of Yr. Riverview High Sch., 1991-92. Mem. Internat. Soc. Bus. Educators, Nat. Bus. Edn. Assn., Am. Vocat. Assn., So. Bus. Edn. Assn., Fla. Bus. Edn. Assn., Fla. Vocat. Assn., Sarasota County Vocat. Adult Assn. (pres. 1989-90), Fla. Assn. for Computers in Edn., Internat. Soc. for Tech. in Edn., Order of Rainbow (mem. adv. bd. 1977—, Grand Cross Color award 1949), Order Ea. Star, Kappa Delta Pi, Delta Pi Epsilon, Alpha Delta Kappa (chpt. treas. 1982-86, chpt. pres. 1986-88, chmn. state ad hoc com. 1989-90, chmn. state candidate qualifications com. 1994-96, chmn. state budget com. 1996—, dist. treas. 1987-92, dist. chmn. 1992-94, State Honoris Causa award 1992). Presbyterian. Avocations: theatre, choreography, dance, family, walking. Home: 4561 Ashton Rd Sarasota FL 34233-3405 Office: Riverview HS One Ram Way Sarasota FL 34231

TATUM, RITA, communications executive; b. Elkhart, Ind., Nov. 30, 1948; d. Edward Anthony and Edith Ann (Chomer) Osowski; m. Michael Ray Tatum, May 22, 1971 (div. 1977). BA in English, St. Mary of the Woods, 1971, BA in Journalism, 1971; postgrad., Loyola U., Chgo., 1977-78. Reporter Stas. WTHI and WTHI-TV, Terre Haute, Ind., 1970-71; assoc. editor Bldg. Design and Constrn., Chgo., 1972-76; editor-in-chief Gorman Pub., Chgo., 1976-79; prin. Tatum Communications, Elkhart, Ind., 1979—; editorial cons. ABA, Aspen Pubs., Bonus Books, Dearborn Fin. Pub., Air Conditioning and Refrigeration Inst., Circle Solutions, Cygnus Corp., EPA GreenLights Program, Envirosense Consortium, FASA Corp., Precept Press, Teach 'Em, Trade Press Pub., others. Author, collaborator: The Alternative House, 1978, Sourcebook of Food and Nutrition, 1980, 2nd edit. 1982, Yearbook of Special Education, 1980, Standard Education Almanac, 1984, 4 edits., Financial Planner's Seminar Kit, 1985, CPA's Guide to Financial Planning, 1985, The Financial Planner: A New Professional, 1986, University Hospital Consortium Recruitment/Orientation Manual, 1989, Ellis Island, 1990; contbr. articles to profl. jours., chpts. to books. Recipient Jesse Neal award Am. Bus. Press, 1976, 2d Place award Soc. Nat. Assn. Publs., 1987, 3d Place award Writer's Digest Writing Competition, 1989. Mem. AAAS, Soc. Profl. Journalists, Nature Conservancy. Office: Tatum Communications 55714 Merle St Elkhart IN 46514-9591

TATUM, RONALD WINSTON, physician, endocrinologist; b. Joplin, Mo., Apr. 29, 1935; s. Dorothy Elizabeth (Messick) T.; m. Phyllis Wainman, June 25 (div. May 1974); children: Jeffrey, Stacey; m. Yvonne Marie Laug, Oct. 8, 1994; children: Christina, Candice. AB, Harvard U., 1957; MD, U. Rochester, 1961. Intern Strong Meml. Hosp., Rochester, N.Y., 1961-62; resident U. Rochester, 1962-64, fellow, 1964-66; clin. endocrinologist in pvt. practice Albuquerque, 1966—; active staff Presbyn. Hosp. and St. Joseph Hosp., Albuquerque, 1966—; med. dir. Cottonwood Treatment Ctr., Albuquerque, 1985-90, N.Mex. Monitored Treatment Program, Albuquerque, 1990—; clin. endocrine cons. Charter Hosp. and Heights Psychiat. Hosp., Albuquerque, 1985—. Contbr. articles to profl. jours. Mem. med. adv. com. Hospice Home Health Care, Albuquerque, 1991—. Mem. Am. Assn. Clin. Endocrinologists (charter), Am. Assn. Internal Medicine, Am. Diabetes Assn. (pres. N.Mex. chpt. 1970, 74), Am. Soc. Addiction Medicine, Assn. for Med. Rsch. in Substance Abuse. Avocations: photography, computer investing. Home: 408 Poinsettia Pl SE Albuquerque NM 87123 Office: 8008 Constitution Pl NE Albuquerque NM 87110-7628

TATUM, WILBERT ARNOLD, editor, publisher; b. Durham, N.C., Jan. 23, 1933; s. Eugene Malcolm Tatum and Mittie Novesta (Spell) Tatum-Smith; m. Susan Kohn, June 17, 1966; 1 child, Elinor Ruth. BS, Lincoln U., 1972; MS, Occidental Coll., 1972; DHL (hon.), Coll. Human Svcs., N.Y.C., 1988. Dep. pres. Borough of Manhattan, N.Y.C., 1970-71; dir. planning and devel. City of N.Y., 1971-77; sr. v.p. Health Ins. Plan of Greater N.Y., N.Y.C., 1978-86; editor, pub., CEO N.Y. Amsterdam News, N.Y.C., 1983—; vice chmn. Inner City Broadcasting, N.Y.C., 1970-73; chmn. bd. Tatum-Kohn Assn., N.Y.C., 1980—, Amnews Corp., N.Y.C., 1983—, Palisades Amsterdam Comm., N.Y.C., 1988—. Cpl. USMC, 1951-54, Far East. Fellow Nat. Urban Fellows, 1971-72. Mem. Nat. Newspaper Pubs. Assn. (bd. dirs.), N.Y. Urban League (Bldg. brick 1993), Wallenberg Com. of U.S. (v.p.). Democrat. Baptist. Home: 34 E 3rd St New York NY 10003-8908 Office: Amnews Corp 2340 Frederick Douglass Blvd New York NY 10027-3619*

TATYREK, ALFRED FRANK, consultant, materials/environmental engineer, analytical/research chemist; b. Hillside, N.J., Jan. 23, 1930; s. Frank Peter and Frances (Luxa) T. BS, Seton Hall U., 1954; postgrad., Rutgers U., 1956-57. Rsch. chemist Bakelite div. Union Carbide, Bloomfield, N.J., 1953-58, U.S. Radium Corp., Morristown, N.J., 1959-62; analytical chemist insp. Chem. Procurement Dist. U.S. Army, N.Y.C., 1962-64; rsch. chemist Picatinny Arsenal U.S. Army, Dover, N.J., 1964-73; chem. materials engr. U.S. Army Armament Rsch., Devel. and Engring. Ctr., N.J., 1973-95; cons. polymer materials, environ. chemistry. Patentee pyrotechnic compositions, chemiluminescent compounds and processes, crank case oil vacuum purification sys. for internal combustion engines; lectr., contbr. articles on mountaineering expdns. and adventures in the great mountain ranges of N.Am., S.Am., Europe and Africa to mags.; contbr. more than 50 sci. and tech. reports. 1st aid instr. ARC, Essex County, N.J., 1969-82; chief 1st aid Maplewood (N.J.) CD, 1971-91; patrol dir. Nat. Ski Patrol, Phoenicia, N.Y., 1978-84, sr. lifetime Nat. Ski patroller So. N.Y. region, 1979—. Recipient comdr.'s award for pub. svc. Dept. of Army, 1996. Mem. Nat. Soc. Inventors, Nat. Assn. Underwater Instrs. (cert. advanced diver and underwater photographer 1971—), Magician's Roundtable, Internat. Magician's Soc., Alpine Club of Can., Appalachian Mountain Club, Sierra Club, The Scientific Rsch. Soc., Sigma Xi (pres. Picatinny chpt. 1974-75, 79-80, 85-86). Roman Catholic. Achievments include 6 patents in field. Also climbed 15,771 feet Mt. Blanc, highest mountain peak in Europe; climbed to highest summit of 19,730 feet on Mt. Kilimanjaro, highest mountian peak in Africa, 1972; leader of climb on Matterhorn and Monte Rosa, Switzerland's highest peak; participant in numerous mountain expdns. in U.S. and Can., including 3 first ascents in No. Cascades of Wash. (S.E. ridge of Mt. Goode, Aug. 1963, Peak 7732 via the Snow Chute, Aug. 1964, East ridge of Bear Mountain Aug. 1964). Home: 27 Orchard Rd Maplewood NJ 07040-1919 *"God has given us a world rich in physical and intellectual beauty as well as intriguing scientific discovery. To earn these rewards we must seek out and meet the challanges of life, not as distastful burdens, but as true opportunities upon which to build where others have failed or left off, using all the infinite resources that God has given to all of us".*

TAUB, AARON MYRON, healthcare administrator, consultant; b. Jersey City, Dec. 21, 1935; s. Isadore and Beatrice (Grotsky) T.; m. Rosemary Elizabeth Dessel, July 24, 1967; children: Michael David, Deborah Anne. BS, Wagner Coll., 1960; PhD, SUNY, Buffalo, 1965. Mgr. med. svcs. Fisons Can., Toronto, 1969-72; mgr., dir. quality control Fisons Corp., Bedford, Mass., 1972-82, dir. regulatory affairs, 1982-84, sr. scientist, 1984, dir. project mgmt., 1985-88; dir. new product coord. Fisons Corp., Rochester, N.Y., 1988-96. Mem., chmn. Bd. of Health, Stow, Mass., 1977-82. With USNR, 1953-55. Predoctoral fellow NIH, SUNY, 1962-64. Mem. Am. Assn. Aerosol Rsch., Sigma Xi. Avocation: reading. Home: 5 Glencannon Trail Pittsford NY 14534

TAUB, EDWARD, psychology researcher; b. Bklyn., Oct. 22, 1931; s. Samuel Hart and Ida Pearl (Kimmel) T.; m. Mildred Allen Taub, Aug. 13, 1959. BA, Bklyn. Coll., 1953; MA, Columbia U., 1959; PhD, NYU, 1969. Rsch. asst. Columbia U., N.Y.C., 1956, Dept. Exptl. Neurology, Jewish Chronic Disease Hosp., N.Y.C., 1957-60; rsch. assoc. Dept. Exptl. Neurology, Jewish Chronic Disease Hosp., 1960-68; dir. Behavioral Biology Ctr., Inst. for Behavioral Rsch., 1968-83; assoc. dir. Inst. for Behavioral Rsch., 1978-83; dir. Feedback Rsch. Ctr., Birmingham, Ala., 1984-91; prof. psychology U. Ala., Birmingham, 1986—, sr. scientist ctr. for aging; guest prof. U. Konstanz, Germany, 1995-96, U. Jena, Germany, 1996-97; asst. prof. dept. psychiatry Johns Hopkins U., Balt., 1972-82; vis. prof. grad. prog. dept. psychology CUNY, 1984-85; vis. prof. U. Tuebingen, U. Trier, U. Muenster, Humboldt U., Germany, 1993—. Contbr. articles to profl. jours.; co-inventor technnique of thermal biofeedback, 1970-71. Recipient Pioneering Rsch. Contbn. award Assn. Applied Psychophysiol. and Biofeedback, 1989, Ireland Prize for Scholarly Distinction U. Ala., Birmingham, 1997; Guggenheim Found. fellow, 1983-84. Fellow AAAS, APA (exec. com. div. 6), Soc. for Behavioral Medicine, Am. Psychol. Soc. (charter, William James Fellow award 1997); mem. Soc. for Neurosci., Biofeedback Soc. Am. (pres. 1978-79, Outstanding Rsch. Contbn. award 1988), Am. Physiol. Soc. (exec. com. neurosci. sect. 1988-91). Office: U Ala at Birmingham 201 Campbell Hall Birmingham AL 35294

TAUB, ELI IRWIN, lawyer, arbitrator; b. N.Y.C., July 6, 1938; s. Max and Belle (Slutsky) T.; m. Nancy Denise Bell, May 15, 1983. 1 child, Jennifer. BA, Bklyn. Coll., 1960; JD, NYU, 1963. Bar: N.Y. 1964, U.S. Dist. Ct. (no. dist.) N.Y. 1979. Ptnr. Silverman, Silverman & Taub, Schenectady, 1971-77; pres. Eli I. Taub, P.C., Schenectady, 1978—; chmn. Bd. Assessment Review, Schenectady, 1972-81; arbitrator Am. Arbitration Assn., Pa., N.Y. Employment Rels. Bd., 1966—; N.Y. State Pub. Employer's Rels. Bd.; hearing officer articles 72 and 75 proceedings N.Y. State/CSEA Arbitration Panel; mem. paralegal adv. com. Schenectady County C.C.; counsel Alcoholism and Substance Abuse Coun., Schenectady County. Chmn. trustees Joseph Egan Supreme Ct. Library, Schenectady, 1980, 81, 84; pres. Schenectady County Republican Club, 1985-86; v.p. Jewish Fedn. Schenectady, 1983-86; mem. surrogate decision making com. N.Y. State Commn. on Quality of Care for the Mentally Disabled; bd. dirs. Jewish Community Ctr., NE Parent and Child Soc., United Jewish Fedn. of N.E. N.Y.; advocate Nat. Coll. of Advocay. Mem. Assn. Trial Lawyers Am., Am. Arbitration Assn., Nat. Orgn. of Social Security Claimant Reps., Indsl. Rels. Research Assn., N.Y. State Bar Assn., N.Y. State Trial Lawyers Assn., Schenectady County Bar Assn., Capital Dist. Trial Lawyers Assn., Injured Workers Bar Assn., B'nai B'rith (pres. 1976-77, spl. award 1982, youth services award 1985). Jewish. Home: 105 N Ferry St Schenectady NY 12305-1610 Office: 705 Union St Schenectady NY 12305-1504

TAUB, JESSE J., electrical engineering researcher; b. N.Y.C., Apr. 27, 1927; s. Julius and Ida (Orlansky) T.; m. Eva Pollack, Dec. 24, 1955 (dec. Nov. 1973); children: Richard Lawrence, Jocelyn Cara, Suzanne Mara; m. Naomi Etta Trachtenberg, June 30, 1974. BEE, CCNY, 1948; MEE, Poly. U., 1949. Group leader microwave electronics, Material Lab. USN, Bklyn., 1949-55; engr. Airborne Instruments Lab., Mineola, N.Y., 1955-58, sect. leader, 1958-61, engring. cons., 1961-75; chief scientist AIL Systems Inc., Melville, N.Y., 1975-93; cons., 1993—. Author: (with others) Microwave Measurements, 1963; contbr. numerous papers to profl. publs.; patentee microwave techniques. With USN, 1945-46. Fellow IEEE (centennial medal 1984, C.A. Fowler award 1993, adminstrv. com. 1972-74, program chmn. microwave symposium, steering com., chmn. L.I. sect.); mem. Archaeology Inst. Am. Democrat. Jewish. Avocations: classical musician, contract bridge, archaeology. Home: 115 Northgate Cir Melville NY 11747-3045 Office: AIL Systems Inc Commack Rd Deer Park NY 11729

TAUB, RICHARD PAUL, social sciences educator; b. Bklyn., Apr. 16, 1937; s. Martin Glynn and Frances (Israel) T.; m. Doris Susan Leventhal, Aug. 14, 1961 (dec. Feb. 1996); children: Neela Robin, Zachariah Jacob. BA, U. Mich., 1959; MA, Harvard U., 1962, PhD in Social Relations, 1966. Asst. prof. sociology Brown U., Providence, 1965-69; from asst. prof. to Paul Klapper prof. of social scis. U. Chgo., 1969—, assoc. dean Coll. of Univ., 1982-86; adv. bd. Neighborhood Preservation Initiative, 1993—; chair adv. bd. Nat. Comty. Devel. Initiative, 1991-95; dir. South Ark. Rural Devel. Study, 1988—. Author: Community Capitalism, Bureaucrats Under Stress, (with D. Garth Taylor and Jan Dunham) Paths of Neighborhood Change, (with Doris L. Taub) Entrepreneurship in India's Small Scale Industries; editor: (with Doris L. Taub) American Society in Tocqueville's Time and Today; co-editor Studies of Urban Soc., 1978—; contbr. articles to profl. jours. Chmn. bd. St. Thomas the Apostle Sch., Chgo., 1983-86; bd. dirs. Hyde Park Kenwood Cmty. Conf., Chgo., 1972-75; bd. seminary Coop Bookstore, Chgo., 1994—. Angell scholar U. Mich., 1956; Woodrow Wilson fellow Harvard U., 1959-60; grantee Am. Inst. Indian Studies, Ford Found., MacArthur Found., NSF, Wieboldt Found., Nat. Inst. Justice. Mem. Am. Sociol. Assn., Midwest Sociol. Soc., Assn. for Asian Studies. Avocations: bicycling, music. Office: Univ Chgo 5845 S Ellis Ave Rm 223 Chicago IL 60637-1476

TAUB, ROBERT ALLAN, lawyer; b. Denver, Nov. 25, 1923; s. Clarence Arthur and Mary Frances (Jones) T.; m. Doris Irene Schroeder, Dec. 22, 1945; children: Amanda, Jonathan, Barbara. BA, U. Chgo., 1944, JD, 1947. Bar: Ill. 1947. Legal staff Marshall Field & Co., Chgo., 1947-50; mgr. exec. compensation Ford Motor Co., Dearborn, Mich., 1950-63; asst. sect. Ford Motor Co., Dearborn, 1963-74, dir. corp. affairs planning, 1974—. Pres. Dearborn Community Arts Council, 1971-72; trustee Internat. Mus. Photography, George Eastman House, Rochester, N.Y., 1976—, chmn., 1979-82; mem. adv. bd. U. Mich. Dearborn, 1980—, Met. Mus. Art, N.Y.C., 1987—; trustee Henry Ford Hosp., Detroit, 1983—; chmn. Dearborn Pub. Libr., 1986—; bd. dirs., mem. exec. com., chmn. fin. com., Health Alliance Plan, 1992—. Mem. ABA, Ill. Bar Assn. Presbyterian. Home: 1824 Hawthorne St Dearborn MI 48128-1448 Office: Ford Motor Co The American Rd Rm #950 Dearborn MI 48126

TAUB, THEODORE CALVIN, lawyer; b. Springfield, Mass., Jan. 1, 1935; s. Samuel and Sara Lee (Daum) T.; m. Roberta Mae Ginsburg, Aug. 23, 1959; children: Tracy, Andrew, Adam. AB, Duke U., 1956; JD, U. Fla., 1960. Bar: Fla., 1960, U.S. Supreme Ct. Atty. Broad and Cassel, Tampa; asst. city atty. City of Tampa, 1963-67; city atty. City of Temple Terrace, Fla., 1974—; panelist in field. Contbr. articles to profl. jours. Chmn. Tampa-Hillsborough (Fla.) County Expy. Authority, 1974-84; mem. Hillsborough County Charter Commn., 1966-69, Local Govt. Mgmt. Efficiency Com., 1979, State of Fla. Environ. Efficiency Study Commn., 1986-88; founder Tampa Bay Performing Arts Ctr. Fellow: Am. Bar Found; mem. ABA (chmn. real property litigation com. 1981-86, chmn. com. on housing and urban environ. 1989-91), Am. Coll. Real Estate Lawyers (bd. govs.), Am. Land Title Assn. (lenders' counsel group), Fla. Bar Assn. (bd. cert. real estate lawyer), Fla. Jaycees (pres.), Tau Epsilon Phi. Democrat. Jewish. Home: 4937 Lyford Cay Rd Tampa FL 33629-4828 Office: 100 N Tampa St Ste 3500 Tampa FL 33602-5830

TAUBE, HENRY, chemistry educator; b. Sask., Can., Nov. 30, 1915; came to U.S., 1937, naturalized, 1942; s. Samuel and Albertina (Tiledetski) T.; m. Mary Alice Wesche, Nov. 27, 1952; children: Linda, Marianna, Heinrich, Karl. BS, U. Sask., 1935, MS, 1937, LLD, 1973; PhD, U. Calif., 1940; PhD (hon.), Hebrew U. of Jerusalem, 1979; DSc (hon.), U. Chgo., 1983, Poly. Inst., N.Y., 1984, SUNY, 1985, U. Guelph, 1987; DSc honoris causa, Seton Hall U., 1988; Lajos Kossuth U. of Debrecen, Hungary, 1988; DSc, Northwestern U., 1990; hon. degree, U. Athens, 1993. Instr. U. Calif., 1940-41; instr., asst. prof. Cornell U., 1941-46; faculty U. Chgo., 1946-62, prof., 1952-62, chmn. dept. chemistry, 1955-59; prof. chemistry Stanford U., 1962-90; prof. emeritus chemistry Stanford U, 1990—; Marguerite Blake Wilbur prof. Stanford U., 1976, chmn. dept., 1971-74; Baker lectr. Cornell U., 1965. Hon. mem. Hungarian Acad., Scis., 1988. Guggenheim fellow, 1949, 55; recipient Harrison Howe award, 1961, Chandler medal Columbia U., 1964, F. P. Dwyer medal U. NSW, Australia, 1973, Nat. medal of Sci., 1976, 77, Allied Chem. award for Excellence in Grad. Tchg. and Innovative Sci., 1979, Nobel prize in Chemistry, 1983, Bailar medal U. Ill., 1983, Robert A. Welch Found. award in Chemistry, 1983, Disting. Achievement award Internat. Precious Metals Inst., 1986, Brazilian Order of Sci. Merit award, 1994. Fellow Royal Soc. Chemistry (hon.), Indian Chem. Soc. (hon.); mem. NAS (award in chem. scis. 1983), Am. Acad. Arts and Scis., Am. Chem. Soc. (Kirkwood award New Haven sect. 1965, award for nuclear applications in chemistry 1955, Nichols medal N.Y. sect. 1971, Willard Gibbs medal Chgo. sect. 1971, Disting. Svc. in Advancement Inorganic Chemistry award 1967, T.W. Richards medal NE sect. 1980, Monsanto Co. award in inorganic chemistry 1981, Linus Pauling award Puget Sound sect. 1981, Priestley medal 1985, Oesper award Cin. sect. 1986, G.M. Kosolapoff award Auburn sect. 1990), Royal Physiographical Soc. of Lund (fgn. mem.), Am. Philos. Soc., Finnish Acad. Sci. and Letters, Royal Danish Acad. Scis. and Letters, Coll. Chemists of Catalonia and Beleares (hon.), Can. Soc. Chemistry (hon.), Hungarian Acad. Scis. (hon. mem.), Royal Soc. (fgn. mem.), Brazilian Acad. Scis. (corr.), Engring. Acad. Japan (fgn. assoc.), Australian Acad. Scis. (corr.), Chem. Soc. Japan (hon. mem. 1993), Phi Beta Kappa, Sigma Xi, Phi Lambda Upsilon (hon.). Office: Stanford U Dept Chemistry Stanford CA 94305-5080

TAUBENFELD, HARRY SAMUEL, lawyer; b. Bklyn., June 27, 1929; s. Marcus Isaac and Anna (Engelhard) T.; m. Florence Spatz, June 17, 1956; children: Anne Gail Weisbrod, Stephen Marshall. BA, Bklyn. Coll., 1951; JD, Columbia U., 1954. Bar: N.Y. 1955, U.S. Supreme Ct. 1965, U.S. Dist. Ct. (so. and ea. dists.) N.Y. 1976. Assoc. Benjamin H. Schor, Bklyn., 1955-58; ptnr. Zuckerbrod & Taubenfeld, Cedarhurst (N.Y.), N.Y.C., 1958—; bd. dirs. Cornerstone Real Estate Income Trust, 1993—, Next Generation Mktg., Inc., 1996—; village atty. Village of Cedarhurst, 1977-88, trustee, 1989—; mem. bd. Downtown Cedarhurst Bus. Improvement Dist., 1993; legis. chmn., counsel Nassau County Village Ofcls., 1979-86, v.p., 1991-93, pres., 1993-94, mem. exec. com., 1989—, chmn. intergovtl. liaison com., 1991-93; mem. legis. com. N.Y. State Conf. Mayors, 1979-87, 92-93; mem. exec. bd. Tri-County Village Ofcls., 1991-95, pres., 1993-94; arbitrator Am. Arbitration Assn. Dist. Ct. Nassau County, 1980—, Assessment Rev. Panel, Supreme Ct., Nassau County, 1981—; mem. Constl. Bicentennial Com., 1987-89; bd. dirs. Am. Friend of Israel Cmty. Devel. Fund; bd. trustees Cong. Beth Shalom, Lawrence, N.Y.; nat. bd. dirs. Zionist Orgn. Am. Assoc. chmn. Am. Zionist Fedn., 1985-87; pres. Herut Zionists Am., 1977-79; v.p. Hartman YMHA, 1983-87; del. World Zionist Congress, 1977, 82, 87; mem. Zionist Gen. Coun., 1977-83; bd. govs. Jewish Agy., 1983-92; mem. exec. com. World Zionist Orgn., 1983-92; trustee United Jewish Appeal, 1986-91; bd. dirs. United Israel Appeal, 1986-91; hon. vice chmn., bd. dirs. Jewish Nat. Fund, 1987-89; nat. bd. dirs. Am. for a Safe Israel; hon. pres. World Coun. Herut Hatzoa, Jerusalem, Internat. Bd. Youthtown of Israel. Recipient Centenial award Jabotinsky Found. 1981, Betar Youth award World Betar 1982, award Internat. League for Repatriation of Russian Jews 1977, Youth Towns of Israel Leadership award 1973, Israel Bonds Leadership award 1976, Life Time Achievement award Israel Bonds 1991, Defender of Jerusalem award 1991. Mem. Internat. Assn. Jewish Lawyers and Jurists, Jewish War Vets., B'nai B'rith, Nordau Circle Club, Zionist Orgn. of Am., Cong. Beth. Shalom (Lawrence, N.Y.). Home: 288 Leroy Ave Cedarhurst NY 11516-1424 Office: PO Box 488 575 Chestnut St Cedarhurst NY 11516-2223

TAUBER, ALFRED IMRE, hematologist, immunologist, philosopher of science; b. Washington, June 24, 1947; s. Laszlo Nandor Tauber and Lilly Katherine (Manovill) Endrei; m. Susan Alice Swerdlow, Dec. 22, 1966; children: Joel, Dylan, Benjamin, Hannah. BS, Tufts U., 1969, MD, 1973. Intern, resident in internal medicine U. Wash., Seattle, 1973-75; clin. and research fellow in hematology Tufts-N.Eng. Med. Ctr., Boston, 1975-77; instr. in medicine Harvard Med. Sch., Boston, 1978-80; jr. assoc. in medicine Brigham and Women's Hosp., Boston, 1979-82; research assoc. Robert B. Brigham Hosp., Boston, 1979-82; asst. prof. medicine Harvard Med. Sch., Boston, 1980-82; assoc. prof. medicine, assoc. rsch. prof. biochemistry Boston U. Sch. Medicine, 1982-86, prof. medicine, 1986—, assoc. prof. pathology, 1985-87, prof. pathology, 1987—; prof. philosophy Boston U., 1992—, dir. Ctr. for Philosophy and History of Sci., 1993—; assoc. vis. physician Boston City Hosp., 1982-87, vis. physician, 1988—, chief hematology and oncology, 1982-91. Author: The Immune Self: Theory or Metaphor?, 1994; co-author: Metchnikoff and the Origins of Immunology, 1991; editor: Organism and the Origins of Self, 1991, The Elusive Synthesis: Aesthetics and Science, 1996, Science and the Quest for Reality, 1997; contbr. more than 150 articles on neutrophil biochemistry and history/philosophy of biology to profl. jours. Fellow Brandeis U. Waltham, Mass., 1978. Fellow ACP; mem. Am. Soc. Hematology, Reticuloendothelial Soc., Am. Assn. Immunology, Am. Soc. Cell Biology, Am. Assn. Biol. Chemistry and Molecular Biology, Am. Soc. Clin. Investigation, Assn. Am. Physicians, History of Sci. Soc., Am. Assn. History of Medicine, Am. Philos. Assn., Philosophy of Sci. Assn. Jewish. Office: Boston Univ 745 Commonwealth Ave Boston MA 02215-1401

TAUBER, JOEL DAVID, manufacturing company executive; b. Detroit, June 28, 1935; s. Benjamin and Anne (Merliss) T.; m. Shelley Tauber; children: Julie, Ellen, Benjamin Brian, Melissa, Juliana. B.B.A., U. Mich., 1956, J.D., 1959, M.B.A., 1963. Bar: Mich. 1959. Pres. Key Internat. Mfg. Inc., Southfield, Mich., 1969-86; pres. Tauber Enterprises, 1986—; trustee Nat. Indsl. Group Pension Plan, 1980; chmn. bd. dirs. Key Plastics, Inc., Keywell Corp.; established Tauber Mfg. Inst., U. Mich., 1995. Pres. Jewish Welfare Fedn., Detroit, 1983-86, Jewish Cmty. Ctr., 1978-80; nat. chmn. United Jewish Appeal, 1992-94, pres., 1994-96; treas. Coun. of Jewish Fedns., 1996—; bd. dirs. United Found., 1980—, v.p., 1986—; co-chmn. Detroit Round Table-Nat. Coun. Christians, Jews and Muslims, 1989-91; trustee, vice-chmn. Sinai Hosp., Detroit, 1980-91; mem. Fed. Judges Selection Panel Ea. Dist. Mich., 1978; mem. U. Mich. Devel. Adv. Bd., 1986-96, vis. com., 1996—; trustee Growth Fund, 1988—. Recipient Frank A. Wetsman Meml. Leadership award Jewish Welfare Fedn., 1970, Butzel award, 1990; named Entrepreneur of Yr., 1990, Socially Responsible Entrepreneur of Yr., 1993. Mem. Mich. Bar Assn., World Bus. Coun., Franklin Hills Country Club, Detroit Athletic Club, U. Mich. Alumni Club, U. Mich. Victors Club, Masons. Office: Tauber Enterprises 27777 Franklin Rd Ste 1850 Southfield MI 48034-8268 *To give life meaning and fulfillment one must live life to its fullest everyday and do one's best each of these days.*

TAUBER, MARK J., lawyer; b. Detroit, Mar. 25, 1949; s. Max M. and Beatrice R. (Roth) T.; m. Anita L. Tilben, June 23, 1970; children: Melissa A., Benjamin M., Allison B. BA, U. Mich., 1970; JD, George Washington U., 1973. Bar: D.C. 1973, Md. 1974, U.S. Supreme Ct. 1980. Assoc. Pierson, Ball & Dowd, Washington, 1973-79, ptnr., 1980-82; ptnr. Piper & Marbury, Washington, 1982—. Home: 11515 Big Piney Way Potomac MD 20854-1365 Office: Piper & Marbury 1200 19th St NW Washington DC 20036-2412

TAUBITZ, FREDRICKA, financial executive; b. Los Angeles, Feb. 25, 1944; d. Ferdinand C. and Marie L. (Stewart) T. AA, Pasadena City Coll., 1963; BSBA, U. Calif., Berkeley, 1965; MSBA, UCLA, 1967; grad. advanced mgmt. program, Harvard U., 1980-81. CPA, Calif. Acct. Coopers & Lybrand, Los Angeles, 1965-75, ptnr., 1976-85; exec. v.p., chief fin. officer Zenith Nat. Ins. Corp., Woodland Hills, Calif., 1985—; founding dir. First Women's Bank Calif., Los Angeles, 1974-76; mem. audit com. L.A. Unified Sch. Dist. Bd. dirs. Soroptimist Found. Los Angeles, 1978-79; bd. dirs. Girls' Club, Pasadena, Calif., 1973-84, pres., 1981-83; mem. Calif. Mus. Found. Adv. Bd., 1978-81. Recipient Outstanding Young Bus. Leader award Los Angeles Jr. C. of C., 1978, Internat. Achievement award Soroptimist Internat., 1977. Mem. AICPA (ins. coms. com. 1990-93), Calif. Soc. CPAs, L.A. C. of C. (bd. dirs. women's coun. 1978-81), Fin. Execs. Inst., Phi Beta Kappa. Office: Zenith Nat Ins Corp 21255 Califa St Woodland Hills CA 91367-5005

TAUBMAN, A. ALFRED, real estate developer; b. Pontiac, Mich., Jan. 31, 1925; s. Philip and Fannie Ester (Blustin) T.; m. Reva Kolodney, Dec. 1, 1949 (div. July 1977); children: Gayle Kalisman, Robert S., William S.; m. Judith Mazor, June 17, 1982. Student, U. Mich., 1945-48, LLD (hon.), 1991; student, Lawrence Inst. Tech., 1948-49, DArch (hon.), 1985; D in Bus. (hon.), Eastern Mich. U., 1984; D in Edn. (hon.), Mich. State U., 1993; HHD (hon.), No. Mich. U., 1995. Chmn. The Taubman Co., Bloomfield Hills, Mich., 1950—, Taubman Ctrs., Inc., Bloomfield Hills, Mich., 1992—; chmn. Sotheby's Holdings, Inc., N.Y.C., 1983—; bd. dirs. Live Entertainment of Can., Inc. Trustee Ctr. for Creative Studies, Detroit, Harper-Grace Hosps., Detroit; chmn. emeritus Archives Am. Art Smithsonian Inst., Washington, U. Pa. Wharton Real Estate Ctr., Phila.; pres. Arts Commn. of Detroit; mem. nat. bd. Smithsonian Assocs.; established Taubman Ctr. for State and Local Govt. Harvard U., Cambridge, Mass., chmn. Mich. Partnership for New Edn., Program in Am. Instns., U. Mich., Brown U.'s Pub. Policy and Am. Instns. Program; prin. benefactor A. Alfred Taubman Health Care Ctr. and A. Alfred Taubman Med. Libr., U. Mich.; bd. dirs. Detroit Renaissance, Inc., Friends of Art and Preservation in Embassies, Washington; active State of Mich. Gaming Commn. Recipient Bus. Statesman award Harvard Bus. Sch. Club of Detroit, 1983, Sportsman of Yr. award United Found. Detroit, SE Mich. Chpt. March of Dimes Birth Defects, 1983; named Michiganian of Yr. The Detroit News, 1983. Mem. Urban Land Inst. (trustee), Nat. Realty Com. (bd. dirs.).

TAUBMAN, JANE ANDELMAN, Russian literature educator; b. Boston, Oct. 23, 1942; d. Hyman M. and Esther (Rosenthal) Andelman; m. William Chase Taubman; children: Alexander, Phoebe. BA, Radcliffe Coll., 1964; MA, Yale U., 1968, PhD, 1972. Instr. Russian Smith Coll., Northampton,

Mass., 1968-72; asst. prof. Russian Amherst (Mass.) Coll., 1973-83, assoc. prof. Russian, 1983-89, prof. Russian, 1989—. Author: A Life Through Poetry: Marina Tsvetaeva's Lyric Diary, 1989; co-author: Moscow Spring, 1989; co-editor: Marina Tsvetaeva: One Hundred Years, 1994; contbr. articles to profl. jours. Woodrow Wilson Found. fellow, 1964—, Am. Coun. Learned Socs.-SSRC, 1974, trustee-faculty fellow Amherst Coll., 1978, fellow Nat. Def. Title VI, 1965-68; grantee Am. Philos. Soc., 1975, Amherst Coll., 1991, 94, IREX grantee USSR, 1988. Mem. AAUP, Modern Langs. Assn., Am. Assn. Tchrs. Slavic and East European Langs., Am. Assn. Slavic Studies, Am. Coun. Tchrs. of Russian, Am. Assn. Tchrs. of Slavic and East European Langs. Office: Amherst Coll Dept Russian Amherst MA 01002

TAUBMAN, MARTIN ARNOLD, immunologist; b. N.Y.C., July 10, 1940; s. Herman and Betty (Berger) T.; m. Joan Petra Mikelbank, May 30, 1965; children: Benjamin Abby, Joel David. B.S., Bklyn. Coll., 1961; D.D.S., Columbia U., 1965; Ph.D., SUNY, Buffalo, 1970. Asst. mem. staff Forsyth Dental Center, Boston, 1970—; head immunology dept. Forsyth Dental Center, 1972—, assoc. mem. staff, 1974-80, sr. staff mem., 1980—; asst. clin. prof. oral biology and pathophysiology Harvard U. Sch. Dental Medicine, 1976-79, assoc. clin. prof., 1979-97, prof. oral biology, 1997—; mem. oral biology and medicine study sect. NIH, 1980-84. Editor: (with J. Siots) Contemporary Microbiology and Immunology; contbr. articles to profl. jours, chpts. to books. Recipient Rsch. Career Devel. award, 1971-76, Fred Birnberg Alumni award for disting. dental rsch. Columbia U. Assn. Dental Alumni, Disting. Faculty award Harvard Sch. Dental Medicine, 1990, MERIT award NIH, 1991; USPHS fellow, 1962-63; postdoctoral fellow, 1966-70. Mem. Am. Soc. Microbiology, Soc. Mucosal Immunology, Internat. Assn. Dental Research (Oral Biology award 1991), Am. Assn. Immunologists, Am. Assn. Dental Research (v.p. 1987—, pres. elect 1988, pres. 1989). Office: Forsyth Dental Ctr 140 Fenway Boston MA 02115-3782

TAUBMAN, WILLIAM CHASE, political science educator; b. N.Y.C., Nov. 13, 1941; s. Howard and Nora (Stern) T.; m. Jane Dea Andelman, May 18, 1969; children—Alexander, Phoebe. A.B., Harvard U., 1962; M.A., Columbia U., 1965, cert. of Russian Inst., 1965, Ph.D., 1969; M.A. (hon.), Amherst Coll., 1978. Instr. Amherst Coll., Mass., 1967-69; asst. prof. Amherst Coll., 1969-73, assoc. prof., 1973-78, prof. dept. polit. sci., 1978-83, Bertrand Snell prof., 1983—; mem. planning staff U.S. Dept. State, Washington, 1970-71; mem. bd. Internat. Rsch. and Exch. Bd., N.Y.C., 1971-74, mem. selection com., 1984-85; vis. assoc. prof. Yale U., New Haven, spring 1975; chmn. adv. com. Cold War Internat. History Project, Woodrow Wilson Ctr., Washington, 1993—; mem. Internat. Acad. Adv. Group, Russian Fgn. Ministry Archives, 1992—. Author: The View from Lenin Hills, 1967; Governing Soviet Cities, 1973; Stalin's American Policy, 1982; co-author: (with Jane Taubman) Moscow Spring, 1989; editor, translator: Khrushchev on Khrushchev (Sergei N. Khrushchev), 1990; editor: Globalism and Its Critics, 1973. Woodrow Wilson Nat. Found. fellow, 1962; Ford Found. fellow, 1963-67; Council Fgn. Relations fellow, 1970-71; Rockefeller Found. fellow, 1983; Columbia U. Harriman Inst. sr. fellow, 1987; grantee Nat. Council Soviet and East European Research, 1984; Fulbright-Hays Faculty Rsch. fellow, 1988, NEH fellow, 1992. Fellow Russian Research Ctr. Harvard U.; mem. Council Fgn. Relations, Authors Guild. Home: 43 Hitchcock Rd Amherst MA 01002-2500 Office: Amherst Coll Dept Polit Sci Box 2259 Amherst MA 01002-5000

TAUC, JAN, physics educator; b. Pardubice, Czechoslovakia, Apr. 15, 1922; came to U.S., 1969, naturalized, 1978; s. Jan and Josefa (Semonska) T.; m. Vera Koubelova, Oct. 18, 1947; children: Elena (Mrs. Milan Kokta), Jan. Ing.Dr. in Elec. Engring., Tech. U. Prague, 1949; RNDr., Charles U., 1956; Dr.Sc. in Physics, Czechoslovak Acad. Scis., 1956. Scientist microwave research Sci. and Tech. Research Inst., Tanvald and Prague, 1949-52; head semiconductor dept. Inst. Solid State Physics, Czechoslovak Acad. Scis., 1953-69; prof. exptl. physics Charles U., 1964-69, dir. Inst. Physics,, 1968-69; mem. tech. staff Bell Telephone Labs., Murray Hill, N.J., 1969-70; prof. engring. and physics Brown U., 1970-83, L. Herbert Ballou prof. engring. and physics, 1983-92, L. Herbert Ballou prof. emeritus, 1992—, dir. material research lab., 1983-88; dir. E. Fermi Summer Sch., Varenna, Italy, 1965; vis. prof. U. Paris, 1969, Stanford U., 1977, Max Planck Inst. Solid State Research, Stuttgart, Germany, 1982; UNESCO fellow, Harvard, 1961-62. Author: Photo and Thermoelectric Effects in Semiconductors, 1962, also numerous articles; editor: The Optical Properties of Solids, 1966, Amorphous and Liquid Semiconductors, 1974; co-editor: Solid State Communications, 1963-92. Recipient Nat. prize Czechoslovak Govt., 1955, 69; Sr. U.S. Scientist award Humboldt Found., 1981, Silver medal Union of Czechoslovak Mathematicians and Physicists, 1992. Fellow AAAS, Am. Phys. Soc. (Frank Isakson prize 1982, David Adler award 1988); mem. NAS, European Phys. Soc. (founding), Czechoslovak Acad. Scis. (corr. 1963-71, 90-91, fgn. 1991-92, Hlavka medal 1992). Office: Brown U Divsn Engring Providence RI 02912

TAUCHERT, THEODORE RICHMOND, mechanical engineer, educator; s. Elwyn Harding and Eleanor (Richmond) T.; m. Ann Dudley Bradlee, May 10, 1958; children: Amy T. Teicher, Sarah T. Rushing, Rebecca T. McGowan, Charles W., Macy G. Casperson. B.S.E., Princeton U., 1957; M.Eng., Yale U., 1960, D.Eng., 1964. Structural engr. Sikorsky Aircraft, Stratford, Conn., 1957-61; research assoc., lectr. Princeton U., N.J., 1964-65, asst. prof., 1965-70; assoc. prof. U. Ky., Lexington, 1970-76, prof. engring. mechanics, 1976—, chmn. dept., 1980-84, 88-94. Editorial bd.: Acta Mechanica, 1976—, Jour. Thermal Stresses, 1981—; author: Energy Principles in Structural Mechanics, 1974; contbr. articles to profl. jours. Served to 2d lt. U.S. Army, 1957-58. Mem. ASCE, ASME, Am. Soc. Engring. Edn., Soc. Engring. Sci., Sigma Xi. Home: 1620 Richmond Rd Lexington KY 40502-1620 Office: U Ky Dept Mech Engring Lexington KY 40506

TAURO, JOSEPH LOUIS, federal judge; b. Winchester, Mass., Sept. 26, 1931; s. G. Joseph and Helen Maria (Petrossi) T.; m. Elizabeth Mary Quinlan, Feb. 7, 1959 (dec. 1978); children—Joseph L., Elizabeth H., Christopher M.; m. Ann Lefavour Jones, July 12, 1980. AB, Brown U., 1953; LLB, Cornell U., 1956; JD (hon.), U. Mass., 1985, Suffolk U., 1986, Northeastern U., 1990, New Eng. Sch. Law, 1992, Boston U., 1997. Bar: Mass. 1956, D.C. 1960. Assoc. Tauro & Tauro, Lynn, Mass., 1958-59; asst. U.S. atty. Dept. Justice, Boston, 1959-60; ptnr. Jaffee & Tauro, Boston and Lynn, Mass., 1960-71; chief legal counsel Gov. of Mass., Boston, 1965-68; U.S. atty. Dept. Justice, Boston, 1972; judge U.S. Dist. Ct., Boston, 1972—; chief judge U.S. Dist. Ct., Mass., 1992—; mem. exec. com. Cornell Law Assn., Ithaca, N.Y., 1968-71; mem. adv. coun. Cornell Law Sch., Ithaca, 1975-80; adj. prof. law Boston U. Law Sch., 1977—; mem. Jud. Conf. U.S., 1994—, mem. com. on operation of jury sys., 1979-86, mem. adv. com. on codes of conduct, 1988-94. Trustee Brown U., 1978—, Mass. Gen. Hosp., Boston, 1968-72, Children's Hosp. Med. Ctr., Boston, 1979-94. 1st lt. U.S. Army, 1956-58. Recipient Disting. Alumnus award Cornell U. Law Sch., 1992, Brown Bear award Brown U., 1993; named one of 10 Outstanding Young Men, Greater Boston Jaycees, 1966. Fellow Am. Bar Found.; mem. Mass. Bar Assn., Boston Bar Assn. (coun. 1968-71), D.C. Bar Assn., Boston Yacht Club (Marblehead, Mass.). Republican. Roman Catholic. Avocations: sports; reading; music; films; theater. Office: US Dist Ct Ste 1615 Boston MA 02109

TAUSCHER, ELLEN O., congresswoman; b. Newark, N.J., 1951; m. William Y. Tauscher; 1 child, Katherine. BS in early Childhood Edn., Seton Hall U., 1974. With Bache Securities, N.Y.C., N.Y. Stock Exchange; dir. Tauscher Found.; mem. 105th Congress from 10th Calif. dist., 1997—; founder The ChildCare Registry; bd. regents Seton Hall U.; co-chair Delaine Eastin's State Supt. Pub. Instrn. Campaign, 1994; transp. and infrastructure com., surface transp. and water resources and environ. Author: The Child-Care Sourcebook, 1996. Active The Coalition, New Dem. Coalition, Bipartisan Freshman Campaign Fin. Reform Task Force, House Cancer Awareness Working Group, Congl. Caucus on the Arts; vice-chair Calif. Dem. Del.

TAUSCHER, JOHN WALTER, retired pediatrician, emeritus educator; b. LaSalle, Ill., Feb. 3, 1929; s. John Robert and Ella (Danz) T.; m. Mary Claire Cline, June 19, 1954 (dec. 1989); children—Michael, John, Claire, Mark, Matthew. B.S., U. Ill., 1952, M.D., 1954. Diplomate Am. Bd. Pediatrics. Intern Cook County Hosp., Chgo., 1954-55; resident in pediatrics Hurley Hosp., Flint, Mich., 1958-60; practice medicine specializing in pediatrics Flint, 1960-75; assoc. prof. human devel. Coll. Human Medicine, Mich. State U., East Lansing, 1975-80, prof. pediatrics and human devel., 1980-94, prof. emeritus, 1994; ret., 1994; v.p. After Hours Pediatric Care, P.C., Flint, 1972-87; chmn. pediatrics Hurley Med. Ctr., 1980-90, dir. pediatric edn., dir. primary care pediatrics, 1991-94; dir. clin. svcs. Mott Children's Health Ctr., 1981-85, v.p. health affairs, 1985-91. Served with USAF, 1955-58. Recipient Outstanding Teaching award Coll. Human Medicine, Mich. State U., 1977, 84, 85, Clin. Instr. of Yr. award St. Joseph Hosp., 1977, Disting. Community Faculty award Mich. State U., 1989. Mem. AMA, Genesee County Med. Soc. (pres. 1990), Mich. State Med. Soc., Northeastern Mich. Pediatric Soc., Am. Acad. Pediatrics. Roman Catholic. Home: 1069 Rayna Dr Davison MI 48423-2845 Office: Dept Pediatric Edn One Hurley Plaza Flint MI 48503-5905

TAUSSIG, JOSEPH KNEFLER, JR., retired government official, lawyer; b. Newport, R.I., May 28, 1920; s. Joseph Knefler and Lulie Augusta (Johnston) T.; m. Betty Carney, Dec. 2, 1943; children: Joseph Knefler III, Susan Taussig Graves (dec.). B.S., U.S. Naval Acad., 1941; J.D. with honors, George Washington U., 1949. Bar: U.S. Supreme Ct., 1975. Commd. U.S. Navy, 1937, advanced through grades to capt., 1954, ret., 1954; exec. sec. U.S. Naval Inst., Annapolis, Md., 1954-56; also pub. books, mags. U.S. Naval Inst., 1952-56; in various positions Westinghouse, Joy Mfg., Raytheon, Washington, 1956-62; pres. Taussig-Tomb & Assocs., Washington, 1962-81, 93—; dep. asst. sec. Dept. Navy, Washington, 1981-85; asst. dep. undersec. for safety and survivability Dept. Navy, Arlington, Va., 1985-93. Contbr. numerous articles to various publs., 1942—. Candidate for U.S. Congress from Md., 1956; pres. Md. Easter Seal Soc., 1968-74; pres. Internat. Assn. Pollution Control, Washington, 1970-74; active Nat. Amputation Found. Decorated Navy Cross, 2 Navy Disting. Pub. Svc. medals; recipient commendation U.s. Atty. Gen., 1994, Pres.'s award Ret. Officers Assn., 1966, 68. Mem. Naval Hist. Found. (trustee 1980—), U.S. Naval Inst. (sec.-treas. 1952-56), U.S. Naval Acad. Alumni Assn. (trustee 1956-60), Navy League (local bd. dirs. 1962-64). Republican. Episcopalian. Club: Army-Navy (treas. 1974-80) (Washington). Lodge: Rotary (bd. dirs. local club 1954-58). Avocations: philately; boating; piano playing. Home: 400 Ridgely Ave Annapolis MD 21401-1306

TAUSSIG, LYNN MAX, healthcare administrator, pulmonologist, pediatrician, educator; b. Milw., July 19, 1942; m. Lisa Peter; children: Heather, Jennifer. AB cum laude, Harvard U., 1964; MD, Washington U., St. Louis, 1968. Diplomate Am. Bd. Pediat., Nat. Bd. Med. Examiners, Am. Bd. Pediat. Pulmonary. Rsch. asst. dept. neuroanatomy Marquette U., Milw., 1965; intern in pediat. St. Louis Children's Hosp., 1968-69; resident in pediat. U. Colo. Med. Ctr., Denver, 1969-70; clin. assoc. pediat. metabolism br. Nat. Inst. Arthritis, Metabolism, and Digestive Diseases, NIH, Bethesda, Md., 1970-72; pulmonary fellow Montreal (Que., Can.) Children's Hosp., 1972-74; asst. prof. pediat. Ariz. Health Scis. Ctr., Tucson, 1974-77, cystic fibrosis ctr. dir., 1974-85, assoc. chief pulmonary function labs., 1974-85, dir. pulmonary sect., 1974-85, asst. dir. divsn. respiratory scis., 1976-92, assoc. prof. pediat., 1977-81, assoc. head dept. pediat., 1979-84, prof., 1981-93, head dept. pediat., 1985-93, dir. Steele Meml. Children's Rsch. Ctr., 1986-93; prof. pediats. U. Colo. Health Scis. Ctr., Denver, 1993—; pres., CEO Nat. Jewish Ctr. for Immunology and Respiratory Medicine, Denver, 1993—; Frank Stevenson vis. prof. U. Con., 1977, 82; Robert Chinnock Meml. lectr. Loma Linda U., Calif., 1983; Jour. Pediats. vis. prof. U. Chgo., 1984; Brennenman lectr. L.A. Pediat. Soc., 1988, 94; Danis Meml. lectr. St. Louis U., 1989; Talamo Meml. lectr. Johns Hopkins U., Balt., 1989; Anna Zager vis. lectr. in pediats. Technion U., Haifa, Israel, 1990; Sir Clavering Fison vis. prof. Inst. Child Health, U. London, 1992; Benjamin Meaker vis. prof. U. Bristol, Eng., 1992; Ben Kagan vis. lectr. Cedars-Sinai Hosp., L.A., 1993. Mem. editl. bd. Chest, 1983-88, Am. Rev. Respiratory Diseases, 1983-89; contbr. articles to profl. jours. Trustee Congregation Anshei Israel, 1978-80; bd. dirs. Jerwish Cmty. Ctr., 1982-90, sec., 1984-86, v.p., 1987-89; mem. allocations com. Jewish Fedn. So. Ariz., 1985, 88, Allied Jewish Fedn. Denver, 1996—; bd. dirs. Colo. Biomed. Venture Ctr., 1994—, Congregation Rodef Shalom, 1996—; active Martin Luther King Jr. Minority Scholarship Program, 1994—, Colo. Concern, 1995—. Cystic Fibrosis Found. Clin. fellow, 1972-74, Sr. Internat. fellow Fogarty Internat. Ctr., 1980-81; Young Investigator Pulmonary Rsch. grantee Nat. Heart and Lung Inst., 1974-76, and numerous other med. grants; Pfizer Labs. Med. scholar, 1966; recipient Lang Med. Book award, 1966. Mem. Am. Acad. Pediat. (mem. exec. com. sect. on diseases of chest 1978-80, mem. ad hoc com. for pediat. pulmonary bds., sect. on diseases of chest 1978-85), Am. Pediat. Soc., Am. Thoracic Soc. (mem. com. to advise pres. 1975-76, sec. sci. assembly for pediats. 1975-77, mem. respiratory care com. 1976-78, mem. nominating com. 1977, 84-85, chmn. prograom com. 1979-81, mem. ann. meeting com. 1979-81, mem. rsch. rev. com. 1981-82, chmn. publs. policy com. 1988-89, 90-92, mem. exec. com. 1989-90, sec.-treas. 1989-90, active many other coms.), Am. Coll. Chest Physicians (mem. steering group for com. on cardiopulmonary diseases in children 1977-79), Ariz. Pediat. Soc., Ariz. Lung Assn., Pima County Pediat. Soc., Soc. Pediat. Rsch. (founder Lung Club 1985), Western Soc. Pediat. Rsch. (mem. nominating com. 1979-80, elected to coun. 1994—), Rotary, Harvard Club of So. Ariz. (schs. com. 1982-93, sec.-treas. 1989-93), Alpha Omega Alpha. Office: Nat Jewish Ctr for Immunology and Respiratory Medicine 1400 Jackson St Denver CO 80206-2761

TAUZIN, W. J. BILLY, II (WILBERT J. TAUZIN), congressman; b. Chackbay, LA, June 14, 1943; s. Wilbert Joseph and Enola (Martinez) T.; m. Cecile Bergeron, May 29, 1993; children: Kristie René, Wilbert J. III, John Ashton, Thomas Nicholas, Michael James. BA, Nicholls State U., 1964; JD, La. State U., 1967. Bar: La. 1967. Practice Houma and Thibodaux, La., 1967-80; mem. firm Marcel Fanguy & Tauzin, 1967-72, Tauzin-Sonnier, 1972-80; mem. La. Ho. of Reps., 1971-80, house floor leader, 1974-79, chmn. Teche Clearinghouse Rev. Bd., 1975-78, chmn. house natural resources com., 1975-80; mem. 96th-105th Congresses from 3d La. Dist., 1980—; mem. energy, commerce, merchant marine, fisheries coms., subcoms. energy, power, telecom., coast guard, navigation, wildlife conservation, environment. Mem. Thibodaux Playhouse, 1967-75; mem. Criminal Justice Inst. Recipient Thibodaux Outstanding Young Man award, 1971. Mem. ABA, La. State Bar Assn., Lafourche Parish Bar Assn. (past pres.), Chackbay-Choupic Jr. C. of C. (past pres.), Nicholls Alumni Council (v.p.). Lodges: Kiwanis; K.C. Home: Rienzi B-5 PO Box 1407 Thibodaux LA 70302-1407 Office: 2183 Rayburn US Ho Reps Washington DC 20515-1803*

TAVARES, TONY, professional hockey team executive; b. Fall River, Mass., Oct. 17, 1949; m. Elizabeth Tavares; children: Sheila, Kristen, Mark. BS in Acctg., Roger Williams Coll. Comptroller, acting dir. Providence Civic Ctr.; with Centrum, Worcester, Mass., New Haven Vets. Meml. Coliseum, Nassau Vets. Meml. Coliseum, Uniondale, N.Y.; with Spectacor Mgmt. Group, pres., CEO; cons. Walt Disney Co.; pres. Disney Sports Enterprises, Inc., Anaheim, Calif., 1993—; pres., alt. gov. Mighty ducks of Anaheim, 1993—. Mem. Internat. Assn. Auditorium Mgrs. Office: Mighty Ducks of Anaheim PO Box 61077 2695 E Katella Ave Anaheim CA 92803-6177*

TAVEGGIA, THOMAS CHARLES, management educator, management consultant; b. Oak Lawn, Ill., June 15, 1943; s. Thomas Angelo and Eunice Louise (Harriss) T.; m. Brigitte I. Adams, Jan. 23, 1965; children: Michaela, Francesca. BS, Ill. Inst. Tech., 1965; MA, U. Oreg., 1968, PhD, 1971. Prof., U. Oreg., Eugene, 1970, U. B.C. (Can.), Vancouver, 1970-73, U. Calif.-Irvine, 1973-74, Ill. Inst. Tech., Chgo., 1974-77; mgmt. cons. Towers, Perrin, Forster & Crosby, Chgo., 1977-80; ptnr. Manplan Cons., Chgo., 1980-81; ptnr. Coopers & Lybrand, San Francisco, 1981-86; ptnr. Touche Ross, San Francisco, 1986-88; prof. Calif. Sch. Profl. Psychology, Berkeley, 1988—. NDEA Title IV fellow, 1967-71; U. B.C. faculty rsch. grantee, 1970, 71, 73. Faculty Rsch. grantee Calif. Sch. Profl. Psychology, 1993—ss. Mem. Acad. Mgmt. Soc., Am. Sociol. Assn., Nat. Bur. Profl. Mgmt. Cons., Human Resource Mgmt. Soc., Inst. Mgmt. Cons. Presbyterian. Author: (with R. Dubin and R. Arends) From Family and School To Work, 1967; (with Dubin) The Teaching-Learning Paradox: A Comparative Analysis of College Teaching Methods, 1968; (with Dubin and R.A. Hedley) The Medium May Be Related to the Message: College Instruction by TV, 1969; contbr. numerous articles to books and profl. jours. Home: 2188 Lariat Ln Walnut Creek CA 94596-6515 Office: Calif Sch Profl Psychology 1005 Atlantic Ave Alameda CA 94501-1148

TAVEL, MARK KIVEY, money management company executive, economist; b. Cambridge, Mass., May 9, 1945; s. Bernard Benjamin and Elizabeth (Rogers) T.; m. Susana Sara Doño, Dec. 14, 1980; children: Sarah Emily, Rachel Florence, Amanda Victoria, Nathaniel Benjamin, Roberto Aaron Doño. BA cum laude, Harvard U., 1967; MBA, Columbia U., 1968. Sr. mngh. dir. Rothschild Asset Mgmt., Inc., N.Y.C.; bd. dirs. N. M. Rothschild Internat. Asset Mgmt., London; bd. dirs. Rothschild Asset Mgmt., Inc. Trustee The Day Sch. of the Ch. of the Heavenly Rest, N.Y.C. Mem. Harvard Club (N.Y.C.). Home: 110 Riverside Dr New York NY 10024-3715 Office: Rothschild Inc 1251 Avenue Of The Americas New York NY 10020-1104

TAVEL, MORTON ALLEN, physics educator, researcher; b. Bklyn., June 14, 1939; s. Irving and Sylvia (Cutler) T.; m. Judith Carol Fibkins, June 29, 1969; 1 child, Phillip Alden. B.S., CCNY, 1960; M.S., Stevens Inst., 1962; Ph.D., Yeshiva U., 1964. Asst. scientist Brookhaven Nat. Lab., Upton, N.Y., 1964-67; asst. prof. Vassar Coll., Poughkeepsie, N.Y., 1967-69, assoc. prof., 1970-75, prof. physics, 1975—; vis. prof. Va. Poly., Blacksburg, Va., 1971-72, SUNY-Stony Brook, 1976-77; mem. summer faculty IBM, Poughkeepsie, N.Y., 1978-80, engring. cons., 1980—. Author: Introduction to Electricity and Magnetism I and II, 1971, Information Theory, 1989. NSF fellow, 1962-64. Mem. IEEE (sr.), Am. Phys. Soc., Soc. Wine Educators, Sigma Xi. Avocation: oenology. Home: Vassar Coll 437 Hillside Lake Rd Wappingers Falls NY 12590 Office: Vassar Coll PO Box 471 Poughkeepsie NY 12604-0471

TAVENAS, FRANÇOIS, civil engineer, educator; b. Bourg de Péage, Drôme, France, Sept. 12, 1942; arrived in Can., 1966; s. Adrien and Marie Thérèse (Bazin) T.; m. Gundula Schlichting, Apr. 27, 1963; children: Anne Catherine, Philippe, Sophie. BCE, Inst. Nat. des Scis. Appliquées, Lyon, France, 1963; PhD, U. Grenoble, France, 1965. Registered profl. engr., Que. Engr. Piette & Assocs., Que., Can., 1966-70; asst. prof. civil engring. Laval U., Que., 1970-73, assoc. prof., 1973-79, prof., 1979-85, dean, 1985-89; vice prin. planning and resources McGill U., Montreal, Que., 1988-97; rector Laval U., Que., Can., 1997—; cons. Golder & Assocs., Toronto, Ont. Can., 1973-75, Terratech, Montreal, 1975-85, Soc. d'Energie de la Baie James, Montreal, 1980-84; mem. coun. Natural Scis. and Engring. Rsch. Coun. Can., 1989-95. Author: (with others) Embankments On Soft Soils, 1985; contbr. articles to profl. jours. Mem. Can. Geotech. Soc. (v.p. 1982-85, pres.-elect 1990, pres. 1991-92), Internat. Soc. Soil Mechanics and Found. Engring., Assn. Can. Francaise pour L'Avancement de la Sci. (pres. 1997—). Avocations: tennis, travel, sailing. Office: McGill U, 845 Sherbrooke St W # 536, Montreal, PQ Canada H3A 2T5

TAVERAS, JUAN MANUEL, physician, educator; b. Dominican Republic, Sept. 27, 1919; came to U.S., 1944, naturalized, 1950; s. Marcos M. and Ana L. (Rodriguez) T.; m. Bernice Helen McGonigle, June 12, 1947 (dec. 1990); children: Angela Forbes Summers, Louisa Helen Taveras Koranda, Jeffrey Lawrence; m. Mariana Margarita Bucher, Mar. 18, 1991. BS, Normal Sch. Santiago, Dominican Republic, 1937; MD, U. Santo Domingo, Dominican Republic, 1943, U. Pa., 1949; MS honoris causa, Harvard Med. Sch., 1971; Dr. honoris causa, Univ. Nacional Pedro Henriquez Ureña, Dominican Republic, 1987; Doctor Honoris Causa, U. Catolica Madre Y Maestra, Santiago, Dominican Republic, 1992. Diplomate: Am. Bd. Radiology. Instr. anatomy U. Santo Domingo, 1943-44; fellow radiology Grad. Hosp. U. Pa., 1945-48; rotating intern Misericordia Hosp., Phila., 1949-50; asst. radiologist Presbyn. Hosp., N.Y.C., 1950-52; asst. attending radiologist Presbyn. Hosp., 1953-56, assoc. attending radiologist, 1956-60, attending radiologist, 1960-65; dir. radiology Neurol. Inst., N.Y.C., 1952-65; cons. USPHS Hosp., S.I., N.Y., 1952-65, Morristown (N.J.) Meml. Hosp., 1957-65, St. Barnabas Hosp., N.Y.C., 1959-65, VA Hosp., Bronx, N.Y., 1960-65; asst. instr. radiology U. Pa. Sch. Medicine, 1947-48; faculty Columbia Coll. Phys. and Surg., 1950-65, prof. radiology, 1959-65; prof. radiology, chmn. dept., dir. Mallinckrodt Inst. Radiology, Washington U. Sch. Medicine, St. Louis, 1965-71; radiologist-in-chief Barnes and Allied Hosps., St. Louis, 1965-71; cons. neuroradiology service Unit 1 St. Louis City Hosp., 1966-71; cons. radiology Jewish Hosp., St. Louis, 1966-71; prof. radiology Harvard Med. Sch., 1971-89, prof. radiology emeritus, 1989—; radiologist-in-chief Mass. Gen. Hosp., Boston, 1971-88; pres. VII Symposium Neuroradiologieum, 1964. Author: Neuroradiology, 1996; (with Ross Golden) Roentgenology of the Abdomen, 1961, (with Ernest H. Wood) Diagnostic Neuroradiology, 1964, 2d edit., 1976, (with Norman Leeds) Dynamic Factors in Diagnosis of Supratentorial Brain Tumors by Cerebral Angiography, 1969, (with F. Morello) Normal Neuroradiology, 1979, (with James Provenzale) Clinical Cases in Neuroradiology, 1994, (with Laszlo Szlavy) Noncoronary Angioplasty, 1994; editor: (with others) Recent Advances in the Study of Cerebral Circulation, 1970, Cysticercosis of the Central Nervous System, 1983, Radiology: Diagnosis, Imaging, Intervention, 1986; chief editor: Am. Jour. Neuroradiology, 1980-89; contbr. numerous articles to profl. jours. Bd. dirs. Edward Mallinckrodt, Jr. Found., 1980—. Decorated knight Order of Duarte Sanchez y Mella (Dominican Republic) 1972; Juan M. Taveras professorship established in his honor Harvard Med. Sch., 1988. Fellow Am. Coll. Radiology (gold medal 1985); mem. AMA, Am. Neurol. Assn., Am. Roentgen Ray Soc. (gold medal 1988), Radiol. Soc. N.Am. (gold medal 1981), Mass. Med. Soc., Inter-Am. Coll. Radiology, World Fedn. Neurology, Am. Soc. Neuroradiology (pres. 1962-64, gold medal, 1995), N.Y. Acad. Scis., Am. Assn. Neurol. Surgeons (assoc.), Assn. U. Radiologists (gold medal 1985), Mass. Radiol. Soc., New Eng. Roentgen Ray Soc.; pres. Iberian Latin Am. Soc. of Neuroradiology 1988-91, pres. IV Congress of Iberian Latin Am. Soc. of Neuroradiology 1992, hon. mem. Phila. Roentgen Ray Soc., Radiol. Soc. Venezuela, Rocky Mountain Radiol. Soc., Tex. Radiol. Soc., Radiol. Assn. Ctrl. Am. and Panama, Hungarian Radiologic Soc., European Soc. Neuroradiology (hon.), Alpha Omega Alpha. Republican. Home: 122 Glen Rd Wellesley MA 02181-1551 Office: Mass Gen Hosp Boston MA 02114

TAVLIN, MICHAEL JOHN, telecommunications company executive; b. Lincoln, Nebr., Dec. 16, 1946. BEd, Oklahoma City U., 1970; JD, U. Nebr., 1973; LLM in Taxation, Washington U., St. Louis, 1977. Bar: Nebr. 1973, Mo. 1974. Ptnr. Nelson & Harding, Lincoln, 1973-77; sr. tax. mgr. Touche Ross & Co., Lincoln and Tulsa, 1979-84, Coopers & Lybrand, Tulsa, 1984-86; v.p., treas., sec. Aliant Comm. Inc. and subs., 1986—. Named Disting. Alumnus Oklahoma City U., 1995. Office: Aliant Comm Inc 1440 M St Lincoln NE 68508-2513

TAVON, MARY E., public relations, marketing and communications executive; b. Montreal, Apr. 4, 1958. Student, Marianopolis Coll. Lit. and Langs., 1977; BA in English, Theatre and Film, McGill U., 1980. Mktg. analyst Korea Trade Promotion Assn., 1980-82; advt., pub. rels. asst. Ann Taylor, 1983-84; acct. exec. Michael Klepper Assocs., N.Y.C., 1984-86, acct. supr., 1986-88, v.p., 1988-89, pres., exec. prodr., 1989. Recipient cert. merit Chgo. Internat. Film Festival, 1990. Office: Michael Klepper Assoc Inc 805 3rd Ave New York NY 10022-7513

TAVROW, RICHARD LAWRENCE, lawyer, corporate executive; b. Syracuse, N.Y., Feb. 3, 1935; s. Harry and Ida Mary (Hodess) T.; m. Barbara J. Silver, Mar. 22, 1972; children—Joshua Michael, Sara Hallie. A.B. magna cum laude, Harvard U., 1957, LL.B., 1960, LL.M., 1961; postgrad., U. Copenhagen, 1961-62, U. Luxembourg, 1962. Bar: N.Y. bar 1961, U.S. Supreme Ct. bar 1969, Calif. bar 1978. Atty. W.R. Grace & Co., N.Y.C., 1962-66; asst. chief counsel Gen. Dynamics Corp., N.Y.C., 1966-68; chief counsel office of fgn. direct investments U.S. Dept. Commerce, Washington, 1969-71; ptnr. Schaeffer, Dale, Vogel & Tavrow, N.Y.C., 1971-75; v.p., sec., gen. counsel Prudential Lines, Inc., N.Y.C., 1975-78, also bd. dirs.; v.p., sec., gen. counsel Am. Pres. Lines, Ltd., Oakland, Calif., 1978-80, sr. v.p., sec., gen. counsel, 1980-91, also bd. dirs.; sr. v.p., sec., gen. counsel Am. Pres. Cos., Ltd., Oakland, 1983-91; also bd. dirs. Am. Pres. Cos., Ltd., Oakland, Calif.; sr. ptnr. Law Offices of R.L. Tavrow, 1991—; chmn., pres., CEO Diabetes Healthcare & Life Enhancement Ltd., 1996—; instr. Harvard Coll., 1959-61; lectr. Am. Mgmt. Assn., Practising Law Inst., other assns. Recipient Silver Medal award Dept. Commerce, 1970; Fulbright scholar, 1961-62. Mem. ABA, State Bar Calif., Internat. Bar Assn., Am. Soc. Internat. Law, Am. Corp. Counsel Assn., Am. Soc. Corp. Secs. Inc., Harvard Law Sch. Assn., Navy League, Harvard Club (N.Y.C.). Democrat. Jewish.

TAW, DUDLEY JOSEPH, sales executive; b. Cleve., Mar. 11, 1916; s. William C. and Ella (Gedeon) T.; m. Louise E. Forshey, Sept. 10, 1938; children: Judith (Mrs. William W. Beck, Jr.), Dudley Joseph. Student, Hiram Coll., 1938. With McKesson & Robbins, Inc. (pharm. co.), after 1937; sales mgr. McKesson & Robbins, Inc. (pharm. co.), Boston, 1947; v.p. sales McKesson & Robbins, Inc. (pharm. co.), N.Y.C., 1953-60; v.p. Revlon, Inc., N.Y.C., 1960-64; v.p. mktg. East Ohio Gas Co., Cleve., 1964-74, pres., 1975-81, chmn., 1981-82; chmn. Middtaw, Ltd., Inc., 1982; bd. dirs. No. New England Gas Corp., First Union Mgmt. Co., Biskind Devel. Co., Vt. Gas Systems Inc. Mem. Better Bus. Bur., Cleve., chmn., 1973; trustee Lakewood Hosp.; treas. Salvation Army, Cleve. With USNR, 1946-47. Named Sales Exec. of Year Sales and Mktg. Execs. Cleve., 1966, Man of Year, 1977. Mem. Sales and Mktg. Execs. Cleve. (pres. 1969-70), Westwood Country Club, Union Club, Pepper Pike Club, Rotary (pres. Cleve. 1972-73). Methodist. Home (summer): 20975 Avalon Dr Cleveland OH 44116-1303 Home (winter): 6050 Bahia Del Mar Cir Bldg 3 Saint Petersburg FL 33715-3304 Office: 806 Statler Office Tower Cleveland OH 44115

TAWAKA, PATRICE, public relations executive. CEO, creative dir. Patrice Tawaka & Co., N.Y.C. Office: Patrice Tawaka & Co Inc 320 W 13th St Fl 7 New York NY 10014-1200

TAWG, MANYIN, editor, periodical. Editor Western Real Estate News, South San Francisco, Calif. Office: Western Real Estate News 500 S Airport Blvd South San Francisco CA 94080-6912

TAYAR, MEMDUH ALI, architect; b. Istanbul, Turkey, Nov. 16, 1959; came to U.S., 1983; s. Omer Tayyar and Ilhan (Cekmegil) T. Diploma in engring., U. Stuttgart, Germany, 1983; MS in Architecture Studies, MIT, 1986. Registered architect, N.Y. Mem. project team Lev Zetlin Assocs., N.Y.C., 1986-88; project architect FTL Assocs., N.Y.C., 1988-91; prin. Parallel Design Partnership Ltd., N.Y.C., 1991—; lectr. MIT, Cambridge, 1985, Ill. Inst. Tech., Chgo., 1992, CUNY, 1993; guest critic Columbia U., N.Y.C., N.J. Inst. Tech., Newark, U. Pa., N.J. Exhibited in group shows at Jacob Javits Ctr., N.Y.C., 1993, 94, Gallery Neotu, Paris, 1994, Mus. Modern Art, N.Y., 1995; featured in N.Y. Times, 1990, Elle Decor, 1994, Internat. Design Yearbook, 1994, Elle Deco Japan, 1995, etc.; contbr. articles to profl. jours. Design grantee NEA, 1995. Achievements include design patent for aluminum parallel ruler, design patent for aluminum shelving system. Office: Parallel Design Partnership Ltd 430 W 14th St Rm 408 New York NY 10014-1020

TAYLER, IRENE, English literature educator; b. Abilene, Tex., July 13, 1934; d. B. Brown and Madeline (Bowron); m. Edward W. Tayler, June 3, 1961 (div. 1971); children: Edward Jr., Jesse; m. Saul Touster, Jan. 14, 1978. BA in Philosophy, Stanford U., 1956, MA in Am. Lit., 1961, PhD in English Lit., 1968. Tchr. Breadloaf Sch. of Eng., Middlebury, Vt., 1970, 71, 75, 76; teaching asst. Stanford U., Calif., 1958-60; lectr. Columbia U., N.Y., 1961-71; asst. prof. CUNY, 1971-73, assoc. prof., 1973-76; assoc. prof. MIT, Cambridge, 1976-82, prof., 1982—, sec. of the faculty, 1993-95; chair gov. com. The English Inst., 1981. Author: (book) Blake's Illustrations to the Poems of Gray, 1971, Holy Ghosts: The Male Muses of Emily and Charlotte Bronte, 1990; contbr. numerous articles to profl. jours. Faculty Rsch. Found. grantee CUNY, 1972-73, Study grantee ACLS, 1968-69; Mac Vicar Faculty fellow MIT, 1993—, Sr. Scholar fellow NEH, 1980, Wilson fellow Stanford U., 1961-62, Internat. Inst. fellow U. Munich, 1957-58. Office: M I T 14 N 412 Cambridge MA 02139

TAYLOR, ALFRED RALEIGH, geologist; b. Eure, Gates County, N.C., July 7, 1928; s. Raleigh Jackson and Annie B. Taylor; m. Eugenia Dare Eure, Nov. 9, 1946; children: Patricia Dare, Teri Ann. BS in Geology, U. N.C., 1955. Cert. geologist Va. Geologist U.S. Geol. Survey, Worldwide, 1955-81, Minerals Mgmt. Svc., Reston, 1981-82, Bur. Land Mgmt., Reston and Washington, 1982-83; geol. cons. Somerset, Ky., 1984-87; sr. geologist Va. Divsn. of Mineral Resources, Cedar Bluff, Va., 1988-89; geol. cons. Cedar Bluff, 1989; supr. geologist Va. Divsn. Min. Resources, Dept. Mines, Minerals & Energy, Abingdon, Va., 1990—; adj. faculty in geology and geography Somerset C.C. of U. Ky., Somerset, 1968-77, 86-88. Contbr. over 50 articles and chpts. to books and profl. jours. S/sgt. USMC, PTO, ATO; lt. USNR. Recipient Antarctic Svc. medal, commendation U.S. Dept. Interior, 1961, citations U.S. Geol. Survey; Alfred Taylor Mountain in Antarctica named for him; named Ky. Col. Mem. Am. Assn. Petroleum Geologists, Am. Inst. Profl. Geologists (cert. prof. geologist), Geol. Soc. Washington, Geol. Soc. Ky., Fleet Res. Assn., VFW (life), Am. Legion, Naval Res. Assn., Sigma Gamma Epsilon. Office: Va Divsn Mineral Resources PO Box 144 Abingdon VA 24212-0144

TAYLOR, ALLAN BERT, lawyer; b. Cin., June 28, 1948; s. H. Ralph and Henrietta Irene (Medalia) T.; m. Sally Ann Silverstein, June 6, 1971; children: Rachel Elizabeth, Karen Ruth. AB, Harvard U., 1970, M in Pub. Policy, 1975, JD, 1975. Bar: Conn. 1975, U.S. Ct. Appeals (D.C. cir.) 1977, U.S. Dist. Ct. Conn. 1978, U.S. Dist. Ct. (so. dist.) N.Y. 1979, U.S. Ct. Appeals (2d cir.) 1979, U.S. Supreme Ct. 1979, U.S. Ct. Appeals (1st and 10th cirs.) 1991. Law clk. to J. Skelly Wright D.C. Cir., Washington, 1975-76; law clk. to Thurgood Marshall U.S. Supreme Ct., Washington, 1976-77; assoc. Day, Berry & Howard, Hartford, Conn., 1977-83, ptnr., 1983—; overseer Bushnell Meml. Hall Corp., Hartford, 1992—. Elected mem. Hartford City Coun., 1981-87, Hartford Bd. Edn., 1989-93, v.p., 1991-93, pres., 1992-93; mem. Conn. State Bd. Edn., 1994—; bd. dirs. Conn. Assn. Bds. Edn., Hartford, 1989-93, Hartford Infant Action Project, 1990—, Hartford Stage Co., 1993—. Mem. ABA, Conn. Bar Assn., Hartford County Bar Assn., Phi Beta Kappa. Democrat. Jewish. Avocations: astronomy, reading. Home: 238 Whitney St Hartford CT 06105-2270 Office: Day Berry & Howard City Place Hartford CT 06103

TAYLOR, ALLAN RICHARD, retired banker; b. Prince Albert, Sask., Can., Sept. 14, 1932; s. Norman and Anna Lydia (Norbeck) T.; m. Shirley Irene Ruston, Oct. 5, 1957; children: Rodney Allan, Leslie Ann. LLD (hon), U. Regina, Sask., 1987, Concordia U., Montreal, Can., 1988; DBA (hon.), Laval U., Quebec City, Can., 1990; LLD (hon.), Queen's U., Kingston, Ont., 1991; Doctorate of Univ. (hon.), U. Ottawa, 1992. With Royal Bank of Can., Toronto, Ont., Can., 1949-95; pres., COO, dir. Royal Bank of Can., Toronto, 1983-86, chmn., CEO, dir., 1986-94, chmn., 1994-95, ret., 1995; bd. dirs. Royal Bank of Can., TransCan. Pipelines Ltd., Toronto, Can.-Pacific Ltd., GM Can. Ltd., Oshawa, Ont., United Dominion Industries, Can. Inst. for Advanced Rsch., Toronto, NeuroScience Network, Montreal; exec. advisor Pub. Policy Forum, Ottawa; ; mem. adv. coun. Can. Exec. Svc. Overseas; former chmn. Can. Bankers Assn.; past pres. Internat. Monetary Conf. Hon. mem. Corp.-Higher Edn. Forum; chmn. Coun. Patrons, Outward Bound of Can.; past chmn., bd. dirs. Jr. Achievement Can.; gov. Olympic Trust, Can.; former chmn. corp. program IMAGINE; mem. adv. bd. Can. Found. AIDS Rsch.; chmn. hon. adv. bd. Can. Assn. for Cmty. Living. Decorated officer Order of Can. Address: 200 Bay St 18th Fl North Tower, Toronto, ON Canada M5J 2J5

TAYLOR, ALLAN ROSS, linguist, educator; b. Palisade, Colo., Dec. 24, 1931; s. Athel Ross and Marjorie Verle (Walters) T.; m. Mary Callas, Sept. 8, 1958; children: Artemisia, Anthony, Peter, Anna, Yoana. AB, U. Colo., Boulder, 1953; PhD (Woodrow Wilson fellow, Fulbright fellow, NDEA fellow), U. Calif., Berkeley, 1969. Teaching asst., lectr. U. Calif., Berkeley, 1958-63; instr. U. Colo., 1964-65, asst. prof., 1965-70, assoc. prof., 1970-77, prof., 1977-93, prof. emeritus, 1993—, also past chmn. dept. linguistics, dept. French and Italian; cons. bilingual edn. for Native Ams. Active Dem. Party and in environ. issues. With U.S. Army, 1954-57. NEH grantee, 1972-76, 80-82, 87-90, 89-93. Mem. Linguistic Soc. Am., Am. Anthrop. Assn. Home: 787 17th St Boulder CO 80302-7601 Office: U Colo Dept Linguistics PO Box 295 Boulder CO 80309-0295 *Reading in physical anthropology and genetics, and many years of an advocacy role in environmental issues, have convinced me that man's highest calling is custodial: to protect, preserve, and pass on inviolate the world and all of its inhabitants, even when it may appear to be against our own short-term interest to do this. For the grand plan, if there is any, is to allow diversity to make the choices which prove ultimately to be the only viable ones.*

TAYLOR, ALLEN M., community foundation executive; b. Cedar Rapids, Iowa, Dec. 22, 1923. AB, Princeton U., 1946; LLB, Yale U., 1949. Bar: Wis. Assoc. Foley & Lardner, Milw., 1949-57, ptnr., 1957-88, sr. ptnr., 1988-93, of counsel, 1993; chmn., CFO The Chipstone Found., Milw., 1994—; vice-chmn., bd. dirs. The Lynde and Harry Bradley Found.; bd. dirs. Stark Hosp. Found., Med. Coll. Wis. Health Policy Inst.; adv. bd. dirs. Med. Coll. Wis. Mem. The Greater Milw. Found.; chmn. capital fund drive Milw. Symphony Orch.; steering com. Pabst Theatre Reconstruction Campaign. With USMC, 1942-45. Mem. ABA, Wisconsin Bar Assn., Assn. Bank Holding Cos. (past chmn. lawyers com.), Milw. Country Club (past pres., sec., bd. dirs.), The Milw. Club, Cap and Gown Princeton, Princeton Club N.Y. Home: 2825 E Newport Ave Milwaukee WI 53211 Office: The Chipstone Found 777 E Wisconsin Ave Milwaukee WI 53202-5302

TAYLOR, ANDREW C., rental leasing company executive; b. 1947. Degree, Denver U., 1970. With Enterprise Rent-A-Car, St. Louis, 1972—, now CEO. Office: Enterprise Rent-A-Car 600 Corporate Park Dr Saint Louis MO 63105-4204*

TAYLOR, ANNA DIGGS, federal judge; b. Washington, Dec. 9, 1932; d. Virginius Douglass and Hazel (Bramlette) Johnston; m. S. Martin Taylor, May 22, 1976; children: Douglass Johnston Diggs, Carla Cecile Diggs. BA, Barnard Coll., 1954; LLB, Yale U., 1957. Bar: D.C. 1957, Mich. 1961. Atty. Office Solicitor, Dept. Labor, W, 1957-60; asst. prosecutor Wayne County, Mich., 1961-62; asst. U.S. atty. Eastern Dist. of Mich., 1966; ptnr. Zwerdling, Maurer, Diggs & Papp, Detroit, 1970-75; asst. corp. counsel City of Detroit, 1975-79; U.S. dist. judge Eastern Dist. Mich. Detroit, 1979—. Hon. chair, United Way Cmty. Found., S.E. Mich. Found. Soc., Detroit Inst. Arts, Greater Detroit Health Coun., Eastern Region Henry Ford Health Sys.; co-chair, vol. Leadership Coun. for S.E. Mich.; trustee Herlong Cathedral Sch. Mem. Fed. Bar Assn., State Bar Mich., Wolverine Bar Assn. (v.p.), Yale Law Assn. Episcopalian. Office: US Dist Ct 740 US Courthouse 231 W Lafayette Blvd Detroit MI 48226-2720

TAYLOR, ARTHUR ROBERT, college president, business executive; b. Elizabeth, N.J., July 6, 1935; s. Arthur Earl and Marion Hilda (Scott) T.; m. Kathryn Pelgrift; 3 daus. by previous marriage. B.A. magna cum laude, Brown U., 1957, M.A. in Am. Econ. History, 1961; H.H.D. (hon.), Bucknell U., 1975, Allentown Coll. of St. Francis de Sales; L.H.D. (hon.), Rensselaer Poly. Inst., 1975, Simmons Coll., 1975; LL.D. (hon.), Mt. Scenario Coll., 1975. Asst. dir. admissions Brown U., Providence, 1957-61; with First Boston Corp., N.Y.C., 1961-70, asst. v.p., 1964-66, v.p., 1966-70, also dir.; v.p. fin. Internat. Paper Co., N.Y.C., 1970-71, exec. v.p., dir., 1971-72; pres. CBS Inc., N.Y.C., 1972-76, also dir.; pres. Muhlenberg Coll., Allentown, Pa., 1992—; chmn. Arthur Taylor & Co., Inc., 1977—; chmn. The Enterntainment Channel, 1980-83; dean faculty of bus. Fordham U., 1985-92; bd. dirs. Nomura Pacific Basin Fund, Pitney Bowes, La. Land & Exploration Co., Jakarta Growth Fund, Japan OTC Equity Fund; mem. adv. com. Toshiba Internat. Mem. Population Resource Ctr., Nat. Commn. of Civic Renewal; trustee Brown U. Mem. Coun. Fgn. Rels., Trilateral Commn., Phi Beta Kappa. Congregationalist. Clubs: Century (N.Y.C.); Met. (Washington); California (L.A.). Office: Muhlenberg Coll Office of Pres 2400 W Chew St Allentown PA 18104-5564

TAYLOR, AUBREY ELMO, physiologist, educator; b. El Paso, Tex., June 4, 1933; s. Virgil T. and Mildred (Maher) T.; m. Mary Jane Davis, Apr. 4, 1953; children: Audrey Jane Hildebrand, Lenda Sue Brown, Mary Ann Smith. BA in Math. and Psychology, Tex. Christian U., 1960; PhD in Physiology, U. Miss., 1964; Postdoctoral fellow biophysics lab. Harvard U. Med. Sch., Boston, 1965-67; from asst. prof. to prof. dept. physiology U. Miss. Coll. Medicine, Jackson, 1967-77; prof., chmn. dept. physiology U. South Ala. Coll. Medicine, Mobile, 1977—, Louise Lenoir Locke eminent scholar; mem. pulmonary score com. Nat. Heart, Lung and Blood Inst., 1976; with Surgery and anesthesiology, 1979-82, and Manpower Com., 1985-95; chmn. RAP, 1983. Author 7 books; contbr. chpts. to books, 700 articles to profl. jours; assoc. editor Jour. Applied Physiology, 1984-94, Critical Care medicine, 1997; editor Clin. Medicine, 1992-97; mem. editl. bd. Circulation Rsch. Am. Jour. Physiology, Microvascular Rsch., Internat. Pathophysiology, Microcirculatory and Lymphatic Rsch., Microcirculation, Chinese Jour. of Physiology Jour. Biomed. Science, Jour. Biomed. Rsch., Am. Rev. Resp. and Critical Care Clin. Scis., Jour. Internat. Soc. of Pathology. Served with U.S. Army, 1953-55. NIH grantee, 1967—; recipient Lederle Faculty award, 1967-70, Philip Dow award U. Ga., 1984, NIH Merit award, 1988—, Lucian award McGill U., 1988, John Whitney award U. Ark., 1990, Gelen award Intestinal Shock Soc., 1991; named Disting. Physiologist Am. Coll. Chest Physicians, 1994. Fellow AAAS, Am. Heart Assn. (circulation, coun., cardiopulmonary and critical care coun. 1977—, chmn. elect, chmn., 1993—. So. regional rev. com. 1977-81, EIA Review Com. 1986-95, mem. pulmonary and devel. rev. com. 1987-95, chmn. grant/review com., 1994-95, chmn. med. student rsch. award com. 1992-94, nat. rsch. com. 1990-95, coun. affairs com. 1994—, Dickson Richards award 1988, Bronze award Miss. AHA, 1976, Outstanding Alabaman AHA program 1993, sci. coun. achievement award, 1995, ACDP Svc. award, 1995), Royal Soc. Medicine, NAS (mem. com. for Internat. Union Physiol. Sci.); mem. Am. Physiol. Soc. (hon. 1993-96, coun. 1984-87, chmn. membership com. 1985-87, pres. 1987-90, Wiggers award 1987, chmn. Perkins fellow com., 1996—, AGDP exec. com. 1996—), Microcirculatory Soc. (coun. 1977-81, pres. 1981-83, Landis award 1985), Ala. Acad. Scis. (State Rsch. award 1988), Internat. Lymphology Soc., N.Am. Soc. Lymphology (pres. 1988-90, recipient First Cecil Drinker award 1988), Internat. Pathophysiology Soc. (v.p. 1991—), N.Y. Acad. Scis., Biophys. Soc., Fedn. Am. Socs. for Exptl. Biology (bd. dirs. 1988-90, reorganizing com.), Am. Thoracic Soc., European Soc., Alpha Omega Alpha, Sigma Xi. Democrat. Presbyterian. Current work: Cardio-pulmonary physiology; fluid balance, edema, microcirculation and capillary exchange of solute and water. Subspecialties: Physiology (medicine); Pulmonary medicine. Home: 11 Audubon Pl Mobile AL 36606-1907

TAYLOR, BARBARA ALDEN, public relations executive; b. Dallas, Aug. 21, 1943; d. Harold Earl and Sally Alden (Howard) T.; BA, Smith Coll., 1965; MA, Antioch Coll., 1971. Vol., Peace Corps, India, 1966-68; tchr. Upper Merion Sch. Dist., King of Prussia, Pa., 1969-70; tchr. Cheltenham Sch. Dist., Elkins Park, Pa., 1970-74; pub. relations dir. Princess Hotels Internat., N.Y.C., 1974-75; chmn. Taylor & Hammond Ltd., N.Y.C., 1975-84; pres. Doremus/Marketshare, 1984-86; exec. v.p. Porter/Novelli, N.Y.C., 1986-90; sr. v.p. Hill and Knowlton, Inc., N.Y.C., 1990-93; sr. v.p. corp. comm. Lancaster Group Worldwide, 1993-95; sr. v.p. Coty Inc. and Benckiser Group, 1995-97; sr. v.p. corp. comms. Voyater Expanded Learning, Dallas, 1997—. Mem. adv. bd. York Theater Co., 1991—; bd. dirs. Madison Square Boys' and Girls' Club N.Y., 1978—, also mem. women's bd. Boys' Club N.Y. Named to Acad. of Women Achievers YWCA, 1985; bd. dirs. Up With People, Tucson, 1990—. Mem. Women in Communications, Pub. Relations Soc. Am. (counselors acad.), Internat. Women's Forum, Advt. Women N.Y., Cosmetic Exec. Women, Fashion Group, Doubles Internat, Smith Coll. Alumnae Assn. (bd. dirs. 1993—), Club N.Y., Lyford Cay Club, Jr. League City N.Y. Avocations: tennis, walking. Office: Voyager Expanded Learning 2200 Ross Ave Ste 3800 Dallas TX 75201

TAYLOR, BARBARA ANN, educational consultant; b. St. Louis, Feb. 8, 1933; d. Spencer Truman and Ann Amelia (Whitney) Olin; m. F. Morgan Taylor Jr., Apr. 5, 1954; children: Frederick M. III, Spencer O., James W., John F. AB, Smith Coll., 1954; M of Mgmt., Northwestern U., 1978, PhD, 1984; LHD, U. New Haven, 1995. Mem. faculty Hamden (Conn.) Hall Country Day Sch., 1972-74; cons. Booz, Allen & Hamilton, Inc., Chgo., 1979; program assoc. Northwestern U., Evanston, Ill., 1982; co-founder, exec. dir. Nat. Ctr. Effective Schs. Rsch. & Devel., Okemos, Mich., 1986-89, rsch. assoc., 1987; cons. on effective schs. rsch. and reform Nat. Ctr. Effective Schs. R&D, U. Wis., Madison, 1990-96; pres. Excelsior! Found., Chgo., 1994—; mem. exec. com. Hudson Inst., New Am. Schs. Devel. Corp. Design Team, 1990-94; Danforth Disting. lectr. U. Nebr., Omaha, 1993. Co-author: Making School Reform Happen, 1993, Keepers of the Dream, 1994, The Revolution Revisited: Effective Schools and Systemic Reform, 1995; editor: Case Studies in Effective Schools Research, 1990; contbr. articles to profl. jours. Pres. Jr. League of New Haven, 1967-69; pres. NCCJ, New Haven, 1971-73; co-chair Coalition Housing and Human Resources, Hartford-New Haven, 1970-73; co-chair steering com. Day Care Conn., Hartford, 1971-73; bd. dirs. U. New Haven, 1961-71, Smith Coll., Northampton, Mass., 1984-90, Choate Rosemary Hall Sch., 1973-78, Lake Forest Coll., 1996—. Recipient Humanitarian award Mt. Calvary Bapt. Ch., 1988, Outstanding Alumna award John Burroughs Sch., 1994. Mem. ASCD, Nat. Commn. Citizens Edn. (bd. dirs. 1980-86), Nat. Staff Devel. Coun., Phi Delta Kappa. Episcopalian. Office: Nat Ctr Effective Schs Rsch & Devel 222 E Wisconsin Ave Ste 301 Lake Forest IL 60045-1723

TAYLOR, BARBARA JO ANNE HARRIS, government official, librarian, educator, civic and political worker; b. Providence, Sept. 9, 1936; d. Ross Cameron and Anita (Coia) Harris; m. Richard Powell Taylor, Dec. 19, 1959; 1 child, Douglas Howard. Student, Tex. Christian U., 1952, Salve Regina Coll., 1952-53; Student, Our Lady of the Lake Coll. and Convent, 1953-54, St. Mary's U., 1954, Incarnate Word Coll., 1954-55, Georgetown U., 1956-59, 62-63; BS cum laude, Georgetown U., 1963. Adminstrv. asst. profl. devel. and welfare NEA, Washington, 1956-59; asst. to dir. Georgetown U., Washington, 1956-59; exec. asst. All Am. Conf. to Combat Communism, Washington, 1960; spl. legis. asst. mil. affairs to chmn. mil. R & D subcom. U.S. Senate Armed Svcs. Com., 1971-72; U.S. nat. commr. UNESCO, 1982—, mem. exec. com. U.S. nat. commn., 1983—, sr. advisor 22d gen. conf., 1983; speaker in field. Contbr. articles to profl. jours. Del. numerous internat. confs.; U.S. commr. Nat. Commn. Librs. and Info. Sci., 1985-96, mem. various coms.; gen. chmn. George Bush for Pres. Md. State Steering Com., 1987-88; co-chmn. Md. del. Rep. Nat. Conv., 1988, 92; dep. chmn. Md. Victory '88, Bush-Quayle Campaign; mem. Nat. Fin. Com. Reagan for Pres., 1980, Reagan-Bush, 1984; state fin. chmn. Md. Rep. Party, 1980; mem. Nat. Rep. Club; mem. exec. bd. Salvation Army Aux., Washington, 1967-75, chmn. membership com., 1969-70, chmn. fund-raising com., 1968-69, mem. exec. com. of exec. bd., 1970-75, treas., mem. fin. com., 1970-71, v.p., 1971-72, historian, 1972-73, editor newsletter, 1968-69, chmn. nominating com., 1974-75, spl. awards. for exceptional vol. svc., 1969, 72; mem. exec. bd. Welcome to Washington Internat., 1969-74, bd. advisers, 1969-74, dir. workshop, 1969-74; exec. bd. Am. Opera Sch. Soc., Washington, 1970—, v.p., 1974—; mem. Episc. Ch. Home for Aged Women's Aux., 1970-75, Episc. Ctr. for Emotionally Disturbed Children Women's Aux., 1970-75; exec. bd. St. David's Episc. Ch. Aux., 1970-72, 73-74; bd. dirs., treas. Spanish-Portuguese Study Group, 1970-72; mem. exec. bd. League Rep. Women D.C., 1964-67, 75-77, treas., 1964-67; mem. nat. coun. Women's Nat. Rep. Club, N.Y.C., 1969—, chmn. Washington-Md.-Va. legis. com., 1970-75; mem. Nat. Fedn. Rep. Women, 1964—; mem. nat. fin. com. Reagan for Pres., 1979-80; mem. governing bd. Capital Speakers Club, 1973-75, chmn. by-laws com., 1973-74; mem. exec. bd. Nat. Vols. in Action, 1975-77; mem. adv. com. Rock Creek Found. Mental Health, 1982-87; mem. 50th anniversary com. Save the Children; mem. fund-raising com. Washington Choral Arts Soc., 1982-84; state fin. chmn. Reagan-Bush campaign Md. Rep. Com., 1980; Md. coord. Nat. Inaugural Com., 1981, 85; trustee Crossnore Sch., Inc., N.C., 1983—, vice chmn. bd; trustee Kate Duncan Smith DAR Sch., Grant, Ala., 1983-86, Tamassee (S.C.) DAR Sch., 1983-86; adviser Bacone Am. Indian Coll., Inc., Muscogee, Okla., 1983-88. Mem. ALA, Spl. Librs. Assn., Coun. on Libr. Resources (commn. on preservation and access), Am. Libr. Trustees Assn., Libr. Adminstrn. and Mgmt. Assn., Assn. Coll. and Rsch. Librs., Am. Antiquarian Soc., Internat. Platform Assn., Spanish-Portuguese Study Group, Nat. Lawyers' Wives, Nat. Capital Law League, Nat. Soc. DAR (chmn. nat. resolutions com. 1980-83, chmn. nat. Nat. Soc. DAR sch. com. 1983-86; state historian 1978-80, mem. state bd. mgmt. 1973—, Nat. Soc. DAR libr. gen., mem. exec. com. and nat. corp. bd. mgmt. 1986-89, chmn. nat. commemorative events com. 1992-95, chmn. nat. Nat. Soc. DAR libr. centennial com. 1995—), Nat. Soc. Children Am. Revolution (sr. nat. asst. registrar 1978-80, mem. sr. nat. bd. mgmt. 1978-80, sr. nat. exec. com. 1978-80), Nat. Assn. Parliamentarians, World Affairs Coun., League of Rep. Women, Md. Fedn. Rep. Women, Women's Nat. Republican Club, Nat. Fed. Rep. Women, Commn. on Preservation and Access, Lit. Vols. Am. (Washington Met. area affiliate), Exec. Women in Govt., Am. News Women's Club, Internat. Club, Capitol Hill Club, Univ. Club Washington, Washington Club, Congl. Country Club (Potomac, Md.).

TAYLOR, BARRY LLEWELLYN, microbiologist, educator; b. Sydney, Australia, May 7, 1937; came to U.S., 1967; s. Fredrick Llewelyn and Vera Lavina (Clarke) T.; m. Desmyrna Ruth Tolhurst, Jan. 4, 1961; children: Lyndon, Nerida, Darrin. BA, Avondale Coll., Cooranbong, New South Wales, 1959; BSc with honors, U. New South Wales, Sydney, 1966; PhD, Case Western Res. U., 1973; postgrad., U. Calif., Berkeley, 1973-75. Vis. postdoctoral fellow Australian Nat. U., Canberra, 1975-76; asst. prof. biochemistry Loma Linda (Calif.) U., 1976-78, assoc. prof. biochemistry, 1978-83, prof. biochemistry, 1983—, prof., chmn. dept. microbiology and molecular genetics, 1988—, interim dir. Ctr. for Molecular Biology, 1989-94. Contbr. articles to profl. publs. Rsch. grantee Am. Heart Assn., 1978-85, 96—, NIH, 1981—. Mem. Am. Soc. Microbiology, Am. Soc. Biochemistry and Molecular Biology. Office: Loma Linda U Dept Microbiology & Molecular Genetics Loma Linda CA 92350

TAYLOR, BARRY NORMAN, physicist; b. Phila., Mar. 27, 1936; s. Morris and Sarah (Weiss) T.; m. Sheila Anne Cohen, Dec. 28, 1958; children: Deborah Susan, David Joel, Denise Beth. AB, Temple U., Phila., 1957; MS, U. Pa., 1960, PhD, 1963. Instr., then asst. prof. physics U. Pa., 1963-66; mem. tech. staff RCA Rsch. Labs., 1966-70; chief absolute elec. measurements sect. Nat. Bur. Standards (name changed to Nat. Inst. of Standards and Tech. 1988), Gaithersburg, Md., 1970-74, adminstr. NIST Precision Measurement Grants Program, 1974—, chief electricity divsn., 1974-89; mgr. Fundamental Cons. Data Ctr., 1989—; instr. Rider Coll., Trenton, N.J., 1969-70; mem., chairperson nat. and internat. tech. coms. Co-author: Fundamental Constants and Quantum Electrodynamics, 1969; co-editor: Precision Measurement and Fundamental Constants, 1971; Co-editor: Precision Measurement and Fundamental Constants II, 1984; contbr. articles to sci. jours. Recipient Silver medal U.S. Dept. Commerce, 1975, Gold medal, 1989, John Price Wetherill medal Franklin Inst., 1975. Fellow IEEE, Am. Phys. Soc. (chair topical group on fundamental constants and precise tests of phys. laws 1990-92), Washington Acad. Scis.; mem. Sigma Xi. Office: Nat Inst of Stds and Tech Bldg 225 Rm B161 Gaithersburg MD 20899-0001

TAYLOR, BENJAMIN B., newspaper publishing executive; b. 1947; s. John I. T.; m. Katherine Taylor; children: Abigail, Samuel, William. Grad., Harvard U. Various positions including asst. mng. editor/local news, consumer affairs reporter, polit. reporter Boston Globe, 1972-88, exec. editor, 1988; v.p. Globe Newspaper Co., 1991, exec. v.p., 1992, pres., 1993—, COO, 1994—. Trustee Radcliffe Coll., Park Sch., Brookline, Mass. Office: Globe Newspapers Co PO Box 2378 135 Morrissey Blvd Boston MA 02107-2378*

TAYLOR, BERNARD J., II, banker; b. Phila., Nov. 10, 1925; s. Bernard and Marie (Pearce) T.; m. Barbara Silverstein; children: Dorothy Taylor Tomlinson, Lawrence Dean, David Stewart. B.S., U. Pa., 1949. Asst. mgr. McCrory Stores Corp., Phila., 1949-51; fin. analyst Fidelity Bank, Phila., 1951-57; asst. to v.p. investments Fidelity Bank, 1957-59, asst. to pres., 1959-60, corp. sec., 1960-63, v.p., sec., 1963-66, sr. v.p. in charge adminstrn. dept., 1966-72, exec. v.p., 1972-74; v.p. Fidelcor, Inc. (parent co. Fidelity Bank), 1969-72, exec. v.p., 1973-76; sr. exec. v.p., 1976-79; pres., dir. Fidelity Bldg. Corp., 1970-79; pres., CEO Wilmington (Del.) Trust Co., Del., 1979-92; dir. Wilmington (Del.) Trust Co., 1979—, chmn., 1980-92; ptnr. Golf Ptnrs. (Hartefield Nat. Golf Course), 1993—. Pres. Savoy Opera Co., Phila., 1961-63, prodn. mgr., dir., 1970-75; pres., bd. dirs. Pa. Opera Theatre, 1975-80, treas., bd. dirs., 1980-93; mem. adv. bd. mgrs. Inglis House Phila., 1967-70; mem. Del. Round Table, 1980-92; bd. dirs. Greater Wilmington Devel. Coun., 1980-84, Sta. WHYY, PBS-TV, Phila., 1980-92; bd. dirs., 1986-91; bd. dirs. Del. Theatre Co., 1987-91. With AUS, 1944-46, PTO. Clubs: Orpheus (Phila); Wilmington Country. Home: 6 Hillspur Rd Kennett Square PA 19348-2702

TAYLOR, BEVERLY LACY, stringed instrument restorer, classical guitarist; b. Denver, Mar. 1, 1928; d. Frederick Thurlow and Ruth (Rogers) Lacy; m. Arthur D. Taylor, Mar. 18, 1967. BA, Wheaton Coll., Norton, Mass., 1949; postgrad., U. Denver, 1951-53, U. Colo., 1953. Scene designer, tech. dir. Piper Players, Idaho Springs, Colo., 1949-51; art instr. Denver Art Mus., 1952; craft and speech instr. Wallace Sch., Denver, 1953; illustrator dept. native art Denver Art Mus., 1954-56; designer, owner The Art Studio, Santa Fe, 1956-58; instr., owner Classic Guitar Studio, Santa Fe, 1959—; instr. classical guitar Santa Fe Conservatory of Music, 1966-67, Coll. Sante Fe, 1971-72; stringed instrument restorer Lacy Taylor Studio, Santa Fe, 1967—. One-woman shows of mosaic panels include Mus. N.Mex., Santa Fe, 1959; exhibited in group shows at Mus. New Mex., 1962, 63; executed mosaic panels Denver Art Mus. Recipient Miriam Carpenter Art prize Wheaton Coll., 1949, prize N.Mex. State Fair, 1959, 61. Mem. Guild Am. Luthiers, Assn. String Instrument Artisans. Avocations: drawing, gardening, dog training. Home: 1210 Canyon Rd Santa Fe NM 87501-6128

TAYLOR, BILLIE WESLEY, retired secondary education educator; b. Charleston, W.Va, Aug. 14, 1940; s. Billie W and Effie (Adams) T.; m. Elisabeth Julia Coler, Jan. 27, 1960; 1 child, Rose Letitia Taylor Allen. BA, Wilmington Coll., 1961; MA, Ohio State U., 1963; PhD, Columbia Pacific U., 1993. Cert. secondary tchr., prin., Ohio. Tchr. Columbus Pub. Schs., Ohio, 1961-64; records, forms, mgnt. officer VI U.S. Army Corps, Battle Creek, Mich., 1964-65; production planner Hoover Ball & Bearing Co., Ann Arbor, Mich., 1965-66; dist. exec. Boy Scouts of Am., Detroit, 1966-72; sales tng. Standard Register Co., Dayton, Ohio, 1972-74; tchr. Dayton Pub. Schs., Dayton, Ohio, 1974-95, curriculum specialist for computer tech., 1989-93. Author: History of the D-MC Park District, 1988, Classroom Discipline, 1987. Pres., Johnson Sch. Parent Tchrs. Assoc., Taylor, Mich., 1966-67; dist. chmn., Boy Scouts of Am., Dayton, 1974-79; bd. mem., Southeast Dayton Priority Bd., Dayton, 1976-77. Recipient Pres. trophy Boy Scouts of Am., 1970; Jenning's scholar Martha Holden Jennings Found., 1980-81. Mem. Nat. Geographic Soc. (life), Nat. Audubon Soc., Smithsonian Nat. Assocs. (charter mem.), Libr. of Congress Assocs. (charter), Nat. Mus. of the Am. Indian (charter), Western Ohio Edn. Assn. (del.), Am. Birding Assn., The Nature Conservancy (life), Am. Assn. Individual Investors (life), Masons. Avocations: birding, motorhoming, foreign travel, reading, investing. Home: 131 Snow Hill Ave Kettering OH 45429-1705

TAYLOR, CALVIN LEE, public administrator; b. Marietta, Ohio, Dec. 27, 1946; s. Fred O. and Wilma B. Taylor; m. Nancy Downs, Mar. 29, 1969; children: Christina, Matthew. BSc in Natural Resources, Ohio State U., 1969, PhD in Environ. Scis., 1977; MPA, Golden Gate U., 1973. Project officer Corps of Engrs. Sacramento (Calif.) Dist., 1970-73; asst. planning chief Ohio EPA, Columbus, 1973-74; acad. advisor Ohio State U. Sch. of Natural Resources, Columbus, 1974-75; asst. to dir. Ohio Water Resources Ctr., Columbus, 1975-76; adminstr. Ohio Dept. Natural Resources, Columbus, 1976-82; chief of pub. rels. Ohio Adj. Gen.'s Dept., 1982-88; chief ops. and tng. Ohio Emergency Mgmt. Agy., Columbus, 1988-94; chief of emergency preparedness State of Ohio, Columbus, 1994—; lectr. in field. Contbr. articles to profl. jours. Chmn., mem. Worthington Planning Commn./Archl. Rev. Bd., 1976-82, active coms. Worthington United Meth. Ch., 1980—. Lt. col. U.S. Army Res., 1970—. Named Outstanding Young Man of Am. U.S. Bd. Jaycees, 1981. Mem. ARC, Ohio Acad. Sci., Ohio State U. Alumni Assn. (pres. natural resources 1979-80), Ohio State U. Army ROTC Alumni Assn. (v.p., pres.), Columbus Acad. Fathers' Assn. Avocations: snow skiing, water skiing, jogging, corporate real estate management. Home: 701 Morning St Worthington OH 43085-3772 Office: Ohio Emergency Mgmt Agy 2855 W Granville Rd Columbus OH 43235

TAYLOR, CARL ERNEST, physician, educator; b. Landour, Mussoorie, India, July 26, 1916; s. John C. and Elizabeth (Siehl) T.; m. Mary Daniels, Feb. 14, 1943; children—Daniel, Elizabeth, Henry. B.S., Muskingum Coll., 1937, D.Sc., 1962; M.D., Harvard, 1941, M.P.H., 1951, D.P.H., 1953; L.H.D. (hon.), Towson U., 1974. Diplomate: Am. Bd. Preventive Medicine. Intern, resident pathology, surg. staff, tropical disease research Gorgas Hosp., Panama C.Z., 1941-44; charge med. service Marine Hosp., Pitts., 1944-46; supt. Meml. Hosp., Fategarh, India, 1947-50; research assoc. Harvard Sch. Pub. Health, Boston, 1950-52; asst. prof. epidemiology Harvard Sch. Pub. Health, 1957-59, assoc. prof., 1959-61; prof. preventive and social medicine Christian Med. Coll., Ludhiana, Punjab, India, 1953-56; prof. internat. health Johns Hopkins Sch. Hygiene and Pub. Health, Balt., 1961-83; prof. emeritus Johns Hopkins Sch. Hygiene and Pub. Health, 1984—, chmn. dept. internat. health, 1961-83; Cons. AID, 1959—; UNICEF country rep. in China, 1984-87; mem. expert com. WHO, 1963, 66, 67, 70, 71, 72, 73, 75; mem. Inst. Medicine, Nat. Acad. Medicine, Nat. Adv. Commn. Health Manpower; chmn. Nat. Council for Internat. Health. Contbr. numerous articles to profl. jours. Fellow Royal Coll. Physicians (Can.), Royal Soc. Tropical Medicine and Hygiene, Am. Pub. Health Assn.; mem. Assn. Tchrs. Preventive Medicine, Am. Soc. Tropical Medicine and Hygiene, Indian Assn. for Advancement Med. Edn. Research on rural health, population dynamics, nutrition, epidemiology of leprosy. Home: Bittersweet Acres 1201 Hollins Ln Baltimore MD 21209-2209 *The growing complexity of human relationships around this increasingly crowded world presents new challenges to concerned scientists. Solutions to our problems must come from new collaborative styles of work bridging the usual boundaries between people, since the problems we face are mutual.*

TAYLOR, CAROLYN L., principal. Prin. James Madison High Sch., Madison, Wis. Recipient Blue Ribbon award U.S. Dept. Edn., 1990-91. Office: James Madison Meml High Sch 201 S Gammon Rd Madison WI 53717-1404*

TAYLOR, CARSON WILLIAM, electrical engineer; b. Superior, Wis., May 24, 1942; s. William Stanley and Elizabeth Marie (Christophersen) T.; m. Gudrun Renate Leistner, Dec. 28, 1966; 1 child, Natasha Marie. BSEE, U. Wis., 1965; M in Engring., Rensselaer Poly. Inst., 1969. Elec. engr. U.S. Bur. Reclamation, Billings, Mont., 1967-68; elec. engr. Bonneville Power Adminstrn., Portland, Oreg., 1969-89, prin. engr., 1989—; prin. Carson Taylor Seminars, Portland, 1986—. Author: Power System Voltage Stability, 1994; contbr. papers to profl. publs.; patentee in field. Lt. U.S. Army, 1965-67. Lt. U.S. Army, 1965-67. Fellow IEEE (chmn. subcom. 1982—); mem. Conférence Internationale des Grands Réseaux Électriques a Haute Tension (CIGRE), Eta Kappa Nu. Lutheran. Avocations: fishing, hunting, woodworking, reading, computers. Office: Bonneville Power Adminstrn PO Box 3621 Portland OR 97208-3621

TAYLOR, CECIL PERCIVAL, pianist, composer, educator; b. N.Y.C., Mar. 15, 1933; s. Percy Clinton and Almeida (Maitie) Ragland. Studied music privately; studied music, N.Y. Coll. Music, New Eng. Conservatory. Music intructor U. of WI, 1970-71, Antioch Coll., Yellow Springs, OH, 1972-74, Glassboro State College; instr. U. Wis., 1970-72, Antioch Coll., 1972-74, Glassboro State Coll. Played with Hot Lips Page, Lawrence Brown; formed own quartet in late 1950's; performed with Archie Shepp and Jimmy Lyons, 1961; recorded and performed as solo pianist and with quartet including Jimmy Lyons, Andrew Cycille, Sam Rivers; compositions include Indent; albums include: Jazz Advance, 1956, Nefertiti, the Beautiful One Has Come, 1962, Unit Structures, 1966, Conquistador!, 1966, Silent Tongues, 1974, Air Above Mountains, 1976, Cicil Taylor, 1978, 3 Phasis, 1978, One Too Many Salty Swift and Not Goodbye, 1986, For Olim, 1986, Garden, 1986, The Eight, 1987, Cecil Taylor in Berlin '88, 1988, Looking, 1989, In Florescence, 1990, Dark to Themselves, 1990, Looking Ahead, 1990, Olu Iwa, 1994, The Great Paris Concert, 1996, Dark to Themselves, 1996, Crossing, 1996, Ow, 1996. Recipient Record of Year Downbeat Critics Poll, 1975; winner Down Beat Critics Poll for best acoustic piano, 1984; recipient Piano Player of Year award, 1972, 79; named to Downbeat Hall of Fame, 1975; Guggenheim fellow, 1973. Office: Koch Internat LP Enja Records 2 Tri-Harbor Ct Port Washington NY 11050*

TAYLOR, CELIANNA ISLEY, information systems specialist; b. Youngstown, Ohio; d. Paul Thornton and Florence (Jacobs) Isley; divorced; children: Polly, Jerry, Jim. BA in Philosophy, Denison U., 1939; MLS, Western Res. U., 1942. Worked in several pub. librs. and univ. librs., 1939-50; head Libr. Cataloging Dept. Battelle Mem. Inst., Columbus, Ohio, 1951-53; head pers. office, assoc. prof. libr. adminstrn. Ohio State U. Librs., Columbus, 1954-65; coord. info. svcs., assoc. prof. libr. adminstrn. Nat. Ctr. for Rsch. in Vocat. Edn., Ohio State U., Columbus, 1966-70; sr. rsch. assoc., adminstrv. assoc., assoc. prof. libr. adminstrn. dept. computer and info. sci. Ohio State U., Columbus, 1970-86, assoc. prof. emeritus Univ. Librs., 1986—; mem. Task Force on a Spl. Collections Database, Ohio State U. Librs., Columbus, 1988-89, comm. systems and recs. coord. Ohio State U. Retirees Assn., Columbus, 1992-93; cons. for several profl. orgns. including Ernst & Ernst CPA's and Oreg. State Sys. of Higher Edn., 1961-82. Author: (with J. Magisos) book, Guide for State Voc-Tech Edn. Dissemination Systems 1971, (with A.E. Petrarca, and R.S. Kohn) book, Info. Interaction 1982; several articles for profl. jours.; designer: info. systems, CALL System, 1977-82, Channel 2000 Proj. Home Info. Svc., 1980-81, Continuing Education Info. Ctr., 1989-90, Human Resources (HUR) System, 1976-77,1979-82, DECOS, 1975-86, Computer-asst. libr. System, Optical Scan System, 1972-73, ERIC Clearinghouse for vocat. edn., 1966-70. Bd. dirs. Columbus Reg. Info. Svc., 1974-78, Cmty. Info. Referral Svc., Inc. 1975-81; chmn. subcom. on design, info. and ref. com. Columbus United Cmty. Coun., 1972-73; dir. Computer Utility for Pub. Info. Columbus, 1975-81; acct. coord. Greater Columbus Free-net, 1994—. Mem. ALA, Assn. Computing Machinery (Ctrl. Ohio chpt.), Am. Soc. Info. Sci.,Assn. Faculty and Profl. Women Ohio State U., Columbus Metro Club, Coun. for Ethics in Econs., Olympic Indoor Tennis Club. Avocations: bicycling, bird watching, gourmet cooking, tennis, water aerobics. Home and Office: 3471 Greenbank Ct Columbus OH 43221-4724

TAYLOR, CHARLES ELLETT, biologist; b. Chgo., Sept. 9, 1945; s. Stewart Ferguson and Barbara (Ellett) T.; m. Minna Glushiens, June 22, 1969. AB, U. Calif., 1968; PhD, SUNY, Stony Brook, 1973. Prof. U. Calif., Riverside, 1974-80, UCLA, 1980—; cons. artificial life and population genetics; dir. UCLA Cognitive Sci. Rsch. Program, 1990—; adv. bd. Computer Mus. Fishtank. Co-author: Artificial Life II; editor Artificial Life, 1997—; contbr. articles to profl. publs. Mem. Santa Fe Inst. Office: Dept Biology UCLA Box 951606 Los Angeles CA 90095-1606

TAYLOR, CHARLES H., congressman; b. Brevard, N.C., Jan. 3, 1941; m. Elizabeth Owen; 3 children. BA, Wake Forest U., 1963, JD, 1966. Mem. N.C. Ho. of Reps., Raleigh, 1967-73, minority leader, 1969-73; mem. N.C. Senate, Raleigh, 1973-75, minority leader, 1973-75; mem. 102nd-105th Congresses from 11th N.C. dist., Washington, 1991—; mem. appropriations subcoms. commerce, justice, state jud. and related agys., legis. com., subcom. on interior; tree farmer N.C. Baptist. Office: U S Ho of Reps 231 Cannon HOB Washington DC 20515 also: 22 S Pack Sq Ste 330 Asheville NC 28801-3524*

TAYLOR, CHARLES HENRY, psychoanalyst, educator; b. Boston, Oct. 2, 1928; s. Charles Henry and Rosamond (Stewardson) T.; m. Diana Burgess, 1950; children: Stephen, Diana Beth, Charles S., Eleanor; m. Patricia Finley, 1988. BA, Yale U., 1950, MA, 1952, PhD, 1955; postgrad., Cambridge (Eng.) U., 1950-51. From instr. to asst. prof. English Ind. U., 1955-61; from asst. dean to assoc. dean, also assoc. prof. English Yale U., 1961-63, acting provost, 1963-64, provost, prof. English,, 1964-72, pres. rep., 1972-76; grad. C.G. Jung Inst., N.Y., 1979; pvt. practice, 1976—; bd. dirs. Globe Newspaper Co. Inc., Meridian Audio, Ltd. Author: The Early Collected Editions of Shelley's Poems, 1958; editor: Essays on the Odyssey, 1963; contbr. articles to profl. jours. Mem. com. on libr. Yale U. Coun., 1990-95; trustee Hampshire Coll., 1988-93. Mem. Internat. Assn. Analytical Psychology, Archive for Rsch. in Archetypal Symbolism (pres. 1987-93, treas. 1993—), N.Y. Assn. Analytical Psychology, Nat. Assn. for Advancement Psychoanalysis, Phi Beta Kappa. Home: 40 Rogers Ave Milford CT 06460-6435

TAYLOR, CLAUDE J., sales executive, consultant; b. Winston-Salem, N.C., Apr. 29, 1943; s. Claude V. and Jessie K. T.; m. Frances T. Denty, Dec. 22, 1962; children: Joseph Vinston, Jeffrey Alan, Marc David, Michael Edward. Student, U.S. Army Schs., 1961-62; AS in Aircraft Comms., Nat. Inst., 1966-68, AS in Indsl. Electronics, 1968-71; student, Palm Beach Jr. Coll., 1971-73. Inside salesman and office ops. Graybar Electric Co., West Palm Beach, Fla., 1964-66; mgr. Lewisville (N.C.) Shell Svc., 1966-67; salesman Joyce Foods, Inc., Lewisville, 1967-69; instrument tech. Pratt-Whitney Aircraft, West Palm Beach, 1969-73; tech. resp., instr., tech. mgr. Siemens Med. Systems, Iselin, N.J., 1973-87; salesman, mfr. rep. Ohmeda div. BOC, LIttleton, Colo., 1987-88; dist. sales mgr. Planmeca, Inc. and Planmed, Wood Dale, 1988-93; owner, pres. dental and medical sales Tech. Splty. Mktg., Jupiter, Fla., 1993—; cons. Instrumentarium Imaging, Inc., Milw., 1993—. With U.S. Army, 1961-64. Home: PO Box 1443 Jupiter FL 33468-1443 Office: Tech Splty 16220 128th Trl N Jupiter FL 33478-6527

TAYLOR, CLAYBORNE DUDLEY, engineering educator; b. Kokomo, Miss., July 15, 1938; s. Dudley Clayborne and Winnie Lee (Holmes) T.; m. Mary Jean Blue, June 23, 1963; children: Clayborne Dudley Jr., David Edward, Rebecca Lynn Taylor Burg. BS in Physics, Miss. State U., 1961; MS in Physics, N.Mex. State U., 1964, PhD in Physics, 1965. Registered profl. engr., Miss. Tech. staff mem. Sandia Labs., Albuquerque, 1965-67; assoc. prof. Miss. State U., Starkville, 1967-69, 1969-71, prof. elec. engring., 1972-86, 88-91, assoc. dean. engring., 1991—; prof. elec. engring. U. Miss., Oxford, 1971-72; vis. Stocker prof. Ohio U., Athens, 1986-88; cons. Phillips Lab., Albuquerque, 1972—. Author: High-Power Microwave Systems and Effects, 1994; contbr. articles to tech. jours. Recipient Cert. of Recognition, NASA, 1986; Electromagnetic Pulse Tech. fellow Summa Found., 1988. Mem. IEEE (sr.), Internat. Union of Radio Scientists, Am. Soc. Engring. Edn. Presbyterian. Home: 517 Greensboro St Starkville MS 39759-2861 Office: Miss State U Coll Engring 106 McCain Bldg PO Box 9544 Mississippi State MS 39762

TAYLOR, CLAYTON CHARLES, management and political legislative consultant; b. Douglas, Ariz., Feb. 9, 1952; s. Clay Arvle and Nellie Josephine (Swaggart) T.; m. Marian Jane Brehmer, July 18, 1981; children: Clayton Charles Jr., Gardner Clark. BSBA, Oklahoma State U., 1974. Lyndon Baines Johnson intern U.S. Ho. Reps., Washington, 1972; asst. to Congressman Clem McSpadden, 1972; asst. to Congressman Gillis Long U.S. Ho. of Reps., Washington, 1975, legis. dir. to Congressman Risenhoover, 1976, adminstrv. asst. to Congressman Hubbard, 1976-77; dir. fed. govt. rels. McDonald's Corp., Chgo., 1978-81; dir. govt. rels. Phillips Petroleum Co., Okla. City, 1982-85; western states dir. govt. rels. Phillips Petroleum Co., Denver, 1986-87; dir. govt. rels. and pub. affairs Phillips Petroleum Co., Oklahoma City, 1988-91; v.p. corp. affairs Coastal Aruba, San Nicolas, Aruba, Dutch West Indies, 1991-93; v.p. govt. affairs Coastal Corp., Houston, 1993-94; pres. The Taylor Consulting Group, Okla. City, 1994—, The Taylor Group. Campaign dir. 2d Dist. Congl. Campaign, Muskogee, Okla., 1976, Congressman Brewster, 3d Congl. Dist., 1994; agrl. cons. U.S.-Egyptian pvt. venture, Cairo and Washington, 1977; pres. alumni assn., bd. dirs. Leadership Okla., pres., 1991-92; founding chmn. Okla. Leadership Congress, 1989; v.p. Ballet Okla., 1989; bd. dirs. Better Bus. Bur., Okla. Energy Found., Internat. Sch. Aruba, chmn. internat. staff recruitement; mem. alumni bd. dirs. Okla. State U. Coll. Bus. Adminstrn.; found. bd. dirs., nat. program adv. com. South/West Energy Coun.; bd. dirs., state pres. coun. Okla. 4-H Club Found.; bd. dirs. Okla. City Met. Libr. Commn.; mem. nat. meeting adv. com. Nat. Conf. State Legislatures; nat. co-chmn., states coun. Consumers for Competitive Fuels. Recipient Nat. Leadership Excellence award Nat. Assn. Cmty. Leadership; named Outstanding Cmty. Leader Aruba, 1992-93. Fellow Amundsen Inst. for U.S.-Mex.; mem. Aruba Industry and Trade Assn. (mem. exec. bd. 1993-94), Okla. Mid-Continent Oil and Gas Assn. (exec. com. 1991), Okla. State U. Bus. Coll. Alumni Assn. (bd. dirs. 1987-89), Petroleum Club Oklahoma City, Houston City Club. Home: 3212 N Harvey Pky Oklahoma City OK 73118 Office: Bar 7 Ranch RR 1 Box 1785 Oktaha OK 74450-9768

TAYLOR, CLYDE CALVIN, JR., literary agent; b. Anderson, S.C., July 27, 1936; s. Clyde Calvin and Ellen Letitia (Hamilton) T.; m. children: Katie Taylor Legnini, Emily Taylor Bradley, Andrew Hamilton. A.B., Wofford Coll., 1958. Tchr. Westminster Schs., Atlanta, 1958; advt. copywriter Harper and Row, 1960, Macmillan & Co., 1961; advt. mgr. Collier-Macmillan Library Div., 1962; asst. bus. mgr. book div. Am. Heritage Pub. Co., 1963-65; dir. subs. rights G.P. Putnam's Sons, 1965-69; v.p. World Pub. Co., 1970; v.p., gen. mgr. G.P. Putnam's Sons, N.Y.C., 1972-74; v.p., pub. G.P. Putnam's Sons, 1974-77, exec. v.p., pub., 1977; pres. Clyde Taylor Lit. Agy., Inc., 1978-79; v.p. Curtis Brown Ltd., 1980-94; lit. agt. affiliated with Knox Burger Assocs., Ltd., 1994-96; v.p. Curtis Brown Ltd., 1996—. Home: 216 E 6th St New York NY 10003-8212

TAYLOR, D. LANSING, cell biology educator; b. Balt., Dec. 26, 1946. BS, U. Md., 1968; PhD in Biology, SUNY, Albany, 1973. Fellow biophysics Marine Biol. Labs., 1973-74; asst. prof. biology Harvard U., 1974-78, assoc. prof., 1978-82; prof. biology Carnegie-Mellon U., Pitts., 1982—. Editor Jour. Cell Biology, 1981—, Jour. Cell Motility, 1981—. Mem. Am. Soc. Cell Biology, Biophys. Soc., N.Y. Acad. Sci. Achievements include research in molecular basis of amoeboid movements, utilizing biochemical, cell biological and biophysical approaches and fluorescence spectroscopy. Office: Carnegie Mellon U Dept Biomed Engring Program 4400 5th Ave Pittsburgh PA 15213-2617*

TAYLOR, D(ARL) CODER, architect, engineer; b. Ft. Wayne, Ind., July 18, 1913; s. Frank A. and Edith (Zook) T.; m. Audrey Helen Larkin, June 5, 1944; children: Barbara Helen Taylor Reddy, Thomas Coder, Julie Marie Taylor Hitchins; m. Harriett Pribble Sinding, July 27, 1985. BArch, Carnegie Inst. Tech., 1935; spl. student, U. Wash., 1933. Draftsman Chgo., 1935; partner Zook & Taylor, architects, Chgo., 1939-42, Holsman, Holsman, Klekamp & Taylor, architects, Chgo., 1948-52, Yost & Taylor, architects and engrs., Kenilworth, Ill., 1952-60; chmn. Coder Taylor Assos., Inc., architects-engrs.-planners, Kenilworth, 1960-78; chmn. bd. Coder Taylor Assos., Inc., 1978-81, spl. cons., 1981—; cons. in field, 1935—. Prin. works include Mcpl. Bldg., St. Charles, Ill., 1940, listed Nat. Register Hist. Places, 1990, Prize Home No. 1, 1946 (Chgo. Tribune prize home competition), Sherman Garden Apts., 1951 (Chgo. chpt. AIA honor award), Kincheloe AFB, Mich., 1962 (Best Family Housing Project No. Area), Chanute AFB, Ill., 1959 (Best Family Housing Project Cen. Area), U.S. Naval Tng. Ctr., Great Lakes, Ill., 1964 (Merit award FHA), Swimming Pool House, Northfield, Ill., 1967 (Chgo. chpt. AIA-Chgo. Assn. Commerce and Industry Disting. Bldg. award), 510 Green Bay Rd. Bldg., Kenilworth, Ill. (AIA-Chgo. Assn. Commerce and Industry award 1967), Roberts Residence, Lake Forest, Ill., 1968 (AIA-Chgo. Assn. Commerce and Industry Disting. Bldg. award), Glenview Pub. Libr., 1970 (Chgo. chpt. AIA-Chgo. Assn. Commerce and Industry Disting. Bldg. award), Kroch's & Brentano's stores, Chgo., 1961-77, Des Plaines Pub. Libr., 1974 (Des Plaines C. of C. Outstanding Achievement award), Wilmette (Ill.) Park Dist. Recreation Ctr., 1974, Wilmette Village Adminstrn. Bldg., 1975, Glenview Cen. Fire Sta., 1976 (Glenview Appearance Commn. Outstanding Bldg. and Landscape award), Internat. Hdqrs. Alpha Phi Frat., Evanston, Ill., 1975, Barrington Area Pub. Libr., 1977; represented in spl. exhbns. and permanent collections Art Inst. Chgo., Chgo. Hist. Soc., Wilmette Hist. Soc., Evanston Hist. Soc., Graham Found.; author: Oral History of D. Coder Taylor, 1989; contbr. articles to profl. jours. Mem. Glenview (Ill.) Planning Commn., 1962-65; chmn. Glenview Appearance Commn., 1968-72, Picasso Day Com., Chgo., 1967; mem. fine arts com. Ill. Sesquicentennial Commn., 1967-68; exec. com., treas. Fedn. Open Lakefront, 1966-68; mem. tech. studies adv. com. NAS-NRC, 1962—; mem. tech. panel, adv. com. HUD, NAS, NAE, 1969; nat. panel arbitrators Am. Arbitrators Assn., 1952—. Lt. comdr. Civil Engr. Corps USNR, 1942-45. Recipient merit award for archtl. accomplishments Carnegie-Mellon U. Alumni Assn., 1982. Fellow AIA (dir. Chgo. chpt. 1965-66, pres. 1967, v.p. Ill. council 1968); mem. Ill. Assn. Professions (dir. 1968), Mich. Soc. Architects, Nat. Assn. Redevel. Ofcls., Tau Sigma Delta (pres. 1934- 35), Sigma Phi Epsilon (pres. 1934-35), Scarab (1934-35). Methodist. Club: North Shore Country (Glenview, Ill.). Home and Office: 727 Redwood Ln Glenview IL 60025-4460 *" Early in my professional career, I decided that quality of work created was more important than quantity. To have the largest practice was not to be the goal, but rather to have personal involvement in the work produced, which would result in less work, but work of high class and character.". Architecture has been the focus of my life from childhood to the present day! Its interesting history dates to the earliest of times, with design appearances reflecting society, religion, geography, economy, and materials. My lifelong practice has given me a wonderful, rewarding and pleasurable existence, and it has been most gratifying to be able to make some contribution.*

TAYLOR, DAVID, clergy member, religious administrator. Dir. World Witness Dept. of the Pentecostal Free Will Baptist Ch., Dunn, N.C. Office: The Pentecostal Baptist Ch PO Box 1568 Dunn NC 28335-1568

TAYLOR, DAVID BROOKE, lawyer, banker; b. Salt Lake City, Oct. 14, 1942; s. Lee Neff and June Taylor; m. Carolyn Kaufholz, May 29, 1965; children: Stewart, Allison. BA, U. Utah, 1964; JD, Columbia U., 1967. Bar: N.Y. 1967, N.C. 1995. Ptnr. Wickes, Riddell, Bloomer, Jacobi & McGuire, N.Y.C., 1967-79, Morgan, Lewis & Bockius, N.Y.C., 1979-89; banker, lawyer Chase Manhattan Bank, N.A., N.Y.C., 1989-92; pres. Geoenertec Corp., N.Y.C., 1992-93; ptnr. Fennebresque, Clark, Swindall & Hay, Charlotte, N.C., 1994—. Mem. ABA, N.Y. State Bar Assn., Internat. Bar Assn. Home: 3815 Beresford Rd Charlotte NC 28211 Office: Fennebresque Clark Swindell & Hay 100 N Tryon St Ste 2900 Charlotte NC 28202-4000

TAYLOR, DAVID GEORGE, retired banker; b. Charlevoix, Mich., July 29, 1929; s. Frank Flagg and Bessie (Strayer) T.; m. Robyne T. McCarthy, July 28, 1990; children from previous marriage: David, Amy, Jeanine. BS, Denison U., 1951; MBA, Northwestern U., 1953. With Continental Ill. Nat. Bank and Trust Co. Chicago, 1958-86, asst. cashier, 1961-64, 2d v.p., 1964-66, v.p., 1966-72, sr. v.p., 1972-74, exec. v.p., 1974-80, exec. v.p., treas., 1980-83, vice chmn., 1983-84, chmn., chief exec. officer, 1984; vice chmn. Irving Trust Co., N.Y.C., 1986-89; group exec. Chem. Bank, N.Y.C., 1989-94, ret., 1994. Mem. Dealer Bank Assn. Com. on Glass-Steagall Reform, 1985-86. Bd. dirs. Evanston Hosp., Glenbrook Hosp.; trustee Art Inst. Chgo., 1981-86; advisor J.L. Kellogg Grad. Sch. Mgmt., Northwestern U., 1984—; bd. dirs. CNA Income Shares. Served to lt. USN, 1953-56. Mem. Pub. Securities Assn. (bd. dirs. 1977-78, chmn. 1977, treas. 1978), Govt. and Fed. Agys. Securities Com. (chmn. bd. dirs. 1982-83), Assn. Res. City Bankers (asset/liability com/govt. relations com. 1983—). Republican. Presbyterian.

TAYLOR, DAVID KERR, international business educator, consultant; b. Oxford, N.C., Oct. 11, 1928; s. David Kerr and Myrtle Norman (Shamburger) T.; m. Isabel de Sousa Botelho de Albuquerque, Apr. 23, 1960; children: Anne de Albuquerque Taylor Grave, Katherine Rowena Taylor. BA, Duke U., 1947, JD, 1949. Bar: N.Y., N.C. Atty. Ins. Co. N.Am., N.Y.C., 1949-51, Milbank, Tweed, Hadley & McCloy, N.Y.C., 1954-55; internat. exec. Mobil Corp., N.Y.C., Washington, Can., Portugal, Nigeria, France, others, 1955-86; rsch. prof. internat. affairs, sr. fellow intrnat. bus. Georgetown U. Sch. Fgn. Svc., Washington, 1987—; pres. Luso-Am. Bus. Coun., 1987-89; bd. visitors Duke U. Law Sch. 1st lt. U.S. Army, 1951-54, Germany. Mem. Am. Portuguese Soc. (bd. dirs., pres. 1968-70, 76-80), Washington Export Coun., Textile Mus. Adv. Coun., Washington Inst. Fgn. Affairs, Cosmos Club, Phi Beta Kappa. Avocations: piano playing, singing. Home: 2737 Devonshire Pl NW Washington DC 20008-3479 Office: Georgetown U Sch Fgn Svc Washington DC 20057

TAYLOR, DAVID WYATT AIKEN, retired clergyman; b. Tsingkiangpu, Kiangsu, China, Dec. 13, 1925; s. Hugh Kerr and Fanny Bland (Graham) T.; m. Lillian Ross McCulloch, Aug. 25, 1951; children: Frances Bland, David Wyatt. B.A., Vanderbilt U., 1949; B.D. cum laude, Union Theol. Sem. Va., 1952; Th.M., Princeton Theol. Sem., 1953; D.D. (hon.), King Coll., Bristol, Tenn., 1959. Ordained to ministry Presbyn. Ch. U.S., 1952. Pastor chs. Elkton, Va., 1953-55, Bristol, Va., 1955-62; ednl. sec. bd. world missions Presbyn. Ch. U.S., 1962-68, program div. dir., 1968-73; ecumenical officer gen. assembly mission bd. Presbyn. Ch. U.S., Atlanta, 1973-82; pastor Orange Park Presbyn. Ch., Orange Park, Fla., 1982-86; gen. sec. for strategy and interpretation Consultation on Ch. Union, Princeton, N.J., 1986-88, gen. sec., 1988-93; ret., 1993; instr. Bible Presbyn. Jr. Coll., Maxton, N.C., 1951; mem. program bd., div. Christian edn. Nat. Council Chs., 1965-69, bd. mgrs., dept. edn. for mission, 1962-68, mem. program bd., div. overseas ministries, 1968-78, mem. governing bd., 1976-80, chmn. governing bd. credentials com., 1978; chmn. Church World Service, Inc., 1973-75; mem. adminstrn. and fin. com. Nat. Council Chs., 1973-75, mem. commn. on faith and order, 1978-93; mem. commn. on interchurch aid World Council Chs., 1973-75; mem. 5th Assembly, 1975; rep. Presbyn. Ch. U.S. to World Alliance Ref. Chs., 1976-82; bd. dirs. Presbyn. Survey mag., 1963-68; mem. Consultation on Ch. Union, 1974-93; chmn. Nat. Ecumenical Officers Assn., 1978-81. Bd. dirs. Abingdon Presbytery's Children's Home, Wytheville, Va., 1958-62. Served with AUS, 1944-46, PTO. Mem. Sigma Chi. Home: PO Box 1898 Elizabethtown NC 28337-1898

TAYLOR, DENNIS DEL, marketing executive; b. St. Louis, Oct. 23, 1946; s. James Henry and Helen Ruby (Dell) T.; m. Dorothy June Henthorn, July 26, 1968; 1 child, Keith Gregory. BSBA, U. Mo., 1970; MBA, Fontbonne Coll., 1994. Dept. mgr. Famous-Barr Co., St. Louis, 1965-69; acct. exec. Union Central Life Ins. Co., Cin., 1969-71; dist. sales mgr. Hallmark Cards, Inc., Kansas City, Mo., 1971-80, Steelcase, Inc., Grand Rapids, Mich., 1980-81; v.p. sales and mktg. Holscher-Werning, Inc., St. Louis, 1981-84, Bus. Interiors, Inc., St. Louis, 1984-91; nat. sales mgr. Harvard Ind., St. Louis, 1991-93; v.p. sales and mktg. Tiffany Office Furniture, St. Louis, 1993-94,

Berco Industries, St. Louis, 1994—. Mem. exec. coun. Luth. Family and Children's Svcs., 1989. Mem. Nat. Office Products Assn., Downtown St. Louis, Sales and Mktg. Execs. St. Louis, Optimists, Mo. Athletic Club, Hidden Valley Golf Club. Republican. Mem. Assembly of God Ch. Avocations: golf, boating, skiing, hunting. Home: 2215 Kehrsglen Ct Chesterfield MO 63005-6518 Office: Berco Industries 1120 Montrose Ave Saint Louis MO 63104-1828

TAYLOR, DONALD, retired manufacturing company executive; b. Worcester, Mass., June 2, 1927; s. John A. B. and Alice M. (Weaver) T.; m. Ruth L. Partridge, June 24, 1950; children: Linda Taylor Robertson, Donald, Mark, John. BSME, Worcester Poly. Inst., 1949; grad., Northeastern U. Mgmt. Devel. Program, 1962, Harvard Bus. Sch. Advanced Mgmt. Program, 1979. Registered profl. engr., Mass. With George J. Meyer Mfg. Co., Milw., 1954-69; pres. mfg. div. A-T-O, Inc., 1969; exec. v.p. Nordberg div. Rex Chainbelt, Inc., Milw., 1969-73; v.p. ops. Rexnord Inc., Brookfield, Wis., pres., chief operating officer, 1978-85, chief exec. officer, from 1985, chmn., 1985-88; pres. Nordberg Machinery Group, Milw., 1973-78; dir. Harnischfeger Corp., Johnson Controls, Inc., Banta Corp. Bd. dirs. Blood Ctr. Southeastern Wis., Greater Milw. Com., Met. Milw. YMCA; bd. dirs. Milw. Symphony Orch. Served with USNR, 1951-54. Mem. ASME. Clubs: Milw. Country, Milw. Athletic, Town, Univ., Masons. Office: 7850 N Club Cir Milwaukee WI 53217-2939

TAYLOR, DONALD ARTHUR, marketing educator; b. Windsor, Ont., Can., Sept. 27, 1923; came to U.S., 1947, naturalized, 1955; s. David Cameron and Eva (Perry) T.; m. Shirley Marion Jenner, 1949; children: John Cameron, Stephen Bruce, Michael James. B.A., U. Western Ont., 1947; M.B.A., U. Mich., 1949, Ph.D. (Horace H. Rackham fellow), 1955. Asst. prof. marketing Mich. State U. at, East Lansing, 1955-58; asso. prof. Mich. State U. at, 1958-62, prof., 1962—, chmn. dept. marketing and transportation adminstrn., 1969-81, prof., 1981-84, chmn. dept. mktg. and transp. adminstrn., 1984-86, chmn., prof. emeritus, 1986—; adviser, chief of party to mission at various univs., Brazil, 1956-58, 62-64; dir. Latin Am. Studies Center, 1968-69; also co-dir. Latin-Am. Market Planning Center, sr. cons. food distbn. studies, N.E. Brazil, Colombia; cons. Geigy Agrl. Chems., Johnson & Johnson Domestic Operating Co., Ford Motor Co., Westinghouse Electric Corp., Whirlpool Corp., Burroughs Corp.; dir. Clark-Graveley Corp., 1972-77. Author: (with D.J. Luck, D.A. Taylor, H. Wales, R. Rubin) Marketing Research, 6th edit, 1982, (with T.A. Staudt, D.A. Taylor and D.J. Bowersox) A Managerial Introduction to Marketing, 3d edit, 1976, (with D.A. Taylor) Institution Building in Business Administration: The Brazilian Experience, 1968, (with Bowersox, Cooper, Lambert and Taylor) Management in Marketing Channels, 1980. Mem. bd. edn. Holt Sch. Dist., 1960-62. Recipient Homenagen Especial award 1st graduating class Escola de Administracao de Empresas, Sao Paulo, Brazil, 1958; named hon. prof., 1964. Mem. Am. Marketing Assn. (bd. dirs. 1969). Home: 3724 Harolds Rd Traverse City MI 49686-9435

TAYLOR, DONNA BLOYD, vocational rehabilitation consultant; b. Louisville, Ky., July 15, 1958; d. Donald Ray Bloyd and Georgia Carmen (Bryant) Whitehead; 1 child, Stephanie Micah Taylor; m. Douglas A. Garner, June 6, 1992. BS, U. Louisville, 1981, MEd, 1982. Lic. profl. counselor, qualified rehab. provider, Ohio; cert. rehab. counselor U.S. Dept. Labor; qualified rehab. coord., Ky.; cert. disability mgmt. specialist; cert. case mgr., vocat. evaluator, nat. counselor; diplomate Am. Bd. Vocat. Experts; qualified mental retardation profl.; cert. vocat. evaluator, RAS. Program coord. Hazelwood ICF-MR, Louisville, 1981-83; lead vocat. therapist Rehab. Ctr. Southeastern Ind., Clarksville, 1983-85; regional supr., vocat. cons. Rehab. Coords., Inc., Louisville, 1985; asst. mgr., rehab. cons. Nat. Rehab. Cons., Cin., 1985-88; dist. mgr., vocat. cons. Recovery Unlimited, Inc., Cin., 1988-92; pvt. practice, Lawrenceburg, Ind., 1992—; vocat. expert Social Security Adminstrn. Co-author: (with Timothy Field and others) Study Guide to the CIRS Exam, 1992, The St. Thomas Resource on Certification, Ethics and Training for Private Sector Rehabilitation, 1993, CCM Study Guide, 1994. Vol. Am. Cancer Soc., mem. Rape Crisis Intervention Team. Mem. Nat. Assn. Rehab. Profls. in Pvt. Sector (past pres. Ky. chpt., SCRB com., co-chair internat. affairs divsn.), Nat. Rehab. Assn., Nat. Forensic Ctr., Nat. Disting. Svc. Registry, Individual Case Mgmt. Assn., U. Louisville Alumni Assn., Disability Network Ohio-Solidarity, Rehab. Referral Network, Rehab. Internat., Phi Kappa Phi. Democrat. Methodist. Office: 15 Mary St Lawrenceburg IN 47025-1919

TAYLOR, DONNA LYNNE, adult education coordinator; b. Balt., July 1, 1944; d. Noel Leroy and Dorothy Anna (Henry) Welsh; 1 child, Tom A., Jr. BS, Okla. State U., 1965, EdD, 1992; MS, Phillips U., 1984. Cert. vocat. bus. and trade and indsl. edn. tchr., prin., supt., vocat. adminstr., Okla. Retail sales Tulsa, 1961-62; secretary Okla. State U. Coop. Extension Svc., Stillwater, 1965-67; secondary instr. social studies Waller Jr. High, Enid, Okla., 1967-69; substitute instr. Autry Tech. Ctr., Enid, 1971-78, instr. vocat. bus. part-time, 1978-84, instr. vocat. bus. full time, 1984-94, coord. adult edn., 1994—; small bus. owner Lynne's Country Crafts, Enid, 1975-85; coord. adult edn. Autry Tech. Ctr., Enid, 1994—; adult educator Sch. Continuing Edn., Enid, 1981-85; mem. strategic planning com. and policy and procedures com. Staff Devel. Affirmative Action, Enid, 1989—; presenter ann. confs. and meetings Okla. State Dept. Vocat. Tech., Stillwater, 1991-92; coord., chair Articulation Agreement Com., Enid, 1991-93; advisor FBLA/Phi Beta Lambda, Enid, 1990-94; mem. North Ctrl. Accreditation Steering Com., 1992-93, staff devel. chair, 1993-94. Bd. dirs. Sch. Continuing Edn., Enid, 1975-85; mem. vol. YWCA, March of Dimes, Am. Heart Assn., MS Soc., Am. Diabetes Assn., Enid Art Assn., 1985—; deacon Christian Ch., Enid, 1986-88, elder, 1988-92, 95-96; active Leadership Greater Enid. Recipient Women of Achievement award March of Dimes, 1992; named Okla. Bus. Tchr. of Yr., 1994. Mem. Am. Vocat. Assn., Okla Vocat. Assn., Enid C. of C. (edn. com. 1991-92), Phi Delta Kappa (sec. 1992—), PEO Sisterhood. Republican. Avocations: art, volunteering, reading. Home: 2110 Appomattox Enid OK 73703-2008 Office: Autry Tech Ctr 1201 W Willow Rd Enid OK 73703-2506

TAYLOR, DORIS DENICE, physician, entrepreneur; b. Indpls., Sept. 19, 1955; d. Eugene and Mary Catherine (Ryder) T. BA, U. Minn., 1976, cert. behavior analyst, 1977, MD, 1983; BS, Purdue U., 1979. Diplomate Nat. Bd. Med. Examiners. Pvt. practice Locumtenens, 1989—; mng. dir. Sebree-Watkins-Ovbokhan Meml. Cancer Fund, Indpls.; pres., CEO Taylors of Indy Corp., Indpls.; oncologic svcs. cons. and developer. Lange scholar, U. Minn., 1980, Joseph Collins Found. scholar, 1980-81, Nat. Med. Fellowship scholar, 1980-81. Mem. AMA, Am. Soc. for Therapeutic Radiology and Oncology, Am. Soc. Clin. Oncologists. Office: Taylors of Indy Corp 55 Monument Cir Ste 814 Indianapolis IN 46204-2951

TAYLOR, DUNCAN PAUL, research neuropharmacologist; b. Bremerton, Wash., Feb. 4, 1949; s. Alan Earl and Barbara Eleanor (Thiel) T.; m. Jeanne Louise Damgaard, Apr. 8, 1972; 1 child, Aubrey Elizabeth. BS in Chemistry, Calif. Inst. Tech., 1971; PhD in Biochemistry, Oreg. State U., 1977. Technician analytical svcs. Carnation Co. Rsch. Labs., Van Nuys, Calif., 1967-70; Peace Corps vol. Princess Margaret Secondary Sch., St. Johns, Antigua and Barbuda, 1971-73; grad. teaching and rsch. asst. biochemistry and biophysics Oreg. State U., Corvallis, 1973-77; rsch. assoc. sect. biochemistry and pharmacology NIMH, Bethesda, Md., 1977-79; scientist, neuropharmacologist, rsch. assoc. Pharm. div. Mead Johnson & Co., Evansville, Ind., 1979-80, sr. scientist, group leader, 1980-82; sr. scientist, group leader, neuropharmacologist Pharm. R & D div. Bristol-Myers Co., Evansville, 1982-83; sr. rsch. scientist, mgr. Pharm. R & D div. Bristol-Myers Co., 1983-85, rsch. fellow preclin. cen. nervous system rsch., 1985-89; sr. rsch. fellow preclin. cen. nervous system rsch. Pharm. Rsch. Inst. Bristol-Myers Squibb Co., Wallingford, Conn.; dir. pharmacology Symphony Pharms., Malvern, Pa., 1994-95; cons., 1995-96; analyst bus. devel. Pharmacia & Upjohn, Kalamazoo, Mich., 1996—; mem. external adv. bd. dept. chemistry U. So. Miss.; grant reviewer NSF, 1981, 2, Med. Rsch. Coun. Can., 1987, 88; frequent presenter to profl. confs. Contbr. numerous articles and abstracts to profl. jours. Bd. dirs. Posey County chpt. Am. Cancer Soc., 1983-85; mem. chancel choir 1st United Meth. Ch., Mt. Vernon, Ind., 1979-86, mem. adminstrv. bd., 1980-83, 84-86; mem. Tri-State Cursillo Community; mentor Horizons Leadership Acad., Evansville-Vanderburgh Sch. Corp., 1985; mem. adult choir South Congl. Ch., Middletown, Conn., 1986-96, deacon, 1987-90, 95-96, co-chmn., 1989-90, 96, mem. coun., 1989-90, mem. task force on long-range planning, 1989-90; mem. adult choir 2d Reformed Ch., Kalamazoo, 1997—, Handbell Choir, 1997—; cons. Project Bus., Jr. Achievement, 1988. Scholar Carnation Co., 1967-70, Calif. State scholar, 1967-68, 70; rsch. fellow NSF, 1970, Cold Spring Harbor Labs., 1974. Fellow Am. Inst. Chemists; mem. AAAS, Am. Chem. Soc., Am. Soc. for Pharmacology and Exptl. Therapeutics, Soc. for Neurosci. (v.p. Conn. chpt. 1989-93), Brit. Brain Rsch. Assn., European Brain and Behavior Soc., Fedn. Am. Socs. for Exptl. Biology, Internat. Brain Rsch. Orgn.-World Fedn. Neuroscientists, Sigma Xi, Phi Lambda Upsilon. Democrat. Achievements include patent for method and treatment of ischemia in the brain; made significant efforts in identification and development of new antipsychotics and antidepressants; identification of potential mechanism of action of the antipsychotic BMY14802; research in receptors, in etiology, expression and pharmacotherapy of psychiatric disorders. Home: 8722 W F Ave Kalamazoo MI 49009-8895

TAYLOR, EDNA JANE, employment program representative; b. Flint, Mich., May 16, 1934; d. Leonard Lee and Wynona Ruth (Davis) Harvey; children: Wynona Jane MacDonald, Cynthia Lee Zellmer. BS, No. Ariz. U., 1963; MEd, U. Ariz., 1967. Tchr. high sch. Sunnyside Sch. Dist., Tucson, 1963-68; employment program rep. employment devel. State of Calif., Canoga Park, 1968—. Mem. adv. coun. Van Nuys Cmty. Adult Sch., Calif., 1983—, steering com., 1989-91, leadership coun., 1991-92; mem. adv. coun. Pierce C.C., Woodland Hills, Calif., 1979-81; first aid instr., recreational leader ARC. Mem. NAFE, Internat. Assn. of Pers. in Employment Security, Calif. Employment Counselors Assn. (state treas. 1978-79, state sec. 1980), Delta Psi Kappa (life). Avocations: writing, tennis, health and fitness. Office: State of Calif Employment Devel Dept 21010 Vanowen St Canoga Park CA 91303-2804

TAYLOR, EDWARD CURTIS, chemistry educator; b. Springfield, Mass., Aug. 3, 1923; s. Edward Curtis and Margaret Louise (Anderson) T.; m. Virginia Dion Crouse, June 29, 1946; children: Edward Newton, Susan Raines. Student, Hamilton Coll., 1942-44, DSc (hon.), 1969; AB, Cornell U., 1946, PhD, 1949. Postdoctoral fellow Nat. Acad. Scis., Zurich, Switzerland, 1949-50; DuPont postdoctoral fellow chemistry U. Ill., 1950-51, faculty, 1951-54, asst. prof. organic chemistry, 1952-54; faculty Princeton U., 1954—, prof. chemistry, 1964—, A. Barton Hepburn prof. organic chemistry, 1966—, chmn. dept. chemistry, 1974-79; vis. prof. Technische Hochschule, Stuttgart, Fed. Republic Germany, 1960, U. East Anglia, 1969, 71; Disting. vis. prof. U. Buffalo, 1968, U. Wyo., 1977; Backer lectr. U. Groningen, Holland, 1969; mem. chemistry adv. com. Office Sci. Research, USAF, 1962-73, Cancer Chemotherapy Nat. Service Ctr., 1958-62; mem. internat. adv. bd. Ctr. Medicinal Chemistry, Bar-Ilan U., Israel, 1994—; cons. rsch. divs. Procter & Gamble, 1953-80, Eastman Kodak Co., 1965-83, Tenn. Eastman Co., 1968-83, Eli Lilly & Co., 1970—, Burroughs Wellcome Co., 1983-95, E.I. duPont de Nemours & Co., 1986-90, Polaroid Corp., 1986—, Dow Elanco Co., 1989—, DuPont Merck Pharm. Co., 1990—. Author: (with McKillop) Chemistry of Cyclic Enaminonitriles and o-Aminonitriles, 1970, Principles of Heterocyclic Chemistry: film and audio courses, 1974; editor (with Raphael and Wynberg) Advances in Organic Chemistry, vols I-V, 1960-65, (with Wynberg) Vol VI, 1969, vols. VII-IX, 1970-79 (with W. Pfleiderer) Pteridine Chemistry, 1964, The Chemistry of Heterocyclic Compounds, 1968—, General Heterocyclic Chemistry, 1968—; organic chemistry editl. advisor John Wiley & Sons, Inc., 1968—; mem. editl. adv. bd. Jour. Medicinal Chemistry, 1962-66, Jour. Organic Chemistry, 1971-75, Synthetic Communications, 1971—, Heterocycles, 1973—, Chm. Substructure Index, 1971—, Advances in Heterocyclic Chemistry, 1983—, Pteridines, 1989—. Recipient rsch. awards SmithKline and French Found., 1955, Hoffmann-LaRoche Foun., 1964-65, Ciba Found., 1971, Disting. Hamilton award, 1977, U.S. Sr. Scientist prize Alexander von Humboldt Found., 1983, Disting. Alumni medal Hamilton Coll., 1990, F. Gowland Hopkins medal, 1993; sr. faculty fellow Harvard U., 1959; Guggenheim fellow, 1979-80. Fellow N.Y. Acad. Scis., Am. Inst. Chemists; mem. Am. Chem. Soc. (award for creative work in synthetic organic chemistry, 1974, chmn. organic chemistry div. 1976-77, Arthur C. Cope scholar award 1994), German Chem. Soc., Chem. Soc. London, Internat. Soc. Heterocyclic Chemistry (5th Internat. award 1989), Phi Beta Kappa, Sigma Xi, Phi Kappa Phi. Home: 288 Western Way Princeton NJ 08540-5337

TAYLOR, EDWARD MICHAEL, insurance and risk management consultant; b. Cambridge, Mass., June 26, 1947; s. Edward D. and Rita P. (Collins) T.; children from previous marriage: Philip A., Donandrea M.; m. Leslie Foxen, 1996; children: Erica Ingraham, Lindsay Ingraham. BSA, Bentley Coll., Waltham, Mass., 1970. V.p. J.H. Albert Internat. Ins. Advisors, Needham, Mass., 1974-80; prin., exec. v.p. Pine Ins. Agy., Melrose, Mass., 1980-83; pres., chief exec. officer, founder Taylor Risk Mgmt. Assocs., New Bedford, Mass., 1983-92; sr. v.p. Kevin F. Donoghue and Assocs., Boston, 1992—. 2d lt. USNG, 1971-76. Decorated Internat. Order of Merit; recipient Leadership award for contbns. to risk mgmt. profession. Mem. Internat. Ins. Soc., Soc. Risk Mgmt. Cons., Risk and Ins. Soc. Am., Am. Biog. Inst. (Disting. Leadership award 1988, apptd. hon. mem. rsch. bd. advisors 1988), Am. Arbitration Assn. (appointed to nat. panel of arbitrators), Am. Fin. Assn., KC (dep. grand knight), Assn. of Contingency Planners. Office: Kevin F Donoghue & Assocs 200 Lincoln St Boston MA 02111-2418

TAYLOR, EDWARD STEWART, physician, educator; b. Hecla, S.D., Aug. 20, 1911; s. Robert Stewart and Sylvia Frances (Dewey) T.; m. Ruth Fatherson, June 15, 1940; children: Edward Stewart, Elizabeth Dewey Taylor Bryant, Catherine Wells Taylor. B.A., U. Iowa, 1933, M.D., 1936. Diplomate Am. Bd. Ob-Gyn (dir. 1962-69). Intern, Hurley Hosp., Flint, Mich., 1936-37; splty. tng. ob-gyn L.I. Coll. Hosp., 1937-41; prof. ob-gyn, chmn. dept. Sch. Medicine, U. Colo., 1947-76, clin. prof., 1976-81, prof., chmn. emeritus, 1981—; nat. cons. ob-gyn to surg. gen. USAF, 1958-62. Author: Manual of Gynecology, 1952, Essentials of Gynecology, 4th edit.; editor: Beck's Obstetrical Practice, 10th edit.; editor-in-chief for obstetrics: Obstetrical and Gynecol. Survey, 1967-92. Trustee Denver Symphony Orch., 1979-85. Served to lt. col. AUS, 1942-45. Fellow ACS, Am. Coll. Obstetricians and Gynecologists (Disting. Svc. award 1984); mem. AMA, Am. Gynecol. Soc. (v.p. 1974-75), Am. Assn. Obstetricians and Gynecologists (pres. 1970-71), Ctrl. Assn. Obstetricians and Gynecologists, S.W. Obstet. and Gynecol. Soc. (hon.), Am. Gynecol. and Obstet. Soc., Assn. Profs. Ob-Gyn (pres. 1974-75), Western Surg. Soc., Finnish Gynecol. Soc. (hon.), University Club (Denver), Alpha Omega Alpha. Congregationalist. Club: University (Denver). Home: 80 S Dexter St Denver CO 80222-1051

TAYLOR, ELDON, psychologist researcher; b. Anchorage, Utah, Jan. 27, 1945; s. Blaine Eldon and Helen Gertrude (George) T.; children: Roy, Angela, Eric, Cassandra, Hillarie, Preston. Student, Weber State Coll., Ogden, Utah, 1971-74; BS, MS, DD, U. Metaphysics, L.A., PhD in Pastoral Psychology, 1986; PhD in Clin. Psychology, St. John's U., Springfield, La., 1990; HHD (hon.), Sem. Coll., 1987; PhD in Pastoral Psychology (hon.), World U. Roundtable, Benson, Ariz., 1988. Dir. Bulwark, Salt Lake City, 1977-84; pres., dir. Progressive Awareness Rsch., Spokane, Wash., 1984—; bd. dirs. World U. Roundtable, Benson, Ariz.; co-founder Creative Living Inst., 1993; mem. adj. faculty St. John's U., 1989—. Author: Thinking Without Thinking, 1995, Subliminal Communication, 1986, Subliminal Learning, 1988, Simple Things and Simple Thoughts, 1989, Wellness: Just a State of Mind, 1993, others; contbr. numerous articles and poetry to various publs.; author numerous audiocassettes on self-improvement; patentee whole brain info. audio processor. Spiritual advisor Intermountain Hospice Ctr., Salt Lake City, 1987-88; counselor Utah State Prison, Draper, 1986-88; sports motivation trainer U.S. Judo Team, Colorado Springs, Colo., 1989—. Named Ky. Col., State of Ky., 1984; recipient Golden Poet award Am. Poetry Soc., 1985-87. Fellow Nat. Assn. Clergy Hypnotherapists; mem. Am. Psychol. Practitioners Assn., Am. Law Enforcement Officers Assn., Internat. Assn. for Forensic Hypnosis, Am. Counselors Soc., Internat. Soc. Stress Analysts, Am. Assn. Religious Counselors. Avocations: physics, horses. Home: PO Box 13249 Spokane WA 99213-3249 Office: Progressive Awareness Rsch 21203 W Beechwood Rd Medical Lake WA 99022-8630

TAYLOR, ELDON DONIVAN, government official; b. Holdenville, Okla., July 29, 1929; s. Rome B. and Alma (Collins) T.; m. Hypatia Ethel Roberts, Feb. 7, 1953; 1 child, Teresa Lynn. Student, Murry State A. and M. Coll., 1948-49, George Washington U., 1949-50; B.S. cum laude, Am. U., 1959, M.A., 1966, postgrad., 1966-68. Research budget analyst, budgetary adminstrn. Office Naval Research, Navy Dept., Washington, 1949-51, 55-56; chief research and devel. budget sect., research and devel. planning adminstrn. Bur. Ordnance, 1956-60; dir. program rev. and resources, mgmt. div. research, devel. planning and adminstrn. Office Space Scis., NASA, Washington, 1960-70; dep. asst. adminstr. for resources mgmt. EPA, 1970-73; asst. dir. adminstrn. NSF, 1973-79; insp. gen. NASA, 1979-80; dir. adminstrn. Va. Ctr. Innovative Tech., 1984-85; v.p. Assn. Univs. for Research in Astronomy, 1985-86; pres. Taylor Mgmt. Assistance Inc., 1987—. Served with USAF, 1951-55. Recipient Commendation award for outstanding performance Dept. Navy, 1958; William A. Jump Meritorious award for achievement in pub. adminstrn., 1964; Exceptional Service award NASA, 1969; Disting. Service award NSF, 1978. Mem. Am. Soc. Pub. Adminstrn. (past sec. com. research pub. adminstrn.), Assn. Univs. for Research in Astronomy, Pi Sigma Alpha, Phi Theta Kappa. Home and Office: 7931 Wolf Run Hills Rd Fairfax Station VA 22039-2101

TAYLOR, ELISABETH COLER, secondary school educator; b. N.Y.C., Jan. 24, 1942; d. Gerhard Helmut and Judith (Horowitz) C.; m. Billie Wesley Taylor II, Jan. 27, 1960; children: Letitia Rose, Billie Albert. Student, Wilmington Coll., 1959-60; BS, Wayne State U., Detroit, 1969; MS, The Ohio State U., 1980; postgrad., Wright State U., Dayton, Ohio, 1989—. Cert. home economist. H.s. tchr. home econs., computer sci., lang. arts Dayton (Ohio) City Schs., 1972—. Bd. mem. Camp Fire Girls, 1970-71, vol. Detroit Mus. of Art, 1970-71, group leader Camp Fire Girls, Boy Scouts, Detroit, 1968-74. Mem. AAUW (life), NEA, Ohio Edn. Assn., Dayton Edn. Assn. Avocations: birding, travelling, needlework. Home: 131 Snow Hill Ave Dayton OH 45429-1705

TAYLOR, ELIZABETH ROSEMOND, actress; b. London, Feb. 27, 1932; d. Francis and Sara (Sothern) T. Student, Byron House, Hawthorne Sch., Metro-Goldwyn-Mayer Sch. Motion pictures include There's One Born Every Minute, 1942, Lassie Come Home, 1943, The White Cliffs of Dover, 1944, Jane Eyre, 1944, National Velvet, 1944, Courage of Lassie, 1946, Cynthia, 1947, Life with Father, 1947, A Date with Judy, 1948, Julia Misbehaves, 1948, Little Women, 1950, Conspirator, 1950, The Big Hangover, 1950, Father of the Bride, 1950, Father's Little Dividend, 1951, A Place in the Sun, 1951, Callaway Went Thataway, 1951, Love Is Better Than Ever, 1952, Ivanhoe, 1952, The Girl Who Had Everything, 1953, Elephant Walk, 1954, Rhapsody, 1954, Beau Brummel, 1954, The Last Time I Saw Paris, 1954, Giant, 1956, Raintree County, 1957, Cat on a Hot Tin Roof, 1958, Suddenly Last Summer, 1959, Scent of Mystery, 1960, Butterfield 8, 1960 (Acad. award best actress), Cleopatra, 1963, The V.I.P.'s, 1963, The Sandpiper, 1965, Who's Afraid of Virginia Woolf?, 1966 (Acad. award best actress), The Taming of the Shrew, 1967, The Comedians, 1967, Reflections in a Golden Eye, 1967, Dr. Faustus, 1967, Boom!, 1968, Secret Ceremony, 1968, The Only Game in Town, 1970, Under Milkwood, 1971, X, Y and Zee, 1972, Hammersmith Is Out, 1972, Night Watch, 1973, Ash Wednesday, 1973, That's Entertainment, 1974 (guest star), The Driver's Seat, 1974, Blue Bird, 1975, Winter Kills, 1977, A Little Night Music, 1977, The Mirror Crack'd, 1980, Young Toscanini, 1988, The Flintstones, 1994; TV appearances include Divorce His/Divorce Hers, 1973, Victory at Entebbe, 1977, Return Engagement, 1979, Between Friends, 1982, Hotel (series), 1984, Malice in Wonderland, 1986, North and South (miniseries), 1986, There Must Be a Pony, 1986, Poker Alice, 1987, Sweet Bird of Youth, 1989; theatre appearances in The Little Foxes, 1981 (Broadway debut), Private Lives, 1983; narrator film documentary Genocide, 1981; author: (with Richard Burton) World Enough and Time, poetry reading, 1964, Elizabeth Taylor, 1965, Elizabeth Taylor Takes Off: On Weight Gain, Weight Loss, Self Esteem and Self Image, 1988; lics. (fragrances) Elizabeth Taylor's Passion, Passion for Men, White Diamonds/Elizabeth Taylor, Elizabeth Taylor's Diamonds & Emeralds, Diamonds & Rubies, Diamonds & Sapphires, (jewelry) The Elizabeth Taylor Fashion Jewelry Collection for Avon. Active philanthropic, relief, charitable causes internationally, including Israeli War Victims Fund for the Chaim Sheba Hosp., 1976, UNICEF, Variety Children's Hosps., med. clinics in Botswana; initiated Ben Gurion U.-Elizabeth Taylor Fund for Children of the Negev, 1982; supporter AIDS Project L.A., 1985; founder, nat. chmn. Am. Found. for AIDS Rsch. (AmFAR), 1985—, internat. fund, 1985—; founder Elizabeth Taylor AIDS Found., 1991—. Named Comdr. Arts Letters (France), 1985; recipient Legion of Honor (France), 1987 (for work with AmFAR), Aristotle S. Onassis Found. award, 1988, Jean Hersholt Humanitarian Academy award, 1993 (for work as AIDS advocate), Life Achievement award Am. Film Inst., 1993; honored with dedication of Elizabeth Taylor Med. Ctr. Whitman-Walker Clinic, Washington, 1993. Address: care N Rubin & Co 245 Fifth Ave New York NY 10016

TAYLOR, ELLEN BORDEN BROADHURST, civic worker; b. Goldsboro, N.C., Jan. 18, 1913; d. Jack Johnson and Mabel Moran (Borden) Broadhurst; student Converse Coll., 1930-32; m. Marvin Edward Taylor, June 13, 1936; children: Marvin Edward, Jack Borden, William Lambert. Bd. govs. Elizabethan Garden, Manteo, N.C., 1964-74; mem. Gov. Robert Scott's Adv. Com. on Beautification, N.C., 1971-73; mem. ACE nat. action com. for environ. Nat. Coun. State Garden Clubs, 1973-75; bd. dirs. Keep N.C. Beautiful, 1973-85; mem. steering com., charter mem. bd. dirs. Keep Johnston County (N.C.) Beautiful, 1977-92; life judge roses Am. Rose Soc.; chmn. local com. that published jointly with N.C. Dept. Cultural Resources: An Inventory of Historic Architecture, Smithfield, N.C., 1977; co-chmn. local com. to survey and publish jointly with N.C. Div. Archives and History: Historical Resources of Johnston County, 1980-91; charter life mem. N.C. Mus. History Assocs., 1994; charter mem. founder's circle New Mus. History Bldg., Raleigh, 1994. Mem. Nat. Coun. State Garden Clubs (life; master judge flower shows), Johnston County Hist. Soc. (charter), Johnston County Arts Coun. (Spl. award for 1987 projects of Pub. Libr. Johnston County & Smithfield 1965-87), N.C. Geneal. Soc. (charter), Johnston County Geneal. Soc. (charter), Hist. Preservation Soc. N.C. (life), N.C. Art Soc. (life). Democrat. Episcopalian. Clubs: Smithfield (N.C.) Garden (charter; pres. 1969-71), Smithfield Woman's (v.p. 1976), DAR (organizing vice-regent chpt. 1976), Gen. Soc. Mayflower Descs. (life), Descs. of Richard Warren, Nat. Soc. New Eng. Women (charter mem. Carolina Capital chpt.), Colonial Dames Am. (life), Magna Charta Dames, Nat. Soc. Daus. of Founders and Patriots Am. Home: 616 Hancock St Smithfield NC 27577-4008

TAYLOR, ELOUISE CHRISTINE, artist; b. Berkeley, Calif., Sept. 17, 1923; d. Charles Vincent and Lola Lucile (Felder) T.; m. P.S. Carnohan, Sept. 8, 1947 (div. 1982); children: Marcus Jay, Max Todd, Cecilia Ann. Student, Chgo. Opera Ballet Sch., Hollywood, Calif., 1941, San Francisco Opera Ballet Sc., Oukrainsky Ballet Sch., 1938-41, San Francisco Opera Ballet Sc. Featured skater Sonja Henie Hollywood Ice Revue, 1941-51, Ctr. Theater, N.Y.; artist Reno, Nev.; instr. figure skating and painting. Oil paintings featured in numerous group and one-woman shows; portrait of Sonja Henie and several others in permanent collection at World Figure Skating Hall of Fame and Mus., Colorado Springs, Colo.; paintings exhibited local shows Los Altos, Calif., 1970-74, Santa Rosa, 1974-79, also Half Moon Bay-Shoreline Sta. Gallery & art shows, 1981, 82, Parklane Mall, Reno, Nev., 1993; numerous commd. paintings; skated as double for Ann Rutherford in film, 1945. Avocations: designing and hand knitting, designing/hand-carving rubber stamps, swimming, dancing, skating.

TAYLOR, ESTELLE WORMLEY, English educator, college dean; b. Washington, Jan. 12, 1924; d. Luther Charles and Wilhelmina Wormley; m. Ivan Earle Taylor, Dec. 26, 1953. BS magna cum laude, Miner Tchrs. Coll., 1945; MA, Howard U., 1947; PhD, Cath. U. Am., 1969. Instr. English Howard U., 1947-52; tchr. Langley Jr. H.S., Washington, 1952-55, Eastern Sr. H.S., Washington, 1955-63; from instr. to prof. D.C. Tchrs. Coll., 1963-91, prof. English emerita, 1991—, acad. dean, 1975-76; assoc. provost Fed. City Coll., Washington, 1974-75; prof. Howard U., 1976-91, chmn. dept. English, 1976-85; assoc. dean Howard U. Coll. Liberal Arts, 1985-86; dir. expository writing program Grad. Sch. Arts and Scis., 1988-91; mem., sec. Edn. Licensure Commn. of D.C., 1993—; mem. Commn. on Higher Edn., Mid. States Assn. Colls. and Schs., 1984-87, 88-90, co-chair steering com. to revise Characteristics of Excellence, 1992-93; mem. ctrl. exec. com. Folger Inst. Renaissance and 18th Century Studies, 1982-91; adv. bd. Humanities Inst. Montgomery Coll., 1997—. 1st v.p. Order Daus. of King Episc. Ch. Diocese, Washington, 1994—; commr. Edn. Licensure Com. of D.C., 1993—, also sec., vice chmn., 1995—; trustee U. D.C., 1979-83, vice chmn., 1983; mem. D.C. Cmty. Humanities Coun., 1990-91; co-chmn. planning com.

Centennial Celebration of the Andrew Rankin Chapel Howard U., 1994. Named Disting. Alumni, Howard U., 1995, Alumni award for Disting. Postgrad. Achievement in Edn. and Lit., 1997; So. fellow, 1968-69; Rockefeller/Aspen Inst. fellow, 1978-79. Mem. MLA (del. assembly 1994—), Nat. Assn. for Equal Opportunity in Higher Edn., Coll. Lang. Assn., Shakespeare Assn. Am., Pub. Mems. Assn. Fgn. Svc. Dept. of State, Links (v.p. Capital City chpt. 1979-81, corr. sec. 1989, rec. sec. 1991-93, 95—). Democrat. Home: 3221 20th St NE Washington DC 20018-2421 *Throughout my career I have been climbing a giant ladder, invisible to all but me. The challenging but humbling feature of this ladder is that whenever I get the feeling that I have almost reached the top, several additional rungs attach themselves to my Jacob's Ladder. Thus, that thing called success is for me forever a goal to be reached. As long as I continue to feel a restlessness and a yearning to climb another rung, I shall know that I am alive.*

TAYLOR, FOSTER JAY, retired university president; b. Gibsland, La., Aug. 9, 1923; s. Lawrence Foster and Marcia Aline (Jay) T.; m. Lou Kavanaugh; 1 son, Terry Jay. Student, La. Poly. Inst., 1940-42; BA, U. Calif., Santa Barbara, 1948; MA, Claremont (Calif.) Grad. Sch., 1949; PhD, Tulane U., 1952. Assoc. prof. history, dean men. La. Coll., Pineville, 1952-56; prof. La. Coll., 1956-62, dean coll., 1960-62; pres. La. Tech. U., Ruston, 1962-87, pres. emeritus, 1987—; past chmn. La. Labor Mediation Bd.; arbitrator Am. Arbitration Assn., Fed. Mediation and Conciliation Svc.; former mem. La. Adv. Coun. on Vocat.-Tech. Edn.; bd. dirs. Michael;s Stores, Pizza Inn, Inc., Ill. Ctrl. R.R. Author: The United States and the Spanish Civil War, 1936-39, 1956, Reluctant Rebel, The Secret Diary of Robert Patrick, 1861-1865, 1959. Served to lt. comdr., aviator USNR, 1942-46. Mem. Am. Hist. Assn., Miss. Valley Hist. Assn., So. Hist. Assn., Nat. Acad. Arbitrators., Phi Alpha Theta. Club: Rotary. Home: 2502 Tanglewood Dr Ruston LA 71270-2244

TAYLOR, FRED, retired basketball coach; b. Zanesville, Ohio, Dec. 3, 1924. Baseball player Washington Senators; coach Ohio State U., 1958-76; Mgr. U.S. Nat. Team, FIBA World Championships, 1978, Pan Am. Games, 1979. Named Coach of Yr., USBWA, 1961, UPI, 1962, Basketball Hall of Fame, 1986. Achievements include coach of NCAA Championship Team, 1960, NCAA Finalist Team, 1961, 62, seven-time Big 10 Title Team. Office: care Basketball Hall of Fame PO Box 179 Springfield MA 01101-0179

TAYLOR, FREDERICK WILLIAM, JR. (FRITZ TAYLOR), lawyer; b. Cleve., Oct. 21, 1933; s. Frederick William Sr. and Marguerite Elizabeth (Kistler) T.; m Mary Phyllis Osborne, June 1, 1985. BA in History, U. Fla., 1957; MA in Near East Studies, U. Mich., 1959; JD cum laude, NYU, 1967. Bar: N.Y. 1968, Calif. 1969, U.S. Dist. Ct. (cen. dist.) Calif. 1969. Govt. rels. rep. Arabian Am. Oil Co., Dhahran, Saudi Arabia, 1959-63; oil supply coord. Arabian Am. Oil Co., N.Y.C., 1963-68; sr. counsel Arabian Am. Oil Co., Dhahran, 1969-71, gen. mgr. govt. rels. orgn., 1971-74, v.p. indsl. rels., 1974-78; assoc. O'Melveny & Myers, L.A., 1968-69; ptnr. Burt & Taylor, Marblehead, Mass., 1978-80; pres., chief exec. officer Nat. Med. Enterprises Internat. Group, L.A., 1980-82; counsel Chadbourne, Parke & Afridi, United Arab Emirates, 1982-84; ptnr. Sidley & Austin, Cairo, 1984-87, Singapore, 1987-93; spl. counsel Heller Ehrman White & McAuliffe, L.A. and Singapore, 1993-95; corp. counsel law divsn. Lucent Techs. Internat. Inc., Riyadh, Saudi Arabia, 1995—. Contbr. articles to profl. jours. Mem. ABA, Calif. Bar Assn., Order of Coif, Singapore Cricket Club, Tanglin Club, Changi Sailing Club, Singapore Am. Club, Dirab Golf Club. Home: Box 6942 Taos NM 87571 Office: Lucent Techs Intl Inc, PO Box 4945 Khurais Rd, Riyadh 11412, Saudi Arabia

TAYLOR, GARY L., federal judge; b. 1938. AB, UCLA, 1960, JD, 1963. Assoc. Wenke, Taylor, Evans & Ikola, 1965-86; judge Orange County Superior Ct., 1986-90, U.S. Dist. Ct. (ctrl. dist.) Calif., Santa Ana, 1990—. With U.S. Army, 1964-66. Mem. Am. Coll. Trial Lawyers, State Bar Calif., Orange County Bar Assn. (bd. dirs. 1980-82, founder, chmn. bus. litigation com., Disting. Svc. award 1983). Office: US Dist Cts 751 W Santa Ana Blvd Rm 801 Santa Ana CA 92701-4509*

TAYLOR, GENE, congressman; b. New Orleans, La., Sept. 17, 1953; m. Margaret Gordon; children: Sarah, Emily, Gary. BA, Tulane U.; grad., U. So. Miss. Sales rep. Stone Container Corp.; U.S. senator from Miss., dist. 46, 1984-89; mem. 101st-104th Congresses from 5th Miss. dist., 1989—; mem. govt. reform & oversight com., ranking minority mem. merchant marine. With USCGR. Mem. Lions, Rotary, Kappa Sigma. Roman Catholic. Office: US House of Reps 2447 Rayburn Washington DC 20007-7820

TAYLOR, GEORGE ALLEN, advertising agency executive; b. Lake City, Iowa, Oct. 26, 1906; s. Bertrand Franklin and Mabel (Minard) T.; m. Regina Helen Wickland, July 3, 1938 (div. 1956). PhB in Fine Arts, Northwestern U., 1947, MEd, 1951, postgrad., 1951-54; art edn. diploma, U. No. Iowa, 1926. Art supr. pub. schs. Indianola, Iowa, 1926-29; instr. art Simpson Coll., Indianola, 1926-29; designer Modern Art Studios, Chgo., 1929-30; display designer W.J. Rankin Corp., Chgo., 1930-35; creative dir. Arthur Meyerhoff Assocs., Inc., Milw., 1935-38; br. mgr. Arthur Meyerhoff Assocs., Inc., L.A., 1938-42; account exec. Arthur Meyerhoff Assocs., Inc., Chgo., 1942-59, account supr., 1959-61, v.p. adminstrn., 1961-65, vice chmn., 1965-80; pres. GATA Ltd.; lectr. semantics Ill. Inst. Tech., Chgo., 1947-50, Northwestern U. Sch. Commerce, 1948. Lyricist popular songs. Reader Recs. for Blind, Inc., 1956-94, CRIS Radio, 1981-85; mem. Chgo. Architecture Found., Landmarks Preservation Coun. Ill. Recipient 1st place awards in copy and layout L.A. Advt. Club, 1940. Mem. AAAS, Friends of Downtown, Art Inst. Chgo. Home (summer): 1212 N Lake Shore Dr Apt 29a-s Chicago IL 60610 Home (winter): 4767 Ocean Blvd Apt 201 San Diego CA 92109-2475

TAYLOR, GEORGE FREDERICK, newspaper publisher, editor; b. Portland, Oreg., Feb. 28, 1928; s. George Noble and Ida Louise (Dixon) T.; m. Georga Bray, Oct. 6, 1951; children—Amelia Ruth, Ross Noble. B.S., U. Oreg., 1950. Reporter Astoria (Oreg.) Budget, 1950-52, Portland Oregonian, 1952-54; copy reader Wall St. Jour., 1955-57, reporter, 1957-59, Detroit Bur. chief, 1959-64, Washington corr., 1964-68; asst. mng. editor Wall St. Jour., San Francisco, 1968-69; mng. editor Wall St. Jour., N.Y.C., 1970-77, exec. editor, 1977-86; pub. North Bend (Oreg.) News, 1986—, Prime Time, 1987—, Coquille Valley Sentinel, 1989—. Served to lt. USAF, 1955-57. Office: 1 Bartons Aly Coquille OR 97423-1270

TAYLOR, GEORGE KIMBROUGH, JR., lawyer; b. Atlanta, Aug. 28, 1939; s. George Kimbrough and Helen Whiteside (Shepard) T.; m. Carol Ann McKinney, July 1, 1961 (div. 1976); children: George Kimbrough III, Thomas Haynes; m. Triska Ashley Drake, Oct. 2, 1981. BA, Emory U., 1961; LLB, U. Va., 1964. Bar: Ga. 1964, U.S. Dist. Ct. (no. dist.) Ga. 1964, U.S. Ct. Appeals (11th cir.) 1964. Assoc. Kilpatrick & Cody, Atlanta, 1964-70, ptnr., 1970-96; ptnr. Kilpatrick Stockton LLP (formerly Kilpatrick & Cody), 1997—; bd. dirs. Ont. Reins. Co. Ltd., Cayman Islands; pres., bd. dirs. Rugby Holdings, Inc., Atlanta, 1984-94, Norcros U.S.A., Inc., Atlanta, U.S. Properties, Inc., Atlanta, 1983-92. Chmn. bd. dirs. Spl. Audiences, Inc., Atlanta, 1985-87; bd. dirs. Atlanta Symphony Orch., 1986—, treas., 1995—; bd. dirs. Atlanta Opera, 1995—, Ga. Humanities Coun., Atlanta, 1986-93, Ga. Conservancy, 1979-85; bd. dirs. Ga. Coun. Internat. Visitors, Atlanta, 1987-94, pres., 1993; bd. dirs. Brit.-Am. Bus. Group, 1989—, pres., 1994; bd. visitors Emory U., Atlanta, 1993-96, Brit.-Am. Bus. Coun., 1997—; mem. alumni coun. U. Va. Law Sch.; active Leadership Atlanta. Woodrow Wilson fellow, 1961. Mem. ABA, Internat. Bar Assn., Atlanta Bar Assn., Order of Coif, Soc. Internat. Bus. Fellows, Phi Beta Kappa, Omicron Delta Kappa. Democrat. Clubs: Capital City, World Trade (Atlanta). Avocations: sailing, skiing. Office: Kilpatrick & Stockton LLP Ste 2800 1100 Peachtree St NE Atlanta GA 30309-4528

TAYLOR, GLEN, professional sports team executive, printing and graphics company executive. State senator Minnesota Senate, 1980-90; pres. Taylor Corp., Mankato, Minn.; owner Minnesota Timberwolves, Minneapolis, Minn., 1994—. Office: Taylor Corp 1725 Roe Crest Dr Mankato MN 56003-1807 Office: Minnesota Timberwolves Target Ctr 600 1st Ave N Minneapolis MN 55403-1400*

TAYLOR, GRACE ELIZABETH WOODALL (BETTY TAYLOR), lawyer, law educator, law library administrator; b. Butler, N.J., June 14, 1926; d. Frank E. and Grace (Carlyon) Woodall; m. Edwin S. Taylor, Feb. 4, 1951 (dec.); children: Carol Lynn Taylor Crespo, Nancy Ann Filer. AB, Fla. State U., 1949, MA, 1950; JD, U. Fla., 1962. Instr. asst. librarian U. Fla., 1950-56; asst. law librarian Univ. Libraries, U. Fla., 1956-62; dir. Legal Info. Ctr., 1962—, prof. law, 1976—; Clarence J. TeSelle prof. of law U. Fla., 1994—; trustee Nat. Ctr. for Automated Rsch., N.Y.C., 1978-96; past chmn. joint com. on LAWNET, Am. Assn. Law Librs., Am. Assn. Law Schs. and ABA, 1978—; cons. to law librs., 1975—; mem. adv. com. N.E. Regional Data Ctr., U. Fla., 1990—. Co-author: American Law Publications, 1986, 21st Century: Technology's Impact, 1988, Law in the Digital Age: The Challenge of Research in Legal Information Centers, 1996, also articles. Recipient 1st Disting. Alumni award Fla. State U. Libr. Sch., 1983; Lewis Scholar Fla. Legislature, 1947-50; grantee NEH, 1981-82, Coun. Libr. Resources, 1984-86. Mem. ABA (Law Libr. Congress facilities com. 1991-97), Am. Assn. Law Librs. (exec. bd. 1981-84, Marian Gould Gallagher Disting. Svc. award 1997, Aspen Law and Bus. Rsch. grant 1997), Am. Assn. Law Schs. (accreditation com. 1978-81), OCLC Users Coun. (pres. 1983-86), Phi Beta Kappa (v.p. U. Fla. chpt. 1994-95, pres. 1995-96—), Beta Phi Mu. Democrat. Methodist. Avocations: computers, genealogy, crafts, gardening, grandchildren. Office: U Fla Legal Info Ctr Gainesville FL 32611

TAYLOR, GUY WATSON, symphonic conductor; b. Anniston, Ala., Dec. 25, 1919; s. Stokely Brackston and Ola Mae (Shaw) T.; m. Renee Lifton, Oct. 19, 1947; children: Eric Anthony, Ellen Jane. Diploma, Birmingham Conservatory of Music, 1941, Juilliard Sch. Music, 1948; pvt. studies and workshops with, Dimitri Mitropoulos, 1941-42, L'Ecole Monteux, 1949, Eugene Ormandy, 1953, George Szell, 1956. Conductor Springfield (Ohio) Symphony Orch., 1948-51, Nashville Symphony Orch., 1951-59, Phoenix Symphony Orch., 1959-69, Fresno Philharmonic Orch., 1969-84; guest conductor, U.S., Gt. Britain, Philippines, P.R., Can. and Mexico City; musical commentator Springfield News & Sun, 1948-51, Ariz. Republic, 1959-61, Fresno Bee, 1970-76. Has appeared on, BBC Radio, CBS-TV. Served with AUS, 1942-45. Recipient Conductor Recognition award Am. Symphony Orch. League, 1960, Alice M. Ditson Orch. award, 1961, citation for adventuresome programming of contemporary music ASCAP, 1977. Mem. Am. Symphony Orch. League, Phi Mu Alpha Sinfonia.

TAYLOR, HAROLD ALLEN, JR., industrial mineral marketing consultant; b. San Jose, Calif., June 27, 1936; s. Harold Allen and Marie Anna (Briody) T.; B.A., Brown U., 1958; M.A., U. Minn., 1968; m. Theresa Josephine Kustritz, Aug. 29, 1963; children: Harold A., III, Ruth F. Cook, Jonathan L.E. Project leader office Mineral Supply, U.S. Bur. Mines, Mpls., 1968-70, commodity specialist div. ferrous metals, Washington, 1970-74; commodity analyst U.S. Internat. Trade Commn., Washington, 1974-80; sr. commodity specialist br. indsl. minerals U.S. Bur. Mines, Washington, 1980-95; pres. Basic/Mines, Summit Point, W.Va., 1995—. Pres. Arlington (Va.) Interfaith Coun., 1994, 95. Mem. AIME (sec. 1983-84, first vice chmn. 1984-85, chmn. 1985-86, exec. adv. bd. mineral econs. subsect. 1981-83, 87-91), Am. Soc. Testing and Materials (chair subcom. nomenclature of com. on dimension stone 1987—, sec. com. dimension stone 1990-95), Soc. Govt. Economists (chmn. materials policy panels 1979-84), Toastmasters (pres. 1978, 81, 87, 91, asst. area gov. 1978-79, area gov. 1979-80, dep. div. lt. gov. 1989-90), Capitol Metals Forum (steering com. 1979-85), Sigma Gamma Epsilon. Contbr. articles to profl. jours. and encys. Address: PO Box 185 Summit Point WV 25446-0185

TAYLOR, HELEN LAVON HOLLINGSHED, association executive, early childhood consultant; b. Fort Valley, Ga., July 27, 1942; d. Earl Herman Hollingshed and Helen (Flowers) Southall; m. Robert Joseph Taylor, Sept. 11, 1965. BA, Howard U., 1964; MA, Cath. U., 1973; cert. mgmt., Tex. Tech. U., 1985, UCLA, 1991. Grad. asst. Howard U., Washington, 1964-65; social worker Nat. Child Day Care Assn., Washington, 1966-68, head start program dir., 1968-70, preschool project dir., 1971-78, exec. dir., chief exec. officer, 1979-83; mem. early childhood cons. various orgns., 1970—; founder, bd. dirs. Washington Child Devel. Coun., 1975—; mem. child care adv. com. Nat. Black Child Devel. Inst., Washington, 1988—; assoc. commr. Head Start Bur., DHHS, 1994—. Chairperson D.C. Coun. Adv. Com. on Child Care Facilities, Washington, 1974-78, Mayor's Adv. Com. for Early Childhood Devel., Washington, 1986—; chair pers. com. Bright Beginnings, Inc., Washington, 1991-92. Recipient Svc. award Adminstrn. for Children, Youth and Families, Washington, 1986, Svc. award Nat. Head Start Assn., Alexandria, Va., 1988, Cmty. Svc. award D.C. Dept. Consumer and Regulatory Affairs, Washington, 1990, Guardian award Nat. Black Child Devel. Inst., 1994, Martin Luther King Cmty. Svc. award, United Planning Orgn., 1994. Mem. Nat. Assn. for Edn. Young Children (conf. chairperson 1982, bd. mem. 1991—), Assn. for Childhood Edn. Internat. (publ. com. 1983-85), Washington (D.C.) Assn. for Edn. Young Children (co-chairperson 1978-80, Svc. award 1991), Delta Sigma Theta, Inc. (chair arts and letters com. 1984-86), Coalition of 100 Black Women). African Methodist Episcopal. Office: Nat Child Day Care Assn 1501 Benning Rd NE Washington DC 20002-4532

TAYLOR, HENRY ROTH, sales and marketing executive; b. Phila., Sept. 25, 1940; s. Henry and Helen Jacquelyn (Roth) T.; B.S., Millersville State Coll., 1962; postgrad., Pa. State U., 1963-65; MS, Temple U., 1966; postgrad., Queens Coll., Oxford U., summer 1973; m. Cynthia Mary DeMarco, Aug. 17, 1968; children: Christopher, Peter, Brett, Melissa. Mng. editor Montgomery Newspapers, Ft. Washington, Pa., 1962-66; news bur. dir. Drexel U., Phila., 1966-68, ann. fund dir., 1971-72; dir. pub. relations Ursinus Coll., Collegeville, Pa., 1968-71, Widener U., Chester, Pa., 1972-74; asst. v.p., dir. athletics Spring Garden Coll., Phila., 1974-87, lectr. mass media, 1979-87; exec. dir. Phila. sect. Profl. Golfers Assn., 1987-89; dir. Athletics, chmn. physical edn. Phila. Coll. Textiles and Sci., 1989-92; v.p. sales and pub. rels. Fleer/Sky Box Internat. Corp., Mt. Laurel, N.J., 1992—; mem. exec. com. Eastern Pa. Athletic Conf., 1982-86; pres. Eastern States Athletic Conf., 1985-87; part-time sportscaster, talk show host, announcer Sta. WIFI, Phila., 1965-70; with Ted Taylor Assocs., Abington, Pa., part-time 1965-74; part-time sportscaster and announcer WIBF Radio, Jenkintown, Pa., 1970-74, Sta. WNPV, Lansdale, Pa., 1983-88; host collectibles syndicated radio show, Sports By-Line USA, 1992—. Founding pres. Glenside Boys Athletic Club, 1958-63; commr. Keystone State Football Conf., 1959-62; dir. Pop Warner Found., 1963-65; pres. Warminster Youth 963-65; pres. Warminster Youth Activities Orgn., 1965-71; mem. Abington Twp. Spl. Police, 1974-81, sec., 1977-78; exec. com. Highland Sch. PTA, 1974-81; mem. Abington Twp. Police Rev. Bd., 1977-81; co-chmn. Phila. Baseball Card and Sports Memorabilia Shows, 1975-82, Ocean City (N.J.) Shows, 1981-84, North Penn. Shows, 1991-92. Named Man of Yr., Hatboro Jr. C. of C., 1962, Suburban Bucks Jr. C. of C., 1967, Citizen of Yr., Southampton Kiwanis, 1972, One of 100 Outstanding Grads. in 100 Yrs., Cheltenham (Pa.) High Sch., 1984; recipient Ursinus Coll. Varsity Club award, 1970; Piece of the Walk civic award Ocean City, N.J., 1981. Mem. Council for Advancement and Support of Edn., Pa. Assn. Colls. and Univs., Phila. Pub. Relations Assn., Pub. Relations Soc. Am., Suburban Pub. Relations Club, Phila. Sportswriters Assn., Coll. Sports Info. Dirs. Am., Eastern Pa. Sports Collectors Club (pres. 1978-82), Phila. Athletics Hist. Soc. (pres. 1996—). Republican. Presbyterian. Lodge: Rotary. Author: (with Robert E. Schmierer) Phillies Checklist Book, 1979, World Series Baseball Cards, 1987, The Rookie Book, 1988, 300 All-Time Baseball Stars, 1988, Encyclopedia of Baseball Cards, 1988, Sports Card Explosion, 1993; assoc. editor Sports Collectors Bible, 1978; columnist Sports Collectors Digest, 1980-92, Phila. Daily News, 1991—; contbr. articles to profl. jours. Home: 1527 Edgehill Rd Abington PA 19001-2609 Office: Fleer/Sky Box Internat Exec Plz 1120 Route 73 Mount Laurel NJ 08054-5113

TAYLOR, HENRY SPLAWN, literature educator, poet, writer; b. Loudoun County, Va., June 21, 1942; s. Thomas Edward and Mary Marshall (Splawn) T.; m. Sarah Spencer Bean, June 12, 1965 (div. 1967); m. Frances Ferguson Carney, June 29, 1968 (div. 1995); children: Thomas Edward, Richard Carney; m. Sarah Spencer, June 11, 1995. BA, U. Va., 1965; MA, Hollins (Va.) Coll., 1966. Instr. English Roanoke (Va.) Coll., 1966-68; asst. prof. U. Utah, 1968-71; mem. faculty Am. U., Washington, 1971—, prof. lit., 1976—, co-dir. MFA program in creative writing, 1982—, dir. Am. studies program, 1983-84; dir. U. Utah Writers' Conf., 1970-72; writer-in-residence Hollins Coll., spring 1978; poet-in-residence Wichita State U., 1994. Author: (poems) The Horse Show at Midnight, 1966, Breakings, 1971, An Afternoon of Pocket Billiards, 1975, Desperado, 1979, The Flying Change, 1985 (Pulitzer prize 1986), (essays) Compulsory Figures: Essays on Recent American Poets, 1992, (textbooks) Poetry: Points of Departure, 1974, The Water of Light: A Miscellany in Honor of Brewster Ghiselin, 1976, (cassette album) Landscape with Tractor, 1985, co-translator: The Children of Herakles, 1981, (poems) Understanding Fiction: Poems 1986-96, 1996; contbg. editor: Hollins Critic, 1971-78, 97—; editl. cons. Magill's Literary Ann., 1972-90; cons. editor Poet Lore, 1977-84; translator: The Weevil, 1995, Sophocles' Electra, 1997. Fellow creative writing Nat. Endowment Arts, 1978, 86; grantee Nat. Endowment Humanities, 1980-81. Mem. PEN, Agrl. History Soc., Am. Lit. Translators Assn. Democrat. Mem. Soc. of Friends. Home: PO Box 23 Lincoln VA 20160-0023 Office: Am U Dept Lit Washington DC 20016

TAYLOR, HUGH PETTINGILL, JR., geologist, educator; b. Holbrook, Ariz., Dec. 27, 1932; s. Hugh Pettingill and Genevieve (Fillerup) T.; m. Candis E. Hoffman, 1982. B.S., Calif. Inst. Tech., 1954; A.M., Harvard U., 1955; Ph.D., Calif. Inst. Tech., 1959. Asst. prof. geochemistry Pa. State U., 1960-62; mem. faculty div. geol. and planetary scis. Calif. Inst. Tech., 1962—, now prof. geology, Robert P. Sharp prof., 1981; Crosby vis. prof. M.I.T., 1978; vis. prof. Stanford U., 1981; William Smith lectr. Geol. Soc. London, 1976; Hofmann lectr. Harvard U., 1980; Cloos lectr. Johns Hopkins U., 1986; with U.S. Geol. Survey, Saudi Arabia, 1980-81. Author: The Oxygen Isotope Geochemistry of Igneous Rocks, 1968, Stable Isotopes in High Temperature Geological Processes, 1986, Stable Isotope Geochemistry, 1991; assoc. editor Bull. Geol. Soc. Am, 1969-71, Geochimica Cosmochimica Acta, 1971-76; editor Chem. Geology, 1985-91. Recipient Day medal Geol. Soc. Am., Urey medal European Assn. Geochem., 1995. Fellow NAS, Soc. Econ. Geol., Geol. Soc. Am., Am. Geophys. Union, Mineral. Soc. Am. (councillor), Am. Acad. Arts and Scis.; mem. Geochem. Soc. (councillor). Republican.

TAYLOR, HUMPHREY JOHN FAUSITT, information services executive; b. Meshed, Iran, Sept. 6, 1934; came to U.S., 1976; s. Geoffrey Fausitt and Frances Margaret (Kenyon) T.; m. Penelope Helen Taylor, Dec. 19, 1970; children: Zanthe, Helena. BA with honors, Cambridge (Eng.) U., 1958. Dist. officer Govt. of Tanganyika, 1959-62; mktg. and opinion researcher Nat. Opinion Poll, Eng., 1963-66; mng. dir. Opinion Rsch. Ctr., Eng., 1966-76; with Louis Harris and Assocs., N.Y.C., 1976-81; pres. Harris and Assocs., N.Y.C., 1981—, CEO, 1992—. Trustee U.S. com. UNICEF, N.Y.C., 1981-87, Overseas Devel. Coun., Washington, 1987—, Am. Health Found., 1988-91, chmn.; trustee Royal Soc. Medicine Found., 1992—. 2d lt. Brit. Army, 1953-55. Mem. Nat. Coun. Pub. Polls (chmn.), Am. Acad. Opthalmology (trustee). Avocations: history, biographies, skiing, tennis, travel. Address: Louis Harris & Assoc 111 Fifth Ave Fl 8 New York NY 10003-1005

TAYLOR, JACK C., rental and leasing company executive; b. 1922. With Lindburg Cadillac, St. Louis, 1944-50, Forrest Cadillac, St. Louis, 1951-56; chmn. bd. Enterprise Rent-A-Car, St. Louis, 1980—. With USN, ret. Office: Enterprise Rent-A-Car 600 Corporate Park Dr Saint Louis MO 63105-4204*

TAYLOR, JACK G., JR., art director. Art dir.: (films) Nine to Five, 1980, Looker, 1981, Uncommon Valor, 1983, Nightmares, 1983, Star 80, 1983, Real Genius, 1985, Gung Ho, 1986, Cape Fear, 1992, A Perfect World, 1993; prodn. designer: (films) Million Dollar Mystery, 1987. Office: Society of Motion Pic & TV Dir 11365 Ventura Blvd Ste 315 Studio City CA 91604-3148*

TAYLOR, JACQUELINE SELF, state legislator; b. Thomas, Okla., Feb. 16, 1935; d. MArtin Richard and Bertha Inez (Murray) Self; m. Nelson Edwin Taylor, May 17, 1952; children: Lucinda Susan Shannon, Robin Melinda. BA in Social Work, Boise State U., 1971. Lic. social worker Idaho. Dir. vol. svcs. Idaho Dept. of Health & Welfare, Caldwell, 1971-77; dir. Clatsop County Assn. REtarded Citizens, Astoria, Oreg., 1980-81; ptnr., owner Johnson Drug Store, Warrenton, Oreg., 1984-92; mem. Clatsop County Commn., Warrenton, 1994; state rep. Legis. Assembly State of Oreg., 1991-93, 95—. Bd. dirs. Pioneer House, Warrenton, 1992, Astoria C. of C., 1988-91, treas., 1988-91; civil svc. com. City of Astoria, 1988-91; mem. North Coast Women's Polit. Caucus, 1988 (named Outstanding Woman 1988), Oreg. Women's Polit. Caucus. Democrat. Avocations: gardening, history, tribal work. Home: 1324 Miller Ln Astoria OR 97103-3947 Office: Oreg State Legis State Capitol Salem OR 97310

TAYLOR, JAMES, JR., lawyer; b. Florence, S.C., Dec. 6, 1942; s. James and Thelma (Baker) T.; m. Jayne S.C. Bridge, May 19, 1974; children: James Robson, Ashley Baker. BA cum laude, U. of the South, 1965; JD, Georgetown U., 1973. Bar: D.C. 1973, U.S. Ct. Internat. Trade 1977, U.S. Ct. Appeals (fed. cir.) 1982, U.S. Supreme Ct. 1978. Assoc. Busby Rivkin Sherman Levy and Rehm, Washington, 1973-76, Busby and Rehm, Washington, 1977-78; ptnr. Busby Rehm and Leonard, Washington, 1979-87, Dorsey & Whitney, Washington, 1988-92, Stroock & Stroock & Lavan, Washington, 1992-95, Abondi, Foster, Sobin & Davidow, P.C., Washington, 1996—. Lt. USN, 1967-70; Vietnam. Mem. ABA, D.C. Bar Assn., Club Interallié (Paris). Episcopalian. Avocations: skiing, fishing, languages. Home: 3319 Cleveland Ave NW Washington DC 20008-3456 Office: Abondi Foster Sobin Davidow 1130 Connecticut Ave NW Ste 500 Washington DC 20036-3919

TAYLOR, JAMES B., securities trader, financial planner; b. Kenosha, Wis., June 23, 1944; s. George R. and Virginia Dare (Scenters) T.; m. Rebecca Matthew, Feb. 14, 1983; children: Joseph F., Jennifer R., Jessica J. Cert., Ky. Bus. Coll., Lexington, 1969; student, U. Wis., 1970-72. Lic. NASD Securities Broker, Tex. Securities Exchange Commn. Lab. technician Allen-Bradley Co., Inc., Milw., 1962-65; mktg. Jaeger Oils, Inc., Milw., 1965-68; mktg., retail mgmt. G.W. Taylor Co., Inc., Williamson, W.Va., 1968-69; acct. RTE Corp., Waukesha, Wis., 1969-72; mktg. new product introduction Victor Comptometer, Milw., Chgo., 1972-76; account exec., personal fin. mgmt. Merrill Lynch Pierce Fenner & Smith, Houston, 1977-80, Rotan Mosle Inc. (merger with Paine Webber Corp.), Houston, 1980-84, Paine Webber Corp./Rotan Mosle Inc., Houston, 1984—; instr. investing and personal fin. mgmt., Merrill Lynch, Houston. 1976-80, Paine Webber, Houston, 1980—; internat. stockbroker. Author articles on personal investing and fin. mgmt. for bus. mags., profl. newsletters, and internat. newspapers; prin. works exhibited in numerous galleries including Art Cetera, Houston, Harris County Coll. Gallery, Houston, Wimberly (Tex.) Galleries; paintings and photographs represented in pvt. collections in Europe and the U.S.; contbr. photos to local newspapers. Parrish coun. Catholic Ch., Livingston, Tex., 1979, 80, 81; dir. Hispanic Arts Group, Houston, 1990-91; active election campaign Ronald Reagan, Jack Fields. Mem. Stockbroker Soc. Am., Visual Arts Alliance. Avocations: art, photography, travel. Office: Paine Webber/Rotan Mosle Inc 16945 Northchase Dr Ste 100 Houston TX 77060-2133

TAYLOR, JAMES BLACKSTONE, aviation company executive; b. N.Y.C., Dec. 14, 1921; s. James Blackstone Taylor, Jr. and Aileen (Sedgwick) Taylor Lippincott; m. Margaret Krout, May 3, 1947; children—James Blackstone IV, Ray K., Jane A., W. Thorne. Grad., Taft sch., Watertown, Conn. Pres. Upressitmetal Cap Corp., N.Y.C., 1948-59; v.p. Am. Flange, N.Y.C., 1959-62, Pan Am. World Airways, N.Y.C., 1962-69, Cessna Aircraft, Wichita, Kans., 1969-76; pres., CEO Canadair, Inc., Westport, Conn., 1976-85; pres., chief exec. officer, dir. Gates Learjet Corp., Tucson, 1985-88; pres. James B. Taylor Assoc., Westport, Conn., 1988—. Served to lt. naval aviator USNR, 1942-46. Named Runner Up World Skeet Shooting Championship, 1962, 83; recipient Meritorious Svc. to Aviator award NBAA, 1992, Elder Statesman of Aviation award, 1992; named Man of Yr. Gathering of Eagles, 1984. Mem. Nat. Aviation Club, Wings Club (v.p., bd. dirs. 1965-67, 83-87), Country Club of Fairfield, Weston Gun Club, Nat. Aviation Assn. (bd. dirs.), Assn Naval Aviation, USS Yorktown Assn. and Found. Republican. Episcopalian. Home: 287 Taintor Dr Southport CT 06490

TAYLOR, JAMES DAVID, health care executive; b. Pitts., Oct. 3, 1947; s. Howard Alvin and Florence Elizabeth (Dale) T.; m. Helen Blair, Apr. 14, 1973; children: Megan, Brian. BA, Westminster Coll., 1969; MBA, Duquesne U., 1972; MPH, U. Pitts., 1974. Fin. trainee Gen. Electric Co., Erie, Pa., 1969-70; adminstrv. trainee Presbyn. U. Hosp., Pitts., 1972; adminstrv.

resident Montefiore Hosp., Pitts., 1973-74; mgr. Geisinger Med. Ctr., Danville, Pa., 1974-76, adminstrv. officer, 1976-78; asst. adminstr. Scott & White, Temple, Tex., 1978-81; dir. Scott & White co., Temple, Tex., 1982-91; prin. Inova, Temple, Tex., 1991-93; exec. dir. Christie Clinic Assn., Champaign, Ill., 1993—; chmn. of bd. Personal Care Health Mgmt. Inc., 1993—; fellowship preceptor Scott & White, Temple, Tex., 1985—; chmn. Joint Am. Coll. of Health Care Execs. and Med. Group Mgmt. Nat. Com., Chgo. and Denver, 1986-87; bd. dirs. Personal Care HMO and Covenant Med. Ctr. Contbr. articles to profl. jours. Bd. dirs. Columbia-Montour Home Health, Bloomburg, Pa., 1976-78; chmn. Grace Sch., Temple, 1980-86; elder Grace Presbyn. Ch., Temple, 1985-87. Recipient Third Place Nat. award Health Industry Mfg. Assn., 1975. Fellow Am. Coll. Healthcare Execs., Am. Coll. Med. Group Adminstrs.; mem. Med. Group Mgmt. Assn. (chmn. joint Am. Coll. Healthcare Execs. nat. com. 1986-87), Beta Gamma Sigma, Omicron Delta Epsilon. Republican. Avocations: golfing, running, coin collecting. Home: 2003 O Donnell Dr Champaign IL 61821-6466 Office: Christie Clinic Assos 101 W University Ave Champaign IL 61820-3909

TAYLOR, J(AMES) HERBERT, cell biology educator; b. Corsicana, Tex., Jan. 14, 1916; s. Charles Aaron and Delia May (McCain) T.; m. Shirley Catherine Hoover, May 1, 1946; children: Lynne Sue, Lucy Delia, Michael Wesley. B.S., So. Okla. State U., 1939; M.S., U. Okla., 1941; Ph.D., U. Va., 1944. Asst. prof. bacteriology and botany U. Okla., Norman, 1946-47; assoc. prof. botany U. Tenn., Knoxville, 1948-51; asst. prof. botany Columbia U., N.Y.C., 1951-54; assoc. prof. Columbia U., 1954-58, prof. cell biology, 1958-64; prof. biol. sci. Fla. State U., Tallahassee, 1964-83, Robert O. Lawton disting. prof. biol. sci., 1983-90, prof. emeritus, 1990—; assoc. dir. Inst. Molecular Biophysics, Fla. State U., 1970-79; dir. Inst. Molecular Biophysics, 1980-85; cons. Oak Ridge Nat. Lab., 1949-51; research collaborator Brookhaven Nat. Lab., 1951-58; nat. lectr. Sigma Xi Research Soc. Author: Molecular Genetics, Vol. 1, 1963, Vol. 2, 1965, Vol. 3, 1979; DNA Methylation and Cellular Differentiation, 1983; also papers on molecular genetics; contbr. over 100 articles in field to profl. jours. Pres. Unitarian Ch. Tallahassee, 1968-70. Served with M.C. U.S. Army, 1944-46, PTO. Recipient Meritorious Research award Mich. State U., 1960; Guggenheim fellow Calif. Inst. Tech., 1958-59. Mem. Nat. Acad. Scis., AAAS, Am. Inst. Biol. Sci., Am. Soc. Cell Biologists (pres. 1969-70), Biophysics Soc., Genetics Soc. Am. Democrat. Office: Fla State U Inst Molecular Biophysics Tallahassee FL 32306

TAYLOR, JAMES JOHN, academic adminstrator; b. Mpls., July 26, 1940; s. James John and Mary Elizabeth (Mason) T.; m. Margaret Claire Zacha, Dec. 28, 1976; children: Jerry William, John Allen. BA, Oblate Coll. of S.W., 1966; MEd, St. Louis U., 1969, MBA in Fin., 1972; cert. of advanced studies, Harvard U., 1977. Dept. head, tchr. Althoff High Sch., Belleville, Ill., 1966-71; asst. to controller U. of South Fla., Tampa, 1972-79; project mgr. W.Va. Bd. of Regents, Morgantown, 1979-83; prin., project dir. Am. Mgmt. Systems, Arlington, Va., 1983-90; mng. cons. Taylor Mgmt. Group, Arlington, 1990-91; v.p. bus. and finance Guam Community Coll., 1991—; founder, treas. Guam Ednl. Radio Found., KPRG-FM; organizer first meeting Chief Bus. Officers of the Pacific, 1997. Member adv. com. on spl. edn. Arlington Sch. Bd., 1981-83; founder, producer St. Louis High Sch. Film Makers Festival, 1968-72; contbr. articles to profl. jours. Founding mem. Harvard Club at Nat. Press Club; mem. Phi Delta Kappa. Avocations: photography, duplicate bridge, scuba diving. Home: 29 Cruz Hts Talofofo GU 96930-4736

TAYLOR, JAMES MARION, II, automotive wholesale executive; b. Andalusia, Ala., Jan. 20, 1926; s. Marion Doby and Catherine (Hill) T.; m. Abbie Chapman Henderson, Mar. 22, 1947; children: Cathy, James III, Merrily, Abbie, John. Student, U.S. Merchant Marine Acad., 1944-46, Auburn U., 1946-47. Salesman Taylor Parts, Inc., Andalusia, 1947-49, salesman, dir., 1950, v.p., sales mgr., 1950-61, v.p., gen. mgr., 1961-62, pres., 1962-88, chmn., chief exec. officer, 1988-92; bd. dirs. Covington County Bank, Andalusia; chmn. Southern Nat., Andalusia, 1986—; mem. adv. bd. Shatterproof Glass Co., Detroit, 1968, AC-Delco, Detroit, 1966-67, Walker (Tenneco), Racine, Wis., 1985. Bd. dirs. Ala. Wildlife Fedn., Montgomery, 1974-77, pres., 1977-78; bd. dirs. Lurleen B. Wallace Jr. Coll. Found., Andalusia, 1986-89, Covington County Bd. Edn., Andalusia, 1960-74, City of Andalusia Downtown Devel. Authority, 1989-96, City of Andalusia Indsl. Devel. Bd., 1969-71. Mem. Nat. Assn. Wholesalers (bd. dirs. and 1st vice chmn. 1988-90, chmn.-elect 1991, chmn. 1992, treas. 1993-94), Automotive Hall of Fame (Midland, Mich. bd. dirs. 1986-94), Automotive Info. Coun. (bd. dirs. 1987-92), Andalusia C. of C. (bd. dirs. 1960-62, 89-92), Auburn Alumni Assn. (life), Kiwanis (pres. Andalusia club 1969-70), Am. Legion. Republican. Baptist. Avocations: hunting, fishing, gun collecting. Home: 104 S Ridge Rd Andalusia AL 36420-4214 Office: Taylor Parts Inc PO Box 1068 Andalusia AL 36420

TAYLOR, JAMES VERNON, musician; b. Boston, Mar. 12, 1948; s. Isaac M. and Gertrude (Woodard) T.; children: Sarah Maria, Benjamin Simon. Student, Milton Acad., Mass., 1962-66, Arlington Sch., Belmont, Mass., 1966-67. Recorded for Apple Records, 1968, Warner Bros. Records, 1970-77, CBS Records, 1977; numerous concert appearances; composer, performer: (albums) Sweet Baby James, 1970, Mud Slide Slim and The Blue Horizon, 1971, One Man Dog, 1972, Walking Man, 1974, Gorilla, 1975, In the Pocket, 1976, James Taylor's Greatest Hits, 1977, J.T., 1977, Flag, 1979, Dad Loves His Work, 1981, That's Why I'm Here, 1985, Never Die Young, 1986, New Moon Shine, 1991, James Taylor (Live), 1993, Hourglass, 1997. Recipient 13 Gold Album awards, 4 Platinum Album awards, 3 Gold Single awards, Grammy award; named Best Pop Vocal Male, 1971, 77. Office: care PAM Artist Mgmt 644 N Doheny Dr West Hollywood CA 90069-5526

TAYLOR, JAMES WALTER, marketing consultant; b. St. Cloud, Minn., Feb. 15, 1933; s. James T. and Nina C. Taylor; m. Joanne Syktte, Feb. 3, 1956; children: Theodore James, Samuel Bennett, Christopher John. BBA, U. Minn., 1957; MBA, NYU, 1960; DBA, U. So. Calif., 1975. Mgr. research div. Atlantic Refining, Phila., 1960-65; dir. new product devel. Hunt-Wesson Foods, Fullerton, Calif., 1965-72; prof. mktg. Calif. State U., Fullerton, 1972-95; mng. dir. Innovative Mgmt. Devel. Co., Laguna Beach, Calif., 1995—; cons. Smithkline Beecham Corp., Tokyo, Govt. of Portugal, Lisbon, Austrade, Govt. of Australia, Hagenfeldt-Affarerna AB, Stockholm. Author: Profitable New Product Strategies, 1984, How to Create a Winning Business Plan, 1986, Competitive Marketing Strategies, 1986, The 101 Best Performing Companies in America, 1987, The Complete Manual for Developing Winning Strategic Plans, 1988, Every Manager's Survival Guide, 1989, Developing Winning Strategic Plans, 1990, How to Develop Successful Advertising Plans, 1993, Marketing Planning: A Step by Step Guide, 1996. Fulbright scholar Ministry of Industry, Lisbon, Portugal, 1986-87, U. We. Sydney, Australia, 1989-90; recipient Merit award Calif. State U., 1986-90. Mem. The Planning Forum, Am. Mktg. Assn., Strategic Mgmt. Assn., Assn. for Consumer Rsch., Acad. Mktg. Sci. Home: 3190 Mountain View Dr Laguna Beach CA 92651-2056

TAYLOR, JANELLE DIANE WILLIAMS, writer; b. Athens, Ga., June 28, 1944; d. Alton L. and Frances (Davis) Williams; m. Michael H. Taylor, Apr. 8, 1965; children: Angela Michelle, Alisha Melanie. Student, Augusta Coll., 1980-81. Orthodontic nurse Dr. W.H. Williams, Athens, 1962-65, Dr. James Metts, Augusta, Ga., 1969-72, Dr. Jack Carter, Augusta, 1973; med. research technologist Med. Coll. Ga., Augusta, 1975-77; writer Ga., 1977—; bd. dirs. Jo Beth Williams Romance Screenplay Award; lectr. writing Augusta Coll., other schs. and workshops, 1982—. Author: Savage Ecstasy, 1981, Valley of Fire, 1984, First Love, Wild Love, 1984 (Maggie awd. 1984), Golden Torment, 1984 (Reviewer's Choic awd. Romantic Times 1984), Savage Conquest, 1985, Stolen Ecstasy, 1985, Moondust and Madness, 1986, Sweet, Savage Heart, 1986 (Golden Pen cert. 1986), Destiny's Temptress, Defiant Ecstasy, 1982, Forbidden Ecstasy, 1982, Brazen Ecstasy, 1983, Tender Ecstasy, 1983, Love Me With Fury, 1983, Bittersweet Ectasy, 1987, Wild Is My Love, 1987, Fortune's Flames, 1988, Passions Wild and Free, 1988, Wild Sweet Promise, 1989, Kiss of the Night Wind, 1989, Whispered Kisses, 1990, Follow the Wind, 1990 (Romantic Times Reviewers Choice award 1990-91), Forever Ecstacy, 1991, Promise Me Forever, 1991, Christmas Rendezvous, 1991, Sharing Christmas, 1991, Stardust and Shadows, 1992, Midnight Secrets, 1992, Taking Chances, 1993, Janelle Taylor Three Complete Novels, 1993, The Last Viking Queen, 1994, Chase The Wind, 1994, Starlight And Splendor, 1994, The New Janelle Taylor Three Novel Collection, 1994, 1996, Destiny Mine, 1995, Anything for Love, 1995, Moonbeams and Magic, 195, Janelle Taylor Three Novel Collection #3, 1996, Defiant Hearts, 1996, Love with a Stranger, 1996, Wild Winds, 1997, By Candlelight, 1997, Summer Love, 1997; contbr. How to Write a Romance and Get It Published, 1983, 2d edit., 1984, Candlelight, Romance and You, 1983, My First Real Romance, 1985, Booksellers' Cookbook, 1988. Recipient trophy award for Indian series Romantic Times, 1985, Sioux Sacred Medicine Wheel and Cheyenne Red-tail Hawk Feather Coup hon. Gray Eagle Siouc Indian series, 1983-84; cert. Vocat. Indsl. Clubs Am., 1986, cert. of merit AAUW, 1986, Bronze Pen award, 1988, Silver Pen award, 1989; named to Writers' Hall of Fame, Romantic Times, 1988, Cowboy Hall of Fame; named hon. flying col. Delta Airlines, 1987. Mem. Romance Writers Am., Novelists Inc., Western Writers Am., Ga. Romance Writers Am., Aughors League/Authors Guild, Ga. Writers Coalition for Literacy, Augusta Author's Club. Republican. Baptist. Avocations: collecting spoons and coins, swimming, fishing, genealogy, English, Indian and American history. Office: PO Box 211646 Augusta GA 30917-1646

TAYLOR, JANET WINONA MILLS, secondary school educator; b. Shelby, N.C., Aug. 3, 1948; d. Robert Lee Sr. and Janet Elizabeth (Plair) Mills; m. Bernard D. Taylor, Dec. 31, 1983; 1 child, Adam Jason. BS in Health Edn., Morgan State Coll., 1974; MS in Ednl. Leadership, Morgan State U., 1986, EdD in Ednl. Adminstrn., 1994. Md. State Dept. Edn. Advanced Profl. cert. for supt., supr., secondary prin., health and gen. sci. tchr. grades 5-12. Tchr. Baltimore (Md.) City Pub. Schs., 1973-78; health educator Morgan State Coll., Balt., 1978-79; tchr. Montgomery County Pub. Schs., Rockville, 1979—; tech. writer, cons. The Assignment Group, Rockville, Md., 1990—; rsch. cons., rsch. assoc. Inst. for Urban Rsch., Morgan State U., 1992-93; libr. adv. bd. mem. Morgan State U., Balt., 1993—; grant cons. United Missionary Bapt., Inc., Balt., 1993—; GED test adminstr. Md. State Dept. Edn., Balt., 1993-94; co-dir. for grants and proposals United Missionary Bapt. Devel. Corp. Md., Balt., 1993—; mem. selection and evaluation adv. com. Montgomery County Pub. Schs., Rockville, 1993—. Editor (monthly jour.) The Doorkeeper, 1987-88. Dir. youth ministry Mt. Hebron Bapt. Ch., Balt., 1990-94; co-dir. children's ministry Bapt. Congress Christian Edn., Balt., 1992-94; corr. sec. Bapt. Congress Christian Edn., Balt., 1993—. Sgt. USAR, 1975-80. Mem. AERA, Zeta Phi Beta. Baptist. Avocations: reading, traveling, playing computer games and chess. Home: 1822 Wadsworth Way Baltimore MD 21239-3109

TAYLOR, JEAN MULL, home economics educator, secondary educator; b. Clover, Va., Feb. 18, 1953; d. Albert Herman and Helen (Jones) Mull; m. Derek Lester, June 28, 1975; children: Jennifer, Brian. BS, Longwood Coll., 1975; postgrad., Clemson U., 1984, U. S.C., 1986, U. Va., 1991, Va. Poly. and Tech. U., Blacksburg. Cert. tchr., nutritionist, Va., S.C. Tchr. home econs. Bluestone Sr. High Sch., Skipwith, Va., 1975, Whitlock Jr. High Sch., Spartanburg, S.C., 1976-80, McCracken Jr. High Sch., 1984-85, James F. Byrnes High Sch., 1985-87; tchr. occupational home econs. Park View Sr. High Sch., South Hill, Va., 1987—; state officer advisor, master advisor FHA/HERO, Va., 1990-94, advisor mentor, 1992-93; cons. home econs.; mem. adv. bd. Va. Assn. Future Homemakers Am.-Home Econs. Related Occupations, Richmond, Va., 1989—; journalist cmty. newspaper, Spartanburg, 1983-87. Pres. Upsy Daisy Garden Club, Spartanburg, 1980; moderator Presbyn. Women, Chase City, Va., 1989-91; enabler Presbyn. Women, Presbytery of the James, 1991-95; lead tchr., coord. Cmty. of Caring. Student Body Nutrition Edn. grantee Va. Dept. Edn., 1991-92. Mem. Va. Home Econs. Tchr. Assn. (pres. elect 1992-93, South Ctrl. Tchr. of Yr. 1991, pres. 1993-94, Tchr. of Yr. 1993), Am. Vocat. Assn., Va. Vocat. Assn., Am. Home Econs. Assn., Va. Home Econs. Assn., Garden Clubs S.C. (life), Nat. Fedn. of Garden Clubs. Avocations: boating, gardening, collecting books and antiques, cooking. Home: PO Box 283 Frisco NC 27936 Office: Park View Sr High Sch RR 1 Box 118 South Hill VA 23970-9506 also: Cape Hatteras Sch Career Devel Ctr Buxton NC 27920

TAYLOR, JOB, III, lawyer; b. N.Y.C., Feb. 18, 1942; s. Job II and Anne Harrison (Flinchbaugh) T.; m. Mary C. August, Oct. 24, 1964 (div. 1978); children: Whitney August, Job IV; m. Sally Lawson, May 31, 1980; 1 child, Alexandra Anne. BA, Washington & Jefferson Coll., 1964; JD, Coll. William and Mary, 1971. Bar: N.Y. 1972, U.S. Dist. Ct. (no., so. ea. and we. dists.) N.Y. 1973, U.S. Ct. Appeals (2d cir.) 1973, U.S. Ct. Claims 1974, U.S. Tax Ct. 1974, U.S. Supreme Ct. 1975, U.S. Ct. Appeals (9th cir.) 1976, U.S. Ct. Mil. Appeals 1977, U.S. Ct. Appeals (D.C. and 10th cirs.) 1977, D.C. 1981, U.S. Ct. Internat. Trade 1981, U.S. Ct. Appeals (fed. cir.) 1982, U.S. Dist. Ct. (no. dist.) Calif. 1983, U.S. Ct. Appeals (6th cir.) U.S. Dist. Ct., 1987, U.S. Ct. Appeals (3d cir.) 1990, U.S. Dist. Ct. Conn. 1996. Ptnr. Olwine, Connelly, Chase, O'Donnell & Weyher, N.Y.C., 1971-85, Latham & Watkins, N.Y.C., 1985—. Served to lt. USN, 1964-68. Mem. ABA, Assn. Bar City N.Y., La Confrerie des Chevaliers du Tastevin, Racquet and Tennis Club, Wee Burn Country Club (Darien, Conn.), New Canaan Country Club.. Republican. Episcopalian. Avocations: squash, tennis, golf, reading. Office: Latham & Watkins 885 3rd Ave New York NY 10022-4834

TAYLOR, J(OCELYN) MARY, museum administrator, zoologist, educator; b. Portland, Oreg., May 30, 1931; d. Arnold Llewellyn and Kathleen Mary (Yorke) T.; m. Joseph William Kamp, Mar. 18, 1972 (dec.). B.A., Smith Coll., 1952; M.A., U. Calif., Berkeley, 1953, Ph.D., 1959. Instr. zoology Wellesley Coll., 1959-61, asst. prof. zoology, 1961-65; assoc. prof. zoology U. B.C., 1965-74; dir. Cowan Vertebrate Mus., 1965-82, prof. dept. zoology, 1974-82; collaborative scientist Oreg. Regional Primate Research Ctr., 1983-87; prof. (courtesy) dept. fisheries and wildlife Oreg. State U., 1984—; dir. Cleve. Mus. Nat. History, 1987-96, dir. emeritus, trustee, 1996—; adj. prof. dept. biology Case Western Res. U., 1987-96. Assoc. editor Jour. Mammalogy, 1981-82. Contbr. numerous articles to sci. jours. Trustee Benjamin Rose Inst., 1988-93, Western Res. Acad., 1989-94, U. Circle, Inc., 1987-96, The Cleve. Aquarium, 1990-93, Cleve. Access to the Arts, 1992-96. Fulbright scholar, 1954-55; Lalor Found. grantee, 1962-63; NSF grantee, 1963-71; NRC Can. grantee, 1966-84; Killam Sr. Research fellow, 1978-79. Mem. Soc. Women Geographers, Am. Soc. Mammalogists (1st v.p. 1978-82, pres. 1982-84, Hartley T. Jackson award 1993, Lake County environ. award 1996), Australian Mammal Soc., Cooper Ornithol., Assn. Sci. Mus. Dirs. (v.p. 1990-93), Rodent Specialist Group of Species Survival Commn. (chmn. 1989-93), Sigma Xi. Episcopalian. Home: 2718 SW Old Orchard Rd Portland OR 97201

TAYLOR, JOE CLINTON, judge; b. Durant, Okla., Mar. 28, 1942; s. Luther Clinton and Virena (Parker) T.; m. Margaret Pearl Byers, June 8, 1963; children: Marna Joanne, Leah Alison, Jocelyn Camille. Student, Southeastern State Coll., 1960-62; B.A., Okla. State U., 1965; J.D., U. Okla., 1968. Bar: Okla. 1968. Practice law Norman, Okla., 1968-69; apptd. spl. dist. judge Durant, 1969-72; assoc. dist. judge Bryan County, Okla., 1972-76; dist. judge, chief judge 19th Dist. Ct., 1976-93; presiding judge Southeastern Okla. Jud. Adminstrv. Dist., 1984-92, Choctaw Tribal Ct., 1979-83; pres. Okla. Jud. Conf., 1987-88; chmn. Assembly Presiding Judges, 1989-90; presiding judge trial div. Okla. Ct. on the Judiciary, 1991-93; Okla. Ct. of Tax Rev., 1992—; judge Okla. Ct. of Civil Appeals, Tulsa, 1993—, vice chief judge, 1997—. Chmn. bd. dirs. Durant Youth Svcs., 1976-93; bd. dirs. Bryan County Youth Svcs., Inc., 1971-93. Mem. Phi Sigma Epsilon, Delta Theta Phi. Mem. Ch. of Christ. Club: Lion. Home: PO Box 329 Durant OK 74702-0329 Office: Ct Civil Appeals 601 State Bldg 440 S Houston Ave Tulsa OK 74127-8922

TAYLOR, JOEL SANFORD, lawyer; b. Hazleton, Pa., Oct. 8, 1942; s. Robert Joseph and Alice Josephine (Sanford) T.; m. Donna Rae Caron, Mar. 26, 1967; children: Jason, Adam, Jeremy. BA, Swarthmore Coll., 1965; LLB, Columbia U., 1968. Bar: N.Y. 1969, U.S. Dist. Ct. (so. and ea. dists.) N.Y. 1970, U.S. Ct. Appeals (2d cir.) 1970, Ohio 1973, U.S. Dist. Ct. (no. dist.) Ohio 1974, U.S. Supreme Ct. 1974, U.S. Dist. Ct. (so. dist.) Ohio 1975, U.S. Ct. Appeals (6th cir.) 1975, U.S. Dist. Ct. (ea. dist.) Ky. 1979. Law clk. hon. Constance B. Motley U.S. Dist. Ct., N.Y.C., 1968-69; assoc. Paul, Weiss, Rifkind, Wharton & Garrison, N.Y.C., 1969-72; exec. asst. Ohio Office of Budget & Mgmt., Columbus, Ohio, 1972-74; asst. atty. gen. Ohio Atty. Gen., Columbus, 1974-83, chief counsel, 1983-91; ptnr. Dinsmore & Shohl, Columbus, 1991—; pres. Ohio Sundry Claims Bd., Columbus, 1972-74, Ohio State Controlling Bd., Columbus, 1973-74; mem., bd. trustees Ohio State Tchrs. Retirement System, Columbus, 1986-91. Mem. ABA, Ohio State Bar Assn., Columbus Bar Assn., Environ. Law Inst., Columbia Law Alumni Assn., Ohio Sierra Club. Office: Dinsmore & Shohl 175 S 3rd St Ste 1000 Columbus OH 43215-5134

TAYLOR, JOHN BRIAN, economist, educator; b. Yonkers, N.Y., Dec. 8, 1946; s. John Joseph and Lorraine (Crowley) T.; m. Raye Allyn Price, Dec. 30, 1972; children: Jennifer Lynn, John Andrew. AB in Econs. summa cum laude, Princeton U., 1968; PhD, Stanford U., 1973. Asst. prof. econs. Columbia U., N.Y.C., 1973-77, assoc. prof., 1977-79, prof., 1979-80; prof. econs. and pub. affairs Princeton U., 1980-84; prof. econs. Stanford U., 1984—, dir. ctr. for Econ. Policy Rsch., 1994—; vis. prof. econs. Yale U., 1980; sr. staff economist Pres.'s Coun. Econ. Advisers, 1976-77, mem., 1989-91; econometric cons. Townsend-Greenspan and Co., N.Y., 1978-81; rsch. advisor Fed. Res. Bank Phila., 1981-84; rsch. assoc. Nat. Bur. Econ. Rsch., 1980—; exec. com. Am. Econ. Assn., 1991-94; rsch. economist Bank Of Japan, Tokyo, 1987; hon. adviser, 1994—; panel of econ. advisers Congl. Budget Office, 1995—. Author: Macroeconomics, 1986; Macroeconomic Policy in the World Economy, 1993, Economics, 1995; co-editor Am. Econ. Rev., 1985-89; assoc. editor Econometrica, 1981-85, Jour. Econ. Dynamics and Control, 1978-85, Jour. Monetary Econs., 1978-83; contbr. articles to profl. jours. NSF grantee, 1979-81, 81-83, 83-86, 86-89, 92-95; Guggenheim Found. fellow, 1983-84; sr. fellow Hoover Instn., 1996. Fellow Econometric Soc., Am. Acad. of Arts and Sci. Office: Stanford U Dept Econs Stanford CA 94305

TAYLOR, JOHN CHESTNUT, III, lawyer; b. N.Y.C., Jan. 7, 1928; s. John Chestnut and Jean Elizabeth (Willis) T.; m. Dolores Yvonne Sunstrom, Nov. 17, 1950; children: Jane Willis Taylor Salem, John Sunstrom, Anne Holliday Taylor Bambino. B.A., Princeton U., 1947; LL.B., Yale U., 1950. Bar: N.Y. 1950, D.C. 1972. Assoc. Paul, Weiss, Rifkind, Wharton & Garrison, N.Y.C., 1950, 52-60, ptnr., 1961-85, 87-91, of counsel, 1986-87, 92—; exec. v.p., dir. AEA Investors Inc., N.Y.C., 1985-86, pres., 1986-87. Bd. dirs. AFS Intercultural Programs, Inc., N.Y.C., 1972-80, trustee, 1973-79, chmn., 1975-79; trustee Carnegie Corp. N.Y., N.Y.C., 1975-84, chmn., 1979-84; trustee, mem. exec. com. Devereux Found., 1992—, vice chmn., 1994—. Served to capt. JAGC, AUS, 1950-52. Mem. Assn. of Bar of City of N.Y., Order of Coif, Phi Beta Kappa, Phi Delta Phi. Democrat. Home: 1 Hammock View Ln Savannah GA 31411-2603 Office: Paul Weiss Rifkind Wharton & Garrison 1285 Avenue Of The Americas New York NY 10019-6028

TAYLOR, JOHN JACKSON (JAY), writer, international consultant, retired foreign service officer; b. Little Rock, Dec. 4, 1931; s. Alfred Wesley and Annie Laurie (Cain) T.; m. Elizabeth Rose, July 9, 1954; children: John Jr., Laurie, Amy, Cynthia. BA, Vanderbilt U., 1952; MA, U. Mich., 1968. 3d sec. U.S. Fgn. Service, Accra, Ghana, 1957-59; 2d sec. U.S. Fgn. Service, Taichung and Taipei, Republic of China, 1960-65; Chinese affairs analyst Dept. State, Washington, 1966-67; staff assoc. Ctr. for Chinese Studies, U. Mich., Ann Arbor, 1967-68; U.S. consul Kuching, Malaysia, 1968-70; chief external reporting U.S. Consulate Gen., Hong Kong, 1970-74; officer-in-charge Chinese affairs Dept. State, Washington, 1974-75; staff mem. Asian affairs Nat. Security Council, Washington, 1975-77; polit. counselor U.S. Embassy, Pretoria/Capetown, 1977-80; polit. cons. U.S. Embassy, Peking, 1980-82; rsch. fellow Fairbanks Ctr. for East Asian Studies Harvard U., Cambridge, Mass., 1982-83; dir. East Asian analysis Dept. State, Washington, 1983-85; dep. asst. sec. state Bur. Intelligence and Research, Dept. State, Washington, 1986-87; chief of mission U.S. Interests Sect., Havana, Cuba, 1987-90; diplomat in residence Carter Presdl. Ctr., Emory U., 1990-92; sr. mem. State Task Force 2000, 1992-93; sr. assoc. Global Bus. Access; assoc. in rsch. Fairbank Ctr. for East Asian Studies, Harvard U.; exec. producer Wye Productions; guest faculty Emory U. and Spelman Coll. Author: China and Southeast Asia, 1974, 76, The Dragon and the Wild Goose, 1987, 90, The Rise and Fall of Totalitarianism, 1993; contbr.: China and National Security, 1985. Served as Naval Aviator with USMC, 1953-57. Mem. Fgn. Svc. Assn., Asian Soc., Royal Asian Soc., Acad. of Polit. Sci. Unitarian.

TAYLOR, JOHN JOSEPH, nuclear engineer; b. Hackensack, N.J., Feb. 27, 1922; s. John J.D. and Johanna F. (Thibideau) T.; m. Lorraine Crowley, Feb. 5, 1943; children: John B., Nancy M., Susan M. BA, St. John's U., Jamaica, N.Y., 1942, DSc (hon.), 1975; MS, U. Notre Dame, 1947. Mathematician Bendix Aviation Corp., Teterburo, N.J., 1946-47; engr. Kellex Corp., N.Y.C., 1947-50; v.p. water reactor div. Westinghouse Electric Corp., Pitts., 1950-81; v.p. nuclear power Electric Power Rsch. Inst., Palo Alto, Calif., 1981-95; energy cons., 1995—; mem. adv. com. Oak Ridge (Tenn.) Nat. Lab., 1973-83, Brookhaven Nat. Lab., Upton, N.Y., 1986-92, Inst. for Nuclear Power Ops., 1988-95; mem. adv. com. Argonne (Ill.), Nat. Lab., 1980-86, bd. dirs.; cons. Office Tech. Assessment, Washington, 1975-93; mem. internat. adv. group IAEA, Vienna, Austria, 1992-95; mem. nuclear rsch. rev. com. NRC, 1995—; mem. U.S.-Russian Commn. on Weapons Plutonium Disposition, 1996—. Co-author: Reactor Shielding Manual, 1953, Naval Reactor Physics Manual, 1956, Nuclear Power, Policy and Prospects, 1987, Management and Disposition of Excess Weapons Plutonium; contbr. articles to profl. jours. Bd. regents St. Mary's Coll., Moraga, Calif. Lt. (j.g.) USN, 1942-45. Recipient Order of Merit, Westinghouse Electric Corp., 1957, George Westinghouse Gold medal ASME, 1990. Fellow AAAS, Am. Phys. Soc., Am. Nuclear Soc. (bd. dirs. Walter Zinn award 1993); mem. NAE, Nat. Acad. Engring., Cosmos Club (Washington). Republican. Roman Catholic. Home: 15 Oliver Ct Menlo Park CA 94025-6685 Office: Electric Power Research Inst PO Box 10412 3412 Hillview Ave Palo Alto CA 94304-1395

TAYLOR, JOHN L., communications executive; b. 1951. BS, U. N.C., Charlotte, 1976. With Deloitte Haskins & Sells, Charlotte, 1976-84, Video Vision, Inc., Charlotte, 1986; various positions, pres., CEO Ingram Entertainment Inc., La Vergne, Tenn., 1986—; CEO, pres. Moovies Inc., Greenville, SC, 1994—. Office: Moovies Inc 201 Brookfield Pkwy Ste 200 Greenville SC 29607-5744

TAYLOR, JOHN LOCKHART, city official; b. N.Y.C., Nov. 4, 1927; s. Floyd and Marian (Lockhart) T.; m. Barbara Becker, July 19, 1952; children: Catherine Fair, Robert, William, Susan. A.B., Middlebury Coll., 1952; M.Govtl. Adminstrn., U. Pa., 1956. Reporter Providence Jour.-Bull., 1952-54; adminstrv. intern City of Xenia, Ohio, 1955-56; mcpl. mgr. Borough of Narberth, Pa., 1956-60, Twp. of Lakewood, N.J., 1960-64; asst. city mgr. Fresno, Calif., 1964-65; city mgr., 1965-68, Kansas City, Mo., 1968-74, Berkeley, Calif., 1974-76; lectr. U. Pa., 1957-58, Golden Gate U., 1977; sr. urban mgmt. specialist Stanford Research Inst., 1977-80; dir. Internat. Devel. Center, 1980-82; clk. of bd. suprs. City of San Francisco, 1982—; pres. Calif. Clks. Bd. Suprs. Assn., 1988-89. Served with USN, 1945-48. Mem. Internat. City Mgrs. Assn., Am. Soc. Pub. Adminstrn., Mcpl. Execs. Assn. (pres. 1991-93). Office: City Hall Rm 308 401 Van Ness Ave Ste 308 San Francisco CA 94102-4527

TAYLOR, JOHN WILKINSON, education educator; b. Covington, Ky., Sept. 26, 1906; s. John Wesley and Ethel (Wilkinson) T.; m. Katherine Willis Wright; 1 child, Walter Bradford; m. Helen Hutchinson Greene (dec. Jan. 1966); stepdau., Patricia (Mrs. H.E. Thornber, Jr.); m. June Cornell Fairbank (dec. Oct. 1986); step-children: Margaret, (Mrs. Terrill K. Jory) (dec. Aug. 1985), Laura (Mrs. Louis C. Sudler, Jr.), Kellogg III, Susan (Mrs. Walter B. Taylor), Elizabeth (Mrs. John W. Cameron), David. A.B., Columbia, 1929, A.M., 1930, Ph.D., 1936; H.D., St. Joseph Coll., 1970. Asst. curriculum research Tchrs. Coll., Columbia, 1927; asst. elementary edn. Tchrs. Coll., 1928, asst. curriculum, 1929, asst. secondary edn., 1929-30, instr. comparative edn., 1930; tchr. English Kaiser Friederich Realgymnasium, Berlin-Neukoeln, Germany, 1930-31; ednl. adviser to pres. John Day Co., 1932-33; asso. in edn., dir. fgn. study Columbia, 1934-35; also asst. to chmn. Columbia (New Coll.), 1935-37; chmn. admissions, scholarship, loan, curriculum and personnel guidance coms., 1937-38; assoc. prof. comparative edn. and sec. instnl. survey com., adminstrv. asst. to pres. La. State U., 1938-40, dir. bur. ednl. research, 1941-43; pres. U. Louisville, 1947-50; dep. dir.-gen. UNESCO, 1951-54, acting dir.-gen., 1952-53; exec. dir. Chgo. Ednl. TV Assn., 1954-71, bd. mem., 1969-73; acting pres. Learning Resources Inst., N.Y.C., 1960-63; pres. Learning Resources Inst., Chgo., 1963-70; dir. Midwestern Ednl. Television Network, Inc., 1966-70; bd. dirs. Fed. Res. br.

Bank Louisville, 1948-50; spl. cons. on ednl. TV N.Y. U., 1958; Dir. Adult Edn. Council Greater Chgo., 1956-62, vice chmn., 1959-60; mem. Chgo. Council on Fgn. Relations, 1954-72, bd. mem., 1970-72; citizens bd. U. Chgo., 1956-80; adv. com. Midwest Office Inst. Internat. Edn., 1954-58; S.E. Chgo. Commn., 1955-63; mem. Midwest Council on Airborne TV Instrn., 1959-62; Exec. sec. to Am. Council on Edn. Commn., survey U. Ill., 1942; on leave from La. State U.; mem. Round Table Meeting on Peace UNESCO, Paris, 1966; Bd. dirs. Chgo. Area Sch. TV, 1964-70, Sight Systems Inst., 1974-78; mem. Mass. Edn. Study, 1963-64; Mem. bus. adv. council Chgo. City Jr., 1964-66; chmn. bd. Chgo. City Coll., 1966-84; bd. dirs. North River Commn., 1967-70; Bd. dirs. Internat. Inst. Adminstrv. Scis., 1951-55; council advisors U.S. Commr. Edn., 1950-52; adv. panel Comptroller Army, 1950-53. Author: Youth Welfare in Germany, 1936, also survey reports.; contbr. articles to edn. profl. jours. Mem. Supts. Roundtable No. Ill., 1954-71, Tri-county Ednl. TV Coun., 1955-63, Citizens Com. U. Ill., 1959-73, Chgo. Civic Com. World Refugees, 1960-69. Commd. capt. O.R.C. AUS; div. mil govt. occupied countries, 1943; maj., 1944; lt. col., 1945, promoted to brig. gen. (assimilated rank), 1946, NATOUSA; North Africa asst. dir., then dir. studies Mil. Govt. Sch. and Holding Ctr., 1943-44; chief edn. and religious affairs br. U.S. Mil. Govt. for Germany (planning unit in Eng., 1944-45, operational unit in Berlin, 1945-47); U.S. rep. on Quadripartite Edn. Com. for Germany 1945-47, Berlin. Decorated Legion of Merit; chevalier French Legion of Honor; officer French Legion of Honor; named Man of Year Louisville, 1950, Chicagoan of Yr. in Edn. Jr. C. of C., 1962; recipient Chgo. medal for merit, 1972, Disting. Alumnus award Peabody Demonstration Sch.-Univ. Sch. Nashville, 1990. Mem. NEA, Am. Acad. Polit. and Social Sci., Am. Legion, Chgo. Assn. Commerce and Industry (chmn. edn. com. 1959-69), Internat. Platform Assn., Acad. TV Arts and Scis. (gov. Chgo. 1958-71), Omicron Delta Kappa, Phi Delta Kappa, Kappa Delta Pi, Phi Kappa Phi. Presbyn. Clubs: Executives (Louisville), Filson (Louisville), Arts (Louisville), Rotary (Louisville), Salmagundi (Louisville), Pendennis (Louisville); Allied Circle (London); Union League (Chgo.), Wayfarers (Chgo.), Casino (Chgo.), Commercial. (Chgo.). Home and Office: 2960 N Lake Shore Dr Apt 2706 Chicago IL 60657-5662

TAYLOR, JONATHAN FRANCIS, agribusiness executive; b. Kampala, Uganda, Aug. 12, 1935; came to U.S., 1980; s. Reginald William and Ruth (Tyson) T.; m. Anthea Gail Proctor, May 1965; children: Luke Augustus James, Matthew Justinian Robert, James Maximillian Rex. BA, Oxford U. (Eng.), 1957, MA, 1959. Adminstrv. sec. Booker Agribusiness Ltd., London, 1960-64; mgr. projects Booker Agribusiness Ltd., Nigeria, Kenya, Indonesia & others, 1964-76; chmn. Booker Agribusiness Ltd., 1976-84; chief exec. Booker PLC, London, 1984-93, chmn., 1993—; bd. dirs. Arbor Acres Farm Inc., Glastonbury, Conn., Tate & Lyle PLC, London, MEPC PLC, London, Equitable Life Assurance Soc.; chmn. Ellis & Everard PLC, Bradford. Chmn. devel. com. Bodleian Libr.; bd. govs. Sch. Oriental and African Studies London U., Royal Agrl. Soc.; chmn. Found. Devel. of Polish Agr.; dir. Internat. Agribus. Mgmt. Assn., Winrock Internat. Inst. Agrl. Devel.; mem. coun. Overseas Devel. Inst. Hon. fellow Corpus Christi, Oxford. Clubs: Knickerbocker (N.Y.C.); Travellers (London). Office: Booker PLC, 85 Buckingham Gate, London SW1E 6PD, England

TAYLOR, JOSEPH HOOTON, JR., radio astronomer, physicist; b. Phila., Mar. 29, 1941; s. Joseph Hooton and Sylvia Hathaway (Evans) T.; m. Marietta Bisson, Jan. 3, 1976; children: Jeffrey, Rebecca, Anne-Marie. BA in Physics, Haverford Coll., 1963; PhD in Astronomy, Harvard U., 1968; DSc (hon., U. Chgo., 1985, U. Mass., 1994. Research fellow, lectr. Harvard U., 1968-69; asst. prof. astronomy U. Mass., Amherst, 1969-72; assoc. prof. U. Mass., 1973-77, prof., 1977-81; prof. physics Princeton U., 1980—, James McDonnell Disting. prof. physics, 1986—. Author: Pulsars, 1977. Recipient Dannie Heineman prize in astrophysics Am. Inst. Physics/Am. Astron. Soc., 1980, Tomalla Found. prize in gravitation and cosmology, 1985, Magellanic Premium award Am. Philos. Soc., 1990, Einstein prize laureate Albert Einstein Soc., 1991, Wolf Prize in Physics, Wolf Found., 1992, Nobel Prize in Physics, Nobel Foundation, 1993; MacArthur fellow, 1981. Fellow Am. Acad. Arts and Scis., Am. Phys. Soc.; mem. NAS (Henry Draper medal 1985, John J. Carty medal Advancement Sci. 1991), Am. Philos. Soc., Am. Astron. Soc., Internat. Sci. Radio Union, Internat. Astron. Union. Mem. Soc. of Friends. Home: 272 Hartley Ave Princeton NJ 08540-5656 Office: Princeton U Dept Physics Jadwin Hall PO Box 708 Princeton NJ 08544*

TAYLOR, JOYCE, religious organization executive. Pres. Youth Dept. of Ch. of God in Christ Internat. Office: 137-17 135th Ave Jamaica NY 11436-2146

TAYLOR, JUDITH ANN, marketing and sales executive; b. Sheridan, Wyo., July 9, 1944; d. Milo G. and Eleanor M. (Wood) Rinker; m. George I. Taylor, Sept. 15, 1962; children: Monte G., Bret A. Fashion dept. mgr. Montgomery Ward, Sheridan, 1968-73; pers. mgr., asst. mgr. Dan's Ranchwear, Sheridan, 1973-80; sales/prodn. coord. KWYO Radio, Sheridan, 1981-83; sales mgr., promotions coord. KROE Radio, Sheridan, 1984-96; mng. editor BOUNTY Publ., 1993-96; dir. sales and marketing Best Western Sheridan Ctr., 1996—; notary pub. State of Wyo., 1985—; lectr., instr. BSA Merit U.; lectr. acad. achievement LVA Adv. Bd., 1993—, instr. Tongue River Middle Sch. Academic Enrichmen t Program, 1994-95; S.C. Ambs., 1980—, pres., 1995-96. Mng. editor BOUNTY Publ., 1993-96. Sec.-treas. Sheridan County Centennial Com., 1986-89; local sec.-treas. Wyo. Cenntennial Com., Sheridan, 1986-90; exec. dir. Sheridan-Wyo. Rodeo bd., 1983—; bd. dirs. Sheridan County Fair Bd., 1991-96, treas., 1995—; bd. dirs. "Christmas in April" Sheridan County, 1992—; mem. WJTP Coun., Cheyenne, 1990-92; mem. adv. coun. Tutor-Literacy Vols. of Am., 1993—; Sheridan High Sch. Key Club sponser, 1994—; Sheridan Jr. High Sch. Builders Club sponser, 1996—; City of Sheridan CVB bd.; Mrs. Santa Claus for local groups; vol. coord. AIDS Quilt; local chmn. March of Dimes Walkamerica, 1997—. Mem. Wyo. Assn. Broadcasters, S.C. C. of C. (dir. 1988—, pres. 1989-91), UMWA Aux. (pres. 1982-89), Kiwanis (v.p. 1992—, pres.-elect 1993, pres. 1994), S.C. Ambassadors (pres. 1995-96), Ft. Phil Kearney/Bozeman Trail (bd. dirs. 1995—). Democrat. Christian Ch. Office: Best We Sheridan Ctr PO Box 4008 Sheridan WY 82801

TAYLOR, JUDITH CAROLINE, entrepreneur; b. Quincy, Ill., June 23, 1948; d. Earl George and Caroline Clara (Knuffman) Schenk; m. Richard Odell Taylor, Nov. 28, 1970; children: Alexander James and Nicholas James (twins). BA, Quincy (Ill.) U., 1985; grad., Unity Sch. Religious Studies, 1997. Ordained Unity minister, 1997. Resident mgr. Landing Heights Apts., Brighton, N.Y., 1973-75; facilitator adult student program Quincy U., 1983-85; dist. mgr. Creative Expressions, 1981-85; mgr. mem. svcs. Quincy Conv. and Visitors Bur., 1985; sales dir. Motor Inn Hotel, Quincy, 1986; entrepreneur Taylor Enterprises, Quincy, 1985—; exec. dir. The Kensington, Quincy, 1987-90; mgr., salesperson, cons. Taylor's Fine Furniture & Gifts, Quincy, 1990-95; cons., freelance designer. Designed, marketed series I and II Quincy Postcards, 1987, 90; photo show John Wood C.C., 1993. House tour chairperson Quincy Perserves Bd., 1989; pres. Quincy Newcomers Club, 1980; pres. Great Rivers Mothers of Twins, Quincy, 1979; student min. Unity Ch., Quincy, 1996, 97. Recipient Americanism award VFW, Quincy, 1966. Mem. AAUW, Older Womens League (pres. 1988), The Atlantis Study Group, Quincy Conv. and Visitors Bur., Altrusa Club. Mem. Unity Ch. Avocations: photography, poetry writing, spirituality. Home: 1461 Maine St Quincy IL 62301-4260 Office: Taylors Fine Furniture & Gifts 123 N 4th St Quincy IL 62301-2913

TAYLOR, JUNE RUTH, retired minister; b. Annapolis, Md., June 27, 1932; d. Benjamin and Naomi Medora (Dill) Michaelson; m. Thomas Wayne Taylor, Mar. 20, 1954; children: Rebecca Susan Taylor DeLameter, Michael Steven. AB, Goucher Coll., 1952; MRE, Presbyn. Sch. of Christian Edn., Richmond, Va., 1954; MDiv., McCormick Theol. Sem., 1978. Ordained to ministry Presbyn. Ch. (U.S.A.), 1976. Min. Christian Edn. Congl. United Ch. of Christ, Arlington Heights, Ill., 1974-79; dir. pastoral svcs. Presbyn. U. Hosp., Pitts., 1979-89; dir. chaplaincy svcs. Ephrata (Pa.) Community Hosp., 1991-96; ret., 1996; chaplain Rush-Presbyn. St. Luke's Med. Ctr., Chgo., 1976-78; chair exec. com. Presbyn. Assn. Specialized Pastoral Ministries, Louisville, 1987-89; bd. dirs. Cocalico Place. Book reviewer in field. Fellow Coll. Chaplains (sec. exec. com. 1985-87); mem. Soc. Chaplains, Hosp. Assn. Pa. (pres. 1983), Assn. Mental Health Clergy, Assn. for Clin. Pastoral Edn. (clin.), Rotary (liaison to Boys and Girls Club S.W. Pitts. chpt. 1990-91, program chair Denver-Adamstown club 1996-97), Gamma Phi Beta Alumnae Club (pres. 1990-91).

TAYLOR, KAREN ANNETTE, mental health nurse; b. Kinston, N.C., Oct. 7, 1952; d. Emmett Green and Polly Ann (Taylor) Tyndall; m. Paul Othell Taylor Jr., June 24, 1979 (div. 1996); 1 child, Clarissa Anne. AA, Lenoir C.C., Kinston, 1972; Diploma, Lenoir Meml. Hosp. Sch. of, Nursing, 1984; student, St. Joseph's Coll., Windham, Maine, 1993-94. RN, N.C. Staff nurse Lenoir Meml. Hosp., 1984-86; staff nurse, relief patient care dir. Brynn Marr Hosp., Jacksonville, N.C., 1987-90; staff nurse, quality assurance Naval Hosp., Camp Lejeune, N.C., 1990-92. Recipient Meritorious Unit Commendation Am. Fedn. of Govt. Employees, 1992. Baptist. Avocations: reading, crochet.

TAYLOR, KATHLEEN (CHRISTINE), physical chemist; b. Cambridge, Mass., Mar. 16, 1942; d. John F. and Anna M. (Maloney) T. BA in Chemistry, Douglass Coll., New Brunswick, N.J., 1964; PhD in Phys. Chemistry, Northwestern U., 1968. Postdoctoral fellow U. Edinburgh, Scotland, 1968-70; assoc. sr. rsch. chemist Gen. Motors Rsch. Labs., Warren, Mich., 1970-74, sr. rsch. chemist, 1974-75, asst. phys. chemistry dept. head, 1975-83, environ. sci. dept. head, 1983-85, phys. chemistry dept. head, 1985-96, physics and phys. chemistry dept. head, 1995—. Recipient Mich. Sci. Trailblazer award Detroit Sci. Ctr., 1986. Fellow AAAS, mem. NAE, Am. Chem. Soc. (Garvan medal 1989), Materials Rsch. Soc. (treas. 1984, 2d v.p. 1985, 1st v.p. 1986, pres. 1987), Soc. Automotive Engrs., The Catalysis Soc., Sigma Xi. Office: Gen Motors R&D Ctr Physics and Phys Chemistry Dept 30500 Mound Rd Warren MI 48092-2031

TAYLOR, KENARD LYLE, JR., director training; b. Syracuse, N.Y., Dec. 22, 1943; s. Kenard Lyle and Nina T.; m. Sharon Lee Stookey, Dec. 31, 1965; children: Kimberly, Kenard III. BSCE, Ind. Tech. U., 1968; postgrad., Purdue U., 1970-72. Process engr. ARCO, East Chicago, Ind., 1968-71; plant engr. Kiel Chem., Hammond, Ind., 1971-72; mgr. ops. tng. ARCO, 1972-76; dir. Mfg. Tech., St. Louis, 1976—; chmn. bd. dirs. Mfg. Tech., dir. Warren Forthought. Author 210 plant tng. workbooks and articles, 1976-97. City coun. mem. City of Valparaiso (Ind.), 1978-83; campaign mgr. Rep. Candidates Porter County, Ind., 1976-97; Center Twp. Rep. chmn., Porter County, Ind., 1993-97; v.p. Ind. JCI Senate, 1978, Ind. Jaycees, 1976; pres. Valparaiso Jaycees, 1974. Mem. Great Lakes API Com. Tng. (assoc.). Republican. Avocations: golf, fishing. Office: Mfg Tech 306 Napoleon St Valparaiso IN 46383-4744

TAYLOR, KENDRICK JAY, microbiologist; b. Manhattan, Mont., Mar. 17, 1914; s. William Henry and Rose (Carney) T.; BS, Mont. State U., 1938; postgrad. (fellow) U. Wash., 1938-41, U. Calif. at Berkeley, 1952, Drama Studio of London, 1985; m. Hazel Marguerite Griffith, July 28, 1945; children: Stanley, Paul, Richard. Rsch. microbiologist Cutter Labs., Berkeley, Calif., 1945-74; microbiologist Berkeley Biologicals, 1975-86. Committeeman Mount Diablo coun. Boy Scouts Am., 1955, dist. vice-chmn., 1960-61, dist. chmn., 1962-65, cubmaster, 1957, scoutmaster, 1966; active Contact Ministries, 1977-80; bd. dirs. Santa Clara Community Players, 1980-84; vol. instr. English as a Second Lang., 1979-80; vol. ARC Blood Ctr., VA Hosp., San Jose; life mem. PTA; census taker, 1980; mem. Berkely Jr. C. of C., 1946-49. Served with AUS, 1941-46, lt. col. Res., ret. Recipient Scout's Wood badge Boy Scouts Am., 1962; recipient Golden Diploma Mont. State U., 1988. Mem. Am. Soc. Microbiology (chmn. local com. 1953, v.p. No. Calif. br. 1963-65, pres. 1965-67), Sons and Daus. Mont. Pioneers, Mont. State Univ. Alumni Assn., Mont. Hist. Soc., Gallatin County Hist. Soc., Headwaters-Heritage Hist. Soc., Am. Legion Post 89, Parent-Tchrs. Assn. Calif. (life). Presbyterian (trustee 1951-53, elder 1954—). Home: 550 S 13th St San Jose CA 95112-2361

TAYLOR, KENNETH BYRON, JR., librarian, minister, religion educator; b. Russellville, Ala., Dec. 25, 1953; s. Kenneth Byron Sr. and Willene Martha (Sudduth) T.; m. Sheila Carol Mashburn, May 24, 1975; children: Justin, Jonathan, Jordan, Jessica. BS, U. North Ala., 1975; JD, U. Ala., 1978; MDiv, New Orleans Bapt. Theol. Sem., 1986, PhD, 1993; MLIS, La. State U., 1994. Bar: Ala. 1979; ordained to ministry Bapt. Ch., 1987. Staff atty. Legal Svcs. Corp. Ala., Florence, 1979-83; assoc. pastor Elysian Fields Ave. Bapt. Ch., New Orleans, 1984-87, pastor, 1987—; dir. libr. New Orleans (La.) Bapt. Theol. Sem., John T. Christian Libr., 1991—, asst. prof. Evangelism, 1993—. Avocations: hiking, gardening. Office: New Orleans Bapt Theol Sem John T Christian Libr 4110 Seminary Pl New Orleans LA 70126-4619

TAYLOR, KENNETH GRANT, chemistry educator; b. Paterson, N.J., May 12, 1936; s. Ulysses Grant and Susan (De Haan) T.; m. Carla May Rydell, June 17, 1961; children: Koren Lynn, Kevin Grant, Kaylyn Jo. BA, Calvin Coll., 1957; PhD, Wayne State U., 1963. Rsch. assoc. MIT, Cambridge, 1963-64; sr. rsch. assoc. Wayne State U., Detroit, 1964-66; from asst. to assoc. prof. chemistry U. Louisville, 1966-73, prof., 1974—, acting chmn., 1973-74, vice chmn., 1976-78, chmn., 1978-87, assoc. dean. Rsch., Arts and Scis., 1991—; prof. associé Univ. de Nancy I, Nancy Cedex, France, 1974-75, 82-83; vis. prof. U. Lund, Sweden, 1991. Contbr. numerous articles to profl. jours.; co-author, presentor numerous papers at sci. meetings. Rsch. and teaching grantee NIH, NSF, Am. Cancer Soc., Am. Chem. Soc., Dept. Interior, U. Louisville, 1966—. Fellow AAAS; mem. Am. Chem. Soc., Ky. Acad. Sci. Democrat. Presbyterian. Home: 1838 Yale Dr Louisville KY 40205-2031 Office: U Louisville Dept Chemistry Louisville KY 40292

TAYLOR, KENNETH J., diagnostic sonologist; b. Rochford, Essex, Eng., Mar. 8, 1939; s. William Albert and Florence (Soulsby) T.; m. Anne Bowen Simpkins, Apr. 8, 1964 (div. Nov. 1968); 1 child, Sally-Anne; m. Caroline Rix, May 17, 1975; children: Andrew, Ian. BSc, London U., 1961; MBBS, London U./Guys Hosp., Eng., 1964, PhD, 1972; MD, U. London, 1975; MA, Yale U., 1979, FACP, 1979. House surgeon Royal Surrey Hosp., Guildford, U.K., 1964-66; sr. house surgeon Guys Maudsley Hosp., London, 1966-67; jr. lectr. Guys Hosp. Med. Sch., London, 1967-70, lectr., 1970-72; sr. fellow Royal Marsden Hosp., Sutton, Surrey, U.K., 1973-75; assoc. prof. radiology Yale U., New Haven, Conn., 1975-77, tenured assoc. prof., 1977-79, tenured prof., 1979—; co-dir. Yale Ctr. for Ultrasonics and Sonics, New Haven, 1992—; dir. Exptl. Lab. Yale Radiology, 1991—, Yale Vascular Lab., 1992—; ad hoc adv. bd. NIH, Washington. Chmn. editl. bd. Clinics in Diagnostic Ultrasound, 1978—; co-editor: Doppler in Clinic Diagnosis, 1988, 2d edit., 1995; assoc. editor Radiology Jour., 1992—; author: Atlas of Ultrasound, 1978, 2d edit., 1984. Bd. dirs. Friends of Hospice, New Haven, 1980. Lt. Royal Navy Res., 1962-65. Rsch. grantee Am. Cancer Soc., N.Y., 1976, 82, NIH Cancer Inst., Washington, 1988-89, 88-91. Fellow Am. Inst. Ultrasound Med. (bd. gov. 1978-82), Am. Coll. Physicians; mem. Radiol. Soc. N.Am. Achievements include pioneering applications for grey scale ultrasound, applications of Doppler ultrasound; ultrasonic contrast agents main chemical interests. Avocations: travel, classical music, swimming, cycling, Italian culture. Home: 1611 Great Hill Rd Guilford CT 06437-3647 Office: 333 Cedar St New Haven CT 06510-3206

TAYLOR, KENNETH NATHANIEL, publishing executive, author; b. Portland, Oreg., May 8, 1917; s. George Nathaniel and Charlotte Bodwell (Huff) T.; m. Margaret Louise West, Sept. 13, 1940; children: Becky, John, Martha, Peter, Janet, Mark, Cynthia, Gretchen, Mary Lee, Alison. BA, Wheaton Coll., 1938, DLitt (hon.), 1965; student, Dallas Theol. Sem., 1940-43; ThM, No. Bapt. Theol. Sem., 1944; DLitt (hon.), Trinity Evang. Div. Sch., 1972; LHD (hon.), Huntington Coll., 1974, Taylor U., 1989. With Moody Press (pub. protestant religious lit.), Chgo., 1947-63; dir. Moody Press (pub. protestant religious lit.), 1948-62, Moody Lit. Mission (prodn. and distbn. lit.), 1948-62; pres. Tyndale House Publishers, 1963-84, chmn. bd., 1984—; chmn. bd. Coverdale House Pubs., London, Eng., 1969-79; pres. Tyndale House Found., 1964-79, bd. dirs., 1964—; dir. Inter-Varsity Christian Fellowship, 1956-59, Evang. Lit. Overseas, 1951-70, Short Terms Abroad, 1963-77; pres. Living Bibles Internat., Wheaton, Ill., 1968-77, internat. pres., 1977-90, internat. chmn. emeritus, 1990-92; chmn. Unilit., Inc., Portland, 1972-73. Author: Is Christianity Credible, 1946, Living Letters: The Paraphrased Epistles, 1962; juveniles Stories for the Children's Hour, 1953, Devotions for the Children's Hour, 1954, I See, 1958 (reprinted as Small Talks About God, 1995), Bible in Pictures for Little Eyes, 1956, Lost on the Trail, 1959, Romans for the Children's Hour, 1959; Living Prophecies - The Minor Prophets Paraphrased, 1965, Living Gospels, 1966, Living Psalms and Proverbs With the Major Prophets Paraphrased, 1967, The Living New Testament, 1967, Almost 12, 1968, revised, 1995, Living Lessons of Life and Love, 1968, Living Books of Moses, 1969, Living History of Israel, 1970, The Living Bible, 1971, Taylor's Bible Story Book, 1970; juveniles What High School Students Should Know About Creation, 1983, What High School Students Should Know About Evolution, 1983, Big Thoughts for Little People, 1983, Giant Steps for Little People, 1985, Wise Words for Little People, 1987, Next Steps for New Christians (originally How To Grow), 1989, My First Bible in Pictures, 1989 (ann. Angel award 1990, Platinum Book award 1990), The Good Samaritan, 1989, Jesus Feeds A Crowd, 1989, The Lost Sheep, 1989, The Prodigal Son, 1989; Good News for Little People, 1991 (ann. Angel award 1992), My Life, A Guided Tour, 1991, Daniel and the Lions' Den, 1992, Noah's Ark, 1992, Family-Time Bible in Pictures, 1992, A Boy Helps Jesus, 1994, The Good Neighbor, 1994, Noah Builds a Boat, 1994, A Very Special Baby, 1994, The Story of Noah's Ark, 1994, Small Talks About God, 1995, Everything a Child Should Know About God, 1996; co-editor: The Bible for Children, 1990 (ann. Angel award 1991); pub. The Christian Reader, 1964-92, Have a Good Day, 68—. Bd. dirs. Christian Libr. Svc., 1972-75, InterSkrift forlage Aktiebolag, Sweden, Internat. Bible Soc., 1992-94; trustee Living Bible Found., Fuller Theol. Sem.; mem. adv. bd. Internat. Bible Reading Assn. Recipient citation Layman's Nat. Bible Com., 1971; award Religious Heritage Am., 1972; disting. svc. citation Internat. Soc. Christian Endeavor, 1973; Nelson Bible award, 1973; Better World award VFW Aux., 1974; disting. pub. svc. award 1974; Recognition award Urban Ministries, Inc., 1977; Svc. award Wheaton Coll. Alumni Assn., 1977; Crusader award Wheaton Coll., 1979; Gutenberg award Chgo. Bible Soc., 1981; Internat. Christian Edn. Assn. award, 1983; Inducted into DuPage County Heritage Gallery, 1983; named Man of Yr. Com. Internat. Goodwill, 1983; recipient 1st Ann. Lit. award Evang. Lit. Overseas, 1983; Svc. award YFC/USA, 1984; Gold Medallion Achievement award Evang. Pubs. Assn., 1984; named to Christian Booksellers Hall of Fame, 1989; recipient Ann. James DeForest Murch award Nat. Assn. Evangelicals, 1995, Annual Golden Word award Internat. Bible Soc., 1996. Mem. Wheaton Coll. Scholastic Honor Soc. Home: 1515 E Forest Ave Wheaton IL 60187-4469 Office: 351 Executive Dr Carol Stream IL 60188-2420 *Who but God could make an unending universe, sized by billions of light years? And who could dream of knowing such a God personally? I am one who believes this, and have based my life on the Bible as God's message to mankind, and to you and me. But how to manage Bible reading when it is in such an ancient language? How to crack the shell of the coconut and find the milk and meat? That is why I spent 16 years translating the Bible into living English, with 37 million copies now in print.*

TAYLOR, KRISTIN CLARK, media specialist; b. Detroit, Mar. 26, 1959; d. James W. and Mary Elizabeth (Moore) Clark; m. Lonnie Paul Taylor; children: Lonnie Paul II, Mary Elizabeth. BA in Classical Lit., Mich. State U., 1982. Editor, writer USA Today, Washington, 1982-86; asst. press sec. to Vice President Bush White House, Washington, 1987-88, spl. asst. to Vice President Bush for press rels., 1988-89; dir. White House media rels., 1989-90; dir. comm. BellSouth Corp., Washington, 1990-94; v.p. external affairs Student Loan Mktg. Assn. (Sallie Mae), Washington, 1994—. Author: The First To Speak, A Woman of Color Inside the White House, 1993. Republican.

TAYLOR, LANCE JEROME, economics educator; b. Montpelier, Idaho, May 25, 1940; s. Walter Jerome and Ruth (Robinson) T.; m. Yvonne S.M. Johnsson, May 31, 1963; children: Ian Lance, Signe Marguerite. BS with honors, Calif. Inst. Tech., 1962; PhD, Harvard U., 1968. Instr. econs. Harvard U., Cambridge, Mass., 1967-68; asst. prof., assoc. prof. Harvard U., 1970-74; research assoc. MIT, Cambridge, 1968-70; prof. econs. MIT, 1974-93, New Sch. for Social Rsch., N.Y.C., 1993—; vis. prof. U. Brasilia, 1974, Pontifical Cath. U. Rio de Janeiro, 1981, U. Delhi, 1987-88, Stockholm Sch. Econs., 1990; Marshall lectr. Cambridge U., 1986-87; cons. World Bank, UN, various fgn. govts. Author: Macro Models for Developing Countries, 1979, Models of Growth and Distribution for Brazil, 1980, Structuralist Macroeconomics, 1983, Varieties of Stabilization Experience, 1988, Income Distribution, Inflation, and Growth, 1991, The Market Meets its Match: Restructuring the Economies of Eastern Europe, 1994. Fulbright fellow, 1962-63. Mem. Am. Econ. Assn., Royal Econ. Soc. Home: PO Box 378 Washington ME 04574-0378 Office: New School for Social Rsch Grad Faculty 65 Fifth Ave New York NY 10003-3003

TAYLOR, LAWRENCE PALMER, diplomat; b. Cleve., Apr. 18, 1940; s. Sheldon A. and Juanita (Springer) T.; m. Lynda Ellen Gorham; children: Lori, Tracey, Scott. AB, Ohio U., 1963; MA, Am. U., 1969; MPA, Harvard U., 1977. Consular officer Zagreb, Yugoslavia, 1972-73; econ. officer U.S. Embassy, Belgrade, Yugoslavia, 1973-76; petroleum attache U.S. Embassy, Jakarta, Indonesia, 1976-79; energy officer U.S. Embassy, Ottawa, Can., 1980-84; econ. minister U.S. Embassy, Ottawa, Ont., Can., 1989-92; econ. counselor U.S. Embassy, London, 1985-89; dir. Fgn. Svc. Inst., Washington, 1992-95; amb. to Estonia, 1995—. Avocation: collecting polit., military ephemera, maps. Home: 2025 Mummasburg Rd Gettysburg PA 17325-7465 Office: Am Embassy Tallinn Dept of State Washington DC 20521-4530

TAYLOR, LEIGH HERBERT, college dean; b. Chgo., Oct. 23, 1941; s. Herbert and Leona Taylor; m. Nancy E. Young; children: Jennifer, Jeremiah. BA, U. Tulsa, 1964, JD, 1966; LLM, NYU, 1969. Bar: Okla. 1966, Ill. 1976. Trial atty. Civil Rights div. Dept. Justice, Washington, 1966-68; prof. DePaul U. Coll. Law, Chgo., 1969-77; asst. dean DePaul U. Coll. Law, 1972-73, assoc. dean, 1973-77; dean Coll. Law, Ohio No. U., Ada, 1977-78, Sch. Law Southwestern U., L.A., 1978—; mem. adv. bd. 1st Woman's Bank of L.A., 1981-85; dir. Law Sch. Admissions Svcs., Inc., 1982-86; chmn. audit com. Law Sch. Admissions Coun., 1989-91, trustee, 1991-98, chair-elect, 1994-95, chair, 1995-97; mem. bd. trustees Coun. on Legal Edn. Opportunity, 1993-96. Editor-in-chief Tulsa Law Jour., 1966; author: Strategies for Law-Focused Education, 1977; (with others) Law in a New Land, 1972; mem. editorial bd. Family Law Quarterly, 1977-78. Bd. dirs. Criminal Def. Consortium Cook County (Ill.), Inc., 1975-77, L.A. Press Club Found. With AUS, 1959. Fellow Am. Bar Found.; mem. ABA (accreditation com. 1991-95), Law in Am. Soc. Found., Ill. Bar Assn., Chgo. Bar Assn. (rec. sec.), L.A. County Bar Assn., Okla. Bar Assn. Office: Southwestern U Sch Law Office of Dean 675 S Westmoreland Ave Los Angeles CA 90005-3905

TAYLOR, LEONARD STUART, engineering educator, consultant; b. N.Y.C., Dec. 28, 1928; m. Lillian Rachel Schlang, Apr. 12, 1954; children: Robin Jolie, Allyn Lise. AB, Harvard Coll., 1951; MSc, N.Mex. State U., 1955, PhD, 1960. Microwave engr. Raytheon Mfg. Co., Bedford, Mass., 1950-55; research physicist Gen. Electric Co., Phila., 1960-63; assoc. prof. Case Western Res. U., Cleve., 1964-67; prof. U. Md., College Park, Md., 1967-96; prof. emeritus U. Md., College Park, 1996—; cons. USN, Silver Spring, Md., 1967-96. Contbr. articles to profl. jours; inventor Microwave Scalpel, Implantable Microwave Hyperthermia Applicator and numerous others. Recipient Disting. Alumni N.Mex. State U. 1975. Fellow IEEE (life), Am. Soc. for Laser Medicine and Surgery; mem. Am. Phys. Soc., Optical Soc. of Am., Bioelectromagnetics Soc. Avocations: tennis, music. Office: U Md EE Dept College Park MD 20742

TAYLOR, LEWIS JEROME, JR., priest; b. Norfolk, Va., Feb. 22, 1923; s. Lewis Jerome and Roberta Page (Newton) T.; m. Pauline Rector Green, Nov. 24, 1945; children: Lewis J. III, Michael R., John B., Mary F., Joan E. BS in Engring., U.S. Naval Acad., 1944; MDiv, Seabury-Western Theol. Sem., Evanston, Ill., 1961; PhD in Religion, Duke U., 1972. Ordained priest Episcopal Ch., 1962. With George R. Green, Inc., White Post, Va., 1949-52, Travelers Ins. Co., Norfolk, 1956-58; chaplain Coll. William and Mary, Williamsburg, Va., 1961-63; rector St. Aidan's Episc. Ch., Virginia Beach, Va., 1963-68; prof. theology St. Andrews Sem., Manila, The Philippines, 1971-76; rector Ch. of the Messiah, Chester, N.J., 1978-86; interim rector of various parishes Diocese of Southern Va., 1986-93; instnl. chaplain Indian Creek Correctional Ctr., Chesapeake, Va., 1993—; mem. Dept. Missions Diocese of Newark, 1965-68, Commn. on Ministry, Newark, 1979-82; dean Lay Sch. of Christian Studies, Newark, 1977-82; chmn. Commn. on Racism, Southern Va., 1992-95. Author: In Search of Self: Life, Death, and Walker Percy, 1985; contbr. articles to profl. jours. Bd. dirs. Samaritan House, Virginia Beach, 1995—. Comdr. USN, 1944-49, 52-56; PTO. Trinity Inst. grantee, 1986. Mem. Rotary (pres. 1980-86). Democrat. Avocations: tennis, camping, reading.

TAYLOR, LINDA RATHBUN, investment banker; b. Rochester, N.Y., May 25, 1946; d. Lewis Standish and Elizabeth Florence (Hunt) Rathbun; m. Donald Gordon Taylor, Mar. 1, 1975; children: Alexander Standish, Abigail Elizabeth, Elizabeth Downing. BA, Vasser Coll., 1968; MBA, Harvard U., 1973. Chartered fin. analyst. Assoc. corp. fin. Donaldson, Lufkin & Jenrette, N.Y.C., 1973-75; cons. IBRD, Washington, 1975; fin. analyst U.S. Treas. Dept., Washington, 1976-78; chief investment officer United Mine Workers Fund, 1978-85; investment mgr. Cen. Pension Fund Internat. Union Oper. Engrs., Washington, 1985-86; investment banker Saranow Co., 1986-89; pvt. investor, 1990—; pres. Pony Prodns., Inc. Trustee Montgomery County (Md.) Employees' Retirement Sys., 1987-93, Washington Internat. Horse Show, bd. dirs., 1995—; com. mem. Vassar Coll. Endowment Fund, 1992—; elder Bradley Hills Presbyn. Ch., 1992—; bd. pensions Presbyn. Ch. U.S.A., 1996—. Contbr. articles to profl. jours. Recipient Disting. Alumni award Carolina Day Sch., 1996. Mem. Jr. League Washington, Washington Soc. Investment Analysts (bd. dirs. 1984-85), Fin. Analyst Fedn. Republican.

TAYLOR, LYLE DEWEY, economic development company executive; b. Traer, Iowa, Sept. 26, 1934; s. John Dewey and Lorriane (Burrows) T.; m. Margaret Conn, Dec. 29, 1955; children: Lylette, Robin, Carla, Pennie. Student, LaJunta Jr. Coll., 1951-52. Plant worker Rath Packing Co., Waterloo, Iowa, 1952-61; rec. sec. local 46 United Food & Comml. Workers Union, 1961-69, pres. local 46, 1969-82, exec. v.p., 1982-83; pres., chief exec. officer Rath Packing Co., 1983-85; v.p. Blackhawk Holding Co., Waterloo, 1985-88; pres. Black Hawk Econ. Devel. Co., Waterloo, 1988—; pres. Ray Price Cherokee Farms, 1986-89; dir. Am. Meat Inst., Washington, 1983. Sec. Cedar Valley Partnership, 1989-95; past mem. Gov.'s Adv. Com. on OSHA, Iowa U. Alumni Adv. Bd., Ames; past bd. dirs. Goodwill, Inc., Waterloo, Adult's Care, Exceptional Persons; bd. dirs. Iowa Northland Regional Econ. Devel. Commn., 1995—, Airport Area Devel. Auth., 1996—. With USAR, 1956-64. Democrat. Baptist. Home: 826 Skyview Rd Waterloo IA 50703-9301 Office: Black Hawk Econ Devel Co 403 Jefferson St PO Box 330 Waterloo IA 50704-0330

TAYLOR, MARK CHANDLEE, choreographer; b. Wichita Falls, Tex., Apr. 26, 1953; s. William Mottu and Vonna (Gigoux) T.; m. Barbara Winfield Sieck, Mar. 1, 1980. BA in Medieval Studies, Swarthmore (Pa.) Coll., 1975. Artistic dir. Mark Taylor & Friends, N.Y.C., 1981-91, Dance Alloy/Mark Taylor, Pitts., 1991—; dancer, performer Rosalind Newman and Dancers, N.Y.C., 1976-79; lectr. dance Princeton (N.J.) U., 1984-91; freelance choreographer Paris Opera Ballet, 1986; movement cons. CSC Repertory Theater, N.Y.C., 1989-90. Recipient Fellowships, N.Y. Found., 1985, Nat. Endowment for Arts, 1988, Gulkentian Found., Ireland, 1986. Mem. Dance Theater Workshop. Mem. Soc. of Friends. Office: Dance Alloy/ Mark Taylor 5530 Penn Ave Pittsburgh PA 15206-3525*

TAYLOR, MARK DOUGLAS, publishing executive; b. Geneva, Ill., Jan. 16, 1951; s. Kenneth Nathaniel and Margaret Louise (West) T.; m. Carol E. Rogers, May 28, 1973; children: Jeremy Peter, Kristen Elizabeth, Margaret Louise, Rebecca Cynthia, Stephen Rogers. BA, Duke U., 1973. Exec. dir. Tyndale House Found., Wheaton, Ill., 1973-78; v.p. Tyndale House Pubs., Wheaton, Ill., 1978-84; pres., chief exec. officer Tyndale House Pubs., 1984—; dir. Living Bibles Internat. U.S., Naperville, Ill., 1972-92. Author The Complete Book of Bible Literacy, 1992. Mem. Wheaton Liquor Control Commn., 1986—, chmn., 1994—; chmn. bd. dirs. Outreach Cmty. Ctr., 1986-93. Mem. Internat. Bible Soc. (bd. dirs. 1992—). Office: Tyndale House Publishers Inc 351 Executive Dr Box 80 Wheaton IL 60189 *What we accomplish in life is soon forgotten. Our best legacy is to pass on to our children and grandchildren our positive values.*

TAYLOR, MARTHA CROLL, nursing administrator; b. Ohio, July 10, 1964; d. Gaylord William and Geraldine Croll; m. Rodney Alden Taylor, Sept. 17, 1994. BSN, Capitul U., 1986; MSN, Duke U., 1993. On-call rsch. nurse, staff nurse Critical Care Unit Duke U. Med. Ctr., Durham, N.C., 1986-91, rsch. nurse coord., 1989-91, nurse clinician Critical Care Unit, 1990-91, clin. nurse educator, 1992-95, dir. Heart Ctr. Nursing, 1995-97, dir. Heart Ctr. Nursing and Adminstv. Svcs., 1997—; regional clin. coord. Genentech, Inc., Durham, 1991-92. Mem. edn. com. Am. Heart Assn., Durham, 1993—, bd. dirs., 1994—. Mem. AACN (pres. 1993), Sigma Theta Tau. Republican. Lutheran. Avocations: reading, boating. Home: 3018 Little River Dr Hillsborough NC 27278

TAYLOR, MARY D., counselor; b. Manitow, Okla., July 24, 1936; d. Hoye S. and Grace (Herrell) Rayburn; m. Arch Taylor; children: James, Joel, Paul, Steven, Denise. AA in Mental Health, Arts and Scis., Pierce Coll., 1978; BA, cert. in social welfare, child and family welfare, Pacific Luth. U., 1979. Registered counselor; cert. tchr., property mgr. Instr., trainer Tahoma Industries, Tacoma; supr. Sr. Ctr., City of Tacoma; counselor Episcopal Svc. for Youth, Tacoma, Rainier State Sch., Buckley, Wash.; owner, mgr. Taylor Apts., Tacoma. Advocate for mental illness; past bd. dirs. group health Larchmont Sr. Ctr.; mem. Neighborhood Safe Streets. Recipient award Ret. Sr. Vol. Program. Mem. DAV Women's Aux., AARP, ARC (life), Nat. Mental Health Illness Assn., Wash. State Mental Illness Assn., Am. Legion (honor guard), Eagles, Nat. Apt. Owners Assn., Pierce County Rental Housing Assn. Address: 7629 Pacific Ave Tacoma WA 98408-7014

TAYLOR, MARY KAY, geriatrics nurse; b. Knoxville, Iowa, Jan. 26, 1954; d. Wendell Shawver and Margery Ethel (Beebe) Kubli; m. Gregory Taylor, Sept. 4, 1993. ADN, Indian Hills Community Coll., 1979; BSN, Teikyo Marycrest U., 1993. RN, Iowa. Staff nurse Mercy Hosp., Des Moines, 1979-81, Knoxville Area Community Hosp., 1981-83, VA Med. Ctr., Knoxville, 1983—. Home: PO Box 646 Knoxville IA 50138-0646

TAYLOR, MARYANN COURTNEY, elementary education educator; b. Lynn, Mass., May 6, 1948; d. Wilfred Rosario and Mary Evelyn (Brennan) LaFrance; m. Leonard Dwelley Taylor, Apr. 19, 1969; 1 child, Leonard Dwelley III. BS, Bridgewater State Coll., 1970, MEd, 1972; cert. in paralegal studies, Northeastern U., Boston, 1987; postgrad., New Eng. Sch. Law, 1987-88, Oxford (Eng.) U., 1989, Fairfield U., Boston U., Lesley Coll., Boston Archtl. Ctr., 1980—. Cert. tchr., Mass. Tchr. Plymouth (Mass.) Pub. Schs., 1970—; retail lumber sales Taylor Lumber Co., Inc., Marshfield, Mass., 1981-94; owner, pres. Taylor Forest Products, Inc., 1993—. Editor newsletter Cub Scout Pack 212, 1979-83. Vol. South Shore Sci. Ctr., Norwell, Mass., 1980-81, March of Dimes, Marshfield, 1982-85. Mem. NEA, Mass. Tchrs. Assn., Edn. Assn. Plymouth-Carver (union rep. 1989—), Better Bus. Bur. (vol.). Avocation: extensive travel. Home: PO Box 1206 124 Ferry St Marshfield MA 02050 Office: Plymouth Pub Sch System Lincoln St Plymouth MA 02360

TAYLOR, MICHAEL ALAN, psychiatrist; b. N.Y.C., Mar. 6, 1940; s. Edward D. and Clara D. T.; m. Ellen Schoenfield, June 28, 1963; children—Christopher, Andrew. B.A., Cornell U., 1961; M.D., N.Y. Med. Coll., 1965. Intern Lenox Hill Hosp., N.Y.C., 1965-66; resident N.Y. Med. Coll., 1966-69, asst. prof. psychiatry, 1971-73; asso. prof. SUNY Med. Sch., Stony Brook, 1973-76; prof. psychiatry Univ. Health Scis., Chgo. Med. Sch., 1976—, dept., 1976-94. Author: The Neuropsychiatric Mental Status Examination, 1981; sr. author: General Hospital Psychiatry, 1985, The Neuropsychiatric Guide to Modern Everyday Psychiatry, 1993; editor-in-chief Neuropsychiat., Neuropsychology and Behavioral Neurology Jour.; also numerous articles. Served to lt. comdr. M.C. USNR, 1969-71. Grantee NIMH, 1971-73; Grantee Ill. Dept. Mental Health, 1976-81; VA grantee, 1985-93. Mem. Am. Psychopath. Assn. Office: FUHS Chgo Med Sch 3333 Green Bay Rd North Chicago IL 60064-3037

TAYLOR, MICHAEL LESLIE, lawyer; b. Boonville, Mo., Nov. 2, 1954; s. Paul Howard and Nora Lee T.; m. Janet S. Finke, June 23, 1990. AA, Kansas City Communtiy Coll., 1977; BGS, U. Kans., 1979, JD, 1982. Bar: Mo. 1982, U.S. Dist. Ct. Mo. 1982, U.S. Ct. Appeals (10th cir.) 1986, U.S. Ct. Appeals (8th cir.) 1987. Assoc. atty. Watkins, Boulware, Lucas & Miner, St. Joseph, Mo., 1982-85, ptnr., 1986-87; named ptnr. Watkins, Boulware, Lucas, Miner, Murphy & Taylor, St. Joseph, Mo., 1987—; instr. Mo. Western State Coll., St. Joseph, 1985-94. Bd. mem. Midland Empire Diabetes Assn., St. Joseph, 1984; mem. United Way Allocations Com., St. Joseph, 1985-86; pres. East Hills Homes Assn., St. Joseph, 1987-89; co-chair Leadership Tomorrow, St. Joseph, 1985-88. Recipient Outstanding Vol. Svc. to the City Vol. award City St. Joseph, 1985, Lon O. Hocker Meml. Trial LAwyer award Mo. Bar Found., 1989. Fellow Am. Acad. Matrimonial Lawyers; mem. ABA, Mo. Bar Assn., St. Joseph Bar Assn. Avocations: reading, tennis, weightlifting. Office: Watkins Boulware Lucas Miner Murphy & Taylor 3101 Frederick Ave Saint Joseph MO 64506-2911

TAYLOR, MILDRED D., author; b. Jackson, Miss., Sept. 13, 1943; d. Wilbert Lee and Deletha Marie (Davis) Taylor. BA in Edn., U Toledo, 1965; MA, U Colo., 1969. Vol., tchr. English and history Peace Corps, Ethiopia, 1965-67; then recruiter Peace Corps, U.S., 1967-68; study skills coord. black edn. program U. Colo., 1969-71. Author: (children's fiction) Song of the Trees, 1975, Roll of Thunder, Hear My Cry, 1976, Let the Circle Be Unbroken, 1981, The Gold Cadillac, 1987, The Friendship and Other Stories, 1987, Mississippi Bridge, 1990, The Road to Memphis, 1990, The Well, 1995 (winner Jane Addams book award, 1996). Address: care Dial Books For Young Readers 375 Hudson St New York NY 10014-3658

TAYLOR, MINNA, lawyer; b. Washington, Jan. 25, 1947; d. Morris P. and Anne (Williams) Glushien; m. Charles Ellett Taylor, June 22, 1969; 1 child, Amy Caroline. BA, SUNY, Stony Brook, 1969; MA, SUNY, 1973; JD, U. So. Calif., 1977. Bar: Calif. 1977, U.S. Dist. Ct. (cen. dist.) Calif. 1978. Extern to presiding justice Calif. Supreme Ct., 1977; field atty. NLRB, L.A., 1977-82; dir. employee rels., legal svcs. Paramount Pictures Corp., L.A., 1982-85, v.p. employee rels. legal svcs., 1985-89; dir. bus. and legal affairs Wilshire Ct. Prodns., L.A., 1989-91; sr. counsel Fox Broadcasting Co., L.A., 1991-92, v.p. legal affairs, 1992-97, sr. v.p. legal affairs, 1997—. Editor notes and articles: U. So. Calif. Law Rev., 1976-77. Mentor MOSTE, L.A., 1986-87, 88-89; pres. Beverly Hills chpt. ACLU, L.A., 1985. Fellow ABA, Calif. State Bar (mem. copyright subcom. 1994-95), L.A. County Bar Assn.; mem. Beverly Hills Bar Assn., L.A. Bead Soc. (membership sec. 1992-94, mem. bd. dirs. 1994-95), Order of Coif. Office: Fox Broadcasting Co 10201 W Pico Blvd Los Angeles CA 90064-2606

TAYLOR, MORRIS ANTHONY, chemistry educator; b. St. Louis, July 10, 1922; s. Henry Clay Nathaniel and Georgia Lee Anna (Kenner) T.; m. Millie Betty Fudge, July 17, 1948 (dec. Jan. 1969); children: Carla Maria, Morris Jr.; m. Veonnia Joyce McDonald, Aug. 4, 1973; children: Dorcas Lynnea, Demetrius Sirrom. BS in Chemistry, St. Louis U., 1952. Rsch. chemist Universal Match Corp., Ferguson, Mo., 1952-54; mfg. chemist Sigma Chem., St. Louis, 1954; clin. chemist 5th Army Area Med. Lab., St. Louis, 1955-56; analytical chemist U.S. Dept. Agr.-Agrl. Rsch. Svc. Meat & Poultry Inspection, St. Louis, 1956-67; supervisory chemist U.S. Dept. Agr.-Food Safety and Quality Svc., St. Louis, 1967-76, chemist in charge, 1976-79; adj. prof. chemistry St. Louis Community Coll., 1981—; rating panel mem. Bd. CSC, St. Louis, 1969-79; reviewer Assn. Ofcl. Analytical Chemists, St. Louis, 1969-79; collaborator FDA Labs. on Analytical Methods, St. Louis, 1969-79. Bd. mem. Draft Bd. III, St. Louis, 1970-76. With U.S. Army, 1942-46. Fellow Am. Inst. Chemists; mem. Am. Chem. Soc., Internat. Union Pure and Applied Chemistry, St. Louis U. Alumni Chemists (Pioneer award 1994). Roman Catholic. Home: 10410 Monarch Dr Saint Louis MO 63136-5612 Office: Saint Louis CC 5600 Oakland Ave Saint Louis MO 63110-1316

TAYLOR, NICOLE RENÉE, model; b. Miami, Fla.; d. Ken and Barbara T. With Irene Marie, Miami, 1989; contracts with L'Oreal, 1990-92, Cover Girl Makeup; appeared in Seventeen (cover girl) 1989, Vogue, Elle, Mademoiselle, Harper's Bazaar; modeled for Yves Saint Laurent, Karl Lagerfeld. Office: IMG Models 170 5th Ave Fl 10 New York NY 10010-5911*

TAYLOR, NIGEL BRIAN, financial planner; b. Winchester, June 17, 1953. Grad., Coll. Fin. Planning, Denver, 1993. Cert. Fin. Planner; lic. NASD Series 6, 7, 24; registered prin.; lic. to practice in European Cmty. Owner Family Trust Planners, domestic and internat. retirement, estate planning, asset protection, L.A. and Santa Monica, Calif., 1988—; mgr. Fin. Planning Expo '96, L.A. Author: Domestic and International Estate and Asset Protection for the Resident Alien, 1996; mem. editl. rev. bd. Jour. Fin. Planning. Mem. Santa Monica Bar (assoc.), Inst. CFPs (registered practitioner, bd. dirs. L.A. Soc.). Office: 1011 4th St Apt 209 Santa Monica CA 90403-3843

TAYLOR, NORMAN FLOYD, computer educator, administrator, band director; b. Dover, Ohio, Oct. 29, 1932; s. James Benton and Lela Augusta (Sinden) T.; m. Peggy Ann Cox, Sept. 7, 1952; children: Norman Dudley, Steven Dexter, Gregory Dennis. BS, U. Houston, 1954; MEd, Kent State U., 1963, EdS, 1977. Band dir. Ashtabula (Ohio) Area City Schs., 1958-70, prin., 1970-74; prin. Shaker Heights (Ohio) City Schs., 1974-81, Perry (Ohio) Local Schs., 1981-85; treas. Jos. Badger Local Schs., Kinsman, Ohio, 1987-89; supr. computer instrn. support svcs. Ashtabula (Ohio) Area City Schs., 1989-93, computer instr., 1993—; asst. prof. Computer Sci. Kent State U., Burton, Ohio, 1982-86, Ashtabula, 1987-88. Contbr. articles to profl. jours. Dir. Ashtabula Ch. Choir, 1958-78; mem. Ludlow Community Assn., Shaker Heights, 1974-81. Mem. NEA, Ohio Edn. Assn., Ohio Asn. Elem. Sch. Adminstrs., Shaker Heights Elem. Prins. Assn. (pres. 1980-81), Ashtabula Mid. Mgmt. Assn. (pres. 1973-74), Kiwanis Club, Phi Delta Kappa. Presbyterian. Avocations: music, golf, skiing. Home: 2501 Southwood Dr Painesville OH 44077-4956 Office: Ashtabula Area City Schs 401 W 44th St Ashtabula OH 44004-6807

TAYLOR, NORMAN WILLIAM, economics educator; b. Wigan, Eng., Jan. 9, 1923; s. Albert and Jessie (Slonker) T.; m. Eleanor Dorothy Harper, July 18, 1953; children—David Gordon, Laurie Elizabeth. B.Sc., U. London, 1950; M.A., Yale, 1954, Ph.D., 1958; LLD (hon.), Tohoku Gakuin U., Japan, 1988. Clk. London, Midland & Scottish Ry. Co., Preston, Eng., 1939-40; clk. City Treas. Office, Wigan, 1940-42, 47-48; exec. officer War Office, U.K., 1948-49; asst. instr. econs. Yale, 1955-57, instr. econs., 1957-59; asst. prof. econs. Lawrence U., 1959-62; vis. asst. prof. econs. U. Wis., 1961-62; assoc. prof. econs. Franklin and Marshall Coll., Lancaster, Pa., 1962-69; prof. econs. Franklin and Marshall Coll., 1969-80, Charles A. Dana prof. econs., 1980-88, emeritus, 1988—, chmn. dept., 1964-79, 81-84; vis. prof. Tunghai U., Taiwan, 1967-68. Contbr. articles profl. jours. Served to capt. Brit. Army, 1942-47. Recipient Lindback award for disting. teaching, 1981. Mem. Am. Econ. Assn.

TAYLOR, PAUL, choreographer; b. Allegheny County, Pa., July 29, 1930; s. Paul B. and Elizabeth (Rust) T. Student, Syracuse U., 1949-52, Juilliard Sch. Music, 1952-53; hon. doctoral degrees include, Duke U., 1983, Conn. Coll., 1983, Syracuse U., Juilliard, SUNY at Purchase; doctorate (hon.), Skidmore U., 1995. Artistic dir. Paul Taylor Dance Co., 1957—; dancer Merce Cunningham Co., 1954, Martha Graham, 1955-60. Paul Taylor Dance Co. has performed in over 300 U.S. cities and made 34 overseas tours; participated numerous arts festivals in 36 nations; PBS TV appearances include Dance in America, Live From the American Dance Festival, Two Landmark Dances, Three Modern Classics, The Taylor Company: Recent Dances; choreographer over 100 works including Aureole, 1962, Private Domain, 1969, Esplanade, 1975, Cloven Kingdom, 1976, Airs, 1978, Le Sacre du Printemps (the Rehearsal), 1980, Arden Court, 1981, Mercuric Tidings, 1982, Sunset, 1983, Roses, 1985, Last Look, 1985, Musical Offering, 1986, Ab Ovo Usque ad Mala, 1986, Syzygy, 1987, Kith and Kin, 1987, Minikin Fair, 1989, Speaking in Tongues, 1989, Company B, 1991, Spindri Ft., 1993, A Field of Grass, 1993, Oz, 1993, Moonbine, 1994, Aureole, 1994; author: (autobiography) Private Domain, 1987 (Nat. Book Critics Circle award for biography 1987). Decorated Chevalier des Arts et Lettres, France, elevated to officier, 1984; Guggenheim fellow, 1961, 66, 83, MacArthur Found. fellow, 1985; recipient Internat. Circle of Criticism for Artistic Rsch. and Cultural Exch. award Festival Nations, Paris, 1962, Best Fgn. Attraction prize Critics of Chile, 1966, Capezio Dance award, 1967, Creative Arts award Brandeis U., 1978, Dance Mag. award, 1980, Samuel H. Scripps Am. Dance Festival award. 1983, Arts award State N.Y., 1987, Lions of Performing Arts award N.Y. Pub. Libr., 1989, Emmy award Speaking in Tongues, 1992,Kennedy Ctr. Honors award, 1992, Am. Soc. Graphic Artists award, 1992,Nat. Medal Arts, 1993, Meadows award So. Meth. U., 1995; named Dancer of Yr. London's Dance and Dancers, 1965, Nat.Mus. Dance Hall of Fame, 1995. Office: Paul Taylor Dance Co 552 Broadway New York NY 10012-3922*

TAYLOR, PAUL ALBERT, banker; b. St. John, N.B., Can., June 17, 1943; s. Albert and Mary Kathleen (McCullough) T.; children—Beth E., Brian P., Stephen C. B.A. in Econs., U. Western Ont., 1966; M.B.A. in Fin., U. Windsor, 1971. Area exec. Orion Bank Ltd., London, 1974-76, exec. dir., 1977-78; sr. mgr. Global fin. Royal Bank of Can., Montreal, Que., 1978-80, asst. gen. mgr. Global Fin., 1980; asst. gen. mgr. national accts. Royal Bank of Can., Toronto, Ont., 1980-82, sr. v.p. national accts., 1982-83, sr. v.p. world corp. banking, 1983-86; sr. v.p. investment banking, internat. and dep. chmn. Orion Royal Bank, London, 1986-88; exec. v.p. investment banking head office Royal Bank Can., Toronto, Ont., 1988-90, exec. v.p. treasury and investment banking head office, 1990-95, exec. v.p. trading head office, 1995—; bd. dirs. RBC Dominion Securities Ltd.; co-chmn. fin. sector Can. Japan Bus. Com. Mem. Halton Prog. Conservative Assn., Founders Club, Zeta Psi. Roman Catholic. Office: RBC DS Global Markets S Tower, 200 Bay St Royal Bank Plz, Toronto, ON Canada M5J 2W7

TAYLOR, PAUL PEAK, pediatric dentist, educator; b. Childress, Tex., May 11, 1921; s. Noah Peak and Lois T. (Vinson) T.; m. LaVerne Countryman, Aug. 11, 1945; children: Scott, Peri Ann. Student, W. Tex. State Coll., 1938-40; DDS, Baylor U., 1944; MS, U. Mich., 1951. Diplomate Am. Bd. Pediatric Dentistry (examining mem. 1977-84, chair 1983). Prof. Baylor U. Coll. Dentistry, Dallas, 1958-86, chmn. grad. pediatric dentistry, 1960-69, chmn. dept. pediatric dentistry, 1969-86, prof. emeritus, 1986—; dir. dental svcs. Children's Med. Ctr., Dallas, 1965-86, dir. emeritus dental svcs., 1986—; dir. dental svcs. Tex. Scottish Rite Hosp. for Children, Dallas, 1965-86, dir. emeritus dental svcs., 1986—. Contbr. articles to Jour. of Dentistry for Children, 1960-82; author (with others) Pediatric Dentistry, 1986, Current Therapy in Pediatric Infectious Disease, 1989; mem. edtl. and publs. com. Jour. Dentistry for Children. Capt. U.S. Army, 1951-53. Fellow Mott Found., 1949-51. Fellow Am. Coll. of Dentists (life); life mem. Am. Dental Assn., Tex. Dental Assn., Dallas County Dental Assn., Masons (life, Scottish Rite 32d degree Shriner). Episcopalian. Avocation: golf. Home: 2615 Briarcove Plano TX 75074

TAYLOR, PETER VAN VOORHEES, advertising and public relations consultant; b. Montclair, N.J., Aug. 25, 1934; s. John Coard and Mildred (McLaughlin) T.; m. Janet Kristine Kirkebo, Nov. 4, 1978; 1 son, John Coard III. BA in English, Duke U., 1956. Announcer Sta. WQAM, Miami, 1956; announcer, program dir. Sta. KHVH, Honolulu, 1959-61; promotion mgr. Sta. KPEN, San Francisco, 1962; with Kaiser Broadcasting, 1962-74, GE Broadcasting Co., 1974-78; program/ops. mgr. Sta. KFOG, San Francisco, 1962-66; mgr. Sta. WXHR AM/FM, Cambridge, Mass., 1966-67; gen. mgr. Sta. WJIB, Boston, 1967-70; v.p., mgr. FM div. Kaiser Broadcasting, 1969-72; v.p., gen. mgr. Sta. KFOG, San Francisco, 1970-78; pres. Taylor Communications, 1978-90, 97—, Baggott & Taylor, Inc., 1990-91, Taylor Advt. & Pub. Rels., 1991-96, Broadcast Skills Bank, 1975-76, Roast Host, 1993—. Trustee, WDBS, Inc., Duke U., 1974-80; bd. dirs. San Francisco BBB, 1976-78, 89-94, Calif. Broadcasters Assn., 1982-84, San Francisco Boys & Girls Club, 1991-93, Coast Guard Found., 1991—, Leukemia Soc., San Francisco, 1992-93, Duke Devel. Coun., 1992-96, Golden Gate Breakfast Club, 1995-96, v.p., 1995-96; bd. dirs. Commencement Bay Rowing Club, 1997—. Mem. Nat., Internat. and Long Wave Radio Clubs, Worldwide TV/FM Dx Assn., Rotary (San Francisco - bd. dirs. 1988-93, 1st v.p. 1990-91, pres. 1991-92, dist. 5150 - pub. rels. chmn. 1986-89, conf. chmn. 1990, area rep. 1992-93, bd. dirs. 1994-95, dist. governor nom., 1995-96), Golden Gate BUFST Club (bd. dirs., v.p. 1995-96), Commencement Bay Rowing Club. Lt. USCGR, 1957-63. Home and Office: 6002 Bayview Dr NE Tacoma WA 98422-1227

TAYLOR, PEYTON TROY, JR., gynecologic oncologist, educator; b. Tuscaloosa, Ala., July 21, 1941; s. Peyton Troy Sr. and Frances (Sutter) T.; m. Helena Ström, Sept. 23, 1967; children: Annika, Karin, Sarah. BS, U. Ala., 1963; MD, Med. Coll. Ala., 1968. Intern U. Va. Hosp., Charlottesville, 1968-69, resident, 1969-70, 72-75; asst. prof. ob-gyn U. Va., Charlottesville, 1976-79, assoc. prof., dir. divsn. ob-gyn., 1981-87, Richard N. and Louise R. Crockett prof., 1987—; prof. ob-gyn., dir. divsn. ob-gyn. U. Va. Health Scis. Ctr., Charlottesville, 1987—; med. dir. Cancer Ctr. U. Va., 1996—; clin. assoc. surgery Nat. Cancer Inst., Bethesda, Md., 1970-72; assoc. prof. U. Ala., Birmingham, 1979-81. Contbr. articles to profl. jours. Served with USPHS, 1970-72. Fellow ACS, Am. Coll. Obstetricians and Gynecologists; mem. Assn. Acad. Surgeons, Soc. Gynecol. Oncologists, Soc. Surg. Oncology, Am. Soc. of Clin. Oncology, Am. Assn. for Cancer Rsch., Internat. Gynecol. Cancer Soc. Episcopalian. Office: U Va PO Box 10016 Charlottesville VA 22906

TAYLOR, PRESTON M., JR., federal agency administrator; m. Audrey Taylor; children: Christopher, Cinthia. BA, Pepperdine U.; MA, Ctrl. Mich. U.; grad., Indsl. Coll. of Armed Forces, Air Command and Staff Coll., Air Force Squadron Officer's Sch. Commd. USAF, advanced through grades to brig. gen.; with Air Nat. Guard; supr. naval aircraft engine and avionics logistics sect. Naval Air Warfare Ctr., Lakehurst, N.J.; dep. adj. gen. of N.J., ret., 1993, asst. sec. of Labor for Vets.' Employment and Tng., 1993—. Decorated Legion of Merit, Air Force Commendation medal, Air Force Orgnl. Excellence award, Armed Forces Res. medal, N.J. Medal of Honor, N.J. Merit award. Office: Vet Employment & Training Svcs 200 Constitution Ave NW Washington DC 20210-0001

TAYLOR, QUINCY, professional boxer; b. Dallas, July 18, 1963. Named WBC Middleweight Champion, 1995-96. Achievements include record of 26 wins and 4 losses, with 22 knock-outs. Office: care Consejo Mundial de Boxeo, Genova 33 Despacho # 503, 06600 Mexico City Mexico

TAYLOR, R. WILLIAM, foundation administrator; m. Suzanne Monique Olson; children: Jessica, Kelsey. B, Acadia U., Wolfville, Nova Scotia, 1983; student, St. Francis Xavier U., 1983-85. Mgr. pub. info., affiliate svcs. Atlantic Salmon Fedn., St. Andrews, Can., 1988-91; exec. dir. comm., pub. policy Atlantic Salmon Fedn., St. Andrews, 1991-95, pres., CEO, 1995—; mem. adv. bd. Can.'s Atlantic Salmon; gov. Can. Coalition Acid Rain; spl. adv. fisheries Can. Wildlife Fedn.; Can. del. N. Atlantic Salmon Conservation Orgn., 1996—. Contbr. articles to profl. jours. Recipient Ted Williams award Miramichi Salmon Assn., 1990. Mem. Can. Soc. Assn. Execs., Am. Fisheries Soc., Audubon, Can. Wildlife Fedn., Trout Unlimited. Avocations: fly fishing, canoeing, camping, downhill skiing. Office: Atlantic Salmon Fedn, PO Box 429, Saint Andrews, NB Canada E0G 2X0

TAYLOR, RALPH ARTHUR, JR., lawyer; b. Washington, Jan. 19, 1948; s. Ralph Arthur Sr. and Mary Florence Taylor; m. Joanna Lamb Moorhead, Jan. 30, 1988; children: Alison M., John Duncan. BS in Engring. with honors, Princeton, 1970; JD, U. Va., 1975. Bar: Va. 1975, D.C. 1976, Md. 1989, U.S. Dist. Ct. D.C. 1977, U.S. Dist. Cts. (ea. and we. dists.) Va. 1986, U.S. Dist. Ct. Md. 1988, U.S. Ct. Appeals (4th cir.) 1991, U.S. Ct. Appeals (D.C. cir.) 1977, U.S. Ct. Appeals (6th cir.) 1991, U.S. Ct. Claims 1985, U.S. Supreme Ct. 1980. Program advisor U.S. EPA, Boston, 1970-72; assoc. Steptoe & Johnson, Washington, 1975-84; assoc. Shaw, Pittman, Potts, & Trowbridge, Washington, 1984-86, ptnr., 1986—, leader tech. & intellectual litigation group. Assoc. editor Litigation News, 1985—; notes editor Va. Law Rev., 1974-75; contbg. author: International Technology Transfers, 1995. Pres. Cloisters West Homeowners Assn., Washington, 1989, 90; pres. 1625 Q St. Condominium Assn., Washington, 1982-86. Lt. USPHS, 1970-72. Mem. Order of the Coif, Met. Club (Washington), Kenwood Golf and Country Club, Barristers, Princeton Club (Washington). Protestant. Avocations: sailing, skiing, tennis, squash, amateur radio. Office: Shaw Pittman Potts & Trowbridge 2300 N St NW Washington DC 20037-1122

TAYLOR, RAY, state senator; b. Steamboat Rock, Iowa, June 4, 1923; s. Leonard Allen and Mary Delilah (Huffman) T.; student U. No. Iowa, 1940-41, Baylor U., 1948-49; m. Mary Allen, Aug. 29, 1924; children—Gordon, Laura Rae Taylor Hansmann, Karol Ann Taylor Rogers, Jean Lorraine Taylor Mahl. Farmer, Steamboat Rock, Iowa, 1943—; mem. Iowa Senate, 1973-95; bd. dirs., sec. Am. Legis. Exchange Council, 1979-94 . Sec., Hardin County Farm Bur., 1970-72; mem. Iowa div. bds. Am. Cancer Soc.; chmn. Am. Revolution Bicentennial Com. Mem. Steamboat Rock Community Sch. Bd., 1955-70; coordinator Republican youth, 1968-72. Chmn. bd. Faith Bapt. Bible Coll.; pres. Am. Council Christian Chs.; chmn. Iowans for Responsible Govt. Named Guardian of Small Bus., NFIB/Iowa, 1989-90, for outstanding support for good govt. and accessible, affordable health care in Iowa, Iowa Physician Assistant Soc., 1991, bd. dirs. Iowans for Tax Relief, 1995—. Ind. Bapt. fellow of the Midwest, Christian Patriots, 1994, Hon. alumnus Faith

Bapt. Bible Coll. & Theol. Sem., 1995; recipient Contenders award Am. Coun. Christian Chs., 1991, Legislator of Yr. award Iowa Soc. of Friends, 1991-92. Mem. Wildlife Club, Eldora Rotary. Baptist. Home: 31363 185th St Steamboat Rock IA 50672-8107

TAYLOR, RAYMOND ELLORY, engineering executive; b. Ames, Iowa, Oct. 19, 1929; s. Alva A. and Maude Marguerite (Crowe) T.; m. Elfa M. Shaffer, Apr. 22, 1952; children, Wayne, David. BS in Chem. Tech., Iowa State U., 1951; MS in Phys. Chemistry, U. Idaho, 1956; PhD in Solid State Tech., Pa. State U., 1967. Chemist, supr. GE, Richland, Wash., 1951-56; sr. rsch. engr. Atomics Internat., Canoga Park, Calif., 1957-64; assoc. sr. rschr. Thermophysical Properties Rsch. Lab/Purdue U., West Lafayette, Ind., 1967-75, dir., 1975-95; pres. Thermophysical Properties Rsch. Lab., West Lafayette, Ind., 1996—; cons. Ordinance Enrging. Assocs., GE, Sandia Nat. Labs., Lockheed Missle and Space Co., Atomic Energy Commn. Can., Bendix Brake Divsn., Theta Industries, Technometrics, Air Force Materials Lab., Combustion Engring. Co., Supertemp Co., Argonne Nat. Lab., GM, Office Naval Rsch., Pennwalt Corp., Vesuvius Crucible Co., Gibson Electric Co., Proctor and Gamble, ALCOA, Corning Glass Co., Dept. Energy, Naval Surface Weapons Ctr., Bethlehem Steel, Cohart Refractories Co., Corp., Roll Mfrs. Inst., Carborundum Co., Areospace Corp., Sandvik Corp., Cummings Engine Corp., Travenol Labs., Sloan Kettering, Dana Perfect Circle, Teledyne Energy Systems, Pfizer Inc., Hughes Aircraft, Allegheny Ludlum Steel Co., CMW Inc., We. Electric Co., Reliance Universal Inc., AMP Inc., Kock Rsch. and Tech. Ctr., Ctrl. Inst. Indsl. Rsch., Semi-Alloys, Gen. Scis. Inc., Carpenter Techs., Hercules Aerospace Co., Bush-Wellman, Brunswick Corp., North Am. Refractories, Zicar Corp., Hayes Internat., E. I. DuPont, Ferro Corp., Storgae Techs., CTS, IBM Inc., Sci. Applications, Outboard Marine Corp.; presenter in field. Editor Review Sci. Instruments; contbr. numerous articles and reports to sci. jours.; co-inventor direct heating flash diffusivity apparatus, device and techniques to measure thermal diffusivity/conductivity of thin films; research in transport properties at high tempuratures, diffusivity of composite materials, transport properites, multiproperty measurements, thermophotovoltaic energy conservation work, computer applications in the laboratory, high tempurature thermal conductivity reference standards, sonic measurements of insulations; inventor automatic nondestructive aircraft brake discs. Mem. ASTM (governing bd.), North Am. Thermal Analysis Soc., Internat. Thermal Expansion Symposium (governing bd., by-laws com.), Sigma Xi, Phi Lambda Upsilon, Phi Eta Sigma, Phi Kappa Phi. Home: 618 Essex St Lafayette IN 47906-1531 Office: Thermophys Properties Rsch Lab 2595 Yeager Rd West Lafayette IN 47906-1335

TAYLOR, REESE HALE, JR., lawyer, former government administrator; b. Los Angeles, May 6, 1928; s. Reese Hale and Kathryn (Emery) T.; m. Lucille Langdon, Dec. 29, 1948 (div. 1959); children: Reese Hale (dec.), Stuart Langdon, Anne Kathryn, Lucille Emery; m. Jolene Yerby, June 30, 1972. B.A. with distinction, Stanford U., 1949; LL.B., Cornell U., 1952. Bar: Calif. 1954, Nev. 1966. Assoc. Gibson, Dunn & Crutcher, Los Angeles, 1952-58; pvt. practice Los Angeles, 1958-65; assoc. Wiener, Goldwater & Galatz, Las Vegas, Nev., 1966-67; chmn. Nev. Pub. Service Commn., Carson City, 1967-71; ptnr. Laxalt, Berry & Allison, Carson City, 1971-78, Allison, Brunetti, MacKenzie & Taylor, Carson City, 1978-81; chmn. ICC, Washington, 1981-85; ptnr. Heron, Burchette, Ruckert & Rothwell, Washington, 1986-90, Taylor & Morell, Washington and Long Beach, Calif., 1990-91, Taylor, Morell & Gitomer, Washington and Long Beach, 1992-94; of counsel Keesal, Young & Logan, Long Beach, 1994—; vice chmn. Nev. Tax Commn., Carson City, 1967-69; mem. Nev. Gov.'s Cabinet, Carson City, 1967-70, Carson City Bd. Equalization, 1979-81, chmn., 1979-80; bd. dirs. U.S. Rail Assn., Washington, 1981-85. Del. Republican Nat. Conv., Kansas City, Mo., 1976, mem. platform com., 1976, alt. del., Detroit, 1980; mem. Rep. Nat. Com., 1980-81. Mem. ABA, Am. Judicature Soc., Capitol Hill Club, Cornell Club (N.Y.), Order of Coif, Phi Gamma Delta, Phi Delta Phi. Episcopalian. Office: Keesal Young & Logan Union Bank Bldg 400 Oceangate PO Box 1730 Long Beach CA 90801-1730

TAYLOR, RICHARD, philosopher, educator; b. Charlotte, Mich., Nov. 5, 1919; s. Floyd Clyde and Marie Louise (Milbourn) T.; m. Thelma Maxine Elworthy, Jan. 14, 1944 (div. 1961); children: Christopher, Randall; m. Hylda Carpenter Higginson, Dec. 26, 1961 (div. 1985); 1 step dau., Molly; m. Kim Fontana, Oct. 8, 1985; children: Aristotle, Xeno. A.B., U. Ill., 1941; A.M., Oberlin Coll., 1947; Ph.D., Brown U., 1951. Faculty Brown U., 1951-52, 53-63, prof. philosophy, 1958-63, chmn. dept., 1959-60, William Herbert Perry Faunce prof. philosophy, 1959-63; prof. philosophy grad. faculty Columbia, 1963-66; prof. philosophy U. Rochester, N.Y., 1966—; chmn. dept. U. Rochester, 1966-69; Faculty Swarthmore Coll., 1953, Ohio State U., summer 1959, Cornell U., summer 1961; vis. prof. philosophy Columbia, 1962, Ohio State U., 1963; vis. Robert D. Campbell prof. philosophy Wells Coll., 1967-68; vis. Robert H. Truax prof. philosophy Hamilton Coll., 1971; vis. Melvin Hill prof. humanities Hobart-William Smith Colls., 1974; Leavitt-Spencer adj. prof. philosophy Union Coll., 1981-89; Disting. resident philosopher Hartwick Coll., 1989—. Author: Metaphysics (Spanish, Dutch, Japanese, Portuguese, Korean transl.), 1963, rev. edit., 1974, 83, 91, Action and Purpose, 1965, Good and Evil, 1970, Freedom, Anarchy and the Law, 1973, With Heart and Mind, 1973, Having Love Affairs, 1982, 2d edit., 1990, rev. edit., 1997, Ethics, Faith and Reason, 1985, Restoring Pride, 1996; editor: Theism (J.S. Mill), 1957, Selected Essays (Schopenhauer), 1963; assoc. editor: Am. Philos. Quar., 1972-81; contbr. articles to publs., U.S., Eng., Australia. Served to lt. USNR, 1943-47. Mem. Am. Philos. Assn., Phi Beta Kappa. Address: PO Box 352 Interlaken NY 14847-0352

TAYLOR, RICHARD EDWARD, physicist, educator; b. Medicine Hat, Alta., Can., Nov. 2, 1929; came to U.S., 1952; s. Clarence Richard and Delia Alena (Brunsdale) T.; m. Rita Jean Bonneau, Aug. 25, 1951; 1 child, Norman Edward. B.S., U. Alta., 1950, M.S., 1952; Ph.D., Stanford U., 1962; Docteur honoris causa, U. Paris-Sud, 1980; DSc, U. Alta., 1991; LLD (hon.), U. Calgary, Alta., 1993; DSc (hon.), U. Lethbridge, Alta., 1993, U. Victoria, B.C., Can., 1994. Boursier Lab. de l'Accelerateur Lineaire, Orsay, France, 1958-61; physicist Lawrence Berkeley Lab., Berkeley, Calif., 1961-62; staff mem. Stanford (Calif.) Linear Accelerator Ctr., 1962-68, assoc. dir., 1982-86, prof., 1968—. Fellow Guggenheim Found., 1971-72, von Humboldt Found., 1982; recipient Nobel prize in physics, 1990. Fellow AAAS, Am. Acad. Arts and Scis., Am. Phys. Soc. (W.K.H. Panofsky prize div. particles and fields 1989), Royal Soc. Can., Royal Soc. London; mem. Can. Assn. Physicists, Nat. Acad. Scis. (fgn. assoc.). Office: Stanford Linear Accelerator Ctr PO Box 4349, M/S 96 Stanford CA 94309

TAYLOR, RICHARD POWELL, lawyer; b. Phila., Sept. 13, 1928; s. Earl Howard and Helen Moore (Martin) T.; m. Barbara Jo Anne Harris, Dec. 19, 1959; 1 child, Douglas Howard. BA, U. Va., 1950, JD, 1952. Bar: Va. 1952, D.C. 1956. Law clk. U.S. Ct. Appeals for 4th Circuit, 1951-52; assoc. Steptoe & Johnson, Washington, 1956-61, ptnr., 1962—, chmn. transp. dept., 1978—; sec., corp. counsel Slick Corp., 1963-69, asst. sec., 1969-72, also bd. dirs., 1965-68; sec., corp. counsel Slick Indsl. Co., 1963-72; sec., bd. dirs. Slick Indsl. Co. Can. Ltd, 1966-72; bd. dirs. Intercontinental Forwarders, Inc., 1969-72. Mem. Save the Children 50th Anniversary Com., 1982; gen. counsel Am. Opera Scholarship Soc., 1974—; mem. lawyer's com. Washington Performing Arts Soc., 1982—; mem. adv. com. Rock Creek Found. Mental Health, 1982—; mem. nat. adv. bd. DAR, 1980-83, chmn., 1983—; mem. men's com. Project Hope Ball, 1980—; nat. vice chmn. for fin. Reagan for Pres., 1979-80; mem. exec. fin. com. 1981 Presdl. Inauguration; mem. President's Adv. Com. for Arts, 1982—, Rep. Nat. Com., 1983—; Md. fin. chmn. Reagan-Bush '84, Bush-Quayle '88. Served to lt (j.g.), Air Intelligence USNR, 1952-56. Mem. ABA (co-chmn. aviation com. 1964-76, chmn. 1976-77), Fed. Bar Assn., D.C. Bar Assn., Va. Bar Assn., Fed. Energy Bar Assn., Am. Judicature Soc., Assn. Transp. Practitioners, Internat. Platform Assn., Raven Soc., Order of Coif, Univ. Club, Capital Hill Club, Nat. Aviation Club, Aero Club, Congl. Country Club (Washington), Potomac (Md.) Polo Club. Episcopalian. Home: 14914 Spring Meadows Dr Germantown MD 20874-3444 Office: Steptoe & Johnson 1330 Connecticut Ave NW Washington DC 20036-1704 *Everyone should devote a portion of his or her life to efforts which help ensure that our country remains free and strong and that its concept of government under law is maintained and expanded throughout the world.*

TAYLOR, RICHARD TRELORE, retired lawyer; b. Kewanee, Ill., Aug. 5, 1917; s. Earl G. and Lucile (Cully) T.; m. Maureen Hoey, Feb. 9, 1946. B.S., U. Ill., 1939, J.D., 1946; LL.M., Columbia U., 1947. Bar: Ill. 1946, N.Y. 1947. Assoc. Cadwalader, Wickersham & Taft, N.Y.C., 1947-57, ptnr., 1957-87, presiding ptnr., 1977-87, of counsel, 1988-89. Trustee Marlboro Coll., Vt. Served with U.S. Army, 1941-45. Decorated Bronze Star. Mem. ABA, Univ. Club (N.Y.C.). Home: 870 United Nations Plz New York NY 10017-1807

TAYLOR, RICHARD WILLIAM, investment banker, securities broker; b. Toledo, Sept. 16, 1926; s. Everett Ellsworth and Hazel (Broer) T.; m. Lyn Westerlund, Sept. 11, 1954; children: Julie Everett, Richard William, Alison Nichols, Jennifer Broer, Liane Westerlund. BS, U.S. Naval Acad., 1949; postgrad., U. Calif., 1952. Mem. Ohio Ho. of Reps. (100th gen. assembly from 9th Dist.); asst. mgr. Navy sales Martin Aircraft, Balt., 1953-56; with McKinsey & Co. (mgmt. cons.), N.Y.C., 1956-60; asst. to v.p. Cerro Corp., N.Y.C., 1960-62, spl. asst. to pres., 1965; pres. Cerro Aluminum Co., N.Y.C., 1962-65; successively v.p., exec. v.p., pres. and CEO Carter, Walker & Co., Inc., 1967-69; pres., CEO Burton, Dana, Westerlund, Inc., N.Y.C., 1969—; v.p. Sterling, Grace & Co., Inc., 1971-74, sr. v.p. corp. fin., 1980-81; v.p. corp. fin. Moseley, Hallgarten, Estabrook & Weeden Inc., 1975-80; v.p. Kidder, Peabody & Co. Inc., 1981-93, Oppenheimer & Co., Inc., 1993—. Bd. dirs., pres., chmn. fin. com. YWCA Retirement Fund, Inc. With USN, 1944-52. Decorated Air medal, Navy Commendation medal. Mem. U.S. Naval Acad. Alumni Assn. Home: Elmwood Orange VA 22960 Office: Oppenheimer & Co Inc Oppenheimer Tower World Financial Ctr New York NY 10281

TAYLOR, RICHARD WIRTH, political science educator; b. Cleve., Jan. 15, 1923; s. Robert and Irmgard (Wirth) T.; m. Sadie White, Sept. 19, 1946; children: Peter, Karla, Mark, Stephen. B.A., U. Ill., 1947, M.A., 1948, Ph.D., 1950. Instr. polit. sci. U. Minn., Mpls., 1950-52; asst. prof. polit. sci. Lehigh U., Bethlehem, Pa., 1952-55, Wis. State U., Stevens Point, 1955-56; vis. asst. prof. Northwestern U., Evanston, Ill., 1956-57; assoc. prof. Coe Coll., Cedar Rapids, Iowa, 1957-60, chmn., prof., 1960-67; prof. polit. sci. Kent State U., Ohio, 1967-92, prof. emeritus, 1992—, chmn., 1974-82; vis. prof. Karl-Marx-Universität, Leipzig, Fed. Republic Germany, 1990. Co-exec. editor Peace and Change, 1986-87. Mem. policy com. Friends Com. Nat. Legis., Washington, 1964-85, exec. com., 1986-87; mem. acad. adv. com., ombudsman com. Internat. Bar Assn., Edmonton Alta., Can., 1980—; mem. Friends World Com. on Consultation, 1991—. Home: 115 Kendal Dr Oberlin OH 44074-1905

TAYLOR, ROBERT BROWN, medical educator; b. Elmira, N.Y., May 31, 1936; s. Olaf C. Taylor and Elizabeth (Place) Brown; m. Anita Dopico; children: Diana Marie, Sharon Jean. Student, Bucknell U., 1954-57; MD, Temple U., 1961. Diplomate Am. Bd. Family Practice. Gen. practice medicine New Paltz, N.Y., 1964-78; faculty physician Bowman Gray Sch. Medicine Wake Forest U., Winston-Salem, N.C., 1978-84; prof., chmn. dept. family medicine Oreg. Health Scis. U. Sch. Medicine, Portland, 1984—; mem. comprehensive part II com. Nat. Bd. Med. Examiners, Phila., 1986-91. Author: Common Problems in Office Practice, 1972, The Practical Art of Medicine, 1974; editor: Family Medicine: Principles and Practice, 1978, 4th edit., 1994, Health Promotion: Principles and Clinical Applications, 1982, Difficult Diagnosis, 1985, Difficult Medical Management, 1991, Difficult Diagnosis II, 1992, Fundamentals of Family Medicine, 1996, Manual of Family Practice, 1997; contbg. editor Physicians Mgmt. Mag., 1972—; editl. bd. The Family Practice Rsch. Jour., 1980-90, The Female Patient, 1984—, Frontiers of Primary Medicine, 1983—, Am. Family Physician, 1990—, Jour. of Family Practice, 1990-93, Me. Tribune, 1993—. Served as surgeon USPHS, 1961-64. Fellow Am. Acad. Family Physicians (sci. program com.), Am. Coll. Preventive Medicine; mem. Soc. Tchrs. Family Medicine (bd. dirs. cert. of excellence), Assn. Am. Med. Colls., Am. Assn. for Study Headache, City Club, Multnomah Athletic Club, Phi Beta Kappa, Alpha Omega Alpha.. Home: 1414 SW 3rd Ave #2904 Portland OR 97201 Office: Oreg Health Scis U Sch Medicine Mail Code FP 3181 SW Sam Jackson Park Rd Portland OR 97201-3011

TAYLOR, ROBERT DALTON, microbiologist; b. Greenville, Ala., June 29, 1950; s. William Walter and Una Valise (Black) T.; m. Patricia Ann Dunhardt, Mar. 16, 1983. BS, Southeastern La. Univ., 1972, MS, 1973; PhD, La. State U., 1979. NIH postdoctoral fellow Va. Polytechnic Inst., Blackburg, 1979-82; asst. prof. microbiology U. So. Miss., Hattiesburg, 1982-83, asst. prof. biol. sci., 1983-87, assoc. prof. biol. sci., 1987; environmental microbiologist Krug Life Scis. at Johnson Space Ctr., Houston, 1987-89, group mgr. biomed. ops. and rsch. group, 1989-91, asst. to gen. mgr., 1991—; cons. Nat. Marine Fisheries Svc., Pascagoula, Miss., 1985-87; reviewer Soc. for Automotive Engring., 1988-92; mem. tech. staff The MITRE Corp., 1992-94; sr. assoc. Booz-Allen & Hamilton Inc. Contbr. articles to profl. jours. Mem. AAAS, Am. Soc. Microbiology, Air and Waste Mgmt. Assn., Am. Soc. for Testing and Materials, Inst. Food Tech., N.Y. Acad. Scis., Miss. Acad. Scis., Project Mgmt. Inst., Nat. Mgmt. Assn., Civitan, Sigma Xi. Home: PO Box 35514 San Antonio TX 78235-0514 Office: Booz-Allen & Hamilton Inc 300 Convent St Ste 1250 San Antonio TX 78205-3710

TAYLOR, ROBERT HOMER, quality assurance professional, pilot; b. Rochester, N.Y., Mar. 18, 1922; s. C. Gilbert and Josephine Mary (Woodward) T.; m. Mignon Jane Beight, Aug. 1945; children: Robert Jr., Douglas Beight, Scott Woodward, Sondra Lee. BSME, Case Western Res. U., 1947. Commd. 2d lt. USAF, 1944, advanced through grades to lt. col., 1975; v.p., gen. mgr. Taylor Corp., 1947-53; mgr. quality assurance Spectra Physics Laserplane, Dayton, Ohio, 1976-89; pres., gen. mgr. CON-AV Corp., Tipp City, Ohio, 1989—; chief quality assurance staff on NASA Mercury Booster for USAF, Cape Canaveral, Fla., 1961-63; mgr. nuc. tng. weapons devel. USAF Weapons Lab., 1964-67; CAT I test mgr. F-111, 1967-68; instr. pilot C-7, tng. officer, Vietnam, 1969; project element monitor T-43, attache, A-37, C-130 aircraft, Pentagon, 1970-74; br. chief WPAFB, 1974-75. Advisor Aero Scis. Alternatives, Tipp City, 1990—. Lt. col. CAP. Decorated Air medal with three oak leaf clusters, DFC; named to Aviation Hall of Fame, 1986. Mem. VFW, Exptl. Aircraft Assn., Flying Angels, Inc. (pres. 1991), Masons, Beta Theta Pi (Case chpt. pres. 1942), Theta Tau, Early Birds. Episcopalian. Avocations: boating, flying, fishing, refurbishing antique aircraft. Home: 5855 Us Route 40 Tipp City OH 45371-9419 Office: CON-AV Corp 5855 Us Route 40 Tipp City OH 45371-9419

TAYLOR, ROBERT LEE, financial services and sales executive, information systems account executive, educator; b. Adrian, Mich., Jan. 9, 1944; s. Jack Raleigh and Virginia Dixon (Oakes) T.; m. Janice Grace George, Dec. 9, 1961; children—Robin, Lynne, David. A.A., Siena Heights Coll., 1974, B.A., 1976. With computer operation Gen. Parts div. Ford Motor Co., Rawsonville, Mich., 1965-66, prodn. monitoring supr., Saline Plant, Mich., 1966-75, methods and systems analyst, Ypsilanti Plant, Mich., 1975-77, data processing supr. Milan Plant, Mich., 1977-82, sr. systems analyst, Plastics, Paint and Vinyl div., Wixom, Mich., 1982-85; systems engr. Electronic Data Systems, Warren, Mich., 1985-86, systems engr. mgr. Romulus (Mich.) Parts Distbn. Ctr. Plant, 1986-87, customer service mgr., Toledo, Ohio, 1987-88; project mgr. Computer Task Group, Southfield, Mich., 1988-89; tech. svcs. mgr., 1989-92, spl. agent Prudential, Tecumseh, Mich., 1992-94; ret. plan specialist Variable Annuity, Life Ins. Co., Tecumseh, Mich., 1994—; instr. data processing Siena Heights Coll., Adrian, 1985-86; bd. dirs. Lenawee Area Life Underwriters, 1993—, pub. chmn., 1993, nat. committeeman, 1994, pres-elect 1995, 1996-97. Commr. Tecumseh Planning Commn., Mich., 1976-80, vice-chmn., 1981-82; trustee Tecumseh Bd. Edn., 1981-82, sec., 1983-84, chmn. citizens adv. com., 1983, chmn. computer adv. com., 1984, chmn. policy com., 1983-84; chmn. Tecumseh Area Laymen's Assn., 1983; mem. exec. com. Lenawee County Republican party, 1982-88, precinct del., 1982-88, chmn. computer com., 1984-86; state del. State of Mich., 1983-85, 87; founding advisor Ewang. Free Ch. Adrian-Tecumseh, 1984-85, elder, 1986-88, 90-92, 94—, Sunday Sch. supt., 1984-87, 89-90, chmn. Christian edn., 1986-89, 90-91, chmn. planning-bldg. com., 1987-93; asst. Sunday Sch. supt. Berean Baptist Ch., Adrian, 1980-83; tchr. mentally impaired, 1977-83; deacon, Sunday Sch. supt., Grace Bible Ch., Tecumseh, 1973-76; chmn. bd. deacons First Bapt. Ch., Tecumseh, 1970-71, youth advisor, 1968-71, Layman of Yr., 1970; vice chmn. Tecumseh Area Crusade for Christ, 1973, facilities chmn. Lenawee County Crusade for Christ, 1986; chmn. Life Action Crusade, 1987; men's div. chmn. Lenawee Area Celebration, 1996. Served with USAF, 1961-65. Mem. Computer & Automated Systems Assn. (sr.) Mfg. Automation Protocol, Lenawee Assn. Life Underwriter, Nat. Assn. Life Underwriters, Mich. Assn. Life Underwriters, Soc. Mfg. Engrs. Avocations: golf, geneaology. Home: 603 Outer Dr Tecumseh MI 49286-1446 Office: VALIC 603 Outer Dr Tecumseh MI 49286-1446

TAYLOR, ROBERT LEWIS, academic administrator; b. Pitts., Dec. 10, 1939; s. Robert William and Elinor (Miller) T.; m. Linda Taylor Shapiro, Oct. 28, 1988; 1 child, Kara; children by previous marriage: Rob, Mike. AB in Am. Studies, cum laude, Allegheny Coll., 1961; MBA, Ohio State U., 1966; D in Bus. Adminstrn., Mgmt., Ind. U., 1972. Asst. prof., dir. rsch. USAF Acad., Colorado Springs, Colo., 1971-77, assoc. prof., dir. instrn. dept. econ., geography, mgmt., 1977-79, prof. mgmt., head dept. econs., geography, mgmt., 1980-81; assoc. dean Coll. Letters and Sci., head div. Bus. and Econs., Carl N. Jacobs Prof. of Bus. U. Wis., Stevens Point, 1981-84; dean Coll. Bus. Pub. Adminstrn. U. Louisville, 1984—; chmn. bd. dirs. Ky. Wood Floors, Louisville; bd. dirs. Pvt. Industry Coun., Louisville, Banc One Ky. Corp., Louisville; cons., advisor Kellogg Nat. Fellowship program Kellogg Found., Battle Creek Mich., 1985-89. Co-author, editor: Contemporary Issues in Leadership: In Pursuit of Excellence, 1984, 3d edit., 1996, Leadership Challenges for Today's Manager, 1988; contbr. articles to profl. jours. Chmn. Mayor's Strategic Planning Group, Louisville, 1986—; mem. Gov.'s Econ. Devel. Com., Frankfort, Ky., 1987-89, exec. com. Bus. Advs., 1988-92, task force on econ. devel. Ky. Legis. Rsch. Coun., 1991, Leadership Louisville, 1986, Leadership Ky., 1987. Mem. Acad. Mgmt. (proceedings editor 1976-77, newsletter editor 1983-86), Louisville C. of C. (bd. dirs., exec. com 1990—), Sigma Xi, Beta Gamma Sigma, Pi Gamma Mu. Mem. Eastern Orthodox Ch. Avocations: travel, walking, stamp collecting, reading. Home: 1516 Sylvan Way Louisville KY 40205-2408 Office: U Louisville Coll Bus & Pub Adminstrn Louisville KY 40292

TAYLOR, ROBERT M., minister; b. Englewood, N.J., Mar. 5, 1932; s. Robert M. and Irene Maude (Benner) T.; m. Anna Elizabeth Taylor, Dec. 27, 1953 (dec. Sept. 1970); m. Beverly Ann Taylor, Nov. 7, 1971; children: Robert M., William Harrison, Joanne Elizabeth, Susan Ruth. BA cum laude, Lafayette Coll., 1953; MDiv, Princeton Seminary, 1956. Ordained to ministry Presbyn. Ch., 1956. Pastor Mahoning Presbyn. Ch., Danville, Pa., 1956-59; asst. pastor Harundale Presbyn. Ch., Glen Burnie, Md., 1959-62; pastor Cen. Presbyn. Ch., Downingtown, Pa., 1962-69; sr. pastor The Presbyn. Ch., New Brunswick, N.J., 1969-75, Rosedale Gardens Presbyn. Ch., Livonia, Mich., 1975-79, Immanuel Presbyn. Ch., Albuquerque, 1979-85; interim pastor Community Presbyn. Ch., Mountainside, N.J., 1985-86; interim sr. pastor First Presbyn. Ch., Matawan, N.J., 1986-88; pastor Christ Ch. on Quaker Hill, Pawling, N.Y., 1988-94, Hope Presbyn. Ch., Lakewood, N.J., 1994-97; retired, 1997; commr. Gen. Assembly/Presbyn. Ch., Mpls., 1968; supr. Princeton Sem. Tchg. Ch., New Brunswick, N.J., 1969-75; v.p. Inter-Ch. Coalition on Mission in Southwest, Phoenix, 1984; mem. Monmouth Presbytery, 1994—; mem. ethics com. Harlem Valley Psychiat. Ctr.; mem. Interfaith Clergy Coun.; bd. dirs., v.p. Cmty. Resource Ctr. Pawling, 1988-94. Mem. United Fund Bd. Govs., Downingtown, 1969, Citizen's Adv. Com., 1969, Mayor's Youth Adv. Com., East Brunswick, 1973; sec. Coll. Scholarship Found., 1975. Fellow in Pastoral Leadership Devel., Princeton Theol. Seminary, 1973. Mem. Rotary, Alpha Chi Rho (pres. 1952-53). Home: 1043 Waldorf Ter Lakewood NJ 08701-5547 *Life is a marvelous journey of caring and sharing with continual opportunities for growth. The challenge is to remain open to God's leading, even when the necessary hurdles are many.*

TAYLOR, ROBERT MORGAN, electronics executive; b. Orange, N.J., May 13, 1941; s. Morgan H. M. Taylor and Grace Anna (Bonynge) Loding; m. Sandra Ruth Cox, Sept. 11, 1965; children: Scott Joseph, Karen Lynne. BA in Chemistry, Williams Coll., 1963; PhD in Chemistry, Pa. State U., 1968; MBA, Drexel U., 1973. Scientist Leeds & Northrup Co., North Wales, Pa., 1968-70, sr. scientist, 1970-72, prin. scientist, 1972-84, corp. scientist, 1984-85, dir. R&D, 1985-92, dir. analytical mktg., 1990-93; v.p. products The Capital Controls Group, Colmar, Pa., 1993—. Contbr. articles to profl. jours.; 3 patents in dissolved oxygen sensing. Chmn. indsl. com. Montgomery County (Pa.) Sci. Rsch. Competition, 1987—. Mem. IEEE, Electrochem. Soc. (fin. com. 1971-73, controlling mems. com. 1977), Am. Chem. Soc., Instrument Soc. Am. (sr.), Indsl. Rsch. Inst. (rep.). Republican. Presbyterian.

TAYLOR, ROBERT P., lawyer; b. Douglas, Ariz., May 6, 1939; s. Paul Burton and Mary Ruth (Hart) T.; m. Sybil Ann Cappelletti, May 30, 1963 (div. Apr. 1974); children: David Scott, Nicole; m. Anne Dale Kaiser, Sept. 21, 1991. BSEE, U. Ariz., 1961; JD, Georgetown U., 1969. Bar: U.S. Ct. Appeals (9th circ.) 1969, U.S. Ct. Appeals (1st, 2d, 3d, 6th, and Fed. circs.), U.S. Supreme Ct., 1975. Elec. engr. Motorola Corp., Phoenix, 1961, Bell & Howell, Pasadena, Calif., 1964-65; examiner U.S. Patent Office, Washington, 1966-69; atty. Pillsbury Madison & Sutro, San Francisco, 1969-96, Howrey & Simon, Palo Alto, Calif., 1996—; mem. adv. commn. Patent Law Reform, Washington, 1990-92; mem. adv. bd. Litigation Risk Analysis, Palo Alto, Calif., 1985—. Contbr. articles to profl. jours. Dir. Ind. Colls. of No. Calif., San Francisco, 1982-96, officer, 1988-96. Fellow Am. Coll. Trial Lawyers; mem. ABA (chair sect. antitrust 1991-92), Am. Law Inst. Avocations: Bicycling, cooking, hiking. Office: Howrey & Simon 301 Ravenswood Ave Menlo Park CA 94025

TAYLOR, ROBERT SUNDLING, English educator, art critic; b. Newton, Mass., Jan. 19, 1925; s. Frank Millikan and Elsie (Sundling) T.; m. Brenda K. Slattery, June 20, 1964; children: Gillian, Douglas. A.B., Colgate U., 1947; postgrad., Brown U. Art, music, film and theatre critic Boston Herald, 1948-67; editor publs. Inst. Contemporary Art, Boston, 1967; art critic Boston Globe, 1967-90, arts editor, 1973-76, book columnist, 1978—; prof. English, Wheaton Coll., Norton, Mass., 1961-96; fiction coord. Ea. States Writers Conf., Salem (Mass.) State Coll., 1979-80. Author: (novel) In Red Weather, 1961, Saranac: America's Magic Mountain, 1986, Fred Allen: His Life and Wit, 1989, New England: The Home Front, WWII, 1991; co-author: Treasures of New England, 1976. Trustee, Abbot Public Library, Marblehead, Mass., 1980-83. Served with USN, 1943-46. Mem. Mass. Hist. Soc. Club: St. Botolph (Boston). Home: 1 Thomas Cir Marblehead MA 01945-1203 Office: Wheaton Coll Norton MA 02766

TAYLOR, ROBERT WILLIAM, professional society administrator; b. Brownsville, Tenn., July 28, 1929; s. Charles William and Annie Laura (Taliaferro) T.; m. Jeanette Henshaw, Jan. 4, 1953; children: Robert William, Teresa, Mark Thomas. B.S. in Chemistry, Murray (Ky.) State U., 1949; M.S. in Journalism, Ohio U., 1950. Asst. editor Jour. Petroleum Tech., 1953, editor, 1954-63; exec. dir., sec. AIME, 1963-68; exec. v.p., gen. mgr. Soc. Mfg. Engrs., 1968-81; publishing dir. Mfg. Engring., 1968-81; pres. Am. Soc. Assn. Execs., Washington, 1981—, ASAE Found., Washington, 1981—, ASAE Service Corps., Washington, 1981—, ASAE Ins. Co., 1993—; bd. dirs. Inst. Orgn. Mgmt., Points of Light Fedn. Assoc. editor: Petroleum Prodn. Handbook, 1961. Past bd. dirs. One to One Found., Mfg. Engring. Edn. Found.; hon. co-chmn. Clinton/Gore Inaugural. Served to 2d lt. USAF, 1951-53. Fellow Soc. Mfg. Engrs., Jr. Engring. Tech. Soc. (past dir.), Am. Soc. Engring. Edn. (past dir.), Council Engring. and Sci. Soc. Execs. (past pres.), Am. Assn. Engring. Socs. (past dir.). Club: City of Washington (dir.). Home: 1401 N Oak St Apt 605 Arlington VA 22209-3648 Office: Am Soc of Assoc Executives 1575 I St NW Washington DC 20005-1105

TAYLOR, ROBIN LYNN, anchorperson, reporter; b. Pittsfield, Mass., May 11, 1964; d. Orley R. and Toni Taylor. BA, U. Wis., 1986. Anchor, reporter Sta. KAAL-TV, Austin, Minn., 1987-88, Sta. WROC-TV, Rochester, N.Y., 1988-94, Sta. WITI-TV, Milw., 1994—. Participant Day of Caring, United Way, Rochester, 1994; fundraiser Cystic Fibrosis, Milw., 1995, Muscular Dystrophy Assn., 1996; telethon vol. Muscular Dystrophy Assn., Milw., 1995. Recipient hon. mention for best newscast AP, 1992, Excellence in Journalism award Radio TV News Dirs.' Found., 1994, Emmy nomination, 1994, First Place Spots News Coverage award Wis. Broadcasters Assn., 1995, First Place Spot News Coverage award AP, 1996, Spl. Merit award for Spot News Coverage, N.W. Broadcast News Assn., 1996, First Place Planned News Coverage award Milw. Press Club, 1996, Spl. Merit award for Spot News Coverage Wis. Broadcasters Assn., 1996. Office: Sta WITI-TV 9001 N Green Bay Rd Milwaukee WI 53209-1204

TAYLOR, ROGER CONANT, writer; b. Newport, R.I., Nov. 18, 1931; s. Conant and Marjorie Perry (Buffum) T.; m. Priscilla Greene, June 12, 1953; children: Roger Conant, John Dean, Rebecca Buffum, Stephen Greene; m. 2d, Kathleen Elizabeth Carney, Aug. 17, 1991. AB, Harvard U., 1953; MS, Boston U., 1966. Commd. ensign USN, 1953, advanced through grades to comdr. Res., 1967, ret., 1975; served in destroyers and submarines; editorial dir. U.S. Naval Inst., Annapolis, Md., 1960-69; pres. Internat. Marine Pub. Co., Camden, Maine, 1969-86. Author: Good Boats, 1977, More Good Boats, 1979, Still More Good Boats, 1981, The Elements of Seamanship, 1982, The Fourth Book of Good Boats, 1984, Knowing the Ropes, 1989, Thirty Classic Boat Designs, 1992. Mem. U.S. Naval Inst. (life). Home: RR3 Box 5365 Union ME 04862

TAYLOR, ROGER LEE, lawyer; b. Canton, Ill., Apr. 6, 1941; s. Ivan and Pauline Helen (Mahr) T.; m. E. Anne Zweifel, June 13, 1964. BA, Knox Coll., 1963; JD cum laude, Northwestern U., 1971. Bar: Ill. 1971, U.S. Dist. Ct. (no. dist.) Ill. 1971, U.S. Dist. Ct. (no. dist.) Tex. 1975, U.S. Dist. Ct. (no. dist.) Ill. 1982, U.S. Ct. Appeals (7th cir.) 1972, U.S. Ct. Appeals (5th and 11th cirs.) 1981, U.S. Supreme Ct. 1975. Assoc. Kirkland & Ellis, Chgo., 1971-78, ptnr., 1978—. Trustee Knox Coll. Lt. USNR, 1964-68. Mem. ABA, Chgo. Council Lawyers, Ill. Bar Assn., Order of Coif, Univ. Club, Mid-Am. Club Chgo. Office: Kirkland & Ellis 200 E Randolph St Chicago IL 60601-6436

TAYLOR, RONALD FULFORD, physician; b. Bethesda, Md., Mar. 23, 1956; s. Harold Bernard and Evelyn (Stansbury) T.; m. Sharon Delyn Stevenson, Mar. 7, 1987. BS, Frostburg (Md.) State Coll., 1978; MD, Med. Coll. Va., 1982. Intern Vanderbilt U., Nashville, 1982-83, resident, 1983-85, fellow in pulmonary and critical care medicine, 1985-87; practice pulmonary and critical care medicine Jackson (Tenn.) Clinic, 1987—. Contbr. articles to profl. jours. Bd. dirs. Am. Lung Assn. of Tenn., Nashville, 1987-95. Mem. AMA, Am. Coll. Chest Physicians. Office: Jackson Clinic 616 W Forest Ave Jackson TN 38301-3902

TAYLOR, RONALD LEE, school administrator; b. Urbana, Ill., Nov. 11, 1943; s. Lee R. and Katherine L. (Becker) T.; m. Patricia D. Fitzsimmons, Mar. 10, 1973; children: Jamie, Lara, Meredith, Dana. AB, Harvard U., 1966; MBA, Stanford U., 1971. Asst. contr. Bell & Howell, Chgo., 1971-73; pres. DeVry Inc./Keller Grad. Sch., Chgo., 1973—; bd. dirs. Precision Plastic, Columbia City, Ind., L. Karp & Sons, Elk Grove Village, Ill., Chernin's Shoes, Inc., Chgo., SPR Inc., Oak Brook, Ill. Pres. Hinsdale (Ill.) Sch. Bd., 1983-91; com. chmn. Ill. Bd. Higher Edn., Springfield, 1985—; state chmn. Employer Support of Guard and Res. Mem. Ill. State C. of C. (mem. edn. com. 1987—). Office: DeVry Inc 1 Tower Ln Villa Park IL 60181-4671

TAYLOR, ROSE PERRIN, social worker; b. Lander, Wyo., Feb. 11, 1916; d. Wilbur Rexford Perrin and Agatha Catherine (Hartman) Perrin DeMars; m. Louis Kempf Kugland, Sept. 1942 (div. 1951); children: Mary Louise, Carolyn Kugland McElhany; m. Wilfred Taylor, Oct. 13, 1962 (dec. 1991). AB, U. Mich., 1937; MSW, U. Denver, 1956; student, Columbia U., 1936, Santa Rosa Jr. Coll., 1974-93, Coll. of Marin, 1995-97. Group worker Dodge Community House, Detroit, 1937-38; case worker Detroit Welfare Dept., Detroit, 1938-40; child welfare worker Fremont County Welfare Dept., Lander, Wyo., 1940-42; worker children's svcs. Laramie County Welfare Dept., Cheyenne, Wyo., 1951-57, dir., 1957-58; supr. San Mateo (Calif.) County Health & Welfare, 1958-74; dir. Fed. Day Care Project, San Mateo, 1964—; tchr. Sch. Pub. Health Nursing, U. Wyo., 1951-55; tchr. Sch. Social Work, U. Calif., San Jose, 1962-63; workshop leader NIMH, Prescott, Ariz., 1961, Ariz. State U., Phoenix, 1962, Oreg. State Welfare Dept., Otter Crest, 1973; cons. day care workshops. Contbr. articles to profl. jours. Adminstrv. vol. Buck Ctr. for Rsch. in Aging, Marin County, 1994-95, vol. epidemiol. rschr. nutrition validation study for people in their 80's and 90's, 1995. Recipient Resolution of Commendation, Calif. State Senate, 1974; Annual Rose Taylor award San Mateo Child Care Coordinating Coun., 1982. Mem. NASW. Democrat. Mem. United Ch. of Christ. Avocations: artist, writer children's fiction, poetry. Home: The Redwoods # 10105 40 Camino Alto Mill Valley CA 94941-2943

TAYLOR, ROSEMARY, artist; b. Joseph, Oreg.; d. Theodore and Sarah A. (Lambright) Resch; student Cleve. Inst. Art, 1937-40, NYU, 1947; m. Robert Hull Taylor; children: Barbara Taylor Ryalls, Robert H. Tchr. pottery Rahway (N.J.) Art Center, 1950-55; one-woman shows: Paterson (N.J.) Coll., 1964, Westchester (Pa.) Coll., 1970, Gallery 100, Princeton, N.J., 1967, George Jensen's, N.Y.C., 1972, Artisan Gallery, Princeton, 1974, Am. Crafts (Ohio), 1979-97, Guild Gallery, 1986-91, Little Art Gallery, N.C., 1985-97, Olde Queens Gallery (N.J.), 1987, N.J. Designer Craftsmen, 1990, 97 (bd. dirs. 1986-87, standard chmn., 1994), Creative Hand, 95, 97, Princeton, 1994; group shows include: Mus. Natural History, N.Y.C., Newark Mus., Trenton (N.J.) Mus., Montclair (N.J.) Mus., Phila. Art Alliance, Pa. Horticulture Soc., 1988, Nat. Design Center, N.Y.C., Michener Mus., Pa., 1996; represented in permanent collection Westchester Coll.; pottery cons. McCalls Mag., 1962-72. Bd. dirs. Solebury Community Sch.; mem. Fulbright award com., 1982, 83. Mem. LWV (pres. Plainfield, N.J. chpt.). Mem. Am. Craft Council, N.J. Designer-Craftsmen, Phila. Craft Group, Bucks County (Pa.) C. of C., Visual Artists and Galleries Assn., Nat. Assn. Am. Penwoman, Michener Mus., Doylestown, Pa., Women in the Arts (charter). Democrat. Unitarian. Home: PO Box 46 Lumberville PA 18933-0046 Office: PO Box 282 Stockton NJ 08559-0282

TAYLOR, ROY LEWIS, botanist, educator; b. Olds, Alta., Can., Apr. 12, 1932; s. Martin Gilbert and Crystal (Thomas) T. B.Sc., Sir George Williams U., Montreal, Que., Can., 1957; Ph.D., U. Calif. at Berkeley, 1962; DSc (hon.), U. B.C., Vancouver, Can. Pub. sch. tchr. Olds Sch. Div., 1949-52; jr. high sch. tchr. Calgary Sch. Bd., Alta., 1953-55; chief taxonomy sect., research br. Can. Agrl. Dept., Ottawa, Ont., 1962-68; dir. Bot. Garden, prof. botany, prof. plant scis. U. B.C., Vancouver, 1968-85; pres., CEO Chgo. Horticultural Soc., 1985-94; dir. Chgo. Bot. Garden, Glencoe, Ill., 1985-94; exec. dir. Rancho Santa Ana Bot. Garden, Claremont, Calif., 1994—; prof. botany, chmn. botany program Claremont Grad. Sch., 1994—; pres. Western Bot. Svcs. Ltd. Author: The Evolution of Canada's Flora, 1966, Flora of the Queen Charlotte Islands, Vols. I and II, 1968, Vascular Plants of British Columbia: A Descriptive Resource Inventory, 1977; The Rare Plants of British Columbia, 1985. Mem. State of Ill. Bd. Natural Resources and Conservation, 1987-94; trustee Nature Ill. Found., 1990-94. Fellow Linnean Soc. London; mem. Can. Bot. Assn. (pres. 1967-68), Biol. Coun. Can. (pres. 1973-74), Am. Assn. Mus. (accreditation com. 1980-85, chmn. 1985-91, chmn. ethics commn. 1991-93), Am. Assn. Bot. Gardens and Arboreta (pres. 1976, 77, award of merit 1987), Claremont C. of C. (bd. dirs. 1995-98), Ottawa Valley Curling Assn. (pres. 1968-69), B.C. Soc. Landscape Archs. (hon.), U. B.C. Bot. Garden (hon.), Chgo. Hort Soc. (life, medal 1994), Gov. Gen.'s Curling Club Can. (life), Univ. Club Claremont, Men's Garden Club L.A. Office: Rancho Santa Ana Bot Garden Claremont CA 91711-3157

TAYLOR, SAMUEL A., playwright; b. San Francisco, June 13, 1912; m. Suzanne Combes, June 4, 1940; children: Ellinor, Michael, David. Student, U. Calif., Berkeley. Ind. playwright, 1950—; chmn. emeritus Dramatists Play Svc., Inc., N.Y.C. Playwright: The Happy Time, 1950, Sabrina Fair, 1953, The Pleasure of His Company, 1958, First Love, 1961, No Strings (mus. with Richard Rodgers), 1962, Beekman Place, 1964, Avanti!, 1968, A Touch of Spring, 1975, Legend, 1976, Perfect Pitch, 1978, Flying Colours, 1985, Three by Three, 1988. Mem. Dramatists Guild, Authors Guild, Writers Guild Am., Acad. Motion Picture Arts and Scis. Club: Century Assn. (N.Y.C.). Home: Meadow Rue East Blue Hill ME 04629

TAYLOR, SHARON KAY, elementary school counselor; b. Ft. Worth, Oct. 13, 1954; d. Cecil James and Mary Evelyn (Careathers) Owens; m. Kenneth Carroll Taylor, May 21, 1977; children: Anna Marie, Scott Owens. BS, Howard Payne U., 1976; MEd, North Tex. State, 1986. Tchr. Elem. Pub. Sch., Belton, Tex., 1979-89; counselor Kelley Elem. Sch., Denver City, Tex., 1989—. Mem. Tex. Assn. Counseling and Devel., Tex. Sch. Counselors Assn., Assn. for Play Therapy, Beta Sigma Phi. Democrat. Baptist. Avocations: compiling scrapbooks, gardening. Home: PO Box 486 Denver City TX 79323-0486 Office: Kelley Elementary School 500 N Soland Ave Denver City TX 79323-2824

TAYLOR, SHERRIL WIGHTMAN, broadcasting company executive; b. Salt Lake City, Jan. 4, 1924; s. Kenneth E. and Florence May (Wightman) T.; m. Josephine Vermillion, May 2, 1970; 1 child by previous marriage, Sarah. Student, U. Utah, 1943-46; BJ, U. Mo., 1947; postgrad., Yale U. Promotion mgr. KSL Radio, Salt Lake City, 1947-51; sales promotion mgr. CBS, Hollywood, Calif., 1951-53; CBS radio sales CBS, N.Y.C., 1953-56; dir. sales promotion and advt. CBS Radio, N.Y.C.; also v.p. Radio Advt. Bur., N.Y.C., 1956-58; sr. group head J. Walter Thompson, Chgo., 1958-61; ind. TV producer Kukla, Fran, and Ollie Show, N.Y.C., 1961-64; v.p. Nat. Assn. Broadcasters, Washington, 1964-67; dir. Nat. Assn. Broadcasters, 1969-78; v.p. affiliate relations CBS, 1967-79; cons. Bonneville Internat. Corp., 1979-85; pres. Taylor Co., 1985-91; vice chmn. Coltrin & Assoc., 1991—; pvt. sector coordinator USIA, Washington, 1982, cons., 1982—; chmn. adv. com. Voice of Am., Washington, 1989—; vis. lectr. Brigham Young U., Provo, Utah, 1980—, Emerson Coll., Boston, Mich. Central U., Southern Vt. Coll.; adv. faculty-industry seminar, 1980, 81; bd. dirs. Am. Communications Inc., Utica-Rome TV Svcs. Inc., 1988—. Author: Radio Programming in Action, 1967. Mem. Carnegie Hall com. for Utah Symphony, Park Avenue Preservation Com.; chmn. Freedoom of Info. Fund, U. Mo.; past trustee The Helene Toolen Inst. Med. Rsch., Bennington, Vt., 1985—; mem. futures com. Bennington Mus., 1985—; bd. dirs. Nautical Ventures Inc., N.Y.C., 1987—. Mem. So. Calif. Broadcasters Assn. (dir.), Internat. Radio and TV Soc. (v.p., bd. dirs., pres., chmn., bd. dirs. found.), Broadcasters' Found. (dir.), Food and Wine Soc. (N.Y. chpt.), Am. Values Inc. (officer, bd. dirs.), Belleair (Fla.) Country Club, Yale Club of N.Y., Sigma Chi. Episcopalian. Home: 430 E 86th St New York NY 10028-6441

TAYLOR, SHERRILL RUTH, management educator; b. Endwell, N.Y., July 9, 1943; d. Wallace Bixby and Lillie Mary (Sprague) Ingalls; m. William Leon Taylor, July 18, 1964; children: Mark William, Tammie Ann. BBA, Tex. Women's U., 1983, MBA, 1986. Cert. sr. profl. human resources. Pers. rep. Tex. Women's U., Denton, Tex., 1986-87; fleet upgrade coord. Xerox Corp., Oakland, Calif., 1987-88; with Sun Diamond Growers, Pleasanton, Calif., 1988-90; mgmt. lectr. Tex. Women's U., 1990—, dir. Small Bus. Inst., 1993—; co-fellow Sam Walton Students In Free Enterprise. Mem. Denton Pers. Assn., Small Bus. Inst. Dirs. Assn. (nat. v.p. publs. 1997—), Southwestern Small Bus. Inst. Assn., Internat. Credit Assn. Denton County (sec. 1995-97), Dallas Human Resource Mgmt. Assn., Inc. Methodist. Avocation: Sweet Adelines Chorus. Office: Tex Women's U Dept Bus PO Box 425738 Denton TX 76204

TAYLOR, STEPHEN EMLYN, publishing executive; b. Cambridge, Eng., Apr. 28, 1951; s. Charles Henry and Diana (Burgess) T.; m. M. E. Malone, May 24, 1987; children: Maxwell, Conrad. BA in Psychology, Yale U., 1973. U.S. sales mgr., tech. advisor Snapir Ltd., Conn., 1973-74; mgr., sail designer North Sails, Boston, 1974-80; mgmt. trainee Boston Globe, 1980-82, asst. to bus. mgr., 1980-82, dir. info. svcs., 1982-86, asst. bus. mgr., 1986-88, bus. mgr., 1988-91, v.p., 1991-93, exec. v.p., 1993—. Bd. dirs. Greater Boston Food Bank, 1991—; mem. corp. Woods Hole (Mass.) Oceanographic Inst., 1993—; mem. U.S. Olympic Yachting Com., 1980-84. Mem. New Eng. Newspaper Assn. (bd. dirs.), Yale Sailing Assocs. (treas., trustee), Cruising Club Am., N.Y. Yacht Club, New Bedford Yacht Club. Home: 18 Webster Rd Milton MA 02186-5318 Office: Globe Newspaper Co PO Box 2378 Boston MA 02107-2378*

TAYLOR, STEPHEN HOSMER, sports entertainment executive, photographer; b. Syracuse, N.Y., Jan. 10, 1955; s. Robert W. and Shirley (Hosmer) T.; m. Angie Gulliver Taylor, May 5, 1979; children: Christopher, Jessica, Matthew. AA in Liberal Arts, Auburn C.C., 1975. Chief photographer Auburn (N.Y.) Pubs., 1975-83; dir. photography Titan Sports, Inc., Stamford, Conn., 1983-92; v.p. event ops. Titan Sports Inc., Stamford, Conn., 1992—; ofcl. photographer World Wrestling Fedn., 1983-92, stringer UPI, 1978-82. Recipient Sports Photo award UPI, N.Y., 1982. Mem. Nat. Press Photographers Assn. Address: 1241 E Main St Stamford CT 06902-3521

TAYLOR, STEPHEN LLOYD, food toxicologist, educator, food scientist; b. Portland, Oreg., July 19, 1946; s. Lloyd Emerson and Frances Hattie (Hanson) T.; m. Susan Annette Kerns, June 23, 1973; children: Amanda, Andrew. BS in Food Sci. Tech., Oreg. State U., 1968, MS in Food Sci. Tech., 1969; PhD in Biochemistry, U. Calif., Davis, 1973. Research assoc. U. Calif., Davis, 1973-74, research fellow, 1974-75; chief food toxicology Letterman Army Inst., San Francisco, 1975-78; asst. prof. food toxicology U. Wis., Madison, 1978-83, assoc. prof., 1983-87; head dept. food sci. technology, dir. Food Processing Ctr. U. Nebr., Lincoln, 1987—; cons. in field, 1978—. Contbr. articles to profl. jours. Fellow Nat. Inst. Environ. Health Sci., Nat. Acad. Scis. (chair food chems. codex com., bd. food and nutrition), Inst. Food Technologists (divsn. chmn. 198182, sect. chmn. 1984-85, exec. com. 1988-91); mem. Am. Acad. Asthma, Allergy and Immunology, Am. Chem. Soc. Democrat. Presbyterian. Home: 941 Evergreen Dr Lincoln NE 68510-4131 Office: U Nebr Dept Food Sci Tech Lincoln NE 68583-0919

TAYLOR, STEVE HENRY, zoologist; b. Inglewood, Calif., Mar. 18, 1947; s. Raymond Marten and Ardath (Metz) T.; 1 child, Michael Travis; m. Sarah Margaret Young, May 14, 1993. BA in Biology, U. Calif.-Irvine, 1969. Animal keeper Los Angeles Zoo, 1972-75, assoc. curator, 1975-76; children's zoo mgr. San Francisco Zoo, 1976-81; zoo dir. Sacramento Zoo, 1981-88; dir. Cleve. Met. Zoo, 1989—. Bd. dirs. Sacramento Soc. Prevention Cruelty to Animals, 1983-87, Sacramento Red Cross, 1988-89, Conv. and Visitor Bur. of Greater Cleve., 1995—, Leadership Cleveland Class 1997. Fellow Am. Assn. Zool. Parks and Aquariums (infant care diet advisor 1979, 85, bd. dirs. 1987-93, pres. 1991-92, chmn. pub. edn. com. 1987-89, bd. regents, mgmt. sch., Outstanding Svc. award); mem. Captive Breeding Specialist Group, Internat. Union of Dirs. Zool. Gardens, The Wilds (bd. dirs. Ohio club), Sierra Club, Audubon Soc. Democrat. Home: 1265 Elmwood Rd Rocky River OH 44116-2236 Office: Cleveland Metroparks Zoo 3900 Brookside Park Dr Cleveland OH 44109-3132

TAYLOR, STEVEN BRUCE, agriculture company executive; b. Salinas, Calif., Dec. 29, 1954; s. Edward Horton and Joanne (Church) T.; m. Kathryn Hagler, Dec. 17, 1978; children: Meghan Jean, Kyle Hagler, Christian Steven. BA, U. Calif., Berkeley, 1978; MBA, Harvard U., 1985. Pres. Fresh Concepts, San Marino, Calif., 1985-87; mktg. staff Bruce Church, Inc., Salinas, Calif., 1987-91; pres. Fresh Express Retail Mktg., Salinas, 1991—; pres. Fresh Internat., Salinas, 1991—, CEO; v.p. Salinas Valley Lettuce Co-op, Salinas, 1990—; bd. dirs. Produce for Better Health, Del., 1991—. Bd. Elders First Presbyn. Ch., Salinas, 1989-92, personnel com. 1989-94, bldg. com. 1990—; founding mem. Lincoln Club of Monterey County, Salinas, 1990. Avocations: basketball, skiing, soccer coach, bible study, board games. Home: 515 Santa Paula Dr Salinas CA 93901-1517 Office: Fresh Internat 1020 Merrill St Salinas CA 93901-4409*

TAYLOR, STUART ROSS, geochemist, author; b. Ashburton, New Zealand, Nov. 26, 1925; s. Thomas Stuart and Anne Grace (Lloyd) T.; m. Noel Elvie White, May 21, 1958; children: Susanna, Judith, Helen. BSc, U. New Zealand, 1948, MSc, 1951; PhD, Ind. U., 1954; DSc, Oxford U., 1978. Lectr. U. Oxford, Eng., 1954-58; sr. lectr. U. Cape Town, South Africa, 1958-60; professorial fellow Australian Nat. U., Canberra, 1961-90, vis. fellow, 1990-97, prof. emeritus, 1997; prof U. Vienna, 1992, 96; vis. scientist Lunar and Planetary Inst., Houston, 1969-90. Author: Lunar Science: Post-Apollo View, 1975, Planetary Science, 1982, Solar System Evolution, 1992, (with others) Continental Crust, 1985; contbr. more than 200 articles to profl. jours. Recipinet Goldschmidt medal Geochem. Soc., 1993, Gilbert award Geol. Soc. Am., 1994. Fellow Royal Soc. New Zealand (hon.), Australian Acad. Sci., Geol. Soc. London (hon.), Geol. Soc. India (hon.); mem. NAS (frgn. assoc.), Meteoritical Soc. (pres. 1989-90). Office: Australian Nat U, Dept Nuclear Physics, Canberra 0200, Australia

TAYLOR, SUSAN L., editor, magazine; b. N.Y.C., Jan. 23, 1946; d. Lawrency and Violet (Weekes) T.; m. William Bowles (div.); 1 child, Shana-Nequai; m. Khephra Burns, 1989—. BA in Sociology, Fordham U., 1991, postgrad. Freelance beauty editor Essence Mag., N.Y.C., 1971-81, editor, 1981—; host, exec. prod. weekly tv show Essence, 1983-87; driving force behind Essence Awards; v.p. Essence Comm., Inc., N.Y.C., 1986—. Author: In the Spirit: The Inspirational Writings of Susan L. Taylor, 1993, Lessons in Living, 1995. Office: Essence 1500 Broadway New York NY 10036-4015

TAYLOR, TELFORD, lawyer, educator; b. Schenectady, Feb. 24, 1908; s. John Bellamy and Marcia Estabrook (Jones) T.; m. Mary Eleanor Walker, July 2, 1937 (dec.); children: Joan, Ellen, John Bellamy II, Ursula Taylor Rechnegal; m. Toby Barbara Golick, Aug. 9, 1974; children: Benjamin Waite, Samuel Bourne. AB, Williams Coll., 1928, AM, 1932, LLD, 1949; LLB, Harvard U., 1932; LHD (hon.), Yeshiva U., 1987; D in Civil Law (hon.), Union U., 1987; LLD (hon.), Brandeis U., 1988. Instr. history and polit. sci. Williams Coll., 1928-29; law clk. to U.S. circuit judge N.Y.C., 1932-33; asst. solicitor U.S. Dept. Interior, Washington, 1933-34; sr. atty. A.A.A., 1934-35; assoc. counsel U.S. Senate com. on inter-state commerce, 1935-39; spl. asst. to atty. gen. U.S., 1939-40; gen. counsel FCC, 1940-42; practiced with Taylor, Scoll, Ferencz & Simon; vis. lectr. Yale U. Law Sch., 1957-76; vis. lectr. Columbia U. Law Sch., 1958-63, prof. law, 1963-74, Nash prof., 1974-76, emeritus, 1976—; prof. Cardozo Law Sch., 1976-77, 78—; vis. prof. Harvard U. Law Sch., 1977-78; Fed. Spl. master U.S. Dist. Ct. for So. Dist. N.Y., 1977-82; Adminstr. Small Def. Plants Adminstrn., 1951-52; counsel Joint Council for Edn. TV, 1951-61; chmn. N.Y.C. Adv. Bd. Pub. Welfare, 1960-63, mem., 1963-66. Author: Sword and Swastika, 1952, Grand Inquest, 1954, The March of Conquest, 1958, The Breaking Wave, 1967, Two Studies in Constitutional Interpretation, 1969, Nuremberg and Vietnam, 1970, Courts of Terror, 1976, Munich: The Price of Peace, 1979 (Nat. Book Critic's Circle award 1980), The Anatomy of the Nuremberg Trials; also articles on polit., legal, mil. subjects. Commd. maj. M.I. service U.S. Army, 1942; lt. col. Gen. Staff Corps, 1943; col. (assigned as mil. intelligence officer ETO, 1943-45) assoc. counsel, U.S. rep. for prosecution of war criminals, brig. gen. 1946; U.S. chief of counsel for war crimes Office Mil. Govt., 1946-49, U.S. Decorated DSM; Order Brit. Empire; French Legion of Honor; Polonia Restituta Poland; comdr. Order of Orange-Nassau, Netherlands, 1950; Lateran Cross, 3d class Vatican); recipient Nat. critics prize for non-fiction, 1979; Overseas fellow Churchill Coll., Cambridge, 1969. Fellow Am. Acad. Arts and Scis.; mem. Assn. of Bar of City of N.Y., Am. Law Inst., ASCAP, Res. Officer's Assn., Author's Guild, Mil. Order World Wars, Theta Delta Chi. Democrat. Club: Harvard. Home: 54 Morningside Dr New York NY 10025-1740

TAYLOR, TERRY R., editor, educator; b. Valley Forge, Pa., Oct. 4, 1952; d. Thomas R. and Anna P. (Bystrek) T. BA in Journalism, Temple U., 1974. Reporter gen. assignments, sch. news Charlotte (N.C.) News, 1974-77; supr., writer AP, Phila., 1977-81; supr., writer sports desk AP, N.Y.C., 1981-85, asst. editor sports, 1985-87, dep. editor sports, 1987-91, asst. chief bur., 1991-92, editor sports, 1992—; asst. editor sports N.Y. Times, 1991; assoc. in journalism Columbia U., N.Y.C., 1991-95; adv. bd. Honda Awards, 1996—. Recipient John A. Domino Meml. award St. Bonaventure U., 1996. Roman Catholic. Office: AP Sports 50 Rockefeller Plz New York NY 10020-1605

TAYLOR, THEODORE BREWSTER, physicist, business executive; b. Mexico City, July 11, 1925; s. Walter Clyde and Barbara (Howl) T.; m. Caro Dwight Arnim, June 13, 1948; children: Clare E. Taylor Hastings, Katherine W. Taylor Robertson, Christopher H., Robert P., Jeffrey J. B.S., Calif. Inst. Tech., 1945; Ph.D., Cornell U., 1954. Theoretical physicist U. Calif. Radiation Lab., Berkeley, 1946-49, Los Alamos Sci. Lab., 1949-56; sr. research adviser Gen. Atomic div. Gen. Dynamics Corp., San Diego, 1956-64; dep. dir. (sci.) Def. Atomic Support Agy., Dept. Def., 1964-67; chmn. bd. Internat. Research & Tech. Corp., 1967-76; vis. lectr. Princeton U., 1976-80; pres. Appropriate Solar Tech. Inst., 1980-87, Nova, Inc., 1980—; also bd. dirs.; pres. So. Tier Environ. Protection Soc., 1990—; mem. Pres.'s Commn. on Accident at Three-Mile Island, 1979; cons. Los Alamos Sci. Lab., 1956-64, Aerospace Corp., 1960-61, Air Force Sci. Adv. Bd., 1955-58, AEC, 1966-70, Def. Atomic Support Agy., 1966-69, U.S. Army Sci. Adv. Panel, 1967-71, Office of Tech. Assessment, 1976—, Rockefeller Found., 1977-80, Princeton U., 1980—, Fedn. Am. Scientists, 1986—; chmn. Los Alamos Study Group, Air Force Space Study Com., 1961; mem. panel outer space ACDA, 1961; mem. adv. bd. Solar Energy Research Inst., 1980-81. Served to ensign USNR, 1942-46. Recipient Ernest Orlando Lawrence award, 1965. Home and Office: PO Box 662 Wellsville NY 14895-0662

TAYLOR, THEODORE LANGHANS, author; b. Statesville, N.C., June 23, 1921; s. Edward Riley and Elnora Alma (Langhans) T.; m. Gweneth Ann Goodwin, Oct. 25, 1946; children: Mark, Wendy, Michael; m. Flora Gray Schoenleber, Apr. 18, 1981. Student, Fork Union Mil. Acad., 1939-40, U.S. Mcht. Marine Acad., 1942-44. Reporter Portsmouth (Va.) Star, 1941-42, Bluefield (W.Va.) News, 1946-47; sportswriter NBC-Radio, N.Y.C., 1942; asst. dir. pub. relations N.Y. U., 1947-48; dir. pub. relations YMCA Schs. and Colls., N.Y.C., 1948-50; publicist Paramount Pictures, Hollywood, Calif., 1955-56; assoc. producer Perlberg-Seaton Prodns., Hollywood, 1956-61. Free lance writer 1961—; author: The Magnificent Mitscher, 1954, Fire on the Beaches, 1957, People Who Make Movies, 1968, The Cay, 1969 (Jane Addam's Children's Book award 1970), The Children's War, 1971, Air Raid: Pearl Harbor, 1971, The Maldonado Miracle, 1973, Rebellion Town, 1973, Showdown, 1973, Teetoncey, 1974, Teetoncey and Ben O'Neal, 1975, Battle in the Arctic Seas, 1976, The Odyssey of Ben O'Neal, 1977, A Shepherd Watches, A Shepherd Sings, 1977, Jule, 1979, Battle of Midway Island, 1981, The Trouble with Tuck, 1981, Sweet Friday Island, 1981, HMS Hood vs Bismarck, 1982, Battle in the English Channel, 1983, The Cats of Shambala, Rocket Island, 1985, Walking Up a Rainbow, 1986, The Stalker, 1987, The Hostage, 1988, Monocolo, 1989, Sniper, 1989, Tuck Triumphant, 1991, The Wierdo, 1991, Maria, 1992, To Kill the Leopard, 1993, Timothy of the Cay, 1993, The Bomb, 1995, Rogue Wave, 1996. Served with USNR, 1945-46, 50-55. Recipient Lewis Carroll Shelf award, 1970, Silver medal Commonwealth Club, 1970, Best Book award So. Calif. Coun. on Children's Lit., 1970, Best Book award U. Calif. at Irvine, 1970, 74, Best Non-Fiction award Western Writers Am., 1977, Young Reader's Medal Calif. Reading Assn., 1984, 92, Edgar Allan Poe award, 1992, Utah Young Adult Book award, 1993, Md. Children's Book award, 1994, Scott O'Dell Best Hist. Fiction award, 1995, The Kerlan Body of Work award, 1997. Mem. Calif. Writers Guild, Acad. Motion Picture Arts and Scis., Screen Writers Guild. Republican. Lutheran. Address: 1856 Catalina Laguna Beach CA 92651-3340

TAYLOR, THERESA EVERETH, registered nurse, artist; b. Carthage, N.Y., Aug. 9, 1938; d. Michael Patrick and Angelina (Cerroni) Evereth; m. James Edgar Taylor II, Mar. 12, 1966; children: Britt, Priscilla, Blackwell. Diploma in nursing, House of Good Samaritan Sch. Nursing, Watertown, N.Y., 1959; BFA summa cum laude, Ursuline Coll., 1992, MA in Art Therapy, 1997. RN, N.Y., Ohio. Home health nurse DON Brason's Willcare, Cleve., 1995—; intern in art therapy Hospice of the Western Res., Ohio, 1996-97. Exhbns. in group shows. Pres. Wasmer Gallery Coun., Pepper Pike, Ohio, 1992-96; clk. vestry St. Christophers by the River, Gates Mills, 1979-81; treas. Welcome Wagon, Chesterland, Ohio, 1984-85; vol. artist Cleve. Ctr. Contemporary Art, 1993—; hospice vol.; art therapy intern. Avocations: art, political activism, medical AIDS activities. Home: 12060 Caves Rd Chesterland OH 44026-2104 Office: 6151 Wilson Mills Rd Highland Hgts OH 44143-2128

TAYLOR, THOMAS WILLIAM, lawyer; b. Columbus, Ind., Feb. 11, 1943; s. Virgil W. and Margaret Emma (Voiles) T.; m. Linda Kay Followell, Jan. 1, 1964; children: Pamela Kay, William Lansing. AB with honors, Ind. U., 1965; LLB cum laude, Harvard U., 1968. Bar: Mass. 1968, U.S. Dist. Ct. Mass. 1969. Assoc. Ropes & Gray, Boston, 1968-78, ptnr., 1978—; lectr. Pres.'s urban policy program seminars U.S. Coun. of Mayors, 1982; chmn. tax panel nat. workshop Coun. of Infrastructure Financing Authorities, 1993. Mem. Nat. Assn. Bond Lawyers (opinions com., chmn. securities law panel Washington workshop 1992, lectr. atty.'s workshop Chgo. 1983—), Am. Coll. Bond Counsel (founding fellow). Avocations: rock climbing, snowboarding, orienteering, trumpet playing. Office: Ropes & Gray 1 International Pl Boston MA 02110-2602

TAYLOR, TONY S., research scientist. Head stability physics group Gen. Atomics, San Diego. Recipient Excellence in Plasma Physics Rsch. award Am. Phys. Soc., 1994. Office: General Atomics PO Box 85608 San Diego CA 92186-9784

TAYLOR, VESTA FISK, real estate broker, educator; b. Ottawa County, Okla., July 15, 1917; d. Ira Sylvester and Judie Maude (Garman) Fisk; m.

George E. Taylor, Aug. 17, 1957 (dec. Oct. 1963); stepchildren: Joyce, Jean, Luther. AA, Northea. Okla. A&M, 1931; BA, N.E. State U., Tahlequah, Okla., 1937; MA, Okla. State U., 1942. Life cert. Spanish, English, history, elem. Tchr. rural sch. grades 1-4 Ottawa County, Okla., 1931-33; tchr. rural sch. grades 1-8 Ottawa County, 1933-38; tchr. H.S. Spanish, English Wyandotte, Okla., 1938-42; tchr. H.S. Spanish, English, math. Miami, Okla., 1942-57; tchr. H.S. Spanish Jacksonville, Ill., 1960-65; tchr. H.S. Spanish, English Miami, 1965-79; owner, broker First Lady Realty, Miami, 1979—; tchr. real estate for licensing N.E. Okla. Vocat.-Tech., Afton, 1980-94; radio spellmaster weekly-county groups Coleman Theater Stage, 1954-57, radio program weekly 4-H, Miami, 1953-57. Author: (poem) The Country School, 1994. Vol. sec. Ottawa County Senior's Ctr., 1993—; mem. restoration com. Friends of Theater, 1993—; mem. Friends of the Libr. Named Outstanding Coach Ottawa County 4-H Clubs, Miami, 1955, 67, Outstanding Alumnus All Yrs. H.S. Reunion, Wyandotte, Okla., 1992, Champion Speller N.E. Okla. Retirees, Oklahoma City, 1991. Mem. AAUW (pres. 1978-80, treas. 1994—), Ottawa Coutny Ret. Educators (treas. 1990—), Miami Classroom Tchr. (v.p. 1973-77), Tri-state Travel Club (purser 1989—). Democrat. Baptist. Avocations: gardening, reading, travel, volunteering. Home: 821 Jefferson Blvd Miami OK 74354-4910 Office: First Lady Realty 821 Jefferson St Miami OK 74354-4910

TAYLOR, VOLNEY, information company executive; b. Portsmouth, Ohio, Dec. 6, 1939; s. Lafayette and Martha Louise (Frederick) T.; m. Kathleen Ann MacMahon, May 17, 1969; children—Lafayette, Lloyd MacMahon, Kerry Erin, Frederick Daly. B.S. in Indsl. Engrng, Ohio State U., 1962; M.B.A., Harvard U., 1966. Asso. mem. McKinsey & Co., Inc. (mgmt. cons.), N.Y.C., 1966-72; exec. v.p., dir. Funk & Wagnalls, Inc., N.Y.C., 1972-74; v.p. fin. Reuben H. Donnelley Co., N.Y.C., 1974-76; dir. corp. planning Dun & Bradstreet Corp., N.Y.C., 1976-77, v.p. corp. planning, 1977-78, corp. v.p., 1979-80, sr. v.p., 1980-82, exec. v.p., 1982-96; gen. mgr. Official Airline Guides, Oak Brook, Ill., 1978-79; chmn. bd. dirs. Dun & Bradstreet Info. Svcs., Murray Hill, N.J., 1991—; chmn. bd., CEO Dun & Bradstreet Corp., 1996—; bd. dirs. Dun & Bradstreet, Inc., Dun & Bradstreet Europe, Dun & Bradstreet Internat., Dun's Mktg. Svcs., Inc., Moody's Investors Svc.; bd. dirs. Reuben H. Donnelley Corp., pres., 1988-90. Served to lt. (j.g.) USNR, 1962-64. Mem. Harvard Bus. Sch. (N.Y.C.) Club, Beta Theta Pi. Office: Dun & Bradstreet Corp 1 Diamond Hill Rd New Providence NJ 07974-1200

TAYLOR, W. O. (BILL TAYLOR), state legislator, business consultant; b. Zanesville, Ohio, July 29, 1932; s. Henry Ray and Lorena Louise (Winkler) T.; m. Shirley Ann Jacobs, Mar. 11, 1951; children: Bill, Larry, Sallie, Charles, Richard, Julie. AA in Bus. Adminstrn., Jacksonville (Fla.) U., 1957; B of Sci. Edn., Midwestern State U., Wichita Falls, Tex., 1968, MEd, 1972. Advanced secondary cert., Idaho. Acct. Swift & Co., Jacksonville, 1955-58; v.p. Taylor Bros. Inc., Baton Rouge, 1958-60; pres. Carter Paint Co., Inc., Wichita Falls, 1960-68; tchr. econs. Wichita Falls Pub. Sch., 1968-78; pres. Taylor Enterprises, Inc., Nampa, Idaho, 1978—; mem. Ho. of Reps, State of Idaho, Boise, 1986—, chmn. bus. com., 1994. Bishop Ch. of Jesus Christ of Latterday Saints, Wichita Falls, 1964-69. Served to sgt. USMC, 1950-53, Korea. Named Republican of Yr., Canyon County Rep. Ctrl. Com., 1987. Mem. DAV, Sertoma (life, pres. 1965, Sertoman of Yr. award 1964). Republican. Avocations: history, geneaology. Home: 1225 Virginia Cir Nampa ID 83687 Office: Idaho Ho of Reps State Capitol Boise ID 83720

TAYLOR, WALTER WALLACE, lawyer; b. Newton, Iowa, Sept. 18, 1925; s. Carrol W. and Eva (Greenly) T.; A.A., Yuba Coll., 1948, A.B., 1950; M.A., U. Calif., 1955, J.D., McGeorge Coll. Law, 1962; m. Mavis A. Harvey, Oct. 9, 1948; children—Joshua Michael (dec. 1980), Kevin Eileen, Kristin Lisa, Jeremy Walter, Margaret Jane, Melissa E., Amy M. Adminstrv. analyst USAF, Sacramento, 1951-53; personnel, research analyst Calif. Personnel Bd., Sacramento, 1954-56; civil service, personnel analyst, chief counsel, gen. mgr. Calif. Employees Assn., Sacramento, 1956-75; staff counsel, chief profl. standards Calif. Commn. Tchr. Credentialing, 1975-88, ret. 1988; staff counsel State Office Real Estate appraiser Licensing and Certification, 1992-94, ret.; tchr. discipline civil service, personnel cons. Served USCGR, 1943-46. Mem. Calif. State Bar, Am., Sacramento County bar assns. Democrat. Author: Know Your Rights, 1963-64. Home: 4572 Fair Oaks Blvd Sacramento CA 95864-5336

TAYLOR, WATSON ROBBINS, JR., investment banker; b. Montgomery, Ala., Mar. 16, 1956; s. Watson Robbins and Ernestine (Jenkins) T.; m. Davis Anne Denson, July 12, 1980; children: Watson Robbins III, Caroline Davis, Davis Denson. BS, Auburn U., 1979, MBA, 1982. Ranch foreman Johnston & Sons, Letohatchee, Ala., 1975-76; estimator Standard Roofing Co., Montgomery, Ala., 1976-78; v.p. Standard Roofing Co., 1978-84; pres. Standard Roofing USA, Inc., Montgomery, 1984-93, Standard-Taylor Industries, 1990-93; ptnr. First Commerce Capital, Inc., Montgomery, 1993—; bd. dirs. Auburn U. Sch. Bus., Montgomery, Montgomery Acad. Fin. chmn. Ala. Rep. Com., Birmingham, 1989; trustee YMCA Endowment Found., Montgomery, 1989; bd. dirs. ARC, 1989, Montgomery coun. Boy Scouts Am., 1989. Mem. Montgomery Area C. of C. (bd. dirs. 1989-92), Ala. Alliance Bus. and Industry (bd. dirs. 1989-92), Rotary (past dir.), Young Pres.'s Assn. (Rebel chpt.), Montgomery Country Club. Episcopalian. Avocations: tennis, hunting, fishing, travel. Home: 3809 Colline Dr Montgomery AL 36106

TAYLOR, WELFORD DUNAWAY, English language educator; b. Caroline County, Va., Jan. 3, 1938; s. George Welford and Minnie (Durrette) T.; m. Carole Virginia Wickham, Jan. 19, 1942; 1 child, Virginia Welford. BA, U. Richmond, 1959, MA, 1961; PhD, U. Md., 1966. Tchr. Randolph-Macom Acad., Front Royal, Va., 1959-60, St. Christopher's Sch., Richmond, Va., 1960-61; instr. English Va. Commonwealth U., Richmond, 1961-63; prof. English U. Richmond (Va.), 1964—; chmn. English dept. U. Richmond, 1978-86, James H. Bostwick chair English, 1991—; book reviewer Richmond Times-Dispatch, 1986—. Author: Amèlie Rives (Princess Troubetzkoy), 1973, Sherwood Anderson, 1977, Robert Frost and J. J. Lankes: Riders on Pegasus, 1996, The Woodcut Art of J. J. Lankes, 1997; editor: The Buck Fever Papers, 1971, The Newsprint Mask, 1991, Our American Cousin/The Play That Changed History, 1990. Mem. Poe Found. (pres. 1996), Sherwood Anderson Soc. (founder 1976), Va. Writers Club, English-Speaking Union, Country Club Va. (Richmond). Republican. Episcopalian. Avocations: book collecting, art collecting. Home: 5 Calycanthus Rd Richmond VA 23221-3101 Office: U Richmond Dept English Richmond VA 23173

TAYLOR, WESLEY ALAN, accountant, consultant; b. Johnson City, Tenn., Oct. 27, 1958; s. Wesley Wentworth and Charlotte Marie (Holly) T. BS in Acctg., U. Tenn., 1980. CPA, Tenn., Va.; registered rep. Nat. Assn. Securities Dealers; cer. pvt. pilot FAA. Staff acct. Wesley W. Taylor CPA, P.C., 1980-85; sr. acct. Blackburn, Childers & Stegall, CPAs, Elizabethton, Tenn., 1985-88; acct., mgr. BCS & Co., CPAs, Bristol, Tenn., 1988-89; pvt. practice, Elizabethton, 1989; tax sr. Brown, Edwards & Co., CPAs, Abingdon and Bristol, Va., 1989-91; pvt. practice Elizabethton, Tenn., 1991—. Auditor for various local Miss Am. preliminary pageants, 1985-97, local state fair pageant judge, 1992, local parade judge, 1994-95. Mem. AICPA, Johnson City Jaycees (pres., v.p., treas., Keyman of Yr., Jaycee of Yr., Presdl. award of excellence, others), Tenn. Jaycees (state sec.-treas.), Aircraft Owners and Pilots Assn. (pvt. pilot 1996—), Nat. Aeronautic Assn., Pilots Internat. Assn., Profl. Assn. Diving Instrs. (open water diver 1988), Am. Motorcyclist Assn. Republican. Avocations: water- and snow-skiing, motorcycling, boating, aviation, scuba diving. Home: Unit 1 122 Mountain View Dr Johnson City TN 37601 Office: 308 E F St Elizabethton TN 37643-3270

TAYLOR, WESLEY BAYARD, JR., retired army officer; b. Covington, Ky., June 5, 1944; s. Wesley B. Sr. and Varina Martha (Morgan) T.; m. Linda L. Taylor, June 2, 1967; children: Kathleen C., Clint C. BS, U.S. Mil. Acad., 1965; MA in Internat. Rels., U. Calif., Santa Barbara, 1973; student, U.S. Army War Coll., 1985-86. Commd. 2d lt. U.S. Army, 1965, advanced through grades to brig. gen., 1990; asst. bn. advisor, sr. bn. advisor Airborne Divsn. Adv. Detachment, U.S. Mil. Assitance Command, Vietnam, 1967-68; staff officer Dept. of Army, Washington, 1980-81; bn. comdr. 3rd Bn., 5th Inf. U.S. Army, Republic of Panama, 1981-83; bn. comdr. 1st Ranger Bn. Hunter Army Airfield, Ga., 1983-85; strategic fellow U.S. Army War Coll., Carlisle Barracks, Pa., 1986-87; regimental comdr. 75th Ranger Regiment, Ft. Benning, Ga., 1987-89; asst. divsn. comdr. 1st Armored Divsn., Germany, 1989-91; dep. dir. ops, readiness and mobilization Dept. of Army, Washington, 1991-92; dep. asst. sec. of def. for policy and missions Office Sec. of Def. for Spl. Ops. and Low Intensity Conflict, Washington, 1992-94; pres., CEO Cal Farley's Boys Ranch & Affiliates, U.S.A., Amarillo, Tex., 1995—. Dist. commr. Boy Scouts Am., Germany, 1989-91. Decorated DSM, Def. Superior Svc. medal, Silver Star, Legion of Merit, Def. Meritorious Svc. medal, Bronze Star medal with oak leaf cluster, Air medals. Mem. Assn. U.S. Army, U.S. Army Ranger Assn., 75th Ranger Regiment Assn., Soc. Vietnamese Airborne Advisors, Soc. 173rd Airborne Brigade. Methodist. Avocations: fishing, hunting. Office: Cal Farleys Boys Ranch & Affiliates PO Box 1890 Amarillo TX 79174-0001

TAYLOR, WILLIAM AL, church administrator; b. Danville, Va., Sept. 26, 1938; s. Preston Floyd and Helen Elizabeth (Doss) T.; m. Brenda Flo Owen, June 4, 1961; children: Fawnia Rae Ricks, Albert Todd, Athena Dawn Jarman. AA, Lee Coll., 1957; postgrad., U. Calif., Santa Barbara, 1980. Br. mgr. Ency. Britannica, Greensboro, N.C., 1960-62; divsn. trainer Ency. Britannica, Mpls., 1963; dist. mgr. Ency. Britannica, Omaha, 1964-72; adminstrv. asst. Forward in Faith Internat. Broadcast, Cleveland, Tenn., 1972-80; gen. mgr. Sta. WQNE-FM, Cleveland, 1980—; dir. stewardship Ch. of God Internat. Offices, Cleveland, 1980—; pres. Pathway Credit Union, Cleveland, 1985—, Vision Found., Cleveland, 1985—, exec. dir., 1979-80; chmn. Internat. Commn. on Prayer, Cleveland, 1986—. Author: Proving God, 1991, Days of Heaven on Earth, 1993, Stewardship Masterplanning, 1993. Pres. Clean Water Soc., Gastonia, N.C., 1974-75; state Citizens Against Legalized Liquor, Bradley County, Tenn., 1973, 75; advisor Mothers on March, Cleveland, 1976; active Nat. Conf. on Drug Abuse, Washington, 1978; master of ceremonies Nat. Religious Leaders Conf. on Alcohol and Drug Abuse, Indpls., 1979. Recipient Mass Communications award Ch. of God Media Ministries, 1980, Stephen award Ch. of God Lay Ministries, 1990. Mem. Nat. Assn. Evangelicals (bd. adminstrs. 1985—, chmn. stewardship commn. 1985-89), Christian Stewardship Assn. (bd. dirs. 1990-94). Avocations: flying, travel, racquetball. Office: Ch of God Dept Stewardship 2490 Keith St NW Cleveland TN 37311-1309 *We are all spending the precious gift of life, and we have been given the privilege to decide upon what we shall spend it. I have found the most worthy and fulfilling investment of life is God's stated purpose, "that we be conformed to the image of His son Jesus Christ."**

TAYLOR, WILLIAM AL, judge; b. Lusk, Wyo., Nov. 2, 1928; m. Jane Y.; 3 children. BA, U. Wyo., 1951, LLB, 1959. Bar: Wyo. 1959. Teacher Lusk, 1950-51,54-55, pvt. practice, 1959-78; city atty. Town of Lusk, 1962-74; atty. Niobrara County, Wyo., 1964-77; judge Wyo. Dist. Ct. (8th dist.), Cheyenne, 1980—; justice Wyoming Supreme Ct., 1993—, chief justice, 1996—; Exec. dir. Wyo. State Bar, 1977-80. Staff sgt. U.S. Army, 1951-53. Mem. Wyo. State Bar (Civil Rules com.), Wyo. Judicial Conf. (chmn. 1984-85),Tenth Cir. Bar Assn., Nat. Trial Judges, Am. Legion, Sigma Alpha Epsilon. Office: Wyo Supreme Ct PO Box 66 Cheyenne WY 82003-0066

TAYLOR, WILLIAM BERLEY, history educator; b. L.A., Mar. 23, 1943; s. James Chapman and Alma (Berley) T.; m. Barbara E. Tresch, June 17, 1964; children: Karin Elise, Jill Linda. BA, Occidental Coll., L.A., 1964; MA, U. of Ams., Mexico City, 1965; PhD, U. Mich., 1969. Asst. prof. history U. Colo., Denver/Boulder, 1969-72; assoc. prof. history U. Colo., Boulder, 1972-77; prof. history U. Colo., 1977-82; Edward F. Arnold Disting. prof. Whitman Coll., Walla Walla, Wash., 1980; vis. prof. history Harvard U., Cambridge, Mass., 1981; prof. history, Commonwealth prof. U. Va., Charlottesville, 1982-93; Edmund and Louise Kahn prof. history So. Meth. U., Dallas, 1993—; nat. adv. coun. John Carter Brown Libr., Providence, 1986-89; internat. adv. bd. The Mesoamerican Archive, Princeton U., 1989—; cons., expert witness Cochiti Pueblo, 1979-85, U.S. Dept. Justice, 1974-82. Author: Magistrates of the Sacred..., 1996, Drinking, Homicide and Rebellion..., 1979, Landlord and Peasant in Colonial Oaxaca, 1972. Nat. Humanities Ctr. fellow, 1990-91, Inst. for Advanced Study fellow, 1987, Guggenheim fellow, 1979-80, NEH fellow, 1974-75, U. Colo. tchg. awardee, 1974. Mem. Am. Hist. Assn., Conf. on Latin Am. History, Phi Beta Kappa. Office: So Meth Univ Dallas TX 75275

TAYLOR, WILLIAM DANIEL, biophysics educator, university dean; b. Cardiff, Wales, May 25, 1934; came to U.S., 1959; m. Andrea M. Mastro, Nov. 24, 1973; children: Maria, Daniel, Timothy. BSc in Chemistry with honors, Manchester (Eng.) U., 1956, PhD in Phys. Chemistry, 1959. Postdoctoral fellow physics dept. Pa. State U., University Park, 1959-61, from asst. prof. to assoc. prof. biophysics, 1963-71, prof., 1971—, head dept., 1971-75, assoc. chmn. dept. molecular and cell biology, 1975-83, mem. Environ. Resources Rsch. Inst., 1987-90, assoc. dean for rsch. and grad. edn., 1989-91, acting dir. Biotech. Inst., 1990-92, dir. intercoll. rsch. program, 1991—, chmn. faculty senate, 1972-73; acting dir. Intercoll. Materials Rsch. Lab., University Park, 1993-96, acting dean Pa. State U. Grad. Sch., 1995-96; vis. lectr. Donner Lab., Berkeley, Calif., summer 1967; vis. scientist Imperial Cancer Rsch. Fund Lab., London, 1973-74, Biochemistry Inst., German Cancer Rsch. Ctr., Heidelberg, 1985-86. Contbr. articles to sci. jours., chpts. to books. Scholar Glamorganshire County, 1953-57; Courtaulds rsch. fellow, 1957-59, NIH postdoctoral fellow Pa. State U., 1959-61; grantee Pa. State U., 1969-70, Nat. Inst. Gen. Med. Scis., 1972-77, Nat. Cancer Inst., 1976-81, NASA, 1982-87, USPHS, 1988-92, also others. Mem. AAAS, Radiation Rsch. Soc., Biophys. Soc., Am. Soc. for Photobiology, Am. Soc. Biol. Chemists, Am. Soc. for Microbiology. Office: Pa State U Intercollege Rsch Programs 205 Kern Bldg University Park PA 16802-3301

TAYLOR, WILLIAM JAMES (ZAK TAYLOR), lawyer; b. Milw., Jan. 26, 1948; s. William Elmer and Elizabeth Emily (Lupinski) T.; m. Marlou Belyea, Sept. 20, 1975; children: Danielle Belyea, James Zachary Belyea. BA in Econs., Yale U., 1970; JD, Harvard U., 1976. Bar: Calif. 1976, U.S. Dist. Ct. (cen. dist.) Calif. 1976, U.S. Dist. Ct. (no. dist.) Calif. 1977, U.S. Ct. Appeals (9th cir.) 1977, U.S. Dist. Ct. (ea. dist.) Calif. 1980, U.S. Supreme Ct. 1980, U.S. Tax Ct. 1988. Law clk. to hon. Shirley M. Hufstedler U.S. Ct. Appeals (9th cir.), L.A., 1976-77; assoc. Broebeck, Phleger & Harrison, San Francisco, 1977-83; ptnr. Broebeck, Phleger and Harrison, San Francisco, 1983-95; shareholder Taylor & Jenkins, P.C., Oakland, Calif., 1995-96, Chilvers & Taylor, P.C., Oakland, 1996—; bd. dirs. Berkeley (Calif.) Law Found., 1988-91, Legal Svcs. for Children (recipient Jean Waldman Child Advocacy award, San Francisco 1988), 1983-89; co-chmn. Attys. Task Force for Children, San Francisco, 1983-89. Editor-in-chief Harvard Civil Rights, Civil Liberties Law Rev., 1976; bd. editors No. Dist. Calif. Digest, 1978-83; co-author: California Antitrust Law, 1991; contbg. editor: Calif. Bus. Law Reporter, 1995-96, Antitrust Law Developments, 1997. With U.S. Army, 1970-73. Mem. ABA, Bar Assn. San Francisco (bd. dirs. 1986-87, chair antitrust sect. 1987, chair fed. cts. sect. 1995—), Am. Bus. Trial Lawyers Assn., Nat. Health Lawyers Assn., Barristers of San Francisco (bd. dirs. 1980-82, v.p. 1982-83), Nat. Health Lawyers Assn. Democrat. Office: Chilvers & Taylor PC 2030 Franklin St Fl 5 Oakland CA 94612-2908

TAYLOR, WILLIAM JAMES, III, federal official; b. Petersburg, Va., Feb. 12, 1954; s. William James Jr. and Erma Glenn (Brown) T.; m. Elneita Sylvia Hutchins, Dec. 11, 1982; children: Royce Alan, Christian Alexander, Kellye Audrey. BA in Mass Comm., Howard U., 1977; JD, U. Tex. Sch. Law, 1981. Bar: Tex., 1981. Adminstrv. asst. Office Hon. William P. Hobby, Lt. Gov., Tex., 1980-81; staff atty. II Tex. Edn. Agy., 1981-82; campaign coord. Bill Hobby Campaign, 1982; exec. asst. county atty. Office Harris County Atty. Mike Driscoll, 1983; coun. coord. Office former Houston Councilman Rodney Ellis, 1984; divsn. chief Office Harris County Atty. Mike Driscoll, 1983; adminstrv. asst., legal coun. Office late congressman Mickey Leland, 1985-88; atty. Hutcheson & Grundy L.L.P., 1989-93; asst. sec. congl. and intergovernmental affairs Dept. Energy, Washington, 1993-95; counsellor to the Sec. of Commerce Dept. of Commerce, Washington, 1995—. mem. bd, regents East Tex. State U., 1991-93; v.p. Houston Housing Fin. Corp., 1992-93; pres. Tex. Black Leadership Congress, 1988-93; mem. bd. dirs. Juvenile Ct. Vols. Harris County, 1989-92, Tex. Lyceum Assn., Inc., 1989, NAACP, 1991-93, Ctr. for the Retarded, 1991-93, Houston Prep. Acad., 1991-93; com. cons., chmn. legis. com. Houston Mus. Fine Arts, 1989-93; lectr. CLE programs U. Houston Law Ctr., 1990-91; mem. citizens adv. com. Tex. Lottery Startup, 1991; mem. adv. bd. The Chinquapin Sch., 1992-93. Mem. Thurgood Marshall Legal Soc. (pres. 1980). Avocations: basketball, skiing. Office: Counsellor to the Sec Dept of Commerce 14th & Constitution Ave NW Washington DC 20230*

TAYLOR, WILLIAM JAPE, physician; b. Booneville, Miss., Sept. 5, 1924; s. William Melton and Cora Leona (Smith) T.; m. Audrey Y. Dennison, Jan. 31, 1948; children—J. Holley, Andrew D., Richard M., D. Lee. B.S., Yale U., 1944; M.D., Harvard U., 1947. Intern in internal medicine Boston City Hosp., 1947-48; resident in internal medicine Duke U. Hosp., 1948-50, fellow in cardiology, 1950-52, 54-55; instr. Duke U. Med. Sch., 1954-55, U. Pitts. Med. Sch., 1955-58; mem. faculty U. Fla. Coll. Medicine, Gainesville, 1958-95; prof. medicine U. Fla. Coll. Medicine, 1964-74, chief cardiology, 1958-74, disting. service prof. medicine, 1974-95; emeritus, 1995—; vis. prof. U. Ife (Nigeria) Med. Sch., 1974-75; bd. dirs. PSRO, Fla. Area II, 1977-81. Author papers in field, chpts. in books. Mem. human rights advocacy com. mentally retarded Fla. Dist. III, 1977-81; bd. dirs. Gainesville-Natagalpa Sister City, 1988—. Fellow ACP (rsch. fellow 1950-51), Am. Coll. Cardiology; mem. Assn. U. Cardiologists, Am. Heart Assn. (fellow coun. clin. cardiology), Am. Fedn. Clin. Rsch., So. Soc. Clin. Investigation (pres. 1972-73), Fla. Heart Assn. (Disting. Svc. award 1975), Am. Soc. Tropical Medicine and Hygiene, Physicians for Social Responsibility (ho. of dels. 1985-90). Democrat. Home: 500 NW 80th Blvd Gainesville FL 32607-1531 Office: U Fla Med Sch Dept Medicine Gainesville FL 32610

TAYLOR, WILLIAM JESSE, JR., international studies educator, research center executive; b. Florence, S.C., Dec. 28, 1933; s. William J. and Dorothy (Byrd) T.; m. Louise Inger Haegerstrom, Apr. 9, 1977; 1 child, Nicolaus; children by previous marriage: Juliana C., William J. III, L. Scott, Christopher B., Helen B. B.S., U. Md., 1962; M.A., Am. U., 1964, Ph.D., 1967. Enlisted U.S. Army, commd. 2d lt., 1955, advanced through grades to col., 1976; prof. U.S. Mil. Acad., West Point, N.Y., 1970-81; vis. prof. U.S. Nat. War Coll., 1975-76; ret. U.S. Army, 1981; dir. polit. mil. studies Ctr. for Strategic and Internat. Studies Georgetown U., Washington, 1980-83; exec. dir., chief operating officer Ctr. for Strategic and Internat. Studies, 1983-87, v.p. internat. security programs, 1987-92; pres. Taylor Assocs. Inc., 1984—; sr. v.p. Internat. Security Affairs, 1992—; internat. lectr., debater, T.V. mil. analyst, 1970—. Author: Future of Conflict: U.S. Interests, 1982, Future of Conflict into the 21st Century, 1987; co-author: American National Security: Policy and Process, 1981, 83, 89, 93; co-editor: Defense Manpower Planning, 1980, The Future of Conflict in the 1980's, 1982, Strategic Requirements for the Army to the Year 2000, 1983, Strategic Responses to Conflict in the 1980's, 1984, Nordic Defense: Comparative Decisionmaking, 1985, Strategic Dimensions of Military Manpower, 1987, The Future of U.S.-Republic of Korea Security Ties, 1989, The Korean Peninsula: Prospects for Arms Control, 1990, Korea 1991: The Road to Peace, 1991, Elvis in The Army, 1995, 97. Mem. Presiding Bishop's Nat. Episc. Roundtable, 1983-86. Decorated Bronze Star with oak leaf cluster, Legion of Merit (2), Air Medal (3), Air medal for valor, Vietnam Cross of Gallantry, Combat Infantry Badge; recipient Pitman Potter Medal Am. U., 1964; named to Infantry Officer Hall of Fame, 1976; named Disting. Alumnus, Episcopal Acad., 1995. Mem. Council on Fgn. Relations, Internat. Inst. Strategic Studies, St. Anthony Club. Republican. Episcopalian. Office: Ctr for Strategic & Intl Studies 1800 K St NW Washington DC 20006-2202

TAYLOR, WILLIAM MALCOLM, environmentalist, educator; b. South Hiram, Maine, June 18, 1933; s. William Myers and Gladys Marie (Weldy) T.; stepmother Edna (Tyson) Taylor; m. Carrie Mae Fiedler, Aug. 31, 1957 (div. Sept. 1980); children: William Stephan, Alyson Marie, Eric Fiedler; m. Elizabeth Van Horn, June 18, 1983. Student, George Sch., 1948-50; BA in Liberal Arts, Pa. State U., 1956; MEd, U. N.C., 1962. Instr. ESL Anatolia Coll., Am. Lang. Ctr., Salonica, Greece, 1956-58; tchr. biology-chemistry Coral Shores H.S., Tavernier, Fla., 1961-62; pk. naturalist Everglades Nat. Pk., Fla., 1962-65; tech. editor Nat. Pk. Svc., Washington, 1965-67; chief interpretation Canyonlands Nat. Pk., Utah, 1967-71; environ. edn. specialist western regional office Nat. Pk. Svc., Calif., 1971-77; dir. program devel. Living History Ctr., Novato, Calif., 1981-83; exec. recruiter, ptnr. Van Horn, Taylor & Assocs, Biotech-Biomed. Rsch., Santa Cruz, Calif., 1983-95; mem. 2d World Conf. on Nat. Parks and Equivalent Reserves, 10th Internat. Seminar on Nat. Parks, U.S., Can., Mex. Author: The Strands Walk, Exercises in Guided Inquiry for Children; founder, developer (with Sally Berlant) ednl. program Environ. Living Program, 1973 (Calif. Bicentennial Commn. award 1974, Don Perryman award Calif. Social Studies Coun., 1975, Nat. Bicentennial Adminstrn. sponsorship 1976). Bd. dirs. Internat. Sononan Desert Alliance, 1996-97; with Novato Environ. Quality Com., 1973-76; mem. Calif. Conservation Com., 1973-76; mem. Utah Environ. Com., 1968-71; vol. AZ Sonora Desert Mus. Mem. Am. Bonanza Soc., Lighthawk, Flying Samaritans, Tucson Soaring Club, Mensa. Avocations: flying, birding, natural history. Home: 2321 S Circle X Pl Tucson AZ 85713

TAYLOR, WILLIAM OSGOOD, newspaper executive; b. Boston, July 19, 1932; s. William Davis and Mary (Hammond) T.; m. Sally Coxe, June 20, 1959; children: William Davis II, Edmund C., Augustus R. B.A., Harvard U., 1954. With Globe Newspaper Co., Boston, 1956—, treas., 1963—, bus. mgr., 1965-69, gen. mgr., 1969—; now chmn. bd., pub. Boston Globe. Trustee Boston Pub. Libr.; bd. dirs. United Way New Eng., Boston Adult Literacy Fund; trustee Mus. of Fine Arts. With U.S. Army, 1954-56. Mem. Newspaper Assn. Am. (bd. dirs.). Office: Globe Newspaper Co PO Box 2378 135 Morrissey Blvd Boston MA 02107-2378*

TAYLOR, WILLIAM WOODRUFF, III, lawyer; b. Richmond, Va., July 30, 1944; s. William Woodruff Jr. and Ida (Winstead) T.; m. Susan Broadhurst, Sept. 29, 1984; children: Katherine Lowell, Matthew Gordon. AB, U. N.C., 1966; LLB, Yale U., 1969. Bar: N.C. 1969, D.C. 1970, U.S. Ct. Appeals (2nd, 4th, 5th and 11th cirs.), U.S. Supreme Ct. Law clk. to judge U.S. Dist. Ct. Del., Wilmington, 1969-70; staff atty. Pub. Defender Service, Washington, 1970-75; assoc. Ginsburg, Feldman and Bress, Washington, 1975-78; ptnr. Zuckerman, Spaeder, Goldstein, Taylor & Kolker, Washington, 1978—; instr. dept. forensic sci. George Washington U., Washington, 1973-74; adj. prof. Columbus Sch. Law, Cath. U. Am., Washington, 1973-76; mem. D.C. Commn. on Jud. Disabilities and Tenure, 1978-83, chmn., 1979-83; vis. prof. U. N.C. Law Sch., fall 1991. Fellow Am. Coll. Trial Lawyers; mem. ABA (criminal justice sect., vice chmn. for govtl. affairs 1989-92, chair criminal justice sect. 1996-97), Nat. Inst. for Trial Advocacy (faculty 1978—, chmn. pub. defender svc. assn. 1984-89). Episcopalian. Avocations: fly fishing, tennis. Office: Zuckerman Spaeder et al 1201 Connecticut Ave NW Washington DC 20036-2605

TAYLOR, WILSON H., diversified financial company executive. Grad., Trinity Coll. With Conn. Gen., 1954-82, sr. v.p., chief fin. officer, 1980-82; v.p. Aetna Ins. Co., 1975; exec. v.p. Cigna Corp., Phila., 1982-88, pres. property casualty group, 1983-88, corp. vice-chmn., chief operating officer, from 1988, chief operating officer, 1988, pres., chief exec. officer, 1988—, then chmn., pres., chief exec. officer, now chmn., chief exec. officer. Phi Beta Kappa. Office: Cigna Corp 1 Liberty Plz Philadelphia PA 19192-1550

TAYLOR-PICKELL, LAVONNE TROY, editor; b. Riverside, Calif., May 20, 1941; d. Troy Virgil Bradstreet and R. Victoria (Freeman) Chambers; m. Robert Martin Taylor, May 15, 1958 (div. 1975); children: Dana Freeman, Timothy Rene; m. Herman Pickell, Feb. 14, 1985; children: Marianne, Barry, David. Reporter Thousand Oaks (Calif.) Chronicle; with prodn. News Chronicle, Thousand Oaks, prodn. supr., 1979-81; with prodn. Ind. Jour., Thousand Oaks, Herald Examiner, L.A., L.A. Times; asst. mgr. Pub. Typography, Agoura, Calif., 1981-85; owner Excellence Enterprises, L.A., 1982—; sr. editor arts Glencoe/McGraw-Hill Sch. Pub., Mission Hills, Calif., 1987-96; actress, 1997—; contbg. editor Sharpe mag.; speaker various writers clubs;. Editor, pub. L.A. My Way, 1991, On the Wings of Song, 1994; mng. editor The BookWoman, 1991-93. Mem. pub. rels. com. Conejo Players Theatre, Thousand Oaks, 1970-75, Betty Mann for 38th Assembly Dist., Agoura, 1975-76. Mem. NAFE, Nat. Writers Club (pres. 1990-91, Merit Svc. award 1991), Women's Nat. Book Assn. (L.A. chpt. pres. 1992-93, newsletter editor, bd. dirs.). Avocations: reading, writing, gardening, music, art.

TAYS, GLENNY MAE, secondary education educator; b. Presho, S.D., Mar. 12, 1933; d. Glen Harold and Grayce Agnes (LaVelle) Trimble; m.

Richard Ray Tays, May 29, 1954; children: Robert Glen, Thomas Gene. BA, Dakota Wesleyan U., 1956; MEd, U. Mont., 1961. Cert. secondary sch. tchr. and prin. Bus. tchr. Kimball (S.D.) H.S., 1956-58; English/bus. tchr. Burke (S.D.) H.S., 1962-65; Bus. Inst. dept. head DesMoines Area C.C., Boone, Iowa, 1966-78; English/journalism tchr. St. Martin's Acad., Rapid City, S.D., 1979-82; English tchr., dept. head Todd County H.S., Mission, S.D., 1982-95; sch. dist. media specialist C EB, Eagle Butte, S.D., 1995—; pres. Des Moines Area C.C. Faculty Assn., Boone, 1968, 68, 69, 70; pres.-elect Iowa Bus. Edn. Assn., State of Iowa, 1972-73, pres., 1973-74; editor North Ctrl. Bus. Edn. Conv. Bull., Des Moines, 1972; part time tchr. Bus. Inst., Black Hills State U. Br. Campus, Rapid City, S.D., 1981-82, Sinte Gleska U., Mission, S.D., 1983-84. Pres. Burke (S.D.) Women's Club, 1961-63; vol. ARC, Easter Seals, United Fund, Boone, 1965; coord. Country Club Jr. Golf Program, Boone, 1968-74; golf mother Booster Club, Boone (Iowa) H.S., 1972-73; spl. projects chmn. Soroptimist Club Internat., Boone, 1973. Named Outstanding Young Women in Am., 1970. Mem. ASCD, NEA, Nat. Coun. Tchrs. English, Cath. Daus. Am., Delta Kappa Gamma (com.). Democrat. Roman Catholic. Avocations: reading, writing, antiquing, collecting pre-1900 books, golfing. Home: PO Box 329 Eagle Butte SD 57625-0329 Office: C-EB School Dist Box 260 Eagle Butte SD 57625

TCHOBANOGLOUS, GEORGE, civil engineering educator; b. Patterson, Calif., May 24, 1935; s. Christo and Penelope (Megdani) T.; m. Rosemary Ash, June 16, 1957; children—Kathryn, Lynn, Julianne. B.C.E., U. Pacific, 1958; M.C.E., U. Calif., Berkley, 1960; Ph.D., Stanford U., 1969. Registered profl. engr., Calif., Mont. Research engr. U. Calif.-Berkeley, 1960-62; cons. Metcalf & Eddy Engrs., Palo Alto, Calif., 1963-81, Nolte & Assocs., Sacramento, 1981—, Calif. Water Resources Control Bd., 1972-80; assoc. prof. U. Calif.-Davis, 1970-76, prof. engring., 1976—. Prin. author: Wastewater Engineering: Collection, Treatment, Disposal, 1972; author: (with R. Smith and R. Crites) Wastewater Management: A Guide to Information Sources, 1976, (with H. Theisen and R. Eliassen) Solid Wastes: Engineering Principles and Management Issues, 1977, (with Schroeder) Water Quality: Characteristics, Modeling, Modification, 1985, (with Peavy and Rowe) Environmental Engineering, 1985, (with H. Theisen, S.A. Vigil) Integrated Solid Waste Management: Engineering Principles and Management Issues, 1993; co-author: Wastewater Engineering: Treatment, Disposal, Reuse, 1991; author, editor: Wastewater Engineering: Collection and Pumping of Wastewater, 1981; co-editor: Pumping Station Design, 1989; contbr. numerous articles to profl. jours. Mem. bd. Calif. Integrated Waste Mgmt.; lectr. T.R. Camp, 1990. Mem. AAAS, ASCE, Assn. Environ. Engring. Profs. (bd. dirs., past pres.), Am. Acad. Environ. Engrs., Water Environ. Fedn. (Gordon Masken Fair medal 1985), Am. Water Works Assn. (Thomas R. Camp lectr. 1991), World Mariculture Soc., Sigma Xi. Home: 662 Diego Pl Davis CA 95616-0123

TCHOUNWOU, PAUL BERNARD, environmental health specialist, educator; b. Bangou, Cameroon, Aug. 14, 1960; came to U.S., 1985; s. Maurice and Christine (Kouanang) Seumo; m. Martha Namondo Mondoa, Aug. 3, 1990; children: Christine K., Hervey M. BSc, U. Yaounde, Cameroon, 1983, MSc, 1984; MS in Pub. Health, Tulane U., 1986, ScD, 1990. Cert. toxicologist Nat. Environ. Health Assn.; registered sanitarian La. State Bd. Examiners for Sanitarians. Tchg. asst. Tulane Sch. Pub. Health, New Orleans, 1988-90; med. rschr. Inst. Med. Rsch., Yaounde, 1991-94; asst. prof. Faculty Medicine, Yaounde, 1992-94; rsch. assoc. Xavier & Tulane Univs., New Orleans, 1994-96; assoc. prof., dir. environ. sci. PhD program Jackson State U., Jackson, 1996—; environ. health cons. Orstom & UNICEF, Yaounde, 1992-93, U.S. AID, Kaele, 1991-93; rsch. supr. Tulane Sch. Pub. Health, New Orleans, 1994—; tng. and rsch. fellow U.S. AID, Washington, 1985-90. Editl. bd. Internat. Jour. Environ. Toxicology and Water Quality, 1994—; contbr. articles to profl. jours. Grantee Internat. Devel. Rsch. Ctr., Ottowa, 1992-93. Mem. APHA, Water Environ. Fedn., Cameroon Bioscis. Soc., Cameroon Assn. Epidemiology, Nat. Environ. Health Assn., Delta Omega. Roman Catholic. Avocations: travel, playing tennis, watching TV sport programs. Home: Apt 1602 2315 McFadden Rd Jackson MS 39204 Office: Jackson State U Sch Environ Sci & Tech PO Box 18540 Jackson MS 39217

TEACHOUT, NOREEN RUTH, writer; b. Oak Park, Ill., July 12, 1939; d. Anselm Uriel and R. Lydia (Bagne) Asp; m. Willem Heyneker, Nov. 20, 1958 (dec. 1968); children: Carolyn Heyneker Fors, Diana Heyneker Olds; m. Richard Kenneth Teachout, Jan. 21, 1966 (div. 1982); children: Jill, Janelle. BS, U. Minn., 1965; postgrad., Am. Inst. Holistic Theology, 1996—. Tchr. Bloomington (Minn.) Pub. Schs., 1965-85; writer, pubr., CEO The Peace Curriculum, Mpls., 1986—; educator Stockton & Franks Chiropractors, Burnsville, Minn., 1986-92; edn. svcs. dept. coord. Dame Comms., Plymouth, Minn., 1990-94; cons., workshop leader Dame Comms.; writer U. Calif., Berkeley, 1967, Environ. Sci. Ctr., Mpls., 1968-69; educator, presenter Women's World Peace Conf., Dallas, 1988, World Peace Conf., San Jose, Costa Rica, 1989, 92; sponsor Therapeutic Humor Inst. Minn., Colo., 1996; dir. Wellness NOW, A Learning Place, Colo., 1996; tchr. five ancient rites of Tibet and endorphin stimulation. Author curriculum programs, health and revitalization programs, also poems; author: Endorphins in My Health, 1997, The How of Now: Endorphin Annies Energizing Answers, 1997. Avocations: ballroom dancing, reading, gardening, horsepersonship.

TEAGAN, JOHN GERARD, newspaper executive; b. Detroit, Sept. 23, 1947; s. Stanley John and Margaret Suzanne (Sullivan) T.; m. Carla Kay Eurich, Sept. 13, 1975; 1 child, Elizabeth Margaret. B.B.A., U. Notre Dame, 1969. C.P.A., Mich. Audit supr. Ernst & Whinney (C.P.A.s), Detroit, 1969-73; acctg. mgr. Detroit Free Press, 1973-77, treas., controller, 1977-83, v.p. fin., treas., 1983-89, v.p., bus. mgr., 1989—. Adv. bd. Providence Hosp., Southfield, Mich., 1984—, sec., 1989, vice chmn. 1990, chmn., 1991; trustee Grosse Pointe (Mich.) Acad., 1990-96, Children's Home Detroit, Grosse Pointe, 1997—. Mem. AICPA, Internat. Newspaper Fin. Execs., Mich. Assn. CPAs, Detroit Club, Notre Dame Club (Detroit dir. 1970-76, 92—, treas. 1993-94, sec. 1994-95, pres.-elect 1995-96, pres. 1996-97). Roman Catholic. Office: Detroit Free Press Inc 321 W Lafayette Blvd Detroit MI 48226

TEAGUE, HYMAN FARIS, former publishing company executive; b. San Angelo, Jan. 14, 1916; s. John Henry and Minnie Adele (Gauldin) T.; m. Sophia Golda Harvey, Dec. 26, 1944; children: Carl Robin, Alan Cole. B.A., McMurry U., 1935, postgrad., 1940; postgrad, Hardin Simmons U., 1935-36. Tchr., public schs. Tex., 1935-43; prodn. mgr. Steck Vaughn Co. (and predecessor co.), Austin, 1946-57; editor in chief Steck Vaughn Co. (and predecessor co.), 1957-65, v.p., 1964-65, pres., 1965-80, chmn., 1981-82, dir., 1965-82; v.p. Intext Inc., Scranton, Pa., 1975-80. Served with USNR, 1943-46. Democrat. Baptist. Clubs: Austin, Rotary. Home: 4906 Rollingwood Dr Austin TX 78746-5527

TEAGUE, LARRY GENE, editor; b. Victoria, Tex., May 13, 1954; s. Edward Marvin and Nettie Naomi (Welch) T. BJ, U. Houston, 1980. Outdoor correspondent Houston Post, 1977-80; editor Gulf Tide mag. Gulf Coast Conservation Assn., Houston, 1980-85; editor Southern Outdoors mag. Bass Anglers Sportsmans Soc., Montgomery, Ala., 1985—; cons. editor So. Outdoor Saltwater mag., 1986-87. Served with U.S. Army, 1972-75. Recipient writing, photography awards. Avocations: fishing, hunting, gardening, photography. Home: 5832 Red Barn Rd Montgomery AL 36116-1034 Office: Southern Outdoors 5845 Carmichael Rd Montgomery AL 36117-2329

TEAGUE, LAVETTE COX, JR., systems educator, consultant; b. Birmingham, Ala., Oct. 8, 1934; s. Lavette Cox and Caroline Green (Stokes) T.; student Auburn U., 1951-54; B.Arch., MIT, 1957, M.S.C.E., 1965, Ph.D., 1968; MDiv with distinction Ch. Div. Sch. Pacific, 1979. Cert. computer profl. Inst. Cert. of Computer Profls. Archtl. designer Carroll C. Harmon, Birmingham, 1957, Fred Renneker, Jr., Birmingham, 1958-59; architect Rust Engring. Co., Birmingham, 1959-62, Synergetics, Inc., Raleigh, N.C., 1962-64, Rust Engring. Co., Birmingham, 1964-68; research asst., inst., research assoc. MIT, Cambridge, 1964-68; dir. computer services Skidmore, Owings & Merrill, San Francisco, Chgo., 1968-74; postdoctoral fellow UCLA, 1972; adj. assoc. prof. architecture and civil engring. Carnegie-Mellon U., Pitts., 1973-74; archtl. systems cons., Chgo., 1974-75, Berkeley, Calif., 1975-80, Pasadena, Calif., 1980-82, Altadena, Calif., 1982—; lectr. info. systems Calif. State Poly. U., Pomona, 1980-81, prof., 1981—, asst. chair, 1990-91, chair, 1991-93, 96—. Fulbright lectr., Uruguay, 1985. Co-author: Structured Analysis Methods for Computer Information Systems, 1985. Recipient Tucker-Voss award M.I.T., 1967; Fulbright scholar, 1985. Mem. AIA (Arnold W. Brunner scholar 1966), Assn. Computing Machinery, Sigma Xi, Phi Eta Sigma, Scarab, Scabbard and Blade, Tau Beta Pi, Chi Epsilon, Beta Gamma Sigma. Episcopalian. Home: 1696 N Altadena Dr Altadena CA 91001-3623 Office: 3801 W Temple Ave Pomona CA 91768-2557

TEAGUE, PEYTON CLARK, chemist, educator; b. Montgomery, Ala., June 26, 1915; s. Robert S. and Sara McGehee (Clark) T.; m. Patricia Cussons Lamb, June 12, 1937; 1 dau., Norah Teague Grimball. Student, Huntingdon Coll., 1932-34; B.S., Auburn U., 1936; M.S., Pa. State U., 1937; Ph.D., U. Tex., 1942. Research chemist Am. Agrl. Chem. Co., Newark, 1937-39; instr. dept. chemistry Auburn U., Ala., 1941-42, asst. prof., 1943-45; research chemist U.S. Naval Research Lab, 1942-45; asst. prof. U. Ga., Athens, 1945-48, U. Ky., Lexington, 1948-50; assoc. prof. dept. chemistry U. S.C., Columbia, 1950-56, prof., 1956-82, disting. prof. emeritus, 1982—, assoc. dean grad. sch., 1966-68, chmn. grad. council, 1980-81, dept. dir. grad. studies, 1971-82; sec. grad. admission com. U. S.C., 1982—; vis. prof. Univ. Coll., Dublin, Ireland, 1963-64, 77; dir. Teague Hardware Co., Montgomery, Ala., 1955-74. Contbr. articles to sci. jours. Vestryman Trinity Episcopal Cathedral, 1968-71, lay reader, 1963—; bd. dirs. S.C. chpt. Arthritis Found., 1983-86; bd. dirs. Columbia Town Theatre, 1984-91. Recipient Outstanding Tchr. award U. S.C., 1976. Mem. Am. Chem. Soc. (chmn. S.C. sect. 1958-59), Phytochem. Soc. N.Am. (pres. 1969-70), S.C. Acad. Sci., Blue Key, Sigma Xi (pres. U. S.C. chpt. 1962-63), Phi Kappa Phi, Phi Lambda Upsilon, Phi Delta Theta. Club: Forest Lake Country. Lodge: Kiwanis. Home: 1550 Adger Rd Columbia SC 29205-1408 Office: U SC Dept Chemistry Columbia SC 29208

TEAGUE, RANDAL CORNELL, SR., lawyer; b. Durham, N.C., May 19, 1944; s. Roy M. Sr. and Lottie (Rhew) T.; children: R. Cornell, R. Townsend, Mary Robb Durham, James K.B. BA, Am. U., 1967; JD, George Washington U., 1971, LLM with highest honors, 1972; LLD (hon.), Allen U., 1973. Bar: Fla. 1972, D.C. 1972, U.S. Dist. Ct. D.C. 1972, U.S. Tax Ct. 1972, U.S. Ct. Mil. Appeals 1972, U.S. Ct. Appeals (D.C. and fed. cirs.) 1972, U.S. Ct. Appeals (5th cir.) 1973, U.S. Supreme Ct. 1975, Mass. 1979, U.S. Ct. Appeals (1st cir.) 1979, U.S. Dist. Ct. Mass. 1979, U.S. Ct. Internat. Trade. Coordinator policy devel. OEO, Washington, 1971-73; adminstrv. asst., legis. counsel to Rep. Jack F. Kemp Ho. of Reps., Washington, 1973-79; div. counsel Cabot Corp., 1979-81; counsel Vorys, Sater, Seymour & Pease, Washington, 1981-83, ptnr., 1984—. Pres. Internat. Exch. Coun., 1984—; trustee Fund Am. Studies, Washington, 1976—, Air Force Acad. Found., Colorado Springs, Colo., 1983—; chmn. adv. com. voluntary aid U.S. AID, 1987-91; trustee Agrl. Coll. Humid Tropics, Costa Rica, 1987—; councillor Atlantic Coun. of U.S., 1990—; co-founder Am. Inst. on Polit. and Econ. Sys., Charles U., Prague, 1993—; founder Internat. Inst. Polit. and Econ. Studies, Athens, Greece, 1996—. Named one of Outstanding Young Men Am., 1973; recipient George Washington medal Freedoms Found., 1978. Mem. ABA, FBA, Fla. Bar Assn. Republican. Episcopalian. Club: University (Washington). Office: Vorys Sater Seymour & Pease 1828 L St NW Ste 11 Washington DC 20036-5104

TEAGUE, SAM FULLER, association executive, educator,; b. Birmingham, Ala., Aug. 2, 1918; s. Sam Fuller and Virginia (White) T.; m. Frances Middleton, July 2, 1939; children: John Russell, Melanie Olivia. B.S., Auburn U., 1939. Chemist Sloss-Sheffield Steel & Iron Co., Birmingham, 1939-40; asst. dir. sales Monsanto Chem. Co., St. Louis, 1945-60; gen. mgr. sales ITT Rayonier, Inc., N.Y.C., 1960-67; v.p. planning and devel. ITT Rayonier, Inc., 1967-68, sr. v.p., 1968-72, v.p., product mgr., paper and splty. pulp sales, 1972-78, v.p., dir. pulp sales, 1978-80, v.p. prodn./mktg. devel., 1981-83, ret., 1983, also dir.; exec. dir. Rayon/Acetate Council, Inc., Auburn, Ala., 1983-93; adj. prof. textile engring. Auburn U., 1983-96; dir., mem. exec. com. Rayonier Can. Pres. Auburn Heritage Assn., 1985-86; v.p. Auburn Beautification Council, 1985-86; councilman, mayor pro tem City of Auburn, 1986—; vestryman and sr. warden Holy Trinity Episcopal Ch., 1985-86. Served to lt. col. AUS, 1940-45. Decorated Bronze Star with oak leaf cluster. Mem. Am. Chem. Soc., Salesmen's Assn. Am. Chem. Industry (past dir.), Auburn C. of C. (treas. and bd. dirs. 1986, pres. 1989, bd. dirs. 1994). Clubs: Town (Newcastle) (past sec., dir.); Whippoorwill (Armonk, N.Y.) (pres. 1968-69, gov.); Chemists (N.Y.C.) (trustee 1970, pres. 1976-77). Home: 1349 Burke Ln Auburn AL 36830-5140 Office: Auburn U Textile Bldg Auburn AL 36849 *My career is based on honesty, fairness, consideration for my fellow man, trust in God, and always trying to follow the principles set forth by Jesus Christ. I've always felt that people are the most important element of any organization. Whereas bricks and mortar can be bought, people must be considered as individuals.*

TEARE, BERNICE ADELINE, elementary school educator, reading specialist; b. Camden, N.J., May 31, 1942; d. Harry Kenneth and Lorraine P. (Blazer) Schwab; m. Paul A. Teare, Aug. 19, 1967; 1 child, Paul Brian. BA, Glassboro State Coll., 1964, MA, 1967; cert. prin./supr., Trenton State Coll., 1977, MEd, 1979, cert. reading specialist, 1979. Cert. tchr., N.J.; cert. reading specialist, N.J. Elem. tchr. Cherry Hill (N.J.) Pub. Schs., 1964-86, reading specialist, 1986—; conf. presenter West Jersey Reading Coun., Marlton, 1992-94, Reading Coun. South Jersey, Marlton, 1992-94, ASCD, 1993, 97, Internat. Reading Assn., Toronto, 1994, Anaheim, Calif., 1995, New Orleans, 1996, Atlanta, 1997; staff devel. trainer Cherry Hill Sch. Dist., 1991-96. Author: Update '93 Resource Book, 1992, First Grade Resource Book, 1993, Second Grade Resource Book, 1994, Primary '94 Resource Book, 1994, Kindergarten Resource Book, 1996; contbr. articles to profl. jours. Mem. Internat. Reading Assn., N.J. Reading Assn., Reading Coun. South Jersey, West Jersey Reading Coun., Kappa Delta Pi. Avocations: reading, travel, teddy bear collecting, children's literature, computers. Office: Kingston Sch Kingston Rd Cherry Hill NJ 08034

TEARE, IWAN DALE, retired research scientist; b. Moscow, Idaho, July 24, 1931; s. Mylrea Henry and Crystal Ann (Atkinson) T.; m. Claudia Joy Patterson, Sept. 14, 1952; children: Steven, Bradley, Kurtis, Kelly. BS in Agronomy, U. Idaho, 1953; MS in Agronomy, Wash. State U., 1959; PhD, Purdue U., 1963. Instr. agronomy Purdue U., West Lafayette, Ind., 1961-63; asst. prof. agronomy Wash. State U., Pullman, 1963-69; prof. agronomy Kans. State U., Manhattan, 1969-79; dir. Agrl. Rsch. and Edn. Ctr., U. Fla., Quincy, 1979-82; rsch. scientist U. Fla., Quincy, 1982-96; ret., 1996. Active Boy Scouts Am. Served to 1st lt. U.S. Army, 1954-56. Recipient Disting. Grad. Faculty award Kans. State U., 1974; U. Fla. scholar. Fellow Am. Soc. Agronomy; mem. Am. Soc. Crop Sci., Sigma Xi, Phi Kappa Phi, Gamma Sigma Delta. Mem. Ch. Jesus Christ of Latter-Day Saints. Assoc. editor Agronomy Jour., 1979-85, tech. editor, 1986-92; co-editor: Crop-Water Relations, 1983; assoc. editor Contemporary Issues, Jour. Prodn. Agr., 1996—; editor symposium, conf. proceedings; contbr. numerous articles to profl. jours. Home: 420 Maxwell Dr Cairo GA 31728-3554 Office: N Fla Rsch & Edn Ctr Univ of Fla RR 3 Box 4370 Quincy FL 32351-9500

TEARE, RICHARD WALLACE, ambassador; b. Cleve., Feb. 21, 1937; m. Jeanie Walter; 3 children. BA, Harvard U., 1958; student, Naval War Coll., 1977-78. Joined Fgn. Svc., 1959; vice consul U.S. Consulate, Bridgetown, Barbados, 1960-62; consular officer U.S. Embassy, Manila, The Philippines, 1962-64; polit. officer U.S. Embassy, Saigon, Vietnam, 1965-67, Mexico City, 1971-74; counselor for polit. affairs U.S. Embassy, Vientiane, Laos, 1974-76; dep. chief mission U.S. Embassy, Wellington, New Zealand, 1983-86, Canberra, Australia, 1986-89; dep. and acting prin. officer U.S. Consulate Gen., Nha Trang, Vietnam, 1973; intelligence and rsch. specialist Vietnam Working Group Dept. State, 1967-69, desk officer, 1969-71, spl. asst. to asst. sec. for East Asian and Pacific Affairs, 1976-77, dep. dir. Office Philippine Affairs, 1978-80, dep. and acting U.S. rep. for Micronesian Status Negotiations, 1980-83, dir. Office of Indonesia, Malaysia, Brunei and Singapore Affairs, 1989-92, spl. projects officer Office of Dir. Gen., 1992-93, U.S. amb. to Papua New Guinea, Solomon Islands and Vanuatu, 1993-96; fgn. policy advisor to the Commander in Chief U.S. Pacific Command, Camp Smith, Hawaii, 1996—. Mem. Am. Fgn. Assn., Sr. Fgn. Svc. Assn., Asia Soc., Malaysia-Am. Soc., Indonesian-Am. Soc., Nat. Trust Hist. Preservation. Office: HQ USCINCPAC/FPA Box 64028 Camp Smith HI 96861-4028

TEASDALE, KENNETH FULBRIGHT, lawyer; b. St. Louis, Nov. 8, 1934; s. Kenneth and Ann (Fulbright) T.; m. Elizabeth Driscol Langdon, June 13, 1964; children: Caroline, Doug, Cindy. AB, Amherst Coll., 1956; LLB, Washington U., St. Louis, 1961. Bar: Mo. 1961. Atty. antitrust div. U.S. Dept. Justice, Washington, 1961-62; asst. counsel Dem. Policy Com. U.S. Senate, Washington, 1962-63, gen. counsel Dem. Policy Com., asst. to majority leader, 1963-64; assoc. Armstrong, Teasdale, Kramer & Vaughan, St. Louis, 1964-67, ptnr., 1967-86; mng. ptnr. Armstrong, Teasdale, Schlafly & Davis, St. Louis, 1986-93, chmn. of firm, 1993—. Trustee United Way Greater St. Louis, Sci. Ctr. St. Louis, St. Louis Art Mus. ; trustee, chmn. bd. regents St. Louis U.; mem. nat. coun. Washington U. Law Sch., 1988—. Mem. ABA, Bar Assn. Mo., Bar Assn. St. Louis, Racquet Club, Noonday Club, Old Warson Country Club. Presbyterian. Office: Armstrong Teasdale Schlafly & Davis Metropolitan Sq Saint Louis MO 63106

TEASE, JAMES EDWARD, judge; b. Sheffield, Ala., Dec. 28, 1939; s. James Albert and Hattie Wayne (Counts) T.; m. Anne Elizabeth Gilley, Sept. 2, 1972. B.S., Florence State U., 1961; LL.B., U. Ala., 1964; grad., Nat. Coll. State Judiciary, 1971. Bar: Ala. 1964. Gen. practice law Florence, 1965-67, city prosecutor, 1966-67; dep. dist. atty. Lauderdale County, Ala., 1967-71; circuit judge 11th Jud. Cir. Ala., Florence, 1971-89; extra judge Ala. Ct. Civil Appeals, 1989; U.S. adminstrv. law judge Social Security Adminstrn., Office Hearings & Appeals, Florence, Ala., 1989—; Mem. Ala. Constl. Commn.; chmn. Ala. Citizens Adv. Com. on Election Reform; mem. Ala. Ct. of Judiciary, 1981-89. Bd. dirs. Regional Library System. Served with AUS, 1964-65. Named Florence Outstanding Young Man Jaycees, 1974, Alumnus of Year U. N. Ala., 1975. Mem. Am. Judicature Soc., Nat. Conf. State Trial Judges, Ala. Assn. Circuit Judges (pres. 1986), Lauderdale County Bar Assn. (pres.), Am. Legion, Sigma Delta Kappa. Baptist. Home: 1926 Monticello Rd Florence AL 35630-2740 Office: Walnut St Exec Ctr 205 S Walnut St Ste D Florence AL 35630-5723

TEATER, DOROTHY SEATH, county official; b. Manhattan, Kans., Feb. 11, 1931; d. Dwight Moody and Martha (Stahnke) Seath; m. Robert Woodson Teater, May 24, 1952; children: David Dwight, James Stanley, Donald Robert, Andrew Scott. BS, U. Ky., 1951; MS, Ohio State U., 1954. Home econs. tchr. Georgetown (Ky.) City Schs., 1951-53; extension specialist Ohio Coop. Extension, Columbus, 1967-73; consumer affairs adminstr. City of Columbus, 1974-79, Bank One Columbus NA, 1980-85; councilmember Columbus City Coun., 1980-85; commr. Franklin County, Columbus, Ohio, 1985—; mem. Columbus Met. Area Cmty. Action Orgn., Land Policy and Boom Bust Real Estate Markets, 1994, Lincoln Inst. Land Policy; mem. adv. bd. Ohio Housing Trust; mem. Franklin County Children's Cabinet. Bd. dirs. BBB; mem. hon. adv. bd. Girl Scouts. Recipient Outstanding Alumnus award U. Ky., 1989, Women of Achievement award YWCA, 1995, Disting. Svc. award Ohio State U., 1997; named Disting. Alumni, Ohio State U., 1977. Mem. County Commrs. Assn. Ohio (pres. 1994), Columbus Met. Club, Greater Columbus C. of C. (Columbus award 1997). Republican. Methodist. Avocations: gardening, sewing. Office: Franklin County Commrs 373 S High St Columbus OH 43215-4591

TEATES, CHARLES DAVID, radiologist, educator; b. Luray, Va., July 1, 1936; s. Gilbert Grove and Mae Frankie (Pierce) T.; m. Mary Bruce Bucher, June 6, 1958; children—Elizabeth Susan, David Bruce, Mary Catherine. B.S., Lebanon Valley Coll., Annville, Pa., 1958; M.S., U. Va., Charlottesville, 1963, M.D., 1963. Diplomate Am. Bd. Radiology, Am. Bd. Nuclear Medicine. Intern U. Kans. Med. Ctr., 1963-64; resident in radiology U. Va. Med. Ctr., 1964-67; Asst. prof. radiology U. Va., Charlottesville, 1969-73, assoc. prof., 1973-79, prof., 1979—. Contbg. author books on radiology and nuclear medicine. Served to maj. M.C., U.S. Army, 1967-69, Vietnam. Mem. Am. Coll. Radiology (pres. Va. chpt. 1984-85), Soc. Nuclear Medicine (pres. Mid-Eastern chpt. 1984-86), AMA, Alpha Omega Alpha. Home: 4635 Watts Passage Charlottesville VA 22911 Office: U Va Med Ctr PO Box 170 Charlottesville VA 22908

TEBBEL, JOHN, writer, educator; b. Boyne City, Mich., Nov. 16, 1912; s. William and Edna (Johnston) T.; m. Kathryn Carl, Apr. 29, 1939; 1 child, Judith. A.B., Central Mich Coll. Edn., 1935; M.S., Columbia U., 1937. City editor Isabella Co. Times-News, Mt. Pleasant, Mich., 1935-36; writer Newsweek mag., 1937; reporter Detroit Free Press, 1937-39; feature writer, roto news editor Providence Jour., 1939-41; mng. editor Am. Mercury, 1941-43; Sunday staff writer N.Y. Times, 1943; assoc. editor E.P. Dutton & Co., 1943-47; asst. in journalism Sch. Journalism Columbia U., 1943-45; chmn. dept. journalism N.Y. U., 1954-65, prof. journalism, 1965—; Cons. Ford Found., 1966—. Author: An American Dynasty, 1947, The Marshall Fields, 1947, George Horace Lorimer and the Saturday Evening Post, 1948, Battle for North America, 1948, Your Body, 1951, The Conqueror, 1951, Touched With Fire, 1952, The Life and Good Times of William Randolph Hearst, 1952, George Washington's America, 1954, A Voice in the Street, 1954, The Magic of Balanced Living, 1956, The American Indian Wars, 1960, The Inheritors, 1962, The Epicure's Companion, 1962, David Sarnoff, 1963, Compact History of the American Newspaper, 1964, From Rags to Riches, 1964, Open Letter to Newspaper Readers, 1968, Compact History of American Magazines, 1969, A History of Book Publishing in the United States, 4 vols, 1972, 75, 78, 81, The Battle of Fallen Timbers, 1972, The Media in America, 1975, The Press and the Presidency, 1985, Between Covers, 1987, A Certain Club, 1989, The Magazine in America, 1991, Turning the World Upside Down, 1993, America's Great Patriotic War with Spain, 1996; contbr. to Sat. Rev., other mags. Named to Pub. Hall of Fame. Home: 4033 The Forest at Duke 2701 Pickett Rd Durham NC 27705-5654 *From the time my writing career began, at 14, I have tried to write as well and clearly and accurately as I can, so that I could best inform the people who read my books and articles about the world they live in. To me it is the obligation of every writer to recognize the responsibility his talent imposes on him, and understand that he is one of the transmitters of knowledge upon whom the world depends for advancement and the betterment of human society.*

TECCO, ROMUALD GILBERT LOUIS JOSEPH, violinist, concertmaster; b. Toulon, Var, France, May 1, 1941; came to U.S., 1960; s. Raymond Charles and Angele (Cornille) T. Student, Paris Conservatoire, 1954-60; diploma, postgrad. diploma, Juilliard Sch. Music, 1967-68. Mem. N.Y. String Quartet, 1969-72; concertmaster Juilliard Ensemble, N.Y.C., 1969-72, St. Paul Chamber Orch., 1972—; soloist Chgo. Symphony, Bavarian Radio Orch., Orch. of Mex., Orchestre Colonne, Paris, Rotterdam Philharm.; performer numerous festivals, Sweden, Finland, France, Italy, U.S. Recs. with Aaron Copland and Lou Harrison Chamber Music. Served with French Navy, 1964-65, NATO hdqrs. Recipient first prize in violin Conservatoire Paris; recipient first prize chamber music Conservatoire Paris. Mem. St. Paul Univ. Club. Office: St Paul Chamber Orch 408 Saint Peter St Saint Paul MN 55102-1130

TECLAFF, LUDWIK ANDRZEJ, law educator, consultant, author, lawyer; b. Czestochowa, Poland, Nov. 14, 1918; came to U.S., 1952, naturalized, 1958; s. Emil and Helena (Tarnowska) T.; m. Eileen Johnson, May 30, 1952. Mag Iuris, Oxford (Eng.) U., 1944; MS, Columbia U., 1955; LLM, NYU, 1961, JSD, 1965. Attaché Polish Fgn. Ministry, London, 1943-46; consul in Ireland, Polish Govt. in London, 1946-52; student libr. Columbia U. Sch. Libr. Sci., 1953-54; libr. Bklyn. Pub. Libr., 1954-59; rsch. librar. Fordham U. Sch. Law, 1959-62, asst. prof. law, 1962-65, assoc. prof. law, 1965-68, prof. 1968-89, prof. emeritus, 1989—, dir. law libr., 1962-86; cons. in field. With Polish Army, 1940-43, France, Eng. Recipient Clyde Eagleton award in internat. law NYU, 1965. Mem. Am. Soc. Internat. Law, Internat. Law Assn., Am. Law Librs. Assn., Internat. Coun. Environ. Law, Internat. Water Law Assn. Roman Catholic. Author: The River Basin in History and Law, 1967; Abstraction and Use of Water, 1972; Legal and Institutional Responses to Growing Water Demand, 1978; Economic Roots of Oppression, 1984, Water Law in Historical Perspective, 1985; editor: (with Albert E Utton) International Environmental Law, 1974, Water in a Developing World, 1978, International Groundwater Law, 1981, Transboundary Resources Law, 1987; contbr. articles on water law, law of the sea and environ. law to law jours. Office: Fordham U Sch Law 140 W 62nd St New York NY 10023-7407

TEDDER, DANIEL WILLIAM, chemical engineering educator; b. Orlando, Fla., Apr. 13, 1946; s. Daniel Webster and Adelaide Katheryn (Bruechert) T.; m. Wendy Elizabeth Widhelm, Aug. 3, 1968; children: Lisa Christine, Rachel Marie. Student, Kenyon Coll., 1964-67; B Chem. Engring. with highest honors, Ga. Inst. Tech., 1972; MS, U. Wis., 1973, PhD, 1975. Registered profl. engr., Tenn., Ga. Lab. technician Agrico Chem. Co., Pierce, Fla., 1965-67, Puritan Chem. Co., Atlanta, 1967-68; engr. Humble Oil and Refining Co., Baytown, Tex., summer 1972; staff engr. Oak Ridge (Tenn.) Nat. Lab., 1975-79; asst. prof. chem. engring. Ga. Inst. Tech., Atlanta, 1979-84, assoc. prof., 1984—; organizer symposia Emerging Techs. for Hazardous Waste Mgmt.; conf. presenter in field, 1977—; engring. cons. BCM Techs., Inc., Amherstberg, Ont., Can., 1985, Nat. Bur. Standards, U.S. Dept. Commerce, 1986—, Thermax Inc., Atlanta, 1987-88, Exxon R & D Lab., Baton Rouge, 1989—, Waste Policy Inst., Blacksburg, Va., 1992—, Geotech ChemNuclear, Golden, Colo., 1992—, Martin Marietta, Oak Ridge, 1992—, Resource Preservation Corp., Union City, Ga., 1992—; reviewer Jour. Phys. Chemistry, 1993—; others. Sr. series editor: Radioactive Waste Management Handbook; exec. editor Toxic and Hazardous Substance Control; assoc. editor Solvent Extraction and Ion Exchange; editor: (with F.G. Pohland) Emerging Technologies in Hazardous Waste Management, 1989, I, 1990, II, 1991, III, 1993, IV, 1994, V, 1995; contbr. numerous articles to profl. jours., chpts. to books. Mem. AIChE (pub. awareness com. Knoxville 1978-79), Am. Chem. Soc. (symposium chmn. I&EC divsn. 1989—), Am. Nuclear Soc., Water Pollution Control Fedn. Achievements include patents in process producing absolute ethanol by solvent extraction and vacuum distillation, fractional distillation of C2/C3 hydrocarbon at optimum pressures, others. Office: Ga Inst Tech Sch Chem Engring 778 Atlantic Dr Atlanta GA 30332-0100

TEDDER, THOMAS FLETCHER, immunology educator, researcher; b. Chateauroux, France, May 14, 1956; came to U.S. 1959; s. Raymond Percy and Barbara (Hagemann) T. AA, Okaloosa-Walton Community Coll, Niceville, Fla., 1976; BS with honors, U. Fla., 1978, MS, 1980; PhD, U. Ala., Birmingham, 1984. Rsch. fellow in pathology Harvard Med. Sch., Boston, 1984-85, instr. pathology, 1986-88, asst. prof. pathology, 1988-93; assoc. prof. pathology Harvard U. Med. Sch., Boston, 1993; prof. immunology Duke U. Med. Ctr., Durham, N.C., 1993—, chmn. dept., 1993—; Alter Geller prof. rsch. in immunology Duke U. Med. Ctr., 1997. Assoc. editor Jour. Immunology, 1989-93, sect. editor, 1993—; contbr. numerous articles to med. jours., including Jour. Immunology, Nature, Lancet, Jour. Gen. Virology. Recipient LeRoy Collins Disting. Alumnus award Fla. Assn. C.C.'s; named 25th Anniversary Disting. Alumnus, Okaloosa-Walton C.C., 1989; Damon Runyon-Walter Winchell rsch. fellow, 1985-87; scholar Leukemia Soc. Am., 1991-96, Stohlman scholar, 1995-96. Mem. Am. Soc. for Microbiology (Pres. Fellow 1982), Am. Assn. Immunologists, Sigma Xi, Phi Kappa Phi. Achievements include identification and determination of structure and function of many human B lymphocyte cell-surface molecules. Office: Duke U Med Ctr Dept Immunology PO Box 3010 Durham NC 27710

TEDESCHI, ERNEST FRANCIS, JR., retired naval officer, naval company executive; b. New Britain, Conn., Mar. 28, 1942; s. Ernest and Rose (Malucci) T.; m. Christine Ann DiEleuterio, Apr. 15, 1972; children: Gina, Ernest. BS in Marine Engring., U.S. Naval Acad., 1965; MS in Mgmt., Salve Regina U., 1987. Commd. ensign USN, advanced through grades to rear adm., 1992; weapons officer USS Gridley (CG 21), San Diego, 1974-76; operational test & evaluation force Pacific USS John Paul Jones (DDG 32), 1978-81; commdg. officer USS Duncan (FFG 10), Long Beach, Calif., 1982-85; instr. Surface Warfare Officers Sch., Newport, R.I., 1985-87; sponsor, chief of naval ops. Aegis Program, Washington, 1987-89; commdg. officer USS Valley Forge (CG 50), San Diego, 1990-91; dir. plans and policy Supreme Allied Commdr. Atlantic NATO, Norfolk, Va., 1991-93; commdr. naval base, combat logistics group 1 USN, San Francisco, 1993-97; ret. USN, 1997; gen. mgr. San Diego ops. Hughes Naval and Maritime Sys., 1997—; weapons officer USS Brownson (DD 868), Newport, R.I., 1970-72; exec. com. Fed. Exec. Bd., Oakland, Calif., 1993-94. Bd. dirs. ARC, San Francisco, 1993-94; regional chmn. Navy/Marine Corps Relief Soc., No. Calif., 1993-94. Decorated Disting. Svc. medal, Meritorious Svc. medal with gold star, Bronze Star with combat "V", Legion of Merit with gold star, Def. Superior Svc. medal. Mem. Ret. Officer's Assn., Surface Navy Assn., San Francisco C. of C. (exec. bd. 1993-95). Roman Catholic. Avocations: tennis, basketball, jogging, baseball. Home: 12687 Mengibar Ave San Diego CA 92129-3053

TEDESCHI, JOHN ALFRED, historian, librarian; b. Modena, Italy, July 17, 1931; came to U.S., 1939, naturalized, 1944; s. Caesar George and Piera (Forti) T.; m. Anne Wood Christian, Sept. 8, 1956; children: Martha, Philip, Sara. BA, Harvard U., 1954, MA, 1960, PhD, 1966. Bibliographer European history and lit. Newberry Library, Chgo., 1965-84, curator rare books and manuscripts, head dept. spl. collections, 1970-82, dir. Ctr. Renaissance Studies, 1979-84; curator rare books and spl. collections Meml. Library U. Wis.-Madison, 1984-96; lectr. history U. Chgo., 1969-71; vis. prof. U. Ill.-Chgo., 1972-73, adj. prof., 1979-84. Co-editor: (series) Corpus Reformatorum Italicorum, 1968—; editor-in-chief: Bibliographie Internat. de L'Humanisme et de la Renaissance, 1977-82; editor: Italian Reformation Studies in Honor of Laelius Socinus, 1965, (with Anthony Molho) Renaissance Studies in Honor of Hans Baron, 1971, (with Gustav Henningsen) The Inquisition in Early Modern Europe: Studies on Sources and Methods, 1986, The Prosecution of Heresy: Collected Studies on the Inquisition in Early Modern Italy, 1991, Tomasso Sassetti, Il Massacro di San Bartolomeo, 1995; translator: (with Anne Tedeschi) The Cheese and the Worms. The Cosmos of a Sixteenth-Century Miller (Carlo Ginzburg), 1980 (named an Outstanding Acad. Book by Choice mag.), The Night Battles. Witchcraft and Agrarian Cults in the Sixteenth and Seventeenth Centuries (Carlo Ginzburg), 1983, Clues, Myths, and the Historical Method (Carlo Ginzburg), 1989, Hans Urs von Balthasar: A Theological Style (Angelo Scola), 1995, Domenico Scandella Known as Menocchio: His Trials Before the Inquisition (1583-1599) (Andrea Del Col), 1996; mem. editl. com.: Index des Livres Interdits (Sherbrooke), Collected Works of Erasmus (Toronto); mem. editl. bd.: Studi e Testi per la Storia Religiosa Italiana del '500 (Florence); contbr. articles to profl. jours. Served with U.S. Army, 1954-56. Grantee Am. Philos. Soc., 1961; grantee NEH, 1967; Old Dominion fellow Harvard U. Ctr. Renaissance Studies, Florence, Italy, 1967-68; fellow Inst. Research in Humanities, U. Wis.-Madison, 1976-77; Huntington Library fellow, 1984. Mem. Am. Soc. Reformation Research (pres. 1972), Renaissance Soc. Am. (exec. bd. 1971-77), 16th Century Studies Conf. (pres. 1987), Am. Hist. Assn. Home: RR 1 Box 169 Ferryville WI 54628-9749

TEDESCO, FRANCIS JOSEPH, university administrator; b. Derby, Conn., Mar. 8, 1944; s. Lena (Tufano) Tedesco; m. Luann Lee Ekern, Aug. 1, 1970; 1 child, Jennifer Nicole. BS cum laude, Fairfield U., 1965; MD cum laude, St. Louis U., 1969. Asst. instr. Hosp. of U. Pa., Phila., 1971-72; asst. prof. Washington U. Sch. Medicine, St. Louis, 1974-75; asst. prof. U. Miami (Fla.) Sch. Medicine, 1975-77, co-dir. clin. research, 1976-78, assoc. prof., 1977-78; assoc. prof. Med. Coll. Ga., Augusta, 1978-81, chief of gastroenterology dept., 1978-88, prof., 1981—, acting v.p. clin. activities, 1984, v.p. for clin. activities, 1984-88, Interim dean Sch. of Medicine, 1986-88, pres., 1988—; cons. Med.-Letter/AMA div. drugs, Dwight D. Eisenhower Army Med. Ctr., Ft. Gordon, Ga., VA Med. Ctr., Augusta, Walter Reed Army Med. Ctr., Washington; mem. gastroenterology spl. study sect. NIH, Washington, 1982—, mem. nat. digestive disease adv. bd., 1985-88, vice chmn., 1986-87, chmn., 1987-88. Contbr. numerous articles to profl. jours. Bd. dirs. Augusta Country Day Sch., 1981-83, Am. Cancer Soc., Augusta, 1985—, v.p., 1986—; bd. dirs., exec. com. Ga. Coalition for Health, 1995—; chmn. Gov.'s Health Strategies Coun., 1992—. Capt. N.G., 1970-72. Recipient Eddie Palmer award for gastrointestinal endoscopy, 1983, cert. of appreciation Am. Cancer Soc., 1986, Outstanding Faculty award Med. Coll. Ga. Sch. Medicine, 1988, Profl. Achievement award Fairfield U., 1993, alumni merit award St. Louis U. Sch. Medicine, 1996; Avalon Found. scholar St. Louis U., 1968-69, Paul Harris fellow Rotary, 1990. Fellow ACP, Am. Fedn. Clin. Investigation, Am. Gastroent. Assn., Am. Soc. Gastrointestinal Endoscopy (treas. 1981-84, pres.-elect 1984-85, pres. 1985-86, Rudolph Schindler award 1993); mem. Am. Coll. Gastroenterology, So. Soc. Clin. Investigation, Richmond County Med. Soc., Med. Assn. Ga. Roman Catholic. Avocations: reading, swimming. Home: 920 Milledge Rd Augusta GA 30912-7600 Office: Med Coll Ga Office Pres 1120 15th St Augusta GA 30912-0004

TEDESCO, PAUL HERBERT, humanities educator; b. Nashua, N.H., Dec. 28, 1928; s. Steven R. and Ruth (Weaver) T.; m. Eleanor Martha Hollis, Jan. 24, 1953; children: Steven Anthony, Sara Adams Tagget, James Beattie. AB in History, Harvard Coll., 1952; AM in History, Boston U., 1955, PhD in History, 1970; CAGS in Adminstrn., Northeastern U., Boston, 1974. Instr. humanities Mich. State U., East Lansing, 1955-60; tchr. history Great Neck (N.Y.) North H.S., 1960-62; chair dept. social studies Canton (Mass.) H.S., 1962-65; prof./chair edn. Northeastern U., Boston, 1965-87; Fulbright prof. history Peking U., Beijing, China, 1988-89; historian-in-residence City of Haverhill, Mass., 1989-90; lectr. bus., history, govt. edn. Asian divsn. U. Md., Korea, Japan, Guam, 1990-94; team leader/lectr. Joint Siberian-Am. Faculty, Irkutsk State U., Siberia, 1994-95; edn. coord. Asian divsn. U. Md., 1995—; nat. dir. BHelp (Bus., History and Econ. Life Program), Boston, 1968—; cons. in field. Author: Teaching with Case Studies, 1978, A New England City: Haverhill Massachusetts, 1987, Attleboro, Massachusetts: The Hub of the Jewelry Industry, 1979, Protection, Patriotism and Prosperity: James M. Swank, the AISA, and the Tariff, 1872-1913, 1985; author, editor: The Creative Social Science Teacher, 1970, The Thunder of the Mills, 1981. Mem. Town Fin. Com., Canton, Mass., 1966-68. With U.S. Army, 1952-54. Recipient FEI Nat. collegiate award, 1985, Freedoms Found. George Washington medal for econ. edn., 1984. Mem. New Eng. History Tchrs. Assn. (past pres., Kidger award 1975).

TEDFORD, CHARLES FRANKLIN, biophysicist; b. Lawton, Okla., June 26, 1928; s. Charles E. and Loula B. (Waters) T.; m. Julie Reme Sauret, Sept. 15, 1951; children: Gary Franklin, Mark Charles, Philip John. BS with distinction in Chemistry, S.W. Tex. State U., 1950, MS, 1954; postgrad. in radiobiology Reed Coll., 1957, in biophysics U. Calif., Berkeley, 1961-63. Enlisted USN, 1945-47, commd. ensign, 1950, advanced through grades to capt., 1968; biochemist U.S. Naval Hosp., San Diego, 1953-54, U.S. Naval Biol. Lab., Oakland, Calif., 1954-56; sr. instr., radiation safety officer Nuclear, Biol. and Chem. Warfare Def. Sch., Treasure Island, Calif., 1956-61; asst. chief nuclear medicine div. Navy Med. Sch., Bethesda, Md., 1963-66; adminstrv. program mgr. radiation safety br. Bur. Medicine and Surgery, Washington, 1966-72; dir. radiation safety and health physics program Navy Regional Med. Center, San Diego, 1972-74; mgr. Navy Regional Med. Clinic, Seattle, 1974-78, ret., 1978; dir. radiation health unit Ga. Dept. Human Resources, Atlanta, 1978-79; dir. Ariz. Radiation Regulatory Agy., Tempe, 1979-91; chief, Radiological Health Prog., Juneau, Alaska, 1991-93, ret. 1993; cons. 1993—. elected chmn. Conf. Radiation Program Dirs., 1987; named Ariz. Southwestern Low Level Radioactive Waste Compact Commr., 1990. Recipient Ariz. Adminstr. of Yr. award Ariz. Adminstrs. Assn., 1988; decorated Legion of Merit, Meritorious Service medal. Mem. Health Physics Soc., Am. Nuclear Soc. Contbr. articles on radiation safety to profl. publs.

TEDLOCK, BARBARA HELEN, anthropologist, educator; b. Battle Creek, Mich., Sept. 9, 1942; d. Byron Taylor and Mona Gerteresse (O'Connor) McGrath; m. Dennis E. Tedlock, July 19, 1968. BA in Rhetoric, U. Calif., 1967; MA in Anthropology, Wesleyan U., 1973; PhD in Anthropology, SUNY, Albany, 1978. Lectr. in music Tufts U., Medford, Mass., 1977-78, asst. prof. anthropology, 1978-82, assoc. prof., 1982-87; assoc. prof. anthropology SUNY, Buffalo, 1987-89, prof. anthropology, 1989—. Author: Time and the Highland Maya, 1982, The Beautiful and the Dangerous Encounters with Zuni Indians, 1992; editor: Dreaming: Anthropological and Psychological Interpretations, 1987; co-editor: Teaching From the American Earth, 1975; assoc. editor Jour. of Anthropol. Rsch., 1987-93; sr. editor Dreaming, 1990-95; assoc. editor Latin Am. Rsch. Rev., 1992—' mem. editl. adv. bd. Encyc. Cultural Anthropology, 1993-95. Adv. bd. Mus. of Indian Arts, Santa Fe, 1991-95; mem. Roycrofters-at-large East Aurura, N.Y., 1989—; mem. humanities panel WGBH, Boston, 1983-84; judge pottery Southwestern Assn. on Indian Affaris, Santa Fe, 1981-83. Fellowships NEH, 1986, 93, sr. fellowship Am. Coun. of Learned Socs., 1994, Wetherhead fellowship Sch. of Am. Rsch., 1980; recipient Charles Bordon, Geoffrey Bushnell Juan Cosmos Prize in linguistics Internat. Congress of Americanists, 1979. Fellow Am. Anthropol. Assn. (bd. dirs. 1991-93, editor-in-chief Am. Anthropologist 1994—), Soc. for Cultural Anthropology; mem. PEN (elected), Soc. for Humanistic Anthropology (pres. 1991-93, Writing prize 1986), Soc. for Psychol. Anthropology (bd. dirs. 1993-96), Assn. for Study of Dreams (bd. dirs. 1990-95), Soc. for Ethnohistory (exec. bd. 1980-82), Am. Studies Assn. (exec. bd. 1983-85). Avocations: skiing, running, swimming, dancing, videoing. Office: SUNY Buffalo Dept Anthropology Buffalo NY 14261

TEDLOCK, DENNIS, anthropology and literature educator; b. St. Joseph, Mo., June 19, 1939; s. E.W. Tedlock and Agnes Gertrude Peterson; m. Barbara Tedlock, July 19, 1968. BA, U. N.Mex., 1961; PhD in Anthropology, Tulane U., 1968. Asst. prof. anthropology Iowa State U., 1966-67; asst. prof. rhetoric U. Calif., Berkeley, 1967-69; research assoc. Sch. Am. Research, 1969-70; asst. prof. anthropology Bklyn. Coll., 1970-71; asst. prof. Yale U., 1972-73; assoc. Univ. prof., anthropology and religion Boston U., 1973-82, Univ. prof., anthropology and religion, 1982-87; James H. McNulty prof. dept. English SUNY, Buffalo, 1987—, rsch. prof. dept. anthropology, 1987—; vis. asst. prof. Wesleyan U., 1971-72; adj. prof. U. N.Mex., 1980-81; mem. Inst. for Advanced Study, 1986-87. Author: Finding the Center: Narrative Poetry of the Zuni Indians, 1972, The Spoken Word and the Work of Interpretation, 1983, Days from a Dream Almanac, 1990 (Victor Turner prize 1991), Breath on the Mirror: Mythic Voices and Visions of the Living Maya, 1993; co-editor: Teachings from the American Earth, 1975, The Dialogic Emergence of Culture, 1996; co-editor-in-chief Am. Anthropologist, 1994—; contbr. articles to profl. jours. and lit. mags. Dumbarton Oaks fellow in pre-Columbian Studies, 1993-94, Guggenheim fellow, 1986; recipient PEN transl. prize for Popol Vuh: The Mayan Book of the Dawn of Life, 1986. Office: SUNY Buffalo Dept English Buffalo NY 14260

TEDROS, THEODORE ZAKI, educator, real estate broker, appraiser; b. Cairo, June 25, 1910; Naturalized, 1966; s. Zaki and Faika (Lotfi) T.; married 1962; 1 child, Samuel N. BA in Math., Tex. Christian U., 1957, MEd with honors, 1958; postgrad., Fla. State U., 1961. Tchr. pub. schs., Addis Ababa, Ethiopia, 1947-56, The American Inst., Addis Ababa, Ethiopia, 1952-56; instr. math. Fla. State U., Tallahassee, 1958-59; tchr. math. Fla. Mil. Sch. and Coll., Deland, Fla., 1961-64; tchr. Volusia County Bd. Instrn., Deland, 1964-75; real estate broker Daytona Beach, Fla., 1975—, appraiser, 1978-92; prof. edn. sociology U. Man., Winnipeg, Can., summers 1962-64. Sunday sch. tchr., Fla.; mem. Nat. Coun. Math. Tchrs., 1959-75, Phi Delta Kappa, 1960-80. Mem. Nat. Assn. Master Appraisers (v.p. 1985-86), Fla. Assn. Realtors, Daytona Beach Area Bd. Realtors, Nat. Assn. Realtors (cert. 1978-90). Democrat. Home: 227 Kensington Ave Deland FL 32724-2321

TEDROW, JOHN CHARLES FREMONT, soils educator; b. Rockwood, Pa., Apr. 21, 1917; s. John Wesley and Emma Grace (Younkin) T.; m. Mary Jane Lough, Mar. 20, 1943 (dec. Mar. 1991); children: John Charles Fremont, Thomas Lough. BS, Pa. State U., 1939; MS, Mich. State U., 1940; PhD, Rutgers U., 1950. Jr. soil technologist Dept. Agr., 1941-42, soil scientist, 1946-47; instr. Rutgers U., New Brunswick, N.J., 1947-50, asst. prof., 1950-53, assoc. prof., 1953-57, prof. soils, 1957-84, prof. emeritus, 1984—; cons. N.S. Research Found., 1949—; sr. pedologist Boston U., 1953—; prin. investigator Arctic Inst. N.Am., Washington, 1955-68, NSF, 1961-62, Atomic Energy Commn., Washington, 1961-63; cons. to govt. and industry. Author: (with R.C. Murray) Forensic Geology: Earth Sciences and Criminal Investigation, 1974, Soils of the Polar Landscapes, 1977, (with K.A. Linell) Soil and Permafrost Surveys in the Arctic, 1981, Soils of New Jersey, 1986, (with R.C. Murray) Forensic Geology, 1991; editor in chief Soil Science, 1968-79; editor: Antarctic Soils and Soil Forming Processes, 1966. Served to lt. USNR, 1942-46. Recipient Lindback Research award Rutgers U., 1978, Antarctic Service medal. Fellow Am. Soc. Agronomy, Soil Sci. Soc. Am., Arctic Inst. N.Am.; mem. Internat. Soc. Soil Sci., Am. Geophys. Union, Am. Arbitration Assn., Sigma Xi, Alpha Zeta (hon.), Phi Mu Delta. Investigator polar soils in Alaska, Can., Greenland, Scandinavia, Siberia and Antarctica. Home: 5 Bluebird Ct Edison NJ 08820-3677 Office: Rutgers U Ecology Evolution and Natural Resources PO Box 231 New Brunswick NJ 08903-0231

TEEGARDEN, KENNETH LEROY, clergyman; b. Cushing, Okla., Dec. 22, 1921; s. Roy Albert and Eva B. (Swiggart) T.; m. Wanda Jean Strong, May 28, 1944; children: David Kent, Marshall Kirk. Student, Okla. State U., 1938-40; A.B., Phillips U., 1942, M.A., 1945, D.D., 1963; B.D., Tex. Christian U., 1949, D.D., 1976; D.D., Bethany Coll., 1974; LL.D., Lynchburg Coll., 1975; L.H.D., Culver-Stockton Coll., 1975. Ordained to ministry Christian Ch. (Disciples of Christ), 1940; pastor in Chandler, Okla., 1944-47, Texas City, Tex., 1947-48, Healdton, Okla., 1948-49, Vernon, Tex., 1949-55, Fort Smith, Ark., 1955-58; exec. minister Christian Ch. in, Ark., 1958-65; asst. to pres. Christian Ch. in U.S. and Can., Indpls., 1965-69; exec. minister Christian Ch. in Tex., 1969-73; gen. minister, pres. Christian Ch. in U.S. and Can., 1973-85; faculty Brite Div. Sch., Tex. Christian U., 1985-89; mem. governing bd. Nat. Council Chs., 1973-85; del. 5th Assembly of World Council Chs., Nairobi, Kenya, 1975, 6th Assembly, Vancouver, B.C., Can, 1983; rep. Nat. Council Chs. in Exchange of Ch. Leadership with Soviet Union, 1974. Author: We Call Ourselves Disciples, 1975. Named Disting. Alumnus Tex. Christian U., 1973, Phillips U., 1975; Outstanding Citizen Vernon, Tex., 1954. Home: 7013 Serrano Dr Fort Worth TX 76126-2317

TEEGUARDEN, DENNIS EARL, forest economist; b. Gary, Ind., Aug. 21, 1931; s. Gary Leon and Mary Dessa (Pursifull) T.; m. Sally Annette Gleason, Dec. 23, 1954; children—Jason Earl, Julie Annette, Justin Gary. B.S. in Forestry with honors, Mich. Tech. U., Houghton, 1953; M.Forestry, U. Calif., Berkeley, 1958, Ph.D. in Agrl. Econs. (Bidwell research fellow 1962-63), 1964. Rsch. aid U.S. Forest Service, 1957; asst. rsch. specialist U. Calif., Berkeley, 1958-64, mem. faculty, 1964-91, prof. forestry econs. Sch. Forestry, 1964-91, S.J. Hall prof. forest econs., 1989-91, prof. emeritus, 1991—, chmn. dept. forestry and resource mgmt., 1978-86, acting dir. forest products lab., 1987-88, assoc. dean for acad. affairs, 1990-92, assoc. dean rsch. and extension, 1992-93; mem. Calif. Commn. on Agr. and Higher Edn., 1993-95; mem. com. scientists Dept. Agr., 1977-80; cons. in field; mem. adv. bd. U. Calid. Forest Products Lab., 1994—. Co-author: Forest Resource Management: Decision-Making Principles and Cases, 1979; contbr. articles to profl. jours. Trustee Mich. Tech. Fund, Mich. Tech. U., Houghton, 1994—. Lt. USNR, 1953-57, Korea. Recipient Outstanding Alumnus award Mich. Tech. U., 1993, Berkeley citation U. Calif., Berkeley, 1994; grantee U.S. Forest Svc., Bur. Land Mgmt.; named to Honor Acad. Sch. Forestry and Wood Products, Mich. Tech. U., 1995. Fellow Am. Foresters; mem. Western Forest Economists, Calif. Water Fowl Assn. Home: 4732 Westwood Ct Richmond CA 94803-2441 Office: U Calif Coll Natural Resources Berkeley CA 94720

TEEL, JAMES E., supermarket and drug store retail executive; b. 1930. V.p. Raley's, West Sacramento, 1950-1991; co-chmn., dir., 1991—. Office: Raleys & Belaire 500 W Capitol Ave West Sacramento CA 95605-2624*

TEEL, JOYCE, supermarket and drugstore retail executive; b. 1930. Dir. Raley's, West Sacramento, 1950—; co-chmn., 1991—. Office: Raleys & Belaire 500 W Capitol Ave West Sacramento CA 95605-2624*

TEELE, CYNTHIA LOMBARD, lawyer; b. Boston, Oct. 11, 1961; d. John Hughes and Patricia Jeanne (Linder) T. AB in Urban Studies magna cum laude, Brown U., 1983; JD, U. Va., 1986. Bar: Calif. 1986. Assoc. Lillick McHose & Charles, L.A., 1986-87, Wyman Bautzer Kuchel & Silbert, L.A., 1987-91; sr. atty. Paramount Pictures Corp.-TV Divsn., Hollywood, Calif., 1991-92, dir., legal, 1992-94, v.p., legal, 1994—. Office: Paramount Pictures Corp 5555 Melrose Ave Los Angeles CA 90038-3112

TEELE, THURSTON FERDINAND, economist; b. New Rochelle, N.Y., Mar. 27, 1934; s. Stanley Ferdinand and Dorothy Thurston (Newman) T.; m. Shari May Barton, June 15, 1957 (div. 1965); children: Edward B., Stacia L.; m. Dorothy Locy, Aug. 1967 (div. 1980); children: Kristy A., Allen F.; m. Barbara Mangrum Carmichael, Feb. 7, 1982. BA, Amherst Coll., 1956; MA, Tufts U., 1962; PhD, Georgetown U., 1964. Fgn. svc. officer U.S. Dept. State, Washington and Athens, Greece, 1956-64; cons. economist, chief party Checchi. Co., Washington and overseas, 1964-75; pres., CEO Chemonics Internat., Washington, 1975—, Chemonics Industries (Holding Co.), 1996—; vice chmn. Profl. Svc. Coun. AID Task Force, Washington, 1992—. With U.S. Army, 1957-58. Democrat. Mem. United Ch. of Christ. Avocations: travel, reading, working out. Home: 2231 Q St NW Washington DC 20008-2825 Office: Chemonics Internat 1133 20th St NW Washington DC 20036-3402

TEEM, JOHN MCCORKLE, retired association executive; b. Springfield, Mo., July 23, 1925; s. Lon Vester and Judith (McCorkle) T.; m. Sylvia Victoria Konvicka; children—Judith Majka Teem Donald, Paul Norman. A.B., Harvard U., 1949, M.A., 1951, Ph.D., 1954. Sr. research fellow Calif. Inst. Tech., Pasadena, 1954-60; v.p., chief scientist Electro Optical Systems, Pasadena, 1960-67; dir. tech. staff, research and devel. Xerox Corp., Stamford, Conn., 1967-72; asst. gen. mgr., dir. phys. research AEC, Washington, 1973-75; asst. adminstr. ERDA, Washington, 1975-76; pres. Assn. Univs. for Research in Astronomy, Washington, 1977-86. Served with U.S. Army, 1943-46. Recipient Disting. Service medal AEC, 1975; named Fairchild Disting. scholar Calif. Inst. Tech., 1976-77. Fellow AAAS; mem. Am. Astron. Soc. Democrat. Roman Catholic. Home: 3800 Fairfax Dr Apt 1710 Arlington VA 22203-1706

TEEM, PAUL LLOYD, JR., savings and loan executive; b. Gastonia, N.C., Mar. 10, 1948; s. Paul Lloyd Sr. and Ruth Elaine (Bennett) T. BA, U. N.C., 1970; Cert., Inst. Fin. Edn., Chgo., 1984, Diploma, 1985, Degree of Distinction, 1989. Cert. tchr. N.C., cert. consumer credit exec.; lic. real estate broker. Exec. v.p., sec. Gaston Fed. Savs. and Loan Assn., Gastonia, N.C., 1983—; exec. v.p., sec., bd. dirs. Gaston Fin. Svcs., Inc., Gastonia, 1988—. Bd. dirs. Gastonia Mchts. Assn., Inc., 1981-83; lay reader Episcopal Ch. Decorated Order Purple Cross, Legion of Honor; named Ky. Col., 1995. Fellow Soc. Cert. Credit Execs.; mem. SAR, Sons of Confederate Vets., Mil. Order of Stars and Bars, Masons (32d degree, bd. dirs. 1981—, Disting. Svc. award 1987, Gold Honor award 1988, Active Legion of Honor 1989, Order of the Purple Cross of York 1990), Shriners, KT, Royal Order of Scotland, Hon. Order Ky. Cols., Phi Alpha Theta. Democrat. Avocation: genealogy. Home: 1208 Poston Cir Gastonia NC 28054-4634 Office: Gaston Fed Savs and Loan Assn 245 W Main Ave PO Box 2249 Gastonia NC 28053-2249

TEEPEN, THOMAS HENRY, newspaper editor, journalist; b. Nashville, Jan. 19, 1935; s. Albert George and Elizabeth Blanche (Winfree) T.; m. Nancy Irene Roux, Feb. 2, 1957 (div. 1974); children—Kristina Lynn, Jeremy Roux; m. Sandra Jean Richards, May 14, 1975; 1 stepchild, Jennifer Koerlin. B.S. in Journalism, Ohio U., 1957. Reporter Urbana (Ohio) Daily Citizen, 1957-58; asst. editor Kettering-Oakwood Times, Dayton, Ohio, 1958-59; from reporter to editorial writer Dayton Daily News, 1959-68, editorial page editor, 1968-82; editorial page editor Atlanta Constitution, 1982-92; nat. corr. Cox Newspapers, Atlanta, 1992—. Contbg. columnist Liberal Opinion Week. Former pres. Joel Chandler Harris Assn., Atlanta; mem. Atlanta Opera, 1985—, Joint Internat. Observer Group, Ethiopian Elections, 1992; mem. internat. adv. com. The African-Am. Inst., N.Y.C., 1985—; bd. dirs. Capital Area Mosaic, Genesis Shelter. Profl. journalism fellow Stanford Univ., 1967. Home: 900 Charles Allen Dr NE Atlanta GA 30308-1722 Office: Cox Newspapers care The Atlanta Constn Box 4689 Atlanta GA 30302

TEEPLE, FIONA DIANE, librarian, lawyer; b. St. Thomas, Ont., Can., Jan. 9, 1943; d. William Lloyd and Grace (Hathaway) T. BA, U. Western Ont., London, 1964; BLS, U. B.C., Vancouver, 1965; MLS, U. Toronto, Ont., 1976; LLB, York U., Toronto, 1980. Bar: Ont., 1985. Asst. law librarian U. Western Ont., London, 1965-70; reference librarian York U. Law Library, Toronto, 1971-77; adminstrv. asst. Ont. Legis. Library, Toronto, 1980, exec. asst., 1981-83; chief librarian Supreme Ct. of Can., Ottawa, 1983-90, dir. libr., 1990—. Editor: Practitioner's Desk Book, 1976-80; mng. editor CALL Newsletter, 1973-75; contbr. articles, revs., book chpts. in field. Mem. Can. Assn. Law Librs., Law Soc. Upper Can. Mem. United Ch. Can.

TEES, RICHARD CHISHOLM, psychology educator, researcher; b. Montreal, Que., Can., Oct. 31, 1940; s. Ralph Charles and Helen Winnifred (Chisholm) T.; m. Kathleen F. Coleman, Sept. 1, 1962; children: Susan M., Carolyn V. B.A., McGill U., 1961; Ph.D., U. Chgo., 1965. Asst. prof. U. B.C., Vancouver, 1965-67, assoc. prof., 1969-75, prof. psychology, 1975—; head dept. psychology U. B.C., 1984-94; rsch. prof. U. Sussex, Brighton, Eng., 1972-73, 77-78; chmn. grant selection panel Nat. Scis. and Engring. Rsch. Coun. Can., Ottawa, 1993-96, B.C. Health Care Rsch. Found., Vancouver, 1984-87; chmn. studentship com. Med. Rsch. Coun., Ottawa, 1985-92. Author: (with Kolb) Cerebral Cortex of the Rat, 1990; mem.

editorial bd. Can. Jour. Exptl. Psychology, 1975-84, 87—; contbr. articles to profl. jours., chpts. to books. Research fellow Killam Found., 1972-73, 77-78; research fellow Can. Council, 1972-73. Fellow APA, Am. Psychol. Soc., Can. Psychol. Assn.; mem. Soc. for Neurosci., Psychonomic Soc., U. B.C. Senate, Faculty Club. Home: 1856 Acadia Rd, Vancouver, BC Canada V6T 1R3 Office: U BC, Dept Psychology, Vancouver, BC Canada V6T 1Z4

TEETER, DWIGHT LELAND, JR., journalism educator; b. L.A., Jan. 6, 1935; s. Dwight Leland and Ruth Elizabeth (Sauer) T.; m. Letitia Ruth Thoreson, July 7, 1956; children: Susan Letitia Hall, John Thoreson, William Weston. A.B. in Journalism, U. Calif.-Berkeley, 1956, M.J., 1959; Ph.D. in Mass Communications, U. Wis., 1966. Reporter Waterloo Daily Courier, Iowa, 1957-60; asst. prof. Iowa State U., Ames, 1964-66; asst. to assoc. prof. U. Wis., Madison, 1966-72; assoc.prof. to prof. U. Ky., Lexington, 1972-77, dir. journalism dept., 1975-77; prof. journalism, chmn. dept. journalism U. Tex., Austin, 1977-84, William P. Hobby Centennial prof. communication, 1983-87; prof., dept. mass communications U. Wis., Milw., 1987-91; dean, prof. Coll. Communications U. Tenn., Knoxville, 1991—; vis. assoc. prof. U. Wash., Seattle, 1969-70; treas. Journalism Council, Inc., N.Y.C., 1972-81. Author: (with Don R. Le Duc) Law of Mass Communications, 8th edit., 1995, (with Jean L. Folkerts) Voices of a Nation: A History of Media in the United States, 2d edit., 1994; contbr. articles to legal, hist., comm. jours. Chair Headliners Club of Tex. Media Contest, 1979-83; judge Tex. Bar Assn. Media Contest, 1981-85; mem. pub. affairs com. Tex. State Bar, 1985-87. Recipient Tex. Excellence in Teaching award Tex. Ex-Students' Assn., 1983, Harold L. Nelson award U. Wis., 1985. Mem. Assn. for Edn. in Journalism and Mass Comm. (chmn. prof. freedom and responsibility com. 1971-73, pres. 1985-86), Soc. Profl. Journalists (Disting. Tchr. award 1991), Phi Kappa Phi, Kappa Tau Alpha. Office: U Tenn Coll Comm Knoxville TN 37996*

TEETER, KARL VAN DUYN, retired linguistic scientist, educator; b. Berkeley, Calif., Mar. 2, 1929; s. Charles Edwin and Lura May (Shaffner) T.; m. Anita Maria Bonacorsi, Aug. 25, 1951; children—Katharine Emilie, Judith Ann, Teresa Maria, Martha Elisabeth. AB in Oriental Langs. with highest honors, U. Calif., Berkeley, 1959, PhD Linguistics, 1962; AM (hon.), Harvard U., 1966. From instr. to prof. linguistics Harvard U., 1962-89, prof. emeritus, 1989—, chmn. dept. linguistics, 1966-69, 70-71, 77-78; assoc. Kirkland Ho., Harvard U., 1977-82, fellow, 1983-89, hon. assoc., 1989—; guest rsch. fellow Rsch. Inst. Logopedics and Phoniatrics, Faculty of Medicine, Tokyo U., 1969-70; mem. summer faculty U. Mich., 1962, UCLA, 1966, U. N.C., 1972. Author: Maliseet Texts, 1963, The Wiyot Language, 1964, Wiyot Handbook, I and II, 1993; editor: In Memoriam Peter Lewis Paul, 1902-89, 1993. Bd. dirs. Mass. Found. for Humanities and Pub. Policy, 1984-90, exec. com., 1985-89; bd. dirs. New Eng. Found. for Humanities, 1986-93; active New Eng. Native Am. Inst., 1992—. Served with AUS, 1946, 51-54. Fulbright rsch. fellow Japan, 1969-70; NSF grantee, 1990—. Mem. Linguistic Soc. Am. (life mem., long range planning com. 1969-73, lang. rev. com. 1980-82), Soc. Study Indigenous Langs. of the Ams., Phi Beta Kappa, Sigma Xi. Home: 14 Half Woodbridge St Cambridge MA 02140-1220 Office: Harvard Univ Widener T Cambridge MA 02138

TEETER, ROB R., regulatory affairs specialist; b. Rexburg, Idaho, Oct. 4, 1957; s. LaVerl Edward and Kita Dawn (Burns) T. Grad., DeVry Inst. of Tech., 1979. Quality control technician I Sundstrand Data Control, Redmond, Wash., 1979-81; quality control technician I Physio Control Corp., Redmond, 1981-82, quality control technician II, 1982-83, quality control technician II lead, 1983-85, quality control coord., 1985-86, quality control technician III, 1986-90, tech. ops. specialist surface mount tech., 1990-92, calibration supr., 1992-93, tech. assoc. calibration lab., 1993-95, assoc. regulatory affairs specialist, 1995—. Office: Physio Control Co 11811 Willows Rd NE Redmond WA 98052-2003

TEETERS, JOSEPH LEE, mathematician, consultant; b. Caney, Kans., Dec. 10, 1934; s. Jesse L. and Marie (Tapper) T.; m. Janet L. Hamm, June 18, 1984; children: Jeffrey, Susan, Christopher. Student, Colo. Sch. Mines, 1956, U. Kans., 1957; MA in Math., U. No. Colo., 1960, EdD in Math., 1968. Cert. secondary sch. tchr., Colo., Ill., hazard waste profl., OSHA. Exploration geologist Ohio Oil Co., Rawlings, Wyo., 1956-57; instr. Stout State U., Menomonie, Wis., 1960-62; asst. prof. Baker U., Baldwin City, Kans., 1962-65; temp. instr. U. No. Colo., Greeley, 1965-68; asst. prof. Western State Coll., Gunnison, Colo., 1968-69; prof. U. Wis., Eau Claire, 1969-88; cons. assoc. Delphi Data, Corona, Calif., 1989—; land surveying cons. Donaldson Engring., Menomonie, 1960-62; land boundary cons. ACLU, Eau Claire, 1974; lectr., spkr., cons. in field. Author: Creating Escher-Type Drawings, 1977; designer tessellation art; contbr. cover designs for profl. publs. Active Forest Lake (Ill.) Cmty. Assn., 1990—; sr. citizen trainer Marathon Challenge, St. Louis, 1994; mem. Golden Colo. Civic Orch., 1956; unicyclist Kans. State Sunflower State Games. Grantee NSF, 1965, U. New Orleans, 1987. Mem. Internat. Assn. for Math. Geology, Internat. Platform Assn., Stanton County Kans. Hist. Assn., Santa Fe Trail Assn., Kans. Trails Assn., Am. Volkssport Assn. (triathlete), Colo. Sch. of Mines Assn., Tiblow Trailblazers (sports cons. 1994—), Kappa Kappa Psi, Sigma Gamma Epsilon, Phi Delta Kappa. Achievements include creation of magnetic fishing tool for small sand screen well openings, and two successful completions of the Boston Marathon as well as six other 26.2 mile running events. Avocations: raising St. Bernards, designing birdhouses. Home: 21635 W Ravine Rd Lake Zurich IL 60047-8890 Office: Delphi Data 21635 W Ravine Rd Lake Zurich IL 60047-8890

TEETERS, NANCY HAYS, economist; b. Marion, Ind., July 29, 1930; d. S. Edgar and Mabel (Drake) Hays; m. Robert Duane Teeters, June 7, 1952; children: Ann, James, John. A.B. in Econs., Oberlin Coll., 1952, LL.D. (hon.), 1979; M.A. in Econs., U. Mich., 1954, postgrad., 1956-57, LL.D. (hon.), 1983; LL.D. (hon.), Bates Coll., 1981, Mt. Holyoke Coll., 1983. Tchg. fellow U. Mich., 1954-55, instr., 1956-57; instr. U. Md. Overseas, Germany, 1955-56; staff economist govt. fin. sect. Bd. Govs. of FRS, Washington, 1957-66; mem. bd. Bd. Govs. of FRS, 1978-84; economist (on loan) Coun. Econ. Advs., 1962-63; economist Bur. Budget, 1966-70; sr. fellow Brookings Instn., 1970-73; sr. specialist Congl. Rsch. Svc., Library of Congress, Washington, 1973-74; asst. dir., chief economist Ho. of Reps. Com. on the Budget, 1974-78; v.p., chief economist IBM, Armonk, N.Y., 1984-90; bd. dirs., trustee Prudential Mut. Funds, 1985—; bd. dirs. Inland Steel Industries; mem. Coun. on Fgn. Rels., Forum for World Affairs, Women in Mgmt. Author: (with others) Setting National Priorities: The 1972 Budget, 1971, Setting National Priorities: The 1973 Budget, 1972, Setting National Priorities: The 1974 Budget, 1973; contbr. articles to profl. publs. Recipient Comfort Starr award in econs. Oberlin Coll., 1952; Disting. Alumnus award U. Mich., 1980. Mem. Nat. Economists Club (v.p. 1973-74, pres. 1974-75, chmn. bd. 1975-76, gov. 1976-79), Am. Econ. Assn. (com. on status of women 1975-78), Am. Fin. Assn. (dir. 1969-71). Democrat. Home: 243 Willowbrook Ave Stamford CT 06902-7020

TEETS, JOHN WILLIAM, retired diversified company executive; b. Elgin, Ill., Sept. 15, 1933; s. John William and Maudie Teets; m. Nancy Kerchenfaut, June 25, 1965; children: Jerri, Valerie Sue, Heidi Jayne, Suzanne. Student, U. Ill.; LLD (hon.), Trinity Coll., 1982; DBA in Foodsvc. Mgmt. (hon.), Johnson and Wales U., 1991; D in Comml. Sci. (hon.), Western Internat. U., 1992. Pres., ptnr. Winter Garden Restaurant, Inc., Carpenterville, Ill., 1957-63; v.p. Greyhound Food Mgmt. Co.; pres. Post Houses, Inc., and Horne's Enterprises, Chgo., 1964-68; pres., chief operating officer John R. Thompson Co., Chgo., 1968-71; pres., corp. v.p. pub. restaurant divsn. Canteen Corp., Chgo., 1971-75; divsn. pres. Jacques Restaurant Group, 1975; exec. v.p., CEO Bonanza Internat. Co., Dallas, 1975; group v.p. food svcs., pres. Greyhound Food Mgmt., Inc. (now named Restaura), Phoenix, 1975; vice chmn. The Greyhound Corp., Phoenix, 1980; chmn., CEO Greyhound Corp. (now The Dial Corp), Phoenix, 1981-96; chmn., pres., CEO The Dial Corp, Phoenix, 1996-97; vice chmn. Pres.' Conf. on Foodservice Industry. Recipient Silver Plate award, Golden Plate award Internat. Foodsvc. Mgrs. Assn., 1980, Bus. Leadership award Harvard Bus. Sch. Club Ariz., 1985, Order of the Crown, Kingdom of Belgium, 1990, Ellis Island medal of honor Nat. Ethnic Coalition of Orgns. Found., 1995; named Top Bus. Spkr. of Yr., Forbes Mag., 1990, Capt. of Achievement, Acad. of Achievement, 1992, CEO of Yr., Leaders Mag., 1986. Mem. Nat. Inst. Foodsvc. Industry (trustee), Am. Mgmt. Assn., Christian Businessmen's Assn. (chmn. steering com. 1977). Office: JW Teets Enterprises LLC 1850 N Central Ave Phoenix AZ 85004-4527

TEEVAN, RICHARD COLLIER, psychology educator; b. Shelton, Conn., June 12, 1919; s. Daniel Joseph and Elizabeth (Halliwell) T.; m. Virginia Agnes Stehle, July 28, 1945; children—Jan Elizabeth, Kim Ellen, Clay Collier, Allison Tracy. B.A., Wesleyan U., Middletown, Conn., 1951; M.A., U. Mich., 1952, Ph.D., 1955. Rubber buffer Sponge Rubber Product Co., Derby, Conn., 1939-41; with U. Mich., 1951-57, teaching fellow, 1951-53, instr., 1953-57; asst. prof. Smith Coll., 1957-60; assoc. prof. Bucknell U., 1960-64, prof., 1964-69; chmn. psychology, prof. SUNY-Albany, 1969—; pres. Teevan Assocs., Cons., 1991—; cons. on coll. teaching, 1989—. Author: Reinforcement, 1961, Instinct, 1961, Color Vision, 1961, Measuring Human Motivation, 1962, Theories of Motivation in Learning, 1964, Theories of Motivation in Personality and Social Psychology, 1964, Motivation, 1967, Fear of Failure, 1969, Readings in Elementary Psychology, 1973; contbr. articles to sci. jours. Served to capt. AUS, 1941-47; prisoner of war 1943-45, Ger. Office Naval Research grantee, 1958-72; recipient Lindbach award Bucknell U., 1966. Mem. AAAS, AAUP, Am. Psychol. Assn. (Disting. visitor 1981-85), Eastern Psychol. Assn., Phi Beta Kappa, Sigma Xi. Home: 45 Pine St Delmar NY 12054-3413 Office: SUNY Dept Psychology 1400 Washington Ave Albany NY 12222-0100

TEGTMEYER, RENE DESLOGE, lawyer; b. St. Louis, Jan. 5, 1934; s. Adolph Henry and Elise (Desloge) T.; m. Joan Lynch, Aug. 2, 1969; children: Stephen W., Jean M. BSME, Wash. U., 1956; JD, George Washington U., 1963. Bar: Va., D.C., U.S. Ct. Appeals (Fed. cir.). Patent examiner U.S. Patent and Trademark Office, Washington, 1959-64; specialist legis. and internat. affairs U.S. Patent and Trademark Office, 1964, dir. legis. and internat. affairs, 1964-71, asst. commr. for appeals legis. and trademarks, 1971-73, asst. commr. for trademarks, 1973-75, asst. commr. for patents, 1975-89; ptnr. Fish & Richardson, Washington, 1989-95, of counsel, 1996—. Contbr. articles to profl. jours. Lt. USAF, 1956-59; with Res. 1960-68. Congl. fellowship Am. Polit. Sci. Assn., 1967-68. Mem. ABA, Am. Intellectual Property Law Assn., Fed. Bar Assn., N.J. Patent Law Assn. (Jefferson medal 1985), Pi Tau Sigma, Tau Beta Pi. Republican. Roman Catholic. Avocations: reading, skiing. Home: 85 Woodchuck Pl Ridgway CO 81432 Office: Fish & Richardson 601 13th St NW Washington DC 20005-3807

TEGUH, COLLIN, osteopathic physician, educator; b. Medan, Indonesia, Aug. 25, 1957; s. Tonga and Tsit Wati (Salim) T.; m. Lisa Hom; children: Justen W., Branden C. BA, U. Calif. San Diego, 1983; DO, U. Osteo. Medicine Des Moines, 1991. Rsch. asst. Scripp Meml. and Whittier Inst. for Endocrinology & Diabetes, LaJolla, Calif., 1983-87, U. Osteo. Medicine and Health Scis., Des Moines, 1988-90; intern, resident San Bernardino (Calif.) County Med. Ctr., 1991-93; staff physician, com. mem. Family Practice Assn. Med. Mgmt., San Diego, 1994—; asst. clin. prof. U. Calif. San Diego, LaJolla, 1995—, Coll. Osteo. Medicine, Pomona, Calif., 1995—. Contbr. articles to profl. jours. Mem. Am. Osteo. Assn., Am. Acad. Family Physician, San Diego Osteo. Med. Assn., San Diego Acad. Family Physicians, U. Calif. San Diego Alumni Assn., U. Osteo. Medicine and Health Scis. Alumni Assn. Avocations: snorkeling, hiking, reading, horticulture, travel. Office: Family Practice Assoc 3780 El Cajon Blvd San Diego CA 92105-1033

TEHRANI, FLEUR TAHER, electrical engineer, educator, researcher; b. Tehran, Iran, Feb. 16, 1956; came to U.S., 1984; d. Hassan and Pourandokht (Monfared) T. BS in Elec. Engring., Sharif U. of Tech., Tehran, 1975; DIC in Comm. Engring., Imperial Coll. Sci. and Tech., London, 1977; MSc in Comm. Engring., U. London, 1977, PhD in Elec. Engring., 1981. Registered profl. engr., Calif. Comm. engr. Planning Orgn. of Iran, Tehran, 1977-78; lectr. A elec. engring. Robert Gordon's Inst. Tech., Aberdeen, U.K., 1982-83; lectr. II elec. engring. South Bank U., London, 1984; asst. prof. elec. engring. Calif. State U., Fullerton, 1985-91, assoc. prof. elec. engring., 1991-94, prof. elec. engring., 1994—; vis. assoc. prof. elec. engring. Drexel U., Phila., 1987-88; sys. cons. Telebit Corp., Cupertino. Calif., 1985; engring. cons. PRD, Inc., Dresher, Pa., 1989-92; mem. NASA/Am. Soc. Engring. Edn. summer faculty Jet Propulsion Lab., Calif. Inst. Tech., Pasadena, 1995, 96. Contbr. articles to profl. jours.; patentee in field. Recipient Best Ann. Rsch. Manuscript award Assn. for the Advancement of Med. Instrumentation, 1993, Outstanding Excellence in Rsch. Faculty award Calif. State U., 1993. Mem. IEEE, Women in Sci. and Engring. (chair Calif. State U. chpt. 1990-91), Assn. Profs. and Scholars of Iranian Heritage (pres. 1991-92), Sigma Delta Epsilon. Avocations: music, literature, poetry, stamp collecting. Office: Calif State U Dept Elec Engring 800 N State College Blvd Fullerton CA 92831-3547

TEHRANIAN, MAJID, political economy and communications educator; b. Iran, Mar. 22, 1937; m. Katharine Kia; children: Terrence, Yalda, John, Maryam. BA in Govt., Dartmouth Coll., 1959; MA in Middle Eastern Studies, Harvard U., 1961, PhD in Polit. Economy and Govt., 1969. Asst. prof. econs. Lesley Coll., 1964-69; assoc. prof. polit. sci. New Coll. U. South Fla., 1969-71; dir. social planning Plan Orgn. of Iran, 1971-72; sr. analyst, dir. rsch. Indsl. Mgmt. Inst., 1972-74; dir. prospective planning project Nat. Iranian Radio & TV, 1974-75; prof., founding dir. Iran Communications & Devel. Inst., 1976-78; program specialist communication planning and studies Div. Devel. of Communication Systems UNESCO, Paris, 1979-80; fellow Communication Inst., East West Ctr., 1981-82; chair dept. communication U. Hawaii, Manoa, 1986-88, prof. dept. communication, 1981—, dir. Matsunaga Inst. Peace, 1990-92, dir. Toda Inst. Global Peace Policy Rsch., 1996—; vis. scholar Inst. for Communication Rsch., Stanford U., 1977; vis. fellow St. Anthony's Coll., Oxford U., 1978-79; vis. scholar Ctr. for Internat. Affairs MIT, 1980-81, Can., U.S. and USSR universities, 1988; rsch. affiliate Ctr. for Middle Eastern Studies, Harvard U., 1980-81; vis. prof. dept. govt. Harvard Summer Sch., 1989-90; dir.-elect and dir. Inst. for Peace, U. Hawaii, coun. and exec. com., 1986—; rsch. fellow Social Sci. Rsch. Inst., U. Hawaii, Manoa, 1982-83, 84-86; lectr. in field. Author: Towards a Systematic Theory of National Development, 1974, Socio-Economic and Communications Indicators in Development Planning, 1981, Technologies of Power, 1990; co-author: The Middle East: Its Government and Politics, 1972, The Global Context of the Formation of Domestic Communications Policies, 1975, Policy Towards Social Sciences in Asia and Oceania, 1978, Human Security and Global Governance, 1996, many others; editor Communications Policy for Development, 1977, Letters from Jerusalem, 1990, Deconstructing Paradise: Dependency, Development and Discourse in Hawaii, 1990; co-editor: Restructuring for World Peace: On the Threshold of the 21st Century, 1992, Globalism and Its Discontent, 1997; contbr. articles to profl. jours.; reviewer in field. Scholar Dartmouth Coll., 1955-59, Fujio Matsuda scholar, 1990-91; Jane Addams Peace Found. fellow, 1961, Ford Found. fellow Harvard U., 1959-61, fellow St. Anthony's Coll., Oxford, 1978-79, fellow East West Ctr. Communication Isnt., 1977, 81, 82; rsch. grantee Social Sci. Rsch. Inst., U. Hawaii, Manoa, 1982-85, UNESCO rsch. grantee, 1983-84, Can. Studies Faculty Enrichment grantee, 1988, Hawaii Interactive TV System Curriculum Devel. grantee, 1989; recipient Dartmouth Colby & Grimez Prizes, 1959, Excellence in Teaching award 1989, Soka U. award of highest honor. Fellow World Acad. Art & Sci.; mem. Internat. Inst. Communications (bd. trustees 1979-81), Internat. Communication Assn. (conf. theme chair for Asia 1989), Pacific Telecommunication Coun., Middle East Studies Assn. N.Am., Middle East Econs. Assn. (nat. adv. bd.), Soc. for Iranian Studies (founding exec. sec. 1967-71), Worldview Internat. Found. Avocations: swimming, tennis, chess, poetry. Home: 2627 Manoa Rd Honolulu HI 96822-1767 Office: U Hawaii Dept Communication Honolulu HI 96822 also: Toda Inst 1600 Kapiolaini Blvd Ste 1111 Honolulu HI 96814

TEICH, MALVIN CARL, electrical engineering educator; b. N.Y.C., May 4, 1939; s. Sidney R. and Loretta K. Teich. S.B. in Physics, MIT, 1961; M.S.E.E., Stanford U., 1962; Ph.D. in Quantum Electronics, Cornell U., 1966. Research scientist MIT Lincoln Lab., Lexington, Mass., 1966-67; prof. engring. sci. Columbia U., N.Y.C., 1967-96; prof. emeritus Columbia U., N.Y.C, 1996—; chmn. dept. elec. engring. Columbia U., N.Y.C., 1978-80, mem. Columbia Radiation Lab./faculty applied physics dept.; prof. biomed. engring., cognitive and neural systems Boston U., 1995—; mem. Ctr. Photonics Rsch., Hearing Rsch. Ctr.; mem. sci. bd. Inst. Physics, Czech Acad. Scis., Prague. Author: (with B.E.A. Saleh) Fundamentals of Photonics, 1991; dep. editor Quantum Optics, 1988-92; bd. editors Jour. Visual Comm. and Image Representation, 1989-92, Jemná Mechanika a Optika, 1994—; contbr. articles to profl. jours.; patentee in field. Recipient Citation Classic award Inst. for Sci. Info., 1981; Meml. Gold medal of Palacky U., Czech Republic, 1992; Guggenheim Meml. Found. fellow, 1973. Fellow AAAS, IEEE (Browder J. Thompson Meml. prize 1969, Morris E. Leeds award, 1997), Optical Soc. Am. (editl. adv. panel Optics Letters 1977-79), Am. Phys. Soc., Acoustical Soc. Am.; mem. Assn. Rsch. in Otolaryngology, Biomed. Engring. Soc., Sigma Xi, Tau Beta Pi. Office: Boston U Dept Elec and Computer Engr 44 Cummington St Boston MA 02215-2407

TEICHER, MORTON IRVING, social worker, anthropologist, educator; b. N.Y.C., Mar. 10, 1920; s. Sam and Celia (Roth) T.; m. Mildred Adler, Oct. 4, 1941; children: Phyllis Margaret, Oren Jonathan. B.S. in Social Sci., CCNY, 1940; M.S.W., U. Pa., 1942; Ph.D., U. Toronto, 1956. Chief social worker in New Eng. VA, 1946-48; asst. prof., clin. tchr. U. Toronto, 1948-56; cons. Oppenheimer Coll., No. Rhodesia (Zambia), 1962-63; dean Sch. Social Work, Yeshiva U., 1956-72, prof., 1956-72; prof. Sch. Social Work, U. N.C., Chapel Hill, 1972-81, 83-85; dean Sch. Social Work, U. N.C., 1972-81; adj. prof. dept. anthropology, 1972-85; dean emeritus Sch. Social Work, U. N.C., 1985—; prof. sociology and psychiatry, dir. Center on Aging, U. Miami, Coral Gables, 1981-83; instr. Elders Inst. Fla. Internat. U., 1987-88; faculty mentorr Walden U., 1993—; seminar assoc. creativity in sci. NYU, 1959-73; cons. Bar Ilan U., Israel, 1965-69, VA, 1965-69; cons., vis. prof. Henrietta Szold Inst., Jerusalem, 1975; preceptor Ctrl. Inst. Mgmt., Sr. Civil Svc., Israel, 1975; external examiner U. Zambia, 1968-69; cons. in field, 1950—; cons. U. W.I., 1982; chmn. U.S. com. Internat. Coun. Social Welfare, 1978-79; mem. adminstrv. bd. Sch. Pub. Health, U. N.C., 1974-79. Author: Windigo Psychosis, 1960, Looking Homeward: A Thomas Wolfe Photo Album, 1993; co-author Distant Partners, 1990; sr. editor Inside Books, 1988-89; co-editor: Reaching the Aged, Data-Based Planning in the Field of Aging, 1982; book rev. editor: Jour. Jewish Communal Service, 1961-68, Jewish Floridian, 1982-86; mem. editorial bd. Human Orgn., 1963-66, Jour. Am. Soc. Cybernetics, 1970-72, Ednl. Gerontology, 1978-84; book reviewer South Fla. Jewish Jour., Phila. Jewish Exponent, Metrowest Jewish News, Jerusalem Post; also contbr. numerous articles to profl. jours., books. Rsch. chmn. Westchester Dem. Com., 1958-62; bd. dirs. Lake Success Capital Corp., 1967-71; trustee Wurzweiler Found., 1966-90, Coler Found., 1970-72; participant Fla. Gov.'s Challenge Program, 1981; exec. sec. Nat. Conf. Jewish Communal Svc., 1968-70; mem. exec. com. Miami chpt. Am. Jewish Com., 1981-83, mem.-at-large nat. exec. coun., 1980-82; bd. dirs. N.Y. Social Work Recruiting Ctr., 1960-70; mem. policy bd. Carolina Population Ctr., 1973-77; bd. dirs. Internat. Conf. Jewish Communal Svc., 1965-85, Hillel, U. Miami, 1981-83, Beth David Synagogue, Miami, 1991—; pres. Durham-Chapel Hill Jewish Fedn., 1980; mem. planning and budgeting com. Project Renewal Commn., Miami Jewish Fedn., 1981—; adv. coun. Sch. Social Work Barry U., 1986—. 1st lt. AUS, 1942-46, CBI. Recipient Disting. Alumnus cert. U. Pa., 1979; Louis Round Wilson Libr. fellow U. N.C., 1995—. Fellow Am. Anthropol. Assn.; mem. AAUP, Am. Assn. Ret. Persons (v.p. South Miami Beach chpt. 1992), Acad. Cert. Social Workers, Nat. Assn. Social Workers (chmn. Westchester chpt. 1960-62, mem. commn. ethics 1964-67, mem. exec. com. Ea. N.C. chpt. 1972-74, chmn. profl. advancement travel com. 1980-83), Thomas Wolfe Soc. (dir. 1981—, v.p. 1985-87, pres. 1987-91, Citation of Merit 1992). Anthrop. field work among the Eskimo and Iroquois; tour leader to internat. social welfare confs. in Athens, Helsinki, Nairobi, The Hague, San Juan, Jerusalem, Hong Kong, and Brighton, Eng. Home: Jockey Club III Apt 1851 11111 Biscayne Blvd Miami FL 33189-3494

TEICHNER, LESTER, management consulting executive; b. Chgo., Apr. 21, 1944; s. Ben Bernard and Eva Bertha (Weinberg) T.; m. Barbara Rae Bush, Jan. 30, 1966 (div. Aug. 1969); m. Doris Jean Ayres, Jan. 31, 1980; children: Lauren Ayres, Caroline Ayres. BSEE, U. Ill., 1965; MBA in Mktg. and Fin., U. Chgo., 1969. Sales engr. Westinghouse Electric Corp., Chgo., 1965-69; v.p. ops. Intec Inc., Chgo., 1969-74; pres., CEO The Chgo. Group Inc., 1974—, also bd. dirs.; bd. dirs. Strategic Processing Inc., N.Y.C., Dees Communications Ltd., Vancouver, B.C., Maxcor Mfg. Co., Colorado Springs; CEO, bd. dirs. Axcess Worldwide Ltd., Coal Gasification, Inc., Chgo.; guest lectr. U. Chgo. Grad. Sch. Bus., 1982-95. Co-inventor U.S. patent electronic marketplace; contbr. articles to profl. publs. Mem. The Chgo. Forum, 1976—; bd. dirs. Am. Israeli C. of C. Mem. Am. Mgmt. Assn., Am. Mktg. Assn., Midwest Planning Assn. (bd. dirs. 1981). Republican. Jewish. Avocations: comml. renovation, astronomy, skiing, venture capital investment. Home: 2230 N Seminary Ave Chicago IL 60614-3507 Office: Chgo Group Inc 744 N Wells St Chicago IL 60610-3521

TEICHROB, CAROL, Canadian provincial official; b. Sask., Can., Aug. 27, 1939; d. J. Delbert and Elizabeth (Spenst) Sproxton; m. Donald P. Teichrob, Mar. 1, 1958; children: Lori, Sharon, James. Sr. matriculation, Notre Dame Convent, Morinville, Alta., Can. Cert. profl. ct. reporter, exec. mem. Can. and Saskatchewan Fedns. Agriculture, 1976-81; chmn. Can. Turkey Mktg. Agy., 1980-81, Plains Poultry Wynyard, Sask., 1981-88; founding ptnr. Primrose Books, Saskatoon, Sask., 1988—. Reeve, Rural Municipality of Corman Park, Saskatoon, 1981-91; active U. Sask. Senate, 1981-86; mem. legis. assembly N.D.P. Caucus, 1991-96; appointed to cabinet as Min. of Edn., 1991-93, Min. of Mcpl. Govt. responsible for Sasktel, 1995—. Recipient Golden Wheel award Sask. Rotary, 1990; named Woman of Yr. in Bus., Sask. YWCA, 1981, Woman of Yr., 1982. Mem. Saskatoon C. of C. Office: Min Mcpl Govt, Legis Bldg Rm 307, Regina, SK Canada S4S 0B3

TEILLON, L. PIERRE, JR., lawyer; b. N.Y.C., Nov. 15, 1943. AB, Yale U., 1965; LLB, Columbia U., 1968. Bar: Pa. 1968. Mem. Heckscher, Teillon, Terrill & Sager, P.C., West Conshohocken, Pa. Mem. ABA (real property, probate and trust sects.), Am. Coll. Trust and Estate Counsel, Pa. Bar Assn. (real property, probate and trust sects.), Phila. Bar Assn. (past chmn. probate sect.). Office: Heckscher Teillon Terrill & Sager 100 Four Falls Corp Ctr Ste 300 West Conshohocken PA 19428

TEIMAN, RICHARD B., lawyer; b. Bklyn., May 19, 1938. AB, Princeton U., 1959; LLB, Harvard U., 1962. Bar: N.Y. 1963. Ptnr. Winston & Strawn and predecessor Cole and Deitz, N.Y.C., 1968—. Trustee Citizens Budget Commn., 1993—. Mem. Assn. Bar City N.Y. (com. Admiralty 1975-78, 87, chair 1988-91), Maritime Law Assn. (com. Maritime Financing 1980—, chmn. subcom. Recodification U.S. Ship Mortgage Act 1986-91, chmn. subcom. U.S. Coastguard, Citizenship and Related Matters 1988-94), Phi Beta Kappa. Home: 5 Pryer Ln Larchmont NY 10538-4012 Office: Winston & Strawn 200 Park Ave New York NY 10166-0005

TEIRSTEIN, PAUL SHEPHERD, physician, health facility administrator; b. N.Y.C., July 5, 1955; s. Alvin Stanley and Alice Teirstein. BA in Biology, Vassar Coll., 1976; MD, CUNY, 1980. Diplomate Am. Bd. Internal Medicine and Cardiovascular Diseases. With Lab. of Vision Rsch. NIH, Bethesda, Md., 1977-79; intern and resident Brigham & Women's Hosp., Boston, 1980-83; fellow in cardiology Stanford (Calif.) U., 1983-86; fellow in advanced coronary angioplasty Mid-Am. Heart Inst., Kansas City, Mo., 1986-87; fellow in stents, artherectomy and lasers NIH, Bethesda, 1987; dir. interventional cardiology Scripps Clinic and Rsch. Found., La Jolla, Calif., 1987—; presenter at Am. Coll. Cardiology, 1987-94, Am. Heart Assn., 1990-93, The French Hosp., San Luis Obispo, Calif., 1989, St. Luke's Med. Ctr., Phoenix, 1989, Cardiology for the Cons., Rancho Santa Fe, 1989, U. Calif., Irvine, 1989, ACP, Scottsdale, Ariz., 1989, Presbyn. Hosp., Whittier, Calif, 1989, St. Jude Med. Ctr., Fullerton, Calif., 1990, Oscala Med. Ctr., Osaka, Japan, 1992, Cedars-Sinai Med. Ctr., L.A., 1993, European Congress of Cardiology, Nice, France, 1993, Tokyo U., 1993, Lenox Hill Hosp., N.Y., 1993, Japanese Soc. Internat. Cardiology, 1994, Nat. Hindu Hosp., Bombay, 1994, G.B. Pant Hosp., Delhi, India, 1994, Escort's Hosp., 1994, B.M. Birla Hosp., Calcutta, 1994, Shaare Zedek Med. Ctr., Jerusalem, 1994, XV Congresso da Sociedad de Cardiologie de Sao Paulo, Ribeirao Preto, Brazil, 1994, and others. Grantee NSF, 1975. Fellow Am. Coll. Cardiology, Assn. for Rsch. in Vision and Ophthalmology, Beta Beta Beta, Alpha Omega Alpha. Office: Scripps Clinic & Rsch Found 10666 N Torrey Pines Rd La Jolla CA 92037-1027

TEITEL, SIMON, economist, educator; b. Buenos Aires, Dec. 5, 1928; came to U.S., 1961; s. Gregorio and Regina (Tarnorudzka) T.; m. Raquel Schenkolewski, June 20, 1954; children: Rut Gabriela, Ariel Dan. BS in Indsl. Engring., U. Buenos Aires, 1956, MS in Indsl. Engring., 1963; PhD in

Econs., Columbia U., 1969. Econ. affairs officer Ctr. for Indsl. Devel., UN, N.Y.C., 1963-67; sr. indsl. devel. officer policies and programming div. UN Indsl. Devel. Orgn., Vienna, Austria, 1967-68; sr. cons. Office Program Advisor to Pres., Inter-Am. Devel. Bank, Washington, 1968-76, sr. econ. advisor econ. and social devel. dept., 1976-89; sr. rsch. adv., 1989-92; rsch. cons. World Bank, Washington, 1992-94; econ. cons. UN, 1994—; adj. assoc. prof. econs. Cath. U. Am., Washington, 1971-77, adj. prof., 1977-81, prof., 1981-88; adj. prof. Am. U., 1992; professorial lectr. Georgetown U., Washington, 1996—; vis. lectr. internat. econs. Yale U., New Haven, 1977-78; lectr. to numerous profl. assns. and univs.; occasional referee Econ. Devel. and Cultural Change, Jour. Devel. Econs., World Devel., L.Am. Rsch. Rev.; mem. spl. internat. panel on appropriate techs. for developing countries Bd. on Sci. and Tech. for Internat. Devel., NAS-NAE, 1974-77. Author: Politica Economica en Centro y Periferia, 1976, Integracion Economica, 1977, Trade, Stability, Technology and Equity in Latin America, 1982, Symposium on Technological Change and Industrial Development, 1984, Growth, Reform and Adjustment: Latin America's Trade and Macroeconomic Policies in the 1970s and 1980s, 1986, Handbook of Latin American Studies, Library of Congress, Economics: Argentina, 1989, Towards a New Development Strategy for Latin America, 1992, Industrial and Technological Development, 1993, Technology and Enterprise Development, 1994, From Autarky to Competition-Technology and Skills in Zimbabwe's Manufacturing, 1997, Resource Endowments, Industrialization and Exports of Manufactures, 1997; contbr. articles to profl. jours. Mem. Am. Econ. Assn. Jewish. Home: 5610 Wisconsin Ave Apt 606 Chevy Chase MD 20815-4417

TEITELBAUM, LEE E., law educator; b. New Orleans, Nov. 4, 1941. BA magna cum laude, Harvard Coll., 1963; LLB, Harvard U., 1966; LLM, Northwestern U., 1968. Bar: Ill. Staff atty. Chgo. Lawyer Project, 1966-68; asst. prof. law U. N.D., 1968-70; assoc. prof. law SUNY, Buffalo, 1970-73; vis. assoc. prof. law U. N.Mex. Law Sch., 1972, assoc. prof. law, 1973-74, prof. law, 1974-87; prof. law, dir. Ctr. for the Study of Legal Policy Relating to Children Ind. U. Law Sch., 1980-81, vis. prof., 1987; vis. prof. U. Utah Coll. Law, 1985, prof. law, 1986—, assoc. dean acad. affairs, 1987-90, acting dean, 1988, dean, 1990—, Alfred C. Emery prof. law, 1994—; fellow legal history program U. Wis., Madison, 1984; mem. test audit subcom. Law Sch. Admissions Coun. Author: (with A. Gough) Beyond Control: Status Offenders in the Juvenile Court, 1977 (with W.V. Stapleton) In Defense of Youth: The Role of Counsel in American Juvenile Courts, 1972; contbr. articles to profl. jours.; bd. editors Law & Soc. Rev., 1982-87, Law & Policy, Jour. Legal Edn., 1990-92. Fellow ABA (reporter ABA-IJA project on standards for juvenile justics, standards relating to the role of counsel for pvt. parties 1979); mem. Law & Soc. Assn. (bd. trustees 1977-80), Utah Minority Bar Assn. (award), Assn. Am. Law Schs. Office: Univ of Utah Office Dean Coll Law Salt Lake City UT 84112*

TEITELBAUM, MARILYN LEAH, special education educator; b. Bklyn., June 12, 1930; d. Abraham and Fay (Ingis) Nober; m. Harry Teitelbaum, Nov. 7, 1953; children: Mark, David, Deborah. BA, Bklyn. Coll., 1953; MS, Queens Coll., 1968, L.I. U., 1982. Cert. tchr., N.Y. Elem. and spl. edn. tchr. Franklin Square, Franklin's Square, N.Y., 1955-57; elem. tchr. Manetto Hill Sch., Plainview, N.Y., 1968-70; elem. tchr. Northport (N.Y.) Sch. Dist., 1970-78, spl. edn. tchr., 1978-87; pvt. spl. edn. tchr. Laguana Niguel, Calif., 1988—. Author: Teachers as Consumers-What They Should Know About the Hearing Impaired Child, 1981. V.p. Friends of Libr., Laguna Niguel Pub. Libr., 1988—. Recipient outstanding tchr. award Northport PTA, 1987. Mem. NEA, Coun. Exceptional Children, United Tchrs. Northport, Orange County Dyslexic Soc. Avocations: reading, travel, painting, piano. Home: 29562 Avante Laguna Niguel CA 92677-7949

TEITELBAUM, PHILIP, psychologist; b. Bklyn., Oct. 9, 1928; s. Bernard and Betty (Schechter) T.; m. Osnat Boné; children: Benjamin, Daniel, David, Jonathan, Gideon. B.S., CCNY, 1950; M.A., Johns Hopkins U., 1952, Ph.D., 1954. Instr., asst. prof. physiol. psychology Harvard U., 1954-59; assoc. prof. psychology U. Pa., Phila., 1959-63; prof. U. Pa., 1963-73; prof. psychology U. Ill.-Urbana-Champaign, 1973-85, emeritus prof., 1985—, Disting. prof. Ctr. Advanced Studies, 1980-85; grad. research prof. U. Fla., Gainesville, 1984—. Author: Fundamental Principles of Physiological Psychology, 1967; editor: (with E. Satinoff) Motivation: Handbook Behavioral Neurobiology, 1983. Contbr. chpts. to books, articles to profl. jours. Fellow Ctr. for Advanced Study in Behavorial Scis., Stanford U., 1975-76, Fulbright fellow Tel Aviv U., 1978-79, Guggenheim fellow, 1984-85, Carnegie Found. fellow Inst. Neurol. Scis., U. Pa. Med. Sch., 1958-59. Fellow APA (pres. div. physiol. psychology, disting. sci. contbn. award 1978), Am. Psychol. Soc. (William James fellow); mem. NAS, AAAS, Am. Physiol. Soc., Soc. for Neurosci., Soc. Exptl. Psychology. Home: 2239 NW 17th Ave Gainesville FL 32605-3909 Office: U Fla Dept Psychology Gainesville FL 32611

TEITELBAUM, STEVEN LAZARUS, pathology educator; b. Bklyn., June 29, 1938; s. Hyman and Rose Leah (Harnick) T.; m. Marilyn Ruth Schaffner; children: Caren Beth, Aaron Michael, Rebecca Lee. BA, Columbia U., 1960; MD, Washington U., St. Louis, 1964. Intern Washington U. Sch. Medicine, St. Louis, 1964-65, 3d. yr. asst. resident, ACS clin. fellow, 1967-68; intern NYU, 1965-66, 2d yr. resident, 1966-67; assoc. pathologist Jewish Hosp. at Washington U. Med. Ctr., St. Louis, 1969-89, pathologist-in-chief, 1987-96; asst. pathologist Barnes Hosp., St. Louis, 1986—; pathologist St. Louis Shriners Hosp. for Crippled Children, 1986—; Wilma and Roswell Messing prof. pathology Washington U. Sch. Medicine, St. Louis, 1987—; mem. Orthopedics and Musculoskeletal Study Sect. NIH, 1983-87. Contbr. numerous sci. articles to med. jours., 1965—, 12 chpts. to med. books and texts, 1976—; mem. editorial bd. Calcified Tissue Internat., 1980-85, 89-91, Human Pathology; mem. bd. assoc. editors Jour. Orthopaedic Rsch., Jour. Cellular Biochemistry. Mem. Am. Soc. Clin. Investigation, Assn. Am. Physicians, Am. Acad. Orthopaedic Surgeons (Ann Doner Vaughan Kappa Delta award 1988), Paget's Disease Found. (adv. panel), Am. Soc. for Bone and Mineral Rsch. (pres.). Office: Washington U Sch Medicine 216 S Kingshighway Blvd Saint Louis MO 63110-1026

TEITELBAUM, STEVEN USHER, lawyer; b. Chgo., Nov. 29, 1945; s. Jerome H. and Marion Judith (Berlin) T.; m. Cathy Ann Rosenblatt, Mar. 11, 1984. A.B., Boston U., 1967; J.D., Union U., 1975. Bar: N.Y. 1976, U.S. Dist. Ct. (no. dist.) N.Y. 1976, U.S. Supreme Ct. 1980, U.S. Ct. Appeals (2d cir.) 1993; cert. arbitrator. Sr. atty. N.Y. State Dept. Health, Albany, 1976-79; counsel N.Y. State Office Bus. Permits, Albany, 1979-83; sole practice, Albany, 1983-95; dep. commr., gen. counsel N.Y. State Dept. Taxation and Fin., 1995—; staff judge advocate U.S. Army Res. Watervliet Arsenal, N.Y., 1978-84. Author: Streamlining the Regulatory Procedures of the Department of Agriculture, 1982. Active Found. Bd. Ctr. for Disabled, Empire State Performing Arts Ctr., Nat. Alumni Coun. Albany Law Sch.; bd. dirs. Nat. Kidney Found. Northeastern N.Y. Served with U.S. Army, 1968-69. Mem. Am. Arbitration Assn. (arbitrator 1979—), N.Y. State Bar Assn. (com. on pub. health 1976-80, faculty on adminstrv. law 1980, com. on adminstrv. law 1980-84, 93—, labor and employment sect., taxation sect. 1985—), Faculty State Local Tax Inst. Clubs: Fort Orange (Albany), Country Club Troy (N.Y.). Home: 17 Carstead Dr Slingerlands NY 12159-9266 Office: WA Harriman Office Campus Bldg 9 Rm 205 Albany NY 12227

TEITELL, CONRAD LAURENCE, lawyer, author; b. N.Y.C., Nov. 8, 1932; s. Benson and Belle (Altman) T.; m. Adele Mary Crummins, May 26, 1957; children: Beth Mary, Mark Lewis. A.B., U. Mich., 1954; LL.B., Columbia U., 1957; LL.M., N.Y. U., 1968. Bar: N.Y. 1958, D.C., 1968. Mem. Prerau & Teitell, White Plains, N.Y., 1964-96, Cummings & Lockwood, Stamford, Conn., 1996—; dir. Philanthropy Tax Inst., Old Greenwich, Conn., 1964—. Author: Philanthropy and Taxation, 5 vols., 1993-96; editor, pub. Taxwise Giving, 1964—; contbr. articles to legal jours. Served with U.S. Army, 1957. Recipient Disting. Svc. to Higher Edn. award Am. Coll. Pub. Relations Assn., 1970, Disting. Svc. award Nat. Com. on Planned Giving, 1990, Harrison Tweed Spl. Merit award Am. Law Inst./ABA, 1992. Fellow Am. Coll. Trust and Estate Counsel; mem. ABA (former co-chmn. com. charitable giving, trusts, founds.), Assn. of Bar of City of N.Y., Nat. Assn. Coll. Univ. Attys. Home: 16 Marlow Ct Riverside CT 06878-2614 Office: Cummings & Lockwood 4 Stamford Plz Stamford CT 06904 also: PO Box 299 Old Greenwich CT 06870-0299

TEIXEIRA, ARTHUR ALVES, food engineer, educator, consultant; b. Fall River, Mass., Jan. 30, 1944; s. Arthur Araujo and Emelia (Alves) T.; m. Jean E. Lamb, Dec. 26, 1966 (dec. Dec. 1983); children: A. Allan, Scott C.; m. Marjorie St. John, June 28, 1986; 1 stepchild, Craig St. John. PhD, U. Mass., 1971. Profl. engr., Fla., Mass. Rsch. engr. Ross Labs., Columbus, Ohio, 1971-73, R&D group leader, 1973-77; sr. cons. Arthur D. Little, Inc., Cambridge, Mass., 1977-82; assoc. prof. U. Fla., Gainesville, 1982-89, prof., 1989—; sci. advisor Escola Superior de Biotecnologia, Porto, Portugal, 1991-96, FMC Corp., Santa Clara, Calif., 1989-92; internat. cons., Brazil, Cuba, Hungary, Poland, Portugal, Romania, and Bulgaria; reviewer USDA, Washington, 1991—. Author: Computerized Food Processing Operations, 1989; contbr. 8 chpts. to books, 30 articles to profl. jours. Judge Internat. Sci. Fair, Orlando, Fla., 1991. Sr. Guest fellow NATO, 1988, 89; Fulbright grantee U.S. Info. Agy., 1990-91. Fellow Am. Soc. Agrl. Engrs. (dir. 1988-90, Paper awards 1988-89, assoc. editor Transactions of ASAE 1985—); mem. AICE, Inst. Food Technologists (mem. editl. bd. 1980-83), Am. Soc. Engring. Edn., Inst. Thermal Process Specialists, Coun. on Agrl. Sci. and Tech., R & D Assocs. Republican. Roman Catholic. Achievements include design of on-line process control system to assure safety of sterilized canned foods; tech. and econ. feasiblity for radiation sterilization of disposable feeding devices; research in computer optimization and control of food sterilization processes. Office: U Fla Rogers Hall Gainesville FL 32611-0570

TEIXEIRA, JOSEPH, advertising executive; b. Azores, Portugal, Aug. 11, 1949; came to U.S., 1961, naturalized, 1968; s. Fernando J. and Luisa M. (Mendonca) T.; m. Angelica Maria Cabral, Oct. 12, 1974; children: Christine, Debora. B.S. Bently Coll., 1975. Vice pres. Arnold & Co., Boston, 1978-80, sr. v.p., 1980-82, exec. v.p., 1982-95, exec. v.p., CFO, 1995—. Served with U.S. Army, 1969-71. Roman Catholic. Office: Arnold Comms Inc 101 Arch St Boston MA 02110-1130

TEJA, AMYN SADRUDIN, chemical engineering educator, consultant; b. Zanzibar, Tanzania, May 11, 1946; came to U.S., 1980; s. Sadrudin N. and Amina (Dharsi) T.; m. Carole Rosina Thurlow, July 3, 1971; children: Kerima Amy, Adam Riaz. BSc in Engring., U. London, London, 1968; PhD, U. London, 1972. Intern Warren Springs Lab., Stevenage, Eng., summer 1966, Brit. Gas Corp., London, summer 1968; rsch. fellow in chem. engring. Loughborough (U.K.) U. Tech., 1971-74; chem. engring. lectr. Loughborough (Eng.) U. Tech., 1974-80; assoc. prof. chem. engring. Ga. Inst. Tech., Atlanta, 1980-83, prof., 1984-90, regents prof. Woodruff Sch. Mech. Engring., 1991—, regents prof. Sch. Chem. Engring., 1990—, dir. Fluid Properties Rsch. Inst., 1985—, co-dir. Specialty Separations Ctr., 1992—, assoc. dir. grad. studies, 1994—; vis. assoc. prof. chem. engring. U. Del., Newark, 1978-79, Ohio State U., 1980; cons. Laporte Chems., Eng., 1971, Mobil Rsch. and Devel. Co., N.J., 1979, Conoco Ltd., Humberside Refinery, Eng., 1980, Milliken Chem. Co., Spartanburg, S.C., 1981-83, Hoechst Celanese Corp., Corpus Christi, Tex., 1984, Charlotte, 1992. Philip Morris U.S.A., Richmond, Va., 1984-87, DuPont Co., 1988, Union Carbide Corp., South Charleston, W.Va., 1989—, Shell Oil Co., 1989-93; presenter in field, reviewer various jours. Editor: Chemical Engineering and the Environment, 1981; mem. editl. bd. Reports on the Progress of Applied Chemistry, 1972-76, Critical Reports on Applied Chemistry, 1976-80, Jour. Chem. and Engring. Data, 1991—, Chem. Engring. Rsch. Compendium, 1990—, Jour. Supercritical Fluids, 1990—; assoc. editor The Chem. Engring. Jour., 1973—; contbr. more than 170 articles to profl. jours. Recipient Hinchley medal Instn. Chem. Engrs., 1968, IBM Rsch. scholarship, 1968-71, Gas Coun. Rsch. scholarship, 1968-71, Brit. Coun. Younger Rsch. Workers award, 1977, Outstanding Tchr. award Omega Chi Epsilon, 1990. Mem. AIChE (pub. com. 1992—, jour. rev.), Am. Soc. Engring. Edn., Am. Chem. Soc., Sigma Xi (v.p. Ga. Tech. chpt. 1991-92. pres. 1992-93, Supr. Outstanding MS Thesis in Engring. 1984, 90, Supr. Outstanding PhD Thesis 1993, 96, Sustained Rsch. award 1987). Avocations: tennis, science fiction. Home: 6282 Indian Field Norcross GA 30092-1372 Office: Ga Inst Tech Dept Chem Engring Atlanta GA 30332-0100

TEJADA, FRANCISCO, physician, educator; b. Moyobamba, San Martin, Peru, July 25, 1942; s. Francisco Tejada and Semiramis Reatequi; m. Barbara Ann Kotowski, Feb. 1, 1970; children: Anamaria, Semiramis, Barbara Lee, Francisco, James. BS, U. Nacional Mayor de San Marcos, Lima, Peru, 1961; MD, U. Peruana Cayetano Heredia, Lima, 1967. Diplomate Am. Bd. Internal Medicine, Am. Bd. Oncology. Resident in medicine Johns Hopkins U., Balt., 1969-72; sr. cancer researcher Nat. Cancer Inst., NIH, Bethesda, Md., 1972-75; asst. clin. dir. Comprehensive Cancer Ctr. Fla., Miami, Fla., 1975-80; asst. prof. U. Miami, 1975-79, assoc. prof., 1979-85, prof., 1985—; vis. prof. U. Peruana Cayetano Heredia, Lima, 1994—; sr. ptnr. Oncology Assocs., Miami, 1980-85; chief cancer control Papanicolaou Cancer Ctr., Miami, 1984-86; assoc. dir. AMC Cancer Rsch. Ctr., Denver, 1986-87; pres. Am. Oncology Ctrs., Miami, 1985—; prof. U. San Agustin, Arequipa, Peru, 1992—, U. Peruana Cayetano Heredia, Lima, Peru, 1994—; oncology expert Pan Am. Health Orgn., Washington, 1975-85, Nat. Cancer Inst., Bethesda, Md., 1984-86; dir. Miami Cancer Inst., 1980—; dir. Peruvian-Am. Endowment Inc., 1993—, v.p., 1995—. Editor Miami Med. Letter, 1986—; inventor cancer risk assessment. Mem. Beacon Coun., Miami, 1984, Latin Am. Cancer Info., Washington, 1976, Hispanic Cancer Rsch. Network, Washington, 1990; chpt. pres. Peruvian Am. Med. Soc., Miami, 1986. Lt. Peruvian Army, 1966-67. Recipient Gold Medal Merit award Ministry of Edn., Lima, 1959, Hipolito Unanue award Hipolito Unanue Inst., Lima, 1968. Fellow ACP, Johns Hopkins U., Nat. Cancer Inst.; mem. Colegio Medico del Perú, Am. Assn. Cancer Rsch., Am. Soc. Clin. Oncology, Am. Soc. Hematology, Bolivian Cancer Soc. (hon. mem.), Peruvian Cancer Soc. (hon. mem.), Chilean Soc. Cancer (hon. mem.), Argentinian Soc. Head and Neck Pathology (hon. mem.). Roman Catholic. Avocations: hiking, photography, reading. Office: 1321 NW 14th St Ste 401 Miami FL 33125-1655

TE KANAWA, KIRI, opera and concert singer; b. Gisborne, N.Z., Mar. 6, 1944; d. Thomas and Eleanor Te Kanawa; m. Desmond Park, Aug. 30, 1967; children—Antonia Aroha, Thomas Desmond. Student, St. Mary's Coll., Auckland, N.Z., 1957-60, London Opera Centre, 1966-69; DMus (hon.), Oxford U., 1983; DLitt (hon.), U. Warwick, Coventry, England, 1989. Joined Royal Opera House, London, 1971; appeared in role of Countess in Le Nozze di Figaro, 1973; U.S. debut in Santa Fe Festival, 1971; Met. Opera debut as Desdemona in Otello, 1974; appears regularly with all major European and Am. opera houses, including Australian opera cos., Royal Opera House, Covent Garden, London, Paris Opera, Houston Opera, Munich Opera, La Scala, others; opera appearences include Boris Gudonov, Carmen, Don Giovanni, the Magic Flute, Eugene Onegin, La Boheme, Manon Lescaut, many others; appeared in film Don Giovanni as Elvira, 1979; recs. include Blue Skies, 1986, Kiri Sings Gershwin, 1987, Kiri Te Kanawa: Italian Opera Arias, 1991, Kiri Her Greatest Hits, Ave Maria (Sacred and Devotional Music By Handel, Gounod, et. al., Kiri on Broadway, The Kiri Selection, Kiri Side Tracks, My Fair Lady (with Jeremy Irons, Warren Mitchell, John Gielgud, et. al.; PBS appearance: Great Performances: West Side Story, 1985; author: Land of the Long White Cloud, 1989. Decorated comdr. Order Brit. Empire, 1973, Dame Comdr. Brit. Empire, 1983, Order of New Zealand, 1995. Office: care IMG Artists (N Am) 420 W 45th St New York NY 10036

TELENCIO, GLORIA JEAN, elementary education educator; b. Trenton, N.J., Sept. 3, 1955; d. John and Anne (Tymoch) T. BA cum laude, Georgian Ct. Coll., 1977. Cert. elem. edn. Math and sci. tchr. grade 8 St. Anthony's Grammar Sch., Trenton, 1977-78; elem. tchr. grade 7 St. Mary's Assumption Sch., Trenton, 1978-79; elem. tchr. grade 2 Hamilton Twp. Bd. Edn., Trenton, 1979-85, elem. tchr. grade 1, 1985—; sch. coord. Regional Curriculum Svc. Unit, Learning Resource Ctr.-Ctrl., 1990-95. Recipient State of N.J. Gov.'s Tchr. Recognition award State of N.J., 1991, Resolution of Commendation, Town Coun. of the Twp. of Hamilton, 1991; mini-grantee Bd. Edn., 1987-88. Mem. NEA, N.J. Edn. Assn., Hamilton Edn. Assn., Sunnybrae PTA (tchr. rep. exec. bd. 1981-91, co-chair PTA 25th Anniversary com. 1990-91), Kappa Delta Pi, Sigma Tau Delta, Pi Delta Phi, Delta Tau Kappa. Republican. Byzantine Catholic. Avocations: reading, theatre, music. Home: 31 Newkirk Ave Trenton NJ 08629-1429 Office: Sunnybrae Elem Sch 166 Elton Ave Yardville NJ 08620-1622

TELESCA, FRANCIS EUGENE, architect; b. Dunmore, Pa., Oct. 22, 1921; s. Joseph J. and Bernetta (Bocchiccio) T.; children: Celeste Ann Sullivan, Anthony, Francis Eugene II (Gino), Tina Le; m. Alyce G. Wuenstel, July 28, 1992. B.Arch. summa cum laude, Catholic U. Am., 1953. Designer-draftsman, architect various archtl. and engring. firms Washington and Miami, Fla., 1951-59; pvt. practice architecture Miami, 1959-63; pres. Greenleaf/Telesca, engrs., planners and architects, Miami, 1964-85; exec. v.p. Genesis III, Miami Lakes, Fla., 1985-87; chief programming Miami Internat. Airport, 1987—; dir. Greenleaf Enterprises, Inc., Bonefish Towers, Inc.; mem. Nat. Com. Architecture for Commerce and Industry, 1965-66, Fla. Planning and Zoning Assn., 1960—, Met. Dade County Uniform Code Enforcement Com., 1963-64; bd. dirs. South Fla. Inter-Profl. Council, 1965; planning com. U. Miami Inst. Urban Affairs, 1965; adv. com. City Miami Coconut Grove Zoning, 1965; adv. com. dept. architecture and bldg. constrn. Miami Dade Jr. Coll., 1966. (award of merit Fla. chpt. AIA for Miami Lakes Sr. High Sch., award of excellence for 20th St. Transfer Sta., Dade County 1980, Archtl. award of excellence for Hangar 2, Miami Internat. Airport, Am. Inst. Steel Constrn. 1974, also Grand Conceptor award Am. Cons. Engrs. Council 1974, award of excellence for Primera Casa, Fla. Internat. U., Fla. Concrete and Products Assn. 1973, award for outstanding concrete structure for Acad. One Bldg., Fla. Internat. U. 1980). Past pres., dir. Coconut Grove Assn. (arts festival), Grove House (sch. and marketplace for Fla. craftsmen). Served with AUS, 1940-45, 50-51. Decorated Bronze Star; recipient Grand Nat. award Nat. Community Fallout Shelter competition (shopping center), 1964. Mem. AIA (pres. Fla. South chpt. 1965, dir. Fla. 1966-69), Coconut Grove C. of C. (past pres., dir.), Greater Miami C. of C. (mem. aviation com.), Phi Eta Sigma. Roman Catholic. Home: 3509 Estepona Ave Miami FL 33178-2952 Office: Miami Internat Airport Aviation Dept PO Box 592075 Miami FL 33159

TELESCA, MICHAEL ANTHONY, federal judge; b. Rochester, N.Y., Nov. 25, 1929; s. Michael Angelo and Agatha (Locurcio) T.; m. Ethel E. Hibbard, June 5, 1953; children: Michele, Stephen. A.B., U. Rochester, 1952; J.D., U. Buffalo, 1955. Bar: N.Y. 1957, U.S. Dist. Ct. (we. dist.) N.Y. 1958, U.S. Ct. Appeals (2d cir.) 1960, U.S. Supreme Ct. 1967. Ptnr. Lamb, Webster, Walz, Telesca, Rochester, N.Y., 1957-73; surrogate ct. judge Monroe County, N.Y., 1973-82; judge U.S. Dist. Ct. (we. dist.) N.Y., Rochester, 1982—, chief judge, 1989-95; bd. dirs. Fed. Jud. Ctr. Bd. govs. Genesee Hosp., Rochester; mem. adv. bd. Assn. for Retarded Citizens, Al Sigl Ctr., Rochester. Served to 1st lt. USMC, 1955-57. Recipient Civic medal Rochester C. of C., 1983, Hutchinson medal U. Rochester, 1990. Mem. ABA, Am. Judicature Soc., Am. Inns. of Ct. (founder, pres. Rochester chpt.), Justinian Soc. Jurists, N.Y. State Bar Assn., Monroe County Bar Assn. Republican. Roman Catholic. Office: US Dist Ct 272 US Courthouse 100 State St Rochester NY 14614-1309

TELESETSKY, WALTER, government official; b. Boston, Jan. 22, 1938; s. Keril and Nellie (Krelka) T.; m. Sharron-Dawn Lamp, July 15, 1961; children: Stephanie Ann, Anastasia Marie. BS in Mech. Engring., Northeastern U., 1960; MBA, U. Chgo., 1961; postgrad., Harvard U., 1977. Engr. trainee Chrysler Corp., Detroit, 1956-59; rsch. asst. Microtech Rsch. Co., Cambridge, Mass., 1959-60; engr. Allis Chalmers Mfg. Co., Milw., 1960-61; mem. tech. staff The Mitre Corp., Bedford, Mass., 1962-68; sr. mem. tech. staff Data Dynamics, Inc., Washington, 1969; phys. scientist NOAA, Rockville, Md., 1970-71, U.S. Gate Project coord., 1972-74, dir. U.S. Global Weather Experiment Project Office, 1974, dir. Program Integration Office, 1975-77, dir. Programs and Tech. Devel. Office, 1977-79, dir. Programs and Internat. Activities Office, 1979-81; dep. assoc. dir. for tech. svcs., chief AFOS ops. div. Nat. Weather Svc., Silver Spring, Md., 1981-86, dir. Office of Systems Ops., 1986—; liaison to NAS coms. on atmospheric scis., geophysics studies and internat. environ. programs, 1975-81; U.S. coord. U.S./Japan Coop. Program in Natural Resources, 1980-88; chmn. U.S.-Japan Marine Resources and Engring. Coordination Com., 1980-88; U.S. del. governing coun. UN Environ. Program and World Meteorol. Orgn.; mem. commn. for Basic Systems World Meteorol. Orgn., 1988—; speaker in field. Contbr. articles to profl. publs. Recipient Silver medal Dept. Commerce, 1975. Mem. AAAS, Am. Geophys. Union, Am. Meteorol. Soc., Am. Soc. Mech. Engrs., Marine Tech. Soc. Home: 16 Eton Overlook Rockville MD 20850-3003 Office: 1325 E West Hwy Silver Spring MD 20910-3280

TELFER, MARGARET CLARE, internist, hematologist; b. Manila, The Philippines, Apr. 9, 1939; came to U.S., 1941; d. James Gavin and Margaret Adele (Baldwin) T. BA, Stanford U., 1961; MD, Washington U., St. Louis, 1965. Diplomate Am. Bd. Internal Medicine, Am. Bd. Hematology, Am. Bd. Oncology; lic. Ill., Mo. Resident in medicine Michael Reese Hosp., Chgo., 1968, fellow in hematology and oncology, 1970, assoc. attending physician, 1970-72, dir. Hemophilia Ctr., 1971—, interim dir. div. hematology and oncology, 1971-74, 81-84, 89—, attending physician, 1972—; asst. prof. medicine U. Chgo., 1975-80, assoc. prof. medicine, 1980-85, assoc. prof. clin. medicine, 1985-89; assoc. prof. medicine U. Ill., Chgo., 1990—; mem. med. adv. bd. Hemophilia Found. Ill., 1971, chmn., 1972-83, lectr. annual symposium, 1978-84; mem. med. adv. bd. State of Ill. Hemophilia Program; dir. hematology-oncology fellowship program Michael Reese Hosp., 1971-75, 81-84, 89—, lectr. and mem. numerous coms.; lectr. Cook County Grad. Sch. Medicine, 1980-85, U. Chgo., ARC. Contbr. articles to profl. jours. Fellow ACP; mem. Am. Soc. Clin. Oncology, Am. Assn. Med. Colls., Am. Soc. Hematology, World Fedn. Hemophilia, Blood Club (Chgo.), Thrombosis Club (Chgo.). Office: Michael Reese Hosp 29th & Ellis Rm 1200 RC Chicago IL 60616

TELFORD, IRA ROCKWOOD, anatomist, educator; b. Lincoln, Idaho, May 6, 1907; s. John Witt and Martha Starr (Rockwood) T.; m. Thelma Challis Shrives, June 13, 1933; children—Ira Ralph, John Larry, Kent Matthews, Martha Ann. Student, Ricks Coll., 1924-26; A.B., U. Utah, 1931, A.M., 1933; student, U. Calif. at Berkeley, 1937-40; Ph.D., George Washington U., 1942. High sch. adminstr., 1933-37; instr., asst. prof. anatomy George Washington U., 1940-47, prof., exec. officer dept. anatomy, 1946-47, prof., chmn. dept., 1953-72; prof., chmn. dept. anatomy U. Tex. Dental Br., 1947-53; cons. anatomy (Univ. Hosp.), 1953-72; prof. anatomy Georgetown U., Washington, 1972-78; vis. prof. anatomy Uniformed Services U., Bethesda, Md., 1978-93, ret., Jan. 1995. Contbr. articles to biol., med. jours. Fulbright scholar Gt. Britain, 1960. Fellow AAAS (council 1958-60); mem. Am. Assn. Anatomists, Soc. Exptl. Biology and Medicine, Am. Acad. Neurology, Tex. Acads. Sci., Internat. Soc. Dental Research, AMA (asso.), Sigma Xi (chpt. pres. 1958-59), Phi Sigma (chpt. pres. 1932-33). Mem. Ch. of Jesus Christ of Latter-day Saints. Home: 3424 Garrison St NW Washington DC 20008-2037

TELL, WILLIAM KIRN, JR., oil company executive, lawyer; b. Evanston, Ill., Feb. 27, 1934; s. William Kirn and Virginia (Snook) T.; m. Karen Nelson, July 16, 1960; children—Catherine, Caroline, William F. B.A. in Govt., Dartmouth Coll., 1956; J.D., U. Mich., 1959. Bar: Ohio, 1960, D.C., 1979. Atty. Texaco Inc., N.Y.C., 1968-70, asst. to v.p., gen. counsel, 1970, assoc. gen. counsel, 1970-73, asst. to chmn., 1973; v.p. Texaco Inc., Washington and N.Y.C., 1973-79, sr. v.p., 1979—; pres. Texaco Corp. Communications Div., 1989—. Mem. adv. bd. dirs. Met. Opera, N.Y.C., 1983—. Mem. Am. Petroleum Inst. (bd. dirs. 1980—), Greenwich Country Club, Congressional Club, Metropolitan Club, Everglades Club. Home: 320 Old Church Rd Greenwich CT 06830-4824 Office: Texaco Inc 2000 Westchester Ave White Plains NY 10650-0001

TELLEEN, JOHN MARTIN, retired judge; b. Cambridge, Ill., Dec. 16, 1922; s. Leonard E. and Vina (Elm) T.; m. Nell Joanne Larson, June 17, 1950 (dec. 1987); children—Jane, Mary, John D., Thomas; m. Kari Arentzen Larson, May 29, 1988. A.B., Augustana Coll., 1947; LL.B., U. Ill., 1950. Bar: Ill. 1950. Practice in Moline, 1950-53, Rock Island, 1953-81; partner firm Katz, McAndrews, Durkee & Telleen, Rock Island, 1953-81; judge 14th Judicial Circuit, 1981-94; ret., 1994; mem. exec. com. Ill. Jud. Conf., 1986-92; former counsel Luth. Hosp., Moline. Bd. dirs. Augustana Coll., Rock Island, 1968-76, sec., 1968-70, vice chmn., 1970, chmn., 1971-76; bd. dirs. Luth. Hosp., 1957-68. Served with USNR, 1943-46. Mem. ABA, Ill. Bar Assn., Rock Island County Bar Assn. (pres. 1970). Home: 4 Windy Pt Rock Island IL 61201-9219

TELLEM, SUSAN MARY, public relations executive; b. N.Y.C, May 23, 1945; d. John F. and Rita C. (Lietz) Cain; m. Marshall R.B.. Thompson; children: Tori, John, Daniel. BS, Mt. St. Mary's Coll., L.A., 1967. Cert. pub. health nurse; RN. Pres. Tellem Pub. Rels. Agy., Marina del Rey,

Calif., 1977-80, Rowland Grody Tellem, L.A., 1980-90; chmn. The Rowland Co., L.A., 1990—; pres., CEO Tellem, Inc., L.A., 1992-93; instr. UCLA Extension, 1983—; speaker numerous seminars and confs. on pub. rels. Editor: Sports Medicine for the '80's, Sports Medicine Digest, 1982-84. Bd. dirs. Marymount High Sch., 1984-87, pres., 1984-86; bd. dirs. L.A. Police Dept. Booster Assn., 1984-87; mem. Cath. Press Coun.; mem. pres.'s coun. Mus. Sci. and Industry. Mem. Am. Soc. Hosp. Mktg. and Pub. Rels., Healthcare Mktg. and Pub. Rels. Assn., Pub. Rels. Soc. Am. (bd. dirs. 1994—), L.A. Counselors, PETA, Am. Lung Assn. (chair comm. com. L.A. chpt.) Soc. for Prevention of Cruelty to Animals (chair PetSet), Sports Club (L.A.). Roman Catholic. Avocations: reading, tennis, aerobic dance. Office: Tellem Inc Museum Sq 5757 Wilshire Blvd Ste 655 Los Angeles CA 90036-3686

TELLEP, DANIEL MICHAEL, aerospace executive, mechanical engineer; b. Forest City, Pa., Nov. 20, 1931; m. Pat. Tellep; 6 children. B.S. in Mech. Engring. with highest honors, U. Calif., Berkeley, 1954, M.S., 1955; grad. Advanced Mgmt. Program, Harvard U., 1971. Prin. scientist Lockheed Missiles & Space Co., 1955-69, chief engr. missile systems div., 1969-75, v.p., asst. gen. mgr. advanced systems div., 1975-83, exec. v.p., 1983-84, pres., 1984—; pres. Lockheed Missiles & Space Systems Group, 1986—; chmn., chief exec. officer Lockheed Corp., 1989-95; chmn. bd. Lockheed Martin Corp., Bethesda, Md., 1996, retired chm., 1997; cons. in field; bd. dirs. Wells Fargo, SCE Corp. Contbr. article to profl. jours. Bd. govs. Music Ctr. L.A. County, 1991-95; mem. adv. bd. U. Calif. Berkeley Sch. Engring.; mem. Calif. Bus. Roundtable, 1992—; nat. chmn. vol. com. U.S. Savs. Bond Campaign, 1993. Recipient Tower award San Jose State U., 1985, Aeronautics and Propulsion Laurels award Aviation Week and Space Tech., 1993, John R. Alison award, 1993; named Exec. of Yr., Nat. Mgmt. Assn., 1993, James V. Forrestal award, 1996, award Calif . Mfrs., 1996, Nat. Engring. award Am. Assn. Engring. Socs., 1996, award Internat. Acad. Astronautics, 1996, John W. Dixon medal AUSA, 1996. Fellow AIAA (hon., Lawrence Sperry award 1964, Missile Sys. award, 1986), Am. Astronautical Soc. (Indsl. Leadership award 1992); mem. NAE, Nat. Aero. Assn., Soc. Mfg. Engrs., Sigma Xi, Pi Tau Sigma. Office: Lockheed Martin Corp 6801 Rockledge Dr Bethesda MD 20817-1836

TELLER, EDWARD, physicist; b. Budapest, Hungary, Jan. 15, 1908; naturalized, 1941; s. Max and Ilona (Deutch) T.; m. Augusta Harkanyi, Feb. 26, 1934; children: Paul, Susan Wendy. Student, Inst. Tech., Karlsruhe, Germany, 1926-28, U. Munich, 1928; Ph.D., U. Leipzig, Germany, 1930; D.Sc. (hon.), Yale U., 1954, U. Alaska, 1959, Fordham U., 1960, George Washington U., 1960, U. So. Calif., 1960, St. Louis U., 1960, Rochester Inst. Tech., 1962, PMC Colls., 1963, U. Detroit, 1964, Clemson U., 1966, Clarkson Coll., 1969; LL.D., Boston Coll., 1961, Seattle U., 1961, U. Cin., 1962, U. Pitts., 1963, Pepperdine U., 1974, U. Md. at Heidelberg, 1977; D.Sc., L.H.D., Mt. Mary Coll., 1964; Ph.D., Tel Aviv U., 1972; D.Natural Sci., DeLaSalle U., Manila, 1981; D. Med. Sci. (n.c.), Med. U. S.C., 1983. Research assoc. Leipzig, 1929-31, Goettingen, Germany, 1931-33; Rockefeller fellow Copenhagen, 1934; lectr. U. London, 1934-35; prof. physics George Washington U., Washington, 1935-41, Columbia, 1941-42; physicist U. Chgo., 1942-43, Manhattan Engr. Dist., 1942-46, Los Alamos Sci. Lab., 1943-46; prof. physics U. Chgo., 1946-52; prof. physics U. Calif., 1953-60, prof. physics-at-large, 1960-70, Univ. prof., 1970-75; Univ. prof. emeritus, chmn. dept. applied sci. U. Calif., Davis and Livermore, 1963-66; asst. dir. Los Alamos Sci. Lab., 1949-52; cons. Livermore br. U. Calif. Radiation Lab., 1952-53; asso. dir. Lawrence Livermore Lab., U. Calif., 1954-58, 60-75; dir. Lawrence Livermore Radiation Lab., U. Calif., 1958-60; now dir. emeritus, cons. Lawrence Livermore Nat. Lab., U. Calif., Manhattan Dist. of Columbia, 1942-46; also Metall. and Lab. of Argonne Nat. Lab., U. Chgo., 1942-43, 46-52, and Los Alamos, N.Mex., 1943-46; also Radiation Lab., Livermore, Calif., 1952-75; sr. research fellow Hoover Instn. War, Revolution and Peace, Stanford U., 1975—; mem. sci. adv. bd. USAF; bd. dirs. Assn. to the Unite the Democracies; past mem. gen. adv. com. AEC; former mem. Pres.'s Fgn. Intelligence Adv. Nat. Space Coun. Bd. Author: (with Francis Owen Rice) The Structure of Matter, 1949, (with A.L. Latter) Our Nuclear Future, 1958, (with Allen Brown) The Legacy of Hiroshima, 1962, The Reluctant Revolutionary, 1964, (with G.W. Johnson, W.K. Talley, G.H. Higgins) The Constructive Uses of Nuclear Explosives, 1968, (with Segre, Kaplan and Schiff) Great Men of Physics, 1969, The Miracle of Freedom, 1972, Energy: A Plan for Action, 1975, Nuclear Energy in the Developing World, 1977, Energy from Heaven and The Earth, 1979, The Pursuit of Simplicity, 1980, Better a Shield than a Sword, 1987, Conversations on the Dark Secrets of Physics, 1991. Past bd. dirs. Def. Intelligence Sch., Naval War Coll.; bd. dirs. Fed. Union, Hertz Found., Am. Friends of Tel Aviv U.; sponsor Atlantic Union, Atlantic Council U.S., Univ. Ctrs. for Rational Alternatives; mem. Com. to Unite Am., Inc.; bd. govs. Am. Acad. Achievement. Recipient Joseph Priestley Meml. award Dickinson Coll., 1957, Harrison medal Am. Ordnance Assn., 1955; Albert Einstein award, 1958; Gen. Donovan Meml. award, 1959; Midwest Research Inst. award, 1960; Research Inst. Am. Living History award, 1960; Golden Plate award Am. Acad. Achievement, 1961; Gold medal Am. Acad. Achievement, 1982; Thomas E. White and Enrico Fermi awards, 1962; Robins award of Am., 1963; Leslie R. Groves Gold medal, 1974; Harvey prize in sci. and tech. Technion Inst., 1975; Semmelweis medal, 1977; Albert Einstein award Technion Inst., 1977; Henry T. Heald award Ill. Inst. Tech., 1978; Gold medal Am. Coll. Nuclear Medicine, 1980; A.C. Eringen award, 1980; named ARCS Man of Yr., 1980, Disting. Scientist, Nat. Sci. Devel. Bd., 1981; Paul Harris award Rotary Found., 1980; Disting. Scientist Phil-Am. Acad. Sci. and Engring., 1981; Lloyd Freeman Hunt Citizenship award, 1982; Nat. medal of Sci., 1983; Joseph Handleman prize, 1983, Sylvanus Thayer Medal, 1986; Shelby Cullom Davis award Ethics & Pub. Policy Assn., 1988; Presdl. Citizen medal Pres. Reagan, 1989; Ettore Majorana Erice Scienza Per La Pace award, 1990; Order of Banner with Rubies of the Republic of Hungary, 1990. Fellow Am. Nuclear Soc., Am. Phys. Soc., Am. Acad. Arts and Scis., Hungarian Acad. Scis. (hon.); mem. Nat. Acad. Scis., Am. Geophys. Union, Soc. Engring. Scis., Internat. Platform Assn. Research on chem., molecular and nuclear physics, quantum mechanics, thermonuclear reactions, applications of nuclear energy, astrophysics, spectroscopy of polyatomic molecules, theory of atomic nuclei. Office: Stanford U Hoover Inst Stanford CA 94305 also: PO Box 808 Livermore CA 94551-0808*

TELLIER, HENRI, retired Canadian military officer; b. Montreal, Que., Can., Sept. 1, 1918; s. Henry Joseph and Jeanne (St. Cyr) T.; m. Virginia Wright, July 23, 1945; children: Pierre, Michele, Suzanne, John, Nicole. Student, U. Montreal, 1935-40, U. Ottawa, 1946-47, Canadian Army Staff Coll., 1942-43, Imperial Def. Coll., London, Eng., 1966, Dept. Def. Computer Inst., Washington, 1968. With Robert Howard & Co. (ins. brokers), Montreal, 1937-40; commd. 2d lt. Canadian Army, 1940, advanced through grades to lt. gen., 1973; asst. sec. to minister (Nat. Def.), 1945-48; comdg. officer (Royal 22d Regt.), 1948-51; instr. (Canadian Army Staff Coll.), 1951-54; army mem. (Joint Intelligence Staff), 1954-57; mil. adviser Vietnam, 1957-58; chief of staff (Que. Mil. Dist.), 1958-60; mil attache Rome, Italy, 1960- 63; dir. mil. ops. and plans Army, 1963-64, dir. internat. plans, 1964-65; comdr. (Canadian Contingent), Cyprus, 1965-66; dir. gen. plans (Forces Hdqrs.), Ottawa, Ont., 1967-70; dep. chief plans (Forces Hdqrs.), 1970-71; Canadian mil. rep. to mil. com. (NATO Hdqrs.), Brussels, Belgium, 1971-73; ret., 1973; assoc. nat. commr. Canadian Red Cross Soc., Toronto, Ont., 1973-75, nat. commr., 1975, sec.-gen., 1981-83, hon. v.p.; pvt. mem. Refugee Status Adversary Com., 1984-89; chmn. Canadian sect. Mil. Coop. Com. Can.-U.S., Joint Permanent Bd. Def. Can.-U.S.; commr. Commn. for Strategic and Internat. Studies; mem. adv. council Can. Exec. Services Orgn. Decorated Disting. Service Order (Canada); Queens medal Netherlands; comdr. Order of Merit (Italy), officer Order of Red Cross; named to Order of Can. Mem. Canadian Inst. Internat. Affairs., Can. Exec. Svc. Orgn., Inst. Assn. Execs., The Empire Club of Can., Royal 22 Regiment Assn., UN Assn. Office: 19 Bay Hill Ridge, Stittsville, ON Canada K2S 1B9

TELLIER, PAUL M., Canadian railway transportation executive; b. Joliette, Que., Can., May 8, 1939; s. Maurice J. and Eva M. (Bouvier) T.; m. Andree Poirier, June 6, 1959; children: Claude, Marc. BA, U. Ottawa, 1959, LLL, 1962; BLitt, Oxford U., 1966; LLD (hon.), U. Alta., Can., 1996. Bar: Que. bar 1963. Sr. gov. official Can., 1967-92; dep. minister Indian affairs and no. devel., 1979-82, dep. minister energy, mines and resources, 1982-85; chmn. governing bd. Internat. Energy Agy., 1985-92; clk. of Privy Council and sec. to Cabinet Govt. of Can., Ottawa, 1985-92; dir. Petro Can., 1985-92; pres., CEO Canadian Nat. Railway Co., 1992—; bd. dirs. Manulife Fin., Toronto, Grand Trunk Corp., Detroit, Bell Can., Montreal, Can., SNC-Lavalin Group Inc., Montreal, McCain Foods Ltd., Florenceville, Can., Bombadier, Montreal; chmn. Conf. Bd. Canada. Decorated companion Order of Can.; recipient Pub. Svc. Outstanding Achievement award, 1989, Pub. Policy Forum Achievement award, 1989; named to Queen's Privy Coun., Her Majesty Queen Elizabeth, 1992; Queen's counsel, 1981; named Transp. Man of Yr., 1997, Railroader of Yr., 1997. Mem. Que. Bar, Railway Assn. Can. (dir.), Assn. Am. Railroads (dir.). Roman Catholic. Office: Can Nat Railway Co, 935 De La Gauchetiere St West, Montreal, PQ Canada H3B 2M9 also: PO Box 8100, Montreal, PQ Canada H3C 3N4

TELLIER, RICHARD DAVIS, management educator; b. Darby, Pa., Feb. 18, 1942; s. Joseph Campbell and Jane Grace (Davis) T.; m. Susan Gammon, June 10, 1974; children: John-Jo and Tiekka (twins). BSEE, Drexel U., 1967; MBA, Fla. State U., 1971, DBA, 1973. Elec. engr. Philco-Ford Corp., Phila., 1960-67; aerospace sys. engr. GE, Cape Canaveral, Fla., 1967-70; lectr. Fla. State U., Tallahassee, 1970-73; prof. mgmt. Calif. State U., Fresno, 1973—, chmn. dept. mgmt. and mktg., 1979-84, assoc. dean Sch. Bus., 1984-85, asst. dean, 1990-92, assoc. provost acad. resources, 1995—; cons. ops. mgmt., market rsch. orgnl. behavior. Author: Operations Management: Fundamental Concepts and Methods, 1978, Production and Operations Management Test Bank, 1990 ; contbr. articles to profl. jours. Grantee 1975; recipient Meritorious Performance award, 1987, 88, 90. Mem. Ops. Research Soc. Am., Phi Kappa Phi. Home: 8294 N Academy Ave Clovis CA 93611-9454 Office: Calif State U Shaw and Maple Aves Fresno CA 93740-0007

TELLING, EDWARD RIGGS, former retail, insurance, real estate and financial services executive; b. Danville, Ill., Apr. 1, 1919; s. Edward Riggs and Margaret Katherine (Matthews) T.; m. Nancy Hawkins, Dec. 29, 1942 (dec. 1996); children: Edward R. III, Pamela Telling Grimes, Kathryn Telling Bentley, Nancy Telling O'Shaughnessy, Thomas Cole. PhB, Ill. Wesleyan U., 1942, LLD, 1978; LLD, St. Norbert Coll., 1985. With Sears, Roebuck & Co., 1946-85, store mgr., 1954-59, zone mgr., 1960-64, mgr. met. N.Y.C. area ops., 1965-67; adminstrv. asst. to v.p. Ea. ter. Sears, Roebuck & Co., Phila., 1968, v.p. Ea. ter., 1969-74; exec. v.p. Midwestern ter. Sears, Roebuck & Co., Chgo., 1974-75, sr. exec. v.p. field, 1976-77, chmn., CEO, 1978-85. Lt. USNR, 1941-45. Mem. Bus. Coun., Chgo. Club, Old Elm Club, Seminole Club, Lost Tree Club (Fla.). Office: Sears Tower PO Box 06619 Sears Tower 9800 Chicago IL 60606

TELLINGTON, WENTWORTH JORDAN, engineer; b. Gorham, N.H., Oct. 11, 1916; s. Jesse James and Myrtle Meneleh (Jordan) T.; m. Elizabeth Haman-Ashley, Apr. 29, 1939 (div. 1956); children: Wentworth J. Jr., Joan Elizabeth Gabert. Grad., Phillips Andover Acad., 1935; student, Norwich U., 1939; AB, Columbia U., 1940, postgrad., 1946-47; postgrad., U. So. Calif., 1957-59, UCLA, 1959. Instr. U.S. Mil. Acad., West Point, N.Y., 1941-45; field supr. Century Geophys. Corp., Tulsa, 1946-48; chief geophysicist Pacific Petroleums Ltd., Calgary, Alberta, Can., 1949-51; exec. v.p. Overland Inds. Ltd., Edmonton, Alberta, Can., 1952-55; head math. dept. Chadwick Sch., Rolling Hills, Calif., 1956-60; proprietor Pacific Coast Equestrian Rsch. Farm, Badger, Calif., 1961-70, Whitehurst Products Co., San Francisco, 1970-75, Deep Moon Gold Mine, Downieville, 1982-92; CEO Seadeck Corp., Tucson, 1995—, 1995—; adj. prof. Prescott (Ariz.) Coll., 1972-75. Author: (books) Military Maps and Air Photos, 1979, Endurance and Competitive Trail Riding, 1979, Gold and a Hideaway of Your Own, 1993, Crazy in America, 1994; inventor: vehicle tracker, device for tracking and recording locations, 1944, floating airport, 1995, floating platform, 1996. Engr. ethics com. Soc. Profl. Engrs., Can., 1953-54; bd. govs. Western States Trail Assn., Auburn, Calif., 1962-80. Recipient Creative Citizenship in Calif. award Gov. Ronald Reagan, 1968. Mem. Am. Assn. Petroleum Geologists. Republican. Congregationalist. Achievements include patents for Vehicle Tracker, device for tracking and recording locations, 1944, Floating Airport, 1995, Floating Platform, 1996. Avocations: tennis, riding, aerobatic flying. Office: Airdock Enterprise PO Box 68291 Tucson AZ 85737

TELMER, FREDERICK HAROLD, steel products manufacturing executive; b. Edmonton, Alta., Can., Dec. 28, 1937; Ingar and Gertrude Bernice (Floen) T.; m. Margaret Goddard Hutchings, Oct. 30, 1959; children: Christopher, Kevin, Colin. BA in Econs., U. Alberta, 1961, MA in Econs., 1964. With Stelco, Inc., Hamilton, Ont., Can., 1963—, gen. mgr. corp. affairs and strategic planning, 1984-85, v.p. corp. affairs and strategic planning, 1985-87, pres. Stelco Steel, 1988-90, dir., 1989, chmn., chief exec. officer, 1991-97; chmn. Stelco, Inc., Hamilton, Can., 1997—; dir. Inco Ltd., CT Fin. Svcs., Inc.; founding dir. Japan Soc.; vice chmn. Inst. for Work & Health, Can.-Japan Bus. Com. Mem. Toronto Club, Hamilton Club, Burlington Golf and Country Club, Hamilton Golf and Country Club, Delta Kappa Epsilon. Avocations: golf, woodworking, tennis, skiing, piano. Office: Stelco Inc, PO Box 2030, Hamilton, ON Canada L8N 3T1

TELTSER, MICHAEL, chemical engineer; b. Orange, N.J., Jan. 28, 1958; s. Milton and Belle Teltser. BSChemE and BiochemE, Rutgers U., Piscataway, 1995. Cert. in phlebotomy Am. Soc. Clin. Pathologists; cert. emergency med. technician N.J. Cons. Breakers Realty, Springfield, N.J., 1984—; phlebotomy cons. Robert Wood Johnson Trauma Ctr., New Brunswick, N.J., 1992-94; validation engr. Merck & Co., Inc., West Point, Pa., 1995—. Author: Validation of Biotechnology Products and Processes, 1995. Mem. AIChE, Internat. Soc. Pharm. Engrs., Am. Soc. Law Enforcement Trainers. Avocations: martial arts, skiing, weightlifting. Home: 115 Redwood Rd Springfield NJ 07081 Office: Merck & Co Inc PO Box 4 WP14 West Point PA 19486

TEMA-LYN, LAURIE, management consultant; b. Bklyn., Mar. 25, 1951; d. Morton and Jeanne (Lite) Carlin. BA, Bklyn. Coll., 1972. Mgmt. supr. Rapp & Collins, Inc., N.Y.C., 1972-78, v.p., 1978-80; assoc. Synectics, Cambridge, Mass., 1980-83; founder, gen. ptnr. IdeaScope Assocs., Cambridge, 1983-95; prin. Practical Imagination Enterprises, Carlisle, Mass., 1995—; presenter European Conf. on Innovation and Creativity, 1987, 94. Contbr. articles to bus. publs. Bd. dirs. Arica Inst., N.Y.C., 1979-80; v.p. bd. dirs. Savoyand Light Opera Co. Mem. Creative Problem Solving Inst. (presenter, leader), Am. Mktg. Assn., Direct Mktg. Assn. (presenter), Product Devel. Mgmt. Assn., Creative Edn. Found., New Eng. Bus. Assn. for Social Responsibility, Mgmt. Roundtable, Sharing a New Song. Office: Practical Imagination Enterprises PO Box 693 Carlisle MA 01741-0693

TEMAM, ROGER M., mathematician; b. Tunis, Tunisia, May 19, 1940; s. Ange M. and Elise (Ganem) T.; m. Claudette Cukorja, Aug. 21, 1962; children: David, Olivier, Emmanuel. M in Math., U. Paris, 1962, DSc, 1967. Asst. prof. math. U. Paris, 1960-67, prof., 1967—; prof. Ecole Polytechnique, Paris, 1968-85. Author: Numerical Analysis, 1969, Navier-Stokes Equations, 1977, 79, Mathematical Problems in Plasticity, 1983, Infinite Dimensional Dynamical Systems in Mechanics and Physics, 1988, 2nd edit., 1997; contbr. over 230 articles to sci. jours.; editor Math. Model. and Num. Analysis, Physica D, assoc. editor other profl. jours. Recipient Grand Prix Joannidès, Acad. Sci. Paris, 1993. Mem. AAAS, Am. Math. Soc., Am. Physical Soc., N.Y. Acad. Scis., Soc. Indsl. and Applied Math., Soc. Math. Applications of Industry (founding pres. 1983-87).

TEMELES, MARGARET STEWART, psychiatrist; b. Somerville, Mass., May 29, 1922; d. Henry Malcolm Stewart and Margaret Louise Nuttall; m. Lawrence Temeles; children: Gretchen Lee, Ethan Joel, Daniel Stewart. BS, Tufts U., 1943, MD, 1948. Diplomate Nat. Bd. Med. Examiners. Psychiat. cons. Camden Youth Detention Ctr., Lakeland, N.J., 1952-53; asst. chief of staff (now emeritus) Phila. Psychiat. Ctr. (name changed to Belmont Ctr.), 1952—; sr. psychiat. cons. Bryn Mawr (Pa.) Coll., 1964-86; clin. assoc. prof. Hahnemann Med. Coll., Phila., 1966—; cons. Disability Det. Svcs., Augusta, Maine, 1986-95. Author: (with others) Frontiers of Infant Psychology, 1983, Vulnerable Child, vol. III, 1997; editor: Bemoaning the Lost Dream, 1984; contbr. articles to profl. jours. Rsch. grantee Bryn Mawr Coll., 1982. Mem. Am. Psychiat. Assn., Am. Assn. Psychoanalysis, Internat. Assn. Psychoanalysis, World Assn. Infant Psychiatry, Assn. Child Psychoanalysis (recorder Phila. area study group 1980-85), Phila. Assn. Psychoanalysis (child study group 1962-86, child and adult faculty 1967-86, editor jour. 1979-85). Avocations: gardening, music. Home and Office: 206 E Pleasant St Amherst MA 01002-1507

TEMERLIN, LIENER, advertising agency executive; b. Ardmore, Okla., Mar. 27, 1928; s. Pincus and Julie (Kahn) T.; m. Karla Samuelsohn, July 23, 1950; children: Dana Temerlin Crawford, Lisa Temerlin Gottesman, Hayden Crawford, Sandy Gottesman. BFA, U. Okla., 1950. Assoc. editor Sponsor Mag., N.Y.C., 1950-51; copywriter Glenn Advt. Inc., Dallas, 1952-54, creative dir., 1954-70, chief oper. officer, 1970-74; pres. Glenn, Bozell & Jacobs, Inc., 1974-79; chmn. bd. dirs. Bozell & Jacobs Inc., 1979-86, Bozell, Jacobs, Kenyon & Eckhardt, Dallas, 1986-89; chmn. Bozell, 1989-92, Temerlin McClain, 1992—. Chmn. Winston Churchill Found. award dinner, 1986; chmn. Dallas Symphony Assn., 1986-88, pres., 1984-86, mem. bd. govs., 1982-84, pres. coun., 1989—; mem. Blair House Restoration Com., 1987-88; vice chmn. Am. Film Inst., 1992-93, bd. trustees, 1992—; bd. dirs. United Way of Met. Dallas Exec. Com., 1986-89, Dallas Bus. Com. for Arts, 1989, Dallas Citizen's Coun., 1984-86, 92; trustee Southwestern Med. Found., 1988—, bd. trustees, 1992—, So. Meth. U., trustee com. Univ. devel., 1988, exec. bd., 1990-91; trustee and chmn. of devel. com. Dallas Mus. Art, 1993-96; mem. steering com. Susan G. Komen Found., 1989-91, art acquisition com. Meyerson Symphony Ctr., 1989-92, exec. coun. Daytop/Dallas, 1989—; chmn. grand opening fortnight Morton H. Meyerson Symphony Ctr., 1989; mem. Madison Coun. Libr. Congress, Washington, 1991—; hon. chair 2d ann. rsch. dinner Am. Lung Assn. Tex., 1996. Recipient Bill D. Kerss award Dallas Advt. League, 1983, Brotherhood award NCCJ, 1984, Susan G. Komen Found. for Breast Cancer Rsch. Community award, 1989, James K. Wilson Silver Cup award, 1990, Linz award 1990, Silver Medal award Dallas Advt. League, 1991, Vol. Fundraiser of Yr. award Nat. Soc. Fundraising Execs., 1991, Best Man in Advt. award McCall's Mag., 1992; named Dallas Father of Yr., 1991.

TEMES, GABOR CHARLES, electrical engineering educator; b. Budapest, Hungary, Oct. 14, 1929; s. Erno and Rozsa (Angyal) Wohl-Temes; m. Ibi Kutasi-Temes, Feb. 6, 1954; children: Roy Thomas, Carla Andrea. Dipl.Ing., Tech. U. Budapest, 1952, DSc (hon.), 1991; Dipl. Phys., Eotvos U., Budapest, 1954; Ph.D., U. Ottawa, Ont., Can., 1961. Asst. prof. Tech. U. Budapest, 1952-56; project engr. Measurement Engring. Ltd., 1956-59; dept. head No. Electric Co. Ltd., 1959-64; group leader Stanford Linear Accelerator Center, 1964-66; corp. cons. Ampex Corp., 1966-69; prof. elec. engring. UCLA, 1969-90, chmn. dept., 1975-80; dept. head Oreg. State U., Corvallis, 1990—; cons. Xerox Corp., ANT GmbH. Author: (with others) Introduction to Circuit Synthesis and Design, 1977, Analog MOS Integrated Circuits for Signal Processing, 1986; assoc. editor: (with others) Jour. Franklin Inst, 1971-82; co-editor, contbg. author: (with others) Modern Filter Theory and Design, 1973, Oversampling Delta-Sigma Data Converters, 1991. Recipient Western Electric Fund award Am. Soc. Engring. Edn., 1982, Humboldt Sr. Rsch. award, 1991; NSF grantee, 1970—. Fellow IEEE (editor Transactions on Circuit Theory 1969-71 Best Paper award 1969, 81, 85, Centennial medal 1984, Edn. award 1987, Tech. Achievement award 1989). Home: 7100 NW Grandview Dr Corvallis OR 97330-2708 Office: Oreg State U Dept Elec Engring Corvallis OR 97330

TEMIN, MICHAEL LEHMAN, lawyer; b. Phila., July 18, 1933; s. Henry and Annette (Lehman) T.; divorced; children—Aaron Lehman, Seth Lehman. B.A. magna cum laude, Yale U., 1954; LL.B. cum laude, U. Pa., 1957. Bar: Pa. 1958, U.S. Ct. Appeals (3d cir.) 1958, U.S. Supreme Ct. 1969, U.S. Ct. Appeals (2d cir.) 1986, U.S. Ct. Appeals (9th cir.) 1992. Asst. U.S. atty. U.S. Atty.'s Office, Phila., 1958-59; assoc. Wolf, Block, Schorr and Solis-Cohen, Phila., 1959-66, ptnr., 1966—; lectr. Law Sch., U. Pa., Phila., 1982-90, adj. prof., 1990-93, 94-95; Thomas A. O'Boyle vis. disting. practitioner, 1985, I. Grant Irey lectr., 1988. Editor U. Pa. Law Rev., 1955-57. Vice chmn. Ednl. Nominating Panel, Phila., 1981-83; bd. dirs. Citizens Com. in Pub. Edn., Phila., 1970—, pres. 1980-82. Fellow Am. Coll. Bankruptcy; mem. Phila. Bar Assn. (chmn. bankruptcy com., sect. corp., banking and bus. law 1979-86, chmn. profl. guidance com. 1985, sec. sect. corp. banking and bus. law 1985, treas. sect. corp. banking and bus. law 1986, vice chmn. sect. corp. banking and bus. law 1987, chmn. sect. corp. banking and bus. law 1988), Pa. Bar Assn. (ho. of dels. 1985-89, 90—), ABA (bus. bankruptcy com. of sect. corp. banking and bus. law chmn. rules subcom., 1985-92, vice chmn. chpt. 11 subcom. 1992-96, vice chmn. ea. dist. Pa. bankruptcy conf. 1994-95, chmn. ea. dist. Pa. bankruptcy conf., 1995-96), Order of Coif. Jewish. Office: Wolf Block Schorr & Solis-Cohen 12th Fl Packard Bldg Philadelphia PA 19102

TEMIN, PETER, economics educator; b. Phila., Dec. 17, 1937; s. Henry and Annette T.; m. Charlotte Brucar Fox, Aug. 21, 1966; children: Elizabeth Sara, Melanie Wynn. B.A., Swarthmore (Pa.) Coll., 1959; Ph.D., Mass. Inst. Tech., 1964. Mem. faculty MIT, 1965—, prof. econs., 1970—. Author: Iron and Steel in Nineteenth Century America, 1964, The Jacksonian Economy, 1969, Casual Factors in American Economic Growth in the 19th Century, 1975, Did Monetary Forces Cause the Great Depression?, 1976, Taking Your Medicine: Drug Regulation in the United States, 1980, The Fall of the Bell System, 1987, Lessons from the Great Depression, 1989, Inside the Business Enterprise, 1991. Mem. Am. Econ. Assn., Econ. History Assn., Econ. History Soc., Phi Beta Kappa. Home: 15 Channing St Cambridge MA 02138-4713 Office: MIT Dept Econs Cambridge MA 02139

TEMKIN, HARVEY L., lawyer; b. Madison, Wis., Jan. 1, 1952; s. Joe L. and Sylvia (Libanoff) T.; m. Barbara Jean Myers, June 13, 1976; children: James, Daniel, Eli. BA, U. Wis., 1974; JD, U. Ill., 1978. Bar: Wis. 1978. Assoc. Foley & Lardner, Madison, 1978-83; prof. Tulane Law Sch., New Orleans, 1983-87; ptnr. Foley & Lardner, Madison, 1987—; lectr. U. Wis. Law Sch.; mem. U.S. Senator Feingold's Bus. Adv. Group. 1st v.p. Hillel Found., Madison, 1982-83, bd. dirs., 1987—; chmn. edn. com. Beth Israel Synagogue, Madison, 1980-82; chmn. Downtown Madison, Inc., 1989-91; chmn. Jewish edn. panel Madison Jewish Community Coun., 1993—. Fellow Am. Coll. Real Estate Lawyers; mem. ABA (real property probate and trust sect., reporter significant legis. panel 1983-85, significant lit. panel 1985-87). Home: 6609 Inner Dr Madison WI 53705-4218 Office: Foley & Lardner PO Box 1497 150 E Gilman St Madison WI 53701-1497

TEMKIN, LARRY SCOTT, philosopher, educator; b. Milw., May 29, 1954; s. Blair Huntly and Leah Dahlia (Sigman) T.; m. Margaret Ellen Grimm, May 26, 1975; children: Daniel Eric, Andrea Beth, Rebecca Leigh. BA-Honors degree in Philosophy, U. Wis., 1975; student, Oxford U., Eng., 1978-79; PhD, Princeton U., 1983. Instr. philosophy Rice U., Houston, 1980-83, asst. prof., 1983-89, assoc. prof., 1989-95, prof., 1995—; vis. appointment U. Pitts., 1986; speaker in field. Author: Inequality; contbr. articles to profl. jours. Recipient Phi Beta Kappa Outstanding Tchr. award, George R. Brown awards for superior teaching, George R. Brown awards for excellence in teaching; Danforth fellow, Nat. Humanities Ctr. fellow, Weiner fellow, Harvard fellow for Program in Ethics and the Professions. Mem. Am. Philos. Assn., Phi Beta Kappa. Avocations: camping, sports. Home: 4924 Valerie St Bellaire TX 77401-5708 Office: Rice U Dept Philosophy 6100 Main St Houston TX 77005-1827

TEMKIN, ROBERT HARVEY, accountant; b. Boston, Oct. 21, 1943; s. Max and Lillian (Giller) T.; m. Ellen Phyllis Band, Sept. 25, 1966; children: Aron, Rachel, Joshua. BBA, U. Mass., 1964. CPA, Mass., N.Y. With Ernst & Young, 1964-72, 73—, ptnr., 1976—; nat. dir. auditing standards Arthur Young & Co., CPAs, 1980-88; assoc. prof. NYU, 1982. Bd. dirs. Jewish Home for Elderly of Fairfield County, 1979-94, pres., 1985-87; mem. Bd. Edn., Weston, Conn., 1983-87; dir. United Synagogue of Conservative Judaism; mem. bus. adv. coun. U. Mass., chmn. acctg. alumni advisory coun.; bd. dirs. Jewish Cmty. Ctrs. of Greater Boston, Combined Jewish Philanthropies of Greater Boston, exec. com., 1995—; mem. exec. bd. N.E. region Anti-Defamation League; treas. Synagogue Coun., Mass., 1988-93; bd. dirs. Temple Reyim, Newton, Mass., 1995-97. Recipient Acctg. Alumni award U. Mass., 1978, Alumnus Award Sch. Mgmt. U. Mass., 1986. Mem. AICPA (staff dir. commn. on auditors responsibilities 1976-78, mem. task force on auditor's report 1978-81, peer rev. com. 1982-84, auditing stds. bd. 1984-88, chmn. internat. auditing task force 1988-90), Mass. Soc. CPAs (Silver medal 1964), N.Y. State Soc. CPAs, Mass. Bd. Pub. Accountancy (sec. 1996, chmn. 1997), N.E.-Israel C. of C. (bd. dirs.), Bostonian Club (adv. bd.). Home: 1611 Commonwealth Ave Newton MA 02165-2800 Office: Ernst & Young 200 Clarendon St Boston MA 02116-5021

TEMKO, ALLAN BERNARD, writer; b. N.Y.C., Feb. 4, 1924; s. Emanuel and Betty (Alderman) T.; m. Elizabeth Ostroff, July 1, 1950 (dec. Aug.

1996); children: Susannah, Alexander. AB, Columbia U., 1947; postgrad, U. Calif., Berkeley, 1949-51, Sorbonne, 1948-49, 51-52. Lectr. Sorbonne, 1953-54, Ecole des Arts et Metiers, Paris, 1954-55; asst. prof. journalism U. Calif., Berkeley, 1956-62, lectr. in city planning and social scis., 1966-70, lectr. Grad. Sch. Journalism, 1991; prof. art Calif. State U., Hayward, 1971-80; lectr. art Stanford U., 1981, 82; architecture critic San Francisco Chronicle, 1961-93, art editor, 1979-82; archtl. planning cons.; chmn. Yosemite Falls Design Workshop, 1992; Pulitzer Prize juror, 1991-92. Author: Notre Dame of Paris, 1955, Eero Saarinen, 1962, No Way To Build a Ballpark and Other Irreverent Essays on Architecture, 1993; contbr. articles to U.S. and fgn. mags. and newspapers; West Coast editor, Archtl. Forum, 1959-62. Served with USNR, 1943-46. Recipient Gold medal Commonwealth Club Calif., 1956, Silver medal, 1994, Journalism award AIA, 1961, Silver Spur award San Francisco Planning and Urban Renewal Assn., 1985, AIA Inst. Honor award, 1991, Nathaniel A. Owings award AIA Calif. Coun., 1995, 1st prize in archtl. criticism Mfrs. Hanover/Art World, 1986, Critic's award Mfrs. Hanover/Art World, 1987, Profl. Achievement award Soc. Profl. Journalists, 1988, Pulitzer Prize for criticism, 1990; grantee Rockefeller Found., 1962-63, 20th Century Fund, 1963-66, NEA, 1988, Graham Found., 1990; Guggenheim fellow, 1956-57. Home: 1015 Fresno Ave Berkeley CA 94707-2517 *My chief intellectual and professional goal has always been to create excellence in a democratic America and, where possible, in the world at large. This Jeffersonian aim, which came to me directly from Lewis Mumford, naturally includes architecture, environmental planning, the fine arts, and literature. Through education, in which history, criticism, and serious journalism play important roles, I think it is still possible to attain such excellence despite the complex problems of technological civilization.*

TEMKO, STANLEY LEONARD, lawyer; b. N.Y.C., Jan. 4, 1920; s. Emanuel and Betty (Alderman) T.; m. Francine Marie Salzman, Mar. 4, 1944; children: Richard J., Edward J., William D. AB, Columbia U., 1940, LLB, 1943. Bar: N.Y. 1943, D.C. 1951. Practice in N.Y.C., 1943, 46-47; law clk. Mr. Justice Wiley Rutledge, U.S. Supreme Ct., Washington, 1947-48; asso. firm Covington & Burling, Washington, 1949-55; ptnr. Covington & Burling, 1955-90, sr. counsel, 1990—. Editor-in-chief: Columbia Law Rev, 1942-43. Trustee Beauvoir Sch., 1963-69; trustee Columbia U., 1980-91, trustee emeritus, 1991—, mem. bd. visitors Sch. Law, 1961—; mem. bd. govs. St. Albans Sch., 1967-73, chmn., 1971-73. 2nd lt. U.S. Army, 1943-46. Decorated Bronze Star; recipient medal for conspicuous alumni svc. Columbia U., 1979. Fellow Am. Bar Found. (chmn. rsch. com. 1970-72); mem. ABA, Am. Law Inst., D.C. Bar Assn., Columbia U. Sch. Law Alumni Assn. (pres. 1982-84), Met. Club, Nat. Press Club, City Tavern Club, Phi Beta Kappa. Home: 4811 Dexter Ter NW Washington DC 20007-1020 Office: Covington & Burling 1201 Pennsylvania Ave NW PO Box 7566 Washington DC 20044

TEMPEL, JEAN CURTIN, venture capitalist; b. Hartford, Conn., Mar. 23, 1943; d. John J. and Sally (Miller) Curtin Jr.; m. Louis J. Tempel, Nov. 23, 1968 (div. 1978); m. Peter A. Wilson, May 10, 1980. BA in Math., Conn. Coll., 1965; MS in Computer Sci., Rensselaer Poly. Inst., 1970; advanced mgmt. program cert., Harvard U., 1979. Various sr. mgmt. positions Conn. Bank and Trust Co., 1965-80; mgr. strategic planning and mktg. Bank New Eng., 1980-82; sr. v.p., mgr. of custody The Boston Co., 1983, pres. Boston Safe Clearing Corp.,, 1984-90, exec. v.p., chief ops., info. officer, 1985, exec. v.p., COO, 1988-90; prin. Tempel Ptnrs. Inc., Boston, 1991; pres., COO Safeguard Scientifics Inc., Wayne, 1992-93, bd. dirs.; gen. ptnr. TL Ventures LP, Boston, 1994—; bd. dirs. Cambridge (Mass.) Tech. Ptnrs., Cambridge, Mass., Centocor, Malvern, Pa., Sonecta Internat. Hotels, Inc., Boston; trustee Scudder Funds, Boston; overseer Northeastern U.; trustee Conn. Coll. Mem. Internat. Women's Forum (dir.). Avocations: skiing, bicycling, sailing. Office: Safeguard Scientifics Inc 10 Post Office Sq Ste 1325 Boston MA 02109-4603

TEMPELIS, CONSTANTINE HARRY, immunologist, educator; b. Superior, Wis., Aug. 27, 1927; s. Harry and Thelma Marie (Hoff) T.; m. Nancy Louise Foster, Aug. 27, 1955; children: William H., Daniel S. BS, U. Wis.-Superior, 1950; MS, U. Wis.-Madison, 1953, PhD, 1955. Project assoc. immunology U. Wis., Madison, 1955-57; instr. immunology U. W.Va., Morgantown, 1957-58; asst. rsch. immunologist U. Calif., Berkeley, 1958-66, assoc. prof. immunology, 1966-72, prof., 1972-95, prof. emeritus, 1995—, prof. grad. sch., 1996—; vis. scientist Wellcome Rsch. Labs., Beckenham, Kent, Eng., 1977-78, U. Innsbruck, Austria, 1985, 90, 91; cons. in field. Contbr. articles to profl. jours. Served with USNR, 1945-46. Recipient Rsch. Career Devel. award, 1965-70; Fogarty sr. internat. fellow NIH, 1977-78. Mem. AAAS, N.Y. Acad. Scis., Am. Assn. Immunologists, Fedn. Am. Soc. Exptl. Biology, Sigma Xi. Office: U Calif Sch Pub Health Berkeley CA 94720

TEMPLE, DONALD, allergist, dermatologist; b. Chgo., May 21, 1933; s. Samuel Leonard and Matilda Eve (Riff) T.; m. Sarah Rachel Katz, Sept. 29, 1957; children: Michael A., Matthew D., Madeline B. AB in Biology cum laude, Harvard U., 1954; MD, U. Chgo., 1958. Am. Bd. Allergy and Immunology, Am. Bd. Dermatology, Nat. Bd. Med. Examiners; lic. Intern Michael Reese Hosp., Chgo., 1958-59; resident in dermatology U. Chgo. Hosps., 1959-62; clin. asst., dept. dermatology Boston U. Sch. Medicine, 1963-64; clin. instr. dermatology Stanford U. Sch. Medicine, 1965; preceptee in allergy Offices of Leon Unger, M.D., and Donald Unger, M.D., Chgo., 1965-69; practice medicine specializing in allergy and dermatology Des Plaines, Ill., 1969-76; mem. allergy dept. Glen Ellyn (Ill.) Clinic, 1972—; mem. dermatology and allergy staff, Louis A. Weiss Hosp., Chgo., 1965-73, allergy sect. Loyola U. Med. Ctr., Maywood, Ill., 1977-80, exec. and contract medicine coms. Glen Ellyn; clin. asst. prof. dermatology Abraham Lincoln Sch. Medicine, U. Ill., 1972-75; clin. asst. prof. medicine sect. allergy and dermatology, Loyola U., 1977-85; mem. staff Cen. DuPage Hosp., Winfield, Ill., 1973—, Glen Oaks Med. Ctr., Glendale Heights, Ill., Glendale Heights Community Hosp., 1980-92. Contbr. articles to profl. jours. Bd. dirs. Am. Lung Assn., DuPage, McHenry counties, 1980-91; chmn. Contract Medicine, HMO Com., Glen Ellyn Clinic, 1985, mem. exec. com., 1988-92. Fellow Am. Coll. Chest Physicians, Am. Assn. Cert. Allergists, Am. Coll. Allergists, Am. Acad. Allergy, Ill. Soc. Allergy and Clin. Immunology, Chgo. Dermatol. Soc.; mem. AMA, Ill. State Med. Soc., DuPage County Med. Soc., Chgo. Med. Soc. Jewish. Avocations: sailing, investing. Home: 110 E Delaware Pl Apt 2004 Chicago IL 60611-1440 Office: Glen Ellyn Clinic 454 Pennsylvania Ave Glen Ellyn IL 60137-4418

TEMPLE, JOSEPH GEORGE, JR., retired pharmaceutical company executive; b. Bklyn., Aug. 29, 1929; s. Joseph George and Helen Frances (Beney) T.; m. Ann Elizabeth McFerran, June 21, 1952; children: Linda Jo, James, John. BSChemE, Purdue U., 1951, DEng (hon.), 1988. With Dow Chem. Co., Midland, Mich., 1951-89, v.p. mktg., 1976-78, dir., 1979-94; pres. Dow Chem. Latin Am., Coral Gables, Fla., 1978-80; group v.p. human health Dow Chem. Co., Cin., 1980-83; chief exec. officer, pres. Merrell Dow Pharms. Inc., Cin., 1983-87; exec. v.p. Dow Chem. Co., 1983-89; chief exec. officer, chmn. bd. dirs. Merrell Dow Pharms. Inc., Cin., 1988-89; chmn., chief exec. officer Marion Merrell Dow, Inc., Kansas City, Mo., 1989-92, also bd. dirs.; chmn. Marion Merrell Dow Pharms. Inc., 1992-94; vice chmn., 1994-95, ret., 1995; former trustee Com. for Economic Devel. Mem. pres.'s coun. Purdue U., 1978—; bd. fellows Saginaw Valley State U., 1987-89. Recipient Disting. Engr. Alumni award Purdue U., 1978, Outstanding Chem. Engr. award Purdue U., 1993. Mem. Am. Inst. Chem. Engrs., Soc. Plastics Industry (bd. dirs. 1980-82), Pharm. Mfrs. Assn. (bd. dirs. 1981-83), Mgmt. Assn. (Silver Knight award 1976, Gold Knight award 1982). Episcopalian.

TEMPLE, LARRY EUGENE, lawyer; b. Plainview, Tex., Dec. 26, 1935; s. Herman Edward and Grace Eileen (Ivey) T.; m. Laura Louann Atkins, Feb. 23, 1963; children: Laura Allison, John Lawrence. BBA, U. Tex., 1957, LLB with honors, 1959; LLD (hon.), Lamar U., 1985. Bar: Tex., U.S. Dist. Ct. (we. dist.) Tex., U.S. Ct. Appeals (5th cir.), U.S. Supreme Ct. Law clk. to justice Tom Clark U.S. Supreme Ct., Washington, 1959-60; assoc. Powell, Rauhut, McGinnis, Reavley & Lochridge, Austin, Tex., 1960-63; legal adminstrn. asst., exec. asst. Tex. Gov. John B. Connally, Austin, 1963-67; spl. counsel to pres. Lyndon Baines Johnson, Washington, 1967-69; pvt. practice Austin, 1969—; bd. dirs. Temple-Inland, Inc., Guaranty Fed. Bank. Mem. U. Tex. Cancer Found., Houston, 1978-84, U. Tex. Devel. Bd., Austin, 1980-85, 90—, chmn., 1993-95; pres. U. Tex. Ex-Students Assn., 1997-98; mem. Tex. Higher Edn. Coordinating Bd., Austin, 1983-89, chmn., 1983-87; chmn. Select Com. for Higher Edn., Austin, 1985-87; bd. dirs. Lyndon B. Johnson Found., 1986—, vice chmn., 1989—; trustee U. Tex. Law Sch. Found., 1989—. Recipient Faculty award U. Tex. Law Sch., 1987, Humanitarian award Austin region NCCJ, 1988, Santa Rita award U. Tex. System, 1989, Disting. Alumnus award U. Tex., Austin, 1990. Fellow Tex. Bar Found.; mem. ABA, Tex. Bar Assn. (chmn. legis. com. 1980, 83-86), Tex. Jr. Bar Assn. (chmn. bd. dirs. 1967), Austin Jr. Bar Assn. (pres. 1962-63). Democrat. Episcopalian. Home: 2606 Escondido Cv Austin TX 78703-1610 Office: 400 W 15th St Ste 1510 Austin TX 78701-1648

TEMPLE, LEE BRETT, architect; b. Balt., June 7, 1956. BArch, Cornell U., 1979. Cert. Nat. Coun. Archtl. Registration Bds. Gen. ptnr. Temple Gebelein Partnership, Ithaca, N.Y., 1981-91; prin. and sole propr. Lee Temple Architect AIA, Ithaca and Crestone, Colo., 1985—; founder, dir. Temple Mountain Music, Ithaca, 1996—; vis. critic dept. architecture Cornell U., Ithaca, 1981; vis. prof. architecture Hobart Coll., 1981-82, prof., 1992-93; asst. prof. architecture Syracuse (N.Y.) U., 1982-87. Prin. works include Athena Residence, Chapelle Frontenac; author: Medieval Town Study, 1981. Chmn. social justice com. Cornell Cath. Cmty., Ithaca, 1989-92, trustee parish coun., 1989-90; mem. founding bd. dirs. Eco Village at Ithaca, 1991-93; mem. steering com. Tibetan Resettlement Project at Ithaca, 1991-92; founder Sustainable Resource Ctr., Crestone, 1993; founder Temple Mountain Music, 1996. Recipient 1st prize Storey Com. Compact House Competition, 1983; Eidlitz fellow dept. arch. Cornell U., 1979, 81. Mem. AIA (design excellence award 1987, residential design award 1987, Ctrl. N.Y. chpt.), ASCAP, AIA Colo., N.Y. State Assn. Architects, Cousteau Soc. Home and Office: PO Box 220 Crestone CO 81131

TEMPLE, WAYNE CALHOUN, historian; b. nr. Richwood, Ohio, Feb. 5, 1924; s. Howard M. and Ruby March (Calhoun) T.; m. Lois Marjorie Bridges, Sept. 22, 1956 (dec. Apr. 1978); m. Sunderine Wilson, Apr. 9, 1979; 2 stepsons, James C. Mohn, Randy E. Mohn. A.B. cum laude, U. Ill., 1949, A.M., 1951, Ph.D., 1956; Lincoln Diploma Honor, Lincoln Meml. U., Harrogate, Tenn., 1963. Rsch. asst. history U. Ill., 1949-53, teaching asst., 1953-54; curator ethnohistory Ill. State Mus., 1954-58; editor-in-chief Lincoln Herald, Lincoln Meml. U., 1958-73, assoc. editor, 1973—, also dir. dept. Lincolniana, dir. univ. press, John Wingate Weeks prof. history, 1958-64; with Ill. State Archives, 1964—, now chief dep. dir.; lectr. U.S. Mil. Acad., 1975; Sec.-treas. Nat. Lincoln-Civil War Council, 1958-64; mem. bibliography com. Lincoln Lore, 1958—; hon. mem. Lincoln Sesquicentennial Commn., 1959-60; advisory council U.S. Civil War Centennial Commn., 1960-66; maj. Civil War Press Corps, 1962—; pres. Midwest Conf. Masonic Edn., 1985. Author: Indian Villages of the Illinois Country: Historic Tribes, 1958, rev. edits., 1966, 77, 87, Lincoln the Railsplitter, 1961, Abraham Lincoln and Others at the St. Nicholas, 1968, Alexander Williamson-Tutor to the Lincoln Boys, 1971, (with others) First Steps to Victory: Grant's March to Naples, 1977, Lincoln and Grant: Illinois Militiamen, 1981, Stephen A. Douglas: Freemason, 1982, Lincoln as a Lecturer, 1982, By Square and Compasses: The Building of Lincoln's Home and Its Saga, 1984, Lincoln's Connections with the Illinois and Michigan Canal, 1986, Dr. Anson G. Henry: Personal Physician to the Lincolns, 1988, Abraham Lincoln: From Skeptic to Prophet, 1995, Thomas and Abraham Lincoln as Farmers, 1996; co-author: Illinois's Fifth Capitol: The House that Lincoln Built, 1988; contbg. author: Capitol Centennial Papers, 1988; editor: Campaigning with Grant, 1961, 72, The Civil War Letters of Henry C. Bear, 1961; 71 radio scripts A. Lincoln 1809-1959, Indian Villages of the Illinois Country: Atlas Supplement, 1975; editorial advisory bd. Am. Biog. Inst., 1971—, Ency. Indians of Ams., 1973—; contbr. to profl. jours., encys. Sponsor Abraham Lincoln Bay, Washington Nat. Cathedral; mem. Ill. State Flag Commn., 1969—; bd. dirs. Vachel Lindsay House; trustee, regent Lincoln Acad. Ill., 1970-82; bd. govs. St. Louis unit Shriners Hosps. for Crippled Children, 1975-81; mem. commissioning com., hon. crew mem. and plank owner USS Springfield submarine, 1990—; hon. crew mem. USS Abraham Lincoln aircraft carrier, 1989—. With U.S. Army, 1943-46, gen. Res. (ret.). Decorated Bronze Star Medal, Silver Citizenship medal SAR, 1993, Literary Merit Gold medal Ill. Lodge of Rsch., 1993; recipient Order of Arrow Boy Scouts Am., 1957, Scouters award, 1960, Scouter's Key, also medallion, 1967, Lincoln medallion Lincoln Sesquicentennial Commn., 1960, award of Achievement U.S. Civil War Centennial Commn., 1965, Algernon Sydney Sullivan medallion, 1969, Distinguished Service award Ill. State Hist. Library, 1969, 77, I.H. Duval Distinguished Service award, 1971, legion of honor Internat. Supreme Council, Order of De Molay, 1972, Disting. Service award Civil War Round Table of Chgo., 1983, 91, Cert. Excellence Ill. State Hist. Soc., 1985; named Hon. Ky. Col., Marshall of Okla. Territory. Fellow Royal Soc. Arts (life); mem. Lincoln Group D.C. (hon.), U. Ill. Alumni Assn., Ill. State Hist. Soc., Board of Advisors, The Lincoln Forum, Ill. Profl. Land Surveyors Assn., Ill. State Dental Soc. (citation plague 1966), Res. Officers Assn., Lincoln Fellowship of Wis., NRA (endowment), Iron Brigade Assn. (hon. life), Mil. Order Loyal Legion U.S. (hon. companion), Masons (33 degree, meritorious svc. award, Red Cross of Constantine, grand rep. to Grand Lodge of Colo.), Shriners, K.T., Kappa Delta Pi, Phi Alpha, Phi Alpha Theta (Scholarship Key award), Chi Gamma Iota, Tau Kappa Alpha, Alpha Psi Omega, Sigma Pi Beta (Headmaster), Sigma Tau Delta (Gold Honor Key award for editorial writing). Presbyterian (elder). Home: 1121 S 4th Street Ct Springfield IL 62703-2200 Office: Ill State Archives Springfield IL 62756 *Only in America could a poor farm boy from Ohio work his way through a great university, like the University of Illinois, and receive a doctor's degree. Life has been kind to me, and I have tried hard and worked hard. I am proud to be an American.*

TEMPLE, WICK, journalist; b. Little Rock, Oct. 24, 1937; s. Robert Wickliffe and Lorene (Bullard) T.; m. Margaret A. McCay, May 27, 1989; children by previous marriage: Wick III, Ellen Wallace, Carol Halter, Shawn Temple. A.A., Texarkana Coll., 1957; postgrad., U. Tex., 1958-59. Reporter, sports editor Texarkana (Tex.) Gazette-News, 1954-58; reporter Austin (Tex.) American-Statesman, 1958-59; reporter, news editor AP, Little Rock, 1959-65; corr. AP, St. Louis, 1965-66; bur. chief AP, Helena, Mont., 1966-68, Seattle, 1968-73; sports editor AP, N.Y.C., 1973-80, mng. editor, 1980-85, dir. human resources, 1985-88, v.p., 1988, dir. newspaper membership, 1988—. Home: 10 Berkeley Rd Millburn NJ 07041-2012 Office: AP 50 Rockefeller Plz New York NY 10020-1605

TEMPLETON, ALAN ROBERT, biology educator; b. Litchfield, Ill., Feb. 28, 1947; s. John Smith and Lois Arlene (McCormick) T.; m. Bonnie A. Altman, Dec. 20, 1969; children: Jeremy Alan, Jeffrey Alan. BA, Washington U., 1969; MS in Stats., U. Mich., 1972, PhD in Genetics, 1972. Jr. fellow Mich. Soc. Fellows, Ann Arbor, 1972-74; asst. prof. U. Tex., Austin, 1974-77; assoc. prof. Washington U., St. Louis, 1977-81, prof., 1981—; cons. St. Louis Zool. Park, 1979—; founding mem., dir. Soc. for Conservation Biology, 1985—. Editor: Theoretical Population Biology, 1981-91; mem. editorial bd. Molecular Phylogenetics & Evolution, 1991—, Brazilian Jour. of Genetics, 1991—; contbr. numerous article to profl. jours. Grantee NSF, 1974-80, 90—, NIH, 1980—, Nixon Griffis Fund for Zool. Rsch., 1986-87. Mem. Soc. for Study Evolution (v.p. 1982, pres. 1996-97), Genetics Soc. Am., Soc. Conservation Biology (bd. dirs. 1985-88), Nature Conservancy (trustee Mo. chpt. 1988—). Avocations: hiking, caving, music, ethnomusicology, scuba diving, flying. Office: Washington U Dept Biology Saint Louis MO 63130-4899

TEMPLETON, CARSON HOWARD, engineer, policy analyst; b. Wainwright, Alta., Can., Sept. 9, 1917; s. Samuel Howard and Ellen Florence T.; m. Laurie Jean MacLachlan, May 29, 1948; children—Colleen, Neil. B.S., U. Alta., 1943. L.L.D. (hon.), U. Man., 1982; D.E.S. (hon.), U. Waterloo, 1983. Registered profl. engr., B.C., Alta., Man. Chief engr. Greater Winnipeg Dyking Bd., Can., 1948-50; sr. ptnr. Templeton Engring. Co., Winnipeg, 1955-81; pres. Templeton Facilities Ltd., Winnipeg, 1958—; v.p. Teshmont Cons., Inc., Winnipeg, 1970-81; cons. Pub. Utilities Bd. Man., 1962-70. Bd. dirs. Childrens Hosp. Winnipeg, 1958-70; vice chmn. bd. govs. U. Man. Recipient Gzowski medal Engring. Inst. Can., 1951, fellow, 1978; named Officer of the Order of Can. Gov. Gen. of Can., 1978. Mem. Assn. Profl. Engrs. Man. (recipient merit award, named for outstanding service), Assn. Cons. Engrs. Can. (pres. 1968-69).

TEMPLETON, IAN MALCOLM, retired physicist; b. Rugby, Eng., July 31, 1929; emigrated to Can., 1957, naturalized, 1967; s. William and Eleanor Clayton (Butcher) T.; m. Elsa Wood, Aug. 11, 1956; children—Nicola Jean, Jennifer Jane. M.A., Univ. Coll., Oxford, Eng., 1950, D.Phil., 1953. Fellow NRC Can., Ottawa, Ont., 1953-54; asst. rsch. officer NRC Can., 1957-60, assoc. rsch. officer, 1960-64, sr. rsch. officer, 1964-71, prin. rsch. officer, 1971-94, joint head metal physics group, 1969-76, head electronic structure and calorimetry group, 1976-87; mem. staff rsch. lab. Associated Elec. Industries, Rugby, Eng., 1955-57. Contbr. articles to profl. jours. Fellow Inst. Physics, Royal Soc. Can. Home: 17 Dunvegan Rd, Ottawa, ON Canada K1K 3E8

TEMPLETON, JOHN ALEXANDER, II, coal company executive; b. Chgo., Mar. 31, 1927; s. Philip Henry and Florence (Moore) T.; B.S., Ind. U., 1950; m. Norma Frazier, Aug. 10, 1949; children—Lori, Linda, Leslie, Sally. Agt., Conn. Mut. Life Ins. Co., Terre Haute, Ind., 1949-51; ptnr. Miller, Templeton, Scott Ins. Agy., Terre Haute, 1951-64; exec. v.p. Templeton Coal Co., Inc., Terre Haute, 1964-72, pres., 1972-94, elected chmn. 1994, also dir.; pres. Sherwood Templeton Coal Co., Inc., Indpls., 1968—, also dir.; bd. dirs. Plumb Supply Co., Des Moines, 1965—, Dicksons, Inc., Seymour, Ind., 1986—, Franklin (Ind.) Plastic Products Co., 1986; dir. Mchts. Nat. Bank of Terre Haute. Chmn., Vigo County Goldwater for Pres. Com., 1964; trustee Union Hosp., 1968—, v.p., 1975—, chmn. bd. dirs., 1986—; bd. dirs. Ind. State U. Found., 1970—; trustee U. Evansville, 1974-77; bd. of assocs. Rose-Hulman Inst. Tech., 1977; v.p., trustee Ind. Asbury Towers, Greencastle, Ind., 1980-83. Served with U.S. Army, 1946-48. Mem. Ind. Assn. Ins. Agts. (pres. 1959-60), Ind. Coal Assn. (dir.), Lynch Coal Ops. Reciprocal Assn., Interstate Coal Conf., Ind. State C. of C. (bd. dirs. 1981—), Ind. U. Alumni Assn. (exec. council 1983-86). Republican. Methodist. Clubs: Masons, Elks, Scottish Rite.

TEMPLETON, JOHN MARKS, investment counsel, financial analyst; b. Winchester, Tenn., Nov. 29, 1912; s. Harvey Maxwell and Vella (Handly) T.; m. Judith Dudley Folk, Apr. 7, 1937 (dec. Feb. 1951); children: John Marks, Anne Dudley, Christopher Winston; m. Irene Reynolds Butler, Dec. 31, 1958 (dec. Nov. 1993). A.B., Yale U., 1934; M.A. (law) (Rhodes scholar), Balliol Coll., Oxford, Eng., 1936; LLD (hon.), Beaver Coll., 1965, Marquette U., 1980, Jamestown Coll., 1983, Maryville Coll., 1984, Babson Coll., 1992, Rhodes Coll, 1992, U. Rochester, 1992, La. Coll., 1993, Moravian Coll., 1994; D.Litt. (hon.), Wilson Coll., 1974; D.D. (hon.), Buena Vista Coll., 1979; D.C.L. (hon.), U. of South, 1984; DLitt (hon.), Manhattan Coll., 1990; LHD, U. Dubuque, 1992, Fla. Southern Coll., 1992; DLitt (hon.), Campbell U., 1993; LLD, Moravian Coll., 1994; DPhil (hon.), Stonehill Coll., 1995; LHD (hon.), Furman U., 1995; LLD (hon.), Notre Dame U., 1996, Methodist Coll., 1997. Chartered fin. analyst. Sec.-treas., v.p., dir. Nat. Geophys. Co., Dallas and N.Y.C., 1937-41; pres., dir. Templeton, Dobbrow & Vance, Inc., N.Y.C., 1941-65; chmn. Templeton Damroth Corp., 1959-62; v.p., dir. First Trust Bank Ltd., Bahamas, 1963—; pres., dir. Templeton Funds Inc., 1977-86, Templeton Global Funds Inc., 1981-86, Templeton Growth Fund Can., Ltd., Toronto, 1954-85; chmn Templeton Galbraith & Hansberger Ltd, 1986-92. Author: The Humble Approach, 1981; co-author: The Templeton Touch, 1985, The Templeton Plan, 1987, Global Investing, 1988, The God Who Would Be Known, 1989, Riches for the Mind and Spirit, 1990, Looking Forward, 1993, Discovering the Laws of Life, 1994, Is God the Only Reality?, 1994, Evidence of Purpose, 1994, Future Agenda, 1995; contbr. articles to fin. publs. Past pres. Lyford Cay (Bahamas) Property Owners Assn.; Chmn. YMCA Bergen County, 1952-54; dir., campaign chmn. Englewood Community Chest, 1953-54; trustee Englewood Hosp., 1953-56, Soc. for Promoting Christian Knowledge, 1984-87, Balliol Coll. Endowments (Oxford), Templeton Project Trust (Eng.); chmn. bd. trustees Princeton Theol. Sem., 1967-73, 79-85, trustee for restoration of Westminster Abbey, 1991—; trustee Wilson Coll., 1941-73, Buena Vista Coll., 1981—, Templeton Found. Inc., 1952—, John Templeton Found. Inc., 1987—, council on theol. sems. United Presbyn. Ch. U.S.A., 1946-83; mem. Ctr. Theol. Inquiry, 1979-92, Commn. on Ecumenical Mission, 1961-70; bd. corporators Presbyn. Ministers Fund, Inc., 1960-93; bd. visitors Harvard Div. Sch., 1981-88; adv. bd. Harvard Ctr. for the study of World Religions, 1975-89; bd. mgrs. Am. Bible Soc., 1972-92; mgmt. Council Templeton Coll. (Oxford); pres. Templeton Theol. Sem., Bahamas, 1984-88; hon. rector Dubuque U., 1982-92, Chancellor Fla. Southern Coll., 1992. Decorated knight Order of Brit. Empire, Knight of St. John; recipient Churchman of Yr. award Religious Heritage Am., 1979, Internat. Churchman of Yr. award, 1981, Ecumenical Patriarch's Hon. Order of Mt. Athos, Free Enterprise award Palm Beach Atlantic Coll., 1984, Centennial medal N.Y. Mayflower Soc., 1987, award USA Today, 1991, award for excellence in investment mgmt., 1991, Benjamin Franklin award Royal Soc. Arts, 1994, Lifetime Achievement award Laymans Nat. Bible Assn., 1995, Nat. Bus. Hall of Fame award Jr. Achievement Assn., 1996; named to Wall Street Week Hall of Fame, 1990. Mem. Soc. Security Analysts, World Pres. Orgn., Chief Execs. Orgn. (pres. 1968-69), Bahamas C. of C. (bd. dirs. 1976-79), Internat. Acad. Religious Scis., Mt. Pelerin Soc., Elihu Club, Elizabethan Club (New Haven), Yale Club, University Club (N.Y.C.), Lyford Cay Club of Bahamas (dep. chmn. 1980-86), Lansdowne Club, Royal Overseas League, Athenaeum (Eng.), United Oxford and Cambridge Univs. Club (Eng.), White's Club (Eng.), Rotary (Bahamas), Phi Beta Kappa., Zeta Psi. Office: Box N7776, Nassau Bahamas

TEMPLETON, JOHN MARKS, JR., pediatric surgeon, foundation executive; b. N.Y.C. Feb. 19, 1940; s. John Marks and Judith Dudley (Folk) T.; BA, Yale Coll., 1962; MD, Harvard U., 1968; m. Josephine J. Gargiulo, Aug. 2, 1970; children: Heather Erin, Jennifer Ann. Intern, Med. Coll. Va., Richmond, 1968-69, resident, 1969-73; prof. pediatric surgery U. Pa. and Children's Hosp. of Phila., 1995, dir. trauma program, 1989-95; chmn. bd. Templeton Growth Fund, Ltd. Assoc. editor: Textbook of Pediatric Emergencies, 1993. Chmn. health and safety, exec. bd. Cradle of Liberty Coun. Boy Scouts Am.; Ea. Coll., Nat. Recreation Found., Melmark Charitable Found.; nat. bd. dirs., pres. Pa. div. Am. Trauma Soc.; bd. dirs. Layman's Nat. Bible Assn.; pres. John Templeton Found. Served with M.C., USNR, 1975-77. Barclay fellow Templeton Coll. Oxford U. Mem. ACS, AMA, Am. Pediatric Surg. Assn., Am. Acad. Pediatrics, Am. Assn. Surgery of Trauma, Ea. Assn. Surgery of Trauma, Phila. Coll. Physicians, Union League, Merion Cricket Club. Republican. Evangelical. Office: 2 Radnor Corp Ctr Ste 320 Radnor PA 19087-4514

TEMPLETON, ROBERT EARL, engineering and construction company executive; b. Pitts., June 21, 1931; s. Robert James and Alice Wilma (Schepple) T.; m. Barbara Ann McDonald, June 9, 1956; children: Shirley Anne (dec.), Susan Elaine, Sally Irene. BSCE, Carnegie Mellon U., 1953, MSCE, 1954; MBA in Mgmt., NYU, 1960. Registered profl. engr., N.Y. With M.W. Kellogg Co., Houston, 1954-93, project engr., 1963-66, mgr. contract status, 1966-68, mgr. sales forecasting, 1968-72, mgr. market forecasting, 1972-73; mgr. Venture Analysis, Houston, 1973-74, mgr. analysis and methods div., 1974-76, mgr. Project Cost Services div., 1976-81, mgr. Cost Mgmt. Services div., 1981-85, project control mgr., 1985-93; pres. Templeton Enterprises, Houston, 1993—; project mgmt. profl. cons. Steege Kingston & Assocs., Inc., Houston, 1993-96, Team Assocs. Inc., Houston, 1996—; cons. project mgmt. profl., total cost mgmt., work process improvement, reengring., benchmarking, electronic data interchange, Internat. Stds. Orgn., 9000 Quality Sys. Stds., Houston, 1993—. Mem. editl. bd. Engring. and Process Econs., 1976-85. Area chmn. United Campaign, Summit, N.J., 1969-70; v.p. Jefferson Sch. PTA, Summit, 1965-67, pres., 1967-69; security chmn. Fonn Villas Civic Assn., Houston, 1973, chmn. archtl. stds. com., 1974, v.p., 1975, pres., 1976; mem. exec. com., bd. dirs. Houston Advs. for Mentally Ill Children; active Can Care of Houston Inc., For-By-To Cancer Survivors (ch. ministry), Income Tax Assistance (VITA), Tax Counseling for the Elderly (TCE), AARP, Houston. J. Waldo Smith Hydraulic fellow ASCE, 1953-54. Fellow Am. Assn. Cost Engrs. (award of merit 1977, award of recognition 1980, cert. cost engr.; nat. pres. 1971-72, nat. adminstrv. v.p. 1970-71, nat. adv. staff 1973—, spl. projects chmn. 1974-75, cert. bd. chmn. 1976-79, chmn. assn. standards and recommended practices com. 1985-89, chmn. quality mgmt. com. 1988—, chmn. inter-orgnl. liaison com. 1995—); mem. N.Am. Soc. Corporate Planners (program dir. 1974, chmn. ad hoc cert. com. 1986—), Am. Assn. Engring. Socs., Project Mgmt. Inst. (cert. project mgmt. profl., v.p. certification Houston chpt. 1993-94, v.p. edn. 1985-86, 87-88, 91-92, pres. 1988-89, chmn. advisor 1989-90), Sigma XI (Sec. M.W. Kellogg br. 1973-74), Sigma Xi (2d v.p. 1976-77, 84-85, 1st v.p. 1985-86), Houston Comml. Bridge League (v.p. 1973-75), Houston C. of C. (life mem., dir. engring. and constrn. internat. bus. network exec. com.), Am. Mktg. Assn., Acad. for Health Services Mktg. (profl. mem.), Health Services Mktg. Soc. (bd. dirs.), Tau Beta Pi, Beta Theta Pi. Republican. Presbyterian (deacon

1956-59, elder 1980-82). Club: M.W. Kellogg Quarter Century (pres. 1986-87). Home and Office: 12718 Old Oaks Dr Houston TX 77024-4016

TEMPLIN, JOHN LEON, JR., healthcare consulting executive; b. New Brunswick, N.Y., Aug. 5, 1940; s. John Leon and Theresa Veronica (Revolinski) T.; m. Barbara Maria Ribley, Sept. 12, 1970; children: John, Joseph, Kevin, Nan, Danielle, Christopher. BS in Mgmt. Engring., Rensselaer Poly. Inst., 1962, MS in Mgmt., 1969. Cert. healthcare cons. Am. Assn. Healthcare Cons. Mgr. customer svc. Norton Abrasives, Troy, N.Y., 1968-70; cons., sr. cons. Hosp. Assn. N.Y. State, Albany, 1970-79, dir. mgmt. svcs., 1979-80, sr. dir. mgmt. svc., 1981-83; dir. productivity improvement Applied Leadership Technologies, Inc., Greenfield Center, N.Y., 1983-84, v.p., productivity improvement div., 1984-85, pres., 1985-86; pres. Templin Mgmt. Assocs., Inc., Greenfield Center, 1987—, The Northeastern Cons. Alliance, Albany, N.Y., 1995—. Editor quar. jour. Healthcare Supr., 1983—; mem. editorial com. ann. Manual for Workload Recording, 1978-91. Mem. budget com. Greater Saratoga Sch. Dist., Saratoga Springs, N.Y., 1978-79; mem. energy com. Blue Cross Assn., Chgo., 1978-81; mem. Gov.'s Task Force on Nursing, Albany, 1980; mem. parish coun. St. Joseph's Ch., Greenfield Center, 1981-87. Capt. U.S. Army, 1962-64. Fellow Am. Coll. Healthcare Execs., Healthcare Info. and Mgmt. Sys. Soc. (liaison Coll. Am. Pathologists 1978-91, chair edn. com. 1995-96); mem. Am. Hosp. Assn. (seminar spkr. 1980-93), Clin. Lab. Mgmt. Assn. (bd. dirs. 1980-84), KC. Republican. Roman Catholic. Avocations: golf, computers, gardening, fishing. Home and Office: Templin Mgmt Assocs Inc 265 Locust Grove Rd Greenfield Center NY 12833-1501

TEMPLIN, KENNETH ELWOOD, paper company executive; b. Mason City, Nebr., Jan. 26, 1927; s. Otto Rudolph and Marianna (Graf) T.; m. Harriet Elaine Ressel, Aug. 24, 1951; children: Steven, David, Daniel, Benjamin, Elizabeth. B.S. in Bus. Adminstrn, U. Nebr., 1950; M.B.A., Wayne State U., 1961. Fin. analyst Ford Motor Co., 1950-54; fin. analyst, corp. staff Chrysler Corp., 1955-60, div. controller marine engine div., 1961-63, gen. sales mgr., 1964-65; v.p. Marsh and Templin, N.Y.C., 1966-69; v.p., gen. mgr. operating group Saxon Industries, N.Y.C., 1970-79; group v.p. Saxon Industries, 1979-82, sr. v.p., 1982-85; v.p.-converting Paper Corp. Am., Wayne, Pa., 1985-86; exec. v.p. Quality Park Products Inc., St. Paul, 1986-88, 1986-88, pres., 1988-96, ret., 1996; mem. exec. com. Single Service Inst., 1971-79. Regional chmn. Minn. devel. com. Nat. Multiple Sclerosis Soc., 1970-71; co-pres. Home and Sch. Assn., Bernardsville, N.J., 1975-76; bd. dirs. West Hennepin Counseling Svcs., Inc., 1996—. Served with U.S. Army, 1945-47, 50-51. Mem. Envelope Mfrs. Assn. Am. (postal affairs com. 1989-96, fin. com. chmn. 1994-95, bd. dirs. 1990-91, 93-95), Small Bus. Adminstrn. (Mpls. Score chpt. 2). Presbyterian. Home: 3993 County Road 42 NE Alexandria MN 56308-6621

TEN CATE, ARNOLD RICHARD, dentistry educator; b. Accrington, Lancashire, Eng., Oct. 21, 1933; s. Gys Johan and Lien (Dalenoord) Ten C.; m. Alice Mitchell, Apr. 7, 1956 (dec.); children: Pauline Ann, Jill Elaine, Ian Richard. B.Sc., U. London, 1955, Ph.D. in Anatomy, 1957, B.D.S., 1960; DSc (hon.), McGill U., 1989, U. Western Ont., 1989; DDS (hon.), Nihon U., 1995. Leverhulme fellow in dental sci. Royal Coll. Surgeons, Eng., 1961-63; sr. lectr. in anatomy in relation to dentistry Guy's Hosp. Med. Sch., U. London, 1963-68; prof. dentistry Faculty Dentistry, U. Toronto, Ont., Can., 1968-77; chmn. div. biol. scis. Faculty Dentistry, U. Toronto, 1971-77, dean, 1977-89, vice provost health scis., 1989-94; Chmn. bd. dirs. Aboutface, Oralife Group. Author: Advanced Dental Histology, 4th edit., 1983, Oral Histology, Development, Structure and Function, 1980, 4th edit., 1994; others, also articles. Recipient Colyer prize Royal Soc. Medicine, 1962; Mil. Hellman award Am. Assn. Orthodontists, 1975. Mem. Internat. Assn. Dental Research (pres. 1984, Isaac Schour Meml. award 1978). Conservative. Mem. Christian Ch. Home: 50 Squire Baker's Ln, Markham, ON Canada L3P 3G9 Office: Faculty of Dentistry, 123 Edward St, Toronto, ON Canada M5G 1G6

TENDLER, DAVID, international trade company executive; b. N.Y.C., Jan. 15, 1938; s. Philip and Pearl (Berman) T.; m. Beatrice Weisberg, Oct. 11, 1958; children: Pearl, Karen. BBA in Internat. Econs., CCNY, 1959. With Philipp Bros. Co., 1960—, mgr. Far Eastern ops., 1968-75; pres. Philipp Bros. Co., N.Y.C., 1975—; dir. parent corp. Engelhard Minerals & Chems. Corp. (name changed to Phibro Corp. 1981), N.Y.C., 1975-85; vice chmn. bd. Engelhard Minerals & Chems. Corp. (name changed to Phibro Corp. 1981), 1979-81, chmn. bd., chief exec. officer, 1981—; co-chmn., co-chief exec. officer Phibro-Salomon Inc., 1983-84; founder Tendler Beretz Assocs. Ltd., 1985—; chmn. subcom. trade U.S.-German Dem. Rep. Trade and Econ. Coun., 1978-84; bd. dirs., mem. exec. com. U.S./USSR Trade and Econ. Coun., 1979-85, U.S.-China Bus. Coun., 1983-94; bd. dirs. Biotech. Gen. Corp., Iselin, N.J.; chmn. bd. dirs. V.I. Technologies, Inc., L.I., N.Y. Mem. bd. overseers NYU Grad. Sch. Bus., 1981-85; trustee Lenox Hill Hosp., 1981-94; mem. exec. com. N.Y. Blood Ctr., 1987—; bd. dirs., mem. exec. com. Fgn. Policy Assn., 1983-96. Recipient Torch of Liberty award metals and metal products div. Anti-Defamation League, 1976, Edith and Herbert Lehman award Henry St. Settlement, 1982; named Man of Yr., Fgn. Trade Soc., Baruch Coll., CUNY, 1985. Office: Tendler Beretz Assocs 150 E 52nd St New York NY 10022-6017

TENENBAUM, BARBARA APPELL, specialist in Mexican culture; b. Phila., June 9, 1946; d. Eugene and Rose Appell; m. Heinz Heinemann, Apr. 23, 1995. BA magna cum laude, Brandeis U., 1968; MA, HArvard U., 1969, PhD, 1973. Asst. prof. history, dir. L.Am. studies progra, Vassar Coll., 1973-78, U. S.C., 1978-86; specialist Mexican culture Libr. Congress, Hispanic divsn., 1992—; vis. assoc. prof. history Howard U., 1988-89, vis. asst. prof. history Cath. U., 1987-91; chair Mexican studies com. Conf. L.Am. History, 1989-90. Author: México en la época de los agiotistas, 1821-1857, 1985, The Politics of Penury: Debts and Taxes in Mexico, 1821-1856, 1986; co-editor: (with Vincent Peloso) Liberals, Politics and Power: State Formation in Nineteenth Century Latin America, 1996; contbg. editor: Handbook of Latin American Studies, 1988—; editor-in-chief Ency. of Latin Am. History and Culture, 5 vols., 1996; asst. editor The Americas, 1987—; contbr. articles to profl. jours. Bd. advisors History House; lit. adv. bd. GALA Hispanic Theater, Washington; exec. bd. Nat. Hispanic Quincentennial Commn., Washington, v.p., 1989-93. Rockefeller Found. fellow, 1991-92; recipient Waldo G. Leland prize Am. Hist. Soc., 1997, Outstanding Svc. award Conf. L.Am. History, 1997. Office: Libr Congress Hispanic Divsn Washington DC 20540-4850

TENENBAUM, JEFFREY MARK, academic librarian; b. Phila., Apr. 10, 1945; s. Paul and Hansi (Barber) T. BA, Pa. State U., 1966; MLS, McGill U., 1968. Documents librarian, then reference librarian U. Toronto (Ont., Can.) Library, 1968-72; reference librarian U. Mass. Library, Amherst, 1973—; mem. Info. Access Co. Acad. Libr. Product Adv. Bd., Foster City, Calif., 1992-94. Mem. Amherst Pub. Art Commn., 1994—. Mem. ALA, Assn. Can. Studies in U.S., Am. Coun. Que. Studies, Mid-Atlantic and New Eng. Conf. for Can. Studies (sec. 1992-96), Pioneer Valley Assn. Acad. Librs. (pres. 1989-90), Assn. Coll. and Rsch. Librs., Beta Phi Mu, Phi Alpha Theta, Pi Gamma Mu. Jewish. Home: 48 Riverside Park Amherst MA 01002-4011 Office: U Mass Univ Libr Amherst MA 01003-4710

TENENBAUM, MICHAEL, steel company executive; b. St. Paul, July 23, 1913; s. Harry and Ida Vivian (Kolohoski) T.; m. Helen Zlatovski, Aug. 16, 1941 (div. 1981); children: Susan Rose Tenenbaum Uyama, Anne Louise Benjamin; m. Martha Smith Berner, July 30, 1982. Met.E., U. Minn., 1936, M.S., 1937, Ph.D., 1940; D.Sc. hon., Northwestern U., 1976. Metallurgist Inland Steel Co., East Chicago, Ind., 1940-50, mgr., 1950-65; v.p. Inland Steel Co., Chgo., 1965-71, pres., 1971-78, dir., 1971-84; cons., 1984—. Fellow AIME (hon., Hunt and Raymond award 1949), Am. Soc. Metals (disting. mem.); mem. The Metall. Soc. (pres.), Western Soc. Engrs. (Washington award 1976), Brit. Metals Soc. (Bessemer Gold medal 1980), Assn. Iron and Steel Engrs., Am. Iron and Steel Inst., Nat. Acad. Engring. Home: 4049 220th Pl SE Issaquah WA 98029-7212

TENER, CAROL JOAN, retired secondary education educator; b. Cleve., Feb. 10, 1935; d. Peter Paul and Mamie Christine (Dombrowski) Manusack; m. Dale Keith Tener, Feb. 13, 1958 (div. Aug. 1991); children: Dean Robert, Susan Dawn. Student, Cleve. Mus. Art, 1948-53, Cleve. Art Inst., 1953-54; BS in Edn. cum laude, Kent State U., 1957; MS in Supervision, Akron U., 1974; postgrad., Kent State U., 1964, 81, 88-90, Akron U., 1975, 79, John Carroll U., 1982, 83, 85-86, Ohio U., 1987, Baldwin Wallace Coll., 1989. Cert. permanent K-12 tchr., Ohio. Stenographer Equitable Life Iowa, Cleve., 1953-54; tchr. elem. art Cuyahoga Falls (Ohio) Bd. Edn., 1957-58, 62-63, 1965-68, tchr. jr. h.s., 1968-69; tchr. h.s. Brecksville (Ohio)-Broadview Heights Sch. Dist., 1969-94; chmn. dept. art Brecksville-Broadview Heights (Ohio) H.S., 1979-94; ret., chmn. curriculum devel., 1982, 89; instr. for children Kent State U., 1956; advisor, prodr. cmty. svc. in art Brecksville Broadview Heights Bd. of Edn., 1969-94; former tchr. recreation and adult art edn. 1967-68, City of Cuyahoga Falls, 1967-68; com. mem. North Ctrl. Evaluation Com., Nordonia City, Ohio, 1978, Solon City, Ohio, 1989; chmn. north ctrl. evaluation com. Garfield Heights H.S., 1991; chair pilot program curriculum devel. com. in art/econs. Brecksville-Broadview Heights H.S., 1985, 86. Contbr. articles to newspapers, brochures, mags.; commd. artist for mural Brecksville City's Kids Quarters, 1994, Christopher Columbus/John Glen portraits in relief commemorating Columbus Day, 1961, Wooster (Ohio) Products Co. Chmn. Artmart Invitational Exhibit PTA, 1982-94; active Meals on Wheels, 1995-96, Brecksville Broadview, Cancer, 1993-95, Leukemia, 1995, Heart Disease collection, 1995, Stow-Glen Assisted Living Visitations, 1994-95, NCR Assisted Living transp. provision to hosps. and dr. in neighboring county; trustee, sec. Gettysburg Devel. Block Group Parma, 1995-96, Kids Quarters, 1994. Recipient Ohio Coun. on Econ. Edn. award, 1985-86, award for significant svc. to cmty. Retired and Sr. Vol. Program of USA, 1996; Pres.'s scholar Kent State U., 1954-57. Mem. AAUW, ASCD, NAFE, Nat. Art Edn. Assn., Ohio Ret. Tchrs. Assn. (registration chair Greater Cleve. chpt. 1997), Internat. Platform Assn., Brecksville Edn. Assn., Acad. Econ. Edn., Cleve. Mus. Art, Nat. Mus. Women in Arts, S.W. Area Retired Educators (program chair 1996—), Phi Delta Kappa Pi. Roman Catholic. Avocations: European and American museum tours, photography, collecting books on architecture, painting. Home: 7301 Sagamore Rd Parma OH 44134-5732

TENG, JULIET, artist; d. Teng Lenten and Ho Wai Yu; children: Brendan, Trish, Jamie, Stacy, Phaeleau. B Commerce, U. Rangoon. Programmer First Boston Corp., N.Y.C.; systems programmer Chase Manhattan, N.Y.C., Merrill Lynch, Pierce, Fenner & Smith, Inc., N.Y.C.; artist/painter, 1976—. Exhbns. include Prince St. Gallery, N.Y.C., Nat. Arts Club, N.Y.C., Pastel Soc. Am., N.Y.C., Audubon Artists Soc., N.Y.C., Catherine Lorrilard Wolf Art Club, N.Y.C., Painters and Sculptors Soc. N.J., N.Y.C., Knickerbocker Artists Am. Soc., N.Y.C., Keene-Mason Galleries, N.Y.C., Nat. Art Ctr., N.Y.C., Hudson Valley Art Assn., Westchester, N.Y., Manchester Art Ctr., Vt., Five Point Gallery, East Chatham, N.Y., Connoisseur Gallery, Rhinebeck, N.Y., Ridgewood Art Inst., N.J., The New England Fine Art Inst., Boston, The Salmagundi Club, N.Y.C., Prince Street Gallery, Soho, N.Y.C., numerous others. Mem. Nat. Arts Club, Art Students League. Avocations: Flamenco dance, ballroom dance, fashion designing, T'ai Ch'i Chuan, carpentry. Home: 34 Sesame St Old Chatham NY 12136

TENGI, FRANK R., lawyer, insurance company executive; b. Garfield, N.J., Aug. 11, 1920; s. John and Mary (Fedush) T.; m. Shirley H. Mitchell, May 17, 1952; children: Christopher, Nancy. BS, Georgetown U., 1946; LLD, Fordham U., 1951. CPA, N.J.; lic. ins. broker, N.Y. Bar: N.Y. 1955, U.S. Supreme Ct. 1967, U.S. Ct. Claims 1967, U.S. Dist. Ct. (so. dist.) N.Y. 1967, U.S. Dist. Ct. (ea. dist.) N.Y., 1967, U.S. Tax Ct. 1968. Asst. sec. Am. Internat. Aviation Agy., Inc., N.Y.C., 1961-69; assoc. Lee Mulderig & Celentano, N.Y.C., 1965-70; asst. sec. Am. Internat. Underwriting Corp., N.Y.C., 1965—, Am. Internat. Underwriters Assn., 1965—, Starr Tech. Risks Agy., Inc., 1967-78; asst. comptroller taxation A.I.G., Inc., N.Y.C., 1971-75; asst. sec. C.V. Starr & Co., Inc., N.Y.C., 1965—; pres. Estate Maintenance Co., Inc., N.Y.C., 1969-71; mgr. reinsurance security Worldwide, Am. Internat. Group, Inc., N.Y.C., 1978-96, reins. security adv., 1996—. Mem. Mayor's Budget Adv. Com. Plainfield, 1980-81. Treas., Starr Found., 1970—. Served with U.S. Army, 1941-46; ETO. Mem. N.Y. State Bar Assn., Tax Execs. Inst. Home: 17 Madison Ave Apt 58 Madison NJ 07940-1466 Office: 70 Pine St New York NY 10270-0002

TENHOEVE, THOMAS, academic administrator; b. Bklyn., Oct. 1, 1935; s. Thomas and Adeline Ruth (Vander Hill) T.; m. Suzanne Underwood, June 7, 1957; children: Thomas III, Carol, Timothy. AB, Hope Coll., 1956; MA, U. Mich., 1957; PhD, U. Toledo, 1965; postgrad., U. Western Mich. Biology tchr. South Haven. Mich. Pub. Schs., 1957-58; biology instr. Northwestern Coll., Orange City, Iowa, 1958-63; supr. biology students U. Toledo, Ohio, 1963-65; acad. dean, acting pres. Northwestern Coll., Orange City, 1965-70; pres. Butler (Pa.) County Community Coll., 1970-84, Oakton Community Coll., Des Plaines, Ill., 1984-95. Bd. dirs. Sister Cities, 1986-95; trustee Northwestern Coll., 1988-95; mem. Ill. C.C. State Found. Bd., 1993-95, Ill. Math. and Sci. Acad. Selection Bd., 1986, 87, Cook County Sheriff's Scholarship Panel; exec. com. Golden Corridor, 1986-92. Recipient Pacesetter award Nat. Coun. for Community Rels., 1986, Orchard Village award. Mem. Am. Coun. on Internat. Intercultural Edn. (chmn. 1992-95), Coun. North Ctrl. Two-Yr. Colls. (state rep. 1988-92, exec. bd. 1989-95, 2d v.p. 1990-91, 1st v.p. 1991-92, pres. 1992-93).

TENNANT, JOHN RANDALL, management advisory company executive; b. North Bend, Wash., Aug. 23, 1940; s. Maurice Andrew and Jane Downing (Vinnedge) T.; m. Nikki Mae Priem, July 17, 1965 (div.); children: Ann Elizabeth, Randall Warren; m. Deborah Ann Francis, Oct. 25, 1986 (div.); 1 child, Alyssa Jane. B.S. in Indsl. Engring., Stanford U., 1962; M.B.A., U. Wash., 1966. Registered profl. engr., Wash. Sr. research engr. Boeing Co., Seattle, 1962-68; mgr. Price Waterhouse, Seattle, 1968-73; ptnr. Price Waterhouse, Tokyo, 1973-79, Los Angeles, 1979-89; founder, chief exec. officer Manex, Inc., Newport Beach, Calif., 1989—; dir. subs. Price Waterhouse Assocs., Pacific region, 1975-79. Mem. John Tracy Clinic Men's Com., Santa Catalina Island Conservancy, pres., 1985-87. Mem. NSPE, Japan Computer Assn. (founder, pres. 1976-77), Japan Modapts Assn. (founder), Japan Am. Soc., Inst. Mgmt. Cons., Am. Inst. Indsl. Engrs. (pres. Seattle chpt. 1970-71), Data Processing Mgmt. Assn., Tokyo Lawn and Tennis Club, L.A. Country Club, Jonathan Club, Empty Saddle Club, Los Rancheros Visitadores Club, Los Caballeros Club. Home: 2758 Forrester Dr Los Angeles CA 90064

TENNANT, THOMAS MICHAEL, lawyer; b. Anniston, Ala., July 23, 1948; s. Thomas Edward and Mary Eugenia (Warren) T.; m. Sharon Leigh Ebert, Mar. 21, 1970; children: Sharon Michelle, Michael Ebert. BS, Auburn U., 1970; JD, Walter F. George Sch. Law, 1973. Assoc. Webb, Fowler & Tanner, Lawrenceville, Ga., 1973-76, ptnr., 1976-77; mng. ptnr. Tennant, Andersen & Davidson, P.C., Lawrenceville, 1978-81, Tennant, Andersen, Davidson & Edmondson, P.C., Lawrenceville, 1982-85, Tennant, Davidson & Edmondson, P.C., Lawrenceville, 1985-86, Tennant, Davidson & Thompson, P.C., Lawrenceville, 1986-87, Tennant, Davidson, Thompson & Sweeny, Lawrenceville, 1987-89, Tennant, Thompson & Sweeny, 1990, Alston & Bird, Atlanta, 1991—; judge Recorder's Ct., Lawrenceville, 1979-80; mem. State Disciplinary Bd., 1988-91. Bd. dirs. Gwinnett Found., Inc., Lawrenceville, 1984—. Served to 1st lt. U.S. Army, 1970-78. Mem. State Bar Ga. (chmn. lawyer ethics com. young lawyers sect. 1979-80, bd. govs. 1986-92), Gwinnett County Bar Assn. (pres. 1978), Ga. Trial Lawyers Assn., Atlanta Lawyers Club, Gwinnett County C. of C. (pres. 1986). Presbyterian. Home: 4069 Nobleman Pt Duluth GA 30136-2363 Office: Alston & Bird One Atlantic Ctr 1201 W Peachtree St NW Atlanta GA 30309-3400

TENNE, DONALD PAUL, financial planner; b. Bronx, N.Y., Nov. 28, 1954; s. Gerard Lawrence and Rita Rose (Delli Bovi) T.; m. Marybeth Rose Taylor, Oct. 12, 1985; 1 child, Melissa Rose. Grad., Adirondack C.C., 1973-75. Account rep. Met. Ins. Co., Glens Falls, N.Y., 1982-87; fin. planner MetLife Securities, Inc., Glens Falls, N.Y., 1987—; fin. editor Sta. WCKM Radio, Lake George, N.Y., 1994—; instr. Skidmore Coll., Saratoga, N.Y., 1989—, Boces, Hudson Falls, N.Y., 1989—; Metlife Leaders Conf. qualifier, 1993-95; Metlife Pres. Conf. qualifier, 1996. Guest columnist Glens Falls Bus. Jour., 1990. Fund raising com. Literacy Vols. of Glens Falls, 1990-93. Mem. Glens Falls Masons (master), Fort Edward/Hudson Falls Elks, Nat. Assn. of Life Underwriters, Internat. Assn. of Fin. Planners. Avocations: racketball, golf, reading. Office: MetLife Securities Inc PO Box 788 333 Glen St Ste 302 Glens Falls NY 12801-2929

TENNENT, VALENTINE LESLIE, accountant; b. Apia, Western Samoa, Apr. 5, 1919; came to U.S., 1922; s. Hugh Cowper and Madge Grace (Cook) T.; m. Jeanne Marie Elder, Dec. 10, 1941; children: Madeline Jeanne Walls, Hugh Cowper II, Michael Waller, Val Leslie, Paul Anthony. Student, U. Calif., Berkeley, 1938-40. CPA, Hawaii, La. Mgr. Tennent & Greaney, CPAs, Hilo, Hawaii, 1945-50; ptnr. Cameron, Tennent & Dunn, CPAs, Honolulu, 1950-56; ptnr. KPMG Peat Marwick LLP, Honolulu, 1956-79, cons., 1979-84; ind. rschr. pub. fin. and banking, politico-econ. sci., moral philosophy, San Diego, 1984—. Founding trustee, pres., treas. Tennent Art Found., Honolulu, 1955-77; trustee, treas. Watumull Found., Honolulu, 1963-90; bd. dirs. Iolani Sch., Inst. for Human Svcs., Honolulu, Lyman Mus., Hilo. Capt. USAF, 1941-45. Recipient Bishop's Cross for disting. svc. Protestant Episcopal Ch., Dist. Hawaii, 1965, G.J. Watumull award for disting. achievement Watumull Found., Honolulu, 1982. Mem. AICPA (governing coun. 1961-64), Hawaii Soc. CPAs (pres. 1960). Episcopalian. Avocations: swimming, fine arts, music, literature. Home and Office: 700 Front St Apt 1607 San Diego CA 92101-6011 *Joy in life comes from knowing the things you want to accomplish within God's overall purpose, pursuing them to the end regardless of difficulties, and accepting full responsibility for inevitable failures.*

TENNEY, DUDLEY BRADSTREET, lawyer; b. N.Y.C., July 13, 1918; s. Parker Gillespie and Josephine (Keeler) T.; m. Margaret Carter, June 13, 1941 (div. Oct. 1977); children: Ann, Janet Greene; m. Dorothy Walsh, Jan. 7, 1978 (dec. Sept. 1982); m. Joyce McPherson, Jan. 4, 1986. A.B. summa cum laude, Oberlin Coll., 1939; J.D. magna cum laude, Harvard U., 1942. Bar: N.Y. 1948. Assoc. firm Cahill, Gordon & Reindel, N.Y.C., 1946-54, ptnr., 1955-86. Pres.: Harvard U. Law Rev., 1941-42. Served to maj. AUS, 1942-46, CBI. Mem. ABA, Assn. Bar City of N.Y., World Trade Ctr. Club (N.Y.C.), Manhasset Bay Yacht Club (Port Washington, N.Y.). Home: Wood Rd Harbor Acr Port Washington NY 11050 Office: Cahill Gordon & Reindel 80 Pine St New York NY 10005-1702

TENNEY, LISA CHRISTINE GRAY, healthcare administrator; b. Pitts., Feb. 5, 1952; d. Elmer Burtt and Elizabeth (Scharding) Gray; m. Robert Howard Tenney, Mar. 8, 1972; children: Brian, David, Michael. BSN, W.Va. U., 1974. Cert. emergency nurse; cert. ACLS instr., CPR instr./trainer. Staff nurse Suburban Hosp., Bethesda, Md., 1979-80; pvt. practice nursing Gaithersburg, Md., 1982-88; staff nurse Holy Cross Hosp., Silver Spring, Md., 1980—, asst. nurse mgr. emergency dept., 1995—; co-founder, assoc. dir. Md. Profl. Staffing Svcs., Bethesda, 1987-94; speaker in field. Contbr. articles to profl. jours. Mem. Emergency Nurses Assn., Sigma Theta Tau. Home: 9226 Bluebird Ter Gaithersburg MD 20879-1739

TENNEY, PATRICIA ANN, psychotherapist, nurse; b. Hartford, Conn., Oct. 15, 1942; d. Adam Edward Waite and Catherine Helen Russell; m. John Lawrence Tenney, Nov. 25, 1967; children: Jeffrey Russell, Kate Theresa. Grad. in nursing, Cooley Dickinson Hosp., Northampton, Mass., 1964; BS in Sociology cum laude, Bridgewater State Coll., 1987; MA in Rehab. Counseling, Assumption Coll., Worcester, Mass., 1990. RN cert.; cert. in adult psychiatry; cert. forensic counselor, addiction counselor. Head nurse, acting supr. Medfield State Hosp., Harding, Mass., 1964-67; supr. Bridgewater (Mass.) State Hosp., 1967-90, asst. DON, 1990-93; pvt. practice psychotherapy, behavioral cons., Taunton, Mass., 1993—; ct. apptd. guardian, Taunton, 1993—; facilitator S.E. Lung Assn., Middleboro, Mass., 1993—. Pres. St. Mary's Guild, Taunton, 1989-91; appointed nursing rep. to bd. dirs. Taunton Nursing Home. Mass. Mental Health Nurses Assn. scholar, 1994. Mem. Mass. Nurses Assn. (nursing practice com. dist. IIII 1967—, bd. dirs. 1992-95, pres. unit 7, 1990-93, del. to ANA conv. 1990-95), Mass. Mental Health Nurses Assn. (v.p. 1987-88), Mass. Mental Health Orgn. (lic.), Marriage and Family Therapists (lic.), Taunton C. of C. Democrat. Roman Catholic. Avocations: travel, reading, church activities. Home: 3 Lewis Dr Berkley MA 02779 Office: Behavioral Cons 135 Washington St Taunton MA 02780-2528

TENNEY, RUTH DAWN, medical/surgical nurse; b. Saginaw, Mich., Oct. 16, 1940; d. Grover L. and Nora L. (Schlappi) Wolfgang; m. Jay Beach Tenney, Dec. 4, 1979; children: Gary Lee Seibert, Floyd Eric Seibert, Rodney Grover Seibert, Steven J. Tenney, John J. Tenney, Barbara Luongo, Julie Tenney. ADN, Delta Coll., 1974; BS in Mgmt., Ctrl. Mich. U., 1994. Cert. med.-surg. nurse, cert. gerontol. nurse. Staff nurse med.-surg., instr., unit edn. coord. VA Hosp., Saginaw, 1974-78, 87—; charge nurse obstetrics, prenatal instr. Saginaw Osteo. Hosp., 1978-86; mem. nurse profl. stds. bd. VA Hosp., Saginaw.

TENNEY, STEPHEN MARSH, physiologist, educator; b. Bloomington, Ill., Oct. 22, 1922; s. Harry Houser and Caroline (Marsh) T.; m. Carolyn Cartwright, Oct. 18, 1947; children: Joyce B., Karen M., Stephen M. AB, Dartmouth; MD, Cornell U.; ScD (hon.), U. Rochester. From instr. to assoc. prof. of medicine and physiology U. Rochester Sch. Medicine, 1951-56; prof. physiology Dartmouth Med. Sch., Hanover, N.H., 1956-74; dean Dartmouth Med. Sch., 1960-62, acting dean, 1966, 73, dir. med. scis., 1957-59, chmn. dept. physiology, 1956-77, Nathan Smith prof. physiology, 1974-88, Nathan Smith prof. emeritus, 1988—; med. dir. Parker B. Francis Found., 1975-83, exec. v.p., 1984-89; Chmn. physiology study sect. NIH, 1962-65; tng. com. Nat. Heart Inst., 1968-71; mem. exec. com. NRC; mem. physiology panel NIH study Office Sci. and Tech.; mem. regulatory biology panel NSF, 1971-75; chmn. bd. sci. counselors Nat. Heart and Lung Inst., 1974-78; chmn. Commn. Respiratory Physiology Internat. Union Physiol. Scis. Asso. editor: Jour. Applied Physiology, 1976—, Handbook of Physiology; notes editor: News in Physiol. Sci., 1989—; editorial bd.: Am. Jour. Physiology, Circulation Research, Physiol. Revs; Contbr. articles to sci. jours. Served with USNR, 1947-49; sr. med. officer Shanghai. Markle scholar in med. sci., 1954-59; recipient Disting. Achievement award Dartmouth, 1994. Fellow Am. Acad. Arts and Scis., AAAS; mem. Inst. Medicine of Nat. Acad. Scis., Am. Physiol. Soc., Am. Soc. Clin. Investigation, N.Y. Acad. Scis., Gerontol. Soc., Am. Heart Assn., Assn. Am. Med. Colls., , Alpha Omega Alpha, Sigma Xi.

TENNEY, TOM FRED, bishop; b. DeRidder, La., Dec. 6, 1933; s. Fred and Jenny Veve (Nichols) T.; m. Thetus Pearl Caughron, Dec. 27, 1952; children: Tom Gregory, Teri Denise Tenney Spears. Student, Apostolic Bible Inst., St. Paul, 1952; DD (hon.), 1992. Ordained to ministry United Pentecostal Ch., 1954. Pastor United Pentecostal Ch., Monroe, La., 1953-56, DeRidder, 1976-78; youth pres. La. dist. United Pentecostal Ch., 1953-60; dist. supt. for La. United Pentecostal Ch., Tioga, 1978—; youth pres. United Pentecostal Ch., Internat., St. Louis, 1960-69, dir. fgn. missions, mem. exec. bd., 1969-76, mem. gen. bd., 1978—; internat. radio speaker Harvestime, St. Louis, 1976-78. Author: Pentecost: What's That?, 1975, The Flame Still Burns, 1989, The Main Thing, 1993, Advice to Pastors and Other Saints, 1995, Beyond Sunrise, 1996. Trustee Tupelo (Miss.) Children's Mansion, Spirit of Freedom, Metairie, La., Lighthouse Ranch for Boys, Hammond, La. Democrat. Home and Office: PO Box 248 Tioga LA 71477-0248

TENNIES, ROBERT HUNTER, headmaster; b. Bogotá, Colombia, Aug. 19, 1952; s. Leo C. and Ruth (Winston) T.; m. Ruth Ellen Fischer, June 14, 1975; children: Debbie, Julie. BS, Wheaton (Ill.) Coll., 1973; MA, U. South Fla., 1975; EdS, Fla. Atlantic U., 1978, EdD, 1982. Sci. tchr. Cypress Lake Middle Sch., Ft. Myers, Fla., 1973-77; sci. tchr. Boca Raton (Fla.) Christian Sch., 1977-78, asst. administr., 1978-84, headmaster, 1984—, min. of children, 1984-90; interim. min. of edn., 1991-93; Spkr. Internat. Conf. Religious Edn., Petrozavodsk, Russia. Recipient Excellence in Edn. award Nat. Assn. Elem. Prins., 1990. Mem. Nat. Sci. Tchrs. Assn., Assn. of Christian Schs. Internat. (accreditation commn.), Nat. Assn. Elem. Sch. Prins. Avocation: camping. Home: 2415 NW 30th Rd Boca Raton FL 33431-6214 Office: Boca Raton Christian Sch 315 NW 4th St Boca Raton FL 33432-3670

TENNIS, CALVIN CABELL, bishop. Bishop Episcopal Ch., Wilmington, Del., 1986—. Office: Diocesan Office 2020 N Tatnall St Wilmington DE 19802-4821*

TENNSTEDT, KLAUS, conductor; b. Merseburg, Germany, June 6, 1926. Formerly gen. music dir. Dresden Opera, and dir., State Orch. and Theatre in Schwerin, Ger.; gen. music dir. and resident condr. Buehnen der Landeshauptstadt Kiel, Ger., N.Am. debut, Toronto Symphony, U.S. debut, Boston Symphony, 1974; named prin. guest condr. Minn. Orch., 1978, has since conducted all major orchs. of world including Cleve. Symphony, Phila. Orch., N.Y. Philharm., Chgo. Symphony, Berlin Philharm., Israel Philharm.,

Swedish Radio Orchestra,, Metropolitan Opera; prin. guest condr. The London Philharm., music dir. 1983-87, condr. laureate, 1987—; chief condr. Norddeutscher Rundfunk Orchestra, 1979; recordings include Complete Symphonies of Mahler. Home: Roesoll 13, Heikerdorf 2305 Kiel Germany Office: The London Philharm, 35 Doughty St, London WC1N 2AA, England*

TENNYSON, G(EORG) B(ERNHARD), English educator; b. Washington, July 13, 1930; s. Georg B. and Emily (Zimmerli) T.; m. Elizabeth Caroline Johnstone, July 13, 1953; children: Cameron, Holly. BA, George Wash. U., 1953, MA, 1959; MA, Princeton U., 1959, PhD, 1963. Instr. English U. N.C., Chapel Hill, 1962-64; asst. prof. to prof. English UCLA, 1964—. Author: Sartor Called Resartus, 1965, An Introduction to Drama, 1969, Victorian Devotional Poetry, 1981, Owen Barfield on C.S. Lewis, 1990, Literary Language, 1991, A Carlyle Reader, 1984, Nature and the Victorian Imagination, 1977, An Index to Nineteenth-Century Fiction, 1977, Religion and Modern Literature, 1975, Victorian Literature: Prose and Poetry (2 vols.), 1976; author, prodr. video film Owen Barfield: Man and Meaning, 1995; contbr. articles to profl. jours.; editor: Nineteenth Century Fiction, 1971-73, Nineteenth Century Literature, 1983—. With U.S. Army, 1954-56. Fullbright fellow, Freiburg, Germany, 1953-54, Guggenheim fellow, Guggenheim Found., London, 1970-71. Mem. MLA (chmn. Victorian sect. 1973), Philological Assn. of Pacific Coast (chmn. English 2 1969), Carlyle Soc. (Edinburgh). Republican. Anglican. Office: UCLA Dept of English Los Angeles CA 90095-1530

TENNYSON, PETER JOSEPH, lawyer; b. Winona, Minn., Mar. 18, 1946; s. Richard Harvey and Sylvia Josephine (Jadrich) T.; m. Mary Eileen Fay, Jan. 3, 1970; children: Mark Christian, Rachel Christine, Matthew Patrick, Erica Ruth/. BA, Purdue U., 1968; JD, U. Va., 1975. Bar: Calif. Assoc. atty. O'Melveny & Myers, L.A., 1975-82; v.p., gen. counsel Cannon Mills Co., Kannapolis, N.C., 1982-84; ptnr. Stradling, Yocca, Newport Beach, Calif., 1984-89, Jones, Day, Reavis & Pogue, Irvine, Calif., 1990-95, Paul, Hastings, Janofsky & Walker, Costa Mesa, Calif., 1995—; mem. Calif. Commn. on Future of Legal Profession and State Bar, 1994; lectr. in field. Mem. St. Joseph Hosp. Benefit, Orange, Calif., 1987-93; bd. dirs. Lincoln Club Orange County, 1991-93, South Coast Symphony, 1989-92. Capt. U.S. Army, 1968-72. Mem. Orange County Bar Assn., Performing Arts Bus. Alliance South Coast Repertory Silver Circle. Roman Catholic. Avocations: down hill skiing, swimming. Home: 2621 Circle Dr Newport Beach CA 92663-5616 Office: Paul Hastings Janofsky & Walker LLP 695 Town Center Dr 17th Fl Costa Mesa CA 92626

TENNYSON, RODERICK C., aerospace scientist; b. Toronto, Ont., Can., June 7, 1937; m. Judith Grace Williams, June 17, 1961; children: Shân, Marc, Kristin. BA, U. Toronto, Ont., 1960, MA, 1961, PhD, 1965. Prof. inst. aerospace studies U. Toronto, 1974—, dir., 1985—, chmn. dept. engring. sci., 1982-85; selected as Can. experimimenter on space shuttle flights; dir. ctr. excellence for Inst. Space & Terrestrial Sci.; chmn. Can. Found. for Internat. Space U.; cons. in field. Contbr. numerous articles to profl. jours., chpts. to books. Fellow Can. Aeronautic and Space Inst. Avocations: sailing, writing, recreations. Home: 104 McClure Dr, King City, ON Canada M3H 5T6 Office: Inst Aerospace Studies, 4925 Dufferin St, Downsview, ON Canada M3H 5T6

TENUTA, JEAN LOUISE, sports reporter, medical technologist; b. Kenosha, Wis., Apr. 12, 1958; d. Fred and Lucy Ann (Taylor) Tenuta; m. Robert Louis Bennett, Nov. 22, 1989. BS in Biology, U.Wis., 1979; BA in Journalism, Marquette U., 1983; MS in Print Journalism, Northwestern U., 1989. Sports reporter Kenosha News, 1978-84, Washington Post, 1984-86, Jour. Messenger, Manassas, Va., 1986, Jour. Times, Racine, Wis., 1988-89; med. technologist St. Therese Med. Ctr., Waukegan, Ill., 1980-83, 86-87, Suburban Hosp., Bethesda, Md., 1985-86, Group Health Assn., Washington, 1985-86, St. Francis Hosp., Milw., 1988-89; sports reporter Jour.-Gazette, Ft. Wayne, Ind., 1989-90; med. technologist Columbia Hosp., Milw., 1991; tech. assoc. Coll. Am. Pathologists, 1991—; manuscript reviewer Laboratory Medicine, 1995—. Recipient 1st place in sports writing Capital Press Women, 1986, 87, Women's Press Club of Ind., 1990, 91, Nat. Fedn. Press Women, 1986, 91. Mem. Am. Assn. for Clin. Chemistry (tox/TDM sect.), Am. Soc. Clin. Pathologists, Am. Mgmt. Assn., AAUW, Assn. Women in Sports Media (v.p. adminstrn. 1995-97, Midwest region coord. 1990-95, v.p. adminstrn. 1995—), Nat. Fedn. Press Women (treas. Capital area 1985-87, 1st pl. in sports writing 1986, 91), Soc. Profl. Journalists, Women in Comms. (v.p., sec. Milw. chpt.), Nat. Writers Club, Midwest Assn. for Toxicology & Therapeutic Drug Monitoring (sec., treas. 1995—, newsletters editor 1995—), Italian Geneaol. Soc. of Am., DAR (publicity chmn. mag. chmn. Kenosha chpt. 1994—), Friends of Kenosha Pub. Libr. (life). Democrat. Avocations: computers, reading, baseball. Home: 9110 32nd Ave Kenosha WI 53142-5426 Office: Coll Am Pathologists 325 Waukegan Rd Northfield IL 60093-2719

TEPHLY, THOMAS ROBERT, pharmacologist, toxicologist, educator; b. Norwich, Conn., Feb. 1, 1936; s. Samuel M. and Anna (Pieniadz) T.; m. Joan Bernice Clifcorn, Dec. 17, 1960; children: Susan Lynn, Linda Ann, Annette Michele. B.S., U. Conn., 1957; Ph.D., U. Wis., 1962; M.D., U. Minn., 1965. Research asst. U. Wis., Madison, 1957-62, instr., 1962; asst. prof. U. Mich., Ann Arbor, 1965-69, assoc. prof., 1969-71; prof. pharmacology U. Iowa, Iowa City, 1971—. Contbr. articles to profl. jours. Rsch. scholar Am. Cancer Soc., 1962-65; recipient John Jacob Abel award, 1971, Kenneth P. Dubois award, 1992; Fogarty sr. internat. fellow NIH, 1978; rsch. grantee NIH, 1966. Mem. Am. Soc. Pharmacology and Exptl. Therapeutics, Soc. Toxicology, AAAS, Am. Soc. Biol. Chemists, Research Soc. on Alcholism. Home: 6 Lakeview Dr NE Iowa City IA 52240-9142 Office: U Iowa Dept Pharmacology Iowa City IA 52242

TEPLOW, THEODORE HERZL, valve company executive; b. Brockton, Mass., Apr. 14, 1928; s. Edward Abraham and Evelyn (Stone) T.; m. Charlotte Leah Savitz, June 14, 1953; children: Rachel P., David I., Deborah R., Evan S., Jonathan P. BS, U.S. Mcht. Marine Acad., 1950; MBA, Harvard U., 1953. Mgmt. trainee to pres. Crosby Valve Inc. an FMC Corp. subs., Wrentham, Mass., 1953-82, cons., 1982—; dir. Emerson Investment Mgmt., Inc., Boston, 1985—; cons. Firesafe Products Corp., N.Y.C., 1982-96. Trustee Am. Mcht. Marine Mus. Found., Kings Point, N.Y., 1988—, Rofeh Internat., Boston, 1990—, Hebrew Coll., Brookline, Mass., 1971—, chmn., 1992—; trustee Kings Point Challenge, 1997—; v.p., bd. dirs. Internat. Catacomb Soc., Boston, 1982—; bd. dirs. Cong. Beth El-Atereth Israel, Newton Center, Mass., 1975-85, Beth El Cmty. Hebrew Sch., Newton Center, 1965-85, USMMA Found., Kings Point, 1988—; asst. treas., dir. Am. Com. for Weizmann Inst. Sci., N.Y., 1987—; gov. Weizmann Inst. Sci., Rehovoth, Israel, 1991—; bd. dirs. Wilstein Inst. Jewish Policy Studies, L.A., 1993—, Stone Charitable Found., 1982—; dir. Archives for Hist. Documentation, Boston, 1994—. Comdr. USNR, ret. Recipient Outstanding Profl. Achievement award U.S. Mcht. Marine Acad. Alumni Assn., 1970, Meritorious Alumni Svc. award, 1990, Disting. Svc. award, 1995. Democrat. Office: Crosby Valve Inc 43 Kendrick St Wrentham MA 02093-1554

TEPPER, CLIFFORD, allergist, immunologist, educator; b. Schenectady, N.Y., Oct. 26, 1922; s. Solomon B. and Annette (Lifset) T.; m. Cynthia S. Tepper; children: Stewart, Nancy, Henry, Audrey. Chief allergy dept. Ellis Hosp., Schenectady, 1990—; chief allergy and immunology, clin. med. pharmacy dir. Comty. Health Plan, Latham, N.Y., 1992—; prof. pediatrics Albany (N.Y.) Med. Coll., 1973—; cons. allergist, clin. med. pharmacy dir. Cmty. Health Plan, Latham, N.Y. Trustee Schenectady Mus., 1987—, Schenectady Pub. Libr., 1985—. Mem. Coll. Allergy and Immunology, Am. Acad. Pediatrics, Am. Acad. Allergy and Immunology, New Eng. Soc. Allergy (pres. 1990-92), N.Y. State Allergy Soc. (treas. 1994—), Physicians for Social Responsibility. Avocations: bird watching, art history. Home: 2216 Stone Ridge Rd Niskayuna NY 12309 Office: Cmty Health Plan 1201 Troy Schenectady Rd Latham NY 12110-1007

TEPPER, LLOYD BARTON, physician; b. L.A., Dec. 21, 1931; m. Lamonte Leverage; children: Jeffrey Hamilton, Evan Clothier. AB, Dartmouth Coll., 1954; MD, Harvard U., 1957, MIH, 1960, ScD in Hygiene, 1962. Diplomate in occupational medicine Am. Bd. Preventive Medicine. Rsch. fellow Harvard Med. Sch., Boston, 1958-59; clin. fellow Mass. Gen. Hosp., Boston, 1958-60; rsch. assoc. MIT, Cambridge, 1959-61; physician U.S. AEC, Washington, 1962-65; prof. environ. health U. Cin., 1965-72; assoc. dir. Kettering Lab., Cin., 1965-72; assoc. commr. U.S. FDA, Washington, 1972-76; corp. med. dir. Air Products and Chems., Inc., Allentown, Pa., 1976—; dir. Chem. Industry Inst. Toxicology, Research Triangle Park, N.C., 1982-89; trustee Am. Bd. Preventive Medicine, vice chair, 1986-94. Editor Jour. Occupational Medicine, 1979-91. Fellow Am. Coll. Occupational and Environ. Medicine, Am. Acad. Occupational Medicine (pres. 1980-81). Office: Air Products and Chems Inc 7201 Hamilton Blvd Allentown PA 18195-1526

TEPPER, LYNN MARSHA, gerontology educator; b. N.Y.C., Mar. 16, 1946; d. Jack Mortimer and Ida (Golembe) Drukatz; m. William Chester Tepper, Aug. 27, 1967; children: Sharon Joy, Michelle Dawn. BS, SUNY, Buffalo, 1967; MA, Wayne State U., 1971; MS, Columbia U., 1977, EdM, 1978, EdD, 1980. Instr. John F. Kennedy Sch., Berlin, 1967-68, ednl. counselor, 1968-69; ednl. coordinator Army Edn. Ctr., Berlin, 1969-71; psychologist U.S. Dept. Def., Berlin, 1971-73; prof. Gerontology L.I. U., Dobbs Ferry, N.Y., 1979—, Columbia U., N.Y.C., 1982—; cons. NATO, Belgium, Naples, Italy, 1969-71, numerous nursing homes, N.Y.C., 1978—, Found. for Long Term Care, 1992—; prof. gerontology Mercy Coll., Dobbs Ferry, 1979—; dir. Gerontology Resource Ctr., Ctr. for Geriatrics and Gerontology, Columbia U., N.Y.C., 1980-85, dir. divsn. behavioral sci., 1982—; del. White House Conf. on Aging, 1980. Author: (textbooks) Long Term Care, 1993, Respite Care, 1993; contbr. articles to profl. jours. and textbooks. Advisor Office on Aging, State of N.Y., Albany, 1980—; dir. Mercy Coll., Inst. Gerontology, 1990—; trustee St. Cabrini Nursing Home, 1991-97. Brookdale Inst. on Aging fellow, 1983; Grantee U.S. Dept. Edn., U.S. Bur. Health Professions, interdisciplinary geriat. tng. U.S. Dept. Health Resources Svcs. Adminstrn. Fellow Gerontol. Soc. Am.; mem. Northeastern Gerontol. Soc., N.Y. Assn. Gerontol. Edn., Am. Psychol. Assn. Avocations: physical fitness. Home: 50 Burnside Dr Hastings On Hudson NY 10706-3013 Office: Columbia U Med Campus Box 20 630 W 168th St New York NY 10032

TEPPER, MARVIN B., professional sports team executive. Mem. bd. dirs. N.Y. Mets. Office: NY Mets 12310 Roosevelt Ave Flushing NY 11368-1600*

TEPPER, MICHAEL HOWARD, publishing company executive; b. Balt., Sept. 4, 1941; s. Jack and Betty Lee (Chodak) T.; m. Veronica Ann Schofield, Nov. 15, 1972; children: Alex, Megan, Sarah. B.A., U. Md., 1963; M.A., NYU, 1965, Ph.D., 1970. Pres., mng. editor Geneal. Pub. Co., Inc., Balt., 1971—. Author: American Passenger Arrival Records, 1988; editor: The Famine Immigrants (7 vols.), 1983-86, Passenger Arrivals at the Port of Philadelphia 1800-1819, 1986, Passenger Arrivals at the Port of Baltimore 1820-1834, 1982, New World Immigrants (2 vols.), 1979, Immigrants to the Middle Colonies, 1978, Passengers to America, 1977, Emigrants to Pennsylvania, 1975. Recipient Founders' Day award NYU, 1970. Office: Geneal Pub Co Inc 1001 N Calvert St Baltimore MD 21202-3823

TERAN, TIMOTHY ERIC ALBA, marketing professional; b. N.Y.C., Apr. 11, 1956; s. Eric Henry Alba and Patricia (Wheel) T. BA in Market Psychology, Oberlin Coll., 1978. Rsch. intern Needham Harper & Steers, Chgo., 1977; rsch. exec. Grey Advt., N.Y.C., 1979-80, sr. rsch. exec., 1981, asst. rsch. dir., 1982-83, assoc. rsch. dir., 1984, v.p. assoc. rsch. dir., 1985-88, v.p. sr. assoc. dir. strategic svcs., 1989-92, sr. v.p., deputy dir. strategic svcs., 1992—. Home: 13 Gramercy Park S New York NY 10003-1755 Office: Grey Advt 777 3rd Ave New York NY 10017

TERAO, TOSHIO, physician, educator; b. Shimizu, Japan, Jan. 18, 1930; s. Eiji and Mitsuko (Katagiri) T.; m. Setsuko Nishigaki, Nov. 13, 1961; children: Toshiya, Yasuo, Yoshio. Diploma U. Tokyo, 1953, M.D., 1960. Intern, Tokyo U. Hosp., 1953-54; sr. scientist Nat. Inst. Radiol. Sci., Chiba, Japan, 1963-67; research assoc. Mayo Clinic, Rochester, Minn., 1970-72; asst. U. Tokyo, 1972-77, lectr. in medicine 1977-79; prof. medicine Teikyo U., 1980-91, prof. neurology, 1991—; pres. Teikyo U. Med. Hosp., 1987-93, dean, 1993-95, pres. North Tokyo Jueien, 1995—. Author, editor in field. Mem. Am. Acad. Neurology, Japanese Soc. Internal Medicine, Japanese Soc. Neurology, Japanese Soc. Neuropathology, Japanese Soc. EEG and Electromyography, Japanese Soc. Psychiatry and Neurology, Japanese Soc. Cerebrovascular Disease, Sigma Xi. Office: Teikyo U, 2-11-1 Kaga Itabashiku, Tokyo 173, Japan

TERASMAE, JAAN, geology educator; b. Estonia, May 28, 1926; s. Enn and Virge (Lepik) T.; m. Vaike Jurima, July 31, 1954. Phil. Cand., U. Uppsala, Swden, 1951; Ph.D., McMaster U., Can., 1955. Head palynology lab. Geol. Survey of Can., 1955-67, head paleoecology and geochronology sect., 1968; prof. dept. geology Brock U., St. Catharines, Ont., Can., 1968-91; prof. emeritus Brock U., St. Catharines, Ont., 1991—; chmn. dept. geology Brock U., St. Catharines, Ont., Can., 1969-73, 75-76. Contbr. numerous articles to profl. jours. Fellow Geol. Assn. Can., Geol. Soc. Am., Royal Soc. Can.; mem. Am. Assn. Stratigraphic Palynologists, Am. Quaternary Assn., Arctic Inst. N.Am., Can. Assn. Palynologists (pres. 1984-85), Can. Quaternary Assn. (William A. Johnston medal 1990), Internat. Assn. Gt. Lakes Rsch., Internat. Glaciological Soc., Internat. Limnological Soc., Internat. Orgn. Palaeobotany, Tree-Ring Sooc., Royal Can. Geog. Soc. Lutheran. Avocation: photography. Home: 196 Woodside Dr, Saint Catharines, ON Canada L2T 1X6 Office: Brock U, Dept Geol Sciences, Saint Catharines, ON Canada L2S 3A1

TERENZIO, PETER BERNARD, hospital administrator; b. N.Y.C., Mar. 6, 1916; s. Vincent and Marianna (Piantino) T.; m. Eileen Alma Mosher, May 29, 1941; children—Mary Ellen Alecci, Vincent, Nancy Britton, Peter Bernard. Student, Yale U., 1934-37; J.D., U. Conn., 1940; M. Hosp. Adminstrn., Northwestern U., 1950. Bar: Conn. bar 1941. Practice in New Haven, 1945-48; with standardization div. A.C.S., Chgo., 1948-49; adminstrv. resident Evanston (Ill.) Hosp., 1949-50; asst. dir. Roosevelt Hosp., N.Y.C., 1950-52; exec. v.p., dir. Roosevelt Hosp., 1953-76, cons., 1976-81; pres. Hosp. Bur. Inc., Pleasantville, N.Y., 1977-81; dir. Greenville (S.C.) Gen. Hosp., 1952-53; cons. to surgeon gen. USPHS, 1960-65, 66-69; to commr. Dept. Hosps., N.Y.C., 1961-68; prof. clin. dentistry community Sch. Dental and Oral Surgery, Columbia U., 1963-84; univ. lectr. pub. health and adminstrv. medicine; adj. prof. Pace U., 1978-82, New Sch. Social Research 1977-85; Mem. facilities planning com. Hosp. Rev. and Planning Council of So. N.Y., 1963-69; mem. vol. adv. staff N.Y. State Health and Mental Retardation, 1966-69. Adv. editorial bd., Hosp. and Health Services Adminstrn. Bd. dirs., exec. com. Asso. Hosp. Service N.Y., 1970-74, N.Y. Coll. Podiatry, 1971-73; bd. dirs. Blue Cross-Blue Shield Greater N.Y., 1974-78, Abacus, 1965-86, Dominican Sisters Home Health Agy., 1977-82, Health Services Improvement Fund, 1978-85; mem. exec. adv. bd. Hosp. Home Care Santa Ana, Calif., 1984-86; vol., assoc., Sr. Friendship Health Ctr., Naples, Fla., 1986—, mem. adv. bd., 1992—. Capt., Med. Adminstrn. Corps AUS, 1941-45. Fellow Am. Coll. Hosp. Execs. (gov. 1964-65, regent 2d dist. 1960-64, pres. 1966-67, chmn. bd. dirs.), Am. Pub. Health Assn.; mem. Am. Hosp. Assn. (ho. of dels. 1969-76, rep. Am. Blood Commn., trustee liaison com. podiatry), Hosp. Research and Devel. Inst., N.Y. Acad. Medicine, Pub. Health Assn. N.Y.C. (dir., v.p. 1973-74, pres. 1976-77), Roosevelt Hosp. Alumni Assn. (asso.), Hosp. Assn. N.Y. (pres. 1970-71), Middle Atlantic Hosp. Assembly (bd. govs.), Hosp. Adminstrs. Study Soc., Am. Bar Assn., Greater N.Y. Hosp. Assn. (pres. 1960), Hosp. Adminstrs. Club (pres. 1959), Hosp. Soc. (pres. 1965), Coquina Club of Naples, Inc. (sec., treas. 1984-86, pres. 1987-90). Roman Catholic. Home and Office: 122 Moorings Park Dr Apt G608 Naples FL 34105-2169

TERESI, JOSEPH, publishing executive; b. Mpls., Mar. 13, 1941; s. Cliff I.A. and Helen Ione (Leslie) T.; divorced; 1 child, Nicholas. Chief exec. officer Jammer Cycle Products Inc., Burbank, Calif., 1968-80, Paisano Pubs. Inc., Agoura Hills, Calif., 1970—; promoter motorcycle events; prodr. Easyriders Video mag. Pub. (mags.) Easyriders, 1971—, In the Wind, 1974—, Biker Lifestyle, 1986—, Tatto, 1986—, Am. Rodder, 1987, Womens Enterprise, 1987-89, Eagles Eye, 1989—, Tattoo Flash, 1993—, Tattoo Savage, 1993—, VQ, 1994—, Early-Riders, 1994-96, Quick Throttle, 1995—, Roadware, 1995—. Holds world speed record for motorcycles set at 322 miles per hour, 1990. Avocations: motorcycles, race cars, boats, marlin fishing, skiing. Office: Paisano Pubs Inc PO Box 3000 Agoura Hills CA 91376-3000

TERHORST, JERALD FRANKLIN, public affairs counsel; b. Grand Rapids, Mich., July 11, 1922; s. John Henry and Maude (Van Strien) ter H.; m. Louise Jeffers Roth, Jan. 20, 1945; children: Karen Bayens Morris, Margaret Fulton Robinson, Peter Roth, Martha Morgan Lubin. Student, Mich. State U., 1941-42; A.B., U. Mich., 1947. Reporter Grand Rapids Press, 1946-51; mem. staff Detroit News, 1953-74, city and state polit. writer, 1953-57, Washington corr., 1958-60; chief Detroit News (Washington bur.), 1961-74; White House press sec. to Pres., 1974; columnist Detroit News/Universal Press Syndicate, 1974-81; nat. dir. public affairs Ford Motor Co., 1981-91; fgn. assignments include Berlin crisis Geneva Fgn. Ministers Conf., Yugoslavia, 1959, 70, Israel, 1960, Eng., Ireland, Germany, Italy and France, 1963, 69, Vietnam, India and Pakistan, 1966, 70, China, 1972, Moscow, 1974, Africa, 1978; writer N.Am. Newspaper Alliance, 1958-74. Author: Gerald Ford and Future of the Presidency, 1974, The Flying White House: The Story of Air Force One, 1979; contbr. to mags. and TV documentaries. Bd. dirs. Nat. Press Found., Gridiron Found., WETA-TV (Channel 26), Grad. Sch. Polit. Mgmt., George Washington U., Washington, Handgun Control, Inc. Officer USMCR, 1943-46, 51-52. Mem. Pub. Rels. Soc. Am., Soc. Profl. Journalists, Psi Upsilon. Presbyterian (elder). Clubs: Gridiron, Nat. Press. Overseas Writers.

TERHUNE, ROBERT WILLIAM, optics scientist; b. Detroit, Feb. 8, 1926; married; 2 children. BS, U. Mich., 1947, PhD in Physics, 1957; MA, Dartmouth Coll., 1948. Supr. digital computation and logic design sect. Willow Run Labs. U. Mich., 1951-54, rsch. physicist, 1954-59, mgr. Solid State Physics Lab., 1959-60; rsch. physicist Sci. Lab. Ford Motor Co., Dearborn, Mich., 1960-65, mgr. physics electronics dept., 1965-75, sr. staff scientist engring. and rsch. staff, 1976-87; sr. mem. tech. staff JPL Calif. Tech., 1988-94, cons., 1995—; vis. scholar Stanford U., 1975-76. Editor Optics Let. Jour., 1977-83. Recipient Sci. and Engring. award Drexel Inst. Tech., 1964, Frederic Ives Medal, 1992, Optical Soc. Am. Mem. IEEE, Optical Soc. Am. (editor jour. 1984-87, Frederic Ives medal 1992), Am. Phys. Soc. Achievements include research in quantum electronics, nonlinear optics, optical properties of solids and surfaces, molecular spectroscopy, advanced instrumentation. Office: 4002 Tall Oaks Dr Blacksburg VA 24060-8115

TERILLI, JOSEPH ANTHONY, secondary education educator; b. Winthrop, Mass., June 14, 1948; s. Joseph Anthony and Mary Grace (Colontuoni) T.; m. Carol Ann Saccardo, Oct. 8, 1971; 1 child, Joseph Anthony III. BS, Boston Coll., 1970, MEd, 1973. Tchr., adminstr. Boston Pub. Schs., 1972-77; tchr. Coolidge Jr. H.S., Reading, Mass., 1977-84; tchr. Reading Meml. H.S., 1984—, mentor tchr., 1988—; pres., CEO Terilli Enterprises Devel. Corp., Aruba, 1986—; mem. Profl. Devel. Com., Reading, 1988-92. Author: Blood on the Chalkboard, How Children Succeed, also newspaper articles, booklets, monographs and mock trial; pub. (newsletter) Political Action Network (PAN). Mem. exec. bd., Mass. state chair Dem. Party (New Dems.). Mem. C. of C., Kiwanis (past sec.). Roman Catholic. Avocations: politics, travel, writing, collecing comic books. Home: 27 Lawndale Rd Stoneham MA 02180-1014 Office: Reading Meml HS 62 Oakland Rd Reading MA 01867-1613

TERILLI, SAMUEL A., JR., newspaper publishing executive. Gen. Coun. The Miami Herald, Fla. Office: The Miami Herald 1 Herald Plz Miami FL 33132-1609*

TERKEL, STUDS (LOUIS TERKEL), author, interviewer; b. N.Y.C., May 16, 1912; s. Samuel and Anna (Finkel) T.; m. Ida Goldberg, July 2, 1939; 1 son, Dan. PhB, U. Chgo. 1932, JD, 1934. Stage appearances include Detective Story, 1950, A View From the Bridge, 1958, Light Up the Sky, 1959, The Cave Dwellers, 1960; moderator: (TV program) Studs Place, 1950-53, (radio programs) Wax Museum, 1945— (Ohio State Univ. award 1959, UNESCO Prix Italia award 1962), Studs Terkel Almanac, 1952—, Studs Terkel Show, Sta. WFMT-FM, Chgo.; master of ceremonies Newport Folk Festival, 1959, 60, Ravinia Music Festival, 1959, U. Chgo. Folk Festival, 1961, others; panel moderator, lectr., narrator films; author: (books) Giants of Jazz, 1957, Division Street: America, 1967, Hard Times: An Oral History of the Great Depression, 1970, Working: People Talk about What They Do All Day and How They Feel about What They Do, 1974 (Nat. Book award nomination 1975), Talking to Myself: A Memoir of My Times, 1977, American Dreams: Lost and Found, 1980, The Good War: An Oral History of World War II (Pulitzer prize in nonfiction 1985), Chicago, 1986, The Great Divide: Second Thoughts On The American Dream, 1988, Race: How Blacks and Whites Think and Feel About the American Obsession, 1992, Coming of Age, 1995, My American Century, 1997; (play) Amazing Grace, 1959; also short stories. Named Communicator of Yr. U. Chgo. Alumni Assn., 1969. Office: WFMT Radio 5400 N St Louis Ave Chicago IL 60625-4623*

TERKLA, LOUIS GABRIEL, retired university dean; b. Anaconda, Mont., Mar. 24, 1925; s. George G. and Blanche (Wareham) T.; m. Phyllis Jean Cohn, Aug. 21, 1949; children—David G., Linda J. Student, U. Mont., 1946-48; D.M.D., U. Oreg., 1952. Mem. faculty U. Oreg. Dental Sch., 1952—, prof., asst. to dean acad. affairs, 1961-67, dean, 1967-84, rsch. prof. and dean emeritus, 1984—. Author: (with others) Partial Dentures, 3d edit, 1963; also articles, chpts. in books. Served with inf. AUS, World War II. Fellow AAAS, Am. Coll. Dentists (pres. 1973-74), Acad. Gen. Dentistry (hon.); mem. Am. Dental Assn., Oreg. Dental Assn., Am. Assn. Dental Schs. (pres. 1975-76), Western Conf. Dental Examiners and Dental Sch. Deans (pres. 1975-76), Omicron Kappa Upsilon. Home: 1215 SW Kari Ln Portland OR 97219-6446 *Much of my success as a school of dentistry administrator can be attributed to a willingness to listen patiently to the problems borne by faculty, students and staff and to make a sincere effort toward their resolution. This requires an absolutely open-door administrative style, integrity and dedication to being a service agent to the people who make the school live.*

TERMAN, LEWIS MADISON, electrical engineer, researcher; b. San Francisco, Aug. 26, 1935; s. Frederick Emmons and Sibyl (Walcott) T.; m. Barbara Chertok, Aug. 28, 1958. BS in Physics, Stanford U., 1956, MSEE, 1958, PhD, 1961. Mem. rsch. staff T.J. Watson Rsch. Ctr., IBM, Yorktown Heights, N.Y., 1961-89, sr. mgr., 1989-91, sr. mem. tech. planning staff, 1991-93; mgr. VLSI processor design IBM, Yorktown Heights, N.Y., 1993-94; program mgr., 1994—; co-chmn. Symposium on Very Large Scale Integrated Technology, Systems and Application, Taiwan, 1989, 91, 93, 95, 97, tech. program co-chmn., 1985, 87; tech. program chmn. Internat. Solid State Cirs. Conf., N.Y.C., 1983; chmn. Symposium on Very Large-Scale Integrated Tech., Kobe, Japan, 1985, San Diego, 1986, Symposium on Very Large-Scale Integrated Cirs., Karuizawa, Japan, 1988, Kyoto, Japan, 1989, Symposium on Low Power Electronics, San Diego, 1994. Contbr. articles to profl. jours.; holder 24 patents. Pres. Twin Lakes Water Works Corp., S. Salem, N.Y., 1980—. Recipient IEEE Solid-State Cirs. Tech. Field award, 1995. Fellow AAAS; mem. IBM Acad. Tech. (chair components and processes com., tech. coun. 1996—, co-chair of tech. program com. 1996), Electron Devices Soc. of IEEE (v.p. 1988-89, pres. 1990-91, Disting. Svc. award 1995), Solid State Circuits Coun. of IEEE (treas. 1988-89, editor jour. 1974-77, v.p. 1996-97), IEEE Tech. Activities Bd. (chmn. tech. mtgs. coun. 1993-94, treas. 1995-97), Circuits and Sys. Soc. of IEEE (adminstrv. com. 1981-83); Nat. Academy of Engrin., 1996. Avocations: music, theatre, opera, hiking. Home: 61 Twin Lakes Rd South Salem NY 10590-1012 Office: IBM TJ Watson Rsch Ctr PO Box 218 Yorktown Heights NY 10598-0218

TERMEER, HENRICUS ADRIANUS, biotechnology company executive; b. Tilburg, Holland, Feb. 28, 1946; s. Jacques and Mary (Van Gorp) T.; came to U.S., 1971. Student, Ekonomisch Hogeschool, Rotterdam, Netherlands, 1969; MBA, U. Va., 1973. Mgr. mgmt. svcs. Norvic Co., Norwich, England, 1969-71; mgr. internat. product planning Baxter Travenol, Inc., Deerfield, Ill., 1973-74, internat. mktg. mgr., 1975-76; gen. mgr. Travenol GMBH, Munich, W.Ger., 1976-79, v.p. Hyland Therapeutics div. Baxter Travenol, Glendale, Calif., 1979-81, exec. v.p., 1981-83 ; pres. Genzyme Corp., Inc., Boston, 1983—, COO, 1983-85, CEO, 1986—, chmn., 1988—; dir. Geltex Corp., Autoimmune Corp. Abiomed, Mass. Cystic Fibrosis Found., Genzyme Transgenetics Corp.; dir. Biotech. Industry Orgn., Mass. High Tech. Coun. Trustee Hambrecht & Quist Healthcare Investors Fund, Mus. of Sci., Boston, Darden Bus. School U. of Virginia. Served to 1st lt. Netherlands Royal Air Force, 1966-67. Office: Genzyme Corp 1 Kendall Sq Cambridge MA 02139-1562

TERMINELLA, LUIGI, critical care physician, educator; b. Catania, Italy, Nov. 15, 1960; came to U.S., 1961; s. Roberto and Josephine (Bartolotta) T. MD summa cum laude, U. Catania, 1986. Pathology asst. Brotman Med. Ctr., Culver City, Calif., 1987-89; transitional resident Miriam Hosp./Brown U., Providence, 1989-90; resident in internal medicine U. Hawaii, Honolulu, 1990-92; tng. in critical care/internal medicine U. Hawaii/Queen's Med. Ctr., Honolulu, 1992-93; transfusion svc. physician Blood Bank of Hawaii, Honolulu, 1992-93; internal medicine physician Hawaii Physician Svcs., Honolulu, 1993—; critical care physician Queen's Med. Ctr., Honolulu, 1993—; mem. clin. faculty John H. Burns Sch. Medicine, U. Hawaii, Honolulu, 1994—; pres. Pualani Family Health, SRL, Corp., Honolulu. Recipient Clementi award U. Catania, 1986, others. Mem. ACP, AMA, Am. Soc. Internal Medicine, Hawaiian Soc. Critical Care, Soc. Critical Care Medicine. Avocations: photography, law, architecture. Office: Queen's Med Ctr 1301 Punchbowl QET 4B Honolulu HI 96813

TERMINI, DEANNE LANOIX, research company executive; b. New Orleans, May 2, 1943; d. Albert Oliver and Freida (Fisher) Lanoix; m. Raymond Joseph Termini, Sept. 4, 1965; 1 dau., Andrea. BA, Tulane U., 1964; MA, U. Tex., Austin, 1968. Research analyst Belden Assocs., Dallas, 1968-70, research assoc., 1970-75, v.p., 1975-79, sr. v.p., 1979-87, exec. v.p., 1987-89, pres., 1989—; discussion leader Am. Press Inst., Reston, Va., 1983—. Author research reports. Speaker European and Latin confs., 1986—. Mem. Am. Mktg. Assn., Newspaper Assn. Am., Internat. Newspaper Mktg. Assn., Coun. Am. Survey Rsch. Orgns. Home: 13641 Far Hills Ln Dallas TX 75240-5533 Office: Belden Assocs 3102 Oak Lawn Ave Ste 500 Dallas TX 75219-4260

TERMINI, ROSEANN BRIDGET, lawyer; b. Phila., Feb. 2, 1953; d. Vincent James and Bridget (Marano) T. BS magna cum laude, Drexel U., 1975; MEd, Temple U., 1979, JD, 1985. Bar: Pa. 1985, U.S. Dist. Ct. (ea. dist.) Pa. 1985, D.C. 1986. Jud. clk. Superior Ct. of Pa., Allentown, 1985-86; atty. Pa. Power & Light Co., Allentown, 1986-87; corp. counsel food and drug law Lemmon Co., Sellersville, Pa., 1987-88; sr. dep. atty. bur. consumer protection plain lang. law Office of Atty. Gen., Harrisburg, Pa., 1988-96; prof. Villanova U. Sch. Law, 1996—; Contbr. articles to profl. jours., law revs.; spkr. continuing legal edn.-plain lang. laws, environ. conf.; adj. prof. Widener U. Sch. Law, 1993—, Dickinson Sch. Law. Contbr. articles to profl. jours, law revs.; speaker environ. conf. Active in Sr. Citizens Project Outreach, Hospice, 1986—; mem. St. Thomas More Law Bd. Named Outstanding Young Women of Yr., Dauphin County Bar Assn., 1987; Edn. fellow Temple U., 1978-79. Mem. ABA (various coms.), Bar Assn. D.C., Pa. Bar Assn. (ethics, exceptional children and environ. sects.), Temple U. Law Alumni Assn., Drexel U. Alumni Assn., Omicron Nu, Phi Alpha Delta. Avocations: tap dancing, hiking, cross-country skiing. Home: 1614 Brookhaven Rd Wynne Wood PA 19096 Office: Villanova U Law Sch Villanova PA 17120 *Notable cases include: Waste Conversion case, 1990, violation of Pa. Solid Waste Mgmt. Act.*

TERNBERG, JESSIE LAMOIN, pediatric surgeon; b. Corning, Calif., May 28, 1924; d. Eric G. and Alta M. (Jones) T. A.B., Grinnell Coll., 1946, Sc.D. (hon.), 1972; Ph.D., U. Tex., 1950; M.D., Washington U., St. Louis, 1953; Sc.D. (hon.), U. Mo., St. Louis, 1981. Diplomate: Am. Bd. Surgery. Intern Boston City Hosp., 1953-54; asst. resident in surgery Barnes Hosp., St. Louis, 1954-57; resident in surgery Barnes Hosp., 1958-59; research fellow Washington U. (Sch. Medicine), 1957-58; practice medicine specializing in pediatric surgery St. Louis, 1966—; instr., trainee in surgery Washington U., 1959-62, asst. prof. surgery, 1962-65, assoc. prof., 1965-71, prof. surgery in pediatrics, 1975-96, prof. surgery, 1971-96, chief div. pediatric surgery, 1972-90, prof. emeritus, 1996—; mem. staff Barnes Hosp., 1974-90, pediatric surgeon in chief, 1974-90, mem. operating room com., 1971-90, mem. med. adv. com., 1975-90; mem. staff Children's Hosp., dir. pediatric surgery, 1972-90. Contbr. numerous articles on pediatric surgery to profl. jours. Trustee Grinnell Coll., 1984—. Recipient Alumni award Grinnell Coll., 1966, Faculty/Alumni award Washington U. Sch. Medicine, 1991, 1st Aphrodite Jannopaulo Hofsommer award, 1993. Fellow ACS; mem. AAAS, SIOP, Am. Pediatric Surg. Assn., We. Surg. Assn. (2d v.p. 1984-85), St. Louis Med. Soc., Soc. Surgery of the Alimentary Tract, Am. Acad. Pediatrics, Soc. Pelvic Surgeons (v.p. 1991-92), Brit. Assn. Paediatric Surgeons, Assn. Women Surgeons (disting. mem. 1995), Mo. State Surg. Soc., St. Louis Surg. Soc. (pres. 1980-81), St. Louis Pediatric Soc., Soc. Surg. Oncology, Pediatric Oncology Group (chmn. surg. discipline 1983-96), St. Louis Childrens Hosp. Soc. (pres. 1979-80), St. Louis Met. Med. Soc. (councilor, trustee), Barnes Hosp. Soc., Phi Beta Kappa, Sigma Xi, Iota Sigma Pi, Alpha Omega Alpha. Office: St Louis Childrens Hosp 1 Childrens Pl Saint Louis MO 63110

TERP, DANA GEORGE, architect; b. Chgo., Nov. 5, 1953; s. George and June (Hansen) T.; m. Lynn Meyers, May 17, 1975; children: Sophia, Rachel. BA in Architecture, Washington U., St. Louis, 1974; postgrad., Yale U., 1975-76; MArch, Washington U., 1977. Registered architect, Ill., Calif., Fla. Architect Skidmore Owings & Merrill, Chgo., 1976, 1978-84, Terp Meyers Architects, Chgo., 1984—; prin. Arquitectonica Chgo. Inc., 1986—. Exhibited in group shows at Moming Gallery, Chgo., 1980, Printers Row Exhibit, 1980, Frumkin Struve Gallery, Chgo., 1981, Chgo. Art Inst., 1983; pub. in profl jours. including Progressive Architecture, Los Angeles Architect; work featured in various archtl books; exhibited 150 Yrs. of Chgo. Architecture. Bd. dirs. Architecture Soc. Art Inst. Chgo. Recipient hon. mention Chgo. Townhouse Competition, 1978, award Progressive Architecture mag., 1980, Archtl. Record Houses, 1989, GLOBAL Architecture Ga. Houses/26, 1989, Casa Vogue, 1989, 2d place award Burnham Prize Competition, 1991. Office: Terp Meyers Architects 919 N Michigan Ave Ste 2402 Chicago IL 60611-1664

TERP, THOMAS THOMSEN, lawyer; b. Fountain Hill, Pa., Aug. 12, 1947; s. Norman T. and Josephine (Uhran) T.; m. Pamela Robinson; children: Stephanie, Brian, Adam; step-children: Taylor Mefford, Grace Mefford. BA, Albion (Mich.) Coll., 1969; JD, Coll. of William and Mary, 1973. Bar: Ohio 1973, U.S. Dist. Ct. (so. dist.) Ohio 1973, U.S. Ct. Appeals (6th cir.) 1973, U.S. Supreme Ct. 1979. Assoc. Taft, Stettinius & Hollister, Cin., 1973-80, ptnr., 1981—; bd. dirs. Starflo Corp., Orangeburg, S.C., Attorney's Liability Assurance Soc., Ltd., Hamilton, Bermuda, ALAS, Inc., Chgo. Editor-in-chief William & Mary Law Rev., 1972-73; mem. bd. editors Jour. of Environ. Hazards, 1988—, Environ. Law Jour. of Ohio, 1989—. Mem. Cin. Athletic Club, Coldstream Country Club, Epworth Assembly (Ludington, Mich.), Lincoln Hills Golf Club (Ludington). Avocations: tennis, golf, travel. Office: 1800 Star Bank Ctr 425 Walnut St Cincinnati OH 45202

TERPENING, VIRGINIA ANN, artist; b. Lewistown, Mo., July 17, 1917; d. Floyd Raymond and Bertha Edda (Rodifer) Shoup; m. Charles W. Terpening, July 5, 1951; 1 child by previous marriage, V'Ann Baltzelle Deatrick. Studies with William Woods, Fulton, Mo., 1936-37; student Washington U. Sch. Fine Arts, St. Louis, 1937-40. Exhibited in one-woman shows at Culver-Stockton Coll., Canton, Mo., 1956, Creative Gallery, N.Y.C., 1968, The Breakers, Palm Beach, Fla., 1976; others; exhibited in group shows Mo. Ann., City Art Mus., St. Louis, 1956, 65, Madison Gallery, N.Y.C., 1960; Ligoa Duncan Gallery, N.Y.C., 1964, 78, Two Flags Festival of Art, Douglas, Ariz., 1975, 78-79, Internat. Art Exhibit, El Centro, Calif., 1977, 78, Salon des Nations, Paris, 1985, UN World Conference of Women, Narobi, Kenya, 1985, William Woods Coll., Fulton, Mo., 1992-95, La Junta Coll. Art League Internat., 1992, 94, Coffret Musee, Paris, 1995; represented in permanent collection Nat. Mus. Women in Art., 1990; lectr. on art; jurist for selection of art for exhibits Labelle (Mo.) Centennial, 1972; chmn. Centennial Art Show, Lewiston, 1971, Bicentennial, 1976; dir. exhibit high sch. students for N.E. Mo. State U., 1974; supt. ann. art show Lewis County (Mo.) Fair, 1975-90; executed Mississippi RiverBoat, oil painting presented to Pres. Carter by Lewis County Dem. Com., Canton, 1979. Mem. Lewistown Bicentennial Hist. Soc.; charter mem. Canton Area Arts Coun. N.E. Mo. Recipient cert. of merit Latham Found., 1960-63, Mo. Women's Festival Art, 1974, Bertrand Russell Peace Found., 1973, Gold Medallion award Two Flags Festival Art, 1975, Safeco purchase award El Centro (Calif.) Internat. Art exhibit, 1977, 1st pl. award LaJunta (Colo.) Fine Arts League, 1981, diploma Universita Delle Arti, Parma, Italy, 1981, Purchase award Two Flags Art Festival, 1981, award Assn. Conservation and Mo. Dept. Conservation Art Exhbt., 1982, Purchase award Canton Area Arts Coun., 1988, Colorado Springs Art Festival, 1989; paintings selected for Competition '84 Guide by Nat. Art Appreciation Soc., 1984; 1st pl. award New Orlean Internat. Art Exhibit, 1984, with Am. Women Artists at United Nations Conf. on Women, Nairobi, Kenya, 1985, Two Flags Festival of Art, 1986, Sunflower Judges award Harlin Mus., West Plains, Mo., 1994; named artist laureate, Nepenthe Mondi Soc., 1984, cert. on Arts for the Parks Nat., 1987. Mem. Artist Equity Assn., Inc., Internat. Soc. Artists, Internat. Platform Assn., Nat. Mus. Women in Art (charter), Animal Protection Inst. Mem. Disciples of Christ Ch.

TERPSTRA, VERN, marketing educator; b. Wayland, Mich., Aug. 20, 1927; s. Benjamin and Lucy (Jonker) T.; m. Bonnie Lou Fuller; children: Benjamin Mark, Kathryn Ann, James Richard. BA, U. Mich., 1950, MBA, 1951, PhD, 1965. Dir. normal sch. Grace Mission, Zaire, 1952-61; rsch. asst. Mktg. Sci. Inst., Phila., 1963-66; asst. prof. mktg. Wharton Sch. U. Penn., Phila., 1964-66; prof. Sch. Bus. U. Mich., Ann Arbor, 1967-92, prof. emeritus, 1992—; cons. govt., bus. and acad. orgns., 1972—. Author: The Cultural Environment of International Business, 1978, 3d edit., 1991, International Marketing, 1972, 7th edit., 1997. Fellow Ford Found., Mktg. Sci. Inst., Acad. Internat. Bus.; mem. Am. Mktg. Assn., Acad. Internat. Bus. Presbyterian. Avocations: tennis, travel, theatre, reading. Office: U Mich Bus Sch Ann Arbor MI 48109-1234

TERR, ABBA ISRAEL, allergist, immunologist; b. Cleve., 1930. MD, Case Western Res. U., 1956. Cert. in allergy and immunology; cert. internal medicine. Intern U. Wis. Hosps., Madison, 1956-57; resident in internal medicine U. Mich. Med. Ctr., Ann Arbor, 1957-60, fellow in allergy, 1960-62; physician Stanford (Calif.) U. Med. Ctr.; clin. prof. medicine Stanford U. Fellow ACP, Am. Acad. Allergy, Asthma, and Immunology; mem. Am. Thoracic Soc. Address: 450 Sutter St Rm 2534 San Francisco CA 94108-4204

TERR, LENORE CAGEN, psychiatrist, writer; b. N.Y.C., Mar. 27, 1936; d. Samuel Lawrence Cagen and Esther (Hirsh) Cagen Raiken; m. Abba I. Terr; children: David, Julia. AB magna cum laude, Case Western Res. U., 1957; MD with honors, U. Mich., 1961. Diplomate Am. Bd. Psychiatry and Neurology. Intern Med. Ctr. U. Mich., Ann Arbor, 1961-62, resident Neuropsychiat. Inst., 1962-64, fellow Children's Psychiat. Hosp., 1964-66; from instr. to asst. prof. Med. Sch. Case Western Res. U., Cleve., 1966-71; pvt. practice Terr Med. Corp., San Francisco, 1971—; from asst. clin. prof. to clin. prof. psychiatry Sch. Medicine U. Calif., San Francisco, 1971—; lectr. law, psychiatry U. Calif., Berkeley, 1971—, U. Calif., Davis, 1974-88; bd. dirs. Am. Bd. Psychiatry and Neurology, Deerfield, Ill., 1988-96. Author: Too Scared to Cry, 1990, Unchained Memories, 1994; contbr. articles to profl. jours. Rockefeller Found. scholar-in-residence, Italy, 1981, 88; project grantee Rosenberg Found., 1977, 80-81, William T. Grant Found., 1986-87; recipient Career Tchr. award NIMH, 1967-69, Child Advocacy award, APA, 1994. Fellow Am. Psychiat. Assn. (Child Psychiatry Rsch. award 1984, Clin. Rsch. award 1987), Am. Coll. Psychiatrists (program chair 1991-92, Bowis award 1993), Am. Acad. Child and Adolescent Psychiatry (coun. 1984-87); mem. Phi Beta Kappa, Alpha Omega Alpha. Avocations: piano, walking, travel. Office: Terr Med Corp 450 Sutter St Rm 2534 San Francisco CA 94108-4204

TERRACCIANO, ANTHONY PATRICK, banker; b. Bayonne, N.J., Oct. 27, 1938; s. Patrick and Grace Terracciano; m. Rita Cuddy, Apr. 20, 1963; children: Laura, Karen, Kenneth. BS in Econs. St. Peter's Coll., Jersey City, N.J., 1960; MA in Philosophy, Fordham U., 1962. with Chase Manhattan Bank, N.Y.C., 1964—, exec. v.p. internat., 1974-76, 84-85, exec. v.p., treas., 1976-80, exec. v.p. ops. trusts and systems dept., 1980-83, exec. v.p., chief fin. officer, 1983-84, vice chmn. global banking, 1985-87, pres., chief operating officer, Mellon Bank Corp., Pitts., 1987-90, chmn., pres., chief exec. officer, First Fidelity Bancorp., Newark, N.J., 1990—; CEO First Union Nat. Bank, Summit, N.J.; dir. N.J. Bell Tel. Co., Pitcairn Co. Dir. N.J. Performing Arts Ctr. Corp., N.Y. Philharm., Metro Newark C. of C.; mem. exec. coun. Better Bus. Bur., Newark; trustee Renaissance Newark, Inc.; mem. Coun. on Fgn. Rels. 1st lt. U.S. Army, 1962-64. Mem. N.J. Banker's Assn. (exec. com.). Avocations: music, reading. Office: First Union Nat Bank 190 River Rd Summit NJ 07901*

TERRACINA, ROY DAVID, retired food executive; b. Chgo., Aug. 24, 1946; s. Angelo R. and Josephine T.; m. Dana Wheeler, July 6, 1984; children: Joseph, Vincent, Angela, Peter, Paul. BS in Fin., Marquette U., 1968, MBA, 1972. Officer First Wis. Nat. Bank, Milw., 1968-71; account exec. Robert W. Baird Co., Milw., 1971-74; v.p. mktg. Midwest Retail Group, Milw., 1974-76; mgmt. cons. Anderson-Roethle, Milw., 1976-77; v.p., treas. Farm House Foods Corp., Milw., 1977-84; pres. Sterling Foods, Inc., San Antonio, 1984-93, pvt. investor, 1994—; instr. personal fin. Marquette U.; instr. fin. Trinity U.; bd. dirs. Tex. Commerce Bank, Security Trust, U.S. Global Investors, Norwood Promotional Products Inc., Tex. Commerce Bank; chmn. Life Directions of San Antonio; entrepreneur in residence St. Mary's U. Bd. dirs. YMCA, San Antonio; chmn. Tex. Spl. Olympics. Mem. Young Pres.'s Orgn., Marquette U. Alumni Assn. (pres. 1977-78), Lions Internat. (pres. 1975-76). Roman Catholic. Office: 7900 Callaghan Rd San Antonio TX 78229-2327

TERRAGNO, PAUL JAMES, information industry executive; b. Ogden, Utah, May 17, 1938; s. Charles L. and Florence E. (Gabardi) T.; m. Nancy Robinson, Aug. 26, 1961; children—Thomas C., Paul A., Teresa A. B.A., U. Utah, 1960; M.S., U. Wyo., 1962. Vice pres. Westat, Inc., Rockville, Md., 1962-70; vice pres. Remac Information, Gaithersburg, Md., 1970-76; dir. U.S. Patent Office, Washington, 1976-80; v.p. Pergamon Internat., McLean, Va., 1980-84; pres. Pergamon InfoLine, McLean, Va., 1984-87, Pergamon ORBIT InfoLine, McLean, 1987-89, Maxwell Online, Inc., 1989-92; pres. Pergamon Orbit InfoLine, Ltd., London, 1984-89, Pergabase, Inc., Gainesville, Fla., 1985-92, pres. Topate Information Svcs. Inc., 1992—. Contbr. articles to various publs. Mem. Am. Soc. Info. Sci. Roman Catholic. Home: 10607 Vantage Ct Rockville MD 20854-4244 Office: Topate Info Svcs 10607 Vantage Ct Potomac MD 20854-4244

TERRAS, AUDREY ANNE, mathematics educator; b. Washington, Sept. 10, 1942; d. Stephen Decatur and Maude Mae (Murphy) Bowdoin. BS with high honors in Math., U. Md., 1964; MA, Yale U, 1966, PhD, 1970. Instr. U. Ill., Urbana, 1968-70; asst. prof. U. P.R., Mayaguez, 1970-71; asst. prof. Bklyn. Coll., CUNY, 1971-72; asst. prof. math. U. Calif.-San Diego, La Jolla, 1972-76, assoc. prof., 1976-83, prof., 1983—, vis. positions MIT, fall 1977, 83, U. Bonn (W.Ger.), spring 1977, Inst. Mittag-Leffler, Stockholm, winter, 1978, Inst. Advanced Study, spring 1984, Math. Scis. Rsch. Inst., Berkeley, Calif., winter 1992, spring 1995; dir. West Coast Number Theory Conf., U. Calif.-San Diego, 1976, AMS joint summer rsch. conf., 1984; lectr. in field. Author: Harmonic Analysis on Symmetric Spaces and Applications, Vol. I, 1985, Vol. II, 1988. Contbr. articles and chpts. to profl. publs. Woodrow Wilson fellow, 1964; NSF fellow, 1964-68; NSF grantee Summer Inst. in Number Theory, Ann Arbor, Mich., 1973; prin. investigator NSF, 1974-88. Fellow AAAS; mem. AAAS (nominating com. math. sect. project 2061), Am. Math. Soc. (com. employment and ednl. policy, com. on coms., council, transactions editor, com. for the yr. 2000), Math. Assn. Am. (program com. for nat. meeting 1988-90, chair joint com. Am. Math. Soc. and Math. Assn. Am. 1991), Soc. Indsl. and Applied Math., Assn. for Women in Math. (travel grants com. 1996), Assn. for Women in Sci. Research in harmonic analysis on symmetric spaces and number theory. Office: U Calif San Diego Dept Math La Jolla CA 92093-0112

TERRAS, VICTOR, Slavic languages and comparative literature educator; b. Poltsamaa, Estonia, Jan. 21, 1921; came to U.S., 1952, naturalized, 1956; s. Evald and Elena (Rosenberger) T.; m. Rita Schubert, 1951; 1 child, Alexander. Mag. Phil., U. Tartu, Estonia, 1942; Ph.D., U. Chgo., 1963. Lectr. U. Tartu, 1943-44; instr. to assoc. prof. U. Ill., Urbana, 1959-64, prof. Slavic langs., 1965-66; prof. U. Wis., Madison, 1966-70; prof. Slavic langs. and comparative lit. Brown U., Providence, 1970-88, prof. emeritus, 1988—. Author: The Young Dostoevsky: A Critical Study, 1969, Belinskij and Russian Literary Criticism, 1974, A Karamazov Companion, 1981, Vladimir Mayakovsky, 1983; editor: Handbook of Russian Literature, 1984, The Idiot: An Interpretation, 1990, A History of Russian Literature, 1991. Mem. Am. Assn. Advancement Slavic and East European Studies, Am. Assn. Tchrs. Slavic and East European Langs. (pres. 1981-82), Internat. Dostoevsky Soc. (v.p. 1983—). Home: 128 Maple Ave Little Compton RI 02837-1714 Office: Brown U Box E Providence RI 02912

TERREAULT, R. CHARLES, engineer, management educator, researcher; b. Montreal, Que., Can., Mar. 21, 1935; s. Charles Terreault and Antonia Clark; m. Marie Rolland, Sept. 10, 1960; children: Genevieve, François, Patrick, Olivier-Hugues. BA, Coll. Stanislas, Montreal, 1954; BA in Sci., Ecole Poly., Montreal, 1959; hon. doctorate, U. Que., 1986. Engr. Bell Can., Montreal, 1959-65, staff engr., 1967-69, chief engr., 1971-73, asst. v.p. rsch., 1978-91; researcher Bell Telephone Labs., Holmdel, N.J., 1965-67; dir. planning Bell No. Rsch., Ottawa, Ont., Can., 1969-71; v.p. systems engring. Bell No. Rsch., Montreal, 1973-78; Jvr Cyr prof. mgmt. tech. Ecole Poly., Montreal, 1991-96; bd. dirs. Visiocom Inc.; bd. dirs. Natural Scis. and Engring. Rsch. Coun. Can., Ottawa, 1989-96. Contbr. articles to profl. jours. Fellow IEEE (Armstrong award 1984), Canadian Acad. Engring., Ordre Ingénieurs de Que., Inst. Mgmt. Sci. (chmn. Computer Rsch. Inst. Montreal Scientific Com.), Que. Assn. Indsl. Rsch. (Annual award 1992). Avocations: computers, classical music, skiing. Home and Office: 1665 Victoria Ave # 804, Saint Lambert, PQ Canada J4R 2T6

TERREL, RONALD LEE, civil engineer, business executive, educator; b. Klamath Falls, Oreg., Sept. 2, 1936; s. Theodore Thomas and Ruth Margaret (Fausset) T.; m. Susan Laura Harrower, Feb. 28, 1959 (div. July 1981); children: Douglas Scott, Nancy Dawn, Janet Lynn; m. 2d Alice Marie Blanchard, July 23, 1981. B.S.C.E., Purdue U., 1960, M.S., 1961; Ph.D., U. Calif.-Berkeley, 1967. Estimator J.H. Pomeroy & Co., San Francisco, 1955; lab. asst. Purdue U., 1956-60; asst. field geologist Bear Creek Mining Co., Mpls., 1957-58; materials engr. U.S. Bur. Reclamation, Denver, 1960-64; project engr. J.H. Pomeroy & Co., Antigua, B.W.I. and, Calif., 1964-65; research asst. U. Calif.-Berkeley, 1965-67; asst. prof. civil engr. U. Wash., Seattle, 1967-70, assoc. prof., 1970-75, prof., 1975-85, prof. emeritus, 1985—, head Transp. Constrn. and Geometronics divsn., 1976-79; prof., sr. researcher Oreg. State U., 1989-94; pres. Pavement Systems Inc., 1970-82; exec. v.p. Seattle Engring. Internat., Inc., 1979-81; pres. Terrel Assocs., Inc., 1981-85; owner Terrel Research, 1986—; v.p. Pavement Technologies Inc., 1985-86; chmn., CEO RL Techs. Ltd., 1996—; bd. dirs., v.p. Hydrogenesis, Inc.; cons. in field. Patentee in field. Co-founder, dir. Wash. State Transp. Ctr., 1981-84. Nominated Constrn. Man of Yr. Engring. News-Record, 1972; Purdue Alumni scholar, 1959-60; Ford fellow, 1965-67. Mem. ASTM, ASCE, Tranps. Rsch. Bd., Assn. Asphalt Paving Technologists (bd. dirs. 1979-83, Emmons award 1983, 95, award of merit 1990), Triaxial Inst. (chmn. 1971-73), Can. Tech. Asphalt Assn., Internat. Soc. for Asphalt Pavements (founding mem. 1987), Sigma Xi, Tau Beta Pi, Chi Epsilon, Sigma Gamma Epsilon. Office: 9703 241st Pl SW Edmonds WA 98020-6512

TERRELL, DOMINIQUE LARA, dramatic soprano, actress, real estate and marketing executive; b. South Bend, Ind., Apr. 26; d. Harold J. Metzler and Margaret Terrell (Whiteman) Metzler Fogarty. BA, Ithaca Coll., 1960; diploma, Brown's Bus. Coll., Decatur, Ill., 1960; postgrad. in real estate sales, NYU, 1984. Lic. securities dealer, real estate salesperson. Exec. legal asst. Carb Luria Glassner Cook & Kufeld, N.Y.C., 1962-64; Exec. legal asst. Graubard Moskovitz McGoldrick Dannett & Horowitz, N.Y.C., 1964-79; opera and concert singer N.Y.C.; real estate salesperson Rosemary Edwards Realty, N.Y.C., 1985, Kenneth D. Laub & Co., Inc., N.Y.C., 1987-89, GSW Realty, Inc., N.Y.C., 1990-91, Kuzmuk Realty, Inc., 1992-94, Gala 72 Realty, Inc., 1994—; bd. dirs., singer Broadway-Grand Opera, 1992—; pres. Mystique of Dominique, Whiteman and Stewart Prodns., DharMacduff Publs.; corr. sec., bd. dirs. Community Opera, Inc., N.Y.C., 1984—. Mem. internat. affairs com. and other coms. Women's Nat. Rep. Club, N.Y.C., 1968-82; active Rep. County Vols., N.Y.C., 1976-82; mem. nominating com. Ivy Rep. Club, N.Y.C., 1983-87; bd. dirs. Am. Landmark Festivals, 1986—. Named Female Singer of Yr., Internat. Beaux Arts, Inc., 1978-79, Princess Nightingale, Allied Indian Tribes N.Am. Continent-Cherokee Nation, 1985. Mem. Wagner Internat. Instn. (dir. pub. rels. 1982-84), Navy League U.S. (life, mem. N.Y. coun.), Assn. Former Intelligence Officers (assoc.), Friends of Spanish Opera (bd. dirs. 1982—), Finlandia Found., Inc. (life), The Bohemians, Nat. Arts Club (music com. 1983-87), N.Y. Opera Club. Avocations: tennis, swimming, dancing, travel, antiques.

TERRELL, G. IRVIN, lawyer; b. Houston, Sept. 28, 1946; s. George I. and Adella (Weichert) T.; m. Karen Steenberg, Jan. 8, 1984; 1 child, Katharine. BA, U. Tex., 1968, JD, 1972. Bar: Tex., U.S. Supreme Ct., U.S. Ct. Appeals (5th cir.), U.S. Dist. Ct. (so. dist.) Tex. Assoc. Baker & Botts, Houston, 1972-79; ptnr. Baker & Botts, 1980—. Mem. ABA, Houston Bar Assn., Internat. Soc. Barristers. Office: Baker & Botts 3000 One Shell Pla 910 Louisiana St Houston TX 77002-4916

TERRELL, J. ANTHONY, lawyer; b. N.Y.C., Sept. 20, 1943; s. Claude M. and Kathleen L. (Prevost) T.; m. Karen E. Terrell, Aug. 8, 1969; 1 child, Elizabeth S. BA, NYU, 1965, LLM in Taxation, 1975; JD, Villanova U., 1968. Bar: N.Y. With Frueauff, Farrell, Sullivan & Bryan, N.Y.C., 1970-74, ptnr., 1974; assoc. Reid & Priest, N.Y.C., 1974-76, ptnr., 1977—. Mem. ABA (sect. bus. law, sect. taxation, sect. pub. utility, comm. and transp. law, vice chmn. corp. finance com.), Internat. Bar Assn. (bus. law sect.), Nat. Assn. Bond Lawyers, Belle Haven Club, Met. Club, Coral Beach and Tennis Club. Home: Indian Harbor Greenwich CT 06830 Office: Reid & Priest 40 W 57th St New York NY 10019-4001

TERRELL, (NELSON) JAMES, physicist; b. Houston, Aug. 15, 1923; s. Nelson James Sr. and Gladys Delphine (Stevens) T.; m. Elizabeth Anne Pearson, June 9, 1945; children—Anne (dec.), Barbara, Jean. B.A., Rice U., 1944, M.A., 1947, Ph.D., 1950. Research asst. Rice U., Houston, 1950; asst. prof. physics Western Res. U., Cleve., 1950-51; mem. staff Los Alamos Nat. Lab., U. Calif., 1951-89, assoc., 1989-94; affiliate, 1994—. Producer (computer generated movie) The X-Ray Sky, 1969-76; contbr. articles to profl. jours. and encys. Served to 1st lt. AUS, 1944-46. Graham Baker scholar, 1943-44; fellow Rice U., 1946-48, AEC, 1948-50. Fellow Am. Phys. Soc., AAAS; mem. Am. Astron. Soc., Internat. Astron. Union, Phi Beta Kappa, Sigma Xi. Research in relativity, quasars, x-ray and gamma ray astronomy, nuclear physics, lasers. Home: 85 Obsidian Loop Los Alamos NM 87544-2528 Office: Los Alamos Nat Lab Mail Stop D436 Los Alamos NM 87545

TERRELL, JAMES DANIEL, lawyer; b. Kansas City, Oct. 22, 1956; s. D. Ronald and Bobbie L. (Graham) T.; m. Lori J. McAlister, May 31, 1980; children: Justin Daniel, Christopher James, Alexander Graham. BS, Ctrl. Mo. State U., 1979; JD, U. Mo., 1982. Bar: Mo. 1982, U.S. Dist. Ct. (we. dist.) 1982, U.S. Dist. Ct. (ea. dist.) Mo. 1984. Assoc. Wasinger, Parham & Morthland, Hannibal, Mo., 1982-87; ptnr. Wasinger, Parham, Morthland Terrell & Wasinger, Hannibal, 1987—. Bd. dirs. Marion County Svcs. for the Developmentally Disabled, Hannibal, 1989—. Mem. Mo. Bar Assn. (family law sect.), 10th Jud. Cir. Bar Assn., U. Mo. Alumni Assn. (life), Phi Delta Phi. Office: Wasinger Parham Morthland Terrell & Wasinger 2801 Saint Marys Ave Hannibal MO 63401-3775

TERRELL, PAMELA SUE, pharmacist; b. Richmond, Ind., Feb. 1, 1965; d. Kenneth Duane and Phyllis J. (Preston) T. BS in Pharmacy with honors, PharmD, Purdue U., 1991. Registered pharmacist, Ind. Pharmacist Reid Hosp. and Health Care Svcs., Richmond, 1992-94, Owl Drugs, Muncie, Ind., 1994-95, Ball Meml. Hosp., Muncie, Ind., 1996—; resident in pharmacy practice Meth. Hosp. Ind., Indpls., 1995-96; adj. instr. pharmacy practice Butler U. Sch. Pharmacy and Health Scis., Indpls., 1995-96; cons. pharmacist H&R Healthcare Cons., Muncie, 1994-95. Mem. Am. Coll. Clin. Pharmacy (assoc.), Am. Soc. Health-Sys. Pharmacists, Ind. Soc. Hosp. Pharmacists, Fellowship of Christian Pharmacists Internat., Ind. Coll. Clin. Pharmacy, Rho Chi, Phi Kappa Phi. Avocations: needlework, travel, cooking. Home: 2917 W Applewood Ct Muncie IN 47304-7502 Office: Ball Meml Hosp 2401 W University Ave Muncie IN 47303-3428

TERRELL, SUZANNE HAIK, lawyer; b. New Orleans, July 8, 1954; d. George Michel and Isabel (Saloom) Haik; m. Walter Lee, Apr. 23, 1976; children: Catherine Julie, Elizabeth Lee, Christine Alyce. BA in Art History, Tulane U., 1976; JD, Loyola U., New Orleans, 1984. Jud. law clk. La. 4th Cir. Ct. Appeals, New Orleans, 1984-85, 86-88, La. Supreme Ct., New Orleans, 1985-86; atty. Baldwin & Haspel, New Orleans, 1988-91, Wootan & Saunders, New Orleans, 1991-93; city coun. mem., chmn. telecomm. com. City of New Orleans, 1994—; advisor Teen Ct. Project, New Orleans; legis. strategist La. Opthalmology Assn., New Orleans; adj. faculty mem. Univ. Coll. Tulane U., New Orleans. Trustee Metalrie Park Country Day Sch., New Orleans Mus. Art; bd. dirs. Eye Found. Am., Met. Area Com., Charity

Hosp. New Orleans. Recipient award Loyola Law Alumni Assn., 1983. Mem. ABA, Fed. Bar Assn., Assn. Women's Atty., Coun. Young Children, La. Bar Assn., Jr. League New Orleans, Young Leadership Coun.,. Republican. Home: 170 Audubon Blvd New Orleans LA 70112 Office: New Orleans City Coun 1300 Perdido St Rm 2w80 New Orleans LA 70112-2112

TERRELL, W(ILLIAM) GLENN, university president emeritus; b. Tallahassee, May 24, 1920; s. William Glenn and Esther (Collins) T.; m. Gail Strandberg Terrell; children by previous marriage: Francine Elizabeth, William Glenn III. BA, Davidson Coll., 1942, LLD (hon.), 1969; MS, Fla. State U., 1948; PhD, State U. Iowa, 1952; LLD (hon.), Gonzaga U., 1984, Seattle U., 1985. Instr., then asst. prof. Fla. State U., Tallahassee, 1948-55; asst. prof., then assoc. prof., chmn. dept. psychology U. Colo., Boulder, 1955-59, assoc., acting dean Coll Arts and Scis., 1959-63; prof. psychology, dean Coll. Liberal Arts and Scis., U. Ill. at Chgo. Circle, 1963-65, dean faculties, 1965-67; pres. Wash. State U., Pullman, 1967-85, pres. emeritus, 1985—; Pres. Nat. Assn. State Univs. and Land-Grant Colls., 1977-78; cons. The Pacific Inst., Seattle, 1987—. Contbr. articles to profl. jours. Served to capt. inf. U.S. Army, 1942-46, ETO. Recipient Disting. Alumnus award U. Iowa, 1985. Fellow APA, Soc. Rsch. in Child Devel.; mem. AAAS, Sigma Xi, Phi Kappa Phi. Avocations: golf, reading, traveling. Home: 2438 36th Ave W Seattle WA 98199-3704 Office: The Pacific Inst 1709 Harbor Ave SW Seattle WA 98126-2049

TERRELL-MCDANIEL, ROBIN F., cardiac rehabilitation and critical care nurse; b. Charlton Heights, W.Va., May 9, 1961; d. Clarence E. Sr. and Dorothy Mae (Smith) T.; m. Charles Kevin McDaniel, Aug. 4, 1990. ADN, W.Va. Inst. Tech., 1982; BSN, W.Va. U., 1987. Emergency room charge nurse Montgomery (W.Va.) Gen. Hosp., 1982-87, nursing supr., 1987-88; coord. utilization rev. MedCert, Charleston, W.Va., 1988-89; vis. asst. prof. nursing W.Va. Inst. Tech., Montgomery, 1989-90; critical care nurse W.Va. Gen. Hosp., Montgomery, 1990-97, cardiac rehab. nurse, 1995-97, dir. acute care nursing, cardiac rehab., 1997—. Mem. Am. Assn. Cardiovascular and Pulmonary Rehab. Home: PO Box 345 Pratt WV 25162-0345

TERRILL, CLAIR ELMAN, animal scientist, geneticist, consultant; b. Rippey, Iowa, Oct. 27, 1910; s. Otis Wallace and Mary Irene (Grow) T.; m. Zola Mae Alexander, June 9, 1932; children: Ronald Lee (dec.), Richard Eugene. BS, Iowa State U., 1932; PhD, U. Mo., 1936. Rsch. asst. U. Mo., 1932-36; asst. animal husbandman Ga. Expt. Sta. USDA, 1936; animal husbandman Agrl. Rsch. Svc. USDA, Dubois, Idaho, 1936-53, dir. U.S. Sheep Expt. Sta., 1953-55; chief sheep and fur animal rsch. br. USDA, Beltsville, Md., 1955-72, staff scientist nat. program staff Agrl. Rsch. Svc., 1972-81, collaborator nat. program staff, 1981—; Mem. sub-panel Pres.'s Sci. Adv. Com. World Food Supply, 1966; adj. prof. Utah State U., Logan, 1986-87; cons. FAO, 1984. Contbr. chpts. to several books. Recipient Silver Ram award Am. Sheep Industry, 1975, Saddle and Sirloin Portrait award, 1989; inductee Internat. Stockmen's Hall of Fame, 1987, Agrl. Rsch. Svc. Hall of Fame, 1993; Fulbright grantee U NSW, Kensington, Australia, 1969. Fellow AAAS, Am. Soc. Animal Sci. (pres. Western sect. 1951, chmn. com. rsch. 1950-52, com. monographs 1955-60, editorial bd. 1954-57, sec.-treas. 1960-62, v.p. 1963, pres. 1964, bd. dirs.); mem. World Assn. Animal Prodn. (coun. 1965-68), Am. Forage and Grasslands Coun. (bd. dirs. 1963-68), Am. Registry Profl. Animal Scientists, Internat. Goat Assn. (bd. dirs.), Genetic Soc. Am., Am. Genetic Assn. (coun. 1965-68, v.p., pres. 1970), Am. Meat Sci. Assn., Am. Assn. Anatomists, Am. Inst. Biol. Scis., Soc. Study Reprodn., Sigma Xi, Alpha Zeta, Gamma Sigma Delta. Home: 318 Apple Grove Rd Silver Spring MD 20904-2745 Office: USDA Nat Program Staff Agrl Rsch Svc Barc W # 005 Beltsville MD 20705

TERRILL, JULIA ANN, elementary education educator; b. St. Joseph, Mo., Nov. 24, 1954; d. Jule Holmes and Beverly Jean (Brown) T. BS in Elem. Edn., N.W. Mo. State U., 1976, MEd, 1980. Tchr. learning disabilities Nodaway-Holt, Maitland, Mo., 1976-79; tchr. learning disabilities Lexington (Mo.) R-V, 1979-84, classroom tchr., 1984—. Mem. Young Citizens for Jerry Litton, Chillicothe, Mo., 1972, 76; mem., historian PTO, 1993-94, 94-95; mem. Leslie Bell Tchr. Support Team, 1995-96, 96-97. Mem. ASCD, Mo. State Tchrs. Assn., Comty. Tchrs. Assn. (sec. 1992-93), Order Ea. Star, Delta Kappa Gamma. Baptist. Avocations: reading, playing piano and giving lessons, swimming, walking, traveling. Office: Lexington R-V Sch Leslie Bell 400 S 20th St Lexington MO 64067-1844

TERRILL, ROBERT CARL, hospital administrator; b. Oklahoma City, Dec. 10, 1927; s. D. Willard and Velma (Mitchell) T.; m. Jessica Doe, Dec. 14, 1957; children—Thane Bennett, Sarah Haven. BA, U. Okla., 1948, MA in History, 1961; MA in Hosp. Adminstrn., State U. Iowa, 1954; EdD in Ednl. Adminstrn., Ind. U., 1978. Adminstrv. resident Mary Fletcher Hosp., Burlington, Vt., 1953-55; asst. adminstr., personnel dir. Mary Fletcher Hosp., 1955-65, assoc. adminstr., 1965-72; adminstr. Hosps. of U. Okla., Oklahoma City, 1972-77; dir. Ind. Univ. Hosps., Indpls., 1972-76; assoc. prof. Coll. Mgmt. U. Mass., Boston, 1977-87; preceptor in hosp. adminstrn. Washington U., St. Louis, Trinity U., San Antonio; asst. prof. U. Okla. Health Scis. Center.; pub. edn. planning svcs. corp., 1987—. Fellow Am. Coll. Hosp. Adminstrs.; mem. Mass. Hosp. Assn., Am. Hosp. Assn., Assn. Programs in Hosp. Adminstrn., Pub. Health Assn., New Eng. Hosp. Assembly, Nat. League for Nursing, State U. Iowa. Alumni Assn., Ind. U. Alumni Assn. Club: Rotarian. Home: 26 Grove St Sandwich MA 02563-2125 Office: 93 Old Kings Hwy Sandwich MA 02563-1877

TERRILL, ROSS GLADWIN, author, educator; b. Melbourne, Australia; Came to U.S., 1965, naturalized, 1979; s. Frank and Miriel (Lloyd) T. B.A. with 1st class honors, U. Melbourne; Ph.D., Harvard U., 1970. Tutor in polit. sci. U. Melbourne, 1962-63; staff sec. Australian Student Christian Movement, 1964-65; teaching fellow Harvard, 1968-70, lectr. govt., 1970-73, asso. prof., 1974-78, research fellow East Asian studies, 1970—; dir. student programs Harvard (Center Internat. Affairs), 1974-78; contbg. editor Atlantic Monthly, 1970-84; research fellow Asia Soc., 1977-79. Author: China Profile, 1969, China and Ourselves, 1971, 800,000,000: The Real China, 1972, R.H. Tawney and His Times, 1973, Flowers on an Iron Tree, 1975, The Future of China, 1978, The China Difference, 1979, Mao: A Biography, 1980, revised 1993, 97, White-Boned Demon, 1984, The Australians, 1987, Madam Mao, 1992, revised, 1993, 97, China in Our Time, 1992; contbr. numerous articles to profl. jours. Recipient Nat. Mag. award, 1972; George Polk Meml. award outstanding mag. reporting, 1972; Sumner prize, 1970. Mem. Authors Guild, PEN. Club: Harvard of N.Y.C. Home: 200 Saint Botolph St Boston MA 02115-4911

TERRILL, THOMAS EDWARD, health facility administrator; b. Mpls., Oct. 4, 1939. BS, U. Minn., 1961; M Health Care Adminstrn., U. Pitts., 1963, DS, 1970. Adminstrv. resicent Homestead (Pa.) Hosp., 1962-63; adminstrv. asst. Truman Med. Ctr.-West, Kansas City, Mo., 1963-65, asst. adminstr., 1965-67; asst. prof. U. Pitts., 1967-73, assoc. prof., 1973-74; dir. mktg. and planning Mountain States Regional Med. Program, Boise, Idaho, 1974-76, divsn. dir., 1976-77; v.p. Hollywood Presbyn. Med. Ctr., L.A., 1977; assoc. dir. Akron (Ohio) City Hosp., 1978-81, v.p. med. affairs, 1981-83; sr. mgr. Peat Marwick Mitchell, Phila., 1983-87; v.p. Network Inc., Randolph, N.J., 1987-90; exec. v.p. Univ. Health Sys., New Brunswick, N.J., 1990-93; pres. Univ. Health Sys., New Brunswick, 1994—. Contbr. articles to profl. publs. Home: 13 Old Mill Rd Holmdel NJ 07733 Office: Univ Health Sys 317 George St New Brunswick NJ 08901-2008

TERRIS, ALBERT, metal sculptor; b. N.Y.C., Nov. 10, 1916; s. Aaron and Fania (Rosenthal) Teraspulsky; children: Susan, Abby, David, Enoch. BSS, CCNY, 1939; postgrad., NYU Inst. Fine Arts, 1939-42. lectr. Met. Mus. Art, 1941-42; tchr. fine arts N.Y.C. High Sch. System, 1947-54; prof. emeritus Bklyn. Coll., 1947-86. Steel sculptures include Non-Fixed Relationship, 1948, Anti-Gravity, 1950, Giraffes, 1953, Short Art, 1953, Pro-Gravity Chains, 1956, Tools, 1956, Crushed Sculpture, 1956, Words, 1957, Discursive-Illegible-Boustrophedon, 1975, Plates of Charlemagne, 1975, Fireharps, 1975, Cycle of Life, 1977, Wipes, 1996; one-man shows: Saidenberg, 1955, Duveen-Graham, 1958, Carnagie Internats., 1958, 62, Bklyn. Mus. Biennale (awarded first prize), 1960, Allan Stone, 1962, Critics Choice, 1972, Artists Space, 1975, Gloria Cortella, 1977, (retrospective) The Artist in the Civil Service Bklyn. Coll. Gallery, 1985; exhibited in group shows at Tanager Gallery, 1952-61, Stable anns., 1952-60, Mus. Modern Art, N.Y.C., 1962, others; represented in permanent collections: Stephen Paine, Boston, Arnold Maremont, Evanston, G. David Thompson Estate, NBC-TV, others. Served with 1st Allied Airborne, 1942-45. Home: 280 S Ocean Ave Freeport NY 11520-4939

TERRIS, MILTON, physician, educator; b. N.Y.C., Apr. 22, 1915; s. Harry and Gussie (Dokshitski) T.; m. Rema Lapouse, Nov. 23, 1941 (dec. Aug. 1970); children—Andrew David, Eugene Charles (dec.); m. Lillian Long, Feb. 6, 1971. A.B., Columbia, 1935; M.D., N.Y.U., 1939; M.P.H., Johns Hopkins, 1944. Intern Harlem Hosp., N.Y.C., 1939-41; resident Bellevue Hosp., N.Y.C., 1941-42; practice medicine specializing in preventive medicine Buffalo, 1951-58, N.Y.C., 1960-80, South Burlington, Vt., 1980—; asst. dean post-grad. edn. Sch. Medicine, U. Buffalo, 1951-58, assoc., 1952-54, asst. prof., 1954-55, assoc. prof. preventive medicine, 1955-58; prof. epidemiology Sch. Medicine, Tulane U., 1958-60; head chronic disease unit dept. epidemiology Pub. Health Research Inst., N.Y.C., 1960-64; prof. preventive medicine N.Y. Med. Coll., 1964-80, chmn. dept. community and preventive medicine, 1968-80; vis. prof. U. Toronto, 1984-93, U. Montreal, 1985—. Author: Goldberger on Pellagra, 1964, La Revolución Epidemiológica y la Medicina Social, 1980; Editor: Jour. Public Health Policy, 1980—. Recipient Abraham M. Lilienfeld award Am. Coll. Epidemiology. Fellow N.Y. Acad. Medicine, Am. Pub. Health Assn. (past pres.; Sedgwick Meml. award 1984); mem. Assn. Tchrs. Preventive Medicine (Duncan Clark award 1984; past pres.), Soc. Epidemiologic Research (past pres.), Nat. Assn. Pub. Health Policy (past pres.), Phi Beta Kappa, Alpha Omega Alpha, Delta Omega. Home and Office: 208 Meadowood Dr South Burlington VT 05403-7401

TERRIS, SUSAN, physician, cardiologist; b. Morristown, N.J., Sept. 5, 1944; d. Albert and Virginia (Rinaldy) T. BA in History, U. Chgo., 1967, PhD in Biochemistry, 1975, MD, 1976. Diplomate Am. Bd. Internal Medicine, Am. Bd. Endocrinology and Metabolism, Am. Bd. Cardiovascular Disease. Resident in internal medicine Washington U., Barnes Hosp., St. Louis, 1976-78; fellow in endocrinology and metabolism U. Chgo., 1978-80, fellow cardiology, 1980-83; fellow cardiology U. Mich., Ann Arbor, 1983-85, instr. cardiology, 1985-86; head cardiac catheterization lab., head cardiology Westland (Mich.) Med. Ctr., 1985. Contbr. articles to Jour. Biol. Chemistry, Am. Jour. Physiology, Am. Jour. Cardiology, Jour. Clin. Investigation, other profl. publs. Grantee Juvenile Diabetes Found., 1978-80, NIH, 1978-79. Mem. AAAS, Am. Heart Assn., N.Y. Acad. Sci., Am. Women in Sci. Achievements include rsch. demonstrating dependence of intracellular degradation of insulin upon its prior receptor-mediated uptake by liver; studies of effects of various drugs on human circulatory system.

TERRIS, WILLIAM, publishing executive; b. Chgo., Sept. 24, 1937; s. William and Evelyn M. (Dykstra) T.; m. Shirley Ann Gellinger, Sept. 8, 1958; 1 child, Bruce Robert. BS in Indsl. Econs., Purdue U., 1959; MS in Psychology, Ill. Inst. Technology, 1962, PhD in Psychology, 1964. Registered psychologist, Ill. Asst. prof. U. Okla., Norman, 1964-67; assoc. prof. DePaul U., Chgo., 1967-86; chmn. bd. London House, Inc., Park Ridge, Ill., 1975-92; pres., CEO PSB Corp., Mundelein, Ill., 1993—; cons. Assoc. Consulting Psychologists, St. Louis, 1975-78. Author: (psychological test) Personnel Selection Inventory, 1979, Employee Theft, 1985. Mem. APA, Am. Soc. for Indsl. Security, Soc. for Human Resource Mgmt., Chgo. Crime Commn. Republican. Baptist. Avocation: reading. Home and Office: PSB Co 21851 Riviera Ct Mundelein IL 60060-5328

TERRITO, MARY C., health facility administrator, oncologist. BS in Biology, Wayne State U., 1965, MD, 1968. Intern/resident in internal medicine Parkland Hosp., Dallas, 1971-73; fellow in hematology/oncology Harbor-U. Calif., L.A., 1973-74, UCLA, 1974-75; rsch. assoc. Wadsworth VA Hosp., L.A., 1975-81; asst. prof. dept. medicine UCLA, 1975-81, assoc. prof., 1981-96, prof., 1996—, dir. bone marrow transplant program Ctr. Health Scis., 1981—. Contbr. articles to profl. jours. Office: UCLA Bone Marrow Transplantation Program Ctr 42-121 CHS 10833 Le Conte Ave Los Angeles CA 90095-3075*

TERRY, BRIAN R., counselor, academic administrator; b. Providence, June 8, 1961; s. Edwin R. and Mary W. (Ahern) T.; m. Stephanie A. Fogli; children: Alexander Brian, Jarrod Stephan. AS in Bus. Adminstrn., Community Coll. of R.I., Warwick, 1982; BS in Bus. Adminstrn., Bryant Coll., 1984; MA in Agy. Counseling, R.I. Coll., 1990. Counselor Whitmarsh Corp., Providence, 1985-87, 87-90, supr., 1990-94; juvenile counselor Dept. of Children, Youth, and Families R.I. Tng. Sch., Cranston, R.I., 1988-90, acting dep. supt. for adminstrn. tng. sch. for youth, 1994—, cottage mgr., 1990—; social caseworker II Dept. for Children, Youth and their Families Divsn. of Direct Svcs., Cranston, R.I., 1990. Mem. Nat. Major Gang Task Force, New Eng. Coun. on Crime and Deliquency; vol. Spl. Olympics.; former mem. Big Brothers. Acad. scholar Esterline Corp., acad. scholar City of Cranton, R.I., Tanner Meml. scholar. Am. Assn. for Counseling and Devel., Pub. Offender Counselor Assn., Nat. Ct. Appointed Spl. Advocate Assn., Am. Correctional Assn., Nat. Inst. for Reality Therapy (assoc., Northeast region), Community Leaders of Am., Juvenile Officers Assn., Phi Theta Kappa. Home: 115 E View Ave Cranston RI 02920-6505

TERRY, CLARK, musician; b. St. Louis, Dec. 14, 1920; m. Pauline Reddon; 2 children. Privately educated. Pres. Etoile Music Prodns., 1955—, Pastel Music, 1958—; v.p. Creative Jazz Composers, Inc., 1972—; itinerant jazz clinician and educator; exec. dir. Internat. of Jazz. Leader, Clark Terry Big Bad Band, 1966—; albums include: The World of Duke Ellington, Vol. 2, Duke Ellington Such Sweet Thunder, The Terry-Brookmeyer Quintet, Cruisin', Cool Blues, Oscar Peterson Trio with Clark Terry, Clark Terry's Big Bad Band Live on 57th Street, The Happy Horns of Clark Terry, Yes, The Blues, 1981, Paris 1960, 1985, Live at the Village Gate, 1991, Reunion with Pee Wee Claybrook and Swing Fever, 1995, (with Red Mitchell) Jive at Five, 1993. Author: Let's Talk Trumpet, 1973, Interpretation of the Jazz Language, 1976, Circular Breathing, 1977. Served with USN, 1942-45. Recipient numerous awards, including Grammy nominations, Pote Distinguished Jazz Artist, Phil., 1989. Office: d'Note Records 14134 NE Airport Way Portland OR 97230-1059*

TERRY, CLIFFORD LEWIS, journalist; b. Highland Park, Ill., Jan. 19, 1937; s. Clifford Lewis and Isabelle (Marlow) T.; m. Patricia West Dickelman, Sept. 1, 1966; children: Christopher West, Scott Marlow. Student, Carleton Coll., Northfield, Minn., 1954-55; BA, Trinity Coll., Hartford, Conn., 1958; postgrad., Columbia U., 1962-63. Tchr., English and history Mt. Hermon (Mass.) Sch., 1958-59; police reporter City News Bur. Chgo., 1959-60; mem. staff Chgo. Tribune, 1960-94, movie critic, 1965-70; assoc. editor Chgo. Tribune (Sunday mag.), 1970-82, feature writer, 1982-85, TV critic, 1985-89, arts feature writer, 1989-94; ind. writer, 1994—. Served with AUS, 1960. Nieman fellow Harvard U., 1969-70. Mem. Phi Beta Kappa.

TERRY, FRANK JEFFREY, bishop. Bishop Diocese of Spokane, Wash., 1991—. Office: Episcopal Diocese of Spokane 245 E 13th Ave Spokane WA 99202-1114*

TERRY, GARY A., lawyer, former trade association executive; b. Ogden, Utah, Apr. 2, 1935; s. Hyrum Aceal and Viola (Sorenson) T.; m. Carole Ann Eitel, June 23, 1962; children—Stephanie Ann, Brendan Gary. B.A. in Polit. Sci., UCLA, 1964; J.D., George Washington U., 1968. Bars: Va. 1969 D.C. 1969. Mem. staff U.S. Ho. of Reps., Washington, 1964-65; Washington staff Bethlehem Steel Corp., 1965-69; atty. HUD, Washington, 1969; exec. v.p. Am. Land Devel. Assn. (now Am. Resort Devel. Assn.), Washington, 1969-82, pres., 1982-91; also dir. Am. Land Devel. Assn. (now Am. Resort Devel. Assn.); with Jones, Waldo, Holbrook & McDonough, Washington, 1991—, St. George, 1995—; dir. Internat. Found. for Timesharing, Washington, 1981-91, mem. consultative council Nat. Inst. Bldg. Scis., Washington, 1982-85; U.S. rep. land use and town planning com. Internat. Real Estate Fedn., Brussels, 1984-91; mem. Found. for Internat. Meetings, Washington, 1984—; del. Lincoln Inst. Land Policy, Harvard U., 1984, 85. Contbr. articles to profl. jours. Asst. to exec. dir. Presdl. Inaugural Com., 1969-70; mem. adv. bd. NOAA, Washington, 1972; bd. dirs. Zacchaeus Free Med. and Legal Clinics, Washington, 1991-95, co-chair lawyers com., 1992-95. Seved with USN, 1953-56. Decorated Am. Spirit of Honor medal. Mem. Va. Bar Assn., D.C. Bar Assn., Am. Soc. Assn. Execs. Mem. LDS Ch. Avocations: music; literature; architectural design; art; travel. Home: 952 E Lizzie Ln Saint George UT 84790 Office: Jones Waldo Holbrook & McDonough 2300 M St NW Ste 900 Washington DC 20037-1434 also: 249 E Tabernacle St Ste 200 Saint George UT 84770-2978

TERRY, GLENN A., retired nuclear chemist; b. St. Paul, Aug. 26, 1922; s. Claude Alexander and Loretta (Glenn) T.; m. Evelyn Jean Lehmann, Aug. 16, 1947; 1 child, Stephen Allan. BS, So. Ill. U., 1947; PhD, U. Wis., 1951. Rsch. chemist Mallinckrodt Chem. Works, St. Louis, 1951-56; process improvement head Mallinckodt Chem. Works, St. Louis, 1956-59; sect. leader Spencer/Gulf, Kansas City, Mo., 1959-68; tech. dir. Nuclear Fuel Svcs., Erwin, Tenn., 1968-73; nuclear process engr. U.S. Nulcear Regulatory Com., Washington, 1973-81, sect. leader, 1981-88, ret., 1988. Contbr. articles to profl. jours.; patentee in field. Lt. (j.g.) USN, 1942-46, PTO. Mem. Am. Chem. Soc. (emeritus), Am. Nuclear Soc. (emeritus), Am. Legion, VFW, Elks. Republican. Achievements include patents in field. Home: 3824 Brooke Meadow Ln Olney MD 20832

TERRY, JAMES JOSEPH, JR., lawyer; b. Yonkers, N.Y., July 2, 1952; s. James Joseph Sr. and Marie Catherine (O'Boyle) T.; m. Marguerite Mary O'Connor, Sept. 29, 1985; 1 child, James Daniel. BA, NYU, 1974; JD, Columbia U., 1977. Bar: N.Y. 1978, U.S. Dist. Ct. (so. and ea. dists.) N.Y. 1978, U.S. Ct. Appeals (2d cir.) 1981, U.S. Ct. Appeals (3d cir.) 1989. Assoc. Cole & Deitz, N.Y.C., 1977-86; ptnr. Winston & Strawn (formerly Cole & Deitz), N.Y.C., 1986—. Mem. ABA, N.Y. State Bar Assn., Def. Rsch. Inst., N.Y. County Lawyers Assn. Democrat. Roman Catholic. Avocations: fishing, reading. Home: 190 Kneeland Ave Yonkers NY 10705-2713 Office: Winston & Strawn 200 Park Ave New York NY 10166-0005

TERRY, JOHN ALFRED, judge; b. Utica, N.Y., May 6, 1933; s. Robert Samuel and Julia Berenice (Collins) T. B.A. magna cum laude, Yale U., 1954; J.D., Georgetown U., 1960. Bar: D.C. 1960. Asst. U.S. atty. for D.C., 1962-67; staff atty. Nat. Commn. Reform of Fed. Criminal Laws, Washington, 1967-68; pvt. practice law Washington, 1968-69; chief appellate div. U.S. Atty.'s Office for D.C., 1969-82; judge D.C. Ct. Appeals, 1982—. Mem. D.C. Bar (bd. govs. 1977-82), ABA, Phi Beta Kappa. Office: DC Ct Appeals 500 Indiana Ave NW Washington DC 20001-2131

TERRY, JOHN HART, lawyer, former utility company executive, former congressman; b. Syracuse, N.Y., Nov. 14, 1924; s. Frank and Saydee (Hart) T.; m. Catherine Jean Taylor Phelan, Apr. 15, 1950; children: Catherine Jean (Mrs. Richard Thompson), Lynn Marie (Mrs. Robert Tacher), Susan Louise (Mrs. Stanley Germain), Mary Carole (Mrs. Stephen Brady). B.A., U. Notre Dame, 1945; J.D., Syracuse U., 1948. Bar: N.Y. bar 1950, D.C. bar 1972. Asst. to partner Smith & Sovik, 1948-59; asst. sec. to Gov. State of N.Y., 1959-61; sr. partner firm Smith, Sovik, Terry, Kendrick, McAuliffe & Schwarzer, 1961-73; sr. v.p., gen. counsel, sec. Niagara Mohawk Power Corp., Syracuse, 1973-87; counsel Hiscock & Barclay, Syracuse, 1987-94; atty. in pvt. practice, 1994—; mem. N.Y. State Assembly, 1962-70, 92d Congress from 34th N.Y. Dist., 1971-73; presdl. elector, 1972. State chmn. United Services Orgn., 1964-73; past pres. John Timothy Smith Found.; Founder, dir. Bishop Foery Found., Inc.; dir. St. Joseph's Hosp. Council; past pres. Lourdes Camp; bd. dirs. N.Y. State Traffic Council; past nat. bd. dirs. Am. Cancer Soc.; mem. adv. council Syracuse U. Sch. Mgmt.; past pres. Cath. Youth Orgn.; bd. dirs. Syracuse Community Baseball Club. Served to 1st lt. AUS, 1943-46. Decorated Purple Heart, Bronze Star; named Man of Year Syracuse Jr. C. of C., 1958, Man of Yr. N.Y. State Jr. C. of C., 1959, Young Man of Yr. U. Notre Dame Club Cen. N.Y., 1959. Mem. ABA (utility law sect.), N.Y. State Bar Assn. (chmn. com. on public utility law), Onondaga County Bar Assn. (chmn. membership and legis. coms.), D.C. Bar Assn., County Officers Assn., Citizens Found., U. Notre Dame, Syracuse U. law assns., Am. Legion, VFW, DAV, 40 and 8, Mil. Order of Purple Heart. Roman Catholic. Clubs: Century, Bellevue Country, Capitol Hill (Washington), Vero Beach Country.

TERRY, JOHN JOSEPH, transportation investor; b. Chgo., July 29, 1937; s. Michael Parnell and Honore (Ryan) T.; m. Terese Rose Mulkern, Dec. 31, 1960; children—Michael P., Gregory, Deirdre. B.S., Loyola U., Chgo., 1959; postgrad., U. So. Fla., 1967. C.P.A., Ill. With Touche, Ross & Co., 1959-65; v.p. Nat. City Lines, Denver, 1965-71; v.p. fin. Pepsico Transp., Inc., Tulsa, 1971-74; v.p. U.S. Rwy. Assn., Washington, 1974-76; chmn. P.I.E. Transport Europe, 1976-79; exec. v.p. IU Internat. Corp., Wilmington, Del., 1976-85; pres. Transp. Mgmt. Investment Group, Inc., Phila., 1985—; v.p.-at-large Am. Trucking Assn., Washington, 1984-85, chmn., internat. competitiveness task force, 1991, tax policy com., 1987—; bd. dirs. Caldwell Freight Lines, Lenoir, N.C., Basin Western, Inc., Roosevelt, Utah, Ampace Corp.; cons. freight transp. World Bank and European Bank for Reconstrn. and Devel., 1986—. Served with U.S. Army, 1960-63. Recipient Best Motor Carrier Rsch. award Transp. Rsch. Forum, 1991. Office: Transp Mgmt Investment Group Inc 103 Eton Rd Yardley PA 19067-7311

TERRY, LEON CASS, neurologist, educator; b. Northville, Mich., Dec. 22, 1940; s. Leon Herbert and Zella Irene (Boyd) T.; m. Suzanne Martinson, June 27, 1964; children: Kristin, Sean. Pharm. D., U. Mich., 1964; MD, Marquette U., 1969; PhD, McGill U., 1982, MBA, U. S. Fla., 1994. Diplomate Am. Bd. Psychiatry and Neurology, Am. Bd. Med. Mgmt. Intern, U. Rochester, N.Y., 1969-70; staff assoc. NIH, 1970-72; resident in neurology McGill U., Montreal, Que., Can., 1972-75, MRC fellow, 1975-78; assoc. prof. U. Tenn., Memphis, 1978-81; prof. neurology U. Mich., Ann Arbor, 1981-89, assoc. prof. physiology, 1982-89; asst. chief neurology VA Med. Ctr., Ann Arbor, 1982-89; prof. neurology and physiology, chmn. dept. neurology Med. Coll of Wis., Milw., 1989—; dir. clin. neurosci. ctr. and multiple sclerosis clinic, Med. Coll. Wis., assoc. dean for amb. care, 1996—; vice chief of staff Froedtert Hosp., 1994-97, chief of staff, 1997—. Contbr. articles to profl. jours., chpts. to books. Served to lt. comdr. USPHS, 1970-72. NIH grantee, 1981-92; VA grantee, 1980-92; VA Clin. Investigator award, 1980-81. Mem. AMA, Am. Soc. Clin. Investigation, Cen. Soc. Clin. Investigation, So. Soc. Clin. Investigation, Am. Neurol. Assn., Am. Coll. Physician Execs. (vice chmn. academic health ctr. soc. 1994-95, chair, 1995—, leader forum health care delivery 1995—), Am. Coll. Healthcare Execs., Endocrine Soc., Am. Acad. Neurology, Internat. Soc. Neuroendocrinology, Internat. Soc. Psychoneuroendocrinology, Soc. Neurosci, Soc. Rsch. Biol. Rhythms, Milw. Acad. Physicians, Wis. Neurol. Assn., Wis. State Med. Soc. (del.- elect 1995-96), Med. Soc. Milw. County, Milw. Neuropsychiatric Soc. (pres.-elect). Avocations: pilot, skiing, scuba diving, computers. Office: Med Coll Wis Dept Neurology Froedtert Hosp 9200 W Watertown Plank Rd Milwaukee WI 53226-3557

TERRY, MARSHALL NORTHWAY, JR., English language educator, author; b. Cleve., Feb. 7, 1931; s. Marshall Narthway and Margaret Louise (Carpenter) T.; m. Antoinette Barksdale, Sept. 5, 1953; children: Antoinette, Terry Bryant, Mary Marshall. Student, Amherst Coll., 1949-50, Kenyon Coll., 1950-51; B.A., So. Meth. U., 1953, M.A., 1954. Teaching fellow English So. Meth. U., Dallas, 1954; dir. pub. relations, lectr. English So. Meth. U., 1957-64, instr. English, 1956, 65-67, asst. dir., 1968, assoc. prof., 1969-71, prof. English, 1972—, chmn. dept., 1971-75, 79-82, dir. creative writing program; book critic Dallas News, 1970-75; pres. faculty senate So. Meth. U., 1993-94, assoc. provost, 1994—. Author: Old Liberty, 1961, Tom Northway, 1968, Dallas Stories, 1986, Ringer, 1987, My Father's Hands, 1993, Land of Hope and Glory, 1996; contbr. short stories to various jours. and mags.; editor Prize Stories, 1986. Past trustee Incarnate Word Coll., San Antonio; sec. bd. trustees Fort Burgwin Research Ctr., Ranchos de Taos, N.Mex. Recipient Jesse H. Jones fiction award Tex. Inst. Letters, 1968, Best Short Story award S.W. Rev., 1973, S.W. Writer of Yr. award, 1988, Willis M. Tate award So. Meth. U., 1990, 94, Lon Tinkle award for continuing excellence in Letters, Tex. Inst. Letters, 1991. Mem. AAUP (chpt. pres. 1971), Coll. Conf. Tchrs. English, South Central MLA, Tex. Inst. Letters (pres. 1977-79, councilor 1980—). Democrat. Methodist. Home: 2717 Lovers Ln Dallas TX 75225-7905 Office: So Meth Univ Dept English Dallas TX 75275

TERRY, MEGAN, playwright, performer, photographer; b. Seattle, July 22, 1932; d. Harold Joseph and Marguerite Cecelia (Henry) Duffy. Student, Banff Sch. Fine Arts, summers, 1950-52, 56, U. Alta., Edmondton, Can., 1952-53; B.Ed., U. Wash., 1956. Founding mem. Open Theater, N.Y.C., 1963; ABC fellow Yale U., 1966-67; founding mem., v.p. N.Y. Theatre Strategy, 1971; adj. prof. theatre U. Nebr., Omaha, until 1977; Hill prof. fine arts U. Minn.-Duluth, spring 1983; Bingham prof. humanities U. Louisville,

1981; vis. artist Emory Univ., 1996, Bucknell Univ., 1996, Tex. Tech., 1996; mem. theatre panel, mem. overview panel Nat. Endowment Arts, 1976-86, mem. opera/music theatre panel, 1985, mem. advancement panel, 1987; mem. theatre panel Rockerfeller Found., 1977-85; mem. performing arts panel Nebr. State Council for Arts, 1977; mem. Nebr. Com. for Humanities, 1983-86; mem. Gov.'s Com. on Film and Telecommunications, 1985-86; founding mem. N.Y. Open Theatre, 1963-73; judge playwrights competition Mass., Wis., Ohio, Oreg., L.A., So. Playwrights Competition; Nat. Endowment Arts vis. artist in residence U. Iowa, 1992. Dir. Cornish Players, Cornish Sch. Allied Arts, Seattle, 1954-56, founding dir. playwrights workshop, Open Theatre, N.Y.C., 1963-68, playwright-in-residence, literary mgr. Omaha Magic Theatre, 1974—; author plays including: Kegger, Comings and Goings, The Magic Realists, Sanibel & Captiva, The People vs. Ranchman, Kepp Tightly Closed in a Cool Dry Place, The Gloaming Oh My Darling, Approaching Simone, Viet Rock, Massachussetts Trust, The Tommy Allen Show, Calm Down Mother, Sleazing Toward Athens, Babes in the Big House, Ex Miss Copper Queen, Mollie Bailey's Traveling Family Circus, Goona-Goona, Retro, Hothouse, Dinner's in the Blender, Objective Love, Katmandu, Fifteen Million Fifteen Year Olds, Fireworks, The Trees Blew Down, Choose a Spot on the Floor, Future Soap, Brazil Fado, Pro Game., Amtrak, Headlights, Breakfast Serial, Do You See What I'm Saying?, The Snow Queen, India Plays, I Forgot How Much I Like You; editor, writer: plays including Sea of Forms, Nightwalk, 1001 Horror Stories of The Plains, Running Gag, Couplings and Groupings, Walking Through Walls, Babes Unchained, Cancel That Last Thought; or See The 270 Foot Woman in Spandex, X-Raydiate: E-Motion in Action, Body Leaks, Sound Fields, Belches on Couches, Star Path Moonstop; photographer/editor: Right Brain Vacation Photos: Production Photographs of Omaha Magic Theatre Productions, 1972-92; mem. performance ensemble Omaha Magic Theatre nat. and internat. performance tours Body Leaks, 1991, Body Leaks, 1992, Sound Fields, 1993, 94, Belches on Couches, 1993, 94; contbr. articles in field to profl. jours. Mem. Nebr. Artist-in-the Schs., 1987—. Recipient Stanley Drama award, 1965, Office of Advanced Drama Rsch. award, 1965, Obie award, 1970, Disting. Contbrn. To and Svc. in Am. Theatre Silver medal Amoco Oil Co., 1977; Dramatists Guild Com. of Women Ann. award, 1983, Nebr. Artist of Yr. 1992; Gov. award Nebr., 1992; Rockefeller grantee, 1968, 87; NEA Lit. fellow, 1973; Guggenheim fellow, 1978; NEA playwriting fellow, 1989, Lifetime Am. Theatre fellow, 1994. Mem. NEA (reporter and panelist for theatre program, 1975-85), Women's Theatre Coun. (founding 1971), Women's Forum (charter), Am. Theatre Assn. (co-chmn. playwriting program 1977, chmn. playwrights project com. 1978-79, C. Crawford playwriting judge of 1987), Theatre Comm. Group (bd. dirs. 1988-92), New Dramatists (alumni, judge nat. playwriting competition 1987-88), ASSISTEJ-USA (bd. dirs. 1986-91). Home: 2309 Hanscom Blvd Omaha NE 68105-3143 Agent's Office: E Marton Agy Rm 612 One Union Sq New York NY 10003-3303

TERRY, PETER ANTHONY, lawyer; b. Sterling, Colo., Nov. 3, 1952; s. Fred Ward and Marian (Conroy) T. BA, U. Ariz., 1975, JD, 1978. Bar: Ariz. 1978, U.S. Dist. Ct. Ariz. 1978, Calif. 1979. Assoc. B. Wells O'Brien, Scottsdale, Ariz., 1978-79; ptnr. Fannin, Terry, & Lemberg, P.A.(formerly Fannin, Terry, Hay & Lemberg, PA, Phoenix, Ariz., 1979-88, Quarles & Brady, Phoenix, 1988—. Mem. Fed. Bar Assn., Ariz. Bar Assn., Calif. Bar Assn. Office: Quarles & Brady 1 E Camelback Rd Ste 400 Phoenix AZ 85012-1668

TERRY, REESE, engineering executive. Pres. Engring. Co., Webster, Tex. Office: 17448 Highway 3 Webster TX 77598-4135

TERRY, RICHARD ALLAN, consulting psychologist, former college president; b. Lincoln, Nebr., June 4, 1920; s. Lester C. and Dorothy (Weeden) T.; m. Z. Inci Incikaya, June 3, 1959; 1 child, Deniz. A.B., U. Notre Dame, 1944; M.S., Catholic U. Am., 1950, Ph.D., 1954. Instr., asst. prof., chmn. psychol. dept. U. Portland, Oreg., 1953-59; prin. scientist, chief advanced research, life scis. North Am. Aviation, Downey, Calif., 1959-63; assoc. prof. indsl. engring., dir. systems research center U. Okla., Norman, 1963-69; prof., head dept. psychology U. Tulsa, 1970-73; prof. psychology SUNY Coll. at Oswego, 1973-75, dean grad. studies and research, 1973-75, acting v.p. acad. affairs, 1973-74; v.p. for instrn. and curriculum SUNY Coll. at Brockport, 1975-78; pres. Quinnipiac Coll., Hamden, Conn., 1978-86; sr. ptnr. Richard Allan Terry Assocs., Cons., Hamden, 1986-91; vis. prof. Hacettepe U., Ankara, Turkey, 1969-70; v.p. Found. for Study of Behavioral Scis., Downey, 1965-68; assoc. fellow Timothy Dwight Coll., Yale U., 1982—; v.p. Conn. Council Higher Edn., 1983-84, pres., 1984-85. Trustee Chamber Orch. of New Eng., 1979-82, chmn. bd., 1982-83; vice chmn. Mgmt. Study Group, Town of Hamden, 1982-83; bd. dirs. Urban League Greater New Haven, 1983-90, sec. 1988-90; chmn. oversight com. Study of Police-Media Rels., 1983-84; mem. steering com. New Haven Initiative for Excellence in Edn., 1986-90, steering com. Town of Hamden Plan for the Future, 1988-91, adv. bd. Conn. Small Bus. Devel. Ctr., 1989-91; mem. Town of Hamden Planning and Zoning Commn., 1991-93. Mem. Am. Psychol. Assn., Conn. Conf. Ind. Colls. (sec.-treas. 1983-86), Greater New Haven C. of C. (bd. dirs. 1982-86, chmn. jobs compact planning com., 1984-85, steering com. 1985-86) Sigma Xi. Democrat. Roman Catholic. Home: 24 Talon Dr Schenectady NY 12309-1839

TERRY, ROBERT DAVIS, neuropathologist, educator; b. Hartford, Conn., Jan. 13, 1924; m. Patricia Ann Blech, June 27, 1952; 1 son, Nicolas Saul. AB, Williams Coll., 1946, DSc (hon.), 1991; MD, Albany (N.Y.) Med. Coll., 1950. Diplomate: Am. Bd. Pathology, Am. Bd. Neuropathology. Postdoctoral tng. St. Francis Hosp., Hartford, 1950, Bellevue Hosp., N.Y.C., 1951, Montefiore Hosp., N.Y.C., 1952-53, 54-55, Inst. Recherches sur le Cancer, Paris, France, 1953-54; sr. postdoctoral fellow Inst. Recherches sur le Cancer, 1965-66; asst. pathologist Montefiore Hosp., 1955-59; assoc. prof. dept. pathology Einstein Coll. Medicine, Bronx, N.Y., 1959-64; prof. Einstein Coll. Medicine, 1964-84, acting chmn. dept. pathology, 1969-70, chmn., 1970-84; prof. depts. neuroscis. and pathology U. Calif.-San Diego, 1984-94, prof. emeritus, 1994—; mem. study sect. pathology NIH, 1964-68; study sects. Nat. Multiple Sclerosis Soc., 1964-72, 74-78; mem. bd. sci. counselors Nat. Inst. Neurol. and Communicative Disorders and Stroke, NIH, 1976-80, chmn., 1977-80; mem. nat. sci. coun. Huntington's Disease Assn., 1978-81; mem. med. and sci. adv. bd. Alzheimer Assn., 1978-88; mem. sci. adv. bd. Max Planck Inst., Martinsried, 1990-96. Mem. editorial adv. bd. Jour. Neuropathology and Exptl. Neurology, 1963-83, 85-88, Lab. Investigation, 1967-77, Revue Neurologique, 1977-87, Annals of Neurology, 1978-82, Ultrastructural Pathology, 1978-86, Am. Jour. Pathology, 1985-89. Served with AUS, 1943-46, ETO. Recipient Potamkin prize for Alzheimer Rsch., 1988, Met. Life Found. award, 1991. Fellow AAAS, Am. Acad. Arts and Sci.; mem. Am. Assn. Neuropathologists (pres. 1969-70, Meritorious Contbn. award 1989), N.Y. Path. Soc. (v.p. 1969-70, pres. 1971-73), Am. Assn. Pathologists, Am. Neurol. Assn., Am. Acad. Neurologists. Achievements include research and publications on Alzheimer's disease and Tay Sachs disease. Office: U Calif San Diego Dept Neurosci La Jolla CA 92093

TERRY, ROBERT MEREDITH, foreign language educator; b. Danville, Va., Dec. 16, 1939; s. Willard Terry and Martha Willeford; m. Anne Reynolds Beggarly, Jan. 30, 1965; children: Michael Reynolds, Christopher Robert, Meredith Anne. BA in French, Randolph-Macon Coll., Ashland, Va., 1962; PhD in Romance Langs., Duke U., Durham, N.C., 1966. Asst. prof. French U. Fla., Gainesville, Fla., 1966-68; assoc. prof. U. Richmond, Richmond, Va., 1968-83, prof., 1983—; pres. Am. Coun. on Tchg. Fgn. Langs., 1994. Co-author: Accent: Conversational French I, 1980, Vous Y Etes!, 1990, Intersections, 1991; editor Dimension, So. Conf. on Lang. Tchg., 1991-97; assoc. editor ACTFL Foreign Language Education Series, 1994, 96; contbr. articles to profl. jours. Recipient Stephen A. Freeman award N.E. Conf. on Teaching Fgn. Lang., 1990, Robert J. Ludwig Nat. Fgn. Lang. Leadership award, 1995. Mem. Am. Coun. on Tchg. Fgn. Langs., Fgn. Lang. Assn. Va., Am. Assn. Tchrs. French, So. Conf. on Lang. Tchg., Pacific N.W. Coun. for Langs., Wis. Assn. Fgn. Lang. Tchrs. Home: 1504 Cloister Dr Richmond VA 23233 Office: Univ Richmond PO Box 25 28 Westhampton Way University Of Richmond VA 23173

TERRY, ROGER, pathologist, consultant; b. Waterville, N.Y., May 8, 1917; s. Orrin and Mary Isabelle (Kennedy) T.; m. Eleanor Virginia, Dec. 13, 1942; children: Robin, Orrin. AB magna cum laude, Colgate U., 1939; MD, U. Rochester, 1944. Cert. anatomic pathologist. Intern then resident Strong Meml. Hosp., Rochester, N.Y., 1944-51; asst. prof. U. Rochester Sch. Medicine, 1951-56, assoc. prof., 1956-61, prof. pathology, 1961-69; prof. pathology U. So. Calif. Sch. Medicine, Los Angeles, 1969-82; pathologist San Gabriel (Calif.) Valley Med. Ctr., 1982—; exec. dir. Calif. Tumor Tissue Registry, Los Angeles, 1969-84. Contbr. articles to profl. jours. Served to capt. USAF, 1954-56. Fellow Am. Soc. Clin. Pathologists, Coll. Am. Pathologists; mem. AMA, Internat. Acad. Pathology (councilor 1973-76), Am. Assn. Pathologists, L.A. Soc. Pathologists, Am. Soc. Cytology, Phi Beta Kappa, Sigma Xi, Alpha Omega Alpha. Republican. Episcopalian. Avocations: ballroom dancing, snorkeling, tandem bike riding. Home: 2841 Shakespeare Dr San Marino CA 91108-2230 Office: San Gabriel Valley Med Ctr 218 S Santa Anita Ave San Gabriel CA 91776-1154

TERRY, RONALD ANDERSON, bank holding company executive; b. Memphis, Dec. 5, 1930; s. John Burnett and Vernon (Lucas) T.; m. Wynoka W. Evans, May 21, 1989; children by previous marriage: Natalie Carol, Cynthia Leigh. B.S., Memphis State U., 1952; postgrad., So. Meth. U., 1961, Harvard U., 1970. Mgmt. trainee First Tenn. Bank, Memphis, 1957; pres. First Tenn. Nat. Corp., Memphis, 1971, chmn., 1973—; chmn. First Tenn. Bank N.A., Memphis, 1979-95, also bd. dirs.; bd. dirs. BellSouth Corp., AutoZone Inc., Delta Life Corp., Promus Hotel Corp., St. Jude Hosp., Blue Eagle Gold Ctrs., Inc., Home Account Network, Inc. Past pres. Boys Clubs Memphis, Future Memphis, Memphis Job Conf.; chmn. adv. com. Bapt. Meml. Hosp.; past Tenn. state chmn. Com. for Econ. Devel.; mem. adv. bd. Memphis Arts Coun. Lt. USN, 1953-57. Mem. Am. Bankers Assn. (treasury adv. com., bd. dirs., past chmn. govt. relations council), Assn. Res. City Bankers (dir., past chmn. govt. relations com. and pub. affairs com.), Assn. Bank Holding Cos. (legis. policy com., past pres. fed. adv. council), Econ. Club of Memphis (past pres.). Office: 6410 Poplar Ave Ste 375 Memphis TN 38119-4839

TERRY, STUART L(EE), research manager; b. Chgo., Apr. 8, 1942; s. Gordon M. and Fredrica (Gordon) T.; m. Linda Jane Littenberg, Aug. 25, 1963 (div. 1974); m. Mary Ann Stames, Feb. 16, 1980; children: Robin D. Andrews, Mark R. Andrews, Marc L. Terry, Robin M. Terry. BSChemE, Cornell U., 1965, PhD, 1968; MS in Mgmt., Rennselear U., 1972. From sr. rsch. engr. to mgr. tech. acquisitions Monsanto Corp., Springfield, Mass., 1968-88; dir. tech. Sonoco Products Co., Hartsville, S.C., 1988—. Mem. Tech. Assn. of Pulp and Paper Industry, Soc. Plastics Engrs., Futures Soc. Office: Sonoco Products Co 1 N 2nd St Hartsville SC 29550-3300

TERRY, WAYNE GILBERT, healthcare executive, hospital administrator; b. Plymouth, Mass., Oct. 2, 1932; s. Lawrence Arthur Terry and Betty Frances (Boutemain) McClellan; m. Barbara Bromwell, Sept. 20, 1980; children: Karleton Wayne, Dale Duane, Kendrick Shane, Kristen Alayne, Tammye Van Clief, Wade Bromwell Delk. AA, Allan Hancock Coll., Santa Maria, Calif., 1960; BBA, U. Hawaii, 1966; M. Hosp. Adminstrn., Med. Coll. Va., 1973. Commd. 2d lt. USAF Med. Svc. Corps, 1967, advanced through grades to maj., 1986; asst. adminstr. for registrar activities USAF Hosp., Orlando AFB, Fla., 1966-67; assoc. adminstr. aeromed. evacuation activities USAF, Hickam AFB, Hawaii, 1967-71; adminstrv. resident USAF Regional Hosp., Langley AFB, Va., 1972-73; CEO USAF Hosp., Columbus AFB, Miss., 1973-75; nat. health edn. and tng. program advisor Office of Surgeon Gen., Dept. of Air Force, Washington, 1975-78; dir. health professions pers. planning and policy divsn. Office of Asst. Sec. Def. for Health Affairs, The Pentagon, Washington, 1978-80; dep. project mgr./adminstrv. dir. King Faisal U. Teaching Hosp., Al-Khobar, Saudi Arabia, 1980-82; dep. project mgr., hosp. dir. North Yemen Healthcare Project, As-Salem Hosp., Sadah, Yemen Arab Republic, 1982-83; hosp. dir., CEO western area Armed Forces Hosps., Khamis Mushayt, Saudi Arabia, 1983-84; chief adminstr./commissioning team chief Orbit Summit Health, Ltd., Riyadh, Saudi Arabia, 1984-85; hosp. dir., adminstrv. dir. Truk State Dept. Health Svcs., Moen, Federated States of Micronesia, 1985-87; assoc. adminstr. support svcs. King Fahad Hosp., Saudi Arabian N.G., Riyadh, 1987-90; project mgr., CEO N.W. Armed Forces Hosps. Program, Tabuk, Saudi Arabia, 1990—; apptd. cons. in healthcare planning Air Force Surgeon Gen., 1979; apptd. preceptor program in healthcare adminstrn. for adminstrv. residents at N.W. Armed Forces Hosps. Programs, Tabuk, Saudi Arabia, 1993; lectr. in field; cons. in field; mem. supervisory bd. Royal Coll. Surgeons in Ireland/Witikar Saudi Arabia Ltd., 1990-97; active various symposium organizing coms. Author books and monographs in field; contbr. articles to profl. jours. Warden to Am. Cmty. N.W. Region of Yemen Arab Republic to Am. Embassy in Sanaa, 1982-83, warden to Am. Cmty. N.W. Region of Saudi Arabia to Am. Embassy in Riyadh, 1990-97; mem. Internat. Sch. Sys. Coord. Com., Tabuk, 1990-97; bd. dirs. Taif Sch. Dist. Sys., Saudi Arabia, 1981-82. Decorated Air medal with 2 oak leaf clusters, Air Force Commendation medal with 2 oak leaf clusters, Republic of Vietnam Gallantry Cross with palm; recipient Citation of Appreciation Nat. Coun. Social Welfare, Seoul, Republic of Korea, 1963, Suchan Province Govt., Choong Nam, Republic of Korea, 1963, Outstanding Rsch. award Med. Coll. Va., 1973, Men of Achievement award, Cambridge, Eng., 1982, Citation of Appreciation Gov. Truk State, Federated States of Micronesia, 1987, Citation of Merit Internat. Red Cross Commn., 1991, N.W. Armed Forces Hosps., Ministry of Def. and Aviation, Tabuk, 1991, Citation of Appreciation Presidency of Gen. Staff Hdqs., 1992, 93, 95, 96, Personality of the South award, 1975. Fellow Am. Coll. Healthcare Execs., Royal Soc. Health; mem. Am. Hosp. Assn., Am. Mgmt. Assn., Air Force Med. Svc. Corps Assn., Air Force Assn., Assn. Mil. Surgeons of U.S. Republican. Baptist. Avocations: tennis, numismatics, travel. Office: NW Armed Forces Hosp Program Unit 62007 APO AE 09810-2007

TERTZAKIAN, HOVHANNES, bishop; b. Aleppo, Syria, Jan. 3, 1924. Philosophy & Theology, Pontifical Gregorian U., Rome, Italy, 1949. ordained priest Sept. 8, 1948. Teacher, then Dean Mekhitarist Sch., Alexandria, Egypt, 1949-56; dean of studies & admin. Mekhitarist Sch., Aleppo, Syria, 1956-60; headmaster Mekhitarist Sch., Aleppo, 1960-70; rector Moorat-Raphael Coll., Venice, Italy, 1970-79, Samuel-Moorat Coll., Sevres, France, 1980-82, St. Ann's Armenian Catholic Cathedral, New York, N.Y., 1986-89; Pro Exarch, 1989-90, Exarchate Chancellor, 1990-95; Apostolic Exarch for Armenian Catholics U.S. and Can., 1995—; mem. Mekhitarist Order of Venice (superior 1960-70, gen. council mem. 1970-76, gen. admin. 1976-79, provincial supr. 1979-80, Abbot Gen. 1982-84). Office: Chancery Office 110 E 12th St New York NY 10003-5375

TERWILLEGAR, JANE CUSACK, librarian, educator; b. Warsaw, N.Y., Nov. 7, 1935; d. James Scott and Estella B. (Ackerman) Cusack; m. Gordon H. Terwillegar, July 26, 1958 (div. Mar. 1989); children: Sarah Ann Terwillegar Smedley, Arne Matthew. BA, Elmira (N.Y.) Coll., 1957; MLS, SUNY, Geneseo, 1960; EdS, U. Ga., 1977. Cert. tchr., Fla. Instr. U. Ga., Athens, 1975-81; libr. Palm Beach County Libr., West Palm Beach, Fla., 1981-83, Palm Beach County Schs., Royal Palm Beach, Fla., 1983-94; dist. libr. media svcs. specialist Palm Beach County Schs., West Palm Beach, 1994—; lectr. Sch. Libr. and Info. Sci., U. South Fla., Tampa, 1987—, Nova U., Ft. Lauderdale, Fla., 1995—; task force mem. SUNLINK project Fla. Dept. Edn., 1995—. Co-author: Commonsense Cataloging, 3d edit. 1983, 4th edit. 1990; reviewer Sch. Libr. Jour., 1986—; contbr. articles to profl. jours. Pres. Staff Assn. Palm Beach Sch. Dist., 1997—. Mem. ALA, AAUW, Am. Assn. Sch. Librs. (exec. bd. 1990-94), Assn. for Libr. Svc. to Children (Newbery com. 1988-89), Fla. Assn. Meda in Edn. (sec. 1988-89, bd. dirs. 1997—), Ednl. Media Assn. Fla. (pres. 1988), Delta Kappa Gamma, Phi Beta Kappa, Delta Kappa Phi, Phi Delta Kappa. Avocations: scuba diving, sports cars. Home: 911 Oak Harbour Dr Juno Beach FL 33408 Office: School Dist of Palm Beach County 1400 N Florida Mango Rd West Palm Beach FL 33409-5240

TERWILLIGER, GEORGE JAMES, III, lawyer; b. New Brunswick, N.J., June 5, 1950; s. George James Jr. and Ruth Nancy (Mellilo) T.; m. Carol Anne Hitchings, Dec. 18, 1976; children: Sarah Katherine, George Zachary Grant, Virginia. BA in Communications, Seton Hall U., 1973; JD, Antioch Law Sch., 1978. Bar: D.C. 1978, U.S. Dist. Ct. D.C., 1979, U.S. Ct. Appeals (D.C. cir.) 1979, U.S. Dist. Ct. (so. dist.) Fla. 1980, U.S. Dist. Ct. Vt. 1981, U.S. Ct. Appeals (2d cir.) 1982, Vt. 1983, U.S. Supreme Ct. 1992, U.S. Ct. Appeals (4th cir.) 1993. Asst. U.S. atty. Office of U.S. Atty., Washington, 1978-81; asst. U.S. atty. Dist. of Vt., Burlington, 1981-86, U.S. atty., 1986-91; dep. atty. gen. Washington, 1992-93; ptnr.-in-charge McGuire, Woods, Battle & Boothe, Washington, 1993—. Mem. ABA, Vt. Bar Assn., D.C. Bar Assn., Rep. Nat. Lawyers Assn. (pres. 1994-95). Republican. Congregationalist. Avocations: skiing, tennis, fishing. Office: McGuire, Woods, Battle & Boothe Army and Navy Club Building 1627 I St NW Washington DC 20006-4007

TERWILLIGER, JULIA ANNE, art educator, artist; b. Orange, N.J., May 17, 1947; d. Walter William and Rosina Marie (Pepe) Klem; m. Bert Alan Terwilliger, Jan. 1981 (div. Apr. 1989); children: Stacie Lea, David James, Christie Lea. BA cum laude, U. South Fla., 1987, MFA, 1990. Asst. to curator Aljira Gallery, Newark, 1991-92; with Met. Mus. Art Bookstore, N.Y.C., 1991-92; studio asst. Elyn Zimmerman, sculptor, N.Y.C., 1991-92; prof. art Hillsborough C.C., Tampa, 1992-93; sabbatical replacement U. Ctrl. Fla., Orlando, 1992-93, adj. prof. art 1993—; exbhn. com. Fla. Ctr. Contemporary Art, Tampa, 1992; presenter in field. One-person shows include Theater Gallery-U. South Fla., The Centre Gallery, UCF, 1997; exhibited in group shows Einstein-Forum, Potsdam, Germany, 1996, Dunedin (Fla.) Fine Art Ctr., 1995, Ruth Eckard Hall, Clearwater, Fla., 1995, The Prince Street Gallery, N.Y.C., 1992, Snug Harbor Cultural Ctr., S.I., 1992, Tampa Mus., 1997; also exhibited in numerous pvt. collections. Artist AIDS Outreach Program, Tampa, 1991-94; vol. Aljira Gallery, Newark, 1990-91. Project grantee New Forms Fla., 1994-95; emerging artist grantee County Arts Coun., Hillsborough, 1990-91; finalist Divsn. Cultural Affairs, Fla., 1992. Mem. Coll. Art Assn. Am., Women's Caucus for Art. Home: 16413 Lake Ln Lutz FL 33549 Office: U Ctrl Fla Coll Arts & Scis Orlando FL 32816-1342

TERZIAN, GRACE PAINE, publisher; b. Boston, Oct. 19, 1952; d. Thomas Fite and Grace Hillman (Benedict) Paine; m. Philip Henry Terzian, Oct. 20, 1979; children: William Thomas Hillman, Grace Benedict Paine. BA in Art History, Williams Coll., 1974. Art dir. The New Republic, Washington, 1976-78; asst. editor The Chronicle of Higher Edn., Washington, 1978-79; rsch. editor Archtl. Digest, L.A., 1982-85; pub. The Women's Quar., Arlington, Va., 1994—; editor Ex Femina, 1996—. Mem. Soc. Colonial Dames in Am., Phi Beta Kappa. Episcopalian. Home: 10505 Adel Rd Oakton VA 22124 Office: The Women's Quarterly 2111 Wilson Blvd Ste 550 Arlington VA 22201-3001

TERZIAN, PHILIP HENRY, journalist; b. Kensington, Md., July 5, 1950; s. L.A. and Louise (Anderson) T.; m. Grace Barrett Paine, Oct. 20, 1979; children: William Thomas Hillman, Grace Benedict Paine. BA, Villanova U., 1973; DTS, Episcopal Theol. Sem., Va., 1995; postgrad., Oxford (Eng.) U., 1976. Desk editor Reuters, Washington, 1973, U.S. News & World Report, Washington, 1973-74; asst. editor The New Republic, Washington, 1974-78; mem. policy planning staff Dept. State, Washington, 1978-79; asst. editor Anniston (Ala.) Star, 1979-80; assoc. editor Lexington (Ky.) Herald, 1980-82; asst. editor of editorial pages L.A. Times, 1982-86; editor of editorial pages Providence Jour., 1986-92; assoc. editor, syndicated columnist Providence Jour. (Knight-Ridder/Tribune News Svc.), 1992—; panelist Washington Week in Review, C-SPAN, etc.; mem. bd. of advisors, Inst. of Am. Values, Nichols Coll. Contbr. articles to newspapers and jours. Pres. Providence Com. Fgn. Rels., 1989-92. Recipient Edn. Writers award Edn. Writers Assn., 1981, Ida Lee Willis Svc. to Preservation award Ida Lee Willis Found., 1982; named finalist Pulitzer prize Disting. Commentary, 1991, Pulitzer Prize juror, 1994-95. Mem. Am. Coun. on Germany, Va. Hist. Soc., St. Andrew's Soc. Washington Theodore Roosevelt Assn., Soc. King Charles the Martyr, Sons of Union Vets. of Civil War, Wolver Beagles, Nat. Press Club, Hope Club, Nat. Beagle Club. Republican. Episcopalian. Avocations: reading, book collecting, riding, music. Home: 10505 Adel Rd Oakton VA 22124-1605 Office: Providence Jour 1325 G St NW Ste 250 Washington DC 20005-3104

TERZIAN, YERVANT, astronomy and astrophysics educator; b. Alexandria, Egypt, Feb. 9, 1939; came to U.S., 1960, naturalized, 1971; s. Bedros and Maria (Kiriakaki) T.; m. Araxy M. Hovsepian, Apr. 16, 1966; children: Sevan, Tamar. BS, Am. U., Cairo, 1960; MS, Ind. U., 1963, PhD, 1965, DSc (hon.), 1989; DSc (hon.) Yerevan State U., 1994, Aristotle U. of Thessaloniki, Greece, 1997. Rsch. assoc. Arecibo Obs., P.R., 1965-67; asst. prof. astronomy and astrophysics Cornell U., Ithaca, N.Y., 1967-72, assoc. prof., 1972-77, prof., 1977—, chmn. dept. astronomy, 1979—, dir. Program in Sci. Edn., 1988—, James A. Weeks prof. in phys. scis., 1990. Editor: Interstellar Ionized Hydrogen, 1968; Planetary Nebulae, 1978; co-editor: Cosmology and Astrophysics, 1982; assoc. editor The Astrophysical Jour., 1989—; contbr. over 190 articles to tech. jours. Recipient Clark Disting. Teaching award Cornell U., 1984. Mem. Internat. Astron. Union, Soc. Sci. Exploration, Internat. Sci. Radio Union, Am. Astron. Soc., Armenian Acad. Sci. (fgn. mem.). Home: 109 Brandywine Dr Ithaca NY 14850-1747 Office: Cornell U Astronomy Dept Space Scis Bldg Ithaca NY 14853

TESAR, DELBERT, machine systems and robotics educator, researcher, manufacturing consultant; b. Beaver Crossing, Nebr., Sept. 2, 1935; s. Louis and Clara (Capek) T.; m. Rogene Kresak, Feb. 1, 1957; children: Vim Lee, Aleta Anne, Landon Grady, Allison Jeanne. B.Sc. in Mech. Engring., U. Nebr., 1958, M.Sc., 1959; Ph.D., Ga. Tech. U., 1964. Assoc. prof. U. Fla., Gainesville, 1965-71, prof., 1972-83, grad. research prof., 1983-84, dir., founder Ctr. Intelligent Machines and Robotics, 1978-84; Curran chair in engring. U. Tex., Austin, 1985—; lectr. in field; mem. rev. panel Nat. Bur. Stds., Gaithersburg, Md., 1982-88; mem. sci. adv. bd. to Air Force, 1982-86; mem. standing com. NRC for Space Sta. (ISSA), 1992-95; interactor with Russian Acad. Sci. on sci. and tech. Author: (with others) Cam System Design, 1975. Patentee in field; contbr. articles to profl. jours.; assoc. editor 3 computer and mfg. jours. Expert witness house sci. and tech. com. U.S. Ho. of Reps., 1978-84. Fellow AAAS; mem. Fla. Engring. Soc. (Outstanding Tech. Achievement award 1982), ASME (machine design award 1987). Avocations: antiques, art, travel. Home: 8005 Two Cove Dr Austin TX 78730-3125 Office: U Tex Dept Mechanical Engineering Austin TX 78712-1063*

TESAR, MILO BENJAMIN, agricultural researcher, educator, and administrator; b. Tobias, Nebr., Apr. 7, 1920; s. Frank and Frances (Cihal) T.; m. Marian Olive Hunt, Sept. 3, 1944; children: Robert, Ann, Joyce, Janet. BSc with distinction, U. Nebr., 1941; MS, U. Wis., 1947, PhD, 1949; ScD (hon.), U. Nebr., 1989. Asst. prof. crop-soil sci. Mich. State U., East Lansing, 1949-53, assoc. prof., 1953-58, prof., 1958-88, prof. emeritus, 1988—, chmn. dept. crop and soil sci., 1964-67; agrl. advisor China (Inner Mongolia), Australia, New Zealand, Scotland, USSR, Okinawa, Japan, Eng., Brazil, Somalia, Egypt, Finland, Uzbekistan, Nepal, Bangladesh, Philippines, Sweden, Ireland. Author: Forage Management, 1982, 2d edit., 1984, 3d edit., 1986; editor: Physiological Basis of Crop Growth and Development, 1988; author: (with others), assoc. editor: Alfalfa Science and Technology, 1972, Alfalfa and Alfalfa Improvement, 1988; contbr. articles to profl. jours.; patentee alfalfa cultivar "Webfoot." Chmn. bd. elders People's Ch., East Lansing, 1966; mem. East Lansing Sch. Bd., 1966-70. Maj. U.S. Army, 1942-46, PTO, Hiroshima, Japan. Decorated Silver Star, Bronze Star; named NATO fellow NSF, Hurley, Eng., 1959-60; recipient King Charles Educator award Nebr Czechs, 1987, Disting. Rsch. award Mich. State U. Coll. Agr., 1985, hon. extension svc. award, 1984, Alumni Achievement award U. Nebr., 1991. Fellow AAAS, Am. Soc. Agronomy (cert. agronomist, crop scientist, Agronomic Achievement award 1984), Crop Sci. Soc. Am. (DeKalb-Prizer Disting. Crop Sci. Career award 1988); mem. Mich. State U. Pres.'s Club, Farm House Fraternity, Sigma Xi, Gamma Sigma Delta. Republican. Home: 2379 Emerald Forest Cir East Lansing MI 48823-7214 Office: Mich State U Dept Crop Soil Sci East Lansing MI 48824

TESAREK, WILLIAM PAUL, business consultant, writer, financial executive; b. Albuquerque, May 6, 1958; s. Dennis George and Caroline Arrena (Myers) T.; m. Nancy Anne Pence, May 12, 1984 (div. Feb. 1991); children: Michelle Marie, Allison Elaine. BS in Econs., U. Houston, 1986, MA in Econs., 1988, MBA in Fin., 1993, PhD, 1994. Instr. econs. U. Houston, 1987-88; sr. sales tax analyst Tex. State Comptroller, Austin, 1988-89; adj. prof. fin. U. Houston, 1989-93; sr. economist Asset Analysis & Mgmt., Houston, 1993; sr. fin. economist Asset Dynamics, Houston, 1993-94; owner The Tesarek Group, Houston, 1994—; cons. in strategic planning and process reengring. mgmt. Author: Housing Price and Regional Real Estate Cycles: Market Adjustments in Houston, 1991; Beyond Counting the Beans: How Chief Financial Executives Use Knowledge to Advance the Corporation, 1995. With USN, 1976-80. Econ. Honors. Soc. Achievement award, 1986. Mem. Am. Econs. Assn., Am. Fin. Assn., Western Econ. Assn., Tex.

Econ. & Demographic Assn., Allied Soc. Sci. Assn., Houston Bus. Process Reengring. Share Group. Republican. Mem. Ch. of Christ. Avocations: wood working, photography. Home and Office: The Tesarek Grp 16011 Silver Valley Dr Houston TX 77084-2960

TESCHNER, DOUGLASS PAUL, state legislator; b. Cambridge, Mass., Oct. 29, 1949; s. Douglass P. Teschner and Mary Elizabeth (Bernt) Teschner Zeller; m. Martha Weaver, Sept. 26, 1981. BS in Forestry, U. Mass., 1971, EdD in Adminstrn., 1985; MS in Botany, U. Vt., 1978. Land surveyor Lincoln Engring. and Burnell Land Surveying, 1974, 78; tchr. White Mountain Sch., 1976; dir. Inst. Exptl. Studies, various locations, 1984-87; fin. officer Becket Acad., East Haddam, Conn., 1984-85; devel. dir. Riverbend Cmty. Mental Health, Concord, 1987—; state rep. N.H. Ho. Reps., Concord, 1988—. Co-editor: Wilderness Challenge: Outdoor Education Alternatives for Youth in Need, 1984; contbr. articles to profl. jours. Mem. Haverhill Hist. Soc.; vol. Peace Corps, 1971-73; trustee Mt. Washington Obs. Mem. Congregational Ch. Avocations: mountaineering, hiking, rock and ice climbing, skiing. Home: RR 2 Box 173 Pike NH 03780-9706 Office: Riverbend Cmty Mental Hlth PO Box 2032 Concord NH 03302-2032

TESH, JOHN, television talk show host; b. Garden City, N.Y., 1953; s. John and Mildred Tesh; m. Connie Sellecca, Apr. 4, 1992; children: Gib, Prima. Co-host Entertainment Tonight, 1986—; host One-On-One with John Tesh, 1991; co-host John and Leeza from Hollywood, 1993. Television appearances include: The U.S. Open Tennis Championship, 1985, Macy's Thanksgiving Day Parade, 1987, Wimbledon, 1991; film appearances include Shocker, 1989, Soapdish, 1991; albums include Tour de France, 1988, The Early Years, 1990, Ironman, 1992, The Games, 1992, Monterey Nights, 1993, A Romantic Christmas, 1993, Wintersong, Sax by the Fire, Sax on the Beach, John Tesh Live at Red Rocks, Discovery, Avalon; composers theme music Bobby's World, 1990, The Knife and Gun Club, 1990, One on One, 1991, NFL Live. Recipient 4 Emmy awards for composing, 2 Emmy awards for reporting. Office: care GTSP Records PO Box 6010-721 Sherman Oaks CA 91413*

TESK, JOHN ALOYSIUS, materials scientist; b. Chgo., Oct. 19, 1934; s. John August and Theresa Mary (Mattea) T.; m. Regina Sophia Budzyn, Dec. 10, 1966; 1 child, John A.W. BS in Engring. Sci., Northwestern U., 1957, MS in Metallurgy, 1960, PhD in Materials Sci., 1963. Asst. prof. U. Ill., Chgo., 1964-67; cons. Argonne (Ill.) Nat. Lab., 1964-67, asst. metallurgist, 1967-70; dir. rsch. Dental, Howmedica Inc., Chgo., 1970-77; dir. edn. svcs. Inst. Gas. Tech., Chgo., 1977-78; gen. phys. scientist, group leader, biomaterials coord. polymers divsn. Nat. Inst. Stds. & Tech., Gaithersburg, Md., 1978—; cons. Dentsply Internat., York, Pa., 1977-78; mem. review bd. Dental Sch. Case Western Res. U., Cleve., 1987-88, Biomaterials Program, Clemson U., 1972-74, Dental Sch., Tokushima U., Japan; chmn. dental stds. ADA, Chgo., 1980-86; leader U.S. Del. Internat. Stds. Orgn., 1980-86; organizer confs. Holder 8 patents; editl. bd. Jour. Dental Materials, 1988-91, Jour. Oral Implantology, 1984—; contbr. chpts. to books and articles to profl. jours. Mem. bldg. com. Divine Savior Parish, Downers Grove, Ill., 1971-72; chmn. troop 737 Cub Scouts, Highland, Md., 1980; adult supr. youth group Saint Louis Parish, Highland, 1982-83. Fellow Acad. Dental Materials (exec. com. 1987-94); mem. Am. Phys. Soc., Am. Soc. Metals (exec. com. 1964-67, 78), Biomaterials Soc. (charter, contbg. editor Biomaterials Forum, co-chair stds. com., liaison com. 1996—), Internat. Assn. Dental Rsch. (treas. dental materials group 1987-94), Tech. Materials Soc. (exec. com. 1965). Roman Catholic. Avocations: gardening, boating, travel, walking. Home: 6759 Cortina Dr Highland MD 20777 Office: Nat Inst Stds & Tech Rm A143 Bldg 224 Gaithersburg MD 20899

TESLER, LAWRENCE GORDON, computer company executive; b. N.Y.C., Apr. 24, 1945; s. Isidore and Muriel (Krechmer) T.; m. Shelagh Elisabeth Leuterio, Oct 4, 1964 (div. 1970); 1 child, Lisa Traci; m. Colleen Ann Barton, Feb. 17, 1987. BS in Math., Stanford U., 1965. Pres. Info. Processing Corp., Palo Alto, Calif., 1963-68; rsch. asst. Stanford U. Artificial Intelligence Lab., 1968-73; mem. rsch. staff Xerox Corp., Palo Alto, 1973-80; sect. mgr. Lisa div. Apple Computer, Inc., Cupertino, Calif., 1980-82, cons. engr., 1983-86, v.p. advanced tech., 1986-90, v.p. advanced products, 1990-92, v.p. engring., 1992-93, chief scientist, 1993—, v.p. AppleNet divsn., 1996-97; bd. dirs. Advanced RISC Machines Ltd.; mem. Computer Sci. and Telecom. Bd., 1991-94. Contbr. articles to profl. jours., various computer software. Bd. dirs. Peninsula Sch., Menlo Park, Calif., 1974-78. Mem. Assn. Computing Machinery (conf. co-chmn. 1987-88). Office: Apple Computer Inc 1 Infinite Loop Cupertino CA 95014-2083

TESORO, GIULIANA CAVAGLIERI, chemistry research educator, consultant; b. Venice, Italy, June 1, 1921; came to U.S., 1939; d. Gino and Margherita (Maroni) Cavaglieri; m. Victor Tesoro, Apr. 17, 1943; children: Claudia, Andrew. PhD, Yale U., 1943. Rsch. chemist Am. Cyanamid Co., Boundbrook, N.J., 1943-44; asst. dir. rsch. Onyx Chem. Co., Jersey City, 1944-58, J. P. Stevens & Co., Inc., Garfield, N.J., 1958-68; dir. chem. rsch. Burlington Industries, Greenboro, N.C., 1968-72; sr. scientist, adj. prof. MIT, Cambridge, 1973-82; rsch. prof. Poly. U., Bklyn., 1982—; Mem. nat. materials adv. bd. NRC, Washington, 1979-82. Contbr. numerous articles to profl. publs.; patentee in field. Recipient Am. Dyestuff Reporter award, 1959, Achievement award Soc. Women Engrs., 1978. Fellow Textile Inst. Gt. Britain; mem. AAAS (co-chmn. polymer combustion and fire retardance conf. 1977), Am. Assn. Textile Chemists and Colorists (Olney medal 1963), Am. Chem. Soc., Am. Inst. Chemists, Info. Coun. Fabric flammability, N.Y. Acad. Sci., Textile Rsch. Inst. (editorial bd.jours.), Fiber Soc. (pres. 1974-75). Democrat. Home: 278 Clinton Ave Dobbs Ferry NY 10522-3007 Office: Poly U 333 Jay St Brooklyn NY 11201-2907

TESSER, ABRAHAM, social psychologist; b. N.Y.C., May 24, 1941; s. Louis and Ruth (Buchholz) T.; m. Marsha Richman Rosenthal, June 4, 1967 (div. Feb. 22, 1983); children: Louis J., Rachel A.; m. Carmen Chaves, Dec. 15, 1990. BA, L.I. U., 1962; MS, Purdue U., 1965, PhD, 1967. Rsch. assoc. Inst. for Behavioral Rsch., U. Ga., 1971-78, assoc. dir., 1978-84, acting dir. Ctr. for Rsch. on Deviance, 1984-86, dir., 1984-94; from asst. prof. to assoc. prof. social psychology U. Ga., 1967-74, prof., 1974-89, rsch. prof. psychology, 1989—; vis. fellow Yale U., 1976-77, Princeton U., spring 1983; fellow Ctr. for Advanced Studies in the Behavioral Scis., Stanford, Calif., 1992-93. Editor Jour. Personality and Social Cognition, 1991-94; contbr. numerous articles to profl. jours. Mem. AAUP, APA, Am. Psychol. Soc., Soc. for Personality and Social Psychology, Soc. Exptl. Social Psychology, So. Soc. for Social Psychology. Office: Univ Ga Dept Psychology Athens GA 30602

TESSING, LOUISE SCIRE, graphic designer; b. Chgo., May 13, 1946; d. Rocco Roy and Ruth Louise (Knueppel) Scire; m. Arvid Victor Tessing, Jan. 18, 1975. BS in Visual Design, Ill. Inst. Tech., Chgo., 1968; MBA in Mktg., Loyola U., Chgo., 1986. Jr. designer Field Mus. of Natural History, Chgo., 1968-69, Charles MacMurray & Assocs., Chgo., 1969-74; designer, art dir. Grant-Jacoby Inc., Chgo., 1974-76, Playboy Enterprises Inc., Chgo., 1976-78, Stevens Biondi Decicco Inc., Chgo., 1978-80; prin., owner Tessing Design Inc., Chgo., 1980—. Lobby treas. Ill. Women's Agenda, Chgo., 1990-92. Mem. Women in Design/Chgo. (founder 1977, pres. 1977-78, 91-93, Friend award 1990), Am. Ctr. for Design (bd. mem. 1971-77, pres. 1976-77), Chgo. Women in Pub., Nat. Assn. Women Bus. Owners. Home and Office: Tessing Design Inc 3822 N Seeley Ave Chicago IL 60618-3912

TESSMANN, CARY ANNETTE, controller; b. Wausau, Wis., Oct. 30, 1956; d. Orin Sidney Olson and Phyllis Olga (Radtke) O. AS, U. Wis., Waukesha, 1986; BBA in Acctg., U. Wis., Whitewater, 1989; MBA in Acctg., U. Wis., 1995. Cert. mgmt. acct., 1994; CPA 1995. Clk.-typist I, II, III Waukesha County Dept. Social Svc., 1974-83; acct. clk. I Northview Nursing Home, Waukesha, 1984; from acct. clk. II, adminstrv. asst.-fiscal mgmt. I, budget technician, sr. fin. analyst to bus. mgr. Waukesha County Health & Human Svcs. Dept., 1984-94; contr. Waukesha County Tech. Coll., Pewaukee, 1994—; mem. acctg. curriculum adv. com. Waukesha County Tech. Coll., 1993—; cons., Sussex, Wis., 1990-93. Vol. Wis. Lutheran Child & Family Svc., Milw., 1989—, Bargain Ctr.-WELS Synod, Milw., 1970-83, Milw. Women's Ctr., 1989-92; vol. tax preparer IRS, Pewaukee, 1989-93; mem. bd. Waukesha Cmty. Housing Initiatives, 1995-97. Recipient Certificate of Spl. Recognition from Christoph Meml. YWCA Women of Distinction Award Program, 1986. Mem. Inst. Mgmt. Accts. (del. Mid-Am. coun. 1992—, chair corp. & acad. devel. 1994-95, co-dir. mem. attendance 1989-90, v.p. comm. 1990-92, v.p. fin. & adminstrn. 1991-92, pres. 1992-93), Southeastern Wis. Fin. Mgrs. Assn. (planning com. 1987-94), Govt. Fin. Officers Assn. (budget reviewer 1994—, award of excellence 1996, com. on govt. budgeting and mgmt. 1996—, contbr. Govt. Fin. Rev. 1996). Avocations: sports, dancing, reading, handicrafts, exercise. Office: Waukesha County Tech Coll 800 Main St Pewaukee WI 53072-4601

TESTA, DOUGLAS, biotechnology company executive; b. Concord, Mass., May 22, 1944; s. Morris and Alice (Crawford) T.; m. Rosemary Adorno, Aug. 20, 1966; children: Jonathan Douglas, Jaymes Andrew. AA, Queensborough Community Coll., 1965; BS, CCNY, 1967, MS in Edn., 1971, PhD, 1976. Cert. tchr. N.Y. Chmn. dept. biology N.Y.C. Pub. Schs., 1967-70; lect. Hunter Coll. CCNY, 1970-76; project leader Ortho Diagnostics, Inc., Raritan, N.J., 1979-80; asst. dir. biologics Hydron Labs., Inc., New Brunswick, N.J., 1980-84; exec. dir. R & D, Interferon Scis., Inc., New Brunswick, 1981-84, v.p. rsch., 1984-87, v.p. R&D, 1987-93, v.p. rsch., devel. and clin. affairs, 1993-95; pres. AAG Inc., Phillipsburg, N.J., 1995-96; prin. Regulated Technologies, Inc., 1996—; adj. asst. prof. Hunter Coll. of CCNY, 1978-81; adj. assoc. prof. Rutgers U., New Brunswick, 1985-89; advisor to molecular biology hons. prog. L.I. U., Bklyn., Middlesex Community Coll., N.J., 1984-87. Contbr. articles to profl. jours.; patentee in field. V.p. Glen Eagles Homeowners Assn., Branchburg, M.J., 1984. Mem. Am. Soc. Biol. Chem., Am. Soc. Microbiology, Internat. Soc. for Hematology, Internat. Soc. for Interferon Research, N.Y. Acad. Scis., Sigma Xi, Phi Sigma. Office: AAG Inc PO Box 6 Phillipsburg NJ 08865

TESTA, MICHAEL HAROLD, lawyer; b. N.Y.C., Sept. 4, 1939; m. Carol Waldenberg, June 16, 1962; 2 children. BS summa cum laude, NYU, 1958, LLB cum laude, 1961, LLM in Taxation, 1967. Bar: N.Y. 1961. Assoc. White & Case, N.Y.C., 1962-71; assoc. Skadden, Arps, Slate, Meagher & Flom, N.Y.C., 1971-72, ptnr., 1972-91; spl. counsel Living Oceans Program, Nat. Audubon Soc., 1993—; advisor U.S. Del. to UN Conf. on Straddling Fish Stocks and Highly Migratory Fish Stocks, 1994-95, U.S. Del. to Kyoto Internat. Conf. on Sustainable Contribution of Fisheries to Food Security, 1995, U.S. Del. to N.W. Atlantic Fisheries Orgn., 1996, U.S. Del. to 22d Session of FAO Com. on Fisheries, 1997; adj. assoc. prof. law NYU Law Sch., 1986; mem. consultative com. to secs. state and commerce N.W. Atlantic Fisheries Conv., 1996—; lectr. in field. Assoc. editor, contbr.: NYU Law Rev., 1960-61; contbr. articles to legal jours. Mem. planning bd. Town of Tuxedo (N.Y.), 1971-76. Served to capt. USAFR, 1961-72. Root-Tilden-Snow scholar, 1958-61. Mem. ABA, N.Y. State Bar Assn. (mem. exec. com. tax sect. 1978-82), Order of Coif. Home: 32 Wildwood Dr Great Neck NY 11024-1246 Office: 919 3rd Ave New York NY 10022

TESTA, RICHARD JOSEPH, lawyer; b. Marlboro, Mass., Apr. 21, 1939; s. Joseph N. and Jeannette (Clement) T.; m. Janet Lavallee; children: Jo-Anne, Richard J. Jr., Nancy, Susan, Karen. AB, Assumption Coll., 1959; LLB, Harvard U., 1962. Bar: Mass. 1962. Sr. ptnr. Testa, Hurwitz & Thibeault, Boston, 1973—. Mem. ABA. Democrat. Roman Catholic. Office: Testa Hurwitz & Thibeault High St Tower 125 High St Boston MA 02110-2704

TESTA, STEPHEN MICHAEL, geologist, consultant; b. Fitchburg, Mass., July 17, 1951; s. Guiseppe Alfredo and Angelina Mary (Pettito) T.; m. Lydia Mae Payne, July 26, 1986; 1 child, Brant Ethan Gage. AA, Los Angeles Valley Jr. Coll., Van Nuys, 1971; BS in Geology, Calif. State U., Northridge, 1976, MS in Geology, 1978. Registered geologist, Calif., Oreg.; cert. profl. geol. scientist., Idaho, Alaska; cert. engring. geologist, Calif.; registered environ. assessor, Calif. Engring. geologist R.T. Frankian & Assocs., Burbank, Calif., 1976-78, Bechtel, Norwalk, Calif., 1978-80, Converse Cons., Seattle, 1980-82; sr. hydrogeologist Ecology Environment, Seattle, 1982-83; sr. geologist Dames & Moore, Seattle, 1983-86; v.p. Engring. Enterprises, Long Beach, Calif., 1986-89; CEO Applied Environ. Svcs., San Juan Capistrano, Calif., 1990-94; pres. Testa Environ. Corp., Foothill Ranch, Calif., 1994—. Author: Restoration of Petroleum Contaminated Aquifers, 1990, Principles of Technical Consulting and Project Management, 1991, Geological Aspects of Hazardous Waste Management, 1994, Reuse and Recycling of Contaminated Soil, 1997; editor Geologic Field Guide to the Salton Basin, 1988, Environmental Concerns in the Petroleum Industry, 1989; contbr. more than 60 articles to profl. jours., a preface and chpts. to books. Mem. AAAS, Am. Inst. Profl. Geologists (mem. profl. devel. com. 1986, mem. continuing edn. com. program chmn., 1988—, mem. nat. screening bd. 1992-94, chmn. 1995—, exec. bd. del. 1993, nat. v.p. 1994, trustee 1995—, honors and awards com. 1996-97, pres.-elect 1997, presdl. Cert. of Merit 1987, 94), L.A. Basin Geol. Soc. (pres. 1991-92), Geol. Soc. Am., Am. Assn. Petroleum Geologists (Pacific sect. environ. com., co-chmn. 1993—, chmn. liaison com. divsn. environ. geoscis. 1997, cert. of merit 1997), Am. Mineral. Soc., South Coast Geol. Soc., Assn. Ground Water Scientists and Engrs., Assn. Engring. Geologists, Assn. Mil. Engrs., Environ. Assessment Assn., Mineral Soc. Can., Hazardous Materials Rsch. Inst., Calif. Water Pollution Control Assn., Sigma Xi. Roman Catholic. Achievements include research igneous and metamorphic petrology, asphalt chemistry; development of methods for subsurface hydrogeologic characterization and remediation, proprietary processes for incorporation of contaminated soil and other materials considered toxic and hazardous via recycling into a variety of cold-mix asphaltic products. Home: 19814 Jesus Maria Rd Mokelumne Hill CA 95245 Office: Testa Environ Corp Ste 1E-446 27641 Portola Pky Foothill Ranch CA 92610-1743

TETELMAN, ALICE FRAN, city government official; b. N.Y.C., Apr. 15, 1941; d. Harry and Leah (Markovitz) T.; m. Martin A. Wenick, Dec. 7, 1980. BA, Mt. Holyoke Coll., South Hadley, Mass., 1962. Rsch. and info. asst. Edn. and World Affairs, N.Y.C., 1963-67; legis. asst. U.S. Sen. Charles Goodell, Washington, 1968-70; land use and energy specialist Citizens Adv. Com. on Environ. Quality, Washington, 1973-74; sr. assoc. prog. mgr. Linton & Co., Washington, 1971-73, 75-76; pub policy cons. Washington, 1977-78; adminstrv. asst. U.S. Congressman Bill Green (N.Y.), Washington, 1978-81; cons. The Precious Legacy Project, Prague, Czechoslovakia, 1982-83; Rep. staff dir. Select Com. on Hunger, U.S. Ho. of Reps., Washington, 1984-85; dir. State of N.J. Washington Office, 1986-90; exec. dir. Coun. of Gov/'s Policy Advisors, Washington, 1991-94; dir. Washington Office The City of N.Y., 1994—. Bd. mem. Republican Women's Task Force, Nat. Women's Polit. Caucus, 1976-80. European Community grantee, 1975. Mem. Ripon Soc. (nat. exec. com. 1971-73). Republican. Office: City of NY 1301 Pennsylvania Ave NW Washington DC 20004-1701

TETHER, ANTHONY JOHN, aerospace executive; b. Middletown, N.Y., Nov. 28, 1941; s. John Arthur and Antoinette Rose (Gesualdo) T.; m. Nancy Engle Pierson, Dec. 27, 1963 (div. July 1971); 1 child, Jennifer; m. Carol Suzanne Dunbar, Mar. 3, 1973; 1 child, Michael. AAS, Orange County C.C., N.Y., 1961; BS, Rensselaer Poly Inst., 1963; MSEE, Stanford (Calif.) U., 1965, PhD, 1969. V.p., gen. mgr. Sys. Control Inc., Palo Alto, Calif., 1968-78; dir. nat. intelligence Office Sec. of Def., Washington, 1978-82; dir. strategic tech. DARPA, Washington, 1982-86; corp. v.p. Ford Aerospace, Newport Beach, Calif., 1986-90, LORAL, Newport Beach, 1990-92; corp. v.p., gen. mgr. Sci. Application Internat., Inc., San Diego, 1992-94; CEO Dynamics Tech. Inc., Torrance, Calif., 1994-96; CEO, pres. Sequoia Group, Newport Beach, Calif., 1996—; chmn., bd. dirs. Condyne Tech., Inc., Orlando, Fla., 1990-92; dir. Orincon, La Jolla, Calif. Contbr. articles to profl. jours. Recipient Nat. Intelligence medal DCI, 1986, Civilian Meritorious medal U.S. Sec. Def., 1986. Mem. IEEE, Cosmos Club, Sigma Xi, Eta Kappa Nu, Tau Beta Pi. Avocations: ham radio, skiing. Home: 4518 Roxbury Rd Corona Del Mar CA 92625-3125

TETLEY, GLEN, choreographer; b. Cleve., Feb. 3, 1926; s. Glenford and Eleanor (Byrne) T. Student, Franklin and Marshall Coll., 1944-46; BS, NYU, 1948; student contemporary dance with, Hanya Holm, Martha Graham, 1946; student classical ballet with, Margaret Craske, Anthony Tudor at Met. Opera Ballet Sch., 1949. guest instr. Yale Dramatic Workshop, 1947-48, Colo. Coll., 1946-49, Hanya Holm Sch. Contemporary Dance, 1946-52, Ballet Rambert, 1966-68, Netherlands Dance Theatre, 1962-65, B. De Rothschild Found., Israel, 1965-67. Featured dancer in Broadway musical Kiss Me Kate, 1949, Out of This World, 1950, Juno, 1958; premiered in Broadway musical Menotti's Amahl and the Night Visitors, NBC Opera, 1951; soloist with Broadway musical, N.Y.C. Opera, 1951-54, John Butler's Am. Dance Theatre, 1951-55, Robert Joffrey Ballet, 1955-56, Martha Graham Dance Co., 1957-59, Am. Ballet Theatre, 1959-61, Jerome Robbins: Ballets USA, 1961-62, Netherlands Dance Theater, 1962-65, own co., 1962-69; made govt.-sponsored tour of Europe, 1969, appearances at Spoleto Festival, all maj. Am. dance festivals; guest choreographer, Netherlands Dance Theatre; artistic dir.: Netherlands Dance Theatre, 1969; guest choreographer, Am. Ballet Theatre, Ballet Rambert, Batsheva Co. Israel, Robert Joffrey Ballet, Alvin Alley Co., U. Utah Repertory Dance Theatre, Vancouver Festival, Royal Danish Ballet, 1969, Royal Ballet Covent Garden, Royal Swedish Ballet, Den Norske Opera, Hamburg State Opera, Stuttgart Ballet; former artistic dir., Stuttgart Ballet Co.; artistic assoc., Nat. Ballet of Canada, Toronto, 1987-89; ballets include Pierrot Lunaire, 1962, Birds of Sorrow, 1962, The Anatomy Lesson, 1964, Sargasso, 1964, Field Mass, 1965, Mythical Hunters, 1965, Ricercare, 1966, Chronochromie, 1966, Tehilim, 1966, Freefall, 1967, The Seven Deadly Sins, 1967, Dithyramb, 1967, Ziggurat, 1967, Circles, 1968, Embrace Tiger and Return to Mountain, 1968, Arena, 1968, Imaginary Film, 1970, Mutations, 1970, Field Figures, 1971, Rag Dances, 1971, Small Parades, 1972, Threshold, 1972, Laborintus, 1972, Strophe-Antistrophe, 1972, The Moveable Garden, 1973, Gemini, 1973, Voluntaries, 1973, Sacre du Printemps, 1974, Tristan, 1974, Strender, 1974, Daphnis and Chloe, 1975, Greening, 1975, Alegrias, 1975, Poeme Nocturne, 1977, Sphinx, 1978, Praeludium, 1979, The Tempest, 1979, Contredances, 1979, Summer's End, 1980, Dances of Albion-Dark Night: Glad Day, 1980, Firebird, 1981, Murder Hope of Women, 1983, Revelation and Fall, 1984, Pulcinella, 1984, Dream Walk of the Shaman, 1985, Alice, 1986, Orpheus, 1987, La Ronde, 1987, Tagore, 1989, Dialogues, 1991, Oracle, 1994; off-Broadway choreographer-dir. ballets including Fortuna, 1961, Ballet Ballads, 1961. Patron Benesh Inst. Choreology; bd. dirs. Tag Found., N.Y.C. Served with USNR, 1944-46. Recipient German critics award for Die Feder; Queen Elizabeth II Coronation award Royal Acad. Dancing, 1981; recipient Prix Italia Rai prize, 1982, Tennant Caledonia award Edinburgh Festival, 1983, Ohioana Career Medal, 1986, achievement award N.Y.U., 1988. Address: 15 W 9th St New York NY 10011-8918

TETLIE, HAROLD, priest; b. Madison, Minn., Aug. 24, 1926; s. H. Ben and Anna (Mauland) T. BA cum laude, St. Olaf Coll., Northfield, Minn., 1951; MBA, U. Denver, 1956; postgrad., Cornell U., 1959-60; MDiv, Luther Sem., St. Paul, 1965. Ordained to ministry Am. Luth. Ch., 1965. Pastor Christ the King Chs. (Evang. Cath. Ch.), Alice, Tex., 1965—, congregation supr., 1969—; cir. parish priest, Nuevo Leon, Tamaulipas, Hidalgo, San Luis Potosi, Mex. Author numerous poems. Coord. Joint Action in Cmty. Svc., Inc., Alice, 1970—. Sgt. U.S. Army, 1945-46, PTO. Recipient Svc. to Mankind award Sertoma Club, Corpus Christi, Regional Vol. of Yr. award Joint Action in Cmty. Svc., 1991, Michael Madhusudan award for poem, Calcutta, 1996; Ky. Col., 1992. Mem. NEA (life), VFW, Am. Legion, 40 et 8, Family Motor Coach Assn., Sons of Norway, Order of Ky. Col., Internat. Platform Assn., Thousand Trails, WWII Tank Destroyer Soc. (chaplain). Home and Office: Christ the King Chs PO Box 1607 Alice TX 78333-1607 *It is by the Power of Jesus Christ: He tells us in John 13:34: "Love one another, even as I loved you."*

TETLOW, EDWIN, author; b. Altrincham, Eng., May 19, 1905; s. William Chadwick and Mary (Entwistle) T.; m. Kathleen Whitworth Brown, Sept. 14, 1932; children: Susan Edwina, Timothy Chadwick. Student, Manchester (Eng.) U., 1924. Trainee journalist Daily Dispatch, Manchester, 1924-30; mem. staff Eve. News. London, 1930-33, Daily Mail, London, 1933-45; naval war corr. Daily Mail, 1940-42, army War corr., 1942-45; Berlin corr. Daily Telegraph, 1945-50, N.Y. corr., 1950-65; freelance author Esopus, N.Y., 1965—. Author: Eye on Cuba, 1966, The United Nations, 1971, The Enigma of Hastings, 1974, 2d edit., 1993, As It Happened, 1990; book reviewer: Christian Sci. Monitor; contbr.: Economist newspaper, Director Mag., London, Telegraph Sunday Mag., London, N.Y. Times, New Republic. Life mem. Fgn. Press Assn. (pres. 1964-65, mem. exec. bd. 1965—). Home: Druids' Dell PO Box 140 Esopus NY 12429-0140

TETRO, CATHERINE ANNE, shop owner; b. Fulton, N.Y., July 26, 1925; d. Sam and Florence Elizabeth (Corsoneti) Froio; m. John Ralph Tetro, Nov. 29, 1969. Grad. H.S., Fulton, N.Y., 1942. Clk. U.S. Post Office Substa., Fulton, N.Y., 1941-53; owner, operator Kay's Tot Shop, Fulton, N.Y., 1953-95. Sec. Fulton Merchants Assn., 1982; mem. parish coun., 1982-85, mem. choir. Mem. Fulton Women's Bowling Assn. (treas., mem. Women's Bowling Hall of Fame).

TETTEGAH, SHARON YVONNE, education educator; b. Wichita Falls, Tex., Jan. 14, 1956; d. Lawrence Guice and Doris Jean (Leak) Oliver; 1 child, Tandra Ainsworth; m. Joseph Miller Zangai, Dec. 22, 1978 (div. 1983); 1 child, Tonia Monjay Zangai; m. George Tettegah, Apr. 28, 1989; children: Nicole Jennifer, Michael Scott. AA, Coll. Alameda, 1985; BA, U. Calif., Davis, 1988, teaching cert., 1989, MA, 1991; PhD in Ednl. Psychology, U. Calif., Santa Barbara, 1997. Cert. elem. tchr., Calif. Clk. II Alameda County Mcpl. Ct., Oakland, Calif., 1976-77; acct. clk. Alameda County Social Svcs., Oakland, 1977-78, eligibility technician, 1978-82; supervising clk. Alameda County Health Care Svcs., Oakland, 1982-84; tchr. Davis (Calif.) Joint Unified Sch. Dist., 1988-89, L.A. Unified Schs., L.A., 1990-92; tchr. Oakland Unified Sch. Dist., Oakland, 1992—, tchr. sci. mentor, 1993—; teaching asst. U. Calif., Santa Barbara, 1993-94; adminstrv. intern Oxnard Unified Sch. Dist., 1994, U. Calif. Cultural Awareness Program, Santa Barbara, 1994—; rsch. cons. to vice chancellor students affairs, cons. tchr. edn. program, facilitor registrar's office U. Calif., Santa Barbara, 1995-96, rsch. asst. Grad. Sch. Edn., 1996—; cons. U. Calif. , Davis, 1988-89, Montessori Ctr. Sch., Santa Barbara, Calif., 1996; multicultural cons. Davis Unified Sch. Dist., 1988-89; edn. cons. Ednl. Testing Svc., Emeryville, Calif., 1994; chair diversity com. of Santa Barbara Village Charter Sch.; mem. academic senate com. undergrad enrollment and admissions U. Calif. Santa Barbara, 1995, tchr. cross-cultural interactions course, summer, 1995; mem. academic affairs affirmative action com. U. Calif. Santa Barbara, 1995-96, grad. sch. of edn., grad. affairs and affirmative action comms. U. Calif. Santa Barbara, 1995-96. Contbr. articles to profl. jours. Mem. U. Calif. Santa Barbara Acad. Senate Bd. Undergraduate Admissions and Records; co-chair Diversity Com. Montecito-Santa Barbara Charter Sch.; pres. African-Am. Grad. and Profl. Students Orgn., Davis, 1988-89. Recipient Charlene Richardson Acad. Honors award Coll. Alameda, 1985; Calif. State Acad. fellow, 1989-91, Grad. Opportunity Acad. Excellence fellow, 1994-95, Vice Chancellors Acad. Achievement fellowship U. Calif. Santa Barbara, 1995-96, Vice Chancellors Acad. Fellowship Grad. Divsn., 1995-96, 96-97. Mem. Am. Ednl. Researchers Assn., Calif. Sci. Tchrs. Assn., Calif. Advocacy for Math and Sci., Calif. Tchrs. Assn., Calif. Media Libr. Educators Assn., PTA, Multicultural Curriculum Assn., Supervision and Curriculum Leadership Assn., Bay Area Sci. and Tech. Educators Corsortium, Pan-African Students Assn., Kappa Delta Pi. Avocations: travelling, reading, preparing gourmet foods, tennis. Home: PO Box 1782 Santa Barbara CA 93116-1782 Office: U Calif Santa Barbara Sch Edn/Ednl Psychology Santa Barbara CA 93106

TETTLEBAUM, HARVEY M., lawyer; m. Ann Safier; children: Marianne, Benjamin. AB, Dartmouth Coll., 1964; JD, Washington U. Sch. Law, 1968, AM in History, 1968. Asst. dean Washington U. Sch. Law, 1969-77; asst. atty. gne., chief counsel Consumer Protection and Anti-Trust Div., 1970-77; pvt. practice Jefferson City, Mo., 1977-90; ptnr., chmn. health care, adminstrv. and govtl. law dept. Husch & Eppenberger, Jefferson City, Mo., 1990—; vice-chmn. Nat. Health Lawyers Long Term Care and the Law Program, mem., bd. dirs., 1993—. Contbr. articles to profl. jours. Treas. Mo. Rep. State Com., 1976—; v.p. Moniteau County R-1 Sch. Dist. Bd., 1991-95, pres., 1995-96; mem. Calif. R-1 Sch. Bd., 1990-96, v.p., 1993-95, pres., 1995-96. Mem. Nat. Health Lawyers Assn. (bd. dirs.), Mo. Bar Assn. (health and hosp. law com., chmn. adminstrv. law com.), Am. Health Care Assn. (legal subcom. 1994—). Home: 56295 Little Mon Tear Rd California MO 65018-9656 Office: Husch & Eppenberger Monroe House Ste 300 235 E High St PO Box 1251 Jefferson City MO 65101-1251

TETZLAFF, CHARLES ROBERT, prosecutor; b. Oct. 15, 1938; s. Donald H. and Harriet (Ranney) T.; m. Joan Seugling, July 1, 1962; children: Julie Lynn Mulrow, Carl Lawrence. BA, U. Vt., 1960; LLB, Boston U., 1963; LLM, NYU, 1964. Bar: Vt. 1964, U.S. Supreme Ct. 1970. Judge advocate USAF, 1965-68; dep. state's atty. Chittenden County, Vt., 1968-70; ptnr. Latham, Eastman, Schweyer and Tetzlaff, 1969-93; U.S. atty. dist. Vt. Office U.S. Atty., Burlington, 1993—; trustee Vt. Legal Aid, 1976-78; chair Dist. 4

Environ. Commn., 1979-83, Gov. Sentencing Study Commn., 1985-86; active Vt. Bd. Bar Examiners, 1980-84, State Police Adv. Commn., 1985-86, Gov. Bail Amendment Task Force. Capt. USAF, 1965-68. Mem. ABA, Vt. Bar Assn., Chittenden County Bar Assn. Office: US Attys Office PO Box 570 11 Elmwood Ave Burlington VT 05402

TETZLAFF, KAREN MARIE, state official; b. Florence, Oreg., Mar. 9, 1950; d. Chester Arthur and Martha Jane (Howell) Mitchell; m. Sterling Franklin Tetzlaff, July 16, 1988; children: Michelle René Davis, André Scott Matney, Derrick Anthony Matney, Anissa Barret. Diploma, Chemeketa C.C., Salem, Oreg., 1981. Notary pub., Oreg. Sec. Oreg. Corrections div., Madras, 1977-78; intake-release data clk. community corrections Oreg. Corrections div., Salem, 1979-80, correctional officer, 1980-83, records mgr., 1983—, instr., 1990—; master facilitator trainer breaking barriers Oreg. Corrections div., 1995—; facilitator, trainer breaking barriers Gordon Graham & Co., Salem, 1992—, developing capable people, Salem, 1993—; instr., law enforcement data system rep. Oreg. Women's Correctional Ctr., Salem, 1984—, facilitator, 1993—. Head usher John Jacobs Evangelistic Assn., Salem, Medford, Redmond, Oreg., 1990-92; youth worship leader South Salem Foursquare Ch., Salem, 1990-92; vol. Driving Under Influence Tng. Task Force, Salem, 1992—; v.p. Salem Gospel Cente Womens Ministry, 1993-95, Marion County chpt. Mothers Against Drunk Driving, 1994-95; dir. Pentecostal Holiness N.W. Dist. Women's Ministry, 1996—; worship and music dir., youth leader Salem Gospel Ctr., 1996—. Recipient 5-yr. outstanding svc. award Law Enforcement Data System, 1990, Investing in People, Svc. to State Tng. award Exec. Dept., 1992, traffic safety award Oreg. Dept. Transp., 1993, Employee of Quarter award Oreg. Women's Correctionala Ctr., 1993. Mem. Am. Correctional Assn., Oreg. Corrections Assn., Nat. Notary Assn., Cognitive Restructuring Network (letter of appreciation 1993). Republican. Avocations: paralegal studies, reading, singing. Office: Oreg Women's Correctional Ctr 2809 State St Salem OR 97310-1307

TETZLAFF, THEODORE R., lawyer; b. Saukville, Wis., Feb. 27, 1944. AB magna cum laude, Princeton U., 1966; LLB, Yale U., 1969. Bar: Ind. 1969, D.C. 1969, Ill. 1974. Legis. asst. to Congressman John Brademas, 1970; exec. dir. Nat. Conf. Police Community Rels., 1970-71; acting dir. U.S. Office Legal Svcs., Office Econ. Opportunity, Washington, 1972-73; counsel, Com. Judiciary U.S. Ho. of Reps., Washington, 1974; v.p., legal and external affairs Cummins Engine Co., 1980-82; gen. coun. Tenneco, Inc., Houston, 1992—, Greenwich, C.T.; ptnr. Jenner & Block, Chgo., 1976-80, 82—; bd. dirs. Case Corp., Racine, Wis., Continental Materials Corp., Chgo. Pres. Chgo. area Found. Legal Svcs., 1983—; commr. Pub. Bldg. Commn. Chgo., 1990—. Reginald Heber Smith fellow, 1969-70. Mem. ABA (chair sect. litigation 1991-92), Ill. State Bar Assn., Ind. State Bar Assn., D.C. Bar. Office: Tenneco Inc 1275 King St Greenwich CT 06831-2936 also: Jenner & Block 1 E Ibm Plz Fl 4200 Chicago IL 60611-3586

TEUBNER, FERDINAND CARY, JR., retired publishing company executive; b. Phila., Sept. 22, 1921; s. Ferdinand Cary Teubner and Esther Roslyn (Test) Alperstein; m. Ruth May Hazen, Nov. 1, 1953; 1 child, Janell Caron Teubner Crispyn. Student, U. Pa., 1940-41; grad., Charles Morris Price Sch. Advt. and Journalism, 1949. Rep. W.H. Hoedt Studios, Inc., Phila., 1945-52; account exec. Patterson Prodns., Inc., Phila., 1955-56, v.p., 1956-57; staff exec. Am. Assn. Advt. Agys., N.Y.C., 1957-59; rep. W.H. Martin & Co., Inc., N.Y.C., 1959-62; advt. salesman Editor & Pub. Co., Inc., N.Y.C., 1962-65, advt. mgr., 1965-76, gen. mgr., treas., 1976-78, treas., pub., 1978-95, dir., 1969-95; sec.-treas., dir. E & P Research, Inc., N.Y.C., 1985-95, ret., 1995. Served with USAAF, 1942-45, ETO; served to maj. U.S. Army, 1952-55, Korea. Decorated Purple Heart; recipient Silver Shovel award Internat. Newspaper Mktg. Assn., 1993. Mem. Sales Execs. Club N.Y.C., Res. Officer Assn. Episcopalian. Clubs: Union League, Lake Valhalla Country. Home: 18 Lenape Dr Montville NJ 07045-9795

TEUSCHER, GEORGE WILLIAM, dental educator; b. Chgo., Jan. 11, 1908; s. Albert Christian and Elizabeth (Klesch) T.; m. Eleanor C. Oeler, Sept. 29, 1934 (div.); children: Carol Ann, John William; m. Eleanor E. Wilson, May, 1968. D.D.S., Northwestern U., 1929, M.S.D., 1936, A.M., 1940, Ph.D., 1942; Sc.D. (hon.), N.Y. U., 1965. Charter mem. Am. Acad. Pedodontics (pres. 1960-61), Am. Bd. Pedodontics. Engaged in gen. practice of dentistry, 1929-34, in pedodontics, 1934-69; instr. pedodontics Northwestern U., 1933-38, asst. prof., 1938-41, asso. prof., 1941; lectr. surgery Northwestern U. Med. Sch., 1945—, prof. pedodontics, 1946—; dean Northwestern U. Med. Sch. (Dental Sch.), 1953-71; mem. staff Wesley Meml. Hosp., 1946-69, chief dental sect. dept. otolaryngology, 1961-69; mem. adv. com. dentistry Smithsonian Instn., 1967—; lectr. on pedodontics and edn. in, U.S. and Can.; cons. Naval Dental Research Inst., Gt. Lakes. Editor: Dental Progress, 1959-63, Jour. Dentistry for Children, 1967—, Jour. Dental Edn, 1970-73; contbr. articles to dental jours. Bd. dirs. Tb Inst. Chgo. and Cook County, 1964-70; regent Nat. Library Medicine, 1968-72; bd. govs. Chgo. Heart Assn., 1967-74; Pres. Gen. Alumni Assn., Northwestern U., 1948-51. Served with Res. Officers Corps, 1929-42. Fellow Am. Coll. Dentists, Inst. Medicine Chgo.; mem. Internat. Assn. Dental Research, Am. Assn. Dental Schs. (pres. 1962-63), Am. Dental Assn. (council dental edn. 1964-70), Ill. Dental Soc., Chgo. Dental Soc. (pres. 1958-59), Odontographic Soc. (pres. 1952-53), Am. Soc. Dentistry for Children (pres. 1952-53, exec. officer 1982—), Am. Dental Soc. Europe (hon.), Xi Psi Phi, Omicron Kappa Upsilon. Clubs: Tavern (Chgo.), Chicago Literary (Chgo.). Home: 730 Blaney Dr Dyer IN 46311-2306

TEUSCHLER, MICHAEL ALEXANDER, computer company executive, consultant; b. Chgo., Nov. 30, 1953; s. Edward Michael and Josephine Anastasia (Bien) T. Assoc. editor Peacock N.W. News, Chgo., 1972-74; polit. activist Citizen's Action Program, Chgo., 1974; stockman Cotter & Co., Chgo., 1974-77; asst. mgr. Cloona Health Ctr., Westport, Ireland, 1977-78; computer programmer Sears Roebuck & Co., Chgo., 1978-90; computer cons. Cap Gemini Am., Milw., 1991—. Pres. Old Town Renaissance Consort, Chgo., 1985-89, 2100 N. Albany Block Club, Chgo., 1988-89; vice chmn. fin. com. St. Philomena Parish, Chgo., 1976. Mem. ASPCA, Wis. Assn. Sys. Mgrs., Morning Star Fellowship of Isis (founding mem.), Internat. Platform Assn., Humane Soc. of U.S., Nat. Arbor Day Soc., World Wildlife Fund, Nat. Audubon Soc., Nat. Wildlife Fedn., Defenders of Wildlife, Leaders Club. Avocations: renaissance dance, ancient religions. Home: 7625 W Wind Lake Rd Wind Lake WI 53185-2253 Office: Cap Gemini Am 330 E Kilbourn Ave Milwaukee WI 53202

TEVRIZIAN, DICKRAN M., JR., federal judge; b. Los Angeles, Aug. 4, 1940; s. Dickran and Rose Tevrizian; m. Geraldine Tevrizian, Aug. 22, 1964; children: Allyson Tracy, Leslie Sara. BS, U. So. Calif., 1962, JD, 1965. Tax acct. Arthur Andersen and Co., Los Angeles, 1965-66; atty., ptnr. Kirtland and Packard, Los Angeles, 1966-72; judge Los Angeles Mcpl. Ct., Los Angeles, 1972-78, State of Calif. Superior Ct., Los Angeles, 1978-82; ptnr. Manatt, Phelps, Rothenberg & Tunney, Los Angeles, 1982-85, Lewis, D'Amato, Brisbois & Bisgaard, Los Angeles, 1985-86; judge U.S. Dist. Ct., Los Angeles, 1986—. Named Trial Judge of the Yr., Calif. Trial Lawyers Assn., 1987, L.A. County Bar Assn., 1994-95. Mem. Calif. Trial Lawyer's Assn. (trial judge of yr. 1987), L.A. County Bar Assn. (trial judge of yr. 1994-95). Office: US Dist Ct Royal Federal Bldg 255 E Temple St Los Angeles CA 90012-3334

TEWELL, JOSEPH ROBERT, JR., electrical engineer; b. Albany, N.Y., May 19, 1934; s. Joseph Robert and Florence Edna (MacKinnon) T.; m. Barbara Ann Johnson, Nov. 20, 1960; children—Patricia Ann, Donna Lynn, Joseph Robert, III. B.E.E., Rensselaer Poly. Inst., 1955, M.E.E., 1958. Rsch. engr. N.Am. Aviation, Inc., Downey, Calif., 1955; assoc. rsch. engr. Lockheed Aircraft Corp., Burbank, Calif., 1956; instr. Rensselaer Poly. Inst., 1957-64; sr. rsch. scientist Martin Marietta Corp., Denver, 1964-79; mgr. advanced programs Martin Marietta Corp., Michoud, La., 1979-87, mgr. shuttle-C project, 1988-90, mgr. computer-aided productivity, 1991-93; mgr. sys. engring. Martin Marietta Corp., Michoud, 1994-96; ret., 1996, pvt. cons., 1996—; founding sponsor Challenger Ctr.; cons. Redford Corp., Scotia, N.Y., 1961. Contbr. articles to profl. jours.; inventor dual action single drive actuator, spacecraft docking and retrieval mechanism. Founding sponsor Challenger Ctr. Served with Army Security Agy., 1957. Recipient NASA Manned Awareness citation, 1970, NASA Skylab Achievement award, 1974, NASA New Tech. award, 1976, Tech. Achievement award Martin Marietta Corp., 1977, Sustained Performance award Martin Marietta Corp., 1981, NASA cert. of recognition, 1977, Author of Yr. award, 1986, also 38 publ. awards, 1965—. Fellow Explorers Club; mem. AIAA, Smithsonian Assocs., Air and Space Mus., Unmanned Vehicle Sys., Nat. Audubon Soc., Sigma Xi, Eta Kappa Nu, Tau Beta Pi, Theta Chi. Home and Office: 619 Legendre Dr Slidell LA 70460-3427

TEWI, THEA, sculptor; b. Berlin, Germany; came to U.S., 1938, naturalized, 1943; d. Jules and Claire (Kochmann) Wittner; m. Charles K. Schlachet; 1 son, Peter. Grad., Nat. Acad. Fine Arts, Berlin; student New Sch., Art Students League, N.Y.C., 1956-57. Pres. League of Present Day Artists, 1964-70; pres. Sculptors League, 1970-88. Exhibited in one-man shows at, Village Art Center, N.Y.C., 1961, La Boetie Gallery, N.Y.C., 1966, 68, 70, Sala Michelangelo, Carrara, Italy, 1969, Lehigh U., Bethlehem, Pa., 1970, U. Notre Dame, 1970, Hallway Gallery, Washington, 1976, 80, Randall Gallery, N.Y.C., 1977, 79, 81, 83, Vorpal Gallery, N.Y.C., 1985, 87, Bklyn. Bot. Garden, 1989, N.Y. Acad. Scis., 1992, 93, others; exhibited in numerous group shows; represented in permanent collections at, Smithsonian Instn., Washington, Cin. Art Mus., Norfolk (Va.) Mus. Arts and Scis., U. Notre Dame, Norton Simon Collection, Citicorp, N.Y., Fort Worth Nat. Bank, Parks Dept. City of N.Y., N.Y. Acad. Scis., Govt. Ecuador; also represented in pvt. collections U.S., France, Italy, Spain, Switzerland, Japan. Recipient numerous awards and purchase awards, including 1st prize Am. Soc. Contemporary Artists, 1971, 75, 76, 78, medal of merit Nat. Arts Club, 1974, Nawa Peabody award Nat. Acad., 1975, medal of merit Knickerbocker Artists, 1975. Mem. Nat. Assn. Women Artists (1st prize, medal of honor 1969), Am. Soc. Contemporary Artists, Sculptors League (founder, pres. 1971-88). Home: 10030 67th Dr Forest Hills NY 11375-3147

TEWKESBURY, JOAN F., film director, writer; b. Redlands, Calif., Apr. 8, 1936; d. Walter S. and Frances M. (Stevenson) T.; m. Robert F. Maguire, III, Nov. 30, 1960 (div.); children: Robin Tewkesbury, Peter Harlan. Student, Am. Sch. Dance, 1947-54, Mt. San Antonio Jr. Coll., Walnut, Calif., 1956-58; drama scholar, U. So. Calif., 1958-60. Dancer in: film Unfinished Dance, 1946; dancer, flying understudy Peter Pan, LosAngeles and N.Y.C., 1954-55; choreographer film, Los Angeles, 1958-70, tchr. dance and drama, U. So. Calif., 1966-69, Immaculate Heart Coll., Los Angeles, 1960-63, Am. Sch. Dance, Los Angeles, 1959-69; tchr. film writing UCLA, 1986; choreographer, dir., actress, U. So. Calif. Repetory Co., 1965-68, London and Edinburgh (Scotland) Festival, 1965-68; scriptgirl: film McCabe and Mrs. Miller, 1970; author: screenplays Thieves Like Us, 1974, Nashville, 1975 (Los Angeles Critics Best Screenplay award), A Night in Heaven, 1983; playwright, dir. Cowboy Jack Street, 1978; dir. film Old Boyfriends, 1979; film writer, dir. TV 10th Month, 1979, The Acorn People, 1981; dir. film documentary Anna Freud, 1976; writer, dir. (TV show) Alfred Hitchcock Presents, from 1986, (TV movie for TNT) Cold Sassy Tree, 1989; screenwriter, dir., scriptwriter, co-exec. producer TV pilot Elysian Fields, 1988; dir. (Time-Life cable TV film) Sudie and Simpson; scriptwriter, dir.(TV) Shannon's Deal; dir. (TV movie) Wild Texas Wind, 1991, The Stranger (HBO), 1992; dir. (TV episodes) Northern Exposure, 1992, Picket Fences, 1992, Doogie Hauser, 1992; dir.(theater) Chippy, 1993; dir. (TV movie Disney Cable) On Promised Land, 1993. Mem. Literacy Vols. Am. Mem. Writers Guild Am., Dirs. Guild Am., ACLU, Nat. Abortion Rights Action League, Calif. Abortion Rights Action League. Office: care Jane Sindell Creative Artists Agy 1888 Century Park E Ste 1400 Los Angeles CA 90067-1718*

TEWKSBURY, ROBERT ALAN, professional baseball player; b. Concord, N.H., Nov. 30, 1960. Student, Rutgers U., St. Leo Coll. With N.Y. Yankees, 1981-87, Chgo. Cubs, 1987-88; pitcher St. Louis Cardinals, 1989-94, Tex. Rangers, 1995, San Diego Padres, 1996, Minn Twins, 1997—; player Nat. League All-Star Game, 1992. Ranked 2d in Nat. League for earned run average, 1992, 3d in Nat. League for wins. *

TEXTOR, ROBERT BAYARD, cultural anthropology writer, consultant, educator; b. Cloquet, Minn., Mar. 13, 1923; s. Clinton Kenney and Lillian (Nickles) T.; divorced; children: Alexander Robertson, Marisa Elizabeth. Student, Lafayette Coll., 1940-41, Antioch Coll., 1941-43; B.A. in Asian Studies, U. Mich., 1945; Ph.D. in Cultural Anthropology, Cornell U., 1960. Civil info. and edn. officer Mil. Govt., Kyoto-Wakayama, Japan, 1946-48; rsch. fellow anthropology and S.E. Asia studies Yale U., 1959-60, assoc., 1960-61; rsch. fellow in stats. Harvard U., 1962-64; assoc. prof. edn. and anthropology Stanford U., 1964-68, prof. edn. and anthropology, 1968-86, prof. anthropology, 1986-90, prof. anthropology emeritus, 1990—; vis. prof. U. Saar, Saarbrücken, Germany, 1984-85; cons. Motorola U., 1991—; mem. S.E. Asia Coun., 1974-77; cons. cultural anthropology to govt. agys., 1957-58, 61-62. Author: (most recent) Roster of the Gods: An Ethnography of The Supernatural in a Thai Village, 6 vols., 1973, Austria 2005: Projected Sociocultural Effects of the Microelectronic Revolution, 1983, Anticipatory Anthropology, 1985, (with Sippanondha Ketudat) The Middle Path for the Future of Thailand, 1990; assoc. editor Jour. Conflict Resolution, 1965-70; mem. editorial bd. Human orgn., 1966-71, Jour. Cultural Futures, 1979-87; adv. editor Behavior Sci. Rsch., 1974-86. Bd. dirs. Vols. in Asia, Stanford, Calif., 1968-73; mem. Metro Portland Future Vision Commn., 1993-95. Served with U.S. Army, 1943-46. Fellow Rockefeller Found., 1951-52, fgn. area tng. fellow Ford Found., Thailand 1955-58, Carnegie fellow, 1958-59, Fulbright West Europe rsch. fellow, 1984-85, East-West Ctr. fellow, 1988-90; NSF grantee, Thailand, U.S., 1969-73, Volkswagen Found. grantee, Thailand and Germany, 1984. Fellow Am. Anthrop. Assn. (life mem.); mem. Siam Soc. (life mem.), Assn. Asian Studies (life mem.), Council on Anthropology and Edn. (pres. 1974-75), AAUP (pres. Stanford chpt. 1975-76), Phi Kappa Phi.

THACHER, CARTER POMEROY, diversified manufacturing company executive; b. 1926. With Wilbur-Ellis Co., San Francisco, 1960—, v.p., 1963-67, pres., from 1967, chmn. bd., 1989—, also bd. dirs. Office: Wilbur-Ellis Co 320 California St Fl 2 San Francisco CA 94104

THACKER, JERRY LYNN, school administrator; b. Mishawaka, Ind., July 7, 1950; s. Burl Willis and Azzie Dell (Davidson) T.; m. Donna Lee, Aug. 11, 1973. BA, Bethel Coll., Mishawaka, Ind., 1972; MS, Ind. U., S. Bend, 1975; EdD, Andrews U., Berrien Springs, Mich., 1987. Tchr., individually guided edn. team leader Penn-Harris Madison Sch. Corp., Osceola, Ind., 1972-85; elem. prin. Twin lakes Sch. Corp., Monticello, Ind., 1985-89, dir. curriculum, 1989-90; dir. curriculum Saginaw (Mich.) Ind. Sch. Dist., 1989-90; dir. elem. edn. MSD Lawrence Twp., Indpl., 1990-96; asst. supt. for Human Resources MSD Lawrence Twp., 1996—. Presenter in field; contbr. numerous articles to profl. publs. Recipient various grants; recipient Award for Svc. to Profession, Ind. Assn. Curriculum Devel., others. Mem. ASCD, Nat. Assn. Elem. Prins., IAEMSP (pres.), AASA, Internat Reading Assn., Pi Lambda Theta, Phi Delta Kappa. Home: 759 Buckeye Ct Noblesville IN 46060-9196

THACKER, STEPHEN BRADY, medical association administrator, epidemiologist; b. Independence, Mo., Dec. 30, 1947; m. 1976; 2 children. AB, Princeton U., 1969; MD, Mt. Sinai Sch. Medicine, 1973; MSc, London Sch. Hygiene and Tropical Medicine, 1984. Chief consolidated surveillance and cmty. activity epidemiol. progress office Ctr. Disease Control, 1978-83, dir. surveillance and epidemiol. studies, 1983-86; asst. dir. sci. Ctr. Environ. Health and Injury Control, 1986-89; dir. epidemiol. program office Ctr. Disease Control, 1989—; acting dir. Nat. Ctr. Environ. Health, 1993-95; mem. steering com. Assn. Behavioral Sci. Med. Edn., 1971-74; assoc. Dept. Cmty. Medicine, Med. Ctr. Duke U., Durham, N.C., 1975-76; lectr. Cmty. Ctr. Mt. Sinai Sch. Medicine, N.Y.C., 1978—, Sch. Medicine Emory U., Atlanta, 1985-86; cons. epidemiology Arab Republic Egypt, 1979-91; clin. asst. prof. cmty. health Sch. Medicine Emory U., 1986—. Editor: Epidemiologic Revs., 1990—. Clin. scholar Robert Wood Johnson Found., 1974-75; recipient Mosby Book award for excellence, 1973, PHS Outstanding Svc. medal, 1987, PHS Meritorious Svc. medal, 1988, Saul Horowitz Jr. Meml. award, 1990, Supervisory award for contbr. advantage of women, 1991, PHS Commendation medal, 1991, PHS Disting. Svc. medal, 1993, PHS Surgeon Gen.'s Exemplary Svc. medal, 1993, William Watson medal of excellence, 1996, PHS Disting. Svc. medal, 1997. Rsch. public health surveillance, infectious disease, environ. health, alcohol abuse, health care delivery, meta-analysis, technology assessment. Office: Ctr for Disease Control & Prevention MS C08 1600 Clifton Rd NE Atlanta GA 30329-4018

THACKERAY, JONATHAN E., lawyer; b. Athens, Ohio, July 30, 1936; s. Joseph Eugene and Betty Rutherford (Boright) T.; m. Sandra Ann McMahon, 1979; children: Jennifer, Sara, Amy, Jonathan. A.B. cum laude, Harvard U., 1958, J.D., 1961. Bar: Ohio 1961, U.S. Dist. Ct. (no. dist.) Ohio 1961, U.S. Supreme Ct. 1972, U.S. Ct. Appeals (6th cir.) 1973, U.S. Ct. Appeals (9th cir.) 1982, N.Y. 1993. Assoc. Vorys, Sater, Seymour & Pease, Columbus, Ohio, 1961; assoc. Baker & Hostetler, Cleve., 1965-72, ptnr., 1973-93; v.p., gen. counsel The Hearst Corp., N.Y.C., 1993—. Served to lt. USNR, 1961-65. Mem. ABA, Ohio Bar Assn., Cleve. Bar Assn., Am. Law Inst. Office: The Hearst Corp 959 8th Ave New York NY 10019-3737 *Notable cases include: administrative proceedings leading to approval of joint newspaper operating agreements in Cincinnati, Seattle and Las Vegas; litigation of newspaper antitrust cases in Cin., Memphis, Trenton and Dallas.*

THACKRAY, ARNOLD WILFRID, historian, foundation executive; b. Eng., July 30, 1939; came to U.S., 1967, naturalized, 1982; s. Wilfrid Cecil and Mary (Clarke) T.; m. Barbara Hughes, 1965 (div. 1990); children: Helen Mary, Gillian Winifrid, Timothy Arnold; m. Diana Schueller, 1994; 1 stepchild, Gregory Jordan. B.Sc., Bristol (Eng.) U., 1960; M.A., Cambridge (Eng.) U., 1965, Ph.D., 1966. Research chemist Robert Dempster and Co., Yorkshire, Eng., 1960-61; research fellow Churchill Coll., Cambridge U., 1965-68; prof. history and sociology of sci. U. Pa., Phila., 1968-96, Joseph Priestley prof. emeritus history/sociology of sci., 1996—, chmn. dept., 1970-77, dir. Beckman Ctr. for History of Chemistry, 1982-96; prof. history, prof. chemistry, dean grad. studies and research U. Md., 1985-86; exec. dir., libr. Chem. Heritage Found., 1987-96, pres., 1996—; vis. lectr. Harvard U., 1967-68; vis. fellow All Souls Coll., Oxford, Eng., 1977-78; mem. Inst. Advanced Study, 1980. Editor: Isis, an Internat. Rev. of History of Science and its Cultural Influences, 1978-85, Osiris, 1985-94, Science After '40, 1992, Constructing Knowledge in the History of Science, 1995, Private Science, 1997, (with others) Science and Values, 1974, Toward a Metric of Science, 1978; author: Atoms and Powers, 1970, John Dalton, 1972, (with others) Gentlemen of Science, 1981-82, Chemistry in America, 1985; mem. editl. bd. Minerva, History of Science; contbr. articles to profl. jours. Recipient Gladstone Essay prize, also pub. speaking prize Churchill Coll., Cambridge U.; Guggenheim fellow, 1971-72, 85-86; Ctr. for Advanced Study in Behavioral Scis. fellow, 1973-74, 83-84. Fellow AAAS, Am. Acad. Arts and Scis., Royal Hist. Soc., Royal Chem. Soc.; mem. Am. Chem. Soc. (Dexter award 1983), Am. Hist. Assn., Manchester LIt. and Philos. Soc. (corr.), History of Sci. Soc., Am. Coun. Learned Socs. (bd. dirs., treas. 1985-96), Soc. for Social Studies of Sci. (pres. 1981-83), Am. Coun. on Edn. (bd. dirs. 1987), Chemists Club (N.Y.C.), Cosmos Club (Washington). Episcopalian.

THACKSTON, EDWARD LEE, engineer, educator; b. Nashville, Apr. 29, 1937; s. Guy Carleton and Sydney Virginia (Adams) T.; m. Betty Tucker, Mar. 19, 1961; children: Carol Elizabeth Thackston Nixon, Leah Virginia Thackston Hawkins. BE summa cum laude, Vanderbilt U., 1961; MS, U. Ill., 1963; PhD, Vanderbilt U., 1966. Registered profl. engr., Tenn. City engr. City of Lebanon, Tenn., 1959; design engr. City of Nashville, 1961-62; instr. Vanderbilt U., Nashville, 1965-66, asst. prof., 1966-69, assoc. prof., 1969-75, prof. engring., 1975—, chmn. dept. civil and environ. engring., 1980—; asst. to gov. for environ. affairs, State of Tenn., 1972-74; cons. in field. Author book, tech. reports; contbr. to profl. publs. Bd. dirs. Tenn. Environ. Coun., Nashville, 1971-76; bd. dirs. Tenn. Conservation League, Nashville, 1974—, v.p., 1977, pres., 1978-80; trustee Cumberland Mus., Nashville, 1986-92; trustee Cumberland U., Lebanon, 1996—, mem. exec. com., 1996—. Named Tenn. Conservationist of Yr., 1974. Fellow ASCE; mem. Am. Water Works Assn. (life), Water Environ. Fedn., Assn. Environ. Engring. Profs., Tenn. Hist. Soc., Tau Beta Pi, Chi Epsilon. Republican. Episcopalian. Avocations: genealogy, history, hiking, photography, basketball. Office: Vanderbilt U PO Box 133 Nashville TN 37235-0133

THADANI, UDHO, physician, cardiologist; b. Hydedrabad, India, Apr. 1, 1941; came to U.S., 1980; s. Vensimal Mulchand and Gopi Thadani; m. Dorothy Ann Thadani, 1974; 1 child, Emma Sarala. MBBS, All India Inst. Med. Scis., New Delhi, 1964. Lic. physician, Okla., Md., Ont., Can., Eng., India; cert. internal medicine, U.K., Can.; cert. cardiology, Can.; diplomate Am. Bd. Internal Medicine, subspecialty cardiovascular diseases. Intern All India Inst. Med. Scis., New Delhi, 1964-65, house physician, surgeon, 1965-66; house physician in medicine Joyce Green Hosp., Dartford, Kent, Eng., 1966-67; sr. house physician in medicine Kingston Gen. Hosp., Hull, Eng., 1967-69, registrar, rsch. fellow in medicine and cardiology, 1969-71; registrar, rsch. fellow in medicine and cardiology U. Leeds (Eng.), The Gen. Infirmary at Leeds, 1971-75; sr. rsch. fellow, clin. asst. medicine Queen's U., Kingston Gen. Hosp., Ont., Can., 1975-78; asst. prof. medicine Queen's U., Kingston 1978-80; staff physician Kingston Gen. Hosp., 1978-80; assoc. prof. medicine U. Okla. Health Scis. Ctr., Oklahoma City, 1980-83; prof. medicine, vice chief cardiovascular sect. Okla. U. Health Scis. Ctr., Oklahoma City, 1983—, mem. cardiology fellowship com., 1980-82; dir. clin. cardiology Okla. U. Health Scis. Ctr. and VA Med. Ctr., Oklahoma City, 1980-87, vice chief cardiovascular sect., 1981—, dir. clin. rsch., 1987—; vice chmn. rsch. and devel. com. VA Med. Ctr., Oklahoma City, 1989-92, chmn. physiology-pharmacology categorical rev. com., 1989-94, chmn. rsch. and devel. com., 1992-94; sr. rsch. fellow Ont. Heart Found., 1978-80, rsch. fellow, 1976-78; rsch. fellow dept. medicine Queen's U., Kingston, Ont., 1975-76; rsch. fellow U. Leeds, Pub. Health and Ciba Found., dept. medicine and cardiovascular sect. Leeds Gen. Infirmary, 1971-75. Editor: Medical Therapy of Ischemic Heart Disease, 1992, Nitrates Updated, 1996; contbr. over 100 articles to profl. jours., chpts. to books; mem. editl. bd. panel Cardiology Drug Facts and Comparison, 1989; contbg. rev. panel Drug Facts and Comparisons, 1989—; mem. editl. bd. Internat. Jour. Cardiology, 1987-93, Cardiovascular Drugs and Therapy, 1987—; reviewer Circulation, Jour. Am. Coll. Cardiology, Am. Jour. Cardiology, Brit. Heart Jour., Internat. Jour. Cardiology, Can. Jour. Cardiology, European Heart Jour., Annals of Internal Medicine, New Eng. Jour. Medicine, Archives of Internal Medicine, Cardiovascular Drugs and Therapy, Drugs, European Jour. Pharmacology, Clin. Pharmacology and Therapeutics. Fellow Royal Coll. Physicians (Can.), Royal Soc. Medicine London, Am. Coll. Cardiology (mem. cardiovascular drug com. 1990-94), Royal Coll. Physicians (London), Clin. Coun. Cardiology Am. Heart Assn. (coun. rep. Okla. 1989—), Royal Coll. Physicians and Surgeons Can., N.Y. Acad. Med. Scis.; mem. Royal Coll. Physicians (U.K.), AAAS, Can. Cardiovascular Soc., Am. Fedn. Clin. Rsch., Phi Kappa Phi (mem. FDA cardiovascular and renal drugs adv. com. 1995—). Avocations: gardening, tennis, travel. Office: Okla U Health Sci Ctr Cardiology Sect 920 SL Young 5SP-300 Oklahoma City OK 73104

THADDEUS, PATRICK, physicist, educator; b. Wilmington, Del., June 6, 1932; s. Victor and Elizabeth (Ross) T.; m. Janice Petherbridge Farrar, Apr. 6, 1963; children: Eva, Michael. B.Sc., U. Del., 1953; M.A., Oxford (Eng.) U., 1955; Ph.D., Columbia U., 1960. Research assoc. Columbia Radiation Lab., 1960-61; research assoc. Goddard Inst. Space Studies, N.Y.C., 1961-63; mem. sci. staff Goddard Inst. Space Studies, 1963-86; mem. faculty Columbia U., 1965-86, adj. prof. physics, 1971-86; prof. astronomy and applied physics Harvard U., 1986—; mem. sci. staff Smithsonian Astrophys. Obs., 1986—; vis. com. Nat. Radio Astronomy Obs., 1973-76, 91-94; mem. Astronomy Survey Com., 1978-80, 89-90; chair task group on Space Astronomy and Astrophysics, 1996-97; Fairchild Disting. Scholar Calif. Inst. Tech., 1994; Russell Marker lectr. Pa. State U., 1989; vis. fellow Inst. Astronomy, Cambridge, Eng., 1983. Author papers on microwave spectroscopy, optical and radio astronomy. Recipient Exceptional Sci. Achievement medal NASA, 1970, 85; John C. Lindsay Meml. award Goddard Space Flight Center, 1976; Alexander von Humboldt award, 1983; Fulbright fellow, 1953-55. Fellow Am. Phys. Soc.; mem. Am. Astron. Soc., Am. Acad. Arts and Scis., Nat. Acad. Scis., Internat. Astronomical Union, Sigma Xi. Address: 58 Garfield St Cambridge MA 02138-1802

THADEN, EDWARD CARL, history educator; b. Seattle, Apr. 24, 1922; s. Edward Carl and Astrid (Engvik) T.; m. Marianna Theresia Forster, Aug. 7, 1952. B.A., U. Wash., 1944; student, U. Zurich, Switzerland, 1948; Ph.D., U. Paris, 1950. Instr. Russian history Pa. State U., 1952-55, asst. prof., 1955-58, asso. prof., 1958-64, prof., 1964-68; vis. prof. Ind. U., 1957, U. Marburg, 1965, U. Ill., Urbana, 1980, U. Halle, German Dem. Republic, 1988, U. Helsinki, Finland, 1990; prof. U. Ill., Chgo., 1968—, chmn. dept. history, 1971-73; editorial cons. Can. Rev. Studies in Nationalism, 1973-78; vis. rsch. scholar USSR Acad. Scis., 1975, 88, 90; Ford Found. project prin. researcher, 1975-78; U.S. rep. to Internat. Congress of Hist. Scis., 1980; project dir. NEH grant, 1980-82. Author: Conservation Nationalism in

Nineteenth-Century Russia, 1964, Russia and the Balken Alliance of 1912, 1965, Russia Since 1801: The Making of a New Society, 1971, Russia's Western Borderlands, 1710-1870, 1984, Interpreting History: collected Essays on Russia's Relations with Europe, 1990, Essays in Russian and East European History: Festschrift in Honor of Edward C. Thaden, 1995; co-author, editor: Russification in the Baltic Provinces and Finland, 1955-1914, 1981; co-author, co-editor: Finland and the Baltic Provinces in the Russian Empire, 1984; mem. editorial bd. Jour Baltic Studies, 1984-93, assoc. editor, 1987-93. Served to lt. (j.g.) USNR, 1943-46. Carnegie Inter-Univ. Com. travel grantee to USSR, 1956; Fulbright research grantee Finland, 1957-58; Fulbright research grantee Germany, 1965; Fulbright research grantee Poland and Finland, 1968; Soc. Sci. Research Council grantee, 1957; Am. Council Learned Socs. grantee, 1963, 65-66; fellow Woodrow Wilson Internat. Center for Scholars, 1980. Mem. Am. Assn. for Advancement Slavic Studies (pres. Midwest br. 1975-76, exec. sec. 1980-82), Chgo. Consortium for Slavic and Ea. European Studies (pres. 1982-84), Baltische Historische Kommission, Göttingen (corr. mem. 1985—), Commn. Internat. des Etudes Historiques Slaves (v.p. 1985-95, pres. 1995-2000). Office: U Ill Dept History 913 UH (M/C 198) 601 S Morgan St Chicago IL 60607-3401

THAGARD, NORMAN E., astronaut, physician, engineer; b. Marianna, Fla., July 3, 1943; s. James E. Thagard and Mary F. Nicholson; m. Rex Kirby Johnson; children: Norman Gordon, James Robert, Daniel Cary. BS, Florida State U., 1965, MS, 1966; M.D., U. Texas Southwest Med. Sch., 1977. Intern, internal medicine Medical U. South Carolina, 1977-78; astronaut NASA, 1978—; mission specialist NASA Space Shuttle Challenger Flight STS-7, deployed satellites (ANIK C-2, PALAPA B-1), operated Remote Manipulator Sys., conducted experiments, 1983, NASA Spacelab-3 Mission STS-51 B, 1985, NASA Space Shuttle Atlantis Flight STS-30, deployed Magellan Venus exploration spacecraft, 1989; payload commander NASA Space Shuttle Discovery Flight STS-42, International Microgravity Lab.-1 module experiments, 1992; crew mem. Space Station MIR-18, 1995. Contbr. articles to profl. jours. With USMC, 1966-70, Capt. 1967-70, in Vietnam flew 163 combat missions. Decorated 11 Air medals, Navy Commednation medal with Combat V, Marine Corps E award, Vietnam Svc. medal, Vietnamese Cross of Gallantry with Palm. Mem. AIAA, Phi Kappa Phi. Avocations: classical music, electronic design; broke U.S. space endurance record of 84 continuous days aboard the Russian space station Mir. Office: Lyndon B Johnson Space Ctr NASA 2101 Nasa Rd 1 Houston TX 77058-3607

THAKOR, HAREN BHASKERRAO, manufacturing company executive; b. Ahmedabad, Gujarat, India, Dec. 12, 1938; came to U.S., 1960; s. Bhaskerrao Balvantrai and Kumud T.; m. Barbara Ann Martin, July 26, 1969; children: Manisha Ann, Sunil Haren. B.Civil Engring., Gujarat U., 1960; M.S. in Structural Engring., U. Ill., 1961; M.B.A., U. Calif.-Berkeley, 1965. Acct. Friden, Inc., San Leandro, Calif., 1965-67; sr. acct. bus. product group Xerox, Rochester, N.Y., 1967-69; mgr. budget and planning Xerox, Chgo., 1969-70; sr. policy analyst Xerox, Stamford, Conn., 1970-72, mgr. intercompany pricing, 1972-74; dir. bus. planning, automotive div. Arvin Industries, Inc., Columbus, Ind., 1974-77, v.p. fin. automotive div., 1977-81, treas., 1981-82, chief fin. officer, dir., 1982-90, pvt. investor, cons. Mem. AICPA, N.C. Assn. CPAs. Club: Chapel Hill Country. Home and Office: The Oaks 1023 Cleland Dr Chapel Hill NC 27514-5619

THAL, HERBERT LUDWIG, JR., electrical engineer, engineering consultant; b. Mt. Vernon, N.Y., Feb. 15, 1932; s. Herbert Ludwig and Mildred (Martinson) T.; m. Joan Madeline Ragsdale, Jan. 30, 1954; children: Herbert Ludwig III, Wayne, Carolyn, David, Eric. BEE, Rensselaer Poly. Inst., 1953, MEE, 1955, PhDEE, 1962. Rsch. assoc. Rensselaer Poly. Inst., Troy, N.Y., 1953-56; project engr. GE, Schenectady, 1956-67; staff engr. GE, King of Prussia, Pa., 1967-77, mgr. electromagnetics, 1977-89; v.p. Microlab/FXR, Livingston, N.J., 1989-92; adj. prof. Drexel U., Phila., 1983-90; adj. assoc. prof. U. Pa., Phila., 1986-87. 2d lt. U.S. Army, 1957. Fellow IEEE, Sigma Xi, Tau Beta Pi, Eta Kappa Nu. Presbyterian.

THAL, LEON JOEL, neuroscientist; b. N.Y.C., June 17, 1944; s. Bernard and Esther (Beller) T.; m. Donna Jean Norbo, June 25, 1967. MD, Downstate Med. Ctr., N.Y.C., 1969. Diplomate Am. Bd. Psychiatry and Neurology. Instr., asst. prof., assoc. prof. neurology Albert Einstein Coll. Medicine, Bronx, N.Y., 1975-85; assoc. prof. neurosci. U. Calif. San Diego, 1985-89, prof. neurosci., 1989—. Editor: Cognitive Disorders, 1992; contbr. chpts. in books and articles to profl. jours. Lt. comdr. USPHS, 1970-72. Home: 402 Brighton Ave Cardiff By The Sea CA 92007-1610 Office: Univ Calif Dept Neuroscience 9500 Gilman Dr La Jolla CA 92093-5003

THAL, STEVEN HENRY, lawyer; b. N.Y.C., Nov. 16, 1942; s. Michael and Mildred (Hirsch) T.; 1 child, Eric Alexander. BA, U. Mich., 1964, JD, 1967; postgrad., U. Tubingen, Fed. Republic Germany, 1967-68, New Sch. Social Rsch., N.Y.C., 1971-72. Bar: N.Y., 1968, U.S. Ct. Appeals (2d cir.) 1969, U.S. Dist. Ct. (so. and ea. dists.) N.Y. 1969, U.S. Supreme Ct. 1973. Assoc. Donovan, Leisure, Newton & Irvine, N.Y.C., 1968-69, Handler, Kleiman & Sukenik, N.Y.C., 1969-72; ptnr. Thal & Youtt, N.Y.C., 1972-84, Kaplan, Russin & Vecchi, N.Y.C., 1984-88, Summit, Rovins & Feldesman, N.Y.C., 1988-90, Oppenheimer Wolff & Donnelly, N.Y.C., 1990-94, LeBoeuf Lamb Greene & MacRae, N.Y.C., 1994—; pres. Export Assist Corp., Ft. Lee, N.J., 1988-94; bd. dirs. German-Am. Partnership Program, German Verein, N.Y.; trusted atty., Consulate Gen. of Fed. Repubic Germany, N.Y.C., 1986—, Austrian Trade Commn., N.Y.C., 1988—. Fulbright scholar, 1967-68; grantee Ford Found., 1967-68, Deutsche Akademisches Austauchdienst, 1967-68. Mem. ABA (internat. law com.), N.Y. State Bar Assn. (internat. law com.), Assn. Bar City N.Y., German Am. Lawyers Assn., Gesellschaft fuer Rechtsvergleichung. Avocations: boating, fishing, camping. Home: 17 Apple Ln New Milford CT 06776-4026 Office: LeBoeuf Lamb Greene & MacRae 125 W 55th St New York NY 10019-5369

THALACKER, ARBIE ROBERT, lawyer; b. Marquette, Mich., Apr. 17, 1935; s. Arbie Otto and Jeanne (Emmett) T.; m. Rita Annette Skaaren, Sept. 11, 1956 (div. July 1992); children: Marc Emmett, Christopher Paul, Robert Skaaren. AB, Princeton U., 1957; JD, U. Mich., 1960. Bar: N.Y. 1961, U.S. Ct. Appeals (2d cir.) 1962. Assoc. Shearman & Sterling, N.Y.C., 1960-68, ptnr., 1968—; dir. Detrex Corp., Detroit, 1981—, chmn. bd., 1993-96. Leader Rep. Dist. Com., 1966-68; v.p., trustee Greenwich Village Soc. for Hist. Preservation; trustee The Naropa Inst.; bd. dirs. Meredith Monk House Found., Shambhala Internat. Mem. ABA, N.Y. Bar Assn., Assn. Bar City N.Y. (securities regulatory commn. 1975-78), Wine and Food Soc. (bd. dirs. 1976-78, 85-93, 94—), Chevaliers du Tastevin, Commanderie de Bordeaux, Siwanoy Country Club (bd. govs. 1976-79), Derby Club, Links Club, Verbank Hunting and Fishing Club. Home: 17 Commerce St New York NY 10014-3763 Office: Shearman & Sterling 599 Lexington Ave New York NY 10022-6030

THALDEN, BARRY R., architect; b. Chgo., July 5, 1942; s. Joseph and Sibyl (Goodwin) Hechtenthal; m. Irene L. Mittleman, June 23, 1966 (div. 1989); 1 child, Stacey. BArch, U. Ill., 1965; M in Land Architecture, U. Mich., 1969. Landscape architect Hellmuth, Obata, Kassebaum, St. Louis, 1969-70; dir. landscape architecture PGAV Architects, St. Louis, 1970-71; pres. Thalden Corp (formerly Saunders-Thalden & Assocs. Inc.), St. Louis, 1971—. Prin. works include Rock Hill Park, 1975 (AIA award 1977), Wilson Residence, 1983 (AIA award), Nat. Bowling Hall of Fame, 1983 (St. Louis RCGA award 1984), Village Bogey Hills (Home Builders award 1985, St. L. ASLA award 1994), St. Louis U. Campus Mall (St. L. ASLA award 1989), Horizon Casino Resort, Lake Tahoe, Nev., St. Louis Airport's Radisson Hotel, Lady Luck, Treasure Bay, Palace Casinos, Biloxi, Miss., Boomtown Casino, New Orleans, Pres. Casino on the Admiral, St. Louis, Plaza of Champions, Busch Stadium, St. Louis. Bd. dirs. St. Louis Open Space Coun., 1973-83; apptd. Mo. Lands Architect Coun., 1990. Named Architect of Yr. Builder Architect mag., 1986. Fellow Am. Soc. Landscape Architects (nat. v.p. 1979-81, pres. St. Louis chpt. 1975, trustee 1976-79, nat. conv. chair 1991); mem. AIA, World Future Soc. (pres. St. Louis chpt. 1984-94, keynote conf. spkr. 1995). Avocations: painting, gardening, tennis, guitar. Home: 8 Edgewater Is Saint Louis MO 63105 Office: Thalden Corp 7777 Bonhomme Ave Ste 2200 Saint Louis MO 63105-1911

THALER, PAUL SANDERS, lawyer, mediator; b. Washington, May 4, 1961; s. Martin S. Thaler and Barbara (Friedman) Mishkin; m. Melinda Ann Frostic, Oct. 12, 1991; children: Rachel Leigh, Daniel Martin. AB, Vassar Coll., 1983; JD, Georgetown U., 1987. Bar: Md. 1987, D.C. 1988, U.S. Ct. Appeals (D.C. and 4th cirs.) 1988, U.S. Dist. Ct. Md. 1988, U.S. Ct. Appeals (fed. cir.) 1989, U.S. Dist. Ct. D.C. 1989, U.S. Ct. Internat. Trade 1990. Assoc. Cooter & Gell, Washington, 1987-93; pres. The Thaler Group, Bethesda, Md., 1993—; ptnr. The Robinson Law Firm, Washington, 1993-96, Thaler & Liebeler, 1996—. Treas. Montgomery Highlands Estates Homeowners Assn., Silver Spring, Md., 1990—; mediator Superior Ct. of D.C., 1991—; mem. adv. com. Vassar Coll. Fund, 1996—. Mem. ABA (sect. dispute resolution, vice chmn. ethics 1994—), D.C. Bar Assn., Md. Bar Assn., Soc. Profls. in Dispute Resolution, Acad. Family Mediators. Home: 3329 Sea Port Way Silver Spring MD 20902-2200 Office: Thaler & Liebeler 1919 Pennsylvania Ave NW Washington DC 20006-3402

THALER, RICHARD WINSTON, JR., investment banker; b. Boston, Apr. 9, 1951; s. Richard Winston and Victoria Louise (Sears) T.; m. Mary Alice Gast, June 28, 1980; children: Julia Davis, Sarah Sears, Hannah Warren. BA in Am. Polit. History cum laude, Princeton U., 1973; MBA, Harvard U., 1978. Salesman Media Networks, N.Y.C., 1973-74; banker Bank of Boston, Rio De Janeiro, Brazil, 1975-77, Boston, 1978-80; mng. dir. investment banking Lehman Bros., N.Y.C., 1980-96, B.T. Securities, N.Y.C., 1996—. Spl. gifts solicitor Princeton U. Ann. Giving, N.Y.C., 1987-88, class agt., 1988-93; trustee Daily Princetonian, 1989—, Episc. Divinity Sch., Cambridge, Mass., 1995—; mem. vestry Chapel of St. James the Fisherman, Wellfleet, Mass.; trustee at large Plimouth Plantation, Plymouth, Mass., 1995—. Mem. Mass. Soc. Mayflower Descendants, Princeton Club, Siwanoy Country Club, University Cottage Club, Bond Club of N.Y. Democrat. Episcopalian. Avocations: gardening, sailing, Am. polit. hist., exotic travel. Office: BT Securities One Bankers Trust Plaza New York NY 10006

THALHOFER, PAUL TERRANCE, lawyer; b. Eugene, Oreg., Oct. 27, 1954; s. Paul Albert and Elizabeth Ann (Wathen) T.; m. Cindy Ann Whitney, Aug. 7, 1977; 1 child, Brian Allen. BA, U. Colo., 1977; JD, U. Oreg., 1986. Disbursing fin. officer USMC, Okinawa, Japan, 1978-79, El Toro, Calif., 1979-80, Tustin, Calif., 1980-83; with law program dept. U. Oreg. USMC, Eugene, 1983-86; prosecuting atty. USMC, Camp Pendleton, Calif., 1986-87, def. atty., 1987, adminstrv. law atty., 1988-90, operational law atty., 1989-90; sr. legal advisor Marine Air Contingency Force USMC, Honduras, 1988; trial team leader Legal Team Delta/USMC, Camp Pendleton, Calif., 1990; legal advisor to commanding gen. USMC Forces/Operation Desert Shield, Saudi Arabia, 1990; legal advisor to comdg. gen. 3d marine aircraft ops. Desert Shield/Storm Wing, Bahrain, Saudi Arabia, 1990-91; trial team leader Legal Team Delta, Camp Pendleton, Calif., 1991-92; civil litigation atty. Bullivant, Houser, Bailey, Pendergrass & Hoffman, Portland, Oreg., 1992-93; assoc. Reif & Reif, Canby, Oreg., 1993-95; ptnr. Reif, Reif & Thalhofer, Canby, 1996—; adv. I Marine Expeditionary Force Augmentation Command Element, Camp Pendleton, Calif., 1996—. Lt. col. USMCR. Mem. Oreg. State Bar Assn., Clackamas County Bar Assn., Vaquero Riding Club (pres. 1983), Phi Delta Phi (v.p. chpt. 1985-86). Avocations: skiing, golf, fishing. Home: 335 SE 7th Way Canby OR 97013-8763 Office: Reif Reif & Thalhofer 273 N Grant St Canby OR 97013-3629

THALL, BURNETT MURRAY, newspaper executive; b. Toronto, Ont., Can., Sept. 27, 1922; s. Henry and Selina (Harris) Rosenthal; m. Eleanor Langbord, Sept. 23, 1945; children: Nelson Spencer, Martin Evan. B.A.Sc., U. Toronto, 1945, M.A.Sc., 1947, Ph.D., 1949. Registered profl. engr., Ont. Spl. lectr. applied sci. and enging. U. Toronto, 1947; cons. engr., then prodn. engr. Toronto Star, 1947-50, v.p., 1958-68, sr. v.p., 1968—, also dir.; chmn. Toronto Star Newspapers Ltd., elected chmn. of bd., 1996. Author articles in field. Trustee Atkinson Charitable Found.; bd. govs., hon. treas. Women's Coll. Hosp., 1963—; bd. dirs. Princess Margaret Hosp., Ont. Cancer Treatment and Research Found.; bd. govs. U. Toronto. Urgent Care Centre named in his honour Women's Coll. Hosp., 1989. Mem. Am. Newspaper Pubs. Assn., Assn. Profl. Engrs. Ont. (Citizenship medal 1991), Can. Daily Newspaper Pubs. Assn. Home: 15 Rosemary Ln, Toronto, ON Canada M5P 3E7 Office: The Toronto Star, 1 Yonge ST, Toronto, ON Canada M5E 1E6

THALL, RICHARD VINCENT, school system administrator; b. San Francisco, Sept. 12, 1940; s. Albert Vincent and Alice Stella (O'Brien) T.; m. Ellyn Marie Wisherop, June 15, 1963; children: Kristen Ellyn, Richard Vincent Jr. AA, City Coll. San Francisco, 1961; BA, San Francisco State Coll., 1964; MA, San Francisco State U., 1971. Cert. elem. tchr., Calif.; cert. secondary tchr., Calif.; cert. community coll. tchr., Calif. Tchr. biology San Francisco Unified Sch. Dist., 1965-66; tchr. biology Mt. Diablo Unified Sch. Dist., Concord, Calif., 1966-79, program dir. water environ. studies program, 1979—; ranger/naturalist State of Calif., Branna Island, 1973-78; naturalist Adventure Internat., Oakland, Calif., 1979-81; lectr. Princess Cruise Lines, 1982-84, Sea Goddess, 1986—, Sun Lines, 1987, Sitmar Lines, 1989, RCCL, 1991-95; spkr. commencements U. Calif., Berkeley, 1989. Author: Ecological Sampling of the Sacramento-San Joaquin Delta, 1976; Water Environment Studies Program, 1986; co-author: Project MER Laboratory Manual, 1982. Mem. Contra Costa County (Calif.) Natural Resources Commn., 1975-78, vice-chmn., 1977-78; active Save Mt. Diablo, Concord, 1969-76, v.p., 1974-75; mem. citizens com. Assn. Bay Area Govt. Water Quality, 1979-82, vice-chmn., 1980-82; active John Marsh Home Restoration Com., Martinez, Calif., 1977-78; mem. edn. adv. com. Marine World/Africa USA, Vallejo, Calif., 1988—; troop com. chmn. Boy Scouts Am., Concord, 1984-86, asst. scoutmaster, 1985-87. Recipient Recognition and Excellence cert. Assn. Calif. Sch. Adminstrs., 1984, Wood Badge award Boy Scouts Am., 1986; grantee State Calif., 1982, 84, San Francisco Estuary Project, 1992, EPA, 1992, Shell Oil Co., 1993. Mem. AAAS, Nat. Assn. Biology Tchrs., Nat., Audubon Soc., Am. Mus. Natural Hist., Nat. Geog. Soc., Smithsonian Instn. (assoc.). Republican. Roman Catholic. Avocations: skiing, jogging, reading, hiking, photography. Home: 1712 Lindenwood Dr Concord CA 94521-1109 Office: Mt Diablo Unified Sch Dist 1936 Carlotta Dr Concord CA 94519-1358

THAMES, EARL GLENN, accounting educator; b. West Monroe, La., Sept. 13, 1925; s. Archie L. and Lila Belle (Drummond) T.; m. Barbara Ann Thomas Yeates, Aug. 17, 1966; children: Edwin Clifton Yeates III, William Thomas Yeates, Earl Glenn Thames Jr. BBA, U. Miss., 1948, MBA, 1950, PhD, 1964. CPA, Miss., La. Acct. Ford Motor Co., Memphis, 1950-55, Deloitte, Touche, CPA's, New Orleans, 1956-60; grad. asst. U. Miss., Oxford, 1961-64; prof. acctg. Northwestern State U., Natchitoches, La., 1964-87, chmn. dept. acctg., 1964-86; prof. acctg. Fred M. Hale Sch. Bus. East Tex. Bapt. U., Marshall, 1987—, interim dean, 1994-95; cons. in field. Author: Investors Guide to Accounting Statements-Copyright, 1989, Essentials of Accounting-Copyright, 1995; contbr. articles to profl. jours. With inf. U.S. Army, 1943-45, ETO. Decorated Purple Heart. Mem. AICPA, Am. Acctg. Assn., La. Soc. CPAs, Am. Legion, U. Miss. Alumni Assn., Rotary. Republican. Methodist. Avocations: amateur historian, reading. Home: 711 Hancock Natchitoches LA 71457 Office: East Tex Bapt U Fred M Hale Sch Bus 1209 N Grove St Marshall TX 75670-1423

THARP, BENJAMIN CARROLL, JR., architect; b. Austin, Tex., Sept. 3, 1919; s. Benjamin Carroll Tharp and Norris (Ophelia) Wallis; m. Mae Sibley; children: Ronald Emery, Carolyn Jeanine Tharp Love. BArch, U. Tex., 1943. Registered architect, Tex. Draftsman Wurdeman & Beckett, L.A., 1944, Richard Neutra, L.A., 1945, Merrill Baird, L.A., 1946, Golemon & Rolfe, Houston, 1947, Milton Foy Martin, Houston, 1948; prin. Koetter & Tharp, Houston, 1949-64, Koetter, Tharp & Cowell, Houston, 1964-78; architect Koetter, Tharp, Cowell and Lockwood, Andrews, Newman, Houston, 1978-81; ret. Lockwood, Andrews, Newman, 1981. Bd. dirs. Harris County Soil and Water Conservation Dist., Houston, 1972-82; pres. Constrn. Industry Coun., Houston, 1970. Recipient 1st Restoration award Red Cedar Shingle and Handsplit Shake Bur./AIA, Seattle, 1975. Fellow AIA, Tex. Soc. Architects (chmn. hist. resources com. 1986); mem. Montgomery (Tex.) Hist. Soc., Optimist Club (pres. Houston chpt. 1970). Republican. Baptist. Home: RR 3 Box 51A Montgomery TX 77356-2323

THARP, ROLAND GEORGE, psychology, education educator; b. Galveston, Tex., June 6, 1930; s. Oswald Roland and Berma Lucille (Keefer) T.; m. Stephanie Dalton; children: Donald Martin, Thomas Roland, David Michael, Julie. Student, Middlebury Coll., 1956, 60; BA cum laude, U. Houston, 1957; MA, U. Mich., 1958, PhD, 1961. Cert. Am. Bd. Examiners in Profl. Psychology. Reporter Tex. City Sun, 1946-47; mgr. Tharp Lumber Co., LaMarque, Tex., 1949-54; intern VA Hosp., Menlo Park, Calif., 1960; asst. prof. U. Ariz., Tucson, 1961-65, assoc. prof., 1965-68; prof., dir. clin. studies, dir. multicultural ctr. for higher edn. U. Hawaii, Honolulu, 1968-87; provost and v.p. for acad. affairs U.S. Internat. U., San Diego, 1987-89; prof. edn., psychology U. Calif., Santa Cruz, 1990—; dir. Nat. Rsch. Ctr. for Diversity, 1995—; dir. Ctr. for Rsch. on Edn., Diversity and Excellence, 1996—; prin. investigator Kamehameha Early Edn. Program, Honolulu, 1969-89; field selection officer Peace Corps, Washington, 1965-67. Author: (poetry) Highland Station, 1978; co-author: (book) Behavior Modification in the Natural Environment, 1969, Self-Directed Behavior, 1980, Rousing Minds to Life, 1988; writer, producer, dir. film Scenes from the Life, 1981 (Purchase prize The Contemporary Mus. 1981). Mem. Bd. Psychologist Examiners, Ariz., 1964-67; pres. Hawaii Literary Arts Coun., Honolulu, 1982. Robert Frost fellow Middlebury Coll., 1960; recipient Am. Film Mag. award for filmmaking Hawaii Internat. Film Festival, 1990, Grawemeyer award edn., 1993. Mem. Am. Ednl. Rsch. Assn., Am. Anthropol. Assn. Episcopalian. Avocations: tennis, painting. Office: University of California CREDE 1156 High St Santa Cruz CA 95064-1077

THARP, TWYLA, dancer, choreographer; b. Portland, Ind., July 1, 1941; m. Peter Young (div.); m. Robert Huot (div.); 1 child, Jesse. Student, Pomona Coll.; BA in Art History, Barnard Coll., 1963; D of Performing Arts (hon.), Calif. Inst. Arts, 1978, Brown U., 1981, Bard Coll., 1981; LHD, Ind. U., 1987; DFA, Pomona Coll., 1987; studied with Richard Thomas, Merce Cunningham, Igor Schwezoff, Louis Mattox, Paul Taylor, Margaet Craske, Erick Hawkins. Dancer Paul Taylor Dance Co., 1963-65; freelance choreographer with own modern dance troupe and various other cos. including Joffrey Ballet and Am. Ballet Theatre, 1965-87; founder, choreographer Twyla Tharp Dance Found., N.Y.C., 1965-87; artistic assoc., resident choreographer Am. Ballet Theatre, N.Y.C., 1987-91; teaching residencies various colls. and univs. including U. Mass., Oberlin Coll., Walker Art Ctr., Boston U.; choreographer White Oak Dance Project. Choreographer: Tank Dive, 1965, Re-Moves, 1966, One Two Three, 1966, Forevermore, 1967, Generation, 1968, Medley, 1969, After Suite, 1969, Dancing in the Streets of London and Paris, 1969, The One Hundreds, 1970, The Fugue, 1970, The Big Pieces, 1971, Eight Jelly Rolls, 1971, The Raggedy Dances, 1972, Deuce Coupe, 1973, As Time Goes By, 1974, Sue's Leg, 1975, Ocean's Motion, 1975, Push Comes to Shove, 1976, Once More Frank, 1976, Mud, 1977, Baker's Dozen, 1979, When We Were Very Young, 1980, Nine Sinatra Songs, 1982, The Catherine Wheel, 1982, Bach Partita, 1984, The Little Ballet, 1984, (with Jerome Robbins) Brahms/Handel, 1984, At the Supermarket, 1984, In the Upper Room, 1987, Ballare, 1987, Stations of the Crossed, 1988, Everlast, 1989, Quartet, 1989, Bum's Rush, 1989, The Rules of the Game, 1990, Brief Fling, 1990, Grand Pas: Rhythm of the Saints, 1991, Deuce Coupe II, 1992, The Men's Piece, 1992, (with Mikhail Baryshnikov) Cutting Up, 1992-93, Demeter and Persephone, 1993, Waterbaby Bagatelles, 1994, Demeter and Persephone, 1994, Red, White & Blues, 1995, How Near Heaven, 1995, I Remember Clifford, 1995, Jump Start, 1995, Americans We, 1995; (film) Hair, 1979, Ragtime, 1981, Amadeus, 1984, White Nights, 1985, Valmont, 1989, I'll Do Anything, 1994; (video spls.) Making Television Dance, 1977, CBS Cable Confessions of a Corner Maker, 1980; (Broadway shows) Sorrow Floats, 1985, Singin' In The Rain, 1985; (TV) Baryshnikov by Tharp (Emmy award Outstanding Choreography 1985, Emmy award Outstanding Writing of Classical Music/Dance Programming 1985, Emmy award Outstanding Directing of Classical Music/Dance Programming 1985), The Catherine Wheel, 1982 (Emmy award nom. Outstanding Choreography 1982); author (autobiography): When Push Comes to Shove, 1992. MacArthur Found. Chgo. fellow, 1992; recipient Creative Arts award Brandeis U., 1972, Dance mag. award, 1981, Univ. Excellence medal Columbia U., 1987, Lions of the Performing Arts award N.Y. Pub. Libr., 1989, Samuel M. Scripps award Am. Dance Festival, 1990.

THARPE, FRAZIER EUGENE, journalist; b. Panama City, Fla., Jan. 10, 1941; s. Henry Clayton and Margaret Jane (Jenkins) T.; m. Barbara Ann Hembree, Oct. 30, 1971. B.A. in Polit. Sci. and History, Vanderbilt U., Nashville, 1963. Reporter Miami (Fla.) News, 1963; reporter U.P.I., Atlanta and Columbia, S.C., 1964; pub. relations exec. Atlanta, 1965-69; fin. editor Atlanta Constn., 1969-73. Editorial assoc., columnist, 1974-83, columnist Helpline, ConsumerWatch, 1983—, Free-lance writer. Office: 72 Marietta St NW Atlanta GA 30303-2804

THATCHER, BLYTHE DARLYN, assistant principal; b. Kansas City, Mo., Aug. 15, 1947; d. Aubria DeVille and Irene Lois (Cowan) Thatcher. AA, Ricks Coll., Rexburg, Idaho, 1967; BS, Brigham Young U., 1971, MEd, 1983, EdS, 1985. Cert. elem., spl. edn., adminstr., Utah. Spl. edn. tchr. K-6 J. Allen Axson Sch. #8, Jacksonville, Fla., 1971-72; resource tchr., dept. chair Westland Elem. Sch., Sandy, Utah, 1972-78; resource English tchr. Mt. Jordan Mid. Sch., Sandy, Utah, 1978-80; resource tchr., dept. chair Butler Mid. Sch., Sandy, Utah, 1980-87, tchr. specialist/English tchr., 1987-89, adminstrv. asst./English tchr., 1989-90; asst. prin. Bonneville Jr. High Sch., Salt Lake City, 1990-93, Granger High Sch., Salt Lake City, 1993-96, Olympus High Sch., 1996—; presenter, instr. state-wide writing confs., workshops, 1987-89. Editor, contbg. author: Heroines of the Restoration, 1997; contbg. author: (poetry book) Where Feelings Flower, 1992, LDS Women's Treasury, 1997; editor The Am. Mother Mag., 1994-95; editor: A Fruitful Season, 1988; contbg. editor: Singular Life, 1987; editl. asst. The Legacy Remembered and Renewed 1914-70, 1982; chmn. nat. editl. bd. Am. Mothers, Inc., 1994-95; exec. editor: Mother Love, 1995. Mem. Utah Office of Edn. Quality Indicates in Utah Schs. Task Force, Salt Lake City, 1989-90; county del. Utah Rep. Party, Salt Lake City, 1978; vol. Am. Cancer Soc., Utah Heart Assn., Detention Ctr., 1977-79. Recipient grant Assn. H.S. Asst. Prins., 1993—. Fellow Utah Prins. Acad.; mem. Granite Assn. of Sch. Adminstrs. (bd. dirs. 1992-94, editor Adminstrv. Advantage 1992-94), Granite Assn. Jr. High Asst. Prins. (pres. 1992-93), Jordan Edn. Assn. (editor, originator Good Apples newsletter 1984-85), Utah Assn. of Women (chpt. and region pres. 1978-79), Parent Tchr. Student Assn. (2nd v.p. 1987-88), Utah Assn. Secondary Sch. Prins., Utah Found., Utah Women's Ednl. Adminstrs. Assn. (secondary dist. rep. 1995—, newsletter editro 1997—), Utah Days of '47 (sub-com. chair Pioneer of Progress awards 1995—), Granite Assn. H.S. Asst. Prins. Mem. LDS Ch. Avocations: writing, editing, poetry, speech writer. Home: 1254 Cove Park Cir Murray UT 84123 Office: Granite Sch Dist 340 E 3545 S Salt Lake City UT 84115-4615

THATCHER, GEORGE ROBERT, banker; b. Austin, Pa., Sept. 18, 1922; S. Walter Robert and Roberta Estelle (Bernard) T.; widowed; children: Georgia Anne Thatcher Faneca, Janie Estelle Thatcher Holmes, Walter Wimberly. BA in English, U. Miss., 1948; grad. diploma in bus., Ind. U., 1973; degree of distinction, Inst. Fin. Edn., Chgo. Enlisted U.S. Army, 1942, advanced through grades to maj., 1948, stationed in Pacific, Korea, ret., 1952; ptnr. Rand-Thatcher Advt. Agy., Gulfport, Miss., 1948-69; COO Coast Fed. Savings, Gulfport, 1969-81; pres. coast divsn. Magnolia Fed. Bank, Gulfport, 1981-92; also bd. dirs Magnolia Fed. Bank, Hattiesburg, Miss.; councilman City of Gulfport, 1989; commisary Anglican Diocese of No. Malawi, 1995—; bd. dirs. Miss. Econ. Coun., Jackson, 1991-94. Author: Misrepresentation in Mississippi, 1954. Chmn. Miss. Arts Commn., Jackson, 1991—; past chmn. United Way, Harrison County, Gulfport Carnegie Libr., Harrison County Libr.; past trustee Gulfport Meml. Hosp. Found.; past pres. Episcopal Laymen of Miss.; past sr. warden, layreader St. Peter's Episcopal Ch., Gulfport; mem., co-chmn. planned giving com. Episcopal Diocese Miss.; past dir. Miss. Hist. Assn.; bd. dirs. So. Arts Fedn., 1996—. Decorated Bronze Star; named Outstanding Citizen, Gulfport Jaycees. Mem. Gulfport Rotary Club (pres. 1995-96, named Citizen of Yr. 1993, Paul Harris fellow), Century Club (pres.), Gulfport Yacht Club (chmn. Olympic Sailing Commn.), Bayou Bluff Tennis Club, Great So. Club., Newcomen Soc. of U.S., Miss. Gulf Coast C. of C. Republican. Avocations: tennis, chess, reading, classical music. Home: 1302 2nd St Gulfport MS 39501-2219 Office: Magnolia Fed Bank 2200 14th St Gulfport MS 39501-2005

THATCHER, REX HOWARD, newspaper publisher; b. Williamston, Mich., Feb. 22, 1932; s. Howard Alden and Emma (Rappuhn) T.; m. Yvonne Lee Taft, Mar. 22, 1954; children: Thomas D., Richard M., Karen L., Dana L. BJ, Mich. State U., 1954. Advt. salesman The Jackson (Mich.) Citizen Patriot, 1964-69, promotion mgr., 1970, mktg. dir., 1971, asst. gen. mgr., 1972; pub. The Saginaw News, 1990—. Bd. dirs. Bay Medical Ctr., 1983—; mem., officer Bay Area C. of C., 1974-83, Bay Area Community

Found., 1982-88. Mem. Mich. Press Assn., Inland Daily Press Assn., Am. Newspaper Pubs. Assn., Rotary. Presbyterian. Avocations: fly fishing, hunting, competitive and postal chess. Office: The Saginaw News 203 S Washington Ave Saginaw MI 48607-1244*

THATCHER, SANFORD GRAY, publishing executive; b. Washington, Aug. 4, 1943; s. Harold Wesley and Genevieve (Harnett) T.; m. Barbara Boal, June 1966 (div.); m. Catherine Dammeyer, May 27, 1980 (div.); m. Robin Glucroft, June 8, 1997; children: Corinne, Christopher. BA summa cum laude, Princeton U., 1965, postgrad., 1966-67; postgrad., Columbia U., 1965-66. Editor manuscript div. Princeton (N.J.) U. Press, 1967-69, editor social sci. divsn., 1969-78, asst. dir., 1978-85, editor in chief, 1985-89; dir. Pa. State U. Press, University Park, 1989—. Author: AAUP Guide to 1976 Copyright Law, 1977; contbr. articles to profl. jours. Mem. Ch. and Soc. Commn., St. Paul's United Meth. Ch., 1990-92; bd. dirs. The Daily Collegian newspaper, Pa. State U., 1991—. Mem. Am. Philos. Assn., L.Am. Studies Assn., Assn. Am. Pubs. (copyright com. 1972—, freedom to read com. 1982-86), Assn. Am. Univ. Presses (chmn. copyright com. 1972, bd. dirs. 1995—), Assn. for Copyright Enforcement (bd. dirs. 1988-93), Copyright Clearance Ctr. (bd. dirs. 1992—). Democrat. Methodist. Avocations: swimming, sailing, tennis, rare book collecting, music. Home: 1239 Circleville Rd State College PA 16803-3111 Office: Pa State U Press 820 N University Dr University Park PA 16802-1012

THATCHER, SHARON LOUISE, medical educator; b. Seattle, Feb. 17, 1942; d. Ralph McDonald and Audra Joy (Clauson) Thatcher. AB, Ga. State Coll., Milledgeville, 1964; degree in med. tech., Spartanburg Gen. Hosp., 1965; MEd, Ga. State U., 1981, EdS, 1987. Technologist chemistry dept. Greenville (S.C.) Gen. Hosp., 1965-66, Emory U. Hosp., Atlanta, 1966; hematology and bone marrow technologist Office of Dr. Spencer Brewer Jr., Atlanta, 1966-67; asst. lab. supr. chemistry dept. Grady Hosp., Atlanta, 1967-69; lab. technologist Ga. Mental Health Inst., Atlanta, 1969-70; chief lab. technologist Habersham County Hosp., Clarksville, Ga., 1970-72; survey officer Ga. Dept. Human Resources, 1972-74; part owner, gen. mgr. Nolan Biology Labs., Stone Mountain, Ga., 1974-75; bacteriology dept. technologist Northside Hosp., Atlanta, 1975-76; sales rep. Curtin Mathison Sci. Products, Atlanta, 1976-78; night supr. labs. Decatur (Ga.) Hosp., 1978; dir., ednl. coord. med. lab. tech. and phlebotomy tech. programs DeKalb Tech. Inst., Clarkston, Ga., 1978—, chairperson dept. allied health, 1980-86; cons. Med. Lab. Cons., Atlanta, 1987—; mem. site survey team Nat. Accrediting Agy. for Clin. Lab. Scis., Chgo., 1980, 85, 91, site survey team coord., 1993, 94, 95, 96; speaker and presenter in field. Named Outstanding Speaker Am. Soc. for Phlebotomy Technicians, 1986. Mem. Am Soc. for Clin. Lab. Scientists (exhibit chair region III 1971-72), Am. Microbiology Soc., Ga. Soc. for Clin. Lab. Scientists (chair membership 1970-71, exhibit chair 1971-72, pres.-elect 1974-75, pres. 1975-76, bd. dirs. 1976-77, convention chair ann. state meeting 1989-90, Omicron Sigma award 1990, Gloria F. Gilbert achievement award 1993), Kappa Delta Pi. Avocations: ceramics, cross-stitch, 5K walks, gardening. Office: DeKalb Tech Inst 495 N Indian Creek Dr Clarkston GA 30021-2359

THAU, WILLIAM ALBERT, JR., lawyer; b. St. Louis, June 22, 1940; s. William Albert and Irene Elizabeth (Mundy) T.; m. Jane Hancock, Sept. 7, 1961; children: William Albert, Caroline Jane, Jennifer Elizabeth. BS in Indsl. Mgmt., Georgia Inst. Tech., 1962; JD, U. Tex., 1965. Bar: Tex. 1965. Ptnr., head of real estate sect. Jenkens & Gilchrist, Dallas, 1965—; chmn. real estate developer/builder symposium S.W. Legal Found, 1975-79; bd. dirs. Southwestern Film Archives, So. Meth. U.; lectr. Practicing Law Inst. Bd. dirs. St. Philips Sch., Tex., Dallas, 1988, So. Meth. U.; trustee Dallas Can. Acad., 1987-88. Mem. ABA, Tex. State Bar Assn. (chmn real estate, probate, trust law sect.), Am. Coll. Real Estate Lawyers, Brook Hollow Golf Club. Republican. Episcopalian. Author: Negotiating the Purchase and Sale of Real Estate, 1975; editor Tex. State Bar Assn. Newsletter on Real Estate, Probate & Trust Law, 1978-81, Best Lawyers in Am., 1983—; contbr. articles to Real Estate Rev., 1983—. Office: Jenkens & Gilchrist 1445 Ross Ave Ste 3200 Dallas TX 75202-2770

THAXTON, MARVIN DELL, lawyer, farmer; b. Electra, Tex., June 1, 1925; s. Montgomery Dell and Ida (Scheurer) T.; m. Carolyn Moore Alexander, Aug. 30, 1949; children: Rebecca Thaxton Henderson, Gail Thaxton Fogleman, Marvin D. Jr. JD, U. Ark., 1949. Bar: Ark. 1949, U.S. Dist. Ct. (ea. dist.) Ark. 1952, U.S. Dist. Ct. (we. dist.) Ark. 1978, U.S. Dist. Ct. (we. dist.) Okla., U.S. Supreme Ct. 1987. Prin. Thaxton Furniture Co., Newport, Ark., 1949-50; ptnr. Thaxton, Hout & Howard, Attys., Newport, 1950-97; spl. assoc. justice Ark. Supreme Ct., 1978, 84; examiner Ark. State Bd. Law Examiners, 1968-73, chmn. 1973. Pres. Newport C. of C., 1956, Newport Sch. Dist. Bd. Edn., 1964; past pres. Ea. Ark. Young Men's Clubs; adult leader Newport area Boy Scouts Am., 1949-94. Officer U.S. Mcht. Marine, 1945-46, PTO. Fellow Ark. Bar Found.; mem. Ark. Bar Assn. (honor cert. 1973), Ark. Trial Lawyers Assn., Newport Rotary Club (past pres., Paul Harris fellow 1990), Sigma Chi. Democrat. Methodist. Avocations: hunting, fishing, boating. Home: 12 Lakeside Ln Newport AR 72112-3914 Office: Thaxton Hout & Howard 600 Third St Newport AR 72112-3218

THAYER, CHARLES J., investment banker; b. Abilene, Kans., Feb. 28, 1944; s. Bruce V. and Neoma (Obermeyer) T.; 1 child, Travis J. Grad., U. Kans., 1967. Exec. v.p., CFO Citizens Fidelity Bank, Louisville, 1977-87; exec. v.p. fin. PNC Bank Corp., Pitts., 1987-89; chmn., mng. dir. Chartwell Capital Ltd., Ft. Lauderdale, Fla., 1989—; interim chmn. Sunbeam-Oster, Providence, 1993; bd. dirs. Sunbeam-Oster, Providence, 1993; bd. dirs. Sunbeam Corp., Ft. Lauderdale, 1990—, vice chmn., 1996—; adv. dir. Keefe Mgrs., Inc., N.Y.C., 1990—; bd. dirs. NRG Generating (U.S.) Mpls., 1996—, Digital Wireless Corp., LA., 1995—. Trustee Cystic Fibrosis Found., Washington, 1980—; chmn. Cystic Fibrosis Svcs., Washington, 1994—. Avocation: sailing. Office: Chartwell Capital Ltd 420 Isle Of Capri Dr Fort Lauderdale FL 33301-2438

THAYER, EDNA LOUISE, medical facility administrator, nurse; b. Madelia, Minn., May 21, 1936; d. Walter William Arthur and Hilda Engel Emily Ann (Geistfeld) Wilke; m. David LeRoy Thayer, Aug. 30, 1958; children: Scott, Tamara, Brenda. Diploma in nursing, Bethesda Luth., 1956; BS in Nursing Edn., U. Minn., 1960; MSN, Washington U., St. Louis, 1966; MS in Counseling, Mankato (Minn.) State U., 1972. Cert. nursing adminstr. advanced ANA. Nurse Bethesda Luth. Hosp., St. Paul, 1956-58, U. Minn. Hosp., Mpls., 1958; from nurse to asst. head nurse supr., edn. dir. Fairmont (Minn.) Community Hosp., 1959-63; instr. Alton (Ill.) Meml. Hosp., 1963-66; from nursing instr. to assoc. prof. and dean Sch. Nursing Mankato State U., 1966-77; asst. adminstr. Rice County Dist. One Hosp., Faribault, Minn., 1977-89; RN, adminstrv. supr. St. Peter (Minn.) Regional Treatment Ctr., 1990-96; spkr., 1996—; nurse surveyor Minn. Dept. Tech. Edn., St. Paul, 1980-93; mem. adv. co. LPN and MA programs Tech. Inst., Faribault, 1977—. Mem. Rice County Ext. Bd., Faribault, 1986-91, adult leader 4-H Club, Rice County and St. Paul, 1971—; advisor Med. Explorers, Faribault, 1977-89; mem. Rep. Rodosovich Health Com., Faribault, 1984-94; coun. mem. Our Savior's Luth. Ch., Faribault, 1984-87; mem. Rep. Boudreau Health Care Adv. Com., 1996—. Recipient alumni award Nat. 4-H Club, 1983, Disting. Friend of Nursing award Mankato State U., 1995. Mem. Minn. Orgn. Nurse Execs. (bd. dirs. 1987-89), Dist. F Nursing Svc. Adminstrs. (pres. 1980-82), Minn. Nurses Assn. (bd. dirs. 1982-87, Pres.'s award 1983, pres. 5th dist. 1974, 75, pres. 13th dist. 1984-86), AAUW, Sigma Theta Tau, Delta Kappa Gamma (pres. Pi chptr. 1982-84, Woman of Achievement award 1985), Hosp. Aux. Republican. Avocations: crafts, volunteer work, theater, plays. Home: RR 1 Box 7B Elysian MN 56028-9731

THAYER, EDWIN CABOT, musician; b. Weymouth, Mass., May 16, 1935; s. Elliot Pierce and Barbara (Senior) T.; m. Joan Peregoy, June 24, 1961; children: Bruce, Laura, Richard, William. MusB cum laude, U. Ill., 1957, MusM with performing honors, 1958. Instr. horn Brevard (N.C.) Music Center, summers 1957, 58, 62; grad. asst. U. Ill., 1957-58; prin. horn Washington Brass Choir, 1958-61, Norfolk (Va.) Symphony, 1961-65, Richmond (Va.) Symphony, 1960-72; assoc. prof. music Va. Commonwealth U. (formerly Richmond Profl. Inst.), Richmond, 1963-72; head piano dept. Va. Commonwealth U., 1965-69, head brass and winds dept., 1969-72, music librarian, 1965-72; prin. horn Washington Nat. Symphony, 1972—; hornist Nat. Symphony Wind Soloists, 1978—, Euterpe Chamber Players, 1981-89, Chamber Soloists Washington, 1986—, Tanglewood (Mass.) Berkshire Music Festival Orch., summers 1955-56; hornist Brass Prins. and Woodwind Prins. Quintets Nat. Symphony Orch., 1988—; solo recitalist, chamber ensemble recitalist, horn soloist; guest artist Internat. Horn Workshops, Hartford, Ct., 1977, Potsdam, N.Y., 1981, Towson, Md., 1985; hornist 20th Century Consort, 1994—; mem. World Philharm. Orch., Rio de Janeiro, 1986, Highlands, N.C. Music Festival, 1995—. Served with AUS, 1958-61. Disting. tchr. White House Commn. on Presdl. Scholars, 1995. Mem. Internat. Horn Soc., Musicians Union, Pi Kappa Lambda, Phi Mu Alpha Sinfonia. Home: 11902 Triple Crown Rd Reston VA 20191-3016 Office: Nat Symphony Orch Kennedy Ctr for Performing Arts Washington DC 20566

THAYER, JANE See WOOLLEY, CATHERINE

THAYER, LEE, educator, author, consultant; b. Grenola, Kans., Dec. 18, 1927; s. Garrett Osborne and Ruth (Ray) T.; m. Suzanne Katherine Schwan, Apr. 27, 1986: children: Joshua Lee, Jessica Sam. B.A. cum laude, U. Wichita, 1953, M.A., 1956; Ph.D., U. Okla., 1963. Instr. U. Okla., 1956-58; with Pratt & Whitney Co., Inc., 1958-59; assoc. prof. adminstrn. and psychology U. Wichita, 1959-64; prof., dir. Center Advanced Study Communication, U. Mo. at Kansas City, 1964-68; George H. Gallup prof. communication research U. Iowa, Iowa City, 1968-73; prof. communication studies Simon Fraser U., Burnaby, B.C., Can., 1973-76; vis. prof. U. Mass., 1976-77; Fulbright prof. U. Helsinki, Finland, 1977; Disting. vis. prof. U. Houston, 1978-80; prof. and past chmn. communication U. Wis.-Parkside, 1978-93, founding dir. Parkside Honors Program, 1983-87; disting. vis. prof. Kuring-gai Coll. Advanced Edn., Sydney, Australia, 1986, Queensland (Australia) U. Tech., 1994; cons. to govt. and industry, 1956—. Author: Administrative Communication, 1961, Communication and Communication Systems, 1968, On Communication: Essays in Understanding, 1988, Pieces: Toward a Revisioning of Communication/Life, 1997, Making High-Performance Organizations: The Logic of Virtuosity, 1997; editor: Communication: Theory and Research, 1967, Communication: Concepts and Perspectives, 1967, Communication: General Semantics Perspectives, 1969, Communication: Ethical and Moral Issues, 1974, Ethics, Morality, and the Media, 1980, Organization-Communication: Emerging Perspectives I, 1985, vol. II, 1987, vol. III, 1995, vol. IV, 1994, editor book series: The Human Context, 1985—; founding editor Communication, 1970-80. Served to lt. USNR, 1953-55. Danforth Found. tchr., 1961-63; Found. Econ. Edn. fellow, 1963-64; Ford Found. fellow, 1963-64, 65, Fulbright fellow U. Helsinki, 1977-78. Home: 908 Melrose Avenue Ext Tryon NC 28782-3223

THAYER, MARTHA ANN, small business owner; b. Santa Fe, N.Mex., May 8, 1936; d. Duren Howard and Lena Odessa (Fox) Shields; m. Norman S. Thayer Jr., Jan. 30, 1960; children: Murray Norman, Tanya Noelle. BS, U. N.Mex., 1960. Child welfare worker State of N.Mex., Farmington and Santa Fe, 1961-64; owner Baskets by Thayer, Albuquerque, 1975-83, Noelle's, Albuquerque, 1985-89; ptnr., co-owner Indian Originals, Albuquerque, 1989-94, Native Design, 1995-96; owner Martha A. Thayer, 1996—; treas. DHS Properties, Inc., 1994—; agt. for Elizabeth Abeyta, Adrian Quintana, Alexandria Rohrscheib, Albuquerque, 1995—; crafts instr. Village Wool, Continuing Edn., Albuquerque, 1975-78; trustee Shields Trust, 1994—. Contbr. articles, revs. to craft publs.; juried show, Mus. of Internat. Folk Arts, 1975; baskets exhibited in group shows at N.Mex. State Fair, 1980 (1st place award), Women's Show, 1983 (1st place award). Campaign mgr. Dem. Candidate for State Supreme Ct., Bernalillo County, N.Mex., 1970; founding mem. Women's Polit. Caucus, Bernalillo County; chmn. Mother's March of Dimes, Bernalilto County, 1974. Mem. Hist. Preservation Soc., Petroleum Club, Genealogy Club of Albuquerque Pub. Libr., Mus. Albuquerque (assoc.). Avocations: genealogy, gardening, anthropology, politics, antiques, Native American art collector.

THAYER, RUSSELL, III, airlines executive; b. Phila., Dec. 5, 1922; s. Russell and Shelby Wentworth (Johnson) T.; m. Elizabeth Wright Mifflin, June 12, 1947; children: Elizabeth, Dixon, Shelby, Samuel, David. Student, St. George's Sch., 1937-42; A.B., Princeton U., 1949. Mgmt. trainee Eastern Air Lines, 1949-52; mgr. cargo sales and service Am. Airlines, Los Angeles, 1952-63; v.p. mktg. Seaboard World Airlines, N.Y.C., 1963-70; sr. v.p. Braniff Airways, Inc., Dallas, 1970-72; exec. v.p. Braniff Airways, Inc., 1972-77, pres., chief oper. officer, 1977-80, vice chmn., 1981-82; dir. (Braniff Airways, Inc.), 1971-82; v.p. Pan Am. World Airways, Inc., N.Y.C., 1982-84, sr. v.p., 1984-88; sr. v.p. Airline Econs., Inc., Washington, 1988—, also bd. dirs., 1988—; dir. Ft. Worth Nat. Bank, 1977-82; vice chmn. Airline Capital Assn; bd. dirs. Kiwi Internat. Airlines, Inc., World Aux. Power Corp. Mem. Trinity Ch. Ushers Guild, Princeton, N.J., 1968—; Trustee Aviation Hall of Fame N.J. Served with USAAF, 1942-45, ETO. Decorated D.F.C., Air medal with 11 oak leaf clusters. Mem. Am. Aviation Hist. Assn., Air Force Assn., Exptl. Aircraft Assn., Nat. Aeros. Assn., Ivy Club (Princeton), Pretty Brook Tennis Club (Princeton), Bay Head (N.J.) Yacht Club, Nassau Club (Princeton), Princeton Club (N.Y.C.), Phila. Club, Delta Psi. Home: Hulfish St Apt 17-I Princeton NJ 08542-3706 Office: Airline Econs Inc 1130 Connecticut Ave NW Ste 675 Washington DC 20036-3917

THAYER, W(ALTER) STEPHEN, III, state supreme court justice; b. N.Y.C., Jan. 13, 1946; s. Walter S. and Dorothy (Pflum) T.; m. Judith O. O'Brien, Dec. 27, 1982. B.A. in Polit. Sci., Belmont Abbey Coll., 1968; J.D., John Marshall Law Sch., Chgo., 1974. Bar: N.H. 1975, U.S. Dist. Ct. N.H. 1975, U.S. Ct. Appeals (1st cir.) 1981. Sole practice Law Offices W. Stephen Thayer, III, Manchester, N.H., 1975-81; U.S. atty. Dist. N.H., Concord, 1981-84; assoc. justice N.H. Superior Ct., 1984-86, N.H. Supreme Ct., 1986—; legal counsel N.H. State Senate, 1978-80, N.H. Rep. State Com., 1977-80; cons. GSA, Washington, 1981. Alt. del. Rep. nat. conv., 1980; presdl. elector electoral coll., 1980. Served to 1st lt. U.S. Army, 1968-71. Decorated Bronze Star. Mem. N.H. Bar Assn., N.H. Trial Lawyers Assn. Roman Catholic. Home: 1943 Elm St Manchester NH 03104-2528 Office: NH Supreme Ct One Noble Dr Concord NH 03301*

THEALL, DONALD FRANCIS, retired university president; b. Mt. Vernon, N.Y., Oct. 13, 1928; s. Harold A. and Helen (Donaldson) T.; m. Joan Ada Benedict, June 14, 1950; children: Thomas, Margaret, John, Harold, Lawrence, Michael. BA with honors, Yale U., 1950; MA with 1st class honors, U. Toronto, 1951, PhD with 1st class honors, 1954. Teaching fellow U. Toronto, 1950-52, mem. faculty, 1952-65, prof. English, chmn. joint depts. English, 1964-65; dir. communication studies York U., also prof. English and communications, 1965-66; dir. English Atkinson Coll., 1965-66; mem. faculty McGill U., Montreal, Que., Can., 1966-79; prof. English McGill U., 1966-79, chmn. dept., 1966-74, Molson prof., 1972-79, dir. grad. program in communications, 1976-79; adj. prof. grad. comm. McGill U., Montreal, Que., Can., 1989-91; pres., vice chancellor, prof. English and cultural studies Trent U., Peterborough, Ont., 1980-87, univ. prof., 1987-94, univ. prof. emeritus, 1994—; cultural exch. prof. Govt. of Can. and China, 1974; mem. adv. bd. Semiotic Inquiry, 1982—; cons. in field. Author: (with Robinson and Wevers) Let's Speak English, 4 vols., 1960-61, The Medium Is the Rear View Mirror: Understanding McLuhan, 1971, (with G.J. Robinson) Studies in Canadian Communications, 1975; Beyond the Word: Reconstructing Sense in the Joyce Era of Technology, Culture, and Communication, 1995, James Joyce's Techno-Poetics, 1997; mem. editl. bd. Sci. Fiction Studies, 1976—, Can. Jour. Comm., 1979—, Jour. Can. Studies, 1980-87. Mem. Greater Peterborough Econ. Council, 1982-87; mem. fed. adv. council to minister employment and immigration for Peterborough area, 1986-87. Recipient awards Social Sci. and Humanities Rsch. Coun., 1991-94, 94-97, 97—, Can. Fedn. Humanities-Aid to Scholarly Publs., 1994, 96; grantee Humanities Rsch. Coun. Can., 1954-56, 73-76, Ont. Dept. Edn., 1956-59, 91, Atkinson Found., 1960, CBC, 1961, Can. Coun., 1966-68, 73-76, Eastman Kodak Corp., Nat. Film Bd. Can., Can. Dept. Industry, Can. Dept. Trade and Commerce, Can. Ctrl. Mortgage and Housing, 1967-69, Que. Ministry Comm., 1977; sr. leave fellow Can. Coun., 1975. Corr. fellow Acad. Medicine (Toronto); mem. Internat. Communications Assn. (dir. 1978-81), Can. Communications Assn. (chmn. com. to investigate formation 1978, pres. 1979-80), MLA, Philol. Soc. Gt. Britain, Can. Assn. Chmn. English (founding chmn. 1971-74), Assn. Can. Univ. Tchrs. English, Internat. Inst. Communications, Soc. Arts Publs. (v.p. 1967-68), Sci. Fiction Research Assn., University Club of Toronto, Yale Club (Toronto), McGill Faculty Club, Elizabethan Club (Yale). Office: Trent Univ, Grad Methodologies Program, Peterborough, ON Canada K9J 7B8

THEE, CHRISTIAN, artist, designer; b. Long Branch, N.J., Sept. 27, 1934; s. Walter Christian and Edith Draper (Steinmetz) T. Degree in arch. and design, U. S.C., 1964; degree in stage/lighting/costume design, Columbia U., 1966; student, Lester Polakov Forum Stage Des, 1968-71; design asst. to Joe Mielziner, Ben Edwards and Howard Bay. Author, illustrator: Behind the Curtain, 1994; commissions include portrait of Prince Andrew of Eng., 1981, mural for Taj Mahal Casino Hotel, Atlantic City, lobby decor of Empire Hotel, N.Y.C., sky ceiling for lobby of LINPRO Corp., Wilmington, Del., Lincoln Post-Hotel, Houston, St. Paul Hotel, New Belvue Stratford, Phila., Clarion Hotel, New Orleans, Belk Dept. Store, Columbia, S.C., Willard Hotel, Washington, Stouffer's Riverview Plaza Hotel, Mobile, Ala., Trompe L'Oeil elevator for Inn at Nat. Hall, Wesport, Conn., mural for Southeastern Frieght, West Columbia, S.C.; designed numerous theatrical prodns. including Rashmon, The Robber Bridegroom, Irma La Douce, Pal Joey, Brigadoon, View from a Bridge, Dracula, The Countess Dracula, You Can't Take it With You, Sweet Bird of Youth, The Prime of Miss Jean Brodie, Monique, The Last of the Red Hot Lovers, Finian's Rainbow, Pajama Game, Old Herbaceous, Cabaret, The Importance of Being Earnest, The Ballad of the Sad Cafe, Richard III, The Miraculous Mandarin, Charlie's Aunt, The Physicists, Androcles and the Lion, Drat, Flight into Egypt, Carnival, Under the Yum Yum Tree, Amican Buffalo, Something's Afoot, A Christmas Carol, The Marriage Go-Around, The Vinegar Tree, Cat on a Hot Tin Roof, The Time of the Coo-Coo, The Visit, and numerous others; theatrical designs for regional and stock cos. including Am. Place Theatre, N.Y.C., Olney (Md.) Theatre, Avondale Playhouse, Indpls., Cafe La Mama, N.Y.C., Equity Libr. Theatre, N.Y.C., Spoleto Festival, Charlestown, S.C., Scott Repertory Theatre, Ft. Worth, and many books and mags. Avocation: performing magic. Office: Christian Thee & Assoc 6196 Eastshore Rd Columbia SC 29206-4310

THEEN, ROLF HEINZ-WILHELM, political science educator; b. Stadthagen, Germany, Feb. 20, 1937; came to U.S., 1956, naturalized, 1962; s. Walter and Gertrud (Tysper) T.; m. Norma Lee Plunkett, June 14, 1959; children: Tanya Sue, Terrell René. B.A. magna cum laude, Manchester Coll., 1959; M.A., Ind. U., 1962, cert. with high distinction Russian and East European Inst., 1962, Ph.D., 1964. Asst. prof. Iowa State U., 1964-67, assoc. prof., 1968-70; assoc. prof. polit. sci. Purdue U., West Lafayette, Ind., 1971-73, prof., 1974—; dir. Purdue U.-Ind. U. study program U. Hamburg, 1980-81; translator, editor U.S. Joint Publs. Research Service. Author: Lenin: Genesis and Development of a Revolutionary, 1973, 74, 79; co-author: Comparative Politics: An Introduction to Seven Countries, 1992, 96; editor, translator: The Early Years of Lenin (N. Valentinov), 1969; editor: The USSR First Congress of People's Deputies: Complete Documents and Records, 4 vols., 1991; contbr. articles to profl. jours., chpts. to books. Recipient Wilton Park award Iowa State U., 1971; Fgn. Area Tng. fellow Russian and East European Inst., 1962-64; grantee Am. Philos. Soc., Inter Univ. Com., Joint Com. Slavic Studies, Fulbright grantee, 1995; NEH sr. fellow, 1974-75, rsch. fellow Kennan Inst. Advanced Russian Studies, Woodrow Wilson Internat. Ctr. for Scholars, 1976, Ctr. Humanistic Studies fellow Purdue U., 1982, 88, 91. Mem. Am. Polit. Sci. Assn., Am. Assn. Advancement Slavic Studies, Am. Acad. Social and Polit. Sci. Mem. Ch. of Brethren. Home: 717 Orchard Dr Lafayette IN 47905-4435 Office: Purdue U Dept Polit Sci Liberal Arts/Edn Bldg 2221 West Lafayette IN 47907-1363

THEEUWES, FELIX, physical chemist; b. Duffel, Belgium, May 25, 1937. Licentiaat physics, Cath. U. Louvain, 1961, DSc in Physics, 1966. Tchr. St. Vincent Sch., Westerlo, Belgium, 1961-64; rsch. fellow CERN, Geneva, 1964-66; rsch. assoc. chemistry U. Kans., 1966-68, asst. prof., 1968-70; rsch. scientist pharm. chemistry Alza Corp., Palo Alto, Calif., 1970-74, prin. scientist, 1974—, v.p. product R & D, 1980-82, v.p.rsch., chief scientist, 1982-94, pres. Tech. Inst., chief scientist, 1994-95, pres. R&D, chief scientist, 1995—; Louis Busse lectr. dept. pharmacology U. Wis., 1981. Named Inventor of Yr., Peninsula Patent Law Assn., 1980. Fellow Am. Assn. Pharm. Scientists (award for advancement of indsl. pharmacy 1983); mem. AAAS, Controlled Release Soc., Internat. Soc. for Chronobiology, Am. Chem. Soc., Acad. Pharm. Sci., N.Y. Acad. Scis. Achievements include research in osmosis, diffusion, solid state physics, cryogenics, high pressure, thermodynamics, pharmacology, pharmacokinetics, calorimetry. Office: Alza Corp PO Box 10950 950 Page Mill Rd Palo Alto CA 94303-0802

THEIL, HENRI, economist, educator; b. Amsterdam, Netherlands, Oct. 31, 1924; s. Hendrik and Hermina (Siegmann) T.; m. Eleonore A.I. Goldschmidt, June 15, 1951. Ph.D. in Econs, U. Amsterdam, 1951; LL.D. (hon.), U. Chgo., 1964; D. honoris causa, Free U., Brussels, 1974, Erasmus U., Rotterdam, 1983; LL.D. (hon.) Hope Coll. 1985. Mem. staff Central Planning Bur. (The Hague), 1952-55; prof. econometrics Netherlands Sch. Econs., Rotterdam, 1953-66; vis. prof. econs. U. Chgo., 1955-56, 64, Stanford U., 1956, 59, Harvard U., 1960, U. So. Calif., 1979, 80, 81, U. Western Australia, 1982; dir. Econometric Inst. (Netherlands Sch. Econs.), 1956-66; prof. U. Chgo., 1965-81, dir. Center Math. Studies in Bus. and Econs., 1965-81; McKethan-Matherly prof. econometrics and decision scis. U. Fla., 1981—. Author: Linear Aggregation of Economic Relations, 1954, Economic Forecasts and Policy, 2d edit., 1961, Optimal Decision Rules for Government and Industry, 1964, Operations Research and Quantitative Economics, 1965, Applied Economic Forecasting, 1977, Economics and Information Theory, 1967, Principles of Econometrics, 1971, Statistical Decomposition Analysis with Applications in the Social and Administrative Sciences, 1972, Theory and Measurement of Consumer Demand, Vol. 1 1975, Vol. 2 1976, Introduction to Econometrics, 1978, The System-Wide Approach to Microeconomics, 1980, System-Wide Explorations in International Economics, Input-Output Analysis, and Marketing Research, 1980, International Consumption Comparisons, 1981, Exploiting Continuity, 1984, Applied Demand Analysis, 1987, International Evidence on Consumption Patterns, 1989, Contributions to Consumer Demand and Econometrics: Essays in Honour of Henri Theil, 1992, Henri Theil's Contributions to Economics and Econometrics, 1992, Studies in Global Econometrics, 1996; editor Mathematical and Managerial Economics, 1964—; co-editor Series on Econometrics and Management Sciences, 1984—. Fellow Am. Acad. Arts and Scis., Royal Netherlands Acad. Scis., Am. Statis. Assn.; mem. Internat. Statis. Inst., Am. Econ. Assn., Ops. Research Soc. Am., Econometric Soc. (pres. 1961), Inst. Mgmt. Scis. (council 1961-64). Home: PO Box 518 Saint Augustine FL 32085-0518

THEILEN, GORDON HENRY, veterinary surgery educator; b. Montevideo, Minn., May 29, 1928; s. Lou Ernst and Ema Kathryn (Schaller) T.; m. Carolyn June Simon, Mar. 6, 1953; children—Kyle, John, Ann. B.S., U. Calif.-Davis, 1953, D.V.M., 1955. Pvt. practice, Tillamook, Oreg., 1955-56; specialist, lectr. U. Calif.-Davis, 1956-57, instr., 1957-58, asst. prof., 1958-64, assoc. prof., 1964-70, prof., 1970-93, prof. emeritus, 1993—, chief clin. oncology, 1970-90. Co-author: Veterinary Cancer Medicine, 1979, 2nd edit., 1987; co-discoverer Feline sarcoma virus and simian sarcoma virus, 1968, 70; patentee Bovine leukemia virus, 1980; feline leukemia virus vaccine, 1977; contbr. articles to profl. jours. Served with U.S. Army, 1946-48. NIH fellow, 1964-66; N.Y. Cancer Immunology fellow, 1972-73; Alexander von Humboldt Sr. Scientist award, 1979-80; Fleishmann Found. award, 1980-85; Ralston Purina award in Small Animal Medicine, 1982, Alumni Achievement award U. Calif.-Davis, 1987. Mem. AVMA, Am. Coll. Vet. Internal Medicine, Assn. Vet. Clinicians, Am. Assn. Cancer Rsch., Vet. Cancer Soc., Internat. Assn. for Comparative Rsch. on Leukemia and Related Diseases (mem. world com. 1990—), Am. Brittany Club (bd. dirs. 1992—), Phi Zeta, Sigma Xi. Democrat. Lutheran. Office: U Calif Surg & Radiol Scis Vet Med Davis CA 95616

THEIS, FRANCIS WILLIAM, business executive; b. Joliet, Ill., July 10, 1920. Student, Joliet Jr. Coll., 1937-39; B.S., Purdue U., 1941. Dir. devel. PPG Industries, Barberton, Ohio, 1951-56; mgr. planning chem. div. PPG Industries, Pitts., 1956-60; pres., chief exec. officer PPG Internat., Pitts., 1960-63, v.p. internat., 1963-65; pres., chief exec. officer Devoe & Raynaolds Co., Louisville, 1965-67; pres. Celanese Chem. Co., N.Y.C., 1967-71; group v.p. Celanese Corp., N.Y.C., 1971-72; exec. v.p. Internat. Paper Corp., N.Y.C., 1972-73; pres., chief exec. officer Hooker Chem. Corp., Stamford, Conn., 1973; dir. Occidental Petroleum Corp., Stamford, 1973; pres., chief exec. officer, dir. Am. Ship Bldg. Co., Cleve., 1975-79; dir., pres., chief operating officer GATX Corp., Chgo., 1979-86. Named Disting. Alumnus Purdue U., 1965. Mem. Shipbuilders Council Am. (dir.), Nat. Maritime Council (bd. govs.). Clubs: Cleve. Athletic (Cleve.), Union (Cleve.); Shaker

Heights (Ohio) Country); Clifton (Lakewood, Ohio); Landmark (Stamford); Sky (N.Y.C.); Chicago. Office: 9 Middleton Rd Savannah GA 31411-1420

THEIS, FRANK GORDON, federal judge; b. Yale, Kans., June 26, 1911; s. Peter F. and Maude (Cook) T.; m. Marjorie Riddle, Feb. 1, 1939 (dec. 1970); children: Franklin, Roger. A.B. cum laude, U. Kans., 1933; J.D., U. Mich., 1936. Bar: Kans. 1937. Since practiced in Arkansas City; sr. mem. firm Frank G. Theis, 1939—; atty. Kans. Tax Commn., 1937-39; chief counsel OPS for Kans., 1951-52; U.S. dist. judge Dist. Kans., 1967—; chief judge, 1977-81, active sr. status, 1981—; Pres. Young Democrats Kan., 1942-46, Kans. Dem. Club, 1944-46; chmn. Kans. Dem. Com., 1955-60; mem. nat. adv. com. polit. orgn. Dem. Nat. Com., 1956-58, nat. committeeman for Kans., 1957-67; chmn. Dem. Midwest Conf., 1959-60; Dem. nominee for Kans., Supreme Ct., 1950, U.S. Senate, 1960. Mem. ABA, Kans. Bar Assn., Kans. Jr. Bar Conf. (pres. 1942), Phi Beta Kappa., Phi Delta Phi, Sachem. Presbyterian. Club: Mason. Office: US Dist Ct 414 US Courthouse 401 N Market St Wichita KS 67202-2000

THEIS, JAMES EDWARD, pastry chef, interior designer; b. Bellville, Ill., May 23, 1963; s. Clement John and Alice Florence (Schoeppner) T. AA, Crafton Hills Coll., 1983; BS in Wildlife Mgmt., Humboldt State U., 1987; A of Occupational Sci. in Culinary Arts, Calif. Culinary Acad., San Francisco, 1994. Wild animal trainer San Diego Zoo, 1983-84, Wild Animal Tng. Ctr., Riverside, Calif., 1980-85; jewelry salesperson J.C. Penney's, West Covina, Calif., 1987-88; display supr. Sherwood Mgmt., Inc., Bell Gardens, Calif., 1989-90; counselor State of Calif. Sch. for Deaf, Riverside, 1990—; mgr. fine jewelry Finlay Fine Jewelry Corp, Monclair, Calif., 1990; interior designer Theis Interiors, Calimesa, Calif., 1990-93; asst. banquet chef Ritz Carlton Hotel, Rancho Mirage, Calif., 1994-95; chef tournat Elcaris Restaurant, Palm Springs, Calif., 1995-97; exec. chef Cottage Garden Restaurant, Palm Springs, 1996—; pastry chef Wolfgang Puck's Cafe, San Diego, 1997—. Scoutmaster Boy Scouts Am., Athens, Greece, 1985-86; fundraiser Desert AIDS Project. Sgt. USAF, 1985-86. Named to Outstanding Young Men Am., 1986. Republican. Roman Catholic. Avocations: water skiing, snow skiing, rock and ice climbing, hiking, outdoor activities. Home and office: Theis Catering 4018 Alabama St Apt 2 San Diego CA 92104-2424

THEIS, PETER FRANK, engineering executive, inventor; b. Chgo., Mar. 21, 1937; s. Frank Victor and Hazel (Ericsson) T.; m. Jill Anne Pendexter, May 9, 1970; children: Juliana, Ethan. B.E. in Elec. Engring., Yale U., 1958; MBA in Fin., U. Chgo., 1966; JD, Ill. Inst. Tech.-Kent Coll Law, Chgo., 1974; postgrad., U. Stockholm. Bar: Ill. 1975. Engr. ASEA, Ludvika, Sweden, 1959, Signode Corp., Glenview, Ill., 1959-61; importer Internat. Idea, Inc., Chgo., 1961-62; systems analyst Continental Ill. Nat. Bank and Trust, Chgo., 1963-64; sales rep. Honeywell, Inc., Chgo., 1964-68; exec. Morgan Industries, Inc., Chgo., 1968-87; pres. Conversational Voice Technologies Corp., Chgo., Gurnee, Ill., 1973-91, Theis Rsch., Inc., Gurnee, 1991—; cons. Ill. Tech. Transfer LLC, 1994—; cons., mng. mem. Theis Rsch. & Engring. LLC, 1994—. Patentee in field. With Air N.G., 1961-66. Mem. Tech. Exec. Roundtable (bd. dirs. 1992—), Licensing Execs. Soc., Execs. Club of Chgo. (bd. dirs. 1972-74), Intellectual Property Creators (bd. dirs. 1993—). Avocations: canoeing, hiking, sailing. Office: Theis Rsch Inc 4223 Grove Ave Gurnee IL 60031-2134

THEIS, STEVEN THOMAS, executive safety director; b. Trenton, N.J., June 16, 1959; s. Thomas Donald and Pauline (Ciko) T.; m. Mary L. Crane. BS, U. So. Calif., L.A., 1981; Cert. German Lang., Johann Wolfgang Goethe U., Frankfurt am Main, Germany, 1983; postgrad., Friedrich Alexander U., Erlangen, Germany, 1983-84. Cert. safety profl., cert. hazardous materials mgr., EMT, N.J. With Henkels & McCoy, Inc., various locations, 1978—; constrn. coord. Henkels & McCoy, Inc., Phoenix, 1982; project mgr. Henkels & McCoy, Inc., Burlington, N.J., 1985-87; safety dir. N.J. div. Henkels & McCoy, Inc., Burlington, 1987-92; staff support coord. corp. office Henkels & McCoy, Blue Bell, Pa., 1992—, corp. dir. safety, 1992—; bd. dirs. Henkels & McCoy, Inc., 1996; safety and health instr. ARC, Woodbury, N.J., 1984—, safety and health instr., trainer, 1990—; basic instr. OSHA constrn. ind. stds. U.S. Dept. Labor, Chgo., 1987—; chairperson safety and health com. Gloucester County ARC, Woodbury, 1991—. Patentee in field. 1st lt. West Deptford Emergency Squad, Thorofare, N.J., 1987-88, capt., 1989-90, hon. mem. 1991—; vice chmn. West Deptford Twp. Bd. Health, 1989-90, v.p. West Deptford Vol. Fire and Ambulance Assn., 1989-90; emergency med. spl. coord. West Deptford Office Emergency Mtmg., 1989-90. Named Mem. of the Yr. West Deptford Emergency Squad, 1988; recipient Cameron award Nat. Safety Coun., 1992-93, 93-94. Mem. ASTM (membership sec. 1994), Am. Soc. Safety Engrs., Am. Welding Soc., Nat. Safety Coun., Am. Mgmt. Assn., Am. Nat. Stds. Inst., Nat. Safety Coun. (pub. utilities divn.), Nat. Electric Safety Code. Republican. Roman Catholic. Avocations: antiques, classical music, model building, fishing. Office: Henkels & McCoy Inc 985 Jolly Rd Blue Bell PA 19422-1903

THEIS, WILLIAM HAROLD, lawyer, educator; b. Chgo., Nov. 8, 1945; s. Clarence M. and Marion K. (McLendon) T.; m. Maria Luisa Belfiore, Dec. 5, 1973; children: Catherine, Elizabeth. AB, Loyola U. Chgo., 1967; JD, Northwestern U., 1970; LLM, Columbia U., 1977, JSD, 1982. Bar: Ill. 1970, D.C. 1971, U.S. Ct. Appeals (7th cir.) 1971, U.S. Supreme Ct. 1974. Assoc. prof. La. State U. Law Ctr., 1972-78; assoc. prof. Loyola U. Law Sch., Chgo., 1978-81; practiced in Chgo., from 1981; now with firm Shellow, Shellow & Glynn, S.C., Milw.; part-time lectr. admiralty Northwestern Sch. Law, Chgo. Served to lt. USNR, 1970-72. Mem. Am. Law Inst. Contbr. articles to legal jours. Office: Shellow Shellow & Glynn 222 E Mason St Milwaukee WI 53202-3602

THEISEN, RUSSELL EUGENE, electrical engineer; b. Norfolk, Va., Aug. 3, 1937; s. Richard Roudolph and Pansie Mae (Garnette) T.; m. Mary Ann Asbury, May 30, 1962; children: Timothy Mark, Yvette Marie. BSEE, Old Dominion, 1962; MBA, Rollins Coll., 1973. Registered profl. engr., N.Y., Fla. Svc. mgr. Mastercraft Elect., Norfolk, 1955-62; design engr. IBM Corp., Endicott, N.Y., 1962-64; plant mgr. Compton Industries, Vestal, N.Y., 1964-66; sr. engr. Martin Marietta Aerospace, Orlando, Fla., 1966-74; sr. project engr. General Dynamics Corp., Longwood, Fla., 1974-76; sr. mem. profl. staff Martin Marietta Aerospace, Orlando, 1976-92; sr. system software analyst SCI Systems Inc., Huntsville, Ala., 1992—; mgr. Worldwide Document Mgmt. and Control Systems, 1996—; nat. dir. Halbert Genealogy, Bath, Ohio, 1987—; pres. Theisen Enterprises Inc., 1996—; cert. mgr., 1996, Nat. Mgmt. Assn.; Ala. chmn. Am. Enterprise Inst., High Teck Valley Coun. Nat. Mgmt. Assn., 1996-97; dir. Nat. Computer Conf., 1967-79, 83-85; POSIX Programming Language Standard IEEE 1986; 1094 Standard for Life Cycle Process 1989. Contbng. author: Reliability And Maintainibility, 1967; contbr. articles to profl. jours., Posix Prgmg. Language Standard IEEE, 1986; 1094 Standard for Life Cycle Process IEEE, 1989. Dir. Theisen Clan Theisen Genealogy Group, 1988-97; dir. Fla. Libr. Adv. Bd., 1967-79; pres. Theisen Enterprises Inc., 1994—, profl., Nat Soc. for Profl. Engrs., 1963-76, bd. dirs. Am. Fedn. Info. Processing Soc., 1983-85. With USMC, 1953-65. Mem. IEEE (v.p. 1983-85, Fla. Coun. pres. 1987-89, sr.), Nat. Mgmt. Assn. (v.p. 1992-95, sr.), ACM (area chmn. 1987-89, sr.). Achievements include developed data bus standard S-100, HPIB, IEEE-488; helped launch IEEE Computer Soc. Mag. Computer PAMI design and test, microsystems software. Design and devel. Data Metrics Sys. for Corp. Info. Sys., Design and Devel. EDM and PDM Sys. for worldwide Facilities in 25 Countries. Office: SCI Systems Inc M/S 102 2101 Clinton Ave Huntsville AL 35807-4035

THEISMANN, JOSEPH ROBERT, former professional football player, announcer; b. New Brunswick, N.J., Sept. 9, 1949; s. Joseph James and Olga (Tobias) T.; m. Chery Lynn Brown, Dec. 5, 1970 (div.); children: Joseph Winton, Amy Lynn, Patrick James. B.A. in Sociology, U. Notre Dame, 1971. With Toronto Argonauts, CFL, 1971-74; with Washington Redskins, 1974-86, punt returner, 1974-79, starting quarterback, 1979-86; analyst CBS Nat. Football League broadcasts, 1987-88, ESPN Nat. Football League broadcasts, 1988—; tchr. Offense-Def. Football Camp; Superstar participant, 1979-80, played in Pro-Bowl, 1983-84; mem. Pres.'s Athletic Adv. Com., 1975; active Pres. Nat. Svc. Adv. Com., 1993. Author: Quarter Backing. Mem. corp. bd. Children's Hosp. Nat. Med. Center, Washington; participant benefits for Multiple Sclerosis children's hosps., Armed Forces Christmas benefits. High sch. All-Am. Football, 1967; All-Am. Coll., 1971; Acad.-All-Am.; All-Pro UPI; recipient Brian Picollo award; played in Pro Bowl, 1982, 83; mem. Super Bowl XVII Championship Team, 1982; cable Ace award, Best Sports Commentator-Analyst, 1994. Mem. Nat. Football Players Assn. Republican. Methodist. Office: JRT Assocs 5912 Leesburg Pike Falls Church VA 22041-2202*

THELEN, BRUCE CYRIL, lawyer; b. St. Johns, Mich., Nov. 24, 1951. BA, Mich. State U., 1973; JD, U. Mich., 1977. Bar: N.Y. 1978, Mich. 1980, Ill. 1992. Assoc. Dewey, Ballantine, Bushby, Palmer & Wood, N.Y.C., 1977-80; assoc. Dickinson, Wright, Moon, Van Dusen & Freeman, Detroit, 1981-83, ptnr., 1984—; mem. U.S. Dept. Commerce-Mich. Dist. Export Coun., 1995—. Contbr. articles to profl. publs. Mem. allocation panel, mem. spkrs. bur., vice chmn. rsch. and tech. com. United Way of Detroit, 1987—; mem. State of Mich. Task Force on Internat. Trade, Lansing, 1990; mem. Detroit Com. on Fgn. Rels., Greater Detroit-Windsor Japan Am. Soc. Mem. N.Y. Bar Assn. (mem. internat. law sect.), Mich. Bar Assn., State Bar Mich. (chmn. internat. law sect. 1990-91), Internat. Bar Assn., Am. Soc. Internat. Law, Ill. Bar Assn. (internat. law sect.), Internat. Law Assn., French-Am. C. of C. of Detroit, German Am. C. of C. of Midwest (bd. dirs. 1992—, pres. Mich. chpt. 1994—), Greater Detroit C. of C. (chmn. European mission com. 1991-92, 95, export com. 1992-95, Leadership Detroit VIII program 1986-87), World Trade Club (exec. com. 1992—). Office: Dickinson Wright Moon Van Dusen & Freeman One Detroit Center 500 Woodward Ave Ste 4000 Detroit MI 48226-3423

THELEN, EDMUND, research executive; b. Berkeley, Calif., May 8, 1913; s. Paul and Alice (Arnold) T.; B.S., U. Calif., Berkeley, 1934; m. Helen Naomi Betton, Oct. 30, 1965; children—Nancy Anne, Joan Arnold Thelen Hanson. Asst. chemist Certain-Teed Products Corp., Richmond, Calif., 1934-35; chemist O. C. Field Gasoline Corp., Santa Maria, Calif., 1936-41; asst. mgr. Eclipse Pioneer div. Bendix Corp., Teterboro, N.J., 1946-47; sr. research chemist Franklin Inst. Research Labs., Phila., 1947-51, mgr. colloids and polymers br., 1951-74, v.p., dir. phys. and life scis. dept., 1974-76, Inst. fellow, sec. com. on sci. and the arts, 1976-82; pres. Safety Surface Corp., 1983-88; mem. Council for Delivery of Dental Care, 1970-85; bd. govs. Franklin-Hahnemann Inst. Occupational and Environ. Health, 1975-80, Mayor's Sci. and Tech. Adv. Com. on Environment, 1973-80; instr. dental medicine Hahnemann Med. Coll. and Hosp., 1964-74; v.p., dir. Pa. Environ. Council, 1974-85; treas. Home Health Services of Chester County and Vicinity, 1981-86; bd. dirs. Neighborhood Vis. Nurse Assn, 1987-93. Served with USN, 1941-45; to comdr. USNR, 1941-66. Recipient spl. recognition award Am. Soc. Landscape Architects, 1974. Mem. Franklin Inst., Sierra Club (Eastern Pa. group chmn. 1968, Atlantic chpt. vice chmn. 1971-73, founding chmn. Pa. chpt. 1974), Retired Officers Assn. (treas. Valley Forge chpt. 1980-85, v.p. 1987, pres. 1988-89, sec. 1994—), Sigma Xi. Clubs: Toastmasters Internat. (dist. gov. 1959-60), Sunday Breakfast Speakers (pres. 1960-61). Patentee asphalts, dropwise condensation, safe fibres to replace asbestos, resilient pavements for play and sports fields; head devel. team, co-author book: Porous Pavement for Runoff Control, 1978; editor Am. Assn. Ret. Persons, Eastern Chester County news letter; contbr. papers to tech. publs. Home: 658 Davis Ln Wayne PA 19087-5418

THELEN, GIL, newspaper editor; b. Chgo.; s. Gilbert Carl and Violet (Okonn) T.; m. Carol Abernathy, July 1966 (div. Apr. 1978); children: Deborah Brooke, Todd Foster; m. Cynthia Jane Struby, Sept. 2, 1979; children: Matthew David, Jonathan Whitfield. BA, Duke U., 1960. Reporter Milw. Jour., 1960-61, AP, Washington, 1965-72; writer Consumer Reports, Mt. Vernon, N.Y., 1972-77; reporter Chgo. Daily News, 1977-78; asst. met. editor Charlotte (N.C.) Observer, 1978-82, met. editor, 1982-83, asst. mng. editor, 1983-87; editor The Sun News, Myrtle Beach, S.C., 1987-90; exec. editor The State, 1990—; adj. prof. U. S.C., Aiken, 1989—. Pres. Montgomery County Big Brothers, Bethesda, Md., 1967-69; co-founder Alpha Group, Myrtle Beach, S.C., 1989. Mem. Am. Soc. Newspaper Editors, S.C. Press Assn., Columbia Rotary Club, Leadership S.C., Leadership Columbia, Phi Beta Kappa, Omicron Delta Kappa. Methodist. Avocations: golf, tennis, reading, classical music. Home: 128 Alexander Cir Columbia SC 29206-4956 Office: The State Newspaper 1401 Shop Rd Columbia SC 29201-4843

THELIN, JOHN ROBERT, academic administrator, education educator, historian; b. West Newton, Mass., Oct. 15, 1947; s. George Willard and Rozalija Katherine (Komarec) T.; m. Anna Sharon Blackburn, June 24, 1978. AB, Brown U., 1969; MA, U. Calif., Berkeley, 1972, PhD, 1973. Rsch. asst. Brown U., Providence, 1968-69; researcher, lectr. U. Calif., Berkeley, 1972-74; asst. prof. U. Ky., Lexington, 1974-77; asst. dean Pomona Coll., Claremont, Calif., 1977-79; from asst. dir. to rsch. dir. Assn. Ind. Calif. Colls. and Univs., Santa Ana, 1979-81; chancellor prof. Coll. William and Mary, Williamsburg, Va., 1981-93, pres. faculty assembly, 1990-91; prof. higher edn. & philanthropy Ind. U., Bloomington, 1993-96; prof. ednl. policy and history U. Ky., Lexington, 1996—; vis. prof. grad. sch. Claremont U., 1978-81; vis. scholar U. Calif., Berkeley, 1995; curator Marquandia Soc., 1971-96; essay rev. editor Rev. of Higher Edn., 1979-91; rsch. cons. NSF, Washington, 1991; mem. faculty senate U. Ky., 1997—. Author: Higher Education and Its Useful Past, 1982, The Cultivation of Ivy, 1976, (with others) The Old College Try, 1989, Higher Education and Public Policy, 1991, Games Colleges Play, 1994; assoc. editor: (jour.) Higher Education: Theory and Research, 1983-91. Pres., bd. dirs. United Way, Williamsburg, 1987-89; pres. Friends of Williamsburg Libr., 1989. Rsch. grantee Spencer Found., 1989-91; Regents fellow U. Calif., 1972. Mem. Assn. for Study of Higher Edn. (bd. dirs. 1988-90, keynote spkr. 1994), History of Edn. Soc. (editl. bd. 1988-91), Phi Beta Kappa. Avocations: long-distance running, history of Los Angeles and California, sports history. Home: 324 Chinoe Rd Lexington KY 40502-2350 Office: U Ky Edn Policy Studies Lexington KY 40503

THEMELIS, NICKOLAS JOHN, metallurgical and chemical engineering educator; b. Athens, Greece. B in Engring., McGill U., Montreal, Que., Can., 1956, PhD, 1961. Registered profl. engr., Conn. Mgr. engring. divsn. Noranda Tech. Ctr., Pointe Claire, Que., 1962-72; v.p. tech. Kennecott Corp., N.Y.C., 1972-80; Stanley-Thompson prof. chem. metallurgy Columbia U., N.Y.C., 1980—. Author 4 books; contbr. articles to profl. jours. Fellow Minerals, Metals and Materials Soc.; mem. NAE, Metallurgical Soc. AIME (3 gold medals). Democrat. Mem. Christian Orthodox Ch. Avocations: sailing, music. Office: Columbia Univ Earth Engring Ctr 500 W 120th St # 1047 New York NY 10027-6623

THEOBALD, EDWARD ROBERT, lawyer; b. Chgo., Feb. 10, 1947; s. Edward Robert Theobald Jr. and Marie (Turner) Logan; m. Bonnie J. Singer, July 18, 1970; children: Debra Marie, Kimberly Ann. BA, So. Ill. U., 1969; JD, Ill. Inst. Tech., 1974. Bar: Ill. 1974, U.S. Dist. Ct. (no. dist.) Ill. 1974. Asst. state's atty. Cook County, Chgo., 1974-79, supr. felony trial divsn., 1980-81; assoc. Conklin, Leahy & Eisenberg, Chgo., 1977; ptnr. Boharic & Theobald, Chgo., 1981-83, owner, ptnr., 1983—; legal adv. Sheriff of Cook County, Ill., 1986-89; spl. state's atty. U.S. Dist. Ct. no. dist. Ill., 1989-91; apptd. spl. corp. counsel City of Chgo., 1994. Mem. Parent adv. bd. Downers Grove (Ill.) South H.S., 1992-94. Named Number One Trial Atty. in Felony Trial Divsn. of Office of Cook County State's Atty., Felony Trial Divsn. Suprs., 1979. Mem. ABA (sect. on tort and ins. law, sect. on labor and employment law, chmn. com. on sentencing alternatives young lawyers sect. 1982-83, tort and ins. practice sect., labor and employment law sect.), ATLA, Chgo. Bar Assn. (mem. bd. mgrs. 1985-87, mem. labor and employment law com. 1983—, mem. com. on coms. 1990-94, mem. membership com. 1990-95), Ill. Bar Assn., Christian Legal Soc. (bd. dirs. Ill. chpt. 1993—), Civil War Roundtable (Chgo. chpt.). Roman Catholic. Home: 7104 Grand Ave Downers Grove IL 60516-3915 Office: 135 S La Salle St Ste 2148 Chicago IL 60603-4401

THEOBALD, H RUPERT, retired political scientist; b. Berlin, Mar. 12, 1930; came to U.S., 1950; s. Hans Herman and Marlene (Rackow) T.; m. Elizabeth Joanna Frisella, Nov. 3, 1951 (dec. Mar. 1996); children: H. Michael, Marlies J., Peter J. MA, U. Wis., 1960, PhD, 1971. Rschr. Wis. Legis. Reference Bur., Madison, 1957-60, coord., 1960-63, acting chief, 1963-64, chief, 1964-94; ret., 1994; lay mem. bd. govs. State Bar Wis., 1994-96. Editor: Laws of Wisconsin, 1991-94; contbr. articles to profl. jours. Mem. Coun of State Governments, 1963-94 (Charles McCarthy award 1986), Com. on Suggested State Legis., 1964-94.

THEOBALD, THOMAS CHARLES, banker; b. Cin., May 5, 1937; m. Gigi Mahon, Jan. 1987. AB in Econs., Coll. Holy Cross, 1958; MBA in Fin. with high distinction, Harvard U., 1960. With Citibank, N.A. div. Citicorp, 1960-87; vice-chmn. Citicorp, N.Y.C., 1982-87; CEO, chmn. Continental Bank Corp., Chgo., 1987-94; chmn. bd. dirs. Continental Bank N.A., Chgo., 1987-94; ptnr. Blair Capital Ptnrs, LLC (formally Blair Capital Mgmt), Chgo., 1994—; bd. dirs. Xerox Corp., Enron Global Power and Pipelines, Anixter Internat., Stein Roe Funds, Mac Arthur Found. Trustee Mut. of N.Y., Northwestern U.; bd. dirs. Assocs. of Harvard Bus. Sch., Chgo. Coun. on Fgn. Rels. Office: Blair Capital Partners, LLC 222 W Adams St Ste 3300 Chicago IL 60606-5307

THEODORE, EUSTACE D., alumni association executive, management consultant; b. Marietta, Ohio, Aug. 4, 1941; s. Demetrios E. and Nicoletta D. T.; m. Carol Nagy, June 13, 1964; children: Kyle James, Graham Clark. B.A., Yale U., 1963; M.A., Cornell U., 1965, Ph.D., 1967. Mem. faculty Hollins Coll., Roanoke, Va., 1967-71, Mt. Holyoke Coll., South Hadley, Mass., 1971-72; dean Calhoun Coll., Yale U., New Haven, 1972-81; exec. dir. Assn. Yale Alumni, 1981—; mgmt. cons., 1965—. Contbr. articles to jours. Recipient NSF-COSIP award, 1966. Mem. Coun. Alumni Assn. Execs. (bd. dirs. 1991—, pres. 1995-96), Coun. for Advancement and Support Edn. (trustee 1993—, chair internat. task force 1994—), CASE (Europe) (trustee 1995—), Commn. on Alumni Rels. (chair 1992-96). Office: Yale U Alumni Assn PO Box 209010 New Haven CT 06520-9010

THEODORESCU, RADU AMZA SERBAN, mathematician, educator; b. Bucharest, Romania, Apr. 12, 1933; emigrated to Can., 1968, naturalized, 1975; s. Dan and Ortensia Maria (Butoianu) T.; children: Dan, Paul, Anne. BSc, U. Bucharest, 1954, DSc, 1967; PhD, Acad. Romania, 1958. Asst. prof. Inst. Math. of Acad., Romania, Bucharest, 1954-57; sr. asst. prof. Inst. Math. of Acad., 1957-60, assoc. prof., sci. sec., 1960-64; prof., head dept. Center Math. Statistics, 1964-68; prof. U. Bucharest, 1968-69, Laval U., Quebec, Que., Can., 1969—; guest prof., lectr. univs. in Europe, N.Am. and Australia. Author: (with G. Ciucu) Processes with Complete Connections, 1960, (with S. Guiasu) Mathematical Information Theory, 1968, Uncertainty and Information, 1971, (with M. Iosifescu) Random Processes and Learning, 1969, (with W. Hengartner) Concentration Functions, 1973, 2d edit., 1980, Monte-Carlo Methods, 1978, (with E. Bertin and I. Cuculescu) Unimodality of Probability Measures, 1997; mem. editorial bd. Annales des Sciences Mathématiques du Québec, Optimization, Statistics and Decisions; contbr. articles to profl. jours. Mem. bd. European Orgn. Quality Control, 1966-69. Recipient prize Acad. Romania, 1960. Fellow Inst. Math. Stats., Am. Soc. Quality Control; mem. Can. Math. Soc., Statis. Soc. Can., Am. Math. Soc., Internat. Statis. Inst. Home: Apt 1603, 9 Jardins MErici, Quebec, PQ Canada G1S 4S8 Office: Laval U, Dept Math and Stats, Quebec, PQ Canada G1K 7P4

THEODORIDIS, GEORGE CONSTANTIN, biomedical engineering educator, researcher; b. Braila, Romania, Dec. 3, 1935; came to U.S., 1959; s. Constantin George and Anastasia (Haritopoulos) T.; m. Lilly Kate Hyman, Sept. 20, 1975; 1 child, Alexander. BS in Mechanical and Elec. Engring., Nat. Tech. U. Athens, 1959; DSc, MIT, Cambridge, Mass., 1964. Rsch. assoc. MIT, Cambridge, Mass., 1964; sr. scientist Am. Sci. Engring., Cambridge, Mass., 1964-68; assoc. prof. in residence U. Calif., Berkeley, 1968-70; biomedical engring. U. Va., Charlottesville, 1970—; prof. elec. engring. U. Patras, Greece, 1976-83; cons. Food and Drug Adminstrn., Washington, 1975-76, Applied Physics Lab, Columbia, Md., 1978-79. Author: Applied Math, 1983; contbr. articles to profl. jours. Den leader Boy Scouts Am., Charlottesville, Va., 1984-85. Fulbright fellow U.S. Govt., MIT, 1959-60; Nato fellow NATO, MIT, 1961-64; Spl. fellow NIH, U. Calif., 1968-70; recipient teaching award GE, MIT, 1963. Mem. Inst. Elec. and Electronics Engrs., Sigma Xi. Greek Orthodox. Avocations: history, travel. Home: 1817 Fendall Ave Charlottesville VA 22903-1613 Office: U Va Dept Biomed Engring Box 377 Medical Ctr Charlottesville VA 22908

THEODORU, STEFAN GHEORGHE, civil engineer, writer; b. Braila, Romania, June 11, 1921; came to U.S., 1965; s. Alexandru and Georgeta (Iovitz) T.; m. Nina Bogos, Jan. 31, 1945; children: Anexander, Radu. Civil engineering degree, Politech. Inst., Bucharest, Romania, 1947. Civil engr. Romanian Govt., Bucharest, 1947-64, Rella et Co., Vienna, Austria, 1964-65, Hydrotech. Corp., N.Y.C., 1965-66, Leon Selzer Assoc. P.E.C.P., N.Y.C., 1966-76, pvt. practice, Long Island City, N.Y.C., 1976—. Author: Fata fara glas, 1993, Teatru, 1993, Meeting in the Twilight, 1994, The Bag of Stars, 1995, Doamna, Teatru Vol. II, 1995, Transylvania, 1995, (haiku) Centum, 1997; author, editor: Versuri Vol. I, 1973, A Wallachian Flag, 1977, Versuri Vol. II, La Lumina, 1993, Odiseea unui cuget, 1993, Un Milionar nebun, 1996, Genius, 1996, Născută în castelul lui Dracula, 1997, Teatru Vol. III, 1997, Mărul din poveste, 1997; co-inventor Patern Registration System, 1979. Mem. Am. Romanian Relief Found., N.Y. Acad. Scis., Romanian Gen. Engring. Assn. (ct. tech. expert 1948, 64), Profl. Internat. Journalists Union Romania, Internat. Writers Assn. Ohio, Internat. Assn. Romanian Writers & Artists Ga. Home: 28-18 29th St Long Island City NY 11102

THEODOSIUS, HIS BEATITUDE METROPOLITAN See LAZOR, THEODOSIUS

THEOHARIDES, THEOHARIS CONSTANTIN, pharmacologist, physician, educator; b. Thessaloniki, Macedonia, Greece, Feb. 11, 1950; s. Constantin A. and Marika (Krava) T.; m. Efthalia I. Triarchou, July 10, 1981; children: Niove, Konstantinos. Diploma with honors, Anatolia Coll., 1968, BA in Biology and History of Sci. and Medicine, Yale U., 1972, MS in Immunology, 1975, MPhil. in Endocrinology, 1975, PhD in Pharmacology Yale U., 1978, MD Yale U., 1983. Asst. in rsch. biology Yale U., 1968-71, asst. in rsch. pharmacology, 1973-78, exec. sec. univ. senate, 1976-78, rsch. assoc. faculty clin. immunology, 1978-83; spl. instr. modern Greek Yale U., 1974, 77; vis. faculty Aristotelian U. Sch. Medicine, Thessaloniki, 1979; asst. prof. biochemistry and pharmacology Tufts U., 1983-88, co-dir. med. pharmacology curriculum, 1983-85, dir. med. pharmacology, 1985-93, assoc. prof. pharmacology, biochemistry and psychiatry, 1989-94, prof. pharmacology and internal medicine, 1995—, dir. grad. pharmacology, 1994—; clin. pharmacologist Commonwealth Mass. Drug Formulary Commn., 1985—; co-chmn. neuro-immunology 2d and 3d World Conf. on Inflammation, Monte Carlo, 1986, 89; mem. internat. adv. bd. 4th, 5th, 6th and 7th World Conf. on Inflammation, Geneva, 1991, 93, 95, 97; spl. cons. Min. of Health, Greece, 1993-95; chmn. Internat. Com. to Upgrade Med. Edn. in Greece, 1994; bd. dirs., spl. cons. Inst. Pharm. Rsch. & Tech., Athens, 1994—. Trustee Anatolia Coll. 1984-85. Author books on pharmacology; mem. editorial bd. numerous jours.; contbr. articles to profl. jours.; patentee in field. Bd. dirs., v.p. for rels. with Greece, Krikos, 1978-79; sec. Assn. Greeks to Yale, 1974-79, pres., 1982-83. Recipient Theodore Cuyler award Yale U., 1972; George Papanicoalou Grad. award, 1977; Med. award Hellenic Med. Soc. N.Y., 1979, 83; M.C. Winternitz prize in pathology Yale U., 1980; Disting. Service award Tufts U. Alumni Assn., 1986, Spl. Faculty Recognition award Tufts U. Med. Sch., 1987, 88. Mem. Hellenic Biochem. and Biophys. Soc., AMA, AAUP, N.Y. Acad. Scis., Am. Inst. History Pharmacy, AAAS, Soc. Health and Human Values, Am. Assn. History Medicine, Am. Soc. Cell Biology, Soc. Neurosci., Am. Fedn. Clin. Research, Conn. Acad. Arts and Scis., Am. Soc. Pharmacology and Exptl. Therapeutics, Hellenic Soc. Cancer Research, Hellenic Soc. Med. Chemistry, Internat. Soc. Immunopharmacology, Am. Soc. Microbiology, Am. Assn. Immunologists, Internat. Soc. History of Medicine, Mass. Med. Soc., N.E. Hellenic Med. Soc. (sec. 1984-85, v.p. 1985-86, 94—, pres. 1986-87), Hellenic Sci. Assn. Boston (bd. dirs. 1985), Internat. Anatolia Alumni Assn. (sec. 1984-85). Alpha Omega Alpha (citation for excellence in teaching 1989, 90, 91, 92, 93, 94, 96), Sigma Xi. Research on mechanisms of release of secretory products; hormonal induction of ornithine decarboxylase and membrane functions of polyamines; pathophysiology of mast cells in neuroimmunoendocrine diseases such as irritable bowel syndrome, interstitial cystitis, migraines and multiple sclerosis. Home: 14 Parkman St Apt 2 Brookline MA 02146-3802 Office: Tufts U Sch Med 136 Harrison Ave Boston MA 02111-1817

THEON, JOHN SPERIDON, meteorologist; b. Washington, Dec. 12, 1934; s. Lewis and Merope (Xydias) T.; m. Joanne Edens, July 31, 1965; children—Christopher James, Catherine. B.S. in Aero. Engring, U. Md., 1957; B.S. in Meteorology, Pa. State U., 1959, M.S., 1962; Ph.D. in Engring. Sci.

and Mechanics, U. Tenn., 1985. Aero. engr. Douglas Aircraft Co., Santa Monica, Calif., 1957-58; engr. U.S. Naval Ordnance Lab., White Oak, Md., 1962; rsch. meterologist, 1962-74; head meterology br. NASA Goddard Space Flight Center, Greenbelt, Md., 1974-77; asst. chief Lab. for Atmospheric Scis., 1977-78, Nimbus project scientist, 1972-78, Landsat discipline leader meteorol. investigations, 1974-78; mgr. global weather research program NASA Hdqrs., Washington, 1978-82, chief Atmospheric Dynamics and Radiation br., 1982-89; Spacelab 3 program scientist NASA Hdqrs., 1979-86, chmn. space shuttle weather adv. panel, 1985-87; chief atmospheric, dynamics, radiation and hydrol. processes, 1989-93, chief phys. climate br., 1993-94, divsn. program scientist, 1994-95, exec. sec. task force on observations and data mgmt., 1994-95; cons. Inst. for Global Environ. Strategies, 1995—, Orbital Scis. Corp., 1995-96. Contbr. articles to profl. jours. Served with USAF, 1958-60. Recipient Nimbus F Instrument Team award NASA-Goddard, 1976, Goddard Exceptional Performance award, 1978, NASA Exceptional Performance award, 1986, Radio Wave award Ministry of Posts & Telecomm. of Japan, 1995; name Disting. Alumnus U. Tenn., 1989. Fellow Am. Meteorol. Soc.; mem. Am. Geophys. Union, Sigma Xi. Presbyterian. Home and Office: 6801 Lupine Ln Mc Lean VA 22101

THERNSTROM, STEPHAN ALBERT, historian, educator; b. Port Huron, Mich., Nov. 5, 1934; s. Albert George and Bernadene (Robbins) T.; m. Abigail Mann, Jan. 3, 1959; children—Melanie Rachel, Samuel Altgeld. B.S., Northwestern U., 1956; A.M., Harvard, 1958, Ph.D., 1962. Instr. history Harvard U., Cambridge, Mass., 1962-66, asst. prof., 1966-67, prof., 1973-81, Winthrop prof., 1981—, chmn. com. on higher degrees in history of Am. civilization, 1985-92; prof. Brandeis U., 1967-69, UCLA, 1969-73; Pitt. prof. Am. history and instns. Cambridge U., 1978-79; dir. Charles Warren Ctr. for Research in Am. History, 1980-83. Author: Poverty and Progress, 1964, Poverty, Planning and Politics in the New Boston, 1969, The Other Bostonians, 1973, History of the American People, 1984, 88; co-author: America in Black and White, 1997; editor: Harvard Ency. Am. Ethnic Groups; co-editor: Harvard Studies in Urban History; Cambridge Interdisciplinary Perspectives on Modern History Series. Recipient Bancroft prize, R.R. Hawkins award, Faculty prize Harvard U. Press, Waldo G. Leland prize; Guggenheim fellow; John M. Olin fellow; ACLS fellow. Office: Harvard U Robinson Hall Cambridge MA 02138

THEROUX, DENNIS ROBERT, engineering executive; b. New Haven, Conn., Aug. 17, 1951; s. Theogene Charles and Theresa Cecile (La Croix) T. BA, U. Conn., 1973; MS, U. Hawaii, Mamoa, 1975; cert. in occupational, safety, health, U. New Haven, 1986-88; postgrad., Columbia Pacific U. Cert. indsl. hygienist, safety profl. Pres. Hamden (Conn.) Pest Control Co., 1975-85; pres. and chief exec. officer Theroux Engring., Hamden, 1985—; regional producer Hartford Pub. Access TV Cable Ch. 5. Author (with others): Radon-The Invisible Threat, 1986. Sponsor St. Francis Home for Children, New Haven, 1986—; co-founder Profl. Coun. for Edn., Hadlyme, Conn., 1990. Mem. Am. Soc. Safety Engrs., Am. Industrial Hygiene Assn., Am. Mgmt. Assn. (pres. assoc. 1990—), Conn. Environ. Health Assn., Conn. Pest Control Assn. Roman Catholic. Avocations: collecting musical instruments, Harley-Davidson touring. Home: PO Box 100 Hadlyme CT 06439-0100 Office: Theroux Engring PO Box 4096 Hamden CT 06514-0096

THEROUX, EUGENE, lawyer; b. Medford, Mass., Apr. 29, 1938; s. Albert and Anne (Dittami) T.; m. Phyllis Grissim, Feb. 13, 1963 (div. 1978); children: Christian, Elizabeth, Justin; m. Colleen Marie Pankratz, Feb. 27, 1982; children: Jean-Paul, Alexandra, Sebastien. Student, Harvard U., 1959, 60; BID, Pratt Inst., 1961, LittD, 1982; JD, Georgetown U., 1968. Bar: D.C. 1969, Mass. 1982, Va. 1985. Ptnr. Baker & McKenzie, Washington, 1969—, mem. policy com., 1992-94; spl. counsel joint econ. com. U.S. Congress, Washington, 1972; adv. prof. Fudan U., Shanghai, People's Republic China, 1986—; adv. bd. Fletcher Sch. Law and Diplomacy, 1987—; trustee Monterey Inst. Internat. Studies. Author: (book) Joint Ventures In USSR, 1989, Business Guide To Moscow, 1990, Business Guide to Mongolia, 1996. Trustee Am. Leprosy Found., Washington, 1987—; v.p. U.S.-China Bus. Coun., Washington, 1973-75, dir., vice chair of bd., 1991—. 1st lt. inf., U.S. Army, 1962-64, MAC/V So. Vietnam, 1968. Mem. ABA (chair Soviet law com. 1989-91), Army and Navy Club, Univ. Club. Roman Catholic. Avocations: drawing, painting, running. Home: Short Hill Mountain Farm Lovettsville VA 22080 Office: Baker & McKenzie 815 Connecticut Ave NW Washington DC 20006-4004

THEROUX, PAUL EDWARD, author; b. Medford, Mass., Apr. 10, 1941; s. Albert Eugene and Anne (Dittami) T.; m. Anne Castle, Dec. 4, 1967 (div. 1993); children: Marcel, Louis; m. Sheila Donnelly, Nov. 18, 1995. BA, U. Mass., Amherst, DLitt, 1988; DLitt, Trinity Coll., Washington, 1980, Tufts U., 1980. Lectr. U. Urbino, Italy, 1963, Soche Hill Coll., Malawi, 1963-65; mem. faculty English dept. Makerere U., Uganda, 1965-68, U. Singapore, 1968-71; vis. lectr. U. Va., 1972-73. Author: (fiction) Waldo, 1967, Fong and the Indians, 1968, Girls at Play, 1969, Murder in Mt. Holly, 1969, Jungle Lovers, 1971, Sinning with Annie, 1972, Saint Jack, 1973, The Black House, 1974, The Family Arsenal, 1976, The Consul's File, 1977, Picture Palace, 1978 (Whitbread prize for fiction), A Christmas Card, 1978, London Snow, 1980, World's End, 1980, The Mosquito Coast, 1981, The London Embassy, 1982, Half Moon Street, 1984, O-Zone, 1986, My Secret History, 1988, Chicago Loop, 1990, Millroy and the Magician, 1993, My Other Life, 1996, Kowloon Tong, 1997, (nonfiction) V.S. Naipaul, 1973, The Great Railway Bazaar, 1975, The Old Patagonian Express, 1979, The Kingdom by the Sea, 1983, Sailing Through China, 1983, Sunrise with Sea Monsters, 1985, The White Man's Burden, 1987, Riding the Iron Rooster, 1988, The Happy Isles of Oceania, 1992, The Pillars of Hercules, 1995, (film script) Saint Jack, 1979. Recipient Editorial award Playboy mag., 1972, 76, 77, 79, Lit. award AAAL, 1977, James Tait Black award, 1982, Yorkshire Post Best Novel award, 1982, Thomas Cook Travel Book prize, 1989. Fellow Royal Soc. Lit., Royal Geog. Soc.; mem. AAAL.

THESEN, ARNE, industrial engineering educator; b. Oslo, May 6, 1943; came to U.S., 1963; s. Gudbrand and Astrid (Siggerud) T.; m. Maria Tan, Jan. 25, 1969 (div. Dec. 1987); children: Anita Mei-Ling, Britt Wei-Ling; m. Sharon W. Foster, June 21, 1991 (div. Mar. 1994). Student, Schous Tekniske Inst., Oslo, 1961-63; B.S., U. Ill., 1965, M.S., 1968, Ph.D., 1972. Systems analyst Bell Telephone Labs., Piscataway, N.J., 1970-72; prof. dept. indsl. engring. U. Wis.-Madison, 1972—; chmn. dept. indsl. engring., 1978-81, 91-95, prof. dept. computer sci., 1981-93; ptnr. Troll Assocs., Madison, 1976-84; prin. Troll Software, Madison, 1984—. Author: Computer Methods in O.R., 1976; co-author: Systems Tools for Planning, 1976, Simulation for Decision Making, 1992; contbr. articles to profl. jours. With Royal Norwegian Air Force, 1965-66. Mem. INFORMS, Assn. Computer Machinery, Inst. for Indsl. Engring. Home: 4310 Fawn Ct Cross Plains WI 53528-9780 Office: Univ Wis Dept Indsl Engring 1513 University Ave Madison WI 53706-1539

THEUNER, DOUGLAS EDWIN, bishop; b. N.Y.C., Nov. 15, 1938; s. Alfred Edwin Kipp and Grace Elizabeth (MacKean) T.; m. Jane Lois Szuhany, May 16, 1959; children: Elizabeth Susan, Nicholas Frederick Kipp. BA, Coll. of Wooster, 1960; BD, Kenyon Coll., 1962; MA, U. Conn., 1968. Ordained to ministry Episcopal Ch. as deacon, then priest, 1962. Curate St. Peter's Episcopal Ch., Ashtabula, Ohio, 1962-65; vicar St. George's Episcopal Ch., Bolton, Conn., 1965-68; rector St. Paul's Episcopal Ch., Wllimantic, Conn., 1968-74, St. John's Episcopal Ch., Stamford, Conn., 1974-86; bishop Diocese of N.H., Concord, 1986—. Chmn. Community Housing Coalition, Stamford, Conn., 1975-86, Instituto Pastoral Hispano, N.Y.C., 1979-86; pres. Holderness (N.H.) Sch., 1987—, White Mountain Sch., Littleton, N.H., 1987—. Mem. N.H. Coun. Chs. (v.p.). Avocations: photography, cooking, hiking, skiing. Office: Concord Diocese Diocesan Office 63 Green St Concord NH 03301-4243*

THEURER, BYRON W., aerospace engineer, business owner; b. Glendale, Calif., July 1, 1939; s. William Louis and Roberta Cecelia (Sturgiss) T.; m. Sue Ann McKay, Sept. 15, 1962 (div. 1980); children: Karen Marie, William Thomas, Alison Lee. BS in Engring. Sci., USAF Acad., 1961; MS in Aero. Sci., U. Calif., Berkeley, 1965; MBA, U. Redlands, 1991. Commd. USAF, 1961, advanced through grades to lt. col., ret. 1978; project officer Space Shuttle Devel. Prog., Houston, 1971-76; chief of test F-15 Systems Prog. Office Wright Patterson AFB, Ohio, 1976-78; sr. engr. Veda, Inc., Dayton, 1979-81, Logicon Inc., Dayton, 1981-83; project mgr. Support Systems Assocs., Inc., Dayton, 1983-84, CTA Inc., Ridgecrest, Calif., 1985-89; owner, operator The Princeton Rev. of Ctrl. Calif., Ridgecrest, 1989-92, San Luis Obispo, 1993—; cons. in field. Decorated Silver Star, D.F.C., Air Medals (16); named Officer of the Yr., Air Force Flight Test Ctr., Edwards AFB, 1970. Mem. Air Force Assn., Assn. Old Crows, USAF Acad. Assn. Grads. (nat. bd. dirs. 1972-75, chpt. pres. 1981-83). Republican. Episcopalian. Avocations: long distance running. Home: PO Box 697 Cayucos CA 93430-0697

THEVENET, PATRICIA CONFREY, social studies educator; b. Norwich, Conn., Apr. 16, 1924; d. John George and Gertrude Pauline (Doolittle) Confrey; m. Rubén Thevenet, Dec. 15, 1945 (dec. Mar. 1983); children: Susanne, Gregory, Richard, R. James. BS, U. Conn., 1944; AM, U. Chgo., 1945; EdM, Columbia U., 1992, EdD, 1994. Cert. elem. tchr., N.J. Counselor testing and guidance U. Chgo., 1945; home economist Western Mass. Electric Co., Pittsfield, 1946; tchr. Unquowa Sch., Fairfield, Conn., 1950-53, Alpine (N.J.) Sch., 1968-86; program asst. soc. studies Tchrs. Coll. Columbia U., N.Y.C., 1987-93; ret., 1993; historian Borough Northvale, N.J., 1987-94; participant summer seminar Smithsonian Instn., Washington, 1984. Del 2d dist. rep. Town Mtg., Trumbull, Conn., 1954-56; pres., trustee Northvale Pub. Libr. Assn., 1957-63; trustee Northvale Bd. Edn., 1963-72, pres. Northvale Bd. Edn., 1969-70; exec. bd. dirs. Bergen County (N.J.) County Bds. Edn., 1965-72; mem. Evening Sch. Comm. No. Valley Regional Dist., Bergen County, 1976-83; trustee Voluntown Libr., 1997. Mem. Am. Hist. Assn., Nat. Coun. Social Studies, Alumni Coun. Tchrs. Coll., Columbia U., Conn. Hist. Soc., Voluntown Hist. Soc., Friends of Slater Mus. (bd. dirs.). Avocations: sailing, swimming, reading. Home: 88 N Shore Rd # B Voluntown CT 06384-1719

THIBADEAU, EUGENE FRANCIS, education educator, consultant; b. N.Y.C., May 18, 1933; s. Eugene Servanis and Lillian (Archer) T.; 1 child, Christine; m. Patricia M. Batchelder, March 16, 1993. BA, NYU, 1959, MA, 1967; MA, NYU, 1968, PhD, 1973. Instr. NYU, N.Y.C., 1968; lectr. in philosophy Dowling Coll., Oakdale, N.Y., 1968-70; prof. edn. Indiana U. of Pa., Indiana, Pa., 1970—; vis. assoc. prof. Adelphi U., Garden City, N.Y., 1974-75; vis. scholar NYU, N.Y.C., 1984-85; vis. prof. Hofstra U., Hempstead, N.Y., 1974, 75, 84, 86; cons. Central Bur. of Ednl. Visits, London, 1980-81, Commonwealth Speakers Bur., Harrisburg, Pa., 1983-85, U.S. Dept. Edn., Washington, 1983-85, Pa. Dept. Edn., Harrisburg, 1988—. Author: Opening Up Education-In Theory and Practice, 1976, Curriculum Theory, 1988, Existentialism in the Classroom, 1994; rev. editor: Focus on Learning, 1973-77, editor, 1977-84; contbg. editor: International Encyclopedia of Education, 2d edit., International Encyclopedia of Teaching and Teacher Education, 2nd edit.; contbr. articles to profl. jours. Active in United Way, Indiana, Pa., 1980—, NAACP, Indiana, 1985—, Red Cross, Indiana, 1985—. Fulbright sr. lectr. Thames Polytechnic, London, 1978-79, Janus Pannonius U., Peces, Hungary, 1990-91; foreign expert Shanghai (China) Tchrs. U., 1988; designated faculty rsch. assoc. Inst. for Applied Rsch. and Pub. Policy, Indiana U. of Pa., 1989; named Commonwealth Teaching fellow, Pa. State Colls. and Univ. Disting. Faculty Awards Com., 1976; recipient Founder's Day award, NYU, 1973. Fellow Am. Philosophy Edn. Soc.; mem. Am. Ednl. Studies Assn., AAUP, The S.W. Philosophy Edn. Soc., ASCD. Avocations: traveling, skiing, tennis, reading, chess. Home: RR 1 Box 103 Penn Run PA 15765-9733 Office: Indiana Univ of Pa 133 Stouffer Hall Indiana PA 15701

THIBAULT, J(OSEPH) LAURENT, service company executive; b. Sturgeon Falls, Ont., Can., Dec. 31, 1944; s. J. Rene and Leone (Doucet) T.; m. Paulette Patricia Lalonde, June 4, 1966; children—Alain, Andre. B.A. in Econs., Laurentian U., Sudbury, 1966; M.A. in Econs., U. Toronto, Ont., 1968. Cons. Kates, Peat & Marwick Co., Toronto, 1968-72; dir. econs. and communications Can. Mfrs. Assn., Toronto, 1972-76; v.p. Can. Mfrs. Assn., 1976-81, sr. exec. v.p., 1981-84, pres., exec. dir., 1985-91; co-chair Can. Labour Force Devel. Bd., Ottawa, Ont., Can., 1991-95; fin. advisor Equion Group, Mississauga, Ont., 1995—. Club: National. Home: 24 Cindebarke Terr, Georgetown, ON Canada L7G 4S5 Office: City Ctr Plz, 1 City Centre Dr Ste 1520, Mississauga, ON Canada L5B 1M2

THIBEAULT, GEORGE WALTER, lawyer; b. Cambridge, Mass., Sept. 21, 1941; s. George Walter and Josephine (Maraggia) T.; m. Antoinette Miller, June 30, 1963; children—Robin M., Holly Ann. B.S., Northeastern U., 1964; M.B.A., Boston Coll., 1966, J.D., 1969. Bar: Mass. 1969. Assoc. Gaston & Snow, Boston, 1969-73; ptnr. Testa, Hurwitz & Thibeault, Boston, 1973—. Mem. ABA, Mass. Bar Assn., Am. Arbitration Assn. Home: 181 Caterina Hts Concord MA 01742-4773 Office: Testa Hurwitz & Thibeault High St Tower 125 High St Boston MA 02110-2704

THIBEDEAU, RICHARD HERBERT, environmental planner, administrator; b. Needham, Mass., Apr. 2, 1942; s. Richard and Mary (Neenan) T.; . Susan McAllister Richardson, Nov. 8, 1986; children: Susan, Richard, Catherine, Julie, Billy. BSFS, Georgetown U., 1964; M of Internat. Rels., U. Pa., 1967; M of Regional Planning, Harvard U., 1974. Field rep. CARE, Sri Lanka, 1967-70; asst. county dir. CARE, Korea, 1971-72; chief pvt. land planning Adirondack Park Agy., Ray Brook, N.Y., 1974-78; dep. dir. Mass. Coastal Zone Mgmt., Boston, 1978-80; chief planner Mass. Divsn. Water Resources, Boston, 1981-87, dir., 1987-90; dir. Bur. Resource Protection Dept. Environ. Mgmt., Boston, 1990—; Reservist Fed. Emergency Mgmt. Agy., 1992—; chmn. Conn. River Flood Control Commn., Vt., N.H., Mass. and Conn., 1993-94. Clk. 45 Trowbridge Condominium Assn., Cambridge, 1991—. 1st lt. U.S. Army, 1964-66, Korea. Recipient Mass. Citation for Outstanding Performance, 1988, Mass. Cert. Performance, State Gov., 1990. Mem. Am. Planning Assn. (Disting. Leadership award N.E. chpt. 1989), Am. Inst. Cert. Planners (cert.), Am. Water Assn., Appalachian Mountain Club (com. chmn. 1986—). Avocations: hiking, sailing, skiing. Home: 15 Village St Marblehead MA 01945-2212 Office: Mass Dept Environ Mgmt 100 Cambridge St Boston MA 02202-0044

THIBERT, ROGER JOSEPH, clinical chemist, educator; b. Tecumseh, Ont., Can., Aug. 29, 1929; s. Charles and Violet (Hebert) T.; m. Audrey M. Wissler, July 10, 1954; children: Mark Roger, Robert Francis. BA, U. Western Ont., 1951; MS, U. Detroit, 1954; PhD, Wayne State U., 1958. Diplomate: Am. Bd. Clin. Chemistry, also past bd. dirs. Mem. faculty U. Windsor, Ont., Can., 1953—; prof. chemistry U. Windsor, 1967-94, dir. clin. chemistry, 1972-94, prof. emeritus, 1994—; prof. pathology Med. Sch. Wayne State U., Detroit, 1972-94; asso. div. head, clin. chemistry Detroit Receiving Hosp., Univ. Health Ctr., 1973-94; mem. med. staff Detroit Receiving Hosp.-Univ. Health Center, 1973-94; cons. med. biochemistry Med. Labs. Windsor, Ont., Can. Contbr. articles on chemistry, biochemistry, analytical chemistry, clin. chemistry to profl. jours. Recipient Smith Kline award Am. Assn. Clin. Chemistry, 1980, Alumni Teaching award U. Windsor, 1988, Alumni Award of Merit, 1994, Teaching award Ont. Confedn. U. Faculty Assns., 1990, Beckman Edn. Excellence award Canadian Soc. Clin. Chemists, 1992; Chem. Inst. Can. fellow, 1968—; Nat. Acad. Clin. Biochemistry fellow, 1978—; recipient grants Natural Scis. and Engring. Rsch. Coun., Can., award Union Carbide, Chem. Inst., Can., 1978. Fellow AAAS, Can. Acad. Clin. Biochemistry; mem. Am. Chem. Soc., Chem. Inst. Can., Assn. Chem. Profession Ont., Am. Assn. Clin. Chemistry, Nat. Acad. Clin. Biochemistry, Can. Soc. Clin. Chemists (Ames award 1988), Ont. Soc. Clin. Chemists, Am. Soc. for Biochemistry and Molecular Biology, Fedn. Am. Socs. Exptl. Biology, Can. Soc. Biochemistry and Molecular Biology, Can. Fedn. Biol. Scis., Can. Soc. for Chemistry, Sigma Xi. Roman Catholic. Home: 4612 Dali Ct, Windsor, ON Canada N9G 2M8 Office: U Windsor, Dept Chemistry/Biochemistry, Windsor, ON Canada N9B 3P4

THIBODEAU, GARY A., academic administrator; b. Sioux City, Iowa, Sept. 26, 1938; m. Emogene J. McCarville, Aug. 1, 1964; children: Douglas James, Beth Ann. BS, Creighton U., 1962; MS, S.D. State U., 1967, S.D. State U., 1970; PhD, S.D. State U., 1971. Profl. service rep. Baxter Lab., Inc., Deerfield, Ill., 1963-65; tchr., researcher dept. biology S.D. State U., Brookings, 1965-76, asst. to v.p. for acad. affairs, 1976-80, v.p. for adminstrn., 1980-85; chancellor U. Wis., River Falls, 1985—; mem. investment com. U. Wis., River Falls Found.; trustee W. Cen. Wis. Consortium U. Wis. System; bd. dirs. U. Wis. at River Falls Found.; mem. Phi Kappa Phi nat. budget rev. and adv. comm., Phi Kappa Phi Found. investment comm., comm. on Agrl. and Rural Devel., steering commn. Coun. of Rural Colls. and Univs., Joint Coun. on Food and Agrl. Scis., USDA. Author: Basic Concepts in Anatomy and Physiology, 1983, Athletic Injury Assessment, 1994, Structure and Function of the Body, 1996, The Human Body in Health and Disease, 1996, Textbook of Anatomy and Physiology, 1996. Mem. AAAS, Sigma Xi, Phi Kappa Phi, Gamma Sigma Delta, Gamma Alpha. Office: U Wis 116 N Hall River Falls WI 54022

THIBODEAU, ROBIN ANN, union official, mail carrier; b. Southington, Conn., Oct. 27, 1956; d. Robert Edward and Irene Josephine (Bendott) Dunbar; m. Roland Leo Thibodeau, Feb. 25, 1978 (div. Aug. 1983); children: Christina Ann Thibodeau, Desilyn Joanne Nelson. Grad. high sch., Southington; grad., Porter & Chesters Auto. Inst. Sec. Bd. of Edn., Southington, 1974-75; cashier, clk. Cumberland Farms, Plantsville, Conn., 1974; acctg. clk. to contr. Waterbury Farrel, Mfg., Cheshire, Conn., 1975-76; machinist Supreme Lake Mfg., Plantsville, 1976-77; auto transmission re-builder Transmission Works, Hartford, Conn., 1978-79; rural carrier substitute Southington Post Office, 1979-81, Terryville (Conn.) Post Office, 1980; regular rural carrier Plainville (Conn.) Post Office, 1981-84, Farmington (Conn.) Post Office, 1984—; local union steward Plainville Post Office, 1981-84; local/area steward Farmington Post Office, 1985-94. Democrat. Avocations: computer bulletin board, RV travel, crafting, gardening. Home: 17 Spruce St Plainville CT 06062-2327 Office: Conn Rural Letter Carrier Assn 210 Main St Farmington CT 06032-9998

THIEDE, RICHARD WESLEY, communications educator; b. Detroit, Mar. 30, 1936; s. Harold Victor and Blanche May (Gross) T. BS, Ea. Mich. U., 1961; MA, U. Ill., 1963; PhD, U. Mo., 1977. Tchg. asst. U. Ill., Urbana, 1961-62; tchr. Ctrl. H.S., Battle Creek, Mich., 1962-63, Shafer H.S., Southgate, Mich., 1963-64, Chadsey H.S., Detroit, 1964-68, Stevenson H.S., Livonia, Mich., 1968-71; part-time instr. Schoolcraft Coll., Livonia, 1969-71; teaching/tech. asst. U. Mo., Columbia, 1971-74; instr. Ottumwa Hts. Coll., Iowa, 1975-76, Midland Luth. Coll., Fremont, Nebr., 1976-77; prof. dept. comm. arts The Defiance (Ohio) Coll., 1978—; tchr. summer sch. Southwestern H.S., Detroit, 1966, Cody H.S., Detroit, 1967, 68; tchr. evening sch. Chadsey H.S., 1965-67, Stevenson H.S., 1969-70. Mem. AAUP, Assn. for Theatre in Higher Edn., Ohio Theatre Alliance, Alpha Psi Omega, Kappa Delta Pi. Democrat. Home: PO Box 1101 Defiance OH 43512-1101 Office: The Defiance Coll 701 N Clinton St Defiance OH 43512-1610

THIEL, ARTHUR WARREN, journalist; b. Hot Springs, Mont., Nov. 27, 1952; s. Robert Harry and Mary (Previs) T.; m. Julia Claire Akoury, July 16, 1988. BA, Pacific Luth. U., 1975. Reporter News Tribune, Tacoma, 1972-76; reporter, asst. sports editor Jour. Am., Bellevue, Wash., 1976-80; reporter, columnist Post-Intelligencer, Seattle, 1980—; commentator, talk-show host Sta. KIRO, Seattle, 1989—; commentator Sta. KZOK-FM, Seattle, 1991-96. Bd. dirs. Alzheimers Assn. Western and Ctrl Wash., Seattle, 1990-96. Named State Sportswriter of Yr., Nat. Sportswriter & Sportscasters Assn., 1990, 92, 96, Disting. Alumnus Pacific Luth. U., 1991. Avocations: sea kayaking, gardening, adventure travel. Office: Seattle Post-Intelligencer 101 Elliott Ave W Seattle WA 98119-4220

THIEL, PHILIP, design educator; b. Bklyn., Dec. 20, 1920; s. Philip and Alma Theone (Meyer) T.; m. Midori Kono, 1955; children: Philip Kenji, Nancy Tamiko, Susan Akiko, Peter Akira (dec.). BSc, Webb Inst. Naval Architecture, 1943; MSc, U. Mich., 1948; BArch, MIT, 1952. Instr. naval architecture MIT, Cambridge, 1949-50; instr. U. Calif., Berkeley, 1954-56, asst. prof., 1956-60; assoc. prof. U. Wash., Seattle, 1961-66; prof. visual design and experiential notation U. Wash., 1966-91; guest prof. Tokyo Inst. Tech., 1976-78; vis. prof. Sapporo (Japan) Sch. of Arts, 1992—; lectr., U.S., Can. Japan, Norway, Denmark, Sweden, Eng., Austria, Switzerland, Peru, Bolivia; cons. FAO, Rome, 1952; co-founder Environment and Behavior, 1969; founder Ctr. for Experiential Notation, Seattle, 1981. Author: Freehand Drawing, 1965, Visual Awareness and Design, 1981, People, Paths and Purposes, 1997; patentee in field. Soc. Naval Architects and Marine Engrs. scholar, 1947; Rehmann scholar AIA, 1960; NIMH grantee, 1967, Nat. Endowment for Arts, 1969, Graham Found., 1995.

THIELE, HOWARD NELLIS, JR., lawyer; b. Dayton, Ohio, June 22, 1930; s. Howard Nellis and Irma Laura (Scheibe) T.; m. Alma Kuhn, Oct. 14, 1995; children: Leslie, Howard III, Craig. AB, Miami U., Oxford, Ohio, 1952; JD with distinction, U. Mich., 1955. Bar: Ohio 1955. Assoc., ptnr. Smith & Schnacke, LPA, Dayton, Ohio, 1957-89; ptnr. Thompson, Hine & Flory, Dayton, 1989-95; ret., 1995. Pres. Dayton Art Inst., 1981-85; bd. dirs. Dayton Area chpt. ARC, 1983—, 1st vice chmn., 1990-91, chmn., 1992-94; bd. dirs. Jr. Achievement. Capt. USAF, 1955-57. Mem. Ohio State Bar Assn., Dayton Bar Assn., Order of the Coif, Engrs. Club, Phi Beta Kappa. Republican. Episcopalian.

THIELSCH, HELMUT JOHN, engineering company executive; b. Berlin, Nov. 16, 1922; came to U.S., 1939, naturalized, 1954; s. Kurt and Anna-Sibylle T.; m. Margaret E. McKenna, Aug. 16, 1952; children: Barbara Anne, Donald Kurt, Deborah Lee, Helmut John. BS, Auburn U., 1943; postgrad., U. Mich., 1943-45, Lehigh U., 1948. Registered profl. engr., R.I., Mass., Maine, N.J., Ga., Calif. Research engr. Allis Chalmers Co., Milw., 1945-46; metall. engr. Black, Sivalls & Bryson, Inc., Kansas City, Mo., 1946-47; research engr. Lukens Steel Co., Coatsville, Pa., 1948-49; engr. Welding Research Council, N.Y.C., 1949-52; dir. research Eutectic Welding Alloys Co., N.Y.C., 1952-53; v.p., dir. research, devel. and engring. ITT Grinnell Corp., Providence, 1954-84; pres. Thielsch Engring., Inc., Providence, 1984—; pres. HiTech Realty Assocs. Inc.; cons. on failure analysis to industry, public utilities, equipment builders, 1954—; lectr. at confs. on failures and failure prevention; mem. component tech. com. Argonne (Ill.) Nat. Lab.; bd. dirs. Ind. Energy, Inc. Author: Defects and Failures in Pressure Vessels and Piping, 1965; contbr. numerous articles to profl. publs.; patentee in field. Recipient Nat. Safety award Nat. Bd. Boiler and Pressure Vessel Insps., 1990. Fellow ASME, Am. Soc. Metals, Am. Soc. Nondestructive Testing, Am. Welding Soc. (Adams Lecture award 1982); mem. TAPPI, Am. Soc. Quality Control, Am. Nuclear Soc., Nat. Assn. Corrosion Engrs., Am. Chem. Soc., Am. Mgmt. Assn., Am. Soc. Profl. Engrs. (Freeman award 1985), Am. Bd. Forensic Examiners. Office: 195 Frances Ave Cranston RI 02910-2211

THIEMANN, CHARLES LEE, banker; b. Louisville, Nov. 21, 1937; s. Paul and Helen (Kern) T.; m. Donna Timperman, June 18, 1960; children: Laura Gerette, Charles Lee, Rodney Gerard, Jeffrey Michael, Matthew Joseph. BA in Chemistry, Bellarmine Coll., 1959; MBA, Ind. U., 1961, DBA, 1963. Mem. rsch. dept. Fed. Res. Bank, St. Louis, 1963-64; with Fed. Home Loan Bank, Cin., 1964—, sr. v.p., then exec. v.p., 1974, pres., 1975—; adj. prof. Grad. Sch. Bus., Xavier U., Cin., mem. bus. adv. coun. Coll. Bus. Adminstrn., chmn. bd. dirs. Office Fin.; trustee Fin. Instns. Retirement Fund, Leadership Group Social Compact; mem. First Step Home; past chmn. bd. Resolution Funding Corp. Directorate. Past chmn. real estate exec. adv. coun. U. Cin. Mem. Cin. C. of C., Queen City Club, Rotary. Roman Catholic. Office: Fed Home Loan Bank 221 E 4th St Cincinnati OH 45202-4124

THIEMANN, RONALD FRANK, dean, religion educator; b. St. Louis, Oct. 4, 1946; s. Frank Joseph and Marie Magdalene (Graeser) T.; m. Beth Arlene Barkow, June 15, 1968; children: Sarah Elizabeth, Laura Kristen. B.A. magna cum laude, Concordia Sr. Coll., Fort Wayne, Ind., 1968; M.Div., Concordia Sem., St. Louis, 1972; M.A., Yale U., 1973, M.Philosophy, 1974, Ph.D., 1976; postgrad., Eberhard-Karls Universitat, Tubingen, W.Ger., 1974-75. Asst. prof. dept. religion Haverford Coll., Pa., 1976-82, assoc. prof. dept. religion, 1982-85, prof. dept. religion, 1985-86, acting provost, 1985, acting pres., 1986; dean Div. Sch. Harvard U., Cambridge, Mass., 1986—; John Lord O'Brian prof. divinity Harvard U., Cambridge, 1986—; vis. prof. honors program Villanova U., 1981; vis. asst. prof. Luth. Theol. Sem., Phila., 1977; mem. Ctr. Theol. Inquiry, Princeton, N.J., 1982-83; mem. consultation on Christianity and Marxism, U.S.A. nat. com. Luth. World Fedn., 1979-83, mem. consultation on civil religion, 1983-86, mem. consultation on problem of common good, 1985-88; bd. dirs. Trinity Press Internat.; mem. exec. com. Assn. Theol. Schs., 1994—. Author: Revelation and Theology, 1985, Constructing a Public Theology: The Church in a Pluralistic Culture, 1991, Religion in Public Life: A Dilemma for Democracy, 1995; editor: The Legacy of H. Richard Niebuhr, 1991; mem. editl. bd. Dialog, 1987—; contbr. numerous articles to profl. jours. Mem. bd. trustees

Buckingham Browne & Nichols Schs., 1988-90; mem. task force on theol. education, Evang. Luth. Ch. in Am., 1989-91, task force on Luth.-Reformed Conversations, Evang. Luth. Ch. Am., 1988-92. Recipient Disting. Teaching award Lindback Found., 1982; Mellon Found. fellow, 1982-83; Deutscher Akademischer Austauschdienst fellow, 1974-75. Mem. Am. Acad. Religion, (chmn. narrative interpretation and theology group 1982-86). Avocations: tennis; squash; piano. Home: 44 Francis Ave Cambridge MA 02138-1912 Office: Harvard Div Sch 45 Francis Ave Cambridge MA 02138-1911

THIER, SAMUEL OSIAH, physician, educator; b. Bklyn., June 23, 1937; s. Sidney and May Henrietta (Kanner) T.; m. Paula Dell Finkelstein, June 28, 1958; children: Audrey Lauren, Stephanie Ellen, Sara Leslie. Student, Cornell U., 1953-56; MD, SUNY, Syracuse, 1960, DSc (hon.), 1987; DSc (hon.), Tufts U., 1988, George Washington U., 1988, Mt. Sinai Sch. Med., 1989, Hahnemann U., 1989, U. Pa., 1994, Dartmouth Coll., 1996; LHD (hon.), Rush U., 1988, Va. Commonwealth U., 1992, Med. Coll. Pa., 1992, Brandeis U., 1994. Diplomate: Am. Bd. Internal Medicine (dir. 1977-85, exec. com. 1981-85, chmn. 1984-85). Intern Mass. Gen. Hosp., Boston, 1960-61; asst. resident Mass. Gen. Hosp., 1961-62, sr. resident, 1964-65, clin. and research fellow, 1965, chief resident, 1966; clin. asso. Nat. Inst. Arthritis and Metabolic Diseases, 1962-64; from instr. to asst. prof. medicine Harvard U. Med. Sch., 1967-69; prof. medicine, health care policy Harvard Med. Sch., 1994—; asst. in medicine, chief renal unit Mass. Gen. Hosp., Boston, 1967-69; asso. prof., then prof. medicine U. Pa. Med. Sch., 1969-72, vice chmn. dept., 1971-74; assoc. dir. med. svcs. Hosp. U. Pa., 1969-71; David Paige Smith prof. medicine Yale U. Sch. Medicine, 1978-81, Sterling prof. medicine, 1981-85, chmn. dept., 1975-85; pres. Inst. Medicine NAS, Washington, 1985-91; pres., Univ. prof. Brandeis U., Waltham, Mass., 1991-94; pres. Mass. Gen. Hosp., Boston, 1994-97; pres. Ptnrs. HealthCare Sys., Inc., Boston, 1994-96, 97—, CEO, 1996—; chief medicine Yale-New Haven Hosp., 1975-85, trustee, 1978-85; bd. dirs. Conn. Hospice, Inc., 1976-82. Mem. editorial bd.: New Eng. Jour. Medicine, 1978-81; Contbr. articles to med. jours. Mem. adv. com. to the dir. NIH, 1980-85. Served with USPHS, 1962-64. Recipient Christian R. and Mary F. Lindback Found. Distinguished Teaching award, 1971. Mem. ACP (bd. regents 1982-85), Assn. Am. Med. Colls. (adminstrv. bd. coun. acad. socs.), John Morgan Soc., Am. Fedn. Clin. Rsch. (pres. 1976-77), Am. Soc. Nephrology, Am. Physiol. Soc., Internat. Soc. Nephrology, Assn. Profs. Medicine, Assn. Am. Physicians, Interurban Clin. Club, Alpha Omega Alpha. Home: 99-20 Florence St Apt 4B Chestnut Hill MA 02167-1927

THIEROLF, RICHARD BURTON, JR., lawyer; b. Medford, Oreg., Oct. 27, 1948; s. Richard Burton Sr. and Helen Dorothy (Rivolta) T. BA, Columbia U., N.Y.C., 1970; JD, U. Oreg., 1976. Bar: Oreg. 1976, U.S. Dist. Ct. Oreg. 1976, U.S. Ct. Appeals (9th cir.) 1977, U.S. Dist. Ct. (no. dist.) Calif. 1980, U.S. Supreme Ct. 1993, U.S. Ct. Fed. Claims 1993. Staff atty. Orgn. of the Forgotten Am., Inc., Klamath Falls, Oreg., 1976-77, exec. dir., 1977-79; ptnr. Jacobson, Jewett & Thierolf, P.C., Medford, 1980—. Mem. City of Medford Planning Commn., 1990-92; mem. Medford Sch. Dist. 549-C Budget Com., 1991-92, chmn., 1991. Mem. ABA, Fed. Bar Assn., Oreg. State Bar (local profl. responsibility com. 1987-89, mem. fed. practice and procedure com. 1994—, sec. 1995—), Jackson County Bar Assn. (sec. 1988). Episcopalian. Avocation: violin. Home: 234 Ridge Rd Ashland OR 97520-2829 Office: Jacobson Jewett & Thierolf PC Two N Oakdale Ave Medford OR 97501

THIERRY, JOHN ADAMS, heavy machinery manufacturing company executive, lawyer; b. Watertown, Mass., May 8, 1913; s. Louis Sidney and Adelaide (Hamlin) T.; m. Mary Mills Hatch, June 6, 1953 (div.); 1 child, Charles Adams; m. Silvie Marie Frère, Dec. 1977. A.B. summa cum laude, Harvard U., 1935, A.M., 1936, J.D., 1940; postgrad. (Sheldon traveling fellow Harvard), U. Cambridge, Eng., 1936-37. Bar: Wis. 1941. With Bucyrus-Erie Co., South Milwaukee, Wis., 1940-82; sec. Bucyrus-Erie Co., 1958-77, gen. atty., 1958-76, v.p., 1960-77, sr. v.p., 1977-78, dir., 1961-79, mem. exec. com., 1967-78; v.p., dir. Bucyrus Erie Co. Can., Ltd., 1959-78; dir. Ruston-Bucyrus, Ltd., Lincoln, Eng., 1964-79, Komatsu-Bucyrus K.K., Japan, 1971-81; former dir. Bucyrus (Australia) Pty. Ltd., Bucyrus Internat., Inc., Brad Foot Gear Works, Inc., Pitts. Gear Co., South Milw. Marine Bank, Atlas Chain & Precision. Dir. Wis. Pub. Expenditure Survey, 1954-78; v.p., bd. dirs. Bucyrus-Erie Found., 1963-78; bd. dirs. Pub. Expenditure Research Found., 1964-78, YMCA, Milw., 1973-78, Milw. Symphony Orch., 1974-78; trustee Wis. Conservatory Music, 1969-78, S.E. Asia Art Found., 1977—; pres. United Performing Arts Fund, Milw., 1969; mem. adv. council Coll. Engrng. U. Wis.-Milw., 1975-78, mem. adv. council Sch. Bus., 1975-78; mem. council Med. Coll. Wis., 1975-78; pres. Milw. Patent Law Assn., 1961-62. Served to capt., C.E. AUS, 1942-46. Recipient Granite State award U. N.H., 1986. Mem. Mass., Wis. patent office bars, Cambridge Union Soc., Phi Beta Kappa. Episcopalian. Club: Harvard (Boston and N.Y.C.). Home: Murray Hill Rd Hill NH 03243-9711

THIES, AUSTIN COLE, retired utility company executive; b. Charlotte, N.C., July 18, 1921; s. Oscar Julius and Blanche (Austin) T.; m. Marilyn Joy Walker, June 26, 1945 (dec. Dec. 1992); children: Austin Cole, Robert Melvin, Marilyn Leone; m. Fay Best Britt, May 7, 1993; stepchildren: Jeff Britt, Mike Britt. BSME, Ga. Inst. Tech., 1943. With Duke Power Co., Charlotte, 1946-86; mgr. steam prodn. Duke Power Co., 1963-65, asst. v.p., 1965-67, v.p. prodn. and operation, 1967-71, sr. v.p., 1971-82, exec. v.p., 1982-86, also dir.; past chmn. prodn. com., engrng. and operating div. Southeastern Electric Exchange; chmn. tech. advisory com. Carolinas Va. Nuclear Power Assos.; chmn. N.C. Air Control Advisory Council. Mem. nat. adv. bd. Ga. Inst. Tech.; pres. Arts and Scis. Council; chmn. bd. dirs. Mercy Hosp.; trustee Alexander Childrens Center; bd. visitors Boy's Town.; 1st v.p. Sci. Museums of Charlotte; bd. dirs. Sci. Mus. Served with USNR, 1943-46. Decorated Purple Heart; named to Ga. Tech. Hall of Fame, 1994. Mem. Edison Electric Inst. (past chmn. engrng. and operating div. exec. com.), IEEE, Charlotte C. of C., ASME (past chmn. Piedmont Carolina sect.), Am. Nuclear Soc., Air Pollution Control Assn., N.C. Soc. Engrs. (past pres., Engr. of Yr. 1985), Charlotte Engrs. Club (Disting. Service award 1984), Nat. Rifle Assn. (life), Kappa Sigma. Presbyterian (elder). Clubs: Rotary (past pres., dir. N. Charlotte), Cowans Ford Country (bd. dirs.), Quail Hollow Country (bd. dirs.), Charlotte City (bd. dirs.), Charlotte Ga. Inst. Tech. (past pres.), Charlotte Rifle and Pistol (past pres.). Home: 2429 Red Fox Trl Charlotte NC 28211-3766 Office: 422 S Church St Charlotte NC 28242-0001

THIES, LYNN WAPINSKI, elementary education educator; b. Pottsville, Pa., Aug. 11, 1946; d. Stanley Walter and Mary Etta (Stevens) Wapinski; m. Wynn Gerrard, June 14, 1969; children: Heather Anne, Kevin Leonard. BA in Edn., Assoc. Libr. Sci., U. S.C., 1968. Tchr. 5th grade Ft. Jackson (S.C.) Elem. Sch., 1968-70; tchr. 4th and 5th grades Groner Elem. Sch., Scholls, Oreg., 1970-72; tchr. 1st grade Welches (Oreg.) Elem., 1980; tchr. 6th grade Sandy (Oreg.) Elem. Sch. Dist. 46, 1983-87, tchr. 3rd grade, 1987-94, tchr. mixed-age class, ages 7 and 8, 1994-96, 2nd grade tchr., 1996—; mem. lang. arts curriculum com. Firwood Elem. Sch., Sandy Elem. Sch. Dist. 46, 1986-87, mem. 21st Century S.I.T.E. com., 1994—, sci. curriculum com., 1995—; active Oreg. Consortium Quality Sci., Portland, 1985-87, Oreg. Cadre Quality Sci. Edn., Sandy, 1987-89, Sci. Curriculum Consortium, Sandy, 1989-92. Leader, mem. Day Camp core staff Girl Scouts U.S., mem. hist. re-enactment group, vol. Columbia River Girl Scout coun., Portland, 1972-92. Eisenhower grantee, 1994, 95, 96, 97, ODE Primary Math Project grantee, 1996-97. Mem. NEA, ASCD, Internat. Reading Assn., Oreg. State Tchrs. Assn., Oreg. Consortium for Quality in Sci. Edn., Oreg. Cadre for Assistance to Tchrs. Sci., Oreg. Sci. Tchrs. Assn., Clackamas County Sci. Tchrs. Assn., Barlow Trail Long Rifles. Democrat. Roman Catholic. Avocations: historical reinactment, percussion rifle competitions, historical memorabilia, research into American history. Home: 51956 E Terra Fern Dr Sandy OR 97055-9415

THIES, MARGARET DIANE, nurse; b. Carrol, Iowa, Oct. 5, 1949; d. George Duane and Elizabeth Lee (Cram) Smith; children: Alicia Kay, Matthew John. Diploma in Nursing, Iowa Luth. Sch. Nursing, Des Moines, 1972; BSN, Creighton U., 1989. RN, Nebr., Iowa, Colo. Staff nurse mental health unit Mary Greely Hosp., Ames, Iowa, 1972-73; staff nurse Kossuth County Hosp., Algona, Iowa, 1973-74, 77-81; staff nurse med.-surg. unit U. Nebr. Hosp., Omaha, 1981-83, 87-89, charge nurse med.-surg. unit, 1983-87, quality assurance com. chairperson med.-surg. unit, 1984-88; quality assurance coord. Share Health Plan of Nebr., Omaha, 1990-91; staff nurse med. Poudre Valley Hosp., Ft. Collins, Colo., 1992-95; quality resource specialist Poudre Valle Hosp., Ft. Collins, 1995—; quality assessment and improvement com. chairperson, 1993-95. Pres. City of Ft. Collins Parks and Rec. Commn., 1995—; mem. Family Support Coun., Foothills Gateway, 1995-96. Recipient Sec.'s Community Health Promotion award, 1990, Physician's award 1994. Mem. Sigma Theta Tau. Home: 2731 Claremont Dr Fort Collins CO 80526-2280 Office: Poudre Valley Hosp Quality Resources Dept Fort Collins CO 80524-3998

THIES, RICHARD BRIAN, lawyer; b. Chgo., Dec. 14, 1943; s. Fred W. and Loraine C. (Mannix) T.; m. Anita Marie Rees, Aug. 5, 1972; children: Emily Marie, Richard Clarke. BA, Miami U., 1966; JD, Loyola U., 1974. Bar: Ill. 1974, U.S. Tax Ct. 1989. Assoc. Wilson & McIlvaine, Chgo., 1974-78; assoc.-ptnr. Isham, Lincoln & Beale, Chgo., 1978-88; ptnr. Wildman, Harrold, Allen & Dixon, Chgo., 1988—. Bd. govs. Chgo. HEart Assn., 1980-87, exec. com., 1982-87; bd. dirs. Juvenile Protective Assn., Chgo., 1984—; v.p. Samaritan Counseling Ctr., Evanston, 1989-94, pres., 1994. Mem. ABA, Chgo. Bar Assn., Chgo. Estate Planning Coun. Avocations: coaching children's sports, photography, music. Home: 305 Driftwood Ln Wilmette IL 60091-3441 Office: Wildman Harrold Allen & Dixon 225 W Wacker Dr Chicago IL 60606-1224

THIESENHUSEN, WILLIAM CHARLES, agricultural economist; b. Waukesha, Wis., Feb. 12, 1936; s. Arthur Henry and Myrtle O. (Honeyager) T.; children—James Waring, Kathryn Hague, Gail Ann. BS, U. Wis., 1958, MS, 1960, PhD, 1965; M.P.A. (Danforth Found. fellow), Harvard U., 1962, postgrad., 1968-69. Instr. agrl. extension U. Wis., Madison, 1959-61; exec. asst. Land Tenure Center and Instituto de Economia Universidad de Chile research team in, Santiago, 1963-65; asst. prof. agrl. econs. Land Tenure Center and Instituto de Economia Universidad de Chile research team in, 1965-68, asso. prof. agrl. econs., 1971-72, asso. prof. agrl. journalism, 1968-72, prof. agrl. journalism and agrl. econs., 1972—; dir. Land Tenure Ctr., 1971-75, 94—; asst. prof. econs. U. Wis., Milw., 1966-67; prof. agrl. econs. Escuela Nacional de Agricultura, Chapingo, Mex.; under AID contract, summer 1965; vis. prof. Universidad Autonoma de Madrid, Fulbright Program, 1977; cons., condr. seminars in field; Fulbright-Hays lectr., 1965, 72. Author: Chile's Experiments in Agrarian Reform, 1966, Reforma Agraria en Chile: Experimentos en Cuatro Fundos de la Iglesia, 1968, Broken Promises: Agrarian Reform and the Latin American Campesino, 1995; editor: Searching for Agrarian Reform in Latin America, 1989; mem. editl. bd. Latin Am. Rsch. Rev., Pakistan Devel. Rev.; contbr. articles to profl. jours. Served with USAR, 1960. Recipient award for best article Am. Jour. Agrl. Econs., 1969; Alpha Zeta nat. fellow, 1957; U. Wis. fellow, 1956; Harvard U. Adminstrn. fellow, 1962. Mem. Am. Agrl. Econs. Assn., Am. Econ. Assn., Latin Am. Studies Assn., Council Internat. Exchange Scholars (chmn. com. econs. selection 1979-80), Inter-Am. Found. (selection bd.), Wis. Acad. Scis., Arts and Letters, Phi Kappa Phi, Alpha Zeta, Sigma Delta Chi. Unitarian. Office: U Wis Land Tenure Ctr 1300 University Ave Madison WI 53706-1510

THIESSEN, DELBERT DUANE, psychologist; b. Julesberg, Colo., Aug. 13, 1932; s. David and Eva Peters (Wetherby) T.; children—Trevor, Theron, Kendell Courtney. B.A. in Psychology with great distinction, San Jose (Calif.) State Coll., 1958; Ph.D., U. Calif., Berkeley, 1963. Extension instr. U. Calif., La Jolla, fall 1964; asst. sect. med. psychology, div. psychiatry and neurology Scripps Clinic and Research Found., La Jolla, 1962-65; mem. faculty U. Tex., Austin, 1965—; prof. psychology U. Tex., 1971—; research cons. NIMH. Author: Gene Organization and Behavior, 1972, The Evolution and Biochemistry of Aggression, 1976, Bitter-Sweet Destiny: The Stormy Evolution of Human Behavior, 1996, Universal Desires and Fears: The Deep History of Sociology, 1997; contbr. articles and chpts. to books. Served with AUS, 1952-54, Korea. Fellow USPHS, 1960-61; recipient Career Devel. award NIMH, 1967-72, grantee, 1967-78; grantee Russel Sage Found.; grantee NSF; grantee U. Tex. Research Inst. Mem. AAAS, Alumni Assn. Roscoe B. Jackson Meml. Lab., Am. Psychol. Assn., Am. Genetic Assn., Psychonomic Soc., Animal Behavior Soc., Southwestern Psychol. Assn., Behavior Genetics Assn., Sigma Xi, Phi Kappa Phi, Psi Chi. Home: 7300 Barcelona Dr Austin TX 78752-2003 Office: Univ Tex Dept Psychology Mezes 330 Austin TX 78712

THIESSEN, GORDON GEORGE, banker; b. South Porcupine, Ont., Can., Aug. 14, 1938; m. Annette Margaret Hillyar, Oct. 3, 1964; 2 children. BA with honours, U. Sask., 1960, MA, 1961; PhD in Econs., London Sch. Econs., 1972.. Lectr. U. Sask., Saskatoon, Can., 1961-62; Economist Bank of Can., Ottawa, Ont., 1963-73; chief monetary and fin. analysis dept. Bank of Can., Ottawa, 1975-79, adviser, 1979-84, dep. gov., 1984-87, sr. dep. gov., 1987-94; gov. Bank of Can., Ottawa, Ont., 1994—; also chmn. bd. dirs. Bank of Can., Ottawa; vis. economist Res. Bank Australia, Sydney, 1973-75. Avocations: sailing; skiing.

THIGPEN, ALTON HILL, motor transportation company executive; b. Kinston, N.C., Feb. 3, 1927; s. Kirby Alton and Alice (Hill) T.; m. Rebecca Ann Braswell, May 16, 1953; children: David Alton, Jennifer Ann, Steven Roy. B.S. in Indsl. Engring, N.C. State U., 1950. With Asso. Transport, Inc., Burlington, N.C., 1950-71; engr. Asso. Transport, Inc., 1950-57; asst. terminal mgr. Asso. Transport, Inc., Phila., 1957-58; terminal mgr. Asso. Transport, Inc., Knoxville, Tenn., 1959; regional mgr. Asso. Transport, Inc., Valley region, 1960-62, South region, 1962-68; v.p.-dir. So. div. Asso. Transport, Inc., 1968-71; v.p. R.S. Braswell Co. Inc., Kannapolis, 1971-80; pres. R.S. Braswell Co. Inc., 1980—, Hartford Motor Inn Inc., North Myrtle Beach, S.C., 1982—, A.T. Developers, Inc., North Myrtle Beach, S.C., 1983—; pres. Cherokee 2 Inc., Shelby, N.C., 1986—, bd. dirs.; bd. dirs. First Union Nat. Bank, Earl Ownsby Studios Inc., Shelby. Bd. regents Berkshire Christian Coll., Lenox, Mass., 1975—; mem. adv. bd. Salvation Army. Served with USNR, 1945-46. Mem. Motor Carriers Va. (pres. 1967-68), N.C. Motor Carriers Assn. (dir. 1968—), Sigma Chi, Tau Beta Pi. Mem. Advent Christian Ch. Club: Mason (32 deg.), Lions. Home: 5395 Mooresville Rd Kannapolis NC 28081-8726 Office: PO Box 1197 Kannapolis NC 28082-1197

THIGPEN, RICHARD ELTON, JR., lawyer; b. Washington, Dec. 29, 1930; s. Richard Elton and Dorothy (Dotger) T.; m. Nancy H. Shand, Dec. 15, 1951; children: Susan B., Richard M. AB, Duke U., 1951; LLB, U. N.C., 1956. Bar: N.C., 1956, U.S. Ct. Appeals (4th cir.) 1960, U.S. Ct. Appeals (5th cir.) 1960, U.S. Ct. Appeals (10th cir.) 1974, U.S. Tax Ct. 1958, U.S. Ct. Claims 1978. Lawyer FTC, Washington, 1956-58, Thigpen & Hines, Charlotte, N.C., 1958-84, Moore & Van Allen, Charlotte, N.C., 1984-88, Poyner & Spruill, Charlotte, N.C., 1988-93; gen. counsel Richardson Sports, 1994—. Dir. Charlotte-Mecklenburg YMCA, 1964-88, Heineman Med. Rsch. Ctr., Charlotte, 1970—, Charlotte C. of C., 1982-85. Lt. USNR, 1951-53. Fellow Am. Bar Found., Am. Coll. Tax Counsel (regent 1989-95, vice chmn. 1992, chmn. 1993-94); mem. ABA, N.C. State Bar, N.C. Bar Assn. (pres. 1988-89, chmn. tax sect. 1976-80), Sports Lawyers Assn. (bd. dirs. 1995—). Avocation: golf, travel. Office: Richardson Sports 800 S Mint St Charlotte NC 28202-1518

THIMM, ALFRED LOUIS, management educator; b. Vienna, Austria, Dec. 10, 1923; came to U.S., 1939, naturalized, 1943; s. Hartwig H. and Olga F. (Felsner) T.; m. Patricia Mullen, Dec. 18, 1954; children: Alfred Louis, Peter H. B.A., NYU, 1948, M.A., 1949, Ph.D., 1959. Asst. prof. econs. St. Lawrence U., Canton, N.Y., 1953-55; research fellow NYU, 1955-56; assoc. prof. Clarkson Coll., Potsdam, N.Y., 1956-59; mem. faculty Union Coll., Schenectady, 1960-81, prof. econs. and indsl. adminstrn., 1968-81, dir. Inst. Adminstrn. and Mgmt., 1968-80, dir. Ph.D. program in adminstrn. and engrng. systems, 1980-81; dean, dir. Sch. Bus. U. Vt., Burlington, 1981-85, prof. mgmt., 1981—; mgmt. cons., 1973-81; cons. in field; vis. prof. Wirtschafts U., Vienna, 1980, 85-86, 89, 92, Inst. Entscheidungs und Organisationsforschung, U. Munich, 1972, 74-75, 90. Author: Economists and Society: From Aquinas to Keynes, 1973, 81, Entscheidungstheorie, 1977, The False Promise of Codetermination, 1980, America's Stake in European Telecommuncation Policies, 1992; contbr. articles to profl. jours., monographs. Grantee NSF, 1951, 61; grantee Ford Found., summers 1960, 62; Fulbright rsch. scholar Austria, 1967-68, 92. Mem. Am. Econs. Assn., Am. Statis. Assn., Inst. Mgmt. Sci. Office: U Vt Sch Bus Burlington VT 05401

THIMOTHEOSE, KADAKAMPALLIL GEORGE, psychologist; b. Karipuza, India, Feb. 11, 1938; came to the U.S., 1976; s. K.G. and Mariamma Varghese; m. Mariamma Thimotheose, May 20, 1968 (div.); children: Geebee, Sonia. MA in Psychology, Kerala U., India, 1967, B in Edn., 1960, MA in Sociology, 1969; MA in History, Kerala U., 1975, PhD in Psychology, 1975; D Therapeutic Philosophy (hon.), World U., 1989. Lic. psychologist, marriage and family therapist, Mich.; diplomate Am. Bd. Med. Psychotherapists, Am. Bd. Psychotherapy, Am. Bd. Sexology, Am. Bd. Forensic Examiners, Am. Bd. Forensic Medicine, Am. Bd. Psychol. Specialities. Lectr., head dept. ednl. psychology S.N. Tchrs. Coll., Trivandrum, India; clin./adminstrv. dir. Alexandrine House, Inc., Detroit, 1976-81; chief exec. officer Cen. Therapeutic Svcs., Inc., Southfield, Mich., 1981—; adv. bd. Trivandrum Med. Coll. Hosps., 1969-75; edn. faculty mem. U. Calicut, Kerala, India, 1969-75; v.p. forum ednl. rsch. and studies Kerala U., 1969-73. Author: Educational Psychology for B.Ed. Students, 1970; editor: Kerala University Journal of Education, 1969-73. Fellow Am. Bd. Med. Psychotherapists, Am. Acad. Clin. Sexologists; mem. APA, Am. Coll. Sexologists (sexologist), Am. Coll. Forensic Examiners, Am. Bd. Sexology (clin. supr.), World U. Round Table (hon. cultural doctorate in therapeutic philosophy). Republican. Avocations: photography, travel, reading, sightseeing. Home: 3048 Brewster Ct West Bloomfield MI 48322-2421 Office: Cen Therapeutic Svcs Inc 17600 W 8 Mile Rd Ste 7 Southfield MI 48075-4316

THIRUMALAI, DEVARAJAN, physical sciences researcher, educator; b. Madras, India, June 6, 1956; s. Sadagopan and Saranayaki Thirumalai; m. Cynthia Kahl, Apr. 15, 1982; children: Alexandra, Samuel. BS, Indian Inst. Technology, Kampur, India, 1977; PhD, U. Minn., 1982. Postdoctoral rsch. fellow Columbia U., N.Y.C., 1982-85; prof. U. Md., College Park, 1985—; guest worker NIST, Gaithersburg, Md., 1990—. Contbr. more than 100 rsch. papers to profl. jours. Named Presdl. Young investigator NSF, 1987; Alfred P. Sloan fellow Sloan Found.,. Home: 9220 Clematis Ct Gaithersburg MD 20882 Office: U Md Inst for Phys Sci & Tech College Park MD 20742

THISSELL, JAMES DENNIS, physicist; b. Lincoln County, S.D., June 1, 1935; s. Oscar H. and Bernice G.J. (Olbertson) T. BA cum laude, Augustana Coll., 1957; MS, U. Iowa, 1963. Rsch. physicist U. Iowa, Iowa City, 1958-64; engr. McDonnell Douglas, St. Louis, 1965-66; scientist E.G. & G., Inc., Las Vegas, Nev., 1967-68; engr. Bendix Field Engrng. Corp. Ames Rsch. Ctr., Moffett Field, Calif., 1970-77, Lockheed Missiles and Space Co., Sunnyvale, Calif., 1978—. Mem. AIAA, IEEE, Am. Phys. Soc., Am. Geophys. Soc., Sigma Xi. Republican. Lutheran. Home: 38475 Jacaranda Dr Newark CA 94560-4727 Office: LMTO 0/28-14 B158 FAC 1 PO Box 61687 Sunnyvale CA 94088-1687

THISTED, RONALD AARON, statistician, educator, consultant; b. L.A., Mar. 2, 1951; s. Dale Owen and Barbara Jean (Walker) T.; m. Linda Jeane Soder, Dec. 30, 1972; 1 child, Walker. BA, Pomona Coll., 1972; PhD, Stanford U., 1977. Asst. prof. statistics U. Chgo., 1976-82, assoc. prof. statistics, 1982-92, assoc. prof. anesthesia and critical care, 1989-92, prof. stats. and anesthesia and critical care, 1992—. Author: Elements of Statistical Computing, 1988; contbr. over 60 articles to profl. jours. Fellow AAAS, Am. Statis. Assn.; mem. Assn. for Computing Machinery, Inst. for Math. Stats., Soc. for Clin. Trials. Office: U Chgo 5734 S University Ave Chicago IL 60637-1514

THISTLETHWAITE, DAVID RICHARD, architect; b. Burlington, Iowa, Aug. 24, 1947; s. Robert and Nona (Binder) T.; m. Carol Anne Armstrong, Aug. 22, 1970. BArch, Iowa State U., 1971. Registered arch., Calif., Minn.; registered Nat. Coun. Archtl. Registration Bds. Designer Morrison Architects, St. Paul, 1971-73, Times Architects, Mpls., 1973-74; project architect Bentz/Thompson Assocs., Mpls., 1974-77; project mgr. Setter Leach Lindstrom, Mpls., 1977-78; project architect Wurster Bernardi Emmons, San Francisco, 1978-79, Strotz & Assocs., Tiburon, Calif., 1979-81, Hood Miller Assoc., San Francisco, 1981-84; prin., ptnr. R S T Architects, San Francisco, 1984-88; prin. Thistlethwaite Archtl. Group, San Francisco, 1988—. Contbr. articles to profl. jours. Mem. AIA (nat. profl. devel. com. 1983-86, treas. San Francisco chpt. 1985-86, chmn. Calif. coun. health facilities com. 1994-96, chmn. design com. Acad. Architecture for Health, 1994-96, mem. Calif. coun. ins. bd. trustees 1988—, mem. Calif. coun. legis. com. 1996—), Am. Soc. Hosp. Engrs., Design Profls. Safety Assn. (bd. dirs.). Office: 250 Sutter St San Francisco CA 94108-4451

THODE, EDWARD FREDERICK, chemical engineer, educator; b. N.Y.C., May 31, 1921; s. E. Frederick and Kathleen V. (McGowan) T.; m. Isobel Zoeller, May 27, 1944; children: Karen (Mrs. Paul M. O'Neil), Stephen Frederick, Jonathan Edward. S.B., M.I.T., 1942, S.M., 1943, Sc.D., 1947. Registered profl. engr., Maine, N.Mex. Chem. engr. Boston Woven Hose & Rubber Co., Cambridge, Mass.; asst. prof. chem. engrng. U. Maine, Orono, 1947-49; asso. prof. U. Maine, 1949-54; sr. research engr. 3M Co., St. Paul, 1954-55; research asso., faculty mem. Inst. Paper Chemistry, Appleton, Wis., 1955-63; mgr. dept. engrng. computer and computer ctr. Inst. Paper Chemistry, 1959-63; prof. chem. engring. N.Mex. State U., Las Cruces, 1963-74; head dept. chem. engrng. N.Mex. State U., 1963-74, prof. mgmt., 1974-86, prof. emertus chem. engrng. and mgmt., 1986—; cons. Am. Cyanamid Co., IBM, Gen. Elec. Co., Bell Telephone Labs.; affiliate staff mem. Los Alamos Sci. Lab., 1965-90; propr. EIT Cons., 1972-91. Contbr. numerous articles to profl. jours. Mem. exec. bd. Yucca council Boy Scouts Am., 1968-72; dir. Mesilla Park Heritage Assn., 1988-93, sec., 1988-89, v.p., 1990, pres. 1991; treas. Mesilla Valley Conf. Chs., 1989; vestryman, lay reader, lay eucharistic minister, warden, 1970, 71, 87, 93, 94. Recipient Disting. faculty award N. Mex. State U., 1981, 83. Mem. AIChE (chmn. Rio Grande sect. 1990), Am. Soc. Engrng. Edn., Masons, Lions, Sigma Xi, Tau Beta Pi, Beta Gamma Sigma, Phi Kappa Phi. Republican. Episcopalian. Home: 905 Conway Ave Apt 45 Las Cruces NM 88005-3775 *To discover God's will for our lives is difficult; the search is worth the effort.*

THOM, JOSEPH M., librarian; b. Bronx, N.Y., Oct. 22, 1919; s. Harry and Jennie T.; m. Lillian Rosenstein, Sept. 1, 1945; children—Janice Eleanor, Eric Frederick. B.A., N.Y.U., 1948, M.A., 1949; M.S. in L.S, Columbia, 1950; postgrad., Washington U., St. Louis, 1951-53, Ohio U., 1958-59. Library asst. N.Y.U., 1940-42, 46-49; library fellow Bklyn. Coll., 1949-50; chief reference dept. Washington U., 1950-53, instr. librarianship, 1950-54; dir. Research Information Service of St. Louis, 1954-55; supr. records and library Goodyear Atomic Corp., 1955-60; dir. libraries Yeshiva U., 1960; librarian Port Jefferson (N.Y.) Schs.; library and multi-media cons. on design and services. Editor: Reference Sources in Education, 1953, Personnel Notes and News; Compiler: Reference Sources in Politcal Science, 1953; Contbr. articles to profl. jours. Served with AUS, 1942-45. Home: PO Box 2514 East Setauket NY 11733-0755

THOM, RICHARD DAVID, aerospace executive; b. St. Louis, Oct. 4, 1944; s. Reginald James and Vlasta (Koukl) T.; m. Linda Marie Hunt, Sept. 9, 1967; children: Elizabeth Marie, Robert James. BS in Physics, U. Mo., Rolla, 1967; MSEE, UCLA, 1971. Co-op engr. McDonnell Aircraft Corp., St. Louis, 1962-67; head advanced tech. group IR systems dept., aerospace group Hughes Aircraft Co., Culver City, Calif., 1967-72; mem. tech. staff Santa Barbara Rsch. Ctr., Hughes Aircraft Co., Goleta, Calif., 1972-76, asst. mgr. R&D Lab., 1976-80, mgr. advanced applications, 1980-83, chief engr., 1984-86, chief scientist, 1986-90, dir. tech., 1990-95; tech. program exec. Hughes Aircraft Co., Goleta, Calif., 1995—. Contbr. articles to profl. jours.; patentee in field. Recipient Hughes Group Patent award for pioneering contbns. in infrared detector tech., 1990. Mem. IEEE, Tau Beta Pi, Sigma Pi Sigma, Delta Sigma Phi. Republican. Avocation: freelance travel writing and photography, specializing in railway travel around the world. Home: 1236 Camino Palomera Santa Barbara CA 93111-1013 Office: Santa Barbara Rsch Ctr 75 Coromar Dr Goleta CA 93117-3088

THOMA, RICHARD WILLIAM, chemical safety and waste management consultant; b. Milw., Dec. 7, 1921; s. Joseph Donath and Margaret Mary (Murphy) T.; A.A., U. Chgo., 1941; BS, U. Wis., Madison, 1947, MS in Biochemistry, 1949, PhD, 1951; m. Ida Mary Scharfschwerdt, Mar. 15, 1952; children: Adele, Richard W., Joseph O., John C. With E. R. Squibb & Sons, Inc., New Brunswick, N.J., 1951-82, sr. rsch. fellow, 1980-82; dir. process devel. New Brunswick Sci. Co., Inc., Edison, N.J., 1982-84; cons., 1984—. Commr. Somerset County Bd. Elections, 1981-84; mem. Bridgewater Town

Coun., 1975-81, Environ. Commn., 1974-75, Sewerage Authority, 1975-76, Police Commn., 1977-81; chmn. Bridgewater Dem. Mcpl. Com., 1980-87; alderman St. Lucie Village, 1996—. Served with AUS, 1942-46. Mem. VFW, Am. Chem. Soc., Am. Soc. Safety Engrs., Nat. Safety Coun., Am. Soc. Microbiology, Am. Acad. Microbiology, N.Y. Acad. Scis., Am. Inst. Biol. Scis., Soc. Indsl. Microbiology, Soc. Gen. Microbiology (U.K.), St. Lucie County C. of C., Phi Beta Kappa, Sigma Xi, Phi Lambda Upsilon. Contbr. articles to sci. jours.; editor Industrial Microbiology, 1977; patentee microbiol. transformation of steroids. Home and Office: 3772 Outrigger Ct Fort Pierce FL 34946-1911

THOMAJAN, ROBERT, lawyer, management and financial consultant; b. N.Y.C., May 4, 1941; s. Leon and Fay T. BS, NYU, 1962; JD, St. John's U., 1965. Bar: N.Y. 1965, U.S. Ct. Appeals (2nd cir.) 1966, U.S. Dist. Ct. (ea. and so. dists.) N.Y. 1967, U.S. Ct. Internat. Trade 1975, U.S. Supreme Ct. 1975, U.S. Ct. Appeals (9th cir.) 1976, U.S. Dist. Ct. (we. dist.) Tex. 1979, Tex. 1987. Atty. Nixon, Mudge, Rose, Guthrie, Alexander & Mitchell, N.Y.C., 1964-68; ptnr. Milgrim, Thomajan & Lee, N.Y.C., 1968-90; mng. dir. Caribbean Capital Ltd., 1994—; pres. Eterna Investments, Austin, Tex., 1995—. Arbitrator Civil Ct., N.Y., 1981-86; mem. adv. bd. Ronald McDonald House, 1988-90; bd. dirs. Big Bros./Big Sisters, 1988-90; mem. World Econ. Forum, 1990-93. Mem. Am. Soc. Internat. Law, Internat. Law Assn. Office: 2900 Westlake Cv Austin TX 78746-1961

THOMAN, G. RICHARD, computer company executive; b. Tuscaloosa, Ala., June 25, 1944; s. Richard S. and Evelyn (Zumwalt) T.; m. Wenke Helina Brier, Aug. 25, 1966 (div. Dec. 1987); children: Camille, Alexis; m. Lynn Susan Bendheim, Sept. 24, 1989; children: Kylie, Max, Amy. BA with honors, McGill U., 1966; diploma, Grad. Inst. Internat. Studies, Geneva, 1968; MA in Internat. Econs., Tufts U., 1967, MA in Law and Diplomacy, 1969, PhD in Internat. Econs., 1971. Exec. trainee Citicorp, N.Y.C., 1968-69; sr. fin. analyst Exxon Corp., N.Y.C., 1968-72; sr. assoc. McKinsey and Co., N.Y.C. and Paris, 1972-79; exec. v.p., CFO Am. Express Travel Related Svcs., N.Y.C., 1979-85, pres., Travel Related Svcs. Internat., 1985-89, chmn., CEO, 1989-92; pres., CEO Nabisco Internat. RJR Nabisco, Inc., N.Y.C., 1992-94; sr. v.p., group exec. IBM Corp., Somers, N.Y., 1994—; now sr. v.p., cfo IBM Corp., Armok, NY; bd. dirs. Union Banque Prive, Geneva. Author: Foreign Investment and Regional Development, 1972. Bd. dirs. Ams. Soc., N.Y.C., 1990—; bd. advisors Fletcher Sch. of Law and Diplomacy, Tufts U., Medford, Mass., 1990—. Recipient Legion of Honors, Govt. of France, 1992. Mem. Coun. on Fgn. Rels. Avocations: tennis, reading, jogging, travel. Office: IBM Corp Old Orchard Rd Armonk NY 10504

THOMAN, HENRY NIXON, lawyer; b. Cin., May 5, 1957; s. Richard B. and Barbara (Lutz) T.; m. Kathleen Brewer Thoman, Aug. 14, 1982; children: Victoria E., Nicholas B. BA, Duke U., 1979; JD, U. Chgo., 1982. Bar: Ohio 1982, U.S. Dist. Ct. (so. dist.) Ohio, 1982. With Taft, Stettinius & Hollister, Cin., 1982-88; sr. atty. John Morrell & Co., Cin., 1988-90; sr. counsel Chiquita Brands Internat. Inc., Cin., 1990-91, corp. planner, 1991-92; sr. dir. CTP ops. Chiquita Brands, Inc., Cin., 1993-94, chief adminstrv. officer Armuelles divsn., 1994-95; corp. counsel The Loewen Group, Covington, Ky., 1995-97; asst. gen. chief, asst. v.p. The Midland Co., Amelia, Ohio, 1997—. Mem. counselors com. U.S. Swimming, Colo., 1983-89; bd. dirs. Friends of Cin. Parks, 1990-93, 96—, Starshine Children's Hospice, 1996—, Cinci. Aquatic Club, 1997—, Mariemont Aquatic Club, v.p., 1992-93; pres. Club Atletico Y Socialde Chiriqui, 1994-95. Mem. ABA, Ohio State Bar, Cin. Bar Assn. Office: The Midland Company 7000 Midland Blvd Amelia OH 45102-2608

THOMAN, JOHN EVERETT, architect, mediator; b. Dixon, Ill., Aug. 6, 1925; s. George Dewey and Agnes Katherine (Fane) T.; m. Paula Ann Finnegan, Oct. 31, 1953; children: Shawn Michael, Brian Gerard, Kevin Charles, Trace Marie, Patricia Ann, Ronan Patrick, Caron Lynn. AA, UCLA, 1948; BArch cum laude, U. So. Calif., 1955. Registered architect, Calif. Project dir. A. Quincy Jones & Frederick E. Emmons, L.A., 1956-57, assoc., 1958, dir. constrn., 1958-73; dir. specifications A. Quincy Jones, FAIA & Assocs., L.A., 1973-77; dir. specifications Albert C. Martin and Assocs., L.A., 1977-79, dir. constrn. and industry rels., 1979-95, assoc., 1979-90, sr. assoc., 1990—, dir. emeritus constrn. and industry rels., 1996—; guest lectr. U. So. Calif. Lusk Sch. Real Estate, UCLA Grad. Sch., also various student, trade and tech. groups. Mem., vice chmn. Culver City (Calif.) Planning Commn., 1959; mem. Calif. Gov.'s Housing Commn., L.A., 1960, Community Redevel. Agy., Culver City, 1992-94. With U.S. Army, 1943-45, USAF, 1950-51. Mem. AIA (chmn. design awards com. L.A. 1960), Constrn. Specifications Inst. (bd. dirs. 1977-80, guest lectr.), Phi Eta Sigma, Tau Sigma Delta. Avocations: fishing, military history. Office: Albert C Martin and Assocs 811 W 7th St Los Angeles CA 90017-3408

THOMAN, MARK EDWARD, pediatrician; b. Chgo., Feb. 15, 1936; s. John Charles and Tasula Mark (Petrakis) T.; AA, Graceland Coll., 1956; BA, U. Mo., 1958, MD, 1962; m. Theresa Thompson, 1984; children: Marilisa Rae, Susan Kay, Edward Kim, Nancy Lynn, Janet Lea, David Mark. Intern, U. Mo. at Columbia, 1962-63; resident in pediatrics Blank Meml. Children's Hosp., Des Moines, 1963-65, chief resident, 1964-65; cons. in toxicology, 1966-67; chief dept. pediatrics Shiprock (N.Mex.) Navajo Indian Hosp., dir. N.D. Poison Info. Center, also practice medicine, specializing in pediatrics Quain & Ramstad Clinic, Bismarck, N.D., 1967-69; dir. Iowa Poison Info. Center, Des Moines, 1969-97; pvt. solo practice pediatrics, Des Moines, 1969—; sr. aviation med. examiner, accident investigator FAA, 1976—, cons., aviation seminars lectr., 1977—; faculty Iowa State U., U. Iowa, U. Osteo. Sci. and Health; dir. Cystic Fibrosis Clinic, 1973-82; dir. Mid-Iowa Drug Abuse Program, 1972-76; mem. med. adv. bd. La Leche League Internat., 1965—; pres. Medic-Air Ltd., 1976—. Editor-in-chief AACTION, 1975-90. Bd. dirs. Polk County Pub. Health Nurses Assn., 1969-77, Des Moines Speech and Hearing Center, 1974-79, Ecumenical Coun. of Iowa, 1990—; bd. govs. Mo. U. Sch. Medicine Alumni, 1988—, pres., 1997—. Served with USMCR, 1954-59; lt. comdr. USPHS, 1965-66; capt. USNR, 1993-96, ret. 1996; dir. Dept. Health Svcs. USNR. Recipient N.D. Gov.'s award of merit, 1969; Cystic Fibrosis Rsch. Found. award, 1975, Am. Psychiat. Assn. Thesis award, Diplomate Am. Bd. Pediatrics, Am. Coll. Toxicology (examiner). 1962. Mem. AMA (del. 1970-88), NRA (life), Assn. Am. Physicians & Surgeons, Polk County Med. Soc., Iowa State Med. Assn., Aerospace Med. Assn., Res. Officers Assn., Civil Aviation Med. Assn., Am. Public Health Assn., 1986—, Soc. Adolescent Medicine, Inst. Clin. Toxicology, Internat. Soc. Pediatrics, Am. Acad. Pediatrics (chmn. accident prevention com. Iowa chpt. 1975—), Cystic Fibrosis Club, Am. Acad. Clin. Toxicology (trustee 1969-90, pres. 1982-84), Am. Assn. Poison Control Centers, U.S. Naval Inst. Republican. Elder mem. Reorganized Latter-Day Saints Ch. Clubs: Flying Physicians, Aircraft Owners and Pilots Assn., Nat. Pilots Assn. (Safe Pilot award), Hyperion Field and Country. Editor in chief AACTION, 1976-90. Home: 6896 Trail Ridge Dr Johnston IA 50131-1322 Office: 1426 Woodland Ave Des Moines IA 50309-3204

THOMAN, MARY E., business and marketing educator, rancher; b. Kemmerer, Wyo., Sept. 14, 1949; d. William J. and Mary A. (Ferentchak) T. AA, Western Wyo. C.C., Rock Springs, 1970; BS in Bus., U. Wyo., 1972; MEd in Mktg., Colo. State U., 1978, PhD in Vocat./Secondary Adminstrn., 1981. Profl. Teaching Cert., Wyo. Bus. edn. Green River (Wyo.) H.S., 1972-75; part time bus. and mktg. instr. Western Wyo. C.C., Green River, 1972-77, Rock Springs, Wyo., 1972-80, Kemmerer, Wyo., 1983—; mktg. and coop. educator Green River H.S., 1975-77; asst. dir. Nev. St. Coun. on Vocat. Edn., Carson City, Nev., 1977; exec. dir. Mont. St. Coun. on Vocat. Edn., Helena, Mont., 1981-82; cattle/sheep rancher Kemmerer, 1981—; sr. sales dir. Mary Kay Cosmetics, Kemmerer, Wyo., 1988—; ednl. cons. past chair Wyo. St. Coun. on Vocat. Edn., Cheyenne, 1984-93; bus. cons. Western Wyo. Coll., Rock Springs, 1983—; sch.-to-work, S.W. Wyo. Collaborative Team; edn. cons. Kemmerer Sch. Dist., 1993—, chair voc/tech prep bus. curriculum com.; mem. Wyo. Agr. in Classroom, 1992-96. Active western range issues; testifier on Range Reform Hearings; mem. Cumberland Allotment Coordinated Resource Mgmt. Team Bur. Land Mgmt.; mem. S.W. Wyo. Resource Rendezvous Steering Com. Ednl./Profl. Devel. Act fellow, 1977-78, Grad. Leadership Devel. awardee, 1978-81. Mem. Kemmerer C. of C. (edn. com., bd. dirs. 1992—). Roman Catholic. Avocations: flying, skiing, gardening, dancing, traveling. Home: PO Box 146 Green River WY 82935-0146

THOMAS, ADRIAN WESLEY, laboratory director; b. Edgefield, S.C., June 23, 1939; s. Hasting Adrian and Nancy Azalena (Bridges) T.; m. Martha Elizabeth McAllister, July 12, 1964; children: Wesley Adrian, Andrea Elizabeth. BS in Agrl. Engring., Clemson U., 1962, MS in Agrl. Engring., 1965; PhD, Colo. State U., 1972. Rsch. scientist USDA-Agrl. Rsch. Svc., Tifton, Ga., 1965-69, Fort Collins, Colo., 1969-72; rsch. leader USDA-Agrl. Rsch. Svc., Walkinsville, Ga., 1972-89; lab. dir. USDA-Agrl. Rsch. Svc., Tifton, 1989—; mem. acad. faculty Colo. State U. Ft. Collins, 1969-72; acad. faculty U. Ga., Athens, 1973—, grad. faculty, 1988—. Contbr. agrl. rsch. articles to profl. jours. With U.S. Army, 1962-63. Mem. Am. Soc. Agrl. Engrs., Am. Soc. Agronomy, Soil and Water Conservation Soc. Am., Soil Sci. Soc. Am., Sigma Xi, Alpha Epsilon, Gamma Sigma Delta, Phi Kappa Phi. Lutheran. Avocations: reading, gardening, yard care, remodeling home, sports. Office: USDA Agrl Rsch Svc PO Box 946 Tifton GA 31793-0946

THOMAS, ALAN RICHARD, natural resources products executive; b. Toronto, Ont., Can., Dec. 14, 1942; s. Ronald H. Thomas and Edna M. Green; m. Jill H.E. Parkinson; children: Kimberley Anne, Michael. B in Commerce, U. Toronto, 1964. Chartered acct., Ont. Ptnr. Ernst & Young, Toronto, 1964-87; CFO Noranda Inc., Toronto, 1987—. Recipient Bronze medal Can. Inst. Chartered Accts., 1967. Mem. Ont. Inst. Chartered Accts., Donalda Club, Toronto Cricket Club, Cambridge Club, Royal Ottawa Golf Club. Mem. United Ch. Can. Office: Noranda Inc, 181 Bay St Ste 4100 PO Box 755, Toronto, ON Canada M5J 2T3

THOMAS, ALLEN LLOYD, lawyer, private investor; b. Orange, N.J., Sept. 15, 1939; s. Richard Lloyd and Dorothy (Carr) T.; m. Virginia Dehnert, June 24, 1961 (div. 1974); children: Sarah Ann, Anne Marjorie; m. Barbara Singer, Mar. 12, 1978; 1 child, Allen Lloyd Jr. BA, Wesleyan U., 1961; LLB, Yale U., 1964. Bar: N.Y. 1965, U.S. Ct. Appeals (D.C. cir.) 1981; solicitor, Eng. and Wales. Ptnr. Paul Weiss Rifkind Wharton & Garrison, N.Y.C., 1964-92; resident ptnr. Hong Kong, 1983-87; dir., gen. counsel Gerard Atkins & Co. Ltd., 1992-94; gen. counsel Gen. Atlantic Group Ltd, 1992-94; chmn. Ockham Holdings PLC; bd. dirs. Penna Holdings PLC, Kingsmead Underwriting Agy. Ltd. Chmn. Urban Bus. Assis. Corp., N.Y.C., 1971-82; chmn. Hong Kong Ballet, 1985-87; co-chmn. Internat. Com., N.Y.C. Ballet, 1986-91; pres. Internat. Salzburg Assn. Am., 1987-92; dir., mem. exec. com., gen. counsel Child Care Action Campaign, 1990-92. Fellow Am. Coll. Investment Counsel, Hartford, Conn. Mem. River Club, N.Y. Met. Club of Washington, Hong Kong Club, Hong Kong Jockey Club, Coral Beach and Tennis Club, Lenox Club, Buck's Club. Home: 3 Chester St, London SW1X 7BB, England

THOMAS, ANN VAN WYNEN, law educator; b. The Netherlands, May 27, 1919; came to U.S., 1921, naturalized, 1926; d. Cornelius and Cora Jacoba (Daansen) Van Wynen; m. A.J. Thomas Jr., Sept. 10, 1948. AB with distinction, U. Rochester, 1940; JD, U. Tex., 1943; post doctoral degree, So. Meth. U., 1952. U.S. fgn. svc. officer Johannesburg, South Africa, London, The Hague, The Netherlands, 1943-47; rsch. atty. Southwestern Legal Found., Sch. Law So. Meth. U., Dallas, 1952-67; asst. prof. polit. sci. Sch. Law So. Meth. U., 1968-73, assoc. prof., 1973-76, prof., 1976-85; prof. emeritus So. Meth. U. Sch. Law, 1985—. Author: Communism versus International Law, 1953, (with A.J. Thomas Jr.) International Treaties, 1950, Non-Intervention—The Law and its Import in the Americas, 1956, OAS: The Organization of American States, 1962, International Legal Aspects of Civil War in Spain, 1936-1939, 1967, Legal Limitations on Chemical and Biological Weapons, 1970, The Concept of Aggression, 1972, Presidential War Making Power: Constitutional and International Law Aspects, 1981, An International Rule of Law—Problems and Prospects, 1974. Chmn. time capsule com. Grayson County Commn. on Tex. Sesquicentennial, 1986-88; co-chmn. Grayson County Commn. on Bicentennial U.S. Constn., 1988-93; co-chmn. com. Grayson County Sesquicentennial, 1994-97; co-chmn. Grayson County Commn. on the Millenium, 1997—. Recipient Am. medal Nat. DAR Soc., 1992. Mem. Tex. Bar Assn., Am. Soc. Internat. Law, Grayson County Bar Assn. Home: Spaniel Hall RR 2, Box 444T Pottsboro TX 75076

THOMAS, BARBARA ANN, record company executive; b. Bklyn., Feb. 5, 1948; d. Wilfred Godfrey and Violet Rose (Howell) Swaby; m. Ronald L. Hannah (div.). Adminstrv. asst. Million Dollar Record Poll, College Park, Ga., 1985-86, Points East Records, College Park, 1986-87, Greer Booking Agy., Atlanta, 1986-87; pres. Gunsmoke Records, College Park, 1988—; v.p. Toroy Mercedes Records, 1994—; mgr. Jesse James, 1983—. Mem. NAFE, COPE, Blues Found., Atlanta Top Star Awards, Nat. Young Black Programmers (bd. dirs.), Nat. Club Owners, Promoters and Entertainment Assn. (bd. dirs. 1996). Democrat. Roman Catholic. Office: Gunsmoke Records 2523 Roosevelt Hwy Ste 3D Atlanta GA 30337-6244

THOMAS, BESSIE, primary education educator; b. Shreveport, La., Nov. 30, 1943; d. Fleen and Tommie Lee (Anderson) Myles; m. Jesse Thomas, May 11, 1968 (dec. 1995). BS, Grambling Coll., 1966; MS, Grambling State U., 1976; postgrad., various colls. and univs., 1967-79. Cert. primary and elem. tchr., La. 1st grade tchr. Pine St. Sch., Hamburg, Ark., 1966-67, Pine Grove Elem. Sch., Shreveport, 1967-70, Mooringsport (La.) Sch., 1970-81; early childhood edn. tchr. Fairfield Elem. Sch., Shreveport, 1981—. Active Word of Faith Christian Ctr. Grantee Caddo Pub. Edn. Found., 1995—. Mem. NEA, Nat. Assn. for Edn. Young Children, ASCD, Reading Tchr., Assn. for Childhood Edn. Internat., PTA. Democrat. Avocations: inspirational reading, painting T-shirts, travel, interacting with children, viewing works of art. Home: 2831 Abbie St Shreveport LA 71103-2130

THOMAS, BROOKS, publishing company executive; b. Phila., Nov. 28, 1931; s. Walter Horstman and Ruth Sterling (Boomer) T.; m. Galen Pinckard Clark, Apr. 15, 1969 (div. 1973). B.A., Yale U., 1953, LL.B., 1956; grad., Advanced Mgmt. Program, Harvard, 1973. Bar: Pa. 1957, N.Y. 1960. With law firm Winthrop, Stimson, Putnam & Roberts, N.Y.C., 1960-68; sec., gen. counsel Harper & Row, Pubs., Inc., N.Y.C., 1968-69; v.p., gen. counsel Harper & Row, Pubs., Inc., 1969-73, exec. v.p., 1973-79, chief operating officer, 1977-81, pres., 1979-87, chief exec. officer, 1981-87, chmn. bd., 1986-87; chmn. bd. Harper & Row, Ltd., London, 1973-87; dir. Harper & Row, Pty. Ltd., Australia, Harla S.A. de C.V., Mex., Harper & Row Pubs. Asia, Pte. Ltd., Singapore. Pres., bd. dirs. Butterfield House, 1968-72, 90-93; trustee, dir. RADG, Inc., 1987-89; dir. Thompson Island Outward Bound Edn. Ctr., 1987-95, Colo. Outward Bound Sch., 1990-96, bd. govs., 1996—; bd. dirs. Young Audiences, Inc., 1977—, chmn., 1985—; trustee Outward Bound USA, 1980—, vice chmn., 1983-84, chmn., 1984-87; chmn. Nat. Book Awards, 1984-85, dir., 1985-87; mem. devel. bd. Yale U., 1985-89; adv. bd. Yale Sch. Orgn. and Mgmt., 1987-96; chmn. Vail Valley Inst., 1989—. Lt. (j.g.) USNR, 1956-59. Mem. Am. Bar Assn., Assn. Bar City of N.Y., Assn. Am. Pubs. (bd. dirs. 1980-85, chmn. 1983-85), Council Fgn. Relations, Yale U. Alumni Assn. (law sch. rep. 1980-83). Clubs: Merion Cricket (Phila.); Century (N.Y.C.), Yale (N.Y.C.), University (N.Y.C.), N.Y. Yacht (N.Y.C.); Essex Yacht (Conn.). Home: 37 W 12th St New York NY 10011-8502 also: 141 Saybrook Rd Essex CT 06426-1412 also: 63 Willow Pl Vail CO 81657-5304

THOMAS, CALVERT, lawyer; b. Balt., Nov. 1, 1916; s. William Douglas Nelson and Elizabeth Steuart (Calvert) T.; m. Margaret Somervell Berry, Sept. 1, 1943; children—Calvert Bowie, Carolyn Brooke Dold. Douglas Mackubin. B.S., Washington and Lee U., 1938; LL.B., U. Md., 1940. Bar: Md. bar 1940, D.C. bar 1972, Mich. bar 1947, N.Y. State bar 1974, Conn. bar 1979. Asso. atty. Legal Aid Bur., Balt., 1940-41; atty. Lehmeyer & Moser, Balt., 1941-42, Solicitor's Office, Dept. Labor, Washington, 1942-43, Tax Ct. of U.S., Washington, 1943-44, Chief Counsel's Office, Bur. Internal Revenue, Washington, 1944-46; atty. legal staff Gen. Motors Corp., Detroit, 1946-72; asst. gen. counsel Gen. Motors Corp., 1972-78; sec., asst. gen. counsel in charge N.Y. legal staff, N.Y.C., 1973-78; chmn. Thomas Cadillac, Inc., 1978—. Councilman, Franklin Village, Mich., 1958-60, pres., 1960-64; Bd. dirs. Franklin Community Assn., 1956-58; vice chmn. Kingswood Sch., Cranbrook, 1968-69, chmn., 1969-71; trustee Cranbrook Schs., 1971-73, Washington and Lee U., 1975—; chmn. Old Guard West Hartford, 1992-93. Mem. Am., Fed., Detroit, Md., D.C., N.Y. bar assns., State Bar Mich. (chmn. tax sect. 1971-72), Am. Soc. Corp. Secs., So. Md. Soc., Soc. Colonial Wars, Lords of Md. Manors, Descendants of the Signers of the Declaration of Independence, Sons of the Am. Revolution, Soc. of the Ark and Dove, Soc. of Founders and Patriots of Am., Beta Theta Pi, Phi Delta Phi, Omicron Delta Kappa. Republican. Episcopalian. Clubs: Orchard Lake (Mich.) Country; Recess (Detroit); Princeton (N.Y.C.); Country of Farmington (Conn.); Hartford, Hartford Golf. Home: 138 Stoner Dr West Hartford CT 06107-1306 Office: 170 Weston St Box 1778 Hartford CT 06144-9999

THOMAS, CARMEN CHRISTINE, physician, consultant administrator; b. Germany, Apr. 15, 1908; came to U.S., 1921; d. Paul Ernest and Huberta (Mohr) T. AB, U. Del., 1929; MD, Woman's Med. Coll. Pa., 1932; DSc, U. Pa., 1940. Diplomate Am. Bd. Dermatology. Asst. chief resident Phila. Gen. Hosp., 1934-35; fellow in dermatology U. Pa., Phila., 1936-39, asst. prof. dermatology, 1940-67; prof. dermatology Woman's Med. Coll. Pa., Phila., 1941-68, dir. dept. oncology, 1952-66, emeritus prof. dermatology, 1968—; chief dermatologist Phila. Gen. Hosp., 1944-77; pvt. practice Phila., 1939-77; cons. Vets. Hosp., Memor Hosp., Phila., 1950-77, Elwyn Inst., Devereux Sch., Delaware County, 1950-69. Contbr. articles to profl. jours. Fellow Phila. Coll. Physicians; mem. Am. Acad. Dermatology (life), Phila. Dermatol. Soc. (life, pres. 1942), Phila. County Med. Soc. (life), Phi Beta Kappa, Alpha Omega Alpha, Sigma Xi. Avocations: travel, photography, music archeology. Home: 600 E Cathedral Rd Apt G305 Philadelphia PA 19128-1929

THOMAS, CAROL TAYLOR, general services coordinator; b. Carthage, N.C., Jan. 13, 1952; d. Elbert Watson and Lela Frances (Reynolds) Taylor; m. Michael Conley Thomas, Sept. 8, 1973; children: Kelli R. Thomas, Melvin Conley Thomas. Student, Sandhills Community Coll., 1970-72. Asst. purchasing officer County of Moore, Carthage, N.C., 1978-83, purchasing officer, 1983—, purchasing officer, airport mgr., 1988—. Mem. Moore County Airport Adv. Com., N.C. Airport Assn., Nat. Purchasing Mgmt. Assn., Purchasing Mgmt. Assn. of Carolinas-Va. Inc. (triangle chpt. 1988—). Presbyterian. Avocations: gardening, exercising, bicycling, go kart racing, family. Office: Moore County Airport Moore County Courthouse PO Box 905 Carthage NC 28327

THOMAS, CAROLYN HARPER, elementary educator; b. Villa Ridge, Ill., June 24, 1950; d. John Nathan Sr and Walterene (Carter) Harper. BS in Edn., Ind. U., Gary, 1977; M in Early Childhood Edn., Edinboro (Pa.) State Coll., 1980. Lic. tchr., Ohio, Ind. Tchr. Ashtabula (Ohio) Area City Schs., 1978-91; program coord. Project Have Hope Mary Chatman Community Ctr., Ashtabula, 1987-90; coord. summer recreation program Ashtabula City Schs. & Job Tng. Partnership Act, summer 1989, 90; tchr. Gary Community Sch. Corp., 1991—; lead tchr. Kids Enrichment Program, Gary, 1992—; program coord. I Can-Tutorial and Enrichment, 1995—; mem. Kneely Mae Fleming Scholarship Selection Com., Ashtabula, 1989-91. Mem. allocations com. United Way, Ashtabula, 1989-90. Mem. Gary Reading Coun., N.W. Ind. Assn. Black Sch. Educators. Pentecostal. also: Kuny Elem Sch 5050 Vermont St Gary IN 46409

THOMAS, CHARLES ALLEN, JR., molecular biologist, educator; b. Dayton, Ohio, July 7, 1927; s. Charles Allen and Margaret Stoddard (Talbott) T.; m. Margaret M. Gay, July 7, 1951; children: Linda Carrick, Stephen Gay. AB, Princeton (N.J.) U., 1950; PhD, Harvard U., 1954. Rsch. scientist Eli Lilly Co., Indpls., 1954-55; NCR fellow U. Mich., Ann Arbor, 1955-56, prof. biophysics, 1956-57; prof. biophysics Johns Hopkins U., Balt., 1957-67; prof. biol. chemistry Med. Sch. Harvard U., Boston, 1967-78; chmn. dept. cellular biology Scripps Clinic & Rsch. Found., La Jolla, Calif., 1978-81; pres., dir. Helicon Found., San Diego, 1981—; founder, CEO The Syntro Corp., San Diego, 1981-82; founder, CEO, now dir. of R&D Pantox Corp., San Diego, 1989—; mem. genetics study sect. NIH, 1968-72; mem. rsch. grants com. Am. Cancer Soc., 1972-76, 79-85. Mem. editorial bd. Virology, 1967-73, Jour. Molecular Biology, 1968-72, BiOPhysics Jour., 1965-68, Chromosoma, 1969-79, Analytic Biochemistry, 1970-79, Biochim Biophys. ACTA, 1973-79, Plasmid, 1977—. With USNR, 1945-46. NRC fellow, 1965-66. Mem. AAAS, Am. Acad. Arts and Scis., Am. Fedn. Biol. Chemists, Genetics Soc. Am., Am. Chem. Soc. Achievements include rsch. in genetic and structural orgn. of chromosomes and devel. of a practical assessment of ind. antioxidant def. system by analytical biochemistry. Home: 1640 El Paso Real La Jolla CA 92037-6304 Office: Helicon Foundation 4622 Santa Fe St San Diego CA 92109-1601

THOMAS, CHARLES HOWARD, II, federal official; b. Buffalo, June 23, 1934; s. John Charles Thomas and Helen (Wright) Cogswell; m. Lourana Swift, Dec. 28, 1956; children: John, Stuart, Jennifer Thomas McGrath, Andrew. AB, Harvard U., 1956; student, Nat. War Coll., 1977-78. Fgn. service officer U.S. Consulate, Cuidad Juarez, Mex., 1960-62, U.S. Embassy, La Paz, Bolivia, 1962-64, Dept. State, Washington, 1964-66; dep. dir. Peace Corps, Tegucigalpa, Honduras, 1966-67; dir. Peace Corps, Montevideo, Uruguay, 1967-69; polit. counselor U.S. Embassy, Lisbon, Potugal, 1974-77; dep. chief of mission U.S. Embassy, Brussels, 1982-85; dir. ops. ctr. Dept. State, Washington, 1970-74, dir. NATO affairs, 1978-82, dep. asst. sec. of state for European and Can. Affairs, 1985-89; amb. to Hungary Dept. State, Budapest, 1990-94; spl. envoy for Burdensharing Bur. Politico-Mil. Affairs Dept. State, Washington, 1994; exec. dir. Spl. Group. on Ea. Europe, 1994; spl. envoy for former Yugoslavia, U.S. rep. on contact group, 1994-95, spl. envoy for Bosnian Fedn., 1995. Served to lt., USN, 1956-59. Recipient Heroism award, Dept. State, 1965. Mem. Am. Fgn. Service Assn. Episcopalian. Avocation: skiing.

THOMAS, CHRISTOPHER YANCEY, III, surgeon, educator; b. Kansas City, Mo., Oct. 27, 1923; s. Christopher Yancey and Dorothea Louise (Engel) T.; m. Barbara Ann Barcroft, June 27, 1946; children—Christopher, Gregg, Jeffrey, Anne. Student, U. Colo., 1942-44; M.D., U. Kans., 1948. Diplomate Am. Bd. Surgery. Intern U. Utah Hosp., Salt Lake City, 1948-49; resident in surgery Cleve. Clinic Found., 1949-52; pvt. practice specializing in surgery Kansas City, Mo., 1954-89; mem. staff St. Luke's Hosp., chief surgery, 1969-70; mem. staff Children's Mercy Hosp.; clin. prof. surgery U. Mo., Kansas City Med. Sch.; pres. St. Luke's Hosp. Edn. Found., 1977-83, Med. Plaza Corp., 1977-79; pres. Midwest Organ Bank, 1977-82. Editor IMTRAC investment adv. letter, 1978—. Served to capt. M.C., U.S. Army, 1952-54. Fellow ACS; mem. AMA, Southwestern Surg. Congress, Central Surg. Assn., Mo. State Med. Soc., Kansas City Surg. Soc. (pres. 1968), Jackson County Med. Soc. (pres. 1971). Republican. Methodist. Club: Kansas City Country. Home: 5830 Mission Dr Shawnee Mission KS 66208-1139 Office: 4210 Shawnee Mission Pky Mission KS 66205-2506

THOMAS, CLARA MCCANDLESS, retired English language educator, biographer; b. Strathroy, Ont., Can., May 22, 1919; d. Basil and Mabel (Sullivan) McCandless; m. Morley Keith Thomas, May 23, 1942; children: Stephen, John. B.A., U. Western Ont., London, 1941, M.A., 1944; Ph.D., U. Toronto, 1962; DLitt (hon.), York U., 1986, Trent U., 1991; LLD (hon.), Brock U., 1992. Instr. English U. Western Ont., London, 1947-61, U. Toronto, 1958-61; asst. prof. English York U., Toronto, 1961-68; prof. York U., 1969-84, prof. emeritus, 1984—; acad. adv. panel Social Scis. and Humanities Research Council, 1981-84; mem. Killam Awards Selection Bd., 1978-81. Author biography of Anna Jameson, 1967, of Egerton Ryerson, 1969, of Margaret Laurence, 1969, 75, of William Arthur Deacon, 1982; Literary criticism (Can.), 1946, 72, 94; mem. editl. bd. Literary History of Can., 1980—, Collected Works of Northrop Frye, 1993—. Recipient Internat. Coun. of Can. Studies prize No. Telecom, 1989; grantee Can. Coun., 1967, 73, Social Sci. and Humanities Rsch. Coun. Can., 1978-80. Fellow Royal Soc. Can.; mem. Assn. Can. Univs., Tchrs. English (pres. 1971-72), Assn. Can. and Que. Lit., Bus. and Profl. Women's Club, Assn. for Can. Studies. New Democratic. Office: York U 305 Scott Libr, 4700 Keele St, Downsview, ON Canada M3J 1P3

THOMAS, CLARENCE, United States supreme court justice; b. Savannah, Ga., June 23, 1948. BA, Holy Cross Coll., 1971; JD, Yale U., 1974. Bar: Mo. Asst. atty. gen. State of Mo., Jefferson City, 1974-77; atty. Monsanto Co., St. Louis, 1977-79; legis. asst. to Sen. John C. Danforth, Washington, 1979-81; asst. sec. for civil rights Dept. Edn., Washington, 1981-82; chmn. U.S. EEOC, Washington, 1982-90; judge U.S. Ct. Appeals, Washington, 1990-91; assoc. justice U.S. Supreme Ct., Washington, 1991—. Office: US Supreme Court Supreme Ct Bldg 1 First St NE Washington DC 20543*

THOMAS, CLAUDEWELL SIDNEY, psychiatry educator; b. N.Y.C., Oct. 5, 1932; s. Humphrey Sidney and Frances Elizabeth (Collins) T.; m. Carolyn

Pauline Rozansky, Sept. 6, 1958; children: Jeffrey Evan, Julie-Anne Elizabeth, Jessica Edith. BA, Columbia U., 1952; MD, SUNY, Downstate Med. Ctr., 1956; MPH, Yale U., 1964. Diplomate Nat. Bd. Med. Examiners, Am. Bd. Psychiatry. From instr. to assoc. prof. Yale U., New Haven, 1963-68, dir. Yale tng. program in social community psychiatry, 1967-70; dir. div. mental health service programs NIMH, Washington, 1970-73; chmn. dept. psychiatry U.M.D.N.J., Newark, 1973-83; prof. dept. psychiatry Drew Med. Sch., 1983—, chmn. dept. psychiatry, 1983-93; prof. dept. psychiatry UCLA, 1983-94, vice chmn. dept. psychiatry, 1983-93, prof. emeritus dept. psychiatry, 1994—; med. dir. Tokanui Hosp., TeAwamutu, N.Z., 1996; cons. A.K. Rice Inst., Washington, 1978-80, SAMSA/PHS Cons., 1991—; mem. L.A. County Superior Ct. Psych. Panel, 1991—. Author: (with B. Bergen) Issues and Problems in Social Psychiatry, 1966; editor (with R. Bryce LaPorte) Alienation in Contemporary Society, 1976, (with J. Lindenthal) Psychiatry and Mental Health Science Handbook; mem. editorial bd. Internat. Jour. Mental Health, Adminstrn. In Mental Health. Bd. dirs. Bay Area Found., 1987—. Served to capt. USAF, 1959-61. Fellow APHA, Am. Psychoanalytic Assn. (hon.), Am. Psychiat. Assn. (life), Royal Soc. Health, N.Y. Acad. Sci., N.Y. Acad. Medicine; mem. Am. Sociol. Assn. Avocations: tennis, racquetball, violin, piano. Home and Office: 30676 Palos Verdes Dr W Palos Verdes Peninsula CA 90274 *Personal philosophy: Integrity sooner or later calls upon courage. If courage is not home integrity goes away.*

THOMAS, CLAYTON JAMES, air force executive; b. St. Joseph, Mo., Oct. 29, 1920; s. Gustave Bernard and Edith May (Eason) T.; m. Jerene Elizabeth Snuffer, Sept. 6, 1942; children: Sherry Kapfer, Theresa D'Alessandro, Ann Russell, Bruce, Julie Canavan. BS in Math., U. Chgo., 1942, MS in Math., 1947. Sr. mathematician, chief evaluation divsn. Inst. Air Weapons, U. Chgo., 1947-55; instr. U. Chgo., Roosevelt Coll., 1947-50; ops. rsch. analyst, chief rsch. group Office Ops. Analysis Hdqrs. USAF, Washington, 1955-71, sci. tech. advisor, chief scientist Studies & Analysis Agy., 1971—. Assoc. editor Mil. Ops. Rsch., 1993—. Mem. PTA, Park Forest, Ill., 1949-55, pres. 1949; mem. PTA, Arlington, Va., 1955-58, Annadale, Va., 1958-67, Great Falls, Va., 1967-83; com. mem., chair pers. com. local coun. Girl Scouts Am., Cook County, Ill., Arlington, Va., 1953-57; hostparent, asst. to area chair Am. Field Svc. Student Exch. Program, Annandale, Great Falls, 1959—. Capt. U.S. Army, 1942-45. Recipient Exceptional Civilian Svc. award USAF, 1975, Citation of Honor Air Force Assn., 1980, Meritorious Exec. award Pres. of U.S., 1991, Lanchester prize Ops. Rsch. Soc. Am., 1958. Fellow AAAS, Mil. Ops. Rsch. Soc. (pres. 1973-74, Wanner award 1988, INFORMS Mil. App. Soc., Steinhardt award 1994); mem. AIAA, Am. Math. Soc., Washington Soc. Engring., N.Y. Acad. Sci., Washington Ops. Rsch. and Mgmt. Sci. Coun., Phi Beta Kappa. Avocations: music (piano), reading (science, math, fiction), Foreign students and languages. Home: PO Box 540 Great Falls VA 22066-0540 Office: Hdqrs USAF AFSAA/SAN 1570 Air Force Pentagon Washington DC 20330-1570

THOMAS, COLIN GORDON, JR., surgeon, medical educator; b. Iowa City, July 25, 1918; s. Colin Gordon and Eloise Kinzer (Brainerd) T.; m. Shirley Forbes, Sept. 14, 1946; children: Karen, Barbara, James G., John F. B.S., U. Chgo., 1940, M.D., 1943. Diplomate Am. Bd. Surgery. Intern U. Iowa Hosp., 1943-44, resident surgery, 1944-45, 47-50; assoc. in surgery U. Iowa Med. Sch., 1950-51, asst. prof., 1951-52; mem. faculty U. N.C. Med. Sch., Chapel Hill, 1952—, prof. surgery, 1961—, Byah Thomason Doxey-Sanford Doxey prof. surgery, 1982—, chmn. dept., 1966-84, chief div. gen. surg., 1984-89, part-time prof., 1991—. Contbr. surg. texts, numerous articles to med. jours. Served to capt., M.C. AUS, 1945-47. Recipient Prof. award U. N.C. Sch. Medicine, 1964, Disting. Svc. award U. Chgo., 1982, Med. Alumni Disting. faculty award U. N.C., 1984; Berryhill lectr. U. N.C., 1989; recipient Fleming Fuller award U. N.C. Hosps., 1994. Mem. AMA, ACS (Disting. Leadership award N.C. chpt. 1990), AAUP, Am. Thyroid Assn., Am. Assn. Cancer Research, Am. Assn. Endocrine Surgeons (pres. 1989-90), Soc. Univ. Surgeons, So. Surg. Assn. (v.p. 1989-90), N.Y. Acad. Scis., Halsted Soc., Ga. Surg. Soc., Soc. Exptl. Biology and Medicine, Am. Surg. Assn., Womack Surg. Soc. (pres. 1981-83), Soc. Internationale de Chirurgie, Soc. Surgery Alimentary Tract, N.C. Surg. Assn., Internat. Assn. Endocrine Surgeons, Alpha Omega Alpha. Episcopalian (warden 1961-62). Home: 408 Morgan Creek Rd Chapel Hill NC 27514-4934

THOMAS, CRAIG, senator; b. Cody, Wyo., Feb. 17, 1933; s. Craig E. and Marge Oweta (Lynn) T.; m. Susan Roberts; children: Peter, Paul, Patrick, Alexis. BS, U. Wyo., 1955. V.p. Wyo. Farm Bur., Laramie, 1959-66; with Am. Farm Bur., 1966-75; gen. mgr. Wyo. Rural Elec. Assn., 1975-89; mem. Wyo. Ho. of Reps., 1984-89, 101st-103rd Congresses from Wyo., Washington, 1989-94; U.S. senator from Wyo., 1995—; mem. energy and natural resources com., environment and pub. works com., fgn. rels. com., Indian affairs com. Former chmn. Natrona County (Wyo.) Rep. Com.; state rep. Natrona County Dist.; del. Rep. Nat. Conv., 1980. Capt. USMC. Mem. Am. Soc. Trade Execs., Masons. Methodist. Office: US Senate 302 Hart Senate Office Bldg Washington DC 20510*

THOMAS, CYNTHIA ELIZABETH, advanced practice nurse; b. Highland, Ind., Sept. 3, 1958; d. James William and Naomi Elizabeth (Rice) T. BS in Animal Sci., Purdue U., 1980; ADN, Purdue U. Calumet, 1986, BSN, 1988, MSN, 1990. RN, Ind.; cert. adult nurse practitioner, family nurse practitioner, clin. specialist in med.-surg. nursing. Med.-surg. open heart ICU/CCU staff nurse, charge nurse Porter Meml. Hosp., Valparaiso, Ind., 1986-94; med.-surg. clin. instr. Purdue U., Westville, Ind., 1993-94; med.-surg. advanced practice nurse Cmty. Health Ctrs. Koontz Lake, LaCrosse, North Judson, Starke Meml. Hosp., Ind., 1994-95; nurse practitioner/office coord. Hanna Family Med. Ctr., LaPorte Hosp./Lakeland Area Health Svcs., 1995-96; nurse practitioner Arnett Clinic, Lafayette, Ind., 1996—; med.-surg. clin. instr. Purdue U., Westville, Ind., 1993-94; nursing instr. Bethel Coll., Mishawaka, Ind., 1995-96. Mem. AACN, Am. Acad. Nurse Practitioners, Alpha Zeta.

THOMAS, DALE E., lawyer; b. New Rochelle, N.Y., Jan. 25, 1947. AB summa cum laude, Princeton U., 1969; MDiv, Yale Divinity Sch., 1973; JD, Yale U., 1974. Bar: Ill. 1975. Law clerk U.S. Ct. Appeals 2d cir., 1974-75; ptnr. Sidley & Austin, Chgo. Mem. ABA, Ill. State Bar Assn., Chgo. Bar Assn., Phi Beta Kappa. Office: Sidley & Austin 1 First Natl Plz Chicago IL 60603-2003

THOMAS, DANIEL FOLEY, telecommunications company executive; b. Washington, Aug. 24, 1950; s. Richard Kenneth and Margaret (Foley) T.; m. Barbara Jane Clark, June 30, 1973; 1 child, Alison Clark. BS in Acctg., Mt. St. Mary's Coll., 1972. CPA, Va. Auditor Deloitte, Haskins and Sells, Washington, 1972-74; various fin. positions Communications Satellite Corp., Washington, 1974-78, asst. treas., 1984-85, treas., 1986-87, controller, 1987-89; controller Comsat Telesystems, Washington, 1978-79; mgr. acctg. and taxes Satellite Bus. Systems, McLean, Va., 1979-81, treas., 1981-84; v.p. fin. Comsat Tech. Products, Inc., Washington, 1985-86, Comsat Video Enterprises, Inc., Washington, 1989-90; sr. v.p. Leasetec Corp., Boulder, Colo., 1990—. Named One of Outstanding Young Men Am., 1981. Mem. AICPA, Va. Jaycees (life), Great Falls Jaycees (pres. 1978). Roman Catholic. Avocations: running, raquetball. Home: 1299 S Teal Ct Boulder CO 80303-1480 Office: Leasetec Corp 1401 Pearl St Boulder CO 80302-5319

THOMAS, DANIEL FRENCH, lawyer; b. Balt., Sept. 9, 1937; s. William Daniel and Lillian Hanway (Thompson) T.; m. Sandra Jean Thomas Ailiff, Dec. 20, 1996. BA, Loyola Coll., Balt., 1959; JD, U. Md., 1962. Bar: Md. 1962, U.S. Dist. Ct. Md. 1963. Law clk. to Hon. William M. Horney Ct. of Appeals of Md., Annapolis, 1962-63; atty. Bregel & Bregel, Balt., 1963-70, Thomas & Kalichman, Balt., 1971—; lectr. Md. Inst. for Continuing Profl. Edn. of Lawyers, Balt., 1980—. Editor: Maryland Divorce and Separation Law, 1987, 92, 96; contbr. articles to profl. jours. Home: 1101 Saint Paul St Apt 2104 Baltimore MD 21202-2673 Office: Thomas & Kalichman 7 Saint Paul St Ste 950 Baltimore MD 21202-1626

THOMAS, DANIEL HOLCOMBE, federal judge; b. Prattville, Ala., Aug. 25, 1906; s. Columbus Eugene and Augusta (Pratt) T.; m. Dorothy Quina, Sept. 26, 1936 (dec. 1977); children: Daniel H., Jr., Merrill Pratt; m. Catharine J. Miller, Oct. 25, 1979. LL.B., U. Ala., 1928. Bar: bar. Pvt. practice Mobile, Ala., 1929; asst. solicitor Mobile County; mem. firm Lyons, Chamberlain & Courtney, Mobile County, 1932-37, Lyons & Thomas, Mobile County, 1937-43, Lyons, Thomas & Pipes, Mobile County, 1946-51; judge U.S. Dist. Ct., Mobile, 1951—, now sr. judge. Mem. exec. bd. Mobile Area council Boy Scouts Am., 1963—, v.p., 1967-69, pres., 1973—, mem. nat. council, 1973—, Trustee dept. archieves and history, State of Ala. Served with USNR, 1943-45. Recipient Silver Beaver award Boy Scouts Am., 1970, Silver Antelope award, 1975. Methodist. Club: Mobile Country. Home: 13 Dogwood Cir Mobile AL 36608-2308 Office: US Dist Ct 459 US Courthouse Mobile AL 36602

THOMAS, DAVID ALBERT, law educator; b. L.A., Feb. 4, 1944; s. Albert Rees and Betty Lou (Adams) T.; m. Paula Rasmussen, Aug. 7, 1967; children: Rebecca, David R., John H., Matthew A., Susannah, Amanda, Christina, Erin. BA, Brigham Young U., 1967; JD, Duke U., 1972; MLS, Brigham Young U., 1977. Jud. clk. U.S. Dist. Ct. Utah, Salt Lake City, 1972-73; pvt. practice Salt Lake City, 1973-74; asst. prof. Law Sch. Brigham Young U., Provo, Utah, 1974-76; assoc. prof. Law Sch. Brigham Young U., Provo, 1976-79, prof. Law Sch., 1979—, dir. law libr. Law Sch., 1974-90; accreditation site insp. ABA, Chgo., 1978—. Author: Utah Civil Procedure, 1980, (with others) A Practical Guide to Disputes Between Adjoining Landowners, 1989, Utah Civil Practice, 1992; prin. author, editor-in-chief: Thompson on Real Property, Thomas Edition, 15 vols., 1994; contbr. articles to profl. jours. With U.S. Army, 1969-71, Vietnam. Mem. ABA (chair real property probate & trust sect. legis. com. 1990—). Home: 188 E 1864 S Orem UT 84058-7864 Office: Law Sch Brigham Young U Provo UT 84602

THOMAS, DAVID ANSELL, retired university dean; b. Holliday, Tex., July 5, 1917; s. John Calvin Mitchell and Alice (Willet) T.; m. Mary Elizabeth Smith, May 18, 1946; 1 dau., Ann Elizabeth. B.A., Tex. Tech. Coll., 1937; M.B.A., Tex. Christian U., 1948; Ph.D., U. Mich., 1956. C.P.A., Tex. Accountant Texaco, Inc., 1937-42; asso. prof. Tex. Christian U., 1946-49; lectr. U. Mich., 1949-53; prof. accounting Cornell U., Ithaca, N.Y., 1953-84; assoc. dean Cornell U. Grad. Sch. Mgmt., 1962-79; acting dean Cornell U. Grad. Sch. Bus. and Pub. Adminstrn., 1979-81; dean Samuel Curtis Johnson Grad. Sch. Mgmt. Cornell U., 1981-84. Author: Accelerated Amortization of Defense Facilities, 1958, Accounting for Home Builders, 1952; Contbr. numerous articles to publs.; Editor: Fed. Accountant, 1956-58. Pres. Exec. Investors, Inc.; exec. dir. Charles E. Merrill Family Found., 1954-57, Robert A. Magowan Found., 1957-60; adminstr. Charles E. Merrill Trust, 1957-81, Ithaca Growth Fund.; Bd. dirs. Ithaca Opera Assn., Cornell Student Agys. Served to capt. USAAF, 1942-46, PTO. Mem. Tex. Soc. C.P.A.'s, Nat. Assn. Accountants, Am. Accounting Assn., Phi Beta Kappa, Beta Alpha Psi. Clubs: Cornell of N.Y, University, Statler (pres., dir.). Home: Devenshire Park 1560 Jasper Ct Venice FL 34292-4336

THOMAS, DAVID PHILLIP, forestry educator, college administrator; b. Wasco, Oreg., July 7, 1918; s. William Phillip and Mabel Josephine (Hulery) T.; m. Geraldine Alaire Culross, Oct. 15, 1943; children: Larry K., Jeffrey A., Glenn R. B.S., U. Wash., 1941, M.F., 1947; postgrad., N.Y. State Coll. Forestry, Syracuse U., 1947-50. Research asso. Engring. Expt. Sta., U. Wash., Seattle, 1946-47; instr. wood tech. N.Y. State Coll. Forestry, 1947-50; mem. faculty U. Wash., Seattle, 1950—; prof. forest resources U. Wash., 1966-84, prof. emeritus, 1984—, spl. asst. to v.p. acad. affairs, 1964-72, dir. Inst. Forest Products, 1966-72, asso. dean Coll. Forest Resources, 1973-75; chmn. mgmt. and social scis. div. U. Wash. (Coll. Forest Resources), 1975-80; Instl. rep. Assn. Naval ROTC Colls., 1966-72; curriculum cons. U.S. Army ROTC program, 1969; program dir. Peace Corps, U. Wash., 1968-72; mem. Chile Forestry Vol. Tech. Support Program, 1968-72; del. Internat. Union Forestry Research Orgns., 1967, 76, World Forestry Congress, 1978. Trustee Nellie Martin Carmen Coll. Scholarship, 1992-96; mem. King County Environ. Devel. Commn., Seattle, 1972-79; mem. exec. bd., chief Seattle coun. Boy Scouts Am., 1957-80, coun. commr., 1965-67; mem. Wash. State Forest Practices Adv. Com., 1974-79, Wash. State Forest Practices Appeals Bd., 1981-85; trustee Keep Wash. Green Assn., 1975-86, adv. com., 1986-90, Wash. State Forestry Conf., 1985-90; bd. dirs. U. Lions Found., 1986-96, chmn., 1991-96. Lt. comdr. USNR, 1941-45. Recipient Silver Beaver award Boy Scouts Am., 1961; Outstanding Service award Wash. State Forestry Conf., 1984; Stewart H. Holbrook Disting. Service award for wild fire prevention Keep Wash. Green Assn., 1987. Fellow Soc. Am. Foresters (chmn. S. Puget Sound chpt. 1977-78, chmn.-elect state soc. 1979-80, chmn. 1980-81 Forester of Yr. award Wash. Soc. 1982); mem. Forest Products Rsch. Soc., Forest History Soc., Soc. Wood Sci. and Tech., Western Forestry and Conservation Assn., U. Wash. Foresters Alumni Assn. (pres. 1978-79, Honored Alumnus award 1985), Am. Forestry Assn. (life), Lions Internat. Svcs. Club, Sigma Xi, Xi Sigma Pi, Phi Sigma. Mem. United Ch. of Christ. Home: 3607 NE 100th St Seattle WA 98125-7818

THOMAS, (CHARLES) DAVIS, editor; b. Detroit, Dec. 20, 1928; s. Charles Richard and Nellie Clare (Davis) T.; m. Karin Ronnefeldt, Apr. 21, 1956; 1 child, Cord Alexander. B.A., U. Mich., 1950. Reporter Detroit News, 1950; reporter Life Mag., N.Y.C., 1954-57; staff corr. Life Mag., Los Angeles, 1957-60; photography editor Saturday Evening Post, Phila., 1961; asst. mng. editor Saturday Evening Post, 1962, mng. editor, 1962-63; editor in chief Ladies' Home Jour., N.Y.C., 1964-65; pub. cons. N.Y.C., Toronto, Geneva, Switzerland, 1965-70; exec. editor Holiday Mag., N.Y.C., 1970, Travel & Leisure Mag., N.Y.C., 1971-75; editor in chief Down East Mag., Camden, Maine, 1976-93, v.p., assoc. pub., 1984-93; editor at large Down East Mag., 1994—. Editor: Moon, Man's Greatest Adventure, 1970 (Annual award Aviation Space Writers' Assn. 1971), (with Karin Ronnefeldt) People of the First Man: Life Among the Plains Indians in their Final Days of Glory, 1976. Served with AUS, 1951-54. Home and Office: 57 Megunticook St Camden ME 04843-1643

THOMAS, DEBI (DEBRA J. THOMAS), ice skater; b. Poughkeepsie, N.Y., Mar. 25, 1967; d. McKinley and Janice Thomas; m. Christopher Bequette, Nov. 1996. BS, Stanford U.; MD, Northwestern U., 1997. Competitive figure skater, 1976-88. Winner U.S. Figure Skating Championship, 1986, 88, World Figure Skating Championship, 1986, World Profl. Figure Skating Championship, 1988, 89, 91. Recipient Am. Black Achievement Award, Ebony mag., named Women Athlete of Yr., 1986; winner Bronze medal Olympic Games, 1988. Address: Mentor Mktg and Mgmt 202 S Michigan St Ste 810 South Bend IN 46601

THOMAS, DEBORAH ALLEN, English educator; b. Biddeford, Maine, Sept. 1, 1943; d. Donald Paine and Marjorie (Thompson) Allen; m. Gordon Albert Thomas, Sept. 10, 1966; 1 child, Allen Mansfield. AB magna cum laude, Brown U., 1965; MA, Duke U., 1966; PhD, U. Rochester, 1972. Assoc. in humanities Eastman Sch. Music U. Rochester, N.Y., 1969-72; adj. asst. prof. English Fairleigh Dickinson U., Madison, N.J., 1973-76; co-adj. asst. prof. English Rutgers U., New Brunswick and Newark, N.J., 1976-80; asst. prof. English Villanova (Pa.) U., 1980-84, assoc. prof. English, 1984-91, prof. English, 1991—; visiting scholar Harvard U., Cambridge, Mass., 1985-86. Author: Dickens and the Short Story, 1982, Thackeray and Slavery, 1993, Hard Times: A Fable of Fragmentation and Wholeness, 1997; editor: Dickens, Selected Short Fiction, 1976; contbr. articles to profl. jours. Scholar Duke U., 1965-66; fellow U. Rochester, 1966-67, NEH fellow, 1985-86; faculty rsch. grantee Villanova U., summer 1984, 87, 92. Mem. MLA, N.E. Victorian Studies Assn., Dickens Soc. (sec., treas. 1979-81), Phi Beta Kappa. Avocations: swimming, hiking, aerobics. Office: Villanova U English Dept Villanova PA 19085

THOMAS, DERRICK VINCENT, professional football player; b. Miami, Fla., Nov. 1, 1967. Student, U. Ala. Linebacker Kansas City Chiefs, 1989—. Named to Sporting News Coll. All-Am. 2d team, 1987, 1st team, 1988, named to Sporting News NFL-All Pro Team, 1990-92; selected to Pro Bowl, 1989-96; recipient Butkus award for outstanding coll. linebacker, 1988. Office: Kansas City Chiefs 1 Arrowhead Dr Kansas City MO 64129-1651*

THOMAS, DUKE WINSTON, lawyer; b. Scuddy, Ky., Jan. 25, 1937; s. William E. and Grace T.; m. Jill Staples, Oct. 24, 1964; children: Deborah L., William E. II, Judith A. BSBA, Ohio State U., 1959, JD, 1964. Bar: Ohio 1964, U.S. Dist. Ct. Ohio 1966, U.S. Ct. Appeals (3d cir.) 1971, U.S. Ct. Appeals (6th cir.) 1972, U.S. Supreme Ct. 1973, U.S. Ct. Appeals (7th cir.) 1979. Ptnr. Vorys, Sater, Seymour and Pease, Columbus, Ohio, 1964—; bd. dirs. Ohio Bar Liability Ins. Co., Columbus, Symix Inc., Columbus. Fellow Am. Coll. Trial Lawyers (chmn. Ohio ho. and senate joint select com. on jud. compensation 1987), Am. Bar Found., Ohio Bar Found., Columbus Bar Found.; mem. ABA (ho. of dels. 1985—, state del. 1989-95, bd. govs. 1995—), Ohio Bar Assn. (pres. 1985), Columbus Bar Assn. (pres. 1978), Pres.'s Club Ohio State U., Golf Club, Worthington Hills Country Club, Columbus Athletic Club. Home: 2090 Sheringham Rd Columbus OH 43220-4358 Office: Vorys Sater Seymour & Pease PO Box 1008 52 E Gay St Columbus OH 43216-1008

THOMAS, DWIGHT REMBERT, writer; b. Savannah, Ga., Dec. 8, 1944; s. Huguenin and Alma (Sanders) T. BA in English with honors, Emory U., 1967; PhD in Am. Lit., U. Pa., 1978. Fellow English dept. U. Pa., Phila., 1971-78; writer Savannah, 1979—; cons. Film Odyssey, Washington, 1988-89. Author: The Poe Log: A Documentary Life of Edgar Allan Poe, 1987. Dir. Edgar Allan Poe Mus., Richmond, Va., 1988-96. With U.S. Army, 1969-71. Mem. MLA, Am. Med. Writers Assn., Mensa (treas. Savannah area 1985-88, local sec. 1989-90), Phi Beta Kappa. Roman Catholic. Avocations: German lang., current cinema, bicycling. Home: 7 E Gordon St Savannah GA 31401-4925

THOMAS, EDWARD DONNALL, physician, researcher; b. Mart, Tex., Mar. 15, 1920; married; 3 children. BA, U. Tex., 1941, MA, 1943; MD, Harvard U., 1946; MD (hon.), U. Cagliari, Sardinia, 1981, U. Verona, Italy, 1991, U. Parma, Italy, 1992, U. Barcelona, Spain, 1994, U. Warsaw, Poland, 1996, U. Jagiellonski, Cracow, Poland, 1996. Lic. physician Mass., N.Y., Wash.; diplomate Am. Bd. Internal Medicine. Intern in medicine Peter Bent Brigham Hosp., Boston, 1946-47, rsch. fellow hematology, 1947-48; NRC postdoctoral fellow in medicine dept. biology MIT, Cambridge, 1950-51; chief med. resident, sr. asst. resident Peter Bent Brigham Hosp., 1951-53, hematologist, 1953-55; instr. medicine Harvard Med. Sch., Boston, 1953-55; rsch. assoc. Cancer Rsch. Found. Children's Med. Ctr., Boston, 1953-55; physician-in-chief Mary Imogene Bassett Hosp., Cooperstown, N.Y., 1955-63; assoc. clin. prof. medicine Coll. Physicians and Surgeons Columbia U., N.Y.C., 1955-63; attending physician U. Wash. Hosp., Seattle, 1963-90; prof. medicine Sch. Medicine U. Wash., Seattle, 1963-90, head divsn. oncology Sch. Medicine, 1963-85, prof. emeritus medicine Sch. Medicine, 1990—; dir. med. oncology Fred Hutchinson Cancer Rsch. Ctr., Seattle, 1974-89, assoc. dir. clin. rsch. programs, 1982-89, mem., 1974—; mem. hematology study sect. NIH, 1965-69; mem. bd. trustees and med. sci. adv. com. Leukemia Soc. Am., Inc., 1969-73; mem. clin. cancer investigation review com. Nat. Cancer Inst., 1970-74; 1st ann. Eugene C. Eppinger lectr. Peter Bent Brigham Hosp. and Harvard Med. Sch., 1974; Lilly lectr. Royal Coll. Physicians, London, 1977; Stratton lectr. Internation Soc. Hematology, 1982; Paul Aggeler lectr. U. Calif., San Francisco, 1982; 65th Mellon lectr. U. Pitts. Sch. Medicine, 1984; Stanley Wright Meml. lectr. Western Soc. Pediatric Rsch., 1985; Adolfo Ferrata lectr. Italian Soc. Hematology, Verona, Italy, 1991. Mem. editl. bd. Blood, 1962-75, 77-82, Transplantation, 1970-76, Proc. of Soc. for Exptl. Biology and Medicine, 1974-81, Leukemia Rsch., 1977-87, Hematological Oncology, 1982-87, Jour. Clin. Immunology, 1982-87, Am. Jour. Hematology, 1985—, Bone Marrow Transplantation, 1986—. With U.S. Army, 1948-50. Recipient A. Ross McIntyre award U. Nebr. Med. Ctr., 1975, Philip Levine award Am. Soc. Clin. Pathologists, 1979, Disting. Svc. in Basic Rsch. award Am. Cancer Soc., 1980, Kettering prize Gen. Motors Cancer Rsch. Found., 1981, Spl. Keynote Address award Am. Soc. Therapeutic Radiologists, 1981, Robert Roesler de Villiers award Leukemia Soc. Am., 1983, Karl Landsteiner Meml. award Am. Assn. Blood Banks, 1987, Terry Fox award Can., 1990, Internat. award Gairdner Found., 1990, N.Am. Med. Assn. Hong Kong prize, 1990, Nobel prize in medicine, 1990, Presdl. medal of sci. NSF, 1990,. Mem. NAS, Am. Assn. Cancer Rsch., Am. Assn. Physicians (Kober medal 1992), Am. Fedn. Clin. Rsch., Am. Soc. Clin. Oncology (David A. Karnoksky Meml. lectr. 1983), Am. Soc. Clin. Investigation, Am. Soc. Hematology (pres. 1987-88, Henry M. Stratton lectr. 1975), Internat. Soc. Exptl. Hematology, Internat. Soc. Hematology, Academie Royale de Medicine de Belgique (corresponding mem.), Swedish Soc. Hematology (hon.), Swiss Soc. Hematology, Royal Coll. Physicians and Surgeons Can. (hon.), Western Assn. Physicians, Soc. Exptl. Biology and Medicine, Transplantation Soc., Nat. Acad. Medicine (hon.). Office: Fred Hutchinson Cancer Ctr 1124 Columbia St Seattle WA 98104-2015

THOMAS, ELAINE FREEMAN, artist, educator; b. Cleve., July 21, 1923; d. Daniel Edquard and Ellen Douglas (Wilson) Freeman; m. Frederick Lindel Thomas, June 28, 1943 (dec. May 1969); children: Janet Thomas Sullen, Frederick L. III. BS, Tuskegee (Ala.) U., 1945; MA, NYU, 1949; postgrad., U. Paris, 1966, U. Poona, India, 1973, Columbia U., 1970. Fellow Northwestern U., Evanston, Ill., 1944; Rosenwald fellow Black Mountain (N.C.) Coll., 1945; faculty, art dept. chair Tuskegee U., 1945-89; fellow Berea (Ky.) Coll., 1956, U. of Ams., Mexico City, 1956; curator George Washington Carver Mus., Tuskegee Inst., 1962-77; mem. Fulbright-Hays Faculty Rsch., Senegal and LaGambia, Africa, 1989; panelist expansion arts Nat. Endowment of Arts, Washington, 1977-79; fgn. svc. officer evaluator U.S. Dept. State, Washington, 1979; mem. exec. com. Ala. Coun. Arts, Montgomery, 1986-91; numerous TV appearances. One-woman exhbn. Hallmark Greeting Cards, Crown Ctr., Kansas City, Mo.; participant TV documentary, 1974, 77, 82, 85, 87, 91, 94; set up George Washington Carver Exhbn., White House. Chmn. nat. screening com. Fulbright Grad. Fellows in Design, Inst. Internat. Edn., N.Y.C.. Named A Woman of Distinction, Auburn (Ala.) U., Ms. Sr. Am. of Ala., 1994, 1st runner up Ms. Sr. Am., 1994; recipient Disting. Svc. award U.S. Dept. Interior, Nat. Park Svc., Bicentennial award Pres. Gerald Ford, Resolution HR 274 award State of Ala. Ho. of Reps., Ms. Sr. Ala. award, 1994; named to 1995 Ala. Sr. Citizens Hall of Fame. Mem. Nat. Mus. of Women Artists, Optimists, Tau Beta Sigma, Delta Sigma Theta, Zeta Phi Beta (Woman of Yr. award 1978). Avocations: music, fashion, cross cultural consulting, retired senior volunteer. Home: 202 Rush Dr Tuskegee AL 36083-2707

THOMAS, ELIZABETH MARSHALL, writer; b. Boston, Sept. 13, 1931; d. Laurence K. and Lorna (McLean) Marshall; m. Stephen Thomas, 1956; children: Stephanie, Ramsay. Student, Smith Coll.; BA in English, Radliffe Coll., 1954. Writer, 1954—. Author: The Harmless People, 1959, Warrior Herdsmen, 1965, Reindeer Moon, 1987, The Animal Wife, 1990, The Hidden Life of Dogs, 1993, The Tribe of the Tiger, 1994; author bi-weekly column about pets USA Today. Office: Simon and Schuster Touchtone Books 1230 Avenue Of The Americas New York NY 10020-1513

THOMAS, ELLA COOPER, lawyer; b. Ft. Totten, N.Y.; d. Avery John and Ona Caroline (Gibson) C.; m. Robert Edward Lee Thomas, Nov. 22, 1938 (dec. Jan. 1985); 1 child, Robert Edward Lee Jr. Student, Vassar Coll., 1932-34, U. Hawaii, 1934-35, George Washington U., 1935-36; JD, George Washington U., 1940. Bar: U.S. Dist. Ct. D.C. 1942, U.S. Ct. Appeals (D.C. cir.) 1943, U.S. Supreme Ct. 1947, U.S. Tax Ct. 1973. Secret maps custodian U.S. Dist. Engrs., Honolulu, 1941-42; contbg. editor Labor Rels. Reporter, Washington, 1942; assoc. Smith, Ristig & Smith, Washington, 1942-45; law libr. George Washington Law Sch., Washington, 1946-53; reporter of decisions U.S. Tax Ct., Washington, 1953-75. Author: Law of Libel and Slander, 1949. Mem. Inter-Am. Bar Assn. (coun. mem. 1973—), D.C. Bar Assn. Avocations: physical fitness, crostics, mote marine lab. vol. computer.

THOMAS, ESTHER MERLENE, elementary education educator; b. San Diego, Oct. 16, 1945; d. Merton Alfred and Nellie Lida (Von Pilz) T. AA with honors, Grossmont Coll., 1966; BA with honors, San Diego State U., 1969; MA, U. Redlands, 1977. Cert. elem. and adult edn. tchr. Tchr. Cajon Valley Union Sch. Dist., El Cajon, 1969—; sci. fair coord. Flying Hills Sch.; tchr. Hopi and Navajo Native Americans, Ariz., Utah, 1964-74, Goose and Gander Nursery Sch., Lakeside, Calif., 1964-66; dir., supt. Bible and Sunday schs. various chs., Lakeside, 1961-87; mem. sci. com., math. coun. Cajon Valley Union Sch. Dist., 1990-91. Author: Individualized Curriculum in the Affective Domain; contbg. author: Campbell County, The Treasured Years, 1990, Legends of the Lakeside; songwriter for Hilltop Records, Hollywood, Calif.; songs released Never Trouble Trouble, Old Glory, Jesus Is Our Lord, Daniel's Prayer, There Lay Jesus; songwriter for Amerecord Records, Hollywood; songs released Born to Win, 1996; songwriter for Hollywood Artists Records, Hollywood; songs released Clear the Path Lord, Aqua Forte, In the Volume of the Book, 1996; contbr. articles to profl. jours. and newspapers. Tem. U.S. Senatorial Club, Washington, 1984—, Conservative Caucus, Inc., Washington, 1988—, Ronald Reagan Presdl. Found., Ronald Reagan Rep. Ctr., 1988, Rep. Presdl. Citizen's Adv. Commn., 1989—, Rep. Platform Planning Com., Calif., 1992, at-large del. representing dist. #45, Lakeside, Calif., 1992, 1995—, Am. Security Coun., Washington, 1994, Congressman

Hunter's Off Road Adv. Coun., El Cajon, Calif., 1994, Century Club, San Diego Rep. Century Club, 1995; mem. health articulation com. project AIDS, Cajon Valley Union Sch. Dist., 1988—, Concerned Women Am., Washington, Recruit Depot Hist. Mus., San Diego, 1989, Citizen's Drug Free Am., Calif., 1989—, The Heritage Found., 1988—; charter mem. Marine Corps Mus.; mem. Lakeside Centennial Com., 1985-86; hon. mem. Rep. Presdl. Task Force, Washington, 1986; del. Calif. Rep. Senatorial Mid-Term Conv., Washington, 1994; mus. curator Lakeside Hist. Soc., 1992-93. Recipient Outstanding Svc. award PTA, 1972-74; recognized for various contbns. Commdg. Post Gen., San Diego Bd. Edn., 1989. Mem. Tchrs. Assn., Calif. Tchrs. Assn., Cajon Valley Educators Assn. (faculty advisor, rep. 1980-82, 84-86, 87-88), Nat. Trust for Hist. Preservation, Christian Bus. and Profl. Women, Trust for Hist. Preservation, Nashville Songwriters Assn., Capitol Hill Women's Club, Am. Ctr. for Law and Justice, Internat. Christian Women's Club (Christian amb. to Taiwan, Korea, 1974). Republican. Avocations: world traveling, Christian teaching, vocal music, piano, guitar. Home: 13594 Hwy 8 # 3 Lakeside CA 92040-5235 Office: Flying Hills Elem Sch 1251 Finch St El Cajon CA 92020-1433

THOMAS, EVERETTE EARL, federal judge; b. Knoxville, Tenn., Nov. 13, 1935; s. Vaughn Lewis and Anna (Marsee) T.; m. Joy Valante, Aug. 29, 1964. BS, U. Tenn., 1958, JD, 1968. Bar: Tenn. 1968, Va. 1972, D.C. 1972, U.S. Ct. Appeals (D.C. cir.) 1972. Trial atty. Fed. Trade Commn., Washington, 1968-73, regional dir., 1973-77; adminstrv. law judge U.S. Dept. Labor, Washington, 1977-80, dep. chief judge, 1980-87; dist. chief judge U.S. Dept. Labor, Ft. Lauderdale, Fla., 1987—. Author: (monograph) Administrative Law Judges, The Corps Issue, 1987; contbr. articles to profl. jours. Pres. Lake Bancroft Commn. Assn., Falls Church, Va., 1982. Lt. USN, 1959-64. Recipient scholarship NSF, 1957. Mem. ABA (exec. com. Nat. Conf. Adminstrv. Law Judges 1982-90, chmn. 1990-91). Avocations: scuba diving, boating, sport fishing. Home: 11683 6th Ave Marathon FL 33050 Office: Office Adminstrv Law Judges Ste 530 111 Veterans Memorial Blvd Metairie LA 70005-3033

THOMAS, FRANK EDWARD, professional baseball player; b. Columbus, Ga., May 27, 1968. Student, Auburn U. With Chgo. White Sox, 1990—. Named to Sporting News All-Star Coll. All Am. team, 1989; Sporting News All-Star team, 1991, 93-94; recipient Silver Slugger award, 1991, 93, 94; mem. Am. League All-Star Team, 1993-95; recipient Am. League MVP award, 1994; named Major League Player of Yr., Sporting News, 1993. Office: Chgo White Sox Comiskey Park 333 W 35th St Chicago IL 60616-3621*

THOMAS, FRANKLIN AUGUSTINE, foundation executive; b. Bklyn., May 27, 1934; s. James and Viola (Atherley) T.; divorced; children: Keith, Hillary, Kerrie, Kyle. B.A., Columbia U., 1956, LL.B., 1963; LL.D. (hon.), Yale U., 1970, Fordham U., 1972, Pratt Inst., 1974, Pace U., 1977, Columbia U., 1979. Bar: N.Y. 1964. Atty. Fed. Housing and Home Finance Agy., N.Y.C., 1963-64; asst. U.S. atty. for So. Dist. N.Y., 1964-65; dep. police commr. charge legal matters N.Y.C., 1965-67; pres., chief exec. officer Bedford Stuyvesant Restoration Corp., Bklyn., 1967-77; pres. The Ford Found., 1979-96; atty., cons., 1996—; bd. dirs. Citicorp/Citibank, ALCOA, Cummins Engine Co., Lucent Techs., PepsiCo, Inc. Trustee Columbia U., 1969-75. Served with USAF, 1956-60. Recipient LBJ Found. award for contbn. to betterment of urban life, 1974, medal of excellence Columbia U., 1976, Alexander Hamilton award Columbia U., 1983.

THOMAS, FREDERICK BRADLEY, lawyer; b. Evanston, Ill., Aug. 13, 1949; s. Frederick Bradley and Katherine Kidder (Bingham) T.; m. Elizabeth Maxwell, Oct. 25, 1975; children: Bradley Bingham, Stephens Maxwell, Rosa Macaulay. AB, Dartmouth Coll., 1971; JD, U. Chgo., 1974. Bar: Ill. 1974. Law clk. to hon. judge John C. Godbold U.S. Ct. Appeals (5th cir.), Montgomery, Ala., 1974-75; assoc. Mayer, Brown & Platt, Chgo., 1975-80, ptnr., 1981—. Bd. dirs. St. Gregory Episcopal Sch., 1989—; bd. trustees La Rabida Children's Hosp., 1990—. Mem. ABA, Chgo. Council Lawyers. Republican. Episcopalian. Office: Mayer Brown & Platt 190 S La Salle St Chicago IL 60603-3410

THOMAS, GARETH, metallurgy educator; b. Maesteg, U.K., Aug. 9, 1932; came to U.S., 1960, naturalized, 1977; s. David Bassett and Edith May (Gregory) T.; 1 child, Julian Guy David. B.Sc., U. Wales, 1952; Ph.D., Cambridge U., 1955, Sc.D., 1969; DCs (hon.), Lehigh U., 1996. I.C.I. fellow Cambridge U., 1956-59; asst. prof. U. Calif., Berkeley, 1960-63; asso. prof. U. Calif., 1963-67, prof. metallurgy, 1967—, assoc. dean grad. div., 1968-69, asst. chancellor, acting vice chancellor for acad. affairs, 1969-72; founder, sci. dir. Nat. Ctr. Electron Microscopy, 1982-93; cons. to industry. Author: Transmission Electron Microscopy of Metals, 1962, Electron Microscopy and Strength of Crystals, 1963, (with O. Johari) Stereographic Projection and Applications, 1969, Transmission Electron Microscopy of Materials, 1980; editor-in-chief: Acta and Scripta Mat., 1995—; contbr. articles to profl. jours. Recipient Curtis McGraw Rsch. award Am. Soc. Engring. Edn., 1966, E.O. Lawrence award Dept. Energy, 1978, I-R 100 award R & D mag., 1987, Henry Clifton Sorby award Internat. Metallographic Soc., 1987, Albert Sauveur Achievement award, 1991; Guggenheim fellow, 1972. Fellow Am. Soc. Metals (Bradley Stoughton Young Tchrs. award 1965, Grossman Publ. award 1966), Am. Inst. Mining, Metall. and Petroleum Engrs.; mem. Electron Microscopy Soc. Am. (prize 1965, pres. 1976), Am. Phys. Soc., Nat. Acad. Scis., Nat. Acad. Engring., Brit. Inst. Metals (Rosenheim medal 1977), Internat. Fedn. Electron Microscopy Socs. (pres. 1986-90), Brit. Iron and Steel Inst. Club: Marylebone Cricket (Eng.). Patentee in field. Office: U Calif Dept Materials Sci/Engring 561 Evans Hall Berkeley CA 94720-1760

THOMAS, GARTH JOHNSON, psychology educator emeritus; b. Pittsburg, Kans., Sept. 8, 1916; s. Leslie Homer and Lou Opal (Johnson) T.; m. Mary Mona Gee, Sept. 21, 1945; children—Gregory Allen, Barbara Elizabeth. A.B., Kans. State Tchrs. Coll. at Pittsburg, 1938; M.A., U. Kans., 1941, Harvard, 1943; Ph.D., Harvard, 1948. Instr., asst. prof. U. Chgo., 1948-54; asso. prof. U. Ill. Med. Sch., 1954-57; research prof. physiology and elec. engring. U. Ill., Urbana, 1957-66; prof. U. Rochester, N.Y., 1966-82, dir. Ctr. for Brain Rsch., 1970-77, prof. emeritus, 1982—; mem. rev. com. Exptl. Psychology Fellowship panel NIMH, 1965-70, chmn., 1970; mem. psychobiology panel NSF; cons. editor Sinauer Press, Inc. Cons. editor: Jour. Comparative and Physiol. Psychology, 1969-75, 82-91, editor, 1975-81; cons. editor: McGraw Hill Ency. of Sci. and Tech.; contbr. articles to profl. jours. Served to 1st lt. AUS, 1944-47. Recipient research grants NSF, research grants NIMH, research grants U.S. Army, 1951—; Alumni Meritorious Achievement award Kans. State Coll. at Pittsburg, 1976. Mem. Am. Psychol. Assn., Animal Behavior Soc., AAAS, Psychonomic Soc., Soc. Exptl. Psychology, Soc. for Neurosci. Home: 186 Buckland Ave Rochester NY 14618-2139

THOMAS, GARY EDWARD, science educator, researcher; b. Lookout, W.V., Oct. 25, 1934; s. Garland Eugene Thomas and Dorothy Mae (Fish) Johnson; m. Susan Jude Cherup, Jan. 20, 1963; 1 child, Jennifer Ann. BS, N.Mex. State U., 1957; PhD, U. Pitts., 1963. Rsch. assoc. Svc. d'Aeronomie du CNRS, Paris, France, 1962-63; staff scientist Aerospace Corp., El Segundo, Calif., 1965-67; prof. U. Colo., Boulder, 1967—; sec. Internat. Comm. on Meteorology of the Upper Atmosphere, 1988-95; disting. vis. prof. U. Adelaide, Australia, 1995. Assoc. editor Jour. Geophys. Rsch., 1992&; contbr. more than 100 articles to profl. jours. 1st lt. Signal Corps U.S. Army, 1963-65. Recipient Award Rsch. Excellence U. Colo., 1994; fellowship U. Colo., 1974-75. Mem. Am. Geophysical Union (assoc. editor 1992). Office: U Colo CB 392 Boulder CO 80309-0392

THOMAS, GARY L., academic administrator; b. Willows, Calif., May 12, 1937; s. Leonel Richard and Myrtle Blanch (Moncur) T.; m. Margaret Anderson, Aug. 11, 1960 (div. 1975); children: Katelin, Elizabeth Ann, Derek Alan. AA, Modesto Jr. Coll., 1958; BS in Elec. Engring., U. Calif., Berkeley, 1960, MA in Physics, 1962, PhD in Elec. and Computer Engring., 1967. Acting asst. prof. U. Calif., Berkeley, 1967; asst. prof. elec. engring. SUNY, Stony Brook, 1967-70, assoc. prof. elec. engring., 1970-73, assoc. dean grad. sch., 1973-74, chairperson, prof. elec. engring., 1975-79; congl. fellow A.A.A.S., Washington, 1974-75; provost, vp.p acad. affairs N.J. Inst. Tech., Newark, 1980—; student asst. bd. Dept. Higher Edn., N.J., 1980-97; chairperson rsch. adv. bd. PSE & G, Newark, 1986-90, Regional Transp. Rsch. Bd., N.Y. and N.J., 1987-90; mem. Kessler Inst. for Rehab., West Orange, N.J., 1988—. Author, editor: Fundamentals of Electrical and Computer Engineering, 1983. State of Calif. scholar, 1960, Schumberger scholar, 1961; NSF grantee, 1973-79. Home: 209 Gregory Ave West Orange NJ 07052-4529 Office: NJ Inst Tech University Heights Newark NJ 07102

THOMAS, GARY LYNN, financial executive; b. Port Vue, Pa., May 15, 1942; s. Willis L. and Luella M. (Rorabaugh) T.; m. Sharen A. Gibbons, May 13, 1967; children—Gregory Scott, Tara Elizabeth. B.S. in Bus. Adminstrn, Pa. State U., 1964; grad., Sch. Bank Adminstrn., U. Wis., 1973. CPA, Pa. Sr. auditor Arthur Andersen & Co., Los Angeles and Pitts., 1964-69; v.p. and dep. comptroller Pitts. Nat. Bank, 1969-77; v.p. and treas. Md. Nat. Corp., Balt., 1977-80; v.p., mgr. corp. fin. div. Md. Nat. Bank, Balt.; exec. v.p. adminstrn. Peterson, Howell & Heather, Hunt Valley, Md., 1980-82; v.p. fin. Am. TeleServices, Inc, a Metromedia co., Balt., 1983-85; chief fin. officer First Cellular Group, Inc., Balt., 1985-88, Schelle, Warner, Murray & Thomas, Inc., Balt., 1988—; mng. dir. Schelle Cellular Group, Inc., 1989—; pres. Ruxton Capital Group, Inc., 1989—; chief fin. officer Am. Personal Communications, Inc., Balt. and D.C., 1990—; adj. instr. Sch. Bank Adminstrn., U. Wis., 1975-80; speaker 14th ann. Bank Tax Inst., 1978. Mem. adv. bd., fin. com. St. Joseph Hosp., Balt.; bd. dirs. industry luncheon club Towson State U. Served with USAR, 1968. Inducted into McKeesport H.S. Hall of Fame, 1994. Mem. AICPA, Pa. Inst. CPAs, Md. Assn. CPAs (prior chmn. mems. in industry com.). Republican. Methodist. Home: 575 18th Ave S Naples FL 34102

THOMAS, HAROLD ALLEN, JR., civil engineer, educator; b. Terre Haute, Ind., Aug. 14, 1913; s. Harold A. and Katherine (Sass) T.; m. Gertrude A. Grim, July 2, 1935; children—Harold Allen III, Stephen C., Calvin R. B.S. in Civil Engring, Carnegie Inst. Tech., 1935; S.D., Harvard, 1938. Faculty mem. Harvard, 1939—, successively instr., asst. prof., asso. prof., 1939-56, Gordon McKay prof. civil and san. engring., 1956-84, prof. emeritus, 1984—; profl. cons. HEW, 1949—; div. med. scis. NRC-Nat. Acad. Scis., 1943-63, also Dept. Def., AEC; cons. Exec. Office Pres., also Dept. Interior, 1961—; Mem. sci. bd. for Middle East and Southeast Asia, Nat. Acad. Scis., 1964-66, exec. com. social consequences of population changes, 1968—. Co-author: Design Water Resource Systems, 1961, Models for Managing Regional Water Quality, 1973. Fellow Am. Acad. of Arts and Scis.; mem. Am. Geophys. Union (RE Horton medal 1978), ASCE, Nat. Acad. Engring., Boston Soc. C.E. Home: 61 Cotuit Rd Sandwich MA 02563-2654 Office: Harvard U Dept Civil Engring Cambridge MA 02138

THOMAS, HAROLD WILLIAM, avionics systems engineer, flight instructor; b. Cle Elum, Wash., Sept. 29, 1941; s. Albert John and Margaret Jenny (Micheletto) T.; children: Gregg Wallace, Lisa Michele. BS, U. Wash., 1964; M of Engring., U. Fla., 1968; Cert. Aviation Safety, U. So. Calif., 1994. Sci. programmer Aerojet Gen. Corp., Sacramento, Calif., 1964-65; systems analyst GE Co., Daytona Beach, Fla., 1965-69; systems engr. GE Co., Phoenix, 1969-70; sr. software engr. Sperry Flight Systems, Phoenix, 1970-77; sr. systems engr. Honeywell, Inc., Phoenix, 1977-80; engr. section head Sperry Flight Systems, Phoenix, 1980-87; free lance flight instr., 1981—; tech. staff engr. Honeywell, Inc., Phoenix, 1987—; designated engring. rep. Fed. Aviation Adminstrn., Long Beach, 1987—. Mem. AIAA, SAE Internat. Internat. Soc. Air Safety Investigators, Am. Mensa Ltd. Achievements include patent for rotating round dial aircraft engine instruments, patent for dynamic approach display format with plan and profile views. Home: 2514 W Pershing Ave Phoenix AZ 85029-1445 Office: Honeywell INc 21111 N 19th Ave Phoenix AZ 85027-2708

THOMAS, HELEN A. (MRS. DOUGLAS B. CORNELL), newspaper bureau executive; b. Winchester, Ky., Aug. 4, 1920; d. George and Mary (Thomas) T.; m. Douglas B. Cornell. BA, Wayne U., 1942; LLD, Eastern Mich. State U., 1972, Ferris State Coll., 1978, Brown U., 1986; LHD, Wayne State U., 1974, U. Detroit, 1979; LLD, St. Bonaventure U., 1988, Franklin Marshall U., 1989, No. Michigan U., 1989, Skidmore Coll., 1992; Susquehanna U., 1993, Sage Coll., 1994, U. Mo., 1994; LLD, Northwestern U., 1995, Franklin Coll., 1995; Hon. degree, Mich. State U., 1996. With UPI, 1943—; wire svc. reporter UPI, Washington, 1943-74; White House bur. chief UPI, 1974—. Author: Dateline White House. Recipient Woman of Yr. in Comm. award Ladies Home Jour., 1975, 4th Estate award Nat. press Club, 1984; Journalism award U. Mo., Dean of Sch. Journalism award, Al Newharth award, 1990, Ralph McGill award, 1995. Mem. Women's Nat. Press Club (pres. 1959-60, William Allen White Journalism award), Am. Newspaper Women's Club (past v.p.), White House Corrs. Assn. (pres. 1976), Gridiron Club (pres. 1993), Sigma Delta Chi (fellow, Hall of Fame), Delta Sigma Phi (hon.). Home: 2501 Calvert St NW Washington DC 20008-2620 Office: UPI World Hdqrs 1510 H St NW Washington DC 20005-1008

THOMAS, HENRY LEE, JR., professional football player; b. Houston, Jan. 12, 1965. Student, La. State U. Defensive tackle Minnesota Vikings, 1987-97, Detroit Lions, 1997—. Played in Pro Bowl, 1991, 92. Office: Detroit Lions 1200 Featherstone Rd Pontiac MI 48342*

THOMAS, HERMAN L., school system administrator. Asst. supt. Arkadelphia (Ark.) Sch. Dist. Recipient Blue Ribbon Sch. Award, 1990-91. Office: Arkadelphia Sch Dist 235N 11th St Arkadelphia AR 71923*

THOMAS, HOWARD PAUL, civil engineer, consultant; b. Cambridge, Mass., Aug. 20, 1942; s. Charles Calvin and Helen Elizabeth (Hook) T.; m. Ingrid Nybo, Jan. 4, 1969; children: Kent Michael, Lisa Karen, Karina Michelle. BS in Engring., U. Mich., 1965, MS in Engring., 1966. Registered profl. engr., Alaska, Calif. Engr. Ove Arup & Ptnrs., London, 1966-67; project engr. Woodward-Clyde Cons., San Francisco, 1967-73; assoc. Woodward-Clyde Cons., Anchorage, 1975-89; spl. cons. Cowiconsult Cons., Copenhagen, 1973-75; prin. engr. Harding-Lawson Assocs., Anchorage, 1989-90; v.p., chief engr. EMCON Alaska, Inc., Anchorage, 1991-94; gen. mgr. Internat. Tech. Corp., Anchorage, 1994-96; assoc. GeoEngrs., Inc., Anchorage, 1996—; mem. Anchorage Mayor's Geotech. Adv. Commn., 1997—; chmn. Nat. Tech. Coun. Cold Regions Engring., 1988-89, chmn. com. program and publs., 1982-84; chmn. 4th Internat. Conf. Cold Regions Engring., Anchorage, 1986; liaison NAS/Nat. Rsch. Coun. Polar Rsch. Bd., 1989—; mem. Achorage Mayor's Geotech. Adv. Commn., 1997—. Contbr. articles to profl. jours. French horn musician Anchorage Civic Orch. Named Alaskan Engr. Yr., 1986. Fellow ASCE (pres. Anchorage chpt. 1985-86, chair mgmt. group A. 1996-97); mem. Soc. Am. Mil. Engrs., Cons. Engrs. Coun. Alaska (pres. 1989-90), Am. Cons. Engrs. Coun. (nat. dir. 1990-91), Project Mgmt. Inst. (v.p. Alaska chpt. 1991-95), Toastmasters (pres. Anchorage club 1984), Sons of Norway (v.p. Anchorage lodge 1997). Lutheran. Avocations: playing French Horn in Anchorage Civic Orchestra, travel, skiing, sailing. Home: 2611 Brittany Dr Anchorage AK 99504-3332

THOMAS, IAN LESLIE MAURICE, publisher; b. Bearsden, Scotland, May 10, 1937; came to U.S., 1989; s. Maurice and Fanny Olive (White) T.; m. Margaret June Thomas, Aug. 13, 1960; children: Fiona, Diana, Ian. BSc with honours, U. Glasgow, Scotland, 1960; ARCST with honors, U. Strathclyde, Scotland, 1960. Chartered engr., U.K. Indentured apprentice Brit. Polar Engines, Scotland, 1955-60; installation engr. Free Piston Engine Co., Singapore, 1960-62; prodn. mgr. Imperial Chem. Industries, Eng., 1962-73; gen. mgr. wall coverings Reed Internat., 1973-78; mng. dir. Odhams (Watford) Ltd., 1979-82; CEO Reed Travel Group, Eng., 1983-92, Reed Telepublishing, Secaucus, N.J., 1983—; bd. dirs. Reed Internat. PLC, Reed Elsevier PLC. Mem. Instn. Mech. Engrs. Avocations: sailing, rugby. Office: Reed Travel Group 500 Plaza Dr Secaucus NJ 07094-3619

THOMAS, ISIAH LORD, III, former professional basketball player, basketball team executive; b. Chgo., Apr. 30, 1961. Grad. in Criminal Justice, Ind. U., 1987. With Detroit Pistons, 1981-94; v.p. Toronto Raptors, 1994—, now v.p. basketball ops., owner, exec. v.p.; mem. U.S. Olympic Basketball Team, 1980, NBA Championship Teams, 1989-90. Named to All-Star team, 1982-93, All NBA First Team, 1984, 85, 86; recipient All-Star team MVP award, 1984, 86, NBA Playoff MVP award, 1990, NBA Finals MVP, 1990. Named to NBA All-Rookie team 1982. Office: Toronto Raptors, 20 Bay St Ste 1702, Toronto, ON Canada M5J 2N8*

THOMAS, ISSAC DAVID ELLIS, clergy member; b. Llandovery, Wales, U.K., Apr. 30, 1921; came to U.S. 1972; s. David and Blodwen T.; m. Mildred Stevenson, Feb. 14, 1972. BA, U. Wales, 1943, BD, 1946; PhD, Calif. Grad. Sch. Theology, 1971, DLitt, 1989. Ordained to ministry Baptist Ch., 1946. Pastor Bapt. Ch., Glanaman, Wales, 1946-52, Caernarvon, Wales, 1952-58; pastor Zion Ch., Llanelli, Wales, 1958-62; free-lance evangelist, 1962-72; pastor First Bapt. Ch., Maywood, Calif., 1973—; commentator B.B.C., 1973—; prof. Calif. Grad. Sch. Theology, 1972-89, internat. pres., 1989-90, pres., 1991-92; provost St. Charles U., La., 1993—. Author: Golden Treasury of Puritan Quotations, 1975, A Word from the Wise, 1978, The Omega Conspiracy, 1984, Puritan Power, 1990. Named Citizen of the Yr. City of Maywood, 1981; recipient Cert. Freedom Found. of Valley Forge, 1973. Mem. Lions (pres. 1976). Avocations: reading, travel. Home: 2170 Century Park E Apt 1002 Century City CA 90067-2221

THOMAS, J. EARL, physicist; b. Seattle, Sept. 7, 1918; s. Jacob Earl and Ursula May (Johnson) T.; m. Margaret Louise Johnston, June 15, 1977; children—Richard Bruce, Jacob Earl, John Calvin, James Hayden, Denise May, Stillman Jefferson. A.B., Johns Hopkins U., 1939; Ph.D., Calif. Inst. Tech., 1943. Group leader rocket devel. Calif. Inst. Tech., Pasadena, 1942-45; group leader Manhattan Project, U. Calif., Los Alamos, 1945-46; asst. prof. elec. engring. M.I.T., Cambridge, 1946-51; mem. tech. staff Bell Telephone Labs., Murray Hill, N.J., 1951-52; group leader M.I.T. Lincoln Labs., Lexington, 1952-55; prof., chmn. dept. physics Wayne State U., Detroit, 1955-59; dir. research Sylvania Electric, Woburn, Mass., 1959-62; mgr. solid state devel. IBM, Poughkeepsie, N.Y., 1962-64; mgr. new product devel. Gen. Instrument Co., Newark, 1964-67; v.p. Carman Sapphire Co., Reseda, Calif., 1967-70; cons. Warnecke Electron Tubes, Des Plaines, Ill., 1970-71; dir. components research Victor Comptometer Co., Des Plaines, 1971-75; mgr. advanced devel. NCR Corp., Ithaca, N.Y., 1975-84; cons. pvt. cos. and govt. agys. Contbr. articles to sci. jours. Active S.E. Asian refugee resettlement program. Recipient Service award U.S. Office Sci. Research and Devel., 1946. Fellow IEEE, Am. Phys. Soc.; mem. Sigma Xi, Phi Beta Kappa, Tau Beta Pi. Democrat. Presbyterian. Patentee in field. Home: 323 Savage Farm Dr Ithaca NY 14850

THOMAS, JACQUELINE MARIE, journalist, editor; b. Nashville, Aug. 31, 1952; d. John James and Dorothy Jacqueline (Phillips) T. B.A., Briarcliff Coll., 1972; M.Internat. Affairs, Columbia U., 1974. Reporter Chgo Sun-Times, 1974-85; assoc. editor Courier-Jour. and Louisville Times, 1985-86, Detroit Free Press, 1986-93; deputy bureau chief, news editor Detroit News, Washington Bureau, 1993-94, bur. chief, 1994-97; editl. page editor The Balt. Sun, 1997—; instr. Roosevelt U., Chgo., 1983. Nieman fellow Harvard U., 1983. Mem. Chgo. Assn. Black Journalists (Print Journalist of Yr. 1982), Nat. Assn. Black Journalists, Nat. Press Found. (bd. mem.), Am. Soc. Newspaper Editors. Office: Detroit News Washington Bur 1148 National Press Building Washington DC 20045-2101

THOMAS, JACQUELYN MAY, librarian; b. Mechanicsburg, Pa., Jan. 26, 1932; d. William John and Gladys Elizabeth (Warren) Harvey; m. David Edward Thomas, Aug. 28, 1954; children: Lesley J., Courtenay J., Hilary A. BA summa cum laude, Gettysburg Coll., 1954; student U. N.C., 1969; MEd, U. N.H., 1971. Libr. Phillips Exeter Acad., Exeter, N.H., 1971-77, acad. libr., 1977—, chair governing bd. Child Care Ctr., 1987-91; chair Com. to Enhance Status of Women, Exeter, 1981-84; chair Loewenstein Com., Exeter, 1982—; pres. Cum Laude Soc., Exeter, 1984-86; James H. Ottaway Jr. prof., 1990—. Editor: The Design of the Libr.: A Guide to Sources of Information, 1981, Rarities of Our Time: The Special Collections of the Phillips Exeter Academy Libr. Trustee, treas. Exeter Day Sch., 1965-69; mem. bd. Exeter Hosp. Vols., 1954-59; mem. Exeter Hosp. Corp., 1978—; mem. bldg. com. Exeter Pub. Libr., 1986-88; chair No. New Eng., Coun. for Women in Ind. Schs., 1985-87; chmn. Lamont Poetry Program, Exeter, 1984-86; dir. Greater Portsmouth Community Found, 1990—; active AAC&U, On Campus with Women, Wellesley Coll. Ctr. for Rsch. on Women. N.H. Coun. for Humanities grantee, 1981-82; NEH grantee, 1982; recipient Lillian Radford Trust award, 1989. Mem. ALA, Internat. Assn. Sch. Librs., New Eng. Libr. Assn., N.H. Ednl. Media Assn., New Eng. Assn. Ind. Sch. Librs., Am. Assn. Sch. Librs. (chmn. non-pub. sch. sect.), Phi Beta Kappa. Home: 16 Elm St Exeter NH 03833-2704 Office: Acad Libr Phillips Exeter Acad 20 Main St Exeter NH 03833-2438

THOMAS, JAMES BERT, JR., government official; b. Tallahassee, Mar. 16, 1935; s. James Bert and Stella E. (Lewis) T.; m. Sharon Mae Kelly, June 16, 1962; children: James Bert III, Mary Elizabeth, John Christopher. B.S., Fla. State U., 1957. C.P.A., Fla. Spl. auditor Office State Comptroller, Jacksonville, Fla., 1958; jr. auditor J.D.A. Holley & Co., C.P.A.'s, Tallahassee, 1959; sr. auditor Office of the State Auditor, Tallahassee, 1959-60; trainee, audit dir. HUD audit div., Washington, 1960-71; asst. dir. Bur. Accounts ICC, Washington, 1972-75, dir. Bur. Accounts, 1977-80; inspector gen. U.S. Dept. HUD, Washington, 1975-77, U.S. Dept. Edn., Washington, 1980-95; dir. auditing Office of the Gov., State of Fla., Tallahassee, 1995—; mem. Pres.'s Coun. Integrity and Efficiency, chmn. audit stds. subcom., 1984-95, chmn. audit com., 1989-90. Mem. AICPA (strategic planning com. 1987-90, chmn. govt. auditing standards adv. coun. 1991—), Inst. Internal Auditors (trustee Rsch. Found. 1991-92), Assn. Govt. Accts. (chmn. fin. mgmt. standards bd. 1985-86), Accts. Roundtable. Roman Catholic. Home: Unit 601 4737 Tory Sound Ln Tallahassee FL 32308 Office: Exec Office of Governor Rm 2107 The Capitol Tallahassee FL 32399-0001

THOMAS, JAMES EDWARD, JR., brokerage house executive; b. Atlanta, Apr. 23, 1950; s. James Edward and Dortha Jean (White) E.; m. Leslie Ann Stagmaier, Sept. 6, 1975; children: Steele Stagmaier, Katherine Mills. BA magna cum laude, U. Ga., 1972, JD cum laude, 1975. Mgr. Genuine Parts Co., Atlanta, 1975-77; v.p. Robinson Humphrey Co., Atlanta, 1977-94; ptnr. J.C. Bradford and Co., Atlanta, 1994—; bd. dirs. Enstar Comm. Corp., The Kinston Group, Inc., Atlanta, Tophat Soccer Club, Atlanta, Hall's Boathouse, Inc., Lakemont, Ga., Vista Environ. Info., Inc., San Diego. Pres. Castlewood Civic Orgn., Inc., Atlanta; mem. Lake Rabun Homeowners Assn., Lakemont, Ga. Mem. Internat. Platform Assn., Ga. Bar Assn., La Societe des Tetes Grandes, Capital City Club. Republican. Episcopalian. Avocations: boating, tennis. Office: JC Bradford 3060 Peachtree Rd NW 1 Buckhead Loop NE Ste 1200 Atlanta GA 30326-1500

THOMAS, JAMES LEWIS, biomedical research scientist; b. Atlanta, May 18, 1949; s. Ruble Anderson and Mary Jo (Bass) T.; m. Kathleen Lee Hunter, Aug. 18, 1979; children: Jack, Mary Kate. BA, Emory U., 1971; PhD, U. Ala., Birmingham, 1981. Rsch. assoc. Washington U. Med. Sch., St. Louis, 1981-85, rsch. instr., 1985-91, rsch. asst. prof., 1991—. Contbr. articles to profl. jours. Mem. AAAS, Endocrine Soc., Soc. for Study of Reprodn., Pi Alpha, Delta Tau Delta. Achievements include research on structure/function relationships of enzyme catalytic amino acids; how changes in enzyme conformation participate in reaction mechanisms. Home: 7210 Stanford Ave Saint Louis MO 63130-3029 Office: Washington U Sch Medicine Dept Ob-Gyn 4911 Barnes Plz Saint Louis MO 63110

THOMAS, JAMES PATRICK, special education educator; b. Chgo., Sept. 24, 1946; s. Jacque Anthony and Dorothy Lucille (Brown) T.; m. Cathy E. Hanks, Sept. 29, 1979 (div. Aug. 1990); 1 child, Nicholas Jacque. BA in History and Polit. Sci., Drake U., 1973; MS in Pub. Adminstrn., Troy State U., 1983; MS in Spl. Edn., Johns Hopkins U., 1994, Cert. advanced grad. studies, 1994. cert. spl. educator. Commd. 2nd lt. USAF, 1973, advanced through grades to maj., 1985; missile launch officer, instr., crew comdr., contr. 91st Strategic Missile Wing, Minot, N.D., 1974-78; exec. officer, asst. ops. officer, resource advisor 6916th Electronic Security Squadron, Hellenikon Air Base, Greece, 1978-81; chief programs br. 6940th Electronic Security Wing, Ft. Meade, Md., 1981-82; program mgr. USAF Ops. Security Hq USAF/XOEO Directorate of Electronic Combat, Washington, 1982-85; intelligence collection activities mgr./chief Hdqrs. U.S. European Command, Stuttgart, Germany, 1986-88; signals intelligence planning staff officer Nat. Security Agy., Ft. Meade, 1988-90; cons. spl. edn. Balt., 1991—; adj. faculty mem. Catonsville (Md.) C.C., 1991—; spl. educator Howard County Sch. System, Columbia, 1992-94, Boonsboro (Md.) Middle Sch., 1994-96, Huatt Mid. Sch., Des Moines. Author: (pamphlet) Your Rights to Legal Advice, 1994. Pres. Cath. Men Parish Athens, Greece, 1979-81, Minot AFB, N.D., 1975-78; asst. den leader, vice den leader Cub Scouts, Boy Scouts Am., Ellicott City, Md., 1987-90. With USN, 1964-73. Decorated Purple Heart, 2 Def. Meritorious Svc. medals, Meritorious Svc. medals, Air Force Commendation medal. Mem. Phoenix Soc., Mil. Order Purple Heart (life), Am.

Legion China Post 1, Ret. Officers Assn. (life), Vets. Vietnam War, Soaring Assn. Am., Swiftboat Sailors Assn. Inc. (pres. 1995—), Phi Delta Gamma (v.p. Gamma chpt.). Roman Catholic. Avocations: pilot of sailplanes, sailing, snorkeling, golf, running, photography. Home: 1110 N Farnsworth Ave Apt 213 Aurora IL 60505-2043

THOMAS, JAMES WILLIAM, lawyer; b. N.Y.C., May 12, 1949; s. Howard and Alice (Brennan) T.; m. Cecilia Coleman Goad, July 7, 1973; children: James William Jr., Brennan McKinney. BS, U. Dayton, 1971; JD, Ohio No. U., 1974. Bar: Ohio 1974, U.S. Dist. Ct. Ohio 1976. Ptnr., Earley & Thomas, Eaton, Ohio, 1974-89; pvt. practice, Eaton, 1989—; village solicitor Village of Lewisburg (Ohio), 1977-81, Village of Verona (Ohio), 1979-81; asst. pros. atty. Preble County (Ohio), 1980-81. Mem. Preble County Cmty. Corrections Planning Bd. Fellow Ohio State Bar Found.; mem. ABA, Ohio State Bar Assn., Ohio Acad. Trial Lawyers, Ohio Assn. Criminal Def. lawyers, Preble County Bar Assn. (pres. 1982-84), Community Improvement Corp. Republican. Roman Catholic. Club: Eaton Country. Lodge: Rotary (dir. 1980-87, pres. 1987-88). Avocations: boating, tennis. Home: 761 Vinland Cv Eaton OH 45320-2536 Office: 112 N Barron St Eaton OH 45320-1702

THOMAS, JANEY SUE, elementary school principal; b. Clarksville, Tenn., Feb. 10, 1949; d. James Ernest and Ethel Mae (Evans) Kirkland; m. Tony Lee Thomas, Oct. 9, 1965; children: Jeff, Kelli. BS in Elem. Edn., Austin Peay State U., 1979, MA in Elem. Edn. Adminstrn., 1982, postgrad., 1987-89. Tchr. Charlotte (Tenn.) Jr. High Sch., 1979-86; prin. Vanleer (Tenn.) Elem. Sch., 1986-91, Oakmont Elem. Sch., Dickson, Tenn., 1991—. Ednl. rep. Concerned Citizens for Edn., Dickson County, 1988; mem. com. United Way Med. Tenn., Dickson County, 1990-91, bd. dirs., 1992-93. Recipient Nat. Sch. of Recognition award U.S. Dept. Edn., 1990. Mem. NAESP (Excellence in Edn. award 1989-90), Tenn. Assn. Elem. Sch. Prins. (Nat. Exemplary Sch. award 1989-90), Dickson County Edn. Assn. (pres. 1989-90). Baptist. Avocations: reading, traveling, shopping. Home: 226 Druid Hills Dr Dickson TN 37055-3331 Office: Oakmont Elem Sch 630 Highway 46 S Dickson TN 37055-2552*

THOMAS, JERRY, pharmacist; b. Milan, Ga., Oct. 2, 1942; s. Robert Guy and Myrtice (Hinson) T.; m. Marianne Norris, Nov. 14, 1964; children: Angela, Tammy, Melanie, Jamey, Jason. BS in Pharmacy, Auburn (Ala.) U., 1966. Lic. pharmacist, Ala. Pharmacist Harco Drug Inc., Tuscaloosa, 1966-75, v.p., 1975-79, exec. v.p., 1979-93, pres., 1993—. Bd. dirs. West Ala. Easter Seal Rehab., 1994-95, Salvation Army, 1993-95, fin. chmn. Mem. Am. Pharm. Assn. (legis. affairs com.), Ala. Pharm. Assn. (A.A. Ribbon Bowl of Hygiene 1989), Lions (pres. 1987). Baptist. Avocations: jogging, reading. Home: 4929 Emerald Bay Dr Northport AL 35476-5315 Office: Harco Drug Inc 3925 Rice Mine Rd NE Tuscaloosa AL 35406-1523

THOMAS, JIM, professional basketball team executive. Mng. gen. ptnr. Sacramento Kings. Office: Sacramento Kings 1 Sports Pky Sacramento CA 95834-2300*

THOMAS, JIMMY LYNN, financial executive; b. Mayfield, Ky., Aug. 3, 1941; s. Alben Stanley and Emma Laura (Alexander) T.; m. Kristin H. Kent, Oct. 1986; children: James Nelson, Carter Danforth. BS, U. Ky., 1963; MBA, Columbia U., 1964. Fin. analyst Ford Motor Co., Detroit, 1964-66; asst. treas. Joel Dean Assocs., N.Y.C., 1966-67; asst. contr. Trans World Airlines, N.Y.C., 1967-73; sr. v.p. fin. svcs., treas. Gannett Co., Inc., Arlington, Va., 1973—; bd. dirs. Marine Midland Bank, Rochester, Arkwright Boston Mut. Ins. Co-Atlantic Region, Tremont Ptnrs., Brown Devel. Co., Newspaper Printing Corp., Pacific Media, Inc., Guam Publs., Gannett Supply Corp., Gannett Fla. Corp., Gannett Pacific Corp. With U.S. Army, 1966-72. Ashland Oil Co. scholar, 1959-63, McKinsey scholar 1964; Samuel Bronfman fellow, 1963-64. Mem. Nat. Assn. Corp. Treas., U. Ky. Alumni Assn., Columbia U. Alumni Assn., Fin. Execs. Inst., Inst. Newspaper Contrs. and Fin. Officers, Country Club of Rochester, Genessee Valley Club, Georgetown Club, Washington Golf and Country Club, Beta Gamma Sigma, Omicron Delta Kappa, Sigma Alpha Epsilon. Democrat. Mem. Christian Ch. (Disciples of Christ). Home: 100 Gibbon St Alexandria VA 22314-3836 Office: Gannett Co Inc 1100 Wilson Blvd Arlington VA 22209-2297

THOMAS, JOAB LANGSTON, academic administrator, biology educator; b. Holt, Ala., Feb. 14, 1933; s. Ralph Cage and Chamintney Elizabeth (Stovall) T.; m. Marly A. Dukes, Dec. 22, 1954; children: Catherine, David, Jennifer, Frances. AB, Harvard U., 1955, MA, 1957, PhD, 1959; DSc (hon.), U. Ala., 1981; LLD (hon.), Stillman Coll., 1987; LHD (hon.), Tri-State U., 1994. Cytotaxonomist Arnold Aboretum, Harvard, 1959-61; faculty U. Ala., University, 1961-76, prof. biology, 1966-76, 88-91, asst. dean Coll. Arts and Scis., 1964-65, 69, dean for student devel. Coll., 1969-74, v.p., 1974-76, dir. Herbarium, 1961-76, dir. Arboretum, 1964-65, 66-69; pres. U. Ala., Tuscaloosa, 1981-88; chancellor N.C. State U., Raleigh, 1976-81; pres. Pa. State U., University Park, 1990-95, pres. emeritus, 1995—; bd. dirs. Blount, Inc., Lukens, Inc., Mellon Corp.; intern acad. adminstrn. Am. Coun. on Edn., 1971. Author: A Monographic Study of the Cyrillaceae, 1960, Wildflowers of Alabama and Adjoining States, 1973, The Rising South, 1976, Poisonous Plants and Venomous Animals of Alabama and Adjoining States, 1990. Bd. dirs. Internat. Potato Ctr., 1977-83, chmn. 1982-83; bd. dirs. Internat. Svc. for Nat. Agrl. Rsch., 1985-91. Named Ala. Acad. Honor, 1983, Citizen of Yr., Tuscaloosa, 1987; recipient Palmer Mus. Art medal. Mem. Golden Key, Phi Beta Kappa, Sigma Xi, Omicron Delta Kappa, Phi Kappa Phi. Office: Univ Ala 424 Biology Bldg Tuscaloosa AL 35487

THOMAS, JOE CARROLL, human resources director; b. Belmont, N.C., Nov. 2, 1931; m. Ruth Stone, June 17, 1951; children: Joe, Jerry, Angela. BA, Belmont Abbey Coll., 1954; MS, Cornell U., 1961. Mgr. terr. sales Gen. Foods Corp., San Antonio, 1954-62; asst. dir. personnel textiles divsn. Kendall Co., Charlotte, N.C., 1962-64; dir. personnel S.E. region Gifford Hill & Co., Charlotte, 1964-71; dir. mgmt. svcs. Ervin Industries, Charlotte, 1971-75; v.p. indsl. rels. Crompton & Knowles, Charlotte, 1975-76; exec. v.p., dir. human resources Barclays Group Inc. (USA), Charlotte, 1976-97; mem. adv. coun. Sch. Bus., Western Carolina U., Cullowhee, N.C., 1980-84. Vice chmn. bd. trustees Belmont Abbey Coll., 1982-88; chmn. fundraising campaign Charlotte chpt. Am. Heart Assn., 1984; mem. bd. visitors Mercy Hosp., Charlotte, 1984-87; bd. dirs. Mercy Health Svcs., Charlotte, 1988-96; bd. dirs. Jr. Achievement Charlotte, 1985-88; chmn. bd. dirs. INROADS div. Charlotte, Inc., 1987-88; bd. visitors Johnson C. Smith Univ., 1989-92. Mem. Soc. for Human Resource Mgmt., The Employers Assn. (bd. dirs. 1993—, exec. com. 1995), Charlotte Athletic Club (pres. 1982-83), Charlotte Rotary, Charlotte C. of C. (bd. advisors 1992—). Democrat. Methodist.

THOMAS, JOHN CHARLES, lawyer, former state supreme court justice; b. Norfolk, Va., Sept. 18, 1950; s. John and Floretta V. (Sears) T.; m. Pearl Walden, Oct. 9, 1982; children: John Charles Jr., Ruby Virginia, Lewis LeGrant. B.A. in Am. Govt. with distinction, U. Va., 1972, J.D., 1975. Bar: Va. 1975, U.S. Dist. Ct. (ea. and we. dists.) 1976, U.S. Ct. Appeals (4th cir.) 1976, U.S. Supreme Ct. 1979, U.S. Ct. Appeals (D.C. cir.) 1980, U.S. Ct. Appeals (10th cir.) 1991, U.S. Ct. Appeals (11th cir.) 1992. Assoc. Hunton & Williams, Richmond, Va., 1975-82, ptnr., 1982-83, 89—; justice Supreme Ct. of Va., Richmond, 1983-89; mem. adv. con. on appellate rules U.S. Jud. Conf. Bd. dirs. U. Va. Law Sch. Found., Thomas Jefferson Meml. Foun. Master John Marshall Inn of Ct. (exec. com.); fellow Am. Bar Found., Va. Bar Found.; mem. Am. Arbitration Assn. (bd. dirs., exec. com.), Am. Acad. Appellate Lawyers, Va. State Bar, Va. Bar Assn., Bar Assn. City of Richmond, Old Dominion Bar Assn., Omega Psi Phi. Office: Hunton & Williams Riverfront Plz East Tower 951 E Byrd St Richmond VA 23219-4040

THOMAS, JOHN DAVID, musician, composer, arranger, photographer, recording engineer, producer; b. Muncie, Ind., Mar. 30, 1951; s. John Charles and Phyllis Lorraine (Wear) T.; m. Rosalie Faith Baldwin, July 27, 1974 (div. 1991); children: Bethany Carol, Mark David. Student, Purdue U., 1969-71, Jordan Coll. of Music, Indpls., 1961-65; BS in Music Theory and Composition, Ball State U., 1976. Musician, composer, 1955—; cellist The Howe String Quartet (with Ann Pinney, Mary Ann Tilford, Anne Wuster), Indpls., 1967-68; keyboardist, vocalist, cellist Fire and The Rebel Kind rock bands, Indpls., 1967-69, Good Conduct rock band, Muncie, Ind., 1972-73; pianist The Pavillion at Olde Towne, Los Gatos, Calif., 1969; radio announcer John David's Late Night Rock Show WCCR-AM, West Lafayette, Ind., 1969-70; photographer Indpls., 1964-84, 91—; budget analyst Office of Comptr. USAFAC, Indpls., 1976-84; co-leader, keyboardist, composer, arranger, vocalist, sound technician JETSTREAM Band, Carmel, Indpls., Kokomo, Columbus, Bloomington, Ind., 1979-83; co-leader, keyboardist, vocalist, sound technician The Thomas Bros., King's Crown Inn, Kokomo, 1979; sound/audio visual technician Valley Cathedral Ch., Phoenix, 1987; solo pianist Cascade Club, Everett, Wash., 1990; pianist, synthesist Paul Thomas and Night and Day, The Tim Barnett Band, Indpls. Mus. Art, 1992, Radisson Hotel and Broadmoor Country Club, Indpls., 1991, Highland Country Club, Indpls., The Ritz Charles Hotel and Summertrace, Carmel, Ind., Stonehenge Resort, Bedford, Ind., 1991; solo pianist Terranova Mansion, Paradise Valley, Ariz., 1987, Wrigley Mansion, Phoenix, 1988, Boulders Resort, Carefree, Ariz., 1987, Clarion Inn/McCormick's Ranch Resort, Scottsdale, Ariz., 1986, China Gate, Phoenix, 1988, Victor's, Phoenix, 1988; keyboardist, synthesist, key bassist, The Guich Gang, Pinnacle Peak Patio, Scottsdale, 1984, Dee Dee Ryan, The Longhorn Saloon, Apache Junction, Ariz., 1984-86, The Last Straw Band, Country City saloon, Mesa, Ariz., 1986; keyboardist, pianist, vocalist with Peter, Paul and John, Anderson Coll., Anderson, Ind., 1977; CEO, composer, arranger, prodr., musician, engr. John David Thomas Prodns., Indpls., 1993—. Composer, lyricist of over 200 classical, religious, comml., rock, jazz, popular and avante garde/futuristic compositions, including Infinity, 1970-71, Death of Rock and Roll, 1970, Night Visions, 1972, First Things First, 1972, Two Nudes and a Fire Hydrant, 1972-73, Zeitgeist: The Spirit of the Time, 1974, The Little Prince, 1973, When We Dead Awaken, 1973, Pray, 1972, Apogee, 1974, Chinese Baby, 1973, Alabama DA (Top Forty recording), 1973, Angel, 1974, Music for French Horn, Cello, and Piano, 1976, Cruising Beyond, 1979, Jetstream Theme, 1979, Chrissy, 1979, Night Visions, 1979, In Your Heart, 1983, Future Music, 1987, The Recurrent New Millenium Orchestral Olympic Disco Festival Dance, 1989, Jubilee in F, 1989, Praise Him, The King Liveth, 1989, Love Flowers: Reflections and Meditations on Beauty and Truth, 1990, Sheena's Theme, 1992, I Want You Forever You're My Miracle, 1992, My Pseudo-Erotic, Sensual, Exotic Musical Fantasy and Romance for Our Heavenly Nocturnal Starry-Skied Carpet Ride to Paradise in Istanbul and Constantinople, 1992, I'm in Love with Someone Beautiful, 1992, Improvisations for Sheena, 1992, Music for Baritone Vocal and String Orch., 1995, Meditaton for Pipe Organ, 1996, Trumpet Voluntary in F, 1996; (albums) The Journey of Life, Destiny's Calling: Improvisations, 1994, Musical Essences, 1995, Pathway to Love, 1996, (broadcast) Hometown Hour, Sta. WFBQ-FM, Indpls., 1979-80; performed orginal composition, Someday, WFBM-TV, Indpls., 1969; designer automotive concepts and popular fashions; recordings of over 45 original songs and compositions, Ind., Ariz., Wash., 1970—; author (poetry with others) Mind, 1993, 96. Musician, vocalist, composer Downey Ave. Christian Ch., Indpls., 1961-69, Univ. Presbyn. Ch., West Lafayette, Ind., 1969-71, Castleview Bapt. Ch., Indpls., 1974-84, Valley Cathedral Ch., Phoenix, 1986-87, Edmonds (Wash.) Christian Ch., 1988-90, Edmonds United Meth. Ch., 1989-90; page to speaker Ho. of Reps. Ind. State Legislature, 1963; active All Souls Unitarian Ch., Indpls., 1994-96. GM scholar Purdue U., 1969-70, Hoosier scholar, 1969, Palmer Meml. Music scholar Ball State U., 1971-74; named to Ind. All-State Orch. (cellist), 1968; recipient 1st place award (cellist) Ind. State Music Contest, 1968, God and Country award, 1965, Outstanding Musician award Irvington Music Club, Indpls., 1969, Purdue U. Symphonette, 1970, Hometown Hour award WFBQ-FM Radio Sta., Indpls., 1979. Mem. ASCAP, Audio Engring. Soc., Mensa, Amnesty Internat. Avocations: concerts, cd's, listening to music, travel, collectibles. Home and Office: 2704 Central Ct Indianapolis IN 46280-1930

THOMAS, JOHN EDWIN, retired academic administrator; b. Fort Worth, Tex., Apr. 23, 1931; s. John L. and Dorothy F. T.; m. Janice Paula Winzinek, Jan. 29, 1967; children—John L., Christa T., Scott A., Brandon F. BSEE, U. Kans., 1953; JD, U. Mo., Kansas City, 1961; MS, Fla. State U., 1965, DBA, 1970. With Wagner Electric Corp., St. Louis, 1955-63; mgr. elec. apparatus div. Wagner Electric Corp., Atlanta, 1961-63; with NASA, Cape Kennedy, Fla., 1963-70; chief requirements and resources office, dir. tech. support NASA, 1966-70; prof., head gen. bus. dept. East Tex. State U., 1970-72; dean (Coll. Scis. and Tech.), 1972-74; vice chancellor for acad. affairs Appalachian State U., Boone, N.C., 1974-79; chancellor Appalachian State U., 1979-93; ret. N.C. Utilities Commn., Raleigh, 1993; spl. advisor for sci., tech. & higher edn. Gov. State of N.C., Raleigh, 1994, ret., 1994; chair N.C. Utilities Commn., 1993-94; spl. advisor to Gov. of State of N.C. on sci./tech. and higher edn., 1994; edn./comm. cons. and chancellor emeritus, Appalachian State U., 1994—. Mem. N.C. Agy. for Pub. Telecommunications. Served with USN, 1949-50, USMC, 1953-55. NDEA fellow, 1968. Mem. Fed. Bar Assn., Soc. Advancement Mgmt., So. Mgmt. Assn., Phi Delta Kappa, Pi Sigma Epsilon, Delta Gamma Sigma., Phi Kappa Phi. Methodist. Club: Kiwanis. Home: 342 Wildwood Run Daisy Ridge Banner Elk NC 28604

THOMAS, JOHN HOWARD, astrophysicist, engineer, educator; b. Chgo., Apr. 9, 1941; s. William Whitney and Dorothy Loretta (Derris) T.; m. Lois Ruth Moffit, Aug. 11, 1962; children: Jeffrey, Laura. B.S. in Engring. Sci., Purdue U., 1962, M.S. in Engring. Sci., 1964, Ph.D. in Engring. Sci., 1966. Lic. profl. engr., N.Y. NATO postdoctoral fellow U. Cambridge, Eng., 1966-67; asst. prof. mech. and aerospace sci. U. Rochester, 1967-73, assoc. prof., 1973-81, prof., 1981—, prof. astronomy, 1986—, assoc. dean for grad. studies Coll. Engring. and Applied Sci., 1981-83, univ. dean grad. studies, 1983-91; vis. astronomer Nat. Solar Obs., Sunspot, N.Mex.; vis. scientist Max-Planck Inst. for Physics and Astrophysics, Munich, 1973-74, High Altitude Obs., Boulder, Colo., 1985; vis. fellow Worcester Coll, vis. prof. dept. theoretical physics Oxford (Eng.) U., 1987-88; affiliate scientist Nat. Ctr. for Atmospheric Rsch., Boulder, 1989—; vis. prof. Rsch. Ctr. for Theoretical Astrophysics, U. Sydney, Australia, 1991, Sch. Math. and Stats., 1993; prin. investigator NASA, NSF, USAF, Office Naval Rsch. Editor: Physics of Sunspots, 1981, Sunspots: Theory and Observations, 1992; assoc. editor Astrophys. Jour., 1993-96, sci. editor, 1996—; author articles on astrophysics, solar physics and fluid dynamics. NSF fellow, 1963-66; Guggenheim fellow, 1993-94. Mem. AAAS, Am. Astron. Soc. (chair solar physics divsn. 1995-97), Internat. Astron. Union, Am. Phys. Soc., Am. Geophys. Union, Sigma Xi, Tau Beta Pi, Sigma Delta Chi. Office: U Rochester 223 Hopeman Bldg Rochester NY 14627

THOMAS, JOHN KERRY, chemistry educator; b. Llanelli, Wales, May 16, 1934; came to U.S., 1960; s. Ronald W. and Rebecca (Johns) T.; m. June M. Critchley, Feb. 28, 1959; children: Delia, Roland, Roger. BS, U. Manchester, Eng., 1954, PhD, 1957, DSc, 1969. Rsch. assoc. Nat. Rsch. Coun. Can., Ottawa, 1957-58; sci. officer Atomic Energy. U.K., Harwell, Eng., 1958-60; rsch. assoc. Argonne (Ill.) Nat. Lab., 1960-70; prof. chemistry U. Notre Dame, Ind., 1970-82, Nieuwland prof. chemistry, 1982—. Author: Chemistry of Excitation at Interfaces, 1984; mem. editorial bd. Macromolecules Langmuir, Jour. of Colloid and Interface Soc. Recipient of Rsch. Awd., 1994, Radiation Rsch, Am. Chem. Soc. award in Colloid or Surface Chemistry, 1994. Fellow Royal Soc. Chemistry; mem. Am. Chem. Soc. (award in colloids and surface 1994), Radiation Rsch. Soc. (editorial bd. jours., rsch. award 1972, 1994), Photochem. Soc. Home: 17704 Waxwing Ln South Bend IN 46635-1327 Office: Univ Notre Dame Dept Chemistry Notre Dame IN 46556

THOMAS, JOHN MELVIN, retired surgeon; b. Carmarthen, U.K., Apr. 26, 1933; came to U.S., 1958; s. Morgan and Margaret (Morgan) T.; m. Betty Ann Mayo, Nov. 3, 1958; children: James, Hugh, Pamela. MB, BChir, U. Coll. Wales, U. Edinburgh, 1958. Intern Robert Packer Hosp., Sayre, Pa., 1958-59, chief surg. resident, 1963, pres. med. staff, 1968; assoc. surgeon Guthrie Clinic Ltd., Sayre, 1963-69, chmn. dept. surgery, 1969-91; vice chmn. Guthrie Healthcare System, 1995—; pres. bd. dirs. Guthrie Clinic Ltd., 1972-89; trustee Robert Packer Hosp.; chmn. exec. com. Guthrie Healthcare Sys., 1990-92, dir., 1994—; guest examiner Am. Bd. Surgery, 1979, 81, 85; bd. dirs. Measurement Innovations Corp., Citizen Fin. Bank, Mansfield, Pa., Trianalytics Corp.; cons. The Hunter Group, 1995—. Bd. dirs. Donald Guthrie Found. for Rsch., pres., 1983—; bd. dirs. Pa. Trauma Sys. Found., 1984-90, pres., 1988, 89; chmn. licensure and accountability Gov.'s Conf., 1974; bd. dirs. Vol. Hosps. Am., 1993-95; trustee Mansfield (Pa.) U. Found., 1991—; trustee Mansfield Univ. Found., 1991-95. Mem. ACS (gov. 1985-91), AMA, Am. Group Practice Assn., Soc. for Surgery Alimentary Tract, Pa. Med. Soc., Bradford County Med. Soc., Cen. N.Y. Surg. Soc., Internat. Soc. Surgery, Soc. Surgery Alimentary Tract, Ea. Vascular Soc., Ithaca Country Club, Moselem Springs Golf Club. Presbyterian. Home: 383 Lansing Station Rd Lansing NY 14882-8606

THOMAS, JOHN RICHARD, chemist; b. Anchorage, Ky., Aug. 26, 1921; s. John R. and Mildred (Woods) T.; m. Beatrice Ann Davidson, Dec. 7, 1944; children: Jonnie Sue Jacobs, Richard G. B.S., U. Calif., Berkeley, 1943, Ph.D., 1947. With U.S. AEC, 1949-51; rsch. chemist Chevron Rsch. Co., Richmond, Calif., 1948-49; sr. rsch. assoc. Chevron Rsch. Co., 1951-60, sr. rsch. scientist, 1961-67, pres., also bd. dirs., 1970-86; v.p. petroleum rsch. Chevron Corp., 1984-86, ret., 1986; mgr. R&D Ortho div. Chevron Chem. Co., Richmond, 1967-68; asst. sec. Standard Oil Co., Calif., 1968-70. Contbr. articles to profl. jours. Mem. Am. Chem. Soc. Republican. Patentee in field. Home: 847 McEllen Way Lafayette CA 94549-5134 Office: Chevron Research Co 576 Standard Ave Richmond CA 94801-2016

THOMAS, JOHN THIEME, management consultant; b. Detroit, Aug. 21, 1935; s. John Shepherd and Florence Leona (Thieme) T.; m. Ellen Linden Taylor, June 27, 1959; children: Johnson Taylor, Evan Thurston. BBA, U. Mich., 1957, MBA, 1958. Mfg. dept. mgr. Procter & Gamble Co., Cin., 1958-60, brand mgr., 1960-63; sr. cons. Glendinning Cos. Inc., Westport, Conn., 1964-66; v.p. Glendinning Cos. Inc., London, 1967-69; exec. v.p. Glendinning Cos. Inc., Westport, 1970-74; also bd. dirs.; exec. v.p., chief operating officer Ero Industries, Chgo., 1974-76; v.p. Lamalie Assocs. Inc., Chgo., 1977-81; pres. Wilkins & Thomas Inc., Chgo., 1981-87; ptnr. Ward Howell Internat., Chgo., 1987—, mng. dir., cons. practice, 1992—, chief of staff, 1995—; also bd. dirs.; exec. com. Procter & Gamble Alumni Assn., Chgo., 1981—. Pub. Proctor & Gamble Mfg. Alumni directory, 1981—; author articles in profl. jours. Chmn. bd. dirs. Winnetka (Ill.) Youth Orgn., 1986—; selector Winnetka Town Coun., 1978, 80, 84. Mem. Nat. Assn. Corp. & Profl. Recruiters, Assn. Exec. Search Cons., Am. Soc. Personnel Adminstrn. Club: Fairfield (Conn.) Hunt (treas. 1971-74). Avocations: gardening, music, playing tuba. Home: 525 Ash St Winnetka IL 60093-2601 Office: Ward Howell Internat 300 W Wacker Dr Chicago IL 60606

THOMAS, JOSEPH ERUMAPPETTICAL, psychologist; b. Piravom, Kerala, India, Feb. 11, 1937; came to U.S., 1971; s. Iype Erumappettiyil and Kunjamma M. (Padiyil) T.; m. Chinnamma Kavatt, Nov. 23, 1964; children: Joseph Jr., Kurian, Elizabeth. BA, Kerala U., India, 1957, MA, 1960, PhD, 1969. Diplomate Internat. Acad. Behavioral Medicine, Counseling, and Psychotherapy; lic. psychologist; cert. biofeedback therapist. Lectr. psychology U. Kerala, Trivandrum, India, 1967-70; postdoctoral fellow in psychology Northwestern U. Med. Sch., Chgo., 1971-72; psychologist U. Chgo., 1972-74; instr. psychiatry Northwestern U. Med. Sch., Chgo., 1972-76, asst. prof. dept. psychiatry, 1977—; psychologist Northwestern Meml. Hosp., Chgo., 1974-80; pvt. practice psychology Chgo., 1980—; cons. Michael Reese Hosp., Chgo., 1980-86; founding mem. Inst. Psychiatry, Northwestern U., Chgo.; cons. psychologist Block Med. Ctr., Evanston, 1995—. Contbr. articles to profl. jours. Mem. Dupage County Health Planning Com., Wheaton, Ill., 1984; founding mem., trustee St. Thomas Ch. Chgo., St. Gregorios Orthodox Ch., Oak Park, Ill. Commonwealth fellow Govt. U.K., U. Glasgow, 1970. Mem. Am. Psychological Assn., Mental Health Assn. DuPage County (bd. dirs. 1982-84), Biofeedback Soc. Ill. (pres. 1984-85). Home: 16 W 731 89th Pl Hinsdale IL 60521 Office: 1776 S Naperville Rd Ste B 103 Wheaton IL 60187-8133

THOMAS, JOSEPH FLESHMAN, architect; b. Oak Hill, W.Va., Mar. 23, 1915; s. Robert Russel and Effie (Fleshman) T.; m. Margaret Ruth Lively, Feb. 28, 1939 (dec.); children: Anita Carol, Joseph Stephen; m. Dorothy Francene Root, Apr. 29, 1967 (div.); m. Bonnie Abbott Buckley, June 15, 1991. Student, Duke, 1931-32; B.Arch., Carnegie-Mellon U., 1938. Practice architecture various firms W. Va., Va., Tenn., Calif., 1938-49; staff architect Calif. Div. Architecture, Los Angeles, 1949-52; prin. Joseph F. Thomas, architect, Pasadena, Calif., 1952-53; pres. Neptune & Thomas (architects-engrs.), Pasadena and San Diego, 1953-78; Mem. Pasadena Planning Commn., 1956-64, chmn., 1963-64; pres. Citizens Coun. for Planning, Pasadena, 1966-67; mem. steering com. Pasadena NOW, 1970-74; mem. Pasadena Design Com., 1979-86; mem. adv. bd. Calif. Office Architecture and Constrn., 1970-72; mem. archtl. adv. com. Calif. State U. System, 1981-84; mem. adv. coun. Sch. Environ. Design Calif. Poly. Inst., 1983—; mem. outreach for architecture com. Carnegie Mellon U., 1989—, pres.'s devel. com., 1991—. Prin. works include Meth. Hosp., Arcadia, Calif., Foothill Presbyn. Hosp., Glendora, Calif., master plans and bldgs., Citrus Coll., Azusa, Calif., Riverside (Calif.) Coll., Westmont Coll., Monticeto, Calif., Northrop Inst. Tech., Inglewood, Calif, Indian Valley Coll., Marin County, Calif., Pepperdine U., Malibu, Calif., UCLA, U. Calif., San Diego, Long Beach (Calif.) State U., Calif. Inst. Tech., Pasadena, Calif., other coll. bldgs. Pacific Telephone Co., Pasadena, L.A. County Superior Ct. Bldg., U.S. Naval Hosp., San Diego. Trustee Almansor Edn. Ctr., 1986-92; bd. dirs., co-founder Syncor Internat., 1973-83; founding dir. Bank of Pasadena, 1962-65. Lt. (j.g.) USNR, 1943-46. Recipient Service award City of Pasadena, 1964; Disting. Service award Calif. Dept. Gen. Services, 1972; Gold Crown award Pasadena Arts Council, 1981. Fellow AIA (4 awards honor, 13 awards merit 1957-78, dir. Calif. coun. 1966-68, exec. com. 1974-77, pres. Pasadena chpt. 1967, chmn. Calif. sch. facilities com. 1970-72, mem. nat. jud. bd. 1973-74, nat. dir. 1974-77, treas. 1977-79, exec. com., planning com., chmn. finance com.); mem. Breakfast Forum (chmn. 1983), Annandale Golf Club, Pi Kappa Alpha. Republican. Methodist. Home: 330 San Miguel Rd Pasadena CA 91105-1446

THOMAS, JOSEPH PAUL, psychiatrist; b. Bioloxi, Miss., Oct. 11, 1947; s. William Lloyd and Myrtis (Farmer) T.; m. Sandra Kay Elam, Dec. 20, 1973; children: Stephen Paul, Ashlie Lauren, Emily Grace. BA, U. Ala., Tuscaloosa, 1968; MA, U. Ala., 1971; MD, U. Ala., Birmingham, 1979. Diplomate Am. Bd. Psychiatry and Neurology with added qualification in geriat. psychiatry, addiction psychiatry, forensic psychiatry, Am. Bd. Adolescent Psychiatry; cert. Am. Soc. Addiction Medicine. Tchr. Gadsden (Ala.) Pub. Schs., 1968-69, Birmingham Bd. Edn., 1969-75, 80; resident Univ. Hosps., Birmingham, 1980; intern Mayo Grad. Sch. Medicine, Rochester, Minn., 1980-81; resident Johns Hopkins Hosp., Balt., 1981-84; psychiatrist The Thomas Clinic, P.C., Mobile, Ala., 1984, Neuropsychiatric Assocs. of South P.C., Mobile, 1984—. Fellow Am. Psychiat. Assn.; mem. Ala. Psychiat. Soc. (pres. 1993-94), Am. Acad. Psychaitry and Law, Med. Soc. Mobile County (bd. censors). Office: Neuropsychiat Assocs South PO Box 8309 Mobile AL 36689-0309

THOMAS, KAREN P., composer, conductor; b. Seattle, Sept. 17, 1957. BA in Composition, Cornish Inst., 1979; MusM in Composition, Conducting, U. Wash., 1985. Condr. The Contemporary Group, 1981-85; condr., music dir. Wash. Composers Forum, 1984-86; artistic dir., condr. Seattle Pro Musica, 1987—. Conducting debut Seattle, 1987; composer: Four Delineations of Curtmantle for Trombone or Cello, 1982, Metamorphoses on a Machaut Kyrie for Strong Orch. or Quartet, 1983, Cowboy Songs for Voice and Piano, 1985, There Must Be a Lone Range for Soprano and Chamber Ensemble, 1987, Brass Quintet, 1987, Four Lewis Carroll Songs for Choir, 1989, (music/dance/theater) Boxiana, 1990, Elementi for Clarinet and Percussion, 1991, (one-act children's opera) Coyote's Tail, 1991, Clarion Dances for Brass Ensemble, 1993, Roundup for Sax Quartet, 1993, Three Medieval Lyrics for Choir, 1992, Sopravvento for Wind Quartet and Percussion, 1994, When Night Came for Clarinet and Chamber Orch. or Clarinet and Piano, 1994, also numerous others. Recipient Composers Forum award N.W. Chamber Orch., 1984, King County Arts Commn., 1987, 90, Artist Trust, 1988, 93, 96, Seattle Arts Commn., 1988, 91, 93, New Langton Arts, 1988, Delius Festival, 1993, Melodious Accord award 1993; fellow Wash. State Arts Commn., 1991; Charles E. Ives scholar AAAl. Mem. Broadcast Music, Am. Music Ctr., Internat. Alliance for Women in Music, Soc. Composers, Chorus Am., Conductors Guild. Office: 4426 1st Ave NW Seattle WA 98107-4306

THOMAS, KATHERINE JANE, newspaper business columnist; b. Bryan, Tex., Mar. 22, 1942; d. William Holt Jr. and Mary Anne (McCasland) Oliver; m. Robert Wayne Thomas, June 1, 1968; children: Jennifer Ann, Michael Frederick. BA, U. Tex., 1964. News reporter Abilene Reporter, Tex., 1964-67; with Ralston Purina Co., 1967-68; journalist The Eagle, Bryan, Tex., 1969-72, Wall St. Jour., Houston Bus. Jour., 1976-80; bus. columnist Houston Post, 1980-95; freelance bus. columnist Daily Ct. Rev.,

West U. Jour. Judge Houston Women on the Move Sect. Com., 1989-90, 91; judge Houston Area Inc. Mag. Entrepreneur of Yr., 1995; vol. judge out-of-state journalism competitions. Recipient Writing awards Tex. Press Assn., 1978-79, AP, 1966, 88, 91, Dallas Press Club Katie Finalist, 1990, 94, Matrix, 1989-90, Press Club of Houston, 1987, 89, 90, 91, 95, 96, Sierra Club of Houston, 1989, St. Louis United Fund, 1968, Abilene C. of C., 1965. Mem. Press Club of Houston (bd. dirs., sec. 1991), Press Club of Houston Ednl. Found. (treas. 1991, bd. dirs.). Episcopalian. Avocations: sailing, entertaining, walking, reading.

THOMAS, KENNETH EASTMAN, cardiothoracic surgeon; b. Evanston, Ill., Mar. 3, 1934; s. Kenneth Henry and Eloise (Eastman) T.; m. Sara Anne Stephens, Aug. 14, 1971; children: Diana, Allison, Michael. BA, Dartmouth Coll., 1956; MD, Stanford U., 1959. Med. diplomate, Ga. Med. intern dept. medicine U. Minn. Hosp., Mlps., 1959-60; med. resident dept. medicine U. Minn. Med. Sch., Mlps., 1960-61; surg. resident dept. surgery W.Va. U. Sch. Medicine, Morgantown, 1961-66, cancer rsch. fellow dept. surgery, 1966; clin. instr. thoracic surgery Med. Coll. Va., Richmond, 1969-71, fellow thoracic and cardiovascular surgery, 1969-71; ptnr., officer Peachtree Cardiovascular and Thoracic Surgeons, Atlanta, 1972—; bd. trustees St. Joseph's Hosp., Atlanta, 1990—, chmn. and dir. cardiothoracic surgery, 1992-94; active staff St. Joseph's Hosp., Piedmont Hosp., Ga. Bapt. Hosp; courtesy hosp. staff Northside Hosp., Dunwoody Med. Ctr. Contbr. articles to profl. jours. Participant Talented and Gifted Program of Fulton County Schs., Atlanta, 1985—, Cross Connection Mission Heart Surgery, El Salvador, 1995—; mem. adv. bd. Atlanta (Ga.) Heart Ball, 1993—. Capt. USAF-Med. Corp., 1966-69, Vietnam. Decorated Bronze star USAF, Vietnam, 1969. Mem. ACS, AMA, Med. Assn. Ga., Med. Assn. Atlanta, Am. Heart Assn., Ga. Heart Assn., Soc. Thoracic Surgeons, Ga. Thoracic Soc., Am. Coll. Cardiology, So. Thoracic Surg. Assn., Am. Coll. Chest Physicians, N.Am. Soc. of Pacing and Electrophysiology, Rotary. Republican. Episcopalian. Avocations: golf, travel, investments. Office: Peachtree Cardiovascular 5669 Peachtree Dunwoody Rd NE Atlanta GA 30342-1786

THOMAS, KENNETH GLYNDWR, mining executive; b. Llanelli, Wales, June 25, 1944; arrived in Can., 1980; m. Elizabeth June Hickman, Sept. 25, 1976; children: Louise June, Kelly Jane. BSc in Metallurgy, U. Wales, Cardiff, 1970; MSc in Mgmt. Sci., U. London, 1971; PhD in Tech. Sci., U. of Delft, The Netherlands, 1994. Chartered engr., U.K.; registered profl. engr., Ont., Can. Metallurgist Brit. Steel Corp., Wales, 1959-67, Anglo Am. Corp., Kitwe, Zambia, 1971-75; plant supt. Anglo Am. Corp., Klerksdorp, South Africa, 1975-80; design metallurgist Kilborn Engring., Toronto, Ont., 1980-85; mill supt. Giant Yellowknife (Can.) Mines Ltd., N.W.T., 1985-87; sr. v.p. metallurgy and constrn. Barrick Gold Corp., Toronto, 1987-95, sr. v.p. tech. svcs., 1995—. Contbr. articles to tech. jours.; co-patentee in field. Mem. Inst. Materials (U.K.), Can. Inst. Mining, Metallurgy and Petroleum (Mill Man of Yr. award 1990). Office: Barrick Gold Corp, Royal Bank Pla S Twr 200 Bay St, Toronto, ON Canada M5J 2J3

THOMAS, LAWRENCE ELDON, mathematics educator; b. Columbus, Ohio, Mar. 15, 1942; s. Bertram D. and Glorian (Butler) T.; m. Rebecca Nolan, June 13, 1970; children: David Nolan, Kathleen Rebecca. BS, U. Mich., 1964; PhD, Yale U., 1970. Rsch. asst. math. dept. Swiss Fed. Inst. Tech., Zurich, 1970-72; rsch. asst. physics dept. U. Geneva, 1972-74; asst. prof. math. U. Va., Charlottesville, 1974-76, assoc. prof., 1976-82, prof., 1982—, chmn. dept., 1989-93. Contbr. articles on theory of Schrodinger operators, statis. mechanics and stochastic processes to profl. jours. Mem. Am. Math. Soc., Am. Physics Soc., Internat. Nat. Math. Physics, Phi Beta Kappa. Avocations: sailing, tennis. Home: 2308 Glenn Ct Charlottesville VA 22901-2913 Office: U Va Dept Math Cabell Dr Charlottesville VA 22903

THOMAS, LEE, professional sports team executive. Sr. v.p., gen. mgr. Phila. Phillies. Office: Phila Phillies PO Box 7575 Philadelphia PA 19101-7575*

THOMAS, LEELAMMA KOSHY, women's health care nurse; b. Kerala, Kozhencherry, India, Feb. 10, 1936; naturalized Am. citizen, 1977; d. V.T. and Kunjamma (Koruth) Koshy; m. C.A. Thomas, Oct. 26, 1967; children: Linda Thomas Mathew, Lucie Thomas, John Thomas. BS in Nursing with honors, Coll. Nursing, Delhi, 1960; MA, Karnatak U., Dharwar Karnataka, Mysore, 1968. RN, Punjab, India, Tex.; RNC. PHN operational rsch. Nat. Tuberculosis Inst., Banglore, Mysore State, India, 1960-67; lectr. nursing Armed Forces Med. Coll., Maharstra State, India, 1971—; nurse labor and delivery U. Tex. Med. Br., nurse infant spl. care unit, nursing care coord. ob-gyn; head nurse U. Tex. Med. Br., Galveston, 1980-92, nurse clinician IV women and infants, 1993—; clin. instr. U. Tex. Sch. Nursing, Galveston, 1982—; presenter in field. Contbr. articles to profl. jours. Sunday sch. tchr. First Bapt. Ch., Galveston, Tex., 1982—. Recipient U. Tex. Med. Br. Maternal Health Coun. award, 1984; Am. Women's scholar. Mem. Sigma Theta Tau. Avocation: born-again Christian/ch. activities. Office: U Tex Med Br Ob-Gyn Nursing Svc Galveston TX 77550 also: U Tex Sch Nursing Galveston TX 77550

THOMAS, LEO J., retired imaging company executive; b. St. Paul, Oct. 30, 1936; s. Leo John and Christal (Dietrich) T.; m. Joanne Juliani, Dec. 27, 1958; children: Christopher, Gregory, Cynthia, Jeffrey. Student, Coll. St. Thomas, 1954-56; BS, U. Minn., 1958; MS, U. Ill., 1960, PhD, 1961. Rsch. chemist Eastman Kodak Co., Rochester, N.Y., 1961-67, lab. head, 1967-70, asst. div. head color photography div., 1970-72, tech. asst. to dir., 1972-75, asst. dir., 1975-77, v.p., dir., 1977-78, sr. v.p., dir., 1978-84; sr. v.p., gen. mgr. Life Scis., Rochester, N.Y., 1985-88; vice-chmn., chmn. Sterling Drug Inc., N.Y.C., 1988-89; group v.p., gen. mgr. Health Eastman Kodak Co., Rochester, 1989-91, group v.p., pres. imaging, 1991-94; exec. v.p. Eastman Kodak Co., Rochester, N.Y., 1994-96, ret., 1996; bd. dirs. Frontier Corp., John Wiley and Sons, Inc., N.Y.C. Mem. AIChE, Am. Acad. Arts and Scis., Am. Inst. for Med. and Bioengring, Nat. Acad. Engring.

THOMAS, LEONA MARLENE, health information educator; b. Rock Springs, Wyo., Jan. 15, 1933; d. Leonard H. and Opal (Wright) Francis; children: Peter, Paul, Patrick, Alexis. BA, Govs. State U., 1982, MHS, 1986; cert. med. records adminstrn., U. Colo., 1954. Dir. med. records dept. Meml. Hosp. Sweetwater County, Rock Springs, Wyo., 1954-57; staff assoc. Am. Med. Records Assn., Chgo., 1972-77, asst. editor, 1979-81; statistician Westlake Hosp., Melrose Park, Ill., 1982-84; asst. prof. Chgo. State U., 1984—, acting dir. health info. adminstrn. program, 1991-92; acting dir. health info. Internat. Coll., Naples, Fla., 1994; dir. health info. adminstrn. program Chgo. State U., 1994—; chairperson Coll. Allied Health Pers., 1986-88; mem. rev. bd. network Newsletter of Assembly on Edn. Co-pres. Ill. Dist. 60 PTA, Westmont; liaison Ill. Trauma Registry, 1991; mem. adv. com. Health Info. Tech. Program Morraine Valley Cmty. Coll., Palos Hills, Ill., 1995—, Health Info. Tech. Program Robert Morris Coll., Orland Pk., Ill., 1995—, Wellness Ctr., Chgo. State U. Mem. Assembly on Edn., Am. Health Info. Mgmt. Assn., Am. Pub. Health Assn., Ill. Pub. Health Assn., Chgo. and Vicinity Med. Records Assn. (publicity com. 1989-90), Ill. Assn. Allied Health Profls., Gov.'s State Alumni Assn. Democrat. Methodist. Home: 6340 Americana Dr Apt 1101 Clarendon Hills IL 60514-2249 Office: Chgo State U Coll Nursin & Allied Health 95th at King Dr Chicago IL 60628

THOMAS, LINDSEY KAY, JR., research biologist, educator, consultant; b. Salt Lake City, Apr. 16, 1931; s. Lindsey Kay and Naomi Lurie (Biesinger) T.; m. Nancy Ruth Van Dyke, Aug. 24, 1956; children: Elizabeth Nan Thomas Cardinale, David Lindsey, Wayne Hal, Dorothy Ann Thomas Brown. BS, Utah State Agrl. Coll., 1953; MS, Brigham Young U., 1958; PhD, Duke U., 1974; Habilitate D, Warsaw (Poland) U. Tech., 1996. Park naturalist Nat. Capital Parks, Nat. Park Svc., Washington, 1957-62, rsch. park naturalist Region 6, Washington, 1962-63, rsch. park naturalist Nat. Capital Region, Washington, 1963-66, rsch. biologist S.E. Temperate Forest Park Areas, Washington, 1966, Durham, N.C., 1966-67, Great Falls, Md., 1967-71, rsch. biologist Nat. Capital Parks, Great Falls, 1971-74, rsch. biologist Nat. Capital Region, Triangle, Va., 1974-93, Washington, 1985-93, Nat. Biol. Svc., Washington and Triangle, 1993-96; resource mgmt. specialist Balt.-Washington Pky., Greenbelt, Md., 1996, Nat. Capital Parks-East, 1996—; bd. dirs. Prince William County (Va.) Svc. Authority, 1996—; adj. prof. George Mason U., Fairfax, Va., 1988—, George Washington U., Washington, 1992—; instr. Dept. Agr. Grad. Sch., 1964-66; aquatic ecol. cons. Fairfax Count (Va.) Fedn. Citizens Assns., 1970-71; guest lectr. U. D.C., 1976. Bd. dirs. Prince William County (Va.) Svc. Authority; wildlife mgmt. cons. Girl Scouts Am., Loudoun County, Va., 1958; asst. scoutmaster and scoutmaster, merit badges counselor Boy Scouts Am., 1958—, Scouters Tng. award, 1961. Recipient incentive awards Nat. Park Service, 1962; research grantee Washington Biologists' Field Club, 1977, 82. Mem. AAAS, Bot. Soc. Washington, Ecol. Soc. Am., George Wright Soc., Nature Conservancy, Soc. Early Hist. Archaeology, So. Appalachian Bot. Soc., Washington Biologists' Field Club, Sigma Xi. Mormon. Contbr. articles profl. jours. Home: 13854 Delaney Rd Woodbridge VA 22193-4654 Office: Balt-Washingtn Pky 6565 Greenbelt Rd Greenbelt MD 20770-3207 also: Prince William Forest Park 18100 Park Hdqs Rd Triangle VA 22172

THOMAS, LLOYD BREWSTER, economics educator; b. Columbia, Mo., Oct. 22, 1941; s. Lloyd B. and Marianne (Moon) T.; m. Sally Leach, Aug. 11, 1963; 1 child, Elizabeth. AB, U. Mo., 1963, AM, 1964; PhD, Northwestern U., 1970. Instr. Northwestern U., Evanston, Ill., 1966-68; asst. prof. econs. Kan. State U., Manhattan, 1968-72, assoc. prof., 1974-81, prof., 1983—; asst. prof. Fla. State U., Tallahassee, 1973-74; vis. prof. U. Calif., Berkeley, 1981-82, U. Del., 1993; prof., chair dept. econs. U. Idaho, 1989. Author: Money, Banking and Economic Activity, 3d edit., 1986, Principles of Economics, 2d edit, 1993, Principles of Macroeconomics, 2d edit,, 1993, Principles of Microeconomics, 2d edit, 1993, Money, Banking and Financial Markets, 1997; contbr. articles to profl. jours. Mem. Am. Econs. Assn., Midwest Econs. Assn., So. Econs. Assn., Western Econs. Assn., Phi Kappa Phi. Avocations: tennis, classical music. Home: 1501 N 10th Ct Manhattan KS 66502

THOMAS, LOWELL, JR., author, lecturer, former lieutenant governor, former state senator; b. London, Oct. 6, 1923; s. Lowell Jackson and Frances (Ryan) T.; m. Mary Taylor Pryor, May 20, 1950; children: Anne Frazier, David Lowell. Student, Taft Sch., 1942; B.A., Dartmouth Coll., 1948; postgrad., Princeton Sch. Pub. and Internat. Affairs, 1952. Asst. cameraman Fox Movietone News, S.Am., 1939, Bradford Washburn Alaskan mountaineering expdn., 1940; illustrated lecturer, 1946—; asst. economist, photographer with Max Weston Thornburg, Turkey, 1947, Iran, 1948; film prodn. Iran, 1949; Tibet expdn. with Lowell Thomas, Sr., 1949; field work Cinerama, S.Am., Africa, Asia, 1951-52; travels by small airplane with wife, writing and filming Europe, Africa, Middle East, 1954-55; mem. Rockwell Polar Flight, first flight around the world over both poles, Nov., 1965; mem. Alaska State Senate, 1967-74; lt. gov. State of Alaska, 1974-79; owner Talkeetna Air Taxi, Inc., air contract carrier, Anchorage, Alaska, 1980-94. Producer series of films Flight to Adventure, NBC-TV, 1956; producer, writer TV series High Adventure, 1957-59; producer documentary film Adaq, King of Alaskan Seas, 1960; producer two films on Alaska, 1962, 63, film on U. Alaska, 1964, South Pacific travel documentary, 1965, film on Arctic oil exploration, Atlantic-Richfield Co., 1969. Author: Out of this World, A Journey to Tibet, 1950, (with Mrs. Lowell Thomas, Jr.) Our Flight to Adventure, 1956, The Silent War in Tibet, 1959, The Dalai Lama, 1961, The Trail of Ninety-Eight, 1962, (with Lowell Thomas Sr.) More Great True Adventures, 1963, Famous First Flights that Changed History, 1968. past pres. Western Alaska coun. Boys Scouts Am.; bd. dirs. Anchorage unit Salvation Army, Alaska Conservation Found. 1st lt. USAAF, 1943-45. Mem. Nat. Parks and Conservation Assn. (bd. dirs.), Alaska C. of C., Aircraft Owners and Pilots Assn. Clubs: Explorers, Marco Polo, Dutch Treat (N.Y.C.); Rotary, (Anchorage), Press (Anchorage); Dartmouth Outing; American Alpine. Address: 10800 Hideaway Lake Dr Anchorage AK 99516-1145

THOMAS, MABLE, communications company executive, former state legislator; b. Atlanta, Nov. 8, 1957; d. Bernard and Madie Thomas. BS in Pub. Adminstrn., Ga. State U., 1982, postgrad., 1983—. With acctg. dept. Trust Co. Bank, Atlanta, 1977; recreation supr. Sutton Cmty. Sch., Atlanta, 1977-78; data transcriber Ga. Dept. Natural Resources, Atlanta, 1978-79; clk. U.S. Census Bur., Atlanta, 1980; laborer City of Atlanta Parks and Recreation, 1980-81; student asst. Ga. State U., Atlanta, 1981-82; mem. Ga. Ho. Reps., Atlanta, 1984-94; pres. Master Comms. Inc., Atlanta, 1994—; mem. exec. com. Ga. Legis. Black Census, Atlanta, 1985—. Mem. adv. youth coun. Salvation Army Bellwood Club, 1975; founder, pres. Greater Vine City Opportunities Program Inc., 1996; founder Vine City Cmty. improvement Assn., Atlanta, 1985; mem. neighborhood planning unit adv. bd. of comprehensive youth svcs. Ga. State U., 1988—; mem. Nat. Black Woman's Health Project, Ga. Housing Coalition; bd. dirs. Ga. Coalition Black Women, 1996, Am. Cancer Soc., 1988—. Recipient Bronze Jubilee award City of Atlanta Cultural Affairs, 1984, Disting Svc. award Grady Hosp., 1985, Human Svc. award for cmty. and polit. leadership for disadvantaged, 1986, Exceptional Svc. award Young Cmty. Leaders, 1986, Citizenship award Salvation Army Club, Leadership and Achievement award Ga. Breast Cancer Prevention Coalition, 1994, Adopt a Sch. Appreciation award Atlanta Pub. Schs., 1996; named Outstanding Freshman Legislator, 1986, one of Outstanding Young People of Atlanta, 1987. Mem. Nat. Polit. Congress Black Women (bd. dirs., Fannie Lou Hamer award Phila. chpt. 1995), Conf. Minority Pub. Adminstrn. (Outstanding Svc. award), Ga. Assn. Black Elected Ofcls. (mem. housing and econ. devel. com.). Democrat. Methodist. Home: PO Box 573 Atlanta GA 30301-0573

THOMAS, MARGARET JEAN, clergywoman, religious research consultant; b. Detroit, Dec. 24, 1943; d. Robert Elcana and Purcella Margaret (Hartness) T. BS, Mich. State U., 1964; MDiv, Union Theol. Sem., Va., 1971; DMin, San Francisco Theol. Sem., 1991. Ordained to ministry United Presbyn. Ch., 1971. Dir. rsch. bd. Christian edn. Presbyn. Ch. U.S., Richmond, Va., 1965-71; dir. rsch. gen. coun. Presbyn. Ch. U.S., Atlanta, 1972-73; mng. dir. rsch. div. support agy. United Presbyn. Ch. U.S.A., N.Y.C., 1974-76; dep. exec. dir. gen. assembly mission coun. United Presbyn. Ch. U.S.A., 1977-83; dir. N.Y. coordination Presbyn. Ch. (U.S.A.), 1983-85; exec. dir. Minn. Coun. Chs., Mpls., 1985-95; synod exec. Synod of Lakes and Prairies Presbyn. Ch. (U.S.A.), Bloomington, Minn., 1995—; mem. Permanent Jud. Commn., Presbyn. Ch. (U.S.A.), 1985-91, moderator, 1989-91, mem. adv. com. on constn., 1992—, moderator, 1996—; sec. com. on ministry Twin Cities Area Presbytery, Mpls., 1985-91, vice moderator, 1991-92, moderator, 1992-93; mem. joint religious legis. coalition, 1985-95; mem. Commn. on Regional and Local Ecumenism Nat. Coun. Chs., 1988-91, officer Ecumenical Networks, 1992-95, mem. Unity and Rels. unit, 1992-93; treas., chair adminstrn. and fin. com. Nat. Coun. of Chs., 1996—; mem. nat. planning com. Nat. Workshop on Christian Unity, 1992-95; bd. dirs. Franklin Nat. Bank, Mpls., 1987—. Contbr. articles to profl. jours. Mem. adv. panel crime victims svcs. Hennepin County Atty.'s Office, 1985-86, Police and Cmty. Rels. Task Force, St. Paul, 1986; mem. adv. panel Hennepin County Crime Victim Coun., 1990-93, chmn., 1990-93; bd. dirs. Minn. Foodshare, 1985-95, Minn. Coalition on Health, 1986-92, Minn. Black-on-Black Crime Task Force, 1988, Twin Cities Coalition Affordable Health Care, 1986-87, Presbyn. Homes of Minn., 1995—, Clearwater Forest, Deerwood, Minn., 1995-96; co-chmn. Minn. Interreligious Com., 1988-95; bd. dirs. Abbott Northwestern Pastoral Counseling Ctr., 1988-91, chmn., 1990-91. Recipient Human Rels. award Jewish Community Rels. Coun./Anti-Defamation League, 1989, Gov.'s Cert. of Commendation for Women's Leadership, 1993. Mem. NOW (Outstanding Woman of Minn. 1986). Mem. Democrat-Farm-Labor Party. Office: Synod of Lakes and Prairies Presbyn Ch USA 8012 Cedar Ave S Bloomington MN 55425-1204

THOMAS, MARIANNE GREGORY, school psychologist; b. N.Y.C., Dec. 10, 1945. BS, U. Conn., 1985; MS, So. Conn. State U., 1987. Cert. sch. psychologist, Conn., N.Y. Sch. psychology intern Greenwich (Conn.) Pub. Schs., 1986-87; sch. psychologist Hawthorne (N.Y.)-Cedar Knolls, U.F.S.D., 1987-88, Darien (Conn.) Pub. Schs., 1988—. Mem. AAUW, NASP (cert.), Conn. Assn. Sch. Psychologists. Home: 154 Indian Rock Rd New Canaan CT 06840-3117

THOMAS, MARILYN JANE, insurance company executive; b. Fremont, Ohio, Dec. 11, 1944; d. Myron Elwood and Elvira Evelyn (Plagman) Magsig; m. William E. Thomas, Jr., Nov. 7, 1992; stepchildren: Dana Lauren Thomas, Keira Anne Schwartz. BS in Edn., Capitol U., Columbus, 1966; postgrad., U. Calif., Irvine, Fullerton, 1969-70. Tchr. pub. schs., Ohio, Calif., La., 1966-71; underwriter Tenn. Life Ins. Co., Houston, Tex., 1971-73; supr., mgr. contracts adminstrn. Phila. Life Ins. Co. (merger with Tenn. Life Ins. Co.), Houston, 1973-80; systems analyst Phila. Life Ins. Co., Houston, 1980-84; dir. market research/product devel. Phila. Am. Life Ins. Co. (merger Phila. Life Ins. Co.), Houston, 1984-87; 2d v.p. mktg. Phila. Am. Life Ins./New Era Life, Houston, 1987—. Vol. Spl. Olympics, Houston; tchr. Project Business, 1981. Recipient Outstanding Woman award, Houston YWCA, 1984. Mem. Am. Bus. Women's Assn. (chmn. edn. com. 1987-88), Soc. Group Contract Analysts (chmn. com. 1977-80), Houston Assn. Health Underwriters. Republican. Lutheran. Avocation: cooking. Office: Phila Am Life Ins/New Era Life 200 Westlake Park Blvd Houston TX 77079-2663

THOMAS, MARLIN ULUESS, industrial engineering educator, academic administrator; b. Middlesboro, Ky., June 28, 1942; s. Elmer Vernon and Helen Lavada (Banks) T.; m. Susan Kay Stoner, Jan. 18, 1963; children: Pamela Claire Thomas Davis, Martin Phillip. BSE, U. Mich., Dearborn, 1967; MSE, U. Mich., Ann Arbor, 1968, PhD, 1971. Registered profl. engr., Mich. Asst. and assoc. prof. dept. ops. rsch. Naval Postgrad. Sch., Monterey, Calif., 1971-76; assoc. prof. systems design dept. U. Wis., Milw., 1976-78; mgr. tech. planning and analysis vehicle quality-reliability Chrysler Corp., Detroit, 1978-79; prof. dept. indsl. engring. U. Mo., Columbia, 1979-82; prof. indsl. engring., chmn. dept. Cleve State U., 1982-88, acting dir. Advanced Mfg. Ctr., 1984-85; prof., chmn. indsl. engring. Lehigh U., Bethlehem, Pa., 1988-93; prof., head Sch. Indsl. Engring. Purdue U., West Lafayette, Ind., 1993—; program dir. NSF, Washington, 1987-88. Contbr. numerous articles on indsl. engring. and ops. rsch. to profl. jours. With USN, 1958-62; capt. USNR, 1971—. Named Outstanding Tchr., U. Mo. Coll. Engring., 1980, Coll. Man of Yr, Cleve. State U. Coll. Engring., 1985. Fellow Inst. Indsl. Engrs; mem. Ops. Rsch. Soc. Am., Am. Soc. for Engring. Edn., Am. Soc. Quality Control, Am. Statis. Assn., Soc. Am. Mil. Engrs., VFW. Office: Purdue U Sch Indsl Engring 1287 Grissom Hall West Lafayette IN 47907-1287

THOMAS, MARLO (MARGARET JULIA THOMAS), actress; b. Detroit, Nov. 21, 1943; d. Danny and Rose Marie (Cassanti) T.; m. Phil Donahue, May 21, 1980. Ed., U. So. Calif. Theatrical appearances in Thieves, Broadway, 1974, Barefoot in the Park, London, Social Security, Broadway, 1986, The Shadow Box, Broadway, 1994; star: TV series That Girl, 1966-71 (Golden Globe award Best TV actress, 1967); appeared in TV films: The Body Human: Facts for Girls (Emmy award Best Performer Children's Program), 1981, The Last Honor of Kathryn Beck, 1984 (also exec. prodr.), Consenting Adults, 1985, Nobody's Child, 1986 (Emmy Best Dramatic Actress), Held Hostage: The Sis and Jerry Levin Story, 1991, Ultimate Betrayal, 1994, Reunion, 1994, A Century of Women, 1994; guest star Friends, 1995; conceived book and record, starred in TV spl. Free to Be. . . You and Me, 1974 (Emmy for best children's show); films include Thieves, 1977, In the Spirit, 1991, Jenny, 1963; conceived book, record and TV spl. Free to Be A Family (Emmy Best Children's Show). Recipient 4 Emmys, Golden Globe award, George Foster Peabody award, Tom Paine award Nat. Emergency Civil Liberties Com. Mem. Ms. Found., Nat. Women's Polit. Caucus.

THOMAS, NATHANIEL CHARLES, clergyman; b. Jonesboro, Ark., June 24, 1929; s. Willie James and Linnie (Elias) T.; B.A., Miss. Indsl. Coll., Holly Springs, 1951; B.D., Lincoln U., 1954, M.Div., 1974; student Lancaster (Pa.) Theol. Sem., 1952-53; D.Div., Tex. Coll., Tyler, 1981; m. Juanita Fanny Jefferson, May 20, 1961 (dec. 1970); children—Gina Charlise, Nathaniel Charles, Keith Antony; m. 2d, Mary Elizabeth Partee, June 8, 1971. Ordained to ministry Christian Meth. Episcopal Ch., 1954; dir. Christian edn. 8th dist. Christian Meth. Episc. Ch., 1954-58; pastor in Waterford, Miss., 1949-51, Wrightville, Ark., 1955-57, Hot Springs, Ark., 1957-60, Little Rock, 1960-62, Mt. Pisgah Christian Meth. Episc. Ch., Memphis, 1966-67, Greenwood Christian Meth. Episc. Ch., Memphis, 1980-81; dir. Christian edn., adminstrv. asst. to Bishop B. Julian Smith, Christian Meth. Episc. Ch., Memphis, 1954-74, presiding elder South Memphis dist., 1971-74, sec. gen. conf. of ch., 1970-82, gen. sec. gen. bd. personnel services, 1978—, also mem. gen. connectional bd., program adminstr. ministerial salary supplement program, 1974-90, asst. to sec. gen. Gen. Bd. Pensions, 1974-78; program dir. CME Ch. Group Fire & Casualty Ins. Plan, 1978—, Annual CME Convocation and CME Reader Resource Series, 1990—; sec. Ministerial Assn. Little Rock, 1960-62; v.p. youth work sect., div. Christian edn. Nat. Council Chs., del. World Council Chs. Conf., Upsalla Sweden, 1968. Dir. Haygood-Neal Garden Apts., Inc., Eldorado, Ark., 1969—, Smith-Keys Village Apts., Inc., Texarkana, Ark., 1968—, East Gate Village Apts., Inc., Union City, Tenn., 1971—; trustee Collins Chapel Health Care Center, Memphis, 1974—, Tex. Coll., 1981—; bd. dirs. Family Service Memphis, 1972-73, Newsday Coop., Inc., exec. trustee; chmn. bd. dirs. Memphis Opportunities Indsl. Ctr., 1976-78. Mem. NAACP, Urban League, Community on Move for Equality, Memphis Interdenomminational Ministers Alliance, Memphis Ministers Assn., Tenn. Assn. Chs., Ark. Council Chs., Ark. Council Human Relations, Tenn. Council Human Relations, Family Service Memphis, A.B. Hill PTA. Author: Christian Youth Fellow Guide, 8th Episcopal District, 1959; Living Up to My Obligations to the Christian Methodist Episcopal Church, 1956; Steps Toward Developing an Effective Program of Christian Education, 1972; co-author: Worship in the Local Church, 1966; co-author, editor: Coming to Grips with the Teaching Work of the Church, 1966, Discipleship: Creation, Covenant, Community, 1994—. Co-editor: Developing Black Families, 1975; compiling editor: Dedicated . . . Committed-Autobiography of Bishop B. Julian Smith, 1978—. Home: PO Box 9 Memphis TN 38101-0009 Office: PO Box 74 Memphis TN 38101-0074*

THOMAS, ORVILLE C., physician; b. Haynesville, La., Aug. 23, 1915; children—David, Diane, Cody. Pre-med. Student, Marian Mil. Inst., 1932-33, Tulane U., 1933; M.D., Tulane U., 1939. Diplomate Am. Bd. Pediatrics. Diplomate Am. Bd. Allergy and Immunology. Intern Shreveport Charity Hosp., La., 1939-40; asst. resident in pediatrics Children's Meml. Hosp., Chgo., 1946-47, resident in pediatrics, 1947, chief resident in pediatrics, 1948; active staff Tex. Children's Hosp., Houston, 1962—, fellow pediatric allergy, 1963-65, chief allergy sect., 1973-78; fellow in pediatric allergy Baylor Coll. Medicine, Houston, 1963-65; chief pediatrics Schumpert Meml. Hosp., Shreveport, La, 1958-61, chief of staff, 1958; sr. staff pediatrics Confederate Meml. Hosp., Shreveport, La, 1948-61; active staff Highland Hosp., Shreveport, La, 1948-61, North La. Hosp., Shreveport, La, 1948-61, Physicians and Surgeons Hosp., Shreveport, La, 1948-61, Ben Taub Gen. Hosp., Houston, 1962—, Hermann Hosp., Houston, 1966-69; hon. staff St. Luke's Hosp., Houston, 1962—; cons. staff Meth. Hosp., Houston, 1962—, St. Joseph Hosp., Houston, 1966—, Bellaire (Tex.) Gen. Hosp., 1966-86, Rosewood Gen. Hosp., Houston, 1967—, Meml. Bapt. Hosp., Houston, 1968—, Pasadena Bayshore Hosp., Pasadena, Tex., 1970—; instr. pediatrics Northwestern U. Sch. Medicine, Chgo., 1948; assoc. prof. pediatrics La. State U. Postgrad. Sch. Medicine, 1956-61; clin. instr. pediatrics Baylor Coll. Medicine, Houston, 1961-66, asst. clin. prof. pediatrics, 1966-76, assoc. clin. prof. pediatrics, 1977—; assoc. clin. prof. allergy and immunology U. Tex. Grad. Sch. Biomed. Scis., Houston, 1970—. Book reviewer: Venom Diseases; Aspects of Allergy and Applied Immunology. Contbr. articles to profl. jours. Served to maj. USMC AUS, 1942-46. Fellow Am. Coll. Allergy and Immunology (pediatrics com. 1964—, pres. 1978), Am. Acad. Allergy and Immunology, Am. Assn. Cert. Allergists (bd. govs. 1974, pres. 1979); mem. AMA, Am. Acad. Pediatrics, So. Med. Assn. (chmn. allergy sect. 1970-71), Tex. Allergy Research Found. Houston(research and edn. com. 1966-86, chmn. sci. adv. council 1973—), Tex. Pediatric Soc., Harris County Med. Soc., Tex. Med. Assn. (chmn. allergy sect. 1976-77), Am. Assn. for Inhalation Therapy (awards com. 1969-72, spl. edn. com. 1969-72), Greater Houston Allergy Soc. (pres. 1977), Joint Council of Allergy and Immunology, Internat. Assn. of Allergology and Clin. Immunology (U.S. rep. 1981-85). Home: 1111 Bering Dr Apt 704 Houston TX 77057-2320 Office: 6969 Brompton St Houston TX 77025-1611

THOMAS, OWEN CLARK, clergyman, educator; b. N.Y.C., Oct. 11, 1922; s. Harrison Cook and Frances (Arnold) T.; m. Margaret Ruth Miles, June 6, 1981; children: Aaron Beecher, Addison Lippitt, Owen Clark Jr. A.B., Hamilton Coll., 1944, D.D., 1970; grad. student physics, Cornell U., 1943-44; B.D., Episcopal Theol. Sch., Cambridge, Mass., 1949; Ph.D., Columbia U., 1956. Ordained to ministry Episcopal Ch., 1949. Dir. coll. work Episcopal Diocese, N.Y., 1951-52; chaplain to Episcopal students Sarah Lawrence Coll., 1950-52; mem. faculty Episcopal Div. Sch. (formerly Episcopal Theol. Sch.), Cambridge, Mass., 1952—, prof. theology, 1965-93, prof. emeritus, 1993—; chmn. dept. coll. work Episcopal Diocese Mass., 1956-59; vis. prof. Pontifical Gregorian U., 1973-74, N. Am. Coll., Rome, 1982-83. Author: William Temple's Philosophy of Religion, 1961, Science Challenges

Faith, 1967, Attitudes Toward Other Religions, 1969, rev. edit., 1986, Introduction To Theology, 1973, rev. edit., 1983, God's Activity in the World, 1983, Theological Questions: Analysis and Argument, 1983; contbr. chpts. to books. Mem. Cambridge Democratic City Com., 1966-80, 88-93. Served to ensign USNR, 1944-45. Elihu Root fellow Hamilton Coll., 1943; Univ. fellow Columbia U., 1949-50; scholar in residence Rockefeller Found. Study and Conf. Ctr., Bellagio, Italy, 1991. Fellow Soc. Values in Higher Edn.; mem. Am. Theol. Soc., Phi Beta Kappa. Home: 1402 Glendale Ave Berkeley CA 94708

THOMAS, PAMELA ADRIENNE, special education educator; b. St. Louis, Oct. 28, 1940; d. Charles Seraphin Fernandez and Adrienne Louise (O'Brien) Fernandez Reeg; divorced, 1977; m. Alvertis T. Thomas, July 22, 1981. BA in Spanish and EdS, Maryville Coll., 1962; Cert. EdS, U. Ky., 1966-67; MA in Edn., St. Louis U., 1974. Cert. learning disabilities, behavior disorders, educable mentally retarded, Spanish, Mo. Tchr. Pawnee Rock Kans. Sch., 1963-64; diagnostic tchr. Frankfort State Hosp. Sch., Ky., 1964-67; spl. edn. tchr. St. Louis City Pub. Schs., 1968-71, itinerant tchr., 1971-73, ednl. strategist, 1973-74, elem. level resource tchr., 1974-78, secondary resource tchr., dept. head, 1978—; head dept. spl. edn., 1978—; Co-author: Sophomore English Resource for Credit Curriculum Handbook, 1991. Co-author: Teaching Foreign Language to Handicapped Secondary Students, 1990. Pres. Council for Exceptional Children, local chpt. #103, 1982-83, Mo. Division of Mentally Retarded, 1985-87. Mem. Alpha Delta Kappa (St. Louis chpt. pres. 1982-84). Avocations: traveling, reading, swimming, theatre, handicrafts. Home: 4534 Ohio Ave Saint Louis MO 63111-1324 Office: Cen VAP High Sch 3616 N Garrison Ave Saint Louis MO 63107-2501

THOMAS, PAMELLA DELORES, medical director, physician, educator; b. Wetmoreland, Jamaica, May 11, 1947; came to U.S., 1976; d. Wellesley Johnston and Hyacinth Ida Muir; m. Earl A. Thomas, Apr. 9, 1977; children: Ramogi O., Monifa J. MD, U. W.I., 1974; MPH, Med. Coll. Wis., 1990. Diplomate Am. Bd. Preventive Medicine in Occupational Medicine. Intern in surgery Brookdale Hosp., Bklyn., 1976-77, attending physician, 1979-83; resident in surgery Cath. Med. Ctr., Queens, N.Y., 1978-79; staff physician N.Y.C. Transit, Bklyn., 1983-86, asst. med. dir., 1986-89; med. dir. Lockheed Aeronautics, Marietta, Ga., 1989—; asst. adj. prof. Emory Sch. Pub. Health, 1992, chairperson residency adv. com. occupl. medicine program, 1995—; bd. dirs. Lockheed Ga. Employment Fed. Credit Union, sec., 1993—. Bd. dirs. Am. Cancer Soc., Cobb County, Ga., 1989—; mem. Promina N.W. Hosp. Found., 1993—; dir. pub. rels. Cobb Med. Soc., 1993-96; v.p. bd. govs. Atlanta Wellness Alliance, 1993-95. Fellow Am. Coll. Preventive Medicine, Am. Coll. Occupational and Environ. Medicine (pres. Ga. chpt. 1996—); mem. AMA, APHA, Am. Occupational Medicine Assn., Am. Coll. Physicians Execs., Am. Coll. Legal Medicine, Tchrs. Pub. Health Med. Assn. Ga., Am. Aerospace Med. Assn. Avocations: reading, baking, gardening, music. Office: Lockheed Aeronautics 86 S Cobb Dr # 0454 Marietta GA 30063-1000

THOMAS, PATRICIA ANNE, retired law librarian; b. Cleve., Aug. 21, 1927; d. Richard Joseph and Marietta Bernadette (Teevans) T.; BA, Case Western Res. U., 1949, JD, 1951. Admitted to Ohio bar, 1951, U.S. Supreme Ct. bar, 1980; libr. Arter & Hadden, Cleve., 1951-62; asst. libr., then libr. IRS, Washington, 1962-78; libr. dir. Adminstrv. Office, U.S. Cts., 1978-93; ret. 1993. Mem. Am. Assn. Law Libraries, Law Librs. Soc. D.C. (pres. 1967-69), Soc. Benchers (Case We. Res. Law Sch.).

THOMAS, PATRICK ROBERT MAXWELL, oncology educator, academic administrator; b. Exmouth, Devon, Eng., Feb. 23, 1943; came to U.S., 1976; s. Christopher Codrington and Aileen Daphne (Gordon) T.; m. Linda Sharon Rich, June 23, 1986 (dec. 1987), m. Geraldine M. Jacobson, Mar. 2, 1996. Diploma in biochemistry, London U., 1965, MB, BS, 1968. Lectr. Inst. Cancer Rsch., London, 1974-76; assoc. chief clinician Roswell Park Meml. Inst., Buffalo, 1976-79; asst. prof. Washington U., St. Louis, 1979-83, assoc. prof., 1983-89, prof., 1989-90; prof., chmn. Temple U., Phila., 1991—; extramural bd. PDQ, Bethesda, Md., 1989—; mem. in-svc. exam. com. Am. Coll. Radiology, Reston, Va., 1990—; examiner Am. Bd. Radiology, Louisville, 1990—. Fellow Am. Coll. Radiologists, Royal Coll. Physicians of London. Home: 106 Pier Five 7 N Columbus Blvd Philadelphia PA 19106-1422 Office: Temple U 3401 N Broad St Philadelphia PA 19140-5103

THOMAS, PAUL EMERY, mathematics educator; b. Phoenix, Feb. 15, 1927; m. Chi-Yuen Chan, 1958; children: Jenny, Valerie. BA, Oberlin Coll., 1950, Oxford U., Eng., 1952; PhD in Math, Princeton U., 1955. Rsch. instr. Columbia U., 1955-56; asst. prof. math. U. Calif., Berkeley, 1956-60, assoc. prof., 1960-63, prof., 1963-91, prof. emeritus, 1991—; prof. Miller Inst. Basic Rsch. in Sci., 1966-67, mem. exec. com., 1983-89; exec. dir. Miller Inst. Basic Research in Sci., 1987-89; dep. dir. Math. Scis. Rsch. Inst., 1987-90; vis. prof. Princeton U., fall 1971, mem. adv. coun. dept. math., 1987—. Served with USNR, 1945-46. NSF fellow Princeton U., 1955, U. Calif., 1958-59; Guggenheim Meml. Found. fellow, 1961; Rhodes scholar Oxford U., 1950-53. Mem. Am. Math. Soc. (trustee 1980-84, chmn. bd. trustees 1983). Office: U Calif Evans Hall Mathematics Dept Berkeley CA 94720

THOMAS, PAUL LOUIS, health services administrator; b. Hollis, N.Y., Feb. 28, 1950; s. Paul J. and Rita A. (Sheld) T.; m. Elizabeth A. O'Neil, Sept. 24, 1977; children: Alexander, Cassandra, Andrea. BSBA, Calif. State U., San Luis Obispo, 1972; M in Health Care Adminstrn., Va. Commonwealth U., 1983. Commd. 2d lt. USAF, 1973, advanced through grades to lt. col., 1990, ret., 1993; provider rels./network devel. MetLife Healthcare Corp., Richmond, Va., 1994-95; exec. dir. S.W. Ga. Healthcare Assn., Inc., Americus, Ga., 1995—; mem. Nat. Disaster Med. Sys. Adv. Bd., Washington, 1987-91. Recipient Sr. Health Policy fellowship Air Force Inst. Tech. and Am. Hosp. Assn., 1986-87, Cert. of Appreciation, Sec. Dept. Health and Human Svcs., 1990. Fellow Am. Coll. Healthcare Execs. (chmn. recruitment subcom./membership com. 1992-93); mem. Assn. Mil. Surgeons of U.S. (life), Am. Hosp. Assn., Ga. Soc. for Managed Care, Americus/Sumter County C. of C. Avocations: fishing, baseball/sports. Office: SW Ga Healthcare Assn Inc The Windsor Hotel 125 W Lamar St Fl 4 Americus GA 31709-3546

THOMAS, PAUL S., principal. Prin. Passel-Cokato (Minn.) Sr. High Sch. Recipient Blue Ribbon award U.S. Dept. Edn., 1990-91. Office: Dassel-Cokato Sr High Sch Hwy # 12 and Wright County Rd # 100 Cokato MN 55321*

THOMAS, PEARL ELIZABETH, English educator; b. N.Y.C., Feb. 22, 1928; d. Humphrey S. and Frances (Collins) T. BS, CCNY, 1948, MA, 1952; PhD, Columbia U., 1977; postgrad., Union Grad. Sch. Chmn. English dept. N.Y.C. secondary schs.; asst. prof. CUNY, N.Y.C., 1977-83; prin. A.P. Randolph High Sch.; adj. prof. U. Calif., Irvine, 1983—, L.A. Coll., 1988-91. Author: (series) Adventures in Literature, 1980-90, College Video on Native Son, 1991. Recipient awards for Contbn. to Edn. 1976-83. Mem. MLA, Am. Tchrs. English, Global Network in Edn. Home: 5718 Ravenspur Dr Palos Verdes Peninsula CA 90275-3561

THOMAS, PETER M., real estate developer; b. Las Vegas, Nev., Feb. 6, 1950; s. E. Parry and Peggy (Chatterton) T.; m. Nancy Paxman, June 12, 1972; children: David P., Megan, Lindsey, Adam. BS, U. Utah, 1972. V.p. Valley Bank of Nev., Las Vegas, 1977-79, exec. v.p., 1979-82, pres., 1982-92; pres. Bank of Am., Nev., 1992-95, pres., coo, 1992-95; mng. dir. Thomas and Mack Co., 1995—. Mem. long range planning com. United Way, 1982-84; bd. dirs. Friends of Channel 10, 1982-85; mem. Las Vegas Conv. and Visitor's Authority, 1984-88, sec./treas., 1985-86, treas./v.p., 1987-88; chmn. Las Vegas Met. Police Dept. Com. Fiscal Affairs, 1994—, Citizen's Adv. Com. on Downtown Redevel., 1986—, Nev. Bankers Legislative Com., Nev. Devel. Authority, (mem. exec. com. 1986—, trustee 1986-90, chmn.-elect 1992—); mem. Downtown Progresss Assn., 1986-90, Nev. Nuclear Projects Commn., 1993—, Am. Bankers Assn. Govt. Rels. and Adminstrv. Coms., Las Vegas Mayor's Multi-jurisdictional Cmty. Empowerment Commn.; mem. vision project exec. coun. U. Nev., 1988-90, Pres.'s Assn., 1988—; bd. trustees U. Nev. Las Vegas Found., 1994—. Mem. Nev. Bar Assn., Utah Bar Assn., D.C. Bar Assn., Las Vegas C. of C., Nev. Bankers Assn. (pres. 1987-89, chmn. legis. com. 1988—), Am. Bankers Assn. (govt. rels. coun. mgmt. com. 1988—), Young Pres.'s Orgn. Office: Thomas and Mack Co 2300 W Sahara Ave Ste 1 Las Vegas NV 89102-4353

THOMAS, PHILIP STANLEY, economics educator; b. Hinsdale, Ill., Oct. 23, 1928; s. Roy Kehl and Pauline (Grafton) T.; m. Carol Morris, Dec. 27, 1950; children: Lindsey Carol, Daniel Kyle, Lauren Louise, Gay Richardson. B.A., Oberlin Coll., 1950; M.A., U. Mich., 1951, Ph.D., 1961; postgrad., Delhi U., 1953-54. Instr. U. Mich., 1956-57; asst. prof. Grinnell (Ia.) Coll., 1957-63, assoc. prof., 1963-65; assoc. prof. econs. Kalamazoo Coll., 1965-68, prof. econs., 1968-94, prof. emeritus, 1994—; econ. advisor Pakistan Inst. Devel. Econs., 1963-64, USAID, 1965, 66, 67, 68, 71, Planning Commn., Pakistan, 1969-70, Ctrl. Bank of Swaziland, 1974-75, Ministry of Planning, Kenya, 1980-81, 83, 84, 85, 86-88, Ministry of Fin., Swaziland, 1990, Kenya, 1991, 92, Ministry Indsl. Devel., Sri Lanka, 1997. Contbr. articles to profl. jours. Mem. alumni coun. Oberlin Coll., 1961-63, 74-76, 83-86, 95—. Served with AUS, 1954-56. Fulbright scholar; Ford Found. overseas fellow India, 1953-54. Mem. Am. Econs. Assn., Phi Beta Kappa. Home and Office: 313A S Shabwasung St Northport MI 49670-9604

THOMAS, RHONDA CHURCHILL, lawyer; b. 1947; m. J. Regan Thomas; children: Ryan, Aaron, Evan. BA, Drury Coll., 1969; JD, U. Mo., 1972, Yale U., 1973. Bar: Mo. 1973. Newswoman Sta. KFRU Radio, Columbia, Mo., 1969-70; law clk. to Hon. Robert E. Seiler Supreme Ct. of Mo., Jefferson City, 1973-74; asst. city counselor City of Columbia, 1974-76, city counselor, chief legal advisor to city coun., dept. heads, 1976-79; assoc. prof. law U. Mo., 1979-82; ptnr. Thompson Coburn, St. Louis, 1985—; past chmn. franchise com. Nat. Inst. Mcpl. Law Officers. Contbr. articles to profl. jours. Past chmn. Boone County Home Rule Charter Commn.; past pres. Boone County Indsl. Devel. Authority. Mem. ABA (local govt. law sect., taxation sect.), Mo. Bar Assn. (mem. edn. law com., mem. local govt. law com., mem. med.-legal rels. com., past mem. spl. com. on quality and methods of practice), St. Louis Bar Assn., Nat. Assn. Bond Lawyers, Mo. Mcpl. Attys. Assn. (past pres.). Office: Thompson Coburn 1 Mercantile Ctr Ste 3400 Saint Louis MO 63101-1623

THOMAS, RICHARD, actor; b. N.Y.C., June 13, 1951; s. Richard and Barbara (Fallis) T.; m. Alma Gonzalez, Feb. 14, 1975 (div.); children: Richard F., Barbara, Gwyneth and Pilar (triplets); m. Georgiana Bischoff, Nov. 20, 1995; 1 child, Montana; children from previous marriage: Brooke, Kendra. Student, Columbia U. Owner, prin. Melpomene Prodns. Made Broadway debut at age 7 in Sunrise at Campobello, 1958; regular on children's series One, Two, Three - Go!, 1961-62, regular on TV series The Waltons, 1972-77 (Emmy award 1973); films include Winning, 1969, Last Summer, 1969, You Can't Have Everything, 1970, Red Sky at Morning, 1971, The Todd Killings, 1971, Cactus in the Snow, 1971, You'll Like My Mother, 1972, 9/30/55, 1977, Battle Beyond the Stars, 1980; stage appearances include Sunrise at Campobello, 1958, Whose Life Is It Anyway?, 1980, The Fifth of July, 1981, The Sea Gull, 1984, The Count of Monte Cristo, 1985, Citizen Tom Paine, 1986, The Front Page, 1986, Hamlet, 1987, Peer Gynt, 1989, Love Letters, 1989-90, Square One, 1990, Lisbon Traviata, 1990, Danton's Death, 1992, Richard II, 1993, Richard III, 1994; author: Poems by Richard Thomas, Vols. I and 2, 1974; TV dramatic spl. and movies The Homecoming— A Christmas Story, 1971, The Red Badge of Courage, 1974, The Silence, 1975, All Quiet on the Western Front, 1979, The Hank Williams Jr. Story, 1983, Hobson's Choice, 1984, The Master of Ballantrae, 1984, Glory!, Glory!, 1990, Andre's Mother, 1990, It, 1990, Mission of the Shark, 1991, Yes, Virginia, There Really Is a Santa Claus, 1991, I Can Make You Love Me: The Stalking of Laura Black, 1993, A Walton's Thanksgiving Reunion, 1993, Death in Small Doses, 1993, Linda, 1993, A Walton Wedding, 1995, A Christmas Box, 1995, What Love Sees, 1996, A Walton Easter, 1998, Swiss Family Robinson, 1997; host children's spl. H.M.S. Pinafore, 1973. Nat. chmn. Better Hearing Inst., 1987—. Office: care Springer Assoc 1501 Broadway Ste 1314 A New York NY 10036-5601

THOMAS, RICHARD EMERY, federal government official; b. Laconia, N.H., Dec. 12, 1929; s. Emery Everett and Zera Mae (Bean) T.; m. Blythe Ann Jamieson, June 14, 1952; children—Karen, Douglas, Kathryn, Jeffrey. B.S., U. N.H., 1952, M.S., 1954; postgrad. U. Md., 1954-56; postgrad. Cornell U., 1961-63. Research scientist Pub. Health Service, Cin., 1957-67; sr. research scientist Fed. Water Quality Adminstrn., Ada, Okla., 1967-77; sr. program scientist EPA, Washington, 1977-82, program coordinator, 1983-86, environ. cons., 1987—. Editor, author design manual: Land Treatment of Municipal Wastewater, 1977, rev. edit., 1981, supplement, 1984. Contbr. articles to profl. jours., chpts. to books. Mem. troop com. Arbuchle council Boy Scouts Am., 1971-73, pack master, 1968-69. Recipient Cert. Appreciation, Boy Scouts Am., Ada, 1973; Bronze medal, EPA, 1975, Outstanding Performance award, 1984, Disting. Career award, 1986. Mem. Water Environ. Fedn., Irrigation Assn., Council for Agrl. Sci. and Tech. Republican. Methodist. Avocations: softball, bowling, swimming, hiking, golf.

THOMAS, RICHARD IRWIN, lawyer; b. Pitts., Jan. 28, 1944; s. Donald Martin and Mary Jane (Smith) T.; m. Karen Rose Sorg, July 31, 1966 (dec. Aug. 1979); children: Amy, Joe, Mike, Jim, Mauri, Mark, John. Student, Georgetown U., 1961-62; BA, W.Va. Wesleyan Coll., 1965; JD, Duquesne U., 1972. Bar: Pa. 1972, U.S. Dist. Ct. (we. dist.) Pa. 1972, U.S. Ct. Appeals (3d cir.) 1974, U.S. Dist. Ct. (ea. dist.) Pa. 1976, U.S. Supreme Ct. 1977, U.S. Ct. Appeals (6th cir.) 1981. Asst. personnel mgr. Continental Can Co., Pitts., 1966; mgr. labor relations U.S. Steel Corp., Pitts., 1966-72; ptnr. Thorp, Reed & Armstrong, Pitts., 1972—; adj. prof. Duquesne U., Pitts., 1974-76; jud. mgr. Allegheny County Common Pleas Ct., Pitts., 1985; bd. dirs. Gen. Roofing Co., Bridgeville, Pa. Coach Upper St. Clair (Pa.) Athletic Assn., 1977-85; firefighter Upper St. Clair (Pa.) Vol. Fire Co., 1977-84. Named one of Outstanding Young Men in Am., 1973. Mem. ABA, Pa. Bar Assn., Allegheny Bar Assn. Republican. Roman Catholic. Avocations: skiing, white water rafting, golf, athletics. Home: 287 Mcmurray Rd Pittsburgh PA 15241-1613 Office: Thorp Reed & Armstrong 1 Riverfront Ctr Pittsburgh PA 15222-4800

THOMAS, RICHARD LEE, banker; b. Marion, Ohio, Jan. 11, 1931; s. Marvin C. and Irene (Harruff) T.; m. Helen Moore, June 17, 1953; children: Richard L., David Paul, Laura Sue. BA, Kenyon Coll., 1953; postgrad. (Fulbright scholar), U. Copenhagen, Denmark, 1954; MBA (George F. Baker scholar), Harvard U., 1958. With First Nat. Bank Chgo., 1958—, asst. v.p., 1962-63, v.p., 1963-65; v.p., gen. mgr. First Nat. Bank Chgo. (London br.), 1965-66; v.p. term loan divsn. First Nat. Bank, Chgo., 1968; sr. v.p., gen. mgr. First Chgo. Corp., 1969-72, exec. v.p., 1972-73, vice chmn. bd., 1973-75, pres., 1975-92, chmn., pres., CEO, 1992-95; chmn. First Chgo. NBD Corp., 1995-96, ret. chmn., 1996; dir. CNA Fin. Corp., Sara Lee Corp., IMC Global Inc., PMI Group Inc. Trustee, past chmn. bd. trustees Kenyon Coll.,Orchestral Assn.; trustee Rush-Presbyn.-St. Luke's Med. Ctr.; trustee Northwestern U. With AUS, 1954-56. Mem. Chgo. Coun. Fgn. Rels., Sunningdale Golf Club (London), Econ. Club (past pres.), Comml. Club (chmn.), Chgo. Club, Casino Club, Mid-Am. Club, Indian Hill Club (Winnetka, Ill.), Old Elm Club (Highland Park, Ill.), Phi Beta Kappa, Beta Theta Pi. Office: First Chgo NBD Corp 1 First Natl Plz Chicago IL 60603-2003

THOMAS, RICHARD O., civilian military employee; b. Boise, Idaho, May 29, 1941; s. Ormond and Mary Lacey T.; m. Linda Hill, Oct. 5, 1963; children: Lauren, Sharon, Steven. BS Aeronautical Engrng., Rensselaer Polytech. Inst., 1963; MS Ops. Rsch., George Washington U., 1973; postgrad. program for sr. execs., MIT, 1986. Rschr. David Taylor Rsch. Ctr., Carderock, Md., 1963-68; head support forces, logistic sect. Office Naval Ops., 1969-75; mgr. Am. Mgmt. Systems Inc., 1976-77; dir. Office Policy and Plans Maritime Adminstrn. (U.S. Dept. Commerce, now U.S. Dept. Transp.), Washington, 1978-82; dir. resources and policy evaluation Office Asst. Sec. Navy U.S. Dept. Navy, 1983-90, dep. asst. sec. Shore Resources, 1991—. Office: Installations & Environment 1000 Navy Pentagon Washington DC 20350-1000

THOMAS, RITCHIE TUCKER, lawyer; b. Cleve., Aug. 12, 1936; s. Myron F. and Marjorie (Ritchie) T.; m. Elizabeth Blackwell Haynes Main, Jan. 1, 1994. BA, Cornell U., 1959; JD, Case-Western Res. U., 1964. Bar: Ohio 1964, U.S. Dist. Ct. (no. dist.) Ohio 1964, U.S. Ct. Appeals (D.C. cir.) 1971, U.S. Ct. Appeals (fed. cir.) 1973, U.S. Ct. Internat. Trade 1976, U.S. Ct. Appeals (9th cir.) 1985. Assoc. office of gen. counsel U.S. Tariff Commn., Washington, 1964-67; assoc. Squire, Sanders & Dempsey, Cleve., 1967-69, Cox, Langford & Brown, Washington, 1969-74; ptnr. Squire, Sanders & Dempsey, Washington, 1974—; mem. exec. com. Meridian House Internat., Washington, 1977-94; Washington rep. Am. C. of C. in Germany, 1984—; v.p. bd. dirs. Belgian Am. Assn., 1989—. Assoc. editor Western Res. U. Law Rev., 1964; contbr. articles to profl. jours. Recipient various book award West Pub. Co., 1964. Mem. Fed. Bar Assn., Ohio Bar Assn., D.C. Bar Assn., Order of Coif. Home: 6700 Bradley Blvd Bethesda MD 20817-3045 Office: Squire Sanders & Dempsey 1201 Pennsylvania Ave NW PO Box 407 Washington DC 20044

THOMAS, ROBERT ALLEN, environmental policy administrator, educator; b. Luling, Tex., Apr. 10, 1946; s. Julian H. and Katie (Schneider) T.; m. Paulette M. Jung, Aug. 17, 1968; children: Jennifer Leigh, Aimee Kathryn, Patrick Julian. BS, U. Southwest La., 1970; MS, Tex. A&M U., 1974, PhD, 1976. Lectr. Tex. A&M U., College Station, 1976-77; instr. La. State U. Med. Ctr., New Orleans, 1977-78; exec. dir. La. Nature and Sci. Ctr., New Orleans, 1978-94; v.p. environ. policy The Audubon Inst., 1994; adj. prof. biol. sci. U. New Orleans, 1979—; sr. scientist Audubon Ctr. for Rsch. of Endangered Species, 1996—; chmn. environ. comm. Loyola U., 1996—, New Orleans; cons. for environ. issues, New Orleans. Contbr. articles to profl. jours.; columnist. Recipient Elsie Naumburg award Nat. Sci. for Youth Found., 1983; Margaret Stone medal The Garden Club Am., 1994. Mem. Soc. for Study of Amphibians and Reptiles, Herpetologists League, Am. Soc. Ichthyologists and Herpetologists, La. Assn. Mus. (pres. 1986-88), Am. Assn. Mus. (mem. accreditation commn. 1992-96), Southwestern Assn. Naturalists (mem. bd. govs. 1982-85), East New Orleans C. of C. (mem. exec. com.). Roman Catholic. Lodge: Rotary (pres. 1984-85, 94-96). Avocations: tennis; writing. Office: Loyola Univ Dept Comm New Orleans LA 70118-3265

THOMAS, ROBERT EGGLESTON, former corporate executive; b. Cuyahoga Falls, Ohio, July 28, 1914; s. Talbott E. and Jane S. (Eggleston) T.; children: Robert Eggleston, Barbara Ann. B.S. in Econs, U. Pa., 1936. Asst. to gen. mgr., sec., mgr. r.r. investments Keystone Custodian Funds, Boston, 1936-53; v.p. Pennroad Corp., N.Y.C., 1953-59; chmn. exec. com., dir. M.-K.- T. R.R., 1956-65; mem. exec. com. MAPCO Inc., 1960-84, dir., chief exec. officer, 1960-80, pres., 1960-76, chmn. bd., 1973-84; adv. bd. BancOkla. Corp. Mem. Am. Petroleum Inst. (hon. dir.), Nat. Mining Assn. (hon. dir.), Newcomen Soc., Chgo. Club, So. Hills Country Club (Tulsa), San Diego Yacht Club, Desert Horizons Country Club (Indian Wells, Calif.), Wianno (Mass.) Club, Teton Pines Country Club (Jackson Hole, Wyo.). Episcopalian. Office: MAPCO Inc PO Box 645 Tulsa OK 74101-0645

THOMAS, ROBERT JOSEPH, columnist, author; b. San Diego, Jan. 26, 1922; s. George H. and Marguerite (Creelman) T.; m. Patricia Thompson, Sept. 6, 1947; children: Nancy Katherine, Janet Elizabeth, Caroline Brooke. Student, UCLA, 1943. With AP, 1943—, Hollywood columnist, 1944—; radio, TV, lecture appearances; editor Action Mag., 1968-74. Author: The Art of Animation, 1958; (novel) Flesh Merchants, 1959; The Massie Case, 1966, King Cohn, 1967, Walt Disney: Magician of the Movies, 1967, Will Penny, Star, 1968, Thalberg, 1969, Selznick, 1970, The Heart of Hollywood, The Secret Boss of California, Winchell, 1971; (novel) Weekend '33, 1972; Marlon, 1974, Walt Disney, An American Original, 1976, Bud and Lou, The Abbott and Costello Story, 1977, The Road to Hollywood (with Bob Hope), 1977, The One and Only Bing, 1977, Joan Crawford, 1978, Golden Boy, the Untold Story of William Holden, 1983, Astaire, 1984, I Got Rhythm, The Ethel Merman Story, 1985; also numerous mag. articles. Mem. Beta Theta Pi. Office: Associated Press 221 S Figueroa St Ste 300 Los Angeles CA 90012-2552*

THOMAS, ROBERT LEE, financial services company executive, consultant; b. San Antonio, Dec. 29, 1938; s. Lawrence Grant and Mabel Louise (Carlson) T.; m. Terry Eileen Morgan, Dec. 14, 1972; 1 child, Evan Grant. Cert., Am. Coll., 1984, 85, cert. in fin. planning, 1990, cert. in health underwriting, 1991; postgrad., Northeastern U., 1991—. Cert. fin. planner, investment specialist; designated registered employee benefit cons. Various middle mgmt. positions Gen. Fin. Corp., Dallas, 1962-65; full charge mgmt. positions TransAm. Fin. Corp., Dallas, 1965-74; sr. agt. Am. Security Life, San Antonio, 1974-81; chmn., pres. Thomas Fin. Svcs., Inc., Dallas, 1981—; bd. dirs. Cherokee Children's Home; mem. adv. bd. Am. Security Life, 1977—; frequent guest on internat. and nat. radio and TV talk shows; host radio program, 1986—; nat. and internat. spkr. in field; initiator/tchr. fin. planning course for H.S. students. Mem. fin. profl. adv. panel Digest of Financial Planning Ideas mag., 1984; designer, creator Mortgage Pre-Payment System, 1990, Mortgage Management Software, 1990; author: Cost Cutter Mortgage Management Manual, 1990; creator Commercial Debt Expense Reduction System and Debt Cash Flow Analysis Software, 1991; columnist Jour. Shepherding group leader Meadowview Ch. Christ, Mesquite, Tex., 1983—, Bible class tchr., 1978—, deacon, 1987—; regular spokesman pub. svc. and promotional messages various civic orgns.; chmn. charity telethon Million Dollar Round Table; leader internat. missions ministry, Papau, New Guinea, 1989, S.E. Asia, 1990; team mem. for tribal contact, New Guinea, 1991-94, team leader, 95, 96; dir. Sr. Info. Svcs. of Am., 1994—; bd. dirs. Cherokee Home for Children, 1994—; team leader group exploring un-charted region of South Pacific Island of New Guinea, 1995-96. Recipient Lone Star Leader award Tex. Assn. Life Underwriters, 1982—, Nat. Sales Achievement award, Nat. Quality award Nat. Assn. Life Underwriters, 1976—. Fellow Life Underwriting Tng. Coun.; mem. Dallas Estate Planning Coun., Dallas Assn. Life Underwriters (chmn. health com. 1979-80, president's cabinet 1989—, pub. rels. com. 1992—), Internat. Assn. Registered Fin. Planners, Internat. Assn. Fin Planning, Am. Soc. CLUs, Am. Inst. Cert. Fin. Planners, Am. Assn. Fin. Profls., Am. Health Ins. Assn., Investment Rsch. Inst., Million Dollar Round Table (life), Dallas Assn. Life Underwriters (mem. steering com. 1992—), Tex. Assn. Life Underwriters (nat. sales achievement award 1976—, nat. quality award 1976—), Am. Arbitration Assn (nat. arbitration panel, securities arbitrator 1989—), Better Bus. Bur. (sr. arbitrator nat. panel), Gen. Agts. and Mgmt. Assn. (yearling achievement 1975), Internat. Platform Assn., Internat. Assn. Registered Fin. Planners, Tex. Investment Mgmt. Coun., Aircraft Owners and Pilots Assn. Avocations: diving, travel, exploration, flying. Office: Thomas Fin Svcs Inc Ste 221 1221 Abrams Rd Richardson TX 75081

THOMAS, ROBERT MORTON, JR., lawyer; b. Kansas City, Kans., Jan. 1, 1941; s. Robert Morton Sr. and Arlowyne Edith (Arganbright) T.; m. Rebecca Ann Myers, Aug. 21, 1965; children: Brooke J., Austin B. BA, U. Kans., 1962; LLB, Harvard U., 1966. Bar: N.Y., U.S. Dist. Ct. (so. dist.) N.Y., U.S. Ct. Appeals (2nd cir.). Local govt. advisor Republic of Botswana, Gaborone, 1966; dist. officer Republic of Botswana, Serowe, 1967; dist. commr. Republic of Botswana, Maun, 1968; assoc. Sullivan & Cromwell, N.Y.C., 1969-75, ptnr., 1975—; ptnr.-in-charge Sullivan & Cromwell, London, 1979-82; mng. ptnr. gen. practice group Sullivan & Cromwell, N.Y.C., 1986-91. Mem. ABA, N.Y. State Bar Assn., Assn. of Bar of City of N.Y., Internat. Bar Assn., India House, Buck's Club, Harvard Club, Mill Reef Club, Verbank Hunting and Fishing Club (dir., sec.). Republican. Presbyterian. Office: Sullivan & Cromwell 125 Broad St New York NY 10004-2400

THOMAS, ROBERT MURRAY, educational psychology educator; b. Cheyenne, Wyo., July 28, 1921; s. Robert MacDonald and Elizabeth (Carson) T.; m. Shirley Louise Moore, July 3, 1948; children: Robert Gilmour, Kathryn Elizabeth. A.B., Colo. State Coll., 1943, M.A., 1944; Ph.D., Stanford U., 1950. Tchr. Kamehameha Schs., Honolulu, 1944-45; Tchr. Mid-Pacific Inst., Honolulu, 1945-47; instr. San Francisco State Coll., 1949-50; prof. State U. Coll., Brockport, N.Y., 1950-58, Padjadjaran (Indonesia) U., 1958-61, 64-65; prof. ednl. psychology U. Calif. at Santa Barbara, 1961-64, 69-91, prof. emeritus ednl. psychology, 1992—; dean U. Calif. at Santa Barbara (Grad. Sch.), 1965-69. Author: Judging Student Progress, 2d edit, 1960, Ways of Teaching, 1955, Integrated Teaching Materials, 2d edit, 1963, Individual Differences in the Classroom, 1965, Social Differences in the Classroom, 1965, Aiding the Maladjusted Pupil, 1967, A Chronicle of Indonesian Higher Education, 1973, Comparing Theories of Child Development, 1979, 4th edit., 1996, Japanese edit., 1985, Education in American Samoa-1700 to 1980, 1987, The Puzzle of Learning Difficulties-Applying a Diagnostic and Treatment Model, 1989, Counseling and Life-span Development, 1990, Classifying Reactions to Wrongdoing, 1995, An

Integrated Theory of Moral Development, 1997, Moral Devel. Theories-Secular and Religious, 1997 and numerous others; editor: Strategies for Curriculum Change: Cases from 13 Nations, 1968, Politics and Education: Cases from 11 Nations, 1983, Ency. of Human Development and Education, 1990, International Comparative Education, 1990, Education's Role in National Development Plans, 1992; co-author: Decisions in Teaching Elementary Social Studies, 1971, Curriculum Patterns in Elementary Social Studies, 1971, Penggunaan Statistik Dalam Ilmu Pengetahuan Sosial, 1971, Teaching Elementary Social Studies: Readings, 1972, Indonesian Education: An Annotated Bibliography, 1973, Social Strata in Indonesia, 1975, Political Style and Education Law in Indonesia, 1980, Schooling in the ASEAN Region, 1980, Schooling in East Asia, 1983, Schooling in the Pacific Islands, 1984, Die Entwicklung des Kindes, 1986, Educational Technology, 1987, Oriental Theories of Human Development, 1988, What Wrongdoers Deserve, 1993, Etude Comparée des Théories du Dévelopment de l'Enfant, 1994, Prevent, Repent, Reform, Revenge, 1995. Home: 1436 Los Encinas Dr Los Osos CA 93402-4520

THOMAS, ROBERT RAY, management consultant; b. Columbus, Ohio, Dec. 14, 1926; s. Robert Ray and Esther Susan (Wolfe) T.; BS in TV Engring., Am. Inst. of Tech., 1950; m. Ann Lee Estes, Nov. 24, 1973; children: Sandra Ann, Robert Ray; 1 child by previous marriage, Margo Lynne. Electronic engr. Oakton Engring. Co., Evanston, Ill., 1949-50, Stewart Warner Corp., Chgo., 1950-51, Gen. Transformer Co., Homewood, Ill., 1951-53; electronic sales engr. Electronic Components Inc., Chgo., 1953-54; gen. mgr. West Coast, Miller Calson Services, Los Angeles, 1954-55; sales engr. R. Edward Steem Co., Chgo., 1955-59; dist. sales mgr. Motorola Semiconductor div. Motorola, Inc., Chgo. and Dallas, 1959-61; pres., chmn. bd. Enterprises Ltd. Co., Inc., Dallas, 1961—, pres. subs. Robert R. Thomas Co., 1961—, Rep. Mgmt. & Mktg. Counselors, 1969—; pres. Press Insulator Co., 1978-92; co-founder CH&T Transformers Inc., 1983-85; owner, pres. Westwood Creations, Inc., 1986-89; co-founder, pres. Data MAXX Corp., 1994—. Served with USAAF, 1945-46. Named Boss of Year, Big D chpt. Am. Bus. Womens Assn., 1965, Super Salesman by Purchasing Mag., Oct. 1975. Mem. Mfrs. Electronic Reps. Assn. (dir. S.W. chpt. 1964-69, pres. S.W. chpt. 1968-69), Sales and Mktg. Execs. of Dallas pres. (1977-78), S.W. Found. for Free Enterprise in Dallas (pres. 1976-77), TESS (founder, pres.), Masons, Shriner. Baptist. Office: 4620 Sunbelt Dr Dallas TX 75248-6923

THOMAS, ROBERT WILBURN, broadcasting and advertising executive; b. Athens, Ga., Nov. 20, 1937; s. Ernest Wilburn and Bobbie (Morton) T.; m. Betsey Ruth Thorne, Sept. 6, 1958; children: Richard Gregory, Coleen Suzanne. BS in Speech, Northwestern U., 1960, MA, 1961. Producer radio, TV broadcasts Northwestern U., Evanston, Ill., 1961-68, instr., 1967-68; exec. producer Sta. WCNY-TV, Syracuse, N.Y., 1968-70; gen. mgr., v.p. Sta. WEKT-FM, Hammondsport, N.Y., 1970-71; gen. mgr. Sta. KWMU-FM, St. Louis, 1971-76; dir. broadcasting Sta. KWIT, Sioux City, Iowa, 1976-79; sta. expansion mgr. Corp. for Pub. Broadcasting, Washington, 1979-82; exec. dir. Cable Comm. Prince Georges County (Md.), 1982-83; cable adminstr. City of Raleigh (N.C.), 1983-86; pres. B&B Media, Inc. (advt. and pub. rels. agy.), 1986—; co-owner, gen. mgr. Sta. WBLB, Pulaski, Va., 1986-89; co-innkeeper Claytor Lake Homestead Inn, Draper, Va., 1990-91; news, pub. affair dir. Sta. WRAD-WRIQ, Radford, Va., 1993-94; bd. dirs. S.W. Devel. Financing, Inc., chmn., 1993—, chair, 1996; mem. Emmy awards com. Chgo. chpt. Nat. Acad. TV Arts and Scis., 1962-65; mem. radio adv. com. Ill. Telecommunications Commn., 1968; chmn. radio divsn. Midwest Telecommunications Conf., Nat. Assn. Ednl. Broadcasters, 1972; mem. Va. News Network adv. bd., 1987-89; co-founder, bd. dirs. Pulaski County HOSTS, pres. 1991; bd. dirs. New River Valley HOSTS, pres., 1992-93. Mem. pack com. Cub Scouts Am., Florissant, Mo., 1971-72; chmn. Mo. Jr. Miss Pagent, 1971-72, co-chmn., 1972-73, exec. dir., 1973-76; past bd. dirs. Sioux City Youth Orch. Assn., Siouxland Arts Coun., Sioux City Chamber Music Assn.; founding mem. Pub. Radio in Mid. Am., program chmn., 1976-77; bd. dirs. Pulaski County United Way, 1987-92, pub. rels. chmn., 1987-89; bd. dirs. Salvation Army, 1987-90, pub. rels. chmn., 1987, v.p., 1988; bd. dirs. Count Pulaskifest, 1987-90, prodr., dir. Ms. Va. Sr. Citizen Pageant, 1993—; bd. dirs. Pulaski County Emergency Needs Task Force, 1989-92, Radford Heritage Found., pub. rels. chmn., 1993—; chmn. Environ. Commn. City of Radford, 1995—. Recipient award Freedoms Found., 1963, 65, Outstanding Program award Ill. Med. Soc., 1965; named Outstanding State chmn. in Nation America's Jr. Miss Pageant, 1974. Mem. Mo. Pub. Radio Assn. (pres. 1975-76), Nat. Assn. Telecom. Officers and Advisors (bd. dirs. 1982-86, sec. 1983-85, v.p. 1985-86), Pulaski County C. of C. (bd. dirs. 1987-89), Pulaski Mchts. Assn. (chmn. promotions com. 1986-89, bd. dirs. 1987-89, 4th of July com. 1987, 91, town hist. com. 1987-89), Pulaski Main St. (chmn. corp. rels. com. 1988-89), Rotary (v.p. Radford 1993-94, pres.-elect 1994-95, pres. 1995-96, Paul Harris fellow 1990). Home and Office: 1006 3rd St Radford VA 24141-1306 *Without belief in and enthusiasm for the undertakings of life, achievement is slowed, if not actually blocked.*

THOMAS, ROBERTA WILL, home care agency administrator; b. Knoxville, Tenn., July 13, 1950; d. Robert Spicer Thomas and Naoma Kathleen (Burchell) Winningham; 1 child, Lindsey Kelly. BS in Edn., U. Tenn., 1974, ADN, 1979; MS in Health Svcs. Adminstrn., Coll. of St. Francis, Joliet, Ill., 1991. Staff nurse clin. rsch. Vanderbilt U. Med. Ctr., Nashville, 1979-80; charge nurse surg. gynecology Owensboro (Ky.)-Davies County Hosp., 1980-81; nurse mgr. med./surg. Nashville Meml. Hosp., 1981-84; dir. nursing edn. Clover Bottom Devel. Ctr., 1984-92; edn. coord. Physician's Home Health Care, 1992-93; dir. infusion svcs. Home Tech. Healthcare-Mid South, 1993-96; adminstr. Home Tech. Healthcare-Tenn., 1994-96; case mgr., provider contracting rep. Nat. Healthcare, Hendersonville, Tenn., 1996—; CPR instr. AHA and ARC, Nashville, 1981—; guest lecr. Tenn. Assn. Home Care, 1991—; ind. trainer various mental retardation facilities, Tenn., 1992—. Author, implementor tng. program Medication Administration Training for Medicaid Waiver Group Homes, 1985. Mem. Mid. Tenn. Assn. Healthcare Quality, Mid. Tenn. Orgn. Nurse Execs. Office: Nat Healthcare 236 Sterling Rd Hendersonville TN 37075-5329

THOMAS, ROGER MERIWETHER, lawyer; b. Hartford, Conn., Feb. 28, 1930; s. Frederick Metcalf and Helen Meriwether (Lewis) T.; m. Mary Dorothea Wyman, Dec. 4, 1965; children—Donald Wyman, Helen Dorothea. A.B., Princeton U., 1952; LL.B., Va. U., 1957; LL.M., Boston U., 1964. Bar: N.Y. 1958, Mass. 1960, U.S. Dist. Ct. (Mass) 1965, U.S. Tax Ct. 1965, U.S. Supreme Ct. 1967. Assoc. Angulo, Cooney, Marsh & Ouchterloney, N.Y.C., 1957-60; assoc., then ptnr. Gaston & Snow, Boston, 1960-91; counsel Condit & Assocs., P.C., Boston, 1992-94; outline author and lectr. Mass. Continuing Legal Edn., Inc., Boston; past panelist New Eng. Law Inst. Estate Planning Forums, Boston. Trustee Buckingham Browne & Nichols Sch., Cambridge, Mass., 1967-69. Served to 1st lt. U.S. Army, 1952-54, Korea. Mem. Am. Coll. Trust and Estate Counsel, Boston Bar Assn., Mass. Bar Assn. Avocations: reading; sports; old movies. Home: 40 Byron Rd Weston MA 02193-2229

THOMAS, ROGER WARREN, lawyer; b. South Weymouth, Mass., Sept. 17, 1937; s. Clement Rogers and Beatrice (Merritt) T.; m. Maria Sava Brenner, July 5, 1968; children: Caroline, Andrew, Phillip. BA, U. N.H., 1959; postgrad. (Rotary Internat. fellow), Free U. Berlin, 1960; LLB (Root-Tilden scholar), NYU, 1963, LLM (Ford Found. grantee), 1965; postgrad., U. Chile, Santiago, 1965. Bar: N.Y. 1964. Assoc. Cleary, Gottlieb, Steen and Hamilton, N.Y.C., 1965-66, 69-74; partner Cleary, Gottlieb, Steen and Hamilton, 1974—; mem. Harvard-Chile Tax Reform Project, 1966-68, head project in Chile, 1968-69; cons. to UN, Santiago, 1969; adj. prof. taxation NYU, 1974-96. Co-author: El Impuesto a la Renta, 1969. Bd. dirs. Spanish Repertory Theatre. Mem. ABA, Am. Fgn. Lawyers Assn. (dir.), N.Y. State Bar Assn., N.Am.-Chilean C. of C. (pres. 1984-96), Am. Soc., Coun. of Am., Down Town Assn. N.Y.C., Knickerbocker Club. Home: 1165 Fifth Ave New York NY 10029-6931 Office: 1 Liberty Plz New York NY 10006-1404

THOMAS, S. BERNARD, history educator; b. N.Y.C., Oct. 17, 1921; s. Hyman and Rose (Samilow) T.; m. Evelyn Green Hechtlinger, Dec. 28, 1955; 1 child, Ruth Thomas; stepchildren: Ira, John. BS in Social Sci., CCNY, 1942; MA, Columbia U., 1947, cert. East Asian Inst., 1951, PhD, 1964. Rsch. assoc. internat. secretariat Inst. Pacific Rels., 1950-55; chmn. social studies Colby Acad., N.Y.C., 1955-58; tchr. social studies Forest Hills (N.Y.) High Sch., 1958-65; asst. prof. history Oakland U., Rochester, Mich., 1965-67, assoc. prof., 1967-71, prof., 1971-89, prof. emeritus, 1989—, chmn. area studies programs, 1967-71, chmn. dept. history, 1984-87. Author: Government and Administration in Communist China, 1953, reprinted 1972, Labor and the Chinese Revolution, 1983, Season of High Adventure: Edgar Snow in China, 1996; contbr. numerous articles and revs. to profl. jours. With Signal Corps, AUS, 1942-46. East Asian Inst. fellow, 1962, Fulbright fellow, 1969-70. Mem. Assn. Asian Studies, Fulbright Assn. Home: 926 Norwich Rd Troy MI 48084-2671 Office: Oakland U Dept History Rochester MI 48309-4401

THOMAS, SARAH ELAINE, elementary music educator; b. Little Rock, Aug. 8, 1947; d. William and Madie Murle (Stout) Collins; m. Gary Wayne Thomas Aug. 8, 1970 (dec. Nov. 1991). MusB in Edn., U. N. Tex., 1970; postgrad., Dallas Bapt. U. Cert. tchr.-all-levels, Tex. Music tchr. Winnetka Elem., Dallas, 1970-82, L. K. Hall Elem., Dallas, 1982-94; Kleberg Elem. and Seagoville Mid. Sch., Dallas, 1994—; staff. devel. presenter Dallas Ind. Sch. Dist., 1977-97; workshop presenter Tex. Arts Coun., Austin, 1990-94. Bd. dirs. Dallas PTA, 1980-82; bd. dirs. Dallas All-City Elem. Choir, 1995—, chair, 1991—. Named Class Act Teacher, Sta. KDFW-TV, Dallas, 1992. Mem. PTA (life), Am. Fedn. Tchrs., Tex. Music Educators Assn., Dallas Music Educators Assn. (v.p. 1992), Am. Orff-Schulwerk Assn. Avocations: cooking, sewing, gardening, travel. Home: 2407 Norwich Ct Arlington TX 76015-3262 Office: Kleberg Elem 1450 Edd Rd Dallas TX 75253-4801

THOMAS, SCOTT E., federal government executive, lawyer; b. Buffalo, Wyo., Mar. 5, 1953; s. Ralph E. and Bonnie E. (Kaan) T.; m. Elena W. King, Apr. 28, 1984. BA, Stanford U., 1974; JD, Georgetown U., 1977. Bar: D.C., U.S. Ct. Appeals (9th cir.) 1980, U.S. Supreme Ct. 1981. Atty. Office of Gen. Counsel, Fed. Election Commn., Washington, 1977-80, asst. gen. counsel, 1980-83; exec. asst. to commr. Fed. Election Commn., Washington, 1983-86, commr., 1986—. Mem. D.C. Bar Assn. Office: Fed Election Commn 999 E St NW Washington DC 20463-0001

THOMAS, SHIRLEY, author, educator, business executive; b. Glendale, Calif.; d. Oscar Miller and Ruby (Thomas) Annis; m. W. White, Feb. 22, 1949 (div. June 1952); m. William C. Perkins, Oct. 24, 1969. BA in Modern Lit., U. Sussex, Eng., 1960, PhD in Comm., 1967; diploma, Russian Fedn. Cosmonautics, 1995. Actress, writer, producer, dir. numerous radio and TV stas., 1942-46; v.p. Commodore Prodns., Hollywood, Calif., 1946-52; pres. Annis & Thomas, Inc., Hollywood, 1952—; prof. technical writing U. So. Calif., L.A., 1975—; Hollywood corr. NBC, 1952-56; editor motion pictures CBS, Hollywood, 1956-58; corr. Voice of Am., 1958-59; now free lance writer; cons. biol. scis. communication project George Washington U., 1965-66; cons. Stanford Rsch. Inst., 1967-68, Jet Propulsion Lab., 1969-70. Author: Men of Space vols. 1-8, 1960-68, Spanish trans., 1961, Italian, 1962; Space Tracking Facilities, 1963, Computers: Their History, Present Applications and Future, 1965; The Book of Diets, 1974. Organizer, chmn. City of L.A. Space Adv. Com., 1964-73, Women's Space Symposia, 1962-73; founder, chmn. aerospace hist. com. Calif. Mus. Sci. and Industry; chmn. Theodore von Karman Postage Stamp Com., 1965—, stamp issued 1992; bd. dirs. World Children's Transplant Fund. Recipient Aerospace Excellence award Calif. Mus. Found. 1991, Nat. Medal Honor DAR, 1992, Yuri Gagarin Medal Honor, 1995. Fellow Brit. Interplanetary Soc.; mem. AIAA, AAAS, Internat. Soc. Aviation Writers, Air Force Assn. (Airpower Arts and Letters award 1961), Internat. Acad. Astronautics, Nat. Aero. Assn., Nat. Asn. Sci. Writers, Soc. for Tech. Communications, Am. Astronautical Soc., Nat. Geog. Soc., Am. Soc. Pub. Adminstrn. (sci. and tech. in govt. com. 1972—), Achievement Awards for Coll. Scientists, Muses of Calif., Theta Sigma Phi, Phi Beta. Home: 8027 Hollywood Blvd Los Angeles CA 90046-2510 Office: U So Calif Profl Writing Program University Park Waite-Phillips Hall 404 Los Angeles CA 90089-4034

THOMAS, SIDNEY, fine arts educator, researcher; b. N.Y.C., Dec. 21, 1915; s. Hyman and Rose (Samilowitz) T.; m. Rae Dinkowitz, May 26, 1940; children: David Phillip, Deborah Rose. B.A., CCNY, 1935; M.A., Columbia U., 1938, Ph.D., 1943. Tutor in English CCNY, N.Y.C., 1939-43; instr. English Queens Coll., N.Y.C., 1946-54; self-employed as editor, 1954-58; asst. editor Merriam-Webster, Springfield, Mass., 1958-61; assoc. prof. fine arts Syracuse U. (N.Y.), 1961-66, prof., 1966-85, prof. emeritus, 1985—, dir. humanities doctoral program, 1964-72, chmn. dept. fine arts, 1969-73; bibliographer Shakespeare Assn., N.Y.C., 1949-54. Author: The Antic Hamlet, 1943; co-editor: The Nature of Art, 1964; editor: Images of Man, 1972. Served to sgt., inf. U.S. Army, 1943-45, ETO. Research fellow Folger Shakespeare Library, Washington, 1947-48. Fellow Royal Soc. Arts (London); mem. MLA (life), Shakespeare Assn. Am., Internat. Shakespeare Assn., AAUP (pres. Syracuse U. chpt. 1974), ACLU, Phi Beta Kappa. Office: Syracuse U Dept Fine Arts Syracuse NY 13210

THOMAS, STEPHEN J., anesthesiologist; b. Washington, 1943. Intern San Francisco Gen. Hosp., 1968-69; resident in anesthesiology Mesa Gen. Hosp., Boston, 1971-73, fellow, 1973-74; assoc. prof. NYU Med. Ctr.; vice chmn., prof. dept. anesthesiology N.Y. Hosp. Cornell Med. Ctr., 1989—. Office: NY Hosp Cornell Med Ctr Dept Anesthesiology 525 E 68th St New York NY 10021*

THOMAS, STEPHEN PAUL, lawyer; b. Bloomington, Ill., July 30, 1938; s. Owen Wilson and Mary Katherine (Paulsen) T.; m. Marieanne Sauer, Dec. 7, 1963 (dec. June 1984); 1 child, Catherine Marie; m. Marcia Aldrich Toomey, May 28, 1988; 1 child, Ellen Antonia. BA, U. Ill., 1959; LLB, Harvard U., 1962. Bar: Ill. 1962. Vol. Peace Corps, Malawi, Africa, 1963-65; assoc. Sidley & Austin and predecessor firms, Chgo., 1965-70, ptnr., 1970—; lectr. on law Malawi Inst. Pub. Adminstrn., 1963-65. Pres. Hyde Park-Kenwood Cmty. Conf., Chgo., 1988-90; trustee Chgo. Acad. for Arts, 1991—, chmn., 1992—; bd. dirs. Ctr. for Ethics Garrett-Evang. Theol. Sem., Evanston, Ill., 1995—. Recipient Paul Cornell award Hyde Park Hist. Soc., 1981. Mem. ABA, Chgo. Bar Assn., Chgo. Fedn. of Musicians, Legal and Law Clubs Chgo., Union League Club Chgo. Democrat. Roman Catholic. Avocation: jazz piano playing. Home: 5740 S Harper Ave Chicago IL 60637-1841 Office: Sidley & Austin 1 First Natl Plz Chicago IL 60603-2003

THOMAS, TED, SR., minister; b. Raeford, N.C., Oct. 19, 1935; s. Simuel and Nancy Anna (McPhatter) T.; m. Charletta Virginia Clifton, May 30, 1957; children: Ted, Christopher, Marc, Charles, Jonathan, Reuben. BS, Norfolk State Coll., 1959; MA in Math., Edn. and Secondary Edn., Hampton Inst., 1972. Ordained to ministry Ch. of God in Christ Inc., 1957. Pastor New Community Ch. of God in Christ, Churchland, Portsmouth, Va., 1967—; State project dir. Chs. of God in Christ, Va. Jurisdiction 1, 1965—; supt. cen. dist. Chs. of God in Christ, Va., 1964—; asst. prin. Ruffner Jr. High Sch., Norfolk, Va., 1983-84; past pres. young people Willing Works, 1962-66; Sunday sch. supt., 1970-73; asst. bishop 1st jurisdiction Chs. of God in Christ Inc. of Va., 1977-84, State Bishop, 1984—. Mem. NEA, Va. Edn. Assn., Edn. Assn. Norfolk. Home: 4145 Sunkist Rd Chesapeake VA 23321-3131 Office: Ch of God in Christ 3615 Tyre Neck Rd Portsmouth VA 23703-3125*

THOMAS, THOMAS DARRAH, chemistry educator; b. Glen Ridge, N.J., Apr. 8, 1932; s. Woodlief and Jean (Darrah) T.; m. Barbara Joan Rassweiler, Sept. 8, 1956; children: David, Steven, Kathleen, Susan. BS, Haverford Coll., 1954; PhD, U. Calif., Berkeley, 1957. Instr. chemistry U. Calif., Berkeley, 1957-58, asst. prof., 1958-59; research assoc. Brookhaven Nat. Lab., Upton, N.Y., 1959-61; asst. prof. Princeton (N.J.) U., 1961-66, assoc. prof., 1966-71; prof. Oreg. State U., Corvallis, 1971-89, disting. prof., 1989-97, chmn. dept. chemistry, 1981-84, dir. Ctr. Advanced Materials Research, 1986-91, Disting. prof. emeritus, 1997—; cons. Los Alamos (N.Mex.) Sci. Lab., 1965. Contbr. articles to profl. jours. Fellow Alfred P. Sloan Found., 1966-68, Guggenheim Found., 1969, U. Liverpool, Eng., 1984-85. Fellow AAAS, Am. Phys. Soc.; mem. Am. Chem. Soc., Sigma Xi, Phi Beta Kappa. Home: 1470 NW Greenwood Pl Corvallis OR 97330-1827 Office: Oreg State U Dept Chemistry Gilbert Hall # 153 Corvallis OR 97331-4003

THOMAS, THURMAN, professional football player; b. Houston, May 16, 1966. Student, Okla. State U. With Buffalo Bills, 1988—. Named to Pro-Bowl team, 1989-93, Sporting News All-Pro team, 1990, 91; named MVP, NFL, 1991, Player of Yr., Sporting News, 1991. Office: care Buffalo Bills 1 Bills Dr Orchard Park NY 14127-2237*

THOMAS, TOM, retired plastics company executive; b. Malang, Java, Indonesia, Feb. 15, 1932; arrived in Can., 1954; s. Ferdinand and Elfrieda Emma (Macht) T.; m. Jannie Chine Sneep, Jan. 19, 1956; children: Gregory John, Renée Sonja Elfrieda, Michael Grant, Thomas. Grad. high sch., The Hague, Holland. Jr. mgr. Lever Bros. Ltd., Toronto, Ont., Can., 1954-60; sr. mgr. Impac & Somerville Plastics, Toronto, Ont., Can., 1960-64; founder, C.E.O. Can. Cup Inc., Toronto, Ont., Can., 1964—, also bd. dirs., 1964-93; ret., 1993; Inventor in field. Trustee Frazer Inst., Vancouver, B.C., Can., 1977-93; gov. Massey and Roy Thomson Hall, Toronto, 1991-92; bd. dirs. Toronto Symphony, 1986-92, mem. Maestro's Club, 1984, mem. pres.'s coun. Can. Opera Co., 1980, adv. coun. Toronto Symphony, 1995, pres. Coun. Can. Opera, 1980-95. Avocations: sailing, history, classical music, chess.

THOMAS, VINCENT COX, editor; b. Louisville, July 5, 1920; s. Vincent Cox and Mary Tuley Thomas; m. Violette McLaughlin, Aug. 26, 1945; children: Dian Speed, Sheilah Nehan, Vincent Cox III, Jeanne-Marie Stuart. BA, Centre Coll., Danville, Ky., 1941; postgrad., U. Louisville, 1946-47. With Louisville Courier-Jour., 1946-50; commd. ensign USN, 1942, advanced through grades to capt., 1962, commdg. officer ops., pub. affairs officer, 1950-70, spl. asst. pub. affairs to chief of naval ops., 1961-64, dir. pub. affairs U.S. European Command, 1964-66, fleet pub. affairs officer U.S. Pacific Fleet, 1966-69; dir. community rels. Office Sec. Def., 1969-70; dir. pub. affairs, exec. dir. Navy League U.S., 1970-82; editor Almanac of Seapower, Summerland Key, Fla., 1983—. U.S. Editor Jane's fighting Ships, 1985—; contbg. editor Sea Power mag., 1983—. Decorated Legion of Merit (3), others. Republican. Episcopalian. Avocations: swimming, canoeing, sports. Home and Office: 919 Bay Dr Summerland Key FL 33042-4837

THOMAS, VIOLETA DE LOS ANGELES, real estate broker; b. Buenos Aires, Dec. 21, 1949; came to U.S., 1967; d. Angel and Lola (Andino) de Rios; m. Jess Thomas, Dec. 23, 1974; 1 child, Victor Justin. Student, Harvard U. and U. Buenos Aires, 1967-73. Mgr. book div. Time-Life, N.Y.C., 1985-94; real estate broker First Marin Realty, Inc., Mill Valley, Calif., 1996-97; assoc. broker Trump Corp., N.Y.C., 1997—, Brown Harris Stevens, N.Y.C., 1997—; pres. Principia Coll., Elsah, Ill., 1997—, rep. N.Y.C. Bd. dirs. Alliance Francaise, St. Louis, 1995-96, City of Tuburon, Calif., 1987-93, Art and Heritage Commn., Tiburon. Named Woman of Yr., City of Buenos Aires, 1977, Broker of Yr., Marin County and San Francisco, 1987-92. Home: 721 Fifth Ave Apt 57 C New York NY 10022 Office: 655 Madison Ave New York NY 10021-8043

THOMAS, W. DENNIS, paper company executive, former government official; b. Balt., Dec. 8, 1943; s. George Crosby and Justa Mae (Witherspoon) T.; m. Dawn Frances Haines, 1965; 1 son, William David. B.S., Frostburg State Coll., 1965; M.S.W., U. Md., 1967. Asst. to Hon. J. Glenn Beall, Jr., Washington, 1969-71, spl. asst., 1971-73, adminstrv. asst., 1973-77; adminstrv. asst. to Hon. William V. Roth, Jr., Washington, 1977-81; asst. sec. legis. affairs Dept. Treasury, Washington, 1981-83; dep. asst. to Pres. legis. affairs White House, 1983-85; ptnr. Touche Ross and Co., Inc., 1985; asst. to Pres., The White House, 1985-87; v.p. pub. affairs Internat. Paper Co., Washington, 1987—. Republican. Office: Internat Paper 1101 Pennsylvania Ave NW Washington DC 20004-2514

THOMAS, WALTER DILL, JR., forest pathologist, consultant; b. St. Louis, July 3, 1918; s. Walter D. and Helen (Gardner) T.; m. Dolores B. Thomas, Dec. 31, 1939 (div. May 1984); children: Sandra Thomas Bosworth, Arthur D; m. Nancy McCarthy, Feb. 15, 1985. BS, Colo. State U., 1939; MS, U. Minn., 1943, PhD, 1947. Diplomate Am. Bd. Forensics Examiners. Prof. plant pathology Colo. State U., Ft. Collins, 1947-55; supr. biol. research Chevron Chem. Co., Richmond, Calif., 1955-70; v.p. rsch. Nat. Resource Mgmt., Eureka, Calif., 1970-72; pres. Forest Ag Corp., Lafayette, Calif., 1972-86; coord. bd. forest stewardship Calif. Dept. Forestry and Fire Control, 1990-94; cons. in field, 1986—. Author: Field Manual of Forest and Shade Tree Diseases, 1947, Not Long Apart, 1965, Maugat Field Manual: Insects and Diseases of Shade Trees, 1995. commr. Park and Recreation Com., Ft. Collins, 1949-54, Concord, Calif., 1959-65; city forester, Ft. Collins, 1950-55. Comdr. USNR, 1944-80. Fellow AAAS (life); mem. Am. Phytopathol. Soc., Soc. Am. Foresters, Foresters Assn. (Calif. lic.), Pesticide Applicators Profl. Assn., Internat. Soc. Arboriculture, Nat. Forensic Soc., Bd. Forensics Examiners, Assn. Cons. Foresters, Am. Soc. Cons. Arborists, Soc. Tech. Comms. (sr. mem.), VFW, Elks, Lions. Republican. Avocations: swimming, writing, music. Home and Office: 2435 Heatherleaf Ln Martinez CA 94553-4337 *It is better to fail humbly while trying to succeed than to never even try.*

THOMAS, WAYNE LEE, lawyer; b. Tampa, Sept. 22, 1945; s. Willard McSwain and June Frances (Jones) T.; m. Patricia H., Mar. 16, 1968; children: Brigitte Elisabeth, Kate Adelaide. BA, U. Fla., 1967, JD cum laude, 1971. Bar: Fla., 1971, U.S. Supreme Ct., 1975, U.S. Ct. Appeals (5th cir.), 1975, U.S. Ct. Appeals (11th cir.), 1981, U.S. Ct. Claims 1976, U.S. Dist. Ct. (mid. dist.) Fla., 1973, U.S. Dist. Ct. (so. dist. trial bar) Fla., 1975; cert. mediator. Law clk. U.S. Dist. Ct. (mid. dist.) Fla., 1971-73; assoc. Trenam, Simmons, Kemker, Scharf, Barkin, Frye & O'Neill, P.A., Tampa, 1973-77, ptnr., 1978-81; founder, pres. McKay & Thomas, P.A., Tampa, 1981-89; ptnr. Carlton, Fields, Ward, Emmanuel, Smith & Cutler, P.A., 1989-95; pvt. practice, Tampa, 1995—. Mem. Fla. Bar (chmn. sect. gen. practice, 1981-83, mem. ethics com., vice chmn. unauthorized practice law com. 1994—, vice chmn. fed. practice com. 1995-96, chmn. 1996-97, mem. bd. bar examiners 1986-91, chmn. 1990-91), ABA, Hillsborough County Bar Assn. (chmn. grievance com. 1985-86), Order of Coif, Fla. Blue Key, Phi Kappa Phi, Omicron Delta Kappa. Democrat. Office: 707 N Franklin St Fl 10 Tampa FL 33602-4430

THOMAS, W(ILLIAM) BRUCE, retired steel, oil, gas company executive; b. Ripley, Mich., Oct. 25, 1926; s. William and Ethel (Collins) T.; m. Phyllis Jeanne Smith, June 25, 1950; 1 son, Robert William. BA magna cum laude, Western Mich. U., 1950; JD with distinction, U. Mich., 1952; postgrad., Law Sch., NYU, 1953. Bar: Mich. 1952. With USX Corp. (formerly U.S. Steel) and subs., various locations, 1952-91; tax atty. Oliver Iron Mining Div., Duluth, Minn., 1952-53; tax atty., tax supr., comptroller Orinoco Mining Co., N.Y.C. and Venezuela, 1953-64, dir., v.p. taxes, 1967-70, v.p., asst. treas., 1970-71, v.p., treas., 1971-75; exec. v.p., CFO, dir. USX Corp., Pitts., 1975-82, vice chmn., CFO, dir., 1982-91; bd. dirs. Chase Manhattan Corp. and Chase Manhattan Bank. Bd. dirs. Duquesne U., Allegheny Gen. Hosp.; trustee Kenyon Coll. With USAAF, 1943-45. Mem. ABA, Mich. Bar Assn., Fin. Execs. Inst., Order of Coif, Duquesne Club, Pitts. Club, Laurel Valley Golf Club, Rolling Rock Club, Allegheny Country Club, Sky Club, Links, Belleair Country Club, Phi Alpha Delta. Methodist. Home: Blackburn Rd Sewickley PA 15143 Office: USX Corp 600 Grant Building Ste 6200 Pittsburgh PA 15219-2203

THOMAS, WILLIAM ERIC, biochemistry educator; b. Nashville, Aug. 2, 1951; s. Andrew Johnson and Alphonsa Lucille (Williams) T.; children: Kimberly, Renee, Jenee, Erica, Ricky. BS in Biology, Tenn. State U., 1973, MS in Biology, 1975; PhD in Biochemistry, Meharry Med. Coll., 1980. Rsch. assoc. dept. physiology and biophysics U. Ill., Chgo., 1980; postdoctoral fellow dept. neurobiology Harvard Med. Sch., Boston, 1980-82; asst. prof. dept. physiology Meharry Med. Coll., Nashville, 1982-87; assoc. prof. dept. oral biology Ohio State U., Columbus, 1988-92; prof., chmn. dept. biology Howard U., Washington, 1992-94; prof., v.p. Miss. Valley State U., Itta Bena, 1994—; ad hoc reviewer NSF, Washington, 1989—; site visit team Minority Biomedical Rsch. Support Program, Rust Coll., Holly Springs, Miss., Tougaloo Coll., Jackson, Miss., 1989—; review panelist Dept. Edn., 1989—; vis. scientist FASEB, 1990—. Contbr. numerous papers, abstracts to sci. jours. Grantee Sandoz Pharm. Co., 1975, 77, Meharry Pre-alumni Assn., 1975, Minority Biochemical Rsch. Support Project, 1983-86, 86-87, NSF, 1983-87, 86-89, 87-92, 91-92, Southern Ctr. Elec. Engring. Edn., 1984-85, Office Naval Rsch, 1986-89, Epilepsy Found. Am., 1993-94; Klingenstein Found. fellow, 1988-91. Mem. AAAS, AAUP, Soc. Neuroscience, N.Y. Acad. Scis., Am. Aging Assn., Am. Soc. Cell Biology, Am. Assn. Dental Rsch., Sigma Xi. Democrat. Baptist. Avocations: reading, racquet ball, fishing. Office: Miss Valley State U 14000 Highway 82 W #7269 Itta Bena MS 38941-1400

THOMAS, WILLIAM GERAINT, museum administrator; b. Columbo, Sri Lanka, June 27, 1931; came to U.S., 1941; s. Cecil James and Iris Katharine

(Evans) T.; m. Maria Alcalde, Jan. 2, 1976; 1 child, Laura. BA, U. Calif., Berkeley, 1952. Reporter, editor San Francisco Chronicle, 1952-64; asst. to mayor City of San Francisco, 1964-66; chief cons. majority caucus Calif. State Assembly, Sacramento, 1966-68; adminstrv. asst. U.S. Congressman Phillip Burson, Washington, 1968-70; cons. interior com. U.S. Ho. of Reps., Washington, 1970-72; ptnr. Thomas & Iovino, San Francisco, 1972-78; asst. regional dir. Nat. Park Svc., San Francisco, 1978-89; supt. San Francisco Maritime NHP, 1989—. Mem. Nat. Dem. Club; bd. dirs. Nat. Libery Ship Meml., 1978-80. Sgt. U.S. Army, 1952-54, Korea. Mem. Nat. Maritime Mus. Assn., Nat. Maritime Hist. Soc., Press Club of San Francisco (pres. 1973-74, Best News Story 1963). Episcopalian. Avocation: sailing. Office: San Francisco Maritime Bldg 201 Ft Mason San Francisco CA 94123

THOMAS, WILLIAM GRIFFITH, lawyer; b. Washington, Nov. 1, 1939; s. Henry Phineas and Margaret Wilson (Carr) T.; m. Suzanne Campbell Foster, June 7, 1960. Student Williams Coll., 1957-59, Richmond Coll., 1960; J.D., U. Richmond, 1963. Bar: Va. 1963. Mem., pres. Hazel & Thomas, P.C., Alexandria, Va., 1987—; Va. Electric and Power Co., Richmond. Sec., Va. Dem. Com., 1968-70, chmn., 1970-72. Mem. ABA, Va. State Bar Assn., Alexandria Bar Assn., Am. Law Inst., Am. Coll. Real Estate Lawyers. Home: 200 S Fairfax St # 14 Alexandria VA 22314-3331 Office: Hazel & Thomas 510 King St Ste 200 Alexandria VA 22314-3132

THOMAS, WILLIAM HARRISON, professional football player; b. Amarillo, Tex., Aug. 13, 1968. Student, Tex. A&M U., 1987-91. Linebacker Phila. Eagles, 1991—. Selected to Pro Bowl, 1995. Office: Philadelphia Eagles 3501 S Broad St Philadelphia PA 19148-5249*

THOMAS, WILLIAM KERNAHAN, federal judge; b. Columbus, Ohio, Feb. 15, 1911; m. Dorothy Good, 1936 (dec.); children: John R., Richard G., Stephen G., Cynthia G. B.A., Ohio State U., 1932, LLB, JD, 1935. Bar: Ohio 1935. Practiced in Cleve., until 1950; judge Ct. Common Pleas, Geauga County, Ohio, 1950-53, Ct. of Common Pleas, Cuyahoga County, Cleve., 1953-66; now judge U.S. Dist. Ct., No. Dist. Ohio, Eastern div., Cleve., sr. judge, 1981—. Served with USNR, 1944-46. Mem. Common Pleas Judges Assn. (pres. 1959-60), Nat. Conf. State Trial Judges (chmn. sociopathic offender com. 1963-66), 6th Circuit Dist. Judges Assn. (pres. 1981-82), Jud. Conf. U.S. (com. on adminstrn. bankruptcy system 1968-71, com. on operation of jury system in U.S. 1971-77, subcom. on fair trial free press 1977—), Ohio State Bar Assn. (Ohio Bar medal 1994). Office: US Dist Ct Key Tower 127 Public Sq Fl 33 Cleveland OH 44114-1216*

THOMAS, WILLIAM LEROY, geography educator, cruise lecturer; b. Long Beach, Calif., Mar. 18, 1920; s. William LeRoy and Margaret Lucile (Young) T.; m. Mildred Phyllis Smith, Apr. 10, 1942 (div.); children: Barbara Jean, Lawrence Charles, Virginia Jane, Margaret Joan, Pamela June; m. Loida Ayson Aquino, Aug. 29, 1964 (dec.); children: William John Aquino, Lloyd Aquino; m. Rosalinda Zuñiga Valencia, July 4, 1986; 1 adopted child, Don Valencia. A.B., UCLA, 1941, M.A., 1948; Ph.D., Yale U., 1955. Instr. geography Rutgers U., 1947-50; research asst. S.E. Asia studies Yale U., 1949-50; asst. dir. research Wenner-Gren Found. Anthrop. Research, N.Y.C., 1950-57; asst. to assoc. prof. geography U. Calif., Riverside, 1957-63; prof. anthropology and geography Calif. State U., Hayward, 1963-71, chmn. dept. anthropology and geography, 1963-66, prof. geography and Southeast Asian studies, 1971-91, prof. emeritus, 1983—, chmn. dept. geography, 1971-74; assoc. dir. Ctr. for Filipino Studies Calif. State U., 1990-91; v.p. rsch. and devel. Heritage Tours, Ltd., Oakland, Calif., 1981-83; v.p. rsch. and devel., chmn. bd. Geo-Expdns. Internat., Inc., 1981-83; pres. Thomas Opportunity Program Services, 1983-90; vis. prof. La. State U., spring 1966, U. Hawaii, summer 1966, U. Wis., fall 1966, U. Toronto, Canada, fall 1968, 69, Georgetown U., 1992; vis. research assoc. Inst. Philippine Culture, Ateneo de Manila U., Quezon City, 1970, 76-77; Fulbright lectr. Centre for Asian Studies, U. Western Australia, Nedlands, 1974; Fulbright sr. research scholar Mariano Marcos State U., Batac, Ilocos Norte, Philippines, 1984-85; organizer internat. symposium Man's Role in Changing the Face of the Earth, Princeton, N.J., 1955; cons. Nat. Acad. Scis.-NRC, in orgn. of sect. 6th Nat. Conf. UNESCO, 1957; mem. tech. cons. group Calif. Pub. Outdoor Recreation Plan Com., 1958-60; geog. cons. Pacific Missile Range, Pt. Mugu, Calif., 1958-60; organizer geography sect. 10th Pacific Sci. Congress, 1961; foreign field research, Philippines, 1961-62, Philippines, Thailand, Burma, 1970, Australia, Indonesia, 1974, Philippines, 1976-77, 84-85, 86, French Polynesia, 1992, 93, Thailand, Malaysia, Indonesia, Singapore, 1993, Indonesia, 1994, 95 Northern Australia, 1995; mem. ad hoc com. on geography Nat. Acad. Scis.-NRC, 1963-65, cons. effects of herbicides in, Vietnam, 1972-74; chmn. Asian studies council Calif. State Colls., 1971-72; mem. com. internat. symposium earth as transformed by human action Clark U., Worcester, Mass., 1987; invited speaker V.I. Vernadsky anniversary symposium USSR Acad. Scis., Leningrad, Kiev, Moscow, 1988; guest lectr. Cunard Line 'Vistafjord' cruise, Feb. 1992, Royal Viking Line 'Sun' Cruise, 1992, Paquet Cruise Company 'Ocean Pearl' cruise, 1993, Cunard Line 'Sagafjord' cruise, 1993, Seven Seas Cruise Line 'Song of Flower' cruise, 1993-94, Cunard Line 'Vistafjord' Cruise, 1994, Crystal Cruises 'Crystal Harmony' Cruise, 1994, Regency Cruises 'Regent Sea' Cruise, 1994, Orient Line 'Marco Polo' Cruise, 1994, Holland-Am. Line 'Rotterdam' Grand World Voyage Cruise, 1995, Orient Line 'Marco Polo' Cruise, 1995, Royal Caribbean Cruises on Sun Viking, Far East, 1996. Author: (with J. F. Embree) Ethnic Groups of Northern Southeast Asia, 1950, Land, Man and Culture in Mainland Southeast Asia, 1957, (with J.E. Spencer) Cultural Geography, 1969, Asia, East by South, 2d edit, 1971, Introducing Cultural Geography, 1973, 2d edit., 1978; Editor: (with Anna M. Pikells) International Directory of Anthropological Institutions, 1953, Yearbook of Anthropology, 1955, Current Anthropology, 1956, Man's Role in Changing the Face of the Earth, 1956, Am. Anthrop. Assn. Bull, 1958-60, Man, Time, and Space in Southern California, 1959;paperback series Man-Environment System in The Late 20th Century, 1969-75. Moderator United Ch. Hayward, 1988-90. 1st lt. C.E., AUS, 1942-45. Mem. Assn. Asian Studies, Asian Studies on Pacific Coast (chmn. standing com. 1979-80, conf. chmn. 1980), Pacific Sci. Assn. (U.S. mem. sci. com. on geography), Assn. Am. Geographers (Pacific Coast regional councilor 1971-74, citation for meritorious contbn. to geography 1961), Assn. Pacific Coast Geographers (v.p. 1976-77, pres. 1977-78, Disting. Svc. award 1988), Calif. Geog. Soc. (pres. 1967-68, Outstanding Educator award 1986). Democrat. Address: 307 Shalako Dr Oakdale CA 95361-9683

THOMAS, WILLIAM MARSHALL, congressman; b. Wallace, Idaho, Dec. 6, 1941; s. Virgil and Gertrude Thomas; m. Sharon Lynn Hamilton, Jan. 1968; children: Christopher, Amelia. B.A., San Francisco State U., 1963, M.A., 1965. Mem. faculty dept. Am. govt. Bakersfield (Calif.) Coll., 1965-74, prof., 1965-74; mem. Calif. State Assembly, 1974-78, 96th-105th Congress from 18th, now 21st Calif. Dist., 1979—; vice chmn. of House Task Force on Campaign Fin. Reform; mem. Ho. of Reps. Ways and Means Com.; chmn. Com. on House Oversight, Ways & Means Health Subcom.; mem. Ways & Means subcom on Trade; mem. del. to Soviet Union, by Am. Council Young Polit. Leaders, 1977; chmn. Kern County Republican Central Com., 1972-74; mem. Calif. Rep. Com., 1972-80; del. Republican Party Nat. Conv., 1980, 84, 88; mem. Rep. Leader's Task Force on Health Care Reform. Office: Ho of Reps 2208 Rayburn Ho Office Bldg Washington DC 20515

THOMAS, WYNN P., art director, production designer. Art dir.: (films) Beat Street, 1984, She's Gotta Have It, 1986; prodn. designer: (films) Eddie Murphy Raw, 1987, School Daze, 1988, Do the Right Thing, 1989, Mo' Better Blues, 1990, The Five Heartbeats, 1991, Jungle Fever, 1991, Malcolm X, 1992, A Bronx Tale, 1993, Crooklyn, 1994. Office: care Art Directors Guild 11365 Ventura Blvd Ste 315 Studio City CA 91604-3148 ADDRESS: 535 W 110th St # 15-F New York NY 10025*

THOMASCH, ROGER PAUL, lawyer; b. N.Y.C., Nov. 7, 1942; s. Gordon J. and Margaret (Molloy) T.; children: Laura Leigh, Paul Butler. BA, Coll. William and Mary, 1964; LLB, Duke U., 1967. Bar: Conn. 1967, Colo. 1974. Assoc. atty. Cummings & Lockwood, Stamford, Conn., 1967-70; trial atty. U.S. Dept. Justice, Washington, 1970-73; ptnr. Roath & Brega, Denver, 1975-87; mng. ptnr. Denver office of Ballard, Spahr, Andrews & Ingersoll, 1987—; vis. assoc. prof. of law Drake U. Sch. Law, Des Moines, 1973-74; frequent lectr. in field, U.S. and Can.; adj. faculty mem. U. Denver Coll. Law, 1976-80. Recipient Leland Forrest Outstanding Prof. award, Drake U. Sch. Law, 1973. Fellow Colo. Bar Found.; mem. ABA, Colo. Bar Assn., Denver Country Club, Univ. Club, Denver Athletic Club. Office: Ballard Spahr Andrews & Ingersoll 1225 17th St Denver CO 80202-5534

THOMASHOW, BYRON MARTIN, pulmonary physician; b. Bklyn., Apr. 19, 1949; s. Alexander Irwin and Emma (Zaslow) T.; m. Laurie Jo Kasoff, July 2, 1972; children: Samantha, Michael. BA, Columbia U., 1970, MD, 1974. Diplomate Nat. Bd. Med. Examiners, Am. Bd. Internal Medicine, subspecialty in pulmonary medicine. Med. intern Roosevelt Hosp., N.Y.C., 1974-75, med. resident, 1975-77, med. chief resident, pulmonary fellow, 1977-78; sr. pulmonary fellow Harlem Hosp., N.Y.C., 1978-79; asst. attending physician Presbyn. Hosp., Columbia Presbyn. Med. Ctr., N.Y.C., 1979-90, assoc. attending physician, 1991—; physician in charge Tbc Clinic Presbyn. Hosp., N.Y.C., 1983-90, attending physician Chest Clinic, 1979—; asst. prof. clin. medicine Columbia U., N.Y.C., 1979-90, assoc. clin. prof. medicine, 1990—; lectr. Englewood Hosp., 1988, ACP, 1986-92, Harlem Hosp., 1984, 93, Roosevelt Hosp., 1978, 86, 87, 88, 91, Columbia Presbyn. Hosp., 1980, 82-88, 90, 92, 93, 94, 95, 96, N.Y. Trudeau Soc., 1982, Columbia U. Coll. Physicians and Surgeons, 1980-96, Med. House staff Pulmonary Bd. Rev., 1980—, Emergency Med. Course, 1981—; mem. Presbyn. Hosp. Med. Bd., 1995—; med. co-dir. emphysema lung reduction program Columbia Presbyn. Med. Ctr., 1995—. Stony Wold-Herbert Fund fellowship grantee, 1978-79. Fellow ACP, Am. Coll. Chest Physicians; mem. NIH (steering com. 1997), Am. Thoracic Soc., N.Y. Trudeau Soc. (exec. com. 1992-94, chmn. membership com. 1992-94), Soc. Practitioners (exec. com. 1994—, chmn. quality care com. 1995—). Office: 161 Fort Washington Ave New York NY 10032-3713

THOMAS-MYERS, SUSAN JANE, executive sales representatives group; b. Marin County, Calif., Sept. 12, 1967; d. William Richard and Jane Dunning (Lasher) Thomas; m. Collin Allen Myers, Aug. 26, 1995. Student gen. edn., Mesa Coll., 1985-87; BA in Liberal Arts and Scis., San Diego State U., 1990. Asst buyer Robinson's Dept. Store, L.A., 1990-91; buyer Helen's Cycles Stores, Santa Monica, 1991-93; pres. Thomas Promotional Group, Manhattan Beach, Calif., 1993—; coord. sponsorship Manhattan Beach (Calif.) Grand Prix, 1995. Named Rookie of Yr. J&B Importers, Washington, 1993. Lutheran. Avocations: travel, cooking, biking, reading.

THOMASON, SCOTT, automobile executive; b. 1953. Prin. Thomason Toyota, Gladstone; pres. Dee A. Thomason Ford Co., Gladstone, 1974—, Thomason Nissan Inc., Gladstone, 1990—, Heritage Auto Ctr. Inc., Kirkland, Wash., 1991—, Thomason Auto Group, Gladsone. Office: Thomason Auto Group 19405 McLoughlin Blvd Gladstone OR 97027-2621*

THOMASSEN, PAULINE F., medical and surgical nurse; b. Cleve., Jan. 19, 1939; d. Henry Clifford and Mabel Pauline (Hill) Nichols; m. Ruben Thomassen, Nov. 10, 1979; children: Rhonda, Terry, Diana, Philipp, Jody, Barbara. AA in Nursing, So. Colo. State Coll., 1974, BA in Psychology with distinction, 1975; BSN magna cum laude, Seattle Pacific U., 1986. RN, Wash. Staff nurse III orthopedic unit, preceptor orientation RNs and student RNs Swedish Hosp. Med. Ctr., Seattle, 1975—; mem. planning task force and faculty National Nurses Conference, The Nurse and Spinal Surgery, Cleve. Author: Spinal Disease and Surgical Interventions. Mem. Nat. Assn. Orthop. Nurses.

THOMASSON, PATSY, federal official. BA, Henderson State U.; MA, U. Mo. Staff asst. to congressman Wilbur D. Mills U.S. House Reps., Washington, Ark., 1969-71, 72-74; exec. dir. Dem. Party Ark.; assoc. adminstr. Doctors Hosp., Little Rock; pres. So. Mgmt. Assn.; exec. v.p., pres. Phoenix Group; spl. asst. to pres., dir. Office adminstrn. Mgmt. and Adminstrn., Washington, 1993—; dep. asst. to the pres., dep. dir. Washington. Overseer Coord. Campaign Ark. Mem. Am. Assn. State Highway and Transp. Officials. Office: The White House Office of Presidential Personnel 1600 Pennsylvania Ave NW Washington DC 20503-0001*

THOMLINSON, RALPH, demographer, educator; b. St. Louis, Feb. 12, 1925; s. Ralph and Ora Lee (Barr) T.; m. Margaret Mary Willits, Dec. 21, 1946; children: Elizabeth Barr, William Lockwood. BA, Oberlin Coll., 1948; postgrad., U. Pitts., 1943-44, Harvard U., 1948; MA, Yale U., 1949; PhD, Columbia U., 1960. Asst. town planner Montclair, N.J., 1949-50; asst. city planner Paterson, N.J., 1950; research asst. Bur. Applied Social Research, N.Y.C., 1952; med. statistics asst. actuarial dept. Met. Life Ins. Co., N.Y.C., 1952-53; instr. statistics and population U. Wis., 1953-56; instr. sociology and anthropology Denison U., Granville, Ohio, 1956-59; asst. prof. sociology Calif. State U., L.A., 1959-62; assoc. prof. Calif. State U., 1962-65, prof., 1965-88, prof. emeritus, 1988—, chmn. dept. sociology, 1967-69; vis. prof. sociology U. Alta., Can., 1966; vis. prof. biostatistics U. N.C., Chapel Hill, 1972-73; demographic adviser Inst. Population Studies, Chulalongkorn U., Bangkok, Thailand, 1969-71; cons. Nat. Family Planning Program, Thailand, Census of Thailand, 1970-71, Population/Food Fund, 1977-79, also various research centers abroad, 1969-73; cons. to fourteen book pubs., 1965—; field assoc. Population Coun., N.Y.C., 1969-71; rsch. adviser Ctr. for Rsch. and Demographic Studies, Rabat, Morocco, 1972-73; acad. visitor Population Investigation Com., London Sch. Econs., 1973; vis. scholar Nat. Inst. Demographic Studies, Paris, 1973-74. Author: A Mathematical Model for Migration, 1960, Population Dynamics, 2d edit, 1976, Sociological Concepts and Research, 1965, Demographic Problems, 2d edit, 1975, Urban Structure, 1969, Thailand's Population, 1971, (with others) The Methodology of the Longitudinal Study of Social, Economic and Demographic Change, 1971; editor: (with Visid Prachuabmoh) The Potharam Study, 1971; adv. editor: Sociol. Abstracts, 1963-67, Sociology Quar, 1978-84; cons. editor: As-Soukan, 1972-73; assoc. editor: Pacific Sociol. Rev, 1976-83; Sociol. Perspective, 1983-85; chmn. editorial bd. Calif. Sociologist, 1981-84; cons.: Dictionary of Modern Sociology, 1969; contbr. to: Dictionary of Demography, 5 vols., 1985-86; books, profl. jours. Served with AUS, 1943-45, ETO. Mem. Population Assn. Am., Internat. Union for Sci. Study Population, Am. Sociol. Assn., Internat. Assn. Survey Statisticians, Assn. Asian Studies. Home: 712 Coronado Ln Foster City CA 94404-2925

THOMOPULOS, GREGS G., consulting engineering company executive; b. Benin City, Nigeria, May 16, 1942; s. Aristoteles and Christiana E. (Ogiamien) T.; m. Patricia Walker, Sept. 4, 1966 (div. 1974); 1 child, Lisa; m. Mettie L. Williams, May 28, 1976; children: Nicole, Euphemia. BSCE with highest distinction, U. Kans., 1965; MS in Structural Engring., U. Calif., Berkeley, 1966; PhD (hon.), Teikyo Marycrest U., 1996. Sr. v.p. internat. div. Stanley Cons., Inc., Muscatine, Iowa, 1978-84, sr. v.p. project divsn., 1984-87; pres. Stanley Consultants, Inc., Muscatine, Iowa, 1987—; exec. v.p. SC Co., Inc., Muscatine, 1992—, also bd. dirs.; chmn., CEO Stanley Environ., Inc., Chgo., 1991—, also bd. dirs.; chmn., CEO SC Power Devel., Inc., 1992—; chmn., CEO Stanley Design-Build, Inc., 1995—; bd. dirs. Stanley Cons., Inc., Muscatine. Bd. dirs. Goodwill Industries Ea. Iowa, 1987—, pres., 1992-94; mem. adv. bd. U. Iowa Coll. Engring. Fellow ASCE, Am. Cons. Engring. Coun.; mem. NSPE, 33 Club (pres. 1987), Rotary. Presbyterian. Avocations: tennis, computers, music. Home: 1002 Estron St Iowa City IA 52246-4602 Office: Stanley Cons Inc 225 Iowa Ave Muscatine IA 52761-3730

THOMPSON, ALICE M. BROUSSARD, special education administrator; b. Opelousas, La., May 15, 1950; d. Melvin and Roseanna (Joseph) Broussard; m. Samuel Joe Thompson; 1 child, Tameka Rose Thompson. BS in Vocat. Home Econs., McNeese State U., 1973; MEd in Spl. Edn., U. Mo., St. Louis, 1993; cert. in mid-mgmt., Tex. So. U., 1993; completed studies, Harvard U., 1995. Food svc. supr. Parkland Meml. Hosp., Dallas, 1982-83; tchr. home econs. Milw. pub. Schs., 1984-85; tchr. career lab. Ft. Bend Ind. Sch., Sugarland, Tex., 1985-87; tchr. home econs. Epworth Pvt. Sch., Webster Grove, Mo., 1988-91; tchr. resource math. Ft. Bend Ind. Sch. Dist., Sugarland, 1991-92, coord. spl. edn., 1993—; cons. Inclusion, Tex., 1993; coord. Inclusion Adv. Bd., Sugarland, 1993—; mem. Inclusion Works Adv. Bd., Austin, 1994—. Mem. NAFE, ASCD, Coun. for Exceptional Children, Nat. Assn. Black Educators, Alpha Kappa Alpha (dean of pledges 1973). Avocations: reading, tennis, traveling. Home: 2811 Plantation Wood Ln Missouri City TX 77459-4253 Office: Ft Bend Ind Sch Dist PO Box 1004 Sugar Land TX 77487-1004

THOMPSON, ANNA BLANCHE, retired educator; b. Ft. Worth, Oct. 8, 1914; d. George Lewis and Gula Gertrude (Cook) Turnbow; m. Jess Lee, May 27, 1939; children: Jess Lee II, Mary Ann Thompson Archbold. BA in Edn., Ariz. State U., Tempe, 1935; postgrad., U. Ariz., 1940, U. Hawaii, 1964, Pepperdine U., 1967. Tchr. Parke (Ariz.) Elem. Sch., 1935-40; tchr. music Parker High Sch., 1940-42; tchr. Scottsdale (Ariz.) Elem. Sch., 1948-71; tchr. U. Hawaii, Laie, 1971-72; tchr. U. Hawaii, 1972-79, ret., 1979. Mem. edn. bd. Phoenix Women's Club, 1983-84; pres. Ariz. Res. Officers Ladies, Phoenix, 1982-84, state pres., 1986-87; pres. Ladies of the Ribbon, Phoenix, 1987-90, Tempe Garden Club, 1987-88. Recipient Mus. plaque Phoenix Symphony Symphonette, 1982-83, Cert. of Appreciation, St. Luke's Hosp. Aux., 1985, Cert. of Appreciation, Mil. Order of World Wars, 1989. Mem. Ariz. Res. Officers Ladies (state sec. 1990—), Tri-City Angels of Ariz. (pres. 1984—), Collectors Club Am. (nat. pres. 1987—), Ikebana Internat., AAUW (historian Tempe chpt. 1987-90), Delta Kappa Gamma (pres. Phoenix chpt. 1974-76, 88-90, parliamentarian 1990—). Avocations: needlepoint, travel. Home: 533 E Fairmont Dr Tempe AZ 85282-3722

THOMPSON, ANNE ELISE, federal judge; b. Phila., July 8, 1934; d. Leroy Henry and Mary Elise (Jackson) Jenkins; m. William H. Thompson, June 19, 1965; children: William H., Sharon A. BA, Howard U., 1955, LLB, 1964; MA, Temple U., 1957. Bar: D.C. bar 1964, N.J. bar 1966. Staff atty. Office of Solicitor, Dept. Labor, Chgo., 1964-65; asst. dep. public defender Trenton, N.J., 1967-70; mcpl. prosecutor Lawrence Twp., Lawrenceville, N.J., 1970-72; mcpl. ct. judge Trenton, 1972-75; prosecutor Mercer County, Mercer County, Trenton, 1975-79; judge U.S. Dist. Ct. N.J., Trenton, 1979—, now chief judge; vice chmn. Mercer County Criminal Justice Planning Com., 1972; mem. com. criminal practice N.J. Supreme Ct., 1975-79, mem. com. mcpl. cts., 1972-75; v.p. N.J. County Prosecutors Assn., 1978-79; chmn. juvenile justice com. Nat. Dist. Attys. Assn., 1978-79. Del. Democratic Nat. Conv., 1972. Recipient Assn. Black Women Lawyers award, 1976, Disting. Service award Nat. Dist. Attys. Assn., 1979, Gene Carte Meml. award Am. Criminal Justice Assn., 1980, Outstanding Leadership award N.J. County Prosecutors Assn., 1980, John Mercer Langston Outstanding Alumnus award Howard U. Law Sch., 1981; also various service awards; certs. of appreciation. Mem. Am. Bar Assn., Fed. Bar Assn., N.J. Bar Assn., Mercer County Bar Assn. Democrat. Office: US Dist Ct US Courthouse 402 E State St Trenton NJ 08608-1507*

THOMPSON, ANNIE FIGUEROA, academic director, educator; b. Río Piedras, P.R., June 7, 1941; d. Antonio Figueroa-Colón and Ana Isabel Laugier; m. Donald P. Thompson, Jan. 23, 1972; 1 child, John Anthony. BA, Baylor U., 1962; MSLS, U. So. Calif., 1965; AMD, Fla. State U., 1978, PhD, 1980. Educator Mayan Sch., Guatemala City, Guatemala, 1962-63; cataloger libr. system U. P.R., Río Piedras, 1965-67, head music libr., 1967-81, assoc. prof. librarianship, 1981-85; dir. grad. sch. libr. info. sci. U. P.R., Rio Piedras, 1986-93, prof., 1986-96; ret., 1996. Author: An Annotated Bibliography About Music in Puerto Rico, 1975; co-author: Music and Dance in Puerto Rico from the Age of Columbus to Modern Times, An Annotated Bibliography, 1991; contbr. articles to profl. jours.; performed song recitals Inst. of P.R. Culture and U. P.R. Artist Series, 1974-78; soloist with P.R. Symphony Orch., San Juan, 1978; performed in opera, on radio and TV, San Juan, 1968-81;. Sec. P.R. Symphony Orch League, San Juan, 1982-84; mem. pub. libr. adv. com. Adminstrn. for Devel. of Arts and Culture, P.R., 1982-84, Pub. Libr. Adv. Bd., 1989-94. Recipient Lauro a la Instrucción Bibliotecaria Sociedad de Bibliotecarios de P.R., 1985, Lauro a la Bibliografía Puertorriqueña, 1993. Mem. ALA, Assn. Libr. and Info. Sci., San Juan Rotary, Sociedad de Bibliotecarios de P.R. (pres. 1994-96), Music Libr. Assn., Sigma Delta Kappa, Mu Phi Epsilon, Beta Phi Mu. Episcopalian. Home: N-64 Acadia St Park Gardens Rio Piedras San Juan PR 00926

THOMPSON, ANNIE LAURA, foreign language educator; b. Henderson, Tenn., July 8, 1937; d. Wesley Sylvester and Letha Irene (Jones) T.; m. Edward L. Patterson, June 7, 1980. BA, U. Ala., 1959; MA, Duke U., 1961; PhD, Tulane U., 1973. Instr. Spanish lang. U. Miss., Oxford, 1960-64; instr. Auburn (Ala.) U., 1964-66; tchg. asst. Tulane U., New Orleans, 1966-70; prof. Spanish lang. Delgado C.C., New Orleans, 1970—; instr. Spanish for Physicians and Med. Persons Tulane U., La. State U. Med. Eye Ctr., Ochsner Clinic and Hosp. Author: Religious Elements in the Quijote, 1960, The Attempt of Spanish Intellectuals to Create a New Spain, 1930-36, 1973, The Generation of 1898: Intellectual Politicians; asst. editor The Crusader, 1961-64. Rep. candidate for gov. State of La., 1991, 95, for 1st Dist. U.S. Congress, 1992; alt. mem. La. Coastal Commn., 1984—; del. Women's State Rep. Conv., 1987, La. State Rep. Conv., 1990, 93; active Women for Better La., 1986-89, La. Coastal Adv. Coun., 1988, Pan Am. Commn., 1992-95; v.p. pub. rels. Alliance for Good Govt., 1990. Recipient Outstanding Tchr. award Delgado Coll. Student Govt. Assn., 1974; Woodoow Wilson fellow, 1959-60; NDEA fellow, 1968-69. Mem. Pachyderm Club, Women's Rep. Club, Phi Beta Kappa, Phi Alpha Theta, Sigma Delta Pi. Republican. Mem. Ch. of Christ. Home: PO Box 24399 New Orleans LA 70184-4399 Office: Delgado Coll Isaac Delgado Hall 113W-1 615 City Park Ave New Orleans LA 70119-4326

THOMPSON, ANTHONY RICHARD, electrical engineer, astronomer; b. Hull, Yorkshire, Eng., Apr. 7, 1931; came to U.S., 1957; s. George and Ada Mary (Laybourn) T.; m. Sheila Margaret Press, Oct. 12, 1963; 1 child, Sarah Louise. BSc in Physics with honors, U. Manchester, Eng., 1952, PhD, 1955. Engr. E.M.I. Electronics Ltd., Feltham, Eng., 1956-57; rsch. fellow Coll. Obs. Harvard U., Cambridge, Mass., 1957-62; sr. rsch. assoc. Radio Astronomy Inst. Stanford (Calif.) U., 1962-72; head electronics divsn., VLA and VLBA projects Nat. Radio Astronomy Obs., Charlottesville, Va., 1973-92, dep. head Ctrl. Electronics Lab., 1993—; vis. sr. rsch. fellow Owens Valley Radio Obs., Calif. Inst. Tech., Pasadena, 1966-72; mem. Com. on Radio Frequencies NAS, Washington, 1980-91; sec. Interunion Commn. on Frequency Allocations for Radio Astronomy and Space Sci., 1982-88, mem., 1991—; guest lectr. in radio astronomy Ukrainian Acad. Sci., 1988. Prin. author: (monograph) Interferometry and Synthesis in Radio Astronomy, 1986; contbr. articles to Astrophys. Jour., Astron. Jour., Proceedings of IEEE, Sci., Radiosci. Fellow IEEE; mem. Internat. Telecom. Union (radiocommunication sector, chmn. working group on radio astronomy U.S. Study group 7 1978—), Am. Astron. Soc., Internat. Astron. Union. Achievements include research in astronomy and contributions to system design of the VLA and VLB array; design of instruments: frequency coordination for radio astronomy. Office: Nat Radio Astronomy Obs 520 Edgemont Rd Charlottesville VA 22903-2454

THOMPSON, ANTHONY WAYNE, metallurgist, educator, consultant; b. Burbank, Calif., Mar. 6, 1940; s. William Lyman and Mary Adelaide (Nisbet) T.; m. Mary Ruth Cummings, Aug. 24, 1963; children: Campbell Lyman, Michael Anthony. BS, Stanford U., 1962; MS, U. Wash., 1965; PhD, MIT, 1970. Research engr. Jet Propulsion Lab., Pasadena, Calif., 1962-63; mem. tech. staff Sandia Labs., Livermore, Calif., 1970-73, Rockwell Sci. Ctr., Thousand Oaks, Calif., 1973-77; assoc. prof. Carnegie Mellon U., Pitts., 1977-79, prof., 1980-94, dept. head, 1987-90; staff scientist Lawrence Berkeley Lab., Berkeley, Calif., 1994—; vis. scientist U. Cambridge, Eng., 1983, Risø, Denmark, 1987, U. Calif., 1991; cons. Sandia Labs., 1977—, GE, 1988—. Editor: Work Hardening, 1976, Metall. Transactions, 1983-88; coeditor: Hydrogen in Metals, 1974, Hydrogen Conf. Proc., 1976, 81, 89, 94; mem. editl. bd. Internat. Metals Revs., 1980-88; contbr. articles to profl. jours. Overseas fellow Churchill Coll. Cambridge U., 1982. Fellow Am. Soc. Metals; mem. AAAS, AIME, Sigma Xi. Democrat. Clubs: Sierra, Nat. Model R.R. Assn. Home: 2942 Linden Ave Berkeley CA 94705-2328 Office: Lawrence Berkeley Lab Material Sci Divsn Berkeley CA 94720

THOMPSON, ARLENE RITA, nursing educator; b. Yakima, Wash., May 17, 1933; d. Paul James and Esther Margaret (Danroth) T. BS in Nursing, U. Wash., 1966, Masters in Nursing, 1970, postgrad., 1982—. Staff nurse Univ. Teaching Hosp., Seattle, 1966-69; mem. nursing faculty U. Wash. Sch. Nurses, Seattle, 1971-73; critical care nurse Virginia Mason Hosp., Seattle, 1973—; educator Seattle Pacific U. Sch. Nursing, 1981—; nurse legal cons. nursing edn., critical care nurse. Contbr. articles to profl. jours. USPHS grantee, 1969; nursing scholar Virginia Mason Hosp., 1965. Mem. Am. Assn. Critical Care Nurses (cert.), Am. Nurses Assn., Am. Heart Assn., Nat. League Nursing, Sigma Theta Tau, Alpha Tau Omega. Republican. Presbyterian. Avocations: sewing, swimming, jogging, bicycle riding, hiking. Home: 2320 W Newton St Seattle WA 98199-4115 Office: Seattle Pacific U 3307 3rd Ave W Seattle WA 98119-1940

THOMPSON, BARBARA STORCK, state official; b. McFarland, Wis., Oct. 15, 1924; d. John Casper and Marie Ann (Kassabaum) Storck; m. Glenn T. Thompson, July 1, 1944; children—David C., James T. B.S., Wis. State U., 1956; M.S., U. Wis., 1959, Ph.D., 1969; L.H.D. (hon.), Carroll Coll., 1974. Tchr. pub. schs. West Dane County, Mt. Horeb, Wis., 1944-56; instr. Green County Tchrs. Coll., Monroe, Wis., 1956-57; coordinator curriculum Monroe Pub. Schs., 1957-60; instr. U. Wis., Platteville, 1960; supr. schs. Waukesha County Schs., Wis., 1960-63; supt. schs. Waukesha County Schs., 1963-65; prin. Fairview Elem. Schs., Brookfield, Wis., 1962-64; adminstrv. cons. Wis. Dept. Pub. Instrn., Madison, 1964-72; state coordinator Wis. Dept. Pub. Instrn., 1971-72; instr. U. Wis., Madison and Green Bay, 1972; supt. pub. instrn. Madison, State of Wis., 1973-81; mem. Wis. State Bd. Vocat. Edn., 1973-81, Wis. Edn. Comm. Bd., 1973-81. Author: A Candid Discussion of Critical Issues, 1975; Mem. editorial bd.: The Education Digest, 1975—; Contbr. articles to profl. jours. Mem. White House Conf. Children, 1970, Gov.'s Com. State Conf. Children and Youth, 1969-70, Manpower Council, 1973-81; bd. dirs. Vocational, Tech. and Adult Edn., 1973-81, Ednl. Communications, 1973-81, Higher Edn. Aids, 1973-81, Agy. Instructional TV, 1975-81; mem. nat. panel on SAT score decline; bd. regents U. Wis., 1973-81. Recipient State Conservation award Madison Lions CLub, 1956; Waukesha Freeman award, 1961. Mem. Nat. Council Adminstrv. Women in Edn. (named Woman of Year 1974), Nat. Council State Cons. in Elementary Edn. (pres. 1974-75), Wis. Assn. Sch. Dist. Adminstrs., Assn. Supervision and Curriculum Devel., Wis. Assn. Supervision and Curriculum Devel., Southwestern Wis. Assn. Supervision and Curriculum Devel., Southeastern Wis. Assn. Supervision and Curriculum Devel. (mem. exec. council 1972-73), Dept. Elementary Sch. Prins., Wis. Elementary Sch. Prins. Assn., NEA, Wis. Edn. Assn. (pres. local chpt. 1970-71); life mem. So. Wis. Edn. Assn., Wis. Ednl. Research Assn., Dept. Elementary-Kindergarten-Nursery Edn., Assn. Childhood Edn. Internat., Assn. Childhood Edn., Council Chief State Sch. Officers, Edn. Commn. of States, Nat. Council State Cons. in Elementary Edn. (pres. 1974-75), Am. Assn. Sch. Dist. Adminstrs. (chmn. policy com. 1963-81), Delta Kappa Gamma. Office: 204 3rd St W Bradenton FL 34205-8856

THOMPSON, BENNIE, professional football player. Student, Grambling State. Safety Kansas City Chiefs, Mo., 1989-94; with Cleveland Browns, 1994—. Played in Pro Bowl, 1991. Office: Cleveland Browns/Baltimore Ravens 11001 Owings Mills Blvd Owings Mills MD 21117-2857*

THOMPSON, BENNIE G., congressman; b. Bolton, Miss.. BA Polit. Sci., Tougaloo Coll.; MS Ednl. Adminstrn., Jackson State U., Miss.; grad., U. So. Miss. Alderman Bolton, Miss., 1970-74, mayor, 1974-80; supr. dist. 2 Hinds County Bd., Miss., 1980-93; mem. 103d-105th U.S. Congress from 2d dist. Miss., 1993—; mem. agr. com., 1993—, mem. Small Bus. Com.; Presdl. appointee Nat. Coun. Health Planning and Devel. Bd. trustees Tougaloo Coll.; bd. dirs. So. Regional Coun., Housing Assistance Coun. Mem. Miss. Assn. Black Mayors (founder), Miss. Assn. Black Suprs. Democrat. Original plaintiff in 1975 Ayers case. Office: 1408 Longworth Bldg Ofc Bl Washington DC 20515-2402*

THOMPSON, BERNIDA LAMERLE, principal, consultant, educator; b. Tuskeegee, Ala., July 5, 1946; d. Berry James Sr. and Doris LaMerle (Askey) T.; m. Rolando Amerson, June 15, 1968 (div. Aug. 1988); children: Afriye Amerson, Mwando Amerson. BS in Elem. Edn., Cen. State U., 1968; MEd in Adminstrn. and Curriculum, Miami U., Oxford, Ohio, 1971; EdD in Early and Mid. Childhood Edn., Nova U., 1992. Classroom elem. sch. tchr. Dayton Pub. Schs.; asst. prin., intern St. James Cath. Sch., Dayton, Ohio; tchr. St. Augustine Cath. Sch., Washington; sci. resource tchr. D.C. Pub. Schs., Washington; prin., co-founder, tchr. Roots Activity Learning Ctr., Washington; multicultural advisor HBJ 1992 Reading Textbook. Author: Black Madonnas and Young Lions a Rite of Passage for African American Adolescents, 1992, Africentric Interdisciplinary Multi-Level Hands On Science, 1994; contbr. articles to profl. jours. Mem. Nat. Assn. Edn. Young Children, World Coun. Curriculum Instrn., Coun. Ind. Black Inst., Nat. Alliance Black Sch. Educators, Nat. Black Child Devel. Inst. Office: Roots Activity Learning Ctr 6222 N Capitol St NW Washington DC 20011-1408

THOMPSON, BERT ALLEN, retired librarian; b. Bloomington, Ind., Dec. 13, 1930; s. James Albert and Dorothy Fern (Myers) T.; m. Martha Ellen Palmer; children—John Carter II, Anne Palmer, Paul Julian. BS, Ball State Tchrs. Coll., 1953; AM, Ind. U., 1960; certificate in archival adm., U. Denver, 1967. Tchr., libr. Ind. pub. schs., 1953-55; ref. asst. Indpls. Pub. Libr., 1956-59; head ref. svc. Mankato (Minn.) State Coll., 1959-61; instr. Grad. Libr. Sch. No. Ill. U., Dekalb, 1961-63; dir. libs., asst. prof. ednl. media U. Nebr. at Kearney, 1963-69; dir. libr. svc. Benedictine U., Lisle, Ill., 1969-90; spl. collections libr. Ill. Benedictine Coll., Lisle, Ill., 1990-92. Mem. exec. bd. Ill. regional Libr. Coun., 1976-79. Recipient 1st Melvin R. George LIBRAS award for Outstanding Svc. to Libr. Cooperation, 1993. Mem. Ill. (de Lafayette Reid Research scholar 1976), Cath. Libr. Assn. (treas. Ill. chpt. 1973-75, nat. sec.-treas. coll./univ. sect. 1981-85, nat. bd. dirs. 1987-93), Nebr. Libr. Assn, chmn. coll. and univ. sect. 1963-64). Episcopalian. Home: 1011 N Cross St Wheaton IL 60187-3587

THOMPSON, BERTHA BOYA, retired education educator, antique dealer and appraiser; b. New Castle, Pa., Jan. 31, 1917; d. Frank L. and Kathryn Belle (Park) Boya; m. John L. Thompson, Mar. 27, 1942; children: Kay Lynn Thompson Koolage, Scott McClain. BS in Elem. & Secondary Edn., Slippery Rock State Coll., 1940; MA in Geography and History, Miami U., 1954; EdD, Ind. U., 1961. Cert. elem. and secondary edn. tchr. Elem. tchr., reading specialist New Castle (Pa.) Sch. System, 1940-45; tchr., chmn. social studies Talawanda Sch. System, Oxford, Ohio, 1954-63; assoc. prof. psychology and geography, chair edn. dept. Western Coll. for Women, Oxford, 1963-74; assoc. prof. edn., reading clinic Miami U., Oxford, 1974-78, prof. emeritus, 1978—; pvt. antique dealer, appraiser Oxford, 1978—. Contbr. articles to profl. jours. Mem. folk art com. Miami U. Art Mus., Oxford, 1974-76; mem. adv. com. Smith libr., Oxford Pub. Libr., 1978-81. Mem. AAUP, Nat. Coun. Geographic Edn. (exec. bd. dirs. 1966-69), Nat. Soc. for Study Edn., Assn. Am. Geographers, Soc. Women Geographers, Nat. Coun. for the Social Studies, Pi Lambda Theta, Zeta Tau Alpha, Pi Gamma Mu, Gamma Theta Upsilon, Kappa Delta Pi. Avocations: antique collecting, reading, travel, tennis. Home: 6073 Contreras Rd Oxford OH 45056-9708

THOMPSON, BONNIE RANSA, secondary educator, chemistry educator; b. Charleroi, Pa., Oct. 12, 1940; d. William Edward and Edith Lorraine Ransa; m. Joel E. Thompson, June 15, 1963 (div. Dec. 1980). BA, Seton Hill Coll., Greensburg, Pa., 1963; MEd, Ariz. State U., 1979, postgrad. Cert. in secondary chemistry, anthropology, and gifted edn., Ariz. Tchr. chemistry Scotch Plains (N.J.)-Fanwood High Sch., 1963-74; tchr. chemistry and anthropology Tolleson (Ariz.) Union High Sch., 1974-93; tchr. chemistry Westview High Sch., Phoenix, 1992—; owner Drenen Solutions, Inc.-Material Handling Systems, 1996—; instr. anthropology and archaeology Rio Salado C.C., Sun City, Ariz., 1981-88; instr. chemistry Glendale (Ariz.) C.C., 1988—, Estrella Mt. Cmty. Coll., 1996—; pres. Brite Ednl. Programs, Ltd., Phoenix, 1988-91; mem. Ariz. Reagent and Task Force on Lab. Sci., Tempe, 1987; tchr., cons. Pitts. SuperComputer Project, Tolleson, 1992—; amb. People to People Sci. Exchange, Russia, Australia, New Zealand, summer 1989-92; rsch partnership High Sch./Coll. Flinn Found. Rsch. Corp., 1988-91. Editor: Starting at Ground Zero, 1988, others; editor: Energy Education Kits, 1985; contbr. articles to mags. V.p. Villa Casitas Townhouse Assn., Phoenix, 1991-92, pres., 1993—; vol. Perot Orgn. for Pres., Phoenix, 1992. Woodrow Wilson fellow, 1983; recipient Golden Bell award Ariz. Sch. Bd. Assn., 1985, 88; recipient Growth Incentives for Tchrs. award GTE Corp., 1987, Tech. Scholar award Tandy Corp., 1990; named Outstanding High Sch. Sci. Tchr. Ariz. Coun. for Engring. and Scientific Assocs., 1993. Mem. NEA, Ariz. Edn. Assn., Tolleson Edn. Assn. (pres. 1981-83), Nat. Sci. Tchrs. Assn., Ariz. Sci. Tchrs. Assn., Ariz. Alliance for Math., Sci. and Tech., S.W. Archeol. Team. Avocations: reading, touring motorcycles. Office: Westview High Sch 10850 W Garden Lakes Pkwy Avondale AZ 85323-3718

THOMPSON, BRIAN JOHN, university administrator, optics educator; b. Glossop, Eng., June 10, 1932; came to U.S., 1962; s. Alexander William and Edna May (Gould) T.; m. Joyce Emily Cheshire, May 31, 1956; children: Karen Joyce, Andrew Derrick. B of Sci. Tech., U. Manchester, Eng., 1955, PhD, 1959. Demonstrator in physics Dept. Tech., U. Manchester, 1955-56, asst. lectr., 1957-59; lectr. physics U. Leeds, Eng., 1959-62; sr. physicist Tech. Optics, Inc., Burlington, Mass., 1963-65, dir. dept. optics, 1966-67, mgr. tech. ops. west, tech. dir., 1967-68; prof. Inst. Optics U. Rochester, N.Y., 1968-94, dir. Inst. Optics, 1968-75, dean Coll. Engring. and Applied Scis., 1975-84, Wm. F. May prof. engring., 1982-85, provost, 1984-94, provost emeritus, Disting. univ. prof., 1994—. Internat. editor; Optics and Laser Tech., 1969—; assoc. editor: Optical Engring., 1972-76, Optics Comm., 1978-86; Am. editor: Optica Acta, 1981-85; editor: Optical Engineering Series, vols. 1-57, 1980—; mem. editl. adv. bd. Laser Focus, 1970—, Particle Characterization, 1984-95, Optics and Lasers in Engring., 1985, Milestone Series of Selected Papers, vols. 1-135, 1984—, Optical Engring., 1991—; chmn. adv. bd. Marquis Who's Who Directory Optical Scientists and Engrs., 1983-86; contbr. articles to profl. jours. With Brit. Army, 1950-52. Fellow Optical Soc. Am. (bd. dirs. 1969-72, exec. com. 1970-73, assoc. editor jour. 1966-77), Inst. Physics and Phys. Soc. (Gt. Britain 1955), Soc. Photo-Optical Instrumentation Engrs. (life, pres. 1974, 75-76, gen. editor series of selected papers 1983—, editor Optical Engring. Jour., 1991—, Pres.'s award 1967, Pezzuto award 1978, Kingslake medal 1978, Gold medal 1986); mem. AAAS, Am. Phys. Soc. Home and Office: 692 Mount Hope Ave Rochester NY 14620-2731

THOMPSON, BRUCE EDWARD, JR., brokerage house executive, former government official; b. Cleve., June 5, 1949; s. Bruce Edward and Mary Ruth (Miller) T.; m. Kathleen Ann Vaughn, May 27, 1972; children: Lesley, Bret. B.S.B.A. in Fin., Georgetown U., 1971. Sr. analyst Govt. Research Corp., Washington, 1971-74; legis. asst. U.S. Sen. William V. Roth Jr., 1974-81; dep. asst. sec. legis. affairs U.S. Treasury Dept., 1981-83, asst. sec. bus. and consumer affairs, 1983-84, asst. sec. legis. affairs, 1984-86; v.p., dir. govt. rels. Merrill Lynch & Co., Inc., 1986—. Staff dir. fiscal and monetary affairs subcom. Republican Platform Com., 1980; adviser Pres. Reagan's Tax Policy Task Force; asst. Pres. Reagan's Transition Hqrs., 1980. Recipient Alexander Hamilton award, 1986. Roman Catholic. Office: Merrill Lynch & Co Inc 3000 K St NW Ste 620 Washington DC 20007-5115

THOMPSON, CAROLINE WARNER, film director, screenwriter; b. Washington, Apr. 23, 1956; d. Thomas Carlton Jr. and Bettie Marshall (Warner) T.; m. Alfred Henry Bromell, Aug. 28, 1982 (div. 1985). BA summa cum laude, Amherst Coll., 1978. Author: First Born, 1983; screenwriter: (films) Edward Scissorhands, 1990, The Addams Family, 1991, Homeward Bound: The Incredible Journey, 1993, The Secret Garden, 1993, Tim Burton's The Nightmare Before Christmas, 1993; screenwriter, dir.: Black Beauty, 1994. Mem. Phi Beta Kappa. Avocation: horseback riding. Office: William Morris Agency Inc 151 S El Camino Dr Beverly Hills CA 90212-2704*

THOMPSON, CARSON R., retail, manufacturing company executive; b. Wilson, Okla., Feb. 10, 1939; s. Silas and Della (Woods) T.; m. Charlotte Arwine, Dec. 26, 1959; children—Shelley Elaine, Susan Denise. B.S., Tex. Wesleyan U., 1962, D Bus. and Fin. (hon.). Leather buyer, mdse. mgr. Tandy Leather Co., Ft. Worth, 1970-74, 74-77; pres. Tex Tan Welhausen Co., Yoakum, Tex., 1978; v.p. Tandy Brands Corp., Fort Worth, 1981—, chmn., CEO, 1982—; pres., CEO Bombay Co., Inc. (formerly Tandy Brands, Inc.), 1996—; chmn. bd., pres., CEO CRT Group, Inc., 1991—. Home: 1801 Sanguinet St Fort Worth TX 76107-3765 Office: PCI Capital Corp 301 Commerce St Ste 3600 Fort Worth TX 76102-4140

THOMPSON, CATHERINE RUSH, physical therapist, educator; b. Kansas City, Mo., Feb. 26, 1954; d. John Adams and Jacqueline (Richard) Rush; m. Gerald Lathen Thompson, Aug. 4, 1979; children: Richard Lathen, Eric Rush. BS in Phys. Therapy with distinction, U. Colo., Denver, 1976; MS in Spl. Edn. with distinction, U. Kans., 1981; postgrad., U. Kans. Med. Ctr., 1990—. Cert. phys. therapist, Kans., Mo. Sch. phys. therapist Easter Seal Soc., Miami, Fla., 1976, Taylor Rehab. Ctr., Cedar Rapids, Iowa, 1977-79; cons. B.W. Shepard State Schs., Kansas City, Mo., 1979-86; pediatric phys. therapist Consol. Sch. Dist. 1, Kansas City, Mo., 1986-94, Spina Bifida Clinic-U. Kans. Med. Ctr., Kansas City, Kans., 1991-94; instr. phys. therapy U. Kans. Med. Ctr., Kansas City, Kans., 1990—; phys. therapy cons. Lakemary Ctr., Paola, Kans., 1991—; mem. desegregation monitoring com. Kansas City (Mo.) Sch. Dist., 1991—; chair Kansas City (Mo.) Pediatric Alliance, 1981-84; adv. com. Ctr. for Devel. Disabled, Kansas City, Mo., 1982-85; pres. Rush Assocs., Inc., 1980-85; speaker at profl. confs. Festival chair Hyde Park Neighborhood Assn., Kansas City, Mo., 1985; parent rep. sch. adv. com. Faxon Montessori Sch., Kansas City, Mo., 1987; summer tchr. Trinity United Meth. Ch., Kansas City, Mo., 1991; grants chair sch. adv. com. Ecole Longan, Kansas City, Mo., 1991. Arthur Mag fellow U. Mo., 1989. Mem. Am. Phys. Therapy Assn. (abstract editor pediatric sect. 1981-83), Kans. Phys. Therapy Assn. (rsch. com. 1989-94), Spina Bifida Assn., Kansas City Soc. Neurosci., Ind. Therapy Svcs. (pres. 1982-86). Avocations: wellness, historic preservation, gardening, poetry. Home: 711 Manheim Rd Kansas City MO 64109-2633 Office: Univ Kans Med Ctr 104 Hinch Hall Kansas City KS 66103

THOMPSON, CHARLES KERRY, company executive; b. Chgo., Sept. 11, 1943; s. Charles Edward and Rose Elizabeth (Peacock) T.; children: Charles Edward, Tiffany Shaffer, Rebecca Lynn. Student, Parsons Coll., 1961-62. Dept. mgr. Montgomery Ward, Chgo., 1962-65; gen. mgr. Jackie's Smartwear, Inc., Niles, Ill., 1965-76; pres. Am. Woman, Inc., Richardson, Tex., 1976-79; zone mgr. The Southland Corp., Dallas, 1979-86; pres. Printelligence Inc. (formerly Graphic Telesis, Inc.), Dallas, 1986-92, Cybersearch, Inc., 1995—; mktg. dir. Nova Internet Svcs., Inc., 1996—; pres. Charles K. Thompson Mktg. and Promotional Cons., NeoMail, Inc., 1992-95. Contbr. articles to profl. jours. Chmn. Muscular Dystrophy, Southland, N. Tex., 1982-86, March of Dimes, 1982-86. Mem. Intertel, Mensa, Jaguar Club (pres. 1972-74). Republican. Avocations: photography, cooking, hunting, cabinetry, furniture refinishing. Home: 4067 Beltway Dr Apt 126 Dallas TX 75244-2629

THOMPSON, CHARLES MURRAY, lawyer; b. Childress, Tex., Oct. 13, 1942; s. Walter Lee and Lois S. (Sheehan) T.; children: Murray McKay, McLean Ann. BS with honors, Colo. State U., 1965; JD cum laude, U. S.D., 1969, LLD (hon.), 1995. Bar: S.D. 1969, U.S. Dist. Ct. S.D. 1969, U.S. Ct. Claims 1989, U.S. Ct. Appeals (8th cir.) 1972, U.S. Supreme Ct. 1973. Ptnr. May, Adam, Gerdes & Thompson, Pierre, S.D., 1969—; spkr. at trial lawyer and state bar seminars; bd. dirs. Bank West, Pierre, S.D.; dir. Delta Trust, Pierre. Editor S.D. Law Rev., 1969. Pres. S.D. Council Sch. Attys., 1984-86. Fellow Am. Bar Found. (chmn. 1991-92, bd. dirs. 1989-92), Coll. Law Practice Mgmt., Am. Coll. Trial Lawyers; mem. ABA (ho. of dels. 1978-96, bd. govs. 1983-86), ATLA, Am. Bd. Trial Advs., Am. Counsel Assn., Am. Judicature Soc. (bd. dirs. 1981-85), Am. Bar Endowment (bd. dirs. 1991—), Nat. Conf. Bar Pres.'s (exec. coun. 1986-94, pres. 1992-93), State Bar S.D. (pres. young lawyers sect. 1974-75, pres. 1986-87), S.D. Bar Found. (pres. 1991), S.D. Trial Lawyers Assn. (pres. 1980-81), Jackrabbit Bar Assn. (chancellor 1981-82), Kiwanis (pres. local club 1977). Democrat. Avocations: flying, ranching. Home and Office: PO Box 160 Pierre SD 57501-0160

THOMPSON, CHARLOTTE ELLIS, pediatrician, educator, author; b. Sept. 5, 1928; d. Robert and Ann Ellis; divorced; children: Jennifer Ann, Geoffrey Graeme. BA, Stanford U., 1950, MD, 1954. Diplomate Am. Bd. Pediat. Intern Children's Hosp., San Francisco, 1953-54; resident UCLA, 1960-61, L.A. Children's Hosp., 1962-63; pvt. practice La Jolla, Calif., 1963-75; dir. Muscle Disease Clinic, Univ. Hosp.-U. Calif. Sch. Medicine, San Diego, 1969-80, asst. clin. prof. pediat., 1969—; dir. Ctr. for Handicapped Children and Teenagers, San Francisco, 1981—; cons. U.S. Naval Hosp., San Diego, 1970-91; dep. dir. Santa Clara County Child Health and Disability, Santa Clara, Calif., 1974-75; dir. Ctr. for Multiple Handicaps, Oakland, Calif., 1976-81; co-dir. Muscle Clinic Children's Hosp., San Diego, 1963-69. Author: Raising a Handicapped Child: A Helpful Guide for Parents of the Physically Disabled, 1986, 4th edit., 1991, Allein leben: Ein umfassendes Handbuch für Frauen, 1993, Making Wise Choices: A Guide for Women, 1993; contbr. articles to med. jours., including Clin. Pediat., New Eng. Jour. Medicine, Neurology, Jour. Family Practice, Mothering, Jour. Pediatric Orthopedics, Pediatrician, Am. Baby, Pediatric News, also chpts. to books. Mem. Calif. Children's Svc. Com., 1977—. Fellow Am. Acad. Pediatrics; mem. Am. Women's Med. Assn., Internat. Music Box Soc. Avocations: tennis, ice skating, opera. Office: Ctr for Handicapped Children and Teenagers 2000 Van Ness Ave Ste 307 San Francisco CA 94109-3020

THOMPSON, CHERYL ANN, special education educator; b. Berlin, Sept. 15, 1967; d. Edward Joseph and Kathleen (Snay) T. BS in Spl. Edn., Westfield (Mass.) State Coll., 1989; MEd, R.I. Coll., 1994. Spl. edn. tchr. Behavior Rsch. Inst., Providence, R.I., 1989-92, Boston Ctr. for Blind Children, 1993-94, Barnstable Pub. Schs., Hyannis, Mass., 1996—; day program supr. Residential Rehab. Ctrs. Inc., Brewster, Mass., 1994-96; spl. edn. tchr. Barnstable Pub. Schs., Hyannis, Mass., 1996—. Mem. Assn. for Persons with Severe Handicaps, Am. Assn. on Mental Retardation, Prader-Willi Syndrome Assn. Democrat. Roman Catholic. Avocations: collecting clowns, reading, softball, animals. Home: 365 Rt 6 PO Box 1247 Eastham MA 02642

THOMPSON, CLAIRE LOUISA, nurse, educator, administrator; b. Columbus, Ohio, Sept. 29, 1938; d. Harry Edgar and Clara Etta (Brackenbusch) McKeever; m. Roger Lee Thompson, Dec. 20, 1958 (div. 1988); children: Jeffrey, Michael. Diploma, Bethesda Hosp. Sch. Nursing, Cin., 1959; student, Ball State, 1970, Ind. U., 1981, Purdue U., 1982-83. RN, Ohio, Ind., Calif.; cert. ins. rehab. specialist, 1985, CCM case mgr., 1993. Oper. rm./emergency rm. nurse Greene Meml. Hosp., Xenia, Ohio, 1959-60; med.-surg. nurse, charge nurse Bethesda Hosp., 1960-64; med.-surg. nurse Porter Meml. Hosp., Valparaiso, Ind., 1965-66; staff and charge nurse Mercy Hosp., Elwood, Ind., 1968-74; gen. practice nurse W. A. Scea, MD, Elwood, 1970-74; exec. dir. Vis. Nurse Assn., Elwood, 1974-78; analyst Blue Cross/Blue Shield of Indpls., 1978; supr. Meth. Hosp. Clinic, Indpls., 1979-80; dir. nursing Upjohn Health Care, Indpls., 1980; staff nurse Americana Health Care Ctr., Indpls., 1981; instr. health occups. Washington Twp. Schs., Indpls., 1981-84; br. mgr. health & rehab. Crawford & Co., Indpls., 1984-88; regional med. svcs. advisor western region Crawford & Co., San Francisco, 1988-92; br. mgr. Crawford & Co., Health Care Mgmt., Modesto, Calif., 1992-94; ret., 1994; developer in case mgmt. nursing svcs., 1974-94. Founder Meals on Wheels, Elwood, 1975, Vis. Nurses Assn., Elwood, 1976. Mem. NLN, Assn. Rehab. Nurses (pres. Ind. chpt. 1987-88), Nat. Ins. Womens Assn., Case Mgmt. Soc. Am., San Francisco Ins. Womens Assn., Rehab. Ins. Nurses Group. Roman Catholic. Avocations: the arts, photography, rose gardening, cats, family. Home: PO Box 1263 Westerville OH 43086-1263

THOMPSON, CLEON F., JR., university administrator. BS in Biology, N.C. Cen. U., 1956, MS in Biology, 1958; PhD in Edn. Adminstrn., Duke U., 1977. Vice-pres. student services and spl. programs U. N.C., to 1985; chancellor Winston-Salem State U., N.C., 1985—. Office: Winston Salem State U Office of Chancellor Winston Salem NC 27110

THOMPSON, CLIFTON C., chemistry educator, university administrator; b. Franklin, Tenn., Aug. 16, 1939; s. Clifton C. and Ruby M. (Moore) T.; m. Sarah Ellen Gaunt, Dec. 1, 1978; children: Brenda Kay, Victoria Lea. BS, Middle Tenn. State U., 1961; PhD, U. Miss., 1964. Asst. prof. Rutgers U., New Brunswick, N.J., 1965, Marshall U., Huntington, W.Va., 1965-66; assoc. prof. Middle Tenn. State U., Murfreesboro, 1966-68, Memphis State U., 1968-74; prof. chemistry, dept. head, dean Coll. Sci. and Math., dir. Ctr. for Sci. Rsch., assoc. v.p. for grad. studies and rsch. S.W. Mo. State U., Springfield, 1974-96; prof. chemistry Cen. Mich. U., Mt. Pleasant, 1996—; research assoc. U. Tex., Austin, 1964-65; research Oak Ridge Nat. Lab., 1968; cons. Mid-South Research Assocs., Memphis, 1969-71; mem. med. tech. rev. com. Nat. Accrediting Agy. for Clin. Lab. Sci., Chgo., 1974-80. Author: Ultraviolet-Visible Absorption Spectroscopy, 1974. Mem. health care com. Springfield C. of C., 1978-79, mem. econ. devel. com., 1983-89; bd. dirs. United Hebrew Congregation, Springfield, 1983-86, United Hebrew Found., Inc., 1994-96. NSF fellow, 1961-64; Sigma Xi grantee-in-aide, 1970; NSF sr. fgn. scientist grantee, 1971; NSF coop-coll. sch. sci. grantee, 1972; Higher Edn. Applied Projects grantee, 1987-90. Mem. Am. Chem. Soc., Royal Soc. Chemistry, AAAS, Sigma Xi, Phi Kappa Phi. Jewish. Office: Central Mich Univ Dept Chemistry Mount Pleasant MI 48859

THOMPSON, CRAIG DEAN, sports association executive; b. Estherville, Iowa, Aug. 1, 1956; s. Maurice Ray and Dorothy Jean (Ross) T.; m. Carla Kaye Nealy, July 30, 1983; 1 child, Theodore Edgar. BA, U. Minn., 1978. Asst. sports info. dir. Kans. State U., Manhattan, 1978-80; dir. pub. rels. and promotions Kansas City Kings, Mo., 1980-83; dir. of comms. Metro Conf., Atlanta, 1983-87; commr. Am. South Conf., New Orleans, 1987-91, Sun Belt Conf., New Orleans, 1991—; mem. 1993 NCAA Final Four Exec. Planning Com., New Orleans. Mem. Collegiate Commrs. Assn. (past v.p.), NCAA Divsn. I Mens Basketball Com. Republican. Presbyterian. Avocation: coin collecting.

THOMPSON, CRAIG SNOVER, corporate communications executive; b. Bklyn., May 24, 1932; s. Craig F. and Edith (Williams) T.; m. Masae Sugizaki, Feb. 21, 1957; children: Lee Anne, Jane Laura. Grad., Valley Forge Mil. Acad., 1951; B.A., Johns Hopkins U., 1954. Newspaper and radio reporter Easton (Pa.) Express, 1954-55, 57-59, Wall St. Jour., 1959-60; account exec. Moore, Meldrum & Assocs., 1960; mgr. pub. relations Cen. Nat. Bank of Cleve., 1961-62; account exec. Edward Howard & Co., Cleve., 1962-67; v.p. Edward Howard & Co., 1967-69, sr. v.p., 1969-71; dir. pub. relations White Motor Corp., Cleve., 1971-76; v.p. pub. relations No. Telecom Inc., Nashville, 1976-77, White Motor Corp., Farmington Hills, Mich., 1977-80; v.p. corp. communications White Motor Corp., 1980-81; dir. exec. communications Rockwell Internat. Corp., Pitts., 1981-86, El Segundo, Calif., 1986-91; dir. exec. communications Rockwell Internat. Corp., Seal Beach, Calif., 1992-97, sr. communications exec., 1997—. Bd. dirs. Shaker Lakes Regional Nature Center, 1970-73. Served to 1st lt., inf. U.S. Army, 1955-57. Mem. Pub. Rels. Soc. Am. (accredited), Alumni Assn. Valley Forge Mil. Acad. (bd. dirs. 1988-94). Office: Rockwell Internat Corp 2201 Seal Beach Blvd Seal Beach CA 90740-5603

THOMPSON, DAVID ALFRED, industrial engineer; b. Chgo., Sept. 9, 1929; s. Clifford James and Christobel Eliza (Sawin) T.; children: Nancy, Brooke, Lynda, Diane, Kristy. B.M.E., U. Va., 1951; B.S. in Indsl. Engring, U. Fla., 1955, M.S. in Engring, 1956; Ph.D., Stanford U., 1961. Registered profl. engr., Calif; cert. profl. ergonomist. Research asst. U. Fla. Engring. and Industries Exptl. Sta., Gainesville, 1955-56; instr. indsl. engring. Stanford U., 1956-58, acting asst. prof., 1958-61, asst. prof., 1961-64, asso. prof., 1964-72, prof., 1972-83, prof., asso. chmn. dept. indsl. engring., 1972-73, prof. emeritus, 1983—; mem. clin. faculty occupational medicine U. Calif. Med. Sch., San Francisco, 1985—; pres., chief scientist Portola Assocs., Palo Alto, Calif., 1965—; prin. investigator NASA Ames Research Center, Moffatt Field, Calif., 1974-77; cons. Dept. State, Fed. EEO Commn., maj. U.S. and fgn. cos.; cons. emergency commn. ctr. design Santa Clara County Criminal Justice Bd., 1974, Bay Area Rapid Transit Control Ctr., 1977, Govt. of Mex., 1978, Amadahl Corp., 1978-79, Kerr-McGee Corp., 1979, Chase Manhattan Bank, 1980, St. Regis Paper Co., 1980-82, Pacific Gas & Electric, 1983-85, Pacific Bell, 1984-86, 89-93, IBM, 1988-91, Hewlett-Packard, 1990-91, Reuter's News Svc., 1990-92, Safeway Corp., 1992—, New United Motors Mfg., 1993-95, Sun Microsys., 1993-94, Microsoft, 1995—; mem. com. for office computers Calif. OSHA. Dir., editor: documentary film Rapid Answers for Rapid Transit, Dept. Transp., 1974; mem. editorial adv. bd. Computers and Graphics, 1970-85; reviewer Indsl. Engring. and IEEE Transactions, 1972-86; contbr. articles to profl. jours. Served to lt. USNR, 1951-54. HEW grantee, 1967-70. Mem. IEEE,. Home: PO Box 6685 Incline Village NV 89450 Office: Portola Assocs 2600 El Camino Real Ste 414 Palo Alto CA 94306-1705

THOMPSON, DAVID B., bishop. Ordained priest, 1950; consecrated bishop, 1989. Coadjutor bishop Diocese of Charleston, S.C., 1989-90, bishop, 1990—. Office: Bishop of Charleston 119 Broad St Charleston SC 29401-2435

THOMPSON, DAVID O'NEAL, retired basketball player; b. Shelby, N.C., July 13, 1954. BS in Sociology, N.C. State U., 1975. With Denver Nuggets, 1975-82, Seattle SuperSonics, 1982-84. Named Athlete of Yr., ACC, 1973, 75, Player of Yr., ACC, 1973-75, Most Valuable Player, NCAA Tournament, Player of Yr., Naismith, 1975, Rupp, 1975, AP, 1975, UPI, 1975, Eastman Kodak, 1975, The Sporting News, 1975, N.C. Sports Hall of Fame, 1982, Most Valuable Player, 1979 All-Star Game, Basketball Hall of Fame, 1996, Colo. Sports Hall of Fame, 1996, Sport Mag. Performer of Yr./

Basketball, 1978; recipient Joe Mallamo Humanitarian award 1994, others. Achievements include three-time First-Team All-Am., Three-time All-ACC selection; mem. Championship Team, 1974, NCAA All-Decade Team, 1970's; First Team All-NBA selection, 1977, 78, four-time NBA All-Star. Office: care Basketball Hall of Fame PO Box 179 Springfield MA 01101-0179

THOMPSON, DAVID RENWICK, federal judge; b. 1930. BS in Bus., U. So. Calif., 1952, LLB, 1955. Pvt. practice law with Thompson & Thompson (and predecessor firms), 1957-85; judge U.S. Ct. Appeals (9th cir.), 1985—. Served with USN, 1955-57. Mem. ABA, San Diego County Bar Assn., Am. Bd. Trial Lawyers (sec. San Diego chpt. 1983, v.p. 1984, pres. 1985). Office: US Ct Appeals 940 Front St San Diego CA 92101-8994*

THOMPSON, DAVID RUSSELL, engineering educator, academic dean; b. Cleve., Apr. 4, 1944; s. Dwight L. and Ella Caroline (Wolff) T.; m. Janet Ann Schall, Aug. 27, 1966; children: Devin Mathew, Colleen Michelle, Darin Michael. BS in Agrl. Engring., Purdue U., 1966, MS in Agrl. Engring., 1967; PhD in Agrl. Engring., Mich. State U., 1970. Asst. prof. agrl. engring., food sci. and nutrition depts. U. Minn., St. Paul, 1970-75, assoc. prof., 1975-81, prof., 1981-85; prof. agrl. engring., head dept. Okla. State U., Stillwater, 1985-91, assoc. dean Coll. Engring., Architecture and Tech., 1991—; engr. ops. dept. Green Giant Co., La Sueur, Minn., 1978-79; reviewer Colo. State U., CRS, USDA, Ft. Collins, 1989, foods, feeds and prodn. cluster U. Mo., Columbia, 1989, 93, dept. agrl. engring. Pa. State U., University Park, 1990, Tex. A&M U., College Station, 1992, Utah State U., Logan, 1993, USAF, Tyndall, Fla. and San Angelo, Tex., 1994, 95, 97, Washington State U., Pullman, 1995, U. Ga., Athens, 1996, others; reviewer USDA, 1983; vis. scholar Va. Poly. Inst. and State U., Blacksburg. Author: The Influence of Materials Properties on the Freezing of Sweet Corn , 1984, Mathematical Model for Predicting Lysine and Methionine Losses During Thermal Processing of Fortified Foods; contbr. over 50 articles to sci. jours., including Jour. Food Sci. Fellow Am. Soc. Agrl. Engrs. (div. chmn. 1976-77, bd. dirs. 1981-84, 87-89, v.p. 1994—, FIEI Young Rschr. award 1983, Pres.'s citation 1989); mem. ASHRAE, NSPE (chair Okla. mid-north sect. 1994-95), Inst. Food Technologists (program com. 1982-85, state officer 1987-89), Am. Soc. Engring. Edn. (chair Midwest sect. 1994-95), Sigma Xi Phi Kappa Phi, Tau Beta Pi, Alpha Epsilon, Phi Eta Sigma, Gamma Sigma Delta. Office: Okla State U Coll Engring Arch & Tech 111 Engineering N Stillwater OK 74078-5010

THOMPSON, DAVID WILLIAM, business educator; b. Ft. Wayne, Ind., Sept. 3, 1914; s. William Byron and Georgia Louise (Davis) T.; m. M. Miriam Vollmer, Dec. 21, 1956 (dec.). B.S., Ind. U., 1938, M.S., 1940. C.P.A., N.Y., Ill., Ind., Va., N.C., N. Mex., La. Prof. Samford U., Birmingham, Butler U., Indpls., 1941-42, Ind. U., Bloomington, 1942-54; cons. Gen. Electric Co., N.Y.C., 1954-56; ptnr. KPMG Peat Marwick, N.Y.C., 1956-76; Frank S. Kaulback Jr. prof. commerce McIntire Sch. Commerce U. Va., Charlottesville, 1976—; chmn. State Bd. Examiners C.P.A.s, N.Y.C., 1966-70, State Bd. Pub. Accountancy, N.Y.C., 1974-76. Dir. Univ. of the Ams., Mexico City, U. of the Ams. Found., San Antonio. Mem. AICPA, Ind. U. Acad. Alumni Fellows, Indpls. Athletic Club, India House Club N.Y.C., Univ. Club N.Y.C., Farmington Country Club Charlottesville Va., Beta Gamma Sigma (dirs. table). Home: Ednam Forest 425 Wellington Dr Charlottesville VA 22903-4746 Office: U Va Monroe Hall McIntire Sch Commerce Charlottesville VA 22903

THOMPSON, DENISSE R., mathematics educator; b. Keesler AFB, Miss., Aug. 26, 1954. BA, BS, U. South Fla., 1976, MA, 1980; PhD, U. Chgo., 1992. Cert. tchr., Fla. Tchr. Hernando County Schs., Brooksville, Fla., 1977-82; instr. maths. Manatee C.C., Bradenton, Fla., 1982-87; asst. prof. U. South Fla., Tampa, 1991—; cons. in field. Author: Fundamental Skills of Mathematics, 1987, Advanced Algebra, 1990, 2d edit., 1996, (with others) Precalculus and Discrete Mathematics, 1992, Nat. Coun. Tchrs. of Math. Yearbook, 1991, 93, 94, 95; contbr. articles to profl. jours. Recipient Carolyn Hoefer Meml. award Pi Lambda Theta, 1988. Mem. ASCD, Math. Assn. Am., Nat. Coun. Tchrs. Math., Nat. Coun. Suprs. Math., Assn. Women in Maths., Phi Delta Kappa, Phi Kappa Phi. Office: U South Fla College of Edn EDU208B Tampa FL 33620

THOMPSON, DENNIS FRANK, political science and ethics educator, consultant; b. Hamilton, Ohio, May 12, 1940; s. Frank and Florence (Downs) T.; m. Carol Thompson, June 22, 1963; children: Eric, David. BA, Coll. of William and Mary, 1962, Oxford U., 1964; MA, Oxford U., 1968; PhD, Harvard U., 1968; LHD (hon.), Coll. of William and Mary, 1990. Instr. govt. Harvard U., Cambridge, Mass., 1967-68; Alfred North Whitehead prof. Harvard U., 1986—, dir. univ. program in ethics and professions, 1986—; assoc. provost Harvard U., Cambridge, Mass., 1996—; asst. prof. politics Princeton U., N.J., 1968-72, assoc. prof., 1972-75, dept. chmn., 1972-73, 76-79, 82-83, prof., 1975-86; cons. to spl. counsel U.S. Senate Select Com. on Ethics, 1990-91, U.S. Dept. HHS, 1980, FDA, 1993. Author: The Democratic Citizen, 1970, John Stuart Mill and Representative Government, 1976, Political Ethics and Public Office, 1987, Ethics in Congress, 1995, (with A. Gutmann) Democracy and Disagreement, 1996; mem. editl. bd. Polit. Theory, 1974—, Philosophy and Pub. Affairs, 1971—, Am. Polit. Sci. Rev., 1985-88. Trustee Smith Coll., 1994—. Fellow Am. Acad. Arts and Scis.; mem. Am. Soc. Legal and Polit. Philosophy (v.p. 1977-80, pres. 1986-89). Home: 9 Shady Hill Sq Cambridge MA 02138-2035 Office: Harvard Univ 202 Taubman 79 JFK St Cambridge MA 02138-5801

THOMPSON, DENNIS PETERS, plastic surgeon; b. Chgo., Mar. 18, 1937; s. David John and Ruth Dorothy (Peters) T.; m. Virginia Louise Williams, June 17, 1961; children: Laura Faye, Victoria Ruth, Elizabeth Jan. BS, U. Ill., 1957, BS in Medicine, 1959, MS in Physiology, MD, 1961. Diplomate Am. Bd. Surgery, Am. Bd. Plastic Surgery. Intern Presbyn.-St. Lukes Hosp., Chgo., 1961-62; resident in gen. surgery Mayo Clinic, Rochester, Minn., 1964-66, fellow in gen. surgery, 1964-66; resident in gen. surgery Harbor Gen. Hosp., Los Angeles, 1968-70; resident in plastic surgery UCLA, 1971-73, clin. instr. plastic surgery, 1975-82, asst. clin. prof. surgery, 1982—; practice medicine specializing in plastic and reconstructive surgery, Los Angeles, 1974-78, Santa Monica, Calif., 1978—; chmn. plastic surgery sect. St. John's Hosp., 1986-91; mem. staff Santa Monica Hosp., UCLA Ctr. Health Scis.; chmn. dept. surgery Beverly Glen Hosp., 1978-79; pres. Coop. of Am. Physicians Credit Union, 1978-80, bd. dirs., 1980—, chmn. membership devel. com., 1983—, treas., 1985—. Contbr. articles to med. jours. Moderator Congl. Ch. of Northridge (Calif.), 1975-76, chmn. bd. trustees, 1973-74, 80-82; bd. dirs. L.A. Bus. Coun., 1987-90. Am. Tobacco Inst. research grantee, 1959-60. Fellow ACS; mem. AMA (Physicians Recognition award 1971, 74, 77, 81, 84, 87, 90, 93, 96), Calif. Med. Assn., L.A. County Med. Assn. (chmn. bylaws com. 1979-80, chmn. ethics com. 1980-81, sec.-treas. dist. 5 1982-83, program chmn. 1983-84, pres. 1985-86, councilor 1988-96), Pan-Pacific Surgical Assn., Am. Soc. Plastic and Reconstructive Surgeons, Calif. Soc. Plastic Surgeons (chmn. bylaws com. 1982-83, chmn. liability com. 1983-85, councilor 1988-91, sec. 1993-95, v.p. 1995-96, pres.-elect 1996-97, pres. 1997—), L.A. Soc. Plastic Surgeons (sec. 1980-82, pres. 1982-97), Lipoplasty Soc. N.Am., UCLA Plastic Surgery Soc. (treas. 1983-84), Am. Soc. Aesthetic Plastic Surgery, Am. Assn. Accreditation of Ambulatory Surg. Facilities (bd. dirs. 1995—), Western Los Angeles Regional C. of C. (bd. dirs. 1981-84, 86-89, chmn. legis. action com. 1978-80), Phi Beta Kappa, Alpha Omega Alpha, Nu Sigma Nu, Phi Kappa Phi, Delta Sigma Delta, Omega Beta Pi, Phi Eta Sigma. Republican. Office: 2001 Santa Monica Blvd Santa Monica CA 90404-2102

THOMPSON, DIDI CASTLE (MARY BENNETT), writer, editor; b. Terre Haute, Ind., Feb. 7, 1918; d. Robert Langley Bennett and Marjorie Rose (Tyler) Castle; student U. Ill., Champaign, 1935-36, U. Ky., 1936-39; m. Jamie Campbell Thompson, Jr., June 24, 1939; children—Jamie III, Julia King Balko, Langley Stewart Ruede. News editor Glen-Echoes, Glencoe, Ill., 1930; columnist Ky. Kernel, U. Ky., Lexington, 1937-39; radio script writer Modern Am. Music, 1940-42; asst. pub. relations dir. Salem Coll., Winston-Salem, N.C., 1945; pub. relations chmn. Barrington (Ill.) Horse Show, 1959-67; staff writer, columnist Barrington Press Newspapers, 1958-84; editor ECHO, Defenders of the Fox River, Inc. newsletter, 1970-80; travel editor Barrington Press Newspapers, 1973-84; columnist The Daily Herald, Paddock Publs., 1984-86; columnist Rapid City (S.D.) Journal, 1990-95; freelance writer, 1943—. Past bd. mem. Barrington chpt. Lyric Opera Guild Chgo., Barrington Sr. Center, Infant Welfare Soc. Chgo., Art Inst. Chgo., Barrington Assos.; elected trustee Village of Barrington Hills, 1969-73, health, pub. relations chmn., 1969-73; mem. Barrington Hills Plan Commn., 1986. Mem. Women in Communications (past dir.), Citizens for Conservation (past dir.), Barrington Countryside Assn. (past dir.), Barrington Hist. Soc., Spring Creek Basset Hounds Club, Barrington Hills Riding Club (past dir.), Pan Hellenic Council, DAR, Chgo. Press Club, Chi Omega. Episcopalian. Address: 1827 Princess Ct Naples FL 34110

THOMPSON, DONALD CHARLES, electronics company executive, former coast guard officer; b. Hollis, N.Y., Nov. 9, 1930; s. Arthur I. and Gertrude M. (Hauck) T.; m. Jeannie Germaine Kline, Oct. 4, 1952; children: Dennis C., Mitchell L., Sandra J., Janice M., Theresa A., Patrick J. B.S., U.S. Coast Guard Acad., 1952; M.S. (Krannert scholar), Krannert Grad. Sch., Purdue U., 1966. Commd. ensign USCG, 1952, advanced through grades to vice adm., 1986; shipboard navigator and engr., 1952-54, naval flight tng., 1954-55; search and rescue aviator and aircraft maintenance officer Calif., Ill., Alaska and Fla., 1955-65; chief computer-based mgmt. info. div. Elizabeth City, N.C., 1966-70; chief aero. engring. div. USCG Hdqrs., 1970-74; capt. of the port, group comdr., air sta. comdr. San Diego, 1974-76; chief ops. 11th USCG Dist., Long Beach, Calif., 1976-78; chief of staff 11th USCG Dist., 1979; chief office of engring. USCG Hdqrs., Washington, 1979-81; chief office of ops. USCG Hdqrs., 1981-82, chief staff, 1984-86, comdr. Atlantic area, 1986-88; comdr. 7th Coast Guard Dist., Miami, Fla., 1982-84; math. instr. Coll. Albermarle, N.C., 1967-70, Nat. U., San Diego, 1975-76; chmn. Interagy. Com. Search and Rescue, 1981-82; ret. USCG, 1988; v.p. strategic devel. R&E Electronics, Inc., Wilmington, N.C., 1990-93; pres. D.C. Thompson Consulting, Wilmington, 1994—; v.p.'s coordinator for S.E. region Nat. Narcotics Border Interdiction System, 1983-84. Contbr. articles to profl. jours. Coordinator White House South Fla. Task Force on Crime, 1983-84. Decorated DSM with two gold stars, Coast Guard Meritorious Service medal, Def. Superior Service medal, Commendation medal with three gold stars, Legion of Merit with gold star. Mem. Soc. Am. Mil. Engrs. (dir. 1979-81), Am. Soc. Naval Engrs., Am. Helicopter Soc. (dir. 1981-82), Air Force Assn., Naval Inst. Roman Catholic. Clubs: Propeller, Nat. Aviation. Home and office: 1903 Market St Wilmington NC 28403-1015

THOMPSON, DOROTHY BARNARD, elementary school educator; b. Flushing, N.Y., Aug. 14, 1933; d. Henry Clay and Cecelia Minnie Theresa (La Pardo) Barnard; m. Norman Earl Thompson, Aug. 12, 1956; children: Greg, Scot, Henry, Marc, Matthew. BSEd, SUNY, New Paltz, 1953; MS, Hofstra U., 1984. Cert. elem. tchr. K-6th grades, reading specialist K-12th grades, N.Y. Adjunct prof. Suffolk Community Coll., Brentwood, N.Y., 1987—, Nassau Community Coll., Uniondale, N.Y., 1986—; adjunct prof., instr. Ctr. for Acad. Achievement Long Island U., Greenvale, N.Y., 1984-92; tchr. reading, K-5th grades Long Beach (N.Y.) Pub. Schs., 1988—; mem. founding group Parent/Tchr., The Learning Tree, Garden City, N.Y., 1971; founder parent coop. Happy Day Nursery Sch., Bellmore, N.Y., 1975; parent-tchr. Commonwealth Sch., Bay Shore, Oakdale, 1976-82. Mem. NEA, ASCD, Nassau Reading Coun., N.Y. State Tchrs. Assn., Adelphi Tawl. Home: 2385 Warren Ave Bellmore NY 11710-2545 Office: 456 Neptune Blvd Long Beach NY 11561-2400

THOMPSON, EARL ALBERT, economics educator; b. Los Angeles, Oct. 15, 1938; s. Hyman Harry and Sue (Field) T.; m. Velma Montoya, June 9, 1961; 1 son, Bret. B.A., UCLA, 1959; M.A. (fellow), Harvard U., 1961, Ph.D., 1961. Asst. prof. econs. Stanford (Calif.) U., 1962-65; asst. prof. econs. UCLA, 1965-68, assoc. prof., 1968-70, prof., 1970—. Grantee NSF; Grantee Lily Found.; Grantee Found. Research Econs. and Edn. Mem. Am. Econ. Assn. Home: 6970 Los Tilos Rd Los Angeles CA 90068-3107

THOMPSON, EARLENE, civic volunteer; b. Pelzer, S.C., Nov. 12, 1942; d. Tobie and Sallie (Moss) Tate; m. Willie J. Thompson, Apr. 19, 1958; children: Quenton, Quentena, Quenleasa, Quendrida. CEO Neighbor in the Hood Resource Ctr. Foster parent Ventura County DPSS, Simi Valley, Calif., 1969-73, L.A. County, 1983-87; exec. dir. Wilene's Re-Growth Ctr., San Dimas, Calif., 1986—; CEO Wilene's Children of the Village Foster Family Agy. Recipient Woman of Achievement award YWCA, 1991. Mem. Soroptimist (photographer 1988-89). Democrat. Office: Neighbor in the Hood Resource Ctr 637 N Park Ave Pomona CA 91768-3669

THOMPSON, EDWARD IVINS BRAD, biological chemistry and genetics educator, molecular endocrinologist, department chairman; b. Burlington, Iowa, Dec. 20, 1933; s. Edward Bills and Lois Elizabeth (Bradbridge) T.; m. Lynn Taylor Parsons; children: Elizabeth Lynn, Edward Ernest Bradbridge. BA with distinction, Rice U., 1955; postgrad., Cambridge U., 1957-58; MD, Harvard U., 1960. Intern The Presbyn. Hosp., N.Y.C., 1960-61, asst. resident internal medicine, 1961-62; rsch. assoc. Nat. Inst. Mental Health, NIH, Bethesda, Md., 1962-64; rsch. scientist Nat. Inst. Arthritis and Metabolic Diseases, NIH, Bethesda, Md., 1964-68; rsch. scientist Lab of Biochemistry, Nat. Cancer Inst., NIH, Bethesda, Md., 1968-73, sect. chief, 1973-84; I.H. Kempner prof. U. Tex. Med. Br., Galveston, 1984, prof., chmn. dept. human biol. chemistry and genetics, 1984—, prof. internal medicine, 1984—, interim dir. Sealy Ctr. for Molecular Sci., 1996—; attending physician Nat. Naval Med. Ctr., Bethesda, 1978-80; chmn. hormones and cancer task force NIH, Bethesda, 1978-80; co-chmn. Gordon Research Conf., 1980; mem. adv. com. on Biochem. & Chem. Carcinogenesis, Am. Cancer Soc., 1982-86; mem. revision com. Endocrinology adv. panel U.S. Pharmacopoeial Conv., Inc., 1980-85; mem. council for clin. investigation and research awds., Am. Cancer Soc., 1989-93; bd. scientific overseers Pennington Nutrition Rsch. Ctr. La. State U., 1991—; Fulbright prof., Marburg, Germany. 1992-93. Co-editor Gene Expression and Carcinogenesis in Cultured Liver, 1975, Steroid Receptors and the Management of Cancer, 1979, DNA: Protein Interactions and Gene Regulation, other vols. in field; assoc. editor Cancer Rsch. jour., 1976-86; corr. editor Jour. Steroid Biochemistry, 1977-85; founding editor-in-chief Molecular Endocrinology Jour., 1985-92; mem. editl. bd. Steroids & WWW Jour. Biology, 1995—; contbr. over 200 sci. articles to profl. jours. Mem. troop com. Girl Scouts U.S., Rockville, Md., 1970-76; mem. PTA, Rockville, 1967-77, Wilderness Soc., Washington, 1964-75; initiator sci. edn. liaison program Galveston Pub. Schs., 1991; mem. pres.'s cabinet U. Tex. Med. Br. Served as med. dir. USPHS, 1962-84. Grantee NIH, Walls Rsch., Nat. Inst. Diabetes and Digestive and Kidney Diseases, Nat. Cancer Inst.; Am. Cancer Soc. scholar, 1992-93; Fulbright scholar. Mem. Am. Soc. Cell Biology, Am. Assn. Cancer Rsch., Am. Soc. Biol. Chemists, Endocrine Soc., Am. Soc. Microbiology, Am. Coll. Med. Genetics (affiliate), Tissue Culture Assn., S.W. Environ. Mutagen Soc., Rotary Internat., The Yacht Club, Racquet Club, Harvard Club, Pres.'s Clubs of Rice U. and U. Tex. Med. Br., Phi Beta Kappa, Alpha Omega Alpha. Achievements include patent on anti-tumor activity of a modified fragment of glucocorticoid receptor. Office: U Tex Med Br Dept Human Biol Gene Galveston TX 77555

THOMPSON, EDWARD THORWALD, magazine editor; b. Milw., Feb. 13, 1928; s. Edward Kramer and Marguerite Minerva (Maxam) T.; m. Margaret Kessler, 1949; children: Edward T. III, Anne B., Evan K., David S.; m. Nancy Cale, May 28, 1966; 1 child, Julie.; m. Susan L. Jacobson, Nov. 28, 1981. Grad., Lawrenceville Sch., 1945; SB, MIT, 1949. Engr. Mobil Oil Co., Beaumont, Tex., 1949-52; assoc. editor Chem. Engr. mag., N.Y.C., 1952-55; mng. editor Chem. Week mag., N.Y.C., 1955-56; assoc. editor Fortune mag., 1956-60; with Reader's Digest., Pleasantville, N.Y., 1960-84; asst. mng. editor, then mng. editor Reader's Digest., 1973-76, editor-in-chief, mem. exec. com., 1976-84; cons. in pub. Waccabuc, N.Y., 1984—; pres. Thompson Assocs.; bd. dirs. The Quarton Group, Tech. Rev. Mag. Recipient Golden Plate award Am. Acad. Achievement, 1977. Mem. Am. Soc. Mag. Editors, Waccabuc Country Club. Home: 3 Hunt Farm Waccabuc NY 10597-1100

THOMPSON, ELIZABETH JANE, small business owner; b. Ithaca, N.Y., Jan. 11, 1927; d. Merle Godley and Nellie Gray (Trowbridge) T. AB, Syracuse U., 1948, MA, 1962, PhD, 1971. Writer, editor Cornell U., Ithaca, N.Y., 1950-53; dir. pub. rels. Taylor Ward Advt., Ithaca, 1953-54; account exec. Doug Johnson Assocs., Syracuse, N.Y., 1954-58; assoc. in community rels., Youth Devel. Ctr. Syracuse U., 1958-66, grad. asst., 1967-68; from asst. prof. to prof. sociology Shippensburg (Pa.) U., 1968-90, dir. Fashion Archives, 1980-90; owner Timelines & Hemlines Cons. Svc., Shippensburg, 1991—; lectr. on costume, fashion and sociology of dress to numerous civic and ednl. groups. Co-editor: Among the People: Studies of the Urban Poor, 1968; contbr. articles on sociology of dress to numerous publs. Mem. Costume Soc. Am., Am. Sociol. Soc. Dutch Reform. Avocations: vintage clothing, photography, travel, historical architecture. Home and Office: 19 S Prince St Shippensburg PA 17257-1919

THOMPSON, EMMETT FRANK, forestry educator, dean; b. El Reno, Okla., Nov. 6, 1936; m. 1961; 3 children. BS, Okla. State U., 1958; MS, N.C. State U., 1960; PhD in Forest Econs., Oreg. State U., 1966. Registered forester, Ala. Asst. prof. to prof. forestry Va. Poly. Inst., 1962-73; prof. forestry, head dept. Miss. State U., 1973-77; prof. forestry Auburn (Ala.) U., 1977—, head dept., 1977-84, dean Sch. Forestry, 1977—. Contbr. articles to profl. jours. Fellow Soc. Am. Foresters; mem. Forest Products Rsch. Soc., Am. Forests, Ala. Forestry Assn., Ala. Wildlife Fedn., Coun. Forestry Engring., Forest History Soc., Forest Landowners Assn. (bd. dirs.). Office: Auburn U Sch Forestry 108M White Smith Hall Auburn AL 36849-5418

THOMPSON, ERIC THOMAS, manufacturing company executive; b. Warren, Ohio, July 19, 1962; s. Thomas Leroy Thompson and Georgia Kay (Rex) Stafani; 1 stepchild, Eugene Stefani; m. Susan E. Robertson, 1988; children: Sara Rebecca, Eric Thomas Jr., Katlyn Grace. Student., Youngstown State U., 1981, 83-84, Kent State U., 1982. Outside sales rep., disc jockey WTCL Radio Sta., Warren, Ohio, 1979-80; disc jockey WOKG, Warren, Ohio, 1981-82, WMGZ, Sharon, Pa., 1982-83; sales rep. Custom Sound Co., Warren, Ohio, 1983-86, Litco Internat., Youngstown, Ohio, 1986-88; admissions rep. Bryant and Stratton Bus. Inst., Cleve., 1988-89; broker Argent Diamond & Gems, Charlotte, N.C., 1983; asst. sales mgr. Gene and Sons Jewelers, Warren, 1986-87; mgr. sales ops. Internat. Graphics Co., Cleve., 1988; network coord. The Ohio Desk Co., Cleve., 1989-90; account executive Alco Office Furniture, Cleve., 1989-91; high sch. admissions rep. Nat. Edn. Ctr., Cleve., 1992-93; small bus. owner, operator, ptnr. Satolli Carpet Floor Covering, Warren, Ohio, 1993—; Cable TV talk show host Falls Focus Cmty. Program, 1995—; v.p., treas. Northeast Ohio Realty Investors, Inc., Warren, 1996—; disc jockey WSOM-WQXK, Salem, Ohio, 1980-82; host (TV weekly program) Newton Falls Focus, 1995—. Contbr. articles to bus. publs, newspapers and mags. Pres. Brooklyn (Ohio) Rep. club, 1990-93, treas., 1992; team capt. spl. project Am. Heart Assn. N.E. Ohio, 1992; vol. Shoes for Kids, 1991-93, Child Care Task Force, Brooklyn, 1991-93; mem. Greater Cleve. Holiday Lighting Com., 1991-93; st. capt. Mayor's Com. on Recycling, Brooklyn, 1990-93; bd. mem. Trumbull County Govt. Affairs Com., 1996—; cons. Jr. Achievement, Cleve., 1991-93; mem. Rock and Roll Hall of Fame and Mus. Task Force, Clean-Land Ohio Task Force; dir. Broad St. Merchants Group, 1994-95; bd. trustees Newton Falls United Meth. Ch., 1995—; mem. bd. July 4th Com., 1995—; mem. Youngstown-Warren Ohio Better Bus. Bur., 1993—; youth coach Newton Falls (Ohio) Hot Stove Baseball, 1994—; vol. Newton Falls Cmty. Car Show, 1995—. Recipient Outstanding Leadership award Brooklyn Rep. Club, 1990, Coun. of Sml. Bus. Outstanding Effort award, 1991. Mem. Greater Cleve. Growth Assn. (Outstanding Vol. Svc. award 1991, 93), Greater Cleve. Coun. Smaller Enterprises, Ind. C. of C., Cleve. Zool. Soc., Internat. Customer Svc. Assn., Sale and Mktg. Execs., N.E. Ohio Floor Covering Assn., Eagles Bus. and Profl. Orgn., Internat. Brotherhood Magicians, Soc. Am. Magicians, Fellowship Christian Magicians, Eagles, Newton Falls C. of C. (pres. 1994, 95, 96, bd. dirs. 1993-94, Disting. Svc. Honor Leadership award 1995), N.E. Ohio Floor Covering Assn., Youngstown Warren C. of C., Kiwanis Club (v.p. 1994-95, pres. 1995-96, chmn. program com. Newton Falls chpt. 1993-94, July 4th festivities com. 1995), Warren Civic Music Assn. Methodist. Avocations: whitewater rafting, stand up comedy, magic and illusion, travel, reading. Home: 315 Marshall St Newton Falls OH 44444-1426 Office: 367 High St NE Warren OH 44481-1224

THOMPSON, EUGENE MAYNE, retired minister; b. Oxford, N.S., Can., Jan. 5, 1931; s. Curry Allison and Hortense Elsie (Mayne) T.; m. Rhoda Mitchell, May 21, 1955; children: Adrian Calvin, Nancy Lynn, Howard Allison. BA, Acadia U., 1954; MDiv, Acadia Divinity Coll., 1976; D of Ministry, So. Bapt. Theol. Sem., 1979. Pastor South End United Bapt. Ch., Dartmouth, N.S., 1954-58; assoc. sec. of Christian Edn. United Bapt. Conv. of Atlantic Provinces, St. John, N.B., 1958-61, exec. min., 1984-96; area min. for West N.S. United Bapt. Conv. of Atlantic Provinces, Middleton, N.S., 1974-84; pastor Immanuel Bapt. Ch., Truro, N.S., 1961-65, Hillcrest Bapt. Ch., St. John, N.B., 1965-68; area min. for Man. Bapt. Union of Western Can., 1968-74; ret., 1996; coun., exec. mem. Can. Bapt. Ministries, Mississauga, Ont.; bd. dirs. Atlantic Bapt. Sr. Citizen Homes, Inc., Moncton, N.B.; bd. govs Atlantic Bapt. Coll., Moncton; trustee Acadia Div. Coll.; mem. Bapt. Found. Author: Baptist Youth Fellowship Handbook, 1958, New Design for a Dynamic Church, 1973. Avocations: music, gardening, cross country skiing.

THOMPSON, EWA M., foreign language educator; b. Kaunas, Lithuania; came to U.S., 1963; d. Jozef and Maria Majewski; m. James R. Thompson. BA in English and Russian, U. Warsaw, Poland, 1963; MFA in Piano, Sopot Conservatory Music, 1963; MA in English, Ohio U., 1964; PhD in Comparative Lit., Vamderbilt U., 1967. Instr. Vanderbilt U., Nashville, Tenn., 1964-67; asst. prof. Ind. State U., Terre Haute, 1967-68, Ind. U., 1968-70; asst. prof. Rice U., Houston, 1967-73, assoc. prof., 1974-79, prof., 1979—, chair, 1987-90; assoc. prof. U. Va., Charlottesville, 1973-74; cons. NEH, 1973—, The John D. and Catherine T. MacArthur Found., The John Simon Guggenheim Found., U.S. Dept. Edn.; vis. cons. Tex. A&M U.; seminar dir. NEH Summer Inst., Southeastern La. U., 1990; chair Russian lit. conf. Rice U., 1989; lectr. various colls. and univs. Author: Russian Formalism and Anglo-American New Criticism: A Comparative Study, 1971, Witold Gombrowicz, 1979, Understanding Russia: The Holy Fool in Russian Culture, 1987 (Chinese translation 1995), The Search for Self-Definition in Russian Literature, 1991; contbr. articles to profl. jours., chpts. to books. Mellon grant, 1990, Rice U. grant 1990, Internat. Rsch. and Excahnges Sr. Scholar grant, 1991; Hoover Inst. fellow, 1988; scholar Vanderbilt U., 1964-67; recipient Silver Thistle award Houston's Scottish Heritage Found., 1988. Roman Catholic. Office: Rice University PO Box 1892 6100 South Main Houston TX 77251

THOMPSON, FAYE ALISON, minister; b. Georgetown, Guyana, Jan. 31, 1961; came to U.S., 1980; d. Edwin Percival and Ismay Esther Gill; m. Devon Tennyson Thompson, Aug. 24, 1991. B.Bibl. Counseling, Friends Internat. Christian U., Merced, Calif., 1993. Asst. tchr. United Yount Action Day Care Ctr., Bklyn., 1981-84; rsch. analyst Merrill Lynch, Pierce, Fenner & Smith, N.Y.C., 1984-88; counselor Sheltering Arms Children's Svcs., N.Y.C., 1989-91; foster parent Angel Guardian Home, Bklyn., 1990-91; adminstrv. asst. Nat. Cable Advt., N.Y.C., 1992-94; pres. Shammah Pubs., N.Y.C., 1992—; mem. adv. bd. Zoe Ministries, Bklyn., 1994—, dir. youth dept., 1993—; instr. Dominion Bible Acad., N.Y.C., 1995; conv. spkr. Author: From A to Z Come Rhyme with Me, 1993. Pres. women's dept. The Pilgrim Assemblies Internat., Bklyn., 1994—, pres. Dominion jurisdiction women's dept., 1994. Recipient The Phillip and Marjorie Pocock award Mt. St. Joseph Acad., London, Ont., Can., 1977. Avocations: travel, photography, reading, arts and crafts, writing. Office: Shammah Publications PO Box 2989 New York NY 10185-2989

THOMPSON, FRANCIS NEAL, financial services consultant; b. Yonkers, N.Y., Oct. 21, 1940; s. Maury Weldon and Mary Temple (Meacham) T.; m. Patricia Jennings Turner, June 12, 1962 (div. 1980); children: Melissa Temple Thompson, Turner Jennings Thompson; m. Sharon Griffin, May 8, 1982. BA in Econs., Lynchburg Coll., 1962; MBA, U. Richmond, 1966. Chartered life underwriter; ChFC; CFP. Stockbroker Mason & Lee (now Legg, Mason & Co.), Lynchburg and Richmond, Va., 1960-63; pension analyst Southwestern Life Ins. Co., Dallas, 1963-68; v.p., mktg. dir. Fidelity Bankers Life Ins. Co., Richmond, 1968-75; v.p., dir., chmn. exec. com. Wheat Ins. Svcs. Inc. (now Wheat 1st, Butcher Singer Inc.), Richmond, 1975-78; chmn., CEO Corp. Cons. Inc., Richmond, 1978-84; exec. v.p., dir. Fin. Mgmt. Group, Richmond, 1984-88; v.p. mktg. dir. Ind. Fin. Mktg. Group, White Plains, N.Y., 1988-89; spl. projects mgr. The Acacia Group, Washington, 1990-91; ins. cons. Blue Cross/Blue Shield of Va., Richmond, 1992-93; regional sales mgr. Allmerica Fin., State Mut. Life and Provident Mut., 1993-97; founder Fin. Svcs. Consultants, Inc., Richmond, 1994—; cons. Signet Ins., Richmond, 1984-88, Funds of Am., Portland, 1990-91. Author: Assessing Individual Managerial Performing, 1967. Bd. dirs. Emergency Shelter Inc., Richmond, 1991-95, Boy Scouts Am.-Robert E. Lee

Coun., Richmond, 1984-94. With USN, 1955-58. Recipient Disting. Prof. 20 Yr. Svc. award Coll. for Fin. Planning, 1997. Fellow Life Underwriters Tng. Coun. (Ernest E. Cragg Amb. award 1996); mem. Ctrl. Va. Soc. CFP's (bd. dirs. 1991-97, edn. chmn. 1991-92), Richmond Life Underwriters Assn. (bd. dirs. 1994—). Presbyterian. Avocations: sailing, tennis, racketball. Home: 10006 Bellona Ct Richmond VA 23233-2044 Office: PO Box 29634 Richmond VA 23242-0634

THOMPSON, FRANK JOSEPH, political science educator; b. New Ulm, Minn., Mar. 21, 1944; s. Joseph Mariem and Alice Louise (Lindquist) T.; m. Benna Miriam, June 15, 1944; children: Samuel, Aliza, Elizabeth. BA in Polit. Sci., U. Chgo., 1966; MA in Polit. Sci., U. Calif., Berkeley, 1967, PhD in Polit. Sci., 1973. Asst. prof. polit. sci. Calif. State U., Long Beach, 1971-72; asst. prof. U. Ga., Athens, 1972-78, assoc. prof., 1978-83, prof., 1983-88, head dept., 1982-87; prof. pub. adminstrn., policy, polit. sci. and pub. health SUNY, Albany, 1987—, dean Grad. Sch. of Pub. Affairs, 1988—, assoc. provost, 1990—; analyst HEW, Washington, 1968, City Govt. Oakland, Calif., 1968-71; cons. USPHS, 1976-79, 82, U.S. Pres.'s Commn. for Nat. Agenda for 80's, 1980, Am. Pub. Welfare Assn., 1981-83; publ. cons. U.S. Adv. Commn. on Intergovtl. Rels., 1983; mem. task force on exec. and mgmt. devel. U.S. Office Pers. Mgmt., 1990; exec. dir. Nat. Commn. on the State and Local Pub. Svc., 1991—. Author: Personnel Policy in the City, 1975, Health Policy and the Bureaucracy, 1981, Public Administration: Challenges, Choices, Consequences, 1990; editor: Classics of Public Personnel Policy, 1979, 2d edit., 1991, Revitalizing State and Local Public Service, 1993; contbr. articles to profl. jours. Mem. Ga. PTA, Athens, 1980-86, N.Y. PTA, 1989—; bd. dirs. Upper Hudson Planned Parenthood, 1990-96. Pub. adminstrn. fellow U.S. Pub. Health Service, 1975-76, NSF fellow, 1970-71; recipient Simon award Internat. Jour. Pub. Adminstrn., 1981. Fellow Nat. Acad. Pub. Adminstrn.; mem. Am. Pub. Health Assn., Assn. for Pub. Policy Analysis and Mgmt., Am. Soc. for Pub. Adminstrn. (publs. com. 1982-84, William E. Mosher award 1983), Am. Polit. Sci. Assn. (chmn. departmental services com. 1985-87, exec. com. sect. pub. adminstrn. 1985-87, 89—, chair sect. pub. adminstrn. 1990-91, chair Gaus award com. 1991-92), Nat. Assn. Schs. Pub. Affairs and Adminstrn. (peer rev. com. 1984-86, 1st chmn. commn. on peer rev. and accreditation 1986-87, chmn. task force on revitalizing the pub. svc., v.p. 1990-91, pres. 1991-92), N.Y. State Acad. Pub. Adminstrn. (bd. dirs. 1994—). Home: 9 Harvard Ave Albany NY 12208-2019 Office: SUNY Grad Sch Pub Affairs Albany NY 12222

THOMPSON, FRED, senator; b. Sheffield, Ala., Aug. 19, 1942. BS, Memphis State U., 1964; JD, Vanderbilt U., 1967. Asst. U.S. atty. Mid. Tenn., 1969-72; min. counsel Senate Watergate Com., 1973-74; pvt. practice, 1975-94; spl. counsel senate fgn. rels. com. U.S. Intelligence and Fgn. Rels. Coms., 1980; spl. counsel Senate Intelligence Com., 1982; atty. Arent, Fox, Kintner, Plotkin & Kahn, 1991-94; U.S. senator from Tenn., 1994—. Appeared in 18 films including The Hunt for Red October, In the Line of Fire, Cape Fear, 1985-94. Office: US Senate 523 Dirksen Senate Bldg Washington DC 20510-4203

THOMPSON, FRED CLAYTON, engineering executive, consultant; b. Snow Shoe, Pa., Feb. 26, 1928; s. Clayton Alfred and Edna (Pearl) T.; m. M. Joanne Bender; children: Marjorie Ann, Richard Clayton, Scott David, Carol Ann. BSEE, Pa. State U., 1950, MSEE, 1958. Electronics engr. Martin Corp., Balt., 1965-54; tech. dir. HRB System S, State Coll., Pa., 1954-68; v.p. engring. Locus, Inc., State Coll., 1958-78, pres., chmn., 1978-88, cons., 1989—. Patentee in microwave circuitry. Past pres. and dir. Private Industry Coun. With U.S. Army, 1950-52. Named Hon. Alumni Pa. State U., 1987, Disting. Toastmaster, Toastmaster Internat., 1976. Avocation: barbershop quartet singing. Office: care Locus Inc PO Box 740 State College PA 16804-0740

THOMPSON, GARY W., public relations executive; b. Berkeley, Calif., July 15, 1947. BA, Northwestern U., England, 1969—. Acct. exec. Allen & Doward Advt., 1971-74; acct. exec. Hoefer-Amedei Assocs., 1978-81, acct. supr., 1978, v.p., 1978-81; v.p., assoc. dir. Ketchum, 1981-82, sr. v.p., dir., 1982-84, exec. v.p., 1984-87, exec. v.p., dir. we. region, 1987-89, exec. v.p., dir. U.S.A., 1989-90; pres., CEO Hi-Tech Comm., 1990-95, Golin/Harris Techs., 1995—. Mem. Pub. Rels. Soc. Am. (counselors acad., membership chmn. San Francisco chpt. 1983, placement, newsletter chmn. 1985), Internat. Assn. Bus. Communicators,. Office: Golin/Harris Techs 101 Howard St San Francisco CA 94105-1629

THOMPSON, GEORGE ALBERT, geophysics educator; b. Swissvale, Pa., June 5, 1919; s. George Albert Sr. and Maude Alice (Harkness) T.; m. Anita Kimmell, July 20, 1944; children: Albert J., Dan A., David C. BS, Pa. State U., 1941; MS, MIT, 1942; PhD, Stanford U., 1949. Geologist, geophysicist U.S. Geol. Survey, Menlo Park, Calif., 1942-49; asst. prof. Stanford (Calif.) U., 1949-55, assoc. prof., 1955-60, prof. geophysics, 1960—, chmn. geophysics dept., 1967-86, chmn. geology dept., 1979-82, Otto N. Miller prof. earth scis., 1980-89, dean sch. earth scis., 1987-89; part-time geologist U.S. Geol. Survey, Menlo Park, 1949-76; cons. adv. com. on reactor safeguards Nuclear Regulation Commn., Washington, 1974-94; mem. bd. earth sci. NRC, 1986-88, vice chmn. Yucca Mountain Hydrology-tectonics panel NRC, 1990-92; mem. exec. com. Inc. Rsch. Inst. for Seismology, Washington, 1990-92; mem. sr. external events rev. com. Lawrence Livermore Nat. Lab., 1989-93; mem. Coun. on Continental Sci. Drilling, 1990-94; cons. Los Alamos Nat. Lab. on volcano-tectonic processes, 1993-96, S.W. Rsch. Inst., 1993; chair com. to review sci. issues NRC, Ward Valley, Calif., 1994-95; mem. panel on probabalistic volcanic hazard analysis Geomatrix Cons., Inc., 1995-96. Author over 100 research papers. With USNR, 1944-46. Recipient G.K. Gilbert award in seismic geology, 1964; NSF postdoctoral fellow, 1956-57; Guggenheim Found. fellow, 1963-64. Fellow AAAS, Geol. Soc. Am. (coun. mem. 1983-86, George P. Woollard award 1983, v.p. 1995, pres. 1996), Am. Geophys. Union; mem. NAS, Seismol. Soc. Am., Soc. Exploration Geophysicists. Avocation: forestry. Home: 421 Adobe Pl Palo Alto CA 94306-4501 Office: Stanford U Geophysics Dept Stanford CA 94305-2215

THOMPSON, GEORGE LEE, consulting company executive; b. Denver, June 12, 1933; s. George H. and Frances M. (Murphy) T.; m. Patricia M. MacKenzie, Sept. 25, 1993; children: Shannon, Tracy, Bradley. BS in Bus., U. Colo., 1957; postgrad. in advanced mgmt., NYU, 1969. With GTE Sylvania, Denvers, Mass., 1957-65, nat. sales mgr., 1965-67, mktg. mgr., 1967-68; v.p. sales entertainment products Batavia, N.Y., 1968-73; dir. corp. mktg. Stamford, Conn., 1973-74; v.p. mktg. Servomation Corp., N.Y.C., 1974-76, exec. v.p., 1976-78; exec. v.p. Singer Co., Edison, N.J., 1978-81, pres., 1981-83; pres. consumer products SCM Corp., N.Y.C., 1983-86; pres., CEO Smith-Corona Corp., New Canaan, Conn., 1986-89, chmn., CEO, 1989-95; chmn. Mackenzie-Thompson Assocs., Palm City, Fla., 1995—; bd. dirs. Vol. Products, Inc. Bd. dirs. Internat. Tennis Hall of Fame, Am. Jr. Golf Found., United Way of New Canaan, 1989-93; chmn. EC-92 Standards Com. U.S. Dept. Commerce; mem. bus. alumni adv. coun. U. Colo., 1989-94; mem. bd. overseers Sch. Bus. U. Conn.; mem. Pres.'s Export Coun., 1991-93; mem. bd. advisors Jr. league. Recipient Disting. Bus. Alumni award U. Colo., 1990. Mem. Computer and Bus. Equipment Mfg. Assn. (bd. dirs. 1992-94), Sales and Mktg. Execs. Internat. (trustee), Am. Mgmt. Assn. (bd. trustees, exec. com. chmn., gen. mgmt. coun.), St. John Assn. (bd. dirs., pres. 1983-93), New Canaan Field Club, Woodway Country Club, Club at Seabrook Island, Wilton Riding Club (bd. govs. 1980-83), Navesink Country Club (bd. govs. 1983-86), Harbour Ridge Yacht and Country Club, Chi Psi. Episcopalian. Home: 13507 NW Wax Myrtle Trl Palm City FL 34990-4828 Office: Mackenzie Thompson Assocs 13507 NW Wax Myrtle Trl Palm City FL 34990-4828

THOMPSON, GEORGE RALPH, church administrator; b. Barbados, Mar. 20, 1929; s. George Gilbert and Edna (Griffith) T.; m. Imogene Clotilde Barker, July 19, 1959; children: Carol Jean, Linda Mae, Gerald Randolph. BA, Atlantic Union Coll., 1956; MA, Andrews U., 1958, BD, 1962, DD (hon.), 1983. Ordained to ministry Seventh-day Adventists, 1959. Evangelist South Caribbean conf. Seventh-day Adventists, Trinidad and Tobago, 1950-53; tchr., ch. pastor, chmn. dept. theology Caribbean Union Coll., Trinidad and Tobago, 1953-54, 59-64; pres. East Caribbean conf. Seventh-day Adventists, Barbados, 1964-70; pres. Caribbean Union conf. Seventh-day Adventists, Trinidad and Tobago, 1970-75; v.p. Gen. Conf. Seventh-day Adventists, Washington, 1975-80; sec. Gen. Conf. Seventh-day Adventists, Silver Spring, Md., 1980—; host radio shows, Barbados. Office: Gen Conf Seventh-day Adventists Ch 12501 Old Columbia Pike Silver Spring MD 20904-6601

THOMPSON, GERALD E., historian, educator; b. Oakland, Calif., Nov. 27, 1947; s. Norman J. and Margaret L. (Daniels) T.; m. Margaret H. Hood, June 6, 1970. BA, U. Ariz., 1969, MA, 1972, PhD, 1978. Editorial asst. Ariz. and the West, Tucson, 1975-77; asst. editor Ariz. and the West, 1977-78; asst. prof. history U. Toledo, 1978-83, assoc. prof., 1983-88, prof., 1988—; editor The Historian, Toledo, 1983-90; hist. cons. Mescalero Apache Tribe, various pubs.; humanities lectr. U. Toledo, 1993-94; vis. assoc. prof. dept. history U. Ariz., summer 1984; instr. Pima Coll., fall 1977. Author: Army and the Navajo, 1976, Edward F. Beale and the American West, 1983; compiler: A Guide to History-Related Microform Holdings, 1986; contbr. articles to profl. jours., chpts. to books. Counselor Ariz. Dept. Corrections, 1970-71. Served with Ariz. N.G., 1969-75. Recipient Ariz. Hist. Found. award, Exceptional Faculty Mem. award U. Toledo, 1985, 91, Ariz. Sonmichsen award, 1997; Edwin Turville fellow U. Ariz., 1975. Mem. Am. Hist. Assn., Western Hist. Assn., Nat. Assn. Scholars, Soc. Calif. Pioneers, Orgn. Am. Historians, Ariz. Hist. Soc., Ohio Acad. History (publs. awards com. 1982-83), Phi Beta Kappa, Phi Kappa Phi, Phi Alpha Theta (historian 1983-90, merit achievement award 1989). Office: U Toledo Dept History 2801 W Bancroft St Toledo OH 43606-3328

THOMPSON, GERALD LUTHER, operations research and applied mathematics educator; b. Rolfe, Iowa, Nov. 25, 1923; s. Luther and Sylva Carlotta (Larson) T.; m. Dorothea Vivian Mosley, Aug. 25, 1954; children: Allison M., Emily A., Abigail E. B.S. in Elec. Engring, Iowa State U., 1944; M.S. in Math, Mass. Inst. Tech., 1948; Ph.D., U. Mich., 1953. Instr. math. Princeton, 1951-53; asst. prof. math. Dartmouth, 1953-58; prof. math. Ohio Wesleyan U., Delaware, 1958-59; assoc. prof. applied math. and indsl. adminstrn. Carnegie-Mellon U., Pitts., 1959-63; prof. Carnegie-Mellon U., 1963—, IBM prof. systems and operations research, 1980—; E.D. Walker Centennial fellow IC2 Inst. U. Tex., 1985—; cons. Econometric Research Program, Princeton, IBM, Bethlehem Steel Co., Port Authority of Allegheny County, McKinsey & Co., Applied Devices Corp., PPG Industries, Westinghouse Electric Corp., Timken Co., J & L Steel, GM; prin. investigator Mgmt. Scis. Research Group, Carnegie-Mellon U. Co-author, author: Introduction to Finite Mathematics, 1957, Finite Mathematical Structures, 1959, Finite Mathematics with Business Applications, 1962, Industrial Scheduling, 1963, Programming and Probability Models in Operations Research, 1973, Mathematical Theory of Expanding and Contracting Economies, 1976, Optimal Control Theory: Management Science Applications, 1981, Computational Economics: Economic Modeling with Optimization Software, 1992; assoc. editor: Inst. Mgmt. Scis. Jour, 1966-69; Contbr. articles to profl. jours. Rep. of Inst. Mgmt. Scis. to NRC. Served with USNR, 1943-46. Ford Found. research fellow, 1963-64. Mem. AAAS, Math. Assn. Am., Inst. Mgmt. Scis., Operations Research Soc. Am., Phi Beta Kappa, Phi Kappa Phi, Tau Beta Phi, Eta Kappa Nu, Phi Mu Alpha. Home: 15 Wedgewood Ln Pittsburgh PA 15215-1560

THOMPSON, GLENN JUDEAN, library science educator; b. Sioux Falls, S.D., Oct. 16, 1936; s. Carl Melvin and Emma Bertina (Johnson) T.; m. Agnes Myrleen Nord, Aug. 23, 1958; children—Christine Faye, Nathan Glenn. B.S., Augustana Coll., Sioux Falls, S.D., 1958; M.A., U. Minn., 1966; Ed.D., U. S.D., 1969. Cert. music tchr., English tchr., librarian, audiovisual dir., Minn. Music tchr. Wayzata Pub. Schs. (Minn.), 1958-63; librarian, audiovisual dir. Perham Pub. Schs. (Minn.), 1963-66; mem. faculty St. Cloud State Coll., (Minn.), 1966-70; mem. faculty U. Wis.-Eau Claire, 1970—, chmn. dept. library sci. and media edn., 1972-90, prof., 1988—. Mem. ALA, Wis. Library Assn., Wis. Ednl. Media Assn., NEA. Home: N7191 540th St Menomonie WI 54751-5588 Office: U Wis Eau Claire Found & Libr Sci Dept Garfield Ave Eau Claire WI 54702-4004

THOMPSON, GORDON, JR., federal judge; b. San Diego, Dec. 28, 1929; s. Gordon and Garnet (Meese) T.; m. Jean Peters, Mar. 17, 1951; children—John M., Peter Renwick, Gordon III. Grad., U. So. Calif., 1951, Southwestern U. Sch. Law, Los Angeles, 1956. Bar: Calif. 1956. With Dist. Atty.'s Office, County of San Diego, 1957-60; partner firm Thompson & Thompson, San Diego, 1960-70; U.S. dist. judge So. Dist. Calif., San Diego, 1970—, chief judge, 1984-91, sr. judge, 1994—. Bd. dirs. Sharp Meml. Hosp. Mem. Am. Bd. Trial Advocates, ABA, San Diego County Bar Assn. (v.p. 1970), Delta Chi. Club: San Diego Yacht. Office: US Dist Ct 940 Front St San Diego CA 92101-8994

THOMPSON, GORDON WILLIAM, dentist, educator, administrator; b. Vancouver, B.C., Can., Dec. 22, 1940; s. Clarence and Emma Jean T.; m. Marilyn Jean Lust, May 23, 1964; children: Janice Lynne, Phillip Glen, Andrew James. Student, U. B.C., Vancouver, 1958-61; D.D.S., U. Alta., Edmonton, Can., 1965; M.Sc.D., U. Toronto, Ont., Can., 1967, Ph.D., 1971. Practice dentistry Wetaskiwin, Alta., 1965; asst. prof. dentistry U. Toronto, 1969-72, asso. prof., 1972-77, prof., 1977-78; prof., dean Faculty of Dentistry, U. Alta., 1978-89, chmn. dept. dental health care, 1989-94; exec. dir. Alta. Dental Assn., Edmonton, 1994—; condr. rsch. programs in Scotland, Portugal, Ecuador. Editor Ont. Dental Assn. Jour., 1977-78; contbr. over 100 articles and 60 abstracts to profl. jours. Fellow Royal Coll. Dentists (Can., coun. 1988-94), Internat. Coll. Dentists; mem. Alta. Dental Assn., Can. Dental Assn., Internat. Assn. Dental Rsch., Assn. Can. Faculties of Dentistry (pres. 1982-84), Can. Fund. for Dental Edn. (chmn. 1991-93), Dentistry Can. Fund (chmn. 1993-95), Can. Assn. Pub. Health Dentists (pres. 1995-97), Am. Coll. Dentists, Can. Assn. Pub. Health Dentistry, Rotary (Edmonton). Conservative. Mem. United Ch. Canada. Home: 12429 28th Ave, Edmonton, AB Canada T6J 4G4 Office: Alta Dental Assn, 8230 105th St, Edmonton, AB Canada T6E 5H9

THOMPSON, HAROLD JEROME, counselor, mental retardation professional; b. Oklahoma City, May 5, 1947; s. John Caldwell and Marian Louree (Cejda) T.; m. Donna Marie Steed, May 13, 1967 (div. Feb. 1977); children: Treva Marie, Derek Martin; m. Clydia Dee Nichols, Aug. 11, 1984 (div. Apr. 1993). BA, Langston U., 1983; MS, Northea. Okla. State U., 1985. Lic. profl. counselor; qualified mental retardation profl.; cert. behavior analyst. Sales rep. Jones-Newly Supply Co., Oklahoma City, 1969-72, Jones-Newby Supply Co., Tulsa, 1972-74; ins. sales agt. ind. brokers, Tulsa, 1974-77; sales rep. Empire Plumbing Supply, Tulsa, 1977-79, 81-82, Amfac Mech. Supply, Tulsa, 1979-81; chmn. citizens adv. bd. Tulsa Psychiat. Ctr., 1982-83; counselor Horizon Program Shadow Mountain Inst., Tulsa, 1983-90; psychologist Hissom Meml. Ctr., Sand Springs., Okla., 1985-91; pvt. practice Tulsa, 1990—; cons., vol. counselor to mentally retarded, Denver, 1987. With U.S. Army, 1966-68. Mem. Am. Assn. on Mental Deficiency, Nat. Assn. Masters in Philosophy. Republican. Roman Catholic. Office: Behavioral Solutions 7217 S Columbia Tulsa OK 74136

THOMPSON, HAROLD LEE, lawyer; b. Dayton, Ohio, Feb. 17, 1945; s. Harold Edward Thompson and Johnita Dorothy (Cox) Metcalf; children: Aishah T., Aliya S. BS in Acctg., Cen. State U., Wilberforce, Ohio, 1967; JD, U. Conn., 1972. Bar: Ohio 1975, U.S. Dist. Ct. (so. dist.) Ohio 1975, D.C. 1976, U.S. Ct. Appeals (4th cir.) 1990. Acct. Communication Satellite Corp., 1968-69; atty. Ohio State Legal Service, Columbus, Ohio, 1972-74; of counsel Ohio Indsl. Commn., Columbus, 1974-76; sole practice Columbus, 1976—; ptnr. Jones & Thompson, Columbus, 1984-88; prin. H. Lee Thompson Co. L.P.A., Columbus, 1988—; pres. toys and clothing H. Lee Toy Co., Columbus, 1988—; adj. prof. law Columbus State Coll., 1989; instr. Acad. Ct. Reporting, 1989; adj. prof. tax and prins. of acctg. Bliss Coll., 1990-91; mem. Am. Bd. Forensic Examiners. Reginald Heber Smith fellow U.S. Fed. Ct., 1972. Mem. ATLA (exec. mem. birth trauma litigation group), Ohio Bar Assn., Am. Coll. Legal Medicine, Ohio Acad. Trial Lawyers, Franklin County Trial Lawyers Assn., Univ. Club, Columbus Met. Club. Roman Catholic. Avocations: reading, music, jogging. Office: 85 E Gay St Ste 810 Columbus OH 43215-3118

THOMPSON, HENRY NAINOA, hospital administrator; b. Honolulu, July 15, 1921; s. Henry Nainoa Sr. and Irmgard Luukia (Harbottle) T.; m. Pearl Elvina Mary Barbel, Nov. 16, 1946; children: Scott Henry Nainoa, Kirk Leopold Kumulani. Student, U. Wash., 1940-42, Columbia U., 1942-44; BA in Phys. Therapy, Columbia U., 1946, MA in Corrective Phys. Edn. & Rehab., 1950; cert. poliomyelitis, U. So. Calif., L.A., 1950; cert. adminstrn. phys. therapy, Stanford U., 1950; cert. adminstrn. rehab., Inst. Phys. Medicine & Rehab., 1953; cert. adminstrn. pers., U. Hawaii, 1956; cert. job sampling testing, Ins. for Crippled and Disabled, 1958; cert. analysis fin. statements, U. Hawaii, 1960. Phys. therapist VA Regional Office, N.Y.C., 1946; chief phys. therapy Nat. Soc. for Crippled Children and Adults, Honolulu, 1948-49, Kauikeolani Children's Hosp., Honolulu, 1950-53; asst. dir. Rehab. Ctr. Hawaii, Honolulu, 1953-68; adminstr. Wahiawa (Hawaii) Gen. Hosp., 1968-71; hosp. adminstr. The Queen's Med. Ctr., Honolulu, 1971-74; dir. arthritis ctr. U. Hawaii Sch. Medicine, Honolulu, 1974-75; dep. dir. county state hosps. Dept. of Health, State of Hawaii, Honolulu, 1975-82; adminstr. Hawaii State Health Planning and Devel. Agy. State of Hawaii, Honolulu, 1982-86; past dir. Family Medicine, Inc., Honolulu. Past pres. Hawaii Kai Comty. Assn.; past pres., dir. Abilities Unltd. With AUS, 1946-48. Named one of 12 Nat. Phys. Fitness Leaders of Am., Pres.'s Johnson's Program for Phys. Fitness, 1965. Fellow Am. Coll. Hosp. Adminstrs.; mem. APHA, Am. Health Planning Assn., Hosp. Assn. Hawaii (assoc.), Am. Hosp. Assn. (assoc.), Koko Head Athletic Club (past pres.), Hawaii State Health Coun. (past pres.), Nat. Rehab. Assn. (past dir. Hawaii chpt.), Am. Assn. Phys. Therapy (past pres. Hawaii chpt.), Elks. Home and Office: 6815 Niumalu Loop Honolulu HI 96825-1639

THOMPSON, HERBERT, JR., bishop; b. N.Y.C.; m. Ruselle Cross, 1968; children: Herbert, Owen, Kyrie. Grad. cum laude, Lincoln U., 1962; MDiv, Gen. Theol. Sem., N.Y.C., 1965; postgrad., Stony Brook U., Ch. Divinity Sch. of Pacific; D of Ministry, United Theol. Sem., Dayton, Ohio, 1992. Ordained to ministry Episcopal Ch. as deacon, 1965, then as priest. Chaplain Chester County, Pa.; vicar St. Gabriel's Ch., Bklyn.; rector Christ Ch., Bellport, N.Y., 1971-77, Grace Ch., Jamaica, 1977-88; bishop coadjutor Diocese of So. Ohio, 1988-91, bishop, 1992—; exec. dir. Interfaith Svcs., Bklyn.; colloquium moderator Gen. Theol. Sem.; instr., lectr. Mercer Sch. Theology; bd. dirs. Jamaica Devel. Corp. Reader Gen. Ordination Exams.; mem. Presiding Bishop's Commn. on Black Ministries, Coalition for Human Needs; mem. joint standing com. on planning for Gen. Conv., coun. of advice to pres. of Ho. of Deps.; bd. dirs. Cen. Queens YMCA, Queens Fedn. Chs., St. Christopher-Ottilie Home; chmn. Mayor's Commn. on Children, Cin. Served with USAF. Named Hon. Canon Cathedral of the Incarnation Diocese of Long Island, 1985. Mem. Jamaica C. of C. (bd. dirs). Address: 412 Sycamore St Cincinnati OH 45202-4166*

THOMPSON, HERBERT ERNEST, tool and die company executive; b. Jamaica, N.Y., Sept. 8, 1923; s. Walter and Louise (Joly) T.; student Stevens Inst. Tech., 1949-51; m. Patricia Elaine Osborn, Aug. 2, 1968; children: Robert Steven, Debra Lynn. Foreman, Conner Tool Co., 1961-62, Eason & Waller Grinding Corp., 1962-63; owner Endco Machined Products, 1966-67, Thompson Enterprises, 1974—; pres. Method Machined Products, Phoenix, 1967; pres., owner Quality Tool, Inc., 1967-96. Served to capt. USAAF, 1942-46. Decorated D.F.C., Air medal with cluster. Home: 14009 N 42nd Ave Phoenix AZ 85023-5306 Office: 4223 W Clarendon Ave Phoenix AZ 85019-3618

THOMPSON, HERBERT STANLEY, neuro-ophthalmologist; b. Shansi, China, June 12, 1932; came to U.S., 1949, naturalized, 1955; s. Robert Ernest and Ellen (Mulligan) T.; m. Delores Lucille Johnson, June 27, 1953; children: Geoffrey, Peter, Kenneth, Philip, Susan. Student, Methodist Coll., Belfast, No. Ireland, 1947-49; B.A., U. Minn., 1953, M.D., 1961; M.S., U. Iowa, 1966. Diplomate Am. Bd. Ophthalmology (assoc. examiner 1972-88, bd. dirs. 1989-96, chmn. ABO 1996). Intern U. Iowa, Iowa City, 1961-62; resident in ophthalmology U. Iowa, 1962-66; fellow in pupillography Columbia Coll. Physicians and Surgeons, 1962; fellow in clin. neuro-ophthalmology U. Calif., San Francisco, 1966-67; prof. ophthalmology U. Iowa, Iowa City, 1976—; dir. neuro-ophthalmology unit U. Iowa, 1967—; practice medicine specializing in neuro-ophthalmology Iowa City, 1967—. Editor: Topics in Neuro-opthalmology, 1979; assoc. editor Am. Jour. Ophthalmology, 1981-84, book rev. editor, 1984-91; cons. Stedman's Med. Dictionary, 26th edit. Served with AUS, 1954-55. NIH spl. fellow, 1966-67; research career devel. awardee, 1968-72. Fellow Am. Acad. Ophthalmoogy, N.Am. Neuro-ophthalmol. Soc.; mem. Am. Ophthalmol. Soc., Cogan Ophthalmic History Soc. (Charles Snyder lectr. 1995). Primary research interest: movements of the pupil of human eye. Office: U Iowa Dept Ophthalmology Iowa City IA 52242

THOMPSON, HOWARD ELLIOTT, business educator; b. West Allis, Wis., July 30, 1934; s. Leonard Adolph and Hulda Axelina (Granstrom) T.; m. Judith M. Gram, June 30, 1956; children: Linda Kay, Karen Marie, James Howard, John Leonard, Ann Elizabeth. BS, U. Wis., 1956, MS, 1958, PhD, 1964. Mathematician, ops. rsch. analyst A.O. Smith Corp., Milw., 1957-61; asst. prof. Sch. Bus. U. Wis., Madison, 1964-67, assoc. prof., 1967-69, prof., 1969—, Mary Rennebohm prof., 1975-85, Kuechenmeister-Bascom prof., 1985—; vis. prof. Ohio State U., 1970-71; cons. various utilities and utility commns., 1968—; cons. World Bank, 1981-83; Wis. atty. gen., 1973-74; cons. U.S. Energy Info. Adminstrn., 1990—. Author: Applications of Calculus in Business and Economics, 1973, A Brief Calculus with Applications to Business and Economics, 1976, Management Science, 1981, Regulatory Finance, 1991; contbr. articles to profl. jours. Mem. Am. Fin. Assn., Am. Econs. Assn., Ops. Rsch. Soc. Am., Inst. Mgmt. Scis., Am. Inst. Decision Scis., Math. Assn. Am., Pi Mu Epsilon, Beta Gamma Sigma, Alpha Iota Delta, Phi Kappa Phi. Home: 7529 Fox Point Cir Madison WI 53717-1058 Office: Univ Wis Sch Business Grainger Hall 975 University Ave Madison WI 53706-1324

THOMPSON, HUGH LEE, academic administrator; b. Martinsburg, W.Va., Mar. 25, 1934; s. Frank Leslie and Althea T.; m. Patricia Smith; children: Cheri, Linda, Tempe, Vicki. B.S., B.A. in English and Secondary Edn, Shepherd Coll., Shepherdstown, W.Va., 1956; MS, Pa. State U., 1958; Ph.D. in Higher Edn. Adminstrn, Case Western Res. U., 1969. Mem. faculty Pa. State U., 1957-60, Akron (Ohio) U., 1960-62; mem. faculty Baldwin-Wallace Coll., Berea, Ohio, 1962-70, asst. to pres., 1966-69, dir. instl. planning, asst. to pres., 1969-70; coordinator Associated Colls., Cleve., 1970-71; pres. Siena Heights Coll., Adrian, Mich., 1971-77, Detroit Inst. Tech., 1977-80; chancellor Ind. U., Kokomo, 1980-90; pres. Washburn U., Topeka, 1990—; mem. president's adv. coun. Assn. Governing Bds. Univs. and Colls. Mem. Am. Assn. State Colls. and Univs. (coun. of state reps., steering com. urban and met. univs. coun.), North Ctrl. Assn. (evaluator, cons.). Home: 3130 SW Shadow Ln Topeka KS 66604-2541 Office: Washburn U Office of Pres Topeka KS 66621 *I have found that to be successful in any field of endeavor an individual must work very diligently at finding solutions to problems, should be highly goal oriented, honest and forthright, and adhere to the teachings of Christ.*

THOMPSON, HUGH P, justice; b. Montezuma, Ga., July 7, 1943. Grad., Emory U., JD, 1969. Bar: Ga. 1970. Pvt. practice Milledgeville, Ga., 1970-71; judge Recorder's Ct. of Milledgeville, 1971-79, Baldwin County Ct., 1973-79; judge, chief judge Superior Ct. of Ga., 1979-94; justice Supreme Ct. of Ga., Atlanta, 1994—; instr. bus. law Ga. COll., 1971-72. Recipient Disting. Svc. award Baldwin County Jaycees, 1972; named Outstanding Young Man of Baldwin County, 1972. Mem. State Bar Ga., Jud. Coun. Ga., Ocmulgee Jud. Cir. Bar Assn. Avocations: hunting, rose gardening, golf, fishing. Office: Supreme Ct Ga State Judicial Bldg Atlanta GA 30334

THOMPSON, HUNTER STOCKTON, author, political analyst, journalist; b. Louisville, July 18, 1937; s. Jack R. and Virginia (Ray) T.; 1 child, Juan. Carribean corr. N.Y. Herald Tribune, 1959-60; South Am. corr. Nat. Observer, 1961-63; West Coast corr. The Nation, 1964-66; columnist Ramparts, 1967-68, Scanlan's, 1969-70; nat. affairs editor Rolling Stone, 1970—; global affairs corr. High Times, 1977-82; political columnist San Francisco Examiner, 1985—; polit. analyst European mags. London Observer, Tempo, Time Out, Das Magazine, Nieuwe Revu, Die Woche, 1988—; judge Nat. Book Awards, 1975. Author: Prince Jellyfish, 1960, Hell's Angels, 1966, The Rum Diary, 1967, Fear and Loathing in Las Vegas, 1972, Fear and Loathing On the Campaign Trail '72, 1973, The Great Shark Hunt, 1979, (with Ralph Steadman) The Curse of Lono, 1983, Generation of Swine, 1988, Songs of the Doomed, 1990, Screwjack, 1991, Better Than Sex, 1993; creator Gonzo journalism. Mem. president's task force; mem. nat. adv. bd. Nat. Org. for the Reform of Morivanna Laws, 1976—; founder 4th Amendment Found. Mem. NRA, U.S. Naval Inst., Air Force Assn., Hong Kong Fgn. Corrs., Kona Coast Marlin Fisherman's Assn., Vincent Black

Shadow Soc., Woody Creek Rod and Gun Club (exec. dir.), Overseas Press Club, Nat. Press Club. Clubs: Key West Mako, Nat. Press, Hong Kong Fgn. Corrs. Office: Janklow & Nesbit 598 Madison Ave New York NY 10022-1614

THOMPSON, J. ANDY, bank executive; b. Ft. Worth, Sept. 21, 1943; s. Fredrick Dickson and Mary Alice (Rhea) T.; m. Nancy Sealy, Jan. 15, 1966; children: J. Andrew Jr., Christopher Sealy. BBA, U. Tex., 1965. Exec. v.p. Internat. Svc. Ins. Co., Ft. Worth, 1968-83; exec. v.p. Ctrl. Bancorp. Inc., Ft. Worth, 1984-86, pres., 1986-88, chmn., chief exec. officer, 1988—; chmn., chief exec. officer Cen. Bank & Trust, Ft. Worth, 1988—, North Ft. Worth Bank, 1988—; adv. bd. Policy Mgmt. Systems, Columbia, S.C., 1975-83; bd. dirs. Ft. Worth C. of C., 1989—. Mem. adminstrv. bd. First Meth. Ch.; trustee, chmn. Harris Meth. Hosp., Ft. Worth; chmn., trustee Harris Meth. Health System; mem. exec. com., bd. dirs. Lena Pope Home for Children: bd. dirs. James L. West Presbyn. Spl. Care Ctr. Capt. U.S. Army, 1966-68, Vietnam. Mem. Tex. Banker's Assn., Am. Banker's Assn., Ft. Worth Club (pres. 1993—, mem. bd. govs.), Rotary Internat. Republican. Methodist. Avocations: tennis, sailing, golf.

THOMPSON, JACK EDWARD, mining company executive; b. Central City, Nebr., Nov. 17, 1924; s. Ray Elbert and Bessie Fay (Davis) T.; m. Maria del Carmen Larrea, May 8, 1948; children: Jack Edward, Ray Anthony, Robert Davis. Student, Northwestern U., 1942-43, Colo. Sch. Mines, 1943-45; D of Engring. (hon.), Colo. Sch. Mines, 1993. V.p. Cía. Química Comercial de Cuba S.A., 1946-60, Cía. de Fomento Químico S.A., 1946-60; with Newmont Mining Corp., N.Y.C., 1960-86; asst. to pres. Newmont Mining Corp., 1964-67, v.p., 1967-71, dir., 1969-86, exec. v.p., 1971-74, pres., 1974-85, vice chmn., 1985-86, cons., 1986-90. Chmn. bd. trustees Minerals Industry Ednl. Found.; mem. Pres.'s Coun. Colo. Sch. Mines. Recipient Distinguished Achievement medal Colo. Sch. Mines, 1974. Mem. AIME, Mining and Metall. Soc. Am., Mining Found. of S.W. (pres., bd. govs.), Tucson Country Club.

THOMPSON, JAMES AVERY, JR., legal intern; b. Whiteville, N.C., Oct. 3, 1947; s. James Avery and Mary Elizabeth (Davis) T.; m. Julia Lee Stephens Thompson, June 7, 1969 (div. July 1979); 1 child, Marlee Amanda Elizabeth Thompson; m. Susannah Elizabeth Rupp Thompson, May 16, 1987; 1 child, Sarah Mary Elizabeth Thompson. AA (hon.), Marion (Ala.) Mil. Inst., 1967; BA, U. Ala., Tuscaloosa, 1969; MLS, 1973; MBA, So. Calif. Inst., Claremont, 1988; JD, Am. Coll. of Law, 1988. Mus. curator U. Ala., Birmingham, 1972-73, med. libr., 1973-82; asst. law libr. U. Laverne (Calif.) Law Sch., 1985-86; ref. libr. Western State U. Sch. Law, Fullerton, Calif., 1986-88; prof., instr. Am. Coll. Law, Brea, Calif., 1988-89; dir., instr. U. West L.A. Law Libr., 1988-90; legal intern Law Office Frank Phillips, Yorba Linda, Calif., 1990-91, Law Office Susannah Thompson, Temecula, Calif., 1991—. Author numerous periodicals in field. Campaign chmn. Med. Libr. United Way, Birmingham, Ala., 1979-80; mem. Lions Club, Tarrant, Ala., 1975-77; dir., spon. Tennis Assn. Pleasant Grove, Ala., 1980-82. Recipient Eagle Scout award, Order of Arrow Boy Scouts Am., 1963; named pres. Student Bar Assn., Am. Coll. Law, Brea, Calif., 1987-88, editor Law Review Am. Coll. Law, Brea, Calif., 1988. Mem. Royal Numismatic Soc. Can., Royal Philatelic Soc. Can., U.S. Tennis Assn., Am. Numismatic Assn., Delta Theta Phi, Alpha Sigma Phi. Democrat. Methodist. Avocations: numismatics, philately, tennis, anthropology, ice skating. Office: Law Office Susan Thompson 41593 Winchester Rd Ste 201 Temecula CA 92590-4857

THOMPSON, JAMES CLARK, utilities executive; b. St. Louis, Sept. 24, 1939; s. Leonard Andrew and Virginia Evelyn (Clark) T.; m. Gerry Marie Rush, Oct. 2, 1965; children: Ren James, David James. BSBA, Washington U., St. Louis, 1968. Various positions then corp. sec. Union Electric Co., St. Louis, 1982—; sec. Union Electric Devel. Corp., 1982—, also dir. Trustee Laumeier Sculpture Park. Petty officer 2d class USN, 1957-60. Mem. Am. Soc. Corp. Secs. (pres. St. Louis chpt. 1989-90), U.S. Naval Cryptologic Vets. Assn., 1904 World's Fair Soc. (sec. 1987—). Republican. Avocation: collecting 1904 World's Fair and Disney memorabilia. Office: Union Electric Co PO Box 149 Saint Louis MO 63166-0149

THOMPSON, JAMES HOWARD, historian, library administrator; b. Memphis, Aug. 20, 1934; s. Curtis Barnabas and Clara (Terry) T.; m. Margareta Ortenblad, Nov. 24, 1961; children—Ralph, Anna, Howard. B.A. in History, Rhodes Coll., Memphis, 1955; M.A., U. N.C., Chapel Hill, 1957, Ph.D. in History, 1961; M.S. in Library Sci, U. Ill., 1963. Teaching fellow U. N.C., Chapel Hill, 1955-56; departmental asst. U. N.C., 1956-57, reference asst., 1959-61, dir. undergrad. library, lectr. in history, 1968-70; circulation asst. U. Ill., 1961-63; asst. Center for Russian Area and Lang. Studies, 1962-63; cataloger Duke U., 1963-65; asst. prof. history U. S.W. La., 1965-66; asst. prof. U. Colo., 1966-68; dir. libraries, prof. history U. N.C., Greensboro, 1970-94; ret., 1994; bd. dirs. Southeastern Library Network, 1979-82, treas., 1981-82. Contbr. articles, revs. to profl. jours. Ford Found. research fellow, 1957-58; U. Colo. grantee, 1967; U. N.C. at Greensboro grantee, 1977-78, 89. Mem. Phi Beta Kappa (chpt. pres. 1979-80), Beta Phi Mu, Phi Alpha Theta, Chi Beta Phi. Episcopalian. Home: 3006 New Hanover Dr Greensboro NC 27408-6710

THOMPSON, JAMES RICHARD, human resources management consultant; b. Marion, Ohio, June 6, 1933; s. Wallace Wait and Mabel Ann (Maloney) T.; m. Ann Bacon Hallett, Sept. 7, 1973; children: J. Matthew, Mark A. BS in Indsl. Mgmt., U. Dayton, 1956. Pers. asst. wage and salary Gen. Tel. Co. Ohio, Marion, 1957-59, pers. asst. communications and devel., 1959-61; mgmt. devel. adminstr. GTE Svc. Corp., N.Y.C., 1961-62, pers. mgr., 1962-66, pers. adminstr., 1966-67, dir. staffing coordination, Stamford, Conn., 1971-75; dir. pers. GTE Communications, Inc., N.Y.C., 1967-71; dir. labor rels. and compensation Gen. Tel. Co. S.W., San Angelo, Tex., 1975-78, v.p. human resources, 1978-88; asst. v.p. employee rels. and orgn. devel. GTE Tel. Ops., Irving, Tex., 1989-91; asst. v.p. human resources Compañia Dominicana de Teléfonos, Santo Domingo, Dominican Republic, 1991-93; pres. J.R. Thompson & Assocs., Colleyville, Tex., 1993—; v.p. human resources Universal Svc. Telephone Corp., Irving, 1995—. Mem. Dallas Pers. Assn., Soc. for Human Resources Mgmt., Ft. Worth C. of C. Home and Office: 3001 Glen Dale Dr Colleyville TX 76034-4645

THOMPSON, JAMES ROBERT, JR., lawyer, former governor; b. Chgo., May 8, 1936; s. James Robert and Agnes Josephine (Swanson) T.; m. Jayne Carr, 1976; 1 dau., Samantha Jayne. Student, U. Ill., Chgo., 1953-55, Washington U., St. Louis, 1955-56; J.D., Northwestern U., 1959. Bar: Ill. 1959, U.S. Supreme Ct. 1964. Asst. state's atty. Cook County, Ill., 1959-64; assoc. prof. law Northwestern U. Law Sch., 1964-69; asst. atty. gen. State of Ill., 1969-70; chief criminal div., 1969, chief dept. law enforcement and pub. protection, 1969-70; 1st asst. U.S. atty. No. Dist. Ill., 1970-71, U.S. atty., 1971-75; counsel firm Winston & Strawn, Chgo., 1975-77, ptnr., chmn. exec. com., 1991—; gov. Ill., 1977-91; chmn. Pres.' Intelligence Oversight Bd., 1989-93, adv. bd. Fed. Emergency Mgmt. Agy., 1991-93; bd. govs. Chgo. Bd. Trade; bd. dirs. FMC Corp., Jefferson Smurfit Corp., Prime Retail Inc., Am. Nat. Can, Hollinger Internat., Inc., Union Pacific Resources, Inc., Chgo. Mus. Contemporary Art, Chgo. Hist. Soc., Lyric Opera Chgo., Econ. Club Chgo., Civic Com., Comml. Club Chgo., Execs. Club Chgo.; trustee Nat. Coun. Compensation Ins. Co-author: Cases and Comments on Criminal Justice, 2 vols, 1968, 74, Criminal Law and Its Adminstration, 1970, 74. Chmn. Ill. Math. and Sci. Acad. Found.; chmn. Rep. Gov's. Assn., 1982, Nat. Gov.'s Assn., Midwest Gov.'s Assn., Coun. Gt. Lakes Gov's., 1985. Mem. ABA, Ill. Bar Assn., Chgo. Bar Assn. Republican. Office: Winston & Strawn 35 W Wacker Dr Chicago IL 60601-1614

THOMPSON, JAMES WILLIAM, lawyer; b. Dallas, Oct. 22, 1936; s. John Charles and Frances (Van Slyke) T.; BS, U. Mont., 1958, JD, 1962; m. Marie Hertz, June 26, 1965 (dec. 1995); children: Elizabeth, Margaret, John. Acct., Arthur Young & Co., N.Y.C., summer 1959; instr. bus. adminstrn. Eastern Mont. Coll., Billings, 1959-60, U. Mont., Missoula, 1960-61; admitted to Mont. bar, 1962; assoc. Cooke, Moulton, Bellingham & Longo, Billings, 1962-64, James R. Felt, Billings, 1964-65; asst. atty. City of Billings, 1963-64, atty., 1964-66; ptnr. Felt, Speare & Thompson, Billings, 1966-72, McNamer, Thompson & Cashmore, 1973-86, McNamer & Thompson Law Firm PC, 1986-89, McNamer, Thompson, Werner & Stanley, P.C., 1990-93, McNamer Thompson Law Firm PC, 1993—; bd. dirs. Associated Employers of Mont., Inc., 1989—. Mem. Billings Zoning Commn., 1966-69; v.p. Billings Community Action Program (now Dist. 7 Human Resources Devel. Council), 1968-70, pres., 1970-75, trustee, 1975—; mem. Yellowstone County Legal Services Bd., 1969-70; City-County Air Pollution Control Bd., 1969-70; pres. Billings Symphony Soc., 1970-71; bd. dirs. Billings Studio Theatre, 1967-73, Mont. Inst. of Arts Found., 1986-89, Downtown Billings Assn., 1986-90, Billings Area Bus. Incubator, Inc., 1991-94, Found. of Mont. State U., Billings, 1992—; mem. Diocesan exec. council, 1972-75; mem. Billings Transit Commn., 1971-73; mem. City Devel. Agy., 1972-73; bd. dirs. United Way, Billings, 1973-81. CPA, Mont. Mem. ABA, Am. Acad. Estate Planning Attys., Nat. Acad. Elder Law Attys., State Bar Mont., Yellowstone County Bar Assn. (bd. dirs. 1983-87, pres. 1985-86), C. of C., Elks, Kiwanis (pres. Yellowstone chpt. 1974-75), Sigma Chi (pres. Billings alumni assn. 1963-65). Episcopalian. Home: 123 Lewis Ave Billings MT 59101-6034 Office: 300 First Bank Bldg Billings MT 59101

THOMPSON, JANICE M., women's health, pediatrics nurse, educator; b. Stamford, Conn., Apr. 21, 1955; m. Kenneth Thompson, Aug. 13, 1977; children: Scott, Adam, Kenneth, Kyle. ADN, Pace U., Pleasantville, N.Y., 1975; BSN, Mt. St. Mary Coll., Newburgh, N.Y., 1978; MSN magna cum laude, Western Conn. State U., 1989; PhD in Nursing, Adelphi U., 1997. Cert. Lamaze instr.; cert. cmty. health nurse ANCC. Maternal and child health nurse Bridgeport (Conn.) Hosp.; clin. instr. nursing U. Bridgeport; asst. prof. Quinnipiac Coll.; adj. clin. instr. nursing So. Conn. State U., New Haven, Western Conn. State U., Danbury. Mem. Am. Soc. Psychopropylaxis in Obstetrics, Conn. Nurses Assn., Doctoral Assn. N.Y., Sigma Theta Tau.

THOMPSON, JEAN TANNER, retired librarian; b. San Luis Obispo, Calif., June 15, 1929; d. Chester Corey and Mildred (Orr) T.; 1 child, Anne Marie Miller. Student, Whitworth Coll., Spokane, Wash., 1946-49; A.B., Boston U., 1951; postgrad., U. Wis., Eau Claire, 1964-67; M.S.L.S., Columbia U., 1973; Ed.M., U. Va., Charlottesville, 1978. Asst. social sci. librarian Univ. Libraries Va. Polytechnic Inst. and State U., Blacksburg, 1973-77, head social sci. dept. Univ. Libraries, 1977-83; head reference dept. Meml. Library U. Wis., Madison, 1983-86, asst. dir. reference and info. svcs., 1986-91, ret. Contbg. editor: ALA Guide to Information Access, 1994; mem. editorial bd. RQ, 1984-89. Mem. ALA, Assn. Coll. and Research Libraries (edn. and behavioral sci. sect. vice chmn. 1985-86, chmn. 1986-87), Wis. Library Assn., Wis. Assn. of Acad. Librarians. Methodist. Home: 103 S Hunter Ln Troy AL 36079-8206

THOMPSON, JEREMIAH BEISEKER, international medical business executive; b. Harvey, N.D., July 20, 1927; s. Linden Brown and Ferne Althea (Beiseker) T.; m. Paula Maria Ketchum, Feb. 5, 1960; children: Cole, Per, Gover, Susannah. BS, U. Minn., 1949, MD, 1966. Rsch. assoc. U. Colo. Med. Sch., Denver, 1955-56, U. Calif. Med. Sch., San Francisco, 1956-57, Stanford U., 1957-59; applications rsch. scientist Beckman/Spinco Co., Palo Alto, Calif., 1959-61; mgr. Asia and Africa Hewlett Packard Co., Palo Alto, 1966-72; med. cons. Alyeska Pipeline Co., Anchorage, 1973-76; mgr. Asia, Africa, Australasia Corometrics Med. Systems, Wallingford, Conn., 1976-82; dir. internat. ops. Oximetrix (Abbott), Mountain View, Calif., 1982-84, Novametrix Med. Systems, Wallingford, 1984-88; ptnr. TMC Internat., Tokyo and Concord, Calif., 1988—; advisor, cons. Yokogawa-Hewlett Packard, Tokyo, 1966-70; cons. Kupat Holim, Tel Aviv, Israel, 1967-92, Itochu, Tokyo, 1984-97, Nat. Heart-Lung Inst., Beijing, China, 1984-94. Project dir. Comparative Study of Western and Japanese Medicine in Taisho and Showa Eras, 1991—. With USN, 1945-46; PTO. Founding fellow Brit. Interplanetary Soc.; assoc. Japan Found., Assn. Asian Studies; mem. Kokusai Bunka Kaikan, Tokyo, World Affairs Coun., Mechanics Inst. Achievements include cancer research, joint Japan/U.S. project screening and evaluation for anti-cancer activity of halogenated methane derivatives, augmentation of irradiation effects by chemotherapy. Home and Office: TMC Internat 3718 Barrington Dr Concord CA 94518-1614

THOMPSON, JESSE ELDON, vascular surgeon; b. Laredo, Tex., Apr. 7, 1919; s. Jesse Eathel and Sara Gail (Bolton) T.; m. Madeleine Jane Curtis, Sept. 18, 1944; children: Sally C., Jesse E., Janet E., Diane B. BA, U. Tex., 1939; MD, Harvard U., 1943; Rhodes scholar, Oxford U., 1949-50. Intern Mass. Gen. Hosp., Boston, 1943; resident in surgery Mass. Gen. Hosp., 1944-48; practice medicine specializing in surgery, tchr. surgery Boston U., 1949-54; practice medicine specializing in surgery, tchr. vascular surgery Baylor Hosp., Dallas, 1954—; chief vascular surgery Baylor Hosp., 1980-86; clin. prof. surgery U. Tex. Southwestern Med. Sch., Dallas; attending surgeon Baylor Hosp., 1954-92, hon. surgeon, 1992—, chief surgery Baylor Hosp., Dallas, 1982-86; Mem Tex. and Dist. Rhodes Scholar Selection Coms. Author: Surgery for Cerebrovascular Insufficiency, 1968; editorial bd.: Surgery, 1975-89, Jour. Cardiovascular Surgery, 1975—; sr. editor Jour. Vascular Surgery, 1984-86; contbr. numerous articles to profl. jours. Served to capt. M.C. AUS, 1945-47. Fulbright sr. fellow, 1949-50. Fellow ACS (treas.); mem. Am. Surg. Assn., So. Surg. Assn., Tex. Surg. Soc., Soc. Vascular Surgery, Internat. Cardiovascular Soc., Internat. Soc. Surgery, So. Assn. for Vascular Surgery, Dallas Petroleum Club, Dallas Country Club, Masons. Methodist. Home: 3705 Stanford Ave Dallas TX 75225-7204 Office: 712 N Washington Ave Ste 509 Dallas TX 75246-1635

THOMPSON, JILL LYNETTE LONG, congresswoman; b. Warsaw, Ind., July 15, 1952. BS, Valparaiso U.; MBA, Ind. U., PhD. Prof. various colls. and univs.; mem. 101st-103rd Congresses from 4th Ind. dist., 1989-95; mem. agrl. com., mem. vets. affairs com.; under sec. for rural development USDA, 1995—; cons. in small bus. mgmt. Councilwoman City of Valparaiso, Ind.; chair Congrl. Rural Congress. Democrat. Methodist. Office: Rural Development USDA 1400 Independence Ave SW Washington DC 20250-0002

THOMPSON, JOE FLOYD, aerospace engineer, educator; b. Grenada, Miss., Apr. 13, 1939; s. Joe Floyd and Bernice Thompson; m. Emilie Kay Wilson, June 1, 1974; children: Mardi, Douglass. BS, Miss. State U., 1961, MS, 1963; PhD, Ga. Tech., 1971. Aerospace engr. NASA Marshall, Huntsville, Ala., 1963-64; prof. Miss. State U., Starkville, 1964—, Disting. prof. aerospace engring., 1995—; mem. tech. rev. bd. Army Rsch. Lab., Adelphi, Md., 1993-95; dir. computer code Nat. Grid Project 1993—; dir. NSF Engring. Rsch. Ctr. for Computational Field Simulation, 1990-95. Author: Numerical Grid Generation, 1985, (computer code) Eagle Grid System, 1987; sr. assoc. editor Applied Math. and Computation, 1985-94; assoc. editor Numerical Heat Transfer, 1989—; mem. edit. bd. Computational Fluid Dynamics Jour., 1993—, Jour. Computational Physics, 1995—. Recipient Commdr.'s award Army Waterways Exp. Sta., Vicksburg, Miss., 1992. Mem. IEEE, IEEE Computer Soc., AIAA (Aerodynamics award 1992), SIAM. Presbyterian. Achievements include establishment of NSF Engineering Research Center; pioneering work in field of numerical grid generation. Home: Miss State U Box 255 Mississippi State MS 39762 Office: Miss State U PO Box 6176 Mississippi State MS 39762-6176

THOMPSON, JOHN, college basketball coach; b. Washington, Sept. 2, 1941. Student, Providence Coll., 1960-64; M in Counseling and Guidance, U. D.C., 1971; LHD (hon.), St. Peter's Coll., 1982; H.H.D., Wheeling Coll., 1982. Player Boston Celtics, Nat. Basketball Assn., 1964-66; basketball coach St. Anthony High Sch., Washington, 1966-72; basketball coach Georgetown U., Washington, 1972—, presdl. asst. on urban affairs, 1977; founder Summer Basketball Sch. Georgetown U.; mem. Nat. Invitation Tournament Championship Team, 1963, Nat. Basketball Assn. Championship Team, 1965, 66; won NCAA championship, 1984, 2nd place NCAA championship, 1982, 85. Inducted Providence Coll. Hall of Fame, 1974; U.S. asst. coach Olympic Games Montreal, Que., Can., 1976; recipient Pres.'s award, Patrick Healy award Georgetown U., 1982; named U.S. Basketball Writers Assn. Coach of Yr., 1982; recipient other awards; named Coach of Yr., United Press Internat., 1987; Coach U.S. Olympic Games, Seoul, Korea, 1988; recipient bronze medal Olympic Games, 1988. Mem. Nat. Assn. Basketball Coaches (bd. dirs. 1976—, chmn. selection com. for east team, NABC Coach of Yr. 1984-85). Office: Georgetown U Basketball Office 3700 0 St NW Washington DC 20057*

THOMPSON, JOHN ALBERT, JR., dermatologist; b. Austin, Tex., June 5, 1942; s. J. Albert Sr. and Elizabeth (Brady) T. BA, Georgetown U., 1963; MD, Bowman Gray Sch. Medicine, 1967; Dermatology Fellowship, U. N.C., 1971-73. Diplomate Am. Bd. Dermatology. Resident in internal medicine N.C. Baptist Hosp., Winston-Salem, N.C., 1967-69; resident in dermatology N.C. Meml. Hosp., Chapel Hill, N.C., 1971-73; pvt. practice Charlotte, N.C., 1974—; clin. prof. dermatology Dept. Dermatology, U. N.C. Sch. Medicine, Chapel Hill, 1974—. Author profl. papers. Lt. comdr. USNR, 1969-71, Vietnam. Mem. Am. Acad. Dermatology (chmn. subcom. for sch. health edn. 1976-79, task force--nat. health ins.), Carolinas-Va. Dermatology Assn. (adv. bd. council rep. 1976-79), Charlotte Dermatology Assn., Mecklenburg County Med. Soc., N.C. Med. Soc., North Am. Clin. Dermatology Soc. Southern Med. Assn., Southeastern Consortium for Continuing Dermatol. Edn. (steering com. 1983—), South Cen. Dermatol. Congress (organizing com. 1982-86), Am. Soc. Dermatol. Surgery, Am. Dermatol. Soc. Allergy and Immunology, Am. Soc. Laser Medicine and Surgery, Inc. Democrat. Episcopalian. Home: 2633 Richardson Dr Apt 8A Charlotte NC 28211-3346 Office: 2310 Randolph Rd Charlotte NC 28207-1526

THOMPSON, JOHN DOUGLAS, financier; b. Montreal, Que., Can., Sept. 28, 1934; s. William Douglas and Anne F. (Whebby) T.; children: Jacqueline, Catherine, Peter, Anne Marie, Francois. B.Eng., McGill U., 1957; M.B.A., U. Western Ont., 1960. Dep. chmn. bd. Montreal Trustco Inc.; past chmn. bd. dirs. Trust Cos. Assn. of Can., bd. dirs. Domtar, Inc.; J.S. Redpath Holdings Inc., BCE Mobile, Montrusco Assocs. Inc., Axa-Boreal Assurances Inc., Sedgwick, Air Transat, Capital d'Amérique CDPQ Inc., Benvest Capital Inc., Shermag Inc., Manitex Capital Inc., Serviplast Inc. Bd. dirs. MacDonald Stewart Found., Windsor Found., Salvation Army, chmn. Montreal adv. bd.; chmn. Montreal YMCA Found.; mem. audit com. McGill U.; past pres. St. Mary's Hosp. Found.; gov., past pres. St. Mary's Hosp. Ctr. Mem. Assn. Profl. Engrs., Que. and Ont., Mt. Royal Club (Montreal), Royal Montreal Golf Club, Montreal Amateur Athletic Club, Mt. Bruno Country Club Inc., The Forest and Stream Club. Roman Catholic. Office: Montreal Trust, 1800 McGill College Ave 12th Fl, Montreal, PQ Canada H3A 3K9

THOMPSON, JOHN E., principal. Prin. Ardmore (Okla.) Middle Sch. Recipient Blue Ribbon Sch. award U.S. Dept. Edn., 1990-91. Office: Ardmore Mid Sch PO Box 1709 Ardmore OK 73402-1709*

THOMPSON, JOHN HERD, history educator; b. Winnipeg, Man., Can., Sept. 18, 1946; came to U.S. 1989; s. Joseph Whyte and Gladys Kate (Campain) T.; m. Katrin Ann Partelpoeg, Jan. 15, 1977; children: Anne Marie, Mark Thomas. BA with honors, U. Winnipeg, 1968; MA, U. Man., 1969; PhD, Queens U., Kingston, Ont., 1975. Faculty Duke U., Durham, N.C., 1989—. Author: Harvests of War, 1978, Decades of Discord: Canada 1922-1939, 1985, Canada and the United States: Ambivalent Allies, 1994, 2d edit., 1997. Mem. Am. Hist. Assn., Can. Hist. Assn., Soc. for Am. Baseball Rsch., Assn. for Can. Studies in the U.S. Avocation: baseball. Home: Duke Univ Dept History Durham NC 27708

THOMPSON, JOHN KENTON, energy company executive, natural gas engineer; b. McAllen, Tex., Sept. 25, 1947; s. Forrest Arnold and Virginia Lee (Womeldorf) T.; m. Mary Elizabeth White, June 18, 1971; children: Kathleen Ann, John Allen. BS in Natural Gas Engring., Tex. A&M U., Kingsville, 1971. Registered profl. engr., Tex. Gas engr. Sun Oil Co., Oklahoma City, 1972-75; mem. design mgmt. team Sun's 1st cryogenic turboexpander plant, 1974; dist. gas engr. Sun E&P Co., McAllen, 1975-78; OBO plant engr./gas mktg. rep. Sun Gas Co., Dallas, 1978-86; mgr. OBO plants Oryx Energy Co., Dallas, 1986-92; mgr. joint venture plants/pipelines Mitchell Energy & Devel. Corp., The Woodlands, Tex., 1992—; class instr. Petroleum Ext. Svc.- U. Tex., 1995-96; session coord. USN/USMC Radio Svc. Net, Oklahoma City, 1974-75; session chmn. regional mtg. Gas Processors Assn., 1975; corp. ops. rep. to spl. revenue project phase III Sun Gas Co. divsn. Sun Oil Co., 1989-91; engring. aide/surveyor Tex. Hwy. Dept., 1969-70; enging., measurement tech. Transcontinental Gas Pipeline Co., 1970-71. Sect. leader, tchr. Custer Rd. United Meth. Ch., Plano, Tex., 1990; mem. com. Boy Scouts Am., Plano, 1989; co-chmn. edn. and family life com. St. Mark United Meth. Ch., McAllen, 1976; mem. adminstrv. bd. Woodlands (Tex.) Meth. Ch., 1994-96; event co-supr. Tri-Regional Games-Tex. Spl. Olympics, 1995-96; group rep. to United Way Campaign, 1995. Recipient Order of Arrow and Life RAND award Rio Grande coun. Boy Scouts Am., 1965. Mem. Am. Inst. Chem. Engrs., Woodlands Kiwanis (dir. 1993-94, v.p. 94-95, pres.-elect 1995-96, chmn. Key Club/Kiwanis Spl. Fund Event 1995-96), Soc. Petroleum Engrs., SAR. Republican. Avocations: golf, bicycle riding, chess, computers. Home: 10 Gate Hill Dr The Woodlands TX 77381 Office: 2002 Timberloch Pl The Woodlands TX 77380-1153

THOMPSON, JOHN WILLIAM, international management consultant; b. Hurricane, Utah, Oct. 14, 1945; s. Thomas Thurman and Lula (Brinkerhoff) T.; m. Pamela Ruth Williams, Sept. 14, 1991. BSEE, Utah State U., 1969, MBA, 1972; PhD, U. Oreg., 1978. Rsch. asst. Utah State U., Logan, Utah, 1967-69, tching. asst., 1971-72; elec. engr. Collins Radio, Newport Beach, Calif., 1969-72; tching. fellow U. Oreg., Eugene, 1972-78; tng. dir. Lifespring Inc., San Rafael, Calif., 1978-80; pres., CEO Human Factors Inc., San Rafael, Calif., 1980—; chmn. bd. Acumen Internat., San Rafael, Calif., 1985—. Author: The Human Factor: An Inquiry into Communication and Consciousness, 1983, Leadership in the 21st Century in New Traditions in Business, 1992, The Renaissance of Learning in Learning Organizations: Developing Cultures for Tomorrow's Workplace, 1994, The Human Factor, 1996; author of software based management assessment programs, system theory based management development courses, 1980-92. Rockefeller Found. grantee, 1971. Avocations: sailing, breeding Koi, gardening, bicycling, scuba diving. Office: Human Factors Inc 4000 Civic Center Dr Ste 500 San Rafael CA 94903-4171

THOMPSON, JONATHAN SIMS, army officer; b. Ft. Benning, Ga., Nov. 19, 1947; s. Donald Frederick and Gene Elizabeth (Pierce) T.; m. Dinetha Lynn Richards, Aug. 26, 1979; children: Tracy A., Terry A., Jonathan S. II, Tiffany A. BSME, Tex. A&M U., 1970, M Indsl. Engring., 1978; M Bus. Mgmt., Ctrl. Mich. U., 1980; diploma in program mgmt., Def. Sys. Mgmt. Coll., 1987. Registered profl. engr., Tex. Commd. 2d. lt. U.S Army, 1971, advanced through grades to col.; engr. platoon leader 27th Engr. Battalion U.S Army, Ft. Bragg, N.C., 1971-72, staff engr. 5th Spl. Forces Group, 1973-74; engr. instr. Spl. Forces Sch. U.S Army, Ft. Bragg, 1974-75; co. comdr. 2d Engr. Battalion U.S Army, Camp Castle, Korea, 1976-77; project dir. Engr. Strategic Studies Ctr. U.S Army, Rockville, Md., 1978-81; plans and ops. officer 317th Engr. Battalion U.S Army, Eschborn, Germany, 1982-84; engr. staff officer Office of Chief of Staff U.S Army, Washington, 1985-87, ops. rsch. analyst Office of Sec. of Army, 1987-88; battalion comdr. 2d Engr. Battalion U.S Army, Camp Castle, 1989-90; dep. chief of staff Corps. of Engrs. U.S Army, Washington, 1991-92, exec. dir. Office of Chief of Engrs., 1992-93, fellow Ctr. Stratetic/Internat. Studies U.S. Army War Coll., 1993-94; brigade comdr. 20th Engr. Brigade U.S Army, Ft. Bragg, N.C., 1994-96; sr. fellow U.S. Dept. State, 1996—. Editor: Peacetime Defensive Preparations in Europe, 1981 (deMarche award 1985); author govt. study, article in field. Adult leader, asst. scoutmaster Boy Scouts Am., Dale City, Va., 1990-92, chmn. troop advancement com., Ft. Bragg, 1994—; coun. rep. Recreation Ctr. Bd., Dale City, 1985-89. Decorated Legion of Merit with 2 oak leaf clusters; fellow in govt. affairs Coun. for Excellence in Govt., 1991-92. Fellow Soc. Am. Mil. Engrs. (nat. bd. dirs. 1990-92, post pres. 1994—); mem. NSPE, Army Navy Club, Shriners (life mem., Noble), Masons (Companion, Sir Knight). Presbyterian. Achievements include leading the world's largest military engineering task force into Haiti during Operation Uphold Democracy to restore the government and rebuild the infrastructure; principal deputy to engineer commander of 24th infantry "Hail Mary" task force during Operation Desert Storm and the liberation of Kuwait. Avocations: skiing, golf, parachuting. Home: 9710 Dansk Ct Fairfax VA 22032 Office: 4000 Arlington Blvd Arlington VA 22204-1586

THOMPSON, JOSIE, nurse; b. Ark., Apr. 16, 1949; d. James Andrew and Oneda Fay (Watson) Rhoads; m. Mark O. Thompson, Feb. 14, 1980. Diploma, Lake View Sch. Nursing, 1970; student, Danville C.C., 1974-75, St. Petersburg Jr. Coll., 1979. RN, Ill., Wyo. Staff nurse St. Elizabeth Hosp., Danville, Ill., 1970-78, Osteopathetic Hosp., St. Petersburg, Fla., 1980-81, Wyo. State Hosp., Evanston, 1981-83; staff nurse Wyo. Home Health Care, Rock Springs, 1984—, adminstr., 1986-95; pres. Home Health Care Alliance Wyo., 1991-92; staff nurse home health Interim Health Care, Cheyenne, Wyo., 1996-97; staff nurse Rocky Mountain Home Health Care, Green River, Wyo., 1997—. Mem. nursing program adv. bd. Western Wyo.

Community Coll.; mem. Coalition for the Elderly, Spl. Needs Com. Sweetwater County, 1992-93. Home: PO Box 1154 Rock Springs WY 82902 Office: Rocky Mountain Home Health Care 198 Anita Dr Green River WY 82935

THOMPSON, JOYCE ANN, education consultant; b. Little Rock, Mar. 31, 1948; d. James Willie and Mattie Lee (Swope) Wallace; m. Lonnie Thompson, July 24, 1974; children: Nelieta Manoi, Kayle Ayo, Toyin Jean. BA, Okla. Bapt. U., 1970; MA, Calif. State U., Bakersfield, 1983. Cert. secondary tchr., adminstv. svcs. Tchr. bus. edn. Kern High Sch. Dist., Bakersfield, 1970-72, 77-78, 85-87, GED lang. instr., 1987-90, Outreach cons., 1990—; acctg. inst. Santa Barbara Bus. Coll., 1983-85; typing tchr. Greenfield Jr. High Sch., Bakersfield, 1978-83; mem. adv. coun. Foothill High Sch., Bakersfield, 1990—, hearing panel Kern High Sch. Dist., 1991—. Author: Graduation Requires Attendance Daily, 1990, Parent Partners, 1990. Mem. NEA, Kern High Faculty Assn., Kern High Counseling Assn., Calif. Tchrs. Assn., Bus. and Profl. Persons Orgn., Young Women's Christian Coun. Mem. Ch. of God in Christ. Avocations: creative writing, reading. Home: PO Box 10072 Bakersfield CA 93389-0072 Office: Foothill High Sch 501 Park Dr Bakersfield CA 93306-6017

THOMPSON, JOYCE ELIZABETH, arts management educator; b. Pasadena, Tex., Aug. 15, 1951; d. James Little and Ruth Lake (Skinner) Wilkison; divorced; children: Christine Joy, Cassidy Jane. BA in Psychology, David Lipscomb Coll., 1974; MA in Speech, Theater, Murray State U., 1976; postgrad., U. Tex., 1978; MA in Arts Adminstrn., Ind. U., 1981. Asst. prof. speech Vincennes (Ind.) U., 1976-79; asst. dir. mktg. Hartford (Conn.) Ballet, 1981-82; touring dir. Hartford Ballet/Conn. Opera, 1982-84; exec. dir. Wyo. Arts Coun., Cheyenne, 1984-91, South Snohomish County Arts Coun., Lynwood, Wash., 1991-92; asst. prof. arts mgmt. U. Ill., Springfield, Ill., 1992-97; dir. Quad City Arts, Rock Island, Ill., 1997—; adj. instr., Manchester (Conn.) C.C., 1982-84, Chapman Coll., 1990-91, Edmonds C.C., 1992; mem. selection com. Coca-Cola Scholars Found., 1989, 90, 91, 95. Mem. adv. bd. Cheyenne Little Theatre Players, 1986, Cheyenne Civic Ctr., 1987-88; v.p. bd. dirs. Assembly of Ill. Cmty. Arts. Orgns., 1995—. Mem. Assn. Arts Adminstrn. Educators (sec.), Assn. Performing Arts Presenters, Speech Comm. Assn., Western States Arts Fedn. (bd. dirs. 1984-91, chair performing arts com. 1985-87). Democrat. Avocations: singing, theater, reading. Office: Quad City Arts 1715 2nd Ave Rock Island IL 61201

THOMPSON, JOYCE ELIZABETH, retired state education official; b. Pearson, Okla., Nov. 22, 1929; d. Walter Samuel and Clara Gertrude (Davis) T.; m. Gordon Pybas, May 22, 1989. BS, Okla. State U., 1951; M in Home Econs., Okla. U., 1974. Cert. vocat. and gen. home econs., Okla. Home econs. tchr. Wister (Okla.) High Sch., 1951-55, Tishomingo (Okla.) High Sch., 1955-56, Wilson (Okla.) High Sch., 1956-67, Konawa (Okla.) High Sch., 1967-71; dist. supr. State Dept. of Vo-Tech., Oklahoma City, 1971-80; state supr. State Dept. of Vo-Tech., Stillwater, Okla., 1980-88; ret., 1988; mem. adv. com. Future Homemakers Am., Oklahoma City, 1961-68; treas. Nat. Assn. State Suprs., Washington, 1983-87; advisor Nat. Assn. Vocat. Home Econs. Tchrs., Washington, 1986-87. Chairperson Okla. Home Econs. Legis. Network, Stillwater, 1984; mem. fin. com. Wes Watkins for Gov., Stillwater, 1988-90. Named Tchr. of Yr. Ancient Free and Accepted Masons, Wilson, 1960, 65; recipient Grand Cross of Colors, Internat. Order of Rainbow, Wilson, 1964, Hon. membership Future Homemakers of Am., Oklahoma City, 1976, Young Homemakers of Okla., Oklahoma City, 1977, Spl. award of merit Nat. Assn. Vocat. Home Econs. Tchrs., Washington, 1986. Mem. Am. Vocat. Assn. (life mem., membership chair 1981-84), Okla. Vocat. Assn. (life mem., v.p. 1965), Am. Legion Aux., Order Ea. Star. Democrat. Mem. Church of Christ. Avocations: reading, sewing, vol. work, cooking, water skiing. Home: RR 2 Box 113 Wanette OK 74878-9725

THOMPSON, JULIA ANN, physicist, educator; b. Little Rock, Mar. 13, 1943; d. Erwin Arthur and Ruth Evelyn (Johnston) T.; m. Patrick A. Thompson, Mar. 22, 1964 (div. 1974); 1 child, Diane E.; m. David E. Kraus, Jr., June 22, 1976; children: Vincent Szewczyk, Larry Lynch. BA, Cornell Coll., Mt. Vernon, Iowa, 1964; MA, Yale U., 1966, PhD, 1969. Research assoc. Brookhaven Lab., Upton, N.Y., 1969-71; research assoc./assoc. instr. U. Utah, Salt Lake City, 1971-72; asst. prof. physics U. Pitts., 1972-78, assoc. prof., 1978-85, prof., 1986—, dir. undergrad. rsch. program, 1992—; mem. users coms. Brookhaven Nat. Lab., 1983-86; condr. expts. Inst. Nuclear Physics, Novosibirsk, USSR, Ctr. Europeene Recherche Nucleaire, Switzerland, Brookhaven Natl. Lab., L.I.; spokesperson hyperon decay expt BNL, 1972-80. Contbr. articles to profl. jours. Bd. dirs. 1st Unitarian Ch., Pitts., 1980-83; zone councillor Soc. Physics Students, 1986-88; with Nat. Acad. Sci. Exch. to USSR, 1989-90. Woodrow Wilson fellow, 1964-65. Mem. Am. Phys. Soc. (com. on status of women in physics 1983-86, exec. com. forum on physics and soc. 1990—). Democrat. Unitarian. Avocations: promoting effective science education, hiking, reading, music. Achievements include research with W.E. Cleland and D.E. Kraus in optical triggering; with the collaboration with AFS and HELIOS expt. in direct photon and lepton production, leading to modified understanding of the gluon function, and limits on anomalous electron production; studies of rare and semi-rare kaon decays.

THOMPSON, KAY FRANCIS, dentist; b. Pitts.; d. Lony C. and Betha E. (Porter) T.; m. Ralph P. Krichbaum, Jan. 10, 1959. BS, U. Pitts., 1951, DDS, 1953. Pvt. practice dentistry Pitts., 1953—; assoc. prof. U. Pitts., Behavioral Sci., Dentistry, Pitts., 1970-80, W.Va. U. Sch. Dentistry and Sch. of Medicine, Morgantown, 1980—; dentist for handicapped Robinson Devel. Ctr., McKees Rocks, Pa., 1976—; cons. NIH, Washington, 1975-90, VA Hosp., Pitts., 1978—; lectr., educator various med., dental and psychol. assns. Contbr. articles to profl. jours. Chmn. Dental Legis. Fund Pa., Pitts., 1981-83; mem. World Affairs Coun., Pitts., 1980—, Pa. Dental Polit. Action Com., Harrisburg; bd. dirs. Am. Dental Polit. Action Com., Washington, 1985-90; trustee U. Pitts., 1988-91; mem. Amdental Assoc. Govt. Svcs., 1990-93. Recipient Erickson award De Nederlands Vereniging voor Hypnotherapie, 1983, Bicentennial Medallion of Distinction U. Pitts., 1988, Alumnae of Yr. 1991, Erickson Found. Lifetime Achievement award, 1992. Fellow Am. Coll. Dentists, Internat. Coll. Dentists, Am. Soc. Clin. Hypnosis (pres. 1972-73, scientific 1970), Soc. Clin. and Exptl. Hypnosis (exec. bd. 1976-80), Pierre Fauchard Acad.; mem. ADA (trustee 1993—), Am. Assn. Women Dentists (trustee 1982-88, Pres.'s award 1986), Pa. Dental Assn. (sec. 1984-88, pres. 1989-90), U. Pitts. Dental Alumni Assn. (pres. 1988-91). Lutheran. Avocations: mountain climbing, skiing, scuba diving, backpacking, raising Christmas trees. Office: PO Box 16152 Pittsburgh PA 15242-0152

THOMPSON, KENNETH W(INFRED), educational director, author, editor, administrator, social science educator; b. Des Moines, Aug. 29, 1921; s. Thor Carlyle and Agnes (Rorbeck) T.; m. Beverly Bourret; children: Kenneth Caryle, Paul Andrew, James David, Carolyn A. A.B., Augustana Coll., 1943, L.H.D. (hon.), 1986, LLD, 1986; M.A., U. Chgo., 1948, Ph.D., 1950; LL.D., U. Notre Dame, 1964, Bowdoin Coll., 1972, St. Michael's Coll., 1973, St. Olaf Coll., 1974, U. Denver, 1983; L.H.D., W.Va. Wesleyan U., 1970, Nebr. Wesleyan Coll., 1971. Lectr. social scis. U. Chgo., 1948, asst. prof. polit. sci., 1951-53; asst. prof. polit. sci. Northwestern U., 1949-55, chmn. internat. relations com., 1951-55; cons. internat. relations Rockefeller Found., 1953-55, asst. dir. social scis., 1955-57, assoc. dir. social scis., 1957-60, dir. social scis., 1960-61, v.p., 1961-73; dir. higher edn. for devel. Internat. Council for Ednl. Devel., 1974-76; Commonwealth prof. govt. and fgn. affairs U. Va., 1975-78, White Burkett Miller prof. govt. and fgn. affairs, 1979-86; J. Wilson Newman prof. govt. and fgn. affairs, 1986—, dir. White Burkett Miller Ctr. of Public Affairs, 1978—; Riverside Meml. lectr. Riverside Ch., N.Y.C., 1958; Lilly lectr. Duke, 1959; James Stokes lectr. N.Y.U., 1962; Rockwell lectr. Rice U., 1965; Ernest Griffith lectr. Am. U.; Andrew Cecil lectr. U. Tex., 1983; Stuber lectr. U. Rochester, 1984; Morgenthau Meml. lectr., N.Y.C., Mike Mansfield Ctr. lectr., U. Mont.; dir. Inst. Study World Politics, N.Y.C., 1975—. Author, editor: Principles and Problems of International Politics, 1951, 82, Man and Modern Society, 1953, Christian Ethics and the Dilemmas of Foreign Policy, 1959, 81, Conflict and Cooperation Among Nations, 1960, Political Realism and the Crisis of World Politics, 1960, 82, American Diplomacy and Emergent Patterns, 1962, 82, Foreign Policies in a World of Change, 1964, The Moral Issue in Statecraft, 1966, Reconstituting the Human Community, 1972, Foreign Assistance: A View From Private Sector, 1972, 82, Higher Education for National Development, 1972, Understanding World Politics, 1975, Higher Edn. and Social Change, 1976, World Politics, 1976, Truth and Tragedy, 1977, Ethics and Foreign Policy, 1978, Interpreters and Critics of the Cold War, 1978, Foreign Policy and the Democratic Process, 1978, Ethics, Functionalism and Power, 1979, Morality and Foreign Policy, 1980, Masters of International Thought, 1980, The Virginia Papers, vols. 1-29, 1979-96, The President and the Public Philosophy, 1981, Cold War Theories: World Polarization, 1944-53, Vol. I, 1981,91. Winston S. Churchill's World View, 1983, 89, Toynbees's World Politics and History, 1985, Moralism and Morality, 1985, Theory and Practice of International Relations, 1987, Arms Control and Foreign Policy, 1990, Traditions and Values in Politics and Diplomacy, 1992, Fathers of International Thought, 1994, Schools of Thought in International Relations, 1996; editor: Am. Values Series, Vols. I-XX, Presdl. Nominating Process, Vols. I-IV, Portraits of American Presidents, Vols. I-III, Herbert Butterfield: The Ethics of History; The American Presidency, Vols. I-III, 1982-83, Ethics and International Relations, 1985, Moral Dimensions of American Foreign Policy, 1985, 94, The Credibility of Leadership and Institutions, Vols. I-XX, 1983-86, Rhetoric and Political Discourse, Vols.I-XX, Governance, Vols. I-VII, 1990-97, Constitutionalism, Vols. I-VII, 1989-91, Presidency and Science Advising, Vols. I-VIII, 1986-90, Political Transitions and Foreign Policy, Vols. I-IX, 1985-91, A World in Change, Vols. I-VIII, 1989-96, Presidential Disability, Vols. I-III, 1989-96, A New World Order, Vols. I-V, 1991-96, Great American Presidents, 1994, Defeated Presidential Candidates, 1994, Statesmen Who Were Never President, 1996; bd. editors Va. Quar. Rev., Society, Ethics and International Affairs, Interpretation, The Rev. of Politics; contbr. articles to profl. jours. Pres. Dist. of Scarsdale and Mamaroneck (N.Y.) Bd. Edn., 1965-68; trustee Union Theol. Sem., 1967-71, Dillard U., 1975—, Social Sci. Found., U. Denver, 1974-94, Compton Found., 1975—. 1st lt. AUS, 1943-46. Named Va. laureate, 1981; recipient Phi Beta Kappa and Va. Coll. Stores prizes, Va. Social Sci. Assn. ann. award, English Speaking Union award, medal U. Chgo., 1968. Fellow Soc. Religion Higher Edn., Am. Acad. Arts and Scis.; mem. Century Club, Scarsdale Town Club, Raven Soc. (ann. award U. Va.), Phi Beta Kappa (pres.), Omicron Delta Phi. Office: Univ Va Miller Ctr PO Box 5106 Charlottesville VA 22905-5106

THOMPSON, LARRY ANGELO, producer, lawyer, personal manager; b. Clarksdale, Miss., Aug. 1, 1944; s. Angelo and Anne (Tuminello) T.; BBA, U. Miss., 1966, JD, 1968. Bar: Miss. 1968, Calif. 1970. In-house counsel Capitol Records, Hollywood, Calif., 1969-71; sr. ptnr. in entertainment law Thompson, Shankman and Bond, Beverly Hills, Calif., 1971-77; pres. Larry A. Thompson Orgn., Inc., 1977—; co-owner New World Pictures, 1983-85; lectr. entertainment bus. UCLA, U. So. Calif., Southwestern U. Law Sch. Co-chmn. Rep. Nat. Entertainment Com.; apptd. by Gov. of Calif. to Calif. Entertainment Commn. Recipient Show Bus. Atty. of Yr. award Capitol Records, 1971. Mem. Inauguration of Thompson Ctr. for Fine Arts in Clarksdale, Miss., 1986. Served with JAGC, U.S. Army, 1966-72. Mem. ABA, Miss. Bar Assn., Calif. Bar Assn., Inter-Am. Bar Assn., Hon. Order Ky. Colonels, Am. Film Inst., Nat. Acad. Recording Arts and Scis., Acad. TV Arts and Scis. Republican. Roman Catholic. Author: How to Make a Record Deal & Have Your Songs Recorded, 1975, Prime Time Crime, 1982; producer: (TV) Jim Nabors Show, 1977 (Emmy nominee), Mickey Spillane's Margin for Murder, 1981, Bring 'Em Back Alive, 1982, Mickey Spillane's Murder Me, Murder You, 1982, The Other Lover, 1985, Convicted, 1986, Intimate Encounters, 1986, The Woman He Loved, 1988, Original Sin, 1989, Class Cruise, 1989, Little White Lies, 1989, Lucy and Desi: Before The Laughter, 1990, Broken Promises, 1993, Separated By Murder, 1994, Face of Evil, 1996; (motion pictures) Crimes of Passion, 1984, Quiet Cool, 1987, My Demon Lover, 1987, Breaking the Rules, 1992. Recipient Vision award, 1993. Home: 9451 Hidden Valley Pl Beverly Hills CA 90210-1310 Office: Larry A Thompson Orgn 335 N Maple Dr Ste 361 Beverly Hills CA 90210-3857

THOMPSON, LARRY DEAN, lawyer; b. Hannibal, Mo., Nov. 15, 1945; s. Ezra W. and Ruth L. (Robinson) T.; m. Brenda Anne Taggart, June 26, 1970; children: Larry Dean, Gary E. BA cum laude, Culver-Stockton Coll., Canton, Mo., 1967; MA, Mich. State U., 1969; JD, U. Mich., 1974. Bar: Mo. 1974, Ga. 1978. Indsl. rels. rep. Ford Motor Co., Birmingham, Mich., 1969-71; atty. Monsanto Co., St. Louis, 1974-77, King & Spalding, Atlanta, 1977-82; U.S. atty. U.S. Dist. Ct. (no. dist.) Ga., 1982-86; ptnr. King & Spalding, Atlanta, 1986—; mem. lawyer's adv. com. U.S. Ct. Appeals for 11th Cir.; ind. counsel HUD investigation, 1995; mem. Ga. Bd. Bar Examiners. Editor: Jury Instructions in Criminal Antitrust Cases 1976-80, 1982. Chmn. Atlanta Urban League; mem. bd. trustees Met. Atlanta Crime Commn.; bd. dirs. Ga. Rep. Found. Recipient Outstanding Achievement award FBA, 1992. Mem. ABA, Nat. Bar Assn. Presbyterian. Home: 2015 Wallace Rd SW Atlanta GA 30331-7756 Office: King & Spalding 191 Peachtree St NE Atlanta GA 30303-1740

THOMPSON, LAWRENCE HYDE, federal agency official; b. Hamilton, Ohio, Oct. 6, 1943; s. William Hayton and Evelyn (Covault) T.; m. Catherine Crosby, Feb. 3, 1973; children: Bradford Stephen, Sarah Catherine. BS, Iowa State U., 1964; MBA, U. Pa., 1966; PhD, U. Mich., 1971. Economist Office Sec. Health, Edn. and Welfare, Washington, 1974-77, dir. Soc. Security Planning, 1977-79; assoc. commr. Social Security Adminstrn., Washington, 1979-81, dir. rsch., 1981-83; chief economist Gen. Acctg. Office, Washington, 1983-89, asst. comptroller gen., 1989-93; prin. dep. commr. Social Security Adminstrn., 1993-95; sr. fellow The Urban Inst., Washington, 1996—. Contbr. articles to pubs., books. Mem. Am. Economic Assn., Nat. Acad. Social Ins. (dir. 1985-96, sec. 1997—). Avocations: racquetball, choral singing. Office: The Urban Inst 2100 M St NW Washington DC 20037-1207

THOMPSON, LEONARD RUSSELL, pediatrician; b. Columbus, Ohio, Sept. 29, 1934; s. Oliver Bernard and Christina (Nichols) T.; m. Candice Elizabeth Brisken, Dec. 6, 1980; children: Ryan, Deron, Hillary, Jon, Christina, Lisa. BA, Ohio State U., 1956, MD, 1960. Diplomat Am. Bd. Pediatrics. Intern Fitzsimmons Gen. Hosp., Denver, 1960-61, resident, 1961-63; chief pediatrics Ireland Army Hosp., Ft. Knox, Ky., 1965-66; chmn. dept. pediatrics Fresno (Calif.) Med. Group, 1966-80; pediatrician pvt. practice, Fresno, 1990—; pres. med. staff Valley Children's Hosp., Fresno, 1992. Maj. U.S. Army, 1960-66. Fellow Am. Acad. Pediatrics. Office: 5305 N Fremont St #110A Fresno CA 93710

THOMPSON, LEROY, JR., radio engineer, military reserve officer; b. Tulsa, July 7, 1913; s. LeRoy and Mary (McMurrain) T.; B.S. in Elec. Engring., Ala. Poly Inst., 1936; m. Ola Dell Tedder, Dec. 31, 1941; 1 son, Bartow McMurrain. Commd. 2d lt. U.S. Army Res., 1935, advanced through grades to col., 1963; signal officer CCC, 1936-40; radio engr. Officer Hdqrs. 4th C A., 1941; with signal sect. Hdqrs. Western Def. command and 4th Army, San Francisco, 1942, comdg. officer 234th Signal Ops. Co., 1942; asst. chief, chief signal corps ROTC U. Calif., Berkeley, 1942-43; radio engring. officer O.C. SigO War Dept., Washington, 1943; radio engring officer Hdqrs. 3105th Signal Service Co. Hdqrs. CBI, New Delhi, 1944; signal officer Hdqrs. Northern Combat Area Command, Burma, 1944; signal officer Hdqrs. OSS Det 101, Burma, 1945; signal officer Hdqrs. OSS, China, 1945, radio engr., tech. liaison officer, Central Intelligence Group, CIA, 1945-50; chief radio br. Hdqrs. FEC, Tokyo, 1950-53, chief radio engring br. Signal C Plant Engring. Agy., 1953-55; radio cons. to asst. dir. def. research and engring. communications, 1960-62; ret., 1973; pvt. research and devel. on communication and related problems, 1963—; owner Thompson Research Exptl. Devel. Lab. Lic. profl. radio engr., Ga. Mem. IEEE (life sr.), NRA, Vet. Wireless Operators Assn., Am. Radio Relay League, Mil. Order World Wars, Res. Officers Assn., Am. Motorcycle Assn., Nat. Wildlife Fedn. Baptist. Home: 6450 Overlook Dr Alexandria VA 22312-1327

THOMPSON, LESLIE MELVIN, college dean, educator; b. Trinidad, Colo., May 19, 1936; s. J. Roy Thompson and E. Irene (Lance) Campbell; m. Margaret Sue Coward, June 14, 1959; children: Stephen Gregory, Michael Christopher. BA, Wayland Bapt. U., 1959; MA, Tex. Tech U., 1963, PhD, 1965. Cert. health edn. specialist. Instr. Tex. Tech U., Lubbock, 1965; asst. prof., dir. grad. studies in English So. Ill. U., Edwardsville, 1965-68; prof., dir. grad. studies in English Stephen F. Austin State U., Nacogdoches, Tex., 1968-79; dean grad. sch., dir. rsch. Ga. So. U., Statesboro, 1979-84; spl. asst. to pres. Tex. Woman's U., Denton, 1994—; adj. prof. Inst. for Gerontological Studies, Baylor U. Contbr. chpts. to books and articles to profl. jours. Cons. Ga. Endowment for Humanities, 1982-84; mem. budget com. United Way, Nacogdoches, 1975-76; mem. Ptnrs. of Ams., Statesboro, 1981-84; bd. dirs. Home Bound Services, Statesboro, 1982-84. Served with U.S. Army, 1959-61. Named Danforth Assoc. Stephen F. Austin State U., 1969-79; Nat. Def. Edn. Act fellow Office Edn., 1961-65. Mem. Coun. So. Grad. Schs. (pres. 1985-86), Coun. Grad. Schs. (bd. dirs.), Humanities and Tech. Assn. (v.p. 1984-87), Tex. Folklore Soc., Assn. Tex. Grad. Schs. (pres. 1994-95), Soc. for Coll. and Univ. Planners, Tex. Distance Learning Assn., Tex. Telehealth Edn. Assn. (pres. 1996-97), Denton C. of C., Assn. for Advancement of Health Edn., Phi Kappa Phi (pres. Statesboro chpt. 1981-83, chmn. nat. investment com. 1983-89). Democrat. Presbyterian. Avocations: numismatics, antiques. Office: Tex Woman's U Grad Sch PO Box 425649 Denton TX 76204-5649

THOMPSON, LOHREN MATTHEW, oil company executive; b. Sutherland, Nebr., Jan. 21, 1926; s. John M. and Anna (Ecklund) T.; children: Terence M., Sheila M., Clark M. Ed., U. Denver. Spl. rep. Standard Oil Co., Omaha, 1948-56; sales mgr. Frontier REF. Co., 1956-67, v.p. mktg., 1967-68; mgr. mktg. U.S. region Husky Oil Co., Denver, 1968-72; v.p. Westar Stas., Inc., Denver, 1967-70; chmn. bd. Colo. Petroleum, Denver, 1971—. Served with USAAF, 1944-46. Mem. Colo. Petroleum Council, Am. Petroleum Inst., Am. Legion. Lutheran. Clubs: Denver Petroleum, Denver Oilman's, Lodge: Lions. Home: 2410 Spruce Ave Estes Park CO 80517-7146 Office: Colo Petroleum 4080 Globeville Rd Denver CO 80216-4906

THOMPSON, LOIS JEAN HEIDKE ORE, psychologist; b. Chgo., Feb. 22, 1933; d. Harold William and Ethel Rose (Neumann) Heidke; m. Henry Thomas Ore, Aug. 28, 1954 (div. May 1972); children: Christopher, Douglas; m. Joseph Lippard Thompson, Aug. 3, 1972; children: Scott, Les, Melanie. BA, Cornell Coll., Mt. Vernon, Iowa, 1955; MA, Idaho State U., 1964, EdD, 1981. Lic. psychologist, N.Mex. Tchr. pub. schs. various locations, 1956-67; tchr., instr. Idaho State U., Pocatello, 1967-72; employee/orgn. devel. specialist Los Alamos (N.Mex.) Nat. Lab., 1981-84, tng. specialist, 1984-89, sect. leader, 1989-93; pvt. practice indsl. psychology and healthcare, Los Alamos, 1988—; sec. Cornell Coll. Alumni Office, 1954-55, also other orgns.; bd. dirs. Parent Edn. Ctr., Idaho State U., 1980; counselor, Los Alamos, 1981-88. Editor newsletter LWV, Laramie, Wyo., 1957; contbr. articles to profl. jours. Pres. Newcomers Club, Pocatello, 1967, Faculty Womens Club, Pocatello, 1968; chmn. edn. com. AAUW, Pocatello, 1969. Mem. APA, N.Mex. Psychol. Assn. (bd. dirs. divsn. II 1990, sec. 1988-90, chmn. 1990), N.Mex. Soc. Adlerian Psychology (pres. 1990, treas. 1991-97, bd. dirs. 1996—), Soc. Indsl. and Orgn. Psychology. Mem. LDS Ch. Avocations: racewalking, backpacking, skiing, tennis, biking. Home and Office: 340 Aragon Ave Los Alamos NM 87544-3505 *Honesty, dependability, spiritual inspiration, and always doing our best are ingredients that lead to a successful and happy life.*

THOMPSON, LORING MOORE, retired college administrator, writer; b. Newton, Mass., Feb. 17, 1918; s. Henry E. and Ella (Gould) T.; m. Pearl E. Judiesch, Dec. 30, 1949; children—Bruce C., Douglas P. (dec.). B.S. in Indsl. Engring, Northeastern U., 1940; M.S., U. R.I., 1947; Ph.D., U. Chgo., 1956. Instr. U. R.I., 1946; asst. to pres. Assn. Colls. Upper N.Y., 1947-49; assoc. prof. U. Toledo, 1952-59, asst. dean acad. adminstrn., 1958-59; dir. univ. planning Northeastern U., Boston, 1959-63; dean adult programs Northeastern U., 1964-66, v.p. planning, 1967-80, emeritus, 1980—; faculty assoc. continuing edn. Ariz. State U., 1982-84; cons. in field. Author: (with others) Business Communication, 1949; contbr. (with others) articles to profl. publs. Bd. dirs. Back Bay Assn., Boston, 1961-63, v.p., 1963; trustee Huntington Gen. Hosp., Boston, 1970-80; mem. Fenway Project Area Com., 1973-76; mem. Mass. conf. ch. and edn. com. United Ch. of Christ, 1972-78, chairperson, 1973-74, mem. task force on ch. growth, 1978-80; mem. Chandler Area Coun., 1988-89; sec. Interfaith Coun. Greater Sun Lakes, 1993-96. Lt. USNR, 1942-45. Mem. Spiritual Frontiers Fellowship, Tau Beta Pi. Home: 25408 S Sedona Dr Sun Lakes AZ 85248-6636

THOMPSON, LOUIS MILTON, agronomy educator, scientist; b. Throckmorton, Tex., May 15, 1914; s. Aubrey Lafayette and Lola Terry (Frazier) T.; m. Margaret Stromberg, July 10, 1937 (dec. Nov. 1972); children: Louis Milton, Margaret Ann, Glenda Ray (dec.), Carolyn Terry, Jerome Lafayette; m. Ruth Hiatt Phipps, July 7, 1990. BS, Tex. A&M U., 1935; MS, Iowa State U., 1947, PhD, 1950. Soil surveyor Tex., 1935-36, 39-40; instr. Tex. A&M U., 1936-39, 40-42; asst. prof. soils Iowa State U., Ames, 1947-50; prof. soils, head farm operation curriculum Iowa State U., 1950-58, assoc. dean agr. charge resident instrn., 1958-83, emeritus prof. agronomy, 1983—, assoc. dean emeritus, 1984—. Author: Soils and Soil Fertility, rev. edit., 1957, co-author rev. edit., 1978, 83, 93, Russian edit., 1983; contbr. articles on weather-crop yield models and climate change to profl. jours. Elder Presbyn. Ch. With AUS, 1942-46; col. Res. (ret.). Recipient Henry A. Wallace award for Disting. Svc. to Agr., 1982, Faculty citation Iowa State U. Alumni Assn., 1990, Disting. Achievement citation, 1993, Alumni Recognition medal, 1996, Disting. Iowa Scientist award Iowa Acad. Sci., 1991, Agr. Innovator award Iowa State U. Agr. Alumni Soc., 1992, Friends of Agrl. award Iowa Dept. Agr. and Nat. Agrl. Mktg. Assn., 1993, Disting. Svc. to Iowa Agr. award Iowa Farm Bur., 1995; Named one of 150 Iowans Who Made a Difference, Iowa Farm Bur., 1996. Fellow AAAS, Am. Soc. Agronomy, Soil Sci. Soc. Am., Soil and Water Conservation Soc. (pres.'s citation); mem. Am. Meterol. Soc., Farm House (hon.), Rotary (past local pres., Paul Harris fellow), Sigma Xi, Alpha Zeta (Tall Corn award 1957), Gamma Sigma Delta (nat. pres. 1956-58), Phi Kappa Phi (chpt. pres. 1961, Centennial medal 1997). Home: 414 Lynn Ave Ames IA 50014-7318 *To succeed in an academic community one must become an authority on a subject and be able to communicate it.*

THOMPSON, LYNN RENEE, chiropractor; b. Rockford, Ill., Sept. 19, 1955; d. James LeRoy Sturz and Juanita June (Longanecker) Youderian; m. John Michael Thompson, Aug. 27, 1975 (div. Feb. 1985); 1 child, Jennifer Marie. AD med. lab. technologist, Chippewa Valley Tech., 1979; BA, Midwestern State U., 1985; D of Chiropractic, Palmer Coll. Chiropractic, Davenport, Iowa, 1993. Lic. chiropractor Iowa, Ill., Wis. Med. lab. technician Laughlin Osteo. Hosp., Kirksville, Mo., 1979-82; med. technologist Hamilton Hosp., Olney, Tex., 1982-83, Bethania Regional Hosp., Wichita Falls, Tex., 1983-87, St. Clare Hosp., Baraboo, Wis., 1987-88, Samaritan Health Care, Clinton, Iowa, 1993-95; chiropractor Yours For Health Chiropractic, Chippewa Falls, Wis., 1995-97; chiropractor, owner Thompson Chiropractic Clinic, Eau Claire, Wis., 1996—, Foster Chiropractic, Osseo, Wis., 1996—; owner Conant Chiropractic Clinic, LeClaire, Iowa, 1993-96; bd. advisors Iowa Commn. on Persons with Disabilities, Davenport, 1993-94; bd. dirs. Quint Cities Handicap Group, Davenport, 1989-94, Sigma Phi Chi, Davenport, nat. bd. 1993—; chiropractor Gonstead Thompson Chiropractic Clinic, 1996—. Mem. Internat. Chiropractors Assn., Am. Soc. Clin. Pathologists (cert.), Am. Med. Technologists (cert.). Lutheran. Avocations: travel, boating, stock car racing, sports. Office: Gonstead-Thompson Chiropract Clinic 431 E Clairemont Ave Eau Claire WI 54701 also: Foster Chiropractic Clinic E10834 Park Ave Osseo WI 54758

THOMPSON, MACK EUGENE, history educator; b. Burley, Idaho, Feb. 24, 1921; s. Eugene and Nora (McFate) T.; m. Helen Goldhamer, Oct. 30, 1945. A.B., Queen's Coll., CUNY, 1948; M.A., Brown U., 1951, Ph.D., 1955. Instr. history Brown U., 1954-55; asst. prof. Calif. Inst. Tech., 1955-56; asst. prof. U. Calif. at Riverside, 1956-62, assoc. prof., 1962-66, prof., 1966-77; emeritus prof., 1977—; chmn. div. humanities U. Calif. at Riverside, 1961-63, assoc. univ. dean acad. planning, 1965-66, dean, div. undergrad. studies, 1971-74; exec dir. Am. Hist. Assn., Washington, 1974-81; Chmn. editorial bd. Experiment and Innovation: New Directions in Edn., U. Calif., 1966-68. Author: The Ward-Hopkins Controversy and the American Revolution in Rhode Island: An Interpretation, 1959, Moses Brown, Reluctant Reformer, 1962, Causes and Circumstances of the Du Pont Family's Emigration, 1969. Bd. dirs. Harry S. Truman Libr. Inst., 1974-81. With AUS, 1942-45. Home: 1378 River Oaks Ct Oldsmar FL 34677-4828

THOMPSON, MARCIA SLONE, choral director, educator; b. Ary, Ky., June 30, 1959; d. Ray and Wevena (Hall) Slone; m. Randall C. Thompson, Sept. 22, 1979; children: Tiffany, Ashley, Brittany, Alicia, Jessica, Matthew. B in Music Edn., Pikeville Coll., 1981; M in Secondary Edn.,

Morehead State U., 1985. Cert. Rank I supervision, music edn. tchr. with endorsement, grades K-12. Guitarist Slone Family Band, 1970-77; pvt. practice Hindman, Ky., 1977-93; band, choral dir. Pike County Bd. Edn., Pikeville, Ky., 1981-82, Floyd County Bd. Edn., Eastern, Ky., 1982-87; choral dir. Knott County Bd. Edn., Hindman, 1987—, Knott County Central High, Hindman, Ky, 1987—; piano instr. guitar instr., Upward Bound program Pikeville Coll., Hindman, 1977. Albums include Appalachian Bluegrass, 1972, Ramblin' Round with Slone Family, 1977; appeared on the Grand Ole Opry, 1976. Band conductor jr. high divsn. Pike County All-County Festival, Pikeville, 1981; music chair Red White Blue Festival, Martin, Ky., 1982; music judge Floyd County All-County Band, Prestonsburg, Ky., 1982-87; band dir. Ky. Derby Festival Parade, Louisville, 1985; piano accompanist choir 1st Bapt. Ch., Hindman, 1990-91, nursery asst., 1990-93, dir. youth choir, 1992, choral dir. music makers (children's music), 1994, Bapt. young women's hospitality officer, 1995, mem. sch. com.; performer Senator Benny Bailey Salute, Prestonsburg, 1991, Gingerbread Festival, Hindman, 1992-95; active Bapt. Young Women, 1993-95; co-founder Knott County Fine Arts Day Celebration, 1992—, hospitality officer Hindman Baptist Ch. Young Women's Group, 1995. Mem. Nat. Educators Assn., Am. Choral Dirs. Assn., Ky. Educators Assn., Ky. Music Educators. Democrat. Avocations: arranging music, playing piano, guitar, skating, reading. Home: PO Box 15 Hindman KY 41822-0015 Office: Knott County Ctrl High Sch Hindman KY 41822

THOMPSON, MARGARET M., physical education educator; b. nr. Falls Church, Va., Aug. 1, 1921; d. Lesley L. and Madeline (Shawen) T. B.S., Mary Washington Coll., 1941; M.A., George Washington U., 1947; Ph.D., U. Iowa, 1961. Tchr., supr. phys. edn. Staunton (Va.) City Schs., 1941-44; tchr. jr. high sch. phys. edn. Arlington County, Va., 1944-47; instr. women's phys. edn. Fla. State U., Tallahassee, 1947-51; instr., asst. prof., assoc. prof. phys. edn. Purdue U., Lafayette, Ind., 1951-65; dir. gross motor therapy lab. Purdue U., 1963-65; assoc. prof. phys. edn. U. Mo., Columbia, 1965-68; prof. U. Mo., 1968-71, dir. Cinematography and Motor Learning Lab. Dept. Health and Phys. Edn., 1965-71; prof. phys. edn. U. Ill., Champaign-Urbana, 1971-87, prof. emeritus, 1987—. Author: (with Barbara B. Godfrey) Movement Pattern Checklists, 1966, (with Chappelle Arnett) Perceptual Motor and Motor Test Battery for Children, 1968, (with Barbara Mann) An Holistic Approach to Physical Education Curriculum: Objectives Classification System for Elementary Schools, 1977, Gross Motor Inventory, 1976, revised edit., 1980, Developing the Curriculum, 1980, Setting the Learning Environment, 1980, Sex Stereotyping and Human Development, 1980; also film strips, articles. Mem. AAHPER, Internat. Assn. Phys. Edn. and Sports for Coll. Girls and Women. Home: 1311 Wildwood Ln Mahomet IL 61853-9770 Office: U Ill Freer Gymnasium Dept Kinesiology 906 S Goodwin Ave Urbana IL 61801-3841

THOMPSON, MARTIN CHRISTIAN, news service executive; b. Council Bluffs, Iowa, Oct. 25, 1938; s. Ross Kenneth and Mary Ellen (Pierce) T.; m. Janet Ann Morrow, Aug. 4, 1962; children: Chris Michael, Sean Martin. B.A. in Communications, U. Wash., 1960. Newsman Sta. KEDO, Longview, Wash., 1960-61; news dir. Sta. KREW, Sunnyside, Wash., 1961-66; newsman AP, Seattle, 1966-68; corr. AP, Reno, Nev., 1968-70; newsman AP, San Francisco, 1970-72; news editor AP, 1972-75; chief of bur. AP, San Francisco, 1975-86, Los Angeles, 1986-88; mng. editor AP, N.Y.C., 1989-92, dir. state news, 1992—. Mem. Beta Rho Tau, Sigma Delta Chi. Methodist. Office: 50 Rockefeller Plz New York NY 10020-1605

THOMPSON, MARY EILEEN, chemistry educator; b. Mpls., Dec. 21, 1928; d. Albert C. and Blanche (McAvoy) T. B.A., Coll. St. Catherine, 1953; M.S., U. Minn., 1958; Ph.D., U. Calif.-Berkeley, 1964. Math. and sci. tchr. Derham Hall High Sch., St. Paul, 1953-58; faculty Coll. St. Catherine, St. Paul, 1964—, prof., chmn. dept. chemistry, 1969-90; project dir. Women in Chemistry, 1984—. Contbr. articles to profl. jours. Mem. Am. Chem. Soc. (chair women chemists com. 1992-94), Coun. Undergrad. Rsch. (councilor 1991-96), N.Y. Acad. Sci., Chem. Soc. London, AAAS, Sigma Xi, Phi Beta Kappa. Democrat. Roman Catholic. Achievements include research interests in Cr(III) hydrolytic polymers, kinetics of inorganic complexes, Co(III) peroxo/superoxo complexes. Office: Coll St Catherine 2004 Randolph Ave Saint Paul MN 55105-1750

THOMPSON, MARY KOLETA, sculptor, non-profit organization director; b. Portsmouth, Va., Dec. 27, 1938; m. James Burton Thompson, May 5, 1957; children: Burt, Suzan, Kate, Jon. BFA, U. Tex., 1982; postgrad., Boston U., St. Mary's U. of, Minn. Cert. fund raising exec., non-profit mgmt. Pres. The Planning Resource People, Austin, Tex., 1990—; Tex. fin. devel. specialist ARC Tex., 1994—; devel. dir. Very Spl. Arts Tex., 1991-92; dir. devel. ARC, Austin, 1992-94; dir. Tex. Children's Mus., Fredericksburg, 1987-88, Internat. Hdqrs. SHAPE Command Arts and Crafts Ctr., 1985-86; com. chmn. Symposium for Encouragement Women in Math. and Natural Sci., U. Tex., Austin, 1990. Sculptor portrait busts. Bd. dirs. Teenage Parent Coun., Austin, 1990-92. Named U.S. Vol. of Yr., Belgium, 1986; grantee NEA, 1988. Mem. AAUW (life, pres. 1990-92), Women in Comm. (co-chmn. S.W. regional conf.), U. Tex. Ex-Student Assn. (life), Tex. Hist. Found. (life), Leadership Tex. (life), Leadership Tex. Alumnae Assn. (bd. dirs.), Raleigh Tavern Soc. (founder), Austin Antiques Forum (founder). Avocations: writing, lecturing, meeting and strategic planning. Office: San Antonio Area Chpt ARC 3642 E Houston St San Antonio TX 78219-3818

THOMPSON, MORLEY PUNSHON, textile company executive; b. San Francisco, Jan. 2, 1927; s. Morley Punshon and Ruth (Wetmore) T.; m. Patricia Ann Smith, Jan. 31, 1953 (dec.); children: Page Elizabeth Tredennick, Morley Punshon. A.B., Stanford U., 1948; M.B.A., Harvard U., 1950; J.D., Chase Law Sch., 1969; LL.D., Xavier U., 1981. CPA, Ohio. Chmn. Stearns Tech. Textiles Co., Cin., 1985—, Stearns Can., Inc., Cin., 1985—. Bd. dirs. Cin. Inst. Fine Arts. Lt. Supply Corps USNR, 1952-54. Mem. Beta Theta Pi. Office: 100 Williams St Cincinnati OH 45215-4602

THOMPSON, M(ORRIS) LEE, lawyer; b. Hutchinson, Kans., Nov. 29, 1946; s. Morris J. and Ruth W. (Smith) T.; m. M. Susan Morgan, May 26, 1974; children: Deborah, Erin, Andrew, Christopher. BA, Wichita State U., 1968; MA, Emporia State U., 1970; JD, George Washington U., 1974. Bar: Kans., 1974, U.S. Dist. Ct. Kans., 1974, U.S. Ct. Appeals (10th cir.) 1976, U.S. Supreme Ct., 1978. Instr., lectr. Emporia (Kans.) State U., 1969-70; lctr. in speech George Washington U., Washington, 1970-71; asst. to Senator James Pearson Washington, 1971-75; assoc. Martin, Pringle, et al., Wichita, Kans., 1976-78, ptnr., 1979-89; U.S. atty. for dist. of Kans., Dept. Justice, Wichita, 1990-93; mng. ptnr. Triplett, Woolf & Garretson, Wichita, 1993—. Treas. Kansans for Kassebaum, Wichita, 1978-88; mem. Kans. State Rep. Cen. Com., Topeka, 1978-79, 88-90; candidate U.S. Ho. of Reps., Kans., 1988; chmn. civil issues subcom. Atty. Gen.'s Adv. Com. of U.S. Attys., 1992-93. Mem. Kans. Bar Assn. (pres. criminal law sect. 1994-95). Methodist. Office: Triplett Woolf & Garretson 151 N Main St Ste 800 Wichita KS 67202-1409

THOMPSON, MOZELLE WILLMONT, lawyer, federal agency administrator; b. Pitts., Dec. 11, 1954; s. Charles and Eiko (Suzaki) T. AB, Columbia U., 1976; M in Pub. Affairs, Princeton U., 1980; JD, Columbia U., 1981. Bar: N.Y. 1984, D.C. 1984, U.S. Dist. Ct. (ea. dist.) Mich. 1984, U.S. Dist. Ct. (so. and ea. dists.) N.Y. 1985, U.S. Ct. Appeals (11th cir.) 1986. Clk. to presiding judge U.S. Dist. Ct. (so. dist.) Fla., Miami, 1981-82; assoc. Skadden, Arps, Slate, Meagher & Flom, N.Y.C., 1982-90; spl. counsel to supr. Town of Babylon, N.Y., 1988-90; counsel and sec. N.Y. State Housing Fin. Agy., N.Y.C.; counsel, sec. N.Y. State Med. Care Facilities Fin. Agy., N.Y. State Affordable Housing Corp., N.Y. State Mcpl. Bond Bank Agy., N.Y. State Project Fin. Agy., N.Y.C., 1990-93; sr. v.p., gen. coun. N.Y. State Mortgage Agy., N.Y.C., 1993; dep. asst. sec. for govt. fin. policy Dept. of Treasury, Washington, 1993-96; prin. dep. asst. sec. for govt. fin. policy Dept. Treasury, Washington, 1996—; gen. counsel North Amityville Cmty. Econ. Coun., Inc., 1989-90; pres. Greenwich Corp., 1987-93; adj. assoc. prof. Bklyn. Law Sch., 1986-91, Fordham U. Law Sch., 1992—; mem. adv. bd. Udall Ctr., U. Ariz., Tucson, 1994—. Mem. exec. bd. Practicing Attys. for Law Students, N.Y.C., 1986-93. Mem. ABA (coms. litigation, tort and ins. practice 1984—), Nat. Coun. State Housing Agys. (co-chair legal affairs com., disclosure task force, 1991-93), Nat. Coun. Health Care Facilities Fin. Authorities (co-chair advocacy and strategic planning coms., 1991-93) N.Y. State Bar Assn., N.Y. County Lawyers Assn. (com. on fed. cts. 1984-86), D.C. Bar Assn., Assn. of Bar of City of N.Y., Assn. Princeton Grad. Alumni, Assn. Black Princeton Alumni, Columbia Law Sch. Alumni Assn., Columbia Coll. Alumni Assn., Columbia Black and Latino Alumni Assn., Columbia Coll. Class 1976 (pres. 1986—). Avocations: music, theater arts, architecture. Home: 107 6th St NE Washington DC 20002-6243 Office: Dept of Treasury 1500 Pennsylvania Ave NW Washington DC 20005-1007

THOMPSON, MYRON H., federal judge; b. 1947. BA, Yale U., 1969, JD, 1972. Asst. atty. gen. State of Ala., 1972-74; sole practice Montgomery, Ala., 1974-79; ptnr. Thompson & Faulk, Montgomery, 1979-80; judge U.S. Dist. Ct. (mid. dist.) Ala., Montgomery, 1980—, chief judge, 1991—. Mem. ABA, Ala. Bar Assn., Nat. Bar Assn., Ala. Lawyers Assn. Office: US Dist Ct PO Box 235 Montgomery AL 36101-0235*

THOMPSON, NEAL PHILIP, food science and nutrition educator; b. Bklyn., July 18, 1936; s. Thomas I. and Ellenor (Backie) T.; m. Beverly Ethel Godshall, Oct. 4, 1958; children: Erick, Victor, Clifford, Karen, Stuart. BS, Wheaton Coll., 1957; MA, Miami U., 1962; PhD, Princeton U., 1965. Asst. prof. U. Fla., Gainesville, 1965-70, assoc. prof., 1970-76, prof., 1976—, asst. dean, 1980-86, assoc. dean, 1986-93. Capt. USNR, ret. Home: 6510 NW 16th Pl Gainesville FL 32605 Office: U Fla Inst Food & Agrl Scis Food & Environ Toxicology Gainesville FL 32611-0720

THOMPSON, N(ORMAN) DAVID, insurance company executive; b. Rockville Centre, N.Y., July 30, 1934; s. Norman J. and Laurel H. (Johnson) T.; m. Joyce L. Angeletti, June 7, 1958; children: John L., Jennifer L., Sarah S. BA with distinction, Wesleyan U., 1956; LLB, Columbia U., 1959; postgrad., Harvard U., 1973. Bar: N.Y. Pvt. practice law N.Y.C., 1961-62; corp. sec. Gen. Reins. Corp., N.Y.C., 1964-69; v.p. Gen. Reins. Corp., Greenwich, Conn., 1969; v.p., gen. counsel, sec. Gen. Reins. Corp., 1976-77; exec. v.p. N.Am. Reins. Corp., N.Y.C., 1977-78; pres. N.Am. Reins. Corp., 1978-92; chmn., CEO Swiss Reins. Am. Corp. (formerly N.Am. Reins.), 1992-95, Swiss Re Am. Holding Corp. (formerly SwissRe Holding Co.), 1992-97; chmn. SwissRe Group Cos. (U.S.), 1992-95. Dir. Nat. Legal Ctr. for Pub. Interest, chmn., 1992-95; trustee Coll. Ins., 1992. With U.S. Army, 1959-60. Mem. Reins Assn. Am. (chmn. 1982-83), Nat. Assn. Casualty and Surety Execs. (pres. 1986-87), Am. Arbitration Assn. (bd. dirs., chmn. fin. com. 1992-93), Am. Inst. Property and Casualty Underwriters (trustee), Univ. Club (N.Y.C.), Saugatuck Harbor Yacht Club (Westport, Conn.). Home: 47 Kettle Creek Rd Weston CT 06883-2208

THOMPSON, NORMAN WINSLOW, surgeon, educator; b. Boston, July 12, 1932; s. Herman Chandler and Evelyn Millicent (Palmer) T.; m. Marcia Ann Veldman, June 12, 1956; children: Robert, Karen, Susan, Jennifer. BA, Hope Coll., 1953; MD, U. Mich., 1957; MD (hon.), U. Linköping, Sweden, 1995. Diplomate Am. Bd. Surgery. Intern U. Mich., Ann Arbor, 1957-58, resident in surgery, 1959-62, instr., 1962-64, asst. prof., 1964-66, assoc. prof., 1966-71, prof. surgery, 1971-79, Henry King Ranson prof. surgery, 1979—, chief endocrine surg. svc., 1979—. Contbr. articles to profl. jours. Trustee Hope Coll., Holland, Mich., 1973-88. Mem. ACS (gov. 1979-85), Ctrl. Surg. Assn., Western Surg. Assn. (1st v.p. 1992-93, pres. 1994-95), F.A. Coller Surg. Soc. (pres. 1986), Am. Surg. Assn., Am. Thyroid Assn., Soc. Surg. Alimentary Tract, Internat. Assn. Endocrine Surgeons (pres. 1989-91), Internat. Soc. Surgeons (v.p. 1995—), Am. Assn. Endocrine Surgeons (pres. 1980-81, 81-82), Royal Soc. Medicine, Brit. Assn. Endocrine Surgeons, Assn. French Endocrine Surgeons, Scandanvian Surg. Soc., Alpha Omega Alpha. Home: 465 Hillspur Rd Ann Arbor MI 48105-1048 Office: U Mich Med Ctr 2920 Taubman Bldg Ann Arbor MI 48109

THOMPSON, NOVELLA WOODRUM, college administrator, psychotherapist; b. Frankfurt, Germany, Apr. 24, 1968; d. Gary Lynn and Kaye Yvonne (Hickman) Woodrum; m. Philip Drew Thompson, Nov. 12, 1994. BA, W.Va. Wesleyan Coll., Buckhannon, 1992; MA, W.Va. Grad. Coll., Institute, 1994. Counselor, parent educator The Family Ctr., Inc., Beckley, W.Va., 1993; counselor Women's Resource Ctr., Beckley, 1993-94; psychotherapist The Family Inst. of W.Va., Beckley, 1994-95; dean Sch. Acad. Enrichment & Lifelong Learning Coll. W.Va., Beckley, 1995—; guest lectr. W.Va. Grad. Coll., 1994-95; vol. counselor Women's Resource Ctr., Beckley, 1992-93; cons. non-traditional programs Coll. WVa., Beckley, 1995; parent educator & lectr. The Family Ctr. Raleigh County Cmty. Alliance Assn., 1994—. Author: Prior Learning Assessment (PLA), 1996; editor: Experience Counts, 1995. Mem. bd. dirs. The Family Ctr., Beckley, 1993; panelist, speaker Stop Child Abuse Now (SCAN), Beckley, 1994. Recognized for Comty. Svc., Register-Herald "A Celebration of Women." Mem. ACA, W.Va. Counseling Assn., W.Va. Assn. for Specialists in Group Work, Coun. for Adult and Exptl. Learning (state rep. 1996). Avocations: reading, gardening, cross-stitch, decorating, crafts, golf. Home: 1500 Harper Rd Beckley WV 25801 Office: Coll WVa PO Box AG Beckley WV 25802

THOMPSON, OTIS NATHANIEL, JR., professional society executive; b. Balt., Aug. 28, 1923; s. Otis Nathaniel and Mary Willie (Holman) T.; m. Lorraine Cornelia Jones, Mar. 14, 1959; children: Bruce Campbell, Kimberly Ann. B of Journalism, Lincoln U., 1950. Asst. city editor St. Louis Argus Newspaper, 1950-55; pub. rels. assoc. Moss H. Kendrix Orgn., Washington, 1955-61; reporter Assoc. Corr. News Svc., Washington, 1961-63; info. specialist USDA, Washington, 1963-74, chief, 1974-87; exec. dir. Orgn. Profl. Employment USDA, Washington, 1989—. Pres. D.C. chpt. Lincoln U. Alumni Assn., Washington. 1989-92, Whitfield Civic Assn., Lanham, Md., 1966-72. Sgt. U.S. Army Corps Engrs., 1943-46. Methodist. Avocation: collecting historical data on African Am. achievements. Office: OPEDA PO Box 381 Washington DC 20044-0381

THOMPSON, PAUL HAROLD, university president; b. Ogden, Utah, Nov. 28, 1938; s. Harold Merwin and Elda (Skeen) T.; m. Carolyn Lee Nelson, Mar. 9, 1961; children: Loralyn, Kristyn, Shannyn, Robbyn, Daylyn, Nathan. BS, U. Utah, 1964; MBA, Harvard U., 1966, D Bus. Adminstrn., 1969. Rsch. assoc. Harvard U., Cambridge, Mass., 1966-69; asst. prof. Harvard U., Cambridge, 1969-73; assoc. prof. bus. Brigham Young U., Provo, Utah, 1973-78, prof., 1978-84, asst. dean, 1978-81, dean, 1984-89, v.p., 1989-90; pres. Weber State U., Ogden, Utah, 1990—; cons. Goodyear, Hughes Aircraft, Portland GE, Esso Resources Ltd., GE. Co-author: Organization and People: Readings, Cases, and Exercises in Organizational Behavior, 1976, Novations: Strategies for Career Management, 1986; also articles. Named Outstanding Prof. of Yr., Brigham Young U., 1981; Baker scholar Harvard U., 1966. Mem. Am. Assn. State Colls. and Univs. (com. 1991—), Ogden C. of C. (exec. com. 1990—), Rotary (prograam com. Ogden 1991—, Harris fellow 1992—), Phi Beta Kappa. Office: Weber State U 1001 University Cir Ogden UT 84408-1001

THOMPSON, PAUL MICHAEL, lawyer; b. Dubuque, Iowa, Aug. 30, 1935; s. Frank W. and Genevieve (Cassutt) T.; m. Mary Jacqueline McManus, Jan. 30, 1960; children—Anne, Tricia, Paul, Tim, Jim. B.A. magna cum laude, Loras Coll., 1957; LL.B., Georgetown U., 1959. Bar: Iowa 1959, D.C. 1959, Va. 1966. Atty. appellate ct. br. NLRB, Washington, 1962-66; assoc. Hunton & Williams, Richmond, Va., 1966-71, ptnr., 1971—; adj. prof. The T.C. Williams Sch. Law, U. Richmond. Served with JAGC, USAF, 1960-62. Mem. ABA, Va. State Bar, Va. Bar Assn., Internat. Bar Assn., Commonwealth Club. Roman Catholic. Office: Hunton & Williams 951 E Byrd St Riverfront Pla E Tower Richmond VA 23219-4074

THOMPSON, PETER L. H., golf course architect; b. Modesto, Calif., Apr. 26, 1939. BS in East Asian Studies, U. Oreg., 1962, B in Landscape Architecture, 1971, M in Urban Planning, 1971; postgrad., U. Calif., Berkeley, 1975, Nat. U. Registered landscape arch., Calif., Oreg., Wash., Nev. With Oreg. Planning Commn., Lane County, 1965-70; commr. Oreg. Planning Commn., Eugene, 1981-83; sr. assoc. Ruff, Cameron, Lacoss, Eugene, 1971-75; prin. Peter L. H. Thompson & Assocs., Eugene, 1975-83, John H. Midby & Assocs., Las Vegas, Nev., 1983-86, Thompson-Wihlborg, Ltd., Corte Madera, Calif., 1982-89, Thompson Planning Group (now Thompson Golf Planning), Ltd., San Rafael, Calif., 1989—; with Oreg. Planning Commn., commr., 1981-83, Novato, Calif. Planning Commn., commr. 1989-93, pres. 1989-93; spkr. Oreg. Home Builders Conf., 1980, Pacific Coast Builders Conf., 1984, Tacoma Country Club Pro-Pres. Tournament, 1991, Madrona Links Men's Golf Club, 1991, Twin Lakes Country Club Pro-Pres. Tournament, 1992, Golf Expo, Palm Springs, Calif., 1993, 95, Golf Expo, Nashville, 1993, Golf Expo, Monterey, Calif., 1994, others. Contbr. articles to mags. Mem. citizen's adv. bd. City of Eugene, Oreg., City of Las Vegas. Mem. USGA, Am. Soc. Landscape Archs., Am. Assn. Planners, Nat. Golf Found., Urban Land Inst., Rotary Internat. Office: Thompson Golf Planning Ltd 2175 Francisco Blvd E Ste A San Rafael CA 94901-5524

THOMPSON, RALPH GORDON, federal judge; b. Oklahoma City, Dec. 15, 1934; s. Lee Bennett and Elaine (Bizzell) T.; m. Barbara Irene Hencke, Sept. 5, 1964; children: Lisa, Elaine, Maria. BBA, U. Okla., 1956, JD, 1961. Bar: Okla. 1961. Ptnr. Thompson, Thompson, Harbour & Selph (and predecessors), Oklahoma City, 1961-75; judge U.S. Dist. Ct. for Western Dist. Okla., Oklahoma City, 1975—; chief judge U.S. Dist. Ct. (we. dist.) Okla., 1986-93; mem. Okla. Ho. of Reps., 1966-70, asst. minority floor leader, 1969-70; spl. justice Supreme Ct. Okla., 1970-71; tchr. Harvard Law Sch. Trial Advocacy Workshop, 1981—; apptd. by chief justice of U.S. to U.S. Fgn. Intelligence Surveillance Ct., 1990-97; elected to jud. conf. of the U.S., 1997; apptd. to Edward J. Devitt Disting. Svc. Justice award selection com., 1997-99. Rep. nominee for lt. gov., Okla., 1970; chmn. bd. ARC, Oklahoma City, 1970-72; chmn., pres. Okla. Young Lawyers Conf., 1965; mem. bd. visitors U. Okla., 1975-78. Lt. USAF, 1957-60, col. Res., ret. Decorated Legion of Merit; named Oklahoma City's Outstanding Young Man, Oklahoma City Jaycees, 1967, Outstanding Fed. Trial Judge, Okla Trial Lawyers Assn., 1980; recipient Regents Alumni award U. Okla., 1990, Disting. Svc. award, 1993; inducted Okla. Hall of Fame, 1995. Fellow Am. Bar Found.; mem. ABA, Fed. Bar Assn., Okla. Bar Assn. (chmn. sect. internat. law and gen. practice 1974-75), Oklahoma County Bar Assn. (Jud. Svc. award 1988), Jud. Conf. U.S. (com. on ct. adminstrn. 1981-89, com. on fed.-state jurisdiction 1988-91), U.S. Dist. Judges Assn. 10th Cir. (pres. 1992-94), Rotary (hon.), Order of Coif, Am. Inns of Ct. (pres. XXIII 1995-96), Phi Beta Kappa (pres. chpt. 1985-86, Phi Beta Kappa of Yr. 1991), Beta Theta Pi, Phi Alpha Delta. Episcopalian. Office: US Dist Ct 200 NW 4th St Oklahoma City OK 73102-3026

THOMPSON, RALPH NEWELL, former chemical corporation executive; b. Boston, Mar. 4, 1918; s. Ralph and Lillian May (Davenport) T.; m. Virginia Kenniston, Jan. 31, 1942; children: Pamela, Nicholas, Diana. B.S., MIT, 1940. Research engr. Middlesex Products Co., Cambridge, Mass., 1940-42; tech. dir. Falulah Paper Co., Fitchburg, Mass., 1945-48; staff engr. to v.p., div. gen. mgr. Calgon Corp., Pitts., 1948-70; v.p. mktg., corp. devel. Pa. Indsl. Chem. Corp., Clairton, 1970-74; gen. mgr. chem. div. Thiokol Corp., Trenton, N.J., 1974-76; group v.p.-chem. Thiokol Corp., Newtown, Pa., 1976-82; marine artist, specializing in lighthouses and historic sailing vessels, 1982—; dir. Mulford Co. Inc., Mass., 1956-82, Thiokol Can. Ltd., 1975-82, Thiokol Chems., Ltd., Eng., 1976-82, Toray Thiokol Co. Ltd., Japan, 1976-82, Nisso-Ventron K.K., Japan, 1977-82, S.W. Chem. Services Inc., Tex., 1978-82, S.W. Plastics Europe (S.A.), Belgium, 1978-82, Dynachem. Corp., Calif., 1979-82, Carstab Corp., Ohio, 1980-82. Patentee in field. Mem. Mt. Lebanon (Pa.) Civic League, 1950-74. Served with USNR, 1942-45. Recipient Goodreau Meml. Fund medal in chemistry, 1936. Fellow Am. Inst. Chemists; mem. TAPPI (contributor monograph series 1950-65), N.Y. Acad. Scis., Soc. Chem. Industry, Nat. Maritime Soc., Am. Soc. Marine Artists, Mil. Order World Wars, Pa. Soc., Soc. Descs. Colonial Clergy. Republican. Presbyterian.

THOMPSON, RAYMOND EUGENE, JR., education educator; b. Merrillville, Ind., Apr. 19, 1958; s. Mary A. (Be) Thompson. AA, Purdue U., 1979, BS, 1980, MS, 1985. Flight instr. Culver (Ind.) Mil. Acad., 1978; asst. prof. Lewis U., Romeoville, Ill., 1980-81; maintenance supr. Aviation Svcs. FBO, Romeoville, 1981; teaching asst. Purdue U., West Lafayette, Ind., 1979-80, asst. prof. edn., 1982-92, assoc. prof., 1993—; cons. E.G. Composites, Indpls., 1989—, Am. Trans Air, Indpls., 1990—, Am. Corp. Mfg. Learning Ctr., Stuart, Fla., 1992—. Author: Applied Composite Technology, 1992; editor book chpt.; author curriculum in field. Named Outstanding Maintenance Inst., Aviation Tech. Edn. Coun., 1993. Mem. ASM Internat., Great Lake Aviation Tech. Edn. Coun., Soc. for Advancement of Material and Process Engrng., Soc. Mfg. Engrs., Am. Soc. Non-Destructive Testing, Profl. Aircraft Maintenance Assn. Avocations: flying, drama, music, outdoor activities.

THOMPSON, RAYMOND HARRIS, anthropologist, educator; b. Portland, Me., May 10, 1924; s. Raymond and Eloise (MacIntyre) T.; m. Molly Kendall, Sept. 9, 1948; children: Margaret Kelsey Luchetta, Mary Frances. B.S., Tufts U., 1947; A.M., Harvard U., 1950, Ph.D., 1955. Fellow div. hist. research Carnegie Instn., Washington, 1950-52; asst. prof. anthropology, curator Mus. Anthropology, U. Ky., 1952-56; faculty U. Ariz., 1956—, prof. anthropology, 1964—, Riecker Disting. prof., 1980—, head dept., 1964-80; dir. Ariz. State Mus., from 1964; mem. adv. panel program in anthropology NSF, 1963-64, mem. mus. collections program, 1983-85; mem. NSF grad. fellowship panel Nat. Acad. Scis.-NRC, 1964-66; mem. research in nursing in patient care rev. com. USPHS, 1967-69; com. on social sci. commn. edn. in agr. and natural resources Nat. Acad. Scis., 1968-69; mem. anthropology com. examiners Grad. Record Exam., 1967-70, chmn., 1969-70; mem. com. recovery archaeol. remains, 1972-77, chmn., 1973-77; collaborator Nat. Park Service, 1972-76; mem. Ariz. Hist. Adv. Commn., 1966—, chmn., 1971-74, chmn. hist. sites rev. com., 1971-83; chmn. Ariz. Humanities Council, 1973-77, mem., 1979-85; adv. bd. Ariz. Hist. Recors, 1976-84; mem. research review panel for archaeology NEH, 1976-77, mem. rev. panel for museums, 1978, Ariz. Archaeology Adv. Commn., 1985—; cons. task force on archaeology Adv. Council on Historic Preservation, 1978. Author: Modern Yucatecan Maya Pottery Making, 1958; editor: Migrations in New World Culture History, 1958, When is a Kiva, 1990; mem. editl. bd. Science, 1972-77. Trustee Mus. No. Ariz., 1969—; bd. dirs. Tucson Art Mus., 1974-77; cons. Nat. Mus. Act Coun., 1984-86. Served with USNR, 1944-45, PTO. Recipient Pub. Svc. award Dept. Interior, 1990. Fellow AAAS (chmn. sect. H 1977-78), Tree-Ring Soc., Am. Anthrop. Assn. (Disting. Svc. award 1980); mem. Soc. Am. Archaeology (editor 1958-62, exec. com. 1963-64, pres. 1976-77), Am. Soc. Conservation Archaeology (Conservation award 1980), Seminario de Cultura Maya, Am. Assn. Museums (accreditation vis. com. 1972, 82-90, cons. mus. assessment program 1983-89, repatriation task force 1987, steering com. mus. data collection program 1988-93), Internat. Coun. Museums (assoc.), Coun. Mus. Anthropology (dir. 1978-79, pres. 1980-83), Assn. Sci. Mus. Dirs. (sec.-treas. 1978-80), Ariz. Acad. Sci., Ariz. Archaeol. and Hist. Soc. (Byron Cummings award 1993), Mus. Assn. Ariz. (pres. 1983, 84), Phi Beta Kappa, Sigma Xi. Office: Univ Ariz Ariz State Museum Tucson AZ 85721

THOMPSON, RENOLD DURANT, mining and shipping executive; b. Cleve., July 28, 1926; s. James Renold and Gertrude Goldie (Meyers) T.; m. Shirley Ann Sprague, June 24, 1949; children: Renold Durant, Jr., Bradley Sprague, Patricia Sprague Hickey. B.A., Dartmouth Coll., 1946; B.S., Case Inst. Tech., 1948. Metallurgist, U.S. Steel Corp., Cleve. and Duluth, Minn., 1948-52; with Oglebay Norton Co., Cleve., 1952—; sr. v.p. Oglebay Norton Co., 1972-73, exec. v.p. ops., 1973-81, exec. v.p., 1981-82, pres., chief exec. officer, 1982-92, vice chmn., 1992—, also dir.; bd. dirs. 1st Union Mgmt., Inc., Cleve.-Cuyahoga County Port Authority; chmn., CEO Work in N.E. Ohio Coun. Mem. Pepper Pike Club, Chagrin Valley Hunt Club, Union Club. Office: Oglebay Norton Co 1100 Superior Ave E Ste 2000 Cleveland OH 44114-2518

THOMPSON, RICHARD FREDERICK, psychologist, neuroscientist, educator; b. Portland, Oreg., 1930; s. Frederick Albert and Margaret St. Clair (Marr) T.; m. Judith K. Pedersen, May 22, 1960; children: Kathryn M., Elizabeth K., Virginia St. C. B.A., Reed Coll., 1952; M.S., U. Wis., 1953, Ph.D., 1956. Asst. prof. med. psychology Med. Sch. U. Oreg., Portland, 1959-63, assoc. prof., 1963-65, prof., 1965-67; prof. psychobiology U. Calif., Irvine, 1967-73, 75-80; prof. psychology Harvard U., Cambridge, Mass., 1973-74; Lashley chair prof. Harvard U., Cambridge, 1973; prof. psychology, Bing prof. human biology Stanford U., Palo Alto, Calif., 1980-87; Keck prof. psychology and biol. scis. U. So. Calif., L.A., 1987—, dir. neuroscience program, 1989—. Author: Foundations of Physiological Psychology, 1967, (with others) Psychology, 1971, Introduction to Physiological Psychology, 1975; Psychology editor (with others), W.H. Freeman & Co. publs., chief editor, Behavioral Neurosci., 1983—; editor: Jour. Comparative and Physiol. Psychology, 1981-83; regional editor: (with others) Physiology and Behavior; contbr. (with others) articles to profl. jours. Fellow AAAS, APA (Disting. Sci. Contbn. award 1974, governing coun. 1974—), Soc. Neurosci. (councilor

1972-76); mem. NAS, Am. Acad. Arts and Scis., Internat. Brain Rsch. Orgn., Psychonomic Soc. (gov. 1972-77, chmn. 1976), Am. Psychol. Soc. (pres. 1994-95), Western Psychol. Assn. (pres. 1994-95), Soc. Exptl. Psychology (Warren medal). Office: Univ of So Calif Neuroscis Program HNB 122 Univ Park Los Angeles CA 90007

THOMPSON, RICHARD LLOYD, pastor; b. Lansing, Mich., May 8, 1939; s. Lloyd Walter and Gladys V. (Gates) T.; m. Dianne Lee Tuttle, Nov. 14, 1958; children: Matthew, Beth Ann, Douglas. BA, Azusa Pacific U., 1969; MDiv, Concordia Theol. Sem., 1973. Aerospace industry test engr. Hycon Mfg. Co., Monrovia, Calif., 1961-69; pastor Trinity Luth. Ch., Cedar Rapids, Iowa, 1973-84, Billings, Mont., 1984-94; pastor Good Shepherd Luth. Ch., Watertown, Wis., 1994—; chmn. mission com. Iowa E. dist. Luth. Ch. Mo. Synod, 1979-81, 2d v.p. Iowa dist. E., Cedar Rapids, 1981-84, bd. mgr. Concordia plans, St. Louis, 1983-86, bd. dirs., St. Louis, 1986—, chmn. bd. dirs., 1992—; served on various task forces and coms. dealing with structure and vision setting for chs. at local, dist. and nat. level, 1975—. Mem. Nat. Exch. Club, Cedar Rapids, 1982-84, Billings, 1986. With USN, 1957-61. Avocations: attending auctions, yard work, travel, exercise activity. Office: Good Shepherd Luth Ch 1611 E Main St Watertown WI 53094-4109*

THOMPSON, RICHARD STEPHEN, management consultant; b. Des Moines, Oct. 14, 1931; s. Richard Stephen and Mary Ellen (Dailey) T.; m. Nancy Ann Jensen, Apr. 17, 1954; children—Traci Nan, Gregory Christian, Jonathan Richard. B.S.C., State U. Iowa, 1953; M.B.A., Ind. U., 1960. Regional dir. Bristol Meyers Co., N.Y.C., 1969-75; regional dir. Warner Lambert Co., Morris Plains, N.J., 1975-78; exec. v.p. Milton Bradley Co., Milton Bradley Internat., Inc., Springfield, Mass., 1979-83, pres., 1983-84; sr. v.p. internat., dir. Hasbro, Inc., Pawtucket, R.I., 1984-89; pres. Richard Thompson Assocs., London, 1989—. Served to 1st lt. USAF, 1954-55. Republican. Clubs: Chatham Beach Tennis (Mass.); Pilgrims (London and N.Y.); American (London); Roehampton (London). Avocations: tennis; skiing; hiking; reading.

THOMPSON, ROBERT CHARLES, lawyer; b. Council, Idaho, Apr. 20, 1942; s. Ernest Lavelle and Evangeline Montgomery (Carlson) T.; m. Marilyn Anne Wilcox, Jan. 17, 1960 (dec. Mar. 1962); m. Patricia Joan Price, June 1, 1963 (div. 1969); m. Jan Nesbitt, June 29, 1973; 1 child, Tanya. AB, Harvard U., 1963, LLB, 1967. Bar: Mass. 1967, Calif. 1983, U.S. Dist. Ct. (ea. dist.) Mass. 1975, U.S. Ct. Appeals (1st cir.) 1976, U.S. Ct. Appeals (9th cir.) 1984, U.S. Dist. Ct. (no. dist.) Calif. 1983, U.S. Dist. Ct. (ea. dist.) Calif., 1996. Assoc. Choate, Hall & Stewart, Boston, 1967-73; asst. regional counsel EPA, Boston, 1973-75, regional counsel, 1975-82, assoc. gen. counsel, 1979-82; regional counsel EPA, San Francisco, 1982-84; ptnr. Graham & James, San Francisco, 1984-91, LeBoeuf, Lamb, Greene & MacRae, San Francisco, 1992—. Contbr. articles to profl. jours. Bd. dirs. Peninsula Indsl. and Bus. Assn., Palo Alto, Calif., 1986—; chmn. Cambridge (Mass.) Conservation Commn., 1972-74; co-chmn. The Clift Confs. on Environ. Law, 1983-97. John Russell Shaw traveling fellow Harvard Coll., 1963-64; recipient Regional Administrs. Bronze medal EPA, 1976, 84. Mem. ABA (natural resources sect., com. on native Am. natural resources law, spl. com. on mktg.), Natural Resources Def. Coun., Sierra Club, Commonwealth Club, Phi Beta Kappa. Democrat. Episcopalian. Avocations: personal computers, yoga, antiques, wines, cooking. Office: LeBoeuf Lamb Greene & MacRae One Embarcadero Ctr San Francisco CA 94111

THOMPSON, ROBERT JAYE, minister; b. Coffeyville, Kans., Nov. 4, 1951; s. Julis Levi and Verna Belle (Hardrick) T.; m. Carolyn Robinson, Aug. 23, 1971; children: Montie Shannon, Monica Shea, Marquis Shane, Marissa Seana, Terry Dwight, Mycal Shanton. AA in History, Coffeyville Cmty. Jr. Coll, 1971; BA in History, Pittsburg (Kans.) State U., 1973; MDiv cum laude, Memphis Theol. Sem., 1991. Ordained to ministry Bapt. Ch., 1983. Pastor Sweet Home Bapt. Ch., Dardanelle, Ark., 1983-88; assoc. pastor Springdale Bapt. Ch., Memphis, 1988-92; instr. Tenn. Sch. of Religion, Memphis, 1989-92; asst. dean Regular Ark. Bapt. Home and Fgn. Mission Conv., 1994—; chaplain intern Federal Correctional Institution, Memphis, 1990; instr. Nat. Bapt. Congress of Christian Edn., 1994—, Greenfield Presbyn. Ch., Waterford, Miss., 1990-92, New Prospect Bapt. Ch., Russellville, Ark., 1992—; treas. Antioch Dist. Assn., Ft. Smith, Ark., 1987-88, youth min., 1987-89; sec. Ft. Smith Interdenominational Assn., 1984-88; sgt. Guardsmark, Inc., Memphis, 1989-92; program coord. Russellville Area Ministerial Assn., 1994; bd. dirs. Help Network; mem. steering com. Nat. Day of Prayer, Russellville, 1994-95; instr. Regional Ark. Bapt. Congress Christian Edn., 1996—. Dir. gen. Antioch Congress of Christian Edn., 1993-96, Ft. Smith, Ark., 1994—, 2d v.p.; treas. Antioch Dist. Assn., Ft. Smith, 1995—; pres.-elect Russellville Area Ministerial Assn., 1995, pres., 1996; chmn. Nat. Day of Prayer Russellville, 1995-96; block worker Am. Heart Assn., Memphis, 1991; student body pres. Memphis Theol. Sem., 1990-91; bd. dirs. Shelter of Sunshine, Russellville, 1995—, pres.-elect, 1996-97; mem. Bd. of Adjustment, Russellville, 1996—; pres. Race Rels. Task Force, Russellville, 1995—; historian Regional Ark. Bapt. Conv., 1995—. Recipient Benjamin E. Mays fellowship Fund for Theol. Edn., N.Y.C., 1990-91, Disting. Mil. Grad. Pittsburg State U., 1973. Mem. Memphis Bapt. Ministers Assn., Russellville Area Ministerial Assn. (pres. 1996), Downtown Rotary Club. Democrat. Home: 226 S Independence Ave Russellville AR 72801-4960 *It is a good thing that God gives us only one day at a time because it is hard enough to organize that one so that we still look forward to the next with joy.*

THOMPSON, ROBERT L., JR., lawyer; b. St. Paul, Aug. 9, 1944; s. Robert L. and Dorothy R. (Bergstrom) T.; m. Carolyn H. Foss, Aug. 4, 1973; children: Sarah, Kathryn, Jill. BA, Macalester Coll., St. Paul, 1967; JD, U. Oreg., 1973; LLM, NYU, 1988. Bar: Minn. 1973, U.S. Dist. Ct. Minn. 1978, N.Y. 1984. Corp. counsel Northrup King Co., Mpls., 1974-84; assoc. gen. counsel Sandoz Corp., N.Y.C., 1984-88, v.p., gen. counsel, sec., 1989-96; exec. v.p., gen. counsel Novartis Corp., Summit, N.J., 1997—; mem. adv. bd. Allendale Ins. Co., N.Y.C., 1990—; mem. bd. visitors U. Oreg. Law Sch., 1995—. 1st lt. U.S. Army, 1968-70. Mem. ABA, Am. Corp. Counsel Assn., Assn. Bar City N.Y. Republican. Congregationalist. Office: Novartis Corp 556 Morris Ave Summit NJ 07901-1330

THOMPSON, ROBERT LEE, agricultural economist, nonprofit executive; b. Canton, N.Y., Apr. 25, 1945; s. Robert M. and Esther Louise (Weatherup) T.; m. Karen Hansen, Aug. 9, 1968; children—Kristina Marie, Eric Robert. B.S., Cornell U., Ithaca, N.Y., 1967; M.S., Purdue U., West Lafayette, Ind., 1969, Ph.D., 1974. Vol. agriculturalist Internat. Vol. Service, Pakse and Vientiane, Laos, 1968-70; vis. prof. Fed. Univ. Vicosa, Brazil, 1972-73; prof. Purdue U., West Lafayette, Ind., 1974-93, dean of agriculture, 1987-93; rsch. scholar Internat. Inst. for Applied Systems Analysis, Laxenburg, Austria, 1983; sr. staff economist Council Econ. Advisers, Washington, 1983-85; asst. sec. econs. U.S. Dept. Agr., Washington, 1985-87; pres., CEO Winrock Internat. Inst. Agrl. Devel., 1993—; vis. prof. Econ. Rsch. Svc., USDA, 1979-80; bd. dirs. Vigoro Corp., 1993-96, Nat. Coop. Bank, Washington, 1985-97, Commodity Credit Corp., Washington, 1985-87, PSI Resources and P.S.I. Energy, 1987-94; chmn. adv. coun. Nat. Ctr. for Food and Agrl. Policy, Washington, 1987-92; mem. Ind. Commn. on Agr. and Rural Devel., 1989-93, Nat. Commn. on Agrl. Trade and Export Policy, 1985-86, Nat. Commn. Internat. Trade, Devel., and Cooperation, 1996-97; bd. agr. NRC, 1987-92, Internat. Policy Coun. on Agr. and Trade, USDA Joint Coun. on Food and Agrl. Scis., 1994-96; cons. USAID, Agr. Can., Ford Found., Brazilian Agr. Ministry, FAO, World Bank, Internat. Food Policy Rsch. Inst., Internat. Maize and Wheat Improvement Ctr., U.S. Feed Grains Coun., Nat. Planning Assn., USIA, Centre for Internat. Econs., Canberra, Club d'Experts en Economie Agricole Internat., Paris, Danish Coun. Rsch. Policy, FAO, Rome. Contbr. numerous articles to profl. publs. Author monographs, book chpts. Bd. dirs. Ind. 4-H Found., Ind. Inst. Agr. Food and Nutrition, 1987-93, Inst. for Sci. in Soc., 1991-93, USDA Grad. Sch., Washington, 1985-87; mem. nat. adv. coun. Minorities in Agr., Natural Resources and Related Sci.; bd. dirs. Farm Found., 1987-92, chmn. 1991-92. Recipient Agrl. Rsch. award Purdue U., 1983, Outstanding Alumni award Cornell U., 1988, Superior Svc. award USDA, 1989, Justin Smith Morrill award, 1995, Nat. 4-H Alumni award, 1992, Chgo. Farmers Agriculturalist of Yr. award, 1992, Bob Pim Agrl. Vision award Nat. Forum Agr., 1997. Fellow AAAS, Am. Agrl. Econs. Assn. (editorial coun. 1983-85, quality com. award 1979, 91, 93); mem. Internat. Agribus Mgmt. Assn. (bd. dirs.), Am. Econ. Assn., Internat. Assn. Agrl. Economists (pres. 1993-96), Coun. on Fgn. Rels., Bretton Woods Com., Royal Swedish Acad. Agr. and Forestry (fgn.), Ukrainian Acad. Agrl. Scis., Cosmos Club (Washington), Sigma Xi, Alpha Gamma Rho, AlphaZeta, Gamma Sigma Delta. Republican. Avocation: foreign language study. Office: Winrock Internat Inst Agr Devel 38 Winrock Dr Morrilton AR 72110-9370

THOMPSON, ROBERT RANDALL (ROBBY THOMPSON), professional baseball player; b. West Palm Beach, Fla., May 10, 1962. Student, Palm Beach Jr. Coll., Fla. State U. With San Francisco Giants, 1983-96, Cleve. Indians, 1997—; mem. Nat. League All-Star Team, 1988, 93. Named Sporting News Rookie Player of Yr., 1986, Nat. League Leader in Triples, 1989, Nat. League Gold Glove 1993, Silver Slugger Team 1993; named to Sporting News All-Star Team, 1988, 93. Office: Cleve Indians 2401 Ontario St Cleveland OH 44115*

THOMPSON, ROBERT THOMAS, lawyer; b. Pontiac, Ill., Feb. 15, 1930; s. McDuffie and Ivy (Slaughter) T.; m. Elaine Cheshire, Oct. 1, 1950; children: Robert Thomas, Randall C., David L. A.B., Emory U., 1950, J.D. with honors, 1952. Bar: Ga. 1951, S.C. 1964, D.C. 1973. Assoc., ptnr. Wilson, Branch, Barwick & Vandiver, Atlanta, 1952-64; sr. ptnr. Thompson & Hutson, Greenville, S.C., 1964—, Washington, S.C., 1970—; lectr. Law Sch. Emory U.; mgmt. adv. U.S. Del. to Internat. Labor Orgn., 1970; mem., chmn. task force NLRB, 1974-77; mem. pub. Adminstrv. conf. U.S. Bd. vistors Emory U.; chmn. bd. advisors Furman U.; past trustee Buncombe St. United Meth. Ch. Contr. articles to profl. jours. Bd. dirs., v.p. Greenville Symphony Assn. Recipient medal Emory U., 1989. Fellow Am. Bar Found. (life); mem. State Bar Ga. (past pres. young lawyers sect., past bd. govs.), S.C. Bar Assn., Atlanta Bar Assn. (past sec.-treas.), U.S. C. of C. (past chmn. bd. dirs., past chmn. labor rels. and bylaws coms.), S.C. C. of C. (spl. counsel labor rels., adv. com. on labor rels.), Poinsett Club, Commerce Club, Met. Club (Washington and N.Y.C.). also: 1317 F St NW Ste 900 Washington DC 20004-1105

THOMPSON, ROBIN JILL, special education educator; b. Massena, N.Y., Apr. 2, 1958; d. Ronald Michael Thompson and Lucille Joy (Smith) Blinzinger; m. Jon Lavern Spindler, Nov. 1, 1980 (div. Dec. 1985); m. Gregory Ray Savage, May 16, 1992 (div. Nov. 1995). BS, Ind. State U., 1980, MS, 1982. Tchr. autistic adolescents Evansville (Ind.)-Vanderburgh Sch. Corp., 1980-81, tchr. seriously emotionally handicapped, 1981—, gymnastics coach, 1982-85, mgr. athletic equipment, 1985-88, acting asst. athletic dir., 1988-89, homebound tchr., 1984-89; chairperson spl. edn. dept. F.J. Reitz High Sch., Evansville, 1989-97; instr. in community living Res-Care Community Alternatives, S.W., Evansville, 1986-90, asst. athletic dir., 1995—. Scholar Rotary Internat., 1990. Mem. Coun. for Exceptional Children, Coun. for Children with Behavior Disorders, Ind. Interscholastic Athletic Adminstrs. Assn. (bd. dirs. 1996—), World Wildlife Fedn., R-Men's Varsity Club, So. Ind. Athletic Conf. (bd. dirs. 1982-83), Pi Lambda Theta (v.p. 1988-90), Phi Kappa Phi, Kappa Delta Pi. Avocations: needlework, hiking, golf, reading. Home: 7310 Little Schaefer Rd Evansville IN 47720-2741 Office: FJ Reitz High Sch Forest Hills Evansville IN 47712

THOMPSON, ROBY CALVIN, JR., orthopedic surgeon, educator; b. Winchester, Ky., May 1, 1934; s. Roby Calvin and Mary Davis (Guerrant) T.; m. Jane Elizabeth Searcy, May 2, 1959; children: Searcy Lee, Roby Calvin III, Mary Alexandria. BA, Va. Mil. Inst., 1955; MD, U. Va., 1959. Diplomate Am. Bd. Orthopaedic Surgery (mem. bd. 1983). Intern Columbia Presbyn. Med. Center, N.Y.C., 1959-60; asst. resident, then resident in orthopedic surgery Columbia Presbyn. Med. Center, 1963-67; instr. orthopaedic surgery Coll. Phys. and Surg. Columbia U., 1967-68; mem. faculty Med. Sch. U. Va., 1968-74, prof. orthopaedic surgery, vice chmn. dept. Med. Sch., 1973-74; prof., chmn. dept. Med. Sch. U. Minn., 1974-95; chief med. officer U. Minn. Health Sys., 1995-96, clin. affairs provost, 1996—; mem. merit rev. bd. VA, 1977-80; mem. study sect. on applied physiology and orthopedics NIH, 1980-83; adv. council mem. NIH, Nat. Inst. Arthritis, Musculoskeletal Disease and Skin, 1987—. Trustee Jour. Bone and Joint Surgery, 1988—, chmn. bd. trustees, 1991—; contbr. articles to med. jours. Capt. M.C. USAR, 1960-61. Grantee John Hartford Found., NIH. Mem. ACS, Orthopaedic Rsch. and Edn. Found. (bd. trustees 1990-96), Am. Acad. Orthopaedic Surgeons (bd. dirs. 1975-76, 83-90, pres. 1986), Orthopaedic Rsch. Soc. (pres. 1978), Am. Orthopaedic Assn., Musculoskeletal Tumor Soc. (pres. 1988-89), U. Va. Med. Alumni Assn. (bd. dirs. 1979-84), Woodhill Club (Wayzata). Republican. Presbyterian. Club: Woodhill Wayzata, Minn. Office: U Minn Hosps & Clinic PO Box 501 420 Delaware St NW Minneapolis MN 55455*

THOMPSON, RODERICK M., lawyer; b. Chgo., Dec. 11, 1955. BA, Trinity Coll., 1977; JD, U. Calif., San Francisco, 1980. Bar: Calif. 1980. Mem. Pillsbury Madison & Sutro, LLP, San Francisco. Office: Pillsbury Madison & Sutro 235 Montgomery St San Francisco CA 94104-4207

THOMPSON, RONALD EDWARD, lawyer; b. Bremerton, Wash., May 24, 1931; s. Melville Herbert and Clara Mildred (Griggs) T.; m. Marilyn Christine Woods, Dec. 15, 1956; children—Donald Jeffery, Karen, Susan, Nancy, Sally, Claire. B.A., U. Wash., 1953, J.D., 1958. Bar: Wash. 1959. Asst. city atty. City of Tacoma, 1960-61; pres. firm Thompson, Krilich, LaPorte, Tucci & West, P.S., Tacoma, 1961—; judge pro tem Mcpl. Ct., City of Tacoma, Pierce County Dist., 1972—, Pierce County Superior Ct., 1972—. Chmn. housing and social welfare com. City of Tacoma, 1965-69; mem. Tacoma Bd. Adjustment, 1967-71, chmn., 1968; mem. Tacoma Com. Future Devel., 1961-64, Tacoma Planning Commn., 1971-72; bd. dirs., pres. Mcpl. League Tacoma; bd. dirs. Pres. Tacoma Rescue Mission, Tacoma Pierce County Cancer Soc., Tacoma-Pierce County Heart Assn., Tacoma-Pierce County Council for Arts, Econ. Devel. Council Puget Sound, Tacoma Youth Symphony, Kleiner Group Home, Tacoma Community Coll. Found., Pierce County Econ. Devel. Corp., Wash. Transp. Policy Inst.; Coalition to Keep Wash. Moving, precinct committeeman Republican party, 1969-73. Served with AUS, 1953-55; col. Res. Recipient Internat. Community Service award Optimist Club, 1970, Patriotism award Am. Fedn. Police, 1974, citation for community service HUD, 1974, Disting. Citizen award Mcpl. League Tacoma-Pierce County, 1985; named Lawyer of the Yr. Pierce County Legal Secs. Assn., 1992. Mem. Am. Arbitration Assn. (panel of arbitrators), ABA, Wash. State Bar Assn., Tacoma-Pierce County Bar Assn. (sec. 1964, pres. 1979, mem. cts. and judiciary com. 1981-82), Assn. Trial Lawyers Am., Wash. State Trial Lawyers Assn., Tacoma-Pierce County C. of C. (bd. dirs., exec. com., v.p., chmn.), Downtown Tacoma Assn. (com. chmn., bd. dirs. exec. com., chmn.), Phi Delta Phi, Sigma Nu. Roman Catholic. Clubs: Variety (Seattle); Lawn Tennis, Tacoma, Optimist (Tacoma, Internat. Pres. 1973-74). Home: 3101 E Bay Dr NW Gig Harbor WA 98335-7610 Office: 524 Tacoma Ave S Tacoma WA 98402-5416

THOMPSON, RONALD MACKINNON, family physician, artist, writer; b. N.Y.C., Oct. 19, 1916; s. George Harold and Pearl Anita (Hatfield) T.; m. Ethel Joyce Chastant, June 30, 1950; children: Phyllis Anita, Walter MacKinnon, Charles Chastant, Richard Douglas. BS, U. Chgo., 1947, MS, 1948, MD, 1949. Diplomate Am. Bd. Family Practice. Intern U. Mich., Ann Arbor, 1950-51; resident in psychiatry U. Tex., Galveston, 1951-52; pvt. practice, family and internal medicine South Dixie Med. Ctr., West Palm Beach, Fla., 1952-85; instr. Anatomy, U. Chgo., 1946-47, Pharmacology, 1948-49. Contbr. articles to profl. jours.; exhibited in 7 one-man shows (over 30 awards for painting in regional and nat. shows); represented in permanent collections at 5 mus. Mem. Civitan Club W. Palm Beach, Fla., 1951; former bd. dirs. Norton Gallery Mus. of Art, West Palm Beach. Mem. Fla. Nat. Guard, 1936-40; cadet Army Air Force, 1943-44. Over thirty awards for painting in juried regional and nat. shows. Fellow Am. Acad. Family Physicians; mem. AMA, Fla. Med. Assn., Fla. Acad. of Family Physicians, Palm Beach County Med. Soc., Nat. Watercolor Soc., Ariz. Watercolor Soc. Republican. Episcopalian. Avocations: chess, tennis, writing, square and round dancing. Home: 308 Leisure World Mesa AZ 85206-3142

THOMPSON, RONELLE KAY HILDEBRANDT, library director; b. Brookings, S.D., Apr. 21, 1954; d. Earl E. and Maxine R. (Taplin) Hildebrandt; m. Harry Floyd Thompson II, Dec. 24, 1976; children: Clarissa, Harry III. BA in Humanities magna cum laude, Houghton Coll., 1976; MLS, Syracuse U., 1976; postgrad., U. Rochester, 1980, 81; cert., Miami U., 1990. Libr. asst. Norwalk (Conn.) Pub. Libr., 1977; elem. libr. Moriah Cen. Schs., Port Henry, N.Y., 1977-78; div. coord. pediatric gastroenterology and nutrition U. Rochester (N.Y.) Med. Ctr., 1978-81, cons., mem. pediatric housestaff libr. com., 1980-81; dir. Medford Libr. U. S.C., Lancaster, 1981-83; dir. Mikkelsen Libr., Libr. Assocs., Ctr. for Western Studies, mem. acad. computing com., libr. com. Augustana Coll., Sioux Falls, S.D., 1983—, mem. adminstrv. pers. coun., 1989-94; presenter in field. Contbr. articles to profl. jours. Mem. adv. com. S.D. Libr. Network, 1986—, chair, 1989-91, 94—; mem. Sioux Falls Community Playhouse, S.D. Symphony, Sioux Falls Civic Fine Arts Assn.; advisor Minnehaha County Libr., pers. dept. City of Sioux Falls. Named one of Outstanding Young Women Am., 1983; Syracuse U. Gaylord Co. scholar, 1976; recipient YWCA leader award, 1991. Mem. ALA, AAUW, Assn. Coll. and Rsch. Librs. (nat. adv. coun. coll. librs. sect. 1987—), Mountain Plains Libr. Assn. (chair acad. sect., nominating com. 1988-89, pres. 1993-94), S.D. Libr. Assn. (chair interlibr. coop. task force 1986-87, pres. 1987-88, chair recommended minimum salary task force 1988, chair local arrangements com. 1989-90), S.D. Libr. Network (adv. coun. 1986—, exec. com. 1992—, chair adv. coun. 1994—). Office: Augustana Coll Mikkelsen Libr 29th & Summit Sioux Falls SD 57197

THOMPSON, RUFUS E., lawyer; b. Lubbock, Tex., Aug. 15, 1943; s. Glenn Wesley and Naomi Elvina T.; m. Sandra Jean Lemons, Aug. 8, 1965; children—Michael Glenn, Mark Gregory, Matthew Wesley. B.B.A., U. Tex., Austin, 1965, J.D., 1968. Bar: Tex. bar 1968, N.Mex. bar 1969. Assoc. firm Atwood & Malone, Roswell, N.Mex., 1968-71; ptnr. firm Atwood, Malone, Mann & Cooter, Roswell, 1971-78; U.S. Atty. Dist. N.Mex., Albuquerque, 1978-81; now ptnr. firm Modrall, Sperling, Roehl, Harris & Sisk, Albuquerque; mem. Nat. Conf. Commrs. on Uniform State Laws, 1975-79; chmn. N.Mex. Supreme Ct. Com. on Rules of Evidence, 1972-94; U.S. Atty. for N.Mex. Com., 1978-82; mem. U.S. Atty. Gen.'s Adv. Com., 1980—, chmn., 1981. Mem. N.Mex. Democratic Party Central Com., 1972-78; mem. N.Mex. State Senate, 1973-78; mem. Gov's. Commn. on Prevention of Organized Crime, 1985-89. Mem. Am. Bar Assn. (exec. council young lawyers sect. 1972), N.Mex. Bar Assn. (chmn. young lawyers sect. 1970). Baptist. Office: PO Box 607 Albuquerque NM 87103-0607

THOMPSON, SALLY ENGSTROM, state official; b. Spokane, Wash., Feb. 17, 1940; d. Logan C. and Ava Leigh (Phillips) Engstrom; m. Donald Edward Colcun, 1981; children: Lauri Thompson, Tom Thompson, Tami Thompson, Sheri Colcun Trumpfheller. BS magna cum laude, U. Colo., 1975. CPA, Colo. 1976, Kans. 1986. Audit mgr. and mgmt. cons. Touche Ross & Co., Denver, 1975-82; v.p., mgr. planning and fin. analysis United Bank, Denver, 1982-85; pres., chief oper. officer Shawnee Fed. Svgs., Topeka, 1985-90; treas. State of Kans., 1990—. Past editorial advisor New Accountant mag. Bd. dirs. Everywoman's Resource Ctr., Topeka, 1988-92, Community Svc. Found. Kans., Kids Voting Kans. (hon.); v.p., bd. dirs. Downtown Topeka Inc., YWCA, Topeka, 1986-93, Woman of Achievement award, 1984; mem. fin. com. Girl Scouts U.S., Kaw Valley, various coms., United Way of Greater Topeka; chmn. art auction com. KTWU-TV, summer concert, Topeka Civic Theatre. Recipient Disting. Community Leadership award Topeka Pub. Schs., 1989, Disting. Leadership award Nat. Assn. Community Leadership, 1991, 1991 Class Leadership Kans. Mem. AICPAs, Am. Soc. Women Accts., Kans. Soc. CPAs, Kansas C. of C. and Industry, Greater Topeka C. of C. (bd. dirs. 1989-92), Emporia State U. Bus. Sch. Adv. Bd., Nat. Assn. State Auditors, Controllers and Treas., Nat. Assn. State Treas. (v.p., Midwest regional chair), Women Execs. in Govt., Beta Alpha Psi. Democrat. Offices: Office State Treasurer Landon State Office Bldg 900 SW Jackson St Ste 201N Topeka KS 66612-1220*

THOMPSON, SHELDON LEE, refining company executive; b. Mpls., Oct. 7, 1938; s. Wallace E. and Madeline A. (King) T.; m. Karen Beatrice Gallison, Aug. 25, 1962; children: Jeffrey, Paul, Daniel. BS, U. Minn., 1960, MS, 1962; grad. advanced mgmt. program, Harvard U., 1983. Registered profl. chem. engr., Pa. Rsch. engr. Sun Refining & Mktg. Co., Marcus Hook, Pa., 1962-69, assoc. engr., 1969-70, chief engring. rsch., 1970-72, rsch. program mgr. corp. R & D, 1972-74, mgr. venture engring., 1974-77, mgr. R & D chems., 1977-80, dir. R & D, 1980-88; v.p. chems., lubricants and tech. Sun Refining & Mktg. Co., Phila., 1988-91; sr. v.p., chief adminstrv. officer Sun Co., Inc., Phila., 1992—. Inventor 11 patents chems., fuels and lubes processing. Mem. exec. edn. adv. bd. Wharton Sch. Bus., U. Pa.; trustee Acad. Nat. Scis., Phila. Orch., Phila. Coll. Podiatric Medicine. Mem. AIChE, Greater Phila. C. of C. (exec. com.). Republican. Presbyterian. Avocation: music. Office: Sun Co Inc 1801 Market St Philadelphia PA 19103-1628

THOMPSON, STANLEY B., church administrator. Pres., CEO, dir. The Free Meth. Found., Spring Arbor, Mich. Office: The Free Meth Found PO Box 580 Spring Arbor MI 49283-0580

THOMPSON, STEPHEN ARTHUR, publishing executive; b. Englewood, N.J., Jan. 24, 1934; s. Stephen Gerard and Doris Lillian (Evans) T.; m. Joan Frances O'Connor, May 12, 1955 (div. 1978); children: Stephen Andrew, Craig Allen, David John; m. Sandra Rene Fingernut, May 27, 1979. BS, Ohio State U., 1961. Physicist Rocketdyne div. North Am. Aviation, Canoga Park, Calif., 1961-62, Marquardt Corp., Van Nuys, Calif., 1962-63; mem. tech. staff Hughes Rsch. Labs., Malibu, Calif., 1963-69; editor Electronic Engr. mag. Chilton Co., L.A., 1969-72, in advt. sales Instruments and Controls Sys., mag., 1972-77; regional advt. sales Design News mag. Cahners Pub. Co., L.A., 1977-84; sales mgr. Design News mag. Cahners Pub. Co., Newton, Mass., 1984-87, pub. Design News mag., 1987-95, group. pub. mfg. group, 1989-93, sr. v.p. integrated mktg., 1993-94, gen. mgr. Boston divsn., 1995-96, gen. mgr. mfg. mktg. divsn., 1995-97; sr. v.p. tng. Cahners Pub. Co., Newton, 1996-97; founder Design News Engring. Edn. Found., Newton, 1991—; pub. Design News Mag., 1994-95; group pub. Mfg. Group. Author: Basketball for Boys, 1970; contbr. articles to Jour. Spacecraft/Rockets, 1966. Club leader YMCA, Canoga Park, 1963-78; active PTA, Canoga Park, 1961-80; bd. dirs. Chatsworth (Calif.) High Booster Club, 1972-80. 1st lt., jet fighter pilot USAF, 1952-58. Mem. Bus. Profl. Advt. Assn. (Golden Spike award 1980, 81, 82, 83), L.A. Mag. Reps. Assn. (life), Nat. Fluid Power Assn., BPA Internat. (bd. dirs.). Achievements include patents for ion source, system and method for ion implantation of semiconductors. Office: Cahners Pub Co 275 Washington St Newton MA 02158-1646

THOMPSON, STEVE ALLAN, writer; b. Mpls., Sept. 10, 1951; s. John Thomas and Charlotte Joan (Ellis) T.; m. Michele Rae Jones, July 16, 1983; 1 child, Kent Lloyd. Student, U. Minn., 1969-73. Dept. supr. Hennepin County Libr., Edina, Minn., 1973-87; writer, 1987—; cons. Okefenokee Glee & Perloo Inc., Manassa, Va., 1988—, Waycross/Ware County (Ga.) C. of C., 1990—, Phipps Ctr. for Arts, Hudson, Wis., 1996. Author: Walt Kelly Collector's Guide; co-author: Pogo Files for Phophiles, 1992; editor The Fort Mudge Most 1988—; contbr. articles to profl. jours. Mem. Internat. Soc. for Humor Studies, Bibliographical Soc. Am., Walt Kelly Soc. (pres. 1987—), Lewis Carroll Soc., Bakr Street Irregulars. Achievements include international recognized on life and career of Walt Kelly. Home: 6908 Wentworth Ave Richfield MN 55423-2363

THOMPSON, SUSAN A., mayor; b. Winnipeg, Man., Can.. Grad., U. Winnipeg. With Eatons; group dept. mgr. Eatons, Calgary; nat. buyer The Bay, Montreal, Que, 1979-80; mayor City of Winnipeg. Mem. Econ. Coun. of Can., Man. Econ. Adv. Coun., Winnipeg Found., Downtown Winnipeg Assn., Urban Idea Centre, BIZ Task Force, Winnipeg 2000, Interfaith Pastoral Inst.; bd. dirs. Can. West Found., U. Man. Faculty of Mgmt., Winnipeg Symphony Orch. Mem. Rotary. Office: Council Bldg, Civic Ctr 510 Main St, Winnipeg, MB Canada R3B 1B9*

THOMPSON, SUSANNAH ELIZABETH, lawyer; b. Fullerton, Calif., May 20, 1953; d. Harry Lowell and Susannah Elizabeth (Glover) Rupp; m. James Avery Thompson, Jr., May 16, 1987; 1 child, Sarah Mary Elizabeth Thompson. BA, Calif. State U., Fullerton, 1980; JD with hons., Am. Coll. of Law, 1989. Bar: Calif. 1989, U.S. Dist. Ct. (cen. dist.) 1989, U.S. Dist. Ct. (so. dist.) 1991. Legal asst. Minyard & Minyard, Orange, Calif., 1987-89; assoc. Simon & Simon, San Bernardino, Calif., 1989-91; pvt. practice Temecula, Calif., 1991—. Asst. editor Law Rev./Am. Coll. Law, Brea, Calif., 1989. Sec. student bar assn. Am. Coll. Law, 1987-88. Mem. ABA, Riverside County Bar Assn., Calif. Women Lawyers Assn., Inland Empire Bankruptcy Forum, Women Lawyers Assn. (chmn. mem. 1994—), Temecula

C. of C. Republican. Avocations: bowling, Disneyana, reading, skating, tennis. Office: 41593 Winchester Rd Ste 201 Temecula CA 92590-4857

THOMPSON, THEODORE ROBERT, pediatric educator; b. Dayton, Ohio, July 18, 1943; s. Theodore Roosevelt and Helen (Casey) J.;m. Lynette Joanne Shenk; 1 child, S. Beth. BS, Wittenberg U., 1965; MD, U. Pa., 1969. Diplomate Am. Bd. Pediatrics (Neonatal, Perinatal Medicine). Resident in pediatrics U. Minn. Hosp., Mpls., 1969-72, chief resident in pediatrics, 1971-72, fellow neonatal, perinatal, 1974-75, asst. prof., 1975-80, dir. div. of neonatology and newborn intensive care unit, 1977-80, assoc. prof., 1980-85, prof., 1985—, co-dir. Med. Outreach, 1988-91, dir. med. outreach, 1991—, assoc. chief of pediatrics, 1988—; med. dir. U. Minn. Clin. Assocs., 1992—. Editor: Newborn Intensive Care: A Practical Manual, 1983. Bd. dirs. Life Link III, St. Paul, 1987—; cons. Maternal and Child Health, Minn. Bd. Health, 1975—. With USPHS, 1972-74. Fellow Am. Acad. Pediatrics (chmn. perinatal newborn com. Minn. chpt. 1985-92); Gt. Plains Orgn. for Perinatal Health Care (Sioux Falls, S.D., Kunshe award 1989). Lutheran. Office: Box 39 Mayo 420 Delaware St SE Minneapolis MN 55455-0374

THOMPSON, THOMAS HENRY, philosophy educator; b. Sioux City, Iowa, Jan. 10, 1924; s. Elmer Edwin and Ruth Alma (Baker) T.; m. Diane Sargent, Nov. 23, 1955; children: Brenda, Alicia, Mark, Rosemary. B.A., U. Iowa, 1948, M.A., 1950, Ph.D., 1952. Asst., instr. U. Iowa, Iowa City, 1948-52; mem. faculty U. No. Iowa, Cedar Falls, 1952—; prof. philosophy U. No. Iowa, 1969—, head dept., 1969-81, acting dean Coll. Humanities and Fine Arts, 1981-82, dean Coll. Humanities and Fine Arts, 1982-90; prof. emeritus, 1994—. Mem. Sigmund Freud Gesellschaft (Vienna), Am. Philosophy Assn. Home: 2122 California St Cedar Falls IA 50613-4721 Office: U No Iowa Dept Philosophy & Religion Cedar Falls IA 50614-0501

THOMPSON, THOMAS MARTIN, lawyer; b. Albion, Pa., Jan. 7, 1943; s. Donald C. and Mabel Louise (Martin) T.; m. Judith E. Daucher; children: Reid, Chad, Matthew, Molly. AB, Grove City Coll., 1965; JD cum laude, Harvard U., 1968. Bar: Pa. 1968. Ptnr. Buchanan Ingersoll, Pitts., 1968—, chair corp. fin. group; adj. prof. law U. Pitts.; , v.p., dir., past chairperson Pa. Lawyer Trust Acct. Bd. Past pres. Neighborhood Legal Svcs. Assn.; bd. dirs., mem. exec. com. Pitts. Pub. Theater. Mem. ABA, Pa. Bar Assn. (corp., bus. and banking coun., Pro Bono award 1989), Allegheny County Bar Assn. (past chmn. pub. svc. com., past chmn. corp., banking and bus. coun.), Assn. for Corp. Growth (past pres. Pitts. chpt.). Democrat. Home: 1142 Dartmouth Rd Pittsburgh PA 15205-1705 Office: Buchanan Ingersoll One Oxford Ctr 301 Grant St Ste 20 Pittsburgh PA 15219-1408

THOMPSON, THOMAS SANFORD, former college president; b. Lewistown, Mont., Apr. 9, 1916; s. Thomas Swing and Sadie (Mixer) T.; m. Margaret Ann Wiese, June 1, 1941; children—Roger John, Thomas Warren, Pamela Ann, Mary Ann. B.S., Pacific U., 1938, L.H.D., 1966; postgrad., U. Wash., 1939, U. Oreg., 1941; M.Ed., Oreg. State U., 1949. Tchr.-coach Siuslaw Union High Sch., Florence, Oreg., 1938; prin. Siuslaw Union High Sch., 1939-42; coordinator tng. within industry War Manpower Commn., Portland, Oreg., 1942-43; employee utilization dir. North Pacific div. U.S. Army C.E., 1946-47; acting prin. Portland Apprentice Sch., 1947-48; partner Davis Sales Cons., Portland, 1948-51; dir. devel. Lewis and Clark Coll., Portland, 1952-57; dir. sustaining assos. program Washington U., St. Louis, 1957-60; dir. devel. Knox Coll., Galesburg, Ill., 1960-63; v.p. for devel. U. Pacific, Stockton, Calif., 1963-69; pres. Morningside Coll., Sioux City, Iowa, 1969-78; lectr. coll.-univ. devel. adminstrn. Cons. Council on Christian Philanthropy, 1970, Council for Financial Aid to Edn., 1963. Bd. dirs. United Fund, Sioux City, 1969-78, Pacific Med. Center, San Francisco, 1966-68, Marian Health Center, Sioux City, 1977-78, St. Joseph's Hosp., Stockton, 1979-85. Served to lt. col USAAF, 1943-46; Served to lt. col USAF, 1951-52. Mem. Greater Stockton C. of C. (dir. 1967-69), Galesburg C. of C. (dir. 1961-63), Sioux City (dir. 1971-78), Oreg. Mental Health Assn. (pres. 1956-57), Assn. Am. Colls., Am. Colls. Pub. Relations Assn., Royal Rosarians, Phi Delta Kappa. Democrat. Roman Catholic. Club: Rotary (Sioux City) (past pres.). Home: 6879 Atlanta Cir Stockton CA 95219-3233

THOMPSON, TOMMY GEORGE, governor; b. Elroy, Wis., Nov. 19, 1941; s. Allan and Julia (Dutton) T.; m. Sue Ann Mashak, 1969; children: Kelli Sue, Tommi, Jason. BS in Polit. Sci. and History, U. Wis., 1963, JD, 1966. Polit. intern U.S. Rep. Thomson, 1963; legis. messenger Wis. State Senate, 1964-66; sole practice Elroy and Mauston, Wis., 1966-87; mem. Dist. 87 Wis. State Assembly, 1966-87, asst. minority leader, 1972-81, floor leader, 1981-87; self-employed real estate broker Mauston, 1970—; gov. State of Wis., 1987—; alt. del. Rep. Nat. Conv., 1976; chmn. Intergovtl. Policy Adv. Commn. to U.S. Trade Rep.; mem. nat. govs. assn. exec. com.; bd. dirs. AMTRAK. Served with USAR. Recipient med. award for Legis. Wis. Acad. Gen. Practice, Thomas Jefferson Freedon award Am. Legis. Exchange Coun., 1991, Most Valuable Pub. Official award City and State Mag., 1991, Governance award Free Congress Found., 1992. Mem. ABA, Wis. Bar Assn., Rep. Govs. Assn., Phi Delta Phi. Roman Catholic. Office: Office of Gov PO Box 7863 Madison WI 53707-7863*

THOMPSON, VETTA LYNN SANDERS, psychologist, educator; b. Birmingham, Ala., Sept. 7, 1959; d. Grover and Vera Lee (King) S.; m. Cavelli Andre Thompson, May 27, 1990; children: Olajuwon, Malik Rashad, Kimberlyn, Assata Iyana. BA, Harvard U., 1981; MA, Duke U., 1984, PhD, 1988. Cert. psychologist and health svc. provider, State of Mo. Com. Psychologists. Psychology intern Malcolm Bliss Mental Health Ctr., St. Louis, 1985-86; psychotherapist, testing coord. Washington U. Child Guidance Clinic, St. Louis, 1986-87; psychologist, treatment team coord. Hawthorn Children's Psychiatric Hosp., St. Louis, 1987-89; asst. prof. U. Mo., St. Louis, 1989-95, assoc. prof., coord. black studies, 1995—; tchg. asst. Duke U., Durham, N.C., 1982-84, rsch. asst., 1984-85; chair monitoring com. crisis access sys. Ea. Regional Adv. Coun. Dept. Mental Health, St. Louis, 1995-97; chair African Am. Task Force on Mental Health, Jefferson City, Mo., 1995-97; chair budget and planning com. Ea. Regional Adv. Coun., Dept. Mental Health, St. Louis, 1996-97; mem. children's mental health planning group St. Louis Mental Health Bd., 1996-97; bd. dirs. St. Louis Mental Health Assn., mem. Bd. for Respiratory Care. Editl. adv. bd. A Turbulent Voyage: Readings in African American Studies, 1995-96; contbr. articles to profl. jours. Mem. adv. com. on violence prevention and investment in youth Mo. House, Jefferson City, 1995; mem. managed care steering com. Dept. Mental Health, Jefferson City, 1995-96, mem. strategic planning advisory coun., 1997; mem., bd. dirs. St. Louis Mental Health Assn., 1997—; mem. Mo. Bd. for Respiratory Care, 1997—, Dept. Mental Health Strategic Planning Adv. Coun., 1997—. Kellogg Found.-Mo. Youth Initiative fellow, 1991-93; Ctr. for Great Plains Studies fellow U. Nebr., 1995—. Mem. APA (divsns. 1, 45), Assn. Black Psychologists. Methodist. Avocations: aerobics, walking, jazz. Office: U Mo 8001 Natural Bridge Rd Saint Louis MO 63121-4401

THOMPSON, VIRIGINA A., elementary education educator; b. Logan, Ohio, May 4, 1940; d. Charles Frederick and Margaret Frances (Shelton) Wilcoxen; m. Paul Calvin Reed, Sept. 24, 1958 (div. Jan. 1974); children: P. Bradley, John C., Thomas G.; m. James Willard Thompson, Jr., June 11, 1976. BS in Elem. Edn., Ohio State U., 1977; MS in Sch. Counseling, U. Dayton, Ohio, 1990. Cert. in elem. edn. 1-8, elem. guidance and counseling, Ohio. Classroom tchr. Anna (Ohio) Local Schs., 1977—; chair Old Trails Uniserv Coun., Piqua, Ohio, 1982-86. Chair bd. trustees Shelby County Mental Health, Sidney, Ohio, 1989-94; mem. Dem. Ctr. Com. of Shelby County, Sidney, 1992—; mem. com. Black Achievers Scholarship, Sidney, 1988—; treas. Botkins (Ohio) Hist. Soc., 1987—. Recipient Bus. Adv. Coun. Tchr. Yr. award C. of C., Sidney, 1992, Pres.'s Award univ. scholar Ohio State Univ., 1976. Mem. Ohio Edn. Assn. (voting del.), Anna Local Tchrs. Assn. (pres. 1978, 85, 91-94), Ohio State Alumni Assn., Phi Kappa Phi. Democrat. Methodist. Avocations: travel, antiques, theatre. Home: 106 W State St Botkins OH 45306 Office: Anna Local Sch Dist 204 N 2d St Anna OH 45302

THOMPSON, WADE FRANCIS BRUCE, manufacturing company executive; b. Wellington, New Zealand, July 23, 1940; came to U.S., 1961, naturalized, 1990.; m. Angela Ellen Barry, Jan. 20, 1967; children: Amanda and Charles (twins). B in Commerce, Cert. Acctg., Victoria U., Wellington, 1961; MSc, NYU, 1963. Dir. diversification Sperry & Hutchinson, N.Y.C., 1967-72; v.p. Texstar Corp., N.Y.C., 1972-77; chmn. Hi-Lo Trailer Co., Butler, Ohio, 1977—; chmn., pres., chief exec. officer Thor Industries Inc., Jackson Center, Ohio, 1980—. Trustee Mystic Seaport Mus., Conn., 1984—; trustee Wade F.B. Thompson Charitable Found. Inc., 1985—, Mcpl. Art Soc., N.Y.C., 1993—. Mem. Union Club, N.Y. Yacht Club (N.Y.C.). Avocations: tennis, collecting contemporary art. Office: Thor Industries Inc 419 W Pike St Jackson Center OH 45334-9728

THOMPSON, WAYNE WRAY, historian; b. Wichita, Jan. 30, 1945; s. Clarence William and Elaine Maxine (Wray) T. m. Lillian Evelyn Hurlburt, June 28, 1969. BA, Union Coll., Schenectady, 1967; student, U. St. Andrews, Scotland, 1965-66; PhD, U. Calif., San Diego, 1975. Historian USAF, 1975—, Checkmate Air Campaign Planning Group, 1990-91; sr. hist. advisor Gulf War Air Power Survey, 1991-93. Contbr. Congress Investigates (Arthur M. Schlesinger Jr. and Roger Bruns, editors), 1975; editor Air Leadership, 1986; contbr. War in the Pacific (Bernard Nalty, editor), 1991. Served with AUS, 1971-72. Mem. Am. Hist. Assn., Orgn. Am. Historians, Air Force Hist. Found., Air Force Assn., Soc. Historians Am. Fgn. Rels., Soc. for Mil. History, U.S. Commn. on Mil. History, Inter-Univ. Seminar on Armed Forces, Assn. Asian Studies, Asia Soc., World History Assn., Phi Beta Kappa. Home: 9203 Saint Marks Pl Fairfax VA 22031-3045 Office: Hdqrs USAF History Washington DC 20332

THOMPSON, WESLEY DUNCAN, grain merchant; b. Blenheim, Ont., Can., Oct. 18, 1926; s. Wesley Gairdner and Anna Corneil (McCallum) T.; m. Patricia Florence Coatsworth, June 6, 1957; children—Wesley, Jennifer, Frank. B.A., U. Western Ont., London, Can., 1950. Pres., chmn. bd. dirs. W.G. Thompson & Sons Ltd, Blenheim, Can., 1950—. Office: W G Thompson & Sons Ltd, 122 George St, Blenheim, ON Canada N0P 1A0

THOMPSON, WILLIAM, JR., engineering educator; b. Hyannis, Mass., Dec. 4, 1936; s. William and Dinella Helen (Szeliga) T.; m. Martha Marion Cate, July 4, 1959; children: Melanie A., Sharon E., Jennifer L., Keith W. SB, MIT, 1958; MS, Northeastern U., 1963; PhD, Pa. State U., 1971. Staff engr. Raytheon Co., Wayland, Mass., 1958-60; sr. engr. Cambridge (Mass.) Acoustical Assocs., 1960-66; research asst. Applied Research Lab., State College, Pa., 1966-72; asst. prof. engring. sci. Pa. State U., University Park, 1972-78, assoc. prof., 1978-85, prof., 1985—; head transducer group Applied Rsch. Lab., State College, 1971-80; sabbatic leave Naval Rsch. Lab., Orlando, Fla., 1988-89; chairperson IBM Master Tchrs. Team, 1997—. Contbr. articles to profl. jours.; patentee in field. Bd. dirs., treas., past pres. Nittany Mountain chpt. Am. Diabetes Assn., State College, 1979-92; bd. dirs., asst. treas., treas. Mid-Pa. affiliate, Bethlehem, Pa., 1980-90. Recipient Disting. Svc. citation Mid-Pa. Affiliate Am. Diabetes Assn., 1981, and Affiliate Svc. award, 1988. Fellow Acoustical Soc. Am. (patent reviewer of soc. jour. 1990—); mem. IEEE (sr.), Soc. Engring. Sci., Lions (pres. State College 1981-82, 89-90, sec.-treas. 1984-88, 90-92, treas. 1992—, dist. diabetes chmn. 1983-88, 94—, chmn. Ctr. Lions Foresight Commn. 1992—, Melvin Jones fellow 1991). Republican. Avocations: sports, reading, photography. Home: 601 Glenn Rd State College PA 16803-3475 Office: Pa State U Dept of Engring Sci and Mechanics 227C Hammond Bldg University Park PA 16802

THOMPSON, WILLIAM ANCKER, intramural-recreational sports director, educator; b. Syracuse, N.Y., Apr. 26, 1931; s. Frederick Howe Thompson and Ellen (Ensten) Ancker; m. Sally Whitmer; children: Cary, Paige. BS, Springfield (Mass.) Coll., 1953; MA, Calif. State U., Long Beach, 1960; postgrad., U. So. Calif., L.A., 1961-62. Phys. dir. Wendell P. Clark Meml., Winchendon, Mass., 1956-57; dir. intramural/recreational sports Long Beach City Coll., 1958-96, dir. intramural/recreational sports emeritus, 1996—; with promotion and sales div. Calif. Sports, Inc. (L.A. Lakers, Kings), L.A. and Inglewood, 1960-76; v.p. sales Calif. Sports, Inc. (L.A. Lakers, Kings), L.A. and Inglewood, 1970-71. Co-author: Modern Sports Officiating, 1974, 5th rev. edit., 1993. 1st lt. USMC, 1954-56, Korea. Mem. Nat. Intramural-Recreational Sports Assn. (v.p. 1974-76, pres. 1976-77, Honor award 1980), Old Ranch Country Club. Avocations: swimming, golf, writing, reading, avocado grower. Office: Long Beach City Coll 4901 E Carson St Long Beach CA 90808-1706

THOMPSON, WILLIAM BENBOW, JR., obstetrician, gynecologist, educator; b. Detroit, July 26, 1923; s. William Benbow and Ruth Wood (Locke) T.; m. Constance Carter, July 30, 1947 (div. Feb. 1958); 1 child, William Benbow IV; m. Jane Gilliland, Mar. 12, 1958; children: Reese Ellison, Belinda Day. AB, U. So. Calif., 1947, MD, 1951. Diplomate Am. Bd. Ob-Gyn. Resident Gallinger Mun. Hosp., Washington, 1952-53; resident George Washington U. Hosp., Washington, 1953-55; asst. ob-gyn. La. State U., 1955-56; asst. clinical prof. UCLA, 1957-64; assoc. prof. U. Calif.-Irvine Sch. Med., Orange, Calif., 1964-92; dir. gynecology U. Calif.-Irvine Sch. Med., 1977-92; prof. emeritus U. Calif.-Irvine Sch. Med., Orange, 1993—; vice chmn. ob-gyn. U. Calif.-Irvine Sch. Med., 1978-89; assoc. dean U. Calif.-Irvine Coll. Med., Irvine, 1969-73. Inventor: Thompson Retractor, 1976; Thompson Manipulator, 1977. Bd. dirs. Monarch Bay Assn. Laguna Niguel, Calif. 1969-77, Monarch Summitt II A ssn. 1981-83. With U.S. Army, 1942-44, PTO. Fellow ACS, Am. Coll. Ob-Gyn. (life), L.A. Ob-Gyn. Soc. (life); mem. Orange County Gynecology and Obstetrics Soc. (hon.), Am. Soc. Law and Medicine, Capistrano Bay Yacht Club (commodore 1975), Internat. Order Blue Gavel. Avocation: boating. Office: UCI Med Ctr OB/GYN 101 The City Dr S Orange CA 92868-3201

THOMPSON, WILLIAM DAVID, investment banking executive; b. Pitts., Nov. 30, 1921; s. Ross Ephraim and Blanche (Watson) T.; B.S., Yale U., 1944. Asst. advt. mgr. Scovill Mfg. Co., Waterbury, Conn., 1945-48; acctg. supr. James Thomas Chirurg, N.Y.C., 1948-52; mgr. mktg. dept. McCann-Erickson, N.Y.C., 1951-52; exec. v.p. Young & Rubicam, N.Y.C., 1952-89; chmn. Ctr. Devel. Investments, Inc., Greenwich, Conn., 1990; bd. dirs. Recovery Engring., Inc., Mpls. Lt. U.S. Army, 1943-44. Mem. Union League (N.Y.C.), Wee Burn Country Club, Piping Rock Country Club, John's Island Club. Republican. Presbyterian. Avocations: golf, tennis. Home and Office: John's Island Ste 345 650 Beach Rd Vero Beach FL 32963-3394

THOMPSON, WILLIAM DAVID, minister, homiletics educator; b. Chgo., Jan. 11, 1929; s. Robert Ayre and Mary Elizabeth (McDowell) T.; m. Linda Brady Stevenson, Nov. 2, 1968; children—Tammy, Kirk, Lisa, Rebecca, Gwyneth. A.B., Wheaton Coll., Ill., 1950; B.D., No. Baptist Sem., 1954; M.A., Northwestern U., 1955, Ph.D., 1960. Ordained to ministry Am. Baptist Ch., 1954. Instr. speech Wheaton Coll., 1952-55; pastor Raymond Baptist Ch., Chgo., 1956-58; assoc. prof. homiletics No. Bapt. Sem., Chgo., 1958-62; mem. faculty Eastern Bapt. Sem., Phila., 1962-87, prof. preaching, 1969-87; minister 1st Bapt. Ch., Phila., 1983-90; pres. Thompson Comm., 1988—. Author: A Listener's Guide to Preaching, 1966, Recent Homiletical Thought, 1967, Dialogue Preaching, 1969, Preaching Biblically, 1981, Listening on Sunday for Sharing on Monday, 1983, Philadelphia's First Baptists, 1989, Public Speaking for Pleasure and Profit, 1997; editor Professional Speakers Library, 10 vols. Mem. Phila. Hist. Commn., 1984-92. Vis. fellow Cambridge U., 1968-69. Mem. Nat. Speakers Assn., Acad. Homiletics (pres. 1973), Religious Speech Communication Assn. (v.p. 1983, pres. 1984), Union League Club. Democrat. Home: 765 Ormond Ave Drexel Hill PA 19026-2417

THOMPSON, WILLIAM DENNISON, JR., aeronautical consultant; b. Chgo., Jan. 26, 1920; s. William Dennison and Bertha Helen (Lachnit) T.; m. Jeanne Ann Burkholder, Dec. 26, 1942; children: William III, Burk Blair, Constance Gail. BA in Aero. Engring., Purdue U., 1947. Draftsman/engr. Curtis-Wright Airplane Co., St. Louis, 1940-41; army air corps flight instr. Hawthorne Flying Svc., Orangeburg, S.C., 1942-45; flight instr. Purdue Aeronautics Corp., West Lafayette, Ind., 1946-47; engring. test pilot Cessna Aircraft Co., Wichita, Kans., 1947-53, mgr. flight test and aerodynamics, 1953-74; tech. cons. SIAI Marchetti, Sesto Calende, Italy, 1975-77; owner Thompson Aeronautical Cons., Sunriver, Oreg., 1978—; pres. Precise Flight, Inc., Bend, Oreg., 1980-83; owner Thompson Aero Products, Sunriver, 1984—; cons. for aerodynamics and aeronautics coms. NASA, 1969-73. Author: Cessna Wings for the World-The Single-Engine Development Story, 1991, Cessna Kings for the World--Development of the 300 Series Twins and Miscellaneous Prototypes, 1995, A Tes tPilot's Life - An Autobiography; editor (booklets) Cessna Owners Manuals, 1953-74; co-inventor, patentee integrated spoiler/throttle assembly, 1984. Loaned exec. United Fund, Wichita, 1965; designated engring. rep., flight test pilot, flight analyst FAA, Seattle, Washington, 1980-93, Ft. Worth, 1994—. Fellow Soc. Exptl. Test Pilots (1st chmn. Wichita sect. 1962-63); mem. Soc. Automotive Engrs. (chmn. Wichita sect. 1970-71), Exptl. Aircraft Assn. Internat., Internat. 195 Club, Cardinal Club. Republican. Methodist. Avocations: snow skiing, flying, hiking, traveling, writing. Home and Office: 2 Bridgeport Ln Bella Vista AR 72714-5309

THOMPSON, WILLIAM IRWIN, humanities educator, author; b. Chgo., July 16, 1938; s. Chester Andrew and Lillian Margaret (Fahey) T.; m. Gail Joan Gordon, Feb. 3, 1960 (div. Jan. 1979); children: Evan Timothy, Hilary Joan, Andrew Rhys; m. Beatrice Madeleine Rudin, Mar. 1, 1979. B.A. with honors in Philosophy, Pomona Coll., 1962; M.A. (Woodrow Wilson fellow), Cornell U., 1964, Ph.D. (Woodrow Wilson dissertation fellow), 1966. Instr. humanities MIT, Cambridge, 1965-66; asst. prof. MIT, 1966-67, Old Dominion fellow, 1967, assoc. prof. humanities, 1968; assoc. prof. humanities York U., Toronto, Ont., Can., 1968-72; prof. York U., 1973; vis. prof. religion Syracuse (N.Y.) U., 1973; vis. scholar in polit. sci. U. Hawaii, 1981, vis. prof., 1985; vis. prof. Celtic studies U. Toronto, 1984; founding dir. Lindisfarne Assocs., 1972—. Author: Imagination of an Insurrection: Dublin, Easter 1916, 1967, At the Edge of History, 1971, Passages about Earth, 1974, Evil and World Order, 1976, Darkness and Scattered Light, 1978, The Time Falling Bodies Take to Light, 1981, From Nation to Emanation, 1981, Blue Jade from the Morning Star, 1983, Islands Out of Time, 1985, Pacific Shift, 1986, GAIA: A Way of Knowing, 1987, Imaginary Landscape, 1989, Selected Poems 1959-89; GAIA TWO: Emergence, the New Science of Becoming, 1991, Reimagination of the World, 1991, The American Replacement of Nature, 1991, Coming into Being, 1996, Worlds Interpenetrating and Apart, 1996. Hon. colleague and Lindis Farne Scholar of the Cathedral of St. John the Divine, N.Y.C. Recipient Obstfelder prize Oslo Internat. Poetry Festival, 1986; Rockefeller scholar Calif. Inst. Integral Studies, 1993-95; Laurance S. Rockefeller fellow, 1992-96. Address: Cathedral St John the Divine 1047 Amsterdam Ave New York NY 10025

THOMPSON, WILLIAM MOREAU, radiologist, educator; b. Phila., Oct. 20, 1943; s. Charles Moreau and Aileen (Haddon) T.; m. Judy Ann Seel, July 27, 1968; children—Christopher Moreau, Thayer Haddon. B.A., Colgate U., 1965; M.D., U. Pa., 1969. Diplomate Am. Bd. Radiology. Intern, Case Western Res. U., Cleve., 1969-70; resident in radiology Duke U., Durham, N.C., 1972-75, asst. prof. Duke U. Med. Center, 1976-77, assoc. prof., 1977-82, prof. radiology, 1982-86; prof., chmn. dept. radiology, Vilhelmina and Eugene Gedgared chair in Radiology, U. Minn. Hosp. and Clinic, Mpls., 1986—. Served with USPHS, 1970-72. Recipient James Picker Found. Scholar in Acad. Medicine award, 1975-79; research and devel. grantee VA, 1977-86. Fellow Am. Coll. Radiology; mem. AMA, Radiology Soc. N.Am. (program chmn. 1994—), Minn. Med. Soc., Am. Roentgen Ray Soc., Assn. Univ. Radiologists (pres. 1989-90), Soc. Gastrointestinal Radiology (pres. 1995), Sigma Xi. Republican. Presbyterian. Contbr. chpts. to books, articles to profl. jours. Home: 18700 Woolman Dr Minnetonka MN 55345-3164 Office: U Minn Med Sch UMHC Box 292 Harvard Street Rd Minneapolis MN 55455-0361

THOMPSON, WILLIAM REID, public utility executive, lawyer; b. Durham, N.C., Aug. 13, 1924; s. William Reid and Myrtle (Siler) T.; m. Mary Louise Milliken, Aug. 16, 1952; children: Mary Elizabeth, William Reid III, John Milliken, Susan Siler. BS, U. N.C., 1945; LLB, Harvard U., 1949. Bar: N.C. 1949. Ptnr. Barber and Thompson, Pittsboro, N.C., 1949-58; judge Superior Cts. N.C., 1958-60; assoc. gen. counsel Carolina Power & Light Co., 1960-63, v.p., gen. counsel, 1963-67, exec. v.p., 1967-71; chmn. bd., chief exec. officer Potomac Electric Power Co., Washington, 1971-89, chmn. bd., 1989-92; adv. dir. Potomac Elec. Power Co. Bd. dirs. Nat. Symphony Orch. Assn.; mem. Fed. City Coun., N.C. Gen. Assembly from Chatham County, 1955-57. Served to lt. (j.g.) USNR, 1943-45, PTO. Mem. ABA, Edison Electric Inst. (bd. dirs., past chmn.), Southeastern Electric Exchange (past pres.), Assn. Edison Illuminating Cos. (past pres.), Bus. Council, Bus. Roundtable, Phi Beta Kappa, Delta Kappa Epsilon. Democrat. Methodist. Clubs: Met., Burning Tree, Chevy Chase, 1925 F St (Washington). Lodge: Rotary. Office: Potomac Electric Power Co 1900 Pennsylvania Ave NW Washington DC 20068-0001

THOMPSON, WILLIAM SCOTT, lawyer; b. Grand Rapids, Mich., Feb. 6, 1930; s. William Scott Thompson and Mary Louise (Chatel) Kruse; m. Margaret Jane Favier, June 16, 1951; children: William, Michelle, Marta, Rebecca. BSME, U. Mich., 1952; JD, U. Notre Dame, 1959. Bar: Ind. 1959, U.S. Dist. Ct. (so. dist.) Ind. 1959, U.S. Ct. Appeals (Fed. cir.) 1963. Engr. Bendix Corp., South Bend, Ind., 1954-57, patent agt., 1957-59, patent atty., 1959-64, regional patent counsel, Utica, N.Y. and Detroit, 1964-74; patent dept. mgr. Caterpillar Inc., Peoria, Ill., 1974-94; with Internat. Intellectual Property Cons., Ft. Myers, Fla., 1994—. 1st lt. USAF, 1952-54. Mem. Am. Intellectual Property Law Assn. (past pres.), Internat. Patent and Trademark Assn. (v.p.), Assn. Corp. Patent Counsel, ABA.

THOMPSON, W(ILMER) LEIGH, pharmaceutical company executive, physician, pharmacologist; b. Shreveport, La., June 25, 1938; s. Wilmer Leigh and Mary Bissell (McIver) T.; m. Maurice Eugenie Horne, Mar. 29, 1957; 1 child, Mary Linton Bounetheau. BS, Coll. Charleston, 1958; MS in Pharmacology, Med. U. S.C., 1960, PhD, 1963; MD, John Hopkins U., 1965; ScD (hon.) Med. U. S.C., 1994. Diplomate Am. Bd. Internal Medicine. Intern, Johns Hopkins Hosp., 1965-66, resident, 1966-67, 69-70; staff assoc. NIH, Bethesda, Md., 1967-69; asst. prof. medicine and pharmacology Johns Hopkins U., Balt., 1970-74, dir. critical care medicine and emergency medicine, 1970-74; prof. medicine, assoc. prof. pharmacology Case Western Res. U., Cleve., 1974-82, head critical care and clin. pharmacology, 1974-82; prof. medicine Ind. U., 1985—; dir. Lilly Rsch. Labs., Eli Lilly & Co., Indpls., 1982, exec. dir., 1982-86, v.p., 1986-88, group v.p., 1988-91, exec. v.p., 1992-93, chief sci. officer, 1993-94; chmn., CEO Profound Quality Resources Consulting, Charleston, 1995—; mem. bd. dirs. BAS, Corvas Internat., DNX Inc., Ergo Scis., Guilford Pharmaceuticals, Genemedicine, Galileo Labs, Inspire, Ontogeny, La Jolla Pharms., Orphan Medical,, Medarex, Roper Found., Pharmaceutical Development, Inc. Editor: Textbook of Critical Care Medicine, 1984, 89, State of the Art: Critical Care, 1980-83. Served to surgeon USPHS, 1967-69. Burroughs Wellcome Fund scholar 1975-80; recipient Faculty Devel. award Pharm. Mfrs. Assn. Found. Fellow ACP, Am. Coll. Critical Care Medicine; mem. Soc. Critical Care Medicine (pres. 1981-82, hon. life mem. 1987), Cen. Soc. Clin. Rsch., Am. Soc. Pharmacology and Exptl. Therapeutics. Episcopalian and Huguenot. Office: Profound Quality Resources Consulting 54 King St Charleston SC 29401-2731

THOMPSON, WINFRED LEE, university president, lawyer; b. Little Rock, July 28, 1945; s. Vester Lee and Willow Mae (Mills) T.; m. Carmen Angeles Tiongson; children: Emily, Michael. BA, U. Ark., 1967; MA, U. Chgo., 1970, PhD, 1987; JD, George Washington U., 1978. Congl. aide U.S. Ho. of Reps., Washington, 1973-77; exec. asst. to asst. sec. labor U.S. Dept. Labor, Washington, 1977-78; atty. Hatfield and Thompson, Searcy, Ark., 1978-81; dir. devel. Ark. State U., Jonesboro, 1981-82, v.p. for planning and devel., 1982-84; v.p. for fin. and adminstrn. U. Ark. System, Fayetteville, 1984-85; vice chancellor for fin. and adminstrn. U. Ark, Fayetteville, 1985-87; pres. U. Cen. Ark., Conway, 1988—; bd. dirs. Ark. Sci. and Tech. Authority, Little Rock, 1984-89. Bd. dirs. Ark. Symphony Orch., 1991-94. 2d lt. USAR. Woodrow Wilson fellow U. Chgo., 1969-70. Mem. Phi Beta Kappa. Home: 140 Donaghey Ave Conway AR 72032-6252 Office: U Ctrl Ark Office of the President 201 Donaghey Ave Conway AR 72035-5001

THOMPSON, WYNELLE DOGGETT, chemistry educator; b. Birmingham, Ala., May 25, 1914; d. William Edward and Dollie Odessa (Ferguson) Doggett; m. Davis Hunt Thompson, Sept. 17, 1938; children: Carolyn Wynelle, Helen Hunt, Cynthia Carle, Davis Hunt, jr. BS summa cum laude, Birmingham Southern, 1934, MS, 1935; MS, U. Ala., 1956, PhD, 1960. From grad. lab. asst. to instr. chemistry Birmingham (Ala.) Southern Coll., 1934-36,39-44; tchr. Bd. Edn., Sheffield, Ala., 1936-37; jr. chemist Bur. Home Econs. USDA, Washington, 1937-38; instr. chemistry U. Ala. extension ctr., Birmingham, 1950-54; grad. asst. biochemistry U. Ala. Med. Coll., Birmingham, 1954-55; from asst. prof. chemistry to prof. emerita Birmingham (Ala.) Southern Coll., 1955-76; rsch. assoc. U. Ala. Dept. Biochemistry, Birmingham, 1965, 1968, 1969, Dept. Biophysics, 1976-78; adj.

prof. chemistry New Coll. Tuscaloosa, Ala., 1980—. Contbr. articles to profl. jours. Bd. dirs. Cahaba Coun. Girl Scouts U.S. (vol. chmn. troop orgn., camping.). Grantee NSF, Appleton, Wis., Emory U., Atlanta; recipient disting. alumna award Birmingham So. Coll., 1976, medal of svc. award, 1994. Fellow Am. Inst. Chemists; mem. AAUW (bd. dirs., treas.), Am. Chem. Soc. (sec. 1942-44, 72-73, chmn.-elect 1966-67, chmn. 1967-68, 50-Yr. Mem. award 1992), Ala. Acad. Sci. (chmn. edn. sect. 1960-62), Phi Beta Kappa, Sigma Xi (sec. 1970-72), Theta Chi Delta, Delta Phi Alpha, Theta Sigma Lambda, Kappa Delta Epsilon, Delta Kappa Gamma, Kappa Mu Epsilon. Republican. Methodist. Avocations: music, camping, travel, needlework. Home: 1237 Berwick Rd Birmingham AL 35242-7124

THOMPSON-CAGER, CHEZIA BRENDA, literature educator, writer, performance artist; b. St. Louis, Sept. 8, 1951; d. James Henry and Emma Jean (Mack-Anderson) Thompson; m. Lawrence Chris Cager Jr., May 19, 1984; 1 child, Chezia. BA, Washington U., St. Louis, 1973, MA, 1975; ArtsD, Carnegie-Mellon U., 1984. Tchg. asst. Washington U., 1973-76; instr., asst. prof. St. Louis C.C., 1975-79; asst. prof. Clarion (Pa.) State U., 1980-82, U. Md., Catonsville, 1982-86; assoc. prof. Smith Coll., Northampton, Mass., 1986-89; vis. assoc. prof. Bowie (Md.) State U., 1989-90; sr. v.p. Park Heights Devel. Corp., Balt., 1990-92; cons. Balt. City Pub. Sch., Inst. Div., 1992-94; prof. lang. & lit. Md. Inst. Coll. Art, Balt., 1993—; Disting. scholar in residence U. Pa. Dept. Theatre, University Park, 1989; project dir. poetry enrichment program U. City Pub. Sch., 1972; performance artist Artscape, 1996. Author: Jumpin' Rope on the Axis, 1986, Power Objects, 1996 (Artscape Poetry Competition award 1996), The Presence of Things Unseen, 1996, Praise Song for Katherine Dunham Artscape, 1996, numerous poems; dir. dramatic works including Narrator Vachel Lindsay's Congo Visits Langston Hughes, 1989, Jestina's Calypso, 1988, 7 Principles: or how I got ova, 1987, Tribute to Martin Luther King, 1985; contbr. lit. criticisms, articles to profl. jours., freelance for St. Louis Am. News., Pitts. Courier News, Balt. Sun News. Mem. adv. bd. Sexual Assault Recovery Ctr., Balt., 1989-93; site proj. evaluator Nat. Endowment Arts, Washington, 1984; mem. Heritage Art panel Md. State Coun. Arts, 1990-94; cons. Balt. Arrabers Documentation Project, 1992. Recipient Paul Robeson Black Artist award Washington U., 1972, W.E.B. DuBois Svc. award, 1973, Merit for Poetry award Mo. State Coun. Arts, 1974, Mayor's Citizen Citation Poetry award, 1996, Resolution for Literacy award City Coun. Balt., 1996; named Oyo Traditions Pan-African Cultural Innovator, 1996. Mem. NWSA, Nat. Assn. Tchrs. English, Nat. Black Theater Network, African Lit. Assn., Coll. Art Assn. Office: Md Inst Coll Art Dept Lang and Lit 1300 W Mount Royal Ave Baltimore MD 21217-4134

THOMS, DAVID MOORE, lawyer; b. N.Y.C., Apr. 28, 1948; s. Theodore Clark and Elizabeth Augusta (Moore) T.; m. Susan Rebecca Stuckey, Dec. 16, 1972. BA, Kalamazoo Coll., 1970; M in Urban Planning, Wayne State U., 1975, LLM in Taxation, 1988; JD, U. Detroit, 1979. Bar: Mich. 1980, N.Y. 1995. Planner City of Detroit, 1971-75; atty. Rockwell and Kotz, P.C., Detroit, 1980-87; pvt. practice David M. Thoms & Assocs., P.C., Detroit, 1987—; adj. assoc. prof. Madonna U., 1993—; presenter NYU Tax Inst. Editor Case and Comment Law Rev., 1978-79. Mem. program com. Fin. and Estate Planning Coun. Detroit, 1980—; mem. adv. bd., chmn. nominating com., mem. exec. com. Met. Detroit Salvation Army, sec.-treas., vice chmn., 1994-95, chmn., 1995-96; bd. dirs. bylaws and property com., mem. nominating com., devel. com., exec. com. Mich. chpt. ARC; bd. dirs., pres. L'Alliance Française de Grosse Pointe, French Festival of Detroit, Inc.; trustee Detroit Symphony Orch. Hall, Inc., dir., 1996—; trustee Kalamazoo Coll., 1993—, dir., exec. com., 1995—; dir. vis. com. European art DIA, 1995—. Recipient Burton scholarship U. Detroit, 1979; Officier dans l'Ordre des Palmes Academiques. Mem. ABA (chmn. subcom. on probate and estate planning, mem. charitable trust com.), Fed. Bar Assn., Oakland County Bar Assn., Detroit Bar Assn., State Bar Mich., N.Y. Bar Assn., Bar Assn. of City of N.Y., Fedn. Alliances Françaises-U.S.A. (bd. dirs., treas. 1991—), Am. Planning Assn. (Mich. chpt.), Detroit Athletic Club, Renaissance Club, The Grosse Pointe Club. Mem. United Church of Christ. Avocations: tennis, architectural history, music, travel, art history. Office: 400 Renaissance Ctr Ste 950 Detroit MI 48243-1509

THOMS, JEANNINE AUMOND, lawyer; b. Chgo.; d. Emmett Patrick and Margaret (Gallet) Aumond; m. Richard W. Thoms; children: Catherine Thoms, Alison Thoms. AA, McHenry County Coll., 1979; BA, No. Ill. U., 1981; JD, Ill. Inst. Tech., 1984. Bar: Ill. 1984, U.S. Dist. Ct. (no. dist.) Ill. 1984, U.S. Ct. Appeals (7th cir.) 1985. Assoc. Foss Schuman Drake & Barnard, Chgo., 1984-86; assoc. Zukowski Rogers Flood & McArdle, Crystal Lake and Chgo., 1986-92, ptnr., 1992—; bd. dirs. McHenry County Mental Health Bd., 1991—, pres., 1995—; arbitrator 19th Jud. Ct. Ill., 1991—; cert. mediator Acad. Family Mediators, Ill., 1992—. Mem. Women's Adv. Coun. to Gov., State of Ill. Mem. ABA, LWV, Ill. State Bar Assn., Chgo. Bar Assn., McHenry County Bar Assn., Am. Trial Lawyers Assn., Acad. Family Mediators, Women's Network, Phi Alpha Delta. Office: Zukowski Rogers Flood & McArdle 50 N Virginia St Crystal Lake IL 60014-4126 also: 100 S Wacker Dr Chicago IL 60606-4006

THOMS, NORMAN WELLS, cardiovascular and thoracic surgeon; b. Bahrain, Nov. 5, 1934; (parents Am. citizens); m. Anna J. Holmes, June 22, 1962; 3 children. BA, Oberlin Coll., 1955; MD, U. Mich., 1959. Diplomate Am. Bd. Surgery, Am. Bd. Thoracic Surgery. Rotating intern Blodgett Meml. Hosp., Grand Rapids, Mich., 1959-60; resident in gen. surgery Detroit Gen. Hosp., 1960-62, 66-68, resident in thoracic surgery, 1968-70; instr. surgery Wayne State U. Sch. Medicine, Detroit, 1968-70, asst. prof., 1970-74, assoc. prof., 1974-75; pvt. practice, Topeka, 1975—; active staff Stormont-Vail Regional Health Ctr., Topeka, St. Francis Hosp. and Med. Ctr., Topeka; participant state and local med. meetings. Contbr. articles to med. jours. Officer M.C., U.S. Army, 1962-64. Recipient Regents' award for best sci. exhibit Am. Coll. Chest Physicians, 1972, Bal Jeffrey award Stormont-Vail Found., 1995. Fellow ACS; mem. AMA, Internat. Soc. Heart Transplantation, Kans. Med. Soc., Shawnee County Med. Soc., Soc. Thoracic Surgeons. Office: Cardiovasc & Thoracic Surgeons PA 901 SW Garfield Ave Fl 2 Topeka KS 66606-1670

THOMSEN, DONALD LAURENCE, JR., institute executive, mathematician; b. Stamford, Conn., Apr. 21, 1921; s. Donald Laurence and Linda (Comstock) T.; m. Linda Rollins Leach, June 14, 1958; children: Melinda Rollins, Katherine Thomsen Love, Donald Laurence III. Grad., Phillips Exeter Acad., 1938; BA in Math. magna cum laude, Amherst Coll., 1942; PhD, MIT, 1947. Tchg. fellow MIT, 1942, instr., 1943-47; instr., then asst. prof. Haverford (Pa.) Coll., 1947-50; rsch. fellow, then rsch. engr. Jet Propulsion Lab., Calif. Inst. Tech., 1950-52; asst. prof. Pa. State U., 1952-54; with IBM Corp., 1954-72, spl. asst. to dir. edn., 1961-62, dir. profl. activities, 1963-66, corp. dir. engring. edn., 1967-72; pres. Societal Inst. of Math. Scis., New Canaan, Conn., 1973—, also bd. dirs.; mem. vis. com. Coll. Sci., Drexel Inst. Tech., 1969-71; mem. adv. com. for Individualized sci. instrnl. sys. Coll. Edn., Fla. State U., 1973-75; prin. investigator rsch. studies in environ. pollution and human exposure, 1973—; AIDS rschr., 1988—. Author: Higher Transcendental Functions, 3 vols; contbr. articles to profl. jours. Recipient Spl. cert. Milw. Sch. Engring., 1969. Mem. AAAS, Am. Math. Soc., Am. Statis. Assn., Math. Assn. Am. (chmn. com. insts.), Soc. Indsl. and Applied Math. (pres. 1959, chmn. trustees 1960-72, Merit cert. Inst. Math. and Soc. 1972), Am. Fedn. Info. Processing Socs. (chmn. edn. com. 1965-66, chmn. U.S. com. IFIP Congress 1968, 66-69, bd. dirs. 1969-77, exec. com. 1975-77), Assn. Computing Machinery, Am. Ordnance Assn. (chmn. rsch. divsn.), Internat. Fedn. Info. Processing (chmn. exhibits com. N.Y.C. Congress 1965), Conf. Bd. Math. Scis. (chmn. budget and fin. com.), Internat. AIDS Soc., Internat. Soc. Exposure Analysis, Conn. Acad. Arts and Scis., Cosmos Club (Washington), The Princeton Club (N.Y.C.), Woodway Country Club (Darien, Conn.), Phi Beta Kappa, Sigma Xi, Delta Tau Delta. Presbyterian. Home and Office: Societal Inst Math Scis 97 Parish Rd S New Canaan CT 06840

THOMSEN, SAMUEL BORRON, non-profit executive, consultant; b. St. Paul, July 10, 1931; s. Samuel W. and Margaret (View) T.; m. Judith Diane Wolf, June 17, 1961; children: Kathryn G., Samuel P.E., Robert J. BA in Polit. Sci., UCLA, 1957; postgrad., Cornell U., 1966-67. With U.S. Dept. State, Washington, 1960-90, U.S. Consul, Hue, Vietnam, 1964-66; polit. advisor U.S. Marines, Vietnam, 1965-66; dir. Office for Internat. Sci. Coop. Dept. State, Washington, 1980-83; dep. pres.'s rep. Office for Micronesian Status Negotiations, Washington, 1983-87; amb. U.S. Embassy, Majuro, Marshall Islands, 1987-90; pres. The Micronesia Inst., Washington, 1990—; mem. commissioning bd. U.S. Info. Agy., Washington, 1980-86; chmn. Washington tradecraft program Fgn. Svc. Inst., Dept. State, 1995-96, dir. micronesian diplomatic tng. program, 1996—. Mem. editl. bd. Fgn. Svc. Jour., 1961-62. Mem. Rotary, Vientiane, Laos, 1968-70, Gaborone, Botswana, 1974-76. With U.S. Army, 1951-54. Mem. Washington Inst. Fgn. Affairs, Diplomatic and Consular Officers Ret., Asia Soc., World Affairs Coun. Washington, Am. Fgn. Svc. Assn., Am. Legion. Republican. Episcopalian. Avocations: tennis, gardening, computing. Home: 6502 Kerns Ct Falls Church VA 22044 Office: The Micronesia Inst 1275 K St NW Ste 360 Washington DC 20005-4006

THOMSEN, THOMAS RICHARD, retired communications company executive; b. Avoca, Iowa, July 29, 1935; s. Howard August and Edna Mary (Walker) T.; m. Raylene Alice Tomes, Sept. 1, 1956; children: Jeffrey, Cathy. BSME, U. Nebr., 1958; MS, MIT, 1973. Engr. Western Electric Co., Omaha, 1957-64; mgr. Western Electric Co., Columbus, Ohio, 1964-72; v.p. Bell Sales West Western Electric Co., Morristown, N.J., 1979-80; asst. v.p. ops. staff AT&T, Basking Ridge, N.J., 1980-81; exec. v.p. Western Electric Corp., N.Y.C., 1981-82; pres. AT&T Tech. Systems, Berkeley Heights, N.J., 1982-90, ret., 1990; bd. dirs. Transcrypt Internat. Corp., Lithium Tech. Corp., U. Nebr. Tech. Park. Trustee Rensselaer Poly. Inst.; bd. dirs. Tele. Pioneer Found., 1997—. Mem. Telephone Pioneers Am. (former pres.), Pi Tau Sigma, Sigma Tau. Republican. Presbyterian. Avocations: golf, tennis. Home: 26 Bellinghamshire Pl New Hope PA 18938-5657 Office: Lithium Tech Corp 5115 Campus Dr Plymouth Meeting PA 19462-1129

THOMSON, ALEX, cinematographer. Cinematographer: (films) Fear Is the Key, 1973, The Cat and the Canary, 1978, The Class of Miss MacMichael, 1978, Excalibur, 1981 (Academy award nomination best cinematography 1981), The Keep, 1983, Blueshot, 1983, Eureka, 1984, Electric Dreams, 1984, Labyrinth, 1985, Year of the Dragon, 1985, Legend, 1986, Raw Deal, 1986, The Sicilian, 1987, Date with an Angel, 1987, Duet for One, 1987, High Spirits, 1988, Track 29, 1988, Leviathan, 1989, The Rachel Papers, 1989, Mr. Destiny, 1990, Alien 3, 1992, Cliffhanger, 1993, Demolition Man, 1993, Black Beauty, 1994.

THOMSON, BASIL HENRY, JR., lawyer, university general counsel; b. Amarillo, Tex., Jan. 17, 1945; m. Margaret Shepard, May 4, 1985; children: Christopher, Matthew, Robert. BBA, Baylor U., 1968, JD, 1973. Bar: Tex. 1974, U.S. Ct. Mil. Appeals 1974, U.S. Supreme Ct. 1977, U.S. Dist. Ct. (we. dist.) Tex. 1988, U.S. Ct. Appeals (fed. cir.) 1990. Oil title analyst Hunt Oil Co., Dallas, 1971-73; atty., advisor Regulations and Adminstrv. Law div. Office of Chief Counsel USCG, Washington, 1973-77; dir. estate planning devel. dept. Baylor U., Waco, Tex., 1977-80, gen. counsel, 1980—; adj. prof. law Baylor U.; lobbyist legis. Ind. Higher Edn., 71st Session of Tex. Legislature; mem. legis. com. Gov.'s Task Force on Drug Abuse; dir. govtl. relations Baylor U.; speaker at meetings of coll. and univ. adminstrs.; assisted in drafting legis. for Texan's War on Drugs Tex. Legislature. Active Heart O'Tex. coun. Boy Scouts Am., Heart of Tex. Coun. on Alcoholism and Drug Abuse, bd. dirs., 1987-91. Recipient Pres.'s award Ind. Colls. and Univs. of Tex., 1994, Dist. award of merit Boy Scouts Am. Fellow Coll. State Bar Tex.; mem. ABA, FBA, Nat. Assn. Coll. and Univ. Attys. (fin., nominations and elections coms. 1994-95, bd. dirs. 1988-91), Nat. Assn. Ind. Colls. and Univs. (legal svcs. revie panel 1997—), Tex. Bar Assn., Waco Bar Assn., McLennan County Bar Assn., Owners Assn. of Sugar Creek, Inc. (dir. 1995—). Baptist. Avocations: backpacking, running, environ. concerns. Home: 100 Sugar Creek Pl Waco TX 76712-3410 Office: Baylor U PO Box 97034 Waco TX 76798-7034

THOMSON, GEORGE RONALD, lawyer, educator; b. Wadsworth, Ohio, Aug. 25, 1959; s. John Alan and Elizabeth (Galbraith) T. BA summa cum laude, Miami U., Oxford, Ohio, 1982, MA summa cum laude, 1983; JD with honors, Ohio State U., 1986. Bar: Ill. 1986, U.S. Dist. Ct. (no. dist.) Ill. 1986. Teaching fellow Miami U., 1982-83; dir. speech activities Ohio State U., Columbus, 1983-86; assoc. Peterson, Ross, Schloerb & Seidel, Chgo., 1986-87, Lord, Bissell & Brook, Chgo., 1987-94; asst. corp. counsel labor divsn. City of Chgo., 1994—; adj. prof. dept. comm. De Paul U., Chgo., 1988-90; presenter in field. Contbr. articles to profl. jours. Fundraiser Chgo. Hist. Soc., Steppenwolf Theater Co., AIDS Legal Counsel Chgo., Smithsonian Instn., Washington, 1988—, U.S. Tennis Assn., 1990—; bd. dirs. Metro Sports Assn., 1992-94, Gerber-Hart Libr. and Archives, 1993-95, Gay and Lesbian Tennis Alliance Am., 1993-95, Team Chgo., 1994-96; mem. coord. coun. Nat. Gay and Lesbian History Month; mem. Lawyer's Com. for Ill Human Rights; dir. Chgo. Internat. Charity Tennis Classic, 1993, 94, 95. Recipient Spl. Commendation Ohio Ho. of Reps., 1984, 85, Nat. Forensics Assn. award, 1982. Mem. ABA, Chgo. Bar Assn., Lesbian and Gay Bar Assn., Speech Comm. Assn. Am., Mortar Bd., Phi Beta Kappa, Phi Kappa Phi, Omicron Delta Kappa, Delta Sigma Rho-Tau Kappa Alpha, Phi Alpha Delta. Presbyterian. Avocations: tennis, flute, antiques, folk arts and crafts, reading, travel. Home: 2835 N Pine Grove Ave Unit 2S Chicago IL 60657-6109 Office: City of Chgo Dept of Law 30 N La Salle St Ste 700 Chicago IL 60602-2503

THOMSON, GERALD EDMUND, physician, educator; b. N.Y.C., 1932; s. Lloyd and Sybil (Gilbourne) T.; m. Carolyn Webber; children: Gregory, Karen. M.D., Howard U., 1959. Diplomate Am. Bd. Internal Medicine (bd. govs. 1985-92, exec. com. 1988-91, chmn.-elect 1990-91, chmn. 1991-92). Intern SUNY-Kings County Hosp. Center, Bklyn., 1959-60; resident in medicine SUNY-Kings County Hosp. Center, 1960-62, chief resident, 1962-63, N.Y. Heart Assn. fellow in nephrology, 1964-65, asst. vis. physician, 1963-70, clin. dir. dialysis unit, 1965-67; practice medicine specializing in internal medicine N.Y.C., 1963—; attending physician SUNY Med. Bklyn. Hosp., 1966-70; instr. in medicine SUNY, Bklyn., 1963-68; clin. asst. prof. medicine SUNY, 1968-70; asso. chief med. services Coney Island Hosp., Bklyn., 1967-70; attending physician Presbyn. Hosp., 1970—; dir. nephrology Harlem Hosp. Center, N.Y.C., 1970-71; dir. med. services Harlem Hosp. Center, 1971-85, pres. med. bd., 1976-78; assoc. prof. medicine Columbia Coll. Physicians and Surgeons, 1970-72, prof., 1972—, Samuel Lambert prof. medicine, and chief of staff, 1980—; exec. v.p. for profl. affairs, chief of staff Columbia-Presbyn. Med. Ctr., 1985-90; sr. assoc. dean Coll. Physicians and Surgeons, Columbia U., N.Y.C., 1990—; mem. Health Rsch. Coun. City N.Y., 1972-75; mem. med. adv. bd. N.Y. Kidney Found., 1971-82; mem. Health Rsch. Coun., State N.Y., 1975-81; mem. hypertension info. and edn. adv. com. NIH, 1973-74, N.Y. State Adv. Com. on Hypertension, 1977-80; com. on non-pharm. treatment of hypertension Inst. of Medicine, Nat. Acad. Scis., 1980; mem. med. adv. bd. Nat. Assn. Patients on Hemodialysis and Transplantation, 1973-83; mem. adv. bd. Sch. Biomed. Edn., CUNY, 1979-83, Med. News Network, 1993-95; mem. com. on mild hypertension Nat. Heart and Lung Inst., 1976, mem. clin. trials rev. com., 1980-85, mem. rev. panel, 1979; bd. dirs. N.Y. Heart Assn., 1973-81, chmn. com. high blood pressure, 1976-81, Primary Care Devel. Corp.; chmn. com. hypertension N.Y. Met. Regional Med. Program, 1974-76; mem. adv. com. Heart and Hypertension Inst. of N.Y. State, 1984; mem. N.Y. Gov.'s Health Adv. Coun., 1981-84, pub. Health Coun., N.Y., 1983-95, Joint Nat. Com. High Blood Pressure NIH, 1983-84, 87-88, mem. rev. panel hypertension detection and monitoring bd. study cardiovasc. risk factors in young Nat. Heart, Lung and Blood Inst., 1984-90; mem. panel on receiving and withholding med. treatment ACLU, 1984-88; mem. Grad. Med. Edn. Commn., State of N.Y., 1984-86, mem. Commn. on End-State Renal Disease, 1985, 89-90; pres. Washington Heights-Inwood Ambulatory Care Network Corp., 1986-91; bd. dirs. Primary Care Devel. Corp., 1993—. Mem. adv. bd. Jour. Urban Health, 1974-80, Med. News Network, 1993-94. Chmn. ad hoc com. on access to nursing homes Pub. Health Council State of N.Y.; pres. Washington Heights-Inwood Ambulatory Care Network Corp., 1986-91; chmn. Federated Coun. Internal Medicine, 1991-92; mem. Mayor's Commn. Health and Hosps. Corp.; dir. Harlem Ctr. for Health Promotion and Disease Prevention; bd. dirs. Primary Care Devel. Corp. Recipient Nat. Med. award Nat. Kidney Found., N.Y., 1984, Outstanding Alumnus award Howard U., 1987, Dean's Outstanding Tchg. award Coll. Physicians and Surgeons Columbia U., 1986. Fellow ACP (Gov.'s coun. downstate region 1982-89, chmn. com. health pub. policy N.Y. chpt. 1982-89, health care professions com. 1987-90, bd. regents 1990-97, chmn. nat. health and pub. policy com. 1993-94, pres.-elect 1994-95, pres. 1995-96), N.Y. Acad. Medicine (mem. com. medicine in soc. 1974-76); mem. AAAS, N.Y. Soc. Nephrology (pres. 1973-74), Am. Fedn. Clin. Rsch., Federated Coun. for Internal Medicine (chmn. 1991-92, 95-96), Soc. Urban Physicians (pres. 1972-73), Am. Soc. Artificial Internal Organs, Assn. Program Dirs. in Internal Medicine, Pub. Health Assn. N.Y.C. (dir. 1983-86), Physicians for Social Responsibility of N.Y. (dir. 1983-85), Assn. Acad. Minority Physicians (pres. 1988-90), Inst. of Medicine, Nat. Acad. Scis. Home: Premium Pt New Rochelle NY 10801-5327 Office: Coll Physicians & Surgeons Columbia U New York NY 10032

THOMSON, H. BAILEY, editor; b. Aliceville, Ala., Feb. 4, 1949; s. William Joshua and Attie (Kimbrell) T.; m. Reba Kristi Garrison, Nov. 19, 1977; 1 child, Sarah Rachel. BA, U. Ala., 1972, MA, 1974, PhD, 1995. Copy editor Huntsville (Ala.) Times, 1971-72, staff writer, 1975-77; reporter, copy editor Tuscaloosa (Ala.) News, 1972-75; editorial page editor Shreveport (La.) Jour., 1977-86; chief editorial writer Orlando (Fla.) Sentinel, 1986-91; assoc. editor Mobile (Ala.) Press Register, 1992-96; Phifer vis. prof. journalism U. Ala., 1996-97, assoc. prof. journalism, 1997. Author: Shreveport, 1986. vice chmn. La. Endowment Humanities, 1984-85. Profl. journalism fellow Stanford U., 1981-82; finalist Pulitzer prizes for editl. writing, 1995, Green Eyeshade awards, 1988, 1996. Mem. Nat. Conf. Editl. Writers (bd. dirs. 1991-92). Methodist. Avocations: historical writing, reading. Office: Coll of Communication Dept Journalism Box 870172 Tuscaloosa AL 35487

THOMSON, JAMES ALAN, research company executive; b. Boston, Jan. 21, 1945; s. James Alan and Mary Elizabeth (Pluff) T.; m. Darlene Thomson; children: Kristen Ann, David Alan. BS, U. N.H., 1967; MS, Purdue U., 1970, PhD, 1972, DSc (hon.), 1992; LLD (hon.), Pepperdine U., 1996. Research fellow U. Wis., Madison, 1972-74; systems analyst Office Sec. Def., U.S. Dept. Def., Washington, 1974-77; staff mem. Nat. Security Council, White House, Washington, 1977-81; v.p. RAND, Santa Monica, Calif., 1981-89, pres., chief exec. officer, 1989—; bd. dirs. L.A. World Affairs Coun., UCLA Bd. Visitors, Calif. Gov. Pete Wilson's Coun. Econ. Advisors. Contbr. articles to profl. jours. and chpts. to books. Mem. Internat. Inst. for Strategic Studies (council 1985—), Coun. Fgn. Rels. Office: Rand 1700 Main St Santa Monica CA 90401-3208

THOMSON, JOHN CHRISTIAN, financial analyst, portfolio manager; b. Hattiesburg, Miss., Mar. 16, 1965; s. Richard Spotswood and Inez Christina (Heidelberg) T. Student, U. So. Miss., 1985, Mercer U., 1986; grad., Sch. Communication Arts, 1987. Producer, photographer Alternative Art Studios, Mpls., 1987-89; exec. producer, photographer Visual Art Studios, Hattiesburg, 1989-91; dir. Acme Toy Factory Inc., New Smyrna Beach, Fla., 1992—; CEO, portfolio mgr. Fin. Trust Svcs., New Smyrna Beach. Photos exhibited in galleries 1989, 90, Advt. Photographers of Am., Meteor Photo, Atlanta, 1991. Recipient 1st Pl. (state), Honorable Mention (nat.) Nat. Scholastic Art Assn., 1981, 1st Pl. Black & White, Civic Arts Coun., 1989, Cert. of Merit Nat. Fine Arts Video Competition, 1991, Addy award Greater Jackson Advt. Club, 1991. Mem. New Smyrna Yacht Club, Amnesty Internat. (leadership group 1989—). Republican. Episcopalian. Avocations: photography, automobile racing, surfing. Office: Fin Trust Svcs 702 Palmetto St New Smyrna Beach FL 32168-7421

THOMSON, JOHN WANAMAKER, bank executive; b. Sioux Falls, S.D., Oct. 1, 1928; s. John Norman and Muriel Evelyn (Wanamaker) T.; m. Nane A. McConnell, Sept. 16, 1950; children: John L., James R., Ann L. BS in Acctg., U. S.D., 1950; postgrad., U. Wis., 1964. Chmn. First Midwest Bank, Centerville, S.D., 1950—; CEO, pres., chmn. Thomson Holdings, Ind., Centerville, 1986—, Thomson Agy., Inc., Centerville, 1984; chmn. S.D. Banking Commn., Pierre, 1986-95. Mem. S.D. Bankers Assn. (pres. 1980), U. S.D. Found. (bd. dirs.), S.D. Bankers Assn. Found. (chmn. 1990-91), Myrtle Lodge, Masons (treas. 1980-91), Riverview Cemetery Assn., U. S.D. Alumni Assn. (pres. 1990-92). Republican. Avocations: golf, hunting. Office: First Midwest Bank 549 Broadway Centerville SD 57014

THOMSON, KEITH STEWART, biologist, writer; b. Heanor, Eng., July 29, 1938; s. Ronald William and Marian Adelaide (Coster) T.; m. Linda Gailbreath Price, Sept. 27, 1963; children: Jessica Adelaide, Elizabeth Rose. B.Sc. with honors, U. Birmingham, Eng., 1960; A.M., Harvard U., 1961, Ph.D. (NATO fellow), 1963. NATO postdoctoral fellow Univ. Coll., London U., 1963-65; asst. prof. to prof. biology Yale U., 1965-87, dean Grad. Sch., 1979-87; dir. Peabody Mus. Natural History, 1976-79; pres. Acad. Natural Scis., Phila., 1987-95; disting. scientist-in-residence New Sch Social Rsch., N.Y.C., 1996—; dir. Sears Found. Marine Rsch. and Oceanographic History; hon. rsch. fellow Australian Nat. U., 1967; trustee, mem. corp. Woods Hole Oceanographic Inst.; bd. dirs. Wistar Inst., Ctrl. Phila. Devel. Corp., Wetlands Inst., Phila. Cultural Alliance; rschr. in vertebrate evolution. Mem. editl. bd. Paleobiology, Jour. Morphology, 1988, Aspects of Lower Vertebrate Evolution, 1968, Origin of Terrestrial Vertebrates, 1968, Saltwater Fishes of Conn., 1971, 88, Priorities and Needs in Systematic Biology, 1981, Morphogenesis and Evolution, 1988, Living Fossil, 1991, The Common But Less Frequent Loon and Other Essays, 1993, HMS Beagle, 1995. Fellow Linnean Soc. London, Zool. Soc. London; mem. Soc. Vertebrate Palaeontology, Sigma Xi. Office: New Sch Social Rsch 55 W 11th St New York NY 10011-8662

THOMSON, KENNETH R. (LORD THOMSON OF FLEET), publishing executive; b. Toronto, Ont., Can., Sept. 1, 1923; s. Lord Thomson of Fleet; m. Nora Marilyn Lavis, June 1956; children: David Kenneth Roy, Peter John, Lesley Lynne. Student, Upper Can. Coll., Toronto; BA, MA, U. Cambridge, Eng., 1947. With editorial dept. Timmins Daily Press, Eng., 1947; with advt. dept. Cambridge (Galt) Reporter, 1948-50, gen. mgr., 1950-53; owner Thomson Newspapers, Toronto, 1953—; chmn., bd. dirs. Thomson Corp., The Woodbridge Co. Ltd.; pres., bd. dirs. Thomson Works of Art Ltd. With RCAF, World War II. Mem. Granite Club, Hunt Club, National Club, Toronto Club, York Club, York Downs Club. Baptist. Avocations: collecting paintings and works of art, walking. Home: 8 Castle Frank Rd, Toronto, ON Canada M4W 2Z4 Office: Thomson Corp, 65 Queen St W Ste 2400, Toronto, ON Canada M5H 2M8

THOMSON, MARJORIE BELLE ANDERSON, sociology educator, consultant; b. Topeka, Dec. 4, 1921; d. Roy John and Bessie Margaret (Knarr) Anderson; m. John Whitner Thomson, Jan. 4, 1952 (div. June 9, 1963); 1 child, John Coe. Diploma hostess, Trans World Airlines, 1945; diploma, U.Saltillo, Mex., 1945; BS, Butler U., 1957; MS, Ft. Hays Kans. State U., 1966; postgrad., U. Calif., Santa Barbara, 1968, Kans. State U., 1972-73, Kans. U., 1973. Cert. elem. tchr., Calif., Colo., Ind., Kans., jr. coll. tchr. Tech. libr. N.Am. Aviation, Dallas, 1944-45; flight attendant TWA, Kansas City, Mo., 1945-50; recreation dir. U.S. Govt., Ft. Carson, Colo., 1951-52; elem. tchr. Indpls. Pub. Schs., 1954-57; jr. high tchr. Cheyenne County Schs., Cheyenne Wells, Colo., 1958-59; elem. tchr. Sherman County Schs., Goodland, Kans., 1961-62; lectr. Calif. Luth. U., Thousand Oaks, 1967-69; instr. Ft. Hays Kans. State U., 1969-71; dir. HeadStart Kans. Coun. of Agrl. Workers and Low Income Families, Inc., Goodland, 1971-72; supr. U.S. Govt. Manpower Devel. Programs, Plainville, Kans., 1972-74; bilingual counselor Kans. Dept. Human Resources, Goodland, 1975-82; leader trainee Expt. in Internat. Living, Brattleboro, Vt., 1967-71; cons. M. Anderson & Co., Lakewood, Colo., 1982—; participant Internat. Peace Walk, Moscow to Archangel, Russia, 1991, N.Am. Conf. on Ecology and the Soviet Save Peace and Nature Ecol. Collective, Russia, 1992, Liberators-The Holocaust Awareness Inst., Denver, 1992; amb. internat. Friendship Force, Tiblisi, Republic of Georgia, 1991, Republic South Africa, 1995, Republic of Turkey, 1996; presenter State Conv. AAUW, Aurora, Colo., 1992, presenter nat. conv. Am. Acad. Audiology, Denver, 1992; cons. Gov.'s Conf. in Libr. and Info. Svc., Vail, Colo., 1992; presenter annual conf. Nat. Emergency Number 911 Assn., Denver, 1996. Docent Colo. Gallery of the Arts, Littleton, 1989; spkr. Internat. Self Help for Hard of Hearing People, Inc., 1990—, mem. state recreation resource com. for Self Help for Hard of Hearing People Internat. Conv., Denver, 1991; mem. Denver Deaf and Hard of Hearing Access Com., 1991—; spkr. Ret. Sr. Vol. Program, Denver, 1992—; dir. Holiday Project, Denver, 1992; mem. Lakewood Access Com., 1994—, Arvada Ctr.'s Women's Voices com., 1995—; participant women readers com. Rocky Mountain News, Denver, 1995; trustee Internat. Self Help for Hard of Hearing People, Inc., Bethesda, Md., 1995—; Deaf Panel spkr. for Deaf Awareness Week, Denver, 1995; program co-chair Lakewood Woman's Club, 1996, 97; mem. accessibility com. Arvada Ctr. for Arts and

Humanities, 1997; commr. Denver Commn. for People with Disabilities, 1997. Grantee NSF, 1970, 71; recipient Svc. award Mayor of Lakewood, 1995, Honorable Mention Four Who Dare, Colo. Bus. and Profl. Women and KCNC Channel 4, 1995, J.C. Penney Nat. Golden Rule award for cmty. vol. svc., 1996, Cmty. Svc. award Mayor Denver, 1996, City and County of Denver Proclamation for Marjorie Thomason Day, Mayor Wellington E. Webb, April 8, 1997. Mem. AAUW (life, v.p., program chairperson Lakewood br. 1996, Trailblazer award Denver br. 1997), AARP (pres. Denver-Grandview chpt. 1994), VFW Aux. (life), Sociologists for Women in Soc., Bus. and Profl. Woman's Club, Internat. Peace Walkers, Spellbinders, Denver Press Club, Lakewood Woman's Club, TWA Internat. Clipped Wings (cert.), Mile High Wings, Order Ea. Star (life), Sons of Norway, UNESCO, Grange, Toastmasters, PHAMALy, Pi Gamma Mu, Alpha Sigma Alpha (life). Democrat. Presbyterian. Avocations: photography, traveling, whitewater rafting, storytelling, writing. Home: 12313 W Louisiana Ave G Lakewood CO 80228-3829 Office: M Anderson & Co 6941 W 13th Ave Lakewood CO 80215-5285

THOMSON, RICHARD MURRAY, banker; b. Winnipeg, Man., Can., Aug. 14, 1933; s. H.W. and Mary T. BASC in Engring., U. Toronto, 1955; MBA, Harvard U., 1957; fellow course in banking, Queen's U., 1958. With Toronto Dominion Bank, Ont., Can., 1957—, asst. to pres. head office, 1963-68, chief gen. mgr., 1968-71, v.p., chief gen. mgr., dir., 1971-72, pres., 1972-77, pres. and CEO, 1977-78, chmn., 1978—; CEO Toronto Dominion Bank, 1978-97, also bd. dirs., chmn. of bd., 1997—; bd. dirs. C.G.C. Inc., Eatons of Can., S.C. Johnson & Son Inc., The Prudential Ins. Co. Am., The Thomson Corp., Inco Ltd. Bd. dirs. The Hosp. for Sick Children Found. Office: Toronto-Dominion Bank, 55 King St PO Box 1, Toronto, ON Canada M5K 1A2

THOMSON, ROBERT GORDON, JR., environmental engineer; b. Newport News, Va., July 29, 1962; s. Robert Gordon and Barbara Sue (Soar) T.; m. Debra Sue Holzsweig, July 20, 1986. BS in Engring., Va. Tech., 1985; postgrad., Drexel U., 1986—. Registered profl. engr., Pa., Va.; registered assoc. environ. profl., NREP. Engring. tech. Applied Tech. Lab. U.S. Army, Fort Eustis, Va., summers 83, 84; environ. engr., disinfection coord. U.S. EPA, Phila., 1985-90; environ. engr. office of superfund programs U.S. EPA, 1990—; environ. engr. SITE-Blauvelt Engrs., Inc., Mt. Laurel, N.J., 1992—, Stokes Environ. Assocs. Ltd., Norfolk, Va., 1996—. Co-author: West Virginia Ordnance Works Case Study, Hazardous Materials Control Resources Inst., 1993, Ecological Risk Screening To Prioritize Cleanups at Yorktown Naval Weapons Station, Hazardous Materials Control Resources Inst., 1995; contbr. author, editor: Ecology and Restoration of the Delaware River Basin, 1989. Organizer employees Coastweeks, Del. Valley, S. Jersey, 1989-90, Nat. Engrs. Week, EPA, Phila., 1990; mem. Temple Emanuel, Cherry Hill, N.J., 1989—. Recipient U.S. EPA Bronze medal, 1994, U.S. EPA Spl. Act award, 1996. Mem. Soc. Am. Mil. Engrs., Chesapeake Bay Found., Internat. Soc. Explosive Engrs., Am. Littoral Soc., Nat. Arbor Day Found. Jewish. Avocations: lighthouse preservation, forestry, wildlife conservation, hiking. Home: 1516 Squire Ln Cherry Hill NJ 08003-1537 Office: US EPA Region III (3HW50) 841 Chestnut St Philadelphia PA 19107-4414

THOMSON, ROBERT JAMES, natural gas distribution company executive; b. Detroit, Dec. 16, 1927; s. Harold E.J. and Irene L. (Silsbee) T.; m. Doris L. Mullen, Sept. 19, 1953; children—Gregory R., Susan C., Jeffrey S., Arthur J. AB, Mich. State U., 1951, MBA, 1967. CPA, Mich. Mgr. Arthur Andersen & Co., Detroit, 1951-58; v.p. Southeastern Mich. Gas Co., Port Huron, 1961-71, pres., 1971-84, pres., chief exec. officer, 1984-86; pres., CEO Southeastern Mich. Gas Enterprise, Inc., Pt. Huron, 1977-93; chmn. Southeastern Mich. Gas Enterprise, Inc., Port Huron, 1987-95; bd. dirs. Mich. Nat. Bank-Port Huron, 1972-97. Trustee Cmty. Found. St. Clair County, 1972—, pres., 1981-83; bd. dirs. Indsl. Devel. Corp., Port Huron, 1972-86, pres. 1976-78; trustee Port Huron Hosp., 1981-90, vice chmn., 1985-90; bd. dirs. Blue Water Health Svcs. Corp., 1981—, vice chmn., 1981-93, chmn., 1993—; trustee Marwood Manor Nursing Home., 1987-97, chmn. 1996-97; vestryman Grace Episcopal Ch., Port Huron, 1990-93. With USN, 1946-47. Mem. Mich. C. of C. (bd. dirs. 1982-88), Mich. Utilities Assn. (bd. dirs., treas. 1983-85), Renaissance Club, Port Huron Golf Club, Port Huron Yacht Club, Mich. State U. Advanced Mgmt. Program Club, Port Huron/Marysville C. of C. (bd. dirs. 1973-75, v.p. 1975). Home: 3355 Lomar Dr Fort Gratiot MI 48059-4207 Office: Mich Nat Bank Bldg 800 Military St Rm 302 Port Huron MI 48060-5461

THOMSON, SHIRLEY LAVINIA, museum director; b. Walkerville, Ont., Can., Feb. 19, 1930; d. Walter Cull. BA in Art History with honors, U. West Ont., 1952; MA in Art History, U. Md., 1974; PhD in Art History, McGill U., 1981, Doctoris honoris causa, 1989; PhD (hon.), Ottawa U., 1989; D (hon.), Mt. Allison U., 1990, U. West Ont., 1990; PhD (hon.), U. Windsor, Ont., 1996. Editor conf. NATO, Paris, 1956-60; asst. sec.-gen. World Univ. Svc. WUSC, Toronto, 1960-63; asst. sec. gen. Can. Commn. for UNESCO, Ottawa, 1964-67; sec.-gen. Can. Commn. for UNESCO, Montreal, 1985-87; rsch. coord., writer Memoirs of Sen. Thérèse Casgrain, 1968-70; spl. coord. Largillière Exhbn., Mus. Fine Arts, Montreal, 1981; dir. McCord Mus., 1982-85, Nat. Gallery Can., Ottawa, 1987—; dir., dep. commr. UNESCO Pavilion Man and His World, Montreal, 1978-80. Officer Order of Can., 1994. Decorated Chevalier des Arts et Lettres, France, 1977-78; recipient Can. Coun. doctoral award, 1978-79. Mem. Can. Soc. Decorative Arts (coun.), Can. Mus. Assn. (dir.). Office: Nat Gallery Can, 380 Sussex Dr, Ottawa, ON Canada K1N 9N4

THOMSON, THYRA GODFREY, former state official; b. Florence, Colo., July 30, 1916; d. John and Rosalie (Altman) Godfrey; m. Keith Thomson, Aug. 6, 1939 (dec. Dec. 1960); children—William John, Bruce Godfrey, Keith Coffey. B.A. cum laude, U. Wyo., 1939. With dept. agronomy and agrl. econs. U. Wyo., 1938-39; writer weekly column Watching Washington pub. in 14 papers, Wyo., 1955-60; planning chmn. Nat. Fedn. Republican Women, Washington, 1961; sec. state Wyo. Cheyenne, 1962-86; mem. Marshall Scholarships Com. for Pacific region, 1964-68; del. 72d Wilton Park Conf., Eng., 1965; mem. youth commn. UNESCO, 1970-71, Allied Health Professions Council HEW, 1971-72; del. U.S.-Republic of China Trade Conf., Taipei, Taiwan, 1983; mem. lt. gov.'s trade and fact-finding mission to Saudi Arabia, Jordan, and Egypt, 1985. Bd. dirs. Buffalo Bill Mus., Cody, Wyo., 1987—; adv. bd. Coll. Arts and Scis., U. Wyo., 1989, Cheyenne Symphony Orch. Found., 1990—. Recipient Disting. Alumni award U. Wyo., 1969, Disting. U. Wyo. Arts and Scis. Alumna award, 1987; named Internat. Woman of Distinction, Alpha Delta Kappa; recipient citation Omicron Delta Epsilon, 1965, citation Beta Gamma Sigma, 1968, citation Delta Kappa Gamma, 1973, citation Wyo. Commn. Women, 1986. Mem. N.Am. Securities Adminstrs. (pres. 1973-74), Nat. Assn. Secs. of State, Council State Govts. (chmn. natural resources com. Western states 1966-68), Nat. Conf. Lt. Govs. (exec. com. 1976-79). Home: 3102 Sunrise Rd Cheyenne WY 82001-6136

THOMSON, WILLIAM BARRY, retail company executive; b. Morristown, N.J., Dec. 3, 1952; s. James Bruce and Ruth Janet (Hill) T. BA, Drew U., 1974. Dir. spl. projects F.W. Woolworth Co., N.Y.C., 1979-82, asst. sec., 1982-86, sec., 1986-90; v.p. pub. affairs Woolworth Corp. (formerly F.W. Woolworth Co.), N.Y.C., 1990-91, sr. v.p. adminstrn., 1991-93; sr. v.p., chief adminstrv. officer Woolworth Corp., N.Y.C., 1993-96.

THON, WILLIAM, artist; b. N.Y.C., Aug. 8, 1906; s. Felix Leo and Jane (Upham) T.; m. Helen Elizabeth Walters, June 3, 1929. Student, Art Students League, 1924-25; A.F.D., Bates Coll., 1957. Represented in nat. art exhibits at Corcoran Gallery Art, Washington, Art Inst. Chgo., Pa. Acad., Va. Mus., Toledo Mus., Met. Mus., Nat. Acad., Carnegie Inst.; one-man show Farnsworth Mus., Rockland, Me.; included in permanent collections Swope Art Gallery, Terre Haute, Ind., Farnsworth Mus., Bloomington Art Assn., Ency. Brit., Toledo Mus., Am. Acad. Arts and Letters, Mus. of Ann Arbor, Mich., Met. Mus. Art, N.Y.C., Portland Mus. Art, U. Hawaii, Honolulu, Johnson's Wax Collection, Bklyn. Mus., Whitney Mus., Portland Mus., Oqunquet Mus., others.; artist-in-residence Am. Acad., Rome, 1956. Served with USNR, 1942-46. Recipient prize Salmagundi Club, 1941, Dana watercolor medal Pa. Acad., 1950, prize Bklyn. Mus., 1945, Prix de Rome, 1947, Maine State award, 1970, Florence and H. Samuel Slater Meml. award Adirondacks Nat. Exhibit, Arts Guild Old Forge, Inc., 1992, Pulsifer award, 1993, Hardware prize, 1995, Watercolor prize Old Forge, 1996. Mem. NAD (2d Altman prize for landscape 1951, 1st 1954, 67, Palmer Meml. prize 1944, Samuel F.B. Morse medal 1956, Altman prize for landscape 1961, Adolph and Clara Obrig prize 1965, Ranger Fund purchase award 1976, Ogden Pliessner Meml. prize 1988, William A. Patton prize 1991, Adolph and Clara Obrig award 1992), Nat. Inst. Arts and Letters (grantee 1951), Am. Watercolor Soc. (silver medal 1957, 67, Gordon Grant Meml. award 1963, gold medal of honor 1970, 79, Lena Newcastle Meml. award 1976, Caroline Stern award 1986), Audubon Artists (silver medal 1986, Lillian Judith Newman award 1992), Friendship Sloop Soc. Home: Port Clyde ME 04855

THONG, TRAN, biomedical company executive; b. Saigon, Vietnam, Dec. 8, 1951; came to U.S., 1969, naturalized, 1980; s. Vy and Vinh-Thi (Nguyen) T.; m. Thuy Thi-Bich Nguyen, Jan. 12, 1978. BSEE, Ill. Inst. Tech., 1972; MS in Engring., Princeton U., 1974, MA, 1974, PhD, 1975. Rsch. scientist Western Geophys. Houston, 1975-76; computer devel. engr. GE Co., Syracuse, N.Y., 1976-79; dir. electronic system lab. Tektronix, Inc., Beaverton, Oreg., 1980-90, v.p. engring., and digital signal processing gen. mgr., Tektronix Fed. Systems Inc., Beaverton, Oreg., 1990-93, v.p. systems design and devel. Micro Systems Engring., Inc., Lake Oswego, Oreg., 1993—; prin. N.W. Signal Processing, Inc.; adj. asst. prof. Syracuse U., 1979-81, Oreg. State U., Corvallis, 1980-83, U. Portland, Oreg., 1981-83; adj. assoc. prof. Oreg. Grad. Ctr., Beaverton, 1984-95; mem. bd. advisors Biomed. Engring. Inst., U. Erlangen, Germany; founding mem. Pacific Advanced Comm. Consortium, Eugene, Oreg. Founding mem., chmn. Vietnamese Assn. for Computing, Engring. Tech. and Sci., 1994-95, past pres., 1995-96; bd. dirs. S.E. Asia Scholarship Fund, 1984—. Author numerous sci. papers and U.S. patents. Princeton U. fellow, 1974. Fellow IEEE (com. chmn. 1982-88, assoc. editor transaction 1979-81, gen. chmn. 1989, exec. v.p. circuits and sys. 1989); mem. Eta Kappa Nu, Tau Beta Pi, Sigma Xi. Republican. Office: Micro Sys Engring 6024 Jean Rd Lake Oswego OR 97035-5369

THONGSAK, VAJEEPRASEE THOMAS, business planning executive; b. Udonthani, Thailand, Feb. 10, 1935; came to U.S., 1970; s. Chanmar and Pee Vajeeprasee; m. Somchit; 1 child, Rosarine. BS in Sociology, BA in Philosophy, Mahamakut U., Bangkok, 1968; MA in Edn., Kean Coll. of N.J., 1976; MA in Philosophy, NYU, 1989; PhD in Mgmt., AMA Mgmt. Inst., 1987. Tchr. Machimavas Sch., Udonthani, 1958-65; spl. instr. Chana Songkram Sch., Bangkok, 1965-68; tchrs. staff Thai Sripratoom U., Bangkok, 1968-70; salesman Met. Life of N.Y., 1974-76; rep. Mut. Life of N.Y., 1976-78; agt. Equitable Life Ins., N.Y.C., 1983-84; insp. IBI Security Svc. Inc., L.I., 1979-85; security police insp. Brandeis U., Waltham, Mass., 1985-86; U.S. chief legal investigator, pvt. investigator U.S. Legal Investigation, Inc., U.S. Bur.'s Security Agy., Boston, N.Y.C., Fresno, Calif., 1987—; advisor Thai N.E. Assn., N.Y.C., 1980—, Rep. Nat. Com., Washingotn, 1980—; state advisor U.S. Congl. Adv., Washington, 1980; assoc. mem. Nat. Security Ctr., Citizen's Adv. Coun., Washington, 1989; pres., chief security agt. U.S. Bur. Security Agy., 1991; mem. Pres. Pvt. Sector Survey on Cost Control, Washington, 1989—; mem. Am. Security Coun. Adv. Bd., Washington, 1983-88; U.S. chief legal investigator, pvt. investigator U.S. Legal Investigation, Inc., U.S. Bureau's Security Agy. under Million Mutual Corp., Inc. Mem. G.O.P. Republican Conservative Party (recommendation pres. Gerald R. Ford 1977), 1977—, Nat. Republican Congl. Com. Victory Fund, Washington, 1982—, Republican Presdl. Task Force and Comsn. (recommendation chmn. Nat. Republican Senatorial Com. 1982, 93), 1982—, Am. Security Coun. Found., 1978—, Defense Dept., Defense Inst., 1982—, Nat. Rep. Senatorial Com., Washington, Chiefs of Police Nat. Drug Task Force, 1982—, Nat. Law Enforcement Officers Meml. Fund, Washington, 1982—, Natl. Wildlife Fedn., 1982—; apptd. state adviser U.S. Congl. Adv. Bd., 1979, 93; priest asst. U.S.A. Buddhayaram Temple, Bronx, 1970—; pres. S.E. Asia Found., 1970; mem. Citizens Against Govt. Waste, Washington; mem. U.S. Def. Com., Washington, 1982-86; sec. Wat Buddhamonthol United Buddhist Meditation Ctr., 1992—. Recipient Presdl. Seal, Rep. Orgn., 1983, 84, Rep. Presdl. Legion of Merit highest level of Govts. for Lifetime, 1993. Mem. Internat. Assn. Chiefs of Police, President's Club, Senator's Club, Rep. Presdl. Legion of Merit.

THOPPIL, CECIL KOSHEY, pediatrician, educator; b. Trivandrum, India, Aug. 4, 1961; m. Jennifer Carrol Gallego, Apr. 25, 1992; children: Cecilia Ruth, Andrew Obed. Pre-degree, Mar Ivanios Coll., Trivandrum, Kerala, India, 1979; MB, BS, Med. Coll. Hosp., Trivandrum, 1984. Diplomate Am. Bd. Pediat.; cert. instr. neonatal advanced life support, pediat. advanced life support, BLS. Compulsory rotating internship Med. Coll. Hosp., Trivandrum, Kerala, India, 1985-86; postgrad. tng. pediatric medicine dept. child health S.A.T. Hosp., Trivandrum, Kerala, India, 1986-87; postdoctoral rsch. assoc. dept. perinatal pediatrics U. Tex. Med. Br., Galveston, 1987-89; pediatric internship Univ. Hosps. Cleve. Rainbow Babies and Children's Hosp., 1989-90; pediatric residency dept. pediatrics Scott & White Meml. Hosp./Tex. A&M U. Coll. Medicine, Temple, 1990-92; pediatrician Surry County Health Dept., Dobson, N.C., 1992-94, Med. Assocs. of Surry, Carolina Medicorp Inc., Mt. Airy, N.C., 1994—; physician cons. Surry County Sch. Health Adv. Coun., Surry Pre-sch. Interagy. Coun., Surry County Day Care Assn.; pediat. cons. Surry Smart Start Task Force. Contbr. articles to profl. jours. Provider for "Caring" Program; deacon Haymore Bapt. Ch. Recipient Father Kuncheria Goldmedal for First Rank in Loyola Sch. for Matriculation. Fellow Am. Acad. Pediat.; mem. AMA, N.C. Med. Soc., N.C. Pediat. Soc., Surry-Yadkin Med. Soc. Home: 860 Cross Creek Dr Mount Airy NC 27030-9229 Office: Med Assocs of Surry 865 W Lake Dr Mount Airy NC 27030-2157

THOR, LINDA MARIA, college president; b. L.A., Feb. 21, 1950; d. Karl Gustav and Mildred Dorrine (Hofius) T.; m. Robert Paul Huntsinger, Nov. 22, 1974; children: Erik, Marie. BA, Pepperdine U., 1971, EdD, 1986; MPA, Calif. State U., Los Angeles, 1980. Dir. pub. info. Pepperdine U., Los Angeles, 1971-73; pub. info. officer L.A. C.C. Dist., 1974-75, dir. comm., 1975-81, dir. edn. svcs., 1981-82, dir. high tech., 1982-83, sr. dir. occupl. and tech. edn., 1983-86; pres. West Los Angeles Coll., Culver City, Calif., 1986-90, Rio Salado C.C., Phoenix, 1990—; bd. dirs. Coun. for Adult and Experiential Learning, 1990—, Tech. Exch. Ctr., 1986—, Greater Phoenix Econ. Coun., 1994—. Editor: Curriculum Design and Development for Effective Learning, 1973; author: (with others) Effective Media Relations, 1982, Performance Contracting, 1987; contbr. articles to profl. jours. Active Am. Assn. Cmty. Coll. Commn. Acad. and Student Devel., 1995—, Continuous Quality Improvement Network for Cmty. Colls., 1991—, Am. Coun. Edn. Commn. on Leadership Devel., 1995—; mem. Ariz. Gov.'s Adv. Coun. on Quality, 1992-96; pres. Ariz. Cmty. Coll. Pres.'s Coun., 1995-96. Recipient Delores award Pepperdine U., 1986, Alumni Medal of Honor, 1987, Outstanding Achievement award Women's Bus. Network, 1989; named Woman of the Yr., Culver City Bus. and Profl. Women, 1988. Office: 2323 W 14th St Tempe AZ 85281-6950

THOR, PAUL VIETS, computer science educator, software engineer, consultant; b. Schenectady, N.Y., Mar. 10, 1946; s. Donald D. and Eleanor B. (Viets) T.; m. Barbara K. Nelson, Mar. 27, 1982 (div. Dec. 1993). BSME, U. Denver, 1968; MS in Engring. Mgmt., UCLA, 1976; MS in Computer Sci., George Mason U., 1993; postgrad., Colo. Tech. U., 1996—. Engr. Martin Marietta Corp., Denver, 1968-69; commd. 2d lt. USAF, 1969, advanced through grades to maj., 1982; pilot trainee USAF-Williams AFB, Phoenix, Ariz., 1970-71; pilot C141A 15 MAS-Norton AFB, San Bernardino, Calif., 1971-75, pilot C141B, 1981-84; communications and computer officer 2044 CG-Pentagon, Washington, 1977-81; air field mgr. 18TFW-Kadena AB, Okinawa, Japan, 1984-86; pilot C12 1402 MAS-Andrews AFB, Washington, 1986-87; comm. and computer officer 7 Comm. Group-Pentagon, Washington, 1987-89; cons. George Mason U., Fairfax, Va., 1990-93; pvt. practice cons. Colorado Springs, Colo., 1993—; wing flight examiner 63 MAW-Norton AFB, San Bernardino, 1981-84; acquisitions officer 7th Comms. Group-Pentagon, 1987-89; assoc. prof. computer sci. Colo. Tech. U., Colorado Springs, 1993—. Mem. Computer Soc. of IEEE, Assn. Computer Machinery, Air Force Assn. (life), Ret. Officers Assn. Avocations: personal computers, woodworking, crafts, photography, book collector. Home: 5330 Slickrock Dr Colorado Springs CO 80918-7646 Office: Colo Tech U 4435 N Chestnut St Colorado Springs CO 80907-3812

THORBECKE, ERIK, economics educator; b. Berlin, Feb. 17, 1929; s. William and Madelaine (Salisbury) T.; m. Charla J. Westerberg, Oct. 17, 1954; children: Erik Charles, Willem, Jon. Student, Netherlands Sch. Econs., Rotterdam, 1948-51; PhD, U. Calif., 1957; hon. doctorate, U. Ghent, 1981. Asst. prof. econs. Iowa State U., 1957-60, assoc. prof., 1960-63, prof., 1963-73; prof. Cornell U., 1974—, chmn. dept. econs., 1975-78, H.E. Babcock prof. econs. and food econs., 1978—; econ. adviser Nat. Planning Inst., Lima, Peru, 1963-64; asso. asst. adminstr. for program policy AID, Washington, 1966-68, mem. research advisory com., 1976-81; sr. economist world employment program Internat. Labor Office, Geneva, 1972-73; vis. prof. Erasmus U., Rotterdam, 1980-81; mem. com. on internat. nutritional programs NRC-NAS, 1979-81; dir. program on comparative econ. devel., Cornell U., 1988—; sr. rsch. fellow USAID Inst. Policy Reform, 1990—. Author: The Tendency Towards Regionalization in International Trade, 1960, (with Irma Adelman) Theory and Design of Economic Development, 1966, (with K. Fox, J. Sengupta) Theory of Quantitative Economic Policy, 1968, Role of Agriculture in Economic Development, 1968, (with G. Pyatt) Planning Techniques for a Better Future, 1976; (with J. Defourny) Structural Path Analysis and Multiplier Decomposition within a Social Matrix, 1984, (with J. Foster, J. Greer) A Class of Decomposable Poverty Measures, 1984, (with J. Lecaillon, C. Morrisson) Economic Policies and Agricultural Performance of Low Income Countries, 1987, Planning Techniques for Social Justice In: The Balance between Industry and Agriculture in Economic Development, vol. 4, 1989, (with I. Adelman) The Role of Institutions in Economic Development, Special Issue of World Development, 1989, (with others) Adjustment and Equity in Indonesia, 1992, (with T. van der Pluijm) Rural Indonesia: Socio-economic Development in a Changing Environment, 1993; contbr. articles to profl. jours. Mem. Am. Econ. Assn., Am. Assn. Agrl. Econs. (Nat. award for best pub. research 1970). Home: 108 N Sunset Dr Ithaca NY 14850-1460 Office: Cornell U Dept Econs Ithaca NY 14853

THORBURN, DAVID, literature educator; b. N.Y.C., Aug. 14, 1940; s. Frank and Claire (Feller) T.; m. Barbara Ellen Levitan, June 30, 1963; children: Daniel, Adam, Rachel. AB, Princeton U., 1962; MA, Stanford U., 1966, PhD, 1968. Instr., asst. prof., then assoc. prof. dept. English, Yale U., New Haven, 1966-76; prof. lit., dir. film and media studies MIT, Cambridge, 1976—, dir. cultural studies project and comm. forum, 1976—; vis. appointments include U. Calif., Santa Barbara, U. Ill. Author: Conrad's Romanticism, 1974; contbr. articles to profl. jours.; editor scholarly collections; gen. editor Media and Popular Culture, 1986—. Fulbright fellow, Morse fellow, Woodrow Wilson fellow and Rockefeller fellow, 1966-77. Mem. MLA, Popular Culture Assn., Am. Studies Assn., Soc. for Cinema Studies. Democrat. Avocation: basketball. Office: MIT 14N-335 Lit Faculty Cambridge MA 02139

THORBURN, JAMES ALEXANDER, humanities educator; b. Martins Ferry, Ohio, Aug. 24, 1923; s. Charles David and Mary Edna (Ruble) T.; m. Lois McElroy, July 3, 1954; children: Alexander Maurice, Melissa Rachel; m. 2d, June Yingling O'Leary, Apr. 18, 1981. BA, Ohio State U., 1949, MA, 1951; postgrad., U. Mo., 1954-55; PhD, La. State U., 1977. Head English dept. high sch., Sheridan, Mich., 1951-52; instr. English, U. Mo., Columbia, 1952-55, Monmouth (Ill.) Coll., 1955-56, U. Tex., El Paso, 1956-60, U. Mo., St. Louis, 1960-61, La. State U., Baton Rouge, 1961-70; prof. Southeastern La. U., Hammond, 1970-89, ret., named prof. emeritus English and linguistics; testing and cert. examiner English Lang. Inst., U. Mich., 1969—; participant Southeastern Conf. on Linguistics; mem. Conf. Christianity and Lit. Contbg. author: Exercises in English, 1955, also poetry, short stories; book rev. editor: Experiment, 1958-87; editor: Innisfree, 1984-89. With F.A., AUS, 1943-46. Mem. MLA, Linguistic Assn. S.W., Avalon World Arts Acad., Linguistic Soc. Am., Am. Dialect Soc., La. Assn. for Coll. Composition, La. Retired Tchrs. Assn., Internat. Poetry Soc., Internat. Acad. Poets, Sociedad Nacional Hispánica, Sigma Delta Pi, Phi Kappa Phi (named emeritus life), Phi Mu Alpha Sinfonia. Republican. Presbyterian. Home: 602 Susan Dr Hammond LA 70403-3444 Office: Southeastern La U # 739 Hammond LA 70402 *I have always felt that no experience is wasted, if it is not selfish or vicious. Every such experience adds something, I believe, to that inner fund on which one draws, consciously or unconsciously, throughout one's life.*

THORE, STEN ANDERS, economics and aerospace engineering educator; b. Stockholm, Apr. 22, 1930; came to U.S., 1978, naturalized, 1985; s. Eric and Elsa (Ostberg) T.; m. Margrethe Munck; children: Susanne, Alexander, Clementine. M. Commerce, U. Birmingham, Eng., 1954; Filosofie Doktor, U. Stockholm, 1961. Prof. econs. Norwegian Sch. Econs. and Bus. Adminstrn., Bergen, Norway, 1964-78; Gregory A. Kozmetsky Centennial fellow IC2 Inst., U. Tex., Austin, 1984-97, emeritus, 1997—; instr. U. Tex., Austin, Washington, 1996-97; vis. prof. Northwestern U., Carnegie-Mellon U., U. Va., Inst. Superior Tecnico, Lisbon, Portugal. Author: Economic Logistics, 1992, The Diversity, Complexity and Evolution of High Tech Capitalism, 1995; (with G.L. Thompson) Computational Economics, 1991; contbr. articles to profl. jours. Named Hon. Citizen, State of Tex., 1981. Mem. Inst. Mgmt. Scis. Econometric Soc. Home: 113 Cerro Sao Miguel, Vila Vista Alegre Apt 113, 8300 Silves 8300, Portugal Office: Instituto Superior Tecnico, Inst Supr Tecnico Mech Engr, Ave Rovisco Pais, 1096 Lisbon Cedx1096, Portugal

THORFINNSON, A. RODNEY, hospital administrator; b. Kandahar, Sask., Can., Nov. 30, 1934; married. BA, U. Sask., Can., 1958; MA, U. Toronto, 1960. Adminstrv. resident Humber Meml. Hosp., Toronto, 1959-60; cons. Dept. Pub. Health, Regina, Sask., 1960-61; asst. dir. Sask. Hosp. Assn., Regina, 1961-62, exec. dir., 1962-64; asst. dir. Univ. Hosp., Saskatoon, Sask., 1964-65; adminstr. Victoria Hosp., London, Ont., 1966-69; v.p. Comtron Systems, Inc., London, Ont., 1969-70; exec. dir. Victoria Hosp. Corp., London, Ont., 1970-78, pres., 1978-85; pres. Health Scis. Ctr., Winnipeg, Man., 1985—. Office: Health Scis Ctr, 820 Sherbrook St Rm GB127B, Winnipeg, MB Canada R3A 1R9

THORIN, DONALD E., cinematographer. Cinematographer Thief, 1981, An Officer and a Gentleman, 1982, (with Bruce Surtees) Bad Boys, 1983, Against All Odds, 1984, Purple Rain, 1984, Mischief, 1985, Wildcats, 1986, The Golden Child, 1986, American Anthem, 1986, Midnight Run, 1988, Collision Course, 1988, The Couch Trip, 1988, Tango & Cash, 1989, Troop Beverly Hills, 1989, Lock Up, 1989, The Marrying Man, 1991, Out On A Limb, 1992, Scent of a Woman, 1992, Cloak and Diaper, 1992, Undercover Blues, 1993, Little Big League, 1994, Boys on the Side, 1995, Ace Ventura II, 1995, First Wives Club, 1996, Nothing To Lose, 1996. Office: Broder Kurland Webb Uffner Agy 9242 Beverly Blvd Ste 200 Beverly Hills CA 90210-3710*

THORN, ANDREA PAPP, lawyer; b. Greenwich, Conn., May 22, 1960; d. Laszlo G. and Judith (Liptak) Papp; m. Craig Thorn IV, Aug. 27, 1982; children: C. Alexander, Kelsey Amanda. BA, Dartmouth Coll., Hanover, N.H., 1982; JD, Harvard U., 1987. Bar: Mass. 1987, N.H. 1993. Assoc. Bingham Dana & Gould, Boston, 1987-89, Gaffin & Krattenmaker PC, Boston, 1989-90, Phillips, Gerstein & Holber, Haverhill, Mass., 1993-94; spl. asst. to sec. of N.Mex. Dept. of Environment, 1991-92. Mem. ABA, Mass. Bar Assn., N.H. Bar Assn. Home: Phillips Academy Andover MA 01810-4161 Office: Karfunkel & Thorn PA 26 Essex St Andover MA 01810-3714

THORN, GEORGE WIDMER, physician, educator; b. Buffalo, Jan. 15, 1906; s. George W. and Fanny R. (Widmer) T.; m. Doris Weston, June 30, 1931 (dec. Jan. 1984); 1 son, Weston Widmer; m. Claire Steinert, Dec. 28, 1985 (dec. Mar. 1990). Student, Coll. of Wooster, 1923-25; MD, U. Buffalo, 1929; MA (hon.), Harvard U., 1942, DSc (hon.), 1987; DSc (hon.), Temple U., 1951, Suffolk U., 1961, Coll. Wooster, 1963, N.Y. Med. Coll., 1972, Boston U., 1983; LLD (hon.), Dalhousie U., 1950; LLD, Queen's U., Can., 1954; DMed, Cath. U., Louvain, 1960; MD (hon.), U. Geneva, 1965; DSc (hon.), Med. Coll. of Ohio, Toledo, Rockefeller U., 1993; U. Buffalo, 1995. Diplomate Am. Bd. Internal Medicine. House officer Millard Fillmore Hosp., Buffalo, 1929-30; researcher dept. physiology U. Buffalo, 1930-31, asst. researcher dept. physiology and medicine, 1931-34; asst. prof. physiology Ohio State U., Columbus, 1935-36; asst. physician Johns Hopkins Hosp., Balt., 1937-39, assoc. prof. medicine, 1938-42, assoc. physician, 1939-42; mem. med. adv. bd. Howard Hughes Med. Inst., 1955-85, dir., res., 1956-78, chmn. med. adv. bd., 1975-85, mem. exec. com., 1977-84, pres., 1981-84, chmn. bd. trustees, 1984-90; physician-in-chief Peter Bent Brigham Hosp., Boston, 1942-72, physician-in-chief emeritus, 1972—; Samuel A. Levine prof. medicine Harvard U., Cambridge, 1967-72, Samuel A. Levine prof. emeritus,

1972—, Hersey prof. theory and practice physic emeritus, 1972—; Hugh J. Morgan vis. prof. Vanderbilt U., 1967; vis. prof. medicine Columbia Coll. Physicians and Surgeons, 1968, Cornell U. Med. Sch. and N.Y. Hosp., 1970; Wingate Johnson vis. prof. Bownman Gray Sch. Medicine Wake Forest U., 1972; cons. internist Boston Psychopathic Hosp., 1943—; mem. research and devel. adv. bd. Smith, Kline and French Labs., 1953-69; cons. Children's Med. Ctr., USPHA, U.S. Army Med. Services Grad. Sch.; mem. com. stress NRC; mem. Nat. Com. on Radiation, 1958—; mem. drug research bd. NRC-Nat. Acad. Scis., 1972; lectr.U. London, 1957; Jacobaeus lectr., Oslo, 1957; Maurice C. Pincoff lectr. U. Md. Sch. Medicine, 1958; Mellon lectr. U. Pitts., 1959; Banting Meml. lectr. Am. Diabetes Assn., 1959; 1st Lilly lectr. Royal Coll. Physicians, 1966, Soc. Mexicana de Nutricion y Endocrologia, Mexico, 1969; Thayer lectr. Johns Hopkins U., 1967; Billings lectr. AMA, 1968; John C. Leonard Med. lectr. Hartford Med. Soc., 1969; mem. corp. MIT, 1965—, Mus. Sci., 1979—; v.p. Whitaker Health Scis. Fund, Inc., 1974-92; bd. visitors Boston u. Sch. Medicine, 1979—; chmn. sci. adv. bd. Whitaker Found., 1979-93. Editor-in-chief Principles of Internal Medicine, 8th edit., 1974. Pres. Howard Hughes Med. Inst., Boston, 1981-84, chmn. bd. dirs. and trustee, 1984—. Rockefeller fellow in medicine, Harvard U., 1936-37, Johns Hopkins U. Sch. Medicine, 1938, Read Ellsworth fellow in medicine John Hopkins U. Sch. Medicine, 1938; recipient Chancellor's medal U. Buffalo, 1943, Osler oration Can. Med. Assn., 1949, U.S. Pharm. Mfrs. Assn. award 1950, Alvarenga award, 1951, Dr. Charles V. Chapin Meml. award 1956, Ann. Meml. award Buffalo Urol. Soc., 1958, Modern Medicine award, 1961, Oscar B. Hunter Meml. award Am. Therapeutic Soc., 1967, Robert H. Williams award Assn. Profs. of Medicine, 1972, George M. Kober medal Assn. Am. Physicians, 1976, Gold-Headed Can. Soc. award, 1976, Medical Times Physician of Excellence award, 1980, Hubert H. Humphrey Research Ctr. award Boston U., 1980, Gold medal Phi Lambda Kappa, 1981. Fellow Royal Coll. Physicians (London), ACP (master, John Phillips Meml. award 1955); mem. Am. Soc. Clin. Investigation (emeritus), AMA (gold medalist 1932, 39, George Minot award 1963), Assn. Am. Physicians (pres. 1970), Am. Physiol. Soc., Royal Soc. of Medicine (hon. mem. endocronology sect.), Endocrine Soc. (pres. 1962), Am. Clin. and Climatol. Assn. (pres.), Am. Acad. Arts and Scis., Royal Soc. Medicine (hon.), Royal Acad. of Medicine of Belgium, Interurban Clin. Club, John Hopkins Soc. Scholars, Aesculapian Club, Order of Hipolito of Peru (comdr. 1960), Sigma Xi, Nu Sigma Nu, Alpha Omega Alpha. Clubs: Harvard, Harvard Faculty; Country (Brookline); Essex County, St. Botolph, Tavern, Badminton & Tennis, Singing Beach (Manchester). Office: Howard Hughes Med Inst 320 Longwood Ave Enders 661 Boston MA 02115

THORN, JAMES DOUGLAS, safety engineer; b. Tyler, Tex., May 20, 1959; s. Douglas Howard and Patricia Ann (Kolb) T. Student, U. of Mary, Manama, Bahrain, 1982, S.W. Tex. State U., 1984-86, La. State U., 1989, W.Va. Tech., 1991-92, Berlitz Sch. Langs., 1993. Cert. EMT, BTLS, ACLS, CPR instr., hazardous materials ops., hazardous waste ops., hazardous and indsl. waste mgmt. 3d officer Jackson Marine S.A., Manama, 1981; constrn. foreman Brown & Root S.A., Manama, 1982-83; barge officer Rezayat/Brown & Root E.C., Manama, 1983-84; safety insp. Brown & Root U.S.A., Carson, Calif., 1987-88; sr. safety insp. Brown & Root U.S.A., Taft, La., 1988-89; project safety mgr. Brown & Root Braun, Institute, W.Va., 1989-93; mgr. safety and health Brown & Root Braun, Phila., 1993-94; safety supt. Brown & Root, Carson, Calif., 1994; safety/security mgr. L.A. Export Terminal, 1995—; safety cons. Assn. Builders and Contractors, Charleston, W.Va., 1990-93, chmn. safety seminar, 1991-93; drill monitor Kanawha Valley Emergency Preparedness Coun., South Charleston, W.Va., 1990-93; v.p. Arco Contractors Safety Coun., Carson, 1995-96. Youth counsellor Neon League, St. Albans, W.Va., 1991; den leader cub scouts Boy Scouts Am., 1991-93; v.p. Area Contractors Safety Coun., 1995-96; bd. dirs. Johnnie Johnson Tennis Tournament for Boys and Girls Clubs, 1996—. Mem. Am. Soc. Safety Engrs., Nat. Assn. EMTs, Team 911, Great Wall of Tex. Soc., Angels Booster Club (bd. dirs. 1995-97, 1st v.p. 1996-97), Rams Booster Club (bd. dirs. 1995) now NFL Booster Club of Orange County (bd. dirs. 1996—, bd. dirs. Johnnie Johnson Pro/Celebrity Tennis Tournament for Boys and Girls Clubs 1997—). Avocations: snow skiing, scuba diving, bicycle racing, Major League baseball. Office: Brown & Root PO Box 320 Long Beach CA 90801

THORN, ROSEMARY KOST, former librarian; b. N.Y.C., Dec. 15, 1954; d. Stephen John and Henrietta (Rosso) K.; m. Michael Thorn; children: Russell, Stephen. BA in Anthropology, Rutgers U., 1977; MLS, U. N.C., 1980. Head libr. U.S. EPA, Research Triangle Park, N.C., 1980—; EPA. Avocations: running, gardening, travel.

THORN, TERENCE HASTINGS, gas industry executive; b. Takoma, Md., July 6, 1946; s. John Hastings and Norine R. (Freytag) T.; m. Judith Carol Bailey, Aug. 15, 1970; children: Kristin Lynn, Matthew Hastings. BA, U. Md., 1969, MA, 1973. Dir. congl. rels. Am. Gas Assn., Arlington, Va., 1975-79; dir. govt. rels. J. Walter Thompson Co., Washington, 1979-81; v.p. govt. rels. Houston Natural Gas Co., Washington, 1981-85; exec. v.p. Mojave Pipeline Co., Houston, 1986-89; pres., CEO Transwestern Pipeline Co., Houston, 1993—; sr. v.p., exec. mgmt. com. bd. ENRON Corp., 1993—. Bd. dirs. Houston Pops, 1989-90, Pin Oak Charities, Houston, 1991-93, Greater Houston chpt. YMCA, 1994; city alderman, 1992-93; mem. Hermann Soc., 1993—, Energy Industry Sector Adv. Com. U.S. Dept. Commerce; prin. liason Pres.'s Coun. Sustainable Devel.; chmn. internat. com. Bus. Coun. of Sustainable Devel.; mem. adv. com. Commn. for Environ. Cooperation; trustee Tomas Rivera Policy Inst.; vice chmn. Internat. Gas Ctr. Mem. Pacific Coast Gas Assn. (chmn. 1994—), Internat. Gas Union, World Energy Congress. Democrat. Avocation: tennis. Office: ENRON Corp PO Box 1188 Houston TX 77251-1188

THORNBERRY, TERENCE PATRICK, criminologist, educator; b. N.Y.C., Jan. 28, 1945; s. Patrick and Rose (Small) T.; children: Donna Ann, Patrick. BA, Fordham U., 1966; MA, U. Pa., 1971, PhD, 1971. Asst. dir. Ctr. for Studies in Criminology and Criminal Law, U. Pa., Phila., 1971-79; dir. Research Ctr. in Crime and Delinquency, U. Ga., Athens, 1979-84; dean Sch. Criminal Justice, SUNY, Albany, 1984-89; prof. 1984—; dir. Rochester Youth Devel. Study, 1986—; cons. Commn. on Obscenity and Pornography, 1970, Nat. Commn. on Marijuana and Drug Abuse, 1973, Commn. on Rev. of Nat. Policy Toward Gambling, 1975-76; chmn. criminal and violent behavior rev. com. NIMH, 1988-90. Author: Evaluating Criminology, 1978, The Criminology Index, 1978, The Criminally Insane: A Community Followup of Mentally Ill Offenders, 1979 (ABA Gavel award, cert of merit 1980), From Boy to Man: From Delinquency to Crime, 1987; editor: Images of Crime: Offenders and Victims, 1974, Crime and Delinquency: Dimensions of Deviance, 1974; mem. editorial bd.: Jour. Criminal Law and Criminology, Social Forces, Jour. Quantitative Criminology, Criminology: An Interdisciplinary Jour.; contbr. articles to profl. jours. Recipient Appreciation certificate Nat. Inst. Mental Health, 1990. Mem. Am. Soc. Criminology (v.p. 1974-75, exec. counsellor 1974-77, 82, 85—, Presdl. Citation 1975), Am. Sociol. Assn. Home: 188 Jay St Albany NY 12210 Office: SUNY Sch Criminal Justice 135 Western Ave Albany NY 12203-1011

THORNBERRY, WILLIAM M. (MAC THORNBERRY), congressman; b. Clarendon, Tex., July 15, 1958; m. Sally Thornberry; 2 children. BA in History summa cum laude, Tex. Tech U., 1980; JD, U. Tex., 1983. Legis. coun. Rep. Tom Loeffler, 1983-85; chief of staff Rep. Larry Combest, 1985-88; dep. asst. sec. legis. affairs U.S. State Dept., 1988-89; def. atty. Peterson, Farris, Doores & Jones, Amarillo, Tex., 1989—; mem. 104th-105th Congresses from 13th Tex. dist., 1995—; mem. nat. sec. com., resources com.; family rancher. Mem. Tex. and Southwestern Cattle Raisers Assn. Republican. Office: US House Reps 412 Cannon Washington DC 20515-0403*

THORNBURG, FREDERICK FLETCHER, diversified business executive, lawyer; b. South Bend, Ind., Feb. 10, 1940; s. James F. and Margaret R. (Major) T.; children: James Brian, Charles Kevin, Christian Sean, Christopher Herndon; m. Patricia J. Malloy, Dec. 4, 1981. AB, DePauw U., 1963; postgrad., U. Notre Dame, 1965; JD magna cum laude, Ind. U., 1968. Bar: Ind. 1968, U.S. Tax Ct. 1970, U.S. Ct. Appeals (7th cir.) 1970, U.S. Supreme Ct. 1971. Tchr., coach U.S. Peace Corps, Colombia, 1963-65; law clk. to chief judge U.S. Ct. Appeals (7th cir.), 1968-69; assoc. Thornburg, McGill, Deahl, Harman, Carey & Murray, South Bend, 1969-75, ptnr., 1975-80; v.p. systems and svcs. group The Wackenhut Corp., Coral Gables, Fla., 1981-82, sr. v.p. adminstrn., 1982-86, exec. v.p. 1986-88, also bd. dirs.; pres. Wackenhut Internat. Corp. and Wackenhut Svcs., Inc.; v.p. and legal counsel St. Thomas U., 1988-90, adj. prof. law, 1989-90; pres., CEO PropServ, Inc., 1991-94; pres. EPS Ltd., 1995—; CEO Practice Resources Corp., 1996—; cons. Private Freezer Corp., Am. Tel Corp.; legal & mgmt. cons., mem. bd. advisors, Publix Supermarkets, Inc., 1994-95, St. Thomas U.; bd. dirs. Doral Oaks Inc. Assocs., 1993-94; trustee U. Cmty. Hosp. Found., 1991-94; adj. prof. bus. St. Mary's Coll., 1975-78; vis. prof. CTA, 1985-95; vice-chmn., pvt. sec. adv. coun. Fla. Sec. of State, 1985-90. Assoc. editor in chief: Ind. Law Jour., 1967-68; contbr. articles to legal and bus. jours. Bd. dirs. YMCA, Channel 34, Symphony Orch. Assn. Fulbright selectee, Halleck scholar. Mem. ABA, Ind. Bar Assn., Greater Miami C. of C. (former corp. rep. trustee), Elks Club, Doral Park Country Club, Order of Coif, Phi Delta Phi, Alpha Delta Sigma. Office: 10005 NW 52nd Ter Miami FL 33178-2608

THORNBURG, LEE ELLIS, film executive, director; b. Houston, Feb. 16, 1942; s. Richard Ellis and Lucyle (Comstock) T.; m. Jane Kaiser (div. 1981); children: Janette Mattas, Deanne Waddell; m. Patricia Ann Kirkham, June 16, 1987. Tech. svc. engr. Dresser Industries, Houston, 1970-76; pres. Lone Star Pictures Internat., Inc., Dallas, 1976—. Dir. films including Hollywood High Part II, 1981, 6-Pack, 1991, Southwest, 1996, Memo, 1996; prodr. films including Kings of the Hill, 1976, Mr. Mean, 1978. Mem. Am. Film Market Assn. Republican. Methodist. Office: Lonestar Pictures Internat 100 S 6th Ave City Industry CA 91746-2913

THORNBURGH, DICK (RICHARD L. THORNBURGH), lawyer, former United Nations official, former United States attorney general, former governor; b. Pitts., July 16, 1932; s. Charles Garland and Alice (Sanborn) T.; m. Virginia Walton Judson, Oct. 12, 1963; children: John, David, Peter, William. B in Engring., Yale, 1954; LLB, U. Pitts., 1957; hon. degrees, from 30 colls. and univs. Bar: Pa. 1958, U.S. Supreme Ct. 1965. Atty. Kirkpatrick & Lockhart, Pitts., 1959-69, 77-79, 87-88, 91-92, 94—; U.S. atty. for Western Pa. Pitts., 1969-75; U.S. asst. atty. gen. Dept. Justice, Washington, 1975-77; gov. State of Pa., Harrisburg, 1979-87; U.S. atty. gen. Washington, 1988-91; under-sec.-gen. for adminstrn. and mgmt. UN, N.Y.C., 1992-93; del. Pa. Constl. Conv., 1967-68; chmn. State Sci. and Technology Inst. Mem. Coun. Fgn. Rels.; trustee Urban Inst., Henry L. Stimson Ctr., Dole Found. for Employment of People with Disabilities, DeWitt Wallace Fund for Colonial Williamsburg. Fellow Am. Bar Found.; mem. Am. Judicature Soc., Nat. Acad. Pub. Adminstrn. Republican. Office: Kirkpatrick & Lockhart 1800 Massachusetts Ave NW Washington DC 20036-1806

THORNBURGH, RON E., state official; b. Burlingame, Kans., Dec. 31, 1962; m. Annette Thornburgh. Student, Washburn U., 1985. Dep. asst. sec. of state, then asst. sec. of state State of Kans., Topeka, 1985-87, sec. of state, 1995—; asst. sec. of state Sec. of State's Office, Topeka, 1991-95, sec. of state, 1995—; vice chairperson blue ribbon panel on ethical conduct State of Kans., 1989. Mem. Kids Voting Kans. Exec. Com.; mem. adv. com. United Way. Toll fellow Henry Toll Fellowship Program, 1995. Mem. Washburn U. Alumni Bd., 20/30 Club Internat. Methodist. Office: Sec of State 2d Fl Statehouse 300 SW st Topeka KS 66612*

THORNBURY, JOHN ROUSSEAU, radiologist, physician; b. Cleve., Mar. 16, 1929; s. Purla Lee and Gertrude (Glidden) T.; m. Julia Lee McGregor, Mar. 20, 1955; children: Lee Allison, John McGregor. A.B. cum laude, Miami U., Oxford, Ohio, 1950; M.D., Ohio State U., 1955. Diplomate: Am. Bd. Radiology. Intern Hurley Hosp., Flint, Mich., 1955-56; resident U. Iowa Hosps., Iowa City, 1958-61; instr., asst. prof. radiology U. Colo. Med. Center, Denver, 1962-63; practice medicine specializing in radiology Denver, 1962-63, Iowa City, 1963-66, Seattle, 1966-68, Ann Arbor, Mich., 1968-79, Albuquerque, 1979-84, Rochester, N.Y., 1984-89, Madison, Wis., 1989-94; mem. staff U. Wisconsin Hosp., Madison, prof. radiology, chief sect. of body imaging, Med. Sch., 1989-94, prof. emeritus, 1994—; asst. prof. radiology U. Iowa Hosps., 1963-66, U. Wash. Hosp., Seattle, 1966-68; assoc. prof. radiology U. Mich. Med. Ctr., 1968-71, prof. radiology, 1971-79; prof. radiology, chief divsn. diagnostic radiology dept. radiology Sch. Medicine, U. N.Mex., 1979-84; prof. radiology U. Rochester Sch. Medicine, 1984-89, acting chmn., 1985-87; chmn. sci. com. on efficacy studies Nat. Coun. on Radiation Protection, 1980-95; rapporteur/mem. sci. group on indications/limitations of x-ray diagnostic procedures WHO, 1983; cons. com. on efficacy of magnetic resonance nat. health tech. adv. panel Australian Inst. Health, 1986; invited U.S. cons. MRI program, Nijmegen, The Netherlands, 1992; cons., spkr. Royal Australasian Coll. Radiologists, Melbourne, Australia, 1997; lectr. in field; cons. tech. assessment and outcomes rsch., 1994—; cons. to Am. Soc. of Neuroradiology, 1995-98. Co-author/cons. Clin. Efficacy Assessment Project, Am. Coll. Physicians, 1986-89; assoc. editor: Yearbook of Radiology, 1971-82; editorial bd.: Contemporary Diagnostic Radiology, 1977-84, Urologic Radiology, 1977-84. Served to capt., M.C. USAF, 1956-58. Grantee Agy. Health Care Policy and Rsch., 1986-91, U. Rochester, 1986-89, U. Wis., Madison, 1989-91. Fellow Am. Coll. Radiology; mem. Soc. Uroradiology (pres. 1976-77, dir. 1977-79), Assn. Univ. Radiologists (pres. 1980-81), Radiol. Soc. N.Am., Am. Roentgen Ray Soc. (Caldwell medal 1993), Colo. Radiol. Soc., Phi Beta Kappa, Delta Tau Delta, Omicron Delta Kappa, Phi Chi. Republican. Lutheran. Home: 185 Morgan Pl Castle Rock CO 80104-9061 *"Mooring Post" relationships and sharing have been essential to success and achievements in my multi-disciplinary research. "Mooring Post" persons range from expert mentors and stellar colleagues, to the bedrock of a loving and supportive family. Further, to me, Rule One in medicine has always been, "The patient comes first."*

THORNDIKE, EDWARD HARMON, physicist; b. Pasadena, Calif., Aug. 2, 1934; s. Edward Moulton and Louise (Harmon) T.; m. Elizabeth H. Wenger, Sept. 8, 1955; children—Susan Lee, Patricia Lynn, Edward Harmon Jr. A.B., Wesleyan U., Middletown, Conn., 1956; M.S., Stanford U., 1957; Ph.D., Harvard U., 1960. Research fellow Harvard U., Cambridge, Mass., 1960-61; mem. faculty U. Rochester, N.Y., 1961—; asso. prof. physics U. Rochester, 1965-72, prof., 1972—; vis. prof. U. Geneva, 1969-70; vis. scientist CERN, Geneva, 1969-70; mem. adv. coun. Ctr. Environ. Info., Rochester, 1974-93; mem. adv. com. Stanford Linear Accelerator Ctr. Exptl. Program, 1987-89; mem. vis. com. for Fermilab, Univs. Rsch. Assn., 1993-95. Author: Energy and Environment, a Primer for Scientists and Engineers, 1976; contbr. articles to profl. jours. NSF fellow, 1970, Guggenheim fellow, 1987-88. Fellow Am. Phys. Soc. Office: U Rochester Dept Physics/Astronomy Rochester NY 14627

THORNDIKE, JOHN LOWELL, investment executive; b. Boston, Oct. 17, 1926; s. Augustus and Olivia (Lowell) T.; m. Dorothy Wood Dudley, Sept. 16, 1950; 1 child, John Amory Thorndike. BS, Harvard U., 1949. Registered rep Tucker Anthony & Co., Boston, 1950-57; v.p. Putnam Mgmt. Co., Boston, 1957-62; asst. to treas. Harvard U., Cambridge, Mass., 1962-66; v.p. Fiduciary Trust Co., Boston, 1966-92, also bd. dirs.; dir. Fiduciary Co. Inc., 1984-97; trustee Provident Instn. for Savs., Boston, 1965-85; trustee, ptnr. Eaton Vance Mut. Funds, Boston, 1977—. Trustee Boston Symphony Orch., 1960-80, treas., 1965-77, v.p., 1977-80; trustee Brigham and Women's Hosp., 1982-87, Cotting Sch., treas., 1982—; mem. warrant com. Town of Dover, Mass., 1966-69, chmn., 1968-69, town moderator, 1971-75; mem. Mass. Health and Ednl. Facilities Authority, Boston, 1970-88, sec., 1972-84, chmn., 1984-87; mem. cemetery commn. Town of Dover, 1992—; bd. dirs. Mass. Audubon Soc., 1971-89, chmn., 1984-89. With Army Air Corps, 1945. Recipient 1st prize Assn. Town Fin. Coms., 1969. Mem. Boston Security Analyst Soc., Boston Econ. Club, Union Club of Boston (pres. 1978-79), Harvard Club of Boston (pres. 1980-83), Harvard Mus. Assn. (pres. 1988-91). Republican. Episcopalian. Avocations: tennis, bird watching. Home: 10 Main St Dover MA 02030-2022 Office: Fiduciary Trust Co 175 Federal St Boston MA 02110-2210

THORNDIKE, JOSEPH JACOBS, JR., editor; b. Peabody, Mass., July 29, 1913; s. Joseph Jacobs and Susan Ellison (Farnham) T.; m. Virginia Lemont, Sept. 7, 1940; children—John, Alan; m. Margery Darrell, Oct. 3, 1963; 1 son, Joseph Jacobs III. A.B., Harvard, 1934. Asst. editor Time Mag., 1934-36; assoc. editor Life Mag., 1936-46; mng. editor Life, 1946-49; pres. Thorndike, Jensen & Parton, Inc.; co-founder, contbg. editor Am. Heritage Pub. Co. Author: The Very Rich, 1976, The Magnificent Builders, 1978, The Coast, 1993; editor: Seafaring America, 1974, Mysteries of the Past, 1977, Discovery of Lost Worlds, 1979, Mysteries of the Deep, 1980, Three Centuries of American Architects, 1981. Unitarian. Club: Harvard (N.Y.C.). Home: 34 Oak St Harwich MA 02645-2703

THORNDIKE, RICHARD KING, former brokerage company executive; b. Millis, Mass., 1913; s. Richard King and Florence A. (Macy) T.; m. Lucy Saltonstall Rantoul, Sept. 21, 1935 (dec. May 1958); children: Richard III, Rose, Sylvia; m. Mercy Bours Archibald, Oct. 1, 1960. Grad., Harvard, 1935. With F.S. Moseley & Co., Boston, 1935—; asst. analyst F.S. Moseley & Co., 1937-46, partner, 1947-73; v.p. Moseley, Hallgarten, Estabrook & Weeden Inc., 1973-83. Republican. Episcopalian. Clubs: Myopia (Hamilton, Mass.); Ponte Ve dra Inn and Club; Phoenix-SK (Harvard), Lenox (Lenox, Mass.). Home: Apt F-206 1000 Vicars Landing Way Ponte Vedra Beach FL 32082-3127

THORNE, BARBARA LOCKWOOD, guidance counselor, secondary education educator; b. Rochester, N.Y., Nov. 12, 1938; d. Harvey J. and Clara (Lee) Lockwood; m. Marc E. Thorne, July 21, 1962; children: John, Andrew. BA, Westminster Coll., 1960; postgrad., Cornell U., 1961; MS, U. Bridgeport, 1987, 6th Yr. Cert., 1991. Cert. tchr., N.Y., counselor, Conn. Tchr. social studies Greece Olympia High Sch., Rochester, N.Y., 1961-63, East High Sch., Rochester, 1963-64; tchr. recreation Fairfield (Conn.) YMCA, 1965-70; tutor, substitute tchr. Needham (Mass.) Alternate High Sch., 1970-78; tchr. social studies Alternate Learning Program Darien (Conn.) High Sch., 1978-88, team leader, 1982-88, guidance counselor, 1988—, coord. student assistance team, 1991—; locat advisor A Better Chance, Darien, 1989—. Chmn. Youth Commn., Darien, 1982-85; mem. Park and Recreation Commn., Darien, 1985-97, chmn., 1991-97;. Recipient Vol. Svc. award Community Coun., Darien, 1977. Mem. ASCD, AAUW, NEA, LWV (pres., bd. dirs. 1975-85, Sears Found. award 1963, Vol. in Govt. award 1993), Assn. Secondary Sch. Adminstrn., Am. Assn. Counseling and Devel., Nat. Coun. Social Studies, New England Assn. Coll. Admission Counseling, Jr. League Stamford/Norwalk. Democrat. Congregationalist. Avocations: reading, tennis, cross-country skiing.

THORNE, DAVID W., lawyer; b. Walla Walla, Wash., Aug. 9, 1945. BA, Wash. State U., 1967; MBA, U. Wash., 1969, JD, 1974. Bar: Wash. 1974. Mem. Davis Wright Tremaine, Seattle. Mem. ABA, Am. Coll. Real Estate Lawyers, Am. Coll. Mortgage Attys., Am. Land Title Assn. Lender Counsel Group, Wash. State Bar Assn. (past mem. exec. com. real property, probate and trust sect., past chmn. 1991-92), Pacific Real Estate Inst. (past pres. 1994, founding trustee 1989-95), Phi Delta Phi. Office: Davis Wright Tremaine 2600 Century Sq 1501 4th Ave Seattle WA 98101-1662

THORNE, FRANCIS, composer; b. Bay Shore, N.Y., June 23, 1922; s. Francis Burritt and Hildegarde (Kobbé) T.; m. Ann Cobb, Dec. 9, 1942; children: Ann Boughton (Mrs. William F. Niles), Wendy Oakleigh (Mrs. William H. Forsyth, Jr.), Candace Kobbé (Mrs. Anthony M. Canton). B.A. in Music Theory, Yale, 1942. Founder, pres. Thorne Music Fund, Inc., 1965-75; pub. Edward B. Marks Music Corp., 1963—, Gen. Music Pub. Co., 1971—, G. Schirmer/AMP, 1985—, Theodore Presser Co., 1989—; exec. dir. Lenox Arts Center, 1972-76, Am. Composers Alliance, 1975-85; co-founder, pres. Am. Composers Orch., 1976—. Composer: Elegy for Orch., 1964, Burlesque Overture, 1966, Lyric Variations for Orch., 1967, Symphony No. 1, 1963, No. II, 1966, No. III, 1970, No. IV, 1977, Fortuna, 1961-62, Liebesrock, 1969, Sonar Plexus, 1969, Six Set-Pieces, 1969, Contra Band Music, 1970, Antiphonies, 1970, Simultaneities, 1971, Quartessence, 1971, Fanfare, Fugue and Funk, 1972, Lyric Variations II, 1972, Piano Sonata, 1972, Lyric Variations III, 1973, Cantata Sauce, 1973, Evensongs, 1973, Cello Concerto, 1974, Piano Concerto, 1974, Violin Concerto, 1975, String Quartet 1, 1960, 2, 1967, 3, 1976, 4, 1983, Spoon River Overture, 1976, Grand Duo, 1976, Five Set Pieces, 1976, Love's Variations, 1976, Pop Partita, 1978, The Eternal Light for Soprano and Orchestra, 1979, Divertimento for Flute, Strings and Percussion, 1979, Lyric Variations IV for Solo Violin, 1980, Divertimento 2 for Bassoon and Stringed Instruments, 1980, Eine Kleine Meyermusik, 1980, Gems From Spoon River, 1980, Lyric Variations No. 6 for solo clarinet, 1981, Divertimento No. 3, 1982, Praise and Thanksgiving, 1983, Lyric Variations No. 5 for Orch., 1980-81, Symphony No. 5, 1984, Concerto Concertante, 1985, Rhapsodic Variations, No. 2, 1985, Humoresque for Orch., 1985, Rhapsodic Variations No. 3 for Oboe and Strings, 1986, The Affirming Flame for Soprano and Chamber Ensemble, 1987; seven simple syncopations for Piano solo, 1987, Rhapsodic Variations No. 4 For Viol Solo, 1987, Rhapsodic Variations No. 5 for Violins and Piano, 1988, Money Matters for Tenor and Chamber Ensemble, 1988, Piano Concerto No. 3, 1989, Remembering Dizzy for Brass Quintet, 1990, Pop Partita No. 2 for woodwinds and strings, 1991, Mario and The Magician, opera after Thomas Mann, in Prologue and 1 Act, 1991, Symphony No. 6 for Strings, 1992, Symphony No. 7 Along the Hudson for chorus and orch., 1994, Cello Concerto No. 2, 1995, Echo for Soprano and Mixed Chorus, 1996, Clarinet Concerto, 1997; recs. on Composers' Recs., Inc., Serenus, Owl, Louisville Opus One and New World; founder, pres. Am. Composers Orch., 1976. Trustee Am. Symphony Orchestra League, Manhattan Sch. Music, Am. Music Center, MacDowell Colony, Walter W. Naumburg Found., Contemporary Music Soc., Theater Devel. Fund, Group for Contemporary Music., Am. Brass Quintet. Served to lt. USNR, 1942-45. Nat. Endowment Arts grantee, 1966, 73; fellow, 1976, 79; Nat. Inst. Arts and Letters grantee, 1968; N.Y. State Arts Council ballet commn., 1973. Mem. AAAL, BMI, Contemporary Music Soc. (bd. dirs.), Am. Composers Alliance, League Composers, Century Assn. Club: Century Assn. (N.Y.C.). Home: 116 E 66th St New York NY 10021-6504 *Having spent ten years as a businessman, I have been privileged to serve my composer colleagues as an administrator for musical organizations. The practical experience has also served me well as a creative artist in having instilled the virtues of discipline. Serving music as composer and administrator gives the highest sense of satisfaction, from participating in this life-giving world in a total comprehensive way.*

THORNE, FRANK LEADLEY, plastic surgeon; b. Rochester, N.Y., 1933. MD, U. Pa., 1957. Diplomate Am. Bd. Plastic and Reconstructive Surgery. Intern U. Mich., Ann Arbor, 1957-58; resident surgery U. Wash., Seattle, 1962-65; resident plastic surgery Duke U., Durham, N.C., 1965-68; surgeon Swedish Hosp., Seattle; clin. prof. plastic surgery U. Wash., Seattle; pres. Am. Assn. Hand Surgery, 1977-78, Plastic Surgery Ednl. Found., 1988-89; gov. ACS, 1990-96; dir. Am. Bd. Plastic Surgery, 1990-96, vice chmn., 1995-96. Fellow Am. Coll. Surgeons; mem. AMA, Am. Assn. Hand Surgeons, Am. Soc. Plastic and Reconstructive Surgery. Office: 1229 Madison St Ste 790 Seattle WA 98104-1381

THORNE, GARY, sports commentator; b. June 9, 1948. BS in Bus., U. Maine, 1970, JD, 1973; LLD, Georgetown U., 1976. Bar: U.S. Supreme Ct. 1977. Former asst. dist. atty. Bangor, Maine; commentator hockey WBGW-AM, WABI-TV & Radio, 1977-86; NY Mets broadcaster WHN-AM, 1985-88; play-by-play NHL telecasts SportsChannel, 1988-92; play-by-play Nat. Hockey Night ESPN, 1992—; play-by-play major league baseball ESPN, 1990-93, Big East NCAA basketball, 1991, host The Sports Reporters, 1988; play-by-play NY Mets WWOR-TV, 1994—, Chgo. White Sox WFLD-TV, 1989—. Office: ESPN ESPN Plaza Bristol CT 06010

THORNE, JOHN REINECKE, business educator, venture capitalist; b. Pitts., Mar. 25, 1926; s. John Mueller and Louise (Reinecke) T.; m. Barbara Siebert, Aug. 31, 1951 (dec. Feb. 1995); children: John S., Barbara L., Richard W. BS, Brown U., 1947; MSEE, U. Pitts., 1949; MS in Indsl. Adminstrn., Carnegie Mellon U., 1952. Devel. engr. Westinghouse Elec. Corp., Pitts., 1947-50; mgr. fin. analysis Hughes Aircraft Co., L.A., 1952-54; dir. computer systems lab. Litton Industries, L.A., 1954-61; chmn., pres. The Scionics Corp., L.A., 1961-69; cons., L.A., 1969-72; prof. bus. Carnegie-Mellon U., Pitts., 1972—, Morgenthaler prof. entrepreneurship, 1987—, dir. Donald H. Jones Ctr. for Entrepreneurship, 1990—; founder, chmn. Enterprise Corp. Pitts., 1983—; gen. ptnr. Pitts. Seed Fund, 1985—; bd. dirs. Orion Capital Corp., other pvt. corps. Contbr. numerous articles on entrepreneurship to profl. jours. Named Fin. Svcs. Adv. of Yr. by SBA, 1988. Mem. Duquesne Club, Rolling Rock Club, University Club. Unitarian. Home: Furnace Run Laughlintown PA 15655 Office: Carnegie-Mellon U Dept of Bus Schenley Park Pittsburgh PA 15213

THORNE, JOHN WATSON, III, advertising and marketing executive; b. Washington, Jan. 16, 1934; s. John Watson, Jr. and Mary Washington (Tucker) T.; m. Joan Kramer Vail, Mar. 2, 1957; children: Vail Tucker, Tracy Tucker, John Watson, IV. BA in Polit. Sci., George Washington U., 1955; MA in Sociology, New Sch. Social Research, 1974. Asst. account exec. Young & Rubicam, Inc., N.Y.C., 1957-59; advt. mgr. Gen. Electric Co., Decatur, Ill., 1959-63; dir. advt. promotion Brand Names Found., N.Y.C., 1963-66; account exec. Tatham-Laird & Kudner (advt.), N.Y.C., 1966-67; v.p., mgmt. supr. Wells, Rich, Greene, Inc., N.Y.C., 1973-76; v.p., account supr. Batten, Barton, Durstine & Osborn, Inc., N.Y.C., 1967-73, sr. v.p., mgmt. supr., 1976-81, exec. v.p., 1981-87, also dir., mem. operating com.; chmn. Thorne & Assocs., Newtown, Pa., 1987—; pres. Telerx Mktg., Spring House, Pa., 1991-95; chmn. Alliance Telemanagement, Inc., Doylestown, Pa., 1995—; mem. bus. program com. Proprietary Assn., Washington, 1984-85; adj. prof. advt. Syracuse (N.Y.) U. Pres. Hastings-on-Hudson (N.Y.) Bd. Edn.; bd. dirs. Young Concert Artists, N.Y.C.; mem. communications coms. Nat. Urban League, Carnegie Hall. Served as 1st lt. USMCR, 1955-57. Mem. Buckingham Racquet Club. Republican. Roman Catholic. Home: 100 Stoneybrook Rd Newtown PA 18940-2506 Office: Alliance Telemgmt Inc 350 S Main St Ste 119 Doylestown PA 18901-4872

THORNE, JOYE HOLLEY, special education administrator; b. Shreveport, La., Jan. 4, 1933; d. Lockett Beecher and A. Irene (McWilliams) Holley; m. Michael S. Thorne, July 24, 1953; 1 child, Michael S. Jr. BS, Centenary Coll., 1954; MEd, U. Houston, 1969, EdD, 1974. Cert. tchr., Tex. Tchr. Aldine Ind. Sch. Dist., Houston, 1959-66, curriculum cons., 1966-69, dir. spl. edn., 1969—; adj. prof. U. Houston, Clear Lake, Tex., 1974-83, U. St. Thomas, Houston, 1993—; spl. edn. specialist Dept. Def. Dependent Schs., Washington, 1983-84. Recipient Pres.'s award Gulf Coast chpt. Coun. Exceptional Children, Austin, Tex., 1980. Mem. Coun. Exceptional Children (pres. Gulf Coast chpt. 1976-77, pres. Tex. fedn. 1982-83, Pres.'s award 1980), Tex. Coun. Adminstrs. Spl. Edn. (pres. 1985-86, Dir. of Yr. award 1993). Republican. Methodist. Avocations: needlework, quilting, travel. Office: Aldine Ind Sch Dist 1617 Lauder Rd Houston TX 77039-3025

THORNE, LAWRENCE GEORGE, allergist, immunologist, pediatrician; b. Beckley, W.Va., Sept. 9, 1933. MD, Duke U., 1958. Diplomate Am. Bd. Allergy and Immunology, Am. Bd. Pediatrics. Intern Naval Hosp., Bethesda, Md., 1958-59, resident in pediatrics, 1960-62; fellow in immunology Tex. Allergy Rsch. Found., Houston, 1972-74; clin. asst. prof. Baylor Coll. Medicine, 1976—; staff mem. Hermann Hosp., Houston, 1980—, Tex. Children's Hosp., Houston, 1987—, St Joseph Hosp., 1990—; group ptnr., pvt. practice. Mem. Am. Acad. Allergy and Immunology, Am. Acad. Pediatrics, Am. Coll. Allergy and Immunology. Office: 4710 Bellairo Blvd #200 Ballaire TX 77401

THORNE, MELVIN QUENTIN, managed healthcare executive; b. Houston, Feb. 23, 1939; s. Melvin Quentin and Ruby Marie (Bauer Kemper) T.; m. Denise D. Brockman, Dec. 1, 1961 (div. Feb. 1980); children: Dana, Lorrie; m. Peggy J. Ray, Oct. 4, 1980. BS, Sam Houston State U., 1961; MS, U. Tex., 1964. Project cons. Tex. Dept. Mental Health & Mental Retardation, Houston, 1974-75; mental health dir. West Tex. Mental Health & Mental Retardation, San Angelo, 1975-76; exec. dir. Multi-County Mental Health, Tullahoma, Tenn., 1976-80; regional adminstr. Home Health-Home Care, Houston, 1980-84; v.p. Nat. Healthcare Alliance, Houston, 1985-86; regional v.p. Admar Corp., Houston, 1986-89; chief operating officer Managed Healthcare, Houston, 1989-91; pres. Nat. Healthcare Alliance, 1991—; pres. PM Publs., Inc., Houston, 1989—; cons. in field. Recipient gov.'s award for vol. svc. State of Tex., 1984. Mem. Am. Assn. Managed Healthcare (legis. commn. 1993—), Nat. Health Leadership Coun., 1991—. Methodist. Avocations: computers, travel, reading. Home: 1811 Crutchfield Katy TX 77449

THORNE, RICHARD MANSERGH, physicist; b. Birmingham, Eng., July 25, 1942; s. Robert George and Dorothy Lena (Goodchild) T.; children: Peter Baring, Michael Thomas, Thomas Mansergh. BSc, Birmingham U., 1963; PhD, MIT, 1968. Grad. asst. M.I.T., 1963-68; asst. prof. dept. atmospheric scis. UCLA, 1968-71, asso. prof., 1971-75, prof., 1975—, chmn. dept., 1976-79; vis. fellow St. Edmunds Coll., Cambridge (Eng.) U., 1986-87, 92; cons. Jet Propulsion Lab., Aerospace Corp. Contbr. articles to profl. jours. Recipient numerous grants NSF, NASA, NATO, Jet Propulsion Lab. Mem. Am. Geophys. Union. Home: 10390 Caribou Ln Los Angeles CA 90077-2809 Office: UCLA Dept Atmospheric Scis Los Angeles CA 90095

THORNELL, JACK RANDOLPH, photographer; b. Vicksburg, Miss., Aug. 29, 1939; s. Benjamin O. and Myrtice (Jones) T.; divorced; children—Candice, Jay Randolph. Ed. pub. schs. Photographer Jackson (Miss.) Daily News, 1960-64; with A.P., 1964—; assigned A.P., Dominican Republic, 1965, Selma, Ala., 1965; assigned Democratic Nat. Conv., 1968. Served with AUS, 1958-60. Recipient Pulitzer prize for news photography of shooting of James Meredith, 1967; Headliners Photography award, 1967. Home: 6815 Madewood Dr Metairie LA 70003-4529 Office: 3800 Howard Ave New Orleans LA 70140-1002

THORNER, JOHN, professional society administrator; b. Great Neck, N.Y.. BA in History and Polit. Sci., Duke U.; MS in Journalism, Columbia U.; JD, U. Ga. Bar: Ga. 1977, Washington 1978, Pa. 1997. Reporter The Washington Post, 1974-77, The AP, N.Y.C., 1974-77, Atlanta Constn., 1974-77; atty. NLRB, Washington, 1978-87; environ. counsel, dir. comm. Am. Paper Inst., Nat. Forest Products Assn., Washington, 1981-88; dir. pub. affairs, gen. counsel Water Environment Fedn., Washington, 1988-94; exec. dir. Air and Waste Mgmt. Assn., Pitts., 1994—. Office: Air and Waste Management Assn One Gateway Ctr 3d Fl Pittsburgh PA 15222

THORNER, MICHAEL OLIVER, medical educator, research center administrator; b. Beaconsfield, Eng., Jan. 14, 1945; came to U.S., 1977; s. Hans and Ilse T.; m. Prudence Maria Ross, July 7, 1966; children—Benjamin Bruno, Anna Rosa. M.B.B.S., Middlesex Hosp., U. London, 1970. Intern, resident Middlesex Hosp., St. Bartholomeo Hosp., London; lectr. in chem. pathology St. Bartholomews Hosp., London, 1974, research fellow, 1974-75, lectr. in medicine, 1975-77; assoc. prof. medicine U. Va., Charlottesville, 1977-82, prof. medicine, 1982—, head div. endocrinology and metabolism, 1986—, dir. Clin. Research Ctr., 1984—, assoc. dir. CRC, 1981-84, Kenneth R. Crispell prof. in internal medicine, 1990—; mem. FDA Endocrinologic and metabolic drugs adv. com., 1984-88, NIH biochem. endocrinology study sect., 1985-89. Contbr. articles to profl. jours. Recipient Albion O. Bernstein award, 1984, Virginia Scientist of Yr. award, 1985, Gen. Clin. Rsch. Ctrs. program award, 1995, The Pituitary Soc. Annual award for contbns. to understanding pituitary disease, 1995. Fellow Royal Coll. Physicians, ACP; mem. Soc. Endocrinology, Endocrine Soc. (Edwin B. Astwood award 1992), Assn. Am. Physicians, Am. Soc. Clin. Investigations. Home: Mount Ammonett 3140 Plank Rd North Garden VA 22959-9639 Office: U Va Hosps Dept Internal Medicine PO Box 511-66 Charlottesville VA 22908-0001

THORNE-THOMSEN, THOMAS, lawyer; b. El Dorado, Kans., Oct. 22, 1949; s. Fletcher and Barbara (Macoubrey) T.-T. BA, Vanderbilt U., 1972; JD, U. Colo., 1976; LLM in Taxation, NYU, 1983. Bar: Colo. 1976, Ga. 1977, Ill. 1983. Law clk. to Chief Judge Alfred A. Arraj U.S. Dist. Ct. Colo., Boulder, 1976-77; assoc. Alston & Bird, Atlanta, 1977-82; assoc., ptnr. Keck, Mahin & Cate, Chgo., 1983-95; ptnr. Schiff, Harden & Waite, Chgo., 1995—. Bd. dirs. Century Place Devel. Corp., Chgo., 1989—, Sutherland Neighborhood Devel. Corp., Chgo., 1989—, South Shore Neighborhood Devel. Crop. Chgo. 1990—, Argyle Neighborhood Devel. Corp., Chgo., 1991—, Heartland Alliance for Human Rights and Human Need, 1995—, Howard Brown Health Ctr., Chgo., 1991-94; com. mem. Chgo.'s Comprehensive Housing Affordability Strategy, Chgo., 1992—; mem. bond leverage trust fund task force Ill. Housing Authority, 1993. Mem. ABA, Colo. State Bar Assn., Ill. State Bar Assn., Ga. State Bar Assn. Avocations: jogging, biking, swimming, boating, horses. Home: 680 N Lake Shore Dr Apt 1110 Chicago IL 60611-4407 Office: Schiff Harden & Waite 7200 Sears Tower Chicago IL 60606-6327

THORNHILL, ARTHUR HORACE, JR., retired book publisher; b. Boston, Jan. 1, 1924; s. Arthur Horace and Mary Josephine (Peterson) T.; m. Dorothy M. Matheis, Oct. 28, 1944; children: Sandra Susanne Thornhill Brushart, Arthur Horace. AB magna cum laude, Princeton U., 1948. With Little, Brown & Co., Inc., Boston, 1948-88; v.p. Little, Brown & Co., Inc., 1955-58, gen. mgr., 1960-87, chief exec. officer, pres., 1962-87, chmn. bd., 1970-87; chmn., pres., dir. Little, Brown & Co. (Can.), Ltd., 1955-84; v.p. Time, Inc., 1968-87; vice chmn. Time-Life Books, Inc., 1976-86; dir. Conrac Corp., 1971-87; mem. adv. council history dept. Princeton U., 1964-85; trustee, treas. Princeton U. Press, 1972-85; dir. Am. Textbook Pubs. Inst., 1965-68, Grosett & Dunlop, 1965-67, Bantam Books, Inc., 1965-67. Trustee Bennington Coll., 1969-76; fellow emeritus Ctr. for Creative Photography U. Ariz.; bd. dirs. Am. Book Pubs. Council, 1964-67. Served to 1st lt. USAAF, World War II. Decorated Air medal; recipient Princeton U. Press medal, 1985. Mem. Assn. Am. Pubs. (dir. 1978-81), Edgartown Yacht Club, Edgartown Reading Room (pres. 1990-92), Union Club (N.Y.C.), Princeton Club (N.Y.C.), Century Club (N.Y.C.), Publs. Lunch Club (N.Y.C.), Union Club (Boston), St. Botolph (Boston). Home: 50 S School St Portsmouth NH 03801-5258

THORNHILL, BARBARA COLE, marketing executive; b. Rahway, N.J., Sept. 4, 1960; d. Clayton Eugene and Margaret (Fitzgerald) Cole; m. Matthew Thomas Thornhill, Oct. 15, 1983 (div. 1996); children: Allison, Clark. BBA in Mktg., Coll. of William and Mary, 1982. Asst. account exec. March Direct/McCann Direct, N.Y.C., 1983-84, account exec., 1984-86, account supr., 1986-87; dir. comml. client divsn. Huntsinger & Jeffer Direct, Richmond, Va., 1987-89; v.p., account supr. The Stenrich Group, Richmond, 1989-90, sr. v.p., dir. account mgmt., 1990-92, exec. v.p., dir. account mgmt., bd. dirs., 1992-95; exec. v.p. for integrated mktg. comm., mem. exec. com. The Martin Agy., Richmond, 1995-96, exec. v.p., chief adminstrv. officer, 1996—; mem. profit sharing com. The Martin Agy., Richmond, 1993—. Exec. com. bd. trustees Richmond Children's Mus., 1992—, dir. bd. trustees, 1991-92; area coord. William and Mary Alum Admissions Network, Richmond, 1988—; co-chair William and Mary Class of 82 Reunion com., 1997; mem. Leadership Metro Richmond Class of 1997; book fair chairperson Mayberry Elem. Sch., 1997; cookie chairperson Brownie Troop #292, Girl Scouts U.S., 1997. Recipient Silver Echo award Direct Mktg. Assn., 1991, 94, Richmond Area Marketer of Yr. award Am. Mktg. Assn., 1992, 93, 94, Gold Effie award, 1992. Mem. Willow Oaks Country Club. Avocations: travel, family, reading, golf. Office: The Martin Agy One Shockoe Plz Richmond VA 23219-4132

THORNLEY, SHIRLEY BLUMBERG, architect; b. Cape Town, South Africa, Feb. 4, 1952; d. Alec and Anne (Minkowitz) Katz; m. Scott; 1 child, Charles R. Attended, U. Cape Town; BArch (with honors), U. Toronto, 1976. Assoc. Barton Myers Assoc., 1977-87; architect Kuwabara Payne McKenna Blumberg Architects; selected projects with present firm include Hasbro Corp. H.Q. Phase R.I., 1994, King James Place Toronto, 1991, The Design Exch., Toronto, 1994, Minn. Culture, Tourism & Recreation Niagara Falls, 1995, Ammirati & Puris/Lintas Offices, N.Y.C., 1995; adj. asst. prof. U. Toronto, 1987, 90; guest critic Carleton U., U. Waterloo; Hyde chair for excellence Coll. of Architecture U. Nebr., Lincoln, 1994; mem. bd. dirs. Royal Arch. Inst. can., 1990-93, mem. bd. trustees Ont. Sci. Ctr., 1988-91. Recipient Toronto Arts award for Architecture & Design, 1993, Gov. Gen.'s award of Merit King James Place, 1992, Gov. Gen.'s award for Architecture Royal Archtl. Inst. Can., 1992. Mem. Ont. Assn. Architects, Royal Arch. Inst. Can. Office: Kuwarbara Payne McKenna Blumberg, 322 King St W 3rd Fl, Toronto, ON Canada M5V 1J2

THORNLEY, WENDY ANN, educator, sculptor; b. Bolton, Lancashire, Eng., Feb. 28, 1948; came to U.S., 1953; d. Ronald Thornley and Joan Gladys (Hancock) Green. BS, So. Conn. State U., 1970, MS, 1979; MA, Wesleyan U., Middletown, Conn., 1991. Cert. tchr., Conn. Tchr. art New Canaan (Conn.) Pub. Schs., 1970-71, Bristol (Conn.) Pub. Schs., 1972—; adj. faculty Naugatuck Valley Cmty.-Tech. Coll., 1993-96; profl. artists residency Oxbow Summer Sch. Art Inst. Chgo., 1994. Exhibited in nat. and regional juried shows, 1978—, including tour Nat. Assn. Women Artists, 1989; commns. include wall relief Reichhold Chem. Co., 1987, Aetna Ins. Co., 1988, Bank of Boston, 1989, Law Office of Halloran, Sage, Phelon and Hagerty, 1990, Pitney-Bowes, Stamford, Pitney-Bowes Corp., 1996. Summer fellow Skidmore Coll., 1986; recipient 1st prize for sculpture Homestead Show, Fairfield, Conn., 1996. Mem. Nat. Art Edn. Assn., Conn. Art Edn. Assn. (Outstanding Secondary Art Educator award 1995), Nat. Assn. Women Artists, Soc. Conn. Crafts (bd. dirs. 1981-88, Best-in-Show award 1982, 84, 91, Best in Fiber award 1990, Master Craftsman award 1994), Conn. Women Artists (Binney & Smith award 1985, First prize sculpture, Homestead, Fairfield 1996), New Eng. Sculptors Assn. Avocations: photography, reading, travel. Home: 97 Summit Rd PO Box 7094 Prospect CT 06712

THORNLOW, CAROLYN, law firm administrator, consultant; b. Kew Gardens, N.Y., May 25, 1954. 1 child, Johanna Louise Ramm. B.B.A. magna cum laude, Bernard M. Baruch Coll., 1982. Gen. mgr. Richard A. Ramm Assocs., Levittown, N.Y., 1972-78; adminstr. Tunstead Schechter & Torre, N.Y.C., 1978-82, Cowan Liebowitz & Latman, P.C., N.Y.C., 1982-84, Rosenberg & Estis, P.C., N.Y.C., 1984-85; controller Finkelstein, Borah, Schwartz, Altschuler & Goldstein, P.C., N.Y.C., 1986-92; pres. Concinnity Services, Hastings, N.Y., 1984—; instr. introduction to law office mgmt. seminars Assn. Legal Adminstrs., N.Y.C., 1984. Editor: The ABA Guide to Profl. Mgrs. in the Law Office, 1996; contbr. numerous articles to profl. jours. Mem. N.Y. Assn. Legal Adminstrs. (v.p. 1982-83), Internat. Assn. Legal Adminstrs. (asst. regional v.p. 1983-84, regional v.p. 1984-85), Nat. Soc. Tax Profls. (cert. tax profl.), Am. Mgmt. Assn., Adminstrv. Mgmt. Soc. (cert.), ABA, Inst. Cert. Mgmt. Accts., Mensa, Beta Gamma Sigma, Sigma Iota Epsilon. Home and Office: 445 Broadway Hastings On Hudson NY 10706

THORNSBERRY, WILLIS LEE, JR., chemist; b. Sturgis, Ky., Aug. 10, 1940; s. Willis Lee and Jane (Hall) T.; m. Mary Elizabeth Gaswint, June 19, 1965; children: Brian, Michele. BS, Murray State U., 1963; MS, U. Ark., 1967; PhD, Tulane U., 1974. Rsch. chemist Freeport-McMoran Inc., Belle Chasse, La., 1967-74, sr. rsch. chemist, 1974-92; pres. Tech. Devel. Svcs. Inc., Sturgis, Ky., 1992-95, 1995—. Contbr. articles to profl. jours. Coach, leader for youth groups Jefferson Parish Playgrounds, Gretna, La., 1970-84, Boy Scouts Am., Gretna, 1975-82. 1st lt. U.S. Army, 1963-65. Mem. Am. Chem. Soc. (sect. chmn. 1969-82), Sigma Xi (nominating com. 1967—). Democrat. Achievements include numerous patents for process for uranium recovery from phosphoric acid, recovery of silica from hydrofluorosilicic acid, stabilization of gypsum for construction purposes, preparation and use of fertilizer additives. Office: Tech Devel Svcs Inc 1024 N Main St Sturgis KY 42459-1245

THORNTON, ANNA VREE, pediatrics and medical-surgical nurse; b. Chgo., June 10, 1936; d. Edward and Elizabeth Vree; m. George Q. Thornton, June 19, 1982. BA in Edn. Psych., Barrington Coll., 1960; postgrad., NYU, 1960-62; ADN., Dutchess C.C., Poughkeepsie, N.Y., 1986. Tchr. Saugerties (N.Y.) Cen. Schs., 1960-64, Kingston (N.Y.) Consolidated Schs., 1964-66, 68-70; owner BeeVer House, Saugerties, 1970-76; ins. agt. Combined Life Ins. Co., Poughkeepsie, N.Y., 1976-82; staff nurse Putnam County Community Hosp., Carmel, N.Y., 1983-86; charge nurse Calloway County Community Hosp., Murray, Ky., 1986—; tchr. U.S. Peace Corps, Nigeria, 1966-68. Pres. Saugerties Busnessmen's Orgn., 1977. Baha'i'. Avocations: travel, reading, gardening. Home: 4563 Kirksey Rd Kirksey KY 42054-9026 Office: Calloway County Comm Hosp 800 Poplar St Murray KY 42071-2566

THORNTON, BILLY BOB, actor, director; b. Hot Springs, Ariz., Aug. 4, 1955. Appeared in films U-Turn, 1997, A Thousand Miles, 1997, A Simple Plan, 1997, Primary Colors, 1997, Homegrown, 1997, The Apostle, 1997, (screen play) For the Boys, 1991, Indecent Proposal, 1993, Tombstone, 1993, Trouble Bound, 1993, Floundering, 1994, On Deadly Ground, 1994, Some Folks Call It a Slingblade, 1994, Don't Look Back, 1996, A Family Thing, 1996; guest appearence (TV episode) Ellen, 1997, (series), Hearts A Fire, 1992; dir., actor, writer, Sling Blade (AA Best Adapted Screen Play). Office: William Morris Agy 151 El Camino Beverly Hills CA 90212

THORNTON, CAMERON MITCHELL, financial planner; b. L.A., Sept. 30, 1954; s. H. Walter and Naomi L. (Brown) T.; m. Jane Kubasak, June 18, 1978; children: Mitchell, Kathryn, Andrew. BA, U. So. Calif., L.A., 1976; MBA, U. La Verne, 1983. CFP. Planner Lockheed Calif. Co., Burbank, 1980-84; adv. assoc. Fin. Network Investment Corp., Burbank, 1983—, fin. cons., 1983—; prin. Cameron Thornton Assocs., Burbank, 1982—; lic. charitable gift planner Renaissance Inc., 1992—. Author: (manual) Computer Aided Planning System, 1982-83. Mem., vice chair St. Joseph Med. Ctr. Found., 1988-92, chmn. planned giving dept., 1991-92; mem., chair Burbank Police Commn., 1981-85, Burbank Planning Commn., 1989-93; with ARC, Burbank, 1984-88, chmn. 1985-87. Lt. comdr. USN/USNR, 1976-88. Named Friend of Campfire, Camp Fire Coun., Pasadena, Calif., 1989, 92. Mem. Nat. Assn. Renaissance Advisors, Inst. CFP's, Internat. Assn. for Fin. Planning, Cert. Fin. Planner Bd. Standards, Burbank C. of C. Republican. Roman Catholic. Avocations: fishing, reading, snow skiing, water skiing. Office: Cameron Thornton Assocs 290 E Verdugo Ave Ste 205 Burbank CA 91502-1342

THORNTON, CHARLES VICTOR, metals executive; b. Salt Lake City, Feb. 8, 1915; s. Charles Victor and Winnie May (Fitts) T.; m. Margaret Louise Wiggins, Apr. 17, 1937; children: Charles Victor III, Carolyn Louise (Mrs. John J. Moorhouse), David Frank. BS in Civil Engring., U. Utah, 1935; HHD, Ind. Inst. Tech., 1972. Registered profl. engr., Ohio, Tex. Engr. Truscon Steel Co., Youngstown, Ohio, 1935-37; dist. engr. Truscon Steel Co., Washington, 1937-40; chief engr. So. Iron Works, Inc., Alexandria, Va., 1940-45; pres. Thornton Industries, Inc., Ft. Worth, 1945-75; chmn. bd. Thornton Industries, Inc., 1975-88; bd. dirs. Bank Commerce and Comml. Fin. Corp. Author: American Association of Private Railroad Car Owners Roster of Private R.R. Cars, 1991, Autobiography, 1993, Charlie, 1994, Winnie, 1994. Chmn. bd. Southview Corp., 1980—, chmn. emeritus Shriners Hosps. for Crippled Children; mem. nat. adv. coun. U. Utah, 1985-96; chmn. investment com. Longhorn coun. Boy Scouts Am., 1985-88; v.p. campaign chmn. Ft. Worth Arts United, 1989; v.p. Tarrant County Arts Coun., 1989; pres. Tarrant County Water Bd., 1984-88; mem. policy com. Dallas-Ft. Worth Railtran, 1991—; pres. Ft. Worth chpt. Internat. Good Neighbor Coun., 1991-92; bd. dirs. Ft. Worth Opera, 1997; mem. Fort Worth Coun. of World Affairs, 1996. Recipient Salesman of Yr. award Ft. Worth Sales and Mktg. Execs., 1984, Good Neighbor of Yr. award Internat. Good Neighbor Coun., 1984, Merit of Honor award U. Utah, 1986; holder airplane speed record Dallas to Wichita, Kans., 1969. Mem. ASCE (life) (Tex. sect. Svc. to People award 1995), Tex. Assn. Bus. (life), Ft. Forth C. of C. (pres. 1960), Am. Assn. Pvt. R.R. Car Owners (pres. 1982-83), Fort Worth Club, City Club, Exch. Club of Fort Worth (past pres.), La Cima Club, Oxford Club, Grand Coun. (Fort Worth chpt. Confrerie Saint Etienne), Masons (33 degree s.r.), Shriners (past imperial potentate), Kiwanis (past pres.), Elks, Tau Beta Pi. Office: PO Box 136397 Fort Worth TX 76136-0397

THORNTON, CLARENCE GOULD, electronics engineering executive; b. Detroit, Aug. 3, 1925; s. Lorenzo C. and Violet (Gould) T.; m. Gloria Fuchs, June 18, 1949; children: Susan Carol, Richard Scott. BS, U. Mich., 1949, MS, 1950, PhD, 1952. Project engr. Sylvania Electric Co., Woburn, Mass., 1951-52; sect. head to dir. Semiconductor div. Philco Corp., Lansdale, Pa., 1952-60; dir. R&D Philco Corp., Blue Bell, Pa., 1960-72; dir. Electronics Technology and Devices Lab., U.S. Army, Fort Monmouth, N.J., 1972-92; directorate exec. Army Rsch. Lab., 1992-95; mem. Commn. on Engring. and Tech. Sys. Bd. on Army Sci. and Tech., Nat. Rsch. Coun., 1995—; sci., tech., bus. cons. 1995—. Contbr. articles to profl. jours. Mem. Colts Neck Bd. Health, 1974-79. Served with USN, 1944-46. Recipient Local Svc. award Boy Scouts Am., 1963, Sci. Conf. award Dept. Army, 1976, Rsch. and Devel. Achievement award, 1976, Lab. of Yr. award, 1980, 83, 88, Lab. Excellence award, 1981, 85, 86, Sr. Exec. award, 1980-93, Gold medal Armed Forces Comms. and Electronics Assn., 1983, Handicapped Adv. Coun. award of achievement, 1985, Exceptional Civilian Svc. medal Dept. Army, 1985, Presdl. Rank award of Meritorious Svc., 1986, Presdl. Rank award of Disting. Sr. Exec., 1987, Crozier award, 1990, Superior Civilian Svc. medal, 1995, Exceptional Civilian Svc. medal, 1995. Fellow IEEE (Centennial medal 1994, Engring. Leadership Recognition award 1994, Joint Logistics Comdrs. award 1994); mem. AAAS, Electrochemical Soc., Am. Chem. Soc., Armed Forces Electronics Assn., Sr. Execs. Assn. (Exec. Achievement award 1994), Am. Defense Preparedness Assn., Alpha Chi Sigma, Phi Kappa Phi, Phi Lambda Upsilon. Mem. Reformed Ch. Patentee in field of electronics. Home: 28 Glenwood Rd Colts Neck NJ 07722-1015 Office: AMSRL-EP Fort Monmouth NJ 07703

THORNTON, D. WHITNEY, II, lawyer; b. Miami, Fla., Oct. 17, 1946; s. Dade Whitney and Hilda (Bryan) T.; m. Jane Collis, Nov. 27, 1971; children: Bryan Whitney, Elizabeth Jane, Virginia Anne. B.A., Washington and Lee U., 1968, J.D., 1970. Bar: Va. 1970, D.C. 1976, Calif. 1987, U.S. Ct. Appeals (4th cir.) 1978, U.S. Ct. Appeals (9th cir.) 1987, U.S. Sup. Ct. 1980. Atty., Naval Air Systems Command, Dept. Navy, Washington, 1970-73; asst. counsel to comptroller Dept. Navy, 1973-74, asst. to gen. counsel, 1974-76; assoc. Sullivan & Beauregard, Washington, 1976-77, ptnr., 1977-81; ptnr. Bowman, Conner, Touhey & Thornton, Washington, 1981-83; pres. Continental Maritime Industries, Inc., San Francisco, 1983-87; ptnr. Dempsey, Bastianelli, Brown & Touhey, San Francisco, 1987-91; ptnr. Seyfarth, Shaw, Fairweather & Geraldson, San Francisco, 1992—. Mem. ABA (public contract law sect.; chmn. suspension and debarment com. 1977), Fed. Bar Assn. (vice chmn. govt. contracts council; Disting. Service award 1981). Republican. Methodist. Clubs: Washington Golf and Country (Arlington, Va.), Blackhawk Country (Danville, Calif.). Contbr. articles to profl. jours. Office: Seyfarth Shaw Fairweather 101 California St Ste 2900 San Francisco CA 94111-5858

THORNTON, DEAN DICKSON, retired airplane company executive; b. Yakima, Wash., Jan. 5, 1929; s. Dean Stoker and Elva Maud (Dickson) T.; m. Joan Madison, Aug. 25, 1956 (div. Apr. 1978); children—Steven, Jane Thornton; m. Mary Shultz, Nov. 25, 1981; children—Volney, Scott, Peter, Todd Richmond. B.S. in Bus., U. Idaho, 1952. C.P.A., Wash. Acct. Touche, Ross & Co., Seattle, 1954-63; treas., controller Boeing Co., Seattle, 1963-70; various exec. positions Boeing Co., 1974-85; pres. Boeing Comml. Airplane Co., 1985-94, retired, 1994; sr. v.p. Wyly Co., Dallas, 1970-74; bd. dirs. Seafirst Corp., Prin. Fin. Group, Flow Internat. Bd. dirs. YMCA, Seattle, 1966-68, Jr. Achievement, Seattle, 1966-68; chmn. Wash. Council on Internat. Trade, Seattle, 1984-87, Seattle Art Mus., 1994-96. 1st lt. USAF, 1952-54. Named to U. Idaho Alumni Hall of Fame. Mem. Phi Gamma Delta. Republican. Presbyterian. Clubs: Rainier, Seattle Tennis, Seattle Yacht, Conquistadores de Cielo. Avocations: skiing; sailing; fishing. Home: 1602 34th Ct W Seattle WA 98199-3906 Office: Boeing Co 7755 E Marginal Way PO Box 3707 Seattle WA 98124-2207

THORNTON, DOROTHY HABERLACH, artist, photographer; b. Tillamook, Oreg., May 20, 1913; d. Carl Emil and Amanda (Tinnerstet) Haberlach; m. Robert Y. Thornton, Mar. 13, 1937; 1 child, Thomas Wells. BA, U. Oreg., 1934; postgrad., George Washington U., 1936-37, Willamette U., 1940-60, U. Mich., 1943. Draftsman USN, Tillamook, 1942-43; pvt. practice Salem, Oreg., 1952—. Editor Jour. Watermark, 1988-91; photographer (books) Images of Oreg. Women, 1983, N.W. Originals, 1987; photographer for 5 TV documentaries on Japan; rsch. photographer Preventing Crime in America & Japan: A Comparative Study, 1992; exhibited in group show Oreg. Women Artists, 1993. Docent, bd. dirs. Portland Art Mus., 1987—, mentor, 1991—; campaign chmn. Robert Thornton for State Atty. Gen., Oreg., 1952-67, Robert Thornton for Ct. Appeals Judge, Oreg., 1968-80; founder, mem. Mid Valley Art Commn., Salem Art Assn. Guides, Salem Assistance League; active Oreg. Commn. for Humanities; pres. Friends of Libr. Willamette U.; pres. Town and Gown, Willamette U., 1996—. Named Art Citizen of Yr., Oreg. Art Commn., 1991. Mem. AAUW (state pres., nat. bd. dirs., v.p. North Pacific Region States, nat. arts com. chmn. 1970-80, Nat. Endowment Rsch. grantee (hon.)), Photog. Soc. Am. (nat. chmn., pub. rels. com. 1985, hon. Assoc. Photo. Soc. of Am. degree), Arts Oreg. Coun. (bd. dirs., past state chmn.), Watercolor Soc. Oreg. (bd. dirs. 1991—), Oreg. UN Assn. (bd. dirs. 1980—, past state pres.), Ikebana Internat., Alpha Phi. Democrat. Episcopalian. Avocations: civic activities, art consulting, tour docent, photography, artist. Home: 2895 Alvarado Ter S Salem OR 97302-5433

THORNTON, ELAINE SERETHA, oncology nurse; b. N.Y.C., Mar. 25, 1967; d. Jerry Richard and Shelia (Beckford) T. BS, Syracuse U., 1990, postgrad. Cert. in gerontology. Staff nruse, clin. nurse I New Rochelle (N.Y.) Hosp. Med. Ctr., 1990-92, staff nurse, clin. nurse II, 1993-96, staff nurse drug and alcohol detoxification unit, 1996—; RN lab. asst. Sch. Nursing Coll. New Rochelle, 1992—; adj. prof. Coll. New Rochelle, Borough Manhattan C.C., N.Y.C., 1985—; vol. Am. Cancer Soc. Vol. Cancer Info. Svc., N.Y.C., 1991-92, Liz Holzman for Senate, N.Y.C., 1992, Clinton/Gore Presdl. campaign, 1992, Dole for Pres. Campaign, 1995; vol.

providing cancer screening, blood pressure screening Pelham (N.Y.) Sr. Ctr., 1992; pub. info. rep. to economically disadvantaged Am. Cancer Soc., bd. dirs. Westchester divsn., 1993-95, 95—, pres. So. unit; organizer 1st & 2d ann. Cmty. Health Fair, New Rochelle. Recipient Orthobiotech. Quality of Life award, Pub. Educator award Westchester divsn. Am. Cancer Soc. Mem. Oncology Nursing Soc. (Hudson Valley chpt., nominating com. 1992-93, treas. 1993-94, pres. elect Hudson Valley chpt. 1995—), Black Nurses Assn., Am. Psychiat. Nurses Assn., Oncology Nursing Soc. (corr.), CTME (nat. membership). Republican. Home: 50 Guion Pl Apt 5K New Rochelle NY 10801-5517

THORNTON, GEORGE WHITELEY, investment company executive; b. York, Pa., Aug. 11, 1936; s. Henry Moser and Virginia (Whiteley) T.; m. Dianne Fay George, Sept. 9, 1961; children: Sandra Whiteley, William Foster. B.A., U. Va., 1958. Asst. to pres. mfg. Dentsply Internat., York, Pa., 1963-69, v.p. mfg., 1969-79, sr. v.p., 1979-85; pres., bd. dirs. Thornton Group Ltd., 1985—; chmn., chief exec. officer Thornton-White Inc., Charleston, S.C., 1986-92; bd. dirs. Dentsply Internat., York, Commonwealth Nat. Bank (York region). Bd. dirs. United Way, York County, 1974-76; exec. com. Nat. Alliance Businessman, York, 1972-73, chmn., York metro, 1974-75; bd. dirs. Pennsylvanians for Right to Work, 1979-81; bd. trustees Right to Work Def. and Edn. Found., 1979-81. Recipient Dirksen Meml. award Pennsylvanians for Right to Work, 1979, Employer of Yr. award. Mem. Country Club of York (Pa.), Delta Phi. Republican. Presbyterian. Home: 1040 Box Hill Ln York PA 17403-4436

THORNTON, J. RONALD, technology center director; b. Fayetteville, Tenn., Aug. 19, 1939; s. James Alanda and Thelma White (McGee) T.; m. Mary Beth Packard, June 14, 1964 (div. Apr. 1975); 1 child, Nancy Carole; m. Martha Klemann, Jan. 23, 1976 (div. Apr. 1982); 1 child, Trey; m. Bernice McKinney, Feb. 14, 1986; 1 child, Paul Leon. BS in Physics & Math., Berry Coll., 1961; MA in Physics, Wake Forest Coll., 1964; postgrad., U. Ala., 1965-66, Rollins Coll., 1970. Research physicist Brown Engring. Co., Huntsville, Ala., 1963-66; sr. staff engr. Martin Marietta Corp., Orlando, Fla., 1966-75; dep. dir. NASA, Washington, 1976-77; exec. asst. Congressman Louis Frey, Jr., Orlando, 1978; pres. Tens Tec, Inc., Orlando, 1978-79; dir. So. Tech. Applications Ctr. U. Fla., Gainesville, 1979—; bd. dirs., treas. North Fla. Tech. Innovation Ctr., 1994—; mem. light wave tech. com. Fla. High Tech. and Indsl. Coun., Tallahassee, 1986-93, NASA Tech. Transfer Exec. Com., Washington, 1987—, Javits Fellowship Bd., Washington, 1986-91, Gov.'s New Product Award Com., Tallahassee, 1988—, Fla. K-12 Math., Sci. and Computer Sci. Edn. Quality Improvement Adv. Coun., 1989-92, Fla. Sci. Edn. Improvement Adv. Com., 1991-92; bd. dirs. Fla.-NASA Bus. Incubation Ctr., mem. bd. dirs., Tech Transfer Soc., 1996. Pres. Orange County Young Rep. Club, Orlando, 1970-71; treas. Fla. Fedn. Young Reps., Orlando, 1971-72; chmn. Fla. Fedn. Young Reps., Orlando, 1972-74; pres. Gainesville Area Innovation Network, 1988-89. Named Engr. Exhibiting Tech. Excellence and Accomplishment cen. Fla. chpt. Fla. Engring. Soc., 1975, Achievement award NASA, 1977. Mem. IEEE, SME, Tech. Transfer Soc. (bd. dirs. 1996—), Nat. Assn. Mgmt. and Tech. Assistance Ctrs. (bd. dirs. 1988, pres. 1992), Gainesville Area C. of C. Republican. Avocations: music, travel, reading. Home: 17829 NW 20th Ave Newberry FL 32669-2143 Office: U Fla So Tech Applications Ctr 1 Progress Blvd Ste 24 Alachua FL 32615-9536

THORNTON, JOHN S., IV, bishop. Bishop Diocese of Idaho, Boise, 1990—. Office: Episcopal Diocese of Idaho Box 936 510 W Washington St Boise ID 83701*

THORNTON, JOSEPH SCOTT, research institute executive, materials scientist; b. Sewickley, Pa., Feb. 6, 1936; s. Joseph Scott and Evelyn (Miller) T.; divorced; children: Joseph Scott III, Chris P. BSME, U. Tex., 1957, PhD, 1969; MSMetE, Carnegie Mellon U., 1962. Engr. Walworth Valve Co., Boston, 1958; metall. engr. Westinghouse Astronuclear Lab., Large, Pa., 1962-64; instr., teaching assoc. U. Tex., Austin, 1964-67; group leader Tracor Inc., Austin, 1967-69, dept. dir., 1973-75; dept. mgr. Horizons Rsch., Inc., Cleve., 1969-73; chmn., chief exec. officer Tex. Rsch. Internat., Inc. (formerly Tex. Rsch. Inst., Inc.), Austin, 1975—. Contbr. numerous tech. papers to profl. publs.; editor: WANL Materials Manual, 2 vols., 1964; patentee in field. Fellow Alcoa, Austin, 1964, RC Baker Found., 1967. Mem. ASME, ASTM, Am. Soc. Metals Internat. (exec. com. 1965-66), Adhesion Soc. Office: Tex Rsch Internat Inc 9063 Bee Caves Rd Austin TX 78733-6201

THORNTON, LARRY LEE, psychotherapist, author, educator; b. Lake, Miss., Nov. 9, 1937; s. Harvey L. and Onzell (Goodson) T.; children: Matt Alan, Leigh Ann. BA, Miss. Coll., 1959; MDiv, New Orleans Bapt. Theol. Sem., 1963, MRE, 1964; MS, U. So. Miss., 1966, PhD, 1969; postgrad., Harvard U., 1985. Dir. admissions Miss. Coll., Clinton, 1961; sr. prof. psychology Delta State U., Cleveland, Miss., 1968—; founder, dir. Lic. Profl. Counseling, Assocs., Cleveland, 1988—; chmn. Miss. Bd. Lic. Profl. Counselors, 1992-93. Author: Insights into Human Development, 1978. Charter mem. Internat. Devel. Coun., Bapt. Theol. Sem., Rûschlikon, Zurich, Switzerland, 1992. Recipient Panhellenic Outstanding Faculty award, 1996, S.E. Kossman Outstanding Tchr. award, 1991. Mem. APA, ACA. Avocations: golf, tennis, jogging. Home: PO Box 11 104 S 4th Ave Cleveland MS 38732

THORNTON, MAURICE, academic administrator; b. Birmingham, Ala., Dec. 31, 1930; s. William Cullen and Alberta (Jones) T.; m. Elizabeth Ann McDonald, Apr. 15, 1961; children: Karen, Susan, Christopher. BS, Ala. State U., 1952; MEd, Cleve. State U., 1973; EdD, Nova-Southeastern U., 1981. Investigative caseworker, supr. title V Cuyahoga County Welfare Dept., Cleve., 1958-67, coord. neighborhood youth corps, asst. dir. pers. dept., 1958-67; equal employment officer, minority recruiter Cuyahoga C.C., Cleve., 1967-82, dir. equal opportunity, 1967-82; dir. affirmative action compliance SUNY, Albany, 1982—; dir. affirmative action program SUNY Sys. Adminstrn., Albany, 1982—; sec. Capital Dist. Human Rights Adv. Com., Albany; N.Y. mid-Hudson coord. Am. Assn. Affirmative Action Officers, Albany; univ. coord. Capital Dist. Black and Puerto Rican Caucus, Albany; participant Leadership Devel. Program, Cleve. and Albany. Contbr. articles to profl. jours. Active NAACP; fundraiser United Negro Coll. Fund., Albany and Cleve., loaned exec. program United Way, Albany and Cleve.; exec. adv. bd. Boy Scouts Am. Scholar State of Ala., State of Ohio. Mem. VA 369th, 100 Black Men (charter), Omega Psi Phi, Sigma Pi Phi (charter). Avocations: walking, reading, golf, traveling, history buff. Home: 7 Keith Rd Delmar NY 12054-4006 Office: SUNY State University Plz Albany NY 12246

THORNTON, RAY, former congressman; b. Conway, AR, July 16, 1928; s. R.H. and Wilma (Stephens) T.; m. Betty Jo Mann, Jan. 27, 1956; children: Nancy, Mary Jo, Stephanie. B.A., Yale, 1950; J.D., U. Ark., 1956. Bar: Ark. 1956, U.S. Supreme Ct 1956. Pvt. practice in Sheridan and Little Rock, 1956-70; atty. gen. Ark., 1971-73; mem. 93d-95th Congresses from 4th Ark. dist.; exec. dir. Quachita Bapt. U./Henderson State U. Joint Ednl. Consortium, Arkadelphia, Ark., 1979-80; pres. Ark. State U., Jonesboro and Beebe, 1980-84, U. Ark. System, Fayetteville, Little Rock, Pine Bluff, Monticello, 1984-89; mem. 102nd-103rd Congresses from 2d Ark. dist., 1991-96; chmn. Ark. Bd. Law Examiners, 1967-70; Del. 7th Ark. Constl. Conv., 1969-70. Chmn. pres.'s devel. council Harding Coll., Searcy, Ark., 1971-73. Served with USN, 1951-54, Korea. Mem. AAAS (chmn. com. on sci., engring. and public policy 1980). Office: PO Box 826 Little Rock AR 72203*

THORNTON, SPENCER P., ophthalmologist, educator; b. West Palm Beach, Fla., Sept. 16, 1929; s. Ray Spencer and Mae (Phillips) T.; m. Annie Glenn Cooper, Oct. 6, 1956; children: Steven Pitts, David Spencer, Ray Cooper, Beth Ellen. BS, Wake Forest Coll., 1951, MD, 1954. Diplomate: Am. Bd. Ophthalmology. Intern Ga. Bapt. Hosp., Atlanta, 1954-55; resident gen. surgery U. Ala. Med. Center, 1955-56; resident ophthalmology Vanderbilt U. Sch. Medicine, 1960-63; practice medicine specializing in ophthalmic surgery Nashville, 1960—; med. dir. Thornton Eye Ctr., 1995—; mem. staff Bapt. Hosp., chief ophthalmology svc., 1982-87; guest prof., vis. lectr. U. Toronto, 1990, 91, 92, U. Paris, 1989, Rothchilds Inst., Paris, 1992, 94, U. Pretoria, 1991, 93, others; instr. Moscow Inst. Eye Microsurgery, 1981; instr. ophthalmic surgery Am. Acad. Ophthalmology Ann. Courses; lectr. lens implant symposiums Eng., Spain, Australia, Switzerland, Can., Sweden, Greece, Germany, France, Republic of South Africa, Japan; Berzelius lectr. U. Lund, Sweden, 1992; P.J. Hay Gold medal lectr., North of Eng. Ophthal. Soc., Scarborough, 1992. King Features syndicated newspaper columnist, 1959-60, feature writer, NBC radio and TV, 1958-60; author, coauthor textbooks on cataract and refractive surgery; mem. editl. bd. Jour. Refractive and Corneal Surgery, Jour. Cataract and Refractive Surgery, Video Jour. Ophthalmology, Ocular Surgery News (Ophthalmologist of Yr. 1996), Ophthalmic Practice (Can.), Eye Care Tech. Mag. (Lifetime Achievement award 1996); contbr. articles to profl. jours.; inventor instruments and devices for refractive and lens implant surgery. Named among Outstanding Young Men of Yr., U.S. Jaycees, 1965; recipient Honor award Can. Implant Assn., 1993, Outstanding Achievement award Bowman Gray Sch. Medicine, 1995. Named 1 of 100 Best Ophthalmologists in Am., Ophthalmology Times mag., 1996. Fellow ACS, Am. Acad. Ophthalmology (Honor award 1995); mem. Am. Soc. Cataract and Refractive Surgery (pres. 1997-99, chmn. internat. com. stds. and quality control for ophthalmic instruments and devices), Am. Med. Soc. Vienna (life), South African Intraocular Implant Soc. (life), Can. Implant Soc. (life), Tenn. Med. Soc., Nashville Acad. Medicine, Internat. Refractive Surgery Club (v.p. 1994), Phi Rho Sigma, Delta Kappa Alpha. Baptist. Home: 5070 Villa Crest Dr Nashville TN 37220-1425 Office: 2010 Church St Nashville TN 37203-2012

THORNTON, THEODORE KEAN, investment advisor; b. St. Louis, June 4, 1949; s. Leonard Frend and Maxine Belle (McKinley) T.; m. Colleen Bridget Purdy, June 23, 1974; children, Theodore McKinley, Alastair Griffin. BA, MBA, Harvard U. Asst. treas. Chase Manhattan Bank, N.Y.C., 1975-79; asst. treas. Colgate-Palmolive Co., N.Y.C., 1979-84, Sperry Corp., N.Y.C., 1984-85; v.p., treas. Household Internat., Prospect Heights, Ill., 1985-87, v.p. investments, 1987-91, pres., 1991—; pres. Marble Corp., 1991-94. Mem. Am. Fin. Assn. Clubs: Harvard (N.Y.C.). Home: 885 Maplewood Rd Lake Forest IL 60045-2415 Office: 225 W Washington St Ste 1650 Chicago IL 60606-3418

THORNTON, THOMAS NOEL, publishing executive; b. Marceline, Mo., Apr. 23, 1950; s. Bernard F. and Helen F. (Kelley) T.; m. Cynthia L. Murray, Nov. 26, 1971; children: T. Zachary, Timothy. B.J., U. Mo., 1972. Asst. to editor Universal Press Syndicate, Kansas City, Mo., 1972; v.p. Universal Press Syndicate, 1974, dir. mktg., 1976; v.p., dir. mktg. Universal Press Syndicate and Andrews & McMeel, Kansas City, 1976-87; pres. Andrews & McMeel, 1987—; bd. dirs. Andrews McMeel Universal. Office: Universal Press Syndicate 4900 Main St Kansas City MO 64112-2630

THORNTON, WAYNE ALLEN, naval officer, engineer; b. Manchester, Conn., Dec. 17, 1952; s. Warren George and Dorothy Marie (Brooks) T. BS in Ocean Engring. with honors, U.S. Naval Acad., 1974; MS in Mech. Engring., Stanford U., 1980; MA in Nat. Security Studies, Georgetown U., 1991; Grad. with highest distinction, Naval War Coll, 1996. Commd. ensign USN, 1974, advanced through grades to capt., 1995; naval liaison officer to U.S. Senate Office of Legis. Affairs, Washington, 1974; elec./reactor controls officer, combat sys. officer USS Barb, San Diego, 1976-79; rsch. asst. Stanford U., 1980-81; engring. officer USS Gurnard, San Diego, 1981-84; engring. officer submarine group five staff San Diego, 1984-86; engring. officer submarine squadron 11 staff USN, San Diego, 1986; exec. officer USS Pollack, San Diego, 1987-88; br. head undersea manpower, staff ACNO for undersea warfare Washington, 1988-91; commanding officer USS Drum, San Diego, 1991-94; Fed. Exec. fellow Hoover Inst., Stanford U., 1994-95; dept. head undersea warfare Office of Naval Intelligence, Washington, 1995—. Mem. ASME, AIAA, Soc. Naval Architects and Marine Engrs., Stanford Alumni Assn., Georgetown Alumni Assn., Porsche Club of Am., Sigma Xi. Avocations: foreign language, foreign travel, scuba diving, underwater photography, skiing. Office: Office of Naval Intelligence ONI-25 4251 Suitland Rd Washington DC 20395

THORNTON, WILLIAM E., mayor, oral surgeon; b. Abilene, Tex., 1945; m. Carolyn Cleveland Giles; children: Kate, Ted. BS in Biology, Trinity U., 1966; DDS, Baylor Coll. Dentistry, 1969; MSD, Baylor U., 1972. Diplomate Am. Bd. Oral and Maxillofacial Surgeons. Clin. prof. U. Tex. Health Sci. Ctr.; chmn. Bexar County Hosp. Dist., 1981-91; mayor San Antonio, 1995—; chmn. bd. dirs. Greater San Antonio C. of C., 1989. Active San Antonio Symphony Soc., Trinity Baptist Ch., Am. Red Cross, United Way, Am. Cancer Soc., Nat. Conf. Christians and Jews. Office: Office of the Mayor PO Box 839966 San Antonio TX 78283*

THORNTON, YVONNE SHIRLEY, physician, author, musician; b. N.Y.C., Nov. 21, 1947; d. Donald E. and Itasker F. (Edmonds) T.; BS in Biology, Monmouth Coll., 1969; MD, Columbia U., 1973; MPH, 1996; m. Shearwood McClelland, June 8, 1974; children: Shearwood III, Kimberly Itaska. Resident in ob-gyn Roosevelt Hosp., N.Y.C., 1973-77; fellow maternal-fetal medicine Columbia-Presbyn. Med. Center, N.Y.C., 1977-79; commd. lt. comdr. M.C., USN, 1979; asst. prof. ob-gyn Uniformed Svcs. U. Health Scis., 1979-82; assoc. prof. Cornell U. Med. Coll., N.Y.C., 1989-92; dir. clin. svcs. dept. ob-gyn N.Y. Hosp.-Cornell Med. Center, 1982-88; asst. attending N.Y. Lying-In Hosp., 1982-89; assoc. clin. prof. ob-gyn Columbia U., 1995—; dir. Chorionic Villus Sampling Program, 1984-92; dir. perinatal diagnostic testing ctr. Morristown Meml. Hosp., 1992—; staff Nat. Naval Med. Center, Bethesda, Md.; saxophonist Thornton Sisters ensemble, 1955-76.; vis. assoc. physician The Rockefeller U. Hosp., 1986-96. Author: The Ditchdigger's Daughters, 1995, (named best books for young adults ALA, Excellence in Lit. award, N.J. Edn. Assn.) Primary Care for the Obstetrician and Gynecologist, 1997, Woman to Woman, 1997. Diplomate Am. Bd. Ob-Gyn, Nat. Bd. Med. Examiners; Excellence in Literature award, N.J. Edn. Assn., 1996, winner Daniel Webster Oratorical Competition, Internat. Platform Assn., 1996. Fellow ACS, Am. Coll. Obstetricians and Gynecologists; mem. AMA, N.Y. Acad. Medicine, Am. Soc. Human Genetics, Assn. Women Surgeons, Soc. Perinatal Obstetricians, Am. Fedn. Musicians. Am. Coll. Physician Exec., Democrat. Baptist. Office: 100 Madison Ave Morristown NJ 07960-6013

THORON, GRAY, lawyer, educator; b. Danvers, Mass., July 14, 1916; s. Ward and Louisa Chapin (Hooper) T.;m. Pattie Porter Holmes, Dec. 30, 1971; children by previous marriage: Claire, Louisa, Grenville C., Molly D., Thomas G. AB, Harvard U., 1938, LLB, 1941. Bar: N.Y. 1942. Assoc. Sullivan & Cromwell, N.Y.C., 1941-42, 45-48; assoc. prof. law U. Tex., 1948-50, prof., 1950-56; dean Law Sch., Cornell U., Ithaca, N.Y., 1956-63, prof. law, 1956-87, prof. emeritus 1987—; vis. prof. law summers U. Mich., 1951, U. Tex., 1970; mem. faculty Salzburg Seminar in Am. Studies, summer 1959; asst. to solicitor gen. Dept. Justice, Washington, 1954-56; mem. N.Y. State Laporte Legis. Ethics Com., 1964; spl. asst. atty. gen. N.Y. State, 1965. Del. Rep. Nat. Conv., 1952; trustee Concord Acad., 1958-61. Served with inf. AUS, 1942-45. Decorated Silver Star, Bronze Star, Purple Heart with oak leaf cluster. Fellow Am. Bar Found. (life); mem. Am. Law Inst. (life), Am. Judicature Soc., ABA, N.Y. State Bar Assn. (chmn. spl. com. to rev. code of profl. responsibility 1974-77, mem. com. profl. ethics 1965-87, vice chmn. 1973-83, emeritus 1987—), Am. Arbitration Assn. (arbitrator 1965—), Assn. Bar City N.Y., Lawyers Com. for Civil Rights Under Law (trustee 1965-97), Phi Alpha Delta, Phi Kappa Phi. Clubs: Century Assn., Harvard (N.Y.C.). Office: Cornell U Law Sch Myron Taylor Hall Ithaca NY 14853

THORP, BENJAMIN A., III, paper manufacturing company executive; b. Albany, N.Y., May 31, 1938; s. Benjamin A. Jr. and Anna C. (Head) T.; m. Barbara Sue Telloch, Aug. 1, 1964 (div. Mar. 1986); 1 child, Benjamin A. IV; m. Laurie Diane Murdock, Oct. 25, 1987. Student in elec. engring., Rensselaer Poly. Inst., 1956-61, postgrad. in mgmt., 1967-68; BS in Physics, U. Md., 1964; postgrad. in engring., U. Bridgeport, 1966; postgrad. in mktg., U. Tenn., 1970. Product devel. mgr. Huyck Formex div. Huyck, Greenville, Tenn., 1969-71, mktg. mgr., 1971-73, v.p., gen. mgr., 1973-75; v.p., gen. mgr. Huytech Systems div., Wake Forest, N.C., 1975-78; v.p., dir. research Huyck Corp., Rensselaer, N.Y., 1978-80; pres. Benjamin A. Thorp Inc., Albany, 1980-82, POYRY-BEK Inc., Raleigh, N.C., 1982-84; v.p. engring. BE&K Inc., Birmingham, Ala., 1984-85, James River Corp., Richmond, Va., 1984-95; v.p. mfg. tech. Chesapeake Corp., richmond, Va., 1996—; mem. exec. com. Pulp and Paper Found. Bd., Ga. Inst. Tech., 1991-95, pres., 1993-95. Tech. editor Paper Machine Operations, Vol. 7, 3d edit., 1991; contbr. over 50 articles to profl. jours.; patentee in field. Bd. dirs. Richmond Math. and Sci. Ctr., 1987-93, Sic. Mus. of Va. Found., 1989—; chmn. papermaking project adv. com. Inst. Paper Sci. and Tech., 1990-94. Fellow TAPPI (chmn. appermakers com. 1984-86, vice chmn. paper and bd. divsn. 1988-90, chmn. 1990-92, bd. dirs. Leadership award 1994); mem. Paper Industry Mgmt. Assn. (pres. 1996—), Exptl. Aircraft Assn., Meadowbrook Estate Civic Assn. (bd. dirs. 1996—). Presbyterian. Office: Chesapeake Corp PO Box 2350 Richmond VA 23218-2350

THORP, JAMES SHELBY, electrical engineering educator; b. Kansas City, Mo., Feb. 7, 1937; s. Joseph Chester and Ruth Vefe (McNamara) T.; m. Barbara Anne Curit, June 27, 1959 (div. July 1976); children: Jeffrey Barton, Elizabeth Anne; m. Christine Annette Moore, Aug. 10, 1980 (div. 1995); children: Gregory, William. BEE, Cornell U., 1959, MS, 1961, PhD, 1962. Asst. prof. Cornell U., Ithaca, N.Y., 1962-66, assoc. prof., 1966-75, prof., 1975—, assoc. dir. Sch. Elec. Engring., 1991-94, dir. Sch. Elec. Engring., 1994—; faculty intern Am. Electric Power Svc. Corp., N.Y.C., 1976-77; Charles N. Mellowes prof. engring., 1994—; fellow Churchill Coll., U. Cambridge, Eng., 1988—; cons. Am. Electric Power Svc. Corp., 1977-83, Dowty Control Techs., Boonton, N.J., 1988—. Author: Computer Relaying for Power Systems, 1988; contbr. chpts. to books, articles to profl. jours. Fellow IEEE, Nat. Acad. Engring. Avocation: golf. Office: Cornell Univ Phillips Hall Ithaca NY 14853

THORPE, DOUGLAS L., lawyer; b. Wahoo, Nebr., Jan. 25, 1937. BSCE, U. Nebr., 1959; JD cum laude, So. Meth. U., 1968. Bar: Calif. 1969. Mem. Perkins Coie, L.A.; bd. dirs. Pub. Counsel, 1980-83. Mem. ABA (antitrust law sect., corp., banking and bus. law sect., litigation sect., econs. of law practice sect.), State Bar Calif., L.A. County Bar Assn. (del. to State Bar Conf. of Dels. 1981, 1983-84, exec. com. antitrust law sect. 1981-83), Century City Bar Assn. (bd. govs. 1982-85), Order of the Coif, Barristers, Phi Delta Phi, Sigma Tau, Tau Beta Pi, Chi Epsilon. Office: Perkins Coie 1999 Ave Of Stars Fl 9 Los Angeles CA 90067-6022

THORPE, JAMES, humanities researcher; b. Aiken, S.C., Aug. 17, 1915; s. J. Ernest and Ruby (Holloway) T.; m. Elizabeth McLean Daniells, July 19, 1941; children: John D., Sally Jans-Thorpe. A.B., The Citadel, 1936, LL.D., 1971; M.A., U. N.C., 1937; Ph.D., Harvard U., 1941; Litt.D., Occidental Coll., 1968; L.H.D., Claremont Grad. Sch., 1968; H.H.D., U. Toledo, 1977. Instr. to prof. English Princeton, 1946-66; dir. Huntington Libr., Art Gallery and Bot. Gardens, San Marino, Calif., 1966-83; sr. research assoc. Huntington Libr., San Marino, Calif., 1966—. Author: Bibliography of the Writings of George Lyman Kittredge, 1948, Milton Criticism, 1950, Rochester's Poems on Several Occasions, 1950, Poems of Sir George Etherege, 1963, Aims and Methods of Scholarship, 1963, 70, Literary Scholarship, 1964, Relations of Literary Study, 1967, Bunyan's Grace Abounding and Pilgrim's Progress, 1969, Principles of Textual Criticism, 1972, 2d edit., 1979, Use of Manuscripts in Literary Research, 1974, 2d edit., 1979, Gifts of Genius, 1980, A Word to the Wise, 1982, John Milton: The Inner Life, 1983, The Sense of Style: Reading English Prose, 1987, Henry Edwards Huntington: A Biography, 1994, H.E. Huntington: A Short Biography, 1996, A Pleasure of Proverbs, 1996. Served to col. USAAF, 1941-46. Decorated Bronze Star medal.; Guggenheim fellow, 1949-50, 65-66. Fellow Am. Acad. Arts and Scis., Am. Philos. Soc.; mem. MLA, Am. Antiquarian Soc., Soc. for Textual Scholarship. Democrat. Episcopalian. Clubs: Zamorano, Twilight. Home: 1199 Arden Rd Pasadena CA 91106-4143 Office: Huntington Libr San Marino CA 91108

THORPE, LEON FERBER, real estate investment company executive; b. Pitts., May 29, 1940; s. Benjamin and Freda (Ferber) T.; m. Suzanne Rosenthal (div. 1972); children: Joshua Ferber, David Lewis; m. Robin C. Thorpe, 1995. AB, Harvard U., 1961, LLB, 1964. V.p. B. Thorpe & Co., Pitts., 1966-69; pres. Leon Thorpe Realty Co., Pitts., 1969—, Thor Parking Corp., Pitts., 1992—. Mem. com. univ. resources Harvard U., Cambridge, 1983-85; bd. dirs. Chatham Coll., Pitts., 1985-88, investment com. United Jewish Fedn. Western Pa., 1992—; mem. vis. com. Coll. of Harvard U., 1987-92. Mem. Nat. Parking Assn. (bd. dirs. 1978-82, 91-92). Avocations: exercise, travel, piano, reading. Office: Leon Thorpe Realty Co 818 Liberty Ave Pittsburgh PA 15222-3707

THORPE, OTIS HENRY, professional basketball player; b. Boynton Beach, Fla., Aug. 5, 1962. Student, U. Providence. Basketball player Kansas City Kings, 1984-85, Sacramento Kings (formerly Kansas City), 1985-88, Houston Rockets, 1988-94, Portland Trail Blazers, 1994—, now with Detroit Pistons. Mem. NBA championship team 1994. NBA All-Star, 1992. Address: Detroit Pistons Two Championship Dr Auburn Hills MI 48326*

THORSEN, JAMES HUGH, aviation director, airport manager; b. Evanston, Ill., Feb. 5, 1943; s. Chester A. and Mary Jane (Currie) T.; m. Nancy Dain, May 30, 1980. BA, Ripon Coll., 1965. FAA cert. comml. pilot, flight instr. airplanes and instruments. Mem. Am. Assn. Airport Execs. (pres. N.W. chpt.), Rotary (Idaho Falls West club), Mensa, Quiet Birdmen, Sigma Alpha Epsilon. Home: 334 Westmoreland Dr Idaho Falls ID 83402 Office: Mcpl Airport Idaho Falls ID 83402

THORSEN, MARIE KRISTIN, radiologist, educator; b. Milw., Aug. 1, 1947; d. Charles Christian and Margaret Josephine (Little) T.; m. James Lawrence Troy, Jan. 7, 1978; children: Katherine Marie, Megan Elizabeth. B.A., U. Wis., 1969; M.B.A., George Washington U., 1971; M.D., Columbia U., 1977. Diplomate Am. Bd. Radiology. Intern, Columbia-Presbyn. Med. Ctr., N.Y.C., 1977-78, resident dept. radiology, 1978-81; fellow computed body tomography Med. Coll. Wis., Milw., 1981-82; asst. prof. radiology, 1982-87, assoc. prof., 1987-94, prof., 1994—; dir. mammography Waukesha Meml. Hosp. Contbr. articles to profl. jours. Mem. Am. Coll. Radiology, Radiol. Soc. N.Am.

THORSEN, NANCY DAIN, real estate broker; b. Edwardsville, Ill., June 23, 1944; d. Clifford Earl and Suzanne Eleanor (Kribs) Dain; m. David Massie, 1968 (div. 1975); 1 child, Suzanne Dain Massie; m. James Hugh Thorsen, May 30, 1980. BSc in Mktg., So. Ill. U., 1968, MSc in Bus. Edn., 1975; grad. Realtor Inst., Idaho, 1983. Cert. resdl. and investment specialist, fin. instr.; Designated Real Estate Instr. State of Idaho; accredited buyer rep. Personnel officer J.H. Little & Co. Ltd., London, 1969-72; instr. in bus. edn. Spl. Sch. Dist. St. Louis, 1974-77; mgr. mktg./ops. Isis Foods, Inc., St. Louis, 1978-80; asst. mgr. store Stix, Baer & Fuller, St. Louis, 1980; assoc. broker Century 21 Sayer Realty, Inc., Idaho Falls, Idaho, 1981-88, RE/MAX Homestead Realty, 1989—; speaker RE/MAX Internat. Conv., 1990, 94, RE/MAX Stars Cruise, 1993, RE/MAX Pacific N.W. Conv., 1994, Century 21 Austral-Asia, 1995, women's seminar Clemson U., 1996; real estate fin. instr. State of Idaho Real Estate Commn., 1994; founder Nancy Thorsen Seminars, 1995. Bd. dirs. Idaho Vol., Boise, 1981-84, Idaho Falls Symphony, 1982; pres. Friends of Idaho Falls Libr., 1981-83; chmn. Idaho Falls Mayor's Com. for Vol. Coordination, 1981-84; power leader Power Program, 1995; cmty. gifts chair ARC. Recipient Idaho Gov.'s award, 1982, cert. appreciation City of Idaho Falls/Mayor Campbell, 1982, 87, Civitan Disting. Pres. award, 1990; named to Two Million Dollar Club, Three Million Dollar Club, 1987, 88, Four Million Dollar Club, 1989, 90, Top Investment Sales Person for Eastern Idaho, 1985, Realtor of Yr. Idaho Falls Bd. Realtors, 1990, Outstanding Realtors Active in Politics, Mem. of Yr. Idaho Assn. Realtors, 1991, Women of Yr. Am. Biog. Inst., 1991, Profiles of Top Prodrs. award Real Estate Edn. Assn.; named Western Region Power Leader, Darryl Davis Seminars. Mem. Nat. Spkrs. Assn., Idaho Falls Bd. Realtors (chmn. orientation 1982-83, chmn. edn. 1983, chmn. legis. com. 1989, 95—, chmn. program com. 1990, 91), Idaho Assn. Realtors (pres. Million Dollar Club 1988—, edn. com. 1990-93), So. Ill. U. Alumni Assn., Idaho Falls C. of C., Newcomers Club, Civitan (pres. Idaho Falls chpt. 1988-89, Civitan of Yr. 1986, 87, outstanding pres. award 1990), Real Estate Educators Assn. Office: RE/MAX Homestead Inc 1301 E 17th St Ste 1 Idaho Falls ID 83404-6273

THORSON, CONNIE CAPERS, library educator; b. Dallas, July 25, 1940; d. Ewing Ashby and Constance (Romberg) Capers; m. James Llewellyn, June 6, 1970. BA, U. Ark., 1962, MA, 1964; PhD, U. N.Mex., 1970; MS in Library Sci., U. Ill., 1977. Instr. English S.E. Mo. State U., Cape Girardeau, 1963-67; with U. N.Mex., Albuquerque, 1970-71, 79—, acquistitions libr., 1980-94, head reference, 1994-95, assoc. prof. libr., 1984-90, prof., 1990-95; prof., libr. dir. Allegheny Coll., Meadville, Pa., 1995—. Editor: A Million Stars, 1981, Pocket Companion for Oxford, 1989. Mem. South Cen. Soc. for 18th Century Studies (pres. elect 1988-89, pres. 1989-90), Modern Lang.

Assn. Am., Am. Soc. for 18th Century Studies, ALA. Avocations: traveling, reading, walking. Office: Allegheny Coll Pelletier Libr Meadville PA 16335

THORSON, JAMES LLEWELLYN, English language educator; b. Yankton, S.D., Jan. 7, 1934; s. James Albert and Doris Reece (Burgi) T.; m. Barbara Gay Jelgerhuis, Sept. 6, 1957 (div. 1970); m. Connie Capers, June 6, 1970. BS in Edn., U. Nebr., 1956, MA, 1961; PhD, Cornell U., 1966; MA (hon.), Oxford (Eng.) U., 1976. Instr. English U. Nebr., Lincoln, 1961-62; asst. prof. U. N.Mex., Albuquerque, 1965-70; assoc. prof. U. N.Mex., 1970-84; vis. prof. U. Kiril i Metodij, Skopje, Yugoslavia, 1971-72, U. Wurzburg, Wurzburg, Fed. Republic of Germany, 1983; prof. English U. N.Mex., Albuquerque, 1984—; vis. prof. U. Munster, Munster, Fed. Republic of Germany, 1985-86, 92-93; lectr. USIA, Yugoslavia, Switzerland, Denmark, Czechoslovakia, Fed. Republic of Germany, Eng., Belgium, 1971, 85, 93, 95. Editor: Yugoslav Perspectives on American Literature, 1980, Humphry Clinker, 1983, Thomas D'Urfey, Butler's Ghost, 1984, (with Connie Thorson) A Pocket Companion for Oxford, 1988. Lt. USN, 1956-59. Fulbright professorship Skopje, 1971-72, Munster, 1985-86. Mem. MLA, AAUP (pres. U. N.Mex. chpt. 1968-70, mem. nat. coun. 1995—), Old Mems. Jesus Coll. Oxford, Am. Soc. for Eighteenth-Century Studies (patron), Wig and Pen Club (London). Democrat. Avocations: travel, skiing. Home: 1331 Park Ave SW Apt 412 Albuquerque NM 87102-2851 Office: U New Mexico Dept English Albuquerque NM 87131

THORSON, JOHN MARTIN, JR., electrical engineer, consultant; b. Armstrong, Iowa, Dec. 16, 1929; s. John Martin and Hazel Marguerite (Martin) T.; m. Geraldine Carol Moran, Apr. 21, 1956 (dec. 1975); children—John Robert, James Michael; m. Lee Houk, Sept. 24, 1977. B.S.E.E., Iowa State U., 1951. Transmission engr. No. States Power Co., Mpls., 1953-58, system operation relay engr., 1962-74; telephone engr. No. States Power Co., Minot, N.D., 1958-62; utility industry mktg. mgr. Control Data Corp., Mpls., 1974-77, product/program mgr. utilities, 1977-84, sr. cons. energy mgmt. systems, 1984-90; pres. Thorson Engrs., Inc., Chanhassen, Minn., 1991—; inductive coordination cons. SNC Corp., Oshkosh, Wis., 1985—; tech. cons. Power Technologies, Inc., Schenectady, N.Y., 1991—, Control Corp., Osseo, Minn., 1992-93, Control Data, Plymouth, Minn., 1991-92, Hathaway, Denver, 1992-93, Scottish Hydro-Electric, PLC, Perth, Scotland, 1992—, NRG Energy Inc., Mpls., 1993—, Stanford Rsch. Inst., 1995—, Univ. Online, Inc., 1995—, GE, 1996—. Contbr. tech. papers to profl. jours. Dist. commr. Boy Scouts Am., Minn., 1954-58, 64-65, coun. commr. N.D., Mont., 1959-62; mem. coun. St. Philip Luth. Ch., Wayzata, Minn., 1968-69; county del. Rep. Com., Chanhassen, Minn., 1980-82. 1st lt. USAF, 1951-53. Recipient Alumni Service award Iowa State U., 1972. Fellow IEEE (life mem., bd. dirs. 1981-82, dir. region 4, 1981-82, mem. U.S. activities bd. 1981-82, regional activities bd. 1981-82, Centennial medal 1984); mem. Internat. Conf. on Large High Voltage Electric Sys., Iowa State U. Alumni Assn. (v.p., pres. 1963-66). Republican. Avocations: canoeing; back packing; mountain climbing. Home and Office: 7320 Longview Cir Chanhassen MN 55317-7905

THORSON, LEE A., lawyer; b. Seattle, Nov. 10, 1949; s. Theodore Arthur and Irene Mary (Dakers) T.; m. Elizabeth Clayton Hay, June 7, 1975; children: Kirk Hunter, Alex Peter. BA, U. Wash., 1971; JD, U. Pacific, Sacramento, 1975; LLM Taxation, Boston U., 1976. Atty. Dahlgren & Dauenhauer P.S., Seattle, 1976-79, Lane Powell Spears Lubersky, Seattle, 1980-93; shareholder Birmingham Thorson & Barnett, P.C., 1993—; affiliate prof. U. Wash. Grad. Program in Taxation, 1995—. Mem. ABA (health law forum), Internat. Found. Employee Benefits, Employee Benefits and Health Law coms., Wash. State Bar Assn. Avocations: bicycling, skiing. Office: Birmingham Thorson Barnett 601 Union St Ste 3315 Seattle WA 98101-2327

THORSON, OSWALD HAGEN, architect; b. Forest City, Iowa, Dec. 19, 1912; s. Thorwald and Josephine (Hagen) T.; m. Maxine Rustad, Dec. 27, 1941; children: Sigrin, Thorwald. BArch, U. Minn., 1937. Registered architect, Iowa. Ptnr. Thorson & Thorson, Forest City, 1939-52, Thorson & Brom, Forest City, 1952-65, Thorson Brom Broshar Snyder, Waterloo, Iowa, 1965-79, ret. Fellow AIA (nat. sec. 1965-67, Lifetime Achievemnt award Iowa chpt. 1982). Democrat. Home: 919 N Barfield Dr Marco Island FL 34145-2348

THORSON-HOUCK, JANICE HARGREAVES, speech, language pathologist; b. Birmingham, Ala., Oct. 22, 1943; d. Harold Trevelyn and Johnnie Lou (Phillips) Hargreaves; m. William Gerald Thorson, July 4, 1974 (dec. 1984); children: Alice, William, Laura, Elizabeth, Ronald, John; m. Lawrence Clifton Houck, June 25, 1994. BA in Speech/Lang. Pathology, U. Ala., 1969, MA, 1974. Cert. speech/lang. pathologist. Speech/lang. pathologist S.E. Ala. Rehab. Ctr., Dothan, 1969-71, Birmingham City Schs., 1974-90, Midfield (Ala.) City Schs., 1990-95, Birmingham City Schs., 1995—. Cub scout den leader Boy Scouts Am., Birmingham, 1978-79; trustee Nat. Reye's Syndrome Found., Bryan, Ohio, 1985—, nat. sec., 1983-84, pres. Ala. region, 1981-85. Recipient John Dieckman Disting. Svc. award Nat. Reye's Syndrome Found., 1986. Mem. Am. Speech-Lang.-Hearing Assn., Speech and Hearing Assn. Ala. (chair sch. affairs com. 1991-95, Cert. of Appreciation 1986, 90), Pub. Sch. Caucus (sec. 1993-94), Phi Beta Kappa, Delta Kappa Gamma (2d v.p. 1994-96, sec. 1996—). Presbyterian. Avocations: handcrafts, water sports, boating. Home: 3905 Rock Creek Dr Birmingham AL 35223-1683 Office: Birmingham Pub Schs 417 29th St S Birmingham AL 35233-2823

THORSTEINSSON, GUDNI, physiatrist; b. Vestmannaeyjar, Iceland, Aug. 5, 1941; came to U.S., 1971; s. Thorsteinn and Asdis Gudbjörg Einarsson; m. Elin Klein, Apr. 10, 1965; children: Arnar Karl, Asdis Thora. BS, Reykjavik (Iceland) Coll., 1961; candidatus med. et chirurg., U. Iceland, Reykjavik, 1968; MS, U. Minn., 1976. Diplomate Am. Bd. Phys. Medicine and Rehab. Dist physician Icelandic Govt., Djupivogur, 1970-71; resident dept. phys. medicine and rehab. Mayo Found., Rochester, Minn., 1972-75, mem. consulting staff, 1975-80; chair dept. Nat. Hosp., Reykjavik, 1980-81; dir. rehab. Mayo Clinic/St. Mary's Hosp., Rochester, 1981-85; dir. outpatient rehab. Mayo Clinic, Rochester, 1985-88, chair dept., 1987-91; chair dept. phys. medicine and rehab. Mayo Clinic, Jacksonville, Fla., 1991—; physiatrist cons. Mayo Clinic, Rochester, 81-91, Jacksonville, 1991—. Author: (with others) Therapeutic Electricity and Ultraviolet, 1983. Mem. AMA, Am. Acad. Phys. Medicine and Rehab., Am. Acad. Pain Medicine, Fla. Med. Assn., Fla. Soc. Phys. Medicine and Rehab. Office: Mayo Clinic Jacksonville 4500 San Pablo Rd S Jacksonville FL 32224-1865

THORSTEINSSON, RAYMOND, geology research scientist; b. Wynyard, Sask., Can., Jan. 21, 1921; m. Jean Kristjansson, Dec. 23, 1944; children: Eirikur, Anna Ingrid. BA, U. Sask., 1944; MA, U. Toronto, Can., 1950; PhD, U. Kans., 1955. Rsch. scientist Geol. Survey of Can., Calgary, 1952-92, emeritus rsch. sci., 1992—. Contbr. articles, bulletins and papers to various jours. Decorated officer Order of Can.; recipient Founders medal Royal Geog. Soc., London, 1968, Outstanding Achievement in Sci. award Govt. Province of Alta., 1973, Massey medal Royal Can. Geog. Soc., 1981, Commemorative medal 125th Anniversary Can. Confedn., 1992, Massey medal, 1981, R.J.W. Douglas medal Can. Soc. Petroleum Geologists, 1982, Gold medal Sci. Profl. Inst. Pub. Svc. Can., 1987. Fellow Arctic Inst. N.Am., The Royal Soc. Can. (Willet G. Miller medal 1973), Geol. Assn. Can. (Logan medal 1979). Office: Geol Survey Can, 3303 33 St NW, Calgary, AB Canada T2L 2A7

THORSTENBERG, (JOHN) LAURENCE, oboe and English horn player; b. Salt Lake City, Dec. 6, 1925; s. Laurence Nathaniel and Alys Josephine (Blomquist) T. MusB, Curtis Inst. Music, Phila., 1951. Instrumental tchr., 1975-96, New Eng. Conservatory, Boston U., 1980-96; mem. Symphony Orch. Balt., 1951-52, Dallas Symphony Orch., 1952-54, Chgo. Symphony Orch., 1954-63, Boston Symphony Orch., 1964-93; appeared summers, Marlboro (Vt.) Music Festival, 1952-54. Served with U.S. Army, 1944-46, ETO. Mem. Internat. Conf. Symphony and Opera Musicians (emeritus).

THOTTUPURAM, KURIAN CHERIAN, priest, college director, educator; b. Cherianad, Kerala, India; came to U.S., 1971; s. Cherian Koruth and Eliamma (Kandanavila) T.; m. Susan Grace Kompady, Dec. 29, 1969; children: Cherian, Kurian Jr., Theodore-George. BA, St. Joseph's Coll., India, 1964; grad. diploma in theology, Sem. of Lateran U., 1966; MA, Karnatak U., 1970, Mundelein Coll., Chgo., 1973; MEd, Loyola U., Chgo., 1979, PhD, 1981; DD, Notre Dame de Lafayette U., 1993. Ordained subdeacon, 1967, deacon, 1970, priest, 1970, chorbishop, 1986. Tchr. Mt. Tabor - St. Stephen's Monastery Coll., Pathanapuram, India, 1966-70; founder Malankarese Orthodox Syrian Ch., Chgo., 1971—; pastor St. John's Syrian Orthodox Ch., 1971-72; founder, pastor St. Thomas Orthodox Ch., 1972-80, St. Mary's Orthodox Ch., 1982—; counseling psychologist Incentives Inst., Des Plaines, Ill., 1974-76; dir. social svc. Millardogden Ctr., Chgo., 1976-77; ednl. adminstr. ednl. program Chgo. Housing Authority, 1977-81; ecumenical officer Malankarese Orthodox Diocese, Chgo., 1981-85; dir. program planning and devel. Malcolm X Coll., Chgo. City Coll. System, 1985-91; english faculty Truman Coll., 1991-92; exec. dir. International Edn. Cons. and Evaluators of Ill., 1992; dir. curriculum/instrn. S.E.A. Ctr., 1993-94; mem. philosophy faculty Daley Coll., 1993-95, Triton Coll., 1995—; pioneer Malankarese Orthodox Chs., 1971-81; adj. prof. philosophy Coll. of Lake County, 1995-96; pres. Am. Acad. Comparative-Internat. Edn., Chgo., 1993—; mem. Sch. Bd. Coun., 1991-93. Tuthor: Dhyanamitram, 1966, Kalari, 1967, Perumpepadam, 1968, Foundations of Kerala Education, 1981, Bible Reading Guide of the Malankara Orthodox Church, Education and Social Change, 1987; chief editor: The Mystery of Man, 1971, Personality of a Child: A Constant Process of Dualistic Eruption into Monism, 1972, Incarnation: A Theologico-mystical Study, 1981, Holy Spirit: The Life Giver, 1981, An Orthodox Introduction to Sacraments, 1983, The Book of Common Prayer of the Syrian Orthodox Ch., 1985, Voice of Orthodoxy, 1986, Book of Ordinations of the Syrian Orthodox Ch., 1987, Marriage After the Holy Priesthood, 1985, Contraception and Orthodox Theology, 1990, The Orthodox Christian Priesthood: An Anthology of Patristic Writings, 1995, Pre-British European Educational Activities in India, 1989. Chmn. social action Diocese of Niraram, India, 1967-71; mem. Zonal coun. Diocese of Am., 1975-78, Diocesan Coun.; bd. regents Lafayette U., Aurora, Colo., 1989-95; exec. mem. Alleppey DT Kerala Congress, India, 1967-71; pres. Ecumenical Coun. Kerala Chs. Chgo., 1983-97; founder Voice of Orthodox Found., Chgo., 1995. Recipient Taylor award for High Achievement, Greek Orthodox Archdiocese, Schmitt Found. award, 1977, Pub. Svc. award Citizens Cultural Found., 1985. Mem. Am. Ednl. Studies Assn., Midwest History of Edn. Soc., Am. Assn. Biofeedback Clinicians, Internat. Assn. of Mission Studies, Germany. Mem. Eastern Orthodox Ch. Avocations: music, philanthropic work.

THOULESS, DAVID JAMES, physicist, educator; b. Bearsden, Scotland, Sept. 21, 1934; came to U.S., 1979; U.S. citizen, 1994; s. Robert Henry and Priscilla (Gorton) T.; m. Margaret Elizabeth Scrase, July 26, 1958; children: Michael, Christopher, Helen. BA, U. Cambridge, Eng., 1955, ScD, 1986; PhD, Cornell U., 1958. Physicist Lawrence Berkeley Lab., Calif., 1958-59; rsch. fellow U. Birmingham, Eng., 1959-61, prof. math. physics, 1965-78; lectr., fellow Churchill Coll. U. Cambridge, Eng., 1961-65; prof. physics Queen's U., Kingston, Ont., Can., 1978; prof. applied sci. Yale U., New Haven, 1979-80; prof. physics U. Wash., Seattle, 1980—. Author: Quantum Mechanics of Many Body Systems, 2d edit., 1972. Recipient Maxwell medal Inst. Physics, 1973, Holweck prize Soc. Francaise de Physique-Inst. Physics, 1980, Fritz London award for Low temperature physics, Fritz London Meml. Fund, 1984, Wolf prize in physics, 1990, Paul Dirac medal Inst. Physics, 1993; Edwin Uehling disting. scholar U. Wash., 1988—. Fellow Royal Soc., Am. Acad. Arts and Scis., Nat. Acad. Sci. Office: U Wash Dept Physics Box 351560 Seattle WA 98195

THOW, GEORGE BRUCE, surgeon; b. Toronto, Mar. 24, 1930; came to U.S., 1965; s. George and Helen Bruce (Smith) T.; m. Marion Bernice Perry, Sept. 7, 1956; children—Deborah, George, Helen, Catherine. M.D., U. Toronto, 1954. Diplomate Am. Bd. Gen. Surgery, Am. Bd. Colon and Rectal Surgery (pres. 1983-84, adv. coun. 1989—, sr. examiner 1989—). Intern Toronto East Gen. Hosp., 1954-55; gen. practice medicine Toronto, 1955-56; instr. anatomy U. Toronto; resident in gen. and colon and rectal surgery Mayo Postgrad. Sch. Medicine, Rochester, Minn., 1957-63; gen., colon and rectal surgeon Lockwood Clinic, Toronto, 1963-65; founder and dir. colon and rectal residency program U. Ill. Med. Sch. and Carle Found. Hosp., Urbana, 1974-85; dir. dept. colon and rectal surgery Carle Clinic Assocs., Urbana, Ill., 1974-85; clin. assoc. Sch. Basic Med. Scis., U. Ill., Urbana, 1973-77; clin. asst. prof. Coll. Medicine, U. Ill., Urbana-Champaign, 1975-78; clin. assoc. prof. Coll. Medicine, U. Ill., 1978-85; prof. clin. nutrition, dept. food sci. U. Ill., Urbana, 1981-85; practice medicine specializing in colon and rectal surgery Chattanooga, 1985—; vice chmn. Residency Rev. Bd. in Colon and Rectal Surgery, 1980-82; active Am. Bd. Med. Specialties, 1979-84; mem. interspecialty bd. AMA, Chgo., 1974-80. Assoc. editor Diseases of the Colon and Rectum Jour., 1978—; contbr. chpt. to book, numerous articles to profl. publs.; inventor Thow tube, Colovage operative irrigation tube. Cmty. coord. Urbana conv. Inter-Varsity Christian Fellowship, Ill., 1967-84. Recipient Med. Edn. award Carle Found., 1982. Fellow Royal Coll Surgeons (Can.) (cert. 1963), ACS (credentials com. 1980-82); mem. Priestley Surg. Soc., Mid-West Colon and Rectal Surg. Soc. (pres. 1985-86), Can. Assn. Gen. Surgeons, Am. Bd. of Colon and Rectal Surgery (chmn. exam. com.1980-83, pres. 1983-84, adv. coun. 1989), Soc. Surgery Alimentary Tract, Am. Cancer Soc. (pres. Champaign County unit 1975-77, Ill. Top Ten award 1973-74), United Ostomy Assn. (founding mem. Champaign-Urbana chpt.). Presbyterian. Home: 7142 Revere Cir Concord Highlands Chattanooga TN 37421-1205 Office: Univ Surg Assocs Inc Med Ctr Plz North 979 E 3rd St Ste 300 Chattanooga TN 37403-2186

THOW, JOHN H., music educator, composer; b. L.A., Oct. 6, 1949; s. George H. and Marie (Dykes) T.; m. Margaret Wait, June 24, 1971; children: Diana Corinna, Caroline Miranda. BMus in Composition magna cum laude, U. So. Calif., 1971; MA in Music Composition, Harvard U., 1973, PhD in Music Composition, 1977; diploma d'onore (Composition), Accademia Musicale Chigiana, Siena, Italy, 1974. Asst. prof. music theory and composition Boston U. Sch. for the Arts, 1978-80; asst. prof. in music composition U. Calif. Dept. Music, Berkeley, 1981-86, assoc. prof., 1986-90, prof., 1990—. Composer: Madrone (Bklyn. Philharm. commn. 1987), Image Double & Envoi, All Hallows, 1982 (NEA rec. grant 1983, Boston Musica Viva/New Eng. Found. for the Arts Commn. 1981), Breath of the Sun, 1993, Seven Charms for a New Day, Canto del Quetzal, Chinese Poems, Divergences, Trombone Concerto, Songs for the Earth, 1994 (Am. Acad. award 1994), Into the Twilight, 1988 (San Francisco Symphony commn. 1988), Trigon, 1974 (Debut Orchesta award 1976), Live Oak (Musical Elements N.Y. commn. 1983), To Invoke the Clouds (award Nat. Flute Assn. 1997); recs. include Neuma, Music and Arts. Guggenheim fellowship Guggenheim Fdn., 1986, Djerassi Fdn. fellowships, 1986, 87, Regents Jr. Faculty fellowship U. Calif., 1983, Goddard Lieberson fellowship Am. Acad. and Inst. of Arts and Letters, 1983, Dorland Mountain Colony fellow, 1981, Yaddo fellowships, 1976, 1980, John Knowles Paine Travelling fellowship (Harvard), 1976-77, Fulbright Grad. fellowship to Italy, 1973-74; Margaret Jory Fairbanks Copying Assistance grants (The Am. Music Ctr.), 1978, 92, Meet the Composer grants, 1980, 82, 86, 87, 92, 95; Acad. award in Music Composition AAAL, 1994, Newly Published Music award Nat. Flute Assn., 1997. Fellow Am. Academy in Rome (Rome Prize fellowship 1977); mem. BMI, Am. Music Ctr., Am. Composers Forum. Home: 1045 Ordway St Albany CA 94706-2522 Office: Univ of Calif-Berkeley Dept Music 104 Morrison Hall Berkeley CA 94720-1201

THOYER, JUDITH REINHARDT, lawyer; b. Mt. Vernon, N.Y., July 29, 1940; d. Edgar Allen and Florence (Mayer) Reinhardt; m. Michael E. Thoyer, June 30, 1963; children: Erinn, Michael John. AB with honors, U. Mich., 1961; LLB summa cum laude, Columbia U., 1965. Bar: N.Y. 1966, D.C. 1984. Law libr. U. Ghana, Accra, Africa, 1963-64; assoc. Paul, Weiss, Rifkind, Wharton & Garrison, N.Y.C., 1966-75, ptnr., 1975—; mem. TriBar Opinion Com., 1995—. Mem. bd. visitors Law Sch. Columbia U., N.Y.C., 1991—; bd. dirs. Women's Action Alliance, N.Y.C., 1975-89, pro bono counsel, 1975—; mem. Women's Coun. Dem. Senatorial, mem. campaign com., 1993—; organizing com. Alumnae Columbia Law Sch., 1996—. Mem. N.Y. County Lawyers Assn. (mem. securities and exchs. com. 1976—), Assn. of Bar of City of N.Y. (mem. securities regulation com. 1976-79, mem. recruitment of lawyers com. 1980-82, mem. spl. com. on mergers, acquisitions and corp. control contests 1996—). Home: 1115 Fifth Ave Apt 3B New York NY 10128-0100 Office: Paul Weiss Rifkind Wharton & Garrison 1285 Avenue Of The Americas New York NY 10019-6028

THRALL, ARTHUR ALVIN, artist; b. Milw., Mar. 18, 1926; s. Irving and Helen (Fabich) T.; m. Winifred Rogers, 1960; children: Grant, Wade, Sara, Jay. BS, Milw. State Tchrs. Coll., 1950; MS, U. Wis., Milw., 1954; postgrad. (fellow), U. Ill., 1954-55. Tchr. art Lincoln Jr. High Sch., Kenosha, Wis., 1951-54; asst. prof. SUNY, Geneseo, 1955-56; assoc. prof. Milw.-Downer Coll., 1956-64; prof., Farrar-Marrs prof. fine arts Lawrence U., Appleton, Wis., 1964-90; prof. emeritus Lawrence U., Appleton, 1990—. One-man shows include Smithsonian Instn., 1960, U. Dubuque, Iowa, 1993, Mt. Mary Coll., Milw., 1994, St. Norbert Coll, De Pere, Wis., 1995, also others; group shows include Corcoran bienials, Washington, 1951, 53, 55, 57, 62, Bklyn. Mus. annuals, Mus. Modern Art, N.Y.C., NAD, N,Y,C, Audubon Artists, N.Y.C., 1985, S.A.G.A., N.Y.C., 1985; represented in permanent collections Tate Gallery, Victoria and Alberta Mus., Brit. Mus., all London, Phila. Mus., Seattle Mus., Art Inst. Chgo., Bklyn. Mus., others. Served with U.S. Army, 1944-46, ETO. Recipient Bklyn. Mus. print awards 1952, 64; Pa. Acad. Arts award 1960; NAD awards 1956, 68); Louis Comfort Tiffany fellow, 1963. Mem. AAUP, Boston Printmakers (awards 1963, 65), Soc. Am. Graphic Artists (awards 1951, 52, 60, 78), Audubon Artists Inc. (award 1977). Home: 4225 N Woodburn St Milwaukee WI 53211-1504

THRALL, DONALD STUART, artist; b. Detroit, Mar. 29, 1918; s. Ernest Lawrence and Gertrude Marie (Aikenhead) T. B.A., Mich. State U., 1940; M.A., Columbia U. Tchrs. Coll., 1946; summer student, Skowhegan (Maine) Sch. Painting and Sculpture, 1947, Black Mountain (N.C.) Coll., 1948. Instr. painting and design Cass Tech. Sch., Detroit, 1949-55; ednl. coordinator Guggenheim Mus., N.Y.C., 1961-73; Bd. dirs. Mich. Watercolor Soc., 1950-55, Detroit Met. Art Assn., 1948-54; exhibiting mem. Detroit Inst. Arts, 1947-53. One-man exhbn., Contemporary Arts Gallery, N.Y.C., 1961, group exhbns. include, Met. Mus. Art, 1950, Detroit Inst. Arts, 1947-55 (award 1950, 53, 55), Mich. Artists invited survey show, 1951, Butler Inst. Am. Art, Youngstown, Ohio, 1950-52 (1st prize 1951), Whitney Mus., N.Y.C., 1953, Bklyn. Mus., 1961, others, group exhbns. include, Wildenstein Galleries, N.Y.C., 1952 (Hallmark Art prize), Downtown Gallery, N.Y.C., 1950-53, Detroit Artists Market, 1948-54, Scarab Gallery, Detroit, 1948-53 (award 1948, 51, 53, 54), Mich. Watercolor Soc., 1949-55 (award 1950, 52, 53, 55), Mich. State Fair, 1952 (1st prize 1952), Detroit Art Instr. Exhbn., 1946-53 (1st award 1946, 48, 50, 51, 53), 16th Serigraph Internat., N.Y.C., 1955, others; represented in permanent collections, Detroit Inst. Arts, Butler Inst. Am. Art, U. Mich. Mus. Art, Mus. Wayne State U., Cranbrook Acad. Art Mus., Bloomfield Hills, Mich., numerous pvt. collections, U.S. and abroad. Served with AUS, 1941-45. Guggenheim fellow, 1955. Mem. Mich. Acad. Sci., Arts and Letters, Beta Alpha Sigma (pres. 1940). Address: 945 W End Ave New York NY 10025-3566

THRAPP, MARK STEPHEN, executive search consultant; b. Cheyenne, Wyo., Dec. 2, 1949; s. Thomas Albert and Zona Beth (Corwin) T.; divorced; 1 child, Jan Lauren. BS in Psychology, Ga. State U., 1973. Personnel mgr. Davison's R.H. Macy & Co., Inc., Atlanta, 1973-74, Marriot Hotels, Chgo., Boston, 1974-76; cons. Roth Young Am., Atlanta, 1976-78; dir. recruitment Federated Dept. Stores, N.Y.C., 1978-81; v.p. search cons. R.H. Macy & Co., Inc., N.Y.C., 1981-94; mng. dir. Exec. Search Cons. Internat., N.Y.C., 1994-97, Endeavor Capital, N.Y.C., 1997—; ptnr. Endeavor Capital Fin. Adv. Firm, N.Y.C., 1997—. Avocations: antiques, restoration of Victorian homes. Office: Exec Search Cons Internat 350 5th Ave Ste 5501 New York NY 10118-5599

THRASH, EDSEL E., educational administrator; b. Lake, Miss., Aug. 28, 1925; m. Jessie McLendon, Apr. 16, 1949; children—Jane, Catherine, George. B.S. in Bus. Adminstrn, La. State U., 1950, M.B.A., 1951, Ph.D., 1963. Acct. Esso Standard Oil Co., 1951-55; dir. alumni affairs La. State U., 1957-68, mem. dept. econs., 1966-68; exec. sec., dir. bd. trustees State Instns. Higher Learning in Miss., Jackson, 1968-87; Disting. prof. health care econs. U. Miss. Med. Ctr., Jackson, 1987—. Bd. dirs. Miss. Heart Assn., 1970-76; mem. exec. council Andrew Jackson council Boy Scouts Am.; mem. council on ministries United Meth. Ch., Raymond, Miss., 1973—. Recipient Silver Beaver award Boy Scouts Am., 1977, Gold Heart award Miss. Heart Assn., 1976; elected to La. State U. Alumni Hall of Distinction, 1993. Mem. State Higher Edn. Exec. Officers (nat. pres. 1984-85), Omicron Delta Kappa, Alpha Kappa Psi. Office: U Miss Health Care Ctr PO Box 13872 Jackson MS 39236-3872

THRASH, PATRICIA ANN, educational association administrator; b. Grenada, Miss., May 4, 1929; d. Lewis Edgar and Weaver (Betts) T. BS, Delta State Coll., 1950; MA, Northwestern U., 1953, PhD, 1959; cert. Inst. Edn. Mgmt., Harvard U., 1983. Tchr. high sch. English Clarksdale, Miss., 1950-52; head resident Northwestern U., 1953-55, asst. to dean women, 1955-58, asst. dean women, 1958-60, lectr. edn., 1959-65, dean women, 1960-69, assoc. prof. edn., 1965-72, assoc. dean students, 1969-71; asst. exec. sec. Commn. on Instns. Higher Edn., North Central Assn. Colls. and Schs., 1972-73, assoc. exec. dir., 1973-76, assoc. dir., 1976-87, exec. dir., 1988-96; exec. dir. emeritus, 1997—; mem. adv. panel Am. Coun. on Edn., MIVER program evaluation mil. base program, 1991-94; mem. nat. adv. panel Nat. Ctr. Postsecondary Tchg., Learning & Assessment, 1991-95. Author (with others): Handbook of College and University Administration, 1970; contbr. articles to ednl. jours. Mem. Nat. Assn. Women Deans and Counselors (v.p. 1967-69, pres. 1972-73), Ill. Assn. Women Deans and Counselors (sec. 1961-63, pres. 1964-66), Am. Coll. Pers. Assn. (editl. bd. jour. 1971-74), Coun. Student Pers. Assns. in Higher Edn. (program nominations com. 1974-75, adv. panel Am. Coll. Testing Coll. Outcome Measures project 1977-78, staff Coun. on Postsecondary Accreditation project for evaluation nontraditional edn. 1977-78, mem. editl. bd. Jour. Higher Edn. 1975-80, guest editor Mar.-Apr. 1979, co-editor NCA Quar. 1988—, vice-chair regional accrediting dirs. group 1993, exec. com. Nat. Policy Bd. for Higher Edn. Inst. 1993-95), Mortar Bd. (hon.), Phi Delta Theta, Pi Lambda Theta, Alpha Psi Omega, Alpha Lambda Delta. Methodist. Home: 2337 Hartrey Ave Evanston IL 60201-2552

THRASHER, DIANNE ELIZABETH, mathematics educator, computer consultant; b. Brockton, Mass., July 11, 1945; m. George Thomas Thrasher, Jan. 28, 1967; children: Kimberly Elizabeth, Noelle Elizabeth. BA in Math., Bridgewater State Coll., 1967, postgrad., 1984-87. Cert. secondary math., history tchr. Tchr. math. Plymouth/Carver Regional Schs., Plymouth, Mass., 1976-78, Alden Sch., Duxbury, Mass., 1980-82, Marshfield (Mass.) H.S., 1982-84; computer cons. TC2I-Thrasher Computer Cons. and Instrn., Duxbury, Mass., 1988—; dir., owner Internat. Ednl. Franchise, 1991-95; owner Duxbury Math. Ctr. K-Adult, 1995—; owner New Eng. Regional Kumon Ednl. Franchise, 1991-95; Mass. State approved profl. point devel. provider for tchr. cert., 1996. Active U.S. Figure Skating Assn., Colorado Springs, 1978-85; 2d reader First Ch. Christ Scientist, Plymouth, 1971-73; bd. govs. Skating Club of Hingham, Mass., 1978-85, pres., 1983-85, dir. Learn to Skate program, 1983-85; mem. First Ch. Christ Scientist, Boston, 1964—; with New Eng. Regional Kumon Franchise Owners, 1991-95; charter mem. Nat. Adv. Coun. of the U.S. Navy Meml. Found., 1992. Recipient Presdl. Nomination for Excellence in Tng. Math., NSF, 1992, Ed Taylor Meml. Vol. Svc. award Skating Club Hingham, 1995. Mem. NAFE, AAUW, Nat. Coun. Tchrs. Math, Duxbury Bus. Assn., Bostonian Soc., Nat. Hist. Trust & Preservation Soc., Smithsonian. Avocations: antiques, bicycling, skating, sailing. Home: 140 Toby Garden St Duxbury MA 02332-4945

THRASHER, JACK D., toxicologist, researcher, consultant; b. Nashville, Kans., Aug. 13, 1936; s. Harold A. and Margaret E. (Bolin) T.; m. Diane L. Walton, June 29, 1963; children: Traci L., Kristen I. BS, Longbeach State U., 1959; PhD, UCLA, 1964. Asst. prof. U. of Colo. Sch. of Medicine, Denver, 1964-66, UCLA Sch. of Medicine, L.A., 1966-72; application specialist Millipore Corp., Bedford, Mass., 1973-75; cons. Thrasher and Assocs., L.A., 1975-92, Alto, N. Mex., 1992—; mem. faculty E. N. Mex. U., Ruidoso, 1992—; mentor Columbia Pacific U., San Rafael, Calif., 1992—; bd. dirs., chmn. Internat. Inst. Rsch. for Chem. Hypersensitivity, Alto, N. Mex., 1991-94; advisor Chem. Impact Project Mill Valley, Calif., 1993—. Author: (books) Cellular and Molecular Renewal in the Mammalian Body, 1971, The Poisoning of our Homes and Work Places, 1990; editor-in-chief Informed Consent, 1993-94. Grantee: USPHS, NIH, 1966-69. Avocations: golf, fishing, wood working. Home and Office: Thrasher and Assocs PO Box 879 110 Raven Court Alto NM 88312

THRASHER, ROSE MARIE, critical care and community health nurse; b. Urbana, Ohio, Jan. 19, 1948; d. Jesse and Anna Frances (Clark) T. Student, Mercy Med. Ctr. Sch. Med. Tech., 1966-67, Wittenberg U., 1969-70; BSN,

Ohio State U., 1974, BA in Anthropology, 1994, BA in History of Art, 1997. RN, Ohio; cert. cmty. health nurse ANA; cert. provider BCLS and ACLS, Am. Heart Assn., CCRN. Pub. health nurse Columbus (Ohio) Health Dept., 1977-78; critical care nurse VA Med. Ctr., San Francisco, 1981, Staff Builders Health Care Svc., Oakland, Calif., 1975-76, 81-85; supr., case mgr. home health nurse passport program and intermittent care program Interim Health Care (formerly Med. Pers. Pool), Columbus, 1976-77, 85—, chart reviewer, 1996—; chart reviewer Interim Health Care Support Svcs., Columbus, 1997—. Recipient numerous acad. scholarships Wittenberg U. and Ohio State U.; mem. Nat. Women's Hall of Fame. Mem. AACN, ANA (coun. cmty. health nursing), AAUW, N.Y. Acad. Scis., Ohio Nurses Assn., Intravenous Nurses Soc., Ohio State U. Alumni Assn., Am. Anthropol. Assn., Ohio Acad. Sci., Ohio State U. Coll. of Nursing Alumni Soc.

THREADCRAFT, HAL LAW, III, pastor, counselor; b. Birmingham, Feb. 10, 1952; s. Hal L. Jr. and Helen Barbara (Foster) T.; m. Marion Lee Haygood, Aug. 18, 1973; children: Joshua, John Caleb, Anna. BSCE, U. Ala., 1975; ThM, Dallas Theol. Sem., 1979; MA, U. Ala., 1990, PhD, 1992. Lic. profl. counselor, clin. marriage and family therapist, Ala.; nat. cert. counselor. Min. Young Life, Dallas, 1975-79; prof. Evangelische Theologische Facultait, Heverlee, Belgium, 1979-83; preacher at large Christian Brethren, Alberta, Can., 1983-85; sr. pastor Grace Chapel, Halifax, N.S., Can., 1985-88; pvt. practice Tuscaloosa, Ala., 1990—; adj. prof. Beeson Sch. Divinity; vis. lectr. U. Ala., 1992—. Author: Apostle Paul's Principles of Church Growth, 1980. Mem. U. Ala. Counseling and Devel. Assn. (pres. 1989-90), Kappa Delta Pi, Phi Kappa Phi, Chi Sigma Iota, Omicron Delta Kappa. Home: 1011 Berrington Cr Birmingham AL 35242

THREEFOOT, SAM ABRAHAM, physician, educator; b. Meridian, Miss., Apr. 10, 1921; s. Sam Abraham and Ruth Frances (Lilienthal) T.; m. Virginia Rush, Feb. 6, 1954; children: Barbara Jane Stockton Mattingly, Ginny Ruth Threefoot Lindberg, Tracyann Threefoot Esenstad, Shelley Ann Threefoot Cowan. B.S., Tulane U., 1943, M.D., 1945. Diplomate: Am. Bd. Internal Medicine. Intern Michael Reese Hosp., Chgo., 1945-47; asst. vis. physician Charity Hosp. New Orleans, 1947-50, vis. physician, 1950-57, sr. vis. physician, 1957-69, cons., 1969-70, 76—; clin. asst. dept. medicine Touro Infirmary, New Orleans, 1953-56; jr. asst. Touro Infirmary, 1956-60, sr. asst., 1960-63, dir. med. edn., 1953-63, dir. research, 1953-70, sr. dept. medicine, 1963-70; fellow dept. medicine Tulane U., 1947-49, instr., 1948-53, asst. prof., 1953-59, asso. prof., 1959-63, prof., 1963-70, 76-91, prof. emeritus, 1991—, asst. dean, 1979-91, adj. prof. emeritus Sch. Pub. Health & Tropical Medicine, 1993—; chief of staff VA Hosp. (Forest Hills div.), Augusta, Ga., 1970-76; asso. chief staff VA Hosp., New Orleans, 1976-79; chief of staff VA Hosp., 1979-91, cons., 1991—; asst. dean Med. Coll. Ga., 1970-76, prof. medicine, 1970-76; Cons. physician Lallie Kemp Charity Hosp., Independence, La., 1951-53. Editor: Lymphology, 1967-70; Contbr. articles profl. jours. Served with AUS, 1943-45. La. Heart Assn. grantee, 1953-55; John A. Hartford Found. grantee, 1956-74; Am. Heart Assn. grantee, 1959-61; USPHS grantee, 1953-66. Fellow A.C.P., Am. Coll. Cardiology, N.Y. Acad. Sci.; mem. Am. Heart Assn. (v.p. 1970, fellow council on circulation), Central Soc. Clin. Research, So. Soc. Clin. Investigation (pres. 1967), AAAS, Internat. Soc. Lymphology, Soc. Exptl. Biology and Medicine, Soc. Nuclear Medicine, Microcirculatory Conf., Inc., Am. Fedn. Clin. Research, La. Heart Assn. (pres. 1967), Nat. Assn. VA Chiefs of Staff (pres. 1987-88), Phi Beta Kappa, Sigma Xi. Jewish. *I am one of those fortunate individuals who has been able to approach goals set early in life. Although my achievements are far short of my aspirations, at least I have had the opportunity. In dealing with both people and things, I have always felt that no detail was too small to receive attention.*

THREET, JACK CURTIS, oil company executive; b. Dundas, Ill., Aug. 16, 1928; s. Ivy Clemon and Daryl (Curtis) T.; m. Catherine Irene Hall, Mar. 24, 1951; children—Linda Sue, Judith Ann. B.A. in Geology, U. Ill., 1951. Geologist, dist. geologist, div. exploration mgr., area exploration mgr. Shell Oil Co., various locations including Oklahoma City, Amarillo, Tex., Denver, Pitts., Lafayette, La., Billings, Mont., N.Y.C., L.A., 1951-69; gen. mgr. exploration and prodn. Shell Australia Ltd., Melbourne, 1969-71; v.p. internat. exploration and prodn. Shell Can., Calgary, Alta., 1972-74, Shell Oil Co., New Orleans, 1974-75; v.p. internat. exploration and prodn. Houston, 1975-78, corp. v.p. exploration, 1978-87, ret., 1987; v.p., dir., co-founder Energy Exploration Mgmt. Co., Houston, 1988-90; pres., owner Threet Energy, Inc., Houston, 1989—, Threet, Inc., Houston, 1995—. Served with U.S. Army, 1953-55. Mem. Am. Assn. Petroleum Geologists, Lakeside Country Club (Houston), Rotary. Republican. Methodist.

THRELKELD, RICHARD DAVIS, broadcast journalist; b. Cedar Rapids, Iowa, Nov. 30, 1937; s. Robert M. and Lou Jane (Davis) T.; m. Sharon A. Adams, June 11, 1960 (div. 1983); children: Susan Anne, Julia Lynn; m. Betsy Aaron, May 15, 1983. B.A., Ripon Coll., 1959; M.S. in Journalism, Northwestern U., 1961; LHD (hon.), Ripon Coll., 1989. Editor Sta. WHAS-TV, Louisville, 1961; reporter Sta. WMT-TV, Cedar Rapids, Iowa, 1961-66; corr. CBS News, N.Y.C. and San Francisco, 1966-82; nat. corr. CBS News, 1989-96; chief corr. ABC News N.Y., N.Y.C., 1982-89; Moscow corr. CBS News, 1996—. Corr.: TV news documentary Defense of America, 1981 (Emmy award); TV news report Rhodesia Remembered, 1980 (Overseas Press Club award), TV news report Vietnam Remembered, 1985 (Emmy award), TV news series Status Reports, 1984 (Dupont award), TV new report Lebanon-Grenada 1983 (Overseas Press Club award). CBS News fellow, 1964. Mem. AFTRA, Radio-TV News Dirs. Assn., Sigma Delta Chi.

THRIFT, JULIANNE STILL, academic administrator; b. Barnwell, S.C.; m. Ashley Ormand Thrift; children: Lindsay, Laura. BA, U. S.C., MEd; PhD in Pub. Policy, George Washington U. Formerly asst. exec. dir. Nat. Assn. Coll. and Univ. Attys.; ombudsman U. S.C.; exec. dir. Nat. Inst. Ind. Colls. and Univs., 1982-88; exec. v.p. Nat. Assn. Ind. Colls. and Univs., Washington, 1988-91; pres. Salem Acad. and Coll., Winston-Salem, N.C., 1991—. Office: Salem Coll Office of the President Winston Salem NC 27108-0548

THROCKMORTON, JOAN HELEN, direct marketing consultant; b. Evanston, Ill., Apr. 11, 1931; d. Sydney L. and Anita H. (Pusheck) T.; m. Sheldon Burton Satin, June 26, 1982. B.A. with honors, Smith Coll., 1953. Mktg. exec. Lawrence Chait & Co., N.Y.C., 1965; mktg. exec. Cowles Communications, Inc., N.Y.C., 1968-69; founder, chief exec. officer Throckmorton Assocs., Inc., N.Y.C., 1970-83; pres. Joan Throckmorton, Inc., N.Y.C., 1983—; lectr. in field; instr. Direct Mktg. Assn., Sch. Continuing Edn., NYU, N.Y.C., 1985. Author: Winning Direct Response Advertising, 1986, 2d edit., 1996. Trustee Halle Ravine Com. Nature Conservancy, 1985; mem. expetition com. Outward Bound, 1980-83. Recipient Edward N. Mayer Jr. award, Direct Mktg. Edn. Found., 1996, Andi Emerson award John Caples Internat. Awards, Inc., 1996; named Direct Mktg. Women of the Yr., 1986. Mem. Women's Dir. Response Group (founding mem.), Dir. Mktg. Assn. (bd. dirs. 1971-77, exec. com. 1972-77, mem. long-range planning com. 1977-78), Women's Forum, Dir. Mktg. Idea Exchange, Dir. Mktg. Creative Guild (bd. dirs. 1984-85), Jr. League Mexico City, Jr. League N.Y.C., Phi Beta Kappa. Office: Joan Throckmorton Inc PO Box 452 Pound Ridge NY 10576-0452

THRODAHL, MARK CRANDALL, medical technology company executive; b. Charleston, W.Va., Mar. 31, 1951; s. Monte Cordon and Josephine (Crandall) T.; m. Sudie Kenton, Oct. 21, 1978; children: Mary Elizabeth, Anne Katherine, Andrew Kenton. AB, Princeton U., 1973; MBA, Harvard U., Boston, 1975. Various positions Mallinckrodt, Inc., St. Louis, 1975-88; dir. corp. planning Becton Dickinson & Co., Franklin Lakes, N.J., 1988-91; pres. Nippon Becton Dickinson, Becton Dickinson & Co., Tokyo, 1991-94; sector pres. Becton Dickinson & Co., Franklin Lakes, 1994-95, sr. v.p., 1995—. Mem. Old Warson Country Club, Ivy Club. Republican. Episcopalian. Home: 38 Carteret Rd Allendale NJ 07401-1850 Office: Becton Dickinson & Co One Becton Dr Franklin Lakes NJ 07417

THRODAHL, MONTE CORDEN, former chemical company executive; b. Mpls., Mar. 25, 1919; s. Monte Conrad and Hilda (Larson) T.; m. Josephine Crandall, Nov. 6, 1948; children: Mark Crandall, Peter Douglas. B.S., Iowa State U., 1941. With Monsanto Co., St. Louis, 1941-84; gen. mgr. internat. div. Monsanto Co., 1964-66, v.p., 1965-84, dir., 1966-84, group v.p. tech., 1974-77, sr. v.p., 1979-84; v.p., dir. Monsanto Research Corp. Fellow AIChE, AAAS, Am. Inst. Chemists; mem. NAE, Am. Chem. Soc., Comml. Devel. Assn., Soc. Chem. Industry, Old Watson Country Club, St. Louis Club, Univ. Club, Alpha Chi Sigma. Home: 36 Briarcliff Ladue MO 63124-1753 Office: 20 S Central Ave Saint Louis MO 63105-1715

THROGMARTIN, DIANNE, educational foundation executive; b. Indpls., May 3, 1964; d. Roy Don and Suzzane (Jackson) T. Cert., Landmark Coll., 1988, Motivation Inst., 1991; BS in Edn., Butler U., 1992; cert., Fund Raising Sch., Indpls., 1992-93. Product mgr. H.H. Gregg, Indpls., 1982-85, salesperson, trainer, 1988-90; substitute tchr. Camp Delafield Lakeview Temple, Indpls., 1990-91; gen. asst. Robo Group Internat., Indpls., 1992-93, Indpls. Jaycees, 1993-94; pres., founder Dyslexia Ednl. Found. Am., Indpls., 1994—. Pres. bd. Ind. Hugh O'Brian Youth Found., Indpls., 1992-95, Leadership America, 1996. Recipient Cmty. Svc. award Landmark Coll., 1988, 87. Mem. Jaycees (dir. Indpls. chpt. 1993-95, Mem. of Month 1992, Outstanding Com. chmn. 1993, 94, Dir. of Month 1993, Dir. of Yr. 1994, Mgmt. Devel. award 1994), Indpls. C. of C. Republican. Avocations: movies, cooking, spending time in the country, camping, walking. Home: 10424 Ridgeview Cir Fishers IN 46208 Office: Dyslexia Ednl Found Am 4181 E 96th St Ste 120 Indianapolis IN 46240-3814

THRONDSON, EDWARD WARNER, residential association administrator; b. Woodland, Calif., May 22, 1938; s. Edward J. and Arden Warner (Law) T.; m. Marjorie Jean Waite, June 25, 1960 (div. 1993); children: Mark Edward, Kimberly Anne, Sulin Marget; m. Mary Jo Riddell Law, Jan. 13, 1994. BS, Stanford U., 1960; MBA, Harvard U., 1962. Profl. Community Assn. Mgr., Community Assn. Inst. Asst. br. mgr. Pacific Delta Gas, Santa Rosa, Calif., 1962-65; corp. staff asst. Pacific Delta Gas, San Jose, Calif., 1965-72; regional mgr. Pargas, San Jose, 1972-86; gen. mgr., COO The Villages Golf and Country Club, San Jose, 1986-93; sr. v.p. West Coast Community Assocs., Campbell, Calif., 1994-95; assn. mgr. Cmty. Assns. Consulting, Napa, Calif., 1996—. Mem. Cmty. Assns. Inst. (com. chair 1991—, Pres.'s Appreciation award 1991), Calif. Assn. Cmty. Mgrs. (cert., founding mem., com. chair 1992—, author course 1992, 94). Avocations: golf, stamp collecting, geneology.

THRONER, GUY CHARLES, JR., engineering executive, scientist, engineer, inventor, consultant; b. Mpls., Sept. 14, 1919; s. Guy Charles and Marie (Zechar) T.; m. Jean Holt, Dec. 5, 1943; children—Richard, Carol Anne, Steven. BA, Oberlin Coll., 1943; postgrad., UCLA, 1960, 61. Registered profl. engr., Calif. Br. head Naval Weapon Ctr., China Lake, Calif., 1946-53; mgr. ordnance div., mgr. weapon systems div. Aerojet Gen. Corp., Azusa, Calif., 1953-64; v.p., div. mgr. FMC Corp., San Jose, Calif., 1964-74; research dir. Vacu Blast Corp., Belmont, Calif., 1976-78; v.p., devel. mfg. Dahlman, Inc., Braham, Minn., 1978-79; mgr. ordnance systems & tech. Battelle Meml. Inst., Columbus, Ohio, 1979-85; pres. Guy C. Throner & Assocs., tech. and mgmt. cons., 1985—; dir. Omron Corp. Am., Chgo., 1976-77. Inventor, patentee indls., med. and mil. systems design. Served as officer USNR, World War II. Am. Order St. Barbara medal U.S. Army Arty, 1983, Recipient IR-100 award Indsl. Research Mag., Chgo., 1971, Congl. Commendation, 1985, also various commendations. Mem. AIAA, Am. Def. Preparedness Assn. (Bronze medal 1974, Simon award 1985), Lake Wildwood Country Club, Sigma Xi. Republican. Avocations: astronomy; photography; golf. Home and Office: 17992 Jayhawk Dr Penn Valley CA 95946-9206

THROWER, F. MITCHELL, III, advertising executive; b. N.Y.C., Jan. 16, 1968; s. Frederick Mitchell and Lori (Terhorst) T. BA, St. Lawrence Coll., 1990; SA, Yale U., 1989; student, Regent St. Diplomatic Acad., London, 1988. Counselor Open Line Counseling, Westport, Conn., 1985-86; promotions coord. WICC Radio, Bridgeport, Conn., 1986-87; intern Walt Disney World Prodns., Lake Buena Vista, Fla., 1987-88; author, rsch. staff Small Bus. Bur. Conservative Cen. Office, London, 1988-89; pres., chief exec. officer Coll. Connection, Inc., La Jolla, Calif., 1990-97; pres., COO Triathlete and Winning mags., 1997—; cons., educator Staples High Sch., Westport, 1991—. Author: The Small Business Guide to Small Business Awards, 1989, The Passport-A Student's Best Resource Overseas, 1991. Chmn. and coord. UN Student Fellowship, 1991—; advisor Friends of the UN, 1991. Recipient Good Citizenship award DAR 1986, Jan Bruniczka Govt. award Bruniczka Found. 1986, Johanna Lambros award Lambros Found. 1984. Mem. Sigma Chi, Squadron A. Avocations: triathalons, travel, skiing, sailing, diving. Office: College Connection Inc 1295 Prospect St Ste B La Jolla CA 92037-3641

THROWER, NORMAN JOSEPH WILLIAM, geographer, educator; b. Crowthorne, Eng., Oct. 23, 1919; came to U.S., 1947, naturalized, 1957; s. Gordon William and Ethel Daisy (Bayley) T.; m. Elizabeth McPherson Martin, Aug. 9, 1947; children: Mildred Page Mosier, Anne Bayley Leonard, Mary Elizabeth Thrower Kerr. BA with honors, U. Va., 1953; MA, U.Wis., 1955, PhD, 1958. Asst. prof. geography UCLA, 1957-61, assoc. prof., 1961-65, prof., 1965-90, prof. emeritus, 1990—, Clark Libr. prof., 1972-73, dir. William Andrews Clark Meml. Library, 1981-87; founder UCLA Ctr. for 17th and 18th Century Studies, 1985; dir. Columbus Quincentenary Programs UCLA, 1989-93; adv. bd. Guggenheim Found., 1978—. Author 10 books on cartographic subjects; contbr. articles to profl. jours. Vice pres. Sir Francis Drake Commn. of State of Calif., 1973-75, pres., 1975-80. Served with Brit. Army, 1940-47. Decorated Burma Star, Orden del Mérito Civil (Spain), 1992; Guggenheim fellow, 1962-63. Mem. Assn. Am. Geographers, Soc. History of Discoveries (v.p. 1971-72, pres. 1973-74), Hakluyt Soc. (hon. sec. overseas 1993—), Internat. Cartographic Assn. (corr.), Internat. Soc. for History for Cartography, Western Soc. for 18th Century Studies (v.p. 1986-87, pres. 1987-88). Presbyterian. Office: U Calif Dept Geography Los Angeles CA 90024

THRUN, ROBERT READ, architect; b. Ossining, N.Y., June 9, 1949; s. Robert and Roberta Read (Lewis) T.; m. Rita Catherine McDermott, June 15, 1968; 1 child, Zachary. BA, Colby Coll., 1971; MArch, U. Pa., 1974. Registered architect Ohio, N.Y., Pa., Conn., Md., N.J., Ky., Tenn., Wis., Ind., Iowa. Architect Mitchell/Giurgola Assocs., Phila., 1974-75; project architect/designer The Kling Lingquist Partnership, Phila., 1975-83; studio dir., prin designer CUH2A, Princeton, 1983-89; mng. ptnr., prin. designer A.M. Kinney Assocs., Cin., 1989-96. Prin. works include C.C. of Phila., 1979 (AIA medal 1980), Corp. Hdqrs. Bldg. BMW of N.Am., 1986, Rsch. complex Pfizer, Inc., 1989 (City of Groton 1990), European Corp. Hdqrs. Nalco Chem. Co., 1993. Mem. AIA (award for design excellence Ohio chpt. 1993, award 1994). Avocations: cross country skiing, sailing, painting, reading. Office: AM Kinney Assocs 303 Court St Covington KY 41011-1638

THUERING, GEORGE LEWIS, industrial engineering educator; b. Milw., Sept. 2, 1919; s. Louis Charles and Elsie (Luetzow) T.; m. Lillian May Cline, Dec. 7, 1945 (dec.); 1 child; m. Betty L. McBride, Aug. 9, 1975. B.S., U. Wis., 1941, M.E., 1954; M.S., Pa. State U., 1949. Registered profl. engr., Pa. Mfg. engr. Lockheed Aircraft Corp., Burbank, Calif., 1941-47; supr. plant layout Lockheed Aircraft Corp., Marietta, Ga., 1951-52; mem. faculty Pa. State U., University Park, 1947—; assoc. prof. indsl. engring. Pa. State U., 1952-56, prof., 1956-82, prof. emeritus, 1982—, dir. mgmt. engring., 1961-82; cons. engring. Contbr. articles to profl. jours. Fellow Soc. Advancement Mgmt.; mem. ASME (chmn. mgmt. div. 1976-77, mem. exec. com. mgmt. div. 1973-77, chmn. papers rev. com. 1969-73, v.p. gen. engring. 1982-84), Am. Inst. Indsl. Engrs. (dir. students affairs 1972-74), Am. Soc. Engring. Edn. (chmn. indsl. engring. div. 1956-57), Sigma Xi, Tau Beta Pi, Pi Tau Sigma, Alpha Pi Mu. Home: 436 Homan Ave State College PA 16801-6336 Office: 207 Hammond Bldg University Park PA 16802-1401

THUESEN, GERALD JORGEN, industrial engineer, educator; b. Oklahoma City, July 20, 1938; s. Holger G. and Helen S. T.; m. Harriett M. Thuesen; children: Karen E., Dyan L. BS, Stanford U., 1960, MS, 1961, PhD, 1968. Engr. Pacific Tel. Co., San Francisco, 1961-62, Atlantic Richfield Co., Dallas, 1962-63; asst. prof. indsl. engring. U. Tex., Arlington, 1963, 67-68; assoc. prof. indsl. and sys. engring. Ga. Inst. Tech., Atlanta, 1968-76, prof., 1976—. Author: Engineering Economy, 4th edit., 1971, 5th edit., 1977, 6th edit., 1984, 7th edit., 1989, 8th edit., 1993, Economic Decision Analysis, 1974, 2nd edit., 1980; assoc. editor: The Engring. Economist, 1974-80, editor, 1981-91. NASA/Am. Soc. Engring. Edn. summer faculty fellow, 1970. Fellow Inst. Indsl. Engrs. (dept. editor Trans. 1976-80, v.p. publs. 1979-80, divsn. dir. 1978-80, Wellington award 1989, Publs. award 1990), Am. Soc. Engring. Edn. (bd. dirs. 1977-79, Eugene L. Grant award 1977, 89); mem. Sigma Xi. Office: Ga Inst Tech Sch Indsl & System Engring Atlanta GA 30332

THUESON, DAVID OREL, pharmaceutical executive, researcher, educator, writer; b. Twin Falls, Idaho, May 9, 1947; s. Orel Grover and Shirley Jean (Archer) T.; m. Sherrie Linn Lowe, June 14, 1969; children: Sean, Kirsten, Eric, Ryan, Todd. BS, Brigham Young U., 1971; PhD, U. Utah, 1976. Postdoctoral fellow U. Tex. Med. Br., Galveston, 1976-77, asst. prof., 1977-82; sr. rsch. assoc. Parke-Davis Pharms., Ann Arbor, Mich., 1982-88; dir. pharmacology Immunetech Pharms., San Diego, 1988-90; dir. immunopharmacology Tanabe Rsch. Labs., San Diego, 1990-92; v.p. discovery Cosmederm Techs., San Diego, 1992—. Contbr. articles to profl. jours.; patentee in field. Scout leader Boy Scouts Am., Mich., Tex. and Calif., 1979—. NIH grantee, 1978-81. Mem. Am. Acad. Allergy and Clin. Immunology, Am. Assn. Immunologists, Am. Thoracic Soc. Republican. Mormon. Avocations: water skiing, tennis, scuba diving. Home: 12740 Boxwood Ct Poway CA 92064-2643 Office: Cosmederm Techs 3252 Holiday Ct Ste 226 La Jolla CA 92037-1808

THUILLIER, RICHARD HOWARD, meteorologist; b. N.Y.C., Apr. 3, 1936; s. Howard Joseph and Louise (Schilling) T.; m. Barbara Unger (dec. 1992); children: Stephen, David, Lawrence, Daniel. BS in Physics, Fordham U., 1959; MS in Meteorology, NYU, 1963, postgrad., 1963-66. Cert. cons. meteorologist. Instr. SUNY, 1963-66; dir. of research Weather Engrs. of Panama Inc., Panama City, Rep. Panama, 1966-68; cons. Oakland, Calif., 1968—; meteorologist and chief of research and planning Bay Area Air Quality Mgmt. Dist., San Francisco, 1968-76; sr. research meteorologist SRI Internat., Menlo Park, Calif., 1976-80, Pacific Gas & Electric, San Ramon, Calif., 1980—; Note, your military record is listed in your civic section, per style. Capt. USAF, 1959-62. Mem. Am. Meterol. Soc., (pres. Panama Canal Zone chpt. 1967-68, San Francisco Bay chpt. 1971-72, Outstanding Contributions to Advance of Applied Meteorolgy award 1993), Sigma Xi (hon.). Republican. Roman Catholic. Avocations: hiking, bowling, golf, music, art.

THULEAN, DONALD MYRON, symphony conductor; b. Wenatchee, Wash., June 24, 1929; s. Elmer Edward and Mary (Myron) T.; m. Meryl Mary Parnell, Mar. 17, 1951; children—Dorcas Marie, Mark Myron, William Norton. B.A., U. Wash., 1950, M.A. in Music, 1952; Mus.D. (hon.), Whitworth Coll., 1967. Faculty Pacific U., 1955-62; dean Pacific U. (Sch. Music), 1957-62. Assoc. conductor Portland (Ore.) Symphony, 1961-62, conductor, music dir. Spokane Symphony, 1962-84; v.p. artistic affairs, orch. svcs. Am. Symphony Orch. League, 1984—; asst. conductor Seattle Symphony, 1966-69, chorus master, Aspen Music Festival, 1957-61; artistic cons. Title III project in performing arts, Wash., 1966-68, music dir. Tamarack Music Festival, 1971. Served with AUS, 1953-55. Unitarian (trustee). Office: Amer Symp Orchestra League 1156 15th St NW Washington DC 20005-1704

THULIN, WALTER WILLIS, real estate company executive; b. Mpls., Aug. 10, 1929; s. Edwin and Henrietta Helen (Kaupp) T.; m. M. Joan Thulin, Jan. 11, 1952; children: Elizabeth, Joshua K., Edwin K., Justin F. BChemE, U. Minn., 1952, BBA, 1952; MBA, Harvard U., 1954. V.p. internat. mktg. Internat. Flavors & Fragrances, N.Y.C., 1967-78; group v.p. Mallinckrodt, Inc., St. Louis, 1978-88. Home: PO Box 727 Wilson WY 83014-0727 Office: PO Box 2871 Jackson WY 83001-2871

THUMANN, ALBERT, association executive, engineer; b. Bronx, N.Y., Mar. 12, 1942; s. Albert and Ella (Josephy) T.; m. Susan Stock, Jan. 23, 1966; 1 child, Brian. BS, CUNY, 1964; MS in Elec. Engring., NYU, 1967, M.S. in Indsl. Engring, 1970. Registered profl. engr., N.Y., Ga., Ky. Project engring. mgr. Bechtel Corp., N.Y.C., Louisville, 1964-77; exec. dir., founder Assn. Energy Engrs., 1977—; Adj. prof. environmental engring. U. Louisville, 1974-75; lectr. on energy conservation. Author: Electrical Consulting-Engineering and Design, 1973, (with R.K. Miller) Secrets of Noise Control, 1976, Biorhythms and Industrial Safety, 1977, How to Patent Without a Lawyer, 1978, Electrical Design, Safety and Energy Conservation, 1978, 979, 3d edit., 1995, Energy Audit Sourcebook, 1983, Fundamentals of Energy Engineering, 1984, Introduction to Efficient Electrical Systems Design, 3d edit., 1990, (with Goldstick) Waste Heat Recovery, 1986, (with Miller) Introduction to Noise Control Engineering, 1986, Optimizing HVAC Systems, 1988, Lighting Efficiency Applications, 1988, (with James A. Bent) Project Management for Engineering and Construction, 1988, Palnt Engineers and Managers Guide to Energy Conservation, 5th edit., 1991, Handbook of Energy Engineering, 1989, 3d edit., 1994, Energy management Guide for Government Buildings, 1994, (with D. Paul Mehta) Handbook of Energy Engineering, 1995, Plant Engineers and Managers Guide to Energy Conservation, 6th edit., 1996; editor: Emerging Synthetic Fuel Industry, 1981; contbr. articles to profl. jours. Named Young Engr. of Year Ky. Soc. Profl. Engrs., 1974-75, Ky. col.; recipient Disting. Service award Assn. Energy Engrs., 1980. Mem. Nat. Soc. Profl. Engrs., Am. Soc. Assn. Execs., City Coll. Alumni Assn. Creater retng. course for unemployed aerospace engrs. Home: 931 Smoketree Dr Tucker GA 30084-1548 Office: Assn Energy Engrs 4025 Pleasantdale Rd Ste 420 Atlanta GA 30340-4264 *Where am I going and what am I doing, is a phrase which I have repeated many times. Constant appraisal of what one is doing and evaluation of this action with the goal are necessary for achieving one's objective. Salesmanship is the guiding tool which helps to obtain the objective once the course is chosen.*

THUNE, JOHN, congressman; b. Murdo, S.D., Jan. 7, 1961; m. Kimberley Thune; children: Brittany, Larissa. BBA, U. S.D., MBA. Legis. asst. Senator James Abdnor, 1985-87; dep. staff dir. to the ranking rep. Senate Small Bus. Com., 1987-89; exec. dir. South Dakota Rep. Party, 1989-91; state railroad dir. Gov. George Mickelson, 1991-93; exec. dir. S.D. Mcpl. League, 1993-96; mem. 105th Congress from S.D. dist., 1996—; mem. agr. com., transp. and infrastructure com., surface transp. subcom., gen. farm commodities and dept. ops., nutrition and fgn. agr. subcom.; vice-chmn. water resources and environ. subcom. Avocations: basketball, pheasant hunting.

THURBER, CLEVELAND, JR., trust banker; b. Detroit, Aug. 2, 1925; s. Cleveland and Marie Louise (Palms) T.; children: Cleveland III, Elizabeth King Thurber Crawford, David. Student, Purdue U.; B.A., Williams Coll., 1948. Asst. trust officer Comerica Bank-Detroit, 1958-61, trust officer, 1961-63, v.p., 1963-69, sr. v.p., 1969-81, exec. v.p., chief trust officer, 1981-89. Pres. Friends of Grosse Pointe Pub. Libr., 1971-72, Mich. Heart Assn., 1969-74; sec. United Community Svcs., 1968-70; bd. dirs. Cottage Hosp., 1970-94, United Found., 1975-89, Mich. Humane Soc., 1973-89, Elmwood Cemetery, pres., 1995; bd. dirs. Ctr. for Creative Studies, 1976-89, Wm. L. Clements Libr., Ann Arbor. With USMCR, 1943-46. Clubs: Bayview Yacht (Detroit), Yondotega (Detroit), Country (Detroit), Grosse Pointe. Home: 34 Edgemere Rd Grosse Pointe MI 48236-3709 Office: 21 Kercheval Ave Grosse Pointe MI 48236-3601

THURBER, DONALD MACDONALD DICKINSON, public relations counsel; b. Detroit, Feb. 3, 1918; s. Donald MacDonald Dickinson and Fayetta Cecelia (Crowley) T.; m. Margaret Worcester Dudley, June 6, 1964. A.B. magna cum laude, Harvard U., 1940. Pvt. tutor Detroit, 1937-39; house mgr. Cape Playhouse, Dennis, Mass., 1940; exec. sec. youth div. Democratic Nat. Com., 1940; membership sec. Harvard Club, N.Y.C., 1940; project supr. Detroit Council for Youth Service, 1941-43; rep. for Mich., Nat. Found. Infantile Paralysis, 1943-46; sec., administr. Wayne County (Mich.) chpt., 1946-50; exec. dir. Gov. Mich. Study Commn. on Deviated Criminal Sex Offenders, 1950-51; exec. sec. Mayor Detroit Com. Rehab. Narcotic Addicts, 1951-53; sec., asst. treas. Mich. Rotary Press, Inc., Detroit, 1953-54; pres. Mich. Rotary Press, Inc., 1954-58; exec. v.p. Pub. Relations Counselors, Inc., Detroit, 1958-61; pres. Pub. Relations Counselors, Inc., 1961—. Bd. dirs. Clan Donald Found., 1994—; mem. Mich. Crippled Children Commn., 1954-58, vice chmn., 1956-58; planning dir. Episcopal Diocese of Mich., 1958-62, mem. exec. council, 1963-66; cons. to Sec. Interior, 1962-68; mem. Nat. Park Trust Fund Bd., 1963-67; bd. regents U. Mich., 1959-63; mem. Mich. Bd. Edn., 1965-67; mem. bd. overseers com. to visit Harvard Coll., 1964-70; mem. Mich. Citizens Com. for Higher Edn. Planning, 1967-69; chmn. Wayne County Community Coll., 1968-72, trustee, 1968-74; mem. Adv. Com. on Higher Edn. Planning in Southeastern Mich.,

1970-72; advisor Nat. Trust Hist. Preservation, 1972-78; bd. dirs. Nat. Park Found., 1974-80, founder and historian, 1992—; mem. adv. council to Sec. Commerce, 1976-77; former v.p. Detroit Grand Opera Assn.; mem. adv. com. Detroit Urban League; trustee Clan Donald Lands Trust, Isle of Skye, Scotland, 1979—; trustee, vice chmn. St. Gregory's Abbey Found., Three Rivers, Mich., 1984-92; trustee Mich. Hist. Ctr. Found., vice chmn., 1992—; mem. Mich. Hist. Commn., 1984-87; bd. dirs. Blue Cross-Blue Shield of Mich., 1986-92, chmn. bd., 1988-92; Mich. exec. com. United Negro Coll. Fund; bd. dirs. Friends of U. Mich. Libr., 1988-96. Mem. Detroit Symphony Orch. Hall Vol. Coun., Detroit Hist. Soc., Mich. Hist. Soc., Friends of Detroit and Grosse Pointe Pub. Librs., Mich. Natural Areas Coun., Mich. Nature Assn., Clan McDonald-U.S.A. (Gt. Lakes commr. emeritus, Mich. commr. emeritus), Ancient and Honorable Artillery Co., Soc. Colonial Wars, Soc. War of 1812, State Soc. of the Cincinnati of Pa., Mil. Order Loyal Legion U.S., Order Founders and Patriots Am., Colonial Order of Acorn, St. Nicholas Soc., Prismatic Club (Detroit), Detroit Club, Harvard Club (Ea. Mich., N.Y.C., Boston). Democrat. Episcopalian. Office: Pub Rels Counselors Inc 10 Rathbone Pl Grosse Pointe MI 48230-1914

THURBER, JAMES CAMERON, law enforcement officer, consultant, author; b. Boynton Beach, Fla., Oct. 3, 1965; s. John Cameron and JeanAnn (Bridgeman) T. AA, Palm Beach CC, 1986; BS in Criminology, Fla. State U., Tallahassee, 1988, MPA, 1991. Cert. Police Officer, EMT. EMT Atlantic Ambulance Svc., West Palm Beach, 1984-88, Bethesda Ambulance Svc., Boynton Beach, Fla., 1988-92; police officer Lake Worth (Fla.) Police Dept., 1992-94; law enforcement investigator Fla. Divsn. Ins. Fraud, 1994—; vol. aux. police officer Lake Worth Police Dept., 1985-92; cons. Fla. C. of C., Tallahassee, 1991, Fla. Div. Emergency Mgmt., Tallahassee, 1991; intern. Fed. Bureau of Prisons, Tallahassee, 1990, Fla. Dept. Law Enforcement, Pompano Beach, 1987. Contbr. articles to profl. jours. Mem. Lake Worth Pioneer Assn., West Palm Beach, 1965-94, Hist. Soc. Palm Beach County, 1993—; squadron emergency svcs. officer CAP, Lantana, Fla., 1983-89. Recipient Outstanding Academic Achievement award Fraternal Order of Police, Lake Worth, 1992. Mem. Am. Soc. Pub. Adminstrn., Lake Worth Scottish Rite, Masons (Boynton Lodge @ 236), Lambda Chi Alpha, Palm Beach County Seminole Boosters. Episcopalian. Office: Ste 704 1655 Palm Beach Lakes Blvd West Palm Beach FL 33401-2208

THURBER, JOHN ALEXANDER, lawyer; b. Detroit, Nov. 9, 1939; s. John Levington and Mary Anne (D'Agostino) T.; m. Barbara Irene Brown, June 30, 1962; children: John Levington II, Sarah Jeanne. AB in History, U. Mich., 1962, JD, 1965. Bar: Ohio 1965, Mich. 1968. Assoc. Hahn, Loeser and Parks, Cleve., 1965-67, Miller, Canfield, Paddock and Stone, Birmingham, Mich., 1967-73; ptnr. Miller, Canfield, Paddock and Stone, P.L.C., Bloomfield Hills, Mich., 1974—. Treas. Birmingham Community House, 1971-73; pres. Birmingham Village Players, 1983-84; bd. dirs. Oakland Parks Found., Pontiac, Mich., 1984—, pres., 1989-92; mem. capital com. Lighthouse Found. Avocations: reading, theater, walking, sports. Office: Miller Canfield Paddock & Stone PLC 1400 N Woodward Ave Ste 100 Bloomfield Hills MI 48304-2855

THURBER, PETER PALMS, lawyer; b. Detroit, Mar. 23, 1928; s. Cleveland and Marie Louise (Palms) T.; m. Ellen Bodley Stites, Apr. 16, 1955; children—Edith Bodley, Jane Chenoweth, H. Thomas, Sarah Bartlett. B.A., Williams Coll., 1950; J.D., Harvard U., 1953. Bar: Mich., 1954. Ptnr. Miller, Canfield, Paddock and Stone, Detroit, 1953-93, of counsel, 1994—; trustee McGregor Fund, Detroit, 1979—. Bd. dirs. Detroit Symphony Orch., Inc., 1974-93; trustee Community Found. for Southeastern Mich., 1990—, Coun. Mich. Founds., 1991—. With U.S. Army, 1953-55. Fellow Am. Bar Found.; mem. ABA, Mich. Bar Assn. Roman Catholic. Club: Country of Detroit (Grosse Pointe Farms, Mich.). Avocations: reading; traveling; athletics. Home: 28 Provencal Rd Grosse Pointe MI 48236-3038 Office: Miller Canfield Paddock & Stone 150 W Jefferson Ave Ste 2500 Detroit MI 48226-4432

THURBER, ROBERT EUGENE, physiologist, researcher; b. Bayshore, N.Y., Oct. 11, 1932; s. Hallett Elliot and Mary Jean (Winkler) T.; m. Barbara Meyer, June 24, 1953 (div. 1982); children: Robert, Joseph, Karl, Michael; m. Linda Boyd, Mar. 4, 1984; stepchildren: Janet, Barbara, Karen, Robert. BS, Holy Cross Coll., Worcester, Mass., 1954; MS, Adelphi U., 1961; PhD, U. Kans., 1964. Rsch. assoc. Brookhaven Nat. Lab., Upton, N.Y., 1956-61; rsch. asst. Iowa State U., Ames, 1961-62; asst. prof. Med. Coll. Va., Richmond, 1964-69; assoc. prof. Jefferson Med. Coll., Phila., 1969-70; prof., chmn. physiology Sch. Medicine East Carolina, Greenville, N.C., 1970-94, prof., 1994—. Contbr. articles to profl. jours. Sgt. U.S. Army, 1954-56, Korea. Predoctoral fellow USPHS, 1962, postdoctoral fellow NEH, 1977. Mem. Am. Physiol. Soc., Assn. Chairmen Depts. Physiology (councilor 1989-91), Am. Heart Assn. (pres. N.C. affiliate 1979), Greenville Country Club, River Bend Country Club. Avocations: music, sailing. Home: 108 Hyde Ct New Bern NC 28562-3724 Office: E Carolina U Sch Medicine Dept Physiology Greenville NC 27858

THURLBECK, WILLIAM MICHAEL, retired pathologist, retired medical educator; b. Johannesburg, South Africa, Sept. 7, 1929; s. William and Enid Muriel (Mears) T.; m. Elizabeth Anne Tippett, Oct. 28, 1955; children—Sarah Margaret, David William, Alison Mary. B.Sc., U. Cape Town, 1951, M.B., Ch.B., 1953. Intern Groote Schuur Hosp., Cape Town, 1955; research fellow resident in pathology Mass. Gen. Hosp. and Harvard U., 1955-61; asst. prof. to prof. pathology McGill U., 1961-73; sr. investigator Midhurst Med. Research Inst. and Royal Postgrad. Med. Sch., Eng., 1973-75; prof. pathology, head U. Man. and Health Scis. Centre, Winnipeg, 1975-80; prof. pathology U. B.C., 1981—, assoc. dean research and grad. studies, 1981—, pathologist Children's Hosp., 1985—, acting head med. microbiol., 1992—; examiner in pathology Royal Coll. Physicians and Surgeons Can., 1964-70; mem. McGill Interdisciplinary Com. on Air Pollution, 1967-73; cons. Cardiovascular Research Inst., San Francisco; pulmonary diseases adv. com. Nat. Heart and Lung Inst., 1971-74; task force research planning in environ. health scis. NIH, mem. respiration and applied physiology study sect., 1981—; adv. fellow Indsl. Hygiene Found., Pitts., 1967-71, Paul Dudley White fellow in cardiology, 1960-61; Med. Research Council vis. scientist Oxford (Eng.) U., 1970-71; Schering travelling fellow Canadian Soc. Clin. Investigation, 1971. Author: Chronic Airflow Obstruction in Lung Disease, 1976, The Lung: Structure, Function and Disease, 1978; Contbr. articles to med. jours. Fellow Royal Coll. Physicians, Royal Coll. Pathologists, Am. Coll. Chest Physicians (medalist), Royal Coll. Pathology; mem. Am. Assn. Pathologists, Internat. Acad. Pathology, Path. Soc. Gt. Britain and Ireland, Canadian Soc. Clin. Investigation, Am. Thoracic Soc., Fleischner Soc. Clubs: Rondebosch Old Boys, Pluto. Home: 4094 W 37th Ave, Vancouver, BC Canada V6N 2W7

THURM, GIL, lawyer; b. Bklyn., Sept. 26, 1947; s. Isidore Leo and Rosalind (Greenstein) T.; m. Mary-Ellen Driscoll, Oct. 12, 1975; children: Michael Craig, Jennifer Leigh, Jeffrey Bryan. BA, Bklyn. Coll. of CUNY, 1969; JD, George Washington U., 1972, LLM in Taxation, 1974. Bar: D.C. 1973. Sr. tax atty. Arthur Andersen & Co., Washington, 1972-75; v.p., chief of staff and legis. counsel Nat. Assn. Realtors, Washington, 1975-89; of counsel Arent Fox Kintner Plotkin & Kahn, Washington, 1989-92; sr. v.p., chief counsel Internat. Franchise Assn., Washington, 1992-94; v.p., counsel Nat. Assn. Mfrs., Washington, 1994—; lectr. in field. Exec. editor: Franchise Legal Digest, 1992-94; contbg. editor Jour. Real Estate Taxation "Washington Tax Watch" column, 1977-94; editor Jour. Internat. Law and Econs., 1971-72; bd. advisor Housing and Devel. Reporter, 1977-88; contbr. numerous articles to profl. jours. Bd. dirs., pres. Fallswick Homeowners Assn., Potomac, Md., 1988-90; active various local, state and nat. polit. campaigns, 1975—. Recipient Outstanding Leadership award Child Ctr., Inc., 1988. Mem. ABA, FBA (officer tax sect. 1990—, vice chmn. 16th ann. tax law conf. 1992), D.C. Bar Assn., D.C. Bldg. Industry Assn. (bd. dirs. 1990-92), Assn. Global Real Estate Execs., Am. Soc. Assn. Execs. (coun. mem. govt. rels. sect. 1988-90, coun. mem. legal sect. 1991-94), Greater Washington Bd. of Trade, D.C. Assn. Realtors, Greater Washington Soc. Assn. Execs., Internat. Bar Assn. (com. on franchising), Exchequer Club of Washington. Home: 9409 Fox Hollow Dr Potomac MD 20854-2082 Office: Nat Assn Mfrs 1331 Pennsylvania Ave NW Washington DC 20004

THURMAN, ANDREW EDWARD, lawyer; b. Raleigh, N.C., May 11, 1954; s. William Gentry and Peggy Lou (Brown) T.; m. Patricia Thurman, May 19, 1979 (dec. 1989); children: Gentry Brown, Harrison Beauchamp, Andrew Guilford; m. Tracy Fletcher, Nov. 16, 1991; 1 child, Spencer Lee. BA, Columbia U., 1976; JD, Coll. William and Mary, 1979; MPH, U. Okla., 1984. Bar: Va. 1979, Okla. 1980, U.S. Ct. Appeals (10th cir.) 1981, U.S. Supreme Ct. 1985, Pa. 1988. Staff atty. Dept. of Human Services, Oklahoma City, 1979-80; counsel State of Okla. Teaching Hosps., Oklahoma City, 1980-84; mem. Miller, Dollarhide, Dawson & Shaw, Oklahoma City, 1984-87; ptnr. Berkman, Ruslander, Pohl, Lieber & Engel, Pitts., 1988-89; of counsel Buchanan Ingersoll, Pitts., 1989; sr. v.p. and gen. counsel Forbes Health System, Pitts., 1989-96; sr. atty. Allegheny Health Edn. & Rsch. Found., Pitts., 1997—; Pres. Council of Neighborhood Assns., Oklahoma City, 1984, Lincoln Terr. Neighborhood Assn., Oklahoma City, 1984; trustee Rader Trust, Oklahoma City, 1980—; treas. Bd. dirs. State Okla. Tchg. Hosps. Found., Oklahoma City, 1984-87, Newman Meml. Hosp., 1983-87, Willowview Hosp., Spencer, Okla., 1985-87; chair HCWP Ethics Task Force, 1993—. Fellow Am. Acad. Hosp. Attys.; mem. ABA, Nat. Health Lawyers Assn., St. Anthony Hall Club of N.Y.C. (pres. 1976), Rivers Club, Pitts. Athletic Assn. Democrat. Presbyterian. Avocation: reading detective novels. Home: 106 Richmond Dr Pittsburgh PA 15215-1039 Office: AHERF 120 5th Ave Ste 2900 Pittsburgh PA 15222-3001

THURMAN, KAREN L., congresswoman; b. Rapid City, S.D., Jan. 12, 1951; d. Lee Searle and Donna (Altfillisch) Loveland; m. John Patrick Thurman, 1973; children: McLin Searl and Liberty Lee. BA, U. Fla., 1973. Mem. Dunnellon City Council (Fla.), 1974-82; mayor of Dunnellon, 1979-81; mem. Monroe Regional Med. Ctr. Governancy Com.; mem. Comprehensive Plan Tech. Adv. Com.; del. Fla. Dem. Conv.; Dem. Nat. Conv., 1980; mem. Regional Energy Action com.; mem. Fla. State Senate, 1982-1992; mem. 103rd-105th Congress from 5th Fla. dist., 1993—, ranking minority mem. govt. reform & oversight subcom. nat. security, internat. affairs & criminal justice, mem. com. on aging, mem. ways and means com. Recipient Svc. Above Self award Dunnellon C. of C., 1980; Regional Planning Coun. Appreciation for Svc. award. Mem. Dunnellon C. of C. (dir.), Fla. Horseman's Children's Soc. (charter). Episcopalian. Office: US Ho of Reps 440 Cannon Bldg Ofc Bldg Washington DC 20515-1311*

THURMAN, ROBERT, theology, religious studies educator; m. Nena von Schlebrugge. Co-founder Am. Inst. Buddhism, 1973—; founder Tibet House, N.Y., 1987—; scholar, activist, chair religion dept. Columbia U., N.Y.C., 1988—. Named One of the Most Influential Americans, Time Mag. Office: Columbia U Kent Hall Rm 621 New York NY 10027*

THURMAN, UMA KARUNA, actress; b. Boston, Apr. 29, 1970; d. Robert and Nena (von Schlebrugge) T.; m. Gary Oldman (div.). Appeared in films Kiss Daddy Good Night, 1987, Johnny Be Good, 1988, Dangerous Liaisons, 1988, The Adventures of Baron Munchausen, 1989, Where the Heart Is, 1990, Henry and June, 1990, Final Analysis, 1992, Jennifer Eight, 1992, Mad Dog and Glory, 1993, Even Cowgirls Get the Blues, 1993, Pulp Fiction, 1994 (Acad. award nom. Best Supporting Actress), A Month By the Lake, 1995, The Truth About Cats and Dogs, 1996, Beautiful Girls, 1996; TV movies include Robin Hood, 1991. Office: care CAA 9830 Wilshire Blvd Beverly Hills CA 90212-1804

THURMAN, WILLIAM GENTRY, medical research foundation executive, pediatric hematology and oncology physician, educator; b. Jacksonville, Fla., July 1, 1928; s. Horace Edward and Theodosia (Mitchell) T.; m. Peggy Lou Brown, Aug. 11, 1949 (div. 1978); children—Andrew E., Margaret Anne, Mary Allison; m. Gabrielle Anne Martin, Jan. 22, 1980; 1 step child, Stephanie Anne. B.S., U. N.C., 1949; M.S., Tulane U. Sch. Pub. Health, 1960; M.D.C.M., McGill U., Montreal,, 1954. Prof. pediatrics Cornell U. Sch. Medicine, N.Y.C., 1962-64; prof. pediatrics U. Va., Charlottesville, 1964-73; dean sch. medicine Tulane U., New Orleans, 1973-75; provost Health Scis. Ctr. U. Oklahoma, Oklahoma City, 1975-80; pres., chief exec. officer Okla. Med. Research Found., Oklahoma City, 1979—; sr. cons. pediatrics Surgeon Gen. USAF, Washington, 1964—; mem. Diet and Nutrition Study Com., Nat. Cancer Inst., Bethesda, Md., 1969—, Profl. Edn. Com., Am. Cancer Soc., N.Y.C., 1973—. Author: (with others) Bone Tumors in Children, 1963, Pediatric Malignant Disease, 1964; contbr. articles to profl. jours. Bd. dirs. United Way, Oklahoma City, 1977—, chmn., 1994, Community Found., Oklahoma City, 1975—, ARC, Oklahoma City, 1992—; bd. dirs. C. of C., 1984—, chmn. 1995. Served with U.S. Army, 1944-46, ETO. Markle scholar, 1959-64. Fellow Am. Acad. Pediatrics (dir. 1969-72); mem. Am. Pediatric Soc., Soc. Pediatric Rsch. (councillor 1971-75), Soc. Mil. Cons., Assn. Ind. Rsch. Insts. (pres. 1985-87), Oklahoma City C. of C. (dir. 1979, chmn. 1994-95), Alpha Omega Alpha. Baptist. Club: Petroleum. Avocations: physical fitness; sailing. Home: 1213 Larchmont Ln Oklahoma City OK 73116

THURMON, THEODORE FRANCIS, medical educator; b. Baton Rouge, Oct. 20, 1937; s. Theodore Francis and Gertrude Wilhemena (Arnette) T.; m. Virginia Ruth Strange, Sept. 1, 1961 (div. Oct. 1975); children: Penelope, Suzanna; m. Susonne Annette Ursin, Aug. 8, 1981 (div. Aug. 1992); children: Sarah Eileen, Amanda Aislinn; m. Suzanne Greenwood, Sept. 2, 1992. BS, La. State U., Baton Rouge, 1960; MD, La. State U., New Orleans, 1962. Diplomate Am. Bd. Pediatrics, Am. Bd. Med. Genetics. Commd. ensign USNR, 1957; transferred to USN, 1957, advanced through grades to lt. comdr., 1967; intern naval hosp. Pensacola, Fla., 1962-63; resident in pediatrics naval hosp. Phila., 1963-65, trainee in cytogenetics St. Christopher's Hosp., 1964-65; asst. cardiology naval hosp. St. Albans, N.Y., 1965-67; resigned USN, 1968; fellow in med. genetics Johns Hopkins Hosp., Balt., 1968-69; asst. prof. La. State U. Med. Ctr., New Orleans, 1969-72, assoc. prof., 1972-78, prof., 1978-86; prof. La. State U. Med. Ctr., Shreveport, 1986—. Author: Rare Genetic Diseases, 1974, Medical Genetics Primer, 1995; contbr. articles to med. jours. Active birth defects ctr. Nat. Found./ March of Dimes, New Orleans, 1969-81, La. Bd. Regents, New Orleans, 1982, La. Dept. Health, New Orleans, 1984—, La. Cancer & Lung Trust Fund, New Orleans, 1985-86. Fellow Am. Coll. Med. Genetics, Am. Acad. Pediat.; mem. AAAS, Am. Genetic Assn., Am. Soc. Human Genetics, Am. Statis. Assn., Assn. Profs. Human or Med. Genetics, La. Med. Soc., N.Y. Acad. Scis. Home: 1732 Willow Point Dr Shreveport LA 71119-4108 Office: La State U Med Sch Pediat-Genetics 1501 Kings Hwy Shreveport LA 71103-4228

THURMOND, GEORGE MURAT, judge; b. Del Rio, Tex., Oct. 22, 1930; s. Roger H. and Day (Hamilton) T.; m. Elsiejean Davis, June 27, 1959; children: Carolyn Day, Georganna, Sarah Gail. BA, U. of the South, 1952; JD, U. Tex., 1955. Bar: Tex. 1955. Ptnr. Montague & Thurmond, Del Rio, 1955-69; judge Tex. Dist. Ct. (63rd dist.), Del Rio, 1970—; presiding judge 6th Adminstrv. Region, Del Rio, 1983-87; chmn. jud. sect. State Bar Tex., 1988-89. Editor: U. Tex. Law Review, 1955. Rep. Tex. Ho. of Reps., 1955-58. Mem. ABA, Tex. Bar Assn. Democrat. Episcopalian. Avocations: jogging, water sports. Office: 63d Jud Dist of Tex PO Box 1089 243 W Strickland Del Rio TX 78841-1089

THURMOND, JOHN PETER, II, bank executive, rancher, archaeologist; b. Elk City, Okla., Apr. 22, 1955; s. Arthur Leslie and Dorothea Jean (Lee) T.; m. Susan Ide Smith, June 7, 1979; children: Katherine Anne, Allison Lee, Patrick Andrew. BA, U. Tex., 1976, MA, 1979. Pres., chmn. First Nat. Bank of Leedey, Okla., 1984-92, Leedey Bancorporation, Inc., 1984-92, Thurmond Ranch, Inc., Cheyenne, Okla., 1982—; vice chmn. First Nat. Bank & Trust Co., Elk City, 1992—. Author: Archeology of the Cypress Basin, NE Texas, 1981, Late Paleoindian Utilization of the Dempsey Divide, 1990. Emergency med. technician, sec. Leedey Ambulance Svc., Inc., 1981-88. Recipient Hist. Preservation award Okla. Hist. Soc., 1991, 97. Mem. Okla. Anthrop. Soc. (sec., treas. 1988—), Leedey C. of C. (pres. 1982-83), Tex. Archeol. Soc., Plains Anthrop. Soc., Am. Quaternary Assn., Geol. Soc. Am., Okla. Cattlemen's Assn., Okla. Hist. Soc., Cum Laude Soc., Phi Beta Kappa, Phi Kappa Phi. Republican. Episcopalian.

THURMOND, NATHANIEL, retired basketball player; b. Akron, Ohio, July 25, 1941. Student, Bowling Green State U. With San Francisco Warriors, 1963, Golden State Warriors (formerly San Francisco Warriors), 1971-73, Chgo. Bulls, 1974-75, Cleve. Cavaliers, 1975-76. Named to Basketball Hall of Fame, 1984. Achievements include Golden State Warriors all-time leading rebounder, 1963-74; holds single game record for most rebounds in one quarter, 1965; seven-time All-Star Game member, NBA All-Defensive First Team, 1969, 71, NBA All-Defensive Second Team, 1972-74, NBA All-Rookie Team 1964; All-Am., Bowling Green State U. Office: care Basketball Hall of Fame PO Box 179 Springfield MA 01101-0179

THURMOND, STROM, senator; b. Edgefield, S.C., Dec. 5, 1902; s. John William and Eleanor Gertrude (Strom) T.; m. Jean Crouch, Nov. 7, 1947 (dec. Jan. 1960); m. Nancy Moore, Dec. 22, 1968; children: Nancy Moore (dec.), J. Strom, Jr., Juliana Gertrude, Paul Reynolds. B.S., Clemson Coll., 1923; 34 hon. degrees. Bar: S.C. 1930. Tchr. S.C. schs., 1923-29; city atty., county atty., supt. edn. Edgefield County, 1929-33; state senator, 1933-38, circuit judge, 1938-46, gov. of S.C., 1947-51; chmn. So. Govs. Conf., 1950; practiced in Alken, S.C., 1951-55; U.S. senator from S.C., 1955—, pres. pro tem, 1981-87, 95—; del. Nat. Democratic Conv., 1932, 36, 48, 52, 56, 60; chmn. S.C. dels., armed svcs. com.; mem. Judiciary VA com.; mem. Dem. Nat. Com., 1948; States Rights candidate for Pres. U.S., 1948; del. Nat. Republican Conv., 1968, 72, 76, 80, 84, 88, 92, 96. Bd. dirs. Ga.-Carolina council Boy Scouts Am. Served with AUS; attached to 82d Airborne Div. for invasion 1942-46, Europe; maj. gen. Res. Decorated Legion of Merit with oak leaf cluster, Bronze Star with V, Purple Heart, Croix de Guerre France; Cross of Order of Crown Belgium; others; recipient Congl. Medal Honor Soc. Nat. Patriots award, 1974, Presdl. Medal of Freedom, 1993. Mem. S.C. (past v.p.), ABA, Clemson Coll. Alumni Assn. (past pres.), also numerous def., vets., civic, fraternal and farm orgns. Baptist. Office: US Senate 217 Russell Senate Office Bldg Washington DC 20510

THURSBY, JERRY GILBERT, economics educator, consultant; b. Camp Le Jeune, N.C., Aug. 6, 1947; s. Gilbert Earl and Mary Kathleen (Bailey) T.; m. Marie Sloan Currie, Mar. 11, 1972; children: James, Mary. AB, U. N.C., 1969, PhD, 1975. Asst. prof. Syracuse (N.Y.) U., 1975-78; from asst. to assoc. prof. Ohio State U., Columbus, 1978-88; prof. Purdue U., West Lafayette, Ind., 1988—. Contbr. articles to profl. jours. With U.S. Army, 1969-71. Home: 144 Creighton Rd West Lafayette IN 47906-2102 Office: Dept Econs Kran Bldg Purdue Univ West Lafayette IN 47907

THURSTON, DONALD ALLEN, broadcasting executive; b. Gloucester, Mass., Apr. 2, 1930; s. Joseph Allen and Helen Ruth (Leach) T.; m. Oralie Alice Lane, Sept. 9, 1951; children: Corydon Leach, Carolie Lane. Grad., Mass. Radio and Telegraph, 1949; HHD (hon.), North Adams (Mass.) State Coll., 1977; LHD (hon.), Emerson Coll., 1995. Announcer, engr. Sta. WTWN, St. Johnsbury, Vt., 1949-52; v.p., gen. mgr. Sta. WIKE, Newport, Vt., 1952-60; v.p., treas., gen. mgr. Sta. WMNB, North Adams, 1960-66; pres., treas. Berkshire Broadcasting Co., Inc., North Adams, 1966—; bd. dirs. Broadcast Capital Fund, Inc., 1980-96, chmn. bd., 1981-89; dir. Berkshire Bank and Trust Co., 1967-85, Broadcast Music, Inc., N.Y.C., 1990—, chmn. bd., 1994—. Pres. No. Berkshire Indsl. Devel. Corp., 1965-67; commr. Mass. Cmty. Antenna TV Commn., 1972-74; trustee North Adams State Coll., 1991—, vice chmn. bd. trustees, 1993-96, chmn., 1996—. Recipient Laymen's award Vt. Tchrs. Assn., 1958; Laymen's award Mass. Tchrs. Assn., 1962; Abe Lincoln Merit award So. Baptist Radio and TV Commn., 1975; named Man of Yr. Vt. Assn. Broadcasters, 1978. Mem. North Adams C. of C. (Hayden award 1967, pres. 1964-67), Nat. Assn. Broadcasters (dir. 1965-69, 73-77, chmn. radio 1976-77, chmn. bd., chmn. exec. com. 1977-79, Disting. Svc. award 1980), Mass. Broadcasters Assn. (pres. 1964, Disting. Svc. award 1964, 71, 78), Taconic Golf Club (Williamston, Mass.; bd. dirs. 1975-89). Republican. Methodist. Office: 466 Curran Hwy North Adams MA 01247-3901 *My goals have been to better my community, profession and life in general because I was a positive participant, and to provide independence, a sense of responsibility and a love of humanity for my family.*

THURSTON, GEORGE BUTTE, mechanical and biomedical engineering educator; b. Austin, Tex., Oct. 8, 1924; s. Rudolph D. and Olivia Ruth (Lester) T.; m. Carol A. McWharter, Apr. 5, 1947; children—John Douglas, Mary Elizabeth. B.S., U. Tex., Austin, 1944, M.A., 1948, Ph.D., 1952. Registered profl. engr., Tex. Supr. hydroacoustics sect. Def. Research Lab., U. Tex., Austin, 1949-52; asst. prof. physics U. Wyo., Laramie, 1952-53, U. Ark., Fayetteville, 1953-54; physicist Naval Ordnance Test Sta., Inyokern, Calif., 1954-55; assoc. prof. Okla. State U., Stillwater, 1954-59; research physicist U. Mich., Ann Arbor, 1958-59; prof. Okla. State U., Ann Arbor, 1959-68; vis. scientist Centre de Recherche sur les Macromolecules, Strasbourg, France, 1963-64; prof. mech. engring. and biomed. engring. U. Tex., Austin, 1968—; vis. prof. Helmholtz Inst. fur Biomedizinische Technik, Aachen, West Germany, 1975-76; cons. for govt., industry. Contbr. articles to profl. jours. Recipient Brown U. Calculus prize, 1942; Alexander von Humboldt Found. Sr. U.S. Scientist award, 1975; NSF faculty fellow, 1963-64; numerous grants. Fellow Am. Phys. Soc., Acoustical Soc. Am.; mem. ASME, Soc. Rheology, Internat. Soc. Biorheology, Brit. Soc. Rheology, Sigma Xi, Sigma Pi Sigma. Home: 1000 Madrone Rd Austin TX 78746-4320 Office: U Tex Dept Mech Engring Austin TX 78712

THURSTON, JOHN THOMAS, university advancement official; b. Lockport, N.Y., Oct. 24, 1948; s. John Henry and Helen Lenore (Shaffert) Mahar. BA in English and Journalism, So. Ark. U., 1971. Ednl. affairs writer SUNY, Buffalo, 1972-74, sci. editor, 1974-76, news editor, 1976-77, assoc. dir. Univ. New Burs., 1977-78, dir., 1979-83; assoc. dir. pub. affairs SUNY, 1983-86; staff assoc. Univ. Rels. SUNY, Buffalo, 1987-92, budget and pers. officer dept.Univ. Advancement and Devel., 1992—; communications instr., freelance writer, cons. Hockey coach, ofcl., youth baseball, basketball and football, pres. Western N.Y. High Sch. Club, 1983-85; pres. Lockport Tigers Youth Hockey Assn., 1996—. Recipient nat. award Coun. Advancement and Support of Edn., 1975, 78; named Lockport Sportsman of Yr., 1984. Mem. Coun. Advancement and Support Higher Edn., Nat. Assn. Sci. Writers, Constrn. Writers Am., Pub. Rels. Soc. Am., USA Hockey, Prof. Com. Western N.Y. Republican. Roman Catholic. Home: 4 Rogers Ave Lockport NY 14094-2520 Office: SUNY 503 Capen Blvd Buffalo NY 14226-2821

THURSTON, MORRIS ASHCROFT, lawyer; b. Logan, Utah, May 25, 1943; s. Morris Alma and Barbara (Ashcroft) T.; m. Dawna Lyn Parrett, Sept. 10, 1966; children: Morris III, David, Ashley, Tyson. BA, Brigham Young U., 1967; JD, Harvard U., 1970. Bar: Calif. 1971, U.S. Dist. Ct. (cen. dist.) Calif. 1971, U.S. Supreme Ct. 1978. Assoc. Latham & Watkins, Los Angeles, 1970-77, ptnr., 1978—; jud. arbitrator Orange County Superior Ct., Calif., 1980—. Mem. Calif. Bar Assn., Orange County Bar Assn., Assn. Bus. Trial Lawyers. Republican. Mormon. Avocations: writing, basketball, tennis. Home: 9752 Crestview Cir Orange CA 92861-1313 Office: Latham & Watkins 650 Town Center Dr Ste 2000 Costa Mesa CA 92626-1905

THURSTON, STEPHEN JOHN, pastor; b. Chgo., July 20, 1952; s. John Lee and Ruth (Hall) T.; m. Joyce DeVonne Hand, June 18, 1977; children: Stephen John II, Nicole D'Vaugh, Teniece Rael, Christian Avery Elijah. BA in Religion, Bishop Coll., 1975; Hon. degree, Chgo. Baptist Inst., 1986. Copastor New Covenant Missionary Bapt. Ch., Chgo., 1975-79, pastor, 1979—; third v.p. Nat. Bapt. Conv. Am., mem. exec. com. Christian Edn. Congress; pres. Ill. Nat. Bapt. State Conv.; mem. Christian Fellowship Dist. Assn.; lectr. various orgns.; instr. New Covenant Bapt. Ch., Fellowship Bapt. Ch. Co-chmn. religious affairs div. People United to Save Humanity (PUSH); bd. dirs. nat. alumni assn. Bishop Coll.; active NAACP; trustee, fin. chmn. Chgo. Bapt. Inst. Mem. Broadcast Ministers Alliance, Bapt. Ministers Conf. Chgo. (Ministerial Pioneer award). Club: Bishop Coll. (Chgo.). Office: New Cov Miss Baptist Church 740 E 77th St Chicago IL 60619-2553

THURSWELL, GERALD ELLIOTT, lawyer; b. Detroit, Feb. 4, 1944; s. Harry and Lilyan (Zeitlin) T.; m. Lynn Satovsky, Sept. 17, 1967 (div. Aug. 1978); children: Jennifer, Lawrence; m. Judith Linda Bendix, Sept. 2, 1978; children: Jeremy, Lindsey. LLB with distinction, Wayne State U., 1967. Bar: Mich. 1968, N.Y. 1984, D.C. 1986, Colo. 1990, Ill. 1992, U.S. Dist. Ct. (ea. dist.) Mich. 1968, U.S. Ct. Appeals (7th cir.) 1968, U.S. Supreme Ct., 1994. Student asst. to U.S. atty. Ea. Dist. Mich., Detroit, 1966; assoc. Zwerdling, Miller, Klimist & Maurer, Detroit, 1967-68; sr. ptnr. Thurswell, Chayet & Weiner, Southfield, Mich., 1968—; arbitrator Am. Arbitration Assn., Detroit, 1969—; mediator Wayne County Cir. Ct., Mich., 1983—, Oakland County Cir. Ct. Mich., 1984—, also facilitator, 1991; twp. atty. Royal Oak Twp., Mich., 1982—; lectr. Oakland County Bar Assn. People's Law Sch., 1988. Pres. Powder Horn Estates Subdiv. Assn., West Bloomfield, Mich., 1975, United Fund, West Bloomfield, 1976. Arthur F. Lederle scholar

Wayne State U. Law Sch., Detroit, 1964, grad. profl. scholar Wayne State U. Law Sch., 1965, 66. Mem. Mich. Bar Assn. (investigator/arbitrator grievance bd., atty. discipline bd., chmn. hearing panel), Mich. Trial Lawyers Assn. (legis. com. on govtl. immunit, 1984), ATLA (treas. Detroit met. chpt. 1986-87, v.p. 1989-90, pres. 1991-93), Detroit Bar Assn. (lawyer referral com., panel pub. adv. com. judicial candidates), Oakland County Bar Assn. Clubs: Wabeek Country (Bloomfield Hills), Skyline (Southfield, Mich.). Home: 1781 Golf Ridge Dr S Bloomfield Hills MI 48302-1733 Office: Thurswell Chayet & Weiner 1000 Town Ctr Ste 500 Southfield MI 48075-1221

THURSZ, DANIEL, retired service organization executive, consultant; b. Casablanca, Morocco, Jan. 25, 1929; came to U.S., 1941; s. Jonathan and Franka (Gutlas) T.; m. Hadassah Neulander, Feb. 8, 1953; children: Deborah Thursz Bleiweis, David, Deena Thursz Klopman, Tamar Thursz Truland. B.A., Queens Coll., 1949; M.S.W., Catholic U. Am., 1955, D.S.W., 1960; L.H.D. (hon.), U. Md., 1977, Balt. Hebrew U., 1990. Asso. prof. social welfare Sch. Social Service, Cath. U. Am., 1961-63; Assoc. prof. social welfare Sch. Social Work, U. Md., 1963-65; nat. asso. dir. VISTA, OEO, Washington, 1965-67; dean, prof. U. Md. Sch. Social Work and Community Planning, 1967-77; exec. v.p. B'nai B'rith Internat., Washington, 1977-87; pres., CEO, Nat. Coun. on Aging Inc., Washington, 1988-95, pres. emeritus, 1995—; Cardinal O'Boyle prof. social work Catholic U. Am.; cons. social welfare agys.; mem. nat. and state commns. social welfare; internat. v.p. Internat. Fedn. Aging; bd. dirs. Sage Pubs., Thousand Oaks, Calif. Author books, monographs, articles in field.; Co-editor: Meeting Human Needs, Vol. 1, 1975, Vol. 11, 1977, Vol. III, Reaching People, 1978, Vol. IV, Reaching the Aged, 1979. Mem. bd. visitors U. N.C., Asheville. Served with AUS, 1951-53. Alvin Johnson scholar. Mem. Acad. Certified Social Workers, Md. Welfare Conf. (pres. 1969-71), Nat. Assn. Social Workers (1st v.p. 1973-75), Conf. Jewish Communal Service (exec. com., pres. 1988-90), B'nai B'rith (hon. exec. v.p.). Jewish. Home and Office: 8605 Carlynn Dr Bethesda MD 20817-4310

THYDEN, JAMES ESKEL, diplomat, educator; b. L.A., Apr. 10, 1939; s. Eskel A. and Mildred Aileene (Rock) T.; m. Patricia Irene Kelsey, Dec. 15, 1959; children: Teresa Lynn, Janice Kay, James Blaine. BA in Biology, Pepperdine U., 1961; MA in Scandinavian Area Studies, U. Wash., 1992. Cert. secondary tchr., Calif., Wash. Tchr. Gompers Jr. High Sch., L.A., 1962-64; fgn. svc. officer U.S. Dept. State, Washington, 1964-90; rschr. U. Wash., Seattle, 1991-93; exec. dir. Seattle chpt. UN Assn., 1993-96; travel lectr. Cunard Lines' Royal Viking Sun, 1995, and Royal Caribbean's Splendour of the Seas, 1997. Editor govt. report, ann. human rights reports, 1983-86; author, editor in-house govt. reports, documents. Dir. Office of Human Rights, 1983-86; counselor Embassy for Polit. Affairs, Am. Embassy, Oslo, Norway, 1986-90. Named Outstanding Young Man Am., 1969, Alumnus of Yr., Pepperdine U., 1984. Mem. Am. Fgn. Svc. Assn., World Affairs Coun. Seattle, UN Assn. Avocations: travel, reading, gardening. Home: 5631 153rd Pl SW Edmonds WA 98026-4239

THYGESON, NELS MARCUS, physician; b. Palo Alto, Calif., Aug. 12, 1953; s. Robert James Will and Ralda Lee Meyerson; m. Cecelia Alice Thygeson, May 22, 1983 (div. Dec. 1996); 1 child, April Elizabeth. MD, Harvard Med. Sch., 1980; BS, U. Calif., Davis, 1995. Diplomate Am. Bd. Internal Medicine, Gastroenterology. Clin. practice Gastroenterology Assn. of the East Bay, Berkeley, Calif., 1987—; asst. clin. prof. medicine UCSF, San Francisco, 1990—; chmn. dept medicine Alta Bates Med. Ctr., Berkeley, 1995-96; med. dir. Alta Bates Med. Ctr., Emenyville, Calif., 1996—. Office: Alta Bates Med Group PO Box 5039 Berkeley CA 94705-0039

THYRET, RUSS, recording industry executive. Sales person L.A. WEA Br; singles sales mgr. Warner Bros. Records Inc., 1971-73, sales mgr., 1973-75, v.p. sales dept., 1975-76, v.p. promotion, 1976-81, sr. v.p. mktg. dept., 1981-83, sr. v.p. mktg. and promotion, 1983, vice chmn., chmn., CEO, 1995—. Office: Warner Bros Records 3300 Warner Blvd Burbank CA 91505

THYSEN, BENJAMIN, biochemist, health science facility administrator, researcher; b. N.Y.C., July 27, 1932; s. Bernard and Clara (Linietsky) Tissenbaum; m. Joan Albin; children: Julie Ann, Gregory Eden. BS, CCNY, 1954; MS, U. Mo., 1963; PhD, St. Louis U., 1967. Instr. St. Louis U. Med. Sch., 1967-68; sr. research scientist Technicon Instrument Corp., Ardsly, N.Y., 1968-69; group leader Technicon Instrument Corp., Tarrytown, N.Y., 1969-70; asst. prof. lab., med., and ob-gyn depts. Albert Einstein Coll. Medicine, Bronx, N.Y., 1971-86, assoc. prof. lab. med. and ob-gyn depts., 1986—, dir. endocrine labs., 1971—; cons. Technicon Instrument Corp., Tarrytown, 1979-81, Albert Einstein Coll. of Medicine, Bronx, 1969-70; mem. spl. study sect. Nat. Inst. Environ. Health Sci., 1986. Contbr. articles to profl. jours. Served with U.S. Army, 1956-58. Recipient Cancer Research award St. Louis U., 1967-68; fellow NIH, 1963-67. Mem. AAAS, Assn. Clin. Scientists, Soc. Study of Reproduction, Endocrine Soc., Sigma Xi. Office: Albert Einstein Coll Med 1635 Poplar St Bronx NY 10461-2659

TIAHRT, W. TODD, congressman, former state senator; b. Vermillion, S.D., June 15, 1951; s. Wilbur E. and Sara Ella Marcine (Steele) T.; m. Vicki Lyn Holland, Aug. 14, 1976; children: Jessica, John, Luke. Student, S.D. Sch. Mines & Tech., Rapid City, 1969-72; BA, Evangel Coll., 1975; MBA, S.W. Mo. State U., 1989. Property estimator Crawford & Co., Springfield, Mo., 1975-78; project engr. Zenith Electronics, Springfield, 1978-81; cost engr. Boeing, Wichita, Kans., 1981-94; proposal mgr. Boeing, Wichita, 1991-94; state senator State of Kans., Topeka, 1995—; mem. 104th-105th Congresses from 4th Kans. dist., Washington; mem. appropriations com.; chmn. 4th dist. Rep. party, 1990-92; exec. com. Kans. Rep. party, 1990-92, nat. security com., sci. com. Mem. Pachyderm (bd. dirs. 1991-92), Delta Sigma Phi. Republican. Home: 1329 Amity St Goddard KS 67052-9133 Office: 428 Cannon Washington DC 20515-0402*

TIANO, ANTHONY STEVEN, television producer, book publishing executive; b. Santa Fe, Mar. 27, 1941; s. Joseph A. and Marian (Adlesperger) T.; m. Kathleen O'Brien, Dec. 29, 1972; children: Mark A., A. Steven. BA, U. N.Mex., 1969, MA, 1971; LittD (hon.), Calif. Sch. Profl. Psychology, 1985. Dir. programming Sta. KNME-TV U. N.Mex., Albuquerque, 1968-72; sta. mgr. Sta. WHA-TV U. Wis., Madison, 1972-76; exec. dir. Sta. KETC-TV, St. Louis, 1976-78; pres., CEO KQED, Inc., San Francisco, 1978-93; chmn., CEO Santa Fe Ventures, Inc., San Francisco, 1993—. Vice-chair bd. dirs. Calif. Sch. Profl. Psychology, San Francisco, 1985-90. Mem. Nat. Assn. Pub. TV Stas. (vice chair bd. dirs. 1986). Office: Santa Fe Ventures 877 Bryant St # 210 San Francisco CA 94103-4720

TIBBITTS, THEODORE WILLIAM, horticulturist, researcher; b. La Crosse, Wis., Apr. 10, 1929; s. John Wilson and Vivian Sophia (Elver) T.; m. Allison Lou Mahan, Aug. 25, 1956 (dec. June 1975); children: Scott, Tia Anne; m. Mary Florence Olmsted, June 22, 1985. BS, U. Wis., 1950, MS, 1952, PhD, 1953. Asst prof., assoc. prof., and prof. U. Wis., Madison, 1955-96, emeritus prof., 1996—, dir. Biotron, 1987-92; sr. rsch. engr. N.Am. Aviation, L.A., 1965-66; cons. Johnson Space Ctr., Manned Spaceflight Ctr., Apollo Flights, 1969-70; vis. prof. U. Guelph, Ont., Can., 1981; mem. NASA Controlled Ecol. Life Support System Discipline Working Group, Washington, 1989—. Author: Controlled Environment Guidelines for Plant Research, 1979; co-author: Growth Chamber Manual, 1978, 1995; contbr. articles to sci. jours. Elder Covenant Presbyn. Ch., Madison, 1961-65. With U.S. Army, 1953-55. Recipient Rsch. award Dept. Sci. and Indsl. Rsch., New Zealand, 1981. Fellow Am. Soc. Hort. Sci. (assoc. editor, Marion Meadows award); mem. AAAS, Am. Inst. Biol. Sci., Internat. Hort. Soc., Potato Assn. Am., Am. Soc. Gravitational and Space Biology, Am. Soc. Plant Physiologists, Internat. Commn. of Illumination (CIE). Achievements include development of guidelines for controlled environment research, optimizing growth of potatoes for life support in space, patent for use of light-emitting diodes for irradiation of plants; establishment of causal factors for physiological disorders in vegetable species; plant experiment on Biosatellite flights 1966-67, growth chamber experiments on shuttle flight, 1992, 93, 94, 95. Office: U Wis Dept Hort Madison WI 53706

TIBBLE, DOUGLAS CLAIR, lawyer; b. Joliet, Ill., May 26, 1952. BA, DePaul U., 1974; JD, Syracuse U., 1977, MPA, 1978. Bar: Ill., U.S. Dist. Ct. (no. dist.) Ill., U.S. Ct. Appeals (7th cir.), U.S. Supreme Ct. Ptnr. McBride, Baker & Coles, Oakbrook Terrace, Ill., 1996—. Mem. ABA, DuPage County Bar Assn., Chgo. Bar Assn. Office: McBride Baker & Coles 1 Mid America Plz Ste 1000 Oakbrook Terrace IL 60181-4710

TIBLIER, FERNAND JOSEPH, JR., municipal engineering administrator; b. New Orleans, Mar. 11, 1960; s. Fernand Joseph and Dorothy May (Bosworth) T.; m. Janine Therese Cousineau, Sept. 1, 1990; children: Amanda, Christine. BA in Chemistry, Biology, Drury Coll., 1982; MS in Environ. Engring., U. Cen. Fla., 1986. Registered profl. engr., Fla. Rsch. asst. U. Cen. Fla., Orlando, 1983-86; asst. city engr., then acting city engr. City of Longwood, Fla., 1986-92, city engr., 1992-94, dir. pub. works, city engr., 1994-96; city engr. City of Deltona, Fla., 1996—; mem. road impact fee com. Seminole County Citizen Adviser, Sanford, Fla., 1988-89; mem. water resources task force Seminole County Tech. Adviser, Sanford, 1992; advisor Pub. Works Acad. Oak Ridge High Sch., Orlando, 1996—. Lector, youth minister Nativity Ch., Lake Mary, Fla., 1987—; team capt. City of Longwood March of Dimes, 1992; mem. City of Longwood Planning Agy., 1997—. Mem. Am. Water Works Assn., Water Environ. Fedn., Community Leaders/Elected Ofcls. Seminole County. Republican. Roman Catholic. Avocations: home improvement, photography, travel, cooking, reading. Home: 407 Parson Brown Way Longwood FL 32750-4020 Office: City of Longwood 180 E Warren Ave Longwood FL 32750-4266

TICE, CAROL HOFF, middle school educator, consultant; b. Ashville, N.C., Oct. 6, 1931; d. Amos H. and Fern (Irvin) Hoff; m. (div.); children: Karin E., Jonathan H. BS, Manchester Coll., North Manchester, Ind., 1954; MEd, Cornell U., 1955. Cert. tchr., Mich., N.Y., N.J. Tchr. Princeton (N.J.) Schs., 1955-60; tchr. Ann Arbor (Mich.) Schs., 1964—; dir. intergenerational programs Inst. for Study Children and Families Eastern Mich. U., Ypsilanti, 1985—; founder, pres. Lifespan Resources, Inc., Ann Arbor, 1979—; commr. U.S. Nat. Commn. Internat. Yr. of the Child, Washington, 1979-81; del. to White House Conf. on Aging, 1995. Innovator; program, Tch. Learning Intergenerational Communities, 1971; author: Guide Books and articles, Community of Caring, 1980; co-producer, Film, What We Have, 1976 (award, Milan, Italy Film Festival 1982). Trustee Blue Lake Fine Arts Camp, Twin Lake, Mich., 1975—. Recipient Program Innovation award Mich. Dept. Edn., 1974-80, C.S. Mott Found. award, 1982, Nat. Found. Improvement in Edn. award, Washington, 1986, Disting. Alumni award Manchester Coll., 1979, A+ Break the Mold award U.S. Sec. of Edn., 1992; Ford Found. fellow, Ithaca, N.Y., 1955. Mem. AAUW (agt. 1979, Agent of Change award), Generations United (Pioneer award 1989), Optimist Club (Humanitarian award). Democrat. Presbyterian. Office: Scarlett MS 3300 Lorraine St Ann Arbor MI 48108-1970

TICE, DOUGLAS OSCAR, JR., federal judge; b. Lexington, N.C., May 2, 1933; s. Douglas Oscar Sr. and Lila Clayton (Wright) T.; m. Janet N. Capps, Feb. 28, 1959 (div. Sept. 1976); children: Douglas Oscar III, Janet E.; m. Beverley Carole Black, Aug. 8, 1982 (div. Apr. 1995); m. Martha Murdoch Edwards, June 8, 1996. BS, U. N.C., 1955, JD, 1957. Bar: N.C. 1957, U.S. Ct. Appeals (4th cir.) 1964, Va. 1970, U.S. Dist. ct. (ea. dist.) Va. 1976, U.S. Bankruptcy Ct. (ea. dist.) Va. 1976. Exec. sec. N.C. Jud. Coun., Raleigh, 1958-59; assoc. Baucom & Adams, Raleigh, 1959-61; trial atty. Office Dist. Coun., IRS, Richmond, Va., 1961-70; corp. atty. Carlton Industries, Inc., Richmond, 1970-75; ptnr. Hubard, Tice, Marchant & Samuels, P.C., Richmond, 1975-87; judge U.S. Bankruptcy Ct., Richmond, Norfolk, Alexandria, Va., 1987—. Co-author: Monument & Boulevard, Richmond's Grand Avenues, 1996; contbr. articles to profl. jours. Vice pres. Richmond Pub. Forum, 1976-80, com. chmn. Richmond Forum, Inc., 1986—; past pres. Richmond Civil War Roundtable, mem., 1965—; bd. dirs. Epilepsy Assn. Va., Inc., 1976-87. Capt. USAR, 1957-66. Mem. ABA, Va. Bar Assn., City of Richmond Bar Assn., Am. Bankruptcy Inst., Nat. Conf. Bankruptcy Judges, Old Dominion Sertoma (pres. Richmond chpt. 1967). Home: 2037 W Grace St Richmond VA 23220-2003 Office: US Bankruptcy Ct 1100 E Main St Ste 341 Richmond VA 23219-3538

TICE, GEORGE A(NDREW), photographer; b. Newark, Oct. 13, 1938; s. William S. and Margaret T. (Robertson) T.; m. Joanna Blaylock, 1958; m. Marie Tremmel, 1960; children: Christopher, Loretta, Lisa, Lynn, Jennifer. Instr. photography New Sch. Social Research, 1970—. One-man shows, Witkin Gallery, 1970, Met. Mus. Art, 1972, group shows include, Whitney Mus. Am. Art, 1974, Mus. Modern Art, 1979; represented in permanent collections, Mus. Modern Art, Met. Mus. Art, Art Inst. Chgo., Bibliothèque Nationale, Nihon U., Tokyo; books include Fields of Peace, 1970, Goodbye River, Goodbye, 1971, Paterson, 1972, Seacoast Maine, 1973, George A. Tice Photographs, 1953-73, 1975, Urban Landscapes, 1975, Artie Van Blarcum, 1977, Urban Romantic, 1982, Lincoln, 1984, Hometowns, 1988, Stone Walls, Grey Skies, 1991. Served with USN, 1956-59. Recipient Grand prix for best photography book of Year Arles, France, 1973; Guggenheim Found. fellow, 1973-74; Nat. Endowment for Arts fellow, 1973—; Nat. Mus. Photography and Bradford and Ilkley Community Coll. (Eng.) fellow, 1990-91. Address: 323 Gill Ln Apt 9B Iselin NJ 08830-2825

TICE, RAPHAEL DEAN, army officer; b. Topeka, Kans., Dec. 4, 1927; s. Arthur Taylor and Mamie (McDonald) T.; m. Eunice Miriam Suddarth, Dec. 23, 1946; children: Karen Ann Tice Claterbos, William Dean. B.S. in Mil. Sci., U. Md., 1963; M.S. in Bus. Adminstrn, George Washington U., 1970. Served as enlisted man U.S. Army, 1946-47; commd. 2d lt., 1947, advanced through grades to lt. gen., 1981; platoon leader and co. comdr. 1st Inf. div., W.Ger., 1949-52; co. comdr., regimental adj. 8th Inf. div., 1955-56; tng. advisor Vietnam, 1956-57; mem. staff Office of Dep. chief of Staff for Personnel, Dept. Army, 1960-63; chief personnel mgmt. div. Office of Under Sec. of Army, 1963-64; plans Officer So. Command, Panama, 1965-67; dep. brigade comdr. 3d Brigade, 4th Inf. Div., 1967; comdr. 2d Bn., 12th Inf. of 25th Inf. div., Vietnam, 1968; exec. for personnel procurement Office of Sec. Def. for Manpower and Res. Affairs, 1968-69; comdr. 1st Brigade, 1st Inf. div., 1970, chief of staff, 1971; dep. dir. mil. personnel mgmt. Dept. Army, 1972-73; comdg. gen. Berlin Brigade, 1974-76; dep. chief of staff personnel U.S. Army Europe, 1976-77; comdg. gen. 3d. Inf. div., 1977-79; dep. asst. sec. def. for mil. personnel and force mgmt. Dept. Def., 1979-85; exec. dir. Nat. Recreation and Park Assn., 1986—; spl. adviser Pres.'s Council on Phys. Fitness and Sports. Decorated Silver Star, Legion of Merit with 2 oak leaf clusters, Air medal with V and 7 oak leaf clusters, Bronze Star with V, Vietnam Cross of Gallantry with Palm, Purple Heart., Def. Disting. Service medal, Army Disting. Service medal. Mem. Assn. U.S. Army, Am. Chess Found. (hon. pres.). Home: 8655 Gateshead Rd Alexandria VA 22309-4042 Office: Nat Recreation & Park Assn 2775 S Quincy St Ste 300 Arlington VA 22206-2236

TICER, PATRICIA, state senator; m. Jack Ticer; 4 children. Grad., Sweet Briar Coll. Councilwoman City of Alexandria, Va., 1982-84, vice mayor, 1984-90, appointed mayor, 1991-92, mayor, 1992-95; state senator Commonwealth of Va., 1995—; mem. Agrl., Conservation and Natural Resources Com., Transp. Com., Rehab. and Social Svcs. Com., Local Govt. Com., 1995—; chair Metro Washington Coun. of Govts.; bd. dirs. No. Va. Transp. Commn., chmn., 1994. Founding mem. Early Childhood Devel. Commn., No. Va. Housing Coalition, Alexandria Commn. on the Arts; mem. Govs. Coun. on Child Care and Early Childhood Programs; mem. adv. coun. Alexandria Symphony Orch.; active No. Va. AIDS Mins. Office: Rm 2007 City Hall 301 King St Alexandria VA 22314-3211

TIDBALL, CHARLES STANLEY, computer scientist, educator; b. Geneva, Switzerland, Apr. 15, 1928; (parents Am. citizens); s. Charles Taylor and Adele (Desmaison) T.; m. Mary Elizabeth Peters, Oct. 25, 1952. B.A., Wesleyan U., 1950; M.S. (Univ. scholar), U. Rochester, 1952; Ph.D., U. Wis., Madison, 1955; M.D. (Shattuck fellow, Van Noyes scholar), U. Chgo., 1958; LHD (hon.), Wilson Coll., 1994. Rotating intern Madison (Wis.) Gen. Hosp., 1958-59; physician I Mendota State Hosp., Madison, 1959; asst. research prof. physiology dept. George Washington U. Med. Center, Washington, 1959-63; USPHS spl. fellow George Washington U. Med. Center, 1960-61, asso. prof., acting chmn. dept., 1963-64, prof., 1964-65, chmn. dept., 1964-71, Henry D. Fry prof., 1965-84, research prof. med., 1972-80; dir. Office Computer Assisted Edn. George Washington U. Med. Ctr., 1973-75, dir. Office Computer Assisted Edn. and Svcs., 1975-78; Lucie Stern disting. vis. prof. natural scis. Mills Coll., 1980; prof. edn. George Washington U., 1982-84, dir. ednl. computing tech. program Sch. Edn., 1982-84, prof. computer medicine Med. Ctr., 1984-92, prof. emeritus computer medicine, 1992, prof. neurol. surgery, 1990-92, prof. emeritus neurol. surgery, 1992; civil surgeon Immigration and Naturalization Svc., Dept. Justice, Washington, 1986-89; disting. rsch. scholar, co-dir. Tidball Ctr. for Study Ednl. Environments Hood Coll., Frederick, Md., 1994—; trustee in residence Skidmore Coll., 1995. Author: (with others) Consolidated Index to For Thy Great Glory, 1993; editor: (with M. C. Shelesnyak) Frontiers in the Teaching of Physiology: Computer Literacy and Simulation, 1981; mem. editorial bd.: Jour. Applied Physiology, 1966-69, Jour. Computer-Based Instrn., 1974-89, Am. Jour. Physiology; assoc. editor physiology tchr. sect.; The Physiologist, 1979-85; contbr. articles to profl. jours. Trustee Cathedral Choral Soc., 1976-79, Wilson Coll., 1983-92, Everitt-Pomeroy, 1993-96, Population Reference Bur., 1987-94, 96—, chmn. bd. trustees, 1992-94, sec., 1994-97; lay reader St. Albans Parish, 1965-67, Washington Nat. Cathedral, 1967-94, lay eucharist minister, 1994—, clergy asst., 1968—, homilist, 1977—, info. sys. specialist, 1986-93, vol. mgr. info. sys. program, 1982—; mem. commn. Episcopal Diocese Washington, 1976-78; mem. com. mgmt. YMCA Camp Letts, 1968—, chmn., 1972-75, dir., chmn. Endowment Fund, 1977-96; bd. dirs. Met. YMCA, Washington, 1972-84, trustees coun., 1984-91, fin. com., 1972-93, v.p. internat. program, 1974-75, asst. treas., 1975-77, v.p., treas., 1977-79, vice chmn., 1979-80, chmn., 1980-82, pres. of found., 1991-93; bd. dirs., treas. Woodley Ensemble, 1993—; bd. dirs. Mid-Atlantic Region YMCA, 1974-83; bd. dirs., vice-chmn. Cathedral West Condo., 1983-84, chmn., 1984-87, 91-93, fin. com., 1979-94. Recipient award Washington Acad. Scis., 1967, Leader of Yr. award Met. YMCA, Washington, 1974, Red Triangle award, 1976, Service award, 1979; Dakota Indian name Am. Youth Found., 1976; Research Career Devel. award USPHS, 1961-63. Mem. Am. Physiol. Soc. (emeritus). Home: 4100 Cathedral Ave NW Washington DC 20016-3584

TIDBALL, M. ELIZABETH PETERS, physiologist, educator, research director; b. Anderson, Ind., Oct. 15, 1929; d. John Winton and Beatrice (Ryan) Peters; m. Charles S. Tidball, Oct. 25, 1952. BA, Mt. Holyoke Coll., 1951, LHD, 1976; MS, U. Wis., 1955, PhD, 1959; MTS summa cum laude, Wesley Theol. Sem., 1990; ScD (hon.), Wilson Coll., 1973; DSc (hon.), Trinity Coll., 1974, Cedar Crest Coll., 1977; ScD (hon.), U. of South, 1978, Goucher Coll., 1979; DSc (hon.), St. Mary-of-The-Woods Coll., 1986; LittD (hon.), Regis Coll., 1980, Coll. St. Catherine, 1980, Alverno Coll., 1989; HHD (hon.), St. Mary's Coll., 1977, Hood Coll., 1982; LLD (hon.), St. Joseph Coll., 1983; LHD (hon.), Skidmore Coll., 1984, Marymount Coll., 1985, Converse Coll., 1985, Mt. Vernon Coll., 1986. Teaching asst. physiology dept. U. Wis., 1952-55, 58-59; research asst. anatomy dept. U. Chgo., 1955-56, research asst. physiology dept., 1956-58; USPHS postdoctoral fellow NIH, Bethesda, Md., 1959-61; staff pharmacologist Hazleton Labs., Falls Church, Va., 1961; assoc. in physiology George Washington U. Med. Ctr., 1960-62; cons. Hazleton Labs., 1962; asst. research prof. dept. pharmacology George Washington U. Med. Ctr., 1962-64, assoc. research prof. dept. physiology, 1964-70, research prof., 1970-71, prof., 1971-94, prof. emeritus, 1994—; asst. dir. M of Theol. Studies program Wesley Theol Sem., 1993-94; disting. rsch. scholar Hood Coll., Frederick, Md., 1994—; co-dir. Tidball Ctr. for Study of Ednl. Environments Hood Coll., 1994—; Lucie Stern Disting. vis. prof. natural scis. Mills Coll., 1980; scholar in residence Coll. Preachers, 1984, Salem Coll., 1985, Wesley Theol. Sem., 1992; Disting. scholar in residence So. Meth. U., 1985; vis. trustee prof. Skidmore Coll., 1995; cons. FDA, 1966-67, assoc. sci. coord. sci. assocs. tng. programs, 1966-67; mem. com. on NIH tng. programs and fellowships Nat. Acad. Scis., 1972-75; faculty summer confs. Am. Youth Found., 1967-78; founder, dir. Summer Seminars for Women Am. Youth Found., 1987-95; cons. for instl. rsch. Wellesley Coll., 1974-75; exec. sec. com. on edn. and employment women in sci. and engring. Commn. on Human Resources, NRC/NAS, 1974-75, vice chmn., 1977-82; cons., staff officer NRC/Nat. Acad. Scis., 1974-75; cons. Woodrow Wilson Nat. Fellowship Found., 1975—, NSF, 1974-91; bd. mentor Assn. Governing Bds. of Univs. and Colls., 1991—, Gale Fund for the Study of Trusteeship Adv. Comm., 1992—; cons. Assn. Am. Colls. Women's Coll. Coalition Rsch. Adv. Com., 1992—; Single Gender Schooling Working Group, U.S. Dept. Edn., 1992-94; rep. to D.C. Commn. on Status of Women, 1972-75; nat. panelist Am. Coun. on Edn., 1983-90; panel mem. Congl. Office of Tech. Assessment, 1986-87; mem. fellows selection com., fellows mentor Coll. Preachers, 1992—. Columnist Trusteeship, 1993-95; mem. editl. bd. Jour. Higher Edn., 1979-84, cons. editor, 1984—; mem. editl. adv. bd. Religion and Intellectual Life, 1983—; contbr. sci. articles and rsch. on edn. of women to profl. jours. Trustee Mt. Holyoke Coll., 1968-73, vice chmn., 1972-73, trustee fellow, 1988—; trustee Hood Coll., 1972-84, 86-92, exec. com., 1974-84, 89-92; overseer Sweet Briar Coll., 1978-85; trustee Cathedral Choral Soc., 1976-90, pres. bd. trustees, 1982-84, hon. trustee, 1991—; trustee Skidmore Coll., 1988—, mem. exec. com., 1993—; mem. governing bd. Coll. of Preachers, 1979-85, chmn., 1983-85; mem. governing bd. Washington Nat. Cathedral Found., 1983-85, mem. exec. com., 1983-85; bd. vis. Salem Coll., 1986-93; ctr. assoc. Nat. Resource Ctr., Girls Club Am., 1983—. Shattuck fellow, 1955-56; Mary E. Woolley fellow Mt. Holyoke Coll., 1958-59; USPHS postdoctoral fellow, 1959-61; recipient Alumnae Medal of Honor Mt. Holyoke Coll., 1971, Award for Valuable Contbns. Gen. Alumni Assn. George Washington U., 1982, 87, Chestnut Hill Medal for Outstanding Achievement Chestnut Hill Coll., Phila., 1987; named Outstanding Grad. The Penn Hall Sch., 1988. Mem. AAAS, Am. Physiol. Soc. (chmn. task force on women in physiology 1973-80, com. on cons. 1977-80, mem. emeritus 1994—), Am. Assn. Higher Edn., Mt. Holyoke Alumnae Assn. (dir. 1966-70, 76-77), Histamine Club, Sigma Delta Epsilon, Sigma Xi. Episcopalian. Home: 4100 Cathedral Ave NW Washington DC 20016-3584

TIDMAN, DEREK ALBERT, physics researcher; b. London, Oct. 18, 1930; came to U.S., 1957; s. Albert Horace and Florence Violet (Oscar) T.; m. Pauline Harrell Tidman, Apr. 25, 1959; children: Katherine Fleming, Mark Harrell. BSc, London U., 1952; diploma, Imperial Coll. Sci. & Tech., 1956; PhD, 1956. Rsch. fellow U. Sydney, Australia, 1956-57; asst. prof. U. Chgo., Ill., 1957-60; rsch. assoc. prof. U. Md., College Park, 1961-64, rsch. prof., 1964-80; pres. GT-Devices subs. Gen. Dynamics, Alexandria, Va., 1980-94, Utron Inc., Manassas, Va., 1994—; cons. NASA Goddard Space Flight Ctr., Greenbelt, Md., 1961-69, Los Alamos Sci. Lab., 1974-78, Lawrence Livermore Lab., Calif., 1977-80. Co-author: Plasma Kinetic Theory, 1963, Shock Waves in Collisionless Plasmas, 1971; co-editor: Plasma Instabilities in Astrophysics, 1969; assoc. editor: Physics of Fluids, 1970-72, Jour. Math. Physics, 1972-74; contbr. articles to profl. jours.; patentee in field. Recipient Disting. Scientist award Md. Acad. Scis., 1965. Fellow Am. Phys. Soc.; mem. IEEE, AIAA. Office: Utron 8506 Wellington Rd Manassas VA 20109-3915

TIDWELL, GEORGE ERNEST, federal judge; b. Atlanta, Aug. 1, 1931; s. George Brown and Mary (Wooddall) T.; m. Carolyn White, July 1, 1961; children: Thomas George, Linda Carol, David Loran. LL.B., Emory U., 1954. Bar: Ga. 1954. With John J. Westmoreland Sr. and Jr., Atlanta, 1954-58, Slaton, Brookins, Robertson & Tidewell, Atlanta, 1958-66; exec. asst. atty. gen. Atlanta, 1966-68; judge Civil Ct., Fulton County, Ga., 1968-71, Superior Ct., Atlanta Jud. Circuit, 1971-79, U.S. Dist. Ct. (no. dist.) Ga., Atlanta, 1979—; now chief judge. Mem. ABA, State Bar Ga., Am. Judicature Soc., Atlanta Bar Assn. Office: US Dist Ct 1967 US Courthouse 75 Spring St SW Atlanta GA 30335-3309*

TIDWELL, JOSEPH PAUL, JR., technical specialist research and engineering; b. Tuscaloosa, Ala., Oct. 29, 1943; s. Joseph Paul and Jeanette (Steinwinder) T.; m. Susan Kay White, Oct. 3, 1970; children: Joseph Paul III, James Boland, Heather Loran, Shawn Damon. A.S., NYU, 1978, BS, 1984; postgrad. Murray (Ky.) State U., 1984-85; MBA Embry Riddle Aero. U., 1991. Lic. pilot rotorcraft, cert. safety mgr., safety exec. Commd. aviation ops. officer U.S. Army, 1976, advanced through grades to maj., 1985; aviation safety officer Ft. Campbell, Ky., 1982-85, Chun Chon, Korea, 1981-82; chief aviation and product safety/flight safety parts programs McDonnell Douglas Helicopter, Co., Mesa, Ariz., 1985-89, dept. mgr., supplier evaluation and requirements Quality Control div., 1989-91, sr. systems safety engr. Advanced Devel. and Tech. div., 1991-93; rsch. and engring. tech. specialist (aviation and product safety) advanced devel. and engring. divsn. McDonnell Douglas Corp., 1993—. Adj. instr. Embry Riddle Aero. Univ.; developer safety engring., safety cons., safety instr. Webelos den leader Clarksville council Cub Scouts Am., Tenn., 1983-85; asst. scout master Clarksville council Boy Scouts Am., 1983-85, scoutmaster Mesa council, 1985—. Decorated Purple Heart, Meritorious Service medal, recipient Den Leaders Tng. Key Middle Tenn. council Boy Scouts Am., 1985, Woodbadge Beads Middle Tenn. Council Boy Scouts Am., 1985. Named Scoutmaster of Yr.,

Mesa Dist., Theodore Roosevelt Council Boy Scouts Am., 1986, award of merit Mesa Dist. 1988.. Mem. Am. Soc. Safety Engrs. (profl.; Safety Officer of Month award 1985, chmn. awards and elections Ariz. chpt. 1985-87), Army Aviation Assn. Am. (air assault chpt. exec. treas. 1983-85, Aviation Safety Officer of Yr. award 1984), U.S. Army Warrant Officer's Assn. (Ky.-Tenn. chpt. pres. 1984-85, Disting. Service plaque 1984, Cert. of Merit for Disting. Achievement in Youth Leadership Devel. Men of Achievement, Cambridge, Eng., 1987. World Safety Orgn. (affiliate), Internat. Soc. Air Safety Investigators, S.W. Safety Congress and Exposition (bd. govs., conv. and advt. dir., vice chmn. external affairs 1985-88), Aviation Edn. Coun. of Ariz. (bd. govs.), System Safety Soc. (organizer, pres. Ariz. chpt. 1993). Republican. Roman Catholic. Lodge: WIPALA WIKI, Order of Arrow. Avocations: golfing, camping, cycling. Home: 913 E 9th Pl Mesa AZ 85203 Office: McDonnell Douglas Helicopter Co 5000 E Mcdowell Rd Mesa AZ 85215-9707

TIDWELL, MOODY RUDOLPH, federal judge; b. Kansas City, Mo., Feb. 15, 1939; s. Moody R., Jr. and Dorothy T.; m. Rena Alexandra, Jan. 28, 1966; children—Gregory, Jeremy. B.A., Ohio Wesleyan U., 1961; J.D., Am. U., 1964; LL.M., George Washington U., 1972. Bar: U.S. Ct. Appeals (D.C. cir.) 1964, U.S. Dist Ct. D.C. 1965, U.S. Ct. Claims 1972, U.S. Ct. Appeals (10th cir.) 1979. Assoc. solicitor U.S. Dept. Interior, Washington, 1972-80; assoc. solicitor Mine Health and Safety div. Dept. Labor, Washington, 1978-80; deputy solicitor, counsellor to the sec. Dept. Interior, Washington, 1981-83; judge U.S. Ct. Federal Claims, Washington, 1983—; dir., corporate sec. Keco, Inc., Cin. Chmn. Crafts for Econ. Empowerment, Inc., 1996—. Recipient Disting. Service award Sec. of Interior, 1983, Meritorious Service award Sec. of Labor, 1979. Mem. ABA, FBA, D.C. Bar Assn. Office: US Ct Fed Claims 717 Madison Pl NW Washington DC 20005-1011*

TIDWELL, THOMAS TINSLEY, chemistry educator; b. Atlanta, Feb. 20, 1939; s. Charles Speer and Helen (Frazier) T.; m. Sarah Huddleston, July 29, 1971. BS, Ga. Inst. Tech., 1960; AM, Harvard U., 1963, Ph.D., 1964. Research assoc. U. Calif., San Diego, 1964-65; research assoc. U. East Anglia, Norwich, Eng., 1966-67; asst. prof. U. S.C., Columbia, 1965-72; assoc. prof. U. Toronto, 1972-77, prof. chemistry, 1977—, assoc. dean, 1979-82, assoc. chair dept. chemistry, 1991-93; chair Iupac Commn. Phys. Orgn. Chem., 1994—. NATO research fellow, 1978, 83, 89; exch. scientist U.S. Acad. Sci., Bulgaria, 1982, USSR, 1989. Mem. Am. Chem. Soc., Am. Assn. Adv. Sci., Can. Soc. Chemistry. Office: U Toronto, Dept Chemistry, Toronto, ON Canada M5S 3H6

TIECKE, RICHARD WILLIAM, pathologist, educator, association executive; b. Muscatine, Iowa, Apr. 5, 1917; s. Harry Frederick and Nell Eola (McKibben) T. BS, U. Iowa, 1940, DDS, 1942, MS, 1947; Ph.D. pathology, U Chicago, 1949; postgrad. in pathology, U. Chgo., 1947-49. Diplomate Am. Bd. Oral Pathology (bd. dirs., past pres.). Jr. pathologist, asst. pathologist, dep. chief oral pathology div. Armed Forces Inst. Pathology, 1949-54; assoc. prof. pathology Georgetown, 1949-54; prof. pathology Northwestern U. Sch. Medicine, Chgo., 1954-85; prof. emeritus Northwestern U. Sch. Medicine, 1985—, head oral pathology, assoc. cancer coordinator, 1954-62; prof.—dept. oral pathology U. Ill., 1965-80, prof. dept. oral diagnosis, 1980-84; adj. staff Northwestern Meml. Hosps., 1981-85; research fellow Hektoen Inst. Med. Research, Cook County Hosp., Chgo., 1965-80; dir. research inst. Am. Dental Assn., Chgo., 1968-71, asst. exec. dir., 1971-85; lectr. Royal Coll. Surgeons, London, 1958, Royal Coll. Surgeons, Copenhagen, Denmark, 1959, Royal Coll. Surgeons, Helsinki, Finland, 1959; cons. AMA, U.S. Naval Hosp., Great Lakes, Ill., VA Research Hosp., VA West Side Hosp., Pub. Health Hosp., Chgo., City Chgo. Bd. Health; surgeon gen. USPHS; head and neck cancer detection Nat. Center Chronic Disease Control-USPHS, Nat. Cancer Inst. NIH; cons. to surgeon gen. Army, 1969-80. Author: Physiologic Pathology of Oral Disease, 1959, Oral Pathology, 1964, Atlas on Oral Cytology, 1969, also research articles. Served from 1st lt. to col. U.S. Army and AUS, 1942-77; now col. Res. (ret.). Richard W. Tiecke Pathology Lab. named in his honor Northwestern U. Med. Ctr., 1987. Fellow Am. Acad. Oral Pathology (past pres.), Am. Coll. Dentists; mem. ADA (hon., asst. sec. coun. dental therapeutics 1962-68), Ill., Chgo. dental socs., Internat. Assn. Dental Rsch., Psi Omega, Omicron Kappa Upsilon. Home: 5 Major Aly Palm Beach FL 33480-4518

TIEDE, TOM ROBERT, journalist; b. Huron, S.D., Feb. 24, 1937; s. Leslie Albert and Rose (Allen) T.; children: Kristina Anne, Thomas Patrick. B.A. in Journalism, Wash. State U., 1959. Mem. staff Kalispell (Mont.) Daily Interlake, 1960-61, Daytona Beach (Fla.) News Jour., 1961-63; war corr. Newspaper Enterprise Assn., N.Y.C., 1964—; lectr. in field., 1965—. Author: Your Men at War, 1965, Coward, 1968, Calley: Soldier or Killer?, 1971, Welcome to Washington, Mr. Witherspoon, 1979, The Great Whale Rescue, 1986, American Tapestry: Eye Witness Accounts of the 1900's, 1988, The Man Who Discovered Pluto, 1990, Fosser, 1994. Served as lt., inf. AUS, 1960. Recipient Ernie Pyle Meml. award, 1965; Freedoms Found. award, 1966; George Washington medal, 1972. Mem. Internat. Platform Assn., Sigma Delta Chi, Lambda Chi Alpha. Roman Catholic. Clubs: Overseas Press, National Press, Nat. Headliners (award 1966 Atlantic City). Work collected by Boston U. Library. Office: NEA 1090 Vermont Ave NW Washington DC 20005-4905 Address: 316 E Main St Charlottesville VA 22902

TIEDEMAN, DAVID VALENTINE, education educator; b. Americus, Ga., Aug. 12, 1919; s. Walter Dohlen and Edna M(arie) (Komfort) T.; m. Marjorie I(da) Denman, Sept. 26, 1942 (div. Jan. 2, 1973); children—David Michael, Jeffrey Denman; m. Anna Louise Miller, Jan. 6, 1973. A.B., Union Coll., Schenectady, 1941; A.M., U. Rochester, 1943; Ed.M., Harvard, 1948, Ed.D., 1949. Staff mem. NRC com. selection and tng. aircraft pilots U. Rochester, 1941-43; staff mem. test constrn. dept. Coll. Entrance Exam. Bd., 1943-44; assoc. head statistics div. Manhattan Project, 1944-46; Milton teaching fellow, instr. edn. Harvard Grad. Sch. Edn., 1946-48, Sheldon travelling fellow, 1948-49, instr. edn., 1949-51, asst. prof. edn., 1951-52, lectr. edn., 1952-55, assoc. prof., 1955-59, prof., 1959-71, assoc. dir., research assoc. Center for Research in Careers, 1963-66, also chmn. exec. com., info. system for vocat. decisions, 1966-69; prin. research scientist Palo Alto office Am. Insts. for Research, 1971-73; prof. edn. No. Ill. U., DeKalb, 1973-80; dir. ERIC Clearinghouse in Career Edn., 1973-76; coordinator Office Vocat., Tech., and Career Edn., 1978-80; prof. career and higher edn. U. So. Calif., Los Angeles, 1981-84; prof. emeritus higher and post secondary edn. U. So. Calif., 1984—; exec. dir. Nat. Inst. Advancement of Career Edn., 1981-84; pres. Internat. Coll., 1985-86; v.p. Lifecareer Found., 1985—; provost William Lyon U., 1988-91; faculty Walden U., 1992—; mem. Adv. Council on Guidance Dept. Edn. Commonwealth Mass., 1957-63; chmn. commn. on tests Coll. Entrance Exam. Bd., 1967-70; mem. advisory screening com. in edn. Council Internat. Exchange of Scholars, 1975-79, chmn., 1978-79. Co-author 5 books.; editorial assoc.: Jour. Counseling Psychology, 1957-63, Personnel and Guidance Jour., 1960-63, Character Potential: A Record of Research, 1977-82, Jour. Career Edn., 1979-85; contbr. articles to profl. jours., chpts. to books. Bd. dirs. Mass. Com. Children and Youth, 1961-63. Fellow Ctr. for Advanced Study in Behavioral Scis.; spl. fellow NIMH, 1963-64. Fellow Am. Psychol. Soc., APA (prs. divsn. counseling psychology 1965-66); mem. ACA, Nat. Career Devel. Assn. (pres. 1965-66, Eminent Career award 1979), Nat. Coun. Measurement in Edn. (pres. 1962-63), Phi Beta Kappa, Sigma Xi, Phi Delta Kappa, Phi Kappa Phi. Office: Lifecareer Ctr 1078 La Tortuga Dr Vista CA 92083-6441

TIEDEMANN, ALBERT WILLIAM, JR., chemist; b. Balt., Nov. 7, 1924; s. Albert William and Catherine (Madigan) T.; m. Mary Therese Sellmayer, Apr. 6, 1953; children: Marie Therese, Donna Elise, Albert William III, David Lawrence. BS, Loyola Coll., Balt., 1947; MS, NYU, 1949; PhD, Georgetown U., 1958. Teaching fellow N.Y. U., 1947-50; instr. chemistry Mt. St. Agnes Coll., 1950-55; chief chemist Emerson Drug div. Warner Lambert Pharm. Co., Balt., 1955-60; analytical supr. Hercules Powder Co., Allegany Ballistics Lab., Cumberland, Md., 1960-68; tech. svc. supt. Hercules Inc., Radford, Va., 1968-72; dir. Va. Div. Consol. Labs., Richmond, 1972-78; vice-chmn. Va. Toxic Substances Adv. Council, 1978-92; dep. dir. for labs. Va. Dept. Gen. Svcs., 1978-92, cons. 1992—. Mem. sci. adv. com. Longwood Coll., 1983-90. Served to lt. (j.g.) USNR, 1943-46; capt. Res., 1946—. Fellow Am. Inst. Chemists; mem. Soc. Advancement Mgmt. (chpt. v.p. 1983-84, chpt. pres. 1984-85), Am. Soc. Quality Control (chmn. Richmond sect. 1975-76, councilor biomed. divsn. 1978-80), U.S. Naval Inst., Naval Res. Assn. (dist. pres. 1954-57; nat. v.p. 1962-63, 65-69; nat. chmn. Navy Sabbath Program 1969-75, Nat. Meritorious Svc. award 1971, Twice a Citizen award 1978), Cen. Atlantic States Assn. Food & Drug Ofcls. (exec. bd. 1977-84, v.p. 1981-82, pres. 1982-83, CASA award 1986), Nat. Assn. Food & Drug Ofcls. (chmn. sci. and tech. com. 1981-85, sec.-treas. 1985-87), Internat. Assn. Ofcl. Analytical Chemists (editl. bd. 1986-88, bd. dirs. 1987-90), Analytical Lab. Mgrs. Assn., Royal Acad. Pharmacy (elected acad. fgn. mem. Barcelona, Spain 1989—). Home: 10511 Cherokee Rd Richmond VA 23235-1008

TIEDGE-LAFRANIER, JEANNE MARIE, editor; b. N.Y.C., July 24, 1960; d. Richard Frederick and Joan Jean (Gerardo) Tiedge; m. John Daniel Lewis Lafranier, Oct. 8, 1989; children: Katelyn Ellen, John Richard. BA, Drew U., 1982. Asst. Denise Marcil Lit. Agy., N.Y.C., 1982-84; sr. editor New Am. Libr., N.Y.C., 1984-87, Warner Books, N.Y.C., 1987-95; edito-in-chief Disticor News, Ajax, Ont., Can., 1995—. Avocation: equestrian.

TIEFEL, VIRGINIA MAY, librarian; b. Detroit, May 20, 1926; d. Karl and June Garland (Young) Brenkert; m. Paul Martin Tiefel, Jan. 25, 1947; children: Paul Martin Jr., Mark Gregory. B.A. in Elem. Edn., Wayne State U., 1962; M.A. in Library Sci., U. Mich., 1968. Librarian Birmingham Schs., Mich., 1967-68; librarian S. Euclid-Lyndhurst Schs., Cleve., 1968-69; acquisitions-reference librarian Hiram Coll., Ohio, 1969-77; head undergrad. libraries Ohio State U., Columbus, 1977-84, dir. library user edn., 1978-95, faculty outreach coord., 1995—. Contbr. articles to profl. jours. Recipient Disting. Alumnus award U. Mich. Sch. Info. and Libr. Studies, 1993. Mem. ALA (v.p. Ohio sect. 1973-74, pres. 1974-75, Miriam Dudley Bibliographic Instrn. Librarian of Yr. 1986), Acad. Library Assn. Ohio (Outstanding Ohio Acad. Librarian 1984), Assn. Coll. and Research Libraries (chmn. bibliographic instrn. sect. com. on research 1983-84, chmn. com. on performance measures 1984-90). Lutheran. Home: 4956 Smoketalk Ln Westerville OH 43081-4433 Office: Ohio State U Libraries 1858 Neil Ave Columbus OH 43210-1225

TIEFEL, WILLIAM REGINALD, hotel company executive; b. Rochester, N.Y., Mar. 30, 1934; s. William Reginald and Mary Hazel (Cross) T.; m. Vada Morell, Dec. 30, 1985. Student, Williams Coll., 1952-54; B.A. with honors, Mich. State U., 1956; postgrad., Harvard Bus. Sch. Gen. mgr. Marriott Hotels, Arlington, Va., 1964-65, Saddle Brook, N.J., 1966-69, Newton, Mass., 1969-71; regional v.p. Marriott Hotels, Washington, 1971-80; corp. v.p. Marriott Corp., Washington, 1976-89; exec. v.p. Marriott Hotels and Resorts, Washington, 1980-88; pres. Marriott Hotels, Resorts and Suites, 1988-92; exec. v.p., mem. exec. and growth coms. Marriott Corp.,' 1988—; pres. Marriott Lodging Group, 1992—. Bd. visitors Valley Forge Mil. Acad. and Jr. Coll., 1976-79, chmn., 1979, trustee, 1982-88, 89-92; chmn. Campaign for Valley Forge, 1985-88, chmn. com. on trustees, 1989-91. Mem. Am. Hotel and Motel Assn. (dir. Ednl. Inst.). Republican. Roman Catholic. Home: 2426 Wyoming Ave NW Washington DC 20008-1643 Office: Marriott Corp 1 Marriott Dr Washington DC 20058-0001

TIEFENTHAL, MARGUERITE AURAND, school social worker; b. Battle Creek, Mich., July 23, 1919; d. Charles Henry and Elisabeth Dirk (Hoekstra) Aurand; m. Harlan E. Tiefenthal, Nov. 26, 1942; children: Susan Ann, Daniel E., Elisabeth Amber, Carol Aurand. BS, Western Mich. U., 1941; MSW, U. Mich., 1950; postgrad., Coll. of DuPage, Ill., 1988-90. Tchr. No. High Sch., Flint, Mich., 1941-44, Cen. High Sch., Kalamazoo, 1944-45; acct. Upjohn Co., Kalamazoo, 1945-48; social worker Family Svc. Agy., Lansing, Mich., 1948-50, Pitts., 1950-55; sch. social worker Gower Sch. Dist., Hinsdale, Ill., 1962-70; sch. social worker Hinsdale (Ill.) Dist. 181, 1970-89, cons., 1989—; sch. social worker Villa Park (Ill.) Sch. Dist. 45, 1989; addictions counselor Mercy Hosp., 1990-92; asst. prof. sch. social work, liaison to pub. schs. Loyola U., Chgo., 1990—; field instr. social work interns U. Ill., 1979-88; impartial due process hearing officer; mem. adv. com. sch. social work Ill. State Bd. Edn. approved programs U. Ill. and George Williams Coll.; speaker Nat. Conf. Sch. Social Work, Denver, U. Tex. Joint Conf. Sch. Social Work in Ill.; founder Marguerite Tiefenthal Symposium for Ill. Sch. Social Work Interns. Co-editor The School Social Worker and the Handicapped Child: Making P.L. 94-142 Work; sect. editor: Sch. Social Work Quarterly, 1979. Sec. All Village Caucus Village of Western Springs, Ill., mem. village disaster com.; deacon Presbyn. Ch. Western Springs, Sunday sch. tchr., mem. choir; instr. Parent Effectiveness, Teacher Effectiveness, STEP; trainer Widowed Persons Service Tng. Program for Vol. Aides AARP. Recipient Ill. Sch. Social Worker of Yr., 1982. Mem. Nat. Assn. Social Workers (chmn. exec. council on social work in schs.), Ill. Assn. Sch. Social Workers (past pres., past conf. chmn., conf. program chmn.), Sch. Social Workers Supervisors Group (del. to Ill. Commn. on Children), Programs. for Licensure of Social Work Practice in Ill., LWV, DKG, PEO. Avocation: sewing. Home: 4544 Grand Ave Western Springs IL 60558-1545

TIEGS, CHERYL, model, designer. Profl. model, appearing in nat. mags., including, Time, Life, Bazaar, Sports Illustrated, Glamour; appeared weekly on ABC's Good Morning America; also appearing in TV commls., Cheryl Tiegs line of sportswear, Cheryl Tiegs nationally-distributed line of women's eyeglass frames, Cheryl Tiegs Collection of 14k Gold Jewelry, Fashion Watches, Shoes and Hosiery; author: The Way to Natural Beauty, 1980; Sports Illustrated video Aerobic Interval Training with Cheryl Tiegs. Address: care Barbara Shapiro 2 Greenwich Plz Ste 100 Greenwich CT 06830-6353

TIELKE, JAMES CLEMENS, retail and manufacturing management consultant; b. St. Helena, Nebr., May 15, 1931; s. Joseph Hubert and Catherine Josephine (Schmidt) T.; m. Betty Merle Adams, Apr. 18, 1953; children: P.J., Michael J., Dawn M. B.S. in Bus. Adminstrn., U. S.D., 1959, MA in Speech and Econ., 1960. Partner, Tielke Motors, Yankton, S.D., 1952-54; owner Ft. Collins Motors Colo., 1954-56; grad. tchg. asst. U. S.D., 1959-60; mgr. corp. buying paint, lawn and garden, electronics Montgomery Ward, Chgo., 1960-77, v.p. mdse. adminstrn., 1978-81; pres. Midwest div. Structured Approaches, Inc., 1981-82; v.p. nat. accounts Dupli-Color Products, Elk Grove Village, Ill., 1983-85; pres. Black Leaf Products Co., 1985-89; v.p. Hysan Corp., Des Plaines, Ill., 1985-89; v.p. ice melter sales IMC Vigoro, Kenosha, Wis., 1989-97; pres. J.C. Tielke Assocs., Inc., 1997—. Recipient Honors award U. S.D. Sch. Bus., 1977. Mem. Internat. Sanitary Supply Assn. Office: 4500 13th Ct Kenosha WI 53140-2790

TIEMAN, SUZANNAH BLISS, neurobiologist; b. Washington, Oct. 10, 1943; d. John Alden and Winifred Texas (Bell) Bliss; m. David George Tieman, Dec. 19, 1969. AB with honors, Cornell U., 1965; postgrad., MIT, 1965-66, Calif. Inst. Tech., 1971-72; PhD, Stanford U., 1974. Postdoctoral fellow dept. anatomy U. Calif., San Francisco, 1974-77; rsch. assoc. Neurobiology Rsch. Ctr. SUNY, Albany, 1977-90, sr. rsch. assoc., 1990—, assoc. prof. dept. biomed. scis., 1988-95, prof., 1995—, rsch. prof. dept. biol. scis., 1990—. Contbr. articles to profl. jours., chpts. to books in field. Rsch. grantee Nat. Eye Inst., SUNY, Albany, 1979-83, NSF, SUNY, 1983-86, 88-92, 92-97; predoctoral fellow Nat. Eye Inst., U. Calif., San Francisco, 1974-77. Mem. AAAS, Soc. for Neurosci. (steering com. Hudson Berkshire chpt. 1980-81, pres. 1991-93), Assn. Rsch. in Vision and Ophthalmology, Am. Assn. Anatomists, Assn. Women in Sci., Fedn. Am. Socs. Exptl. Biology, Women in Neurosci., Nat. Audubon Soc., Nature Conservancy. Avocations: choral music, folk music, birding, eskimo art. Office: SUNY Neurobiology Rsch Ctr 1400 Washington Ave Albany NY 12222-0100

TIEN, CHANG-LIN, chancellor; b. Wuhan, China, July 24, 1935; came to U.S., 1956, naturalized, 1969; s. Yun Chien and Yun Di (Lee) T.; m. Di-Hwa Liu, July 25, 1959; children: Norman Chihnan, Phyllis Chihping, Christine Chihyih. BS, Nat. Taiwan U., 1955; MME, U. Louisville, 1957; MA, PhD, Princeton U., 1959; PhD (hon.), U. Louisville, 1991, U. Notre Dame, 1992, Hong Kong U. Sci. and Tech., 1993, U. Conn., 1994, U. Waterloo, Can., 1995, U. Ill., 1995. Acting asst. prof. dept. mech. engring. U. Calif., Berkeley, 1959-60, asst. prof., 1960-64, assoc. prof., 1964-68, prof., 1968-88, 90—, A. Martin Berlin prof., 1987-88, 90—, dept. chair, 1974-81, also vice chancellor for research, 1983-85; exec. vice chancellor U. Calif., Irvine, 1988-90; chancellor U. Calif., Berkeley, 1990-97; chair exec. com. Internat. Ctr. for Heat and Mass Transfer, 1980-82; hon. prof., dir. Xi'an Jiatong U. Engring. Thermodynamics Rsch. Inst., 1987—; mem. adv. bd. Hong Kong U. Sci. and Tech., 1991—; chair internat. adv. panel U. Tokyo Inst. Indsl. Sci., 1995; bd. trustees Princeton (N.J.) U., 1991-95, Chiang Indsl. Charity Found., Ltd., Hong Kong, 1991—, The Asia Found., 1993—, U.S. Com. on Econ. Devel., 1994—, Carnegie Found. for Advancement of Tchg., 1994—; tech. cons. Lockheed Missiles and Space Co., GE; gov. bd. dirs. Com. of 100, 1991—; bd. dirs. Berkeley Cmty. Found., Wells Fargo Bank, Raychem Corp., 1996; mem. coun. Foreign Rels., 1996; active Aspen Inst. Domestic Strategy Group. Author one book; editor Internat. Commn. Heat and Mass Transfer, 1981—; editor-in-chief Exptl. Heat Transfer, 1987—; editor twelve vols.; contbr. articles to profl. jours. John Simon Guggenheim fellow, 1965, Sr. U.S. Sci. fellow Japan Soc. for Promotion of Sci., 1980; recipient Sr. U.S. Sci. award Alexander von Humboldt Found., 1979; named Most Disting. Chinese scholar, Soc. Hong Kong Scholars, 1989, Li Ka Shing Disting. Lectr., U. Hong Kong, 1994, Gordon Wu Disting. Lectr., Princeton U., 1995, Martin Martel Lectr., Brown U., 1996. Fellow AAAS (bd. dirs. 1992—), ASME (hon., chair exec. com. heat transfer divsn. 1980-81, v.p. basic engring. 1988-90, Heat Transfer Meml. award 1974, Gustus L. Larson Meml. award 1975, AIChE/ASME Max Jakob Meml. award 1981, Disting. Lectr. award 1987-89), AIAA (Thermophysics award 1977), Am. Acad. Arts and Scis. (hon.), Academia Sinica (hon., Taiwan); mem. NAE (mem. internat. affairs adv. com. 1987-90, chair mech. engring. peer com. 1989-90), Am. Soc. Engring. Edn. (mem. nat. adv. coun. 1993—), Heat Transfer Soc. Japan (hon.), Chinese Acad. Scis. (fgn. mem., Hon. Prof., Inst. Thermophysics 1981—). Office: U Calif Berkeley Chancellor's Office 200 Calif Hall 1500 Berkeley CA 94720-1500

TIEN, H. TI, biophysics and physiology educator, scientist; b. Beijing, China, Feb. 1; came to U.S., 1947; s. Fang-cheng and Wen-tsun (Chow) T.; children: Stephen, David, Adrienne, Jennifer; m. Angelica Leitmannova, 1992. B.Sc., U. Nebr., 1953; Ph.D., Temple U., 1963. Chem. engr. Allied Chem. Corp., Phila., 1953-57; med. scientist Eastern Pa. Psychiat. Inst., Phila., 1957-63; assoc. prof. Northweastern U., Boston, 1963-66; assoc. prof. Mich. State U., East Lansing, 1966-70, prof. biophysics, 1970—, chmn. dept., 1978-82; cons. Hungarian Acad. Sci., Szeged, 1975-76; rsch. prof. Acad. Sinica, Beijing, 1978; cons. prof. Sichuan U., 1984—; cons. Tianjin Econ. Tech. Devel. Area, China; external dir. Ctr. Interface Scis., Slovak Tech. U., Slovakia; cons. prof. Jilin U., Peoples Republic China; frequent lectr. many countries. Author: Bilayer Lipid Membranes, 1974; contbr. chpts. to books. Research grantee NIH, 1964—, NSF, 1978, Dept. Energy, 1980-83, U.S. Naval Rsch. Office, 1985—. Mem. AAAS, Biophys. Soc. (council 1972-75), Nat. Inst. Peer Reviewer. Research interests include membrane biophysics, bioelectrochemistry, photobiology, solar energy conversion via semiconductor septum electrochemical photovoltaic cells (SC-SEP); biomolecular electronic devices. Office: Mich State U Physiology Dept Giltner Hall East Lansing MI 48824

TIEN, PING KING, electronics engineer; b. Chekieng, China, Aug. 2, 1919; came to U.S., 1947; s. N.S. and C.S. (Yen) T.; m. Nancy N.Y. Chen, Apr. 19, 1952; children: Emily-Ju-Psia, Julia Ju-Wen. MS, Stanford U., 1948, PhD, 1951. Fellow emeritus Bell Labs. Lucent Technologies, Holmdel, N.J., 1990—; hon. prof. Jiao-Tong U., Shanghai, China. Editor-in-chief Internat. Jour. High Speed Electronics and Sys.; contbr. sci. and tech. articles to profl. jours. Recipient Achievement award Chinese Inst. Engrs., 1966; fellow AT&T Labs., 1983. Fellow IEEE (Morris N. Liebmann award 1979), Optical Soc. Am.; mem. Nat. Acad. Sci., Nat. Acad. Engring., Inst. Am. Physics, Acad. Sci. Republic of China, Acad. Sci. of Third World, Sigma Xi. Patentee in field. Office: Bell Labs Lucent Technologies Holmdel NJ 07733

TIENDA, MARTA, demographer, educator; b. Tex. Ph.D. in Sociology, U. Tex., 1977. From asst. prof. to prof. rural sociology U. Wis., Madison, 1976-87; vis. prof. Stanford U., 1987; Ralph Lewis prof. sociology U. Chgo., 1994—, chmn. dept. sociology, 1994-96; rsch. assoc. Population Research Ctr., Ogburn-Stouffer Ctr. Co-author: Hispanics in the U.S. Economy, 1985, Hispanic Population of the United States, 1987, Divided Opporunities, 1988; contbr. articles to profl. jours. Trustee Kaiser Family Found., Russell Sage Found., Carnegie Corp. N.Y. Guggenheim fellow. Fellow Am. Acad. Arts and Scis., Ctr. Advanced Study Behavioral Scis.; mem. Am. Sociol. Assn., Am. Econ. Assn., Population Assn. Am., Internat. Union for Sci. Study of Population. Office: Dept Sociology Princeton U 15 Roszel Rd Princeton NJ 08540-6248

TIENKEN, ARTHUR T., retired foreign service officer; b. Yonkers, N.Y., Aug. 5, 1922. B.A., Princeton U., 1947, M.A., 1949. With U.S. Fgn. Svc., 1949-87; dep. chief mission U.S. Fgn. Svc., Tunis, Tunisia, 1973-75, Addis Ababa, Ethiopia, 1975-77; Ambassador to Gabonese Republic and Democratic Republic of Sao Tome and Principe,, Libreville, Gabon, 1978-81; dir. Fgn. Svc. Assignments and Career devel. Dept. State, 1981-85, sr. insp., 1985-87, ret., 1987; diplomat-in-residence Marquette U., 1972-73. Served with U.S. Army, 1943-46.

TIERNEY, BILL, university athletic coach. Head coach Princeton Tigers, 1988—. NCAA Divsn. 1A Champions, 1992, 94, 97; named Morris Touchstone Divsn. 1A Coach of the Yr.; elected to L.I. Lacrosse Hall of Fame, 1995. Office: Princeton U Dillon Gym Princeton NJ 08544*

TIERNEY, BRIAN PATRICK, advertising and public relations executive; b. Bryn Mawr, Pa., Feb. 21, 1957; s. James Richard and Claire Ella (Springfield) T.; married; 2 children. BA, U. Pa., 1979; JD, Widener U., 1987. Field person Rep. Nat. Com., Washington, 1979-82, dir. incumbent programs, 1979-81, dep. dir. edn., 1981-82; polit. dir. GOPAC, Washington, 1982-83; asst. regional adminstr. U.S. SBA, Bala Cynwyd, Pa., 1983-84; pres. Tierney & Co., Phila., 1984-86; pres., chief exec. officer, Lewis, Gilman & Kynett Pub. Rels., Phila., 1986-89; pres., chief exec. officer The Tierney Group, Phila, 1989—; pres., CEO FCB/Tierney, Phila., 1994—. ann. giving chmn. Ingis House for Disabled Persons, Phila.; bd. dirs. Wilma Theater, Phila., Moore Coll. Art and Design, Phila., Sch. Bd. Archdiocese of Phila., Ave. of Arts, Inc., Phila. Police Athletic League, Phila. coun. Boy Scouts Am., fund for Phila., Phila. Festival of Arts. Mem. ABA, Pa. Bar Assn., Phila. Bar Assn., Pub. Rels. Soc. Am., St. Anthony Club, Union League. Roman Catholic. Avocation: skydiving, Bonsai gardening. Office: Foote Cone and Belding of PA Inc 200 S Broad St Fl 10 Philadelphia PA 19102-3803

TIERNEY, GORDON PAUL, real estate broker, genealogist; b. Ft. Wayne, Ind., Oct. 17, 1922; s. James Leonard and Ethele Lydia (Brown) T.; m. Carma Lillian Devine, Oct. 17, 1946; 1 child, Paul N. Student, Ind. U., 1940-41, Cath. U. Am., 1941-42; coll. tng. detachment, Clemson U., 1943. Br. mgr. Bartlett-Collins Co., Chgo., 1956-84; prin., broker Kaiser-Tierney Real Estate, Inc., Palatine, Ill., 1984-89; pres. Tierney Real Estate, Newburgh, Ind. Author: Burgess/Bryan Connection, 1978; assoc. editor Colonial Genealogist Jour., 1976-85. Served in USAC, 1943-45, China. Decorated Legion of Honor. Fellow Am. Coll. Genealogists (pres. 1977—); mem. SAR (v.p. gen. 1984-85, genealogist gen. 1981-83, Silver and Bronze medals 1978-80, Patriot medal 1976, Meritorious Svc. award 1983, Minutemen award 1984), Huguenot Soc. Ill. (state pres. 1978-80), Huguenot Soc. S.C., Nat. Huguenot Soc., Huguenot Soc. Ind. (pres. 1993-95), Nat. Geneal. Soc., Ind. Hist. Soc., Soc. Ind. Pioneers, First Families Ohio, Ohio Geneal. Soc., Va. Geneal. Soc., Md. Geneal. Soc., Augustan Soc., Gen. Soc. War 1812 (state pres. 1985), Sons. and Daus. Pilgrims, Descs. Old Plymouth Colony, Mil. Order Stars and Bars, Soc. Descs. Colonial Clergy, Sons of Union Vets., Sons of Confederate Vets., Pioneer Wis. Families, Welcome Soc. Pa., Pa. Geneal. Soc., Nat. Soc. Archivists, Soc. Colonial Wars in Ill., Soc. Colonial Wars in Ind. (gov. 1992-94), Sons of Am. Colonists (nat. v.p. 1971-74), Mil. and Hospitalier Order St. Lazarus of Jerusalem, Order Descs. Ancient Planters, Hump Pilots Assn., Nat. Bd. Realtors, Ill. Bd. Realtors, Sword Bunker Hill, Tri-State Geneal. Soc., Jamestowne Soc., Baronial Order Magna Charta, Masons, Shriners, Rolling Hill Country Club. Republican. Presbyterian. Home and Office: 8766 Hanover Dr Newburgh IN 47630-9327

TIERNEY, JAMES EDWARD, attorney general; b. Bklyn., Apr. 12, 1947; s. Charles J. and Agnes V. (Quinn) T.; m. Susan Webster, Jan. 26, 1969; children: Adam, Josie, Matthew, Daniel, Kate. B.A. with highest honors, U. Maine, 1969, J.D., 1974. Bar: Maine 1974. Mem. Maine State Ho. Reps., 1972-80, majority leader, 1976-80; atty. gen. State of Maine, 1980-90; cons. state attys. gen., 1994—; bd. dirs. People for the Am. Way, Topsham, Maine, 1991-93; spl. prosecutor investigate Pa. Supreme Ct., 1992-93; mem. bd. commentators Courtroom TV Network. Wasserstein fellow Harvard

Law Sch., 1992-93. Mem. Am. Judicature Soc. (bd. dirs.). Office: PO Box 417 Topsham ME 04086-0417

TIERNEY, JOHN WILLIAM, chemical engineering educator; b. Oak Park, Ill., Dec. 29, 1923; s. John William and Agnes (Shea) T.; m. Patricia A. O'Neill, June 21, 1952; children: John, Patrick, Joseph, Paul. B.S. in Chem. Engring., Purdue U., 1947; M.S. in Chem. Engring., U. Mich., 1948; Ph.D. in Chem. Engring., Northwestern U., 1951. Sr. research engr. Pure Oil Co., Crystal Lake, Ill., 1948-53; asst. prof. Purdue U., West Lafayette, Ind., 1953-56; mgr. dept. Remington Rand Univac, St. Paul, 1956-60; assoc. prof. chem. engring. U. Pitts., 1960-62, prof., 1962—, W.K. Whiteford prof. chem. engring., 1991-94, prof. emeritus, 1995—; vis. prof. U. Técnica Federico Santa Maria, Valparaiso, Chile, 1960-62; lectr. U. Barcelona (Spain), 1968-69. Fellow AIChE (chmn. Pitts. sect. 1982, McAfee award Pitts. sect. 1995); mem. Am. Chem. Soc., Am. Soc. Engring. Edn. Home: 1330 N Sheridan Ave Pittsburgh PA 15206-1760 Office: U Pitts 1230 Benedum Hall Pittsburgh PA 15261-2212

TIERNEY, MICHAEL EDWARD, lawyer; b. N.Y., July 16, 1948; s. Michael Francis and Margaret Mary (Creamer) T.; m. Alicia Mary Boldt, June 6, 1981; children: Colin, Madeleine. BA, St. Louis U., 1970, MBA, 1978, JD, 1978. Bar: Mo. Assoc., law clk. Wayne L. Millsap, P.C., St. Louis, 1977-80; staff atty. Interco. Inc., St. Louis, 1980-83; textile divsn. counsel Chromalloy Am. Corp., St. Louis, 1984-87; v.p., sec. P.N. Hirsch & Co., St. Louis, 1983-84; sr. counsel, asst. sec. Jefferson Smurfit Corp., St. Louis, 1987-92, v.p., gen. counsel, sec., 1993—. Mem. adv. bd. St. Louis Area Food Bank, 1980—. U.S. Army Security Agy., 1970-73. Mem. Racquet Club St. Louis. Republican. Roman Catholic. Avocations: sailing, squash. Home: 10 Twin Springs Ln Saint Louis MO 63124-1139 Office: Jefferson Smurfit Corp 8182 Maryland Ave Saint Louis MO 63105-3786

TIERNEY, MICHAEL STEWART, newspaper editor, journalist; b. Louisville, May 20, 1952; s. James Edmund Jr. and Mary (Mullin) T.; children: Shannon, Meredith, Jordan. BA, U. Ky., 1973. Sports writer, asst. sports editor St. Petersburg Times, 1973-85; asst. sports editor, exec. sports editor, Olympics editor Atlanta Jour.-Constitution, 1986-91, sports editor, 1991-96; mem. nat. recognized sports staffs St. Petersburg Times, Atlanta Jour.-Constitution, Assoc. Press Sports Editors. Recipient various writing awards Assoc. Press Sports Editors, Fla. Sports Writers Assn. Mem. Assoc. Press Sports Editors. Home: 457 Nelson Ferry Rd Decatur GA 30030-2323 Office: Atlanta Journal-Constitution PO Box 4689 Atlanta GA 30302-4689

TIERNEY, PATRICK JOHN, information services executive; b. Denver, Oct. 9, 1945; s. Thomas Michael and Betty Ruth (Fairall) T.; m. Lois Bruce, Jan. 1, 1980; children: Christopher, Blake. BS, U. Colo., 1967, MBA, 1970. Pres. Gould E.P.C. Div., San Diego, 1980-84, Caterpillar Capital, San Diego, 1984-85; v.p., gen. mgr. TRW Info. Svcs., Orange, Calif., 1985-91; CEO Knight-Ridder Info., Mountain View, Calif., 1991-96; group CEO, The Thomson Corp., Stamford, Conn., 1996—. Mem. Info. Industry Assn. (bd. dirs. 1992—). Republican. Office: The Thomson Corp Metro Ctr at 1 Station Pl Stamford CT 06902

TIERNEY, PAUL E., JR., investment company executive; b. Feb. 18, 1943; married. Postgrad., Harvard U. With Peace Corps., Chile, 1964-66, Starwood Corp., 1969-72; v.p., gen. mgr. Continental Ill. Ltd., London, 1972-75; sr. v.p. White Weld & Co., 1975-78; mng. dir. Gollust Tierney & Oliver, Inc., 1987-90; chmn. TW Holdings, Inc., Spartanburg, S.C., 1990-92; founding mem. Devel. Capital, LLC, 1996—; chmn. bd. Technoserve, Inc.; bd. dirs. United Airlines, Liz Claiborne, Inc., Argentine Investment Fund, Straits Corp., Internat. Venture Ptnrs. of Brazil, D.C. Unied. Bd. dirs. St. John's Coll. Office: Development Capital LLC 500 Park Ave Ste 510 New York NY 10022-1606

TIERNEY, RAYMOND MORAN, JR., lawyer; b. Bklyn., Aug. 1, 1932; s. Raymond M. and Alice Mary (Hoag) T.; m. Kathleen Maguire, June 23, 1956; children: Kathleen Snyder, Alicia Johnson, Raymond III, Michael, Christopher. BA, U. Notre Dame, 1954; LLB, Fordham U., 1961. Bar: N.J. 1962. Asst. sec. and credit loaning officer Hanover Bank, N.Y.C., 1956-61; law sec. to Hon. J.J. Francis Supreme Ct. N.J., 1961-62; assoc. Shanley & Fisher P.C., Newark, 1962-67; ptnr. Shanley & Fisher P.C., Morristown, 1967—; adj. prof. Monmouth Coll., W. Long Branch, N.J., 1985-88; master William J. Brennan Jr. Inn of Ct., 1987-92; faculty U. Va. Law Sch. Ann. Trial Inst., 1990—; speaker in field. Bd. adjustment Borough Shrewsbury, 1973-80; councilman Coun. Borough Shrewsbury, 1981-83; commr. Gateway Nat. Park Adv. Commn., 1983-86; trustee Newark Mus., 1990—, St. Peter's Coll., Jersey City, 1990-96, regent, 1996—. 1st Lt. U.S. Marines, 1954-56. Recipient Trial Bar award Trial Attys. N.J., 1989, Thomas More Assn. medal Seton Hall Law Sch., 1991, William J. Brennan award U. Va. Law Trial Advocacy Inst., 1996. Fellow Am. Coll. Trial Attys., Am. Bar Found.; mem. D.C. Bar Assn., N.J. State Bar Found. (chmn. 1990-92, pres. 1992-94), N.J. State Bar Assn. (trustee 1992-94), Monmouth County Bar Assn. Office: Shanley & Fisher 131 Madison Ave Morristown NJ 07960-6086

TIERNEY, THOMAS J., business management consultant; b. San Francisco, Mar. 5, 1954; s. Ralph Thomas and Eleanor Faye (Walker) T.; m. Joy Karen McGee, Sept. 23, 1984; children: Colin McGee, Braden Thomas. BA in Econs. with distinction, U. Calif., Davis, 1976; MBA with distinction, Harvard, 1980. Field engr. Bechtel Internat., Azrew, Algeria, 1976-78; cons. Bain & Co., San Francisco, 1980-82, mgr., 1982-83, v.p., 1983-87, mng. ptnr., 1987-92; pres. Bain & Co. Worldwide, San Francisco, 1992—, CEO, 1993—. Mem. bds. dirs. The Nature Conservancy, Harvard Bus. Sch. Alumni Assn., United Way of Mass. Bay, Woods Hole Oceanographic Inst., Com. for Econ. Devel., The Hoover Inst., Boston Symphony Orch.; active with Young Pres. Org., Conf. Bd. Former dir. Bay Area Coun., Bay Area United Way, U. Calif. at Davis Alumni Assn. Recipient Winslow Meml. award U. Calif. Davis, 1976. Mem. U. Calif. Davis Alumni Assn. (dir. 1984-88), Harvard Bus. Sch. Alumni Assn. Roman Catholic. Avocations: fishing, politics, history and non-profit sector. Home: 45 Old Farm Rd Wellesley MA 02181-1423

TIESZEN, RALPH LELAND, SR., internist; b. Marion, S.D., Sept. 21, 1928; s. Bernard D. and Hulda J. (Thomas) T.; m. Florence Morrill Johnson, July 25, 1952; children: Ralph Leland Jr., Stuart Carl, Stephan Lee. Student, Freeman Jr. Coll., 1946-48; BS, Wheaton Coll., 1950; postgrad., U. S.D., 1950-52; MD, Loma Linda U., 1954. Diplomate Am. Bd. Internal Medicine, Am. Bd. Geriatric Medicine. Intern L.A. County Hosp., 1954-55, resident TB and Chest, 1955-56; commd. 2d lt. med. corps. USAF, 1956, advanced through grades to maj., 1964; chief medicine hosp. USAF, Eglin AFB, 1962-64; ret. USAF, 1979; resident in internal medicine Mayo Found., Rochester, Minn., 1957-60; mem. active staff dept. internal medicine Carraway Meth. Med. Ctr., Birmingham, 1964—, dir. resident program, 1968-72, trustee, 1972-77, pres. staff, 1973-75, exec. com., fin. com., 1974-77, dir. geriatrics, 1989—; pvt. practice Norwood Clinic, Inc., Birmingham, Ala., 1964—; asst. clin. prof. medicine Med. Coll. Ala., 1965-69, asst. clin. prof. dept. endocrinology, 1969-70, clin. assoc. prof. medicine, 1970-81, clin. prof. medicine, 1981—; med. dir. Community Hosp., 1989—; mem. faculty joint commn. accreditation hosps., 1974-78; exec. com. Birmingham Regional Health Systems Agy.; investigator numerous clin. trials. Contbr. articles to profl. jours. Chmn. Birmingham String Quartet, 1970-74; v.p. ticket sales Ala. Symphony Assn., 1979, exec. com.; sec. men's com. Ala. Symphony, 1986-88, pres. 1990-91. Gen. Med. Officer USAR, 197984, comdr. U.S. Army Hosp., Birmingham, 1984-88, col., chief profl. svcs. 5th med. group, Birmingham, 1988-92, ret., 1992. Mem. ACP, AMA, Am. Thoracic Soc. (sr.), Med. Assn. State Ala., Jefferson County Med. Soc. (past bd. censors, del. to state med. assn.), Birmingham Acad. Medicine (pres. 1987-88), Birmingham Internists Soc. (pres. 1972-73). Democrat. Avocations: opera, symphony, philosophy, medical ethics, astronomy. Office: Norwood Clinic Inc PO Box 830230 1528 26th St N Birmingham AL 35234-1911

TIETJEN, JOHN HENRY, biology and oceanography educator, consultant; b. Jamaica, N.Y., June 19, 1940; s. Reinhard L. and Emma (Wilkomm) T.; m. Theresa Mary Martin, Aug., 24, 1968; children: Theresa Emma, Mary Elizabeth. BS, CCNY, 1961; PhD, U. R.I., 1966. Asst. prof. biology CCNY, N.Y.C., 1966-71, assoc. prof., 1971-75, prof., 1975—; ecol. cons. Tex. Instruments, Dallas, 1977-79, S.W. Rsch. Inst., Houston, 1978-80, Henderson and Bodwell Engrs., Bethpage, N.Y., 1982, N.E. Utilities, Hartford, Conn., 1968—, North Atlantic Energy Svc., Seabrook, N.H., 1994—; rsch. assoc. Am. Mus. Natural History, 1993—. Contbr. over 50 articles to sci. jours. V.p., pres. Leonia (N.J.) Bd. Edn., 1977-86. Rsch. grantee NSF, Office Naval Research, Dept. Energy, NOAA. Mem. Estuary Rsch. Found., Sigma Xi. Roman Catholic. Avocations: outdoor activities, reading, travel. Office: CCNY Dept of Biology Convent Ave New York NY 10027-2604

TIETJEN, SCOTT PHILLIPS, computer programmer, analyst; b. West Haven, Conn., May 14, 1960; s. Henry Louis and Ruth Evelyn (Haupt) T. BS in Applied Math. and Computer Sci., Carnegie-Mellon U., 1982; MS in Computer Sci., Marist Coll., 1991. Staff programmer IBM Corp., Poughkeepsie, N.Y., 1982-93; cons. personal computer technician Aerotek, Inc., N.Y.C., 1993; cons. programmer/analyst Data-Based Devel. Sys., East Providence, R.I., 1994; cons. data security analyst Atlantic Search Group, Inc., Stamford, Conn., 1994-95; cons. programmer/analyst Maxim Group, Shelton, Conn., 1995, Keane, Inc., Darien, Conn., 1996—. Treas. Aid Assn. for Luths. Br. 6981. Mem. IEEE (computer soc.), Assn. Computing Machinery, Tall Clubs Internat. (club del.), Tri-County Talls of N.Y. and Conn. (newsletter editor), Rivercity High Soc. (Evansville, Ind.), Atlanta Sky-Hi Club. Republican. Lutheran. Avocations: theatrical and architectural lighting design.

TIETZ, NORBERT WOLFGANG, clinical chemistry educator, administrator; b. Stettin, Germany, Nov. 13, 1926; s. Joseph and Anna (Kozalla) T.; m. Gertrud Kraft, Oct. 17, 1959; children—Margaret, Kurt, Annette, Michael. Student, Tuebingen, Germany, 1945-46; D.Sc., Tech. U., Stuttgart, W.Ger., 1950. Chmn. dept. chemistry Reid Meml. Hosp., Richmond, Ind., 1956-59; prof., dir. clin. chemistry Mt. Sinai Med. Ctr. and Chgo. Med. Sch., Chgo., 1959-76, U. Ky. Med. Ctr., Lexington, 1976-96; prof. pathology U. Calif., San Diego, 1996—; research fellow and asst. U. Munich, W.Ger., 1951-54; research fellow dept. pathology U. Chgo. and St. Luke's Hosp., Chgo., 1955-56, Rockford Meml. Hosp., Ill., 1954-55; cons. Ill. Dept. Pub. Health, 1967-76, VA Hosp., Hines, Ill., 1974-76; prof. biochemistry and pathology Rush Med. Coll., Chgo., 1975-76; vol. cons. VA Hosp., Lexington, 1976-96. Editor: Fundamentals of Clinical Chemistry, 1970, 76, 87, Clinical Guide to Laboratory Tests, 1983, 90, 95, Textbook of Clinical Chemistry, 1986, A Study Guide to Clinical Chemistry, 1987, Applied Laboratory Medicine, 1992; assoc. editor: Dictionary and Encyclopedia of Laboratory Medicine and Technology, 1983; contbr. numerous articles to profl. jours. Recipient A. Dubin award Nat. Acad. Clin. Biochemistry, 1995, Disting. Internat. Svc. award Internat. Fedn. Clin. Chemistry, 1996. Fellow Acad. Clin. Lab. Physicians and Scientists, Am. Inst. Chemists; mem. Am. Assn. Clin. Chemistry (clin. chemist award 1971, award for outstanding efforts in edn. and tng. 1976, Disting. Alumnus award 1977, Steuben Bowl award 1978, Bernard F. Gerulat award N.J. chpt. 1988, award for Outstanding Contbns. to Clin. Chemistry 1989, Donald D. Van Slyke award N.Y. Met. chpt. 1989), AAAS, Am. Chem. Soc., Am. Soc. Clin. Pathologists, Man. Soc. Clin. Chemists (ann. Lectureship award 1987), Sigma Xi. Roman Catholic. Home: 7472 Caminito Rialto La Jolla CA 92037 Office: U Calif Dept Pathology 9500 Gilman Dr La Jolla CA 92093-5003

TIETZE, LUTZ FRIEDJAN, chemist, educator; b. Berlin, Mar. 14, 1942; s. Friedrich and Hete-Irene (Kruse) T.; m. Karin Krautschneider; children: Martin, Maja, Andrea, Julia. Diploma, U. Kiel, 1966, PhD, 1968; habil. for Organic Chemistry, U. Münster, 1975; DSc honoris causa, U. Szeged, Hungary, 1994. Rsch. assoc. MIT, 1969-71; lectr. U. Münster, 1971-76; prof. U. Dortmund, 1977-78; full prof. and inst. dir. U. Göttingen, Göttingen, 1978—; dean and prodean U. Göttingen, 1983-87, 91-95; mem. bd. German Faculties of Chemistry; spkr. Sonderforschungsbereich 416; pres. bd. German Chem. Socs.; adv. bd. Fachinjormationszentien Chemic. Author: Reactions and Syntheses, 1981, (translated into Japanese 1984, 2d edit., 1995, English 1989), 2d edit., 1991, Basic Course in Organic Chemistry, 1993, 2d edit., 1995; contbr. numerous articles to profl. jours.; patentee in field. Recipient Karl-Winnacker award, Hoechst AG, Germany, 1976, Lit. prize, Fonds der Chem. Industry, Germany, 1982; fellow Japan Soc. Promotion Sci. Fellow Royal Soc. Chemists; mem. Gesellschaft Deutscher Chemiker, Am. Chem. Soc., Chem. Soc. Argentina (hon.), German Chem. Soc. (pres.), Academia Scientiarum Göttingen. Home: Stumpfe Eiche 73, D-37077 Göttingen Germany Office: U Göttingen Inst Organic Chemistry, Tammannstrasse 2, D-37077 Göttingen Germany

TIFFANY, JOSEPH RAYMOND, II, lawyer; b. Dayton, Ohio, Feb. 5, 1949; s. Forrest Fraser and Margaret Watson (Clark) T.; m. Terri Robbins, Dec. 1, 1984. AB magna cum laude, Harvard U., 1971; MS in Internat. Relations, London Sch. Econs., 1972; JD, U. Calif., Berkeley, 1975. Bar: U.S. Dist. Ct. (no. dist.) 1975, U.S. Dist. Ct. (ea. dist.) 1977, U.S. Ct. Appeals (9th cir.) 1982. Assoc. Pillsbury, Madison & Sutro, San Francisco, 1975-82, ptnr., 1983—. Mem. ABA (antitrust, intellectual property, litigation sects.), Calif. Bar Assn., Harvard Club. Office: Pillsbury Madison & Sutro 235 Montgomery St San Francisco CA 94104-2902

TIFFANY, SANDRA L., state legislator; b. Spokane, Wash., June 30, 1949; m. Ross M. Tonkens; 1 child, Courtney. Student, U. Calif. Mem. Nev. Assembly, 1993—. Mem. Nev. Rep. Women's Club, Green Valley Cmty. Assn. Home: 75 Quail Run Rd Henderson NV 89014-2151 Office: Nev Assembly State Capitol Carson City NV 89710 Address: 2289 Cassatt Dr Henderson NV 89014*

TIFFT, WILLIAM GRANT, astronomer; b. Derby, Conn., Apr. 5, 1932; s. William Charles and Marguerite Howe (Hubbell) T.; m. Carol Ruth Nordquist, June 1, 1957 (div. July 1964); children: Jennifer, William John; m. Janet Ann Lindner Homewood, June 2, 1965; 1 child, Amy, stepchildren: Patricia, Susan, Hollis. AB, Harvard Coll., 1954; PhD, Calif. Inst. Tech., 1958. Nat. sci. postdoctoral Australian Nat. U., Canberra, 1958-60; rsch. assoc. Vanderbilt U., Nashville, 1960-61; astronomer Lowell Obs., Flagstaff, Ariz., 1961-64; assoc. prof. U. Ariz., Tucson, 1964-73, prof., 1973—. Joint author: Revised New General Catalog, 1973; contbr. over 100 articles to profl. jours. NSF Predoctoral fellow, 1954-58, NSF Postdoctoral fellow, 1958-60; grantee NASA, NSF, ONR, Rsch. Corp. Fellow Am. Astron. Soc.; mem. Internat. Astron. Union. Achievements include discovery of redshift quantization and correlations relating to it, including variability; first to detect voids in mapping of large scale supercluster structure; investigations of three-dimensional time in cosmology and particle physics. Office: U of Arizona Dept of Astronomy Tucson AZ 85721

TIFT, MARY LOUISE, artist; b. Seattle, Jan. 2, 1913; d. John Howard and Wilhelmina (Pressler) Dreher; m. William Raymond Tift, Dec. 4, 1948. BFA cum laude, U. Wash., 1933; postgrad., Art Ctr. Coll., L.A., 1945-48, U. Calif., San Francisco, 1962-63. Art dir. Vaughn Shedd Advt., L.A., 1948; asst. prof. design Calif. Coll. Arts & Crafts, Oakland, Calif., 1949-59; coord. design dept. San Francisco Art Inst., 1959-62. Subject of cover story, Am. Artist mag., 1980, studio article, 1987; one woman shows, Gumps Gallery, San Francisco, 1977, 1986, 90, Diane Gilson Gallery, Seattle, 1978, Oreg. State U., 1981, group shows include, Brit. Biennale, Yorkshire, Eng., 1970, Grenchen Triennale, Switzerland, 1970, Polish Biennale, Crakow, 1972, Nat. Gallery, Washington, 1973, U.S.-U.K. Impressions, Eng., 1988; represented in permanent collections, Phila. Mus. Art, Bklyn. Mus., Seattle Art Mus., Library Congress, Achenbach Print Collection, San Francisco Palace Legion of Honor. Served to lt. USNR, 1943-45. Mem. Print Club Phila., World Print Council, Calif. Soc. Printmakers, Phi Beta Kappa, Lambda Rho. Christian Scientist. Studio: 275 Los Ranchitos Rd Apt 341 San Rafael CA 94903-3692

TIGAR, MICHAEL EDWARD, lawyer, educator; b. Glendale, Calif., Jan. 18, 1941; s. Charles Henry and Margaret Elizabeth (Lang) T.; m. Pamet Ayer Jones, Sept. 21, 1961 (div. Mar. 1973); children: Jon Steven, Katherine Ayer; m. Amanda G. Birrell, Feb. 16, 1980 (div. Aug. 1996); 1 child, Elizabeth Torrey; m. Jane E. Blanksteen, Aug. 22, 1996. BA in Polit. Sci., U. Calif., Berkeley, 1962, JD, 1966. Bar: D.C. 1967, U.S. Ct. Appeals (2d, 4th, 5th, 6th, 7th, 8th, 9th, 10th and D.C. cirs.), U.S. Tax Ct., U.S. Supreme Ct. 1972, N.Y. 1993. Assoc. Williams & Connolly, Washington, 1966-69; editor-in-chief Selective Svc. Law Reporter, Washington, 1967-69; acting prof. law UCLA, 1969-71; pvt. practice law Grasse, France, 1972-74; assoc. William & Connolly, Washington, 1974, ptnr., 1975-77; ptnr. Tigar & Buffone, Washington, 1977-84; prof. law U. Tex., Austin, 1984-87, Joseph D. Jamail centennial chair in law, 1987—; of counsel Haddon, Morgan & Foreman, Denver, 1996—; reporter 5th Cir. Pattern Jury Instrns., Austin, 1988-90. Author: Practice Manual Selective Service Law Reporter, 1968, Law and the Rise of Capitalism, 1977, Federal Appeals: Jurisdiction and Practice, 2d edit., 1993, Examining Witnesses, 1993; contbr. articles to profl. jours. Mem. ABA (vice chair 1987-88, chair elect 1988-89, chair 1989-90 sect. litigation). Avocations: sailing, cooking.

TIGER, IRA PAUL, lawyer; b. Bklyn., Jan. 31, 1936; s. Sidney and Rebecca (Frankel) T.; m. Rosalind Silverman, July 4, 1957 (dec. Nov. 1972); children: Ruth, Lori; m. Ann Mae Gersh, May 5, 1974; stepchildren: Jimmie, Randy, Richard Riesenberg. B.S. in Econs., U. Pa., 1956, J.D. magna cum laude, 1959. Bar: Pa. 1960, U.S. Dist. Ct. (ea. dist.) Pa. 1960, U.S. Ct. Appeals (3d cir.) 1960, U.S. Supreme Ct. 1971. Law clk. 3d cir., 1959-60; assoc. Schnader, Harrison, Segal & Lewis, Phila., 1960-67, ptnr., 1968—, chmn. litigation dept., 1986-90, chmn. standing com. on profl. conduct, 1992—. Research editor U. Pa. Law Rev., 1958-59. Pres. Temple Sinai Synagogue, 1989-91; mem. Planning Adv. Bd. Upper Dublin Twp., 1982-87, mem. ednl. adv. com., 1976-78; legal counsel Phila. Jr. C. of C., 1963-64, bd. dirs., 1962-66, sec. Jewish campus activities bd., 1971-73. Mem. ABA, Am. Judicature Soc., Inst. Jud. Adminstrn., Pa. Bar Assn., Phila. Bar Assn. (chmn. fed. cts. com. 1985), Lawyers Club Phila., Order of Coif (exec. com. Pa. chpt. 1981-83), Beta Alpha Psi, Beta Gamma Sigma. Democrat. Office: Schnader Harrison 1600 Market St Ste 3600 Philadelphia PA 19103-7286

TIGER, LIONEL, social scientist, anthropology consultant; b. Montreal, Que., Can., Feb. 5, 1937; s. Martin and Lillian (Schneider) T.; m. Virginia Conner, Aug. 19, 1964; 1 child, Sebastian Benjamin. BA, McGill U., 1957, MA, 1959; PhD, U. London, 1963. Instr. anthropology U. Ghana, Accra, 1960; asst. prof. dept. anthropology and sociology U. B.C., Vancouver, Can., 1963-68; assoc. prof. anthropology Rutgers U., New Brunswick, N.J., 1969-74, prof. anthropology, 1974—, Charles Darwin prof. anthropology, 1990—; cons., rsch. dir. Harry F. Guggenheim Found., N.Y.C., 1972-84; chmn. bd. social scientists U.S. News and World Report, 1986-88; sci. adv. bd. Am. Wine Inst., San Francisco. Author: Men in Groups, 1969, 2d edit., 1987, (with Robin Rox) The Imperial Animal, 1971, 3d edit., 1997, (with Joseph Shepher) Women in the Kibbutz, 1975, Optimism: The Biology of Hope, 1979, 2d edit., 1994, China's Food, 1985, The Manufacture of Evil: Ethics, Evolution and the Industrial System, 1987; editor: Female Hierarchies, 1978, (with Michael Robinson) Man and Beast Revisited, 1991, The Pursuit of Pleasure, 1992; mem. editl. bd. Social Sci. Info., Ethology and Sociobiology jour., Jour. of Social Distress and the Homeless. Bd. advisors David R. Graham Found., Toronto, Ont., Can. Recipient W.I. Susman award for excellence in tchg., 1985, McNaughton prize for creative writing; Guggenheim fellow, 1969, rsch. fellow ASDA Found., 1985, Can. Coun., fgn. area tng. fellow Ford Found., Can. Coun.-Killam fellow for interdisciplinary rsch., Rockefeller fellow Aspen Inst., 1979, fellow H.F. Guggenheim Found, 1988-89. Fellow Royal Anthrop. Inst. (Eng.); mem. PEN (mem. exec. bd., treas. 1988-91, v.p. 1991-94), Am. Anthrop. Assn., Can. Anthrop. Assn., Can. Humanists Assn. (hon.), Soc. for Study of Evolution, Century Assn. Home: 248 W 23rd St Fl 4 New York NY 10011-2304 also: RR 2 Millbrook NY 12545-0965 Office: Rutgers U Douglas Coll New Brunswick NJ 08903-0270

TIGERMAN, STANLEY, architect, educator; b. Chgo., Sept. 20, 1930; s. Samuel Bernard and Emma Louise (Stern) T.; m. Margaret I. McCurry; children: Judson Joel, Tracy Leigh. Student, MIT, 1948-49; BArch, Yale U., 1960, MArch, 1961. Archtl. draftsman firm George Fred Keck, Chgo., 1949-50, Skidmore, Owings and Merrill, Chgo., 1957-59, Paul Rudolph, New Haven, 1959-61, Harry Weese, Chgo., 1961-62; partner firm Tigerman & Koglin, Chgo., 1962-64; prin. firm Stanley Tigerman & Assos., Chgo., 1964-82; ptnr. Tigerman Fugman McCurry, Chgo., 1982-88, Tigerman McCurry, 1988—; prof. architecture U. Ill.-Chgo., 1967-71, 80-93, dir. Sch. Architecture, 1985-93; vis. lectr. Yale U., 1974, Cornell U., Ithaca, N.Y., 1963, Cooper Union, 1970, U. Calif. at Berkeley, 1968, Cardiff (Wales) Coll., 1965, Engring. U., Bangladesh, 1967; chmn. AIA com. on design, coordinator exhbn. and book Chicago Architects, 1977; Charlotte Shepherd Davenport prof. architecture Yale U., 1979; architect-in-residence Am. Acad. in Rome, 1980; vis. prof. architecture Harvard U., 1982; William Henry Bishop Chair. prof. architecture Yale U., 1984, Sarrinen prof., 1993; dir. post-professional grad. program U. Ill.-Chgo.; co-founder Archeworks, Design Lab., Chgo., 1993; mem. adv. com. Princeton U., 1997. Prin. works include: Fukuoka Apt. Complex, Japan, The Power House, Zion, Ill., The Preserve Clubhouse, New Buffalo, Mich., others; author: Versus, 1982, Architecture of Exile, 1988 (nominated Nat. Jewish Book awar 1989), Stanley Tigerman: Buildings and Projects, 1966-89, 1989; contbg. author: Design of the Housing Site, 1966, Chicago on Foot, 1969, Art Today, 1969, New Directions in American Architecture, 1969, Contemporary Jewelry, 1970, Urban Structures for the Future, 1972, Spaces for Living, 1973, Chicago 1930-70, 1974, Interior Spaces Designed by Architects, 1974, Housing, 1976, Chicago Architects, 1976, 100 Years of Architecture in Chicago, 1976, Architectural Graphics Primer, 1976, 86, Mies Reconsidered, 1986, Chicago Architecture 1872-1922, 1988 (designer exhbn.), others, also numerous articles in newspapers and profl. jours.; exhibited, Venice Biennale, 1976, 80; co-curator, author essay, Calif. Condition exhbn., 1982; curator, designer exhbn., author catalogue Chicago Architecture, The New Zeitgeist: In Search of Closure, 1989. Pres. Yale Arts Assn., 1969-70; mem. advisory com. Yale Archtl. Sch., 1976—; bd. dirs. Bangladesh Found. Served with USN, 1950-54. Recipient Alpha Rho Chi medal Yale, 1961, Advanced Studies in Fine Art grant Graham Fedn., 1965, Archtl. Record award, 1970, Chgo. Masonry award, 1974, Masonry gold medal, 1974, Alumni Art award Yale U., 1985, Design award for Art Inst. Chgo. Schinkel Exhbn., Am. Soc. Interior Designers, 1995. Fellow AIA (chmn. com. design 1976-77, adv. com., Disting. Svc. award Chgo. chpt. 1983, Chgo. Honor awards 1977-79, Nat. Honor award 1982, 84, 87, 91, Nat. Modern Income Housing award 1970, Nat. Homes for Better Living award 1974, 75, Ill. award 1976, Nat. award of Merit 1970, 74, 75, named to Hall of Fame 1990, Disting. Bldg. award for pvt. residence Chgo. chpt. 1991, Chgo. Interior Archtl. Award of Excellence 1981, 83, 87, 91, 92, Nat. Interior Archtl. Award of Excellence 1992-93, Chgo. Disting. Bldg. award 1971, 73, 75, 77, 79, 81, 82, 84, 85, 86, 91, 94, Italian Ceramic Tile Design award 1995, Fukuoka Urban Beautification award 1995, 6 citations of merit Chgo. chpt. 1994, Interior Design award for A.I.C. Schinkel Exhibit 1996); mem. Arts Club of Chgo., Yale Club of N.Y.C., Century Assn. Club, Phi Kappa Phi. Office: Tigerman & McCurry Ltd 444 N Wells St Ste 206 Chicago IL 60610-4522

TIGGES, KENNETH EDWIN, retired financial executive; b. Sandusky, Ohio, Sept. 4, 1927; s. Edwin Ernest and Ruth Dorothea (Krapp) T.; m. Mary Anne Richardson, June 11, 1955. BSBA, Bowling Green State U., 1950. C.P.A., Ohio. With Konopak & Dalton (C.P.A.s), Toledo, 1950-57; with Owens-Illinois, Inc., 1957-84, comptr., 1963-71, v.p., comptr., 1971-84; v.p. fin. The De Vilbiss Co., Toledo, 1984-90, cons., 1990-92. Mem. fin. com. St. Vincent Hosp., Toledo, 1968—, Bowling Green State U. Bus. Adv. Council; bd. dirs. Jr. Achievement, Toledo, 1986-97. Served with U.S. Army, 1946-47. Recipient Acct. of Yr.-Industry award Beta Alpha Psi, 1983. Mem. Am. Inst. C.P.A.s, Ohio Soc. C.P.A.s, Fin. Execs. Inst. (pres. Toledo chpt. 1970-71, v.p., bd. dirs. 1972-73, mem. com. on govt. liaison), Bowling Green State U. Alumni Bd. Dirs., Sigma Chi. Episcopal. Lodge: Rotary. Avocations: golf, reading. Home: 6655 Mill Ridge Rd Maumee OH 43537-9659

TIGHE, JAMES C., publisher; b. Edmonton, Alta., Can., Sept. 30, 1950; s. James Donald and Ellen Grant (Drever) T.; m. Barbara C. Teske, Dec. 2, 1972; children: Teresa M., Jason M. Grad. high sch., Edmonton. Area supr. Edmonton Jour., 1969-73; circulation mgr. Thomson Newspapers, Western Can., 1973-79; dir. circulation Edmonton sun, 1979-81, gen. mgr., 1981-82; gen. mgr. UP Can., Toronto, Ont., 1982-84; pub. Calgary (Alta.) Sun, 1984-88; gen. mgr. Toronto Sun, 1988-89, pub., 1991-94, v.p. corp. planning, 1994-95; pres. Island Pub. Ltd., Can., 1995—. Office: Island Pub Ltd, 1824 Store St, Victoria, BC Canada VAT 4R4*

TIGHE-MOORE, BARBARA JEANNE, electronics executive; b. Wadsworth, Ohio, Jan. 12, 1961; d. Norton Raymond and Laura Alida (Frank) Tighe; m. Derek William Moore, June 26, 1982. AS in Electronic Engring. summa cum laude, Hocking Tech. Coll., 1981; AS in Electronic Data Processing magna cum laude, Sinclair Coll., 1986; BBA Honors Coll. magna cum laude, Kent State U., 1988. Lic. amateur radio operator. Tech. writer computer dept. Sinclair Coll., Dayton, Ohio, 1983; project mgr. O'Neil & Assocs., Dayton, 1983-84; biomed., bio-acoustic real-time flight simulation tempest developer Systems Rsch. Labs., Dayton, 1984-86; owner, pres. Lida Ray Techs., Dayton, 1978—; computer specialist Kent State U. Press, 1987-88; mgmt. analyst Electronic Warfare Frontier Engring. Inc., 1988-89; supr. small computer tech. svcs. Frontier Engring., Inc., 1989-90, project engr., 1990-92; ptnr., bd. dirs. MKCC, Dayton, 1990—; sr. program mgr. C.E.T.A., Dayton, 1992-93; ptnr., bd. dirs. SDCC, Dayton, 1992—; pres. Lida Ray Techs., Dayton; regional mgr. User Tech. Assocs., Dayton, 1993-96; mem. graphics steering com., mem. sanctioned UNIX software adv. team Aero. Sys. Divsn.; program chair IEEE Internat. Wireless LAN Conf.; mem. Engring. Application Support Environ. Security Working Group; proceedings chmn. Nat. Aerospace & Electronics Conf., 1995, 96, 97; bd. dirs. MKCC, Dayton, 1993—, SDCC; spkr. Govt. Land Mobile Commn. Conf., 1993, Internat. Engring. Mgmt. Cons., 1994, Wireless '93, Calgary, Alta., Nat. Aerospace & Electronics Conf., 1995, 96. Author: Job Search Strategies for the 90's, 1993, Through the Glass Ceiling, 1997; co-author: Women on a Wire, 1996; editor: Graphics Directions, 1990-91; pub. Team Advisor, SDCC Cleaning Times, IEEE Update; contbr. poetry to mags. and anthologies; contbr. papers, articles to profl. jours. Counselor Kwam's Kinder Kamp; tchr. Bible Sch.; cook Meals on Wheels; organizer/cook funeral Svcs. Dinners. Recipient Vol. Citizen award Wadsworth C. of C, 1979, Ohio Essayist award, 1979, Virginia Perryman award, 1979, Disting. Leadership award, 1990, 91. Mem. IEEE (former treas., sec. Dayton sect., bd. dirs. 1995-97), Computer Soc. of IEEE (sec. 1991-92, vice chmn. 1992-93, chmn. 1994-95), Engring. Mgmt. Soc. of IEEE, Tech. and Soc. of IEEE, Data Processing Mgmt. Assn., Assn. Computer Machinery, Def. Planning Analysis Soc. (exec. bd.), Assn. Internat. Students Econs. & Commerce (pres. 1986-87), Internat. Film Soc. (pres. 1986-88), Armed Forces Comms. and Electronics Assn. (judge sci. fair western dist. 1992—), Equestrian Team (point rider 1977-87), Fencing Club, Phi Theta Kappa, Mortar Bd., Omicron Delta Kappa, Beta Gamma Sigma. Avocations: travel, investing, equestrian show jumping, soccer. Home: 729 Kyle Dr Tipp City OH 45371-1435

TIGHT, DEXTER CORWIN, lawyer; b. San Francisco, Sept. 14, 1924; s. Dexter Junkins and Marie (Corwin) T.; m. Elizabeth Callander, Apr. 20, 1951; children: Dexter C. Jr., Kathyryn Marie Loken, Steven M., David C. AB, Denison U., 1948; JD, Yale U., 1951. Bar: Calif. 1951. Assoc. Pillsbury, Madison & Sutro, San Francisco, 1953-60; gen. atty. W.P. Fuller & Co., San Francisco, 1960-61; gen. counsel Schlage Lock Co., San Francisco, 1961-77; dir. govt. affairs Crown Zellerbach Corp., San Francisco, 1977-78; sr. v.p., gen. counsel The Gap Inc., San Bruno, Calif., 1978-90, legal, internat. cons., 1990—; gen. coun. The Nature Co., 1990-96; bd. dirs. Shaw-Clayton Plastics, San Rafael, Calif., Granite Rock Co., Watsonville, Calif., Alden Lee Co., Menlo Park, Calif. Chmn. That May See, San Fransisco; trustee Denison U., 1978—, chmn. capital fund dr., 1988-94; trustee Calvary Presbyn. Ch., 1968, 73, elder, 1969-90; elder Valley Presbyn. Ch., 1992—; vol. Internat. Exec. Svc. Corps. 1st lt. U.S. Army, 1943-45, 51-52. Mem. ABA, Calif. Bar Assn., San Francisco Bar Assn. (chmn. various coms.), Commonwealth Club Calif. (past bd. dirs., exec. com.), Menlo Country Club, Bohemian Club (San Francisco), Guardsman Club (1st v.p. 1961), Phi Beta Kappa. Republican. Presbyterian. Avocations: hiking, fishing, tennis, golf, photography. Home: 170 Wildwood Way Redwood City CA 94062-2352

TIJERINA, RAUL MARTIN, physics and mathematics educator; b. Brownsville, Tex., Dec. 10, 1962; s. Gregorio and Maria Olivia (Reyes) T. BS in Physics, U. North Tex., 1987; Cert. in Teaching, U. Tex., Brownsville, 1989. Cert. tchr., Tex. Math., physics tchr. U. Tex., Brownsville, 1988—; math., algebra tchr. Brownsville Ind. Sch. Dist., 1988—. Mem. Nat. Coun. Tchrs. Math., Math. Assn. Am., Am. Inst. Physics. Roman Catholic. Avocations: computers, racquetball, softball. Office: Perkins Mid Sch 4750 Austin Rd Brownsville TX 78521-5455

TILBERIS, ELIZABETH, editor-in-chief; m. Andrew Tilberis, 1971. Student, Jacob Kramer Coll. Arts, Leeds, England; BA in Eng., Leicester (Eng.) Poly. Fashion asst. British Vogue, 1970, fashion editor, 1974, exec. fashion editor, 1984, sr. fashion editor, 1986, editor-in-chief, 1987; dir. Conde Nast Pubs., 1991; editor-in-chief Harper's Bazaar, N.Y.C., 1992—. Recipient 2 Nat. Mag. awards for design, photography, 1993, Coun. Fashion Designers of Am. award, 1994. Office: Harper's Bazaar 1700 Broadway Fl 37 New York NY 10019-5905 also: care Susan Magrino Susan Magrino Agency 167 E 73rd St New York NY 10021-3510*

TILGER, JUSTINE THARP, research director; b. New Point, Ind., Sept. 11, 1931; d. Joseph Riley and Marcella Lorene (King) Tharp; m. Clarence A. Tilger II Aug. 22, 1959 (div. Nov. 1972); children: Evelyn Mary, Clarence Arthur III, Joseph Thomas. AB, U. Chgo., 1951; BA, St. Mary's Coll., Notre Dame, Ind., 1954; MA, Ind. U., 1962; PhD, 1971. Mem. Sisters of the Holy Cross, Notre Dame, 1954-58; teaching fellow Ind. U., Bloomington, 1959-61; asst. editor Ind. Mag. History, Bloomington, 1962-64; bookkeeper Touche Ross, Boston, 1974-77; mgr. account services Harvard U., Cambridge, Mass., 1977-81; dir. research and records Bentley Coll., Waltham, Mass., 1982-84; dir. support services Sta. WGBH-TV, Boston, 1985; dir. research Tufts U., Medford, Mass., 1986—; cons. Laduke Assocs., Framingham, Mass., 1972-74, New Eng. Ballet, Sudbury, Mass., 1981-82. v.p. Potter Rd. Sch. Assn., Framingham, 1968-69; chmn. vols. St. Anselm's, Sudbury, 1970-71. Mem. Coun. for Advancement and Support Edn., Assn. Records Mgmt. Adminstrs., Am. Prospect Rsch. Assn., New Eng. Devel. Rsch. Assn., Mass. Bus. and Profl. Women (sec. 1981-82), Mensa. Roman Catholic. Avocations: dramatics, travel. Home: 15 Auburn St # 6 Framingham MA 01701-4844 Office: Tufts U Dept of Research Pachard Hall Medford MA 02155

TILGHMAN, RICHARD GRANVILLE, banker; b. Norfolk, Va., Sept. 18, 1940; s. Henry Granville and Frances (Fulghum) T.; m. Alice Creech, June 28, 1969; children—Elizabeth Arrington, Caroline Harrison. B.A., U. Va., 1963. Asst. cashier United Va. Bank-Seaboard Nat., Norfolk, Va., 1968-70, asst. v.p., 1970-72; pres., chief adminstrv. officer United Va. Bank, Richmond, 1978-80; asst. v.p. United Va. Mortgage Corp., Norfolk, Va., 1972, v.p., 1972-73, pres., chief exec. officer, 1974-76; pres., chief exec. officer United Va. Leasing Corp., Richmond, Va., 1973-74; sr. v.p. bank related United Va. Bankshares, Inc., Richmond, 1976-78, exec. v.p. corp. banking, 1980-84, vice chmn., 1984-85; pres., chief exec. officer United Va. Bankshares, Inc., now Crestar Fin. Corp., Richmond, 1985—, chmn., 1986—; bd. dirs. Chesapeake Corp., Richmond, 1986—; chmn. Va. Pub. Bldg. Authority, Richmond, 1982-87; prin. Va. Bus. Coun., 1987—; mem. Fed. Adv. Coun., 1994-97, pres. 1996-97. Chmn. bd. dirs. Richmond Symphony, 1984-85; bd. dirs., mem. gen. adv. coun. Sheltering Arms Hosp., Richmond, 1981-89; bd. dirs. Va. Free, 1989-90, Richmond Symphony Found., 1989-91, Va. Found. Ind. Colls., 1988—, Va. Literacy Found., 1986-89; bd. govs. St. Catherine's Sch., 1989-95; bd. dirs. Va. Mus. Found., 1986-92, trustee, 1994—; trustee Randolph Macon Coll., 1985-93, Richmond Renaissance, 1986—, Colonial Williamsburg Found., 1994—; co-chmn. NCCJ. 1st lt. U.S. Army, 1963-66. Mem. Bankers Rountable (dir. 1996—), Am. Bankers Assn., Va. Bankers Assn. (bd. dirs. 1991—, pres. 1996-97). Episcopalian. Clubs: Commonwealth, Country of Va. Office: Crestar Fin Corp PO Box 26665 919 E Main St Richmond VA 23219-4625

TILL, BEATRIZ MARIA, international business consultant, translator; b. Havana, Cuba, Sept. 27, 1952; came to U.S., 1961; d. Thomas Emanuel and Gladys Manuela (Loret de Mola) Alexander; m. John Edwin Till, Oct. 30, 1976. Student, U. Fla., 1970-71, 72-74, U. Ariz., 1988. Translating sales sec. Rozier Machinery, Tampa, Fla., 1976-78; paralegal, interpreter-translator, 1979-83; pres. Beatriz M. Till Translations, 1983—; interpreter-translator Office of Worker's Compensation, State of Fla., Tampa, pvt. attys., 1979—; spl. advisor to Sec. of Commerce, State of Fla.; surveillance audio/video transcription specialist Fed. Ct. State of Fla. (middle dist.); also, expert witness on tape recording transcriptions and translations. Active Navy League of U.S. Mem. Internat. Platform Assn., Fla. C. of C., Tampa Bay Internat. Trade Coun.,Fla. Coun. Internat. Devel. Republican. Avocations: reading, photography, cooking. Home: 12301 Pathway Ct Riverview FL 33569-4122 Office: Beatriz M Till Translations 12301 Pathway Ct Riverview FL 33569-4122

TILL, FRANKLIN L., school system administrator; b. San Diego, Jan. 20, 1947; s. Franklin L. Sr. and Luella Jane (Krough) T.; m. Barbara Jane Till, May 1, 1971; children: Marlo, Jeffrey. BA, San Diego State U., 1969, MA, 1973; EdD, U. So. Calif., 1981. Vice prin. secondary schs. San Diego United Sch. Dist., ops. mgr., prin. mid. level, dep. supt. Contbr. articles to profl. jours. Bd. dirs. YMCA, Cornerstone 2000, Weed and Seed, United Way; mem. exec. bd. ACSA Sch. to Career. Recipient three PTA Hon. Svc. awards. Mem. Assn. of Calif. Sch. Adminstrs. (Disting. Leaders award), Adminstrs. Assn. Home: 5851 Torca Ct San Diego CA 92124-1020

TILL, JAMES EDGAR, medical educator, researcher; b. Lloydminster, Sask., Can., Aug. 25, 1931; s. William and Gertrude Ruth (Isaac) T.; m. Marion Joyce Sinclair, June 6, 1959; children: David William, Karen Sinclair, Susan Elizabeth. BA, U. Sask., 1952, MA, 1954; PhD, Yale U., 1957. Mem. physics divsn. Ont. Cancer Inst., Toronto, 1957-67, with divsn. biol. rsch., 1967-69, divsn. head, 1969-82, with divsn. epidemiology and stats., 1989—; assoc. dean U. Toronto, 1981-84, prof., 1984—. Contbr. articles on biophysics, cell biology and cancer control research to sci. jours. Recipient Gairdner Found. Internat. award, 1969, Order of Can., 1994. Fellow Royal Soc. Can.; mem. Can. Bioethics Soc. Home: 182 Briar Hill Ave, Toronto, ON Canada M4R 1H9 Office: 610 University Ave, Toronto, ON Canada M5G 2M9 *Albert Einstein said: "The most beautiful thing we can experience is the mysterious. It is the source of all true art and science." He also believed that concern for humanity must always form the chief interest of all technical endeavors—"in order that the creations of our mind shall be a blessing and not a curse to mankind." Is there a more eloquent summary of standards for the scientist than this?*

TILLACK, THOMAS WARNER, pathologist; b. Jacksonville, Fla., Nov. 16, 1937; s. Warner S. and Charlotte G. T.; m. Lynne Anne Beam, Oct. 30, 1970; children—Jonathan Allan, Allison Anne. B.A., U. Rochester, 1959; M.D., Yale U., 1963. Diplomate: Diploma Am. Bd. Pathology. Intern Barnes Hosp., St. Louis, 1963-64; resident Barnes Hosp., 1964-66; staff asso. NIH, Bethesda, Md., 1966-69; sr. staff fellow NIH, 1969-71; asst. prof. pathology Washington U., St. Louis, 1971-73; assoc. prof. Washington U., 1973-76; Walter Reed prof., chmn. dept. pathology U. Va. Med. Center, 1976—. Served with USPHS, 1966-69. Mem. Am. Soc. Investigative Pathology, U.S. and Can. Acad. Pathology, Am. Soc. Cell Biology, Assn. Pathology Chairs, Phi Beta Kappa. Research, publs. in cell biology and pathology. Home: PO Box 376 Ivy VA 22945-0376 Office: U Va Med Ctr Dept Pathology PO Box 214 Charlottesville VA 22908-0001

TILLE, JAMES EUGENE, army chaplain; b. Decatur, Ill., July 31, 1951; s. Charles Herman and Alice Elizabeth (Wochner) T.; m. Insuk Kay Ch'oe, Jan. 6, 1976; 1 child, Charles Andrew. BA in Liberal Studies, SUNY, Albany, 1977; Assoc. in Acctg., Ft. Steilacoom Community Coll., 1984; MDiv, Golden Gate Bapt. Theol. Sem., 1988; MA in Counseling, Liberty U., 1990. Nat. cert. counselor; nat. cert. family therapist; cert. mental health counselor, Wash. Enlisted U.S. Army, 1973-82; chaplain candidate U.S. Army, Individual Ready Res., St. Louis, 1985-89; mental health technician Western State Hosp., Ft. Steilacoom, Wash., 1982-89; assoc. pastor Harbor Baptist Ch., Gig Harbor, Wash., 1985-89; battalion chaplain 3-3 FA Bn 2AD, Ft. Hood, Tex., 1989-90, 1-3 FA Bn. 2AD&1CD, Ft. Hood, 1990-91, 3-5CAV Bn, Germany, 1991-94, 14th Engr. Bn, Ft. Lewis, Wash., 1995-96; with 555 CMBT EN GP, Ft. Lewis, 1996—. Decorated Army Meritorious Svc. medal, Army Commendation medal, Army Achievement medal. Mem. ACA, Am. Assn. Christian Counselors, Internat. Assn. Marriage and Family Counselors, 2d Armored Divsn. Hell on Wheels Assn. (life), 1st Cavalry Divsn. Assn. (life). Baptist. Home: 9109 Zircon Dr SW Lakewood WA 98498-4054 Office: HHC 555 CMBT EN GP Fort Lewis WA 98433

TILLER, OLIVE MARIE, retired church worker; b. St. Paul, Dec. 13, 1920; d. Otto William and Myrtle Alice (Brougham) Foerster; m. Carl William Tiller, June 21, 1940; children: Robert W., Jeanne L. Peterson. BS, U. Minn., 1940. Spl. edn. tchr. Prince Georges County, Md., 1955-63; spl. asst. for profl. svcs. Kendall Demonstration Elem. Sch., Gallaudet Coll., Washington, 1971-78; spl. asst. for program Ch. Women United, N.Y.C., 1979-80; exec. asst. to gen. sec. Nat. Coun. Chs. of Christ in U.S.A., N.Y.C., 1981-87; dep. gen. sec. for coop. Christianity Am. Bapt. Chs. of U.S.A., Valley Forge, Pa., 1987-88. Author: (with Carl W. Tiller) At Calvary, 1994. Mem. Human Rels. Commn., Prince George's County, 1967-73; v.p. Am. Bapt. Chs. U.S.A., Valley Forge, 1976-77; bd. dirs. Am. Leprosy Missions, Greenville, S.C., 1981-95, Bapt. Peace Fellowship of N.Am., Junaluska, N.C., 1984-95; mem. Nat. Interreligious Svc. Bd. for Conscientious Objectors, 1991—, treas., 1994—; mem. nat. coun. Fellowship of Reconciliation, 1985-88, 96-97. Recipient Dahlberg Peace award Am. Bapt. Chs., 1991, Valiant Woman award Ch. Women United, 1978, Meeker award Ottawa U., 1995. Mem. Nat. Coun. Fellowship of Reconciliation. Baptist. Home: 100 Norman Dr Apt 283 Cranberry Township PA 16066-4235

TILLERY, RICHARD LEE, television executive; b. Pratt, Kans., Nov. 6, 1940; s. Donald R. and Thelma L. (Keen) T.; m. Naomi Goodman, June 7, 1967 (div. July 1984); children: Richard Craig, Mary Kathrine; m. Julia D. Rockler, June 30, 1985; 1 child, Melissa Beth. Student, Ft. Hays State U., 1958-60, 63-65. Investigative reporter, photographer, editor Sta. KZTV, Corpus Christi, Tex., 1965; asst. news dir., prodr., assignments editor, inv. reporter Sta. KIII-TV, Corpus Christi, 1970; asst. news dir., co-anchor, prodr. Sta. KRIS-TV, Corpus Christi, 1973; asst. news dir., prodr., assignment editor Sta. KETV, Omaha, 1974; news dir. Sta. KHGI-TV, Kearney, Nebr., 1976; acting news dir., exec. prodr. Sta. KWCH-TV, Wichita, Kans., 1980; exec. prodr., dir. spl. projects Sta. KENS-TV, San Antonio, 1984; freelance prodr., investigator Washington, 1986-87; coord. Newsnet satellite feed svc. CBS News, 1987-88; bur. chief The Washington Bur., Washington, 1988—; com. mem. UPI, AP, Soc. of Prof. Journalists; panelist, guest speaker in field; organizer profl. seminars in field. Bd. dirs. ARC, Campfire Girls, Boy Scouts Am., South Tex. Mental Health and Retardation. With U.S. Army, 1960-63. Recipient Pieringer award Tex. Assn. Broadcasters, Headliners award U. Tex., Gavel award Tex. Bar Assn., Sch. Bell award Tex. Classroom Tchrs. Assn., Investigative Reporting award Nat. AP, investigative reporting and regional awards from various orgns. Mem. Nebr. AP Broadcasters (past pres., regional awards), South Tex. Press Club (past v.p., regional awards), Radio and TV News Dirs. Assn. (com. mem., panelist, guest speaker). Office: The Washington Bur 400 N Capitol St NW Ste 363 Washington DC 20001-1511*

TILLERY-TATE, JOHNNIE LEA, mental health and geriatrics nurse; b. San Angelo, Tex., Aug. 25, 1938; d. John A. and M. Inez (Balkum) Whittenberg; m. Leon Tillery, June 1, 1957; children: Valerie Joyce, Tanya Leann; m. Don Tate, Sept. 5, 1992. Student, Angelo State U., San Angelo, 1956; diploma, San Angelo Sch. Vocat. Nursing, 1979; ASN, Eastern N.Mex. U., 1984. Cert. mental health and gerontol. nurse. Staff nurse Permian Gen. Hosp., 1984-87, St. Johns Hosp., 1987, Sterling County Hosp., 1989; unit supr. San Angelo State Sch. Tex. Dept. Mental Health and Mental Retardation, 1987-93; investigator, surveyor Tex. Dept. Health, 1993; nurse, surveyor, qualified mental retardation profl. Tex. Dept. Human Svcs., 1993—. Mem. Tex. Pub. Employees Assn., Am. Assn. Mental Retardation (nursing div.). Home: 7593 Gladiola San Angelo TX 76901

TILLETT, GRACE MONTANA, ophthalmologist, real estate developer; b. Malone, N.Y., Dec. 5, 1924; d. Everett Reed and Althea Adela (Manson) Montana; m. Charles W. Tillett, Aug. 9, 1952; children—Charles, James, Avery. B.A., Syracuse U., 1946, M.D., 1949. Diplomate Am. Bd. Radiology, Am. Bd. Ophthalmology. Intern, Balt. City Hosps., 1949-50, resident, 1950-51; resident Johns Hopkins Hosp., Balt., 1951-53; practice medicine specializing in ophthalmology, Charlotte, N.C., 1957—; v.p. Prof. Optical Service, Charlotte, 1959—; pres. 2200 E. Seventh St. Real Estate Corp., Charlotte, 1965—; mem. staff Presbyn., Mercy, Charlotte Meml. hosps. Bd. dirs. Heart Assn. Charlotte, 1971-73, Dance Charlotte, 1978-79. Mem. Bus. and Profl. Women's Assn., Am. Acad. Ophthalmology, Am. Acad. Radiology, AMA, N.C. Med. Soc., Mecklenburg County Med. Soc., Charlotte Ophthalmol. Soc. Republican. Club: Charlotte Country. Office: 2130 Sharon Ln Charlotte NC 28211-3736

TILLEY, CAROLYN BITTNER, technical information specialist; b. Washington, July 29, 1947; d. Klaud Kay and Margaret Louise (Hanson) Bittner; m. Frederick Edwin Dudley, June 18, 1985. B.S., Am. U., 1975; M.L.S., U. Md., 1976. With NIH, 1965-71; statis. research asst. Health Manpower Edn., Bethesda, Md., 1971-72; tech. info. specialist Nat. Libr. Medicine, Bethesda, Md., 1972-81, head medlars (med. lit. analysis and retrieval system) mgmt. sect., 1981—. Mem. editorial bd.: Med. Reference Services Quar. Mem. CENDI User Edn. Com., Nat. Fed. Abstracting and Info. Svc. Pub. Com. Recipient Merit award NIH, 1984, Rogers award Nat. Libr. Medicine, 1991. Mem. Med. Library Assn. Presbyterian. Avocation: horseback riding. Office: Nat Libr Medicine 8600 Rockville Pike Bethesda MD 20894-0001

TILLEY, NORWOOD CARLTON, JR., federal judge; b. Rock Hill, S.C., 1943; s. Norwood Carlton and Rebecca (Westbrook) T.; m. Greta Medlin, Sept. 25, 1970. BA, Wake Forest U., 1966, JD, 1969. Bar: N.C. 1969, U.S. Dist. Ct. (middle dist.) N.C. 1971. Law clk. to Hon. Eugene A Gordon, U.S. Dist. Judge Middle Dist. N.C., 1969-71; asst. U.S. atty. Mid. Dist. N.C., Greensboro, 1971-73, U.S. atty., 1974-77; U.S. dist. judge Mid. Dist. N.C., Durham, 1988—; ptnr. Osteen, Adams, Tilley & Walker, Greensboro, 1977-88; instr. Wake Forest U. Sch. Law, 1980. Office: US Dist Ct PO Box 3443 Greensboro NC 27402-3443

TILLEY, RICE M(ATTHEWS), JR., lawyer; b. Ft. Worth, June 21, 1936; s. Rice Matthews Sr. and Lucille Geyer (Kelly) T.; children: Marisa Lynn, Angela Ainsworth, Lisa Scott, Rice Matthews III; m. Sandra Cooper, May 13, 1994. BA, Washington & Lee U., 1958; JD, So. Meth. U., 1961; LLM in Taxation, NYU, 1962. Bar: Tex. 1961. Mem. Law, Snakard & Gambill, Ft. Worth, 1964—. Bd. dirs. Van Cliburn Found., Ft. Worth Ballet Assn., Ft. Worth Symphony Orch. Assn.; bd. trustees Tex. Wesleyan Univ.; pres. Ft. Worth Opera Assn. Mem. State Bar Tex. (chmn. real estate, probate and trust law sect.), Ft. Worth C. of C. (chmn. bd.), Century II Club (pres.), Leadership Ft. Worth (chmn. bd. dirs.), Exch. Club of Ft. Worth (pres.). Republican. Office: Law Snakard & Gambill 500 Throckmorton St Ste 3200 Fort Worth TX 76102-3819

TILLINGHAST, CHARLES CARPENTER, JR., aviation and financial consultant; b. Saxton's River, Vt., Jan. 30, 1911; s. Charles C. and Adelaide Barrows (Shaw) T.; m. Lisette Micoleau, Nov. 16, 1935; children: Charles Carpenter III, Elizabeth, Jane, Anne Shaw. Ph.B., Brown U., 1932; J.D., Columbia U., 1935; L.H.D., S.D. Sch. Mines and Tech., 1959; LL.D., Franklin Coll., 1963, U. Redlands, 1964, Brown U., 1967, Drury Coll., 1967, William Jewell Coll., 1973. Bar: N.Y. bar 1935, Mich. 1943. Assoc. Hughes, Schurman & Dwight, 1935-37; dep. asst. dist. atty. N.Y. County, 1938-40; assoc. Hughes, Richards, Hubbard & Ewing, 1940-42; ptnr. Hughes, Hubbard, Blair & Reed (and predecessor firms), N.Y.C., 1942-57; v.p., dir. The Bendix Corp., Detroit, 1957-61; pres., chief exec. officer Trans World Airlines, Inc., 1961-69, chmn. bd., chief exec. officer, 1969-76, dir., 1961-81; dir., vice chmn. bd. White Weld & Co., Inc., 1977-78; mng. dir. Merrill Lynch White Weld Capital Markets Group, 1978-82; bd. dirs. Henry Luce Found., Air Transport Assn., 1961-72, 74-75; mem. exec. com. Internat. Air Transport Assn., 1969-75. Bd. dirs. Cmty. Welfare Fund, Bronxville, 1951-53, pres., 1953; gov. Lawrence Hosp., Bronxville, 1955-59; trustee Brown U., 1954-61, 65-79, chancellor, 1968-79, fellow, 1979—; fellow Midwest Rsch. Inst., 1963-76, the Conf. Bd., 1965-76, People to People Program, 1961-70, Com. for Econ. Devel., 1967—; bd. visitors Sch. Law, Columbia U., 1962-92; bd. govs. John Carter Brown Libr., 1989-96. Mem. ABA, Assn. Bar City N.Y., Brown U. Club (N.Y.C.), Hope Club (R.I.), Sakonnet Golf Club. Home: 355 Blackstone Blvd Apt 530 Providence RI 02906-4953

TILLINGHAST, CHARLES CARPENTER, III, marketing company executive; b. N.Y.C., Nov. 16, 1936; s. Charles Carpenter, Jr. and Lisette (Micoleau) T.; m. Cynthia Branch, Sept. 28, 1974; children by previous marriage: Avery D., Charles W., David C. B.S. in Mech. Engring, Lehigh U., 1958; M.B.A., Harvard U., 1963. Asst. to dir. devel. Lehigh U., Bethlehem, Pa., 1958-61; adminstrv. asst. Boise Cascade Corp., Portland, Oreg., 1963; asst. to v.p. Boise Cascade Corp., Boise, Idaho, 1964-65; gen. mgr. office supply div. Boise Cascade Corp., 1965-67, gen. mgr. paper distbn. div., 1966, v.p. bus. products, 1967-69, sr. v.p. housing group, 1969-71, sr. v.p., 1971-73; pres. CRM div. Ziff-Davis Pub. Co., Inc., Del Mar, Calif., 1971-75; pres., treas. Value Communications, Inc., La Jolla, Calif., 1975-76; pres. Oak Tree Publs., Inc., San Diego, 1976-81; pres. Advanced Mktg. Services Inc., San Diego, 1982-94, chmn., 1994—. Served to 2d lt. AUS, 1959. Home: 1762 Nautilus St La Jolla CA 92037-6413 Office: Advanced Mktg Svcs Inc 5880 Oberlin Dr San Diego CA 92121-4735

TILLINGHAST, DAVID ROLLHAUS, lawyer; b. N.Y.C., Feb. 25, 1930; s. Charles Carpenter and Josephine Dorothy (Rollhaus) T.; m. Phyllis Van Horn, Sept. 24, 1955 (div. Jan. 1984); m. Lisa Sewell, Feb. 25, 1984; children: Gregory Barrett Sewell, Lauren Alexa. AB cum laude, Brown U., 1951; LLB cum laude, Yale U., 1954. Bar: N.Y. 1955, Oreg. 1956, U.S. Supreme Ct. 1978. Assoc. Hughes, Hubbard & Reed, N.Y.C., 1954-55, 57-61; ptnr. Hughes, Hubbard & Reed, 1961-62, 65-90; assoc. King, Miller, Anderson, Nash & Yerke, Portland, Oreg., 1955-57; spl. asst. for internat. tax affairs U.S. Dept. Treasury, Washington, 1962-65; ptnr. Chadbourne & Parke, N.Y.C., 1990—; adj. prof. Sch. Law, NYU, 1977-87; cons. UN Ctr. on Transnat. Corps., 1978-87; reporter Am. Law Inst. Project on Internat. Aspects of U.S. Income Taxation, 1982-91; cons. to reporters Am. Law Inst. Revision of Restatement of Fgn. Relations Law of U.S., 1982-83. Author: Tax Aspects of Internat. Transactions, 1978, 2d edit., 1984; contbr. articles to profl. publs. Mem. transition team Sec. of Treasury W. Michael Blumenthal, 1977. Estab. David L. Tillinghast lectr. on internat. taxation NYU Sch. Law. Mem. Assn. of Bar of City of N.Y. (chmn. com. on taxation 1981-83), Internat. Fiscal Assn. (v.p. U.S. br. 1983—, permanent sci. com. 1983—, vice chmn. 1993-95, chmn. 1995—), Internat. Bar Assn. (vice chmn. com. on taxation bus. law sect. 1984-86), Tax Forum, Coun. on Fgn. Rels. Democrat. Avocations: golf; tennis. Office: Chadbourne & Parke 30 Rockefeller Plz New York NY 10112

TILLINGHAST, JOHN AVERY, utilities executive; b. N.Y.C., Apr. 30, 1927; s. Charles C. and Dorothy J. (Rollhaus) T.; m. Mabel Healy, Sept. 11, 1948; children: Katherine Brickley, Susan Trainor, Abigail Ryan. BSME, Columbia U., 1948, MS, 1949. Registered profl. engr., Ky., Ind., Mich., N.Y., Ohio, Va., W.Va., N.H. With Am. Elec. Power Service Corp., N.Y.C., 1949-79, exec. v.p. engring. and constrn., 1967-72, sr. exec. v.p., vice chmn. engring. and constrn., 1972-79; sr. v.p. tech. Wheelabrator-Frye Inc., Hampton, N.H., 1979-83, Signal Advanced Tech. Group, The Signal Cos., Hampton, N.H., 1983-85; sr. v.p. Allied-Signal Internat., Hampton, 1985-86, Sci. Applications Internat. Corp., San Diego, 1986-88; pres. TILTEC, Portsmouth, N.H, 1987-94; CEO Great Bay Power Corp., Dover, N.H, 1994-97, BayCorp Holdings, Ltd., Dover, N.H, 1997—. Patentee generating unit control system. Elder Reformed Ch., 1976-79. Served with USN, 1944-46. Fellow ASME; mem. IEEE, Nat. Acad. Engring.,Sigma Xi, Tau Beta Pi. Office: Great Bay Power Corp 100 Main St Dover NH 03820-3835

TILLIS, MEL(VIN), musician, songwriter; b. Tampa, Fla., Aug. 8, 1932; m. Judy Edwards, 1979; children: Pam, Connie, Cindy, Melvin Jr., Carrie, Hannah. Student, U. Fla. Founder Sawgrass Music, Sabal Music, Tillis Tunes, Sweet Tater Tunes, Nashville; owner, pres. Mell Tillis Theater, 1990—. Songwriter, Cedarwood Music, Nashville, 20 years, (Named Entertainer of Year, Country Music Assn. 1976), numerous personal and TV appearances; composer over 600 songs recorded by, Webb Pierce, Ray Price, Carl Smith, Brenda Lee, Kenny Rogers, Charlie Pride, Burl Ives, George Strait, others; (with The Statesiders) 56 albums including; Mel Tillis and the Statesiders on Stage, Best of Mel Tillis, Love Revival, Welcome to Country, California Road, 1985, American Originals, 1990, Greatest Hits, 1991, Beyond the Sunset, 1993, The Memory Maker, 1995; author: Stuttering Boy, 1986. Served in USAF, 1951-55. Named Comedian of Yr., Country Music Assn., 1971, 73, 74, 75, 76, 77, Entertainer of Yr., 1976. Office: Mel Tillis Theater Inc PO Box 1626 2527 Hwy 248 Branson MO 65616

TILLIS, PAM, country singer, songwriter; b. Plant City, Fla., 1957; d. Mel and Doris T.; divorced; 1 child, Ben; m. Bob DiPiero, Feb. 14, 1991. Student, U. Tenn. Recording artist Arista Records, 1990—. Singer, songwriter for acts including Highway 101, Gloria Gayner, Dan Seals, Chaka Kahn, Ricky Van Shelton, Suzy Bogguss, Conway Twitty; albums: Put Yourself in My Place, 1991, Homeward Looking Angel, 1992, Pam Tillis Collection, 1994, Sweethearts Dance, 1994, All Of This Love, 1995; 1st single: Every Home Should Have One, 1981; #1 hit record Don't Tell Me What To Do, 1991. Grammy nomination, Best Country Vocal Collaboration for "Romeo" with Dolly Parton, Tanya Tucker, Billy Ray Cyrus, Kathy Mattea & Mary-Chapin Carpenter, 1994. Office: Arista Records 6 W 57th St New York NY 10019-3913*

TILLMAN, ELIZABETH CARLOTTA, nurse, educator; b. Md., Aug. 31, 1929; d. Walter Monroe and Mozelle Virginia (Shugars) Brown; m. Lloyd A. Tillman, Apr. 16, 1949; children: Lloyd A. Jr., William L., Susan E. Tillman Chaires. Diploma, Md. Gen. Hosp. Sch. Nursing, 1950; student, Towson State U., U. Md., Loyola Coll., Balt., Howard C.C. RN. Psychiatric nurse Spring Grove Hosp. Ctr., Catonsville, Md., 1950; pvt. duty home health nurse Md., 1951-60; dir., tchr., nurse Doughoregan Manor Day Sch., Ellicott City, Md., 1960-80; med.-surg. nurse Woman's Hosp., Balt., 1964, Md. Gen. Hosp., Balt., 1980; nursing instr. Howard County Dept. Edn., Ellicott City, 1981-91; nursing educator Howard County Sch. Tech., 1981-91, Howard County Gen. Hosp., 1981-91; geriatric nurse Lorien Columbia (Md.) Nursing & Rehab. Ctr., 1981-91; home health nurse Md., 1992—. Mem. NEA, Md. State Tchrs. Assn., Md. Gen. Hosp. Alumni Assn., Am. Vocat. Assn., Health Occupations Educators, Md. Vocat. Assn., Phi Eta Sigma, Iota Lambda Sigma. Home: 10002 Reed Ln Ellicott City MD 21042-2238

TILLMAN, JOHN LEE, principal; b. Mesa, Ariz., Jan. 31, 1947; s. W.L. and Juanita (Johnson) T.; m. Judith Ann Tuxhorn, May 31, 1980; children Matthew Lee, Andrew Lee. BA, Adams State Coll., 1969, MA, 1975. Cert. tchr., Colo., Va.; cert. adminstr., Colo. Music tchr. Mountain Valley Sch., Saquache, Colo., 1969-70; dir. music Hargrave Mil. Acad., Chatham, Va., 1970-76; music tchr. Sargent Sch. Dist., Monte Vista, Colo., 1976-82; secondary prin. Sargent Sch. Dist., Monte Vista, 1982-95, dir. devel., 1995—; bd. control Colo. H.S. Activities Assn., Denver, 1990-93; alumni bd. dirs. Adams State Coll., Alamosa, Colo., 1990-93. Music dir. Calvary Bapt. Ch., Monte Vista, 1976—. Mem. Am. Assn. Sch. Adminstrs., Colo. Assn. Sch. Execs., Colo. Music Educators Nat. Conf., Phi Delta Kappa. Baptist. Avocations: computers, music, electronics, woodworking. Office: Sargent Sch Dist 7090 N County Road 2 E Monte Vista CO 81144-9756

TILLMAN, JOSEPH NATHANIEL, engineering executive; b. Augusta, Ga., Aug. 1, 1926; s. Leroy and Canarie (Kelly) T.; m. Alice Lavonia Walton, Sept. 5, 1950 (dec. 1983); children: Alice Lavonia, Robert Bertram; m. Areerat Usahaviriyakit, Nov. 24, 1986. BA magna cum laude, Paine Coll., 1948; MS, Northrop U., 1975, MBA, 1976; DBA, Nova U., 1989. Dir. Rockwell Internat., Anaheim, Calif., 1958-84; pres. Tillman Enterprises, Corona, Calif., 1985—; guest lectr. UCLA, 1980-85. Contbr. articles to profl. jours. Capt. USAF, 1948-57, Korea. Recipient Presdl. Citation Nat. Assn. for Equal Opportunity in Higher Edn., 1986. Mem. Acad. Mgmt. (chmn. 1985-86), Soc. Logistics Engrs. (pres. 1985-86), Paine Coll. Alumni Assn. (v.p. 1976—), NAACP (pres. 1984-88). Avocations: duplicate bridge, travel, swimming, skiing, hiking. Office: Tillman Enterprises 1550 Rimpau Ave Trlr 45 Corona CA 91719-3206

TILLMAN, MARY NORMAN, urban affairs consultant; b. Atlanta, Jan. 31, 1926; d. Mary Nellie Shehee; B.A., Morris Brown Coll., 1947; postgrad. U. Minn., 1964, Old Dominion U., 1975—; m. James A. Tillman, Jr., Apr. 11, 1952; children—James A., Gina G. Asst. bus. mgr. Morris Brown Coll., Atlanta, 1947-53; race relations and urban affairs cons. Tillman Assos. Cons. Social Engrs., Atlanta and Syracuse, N.Y., 1963—, sr. ptnr., treas., from 1965, now pres.; bd. dirs. The Tillman Inst. of Human Rels., Inc.; clin. prof. United Theol. Sem., New Brighton, Minn.; adj. prof. Gordon-Conwell Theol. Sem., South Hamilton, Mass. Mem. adv. council to urban ministries dept. So. Bapt. Conv., Community Relations Commission, Atlanta; bd. dirs. Christian Council Met. Atlanta, Tillman Inst. Human Relations. Mem. Tidewater Assn. Public Adminstrs. (dir.), Am. Acad. Consultants, Nat. Black Writers Consortium (v.p.), Joint Ctr. for Polit. Studies. Author: What is Your Racism Quotient?, 1964; (with James A. Tillman, Jr.) Why America Needs Racism and Poverty, 1972; (with J.A. Tillman, Jr.) Black Intellectuals, White Liberals and Race Relations: An Analytic Overview, 1973; What Is Your Exclusivity Quotient, 1978; also articles. Office: 1765 Glenview Dr SW Atlanta GA 30331-2307

TILLMAN, MASSIE MONROE, federal judge; b. Corpus Christi, Tex., Aug. 15, 1937; s. Clarence and Artie Lee (Stewart) T.; m. Karen Wright, July 2, 1993; children: Jeffrey Monroe, Holly. BBA, Baylor U., 1959, LLB, 1961. Bar: Tex. 1961, U.S. Dist. Ct. (no. dist.) Tex. 1961, U.S. Ct. Appeals (5th cir.) 1969, U.S. Supreme Ct. 1969; bd. cert. Personal Injury Trial Law, Tex. Ptnr. Herrick & Tillman, Ft. Worth, 1961-66; pvt. practice, Ft. Worth, 1966-70, 79-87; ptnr. Brown, Herman et al, Ft. Worth, 1970-78, Street, Swift et al, Ft. Worth, 1978-79; U.S. bankruptcy judge Ft. Worth divsn. No. Dist. Tex., 1987—. Author: Tillman's Trial Guide, 1970; Comments Editor/Case Notes Editor; mem. editl. bd. Baylor Law Rev., 1960-63. Fellow Am. Bd. Trial Advocates, Tex. Bar Found.; mem. Ft. Worth/Tarrant County Bar (bd. dirs. 1969-70, v.p. 1970-71), Assn. Trial Lawyers Am., Trial Attys.'s of Am., Nat. Conf. of Bankruptcy Judges, Am. Bankruptcy Inst. Republican. Baptist. Avocations: cutting horses, competition shotgun shooting.

TILLMAN, ROLLIE, JR., university official; b. Lake Wales, Fla., Apr. 11, 1933; s. Rollie and Louise (Johnson) T.; m. Mary Windley Dunn, June 22, 1957; children—Mary Windley, Jane Guion, Rollie. BS, U. N.C., 1955; MBA, Harvard U., 1957, DBA, 1962. Rsch. asst. Harvard Bus. Sch., 1958-60; asst. prof. bus. adminstrn. U. N.C., Chapel Hill, 1960-63, assoc. prof., 1963-65, prof., 1965—, dir. MBA program, 1965-67, dir. exec. program, 1968-77, vice chancellor for univ. relations, 1978-84; trustee chmn. Kenan Inst. Pvt. Enterprise, Chapel Hill, 1985-90, chmn. bd., 1990—; dir. U. N.C. Press, Renfro Inc., Entrepreneur of Yr. Inst., Coun. Entrepreneur Devel., Good Mark Foods, Micell Techs., Inc. Author: (with C.A. Kirkpatrick) Promotion: Persuasive Communication in Marketing, 1964, (with Luther H. Hodges, Jr.) Bank Marketing: Text and Cases, 1968. Trustee St. Mary's Coll., 1968-78; dir., pres. N.C. Mus. of Art Soc. Mem. Am. Mktg. Assn. (dir. 1967-69), Small Bus. Coun., U.S. C. of C. Democrat. Episcopalian. Office: Kenan Inst Pvt Enterprise CB 3490 Chapel Hill NC 27599

TILLSON, JOHN BRADFORD, JR., newspaper publisher; b. Paris, Tex., Dec. 21, 1944; s. John Bradford Sr. and Frances (Ragland) T.; m. Patricia Hunt, June 14, 1966 (div. June 1978); children: John, Karen; m. Cynthia Wornom, Oct. 10, 1981. BA, Denison U., Granville, Ohio, 1966. Reporter Charlotte (N.C.) News, 1969-71; reporter Dayton (Ohio) Daily News, 1971-76, city editor, 1977-80, asst. mng. editor, 1980-82, mng. editor features, 1982-84; editor Dayton Daily News and Jour. Herald, 1984-88, pub., 1988—; lectr. Am. Press Inst., Reston, Va., 1980-84. Exec. com. Vietnam Vets. Meml. Park Fund, Dayton, 1985-86; community bd. advisors Jr. League Dayton, 1986; trustee Dayton Art Inst., 1984—, Victory Theatre, 1986—; trustee Dayton Performing Arts Fund. Mem. Am. Soc. Newspaper Pub. Episcopalian. Home: 4833 Far Hills Ave Dayton OH 45429-2318 Office: Dayton Daily News 45th S Ludlow St Dayton OH 45402*

TILLY, JENNIFER, actress. TV series include: Shaping Up, 1984, Bodyguard, 1990, Key West, 1993; TV movies include: Heads, 1994; films include: No Small Affair, 1984, Moving Violations, 1985, He's My Girl, 1987, Inside Out, 1987, Rented Lips, 1988, High Spirits, 1988, Johnny Be Good, 1988, Remote Control, 1988, The Fabulous Baker Boys, 1989, Let It Ride, 1989, Far From Home, 1989, Scorchers, 1991, Shadow of the Wolf, 1992, Made in America, 1993, At Home With the Webbers, 1993, Double Cross, 1994, Bullets Over Broadway, 1994 (Academy award nomination best supporting actress 1994), The Getaway, 1994, The Pompatus of Love, 1996, Liar, Liar, 1996, House Arrest, 1996, Edie & Pen, 1996, Bound, 1996. Home: Care Carrol Gettko 118 S Beverly Beverly Hills CA 90212

TILLY, LOUISE AUDINO, history and sociology educator; b. Orange, N.J., Dec. 13, 1930; d. Hector and Piera (Roffino) Audino; m. Charles Tilly, Aug. 15, 1953; children: Christopher, Kathryn, Laura, Sarah. BA, Rutgers U., 1952; MA, Boston U., 1955; PhD, U. Toronto, 1974. From instr. to asst. prof. Mich. State U., East Lansing, 1972-75; from asst. prof. to prof. U. Mich., Ann Arbor, 1975-84; prof. history and sociology New Sch. for Social Rsch., N.Y.C., 1984-94, chair com. hist. studies, 1984—, Michael E. Gellert prof. history and sociology, 1994—; assoc. dir. studies Ecole des Hautes Etudes en Scis. Sociales, Paris, 1979, 80, 88; fellow Shelby Cullom Davis Ctr., Princeton (N.J.) U., 1978; vis. mem. Inst. for Advanced Study, Princeton, 1987-88; fellow Ctr. for Advanced Study Behavioral Scis., 1991-92; vis. scholar Russell Sage Found., 1994-95; bd. dirs. Social Scis. Rsch. Coun., N.Y.C., 1983-86. Author: Politics and Class in Milan, 1881-1901, 1992; co-author: The Rebellious Century, 1975, Women, Work and Family, 1978, rev. edit., 1987; co-editor, co-author: Class Conflict and Collective Action, 1981, Women, Politics and Change, 1990; co-editor: The European Experience of Declining Fertility: The Quiet Revolution, 1992, Internation Labor and Working-Class History, 1994—; also articles. Active com. on women's employment and related social issues Nat. Acad. Scis., 1981-86, chmn., co-editor report Panel on Tech. and Women's Employment, 1984-86. Grantee Rockefeller Found., 1974-76, Am. Philos. Soc., 1977-78, 85-86, Russell Sage Found., 1985-86; Guggenheim Found. fellow, 1991-92. Mem. Am. Hist. Assn. (coun. 1985-87, pres. elect. 1992, pres. 1993), Social Sci. History Assn.(pres. 1981-82), Coun. on European Studies (exec. com. 1980-83), Berkshire Conf. Women Historians. Democrat. Home: 5 E 22nd St Apt 5K New York NY 10010-5321 Office: Com on Hist Studies 80 Fifth Ave 5th Fl New York NY 10011-8002

TILLY, MEG, actress; b. Long Beach, Calif., Feb. 14, 1960. Actress: (films) Fame, 1980, Tex, 1982, One Dark Night, 1983, The Big Chill, 1983, Psycho II, 1983, Impulse, 1984, Agnes of God, 1985 (Academy award nomination best supporting actress 1985), Off Beat, 1986, Masquerade, 1988, The Girl in a Swing, 1988, Valmont, 1989, The Two Jakes, 1990, Carmilla, 1990, Leaving Normal, 1992, Body Snatchers, 1994, Sleep with Me, 1994, Journey, 1996, (TV movies) In the Best Interest of the Child, 1990, Trick of the Eye, 1994, (TV series) Winnetka Road, 1993, Fallen Angels, 1993; author: Singing Songs, 1994.

TILNEY, NICHOLAS LECHMERE, surgery educator; b. N.Y.C., Oct. 19, 1935; s. Robert Wallace and Olive van Rensallaer (Gawtry) T.; m. Henriette Beatrice London, Sept. 20, 1958 (div. 1975); children: Rebecca, Louise Moore, Victoria; m. Mary Johanna Graves, June 17, 1978. AB, Harvard U., 1958; MD, Cornell U., 1962. Surg. resident Peter Bent Brigham Hosp., Boston, 1962-71; rsch. fellow U. Oxford, Eng., 1968-69, 71-72; surg. registrar U. Glasgow, Scotland, 1972-73; asst. prof. surgery Harvard Med. Sch., Boston, 1974-76, assoc. prof. surgery, 1977-82, prof. surgery, 1983—, Francis D. Moore prof., 1992—, dir. Surg. Rsch. Lab., 1975—; dir. transplant svcs. Brigham & Womens Hosp., Boston, 1976-92, Transplant Rsch. Ctr., 1992—. Contbr. articles to profl. jours. Lt. comdr. USN, 1966-68. Fellow ACS, Royal Coll. Physicians and Surgeons (Glasgow); mem. Am. Soc. Transplant Surgeons (pres. 1995), Phi Beta Kappa. Avocation: boating. Office: Brigham and Womens Hosp 75 Francis St Boston MA 02115-6110

TILSON, DOROTHY RUTH, word processing executive; b. Bloomsburg, Pa., Mar. 24, 1918; d. Roy Earl and Mary Etta (Masteller) Derr; m. Irving Tilson, Sept. 1949. BS, Bloomsburg U., 1940. Tchr. Madison Consol. Sch., Jerseytown, Pa., 1940-42; gage checker Phila. Ordinance Gage Lab., 1942-43; tabulating asst. Remington Rand, Phila., N.Y.C., 1943-46; copy writer Sears Roebuck, Phila., N.Y.C., 1946-48; statis. asst. Ford Internat., N.Y.C., 1949-56; word processing adminstrv. asst. Coopers & Lybrand, N.Y.C., 1956-91. Life mem. Rep. Senatorial Inner Circle, Washington, 1987—. Mem. Am. Movement for World Govt. (sec. 1991—), N.Y. Theosophical Soc. (libr. 1969—), UN Assn.-USA (mem. global policy project which includes internat. econ. governance and human rights). Home: 435 W 119th St # 9G New York NY 10027-7102

TILSON, JOHN QUILLIN, lawyer; b. New Haven, Aug. 27, 1911; s. John Quillin and Marguerite (North) T.; m. Catherine E. Jackson, Sept. 14, 1934; children—John Quillin III, Thomas D., Rebecca E. BA, Yale, 1933, LLB, 1936. Bar: Conn. bar 1936. Since practiced in New Haven; assoc. Wiggin & Dana, New Haven, 1936-48, ptnr., 1948—; lectr. hosp. law Yale Sch. Medicine, 1959—. Chmn. plan and zoning commn., Hamden, Conn., 1949-51; pres. Conn. Conf. Social Work, 1949-50; Bd. aldermen, New Haven, 1935-37; rep. Conn. Gen. Assembly, 1953; alternate Republican Nat. Conv., 1956, del., 1964; chmn. Hamden Rep. Town Com., 1964-68; Corporator Inst. Living, Hartford, 1959—; bd. dirs. New Haven Vis. Nurse Assn., New Haven United Fund; trustee Yale in China, 1936-62; bd. dirs. Yale New Haven Hosp., Yale Psychiat. Inst.; bd. dels. Am. Hosp. Assn. Served to lt. comdr. USNR, 1943-46, 51-53. Mem. ABA (del.), Conn. Bar Assn. (pres.), New Haven County Bar Assn., Quinnipiack Club, Morys Club. Home: 88 Notch Hill Rd Apt 372 North Branford CT 06471-1853 Office: Wiggin & Dana 1 Century Tower New Haven CT 06510-7013

TILSON, M(ARTIN) DAVID, surgeon, scientist, educator; b. Texarkana, Tex., Aug. 25, 1941; s. M. David and Leta (Martin) T.; m. Joan E. Stanescki, 1974; children: William Thomas, John Wainwright, Martin David III. BA, Rice U., 1963; MD, Yale U., 1967. Diplomate Am. Bd. Surgery, Nat. Bd. Med. Examiners. Surg. intern Yale U., 1967-68; resident in surgery U. New Haven, 1968-72; asst. to assoc. prof. Yale U., New Haven, 1974-83, prof., 1983-89; Alisa Mellon Bruce prof. of surgery Columbia U., N.Y.C., 1989—. Contbr. articles to profl. jours. Maj. USAF, 1972-74. Rsch. grantee NIH, 1983-94. Mem. ACS, Soc. Univ. Surgeons, Am. Surg. Assn., Soc. Vascular Surgery, Internat. Soc. Cadiovasc. Surgery, Halsted Soc. Office: St Lukes Roosevelt Hosp 1000 10th Ave New York NY 10019-1147 Home: 104 Edgemont Rd Scarsdale NY 10583

TILSON THOMAS, MICHAEL, symphony conductor; b. L.A., 1944; s. Ted and Roberta T. Studies with, Ingolf Dahl, U. So. Calif., others; student conducting, Berkshire Music Festival, Tanglewood, Mass.; student conducting (Koussevitsky prize 1968); LL.D., Hamilton Coll.; L.H.D. (hon.), D'Youville Coll., 1976. Asst. condr. Boston Symphony Orch., 1969, assoc. condr., 1970-72, prin. guest condr., 1972-74; also Berkshire Music Festival, summer 1970, 74; music dir., condr. Buffalo Philharmonic Orch., 1971-79; music dir., prin. condr. Great Woods Ctr. for Performing Arts, 1985-88; prin. condr. London Symphony Orch., 1988—; artistic dir. New World Symphony, Fla., 1988—. Condr., dir., N.Y. Philharmonic Young People's Concerts, CBS-TV, 1971-77; vis. condr. numerous orchs., U.S., Europe, Japan; chief condr. Ojai Festival, 1967, dir., 1972-77; opera debut, Cin., 1975; condr.: Am. premiere Lulu (Alban Berg), Santa Fe Opera, summer 1979; prin. guest condr., L.A. Philharm., 1981-85, Am. premiere Desert Music (Steve Reich), 1984; prin. condr. Gershwin festival London Symphony Orch., Barbcan Ctr., 1987; composer: Grace (A Song for Leonard Bernstein), 1988, Street Song (for Empire Brass Quintet), 1988, From the Diary of Anne Frank (for orchestra and narrator Audrey Hepburn and New World Symphony), 1990; commd. by UNICEF for Concerts for Life's European premiere, 1991; recording artist Sony Classical/CBS Masterworks, 1973—; co-artistic dir. Pacific Music Festival, 1990—, with Leonard Bernstein 1st ann. Pacific Music Festival, Sapporo, Japan, 1990; co-artistic dir. 2d ann. Pacific Music festival, 1991, Salzburg Festival, 1991; conducted Mozart Requiem. Named Musician of Year, Musical Am. 1970; recipient Koussevitsky prize, 1968, Grammy award for Carmina Burana with Cleve. Orch., 1976, for Gershwin Live with Los Angeles Philharm., 1983, Grammy nomination, Best Classical Album - Debussy: Le Martyre de Saint Sebastien (with the London Symphony Orchestra), 1994. Office: 888 7th Ave Fl 37 New York NY 10106-3799 Office: San Francisco Symphony Davies Symphony Hall San Francisco CA 94102*

TILSWORTH, TIMOTHY, retired environmental/civil engineering educator; b. Norfolk, Nebr., Apr. 6, 1939; s. Brooke and Mildred (Palmer) T.; m. Joanne Novak, Apr. 19, 1966 (div. Jan. 1984); children: Craig Scott, Patrick Joseph; m. Debbie J. May, July 20, 1984. BSCE, U. Nebr., Lincoln, 1966, MSCE, 1967; PhD, U. Kans, 1970. Registered profl. engr., Alaska; diplomate Inst. Hazardous Materials Mgmt. Instr. U. Nebr., Lincoln, 1967; prof. environ. quality and civil engring. U. Alaska, Fairbanks, 1970-94, dir. program environ. quality engring. and sci., 1972-76, 78-94, asst. to pres. for acad. affairs, 1976-78, head dept. civil engring, 1990-91, chmn. grad. coun., chmn. chancellor search com., 1990-91; co-owner Raven Press Pub. Co., Fairbanks, 1990—; prof. emeritus civil engring. and environ. quality engring., 1994—; pres. faculty senate U. Alaska, 1992-93; owner Alaska Arctic Environ. Svcs., Fairbanks, 1972—, DJT's Shelties Delight, Fairbanks, 1985—, T2 Antiques, 1994—; project mgr. superconducting super collider proposal State of Alaska, Fairbanks, 1987-88. Chmn. exec. com. Cowper for Gov. Alaska, Fairbanks, 1986. Recipient commendation State of Alaska, 1988. Mem. Assn. for Environ. Engring. Profs., ASCE (Outstanding Service award 1975), Am. Water Works Assn. Water Pollution Control Fedn., Chi Epsilon. Roman Catholic. Home and Office: 1900 Raven Dr Fairbanks AK 99709-6661

TILTON, DAVID LLOYD, savings and loan association executive; b. Santa Barbara, Calif., Sept. 21, 1926; s. Lloyd Irving and Grace (Hart) T.; m. Mary Caroline Knudtson, June 6, 1953; children: Peter, Jennifer, Michael, Catharine. A.B., Stanford U., 1949, M.B.A., 1951. With Santa Barbara Savs. & Loan Assn., 1951-90, pres., 1965-84; now pres. Fin. Corp., Santa Barbara; trustee, chmn. Calif. Real Estate Investment Trust, 1988. Served with USNR, World War II. Mem. Calif. Savs. and Loan League (dir. 1980), Delta Chi. Home: 630 Oak Grove Dr Santa Barbara CA 93108-1402 Office: 505 Bath St Ste 102 Santa Barbara CA 93101-3403

TILTON, GEORGE ROBERT, geochemistry educator; b. Danville, Ill., June 3, 1923; s. Edgar Josiah and Caroline Lenore (Burkmeyer) T.; m. Elizabeth Jane Foster, Feb. 7, 1948; children—Linda Ruth, Helen Elizabeth, Elaine Lee, David Foster, John Robert. Student, Blackburn Coll., 1940-42; B.S., U. Ill., 1947; Ph.D., U. Chgo., 1951; D.Sc. (hon.), Swiss Fed. Inst. Tech., Zurich, 1984. Phys. chemist Carnegie Instn., Washington, 1951-65; prof. geochemistry U. Calif.-Santa Barbara, 1965-91, emeritus, 1991—, chmn. dept. geol. scis., 1973-77; guest prof. Swiss Fed. Inst., Zurich, 1971-72; prin. investigator NSF research grant, 1965—; mem. earth scis. panel NSF, 1966-69, 82-85. Assoc. editor Jour. Geophys. Research, 1962-65, Geochimica et Cosmochimica Acta, 1973—; contbr. articles to profl. jours. Served with AUS, 1942-45. Decorated Purple Heart; recipient Sr. Scientist award Alexander von Humboldt Found., 1989. Fellow AAAS, Am. Geophys. Union, Geol. Soc. Am.; mem. Nat. Acad. Scis., Geochem. Soc. (pres. 1981), Sigma Xi. Episcopalian. Home: 2661 Tallant Rd MW-512 Santa Barbara CA 93105 Office: U Calif Dept Geol Scis Santa Barbara CA 93106

TILTON, JAMES FLOYD, theatrical designer, art director; b. Rochelle, Ill., July 30, 1937; s. Norval Bailey T. and Magdeline (Ripplinger) Marelli; m. Helga Strang, Dec. 26, 1962 (div. Nov. 1976). B.A., U. Iowa, 1959. Resident designer John Drew Theater, Easthampton, N.Y., 1963; prin. designer Assn. Producing Artists, N.Y.C., 1965-69, Phoenix Theatre, N.Y.C., 1970-80; freelance designer, 1963—; designer maj. indsl. shows Avon, Coca-Cola, ABC, NBC Affl., N.Y.C., 1974—; designer for TV, 1977—; designer mus. exhibits Guild Hall Mus., East Hampton, 1979—; set and lighting designer 30 Broadway shows including You Can't Take It With You,, 1965, 83, Seascape (nomination for Antoinette Perry award), 1975. Served with U.S. Army, 1960-62. Recipient Carbonelle awards, 1987, 91, 92. Mem. United Scenic Artists 829. Democrat. Roman Catholic. Office: 10 W 15th St New York NY 10011-6838

TILTON, JOHN ELVIN, mineral economics educator; b. Brownsville, Pa., Sept. 16, 1939; s. John Elvin Sr. and Margaret Julia (Renn) T.; m. Elizabeth Martha Meier, June 18, 1966; children: Margaret Ann, John Christian. AB, Princeton U., 1961; PhD in Econs., Yale U., 1965. Staff analyst Office of Sec. of Def., Washington, 1965-67; rsch. assoc. Brookings Inst., Washington, 1967-70; asst. prof. econs. U. Md., College Park, 1970-72; assoc. prof. mineral econs. Pa. State U., University Park, 1972-75, prof., 1975-85; Coulter prof. Colo. Sch. Mines, Golden, 1985-94, dir. Divsn. Econs. and Bus., 1994—; officer econ. affairs commodities divsn. UN Conf. on Trade and Devel., Geneva, 1977; leader rsch. Internat. Inst. Applied Systems Analysis, Laxenburg, Austria, 1982-84; joint dir. mineral econs. and policy Program of Resources for Future, Colo. Sch. Mines, Washington, 1982—; vice chmn. bd. mineral and energy resources NRC, Washington, 1980-83, mem. nat. materials adv. bd., 1987-89. Author: International Diffusion of Technology, 1971, The Future of Nonfuel Minerals, 1977; editor: Material Substitution, 1983, World Metal Demand, 1990, Mineral Wealth and Economic Development, 1992, View from the Helm, 1995; co-editor: Economics of Mineral Exploration, 1987, Competitiveness in Metals, 1992. Capt. U.S. Army, 1965-67. Fulbright scholar Ecole Nat. Supérieure des Mines de Paris, 1992. Mem. Am. Econ. Assn., Am. Inst. Mining Metall. and Petroleum Engrs. (Mineral Econs. award 1985), Mineral Econs. and Mgmt. Soc. (pres. 1993-94), Mining and Metall. Soc. Am. Avocations: skiing, hiking. Office: Colo Sch Mines Divsn Econs and Bus Golden CO 80401

TILTON, WEBSTER, JR., contractor; b. St. Louis, Sept. 11, 1922; s. Webster and Eleanor (Dozier) T.; student St. Marks Prep. Sch., 1936-40, Pawling Prep. Sch., 1940-42; master brewers degree, U.S. Brewers Acad., 1949; m. Grace Drew Wilson, Feb. 14, 1948 (div. Oct. 1959); 1 son, Webster III; m. 2d, Nancy McBlair Payne, Jan. 5, 1963. Asst. brewing technologist F&M Schaffer Brewing Co., Bklyn., 1948-52; factory sales rep. Cole Steel Equipment Co., N.Y.C., 1957-68; dist. sales mgr. Scantlin Electronics, Inc., Washington, 1968-70; sales rep. Comml. Washer & Dryer Sales Co., Washington, 1970-72; propr. Webster Tilton, Jr., contractor, Washington, 1972-86. Served from cadet to chief mate Mcht. Marine Res.-USNR, 1942-45. Episcopalian. Home: RD # 2 Box 634 Cooperstown NY 13326

TILY, STEPHEN BROMLEY, III, bank executive; b. Phila., July 7, 1937; s. Stephen Bromley Jr. and Edith Helen (Straub) T.; m. Janet Anita Walz, July 10, 1965; children: Deborah Powell, Stephen Bromley IV, James Charles II. BS in Econs., Washington and Jefferson Coll., 1960; postgrad., Temple U. Sch. Law, 1963. Trust officer Indsl. Valley Bank & Trust Co., Phila., 1968-71; v.p. Farmers Bank of Delaware, Wilmington, 1971-77; exec. officer G&T, Inc., Ltd., Wilmington, 1977-80; pres., COO DCG&T Co., Wilmington, 1977-91, chmn., CEO, 1991-93, chmn. emeritus, 1993—; chmn. The Declaration Group, Conshohocken, Pa., 1985—; tchr. Am. Inst. Banking, 1970-79. Capt. USAR, 1960-61. Mem. Fin. Analysts of Phila., Internat. Assn. Fin. Planning, Barnegat Light Yacht Club (commodore 1988-89, trustee 1989-92), Kimberton Fish and Game Assn., Waynesborough Country Club, Union League Club of Phila., Merion Golf Club, Ducks Unltd. Republican. Episcopalian. Office: The Declaration Group 555 E North Ln Ste 6160 Conshohocken PA 19428-2233

TIMBERG, SIGMUND, lawyer; b. Antwerp, Belgium, Mar. 5, 1911; came to U.S., 1916, naturalized, 1921; s. Arnold and Rose (Mahler) T.; m. Eleanor Ernst, Sept. 22, 1940; children—Thomas Arnold, Bernard Mahler, Rosamund and Richard Ernst (twins). A.B., Columbia U., 1930, A.M., 1930, LL.B., 1933. Bar: N.Y. 1935, U.S. Supreme Ct. 1940, D.C. 1954. Sr. atty., solicitors' office Dept. Agr., 1933-35, chief, soil conservation sect., 1935-38; staff mem. Temporary Nat. Econ. Com., 1938-39; sr. atty. SEC, 1938-42; chief, property relations and indsl. orgn. div., reoccupation br. Bd. Econ. Warfare and Fgn. Econ. Adminstrn., 1942-44; spl. asst. to atty. gen., antitrust div. Dept. Justice, 1944-45, chief judgments and judgment enforcement sect., 1946-52; sec. UN Com. on Restrictive Bus. Practices, 1952-53; cons. UN, 1953-55, 62-64; pvt. law practice, 1954-88; prof. law Georgetown U. Law School, 1952-54; faculty Parker Sch. Comparative Law, Columbia U., 1967-80; spl. counsel Senate Mil. Affairs Subcom. on Surplus Property Legislation, 1944; mem. Mission for Econ. Affairs, Am. Embassy, London, 1945; del. Anglo-Am. Telecommunications Conf., Bermuda, 1945, Geneva Copyright Conf., 1952; cons. Senate Patents Subcom., 1961, UN Patents Study, 1962-64, OAS, 1970; mem. adv. com. on fed. policy on indsl. innovation, patent and info. policy sub com., 1978-79, adv. com. on internat. investment, tech. and devel., 1979-85. Contbr. articles on antitrust, intellectual property and internat. law to legal periodicals. Mem. ABA, D.C. Bar Assn., Internat. Bar Assn., Internat. Law Assn., Am. Soc. Internat. Law, Washington Fgn. Law Soc., Am. Law Inst., Assn. Bar City N.Y., Copyright Soc. Am., Cosmos Club (Washington), Philosophy Club (Washington). Home: 3519 Porter St NW Washington DC 20016-3177

TIMBERLAKE, CHARLES EDWARD, history educator; b. South Shore, Ky., Sept. 9, 1935; s. Howard Ellis and Mabel Viola (Collier) T.; m. Patricia Alice Perkins, Dec. 23, 1958; children: Mark Brewster, Daniel Edward, Eric Collier. BA, Berea Coll., 1957; Calif. State Teaching Credential, Claremont Grad. Sch., 1958, MA, 1962; PhD, U. Wash., 1968. Tchr. Barstow High Sch., Calif., 1959-60, Claremont City Sch., Calif., 1960-61; teaching, rsch. asst. U. Wash., Seattle, 1961-64; asst. prof. history U. Mo., Columbia, 1967-73, assoc. prof., 1973-81, prof., 1981—, Byler dist. prof., chmn. dept., 1996—, asst. dir. Honors Coll., 1988-90; exch. prof. Moscow State U., 1985, U. Manchester, Eng., 1987-88; hon. prof. history Lanzhou U., China, 1991; edn. coord. Revalba Russian River Cruises, 1992—; vis. prof. Joensuu (Finland) U., 1996. Editor: Essays on Russian Liberalism, 1972, Detente: A Documentary Record, 1978, Religious and Secular Forces in Late Tsarist Russia, 1992, The Fate of Russian Orthodox Monasteries and Convents

Since 1917, 1995, Profiles of Finland series, 1991-94, (microfiche) The St. Petersburg Collection of Zemstvo Publs., 1992—; contbr. chpts. to books, articles to profl. jours. Mem. Citizens Alliance for Progress, Columbia, Mo., 1969-75, pres., 1969-70; founding mem. High Edn. Rescue Operation, Mo., 1983—; mem. Columbians Against Throw-Aways, 1980-83. Fgn. Area fellow, 1965-66, fellow Internat. Rsch. and Exchs. Bd., 1971, 95, Am. Coun. Learned Socs., 1978-79, Fulbright-Hays fellow, 1995; grantee NEH, 1972, 79, 87. Mem. Am. Assn. Advancement Slavic Studies (bd. dirs. 1980-82, 84-86, chmn. council regional affiliates 1981-82, 85-86, chmn. permanent membership com. 1981-84), Western Slavic Conf., Am. Hist. Assn. (exec. council Conf. on Slavic and East European History 1987-89), Central Slavic Conf. (sec.-treas. 1967-68, pres. 1968-69, 76-77, 83-84, 88-89, exec. bd. 1972—, custodian archive 1972—), Mo. Conf. History (pres. 1992, sec.-treas. 1996—), State Hist. Soc. Mo., Rocky Mountain Assn. Slavic Studies, Fulbright Assn. (pres. Mo. chpt. 1997—). Avocations: backpacking, travel, skiing. Home: 9221 S Rt N Columbia MO 65203-9312 Office: U Mo Dept History Columbia MO 65211

TIMBERLAKE, MARSHALL, lawyer; b. Birmingham, Ala., July 25, 1939; s. Landon and Mary (Perry) T.; m. Rebecca Ann Griffin, Aug. 22, 1987; children: Sumner, Jane Ellison. BA, Washington & Lee U., 1961; JD, U. Ala., 1970. Bar: Ala. 1970, Ala. Supreme Ct. 1970, U.S. Dist. Ct. (no., so. and mid. dists.) Ala. 1970, U.S. Supreme Ct. 1976, U.S. Ct. Appeals (11th and 5th cirs.) 1981, U.S. Ct. Appeals (D.C. cir.) 1991. Assoc. Balch & Bingham Law Firm, Birmingham, 1970-76, ptnr., 1976—; pres. Legal Aid Soc., Birmingham, 1980-81; chmn. Ala. Supreme Ct. Commn. on Dispute Resolution, 1994-96, commr., 1996—; trustee Ala. Dispute Resolution Found., 1995—. Pres. Ala. Alcohol and Drug Abuse Coun., 1994-95, dir., 1989—; v.p. Assn. Atty. Mediators, 1994—. Capt. U.S. Army, 1962-66, Vietnam. Fellow Ala. Law Found.; mem. ABA, Ala. State Bar (chmn. corp. banking and bus. law sect. 1981-82, chmn. bar task force on alternative dispute resolution 1992-94, Spl. Merit award 1995, co-chmn. state bar com. on ADR 1996-97, mem. spl. task force on jud. selection 1996—), Birmingham Bar Assn. (chmn. ethics com. 1975-76, chmn. unauthorized practice of law com. 1976-77, chmn. spl. projects com. 1994-95, co-chmn. com. on jud. and legal reform 1996—), Redstone Club (bd. govs. 1977-78), Rotary (Birmingham chpt., chmn. civic club found. 1984), Beaux Arts Krewe, Mountain Brook Club. Republican. Presbyterian. Avocations: tennis, thoroughbred racing, photography. Office: Balch & Bingham 1901 6th Ave N Birmingham AL 35203-2618

TIMBERS, STEPHEN BRYAN, financial services company executive; b. Madison, Wis., Aug. 8, 1944; s. James G. Timbers and Betty A. (Aalseth) Fink; m. Joan Phillips (div.); 1 child, Alexander C. A.; m. Elaine C. Mack, Nov. 17, 1990; children: Christopher B., Brendan C. (dec.), Michele. AB in English Lit., Yale U., 1966; MBA, Harvard U., 1968. Portfolio strategist Mut. Life Ins. Co. of N.Y., N.Y.C., 1970-81; sr. portfolio mgr. Smith Barney, Harris Upham & Co., N.Y.C., 1981-84; chief investment officer The Portfolio Group, Inc., N.Y.C., 1984-87, Kemper Fin. Svcs., Inc., Chgo., 1987-92; pres., COO Kemper Corp., Long Grove, Ill., 1992-96; pres., CEO., CIO Zurich Kemper Investments, Inc.(acquired by Zurich Ins. Group), Chgo., 1996—; bd. dirs. ICI Mut. Ins. Co.; trustee Kemper Mut. Funds and Seperate Accounts; mem. panel on market volatility and investor confidence N.Y. Stock Exch., N.Y.C., 1990. Agt. Yale Alumni Fund, Harvard Bus. Sch. Alumni Fund; active United Way Crusade of Mercy. With U.S. Army, 1968-70. Mem. Investment Analysts Soc. Chgo. (dir. 1992-95), N.Y. Soc. Security Analysts, Yale Club of N.Y.C., Econ. Club of Chgo. (membership com. 1990), Chgo. Club, Glen View Club, The Attic, Racquet Club of Chgo., Castle Pines Golf Club. Office: Zurich Kemper Investments 222 S Riverside Plz Chicago IL 60606-5808

TIMINS, BONITA LEA, interior decorator; b. Scranton, Pa., Nov. 26, 1951; d. Edward Joseph and Mary Loretta (Lake) T. BS in Art Edn., Kutztown U., 1973; MA in Art Edn. magna cum laude, Marywood Coll., 1976, MA in Psychology magna cum laude, 1990; PhD in Metaphysics, Am. Internat. U., 1994. Art tchr. Scranton Sch. Dist., 1974-77; prodn. asst. Garan, Inc., N.Y.C., 1977-78, Marty Gutmacher, Inc., N.Y.C., 1979-81, R.R.J. Industries, N.Y.C., 1981-82; prodn. mgr. Double Dutch Sportswear, N.Y.C., 1982-84; MR/CLA supr. Allied Svcs., Scranton, 1984-86; home health care coord. Scranton, 1986-95; interior decorator Kurlancheek Furniture Gallery, Clarks Summit, Pa., 1995—; ind. curator, Scranton, 1992-94; chemistry tutor U. Scranton, 1994-95. Contbr. articles to profl. jours. Com. woman Dem. Party, Scranton, 1994; fundraiser Am. Cancer soc., Scranton, 1993; mem. Nat. Coun. for Geocosmic Rsch. Recipient Nightingale award Pa. Hosp. Assn., 1995, Outstanding Assoc. Mem. Cmty. Svc. award Lackawanna County Young Dems., 1996, Excellence award Sigma Theta Tau Internat. Nursing Soc., 1995. Mem. Art Student's League N.Y.C. (life), Psi Chi, Kappa Pi. Roman Catholic. Avocations: travel, costume design, oil painting. Home: 2108 Jackson St Scranton PA 18504-1610

TIMLIN, JAMES CLIFFORD, bishop; b. Scranton, Pa., Aug. 5, 1927; s. James C. and Helen E. (Norton) T. A.B., St. Mary's Sem., Balt., 1948; S.T.B., Gregorian U., Rome, Italy, 1950. Ordained priest Roman Catholic Ch., 1951; asst. pastor St. John the Evangelist Ch., Pittston, Pa., 1952-53, St. Peter's Cathedral, Scranton, Pa., 1953-66; asst. chancellor, sec. Diocese of Scranton, 1966-71, chancellor, 1971-77, aux. bishop, vicar gen., 1976-84; pastor Ch. of Nativity, Scranton, 1979-84; bishop Diocese of Scranton, 1984—. Address: 300 Wyoming Ave Scranton PA 18503-1224

TIMM, ROGER K., lawyer; b. Bay City, Mich., May 21, 1947. BS, U. Mich., 1969; JD, Harvard U., 1972. Bar: Mich. 1972. Mem. Dykema Gossett, Detroit. Mem. ABA, State Bar Mich. Office: Dykema Gossett 400 Renaissance Ctr Detroit MI 48243

TIMMCKE, ALAN EDWARD, physician and surgeon; b. Madison, Wis., July 7, 1949; s. Wesley Eugene Timmcke; m. Deborah Cameron Brosseau (div.); m. Teresa Ann Watkins, Dec. 31, 1977; children: Gretchen Kristine, Alan Edward Jr. BS, Dickinson Coll., 1971; MD with honors, Temple U., 1975. Diplomate Am. Bd. Surgery, Am. Bd. Colon and Rectal Surgery; lic. physician, Pa., Maine, Mo., La. Intern in surgery Nat. Naval Med. Ctr., Bethesda, Md., 1975-76, resident in gen. surgery, 1976-79; rsch. fellow in colon and rectal surgery Jewish Hosp./Washington U. Med. Ctr., St. Louis, 1985-86, clin. fellow in colon and rectal surgery, 1986-87; asst. in surgery Washington U. Sch. Medicine, St. Louis, 1985-87; staff colon and rectal surgeon Ochsner Clinic, New Orleans, 1987—; staff surgeon Nat. Naval Med. Ctr., Bethesda, 1979, Naval Regional Med. Ctr., Newport, R.I., 1979-82, dept. colon and rectal surgery Lahey Clinic Med. Ctr., Burlington, Mass., 1984-85; staff surgeon Rumford (Maine) Community Hosp., 1982-84, med. staff v.p., 1983-84; instr. surgery Uniformed Svcs. U. of Health Scis., Bethesda, 1978-79; lectr. in field. Contbr. articles and abstracts to profl. jours. Lt. comdr. M.C., USN, 1975-82. Recipient Harry E. Bacon Found. award for best original paper, 1987; NIH Summer Rsch. fellow, 1972. Fellow ACS, Am. Soc. Colon and Rectal Surgeons; mem. New Orleans Surg. Soc., Surg. Assn. of La., Internat. Soc. Univ. Colon and Rectal Surgeons, Soc. of Am. Gastrointestinal Endoscopic Surgeons, Am. Soc. Gastrointestinal Endoscopy, Alpha Omega Alpha. Office: Ochsner Clinic Dept Colon/Rectal Surgery 1514 Jefferson Hwy New Orleans LA 70121-2429

TIMMER, BARBARA, lawyer; b. Holland, Mich., Dec. 13, 1946; d. John Norman and Barbara Dee (Folensbee) T. BA, Hope Coll., Holland, Mich., 1969; JD, U. Mich., 1975. Bar: Mich. 1975, U.S. Supreme Ct., 1995. Assoc. McCrosky, Libner, VanLeuven, Muskegon, Mich., 1975-78; apptd. to Mich. Women Commn. by Gov., 1976-79; staff counsel subcom. commerce, consumer & monetary affairs Ho. Govt. Ops. Com., 1979-82, 85-86; exec. v.p. NOW, 1982-84; legis. asst. to Rep. Geraldine Ferraro, 1984; atty. Office Gen. Counsel Fed. Home Loan Bank Bd., 1986-89; gen. counsel Com. on Banking, Fin. and Urban affairs U.S. Ho. of Reps., Washington, 1989-92; asst. gen. counsel, dir. govt. affairs ITT Corp., Washington, 1992-96; ptnr. Alliance Capitol, Washington, 1994—; sr. v.p., dir. govt. rels. Home Savs. of Am., Irwindale, Calif., 1996—. Editor: Compliance With Lobbying Laws and Gift Rule Guide, 1996. Recipient Affordable Housing award Nat. Assn. Real Estate Brokers, 1990, Acad. of Women Achievers, YWCA, 1993. Mem. ABA (bus. law, exec. coun. adminstrv. law and regulatory practice sects.), FBA (chair, exec. coun. banking law com.), Women in Housing and Fin. (bd. dirs. 1992-94, gen. counsel 1994—), Supreme Ct. Bar Assn., Supreme Ct. Hist. Soc., Mich. Bar Assn. Episcopalian. Office: Home Savings of America Mail Stop 2500 4900 Rivergrade Rd Irwindale CA 91706-1404

TIMMER, CHARLES PETER, agricultural economist; b. Troy, Ohio, July 29, 1941; s. Thomas Gerhart and Rose Marie (Hoffman) T.; m. Carol Falb, Aug. 31, 1963; children: Anne Carol, Ashley Susan. A.B. in Econs. magna cum laude, Harvard U., 1963, Ph.D. in Econs, 1969. Commodity analyst W.R. Grace and Co., N.Y.C., 1964-66; asst. prof. econs. Food Research Inst., Stanford U., 1968-74, assoc. prof., 1974-75; econ. adv. Indonesian Nat. Planning Agy., Harvard Adv. Group, Jakarta, 1970-71; H.E. Babcock prof. food econs. Cornell U., 1975-77; prof. econs. of food and agr. Sch. Public Health Harvard U., Cambridge, Mass., 1977-80, John D. Black prof. agr. and bus., 1980-86, prof. devel. studies at large, 1986-88, Thomas D. Cabot prof. devel. studies at large, 1988—; Hibbard lectr. U. Wis., 1993; cons. on food and agr. Author: (with others) Choice of Technology in Developing Countries, 1975, (with Perkins et al) Small Scale Rural Industry in the People's Republic of China, 1977, (with Falcon and Pearson) Food Policy Analysis, 1983, (with Nelson et al) Food Aid and Development, 1981, Getting Prices Right: Scope and Limits of Agricultural Price Policy, 1986; editor, contbg. author: Rice Policy in Indonesia, 1974, The Political Economy of Rice in Asia, 1976, The Corn Economy of Indonesia, 1987, Agriculture and the State: Growth, Employment, and Poverty in Developing Countries, 1991; guest editor, contbg. author to Food Policy, 1995. Recipient Bintang Jasa Utama medal Govt. Indonesia, 1992; John Harvard scholar, 1960-63; Fulbright fellow, 1963-64; NSF fellow, 1966-68. Mem. Am. Econ. Assn., Am. Agrl. Econs. Assn., AAAS, Phi Beta Kappa. Home: 15 Winnetaska Rd Newton MA 02168-1424 Office: Harvard U Inst for Internat Devel 1 Eliot St Cambridge MA 02138-5705

TIMMER, STEPHEN BLAINE, lawyer; b. Holland, Mich., May 19, 1962; s. Blaine Edward and Nancy Jean (Mulder) T. BA in Econs., Eckerd Coll., 1984; JD, U. Fla., 1988; LLB (hon.), Kagawa U., Takamatsu, Japan, 1985. Atty. Burditt & Radzius, Chartered, Chgo., 1988—; bd. dirs. The Renaissance Soc. Editor-in-chief Fla. Internat. Law Jour., 1988. Recipient fellowship St. Petersburg, Fla./Takamatsu, Japan Sister City Com., 1986. Mem. ABA, Internat. Young Lawyers Assn., Lawyers for Creative Arts, Chgo. Bar Assn., AIDS Legal Coun. Chgo. (bd. dirs. 1990—), Contemporary Mus. Art, Art Inst. Chgo., Centre du Droit de l'Art (Switzerland). Democrat. Presbyterian. Avocations: sailing, scuba diving, tennis, art collecting. Office: Burditt and Radzius 333 W Wacker Dr Ste 2600 Chicago IL 60606-1227

TIMMER, WAYNE FRANCIS, architectural firm executive. BA in Pre-Architecture with high honors, Clemson U., 1972; MArch in Urban Design, Rice U., 1975, MArch, 1978. Registered architect, Miss., La.; cert. Nat. Coun. Archtl. Registration Bds. Asst. planner/programmer Caudill, Rowlett, and Scott, Architects and Engrs., Houston, 1975; sr. planner divsn. urban design Oklahoma City Dept. Planning, 1976-78; project architect Barlow and Plunkett, Architects and Engrs., Jackson, Miss., 1978-83; prin., project mgr. WFT Architects, P.A., Jackson, 1983—; adj. prof. sch. architecture Miss. State U., 1981—. Mem. adv. com. neighborhood revitalization City of Jackson, 1988, mem. history city hall com., 1990; mem. Save Hist. Burwell Ho. Com., 1990-91; mem. Jackson Hist. Preservation Commn., 1990—, chmn., 1990, 91. Rsch. fellow Rice U. Mem. AIA (bd. dirs. Miss. chpt. 1992-93, sec./treas. 1994, 2nd v.p. 1995, pres. 1997), Nat. Trust Hist. Preservation, Tau Sigma Delta, Phi Kappa Phi. Office: WFT Architects PA PO Box 12344 Jackson MS 39236-2344

TIMMERHAUS, KLAUS DIETER, chemical engineering educator; b. Mpls., Sept. 10, 1924; s. Paul P. and Elsa L. (Bever) T.; m. Jean L. Mevis, Aug. 3, 1952; 1 dau., Carol Jane. BS in Chem. Engring, U. Ill., 1948, MS, 1949, PhD, 1951. Registered profl. engr., Colo. Process design engr. Calif. Rsch. Corp., Richmond, 1952-53; extension lectr. U. Calif., Berkeley, 1952; mem. faculty U. Colo., Boulder, 1953-95, prof. chem. engring., 1961-95, asso. dean engring., 1963-86, dir. engring. rsch. ctr. coll. engring., 1963-86, chmn. aerospace dept., 1979-80, chmn. chem. engring. dept., 1986-89, Patten Chair Disting. prof., 1986-89, presdl. teaching scholar, 1989—; chem. engr. cryogenics lab. Nat. Bur. Standards, Boulder, summers 1955,57,59,61; lectr. U. Calif. at L.A., 1961-62; sect. head engring. div. NSF, 1972-73; cons. in field. Bd. dirs. Colo. Engring. Expt. Sta., Inc., Engring. Measurements Co., both Boulder. Editor: Advances in Cryogenic Engineering, vols. 1-25, 1954-80; co-editor: Internat. Cryogenic Monograph Series, 1965—. Served with USNR, 1944-46. Recipient Disting. Svc. award Dept. Commerce, 1957, Samuel C. Collins award for outstanding contbns. to cyrogenic tech., 1967, Meritorious Svc. award Cryogenic Engring. Conf., 1987, Disting. Pub. Svc. award NSF, 1984; named CASE Colo. Prof. of Yr., 1993. Fellow AAAS, Internat. Inst. Refrigeration (v.p. 1979-87, pres. 1987-95, U.S. nat. commn. 1983—, pres. 1983-86, W.T. Pentzer award 1989), AIChE (v.p. 1975, pres. 1976, Alpha Chi Sigma award for chem. engring. rsch., 1968, Founders award 1978, Eminent Chem. Engr. award 1983, W.K. Lewis award 1987, F.J. Van Antwerpen award 1991, Inst. Lecture award 1995), Am. Soc. for Engring. Edn. (bd. dirs. 1986-88, George Westinghouse award 1968, 3M Chem. Engring. divsn. award 1980, Southwestern and Rocky Mountain divsn. Pres.' award 1989, Engring. Rsch. Coun. award 1990, Delos Svc. award 1991); mem. NAE, Am. Astron. Soc., Austrian Acad. Sci., Cryogenic Engring. Conf. (chmn. 1956-67, bd. dirs. 1956—), Soc. Automotive Engrs. (Ralph Teetor award 1991), Sigma Xi (v.p. 1986-87, pres. 1987-88, bd. dirs. 1981-89), Cryogenic Soc. Am., Sigma Tau, Tau Beta Pi, Phi Lambda Upsilon. Home: 905 Brooklawn Dr Boulder CO 80303-2708

TIMMINS, MICHAEL JOSEPH, communications services company executive; b. Jersey City, Feb. 14, 1952; s. Michael Joseph and Eva Marie (Corti) T.; m. Janice Rose Markham, May 12, 1973; children: Keith Dylan, Christopher Michael, Chelsea Victoria. BA in Econs., Jersey City State Coll., 1977. Securities clk. N.Y. Stock Exch., N.Y.C., 1971-73; rsch. analyst Metro Containers, Kraft Foods, Lyndhurst, N.J., 1973-77; mktg. rep. Infonet div. Computer Scis. Corp., N.Y.C., 1977-80; sales mgr. Infonet div. Computer Scis. Corp., Hackensack, N.J., 1980-82, multinat. mgr., 1982-88, dir. for Europe, 1985-88; v.p. Europe, Africa and Middle East Infonet Svcs. Corp., Hackensack, 1988-91, corp. v.p. internat., 1991-92, exec. v.p. internat. ops., exec. v.p. software sales/svcs., 1992-93, exec. v.p. global bus. devel., 1993—; bd. dirs. Interpac Belgium, S.A., vice chmn., Brussels, Infonet Oy, Helsinki, vice chmn., Infonet/CSCL Ltd., Toronto, vice chmn., Infonet Svenska AB, Stockholm, vice chmn., Osiware, S.A., Paris, chmn., Infonet Nederland B.V., Infocom Joint Venture, Moscow. Mem. Internat. Computers and Communications (planning coord. 1989—). Roman Catholic. Avocation: golf. Home: 677 Palmer Ave Maywood NJ 07607-1521 Office: Infonet Svcs Corp 1 University Plaza Dr Hackensack NJ 07601-6201

TIMMONS, EDWIN O'NEAL, psychologist; b. West Point, Ga., May 12, 1928; s. Robert A. and Lois O. T.; m. Mary Birmingham, June 21, 1952; children: Robert A., Laura W., Jenny O., William B. B.S., Auburn U., 1951; M.A., U. Tenn., 1956, Ph.D., 1959. Staff psychologist Tuscaloosa (Ala.) VA Hosp., 1958-59; clin. psychologist Gulfport (Miss.) VA Hosp., 1960-61; asso. prof., then Alumni prof. psychology La. State U., 1961-78, prof. bus. adminstrn. and Alumni prof. psychology, 1978-83; mem. faculty Sch. Banking of South, 1975—; prin. Timmons & Assos. (Psychol. Cons.), Baton Rouge; mem. faculty So. Meth. U. Grad. Sch. Banking, 1976-83. Author TV-based tng. series on sales, mgmt., human rels., 1979. Served with U.S. Army, 1946-48, 51-53. Mem. Am. Psychol. Assn., La. Psychol. Assn., Southeastern Psychol. Assn., AAAS, AAUP, Sigma Xi. Office: 505 L S U Ave Baton Rouge LA 70808-4643 *Assume we have a given amount of elan vital. If we overinvest it in the past, we reap guilt over what we should or shouldn't have done. If we overinvest it in the future, we gain anxiety over what may happen. How better to invest it mainly in the here-and-now, to live the most fully human life possible for each of us.*

TIMMONS, EVELYN DEERING, pharmacist; b. Durango, Colo., Sept. 29, 1926; d. Claude Elliot and Evelyn Allen (Gooch) Deering; m. Richard Palmer Timmons, Oct. 4, 1952 (div. 1968); children: Roderick Deering, Steven Palmer. BS in Chemistry and Pharmacy cum laude, U. Colo., 1948. Chief pharmacist Meml. Hosp., Phoenix, 1950-54; med. lit. rsch. librarian Hoffman-LaRoche, Inc., Nutley, N.J., 1956-57; staff pharmacist St. Joseph's Hosp., Phoenix, 1958-60; relief mgr. various ind. apothecaries, Phoenix, 1960-68; asst. then mgr. Profl. Pharmacies, Inc., Phoenix, 1968-72; mgr. then owner Mt. View Pharmacy, Phoenix and Paradise Valley, Ariz., 1972—; pres. Ariz. Apothecaries, Ltd., Phoenix, 1976—; mem. profl. adv. bd., bereavement counselor Hospice of Valley, 1983—; mem. profl. adv. bd. Upjohn Health Care and Svcs., Phoenix, 1984-86; bd. dirs. Am. Council on Pharm. Edn., Chgo., 1986-92, v.p. 1988, 89, treas., 1990-91. Author poetry; contbr. articles to profl. jours. Mem. Scottsdale (Ariz.) Fedn. Rep. Women, 1963; various other offices Rep. Fedn.; mem. platform com. State of Ariz., Nat. Rep. Conv., 1964; asst. sec. Young Rep. Nat. Fedn., 1963-65; active county and state Rep. coms.; fin. chmn. Internat. Leadership Symposium:Woman in Pharmacy, London, 1987; treas. Leadership Internat. Women Pharmacy, 1991—. Named Outstanding Young Rep. of Yr., Nat. Fedn. Young Reps., 1965, Preceptor of Yr., U. Ariz./Syntex, 1984; recipient Disting. Public Svc. award Maricopa County Med. Soc., 1962, Disting. Alumni award Wasatch Acad., 1982, Career Achievement award Kappa Epsilon, 1983, Leadership and Achievement award Upjohn Labs., 1985-86, Outstanding Achievement in Profession award Merck, Sharp & Dohme, 1986, award of Merit Kappa Epsilon, 1988, Disting. Coloradoan award U. Colo., 1989, Vanguard award Kappa Epsilon, 1991, Uniform award Kappa Epsilon, 1993, Pharmacist of the Yr. award Profl. Compounding Corp. of Am., 1995, 96. Fellow Am. Coll. of Apothecaries (v.p. 1982-83, pres. 1984-85; chmn. bd. dirs. 1985-86, adv. coun. 1986-92, Chmn. of Yr. 1980-81 Victor H. Morganroth award 1985, J. Leon Lascoff award 1990); mem. Ariz. Soc. of Hosp. Pharmacists, Am. Pharm. Assn. (Daniel B. Smith award 1990, U.S. pharmacoepial conv. expert adv. com. on compounding pharms. 1992—), Ariz. Pharmacy Assn. (Svc. to Pharmacy award 1976, Pharmacist of Yr. 1981, Bowl of Hygeia 1989, 1st Innovative Pharmacy award 1994), Maricopa County Pharmacy Assn. (pres. 1977, Svc. to Pharmacy award 1977), Am. Soc. of Hosp. Pharmacists, Aux. to County Med. Soc. (pres. 1967-68), Am. Aircraft Owners and Pilots Assn., Air Safety Found., Nat. Assn. of Registered Parliamentarians, Kappa Epsilon (recipient Career Achievement award 1986, Vanguard award 1991, Unicorn award 1993). Lodge: Civinettes (pres. Scottsdale chpt. 1960-61). Avocations: flying, skiing, swimming, backpacking, hiking. Office: Mt View Pharmacy 10565 N Tatum Blvd Ste B-118 Paradise Vly AZ 85253-1095

TIMMONS, GERALD DEAN, pediatric neurologist; b. Rensselaer, Ind., June 1, 1931; s. Homer Timmons and Tamma Mildred (Spall) Rodgers; m. Lynne Rita Matrisciano, May 29, 1982; 1 child, Deanna Lynne; children from previous marriage: Jane Christina Timmons Mitchell, Ann Elizabeth, Mary Catherine. AB, Ind. U., 1953, MD, 1956. Diplomate Am. Bd. Psychiatry and Neurology. Intern Lima (Ohio) Meml. Hosp., 1956-57; resident Ind. U. Hosp., Indpls., 1957-59, 61-62; instr. neurology dept. Ind. U., Indpls., 1962-64; practice medicine specializing in psychiatry and neurology Indpls., 1962-64; practice medicine specializing in pediatric neurology Akron, Ohio, 1964—; chief pediatric neurology Children's Hosp. Med. Ctr., Akron, 1964—; chmn. neurology subcouncil Coll. Medicine Northeastern Ohio Univs., Rootstown, 1978—; chief examiner Am. Bd. Neurology and Psychiatry. Contbr. articles to profl. and scholarly jours. Served to capt. USAF, 1959-61. Mem. Summit County Med. Soc., Ohio Med. Soc., AMA, Am. Acad. Pediatrics, Am. Acad. Neurology (practice com. 1980-86), Child Neurology Soc. (chmn. honors and awards com. 1978—), Am. Soc. Internal Medicine, Am. Electroencephalographic Soc. Republican. Methodist. Office: Akron Pediatric Neurology 300 Locust St Ste 460 Akron OH 44302-1804

TIMMONS, STEVE (RED), volleyball player; b. Newport Beach, Calif., Nov. 29, 1958. BA in Comm., U. So. Calif., 1982. Mem. U.S.A. Nat. Olympic Volleyball Team, 1983-88, 92; founder, creator volleyball clothing Redsand, 1985—; profl. volleyball tour player U.S., Il Messaggero, Italian Profl. League, Ravenna. Recipient Gold medal Olympics, 1984, 88, Bronze medal Olympics, 1992; named Most Valuable Player U.S.A. Olympic Volleyball Team, 1984. Mem. Assn. Volleyball Profls. Career-high second at 1991 Off Shore Manhattan Beach Open, 1991; only 3-time Olympic medal winner; led U.S.A. Nat. Team to bronze medal finish Olympics, Barcelona, Spain, 1992, gold medal finishes, 1984, 88; led U.S.A. Nat. Team to first Triple Crown-1984 Olympics, 1985 World Cup, 1986 World Championships; led Il Messaggero to team title, 1991, 2d place finish, 1992; team capt. Team Cup Volleyball champions, 1992; team capt. Team Coca-Cola Superstars Competition, 1993-94. Office: care Assn Volleyball Profls 330 Washington Blvd Ste 600 Marina Del Rey CA 90292*

TIMMONS, WILLIAM EVAN, corporate executive; b. Chattanooga, Dec. 27, 1930; s. Owen Walter and Doris (Eckenrod) T.; m. Mimi Bakshian, Sept. 28, 1966; children: Karen Leigh, Kimberly Anne, William Evan. Grad., Baylor Mil. Acad., Chattanooga, 1949; BS in Fgn. Svc., Georgetown U., 1959; postgrad., George Washington U., 1959-61. Aide to U.S. Senator Alexander Wiley, 1955-62; adminstrv. asst. to U.S. Rep. William Brock, 1963-69; dep. asst. to Pres. Richard M. Nixon, 1969-70, asst., 1970-74; asst. to Pres. Gerald R. Ford, 1974; pres. Timmons & Co. Inc., 1975-86, chmn. exec. com., 1986—; mem. Fed. Property Rev. Bd., 1972-75, Pres.'s Trade Adv. Com., 1975-80; U.S. del. to Internat. Conf. on Viet Nam, Paris, 1973. Exec. dir. Tenn. Rep. Com., 1962; mgr. Brock campaigns, 1962, 64, 66, 68; dir. congl. rels. Nixon-Agnew campaign, 1968; coord. Nixon for Pres.; Rep. Nat. Conv., Miami, Fla., 1968, 72; dir. Pres. Ford com. Rep. Nat. Conv., Kansas City, 1976; nat. conv. dir. Reagan for Pres. Com., Detroit, 1980, Dallas, 1984; mem. adv. com. Rep. Nat. Com. Conv., New Orleans, 1988, San Diego, 1996; mem. exec. com. Nat. Young Reps., 1965-67; nat. polit. dir. Reagan for Pres. Com., 1980; dep. dir. for transition Office of Pres-Elect, 1980-81; presdl. appointee U.S.-Japan Adv. Commn., 1983-85; mem. faculty Nat. Rep. campaign workshops, 1963-69; bd. dirs. Radio Free Europe/Liberty, 1975-82, Georgetown U. Ctr. Strategic and Internat. Studies, 1982-85; sr. adviser Bush for Pres. Com., New Orleans, 1988, Dole for Pres. Com., 1996. With USAF, 1951-55. Named Outstanding Young Rep. of Year Nat. Rep. Com., 1965; recipient 1970 Ann. Achievement award Georgetown Alumni Club; citation for Disting. Service Baylor Mil. Acad. Alumni Assn., 1970. Mem. SCV, SAR, Soc. of the Cin., Soc. of Colonial Wars, Columbia Country Club, George Towne Club, F Street Club, City Club, St. Alban's Tennis Club, Masons (33d degree). Home: 4426 Garfield St NW Washington DC 20007-1142 Office: Timmons & Co 1850 K St NW Washington DC 20006-2213

TIMMONS, WILLIAM MILTON, producer, freelance writer, retired cinema arts educator, publisher, film maker; b. Houston, Apr. 21, 1933; s. Carter Charles and Gertrude Monte (Lee) T.; m. Pamela Cadorette, Dec. 24, 1975 (div. 1977). BS, U. Houston, 1958; MA, UCLA, 1961; PhD, U. So. Calif., 1975. Child actor Houston Jr. Theater, 1945-46; staff announcer Sta. KMCO, Conroe, Tex., 1951-52; prodn. asst. Sta. KUHT-TV, Houston, 1953-54, 56-57; teaching fellow UCLA, 1960-61; ops. asst. CBS-TV, Hollywood, Calif., 1961-62; prof. speech and drama Sam Houston State U., Huntsville, Tex., 1963-67; chmn. dept. cinema Los Angeles Valley Coll., Van Nuys, Calif., 1970-91, ret., 1992; prodr. Sta. KPFK, L.A., 1959-60, 83-95; pub. Acad. Assocs., L.A., 1976; proofreader, cons. Focal Press Pub. Co., N.Y.C., 1983-92. Author: Orientation to Cinema, 1986; contbr. articles to mags.; prodr., dir.: (radio programs) Campus Comments, 1963-67, numerous ednl. films, 1963—; prodr. ednl. series for cable TV, 1993-97. With USNR, 1954-56. Named Hon. Tex. Ranger, State of Tex., Austin, 1946; U. Houston scholar, 1957. Mem. Mensa, U. So. Calif. Cinema-TV Alumni Assn., Red Masque Players, Secular Humanists L.A., Alpha Epsilon Rho, Delta Kappa Alpha. Democrat. Avocations: reading, writing, viewing movies.

TIMMRECK, THOMAS C., health sciences and health administration educator; b. Montpelier, Idaho, June 15, 1946; s. Archie Carl and Janone (Jensen) T.; m. Ellen Prusse, Jan. 27, 1971; children: Chad Thomas, Benjamin Brian, Julie Anne. AA, Ricks Coll., 1968; BS, Brigham Young U., 1971; MEd, Oreg. State U., 1972; MA, No. Ariz. U., 1981; PhD, U. Utah, 1976. Program dir. Cache County Aging Program, Logan, Utah, 1972-73; asst. prof. div. health edn. Tex. Tech U., Lubbock, 1976-77; asst. prof. dept. health care adminstrn. Idaho State U., Pocatello, 1977-78; program dir., asst. prof. health services program No. Ariz. U., Flagstaff, 1978-84; cons., dir. grants Beth Israel Hosp., Denver, 1985; prof. dept. health scis. and human ecology, coordinator grad. studies, coordinator health adminstrn. and planning Calif. State U., San Bernardino, 1985—; pres. Health Care Mgmt. Assocs., 1985—; presenter at nat. confs.; mem. faculty Loretto Heights Coll., Denver, Dept. Mgmt. U. Denver, Dept. Mgmt. and Health Adminstrn. U. Colo., Denver, dept. bus. adminstrn. U. Redlands (Calif.), U. So. Calif., L.A. Author: Dictionary of Health Services Management, rev. 2d edit., 1987, Health Services Cyclopedic Dictionary, 3d edit., An Introduction to Epidemiology, 1994, Planning and Program Development and Evaluation: A Handbook for Health Promotion, Aging, and Health Services, 1995; mem.

editl. bd. Jour. Health Values, 1986—, Basic Epidemiological Methods and Biostats., Dictionary of Epidemiology and Public Health; contbr. numerous articles on health care adminstrn., behavioral health, gerontology and health edn. to profl. jours. Chmn., bd. dirs. Inland Counties Health System Agy.; mem. strategic planning com. chmn. Vis. Nurses Assn. of Inland Counties; bd. dirs. health svc. orgns. With U.S. Army, 1966-72, Vietnam. Mem. Assn. Advancement of Health Edn., Am. Acad. Mgmt., Assn. Univ. Programs in Health Care Adminstrn., Healthcare Forum. Republican. Mormon. Office: Calif State U Dept Health Scis and Human Ecology San Bernardino CA 92407

TIMMS, PETER ROWLAND, art museum administrator; b. Phila., Aug. 26, 1942; s. H. Rowland and Nancy Virginia (Shaub) T.; m. Romayne Julian Dawnay, Jan. 8, 1972; children: Matthew, Zöe, Christopher. B.A., Brown U., 1964; M.A., Harvard U., 1970, Ph.D., 1976. Instr. Internat. Coll., Beirut, Lebanon, 1967-68; dir. Fitchburg (Mass.) Art Mus., 1973—; dir. Spofford Garrison Excavations, 1978; teaching fellow Harvard U., 1969-71, MIT, 1973. Author: Flint Implements of the Old Stone Age, 1974. Mem. Fitchburg Bicentennial Com., 1974; bd. dirs. Cen. Mass. Tourist Coun., 1974-78, Fitchburg chpt. ARC, 1975-79, Spofford Garrison Excavations, 1978, 79, 80, Nashua River Watershed Assn., 1979-81, Nashua Arts and Sci. Ctr., 1983-86; trustee Applewild Sch., 1982-94, Nat. Plastics Ctr. and Mus., 1991—; pres. Fitchburg Cultural Alliance, 1979-83. Capt. USMCR, 1964-67, Vietnam. Mem. Am. Assn. Museums, Fitchburg Hist. Soc. Republican. Episcopalian. Home: 198 Lake Rd Ashburnham MA 01430-1207

TIMONEY, PETER JOSEPH, veterinarian, virologist, educator, consultant; b. Dublin, Ireland, June 5, 1941; came to U.S., 1983; s. John Francis and Evelyn Norah (Whittle) T.; m. Katherine Mary Murphy, Sept. 11, 1971; children: Peter, Caroline, Sarah, David. MVB, Nat. U., Dublin, 1964; MS, U. Ill., 1966; PhD, U. Dublin, 1974. Rsch. assoc. U. Ill., Urbana, 1964-66; rsch. officer Vet. Rsch. Lab., Abbotstown, Ireland, 1966-72; sr. rsch. officer equine diseases sect. Veterinary Rsch. Lab., Abbotstown, Ireland, 1972-79; assoc. prof. diagnostic lab., dept. microbiology Cornell U., Ithaca, N.Y., 1979-81; sci. dir. Irish Equine Ctr., Johnstown, Ireland, 1981-83; assoc. prof. virology vet. sci. dept. U. Ky., Lexington, 1983-87, prof. virology, assoc. chair for rsch., 1987-89, Frederick Van Lennep prof., 1988—, acting chair, 1989-90, chair, dir. Gluck Equine Rsch. Ctr., 1990—; cons. Daryl Labs., Inc., Santa Clara, Calif., 1981-86, Ft. Dodge (Iowa) Lab., 1986-92, 94—. Fellow Royal Coll. Vet. Surgeons, World Equine Vet. Assn. (pres. 1995—); mem. AAAS, Am. Assn. Equine Practitioners, Am. Soc. Microbiology, Am. Soc. Virology, U.S. Animal Health Assn. Avocations: reading, gardening. Office: U Ky Gluck Equine Rsch Ctr 108 Gluck Ctr Lexington KY 40506

TIMOTHY, DAVID HARRY, biology educator; b. Pitts., June 9, 1928; s. David Edgar and Harriett P. (Stein) T.; m. Marian Claire Whiteley, Sept. 5, 1953; children: Marjory J., M. Elisabeth, David W. BS, Pa. State U., 1952, MS, 1955; PhD, U. Minn., 1956. Asst. geneticist Rockefeller Found., Bogota, Colombia, 1956-58; assoc. geneticist Rockefeller Found., Bogota, 1958-61; assoc. prof. N.C. State U., Raleigh, 1961-66, prof., 1966-93, prof. emeritus, 1993—; cons. to fgn. and U.S. govts., also U.S. and internat. sci. orgns.; mem. crop adv. com. on grasses USDA, 1983-87, mem. policy adv. com., sci. and edn. grants program, 1982-84, chief scientist Sci. and Edn. Competetive Rsch. Grants Office, 1985, 86; with Nat. Plant Genetic Resources Bd., 1984-91, vice chmn., 1991; bd. dirs., treas. Genetic Resources Comms. Sys., Inc., 1985-91, pres., 1991-93; mem. bd. on agr. NAS-NRC, work group on U.S. Nat. Plant Germplasm Sys., 1987-89. Co-author monographs, also author articles. With AUS, 1946-48, PTO. Grantee NSF, 1965, 78, Rockefeller Found., 1968, 69, Pioneer Hi-Bred Internat., 1982, 83. Fellow AAAS (electorate nominating com., sect. O, Agr. 1988-90), Am. Soc. Agronomy, Crop Sci. Soc. Am. (editl. bd. 1982-84, assoc. editor Crop Sci. 1982-84, Frank N. Meyer medal for plant genetic resources 1994). Home: 13 Furches St Raleigh NC 27607-7048

TIMOTHY, ROBERT KELLER, telephone company executive; b. Gilcrest, Colo., June 27, 1918; s. Virge and Alice (Patterson) T.; m. Elaine Hurd, Oct. 23, 1941; children: Kristen, Timothy Lankester, Robert Alan. AB, U. No. Colo., 1941, LLD (hon.), 1986. High sch. sci. tchr. Ft. Lupton, Colo., 1941-42; with Mountain States Tel. & Tel. Co., 1946-83, v.p. operations, 1968-69, pres., 1970-82, chmn. bd., 1982-83, also bd. dirs.; past bd. dirs. United Bank Denver, United Banks Colo.; bd. dirs. Rocky Mountain Health Care Corp. Pres., campaign chmn. United Fund, Boise, Idaho, 1962-64; Bd. dirs. Air Force Acad. Found., Bus.-Industry Polit. Action Com., 1975-82, Luth. Med. Center, 1971-84, Nat. Safety Council, 1971-80; trustee U. Denver, 1982-89, Gates Found., 1982-89; pres. Telephone Pioneers Am., 1977-78. Served to capt., Signal Corps U.S. Army, 1943-46. Mem. Newcomen Soc. (chmn. Colo. 1980-84), Civilian/Mil. Inst. (founding bd.), Rotary, Denver Country Club, Univ. Club (Denver). Republican. Home: 2155 E Alameda Ave Denver CO 80209-2710 Office: 931 14th St Denver CO 80202-2903

TIMOUR, JOHN ARNOLD, retired librarian, medical bibliography and library science educator; b. Hartford, Conn., Jan. 20, 1926; s. John Alfred and Karin Elizabeth (Levin) T.; m. Betty Jo Lord, Mar. 23, 1952; children—Jon, David, Alan. B.A., Miami U., Oxford, Ohio, 1951; postgrad., Fla. State U., 1951-52; M.A., George Washington U., 1960; M.L.S., U. Md., 1969. Tng. and Med. Lit. Analysis and Retrieval System liaison officer Nat. Library of Medicine, Bethesda, Md., 1966-69; dir. library services Conn. Regional Med. Program-Yale U., New Haven, 1969-73; dir. Mid-Eastern Med. Library Service Coll. Physicians of Phila., 1973-75; univ. librarian Thomas Jefferson U., Phila., 1975-87; instr. U.S. Army Reserve, Hamden, Conn., 1970-73; lectr. library sci. So. Conn. State Coll., New Haven, 1970-71; adj. prof. library sci. Drexel U., Phila., 1976-78. Contbr. articles to profl. jours. Served to RM2-c USN, 1943-46, PTO; 2d lt. USAF, 1951-53, lt. col. USAR, ret. Mem. Assn. Acad. Health Sci. Libr. Dirs., Am. Med. Writers Assn. (pres. Phila. chpt. 1986-87), Med. Libr. Assn. (bd. dirs. 1978-81, Eliot prize 1974), Acad. of Health Info. Profls. (disting. mem.), Spl. Librs. Assn. (pres. Phila. chpt. 1979-80), Conn. Assn. Health Sci. Librs. (hon. life), Sigma Xi (bull. editor Jefferson chpt. 1980-86, recognition cert. 1982), Beta Phi Mu. Episcopalian. Club: Washington Yacht and Country. Avocations: golfing, sailing, chess, Macintosh computers. Home: 209 Wedgewood Dr Washington NC 27889-9688

TIMPANE, PHILIP MICHAEL, education educator, foundation official; b. Troy, N.Y., Nov. 27, 1934; s. Philip Thomas and Rita (Killeen) T.; m. Genevieve LaGrua, Nov. 30, 1957; children: Michael J., Joseph T., Paul J., David A. AB, Cath. U. Am., 1956, MA, 1964; MPA, Harvard U., 1970; LittD (hon.), Wagner Coll., 1986; LLD (hon.), Catholic U. Am., 1991. Historian Joint Chiefs of Staff Dept. Def., 1961-65; spl. asst. civil rights Office of Sec. Def., 1965-68; edn. policy planner HEW, 1968-72; sr. fellow Brookings Instn., 1972-74; dir. edn. policy ctr. Rand Corp., 1974-77; dep. dir. Nat. Inst. Edn., Washington, 1977-80; dir. Nat. Inst. Edn., 1980-81; prof. edn. Tchrs. Coll. Columbia U., N.Y.C., 1981—, dean, 1981-84, pres., 1984-94; Aspen Inst. Edn. Program, 1974-77, 87—; v.p. and sr. scholar Carnegie Found. for the Advancement of Teaching, Princeton, N.J., 1994—. Author: Corporate Interest in Public Education in the Cities, 1982; co-author: Youth Policy in Transition, 1976, Business Impact on Education and Child Development Reform, 1991; co-editor: Planned Variation in Education, 1975, Work Incentives and Income Guarantees, 1975, Ethical and Legal Issues in Social Experimentation, 1975; editor: Federal Interest in Financing Schooling, 1978. Mem. Arlington (Va.) Sch. Bd., 1972-76, chmn., 1973-74; bd. dirs. Children's TV Workshop, 1989—, Jobs for the Future, 1995—, So. Edn. Found., 1995—. Mem. Cosmos Club. Democrat. Roman Catholic. Office: Carnegie Found Advncmnt of Tchng 5 Ivy Ln Princeton NJ 08540-7218

TIMPANO, ANNE, museum director, art historian; b. Osaka, Japan, June 17, 1950; d. A.J. and Margaret (Smith) T. BA, Coll. William and Mary, 1972; MA, George Washington U., 1983. Program mgmt. asst. Nat. Mus. Am. Art, Washington, 1977-86; dir. The Columbus (Ga.) Mus., 1986-93, DAAP Galleries, U. Cin., 1993—; grant reviewer Inst. Mus. Svcs., Washington, 1988—, Ga. Coun. for Arts, Atlanta, 1988-91. Mem. 1992 Quincentenary Commn., Columbus, 1987-92. Recipient David Lloyd Kreeger award George Washington U., 1980. Mem. Am. Assn. Mus. (surveyor mus. assessment program), Assn. of Coll. and Univ. Mus. and Galleries, Coll. Art Assn., Midwest Mus. Conf. Roman Catholic. Home: 85 Pleasant Ridge Ave Fort Mitchell KY 41017-2861 Office: U Cin PO Box 210016 Cincinnati OH 45221-0016

TIMPERLAKE, EDWARD THOMAS, professional staff member of Congress; b. Perth Amboy, N.J., Nov. 22, 1946; s. James Elwood Timperlake Jr. and Joan Dorothy (Conkling) Maurer; m. Barbette Runckel, Aug. 10, 1969 (div. 1993; children: Tara, Kimberly. BS, U.S. Naval Acad., 1969; MBA, Cornell U., 1977. Commd. 2d lt. USMC, 1969, advanced through grades to lt. col., 1985, resigned, 1975; rsch. asst. peace studies program Cornell U., Ithaca, N.Y., 1976-77; asst. venture mgr. Exxon Enterprise, N.Y.C., 1977-88; sect. mgr. Analytic Svcs. Corp., Arlington, Va., 1978-81; dep. dir. Nat. Dir. Vietnam Vets. Leadership Program, Action Agy., Washington, 1981-83; dir. mobilization plans and requirements Office of Sec. Def., Washington, 1984; campaign staff George Bush for Pres., 1988; asst. sec. Dept. Vets. Affairs, Washington, 1989-93; pres. T-9 Group, 1993-95; profl. staff rules com. U.S. House of Reps., Washington, 1996-97, profl. staff, investigator govt. reform and oversight com., 1997—. Contbr. numerous articles to profl. jours. Bd. dirs. Louis Puller Vietnam Children's Fund. Lt. col. USMCR, 1985-88, ret., 1993. Mem. Naval Acad. Alumni Assn., Army-Navy Club, U.S. Naval Sailing Squadron, N.Y. Yacht Club. Home: 317 Chesapeake Ave Annapolis MD 21403-3201 Office: 2157 RHOB The Capital Washington DC 20515

TIMS, ROBERT AUSTIN, data processing official, pilot; b. Seattle, Dec. 21, 1942; s. Robert Mitchell Tims and Winifred Eileen (Dorgan) Bristol; m. Jane Moore, June 6, 1980. Student, Pacific Union Coll., 1960-61, Alpha Aviation Sch., 1976-77, Ark. State U., 1995—. Lic. comml. and instrument pilot; cert. flight instr. Engring. technician Tex. Instruments, Inc., Ridgecrest, Calif., 1966-67, various projects, Conn., N.Y. and N.J., 1967-70; homesteader Leslie, Ark., 1970-77; chief pilot/flight instr. Sharp Aviation Co., Jonesboro, Ark., 1977-79; chief pilot Pizza Inn of Ark., Jonesboro, 1979-83; data processing mgr., chief pilot Realty Assocs. Brokerage, Inc., Jonesboro, 1983-91, microanalyst, 1991-94; pres., owner ABS Logic, Inc., computers and programming cons., Jonesboro, 1985—. Served with USN, 1962-66. Recipient Nat. Collegiate Bus. Merit award. Mem. CAP (squadron comdr. Jonesboro 1986-93), Am. Philatelic Soc., Data Processing Mgrs. Assn. Avocation: philately. Home and Office: 1616 Alonzo St Jonesboro AR 72401-4802

TINDAL, DOUGLAS, religious organization administrator. Chmn. Religious TV Assocs. Office: Religious TV Assocs, 600 Jarvis St, Toronto, ON Canada M4Y 2J6*

TINDALL, GEORGE BROWN, historian, educator; b. Greenville, S.C., Feb. 26, 1921; s. Goin Roscoe and Nellie Evelyn (Brown) T.; m. Carliss Blossom McGarrity, June 29, 1946; children: Bruce McGarrity, Blair Alston Mercer. AB, Furman U., 1942, LittD, 1971; MA, U. N.C., 1948, PhD, 1951. Asst. prof. history Eastern Ky. State Coll., 1950-51, U. Miss., 1951-52, Woman's Coll. of U. N.C., 1952-53, La. State U., 1953-58; assoc. prof. U. N.C., Chapel Hill, 1958-64, prof., 1964-69, Kenan prof., 1969-90, Kenan prof. emeritus, 1990—; vis. prof. Coll. of Charleston, 1951, Kyoto Am. Studies Sem., 1977; Fulbright guest prof. U. Vienna, 1967-68; mem. Inst. for Advanced Study, 1963-64; mem. Ctr. for Advanced Study in Behavioral Scies., 1979-80. Author: South Carolina Negroes, 1877-1900, 1952, The Emergence of the New South, 1913-1945, 1967 (Jules F. Landry award 1968, Mayflower Cup 1968, Lillian E. Smith award 1968, Charles S. Syndor award 1968), The Disruption of the Solid South, 1972, The Persistent Tradition in New South Politics, 1975, The Ethnic Southerners, 1976, America: A Narrative History, 1984, 4th edit., (with David Shi), 1996, Natives and Newcomers: Ethnic Southerners and Southern Ethnics, 1995; editor: The Pursuit of Southern History, 1964, A Populist Reader, 1966. Guggenheim fellow, 1957-58, Social Sci. Rsch. Coun. fellow, 1959-60, Ctr. for Advanced Study in Behavioral Scis., 1979-80. Mem. Am. Hist. Assn., Hist. Soc. N.C. (pres. 1990), N.C. Lit. and Hist. Soc., Organ. Am. Historians, So. Hist. Assn. (pres. 1973). Home: 305 Burlage Cir Chapel Hill NC 27514-2703

TINDALL, ROBERT EMMETT, lawyer, educator; b. N.Y.C., Jan. 2, 1934; s. Robert E. and Alice (McGonigle) T.; BS in Marine Engring., SUNY, 1955; postgrad. Georgetown U. Law Sch., 1960-61; LLB, U. Ariz., 1963; LLM, N.Y.U., 1967; PhD, City U., London, 1975; children: Robert Emmett IV, Elizabeth. Mgmt. trainee Gen. Electric Co., Schenectady, N.Y., Lynn, Mass., Glen Falls, N.Y., 1955-56, 58-60; law clk. firm Haight, Gardner, Poor and Havens, N.Y.C., 1961; admitted to Ariz. bar, 1963; prin., mem. firm Robert Emmett Tindall & Assocs., Tucson, 1963—; asso. prof. mgmt. U. Ariz., Tucson, 1969—; vis. prof. Grad. Sch. of Law, Soochow U., Republic of China, 1972, Grad. Bus. Centre, London, 1974, NYU, 1991—; dir. MBA program U. Ariz., Tucson, 1975-81; investment cons. Kingdom of Saudi Arabia, 1981—; dir. entrepreneurship program, U. Ariz., Tucson, 1984-86; lectr. USIA in Eng., India, Middle East, 1974; lectr. bus. orgn. and regulatory laws Southwestern Legal Found., Acad. Am. and Internat. Law, 1976-80. Actor community theatres of Schenectady, 1955-56, Harrisburgh, Pa., 1957-58, Tucson, 1961-71; appeared in films Rage, 1971, Showdown at OK Corral, 1971, Lost Horizon, 1972; appeared in TV programs Gunsmoke, 1972, Petrocelli, 1974. Served to lt. USN, 1956-58. Ford Found. fellow, 1965-67; Asia Found. grantee, 1972-73. Mem. Strategic Mgmt. Soc., State Bar of Ariz., Acad. Internat. Bus., Screen Actors Guild, Honourable Soc. of Middle Temple (London), Phi Delta Phi, Beta Gamma Sigma, Assoc. for Corp. Growth. Clubs: Royal Overseas League (London). Author: Multinational Enterprises, 1975; contbr. articles on domestic and internat. bus. to profl. jours. Home: 2020 E Elm St Tucson AZ 85719-4328 Office: Coll Bus and Public Adminstrn U Ariz Dept Mgmt and Policy Tucson AZ 85721

TING, ALBERT CHIA, bioengineering researcher; b. Hong Kong, Sept. 7, 1950; came to U.S., 1957; s. William Su and Katherine Sung (Bao) T.; m. Shirley Roung Wang, July 30, 1988. BA, UCLA, 1973; MS, Calif. State U., L.A., 1975, Calif. Inst. Tech., 1977; PhD, U. Calif., San Diego, 1983. Rsch. asst. Calif. Inst. Tech., Pasadena, 1975-77, U. Calif., San Diego, 1982-83; sr. staff engr. R&D Am. Med. Optics, Irvine, Calif., 1983-86; project engr., rsch. Allergan Med. Optics, Irvine, Calif., 1987-89; sr. project engr., rsch., 1989-92, sr. project engr., engring., 1993-94; bioengr. cons. Pharmacia Iovision, Inc., Irvine, Calif., 1995-97; sr. engr. D & E, 1997—. Inventor med. and optical devices, recipient patent awards 1988, 89, 91, 92, 93, 95; contbr. articles to sci. jours. Mem. AAAS, Biomed. Engring. Soc., Assn. for Rsch. in Vision and Ophthalmology, Biomed. Optics Soc.

TING, JOSEPH K., mechanical engineer; b. Manila, Jan. 23, 1950; s. Manuel and Lourdes (Co) T.; m. Monique Crenn, Sept. 2, 1978; children: Audrey Adrienne, William Alexander. BS in Mech. Engring., De La Salle U., Manila, 1972; MSc, MIT, 1974; MBA, U. Ottawa, Ont., Can., 1986. Registered profl. engr., N.Y., Mass., Ont., Can. Product engr. Brier Mfg. Co., Providence, R.I., 1974-75; plant mgr. Nemo Brier Ltd., Hull, Que., Can., 1975; assoc. engr., asst. rsch. officer Nat. Rsch. Coun., Ont., 1975-86; sr. mech. engr., supr. Dormitory Authority/State of N.Y., Delmar, 1986—; adj. prof. Rensselaer Polytechnic Inst., Troy, N.Y., 1992—; ednl. counselor MIT Admissions, Cambridge, Mass., 1993—. Contbg. author: Canadian Financial Managment, 1983, Essentials of Engineering Economics, 1983, Computer Aided Design Drafting, 1987, ASHRAE Std. 15-1992, 1992; developer Rolls-Royce RB211 jet engine into a gas pumping engine. Pres. Chinese Am. Comm. Ctr., Albany, N.Y., 1993-94, bd. dirs. 1993-96. Grantee E.I. DuPont Co.; recipient Disting. Svc. award Chinese Am. Comm. Ctr., 1991, Outstanding Svcs., 1996. Mem. ASHRAE (chpt. pres. 1991-92, chmn. refrigeration com. 1993-94, regional chmn. northeastern U.S. 1994-97, bd. dirs. Atlanta 1994—, asst. regional chmn. 1992-94, Black Ink award 1990, Golden Gavel award 1992, Disting. Svc. award 1997), MIT Alumni Club (pres. 1992-94, bd. dirs. 1992—). Roman Catholic. Avocations: tennis, swimming, organizing seminars and confs., martial arts. Home: PO Box 234 Delmar NY 12054 Office: Dormitory Authority State of NY 161 Delaware Ave Delmar NY 12054-1310

TING, ROBERT YEN-YING, physicist; b. Kwei-yang, China, Mar. 8, 1942; came to U.S. 1965; s. Chu-yung and Shou-feng (Yang) T.; m. Teresa Yen-chun Ting, June 3, 1967; children: Paul H., Peggy Y. BS, Nat. Taiwan U., 1964; MS, MIT, 1967; PhD, U. Calif., San Diego, 1971. Rsch. engr. U.S. Naval Rsch. Lab., Washington, 1971-77, supervisory engr., 1977-80; supervisory physicist U.S. Naval Rsch. Lab., Orlando, Fla., 1980—; prof. George Washington U., 1972-80. Contbr. over 100 articles in rheology, polymer and acoustics to profl. jours. Fellow Acoustical Soc. Am.; mem. Am. chem. Soc., Am. Ceramics Soc., Am. Inst. Chem. Engrs. Office: US Naval Rsch Lab PO Box 568337 Orlando FL 32856-8337

TING, SAMUEL CHAO CHUNG, physicist, educator; b. Ann Arbor, Mich., Jan. 27, 1936; s. Kuan H. and Jeanne (Wong) T.; m. Susan Carol Marks, Apr. 28, 1985; children: Jeanne Min, Amy Min, Christopher M. BS in Engring., U. Mich., 1959, MS, 1960, PhD in Physics, 1962, ScD (hon.), 1978; ScD (hon.), Chinese U. Hong Kong, 1987, U. Bologna, Italy, 1988, Columbia U., 1990, U. Sci. and Tech., China, 1990, Moscow State U., 1991, U. Bucharest, Romania, 1993. Ford Found. fellow CERN (European Orgn. Nuc. Rsch.), Geneva, 1963; instr. physics Columbia U., 1964, asst. prof., 1965-67; group leader Deutsches Elektronen-Synchrotron, Hamburg, W.Ger., 1966; assoc. prof. physics MIT, Cambridge, 1967-68, prof., 1969—; Thomas Dudley Cabot Inst. prof. M.I.T., 1977—; program cons. divsn. particles and fields Am. Phys. Soc., 1970; hon. prof. Beijing Normal Coll., 1987, Jiatong U., Shanghai, 1987, U. Bologna, Italy, 1988. Assoc. editor: Nuclear Physics B, 1970; mem. editl. bd. Nuc. Instruments and Methods, Mathematical Modeling; advisor Jour. Modern Physics A; contbr. articles to profl. jours. Recipient Nobel prize in Physics, 1976, De Gasperi prize in Sci., Italian Republic, 1988, Ernest Orlando Lawrence award U.S. Govt., 1976, Eringen medal Soc. Engring. Sci., 1977, Gold medal in Sci. City of Brescia, Italy, 1988, Golden Leopard award Town of Taormina, 1988, Forum Engelberg prize, 1996; Am. Acad. Arts and Sci. fellow, 1975. Mem. NAS; mem. Pakistani Acad. Sci., Acad. Sinica, Russian Acad. Sci., Hungarian Acad. Sci., Deutsche Acad. Naturforscher Leopoldina. Office: MIT Dept Physics 51 Vassar St Cambridge MA 02139-4308

TINGELSTAD, JON BUNDE, physician; b. McVille, N.D., Jan. 15, 1935; s. Sophus B. and Mabelle (Bunde) T.; m. Marcia Ayers, Dec. 17, 1960; children: Paul, Catherine, David. B.A., U. N.D., 1957, B.S., 1958; M.D., Harvard U., 1960. Diplomate Am. Bd. Pediatrics. Intern Children's Hosp. Med. Ctr., Boston, 1960-61, resident, 1961-62; resident U. Colo. Med. Ctr., Denver, 1962-63; fellow in pediatric cardiology Children's Hosp., Buffalo, 1965-67; asst. prof. pediatrics Med. Coll. Va., Richmond, 1967-71, assoc. prof., 1971-76; prof., vice chmn. pediatrics East Carolina U. Sch. Medicine, Greenville, N.C., 1976-77, prof., chmn. pediatrics, 1977—. Mem. Greenville City Bd. Edn., 1978-82, chmn., 1981-82. Served to capt. USAF, 1963-65. Fellow Am. Acad. Pediatrics, Am. Coll. Cardiology; mem. AAAS, AMA, So. Soc. Pediatric Rsch., Assn. Med. Sch. Pediatric Dept. Chairmen, Am. Bd. Pediatrics (bd. dirs., chmn.-elect), Phi Beta Kappa, Phi Eta Sigma. Home: 208 Chowan Rd Greenville NC 27858-6321 Office: E Carolina U Sch Med Dept Pediatrics Greenville NC 27858-4354

TINGLE, AUBREY JAMES, pediatric immunologist, research administrator; b. St. Paul, Alta., Can., June 28, 1943; s. Cyril Nisbet Tingle and Margaret Lucy (Fraser) Tarbuck; m. Valerie Jean Anderson, Nov. 2, 1968; children: Heather Lynn, Brian James. MD, U. Alta., Edmonton, 1967; PhD, McGill U., Montreal, Que., Can., 1974. Asst. prof. dept. pediatrics U. B.C., Vancouver, Can., 1974-79, head div. immunology dept. pediatrics, 1974-86, assoc. prof., 1979-86, prof., 1986—, prof. dept. pathology, 1986—; dir. rsch. B.C. Rsch. Inst. for Child and Family Health, Vancouver, 1992—; asst. dean rsch. Faculty of Medicine, U. B.C., Vancouver, 1992—. Fellow Royal Coll. Physicians and Surgeons Can., Soc. Pediatric Research, Am. Acad. Pediatrics; mem. Western Soc. Pediatric Research. Office: BC Childrens Hosp-Pediatrics, 4480 Oak St, Vancouver, BC Canada V6H 3V4

TINGLE, JAMES O'MALLEY, lawyer; b. N.Y.C., June 12, 1928; s. Thomas Jefferson and Mercedes (O'Malley) T. B.S., U. Mont., 1950, B.A., 1952, LL.B., 1952; LL.M., U. Mich., 1953, S.J.D., 1958. Bar: Calif. 1959, Mont. 1952, N.Y. 1961. Asst. prof. law U. Mont., Missoula, 1955-56; atty. Shell Oil Co., N.Y.C., 1957-62; assoc. Pillsbury, Madison & Sutro, San Francisco, 1962-68, ptnr., 1969—. Author: The Stockholder's Remedy of Corporate Dissolution, 1959; editor: State Antitrust Laws, 1974. Served to 1st lt. USAF, 1953-55. William W. Cook fellow U. Mich. Mem. Mont. Bar Assn., Calif. Bar Assn., ABA. Democrat. Office: Pillsbury Madison & Sutro 235 Montgomery St San Francisco CA 94104-2902

TINGLEY, FLOYD WARREN, physician; b. Charlotte, N.C., Nov. 22, 1933; s. Floyd Warren Sr. and Janie (Suggs) T.; m. Sandra Carpenter, Aug. 20, 1955 (div. Dec. 1984); children: Sheryl Tingley Hagen, David Alan; m. Johnette Hill, Apr. 5, 1985. BA in English, Emory U., 1955, MD, 1959. Diplomate Am. Bd. Internal Medicine (bd. govs. 1986-92). Intern USAF Hosp., Lackland AFB, Tex., 1959-60; resident in internal medicine Parkland Meml. Hosp., Dallas, 1963-65, fellow in cardiology, 1965-66; pvt. practice specializing in internal medicine Arlington, Tex., 1966-88; med. dir. southwestern region Met. Life Ins. Co., Irving, Tex., 1988-90; regional practice leader William M. Mercer Inc., 1990-91; v.p., sr. med. dir. Provident Life and Accident Co., Chattanooga, 1991-92; v.p., nat. med. dir. Travelers Ins. Cos., Hartford, Conn., 1992-94; sr. v.p., chief med. officer Kemper Nat. Svcs., Plantation, Fla., 1995—; apptd. Tex. Commn. on Health Care Reimbursement Alternatives, 1987; bd. dirs. Riverside Nat. Bank, Grand Prairie, Tex. Contbr. articles to profl. jours. Pres. Arlington YMCA, 1971; chmn. budget com. Family Services, Ft. Worth, 1973; participant Health Policy Agenda for Am. People, Chgo., 1984-87; trustee Tex. Med. Liability Trust, Austin, 1987-88. Capt. USAF, 1958-63. Fellow ACP (pres. Tex. chpt. 1981); mem. AMA (chmn. sect. coun. internal medicine, 1979-88), Am. Soc. Internal Medicine (pres. 1986-87), Tex. Med. Assn. (treas. 1978-85, alt. del. to AMA 1985-91, commendation 1985), Tarrant County Med. Soc. (pres. Arlington br. 1974, del. to Tex. Med. Assn., Community Svc. award 1983). Presbyterian. Avocations: photography, sailing, gardening, computer hobbies. Home: 7588 NW 51st Pl Coral Springs FL 33067 Office: Kemper Nat Svcs Inc 1601 SW 80th Ter Plantation FL 33324-4034

TINGLEY, WALTER WATSON, computer systems manager; b. Portland, Maine, July 24, 1946; s. Edward Allen Tingley and Ruth Annie (Howard) Tuttle; m. Elizabeth A. Fletcher, May 1970 (div. 1975). BS, U. Md., 1974. Programmer analyst U.S. Ry. Assn., Washington, 1974-80, Digital Equipment Corp., Maynard, Mass., 1980-81, Interactive Mgmt. Systems, Belmont, Mass., 1981; systems designer Martin Marietta Data Systems, Greenbelt, Md., 1982-84; mgr. computer ops. Genex, Rockville, Md., 1984; system mgr. Applied Rsch. Corp., Landover, Md., 1985; programmer analyst Input/Output Computer Svcs., Washington, 1986-87, Lockheed Engring. and Scis., Las Vegas, Nev., 1987-91, Los Alamos (N.Mex.) Nat. Lab., 1992-96. Author tech. book revs., software revs. With USAF, 1964-68. Mem. IEEE Computer Soc., Assn. Computing Machinery. Avocations: skiing, hiking, swimming. Home: PO Box 429 Los Alamos NM 87544-0429

TINKER, H(AROLD) BURNHAM, chemical company executive; b. St. Louis, May 16, 1939; s. H(arold) Burnham and Emily (Barnicle) T.; m. Barbara Ann Lydon, Feb. 20, 1965; children: Michael B., Mary K., Ann E. BS in Chemistry, St. Louis U., 1961; MS in Chemistry, U. Chgo., 1964, PhD in Chemistry, 1966. Sr. research chemist Monsanto, St. Louis, 1966-69, research specialist, 1969-73, research group leader, 1973-77, research mgr., 1977-81; tech. dir. Mooney Chems., Inc., Cleve., 1981-90, v.p. rsch. and devel., 1991-94; v.p. corp. devel., 1994—. Patentee in field; contbr. article to profl. jours. Mem. scis. adv. coun. U. Akron, 1995—. Mem. Am. Chem. Soc. (chmn. bd. St. Louis sect. 1978-79), Cleve. Assn. Rsch. Dirs. (v.p. 1989, pres. 1990, bd. dirs. 1991—). Roman Catholic. Avocation: computers. Home: 2889 Manchester Rd Cleveland OH 44122-2570 Office: OM Group Inc 3800 Terminal Tower Cleveland OH 44113-2204

TINKER, JOHN HEATH, anesthesiologist, educator; b. Cin., May 18, 1941; s. Leonard Henry and Georgia (Reeves) T.; m. Martha Iuen (div. Jan., 1989); children: Deborah H. Lynne, Karen Sue, Juliette Kay; m. Bonnie Howard, Mar. 18, 1989. BS magna cum laude, U. Cin., 1964, MS summa cum laude, 1968. Diplomate Am. Bd. Anesthesiology (sr. examiner 1976—). Surg. intern, resident Harvard Med. Sch., Peter Bent Brigham Hosp., Boston, 1969-70, resident in anesthesiology, 1970-72; cons. anesthesiology Mayo Clinic, Rochester, Minn., 1974-83, chief cardiovascular anesthesiology, 1978-83; prof. anesthesiology U. Iowa Coll. Medicine, Iowa City, 1983-97, chmn. dept., 1983-97; prof., chmn. Med. Ctr. U. Nebr., Omaha, 1997—; mem. pharm. scis. rev. com., NIH, Bethesda, Md., 1986—; dir. Matrix Med. Inc., Orchard Park, N.Y., 1988—; frequent guest lectr. Author: Controversies in Cardiopulmonary Bypass, 1989 (monograph award Soc. Cardiovascular Anesthesiologists); editor: Anesthesia and Analgesia, Jour. Internat. Anesthesiology Rsch. Soc., 1983—; contbr. over 185 articles to profl. jours.

Maj. U.S. Army, 1972-74. NIH grantee, 1977-87. Fellow Royal Coll. Surgeons Australia; mem. Am. Soc. Anesthesiologists (active numerous coms. 1972—), Soc. Cardiovascular Anesthesiologists, Assn. Univ. Anesthetists. Avocations: fishing, golf, modeling ships and airplanes. Office: U Nebr Med Ctr 600 S 42d St Omaha NE 68198-4455*

TINKER, MARK CHRISTIAN, producer, director; b. Stamford, Conn., Jan. 16, 1951; s. Grant Almerin Tinker and Ruth Prince Byerly Fricke; m. Kristin Harmon, Apr. 16, 1988; 1 child, James. BS, Syracuse U., 1973. Producer, dir., writer TV series: The White Shadow, 1978-81, St. Elsewhere, 1981-88 (Emmy, Peabody award, Peoples Choice award); dir. TV Movie: Babe Ruth, 1991, Bonanza: Under Attack, 1995; producer, dir. TV series: Civil Wars, 1991—; dir. episode TV series: ER (Going Home), 1994; dir. TV series: NYPD Blue, 1993—. Mem. Nat. Acad. TV Arts and Scis. *

TINKER, ROBERT EUGENE, minister, educational consultant; b. Lincoln, Kans., June 10, 1915; s. Eugene F. and Mildred Adelaide (Brown) T.; AB, Am. U., 1937; MDiv, Garrett Theol. Sem., 1942; postgrad. Northwestern U., 1942-46; m. Anne Elizabeth Hall, June 13, 1942; children: Anne Terrill, Robert Bruce, MaryBeth. Ordained to ministry Methodist Ch., 1942, Congregational Ch., 1947-77, United Ch. Christ; minister Oxen Hill, Md., Tuxedo, Md., 1934-37, Evergreen Park, Ill., 1940-41; assoc. minister 1st Presbyterian Ch., Evanston, Ill., 1942-44; minister Glenview Meth. Ch. (Ill.), 1944-46, Broadway Meth. Ch., Chgo., 1946-47; with Chgo. Theol. Sem., 1947-58, asst. sec., asst. treas., bd. dirs., 1947-58, asst. bus. mgr., 1947-50, bus. mgr., 1951-55, dir. devel., 1953-55, v.p. charge devel., 1955-58; assoc. Gonser and Gerber, 1958-64; ptnr. Gonser Gerber Tinker Stuhr, ednl. cons. in devel. and public relations, Chgo., 1964-82, cons., 1982—; pres. Tabco Corp., Chgo., 1983-85; lectr. Creighton U., Omaha, summers 1978-80. N.J. State scholar, 1933; Larry Foster scholar, 1933; Wanamaker scholar Lingnon U., Canton, Republic of China, 1935-36; Howes Meml. scholar, 1939-42. Bd. dirs. Hyde Park YMCA, Chgo., Hyde Park Union Ch., Porter Found., U. Chgo., 1947-58, Bryn Mawr Cmty. Ch., Habitat for Humanity, Tucson, 1992—, Phi Sigma Kappa, Phi Beta Zeta, Pi Gamma Mu. Republican. Contbr. articles to profl. books and jours. Mem. Oro Valley Townhouses Improvement Assn. (bd. dirs. 1993-94, pres. 1994). Home: 69 W Oro Pl Oro Valley AZ 85737-7625

TINKHAM, MICHAEL, physicist, educator; b. Green Lake County, Wis., Feb. 23, 1928; s. Clayton Harold and LaVerna (Krause) T.; m. Mary Stephanie Merin, June 24, 1961; children: Jeffrey Michael, Christopher Gillespie. A.B., Ripon (Wis.) Coll., 1951, Sc.D. (hon.), 1976; M.S., MIT, 1951; Ph.D., 1954; M.A. (hon.), Harvard, 1966. NSF postdoctoral fellow at Clarendon Lab., Oxford (Eng.) U., 1954-55; successively research physicist, lectr., asst. prof., asso. prof., prof. physics U. Calif. at Berkeley, 1955-66; Gordon McKay prof. applied physics Harvard U., 1966—, prof. physics, 1966-80, Rumford prof. physics, 1980—, chmn. physics dept., 1975-78; cons. to industry, 1958—; participant internat. seminars and confs.; mem. comm. on very low temperatures Internat. Union Pure and applied Physics, 1972-78; vis. Miller rsch. prof. U. Calif.-Berkeley, 1987; vis. prof. Technical Univ., Delft, The Netherlands, 1993. Author: Group Theory and Quantum Mechanics, 1964, Superconductivity, 1965, Introduction to Superconductivity, 1975, 2d edit., 1996; contbr. articles to profl. jours. Served USNR, 1945-46. Recipient award Alexander von Humboldt Found. U. Karlsruhe, W. Ger., 1978-79; NSF sr. postdoctoral fellow Cavendish lab.; vis. fellow Clare Hall Cambridge (Eng.) U., 1971-72; Guggenheim fellow, 1963-64. Fellow Am. Phys. Soc. (chmn. div. solid state physics 1966-67, Buckley prize 1974, Richtmyer lectr. 1977), AAAS; mem. Am. Acad. Arts and Scis., Nat. Acad. Scis. Home: 98 Rutledge Rd Belmont MA 02178-2633 Office: Harvard Univ Physics Dept Lyman Lab of Physics 326 Cambridge MA 02138

TINNER, FRANZISKA PAULA, social worker, artist, designer, educator; b. Zurich, Switzerland, Sept. 18, 1944; came to U.S., 1969; d. Siegfied Albin and Gertrude Emilie (Sigg) Maier; m. Rolf Christian Tinner, Dec. 19, 1976; 1 child, Eric Francis. Student, U. Del., 1973-74, Va. Commonwealth U., 1974; BFA, U. Tenn., 1984; BA of Arts, U. Ark., Little Rock, 1991, postgrad. Lic. real estate broker. Dominican nun Ilanz, Switzerland, 1961-67; waitress London, 1967-68; governess Bryn Mawr, Pa., 1969; saleswoman, 1970-90, model, 1983; artist, designer Made For You, Kerrville, Tex. and Milw., 1984—; realtor Century 21, Milw., 1987-91; intern Birch Community Ctr., 1992-93. Designer softsculptor doll Texas Cactus Blossom, 1984; author: (poem) The Gang (recorded by Nat. Libr. of Poetry), 1996. Ombudsman Action 10 Consumerline, Knoxville, Tenn., 1983-84; foster mother, Powhatan, Va., 1976-81; vol. ARC, Knoxville, 1979, Va. Home for Permanently Disabled, 1975; vol., counselor Youth For Understanding-Fgn. Exch., Powhatan, Va., 1975-77; tchr. pager/archiving host, mentor, area expert on Am. On Line; vol. Interactive Ednl. Svc. Recipient Art Display award U. Knoxville, 1983, Prof. Choice of Yr. award, 1983, Outstanding Achievemnt award TV Channel 10, Knoxville, 1984, 1st place award for paintings and crafts State Fair Va., Tenn., 1st place award Nat. Dollmakers, 1985. finalist Best of Coll. Photography, 1991, Achievement award Coll. Scholar af Am., 1991, Achievement cert. in technique of anger therapy, 1993, Achievement cert. in crisis response team tng., 1994, Editors' Choice award, Internat. Poetic Soc., 1997; named One of Outstanding 1000 Women, 1995, Woman of Yr., 1995; nominated Poet of Yr., Internat. Soc. Poets, 1997. Mem. NASW, NAFE, Milw. Bd. Realtors, Homemakers Club (pres. 1979-80), Newcomers Club, Bowlers Club (v.p.), Internat. Platform Assn. Avocations: art, cooking, teaching, writing, helping disabled and mentally ill.

TINNING, HERBERT PETER, association executive; b. Hoboken, N.J., Apr. 17, 1928; s. Peter Christian and Emmy Asta (Andersen) T.; divorced; children: Christian, Kirsten; m. Adeline Augusta Falk, Aug. 13, 1990. Degree in mech. engring., Stevens Inst. Tech., 1952. Engr. Good Housekeeping Inst., N.Y.C., 1954-56; dir. membership and sects. Am. Soc. Refrigerating Engrs., N.Y.C., 1956-58; application and sales engr. Dunham Bush Inc., N.Y.C., 1958-61; dir. tech. svcs. ASHRAE, N.Y.C., 1961-69; asst. tech. dir. Assn. Home Appliance Mfrs., Chgo., 1969-71; regional coord., dir. socioecon. program Nat. Assn. Accts., N.Y.C., 1972-77; adminstrv. exec. Compressed Gas Assn., N.Y.C., 1977-79; group dir., tech. affairs ASME, N.Y.C., 1980-93; exec. dir. Devils Foot Soc., Millburn, N.J., 1982—; chmn. heating, refrigeration and air conditioning stds. bd. Am. Nat. Stds. Inst., N.Y.C., 1968-69; presenter in field. Contbr. articles to various publs. Mem. current affairs com. Berkeley Square Civic Assn., Arlington Heights, Ill., 1969-72; mem. pub. rels. and bylaws coms. Citizens Adv. Com., Arlington Heights, 1969-71; mem. mayor's action com. on drugs Village of Arlington Heights, 1970-71; mem. devel. com. Twp. of Weehawken, N.J., 1978-81; chmn. Brotherhood of St. Andrew, Arlington Heights, 1970-72; trustee Seabury-Western Theol. Sem., Evanston, Ill., 1972-75; deacon Episcopal Ch., 1974; fund capt. Stevens Inst. Tech., Hoboken, 1982-87. Recipient award of excellence U.S. Dept. Commerce, 1977. Mem. Am. Soc. Assn. Execs. (life, cert.), N.Y. Soc. Assn. Execs. (life, chmn. awards com., mem. human resources com.), Palisades Nature Assn. (life), Baker Street Irregulars (Horace Harker award 1973), Sherlock Holmes Soc. London, Priory Scholars (hon.), Millburn Old Guard (citation 1995). Avocations: Sherlockian studies, gardening, natural history, reading. Home and Office: 93 Sagamore Rd Millburn NJ 07041-2154

TINSLEY, ADRIAN, college president; b. N.Y.C., July 6, 1937; d. Theodore A. and Mary Ethel (White) T. AB, Bryn Mawr Coll., 1958; MA, U. Wash., 1962; PhD, Cornell U., 1969. Asst. prof. English U. Md., College Park, 1968-72; dean William James Coll., Grand Valley State, Allendale, Mich., 1972-80; assoc. vice chancellor acad. affairs Minn. State U., St. Paul, 1982-85; exec. v.p., provost Glassboro (N.J.) State Coll., 1985-89; pres. Bridgewater (Mass.) State Coll., 1989—; coord. women higher edn. adminstrn. Bryn Mawr (Pa.) & Hers Summer Inst., 1977—. Editor: Women in Higher Education Administration, 1984. Office: Bridgewater State Coll Office of Pres Bridgewater MA 02325-0001

TINSLEY, BARBARA SHER, historian, educator, writer; b. Gloversville, N.Y., Apr. 29, 1938; d. Max and Ruth Ida (Shpritzer) Sher; m. William Earl Tinsley, Dec. 30, 1959; children: Claire Jennifer, Yve Hillary. BA, U. Wis., Milw., 1959; MA, U. Calif., Berkeley, 1960; PhD, Stanford U., 1983. Instr. English and French Stephens Coll., Columbia, Mo., 1963-64; asst. prof. European history San Jose (Calif.) State U., 1969-71; prof. European history Foothill Coll., Los Altos Hills, Calif., 1974—; lectr. in history Santa Clara (Calif.) U., 1977-79; lectr. in western culture Stanford (Calif.) U., 1985, vis. scholar, 1989—. Author: History and Polemics in the French Reformation: Florimond de Raemond Defender of the Church, 1992; co-author (with Lewis S. Spitz) Johann Sturm and Education, 1995; contbr. articles to profl. jours. Woodrow Wilson fellow U. Calif.-Berkeley, 1959-60; NDEA fellow Mich. State U. and Emory U., 1961, 63; Jessie Speyer fellow Stanford U., 1965-67; Fulbright fellow U. Strasbourg, 1983-84; NEH fellow Duke U., 1988, Princeton, 1995. Mem. Am. Hist. Assn., Sixteenth Century Studies Conf., YMCA. Democrat. Avocations: sewing, piano, gardening, swimming, oil painting. Home: 15550 Glen Una Dr Los Gatos CA 95030-2936

TINSLEY, JACKSON BENNETT, newspaper editor; b. Ewing, Tex., Dec. 14, 1934; s. Henry Bine and Sallie Alberta (Jackson) T.; m. Claudia Anne Miller, Oct. 3, 1965; children: Ben, Anna. B.S., Sam Houston State U., 1958. Editor Diboll News-Bull., 1953-54, Corrigan Times, 1954; reporter Lufkin News, 1952, 56; news editor Port Lavaca Wave, 1955; mem. staff Ft. Worth Star-Telegram, 1959-60, 62—, Sunday editor, 1967-71, asst. mng. editor, 1971-74, asst. to editor, 1974-75, exec. editor, 1975-82, v.p., exec. editor, 1982-86, v.p., editor, 1986-90, sr. v.p., editor, chmn., 1990—; info. asst. S.W. Bell Telephone Co., 1960-62; part time instr., editor Tex. Christian U., 1971-72. Com. chmn. United Way Tarrant County, 1970-87, gen. chmn. Tex. Gridiron Show, 1981, 93-95; bd. dirs. Safety Coun. Ft. Worth, 1975-80; pres., bd. dirs. Parenting Guidance Ctr., 1989-90. 2d lt. U.S. Army, 1959. Recipient Nat. Writing award Edn. Writers Assn., 1965, citation Tex. Conf. AAUP, 1965; named Disting. Alumnus, Sam Houston State U., 1984; named to C.E. Shuford Journalism Hall of Honor, U. North Tex., 1987, his bust in U. Tex. Wall of Honor; established Jack B. Tinsley/Fort Worth Star Telegram endowed journalism scholarship. Mem. Soc. Profl. Journalists (pres. Ft. Worth chpt. 1991-92, chmn. journalism adv. com. U. North Tex. and Sam Houston State U. 1988-93), Am. Soc. Newspapers Editors, AP Mng. Editors Assn., Tex. AP Mng. Editors Assn. (pres. 1979-80), Press Club Ft. Worth (pres. 1970-71), Colonial Country Club, Ft. Worth Club, Rotary (v.p. Ft. Worth 1981, pres. 1983-84). Home: 3550 Wind River Ct Fort Worth TX 76116-9329 Office: Ft Worth Star-Telegram 400 W 7th St Fort Worth TX 76102-4701

TINSLEY, TUCK, III, book publishing executive. With Fla. School for the Deaf & Blind, St. Augustine, Fla., 1968-89; pres. American Printing House for the Blind, Louisville, 1989—. Office: Am Print House for the Blind PO Box 6085 1839 Frandfort Ave Louisville KY 40206-0085*

TINSLEY, WALTON EUGENE, lawyer; b. Vanceburg, Ky., Jan. 22, 1921; s. Wilbur Walton and Sarah Edith (Frizzell) T.; m. Joy Mae Matthews, Aug. 31, 1952; children—Merry Walton Tinsley Moore, Troy Eugene, Paul Richard. E.E., U. Cin., 1943; M.S. in Aero. Engring, NYU, 1947; J.D., U. So. Calif., 1953. Bar: Calif. 1954, U.S. Supreme Ct. 1971. Practiced in Los Angeles, 1954—; mem. firm Harris, Wallen, MacDermott & Tinsley, 1958-96; of counsel Pretty, Schroeder & Poplawski, L.A., 1996—. Author: (book) Tasmania: Stamps and Postal History, 1986. Pres. World Philatelic Exhbn., Pacific 97 Inc. Signatory Roll of Disting. Philatelists, 1983. Fellow Royal Philatelic Soc. London; mem. IEEE (assoc.), AIAA, ABA, L.A. County Bar Assn., Am. Philatelic Soc. (v.p. 1965-69, Luff award 1986), S.R., English Speaking Union (dir. L.A. br.), Mensa. Presbyterian (elder, trustee, chmn. trustees 1972). Home: 2210 Moreno Dr Los Angeles CA 90039-3044 Office: Pretty Schroeder et al 444 S Flower St Ste 2000 Los Angeles CA 90071-2921

TINSTMAN, DALE CLINTON, food products company consultant; b. Chester, Nebr., May 19, 1919; s. Clinton Lewis and Elizabeth Golashin (Gretzinger) T.; m. Jean Sundell, Oct. 1, 1942; children: Thomas C., Nancy (Mrs. Ron Remington), Jane C. (Mrs. Stephen Kramer). BS, U. Nebr., 1941, JD, 1947. Bar: Nebr. 1947. Asst. sec., asst. mgr. investment dept. First Trust Co., Lincoln, Nebr., 1947-58; v.p., asst. treas. Securities Acceptance Corp., Omaha, financial v.p., treas. Central Nat. Ins. Group, Omaha, 1958-60; pres., treas. Tinstman & Co., Inc., Lincoln, 1960-61; exec. v.p. First Mid Am., Inc., Lincoln, 1961-68, pres., 1968-74, fin. cons., 1974—; pres., dir. Iowa Beef Processors, Inc., 1976-77, vice chmn., 1977-82, co-chmn., 1982-83, dir., cons., 1983—; chmn., dir. Eaton Tinstman Druliner, Inc., 1983—; bd. dirs. IBP, Inc.; past chmn. Nebr. Investment Council. Trustee, chmn. U. Nebr. Found.; trustee Lincoln Found., Nebr. Council Econ. Edn., Mall Corp., Smith Haye Trust. Served with USAAF, World War II, Korea; to col. Nebr. Air NG. Mem. Nebr. Bar Assn., Neb. Diplomats, Newcomen Soc. N.Am., Am. Legion, Nebr. State Chamber of Commerce, Lincoln Contry Club, Lincoln U. Club, Firethorn Country Club, Alpha Sigma Phi, Phi Delta Phi. Republican. Presbyterian (elder). Home and Office: 40 Bishop Sq Lincoln NE 68502

TINSTMAN, ROBERT ALLEN, construction company executive. BS, Mining Engring., Univ. Wisconsin, Platteville, 1968. Underground engr. Reynolds Mining Corp., Bauxite, Ark., 1966-68, stripping engr., 1968-71, asst. mine superintendant, 1971-73; sr. mine engr. Texasgulf, Aurora, N.C., 1973-74; sr. mine engr. Morrison Knudsen Corp., Boise, Idaho, 1974-75, asst. mgr., mining engr., 1975-77, dir. mining engring., 1977-79, v.p., gen. mgr. mining engring., 1979-85; exec. v.p. Morrison Knudsen Engineers, Inc., Boise, Idaho, 1985-88, pres., 1988-89; pres. mining group Morrison Knudsen Co., Inc., Boise, Idaho, 1989-95; pres, CEO Morrison Knudsen Corp., Boise, Idaho, 1995—; Exec. comm. mem. Morrison Knudsen bd. dirs.; mng. dir. MK Peru; dir., Centennial Engring. Inc.; dir. Natl. Projects Inc. Mem. Natl. Soc. of Professional Engrs., Soc. of Mining Engrs. Office: Morrison Knudsen Corp 720 Park Blvd Boise ID 83712-7714

TIPKA, KAREN, obstetric and women's health nurse; b. Wilmington, Del., Aug. 13, 1946; d. James Spruance and Catherine (O'Connor) T. BA in English, Immaculata Coll., Malvern, Pa., 1969; MA in Psychology, Pa. Dept. Edn., Harrisburg, 1975; postgrad., U. Del., 1995—. Tchr. English Tredyffrin/Easttown Schs., Berwyn, Pa., 1969-76; mental health asst. Psychiatric Unit, Paoli (Pa.) Meml. Hosp., 1977-78; med. asst. Internal Medicine Assocs., Norristown, Pa., 1980-82; crisis counselor Chester County Crisis Intervention, Downingtown, Pa., 1979-82; staff nurse psychiatry Phila. Psychiat. Ctr., 1984; staff nurse labor/delivery Osteopathic Med. Ctr., Phila., 1985, Sacred Heart Med. Ctr., Chester, 1985-86; staff nurse high risk labor/delivery Thomas Jefferson Univ. Hosp., Phila., 1986-87; staff nurse labor/delivery Lankenau Hosp., Phila., 1987-88, Bryn Mawr (Pa.) Hosp., 1987-88; nurse clinician Caremark Women's Health, Malvern, Pa., 1992; clin. educator Holy Family Coll., Phila., 1993-94; perinatal cons., educator Toitu of Am., Wayne, Pa., 1995—; clin. adj. instr. Del. County Community Coll., Media, Pa., 1989-90; William Penn grant minority nursing tutor Gwynedd Mercy Coll., 1992; group facilitator Parkinson's Disease Support Group, Delaware County, Pa., 1989—; selected del. People to People Found. Profl. Nurse Exchange, Norway, Sweden, Czechoslovakia, 1988. Contbr. articles to profl. jours. Safety instr. Girl Scouts U.S., Chester County, 1987-88; guest speaker, ethics St. Joseph's U. Grad. Sch. Health Adminstrn., Phila., 1991. U.S. Dept. Health and Human Svcs. traineeship, 1988-89; Foerderer scholar, 1983-84. Mem. ANA, NAACOG (cert.), Pa. Nurses Assn., Pa. Perinatal Soc., Phila. Perinatal Soc., ANA Coun. Maternal/Child Nurses, Am. Med. Writers Assn. Avocations: reading, sewing, gardening, cooking. Home: 119 Bishop Hollow Rd Newtown Square PA 19073-3220

TIPP, KAREN LYNN WAGNER, school psychologist; b. Chgo., Feb. 15, 1947; d. Harry and Sarah (Damask) Wagner; m. Michael Harvey, Dec. 30, 1973; children: Brenda Alyse, Brandon Philip. BA in Gen. High Sch. Edn., Roosevelt U., 1971; B of Jewish Studies, Spertus Coll., 1973, cert. in sch. psychology, 1981, MA in Jewish Studies, 1993; MS in Ednl. Theory, Nat. Louis U., 1974, CAS, 1981. Cert. psychologist, Ill.; nat. cert. sch. psychologist. Tchr. Niles Twp. High Sch., Skokie, Ill., 1971-72; mgr. travel agy. Chgo., 1983-85; tchr. spl. edn. No. Cook County, Ill., 1972-90; tchr. Hebrew Chgo. Bd. Jewish Edn., 1969-90, interim prin. religious sch., 1989-90; sch. psychologist Chgo. Pub. Schs., 1990—; ind. ednl. therapist, Chgo., 1973—; contract psychologist N.W. Suburban Chgo., 1981-90; cons. learning disabled Chgo. Bd. Jewish Edn., 1983-90; mem. adv. bd. Tchr.'s Task Force, 1993—. Pres. Truman Coll. (City Coll. Chgo.) Coun., 1985-87, 93-95, nom. chair, 1990—; exec. sec. North Town Cmty. Coun., Chgo., 1984-86, pres., 1989-91, v.p., 1991-93, treas., 1993-96, v.p., 1996—; pres. dist. 2 coun. Chgo. Bd. Edn., 1987-89, pres. ednl. chair, 1990-92; exec. sec. North Town Civic League, 1978-80, pres., 1981-84; mem. coop. extension youth coun. U. Ill., sec., 1985-91, exec. coun., 1990-91; charter mem. Hild Culture Ctr., membership chair; beat rep. Chgo. Police Dept.; vice chair Head Start, Salvation Army, Dewey Day Care Evanston, 1972-75, Rogers Park Montessori Sch., 1979-80; corr. sec. Day Care Ctr. Bd.-Evanston, 1978-81, Rogers Park Mental Health Coun.; youth chair Indian Boundary Playground Bldg., 1986-89; mem. steering com. Rogers Park Centennial, 1991-93; mem. state coms. 4-H, 1986-88, Chgo./Cook County 4-H Coun., 1984-95; mem. North Town Post Office Adv. Coun., 1995—. Master Tchr. grantee Jewish Bd. Edn., Chgo., 1981-89, 20 Yr. award, 1990; recipient Cmty. Leadership award Dept. Human Svcs., Chgo., 1985, North Town-Dorothy LeRoy Cmty. Svc. award, 1992; Statewide Mentor of Mentors Transition Project grantee U. Ill. and Family Resource, 1997—. Fellow Am. Orthopsychiat. Assn.; mem. NASP, APA (divsn. 16), Coun. Exceptional Children (liaison 1972-86), Assn. Ednl. Therapist, Ill. Psychol. Assn. (Sch. Psychologist of Yr. 1991), Family Resource Ctr. on Disabilities (spl. edn. com. 1990—, bd. dirs. 1993—), Profls. in Learning Disabilities (legis. chair 1987—), Children with Attention Deficit Disorder, Learning Disabilities Assn., Coun. Exceptional Children (Ill. Computer Educators Pioneers), Ill. Sch. Psychologists Assn. (Practitioner of Yr. 1991, child study com.), Chgo. Assn. Sch. Psychologists (rec. sec. 1995—, v.p. 1996-97, pres. 1997-98), Greater Uptown Youth Network, Ill. 4-H Found., Edn. Therapists, Samoyed Club Am., Prairieland Samoyed Club (legis. chair 1995—, publicity chair 1996—, bd. dirs. 1996-97. Avocations: education, animals, playground building, activities with youth and community, computers. Home: 6730 N Maplewood Ave Chicago IL 60645-4620

TIPPETT, WILLIS PAUL, JR., automotive and textile company executive, retired; b. Cin., Dec. 27, 1932; s. Willis Paul and Edna Marie (Conn) T.; m. Carlotta Prichard, Jan. 24, 1959; children: Willis Paul III, Holly. AB, Wabash Coll., 1953. Brand mgr., advt. supr. Procter & Gamble Co., Cin., 1958-64; advt. and sales promotion mgr. Ford Motor Co., Dearborn, Mich., 1964-65; gen. mktg. mgr. Ford Motor Co., 1965-69; advt. mgr. Ford Motor Co. (Ford div.), 1969-70, advt. and sales promotion mgr., 1970-72; v.p. product and mktg. Philco-Ford Corp., Phila., 1972-73; dir. sales and mktg. Ford of Europe, Inc., Brentwood, Essex, Eng., 1973-75; pres., dir. STP Corp., Ft. Lauderdale, Fla., 1975-76; exec. v.p., dir. Singer Co., N.Y.C., 1976-78; pres., chief operating officer, dir. Am. Motors Corp., Southfield, Mich., 1978-82; chmn., chief exec. officer Am. Motors Corp., Southfield, 1982-85; pres. Springs Industries, Inc., Ft. Mill, S.C., 1985-89; prin. Ann Arbor (Mich.) Ptnrs. Investment Co., 1989—; bd. dirs. Lukens, Inc., Stride Rite Corp., Just Cynthia Inc. With USN, 1953-58. Mem. Univ. Club (N.Y.).

TIPPIN, AARON, country music singer, songwriter; b. Pensacola, Fla., July 3, 1958; married; 1 child, Charla. Various positions including farm hand, welder, airplane pilot, truck driver, heavy equipment operator, factory worker; writer Acuff-Rose, 1987—; recording artist RCA, 1990-97. Albums include You've Got to Stand for Something, 1991 (gold), Read Between the Lines, 1992 (platinum), Call of the Wild, 1993 (gold), Lookin' Back at Myself, 1994 (gold), Toolbox, 1995 (gold), Greatest Hits and Then Some, 1997; No. 1 single There Ain't Nothing Wrong with the Radio, 1992, That's As Close As I'll Get to Lovin You, 1995, Toolbox, 1995 (gold), Greatest Hits and Then Some, 1997; toured with Bob Hope to perform for troops during Persian Gulf War, 1991; 1st singer to perform song You've Got to Stand for Something, anthem of troops. Avocation: body-building (prize winner). Office: Tip Top Entertainment PO Box 41689 Nashville TN 37204

TIPPING, WILLIAM MALCOLM, social services administrator; b. Oak Park, Ill., Mar. 31, 1931; s. William McKinley and Evelyn Amelia (Freier) T.; m. Lois A. Grife, Sept. 18, 1954 (dec. May 1986); children: William, Barbara, Robert; m. Babette J. Cumming, Oct. 10, 1987; children: Christopher Cumming, Courtney Barone. BA, Carleton Coll., Northfield, Minn., 1954. Sales rep. Gen. Mills, Inc., Mpls., 1954-56; account exec. Campbell Mithun, Inc., Mpls., 1956-63; v.p. mgmt., supr. Campbell Mithun, Inc., Mpls. and Chgo., 1965-76; account supr., v.p. Lennen & Newell, Inc., N.Y.C., 1963-65; ptnr., mgr. Heidrick & Struggles, Inc., Chgo., 1976-88; exec. v.p., chief exec. officer Am. Cancer Soc., Atlanta, 1988-91; pres. Tipping and McRae, Inc., Atlanta, 1991-93; mng. dir. Ward Howell Internat., Inc., Atlanta, 1993—. Trustee Carleton Coll., 1986-90; bd. dirs. Nat. Health Coun., N.Y.C., Ga. Conservancy, Families First; mem. fin. com. UICC, Geneva, 1990-91. Recipient Disting. Svc. award Carleton Coll., 1984. Mem. Skokie Country Club (Glencoe, Ill., pres. 1983-84), Capital City Club (Atlanta), Haig Pt. Club (Daufuskie Island, S.C.), Quechee (Vt.) Club. Republican. Episcopalian. Office: Ward Howell Internat Inc 3350 Peachtree Rd NE Ste 1600 Atlanta GA 30326-1040

TIPPINS, SUSAN SMITH, elementary school principal; b. Jacksonville, Fla., Jan. 4, 1961; d. Arthur Thomas and Kathleen May (Blake) Smith; m. John Malcolm Tippins Jr., Apr. 21, 1984; children: Matthew Scott, Paul Blake. AA, Fla. Jr. Coll., Jacksonville, 1980; BA in Edn., U. North Fla., 1983, MEd, 1993. Cert. tchr., Fla. 6th grade tchr. Duval County Sch. Sys., Jacksonville, 1984-87; 3rd grade tchr. Nassau County Sch. Sys., Callahan, Fla., 1987-88, tchr. specific learning disabilities, 1990-92, 1st grade tchr., 1992-96, adminstrv. intern, 1995-96; prin. Bryceville (Fla.) Elem. Sch., 1997—. Mem. ASCD, Internat. Reading Assn., Fla. Reading Assn., Fla. Assn. Computer Edn., Alpha Delta Kappa (pres. 1996), Kappa Delta Pi. Avocation: crafting. Home: Rt 2 Box 1413 Bryceville FL 32009 Office: Bryceville Elem Sch PO Box 3 Church Ave Bryceville FL 32009-9542

TIPPIT, JOHN HARLOW, lawyer; b. Marietta, Okla., July 22, 1916; s. Alva Ney and Edna Pearl (Harlow) T.; m. Ann Morse, Feb. 27, 1943; children—David H., Ann Maurine. B.A., U. Okla., 1940, LL.B., 1940. Bar: Okla., 1940, Colo., 1945, U.S. Supreme Ct., 1960. States atty. Love County, Okla., 1940; sole practice Denver, 1945-77, Boulder, Colo., 1978-83; ptnr. Tippit, Haskell & Welborn, Tippit & Haskell and Tippit & Whittington P.C., Boulder, 1947-48; dir. Buckingham Nat. Bank; pres., mng. ptnr. natural resources cos.; lectr. Rocky Mountain Mineral Law Found.; lectr. various legal confs. Co-author: American Law of Mining; contbr. articles to profl. jours. Vice pres. Denver council Boy Scouts Am.; pres. Red Rocks Assn.; bd. dirs., sec. Acad. Ind. Scholars. Served to lt. col. USAAF, 1940-44. Mem. ABA (chmn. sect. natural resources), Okla. Bar Assn., Colo. Bar Assn. (chmn. mineral law sect.), Denver Bar Assn. (trustee). Republican. Episcopalian. Clubs: Mile High Denver Country (Denver); Boulder Country. Home: 525 Aurora Ave Boulder CO 80302-7127 Office: 305 Park West Bldg 250 Arapahoe Ave Boulder CO 80302-5838

TIPPLES, KEITH HOWARD, research director; b. Cambridge, Eng., Feb. 4, 1936; arrived in Can., 1963; s. Arthur Lyndhurst and Violet Isobel (Brown) T.; m. Maureen Cecilia Mannall, Apr. 23, 1962; children: Neil Anthony, Megan Angela, Graham Arthur. BSc, U. Birmingham, Eng., 1959, PhD, 1962. Rsch. scientist Grain Rsch. Lab., Can. Grain Commn., Winnipeg, Man., 1964-79, dir. rsch., 1979—. Fellow Am. Assn. Cereal Chemists (bd. dirs. 1985-87, Carl Wilhelm Brabender award 1978, William F. Geddes Meml. award 1991). Avocations: choral singing, cross-country skiing, sailing, tennis, cricket. Office: Can Grain Commn Rsch Lab, 1404-303 Main St, Winnipeg, MB Canada R3C 3G8

TIPPO, OSWALD, botanist, educator, university administrator; b. Milo, Maine, Nov. 27, 1911; s. John and Anna (Kimen) T.; m. Emmie Fernas, Sept. 21, 1934; children: Ray Ethan, Denis Robert. BS, U. Mass., 1932, DSc (hon.), 1954; MA, Harvard U., 1933, PhD, 1937; MA (hon.), Yale U., 1955. Austin teaching fellow Harvard U., Cambridge, Mass., 1932-35; teaching asst. Radcliffe Coll., Cambridge, 1935-37; Harvard fellow Atkins Instn. Arnold Arboretum, Cuba, 1937; instr. botany U. Ill., Urbana, 1937-39, assoc. in botany, 1939-41, asst. prof. botany, 1941-47, assoc. prof., 1947-49, prof. botany, 1949-55, acting head dept., 1947-48, chmn. dept., 1948-55, chmn. div. biol. scis., 1949-51, dean grad coll., 1953-55; Eaton prof. botany, chmn. dept. Yale U., New Haven, 1955-60, dir. Marsh Bot. Garden, 1955-60; provost U. Colo., Boulder, 1960-63; exec. dean arts and scis. NYU, 1963-64; provost U. Mass., Amherst, 1964-70, chancellor, 1970-71, Commonwealth prof. botany and higher edn., 1971-82, prof. emeritus, 1982—. Author: (with H.J. Fuller) College Botany, 1949, rev. edit., 1954, (with W.L. Stern) Humanistic Botany, 1977; editor in chief Am. Jour. Botany, 1951-53; chmn. editorial com. in biol. scis. Rinehart & Co., 1958-60; mem. com. on Handbook of Biol. Data, 1953-60; trustee Biol. Abstracts, 1957-63, pres. 1963-64; editor Econ. Botany, 1979-86; contbr. articles to profl. jours. Mem. Harvard U. bd. overseers com. to visit Arnold Arboretum, 1957-62; mem. Mass. bd. Found. for Sci. and Tech., 1970-71; trustee Hampshire Coll., 1970-

71; mem. Commn. on Instns. of Higher Edn., New Eng. Assn. Schs. and Coll., 1977-81; biologist wood sect., test lab. USN Yard, Phila., 1943-45. Fellow AAAS (v.p., chmn. sect. G 1958), Am. Acad. Arts and Scis. (coun. 1967-71, membership com. 1974-76); mem. AAUP (U. Ill. chpt. pres. 1952-53), Am. Inst. Biol. Scis. (chmn. ednl. commn. 1956-60, chmn. steering com. on secondary sch. biology film series 1958-60), Bot. Soc. Am. (pres. 1955, Merit award 1980), Soc. for Econ. Botany (Disting. Econ. Botanist award 1988), Conn. Bot. Soc. (dir. 1955-60), New Eng. Bot. Club, Internat. Assn. Wood Anatomists, Sigma Xi (pres. U. Ill. chpt. 1951-52, Yale U. chpt. 1958), Phi Beta Kappa. Home: 95 Aubinwood Rd Amherst MA 01002-1623 Office: Univ Mass Botany Dept Amherst MA 01003

TIPTON, CLYDE RAYMOND, JR., communications and resources development consultant; b. Cin., Nov. 13, 1921; s. Clyde Raymond and Ida Marie (Molitor) T.; m. Marian Gertrude Beushausen, Aug. 6, 1942; children: Marian Page Ashley, Robert Bruce. BS, U. Ky., 1946, MS, 1947. Research engr. Battelle Meml. Inst., Columbus, Ohio, 1947-49, sr. tech. adviser, 1951-62, coordinator corporate communications, 1969-73, v.p. communications, 1973-75, asst. to pres., 1978-79, v.p., corp. dir. communications and pub. affairs, 1979-86, ret.; staff mem. Los Alamos Sci. Lab., 1949-51; dir. research Basic, Inc., Bettsville, Ohio, 1962-64; asst. dir. Battelle Pacific N.W. Labs., Richland, Wash., 1964-69; pres., trustee Battelle Commons Co. for Community Urban Redevel., Columbus, 1975-78; cons. bus. communications and devel. Columbus, 1986—; secretariat U.S. del. 2d Internat. Conf. on Peaceful Uses Atomic Energy, Geneva, 1958; cons. U.S. AEC in Atoms for Peace Program, Tokyo, 1959, New Delhi, 1959-60, Rio de Janeiro, Brazil, 1961. Author: How to Change the World, 1982; editor: Jour. Soc. for Nondestructive Testing, 1953-57, The Reactor Handbook, Reactor Materials, vol. 3, 1955, vol. 1, 1960, Learning to Live on a Small Planet, 1974; patentee in field. Past pres. Pilot Dogs; bd. dirs., treas. Pilot Guide Dog Found. Served with U.S. Army Air Corp., 1943. Named to U. Ky. Engring. Hall of Distinction, 1997; U. Ky. Haggin fellow, 1947; Otterbein Coll. Sr. fellow, 1978. Mem. NSPE (past pres.), Am. Soc. Metals, Ohio Soc. Profl. Engrs. (past pres., Distin. Svc. award, Uncommon Man award, Outstanding Svc. award), Lions Club, Sigma Xi, Alpha Chi Sigma. Episcopalian. Home and Office: 6475 Strathaven Ct W Columbus OH 43085-2991

TIPTON, DANIEL L., religious organization executive. Gen. supt. Churches in Christ in Christian Union, Circleville, Ohio. Office: Chs of Christ in Christian Union Box 30 1426 Lancaster Pike Circleville OH 43113*

TIPTON, E. LINWOOD, trade association executive; b. Adrian, Mo., Nov. 19, 1934; s. Harlow Acklin and Mary Catherine (Lacy) T.; m. Marjorie A. Wolford, Dec. 17, 1955 (div. June 1983); children: Kelly A., Mark A.; m. Constance E. Eaton Broadstone, Oct. 8, 1983. BS in Agriculture, U. Mo., 1955, MS in Agriculture and Econs., 1956. Economist USDA Fgn. Agy. Svc., Washington, 1956-57, Eastern Milk Prodrs., Syracuse, N.Y., 1960-62; exec. dir. Coop. Dairy Econ. Svc., Boston, 1962-65; v.p., exec. v.p., pres., chief exec. officer Internat. Dairy Foods Assn., Washington, 1965—; founder Nat. Economist Club, Washington, treas., chmn. bd., 1967-73; founder Nat. Economist Ednl. Found., Washington, treas., chmn. bd., 1969-74; chmn. bd. Petlin, Inc., Fredericksburg, Va.; expert witness congl. coms., regulatory agencies; founder Internat. Sweetener Colloquium; apptd. to Nat. Commn. Agrl. Trade and Export Policy, 1984; advisor Sec. Agriculture, U.S. Trade Rep.; co-founder, chmn. bd. restaurant/motel chain, 1967—; chmn. The Food Group, The Ice Cream and Milk Polit. Action Com., Food Processors Steering Com. on Wage and Price Stability. 1st lt. Army Fin. Corp., 1957-60. Recipient Citation of Merit U. Mo. Alumni Assn., 1988. Avocations: tennis, golf. Office: Internat Dairy Foods Assn 1250 H St NW Ste 900 Washington DC 20005-3952

TIPTON, HARRY BASIL, JR., state legislator, physician; b. Salida, Colo., Mar. 14, 1927; s. Harry Basil Sr. and Nina Belle (Hailey) T.; m. Dorothy Joan Alexander, Sept. 16, 1950; children: Leslie Louise, Harry Basil III, Robert Alexander. BA, U. Colo., 1950, MD, 1953. Diplomate Am. Bd. Family Practice. Postgrad. med. tng. Good Samaritan Hosp., Phoenix, Ariz., Maricopa County Hosp., Phoenix; ptnr., dir. Lander (Wyo.) Med. Clinic, 1954—; mem. Wyo. Ho. Reps., Cheyenne, 1981—, chmn. judiciary com., 1986—; cons. Indian Health Svc., Ft. Washakie, Wyo., 1968—; dir NOWCAP Family Planning, Worland, Wyo., 1975-90. Mem., pres. Fremont County Sch. Dist. # 1, Lander, 1958-78. With USMC, 1945-46, capt. USNR Med. Corps, 1950-87. Named Capt. Med. Corps. USNR, 1974. Fellow Am. Coll. Ob.-Gyn., Am. Assn. Family Practice (charter); mem. Wyo. Med. Soc. (Physician of Yr. 1989), Rotary (pres. 1960-61), Elks. Republican. Avocations: fishing, skiing, bird hunting, military history. Office: Lander Med Clin PC 745 Buena Vista Dr Lander WY 82520-3431

TIPTON, JENNIFER, lighting designer; b. Columbus, Ohio, Sept. 11, 1937; d. Samuel Ridley and Isabel (Hanson) T. B.A., Cornell U., 1958. artist in residence Nat. Theater Artist Residency Program at Wooster Group funded by the PEW Charitable Trusts, 1994; assoc. prof. lighting Yale U. Sch. of Drama. Work includes: Paul Taylor Dance Co., Twyla Tharp and Dancers, Am. Ballet Theater, Jerome Robbins, Dana Reitz, Guthrie Theater, Hartford Stage Co., Murder Among Friends, 1975, Rex, For Colored Girls Who Consider Suicide When the Rainbow is Enuf (Drama Desk award), The Landscape of the Body, Newman Theatre, The Cherry Orchard (Drama Desk award, Tony award 1977), Agamemnon, Beaumont Theatre, Happy End, Martin Beck Theatre, Agamemnon, Delacorte Theatre, 1977, Museum, Public Theatre, Runaways, Public Theatre and Plymouth Theatre, All's Well That Ends Well, Taming of the Shrew, Delacorte Theatre, After the Season, Academy Festival Theatre, A Month in the Country, Williamstown Theatre Festival, Mikhail Baryshnikov's Don Quixote, Am. Ballet Theatre, Drinks Before Dinner, Public Theatre, The Pirates of Penzance, Public Theatre, 1978, Lunch Hour, 1980, Billy Bishop Goes to War, 1980, The Sea Gull, 1980, Sophisticated Ladies, 1981, The Wake of Jamie Foster, 1982, Uncle Vanya, 1983, Orgasmo Adulto Escapes from the Zoo, 1983, Baby with the Bathwater, 1984, Hurlyburly, 1984, Whoopi Goldberg, 1984, Endgame, 1984, Jerome Robbins' Broadway (Tony award 1989). Recipient Chgo.'s Joseph Jefferson award, 1976-77, Obie award 1979, Brandeis U. Creative Arts medal in dance, 1982, Mpls. Kudos award 1983, N.Y. Bessie award 1984, (with Dana Reitz), 1987, Guggenheim fellowship, 1986-87, Am. Theater Wing award 1989, Commonwealth award in dramatic arts, 1989, Lawrence Olivier award, 1991, Dance Mag. award, 1991, NEA Disting. Theater Artist award 1991. Home: 11 W 18th St New York NY 10011-4603

TIPTON, JON PAUL, allergist; b. Lynchburg, Ohio, Nov. 8, 1934; s. Paul Alvin and Jeanette (Palmer) T.; m. Martha J. Johnson, Dec. 29, 1968; children: Nicole Ann, Paula Michelle. BS, Ohio U., 1956; MD, Ohio State U., 1960. Resident internal medicine Ohio State U. Hosps., Columbus, 1964-66; fellow in allergy and pulmonary disease Duke U. Med. Ctr., Durham, N.C., 1963-64, 66-67; pvt. practice medicine specializing in allergies Athens, Ohio, 1967-74; pvt. practice medicine specializing in allergy Marietta, Ohio, 1974—; dir. cardio respiratory therapy Marietta Meml. Hosp., 1983, med. dir. pulmonary rehab. program; med. dir. Inhalation Therapy Sch. Wash. State C.C., Marietta, 1996—; cons. Ohio U. Hudson Health Ctr., 1967—, Mariette Coll. Health Ctr., 1974—, United Mine Workers of Am. Funds, 1984—; med. lectr. for physicians groups. Vol. Marietta Rep. Hdqrs., 1978—; mem. choir St. Luke's Luth. Ch., Marietta, 1983—. Served to capt. USAF, 1961-63. Mem. Am. Acad. Allergy, Ohio State Med. Assn., Wash. County Med. Soc., Parkersburg Acad. Medicine. Republican. Methodist. Avocations: yardwork, piano, attending plays, football, basketball. Home: 101 Meadow Ln Marietta OH 45750-1345 Office: 100 Front St Marietta OH 45750-3142

TIPTON, KENNETH WARREN, agricultural administrator, researcher; b. Belleville, Ill., Nov. 14, 1932; s. Roscoe Roy and Martha Pearl (Davis) T.; m. Barbara Adds, Mar. 2, 1957; children: Kenneth Warren Jr., Nancy Tipton O'Neal. BS, La. State U., 1955, MS, 1959; PhD, Miss. State U., 1969. Asst. prof. Agrl. Ctr., La. State U., Baton Rouge, 1959-70, assoc. prof., 1970-75, prof., 1975—; supt. Red River Rsch. Sta., La. Agrl. Expt. Sta. Agrl. Ctr., La. State U., Bossier City, 1975-79; assoc. dir. La. Agrl. Expt. Sta. Agrl. Ctr., La. State U., Baton Rouge, 1979-89, dir. La. Agrl. Expt. Sta., vice chancellor, 1989-96, vice chancellor, dir. emeritus, 1996—; mem. com. nine USDA/Coop. State Rsch. Svc., 1986-88; Expt. State Com. Orgn. Policy, 1988-91. Contbr. articles to Agronomy Jour., Jour. Econ. Entomology, Grain Sorghum Conf. Coach baseball program Am. Legion, 1969-74; scoutmaster Boy Scouts Am., Baton Rouge, 1970-75. Capt. USAF, 1955-58. Mem. Am. Soc. Agronomy, Crop Sci. Soc. Am., Coun. Agrl. Sci. Tech. Achievements include research on inheritance of fiber traits in cotton, resistance of grain sorghum hybrids to bird damage, tannin content of grain sorghum and effects of phosphorus on growth of sorghum. Home: 732 Baird Dr Baton Rouge LA 70808-5916

TIRANA, BARDYL RIFAT, lawyer; b. Geneva, Dec. 16, 1937; s. Rifat and Rosamond English (Walling) T.; m. Anne Prather, June 22, 1985; children by previous marriage: Kyra, Amina. A.B., Princeton U., 1959; LL.B., Columbia U., 1962. Bar: D.C. 1962, Md. 1986, N.Y. 1986, Va. 1986, Pa. 1992. Trial atty. Dept. Justice, 1962-64; assoc. Amram, Hahn & Sundlun, Washington, 1965-68; ptnr. Amram, Hahn & Sundlun, 1969-72; dir., sec. Exec. Jet Aviation, Inc., Columbus, Ohio, 1970-77, Technics, Inc., Alexandria, Va., 1971-77; ptnr. Sundlun, Tirana & Scher, Washington, 1972-77; dir. def. civil preparedness agy. Dept. Def., Washington, 1977-79, mem. armed forces policy coun., 1977-79; chmn. bd. Technics, Inc., San Jose, Calif., 1979-85; of counsel Silverstein and Mullens, Washington, 1982-84, ptnr., 1984-90; pvt. practice law Washington, 1991—. Mem.-at-large D.C. Bd. Edn., 1970-74; trustee Jimmy Carter Inaugural Trust, Washington, 1977-87; co-chmn. 1977 Presdl. Inaugural Com., 1976-77; mem. exec. adv. coun. Calif. Commn. Indsl. Innovation, 1981-82; pres. China/USA Edn. Fund, Inc., Washington, 1981—; dir. Rocky Mountain Inst., Snowmass Colo., 1982-95. Recipient medal for disting. pub. svc. Dept. Def., 1979, Fuess award Phillips Acad., 1991, Svc. Commendation award YWCA of Nat. Capital Area, 1991. Mem. N.Y.C. Racquet and Tennis Club, D.C. Met. Club. Home: 3550 Tilden St NW Washington DC 20008-3121 Office: Connecticut Ave NW Ste 700 Washington DC 20008-2322

TIRELLA, THERESA MARY, special education educator; b. Worcester, Mass., Apr. 22, 1963; d. Samuel Louis and Cecilia Barbara (Trczinski) T. BS, Northeastern U., 1986, MEd, 1989. Acting supr., childcare worker Dr. Franklin Perkins Sch., Lancaster, Mass., 1983-84; sr. recreational counselor Friendly House Inc., Worcester, 1985; adult edn. educator Action for Boston Community Devel., 1986-87; spl. edn. educator Cotting Sch., Lexington, Mass., 1987—; cons. United Cerebral Palsy, Watertown, Mass., 1993, Spl. Needs Advocacy Network Newton, Mass., 1991-93; corrd, bd. dirs. Access Now, Boston, 1991-93. Vol. mem. program planning com. Ptnrs. for Disabled Youth, Boston, 1991-94; vol. tutor Bethel Bapt. Ch., Roxbury, Mass., 1991-92, mem. youth com., 1991-92, mem. choir, 1991-92. Mem. Assn. for Suprevision and Curriculum Devel., Northeastern Univj. Women's Alumni Club, Northeastern U. Alumni Assn. Avocations: reading, graphic arts, crafts, arts, basketball. Home: 17 Seaverns Ave Jamaica Plain MA 02130-2874

TIRICO, MIKE, sportscaster; b. Whitestone, N.Y., Dec. 13, 1966; married. BA in Polit. Sci. and Broadcast Journalism, Syracuse U., 1988. Sports dir. WTVH-TV (affil. CBS), Syracuse, N.Y., 1987-91; reporter ESPN, Bristol, Conn., 1991—, host NFL Prime Monday, co-host GameDay ESPN Sports Radio, anchor SportsCenter, 1993—. Named top local sportscaster Syracuse Jour., 1989; recipient A.P. N.Y. Broadcasters award. Office: ESPN Inc Comms Dept ESPN Plz Bristol CT 06010*

TIRRELL, DAVID A., research scientist, educator; b. Jan. 10, 1953. BS in Chemistry, MIT, 1974; MS in Polymer Sci. and Engring., U. Mass., 1976, PhD in Polymer Sci. and Engring., 1978. Rsch. assoc. Kyoto U., 1978; asst. prof. chemistry Carnegie-Mellon U., 1978-82, assoc. prof. chemistry, 1982-84; assoc. prof. polymer sci. and engring. U. Mass., 1984-87, prof. polymer sci. and engring., 1987-92, Barrett prof. polymer and sci. and engring., 1992—; adj. prof. chemistry U. Mass., 1991; dir. NSF materials rsch. lab., 1991-94, dir. NSF material rsch. sci. and engring. ctr., 1994—; mem. molecular and cellular biology faculty, 1990—; vis. prog. chemistry U. Queensland, Australia, 1987, Inst. Charles Sadron, Strasbourg, 1991; mem. materials rsch. adv. com. NSF, 1988-91; chmn. com. on synthetic hierarchical structures Nat. Rsch. Coun., 1990-94, mem panel on biomolecular materials, 1991—, mem. naval rsch. lab. polymers in biosystems, Oxnard, 1994; co-chmn. grad. polymer rsch. conf. State Coll., Pa., 1994; program com. IUPAC Macromolecular Symposium, 1994; chmn. Gordon Rsch. Conf. on Chemistry of Supramolecules and Assemblies, 1995. Editor Jour. of Polymer Sci., 1988—; assoc. editor New Polymeric Materials, 1986-87; editl. bd. Indsl. and Engring. Chemistry, Product Rsch. and Devel., 1983-86, Jour. of Bioactive and Compatible Polymers, 1986—, Biomaterials, 1986—, New Polymeric Materials, 1987—, Jour. of Macromolecular Sci.-Chemistry, 1990—, Progress in Polymer Sic., 1992—, Macromolecular Reports, 1992, Materials Sci. and Engring., 1993—, Chem. and Engring. News, 1995—; contbr. articles to profl. jours. Univ. fellow, 1974-77, Alfred P. Sloan Rsch. fellow, 1982-84, Rotschild fellow Institut Curie, 1995-97; recipient Presdl. Young Investigator award, 1984-89, Fulbright Sr. scholar award, 1987. Mem. AAAS, Am. Chem. Soc., N.Y. Acad. Scis., Materials Rsch. Soc., Sigma Xi, Phi Lambda Upsilon. Office: University of Massachusetts Silvio Nat'l Ctr Poly Rsch Amherst MA 01003*

TIRRELL, JOHN ALBERT, organization executive, consultant; b. Boston, Feb. 11, 1934; s. George Howard and Helen Sarah (Hitchings) T.; m. Helga Ruth Eisenhauer, Jan. 29, 1966; children: Steffanie Ruth, Sabina Lisette, Monica Susanne. BA in Psychology, The King's Coll., Briarcliff Manor, N.Y., 1961; MEd, U. Ariz., 1975. Various positions for several orgns., 1962-68; analyst instrnl.-ednl. systems GE, Daytona Beach, Fla., 1969-72; dir. curriculum and program devel. Brookdale C.C., Lincroft, N.J., 1972; dir. learning and faculty resources Pima C.C., Tucson, 1972-76; dir. human resources planning and devel. Miami divsn. Cyprus Copper Co., Claypool, Ariz., 1976-79; exec. dir. Calvary Missionary Fellowship, Tucson, 1983-85; interim pastor Sagauro Evang. Ch., Tucson, 1985-86; Midvale Evang. Ch. Midvale Evangelical Ch., Tucson, 1986-87; founder, pres. The Jethro Consultancy, Birmingham, Mich., 1979—; v.p. mgmt. svc. AA Gage, Ferndale, Mich., 1987-88; pastor Desert Hills Bapt. Ch., Tucson, 1993-95; mem. adv. bd. UIM Internat., Flagstaff, Ariz., 1983-92, mem. fin. com., 1983-94, sec. support svcs. field bd., 1993—, sec. personnel com., 1997—, also bd. dirs.; assoc. faculty mem. Gila Pueblo Campus Ea. Ariz. Coll., Globe, 1978; adj. prof. Montclair State Coll., Upper Montclair, N.J., 1972; chmn. Mgmt. and Pers. Com. Wildwood Ranch, Inc., Howell, Mich., 1989-92; interim pres., v.p. programs, v.p. devel. Detroit Rescue Mission Ministries, 1990-92; v.p. corp. planning, tng., productivity George Instrument Co., Royal Oak. Contbr. articles to profl. jours. Mem. Ariz. Coun. for Econ. Conversion, 1992-94; mem. facilities task force Grace Evang. Free Ch., Birmingham, 1989-90, chmn. bylaws revision com., 1989-90, chmn. property devel. com., 1990-92; interim pastor Desert Hills Bapt. Ch., Tucson, 1992-93; elder 1st Evang. Free Ch., Tucson, 1979-81, 86-87, 97—, supt. Sunday sch., 1981-84, supr. adult Sunday sch., 1992-93, chmn. gen. bd., elder bd., 1979-82, short-term missions coord., missions bd., 1992-93; bd. dirs. S.W. Border dist. Evang. Free Ch. Am., 1996—, Clearing House of Operational Resources for Christian Orgns., Royal Oak, Mich., 1991; bd. dirs. Shadow Roc Home-owners Assn., 1996—, treas., 1997—; v.p. parent-tchr. fellowship Palo Verde Christian Sch., Tucson, 1980-81. Staff sgt. USAF, 1952-56. Mem. ASTD (treas., Old Pueblo chpt. 1982, bd. dirs.-at-large 1983, Human Resources Devel. award Valley of the Sun chpt. 1977), Birmingham-Bloomfield C. of C. (mem. profl. devel. edn. com. 1987-91, mem. pub. rels. mktg. com. 1989), King's Coll. Alumni Assn. (class gov. 1988-95). Republican. Avocations: photography, Bible teaching. Home and Office: 1205 E Deer Canyon Rd Tucson AZ 85718-1069

TIRRELL, MATTHEW, chemical engineering/materials science educator; b. Phillipsburg, N.J., Sept. 5, 1950; s. Matthew Vincent Tirrell Jr. and Loraine (Wier) Gonsky; m. Pamela LaVigne, Aug. 1993. BS, Northwestern U., 1973; PhD, U. Mass., 1977. Mem. coop. edn. program Cin. Milacron Chem. Inc., 1970-72; tchg. and rsch. asst. U. Mass., Amherst, 1973-77; asst. prof. U. Minn., Mpls., 1977-81, assoc. prof., 1981-85, prof. chem. engring. and materials sci., 1985—, Shell disting. prof. chem. engring., 1986-91, acting head, 1992-93, Earl E. Bakken prof. biomed. engring., 1993—, head chem. engring. and materials sci., 1995—; dir. Biomed. Engring. Inst., 1995—; sci. advisor BIOSYM Techs., San Diego. Author: Modeling of Polymerization Processes, 1995. Recipient Charles M.A. Stine award, 1996; Guggenheim fellow, 1986. Mem. AIChE (editor jour. 1991—, Profl. Progress award 1994, Allan P. Colburn award 1985), Am. Chem. Soc., Am. Phys. Soc. (John H. Dillon medal 1987), Materials Rsch. Soc. Avocations: gourmet cooking, movies, distance running. Office: U Minn Dept Chem Engring-Mat Sci Minneapolis MN 55455

TIRRO, FRANK PASCALE, music educator, author, composer; b. Omaha, Sept. 20, 1935; s. Frank and Mary Carmela (Spensieri) T.; m. Charlene Rae Whitney, Aug. 16, 1961; children: John Andrew, Cynthia Anne. B.M.E., U. Nebr., 1960; M.M., Northwestern U., 1961; Ph.D., U. Chgo., 1974. Chmn. lab. schs. U. Chgo., 1961-70; fellow of Villa I Tatti Harvard U., Florence, Italy, 1971-72; lectr. U. Kans., Lawrence, 1972-73; asst. prof. music Duke U., 1973-74; dir. Southeastern Inst. Medieval and Renaissance Studies, Durham, N.C., 1978-80; chmn., assoc. prof. music Duke U., Durham, 1973-80; prof. Yale U., New Haven, 1980—, dean, 1980-89; reader, cons. several univ. presses; jurist Parisot Internat. Cello Competition, Sao Paolo, Brazil, 1981. Author: Jazz: A History, 1977, rev. edit., 1993, Renaissance Choirbooks in the Archive of San Petronio in Bologna, 1986, Living With Jazz, 1995, (with others) The Humanities: Cultural Roots and Continuities, 1980, 5th edit., 1997; editor: Medieval and Renaissance Studies No. 9, 1982; mem. editl. bd. Wittenberg Rev.; composer American Jazz Mass, 1960; assoc. editor Am. Nat. Biography, 1994—. Bd. dirs. New Haven Symphony, 1980-89, Neighborhood Music Sch., New Haven, 1982-89, Chamber Orch. New Eng., 1980-82, Ctr. for Black Music Rsch., 1985—. Recipient Standard Composer award Am. Soc. Composers, Authors and Pubs., 1966, Gustavus Fine Arts medal, 1988, Duke Ellington Fellow medal, 1989; travel grantee Am. Coun. Learned Socs., 1967; rsch. grantee Duke U., 1978. Mem. Am. Musicol. Soc. (council 1978-80), Coll. Music Soc. (council 1980-82, mem. exec. bd. 1984-86), Nat. Assn. Schs. of Music, Internat. Soc. Jazz Research, Renaissance Soc. Am., Mory's Club, Yale Club (N.Y.C.). Republican. Lutheran. Office: Yale U Sch Music PO Box 208246 New Haven CT 06520-8246

TIRYAKIAN, EDWARD ASHOD, sociology educator; b. Bronxville, N.Y., Aug. 6, 1929; s. Ashod Haroutioun and Keghinee (Agathon) T.; m. Josefina Cintron, Sept. 5, 1953; children: Edmund Carlos, Edwyn Ashod. BA summa cum laude, Princeton U., 1952; MA, Harvard U., 1954, PhD, 1956; PhD (hon.), U. Rene Descartes, Paris, 1987. Instr. Princeton U., 1956-57, asst. prof., 1957-62; lectr. Harvard U., 1962-65; assoc. prof. Duke U., Durham, N.C., 1965-67, prof., 1967—, chmn. dept. sociology and anthropology, 1969-72, dir. internat. studies, 1988-91; vis. lectr. U. Philippines, 1954-55, Bryn Mawr Coll., 1957-59; vis. scientist program Am. Sociol. Assn., 1967-70; vis. prof. Laval U., Quebec City, Que., Can., 1978, Inst. Polit. Studies, Paris, 1992, Free U., Berlin, 1996; summer seminar dir. NEH, 1978, 80, 93, 89, 91, 96; lectr. Kyoto Am. Studies Summer Seminar, 1985. Author: Sociologism and Existentialism, 1962; Editor: Sociological Theory, Values and Sociocultural Change: Essays in Honor of P.A. Sorokin, 1963, The Phenomenon of Sociology, 1971, On the Margin of the Visible: Sociology, the Esoteric, and the Occult, 1974, The Global Crisis: Sociological Analyses and Responses, 1984; co-editor: Theoretical Sociology: Perspectives and Developments, 1970; New Nationalisms of the Developed West, 1985. Recipient Fulbright rsch. award, 1955; Ford faculty rsch. fellow, 1971-72. Mem. Am. Sociol. Assn., African Studies Assn., Am. Soc. for Study Religion (council 1975-78, pres. 1981-84), Assn. Internationale des Sociologues de Langue Française (v.p. 1985-88, pres. 1988-92), Soc. for Phenomenology and Existential Philosophy, Phi Beta Kappa. Clubs: Princeton, Century Assn. (N.Y.C.). Home: 16 Pascal Way Durham NC 27705-4924 *As a sociological researcher, I have sought to understand on a comparative basis the dynamics of social consciousness in the process of historical change. As a teacher, I have sought to encourage in students—undergraduates, graduates, and postgraduates— a gusto for intellectual curiosity in exploring the myriad of linkages that make up social reality, our human patrimony.*

TISCH, JAMES S., diversified holding company executive; b. Atlantic City, Jan. 2, 1953; s. Laurence A. and Wilma (Stein) T.; m. Merryl Hiat; children: Jessica, Benjamin, Samuel. BA, Cornell U., 1975; MBA, Wharton Grad. Sch., U. Pa., 1976. With Loews Corp., N.Y.C., 1977—, exec. v.p., 1987-94, pres., COO, 1994—, also mem. mgmt. com. Pres. Fedn. Employment and Guidance Svc., N.Y.C., 1985—; trustee Dalton Sch., N.Y.C., 1985—, Mt. Sinai Med. Ctr., N.Y.C., 1988—. Office: Loews Corp 667 Madison Ave New York NY 10021-8029

TISCH, JONATHAN MARK, hotel company executive; b. Atlantic City, Dec. 7, 1953; s. Preston Robert and Joan (Hyman) T. BA, Tufts U., 1976. Cinematographer, producer WBZ-TV, Boston, 1976-79; sales mgr. Loews Hotels, N.Y.C., 1980-81, dir. devel., 1981-82, v.p., 1982-85, exec. v.p., 1985-86, pres., 1986-89, pres., chief exec. officer, 1986—; mem. mgmt. com. Loews Corp.; bd. dirs. N.Y. Giants, 1991—. Trustee Robert Steel Found., N.Y.C., Gunnery Sch., Washington, Conn., 1983—, Tufts U., Medford, Mass., 1986—, Vice Pres.'s Residence Found., 1994; chmn. N.Y.C. host com. for Grammys, 1988, 92, 94; bd. dirs. Pediatric AIDS found.; vice chair econ. devel. com. N.Y.C. Partnership, 1994—. Mem. Am. Hotel and Motel Assn. (officer 1994—), Travel Bus. Roundtable (chmn. 1995—, conf. chmn. 1995—), Friars Club. Avocations: golf, tennis, skiing. Office: Loews Hotels 667 Madison Ave New York NY 10021-8029

TISCH, LAURENCE ALAN, diversified manufacturing and service executive; b. N.Y.C., Mar. 5, 1923; s. Al and Sadye (Brenner) T.; m. Wilma Stein, Oct. 31, 1948; children: Andrew, Daniel, James, Thomas. BSc cum laude, NYU, 1942; MA in Indsl. Engring, U. Pa., 1943; postgrad., Harvard Law Sch., 1946; LLD (hon.), Skidmore Coll., 1994. Pres. Tisch Hotels, Inc., N.Y.C., 1946-74; chmn. bd., co-chief exec. officer Loews Corp., N.Y.C., 1960—; chmn. bd. dirs. CNA Fin. Corp., Chgo.; bd. dirs. Bulova Corp. subs. Loews Corp., N.Y.C., ADP Corp., Petrie Stores Corp. Bd. dirs. United Jewish Appeal-Fedn.; chmn. bd. trustees NYU; trustee Met. Mus. Art, N.Y.C., N.Y. Pub. Libr. Mem. Coun. Fgn. Rels. Home: Island Dr N Manursing Island Rye NY 10580 also: Loews Corp 667 Madison Ave New York NY 10021-8087*

TISCH, PRESTON ROBERT, finance executive; b. Bklyn., Apr. 29, 1926; s. Abraham Solomon and Sayde (Brenner) T.; m. Joan Hyman, Mar. 14, 1948; children: Steven E., Laurie M., Jonathan M. Student, Bucknell U., 1943-44; B.A., U. Mich., 1948. Co-chmn., co-chief exec. officer, dir. Loews Corp., N.Y.C., 1960—; postmaster gen. U.S. Postal Svc., Washington, 1986-88; chmn., co-CEO, half owner N.Y. Football Giants, 1990—; bd. dirs. CNA Fin. Corp., Bulova Watch Co. Chmn. emeritus N.Y. Conf. and Visitors Bur., Nat. Dem. Conv., 1976, 80; trustee NYU; mem. Quadrennial Commn. on Exec., Legis. and Jud. Salaries, 1988; mem. Gov.'s Bus. Adv. Coun. for N.Y. State; pres. Citymeals on Wheels. With AUS, 1943-44. Mem. Rye Racquet Club, Century Country Club, Sigma Alpha Mu. Office: Loews Corp 667 Madison Ave New York NY 10021-8029 also: NY Giants Giants Stadium East Rutherford NJ 07073*

TISCH, STEVEN E., movie producer; b. Lakewood, N.J., Feb. 14, 1949; s. Preston Robert and Joan (Hyman) T.; m. Patricia Keast, Sept. 27, 1981 (div. July 1991); children: Hilary, William. BA, Tufts U., 1971. Pres. Tisch-Avnet Prodns., L.A., 1981-88, Steve Tisch Co., L.A., 1988—. Exec. prodr. (films) The Long Kiss Goodnight, 1996, American History, 1997; prodr. Forrest Gump, 1994, Corrina, Corrina, 1994, Dear God, 1996, Wild America, 1997, The Postman, 1997, Nico the Unicorn, 1997. Chmn. AIDS Project L.A., 1992-94. Office: 3815 Hughes Ave Culver City CA 90232-2715*

TISCHLER, HERBERT, geologist, educator; b. Detroit, Apr. 28, 1924; s. Louis and Hermina (Leb) T.; m. Annette Zeidman, Aug. 10, 1954; children—Michael A., Robert D. B.S., Wayne U., 1950; M.A., U. Calif.-Berkeley, 1955; Ph.D., U. Mich., 1961. Instr. Wayne State U., Detroit, 1956-58; assoc. prof. No. Ill. U., DeKalb, 1958-65; prof. dept. earth scis. U. N.H., Durham, 1965-97, chmn. dept., 1965-90, prof. emeritus dept. earth scis., 1997—; co-dir. No. New Eng. Jr. Sci. and Humanities Symposium, 1979—, mem. nat. adv. com., 1989-92. Trustee Mt. Washington Observatory, 1980-92. With USCG, 1943-46. Fellow Geol. Soc. Am. (sr.). Home: 36 Oyster River Rd Durham NH 03824-3029 Office: U NH Dept Earth Scis James Hall Durham NH 03824

TISCHMAN, MICHAEL BERNARD, lawyer; b. Elizabeth, N.J., Oct. 8, 1937; s. Nathan and Ann (Goldberg) T.; m. Elinor Cohen, Aug. 16, 1959; children: David F., Susan F. BA, U. Pa., 1959; LLB, Harvard U., 1963; LLM in Taxation, NYU, 1968. Bar: N.J. 1964, Fla. 1979, N.Y. 1984. Law sec. Judge Walter J. Freund N.J. Appellate Div., 1963-64; assoc. Schiff, Cummis & Kent, Newark, 1964-67; ptnr. Cummis, Kent, Radin & Tischman, Newark, 1968-70, Sills, Beck, Cummis, Radin & Tischman, Newark, 1971-87, Sills, Cummis, Zuckerman, Radin, Tischman, Epstein & Gross, Newark, 1988—; panel chmn. fee arbitration com. N.J. Supreme Ct. Dist. Essex County, 1987-91. Mem. Mayor's Performing Arts Ctr. Task Force, Newark, 1988—. Mem. N.J. Bar Assn. (com. on ltd. partnership act revisions 1983-88), Phi Beta Kappa. Home: 8 Wedgewood Way Scotch Plains NJ 07076-2727 Office: Sills Cummis Zuckerman Radin Tischman Epstein & Gross One Riverfront Pla Newark NJ 07102

TISDALE, DOUGLAS MICHAEL, lawyer; b. Detroit, May 3, 1949; s. Charles Walker and Violet Lucille (Battani) T.; m. Patricia Claire Brennan, Dec. 29, 1972; children: Douglas Michael, Jr., Sara Elizabeth, Margaret Patricia, Victoria Claire. BA in Psychology with honors, U. Mich., 1971, JD, 1975. Bar: Colo. 1975, U.S. Dist. Ct. Colo. 1975, U.S. Ct. Appeals (10th cir.) 1976, U.S. Supreme Ct. 1979. Law clk. to chief judge U.S. Dist. Ct. Colo., Denver, 1975-76; assoc. Brownstein Hyatt Farber & Madden, P.C. ; ptnr., dir. Brownstein Hyatt Farber & Strickland, P.C., 1976-92; shareholder Popham, Haik, Schnobrich & Kaufman, Ltd., 1992-97, dir. 1995-97; ptnr. Baker & Hostetler, LLP, Denver, 1997—; Home: 4662 S Elizabeth Ct Cherry Hills Village CO 80110-7106 Office: Baker & Hostetler LLP 303 E 17th Ave Denver CO 80203-1235

TISE, LARRY EDWARD, historical organization administrator, historian; b. Winston-Salem, N.C., Dec. 6, 1942; s. Russell Edward and Lena Irene (Norman) T.; children: Larry Edward, Nicholas Allen, William Zane. A.B., Duke U., 1965, M.Div., 1968; Ph.D. (Ford Found. fellow, 1970, Research Triangle fellow, 1971), U. N.C., 1974. Part-time editor John Fries Blair, Pub., Winston-Salem, 1969-72; teaching fellow history dept. U. N.C., Chapel Hill, 1971; instr. U. N.C., 1972-73; dir. hist. publs. N.C. Bicentennial Com., 1973-74; asst. dir. N.C. Div. Archives and History, Raleigh, 1974-75; dir. N.C. Div. Archives and History, 1975-81, N.C. State Hist. Preservation officer, 1975-81; exec. dir. Pa. Hist. and Mus. Commn., 1981-87; Pa. State Hist. Preservation officer, 1981-87; dir. Am. Assn. for State and Local History, Nashville, Tenn., 1987-89; exec. dir. Benjamin Franklin Nat. Meml., Phila., 1989-97; pres., CEO Congress of Disting. Awards, 1997—; adj. prof. grad. sch. fine arts U. Pa., 1984-87; vis. prof. Vanderbilt U., 1988-89, Temple U., 1989-91; mem. Nat. Hist. Publs. and Records Commn., 1982-88; officer Preservation Action; corp. dir. Fedn. N.C. Hist. Socs., Friends of N.C. Archives, Inc., Hist. Preservation Fund of N.C., Inc., Preservation Fund of Pa., Inc., Hist. Preservation Soc. N.C., Inc., Mus. History Assocs., Inc., N.C. Inst. Applied History, Stagville Ctr. Corp., N.C., Inc. Author, co-author writings in fields of archives, hist. preservation, hist. sites and museums, history, society, religion; author: The Southern Experience in the American Revolution, 1978, The Monitor: Its Meaning and Future, 1978, Writing North Carolina History, 1979, A House Not Made with Hands, 1966, The Yadkin Melting Pot: Methodism and the Moravians in the Yadkin Valley, 1750-1850, 1968, Proslavery: The Defense of Slavery in America, 1987, A Book About Children, 1992; gen. editor: writings in fields of archives, hist. preservation, hist. sites and museums, history, society, religion including Winston-Salem in History, 13 vols, 1976; edit. bd. The Public Historian, 1980-86; editor N.C. Hist. Rev., 1974-81, Pa. Heritage, 1981-87, History News, 1987-89, Franklin Gazette, 1989—; contbr. articles to books, newsletters, publs. Recipient William R. Davie History award, 1979, Herbert L. Feis award, Am. Hist. Assn., 1989, Benjamin Franklin Nat. Meml. awards 1990; Nat. Endowment for the Humanities fellow, 1992-93. Mem. Am. Hist. Assn. (various coms.), Orgn. Am. Historians (chmn. coms.), So. Hist. Assn., Soc. Am. Archivists, Am. Assn. State and Local History (mem. coun. and coms.), Nat. Trust for Hist. Preservation, Nat. Assn. State Archives and Records Adminstrs. (pres. 1980-81), Nat. Conf. State Hist. Preservation Officers (bd. dirs. 1976-79, pres. 1979-81), Nat. Coun. on Pub. History (bd. dirs., exec. com. 1979-83, pres. 1983-85), N.C. Hist. Commn. (sec. 1975-81), N.C. Lit. and Hist. Assn. (sec., treas. 1977-81), Pa. Fedn. Hist. Socs. (sec. 1981-87), Friends of Franklin, Inc. (exec. sec. 1989—). Methodist. Home: 705 Corinthian Ave Philadelphia PA 19130-2614

TISE, MARY SHACKELFORD, public librarian; b. Charlottesville, Va., Oct. 26, 1954; d. Alfred Colquitt and Mary Aston (Leavell) Shackelford; m. Frank Peine Tise, July 4, 1981; children: David, Gregory, Joseph. BA, U. Va., 1976; MLS, U. N.C., 1978. Libr. dir. Vaughan Meml. Libr., Galax, Va., 1978-81; reference libr. Concord Pike Libr., Wilmington, Del., 1981-83, divsn. mgr., 1989—; divsn. mgr. Claymont (Del.) Pub. Libr., 1983-89. Mem. ALA, AAUW, Del. Libr. Assn. (pres. 1989-90). Office: Concord Pike Libr 3406 Concord Pike Wilmington DE 19803-5031

TISHLER, WILLIAM HENRY, landscape architect, educator; b. Baileys Harbor, Wis., June 22, 1936; s. William John and Mary Viola (Sarter) T.; m. Betsy Lehner, Sept. 23, 1961; children—William Phillip, Robin Elizabeth. B.S. in Landscape Architecture, U. Wis., 1960; M.L.A., Harvard U., 1964. Urban planner City of Milw., 1961-62; mem. faculty dept. landscape architecture U. Wis.-Madison, 1964—; asso. Hugh A Dega & Assos. (Landscape Architects), 1964-66; prin. Land Plans Inc. (Land and Hist. Preservation Planning Cons.), Madison, 1966—; advisor emeritus Nat. Trust for Hist. Preservation; mem. Door County Land Trust, Inc., 1986-91; bd. dirs. The Hubbard Ednl. Trust. Author: American Landscape Architecture: Designers and Places, 1989; contbr. articles to profl. jours. Served with C.E., U.S. Army, 1960. Recipient Design Arts Program award NEH, 1981; Attingham (Eng.) Program fellow Soc. Archtl. Historians, 1980, Hawthorn award Friends of The Clearing; Dumbarton Oaks sr. fellow, 1990. Fellow Am. Soc. Landscape Architects (Horace Cleve. vis. prof. U. Minn. 1993, merit award 1971, nat. honor award 1980, 89); mem. Assn. Preservation Tech., Wis. Acad. Arts, Letters and Scis., Pioneer Am. Soc. (Henry Douglas award) , Hist. Madison (hon.), Vernacular Architecture Forum (past pres.), Madison Trust for Hist. Preservation, Alliance for Hist. Landscape Preservation (founder), The Clearing Landscape Inst. (co-dir.), Phi Kappa Phi, Sigma Lambda Alpha, Sigma Nu. Lutheran. Home: 3925 Regent St Madison WI 53705-5222 Office: U Wis Dept Landscape Architecture Madison WI 53706

TISHMAN, JOHN L., realty and construction company executive; b. N.Y.C., Jan. 24, 1926; s. Louis and Rose F. (Foreman) T.; m. Suzanne Weisberg; children: Daniel R., Katherine T. Chmn., chief exec. officer. Tishman Realty & Constrn. Co., Inc., N.Y.C. Home: Mianus Riv Rd Bedford NY 10506 Office: Tishman Realty Const Corp NY 666 Fifth Ave New York NY 10103-0001*

TISHNER, KERI LYNN, secondary education educator; b. Santa Ana, Calif., June 1, 1964; d. Albert John, Jr. and Barbara Ann (Milner) Geverink; m. David Jackson Tishner, Apr. 27, 1985. BA in Art with distinction, Calif. State U., Long Beach, 1988, tchg. credentials, 1991; postgrad. in edn.-instructional tech., Calif. State U., San Bernardino, 1994—. State D coaching license Calif. Youth Soccer Assn., 1993. High sch. art tchr. Apple Valley (Calif.) H.S., 1991—. Presenter in field of art. Participant in the Calif. Arts Project, San Bernardino, 1995. Mem. NEA, Nat. Art Edn. Assn., Calif. Tchrs. Assn., Calif. Art Edn. Assn., Los Angeles County Mus. Art, Norton Simon Mus. Art, Apple Valley Unified Tchrs. Assn., Kappa Delta Pi. Avocations: weaving, computers, stamp collecting, painting, playing soccer. Office: Apple Valley HS 11837 Navajo Rd Apple Valley CA 92308-7653

TISINGER, CATHERINE ANNE, college dean; b. Winchester, Va., Apr. 6, 1936; d. Richard Martin and Irma Regina (Ohl) T. BA, Coll. Wooster, 1958; MA, U. Pa., 1962, PhD, 1970; LLD (hon.), Coll. of Elms, 1985. Provost Callison Coll., U. of Pacific, Stockton, Calif., 1971-72; v.p. Met. State U., St. Paul, 1972-75; v.p. acad. affairs S.W. State U., Marshall, Minn., 1975-76, interim pres., 1976-77; dir. Ctr. for Econ. Edn., R.I. Coll., Providence, 1979-80; v.p. acad. affairs Cen. Mo. State U., Warrensburg, Mo., 1980-84; pres. North Adams State Coll., Mass., 1984-91; dean arts and scis. Shenandoah U., Winchester, Va., 1991—; cons. North Cen. Assn. Colls. and Schs., 1980-84, New Eng. Assn. Schs. and Colls., 1978-79, 85—, Minn. Acad. Family Physicians, 1973-77; mem. adv. bd. First Agrl. Bank, North Adams, 1985-91; pres. No. Berkshire Cooperating Colls., 1986-91; v.p. Coll. Consortium for Internat. Studies, 1989-90. V.p. Med. Simulation Found., 1986-88; bd. dirs. Williamstown Concerts, 1988-91, Shawnee coun. Girl Scouts U.S.A., 1992-93, Parents' Choice, 1997—. Mem. No. Berkshire C. of C. (bd. dirs. 1984-89, v.p. 1986-89). Avocations: fiber and textile arts, photography. Office: Shenandoah U 1460 College Dr Winchester VA 22601

TISMA, MARIJA STEVAN, artist; b. Indjija, Serbia, Yugoslavia, Aug. 22, 1950; s. Stevan Ilija and Djurdjinka Steva (Tubic) T.; m. Nenad Ante Rukavina, May 24, 1989; 1 child, Dane. BArch, Belgrade U., 1983. pres. Ardium, BBS for Art & Architecture, Belgrade, 1995—. Exhibited in one man shows at Libertas Gallery, Dubrovnik, Croatia, 1977, Mostar RU Gallery, Bosnia-Hercegovina, 1980, Can. Embassy Gallery, Belgrade, Yugoslavia, 1987, Lazar Vozarevic Gallery, Yugoslavia, 1988, City Mus., Kraljevo, Yugoslavia, 1988, Singigunum Gallery, Belgrade, 1993, others; group shows include Oct. Salon, Belgrade, 1976-87, May Salon, Belgrade, 1977-87, Serbian Contemporary, Brussels, 1978; included in collections at Hotels Intercontinental, Belgrade, McDonald's Corp., Novi Sad, Yugoslavia. Yugoslav Ministry of Edn. grantee, 1978. Fellow Yugoslav Inst. Artists (Grand prize 1979, Great prize 1989); mem. Yugoslav Inst. Architects. Avocations: traveling, books. Home: 690 Fort Washington Ave # 4-J New York NY 10040

TISON-BRAUN, MICHELINE LUCIE, French language educator; b. Arras, France, Apr. 7, 1913; came to U.S., 1947, naturalized, 1964; d. Eugène and Lucie (Duchat) T.; m. Lev Braun, Apr. 1, 1948. Agregée ès lettres, 1937, Docteur ès lettres, 1972. Prof. French Education Nationale, London, 1938-47; translator BBC, London, 1941-45; translator, précis writer UN, N.Y.C., 1947-54; prof. French Lycée N.Y., City U. N.Y. Grad. Ctr. and Hunter Coll., 1961-81. Author: La Crise de l'Humanisme, vol. I, 1957, rev. edit., 1963, vol. II, 1968, Nathalie Sarraute la Recherche de l'Authenticitè, 1971, Dada et le Surréalisme, 1975, Tristan Tzara, 1977, Poetique du Paysage, 1980, L'Introvable Origine, 1981, Ce Monstre Incomparable, A. Malraux et le Probleme de la Personnalite (Prix Jouvenel), 1982, Marguerite Duras, 1983, Le Moi dècapitè Lang, 1989, L'Esprit Createur, 1995. Decorated Palmes Academiques; Guggenheim fellow, 1978-79. Mem. MLA, Am. Assn. Tchrs. French, Pen Club, Gens de Lettres, Société d'Histoire littéraire de la France. Home: 50 Central Park W New York NY 10023-6028

TISSUE, MIKE, medical educator, respiratory therapist; b. Garfield, Wash., Aug. 24, 1941; s. Altha Lester and Fern Adeline (Willard) T.; m. Marjorie Lena Atkinson, Feb. 24, 1961 (div. June 1991); children: Sue Tipton, Pam Kromholtz, Paul, Donna. AAS (4 degrees) with honors, Spokane (Wash.) C.C., 1985; BS in Respiratory Therapy cum laude, Loma Linda (Calif.) U., 1987; MS in Respiratory Care, Ga. State U., 1997. Registered Cardiovascular Technologist (invasive and non-invasive), Nat. Soc. Cardiopulmonary Technol./Cardiovascular Credentialing Internat.; Registered Respiratory Therapist (RRT), Pulmonary Function Technologist, Perinatal/Pediatric Specialist, NBRC; registered Respiratory Care Practitioner, Calif., Ga. Respiratory intern, Level III NICU Therapist Loma Linda (Calif.) U. Med. Ctr., 1985-87; educator, therapist Riyadh (Saudi Arabia) Armed Forces Hosp., 1987-91; dept. head respiratory care Security Forces Hosp., Riyadh, 1991-93; asst. prof., dir. clin. edn. respiratory therapy program Morehead (Ky.) State U., 1993-94; program dir. assoc. degree respiratory therapy Chattahoochee Tech. Inst., Marietta, Ga., 1994—; pres., founder Riyadh Cardiorespiratory Soc., 1988-93; rschr. Loma Linda U., 1987, Riyadh Armed Forces Hosp., 1988; instr. and affiliate faculty ACLS Wash. State Heart Assn., 1983-85, Calif. Heart Assn., 1985-87, Saudi Heart Assn., 1985-87, Ky. Heart Assn., 1993-94, Ga. affiliate, 1994—; instr. and affiliate faculty pediatric advanced life support Saudi Heart Assn., 1987-93; instr. and affiliate faculty basic life support/CPR Wash. State, 1974-85, Calif., 1985-87, Saudi Heart Assn., 1987-93, Ky. Heart Assn., 1993-94, Ga. affiliate, 1994—; cons. ARC, Tacoma, Wash., 1984, instr. advanced 1st aid, standard 1st aid, CPR, 1975—, Inland Empire Chpt., Spokane, Wash., 1975-94, San Bernardino/Redlands Svc. Ctr., Loma Linda, 1985-87, Am. Cmty. Svcs. U.S. Embassy, Riyadh, 1991-93, U.S. Mil. Operation Desert Storm, Riyadh, 1991-93, Ga. affiliate Cobb County chpt., Marietta, 1994—; instr. Freedom From Smoking Clinic Program Am. Lung Assn., Calif., 1985-87, Saudi Arabia, 1987-93, Smyrna, Ga., 1994—; mem. Instl. Effectiveness Com., Campus Computer Com. Chattahoochee Tech. Inst., 1994—. Contbr. articles to profl. jours. Bd. dirs. Am. Heart Assn., Spokane, 1976-83, chair fin. com., 1981-83; chair spkrs. bur. ARC, Inland Empire Chpt., Spokane, 1982-85, chair pub. rels., 1983-85; mem. Calif. affiliate San Bernardino Chpt., Loma Linda, 1985-87, Ga. affiliate Cobb County Chpt., Marietta, 1994—; chair programming and spkrs. bur. Am. Lung Assn., Smyrna, Ga., 1994—, chmn. bd. dirs., 1995—; sec. Cobb County Cmty. Coun., Marietta, 1995-96, spkr., 1995, v.p., 1996—; vol. Ga. Internat. Cultural Exch., 1995; registry exam. sr. proctor Cardiovascular Credentialing Internat./Nat. Bd. Cardiovascular Technologists, Riyadh, 1987-90; commr. Boy Scouts Am., Spokane, 1973-82, wood badge, 1977, commrs. key, 1977, scouters key, 1979. Named Citizen of Day KGA Radio, Spokane, 1983. Mem. AAUP (legislature com. Atlanta 1995—), Am. Assn. Respiratory Care (therapist driven protocol rev. com. 1994, ad hoc com. on patient-driven-protocol rev. com. 1996, ad hoc com. for sects. rev. 1995, 96), Ga. Soc. Respiratory Care (bd. dirs. 1994—, edn. com., smoking and health com.), Phi Delta Kappa (Alpha Nu chpt. Morehead, Ky. 1993-94, Kennesaw Mountain chpt. Atlanta 1994—, Pub. Rels. Com. 1995—). Roman Catholic. Avocations: photography, travel. Home: 1565 Crider Rd SE Apt 12-B Marietta GA 30060-7430 Office: Chattahoochee Tech Inst Respiratory Therapy Program 980 S Cobb Dr SE Marietta GA 30060-3300

TITCOMB, CALDWELL, music and theatre historian; b. Augusta, Maine, Aug. 16, 1926; s. Samuel and Lura Elizabeth (Smith) T. A.B. summa cum laude, Harvard U., 1947, M.A., 1949, Ph.D., 1952. Univ. organist Brandeis U., Waltham, Mass., 1953-70, dir. undergrad. studies music, 1956-84, curator creative arts, library, 1961-64, co-chmn. music dept., 1977-84, from instr. to prof. music, 1953-88, prof. emeritus, 1988—; drama critic Harvard Crimson, 1953-82, Bay State Banner, 1975—, This Month on Stage, 1996— ; trustee Charles Playhouse, Boston, 1966-71. Editor: The Art of Fine Words, 1965, The Furies (Lucien Price), 1988; co-editor: Varieties of Black Experience at Harvard, 1986, Blacks at Harvard: A Documentary History of African-American Experience at Harvard and Radcliffe, 1993; contbr. articles to profl. jours., ency.; composer stage and film music scores. Bd. dirs. Cambridge Civic Symphony Orch., Mass., 1959-70; exec. bd. Mus. Fine Arts Friends Music, Boston, 1959-65; panelist Mass. Commn. Arts and Humanities, 1981-83; mem. selection com. Theater Hall of Fame, 1980—; juror Elliot Norton awards, 1985—; pres. Boston Theater Critics Assn., 1994—. With U.S. Army, 1944-46, PTO; with Mil. Intelligence Res., 1946-50. Mem. AAUP, Coll. Music Soc., Am. Theatre Critics Assn. (charter), New Eng. Theatre Conf. (adv. coun. 1961-81, coll. fellows 1981—), Am. Guild Organists, Am. Musicol. Soc. (coun. 1965-67), Soc. for Ethnomusicology, Hist. Brass Soc., Signet Soc., Sonneck Soc., Phi Beta Kappa (sec. Mu chpt. Mass. 1984—). Avocations: philology; Afro-Am. history and culture. Office: Brandeis U Music Dept South St Waltham MA 02254-9110

TITE, JOHN GREGORY, secondary school educator; b. Southbridge, Mass., Sept. 20, 1941; s. Gregory Louca and Androniq (Zhidro) T. BS, U. Mass., 1963; MEd, Worcester (Mass.) State Coll., 1966; MS, Clarkson Coll. Tech., 1971. Instr. math. Grafton (Mass.) Pub. Schs., 1963-67, math. dept. chairperson, calculus instr., 1967—; adj. prof. calculus Anna Maria Coll., Paxton, Mass., 1986-88; in-svc. instr. metrics for h.s. and elem. tchrs., 1974-76; spkr. in field. Grantee NSF, 1965, 67, 75, Computer Assisted Math Project grant U. Mass., 1985-86. Mem. Assn. of Tchrs. of Math. in Mass. (pres., exhibits chmn. 1970), Nat. Coun. Suprs. of Math., Nat. Coun. of Tchrs. of Math. (chmn. films and filmstrips com. 1973, chmn. sales of materials 1976), Neighborhood Assn. of Math. Dept. Heads (bd. dirs. 1976-79). Avocations: reading, traveling, walking. Home: 12 Arrowhead Ave Auburn MA 01501-2302 Office: Grafton Pub Schs 24 Providence Rd Grafton MA 01519-1178

TITLE, GAIL MIGDAL, lawyer; b. Waldenberg, Germany, May 31, 1946. AB, Wellesley Coll., 1967; JD, U. Calif., Berkeley, 1970. Bar: Calif. 1971. With Rosenfeld, Meyer & Susman, Beverly Hills; adj. prof. law Loyola U., 1976-96. Mem. ABA (litigation sect., forum com. entertainment), Assn. Bus. Trial Lawyers, State Bar Calif. (standing com. pub. interest law 1976—), L.A. County Bar Assn. (del. conf. dels. 1974-76, 88-89), Beverly Hills Bar Assn. Office: Katten Muchin & Zavis 1999 Ave Of Stars Los Angeles CA 90067-6022

TITLE, PETER STEPHEN, lawyer; b. New Orleans, Nov. 24, 1950; s. Harold Benjamin and Beulah (Sterbcow) T.; m. Sheryl Gerber, June 14, 1981. B.A., Columbia U., 1972; J.D., Tulane U., 1975. Bar: La. 1975, U.S. Dist. Ct. (ea., we., mid. dists.) La., U.S. Ct. Appeals (5th cir.). Assoc. Sessions, Fishman, Rosenson, Boisfontaine, Nathan & Winn, New Orleans, 1975-81, ptnr., 1982—; instr. on property Tulane U., 1978; asst. examiner com. on Admissions to Bar, 1980-88, examiner, 1988—; lectr. on real estate. Author: Louisiana Real Estate Transactions, 1991. Mem. ABA, La. Bar Assn. (chmn. sect. on trust estates, probate and immovable property law 1983-84), New Orleans Bar Assn. (chmn. title examinations com., 1992-93), Rep. Am. Judicature Soc., Order of Coif, Phi Delta Phi. Jewish. Lodge: B'Nai Brith. Home: 515 Hillary St New Orleans LA 70118-3833 Office: Sessions & Fishman 201 Saint Charles Ave Fl 35 New Orleans LA 70170-1000

TITLEY, LARRY J., lawyer; b. Tecumseh, Mich., Dec. 9, 1943; s. Leroy H. and Julia B. (Ruesink) T.; m. Julia Margaret Neukom, May 23, 1970; children: Sarah Catherine, John Neukom. BA, U. Mich., 1965, JD, 1972. Bar: Va. 1973, Mich. 1973. Assoc. Hunton & Williams, Richmond, Va., 1972-73, Varnum, Riddering, Schmidt & Howlett, Grand Rapids, Mich., 1973—. Trustee Friends Pub. Mus., 1985-94; bd. dirs. Pub. Mus. Found., 1988—, pres., 1992-95; bd. dirs. Camp Optimist YMCA, 1993—, Peninsular Club, 1994—, v.p., 1996, pres. 1997. Mem. ABA, Mich. Bar Assn., Grand Rapids Bar Assn. Home: 746 San Jose Dr SE Grand Rapids MI 49506-3418 Office: Varnum Riddering Schmidt & Howlett Bridgewater Pl PO Box 352 Grand Rapids MI 49504

TITLEY, ROBERT L., lawyer; b. Tecumseh, Mich., Dec. 15, 1947. AB, U. Mich., 1970; JD, Duke U., 1973. Bar: Wis. 1973, Mich. 1974. Ptnr. Quarles & Brady, Milw. Mem. editorial bd. Duke Law Jour., 1972-73. Mem. ABA, State Bar Mich., State Bar Wis., Order of Coif. Office: Quarles & Brady 411 E Wisconsin Ave Milwaukee WI 53202-4409

TITLOW, LARRY WAYNE, physical education and kinesiology educator; b. Hearne, Tex., Oct. 12, 1945; s. Stanford P. and Mary Ellen (Bostick) T. BS, U. Houston, 1969, MEd, 1970; PhD, Tex. A&M, 1977. Asst. prof. No. Ky. U., Highland Heights, 1977-82; assoc. prof. U. Cen. Ark., Conway, 1982-89, prof., 1989—; fitness cons. Acxiom, Conway, Ark., 1986-91; rsch. cons. U.. Ark., Fayetteville, 1983—. Author: (with D.K. Cobb, W.G. Smith and M.E. Norman) A Resource Manual for Workshops on Presenting the Educational Improvement Plan to the Communnity, 1980, (with M.E. Gray) Lifetime Fitness, 1981, (with A. Machen) Principles of Kinesiology and Physical Education, 1994, (with D.J. Johnson) Research Methods in Kinesiology and Physical Education. Instr. lifesaving ARC, Conway, 1983-91. Rsch. grantee DaVinci Lab., Burlington, Vt., 1980, Ky. Coun. on Higher Edn., Lexington, 1980, U. Cen. Ark. Rsch. Coun., 1985, 89. Mem. Am. Alliance for Health, Phys. Edn., Recreation and Dance (active various coms., assemblies, rsch. coun. so. dist.), Am. Coll. Sports Medicine (Cen. States chpt.), Ark. Assn. Health, Phys. Edn., Recreation and Dance (pres., other offices), others. Avocations: sailing, scuba diving, travel, hunting, fishing. Office: U Cen Arkansas PO Box 4991 Conway AR 72035

TITONE, VITO JOSEPH, judge; b. Bklyn., July 5, 1929; s. Vito and Elena (Ruisi) T.; m. Margaret Anne Viola, Dec. 30, 1956; children: Stephen, Matthew, Elena Titone Hill, Elizabeth. BA, NYU, 1951; JD, St. John's U., 1956, LL.D., 1984. Bar: N.Y. 1957, U.S. Dist. Ct. (ea. and so. dists.) N.Y., 1962, U.S. Supreme Ct. 1964. Ptnr. Maltese & Titone, N.Y.C., 1957-65, Maltese, Titone & Anastasi, N.Y.C., 1965-68; assoc. counsel to pres. pro tem N.Y. State Senate, 1965; justice N.Y. State Supreme Ct, N.Y.C., 1969-75; assoc. justice appellate div. 2d dept., 1975-85; judge N.Y. State Ct. Appeals, Albany, 1985—; adj. prof. Coll. S.I., CUNY, 1969-72, St. John's U., Jamaica, N.Y., 1969-85. Contbr. articles to law jour. Bd. govs. Daytop Village Inc., N.Y.C.; bd. dirs. Boy Scouts Am. With U.S. Army, 1951-53, to col. N.Y. State Guard. Named Citizen of Yr. Daytop Village, N.Y.C., 1969, Disting. Citizen Wagner Coll., S.I., 1983, Outstanding Contbr. Camelot Substance Abuse Network, 1983; recipient citation of merit S.I. Salvation Army Adv. Bd., 1983, Rapollo award Columbian Lawyers Assn., 1983, Disting. Judiciary award Cath. Lawyers Guild Diocese of Bklyn., 1991, Disting. Svc. award N.Y. State Lawyers Assn., Justice William Brennan award N.Y. Assn. Criminal Def. Lawyers, 1993. Mem. ABA, N.Y. State Bar Assn., Richmond County Bar Assn., Supreme Ct. Justice Assn., VFW, Am. Legion (past comdr.), Charles C. Pinckney Tribute Def. Assn. of N.Y., Justinian Soc., K.C. Roman Catholic. Office: NY Ct Appeals 20 Eagle St Albany NY 12207-1004 also: 60 Bay St Fl 9 Staten Island NY 10301-2514

TITTMANN, BERNHARD RAINER, engineering science and mechanics educator; b. Moshi, Tanganjika, East Africa, Sept. 15, 1935; came to U.S., 1950, naturalized, 1956; s. Gustav and Hermine Marie (Polland) T.; m. Katharine Shower, Dec. 17, 1966; children: Christine M., Heidi E., Raymond J., Monica M., Brian P.F. BS, George Washington U., 1957; MS, UCLA, 1961, PhD, 1965. Mem. staff Hughes Aircraft Co., Culver City, Calif., 1957-65; asst. prof. UCLA, 1965-66; mem. staff Rockwell Internat., Thousand Oaks, Calif., 1966-79, dept. mgr., 1979-89; Schell prof. engrng. Pa. State U., University Park, 1989—. Co-author 5 books; contbr. over 200 articles to profl. jours.; patentee in field. George Washington fellow George Washington U., 1953, Howard Hughes fellow Hughes Aircraft Co., 1957. Fellow IEEE (adminstrv. com. for ultrasonics, ferroelectrics, frequency control, nominating chmn. 1988—); mem. Acoustical Soc. Am. (tech. program mem. 1986-89), KC (4th degree), Phi Beta Kappa. Home: 2466 Sassafras Ct State College PA 16803-3366 Office: Pa State U 210 Hallowell Bldg University Park PA 16802-6804

TITUS, ALICE CESTANDINA (DINA TITUS), state legislator; b. Thomasville, Ga., May 23, 1950. AB, Coll. William and Mary, 1970; MA, U. Ga., 1973; PhD, Fla. State U., 1976. Prof. polit. sci. U. Nev., Las Vegas; mem. Nev. Senate, 1989—; alt. mem. legis. commn., 1989-91, mem., 1991-93; minority floor leader, 1993—; chmn. Nev. Humanities Com., 1984-86; mem. Eldorado Basin adv. group to Colo. River Commn.; active Gov. Commn. Bicentennial of U.S. Constn.; former mem. Gov. Commn. on Aging. Author: Bombs in the Backyard: Atomic Testing and American Politics, 1986, Battle Born: Federal-State Relations in Nevada during the 20th Century, 1989. Mem. Western Polit. Sci. Assn., Clark County Women's Dem. Club. Greek Orthodox. Home: 1637 Travois Cir Las Vegas NV 89119-6283 Office: Nev State Senate State Capitol Carson City NV 89710*

TITUS, BRUCE E., lawyer; b. N.Y.C., June 5, 1942. BA, Coll. William and Mary, 1964, JD, 1971. Bar: Va. 1971, D.C. 1972, Md. 1984. Asst. dir. torts br., civil divsn. U.S. Dept. Justice, 1979-81; ptnr. Venable, Baetjer and Howard, LLP, McLean, Va. Exec. editor William & Mary Law Review, 1970-71. Mem. ABA, Va. State Bar, D.C. Bar, Md. State Bar, Phi Delta Phi, Omicron Delta Kappa. Office: Venable Baetjer and Howard LLP 2010 Corporate Rdg Ste 400 Mc Lean VA 22102-7838

TITUS, CHRISTINA MARIA, lawyer; b. Phila., Oct. 31, 1950; d. George Herman and Frieda Anna (Szuchy) T.; m. Richard Christopher Daddario, Jan. 19, 1980; children: Alexandra Daddario, Matthew Daddario, Catharine Daddario. BA, NYU, 1972; JD, Georgetown U., 1977. Bar: N.Y. 1978, U.S. Dist. Ct. N.Y. (so. and ea. dists.) 1979. Assoc. Trubin Sillcocks Edelman & Knapp, N.Y.C., 1977-80; v.p., counsel Merrill Lynch, Hubbard, Inc., N.Y.C., 1980—. Recipient 1st prize Drexel Keyboard Competition, 1968. Mem. ABA, N.Y. State Bar Assn. (mem. com. on real estate financing and liens real property law sect.), Assn. of Bar of City of N.Y. Lutheran.

TITUS, EDWARD DEPUE, psychiatrist, administrator; b. N.Y.C., May 24, 1931; s. Edward Kleinhans and Mary (Brown) Chadbourne; m. Virginia Van Den Steenhoven, Mar. 24, 1963 (div.); m. Catherine Brown, Apr. 22, 1990. BA, Occidental Coll., 1953; MS, U. Wis., 1955; MD, Stanford U., 1962; PhD, So. Calif. Psychoanalytic Inst., 1977. Mng. ptnr. Hacker Clinic Assn., Lynwood, Calif., 1968-90; chief psychiatrist parole outpatient clinic region III Calif. Dept. Corrections, L.A., 1991—; asst. clin. prof. psychiatry U. So. Calif., 1993—; chmn. dept. psychiatry St. Francis Hosp., Lynwood, 1979-80. Fellow Am. Psychiat. Assn.; mem. Calif. Med. Assn. (ho. of dels. 1981-95), So. Calif. Psychiat. Soc. (sec. 1984-85), Los Angeles County Med. Assn. (dist. pres. 1980-81, pres. sect. psychiatry 1990-92). Avocations: photography, backpacking. Office: Parole Outpatient Clinic 307 W 4th St Los Angeles CA 90013-1104

TITUS, JACK L., pathologist, educator; b. South Bend, Ind., Dec. 7, 1926; s. Loren O. and Rutha B. (Orr) T.; m. Beverly Harden, June 18, 1949; children—Jack, Elizabeth Ann Titus Engelbrecht, Michael, Matthew, Joan. B.S., Notre Dame U., 1948; M.D., Washington U., St. Louis, 1952; Ph.D., U. Minn., 1962. Practice medicine Rensselaer, Ind., 1953-57; fellow in pathology U. Minn., 1957-61; assoc. prof. pathology Mayo Grad. Sch., Rochester, Minn., 1961-72; prof. pathology Mayo Med. Sch., 1971-72, coordinator pathology tng. programs, 1964-72; W.L. Moody Jr. prof., chmn. dept. pathology Baylor Coll. Medicine, Houston, 1972-87; chief pathology service Meth. Hosp., Houston, 1972-87; pathologist-in-chief Harris County Hosp. Dist., Houston, 1972-87; chmn. dept. pathology Med. Ctr. Hosp., Conroe, Tex., 1982-87, Woodlands Community Hosp., 1984-87; dir. registry for cardiovascular diseases United Hosp., 1987-95, sr. cons. registry, 1996—; clin. prof. pathology U. Minn., 1987—; adj. prof. pathology Baylor Coll. Medicine, 1987—; sr. cons. in pathology U. Tex. System Cancer Ctr., Houston, 1974—. Mem. editl. bd. Circulation, 1966-72, Am. Heart Jour., 1972-77, Modern Pathology, 1987-95, Human Pathology, 1988—, Am. Jour. of Cardiovascular Pathology, 1987-94, Cardiovascular Pathology, 1991—; contbr. articles to med. jours. Served with U.S. Army, 1945-47. Recipient Billings gold medal AMA, 1968, Hoektoen gold medal, 1969, Disting. Achievement award Soc. Cardiovascular Pathology, 1993, Scholarly Achievement award Houston Soc. Clin. Pathology, 1993. Mem. Internat. Acad. Pathology, Am. Assn. Pathologists, Am. Soc. Clin. Pathologists, AAAS, AMA, Am. Heart Assn., Coll. Am. Pathologists, Minn. Med. Assn., Minn. Heart Assn., Minn. Soc. Clin. Pathologists, Ramsey County Med. Soc., Sigma Xi, Alpha Omega Alpha. Methodist. Office: 255 Smith Ave N Ste 200 Saint Paul MN 55102-2518

TITUS, ROGER WARREN, lawyer; b. Washington, Dec. 16, 1941; s. George R. and Margaret (Merithew) T.; m. Catherine Mary Gaughen, Aug. 16, 1961; children: Paula Titus Laboy, Richard Roger, Mark William. BA, Johns Hopkins U., 1963; JD, Georgetown U., 1966. Bar: Md. 1966, D.C. 1966, U.S. Dist. Ct. Md. 1966, D.C. Dist. 1966, U.S. Ct. Appeals (4th cir.) 1966, U.S. Supreme Ct. 1970. Ptnr. Titus & Glasgow, Rockville, Md., 1966-88, Venable, Baetjer & Howard, Rockville, 1988—; asst. city atty. City of Rockville, 1966-69, city atty., 1970-82; spl. asst. Md. State Bd. of Law Examiners, 1969-72; adj. prof. law Georgetown U., Washington, 1972-78; mem. inquiry com. Atty. Grievance Commn., Annapolis, Md., 1975-80; mem. Trial Cts. Judicial Nominating Commn. Montgomery County, 1979-91; mem. standing com. on rules of practice and procedure Ct. of Appeals of Md., 1989—; mem. Appellate Jud. Nominating Commn., 1991—. Trustee Suburban Hosp., Inc., Bethesda, Md., 1986—, chmn. bd., 1997—. Fellow Am. Coll. Trial Lawyers, Am. Bar Found., Md. Bar Found. (bd. dirs. 1987-93, v.p. 1990-91, pres. 1991-93); mem. ABA (del. 1987-95), Nat. Conf. Bar Pres. (mem. exec. coun. 1990-93), Md. Bar Assn. (sec. 1984-87, pres. 1988-89), Am. Judicature Soc. (bd. dirs. 1995—), Md. Mcpl. Attys. Assn. (pres. 1975), Montgomery County Bar Assn. (exec. com. 1983-84), City Tavern Club. Office: Venable Baetjer & Howard PO Box 1906 1 Church St Ste 1000 Rockville MD 20850-4158

TITUS, VICTOR ALLEN, lawyer; b. Nevada, Mo., Sept. 2, 1956; s. Charles Allen and Viola Mae (Cliffman) T.; m. Laraine Carol Cook, Oct. 13, 1974 (div. Feb. 1982); 1 child, Matthew; m. Deborah Diane Carpenter, Apr. 10, 1984; 1 child, Jacquelynn. BS, Ctrl. Mo. State U., 1978, BA, 1978; JD, U. Mo., 1981. Bar: N.Mex. 1981, U.S. Dist. Ct. N.Mex. 1981, Mo. 1982, U.S. Ct. Appeals (10th cir. 1983), U.S. Supreme Ct. 1986, Colo. 1989. Lawyer Jay L. Faurot, P.C., Farmington, N.Mex., 1981-83; ptnr. Faurot & Titus, P.C., Farmington, N.Mex., 1983-85; lawyer, sole proprietor Victor A. Titus, P.C., Farmington, N.Mex., 1985—; arbitrator in civil disputes Alternative Dispute Resolution-Arbitration; liquor lic. hearing officer City of Farmington, 1989-94. Contbr. articles to profl. jours. Adult Behind Youth, Boys & Girls Club, Farmington, 1987—; mem. hosp. adv. bd. San Juan Regional Med. Ctr., Farmington, 1988-93. Recipient San Juan County Disting. Svc. award N.Mex. Bar Assn., 1984; named one of Best Lawyers in Am., 1995-96. Mem. Assn. Trial Lawyers of Am., N.Mex. Trial Lawyers (bd. pres. 1983—, pres. 1993-94), State Bar of N.Mex. (specialization com. 1992—, legal advt. com. 1990), San Juan County Bar Assn. (pres. 1984), Nat. Assn. Criminal Def. Lawyers, Colo. Trial Lawyers. Democrat. Avocation: sports. Home: 5711 Tee Dr Farmington NM 87402-0933 Office: Victor A Titus PC 2021 E 20th St Farmington NM 87401-2516

TITZE, INGO ROLAND, physics educator; b. Hirschberg, Silesia, Germany, July 8, 1941; came to U.S. 1955; s. Kurt Herrmann and Marta Emma (Bettermann) T.; m. R. Katherine Pittard, July 19, 1969; children: Karin, Michael, Jason, Gregory. BSEE, U. Utah, 1963, MS in Elec. Engring. and Physics, 1965; Ph.D. in Physics, Brigham Young U., 1972. Rsch. engr. N. Am. Aviation, Tulsa, 1965-66, Boeing Co., Seattle, 1968-70; lectr. Calif. State Poly. U., Pomona, 1973-74; asst. prof. U. Petroleum and Minerals Dhahran, Saudi Arabia, 1974-76, Gallaudet Coll., Washington, 1976-79; disting. prof. speech sci. and voice U. Iowa, Iowa City, 1979—; cons. Bell Labs., Murray Hill, N.J., 1977-78; exec. dir. Wilbur James Gould Voice Rsch. Ctr., Denver Ctr. Performing Arts, 1983—; pres. Voice Cons. Inc., 1985—; panelist, site visitor NRC-NAS, 1984—; regular cons. divsn. rsch. grants NIH, 1986—; chmn. task force on voice Nat. Inst. Deafness and Other Comm. Disorders, 1989; adj. prof. Westminster Choir Coll., Princeton, N.J., 1989-94; dir. Nat. Ctr. for Voice and Speech, 1990—. Author: Principles of Voice Production, 1993; editor: Vocal Fold Physiology: Biomechanics, Acoustics and Phonatory Control, 1985, Vocal Fold Physiology: Frontiers in Basic Science, 1992; assoc. editor Jour. of Voice; contbr. articles to profl. jours. Adv. bd. Voice Found., N.Y.C., 1980—; young men's pres. Latter Day Saints Ch. and Boy Scouts Am., Iowa City, 1982—. Jacob Javits Neurosci. Investigator grantee NIH, 1984; recipient William and Harriot Gould Found. award, 1983, Claude Pepper award, 1989, Quintant award Voice Found., 1990, fellow ASHA, 1992, Am. Laryngological Assn. award, 1996. Fellow Acoustical Soc. Am. (tech. council, awards com. 1989); mem. Am. Speech-Hearing-Lang. Assn., Nat. Assn. Tchrs. Singing (research council 1977—, editorial bd. 1986—), Internat. Assn. Research Singing (dir. publs. 1982—). Republican. Avocations: classical singing; tennis; choir directing; home building. Home: 2015 Glendale Rd Iowa City IA 52245-3217 Office: Nat Ctr for Voice & Speech Univ of Iowa 330 Wjshc Iowa City IA 52242-1012

TIVENAN, CHARLES PATRICK, lawyer; b. Newark, Feb. 20, 1954; s. Gerard Charles and Mary Jo (Vogel) T.; m. Mary Katherine Herlihy, Aug. 2, 1980; children: Moire Kathleen, Sean Patrick, Liam Francis, Michala Maureen. BA in Govt., Seton Hall U., 1975, JD, 1980. Bar: N.J. 1982, U.S. Dist. Ct. N.J. 1982, U.S. Supreme Ct. 1995. Law clk. Essex County Prosecutor's Office, Newark, summer 1978, Dwyer Connell & Lisbona, Attys., Montclair, N.J., 1978-79; legal rsch. asst. Inst. Continuing Legal Edn., Newark, 1979; jud. law clk. to Hon. John J. Dios Superior Ct., Newark, 1981-82; assoc. Timothy J. Provost, Atty., Freehold, N.J., 1982-85, Arthur Stein & Assocs., Forked River, N.J., 1985-92; sole practice Bricktown, N.J., 1992—; mediator, Early Settlement panelist Superior Ct. N.J/Ocean County, Toms River, N.J., 1987—. Mem. juvenile conf. com. South Orange (N.J.) JCC, 1974-81; condemnation commr. Ocean County, Toms River, 1986—; conflict atty. Brick Twp., Bricktown, 1994—; candidate Brick Twp. Coun., 1992; active Bricktown Dem. Club, trustee 1995—. Recipient Cert. of Appreciation, Ocean County Superior Ct., 1987—, certs. of appreciation various orgns., 1985—. Mem. ABA, N.J. Bar Assn. (gen. practice, family law 1985—), Am. Trial Lawyers Assn. (N.J. affiliate, lectr. 1985—), Ocean County Bar Assn. (family law com. 1985—), KC (3d degree). Roman Catholic. Avocations: reading, current events/politics, semi-competitive running, computers. Office: Godfrey Lake Profl Bldg 426 Herbertsville Rd Brick NJ 08724-1310

TIZZIO, THOMAS RALPH, brokerage executive; b. Elmont, N.Y., Jan. 9, 1938; s. Anthony Thomas and Ann Marie (Pascale) T.; m. Mary Ann Gentile, Aug. 26, 1962; children: Anthony, Vincent, Thomas. BBA, Bklyn. Coll., 1962. Underwriter W.J. Roberts & Co., N.Y.C., 1957-65; sr. underwriter Atlantic Mut. Ins. Co., 1965-67; various positions AIG Am. Home Assurance Co., N.Y.C., 1967-74, sr. v.p. property underwriting, 1974-78; exec. v.p. AIG Transatlantic Reins. Co., N.Y.C., 1978-80, pres., bd. dirs., 1980-82; sr. v.p. reins. Am. Internat. Group, Inc., N.Y.C., 1982-85, pres. domestic brokerage divsn., 1985-91, pres. Brokerage divsn., 1986-91, pres., 1991—. Mem. Am. Inst. for Property and Liability Underwriters (trustee), Ins. Inst. Am. (trustee). Office: Am Internat Group Inc 70 Pine St New York NY 10270-0002

TJIAN, ROBERT TSE NAN, bichemistry educator, biology resercher, virology researcher; b. Hong Kong, Sept. 22, 1949; naturalized Brit. citizen.; m. 1976. BA, U. Calif., Berkeley, 1971; PhD in Molecular Biology, Harvard U., 1976. Staff investigator molecular virology Cold Spring Harbor Lab., 1976-79, Robertson fellow, 1978; prof. biochemistry U. Calif., Berkeley, 1979—. Named Passano Found. laureate; recipient Lewis S. Rosentiel award for disting. work in basic med. rsch. Brandeis U., 1995. Mem. NAS (Molecular Biology award 1991). Achievements include research in oncogenic viruses and their interctions with the host cell; control of gene expression; simian virus 40; a small DNA containing oncogenic virus, tumor antigen, its structure and function. Office: Univ Calif Dept Biochemistry 401 Barker Hall Berkeley CA 94720-3203

TJOFLAT, GERALD BARD, federal judge; b. Pitts., Dec. 6, 1929; s. Gerald Benjamin and Sarita (Romero-Hermoso) T.; m. Sarah Marie Pfohl, July 27, 1957 (dec.); children: Gerald Bard, Marie Elizabeth. Student, U. Va., 1947-50, U. Cin., 1950-52; LL.B., Duke U., 1957; D.C.L. (hon.), Jacksonville U., 1978; LLD (hon.), William Mitchell Coll. Law, 1993. Bar: Fla. 1957. Individual practice law Jacksonville, Fla., 1957-68; judge 4th Jud. Cir. Ct. Fla., 1968-70, U.S. Dist. Ct. for Middle Dist. Fla., Jacksonville, 1970-75, U.S. Ct. Appeals, 5th Cir., Jacksonville, 1975-81; judge U.S. Ct. Appeals, 11th Cir., Jacksonville, 1996—, chief judge, 1989-96; mem. Adv. Corrections Coun. U.S., 1975-87, Jud. Conf. of U.S., 1989—, Fed. Jud. Ctr. Com. on Sentencing, Probation and Pretrial Svcs., 1988-90; mem. com. adminstrn. probation system Jud. Conf. of U.S., 1972-87, chmn., 1978-87; U.S. del. 6th and 7th UN Congress for Prevention of Crime and Treatment of Offenders. Hon. life mem., bd. visitors Duke U. Law Sch.; pres. North Fla. coun. Boy Scouts Am., 1976-85, chmn., 1985-90; trustee Jacksonville Marine Inst., 1976-90, Episc. H.S., Jacksonville, 1975-90; mem. vestry St. Johns Cathedral, Jacksonville, 1969-71, 73-75, 77-79, 81-83, 85-87, 93, 95-96, sr. warden, 1975, 83, 87, 91, 92. Served with AUS, 1953-55. Recipient Merit award Duke U., 1990, Fordham-Stein prize, 1996. Mem. ABA, Fla. Bar Assn., Am. Law Inst., Am. Judicature Soc. Episcopalian. Office: US Ct Appeals 311 W Monroe St Rm 539 Jacksonville FL 32202

TKACHUK, KEITH, professional hockey player; b. Melrose, Mass., Mar. 28, 1972. With Phoenix Coyotes formerly Winnipeg (Canada) Jets, 1992—. Named to Hockey East All-Rookie team, 1990-91, NHL All-Star second team, 1994-95, Sporting News All-Star team, 1996. Office: Phoenix Coyotes 2 N Central Ste 1930 1 Renaissance Sq Phoenix AZ 85004

TKACZUK, NANCY ANNE, cardiovascular services administrator; b. Cambridge, Mass., Nov. 17, 1949; d. Ralph Aubrey and Eleanor Mae (Godding) Bedley; m. John Paul Tkaczuk, Apr. 9, 1977 (div. Apr. 1983); children: Timothy Aubrey, James Paul. AS in Social Svc., Endicott Coll., 1969; ADN, Clayton Coll., 1975. Coronary care nurse New England Meml. Hosp., Wakefield, Mass., 1975; cardiac cath lab nurse Saint Josephs Hosp., Atlanta, 1976-79; dir. cardiovascular svcs. Northside Hosp., Atlanta, 1979—; founder Mitral Valve Prolapse Support, Atlanta, 1986—; BCLS instr., trainer Am. Heart Assn., 1976—, instr. ACLS, 1990—, pub. spkr., 1975—. Author: Mitral Valve Prolapse, The Heart With A Different Beat, 1986. Mem. Am. Coll. Cardiovascular Adminstrs., Atlanta Health Care Alliance. Methodist. Avocation: tennis. Home: 715 Cranberry Trail Roswell GA 30076 Office: Northside Hosp Cardiology Dept 1000 Johnson Ferry Rd NE Atlanta GA 30342-1606

TLOU, JOSIAH S., education educator; b. Zimbabwe, Dec. 31, 1935; s. Litsila and Mothateho T.; m. Litha T., Sept. 3, 1959; children: Lee, Hla, Joy B., Leeto. BA, Luther Coll., 1968; MA, Ill. State U., 1969; EdD, U. Ill., 1976. Cons. curriculum Glencoe (Ill.) Pub. Schs.; specialist social studies USAID U. Botswana, Gaborone; assoc. prof. Va. Tech., Blacksburg; civic curriculum planner for U.S. AID project Creative Assocs. Internat./Harvard Inst. Internat. Devel., Malawi, 1996—; Cert. tchr., Zimbabwe. Contbr. articles to profl. jours. Recipient Disting. Svcs. award Luther Coll.; Luce-Bergeson rsch. grantee, African-Am., Scholars Coun. grantee, Creative Univ. Rsch. grantee, 1991-92, 94-95. Mem. ASCD, WCCI, Nat. Coun. Social Studies, ASA, AAPRDTW, Botswana Edn. Rsch. Assn., Phi Delta Kappa. Office: USAID Malawi Lilongwe Dept State Washington DC 20521-2280

TOAL, JAMES FRANCIS, academic administrator; b. N.Y.C., June 7, 1932; s. John Joseph and Catherine (Whyte) T. MA, St. John's U., 1966; PhD, Fordham U., 1976. Cert. elem. tchr., N.Y. cert. supt., adminstrn. and supervision, English 7-12. Athletic dir., tchr. English St. Francis Prep. High Sch., N.Y.C., 1957-60; tchr. Bishop Ford High Sch., N.Y.C., 1960-66, chmn. dept. English; prin. St. Francis Central Summer High Sch., N.Y.C., 1966-73, St. Francis Prep. High Sch., N.Y.C., 1966-73; exec. v.p., assoc. prof. dept. edn. adminstrn. and supervision Grad. Sch. St. Bonaventure U., N.Y., 1976-83; pres., prof. Quincy U., Ill., 1983—; also bd. trustees; mem. Springfield Diocesan Bd. of Edn., Provincial Bd. of Edn., Franciscan Friars of Chgo. and St. Louis. Trustee Siena Coll., Loudonville, N.Y., 1977-83; bd. advisors Jamestown Community Coll., Olean, N.Y., 1979-83; bd. dirs. Am. Cancer Soc., Olean, 1981-83; mem. Mental Health Assn., 1981-83; mem. state legis. com. Commn. of Ind. Colls. and Univs., Albany, N.Y., 1980-83; mem. bd. trustees Padua Franciscan High Sch. Grantee Colgate U., 1967; grantee SUNY-Plattsburg, 1968, St. Bonaventure U., 1980. Mem. Am. Coun. on Edn., Associated Colls. of Ill., Ill. Bus. and Edn. Forum, Assn. of Governing Bds., West Ctrl. Ill. Edni. Telecomm. Corp. (bd. dirs. exec. com., fin. com., pers. com.), Fedn. Ind. Ill. Colls. and Univs. (pub. rels. com.), Mid. States Accrediting Assn. (assoc., evaluation team for higher edn.), Nat. Assn. Secondary Sch. Prins., North Ctrl. Accrediting Assn. (evaluation team for higher edn., chair evaluation team 1986—), Soc. Coll. and U. Planning, Quincy C. of C. (transp. com. 1985-96, computer com. 1996—), Rotary, Univ. Club, KC, Phi Delta Kappa. Office: Quincy Univ Office of Pres 1800 College Ave Quincy IL 62301-2670

TOAL, JEAN HOEFER, state supreme court justice, lawyer; b. Columbia, S.C., Aug. 11, 1943; d. Herbert W. and Lilla (Farrell) Hoefer; m. William Thomas Toal; children: Jean Hoefer, Lilla Patrick. BA in Philosophy, Agnes Scott Coll., 1965; JD, U. S.C., 1968; LHD (hon.), Coll. Charleston, 1991; LLD (hon.), Columbia Coll., 1992. Bar: S.C. Assoc. Haynsworth, Perry, Bryant, Marion & Johnstone, 1968-70; ptnr. Belser, Baker, Barwick, Ravenel, Toal & Bender, Columbia, 1970-88; assoc. justice S.C. Supreme Ct., 1988—; mem. S.C. Human Affairs Commn., 1972-74; mem. S.C. Ho. of Reps., 1975-88, chmn. house rules com., constitutional laws subcom. house judiciary com.; mem. parish coun. and lector St. Joseph's Cath. Ch.; chair S.C. Juvenile Justice Task Force, 1992-94; chair S.C. Rhodes Scholar Selection Com., 1994. Mng. editor S.C. Law Rev., 1967-68. Bd. visitors Clemson U., 1978; trustee Columbia Mus. Art. Named Legislator of Yr. Greenville News, Woman of Yr., U. S.C.; recipient Disting. Svc. award S.C. Mcpl. Assn., Univ. Notre Dame award, 1991, Algernon Sydney Sullivan award U. S.C., 1991. Mem. John Belton O'Neill Inn of Ct., Phi Beta Kappa, Mortar Bd., Order of the Coif. Office: Supreme Ct SC PO Box 12456 Columbia SC 29211-2456

TOALE, THOMAS EDWARD, school system administrator, priest; b. Independence, Iowa, Aug. 30, 1953; s. Francis Mark and Clara R. (DePaepe) T. BS in Biology, Loras Coll., 1975, MA in Edni. Adminstrn., 1986; MA in Theology, St. Paul Sem., 1980; PhD in Ednl. Adminstrn., U. Iowa, 1988. Ordained priest Roman Cath. Ch., 1981; cert. tchr., prin., supt., Iowa. Tchr. St. Joseph Key West, Dubuque, Iowa, 1975-77; tchr. Marquette High Sch., Bellevue, Iowa, 1981-84, prin., 1984-86; assoc. supt. Archdiocese of Dubuque, 1986-87, supt. schs., 1987—; assoc. pastor St. Joseph Ch., Bellevue, 1981-84; pastor Sts. Peter and Paul Ch., Springbrook, Iowa, 1984-86, St. Peter, Temple Hill, Cascade, Iowa, 1986—. Mem. Nat. Cath. Edn. Assn. Office: Archdiocese of Dubuque 1229 Mount Loretta Ave Dubuque IA 52003-7826

TOBACCOWALA, RISHAD, marketing professional; b. Bombay, India, 1959. BA in Maths., U. Bombay, 1979; MBA, U. Chgo., 1982. Media buyer Leo Burnett USA, Chgo., 1982-84, account supr., 1984-92, v.p., account dir. direct mkg., 1992-94, dir. interactive mktg., 1994-96; pres. Giant Step, Chgo., 1996—. Office: Giant Step 820 W Jackson Blvd Chicago IL 60607*

TOBACH, ETHEL, retired curator; b. Miaskovka, USSR, Nov. 7, 1921; came to U.S., 1923; d. Ralph Wiener and Fanny (Schechterman) Wiener Idels; m. Charles Tobach, 1947 (dec. 1969). BA, Hunter Coll., 1949; MA, NYU, 1952, PhD, 1957; DSc (hon.), L.I. Univ., 1975. Lic. psychologist, N.Y. Rsch. fellow Am. Mus. Natural History, N.Y.C., 1958-61, assoc. curator, 1964-69, curator, 1969-90, emerita curator; rsch. fellow NYU, N.Y.C., 1961-64; adj. prof. psychology CUNY, N.Y.C., 1964—. Co-editor: (series) T.C. Schneirla Conference Series, 1981, Genes & Gender, 1975; editor: International Jour. Comparative Psychology, 1987-93; assoc. editor: Peace and Conflict: Jour. of Peace Psychology, 1994—. Recipient Disting. Sci. Career, Assn. Women in Sci., 1974, Disting. Sci. Publ., Assn. for Women in Psychology, 1982, Kurt Lewin award Soc. for Psychol. Study of Social Issues, 1993, Gustavus Myers award for outstanding pub. on human rights in N.Am., 1996. Fellow APA (pres. comparative psychology div. 1985); mem. Internat. Soc. Comparative Psychology (sec. 1988-92), Ea. Psychol. Assn. (pres. 1987), N.Y. Acad. Scis. (v.p. behavioral scis. 1973-76). Office: Am Mus Natural History Central Pkwy 79th St New York NY 10024-5192

TOBE, STEPHEN SOLOMON, zoology educator; b. Niagara-on-the-Lake, Ont., Can., Oct. 11, 1944; s. John Harold and Rose T. (Bolter) T.; m. Martha Reller. BSc, Queen's U., Kingston, Ont., 1967; MSc, York U., Toronto, Ont., 1969; PhD, McGill U., Montreal, Que., Can., 1972. Rsch. fellow U. Sussex, Eng., 1972-74; asst. prof. U. Toronto, 1974-78, assoc. prof., 1974-78, prof., 1982—, assoc. dean scis., faculty arts and sci., 1988-93, vice dean faculty arts and sci., 1995-96; vis. prof. U. Calif., Berkeley, 1981, Nat. U. Singapore, 1987, 1993-94, U. Hawaii, 1988; mem. animal biology grant selection com. Natural Scis. and Engring. Rsch. Coun. Can., 1986-89, chair, 1988-89; lectr. Internat. Congress Entomology, Vancouver, B.C., Can., 1988; cons. in hydroponics. Editor Insect Biochemistry, 1987; mem. editl. bd. Jour. Insect Physiology, 1980—, Physiol. Entomology, 1985—, Life Scis. Advances, 1987—, Gen. and Comparative Endocrinology, 1995—; contbr. chpts. to books and articles to profl. jours. Recipient Pickford medal in comparative endocrinology, 1993; E.W.R. Steacie fellow Natural Scis. and Engring. Rsch. Coun. Can., 1982-84. Fellow Royal Soc. Can., Royal Entomol. Soc.; mem. AAAS, Entomol. Soc. Can. (C. Gordon Hewitt award 1982, gold medal 1990), Entomol. Soc. Am., Soc. Exptl. Biology. Avocations: amateur radio, gardening, hydroponics. Home: 467 Soudan Ave, Toronto, ON Canada M4S 1X1 Office: U Toronto Dept Zoology, 25 Harbord St, Toronto, ON Canada M5S 3G5

TOBER, BARBARA D. (MRS. DONALD GIBBS TOBER), editor; b. Summit, N.J., Aug. 19, 1934; d. Rodney Fielding and Maude (Grebbin) Starkey; m. Donald Gibbs Tober, Apr. 5, 1973. Student, Traphagen Sch. Fashion, 1954-56, Fashion Inst. Tech., 1956-58, N.Y. Sch. Interior Design, 1964. Copy editor Vogue Pattern Book, 1958-60; beauty editor Vogue mag., 1961; dir. women's services Bartell Media Corp., 1961-66; editor-in-chief Bride's mag., N.Y.C., 1966-94; chmn. Am. Craft Mus.; pres. Acronym, Inc., N.Y.C., 1995—, The Barbara Tober Found., 1995—; dir. Gen. Brands Corp., sec.-treas.; adv. bd. Traphagen Sch.; coordinator SBA awards; Am. Craft Council Mus. Assoc., 1983—, benefit food com. chmn., 1984-87. Author: The ABC's of Beauty, 1963, China: A Cognizant Guide, 1980, The Wedding . . . The Marriage . . . And the Role of the Retailer, 1980, The Bride: A Celebration, 1984. Mem. Nat. Council on Family Relations, 1966; nat. council Lincoln Center Performing Arts, Met. Opera Guild; mem. NYU adv. bd. Women in Food Service, 1983; NYU Women's Health Symposium: Steering Com., 1983—. Recipient Alma award, 1968, Penney-Mo. award, 1972, Traphagen Alumni award, 1975, Diamond Jubilee award, 1983. Mem. Fashion Group, Nat. Home Fashions League (v.p., program chmn.), Am. Soc. Mag. Editors, Am. Soc. Interior Designers (press mem.), Intercorporate Group, Women in Communications (60 yrs. of success award N.Y. chpt. 1984), Nat. Assn. Underwater Instrs., Pan Pacific and S.E. Asia Women's Assn., Asia Soc., Japan Soc., China Inst., Internat. Side Saddle Orgn., Millbrook Hounds, Golden's Bridge Hounds, Wine and Food Soc., Chaines des Rotisseurs (chargée de press) (bd. dirs.), Dames d'Escoffier, Culinary Inst. Am. Home and Office: 620 Park Ave New York NY 10021-6591*

TOBER, LESTER VICTOR, shoe company executive; b. St. Louis, Dec. 29, 1916; s. Abraham E.M. and Anna (Saifer) T.; m. Sylvia Isenburg, Aug. 4, 1940; children—Neil Steven, Robert Boyd, Cristie Elizabeth. B.S., U. Wis., 1935; postgrad., Washington U., 1936, U. Mo., 1936-39. Sec. Tober-Saifer Shoe Mfg. Co., St. Louis, 1955-65; v.p. Tober-Saifer Shoe Mfg. Co., 1966-68, exec. v.p., 1969-71, pres., 1974—; pres., chief exec. officer Tober Industries, Inc., 1977—; exec. v.p. Crown Shoe Co., 1994—. Active St. Louis Ambassadors, United Fund.; Trustee A.E. Tober Charitable Trust. Served to lt. (j.g.) USNR, 1944-46. Mem. Washington U. Eliot Soc., St. Louis Club, Mo. Athletic Club, Naples (Fla.) Pelican Bay Club, Hideaway Beach Club, Elks, Zeta Beta Tau. Republican. Jewish (pres. temple brotherhood 1957). Home: 19 Maryhill Dr Saint Louis MO 63124-1318 Office: Tober Industries Inc 1520 Washington Ave Saint Louis MO 63103-1817

TOBER, STEPHEN LLOYD, lawyer; b. Boston, May 27, 1949; s. Benjamin Arthur Tober and Lee (Hymoff) Fruman; m. Susan V. Schwartz, Dec. 22, 1973; children: Cary, Jamie. Grad., Syracuse U., 1971, JD, 1974. Bar: N.H. 1974, U.S. Dist. Ct. N.H. 1974, U.S. Supreme Ct. 1978, N.Y. 1981. Assoc. Flynn, McGuirk & Blanchard, Portsmouth, N.H., 1974-79; sole practice Portsmouth, 1979-81; ptnr. Aeschliman & Tober, Portsmouth, 1981-91; prin. Tober Law Offices, P.A., Portsmouth, 1992—; lectr. Franklin Pierce Law Ctr., Concord, N.H., 1978-80. Contbr. articles to law jours. Mem. Portsmouth Charter Commn., 1976, Portsmouth Planning Bd., 1977-81; del. N.H. Constl. Conv., Concord, 1984; city councilman, Portsmouth, 1977-81. Fellow ABA (mem. ho. dels.), Am. Bar Found., N.H. Bar Assn. (pres. 1988-89, chair com. to redraft code of profl. responsibility, Disting. Svc. award, 1986, 94); mem. ATLA (gov. 1980-86), N.H. Trial Lawyers Assn. (pres. 1977), New Eng. Bar Assn. (bd. dirs. 1988-91), Charles Doe Inns of Ct. Democrat. Jewish. Avocations: reading, tennis. Home: 55 T J Gamester Ave Portsmouth NH 03801-5871 Office: Tober Law Offices PA PO Box 1377 Portsmouth NH 03802-1377

TOBEY, ALTON STANLEY, artist; b. Middletown, Conn., Nov. 5, 1914; s. Saul Zilman and Rose (Aaronson) T.; m. Rosalyn S. Caplovitz, Sept. 24, 1950; children: David Seth, Judith Robin. BFA, Yale Sch. Fine Arts, 1937, MFA, 1946. Faculty mem. Yale Sch. of Fine Arts, New Haven, 1946-50, CCNY, N.Y.C., 1951-53; pvt. practice, 1953—; instr. Yale U. Sch. Fine Art, New Haven, City Coll., N.Y.C., 92nd St. Lexington Ave., YMHA, N.Y.C.,; now teaching privately, Larchmont, N.Y. One-man shows include Am. Ctr., Stockholm, Alliance Gallery, Copenhagen, Cape East Gallery, Provincetown, Mass., Pietrantonis Gallery, N.Y.C., Bridge Gallery, White Plains, N.Y., Burliuk Gallery, N.Y.C., Katonah (N.Y.) Gallery, Portrait Gallery, Westport, Conn., Charles Mann Gallery, N.Y.C., Casa de Aquarella, Mexico City, Alice Tully Hall, Lincoln Ctr., N.Y.C., Riverside Mus., N.Y.C., Westchester Art Soc., White Plains, N.Y., Bloomingdales, White Plains, N.Y., U. Pa., Trinity Coll., Yale Art Sch., Sarah Lawrence Coll., U. Maine; permanent collections include Met. Opera Gallery, Lincoln Ctr., N.Y., Norfolk (Va.) Mus., Mus. City of N.Y., Goshen (N.Y.) Hall of Fame, Hillandale Mus., Chadds Ford, Pa., Sea Air Space Mus., N.Y.C., Smithsonian Inst., Washington, West Point (N.Y.) Mus., MacArthur Meml., Norfolk, Va., Jewish Mus., N.Y.C., Tazewell (Va.) Mus.; limited editions include Royal Doulton Plates, London, Lucien Piccard, N.Y.C., Franklin (Pa.) Mint, Numa Ltd., Akron, Ohio; corporate collections include ABC-TV, N.Y.C., Chas. Pfizer Co., N.Y.C., Readers' Digest, Pleasantville, N.Y., Evyan Perfumes, N.Y.C., Ciba Geigy, Ardsley, N.Y., Am. Cyanamid, Bound Brook, N.J., Gen. Foods, White Plains, N.Y.; govt. and other collections include Dept. Commerce, Washington, Am. Machine & Foundry, White Plains, N.Y., Pres. Coun. on Physical Fitness & Sports, Washington, Yonkers (N.Y.) Profl. Hosp., Iona Coll., New Rochelle, N.Y., Am. Bureau of Shipping, N.Y.C., Nat. Acad., N.Y.C., St. Patrick's Cathedral, N.Y.C., St. Francis Hosp., Hartford, Conn., Elmira (N.Y.) Coll., Hofstra Coll., L.I., N.Y.; murals in public bldngs. throughout the U.S.; portraits include Albert Einstein, Pope John Paul II, Ronald Reagan, Robert Frost, Douglas MacArthur, J.F. and Robert Kennedy, Robert Merrill, E. Roland Harriman, Cardinal Cook, Golda Meir. Named Artist of the Year Westchester Council of Arts, 1987; recipient Honorary award Thornton Donovan Sch., 1989. Mem. Nat. Soc. Mural Painters (pres. emeritus 1985-89), Artists Equity N.Y. (pres. emeritus), Hudson River Contemporary Artists (pres. emeritus), Internat. Artists Assn. (v.p.), Mamaronick Artists Guild (pres. emeritus), Proto V, Abraxas, League of Present Day Artists, Fine Arts Fedn. Avocations: pre-Colombian archeology, history of art. Home and Office: 296 Murray Ave Larchmont NY 10538-1239

TOBEY, CARL WADSWORTH, retired publisher; b. Meriden, Conn., Nov. 18, 1923; s. Carl W. and Prudence (Wadsworth) T.; m. Charlotte Butterworth, Aug. 19, 1944; children: Peter Wadsworth, Carl Eric, Cheryl L. Ed., U.S. Mcht. Marine Acad. Regional sales mgr. Northeastern div. Dell Pub. Co., Inc., 1953-58; sales mgr. Dell Books, 1958-64, v.p. co., 1964-68, sr. v.p., 1968, exec. v.p., dir., 1968-76; pres. Dell Pub. Co. Inc., from 1976, chmn., 1981-83; ret., 1983; owner Greater Savannah Travel, Inc.;. With U.S. Mcht. Marine, 1943-46. Mem. Landing Club on Skidaway Island. Democrat. Congregationalist. Office: Greater Savannah Travel 12-D Bishops Ct Trustees Garden Savannah GA 31401

TOBEY, MARTIN ALAN, cardiologist; b. Dallas, Tex., Sept. 24, 1947; s. Nathan Gene and Rose Marcus T.; m. Judith Helane Ross, Mar. 10, 1974; children: Daniel, Rachel. BS with highest distinction, Pa. State U., 1968; MD, Jefferson Med. Coll., 1970. Diplomate Am. Bd. Internal Medicine, Am. Bd. Cardiovascular Diseases. Intern Phila. Gen. Hosp., 1970-71; resident in internal medicine Parkland Meml. Hosp., Dallas, 1971-74; fellow in cardiology U. Tex. Southwestern Med. Sch., Dallas, 1976-78; cardiologist Cardiology Assocs. of Fort Worth, Tex., 1978—; mem. med. bd. Harris Hosp. Meth., Ft. Worth, 1988-90, chmn. cardiology divsn., 1988-90. Author (software) Workshops in Coronary Angioplasty, 1984. Major U.S. Army, 1974-76. Fellow Am. Coll. Cardiology (regional rep. Tex. chpt. 1996—), Am. Heart Assn., Alpha Omega Alpha. Avocations: classical music, bicycling, computers. Office: Cardiology Assocs Ft Worth 1300 W Rosedale St Fort Worth TX 76104-2802

TOBIA, STEPHEN FRANCIS, JR., marketing professional, consultant; b. Bronx, N.Y., Jan. 14, 1955; s. Stephen Francis and Zelinda (Caruso) T.; m. Maureen Patricia Homan, Dec. 31, 1978; children: Michael, Marc. BA, U. Dayton, 1978; MA, Occidental Coll., L.A., 1980. Project mgr. L.A. C. of C., 1978-81; mgr. pub. affairs/communications Coca Cola Bottling Co., L.A., 1981-84, dir. pub. affairs, 1984; v.p. pub. affairs Beatrice Cos. Inc., L.A., 1984-86; pres. Pacific/West Communications, L.A., 1987—, CEO; mem. adv. com. Calif. Mus. Sci. & Industry, L.A., L.A. C. of C. Edn.; guest lectr. mktg. communications UCLA, 1989, 90; panelist Nat. Recycling Congress, 1990; speaker Inst. for Internat. Rsch., 1991, World Recycling Conf. and Expn., 1991. Mem. adv. com. Sch. Pub. Adminstrn., U. So. Calif., L.A., Focus on Youth; chmn. YMCA, East L.A.; bd. dirs. Big Bros. Greater L.A.; mem. Mayor Bradley's Edn. Adv. Com. Pub. Affairs fellow CORO Found., 1978-79. Mem. RecyCAL (founding chmn.), So. Calif. Business Men's Assn. (bd. dirs.), Calif./Nev. Soft Drink Assn. (bd. dirs.), Nat. Soft Drink Assn. (govt. rels. com.), L.A. Pub. Affairs Officer Assn., CORO Assn., Rotary. Office: Pacific/West Communications Group 3435 Wilshire Blvd Ste 2850 Los Angeles CA 90010-2014*

TOBIAS, ANDREW PREVIN, columnist, lecturer; b. N.Y.C., Apr. 20, 1947; s. Seth D. and Audrey J. (Landau) T. BA, Harvard U., 1968, MBA, 1972. Pres. Harvard Agys. Inc., Cambridge, Mass., 1967-68; v.p. Nat. Student Mktg. Corp., N.Y.C., 1969-70; contbg. editor N.Y. Mag., 1972-77, Esquire mag., 1977-83; columnist Playboy mag., 1982-86; contbr. Time mag., 1989—, Worth mag., 1995—. Author: The Funny Money Game, 1972, Fire and Ice, 1976, The Only Investment Guide You'll Ever Need, 1978, rev. edit., 1996, Getting by on $100,000 a Year and Other Sad Tales, 1980, The Invisible Bankers, 1982, Managing Your Money (software), 1984-94, Money Angles, 1984, The Only Other Investment Guide You'll Ever Need, 1987, Kids Say Don't Smoke, 1991, Auto Insurance Alert!, 1993, My Vast Fortune, 1997. Recipient Gerald Loeb award, 1984, Consumer Fedn. of Am. Media Svc. award, 1993.

TOBIAS, BENJAMIN ALAN, portfolio manager, financial planner; b. Bklyn., June 4, 1951; s. Joseph M. and Alma Ruth (Schneider) T.; m. Barbara Anne Biller, July 31, 1977; children: Daniel, Rachel. BBA, CUNY, 1973. CPA, N.Y., Fla.; CFP. Sr. acct. Deloitte & Touche, N.Y.C., Miami, 1973-79; pres. Benjamin A. Tobias, P.A. dba Tobias Fin. Advisors, Pembroke Pines, Fla., 1980—; mem. adj. faculty Rollins Coll., 1996, Nova Southeastern U., 1997. Author weekly newspaper column, Sun Newspapers, 1988-89. Named One of the Top 200 Advisors in U.S., Worth mag., 1996. Mem. AICPAs, Fla. Inst. CPAs (com. on personal and fin. planning 1989-90, 91), Gold Coast Soc. Cert. Fin. Planners (v.p. comm. 1989-90), South Fla. Cert. Fin. Planners (pres. 1992-93, chmn. 1993-94), Inst. Cert. Fin. Planners (mem. nat. com. 1994-95), Rotary (Pembroke Pines chpt., pres. 1986-87). Office: Tobias Fin Advisors 8211 W Broward Blvd Ste 450 Plantation FL 33324-2741

TOBIAS, CHARLES HARRISON, JR., lawyer; b. Cin., Apr. 16, 1921; s. Charles Harrison and Charlotte (Westheimer) T.; m. Mary J. Kaufman, June 15, 1946; children—Jean M., Thomas Charles, Robert Charles. B.A. cum laude, Harvard U., 1943, LL.B., 1949. Bar: Ohio 1949. Assoc. firm Steer, Strauss and Adair, Cin., 1949-56; ptnr. firm Steer, Strauss, White and Tobias, Cin., 1956-90; mem. Kepley MacConnell & Eyrich, Cin., 1990-93; mediator U.S. Ct. Appeals (6th crct.), Cin., 1993—. Bd. dirs. Cin. City Charter Com., 1955-75; mem. Wyoming (Ohio) City Council, 1972-77, vice mayor, 1974-77; bd. govs., sec., past chmn. Cin. Overseers, Hebrew Union Coll.-Jewish Inst. Religion; pres. Met. Area Religious Coalition of Cin., 1977-80, Jewish Fedn. Cin., 1972-74; mem. nat. bd. govs. Am. Jewish Com., 1981-87. With USN, 1943-46. Mem. Cin. Bar Assn., Losantiville Country Club. Home: 1201 Edgecliff Pl Apt 1001 Cincinnati OH 45206-2849 Office: US Ct Appeals Potter Stewart US Courthse 5th and Walnut St Cincinnati OH 45202

TOBIAS, JULIUS, sculptor; b. N.Y.C., Aug. 27, 1915; s. Louis and Anna (Tabachnick) T.; m. Suzanne Tobias. Student, Atelier Fernand Leger, Paris, 1949-52. Pvt. tchr., 1950-63; tchr. Morris Davidson Sch. Modern Painting, 1947-48; instr. N.Y. Inst. Tech., 1966-70; lectr. Rutgers U., Queens Coll., N.Y.C., 1966-67, Ind. U., Bloomington, 1974. One-man shows include Esther Stuttman Gallery, 1959, Bleecker Gallery, 1961, Easthampton Gallery, 1962, 10 Downtown, 1968, Max Hutchinson Gallery, 1970, 71, 72, Alessandra Gallery, 1976, 55 Mercer St. Gallery, 1976, 77, 78, 80, all N.Y.C., Zriny-Hayes Gallery, Chgo., 1979, B4A Gallery, N.Y.C., 1991, The SUNY, Stony Brook, 1992, Artemisia Gallery, Chgo., 1992, Galerie Art In, Nürnberg, Germany, 1994, 96, Pardo-View Gallery, N.Y.C., 1997; group shows include, Provincetown (Mass.) Art Assn., 1946, Roko Gallery, N.Y.C., 1946, Camino Gallery, N.Y.C., 1957, Polari Gallery, Woodstock, N.Y., 1957, Art USA, Coliseum, N.Y.C., 1957, Brata Gallery, N.Y.C., 1957-59, Pa. Acad. Fine Arts, 1958, Gallery Creuze, Paris, 1958, Knoedler Gallery, N.Y.C., 1959, Mus. Modern Art, traveling exhbn. in Tokyo, 1959, New Eng. Exhbn., Silvermine, Conn., 1960, De Aenlle Gallery, N.Y.C., 1961, Bleecker Gallery, N.Y.C., 1962, Staten Island Mus., N.Y.C., 1962, Allan Stone Gallery, N.Y.C., 1962, Easthampton Gallery, N.Y.C., 1962-66, Windham Coll., Putney, Vt., 1963, Rutgers U., 1966, Park Pl. Gallery, N.Y.C., 1967, Tibor Dinagy Gallery, N.Y.C., 1968, Whitney Mus. Annual, N.Y.C., 1968, Parker St. 470, Boston, 1969, Everson Mus., Syracuse, N.Y., 1972, Hunter Gallery, N.Y.C., 1981, Art Park, Lewiston, N.Y., 1981, Jan Weiss Gallery, N.Y.C., 1990, Munson-Williams-Proctor Inst., Utica, N.Y., 1995, Museen Heilbronn, Germany, 1996, numerous others; represented in numerous collections, Europe, N. and S.Am., also pvt. collections. Served to 1st lt. USAAF, 1942-45. Decorated D.F.C., Air medal with 3 oak leaf clusters; grantee Nat. Endowment for Arts, 1975, 81, N.Y. Coun. Found., 1971-78, Adolph and Esther Gottlieb Found., 1980, The Penny McCall Found., 1988; Guggenheim fellow, 1972-73, 78-79, N.Y. Found. for Arts fellow, 1986; recipient Oscar Williams and Gene Derwood award, 1989, award Adolph and Esther Gottlieb Found., 1991, 96, The Pollock-Krasner Found., 1991, Teh Richard A. Florsheim Art Fund. Address: 9 Great Jones St New York NY 10012-1128

TOBIAS, KAL, transportation executive; b. Bklyn., Feb. 1, 1946; m. Karen Liberty, Mar. 11, 1967; children: Kristopher, Kirk. BA, CUNY, Bklyn., 1967. Mgr. dealer devel. Volkswagon Can., Toronto, Ont., 1967-72; pres. cons. firm Toronto, Ont., Can., 1972-78; v.p. Burmah Oil Group, Toronto, Ont., Can., 1978-83; pres., C.E.O. DHL Internat. Express Ltd., Toronto, Ont., Can., 1983—, also bd. dirs., 1983—; bd. dirs DHL Customs Brokerage, Toronto, 1983—, Skyhawk Trans., Toronto, 1988—, Can. Courier Assn., pres., 1987—, C.E.O., 1987—. Office: DHL Internat Express Ltd, 6205 Airport Rd Ste 400, Mississauga, ON Canada L4V 1E1

TOBIAS, LESTER LEE, psychological consultant; b. Bklyn., Oct. 11, 1946; s. Nathan and Charlotte T.; m. Andrea Furmanek, July 10, 1977; children: Lauren A., Julia E. AB, Grinnell Coll., 1967; AM, U. Ill., 1971, PhD, 1972. Instr. dept. univ. extension U. Ill., Urbana, 1970-72, intern Psychol. and Counseling Ctr., 1970-71, clin. counselor, 1971-72; psychologist Jefferson County (Colo.) Mental Health Ctr., Denver, 1972-73, team leader, psychologist, 1973-74;; psychol. cons. to Denver OEO Colo. Dept. Social Svcs., 1973-74; instr. Denver Community Coll., 1973-74; cons. psychologist Nordli, Wilson Assocs., Westborough, Mass., 1974-81; ptnr., cons. psychologist, 1981—; pres. Psychol. Svcs. Internat., Inc., Westborough, 1983—. Author: Psychological Consulting to Management, 1990; contbr. articles to profl. and bus. publs. Bd. dirs. Worcester Big Bros., 1976, PMCS, 1983—. Meuhlstein Found. scholar, 1964-67; USPHS trainee, 1967-68. Fellow APA; mem. Nat. Psychol. Cons. to Mgmt. (Excellence award 1991), Mass. Psychol. Assn. Home: 6 John St Westborough MA 01581-2511 Office: Nordli Wilson Assocs 2000 W Park Dr PO Box 5000 Westborough MA 01581-5000

TOBIAS, PAUL HENRY, lawyer; b. Cin., Jan. 5, 1930; s. Charles H. and Charlotte (Westheimer) T.; 1 child, Eliza L. AB magna cum laude, Harvard U., 1951, LLB, 1958. Bar: Mass. 1958, Ohio 1962. Assoc. Stoneman & Chandler, Boston, 1958-61, Goldman & Putnick, Cin., 1962-75; ptnr. Tobias, Kraus and Torchia, Cin., 1976—; instr. U. Cin. Law Sch., 1975-77. Author: Litigating Wrongful Discharge Claims, 1987; co-author: Job Rights and Survivor Strategies, a Handbook for Terminated Employees, 1987; contbr. articles to profl. jours. Mem. Cin. Bd. of Park Commrs., 1973-81, Cin. Human Rels. Commn., 1980-84, Cin. Hist. Conservation Bd., 1990-91. With U.S. Army, 1952-54. Mem. ABA, Nat. Employment Lawyers Assn. (founder), Nat. Employee Rights Inst. (chmn.), Ohio State Bar Assn., Cin. Bar Assn. (past chmn. legal aid com.), Phi Beta Kappa. Home: 15 Hill And Hollow Ln Cincinnati OH 45208-3317 Office: Tobias Kraus Torchia 911 Mercantile Libr Bldg Cincinnati OH 45202

TOBIAS, RANDALL L., pharmaceutical company executive; b. Lafayette, Ind., Mar. 20, 1942; m. Marilyn Jane Salyer, Sept. 2, 1966 (dec. May 1994); children: Paige Noelle, Todd Christopher; m. Marianne Williams, July 15, 1995; stepchildren: James Russell Ullyot, Kathryn Lee Ullyot. BS in Mktg., Ind. U., 1964; LLD (hon.), Galuedette U.; D of Engring. (hon.), Rose Hulman Inst. Tech., Sagamore of the Wabash, Ind. Numerous positions Ind. Bell, 1964-77, Ill. Bell, 1977-81; v.p. residence mktg. sales and service AT&T, 1981-82, pres. Am. Bell Consumer Products, 1983, pres. Consumer Products, 1983-84, sr. v.p., 1984-85; chmn., CEO AT&T Comm., N.Y.C., 1985-91, AT&T Internat., Basking Ridge, N.J., 1991-93; vice chmn. bd. AT&T, N.Y.C., 1986-93; chmn., CEO Eli Lilly & Co., Indpls., 1993—; bd. dirs. Eli Lilly & Co., Kimberly-Clark, Knight-Ridder, Phillips Petroleum; active U.S.-Japan Bus. Coun., U.S.-China Bus. Coun. Trustee Duke U.; vice chmn. Colonial Williamsburg Found.; bd. govs. Skyline Club, Indpls. Mus. Art; bd. dirs. Indpls. Symphony Orch., Ind. U. Found. (hon.), Econ. Club Indpls. Mem. Bus. Coun., Healthcare Leadership Coun., Indpls. Corp. Cmty. Coun., Coun. Fgn. Rels., Bus. Roundtable, Meridian Hills Country Club (Indpls.), Woodstock Club (Indpls.), Columbia Club (Indpls.), Athletic Club (Indpls.), Univ. Club (Indpls.), Harrison Country Club (Columbus, Ind.), Amwell Valley Conservancy, Theta Chi. Avocations: skiing, fly fishing, shooting. Office: Eli Lilly & Co Lilly Corp Ctr Indianapolis IN 46285

TOBIAS, ROBERT MAX, labor leader, lawyer; b. Detroit, Aug. 4, 1943. BA, U. Mich., 1965, MBA, 1968; JD, George Washington U., 1969. Lawyer Nat. Treasury Employees Union, Washington, 1968-70, gen. counsel, 1970-79, exec. v.p. and gen. counsel, 1979-83, pres., 1983—; lectr. George Washington U. Law Sch., Washington, 1970-90. Contbr. articles to law revs. Sec., treas. Fed. Employee Edn. and Asst. Fund, Washington, 1986. Mem. ABA, Soc. for Labor Relations Profls. (1st Annual Union Leader award, 1987), Fed. Bar Assn., D.C. Bar Assn., Am. Arbitration Assn. (bd. dirs.). Democrat. Episcopalian. Office: Nat Treasury Employees Union 901 E St NW Ste 600 Washington DC 20004-2037

TOBIAS, TOM, JR., elementary school educator; b. July 22, 1932; s. Thomas N. Sr. and Mary A. (Hanton) T.; m. Kathleen A. Black, May 28, 1964; 1 child, Amy. BA, Ea. Mich. U., 1965, MA, 1966; postgrad., Mich. State U., U. Nev. Cert. elem./secondary tchr., Mich. Tchr. Ypsilanti (Mich.) Pub. Schs., 1965—; vis. lectr. Ea. Mich. U., Ypsilanti, 1980-90; mem. edit. bd. Scholastic Pub. Co., N.Y.C. Cartoonist, Mich. Reading Jours.; author teaching materials. Vice pres. Ypsilanti Hist. Soc.; bd. dirs. Ypsilanti Heritage Found. With USAF, 1951-55. Recipient Outstanding Alumnus award Ea. Mich. U., 1985. Mem. Ypsilanti Edn. Assn. (past pres.). Office: Ypsilanti Sch Dist 1885 Packard Rd Ypsilanti MI 48197-1846

TOBIN, AILEEN WEBB, educational administrator; b. Milford, Del., July 9, 1949; d. Wilson Webster Webb and Dorothy Marie (Benson) Rust; m. Thomas Joseph Tobin, Jr., July 31, 1971. BA cum laude, U. Del., 1971, MEd, 1975, PhD, 1981. Cert. tchr. secondary edn., cert. reading specialist, cert. reading cons., Del. Dir. Del. Tutoring Ctr., Wilmington, 1971-74; grad. teaching asst. U. Del., Newark, 1974-81, instr. Coll. Edn., 1978-82; ednl. specialist U.S. Army Ordnance Ctr. & Sch., Aberdeen Proving Ground, Md., 1982-85, chief internal eval. br., 1985-88, chief evaluation divsn., 1988, chief standardization and analysis div., 1988-90, dir. quality assurance, 1990-94, dir. tactical support equipment dept., 1994—; cons. Dorchester County Sch. Dist., Dorchester County, Md., 1977-80; rsch. assoc., Ctr. for Ednl. Leadership, Newark, 1981-82; staff assoc., Rsch. for Better Schs., Inc., Phila., 1981-84. Author: (book chpt.) Approaches Informal Eval. of Reading, 1982, Dialogues in Literary Research, 1988, Cognitive & Social Perspectives for Literary Research & Instruction, 1989; contbr. articles to profl. jours. Recipient Silver award Fed. Exec. Bd., 1992, Comdr.'s award for Civil Svc. Dept. Army, 1994, 96, Order of Samuel Sharpe award Ordnance Corps Assn., 1994, Superior Civil Svc. award Dept. Army, 1995. Mem. Internat. Reading Assn., Nat. Reading Conf., Am. Ednl. Rsch. Assn., Am. Evaluation Assn., Ordnance Corps Assn., Kappa Delta Pi. Methodist. Avocations: travel, reading, tennis, sailing. Home: 4839 Plum Run Ct Wilmington DE 19808 Office: US Army Ordnance Ctr & Sch ATSL DI TSED Aberdeen Proving Ground MD 21005

TOBIN, CALVIN JAY, architect; b. Boston, Feb. 15, 1927; s. David and Bertha (Tanfield) T.; m. Joan Hope Fink, July 15, 1951; children—Michael Alan, Nancy Ann. B.Arch., U. Mich., 1949. Designer, draftsman Arlen & Lowenfish (architects), N.Y.C., 1949-51; with Samuel Arlen, N.Y.C., 1951-53, Skidmore, Owings & Merrill, N.Y.C., 1953; architect Loebl, Schlossman & Bennett (architects), Chgo., 1953-57, v.p., 1953-57; v.p. Loebl, Schlossman & Hackl, 1957—; Chmn. Jewish United Fund Bldg. Trades Div., 1969; chmn. AIA and Chgo. Hosp. Council Com. of Hosp. Architecture, 1968-76. Archtl. works include Michael Reese Hosp. and Med. Ctr., 1954—, Prairie Shores Apt. Urban Redevel., 1957-62, Louis A. Weiss Meml. Hosp., Chgo., Chgo. State Hosp., Ctrl. Cmty. Hosp., Chgo., Gottlieb Meml. Hosp., Melrose Park, Ill., West Suburban Hosp., Oak Park, Ill., Thorek Hosp. and Med. Ctr., Chgo., Water Power Pl., Chgo., Christ Hosp., Oak Lawn, Greater Balt. Med. Ctr., Shriners Hosp. for Crippled Children, Chgo. Hinsdale (Ill.) Hosp., South Chgo. Cmty. Hosp., Chgo., Mt. Sinai Med. Ctr., Chgo., Alexian Bros. Med. Ctr., Elk Grove Village, Ill., Luth. Gen. Hosp., Park Ridge, Ill., Evanston (Ill.) Hosp., Resurrection Med. Ctr., Chgo., New Cook County Hosp., Chgo., also numerous apt., comml. and cmty. bldgs. Chmn. Highland Park (Ill.) Appearance Rev. Commn., 1972-73; mem. Highland Park Plan Commn., 1973-79; mem. Highland Park City Coun., 1974-89, mayor pro-tem, 1979-89; mem. Highland Park Environ. Control Commn., 1979-84, Highland Park Hist. Preservation Commn., 1982-89; bd. dirs. Highland Park Hist. Soc., Young Men's Jewish Coun., 1953-67, pres., 1967; bd. dirs. Jewish Community Ctrs. Chgo., 1973-78, bd. dirs., 1989-93; Ill. Coun. Against Handgun Violence, 1989-94; trustee Ravinia Festival Assn., 1990—. With USNR, 1945-46. Fellow AIA (2d v.p. Chgo. chpt.); mem. U. Mich. Alumni Soc. Coll. Architecture and Urban Planning (bd. govs. 1989-95), U. Mich. Alumni Assn. (bd. govs. 1990-95, v.p. 1993-95, pres. 1997-99, Disting. Alumni Svc. award 1996), Std. Club, Ravinia Green Country Club, Pi Lambda Phi. Jewish. Home: 814 Dean Ave Highland Park IL 60035-4749 Office: Loebl Schlossman & Hackl 130 E Randolph St Chicago IL 60601

TOBIN, CRAIG DANIEL, lawyer; b. Chgo., Aug. 17, 1954; s. Thomas Arthur and Lois (O'Connor) T. BA with honors, U. Ill., 1976; JD with high honors, Ill. Inst. Tech., 1980. Bar: Ill. 1980, U.S. Dist. Ct. (no. dist.) Ill. 1980, U.S. Dist. Ct. (no. dist.) Ind. 1986, U.S. Ct. Appeals (7th cir.) 1986, U.S. Supreme Ct. 1987. Trial atty. Cook County Pub. Defender, Chgo., 1980-82; trial atty. homicide task force Pub. Defender, Chgo., 1982-84; ptnr. Craig D. Tobin and Assocs., Chgo., 1984—; lectr. Ill. Inst. for Continuing Legal Edn., Cook County Pub. Defender, Chgo., 1983, 92, Ill. Pub. Defender Assn., 1987; instr. Nat. Inst. Trial Advocacy. Named One of Outstanding Young Men in Am., 1985. Mem. ABA, Chgo. Bar Assn., Nat. Assn. Criminal Def. Lawyers. Roman Catholic. Office: Craig D Tobin & Assocs 3 First National Plz Chicago IL 60602

TOBIN, DENNIS MICHAEL, lawyer; b. Chgo., June 3, 1948; s. Thomas Arthur and Lois (O'Connor) T.; m. Sue Wynn Henslee, June 14, 1969 (div. 1977); m. Karen Thompson, Oct. 11, 1980; children: Kyle James, Daniel Patrick. BA with honors, U. Ill., 1971; JD, Loyola U., Chgo., 1976. Bar: Ill 1976, Wis. 1989, U.S. Dist. Ct (no. dist.) Ill. 1976, U.S. Ct. Appeals (7th cir.) 1985, U.S. Supreme Ct. 1985. Trial atty. Cook County Homicide Task Force, Chgo., 1976-84; prin. Dennis M. Tobin & Assocs., Chgo., 1984—; gen. counsel Forest Health Systems and Found., Ill., Miss., Hawaii, 1986—, Manages Behavioral Care Inc., Psychiat. Ins. Co. Am. Dir. Forest Health Systems Found.; mem. Chgo. Coun. on Fgn. Rels. Mem. ABA (forum on health law), Chgo. Bar Assn. (com. on health law), Am. Soc. Law and Medicine, Ill. Assn. Criminal Def. Attys. (v.p. 1984-87), Ill. Attys. for Criminal Justice, Wis. Bar Assn., Ill. Assn. Hosp. Attys., Nat. Health Lawyers Assn., U.S. Sporting Clays Assn., Nat. Sporting Clays Assn., Gateway Gun Club. Roman Catholic. Office: Dennis M Tobin and Assocs 18-3 E Dundee Rd Barrington IL 60010-5292

TOBIN, GARY ALLAN, cultural organization educator; b. St. Louis, July 26, 1949. PhD in City and Regional Planning, U. Calif., Berkeley. Dir. Maurice and Marilyn Cohen Ctr. for Modern Jewish Studies, Waltham, Mass., Inst. Cmty. and Religion, San Francisco; rsch. on synagogue affiliation, youth programs in Jewish Cmty. and Jewish Family Founds. Author: Jewish Perceptions of Antisemitism, Church and Synagogue Affiliation. Office: Brandeis U CMJS/ICR 140 Balboa St San Francisco CA 94118-4017

TOBIN, JAMES, economics educator; b. Champaign, Ill., Mar. 5, 1918; s. Louis Michael and Margaret (Edgerton) T.; m. Elizabeth Fay Ringo, Sept. 14, 1946; children: Margaret Ringo, Louis Michael, Hugh Ringo, Roger Gill. AB summa cum laude, Harvard U., 1939, MA, 1940, PhD, 1947, LLD, 1995; LLD (hon.), Syracuse U., 1967, U. Ill., 1969, Dartmouth Coll., 1970, Swarthmore Coll., 1980, New Sch. Social Research, 1982, NYU, 1982, Bates Coll., 1982, U. Hartford, 1984, Colgate U., 1984, Gustavus Adolphus Coll., 1986, Western Md. Coll., 1984, U. New Haven, 1986; Harvard U., 1995; LD in Econs. (hon.), New U. Lisbon, 1980; D in Econs. (hon.), Athens U. Econ. & Bus., 1992; D in Econs. (hon.), Athens U. of Econ. and Bus., 1992; LHD (hon.), Hofstra U., 1983, Sacred Heart U., 1990; Bard Coll., 1995; D in Social Scis. honoris causa, U. Helsinki, 1986. Assoc. economist OPA, WPB, Washington, 1941-42; teaching fellow econs. Harvard U., Cambridge, Mass., 1946-47, with Soc. Fellows, 1947-50; assoc. prof. econs. Yale U., New Haven, 1950-55, prof., 1955—, Sterling prof. econs., 1957-88, prof. emeritus, 1988—; mem. Council Econ. Advisers, 1961-62, Nat. Acad. Scis. Author: National Economic Policy, 1966, Essays in Economics-Macroeconomics, vol. 1, 1972, The New Economics One Decade Older, 1974, Consumption and Econometrics, vol. 2, 1975, Asset Accumulation and Economic Activity, 1980, Theory and Policy, vol. 3, 1982, Policies for Prosperity, 1987; co-author: Two Revolutions in Economic Policy, 1987, National and International, 1996, Full Employment and Growth, 1966, Money, Credit, and Capital, 1997. Served to lt. USNR, 1942-46. Recipient Nobel prize in econs., 1981; Social Sci. Research Council faculty fellow, 1951-54; Grand cordon Order of the Sacred Treasure, Japan, 1988; Centennial medal Harvard Grad. Sch., 1989. Fellow Am. Acad. Arts and Scis., Econometric Soc. (pres. 1958), Am. Statis. Assn., Brit. Acad. (corr.); mem. Am. Philos. Soc., Am. Econ. Assn. (John Bates Clark medal 1955, v.p. 1964, pres. 1971), Acad. Scis. Portugal (fgn. assoc.), Phi Beta Kappa. Home: 117 Alden Ave New Haven CT 06515-2109 Office: Yale U Dept Econs Box 208281 New Haven CT 06520-8281*

TOBIN, JAMES MICHAEL, lawyer; b. Santa Monica, Calif., Sept. 27, 1948; s. James Joseph and Glada Marie (Meisner) T.; m. Kathleen Marie Esty, Sept. 14, 1985. BA with honors, U. Calif., Riverside, 1970; JD, Georgetown U., 1974. Bar: Calif. 1974, Mich. 1987. From atty. to gen. atty. So. Pacific Co., San Francisco, 1975-82; v.p. regulatory affairs So. Pacific Communications Co., Washington, 1982-83; v.p., gen. counsel Lexitel Corp., Washington, 1983-85; v.p., gen. counsel, sec. ALC Communications Corp., Birmingham, Mich., 1985-87, sr. v.p., gen. counsel, sec., 1987-88; of counsel Morrison & Foerster, San Francisco, 1988-90, ptnr., 1990—. Mem. ABA, Calif. Bar Assn., Mich. Bar Assn., Fed. Communications Bar Assn. Republican. Unitarian. Avocations: carpentry, travel. Home: 3134 Baker St San Francisco CA 94123-4303 Office: Morrison & Foerster 425 Market St San Francisco CA 94105

TOBIN, JAMES ROBERT, biotechnology company executive; b. Lima, Ohio, Aug. 12, 1944; s. J. Robert and Doris L. (Hunt) T.; m. Janet Trafton, Dec. 30, 1971; children: James Robert III, Amanda Trafton. BA in Govt., Harvard U., 1966, MBA, 1968. Fin. analyst Baxter Internat., Inc., Deerfield, Ill., 1972-73, internat. contr., 1973-75; mng. dir. Japan Baxter Internat., Inc., Tokyo, 1975-77; mng. dir. Spain Baxter Internat., Inc., Valencia, 1977-80; pres. IV Sys. Divsn. Baxter Internat. Inc., Deerfield, 1981-84; group v.p. Baxter Internat., Inc., Deerfield, 1984-88, exec. v.p., 1988-92, pres., COO, 1992-94; pres., COO Biogen, 1994-97, pres., CEO, 1997—, also bd. dirs.; bd. dirs. Creative Biomolecules, Genovo. Lt. USN, 1968-72. Republican. Home: 33 Huckleberry Hill Rd Lincoln MA 01773 Office: Biogen Inc 14 Cambridge Ctr Cambridge MA 02142-1401

TOBIN, JOAN ADELE, writer; b. N.Y.C., Nov. 24, 1930; d. William and Helen (Steinis) Butler; m. Oct. 15, 1950; children: Patricia, Michael, Eileen. BA, Charter Oak State Coll., 1996. Freelance editor Suffield, Conn., 1980-85; owner, pub. Paper Works, Suffield, Conn., 1984-92. Contbr. over 80 articles to Internat. Mensa Jour., OWL Nat. News, N.Y. Times, N.Y. Mensa, and others. Mem. Am. Mensa, NOW, Universalist-Unitarian Womens Fedn., Internat. Women's Writing Guild. Home: 32 Harmon Dr Suffield CT 06078-2062

TOBIN, MICHAEL EDWARD, banker; b. Newtown Square, Pa., Jan. 17, 1926; s. Michael Joseph and Emma (Roberts) T.; m. Judith Anne Brown; children: Michael E., Allegra, Corey. B.S. in Econs, U. Pa., 1948. Cons. Philco, RCA, Ebasco Services, Inc., 1950-56; sr. cons. Arthur Young & Co., N.Y.C., 1956-59; midwest dir. cons. svcs. Arthur Young & Co., Chgo., 1959-68; pres. Midwest Stock Exch., Chgo., 1968-78; pres. Am. Nat. Bank & Trust Co., Chgo., 1978, chmn. bd., chief exec. officer, 1979-90, chmn. bd., 1990-91, ret. Served with U.S. Army, World War II, ETO.

TOBIN, PAUL EDWARD, JR., naval officer; b. Detroit, Oct. 24, 1940; s. Paul Edward and Mary Margaret (Atkinson) T.; m. Lynne Dawson Carter, June 12, 1963; children: Mary Elizabeth, Patricia Carter. BS in Naval Sci., U.S. Naval Acad., 1963; MS in Computer Sys., U.S. Naval Postgrad. Sch., 1969. Commd. ensign USN, 1963, advanced through grades to rear adm., 1988; commdg. officer USS Tattnall (DDG-19), 1979-81; chief engr. USS Forrestal (CV-59), 1981-83; commdg. officer USS Fox (CG-33), 1984-86, Surface Warfare Officers Sch., 1986-88; dir. USN Info. Sys. Mgmt., 1988-90; commdr. Surface Group Western Pacific, Subic Bay, The Philippines, 1990-92; asst. chief naval pers. USN, Washington, 1992-94; vice commdr. naval edn. and tng. USN, Pensacola, Fla., 1994-96; oceanographer USN, 1996—. Decorated D.S.M., Legion of Merit (3). Mem. U.S. Naval Inst., Surface Navy Assn., Army Navy Country Club. Presbyterian. Avocations: classical music, running, computers, boating. Home: Quarters O Washington Navy Yard Washington DC 20374 Office: Naval Observatory 3450 Massachusetts Ave NW Washington DC 20392-0001

TOBIN, ROBERT G., supermarket chain executive; b. 1938. With Stop & Shop Supermarket Co., 1960—, pres., COO, 1989-93; pres., COO Stop & Shop Cos., Braintree, Mass., 1993—; chmn. Stop & Shop Cos., Quincy, Mass., 1995—. Office: Stop & Stop Cos Inc 1385 Hancock St Quincy MA 02169-5100

TOBIN, THOMAS F., lawyer; b. Chgo., Apr. 12, 1929. BSS, John Carroll U., 1951; JD, Loyola U., 1954. Bar: Ill. 1954. Ptnr. Connelly & Schroeder, Chgo. Office: Connelly & Schroeder 1 N Franklin St Ste 1200 Chicago IL 60606-3421

TOBIN, VINCENT MICHAEL, professional sports team executive; b. Burlington Junction, Mo., Sept. 29, 1943. Def. ends coach Missouri, 1967-70, def. coord., 1971-76; def. coord. Brit. Columbia Lions CFL, 1977-82, Phila./Balt. Stars USFL, 1983-85, Chgo. Bears NFL, 1986-92, Indpls. Colts NFL, 1994-95; head coach Ariz. Cardinals, 1996—. Office: Arizona Cardinals PO Box 888 Phoenix AZ 85000-0888

TOBIS, JEROME SANFORD, physician; b. Syracuse, N.Y., July 23, 1915; s. David George and Anna (Feinberg) T.; m. Hazel Weisbard, Sept. 18, 1938; children: David, Heather, Jonathan. B.S., CCNY, 1936; M.D., Chgo. Med. Sch., 1943. Diplomate: Am. Bd. Phys. Medicine and Rehab. Intern Knickerbocker Hosp., 1943-44; resident Bronx VA Hosp., 1946-48; med. dir. state fever therapy unit USPHS, Brookhaven, Miss., 1944-46; practice medicine N.Y.C., 1948-70; prof. dir. dept. phys. medicine and rehab. N.Y. Med. Coll., Flower and Fifth Av. Hosps., 1948-61; prof. rehab. medicine Albert Einstein Coll. of Medicine, 1963-70; chief div. rehab. medicine Montefiore Hosp., 1961-70; dir. vis. physician Met., Bird S. Coler hosps., 1952-61; prof., chmn. dept. phys. medicine and rehab. Calif. Coll. Medicine, U. Calif. at Irvine, 1970-82, prof., dir. program in geriatric medicine and gerontology, 1980-86; mem. adv. com. Acad. Geriatric Resource program, 1984-86, 95—; mem. expert med. com. Am. Rehab. Found., 1961-70; cons. Dept. Health, N.Y.C., Long Beach VA Hosp., 1970—, Fairview State Devel. Ctr., 1976—; mem. adv. coun. phys. medicine and rehab. for appeals com. Calif. Med. Assn., 1971-74, adv. com. U. Calif. Acad. Geriatric Resource Program, 1995—; NIH Internat. Fogarty fellow, hon. lectr., dept. geriatric medicine U. Birmingham, 1979-80; chair ethics com. U. Calif.-Irvine Med. Ctr., 1986—; mem. rev. panel musculoskeletal diseases NIH, 1996. Mem. editorial bd.: Heart and Lung, 1973-76, Geriatrics, 1975-80, Archives of Phys. Medicine and Rehab, 1958-73. Named Physician of the Year, 1957; recipient Distinguished Alumnus award Chgo. Med. Sch., 1972, Acad. award Nat. Inst. on Aging, 1981-86; named hon. faculty mem. Calif. Zeta chpt. Alpha Omega Alpha, 1981; Leavitt Meml. lectureship Baylor Coll. Medicine, 1983, Griffith Meml. lectureship Am. Geriatric Soc., 1984; Australian Coll. Rehabilitation Medicine, 1984; Jerome S. Tobis Ann. Conf. on Geriatric Medicine established in his name, U. Calif. at Irvine, 1986. Fellow ACP, Am. Coll. Cardiology; mem. AMA (mem. residency rev. com. Coun. Med. Edn. 1973), AAAS, Am. Acad. Cerebral Palsy, Am. Acad. Phys. Medicine and Rehab. (Disting. Clinician award 1993), Am. Congress Rehab. Medicine (pres. 1962), Calif. Coun. Gerontology and Geriatrics (bd. dirs. 1980-86, pres. 1985), N.Y. Acad. Medicine, N.Y. Acad. Sci., Orange County Med. Soc., Assn. U. Calif. Irvine (chair emeritae/i 1996-97). Home: 1115 Goldenrod Ave Corona Del Mar CA 92625-1508 Office: U Calif Dept Phys Medicine & Rehab Irvine CA 92668

TOBISMAN, STUART PAUL, lawyer; b. Detroit, June 5, 1942; s. Nathan and Beverly (Porvin) T.; m. Karen Sue Tobisman, Aug. 8, 1965; children: Cynthia Elaine, Neal Jay. BA, UCLA, 1966; JD, U. Calif., Berkeley, 1969. Bar: Calif. 1969. Assoc. O'Melveny & Myers, L.A., 1969-77, ptnr., 1977—; dir. Burton G. Bettingen Corp. Contbr. articles to profl. jours. Trustee L.A. County Bar Assn., 1983-84. With USN, 1961-63. Fellow Am. Coll. Trust and Estate Counsel; mem. Phi Beta Kappa, Order of Coif. Office: O'Melveny & Myers 1999 Avenue Of The Stars Los Angeles CA 90067-6022

TOBLER, D. LEE, chemical and aerospace company executive; b. Provo, Utah, July 25, 1933; s. Donald and Louise Harriet (Shoell) T.; m. H. Darlene Thueson, Nov. 21, 1956; children—Lisa, Julianne, Curtis, Craig, Denise, Bradley. BA in Fin. and Econs., Brigham Young U., 1957; MBA in Fin., Northwestern U., 1958. Mgr. planning and econs. Exxon, N.Y.C., 1958-72; v.p., treas. Aetna Life & Casualty, Hartford, Conn., 1972-81; group v.p., chief fin. officer Zapata Corp., Houston, 1981-84; exec. v.p., CFO, B.F. Goodrich Co., Akron, Ohio, 1985—, also bd. dirs. Trustee U. Akron, 1996—; exec. v.p. bd. trustees Ohio Ballet, 1995-96, trustee, 1994—, chmn. Akron Regional Devel. Bd., 1992-95, trustee, exec. com., 1990—; trustee Inventure Place, Inc.; pres. Literacy Vols. Conn., Hartford, 1973-81; exec. bd. Sam Houston Area Boy Scouts Am., 1984. Mem. Portage Country Club (Akron), German Am. C. of C. (bd. dirs. Ohio chpt. 1996—). Republican. Mem. LDS Ch. Avocations: gardening; tennis; reading. Home: 2679 Brittany Oaks Blvd Hilliard OH 43026-8574 Office: BF Goodrich Co 4020 Kinross Lakes Pky Richfield OH 44286-9368

TOBY, JACKSON, sociologist, educator; b. N.Y.C., Sept. 10, 1925; s. Phineas and Anna (Weissman) T.; m. Marcia Lifshitz, Aug. 1, 1952 (dec. Jan. 1997); children: Alan Steven, Gail Afriat. B.A., Bklyn. Coll., 1946; M.A. in Econs, Harvard U., 1947, M.A. in Sociology, 1949, Ph.D. in Sociology, 1950. Research assoc. Lab. Social Relations, Harvard, 1950-51; mem. faculty Rutgers U., 1951—, prof. sociology, chmn. dept., 1961-68, dir. Inst. for Criminological Research, 1969-94; cons. Youth Devel. Program, Ford Found., 1959-63. Author: (with H.C. Bredemeier) Social Problems in America, 1960, 2d edit., 1971; contbr. numerous articles to profl. jours., pub. policy jours., N.Y. Times, Wall St. Jour., L.A. Times, Chgo. Tribune, Washington Post. Cons., Pres.'s Commn. Law Enforcement and Adminstrn. Justice, 1967. Recipient numerous research grants. Mem. Am. Sociol. Assn., Am. Soc. Criminology, Univ. Ctrs. for Rational Alternatives, Nat. Assn. Scholars. Spl. research adolescent delinquency in U.S., Sweden, Japan, other countries, on violence and dropouts in Am. public schools. Home: 17 Harrison Ave Highland Park NJ 08904-1813 Office: Rutgers U Dept Sociology Lucy Stone Hall Livingston Campus New Brunswick NJ 08903

TOCCHET, RICK, professional hockey player; b. Scarborough, Ont., Can., Apr. 9, 1964. Selected as underage jr. in 6th round NHL entry draft Phila. Flyers, 1983, right wing, 1984-92; traded Pitts. Penguins, 1992-94, L.A. Kings, 1994—; capt. Phila. Flyers, 1991-92, mem. Stanley Cup Championship Team, 1992; played in NHL All-Star Game, 1989-91, 93. Office: care Los Angeles Kings 3900 W Manchester Blvd Inglewood CA 90305

TOCCO, JAMES, pianist; b. Detroit, Sept. 21, 1943; s. Vincenzo and Rose (Tabbita) T.; 1 child, Rhoya. Prof. music Ind. U., Bloomington, 1977-91; eminent scholar, artist-in-residence U. Cin. Coll.-Conservatory Music, 1991—; prof. Musikhochschule, Lübeck, Ger., 1990—; artistic dir. Great Lakes Chamber Music Festival, 1994—. Debut with orch., Detroit, 1956, since performed with symphony orchs. including Chgo. Symphony, Los Angeles Philharmonic, Cin. Symphony, Detroit Symphony, Nat. Symphony, Balt. Symphony, Atlanta Symphony, Denver Symphony, Montreal Symphony, London Symphony, London Philharm., Berlin Philharm., Moscow Radio-TV Orch., Amsterdam Philharmonic, Munich Philharmonic, Bavarian Radio Orch., Royal Concergebouw Orch., also recitals, U.S. and abroad, and performances, CBS and NBC networks; guest performer, White House; Recs. include the complete preludes of Chopin, collected piano works of Leonard Bernstein, complete piano works of Charles Tomlinson Griffes, 4 piano sonatas of Edward MacDowell, selected piano works of Aaron Copland, complete Bach-Liszt organ transcriptions. Recipient Bronze medal Tchaikovsky Competition, Moscow 1970, Bronze medal Queen Elisabeth of Belgium Competition, Brussels 1972, 1st prize Piano Competition of Americas, Rio de Janeiro 1973, 1st prize Munich Internat. Competition 1973. Office: U Cin Coll-Conservatory Music Cincinnati OH 45221-0003

TOCHIKURA, TATSUROKURO, applied microbiologist, home economics educator; b. Nagaoka, Niigata, Japan, Nov. 15, 1927; s. Tatsujiro and Fuji (Sato) T.; m. Kano Takako, Nov. 8, 1953; children: Momoyo, Tadafumi. BS in Agrl. Chemistry, Kyoto (Japan) U., 1951, PhD, 1960. Cert. indsl. microbiology and microbial biochemistry. Rsch. assoc. dept. agrl. chemistry Kyoto (Japan) U., 1956-61, assoc. prof. dept. agrl. chemistry, 1961-68, prof. dept. food sci. and tech., 1968-91, prof. emeritus, 1991; prof. home econs. Kobe (Japan) Women's U., 1991—; vis. asst. prof. Oreg. State U., 1964-65. Co-author: Microbial Production of Nucleic Acid-Related Substances, 1976, Methods in Carbohydrate Chemistry, 1980, Bioconversion of Waste Materials to Industrial Products, 1991. Mem. Am. Soc. Microbiology, Japan Bioindustry Assn., Japan Soc. for Fermentation and Bioengrng., Japan Soc. for Bioscience Biotech. and Agrochemistry. Office: Kobe Womens Univ, 2-1 Aoyama Higashi-Suma, Kobe 654, Japan

TOCK, JOSEPH, lawyer; b. Cleve., Aug. 22, 1954; s. Julius Joseph and Marianna Yvonne (Carracio) T. BA, Kent State U., 1979; JD, Case Western Res. U., 1983. Bar: Ohio, 1983, U.S. Ct. Mil. Appeals, 1983, Colo. 1988. Commd. 1st lt. USAF, 1983, advanced through grades to maj., 1994; asst. staff judge advocate, chief civil law USAF, McConnell AFB, Kans., 1983-84; asst. staff judge advocate, chief civil law USAF, Yokota Air Base, Japan, 1984-85, area def. counsel 7th cir., 1985-87; dep. staff judge advocate, chief mil. justice USAF, Kelly AFB, Tex., 1987-88; dep. county atty. El Paso County, Colo., 1989-90; pvt. practice Colorado Springs, Colo., 1990-91; staff atty. Guam Legal Svcs. Corp., 1991-92; asst. atty. gen. White Collar unit Prosecution Divsn., Agana, Guam, 1992-95; 1st asst. to chief prosecutor White Collar unit Prosecution Divsn., Agana, Guam, 1994-96; asst. atty. gen. Solicitor's Divsn., Agana, Guam, 1996—; dep. staff judge advocate Peterson AFB, Colo., 1990-91, Andersen AFB, Guam, 1991—; instr. family law Pikes Peak C.C., 1990-91; lectr. Continental Security Divsn., San Antonio, 1987-88, NCO prep course, Kelly AFB, Tex., 1987-88, Profl. Mil. Edn. Ctr., Yokota Air Base, 1984-87. Mem. Internat. Legal Soc. Japan, Am. Legion. Roman Catholic. Avocations: golf, handball, sailing, scuba. Office: Atty Gen Prosecution Divsn Jud Ctr Bldg 120 W O'Brien Dr Ste 2-200E Agana GU 96910-5174

TOCKLIN, ADRIAN MARTHA, insurance company executive, lawyer; b. Coral Gables, Fla., Aug. 4, 1951; d. Kelso Hampton and Patricia Jane (Crook) Cook Atkins; m. Gary Michael Tocklin, Nov. 23, 1974. BA, George Washington U., 1972; JD, Seton Hall U., 1994. Regional claim examiner Interstate Nat. Corp., St. Petersburg, Fla., 1973-74; branch supr. Underwriter's Adjusting Co. subs. Continental Corp., Tampa, Fla., 1974-77, asst. dir. edn. tng. adminstrn., N.Y.C., 1977, asst. regional mgr. adminstrn. ops., Livingston, N.J., 1977-78, br. mgr., Paramus, N.J., 1978-80, sr. v.p. mktg., N.Y.C., Piscataway, N.J., 1980-84, regional v.p., mgr., Livingston, N.J., 1984-86, exec. v.p., 1986-88, also bd. dirs.; sr. v.p. Continental Corp., 1988-92, exec. v.p. 1992-94, pres., N.Y.C., 1994-95; pres. diversified ops. CNA Ins., Chgo., 1995—; pres. bd. dirs. U.S. Protection Indemnity Agy., Inc., N.Y.C.; bd. dirs. Underwriters Adjusting Co., Arbitration Forums, Inc., Tarrytown, N.Y., Continental Ins. Co., Sonat Corp.; trustee George Washington U., 1996—; v.p. Continental Risk Services, Inc., Hamilton, Bermuda, 1983-86; editor-in-chief Profl. Ins. Bulletin Update, N.Y.C., 1977-79. Mem. YWCA Acad. Women Achievers. Mem. Nat. Assn. Ins. Women (Outstanding Ins. Woman in N.Y.C.), NOW. Democrat. Lutheran. Office: CNA Ins CNA Plz Chicago IL 60685

TOCKMAN, RONALD CHESTER, accountant; b. St. Louis, May 18, 1945; s. Ruben J. and Gertrude (Bensky) T.; m. Lois Joyce Koplan, Sept. 1, 1969; children: Neil D., Lee D., Gail B. BS, Suffolk U., 1971. CPA, Mass. Staff acct. Theodore Samet & Co., Boston, 1972-73; sr. acct. Miller Wachman & Co., Boston, 1973-75; pvt. practice Ronald C. Tockman CPA, Boston, 1975-83; tax prin. and v.p. Cooper & Co. P.C., Burlington, Mass., 1983-94; pvt. practice, 1994—; lectr. profl. edn. courses various topics, 1976—. Served with U.S. Army, 1965-68, Vietnam. Recipient two Purple Heart medals, Vietnamese Cross of Gallantry, U.S. Army, 1966. Fellow AICPA (tax div. 1986—), Mass. Soc. CPAs (fed. tax. com. 1979—); mem. KP (Chancellor Comdr. King Solomon Lodge 1979), Handi-Kids, Inc. (dir.). Avocations: bowling, golf. Office: 95 Washington St Ste 213 Canton MA 02021-4005

TODARO, GEORGE JOSEPH, pathologist; b. N.Y.C., July 1, 1937; s. George J. and Antoinette (Piccinni) T.; m. Jane Lehv, Aug. 12, 1962; children: Wendy C., Thomas M., Anthony A. BS, Swarthmore Coll., 1958; MD, NYU, 1963. Intern NYU Sch. Medicine, N.Y.C., 1963-64, fellow in pathology, 1964-65, asst. prof. pathology, 1965-67; staff assoc. Viral Carcinogenesis br. Nat. Cancer Inst., Bethesda, Md., 1967-70, head molecular biology sect., 1969-70; chief Viral Carcinogenesis br. Nat. Cancer Inst. (Lab. Viral Carcinogenesis), 1970-83; sci. dir., pres. Oncogen, Seattle, 1987-90; sr. v.p. exploratory biomed. rsch. Bristol-Myers Squibb Pharm. Rsch. Inst., 1990; adj. prof. pathology U. Wash., Seattle, 1983—, chmn. dept. pathobiology, 1991—; sr. v.p., sci. dir. Pathogenesis Corp., Seattle, 1992-95; mem. Fred Hutchinson Cancer Rsch. Ctr., Seattle, 1991-93. Editor: Cancer Research, 1973-86, Archives of Virology, 1976—, Jour. Biol. Chemistry, 1979—; contbr. articles to profl. jours. Served as med. officer USPHS, 1967-69. Recipient Borden Undergrad. Research award, 1963, USPHS Career Devel. award, 1967, HEW Superior Service award, 1971, Gustav Stern award for virology, 1972, Parke-Davis award in exptl. pathology, 1975; Walter Hubert lectr. Brit. Cancer Soc., 1977. Mem. Nat. Acad. Scis., Am. Soc. Microbiology, Am. Assn. Cancer Research, Soc. Exptl. Biology and Medicine, Am. Soc. Biol. Chemists, Am. Soc. Clin. Investigation. Home: 1940 15th Ave E Seattle WA 98112-2829 Office: U Wash Dept Pathobiology 101 Elliott Ave W Ste 428 Seattle WA 98119-4220

TODD, BRUCE M., mayor. BBA in acctg., U. Tex. CPA, Tex. Former ptnr. Mueller, Todd and Co.; commr. Travis County, Tex., 1987—; mayor City of Austin, Tex., 1991—; City of Austin chair AISD/City Coun. Joint Com., Audit Com., Conv. Ctr. Com., Opportunities for Youth subcom., Joint Debt Advisory Com., Legis. Com., Judicial Com., Policy Planning and Budget Com., Downtown subcom., So. Union Gas Rate Request subcom. bd. dirs. Tex. Mcpl. League, Austin Transp. Study Com., Capital Metro Local Govt. Approval Com.; mem. Mayor's United on Safety, Crime and Law Enforcement; chairperson Balcones Canyonlands Conservation Plan; former pres. Austin-San Antonio Corridor Coun. Mem. Tex. Soc. CPAs (former mem. bd. dirs, exec. com. Austin chpt.). Address: 7629 Rockpoint Dr Austin TX 78731-1438 Office: Office of Mayor 124 W 8th St Austin TX 78701-2302*

TODD, DAVID FENTON MICHIE, architect; b. Middletown, Ohio, Feb. 22, 1915; s. Robert Chalmers and Frances Fenton (Michie) T.; m. Suzanne Williams, Sept. 1, 1942; 1 child, Gregory F.W. A.B., Dartmouth, 1937; B.Arch., U. Mich., 1940. Draftsman J.R.F. Swanson, Birmingham, Mich., 1940-41; archtl. designer W. Ray Yount, Dayton, Ohio, 1941-42; architect Harrison, Ballard & Allen, N.Y.C., 1942-53; architect, prin. Ballard, Todd & Snibbe, N.Y.C., 1957-62, Ballard Todd Assos., 1962-66, David Todd & Assos., 1966—. Works include Manhattan Plaza, N.Y.C., Collegiate Sch, N.Y.C., Rye (N.Y.) Country Day Sch. Past chmn. bd. dirs. Leake & Watts Children's Home, N.Y.C.; chmn. N.Y.C. Landmarks Preservation Commn., 1989-90. Served to 1st lt. AUS, 1942-46. Recipient awards for tennis pavillion, Princeton U. AIA, 1962, Harry B. Rutkins Meml. award N.Y.C. AIA, 1963, Robert Treat Hotel, Newark Asn. Commerce and Industry, 1964, Manhattan Pla. Constrn. Industry Bd., 1978, Andrew Thomas Pioneer in Housing award N.Y.C. AIA, 1986, cert. of merit Mcpl. Art Soc. N.Y.C., 1991,. Fellow AIA (pres. N.Y.C. chpt. 1969-70, chmn. jury of fellows 1971, chmn. task force on housing policy 1974), Constrn. Specifications Inst. (pres. N.Y.C. chpt. 1960-61, regional dir. 1965-66). Clubs: Century Assn, Amateur Comedy. Home and Office: 134 E 95th St New York NY 10128-1705

TODD, ERICA WEYER, lawyer; b. Beacon Falls, Conn., Sept. 22, 1967; d. Richard Burton and Elizabeth Jane (Weyer) T. BA in Biology, U. Bridgeport, 1989, JD, 1992; JD, Quinnipiac Coll. Sch. Law, 1994. Bar: Conn. 1992, U.S. Dist. Ct. Conn. 1993. Assoc. Trotta, Trotta and Trotta, New Haven, 1993—; admissions counselor Quinnipiac Coll. Sch. of Law, Hamden, 1992-93. Recipient Alumni award for Svc. to Law Sch., Quinnipiac Coll. Sch. Law, 1994. Mem. ABA, Conn. Bar Assn. (exec. com. Young Lawyers divsn. 1993—), New Haven Bar Assn. (exec. com. Young Lawyers Assn. 1994—), Def. Rsch. Inst., Assn. Trial Lawyers of Am., Ct. Trial Lawyers Assn. Democrat. Roman Catholic. Avocation: golf. Home: 551 Skokorat Rd Beacon Falls CT 06403-1457 Office: Trotta Trotta & Trotta 195 Church St # 815 817 PO Box 802 New Haven CT 06503-0802

TODD, FRANCES EILEEN, pediatrics nurse; b. Hawthorne, Calif., Aug. 20, 1950; d. James Clark and Jean Eleanor (McGinty) Nailen; m. Steven Charles Todd, Oct. 25, 1975; 1 child, Amanda Kathryn. ASN, El Camino Jr. Coll., 1974; BSN, Calif. State Coll., Long Beach, 1982, postgrad. RN, Calif.; cert. pub. health nurse, Calif.; cert. pediatric nurse practitioner; cert. pediatric advanced life support Am. Heart Assn. Nursing attendant St. Earne's Nursing Home, Inglewood, Calif., 1973; clinic nurse I Harbor-UCLA Med. Ctr., Torrance, Calif., 1974-77, evening shift relief charge nurse, clinic nurse II, 1977-85, pediatric liaison nurse, 1984-90, pediatric nurse practitioner, 1985—; steward Local Union 660, 1995—; tutor Compton (Calif.) C.C., 1988, clin. instr., 1987-88; lectr. faculty dept. pediatrics UCLA Sch. Medicine, 1980—; lectr. in field. Contbr. articles to profl. jours. Co-chair parent support group Sherrie's Schs., Lomita, Calif. Mem. Nat. Assn. Pediatric Nurse Assocs. and Practitioners, L.A. Pediatric Soc., Emergency Nurses Assn., Local 660 (shop steward), Svc. Employees Int. Union, local 660 (union steward), Peruvian Paso Horse Registry N.Am. (co-chair judge's accreditation com. 1989—, judge's Andalusian horses). Avocations: Peruvian Paso horses, orchids. Office: Harbor UCLA Med Ctr 1000 W Carson St PO Box 14-7W Torrance CA 90509

TODD, HAROLD WADE, association executive, retired air force officer; b. Chgo., Jan. 17, 1938; s. Harold Wade and Jeanne (Fayal) T.; m. Wendy Yvonne Kendrick, July 12, 1981; children by previous marriage: Hellen J. Wilson, Kenneth J., Stephen D., Joseph M., Michelle M. Adams, Mark A.; stepchildren: Jamie Y. White, James K. Mills, Timothy S. Emerson. B.S., U.S. Air Force Acad., 1959; grad., Nat. War Coll., 1975. Commd. 2d lt. U.S. Air Force, 1959, advanced through grades to maj. gen., 1982; aide to comdr. (2d Air Force (SAC)), Barksdale AFB, La., 1970-71; exec. aide to comdr.-in-chief U.S. Air Forces Europe, Germany, 1971-74; spl. asst. chief of staff USAF, 1975-76; chief Concept Devel. Div., 1976-77, chief Readiness and NATO Staff Group, Hdqrs. USAF, 1977-78; exec. asst. to chmn. Joint Chiefs Staff Washington, 1978-80; comdr. 25th region N. Am. Aerospace Def. Command McChord AFB, Wash., 1980-82; chief staff 4th Allied Tactical Air Force Heidelberg, 1982-85; commandant Air War Coll., 1985-89; vice comdr. Air U., 1985-89, ret., 1989; ind. cons. Colorado Springs, Colo., 1989-95; pres., CEO, Nat. Stroke Assn., Denver, 1995—. Founder, pres. Bossier City (La.) chpt. Nat. Assn. for Children with Learning Disabilities, 1970-71. Decorated Def. D.S.M., Air Force D.S.M. (2), Legion of Merit (2), D.F.C., Air medal (8), Air Force Commendation medal. Mem. Air Force Assn., USAF Acad. Assn. Grads., Nat. War Coll. Alumni Assn. Home: 1250 Big Valley Dr Colorado Springs CO 80919-1015

TODD, HARRY WILLIAMS, aircraft propulsion system company executive; b. Oak Park, Ill., 1922. BSME, U. So. Calif., 1947, BSIE, 1948, MBA, 1950. With Rockwell Internat., Pitts., 1947-76, former v.p. ops.; pres., chmn., chief exec. officer, bd. dirs. The L.E. Myers Co., Pitts., 1976-80; with Rohr Industries, Inc., Chula Vista, Calif., 1980-90, chief operating officer, 1980-82, pres., chief exec. officer, chmn., 1982-90, retired, 1990; mng. ptnr. Carlise Enterprises, 1990—; bd. dirs. Rohr Industries, Pacific Scientific, Helmerich & Payne, Garrett Aviation Svcs. Trustee Scripps Clinic and Rsch. Found. With U.S. Army, 1944-46. Office: Carlisle Enterprises 7777 Fay Ave La Jolla CA 92037-4327

TODD, J. C. See COOPER, JANE TODD

TODD, JAMES DALE, federal judge; b. Scotts Hill, Tenn., May 20, 1943; s. James P. and Jeanette Grace (Duck) T.; m. Jeanie M. Todd, June 26, 1965; children: James Michael, Julie Diane. BS, Lambuth Coll., 1965; M Combined Scis., U. Miss., 1968; JD, Memphis State U., 1972. Bar: Tenn. 1972, U.S. Dist. Ct. (we. dist.) Tenn. 1972, U.S. Ct. Appeals (6th cir.) 1973, U.S. Supreme Ct. 1975. Tchr. sci., chmn. sci. dept. Lyman High Sch., Longwood, Fla., 1965-68, Memphis U. Sch., 1968-72; ptnr. Waldrop, Farmer, Todd & Breen, P.A., 1972-83; cir. judge div. II 26th Jud. Dist., Jackson, Tenn., 1983-85; judge U.S. Dist. Ct. (we. dist.) Tenn., Jackson, 1985—. Named Alumnus of Yr. Lambuth Coll. Alumni Assn., 1985. Fellow Tenn. Bar Found.; mem. Fed. Judges Assn., Fed. Bar Assn., Tenn. Bar Assn., Jackson Madison County Bar Assn. (pres. 1978-79). Methodist. Office: US Dist Ct 109 S Highland Ave Jackson TN 38301-6123

TODD, JAMES S., surgeon, educator, medical association administrator; b. Hyannis, Mass., 1931. Intern Presbyn. Hosp., N.Y.C., 1957-58, resident in surgery, 1959-63; resident in surgery Delafield Hosp., N.Y.C., 1963; resident ob-gyn. Sloane Womens Hosp., N.Y.C., 1958-59; resident Valley Hosp., Ridgewood, N.J.; clin. asst. prof. surgery U. Medicine and Dentistry N.J., Newark; exec. v.p. AMA, 1993; pres. AMA. Office: American Medical Assocation 515 N State St Chicago IL 60610-4325

TODD, JAMES STILES, surgeon, professional association executive; b. Hyannis, Mass., July 9, 1931; s. Alexander Campbell and Myra Crowell (Stiles) T.; m. Marjorie Patricia Thorn, Sept. 6, 1958; children: Kendall Scott, Christopher James. AB, Harvard U., 1953, MD, 1957. Diplomate Am. Bd. Surgery. Intern Columbia-Presbyn. Med. Ctr., N.Y.C., 1957-58, resident in surgery, 1958-64; pvt. practice Ridgewood, N.J., 1964-85; asst. in surgery Columbia Coll. of Physicians & Surgeons, N.Y.C., 1964—, Columbia-Presbyn. Hosp., N.Y.C., 1964—; sr. dep. exec. v.p. AMA, Chgo., 1985—, exec. v.p., 1990-96; former chmn. bd. N.J. State Med. Underwriters, Inc. Lawrenceville; cons. physician Valley Hosp., Ridgewood, 1985—; mem. bd. overseers Brown U. Sch. Medicine; mem. trustees com. Duke U. Med. Ctr. Author: (with others) DRGs for Physicians, 1983; editor: Intensive Care, 1965; contbr. articles to profl. jours. Pres. Bergen Community Blood Bank, Paramus, N.J., 1978-85; pres. bd. mgrs. County Hosp., 1978-79. Recipient Edward J. Ill Distinguished Physician award, N.J. Acad. Medicine, 1980, Disting. Svc. award N.J. Hosp. Assn., 1984. Fellow ACS; mem. Health Care Execs., Med. Soc. N.J., AMA, pres. Physician Insurers Assn. of Am., Lawrenceville, N.J., 1984-85. Republican. Avocations: clock building and repair, boating.

TODD, JAN THERESA, counselor; b. Mobile, Ala., Mar. 20, 1961; d. Joseph Thomas and Lessie Grey (Sullivan) T. BA, U. Tex., San Antonio, 1983, MA, 1992. Cert. profl. counselor; cert. provisional tchr. English tchr. Bandera (Tex.) High Sch.-Bandera (Tex.) Ind. Sch. Dist., 1987-91; counselor Yorktown (Tex.) High Sch.-Yorktown (Tex.) Ind. Sch. Dist., 1992-93, John F. Kennedy High Sch.-Edgewood Ind. Sch. Dist., San Antonio, 1993-95, Lackland Jr./Sr. H.S., San Antonio, 1995—. Mem. ACA, Tex. Counselors Assn., South Tex. Counselors Assn., Assn. Tex. Profl. Educators. Home: 9415 De Sapin San Antonio TX 78250-6308 Office: Lackland Jr/Sr High School 2460 Bong Ave Bldg 8265 San Antonio TX 78236-1242

TODD, JOE LEE, historian; b. Bartlesville, Okla., Sept. 28, 1946; s. Harold Albert and Mildred Viola Todd. Student, Okla. State U., 1964-66; BA in Anthropology, U. Okla., 1974; postgrad. in Anthropology, U. Tex., Austin, 1979-81. Curator of collections Okla. Hist. Soc., Oklahoma City, 1971-76; dir. 45th Infantry div. mus., Oklahoma City, 1976-78; curator Ft. Hood (Tex.) Mus., 1978-82; oral historian, archivist Okla. Hist. Soc., Oklahoma City, 1982—; cons. Confederate Air Force, Midland, Tex., 1990—, Andersonville (Ga.) POW Ctr., 1991—. Author: Pipe-Tomahawks in the Oklahoma Historical Society, 1976, Native American Interveiws, oral histories, 1985, USS Oklahoma, Remembrance of a Great Lady, 1990. Bd. dirs. Sacred Heart (Okla.) Indian Mission, 1989-95. With U.S. Army, 1966-69, Okla. Nat. Guard, 1975-78, Tex. Nat. Guard, 1978-83, USAR, 1983-86. Decorated Air medal; recipient Humanitarian Svc. medal U.S. Army, 1992, Vietnam Svc. medal, 1969, Kuwaiti Liberation medal, 1991. Republican. Episcopalian. Office: Okla Hist Soc 2100 N Lincoln Blvd Oklahoma City OK 73105-4907

TODD, JOHN, mathematician, educator; b. Carnacally, Ireland, May 16, 1911; came to U.S., 1947, naturalized, 1953; s. William Robert and Catherine (Stewart) T.; m. Olga Taussky, Sept. 29, 1938. B.S., Queen's U., Belfast, Ireland, 1931; research student, St. John's Coll., Cambridge (Eng.) U., 1931-33. Lectr. Queen's U., 1933-37, King's Coll., London, 1937-49; chief computation lab., then chief numerical analysis Nat. Bur. Standards, 1947-57; prof. math. Calif. Inst. Tech., 1957—; Fulbright prof. Vienna, Austria, 1965. Author, editor books on numerical analysis and tables; editor in chief: Numerische Mathematik, 1959—; assoc. editor Aequationes Mathematicae, 1967-85, 89-95, Jour. Approximation Theory, 1967-93. Mem. Am. Math. Soc., Soc. Indsl. and Applied Math., Math. Assn. Am. (gov. 1980-83). Office: Calif Inst Technology Mathematics 253 # 37 Pasadena CA 91125

TODD, JOHN DICKERSON, JR., lawyer; b. Macon, Ga., June 30, 1912; s. J.D. and Hazel (McManus) T.; m. Mellicent McWhorter, Mar. 7, 1943; children—Rosalind (Mrs. Jack Harding Tedards, Jr.), John D. Student, Va. Mil. Inst., 1930-32; LL.B., U. Ga., 1935. Bar: S.C. bar 1935. With firm Hingson & Todd, 1935-51; partner firm Leatherwood, Walker, Todd & Mann, Greenville, S.C., 1952—; now sr. partner; judge Greenville City Ct., 1939; atty. County of Greenville, 1948-56; mem. bd. bar examiners State of

S.C.; chmn. S.C. Judicial Study Commn., 1995. Served to maj. AUS, 1941-45. Mem. ABA, Am. Coll. Trial Lawyers, Am. Bar Found., 4th U.S. Cir. Jud. Conf., S.C. Bar Assn. (bd. govs., pres. 1978—), Greenville Jr. C. of C. (pres.), Greenville County Bar (past pres.), Greenville Kiwanis (past pres.), Greenville Country Club (past pres.), Summit Club, Commerce Club, Phi Delta Phi, Sigma Nu. Baptist. Home: 200 Riverside Dr Greenville SC 29605-1133 Office: 100 E Coffee St Greenville SC 29601-2707

TODD, JOHN JOSEPH, lawyer; b. St. Paul, Mar. 16, 1927; s. John Alfred and Martha Agnes (Jagoe) T.; m. Dolores Jean Shanahan, Sept. 9, 1950; children: Richard M., Jane E., John P. Student, St. Thomas Coll., 1944, 46-47; B.Sci. and Law, U. Minn., 1949, LL.B., 1950. Bar: Minn. bar 1951. Practice in South St. Paul, Minn., 1951-72; partner Thuet and Todd, 1953-72; asso. justice Minn. Supreme Ct., St. Paul, 1972-85; sole practice West St. Paul, 1985-92; of counsel Brenner & Glassman Ltd., Mpls., 1992—. Served with USNR, 1945-46. Mem. state bar assns., VFW. Home: 6689 Argenta Trl W Inver Grove MN 55077-2208 Office: Brenner & Glassman Ltd 2001 Killebrew Dr Ste 170 Minneapolis MN 55425-1884

TODD, JOHN ODELL, insurance company sales professional; b. Mpls., Nov. 12, 1902; s. Frank Chisholm and Mary Mable (Odell) T.; AB, Cornell U., 1924; CLU, Am. Coll., 1933; m. Katherine Sarah Cone, Feb. 21, 1925; children: John Odell, George Bennett. Spl. agt. Equitable Life Assurance Soc., Mpls., 1926-28; ins. broker, Mpls., 1928-31; spl. agt. Northwestern Mut. Life Ins. Co., Mpls., 1931-38, Evanston, Ill., 1938—; ptnr. H.S. Vail & Sons, Chgo., 1938-43, Vail and Todd, gen. agts. Northwestern Mut., Chgo., 1943-44; sole gen. agt., Chgo., 1944-51; pres. Todd Planning and Service Co., life ins. brokers, 1951—; founder, hon. chmn., prin. John O. Todd Orgn., Exec. Compensation Specialists and Cons., 1970-91; faculty lectr. C.L.U. Insts., U. Conn., 1952-53, U. Wis., 1955-57, U. Calif., 1956, U. Hawaii, 1966; host interviewer ednl. Films Series of the Greats, 1973-74. Pres. Evanston (Ill.) 1st. Ward Non-Partisan Civic Assn., 1956-57; trustee Evanston Hist. Soc., 1973-76; bd. dirs. First Congl Ch., Evanston, 1987-89; co-founder MDRT Charitable Found., 1959, pres., 1971, sole lifetime dir. emeritus, 1971—. Recipient Cleary award Best Gen. Agt. Devel., 1948, Golden Plate award Am. Acad. Achievement, 1969; Huebner Gold medal for contbn. to edn., 1978; named Ins. Field Man of Year, Ins. Field Pub. Co., 1965, John Newton Russell award Instn. Life Ins., 1969; Ill. Room in Hall of States dedicated to him by Am. Coll., 1981. Mem. AALU Am. Coll. John O. Nat. Assn. Life Underwriters, Assn. Advanced Life Underwriters (pres. 1963-64), Am. Coll. Life Underwriters (trustee 1957-78), Chgo. Life Underwriters Assn. (dir. 1938-41, Disting. Service award 1984), Northwestern Mut. Spl. Agts. Assn. (pres. 1955-56), Life Agy. Mgrs. Assn. (dir. 1945-48), Northwestern Mut. Assn. Agts. (pres. 1957-58, leader sr. agents 1994), Chgo. Life Trust Council, Million Dollar Round Table (pres. 1951, only 60th yr. consecutive qualifier), Top of Table (charter mem.), Psi Upsilon, Sphinx Head. Republican. Clubs: Evanston Univ.; Glen View. Author: Taxation, Inflation and Life Insurance, 1950; Ceiling Unlimited, 1965, 5th edit., 1984, Never a Dull Day, an Autobiography, 1990, A Lifetime of Opportunities, 1996; contbg. author to text Huebner Foundation, 1951, Secrets of the Master Sellers, Am. Mgmt. assn., 1987.

TODD, JUDITH F., lawyer; b. Chgo., Jan. 25, 1946. Student, Vassar Coll.; AB, U. Mich., 1968; JD cum laude, U. Miami, 1972. Bar: Fla. 1972, Ill. 1977, Ala. 1981. With Sirote & Permutt P.C., Birmingham, Ala. Assoc. editor U. Miami Law Review, 1971-72. Fellow Am. Coll. Trust and Estate Counsel; mem. ABA, Fla. Bar, Ill. State Bar Assn. Office: Sirote & Permutt PC PO Box 55727 2222 Arlington Ave S Birmingham AL 35255

TODD, KATHLEEN GAIL, physician; b. Portland, Oreg., Aug. 31, 1951; d. Horace Edward and Lois Marie (Messing) T.; m. Andrew Richard Embick, March 31, 1980; children: Elizabeth Todd Embick, Margaret Todd Embick. BA, Pomona Coll., 1972; MD, Washington U., St. Louis, 1976. Diplomate Am. Bd. Family Practice. Resident U. Wash. Affiliated Hosps., Seattle, 1976-79; pvt. practice Valdez (Alaska) Med. Clinic, 1980—; chief of staff Valdez Community Hosp., 1986—. Mem. AMA, AAFP, Am. Acad. Family Practice, Alaska State Med. Assn. (counselor-at-large 1986-87). Democrat. Episcopalian. Avocations: skiing, kayaking, camping, music. Office: Valdez Med Clinic PO Box 1829 Valdez AK 99686-1829

TODD, KENNETH S., JR., parasitologist, educator; b. Three Forks, Mont., Aug. 25, 1936; s. Kenneth S. and Anna Louise (Seeman) T. BS, Mont. State U., 1962, MS, 1964; PhD, Utah State U., 1967. Asst. prof. U. Ill., Urbana, 1967-71, assoc. prof., 1971-76, prof. vet. parasitology, 1976-94, chmn. div. parasitology, 1983-90, asst. head vet. pathobiology, 1984-87, prof. vet. programs in agr., 1984-94, acting head vet. pathobiology, 1987-90, head, 1990-94; prof. emeritus, 1994; affiliate scientist Ill. State Natural History Survey, 1987—; adj. prof. microbiology Mont. State U., 1994—. Served with USAF, 1954-58. NSF grad. fellow, 1966-67. Mem. AVMA, Am. Assn. Vet. Parasitologists, Am. Micros. Soc., Am. Soc. Parasitologists, Am. Soc. Tropical Medicine and Hygiene, Helminthologic Soc. Washington, Midwest Conf. Parasitologists, Wildlife Disease Assn., Soc. Protozoologists, Mont. Acad. Scis. Office: Mont State U Dept Microbiology Bozeman MT 59715

TODD, MALCOLM CLIFFORD, surgeon; b. Carlyle, Ill., Apr. 10, 1913; s. Malcolm N. and Grace (Heitmeier) T.; m. Ruth Holle Schlake, June 12, 1945; 1 son, Malcolm Douglas. AB, U. Ill., 1934, MB, Northwestern U., 1934, MD, 1938; DSc (hon.), Brown U., 1975. Diplomate Am. Bd. Surgery. Intern St. Lukes Hosp., Chgo., 1937-38; resident Cook County Hosp., Chgo., 1938-41; instr. surgery Northwestern U., 1939-46; pvt. practice Long Beach, Calif., 1946-90; clin. prof. surgery U. Calif., Irvine, 1964-85, emeritus prof. surgery, 1985—; chief surgery, hon. bd. dirs. Long Beach Meml. Hosp., 1956-57, chief of staff, 1958-60; attending surgeon Long Beach VA Hosp., 1954-80, Los Angeles County Gen. Hosp., 1964-74; bd. dirs. Harbor Bank Long Beach, Spectral Diagnostics, Toronto, Ont., Can. Contbr. sci. and socio-econ. articles to med. jours. Mem. Nat. Adv. Com. on Health Manpower; U.S. del. WHO, 1970-72; dir. Calif. Health Planning Coun., 1966-74; mem. Calif. Regional Med. Programs Coun., 1968-74, Presdl. Commn. on Refugees, 1975, Long Beach Ednl. TV Bd., 1956-70; chmn. Long Beach br. ARC, 1957-58; pres. Forward Long Beach Com., 1978—; trustee Long Beach Meml. Hosp., Sch. Medicine Morehouse U., Atlanta; chmn. Long Beach Community Svcs. Devel. Corp., 1979—; mem. health policy bd. Georgetown U.; bd. dirs. Downtown Long Beach Assocs., Medic Alert Found., Calif. Cancer Soc., Japan Am. Conf. Mayors; regent Uniformed Svcs. Health Scis. U., 1973-80; mem. Nat. Commn. Cost Health Care. Served to maj. AUS, 1942-46. Fellow ACS, Internat. Coll. Surgeons (pres. 1983-84, pres. U.S. sect. 1977), Royal Soc. Medicine, Am. Coll. Gastroenterology, Soc. Internat. Chirugie; mem. AMA (trustee 1973-76, pres. 1974-75, chmn. coun. on health manpower), Calif. Med. Assn. (pres. 1968-69), L.A. County Med. Soc. (hon. pres. 1995), Long Beach Med. Soc. (pres. 1953-54), Karl A. Meyer Surg. Soc. (pres.), Long Beach C. of C. (pres. 1983), Virginia Country Club, Internat. City Club, Torch, Kiwanis, Pi Kappa Alpha (v.p. 1976). Home: 5330 E El Parque St Long Beach CA 90815-4247 Office: 2840 N Long Beach Blvd Long Beach CA 90806-1531

TODD, MARY PATRICIA, nursing administrator; b. Loogootee, Ind., Sept. 5, 1959; d. James Walter and Anna Margaret (Arvin) T.; m. Joe Linville, 1996; 1 child, B.J. BS in Social Work, St. Mary of the Woods Coll., 1982; AS in Nursing, Tenn. State U., 1989; postgrad., Vanderbilt U., 1995—. Cert. disaster nursing ARC. Comty. organizer Rogers Park Tenants Com., Chgo., 1984-85; dir. Nashville Comys. Orgn. for Progress, Nashville, 1986-87, Tenn. Coun. Sr. Citizens, Nashville, 1987-89; staff nurse Nashville VA Med. Ctr., Nashville, 1989-90; charge nurse Hartsville (Tenn.) Convalescent Ctr., 1990-94; quality assurance coord. ABC Home Health, Hartsville, 1992-93; adminstr. ABC Home Health, Lafayette, Tenn., 1994-95; charge nurse Trousdale Med. Ctr., Hartsville, Tenn., 1995—; presenter rural health conf. Meharry Med. Sch., Nashville, 1994; spkr. Tenn. rural Health Assn., 1995. Contbr., pub.: Love Passed On, 1991; contbr.: Photographic History of Martin County, 1993, Voices from the Hills, 1995; organizer, author: (diaster plan) Caring When it Counts, 1994. Bd. dirs., chair membership com. Mid. Cumberland Cmty. Health Agy., Nashville, 1992—; mem. Network, Washington, 1993—; organizer Trousdale County Cmty. Health Coun., Hartsville, 1992—; active Greenpeace, 1990-92; tchr. Confraternity of Christian Doctrine, Holy Family Cath. Ch., 1992, 94. Mem. ANA, Tenn. Nurses Assn., Tenn. Assn. for Home Care, Tenn. Rural Health Assn., Trousdale County C. of C., Amnesty Internat., Health Profls. Network, Rural Tenn. Women's Support Group (organizer 1994), Sigma Delta Tau. Democrat. Avocations: Karate, music, writing. Home: 314 Church St Apt 22 Hartsville TN 37074-1713 Office: Trousdale Medical Center 500 Church St #22 Hartsville TN 37074

TODD, NORMA JEAN ROSS, retired government official; b. Butler, Pa., Oct. 3, 1920; d. William Bryson and Doris Mae (Ferguson) Ross; m. Alden Frank Miller, Jr., Apr. 16, 1940 (dec. Feb. 1975); 1 child, Alden Frank III; m. Jack R. Todd, Dec. 23, 1977 (dec. Sept. 1990). Student, Pa. State U., 1944-46, Yale U., 1954-57. Exec. mgr. Donora (Pa.) C. of C., 1950-57, pres., 1972; exec. mgr. Donora Community Chest, 1950-57; office mgr. Donora Golden Jubilee, 1951; staff writer Herald-Am., Donora, 1957, city editor, 1957-70; assoc. editor Daily Herald, Donora, 1970-73; svc. rep. Pitts. Teleservice Ctr., Social Security Adminstrn., HHS, 1977-83. Mem. Mayor's Adv. Council, Donora, 1965-69, Citizens' Adv. Council, Donora, 1965-69; mem. Donora Bd. Edn., 1954-60, pres., 1960; mem. Donora Borough Council, 1970-72; bd. dirs. Mon Valley chpt. ARC, 1964—, sec. bd., 1966-97, chmn. bd. dirs., 1997—; bd. dirs. Washington County Tourism Agy., 1970-90, sec., 1972-90; bd. dirs. Washington County History and Landmarks Found. 1971-80, 91-92, sec., 1975-80, 91-92; hon. life mem., 1996; bd. dirs. Mon Valley YMCA, 1960-66, Mon Valley council Camp Fire Girls, 1965-79, Mon Valley Drug and Alcoholism Council, 1971-78; hon. life mem. Pa. Congress PTAs; bd. dirs. United Way Mon Valley, 1973-82, chmn. pub. rels., 1973-74. Recipient Fine Arts Festival of Pa. Poetry first prize award Fedn. of Women's Clubs, 1987, 1st and 2nd pl. awards for photography Washington County Fine Arts Festival, County Fedn. of Women's Club, 1990, Disting. Svc. award Donora Rotary Club, 1997; published in Best Poems of 1995 Nat. Library of Poetry, Best Poems of 1996. Mem. AAUW, Svc. Coprs Retired Execs., Pa. Soc. Newspaper Editors, Pitts. Press Club, Donora C. of C. (pres. 1971-72), DAR (regent Monongahela Valley chpt. 1974-77, treas. 1992—), Internat. Platform Assn., World Poetry Soc. Internat., Washington County Poetry Soc. (pres. 1967-69), Donora Hist. Soc. (curator 1990—), Family of Bruce Soc. (descendants of King Robert the Bruce of Scotland 1987—), Washington County Fedn. Women's Clubs (rec. sec. 1964-66, pub. rels. chmn. 1990-92). Clubs: Order Ea. Star (worthy matron 1966-67, treas. 1986-94., bd. dirs. western Pa. Eastern Star Home 1997—), White Shrine of Jerusalem (high priestess 1973-74, treas. 1995—), Order of Amaranth (royal matron 1966, dist. dep. 3 times, grand rep. W.Va. 1979-80), Donora Forecast (pres. 1962-63), Donora Unidon (pres. 1965-66, 56-57), Svc. Corps Ret. Execs. Avocation: genealogy. Home: Overlook Ter Donora PA 15033 also: 1310 Mckean Ave Donora PA 15033-2200

TODD, RICHARD D. R., lawyer; b. Borger, Tex., July 17, 1962; s. William H. and Linda (Brumfield) T.; m. Lisa Ann McCown, Jan. 4, 1986; children: Richard Benjamin, Madison Claire. Student, Tex. Tech. U., Lubbock, 1984; BS in Health Care Adminstrn., Wayland Bapt. U., Plainview, Tex., 1988; JD magna cum laude, Oklahoma City U., 1991. Bar: Tex. 1992, Okla. 1992, U.S. Dist. Ct. (no. dist.) Tex. 1992, U.S. Dist. Ct. (we. dist.) Okla. 1992, U.S. Ct. Appeals (5th cir.) 1993, U.S. Supreme Ct. 1995. Paramedic/ops. mgr. Amarillo (Tex.) Med. Svcs., 1982-89; legal intern Lampkin, McCaffrey & Tawwater, Oklahoma City, 1990-92; pvt. practice Borger, Tex., 1992-95, Wichita Falls, Tex., 1995—; barrister Am. Inn of Ct., Oklahoma City, 1990-92. Editor Oklahoma City U. Law Rev., 1989-91. Percussionist First Bapt. Ch., Wichita Falls. Mem. ABA, Borger Bar Assn., State Bar Tex. (pro bono coll. 1994-95), Phi Delta Phi (vice magister 1991). Baptist. Office: 1417 9th St Wichita Falls TX 76301-4302

TODD, ROBERT FRANKLIN, III, oncologist, educator; b. Granville, Ohio, Apr. 16, 1948; m. Susan Erhard, 1977; children: Currier Nathaniel, Andrew Joseph. AB, Duke U., 1970, PhD, 1975, MD, 1976. Diplomate Am. Bd. Internal Medicine. Intern Peter Bent Brigham Hosp., Boston, 1976-77, resident, 1977-78; fellow in oncology Sidney Farber Cancer Inst., Boston, 1978-80; clin. fellow in medicine Harvard Med. Sch., Boston, 1978-81; postdoctoral fellow divsn. tumor immunology Sidney Farber Cancer Inst., Boston, 1979-81; asst. prof. medicine Harvard Med. Sch., Boston, 1981-84; assoc. prof. internal medicine U. Mich., Ann Arbor, 1984-88, assoc. prof. cellular and molecular biology, 1985-88, assoc. dir. divsn. hematology-oncology internal medicine, 1987-91, prof. internal medicine, 1988—, assoc. chair for rsch. dept. internal medicine, 1989-91, assoc. chair dept. internal medicine, 1991-93, chief divsn. hematology-oncology dept. internal medicine, 1993—; attending physician U. Mich. Hosps., 1984—; chmn. hematology/oncology subsplty chpt. Ctrl. Soc. for Clin. Rsch., 1995-97. Contbr. numerous articles to profl. jours.; patentee in field. Mem. Am. Coll. Physicians, Am. Assn. of Immunologists, Am. Assn. for Cancer Rsch., Am. Soc. of Clin. Oncology, Soc. of Leukocyte Biology (councilor 1996—), Am. Soc. of Hematology, Am. Fedn. for Clin. Rsch. (councilor midwest chpt. 1986-89), Ctrl. Soc. for Clin. Rsch. (councilor 1997—), S.W. Oncology Group, Am. Soc. for Clin. Investigation, The Microcirculatory Soc., Phi Beta Kappa, Alpha Omega Alpha. Office: U of Mich Med Sch Divsn Hematology/Oncology 3119 Taubman Ctr Ann Arbor MI 48109

TODD, RONALD GARY, lawyer; b. Spokane, Wash., Dec. 12, 1946; s. Theodore H. and Dorothea I. (Swanson) T.; m. Natalie A., June 16, 1973; children: Russell E., Brian N., David E. AB, Cornell U., 1969; JD, Columbia U., 1972. Bar: N.Y. 1973, U.S. Dist. Ct. (so. and ea. dists.) N.Y. 1975, U.S. Ct. Appeals (2nd cir.) 1975, U.S. Supreme Ct. 1976, D.C. 1993. Atty. Dewey Ballantine, N.Y.C., 1973-79, Simpson Thacher & Bartlett, N.Y.C., 1980-82; atty., ptnr. Golenbock & Barell, N.Y.C., 1982-89; ptnr. Reid & Priest, N.Y.C., 1989—; instr., guest lectr. NYU Sch. Continuing Edn., 1983-90; adv. bd. Commonwealth Land Title and TransAm. Title Ins. Co., N.Y.C., 1992—. Contbr. articles to profl. jours. Pres., bd. dirs. Seven Bridges Field Club, 1982-85. Mem. ABA (real property sect. 1973—), N.Y. Bar Assn. (real property sect. 1973—), D.C. Bar Assn. (real property sect. 1992—). Avocations: instrumental music, tennis. Office: Reid & Priest 40 W 57th St New York NY 10019-4001

TODD, SHIRLEY ANN, school system administrator; b. Botetourt County, Va., May 23, 1935; d. William Leonard and Margaret Judy (Simmons) Brown; m. Thomas Byron Todd, July 7, 1962 (dec. July 1977). B.S. in Edn., Madison Coll., 1956; M.Ed., U. Va., 1971. Cert. tchr., Va. Elem. tchr. Fairfax County Sch. Bd., Fairfax, Va., 1956-66, 8th grade history tchr., 1966-71, guidance counselor James F. Cooper Mid. Sch., McLean, Va., 1971-88, dir. guidance, 1988-96; chmn. mktg. Lake Anne Joint Venture, Falls Church, Va., 1979-82, mng. ptnr., 1980-82. Del. Fairfax County Republican Conv., 1985. Fellow Fairfax Edn. Assn. (mem. profl. rights and responsibilities commn. 1970-72, bd. dirs. 1968-70), Va. Edn. Assn. (mem. state com. on local assns. and urban affairs 1969-70), NEA, No. Va. Counselors Assn. (hospitality and social chmn., exec. bd. 1982-83), Va. Counselors Assn. (exec. com. 1987), Va. Sch. Counselors Assn., Am. Assn. for Counseling and Devel., Chantilly Nat. Golf and Country Club (v.p. social 1981-82, Centreville, Va.). Baptist. Avocations: golf, tennis. Home: 6543 Bay Tree Ct Falls Church VA 22041-1001

TODD, THOMAS ABBOTT, architect, urban designer; b. North Stonington, Conn., May 5, 1928; s. James Arnold and Isabel Nisbet (Downs) T.; m. Carol Roberts, July 7, 1956; children: Christopher, Suzannah, Cassandra. B.A., Haverford Coll., 1950; M.C.P., U. Pa., 1959, M.Arch. with honors, 1959. Designer Geddes Brecher Qualls Cunningham, Phila., 1961; chief designer Eshbach Pullinger Stevens Bruder, Phila., 1962; partner Grant & Todd, Phila., 1963, Wallace McHarg Roberts Todd, Phila., 1963-79, Wallace Roberts & Todd, Phila., 1979-91. Works include The master plan for Abuja, capitol city of, Nigeria; urban design concept, master plan and public architecture for Balt. Inner Harbor; master plan U.S. Capitol Grounds, McKeldin Sq., Balt., Norfolk waterfront design, (Va.), Atlantic City Conv. Ctr./Rail Terminal, Lower Manhattan Plan, N.Y.C., Downtown L.A. devel. Plan, plan for State facilities, Annapolis, Md., master plan Haverford Coll., 6th St Market Pl., Richmond, Va., Tredegar Galleries Valentine Mus., Richmond, Waterside Festival Market, Norfolk, Va., Liberty State Pk., Jersey City, N.J., Wiggins Waterfront State Pk., Camden, N.J., Downtown Buffalo master plan, Quadrangle Life Care Community, Haverford, Liberty Pl. master plan, Phila., long range devel. plan U. Pa., Performing Arts Ctr., Haverford Coll., Assembly Hall, Germantown Friends Sch., plan for downtown Westerly, R.I., numerous pvt. residences, landscape plans, instl. and pub. master plans; contbr. numerous articles, editorials to profl.jours. Bd. dirs. Germantown Friends Sch., Phila., 1972-74, Green St. Friends Sch., Phila., 1973-75, Phila. Maritime Mus., 1986-90, Philomel Ancient Instruments, Phila., 1986-91, Maxwell Mansion, Phila., 1983-86; v.p. Haverford Coll. Arboretum, 1983; chmn. ann. giving Haverford Coll., 1987; mem. Jamestown (R.I.) Planning Bd.; advisor Ft. Adams Found., Newport, R.I. Theophilus Parsons Chandler fellow, 1959; recipient numerous design awards. Fellow AIA; mem. Am. Inst. Cert. Planners. Republican. Quaker. Home: 118 Highland Dr Jamestown RI 02835-2900

TODD, VIRGIL HOLCOMB, clergyman, religion educator; b. Jordonia, Tenn., June 22, 1921; s. George Thurman and Nellie Mai (Dutton) T.; m. Irene Rolman, Sept. 21, 1941; 1 child, Donald Edwin. BA, Bethel Coll., 1945; BD, Cumberland Presbyn. Sem., 1947; MA, Scarritt Coll., 1948; PhD, Vanderbilt U., 1956. Ordained to ministry Presbyn. Ch., 1944. Minister Cumberland Presbyn. Chs., Tenn. and Ky., 1943-52; assoc. prof. Bethel Coll., McKenzie, Tenn., 1952-54; prof. of Old Testament Memphis Theol. Sem., 1954—; interim minister Presbyn. chs. in Tenn., Ky. and Miss., 1952—; vice-moderator Gen. Assembly Cumberland Presbyn. Ch., 1984-85, moderator, 1985-86. Author: Prophet Without Portfolio (2d Isaiah), 1972, A New Look at an Old Prophet (Ezekiel), 1977, Biblical Eschatology, 1985. Active Shelby (County) United Neighbors, Memphis, 1973-74, United Way of Greater Memphis, 1974-82. Mem. Soc. Bibl. Lit., Memphis Ministers' Assn. Democrat. Lodge: Civitan (chaplain, bd. dirs. local chpt.). Avocations: travel, golf. Office: Memphis Theol Sem 168 E Parkway S Memphis TN 38104-4340

TODD, WILLIAM BURTON, English language and literature educator; b. Chester, Pa., Apr. 11, 1919; s. William Booth and Edith Hawkins (Burton) T.; m. Ann Bowden, Nov. 23, 1969; children by previous marriage: Marilyn Chestnut Todd Guinn, Susan Linda Todd Kramer, Deborah Burton, Terence Kingsley. BA, Lehigh U., 1940, MA, 1947, LHD (hon.), 1975; PhD, U. Chgo., 1949. Prof., head dept. English, Salem (N.C.) Coll., 1949-54; asst. libr. Houghton Libr., Harvard U.; assoc. prof. English U. Tex., Austin, 1958; prof., dir. bibliog. rsch. U. Tex., 1959-82, Kerr Centennial prof. English history and culture, 1982-85, Kerr Prof. emeritus, 1985—, Ransom Ctr. scholar, 1990—; J.P.R. Lyell reader in bibliography Oxford (Eng.) U., 1969-70; Andrew D. Osbord lectr. U. Western Ont., 1978; cons. Nat. Libr. Australia, 1973; D. Nichol Smith lectr. Australian Nat. U., Canberra, 1973; Cecil Oldman Meml. lectr. Leeds (Eng.) U., 1975; mem. adv. bd. rsch. tools program NEH, 1977-78; Internat. Libr. lectr. Leipzig, Germany, 1981; Internat. Lit. lectr., Budapest, 1984; mem. nat. adv. bd. Ctr. for the Book, 1978-88. Author: New Adventures among Old Books, 1958, Prize Books: Awards Granted to Scholars, 1961, Bibliography of Edmund Burke, 1964, Directory of Printers: London 1800-1840, 1972, The White House Transcripts: An Enquiry, 1974, The Gutenberg Bible: New Evidence, 1982; editor: Goldsmith's Prospect of Society, 1954, Burke's Reflections on the Revolution in France, 1959, Thomas J. Wise Centenary Studies, 1959, (with E. Stenbock-Fermor) The Kilgour Collection of Russian Literature, 1959, Guy of Warwick, 1968, Suppressed Commentaries on the Wiseian Forgeries, 1969, Hume and the Enlightenment, 1974, (with R.H. Campbell and A.S. Skinner) Smith's Wealth of Nations, 1976, (with Paul Langford) Writings and Speeches of Burke, 1981-97, Hume's History of England, 1983-85, Papers Bibliog. Soc. Am., 1967-81, Swinburne's Character and Opinions of Dr. Johnson, 1985, (with Ann Bowden) Tauchnitz International Editions in English, 1988; contbr. articles to profl. jours. Served to maj. inf. AUS, 1941-45, ETO. Decorated Bronze Star, Purple Heart; Fulbright fellow U.K., 1952-53, Am. Coun. Learned Socs. fellow, 1961-62, Guggenheim fellow, 1965-66, vis. fellow All Souls Coll., 1970, Zachariah Poulson fellow Libr. Co. Phila., 1990, Peterson fellow Am. Antiquarian Soc., 1992; scholar-in-residence Rockefeller Conf. and Study Ctr., Villa Serbelloni, Bellagio, Italy, 1986, vis. scholar Wolfson Coll., Oxford, England, 1993; recipient Oldman Meml. award and Marc Fitch bibliography prize, 1975. Mem. MLA, Bibliog. Soc. Am. (v.p. 1981-84), Bibliog. Soc. (Eng.), Printing Hist. Soc., Johnsonians (chmn. 1985), Pvt. Librs. Assn. (Eng.) (pres. 1983-86), Assn. Internat. de Bibliophilie (France), Phi Beta Kappa. Club: Grolier. Home: 2803 Scenic Dr Austin TX 78703-1040

TODD, WILLIAM MICHAEL, lawyer; b. Cleve., Dec. 13, 1952; s. William Charles and Jennie Ann (Diana) T.; m. Sara Lynn, Jan. 4, 1986. BA, U. Notre Dame, 1973; JD, Ohio State U., 1976. Bar: Ohio 1976, U.S. Dist. Ct. (so. dist.) Ohio 1977, U.S. Supreme Ct. 1987. Assoc. Porter, Wright, Morris & Arthur, Columbus, Ohio, 1976-82, ptnr., 1983-93; ptnr. Squire, Sanders & Dempsey, Columbus, 1993—. Trustee Callvac Svcs., Columbus, 1985-91, pres. 1988. Mem. ABA (governing com. forum on health law 1988-91), Ohio Bar Assn., Columbus Bar Assn., Am. Soc. Med. Assn. Counsel, Am. Bd. Trial Advocates, Ohio Soc. Hosp. Attys., Nat. Health Lawyers Assn., Worthington Hills Country Club, Columbus Athletic Club. Roman Catholic. Avocations: music, recreational sports. Office: Squire Sanders & Dempsey 41 S High St Columbus OH 43215-6101

TODD, ZANE GREY, retired utilities executive; b. Hanson, Ky., Feb. 3, 1924; s. Marshall Elvin and Kate (McCormick) T.; m. Marysnow Stone, Feb. 8, 1950 (dec. 1983); m. Frances Z. Anderson, Jan. 6, 1984. Student, Evansville Coll., 1947-49; BS summa cum laude, Purdue U., 1951, DEng (hon.), 1979; postgrad., U. Mich., 1965; DHL, U. Indpls., 1993. Fingerprint classifier FBI, 1942-43; electric system planning engr. Indpls. Power & Light Co., 1951-56, spl. assignments supr., 1956-60, head elec. system planning, 1960-65, head substation design div., 1965-68, head distbn. engring. dept., 1968-70, asst. to v.p., 1970-72, v.p., 1972-74, exec. v.p., 1974-75, pres., 1975-81, chmn., chief exec. officer, 1976-89, dir., chmn. exec. com., 1989-94, chief exec. officer, 1981-89; chmn., pres. IPALCO Enterprises, Inc., Indpls., 1983-89, dir., chmn. exec. com., 1989-94; chmn. bd., chief exec. officer Mid-Am. Capital Resources, Inc. subs. IPALCO Enterprises, Inc., Indpls., 1984-89, also bd. dirs., 1984-94; gen. mgr. Mooresville (Ind.) Pub. Svc. Co., Inc., 1956-60; bd. dirs. Nat. City Bank Ind. (formerly Mchts. Nat. Corp.), 1975-94, Am. States Ins. Co., 1976-94; hon. dir. 500 Festival Assocs., Inc., pres. 1987. Originator probability analysis of power system reliability; contbr. articles to tech. jours. and mags. Past pres. adv. bd. St. Vincent Hosp.; bd. dirs. Commn. for Downtown, YMCA Found., Crime Stoppers Cen. Ind., Corp. Community Coun.; past chmn., bd. trustees Ind. Cen. U. (now U. Indpls.); bd. govs. Associated Colls. of Ind.; Nat. and Greater Indpls. adv. bds. Salvation Army; mem. adv. bd. Clowes Hall. Sgt. AUS, 1943-47. Recipient William Booth award Salvation Army, 1994; named Disting. Engring. Alumnus Purdue U., 1976, Outstanding Elec. Engr. Purdue U., 1992, Knight of Malta, Order of St. John of Jerusalem, 1986. Fellow IEEE (past chmn. power sys. engring. com.); mem. ASME, NSPE, Power Engring. Soc., Ind. Fiscal Policy Inst. (bd. govs.), Ind. C. of C., Indpls. C. of C., Mooresville C. of C. (past pres.), PGA Nat. Country Club, Ulen Country Club, Columbia Club, Indpls. Athletic Club (past bd. dirs.), Meridian Hills Country Club (past bd. dirs.), Skyline Club (bd. govs.), Newcomen Soc. (past chmn. Ind.), Rotary, Lions (past pres.), Eta Kappa Nu, Tau Beta Pi. Home: 420 Eagleton Cove Way Palm Beach Gardens FL 33418-8489

TODD COPLEY, JUDITH ANN, materials and metallurgical engineering educator; b. Wakefield, West Yorkshire, Eng., Dec. 13, 1950; came to U.S., 1978; d. Marley and Joan Mary (Birkinshaw) Booth; m. David Michael Todd, June 17, 1972 (div. June 1981); m. Stephen Michael Copley, Aug. 3, 1984; 1 child, Amy Elizabeth. BA, Cambridge (Eng.) U., 1972, MA, PhD, 1977. Research asst. Imperial Coll. Sci. and Tech., London, 1976-78; research assoc. SUNY, Stonybrook, 1978; research engr. U. Calif., Berkeley, 1979-82; asst. prof. materials sci. and mech. engring. U. So. Calif., L.A., 1982-90; assoc. prof. metall. and materials engring. Ill. Inst. Tech., Chgo., 1990—, assoc. chairperson mech. materials and aerospace engring., 1995—; mem. task force Materials Property Coun., N.Y.C., 1979—; prof. Iron and Steel Soc., 1996—. Contbr. articles to profl. jours.; patentee in field. Recipient Brit. Univs. Student Travel award, 1972, Brit. Fedn. Univ. Women award, 1972, Faculty Rsch. award Oak Ridge (Tenn.) Nat. Lab., 1986, Vanadium award British Inst. Materials, 1990; Kathryn Kingswell Meml. scholar, 1972. Fellow Am. Assn. Women in Sci.; mem. AIME (Rsch. award 1983), ASTM, ASM Internat. (chmn. L.A. chpt. 1986-87, coun. mem. materials sci. divsn. 1984-89), ASME (chmn. materials and fabrication com. pressure vessel and piping divsn., assoc. editor Jour. Pressure Vessel & Piping Tech. 1994), Soc. Women Engrs. (sr.), Electron Microscopy Soc., Hist. Metallurgy Soc., Nat. Soc. Corrosion Engrs. (Seed grant award 1983), Microbeam Analysis Soc. Avocation: archaeometry. Home: 307 Briargate Ter Hinsdale IL 60521-2819 Office: Ill Inst Tech Dept Mech Materials & Aerospace Engring Chicago IL 60616

TODER, ERIC JAY, economist; b. N.Y.C., Mar. 16, 1944; s. Saul and Rose (Cohen) T.; m. Susan C. Cote, Aug. 2, 1980. BS, Union Coll., 1964; MA in Econs., U. Rochester, 1967, PhD in Econs., 1971. Asst. prof. econs. Tufts U., Medford, Mass., 1968-73; sr. rsch. assoc. Charles River Assocs., Cambridge, Mass., 1973-76; fin. economist U.S. Dept. Treasury, Washington, 1976-83; dir. fin. and tax analysis U.S. Dept. Energy, Washington, 1980-81; dep. dir. Office Tax Analysis, U.S. Treasury, Washington, 1983-84; dep. asst. dir. Congl. Budget Office, Washington, 1984-88, 91-93; cons. New Zealand Treasury, Wellington, 1988-91; dep. asst. sec. tax analysis U.S. Dept. Treasury, Washington, 1993-96; vis. prof. econs. U. Mich., 1997. Author: Trade Policy and U.S. Auto Industry, 1978; contbr. to econs. publs. Mem. Am. Econ. Assn., Nat. Tax Assn., Assn. Pub. Policy Analysis and Mgmt., Washington Tax Economists Forum. Jewish. Avocations: travel, hiking, music. Office: US Dept Treasury 15th & Pennsylvania Ave NW Washington DC 20220

TODHUNTER, JOHN ANTHONY, toxicologist; b. Cali, Valle, Colombia, Oct. 9, 1949; s. John Arthur and Teresa Maria (Torres) T.; divorced, 1986; children: Jennifer, Julia; m. Donna Kay Wilson, Apr. 19, 1986; 1 child, Jacqueline Rose. BSc, UCLA, 1971; MSc, Calif. State U., 1973; PhD, U. Calif., Santa Barbara, 1976. Diplomate Am. Bd. Toxicology, Am. Bd. Forensic Examiners; regulatory affairs cert. Instr. Calif. State U., L.A., 1972-73; rsch. asst. U. Calif., Santa Barbara, 1973-76; fellow Roche Inst. Molecular Biology, Nutley, N.J., 1976-78; asst. prof. Cath. U. Am., Washington, 1978-81, chmn. Biochemistry Program, 1980-81; asst. adminstr. U.S. EPA, Washington, 1981-83; cons. Sci. Regulatory Svcs. Internat., Washington, 1983-91; pres. SRS Internat. Corp., 1991—, SRS Internat. Health Care Group, 1995—; expert advisor European regional office WHO, Stockholm, 1984; mem. Hazardous Waste Siting Bd., Annapolis, Md., 1980-81. Contbr. articles to profl. jours. Bd. dirs. Reagan Alumni Assn., Washington, 1985—; vol. Am. Cancer Soc., Washington, 1988—; mem. Presdl. Transition Team, Washington, 1980. U. Calif. Bd. Regents fellow, 1975, B.R. Baker Meml. fellow dept. chemistry U. Calif., Santa Barbara, 1976. Fellow Am. Inst. Chemists (dir. at large 1989-92, vice chmn. bd. 1992); mem. Soc. of Toxicology, Am. Chem. Soc., Soc. for Risk Analysis, N.Y. Acad. Sci. Office: SRS Internat 1625 K St NW Ste 1000 Washington DC 20006-1619

TODOROVIC, JOHN, chemical engineer; b. Madison, Wis., Mar. 28, 1961; s. Radmilo A. and Lillian (Djukic) T.; m. Nadja Petranin, June 29, 1991. BSChemE, Tex. A&M U., 1984; MSChemE, Rose-Hulman Inst. Tech., 1987. Process engr. GE Plastics, Pittsfield, Mass., 1989-90; sr. product devel. engr. Rexam Graphics, South Hadley, Mass., 1991—. Pres. Brazos Valley Amateur Soccer Leauge, College Station, 1984. B. Rankovich scholarship B. Rankovich Found., 1986. Mem. AIChe (student chpt. pres. 1985), Sigma Xi, Tau Beta Pi, Alpha Chi Sigma. Serbian Orthodox. Achievements include implemented a new die coating technology that enabled a specialized product to be coated efficiently after several previous unsuccessful attempts. Office: Rexam Graphics 87 Alvord St South Hadley MA 01075-1342

TODREAS, NEIL EMMANUEL, nuclear engineering educator; b. Peabody, Mass., Dec. 17, 1935; s. David and Anna (Gendleman) T.; m. Carol S. Schonberg, June 19, 1958; children: Timothy, Ian. B.S.M.E., Cornell U., 1958, M.S., 1958; Sc.D. in Nuclear Engring., MIT, 1966. Asst. prof. dept. nuclear engring. MIT, Cambridge, 1970-71, assoc. prof., 1971-75, prof., 1975—, Kepco prof. nuclear engring. and prof. mech. engring., 1992—, head dept. nuclear engring., 1981-89. Served to lt. (j.g.) USN, 1958-62. Named Disting. Tchr., Ruth and Joel Spira award MIT Sch. Engring., 1995. Fellow ASME, Am. Nuclear Soc. (Arthur Holly Compton award for outstanding educators in nuclear engring. 1995, Tech. Achievement award for outstanding contbns. to thermal hydraulics 1994); mem. Nat. Acad. Engring., Sigma Xi, Tau Beta Pi, Pi Tau Sigma. Office: MIT 77 Massachusetts Ave # 24-219 Cambridge MA 02139-4301

TODRES, ELAINE MELLER, foundation administrator; m. Rubin Todres; children: Lindsay Meller, Jesse Paul Meller. PhD in Polit. Sci., U. Pitts. Asst. dep. min. Ont. Women's Directorate Min. of Revenue, dep. min. human resources secretariat, chair civil svc. comm, dep. min. culture and comm., dep. min. culture, tourism and recreation, 1993-95, dep. solicitor gen., dep. min. correctional svcs., 1995-97; pres. Baycrest Centre Found., Toronto, 1997—; spkr. in field. Editor-at-large Agy. for Instrnl. Tech.; mem. editl. bd. Can. Inst. Pub. Adminstr., 1992. Office: Ste 400 N Tower, 175 Bloor St E, Toronto, ON Canada M4W 3R8

TOEDT, D(ELL) C(HARLES), III, lawyer; b. Maxwell AFB, Ala., Nov. 17, 1954; m. Maretta A. Comfort. BA with high honors, U. Tex., 1973, JD, 1981. Bar: Tex. 1982, U.S. Patent and Trademark Office 1983, U.S. Dist. Ct. (so. dist.) Tex. 1984, U.S. Ct. Appeals (fed. cir.) 1984, U.S. Supreme Ct. 1991, U.S. Dist. Ct. (no. dist.) Calif. 1996. Atty. Schlanger, Cook, Cohn, Mills & Grossberg, Houston, 1982-83, Arnold, White & Durkee, Houston, 1983—; adj. prof. South Tex. Coll. Law, 1988-90. Sr. assoc. editor Tex. Law Rev., 1981-82; author/editor: Licensing Law Handbook: Computer Software Issues, 1987; author Law and Bus. of Computer Software, 1989—; contbr. articles to law jours. Served to lt. USN, 1974-79. Mem. ABA (chmn. computer-related coms. 1985—). Office: Arnold White & Durkee PO Box 4433 750 Bering Dr Houston TX 77057-2104

TOEDTMAN, JAMES SMITH, newspaper editor, journalist; b. Dayton, Ohio, Dec. 1, 1941; s. James Christian and Ella Barnes (Smith) T.; m. Haydee N. Sicart, Aug. 23, 1969; children—Eric, Kristen. A.B., Coll. Wooster, 1963; postgrad., U. Queensland, Brisbane, Australia, 1964; M.Sc. in Journalism, Columbia U., 1967. Pub. dir. Coll. Wooster, Ohio, 1963, 65; reporter, city editor, Sunday news editor, Washington Bur. news editor Newsday, L.I., N.Y., 1967-79; exec. editor Boston Herald Am., 1979-82; editor Balt. News Am., 1982-86; mng. editor N.Y. Newsday, 1986-95, Washington bur. chief, 1995—. Recipient shared award Silurian Soc., Polk award, N.Y. Pubs. award, Pulitzer Prize, 1970, spl. citation Inter-Am. Press Assn., 1979, best editorial award Md.-Del.-D.C. Press Assn., 1984, 86; Rotary Found. fellow, 1964, Internat. fellow Columbia U., 1966-67. Mem. Coll. of Wooster Alumni Assn. (pres. 1980-81). Methodist. Home: 2604 Geneva Hill Ct Oakton VA 22124 Office: 1730 Pennsylvania Ave NW Washington DC 20006

TOENSING, VICTORIA, lawyer; b. Colon, Panama, Oct. 16, 1941; d. Philip William and Victoria (Brady) Long; m. Trent David Toensing, Oct. 29, 1962 (div. 1976); children: Todd Robert, Brady Cronon, Amy Victoriana; m. Joseph E. diGenova, June 27, 1981. BS in Edn., Ind. U., 1962; JD cum laude, U. Detroit, 1975. Bar: Mich. 1976, D.C. 1978. Tchr. English Milw., 1965-66; law clk. to presiding justice U.S. Ct. Appeals, Detroit, 1975-76; asst. U.S. atty. U.S. Atty.'s Office, Detroit, 1976-81; chief counsel U.S. Senate Intelligence Com., Washington, 1981-84; dep. asst. atty. gen. criminal div. Dept. Justice, Washington, 1984-88; spl. counsel Hughes Hubbard & Reed, Washington, 1988-90; ptnr. Cooter and Gell, Washington, 1990-91; ptnr., co-chmn. nat. white collar group Manatt, Phelps and Phillips, Washington, 1991-95; founding ptnr. diGenova & Toensing, Wasington, 1996—; mem. working group on corp. sanctions U.S. Sentencing Commn., 1988-89; co-chairperson Coalition for Women's Appts. Judiciary Task Force, 1988-92; legal analyst for trial of O.J. Simpson, Am.'s Talking Network, 1995. Author: Bringing Sanity to the Insanity Defense, 1983, Mens Rea: Insanity by Another Name, 1984; contbg. author: Fighting Back: Winning The War Against Terrorism, Desk Book on White Collar Crime, 1991; contbr. articles to profl. jours. Founder, chmn. Women's Orgn. To Meet Existing Needs, Mich., 1975-79; chmn. Republican Women's Task Force, 1979-81; bd. dirs. Project on Equal Edn. Rights, Mich., 1980-81, Nat. Hist. Intelligence Mus., 1987-95, America's Talking Legal Analyst, 1995. Recipient spl. commendation Office U.S. Atty. Gen., 1980, agy. seal medallion CIA, 1986, award of achievement Alpha Chi Omega, 1992; featured on cover N.Y. Time Mag. for anti-terrorism work, April 1991. Mem. ABA (mem. standing com. on law and nat. security, mem. coun. criminal justice sect., mem. adv. com. complex crimes and litigation, vice chmn. white collar crime com., chmn. subcom. on corp. criminal liability).

TOEPFER, SUSAN JILL, editor; b. Rochester, Minn., Mar. 9, 1948; d. John Bernard and Helen Esther (Chapple) T.; m. Lorenzo Gabriel Carcaterra, May 16, 1981; children: Katherine Marie, Nicholas Gabriel. BA, Bennington Coll., 1970. Mng. editor Photoplay Mag., N.Y.C., 1971-72; freelance writer, N.Y.C., 1972-78; TV week editor N.Y. Daily News, N.Y.C., 1978-79, leisure editor, 1979-82, features editor, 1982-84, arts and entertainment editor, 1984-86, exec. mag. editor, 1986-87; sr. writer People Mag., 1987-89, sr. editor, 1989-91, asst. mng. editor, 1991-94, exec. editor, 1994—. Office: People Mag Time-Life Bldg Rockefeller Ctr New York NY 10020

TOEPLITZ, GIDEON, symphony society executive; b. Tel Aviv, Nov. 18, 1944; s. Erich and Ruth (Loeb) T.; m. Gail Ransom, Sept. 2, 1978. B.A., Hebrew U., Jerusalem, 1969; M.B.A., UCLA, 1973. Flutist, Israel Philharm. Orch., 1969-71; asst. mgr. Rochester Philharm., 1973-75; asst. mgr. Boston Symphony, 1975-79, orch. mgr., 1979-81; exec. dir. Houston Symphony Soc., 1981-87, exec. v.p., mng. dir. Pitts. Symph. Orch., 1987—; active Am. Symphony Orchestra League. Mem. Nat. Acad. Rec. Arts and Scis., Am. Jewish Com. (bd. dirs.), Penn S.W. Assn. (bd. dirs.). Home: 2087 Beechwood Blvd Pittsburgh PA 15217-1705

TOEVS, ALDEN LOUIS, management consultant; b. American Falls, Idaho, Jan. 25, 1949; s. Alden Louis and Wilma Christen (Coffee) T.; m. Coralie Norwood Sickels, July 20, 1974. BS, Lewis and Clark Coll., 1971; PhD, Tulane U., 1975. NSF fellow MIT Energy Lab., Boston, 1975-76; prof. econs. La. State U., Baton Rouge, 1976-77, U. Oreg., Eugene, 1978-83; dir. mortgage rsch. Morgan Stanley and Co., N.Y.C., 1983-90; exec. v.p. First Manhattan Cons. Group, N.Y.C., 1990—; vis. scholar Fed. Home Loan Bank, San Francisco, 1983, Fed. Reserve Bank, 1982; dir. capital market research U. Oreg., Eugene, 1982-83; instnl. investor All-Am. Rsch. Team, 1990. Author: Innovations in Bond Portfolio Managements, 1983; editor, bd. dirs. Fin. Analysts Jour., 1983-95, Jour. Portfolio Mgmt., 1984-90; contbr. articles to profl. jours. Recipient Graham and Dodd scroll Fin. Analysts Fed., 1983.

TOEWS, DANIEL PETER, zoologist; b. Grande Prairie, Alta, Can., Dec. 18, 1941; married; three children. BS, U. Alta, 1963, MS, 1966; PhD in Zoology, U. B.C., 1969. Asst. prof. zoology U. Alta, 1969-71; assoc. prof. Acadia U., Wolfville, N.S., Can., 1971-80, prof. biology, 1980—. Mem. Can. Soc. Zoology, Brit. Soc. Expt. Biology. Office: Acadia University, Perry Biological Laboratories, Wolfville, NS Canada B0P 1X0 also: Dept Biology, Acadia Univ, Wolfville, NS Canada B0P 1X0*

TOFEL, RICHARD JEFFREY, communication executive; b. N.Y.C., Feb. 17, 1957; s. Robert Leonard and Carol (Collins) T.; m. Jeanne Helen Straus, Feb. 26, 1983; children: Rachel Straus, Colin Straus. AB, Harvard U., 1979; MPP, JFK Sch. Govt., 1983; JD, Harvard U., 1983. Bar: N.Y. 1984, U.S. Dist. Ct. (so. and ea. dists.) N.Y. 1984, U.S. Ct. Appeals (2d cir.) 1987, U.S. Dist. Ct. (no. dist.) N.Y. 1988, U.S. Supreme Ct. 1990. Assoc. Patterson, Belknap, Webb & Tyler, N.Y.C., 1983-86; exec. dir. Mayor's Commn. Human Svcs. Reorganization, N.Y.C., 1984-85; assoc. Gibson, Dunn & Crutcher, N.Y.C., 1986-89; counsel Dow Jones & Co., Inc., N.Y.C., 1989-91, asst. gen. counsel, 1991-92; asst. mng. editor The Wall St. Jour., N.Y.C., 1992-95; dir. internat. devel. and adminstrn. Dow Jones & Co., Inc., N.Y.C., 1995-97, dir. corp. comms., 1997—. Contbr. articles to profl. jours. Mem. ABA, Assn. of Bar of City of N.Y. Democrat. Jewish. Home: 12 W 96th St # 8a-8B New York NY 10025-6509 Office: Dow Jones & Co Inc 200 Liberty St New York NY 10281-1003

TOFF, NANCY ELLEN, book editor; b. Greenburgh, N.Y., Aug. 29, 1955; d. Ira N. and Ruth (Bluthenthal) T. AB, Radcliffe Coll./Harvard U., 1976. Editor and producer Music Minus One, N.Y.C., 1973-75; researcher Time-Life Books, Alexandria, Va., 1976-80; editor & asst. producer Time-Life Music, Alexandria, Va., 1980-84; production mgr. Vanguard Recording Soc., N.Y.C., 1984-86; editor Grove's Dictionaries of Music, N.Y.C., 1984-85; v.p. & editor-in-chief Chelsea House Pubs., N.Y.C., 1986-89, v.p., dir. book devel., 1990; editorial dir. Julian Messner/Silver Burdett Press, Englewood Cliffs, N.J., 1990-91; editl. dir. children's and young adult books Oxford U. Press, N.Y.C., 1991—; editorial cons., Music Div. Lib. of Congress, 1983; hist. cons., Dept. of Musical Instruments, Met. Mus. of Art, N.Y.C., 1986. Author: The Development of the Modern Flute, 1979, The Flute Book, 1985, 2d edit., 1996, Georges Barrère and the Flute in America, 1994; cons. editor Flutist Quar., 1990—; contbr. articles to profl. jours.; curator Georges Barrère and the Flute in America, N.Y. Pub. Libr., 1994. Bd. dirs., Radcliffe Coll. Alumnae Assn. 1979-80. Mem. Nat. Flute Assn. (asst. sec. 1988-89, sec. 1989-90, bd. dirs. 1990-92)), N.Y. Flute Club (bd. dirs. 1986—, sec. 1991-92, pres. 1992-95, 1st v.p. 1995—). Home: 309 E 87th St Apt 5H New York NY 10128-4812 Office: Oxford U Press 198 Madison Ave New York NY 10016-4308

TOFFEL, ALVIN EUGENE, corporate executive, business and governmental consultant; b. Los Angeles, July 14, 1935; s. Harry and Estelle Charlotte Toffel; m. Neile McQueen; children: Stephanie, Elizabeth, Michelle; step children: Terry, Chad. B.A., UCLA, 1957. Dir. mgmt. systems and organizational planning Rockwell Internat., 1963-69; Exec. Office for the Pres. White House, Washington, 1969-70; nat. chmn., campaign dir. McCloskey for Pres., 1971-72; polit. cons., 1971—; cons. personal bus. and govt. Norton Simon and Norton Simon, Inc., Los Angeles, 1972-80; pres. Norton Simon Found., Pasadena, Calif., 1977-80; cons. exec. asst. to pres. Twentieth Century Fox Film Corp., 1980; bd. dirs. Geometrics, Inc.; pres. So. Shellfish Inc., Atlantic Internat. Ins. Ltd., Toffel Thoroughbred Racing; lectr. mgmt. UCLA, Stanford U. Pres. Norton Simon Mus. Art, Pasadena; vice chmn. U.S. Pension Svcs., Inc. With SAC USAF, 1958-63. Recipient White House Interchange Exec. Outstanding Achievement, 1971; recipient Achievement Am. Advtg. Council, 1972. Mem. Ky. Cols., Presdl. Interchange Execs. Assn., Assn. Old Crows. Developed standard U.S. govt. program performance measurement system, aerospace engring. techniques of program mgmt., aerospace manuals. Home and Office: 2323 Bowmont Dr Beverly Hills CA 90210-1808 *My legacy derives from my grandparents leaving the familiar to come to America. Here, anything can be accomplished if one honestly defines what he wants. It then becomes a matter of choosing among the many ways to accomplish anything. The character of the individual can be seen by the choices he makes.*

TOFIAS, ALLAN, accountant; b. Boston, Apr. 13, 1930; s. George I. and Anna (Seidel) T.; m. Arlene Shube, Aug. 30, 1981; children: Bradley Neil, Laura Jean Silver. BA, Colgate U., 1951; MBA, Harvard U., 1956. CPA, Mass. Sr. acct. Peat, Marwick, Mitchell & Co., Boston, 1956-60; mng. ptnr. Tofias, Fleishman, Shapiro & Co., P.C., Boston, 1960-96; chmn. bd., 1996—. Mem. Brookline (Mass.) Town Meeting, 1970-77, mem. fin. adv. bd., 1975-81; mem. New Eng. Bapt. Health Care Corp., 1985—; bd. dirs. West Newton YMCA, 1986-89; mem. exec. com. Boston Aid to Blind, bd. dirs., 1988—, pres., 1993-94. Lt. USNR, 1951-54. Mem. AICPA (coun. 1995—), Mass. Soc. CPA's (pres. 1995-96), Nat. CPA Group (exec. com. 1983-88, vice chmn. 1985-88), BKR Internat. (world bd. dirs. 1988—, chmn. 1994—), Wightman Tennis Club (treas. 1974-76), Newton Squash and Tennis Club (bd. dirs. 1966—), Masons. Home: 59 Monadnock Rd Wellesley MA 02181-1334 Office: Tofias Fleishman Shapiro & Co PC 205 Broadway Cambridge MA 02139-1901

TOFT, THELMA MARILYN, secondary school educator; b. Balt., Sept. 15, 1943; d. George Edward and Thelma Iola (Smith) Trageser; m. Ronald Harry Toft, Aug. 27, 1966; 1 child, Joanna Lynn. BS in Med. Tech., Mt. St. Agnes Coll., Balt., 1965; BSE, Coll. Notre Dame, Balt., 1972; MEd, Pa. State U., 1983. Recreation dir. Villa Maria, Balt., 1961-65; blood bank supr. Wayman Park NIH, Balt., 1965-68; tchr. Sacred Heart, St. Mary's Govan's, Balt., 1968-74, Lincoln Intermediate Unit # 12, Adams County, Pa., 1979-80, York (Pa.) City Sch. Dist., 1980—; curriculum dir. M.O.E.S.T. Pa. State U., 1991-93; mem. Pa. State Consortium-Pa. Team for Improving Math. and Sc.; grant writer, spkr. in field; writer Project Connections curriculum. Active Girl Scouts USA, Hanover, 1988-92, leader, 1984-87; mgmt. bd. Agrl. Indsl. Mus. Mem. ASCD, AAUW, Nat. Ptnrs. in Edn., Am. Bus. Women's Assn. (edn. com. 1992, sec. 1993, Chpt. Woman of Yr. 1994, York County Woman of Yr. 1995), Phi Delta Kappa. Democrat. Roman Catholic. Avocations: writing, marketing. Home: 30 Panther Dr Hanover PA 17331-8888

TOFTNER, RICHARD ORVILLE, engineering executive; b. Warren, Minn., Mar. 5, 1935; s. Orville Gayhart and Cora Evelyn (Anderson) T.; m. Jeanne Bredine, June 26, 1960; children: Douglas, Scott, Kristine, Kimberly, Brian. BA, U. Minn., 1966; MBA, Xavier U., 1970. Registered environ. assessor, Calif. Sr. economist Federated Dept. Stores, Inc., Cin., 1967-68; dep. dir. EPA, Washington and Cin., 1968-73; mgmt. cons. environ. affairs, products and mktg., 1973-74; prin. PEDCo Environ., Cin., 1974-80; trustee PEDCo trusts, 1974-80; pres. ROTA Mgmt., Inc., Cin., 1980-82; gen. mgr. CECOS, 1982-85, cons., 1985—; v.p. Smith, Stevens & Young, 1985-88; real estate developer, 1980—; pres., CEO Toxitrol Internat., Inc., 1988-89; dir. Environ. Svcs. Belcan Engring. Group, Inc., Cin., 1989-92; prin. exec. cons. Resource Mgmt. Internat., Inc., 1994—; adj. prof. environ. engring. U. Cin., 1975-86; lectr. Grad. fellowship rev. panel Office of Edn., 1978-79; advisor, cabinet-level task force Office of Gov. of P.R., 1973; pvt. investor, 1991—; bd. dirs. EnviroAudit Svcs., Inc., pres., CEO, 1992—; mem. legis. com. Ohio Chem. Coun., 1995—; v.p. environ. engring. CSA Architects & Engrs., 1996—; subcom. Nat. Safety Coun., 1972; mem. exec. environ. briefing panels Andersen Consulting, 1991-92; nominee commr. PUCO, Ohio; chmn. Cin. City Waste Task Force, 1987-88; co-chair Hamilton County Resource Recovery Com., 1989—. Contbr. articles on mgmt. planning and environ. to periodicals, chpts. to books; inventor, developer Toxitrol Waste Minimization; inventor EnviroAudit. With AUS, 1954-57. Mem. Nat. Registry Environ. Profl. Rep., Engring. Soc. Cin., Assn. Corp. Environ. Execs., Cin. C. of C., Global Assn. Corp. Environ. Execs. (charter), Bankers Club. Republican. Lutheran. Home: 9175 Yellowwood Dr Cincinnati OH 45251-1948 Office: 4100 Executive Park Dr Ste 11 Cincinnati OH 45241-4026

TOGASAKI, SHINOBU, computer scientist; b. San Francisco, Aug. 17, 1932; s. Kikumatsu and Sugi (Hida) T.; m. Toshiko Kawaguchi, Nov. 24, 1959; children: John Shinobu, Ann Mariko. BS in Math., Duke U., 1954; postgrad., Stanford U., 1954-56. Math. programmer IBM, 1956-69; sr. programmer IBM, Palo Alto, 1970-87; mgr. applications devel. Service Bur. Corp., Palo Alto, 1961-64, sr. analyst, 1964-68; systems architect devel. lab. Service Bur. Corp., San Jose, Calif., 1968-70; chief fin. officer Robin Hood Ranch, Inc., 1976—; mgr. architecture & strategy Hewlett Packard Corp., Cupertino, Calif., 1987-89, mgr. strategic planning, 1989-93; chief architect MFA Hewlett Packard, 1993—. Mem. Am. Mgmt. Assn., AAAS, Am. Statis. Assn., Assn. Computing Machinery, Inst. Mgmt. Sci., Palo Alto C. of C., Sigma Pi Sigma. Home: 2367 Booksin Ave San Jose CA 95125-4705 Office: 19447 Pruneridge Ave Cupertino CA 95014-0609

TOGERSON, JOHN DENNIS, computer software company executive, retired; b. Newcastle, England, July 2, 1939; arrived in Can., 1949; s. John Marius and Margaret (McLaughlin) T.; m. Donna Elizabeth Jones, Oct. 3, 1964 (div. 1972); children: Denise, Brenda, Judson; m. Patricia Willis, May 5, 1984. BME, GM Inst., Flint, Mich., 1961; MBA, York U., Toronto, Ont., 1971. Sr. prodn. engr. GM of Can., Oshawa, Ont., 1961-69; with sales, investment banking Cochran Murray, Toronto, 1969-72; pres. Unitec, Inc., Denver, 1972-79, All Seasons Properties, Denver, 1979-81, Resort Computer Corp., Denver, 1981—; mng. dir. VCC London (subs. of Resort Computer Corp.), 1992; retired, 1996; bd. dirs. VCC London (sub. of 1st Nat. Bank U.K.), London, 1989—, mng. dir., 1992; pres., bd. dirs. Resort Mgmt. Corp., Dillon, Colo., 1980-81; presenter Assn. of Resort Developers Nat. Conv., 1993, Internat. T.S. Found. Think Tank, 1993, and others. Contbr. articles to profl. jours. Avocations: mountain biking, ice hockey.

TOGNINO, JOHN NICHOLAS, financial services executive; b. N.Y.C., Sept. 20, 1938; s. Gennaro and Catherine (Barbieri) T.; m. Norma Lucille Borrelli, Nov. 7, 1959; children: Katherine Ann, John Nicholas Jr., Michael A. BA in Econs. summa cum laude, Fordham U., 1975. Instnl. sales trader A.G. Becker & Co., N.Y.C., 1970-72; trader Merill Lynch, N.Y.C., 1957-69, instnl. salesman, 1972-74, mgr. over-the-counter sales trading, 1974-83, dir. over-the-counter dept., 1983-87, dir. unlisted trading, 1987-88; mng. dir. nondollar equities Merill Lynch, London, 1988-91; mng. dir. global equities, ret. Merill Lynch, N.Y.C., 1991-93; exec. v.p. Charles Schwab & Co., Inc., Jersey City, 1993-96; pres., CEO Security Traders Assn., N.Y.C., 1996—; bd. dirs. Nat. Assn. Security Dealers Automated Quotations Inc. Contbg. author: Market Maker Sponsorship: A Synergistic Package of Services, 1987. Pres. Ardsley (N.Y.) Rep. Club, 1967-68; mem. Ardsley Bd. Edn., 1977-84, pres. 1979; v.p. Ardsley Sch. Dist. Bd., 1978, 81; mem. exec. com. of laity Archdiocese of N.Y.C., 1988. Named Trader of Yr., Security Traders Monthly mag., 1984, Over-the-Counter Man of Yr., Equities mag., 1986. Mem. Nat. Security Traders Assn. (various offices 1981-88, chmn. fin. com. Found. 1992—), Nat. Assn. Security Dealers (bus. conduct com. 1984-86), Security Traders Assn. N.Y. (various offices 1973-83, pres. 1980-81), St. Andrews Golf Club (Hastings, N.Y.), Grey Oaks Country Club (Naples, Fla.), Alpha Sigma Lambda. Republican. Roman Catholic. Avocations: jogging, tennis, golf. Home: 114 Boulder Rdg Scarsdale NY 10583-3138 Office: Security Traders Association One World Trade Ctr New York NY 10048

TOIBIN, COLM, journalist, writer; b. Ireland, 1955. Journalist, columnist Dublin Sunday Ind., 1985—. Author: Seeing Is Believing: Moving Statues in Ireland, 1985, (travelogue) Walking Along the Border, 1987, Homage to Barcelona, 1990, Dubliners, 1990, (novel) The South, 1990, The Trial of the Generals: Selected Journalism, 1980-90, The Heather Blazing, 1993, Soho Square 6: New Writing from Ireland, 1993, The Sign of the Cross: Travels in Catholic Europe, 1995, (novel) The Story of the Night, 1997; contbr. articles to profl. publs. Recipient E.M. Forster award Am. Acad. of Arts and Letters, 1995. Home: 12 Upper Pembroke St, Dublin 2, Ireland

TOIFEL, RONALD CHARLES, librarian; b. Mobile, Ala., June 4, 1933; s. Leopold Francis and Thelma Teresa (Eckert) T.; m. Peggy Suzanne White, Jan. 15, 1972; children: Ronald Charles Jr., Mark, Lance. BS, Miss. So. Coll., 1957; MSLS, La. State U., Baton Rouge, 1966; EdD in Higher Edn., Fla. State U., 1990. Head bookmobile divsn. Davis Ave. Br. Libr.; asst. head referencedept., head curriculum dept. Internat. Trade Ctr. Libr., Mobile Pub. Libr., 1966-68; asst. libr. dir. Gadsden (Ala.) Pub. Libr., 1968-69; libr. U. West Fla., Pensacola, 1969—. Contbr. articles to profl. jours. Mem. Bagdad Village Preservation Assn., Santa Rosa County Hist. Soc.; chmn. Libr. Faculty Coun., 1994-96. With USAF,1958-65. Mem. ALA (ednl. and behavioral scis. sect./bibliog. instrn. for edn. com., com. on problems of assessment and control of curriculum materials), Southea. Libr. Assn. (sec. online svcs. roundtable), West Fla. Libr. Assn. (pres. 1971-72), Gulfcoast Online and Automated Librs. (pres. 1983-84). Democrat. Avocations: education, civil war history. Home: PO Box 472 4561 Forsyth St Bagdad FL 32530 Office: University of West Florida John C Pace Libr 11000 University Pkwy Pensacola FL 32514-5732

TOKAR, EDWARD THOMAS, manufacturing company executive; b. Passaic, N.J., June 12, 1947; s. Edward Thomas Sr. and Helen (Fabian) T.; m. Frances Deland, Sept. 30, 1972; 1 child, Adam Edward. BS with high honors, U. Md., 1969; MBA, Coll. William and Mary, 1971; postgrad., George Washington U., 1972. CPA, N.J., Md. Audit, cons. Touche Ross & Co., Washington, 1970-73; mgr. fin. div. Nat. Rural Electric Coop. Assn., Washington, 1973-77; v.p. investments Allied-Signal Inc., Morristown, N.J., 1977—; bd. dirs. Morgan Products Ltd., Noel Group Inc.; mem. bd. advisors Saugatuck Capital Co., Stamford, RFE Investment Ptnrs., Stamford, Allen Value Ptnrs.; trustee Morgan Grenfel Investment Trusts; mem. pension adv. com. N.Y. Stock Exch., N.Y.C. Trustee Newark Boys Chorus Sch., 1980-84, Coll. of William and Mary; mem. investment adv. com. Paterson Diocese Roman Cath. Ch., Clifton, N.J. Mem. AICPA, Nat. Econs. Club, Sentinel Pension Inst. (bd. advisors), Investment Tech. Symposium, Fin. Execs. Inst., CIEBA Comm. Avocations: golf, tennis. Office: Allied-Signal Inc PO Box 1219R Morristown NJ 07962-1219

TOKAR, JOHN MICHAEL, oceanographer, ocean engineer; b. Bayonne, N.J., Sept. 13, 1951; s. Thomas and Frances (Fayder) Wargo; m. Virginia De Bellis, Oct. 10, 1976; children: Melina, Laurel. BA in Chemistry, Jersey City State Coll., 1973; MS in Engring., Cath. U., 1989. Chem. oceanographer Atlantic Oceanographic Lab. NOAA, Miami, Fla., 1977-82, ops. officer ship rsch., 1982-83; project engr. Nat. Ocean Svc. engring. staff NOAA, Rockville, Md., 1983-86, quality assurance coord. Office of Oceanography, 1986-88, program mgr. Nat. Ocean Svc., Office of Ocean Svcs., 1988-89, liaison for oceanography Office of Corps. Ops., 1989-91; commdg. officer Ship FERREL NOAA, Norfolk, Va., 1991-93; chief Damage Assessment Ctr. Ops., 1993-96; tech. transfer coord. Office of Rsch. and Tech. Applications, Silver Spring, Md., 1996—. Author: (chpt.) Geotechnical Engineering of Ocean Waste Disposal, 1990; contbr. articles to profl. jours. Mem. AAAS, IEEE, Am. Geophys. Union, Marine Tech. Soc. Achievements include development of fiber optic chemical sensors for ocean applications. Home: 4935 Tall Oaks Dr Monrovia MD 21770-9315 Office: Office Rsch and Tech Appls 1315 E West Hwy Silver Spring MD 20910-3285

TOKER, FRANKLIN K., art history educator, archaeologist, foundation executive; b. Montreal, Apr. 29, 1944; came to U.S., 1964; naturalized, 1983; s. Maxwell Harris and Ethel (Herzberg-Serchuk) T.; m. Ellen Judith Burack, Sept. 3, 1972; children: Sarah Augusta, Maxwell, Jeffrey. BA, McGill U., Montreal, 1964; AM in Fine Arts, Oberlin Coll., 1966; PhD in Fine Arts, Harvard U., 1973. Instr. Boston Sch. Architecture, 1967; archaeol. dir. Florence (Italy) Cathedral excavations, 1969-74; A.W. Mellon vis. prof. Carnegie-Mellon U., Pitts., 1974-76, assoc. prof., 1976-80; assoc. prof. fine arts U. Pitts., 1980-87, prof., 1987—; vis. prof. U. Florence, 1988-89, U. Rome, 1991—, U. Reggio Calabria, 1996; preservation cons. The Carnegie, Pitts., 1981-83; bd. dirs. Allegheny Survey, Pitts. History and Landmarks Found., 1980-85; mem. Inst. for Advanced Study, Princeton, N.J., 1985; fellow Com. to Rescue Italian Art, Florence, 1969; fellow I Tatti-Harvard U. Ctr. for Italian Renaissance Studies, Florence, 1972. Author: Notre Dame in Montreal, 1970 (Alice Davis Hitchcock award 1971), French edit., 1981, 2d English edit., 1991, S. Reparata: l-Antica Cattedrale Fiorentina, 1974, Pittsburgh: An Urban Portrait, 1986 (Pitts. History and Landmarks Found. award 1987), 2d edit., 1995; contbr. articles to profl. jours. Mem. econ. devel. com. Allegheny Conf. Community Devel., Pitts., 1983-85. Kress fellow, 1965; Can. Coun. fellow, 1966; Guggenheim fellow, 1979; NEH grantee 1979, 92, NEH sr. fellow, 1985, fellow Bellagio Study and Conf. Ctr., Rockefeller Found., 1994. Mem. Coll. Art Assn. (life, Arthur Kingsley Porter prize 1980), Medieval Acad. (life), Soc. Archtl. Historians (pres., 1993-94, life mem., bd. dirs. 1985-88), Archaeol. Inst. Am., Internat. Ctr. for Medieval Art. Avocations: creative writing, photography, cycling. Home: 1521 Denniston Ave Pittsburgh PA 15217-1449 Office: U Pittsburgh Dept History Art Archi Pittsburgh PA 15260

TOKER, KAREN HARKAVY, physician; b. New Haven, Conn., Oct. 23, 1942; d. Victor M. and Nedra (Israel) Harkavy; m. Cyril Toker, Sept. 1, 1968; children: David Edward, Rachel Lee. BS in Chemistry, Coll. William and Mary, 1963; MD, Yale U., 1967. Diplomate Am. Bd. Pediatrics, 1974. Intern dept. pediatrics Bronx Mcpl. Hosp. Ctr., Albert Einstein Coll. Medicine, N.Y., 1967-68, asst. resident dept. pediatrics, 1968-69, sr. resident dept. pediatrics, 1969, 70-71, attending pediatrician, 1971-72, 73-76; pediatrician Montgomery Health Dept., Silver Springs, Md., 1976-83; pediatric cons. Head Start Program Montgomery County Pub. Schs., Rockville, Md., 1976-83; pvt. practice gen. pediatrics Rockville, 1983-89; pediatrician Nemours Children's Clinic, Jacksonville, Fla., 1991-95; med. dir. Pearl Plaza Pediatrics, Duval County Pub. Health Unit, 1995—; instr. pediatrics Albert Einstein Coll. Medicine, N.Y., 1971-74, asst. prof. pediatrics, 1974-76; clin. asst. prof. U. Fla., 1995—. Exec. bd. sec. Congregation Har Shalom, Potomac, 1989-91. Fellow Am. Acad. Pediatrics; mem. Fla. Med. Assn., Duval County Med. Soc., Ambulatory Pediatric Assn. Democrat. Jewish. Avocations: piano, opera, ballet, swimming. Home: 6030 Oakbrook Ct Ponte Vedra Beach FL 32082-2052 Office: Pearl Plaza Pediatrics 5220 N Pearl St Jacksonville FL 32208-5118

TOKHEIM, ROBERT EDWARD, physicist; b. Eastport, Maine, Apr. 25, 1936; s. Edward George and Ruth Lillian (Koenig) T.; m. Diane Alice Green, July 1, 1962; children: Shirley Diane, William Robert, David Eric, Heidi Jean. BS, Calif. Inst. Tech., 1958, MS, 1959; Degree of Engr., Stanford U., 1962, PhD, 1965. Rsch. asst. Hansen Labs Physics Stanford (Calif.) U., 1960-65; microwave engr. Watkins-Johnson Co., Palo Alto, Calif., 1965-73, staff scientist, head ferrimagnetic R&D dept., 1966-69; sr. physicist SRI Internat., Menlo Park, Calif., 1973—. Co-author: Tutorial Handbook on X-ray Effects on Materials and Structures, 1992; contbr. articles to Jour. Applied Physics, IEEE Transactions on Magnetics, conf. proceedings on shock compression, and others. Mem. IEEE (sr. mem.), Am. Phys. Soc., Toastmasters, Tau Beta Pi, Sigma Xi. Achievements include discovery of nonreciprocal line-coupled microwave ferrimagnetic filters, optimum thermal compensation axes in YIG and GaYIG ferrimagnetic spheres, various shock wave equation-of-state computational models for porous materials. Office: SRI International 333 Ravenswood Ave Menlo Park CA 94025-3453 Address: 5 Trinity Ct Menlo Park CA 94025-6643

TOKOFSKY, JERRY HERBERT, film producer; b. N.Y.C., Apr. 14, 1936; s. Julius H. and Rose (Trager) T.; m. Myrna Weinstein, Feb. 21, 1968 (div.); children: David, Peter; m. Fiammetta Bettuzzi, 1970 (div.); 1 child, Tatianna; m. Karen Oliver, Oct. 4, 1981. BS in Journalism, NYU, 1957, LLD, 1959. Talent agt. William Morris Agy., N.Y.C., 1953-59; v.p. William Morris Agy., L.A., 1959-64; exec. v.p. Columbia Pictures, L.A., 1964-69; v.p. Paramount Pictures, London, 1970; exec. v.p. MGM, London, 1971; pres. Jerry Tokofsky Prodns., L.A., 1972-82; exec. v.p. Zupnik Enterprises, L.A., 1982-92; pres. Jerry Tokofsky Entertainment, Encino, Calif., 1992—; prof. Sch. TV and Film U. So. Calif. Sch. Bus. Prodr. films: Where's Poppa, 1971, Born to Win, 1972, Dreamscape, 1985, Fear City, 1986, Wildfire, 1988, Glengarry Glen Ross, 1992, The Grass Harp, 1995, American Buffalo, 1995, Double Down, 1997, Life on Mars, 1997, God's Anul and Out on My Feet, 1997. With U.S. Army, 1959, res. 1959-63. Named Man of Yr. B'nai B'rith, 1981; recipient L.A. Resolution City of L.A., 1981. Mem. Variety Club Internat. Avocations: skiing, tennis, golf, chess. *Passion for family, life, work, with patience and intelligence and you have a chance to grab that winning ring.*

TOKUMARU, ROBERTA, principal. Prin. Aikahi Elem. Sch. Recipient DOE Elem. Sch. Recognition award, 1989-90. Office: Aikahi Elem Sch 281 Ilihau St Kailua HI 96734-1657*

TOLAN, DAVID J., insurance corporation executive; b. Detroit, Dec. 27, 1927; s. Joseph James and Helen Barbara (Blahnik) T.; m. Roseann Biwer, Feb. 15, 1958; children: Joseph, David, Julie. AB, Haverford Coll.; JD, U. Mich.; MS, Am. Coll. Bar: Wis.; CLU. Pvt. practice atty. Milw., 1952-57; agt. Northwestern Mut. Ins. Co., Milw., 1957—; prin. Tolan, Schueller & Assoc., Ltd., Milw., 1959—; lectr. AICPAs, Am. Soc. CLUs, Wis. Bar Assn., 1975—; mem. faculty CLU Inst., 1990—. Contbr. articles to profl. jours. Pres. Young Reps. Milwaukee County, 1961; bd. dirs. United Performing Arts Fund, Milw., 1966, 91, 92, Bel Canto Chorus, Milw., 1960—; scoutmaster Boy Scouts Am., 1975-77; mem. Com. for Future of Milw., 1988. With U.S. Army, 1954-57. Recipient Disting. Svc. award Assn. Milw. Assn. Life Underwriters, 1990. Mem. Am. Soc. CLUs, Assn. Advanced Life Underwriters, Estate Counselors Forum, Mid Winter Estate Planning Coun. Republican. Roman Catholic. Club: University (Milw.). Avocations: golf, sailing, scuba, singing. Office: Tolan Schueller and Assocs 770 N Jefferson St Milwaukee WI 53202-3701

TOLAN, ROBERT WARREN, pediatric infectious disease specialist; b. Bowling Green, Ohio, Nov. 20, 1960; s. Robert Warren Tolan and Margaret Delores (Petter) Cardwell; m. Lenita Kay Newberg, May 15, 1983. BA, Ind. U., 1982, MA, 1983; MD, Washington U., St. Louis, 1987. Diplomate Nat. Bd. Med. Examiners, Am. Bd. Pediatrics, sub-bd. of pediat. infectious diseases. Resident in pediatrics Riley Hosp. for Children, Indpls., 1987-90; fellow in infectious diseases St. Louis Children's Hosp., 1990-94. Co-author: Fever of Unknown Origin in Children, 1991; contbr. articles to Clin. Infectious Diseases, Pediatric Infectious Diseases Jour., Infection and Immunity, Jour. Clin. Microbiology. Nat. Merit scholar Pitts. Plate Glass, 1978; Pediatric Scientist Devel. Program fellow, 1990-94. Fellow Am. Acad. Pediatrics; mem. AMA, Am. Soc. Microbiology, Infectious Diseases Soc. Am., Pediatric Infectious Diseases Soc., Soc. for Preservation and Encouragement of Barbershop Quartet Singing in Am., Physicians for Social Responsibility. Democrat. Episcoplian. Achievements include patent for a cloned outer membrane protein from Haemophilus influenzae type b which is being developed as a vaccine candidate; reviews of surgical management of pediatric endocarditis and of toxic shock syndrome and influenza; description of systemic pseudomalignant form of cat-scratch disease in normal children, the cloning of an outer membrane protein from Haemophilus influenzae type b, the lack of epidemiologic utility of analysis of lipopolysaccharide from the same organism. Office: St Louis Childrens Hosp Rm 1102 One Childrens Pl Saint Louis MO 63110-1093

TOLAN, VICKI IRVENA, physical education educator; b. Vancouver, B.C., Can., Apr. 8, 1949; d. James R. and Adah St. C. (Holmes) Butchart; m. John C. Tolan, Mar. 26, 1988; children: Shauna, Jeffrey, Julie, Kelcie. BA in Edn., Western Wash. U., 1971, postgrad., 1972; M of Sports Sci., U.S. Sports Acad., 1988. Cert. tchr., Wash., Calif. Tchr. Pt. Garden Mid. Sch., Everett, Wash., 1971-74; tchr. phys. edn. Deaconnes Children's Home, Everett, 1972; tchr. phys. edn., health, social studies Mid. Sch., Everett, 1971-74; subs. tchr. Everett and Marysville, Wash., 1974-76, Lakewood, Wash., 1976-77; tchr. ESL Pt. Angeles (Calif.) Sch. Dist., 1983-86, tchr. photography, swimming, health, phys. edn., aerobics, 1986-87, phys. edn. and health specialist, 1987-89; tchr. Alta Loma (Calif.) Sch. Dist., 1989—; student tchr. phys. edn., Lynnwood, Wash., 1971, Bellingham, Wash., 1971; soccer coach youth teams. Pt. Angeles Sch. Dist., 1972—, mem. AIDS/drugs curriculum com., 1986—; cheerleader advisor, 1988, 89, tchr. elem. summer sch., 1986, 87; owner Kits Camera, Pt. Angeles, 1974-83; dist. chair phys. edn. dept. Alta Loma Jr. High Sch., 1989—, chmn. phys. edn. dept., 1992-93. Instr. swimming, Kenmore, 1965-72; founder, coord., pres. Olympic Peninsula Women's Soccer League, 1979-86; bd. dirs. Womanfest, 1985, 86; coord. Jump Rope for Heart, Pt. Angeles, 1989. Named Mother of Yr. Pt. Angeles, 1983, 84, Sports Woman of Yr. Pt. Angeles, 1986; recipient State Phys. Fitness award Pres.'s Challenge, 1988, Nat. Phys. Fitness award Pres.'s Challenge, 1988. Mem. AAHPERD, AAUW, Internat. Pageant Assn., Calif. Assn. Health, Phys. Edn., Recreation and Dance, Delta Kappa Gamma. Republican. Roman Catholic. Avocations: photography, reading, soccer, tennis. Office: Alta Loma Jr High Sch 9000 Lemon Ave Alta Loma CA 91701-3357

TOLAND, FLORENCE WINIFRED, printing company executive, retired business educator; b. Paola, Kans., Aug. 6, 1906; d. Frederick W. and Bertha G. (Cartwright) Arzberger; BA, U. Ariz., 1935, MS in Bus. Adminstrn., 1946; m. Jess William Toland, Dec. 23, 1934 (dec. 1954); 1 child, Ronald William. Tchr. grade sch., Dos Cabezos, Willcox and Mascot, Ariz., 1925-32, jr. high and high sch., 1934-36, 38-42, amphitheater sch., Tucson; asst. prof. U. Ariz., Tucson, 1942-71, asst. prof. emeritus, 1971—; co-owner, mgr., pres. Pima Printing Co., Tucson, 1954-97, retired; cons., semi-ret.. Mem. Ariz. Bus. Educators Assn. (life), Nat. Bus. Educators Assn., Western Bus. Educators Assn., Pi Omega Pi, Pi Lambda Theta. Democrat. Club: Order Eastern Star. Co-author: Transcription Method Shorthand, 1946. Home: 5461 N Paseo Espejo Tucson AZ 85718-5229 Office: 110 S Park Ave Tucson AZ 85719-5746

TOLAND, JOHN WILLARD, historian, writer; b. La Crosse, Wis., June 29, 1912; s. Ralph and Helen Chandler (Snow) T.; m. Toshiko Matsumura, Mar. 12, 1960; 1 dau., Tamiko; children by previous marriage: Diana Toland Netzer, Marcia. B.A., Williams Coll., 1936; student, Yale Drama Sch., 1936-37; L.H.D., Williams Coll., 1968, U. Alaska, 1977, Western Conn. U., 1986. Mem. adv. council Nat. Archives. Author: Ships in the Sky, 1957, Battle: The Story of the Bulge, 1959, But Not in Shame, 1961 (Best Book Fgn. Affairs award Overseas Press Club), The Dillinger Days, 1963, The Flying Tigers, 1963, The Last 100 Days, 1966 (Best Book Fgn. Affairs citation Overseas Press Club), The Battle of the Bulge, 1966, The Rising Sun , 1970 (Van Wyck Brooks award for non-fiction, Best Book Fgn. Affairs award Overseas Press Club, Pulitzer prize for non-fiction), Adolf Hitler, 1976 (Best Book Fgn. Affairs award Overseas Press Club, Gold Medal Nat. Soc. Arts and Letters), Hitler, The Pictorial Documentary of His Life, 1978, No Man's Land, 1980 (Best Book Fgn. Affairs citation Overseas Press Club), Infamy, 1982, In Mortal Combat, 1991; (novels) Gods of War, 1985, Occupation, 1987; also short stories. Served to capt. USAAF, 1942-46, 1947-49. Mem. Authors Guild, Accademia del Mediterraneo., Western Front Assn. (hon. v.p.). Home: 101 Long Ridge Rd Danbury CT 06810-8434

TOLBERT, BERT MILLS, biochemist, educator; b. Twin Falls, Idaho, Jan. 15, 1921; s. Ed. and Helen (Mills) T.; m. Anne Grace Zweifler, July 20, 1959; children—Elizabeth Dawn, Margaret Anne, Caroline Joan, Sarah Helen. Student, Idaho State U., 1938-40; B.S., U. Calif. at Berkeley, 1942, Ph.D., 1945; postgrad., Fed. Inst. Tech., Zurich, Switzerland, 1952-53. Chemist Lawrence Radiation Lab., Berkeley, 1944-57; faculty U. Colo., Boulder, 1957-89, prof., 1961-89, prof. emeritus, 1989—, assoc. chmn. dept. chemistry and biochemistry, 1980-88; bd. dirs. Hauser Chem. Rsch., Boulder, 1983—; vis. prof. IAEA, Buenos Aires, Argentina, 1961-62; Biophysicist U.S. AEC, Washington, 1967-68; cons. pvt. cos, govt. agys. Author: (with others) Isotopic Carbon, 1948; contbr. (with others) articles to profl. jours. Fellow AAAS; mem. Am. Chem. Soc., Am. Soc. Biochemistry and Molecular Biology, Radiation Rsch. Soc., Soc. for Exptl. Biology and Medicine. Rsch. on organic chemistry, including use of isotopes in chemistry and biochemistry, radiation chemistry, radiation effects in protein, intermediary metabolism, metabolism of ascorbic acid, nutritional biochemistry, instrumentation in radioactivity. Home: 444 Kalmia Ave Boulder CO 80304-1732

TOLBERT, JAMES R., III, financial executive; b. Amarillo, Tex., Apr. 29, 1935; s. James R. and Mary (Noble) T.; m. Elizabeth McMahan, Dec. 26, 1956; children: James R. IV, Cannon Miles, Elizabeth Nelson, Lee Mitchener. Student, Stanford U., 1953-55; B.A., Okla. U., 1957; M.B.A., Stanford U., 1959. Vice pres. acquisitions Mid-Am. Corp., 1959-64; pres. James R. Tolbert & Assos., Inc., 1964-69; chmn. bd., treas., co-founder Holden Tolbert & Co., 1967—; sr. partner, co-founder Resource Analysis and Mgmt. Group, 1969-80; chmn., pres. First Okla. Corp., 1986—; trustee in bankruptcy Four Seasons Nursing Ctrs. of Am., Inc., 1971-72; pres., treas., chmn. bd. Anta Corp., Oklahoma City, 1972-85; bd. dirs. Sun Healthcare, Inc. Chmn. Okla. Higher Edn. Task Force, 1986, Oklahoma City Arts Coun., 1987-89; chmn. Okla. Futures Commn., 1988-90; trustee Casady Sch., 1989-94, Okla. Found. for Humanities, McGee Eye Inst.; chmn. Myriad Gardens Authority and Found. Recipient Exec. Leadership of Yr. award Oklahoma City U., 1975, 4th Ann. Dean A. McGee award, Downtown Now, 1989, Deans award for disting. cmty. svc. U. Okla. Med. Alumni Assn. Democrat. Home: 2321 Belleview Ter Oklahoma City OK 73112-7740 Office: First Okla Corp PO Box 1533 Oklahoma City OK 73101-1533

TOLBERT, TONY LEWIS, football player; b. Tuskegee, Ala., Dec. 29, 1967; m. Satasha Tolbert. Degree in criminal justice, U. Tex.- El Paso, 1991. Football player Dallas Cowboys, 1989—. Named to Pro Bowl, 1996. Office: care Dallas Cowboys 1 Cowboys Pky Irving TX 75063*

TOLCHIN, JOAN GUBIN, psychiatrist, educator; b. N.Y.C., Mar. 10, 1944; d. Harold and Bella (Newman) Gubin; m. Matthew Armin Tolchin, Sept. 1, 1966; 1 child, Benjamin. AB, Vassar Coll., 1964; MD, NYU, 1972. Diplomate Am. Bd. Gen. Psychiatry, Am. Bd. Child Psychiatry. Rsch. asst. Albert Einstein Coll. Medicine, N.Y.C., 1964-68; instr. psychiatry med. coll. Cornell U., N.Y.C., 1977-78, clin. instr., 1978-86, clin. asst. prof., 1986—. Contbr. articles to profl. jours. Fellow Am. Acad. Child and Adolescent Psychiatry; mem. APA, Am. Acad. Psychoanalysis, N.Y. Coun. Child and Adolescent Psychiatry (bd. dirs. 1992-96, pres. 1994-95), Alpha Omega Alpha. Office: 35 E 84th St New York NY 10028-0871

TOLCHIN, MARTIN, newspaper reporter, author; b. N.Y.C., Sept. 20, 1928; s. Charles T. and Evelyn (Weisman) Tolchin; m. Susan Jane Goldsmith, Dec. 23, 1965; children: Charles, Karen. Student. U. Utah, 1947-49; LL.B., N.Y. Law Sch., 1951. Reporter N.Y. Times, N.Y.C., 1954-94; publisher and editor-in-chief The Hill, Washington, 1994—. Author: (with Susan Jane Tolchin) To The Victor, 1971, Clout-Woman Power and Politics, 1974, Dismantling America-The Rush to Deregulate, 1983, Buying Into America: How Foreign Money is Changing the Face of Our Nation, 1988, Selling Our Security—The Erosion of America's Assets, 1992. Served with U.S. Army, 1951-53. Recipient Schaeffer Gold Typewriter award E.M. Schaeffer Co., 1967; recipient Page One award Newspaper Guild N.Y., 1967, 69, 73, Citizens Budget Commn. award, 1967, Sigma Delta Chi award, 1973, Everett M. Dirksen award for disting. reporting of Congress, 1983. Jewish. Club: Nat. Press (Washington). Home: 5117 Wickett Ter Bethesda MD 20814-5716 Office: The Hill 733 15th St NW Washington DC 20005-2112

TOLCHIN, SUSAN JANE, public administration educator, writer; b. N.Y.C., Jan. 14, 1941; d. Jacob Nathan and Dorothy Ann (Markowitz) Goldsmith; m. Martin Tolchin, Dec. 23, 1965; children: Charles Peter, Karen Rebecca. B.A., Bryn Mawr Coll., 1961; M.A., U. Chgo., 1962; Ph.D., N.Y.U., 1968. Lectr. in polit. sci. City Coll., N.Y.C., 1963-65, Bklyn. Coll., 1965-71; adj. asst. prof. polit. sci. Seton Hall U., South Orange, N.J., 1971-73; assoc. prof. polit. sci., dir. Inst. for Women and Politics, Mt. Vernon Coll., Washington, 1975-78; prof. pub. adminstrn. George Washington U., Washington, 1978—. disting. lectr. Industrial Coll. of the Armed Forces, 1994. Author: (book) The Angry American: How Voter Rage is Changing the Nation, 1996; co-author (with Martin Tolchin): To The Victor: Political Patronage from the Clubhouse to the White House, 1971, Clout-Womanpower and Politics, 1974, Dismantling America-The Rush to Deregulate, 1983, Buying Into America-How Foreign Money Is Changing the Face of Our Nation, 1988, Selling Our Security-The Erosion of America's Assets, 1992. Bd. dirs. Cystic Fibrosis Foun., 1982—; county committeewoman Dem. Party, Montclair, N.J., 1969-73. Dilthey fellow George Washington U., 1983, Aspen Inst. fellow, 1979; named Tchr. of Yr., Mt. Vernon Coll., 1978; recipient Founder's Day award NYU, 1968. Fellow Nat. Acad. Pub. Adminstrn.; mem. Am. Polit. Sci. Assn. (pres. Women's Caucus for Polit. Sci. 1977-78), Am. Soc. Pub. Adminstrn. (chairperson sect. Natural Resources and Environ. Adminstrn. 1982-83). Democrat. Jewish. Office: George Washington U Dept Pub Adminstrn Washington DC 20052

TOLCHINSKY, PAUL DEAN, organization design psychologist; b. Cleve., Sept. 30, 1946; s. Sanford Melvin and Frances (Klein) T.; m. Laurie S. Schermer, Nov. 3, 1968 (div. Jan. 1982); m. Kathy L. Dworkin, June 19, 1988; children: Heidi E., Dana M. BA, Bowling Green State U., 1971; PhD, Purdue U., 1978. Asst. br. mgr., tng. instr. Detroit Bank and Trust, 1971-73; mgr. tng. and devel. nuclear divsn. Babcock and Wilcox Co., Barberton, Ohio, 1973-75; internal cons. food products divsn. Gen. Foods Corp., West Lafayette, Ind., 1975-77; grad. tchg. asst. Krannert Grad. Sch. Mgmt. Purdue U., West Lafayette, 1975-78; asst. prof. mgmt. Coll. Bus. Adminstrn. Fla. State U., Tallahassee, 1978-79, U. Akron, Ohio, 1979-81; pres. Performance Devel. Assocs., Cleve., 1975-94; ptnr. Dannemiller Tyson Assocs., Cleve., 1994—. Contbr. articles to profl. publs. Bd. dirs. Temple Tiferth Israel, Cleve., 195. With U.S. Army, 1966-69, Vietnam. Mem. APA, Acad. Mgmt. Democrat. Jewish. Avocations: running, travel. Office: Dannemiller Tyson Assocs Box 22987 Beachwood OH 44122

TOLEDANO, RALPH DE, columnist, author, poet; b. Internat. Zone of Tangier, Aug. 17, 1916; s. Hayim and Suzanne (Nahon) de T.; m. Nora Romaine, July 6, 1938 (div. 1964); children: James, Paul, Christopher; m. Eunice Marshall, Apr. 19, 1979. Student, Fieldston Sch., N.Y.C., 1928-34; BA, Columbia Coll., 1938; student, Cornell U., 1943. Founder, co-editor Cross-Town, 1932-33; Founder, co-editor Jazz Info., 1938-39; assoc. editor The New Leader, 1941-43; editor The Standard, 1946; mng. editor Plain Talk, 1946-47; pub. dir. Dress Joint Bd., Internat. Ladies Garment Workers Union, 1947-48; asst. editor Newsweek, 1948, nat. reports editor, 1950-60, asst. chief Washington Bur., 1956-60; syndicated columnist King Features, 1960-71, Nat. News Research Syndicate, 1971-74, Copley News Service, 1974-89, Heritage Features Syndicate, 1989-91, Creators Syndicate, 1991—; editor House Republican Leadership report Am. Mil. Strength and Strategy; chief Washington Bur., Taft Broadcasting Co., 1960-61; dir. polit. intelligence Goldwater Presdl. Campaign Com., 1963-64; contbg. editor Nat. Rev., 1960—; pres. Nat. News-Research, 1960—, Anthem Books, 1970; editor-in-chief Washington World, 1961-62; vice chmn. Am. Conserva-Union, 1965-66; mem. 20th Century Fund Task Force on Freedom Press, 1971-72. Author: Seeds of Treason, 1950, Spies, Dupes and Diplomats, 1952, Day of Reckoning, 1955, Nixon, 1956, Lament for a Generation, 1960, The Greatest Plot in History, 1963, The Winning Side, 1963, The Goldwater Story, 1964, RFK: The Man Who Would be President, 1967, America, I-Love-You, 1968, One Man Alone: Richard M. Nixon, 1969, Claude Kirk: Man and Myth, 1970, Little Cesar, 1971, J. Edgar Hoover: The Man in His Time, 1973, Hit and Run: The Ralph Nader Story, 1975, Let Our Cities Burn, 1975, Poems: You & I, 1978, Devil Take Him, 1979, The Apocrypha of Limbo (poems), 1994, Notes from the Underground: The Chambers-Toledano Letters; editor: Frontiers of Jazz, 1947; co-editor: The Conservative Papers, 1962, 64, 93; editor-in-chief: Political Success, 1968-69; mem. adv. bd.: Yale Lit. Mag, 1981-86; contbr. to nat. mags. Bd. dirs. Americans for Constitutional Action, 1966-67, Constructive Action, 1990—. With OSS, AUS, 1943-46. Recipient Freedoms Found. award, 1950, 61, 74; Americanism award VFW, 1953; Heritage Found. Disting. Journalism fellow. Mem. Internat. Mark Twain Soc. (knight), Bibl. Archeology Soc., Dutch Treat Club (N.Y.), Nat. Press Club, Naval and Mil. Club (London), Am. Philatelic Soc., Sigma Delta Chi. Office: 500 23rd St NW Washington DC 20037-2828

TOLEDO, FRANCISCO, painter, printmaker; b. Minatitlan, Oaxaca, Mex., July 17, 1940. Grad., Nat. Inst. Fine Arts, 1959. One-man shows include Martha Jackson Gallery, N.Y., 1975, Everson Mus., Syracuse, N.Y., 1980; retrospective Nat. Mus. Modern Art, Tokyo, 1974, Mus. Modern Art, Mexico City, 1976, Mus. Contemporary Art, Bogota, Colombia, 1977, Mus. Biblioteca Pape, Monslova, 1979, others. Office: care TwoSixtyOne Art Ste 8A 261 Broadway New York NY 10007*

TOLEDO-PEREYRA, LUIS HORACIO, transplant surgeon, researcher, historian, educator; b. Nogales, Ariz., Oct. 19, 1943; s. Jose Horacio and Elia (Pereyra) Toledo; m. Marjean May Gilbert, Mar. 21, 1974; children: Alexander Horacio, Suzanne Elizabeth. BS magna cum laude, Regis Coll., 1960; MD,Nat. U. Mex., 1967, MS in Internal Medicine, 1970; PhD in Surgery, U. Minn., 1976, PhD in Hist. Medicine, U. Minn., 1984. Intern Hosp. Juarez, Nat. U. Mex., 1966; resident in internal medicine Instituto Nacional de la Nutricion, Nat. U. Mex., 1968, 70; resident in surgery U. Minn., 1970-76; resident in thoracic and cardiovascular surgery U. Chgo., 1976-77; dir. surg. research Henry Ford Hosp., Detroit, 1977-79, co-dir. transplantation, 1977-79; chief transplantation, dir. surg. research Mt. Carmel Mercy Hosp., Detroit, 1979-89; chief transplantation, dir. rsch. Borgess Med. Ctr., Kalamazoo, Mich., 1990—; clin. prof. surgery Mich. State U., 1993-96, prof. surgery, 1996—; instr. biochemistry and internal medicine Nat. U. Mex., 1963, 68; adj. prof. Sch. Health Sci. Mercy Coll., Detroit, 1983-91, history Western Mich. U., 1990—, biol. sci., 1991—; prof. surgery Nat. U. Mex., 1990—. Recipient Outstanding Achievement award U. Mex., 1961, 64, 67; Resident Research award Assn. Acad. Surgery, 1974; Cecil Lehman Mayer Research award Am. Coll. Chest Physicians, 1975, Surgery Rsch. Nat. award Mex. Assn. Gen. Surgery, 1993. Mem. AMA, Transplantation Soc., Assn. Acad. Surgery, Am. Soc. Transplant Surgery, Soc. Organ Sharing (pres., founder), Am. Assn. History Medicine, Am. Soc. Nephrology, Am. Assn. Immunologists, Am. Physiol. Soc., Soc. Exptl. Biology and Medicine, Am. Soc. Artificial Organs, Am. Diabetes Assn., European Soc. Study of Diabetes, No. Am. Soc. Dialysis Transplantation (pres., founder), Pan Am. Soc. Dialysis Transplantation (pres. elect, founder), Transplantation Soc. Mich. (pres., exec. bd.). Roman Catholic. Guest editor various med. and transplant jours.; mem. editorial bd. Dialysis and Transplantation, 1979—, Rsch. in Surgery, 1991—, Cirugia Iberoamericana, 1992—, clin. adv. bd. Transpl. Proc., 1993—, Medico Interamericano, 1993—, Cirugia Española, 1994—; assoc. editor Transplantology, 1990—; contbr. over 800 publs. on organ preservation, transplantation, other surg. and med. related areas, and the history of medicine to profl. jours.

TOLENTINO, CASIMIRO URBANO, lawyer; b. Manila, May 18, 1949; came to U.S., 1959; s. Lucio Rubio and Florence (Jose) T.; m. Jennifer Masculino, June 5, 1982; 2 children: Casimiro Masculino, Cristina Cecelia Masculino. BA in Zoology, UCLA, 1972, JD, 1975. Bar: Calif. 1976. Gen. counsel civil rights div. HEW, Washington, 1975-76; regional atty. Agrl. Labor Relations Bd., Fresno, Calif., 1976-78; regional dir. Sacramento and San Diego, 1978-81; regional atty. Pub. Employment Relations Bd., Los Angeles, 1981; counsel, west div. Writers Guild Am., Los Angeles, 1982-84; dir. legal affairs Embassy TV, Los Angeles, 1984-86; sole practice Los Angeles, 1986-87; mediator Ctr. Dispute Resolution, Santa Monica, Calif., 1986-87; asst. chief counsel Dept. of Fair Employment and Housing, State of Calif., 1986-92, adminstrv. law judge dept. social svcs., 1992—. Editor: Letters in Exile, 1976; contbr. articles and revs. to Amerasia Jour. Chmn. adv. bd. UCLA Asian Am. Studies Ctr., 1983-90; chmn. bd. Asian Pacific Legal Ctr., L.A., 1983-93 (Decade award); pres. bd. civil svc. commrs. City of L.A., 1984-85, 90-93; bd. dirs. met. region United Way, 1987-95; bd. dirs. Rebuild L.A., 1992—; mem. Asian-Pacific Am. adv. coun. L.A. Police Commn. Mem. State Bar Calif. (exec. com. labor law sect. 1985-88), Los Angeles County Bar Assn., Minority Bar Assn. (sec. 1984-85), Philippine Lawyers of So. Calif. (pres. 1984-87, Award of Merit 1982). Democrat. Roman Catholic. Avocations: history, photography, travel.

TOLER, ANN PATRICK, public relations executive; b. Washington, Oct. 7, 1948; d. William A. and Marie Violet (Tyer) Patrick; m. Ronald Aubrey Toler, July 4, 1970; 1 child, Bradley Neal. Student, East Carolina U., 1966-68; cert. bank mktg, U. Colo., 1989. Admiting clk. Beaufort County Hosp., Washington, N.C., 1966-69; receptionist then exec. sec. Flanders Filters, Washington, 1969-81; adminstrv. sec. Bank of Va., Richmond, 1981-85, personal svc. assoc., 1985-87; mktg. coord. Signet Bank, Richmond, 1987-89, mktg. officer, 1989-90, asst. v.p., 1990-93, regional pub. rels. exec., 1993-94, regional pub. rels. exec. Va. Cmty. Affairs, 1994—. Dir. tournament Signet Open Va., Richmond, 1986-97; bd. dirs. Easter Seal Soc., Richmond, 1989-95; chair regional conf. Am. Heart Assn., Richmond, 1991; co-chair spl. events com. United Way, Richmond, 1991, chair 1992 ; sec. bd. dirs. Christmas in April, Richmond 1995-96, v.p., bd. dirs., 1996-97. Methodist. Avocations: walking. Office: Signet Bank 800 E Main St Ste 200 Richmond VA 23219-3306

TOLER, RAY EDWARD, conductor, band director; b. Detroit, Feb. 1, 1942; s. Ralph Vivian and Neva Florence (Killough) T.; m. Catherine Virginia Hoff, Aug. 15, 1964; children: Ray Edward Jr., Eric Andrew, Bryan Alan. MusB, Tex. Christian U., 1964; MA summa cum laude, Trenton State Coll., 1975; grad., Air Command and Staff Coll., Maxwell AFB, Ala., 1982, Air War Coll, Maxwell AFB, Ala., 1984. Commd. 2d lt. USAF, 1968, advanced through grades to lt. col., 1984; trombonist 539th Air Force Band USAF, Lackland AFB, Tex., 1966-68; condr., comdr. Air Force Logistics Command Band Wright-Patterson AFB, Ohio, 1968-71; condr., comdr. 13th Air Force Band of the Pacific Clark AFB, The Philippines, 1971-73, Air Force Band of the East, McGuire AFB, N.J., 1973-75; condr., comdr. Mil. Airlift Command Band Scott AFB, Ill., 1975-78; condr., comdr. Air Force Band of the West, Lackland AFB, 1978-81, Band of the Air Force Res., Robins AFB, Ga., 1982-85; chief of bands and music USAF Pentagon, Washington, 1985-88; condr. USAF Band, Washington, 1985-88; ret. USAF, 1988; dir. bands Tex. A&M U., College Station, 1988—; trombonist Ft. Worth Symphony and Opera Co., 1963-65, Stan Kenton Orch. , L.A., 1965, Dallas Symphony Orch., 1965-66; band dir. Weatherford (Tex.) High Sch., 1964-66. Condr. rec. Music of the King, 1971; condr./prodr. rec. Music of West Africa, 1977, Ready Then, Ready Now, 1982, Concert Band Classics, 1983, Recall! Step-Off on Hullabaloo, 1990, Bands of Aggieland, 1993, Texas Aggie Band Centennial, 1994, Texas A&M Univ. Symphonic Band Live At TMEA, 1995; prodr. Comin' At 'Ya, 1984; condr./composer rec. In Concert, 1985; condr. rec. The Best of the Air Force Reserve, 1988; condr., prodr. rec. The University Symphonic Band at the 62nd National ABA Convention Plus, 1996. Deacon 1st Presbyn. Ch., Fairborn, Ohio, 1970; judge Miss Am. Scholarship Pageant, 1992, 94; bd. dirs. Woodcreek Homeowners assn., College Station, 1988-91; bd. dirs. Brazor Valley Symphony Orch., College Station, 1996. Mem. Nat. Assn. Mil. Marching Bands, John Philip Sousa Found. (bd. dirs.), Coll. Band Dirs. Nat. Assn., Tex. Bandmasters Assn., Tex. Music Educators Assn., World Assn. for Symphonic Bands and Ensembles, N.Am. Band Dirs. Coordinating Coun., Internat. Mil. Music Soc., Assn. Concert Bands, USAF Ret. Band Dirs. Soc., Kappa Kappa Psi, Phi Mu Alpha Sinfonia. Republican. Methodist. Avocations: reading, crossword puzzles, fishing, computers. Office: Tex A&M U Adams Band Bldg College Station TX 77843

TOLES, THOMAS GREGORY, editorial cartoonist; b. Buffalo, Oct. 22, 1951; s. George Edward and Rose Elizabeth (Riehle) T.; m. Gretchen Amanda Saarnijoki, May 26, 1973; children: Amanda Laurel, Seth August. B.A. in English, SUNY-Buffalo, 1973. Artist Buffalo Courier-Express, 1973-80, cartoonist, 1980-82; cartoonist Buffalo News, 1982—, UPS, 1982—, The New Republic, 1992-94, U.S. News & World Report, 1994—. Author: (fiction) My School Is Worse than Yours, 1997; (cartoon collections) The Taxpayer's New Clothes, 1985, Mr. Gazoo: A Cartoon History of the Reagan Era, 1987, At Least Our Bombs Are Getting Smarter: A Cartoon Preview of the 1990's, 1991, My Elected Representatives Went to Washington, 1993, Duh, 1996; creator (comic strip) Curious Avenue, 1992. Recipient John Fischetti Editorial Cartoon award Columbia Coll., Chgo., 1984, Pulitzer Prize for editorial cartooning, 1990. Mem. Am. Assn. Editorial Cartoonists. Home: 75 Central Ave Hamburg NY 14075-6219 Office: Buffalo News 1 News Plz Buffalo NY 14203-2930

TOLIA, VASUNDHARA K., pediatric gastroenterologist, educator; b. Calcutta, India; came to U.S., 1975; d. Rasiklal and Saroj (Kothari) Doshi; m. Kirit Tolia, May 30, 1975; children: Vinay, Sanjay. MBBS, Calcutta U., 1968-75. Intern, resident Children's Hosp. Mich., Detroit, 1976-79, fellow, 1979-81, dir. pediat. endoscopy unit, 1984-90, dir. pediat. gastroenterology and nutrition, 1990—; instr. Wayne State U., Detroit, 1981-83, asst. prof., 1983-91, assoc. prof., 1991-97, prof., 1997—. Contbr. articles to profl. jours. Named Woman of Distinction, Mich. chpt. Crohn's and Colitis Found. Am., 1991. Fellow Am. Coll. Gastroenterology, Am. Acad. Pediats.; mem. Am. Gastroenterology Assn., N.Am. Soc. Pediat. Gastroenterology and Nutrition, Soc. Pediat. Rsch. Office: Children's Hosp of Mich 3901 Beaubien St Detroit MI 48201-2119

TOLIVER, LEE, mechanical engineer; b. Wildhorse, Okla., Oct. 3, 1921; s. Clinton Leslie and Mary (O'Neall) T.; m. Barbara Anne O'Reilly, Jan. 24, 1942; children: Margaret Anne, Michael Edward. BSME, U. Okla., 1942. Registered profl. engr., Ohio. Engr. Douglas Aircraft Co., Santa Monica, Calif., 1942, Oklahoma City, 1942-44; engr. Los Alamos (N.Mex.) Sci. Lab., 1946; instr. mech. engring. Ohio State U., Columbus, 1946-47; engr. Sandia Nat. Labs., Albuquerque, 1947-82; instr. computer sci. and math. U. N.Mex., Valencia County, 1982-84; number theory researcher Belen, N.Mex., 1982—. Author: (computer manuals with G. Carli, AF. Schkade) Experience with an Intelligent Remote Batch Terminal, 1972; (with C.R. Borgman, T.I. Ristine) Transmitting Data from PDP-10 to Precision Graphics, 1973, Data Transmission-PDP-10/Sykes/Precision Graphics, 1975. With Manhattan Project (Atomic Bomb) U.S. Army, 1944-46. Mem. Math. Assn. Am., Am. Math. Soc. Achievements include devel. of 44 computer programs with manuals. Home: 206 Howell St Belen NM 87002-6225

TOLIVER, MAXWELL DOEL, hypnotherapist; b. Staten Island, N.Y., Jan. 18, 1959; s. Russell and Estelle (Trower) T.; m. Janice M. Archibald-Toliver, Aug. 28, 1982; children: Ryan Eugene, Kyle Stewart. Student, Coll. Staten Island, 1977-80. Cert. profl. hypnotherapist, behavioral therapist, HIV-AIDS pre and post test counselor, alcohol, drug and sex addiction specialist. Pvt. practice hypnotherapist and behavioral therapist N.Y.C., 1988—; founder and CEO The Toliver's, Staten Island, N.Y., 1996; cons. John Stossel Show 20/20, N.Y.C., 1988, former Mayor Ed Koch's Com. on the Homeless in the Subways, N.Y.C., 1989-90; with Dr. Bruce Eisenberg show Back to Health, N.Y.C., 1991. Mem. The Black Polit. Action Com., S.I., 1990; bd. dirs. Crisis Pregnancy Ctr., S.I., 1991. Mem. AACD, Am. Assn. Beharioral Therapists, Am. Bd. Hyponotherapy, Am. Assn. Profl. Hypnotherapists, Am. Mental Health Counselors Assn., Am. Inst. for Hypnotherapy and Psychotherpaists, Nat. Assn. Alcoholism and Drug Abuse Counselors, Internat. Hypnosis Network, Nat. Guild Hypnotists, Nat. Black Alcoholism Coun. N.Y.C. Democrat. Baptist. Avocations: running, swimming. Home: 22 Windham Loop 3B Staten Island NY 10314

TOLK, NORMAN HENRY, physics educator; b. Idaho Falls, Idaho, Jan. 9, 1938; s. Henry and Merle (Ricks) T.; m. Marilyn Ann Neubauer, Dec. 19, 1961; children: Jeffrey S., Bentley J., David H., Rebecca E., Amy C. AB in Physics, Harvard U., 1960; PhD in Physics, Columbia U., 1966. Rsch. physicist Columbia Radiation Lab., N.Y.C., 1966, rsch. assoc., 1966-67, lectr., mem. staff, 1967-68; adj. asst. prof. Columbia U., N.Y.C., 1968-69; mem. tech. staff Bell Telephone Lab., Murray Hill, N.J., 1968-83, Bell Comms. Rsch., Murray Hill, 1984; prof. physics Vanderbilt U., Nashville, 1984—, prof. dept. radiology, 1993—; adj. prof. physics Fisk U., Nashville, 1991—; cons. Physitron, Inc., Huntsville, Ala., 1993—, Lawrence Livermore Nat. Lab., Livermore, Calif., 1995—. Editor: Inelastic Ion-Surface Collisions, 1977, Desorption Induced by Elec. Trans., 1983, Atomic Collisions in Solids, 1986; N.Am. editor Radiation Effects and Def./Solids, 1987—; contbr. over 160 articles to profl. jours. Alexander von Humboldt sr. scientist, 1987. Fellow Am. Phys. Soc. Home: 314 Appomattox Dr Brentwood TN 37027-4955 Office: Vanderbilt U Dept Physics PO Box 1807 B Nashville TN 37202-1807

TOLL, DANIEL ROGER, corporate executive, civic leader; b. Denver, Dec. 3, 1927; s. Oliver W. and Merle D'Aubigne (Sampson) T.; m. Sue Andersen, June 15, 1963; children: Daniel Andersen, Matthew Mitchell. AB magna cum laude (Pyne prize), Princeton U., 1949; MBA with distinction, Harvard U., 1955. With Deep Rock Oil Corp., Tulsa, 1949-51, asst. mgr. product supply and distbn.; with Helmerich & Payne, Tulsa, 1955-64, roughneck, landman, exploration mgr., pipeline constrn. mgr., v.p. fin., 1961-64; with Sunray DX Oil Co., Tulsa, 1964-69, treas., v.p. corp. planning and devel.; v.p. Sun Oil Co., 1969; with Walter E. Heller Internat. Corp., Chgo., 1970-85, sr. v.p. fin., dir., 1970-80, pres., dir., 1980-85, corp. and civic dir., 1985—; bd. dirs. Brown Group, Inc., Mallinckrodt Group, Inc. (formerly IMCERA Group Inc.), Kemper Nat. Ins. Co., Lincoln Nat. Income Fund, Inc., Lincoln Nat. Convertible Securities, Inc., NICOR, Inc., A.P. Green Industries Inc. Vice chmn. Tulsa Cmty. Chest, 1964-66; v.p., bd. dirs. Tulsa Opera, 1960-69; bd. dirs. Tulsa Little Theatre, 1963-69, Internat. House, Chgo., 1984-87; bd. dirs. Inroads, Inc., 1973-95, nat. vice chmn., 1982-95; bd. dirs. Chgo. Area coun. Boy Scouts Am., 1976-94, pres., 1981-83; mem. Kenilworth (Ill.) Sch. Bd. Dirs. 38, 1975-81, pres., 1978-81; bd. dirs., mem. exec. com., chmn. fin. and hosp. affairs coms. Evanston (Ill.) Hosp., 1982—; bd. dirs. Chgo. Met. Planning Coun., 1989—, pres., 1991-94; bd. dirs. Northwestern Healthcare Network, Inc., 1995—; trustee Princeton U., 1990-94. Lt. (j.g.) USNR, 1951-52. Baker scholar Harvard U., 1955. Mem. Chgo. Assn. Commerce and Industry (bd. dirs. 1979-86), Chgo. Club, Comml. Club, Econ. Club, Harvard Bus. Sch. Club (past pres., bd. dirs. 1971-91), Indian Hill Club (bd. govs. 1987-90), Princeton Club (past pres., bd. dirs. 1985—), Phi Beta Kappa. Home: 1500 Sheridan Rd # 10-i Wilmette IL 60091 Office: 135 S La Salle St Ste 1117 Chicago IL 60603-4501

TOLL, DAVID, pediatrician; b. Cleve., May 6, 1925; s. Herman I. and Mollie (Neuger) T.; B.A., Harvard U.; M.D., Western Res. U., 1948; m. Bridget Ann Fryer; children: Job, Abel, Seth. Intern, Children's Hosp., Boston, 1948-50; resident in pediatrics Mass. Gen. Hosp., 1951-52; practice medicine specializing in pediatrics, St. Johnsbury, Vt., 1952; med. dir. Child Health Center, St. Johnsbury, 1952—; cons. Vt. Health Dept., N.H. Health Dept., 1952—; adj. asst. prof. pediatrics Dartmouth Med. Sch.; preceptor Stanford, Dartmouth, Case Western Res., U. Vt. med. schs. Mem. AMA, Vt. Med. Assn., Am. Acad. Pediatrics, New Eng. Pediatric Soc., Am. Acad. Med. Dirs. Home: RR 2 Saint Johnsbury VT 05819-9802 Office: 95 Main St Saint Johnsbury VT 05819-2211

TOLL, JOHN SAMPSON, university administrator, physics educator; b. Denver, Oct. 25, 1923; s. Oliver Wolcott and Merle d'Aubigne (Sampson) T.; m. Deborah Ann Taintor, Oct. 24, 1970; children: Dacia Merle Sampson, Caroline Taintor. BS with highest honors, Yale U., 1944; AM, Princeton U., 1948, PhD, 1952; DSc (hon.), U. Md., 1973, U. Wroclaw, Poland, 1975; LLD (hon.), Adelphi U., 1978; hon. doctorate, Fudan U., Peoples Republic China, 1987; LHD (hon.), SUNY, Stony Brook, 1990; LLD (hon.), U. Md., Eastern Shore, 1993. Mng. editor, acting chmn. Yale Sci. mag., 1943-44; with Princeton U., 1946-49, proctor fellow, 1948-49; Friends of Elementary Particle Theory Research grantee for study in France, 1950; theoretical physicist Los Alamos Sci. Lab., 1950-51; staff mem., assoc. dir. Project Matterhorn, Forrestal Rsch. Ctr., Princeton U., 1951-53; prof., chmn. physics and astronomy U. Md., 1953-65; pres., prof. physics SUNY, Stony Brook, 1965-78; pres., prof. physics U. Md., 1978-88, chancellor, 1988-89, chancellor emeritus, prof. physics, 1989—; pres. Univs. Rsch. Assn., Washington, 1989-94, Washington Coll., Chestertown, Md., 1995—; 1st dir. SUNY Chancellor's Panel on Univ. Purposes, 1970; physics cons. to editl. staff Nat. Sci. Tchrs. Assn., 1957-61; U.S. del., head sci., secretariat Internat. Conf. on High Energy Physics, 1960; mem.-at-large U.S. Nat. Com. for Internat. Union of Pure and Applied Physics, 1960-63; chmn. rsch. adv. com. on electrophysics to NASA, 1961-65; mem. gov. Md. Sci. Resources Adv. bd., 1963-65; mem., chmn. NSF adv. panel for physics, 1964-67; mem. N.Y. Gov.'s Adv. Com. Atomic Energy, 1966-70; mem. commn. plans and objectives higher edn. Am. Coun. Edn., 1966-69; mem. Hall of Records Commn., 1979-88; mem., chmn. adv. coun. Princeton Plasma Physics Lab, 1979-85; mem. Adv. Coun. of Pres.'s, Assn. of Governing Bds., 1980-88, So. Regional Edn. Bd., 1980-90; mem. exec. com. Washington/Balt. Regional Assn., 1980-89, Nat. Assn. State Univs. and Land Grant Colls., 1980-88, Ctr. for the Study of the Presidency, 1983-84; mem. univ. programs panel of energy rsch. bd. Dept. Energy, 1982-83; mem. SBHE Adv. Com., 1983-89, Md. Gov.'s Chesapeake Bay Coun., 1985; mem. resource com. State Trade Policy Coun. Gov.'s High Tech Roundtable Md. Dept. Econ. Devel., 1986-89; marine divsn. chmn. NASULGC, 1986; bd. trustees Aspen Inst. for Humanities, 1987-89; mem. Commn. on Higher Edn. Middle States Assn. Colls. and Schs., 1987; chmn. adv. panel on tech. risks and opportunities for U.S. energy supply and demand U.S. Office Tech. Assessment, 1987-91; chmn. adv. panel on internat. collaboration in def. tech., U.S. Office Tech. Assessment, 1989-91; mem. Sea Grant Rev. Panel U.S. Dept. Commerce, 1992—, chair, 1996—; vis. prof. Nordic Inst. Theoretical Physics, Niels Bohr Inst., Denmark, U. Lund, Sweden, 1975-76; mem. Math. Scis. Edn. Bd. NAS, 1991-93. Contbr. articles to sci. jours. Recipient Benjamin Barge prize in math. Yale U., 1943, George Beckwith medal for Proficiency in Astronomy, 1944, Outstanding Citizen award City of Denver, 1958, Outstanding Tchr. award U. Md. Men's League, 1965, Nat. Golden Plate award Am. Acad. Achievement, 1968, Copernicus award govt. of Poland, 1973, Stony Brook Found. award for disting. contbns. to edn., 1979, Disting. Svc. award State of Md., 1981, Silver medal Sci. U. Tokyo, 1994; named Washingtonian of Yr., 1985; John Simon Guggenheim Meml. Found. fellow Inst. Theoretical Physics U. Copenhagen, U. Lund, Sweden, 1958-59. Fellow Am. Phys. Soc., Washington Acad. Scis. (pres. 1995-96), N.Y. Acad. Scis.; mem. NSTA, Am. Coun. Edn. (bd. dirs. 1986-89), NAACP (life), Am. Assn. Physics Tchrs., Fedn. Am. Scientists (chmn. 1961-62), Philos. Soc. Washington, Assn. Higher Edn., Yale U. Sci. and Engring. Assn. (award for disting. contbns. 1996), Cosmos Club, Univ. Club (Washington), Phi Beta Kappa, Sigma Xi (Sci. Achievement award 1965), Phi Kappa Phi (disting.), Omicron Delta Kappa (hon.), Sigma Pi Sigma. Achievements include research on elementary particle theory; scattering. Office: U Md Dept Physics College Park MD 20742-4111 also: Washington Coll Pres's Office Chestertown MD 21620 *Throughout my life I have tried mainly to do whatever seemed most important and useful.*

TOLL, PERRY MARK, lawyer; b. Kansas City, Mo., Oct. 28, 1945; s. Mark Irving and Ruth (Parker) T.; m. Mary Anne Shottenkirk, Aug. 26, 1967; children: Andrea Lynne, Hillary Anne. BS in Polit. Sci. and Econs., U. Kans., 1967, JD, 1970. Bar: Mo. 1970 1970, U.S. Dist. Ct. (we. dist.) Mo. 1970, U.S. Tax. Ct. 1979, U.S. Supreme Ct. 1979. With Shughart, Thomson & Kilroy P.C., Kansas City, 1970-94, pres., 1995—; asst. prof. deferred compensation U. Mo., Kansas City, 1979-83; bd. dirs., pres. Heart of Am. Tax Inst., Kansas City, 1975-87. Mem., chmn. Prairie Village (Kans.) Bd. Zoning Appeals, 1977-95. Mem. ABA, Mo. Bar Assn., Nat. Health Lawyers Assn., Am. Agr. Law Assn., Mo. Merchants and Mfrs. Assn., Greater Kansas City Med. Mgrs. Assn., Lawyers Assn. Kansas City, East Kans. Estate Planning Coun. (bd. dirs., pres.), Phi Kappa Tau (bd. dirs.). Office: Shughart Thomson & Kilroy 12 Wyandotte Plz 120 W 12th St Kansas City MO 64105-1917

TOLL, SHELDON SAMUEL, lawyer; b. Phila., June 6, 1940; s. Herman and Rose (Ornstein) T.; m. Roberta Darlene Pollack, Aug. 11, 1968; children: Candice Moore, John Maitland, Kevin Scott. Bar: Pa. 1967, Mich. 1972, Ill. 1990, Tex. 1990, U.S. Dist. Ct. (ea. dist.) Pa. 1968, U.S. Ct. Appeals (3d cir.) 1970, U.S. Supreme Ct. 1971, Mich. 1972, U.S. Dist. Ct. (ea. dist.), U.S. Ct. Appeals (6th cir.) 1973, U.S. Ct. Appeals (5th cir.) 1978, U.S. Dist. Ct. (no. dist.) Calif. 1986, U.S. Ct. Appeals (9th cir.) 1987, U.S. Dist. Ct. (ea. dist.) Wis. 1989. Assoc. Montgomery, McCracken et al, Phila., 1967-72; sr. ptnr. Honigman Miller Schwartz and Cohn, Detroit, 1972—; panelist Bankruptcy Litigation Inst., N.Y.C., 1984—. Author: Pennsylvania Crime Codes, 1972, Bankruptcy Litigation Manual, 1988. Bd. dirs. Southeastern Mich. chpt. ARC, Detroit. Mem. Fed. Bar Assn. (past pres. Detroit chpt.), ABA, Pa. Bar Assn., Phila. Bar Assn., Detroit Bar Assn., Am. Bankruptcy Inst. (cert. bus. bankruptcy law specialist), Franklin (Mich.) Hills Country Club, Phi Beta Kappa. Democrat. Jewish. Office: Honigman Miller Schwartz & Cohn 2290 1st National Bldg Detroit MI 48226

TOLLENAERE, LAWRENCE ROBERT, retired industrial products company executive; b. Berwyn, Ill., Nov. 19, 1922; s. Cyrille and Modesta (Van Damme) T.; m. Mary Elizabeth Hansen, Aug. 14, 1948; children: Elizabeth, Homer, Stephanie, Caswell, Mary Jennifer. BS in Engring., Iowa State U., 1944, MS in Engring., 1949; MBA, U. So. Calif., 1969; LLD (hon.), Claremont Grad. Sch., 1977. Specification engr. Aluminum Co. Am., Vernon, Calif., 1946-47; asst. prof. indsl. engring. Iowa State U., Ames, 1947-50; sales rep. Am. Pipe and Constrn. Co. (name changed to AMERON 1970), South Gate, Calif., 1950-53; spl. rep. Am. Pipe and Constrn. Co. (name changed to AMERON 1970), S.Am., 1952-54; 2nd v.p., mgr. Columbian divsn. Am. Pipe and Constrn. Co. (name changed to AMERON 1970), Bogota, S.Am., 1955-57; divsn. v.p., mgr. Am. Pipe and Constrn. Co. (name changed to AMERON 1970), Calif., 1957-63; v.p. concrete pipe ops. Am. Pipe and Constrn. Co. (name changed to AMERON 1970), Monterey Park, Calif., 1963-65, pres. corp. hdqrs., 1965-67; pres., CEO Ameron Inc., Monterrey Park, Calif., 1967-89; CEO, pres. Ameron Inc., Pasadena, 1989-93, chmn. bd. dirs., 1989-94, ret., 1994; emeritus bd. dirs. Newhall Land and Farming Co., Valencia, Calif.; bd. dirs. The Parsons Corp., Pasadena. Trustee The Huntington Library, Art Gallery and Bot. Gardens; emeritus mem. bd. fellows Claremont U. Ctr.; bd. gov.'s Iowa State U. Found. Mem. Newcomen Soc. N.Am., Calif. C. of C. (bd. dirs. 1977-92), Calif. Club (past pres.), Jonathan Club, San Gabriel Country Club, Bohemian Club, San Francisco Club, Commanderie de Bordeaux Club, L.A. Confrerie des Chevaliers du Tastevin Club, Calif. Club (past pres.), Twilight Club, Lincoln Club, Beavers Club (past pres., hon. dir.), Valley of Montecito Club, Alpha Tau Omega. Republican. Avocations: fishing, hunting, equestrian, philately. Home: 1400 Milan Ave South Pasadena CA 91030-3930 Office: 750 E Green St Ste 301 Pasadena CA 91101-2134

TOLLES, BRYANT FRANKLIN, JR., history and art history educator; b. Hartford, Conn., Mar. 14, 1939; s. Bryant Franklin and Grace Frances (Ludden) T.; m. Carolyn Coolidge Kimball, Sept. 15, 1962; children: Thayer Coolidge, Bryant Franklin III. BA, Yale U., 1961, MA in Teaching, 1962; PhD, Boston U., 1970. Instr. history King Sch., Stamford, Conn., 1962-63; tchr. history St. George's Sch., Newport, R.I., 1963-65; instr., asst. dean Tufts U., Medford, Mass., 1965-71; asst. dir., libr., editor publs. N.H. Hist. Soc., Concord, 1972-74; exec. dir., libr. Essex Inst., Salem, Mass., 1974-84; dir. mus. studies program, assoc. prof. history and art history U. Del., Newark, 1984—; mem. Com. for a New England Bibliography, Inc. Author: New Hampshire Architecture, 1979, Architecture in Salem, 1983, The Grand Resort Hotels of the White Mountains: A Vanishing Architectural Legacy, 1997; editor: Leadership for the Future, 1991; contr. articles to profl. jours. Trustee Mt. Washington Obs., N.H. Ford. Found. fellow Yale, 1962. Mem. Orgn. Am. Historians, Soc. Archtl. Historians, Soc. Indsl. Archaeology, Am. Assn. Mus., New Eng. Mus. Assn., Mid-Atlantic Mus. Assn., Am. Assn. for State and Local History, Wilmington Rowing Club, Appalachian Mountain Club, Univ. Barge Club (Phila.). Home: 1002 Kent Rd Wilmington DE 19807-2820 Office: U Del Mus Studies Program 301 Old Coll Newark DE 19716

TOLLESTRUP, ALVIN VIRGIL, physicist; b. Los Angeles, Mar. 22, 1924; s. Albert Virgil and Maureen (Petersen) T.; m. Alice Hatch, Feb. 26, 1945 (div. Nov. 1970); children: Kristine, Kurt, Eric, Carl; m. Janine Cukay, Oct. 11, 1986. BS, U. Utah, 1944; PhD, Calif. Inst. Tech., 1950. Mem. faculty Calif. Inst. Tech., Pasadena, 1950-77, prof. physics, 1968-77; scientist Fermi Nat. Lab., Batavia, Ill., 1977-93; co-spokesman CDF Collaboration, 1977-93. Co-developer superconducting magnets for Tevatron, Fermi Lab. Served to lt. (j.g.) USN, 1944-46. NSF fellow; Disting. Alumni award Calif. Inst. Tech., 1993. Fellow AAAS, NAS, Am. Phys. Soc. (R.R. Wilson prize 1989, Nat. medal for tech. 1989). Democrat. Home: 29w254 Renouf Dr Warrenville IL 60555-2113 Office: Fermi Nat Lab PO Box 500 Batavia IL 60510-0500

TOLLETT, GLENNA BELLE, accountant, mobile home park operator; b. Graham, Ariz., Dec. 17, 1913; d. Charles Harry and Myrtle (Stapley) Spafford; m. John W. Tollett, Nov. 28, 1928; 1 child, Jackie J., 1 adopted child, Beverly Mae Malgren. Bus. cert., Lamson Coll. Office mgr, Hurley Meat Packing Co., Phoenix, 1938-42; co-owner, sec., treas. A.B.C. Enterprises, Inc., Seattle, 1942—; ptnr. Bella Investment Co., Seattle, 1962—, Four Square Investment Co., Seattle, 1969—, Warehouses Ltd., Seattle, 1970—, Tri State Partnership, Wash., Idaho, Tex., 1972—; pres. Halycon Mobile Home Park, Inc., Seattle, 1979—; co-owner, operator Martha Lake Mobile Home Park, Lynwood, Wash., 1962-73. Mem. com. Wash. Planning and Community Affairs Agy., Olympia, 1981-82, Wash. Mfg. Housing Assn. Relations Com., Olympia, 1980-84; appointed by Gov. Wash. to Mobile Home and RV Adv. Bd., 1973-79. Named to RV/Mobile Home Hall of Fame, 1980. Mem. Wash. Mobile Park Owners Assn. (legisl. chmn., lobbyist 1976-85, cons. 1984, pres. 1978-79, exec. dir. 1976-84, This is Your Life award 1979), Wash. Soc. of Assn. Execs. (Exec. Dir. Service award 1983), Mobile Home Old Timers Assn., Mobile Home Owners of Am. (sec. 1972-76, Appreciation award 1976), Nat Fire Protection Assn. (com. 1979-86), Aurora Pkwy. North C. of C.)sec. 1976-80), Fremont C. of C. Republican. Mormon. Avocations: needlework, gardening, fishing, swimming, trailering. Home: 18261 Springdale Ct NW Seattle WA 98177-3228 Office: ABC Enterprises Inc 3524 Stone Way N Seattle WA 98103-8924

TOLLETT, LELAND EDWARD, food company executive; b. Nashville, Ark., Jan. 21, 1937; s. Vergil E. and Gladys V. (Sturgis) T.; m. Betty Ruth Blew, June 2, 1961; children—Terri Lynn, Gary Dwayne. B.S.A., U. Ark., 1958, M.S.A., 1959. Dir. Research Tyson Foods, Inc., Springdale, Ark., 1959-64, gen mgr. prodn., 1965-66, v.p. prodn., 1966-80, chief operating officer, 1981-83, pres., chief operating officer, 1983-91, chief exec. officer, 1991—, vice chmn., 1993-95, chmn., CEO, 1995—, also bd dirs.; pres., chief oper. officer Spring Valley Farms Inc., Tyson Farms Tex., Inc., Poultry Growers Inc., Lane Processing Inc., Tyson-Carolina Inc., Eagle Distbg. Inc., Lane Farms Inc., Tyson Export Sales Inc.; pres. Louis Kemp Seafood Co., Arctic Alaska Fisheries Corp., Henry House, Inc. Served with USAF, 1961-62. Mem. Nat. Broiler Council (bd. dirs. 1979—). Avocations: hunting; golfing. Home: 6 Samoset Ct Rogers AR 72758-1463 Office: Tyson Foods Inc 2210 W Oaklawn Dr Springdale AR 72762-6900*

TOLLEY, AUBREY GRANVILLE, hospital administrator; b. Lynchburg, Va., Nov. 15, 1924; married. Student, Duke U., 1942-43; M.D., U. Va., 1952. Diplomate Am. Bd. Psychiatry and Neurology. Intern St. Elizabeths Hosp., Washington, 1952-53; asst. resident psychiatry U. Va. Hosp., Charlottesville, 1953-54; resident psychiatry VA Hosp., Roanoke, Va., 1954-56; instr. U. N.C. Sch. Medicine, 1956-61, asst. prof., 1961-66, clin. asst. prof. psychiatry, 1966-72, clin. assoc. prof., 1972-76, clin. prof., 1976—; dir. psychotherapy Dorothea Dix Hosp., Raleigh, 1962-67; dir. hosp. Dorothea Dix Hosp., 1973-88; dir. resident tng. John Umstead Hosp., Butner, N.C., 1966-67; dir. profl. tng. and edn. N.C. Dept. Mental Health, Raleigh, 1967-72, asst. dir., 1972-73; Prin. investigator USPHS grant, 1957-59; cons. VA Hosp., Fayetteville, N.C., 1957-78; sr. cons., supervising faculty, community psychiatry sect. dept. psychiatry U. N.C. Sch. Medicine, 1971—; exec. sec. Multiversity Group, 1968-73. Trustee Found. Hope, Raleigh, N.C., 1984—. Served with USNR, 1943-46. Fellow Am. Psychiat. Assn. (rep. N.C. Dist. bd. 1969-82, 86—, mem. joint commn. on pub. affairs 1984-87, mem. constl. membership com. 1990-96, mem. commn. on subspecialization 1990-94, Warren Williams award 1987), Am. Coll. Psychiatrists; mem. N.C., Durham-Orange County med. socs., N.C. Neuropsychiat. Assn. (pres. 1984-85), N.C. Hosp. Assn. (life), George C. Ham Soc. (Disting. Alumni award 1992). Home and Office: 110 Laurel Hill Rd Chapel Hill NC 27514-4323

TOLLEY, EDWARD DONALD, lawyer; b. San Antonio, Jan. 31, 1950; s. Lyle Oren and Mary Theresa Tolley; m. Beth Dekle Tolley; 1 child, Edward Spencer. BBA, U. Ga., 1971, MBA, 1974, JD, 1975. Bar: Ga. 1975, U.S. Dist. Ct. (5th cir.) 1976, U.S. Supreme Ct. 1978, U.S. Ct. Appeals (11th cir.) 1981. Ptnr. Cook, Noell, Tolley and Wiggins, Athens, Ga., 1975—; lectr. various colls., univs., civic and profl. groups. Mem. Family Counseling Assn. of Athens, Inc., mem. Gov.'s Commn. on Criminal Sanctions and Correctional Facilities, 1988-90; past bd. dirs. Am. Cancer Soc.; pres. Clarke County Bd. Edn., 1992-93. Fellow Ga. Bar Found., Am. Bd. Criminal Lawyers (bd. dirs. 1987, pres. 1996); mem. FBA (sec. 1983, treas. 1985), State Bar Ga. (chmn. law office and econ. com., bd. govs. 1985—, formal adv. opinion bd.), Ga. Trial Lawyers (v.p.), Ga. Assn. Criminal Def. Lawyers (pres. 1985, Indigent Def. award 1983, 88), Athens Bar Assn. (past pres.), Am. Judicature Soc., Order of Barristers. Office: Cook Noell Tolley & Wiggins 304 E Washington St Athens GA 30601-2751

TOLLEY, JERRY RUSSELL, clinical laboratory executive; b. Goldsboro, N.C., Nov. 6, 1942; s. Elva Russell Tolley and Clara (Smith) Tolley-Bunch; m. Joan Morrison, June 8, 1965; children: Jerry R. Jr., Justin Clay. BS, East

Carolina U., 1965, MEd, 1966; EdD, U. N.C., Greensboro, 1982; exec. mgmt. courses, Duke U. Tchr., coach Fayetteville (N.C.) Sr. High Sch., 1966; asst. football coach, head track and tennis coach Elon Coll., N.C., 1967-77, head football coach, 1977-81, dir. athletic sholarship fund, 1982, dir. corp. and ann. resources, 1983, coordinator Pride II Capital Campaign, 1984, assoc. dir. devel., 1985; asst. v.p. tng., nat. dir. tng. & pub. affairs Lab. Corp. of Am., Burlington, N.C., 1986—. Author: Intercollegiate History of Athletics and Elon College, 1982, American Football Coaches Guidebook to Championship Football Drills, 1985; contbg. author: 101 Winning Plays, 1977, Leadership Education: A Source Book, 1989; contbr. articles to profl. jours. Treas. Town of Elon Coll., 1984-87, mayor protem, 1988, mayor, 1990—; convenor City County Govt. Assn., Alamance County, N.C., 1986—; mem. exec. bd. dirs. Cherokee Coun. Boy Scouts Am., 1986, Thomas E. Powell Jr. Biology Found., Alamance Found.; exec. bd. N.C. Health & Fitness Found.; visitors Elon Coll.; mem. exec. com. Alamance County Ptnrs. in Edn. Named one of Outstanding Young Men Am., 1980, Internat. Men of Achievement, 1990, Cmty. Leaders Am., 1990, Mayors Hall of Fame, 1995; recipient Dwight D. Eisenhower award Nat. Football Hall of Fame, 1980, 81, Nat. Collegiate Football Championship award Eastman Kodak, Meritorious Svc. award Tom Sawyer-Huck Finn Tennis Classic, 1986; named Nat. Football Coach of Yr., Nat. Assn. Intercollegiate Athletics, 1980, Elon Coll. Sports Hall of Fame, East Carolina U. Athletic Hall of Fame, 1991. Mem. Am. Football Coaches Assn., Phi Delta Kappa, Sigma Delta Psi. Avocations: writing, racquet sports, jogging. Home: Box 463 1322 Westbrook Ave Elon College NC 27244 Office: Laboratory Corp America 430 S Spring St Burlington NC 27215-5865

TOLLISON, JOSEPH W., family practice physician. Pres. Am. Bd. Family Practice, Lexington, Ky. Office: Am Bd Family Practice 2228 Young Dr Lexington KY 40505*

TOLLMAN, THOMAS ANDREW, librarian; b. Omaha, Mar. 14, 1939; s. James Perry and Elizabeth (McVey) T.; m. Teresa Ramírez, Jan. 4, 1964; children: James Daniel, Lisa Maria. BA, Carleton Coll., 1960; MA, U. Chgo., 1965, U. Minn., 1974; postgrad., U. Ariz., 1977-79. Admissions counselor Carleton Coll., Northfield, Minn., 1960-62; asst. dean of coll. Carleton Coll., Northfield, 1968-73; assoc. prof., reference libr. N.W. Mo. State U., Maryville, 1974-77; adj. instr. U. Ariz., Tucson, 1977-79; chair libr. reference dept. U. Nebr., Omaha, 1979-88, reference libr., 1988—, prof., 1997—; sr. lectr. Fulbright Commn., Quito, Ecuador, 1991. Contbr. articles to profl. jours. Mem. ALA, Nebr. Libr. Assn., Spl. Librs. Assn., Assn. Coll. and Rsch. Librs., Reference and Adult Svcs. Div., Reforma, Nebr. Libr. Assn. (disting. svc. award, 1995). Mem. ALA, Nebr. Libr. Assn. (Disting. Svc. award 1995), Spl. Librs. Assn., Assn. Coll. and Rsch. Librs., Reference and Adult Svcs. Divsn., Reforma. Avocations: running, bicycling. Home: 2121 S 84th St Omaha NE 68124-2222 Office: Reference Libr U Nebr Omaha NE 68182-0237

TOLLNER, ERNEST WILLIAM, agricultural engineering educator, agricultural radiology consultant; b. Maysville, Ky., July 14, 1949; s. Ernest Edward and Ruby Geneva (Henderson) T.; m. Caren Gayle Crane, Sept. 27, 1987. BS, U. Ky., 1972; PhD, Auburn (Ala.) U., 1981. Registered profl. engr., Ga. Rsch. specialist U. Ky., Lexington, 1972-74, rsch. engr., 1974-76; teaching asst. Tex. A&M U., College Station, 1976-77; rsch. specialist Auburn U., 1977-80; asst. prof. U. Ga., Griffin, 1980-85, assoc. prof., 1985-90, prof., 1990—; cons. to govtl. agys. and pvt. indusry; mem. Ga. State Acad. Panel addressing stream sediment transport issues. Contbr. 60 articles to profl. jours. Treas. Condominium Assn., Peachtree City, 1988-91. Mem. Am. Soc. Agrl. Engrs., Am. Soc. Agronomy, Kiwanis. Achievements include first to use an x-ray tomographic scanner devoted solely to agricultural research tasks; pioneered research into the use of vegetative filterstrips for sediment control; pioneered alternative, nonaerobic composting process for farm residue. Home: 1010 Rogers Rd Bogart GA 30622-2723 Office: U Ga Dept Biology and Agrl Engring Driftmeir Engring Ctr Athens GA 30602

TOLMAN, RICHARD ROBINS, zoology educator; b. Ogden, Utah, Dec. 1, 1937; s. Dale Richards and Dorothy (Robins) T.; m. Bonnie Bjornn, Aug. 18, 1964; children: David, Alicia, Brett, Matthew. BS, U. Utah, 1963, MSEd, 1964; PhD, Oreg. State U., 1969. Tchr. sci. Davis County Sch. Dist., Bountiful, Utah, 1964-66; instr. Mt. Hood C.C., Gresham, Oreg., 1968-69; staff assoc., project dir. Biol. Scis. Curriculum Study, Boulder, Colo., 1969-82; prof. zoology Brigham Young U., Provo, Utah, 1982—, chair dept. of zoology, 1994—. Contbr. articles to profl. jours. Scoutmaster Boy Scouts Am., Orem, Utah, 1992. With USAR, 1956-63. Alcuin fellow Brigham Young U., 1991. Mem. Nat. Sci. Tchrs. Assn., Utah Sci. Tchrs. Assn. (exec. sec. 1991—), Nat. Assn. for Rsch. in Sci. Teaching, Nat. Assn. of Biology Tchrs. Mem. Ch. of LDS. Avocations: whitewater rafting, hunting, fishing, hiking. Home: 174 E 1825 S Orem UT 84058-7836 Office: Brigham Young Univ Dept Zoology Provo UT 84602

TOLMAN, STEVEN KAY, lawyer; b. Pocatello, Idaho, Sept. 16, 1946; s. S. Ernest and June (Carver) T.; m. Geraldine Bryne, Dec. 21, 1968 (div.); children: Brett, Shawna, Kelly, Bryce, Haley; m. Donna Arnold Tolman, July 18, 1992. BA, Brigham Young U., 1968; MBA, U. Utah, 1972; JD, U. Idaho, 1975. Bar: Idaho 1975, U.S. Dist. Ct. Idaho 1975, U.S. Ct. Appeals (9th cir.) 1988. Assoc. St. Clair, Hiller, Benjamin, Wood & McGath, Ketchum, Idaho, 1975-77, Parry, Robertson, Daly & Larson, Twin Falls, Idaho, 1977-78; ptnr. Nelson, Rosholt, Robertson, Tolman & Tucker, Twin Falls, 1979-91, Hollifield Tolman & Bevan, Twin Falls, 1991-92, Hollifield & Tolman, Twin Falls, 1992-94; atty. Tolman Law Office, Twin Falls, 1994—. Sch. bd. trustee Twin Falls Sch. Dist. # 411, 1986-95. 1st lt. U.S. Army, 1968-71, Vietnam. Mem. Greater Twin Falls Area C. of C. (bd. dirs. 1985-88). Avocations: tennis, golf, skiing, hunting. Office: Tolman Law Office PO Box 1276 111 Shoshone St N Ste 201 Twin Falls ID 83303

TOLMIE, DONALD MCEACHERN, lawyer; b. Moline, Ill., June 21, 1928; s. Ronald Charles and Margaret Blaine (Kerr) T.; m. Joann Phillis Swanson, Aug. 15, 1953; children: David M., John K., Paul N. AB, Augustana Coll., 1950; JD, U. Ill., 1953. Bar: Ill. 1953, Va. 1968. Atty. Pa. R.R., Chgo., 1953-60; asst. gen. soliciter Pa. R.R., Phila., 1961-67; gen. atty. Norfolk & Western, Roanoke, Va., 1968; gen. soliciter Norfolk & Western, Roanoke, 1968-75, gen. counsel, 1975-82; gen. counsel Norfolk (Va.) So. Corp., 1982, v.p., gen. counsel, 1983-89. Mem. Va. Bar Assn., U.S Supreme Ct. Bar Assn., Harbor Club, Cedar Point Club. Lutheran. Home: 912 Hanover Ave Norfolk VA 23508-1227

TOLMIE, KENNETH DONALD, artist, author; b. Halifax, N.S., Can., Sept. 18, 1941; s. Archibald and Mary Evelyn (Murray) T.; m. Ruth Mackenzie, Aug. 11, 1962; children: Sarah Katherine, Jane Marianna. B.F.A., Mt. Allison U., 1962. Proprietor Tolmie Gallery, Mahone Bay, N.S., St. Albans, Vt.; Chmn. Visual Arts Ottawa, 1975-76; founding mem. Bridgetown and Area Hist. Soc., James House Mus.; bd. dirs. Art Gallery N.S. Author: (children's book) Tale of an Egg, 1974, (art book) A Rural Life: An Artist's Portrait, 1986; 3 TV documentary films produced on his work by CBC and by TV-Ont.; one-man shows include Dorothy Cameron Gallery, Toronto, 1963, Beckett Gallery, Hamilton, 1986, Kaspar Gallery, Toronto, 1988; Mt. Allison Univ. solo cross Can. touring exbn. Bridgetown Series, 1982-84; group shows include Banfer Gallery, N.Y.C., 1963, Nat. Gallery Can., Watercolors Prints and Drawing, 1964, 66, London Art Mus., Ont., 1966, Can. Soc. Graphic Art, 1973, Art Gallery N.S., 1980, 81, N.S. Art Bank, 1981; represented in permanent collections Nat. Gallery Can., Ottawa, Montreal Mus. Fine Arts, N.S. Art Bank, Art Gallery N.S., Confedn. Centre for Arts, Hirshhorn Collection, Washington, Owens Art Gallery, Mt. Allison U., Dofasco Ltd., Husky Oil Ltd., Procter & Gamble Ltd., Slater Steels Ltd., Crownx Ltd. Mem. Writer's Union Can., Writers Fedn. N.S., Visual Arts N.S. Address: PO Box 96 16 Orchard St, Mahone Bay, NS Canada B0J 2E0

TOLOR, ALEXANDER, psychologist, educator; b. Vienna, Austria, Oct. 21, 1928; s. Stanley and Josephine (Kellner) T.; m. Belle Simon, Sept. 2, 1951; children: Karen Beth, Lori Ann, Diana Susan. B.A., NYU, 1949, M.A., 1950, Ph.D., 1954. Diplomate Am. Bd. Profl. Psychologists. Grad. asst. NYU, 1950-52; intern Neurol. Inst., N.Y.C., 1952-53; clin. psychologist Neurol. Inst., 1953-55; sr. clin. psychologist Inst. of Living, Hartford, Conn., 1957-59; dir. psychol. services Fairfield Hills Hosp., Newtown, Conn., 1959-64; clinic dir. Kennedy Center, Bridgeport, Conn., 1964-65; dir. Inst. Human Devel., Fairfield U., 1965-77, assoc. prof. psychology, 1965-68, research prof. psychology, 1968-75, prof. psychology, 1975-89, dir. school psychology div., 1975-77, dir. sch. and applied psychology program, 1982-86, prof. emeritus, 1989—; practice psychology Danbury, Conn., 1960-96; clin. instr. psychology Yale U., 1963-67; cons. West Haven VA Hosp., 1962-66, Bridgeport Bd. Edn., Silver Hill Found., 1972-75, Fairfield Hills Hosp., 1973-94, Hallbrooke Hosp., 1975-92. Author: (with H.C. Schulberg) An Evaluation of the Bender-Gestalt Test, 1963, (with G.G. Brannigan) Research and Clinical Applications of the Bender-Gestalt Test, 1980, (with M. Deignan) Adjustment Problems in Children, 1984; editor: Effective Interviewing, 1985; adv. editor Jour. Cons. and Clin. Psychology; cons. editor Personality: An Internat. Jour.; contbr. articles to profl. jours. Served to 1st lt. USAF, 1955-57. Fellow Am. Psychol. Assn., Soc. Personality Assessment; mem. Conn. Psychol. Assn. (mem. council 1964, pres. 1984), Eastern Psychol. Assn., Psi Chi, Delta Phi Alpha, Beta Lambda Sigma, Phi Delta Kappa. Home: 6 Brittania Dr Danbury CT 06811-2606

TOLSON, JOHN J., editor; b. Montgomery, Ala., June 28, 1948; s. John J. and Margaret Jordan (Young) T.; m. Mary Irene Bradshaw; 1 child, Benjamin Bradshaw. AB, Princeton U., 1972; MA, Am. Univ., 1977. Instr. English and history Asheville (N.C.) Sch., 1972-74, Landon Sch., Bethesda, Md., 1974-77; free-lance writer, critic Washington, 1977-81; lit. editor The Wilson Quar., Washington, 1981-89, editor, 1989—. Author: Pilgrim in the Ruins: A Life of Walker Percy (So. Book Nonfiction award 1992-93, Hugh Holman prize for best work of criticism and scholarship 1992), 1992; editor: The Correspondence of Shelby Foote and Walker Percy; contbr. essays and criticism to The New Republic, The Nation, The Scis., Washington Post, The Times Lit. Supplement, Civilization, other publs. Independent Scholars fellow NEH, Washington, 1989. Mem. Nat. Book Critics Circle. Home: 2010 N Lincoln St Arlington VA 22207-3729 Office: Wilson Quarterly 901 D St SW Washington DC 20024-2169

TOLTZIS, ROBERT JOSHUA, cardiologist; b. Phila., May 6, 1949; s. Louis and Shirley (Weiner) T.; m. Catharina Kolek, 1989; 1 child, Alexander Jonah. AB, Temple U., 1970; MD, Hahnemann U., 1974. Cert. Am. Bd. Internal Medicine, Cardiovascular Diseases. Intern, resident, fellow Peter Bent Brigham Hosp., Boston, 1974-79, Children's Hosp., Boston, 1974-79; chief of service in cardiology Nat. Heart Lung and Blood Inst., Bethesda, Md., 1980-82; assoc. prof. clin. medicine and pediatrics U. Cin., 1982—; cardiologist Christ Hosp., Cin., 1988—; fellow in medicine Harvard U., Boston, 1974-79, instr. 1979-80; dir. coronary care unit U. Hosp., Cin., 1982-88, dir. electrocardiography lab., 1988—. Fellow Am. Coll. Cardiology (coun. clin. cardiology), Am. Heart Assn., Am. Coll. Chest Physicians; mem. Am. Soc. Echocardiography, Alpha Omega Alpha. Home: 7720 Annesdale Dr Cincinnati OH 45243-4058 Office: 2123 Auburn Ave Ste 139 Cincinnati OH 45219-2966

TOMAC, STEVEN WAYNE, state senator, farmer; b. Hettinger, N.D., Nov. 23, 1953; s. Robert and Betty Ann (Schmidt) T. BS, N.D. State U., 1976. Loan officer Bank of N.D., Bismarck, 1976-79; v.p. 1st Southwest Bank, Mandan, N.D., 1979-80; dir. mktg. N.D. Dept. Agr., Bismarck, 1980-81; exec. dir. N.D. Grain Growers, Bismarck, 1981-86; rodeo clown PRCA, Colorado Springs, 1971—; farmer/rancher St. Anthony, N.D., 1982—; state rep. State of N.D., Bismarck, 1986-90, state senator, 1990—. Mem. Accredited Rural Appraisers, Am. Soc. Farm Mgrs. and Rural Appraisers (appraiser 1981—). Democrat. Roman Catholic. Home: RR 1 Box 36 Saint Anthony ND 58566-9801

TOMAIN, JOSEPH PATRICK, dean, law educator; b. Long Branch, N.J., Sept. 3, 1948; s. Joseph Pasquale and Bernice M. (Krzan) T.; m. Kathleen Corcione, Aug. 1, 1971; children: Joseph Anthony, John Fiore. AB, U. Notre Dame, 1970; JD, George Washington U., 1974. Bar: N.J., Iowa. Assoc. Giordano & Halleran, Middletown, N.J., 1974-76; from asst. to prof. law Drake U. Sch. Law, Des Moines, Iowa, 1976-83; prof. law U. Cin. Coll. Law, 1983—, acting dean, 1989-90, dean, 1990—, Nippert prof. law, 1990—; vis. prof. law U. Tex. Sch. Law, Austin, 1986-87. Author: Energy Law in a Nutshell, 1981, Nuclear Power Transformation, 1987; co-author: Energy Decision Making, 1983, Energy Law and Policy, 1989, Energy and Natural Resources Law, 1992, Regulatory Law and Policy, 1993. Pres. bd. trustees Ctr. Comprehensive Alcohol Treatment, Cin., Vol. Lawyers for Poor, Cin.; bd. trustees Student Loan Funding Corp., Cin.; mem. steering com. BLAC/CBA Round Table, Cin. Served with USAR, 1970-76. Mem. ABA, Am. Law Inst., Ohio State Bar Assn. Roman Catholic. Home: 3009 Springer Ave Cincinnati OH 45208-2440 Office: U Cin Coll Law Office of Dean Cincinnati OH 45221-0040

TOMAINO, JOSEPH CARMINE, retail executive, retired postal inspector; b. Danbury, Conn., Dec. 12, 1948; s. Joseph and Lena Marie (LaCava) T.; m. Eileen Pulver (div. Nov. 1977); m. Ann C. Underriner, Sept. 20, 1986; children: Joseph Richard, Robert John. BS, Western Conn. State U., 1970; MBA, Roosevelt U., 1978, MS in Acctg., 1986. Cert. fraud examiner. Post office clk. U.S. Postal Svc., Ridgefield, Conn., 1970-71; postal inspector U.S. Postal Svc., Chgo., 1971-80, supervisory postal inspector, 1980-93; mgr. western ops. loss prevention dept. Walgreen Co., Deerfield, Ill., 1993-96; sr. mgr. litigation svcs. Altschuler, Melvoin & Glasser CPAs, 1996—. Mem. Am. Soc. Indsl. Security, Fed. Law Enforcement Officers Assn., Nat. Assn. Chiefs Police, Ill. Chiefs Police, Spl. Agts. Assn., Ill. Police Assn., Nat. Soc. Pub. Accts., Assn. Cert. Fraud Examiners. Office: Altschuler Melvoin & Glasser CPAs 30 S Wacker Dr Fl 24 Chicago IL 60606-7405

TOMAINO, MICHAEL THOMAS, lawyer; b. Utica, N.Y., Dec. 1, 1937; s. Joseph Michael and Rosemary (Fragetta) T.; m. Beverly A. Meyer, Aug. 29, 1959; children—Mark, Matthew, Andrea, Michael, Julie. B.A., Holy Cross Coll., 1959; J.D., Cornell U., 1962. Bar: N.Y. 1962, U.S. Dist. Ct. (so., ea., no. and we. dists.) N.Y., U.S. Ct. Appeals (2d., 4th and 5th cirs.), U.S. Supreme Ct. 1975. Assoc. Donovan, Leisure, Newton & Irvine, N.Y.C., 1962-64; assoc. Nixon, Hargrave, Devans & Doyle, Rochester, N.Y., 1964-70, ptnr., 1971-95; v.p., sec., gen. counsel Goulds Pumps, Inc., Fairport, N.Y., 1995—. Past pres., hon. trustee Aquinas Inst. of Rochester, 1976—. Mem. ABA, N.Y. State Bar Assn. (past chmn. com. on pub. utility law), Monroe County Bar Assn., Am. Coll. Trial Lawyers. Republican. Roman Catholic. Avocations: squash; tennis; sailing. Home: 135 Taylor Rd Honeoye Falls NY 14472-9732 Office: Goulds Pumps Inc 300 Willowbrook Office Park Fairport NY 14450-4222

TOMAJCZYK, S(TEPHEN) F(RANCIS), author, communications company executive; b. Newport, R.I., Mar. 30, 1960; s. Charles F. and Gretchen (Mintz) T.; m. Joyce J. Welch, June 21, 1991. BS in Natural Resources, U. Mich., 1982. Editor IDG/CW Comms., Peterborough, N.H., 1982-83; assoc. pub. SoftSide Comms., Milford, N.H., 1983-84; mktg. dir. Ultimate Press, Inc., Nashua, N.H., 1984-88; pub. info. officer N.H. Divn. Pub. Health, Concord, N.H., 1988-96; pres. Turning Point Comm., Concord, N.H., 1996—; sr. lectr. Franklin Pierce Coll., Nashua, N.H., 1985-88, Rivier Coll., Nashua, 1988—; comms. cons. Ctrs. for Disease Control and Prevention, Atlanta, 1989-96; guest speaker in field. Author: Eyes on the Gold, 1985, The Children's Writer's Marketplace, 1987, Dictionary of the Modern United States Military, 1996, U.S. Elite Counterterrorist Forces, 1997; mng. editor Am. Jour. Health Comms., 1995—; contbr. to 6 nat. comms. manuals including Public Health Communications Workbook, 1995, HIV/AIDS Mass Communications Handbook, 1989; columnist Running Shorts, 1983-85; contbr. numerous articles to writers and popular mags. and newspapers including Yankee, Writer's Digest, Sportscape, Pico, Lost Treasure, The Telegraph, Treasure Facts, inCider, Commodore; poetry published in poetry jours. and Am. Poetry Assn. Anthology. Judge Harbinger awards Women in Comm., Inc., Nashua, N.H., 1991; exec. bd. mem. Nat. Pub. Health Info. Coalition, 1993—, v.p., 1995, pres., 1995—; mem. com. Author's Guilds' Freedom of Expression Com., 1994—; mem. media com. Partnership for a Drug Free N.H., 1994—; mem. steering com. Nat. Pub. Health Week, 1995—. Numerous awards for pub. svc. print and video including: recipient 1st Place award Pub. Svc. Print Creative Club N.H., 1990, 1st Place award NH Graniteer Awards, 1993, 94, 96, Telly award, 1993, Golden Mike award, 1994. Mem. Author's Guild (freedom of expression com. 1994—), Nat. Writers Union, Nat. Pub. Health Info. Coalition (v.p. 1995, pres. 1995—, region I rep., mem. exec. bd., 1st pl. prize state produced TV 1992, 1st pl. splty. item 1993-94, 1st pl. poster 1994, 1st pl. print info campaign 1995, 1st pl. pub. info. campaign 1996), Author's League Am., Soc. Profl. Journalists, Am. Med. Writers Assn. Home: 120 Hemlock Hill Dr Loudon NH 03301-0703 Office: Turning Point Comm Concord NH 03301

TOMAN, MARY ANN, federal official; b. Pasadena, Calif., Mar. 31, 1954; d. John James and Mary Ann Zajec T.; m. Milton Allen Miller, Sept. 10, 1988; 1 child, Mary Ann III. BA with honors, Stanford U., 1976; MBA, Harvard U., 1981. Mgmt. cons. Bain and Co., Boston, 1976-77; brand mgr. Procter & Gamble Co., Cin., 1977-79; summer assoc. E.F. Hutton, N.Y.C., 1980; head corp. planning The Burton Group, PLC, London, 1981-84; pres., founder Glendair Ltd., London, 1984-86; pres. London Cons. Group, London, Beverly Hills, Calif., 1987-88; mem. U.S. Presdl. Transition Team, Bus. and Fin., 1988-89; dep. asst. sec. commerce, automotive affairs, consumer goods U.S. Dept. Commerce, Washington, 1989-93; commr., chmn. L.A. Indsl. Devel. Authority, 1993-95; dep. treas. State of Calif., Sacramento, 1995—; bd. dirs. U.S. Coun. of Devel. Fin. Agencies, 1994—. Founder, chair Stanford U. Fundraising, London, 1983-88; chair Reps. Abroad Absentee Voter Registration, London, 1983-88; bd. dirs. Harvard Bus. Sch. Assn., London, 1984-87; vol. Bush-Quayle Campaign, 1988; trustee Bath Coll., Eng., 1988—; apptd. by Gov. Wilson to State of Calif. Econ. Devel. Adv. Coun., 1994—; first vice chmn. Rep. Party L.A. County, 1996—. Mem. Stanford Club U.K. (pres. 1983-88), Harvard Club N.Y., Harvard Club Washington. Roman Catholic. Home: 604 N Elm Dr Beverly Hills CA 90210-3421 Office: PO Box 71483 Los Angeles CA 90071-0483

TOMANIC, JOSEPH P(AUL), research scientist; b. Danbury, Conn., Nov. 18, 1943; s. Joseph A. and Helen U. (Drusik) T.; m. Helen G. Brown Gannon, Apr. 15, 1967; children: Sharon A., Karen S. BEE, U. Bridgeport, 1972. Electronic technician Manson Labs., Wilton, Conn., 1964-66; assoc. rsch. scientist Schlumberger-Doll Research, Ridgefield, Conn., 1966—. Contbr. articles to profl. jours. Mem. Inst. Elec. and Electronic Engrs. Roman Catholic. Home: 36 Deepwood Dr Bethel CT 06801 Office: Schlumberger-Doll Research Old Quarry Rd Ridgefield CT 06877-4108

TOMAR, RUSSELL HERMAN, pathologist, educator, researcher; b. Phila., Oct. 19, 1937; s. Julius and Ethel (Weinreb) T.; m. Karen J. Kent, Aug. 29, 1965; children: Elizabeth, David. BA in Journalism, George Washington U., 1959, MD, 1963. Diplomate Am. Bd. Pathology, Am. Bd. Allergy and Immunology, Am. Bd. Pathology, Immunopathology. Intern Barnes Hosp., Washington U. Sch. Medicine, 1963-64, resident in medicine, 1964-65; asst. prof. medicine SUNY, Syracuse, 1971-79, assoc. prof., 1979-88, assoc. prof. microbiology, 1980-84, prof., 1984-88, asst. prof. pathology, 1974-76, assoc. prof., 1976-83, prof., 1983-88, dir. immunopathology, 1974-88, attending physician immunodeficiency clinic, 1982-88, acting dir. microbiology, 1977-78, 82-83, interim dir. clin. pathology, 1986-87; dir. clin. labs., prof. pathology and lab. medicine U. Wis. Ctr. for Health Scis., Madison, 1988-95; dir. div. lab medicine U. Wis., Madison, 1988-95, dir. immunopathology, 1995—; past mem. numerous coms. SUNY, Syracuse, U. Wis., Madison; mem. exec. com., chair and med. cons. AIDS Task Force Cen. N.Y., 1983-88. Assoc. editor Jour. Clin. Lab. Analysis; contbr. articles, rev. to profl. jours. Mem. pub. health com. Onondaga County Med. Soc., 1987-88. Lt. comdr. USPHS, 1965-67. Allergy and Immunology Div. fellow U. Pa. Fellow Coll. Am. Pathologists (diagnostics immunology rsch. com. 1993—, stds. com. 1995—), Am. Soc. Clin. Pathology (com. on continuing edn. immunopathology 1985-91, pathology data presentation com. 1976-79), Am. Acad. Allergy (penicillin hypersensitivity com. 1973-77); mem. AAAS, Am. Assn. Immunologists, Am. Assn. Pathology, Acad. Clin. Lab. Physicians and Scientists (com. on rsch. 1979-81, chairperson immunology 1979), Clin. Immunology Soc. (clin. lab. immunology com., chair coun. 1991-96). Office: U Wis Clinical Sci Ctr Rm B4-251 Madison WI 53792-2472

TOMAS, JEROLD F. V., business executive, management consultant; b. N.Y.C.; s. Samuel and Jean Tomas. BS, U. Bridgeport, 1968; MEd, U. Mass., 1971, D in Organizational Behavior and Mgmt., 1973. Grantee in exec. devel. Ford Found. and Carnegie Found., 1970-73; fellow Ctr. for Leadership, 1970-73; dir. edn. Young Pres.'s Orgn., Inc., N.Y.C., 1975-77; chief rsch. scientist Mgmt. Decision Lab., Grad. Sch. Bus. Administrn. NYU, 1977-78; officer, sr. cons., mgmt. and orgn. J.P. Morgan & Co., N.Y.C., 1978-80; corp. mgr. mgmt. resources planning Pfizer, Inc., N.Y.C., 1981-82; pres. TOMACO, Inc., Cons., N.Y.C., 1982—; mem. sr. faculty advanced mgmt. program Rutgers U., 1984-94; sr. faculty, presenter Mgmt. Confs., U.S., Latin Am., Europe, and Asia Pacific. Contbr. articles to profl. jours. Football scholar U. Bridgeport.

TOMASH, ERWIN, retired computer equipment company executive; b. St. Paul, Nov. 17, 1921; s. Noah and Milka (Ehrlich) T.; m. Adelle Ruben, July 31, 1943; children: Judith Sarada Tomash Diffenbaugh, Barbara Ann Tomash, Bussa. B.S., U. Minn., 1943; M.S., U. Md., 1950. Instr. elec. engring. U. Minn., 1946; assoc. dir. computer devel. Univac div. Remington Rand Corp., St. Paul, 1947-51; dir. West Coast ops. Univac div. Sperry Rand Corp., L.A., 1953-55; pres. Telemeter Magnetics, Inc., L.A., 1956-60; v.p. Ampex Corp., L.A., 1961; founder, pres. Dataproducts Corp., L.A., 1962-71; chmn. bd. Dataproducts Corp., 1971-80; chmn. bd. & dir. Newport Corp., Irvine, Calif., 1982-94; chmn. exec. com. Dataproducts Corp., 1980-89; chmn. Tomash Cons., Inc., cons. to high tech. industry; chmn. bd. Tomash Pubs., pubs. computer and physics works. Founder, chmn. bd. trustees Charles Babbage Found., U. Minn.; dir. and nat. gov. Coro Found., L.A.; trustee Computer Mus., Boston. Served to capt. Signal Corps AUS, 1943-46. Decorated Bronze Star; recipient Outstanding Grad. award U. Minn., 1983. Mem. IEEE (sr., computer entrepreneur award 1988), Assn. Computing Machinery, Am. Soc. for Technion, History of Sci. Soc., Soc. for History of Tech., Assn. Internationale du Bibliophile, Grolier Club. Home: 110 S Rockingham Ave Los Angeles CA 90049-2514

TOMASHEFSKY, PHILIP, biomedical researcher, educator; b. Bklyn., May 4, 1924; s. Harry and Mae (Shapiro) T.; m. Rhoda Tanenbaum, Oct. 31, 1948; children—Clark Steven, Michael Allen. B.S., CCNY, 1947, M.S., 1951; M.S., NYU, 1963, Ph.D., 1969. Chemist Funk Found., N.Y.C., 1947-65; biochemist U.S. Vitamin, N.Y.C., 1966; asst. prof. clin. pathology Columbia U., N.Y.C., 1975-89 . Contbr. articles to profl. jours. Served with U.S. Army, 1943-45, ETO. Mem. N.Y. Acad. Scis., Sigma Xi. Avocations: travel, photography, gardening. Retired. Office: Columbia Univ Dept Urology 630 W 168th St New York NY 10032-3702

TOMASI, DONALD CHARLES, architect; b. Sacramento, Calif., Oct. 24, 1956; s. Thomas M. and Anita (Migliavacca) T.; m. Loretta Elaine Goveia, Feb. 1, 1986; children: Jeffrey, Genna, Michael. AB in Architecture with honors, U. Calif., Berkeley, 1979; MArch, U. Wash., 1982. Registered architect, Calif. Project mgr. Robert Wells and Assocs., Seattle, 1982-84, Milbrandt Architects, Seattle, 1984, T.M. Tomasi Architects, Santa Rosa, Calif., 1984-86; prin. Tomasi Architects, Santa Rosa, 1986-93, Tomasi Lawry Coker De Silva Architecture, Santa Rosa, 1993—. Grad. Leadership Santa Rosa, 1992; mem. design rev. com. Sonoma County, 1988-90; chmn. Santa Rosa Design Rev. Bd., 1990—. Recipient Honor award Coalition for Adequate Sch. Housing, 1991, 93, 96, Merit award, 1991. Mem. AIA (chpt. bd. dirs. 1990-91, Merit award 1986). Avocations: snow skiing, wine, travel.

TOMASI, THOMAS B., cell biologist, administrator; b. May 24, 1927; s. Thomas B. and Ivis (Ratazzi) T.; m. Barbara Betzold, May 27, 1995; children: Barbara, Theodore, Anne. AB, Dartmouth Coll., Hanover, N.H., 1950; MD, U. Vt., Burlington, 1954; PhD, Rockefeller U., 1965. Intern, resident, chief resident Columbia Presbyn. Hosp., N.Y.C., 1954-58, instr. medicine, 1958-60; prof., chmn. div. exptl. medicine U. Vt., Burlington, 1960-65; prof. medicine, dir. immunology SUNY, Buffalo, 1965-73; prof., chmn. immunology dept. Mayo Med. Sch., Rochester, Minn., 1973-81; dir. Cancer Ctr., Disting. Univ. prof., chmn. dept. cell biology U. N. Mex., Albuquerque, 1981-86; pres., CEO Roswell Park Cancer Inst., Buffalo, 1986—, chmn. dept. molecular medicine. Author: The Immune System of Secretions, 1976; contbr. over 200 articles to profl. jours. Served with USN, 1945-46. Mem. Am. Soc. Cell Biology, Am. Assn. Immunologists, Am. Assn. Cancer Research, Am. Soc. Clin. Investigation, Am. Fedn. Clin. Research, Assn. Am. Physicians. Roman Catholic. Avocations: skiing, tennis, hunting, fishing, gardening. Office: Roswell Park Cancer Inst Elm And Carlton St Buffalo NY 14263-0001

TOMASKO, EDWARD A., financial planner; b. Stafford Springs, Conn., Sept. 18, 1943; s. Edward A. Sr. and Gertrude Ann (Burr) T.; m. Helen F.

Flanagan, Oct. 18, 1969; children: Felicia, Joy. BA, Quinnipac Coll., 1966; MBA, Am. U., 1968. CFP. Direct mktg. & sales Iroquois Brands, Stamford, Conn., 1979-81; owner Tomasko Bus. Cons., Bethel, Conn., 1981-82; v.p. mktg. & consulting Excell Mktg., New Canaan, Conn., 1982; market mgr. Stauffer Chem., Westport, Conn., 1982-85; direct mktg. & sales Folz Vending, L.I., N.Y., 1986; registered rep. Moseley Securities, New Haven, 1987-88, Fahnestock & Co. Inc., Danbury, Conn., 1988-90; prin. Titan Value Equities, Hamden, Conn., 1990—. V.p. bd. govs. Quinnipac Coll. Mem. IAFP (pres. So. Conn. chpt. 1993-96, chmn. state conf. 1992-93). Republican. Avocations: photography, choir singing. Home: 20 Spring Hill Ln Bethel CT 06801-2726 Office: Titan Value Equities 2600 Dixwell Ave Ste 1 Hamden CT 06514-1833

TOMASKY, SUSAN, federal officer; b. Morgantown, W.Va., Mar. 29, 1953; m. Ron Ungvarsky; 1 child, Victoria. BA cum laude, Univ. Ky., 1974; JD (hons.), George Washington Univ., 1979. Staff mem. House Com. Interstate and Fgn. Commerce, Washington, 1974-76; with FERC's Office of Gen. Counsel., Washington, 1979-81; ptnr. Van Ness, Feldman & Curtis, Washington, 1981-93; gen. coun. Federal Energy Regulatory Commn.,, Washington, 1993—. Mem. Phi Beta Kappa. Office: Fed Energy Regulatory Commn General Counsel 888 1st St NE Rm 10a-01 Washington DC 20426-0001

TOMASSON, HELGI, dancer, choreographer, dance company executive; b. Reykjavik, Iceland, 1942; m. Marlene Rizzo, 1965; children: Kristinn, Erik. Student, Sigridur Arman, Erik Bidsted, Vera Volkova, Sch. Am. Ballet, Tivoli Pantomime Theatre, Copenhagen. With Joffrey Ballet, 1961-64; prin. dancer Harkness Ballet, 1964-70, N.Y.C. Ballet, 1970-85; artistic dir. San Francisco Ballet, 1985—, also dir. Debut with Tivoli Pantomime Theatre, 1958; created roles in A Season of Hell, 1967, Stages and Reflections, 1968, La Favorita, 1969, The Goldberg Variations, 1971, Symphony in Three Movements, 1972, Coppélia, 1974, Dybbuk Variations, 1974, Chansons Madecasses, 1975, Introduction and Allegro, 1975, Union Jack, 1976, Vienna Waltzes, 1977; choreographer Theme and Variations, Polonaise, Op. 65, 1982, Ballet d'Isoline, 1983, Menuetto (for N.Y.C. Ballet) 1984, Beads of Memory, 1985, Swan Lake, 1988, Handel-a Celebration, 1989, Sleeping Beauty, 1990, Romeo and Juliet, 1994, others. Decorated Knight Order of Falcon (Iceland), 1974, Comdr. Order of Falcon, 1990; recipient Silver medal Internat. Moscow Ballet Competition, 1969, Golden Plate award Am. Acad. Achievement, 1992, Dance Mag. award, 1992. Office: care San Francisco Ballet 455 Franklin St San Francisco CA 94102-4438*

TOMASSONI, RONN, men's ice hockey coach; m. Pam Tomassoni; children: Emily, Keith. Grad., Rensselaer, 1980. Asst. coach to assoc. caoch, 1982-83, 89-90; head hockey coach Harvard U.; head coach bronze medal winning South team U.S. Olympic Festival; asst. coach U.S. squad World Games IV, 1985. Office: Harvard U 60 Jfk St Cambridge MA 02138-4933

TOMASULO, VIRGINIA MERRILLS, retired lawyer; b. Belleville, Ill., Feb. 10, 1919; d. Frederick Emerson and Mary Eckert (Turner) Merrills; m. Nicholas Angelo Tomasulo, Sept. 30, 1952; m. Harrison I. Anthes, March 5, 1988. BA, Wellesley Coll., 1940; LLB (now JD), Washington U., St. Louis, 1943. Bar: Mo. 1942, U.S. Ct. Appeals (D.C. cir.) 1958, Mich. 1974, U.S. Dist. Ct. (ea. dist.) Mo. 1943, U.S. Supreme Ct. 1954, U.S. Tax Ct. 1974, U.S. Ct. Appeals (6th cir.) 1976. Atty. Dept. of Agr., St. Louis and Washington, 1943-48, Office of Solicitor, Chief Counsel's Office, IRS, Washington and Detroit, 1949-75; assoc. Baker & Hostetler, Washington, 1977-82, ptnr., 1982-89, of counsel, 1989, ret., 1989. Sec., S.W. Day Care Assn., Washington, 1971-73. Mem. ABA, Mo. Bar, Fed. Bar, Village on the Green Residents Assn. (fin. com.), Wellesley Club (Ctrl. Fla.). Episcopalian. Home: 570 Village Pl Apt 300 Longwood FL 32779-6037

TOMASZ, ALEXANDER, cell biologist; b. Budapest, Hungary, Dec. 23, 1930; married; 1 child. Diploma, Pazmany Peter U., Budapest, 1953; PhD in Biochemistry, Columbia U., 1961. Rsch. assoc. cytochem. Inst. Genetics hungarian Nat. Acad., 1953-56; fellow, guest investigator in genetics Am. Cancer Soc., 1961-63; from asst. prof. to assoc. prof. genetics and biochemistry Rockefeller U., N.Y.C., 1963-77, prof. microbiology, chmn. dept., 1977—, prof. microbiology, head lab. microbiology. Mem. AAAS, Am. Soc. Microbiology, Am. Soc. Cell Biology, Harvey Soc. Office: Rockefeller U Dept Biology 1230 York Ave New York NY 10021-6307*

TOMASZEWSKI, RICHARD PAUL, market representation specialist; b. Flushing, N.Y., Jan. 8, 1958; s. Francis Richard and Agatha Jean (Corsaro) T.; m. Joann L. Turone, Aug. 2, 1980; children: Elizabeth Jean, Annamaria Concetta. BA in Econs. and Polit. sci. cum laude, Union Coll., Schenectady, N.Y., 1980; MBA in Mktg., Fin., Syracuse U., 1982. Grad. asst. Syracuse (N.Y.) U., 1981; field ops. analyst Ford Motor Co., Charlotte, N.C., 1982-83; zone mgr. Ford Motor Co., Charlotte, 1983-93; market representation specialist Ford Motor Co., Atlanta, 1993—, nat. employee involvement rep. Atlanta region, 1994—. Mem. Ford Motor Co. Polit. Action Com., Atlanta, 1993. Recipient Tidmarsh scholarshp Union Coll., Schenectady, 1977. Mem. Union Coll. Alumni Assn., Syracuse U. Alumni Assn., U.S. Tennis Assn., Atlanta Lawn Tennis Assn., Omicron Delta Epsilon, Alpha Mu Alpha. Republican. Roman Catholic. Avocations: tennis, swimming, basketball, chess, bicycling. Office: Ford Motor Co 1455 Lincoln Pky E Ste 530 Atlanta GA 30346-2209

TOMAZINIS, ANTHONY RODOFLOS, city planning educator; b. Larissa, Greece, June 24, 1929; came to U.S., 1956, naturalized, 1966; s. Rodolfos A. and Christofily (Papamargaritou) T.; m. JoAnn R. Frank, June 24, 1962; children: Christina, Marina, Alexis. BCE, Assoc. Schs. Nat. Tech. U. Greece, 1952; M of City Planning, Ga. Inst. Tech., 1959; PhD in Planning, U. Pa., 1963. Mem. faculty U. Pa., Phila., 1962—, assoc. prof. city planning, 1966-77, prof. city and regional planning and civil engring., 1977—, chmn. transp. research group, inst. environ. studies, 1969-79, dir. Transp. Studies Center, 1969-79, chmn. univ.-wide program in transp. Transp. Studies Center, 1977—, chmn. faculty senate, 1984-87; chmn. grad. liberal studies program U. Pa., 1987-92; chmn. dynamics of orgn. U. Pa., Phila., 1990—; chmn. dept. city and regional planning dept. U. Pa., 1992—; pres. A.R. Tomazinis & Assocs., Inc., 1977-90; pres. Arista Found. Inc., 1991—, chmn. dept. city and regional planning, 1993—; cons. Inst. for Internat. Edn., 1991-92; cons. transp. and urban planning; pres. ARISTA Found., 1991—; transp. planning cons. Del. Valley Regional Commn., 1965-72, Doxiadis & Assocs., Athens, Greece, 1961-64, OECD, Paris, 1970-74, Govt. Iran, 1976; mem. travel forecasting com. transp. Rsch. Bd.; Fulbright prof. city planning U. Paris, 1973-74, chmn. dept. city & regional planning, 1992—; cons. Institut de Recherche des Transports, Paris, 1973-74. Served with Greek Armed Forces, 1953-54. Decorated medal of Meritorious Acts King of Greece, 1949. Mem. Am. Inst. Cert. Planners, Inst. Transp. Engrs. (assoc. editor Jour. Advanced Transp., Transp. Planning and Tech.), Am. Hellenic League (Phila. pres. 1967-71, 81-85, dir. 1971-80), AAAS, Regional Scis. Assn., Am. Soc. Planning Ofcls., Univ. City Arts League, Fedn. Am. Hellenic Socs. of Greater Phila. (pres. 1977-79). Club: Hellenic University. Home: 379 Montgomery Ave Wynnewood PA 19096-1718 Office: U Pa Translab 3400 Walnut St Philadelphia PA 19104-3411 *What we call success in life is indeed relative to what we want in life. My deep commitment to city planning led me to seek gratification in the process of solving urban problems, planning for new cities and sections of older cities, and in educating the young and aspiring planners. Searching not for convention or compromise, the stress is on innovation and accomplishment. What others call success is for me simply a struggle to achieve the best solution possible to each given problem.*

TOMBERLIN, WILLIAM G., principal. Prin. St. Simons (Ga.) Elem. Sch. Recipient DOE Elem. Sch. Recognition Program award, 1989-90. Office: St Simons Elem Sch 805 Ocean Blvd Saint Simons Island GA 31522-5021*

TOMBERS, EVELYN CHARLOTTE, lawyer; b. Phila., Nov. 7, 1956; d. Gerold G. and Margot (Ort) Knauerhase; m. Peter C. Tombers. AS, Temple U., 1976, BA, 1977; JD, Thomas M. Cooley Law Sch., 1991. Bar: Mich. 1991. Dist. intake counselor Fla. Dept. Health Rehab. Svc., Naples, 1985-87; satellite dir. Youth Shelter S.W. Fla., Naples, 1987-88; adj. prof. Thomas M. Cooley Law Sch., Lansing, Mich., 1991-92; jud. law clk. to Justice Patricia J. Boyle Mich. Supreme Ct., Detroit, 1992-94; assoc. Harvey, Kruse, Westen and Milan, Troy, Mich., 1994-95, Bowen, Anderson, Radabaugh, Milton & Brown, Troy, Mich., 1995—. Editor (newsletter) State Bar Mich. Appellate Practice Sect. Named one of Outstanding Women Grads., Women Lawyers Am., 1991. Avocation: golf. Home: 726 Englewood Ave Royal Oak MI 48073-2833 Office: Bowen Anderson Radabaugh Milton & Brown 4967 Crooks Rd Ste 150 Troy MI 48098

TOMBLIN, EARL RAY, state official; b. Logan County, W.Va., Mar. 15, 1952; s. Earl and Freda (Jarrell) T.; m. Joanne Jaeger, Sept. 8, 1979; 1 child, Brent Jaeger. BS, W.Va. U.; MBA, Marshall U.; postgrad., U. Charleston. Former sch. tchr., businessman; mem. W.Va. Ho. Dels., 1974-80; mem. W.Va. State Senate, 1980—, pres., 1995—; lt. gov. State of W.Va., Charleston; chmn. So. Legis. Conf. Former pres., bd. dirs. Appalachia Ednl. Lab., Inc.; mem. Logan County Devel. Authority. Mem. Kappa Alpha. Democrat. Presbyterian. Office: Capitol Bldg Rm 229M Charleston WV 25305 Address: PO Box 116 Chapmanville WV 25508

TOMBLINSON, JAMES EDMOND, architect; b. Flint, Mich., Feb. 12, 1927; s. Carl and Edna Ethel (Spears) T.; m. Betsy Kinley, Sept. 26, 1959; children: Amy Lisa, John Timothy (dec.). B.Arch., U. Mich., 1951. Draftsman firms in Detroit, 1951-53, Flint, 1953-54, 56-57, San Francisco, 1955-56; field engr. Atlas Constructors, Morocco, 1952-53; architect Tomblinson, Harburn, & Assos., Inc. (and predecessors), Flint, 1958—; pres. Tomblinson, Harburn, & Assos., Inc. (and predecessors), 1969-95; chmn. bd. Timblinson, Harburn & Assocs., Inc. (and predecessors), 1995—; chmn. Mich. Bd. Registration Architects, 1975-77; sec. Mundy Twp. Planning Commn., 1974-85, Grand Blanc Planning Commn., City of Mich., 1985—; chmn., 1988—. Pres. Flint Beautification Commn., 1968-69; bd. dirs. Grand Blanc Beautification Commn., 1969-84; founding mem. bd. dirs. Flint YMCA, 1969-75, chmn. camp com., 1971-75; founding mem. bd. dirs. Flint Environ. Action Team, 1971-77, v.p., 1971-73; elder First Presbyn. Ch. Flint, 1983, trustee, 1986—; exec. com. Tall Pine council Boy Scouts Am., 1975—; bd. dirs. New Paths, pres., 1985-86, 94—. Served with AUS, 1945-46. Recipient various civic service awards. Fellow AIA; mem. Mich. Soc. Architects, Flint Area C. of C. Clubs: Greater Flint Jaycees (dir. 1957-63, v.p. 1963), Flint City, U. Mich. (pres. Flint chpt. 1980—). Lodge: Rotary (pres. 1984-85). Home: 686 Applegate Ln Grand Blanc MI 48439-1669 Office: THA Architects Engrs 817 E Kearsley St Flint MI 48503-1913

TOMBRELLO, THOMAS ANTHONY, JR., physics educator, consultant; b. Austin, Tex., Sept. 20, 1936; s. Thomas Anthony and Jeanette Lilian (Marcuse) T.; m. Esther Ann Hall, May 30, 1957 (div. Jan. 1976); children: Christopher Thomas, Susan Elaine, Karen Elizabeth; m. Stephanie Carhart Merton, Jan. 15, 1977; 1 stepchild, Kerstin Arusha. BA in Physics, Rice U., 1958, MA, 1960, PhD, 1961; doctoral degree (hon.), Uppsala U., 1997. Rsch. fellow in physics Calif. Inst. Tech., Pasadena, 1961-62, 64-65, asst. prof. physics, 1965-67, assoc. prof., 1967-71, prof., 1971—, tech. assessment officer, 1996—, William R. Kenan Jr. prof., 1997—; asst. prof. Yale U., New Haven, 1963; cons. in field; disting. vis. prof. U. Calif.-Davis, 1984; v.p., dir. rsch. Schlumberger-Doll Rsch., Ridgefield, Conn., 1987-89; mem. U.S. V.P.'s Space Policy Adv. Bd., 1992; mem. sci. adv. bd. Ctr. of Nanoscale Sci. and Technology, Rice U., 1995—. Assoc. editor Nuc. Physics, 1971-91, Applications of Nuc. Physics, 1980—, Radiation Effects, 1985-88, Nuc. Instruments and Methods B, 1993—. Recipient Alexander von Humboldt award von Humboldt Stiftung, U. Frankfurt, Germany, 1984-85; NSF fellow Calif. Inst. Tech. 1961-62; A.P. Sloan fellow, 1971-73. Fellow Am. Phys. Soc.; mem. AAAS, Materials Rsch. Soc., Phi Beta Kappa, Sigma Xi, Delta Phi Alpha. Avocations: reading, jogging. Democrat. Office: Calif Inst Tech Dept Physics Mail Code 91125 Pasadena CA 91125

TOMBROS, PETER GEORGE, pharmaceutical company executive; b. Oak Hill, W.Va., June 12, 1942; s. George P. and Mary Jane (Boliski) T.; m. Ann Riblett Cullen, June 12, 1965. BS, Pa. State U., 1964, MS, 1966; MBA, U. Pa., 1968. Mktg. asst. Pfizer Labs. div. Pfizer Inc., N.Y.C., 1968; asst. product mgr. Pfizer Inc., N.Y.C., 1969, product mgr., 1970-71, group product mgr., 1972-74, v.p. mktg., 1975-80; sr. v.p., gen. mgr. Roerig div. Pfizer Inc., N.Y.C., 1980-86; exec. v.p. Pfizer Pharms. div. Pfizer Inc., N.Y.C., 1986-90, v.p. corp. strategic planning, 1990-94; also corp. officer Pfizer Inc., N.Y.C.; pres., CEO Enzon, Inc., Piscataway, 1994—, also bd. dirs.; adv. panel Penn State BS/MBA, 1992—, alumni fellow Penn State, 1993; bd. dirs. Pfizer Pharm. Inc., AL Pharma Inc., Oslo, Norway. Bd. dirs. Am. Found. for Pharm. Edn., North Plainfield, N.J., 1980—, past chmn.; trustee Fisk U., Nashville, 1986—, Dominican Coll., Orangeburg, N.Y., 1987—; key campus exec. U. Pa., Phila., 1987—; trustee Bklyn. Borough Hall Restoration, 1987—; mem. corp. devel. com. Cen. Park Conservancy, N.Y.C.; bd. dirs. Vote America, 1990; bd. dirs. Cancer Care; hon. bd. mem. Reflex Sympathetic Dystrophy Assn. Am. Mem. Pharm. Mfrs. Assn. (past chmn. mktg. steering com.), Links Club, Blind Brook Club, Masons. Avocations: marathon running, golf, tennis, skiing, bridge.

TOMEH, AMIN ADNAN, geotechnical engineer, consultant; b. Damascus, Syria, Apr. 17, 1971; came to U.S., 1986; s. Adnan and Souad (Idlibi) T.; m. Rula Edilbi. BSCE, U. Pitts., 1990; MSCE, Ga. Inst. Tech., 1992. Grad. team leader researcher U. Pitts., Pitts., 1989-90; grad. rsch. asst. Ga. Inst. Tech., Atlanta, 1991-92; sr. project engr. R&D Testing & Drilling, Inc., Atlanta, 1992-94, dept. mgr. constrn. svcs., 1994-95; prin. Matrix Engring. Group, Atlanta, 1995—; civil engring. tutor U. Pitts., 1989; project mgr. law/R&D joint venture Atlanta Fed. Blvd., Olympic Equestrian Venue, Atlanta Olympic Stadium, Olympic Shooting Venue. Mem. ASTM, Ga. Tech. Geotech. Soc. (founding, constn. com. 1991—). Achievements include replacement up to 50% of the cement used in normal weight concrete with an oil shale ash (by-product) without affecting the compressive strength; defined aggregate breaking patterns under compaction devices; project engr. Hartsfield Atlanta Internat. Airport Concourse "E" project, Atlanta Olympic Stadium, Olympic Equestrian Venue and Olympic Shooting Venue; project mgr. South Gobb Water Reclamation Facility Expansion project. Office: Matrix Engring Group 3300 Buckeye Rd Ste 525 Atlanta GA 30341-4239

TOMEI, MARISA, actress; b. Bklyn., Dec. 4, 1964. TV appearances include (series) A Different World, 1987, (films) Parker Kane, 1990; film appearances include: The Flamingo Kid, 1984, Playing for Keeps, 1986, Oscar, 1991, Zandalee, 1991, My Cousin Vinny, 1992 (Acad. award best supporting actress 1993), Chaplin, 1992, Untamed Heart, 1993, Equinox, 1993, The Paper, 1994, Only You, 1994, The Perez Family, 1994, Four Rooms, 1995, Unhook the Stars, 1996; theatre appearances include Slavs! Thinking About the Longstanding Problems of Virtue and Happiness, 1994. Office: William Morris Agy 151 S El Camino Dr Beverly Hills CA 90212-2704

TOMEK, LAURA LINDEMANN, marketing executive; b. New Brunswick, N.J., Oct. 21, 1940; d. A. John and Jeanette (Lacey) Lindemann; m. Charles L. Tomek, Oct. 4, 1969 (div. Apr. 1990); 1 child, Gregory C. Student, U. Wis., Milw., 1958-59; BS in Mktg., U. Ariz., 1962. Market rsch. mgr. Procter & Gamble Inc., Cin., 1962-66; nat. buyer, exec. tng. mgr., market rsch. analyst Sears, Roebuck & Co., Chgo., 1966-84; hdqrs. buyer Federated Dept. Stores, Chgo., 1984-85; v.p. O'Bryan Bros., Inc., Chgo., 1985-86; cons. Mktg. Connections, Chgo., 1986-88; regional sales mgr. Fabrican, Inc., Chgo., 1988-90; counsel Crouch & Fitzgerald, Oakbrook, Ill., 1991-93; merchandise mgr. Little Switzerland Corp., 1993-94; merchandising and mktg. cons. Mktg. Connections Internat., 1994; mktg. cons. Kraft Foods, 1994-95, Govt. of Thailand, 1995-96, Mktg. Connections & Info., 1996—; mem. bd. judges Internat. Fashion Group, 1979—. Mem. com. March of Dimes Ann. Corp. Fundraiser, Chgo., 1992. Mem. Internat. Fashion Group Assn., U. Ariz. Alumni (bd. dirs. 1990—), Midwest Soc. Profl. Cons. (membership com. 1996—). Avocations: skiing, sailing, boating, travel, investments. Home: 1360 N Lake Shore Dr # 905 Chicago IL 60610

TOMEK, WILLIAM GOODRICH, agricultural economist; b. Table Rock, Nebr., Sept. 20, 1932; s. John and Ruth Genevieve (Goodrich) T. B.S., U. Nebr., 1956, M.A., 1957; Ph.D., U. Minn., 1961. Asst. prof. Cornell U., Ithaca, N.Y., 1961-66, NSF fellow, 1965, assoc. prof. agrl. econs., 1966-70, prof., 1970—, chmn. dept. agrl. econs., 1988-93; vis. econ. USDA, 1978-79; vis. fellow Stanford U., 1968-69, U. New Eng., Australia, 1988; mem. adv. panel Rev. Agrl. Econs., 1996—. Author: Agricultural Product Prices, 1990; editor: Am. Jour. Agrl. Econs., 1975-77; co-editor: Chgo. Bd. Trade Rsch. Symposia, 1993—; mem. editl. bd. Jour. Futures Markets, 1992-95; contbr. articles to profl. jours. Served with U.S. Army, 1953-55. Recipient Earl Combs Jr. award Chgo. Bd. Trade Found. Mem. Am. Agrl. Econs. Assn. (pres. 1985-86), Am. Econ. Assn., Econometric Soc., Northeastern Agrl. Econs. Assn., Am. Agrl. Econs. Assn. (awards 1981, 89, fellow), Gamma Sigma Delta (rsch. award 1994). Democrat. Methodist. Office: Cornell U Warren Hall Ithaca NY 14853-7801

TOMHAVE, BEVERLY KORSTAD, corporate executive; b. St. Paul, Feb. 17, 1947; d. William Bernard and Dorothy Ann (Danielson) Korstad; m. Jonathan F. Tomhave, Oct. 15, 1977; children: Anna M., William D. Stefan. BA, Grinnell Coll., 1969; postgrad., U. Minn., 1974-76; student, various schs., India, Japan, Thailand, Ethiopia. Researcher Devel. Rsch. Corp., Mpls., 1965-66; researcher dept. biology Grinnell (Iowa) Coll., 1966-69; with dist. office Northwestern Bell, St. Paul, 1969-72; dist. traffic inst. Northwestern Bell, Mpls., 1972-74; v.p., pres. Jonathan Studios, Plymouth, Minn., 1974—; treas. Korridor Capital Investment, Mpls., 1986-95; bd. dirs E.D. Properties. Active Human Rights Commn., St. Paul, 1969, United Fund Commn., St. Paul, 1972; adviser Jr. Achievement, St. Paul, 1973. Recipient Spectrum award Ceramic Tile Distbrs. Assn., 1988. Mem. Townsend Soc. Am., Minn. State Hist. Soc., Sci. Mus. Minn., Clan Douglas Soc. North Am., Minn. Bus. and Profl. Women. Avocations: genealogical research, gardening, travel. Office: Jonathan Studios PO Box 693 Long Lake MN 55356

TOMICH, LILLIAN, lawyer; b. L.A., Mar. 28, 1935; d. Peter S. and Yovanka P. (Ivanovic) T. AA, Pasadena City Coll., 1954; BA in Polit. Sci., UCLA, 1956, cert. secondary teaching, 1957, MA, 1958; JD, U. So. Calif., 1961. Bar: Calif. Sole practice, 1961-66; house counsel Mfrs. Bank, Los Angeles, 1966; assoc. Hurley, Shaw & Tomich, San Marino, Calif., 1968-76; assoc. Driscoll & Tomich, San Marino, 1976—; dir. Continental Culture Specialists Inc., Glendale, Calif. Trustee, St. Sava Serbian Orthodox Ch., San Gabriel, Calif. Charles Fletcher Scott fellow, 1957; U. So. Calif. Law Sch. scholar, 1958. Mem. ABA, Calif. Bar Assn., Los Angeles County Bar Assn., Women Lawyers Assn., San Marino C. of C., UCLA Alumni Assn., Town Hall and World Affairs Council, Order Mast and Dagger, Iota Tau Tau, Alpha Gamma Sigma. Office: 2460 Huntington Dr San Marino CA 91108-2643

TOMIYASU, KIYO, consulting engineer; b. Las Vegas, Nev., Sept. 25, 1919; s. Yonema and Toyono (Kawamura) T.; m. Eiko Nakamizo, Aug. 31, 1947. B.S., Calif. Inst. Tech., 1940; M.S., Columbia U., 1941; M.E.S., Harvard U., 1947, Ph.D., 1948. Instr. Harvard U., 1948-49; head engring. sect. Sperry Gyroscope Co., Gt. Neck, N.Y., 1949-55; with GE, 1955-93; cons. engr. microwave techniques GE Valley Forge Space Ctr., Phila., 1969-93; with Martin Marietta Corp., Phila., 1993-95, Lockheed Martin Corp., Phila., 1995—. Author: The Laser Literature-An Annotated Guide, 1968; articles; patentee in field. Exec. bd. Friendship Hill Civic Assn., Paoli, Pa., 1972-73, pres., 1973. Recipient Steinmetz award Gen. Electric Co., 1977; Mgmt. and Data Systems fellow Martin Marietta Corp., 1993; established Tomiyasu Meml. ann. scholarship Calif. Inst. Tech., 1977. Fellow IEEE (life, hon. life mem. Microwave Theory and Techniques Soc. 1973, tech. activities bd., awards bd., publs. bd., bd. dirs. div. IV 1985-86, ednl. activities bd. 1987-88, Microwave Career award, 1981, Centennial medal 1984, Geosci. and Remote Sensing Outstanding Svc. award 1986, Microwave Disting. Svc. award 1987); mem. Am. Phys. Soc. Patents. Home: 366 Hilltop Rd Paoli PA 19301-1211 Office: Lockheed Martin Corp PO Box 8048 Philadelphia PA 19101-8048

TOMJACK, T.J., wholesale distribution executive. BBA, U. Notre Dame, 1964. With Peat Marwick Mitchell & Co., 1964-71, Potlatch Corp., 1971-85; exec. v.p. sales North Pacific Lumber Co., Portland, Oreg., 1971-85, exec. v.p., COO, 1987, pres., 1988—, chmn., CEO, 1989—. Office: North Pacific Lumber Co PO Box 3915 Portland OR 97208*

TOMJANOVICH, RUDOLPH, professional athletic coach; b. Hamtramck, Mich., Nov. 24, 1948. Scout Houston Rockets, 1981-83, asst. coach, 1983-92, head coach, 1992—. Named to Sporting News All-Am. first team, 1970; coach NBA championship team, 1994-95. Office: Houston Rockets Ste 400 The Summit 2 Greenway Plz Houston TX 77046-3865*

TOMKA, PETER, diplomat; b. Banská, Bystrica, Slovakia, June 1, 1956; s. Ján and Kornélia (Plai) T.; m. Zuzana Halgasová, June 30, 1990. Grad., Charles U., Prague, Czechoslovakia, 1979; PhD in Internat. Law, Charles U., 1985. Lectr. Law Sch., Charles U., Prague, 1980-86, assoc. lectr. in internat. law, 1986-91; asst. legal advisor Fed. Ministry of Fgn. Affairs, Czechoslovakia, 1986-90, head pub. internat. law divsn., 1990-91; counsellor, legal advisor Permanent Mission to UN, N.Y.C., 1991-92, amb., dep. permanent rep. of Slovakia, 1993—, charge d'affaires, 1994—; agt. of Slovakia Internat. Ct. of Justice in Gabcikovo-Nagymaros Project Case, Hungary/Slovakia; mem. Permanent Ct. Arbitration, 1995. Office: Permanent Mission of Slovak Republic 866 UN Plz Ste 585 New York NY 10017

TOMKEWITZ, MARIE ADELE, elementary school educator; b. San Antonio, Feb. 26, 1965; d. David Eugene and Marie Frances (Sergi) T. BS in Elem. Edn., S.W. Tex. State U., 1988. 4th grade tchr. Sinclair Elem. Sch. East Cen. Ind. Sch. Dist., San Antonio, 1990—, chmn. 2d grade, 1992-93; 4th grade tchr. Sinclair Elem. Sch., San Antonio. Mem. Holy Spirit Cath. Ch., San Antonio, 1965—. Mem. Kappa Delta Pi, Alpha Phi. Avocations: reading, tennis. Home: 1119 Melissa Dr San Antonio TX 78213-2028 Office: Sinclair Elem Sch 6126 Sinclair Rd San Antonio TX 78222-2439

TOMKINS, ALAN, art director, production designer. Art dir.: (films) The Empire Strikes Back, 1980 (Academy award nomination best art direction 1980), The Curse of the Pink Panther, 1983, The Keep, 1983, Lassiter, 1984, Lifeforce, 1985, Haunted Honeymoon, 1986, High Spirits, 1988, A Dry White Season, 1989, (with Steve Spence) Heaven and Earth, 1991, (with Derek R. Hill) JFK, 1991, Natural Born Killers, 1994; prodn. designer: (films) National Lampoon's European Vacation, 1985, (TV movies) War and Remembrance, 1989. Office: care Art Directors Guild 11365 Ventura Blvd Ste 315 Studio City CA 91604-3148 Address: 3 Roman Garden Kings, Langley Herts England WD4 8LG*

TOMKINS, CALVIN, writer; b. Orange, N.J., Dec. 17, 1925; s. Frederick and Laura (Graves) T.; m. Grace Lloyd Fanning, Sept. 11, 1948; children: Anne Graves, Susan Temple, Spencer; m. Judy Johnston, Nov. 11, 1961 (div. Feb. 1981); m. Susan Cheever, Oct. 1, 1981; 1 child, Sarah Liley Cheever; m. Dodie Kazanjian, May 28, 1988. B.A., Princeton U., 1948. Assoc. editor Newsweek mag., N.Y.C., 1955-57, gen. editor, 1957-59; staff writer The New Yorker, N.Y.C., 1960—. Author: The Bride and The Bachelors, 1965, Merchants and Masterpieces, 1970, Living Well Is the Best Revenge, 1971, Off the Wall, 1980, Post- to Neo-, 1988, (with Dodie Kazanjian) Alex: The Life of Alexander Liberman, 1993, Duchamp: A Biography, 1997. Bd. dirs. Cunningham Dance Found., N.Y.C., 1963—. Served with USN. Guggenheim fellow, 1978. Mem. Authors League Am. Inc., Pen Am. Ctr. Club: Century (N.Y.C.). Home: 145 E 74th St New York NY 10021-3225 Office: New Yorker Magazine 20 W 43rd St New York NY 10036-7400

TOMKINS, FRANK SARGENT, physicist; b. Petoskey, Mich., June 24, 1915; s. Charles Frederick and Irene Eugenie (Gouin) T.; m. Mary Ann Lynch, Jan. 6, 1964; 1 son, Frank Sargent. B.S., Kalamazoo Coll., 1937; Ph.D. (Parke-Davis fellow), Mich. State U., 1941. Physicist Buick Aviation Engine Div., Melrose Park, Ill., 1941-42; scientist Manhattan Project U. Chgo., 1943-45; sr. scientist Argonne (Ill.) Nat. Lab., 1945—, group leader, 1944—; U.S. del. 2d Internat. Conf. on Peaceful Uses Atomic Energy, 1958; cons. Bendix Corp., Cin., 1963-69; assoc. Harvard Coll. Obs., 1978—; chmn. bd. Pegasus Enterprises, Inc. Contbr. articles to sci. jours. John Simon Guggenheim fellow Laboratoire Aime-Cotton, Bellevue, France, 1960-61; Sci. Rsc. Coun. fellow Imperial Coll., London, 1975; recipient Argonne Univs. Assn. Disting. Appointment, 1975-76, Kalamazoo Coll. Disting. Achievement award, 1990. Fellow Am. Phys. Soc., Optical Soc. Am. (William F. Meggers award 1977); mem. AAAS, Societe Francaise de Physique, N.Y. Acad. Scis., Sigma Xi. Home: 11714 S 83rd Ave Palos Park IL 60464-1015 Office: 9700 Cass Ave Lemont IL 60439-4803

TOMKOVICZ, JAMES JOSEPH, law educator; b. L.A., Oct. 10, 1951; s. Anthony Edward and Vivian Marion (Coory) T.; m. Nancy Louise Abboud,

June 27, 1987; children: Vivian Rose, Michelle Evelene, Henry James. BA, U. So. Calif., 1973; JD, UCLA, 1976. Bar: Calif. 1976, U.S. Dist. Ct. (so. dist.) Calif., U.S. Ct. Appeals (9th and 10th cirs.), U.S. Supreme Ct. Law clk. to Hon. Edward J. Schwartz San Diego, 1976-77; law clk. to Hon. John M. Ferren Washington, 1977-78; atty. U.S. Dept. Justice, Washington, 1979-80; assoc. prof. law U. Iowa, Iowa City, 1982-86, prof., 1986—; vis. prof. U. Iowa, Iowa City, 1981, U. Mich., Ann Arbor, 1992; adj. prof. UCLA, 1981-82. Author: (casebook) Criminal Procedure, 2d edit., 1994; contbr. articles to profl. jours. Mem. Order of Coif, Phi Beta Kappa. Democrat. Roman Catholic. Avocations: running, tennis, softball, creative writing. Office: U Iowa Coll Law Melrose & Byngton Iowa City IA 52242

TOMKOW, GWEN ADELLE, artist; b. Detroit, May 16, 1932; d. Galen A. and Edythe Christine (Barr) Roberts; m. Michael Tomkow, Nov. 14, 1953; children: Eric Michael, Thomas Edward, Nikola Christine, Kit Adair. A of Bus., Detroit Bus. Inst., 1952; student, Birmingham Bloomfield Art, Assn., Mich., 1985-87, Visual Art Assn., Livonia, Mich., 1984-89. Tchr. watercolor Visual Art Assn., Livonia, 1989-97; tchr. workshop Ella Sharp Mus. Jackson Civic Art, Mich., 1996; tchr. watercolor workshop Village Fine Art Assn., Milford, Mich., 1996; slide lectr. Livonia Artist Club, 1995, Palette and Brush Club, Southfield, Mich., 1995, Pontiac (Mich.) Oakland Artists, 1995, Ea. Mich. U. Watercolor Soc., 1994; tchr. watercolor workshop Ann Arbor Women Painters U. Mich. Art Sch., 1997; artist-in-residence Farmington Art Commn., Farmington Hills, 1998. Contbr. articles and photos to books, including: The Artistic Touch, 1994-95, The Artistic Touch 2, 1996, Splash 3, 1994-95, Splash 4, 1996, also Watercolor edit., Am. Artist Mag., 1991; represented in permanent collections E. Carothers Dunnegan Gallery of Art Mus. Recipient Purchase awards U.S.A. Springfield (Mo.) Art Mus., 1990, 93, 94, 1st prize Helen de Roy Competition, Oakland C.C., Farmington, Mich., 1988, 92, Grumbacher Gold medal Farmington Artists Club, Farmington Hills, Mich., 1995. Mem. Mich. Watercolor Soc. (Meml. award 1992), Farmington Art Assn. (pres. 1987-89), Detroit Soc. Women Painters Sculptors (sec. 1994-95), Palette and Brush (v.p. 1982-83). Presbyterian. Avocations: tennis, golf, choir singer, theater.

TOMLIN, LINTON, court reporter; b. Pecos, Tex., July 26, 1953; d. John Frazier and Clara Mae (James) T. Reporter Tex. State Senate, Austin, 1975; sec., clk. Austin Bd. Realtors, 1975; reporter Austin Ct. Reporters, 1976, Waco (Tex.) Ct. Reporters, 1977; offcl. ct. reporter County Ct. at Law, Pecos, 1977-78; sec. Strauss, Jons & Parker Law Firm, Kerrville, Tex., 1979-81; offcl. ct. reporter 198th Jud. Dist. Ct., Kerrville, Tex., 1981—. Mem. Nat. Ct. Reporters Assn., Tex. Ct. Reporters Assn. Home: 208 Ball Dr Kerrville TX 78028 Office: Kerr County Ct House 700 Main St Kerrville TX 78028-5323

TOMLINSON, ALEXANDER COOPER, investment banker, consultant; b. Haddonfield, N.J., May 13, 1922; s. Alexander Cooper and Mary Cooper (Buzby) T.; m. Elizabeth Anne brierley, Jan. 10, 1953 (div.); children: William Brierley, Deborah T. Marple, Alexander Cooper III; m. Margaret L. Dickey, Nov. 15, 1986. BS, Haverford Coll., 1943; postgrad., London Sch. Econs. and Polit. Sci., 1947-48; MBA, Harvard U., 1950; LLD (hon.), Haverford Coll., 1995. With Morgan Stanley & Co., N.Y.C., 1950-76, ptnr., 1958-76, mng. dir., 1970-76; dir., pres. Morgan Stanley Can. Ltd. div., Montreal, Que., 1972-76; chmn. exec. com. First Boston, Inc., N.Y.C., 1976-82, dir., 1976-88; pres. Nat. Planning Assn., Washington, 1982-85; exec. dir. Ctr. for Privatization, Washington, 1985-88; pres. Hungarian-Am. Enterprise Fund, Washington, 1990-93; chmn. Fund for Arts and Culture in Ctrl. and Ea. Europe, 1994—; bd. dirs. Preco Corp., 1989—; mem. U.S. adv. bd. Que. Hydro, 1984-95. Trustee Incorp. Village, Cove Neck, N.Y., 1958-72, 76-82, Cold Spring Harbor Lab., 1976-87, N.Y. Infirmary-Beekman Downtown Hosp., 1968-82, East Woods Sch., Oyster Bay, N.Y., 1962-70, Nature Conservancy, L.I., N.Y., 1970-82, Carnegie Found. for Advancement Tchg., 1984-90; bd. mgrs. Haverford Coll., 1979-92; bd. dirs. Nat. Bldg. Mus., 1987-94, Nat. Planning Assn., 1982-90, Decatur House Coun., 1990-94; chmn. Am. Friends Can., Inc., 1982-91, Harvard Bus. Sch. Fund, 1981-83. Lt. USNR, 1943-46. Mem. Coun. on Fgn. Rels., Metropolitan Club (Washington), Links (N.Y.). Home: 3314 P St NW Washington DC 20007-2701

TOMLINSON, CHARLES WESLEY, JR., advertising executive; b. West Chester, Pa., Oct. 14, 1947; s. Charles Wesley and Kathryn Elizabeth (Madeira) T.; m. Kathy Anne Petersheim, June 7, 1969 (div.); 1 child, Alan Charles (dec.); m. Carol A. Oldfield, Apr. 4, 1986; 1 stepchild, Christie. BS in Comm., Temple U., 1969. Announcer, then sales mgr., air personality sta. WCHE, West Chester, 1966-70; communications specialist West Chester Area Sch. Dist., 1970-71; freelance advt. cons., 1971-73; gen. mgr. sta. WCHE, 1973-75; gen. sales mgr. Sta. WJBR-AM/FM, Wilmington, Del., 1975-84; dir. mktg. svcs. Winner Group, Wilmington, 1984-93; dir. sales and mktg. Del. Today mag. Del. Today mag., Main Line Today mag. Suburban Mktg. Assn., Wilmington, 1994—. Past mem. exec. com. United Fund Greater West Chester. Mem. Advt. Club Phila., Chester County Chambers Commerce Assn. (1st v.p. 1981-82, pres. 1982-84), C. of C. Greater West Chester (pres. 1977). Republican. Lodges: Masons, Elks (past exalted ruler). Office: 407 Homestead Dr West Chester PA 19382-8200

TOMLINSON, GEORGE HERBERT, retired industrial company research executive; b. Fullerton, La., May 2, 1912; emigrated to Can., 1914; s. George Herbert and Irene Loretta (Nourse) T.; m. Frances Fowler, July 17, 1937; children: Peter George, David Lester, Susan Margaret Tomlinson Goff. B.A., Bishop's U., 1931; Ph.D., McGill U., 1935; D.C.L. (hon.), Bishop's U., 1986. Chief chemist Howard Smith Chem. Ltd., Cornwall, Ont., Can., 1936-39; research dir. Howard Smith Paper Mills Ltd., Cornwall, 1939-61, Domtar Ltd., Montreal, Que., 1961-70; v.p. research and environ. tech. Domtar Ltd., 1970-77, sr. sci. adv., 1977-90. Contbr. articles to profl. jours. Recipient Gov. Gen.'s Gold medal, 1931; Laureate of UN Environ. Programme Global 500, June, 1987. Fellow Royal Soc. Can., Internat. Acad. Wood Sci., Chem. Inst. Can., TAPPI (dir. 1976-79, medal 1969, hon. life mem.); mem. Am. Chem. Soc. (emeritus), Can. Pulp and Paper Assn. (hon. life mem.), Chemists Club (N.Y.). Anglican. Patentee in field. Home: 920 Perrot Blvd N, Ile Perrot, PQ Canada J7V 3K1

TOMLINSON, IAN, software engineer; b. St. Johns, Antigua, Sept. 2, 1964; s. Lydia C. (Davis) Ross; m. Averil V. Archibald, Oct. 24, 1992; children: Akil Ian, Jameel Ian. BA in Bus. Adminstrn., cert in data processing, U. V.I., 1988; MS in Info. Systems, Am. U., 1992; postgrad., George Mason U., 1994—. Database adminstr., programmer V.I. Water and Power Auth., 1988-90; programmer, analyst, task leader Data Tree, Inc., 1990-92; sr. cons. Booz-Allen and Hamilton, Inc., 1992—; v.p. software engring. Omni Systems, Inc., 1993—. Joseph and Jenny Alexander scholar, 1983; Gail E. Boggs Data Processing scholar, 1987. Mem. Assn. for Computing Machinery. Avocations: volleyball, scuba diving, motorcycles. Office: Omni Sys Inc 6255 Brandon Ave Ste 260 Springfield VA 22150

TOMLINSON, J. RICHARD, engineering services company executive; b. Newtown, Pa., Mar. 26, 1930; s. Robert K. and Margaret (Wright) T.; m. Barbara Elizabeth Brazill, Apr. 30, 1955; children: Karin Kathleen Tomlinson Pizzitola, Kimberly Ann Tomlinson Donahue. B.A., Swarthmore Coll., 1952; postgrad., George Washington U., 1952-53, U. Mich., 1955-57, Drexel Inst. Tech., 1954-57, Am. U., 1965. Mgmt. analyst Dept. State, Washington, 1952-53; with Old Republic Life Ins. Co., Washington, 1953-54; supr. financial analysis Ford Motor Co., Detroit, 1954-61; cons. McKinsey & Co., Washington, 1961-65; v.p. finance, dir. passenger svcs. Reading Co., Phila., 1965-69; v.p. finance Rollins Internat., Inc., 1969-71; exec. v.p. Amtrak, Washington, 1972-74; ptnr. L.T. Klauder and Assocs., 1974-75, 79-83; exec. v.p. Penn Central Transp. Co., 1975-78; pres. LTK Engring. Svcs., 1984-95. Named Man of Month, Phila. C. of C., 1967. Mem. Union League, Aronomink Golf and Country Club, Phila. Aviation Country Club. Home: 451 Inveraray Rd Villanova PA 19085-1139

TOMLINSON, JAMES FRANCIS, retired news agency executive; b. Long Beach, Calif., Oct. 18, 1925; s. Lilburn Jesse and Margaret (Roemer) T.; m. Sally JoAnne Ryan, Aug. 12, 1967; children—Elizabeth Anne, Victoria Alexandra. B.A., U. Va., 1950; student, Harvard U., Grad. Sch. Arts and Scis., 1950-51; grad., Advanced Mgmt. Program, Harvard U., 1977. With A.P., 1951-92; chief bur. A.P., Newark, 1957-63; bus. news editor A.P., N.Y.C., 1963-67; dep. treas. A.P., 1967-68, treas., 1968-87, v.p., 1972-92, sec., 1978-92, asst. to pres., 1987-92. Served with AUS, 1943-46, ETO. Mem. Phi Beta Kappa, Phi Eta Sigma. Clubs: N.Y. Athletic (N.Y.C.), Harvard (N.Y.C.). Home: 222 E 71st St New York NY 10021-5134

TOMLINSON, JAMES LAWRENCE, mechanical engineer; b. Detroit, Sept. 12, 1935; s. James Emmet and Ethel Pearl (Williams) T.; m. Marilyn Joyce Peterson, Aug. 24, 1957; children: James, Mary, Robert, Susan. BSME, Mich. Tech., 1957. Registered profl. engr., Mich. Design engr. Buick Motor div. GMC, Flint, Mich., 1960-61, project engr., 1961-66, sr. project engr., 1966-71; staff analysis engr. GM Corp., Warren, Mich., 1971-82, sr. staff analysis engr., 1983-88; pres. Eastport (Mich.) Engring., 1989—. Mayor City of Grand Blanc, 1985-89, city councilman, 1969-84, police liaison/commr., 1971-82, planning adv. bd., 1978-80, planning commn., 1985-89; nat. coun. mem. Boy Scouts Am., 1979-90, 93—, regional bd. mem., 1995—, coun. commr., 1979-84, coun. v.p., 1984—, nat. camp sch. staff, 1986-88, regional camp inspector/accreditation team, 1988—; vice chmn. Genesee County Sml. Cities and Villages Assn., 1986, chmn., 1987. Capt. USAF, 1958-60. Recipient Silver Beaver Tall Pine coun. Boy Scouts Am., 1980, Silver Antelope Ctrl. region, 1996. Mem. NSPE (treas. Flint chpt. 1968-72, Engr. of the Yr. Flint chpt. 1990), SAE (mem. com. 1992-94, 96-98), ASME (exec. bd. Saginaw Valley chpt. 1968-70), Friends of Torch Lake Twp., Inc. (pres. 1994—). United Ch. of Christ. Home: 12077 Harris Beach Rd Eastport MI 49627-0025

TOMLINSON, JOHN EDWARD, secret service agent; b. Alexandria, Va., Oct. 7, 1949; s. John Edward and Mary Frances (Higgins) T.; m. Suzanne Miller, Dec. 14, 1979; children: Jessica, C. Samantha, David, Timothy. BS, Va. Commonwealth U., 1971; MS, Ea. Ky. U., 1972; MS in Strategic Planning (hon.), Nat. War Coll., 1993. Police officer, detective Wilmington (Del.) Bur. Police, 1972-78; spl. agt. U.S. Secret Service, Phila., 1978-79, N.Y.C., 1979-85, Washington, 1985—; mem. adj. faculty Brandywine Coll., Wilmington, 1972-74, Wilmington Coll., 1974-76, Salem (N.J.) C.C., 1975-77. Author: Protective Ops. Manual, 1993-94 (Treas. award 1995). Mem. Gift of Peace Charity, 1988—. Recipient Spl. Act award Dept. of Treas., 1985; grad. fellow Dept. of Edn., Ea. Ky. U., 1971-72. Mem. Nat. War Coll. Alumni Assn. (life), U. Md. "M" Club, Alpha Phi Sigma (past sec.), Phi Theta Pi (past sec., v.p.). Roman Catholic. Avocations: jogging, basketball, racquetball, travel. Home: 9421 Copenhaver Dr Potomac MD 20854

TOMLINSON, JOSEPH ERNEST, manufacturing company executive; b. Sycamore, Ill., Apr. 22, 1939; s. Bernie Gilbert and Elizabeth Lowe (Hoffman) T.; m. Judith Ann Worst, Sept. 20, 1969; children: Mark Joseph, Amy Ann. BS in Acctg., U. Ill., 1962. CPA. Staff acct. Price Waterhouse and Co., Chgo., 1962-65, sr. acct., 1965-69; audit mgr. Price Waterhouse and Co., Indpls., 1969-74; corp. contr. Inland Container Corp., Indpls., 1974-82, v.p., treas., contr., 1982—. Congl. chmn. Carmel Luth. Ch., Ind., 1983-86, v.p., 1988-91; mem. bd. dirs. Luth. Child and Family Svcs., Indpls., 1994—. With Ill. N.G. 1963-69. Mem. Fin. Execs. Inst. (treas. Indpls. chpt. 1986-87, sec. 1987-88, 2d v.p. 1988-89, 1st v.p. 1989-90, pres. 1990-91). Republican. Club: Crooked Stick Golf. Home: 2063 Saint Andrews Cir Carmel IN 46032-9547 Office: Inland Container Corp 4030 Vincennes Rd Indianapolis IN 46268-3007

TOMLINSON, WARREN LEON, lawyer; b. Denver, Apr. 2, 1930; s. Leslie Alton and Esther (Hasler) T.; m. Lois Elaine Retallack, Aug. 8, 1953 (div. 1987); children: Stephanie Lynn Huffine, Brett Louis; m. Linda Jane Beville, May 17, 1989. BA, U. Denver, 1951; JD, NYU, 1954. Bar: Colo. 1954, U.S. Dist. Ct. Colo., U.S. Ct. Appeals (10th cir.) 1958, U.S. Supreme Ct.. 1960. Assoc. Holland & Hart, Denver, 1958-63, ptnr., 1963-85, mediator, arbitrator, 1995—. Contbr. numerous articles to profl. jours. Lt. U.S. Army, 1954-58. Mem. ABA (chmn. law practice mgmt. sect. 1988-89, charter fellow Coll. of Law Practice Mgmt. 1994). Republican. Episcopalian. Avocations: skiing, white-water rafting. Home: 5017 Main Gore Dr # 4 Vail CO 81657 Office: Holland & Hart 555 17th St Ste 2900 Denver CO 80202-5555

TOMLINSON, WILLIAM HOLMES, management educator, retired army officer, b. Thornton, Ark., Apr. 12, 1922; s. Hugh Oscar and Lucy Gray (Holmes) T.; m. Dorothy Payne, June 10, 1947 (dec.); children: Jane Axtell, Lucy Gray, William Payne; m. Florence Mood Smith, May 1, 1969 (div.); m. Suzanne Scollard Gill, Mar. 16, 1977. Student, Centenary Coll., 1938-39; BS, U.S. Mil. Acad., 1943; grad. Field Arty. Sch., 1951; grad. Air Command Staff Coll., 1958; MBA, U. Ala., 1960; MS in Internat. Affairs, George Washington U., 1966; grad. U.S. Army War Coll., 1966; grad. Indsl. Coll. Armed Forces, 1968; PhD in Bus. Adminstrn., Am. U., 1974; postgrad. 56th Advanced Mgmt. Program, Harvard U., 1968, 69; BAS, U. N. Fla., 1988. Commd. 2d lt. U.S. Army, 1943, advanced through grades to col., field arty., 1966; combat svc. in Leyte and Cebu, Philippines 246 Field Arty. Bn. Americal Divsn., 1945; aide de camp, comdg. gen. 8th U.S. Army, Japan, 1945-48, ops. officer 9th Divsn. Arty., Germany, 1954-56, Office of Undersec. Army, Pentagon, Washington, 1961-64; comdr. 2d Bn., 8th Arty. and 7th Div. Arty., UN Comd. S. Korea, 1964-65; faculty Indsl. Coll. Armed Forces, Ft. McNair, Washington, 1966-72, ret., 1973; faculty U. North Fla., Jacksonville, 1972—, prof. mgmt., 1993—; vis. prof. U. Glasgow, Scotland, fall 1987; vis. lectr. Moscow Linguistics U., Plekhanov Econ. U., Ulyanovsk U., Russia, fall 1993; mem. Nat. Def. Exec. Res., Fed. Emergency Mgmt. Agy., 1976—. Author: Assessment of the National Defense Executive Reserve, 1974; co-author: International Business, Theory and Practice, 1991; contbr. articles to profl. jours. and books. Exec. bd. Jacksonville Campus Ministry, 1991—. Decorated Bronze Star, Legion of Merit, Philippine Liberation medal, Japanese Occupation; recipient Freedom Found. award, 1967-71, Sr. Profl. in Human Resources, Teaching Incentive award State Univ. Sys., 1994-95. Mem. SAR, Soc. Human Resource Mgmt., Acad. Mgmt., Indsl. Rels. Rsch. Assn., Acad. Internat. Bus., European Internat. Bus. Assn., Internat. Trade and Fin. Assn., Exec. Svc. Corps. Bd., Co. Mil. Historians., Nat. Eagle Scout Assn., Northeast Fla. Employee Svcs. Assn. (charter pres. 1987-89), West Point Soc. N. Fla. (pres. 1976-77), Mil. Order Stars and Bars (comdr. 1980-90), Army Navy Club, Fla. Yacht Club, Mason, Shriner, Rotary, Beta Gamma Sigma (pres. 1988-89), Kappa Alpha. Presbyterian (elder). Home: 1890 Shadowlawn St Jacksonville FL 32205-9430 Office: U North Fla Dept Mgmt 4567 Saint Johns Bluff Rd S Jacksonville FL 32224-2646

TOMLINSON-KEASEY, CAROL ANN, university administrator; b. Washington, Oct. 15, 1942; d. Robert Bruce and Geraldine (Howe) Tomlinson; m. Charles Blake Keasey, June 13, 1964; children: Kai Linson, Amber Lynn. BS, Pa. State U., 1964; MS, Iowa State U., 1966; PhD, U. Calif., Berkeley, 1970. Lic. psychologist, Calif. Asst. prof. psychology Trenton (N.J.) State Coll., 1969-70, Rutgers U., New Brunswick, N.J., 1970-72; prof. U. Nebr., Lincoln, 1972-77; prof. U. Calif., Riverside, 1977-92, acting dean Coll. Humanities and Social Scis., 1986-88, chmn. dept. psychology, 1989-92; vice provost for academic planning and pers. U. Calif., Davis, 1992-97, vice provost for academic initiatives, 1997—. Author: Child's Eye View, 1980, Child Development, 1985; also numerous chpts. to books; articles to profl. jours. Recipient Disting. Tchr. award U. Calif., 1986. Mem. APA, Soc. Rsch. in Child Devel., Riverside Aquatics Assn. (pres.). Office: U Calif V Provost Acad Initiatives 300 Lakeside Dr Fl 18 Oakland CA 94612-3524

TOMLJANOVICH, ESTHER M., judge; b. Galt, Iowa, Nov. 1, 1931; d. Chester William and Thelma L. (Brooks) Moellering; m. William S. Tomljanovich, Dec. 26, 1957; 1 child, William Brooks. AA, Itasca Jr. Coll., 1951; BSL, St. Paul Coll. Law, 1953, LLB, 1955. Bar: Minn. 1955, U.S. Dist. Ct. Minn. 1958. Asst. revisor of statutes State of Minn., St. Paul, 1957-66, revisor of statutes, 1974-77; dist. ct. judge State of Minn., Stillwater, 1977-90; assoc. justice Minn. Supreme Ct., St. Paul, 1990—. Former mem. North St. Paul Bd. Edn., Maplewood Bd. Edn., Lake Elmo Planning Commn; bd. trustees William Mitchell Coll. Law, 1995—. Mem. Minn. State Bar Assn., Bus. and Profl. Women's Assn. St. Paul (former pres.). Office: Supreme Ct MN MN Judicial Ctr Rm 423 25 Constitution Ave Saint Paul MN 55155-1500

TOMMERAASEN, MILES, college president; b. Sioux Falls, S.D., Jan. 30, 1923; m. Marilyn Fladmark, 1945; children: Marsha Tommeraasen Heimann, Mark, Miles. B.A., Morningside Coll., Sioux City, Iowa, 1943; M.B.A., Northwestern U., 1948; Ph.D., U. Nebr., Lincoln, 1964. Tchr. math. secondary sch. Canton, S.D., 1943-45; staff acct. Arthur Andersen & Co., Chgo., 1946-50; mem. faculty Morningside Coll., 1950-64, chmn. dept. econs. and bus., 1951-61, prof., 1952-64, exec. v.p., 1960-64, pres., 1978-93, pres. emeritus, 1993; prof. U. Nebr., Lincoln, 1964-78; asst. dean Coll. Bus. Adminstrn. U. Nebr., 1968-69, vice chancellor for bus. and fin., 1969-78; mem. 5 corporate bds. Bd. dirs. Siouxland Found., Sunrise Manor; mem. mayor's com. Internat. Visitors; mem. Lincoln Downtown program, United Way Bd., Symphony Bd., First Luth. Ch. Mem. Am. Acctg. Assn., Am. Inst. C.P.A.s, Iowa Soc. C.P.A.s, Nebr. Soc. C.P.A.s (dir. 1966-69), Am. Fin. Assn., Fin. Analysts Soc., Inst. Chartered Fin. Analysts, Midwest Bus. Adminstrn. Assn. (pres. 1973-74), Fin. Execs. Inst. (dir. 1975-76), Lincoln C. of C. Office: Morningside Coll 1501 Morningside Ave Sioux City IA 51106-1717*

TOMMEY, CHARLES ELDON, retired surgeon; b. Nashville, Ark., Jan. 13, 1922; s. William Robert and America Anna (Compton) T.; m. Clara Blair Newman, Aug. 28, 1948; children: Robert, Jean, Phillip, Dale, Scott. Student, Henderson State Tchrs. Coll., 1940-42; BSM, U. Ark. Sch. Medicine, 1944, MD, 1945. Diplomate Am. Bd. Surgery. Intern City Hosp., Columbus, Ga., 1945-46; surg. resident Bapt. Hosp., Little Rock, 1948-49, VA Hosp., Cleve., 1950-54; pvt. practice surgery El Dorado, Ark., 1954-95; ret., 1995; asst. clin. instr. surgery U. Ark. Coll. Medicine. Capt. U.S. Army Med. Corps, 1943-45, 46-48. Fellow ACS. Baptist. Avocations: golf, photography. Home: 123 Glenridge Pky El Dorado AR 71730-3117

TOMOEDA, CHERYL KUNIKO, academic researcher; b. Honolulu, Sept. 24, 1958; d. Charles Kunio and Doris Masue (Takehara) T. BS, U. Hawaii, 1980; MS, U. Ariz., 1982. Cert. speech-lang. pathology. Speech pathologist Amphitheater Pub. Schs., Tucson, 1983-84; rsch. asst. U. Ariz., Tucson, 1982-83, rsch. asst. II, 1984-86, rsch. coord., 1985-91, sr. rsch. specialist, 1991—. Author: (test) Ariz. Battery for Comm. Disorders of Dementia, 1991, The Functional Linguistic Communication Inventory, 1994, (book) The ABC/s of Dementia, 1993; prodr. videoconf. series Telerounds. Mem. Acad. Neurologic Communication Disorders and Scis. (acting sec. 1991, sec. 1992-93), Internat. Neuropsychol. Soc., Am. Speech-Lang.-Hearing Assn. Office: U Ariz Nat Ctr Neurogenic Comm Disorders Dept Speech & Hearing Scis Tucson AZ 85721

TOMOMATSU, HIDEO, chemist; b. Tokyo, June 8, 1929; came to U.S., 1959; s. Shinsai Nasu and Suma (Sugawara) T.; m. Yuko Ito, Nov. 12, 1967; 1 child, Tadao. BSChemE., Waseda U., 1952; MS in Chemistry, U. of the Pacific, 1960; PhD in Chemistry, Ohio State U., 1964. Registered profl. engr., Tex., U.S. patent agt. Chem. Hodogaya Chem. Co., Tokyo, 1952-59, Texaco Chems. Co., Austin, Tex., 1964-72; Quaker fellow Quaker Oats Co., Barrington, Ill., 1972-96; cons. Physiol. Functional Food Resources, Escondido, Calif., 1995—. Contbr. articles to profl. jours.; patentee in field. Mem. Am. Chem. Soc., Am. Assn. Cereal Chemists, Inst. Food Technologists. Home: 2555 Seascape Glen Escondido CA 92026

TOMOVIC, MILETA MILOS, mechanical engineer, educator; b. Belgrade, Yugoslavia, Dec. 29, 1955; came to U.S., 1979; naturalized, 1995; s. Milos Nedeljko and Danica Dane (Lemaic) T.; m. Cynthia Lou Bell, Apr. 15, 1994; children: Milos, Senja. BS, U. Belgrade, 1979; MS, MIT, 1981; PhD, U. Mich., 1991. Rsch. asst. MIT, Cambridge, Mass., 1979-81, 83-85; design engr. Foundry Belgrade, 1982-83; sys. engr. Energoprojekt, Belgrade, 1985-86; pres. Canyus, Inc., Que., Can., 1988—; assoc. prof. Purdue U., West Lafayette, Ind., 1991—; cons. Tech. Assistance Program, 1993—. Assoc. editor Foundry, 1995, also conf. procs. in field. Grantee Purdue Rsch. Found., 1994, 95; named Key prof. Foundry Edn. Found., 1991-97. Mem. ASME (chpt. bd. dirs. 1993-95), Am. Soc. Metals (chpt. chmn. 1994-95), Am. Soc. Engring. Educators, Am. Foundrymen Soc. (chpt. bd. dirs. 1995—). Christian Orthodox. Achievements include patents in areas of metalcasting refiner plates for pulp and paper industry, mill balls for cement and metal extraction industry; research on wear and impact resistant materials, new metalcasting technologies. Avocations: tennis, skiing, swimming. Home: 123 Pawnee Dr West Lafayette IN 47906-2167 Office: Purdue U MET Dept Knoy Hall West Lafayette IN 47907

TOMPKINS, CURTIS JOHNSTON, university president; b. Roanoke, Va., July 14, 1942; s. Joseph Buford and Rebecca (Johnston) T.; m. Mary Katherine Hasle, Sept. 5, 1964; children: Robert, Joseph, Rebecca. BS, Va. Poly. Inst., 1965, MS, 1967; PhD, Ga. Inst. Tech., 1971. Indsl. engr. E.I. DuPont de Nemours, Richmond, Va., 1965-67; instr. Sch. Indsl. and Systems Engring., Ga. Inst. Tech., Atlanta, 1968-71; assoc. prof. Colgate Darden Grad. Sch. Bus. Adminstrn., U. Va., Charlottesville, 1971-77; prof., chmn. dept. indsl. engring. W.Va. U., Morgantown, 1977-80, dean Coll. Engring., 1980-91; pres. Mich. Technol. U., Houghton, 1991—; mem. engring. accreditation commn. Accreditation Bd. for Engring. and Tech., 1981-86; mem. Commn. on Engring. Edn., Nat. Assn. State Univs. and Land Grant Colls., 1985-90; cons. corps., govt. agys., ednl. instns.; lectr. various univs.; mem. exec. bd. Engring. Deans Coun., 1985-89, vice chmn., 1987-89; mem. engring. adv. com., chmn. of planning com. NSF, 1988-91, chm. Mich. Univs. pres. coun., 1996-98; bd. dirs. Oak Ridge Assoc. Univs., 1996—, Pres. Coun. Assn. Governing bds. 1996—, Gov's. Workforce Commn.; mem. com. of 100 Coll. Engring., Va. Tech.; mem. engring. adv. bd. U. Cin., 1996—. Author: (with L.E. Grayson) Management of Public Sector and Nonprofit Organizations, 1983, (with others) Maynard's Industrial Engineering Handbook, 1992; contbr. chpt. to Ency. of Profl. Mgmt, 1978, 83. Co-chmn. W.Va. Gov.'s Coun. on Econ. Devel.; bd. dirs. Pub. Land Corp. W.Va., 1980-89; mem. faculty Nat. Acad. Voluntarism, United Way Am., 1976-91; mem. Morgantown Water Commn., 1981-87, Morgantown Utility Bd., 1987-91; mem. steering com. W.Va. Conf. on Environ., 1985-89; chmn. Monogalia County United Way, 1989-90; mem. Mich. Govs. Workforce Commn., 1996—; campaign chmn. Copper Country United Way, 1995-96; mem., bd. dirs. Oak Ridge Associated Univs., 1996—. Fellow Inst. Indsl. Engrs. (life mem., sr. v.p. publs. 1983-85, v.p. edn. and rsch. 1985-87, trustee 1983-90, pres.-elect 1987-88, pres. 1988-89), Am. Soc. Engring. Edn. (chmn. indsl. engring. div. 1981-82, v.p. pub. affairs 1985-87, bd. dirs. 1985-87, 1st v.p., exec. com., fin. com. 1986-87, pres.-elect 1989-90, pres. 1990-91); mem. Am. Assn. Engring. Soc. (bd. govs. 1987-90, exec. com. 1987-90, sec.-treas. 1989-90), Jr. Engring. Tech. Soc. (bd. dirs. 1988-91), Nat. Soc. for Sci., Tech. and Society (bd. dirs. 1991-94), Internat. Hall of Fame of Sci. and Engring. (hon. trustee), Ga. Tech. Coll. Engring. Disting. Alumni Acad. (hon.), Ga. Tech. Sch. Indsl. and Sys. Engring. Disting. Alumni Acad. (hon.), W.Va. U. Dept. Indsl. Engring. Disting. Alumni Acad. (hon.), Blue Key (hon.), Sigma Xi, Phi Kappa Phi, Tau Beta Pi, Alpha Pi Mu. Methodist. Home: 2 Woodland Rd Houghton MI 49931-9746 Office: Mich Technol U 1400 Townsend Dr Houghton MI 49931-1200

TOMPKINS, JAMES RICHARD, special education educator; b. Camden, N.J., Jan. 17, 1935; s. Leo Joseph and Cecelia Nichols; children: Tim, Mark. BA cum laude, Mt. St. Mary's Coll., 1959; postgrad., U. Mich., 1960; MA, Niagara U., 1961; PhD, Cath. U., 1971. Coord. unit on edn. of emotionally disturbed Bur. Edn. Handicapped-USOE, Washington, 1966-71; asst. prof. U. N.C., Chapel Hill, 1971-72; exec. dir. N.C. Govs. Advocacy Commn., Raleigh, 1972-74; prof. spl. edn. Appalachian State U., Boone, N.C., 1974—; cons. edn. of disturbed children N.C. Dept. Human Resources. Contbr. articles to profl. jours. Mem. Coun. Exceptional Children, Coun. Children with Behavior Disorders, Coun. Career Devel., Give Youth a Chance Inc., Arts and Humanities for the Handicapped, N.C. Tchr. Preparation Programs for Emotionally Disturbed Children. Home: 117 Meadowbrook Ln Deep Gap NC 28618-9713

TOMPKINS, JOSEPH BUFORD, JR., lawyer; b. Roanoke, Va., Apr. 4, 1950; s. Joseph Buford and Rebecca Louise (Johnston) T.; m. Nancy Powell Wilson, Feb. 6, 1993; children: Edward Graves, Claiborne Forbes; 1 stepchild, Clayton Tate Wilson. BA in Politics summa cum laude, Washington and Lee U., 1971; M.P.P. in Pub. Policy, Harvard U., 1975, JD, 1975. Bar: Va. 1975, U.S. Dist. Ct. D.C. 1982, U.S. Ct. Appeals (D.C. cir.) 1976, U.S. Ct. Appeals (5th cir.) 1977, U.S. Ct. Appeals (11th cir.) 1982, U.S. Ct. Appeals (3d cir.) 1983, U.S. Ct. Appeals (6th cir.) 1985, U.S. Ct. Appeals (7th cir.) 1991, U.S. Ct. Appeals (4th cir.) 1993, U.S. Supreme Ct. 1977. Assoc. Sidley & Austin, Washington, 1975-79, ptnr., 1982—; assoc. dir. Office of Policy and Mgmt. Analysis, criminal div. U.S. Dept Justice, Washington, 1979-80, dep. chief fraud sect. criminal div., 1980-82. Contbr. articles to legal publs. Mem. Va. Bd. of Health Professions, Richmond, Va., 1984-92, vice chmn., 1984-86, chmn., 1986-88, 90-91. Recipient Spl. Commendation, U.S. Dept. Justice, 1981. Mem. ABA (criminal justice sect., mem. white collar crime com., 1980—, chmn. task force on computer crime 1982-92), Va.

Bar Assn., D.C. Bar Assn., Fed. Bar Assn., Phi Beta Kappa. Democrat. Methodist. Home: 8146 Wellington Rd Alexandria VA 22308-1214 Office: Sidley & Austin 1722 I St NW Washington DC 20006-3705

TOMPKINS, RAYMOND EDGAR, lawyer; b. Oklahoma City, July 13, 1934; s. Charles Edgar and Eva Mae (Hodges) T.; m. Sue Anne Sharpe, June 10, 1963; children: Matthew Stephen, Christopher T., Katherine Anne. BS, Okla. State U., 1956; JD, U. Okla., 1963. Bar: Okla. 1963, U.S. Dist. Ct. (no. dist.) Okla. 1963, U.S. Dist. Ct. (we. dist.) Okla. 1964, U.S. Ct. Appeals (10th cir.) 1965, U.S. Supreme Ct. 1968, U.S. Dist. Ct. (ea. dist.) Okla. 1969, U.S. Ct. Appeals (9th cir.) 1981, U.S. Ct. Appeals (4th cir.) 1986. Adminstrv. asst. U.S. Congress, 1966-68; ptnr. Linn & Helms, Oklahoma City, 1980-90, Daugherty, Bradford, Haught & Tompkins, P.C., Oklahoma City, 1990-94; shareholder Conner & Winters, P.C., Oklahoma City, 1994—. Past chmn. bd. trustees Okla. Ann. Methodist Conf.; past chmn. Okla. Bur. Investigation Commn.; past gen. counsel Rep. State Com., Interstate Oil Compact. Maj. USAR. Recipient award of Honor Oklahoma City Bi-Centennial Commn., 1976. Master Am. Inns of Ct.; mem. ABA, Okla. County Bar Assn. (Pres.'s award 1988), Okla. Bar Assn. (chmn. bench & bar com. 1995—, Law Day award), Am. Judicature Soc., Assn. Atty.-Mediators (panel mem.), Blue Key, Lions (pres. Oklahoma City chpt.). Home: 329 NW 40th St Oklahoma City OK 73118-8419 Office: 211 N Robinson Ave Ste 1700 Oklahoma City OK 73102-7101

TOMPKINS, ROBERT GEORGE, physician; b. Portland, Oreg., May 29, 1923; s. George Henry and Minnie (Davies) T.; m. Rosemarie Nowicki, June 6, 1948 (dec. 1960); children: Timothy Michael, Mary Eileen, George Henry, Robert George. B.S., U. Wash., 1943; M.B., Northwestern U., 1947; M.D., 1949; M.S., U. Minn., 1954. Diplomate Am. Bd. Internal Medicine. Intern King County Hosp., Seattle, 1948-49; resident King County Hosp., 1949-50; fellow, 1st asst. Mayo Found., Rochester, Minn., 1950-54; practice medicine specializing in cardiology and internal medicine Tulsa, 1954—; mem. staff St. Francis Hosp., chief staff, 1964, med. dir., 1968-86; clin. prof. medicine Tulsa Med. Coll. and U. Okla. Med. Coll.; v.p., med. dir. Wiliam K. Warren Med. Rsch. Inst., med. chmn. Guatemala Mission Hosp., Diocese Oklahoma City and Tulsa; coord. planning program Okla. Regional Med. Program; mem. Tulsa Health and Hosp. Planning Coun.; bd. dirs. Okla. Ctr. Molecular Medicine; med. dir. Laureate Hosp. Rsch. Inst.; pres. Tulsa Med. Edn. Found., 1980-82; bd. dirs. Laureate Psychiatric Clinic and Hosp.; founding mem. bd. dirs. Am. Bank and Trust, Tulsa. Contbr. articles to profl. jours; editor: Jour. Okla. State Med. Assn, 1974-86. Pres. Oklahoma Cath. Health Conf., 1981-82; bd. dirs. St. Francis Hosp., Tulsa; mem. ctrs. of excellence com. Okla. Ctrs. for Sci. and Tech., 1989—; mem. adf. bd. dept. psychology U. Tulsa, 1992—. Decorated Knight of the Grand Cross (Equestrian Order Holy Sepulchre of Jerusalem, Knight (Sovereign Mil. Order of Malta); recipient Dean's award U. Okla., 1991, diploma of Merit and Honor, Municipality of Santiago, Atitlan, Guatemala. Fellow ACP, Royal Coll. Medicine, Am. Coll. Cardiology; mem. AAAS, AMA, Am. Diabetic Assn., Am. Acad. Med. Dirs. (bd. dirs.), Am. Heart Assn., Nat. Fedn. Cath. Physicians Guilds (bd. dirs.), Tulsa County Heart Assn. (pres. 1959), Am. Rheumatism Assn., So. Hist. Assn., Mayo Alumni Assn., KC, Alpha Kappa Kappa. Home: 6551 S Darlington Ave Tulsa OK 74136-2002 Office: 6465 S Yale Ave Tulsa OK 74136-7822

TOMPKINS, RONALD K., surgeon; b. Malta, Ohio, Oct. 14, 1934; s. Kenneth Steidley and Mildred Lillian (Loomis) T.; m. Suzanne Colbert, June 9, 1956; children—Gregory Alan, Teresa Susan, Geoffrey Stuart. B.A., Ohio U., 1956; M.D., Johns Hopkins U., 1960; M.S., Ohio State U., 1968; DSc (hon.), U. Bordeaux, 1995. Diplomate: Am. Bd. Surgery. Intern in surgery Ohio State U., 1960-61, resident in surgery, 1964-68, adminstrv. chief resident in surgery, 1968-69, NIH trainee in acad. surgery, instr. physiol. chemistry, 1966-69; asst. prof. surgery UCLA, 1969-73, assoc. prof., 1973-79, prof., 1979—, chmn. basic surg. tng. program, 1970-79, asst. dean student affairs, 1979-82, chief div. gen. surgery, 1982-88, chief gastrointestinal surgery, 1986-97, assoc. dean, 1988-91; cons. VA Hosps. Editor-in-chief World Jour. Surgery, 1993—. Served with M.C. USAF, 1961-64. NIH grantee, 1968-70; John A. Hartford Found. grantee, 1970-79; Royal Soc. Medicine Eng. travelling fellow, 1976-77. Fellow ACS; mem. Am. Surg. Assn., Am. Gastroenterol. Assn., Am. Fedn. Clin. Rsch. Am. Inst. Nutrition, AMA, Assn. Acad. Surgery, Pacific Coast Surg. Assn. (recorder 1986-91, pres. 1995), Soc. Clin. Surgery, Soc. Surgery Alimentary Tract (sec. 1982-85, pres.-elect 1985, pres. 1986, chmn. bd. trustees 1987), Soc. Univ. Surgeons, Societe Internationale de Chirurgie (U.S. chpt. sec. 1990-94, pres. 1996—), Internat. Biliary Assn. (pres. 1979-81), Bay Surg. Soc., L.A. Surg. Soc. (pres. 1981), ACS (So. Calif. chpt. pres. 1987), Robert M. Zollinger/Ohio State U. Surg. Soc. (pres. 1988-90), Longmire Surg. Soc. (pres. 1997—), Phi Beta Kappa, Sigma Xi, Alpha Omega Alpha, Delta Tau Delta. Republican. Research, numerous publs. in gastrointestinal surgery and gastrointestinal metabolism and biochemistry. Office: Dept of Surgery University of California Los Angeles CA 90024

TOMPKINS, TAIN PENDLETON, foreign service official; b. Phila., Apr. 2, 1943; s. Pendleton Souther and Louise Agnes (Mertz) T.; m. Grace Muller, Feb. 26, 1981; children: Ann Louise, Heather Ashley Muller. BA in English, Washington & Lee U., 1964; MA in Internat. Rels., Johns Hopkins U., 1968, MA in English, 1970. Commd. Fgn. Svc., 1969; 3d sec. Am. Consulate, Can Tho, South Vietnam, 1970-71, Am. Embassy, Lisbon, Portugal, 1972-74; ceasefire observer Am. Consulate, Can Tho, South Vietnam, 1974; staff asst. U.S. Dept. State, Washington, 1974-75; fellow Inst. Politics Harvard U., Cambridge, Mass., 1976; 2d sec. Am. Embassy, Beirut, Lebanon, 1977-80; staff asst. Office of Les Aspin, Washington, 1980-81; dep. dir. staff secretariat U.S. Dept. State, 1981-83; 2d sec. Am. Embassy, Harare, Zimbabwe, 1983-85; 1st sec. Am. Embassy, Canberra, Australia, 1987-91; dep. chief of mission Am. Embassy, Bridgetown, Barbados, 1992-95; coun. Econ. Affairs Am. Embassy, Tel Aviv, Israel, 1995—; diplomat in residence U. Tex., Austin, 1991-92. Co-editor: The Challenge of NAFTA, 1992. Mem. Army and Navy Club, Phi Beta Kappa Assoc. Episcopalian. Avocations: tennis, reading. Office: Am Embassy Psc 98 Box 100 APO AE 09830-0002

TOMPSON, MARIAN LEONARD, professional society administrator; b. Chgo., Dec. 5, 1929; d. Charles Clark and Marie Christine (Bernardini) Leonard; m. Clement R. Tompson, May 7, 1949 (dec. 1981); children: Melanie Tompson Kandler, Deborah Tompson Mikolajczak, Allison Tompson Fagerholm, Laurel Tompson Davies, Sheila Tompson Dorsey, Brian, Philip. Student public and parochial schs., Chgo. and Franklin Park, Ill. Co-founder La Leche League (Internat.), Franklin Park, 1956; pres. La Leche League (Internat.), 1956-80, dir., 1956—, pres. emeritus, 1990—; exec. dir. Alternative Birth Crisis Coalition, 1981-85; cons. WHO; bd. dirs. North Am. Soc. Psychosomatic Ob-Gyn, Natural Birth and Natural Parenting, 1981-83; mem. adv. bd. Nat. Assn. Parents and Profls. for Safe Alternatives in Childbirth, Am. Acad. Husband-Coached Childbirth; mem. adv. bd. Fellowship of Christian Midwives; mem. profl. adv. bd. Home Oriented Maternity Experience; guest lectr. Harvard U. Med. Sch., UCLA Sch. Public Health, U. Antioquia Med. Sch., Medellín, Columbia, U. Ill. Sch. Medicine, Chgo., U. W.I., Jamaica, U. N.C., Nat. Coll. of Chiropractic, Am. Coll. Nurse Midwives, U. Parma, Italy, Inst. Psychology, Rome, Rockford (Ill.) Sch. Medicine, Northwestern U. Sch. Medicine; mem. family com. Ill. Commn. on Status of Women, 1976-85; mem. perinatal adv. com. Ill. Dept. Pub. Health, 1980-83; mem. adv. bd. Internat. Nutrition Communication Service, 1980—; bd. cons. We Can, 1984—; exec. adv. bd. United Resources for Family Health and Support, 1985-86. Author: (with others) Safe Alternatives in Childbirth, 1976, 21st Century Obstetrics Now!, 1977, The Womanly Art of Breastfeeding, 3d edit., 1981, Five Standards for Safe Childbearing, 1981, But Doctor, About That Shot..., 1988, Breast Feeding, 5th edit., 1991; author prefaces and forwards in 10 books; columnist La Leche League News, 1958-80; columnist People's Doctor Newsletter, 1977-88, mem. adv. bd., cons., 1988-92; assoc. editor Child and Family Quar., 1967—; mem. med. adv. bd. East West Jour., 1980—; also articles. Recipient Gold medal of honor Centro de Rehabilitacao Nossa Senhora da Gloria, 1975, Night of 100 Stars III Achiever award Actors Fund Am., 1990. Mem. Nat. Assn. Postpartum Care Svcs. (adv. bd.), Chgo. Cmty. Midwives (adv. bd.), World Alliance for Breast Feeding Action (mem. internat. adv. coun. 1997). Office: 1400 N Meacham Rd Schaumburg IL 60173-4808

TOMSICH, ROBERT J., heavy machinery manufacturing executive. Chmn. Blaw Knox Corp., Pitts.; pres., chmn. Nesco, Inc., Cleve. Office: Nesco 6140 Parkland Blvd Cleveland OH 44124*

TONAY, VERONICA KATHERINE, psychology educator; b. LaJolla, Calif., Mar. 28, 1960. BA with honors, U. Calif., Santa Cruz, 1985; MA, U. Calif., Berkeley, 1988, PhD, 1993. Lic. clin. psychologist. Teaching asst. U. Calif.-Berkeley, U. Calif.-Santa Cruz, 1985-88; psychology intern Family Svcs. Assn., Santa Cruz, 1989-90; lectr. psychology U. Calif., Santa Cruz, 1989—, Berkeley, 1992-94; psychology intern Santa Cruz County Children's Mental Health, 1994-95, registered Psychological asst., 1995—; dir. Psychology Field Study Program U. Calif., Santa Cruz, 1994—; counselor, rschr., Santa Cruz. Author: The Creative Dreamer, 1995, The Creative Dreamer's Journal and Workbook, 1997, (video) Subconscious Journeys, 1997. Fellow State of Calif., 1985-89. Mem. APA (program chmn. div. 32 1989-90), Assn. for Study of Dreams (conf. organizer 1987-88, 91-92). Avocations: writing, painting, gardening. Office: U Calif Psychology Dept Santa Cruz CA 95064

TONDEL, LAWRENCE CHAPMAN, lawyer; b. N.Y.C., Apr. 9, 1946; s. Lyman Mark and Jean (Basch) T.; m. Sharyn A. Smith, Aug. 3, 1974; children: Michael Lawrence, Kathryn Chapman. Student, The Lawrenceville Sch., 1964; AB, Wesleyan U., 1968; JD, U. Mich., 1971. N.Y. 1972. Assoc. Brown & Wood, N.Y.C., 1971-79, ptnr., 1980-97, sr. ptnr., 1997—; chmn. Internat. Bus. Comm. Ann. Internat. Forum on Offshore Funds, 1993-97. Trustee Elisabeth Morrow Sch., Englewood, N.J., 1988-93. Mem. ABA, Am. Law Inst., Am. Bar Found., Assn. Bar City N.Y. Republican. Episcopalian. Office: Brown & Wood 1 World Trade Ctr New York NY 10048-0202

TONDEUR, PHILIPPE MAURICE, mathematician, educator; b. Zurich, Switzerland, Dec. 7, 1932; came to U.S., 1964, naturalized, 1974; s. Jean and Simone (Lapaire) T.; m. Claire-Lise Ballansat, Dec. 20, 1965. Ph.D., U. Zurich, 1961. Rsch. fellow U. Paris, 1961-63; lectr. math. U. Zurich, 1963-64, U. Buenos Aires, 1964, Harvard U., Cambridge, Mass., 1964-65, U. Calif., Berkeley, 1965-66; asso. prof. Wesleyan U., Middletown, Conn., 1966-68, U. Ill., Urbana, 1968-70; prof. U. Ill., 1970—; chair, Dept. of Mathematics, U. Ill., 1996—; vis. prof. Auckland U., 1968, Eidg. Techn. Hochschule U. Heidelberg, 1973, U. Zurich, 1982, U. Rome, 1984, Ecole Polytechnique, Paris, 1987, U. Santiago de Compostela, 1987, Max Planck Inst., 1987, U. Leuven, Belgium, 1990, Keio U., Yokohama, Japan, 1993; assoc. mem. Ctr. Advanced Study U. Ill., 1977-78, 91-92. Contbr. articles to profl. jours. Recipient fellowships Swiss Nat. Sci. Found., fellowships Harvard U., fellowships U. Ill. Mem. Am. Math. Soc., Schweiz Math. Gesellschaft, Société Math. de France. Office: Math Dept U Ill Urbana IL 61801

TONE, PHILIP WILLIS, lawyer, former federal judge; b. Chgo., Apr. 9, 1923; s. Elmer James and Frances (Willis) T.; m. Gretchen Altfillisch, Mar. 10, 1945; children: Michael P., Jeffrey R., Susan A. BA, U. Iowa, 1943, JD, 1948. Bar: Iowa 1948, Ill. 1950, D.C. 1950. Law clk. Justice Wiley B. Rutledge, Supreme Ct. U.S., Washington, 1948-49; assoc. firm Covington & Burling, Washington, 1949-50; assoc., ptnr. firm Jenner & Block, Chgo., 1950-72, 80—; judge U.S. Dist. Ct., Chgo., 1972-74, U.S. Ct. Appeals (7th cir.), Chgo., 1974-80; spl. counsel Nat. Commn. on Causes and Prevention of Violence, 1968-69, U.S. Senate subcom. to investigate individuals representing interests of fgn. govts., 1980; Chmn. Ill. Supreme Ct. Rules Com., 1968-71, sec., 1963-68; mem. Com. on Jud. Br. of Jud. Conf. of U.S., 1987-91; gen. counsel U.S. Golf Assn., 1988-92; mem. Fed. Jud. Fellows Commn., 1986-92; chmn. Fed. Jud. Ctr. Found. Contbr. articles to legal periodicals. With AUS, 1943-46. Grad. fellow Law Sch. Yale U., 1948. Fellow Am. Coll. Trial Lawyers (regent 1984-87, pres. 1988-89); mem. ABA, Am. Bar Found., Am. Law Inst., Ill. Bar Assn. (bd. govs. 1960-64), Chgo. Bar Assn. (bd. mgrs. 1966-69), Am. Judicature Soc., Law Club Chgo. (pres. 1979-80), Legal Club Chgo. Office: Jenner & Block One IBM Plz Chicago IL 60611

TONEGAWA, SUSUMU, biology educator; b. Nagoya, Japan, Sept. 5, 1939; came to U.S., 1963; s. Tsutomu and Miyoko (Masuko) T.; m. Mayumi Yoshinari, Sept. 28, 1985; children: Hidde, Hanna, Satto. BS, Kyoto U., Japan, 1963; PhD, U. Calif., San Diego, 1968. Rsch. asst. U. Calif., San Diego, 1963-64, teaching asst., 1964-68; mem. Basel (Switzerland) Inst. Immunology, 1971-81; prof. biology MIT, Cambridge, 1981—; investigator Howard Hughes Med. Inst., 1988—; dir. MIT Ctr. for Memory and Learning, 1994; professorship Amgen, Inc., 1994. Editorial bd. Jour. Molecular and Cellular Immunology. Decorated Order of Culture, Emperor of Japan; recipient Cloetta prize, 1978, Avery Landsteiner prize Gesselschaft für Immunologie, 1981, Louisa Gross Horwitz prize Columbia U., 1982, award Gardiner Found. Internat., Toronto, Ont., Can., 1983, Robert Koch Found. prize, Bonn., Fed. Republic Germany, 1986, co-recipient Albert Lasker Med. Rsch. award, 1987, Nobel prize in Physiology or Medicine, 1987; named Person with Cultural Merit Japanese Govt., 1983. Mem. NAS (fgn. assoc.), Am. Assn. Immunologists (hon.), Scandinavian Soc. Immunology (hon.). Office: MIT 77 Massachusetts Ave Cambridge MA 02139-4301*

TONELLO-STUART, ENRICA MARIA, political economist; b. Monza, Italy; d. Alessandro P. and Maddalena M. (Marangoni) Tonello; m. Albert E. Smith; m. Charles L. Stuart. BA in Internat. Affairs, Econs., U. Colo., 1961; MA, Claremont Grad. Sch., 1966, PhD, 1971. Sales mgr. Met. Life Ins. Co., 1974-79; pres., CEO, ETS R&D, Inc., Palos Verdes Peninsula, Calif., 1977—; dean internat. studies program Union U., L.A. and Tokyo; lectr. internat. affairs and mktg. UCLA Ext., Union U. Pub., editor Tomorrow Outline Jour., 1963—, The Monitor, 1988; pub. World Regionalism-An Ecological Analysis, 1971, A Proposal for the Reorganization of the United Nations, 1966, The Persuasion Technocracy, Its Forms, Techniques and Potentials, 1966, The Role of the Multitnationals in the Emerging Globalism, 1978; developed the theory of social ecology and econsociometry. Organizer 1st family assistance program Langley FB Tractical Air Command, 1956-58. Recipient vol. svc. award VA, 1956-58, ARC svc. award, 1950-58. Mem. Corp. Planners Assn. (treas. 1974-79), Investigative Reporters and Editors, World Future Soc. (pres. 1974-75), Asian Bus. League, Chinese Am. Assn. (life), Japan Am. Assn., L.A. World Trade Ctr., Palos Verdes C. of C. (legis. com.), L.A. Press Club (bd. dirs.), Zonta (chmn. internat. com. South Bay), Pi Sigma Alpha. Avocations: writing, collecting old books and maps, community service, travel.

TONER, MICHAEL F., journalist; b. LeMars, Iowa, Mar. 17, 1944; s. Francis F. and Mary Ann (Delaney) T.; m. Patricia L. Asleson, Aug. 28, 1966; children: Susan Michelle, Sharon Lynn. BA cum laude, U. Iowa, 1966; postgrad., U. Okla., Peru; MS cum laude, Northwestern U., 1967. Reporter UPI, Chgo., 1966-67; bur. chief Miami Herald, Key West, Fla., 1967-68, reporter, 1968-69, asst. city editor, 1970-72; sci./environ. writer Miami (Fla) Herald, 1973-84; sci. editor Atlanta Journal and Constitution, 1984-91, sci. writer, 1991—. Co-author: Florida by Paddle and Pack, 1979; contbr. articles to mags. Recipient Pulitzer Prize for explanatory journalism, 1993; Stanford U. profl. journalism fellow, 1973. Avocations: hiking, swimming, photography, stamp collecting, cooking. Office: Atlanta Journal and Constn 72 Marietta St NW Atlanta GA 30303-2804

TONER, WALTER JOSEPH, JR., transportation engineer, financial consultant; b. Rutherford, N.J., July 22, 1921; s. Walter Joseph Toner and Rhea Virginia Carell; m. Barbara Jean Francis, Sept. 11, 1943; children: Sherry Francis, Walter J. III. Student, Wesleyan U., 1938-39; BS in Engring., U.S. Naval Acad., 1942. Profl. engr. Engring. mgr. Bethlehem Steel Corp., Boston, 1946-75; nuclear cons. Stone & Webster, Boston, 1975-77; v.p. project devel. & mgmt. Sverdrup Corp., Boston, 1977-86; cons., v.p., T.Y. Lin Internat., Boston, 1986—; v.p. Performance Index, Inc., 1991—. Lt. USN, 1942-46. Fellow Soc. Am. Mil. Engrs. (nat. trustee, v.p. 1978-85, life); mem. ASCE (life), DAV (life), Am. Consulting Engrs. Coun., Am. Railway Engrs. Assn., Boston Soc. Civil Engrs. (life), Transp. Rsch. Bd., U.S. Naval Acad. Alumni Assn. (life, nat. trustee), U.S. Naval Inst. (life), Ret. Employees Benefits Coalition, Wardroom Club, Bass River Yacht Club (chair race com.), Wrinkle Point Beach Assn., Masons. Episcopalian. Office: Box 617 37 Garfield Ln West Dennis MA 02670-0617

TONEY, ANTHONY, artist; b. Gloversville, N.Y., June 28, 1913; s. Michael and Susan (Betor) T.; m. Edna Amadon Greenfield, apr. 8, 1947 (dec. Apr. 1993); children: Anita, Karen, Adele Susan. B.F.A., Syracuse U., 1934; M.A., Columbia Tchrs. Coll., 1952, Ed.D., 1955. Instr. art Stevenson Sch., N.Y.C., 1948-52, Hofstra Coll., Hempstead, N.Y., 1953-55, New Sch. Social Research, 1953-96, No. Westchester Ctr. for Arts, Mt. Kisco, N.Y., 1980—; vis. artist Brandeis U., spring 1973, 74. Executed mural Gloversville (N.Y.) High Schs., 1937, Bowne Hall, 1967, Brockway Cafeteria Syracuse U, 1971; one-man shows Wakefield Gallery, 1941, Santa Barbara Mus., 1942, Artists Gallery, 1948, A.C.A. Gallery, 1949, 51, 54, 55, 57, 59, 62, 64, 68, 70, 72, 75, 77, 79, 81, 83, 87, Syracuse Mus., Roswell Mus., Kansas City Art Inst., U. N.Mex., 1956, Berkshire Mus., 1957, 60, S.I. Mus., Rochester Inst. Tech., 1958, U. So. Ill., Tyringham (Mass.) Gallery, 1960, 61, 66, Katonah Gallery, 1982-83, Albany Inst. History and Art, Lenox (Mass.) Art Gallery, Cayuga Mus., Auburn, N.Y., 1959, Harbor Gallery, L.I., N.Y., 1965, Dutchess C.C. , Fordham Coll., 1967, Pace Coll., 1968, New Sch. for Social Rsch., 1970, 77, 83, St. Mary's Coll. Md., 1974, Bridge Gallery, White Plains, N.Y., 1975, Virginia Barrett Gallery, 1978, 80, 86, Amphora, La Jolla, Calif., 1979, Nardin Gallery, Crossriver, N.Y., 1986, Retrospective ACA Gallery, 1987, Rutgers U., 1987, Rose Mus., Brandeis U., 1987, No. Westchester Ctr. for the Arts, 1988, Juniper Gallery, Napa (Calif.) Art Ctr., 1991, Rasmussen Art Gallery, Angwin, Calif., 1991, Herbert Johnson, Cornell Mus., 1991, Notre Dame U., 1991, Tchrs. Coll.-Columbia U., N.Y.C., 1994 (Audubon Artists Annual prize 1994), others; exhibited many group shows including Syracuse Mus., Whitney Mus., U. Ill., U. Nebr., Carnegie Biennial, Pa. Acad., Nat. Acad., Walker Art Center, Nat. Inst. Arts and Letters, Am. Acad. Arts and Letters, Katonah Gallery, St. Lawrence U., Purchase Coll., Brandeis U., Westminster Coll., Rutgers U., Corcoran Biennial, Butler Inst. Am. Art, Youngstown, Ohio, 1979-80, Staatliche Galerie, Moritazburg Halle, Fed. Republic, Germany, 1990, Im Gemeente, J.K. Vanreekum-Museum Apeldoorn, Niederlande, 1991, Autier Gallery, Piermont, N.Y., 1992, Peel Gallery, Danbi, Vt., 1993, Nardin Galleries, Somers, N.Y., 1993-94, Triton Mus. Art, Santa Clara, Calif., 1994; works in permanent collections, U. Ill., Ind. Fine Arts Ctr., Ohio Wesleyan U., Wichita State U. Mus., U. Wyo. Mus. Art, Norton Gallery (Fla.), New Britain (Conn.) Mus., Whitney Mus., Tchrs. Coll. Columbia U., Nat. Acad., Chrysler Mus. at, Norfolk, Montgomery Community Coll., S.I. Mus., Berkshire Mus., Butler Inst. Am. Art, Hofstra Coll., No. Westchester Hosp. Ctr., Lenin Mus., USSR, Anti-War Show, Berlin, New Soc. Fine Arts, No. Westchester Ctr. for the Arts, Bklyn. Mus., Herbert Johnson, Notre Dame, Cornell U., Fordham U., Skidmore Coll., Bennington Coll., SUNY, Fleming Hall Mus. U. Vt., City Hall, Gloversville, N.Y., Katonah (N.Y.) Libr., New Eng. Ctr. Contemporary Art, Putnam Art Coun., The State Mus. N.J., Bklyn. Mus., also pvt. collections; freelance comml. artist, 1945-50; author: Creative Painting and Drawing, 1968, Painting and Drawing, 1978, Leonardo; also articles.; editor: 150 Masterpieces of Drawing, 1963; contbr. to The Tune of the Calliope, 1958, Family Creative Workshop, 1975, The Palette and the Flame, 1979, Funk and Wagnalls Ency., 1980, Political Affairs, 1985. Served as sgt. AUS, 1942-45. Served in Abraham Lincoln Brigade, Spain, 1938-39. Decorated D.F.C. with clusters, Air medal with clusters; recipient purchase prize U. Ill., 1950, 1st prize Artists Equity Assn., 1952, Emily Lowe award, 1955, Mickewiecz Art Competition 1st prize, 1956, Purchase prize S.I. Mus., 1957, Ranger purchase Nat. Acad., 1966, 76, Childe Hassam purchase prize Nat. Inst. Arts and Letters, 1967, 76, Mintz Meml. award, 1974, Benjamin Altman Figure prize Nat. Acad., 1975, 80, Eggers Sr. Alumni award Syracuse U., 1989, Disting. Alumnus award Tchrs. Coll., Columbia U., 1991, 3 1st prizes Putnam Arts Coun., 1994. Mem. NEA, Nat. Soc. Mural Painters (treas. 1973-74), Artists Equity Assn. (nat. dir. 1952-56, 71-72, sec. nat. bd. 1956-57, exec. bd. N.Y. chpt. 1960-62, 71-72), Audubon Artists (mem. bd. 1959, 75-78, Grumbacher award 1954, medal of honor Nat. Show 1967, 75, 87, Judy Brenne Meml. award 1981, Ann. Emily Lowe award 1983, Ralph Fabri award 1984, Ann. Robert Phillips Meml. award 1988, Len G. Everett Meml. award 1989, 91, Silver medal 1993, Stephen Hirsch Meml. award 1995), Nat. Acad. (mem. coun., asst. corr. sec. 1978—, membership com. 1988—), Coll. Art Assn., Kappa Delta Pi. Home: 7 Court Ln Fairfax CA 94930-1402 *I consider persistent struggle in the context of as much awareness of all possible factors of key importance. It is necessary to be as whole as possible in one's understanding of self, life, society and one's individual endeavor. One's goal must be the survival of life, the earth and solar system that makes it possible, and the solution of the problems that threaten human survival and perhaps all existence as we know it.*

TONG, ALEX WAIMING, immunologist; b. Hong Kong, Apr. 8, 1952; came to U.S., 1970; s. Robert S. and Agnes M. (Cheng) T.; m. Susan J. Radtke, May 23, 1980 (div. Mar. 1988); 1 child, Nicole L.; m. S. Quay Mercer, May 13, 1995. BA in Biology, U. Oreg., 1973; PhD in Microbiology and Immunology, Oreg. Health Scis. U., 1980. Undergrad. teaching asst. biology dept. U. Oreg., Eugene, 1972-73; rsch. asst. dept. microbiology and immunology Oreg. Health Scis. U., Portland, 1975-80, teaching asst. Sch. Medicine, 1977-78, rsch. assoc. dept. micrology and immunology, 1981-82; postdoctoral fellow Surg. Rsch. Lab. Portland VA Med. Ctr., 1980-82; rsch. assoc. in immunology Charles A. Sammons Cancer Ctr., Baylor U. Med. Ctr., Dallas, 1982-86; assoc. dir. immunology lab. Baylor U. Med. Ctr., Dallas, Tex., 1986—; asst. prof. Inst. Biomed. Studies, Baylor U., Waco, 1988-97, assoc. prof., 1997—; prin. investigator Nat. Cancer Inst., Bethesda, Md., 1994—; adj. faculty immunology grad. studies program U. Tex. Southwestern Med. Ctr., Dallas, 1982—. Contbr. articles to profl. jours. Tatar rsch. fellow Med. Rsch. Found. Oreg., Portland, 1981-83. Mem. Am. Assn. Immunologists, Am. Assn. Cancer Rsch., Am. Soc. Hematology, Clin. Immunology Soc., Japan Karate Assn. Dallas (dir.), Internat. Traditional Karate Fedn. (cert. coach 1990—, cert. referee 1988—), Am. Amateur Karate Fedn. (dir. S.W. region). Democrat. Avocations: traditional karate, alpine skiing, scuba diving. Office: Baylor U Med Ctr Cancer Immunology Rsch Lab 3500 Gaston Ave Dallas TX 75246-2017

TONG, HING, mathematician, educator; b. Canton, China, Feb. 16, 1922; s. Shen-Beu and Fung-Kam (Cheng) T.; m. Mary Josephine Powderly, Aug. 19, 1956; children—Christopher Hing, Mary Elizabeth, William Joseph, Jane Frances, James John. A.B., U. Pa., 1943; Ph.D., Columbia, 1947; M.A. (hon.), Wesleyan U., Middletown, Conn., 1961. NRC postdoctoral fellow Inst. Advanced Study, Princeton, 1947-48; lectr. Canton (China) U., 1949; Cutting travelling fellow Inst. Henri Poincare, Paris, France, 1950-51; asst. prof. Reed Coll., 1952-53; vis. asst. prof. Barnard Coll., 1953-54; mem. faculty Wesleyan U., 1954-67, prof. math., 1960-67, chmn. dept., 1962-64; prof. math. Fordham U., Bronx, N.Y., 1966—; chmn. dept. Fordham U., 1967-74; mem. U.S. subcom. World Orgn. Gen. Systems and Cybernetics. Contbr. profl. jours. Mem. Phi Beta Kappa, Sigma Xi. Home: 725 Cooper Ave Oradell NJ 07649-2334 Office: Math Dept Fordham U Bronx NY 10458

TONG, ROSEMARIE, medical humanities and philosophy educator, consultant and researcher; b. Chgo., July 19, 1947; d. Joseph John and Lillian (Nedued) Behensky; m. Paul Ki-King Tong, Aug. 15, 1971 (dec. Apr. 1988); children: Paul Shih-Mien Tong, John Joseph Tong; m. Jeremiah Putnam, Aug. 1, 1992. BA, Marygrove Coll., 1970; MA, Cath. U., 1971; PhD, Temple U., 1978; LLD (hon.), Marygrove Coll., 1987; LHD (hon.), SUNY, Oneonta, 1993. Asst. and assoc. prof. philosophy Williams Coll., Williamstown, Mass., 1978-88; vis. disting. prof. humanities Davidson (N.C.) Coll., 1988-89, Thatcher Prof. in med. humanities and philosophy, 1989—; Louise M. Olmstead vis. prof. philosophy and women's studies, Lafayette Coll., Easton, Pa., 1993—; manuscript reviewer Wadsworth Pub. Co., 1985-92; curriculum reviewer philosophy dept. Carlton and Bowdoin Colls., 1986; honors examiner Hobart and William Smith Colls., 1990; dissertation dir., adj. faculty The Union Inst., 1992-93; cons., awards judge, panelist, organizer and speaker in field; mem. numerous U. coms. Author: Women, Sex and the Law, 1984, Ethics in Policy Analysis, 1985, Feminist Thought: A Comprehensive Introduction, 1989, Feminist Philosophies: Problems, Theories, and Applications, 1991, Feminine and Feminist Ethics, 1993, (with Larry Kaplan) Controlling Our Reproductive Destiny, 1994, Feminist Philosophy: Essential Readings in Theory, Reinterpretation and Application, 1994, Feminist Bioethics, 1997; contbr. numerous articles to profl. jours.; mem. various editl. bds. Project reviewer Annenberg/CPB Project, Washington, 1986; policy writer dvsn. health svcs. rsch. and policy U. Minn., 1988, Frank Graham Porter Early Childhood Ctr., U. N.C. Chapel Hill, 1988; mem. Charlotte task force Congl. Task Force Health Care, Congressman Alex McMillan, 1991, standards and ethics com. Hospice N.C., 1991, resource and ethics coms. McMillan-Spratt Task Force Health Care Policy, 1992, pastoral care com. Carolinas Med. Ctr., 1990—, ethics com.

Presbyt. Hosp., 1990—, Cabarrus Hosp., 1991, Nat. Adv. Bd. Ethics in Reproduction, Washington, 1993; active Hastings Ctr. Project Undergrad. Values Edn., Briarcliff Manor, N.Y., 1993, N.C. Found. Humanities and Pub. Policy. Named Prof. of Yr., Carnegie Found. and Coun. Advancement and Support of Edn., 1986. Mem. Am. Cath. Philosophical Assn., Am. Philosophical Assn. (ad hoc com. computers, pub. and role of Am. Philosophical Assn. 1984, adv. com. to program com. 1986-88, nomination com. 1989-91, nat. com. on status of women 1989-93), Am. Legal Studies and Assn., Am. Soc. Pol. and Legal Philosophy, Am. Soc. Law and Medicine, Nat. Coun. Rsch. on Women, Nat. Women Studies Assn., Internat. Assn. Philosophy of Law and Social Philosophy, Assn. Practical and Profl. Ethics, Soc. Health and Human Values (faculty program chairperson 1991—), Society Christian Ethics, Soc. Women in Philosophy, Soc. Philosophy and Tech., Soc. Philosophy and Pub. Affairs, Soc. Study of Women Philosophers, Network Feminist Approaches to Bioethics, The Hastings Ctr., Triangle Bioethics Group, So. Soc. Philosophy and Psychology. Avocations: aerobics, boating, hiking. Home: 20501 Pointe Regatta Dr Davidson NC 28036-8951 Office: Davidson Coll PO Box 1719 Main St Davidson NC 28036

TONGES, MARY CRABTREE, patient care executive; b. Dixon, Ill.; d. John Charles and Marion Rita (Shields) Crabtree; m. James Alan Tonges, may 21, 1983; children: Christina Mary, James John. BSN, U. Iowa, 1973; MSN, U. Ill., Chgo., 1977; MBA, Baruch Coll., 1994, postgrad., 1997—. Cert. in nursing adminstrn. Asst. dir. med.-surg. nursing St. Joseph Hosp., Chgo., 1977-78; dir. specialty nursing Northwestern Meml. Hosp., Chgo., 1979-82; v.p. nursing Clara Maass Med. Ctr., Belleville, N.J., 1983-86, Robert Wood Johnson U. Hosp., New Brunswick, N.J., 1987-91; cons. Ctr. for Case Mgmt., Inc., South Natick, Mass., 1991—. Contbr. articles to profl. jours. Commonwealth Fund nurse exec. fellow, 1991. Mem. Am. Orgn. Nurse Execs. (Rsch. award 1996), Orgn. Nursing Execs. N.J., Sigma Theta Tau. Home: 8 Fairfield St Montclair NJ 07042-4114

TONGUE, PAUL GRAHAM, financial executive; b. Phila., Dec. 30, 1932; s. George Paul and Florence Amelia (Kogel) T.; m. Marjorie Joan Meyers, May 26, 1954; children: Suzanne Marjorie, Douglas Paul. BS in Commerce, Drexel U., 1957; MBA, NYU, 1965. With Chase Manhattan Bank, N.Y.C., 1957-87; chmn. Plus Systems Inc., Denver, 1985; pres. Eppley-Tongue Assocs., Inc., Towson, Md., 1988—; exec. v.p. Veritas Venture Inc., Scotch Plains, N.J., 1990-91; cons. Prime Care Sys., Inc., Newport News, Va., 1995—. Pres. Our Saviour Luth. Ch., Manhasset, N.Y., 1984; bd. dirs. Nassau Symphony Orch. With U.S. Army, 1954-55. Mem. Ford's Colony Country Club. Avocations: golf, classical music.

TONGUE, WILLIAM WALTER, economics and business consultant, educator emeritus; b. Worcester, Mass., May 24, 1915; s. Walter Ernest and Lena (Brown) T.; m. Beverly Harriet Cohan, Dec. 26, 1936; children—Barbara Tongue Duggan, Kathleen Tongue Alligood. A.B., Dartmouth, 1937, M.C.S., 1938; Ph.D., U. Chgo., 1947. Jr. acct. Price, Waterhouse & Co. (C.P.A.'s), N.Y.C., 1938; instr. Coe Coll., Cedar Rapids, Iowa, 1941-42; spl. cons. OSS, 1942; financial economist Fed. Res. Bank Chgo., 1942-44; economist Jewel Companies, Inc., Chgo., 1944-64; prof. econs. and finance U. Ill. Chgo. Circle, 1965-80; prof. emeritus, 1980—; econ. cons. LaSalle Nat. Bank, Chgo., 1968-91; mem. com. CNA Fin. Separate Fund B.; dir. St. Joseph Light & Power Co., Mo., 1965-86; trustee Signode Employees' Savings and Profit Sharing Trust Fund, 1980-89. Author articles; contbr.: to books including How We Can Halt Inflation and Still Keep Our Jobs, 1974. Bd. dirs., v.p. research and statistics Chgo. Assn. Commerce and Industry, 1968-69. Mem. Nat. Assn. Bus. Economists (pres. 1962-63), Conf. Bus. Economists, Am. Statis. Assn. (pres. Chgo. chpt. 1951-52), Econ. Club Chgo., Investment Analysts Assn. Chgo., Inst. Chartered Fin. Analysts (chartered fin. analyst 1963), Midwest Fin. Assn. (pres. 1972-73). Home and Office: 212 Shoreline Dr Park Ridge IL 60068-2934

TONJES, MARIAN JEANNETTE BENTON, education educator; b. Rockville Center, N.Y., Feb. 16, 1929; d. Millard Warren and Felicia E. (Tyler) Benton; m. Charles F. Tonjes (div. 1965); children: Jeffrey Charles, Kenneth Warren. BA, U. N.Mex., 1951, cert., 1966, MA, 1969; EdD, U. Miami, 1975. Dir. recreation Stuyvesant Town Housing Project, N.Y.C., 1951-53; tchr. music., phys. edn. Sunset Mesa Day Sch., Albuquerque, 1953-54; tchr. remedial reading Zia Elem. Sch., Albuquerque, 1965-67; tchr. secondary devel. reading Rio Grande High Sch., Albuquerque, 1967-69; rsch. asst. reading Southwestern Coop. Ednl. Lab., Albuquerque, 1969-71; assoc. dir., vis. instr. Fla. Ctr. Tchr. Tng. Materials U. Miami, 1971-72; asst. prof. U.S. Internat. U., San Diego, 1972-75; prof. edn. Western Wash. U., Bellingham, 1975-94, dir. summer study, 1979-94, prof. emerita, 1994—; dir. summer study at Oriel Coll. Oxford (Eng.) U.; reading supr. Manzanita Ctr. U. N.Mex., Albuquerque, 1968; vis. prof. adult edn. Palomar (Calif.) Jr. Coll., 1974; vis. prof. U. Guam, Mangilao, 1989-90; speaker, cons. in field; invited guest Russian Reading Assn., Moscow, 1992; part-time prof. U. N.Mex., Albuquerque, 1995—. Author: (with Miles V. Zintz) Teaching Reading/Thinking Study Skills in Content Classrooms, 3d edit., 1992, Secondary Reading, Writing and Learning, 1991; contbr. articles to profl. jours. Tng. Tchr. Trainers grantee, 1975; NDEA fellow Okla. State U., 1969. Mem. Am. Reading Forum (chmn. bd. dirs. 1983-85), Adult and Adolescent Literacy Confs. (spkr. 1991-94), Internat. Reading Assn. (mem. travel, interchange and study tours com. 1984-86, mem. non-print media and reading com. 1980-83, workshop dir. S.W. regional confs. 1982, mem. com. internat. devel. N.Am. 1991-96, Outstanding Tchr. Educator 1988-90), U.K. Reading Assn. (spkr. 1977-93), European Conf. in Reading (spkr. Berlin 1989, Edinburgh 1991, Malmo 1993, Budapest 1995), European Coun. Internat. Schs. (The Hague, spkr. 1993), World Congress in Reading Buenos Aires (spkr. 1994), PEO (past chpt. pres.), Phi Delta Kappa, Delta Delta Delta. Avocations: miniatures, tennis, bridge, art, travel.

TONKIN, HUMPHREY RICHARD, academic administrator; b. Truro, Cornwall, Eng., Dec. 2, 1939; came to U.S., 1962; s. George Leslie and Lorna Winifred (Sandry) T.; m. Sandra Julie Winberg, Mar. 9, 1968 (div. 1981); m. Jane Spencer Edwards, Oct. 1, 1983; 1 child, Sebastian George. BA, St. John's Coll., Cambridge, Eng., 1962, MA, 1966; AM, Harvard U., 1966, PhD, 1966. Asst. prof. English U. Pa., Phila., 1966-71, assoc. prof., 1971-80, prof., 1980-83, vice-provost undergrad. studies, 1971-75, coord. internat. programs, 1977-83, master Stouffer Coll. House, 1980-83; pres. State Univ. Coll., Potsdam, N.Y., 1983-88, U. Hartford, Conn., 1989—; vis. prof. English Columbia U., N.Y.C., 1980-81; exec. dir. Ctr. Rsch. and Documentation on World Lang. Problems, Rotterdam and Hartford, 1974—. N.Am. editor: Lang. Problems and Lang. Planning; author: (bibliography) Sir Walter Raleigh, 1971, Esperanto and International Language Problems, 4th edit., 1977, Spenser's Courteous Pastoral, 1972, (with Jane Edwards) The World in the Curriculum, 1981, The Faerie Queene, 1989, (with Allison Keef) Language in Religion, 1989, Esperanto: Language, Literature and Community, 1993; contbr. articles, studies, revs. to profl. jours. Pres. Pa. Coun. Internat. Edn., 1980-81; bd. dirs. World Affairs Coun. Phila., 1979-83, Am. Forum, 1985—, Zamenhof Found., 1987-94, Hartford Symphony Orch., 1989—, World Affairs Coun. Conn., 1989—, Greater Hartford Arts Coun., 1989—, Can.-U.S. Found. Ednl. Exchange, 1997—; chmn. Coun. Internat. Exch. Scholars, 1991-95, Esperantic Studies Found., 1991—, Partnership for Svc.-Learning, 1991-96. Recipient Lindback award for disting. teaching, 1970; Frank Knox fellow Harvard U., 1962-66; Guggenheim fellow, 1974. Fellow Acad. Esperanto; mem. Universal Esperanto Assn. (pres. 1974-80, 86-89, rep. to UN 1974-83, hon. com. 1995—), Spenser Soc. (pres. 1983-84, former dir.), Internat. Acad. Scis. San Marino, Conn. Acad. Arts and Scis., Hartford Club, Cosmos Club, Hartford Golf Club. Home: 85 Bloomfield Ave Hartford CT 06105-1007 Office: U Hartford Office of Pres 200 Bloomfield Ave Hartford CT 06117-1545

TONKIN, LEO SAMPSON, educational foundation administrator; b. Suffern, N.Y., Apr. 2, 1937; s. Leo S. and Ann (Petrone) T. A.B., Johns Hopkins, 1959; postgrad., Sch. Advanced Internat. Studies, 1962-63; J.D., Harvard, 1962; Dr. Pedagogy, St. Thomas Aquinas Coll., 1973. Legis. asst. to U.S. Congressman; then Sen. Charles McC. Mathias, Jr., of Md., 1962-63; asso. counsel U.S. Ho. of Reps. Select Com. on Govt. Research, 1964; spl. cons. Ho. Spl. Subcom. on Edn., 1965-66; exec. dir. D.C. Commrs. Council on Higher Edn., 1965-66; pres. Leo S. Tonkin Assos., Inc., 1966—; founder, dir., chmn. bd. Washington Workshops Found., 1967—; Mem. White House Conf. on Edn., 1965, White House Conf. on Youth, 1971; spl. asst. to chmn. U.S. Ho. of Reps. Select Com. on Crime, 1972; mem. bd. plebe sponsors U.S. Naval Acad., 1977—; v.p. London Fedn. Boys' Clubs, 1980—; mem. adv. panel Nat. Commn. for Protection of Human Subjects of Biomed. and Behavioral Research, HEW, 1976-77. Contbr. articles to mags. Bd. dirs. Washington Choral Arts Soc., 1971-73, Nat. Coordinating Council on Drug Edn., 1973, Nat. Student Ednl. Fund, 1974—; chmn. Wall Street Seminar Found., 1978—; chmn. bd. trustees St. Thomas Aquinas Coll., 1966-73, continuing trustee, 1973-78, trustee, chmn. emeritus, 1978—; chmn. bd. trustees City of Phila. Govt. Honors Program; trustee Southeastern U., 1966-73; asso. bd. trustees Immaculata Coll., 1966-73; mem. advisory bd. Pub. Affairs and Govt. Degree Program, Mt. Vernon Coll., 1971-74; bd. dirs. YMCA, Washington, 1969-71. Recipient Americanism award, Valley Forge Freedoms Found, 1973. Mem. Johns Hopkins Alumni Assn. of Washington (pres. 1969-72). Clubs: Georgetown (Washington), City Tavern (Washington), Nat. Press (Washington), Capitol Hill (Washington), Capitol Yacht (Washington); Harvard (N.Y.C.). Home: 4368 Sunset Ct Warrenton VA 20187 Office: 3222 N St NW Washington DC 20007-2849

TONKS, ROBERT STANLEY, pharmacology and therapeutics educator, former university dean; b. Aberystwyth, Wales; emigrated to Can., 1973; s. Robert Patrick Dennis and Prudence Violet (Williams) T.; m. Diana Mary Cownie; children: Pamela Mary, Julia Rosalind, Robert Michael, Sara Katharine. Student, U. Coll. of South Wales, Welsh Coll. Pharmacy; B.Pharm., Welsh Nat. Sch. Medicine, Cardiff, Ph.D. Organon postdoctoral fellow Med. Sch., Cardiff, Nat. Health Service postdoctoral fellow; Nat. Health Service sr. fellow Cardiff and Nevill Hall Hosp., Abergavenny; lectr. pharmacology U. Wales, Cardiff, 1958-72; vis. fellow Claude Bernard Research Assn., Faculté de Medicine, Paris, 1959; sr. lectr. pharmacology and therapeutics Med. Sch. and U. Wales Hosp., Cardiff, 1972-73; dir., prof. Coll. Pharmacy, Dalhousie U., Halifax, N.S., Can., 1973-77, dean Faculty of Health Professions, 1977-88, prof. geriatric pharmaco-therapeutics, 1988—, acting head divsn. geriatric medicine, 1991-94; cons. pharm. industry in U.K., Govt. of N.B., Can., Health and Welfare Dept. Can.; advisor health manpower Govt. of N.S.; coordinator N.E. Can./Am. Health Coun. co-chmn., 1974-91; emeritus chmn., mem. Health and Welfare Personnel Career Rev. Com., 1991—; pharm. scis. grants com. Med. Rsch. Council Can., chmn.; mem. rev. com. health protection br. fed. govt. div. pharm. chemistry, Can.; chmn. advisory com. N.B. Minister of Health; mem. joint com. on devel. rsch. in nursing Med. Rsch. Coun.-Nat. Health Rsch. Devel. Program; mem. nat. adv. panel on risk/benefit mgmt. of drugs.; adv. com. on restructuring Health Canada's Personnel Career Awards. Contbr. articles on pharmacology and pathology to profl. jours. Fellow Pharm. Soc. Gt. Britain, Inst. Biology; mem. Brit. Pharmacol. Soc., Internat. Soc. Thrombosis and Haemostasis, Canadian Soc. Clin. Investigation, Soc. Pharm. Medicine, Gerontol. Soc. Am., Am. Soc. Clin. Pharm. and Therapeutics, Can. Soc. Geriatric Medicine, Can. Assn. Population Therapeutics (bd. dirs.), Can. Soc. Hosp. Pharmacy (hon.), N.B. Pharm. Soc. (hon.), N.S. Pharm. Soc. (cert. of merit, coord. drug and med. supplies Ethiopia airlift), Med. Soc. N.S. (task force on pharmacare), Welsh Cultural Soc. (past pres.). Anglican. Mailing Address: 62 Kingsway Dr, Stillwater Lake, NS Canada B3Z 1G3 Office: Dalhousie U, Coburg Rd, Halifax, NS Canada

TONKYN, RICHARD GEORGE, retired oil and gas company executive, researcher, consultant; b. Portland, Oreg., Mar. 26, 1927; s. William James and Gladys (Campbell) T.; m. Carol Joan Sloan, May 29, 1948 (div. 1976); children: Michael Stephen, Paula Ruth, David William, John Campbell, James Lewis, Russell George; m. Barbara Ann Friedman, May 27, 1982. BA, Reed Coll., 1948; MA, U. Oreg., 1951; PhD, U. Wash., 1960. Registered patent agt., U.S. Patent and Trademark Office. Chemist Titanium Metals Corp., Henderson, Nev., 1952-54, Allegheny Ludlum Steel, Brackenridge, Pa., 1954-55; rsch. engr. Boeing Airplane Co., Seattle, 1955-59; chemist, project scientist Union Carbide Corp., Bound Brook, N.J., 1961-69; mgr. rsch., group leader Betz Labs., Inc., Trevose, Pa., 1969-76; v.p. rsch. and devel. Mogul div. The Dexter Corp., Chagrin Falls, Ohio, 1976-85, Petrolite Corp., St. Louis, 1985-92. Patentee in field. NSF fellow, 1959, 60-61. Mem. Am. Chem. Soc., Indsl. Rsch. Inst., Cooling Tower Inst. (bd. dirs. 1982-85, pres. 1985), Physical and Chem. Soc., Sigma Xi, Phi Lambda Upsilon. Avocations: tennis, golf.

TONN, ELVERNE MERYL, pediatric dentist, dental benefits consultant; b. Stockton, Calif., Dec. 10, 1929; s. Emanuel M. and Lorna Darlene (Bryant) T.; m. Ann G. Richardson, Oct. 28, 1951; children: James Edward, Susan Elaine Tonn Yee. AA, La Sierra U., Riverside, Calif., 1949; DDS, U. So. Calif., 1955; BS, Regents Coll., U. State N.Y., 1984. Lic. dentist; cert. tchr., Calif., dental ins. cons. Pediatric dentist, assoc. Walker Dental Group, Long Beach, Calif., 1957-59, Children's Dental Clinic, Sunnyvale, Calif., 1959-61; pediatric dentist in pvt. practice Mountain View, Calif., 1961-72; pediatric dentist, ptnr. Pediatric Dentistry Assocs., Los Altos, Calif., 1972-83; pediatric dentist, ptnr. Valley Oak Dental Group, Manteca, Calif., 1987—; from clin. instr. to assoc. prof. U. Pacific, San Francisco, 1964-84; assoc. prof. U. Calif., San Francisco, Calif., 1984-86; ; pediatric dental cons. Delta Dental Plan, San Francisco, 1985—; chief dental staff El Camino Hosp., Mountain View, 1964-65, 84-85; lectr. in field. Weekly columnist Manteca Bull., 1987-92; producer 2 teaching videos, 1986; contbr. articles to profl. jours. Lectr. to elem. students on dental health Manteca Unified Sch. Dist., 1982—; dental health screener Elem. Schs., San Joaquin County Pub. Health, 1989-92; dental cons. Interplast program Stanford U. Sch. Medicine. Capt. U.S. Army, 1955-57. Fellow Internat. Coll. Dentists, Am. Acad. Pediatric Dentistry, Am. Coll. Dentists, Royal Soc. Health (Eng.), Acad. of Dentistry for Handicapped, Pierre Fauchard Acad., Acad. Dental Materials; mem. ADA, Internat. Assn. Pediatric Dentistry, Internat. Assn. Dental Rsch., Fedn. Dentaire Internationale, Am. Soc. Dentistry for Children, Am. Assn. Dental Cons., Calif. Dental Assn., Calif. Soc. Dentistry for Children (pres. 1968), Calif. Soc. Pediatric Dentists, N.Y. Acad. Scis., Calif. Acad. Sci., Rotary Internat., Am. Bd. Quality Assurance and Utilization Rev. Physicians (diplomate, cert. dental benefits cons.), Nat. Assn. for Healthcare Quality. Republican. Avocations: photography, travel, history, medieval. Home: 374 Laurelwood Cir Manteca CA 95336-7122 Office: Valley Oak Dental Group Inc 1507 W Yosemite Ave Manteca CA 95337-5159

TONN, ROBERT JAMES, entomologist; b. Watertown, Wis., June 23, 1927; s. Harry James and Elise (Foogman) T.; m. Noemi C. Tonn; children: Sigrid M., Monica E. BS, Colo. State U., 1949, MS, 1950; MPH, Okla. Med. Sch., 1963; PhD, Okla. State U., 1959. Rsch. assoc La. State U., Costa Rica/New Orleans, 1961-63; dir. Taunton Field Sta., Taunton, Mass., 1963-65; chief PMO unit WHO, various locations, 1965-87; adj. prof. of parasitology U. Tex.-El Paso, 1988—; cons. USAID/VBC, 1987—. Contbr. numerous articles to profl. jours. Mem. Am. Soc. Tropical Medicine, Soc. Vector Ecology (pres. 1984), Am. Mosquito Control Assn., U.S./Mex. Border Health Assn., Royal Soc. Tropical Medicine and Hygiene, Masons. Congregationalist. Home: RR 3 Box 505 Park Rapids MN 56470-9363

TONN, SHERI JEANNE, chemistry educator, dean; b. Dallas, May 13, 1949; d. Harvey C. Bartel and Jeanne Marie (Siddall) Shelton; m. Jeffrey F. Tonn, Aug. 22, 1971. BS in Chemistry, Oreg. State U., 1971; PhD in Chemistry, Northwestern U., 1976; postgrad., U. Minn., 1976-79. Asst. prof. chemistry Pacific Luth. U., Tacoma, 1979-84, assoc. prof. chemistry, 1984-93, prof. chemistry, 1993—, dean natural sci., 1993—; mem. adv. com. Simpson Tacoma Kraft, 1993—. Co-founder, bd. dirs. Citizens for a Healthy Bay, 1991—, past pres.; bd. dirs. People for Puget Sound, Seattle, 1992—; mem. Puget Sound Water Quality Authority, Olympia, Wash., 1985-96; mem. adv. com. State of Wash. Environment 2010, Olympia, 1990-92; bd. trustees Associated Western Univs., Salt Lake City, 1995—, chair elect, 1996; faculty sponsor and state bd. MESA, Wash., 1993—. Eisenhower grantee, 1994, 95, NSF grantee, 1981, 90, 95, Murdock Charitable Trust grantee, 1995—. Mem. Am. Chem. Soc. (various local sect. offices 1971—), N.Y. Acad. Scis., Sigma Xi, Iota Sigma Pi. Avocations: canoeing, scuba diving, sailing. Home: 1201 Garfield St S Tacoma WA 98444-3817 Office: Pacific Luth U Dept Chemistry Tacoma WA 98447

TONNOS, ANTHONY, bishop; b. Port Colborne, Ont., Can., Aug. 1, 1935. Ordained priest Roman Cath. Ch., 1961. Bishop Archdiocese of Hamilton, Ont., Can., 1984—. Office: Roman Catholic Church-Canada, 700 King St W, Hamilton, ON Canada L8P 1C7

TONTZ, ROBERT L., government official; b. Guthrie, Okla., May 18, 1917; s. John and Mabel (Johnson) T.; m. Hazel D. Crothers, June 10, 1944; children: John W., Brenda Kay. BS, Okla. State U., 1940, PhD, 1952; MS, Iowa State U., 1941. Asst. agrl. economist U. Tenn., 1942; assoc. agrl. economist U.S. Dept. Agr., Washington, 1942-45, agrl. economist, 1956-68, supervisory agrl. economist, 1971-80; agrl. statistician U.S. Dept. Commerce, Washington, 1946; asst. prof. Okla. State U., 1947-55; internat. economist Dept. State, Paris, 1968-71; econ. cons. Nat. Assn. Fed. and State Employees, 1980—. Editor: Foreign Agricultural Trade: Selected Readings, 1966; contbr. numerous econ. studies to profl. jours.; sr. joint author: Memberships of General Farmers' Organizations, United States, 1965-89, 1991, U.S. Agricultural Organizations The Voices of Organized Agriculture, 1991, Historical Statistics of Memberships of General Farmers' Organizations United States, 1874-1991, 1992, Organized Agriculture in the United States, 1992. Elder, chmn. bd. dirs. Christian Ch., Falls Church, Va. Recipient Superior Svc. award U.S. Dept. Agr., 1965, 75, Blue Ribbon award, 1972. Mem. Nat. Orgn. Fed.-State Employees (pres. 1988-92), Sigma Xi, Phi Kappa Phi, Alpha Phi Sigma, Alpha Zeta, Phi Eta Sigma. Home: 8712 Braeburn Dr Annandale VA 22003-3970

TOOHEY, BRIAN FREDERICK, lawyer; b. Niagara Falls, N.Y., Dec. 14, 1944; s. Matthew Frederick and Marilyn Gertrude (Hoag) T.; m. Mary Elizabeth Monihan; children: Maureen Elizabeth, Matthew Sheridan, Margaret Monihan, Mary Catherine, Elizabeth Warner. BS, Niagara U., 1966; JD, Cornell U., 1969. Bar: N.Y. 1969, N.Mex. 1978, Ohio 1980. Ptnr. Cohen, Swados, Wright, Hanifin & Bradford, Buffalo, 1973-77; pvt. practice, Santa Fe, 1977-79; of counsel Jones, Day, Reavis & Pogue, Cleve., 1979-80, ptnr., 1981—. Mem. Citizens League Greater Cleve., 1982—. Lt. JAG Corps, USNR, 1970-73. Mem. ABA, N.Y. State Bar Assn., State Bar N.Mex., Ohio State Bar Assn., Greater Cleve. Bar Assn. Roman Catholic. Home: 25 Pepper Creek Dr Cleveland OH 44124-5279 Office: Jones Day Reavis & Pogue N Point 901 Lakeside Ave E Cleveland OH 44114-1116

TOOHEY, JAMES KEVIN, lawyer; b. Evanston, Ill., July 16, 1944; s. John Joseph and Ruth Regina (Cassidy) T.; m. Julie Marie Crane, Nov. 1, 1969 (div. Aug. 1977); children: Julie Colleen, Jeanne Christine; m. Anne Margaret Boettigheimer, May 28, 1983; children: James Robert, Kevin John, Casey Anne. BBA, U. Notre Dame, 1966; JD, Northwestern U., 1969. Bar: Ill. 1969, U.S. Dist. Ct. (no. dist.) Ill. 1971, U.S. Dist. Ct. (ctrl. dist.) Ill. 1991, U.S. Ct. Appeals (7th cir.) 1972, U.S. Ct. Appeals (8th cir.) 1975, U.S. Supreme Ct. 1988. Assoc. Taylor, Miller, Magner, Sprowl & Hutchings, Chgo., 1970-71, Ross, Hardies, O'Keefe, Babcock & Parsons, Chgo., 1974-77; asst. U.S. atty. Office U.S. Atty., Chgo., 1971-74; ptnr. Ross & Hardies, Chgo., 1978—. Bd. dirs., commr. Edgebrook Sauganash Athletic Assn., 1993-96. Mem. Ill. State Bar Assn., Soc. Trial Lawyers, Assn. Advancement of Automotive Medicine, Ill. Assn. Defense Attys., Trial Lawyers Club Chgo. Office: Ross & Hardies 150 N Michigan Ave Ste 2500 Chicago IL 60601-7524

TOOHEY, PHILIP S., lawyer; b. 1943. BA, Hamilton Coll., 1965; JD, Cornell U., 1968. Bar: N.Y. 1968. Law clk. Hon. Louis M. Greenblatt Appellate Divsn., 1968-69; assoc. Phillips, Lytle, Hitchcock, Blaine & Huber, 1969-74, ptnr., 1975-84; sr. bank counsel Marine Midland Banks, Inc., Buffalo, 1984-88, gen. counsel, 1988-91, gen. counsel, sec., 1991—. Mem. N.Y. State Bar Assn. (chmn. bus. law com. of banking, corp. & bus. law sect. 1985-88, sec. bus. law sect. 1988-89, vice chmn., treas. bus. law sect. 1989-90, 1st vice chmn. bus. law sect. 1990-91, chmn. bus. law sect. 1991-92). Office: Marine Midland Bank 1 Marine Midland Ctr Buffalo NY 14203-2842

TOOKER, CARL E., department store executive; b. Allegan, Mich., 1947. Grad., Ferris State Coll., 1970. Chmn. Filene's subs. May Dept. Stores, Boston; pres., CEO Stage Stores Inc., Houston. Office: Stage Stores Inc 10201 Main St Houston TX 77025-5229*

TOOKER, GARY LAMARR, electronics company executive; b. Shelby, Ohio, May 25, 1939; s. William Henry and Frances Ione (Melick) T.; m. Diane Rae Kreider, Aug. 4, 1962; children: Lisa, Michael. B.S.E.E., Ariz. State U., 1962. With Motorola Inc., Phoenix, 1962—, v.p., gen. mgr. internat. semicondr. div., 1980-81, v.p., gen. mgr. semicondr. products sector, 1981-82, sr. v.p., gen. mgr. semicondr. products sector, 1982-83; exec. v.p., gen. mgr. semicondr. products sector Motorola Inc., 1983-86; sr. exec. v.p., chief corp. staff officer Motorola Inc., Schaumburg, Ill., 1986-88, sr. exec. v.p., chief operating officer, 1988-90, pres., chief oper. officer, 1990-93, chief exec. officer, 1993—, also bd. of dirs., now vice chmn., chief exec. officer; mem. engring. adv. council Ariz. State U., Tempe, 1982-86. Bd. dirs. Scottsdale (Ariz.) Boys Club, 1980-86, Jr. Achievement Chgo., 1988—; chief crusader, major. corp. group United Way, Chgo., 1988—; mem. alumni bd., mem. Found. bd. Ariz. State U., 1991—. Named Outstanding Alumni of Yr., Ariz. State U., 1983. Mem. IEEE, Am. Mgmt. Assn., Semicondr. Industry Assn. (bd. dirs. 1981-86, chmn. bd. 1982-86), Ariz. Assn. Industries (bd. dirs. 1981-86), Am. Electronics Assn. (bd. dirs. 1988—, chmn. bd. 1991), Econ. Club of Chgo., Elec. Mfrs. Club. Republican. Office: Motorola Inc 1303 E Algonquin Rd Schaumburg IL 60196-4041*

TOOKER, GEORGE, artist; b. Bklyn., Aug. 5, 1920; s. George Clair and Angela Montejo (Roura) T. BA, Harvard U., 1942; student, Art Students League, N.Y.C., 1943-44. Instr. Art Students League, N.Y., 1965-68. One man shows include Edwin Hewitt Gallery, 1951, 55, Robert Isaacson Gallery, 1960, 62, Durlacher Bros., 1964, 67, Hopkins Center at Dartmouth Coll., 1967, Fine Arts Mus., San Francisco, 1974, Mus. Contemporary Art, Chgo., 1974, Whitney Mus., N.Y.C., 1975, Indpls. Mus. Art, 1975; exhibited in group shows at Whitney Mus., 1947-50, 53, 55-58, 61, 64, 65, 67, 75, Venice Biennale, 1956, Art Inst. Chgo., 1951, 52, 54, 59, Inst. Contemporary Arts, London, 1950, Va. Mus., 1954, 62, Pa. Acad., 1966, Marisa Del Re Gallery, 1985, 88, 92, Spoleto Festival, Gibbes Mus. Art, Charleston, S.C., 1987, Robert Hall Fleming Mus. U. Vt., 1987, Marsh Gallery, U. Richmond, Va., 1989, Addison Gallery of Am. Art, 1994; represented permanent collections at Smithsonian Nat. Mus. of Am. Art, Smithsonian Hirshhorn Mus., Whitney Mus., Dartmouth Coll., Met. Mus., Walker Art Center, Mus. Modern Art, S.C. Johnson & Sons, Inc., Art, U.S.A., Sara Roby Fund Collection Am. Art, Addison Gallery, Ariz. State Univ. Gallery, Bklyn. Mus. Columbus (Ohio) Mus. Recipient Vt. gov.'s award for excellence in arts, 1983; Grantee Nat. Inst. Arts and Letters, 1960. Mem. NAD., Acad. Arts and Letters. Address: PO Box 385 Hartland VT 05048-0385 Office: care DC Moore Gallery 724 5th Ave New York NY 10019-4106

TOOKEY, ROBERT CLARENCE, consulting actuary; b. Santa Monica, Calif., Mar. 21, 1925; s. Clarence Hall and Minerva Maconachie (Anderson) T.; BS, Calif. Inst. Tech., 1945; MS, U. Mich., 1947; m. Marcia Louise Hickman, Sept. 15, 1956; children: John Hall, Jennifer Louise, Thomas Anderson. With Prudential Ins. Co. Am., Newark, 1947-49; assoc. actuary in group Pacific Mut. Life Ins. Co., Los Angeles, 1949-55; asst. v.p. in charge reins. sales and service for 17 western states Lincoln Nat. Life Ins. Co., Ft. Wayne, Ind., 1955-61; dir. actuarial services Peat, Marwick, Mitchell & Co., Chgo., 1961-63; mng. partner So. Calif. office Milliman & Robertson, cons. actuaries, Pasadena, 1963-76; pres. Robert Tookey Assos., Inc., 1977—. Committeeman troop 501 Boy Scouts Am., 1969-72. Served to lt. (j.g.) USNR, 1943-45, 51-52. Fellow Soc. Actuaries, Conf. Consulting Actuaries; mem. Am. Acad. Actuaries, Pacific States Actuarial Club, Pacific Ins. Conf., Rotary Club (Pasadena), Union League Club (Chgo.). Home and office: 3950 San Augustine Dr Glendale CA 91206-1232 also: PO Box 646 La Canada Flintridge CA 91012-0646

TOOLAN, BRIAN PAUL, newspaper editor; b. Carbondale, Pa., June 29, 1950; s. Walter William and Elizabeth (Cleary) T.; m. Maureen Ellen Connolly, Sept. 7, 1974; children: Brendan, Seamus, Bridget, Colin, Molly. BA in English, St. Bonaventure U., Olean, N.Y., 1972. Reporter Scranton (Pa.) Tribune, 1972-79; copy editor Dayton (Ohio) Jour. Herald, 1979-81; layout editor Balt. News Am., 1981; copy editor Phila. Daily News, 1982-84, sports editor, 1984-89, asst. mng. editor, 1989-91, mng. editor, 1991—. Mem. AP Mng. Editors, Am. Soc. Newspaper Editors, Pa. Soc. Newspaper Editors (dir. 1989-92). Roman Catholic. Office: Phila Daily News 400 N Broad St Philadelphia PA 19130-4015*

TOOLE, DAVID GEORGE, pulp and paper products executive; b. Winnipeg, Man., Can., Apr. 22, 1942; s. George Toole; m. Bette Lynn Smith, Aug. 28, 1965; children: Jennifer, Simon. BSME, U. Man., 1964; MS in Adminstrv. Scis., The City U., London, 1968. Mem. corp. devel. Can. Pacific Ltd., Montreal, 1975-79, dir. fin. analysis, 1983-89, v.p. fin. analysis and planning, 1989-90; gen. mgr. Can. Pacific Ltd., Bermuda, 1979-83; sr. v.p., chief fin. officer Can. Pacific Forest Products Ltd., Montreal, 1990-94; pres. White Paper Group, Avenor Inc., Montreal, 1994—. Mem. Alpine Club Can. (sec.), Viking Ski Club (past pres.). Home: 18 Plumstead Ct, Etobicoke, OH Canada M9A 1V5 Office: 2 Kenview Blvd, Brampton, ON Canada L6T 5EH

TOOLE, JAMES FRANCIS, medical educator; b. Atlanta, Mar. 22, 1925; s. Walter O'Brien and Helen (Whitehurst) T.; m. Patricia Anne Wooldridge, Oct. 25, 1952; children: William, Anne, James, Douglas Sean. BA, Princeton U., 1947; MD, Cornell U., 1949; LLB, LaSalle Extension U., 1962. Intern, then resident internal medicine and neurology U. Pa. Hosp., Nat. Hosp., London, Eng., 1953-58; mem. faculty U. Pa. Sch. Medicine, 1958-62; prof. neurology, chmn. dept. Bowman Gray Sch. Medicine Wake Forest U., 1962-83; vis. prof. neuroscis. U. Calif. at San Diego, 1969-70; vis. scholar Oxford U., 1989; mem. Nat. Bd. Med. Examiners, 1970-76; mem. task force arteriosclerosis Nat. Heart Lung & Blood Inst., 1970-81; chmn. 6th and 7th Princeton confs. cerebrovascular diseases; cons. epidemiology WHO, Japan, 1971, 73, 93, USSR, 1968, Ivory Coast, 1977, Japan, 1993; mem. Lasker Awards com., 1976-77; chmn. neuropharmacologic drugs com. FDA, 1979; chair Commn. on Presdl. Disability, 1994-97; cons. NASA, 1966. Author: Cerebrovascular Diseases, 4th edit., 1990; editor: Current Concepts in Cerebrovascular Disease, 1969-73, Jour. Neurol. Sci., 1990-97; mem. editorial bd. Annals Internal Medicine, 1968-75, Stroke, 1972-91, Jour. AMA, 1975-77, Ann. Neurology, 1980-86, Jour. of Neurology, 1985-89. Pres. N.C. Heart Assn., 1976-77. Served with AUS, 1950-51; flight surgeon USNR, 1951-53. Decorated Bronze Star with V, Combat Med. badge. Fellow ACP (life), AAAS (life); mem. AMA, Am. Clin. and Climatol Assn. (life), Am. Heart Assn. (chmn. com. ethics 1970-75), Am. Physiol. Soc., Am. Neurol. Assn. (sec.-treas. 1978-82, pres. 1984-85, archivist, historian 1988—), World Fedn. Neurology (sec.-treas. 1982-89, mgmt. com. 1990—), Am. Acad. Neurology, Am. Soc. Neuroimaging (pres. 1992-94), Internat. Stroke Soc. (exec. com. 1989—, program chmn. 1992, pres. elect 1997), Nat. Stroke Assn. (bd. dirs. 1993—, exec. com. 1994—, chmn. Commn. on U.S. Presdl. Disability 1994—); hon. mem. Assn. Brit. Neurologists, German Neurol. Soc., Austrian Soc. Neurology, Irish Neurol. Assn., Russian Acad. Neurology. Home: 1836 Virginia Rd Winston Salem NC 27104-2316

TOOLE, JOHN HARPER, lawyer; b. Johnson City, N.Y., Apr. 4, 1941; s. Edward Joseph and Anne (Junius) T.; m. Lamar Sparkman, May 30, 1969; children: John Carter, Lucy Bland. BS, U. Va., 1963; JD, Washington Coll. of Law, 1971. Bar: Va. 1971, D.C. 1972. From assoc. to ptnr. Lewis, Mitchell & Moore, Tysons Corner, Va., 1971-77; ptnr. Watt, Tieder, Killian, Toole & Hoffar, Tysons Corner, 1978-82; ptnr., of counsel McGuire, Woods, Battle & Boothe, Tysons Corner, 1983—. 1st. Lt. U.S. Army, 1963-66. Mem. ABA, Va. State Bar, Va. Bar Assn., D.C. Bar Assn. Office: McGuire Woods Battle & Boothe PO Box 9346 8280 Greensboro Dr Ste 900 Mc Lean VA 22102-3892

TOOLE, WILLIAM BELL, III, college dean, retired, writer; b. Augusta, Ga., Sept. 23, 1930; s. William Bell Jr. and Mary Anita (Haverstick) T.; m. Katie Ruth Durham, June 7, 1955; children: Laurel Anita Toole Smith, William Durham. BA, Presbyn. Coll., Clinton, S.C., 1954; MA, Vanderbilt U., 1955, PhD in English, 1963. From instr. to asst. prof. English Presbyn. Coll., 1955-58; instr. English Vanderbilt U., Nashville, 1960-63; asst. prof. English N.C. State U., Raleigh, 1963-66, assoc. prof., 1966-71, prof., 1971—, asst. dean Sch. Humanities and Social Scis., 1971-72, assoc. dean, 1972-84, dean, 1984-95—; retired, 1995—; mem. nat. bd. cons. NEH, 1979—. Author: Shakespeare's Problem Plays: Studies in Form and Meaning, 1966; contbr. short stories to Wis. Rev., Pembroke Mag., So. Humanities Rev., Crucible, St. Andrews Rev., New Laurel Rev., others; contbr. articles to profl. jours. Bd. dirs. Friends of the Libr., Friends of the Gallery; trustee Triangle Univs. Ctr. for Advanced Studies. Served with U.S. Army, 1948-49. Named to Acad. of Outstanding Tchrs., 1967; Carnegie Found. scholar, 1954-55; So. fellow, 1959-60. Mem. Phi Beta Kappa, Alpha Kappa Psi, Phi Kappa Phi. Avocation: tennis. Home: 2515 Kenmore Dr Raleigh NC 27608 Office: NC State U Box 8101 Raleigh NC 27605

TOOMAJIAN, WILLIAM MARTIN, lawyer; b. Troy, N.Y., Sept. 26, 1943; s. Leo R. and Elizabeth (Gundrum) T.; children: Andrew, Philip. AB, Hamilton Coll., 1965; JD, U. Mich., 1968; LLM, N.Y.U., 1975. Bar: N.Y. 1968, Ohio 1978. Mem. firm Cadwalader, Wickersham & Taft, N.Y.C., 1971-77, Baker & Hostetler, Cleve., 1977—. Served to lt. USCG, 1968-71. Mem. ABA, Ohio Bar Assn., Cleve. Bar Assn., Cleve. Tax Club. Home: 3582 Lytle Rd Cleveland OH 44122-4908 Office: Baker & Hostetler 3200 National City Ctr 1900 E 9th St Cleveland OH 44114-3401

TOOMBS, CATHY WEST, assistant principal; b. Lafayette, Tenn., Dec. 9, 1954; d. Frank and Eudrice Estelle (Russell) West; m. Paul E. Toombs, Jr., June 18, 1977. BS, Mid. Tenn. State U., 1975, MEd, 1986, EdS, 1991; postgrad., Tenn. State U., 1991—. Cert. tchr. English, speech, adminstrn., supervision, Tenn. Tchr. spl. edn. Eastside Elem. Sch., McMinnville, Tenn., 1975-76; tchr. English, speech, drama Mt. Juliet (Tenn.) H.S., 1976-90; dir. continuing studies Mid. Tenn. State U., Murfreesboro, 1990-94; asst. prin. Lebanon (Tenn.) H.S., 1994—. Mem. ASCD, Tenn. Assn. Supervision and Curriculum Devel., Alpha Delta Kappa, Phi Kappa Phi. Home: PO Box 595 Mount Juliet TN 37122-0595 Office: Lebanon HS 415 Harding Dr Lebanon TN 37087-3925

TOOMBS, KENNETH ELDRIDGE, librarian; b. Colonial Heights, Va., Aug. 25, 1928; s. Garnett Eldridge and Susie W. (Bryant) T.; m. Ada Teresa Hornsby, Aug. 29, 1949; children—Susan Elizabeth Shealy, Cheri Lynn Morris, Teresa Ann Heilman. A.A., Tenn. Wesleyan Coll., 1950; B.S., Tenn. Poly. Inst., 1951; M.A., U. Va., 1955; M.L.S., Rutgers U., 1956; student, La. State U., 1961-63. Reference asst. Alderman Library, U. Va., 1954-55; research asst. Grad. Sch . Library Sci., Rutgers U., 1955-56; mem. staff and faculty La. State U., 1956-63, asst. dir. charge pub. services, 1962-63; dir. libraries, prof. library sci. U. Southwestern La., 1963-67; dir. libraries U. S.C., Columbia, 1967—; bd. dirs. Southeastern Library Network, 1967-88; disting. dir. of librs. emeritus U. S.C., Columbia, 1988—; vice chmn. Southeastern Library Network, 1973-74, 83-84, chmn., 1974-75, treas., 1984-85; libr. cons. for bldgs. and adminstrn. for 60 colls. and univs. in past 30 yrs.; chmn. librarians sect. La. Coll. Conf., 1965-67; mem. Bd. La. Libr. Examiners, 1966-67; participant Libr. Mgmt. Inst., U. Wash., Seattle, 1969, Libr. Bldg. Problems Inst., UCLA, 1970. Contbr. articles to profl. jours.; editor: Bull. La. Library Assn, 1959-62; mng. editor: SW La. Jour, 1963-67; adv. bd.: Linguistic Atlas Am. Treas. Wesley Found.; v.p. Am. Field Services Internat. Scholarships; bd. dirs. U. S.C. Ednl. Found., 1975-82; Danforth assoc., 1967—; AIA/ALA Bldg. Awards Jury, 1987. Served to 1st lt. AUS, 1946-47, 51-53. Mem. ALA (life), La. Library Assn. (parliamentarian 1962-63, 66-67), Southeastern Library Assn. (Life mem., exec. bd. 1981-85, Rothrock award 1978), Southwestern Library Assn., S.C. Library Assn. (Life mem., pres. 1976, exec. bd. 1981-85), Assn. Southeastern Research Libraries (chmn. 1973-75, adv. com. to OCLC 1979-84), AAUP (sec.), La. Hist. Assn., La. Tchrs. Assn., Soc. Tympanuchus Cupido Pinnatus, South Caroliniana Soc., Nat. Library Bldg. Consultants List (chmn. 1981-84), Tenn. Squire, Assn. of S.C. Retirees (bd. dirs. 1995—), Omicron Delta Epsilon. Methodist. Clubs: Mason (Shriner), Kiwanis. Home: 16 Garden Springs Rd Columbia SC 29209-1716

TOOMBS, RUSS WILLIAM, laboratory director; b. Troy, N.Y., July 11, 1951; s. George John and Olive Catherine (Blodgett) T.; m. Patrice Ann De Paul, Aug. 19, 1972; children: David Christopher, Mark Patrick. BS, Cornell U., 1973. Environ. scientist Wapora, Inc., Washington, 1973-74; bacteriologist N.Y. State Dept. Health, Wadsworth Ctr. for Labs. and Rsch., Albany, N.Y., 1974-76, sr. bacteriologist, 1976-78, assoc. bacteriologist, 1978-86, dir. ops., 1986-90, assoc. dir., 1990-96; asst. dir. Wadsworth Ctr. for Labs. and Rsch., Albany, N.Y., 1996—. Contbr. articles to profl. jours. Mem. AAAS, Am. Soc. Microbiology, N.Y. Acad. Scis., Saratoga Performing Arts Ctr. Roman Catholic. Home: 65 Huntleigh Dr Albany NY 12211-1175 Office: Wadsworth Ctr NY State Dept Health Empire State Plz Albany NY 12201-0509

TOOMEY, JEANNE ELIZABETH, animal activist; b. N.Y.C., Aug. 22, 1921; d. Edward Aloysius and Anna Margaret (O'Grady) Toomey; m. Peter Terranova, Sept. 28, 1951 (dec. 1968); children: Peter Terranova, Sheila Terranova Beasley. Student, Hofstra U., 1938-40; student law sch., Fordham U., 1940-41; BA, Southampton Coll., 1976; postgrad., Monmouth Coll., 1978-79. Reporter, columnist Bklyn. Daily Eagle, 1943-52; with The Fitzgeralds, NBC Radio, N.Y.C., 1952-53; reporter, writer King Features Syndicate, N.Y.C., 1953-55; reporter, columnist N.Y. Jour.-Am., N.Y.C., 1955-61; newsman AP, N.Y.C., 1963-64; stringer; columnist News Tribune, Woodbridge, N.J., 1976-86; editor Calexico (Calif.) Chronicle, 1987-88; editor community sect. Asbury Park (N.J.) Press, 1988; pres., dir. Last Post Animal Sanctuary, Falls Village, Conn., 1991—. Author: Murder in the Hamptons, 1994. Named Woman of the Yr. N.Y. Women's Press Club, 1960. Mem. Newswomen's Club of N.Y., Overseas Press Club, N.Y. Press Club, Silurians. Roman Catholic. Home and Office: 95 Belden St Falls Village CT 06031-1113

TOOMEY, KENT EDWARD, manufacturing company executive; b. Tellico Plains, Tenn., July 3, 1935; s. Edward Carmack and Eunice Erma (Payne) T.; m. Donna Marlene Blair, Mar. 24, 1956; children: Timothy K., Christopher B. BSME, U. Tenn., 1960; student, Maryville (Tenn.) Coll., 1953-55; MBA, Brenau Coll., 1984. V.p. Mfg. Dempster Div. Carrier Corp., Knoxville, Tenn., 1965-77; v.p. Ops. AgriBus. Co. USI, Atlanta, 1977-85, Fontaine Inc., Birmingham, Ala., 1985-88; pres. L.A. Darling Co., Paragould, Ark., 1989—. Mem. Am. Welding Soc., Nat. Mgmt. Assn., Nat. Assn. Store Fixture Mfrs. (bd. dirs.), Ark. Quality Mgmt. Bd. (bd. dirs.), Ark. Bus. and Edn. Alliance (bd. dirs.), Ark. Exec. Network, Assn. for Mfg. Excellence, Ark. C. of C. (bd. dirs.). Avocations: photography, music. Office: LA Darling Co PO Box 970 Hwy 49B North Paragould AR 72450

TOOMEY, PAULA KATHLEEN, financial analyst, consultant; b. Framingham, Mass., July 15, 1959; d. Paul Joseph and Mary Theresa (Coronella) T. AB in Econs., Boston Coll., 1984; postgrad., Harvard U., 1993—, Simmons Coll., 1996—. Office supr. ADIA, Cambridge, Mass., 1985-87; accounts receivable coord. WGBH Ednl. Found., Boston, 1987-88; fin. analyst Sta. WGBH-TV, Boston, 1988-91; unit mgr. Descriptive Video Svc. WGBH Ednl. Found., Boston, 1991—. Vol. cons. Grow Golphybhangyang, Nepal, 1993-95; vol. tchr. Jr. Achievement, Boston, 1987; vol. master's swim coach YMCA, Brighton, Mass., 1990-93; vol. Franciscan Children's Hosp., Brighton, 1991-93; active NOW. Mem. AAUW. Roman Catholic. Avocations: creative writing, photography, trekking, swimming, cycling. Office: Sta WGBH Ednl Found 125 Western Ave Boston MA 02134-1008

TOOMEY, THOMAS MURRAY, lawyer; b. Washington, Dec. 9, 1923; s. Vincent L. and Catherine V. (McCann) T.; m. Grace Donohoe, June 22, 1948; children: Isabelle Marie Toomey Hessick, Helen Marie, Mary Louise, Thomas Murray. Student, Duke U., 1943-44, Catholic U. Am., 1942-43, 47-49; J.D., Catholic U. Am., 1949. Bar: D.C. 1949, Md. 1952. Sole practice Washington and Md., 1949—; bd. dirs. Allied Capital Corp. and subs., Washington and Vero Beach, Fla., Fed. Ctr. Plz. Corp., Donohoe Cos., Inc., Washington, Nat. Capital Bank, Washington. Chmn. aviation and transp. coms. Met. Washington Bd. Trade, 1954-76, bd. dirs., 1962-77; chmn. dedication Dulles Internat. Airport, 1962; trustee Cath. U. Am., 1981—; founding trustee Heights Sch. Served to 1st lt. USMC, 1942-46, 50-52. Recipient Ann. Alumni Achievement award Cath. U., 1977, Most Disting. Alumnus award St. John's Coll. High Sch. D.C., 1994. Mem. ABA, D.C. Bar Assn., Md. Bar Assn., Bar Assn. D.C., Am. Judicature Soc., Comml. Law League Am., Friendly Sons St. Patrick (pre. 1983), Sovereign Mil. Order of Malta (Fed. Assn. U.S.A.), Congl. Golf and Country Club, Kenwood Golf and Country Club, Univ. Club, Army and Navy Club, Tower Club, Lago Mar Beach Club. Home: 6204 Garnett Dr Bethesda MD 20815-6618 also: 2000 S Ocean Dr Apt 1410 Fort Lauderdale FL 33316-3813 Office: 4701 Sangamore Rd Bethesda MD 20816-2508

TOOMRE, ALAR, applied mathematician, theoretical astronomer; b. Rakvere, Estonia, Feb. 5, 1937; came to U.S., 1949, naturalized, 1955; s. Elmar and Linda (Aghen) T.; m. Joyce Stetson, June 15, 1958; children—Lars, Erik, Anya. B.S. in Aero. Engring., B.S. in Physics, MIT, 1957; Ph.D. in Fluid Mechanics, U. Manchester, Eng., 1960. C.L.E. Moore instr. math. dept. MIT, Cambridge, 1960-62; asst. prof. applied math. MIT, 1963-65, assoc. prof., 1965-70, prof., 1970—; fellow Inst. for Advanced Study, Princeton, N.J., 1962-63. Contbr. articles to profl. jours. Guggenheim fellow, 1969-70, MacArthur fellow, 1984-89; Fairchild scholar, 1975, Marshall scholar, 1957-60. Fellow AAAS; mem. Am. Astron. Soc. (Dirk Brouwer award 1993), Internat. Astron. Union, Am. Acad. Arts and Scis., Nat. Acad. Scis. Office: MIT 77 Massachusetts Ave Rm 2-371 Cambridge MA 02139-4301

TOON, MALCOLM, former ambassador; b. Troy, N.Y., July 4, 1916; s. George and Margaret Harcomb (Broadfoot) T.; m. Elizabeth Jane Taylor, Aug. 28, 1943; children: Barbara, Alan, Nancy. A.B., Tufts U., 1937, LL.D. (hon.), 1977; M.A., Fletcher Sch. Law and Diplomacy, 1938; student, Middlebury Coll., 1950, Harvard U., 1950-51; LL.D. (hon.), Middlebury Coll., 1978, Drexel U., 1980, Am. Coll. Switzerland, 1985, Grove City Coll., 1990. Fgn. service officer, 1946-79; assigned successively Warsaw, Budapest, Moscow, Rome, Berlin, Washington, 1946-60; assigned Am. embassy, London, 1960-63; counselor political affairs Am. embassy, Moscow, 1963-67; with Dept. of State, Washington, 1967-69; ambassador to Czechoslovakia, 1969-71, to Yugoslavia, 1971-75, to Israel, 1975-76, to USSR, 1976-79; mem. U.S. del. Nuclear Test Conf., Geneva, 1958-59, Four Power Working Group, Washington, London, Paris, 1959, Fgn. Ministers Conf., Geneva, 1969, Ten Nation Disarmament Com., Geneva, 1960; mem. SALT II del., 1977-79, U.S.-Soviet Summit Conf., Vienna, 1979; Brennen prof. U. N.C., Asheville, 1981; Finch prof. Miami U., Oxford, Ohio, 1982; Allis-Chalmers chair Marquette U., Milw., 1982. Trustee emeritus Tufts U.; bd. overseers Fletcher Sch. Law and Diplomacy, 1992; chmn. U.S. Delegation to Joint U.S. Russian Commn. on POW's, MIA's. Served from ensign to lt. comdr. USNR, 1942-46. Recipient Freedom Leadership award Hillsdale Coll., 1980, Valley Forge Freedom award, 1981, Disting. Honor award Dept. State, 1980, Wallace award, 1984, Gold medal Nat. Inst. of Social Scis., 1987, Degree of Prof., Acad. Natural Scis. of the Russian Fedn., 1996, Silver medal, 1996. Home: 375 Pee Dee Rd Southern Pines NC 28387-2118

TOOR, HERBERT LAWRENCE, chemical engineering educator, researcher; b. Pitts., June 22, 1927; s. Matthew G. and Jean (Mogul) T.; m. Elizabeth Margaret Weir, Dec. 1950; children: Helen Mary, John Weir, William Ramsay. BS, Drexel U., 1948; MS, Northwestern U., 1950, PhD, 1952. Rsch. chemist Monsanto Chems., Ltd., 1952-53; asst. prof. Carnegie Mellon U., Pitts., 1953-57, assoc. prof., 1957-61, prof., 1961—, head chem. engring dept., 1967-70, dean Carnegie Inst. Tech., 1970-79, Mobay prof. chem. engring., 1980-92, Mobay prof. chem. engring. emeritus, 1992-95, engring. univ. prof. emeritus, 1997—; vis. UNESCO prof. U. Madras, India, 1962-63. Contbr. numerous articles to tech. jours. With USNR, 1944-45. Recipient merit award Northwestern U. Alumni, 1973. Fellow AAAS, Am. Inst. Chem. Engrs. (Colburn award 1964); mem. NAE.

TOOTE, GLORIA E. A., developer, lawyer, columnist; b. N.Y.C.; d. Frederick A. and Lillie M. (Tooks) Toote. Student, Howard U., 1949-51; J.D., NYU, 1954; LL.M., Columbia U., 1956. Bar: N.Y. 1955, U.S. Dist. Ct. (so. and ea. dists.) N.Y. 1956, U.S. Supreme Ct. 1956. With firm Greenbaum, Wolff & Ernst, 1957; mem. editorial staff Time mag., 1957-58; asst. gen. counsel N.Y. State Workmen's Compensation Bd., 1958-64; pres. Toote Town Pub. Co. and Town Sound Studios, Inc., 1966-70; asst. dir. Action Agy., 1971-73; asst. sec. Dept. HUD, 1973-75; vice chmn. Pres.'s Adv. Council on Pvt. Sector Initiatives, 1983-85; housing developer, 1976—; pres. Trea Estates and Enterprises, Inc.; newspaper columnist; chairperson The Policy Coun. Former bd. dirs. Citizens for the Republic, Nat. Black United Fund, Exec. Women in Govt., Am. Arbitration Assn., Consumer Alert; bd. overseers Hoover Inst., 1985-95; vice chair Nat. Polit. Congress of Black Women, 1984-92; former mem. Coun. Econ. Affairs, Rep. Nat. Com.; pres. N.Y.C. Black Rep. Coun.; exec. trustee Polit. Action Com. for Equality; mem. NYNEX Consumer Adv. Coun., 1995—. Recipient citations Nat. Bus. League, Alpha Kappa Alpha, U.S. C. of C., Nat. Assn. Black Women Attys. Mem. N.Y. Fedn. Civil Svc. Orgns., Nat. Assn. Real Estate Brokers, Nat. Fed. Mortgage Assn. (bd. dirs. 1992), Nat. Citizens Participation Coun., Nat. Bar Assn.,Delta Sigma Theta, others. Address: 282 W 137th St New York NY 10030-2439

TOOTHE, KAREN LEE, elementary and secondary school educator; b. Seattle, Dec. 13, 1957; d. Russell Minor and Donna Jean (Drolet) McGraw; m. Edward Frank Toothe, Aug. 6, 1983; 1 child, Kendall Erin. BA in Psychology with high honors, U. Fla., 1977, MEd in Emotional Handicaps and Learning Disabilities, 1979. Cert. behavior analysis Fla. Dept. Profl. Regulation. Alternative edn. self-contained tchr. grades 2 and 3 Gainesville Acad., Micanopy, Fla., 1979; emotional handicaps self-contained tchr. Ctr. Sch. Alternative Sch., Gainesville, Fla., 1979-80; learning disabilities resource tchr. grades 2 and 3 Galaxy Elem. Sch., Boynton Beach, Fla., 1980-81, learning disabilities self-contained tchr. grades 1-3, 1981, varying exceptionalities self-contained tchr. grades 3-5, 1981-83, chpt. one remedial reading tchr. grades 3 and 4, 1982-83; sec. and visual display unit operator Manpower, London, 1983-84; dir. sci./geography/social studies program Fairley House Sch., London, 1984-86, specific learning difficulties self-contained tchr. ages 8-12, dir. computing program, 1984-89; specific learning difficulties resource tchr. ages 8-16 Dyslexia Inst., Sutton Coldfield, Eng., 1990; behavior specialist, head Exceptional Student Edn. dept. Gateway High Sch., Kissimmee, Fla., 1990, behavior specialist, head ESE dept., 1991, resource compliance specialist, head ESE dept., 1991-93, tchr. summer youth tng. and enrichment program, 1993; tchr. summer youth tng. and enrichment program Osceola High Sch., Kissimmee, 1992; resource compliance specialist, program specialist for mentally handicapped, physically impaired, occupational and phys. therapy programs St. Cloud (Fla.) Mid. Sch., 1993-96, local augmentative/assistive tech. specialist, 1995—; resource compliance specialist, program specialist physically impaired occupl. and phys. therapy programs, local augmentative/assistive tech. speciali St. Hickory Tree Elem. Sch., 1996—; sch. rep. CREATE, Alachua County, Fla., 1979-80, Palm Beach County South Area Tchr. Edn. Ctr. Coun., 1980-83, chmn., 1982-83; mem. writing team Title IV-C Ednl. Improvement Grant, Palm Beach County, Fla., 1981; mem. math. curriculum writing team Palm Beach County (Fla.) Schs., 1983; mem., co-dir. Fairley House Rsch. Com., 1984-90; co-founder, dir. Rsch. Database, London, 1984-89; co-chmn. computer and behavior/social aspects writing teams Dyslexia Inst. Math., Staines, Eng., 1990; lectr., course tutor Brit. Dyslexia Assn., Crewe, Eng., 1990; mem. Vocat.-Exceptional Com., 1991-93; mem. Osceola Reading Coun., 1991—; mem. sch. adv. com. Gateway High Sch., 1991-93, St. Cloud Mid. Sch., 1993-96; presenter in field. Named Mid. Sch. Profl. of Yr. Osceola chpt. of Coun. Exceptional Children, 1995, 96. Mem. CEC (named local chpt. Mid. Sch. Profl. of Yr. 1995, 96), Fla. Soc. for Augmentative and Alt. Comm., Fla. Profl. Assn. Staffing Specialists, Phi Beta Kappa. Avocations: traveling, reading, physical fitness, scuba diving, arts and crafts. Home: 2175 James Dr Saint Cloud FL 34771-8830 Office: Osceola Dist Schs 817 Bill Beck Blvd Kissimmee FL 34744-4492

TOPAZ, MURIEL, dance educator, author; b. Phila., May 7, 1932; d. Joseph Topaz and Rhea Rebecca Rosenbloom; m. Jacob Druckman, June 5, 1954; children: Karen Druckman Jeanneret, Daniel Druckman. Student, NYU, 1950-51; studies with Martha Graham, Antony Tudor, The Juilliard Sch., 1951-54; student, Dance Notation Bur., N.Y.C., 1954-56. Mem. faculty The Juilliard Sch., N.Y.C., 1959-70, dir. dance div., 1985-92; exec. dir. Dance Notation Bur., 1978-85; co-chmn. First Internat. Congress on Movement Notation Bur., Israel, 1984, 2d Internat. Congress, Hong Kong, 1990; chmn. artistic com. Dance Notation Bur.; adjudicator Reginal Dance/Am., Mid-States 1980, Pacific 1981, N.E. 1996. Author: Changes and New Developments in Labanotation, 1966, Intermediate Reading Studies, 1972, Choreography and Dance: The Notation Issue, 1988, Alvin Ailey, An American Visionary, 1995, Elementary Labanotation, A Study Guide, 1996; author: (with Hackney & Manno) Elementary Study Guide, 1970, Elementary Reading Studies, 1970, (with Edelson) Readings in Modern Dance, 1972, (with Everett) The Best High School and Undergraduate Performing Arts Programs in Preparation; author, sr. editor Dance Mag.; exec. editor Choreography and Dance, Dance Studies; reconstructor: Lilac Garden (Milw. Ballet), Continuo (Paris Conservatory, N.C. Sch. Arts), Notator Moor's Pavane. Mem. May O'Donnell Hon. Com., 1979; chmn. dance panel N.Y. State Coun. on Arts, 1982-83; assessor Can. Coun., 1987; auditor NEA, 1989-95, 97—; chmn. Internat. Coun. Kinetography Laban, 1997—; panel chair Am. Dancing, Kennedy Ctr.; dance cons. Mass. Cultural Coun. Recipient fgn. travel grant Inst. Internat. Edn., 1967; Guggenheim fellow, 1997-98.

TOPAZIO, VIRGIL WILLIAM, university official; b. Middletown, Conn., Mar. 27, 1915; s. Concetto and Corradina (Rizzo) T.; m. Juwil E. Child, July 28, 1941; 1 dau., Jula Diane. B.A., Wesleyan U., Middletown; M.A., Columbia U., 1947, Ph.D., 1951. Lectr. Columbia U., 1947-48; from instr. to prof. French lit. U. Rochester, 1948-65; prof. French, chmn. dept. Rice U., 1965-67, dean humanities and social scis., 1967—, also acad. v.p.; Favrot chair in French lit., 1973; Fulbright vis. lectr. U. Rennes, France, 1964-65. Author: D'Holbach's Moral Philosophy, 1956, Voltaire: A Critical Study of His Major Works, 1967. Served with AUS, 1945-46. Decorated Palmes Academiques France, 1966, 76. Mem. Alliance Francaise (pres. 1963-65), Modern Lang. Assn. (pres. 18th century sect. 1965), Council Fgn. Langs. (v.p. 1967-68). Home: 3 Knoll Pines Ct The Woodlands TX 77381-2690

TOPE, DWIGHT HAROLD, retired management consultant; b. Grand Junction, Colo., Aug. 29, 1918; s. Richard E. and Elizabeth (Jones) T.; m. Carolyn Stagg, Apr. 29, 1949; children: Stephen R., Chris L. AS, Mesa Coll., 1940; student, George Washington U. With Fgn. Funds Control, a Div. of U.S. Treasury Dept.; staff adjuster Fire Cos. Adjustment Bur., Denver, Albuquerque, 1946-48; br. mgr. Gen. Adjustment Bur., Deming, N.Mex., 1948-50; spl. agt. Cliff Kealey State Agy., Albuquerque, 1950-56; pres. Dwight Tope State Agy., Inc., Albuquerque, 1956-84; with Fgn. Funds Control divsn. U.S. Dept. Treasury, Albuquerque; sr. cons. Dwight Tope State Agy., Inc., Albuquerque, 1985-87. Mem. adv. bd. Salvation Army, Albuquerque, 1974—, Meals on Wheels, 1987-97; past chmn. bd., pres. Presbyn. Heart Inst., Albuquerque, 1977-94. Maj. Coast Arty. Anti-Aircraft, 1941-45. Mem. N.Mex. Ins. Assn. (past chmn.), Ins. Info. Inst. (past chmn.), N.Mex. Surplus Lines Assn. (past pres.), Air Force Assn., Assn. of U.S. Army, Am. Legion, Albuquerque C. of C. (mil. rels. com.), Rotary, Masons, Shriners, Albuquerque Country Club, Petroleum Club. Republican. Avocations: boating, fishing, hunting. Home: 1812 Stanford Dr NE Albuquerque NM 87106-2538 Office: 8100 Mountain Rd NE Ste 204E Albuquerque NM 87110-7833

TOPEL, DAVID GLEN, agricultural studies educator; b. Lake Mills, Wis., Oct. 24, 1937; m. Jackie Richardson. BS, U. Wis., 1960; MS, Kans. State U., 1962; PhD, Mich. State U., 1965. Assoc. prof. animal sci. and food tech. Iowa State U., Ames, 1967-73, prof. animal sci. and food tech., 1973-79, dean Coll. Agr., 1988—, dir. agr. and home econs. experiment sta., 1988—; prof., head dept. Auburn U., Ames, 1979-88; cons., presenter, lectr. in field; mem. Gov. of Iowa's Sci. Adv. Coun., 1990—, Gov. of Iowa's Livestock Revitalization Task Force, 1993—; chair Gov.'s Environ. Agr. Com., 1994; mem. Iowa Corn Promotion Bd.; mem. faculty Royal Vet. and Agrl. U., Denmark, 1971-72, 90; vis. prof. Nat. Taiwan U., 1972. Author: The Pork Industry - Problems and Progress, 1968. Secretariat World Food Prize, Iowa State U., Ames, 1991—. Fulbright-Hays scholar Royal Vet. and Agrl. U., 1971-72; recipient award of merit Knights of Ak-Sar-Ben, 1973, Commr.'s award Agrl. Commr. Republic of China, 1977, disting. Achievement award Block and Bridle Club, 1979, Ala. Cattlemen's Assn.,1 984, Hon. State Farmer Degree, Ala., 1986, Harry L. Rudnick Educator's award Nat. Assn. Meat Purveyors, 1989; named hon. prof. Ukrainian State Agrl. U., 1993. Mem. AAAS, Am. Meat Sci. Assn., Am. Soc. Animal Sci. (Disting. Rsch. award in meat sci. 1979), Inst. Food Tech., Iowa Crop Improvement Assn., Iowa State Dairy Assn., Iowa Farm Bur. Fedn. (ex-officio), Iowa Pork Prodrs. Assn. (ex-officio), Iowa Beef Industry Coun., Nat. Coun. for Agrl. Rsch., Mid-Am. Internat. Agrl. Consortium (pres. 1991-92), Extension and Tchg. (pres. North Ctrl. Region 1992), Nat. Assn. State Univs. and Land-Grant Colls. (chair bd. agr. 1993, mem. commn. on food, environ. and renewable resources 1992—), Ukrainian Acad. Agrl. Scis., Sigma Xi (Outstanding Achievement award Iowa chpt. 1993), Alpha Zeta, Gamma Sigma Delta. Presbyterian. Avocations: fishing, golf. Home: 2630 Meadow Glen

Rd Ames IA 50014-8239 Office: Iowa State U 122 Curtiss Hall Ames IA 50011

TOPELIUS, KATHLEEN E., lawyer; b. July 15, 1948. BA, U. Conn., 1970; postgrad., U. Md., 1971-74; JD, Cath. U. Am., 1978. Bar: D.C. 1978, U.S. Supreme Ct. 1988. Atty. office of gen. counsel Fed. Home Loan Bank Bd., 1978-80; ptnr. Morgan, Lewis & Bockius, Washington, 1985-93, Bryan Cave, Washington, 1993—. Office: Bryan Cave 700 13th St NW Washington DC 20005-3960

TOPERZER, THOMAS RAYMOND, art museum director; b. Pitts., Aug. 12, 1939; s. Raymond Otto and Blodwyn (Roberts) T.; m. Carol Jane Reece, June 2, 1961; children: Scott Thomas, Max Otto. Student, West Liberty (W.Va.) State Coll., 1959, Sterling (Kans.) Coll., 1959-61; AB, Southwestern Coll., 1963; MFA, U. Nebr., 1970. Dir. Blanden Meml. Art Mus., Fort Dodge, Iowa, 1970-71, Rochester (Minn.) Art Ctr., 1971-72; curator univ. art gallery Ill. State U., Normal, 1972-73, asst. dir. univ. mus., 1972-73, dir. univ. art mus. and CVA art galleries, 1973-82; coordinator div. fine arts Bethel Coll., St. Paul, 1982-84; dir. Fred Jones Jr. Mus. Art, U. Okla., Norman, 1984—; arts cons. to various corps., Minn., Ill. and Okla., 1972—. Co-chmn. archives sub-com. Oklahoma City Murrah Bldg. Task Force, 1995-97, Okla. Meml. Ctr., Okla. Meml. Found., 1997—. Nelle Cochran Woods fellow U. Nebr., 1969-70. Mem. Assn. Coll. and U. Mus. and Galleries (mem. exec. com. 1986—), Am. Assn. Mus., Coll. Art Assn. Office: Fred Jones Jr Mus Art U Okla 410 W Boyd St Norman OK 73019-3001

TOPEY, ISHMAEL ALOYSIUS, urban planner; b. Port Henderson, St. Catherine, Jamaica, Nov. 10, 1926; s. Ferdinand Aloysius and Amy (Brown) T.; m. Dulcie Rose Clarke, Feb. 24, 1960; children: Patrick F., Robert I., Amy L., George A. Higher edn. cert., St. George's Coll., 1946; AA in Bus. Adminstrn., Wayne County C.C., 1983; BBA, U. Detroit, 1985; MA in Labor Rels., Wayne State U., Detroit, 1987. Cert. profl. cons./advisor; cert. adminstrv. mgr. Mgr. Sea Food Club, Jamaica, West Indies, 1960-75; tchr. Detroit Pub. Schs., 1986-87; urban renewal asst. City of Detroit, 1987—; founder Inter-Galactic Enterprises, Inc., Detroit, 1990—; creator of human math.; econ. devel. specialist; cons. in field. Creator Topeyology Sys. of Speedy Learning, 1987; author: Letter to Stephen Hawking, Debunking the Bell Curve, History of Intelligence. Co-recipient Papal Citation for Social Work, 1985; Jesuit Founders scholar U. Detroit, 1984. Mem. Am. Planning Assn., Buckminster Fuller Inst., World Future Soc. Home: 15700 Mapleridge St Detroit MI 48205-3031 Office: City of Detroit City County Bldg Ste 150 Detroit MI 48226

TOPHAM, SALLY JANE, ballet educator; b. N.Y.C., June 2, 1933; d. William Holroyd Topham and Marian Phyllis (Thomas) Topham Halligan; m. Joseph Vincent Ferrara, Dec. 27, 1958 (div. 1977); children: Gregory Paul, Mark Edward. Student Ballet Theatre Sch., Royal Acad. Dancing, London; trained in Europe. Free-lance profl. dancer ballet, opera ballet, summer stock, 1956-59; founder, dir. Monmouth Sch. Ballet, N.J., 1963-83; dir. Shore Ballet Theatre Sch., 1986-95, free lance tchr., choreographer, 1996—, founder Central Jersey Acad. Ballet, Red Bank, N.J., 1983-85; dir. Westfield Sch. Ballet, N.J., 1976-77; tchr., dir. Mount Allison U. Summer Sch., New Brunswick, Can., 1973-77; prof. ballet Monmouth Coll., West Long Branch, N.J., 1981-83. Choreographer (ballet) Coppelia, 1981, 90, 96; Shubert Songs, 1980; Homage to Bournonville, 1977; Nutcracker, 1985, Cinderella, 1988; staged many ballets and opera ballets. Bd. dirs. Monmouth Arts Found., Red Bank, 1972—, Shore Ballet Co., Red Bank, 1976—; founder, bd. dirs. Monmouth Civic Ballet, Red Bank, 1972-75. Assoc. mem. Royal Acad. Dancing (reg. tchr., advanced tchg. diploma 1979), English Speaking Union. Avocations: sailing, theater, music, books. Office: Shore Ballet Sch 31 E Main St Freehold NJ 07728-2201

TOPIK, STEVEN CURTIS, history educator; b. Montebello, Calif., Aug. 6, 1949; s. Kurt and Gertrude Irene (Kriszanich) T.; m. Martha Jane Marcy, Feb. 3, 1979; children: Julia, Natalia. BA, U. Calif., San Diego, 1971; MA, U. Tex., 1973, PhD, 1978. Asst. prof. Universidade Fed. Fluminense, Rio de Janeiro, 1978-81, vis. prof., 1984—; asst. prof. Colgate U., Hamilton, N.Y., 1981-84; vis. prof. Univ. Ibero Americana, Mexico City, 1982; prof. U. Calif., Irvine, 1984-96; vis. prof. Ecols des Hautes Etudes en Sci. Social, Paris, 1990; chair historydept., 1996—; cons. in field; mem. editorial com. U. Calif. Press, Berkeley, 1987-89. Author: The Political Economy of the Brazilian State, 1987, Trade and Gunboats, The United States and Brazil in the Age of Empire, 1996, The Second Conquest, 1997; contbr. articles, revs. to profl. publs. Mem. Mayor's Adv. Bd. on Sister Cities, Irvine, 1989-90; mem. adv. bd. Orange County (Calif.) Com. on Latin Am., 1989-90. Fellow NEH, 1987, 89-90, Rockefeller Found., 1977, Social Sci. Rsch. Coun. Mexico City, 1982-83, Fulbright-Hayes Found., 1978-79, 84, U. Calif., 1988-89. Mem. Latin Am. Studies Assn., Am. Hist. Assn., Conf. Latin Am. History (com. on hist. statistics, com. on projects and publs., chair Brazilian studies com. 1988-90), Pacific Coast Coun. on Latin Am. Studies (bd. govs. 1987-90).

TOPILOW, ARTHUR ALAN, internist; b. N.Y.C., July 12, 1942; s. Jacob S. and Pearl (Roth) T.; m. Judith Fiedler, Dec. 5, 1967; children: Justin, Evan. AB, Lafayette Coll., Easton, Pa., 1963; MD, N.Y. Med. Coll., 1967. Diplomate Am. Bd. Internal Medicine. Internship, residency Flower & Met. Hosp. Ctr., N.Y.C., 1967-70; fellow in hematology Flower & Met. Hosp. Ctr., N.Y. Med. Coll., 1970-72; pvt. practice Wall Twp., N.J., 1974—; dir. hematology/oncology Jersey Shore Med. Ctr., Neptune, N.J. Maj. U.S. Army, 1972-74. Fellow ACP. Avocations: sailboat racing, profl. jazz pianist. Office: 1707 Atlantic Ave Manasquan NJ 08736-1147 also: Jersey Shore Med Ctr 1945 Rte 33 Neptune NJ 07753-4859

TOPILOW, CARL S., symphony conductor; b. Jersey City, N.J., Mar. 14, 1947; s. Jacob Topilow and Pearl (Roth) Topilow Josephs; m. Shirley; 1 child, Jenny Michelle. B.Mus., Manhattan Sch. of Mus., 1968, M.Mus., 1969. Exxon/Arts Endowment Condr. Denver Symphony Orch., 1976-79, asst. condr., 1979-80; mus. dir. Denver Chamber Orch., 1976-81, Denver Youth Orch., 1977-80, Grand Junction Symphony, Colo., 1977-80, Nat. Repertory Orch., Breckenridge, Colo., 1978—; dir. orchs. Cleve. Inst. Mus., 1981—, condr. Summit Brass 1986—, Cleve. Pops Orch., 1995—. Recipient Conducting fellowship Nat. Orch. Assn., N.Y.C., 1972-75, Aspen Mus. Festival, Colo., 1976; winner 1st place Balt. Symphony Conducting Competition, Md., 1976.*

TOPINKA, JUDY BAAR, state official; b. Riverside, Ill., Jan. 16, 1944; d. William Daniel and Lillian Mary (Shuss) Baar; 1 child, Joseph Baar. BS, Northwestern U., 1966. Features editor, reporter, columnist Life Newspapers, Berwyn and LaGrange, Ill., 1966-77; with Forest Park (Ill.) Rev. and Westchester News, 1976-77; coord. spl. events dept. fedn. comm., AMA, 1978-80; rsch. analyst Senator Leonard Becker, 1978-79; mem. Ill. Ho. of Reps., 1981-84; mem. Ill. Senate, 1985-94; treas. State of Ill., Springfield, 1995—; former mem. judiciary com., former chmn. senate health and welfare com.; former mem. fin. instn. com.; former co-chmn. Citizens Coun. on Econ. Devel.; former co-chmn. U.S. Commn. for Preservation of Am.'s Heritage Abroad, serves on legis. ref. bur.; former mem. minority bus. resource ctr. adv. com. U.S. Dept. Transp.; former mem. adv. bd. Nat. Inst. Justice. Founder, pres., bd. dirs. West Suburban Exec. Breakfast Club, from 1976; chmn. Ill. Ethnics for Reagan-Bush, 1984, Bush-Quayle 1988; spokesman Nat. Coun. State Legislatures Health Com.; former mem nat. adv. coun. health professions edn. HHS; mem., GOP chairwoman Legis. Audit Commn. of Cook County; chmn. Riverside Twp. Regular Republican Orgn., 1994—. Recipient Outstanding Civilian Svc. medal, Molly Pitcher award, Abraham Lincoln award, Silver Eagle award U.S. Army and N.G. Office: JR Thompson Ctr 100 W Randolph St Ste 15-600 Chicago IL 60601-3220

TOPOL, ROBERT MARTIN, retired financial services executive; b. N.Y.C., Mar. 9, 1925; s. Morris and Pearl Topol; m. D'Vera Greene, Oct. 10, 1948; children—Clifford M., Gail S., Martha E. B.A., NYU, 1948. Ptnr. Greene & Co., N.Y.C., 1948-71; dir. Harris Upham & Co, N.Y.C., 1971-76; exec. v.p., dir. Shearson Lehman Bros., N.Y.C., 1976-94; ret., 1995. Served with USMC, 1943-46. Mem. Security Traders N.Y., Nat. Security Traders Assn., N.Y. Security Dealers Assn. (gov. 1961-77), Securities Industry Assn. (v.p. 1981-94), Investment Co. Inst., Chevalier Chaine de Rotisseurs, Hampshire Country Club. Republican. Jewish. Home: 825 Orienta Ave Mamaroneck NY 10543-4314

TOPP, GEORGE CLARKE, soil physicist; b. Canfield, Ont., Can., Nov. 12, 1937; s. G. Ernest and Rhea L. (Mehlenbacher) T.; m. Eleanor Bruce, Dec. 29, 1962; children: Karen, Bruce, Brenda. BS in Agr., U. Toronto, Ont., 1959; MSc, U. Wis., 1962, PhD, 1964. Rsch. asst. U. Wis., Madison, 1959-64; rsch. assoc. U. Ill., Urbana, 1964-65; rsch. scientist Land Resource Rsch. Ctr., Ottawa, Ont., 1965-87, rsch. mgr., 1987-91; rsch. scientist land resource div. Agr. Can., Ottawa, 1991-95, rsch. scientist crop prodn. divsn., 1996—; sessional lectr. Carleton U., Ottawa, 1975-78; vis. assoc. prof. U. Sask., Saskatoon, Can., 1980; vis. scientist Divsns. Environment, Mechanics and Soils Commonwealth Sci. and Indsl. Rsch. Orgn., Canberra, Australia, 1992-93; cons. Can. Internat. Devel. Agy., Islamabad, Pakistan, 1985, Hyderabad, India, 1986, Campinas, Sao Paulo, Brazil, 1988. Editor: Soil Physical Measurements, 1992. Chmn. Ottawa West End Community Chaplaincy, 1984-87, bd. dirs., 1991-92; chmn. Bells Corners United Ch., Nepean, Ont., 1987-89. Fellow Can. Soc. Soil Sci. (sec. 1969-72, pres. 1978), Soil Sci. Soc. Am. (bd. dirs. 1990-91); mem. Am. Geophys. Union. Mem. United Ch. of Canada. Avocations: cross-country skiing, canoeing, sailing. Home: 45 Foothills Dr, Nepean, ON Canada K2H 6K6 Office: Agriculture Canada, 960 Carling Ave, Ottawa, ON Canada K1A 0C6

TOPPING, DONALD M., English language professional, educaor; b. 1929. BA, U. Ky., 1954, MA, 1956; PhD, Mich. State U., 1963. Asst. prof. English Territorial Coll. Guam, 1956-58, asst. prof. and chmn. English dept., 1960-62; instr. English Mich. State U., East Lansing, 1959-60; instr. English Lang. Inst. U. Hawaii, Honolulu, 1962-64, TESL coord. Peace Corps Tng. Ctr., 1962-63, lang. coord., 1963-66, asst. prof. linguistics, 1964-69, assoc. prof. linguistics, dir. Pacific/Asian Linguistic Inst, 1969-74, prof. linguistics, dir. Social Sci. Rsch. Inst., 1974—, dir. PEACESAT Project, 1981—; mem. NDEA Inst. on TESL, Coll. of Guam, summer 1965; linguistics cons. Officer of Internat. Programs, U. Hawaii, 1966-68, project coord. Micronesian Lang. Materials Project, 1967; prin. investigator Chamorro Dictionary Project, NSF, 1968; specialist in linguistics SEAMEO Regional English Lang. Ctr., Singapore, 1968-69; prin. investigator Micronesian Linguistics Rsch. Project, 1970-74; linguistics cons. Chamorro Bilingual Edn. Project on Guam and Rota, Mariana Islands, 1971-74; prin. investigator Palauan-English Dictionary Project, 1973-74, Bilingual Edn. Project for Micronesia, 1974-77, Assess to Govt. Through Neighborhood Bds., HEW, 1977-79, Pacific Area Lang. Materials Devel. Ctr., 1977-83, Carolinian-English Dictionary Project, Trust Territory Govt., 1981-83, Salish Lexicography Project, NEH, 1985-92, Integrated Approach to Hawaii's Drug Policy Issues, Robert Wood Johnson Found., 1994—. Editl. bd. Oceanic Linguistics: Spl. Publs., 1969—, Pacific Islands Monograph Series, 1981—, ISLA: A Jour. of Micronesian Studies, 1992—; editor SSRI Monograph Series, 1974—, PALI Lang. Series: Micronesia, 1974—; co-author: (with D. Crowley) Lessons in Indonesian, 1964; author: Spoken Chamorro, 1969, Chamorro Reference Grammar, 1973, A Chamorro Dictionary, 1975, Spoken Chamorro, rev. edit., 1980; contbr. articles to profl. jours. Office: U Hawaii at Manoa Social Science Rsch Inst Porteus Hall 2424 Maile Way Honolulu HI 96822*

TOPPING, JOHN CARRUTHERS, JR., environmental organization administrator, lawyer; b. Wilkinsburg, Pa., Apr. 18, 1943; s. John Carruthers and Barbara Anne (Murray) T.; m. Linda Marie Thompson, Dec. 1, 1974; children: John Carruthers III, Elizabeth Barrett, Alexandra LaMotte. AB, Dartmouth Coll., 1964; JD, Yale U., 1967. Bar: Mass. 1967, D.C. 1968. Counsel Adv. Coun. for Minority Enterprise, Washington, 1970-73, staff dir., 1972-73; chief counsel office minority bus. enterprise U.S. Dept. Commerce, Washington, 1973-76; ptnr. Topping and Sherer, Washington, 1977-82; cons. U.S. EPA, Washington, 1982-83, staff dir. office air and radiation, 1983-86; ptnr. Topping & Swillinger, Washington, 1986-87; pres. Climate Inst., Washington, 1986—. Co-author: Southern Republicanism and the New South, 1966, Clean Air Handbook, 1987; editor: Preparing for Climate Change, 1988, Coping with Climate Change, 1989. Mem. D.C. adv. com. to U.S. Commn. on Civil Rights, 1974—; pres. Ripon Soc. Washington, 1978-80. Capt. USAF, 1968-70. Recipient Pres.'s award Nat. Bar Assn., 1976. Republican. Presbyterian. Home: 220 Maryland Ave NE Washington DC 20002-5704 Office: Climate Inst 120 Maryland Ave NE Washington DC 20002-5616 *The challenge of democracy is to represent the interests of generations yet to be born. The world in which they will live depends on decisions we make today.*

TOPPING, PETER, historian, educator; b. Milw., May 13, 1916; s. William P. and Anastasia (Makris) Topitzes; m. Eva V. Catafygiotu, June 20, 1951; 1 son, John Themis. B.A., U. Wis., 1937, M.A., 1938; postgrad., U. Cin., 1939-40; Ph.D., U. Pa., 1942. Instr. history U. Wis., 1943-44, Northwestern U., 1944-45; asst. prof. history U. Calif.-Santa Barbara, 1948-53; librarian Gennadeion Am. Sch. Classical Studies, Athens, Greece, 1953-60, mem. mng. com., 1961—; vis. assoc. prof. history, library cons. U. Pa., 1960-61; assoc. prof. history, later Greek studies U. Cin., 1961-64, prof., 1964-67, Charles Phelps Taft prof., 1967-78; fellow Grad. Sch., 1972—; sr. research assoc. Dumbarton Oaks Rsch. Libr. and Collection, Washington, 1978-84; mem. bd. scholars Dumbarton Oaks Center for Byzantine Studies, 1972-74, mem. sr. fellows, 1979-86, hon. sr. research assoc., 1984—; interpreting officer U.S. staff Allied Mission to Observe Greek Elections, 1946; mem. exec. com. Frank L. Weil Inst. in Religion and Humanities, 1964-78. Author: Feudal Institutions as Revealed in the Assizes of Romania, 1949, (with Jean Longnon) Documents sur le régime des terres dans la principauté de Moreé au XIVme siècle, 1969, Studies on Latin Greece A.D. 1205-1715, 1977; contbr. articles, revs. to hist. jours. Advanced fellow Belgian Am. Edn. Found., 1947-48; Fulbright sr. research awardee Greece, 1950-51; sr. fellow NEH, 1974-75. Mem. Am. Hist. Assn., Mediaeval Acad. Am., Soc. Byzantine Studies (Athens, Greece) (hon.), Modern Greek Studies Assn., Phi Beta Kappa. Democrat. Mem. Greek Orthodox Ch. Home: 1823 Rupert St Mc Lean VA 22101-5434

TOPPING, SEYMOUR, publishing executive, educator; b. N.Y.C., Dec. 11, 1921; s. Joseph and Anna (Seidman) Topolsky; m. Audrey Elaine Ronning, Nov. 10, 1949; children: Susan, Karen, Lesley, Rebecca, Joanna. B.J., U. Mo., 1943; Litt.D. (hon.), Rider Coll., 1983. With I.N.S. (China civil war), 1946-47; with AP, 1948-59; corr. AP, Berlin, 1957-59; mem. staff N.Y. Times, 1959-93; chief corr. N.Y. Times, Moscow, 1960-63, Southeast Asia, 1963-66; fgn. editor N.Y. Times, 1966-69, asst. mng. editor, 1969-76, dep. mng. editor, 1976-77, mng. editor, 1977-86; dir. editorial devel. N.Y. Times Regional Newspapers, 1987-93; pres. Am. Soc. Newspaper Editors, 1992-93; prof. Grad. Sch. Journalism Columbia U., N.Y.C., 1993—; Sanpaolo prof. internat. journalism, 1994—; adminstr. Pulitzer Prizes Columbia U., N.Y.C., 1993—; adviser Ctr. Fgn. Journalists, Found. Am. Comm.; juror Pulitzer Prize com.; lectr. in field. Author: Journey Between Two Chinas, 1972. Spl. advisor to Sec.-Gen. UN to Earth Summit, Rio de Janeiro, 1992; mem. Nat. Com. U.S.-China Rels.; bd. dirs. Lamont-Doherty Earth Obs. Served with inf. AUS, 1943-46, PTO. Mem. Coun. Fgn. Rels., Asia Soc., Am. Soc. Newspaper Editors, Internat. Press Inst. (Am. com., bd. dirs.), Century Assn. Home: 5 Heathcote Rd Scarsdale NY 10583-4413

TORAN, KAY DEAN, social services director; b. Birmingham, Ala., Nov. 21, 1942; d. Benjamin and Mary Rose Dean; children: Traci Rossi, John D. Toran. BA, U. Portland, 1964; MSW, Portland State U., 1970. Asst. prof. social work Portland (Oreg.) State U., 1971-76; mgr. Adult and Family Svcs., Salem, Oreg., 1976-79; asst. gov. Office of Gov., Salem, 1979-87; adminstr. purchasing divsn. Dept. Gen. Svcs., Salem, 1987-90; regional adminstr. Children's Svcs. Divsn., Portland, 1991-94, adminstr., 1994—; pres. Walker Inst., Portland, 1990-94, Portland chapter Links, Inc., 1990-92. Bd. trustees Catlin Gabel Sch., Portland, 1980-84, Portland State U. Found., 1980-87; bd. dirs. Oreg. Law Found., 1990-93. Office: Svcs to Children & Families 500 Summer St NE Salem OR 97310-0101

TORBERT, CLEMENT CLAY, JR., state supreme court justice; b. Opelika, Ala., Aug. 31, 1929; s. Clement Clay Sr. and Lynda (Meadows) T.; m. Gene Hurt, May 2, 1952; children: Mary Dixon, Gene Shealy, Clement Clay III. Student, U.S. Naval Acad., 1948-49; B.S., Auburn U., 1951; postgrad., U. Md., 1952; LL.B., U. Ala., 1954. Bar: Ala. 1954. Practiced in Opelika, 1954-77, city judge, 1954-58; partner firm Samford, Torbert, Denson & Horsley, 1959-74; chief justice Ala. Supreme Ct., 1977-89; ptnr. firm Maynard, Cooper & Gale, 1990—; past chmn. Ala. Jud. Study Commn., Jud. Coordination Com.; past pres. Conf. Chief Justices; supervisory bd. Ala. Law Enforcement Planning Agy., 1977-83; bd. dirs. Ala. Criminal Justice Info. Systems, Nat. Inst. for Dispute Resolution, First Nat. Bank Opelika, State Justice Inst., 1986-92, mem. panel of arbitrators Am. Arbitration Assn.; panelist-at-large Ctr. for Pub. Resources; held Leslie S. Wright Chair of Law, Cumberland Sch. Law, 1989, John Sparkman Chair, U. Ala. Sch. Law. Mem. Ala. Ho. of Reps., 1958-62, Ala. Senate, 1966-70, 74-77. Served to capt. USAF, 1952-53. Elected to Ala. Acad. of Honor, 1979; recipient Disting. Svc. award Nat. Ctr. for State Cts., 1989, 1989 award, Am. Judges Assn. Mem. Am. Judicature Soc., Farrah Law Soc., Phi Delta Phi, Phi Kappa Phi, Alpha Tau Omega. Methodist. Lodge: Kiwanis. Home: 611 Terracewood Dr Opelika AL 36801-3850 Office: One Commerce St Ste 302 Montgomery AL 36104

TORCHIA, H. ANDREW, hotel executive. Chmn. bd. Amerihost Properties, Inc, Des Plaines, Ill. Office: Amerihost Properties Inc 2400 E Devon Ave Ste 280 Des Plaines IL 60018-4617

TORCHIA, KARIN G., sports association administrator; b. Camp Springs, Md., June 28, 1969; d. John Anthony and Patricia Gail (Bernotas) DelBuono; m. Karl Victor Torchia, Aug. 7, 1993. BS in Sport Mgmt., W.Va. U., 1991, MS in Sports Adminstrn., 1993. Cert. coach. Asst. dep. polit. dir. GOPAC, Washington, 1990; sports comm. asst. W.Va. U. Athletic Dept., Morgantown, 1990-93; publicity dir. Tonya Knight Enterprises, Long Branch, N.J., 1993-94; asst. to the commr. Atlantic 10 Conf., Cranbury, N.J., 1993-95; dir. championship Metro Atlantic Athletic Conf., Edison, N.J., 1995-97, asst. commr., 1997—, mem. games com.; mem. ECAC softball championship sel. com., ECAC all-star team selection com. Author, editor: The Total Student-Athlete, 1992; feature writer Ironman Mag., 1993, Fitness Mags., 1993. All-Am. scholar U.S. Achievement Acad., 1991. Mem. W.Va. Sport Mgmt. Assn. Roman Catholic. Avocations: reading, playing sports. Office: Metro Atlantic Athletic Conf 1090 Amboy Ave Edison NJ 08837-2847

TORDOFF, HARRISON BRUCE, retired zoologist, educator; b. Mechanicville, N.Y., Feb. 8, 1923; s. Harry F. and Ethel M. (Dormandy) T.; m. Jean Van Nostrand, July 3, 1946; children: Jeffrey, James. B.S., Cornell U., 1946; M.A., U. Mich., 1949, Ph.D., 1952. Curator Inst. of Jamaica, Kingston, 1946-47; instr. U. Kans., 1950-52, asst. prof., 1952-57, assoc. prof., 1957; asst. prof. U. Mich., 1957-59, assoc. prof., 1959-62, prof., 1962-70; former dir. Bell Mus. Natural History; prof. ecology U. Minn., Mpls., 1970-91, dean coll. biol. scis., 1986-87. Contbr. articles in ornithology to profl. jours. Served with USAF, 1942-45. Decorated D.F.C., 17 Air medals. Fellow Am. Ornithologists Union (pres. 1978-80); mem. Nature Conservancy (chmn. bd. Minn. chpt. 1975-77), Wilson Ornithol. Soc. (editor 1952-54), Cooper Ornithol. Soc. Home: 6 Chickadee Ln North Oaks Saint Paul MN 55127 Office: 100 Ecology 1987 Upper Buford Cir Saint Paul MN 55108-6097

TOREN, ROBERT, photojournalist; b. Grand Rapids, Mich., Oct. 9, 1915; s. Clarence J. and Helen (Holcomb) T.; student Winona Sch. Profl. Photography, 1957, West Coast Sch. Photography, 1959-62; m. Miriam Jeanette Smith, July 17, 1940. Photographer, Harris and Ewing, Washington, 1938-39, Versluis Studios, Grand Rapids, Mich., 1939-43, prodn. mgr., 1940-43; owner, photographer Toren Galleries, San Francisco, 1946-70; photographer Combat Tribes of World, Rich Lee Orgn., 1978-84, Darien jungle expdn. Am. Motors, 1979; feature writer Auburn (Calif.) Jour., El Dorado Gazette, 1983-87, Georgetown Gazette, 1983-96. One man shows various univs.; prints in permanent collections: Photog. Hall of Fame, Coyote Point Mus., San Mateo County Hist. Mus.; photog. column San Mateo Times, Georgetown Gazette; lectr. Am. Pres. Lines, Coll. San Mateo, Peninsula Art Assn., Mendicino Art Ctr. Historian City of Foster City; vice chmn. Art Commn. Foster City. Trustee, West Coast Sch.; bd. dirs. Foster City Art League, Hillbarn Theatre, San Mateo County Arts Council; mem. art com. San Mateo County Fair, 1979-87; coord., dir. Georgetown (Calif.) Mountain Mus., 1982-88; founding pres. Music on The Divide, 1989; founder Georgetown CA. Ragtime Concerts, 1996; pres. El Dorado County Arts Coun. Served from pvt. to staff sgt. AUS, 1943-46. Mem. Calif. Writers (br. pres.), Profl. Photographers Am. Presbyn. Author: Peninsula Wilderness. Illustrator: The Tainted Tree, 1963. Editor: The Evolution of Portraiture, 1965; The Western Way of Portraiture, 1965, Conquest of the Darien, 1984, Two Cities, 1996. Home: 3140 Cascade Trl Cool CA 95614-2615

TORESCO, DONALD, automotive executive; b. 1936. With Dom's Auto Sales, Inc., Plainfield, N.J., 1958-91; CEO Toresco Enterprises, Springfield, N.J., 1984—. Office: 170 Rte 22 E Springfield NJ 07081

TORFFIELD, MARVIN, artist; b. Bklyn., July 25, 1943; s. Barnett Philip and Rina (Shapiro) T. B.F.A., Pratt Inst., 1965; M.F.A., Yale U., 1970. Vis. fellow Advanced Ctr. Visual Studies, MIT, 1970; rsch. fellow Harvard U., 1972. One man shows include Jewish Mus. N.Y., 1969, The Seagram Pla., N.Y.C., 1973, Whitney Mus. Am. Art., 1973-74, Paula Cooper Gallery, 1977, Central Park, 1980, Leo Castelli Gallery, 1983, 35th IDCA, 1985, Sert Gallery, Harvard U., 1986; represented in group shows. Mem. Rolling Stones Steel Wheels Tour, N.Am., Japan, Europe, 1989-90. Patentee in field. Fellow Nat. Endowment for Arts, 1970, Guggenheim Found., 1975; Pollock-Krasner Found. grantee, 1986-87; MacDowell Colony residency, Peterborough, N.H., 1988—. Office: PO Box 292 Canal Sta New York NY 10013

TORG, JOSEPH STEVEN, orthopaedic surgeon, educator; b. Phila., Oct. 25, 1934; s. Jay and Elva Dorothy (May) T.; m. Barbara Jane Groenendaal, May 23, 1959; children—Joseph Steven, Elisabeth, Jay Michael. A.B., Haverford Coll., 1957; M.D., Temple U., 1961. Diplomate: Am. Bd. Orthopaedic Surgeons. Intern San Francisco Gen. Hosp., 1961-62; resident in orthopaedic surgery Temple U. Hosp., Phila., 1964-68, Shriners Hosp. for Crippled Children, Phila., 1966-67; asst. surgeon Episcopal Hosp., Phila., 1968-70; surgeon Shriners Hosp. Crippled Children, 1970-78; mem. staff Temple U. Hosp., 1970-78, instr. orthopaedic surgery, 1968-70, asst. prof., 1970-75, assoc. prof., 1976-78; dir. Center for Sports Medicine and Sci., 1974-78; chief orthopaedic sect. St. Christopher's Hosp. for Children, Phila., 1971-74, mem. staff, 1974—; active staff St. Joseph's Hosp., Phila., 1977—; prof. U. Pa., 1978—, active staff hosp., 1978—; dir. Sports Medicine Center, 1978—; prof. orthopaedic surgery Hahnemann U., 1995; mem. active staff Children's Hosp., Phila., 1978; med. cons. Pres.'s Council on Phys. Fitness and Sports. Mem. editorial bd. Sports Medicine, Yearbook of Sports Medicine, Contemporary Orthopaedics, Jour. Clin. Sport Medicine, Am. Jour. Knee Surgery, Orthopaedic Rev.; contbr. articles to profl. jours. Served with M.C. U.S. Army, 1962-64. Recipient Layman Honor award Pa. State Assn. Health, Phys. Edn. and Recreation, 1970, Grad. Honor award, 1975; Commendation of Merit Phila. Public High Sch. Football Coaches, 1974. Fellow Am. Acad. Orthopaedic Surgeons, Am. Coll. Sports Medicine (trustee 1975-78), Phila. Coll. Physicians; mem. AMA, Eastern Orthopaedic Soc., Am. Orthopaedic Soc., Sports Medicine, Phila. County Med. Soc., Phila. Orthopaedic Soc., Pa. State Med. Soc., Pa. State Orthopaedic Soc. Home: 401 Conestoga Rd Wayne PA 19087-4811 Office: Hahnemann U Sports Medicine Center 219 N Broad St Philadelphia PA 19107-1519

TORGERSEN, PAUL ERNEST, academic administrator, educator; b. N.Y.C., Oct. 13, 1931; s. Elnar and Frances (Hansen) T.; m. Dorothea Hildegarde Zuschlag, Sept. 11, 1954; children: Karen Elizabeth, Janis Elaine, James Einar. BS, Lehigh U., 1953, DEng, 1994; MS, Ohio State U., 1956, PhD, 1959. Grad. tchg. asst. Ohio State U., Columbus, 1957, instr., 1957-59; asst. to assoc. prof. Okla. State U., Stillwater, 1959-66; prof., dept. head, dean Coll. Engring. Va. Tech, Blacksburg, 1967-93, pres., 1993—; dir. Roanoke (Va.) Electric Steel, 1986—, Pressure Sys., Hampton, Va., 1988—, Fistr Union Va., Roanoke, 1994—. Author 5 books. Mem. Gov. Charles Robb's Policy Adv. Com. on High Tech., Richmond, Va., 1984-85; rep. So. State Energy Bd., Richmond, 1986-90. 1st lt. USAF, 1953-55. Fellow Am. Soc. Engring. Edn. (Lamme medal 1994), Inst. Indsl. Engring; mem. Nat. Acad. Engring. Avocation: tennis. Office: Va Tech 210 Burruss Hall Blacksburg VA 24061

TORGERSEN, TORWALD HAROLD, architect, designer; b. Chgo., Sept. 2, 1929; s. Peder and Hansine Malene (Hansen) T.; m. Dorothy Darlene Peterson, June 22, 1963. B.S. in Archtl. Engring. with honors, U. Ill., 1951. Lic. architect Ill., D.C., real estate broker, Ill., interior designer, Ill.; registered architect Nat. Coun. Archtl. Registration Bds. Ptnr. Coyle & Torgersen (Architects-Engrs.), Washington, Chgo. and Joliet, Ill., 1955-56; project coord. Skidmore, Owings & Merrill, Chgo., 1956-60; corp. architect, dir. architecture, constrn. and interiors Container Corp. Am., Chgo., 1960-86; prin. in charge of orgn. and adminstrn. Jack Train Assocs. Inc., Chgo., 1987-88; cons. Torwald H. Torgersen, AIA, FASID, Chgo., 1988—; guest lectr. U. Wis. Capt. USNR, 1951-82. Recipient Top Ten Design award Factory mag., 1964. Fellow Am. Soc. Interior Designers; mem. AIA, Naval Res. Assn., Ill. Naval Militia, Am. Arbitration Assn., Am. Soc. Mil. Engrs., Paper Industry Mgmt. Assn. (hon.), Sports Car Club Am., Nat. Eagle Scout Assn. Club: 20 Fathoms. Home and Office: 3750 N Lake Shore Dr Chicago IL 60613-4238

TORGERSON, DAVID FRANKLYN, chemist, research facility administrator; b. Winnipeg, Man., July 11, 1942; m. Dale Rae Evans, May 28, 1966; children: Kristen, Dara, Shauna. BSc with honors, U. Man., 1965, MSc, 1966; PhD, McMaster U., 1969; postgrad., Nat. Def. Coll., Kingston, Ont., 1987-88. Rsch. scientist cyclotron inst. Tex. A&M Univ., College Station, 1969-76; rsch. scientist cyclotron inst. Atomic Energy Can. Ltd. Rsch., Pinawa, Man., 1976-78, head containment analysis sect., 1978-79, head br. rsch. chemistry, 1979-84, dir. reactor safety rsch., 1984-89, v.p. environ. sci. and waste mgmt., 1989-91; v.p. reactor devel. Atomic Energy Can. Ltd. Rsch., Chalk River, Ont., 1991-95; acting pres. Atomic Energy Can. Ltd. Rsch., Ottawa, Ont., 1994; v.p. rsch., product devel. Atomic Energy Can. Ltd., 1995—; chmn. prin. working group Orgn. Econ. Cooperation and Devel./Com. Safety Nuclear Installation, Paris, 1985-87, chmn. task force on source terms, 1986-87. Contbr. articles to profl. jours. Scholar Dow Chem. Can., 1966, Nat. Rsch. Coun. Can., 1967-69. Fellow Chem. Inst. Can. (chmn. Man. sect. 1982, regional councillor 1983), Can. Nuclear Soc. Office: Atomic Energy Can Ltd, Chalk River Labs, Chalk River, ON Canada K0J 1J0

TORGERSON, RICHARD WARREN, investment broker; b. Boston, Nov. 30, 1956; s. Warren S. and Lorraine M. (Almquist) T.; m. Lisa Warren, Jan. 9, 1982; children: Alayna, Carl. BA, Johns Hopkins U., 1980. Registered rep. series 7 and 24 Nat. Assn. Securities Dealers. Field staff organizer Balt. Neighborhoods, Inc., 1981-85; exec. dir. Liberty Neighbors, Randallstown, Md., 1985; investment broker Dean Witter Reynolds, Inc., Balt., 1985-93; registered prin. Torgerson Asset Mgmt., 1993—; mem. divestment adv. com. Balt. City Devel. Commn., 1992. Author: (book) Tenant Organizing, 1983; contbr. articles to publs. Mem. exec. bd. Coll. Dems. of Am., Washington, 1976-78; v.p. Young Dems. of Md., Balt., 1977-78; housing issue advisor Gary Hart Presdl. Campaign, Washington, 1984; fin. chmn. Earth Day-The Chesapeake Campaign, 1991. Mem. Social Investment Forum, Nuclear Free Am. (exec. bd. 1991—, chmn. 1993—), Greater Balt. Environ. Ctr. (vice chmn. 1989-94). Unitarian. Office: 9814 Branchleigh Rd Randallstown MD 21133-2028

TORGET, ARNE ODMUND, retired electrical engineer; b. Cathlamet, Wash., Oct. 10, 1916; s. John B. and Anna J. (Olson) T.; m. Dorothy M. Lackie, Aug. 30, 1941; children: Kathleen, James, Thomas. BSEE, U. Wash., 1940. Registered profl. elec. engr., Calif. Design engr. Boeing, Seattle, 1940-41, asst. group engr., 1941-46; design specialist N.Am. Aviation, L.A., 1946-50, 60-64, elec. supr., 1950-55; design specialist Rocketdyne N.Am. Aviation, Canoga Park, Calif., 1955-60; design specialist Space Div. Rockwell Internat., Downey, Calif., 1964-79; commr. Wahkiakum Count Pub. Utility, Cathlamet, 1985-96; ret., 1996; Bd. dirs. Wash. Pub. Utility Dist. Utility Systems, Seattle, 1985-96, Wash. Pub. Power Supply System, Richland, 1987-96, Wash. Pub. Utility Dist. Assn., Seattle, 1985-96. Mem. AAAS, IEEE, Elks. Republican. Roman Catholic. Home: 166 E Sunny Sands Rd Cathlamet WA 98612-9708

TORGOW, EUGENE N., electrical engineer; b. Bronx, N.Y., Nov. 26, 1925; s. Frank and Blanche Anita (Revzin) T.; m. Cynthia Silver, Mar. 19, 1950; children: Joan, Martha, Ellen. BSEE, Cooper Union, 1946; MSEE, Poly. Inst. Bklyn., 1949; Engr. in E.E., Poly. Inst. N.Y., 1980; postgrad. UCLA, 1983. Rsch. assoc., sect. leader Microwave Research Inst., Poly. Inst. Bklyn., 1947-51, 53-60, instr., 1954-59; mgr. microwave lab. A.B. Dumont Labs, East Patterson, N.J., 1951-53; chief engr., mgr. microwave products Dorne & Margolin, Inc., Westbury, L.I., N.Y., 1960-64; chief engr., dir. research, dir. mktg. Rantec div. Emerson Electric, Calabasas, Calif., 1964-68; with Missile Systems Group, Hughes Aircraft Co., Canoga Park, Calif., 1968-85. assoc. labs. mgr., 1981-85; cons. various electronics firms, N.Y.C., 1956-59; cons., 1986—; cons. Exec. Svc. Corps of So. Calif., 1996—; lectr. Calif. State U., Northridge, 1986-91. Contbr. articles to profl. jours.; patentee in field. Mem. Fair Housing Coun., San Fernando Valley, L.A., 1967—; mem. L.A. County Mus. Assn., 1976—. Served with USAAF, 1946-47. Recipient Engr. '85 Merit award San Fernando Valley Engrs. Coun., 1985. Fellow Inst. for Advancement Engring., IEEE (life); mem. WINCON (bd. dirs. 1984-89, chmn. bd. dirs. 1988-89), Microwave Theory and Techniques Soc. of IEEE (pres. 1966, mem. adminstrn. com. 1962-72, Svc. award 1978), Accreditation Bd. Engring. and Tech. (mem. engring. accreditation com. 1994—), Hughes Mgmt. Club (edn. chmn. 1979-80), Sigma Xi. Democrat. Office: 9531 Donna Ave Northridge CA 91324-1816

TORIAN, HENRY, automotive executive. CEO Tasha. Office: Tasha Inc 43285 Auto Mall Cir Fremont CA 94538-3186*

TORIBARA, TAFT YUTAKA, radiation biologist, biophysicist, chemist, toxicologist; b. Seattle, Apr. 10, 1917; s. Minekichi and Hisano (Miyata) T.; m. Masako Ono., Aug. 28, 1948; children—Lynne Suzanne, Neil Willard. BS in Chem. Engring. summa cum laude, U. Wash., 1938, M.S. in Chem. Engring, 1939; Ph.D., U. Mich., 1942. Rsch. chemist dept. engring. rsch. U. Mich., 1942-48; from asst. prof. to prof. radiation biology and biophysics Sch. Medicine and Dentistry, U. Rochester, N.Y., 1948-89, prof. emeritus toxicology in biophysics, 1989-93; prof. emeritus dept. environ. medicine, 1993—; cons. in field. Editor: Modern Techniques for the Detection and Measurement of Environmental Pollutants, 1978, Polluted Rain, 1980; contbr. articles to profl. jours. Chmn. advancement com. Boy Scouts Am., 1964-67; pres. Jr. High Family Faculty Forum, 1964-66; mem. Gates Library Bd., 1965-75, pres., 1972-74. NIH Spl. Rsch. fellow, 1960-61. Mem. Am. Chem. Soc., AAAS. Inventor ultrafiltration apparatus, 1953. Home: 54 Timpat Dr Rochester NY 14624-2928 Office: EHSC U Rochester Med Ctr Rochester NY 14642 *My life might be summarized by the statement, "Adversity is not always bad".*

TORII, SHUKO, psychology educator; b. Toyohashi, Aichi-ken, Japan, Apr. 5, 1930; m. Toshiko Mochizuki, June 19, 1975. BA, U. Tokyo, 1954, MA, 1956, PhD, 1964. Rsch. asst. Tokyo Inst. Tech., 1959-61, U. Tokyo, 1961-65; assoc. prof. Tokyo U. Agr. Tech., 1965-70; rsch. assoc. U. Mich., Ann Arbor, 1966-68; rsch. assoc. Inst. Molecular Biophysics Fla. State U., 1968-69; from assoc. prof. to prof. psychology U. Tokyo, 1970-91; prof. U. Sacred Heart, Tokyo, 1991—. Author: The World of Vision, 1979, Psychology of Vision, 1982, Visual Perception in the Congenitally or Early Blinded after Surgery, 1992; author, editor: Perception, 1983, Visually Handicapped and Technology of Sensory Substitution, 1984, The Visually Handicapped and Their Cognitive Activity, 1993. Mem. Japanese Psychonomic Soc. (assoc. editor 1981-88, editor 1988-96, pres. 1996—), Japanese Psychol. Assn. (mem. editorial com. 1987-89, editor 1989-92), Optical Soc. Am., Assn. Rsch. in Vision and Ophthalmology. Home: 2-17-26-204 Takada, Toshima, Tokyo 171, Japan Office: U Sacred Heart, 4-3-1 Hiroo, Shibuya Tokyo 150, Japan

TORKELSON, JODIE RAE, executive branch staff member; b. Cudahy, Wis., May 13, 1958; d. Wallace Keith and Delores Helen (Hagen) T. BA in Polit. Sci., Moorhead State U., 1980. Staff asst. Congressman Richard Nolan, Washington, 1980-81; office mgr. Congressman Leon E. Panetta, Washington, 1981-86, adminstrv. asst., 1988-89; acting exec. dir. Life Underwriters for Lutheran Charities, Mpls., 1986-88; dir. adminstrn. com. on budget U.S. Ho. of Reps., Washington, 1989-93, assoc. dir. for adminstrn. Office of Mgmt. and Budget, 1993-94; asst. to pres. for mgmt. and adminstrn. The White House, Washington, 1994—. Lutheran. Office: The White House Office Mgmt & Adminstrn Old Executive Office Bldg Washington DC 20502

TORKILDSEN, PETER G., congressman; b. Milw., Jan. 28, 1958; s. Robert Allan and Mary Ellen (Hill) T.; m. Gail Bloomgarden, Jan. 1996. BA, U. Mass., 1980; MPA, Harvard U., 1990. Mem. Mass. House of reps., 1985-91, 103rd Congress from 6th Mass. dist., 1993-97; pres. Thunder Hill Inc., Peabody, Mass., 1997—. Chmn. Danvers (Mass.) Rep. Town Com., 1983-88; mem. Danvers Town Meeting, 1983-85, Mass. Rep. State Com., Boston, 1984-93. Mem. Am. Legis. Exchange Council, Mass. Legislator's Assn., Nat. Rep. Legislator Assn. Roman Catholic. Lodge: Sons of Norway. Home: 12 Spruce St Danvers MA 01923-2613 Office: Thunder Hill Inc 140 Summit St Peabody MA 01960-5156

TORME, MARGARET ANNE, public relations executive, communications consultant; b. Indpls., Apr. 5, 1943; d. Ira G. and Margaret Joy (Wright) Barker; children—Karen Anne, Leah Vanessa. Student Coll. San Mateo, 1961-65. Pub. rels. mgr. Hoefer, Dieterich & Brown (now Chiat-Day), San Francisco, 1964-73; v.p., co-founder, creative dir. Lowry & Ptnrs., San Francisco, 1975-83; pres., founder Torme & Co. (now Torme & Kenney), San Francisco, 1983—; cons. in communications. Mem. Pub. Rels. Soc. Am., San Francisco C. of C. (outstanding achievement award for women entrepreneurs 1987), Jr. League (adv. bd.), Pub. Rsls Orgn. Internat. (v.p., dir.). Office: 545 Sansome St San Francisco CA 94111-2908

TORME, MEL(VIN) (HOWARD TORME), musician, jazz vocalist; b. Chgo., Sept. 13, 1925; m. Janette Scott (div.); 2 children. Studied drums at age seven. Acted in radio soap operas; sang with Buddy Rogers, other name bands during early years; toured with Chico Marx band, 1942-43; motion picture debut in Higher and Higher, 1943; other motion picture appearances include Pardon My Rhythm, 1944, Words and Music, 1948, Walk Like a Dragon, 1960, A Man Called Adam, 1966, The Land of No Return; leader vocal group, Mel-Tones, Calif.; solo singer, 1947—, co-founder Producers Group Ltd., 1982; numerous compositions including County Fair; solo singer Vaudeville Tour, Eng., 1956, 57; recs. include Live at the Maisonette, Mel Torme and Friends, Recorded at Marty, Back in Town, Songs of New York, Swings Shubert Alley, That's All, Easy to Remember, Velvet Fog, Songs About Love, Round Midnight, Together Again, The London Sessions, 1992, Mel Torme in Hollywood, 1992, Nothing Without You, 1993, Christmas Songs, 1993, Sixteen Most Requested Songs, 1993, Sing, Sing, Sing: Live at the Fujitsu-Concord Jazz Festival, 1993, Jazz 'Round Midnight, 1994, A Tribute to Bing Crosby, 1994, Spotlight on Mel Torme, 1995; author: The Other Side of the Rainbow, 1970, autobiography It Wasn't All Velvet, 1988. Recipient Grammy award Best Male Jazz Vocal Performance, 1983, 84. Address: Capito Records 1750 Vine St Los Angeles CA 90028 also: Internat Ventures Inc Ste 202 23734 Velencia Blvd Valencia CA 91355*

TORMOLLAN, GARY GORDON, health facility administrator, physical therapist; b. Plainfield, N.J., Feb. 23, 1954; s. Gordon William and Doris Evelyn (Palmer) T.; m. Stacey Lee Cole, Aug. 20, 1983; children: Brian, Kristin. BS in Health Edn., Trenton (N.J.) State Coll., 1976; cert. in phys. therapy, Hahnemann U., 1982; MEd, Trenton State Coll., 1987. Lic. phys. therapist, Maine, Pa.; lic. athletic trainer, N.J. Athletic trainer Princeton (N.J.) High Sch., 1976-81; phys. therapist Holy Redeemer Hosp., Huntington Valley, Pa., 1982-83, Phys. Therapy of Princeton, 1984-86; sports medicine coord. Omni-Fit, Mt. Laurel, N.J., 1986-87; dir. rehab. svcs. Med. Coll. of Pa., Phila., 1987-90; dir. phys. therapy Mid-Maine Med. Ctr., Waterville, 1990-92; pres., CEO Maine Phys. Therapy, Waterville, 1993—; cons. Burnt Mill Med. Ctr., Cherry Hill, N.J., 1983; mem. clin. faculty Temple U., Phila., 1989-90; cons., mem. adv. bd. phys. therapy asst. program Kennebec Valley Tech. Coll., Fairfield, Maine, 1990-94. Deacon Ewing (N.J.) Presbyn. Ch., 1989; coach Waterville Little League, Waterville (Maine) Youth Soccer Assn. Mem. Am. Phys. Therapy Assn., Nat. Athletic Trainers Assn., Waterville Rotary. Congregationalist. Avocations: fishing, golf, tennis. Home: 31 Messalonskee Ave Waterville ME 04901-5352 Office: Maine Physical Therapy 28 College Ave Waterville ME 04901-6105

TORNABENE, RUSSELL C., communications executive; b. Gary, Ind., Sept. 18, 1923; s. Samuel Tornabene and Marion (LaVorci) Roush; m. Audrey F. Shankey, June 21, 1952; children—Joseph, Leigh, David, Lynn. A.A., Gary Jr. Coll., 1941, 46-47; B.A., Ind. U., 1949, M.A., 1950. Radio, TV newswriter WRC-AM-TV, Washington, 1951-55; network supr. NBC Network News, Washington, 1955-61; network gen. mgr. NBC Network News, NYC, 1961-75; v.p. NBC News, NYC, 1975-81; exec. officer Soc. Profl. Journalists, Chgo., 1981-87; Midwest dir. Exec. TV Workshop, Chgo., 1987-96; pres. Russell Communications Cons., 1996—. Contbr. articles on news to mags. and newspapers. Mem. N.Y. Catholic Archdiocese Sch. Bd., N.Y.C., 1972. Recipient Disting. Service award, Sigma Delta Chi, 1949; Ernie Pyle scholar, 1949. Mem. Acad. TV Arts and Scis., Radio TV News Dirs. Assn. Club: Overseas Press (former v.p.). Avocation: photography. Office: 626 Sheridan Sq # 2 Evanston IL 60202-3156

TORNEK, TERRY E., real estate executive; b. Bklyn., Nov. 23, 1945; s. Allen Vernon and Gertrude (Slotkin) T.; m. Maria Elizabeth Mascoli, June 25, 1967; children: Joshua, Jessica, Rachel. BA, Princeton U., 1967; MS in Urban Planning, Columbia U., 1971. Urban renewal rep. U.S. Dept. HUD, N.Y.C., 1968-69; prin. planner, dir. Planning Dept., Springfield, Mass., 1971-75; dir. Planning Dept., Pasadena, Calif., 1982-84; adminstr. Pioneer Valley Transit Authority, Springfield, 1975-79; v.p., gen. mgr. Cannon Planning & Devel., Springfield, 1979-82; dir. devel. BWC Devel., L.A., 1984-87; exec. v.p. Haseko (Calif.) Inc., L.A., 1987—. City councillor Springfield (Mass.) City Coun., 1976-77; bd. dirs. Springfield (Mass.) Action Commn., 1975-80; bd. dirs., v.p. Pasadena (Calif.) Neighborhood Housing Svcs., 1982-88. Home: 4910 Burgoyne Ln La Canada CA 91011-3717 Office: Haseko (Calif) Inc 350 S Figueroa St Ste 601 Los Angeles CA 90071-1201

TORNQVIST, ERIK GUSTAV MARKUS, chemical engineer, research scientist; b. Lund, Sweden, Jan. 13, 1924; came to U.S., 1951; s. Gustav Ivar and Anne Marie (Lassen) T.; m. Linnéa Dagmar Lindborg, June 28, 1969; children: Gunvor, Karin, Carl-Erik. MSChemE, Royal Inst. Tech., Stockholm, 1948; MS in Biochemistry, U. Wis., 1953, PhD in Biochemistry/Organic Chemistry, 1955. Registered engr., Sweden. 1st rsch. asst. div. food chemistry Royal Inst. Tech., 1949-51; rsch. asst. dept. biochemistry U. Wis., Madison, 1951-55; rsch. chemist chem. divsn. Esso Rsch. and Engring. Co., Linden, N.J., 1955-58, rsch. assoc., 1958-66, sr. rsch. assoc., 1966-72; sr. rsch. assoc. Exxon Chem. Co., Tech., Linden, 1972-86; internat. cons. Watchung, N.J., 1986-90; pres. PolymErik, Inc., Watchung, 1990—; vis prof. Royal Inst. Tech., 1987; invited prin. speaker Scandinavian Day, Chautauqua (N.Y.) Instn., 1983, 87; invited speaker, chmn. numerous nat. and internat. meetings. Co-editor: Polymer Chemistry of Synthetic Elastomers, 2 vols., 1968, 69; patentee in field; contbr. articles to profl. jours., chpts. to books. Treas. United Swedish Socs., N.Y.C., 1972-86, Swedish Sch. Assn. N.J., 1988-91; bd. govs. Am. Swedish Hist. Mus., Phila., 1974-89; trustee New Sweden Co., Bridgeton, N.J., 1986-89, Kalmar Nyckel Found., Wilmington, Del., 1987-96, hon. trustee, 1996; bd. dirs. Watchung Hills Soccer Assn., Watchung/Warren, N.J., 1989-95. Recipient award 1st Nat. Inventors Day, 1973, gold Bicentennial medal King of Sweden, 1980, John Hanson award for excellence in pub. svc. Am.-Swedish Cultural Found., Mpls., 1981, citation Swedish Coun. of Am., 1983, cert. of appreciation Swedish New Sweden '88 Com., 1989; grad. fellow Roos' Found., Stockholm, 1949, 51, Govt. of Sweden, 1948, State Coun. for Technol. Rsch., Stockholm, 1949, Adelsköld fellow Royal Acad. Sci., 1951, 53, Univ. fellow Sweden-Am. Found., Stockholm, 1951. Mem. N.Y. Acad. Scis., Am. Chem. Soc., Swedish Soc. Chem. Engrs., Swedish Assn. Grad. Engrs., Internat. Union Pure and Applied Chemistry (affiliate), Am. Soc. Swedish Engrs. (life, sec. 1965-68, pres. 1968-72, John Ericsson Gold medal 1984), John Ericsson Soc., Wis. Alumni Assn. (life), KTH Alumni, Swedish-Am. C.of C., Swedish Colonial Soc. (hon. gov. Ad Vitam 1982, gov. 1977-82, 86-89), Am. Scandinavian Soc., Vasa Order Am., Svensk I Världen (life), Schlaraffia, Swedish Ski Club (pres. 1972-74), Phi Lambda Upsilon, Sigma Xi. Lutheran. Avocations: skiing, music, photography, historical research and writing. Home and Office: 38 Mareu Dr Watchung NJ 07060-5025

TOROK, MARGARET LOUISE, insurance company executive; b. Detroit, June 22, 1922; d. Perl Edward Ensor and Mary (Seggie) Armstrong; m. Leslie A. Torok, Aug. 14, 1952; 1 child, Margaret Mary Ryan. Lic. Ins. Agy. From ins. agt. to corp. officer Grendel-Wittbold Ins., Southgate, Mich., 1961-72; pres. of corp. Grendel-Wittbold Ins., Southgate, 1972—; bd. dirs. Ind. Ins. Agts. of Mich., Lansing, 1984-92, Ind. Ins. Agts. of Wayne County, Dearborn, 1979—, pres. 1978. Bd. dirs. So. Wayne County C. of C., Taylor, 1975, CEO, chmn. bd. dirs., 1997—; bd. dirs. City of Southgate Tex. Increment Fin. Authority Dist. and Econ. Devel. Commn., 1987—; leadership chmn. YMCA, Wyandotte, 1980—, Downriver Comty. Alliance; lay chmn. Cath. Svc. Appeal for Archdiocese of Detroit, 1989; co-chair fundraiser Sacred Heart Ch.; mem. bd. MESC Employers Com., 1991-95; mem. com., bd. New Workforce Devel. Com. (gov. appt., charter mem.). Recipient Capital award Ind. Ins. Agts. of Mich., 1988, Lifetime Achievement award, Amb. award, 1994, Woman of Yr. AAUW, 1994, Salute to Excellence award Downriver Coun. of Arts, 1993-94, Chmn. of Yr. award MESC Job. Svc. Employers Com., 1991, Robert Stewart award Wyandotte Svc. Club Coun., 1994, Info. Ctr.-Partnership award, 1996, W.O. Hildebrand award, 1997. Mem. Wyandotte Yacht Club, Soroptimist Club of Wyandotte Southgate Taylor (pres. 1984-86, Advancing Status Women award 1988, Soroptimist of Yr. award 1993-94), Mich. Assn. Ins. Agts. Roman Catholic. Office: Grendel Wittbold Agy Inc 12850 Eureka Rd Southgate MI 48195-1344

TORQUATO, SALVATORE, civil engineering educator; b. Falerna, Calabria, Italy, Feb. 10, 1954; came to U.S., 1955; s. Vincent and Palma (Vaccaro) T.; m. Kim Tracey Hoberock, Nov. 8, 1975; 1 child, Michelle. BSME, Syracuse U., 1975; MSME, SUNY, Stony Brook, 1977, PhD in Mech. Engring., 1980. Rsch. engr. Grumman Aerospace Corp., Bethpage, N.Y., 1975-78; rsch. asst. dept. mech. engring. SUNY, Stony Brook, 1978-80; asst. prof. dept. mech. engring. GM Inst., Flint, Mich., 1981-82; from asst. to assoc. prof. depts. mech., aerospace & chem. engring. N.C. State U., Raleigh, 1982-90, prof. depts. mech., aerospace & chem. engring., 1991-92; prof. Civil Engring. Princeton (N.J.) U., 1992—; vis. prof. Courant Inst. Math. Scis., N.Y.C., 1990-91; cons. Eastman Kodak, Rochester, N.Y., 1989—. Contbr. articles to profl. jours. Grumman Masters fellow, 1975-77; grantee NSF, 1982—, U.S. Dept. Energy, 1986—; recipient Engring. Rsch. Achievement award Alcoa Co., 1987, Disting. Engring. Rsch. award, 1989, Gustus L. Larson Meml. award, 1994. Fellow ASME; mem. Am. Inst. Chem. Engrs., Am. Phys. Soc., Soc. Engring. Sci., Soc. for Indsl. and Applied Math. Avocations: racquetball, reading. Office: Princeton U Princeton Materials Inst Depts Civ Eng & Oper Rsch Princeton NJ 08544

TORRAS, JOSEPH HILL, pulp and paper company executive; b. Americus, Ga., Nov. 14, 1924; s. Fernando Joseph and Nell Wilson (Hill) T.; m. Mary Ravenel Robertson, Sept. 20, 1952; children: Mary Martin, Fernanda Maria, Joseph Hill. S.B., Yale U., 1948; M.B.A., Harvard U., 1950. Asst. to fin. v.p. Seatrian Lines, Inc., 1950-51; with St. Regis Paper Co., 1951-60, sales mgr. printing papers div., 1956-60; exec. v.p. Brown Co., Boston, 1960-64; pres., chmn. bd. Premoid Corp., West Springfield, Mass., 1964-87; pres. Precon, Inc., Ludlow, 1967-87, Lincoln Pulp & Paper Co., Lincoln, Maine, 1968—, Astro Tissue Co., Battleboro, Vt., 1968-72; chmn. bd. Whitman Products, Ltd., West Warwick, R.I., 1976-89; pres., chief exec. officer Preco Corp., Amherst, Mass., 1976—; chmn. Lincoln (Maine) Pulp and Paper Co., 1989—; bd. dirs. Bay Banks, Inc., Boston; chmn. Ea. Fine Paper Inc., Brewer, Maine; adv. dir. Liberty Mut. Ins. Mem. Mass. Gov.'s Bus. Adv. Coun., 1985-88, devel. bd. Yale U., 1989—; bd. govs. Mass. Gen. Hosp.; bd. dirs. Mass. Taxpayers Assn., 1976-86; trustee Hist. Deerfield, 1990—, Piedmont Coll., Ga., 1991—. Lt. (j.g.), aviator USNR, 1943-46. Mem. Tissue Paper Mfrs. Assn. (dir. 1963-64), Am. Pulp and Paper Mill Supts. Assn., Salesman's Assn. Paper Industry, NAM (dir. 1981-85), Colony Club. Independent. Office: Preco Corp 100 University Dr Amherst MA 01002-2232

TORREGROSSA, JOSEPH ANTHONY, lawyer; b. Bklyn., Sept. 23, 1944; s. Joseph and Marie (Faraone) T.; m. Ann S. Gormally, July 11, 1970; children—Brennan, Maresa. A.B., Villanova U., 1966, J.D., 1969. Bar: N.Y. 1970, Pa. 1971, U.S. Dist. Ct. (ea. dist.) Pa. 1971, U.S. Ct. Appeals (3d cir.) 1973, U.S. Supreme Ct. 1975. Law Clk. to judge U.S. Dist. Ct. (ea. dist.) Pa., 1969-71; assoc. Morgan, Lewis & Bockius, Phila., 1971-77; ptnr. Morgan, Lewis & Bockius, Phila., 1977—; lectr. in field. Mem. Phila. Bar Assn., Pa. Bar Assn., ABA. Office: Morgan Lewis & Bockius 2000 One Logan Sq Philadelphia PA 19103

TORRENCE, GWEN, Olympic athlete; b. Atlanta, June 12, 1965; m. Manley Waller Jr.; 1 child, Manley Waller III. 2d place NCAA 100, 1985; 7th place USA/Mobil 100, 1985; 5th place USA/Mobil 200, 1985; champion NCAA 100, 1987, NCAA 200, 1987; 5th place U.S. World Championships 200; winner of sprints World Univ. Games; winner Pan Am. Games 200, 1987; 3rd place in both 100 and 200 Olympic Trials, 1988; 2d place USA/Mobil 100, 1991; winner USA/Mobil 200, 1991; gold medalist 200 Meter, Barcelona, Spain, 1992; winner Mobil Grand Prix 100 meters, 1993; gold medalist 100 meters World Track & Field Championships, Gutenborg, Sweden, 1995; bronze medalist 100 meters Olympic Games, Atlanta, 1996, gold medalist 4x100 meters relay, 1996. Winner 100 meters, 200 meters USA/Mobil Track & Field Championships, 1995, 100 meters World Athletic Championships, 1995, Gold medal 100 meters, 200 meters Goodwill Games, 1995, Gold medal 4 x 100 meter relay Atlanta Olympics, 1996, Bronze medal 100 meters. Achievements include 5th place world ranking at 200 meters Track & Field News, 1987, ranked number 3 sprinter in the world, 1991, ranked 3rd place in world in the 100, 1993, ranked 2d place in world in the 200, 1993, ranked 4th place in world in the 400, 1993. Address: US Track & Field 1 RCA Dome Ste 140 Indianapolis IN 46225*

TORRENS, PEGGY JEAN, technical school coordinator; b. El Dorado, Kans., Oct. 7, 1952; d. Wayne E. and Evelyn M. (Hornbostel) Clark; m. Dennis L. Torrens, May 3, 1975; children: Jason L., Jennifer L. BS in Edn., Emporia State U., 1974, MS, 1975. Cert. secondary tchr., Kans. Instr. reading Burlington (Kans.) High Sch., 1974-75, Lowther Mid. Sch., Emporia, Kans., 1975-76; coord. resouce ctr., tech. prep coord. Flint Hills Tech. Coll., Emporia, Kans., 1976—; TQM team leader Flint Hills Tech. Coll.; mem., chairperson Profl. Devel. Coun., Emporia, Kans., 1990—, applied curriculum inservice presenter; inservice presenter Nat. Tech. Prep., 1996, State Tech. Prep., 1997. Author software programs; reviewer workbook Modern Reading, 1982. Community leader Lyon County 4-H, Emporia, 1988—. Mem. NEA, Emporia Women's Golf Assn. (v.p.). Democrat. Lutheran. Avocations: reading, crafts, quilting, golf. Office: Flint Hills Tech Coll 3301 W 18th Ave Emporia KS 66801-5957

TORRENZANO, RICHARD, public affairs executive. BS, N.Y. Inst. Tech., 1972, LittD (hon.), 1990; postgrad., Standford U. With N.Y. Stock Exch., N.Y.C., 1981-91, sr. v.p., mgmt. com., chief spokesman, 1991-93; sr. v.p., dir. corp. affairs, mem. mgmt. com. SmithKline Beecham, London, 1991-94; CEO, The Torrenzano Group Ltd., N.Y.C., 1994—; coord. Pres. Reagan's Bd. Advisors on Pvt. Sector Initiatives, Washington, 1986-89; pvt. sector adv. com. USIA, Washington, 1983-92; coord. program USSR-N.Y. Stock Exch., Moscow, 1990; lectr. in field. Contbr. articles to profl. jours. Trustee, mem. exec. com. N.Y. Inst. Tech., 1985—. Recipient Silver Anvil award Pub. Rels. Soc. Am., Ellis Island Medal Honor, 1997. Mem. Royal Soc. Medicine (London), Internat. Pub. Rels. Assn. London, Nat. Press Club, N.Y. Press Club, Knights of Malta. Office: The Torrenzano Group Ltd Ste 1400 551 5th Ave Rm 1400 New York NY 10176-1499

TORRES, CYNTHIA ANN, banker; b. Glendale, Calif., Sept. 24, 1958; d. Adolph and Ruth Ann (Smith) T.; m. Michael Victor Gisser, Mar. 11, 1989; children: Spencer Williams Gisser, David Westfall Torres Gisser. AB, Harvard U., 1980, MBA, 1984. Research assoc. Bain & Co., Boston, 1980-82; assoc. Goldman, Sachs & Co., N.Y.C., 1984-88, v.p., 1988; v.p. First Interstate Bancorp, L.A., 1989-92; dir. Fidelity Investments Mgmt. (H.K.) Ltd., Hong Kong, 1993-96; pres. Integrity Fund Consultants, Ltd., 1996—. Mem. judiciary rev. bd. Bus. Sch. Harvard U., Boston, 1983-84. Rockefeller Found. scholar, 1976; Harvard U. Ctr. for Internat. Affairs fellow, 1979-80; recipient Leadership award Johnson and Johnson, 1980; by Council for Opportunity in Grad. Mgmt. Edn. fellow, 1982-84. Mem. Acad. Polit. Sci., Asia Soc., Fin. Women's Assn. Hong Kong (pres.), Harvard Club of Hong Kong. Avocation: sportswriting. Office: Century Tower II, 2/F 1A Treganter Path, Hong Kong SAR, Hong Kong

TORRES, EDWIN, state judge, writer; b. N.Y., 1931; s. Edelmiro and Ramona T.; m. Vickie; 4 children. Degree, City Coll., N.Y., Bklyn. Law Sch. Asst. dist. atty. complaints bur., then homicide bur. Manhattan Dist. Atty's. Office, 1958-61; appt. judge Criminal Ct. Bench, N.Y. State Supreme Ct., 1980—. Author: Carlito's Way, 1975, After Hours, 1979, Q & A, 1977. Office: NY Supreme Ct 12th Judicial Dist 100 Centre St New York NY 10013-4308*

TORRES, ERNEST C., federal judge; b. 1941. AB, Dartmouth Coll., 1963; JD, Duke U., 1968. Assoc. Hinckley, Allen, Salisbury & Parsons, 1968-74; ptnr. Saunders & Torres, 1974-80; assoc. justice R.I. Superior Ct., 1980-85; asst. v.p. Aetna Life and Casualty, 1985-86; ptnr. Tillinghast, Collins & Graham, 1986-87; judge U.S. Dist. Ct. R.I., Providence, 1988—; pres. East Greenwich (R.I.) Town Coun., 1972-74; state rep. R.I. Ho. of Reps., 1975-80, dep. minority leader, 1977-80. Recipient Disting. Svc. award Jaycees, 1974; named Man of Yr., Prince Henry Soc. R.I., 1988, Prince Henry Soc. Mass., 1995; Alfred P. Sloan scholar Dartmouth Coll. Mem. ABA, ATLA, R.I. Bar Assn., Jaycees (Dist. Svc. award 1974), Prince Henry Soc. of R.I., Prince Henry Soc. of Mass. Office: US Dist Ct 1 Exch Ter 216 Federal St Providence RI 02909-1104

TORRES, ESTEBAN EDWARD, congressman, business executive; b. Miami, Ariz., Jan. 27, 1930; s. Esteban Torres and Rena Baron (Gomez) T.; m. Arcy Sanchez, Jan. 22, 1955; children: Carmen D'Arcy, Rena Denise, Camille Bianca, Selina Andre, Esteban Adrian. Student, East Los Angeles Coll., 1960, Calif. State U., Los Angeles, 1963, U. Md., 1965, Am. U., 1966; PhD (hon.), Nat. U., 1987. Chief steward United Auto Workers, local 230, 1954-63, dir. polit. com., 1963; organizer, internat. rep. United Auto Workers (local 230), Washington, 1964; asst. dir. Internat. Affairs Dept., 1975-77; dir. Inter-Am. Bureau for Latin Am., Caribbean, 1965-67; exec. dir. E. Los Angeles Community Union (TELACU), 1967-74; U.S. ambassador to UNESCO, Paris, 1977-79; chmn. Geneva Grp., 1977-78; chmn. U.S. del. Gen. Conf., 1978; spl. asst. to pres. U.S., dir. White House Office Hispanic Affairs, 1979-81; mem. 98th-103rd Congresses from 34th Dist. Calif., 1983—, mem. appropriations com., subcom. fgn. ops., subcom. transp.; campaign coordinator Jerry Brown for Gov., 1974; Hispanic coordinator Los Angeles County campaign Jimmy Carter for Pres., 1976; mem. Sec. of State Adv. Group, 1979-81; v.p. Nat. Congress Community Econ. Devel., 1973-74; pres. Congress Mex.-Am. Unity, 1970-71, Los Angeles Plaza de la Raza Cultural Center, 1974; dir. Nat. Com. on Citizens Broadcasting, 1977; cons. U.S. Congress office of tech. assessment, 1976-77; del to U.S. Congress European Parliament meetings, 1984—; ofcl. congl. observer Geneva Arms Control Talks; chmn. Congl. Hispanic Caucus, 1987; speaker Wrights Del. to USSR, 1987; Dem. dep. Whip, 1990. Contbr. numerous articles to profl. jours. Co-chmn. Nat. Hispanic Dems., 1988—; chmn. Japan-Hispanic Inst. Inc.; bd. visitors Sch. Architecture U. Calif. at Los Angeles, 1971-73; bd. dirs. Los Angeles County Econ. Devel. Com., 1972-75, Internat. Devel. Conf., 1976-78; chmn. Congrl. Hispanic Caucus, 1985-86; pres. Plaza de la Raza Cultural Ctr., 1972-73; trustee Am. Coll. Paris, 1977-79. Served in AUS, 1949-53, ETO. Recipient Congrl. award Nat. Leadership award 1997. Mem. Americans for Dem. Action (exec. bd. 1975-77), VFW Post 6315, Pico Rivera, Calif., Am. Legion, Smithsonian Inst. (regent 1997—), S.W. Voter Inst. Office: House of Representatives Rayburn Bldg Rm 2269 Washington DC 20515-0005

TORRES, MILTON JOHN, industrial engineering educator; b. N.Y.C., July 28, 1931; s. Milton and Vitalia (Cabrera) T.; m. Dorothy Spaugh (div. Feb. 1971); children: Milton J. III, Geoffrey, Vicky L. Lopez; m. Dorothy Roberts. BS in Gen. Engring., U. Okla., 1963, M Aerospace Engring., 1964; DArts in Mech. Engring., U. Miami, 1989. Commd. 2d lt. USAF, 1954, advanced through grades to maj.; chief test control br. Ops. Directorate Air Force Ea. Test Range, Cape Kennedy, Fla., 1968-71; ret. USAF, 1971; indsl. engr., sr. indsl. engr. Pan Am. World Airways, Inc., Miami, Fla., 1972-73; plant supt. Am. Panel Corp., Miami, 1973-77; plant mgr. Dyplast of Fla., 1977-83; asst. prof. indsl. systems dept. Fla. Internat. U., 1983-87, rsch. scientist, lectr. dept. indsl. engring., 1987-94. Contbr. articles to profl. jours., patentee in field. Decorated DFC, Air medal (13), Air Force Meritorious Svc. medal, Air Force Commendation medal. Mem. Tau Beta Pi, Sigma Tau, Sigma Gamma Tau, Alpha Pi Mu. Home: 11200 SW 99th Ct Miami FL 33176-4123

TORRES, RALPH CHON, minister; b. San José, Calif., Oct. 18, 1948; s. Chon Poncé and Dora (Grijalva) T.; m. Pamela Ellen Hansen, Mar. 6, 1971; children: Chon, Brita, Samuel, Sarah. BTh, L.I.F.E. Bible Coll., L.A., 1970. Ordained to ministry Internat. Ch. of the Foursquare Gospel, 1981. Missionary asst. Internat. Ch. of Foursquare Gospel, Mexicali, Mex., 1970; youth pastor Internat. Ch. of Foursquare Gospel, Redondo Beach, Calif., 1971-72, Pueblo, Colo., 1972-74; sr. pastor Internat. Ch. of Foursquare Gospel., Pasadena, Calif., 1984—; youth pastor Ch. on the Way, Van Nuys, Calif., 1975-84; asst., dir. children's camps, Jr. and Sr. High camps for So. Calif. Dist. Foursquare Chs., 1978—; tchr. L.I.F.E. Bible Coll., L.A., 1979-86; bd. dirs. Holy Ghost Repair Svc., Hollywood, Calif., Centrum of Hollywood, Christians in Govt., L.A., Camp Cedar Crest, Running Springs, Calif.; bd. dirs., speaker Mainstream Inc., Tacoma, 1978-83. Composer: Kids of the Kingdom, 1976. Mem. Prop. 98 Sch. Report Card Com., Pasadena, 1989-90; adv. com. Marshall Fundamental Sch., Pasadena, 1989-90, Pasadena Unified Sch. Dist., 1990—. Recipient commendation for svc. Mayor of Pasadena, 1990. Office: Pasadena Foursquare Ch 174 Harkness Ave Pasadena CA 91106-2007*

TORRES, ROBERT ALVIN, dancer, singer, actor, sign language interpreter; b. Camden, N.J., Apr. 4, 1960; s. Pedro Juan and Nora Hilda (Castellanos) T.; m. Karen Lea Dearborn, Nov. 21, 1987; children: Ariane Lea, Ryan Alexander. Grad. high sch., Willingboro, N.J. Dancer Burlington (N.J.) Ballet Co., 1976-78; soloist Harkness Dancers, N.Y.C., 1979; ind. dancer, singer N.Y.C., 1982—; prin. dancer Rod Rogers Dance Co., N.Y.C., 1985, Louis Johnson Dancers, 1986; dance tchr. Muhlenberg Coll., 1993—, Hartford Ballet Sch., 1993—; tchr. Muhlenberg Coll., 1993-94; sign lang. interpreter, 1992—; guest tchr. master classes Mount Holyoke Coll., 1987, Conn. Coll., 1992, Pa. Youth Theatre, 1993, Ethel Walker Sch., 1993, Dance Forum Lehigh Valley, 1994; dance tchr. Cedar Crest Coll. Allentown Acad. Arts; tchr. Lehigh Valley Ballet Guild. Choreographer (restaged) Sundazy by Sandra Machala, 1979, Midsummer Night's Dream, 1990, On The Town, 1991, Peter Pan, 1994, Wake Up The Moon, 1994, Keep on Walking, 1995, Evita, 1995, A Chorus Line, 1995, Keep on Twalking, 1995, Switching Stations, 1996, Seasonal Allianees, 1996, Follow the Beacon, 1996, My Partner, Myself, 1997, Can You See th Bull..., 1997; dancer Busch Gardens, 1980, Kiss Me Kate with Robert Goulet, 1981; dancer, singer Evita nat. tours III and IV, 1982-84, Barnum, 1986, Cats nat. tour IV, 1987, The Star Dust Road Workshop, 1988, Carousel, 1988, Golden Boy, 1989, West Side Story, 1989, My Fair Lady, 1989, The Chocolate Soldier, 1990; dance capt. Evita, 1985, A Chorus Line, 1986; acrobatic cons. A Christmas Carol, 1989, dance capt., 1989, 90; asst. choreographer, actor A Christmas Carol, 1990, Here's Love, 1991; guest artist with the Decatur Dekalb Ballet, 1979, Virginia Beach Ballet, 1980, St. Petersburg Ballet, 1980, Miss. Ballet Theatre, 1980, Rio Grande Valley Co., 1980-81; choreographer, dance capt., dancer, singer Here's Love, 1991, co-choreographer, Oliver; fight dir. Oliver, 1996; sign lang. performance interpreter Come Back to the Five and Dime, Jimmy Dean, Jimmy Dean, 1997, In Search of Cinderella, 1997. Recipient 3d place award N.J. Scholastic State Gymnastic Tournament, 1978. Mem. Actors' Equity Assn. Republican. Avocations: hang gliding, skiing, skating, diving, auto repair. Office: care Torres Family 514 Cambridge Dr Mount Laurel NJ 08054-2804

TORRES-AYBAR, FRANCISCO GUALBERTO, medical educator; b. San Juan, P.R., July 12, 1934; s. Francisco and Maria (Aybar) Torres; m. Elga Arroyo; children: Elga, JoAnn Marie. BS, U. P.R., 1956; MD, U. Barcelona, Spain, 1963. Diplomate Am. Bd. Pediatrics. Chief pediatric cardiology Ponce (P.R.) Dist. Hosp., 1970-91, chmn. dept. pediatrics, 1971-91, med. dir., 1980, prog. dir. pediatric tng. prog., 1970-91; prof., chmn. dept. pediatrics Cath. Univ. Sch. of Medicine, Ponce, 1978-80; chmn., dept. pediatrics Damas Hosp., Ponce, 1985—; prof., chmn. dept. pediatrics Ponce Sch. of Medicine, 1980-96. Mem. editl. bd. Sci.-Ciencia jour., ponce, 1975-95; contbr. articles to profl. jours. Fellow Am. Acad. Pediatrics, Am. Coll. Physicians, Am. Coll. Cardiology, Am. Coll. Internat. Physicians, British Royal Soc. Health, InterAm. Coll. Physicians and Surgeons; mem. AAUP, Phi Delta Kappa. Republican. Roman Catholic. Home: A26 Jacaranda Ponce PR 00731 Office: 13 Calle Mayor Ponce PR 00731-5025

TORRES-LABAWLD, JOSE DIMAS, institutional research director, service company executive, educator; b. Luquillo, P.R., Mar. 25, 1932; s. Antonio Torres Herrera and Maria S. (Labawld) Torres; m. Patricia Ann Zaccaria, Apr. 18, 1959; children: Peter, Michelle, Mary E., Patrick, David, Gwendolyn, Christopher. BA cum laude, Inter-Am. U., San German, P.R., 1957; MPA, Syracuse U., 1959; postgrad., U. Notre Dame, 1961-62; PhD, Ohio State U., 1973; postgrad., Dartmouth Coll., 1995-96. Mgmt. ofcl., adminstr. U.S. state dept. Point IV program Office of Pers., Office of Gov., San Juan, P.R., 1959-61; lectr. Ind. U., South Bend, 1963-64; lectr. NDEA Knox Coll., Galesburg, Ill., 1965; instr. Ohio U., Athens, 1965-69; rsch. assoc. Mershon Ctr. Ohio State U., Columbus, 1970-71; dir. dept. gen. studies Hocking Coll., Nelsonville, Ohio, 1973-75, dir. instl. rsch., 1975—; pres. IMSA, Inc., Athens, 1981—; bus. cons. IMSA, Inc., 1981—. Coord. youth for understanding internat. exchg. program U.S. State Dept., 1966-70; cand. Athens County Cen. Com. Dem., 1974; chmn. fin. com. Ohio U. Christ the King Parish, 1992-97; dir. Transnational Bus. Program, U.S., Mexico, Can., 1995—. Cpl. U.S. Army, Korea, 1951-53. Commonwealth of P.R. fellow Syracuse U., 1959; Hocking Coll. scholar, 1990. Mem. Am. Arbitration Assn., Assn. for Instnl. Rsch., U.S. Hispanic C. of C., World Trade Club, Columbus Area C. of C., VFW, Lions (pres. Athens chpt. 1984), Am. Legion, Phi Alpha Theta. Roman Catholic. Avocations: tennis, golf, piano, painting, chess. Home: 15 Grand Park Blvd Athens OH 45701-1438

TORRES OLIVER, JUAN FREMIOT, bishop; b. San German, P.R., Oct. 28, 1925; s. Luis N. and Amalia (Oliver) Torres. B.A., St. John's Seminary, 1944-50; M.A. Musicology, Catholic U., 1952; LL.B., U. of P.R., 1959; LL.M., St. John's U., 1964, LL.D., 1995. Ordained priest Roman Cath. Ch., 1950. Instr. Catholic U., Ponce, P.R., 1952-56; vice-chancellor Diocesan Curia, 1961-64; prof., assoc. dean Catholic U. Sch. of Law, Ponce, P.R., 1961-64; bishop of Ponce P.R., 1964—; grand chancellor Pontifical Cath. U. P.R., Ponce, 1964—; pres. P.R. Episcopal Conf. 1982-94; Grand Prior, P.R. lieutenancy of Equestrian Order of the Holy Sepulchre of Jerusalem, 1984—. Decorated Cross of Order Juan Pablo Duarte, Dominican Republic. mem. Academia de Artes y Ciencias; Phi Alpha Delta. Home: PO Box 205 Stat 6 CUPR Ponce PR 00732*

TORREY, BARBARA BOYLE, research council administrator; b. Pensacola, Fla., Nov. 27, 1941; d. Peter F. and Elsie (Hansen) Boyle; m. E. Fuller Torrey, Mar. 23, 1968; children: Michael, Martha. BA, Stanford U., 1963, MS, 1970. Vol. Peace Corps, Tanzania, 1963-65; fiscal economist Office Mgmt. and Budget, Washington, 1970-80; dept. asst. sec. HHS, Washington, 1980-81; dir. Ctr. for Internat. Rsch., Census Bur., Washington, 1984-92; pres. Population Reference Bur., Washington, 1992-93; exec. dir. Commn. on Behavioral and Social Scis. and Edn., NRC, NAS, Washington, 1993—; bd. dirs. Luxembourg Income Study, 1984—. Co-editor: The Vulnerable, 1987, Population and Land Use, 1992; contbr. articles to profl. jours. Mem. Population Assn. Am. (bd. dirs. 1993—). Office: NRC 2101 Constitution Ave NW Washington DC 20418-0007

TORREY, CLAUDIA OLIVIA, lawyer; b. Nashville, June 10, 1958; d. Claude Adolphus and Rubye Mayette (Prigmore) T. BA in Econ., Syracuse U., 1980; JD, N.Y. Law Sch., 1985. Bar: N.Y. State 1988. Legal intern Costello, Cooney & Fearon, Syracuse, N.Y., 1979; legal clk. First Am. Corp., Nashville, 1981; legal asst. James I. Meyerson, N.Y.C., 1982-85; jud. law clk. N.Y. State Supreme Ct., N.Y.C., 1985; interim project supr., legal asst. CUNY Ctrl. Office, 1985-86; legal analyst Rosenman & Colin Law Firm, N.Y.C., 1986-87; asst. counsel N.Y. State Legis., Albany, 1988-90; atty., cons. pvt. practice, Nashville, Cookeville, Tenn., 1991—; bd. mem. Children's Corner Day Care Ctr., Albany, N.Y., 1989-90. Ch. rep. FOCUS exec. coun. Westminster Presbyn. Ch., Albany, 1990; v.p. dormitory coun., flr. rep. Syracuse U., 1977-79. Mem. ABA (young lawyers divsn. liaison to ABA forum on health law 1994-96), Internat. Platform Assn., N.Y. State Bar Assn., Alpha Kappa Alpha (treas. Syracuse U. chpt. 1977-78, pres. 1979). Avocations: singing, piano, harp, tennis, art. Home and Office: PO Box 150234 Nashville TN 37215-0234

TORREY, DAVID LEONARD, investment banker; b. Ottawa, Ont., Can., Oct. 6, 1931; s. Arthur Starratt and Josephine Edith (Leonard) T.; divorced; children: Heather Torrey Murphy, John Winthrop, Diana Bruce, Arthur Bruce, David Molson. BA in Econs., St. Lawrence U., 1953; diploma, Grad. Sch. Bus., U. Western Ont., 1954. With Pitfield Mackay Ross Ltd., Toronto, Ont., Can., 1954-84; v.p. Pitfield Mackay Ross Ltd., 1963-73, sr. v.p., 1973-80, vice chmn., 1980-82, pres., 1982-84, also bd. dirs.; vice chmn. Dominion Securities, Inc., 1984-88, RBC Dominion Securities, Inc., 1988-91; chmn. Montreal Stock Exch., 1971-73, Phillips Cables Ltd., 1991-96; bd. dirs. Total Petroleum N.Am. Ltd., Wajax Ltd., Can. Stubbins Engring. and Mfg. Co. Ltd., Provigo Inc., Cuddy Internat., Inc.; mem. adv. bd. I.C.I. Can., Inc.; mem. coun. Montreal Bd. Trade, 1971-72. Chmn. Montreal Downtown YMCA, 1972-74; trustee St. Lawrence U.; bd. dirs. Montreal Gen. Hosp. Found. Mem. Investment Bankers Assn. (gov. 1971-72), Securities Industries Assn. (bd. govs. 1972-73), Multiple Sclerosis Can. (past pres., bd. dirs.), Royal Montreal Golf Club, Mt. Royal (Montreal) Club, Saifish Club Fla. (Palm Beach), Beta Theta Pi. Home: 389 Carlyle Ave, Montreal, PQ Canada H3R 1T3 Office: PO Box 6001, 1 Pl Ville Marie Ste 7S, Montreal, PQ Canada H3C 3A9

TORREY, HENRY CUTLER, physicist; b. Yonkers, N.Y., Apr. 4, 1911; s. John Cutler and Mabel (Kelso) T.; m. Helen Post Hubert, Sept. 11, 1937; children: John Cutler, Meriel Torrey Goodwin. BSc, U. Vt., 1932, DSc (hon.), 1965; PhD, Columbia U., 1937. Instr. physics Pa. State U., State College, 1937-41, asst. prof., 1941-42; mem. staff radiation lab. MIT, Cambridge, 1942-46; assoc. prof. Rutgers U., New Brunswick, N.J., 1946-48, prof., 1948-76, dean grad. sch., 1965-74, prof. emeritus, 1976—; cons. Chevron Rsch. Corp., La Habra Calif., 1952-65; trustee, mem. organizing com. Univs. Space Rsch. Assn., 1968-70; bd. govs. Lunar Sci. Inst., 1969-70. Co-author: Crystal Rectifiers, 1948; mem. editorial bd. Rev. Sci. Instruments, 1963-65. Guggenheim Found. fellow, Paris, 1964-65. Fellow Am. Phys. Soc. Achievements include patents in Oil Well Logging; co-discovery of nuclear magnetic resonance. Home: 413 Monroe St Arbor Glen Bridgewater NJ 08807

TORREY, RICHARD FRANK, utility executive; b. Saratoga Springs, N.Y., Dec. 31, 1926; s. Reginald Frank and Marian (Currey) T.; m. Betty Louise Stetson, July 2, 1949; children: Patricia Ann Torrey Simpkins, Carol Louise Torrey Kress, Barbara Jean Torrey Friedman. BA cum laude, Syracuse U., 1951. News reporter Syracuse (N.Y.) Post Standard, 1947-51; pub. rels. account exec. Syracuse, 1951-53; home sec. 35th Congl. Dist., Syracuse, 1952-53; exec. sec. to mayor Syracuse, 1954-58; dir. area devel. Niagara Mohawk Power Corp., Syracuse, 1958-66; comml. v.p. Niagara Mohawk Power Corp., Buffalo, 1966-68; adminstrv. v.p. Niagara Mohawk Power Corp., 1968-72, v.p., gen. mgr., 1972-76; sr. v.p. Niagara Mohawk Power Corp., Syracuse, 1976-88, ret., 1988; pres. Can. Niagara Power Co. Ltd., Niagara Falls, Ont., Can., 1968-88, dir., 1968-89; pres., dir. Caragh Investments Ltd., 1981-85; pres. Opinac Investments Ltd., Toronto, 1982-88, bd. dirs., 1982-89; pres. Opinac Energy Ltd., Calgary, Alta., 1983-88, bd. dirs., 1983-89. Pres. Syracuse USO, 1959-61, mem. nat. coun., 1959-62, 68-74; co-chmn. Ctrl. N.Y. Interim Coun. Regional Planning, 1965-66; gen. chmn. Dunbar-Huntington Bldg. Fund, Syracuse, 1963; state campaign chmn. N.Y. Job Devel. Authority, 1961; gen. chmn. United Way of Buffalo and Erie County, 1971; mem. Syracuse U. Corp. Adv. Coun., 1972-76; turstee Elmcrest Children's Ctr., 1962-63, Camp Good Will, Syracuse, 1964-66, Syracuse Area Coun. Chs., 1959-64; bd. dirs. United Way Buffalo and Erie County, 1967-76, Greater Buffalo Devel. Found., Kenmore Mercy Hosp., 1970-76, Crouse Irving Meml. Hosp. Found., 1978-87, Nat. Kidney Found., 1987-89, Bon Secours-Venice (Fla.) Hosp. Found., 1992—, vice chmn. 1995-96, chmn. 1996—; bd. dirs. Plantation Cmty. Found., Venice, 1989, pres., 1990-93, pres. emeritus, 1993—; mem. bd. adv. Sisters of St. Joseph, 1967-76; elder Trinity Presbyn. Ch., Venice, 1992-94; assoc. mem. Dewitt Cmty. Ch. Served with Air Corps U.S. Army, 1944-47. Recipient Syracuse Young Man of Yr. award, 1962; Outstanding Citizen award Buffalo Evening News, 1973. Mem. Empire State (v.p., bd. dirs. 1963-80), Buffalo Area (v.p. 1968-72, bd. dirs. 1968-76, pres. 1972-73, chmn. bd. 1973-74, Man of Yr. 1974) C. of C., Associated Industries of N.Y. (bd. dirs. 1978-80), Bus. Coun. N.Y. (bd. dirs. 1980-82), Mfrs. Assn. Cen. N.Y. (bd. dirs. 1977-88), Augusta Villa Assn. (bd. dirs. 1989-92), Buffalo Club (past 2d v.p., dir.), Syracuse Century Club (gov. 1980-83), Onondaga Golf Club, Plantation Golf and Country Club, Automobile Club Western N.Y.(bd. dirs. 1971-73, pres. 1973), N.Y.S. Automobile Assn. (dir. 1975-76), Venice Yacht Club. Home and Office: 6113 Royal Birkdale Jamesville NY 13078-9712

TORREY, WILLIAM ARTHUR, professional hockey team executive; b. Montreal, Que., Can., June 23, 1934. B.S., St. Lawrence U., 1957. Dir. pub. relations to bus. mgr. Pitts. Hornets Am. Hockey League team, 1960-68; exec. v.p. Calif. Golden Seals, 1968-72; pres., gen. mgr. N.Y. Islanders, from 1972, now chmn. bd., gen. mgr.; pres. Florida Panthers, Fort Lauderdale, Flor., 1993—. N.Y. Islanders NHL Stanley Cup Champions, 1980-83. Office: Florida Panthers 100 NE 3rd Ave Fl 10 Fort Lauderdale FL 33301-1155*

TORREZ, NAOMI ELIZABETH, editor, librarian; b. Scranton, Pa., July 3, 1939; d. Sterling E. and Naomi (Reynolds) Hess; m. Lupe F. Torrez, Dec. 23, 1961; children: Sterling Edward, Stanley Marshall. BA, U. Ariz., 1961; MA, U. Calif., Berkeley, 1964, MLS, 1970; DRE, Golden State Sch. Theology, Oakland, Calif., 1988; cert. in travel industry, Vista C.C., 1993. Libr. asst. Oakland Pub. Libr., 1966-67, U. Calif. Libr., Berkeley, 1967-70; tutor-couns. Sonoma State Hosp., Eldridge, Calif., 1973-77, libr. tech. asst., 1977-79; health scis. libr. Kaiser Hosp., Vallejo, Calif., 1979-87; copyright rev. editor, med. libr. Kaiser Dept. Med. Editing, Oakland, 1987—; former instr. Bay Cities Bible Inst., Oakland; mem. faculty Golden State Sch. Theology, Oakland, 1984—; participant Statewide Latino Congress, 1994. Author: Not in My Pew, 1990, GSST Research Manual, 1990; contbr. to Co-op Low Cost Cookbook, 1965. Active Albany 75th Anniversary Com., 1983, Women's Health Initiative, 1995—; officer Ariz. Fedn. of the Blind, Calif. Coun. of the Blind, 1959-66. Woodrow Wilson fellow, 1961; winner Nat. Spelling Bee, 1953; Nat. Merit scholar, 1957-61. Mem. Kaiser Permanente Latino Assn., Kaiser Affirmative Action Com., Kaiser Health Edn. Com., K.P. Regional Librs. Group (chair 1988), Phi Beta Kappa, Phi Kappa Phi. Baptist. Home: 1009 Murrieta Blvd # 15 Livermore CA 94550-4134 Office: Kaiser Dept Med Editing 1800 Harrison St Fl 16 Oakland CA 94612-3429

TORRIANI-GORINI, ANNAMARIA, microbiologist; b. Milan, Italy, Dec. 19, 1918; came to U.S., 1955, naturalized, 1962; d. Carlo and Ada (Forti) Torriani; m. Luigi Gorini (dec. Aug. 1976); 1 child, Daniel. PhD, U. Milan, Italy, 1942. Research assoc. Istituto Ronzoni Chimica-Biochimica, Milan, 1942-48; charge de recherche Institut Pasteur, Paris, 1948-56; research assoc. NYU, 1956-58, Harvard U., Cambridge, Mass., 1958-60; research assoc. MIT, Cambridge, 1960-71, assoc. prof. microbiology, 1971-76, prof., 1976—; prof. emerita, 1989. Recipient NIH Career award, 1962-72; Fulbright fellow, 1956-58. Mem. Am. Soc. Microbiology, Am. Soc. Genetics, Am. Soc. Biochemistry, Soc. Française de Microbiologie (hon.). Home: 115 Longwood Ave Brookline MA 02146-6625 Office: MIT Dept of Biology 68-371 Cambridge MA 02139

TORRICELLI, ROBERT G., senator; b. Englewood, N.J., Aug. 26, 1951. BA, Rutgers U., 1974, JD, 1977; MPA, Harvard U., 1980. Bar: N.J. 1978. Dep. legis. counsel Office Gov. N.J., 1975-77; counsel to Vice Pres. Mondale, Washington, 1978-81; pvt. practice Washington, 1981-82; mem. 98th-104th Congresses from 9th Dist. N.J., Washington, 1983-96, mem. sci., space and tech. com., mem. fgn. affairs com., select com. on intelligence, chmn. Western Hemisphere subcom., 1992-94; mem. rules, govt. affairs, judiciary com. 105th Congress, Senate from N.J.; U.S. senator from N.J., 1996—; mem. govtl. affairs com., judiciary com., rules and adminstrn. com. Mem. bd. govs. Rutgers U., 1977-83. Mem. ABA, N.J. Bar Assn. Democrat. Office: US Senate 728 Hart Senate Bldg Washington DC 20510

TORRUELLA, JUAN R., federal judge; b. 1933. BS in Bus. and Fin., U. Pa., 1954; LLB, Boston U., 1957; LLM, U. Va., 1984; MPA, U. P.R., 1984; LLD, St. John's U., 1995. Judge U.S. Dist. Ct. P.R., San Juan, 1974-82, chief judge, 1982-84; judge U.S. Ct. Appeals (1st cir.), San Juan, 1984-94, chief judge, 1994—; former mem. jud. conf. com. on the Adminstrn. of the Fed. Magistrate Sys; mem. jud. conf. com. on Internat. Jud. Reform. Mem. ABA, Fed. Bar Assn., Assn. Labor Rels. Practitioners P.R. and V.I., D.C. Bar Assn., P.R. Bar Assn. Office: US Ct Appeals PO Box 3671 San Juan PR 00904 also: US Ct Appeals (1st cir) Boston MA 02109*

TORSHEN, JEROME HAROLD, lawyer; b. Chgo., Nov. 27, 1929; s. Jack and Lillian (Futterman) T.; m. Kay Pomerance, June 19, 1966; children: Jonathan, Jacqueline. BS, Northwestern U., 1951; JD, Harvard U., 1955. Bar: Ill. 1955, U.S. Dist. Ct. (no. dist.) Ill. 1955, U.S. Ct. Appeals (7th cir.) 1958, (8th cir.) 1961, (9th and D.C. cirs.) 1972, U.S. Supreme Ct. 1972. Assoc. Clausen, Hirsh & Miller, Chgo., 1955-62; pres. Jerome H. Torshen, Ltd., Chgo., 1963-87, Torshen, Schoenfield & Spreyer Ltd., Chgo., 1987-93, Torshen, Spreyer & Garmisa, Ltd., Chgo., 1994—; spl. asst. atty. gen. Ill., 1965-70; assoc. counsel Spl. Commn. Ill. Supreme Ct., 1969; counsel Ill. Legis. Redistricting Commn., 1971-72; spl. state's atty. Cook County, Ill., 1979-81, 83-86; spl. counsel Met. San. Dist. Greater Chgo., 1977-81, 84-88. Contbr. articles to profl. jours. Counsel Cook County Dem. Cen. Com., Chgo., 1982-87; bd. dirs. Jewish Family and Community Svc., Parents' Coun. Washington U., St. Louis, 1988-92; mem. collectors' group Mus. Contemporary Art; sustaining fellow Art Int. Chgo. Served with U.S. Army, 1951-52. Recipient Torch of Learning award Am. Friends of Hebrew U., 1985, Outstanding Civic Duty award, Union League Club of Chgo., 1967. Fellow Am. Coll. Trial Lawyers; mem. ABA, Chgo. Bar Assn. (commn. on jud. evaluation 1986-90), Bar Assn. 7th Cir. Appellate Lawyers Assn. (founder, pres. 1976-77), Decalogue Soc., Standard Club, Sixty Club of Chgo. Office: 105 W Adams St Ste 3200 Chicago IL 60603-4102

TORTORELLO, NICHOLAS JOHN, public opinion and market research company executive; b. Maspeth, N.Y., Dec. 1, 1948; s. John Anthony and Verla Jean (Odel) T.; m. Joan Elizabeth King, Jan. 13, 1973; children: Kerry Ann, Jennifer Joan. BA in Polit. Sci. with highest honors, Williams Coll., 1971; M Religious Studies, St. Joseph's Sem., Yonkers, N.Y., 1988. Vice pres. Louis Harris & Assocs., N.Y.C., 1971-73, sr. v.p., 1973-79; exec. v.p. DMT Inc., N.Y.C., 1979-83; pres. Tortorello Corp., Pearl River, N.Y., 1983-85; pres. Tortorello group Market Facts Inc.-N.Y., N.Y.C., 1985-86; v.p. Total Rsch. Corp., Princeton, N.J., 1986-88; chmn. Rsch. and Forecasts Inc., N.Y.C., 1989-93; sr. v.p. Roper Starch Worldwide Inc., N.Y.C., 1993—. Editor, author Tortorello Trendline, 1983-85, Rsch. and Forecasts Trendline, 1989-91. Trustee Riverdale (N.Y.) Country Sch., 1982-90, v.p., 1986-89; trustee Marymount Manhattan Coll., N.Y.C., 1986-88; lectr., tchr. religion St. Anthony's Ch., Nanuet, N.Y., 1984-86; mem. CARA Bd. Georgetown U., Washington, 1992-98; active Hosp. Chaplaincy Bd., 1991-97. Recipient Am. Legion award for leadership, scholarship, honor and svc., 1967, Disting. Alumnus of Yr. award Riverdale Country Sch., 1984. Mem. Am. Dirs. Inst. (trustee 1984-87), Coun. Am. Survey Rsch. Orgn. (chmn. publs. com. 1991-94, chmn. pub. rels. com. 1995-97, chmn. mktg. and comms. com. 1997—, bd. dirs.), Am. Assn. Pub. Opinion Rsch., Williams Club. Democrat. Avocations: collecting Lionel trains, collecting stereo equipment, softball, golf. Office: Roper Starch Worldwide Inc 205 E 42nd St New York NY 10017-5706

TORTORICI, PETER FRANK, television executive; b. N.Y.C., June 19, 1949; s. Tony F. and May (Augello); m. Susan Kay Dupar, June 21, 1986; children: Caitlin, Dayna, Thomas. BA, Ohio State U., 1971; JD, St. John's U., 1974. Sr. counsel grievance com. 2nd & 11th Jud. Dists., Bklyn., 1974-80; prodn. asst. ABC Sports, N.Y.C., 1980; dir. program acquisitions CBS Sports, N.Y.C., 1981-83, v.p. program planning and devel., 1983-86, v.p. programming, 1986-87; sr. v.p. program planning CBS Entertainment, L.A., 1987-91; exec. v.p. CBS Entertainment, 1991-94, pres., 1994-95; exec. producer, sr. exec. The Carsey-Werner Co., 1996—. Writer (TV show) Tour de France, 1987 (Emmy nomination). Mem. Hollywood Radio TV Soc. (bd. dirs. 1990-92, pres. 1994). Avocations: golf, skiing, music, N.Y. sports teams. Home: 1148 Napoli Dr Pacific Palisades CA 90272-4040 Office: Carsey-Werner Co 4024 Radford Ave Bldg 3 Studio City CA 91604-2101*

TORY, JOHN A., newspaper publishing executive. Dep. chmn. The Thomson Co., Toronto, Ont., Can. Office: Thomson Newspaper Inc 3150 Des Plaines Ave Des Plaines IL 60018-4205 also: The Thomson Corporation, Toronto Dominion Ctr Box 24, Toronto, ON Canada M5K 1A1*

TOSCANO, JAMES VINCENT, medical institute administration; b. Passaic, N.J., Aug. 8, 1937; s. William V. and Mary A. (DeNigris) T.; m. Sharon Lee Bowers; children: Shawn Olsen, Lauren Bjorklund, David Brendan, Dania. A.B. summa cum laude, Rutgers U., 1959; M.A., Yale U., 1960. Lectr. Wharton Sch., U. Pa., 1961-64; chief opinion analyst Pa. Opinion Poll, 1962-64; mng. dir. World Press Inst., St. Paul, 1964-68; exec. dir. World

Press Inst., 1968-72; dir. devel. Macalester Coll., St. Paul, 1972-74; v.p. resource devel. and public affairs Mpls. Soc. Fine Arts, 1974-79; pres. Minn. Mus. Art, 1979-81; exec. v.p. Park Nicollet Med. Found., 1981-95; corp. sec. Park Nicollet Med. Ctr., 1983-86; sr. v.p. Am. Med. Ctrs., Inc., 1985-87; exec. v.p. Inst. for Rsch. and Edn. Health Sys. Minn., Mpls., 1996—; adj. prof. sch. of mgmt. U. St. Thomas, 1989—. Author: The Chief Elected Official in the Penjerdel Region, 1964; co-author, co-editor: The Integration of Political Communities, 1964. Bd. dirs., exec. com., sec., World Press Ins., 1972—; bd. dirs., chmn. Southside Newspaper Mpls., 1975-79; chmn. com. to improve student behavior St. Paul Pub. Schs., 1977-79; bd. dirs. Planned Parenthood St. Paul, 1965-72, Mpls. Action Agy., 1976-79; emeritus dir. Help Enable Alcoholics Receive Treatment; mem. St. Paul Heritage Preservation Commn., 1979-82, vice chmn., 1981; mem. Citizens Adv. Com. on Cable Comm.; bd. dirs. Citizens League, 1980, Park Nicollet Med. Found., 1981-95, Inst. for Rsch. and Edn., Health Sys. Minn., 1996—, African-Am. Culture Ctr., 1979-82, Minn. Composers Forum, 1981-85, St. Paul Chamber Orch., 1976-80, 83-89, United Theol. Sem., 1985-88; bd. dirs., mem. exec. com., chmn. Med. Alley Assn., 1986-96; mem. task force on tech. assessment Med. Alley, 1992-93; mem. health affairs adv. com. Acad. Health Ctr. U. Minn., 1988-95; bd. dirs. Mother Cabrini House, 1985-92, Minn. Civil Justice Coalition, 1987-91, also chmn.; chmn. Gov.'s Task Force on Health Care Promotion, 1985-86, mem. Gov.'s Com. Promotion Health Care Resources, 1986-87; chmn. bd. Minn. Fin. Counseling Svcs., Inc., 1990-93; mem. task force cost effectiveness Med. Alley, 1994-95; bd. dirs. Meml. Blood Bank, 1995—, mem. exec. com., 1996—. Woodrow Wilson Nat. fellow. Mem. Minn. Newspaper Found. (bd. dirs. 1987-92), Minn. Coun. Nonprofits (bd. dirs. 1989-95, 97—, bd. mem. Plymouth Music series 1993-96, alt. Minn. Healthcare Commn., 1993-95, mem. Minn. Healthcare Commn., 1995-97, chair task force on med. edn. and rsch. costs 1994-96; chair com. on med. rsch. and edn. costs, 1996—, liaison health tech. adv. com. 1993-97), Skylight Club, Informal Club. Address: 1982 Summit Ave Saint Paul MN 55105-1460 Office: Inst for Rsch and Edn Health Sys Minn 3800 Park Nicollet Blvd Minneapolis MN 55416-2527

TOSCANO, SAMUEL, JR., wholesale distribution executive; b. 1948. With Manhattan Drug Co. and Hillside (N.J.) Drug Co., 1967-72; with Neuman Distributors, Inc., Ridgefield, N.J., 1972—, mgr. sales, dir. sales, v.p. sales, CEO, 1979—. Office: Neyman Distributors Inc 175 Railroad Ave Ridgefield NJ 07657-2312*

TOSI, LAURA LOWE, orthopaedic surgeon; b. N.Y.C., Mar. 25, 1949; d. Jerome Richard T. and Deborah Thornton (Prouty) Rogers; m. David S.C. Chu, Apr. 1, 1978. BA, Boston U., 1971; MD, Harvard U., 1977. Orthopaedic surgeon Children's Nat. Med. Ctr., Washington, 1984—; assoc. prof. orthopaedic surgery George Washington U., Washington, 1984—. Fellow Am. Acad. Cerebral Palsy and Devel. Medicine, Am. Acad. Orthopaedic Surgeons (bd. dirs. 1994-95); mem. Acad. Orthopaedic Soc., Pediatric Orthopaedic Soc. N.Am. (bd.dirs. 1990-91), Ruth Jackson Orthopaedic Soc. (treas. 1987-90, v.p. 1990-91, pres. 1991-92), Orthopaedic Rsch. & Edn. Found. (bd. trustees 1995—). Office: Children's Nat Med Ctr 111 Michigan Ave NW Washington DC 20010-2916

TOSTESON, DANIEL CHARLES, physiologist, medical school dean; b. Milw., Feb. 5, 1925; s. Alexis H. and Dilys (Bodycombe) T.; m. Penelope Kinsley, Dec. 17, 1949 (div. 1969); children: Carrie Marias, Heather Tosteson, Tor, Zoe Losada; m. Magdalena Tieffenberg, July 8, 1969; children: Joshua, Ingrid. Student, Harvard U., 1942-44, MD, 1949; DSc (hon.), U. Copenhagen, 1979; Dr. hon. causa, U. Liege, 1983; DSc (hon.), Med. Coll. Wis., 1984, NYU, 1992; DHL (hon.), Johns Hopkins U., 1993; Dr. honoris causa, Cath. U. Louvain, 1996, Duke U., 1996, Emory U., 1996. Fellow physiology Harvard Med. Sch., 1947-48; intern, then asst. resident medicine Presbyn. Hosp., N.Y.C., 1949-51; research fellow medicine Brookhaven Nat. Lab., 1951-53; lab. kidney and electrolyte metabolism Nat. Heart Inst., 1953-55, 57; research fellow biol. isotope research lab. Nat. Heart Inst., Copenhagen, 1955-56; research fellow Physiol. Lab., Cambridge, Eng., 1956-57; assoc. prof. physiology Washington U. Sch. Medicine, St. Louis, 1958-61; prof., chmn. dept. physiology and pharmacology Duke U. Sch. Medicine, 1961-75, James B. Duke Distinguished prof., 1971-75; dean div. biol. scis., dean Pritzker Sch. Medicine U. Chgo., Lowell T. Coggleshall prof. med. scis., v.p. for Med. Center, 1975-77; dean and Caroline Shields Walker prof. cell biology Harvard Med. Sch., Boston, 1977-97, pres. Med. Center, 1977, dean emeritus, 1997—; mem. molecular biology panel NSF, 1959-62; cons. sci. rev. com. NIH, 1964-67, nat. adv. gen. med. scis. coun., 1982-86; mem. U.S. Office Tech. Assessment, 1976; ethics adv. bd. HEW, 1977-80; nat. adv. gen. med. scis. coun. NIH, 1982—; mem. governing bd. NRC, 1977; mem. sci. com. Found. pour l'Etude du Systeme Nerveux Central et Peripherique, 1982—; nat. adv. com. biomed. scis. PEW Scholars Program, 1984-87. Mem. Inst. Medicine NAS (coun. 1975-78, adv. bd. PEW scholars program 1984-85), AAAS, Am. Physiol. Soc. (council 1967-75, pres. 1973-74), Soc. Gen. Physiologists (pres. 1968-69), Biophys. Soc. (council 1970-73), Assn. Am. Med. Colls. (chmn. coun. acad. socs. 1969-70, chmn. assembly 1973-74, chmn. physician supply task force 1988-90, Abraham Flexner award 1991), Assn. Am. Physicians, Red Cell Club, Soc. Health and Human Values, Danish Royal Soc. (fellow), Alpha Omega Alpha. Spl. research cellular transport processes, red cell membranes. Office: Harvard Med Sch 25 Shattuck St Boston MA 02115-6027

TOSTI, SALLY T., artist, educator; b. Scranton, Pa., Jan. 21, 1946; d. Ivan and Helen (Odell) Thompson; m. Robert Matthew Tosti, May 3, 1974; 1 child, Jennifer Marie. BS in Art Edn., Ind. (Pa.) U., 1967; postgrad., Tyler Sch. Art, 1969-70; MFA in Drawing and Painting, Marywood Coll., 1985. Art tchr. Bristol Twp. Schs., Levittown, Pa., 1967-69, Ctrl. Bucks Schs., Doylestown, Pa., 1971; adj. faculty Marywood Coll., Scranton, Pa., 1986-87; art coord. Keystone Coll., LaPlume, Pa., 1991-96, adj. faculty, 1995—. Exhbns. include San Diego Art Inst., 1993-94, Allentown (Pa.) Art Mus., Abercombie Gallerie, 1994, Lakeview Mus., 1995, U. Tex., Tyler, 1995-96, Linder Art Gallery, 1994—, Haggin Mus., Stockton, Calif., 1996, Fla. Printmakers Soc. Traveling Exhbn., 1995-97, So. Graphics Traveling Exhbn., 1996—, Elon Coll., N.C., 1997, Moss-Thorns Gallery Art, 1997, others. Active Countryside Conservancy, Waverly, Pa. Grantee Pa. Coun. Arts, 1995; F. Lammot Belin Arts scholar, 1996. Mem. Waverly Womans Club, Print Ctr. Phila., So. Graphics Coun., Am. Print Alliance, Womens Studio Workshop, Everhart Mus. Democrat. Home: PO Box 776 Waverly PA 18471

TOTENBERG, NINA, journalist; b. N.Y.C., Jan. 14, 1944; d. Roman and Melanie (Shroder) T.; m. Floyd Haskell, Feb. 3, 1979. Student, Boston U.; LLD (hon.), Haverford Coll., Chatham Coll., Gonzaga U., Northeastern U., St. Mary's, SUNY; LHD, Lebanon Valley Coll., Westfield State Coll. Reporter Boston Record Am., 1965, Peabody Times, 1967, Nat. Observer, 1968-71, Newtimes, 1973, Nat. Pub. Radio, Washington, 1974—, Inside Washington, 1992—; reporter Nightline ABC, 1993—. contbr. articles to N.Y. Times Mag., Harvard Law Rev., Christian Sci. Monitor, N.Y. Mag., Parade. Recipient Alfred I. Dupont award Columbia U., 1988, George Foster Peabook award, 1991, George Polk award, 1991, Joan Barne award, 1991, Silver Gavel award ABA, 1991, Woman of Courage award Women in Film, 1991, Athena award, 1994. Mem. Sigma Delta Chi. Office: NPR 635 Massachusetts Ave NW Washington DC 20001-3752

TOTENBERG, ROMAN, violinist, music educator; b. Lodz, Poland, Jan. 1, 1911; came to U.S., 1935; s. Adam and Stanislava (Vinaver) T.; m. Melanie Shroder, July 30, 1941; children: Nina, Jill, Amy. Grad., Chopin Sch. Music, Warsaw, Poland, 1928, Hochschule für Music, Berlin, 1931, Paris Inst. Instrumental Music, 1933. Head violin dept. Peabody Conservatory, Balt., 1943-44, Mannes Coll. Music, N.Y.C., 1951-57; chmn. string dept. Boston U., 1962-78, prof., 1978—, co-chmn. string dept.; Prin. soloist, dir. chamber music Interstate Broadcasting Co., N.Y.C., 1937-42; prin. soloist, head string dept. Music Acad. West, Santa Barbara, Calif., summers 1948-51; with Music Assocs., Aspen, Colo., summers 1951-62; dir. Totenberg Instrumental Ensemble, 1953-60; George Miller vis. prof. U. Ill., 1960-61; head string dept. Boston U. Tanglewood Inst., summers 1966-74; performer, tchr. Kneisel Hall Festival, Blue Hill, Maine, 1975—, acting dir., 1984-87; dir. Longy Sch. Music, Cambridge, Mass., 1978-85; judge Paganini, Wieniawski, Carnegie Hall competitions, Kreisler and Japan Internat. Competition. Performer worldwide concerts and tours; rec. artist with Vanguard, DGG, Mus. Heritage Soc. records, Titanic compact disk, Omega Records, VGR Records. Chmn. Music Project, Newton Tricentenary, 1988. Recipient Mendelssohn prize, 1932, Wieniawski Soc. medal, 1970, Eugene Ysaye Soc. medal, 1975, Polish Nat. medal of Cultural Achievement, 1988. Mem. Am. String Tchrs. Assn. (named Artist-Tchr. of yr. 1983), AAUP, Music Tchrs. Nat. Assn., Phi Kappa Lambda. Avocations: photography, tennis. Office: Boston U 855 Commonwealth Ave Boston MA 02215-1303 *Devotion to human values expressed through music as well as through daily activities in public life.*

TOTH, ROBERT CHARLES, polling consultant, journalist; b. Blakely, Pa., Dec. 24, 1928; s. John and Tillie (Szuch) T.; m. Paula Goldberg, Apr. 12, 1954; children: Jessica, Jennifer, John. B.S. in Chem. Engring., Washington U., St. Louis, 1952; M.S. in Journalism, Columbia U., 1955; postgrad., Harvard U., 1960-61. Started as engr. in Army Ordnance Dept., 1952-54; reporter Providence Jour., 1955-57; sci. reporter N.Y. Herald Tribune, 1957-62, N.Y. Times, 1962-63; mem. staff Los Angeles Times, 1963-93; bur. chief Los Angeles Times, London, 1965-70; diplomatic corr. Los Angeles Times, 1970-71, White House corr., 1972-74; bur. chief Los Angeles Times, Moscow, 1974-77; nat. security corr. Washington bur. Los Angeles Times, 1977-93; cons. opinion poll in U.S. and abroad by Times Mirror Ctr. (now Pew Rsch. Ctr.) for People and Press, 1990, sr. assoc., 1993—. Served with USMC, 1946-48. Recipient Overseas Press Club award, 1977, Sigma Delta Chi award, 1977, George Polk award in Journalism for fgn. reporting L.I. U., 1978, Columbia U. Alumni award, 1978, Wienthal award Fgn. Service Inst., Georgetown U., 1986, Edwin N. Hood award Nat. Press Club, 1986; Pulitzer Travelling scholar, 1955; Nieman fellow Harvard U., 1960-61. Mem. Coun. on Fgn. Rels. Home: 21 Primrose St Chevy Chase MD 20815-4228 Office: Pew Rsch Ctr 1875 I St NW Washington DC 20006

TOTLIS, GUST JOHN, title insurance company executive; b. Highwood, Ill., May 15, 1939; s. John Chris and Agape (Galelis) T.; m. Joyce Elaine Edholm, June 5, 1960; children: Kenneth Chris, Charles Gust. BA, Lake Forest Coll., 1962; MBA, U. Chgo., 1964. Fin. planning mgr. Gen. Foods Corp., Battle Creek, Mich., 1964-68; fin. analyst Irving Trust Co., N.Y.C., 1968-69, asst. sec., 1969-71, asst. v.p., 1971-72, v.p., 1972-75; corp. contr. Irving Bank Corp., N.Y.C., 1975-82; exec. v.p., CFO Fidelity Union Bancorp, Newark, 1982-85, Star Banc Corp (formerly First Nat. Cin. Corp.), Cin., 1985-93; sr. v.p., CFO Chgo. Title and Trust Co., 1993—; bd. dirs. Ticor Title Ins. Co., Security Union Title Ins. Co., Chgo. Tech. Corp., Credit Data Reporting Svcs., Inc., Market Intelligence, Inc., Nat. Flood Info. Svcs., Inc.; chmn. gov. bd. Ill. Coun. Econ. Edn., 1997—. Adv. bd. dirs., treas. Salvation Army, Cin., 1987-93; bd. dirs., pres. Cin. Chamber Orch., 1988-93; pres. May Festival Assn., 1988-93; v.p. Spl. Olympics, 1990-93; vice chmn. United Way, 1991-94; bd. trustees Cin. Inst. Fine Arts, 1991-93. Mem. Fin. Execs. Inst., Univ. club, Kenwood Country Club, Univ. Club Chgo. Presbyterian. Home: 111 E Bellevue Pl Chicago IL 60611-1115

TOTMAN, CONRAD DAVIS, history educator; b. Conway, Mass., Jan. 5, 1934; s. Raymond Smith and Mildred Edna (Kingsbury) T.; m. Michiko Ikegami, Jan. 21, 1958; children: Kathleen Junko, Christopher Ken. B.A., U. Mass., 1958; M.A., Harvard U., 1960, Ph.D., 1964. Asst. prof. U. Calif., Santa Barbara, 1964-66; asst. prof. Northwestern U., Evanston, Ill., 1966-68; assoc. prof. Northwestern U., 1968-72, prof. Japanese history, 1972-84, chmn. dept. history, 1977-80; prof. Japanese history Yale U., New Haven, 1984—; chmn. Council on East Asian Studies, Yale U., 1985-88, acting chmn. Dept. History, 1989-90; prof. Kyoto Ctr. for Japanese Studies, 1992-93. Author: Politics in the Tokugawa Bakufu 1600-1843, 1967, paperback edit., 1988, The Collapse of the Tokugawa Bakufu 1862-1868, 1979 (John K. Fairbank prize Am. Hist. Assn. 1981), Japan Before Perry: A Short History, 1981, Tokugawa Ieyasu: Shogun, 1983, The Origins of Japan's Modern Forests, 1985, The Green Archipelago: Forestry in Preindustrial Japan, 1989, Early Modern Japan, 1993, paperback edit., 1995, The Lumber Industry in Early Modern Japan, 1995. Served with U.S. Army, 1953-56. Recipient Carstensen prize for essay Agrl. History Soc., 1982; Woodrow Wilson nat. fellow, 1958-59; Social Sci. Research Council-Am. Council Learned Socs. fellow, 1968-69; NEH sr. fellow, 1972-73; Fulbright-Hays research grantee, 1968-69; Japan Found. grantee, 1981-82. Mem. Assn. Asian Studies (N.E. Asia coun. 1977-80, chmn. 1978-80, exec. com. 1978-80, pres. New Eng. Conf. 1985-86, coun. of confs. 1992-95), Forest History Soc. Office: Yale U Dept History New Haven CT 06520

TOTO, MARY, elementary and secondary education educator; b. Phila., Mar. 12, 1922; d. John and Piacentina (Rossi) T. BS in Edn., Temple U., 1943; MS in Edn., U. Pa., 1951; MS in LS, Villanova U., 1963. Cert. elem. and secondary tchr., Pa. Tchr. Phila. Sch. Dist., 1943-81. Mem. Dem. Nat. Com., 1995-97. Mem. NEA, AAUW, LWV, Phila. Fedn. Tchrs., Columbus Forum Lodge, Nationalities Svc. Ctr. of Phila., Italian Folk Art Fedn. of Am., Nat. Assn. Retired Tchrs., Pa. Assn. Sch. Retirees, Pa. Edn. Assn., Womens Internat. League Peace and Freedom, United We Stand Am. Roman Catholic. Avocations: needlework, interior decorating, folk dancing, travel. Home: 1210 W Ritner St Philadelphia PA 19148-3524

TOTTEN, GEORGE OAKLEY, III, political science educator; b. Washington, July 21, 1922; s. George Oakley Totten Jr. and Vicken (von Post) Totten Barrois; m. Astrid Maria Anderson, June, 1948 (dec. Apr. 26, 1975); children: Vicken Yuriko, Linnea Catherine; m. Lilia Huiying Li, July 1, 1976; 1 child, Blanche Maluk Lemes. Cert., U. Mich., 1943; AB, Columbia U., 1946, AM, 1949; MA, Yale U., 1950, PhD, 1954; docentur i japanologi, U. Stockholm, 1977. Lectr. Columbia U., N.Y.C., 1954-55; asst. prof. MIT, Cambridge, 1958-59, Boston U., 1959-61; assoc. prof. U. R.I., Kingston, 1961-64; assoc. prof. polit. sci. U. So. Calif., L.A., 1965-68, prof., 1968-92, chmn. dept., 1980-86, prof. emeritus, 1992—; dir., founder Calif. Pvt. Univs. and Colls. Yr.-in-Japan program Weseda U., 1967-73; dir. East Asian Studies Ctr., 1974-77; 1st dir. USC-UCLA Joint East Asian Studies Ctr., 1976-77; sr. affiliated scholar Ctr. for Multiethnic and Transnat. Studies, 1993—; vis. prof. U. Stockholm, 1977-79, 1st dir. Ctr. Pacific Asia Studies, 1985-89, sr. counselor bd. dirs., 1989—. Author: Social Democratic Movement in Prewar Japan, 1966, Chinese edit., 1987, Korean edit., 1997; co-author: Socialist Parties in Postwar Japan, 1966, Japan and the New Ocean Regime, 1984; author, editor: Helen Snow's Song of Ariran, 1973, Korean edit., 1991, Chinese edit., 1993, Kim Dae-jung's A New Beginning, 1996; author, co-editor: Developing Nations: quest for a Model, 1970, Japanese edit., 1975, China's Economic Reform: Administering the Introduction of the Market Mechanism, 1992, Community in Crisis: Korean American. . ., 1994; co-translator: Chien Mu's Traditional Government in Imperial China, 1982; contbr. The Politics of Divided Nations, 1991, Chinese edit., 1995; editl. bd. Koreanicus, 1997—. Mem. U.S.-China People's Friendship Assn., Washington, 1974—; mem. Com. on U.S.-China Relations, N.Y.C., 1975—; chmn. L.A.-Pusan Sister City Assn., L.A., 1976-77; bd. dirs. L.A.-Guangzhou Sister City Assn., 1982—, Japan-Am. Soc. L.A., 1981—; mem. nat. adv. com. Japan Am. Student Conf., 1984—, Assn. of Korean Pol. Studies in N.Am., 1992—, v.p. 1996—; coun. mem. China Soc. for People's Friendship Studies, Beijing, 1991—. 1st lt. AUS, 1942-46, PTO. Recipient Plaque for program on Korean studies Consulate Gen. of Republic of Korea, 1975, Disting. Emeritus award U. So. Calif., 1996; Social Sci. Rsch. Coun. fellow, 1952-53; Ford Found. grantee, 1955-58, NSF grantee, 1979-81, Korea Found. grantee, 1993, Rebuild L.A. grantee, 1993, Philippine Liberation medal, 1994. Mem. Assn. Asian Studies, Am. Polit. Sci. Assn., Asia Soc., Internat. Polit. Sci. Assn., Internat. Studies Assn., Japanese Polit. Sci. Assn., European Assn. Japanese Studies, U. So. Calif. Faculty Ctr., Phi Beta Delta (founding mem. Beta Kappa chpt. 1993—). Episcopalian. Home: 5129 Village Grn Los Angeles CA 90016-5205 Office: U So Calif Ctr Multiethic & Transnat Studies GFS 344 Los Angeles CA 90089-1694 *The two main driving forces in my life have been a desire for world peace and a fascination with Asia. I try to work for the reduction and eventual abolition of armaments and a world-wide decision making process. Within countries, especially my own, I try to promote democracy. I think it can be promoted in both capitalist and socialist nations, and can be compatible with modified communist ideology but not with fascism. Since childhood I have tried to work for friendship with Asian nations, especially China, Japan and Korea. My research has been on better understanding their politics, history and culture.*

TOTTEN, GLORIA JEAN (DOLLY TOTTEN), real estate executive, financial consultant; b. Port Huron, Mich., Sept. 23, 1943; d. Lewis Elmer and Inez Eugenia (Houston) King; m. Donald Ray Totten, Feb. 5, 1961 (div. Apr. 1981); children: D. Erik, Angela J. Totten Sales, Kymberly D. Totten DiVita. Student, Patricia Stevens Modeling Sch., Detroit, 1976-79, Gold Coast Sch., West Palm Beach, Fla., 1988; degree in mktg., St. Clair County Coll., Port Huron, Mich., 1979. Lic. real estate saleswoman, Fla., Mich. Demonstrator, saleswoman Hoover Co., 1969-75; instr., promoter Port Huron Sch. Bus., 1973-75; real estate broker Select Realty, Port Huron, 1979-81, Earn Keim Realty, Port Huron, 1981-83, Schweitzer's Better Homes and Gardens, Marysville, Mich., 1983-86, Coldwell Banker Property Concepts Corp., North Palm Beach, Fla., 1986-94; pres., broker, owner Dolly Totten Real Estate Inc., West Palm Beach, Fla., 1994—; travel agt. Global Access, Lake Park, Fla., 1997—; model, instr. Patricia Stevens Modeling Sch., Troy, Mich., 1972-75; beauty cons. Mary Kay Cosmetics, 1982—; ind. travel agt. Global Access Internat., 1997. Grantee Mich. State U., 1972. Mem. Nat. Assn. Realtors, North Palm Beach Rd. Realtors, Million Dollar Club (Port Huron chpt.), Women's Coun. Realtors (co-founder Port Huron chpt.). Avocations: singing, acting, dancing, horticulture, crafts. Home and Office: 515 Evergreen Dr Lake Park FL 33403

TOTTER, JOHN RANDOLPH, biochemist; b. Saragosa, Tex., Jan. 7, 1914; s. Mathias and Agnes (Smith) T.; m. Elizabeth Margaret Van Sant, Aug. 6, 1938; children—Lorena E. Totter Barfuss, Anita Ruth, John Alan. B.A., U. Wyo., 1934, M.A., 1935; Ph.D., State U. Iowa, 1938. Instr. biochemistry U. W.Va., 1938-39; instr. biochemistry Ark. Sch. Medicine, 1939-42, asst. prof., 1942-45, asso. prof., 1945-52; chemist Oak Ridge Nat. Lab., 1952-56; biochemist AEC, Washington, 1956-58; vis. staff mem. U. of Republic, Montevideo, Uruguay, 1958-60; prof. biochemistry, chmn. div. biol. scis. U. Ga., 1960-62; asst. dir. for biol. scis. div. biology and medicine U.S. AEC, 1962-67, dir., 1967-72, asso. dir. for research, 1963-67; asso. dir. biomed. and environ. scis. Oak Ridge Nat. Lab., 1972-74; vis. staff mem. Inst. for Energy Analysis, Oak Ridge Asso. Univs., 1976-79, staff mem., 1979-87, ret., 1987; Participant nutritional survey, Alaska, 1947. Mem. Am. Chem Soc., Am. Soc. Biol. Chemists, Soc. for Exptl. Biology and Medicine (chmn. S.W. sect. 1950), Sigma Xi. Home: 360 Laboratory Rd Apt 517 Oak Ridge TN 37830-6851 Office: Med Scis Div Oak Ridge Assoc Univs Oak Ridge TN 37830

TOUBORG, MARGARET EARLEY BOWERS, non-profit executive; b. Rome, N.Y., Aug. 12, 1941; d. George Thomas and Margaret Earley (Brown) Bowers; m. Jens Touborg, Sept. 9, 1961 (div. 1985); children: Margaret Earley, Anne Touborg Zimmer, Sarah Touborg Moyers, Peter Nicolai. AB magna cum laude, Radcliffe Coll., 1965; MEd, Harvard U., 1984. Asst. to pres. Radcliffe Coll., Cambridge, Mass., 1984-86, exec. asst. to pres., 1986-87, dir. corp. and found. relations, 1988-89; pres. U. Cape Town Fund, Inc., N.Y.C., 1989—; sr. project dir. Open Soc. Scholars Fund, N.Y.C., 1989—; bd. dirs. Technoserve, Inc. Trustee The Trinity Sch., N.Y.C., 1994—, Bemis Lectr. Series, Lincoln, Mass., 1982-85; nat. cons. Schlesinger Libr. on History of Women in Am., 1995—; assoc. chmn. edn. div. United Way Mass., 1986. Mem. Harvard Club N.Y.C., Phi Beta Kappa (Iota chpt. chmn. com. hon. membership 1976-94), Cosmpolitan Club (N.Y.C.). Episcopalian. Office: 509 Madison Ave Ste 1014 New York NY 10022-5501

TOUBY, KATHLEEN ANITA, lawyer; b. Miami Beach, Fla., Feb. 20, 1943; s. Harry and Kathleen Rebecca (Hamper) T.; m. Joseph Thomas Woodward; children: Mark Andrew, Judson David Touby. BS in Nursing, U. Fla., 1965, MRC in Rehab. Counseling, 1967; JD with honors, Nova U., 1977. Bar: Fla. 1978, D.C. 1978. Counselor, Jewish Vocat. Svc., Chgo., 1967-68; rehab. counselor Fla. Dept. Vocat. Rehab., Miami, 1968-70; spl. asst., asst. U.S. atty. U.S. Dept. Justice, Miami, 1978-80; assoc. firm Pyszka & Kessler, P.A., Miami, 1980-83; ptnr. firm Touby & Smith, P.A., Miami, Fla., 1983-89, Touby, Smith, DeMahy and Drake P.A., 1989-94, Touby & Woodward, P.A., 1994—; chmn. adv. exec. bd. Paralegal Edn. program Barry U., 1986-87; lectr. Food and Drug Law Inst., 1987-89, 91; lectr. environ. law Exec. Enterprises, 1987-88; lectr. trial techniques, Hispanic Nat. Bar Assn., St. Thomas Law Sch.; adj. prof. product liability Can. Govt., U.S. Trade and Mktg. Dept., 1989-95. Co-author (with Smith and O'Reilly) The Environmental Litigation Deskbook, 1989; contbr. articles to profl. jours.; Mem. ABA, Am. Inns of Ct., Dade County Bar Assn., Fed. Bar Assn. (bd. dirs. 1989—, v.p. 1991-92, pres.-elect So. Fla. chpt. 1992-93, pres. 1993-94), Dade County Bar Assn. (legal aid, pub. svcs. com. 1988), Phi Delta Phi (province pres. 1982-85, bd. dirs. 1985-87). Roman Catholic. Home: 450 Sabal Palm Rd Miami FL 33137 Office: Touby & Woodward PA 250 Bird Rd Ste 308 Miami FL 33146-1424

TOUBY, RICHARD, lawyer; b. Sioux City, Iowa, Nov. 17, 1924; s. Louis and Rebecca (Keck) T.; m. Marion Lascher, Aug. 6, 1949; children: Jill Diane, Kim Paula. LLB, U. Miami, 1948; LLM, Duke U., 1950. Bar: Fla. 1948. Faculty U. Miami, Coral Gables, Fla., 1948-63; mem. 8th Air Force Meml. Assn., 305 Bomb Group (H) Assn., 1994—. 1st Lt. USAF, 1943-45. Office: 19 W Flagler St Ste 907 Miami FL 33130-4407

TOUCH, JOSEPH DEAN, computer scientist, educator; b. Bristol, Pa., Apr. 20, 1963; s. Ralph Benjamin and Filomena (Cianfrani) T. BS in Biophysics and Computer Sci., U. Scranton, 1985; MS in Computer Sci., Cornell U., 1987; PhD in Computer Sci., U. Pa., 1992. Cons., indsl. undergrad. rsch. participation program student GTE Labs., Inc., Waltham, Mass., 1983-85; cons. The Software Engring. Inst., Pitts., 1986; rsch. asst. Cornell U., Ithaca, N.Y., 1985-87; cons. Bell Comm. Rsch., Morristown, N.J., 1987-88; grad. rsch. fellow, AT&T Bell Labs. Rsch. assistantship U. Pa., Phila., 1988-92; cons. NASA Goddard Space Flight Ctr., Greenbelt, Md., 1992; computer scientist, project leader U. So. Calif. Info. Scis. Inst., Marina del Rey, Calif., 1992—; rsch. asst. prof. U. So. Calif., L.A., 1994—; mem. U. Scranton Acad. Computing Adv. Coun., 1983-85; univ. coun. com. on comm. U. Pa., 1989-90, com. on rsch. policy, 1990-91, acad. planning and budget com., 1990-91; reviewer various jours.; lectr. in field. Contbr. articles to profl. jours.; patentee in field. Mem. IEEE, Assn. for Computing Machinery (chpt. pres. 1984-85), IEEE Comm. Soc. (tech. program com. 1993), U. Scranton Phila. Alumni Soc. (v.p. 1990-91), Sigma Xi, Alpha Sigma Nu, Sigma Pi Sigma, Upsilon Pi Epsilon. Democrat. Roman Catholic. Avocations: rollerblading, volleyball, guitar, bicycling, sketching. Home: 14005 Palawan Way Ph 23 Marina Del Rey CA 90292 Office: USC Info Scis Inst 4676 Admiralty Way Marina Dl Rey CA 90292-6601

TOUCHY, DEBORAH K. P., lawyer, accountant; b. Pasadena, Tex., Dec. 9, 1957; d. Donald Carl and Bobbie Jo (Jackson) Putzka; m. Harry Roy Touchy, Jr., Feb. 23, 1980. BBA, Baylor U., 1979; JD, U. Houston, 1988. Bar: Tex. 1989; CPA, Tex.; cert. in estate planning and probate law Tex. Bd. Legal Specialization. Sr. mgr. tax KMPG Peat Marwick, Houston, 1980-86; assoc. Fizer Beck Webster & Bentley, Houston, 1989-90; pvt. practice law and acctg. Houston, 1990—. Editor Houston Law Rev., 1988-89, Jr. League Houston, 1992—. Chmn. ticket sales incentives Chi Omega, Houston, 1985; active ticket sales Mus. Fine Arts, Houston, 1984; facilities chmn. Woodland Trails West Civic Orgn., Houston, 1982-83, Jr. League of Houston, 1993—; pres. Women Attys. in Tax & Probate, 1994-95. Mem. ABA (estate-probate sect. 1989—, vice chmn. commn. property com. 1994—), AICPA (taxation sect., estate and gift tax com. 1992-95), Tex. Soc. CPAs (bd. dirs. 1995—, chmn. tax inst. com. 1996-97, estate planning com. 1990-94, 96), Houston Chpg. CPAs (chmn. taxpayer edn. 1985-86, chmn. membership com. 1992-93, v.p. 1993-94, 96-97, chmn. tax forums 1994-95, long range planning com. 1995-96, treas.-elect 1997—), Houston Bar Assn. (estate-probate sect. 1989—), State Bar Tex. (estate-probate sect. 1989—, mem. elder law com. 1991—), Houston Estate and Fin. Forum, Baylor U. Women's Assn. (treas. 1993-94, chmn. fin. com. 1994-95, parliamentarian 1995-96, sec. 1996-97, pres. 1997—), Chief Justice-Advocates, Tex. Bd. Legal Specializations (cert. estate planning, probate law 1994), Order of Coif, Omicron Delta Kappa, Phi Delta Phi. Office: 2932 Plumb St Houston TX 77005-3058

TOUHILL, BLANCHE MARIE, university chancellor, history-education educator; b. St. Louis, Mo., July 1, 1931; d. Robert and Margaret (Walsh) Van Dillen; m. Joseph M. Touhill, Aug. 29, 1959. BA in History, St. Louis U., 1953, MA in Geography, 1954, PhD in History, 1962. Prof. history and edn. U. Mo., St. Louis, 1965-73, assoc. dean faculties, 1974-76, assoc. vice chancellor for acad. affairs, 1976-87, vice chancellor, 1987-90, chancellor, 1991—; bd. dirs. Boatmen's Nat. Bank of St. Louis, Barnes-Jewish Christian Health Hosps. Conglomerate. Author: William Smith O'Brien and His Irish Revolutionary Companions in Penal Exile, 1981, The Emerging University UM-St. Louis, 1963-83, 1985; editor: Readings in American History, 1970, Varieties of Ireland, 1976, adv. editor Victorian Periodicals Rev. Bd. dirs. Sister City Internat., Am. Coun. Fgn. Rels., St. Louis Forum, Network Bd.,

Mo. State Hist. Soc., 1989—, Mo. Bot. Garden, 1980, St. Louis Symphony Soc., 1993—. Named Outstanding Educator St. Louis chpt. Urban League, 1976; recipient Leadership award St. Louis YWCA, 1986. Mem. Nat. Assn. State Univs. and Land Grant Colls. (exec. com. 1988—), Am. Com. on Irish Studies (pres. 1991—), Phi Kappa Phi, Alpha Sigma Lambda. Office: U Missouri- St Louis Office of the Chancellor 8001 Natural Bridge Rd Saint Louis MO 63121-4401*

TOUHILL, C. JOSEPH, environmental engineer; b. Newark, Aug. 27, 1938; s. Charles J. and Caroline A (Lesaius) T.; m. Helen Elizabeth O'Malley, June 11, 1960; children: Gregory Joseph, Stephen Mark, Christopher Alan, Kathleen Elizabeth. BCE, Rensselaer Poly. Inst., 1960, PhD in Environ. Engring., 1964; SM, MIT, 1961. Diplomate Am. Acad. Environ. Engrs. Mgr. water and land resources dept. Battelle Meml. Inst., Richland, Wash., 1964-71; pres. Baker/TSA Inc., Pitts., 1977-90; group sr. v.p. ICF Kaiser Engrs. Inc., Pitts., 1990-94; exec. v.p. EG&G Environ. Inc., Pitts., 1994—; cons. various engring. firms, Washington and Pitts., 1971-77; trustee Am. Acad. Environ. Engrs., Annapolis, 1971-77, 83-86, Kappe lectr., 1992. Co-author: Hazardous Materials Spills Handbook, 1982, Hazardous Waste Management Engineering, 1987; editor: Resource Management in the Great Lakes Basin, 1971; mem. editorial bd. Environ. Progress Jour., 1979-93. Bd. dirs. Suburban Gen. Hosp., Pitts., 1986-96, Pennwood Bancorp, Pitts., 1991—' vice chmn. Franklin Park (Pa.) Authority, 1977-96, chmn. adv. com., dept. Environ. and energy Engring., Polytech Inst., 1996—. Recipient fellow award Rensselaer Alumni Assn., 1994. Fellow ASCE; mem. Am. Inst. Chem. Engrs. (chmn. environ. engring. div. 1977), Am. Chem. Soc. (editorial adv. bd. 1975-77). Office: EG&G Environ Inc 2206 Almanack Ct Pittsburgh PA 15237-1502

TOULMIN, PRIESTLEY, geologist; b. Birmingham, Ala., June 5, 1930; s. Priestley and Catharine Augusta (Carey) T.; m. Martha Jane Slason, Aug. 30, 1952; children: Catharine Bosier (Mrs. Robert G. Gibson), Priestley Chewning. A.B., Harvard U., 1951, Ph.D., 1959; M.S., U. Colo., 1953. With U.S. Geol. Survey, Washington, 1953-56, 57-89; staff geologist for exptl. geology U.S. Geol. Survey, 1966, chief br. exptl. geochemistry, 1966-71, geologist geologic div., 1971-89; geologist geologic div. U.S. Geol. Survey, Reston, Va., 1974-89, ret., 1989; also leader inorganic chemistry team NASA (Viking Project); adj. prof. Columbia U., 1966; research asso. in geochemistry Calif. Inst. Tech., 1976-77; vis. lectr. Am. Geol. Inst.; dir. petrogenesis and mineral resources program NSF, 1985; bd. dirs., treas. 28th Internat. Geol. Congress, 1985-86;. Mng. sci. editor Geochemistry Internat., 1965-68; assoc. editor Am. Mineralogist, 1974-76; contbr. articles to profl. jours. Mem. advisory com. spl. edn., Alexandria, Va., 1977-80. Recipient Exceptional Service medal NASA, 1977; Meritorious Service award U.S. Dept. Interior, 1978. Fellow Geol. Soc. Am., Mineral Soc. Am. (bd. assoc. editors 1974-76), Soc. Econ. Geologists; mem. AAAS, Geol. Soc. Washington (2d v.p. 1977, councillor 1973-74, 90-91, 1st v.p. 1981, pres. 1982), Am. Geophys. Union, Soc. Mayflower Descs., S.R., SAR, Soc. Colonial Wars (D.C.), Aztec Club of 1847, Cosmos Club (pres. 1993-94, found. trustee 1994—, chmn. 1996—), Sigma Xi, Sigma Gamma Epsilon. Home: 418 Summers Dr Alexandria VA 22301-2449 Office: PO Box 183 Alexandria VA 22313-0183

TOULMIN, STEPHEN EDELSTON, humanities educator; b. London, Mar. 25, 1922. BA in Math. and Physics, King's Coll., Cambridge, Eng., 1942; PhD, King's Coll., 1948; D Tech. (hon.), Royal Inst. Tech., Stockholm, 1991. Lectr. in philosophy of sci. Oxford U., Eng., 1949-55; prof., chmn. dept. of philosophy U. Leeds, Yorkshire, Eng., 1955-59; dir. unit for history of ideas Nuffield Found., London, 1960-65; prof. history of ideas and philosophy Brandeis U., Waltham, Mass., 1965-69; prof. philosophy Mich. State U., East Lansing, 1969-72; prof. humanities U. Calif., Santa Cruz, 1972-73; prof. com. social thought U. Chgo., 1973-86; Avalon prof. humanities Northwestern U., Evanston, Ill., 1986-92, Avalon prof. emeritus, 1992—; Henry R. Luce prof.Ctr. Multiethnic and Transnational Studies U. So. Calif., L.A., 1993—; vis. prof. U. Melbourne, Australia, 1954-55, Stanford U., 1959, Columbia U., N.Y.C., 1960, Hebrew U., Jerusalem, 1964, U. South Fla., 1972, Dartmouth Coll., 1979, SUNY, Plattsburgh, 1980, Colo. Coll., 1980, 82, MacMaster U., 1983, Harvard Project Physics Grad. Sch. Edn., Harvard U., 1965; counselor Smithsonian Inst., Washington, 1967-77; cons., staff mem. Nat. Commn. Protection Human Subjects Biomed. Behavioral Rsch., 1975-78; sr. vis. scholar, fellow Inst. Soc. Ethics and Life Scis., Hastings-on-Hudson, N.Y., 1981—; regent's lectr. U. Calif. Med. Sch., Davis, 1985; Mary Flexner lectr. Bryn Mawr Coll., 1977; Reyerson lectr. U. Chgo., 1979, John Nuveen lectr., 1980; Tate-Wilson lectr. So. Meth. U., 1980; Or Emet lectr. Osgoode Hall Law Sch., 1981; McDermott lectr. U. Dallas, 1985; lectr. Sigma Xi, 1965-66, Phi Beta Kappa, 1978-79, Phi Beta Kappa-AAAS, 1984, Thomas Jefferson lectr. NEH, Washington, 1997; guest prof. social and human scis. Wolfgang Goethe Universitat, Frankfurt, Germany, 1987; vis. fellow Internationales Forschungszentrum Kulturwissenschaften (IFK), Vienna, Austria, 1995—. Author: The Place of Reason in Ethics, 1949, The Philosophy of Science: an Introduction, 1953, The Uses of Argument, 1958, Foresight and Understanding, 1961, Human Understanding, vol. 1, 1972, Knowing and Acting, 1976, The Return to Cosmology, 1982, Cosmopolis, 1989; (with J. Goodfield) The Fabric of the Heavens, 1961, The Architecture of Matter, 1963, The Discovery of Time, 1965; (with A. Janik) Wittgenstein's Vienna, 1973; (with R. Rieke and A. Janik) An Introduction to Reasoning, 1978; (with A. Jonsen) The Abuse of Casuistry, 1987; contbr. numerous sci. articles to profl. jours. Recipient Honor Cross 1st class (Austria), 1991; Getty Ctr. for History of Art and Humanities scholar, 1985-86, First Book of the Year prize Am. Soc. Social Philosophy, 1992; Ctr. for Psychosocial Studies fellow, 1974-76. Fellow Am. Acad. Arts and Scis. Office: U So Calif CMTS GFS 344 Los Angeles CA 90089-1694

TOULOUSE, ROBERT BARTELL, retired college administrator; b. Wellsville, Mo., May 8, 1918; s. Walter Eaton and Emma (Schmidt) T.; m. Virginia Lee Danford, Aug. 7, 1948; children—Samuel Phillip, Robert Bartell. Student, Central Coll., 1935-37; B.S., U. Mo., 1939, M.Ed., 1947, Ed.D., 1948. Tchr. sci. and social studies, high sch. Mountain View, Mo., 1939-41; asst. prof. to prof. U. North Tex., 1949-54, dean Grad. Sch., 1954-82, v.p., from 1982; now ret. Contbr. articles profl. jours. State sponsor Future Tchrs. Am. Served from pvt. to lt. col. AUS, World War II. Mem. Assn. Tex. Grad. Schs. (pres.), Assn. Coll. Tchr. Edn. (v.p.), Tex. Assn. Audio-Visual Edn. Dirs. (v.p.), AAUP, NEA, Phi Delta Kappa. Democrat. Methodist. Club: Kiwanis (pres.). Home: 1218 Emerson Ln Denton TX 76201-1104

TOUMEY, HUBERT JOHN (HUGH TOUMEY), textile company executive; b. N.Y.C.; s. William Joseph and Mary Veronica (Drury) T.; m. Dorothy A. Henry, Oct. 16, 1954; children: Donald Joseph, Kenneth Drury. A.B., Fordham U., 1936; M.B.A., Harvard, 1938. With Cannon Mills, Inc., 1938-81, v.p., mgr. towel sales, 1959-60, v.p., gen. sales mgr., 1960-62, exec. v.p., 1962-67, pres., chief adminstrv. and mktg. officer, 1967-81, chmn., chief exec. officer, 1978-81, also dir.; dir. Cannon Mills Co.; Mem. mktg. com. Am. Textile Mfrs. Inst., 1967-81, chmn., 1977-78. Trustee Coll. Mt. St. Vincent, Riverdale, N.Y., 1977-89, chmn., 1979-88. Mem. Assn. Knights of Malta. Home: 29 Bank St Leefair E New Canaan CT 06840

TOUPIN, HAROLD OVID, chemical company executive; b. Hibbing, Minn., Jan. 21, 1927; s. Ovid Pascal and Ellen (Holt) T.; m. Edna F. Sallila, Feb. 8, 1948 (div. Feb. 1973); m. Colleen Beverly Lange, Apr. 18, 1981; children: James, Ronald. BS, U. Minn., 1954, MA, 1955, postgrad, 1968; PhD (hon.), Internat. Acad. Color, Las Vegas, Nev., 1982, U. Mont., 1990. Mgr. Firestone Tire Co., East Los Angeles, Calif., 1948-51; dir. vocat. edn. Hopkins (Minn.) Pub. Schs., 1955-75; with research and devel. Power-o-Peat Co., Gilbert, Minn., 1956-67; chief exec. officer, cons. Color Specialties Inc., Mpls., 1976—; pres., founder travel, meeting planners svc. co., 1990; founder internat. office for color specialties, 1994; bd. dirs. Vu-tek Inc., St. Paul, Airport Auto Sales, St. Paul Color Specialties of Nev., Las Vegas, Instant Air Inc., Mpls., Freedom Fin.; cons. Runs Hot Cons. Svc., 1966-75. Contbr. articles to profl. jours. Bd. dirs. Hopkins Jaycees, 1958-60. Served with USAAF, 1944-47. Mem. Am. Assn. Mfrs., Internat. Assn. Color, Nat. Ret. Tchrs. Assn., Am. Assn. Self Employeed, Met. Area Dist. Edn. Instrs. Assn. (pres.), Mpls. C. of C. (Super Bowl com. 1992), Am. Legion, VFW. Democrat. Roman Catholic. Lodge: Lions (sec. Hopkins club 1956-76). Avocations: traveling, golfing, writing. Office: Color Specialities Inc 6405 Cedar Ave S Minneapolis MN 55423-1836

TOUR, ROBERT LOUIS, ophthalmologist; b. Sheffield, Ala., Dec. 30, 1918; s. R.S. and Marguerite (Meyer) T.; m. Mona Marie Elien, Oct. 3, 1992. Chem.E., U. Cin., 1942, M.D., 1950. Intern, U. Chgo. Clinics, 1950-51; resident U. Calif. Med. Center-San Francisco, 1951-54; practice medicine, specializing in ophthalmology, occupational medicine and plasmapheresis, San Francisco, 1954-76, Fairbanks, Alaska, 1976-79, Phoenix, 1979—; clin. prof. ophthalmology U. Calif.-San Francisco, 1974-76. Maj. AUS, 1942-45. Diplomate Am. Bd. Ophthalmology. Fellow ACS, Am. Acad. Ophthalmology; mem. AMA, MENSA, Ariz. Ophthal. Soc., Phoenix Ophthal. Soc., Calif. Assn. Ophthalmology, Contact Lens Assn. Ophthalmologists, Pacific Coast Oto-Ophthal. Soc., Ariz. Med. Assn., Maricopa County Med. Soc. , F.C. Cordes Eye Soc., Masons, K.T., Lions, Shriners, Sigma Xi, Nu Sigma Nu, Alpha Tau Omega, Tau Beta Pi, Alpha Omega Alpha, Phi Lambda Upsilon, Omicron Delta Kappa, Kappa Kappa Psi. Home: 2201 E Palmaire Ave Phoenix AZ 85020-5633

TOURLENTES, THOMAS THEODORE, psychiatrist; b. Chgo., Dec. 7, 1922; s. Theodore A. and Mary (Xenostathy) T.; m. Mona Belle Land, Sept. 9, 1956; children: Theodore W., Stephen C., Elizabeth A. BS, U. Chgo., 1945, MD, 1947. Diplomate Am. Bd. Psychiatry and Neurology (sr. examiner 1964-88, 90). Intern Cook County Hosp., Chgo., 1947-48; resident psychiatry Downey (Ill.) VA Hosp., 1948-51; practice medicine specializing in psychiatry Chgo., 1952, Camp Atterbury, Ind., 1953, Ft. Carson, Colo., 1954, Galesburg, Ill., 1955-71; staff psychiatrist Chgo. VA Clinic, 1952; clin. instr. psychiatry Med. Sch., Northwestern U., 1952; dir. mental hygiene consultation service Camp Atterbury, 1953-54, Ft. Carson, 1953-54; asst. supt. Galesburg State Research Hosp., 1954-58, supt., 1958-71; dir. Comprehensive Community Mental Health Ctr. Rock Island and Mercer Counties; dir. psychiat. services Franciscan Hosp., 1971-85; chief mental health services VA Outpatient Clinic, Peoria, Ill., 1985-88; clin. prof. psychiatry U. Ill., Chgo. and Peoria, 1955—; preceptor in hosp. adminstrn. State U. Iowa, Iowa City, 1958-64; councilor, del. Ill. Psychiat. Soc.; chmn. liaison com. Am. Hosp. and Psychiat. Assns., 1978-79, chmn. Quality Care Bd., Ill. Dept. Mental Health, 1995-97. Contbr. articles profl. jours. Mem. Gov. Ill. Com. Employment Handicapped, 1962-64; zone dir. Ill. Dept. Mental Health, Peoria, 1964-71; mem. Spl. Survey Joint Commn. Accreditation Hosps.; chmn. Commn. Cert. Psychiat. Adminstrs., 1979-81; pres. Knox-Galesburg Symphony Soc., 1966-68; bd. dirs. Galesburg Civic Music Assn., pres., 1968-70; chair Knox county United Way Campaign, 1989; pres. Civic Art Ctr., 1990-92. Capt. M.C. AUS, 1952-54. Fellow AAAS, AMA, Am. Psychiat. Assn. (chair hosp. and cmty. psychiatry award bd. 1989-90), Am. Coll. Psychiatrists, Am. Coll. Mental Health Adminstrs.; mem. Ill. Med. Soc. (chmn. aging com. 1968-71, coun. on mental health and addictions 1987-89), chair mental health substance abuse com. 1987-89), Ill. Psychiat. Soc. (pres. 1969-70), Am. Pub. Health Assn., Soc. Biol. Psychiatry, Ill. Hosp. Assn. (trustee 1968-70), Am. Coll. Hosp. Adminstrs., Assn. for Rsch. Nervous and Mental, Am. Assn. Psychiat. Adminstrs. (pres. 1980), Ctrl. Neuorpsychiat. Assn. (pres. 1988-89). Home and Office: 138 Valley View Rd Galesburg IL 61401-8524 *Feeling useful and needed is the greatest recognition and reward.*

TOURLITSAS, JOHN CONSTANTINE, radiologist; b. Cavala, Greece, Oct. 4, 1926; came to U.S., 1956; s. Constantine Nacos and Marica Constantine (Athanasiou) T. MD, U. Athens, Greece, 1955. Diplomate Am. Bd. Radiology. Intern Sioux Valley Hosp., Sioux Falls, S.D., 1956-57; resident Midway Hosp., Mpls.-St. Paul, 1957-59, New Eng. Deaconess Hosp., Harvard MEd. Sch., Boston, 1959-60, Boston U. Med. Ctr., Mass. Meml. Hosps., 1960-62; resident Toronto Western Hosp. U. Toronto, Ont., Can., 1961-62, resident Hosp. for Sick Children, 1962, resident Sunnybrook VA Hosp., 1962-63; resident Royal Victoria Hosp., McGill U., Montreal, Can., 1963-65; attending radiologist, vis. radiologist Maimonides Med. Ctr., Coney Island Hosp., Bklyn., 1966-68; attending, cons. radiologist Bronx-Lebanon Hosp. Ctr., Albert Einstein Coll. Medicine, 1968-95; retired, 1995; instr. radiology Albert Einstein Coll. Medicine, 1972-77. Joslin Clinic fellow, Boston, 1959-60; rsch. fellow U. Toronto, 1962. Fellow Am. Coll. Chest Physicians; mem. AMA, Am. Coll. Radiology, Am. Roentgen Ray Soc., Radiol. Soc. N.Am., N.Y. State Med. Soc. Episcopalian. Avocations: reading, walking, travel. Home: 372 5th Ave Apt 8C New York NY 10018

TOURNEY, GARFIELD, psychiatrist, educator; b. Quincy, Ill., Feb. 6, 1927; s. Guy and Rose Dora (Werner) T.; m. Helen Winifred Wohler, Apr. 4, 1950; children: Carolyn Tourney Florek, Patricia Ann, Catherine Tourney Hughes. BS, U. Ill., 1946, MD, 1948; MS, U. Iowa, 1952; DLitt (hon.), Quincy U., 1992. Intern Univ. Hosps., Iowa City, 1948-49; resident in psychiatry Psychopathic Hosp., Iowa City, 1949-52; instr. Colo. Psychopathic Hosp., Denver, 1952-53; instr., asst. prof. U. Miami, Fla., 1953-55; from asst. prof. to prof. Lafayette Clinic, Wayne State U., Detroit, 1955-67; prof. U. Iowa, Iowa City, 1967-71; prof., vice chmn., chmn. dept. psychiatry Wayne State U., 1971-78; prof. dept. psychiatry U. Miss., Jackson, 1978-92, prof. emeritus, 1992—; part-time cons. in psychiatry, 1992—; psychiat. cons. VA hosps. and others, Iowa, Mich., Miss., 1955—; chief dept. psychiatry Harper Hosp., Detroit, 1971-78. Contbr. numerous chpts. to books and articles and revs. to profl. jours. Bd. dirs. Northeast Mental Health Ctr., Detroit, 1974-78. Life fellow Am. Psychiat. Assn. (libr. and history com. 1985-90, chmn. 1989-90, cons. on 150th anniversary 1990-94, Benjamin Rush Cir. 1992, Garfield and Helen W. Tourney Rare Books Rm. of Libr. and Archives dedicated in his honor 1994); mem. AMA, Am. Osler Soc., Mich. Psychiat. Soc. (Presdl. award 1977), Found. for the Advancement of Psychiatry. Avocations: collecting books and art, literature, history, philosophy, William Blake. Home and Office: 106 Cherry Hills Dr Jackson MS 39211-2507

TOURNILLON, NICHOLAS BRADY, trade finance, international investments company executive; b. New Orleans, Sept. 1, 1933; s. Samuel C. and Anna Mae (Brady) T.; m. Audrey Nicosia, Dec. 15, 1956; children: Brady, Linda, Tracy, Jeffrey, Gregory, Lori. B.A., Southeastern La. U., 1958; M.B.A., La. State U., 1960. Loan officer Export Import Bank U.S., Washington, 1960-66; adminstrv. asst. to exec. officers Atlantic Gulf & Pacific Co. of Manila, 1966-68; asst. treas. GTE Internat., Stamford, Conn., 1968-76, treas., 1976-86, v.p., 1978-86; pres. GTE Fin. Corp., 1984-86; asst. treas. GTE Corp., 1985-86; chmn., chief exec. officer Am. and Internat. Investment Corp., 1986—; mgr. Dir. Trade and Investment Advisors Ltd., Hungary, 1992—; bd. dirs. Global Access Corp.; mem. internat. adv. bd. Union Trust Co.; advisor on export fin. to Office of U.S. Pres. (U.S. Trade Rep.). Past chmn. Conn. Dist. Export Council of US Dept. Commerce; mem. monetary com. U.S. Council Internat. Bus.; bd. dirs. Nat. Fgn. Trade Council. Served with USNR, 1953-54, Korea. Named Outstanding Alumnus of Yr., Southeastern La. U., 1976. Mem. Soc. Internat. Treasurers, Acad. Internat. Bus., Phi Kappa Phi. Home: Midwood Dr Greenwich CT 06831-4400 Office: Am and Internat Investment Corp 25 Midwood Dr Greenwich CT 06831-4412 *Perseverance is an often mentioned but never overrated quality—the quality that prevents the substitution of expediency for excellence. Throughout life, persevering effort has been responsible for converting ideas and talents into results and recognition.*

TOURTELLOTTE, CHARLES DEE, physician, educator; b. Kalamazoo, Aug. 28, 1931; s. Dee and Helen May (Lotz) T.; m. Barbara Richwine, June 25, 1955; children: Daniel DeWitt, Elizabeth Anne, William Charles, Scott David. AB, Johns Hopkins U., 1953; MS in Biochemistry, MD, Temple U., 1957. Diplomate Am. Bd. Internal Medicine. Intern, resident in medicine U. Mich. Hosp., Ann Arbor, 1957-60; fellow in rheumatology Temple U. Hosp., Phila., 1960-61; fellow in biochemistry Rockefeller U., N.Y.C., 1961-63; faculty Sch. Medicine, Temple U., 1963—, prof. medicine, 1972—; chief rheumatology Temple U. Hosp., 1966—, pres. med. staff, bd. govs., 1984-86; dir. Greater Delaware Valley Arthritis Control Program, 1974-77; pres. Eastern Pa. chpt. Arthritis Found., 1972-74; mem. active/cons. staff 10 area and regional hosps. Contbr. chpts. to textbooks, articles to profl. jours.; Editorial Bd.: Arthritis and Rheumatism, 1969-77, 19th-24th Rheumatism Revs, 1969-81. Mem. Haddonfield (N.J.) Bd. Edn., 1968-74, pres., 1974; mem. Borough of Haddonfield Environ. Comm., 1975-87, chmn., 1977-85; mem. Haddonfield Civic Assn., 1963—; South N.J. chmn. Johns Hopkins U. Alumni Schs. Com., 1975-90; trustee Bobby Fulton Meml. Fund, 1979—. Served with AUS, 1953-61. Helen Hay Whitney Found. fellow, 1962-63; Arthritis Found. fellow, 1963-66. Fellow ACP, Phila. Coll. Physicians, Am. Coll. Rheumatology (founding fellow); mem. AMA, Am. Fedn. for Clin. Rsch., Am. Soc. Internal Medicine, Pa. Soc. Internal Medicine, Pa. Med. Soc., Phila. County Med. Soc., Babcock Surg. Soc., Phila. Rheumatism Soc. (pres. 1968-69), Pa. Rheumatology Soc. (founding pres. 1985-86), N.J. Soc. of Pa., Huguenot Soc. Pa., Tavistock County Club (N.J.), Little Egg Harbor Yacht Club, Med. Club of Phila. (bd. dirs. 1991—), Sigma Xi, Alpha Omega Alpha, Delta Upsilon, Phi Chi. Presbyterian. Home: 6 Lane of Acres Haddonfield NJ 08033-3505 Office: Temple Univ Hosp Dept Rheumatology Philadelphia PA 19140-5192

TOURTELLOTTE, WALLACE WILLIAM, neurologist; b. Great Falls, Mont., Sept. 13, 1924; s. Nathaniel Mills and Frances Victoria (Charlton) T.; m. Jean Esther Toncray, Feb. 14, 1953; children: Wallace William, George Mills, James Millard, Warren Gerard. PhB, BS, U. Chgo., 1945, PhD, 1948, MD, 1951. Intern Strong Meml. Hosp. U. Rochester (N.Y.) Sch. Medicine and Dentistry, 1951-54; resident in neurology U. Mich. Med. Ctr., Ann Arbor, 1954-57, asst. prof. neurology, 1957-59, assoc. prof., 1959-66, prof., 1966-71; prof. UCLA, 1971—; prof. dept. neurology, 1996—; vis. assoc. prof. Washington U., St. Louis, 1963-64; mem. med. adv. bd. Nat. Multiple Sclerosis Soc., 1968—, So. Calif. Multiple Sclerosis Socs., 1972—; dir. Multiple Sclerosis Rsch. and Treatment Ctr., Nat. Neurol. Rsch. Specimen Bank, 1971—; vice chmn. dept. neurology UCLA, 1971-96, dir. brain rsch. inst.; chief neurology svc. West L.A. VA Med. Ctr., 1971—; Pritchard lectr., Belfast, Ireland, 1996. Editor: Multiple Sclerosis, Clinical and Pathogenetic Basis, 1997; mem. editorial bd. Jour. Neurol. Sci., Revue Neurologica, Italian Jour. Neurol. Sci., Multiple Sclerosis Jour. Lt. (j.g.) M.C., USN, 1952-54. Recipient Disting. Alumni Service award U. Chgo., 1982. Fellow Am. Acad. Neurology (S. Weir Mitchell Neurology Reseach award 1959); mem. Am. Assn. Univ. Neurol. Prof., Am. Neurol. Assn. (counselor 1982—, v.p. 1992), World Fedn. Neurology (founding mem.), Am. Assn. Neuropathologists, Internat. Soc. Neurochemsitry (founding mem.), Am. Soc. Pharmacology and Exptl. Therapeutics, Am. Soc. Neurochemistry (founding mem.), Soc. Neurosci., Conferie de la Chaine des Rotisseur (chevalier Los Angeles chpt.), Argentier du Baillage de Los Angeles, Ordre Mondial des Gourmets Degustateurs Etats-Unis, Pasadena Wine and Food Soc., Physician Wine & Food Soc., Soc. Med. Friends of Wine, Sigma Xi. Republican. Presbyterian. Home: 1140 Tellem Dr Pacific Palisades CA 90272-2244 Office: West Los Angeles VA Med Ctr 11301 Wilshire Blvd Los Angeles CA 90073-1003

TOURTILLOTT, ELEANOR ALICE, nurse, educational consultant; b. North Hampton, N.H., Mar. 28, 1909; d. Herbert Shaw and Sarah (Fife) T. Diploma Melrose Hosp. Sch. Nursing, Melrose, Mass., 1930; BS, Columbia U., 1948, MA, 1949; edn. specialist Wayne State U., 1962. RN. Gen. pvt. duty nurse, Melrose, Mass., 1930-35; obstet. supr. Samaritan Hosp., Troy, N.Y., 1935-36, Meml. Hosp., Niagara Falls, N.Y., 1937-38, Lawrence Meml. Hosp., New London, Conn., 1939-42, New Eng. Hosp. for Women and Children, Boston, 1942-43; dir. H. W. Smith Sch. Practical Nursing, Syracuse, N.Y., 1949-53; founder, dir. assoc. degree nursing program Henry Ford Community Coll., Dearborn, Mich., 1953-74; dir. pioneering use of learning techs. via mixed media USPHS, 1966-71; prin. cons., initial coord. Wayne State U. Coll. Nursing, Detroit, 1975-78; cons. curriculum design, modular devel., instructional media Tourtillott Cons., Inc., Dearborn, Mich., 1974—; condr. numerous workshops on curriculum design, instructional media at various colls., 1966—; mem. Mich. Bd. Nursing, 1966-73, chmn., 1970-72, mem. rev. com. for constrn. nurse tng. facilities, div. nursing USPHS, 1967-70, mem. nat. adv. coun. on nurse tng., Dept. Health Edn. and Welfare, 1972-76. Author: Commitment-A Lost Characteristic, 1982; contbg. co-author: Patient Assessment-History and Physical Examination, 1975-78; contbr. chpts., articles, speeches to profl. publs. Served to capt. Nurse Corps, U.S. Army, 1943-47; ETO. Recipient Disting. Alumnae award Tchrs. Coll. Columbia U., 1974, Spl. tribute 77th Legislature Mich., 1974, Disting. Alumnae award Wayne State U., 1975, Disting. Service award Henry Ford Community Coll., 1982; established and endowed Eleanor Tourtillott Outstanding Student Nurse of Yr. award at Henry Ford C.C., 1993. Mem. DAR, ANA, Nat. League Nursing (chmn. steering com. degree programs 1965-67, bd. dirs. 1965-67, 71-73, mem. assembly constituent leagues 1971-73, council assoc. degree programs citation 1974, Mildred Montag Excellence in Leadership award coun. assoc. degree programs 1994), Mich. League for Nursing (pres. 1969-71), Mich. Acad. Sci., Arts and Letters, Am. Legion, Tchrs. Coll. Alumnae Assn., Wayne State U. Alumnae Assn., Phi Lambda Theta, Kappa Delta Pi.

TOUSIGNANT, JACQUES, human resources executive, lawyer; b. Montreal, Que., Can., Sept. 20, 1948. JD, Sherbrooke U., Que., 1975. Assoc. law firm Pouliot Mercure & Assocs., Montreal, Que., 1975-85; dir. assoc. law firm Montreal Trans. Soc., Montreal, Que., 1985-87; v.p. La Presse Ltee, Montreal, Que., 1987—. Mem. Can. Bar Assn., Que. Bar Assn. Office: La Presse, 7 Rue St Jacques, Montreal, PQ Canada H2Y 1K9

TOUSSAINT, ALLEN RICHARD, recording studio executive, composer, pianist; b. New Orleans, Jan. 14, 1938; s. Clarence Matthew and Naomi (Neville) T.; children: Naomi, Clarence, Alison. Student pub. and pvt. schs., New Orleans. Pres. Sea-Saint Recording Studios, Inc., New Orleans; lectr. in field. Pianist for, Shirley & Lee, 1957, U.S. Army Soldiers Choir, 1963-65; recorded albums Tousan-Wild Sounds of New Orleans, 1958, Life, Love & Faith, 1972, Southern Nights, 1975, Motion, 1978, Connected, 1996; founder, v.p. recorded albums, Sansu Enterprises, Inc., from 1965, pres., Sea-Saint Rec. Studio, Inc., New Orleans, Marsaint Music, Inc., NYNO Music, Inc.; composer: songs Southern Nights (Country Music Assn. Song of Yr., Broadcast Music, Inc., citation of achievement), The Greatest Love, The Optimism Blues, Viva La Money, Whipped Cream, With You In Mind, Working In A Coal Mine, Yes We Can, Can, All These Things, (Broadcast Music, Inc. citation of achievement); stage (Broadway) performer, dir., choreographer, The High Rollers Social and Pleasure Club, 1992; performer, New Orleans Jazz Festival, annually. Served with U.S. Army, 1963-65. Mem. Broadcast Music, Inc., Am. Fedn. Musicians, Contemporary Arts Ctr. Office: Sea-Saint Rec Studio Inc 3264 Frey Pl New Orleans LA 70119-2717*

TOUSTER, SAUL, law educator; b. Bklyn., Oct. 12, 1925; s. Ben and Bertha (Landau) T.; m. Helen Davidson, Nov. 23, 1954 (div. 1967); children: Natasha Ann, Jonathan Bach; m. Irene Tayler, Jan. 14, 1978. A.B. magna cum laude, Harvard U., 1944, J.D., 1948. Bar: N.Y. 1949. Practiced in N.Y.C., 1949-55; prof. law SUNY-Buffalo, 1955-69, asst. to pres., 1966-68, mem. adj. faculty in medicine, edn., psychology, 1964-69; prof. law and social scis. State Coll. at Old Westbury, 1969-71; prof., provost, acad. v.p. CCNY, 1971-73; acting pres. Richmond Coll. City U. N.Y., 1973-74; prof. law CUNY Grad. Sch. also John Jay Coll. of Criminal Justice, 1974-80; prof., dir. legal studies, humanities, professions programs Brandeis U., Waltham, Mass., 1980-93, prof. emeritus, 1993; legis. cons. N.Y. State Law Rev. Commn., 1956-61; vis. prof. U. Brussels, summer, 1968, Boston Coll. Law Sch., 1994. Author: Still Lives and Other Lives, 1966 (Devins Meml. prize 1966); Contbr. articles to legal periodicals. Served to lt. (j.g.) USNR, 1944-46. NEH fellow, 1978; Am. Bar Found. Legal History fellow, 1977-78. Mem. Internat. Inst. Boston (bd. dirs.), Phi Beta Kappa. Home: 180 Beacon St Boston MA 02116-1401 Office: Legal Studies Program Brandeis U Waltham MA 02254

TOVES, JO ANN VILLAMOR, nursing supervisor; b. Tamuning, Guam, May 14, 1955; d. James Gazer and Rosario Villamor; m. Pedro G. Toves, Feb. 8, 1975; children: Peter Justin, Paul Jay Henri, Francisco James. ASN, U. Guam, Mangilao, 1976, BSN magna cum laude, 1991. RN; cert. emergency nurse, cmty. health nurse, BLS, ACLS, neonatal resuscitation program, Pediatric Advanced Life Support, Trauma Nursing Core Course. Nurse Guam Meml. Hosp., Tamuning, 1976-77, LPN, 1977-78, emergency nurse, 1979-86, 92; cmty. health nurse Dept. Pub. Health, Mangilao, 1986-89, emergency nurse supr., 1993-95; clin. assoc. preceptorship program U. Guam, 1996; emergency med. tech., instr. Mem. Father Duenas Booster Club, Mangilao, 1994, GNA Immunization Campaign, 1994, Child Passenger Safety Campaign, 1995. Regents scholar U. Guam, Mangilao, 1990. Mem. Am./Guam Nurses Assn., Emergency Nurses Assn. Roman Catholic. Avocations: reading, gardening, home improvement, volunteering, singing. Home: 128 Etton Ln Sinajana GU 96926-4207

TOVISH, HAROLD, sculptor; b. N.Y.C., July 31, 1921; s. Louis Goodman and Anna (Treffman) T.; m. Marianna Pineda (Packard), Jan. 14, 1946; children: Margo, Aaron, Nina. Student, WPA Art Project, 1938-40,

Columbia U., 1940-43, Ossip Zadkine Sch. Drawing and Sculpture, Paris, France, 1949-50, Acad. De La Grande Chaumiere, Paris, 1950-51. Tchr. sculpture N.Y. State Coll. Ceramics, 1947-49, U. Minn., 1951-54, Sch. of Boston Mus., 1957-66; sculptor in residence Am. Acad. in, Rome, 1966; prof. art Boston U., 1971-85, prof. emeritus, 1986—; vis. prof. U. Hawaii, 1969-70. Group exhbns. include Met. Mus. of Art, 1943, Toledo Mus. Art, 1948, Galerie 8, 1949, Walker Art Center, 1951, Mpls. Inst. Art, 1953, San Francisco Art Assn., 1953, Whitney Mus. Am. Art, 1954, 58, 60, 64, 80, 28th Venice Biennial, 1956, Mus. Modern Art, 1960, Chgo. Art Inst., 1960, Carnegie Internat, 1960, Am. Fedn. Art, 1964, Decordova Mus., 1964, Internat. Exhbn. of Contemporary Medal, Paris, 1967, Boston Visual Artists Union Gallery, 1975, Boston U., 1975, 78, Colby Coll., 1975, Inst. Contemporary Art, Boston, 1975, 76, Skowhegan Sch., 1975, NYU, 1976, Boston Mus. Fine Arts, 1977, Nat. Mus. Am. Art, 1987, Nat. Acad. Design, 1987, DeCordova Mus., 1987, Howard Yezersky Gallery, 1988; one-man shows include, Walker Art Center, 1953, Swetzoff Gallery, Boston, 1957, 60, 65, Dintenfass Gallery, N.Y.C., 1965, 72, Addison Gallery Am. Art, Andover, Mass., 1965, Alpha Gallery, Boston, 1968, 73, 86, Terry Dintenfass, Inc., N.Y.C., 1980, 85, Boston U., 1980, retrospective exhibit, Wheaton Coll., 1967, Howard Yezerski Gallery, Boston, 1993, 95; survey exhibit, Solomon Guggenheim Meml. Mus., 1968, Fed. Res. Bank, Boston, 1991; retrospective exhbn. Addison Gallery Am. Art, 1988; survey exhibit Muscarelle Mus., Williamsburg, Va., 1990; represented in permanent collections Phila. Mus. Art, Whitney Mus. Am. Art, Walker Art Center, Mpls. Inst. Art, Addison Gallery Am. Art, Chgo. Art Inst., Mus. Modern Art, Boston Mus. Fine Art, Guggenheim Mus., Worcester Mus. Art, Hirshhorn Collection, Sara Roby Found., Colby Coll., Muscarelle Mus. William & Mary Coll., Williamsburg, Va., Nat. Gallery Am. Art, Minn. Gallery Art, Nat. Mus. Am. Art, Boston Pub. Library; (Recipient 1st prize sculpture Boston Arts Festival 1957, 1st prize drawing 1958, award Am. Inst. Arts and Letters 1971, sculpture grantee Am. Inst. Arts and Letters 1960). Guggenheim fellow, 1967; research fellow Center for Advanced Visual Studies, MIT, 1967-68. Assoc. mem. NAD.

TOWBIN, A(BRAHAM) ROBERT, investment banker; b. N.Y.C., May 26, 1935; s. Harold Clay and Minna (Berlin) T.; m. Jacqueline de Chollet; children: Minna Joyce Pinger, Abraham Robert Jr., Zachary Harold. B.A., Dartmouth Coll., 1957. With Asiel & Co., N.Y.C., 1958-59; with L.F. Rothschild, Unterberg, Towbin Holdings, Inc. (merged with C.E. Unterberg, Towbin Co. 1977), N.Y.C., 1959-86, vice chmn., 1961-86; mng. dir. Lehman Bros. (formerly Shearson Lehman Bros., Inc.), N.Y., 1987-94; pres. Russian Am. Enterprise Fund., Moscow and N.Y.C., 1994-95; vice chmn. U.S. Russian Investment Fund, Moscow and N.Y.C., 1995; mng. dir. Unterberg Harris, N.Y.C., 1995—; bd. dirs. Bradley Real Estate, Inc., Gerber Sci. Inc., Globalstar Telecom. Ltd., K&F Industries, Columbus New Millenium Fund, London, 1994. Hon. mem. N.Y. State Coun. Arts.; bd. dirs. Marymount Sch. Mem. Securities Industry Assn., Bond Club N.Y., Stock Exch. Luncheon Club, Harmonie Club (N.Y.C.), Nat. Golf Links Am., N.Y. Yacht Club, Antigua Yacht Club, Chelsea Art Club (London), Century Assn. Home: 1010 5th Ave New York NY 10028-0130 Office: Unterberg Harris 10 E 50th St New York NY 10022

TOWE, THOMAS EDWARD, lawyer; b. Cherokee, Iowa, June 25, 1937; s. Edward and Florence (Tow) T.; m. Ruth James, Aug. 21, 1960; children: James Thomas, Kristofer Edward. Student, U. Paris, 1956; BA, Earlham Coll., 1959; LLB, U. Mont., 1962; LLM, Georgetown U., 1965. Ptnr. Towe, Ball, Enright, Mackey & Sommerfeld, Billings, Mont., 1967—; legislator Mont. House of Rep., Billings, 1971-75, Mont. State Senate, Billings, 1975-87, 91-94; served on various coms. Mont. Senate, 1975-87, 91-94. Contbr. articles to law revs. Mem. Alternatives, Inc., Halfway House, Billing, 1977—, pres., 1985-86; mem. adv. com. Mont. Crime Control Bd., 1973-78, Youth Justice Coun., 1981-83; mem. State Dem. Exec. Com., 1969-73; candidate for Congress, 1976; bd. dirs. Mont. Consumer Affairs Coun., Regl. Cmty. Svcs. for the Devei. Disabled, 1975-77, Rimrock Guidance Found., 1975-80, Vols. of Am., Billings, 1984-89, Youth Dynamics Inc., 1989-96, Zoo Mont., 1985—, Inst. for Peace Studies, 1993—, Mont. State Parks Assn., 1993—. Capt. U.S. Army, 1962-65. Mem. Mont. Bar Assn., Yellowstone County Bar Assn., Am. Hereford Assn., Billings C. of C. Mem. Soc. of Friends. Avocation: outdoor recreation. Home: 2739 Gregory Dr S Billings MT 59102-0509 Office: 2525 6th Ave N Billings MT 59101-1338

TOWELL, WILLIAM EARNEST, forester, former association executive; b. St. James, Mo., June 11, 1916; s. Esco Joel and Margaret (Pinto) T.; m. Virginia Ruth Dotter, Aug. 31, 1940; children: Jane Towell Darrough, Linda Towell Pinney. B.S. in Forestry, U. Mich., 1938, M.S. in Silviculture, 1938; D.Sc. (hon.), U. Mo., 1981. With Mo. Dept. Conservation, 1938-67, dir., 1957-67; exec. v.p. Am. Forestry Assn., Washington, 1967-78; adj. prof. forestry N.C. State U., 1979—. Mem. Pres.'s Water Pollution Control Adv. Bd., 1963-66, Sec. Agr. Wildlife Adv.Bd., 1965-69, Lewis and Clark Trail Commn., 1965-67; mem. conservation com. Boy Scouts Am., 1968-78, nat. chmn., 1975-78; nat. chmn. project SOAR, 1970-74; adv. mem. com. interrelations wildlife and agr. NAS, 1965-70, mem. adv. team to Indonesia, 1972; mem. Cradle of Forestry Advisory Commn., Dept. Agr., 1971-76; conservation cons. Walt Disney Prodns., 1969-78; chmn. exec. com. Internat. Assn. Fish and Wildlife Agys., 1964-65, pres., 1965-66; mem. exec. com. Fontana Conservation Roundup, 1969-80; mem. exec. com. Nat. Resources Coun. Am., 1968-78, chmn., 1975-77; bd. dirs. Nat. Wildlife Fedn., 1979-87; Forest History Soc., 1978-88;; mem. study panel Fishery Mgmt. Nat. Marine Fisheries Svc. NOAA, U.S. Dept. Commerce, 1986; mem. adv. bd. Wild Horse and Burro dept. U.S. Dept. of Interior, 1986-87; mem. diocesan coun., past sr. warden Episcopal Ch., pres. The Village Chapel, Pinehurst, N.C., 1988, 91. Lt. USNR, 1943-46. Recipient Merit de Agrico medal France, 1970; Conservationist of Year award Nat. Wildlife Fedn., 1976; Disting. Service award U. Mich. Sch. Natural Resources Alumni Soc., 1978; Lifetime Achievement award Nat. Assn. State Foresters, 1978; John Aston Warder Medal Am. Forestry Assn., 1982; J. Sterling Morton award Nat. Arbor Day Found., 1984. Fellow Soc. Am. Foresters (chmn. Ozark sect. 1950, v.p. 1982-83, pres. 1984, Sir William Schlich Meml. medal 1978); mem. Kiwanis. Democrat. Home: 4 Village Green Cir Southern Pines NC 28387-3209

TOWER, HORACE LINWOOD, III, consumer products company executive; b. New Haven, July 16, 1932; s. Horace Linwood, Jr. and Madeline Elizabeth (Davin) T.; m. Elizabeth Wright, Dec. 29, 1956; children: Cynthia, William, John. BA, Cornell U., 1955, MBA, 1960; DHL (hon.), Westfield (Mass.) State Coll., 1984. With Procter & Gamble Corp., Cin., 1960-62; mgmt. cons. Booz, Allen & Hamilton, N.Y.C., 1962-63; with Gen. Foods Corp., White Plains, N.Y., 1963-67, pres. Maxwell home divsn., 1963-78, pres., CEO, 1978-90; pres., CEO, Stanhome Inc., Westfield, Mass., 1978-90, chmn., 1982—; bd. dirs. Stanhome Inc., Tambrands, Inc., Stanley Park; formerly bd. dirs. Forman Cos. Capt. USAF, 1956-59. Mem. Air Force Assn., Sabre Pilots Assn., Thimble Island Sailing and Lit. Soc., Stony Creek Boating Club, Pi Kappa Phi, Sigma Gamma Epsilon. Office: Stanhome Inc 333 Western Ave Westfield MA 01085-2560

TOWERS, BERNARD LEONARD, medical educator; b. Preston, Eng., Aug. 20, 1922; s. Thomas Francis and Isabella Ellen (Dobson) T.; m. Carole Ilene Lieberman (div. 1992); 1 child, Tiffany Sabrina; children from previous marriage: Helena Marianne, Celia Marguerite, Julie Carole. M.B., Ch.B., U. Liverpool, 1947; M.A., U. Cambridge, 1954. House surgeon Royal Infirmary, Liverpool, 1947; lectr. U. Bristol, 1949-50, U. Wales, 1950-54, Cambridge U., 1954-70; fellow Jesus Coll., 1957-70, steward, 1961-64, tutor, 1964-69; dir. med. studies, 1964-70; prof. pediatrics UCLA, 1971-84, prof. anatomy, 1971-91, prof. psychiatry, 1983-91, prof. emeritus anatomy and psychiatry, 1991—, convenor, moderator medicine and soc. forum, 1974-89; pvt. practice integrative medicine, 1991—; co-dir. Program in Medicine, Law and Human Values, 1977-84; cons. Inst. Human Values in Medicine, 1971-84; adv. bd. Am. Teilhard Assn. for Future of Man, 1971—; v.p. Teilhard Centre for Future Man, London, 1974—. Author: Teilhard de Chardin, 1966, Naked Ape or Homo Sapiens?, 1969, Concerning Teilhard, 1969; also articles, chpts. on sci. and philosophy.; Editor anat. sect.: Brit. Abstracts Med. Scis, 1954-56, Teilhard Study Library, 1966-70; adv. bd.: Jour. Medicine and Philosophy, 1974-84. Served to capt. RAMC, 1947-49. NIH grantee, 1974-78; NEH grantee, 1977-83. Fellow Cambridge Philos. Soc., Royal Soc. Medicine; mem. Brit. Soc. History of Medicine, Soc. Health and Human Values (pres. 1977-78), Anat. Soc. G.B., Worshipful Soc. Apothecaries London, Am. Assn. for Study Mental Imagery, Western Assn. Physicians, Societe Europeene de Culture Venise. Office: 436 N Bedford Dr Ste 302 Beverly Hills CA 90210-4320

TOWERS, JAMES MC, education educator; b. Ames, Iowa, Dec. 3, 1948; s. Charles Mc and Mary Elizabeth (Peck) T.; m. Karen Ruth Lauridsen, Aug. 18, 1973; children: Devon Charles, Jaimee Faye Elizabeth. BA, U. Iowa, 1970, MA, 1974, diploma as Ednl. Specialist, 1976, PhD in Edn., 1985. Instr. English Walgett High Sch., New South Wales, Australia, 1971-73, Am. Sch. of Kuwait, 1974-75; prof. Muscatine (Iowa) Community Coll., 1976-79; program coordinator U. Iowa, Iowa City, 1979-85; dir. Title III Des Moines Area Community Coll., Ankery, Iowa, 1985-86; asst. prof. edn. Monmouth (Ill.) Coll., 1986-88; assoc. prof., chmn. dept. St. Mary's Coll. of Minn., Winona, 1988—, assoc. dean sch. edn., 1993—, dean sch. edn., 1995—; cons. Am. Coll. Testing, Iowa City, 1984-85. Editor: How To Study for Academic Success, 1988; author poems; contbr. articles to profl. jours. Methodist. Avocation: traveling. Office: St Mary's Coll Winona MN 55987

TOWERY, CURTIS KENT, lawyer; b. Hugoton, Kans., Jan. 29, 1954; s. Clyde D. and Jo June (Curtis) T. BA, Trinity U., 1976; JD, U. Okla., 1979; LLM in Taxation, Boston U., 1989. Mem. Curtis & Blanton, Pauls Valley, Okla., 1980-81; lawyer land and legal dept. Trigg Drilling Co., Oklahoma City, 1981-82; adminstrv. law judge Okla. Corp. Commn., Oklahoma City, 1982-85; counsel Curtis & Blanton, Pauls Valley, Okla., 1985-88; adminstrv. law judge Okla. Dept. Mines, Oklahoma City, 1985-88, assoc. gen. counsel, 1989-92; contracts and purchasing adminstr., atty. Okla. Turnpike Authority, Oklahoma City, 1992-93; asst. gen. counsel Okla. Corp. Commn., 1993—; bd. dirs. First Nat. Bank Pauls Valley, 1983-88. Assoc. bd. Okla. Mus. Art, 1985-88, Okla. Symphony Orch., 1987-92; assoc. bd. Ballet Okla., 1987-92, sec., 1990-91, v.p., 1988-89. Mem. ABA, Okla. Bar Assn., Am. Assn. Petroleum Landmen, Internat. Assn. Energy Economists, Men's Dinner Club, Faculty House, Rotary, Elks, Phi Alpha Delta, Sigma Nu. Democrat. Presbyterian. Avocations: flying, golf, traveling, investment analysis. Home: PO Box 14891 Oklahoma City OK 73113-0891 Office: Jim Thorpe Bldg 2101 N Lincoln Blvd Oklahoma City OK 73105-4904

TOWERY, JAMES E., lawyer; b. Los Alamos, N.Mex., July 12, 1948; s. Lawson E. and Irma (Van Apeldorn) T.; m. Kathryn K. Meier, July 20, 1991; 1 child, Mark J. BA, Princeton U., 1973; JD, Emory U., 1976. Assoc. Morgan Beauzay Hammer, San Jose, Calif., 1977-79; ptnr. Morgan & Towery, San Jose, Calif., 1979-89; assoc. Hoge Fenton Jones & Appel, San Jose, Calif., 1989-90, ptnr., 1990—. Chmn. bd. trustees Alexian Bros. Hosp., San Jose, Calif., 1995. Mem. ABA (ho. of dels.), State Bar Calif. (v.p. and chair discipline com. 1994-95, bd. govs. 1992-96, pres. 1995-96, presiding arbitrator, fee arbitration program 1990-92), Santa Clara County Bar Assn. (counsel 1984-85, treas. 1987, pres. 1989). Office: Hoge Fenton Jones 60 S Market St San Jose CA 95113

TOWEY, CARROLL FRANCIS, senior education specialist; b. Boston, Jan. 30, 1932; s. Thomas Patrick and Marietta V. (Alcock) T.; m. Marie Elizabeth Linehan, Aug 24, 1957 (dec. Apr., 1992); children Mary Ellen Roth, Michael Carroll, Kevin James; m. Miriam A. Quinlan, Sept. 4, 1993. BS in Edn., Salem State Coll., 1953; MEd, Boston U., 1957, cert. advanced grad. study (adult edn.), 1967; EdD, U. Mass., 1973. Sr. supr. Mass. Dept. Edn., Boston, 1965-67; sr. program advisor U.S. Dept. Edn., Washington, 1967—; mem. Met. Wash. Assn. for Adult and Continuing Edn., Washington, 1981-85, pres. 1983-84; author: reports to U.S. Dept. Edn. on model programs, evaluation of adult education, and compliance by states to federal regulations; bd. durs. Northern Va. Chpt. Retired Officers Assn., 1997. Mem. Mass. Soc. Washington, D.C., 1982—, v.p. 1993-95, pres. 1995-96, treas., 1996-97. With U.S. Army, 1955-57, Korea. Recipient Appreciation certs. Nat. Defense U., 1990, Nev. Dept. Edn., 1991, Pima County, Ariz., 1992. Mem. KC, Fed. Vocat. Edn. Assn. (pres. 1993-94), Am. Assn. Adult and Continuing Edn. (founding mem., pres. Met. Washington 1983-84, Appreciation cert. 1988), Ret. Officers Assn. (bd. dirs. Nova Troa 1997), Phi Delta Kappa Boston U. Democrat. Roman Catholic. Avocations: gardening, reading, writing, sports. Home: 1016 S Wayne St # 309 Arlington VA 22204 Office: US Dept Edn 600 Independence Ave SW # Wdc Washington DC 20202-0004

TOWEY, RICHARD EDWARD, economics educator; b. Mount Kisco, N.Y., Sept. 22, 1928; s. William Joseph and Anna Margaret (Rumse) T.; m. Mary Ann Franusich, June 12, 1954 (dec. Mar. 1988); 1 child, John Patrick; m. Lorraine T. Miller, July 21, 1990. BS, U. San Francisco, 1954; MA, U. Calif., Berkeley, 1957, PhD, 1967. Economist Fed. Res. Bank of San Francisco, 1957-60; prof. econs. Oreg. State U., Corvallis, 1962-93, emeritus prof., 1993—; economist Fed. Deposit Ins. Corp., Washington, 1968-70. Cpl. U.S. Army, 1948-49, 1950-51. Earhart fellow U. Calif., Berkeley, 1961-62. Mem. Am. Econ. Assn., Am. Fin. Assn., Western Econ. Assn. Roman Catholic. Office: Oreg State Univ Dept. Econ Corvallis OR 97331

TOWLE, LAIRD CHARLES, book publisher; b. Exeter, N.H., Sept. 13, 1933; s. Gerald Charles and Wilma Lois (Buzzell) T.; m. Marlene Ann Towne, Apr. 14, 1956; children: Karen Lee, Joel Andrew, Glenn Corbett, Leslie Kim. BS in Physics, U. N.H., 1955, MS in Physics, 1958; PhD, U. Va., 1962. Rsch. physicist AVCO Corp., Wilmington, Mass., 1962-63, Allis Chalmers Corp., West Allis, Wis., 1963-67; section head Naval Rsch. Lab., Washington, 1967-77, project mgr., 1977-81; chief exec. officer Heritage Books, Inc., Bowie, Md., 1981—. Author: N.H. Genealogical Research Guide, 1973, The Descendants of William Brown and Isabella Kennedy, 1992; editor: Genealogical Periodical Annual Index, 1974—; contbr. articles to profl. jours. Pres. NRL Fed. Credit Union, Washington, 1970-71, treas., 1972-84; pres. Prince George's County General Soc., Bowie, 1970-71; mem. Bowie Adv. Planning Bd., 1987-91. Mem. Nat. Geneal. Soc., N.E. Historic Geneal. Soc., Prince George's County General Soc., Sigma Xi. Avocations: genealogical research, sailing, gardening. Home: 3602 Maureen Ln Bowie MD 20715-2936 Office: Heritage Books Inc 1540 Pointer Ridge Pl Bowie MD 20716-1859

TOWLE, LELAND HILL, retired government official; b. Boston, Mar. 29, 1931; s. Leland and Bertha Mary (Hill) T.; m. Carol Peterson, June 5, 1953; children—Peter Kimball, Gretchen Towle Maynard, Michele. B.S., U. N.H., 1952; M.S., M.I.T., 1953; Cert. in Bus. and Mgmt, U. Calif., Berkeley, 1962. Nuclear chemist Stanford Research Inst., Menlo Park, Calif., 1956-59; community systems economist, economist, nuclear economist Stanford Research Inst., 1959-68, mgr. health scis. research, 1968-74; asst. dir. Nat. Center for Alcohol Edn., Arlington, Va., 1974-75; cons. Medicine in the Pub. Interest, Washington, 1975, Internat. Ctr. for Alcohol Policies, 1995—; vis. scientist Nat. Inst. on Alcohol Abuse and Alcoholism, Rockville, Md., 1975-76, dep. dir. office of program devel. and analysis, 1976-77, assoc. dir. office of program devel. and analysis, 1977-81, dir. internat. and intergovtl. affairs, 1981-95; dir. LHT Assocs., Inc., 1995—. Contbr. articles to profl. jours. Bd. dirs. Med. Resources Found., Palo Alto, Calif., 1972-73. Served with USAF, 1952-56. Mem. Am. Pub. Health Assn., Sci. Research Soc. Am., Am. Nuclear Soc., Am. Chem. Soc., Sigma Xi, Phi Kappa Phi. Home: Rt 663 Burgess VA 22432

TOWLES, DONALD BLACKBURN, retired newspaper publishing executive; b. Lawrenceburg, Ky., Sept. 10, 1927; s. Joseph Sterling and Marjorie (Blackburn) T.; m. Geraldine Gooch, Dec. 20, 1947 (dec. Nov. 1980); children: Sally Blackburn Towles Clark, Rebecca Neale Towles Brown; m. Julia Mason, Dec. 3, 1981. A.B. in Journalism, U. Ky., 1948. Asst. dir. publicity, editor In Ky. Mag. Commonwealth of Ky., Frankfort, 1948-55; pub. service mgr. Courier-Jour. and Louisville Times Co., Louisville, 1956-66, dir. pub. service and promotion, 1966-71, v.p., 1974-92, v.p., dir. circulation, 1971-76, v.p., dir. pub. affairs, 1976-92. Author: The Press of Kentucky 1787-1994; editor: Newspaper Promotion Handbook, 1983. Pres. Heritage Corp. of Louisville, 1982-85; chmn. Louisville area chpt. ARC, 1987-89; chmn. program adv. com. Louisville Devel. Program, 1971-80; mem. adv. bd. Salvation Army; bd. dirs. Louisville Med. Ctr., 1982-97, Thos. D. Clark Found., Christian Church Homes Ky., 1992-96; chmn. Sr. Citizens East, 1996-97. With U.S. Army, 1952-54, Korea. Recipient Comty. Svc. award Louisville Devel. Com., 1980; named Outstanding Chpt. Vol. Louisville area chpt. ARC, 1993, Outstanding State Vol., 1994; inducted into Ky. Journalism Hall of Fame, 1992. Mem. Internat. Newspaper Promotion Assn. (pres. 1980-82, Silver Shovel 1983), Ky. Press Assn. (pres. 1982, Pres.'s Cup Leadership 1982, Disting. Comty. Svc. award 1987), Journalism Alumni Assn. U. Ky. (pres. 1979-94, Outstanding Alumnus award 1976, All-Am. Alumni award 1994), Soc. Profl. Journalists (pres. Louisville chpt. 1991-92). Democrat. Disciple of Christ. Home: 3536 Norbourne Blvd Louisville KY 40207-3753

TOWNE, ALAN RAYMOND, neurologist, educator; b. Malden, Mass., July 9, 1948; s. Allen Newman and Carmelia (Foskin) T.; m. Elizabeth Ann Hull. BA, Hobart Coll., 1970; Cert. d'etudes in French Lit., U. d'Anger, France, 1972; MD with honors, U. Aix-Marseille, France, 1981. Diplomate Am. Bd. Psychiatry and Neurology; lic. MD, Va. Intern in neurology Hosp. Ste. Anne, Toulon, France, 1979-80; fellow in neuroimaging and neurophysiology U. Aix-Marseille, France, 1980-81; rotating intern Med. Coll. Va., Richmond, 1981-82, resident in neurology, chief resident in neurology, 1982-85, 84-85, fellow in neurophysiology, 1985-86, asst. prof. neurology dept. neurology, 1986-94, assoc. prof. neurology, 1994—, co-dir. clin. neurophysiology labs., 1994—, dir. ambulatory EEG svc. monitoring lab., 1988—, attending physician epilepsy monitoring unit, 1988—, dir. status epilepticus rsch. program, 1988—; chmn. dept. neurology residency recruitment program Med. Coll. of Va., 1989—; guest reviewer Epilepsia; guest lectr. in field. Contbr. articles to profl. publs. and chpts. to books. Usher com. Episcopal Ch. of the Redemmer, 1988—, spl. events com., 1992—; organizing com. Boy Scouts Am., Robert E. Lee Coun., 1992; com. chmn. Pack 811, Boy Scouts Am., 1992—. Grantee Abbott Labs., 1990, 92-93, 91-93, 92—, Burrough Wellcome, 1989-90, 90—, Janssen Rsch. Found., 1989-91, Merrell Dow Pharms. Inc., 1990-92, Marion Merrell Dow, 1991-92, 92—, Carter-Wallace Labs., 1992-93, 92—, Dainippon Pharm. Co., 1993—, NIH, 1987—. Mem. Am. Assn. for Study of Headache, Am. Acad. Neurology, Richmond Acad. Medicine, Am. Epilepsy Soc., Va. Neurol. Soc., Soc. for Neurosci., Am. Electroencephalographic Soc., Am. Acad. Clin. Neurophysiology. Episcopalian. Avocations: swimming, cycling, reading. Home: 2120 Christendom Dr Midlothian VA 23113 Office: Va Commonwealth U Med Coll Va Dept Neurology Box 599 Richmond VA 23298

TOWNE, JONATHAN BAKER, vascular surgeon; b. Youngstown, Ohio, Jan. 10, 1942; s. Sandra Green Towne, Aug. 24, 1963; children: Timothy, Heidi, Crista. BS, U. Pitts., 1963; MD, U. Rochester, N.Y., 1967. Chief gen. surgery USAF Hosp., Vandenberg AFB, Calif., 1972-74; asst. prof. surgery Med. Coll. Wis., Milw., 1975-79, assoc. prof., 1979-84, prof., 1984—, chair vascular surgery, 1984—. Editor: Complications Vascular Surgery, 1980, II, 1985, III, 1991. Mem. Soc. Vascular Surgery (sec. 1994—), Ctrl. Surg. Assn. (recorder 1992-97), Assn. Program Dirs. Vascular Surgery (pres. 1997—), Wis. Surg. Soc. (pres. 1991-92). Avocation: photography. Office: Med Coll Wis 9200 W Wisconsin Ave Milwaukee WI 53226-3522

TOWNE, ROBERT, screenwriter; b. 1936; m. Luisa Towne; 2 children. Student, Pomona State Coll. Screenplays include The Last Woman on Earth, 1960, The Tomb of Ligeia, 1965, Villa Rides, 1968, The Last Detail, 1973, Chinatown, 1974 (Acad. award best original screenplay), (with Warren Beatty) Shampoo, 1974 (Acad. award best original screenplay), (with Paul Schrader) The Yazuka, 1975, (also prodr., dir.) Personal Best, 1981, 1981, (with Michael Austin) Greystoke, 1984, (also dir.) Tequila Sunrise, 1988, The Two Jakes, 1990, Days of Thunder, 1990, The Firm, 1992. Office: Creative Artists Agy 9830 Wilshire Blvd Beverly Hills CA 90212-1804

TOWNES, BOBBY JOE, travel agency executive; b. Pickens, S.C., Aug. 29, 1932; s. James Harold and Coda Lenora (Nations) T.; m. Addie Elise Ray, May 2, 1956; children: John William, Robert Scott. Assoc. BA, Mars Hill (N.C.) Jr. Coll., 1952; BA, Furman U., Greenville, S.C., 1955; diploma, Grad. Sch. Banking, Rutgers U., 1969. V.p. Peoples Nat. Bank, Greenville, 1954-73; exec. v.p. Community Bank, Greenville, 1973-76; pres. Piedmont Travel, Inc., Greenville, 1976-93, chmn., 1993—; mng. ptnr. Long Beach Properties, 1992—; chmn. Greenville World of Travel, 1976-80; pres. Piedco Assocs., Greenville, 1973—; mng. ptnr. Cutter Joint Ventures, Hilton Head, S.C., 1972—; pres. Piedco II, 1992—; chmn. Boutique Ltd., 1971-75; instr. Am. Inst. Banking, 1964-70, Charter Life Underwriters, Greenville, 1968; mem. adv. com. KLM Dutch Airlines, Atlanta, 1982, System One Automation, Miami, Fla., 1980, Eastern Airlines, Miami, 1983-87; mem. adv. bd. Mars Plus Data Systems, Miami, 1976-79. Author: Independent Bank Survival, 1968, Townes and Allied Families, 1995. Chmn. United Way, Greenville, 1973; v.p. ARC, Greenville, 1970, Cancer Soc., Greenville, 1966; v.p. Furman U. Alumni Bd., Greenville, 1968-70, Furman U. Paladin Bd., Greenville, 1972-74; mem. Furman U. Com. for Self Study, Greenville, 1976; com. Gov.'s Econ. Coun., Columbia, S.C., 1972; v.p., mem. founders com. Cmty. Concerts, Greenville, 1976; pres. YMCA Youth Guides, Greenville, 1970; v.p., organizer Centurian Club, 1978. Recipient Sertuma Internat. Disting. Club Pres. award, 1967, Outstanding Young Mem. of Am. award, 1968. Mem. Am. Inst. Banking (pres. 1964, bd. dirs. 1966), Young Bankers S.C. (bd. dirs. 1965), S.C. Bankers Assn. (bd. dirs. 1969), Greenville Wine Soc. (pres., organzer 1968, 72), S.C. Hist. Soc., Greenville County Hist. Soc., Poinsett Club, Commerce Club, Colonial Club (v.p. 1989, pres. 1991), Sertoma (v.p. 1982, Gold Honor club 1967). Republican. Episcopalian. Avocation: genealogy. Home: 14 Selwyn Dr Greenville SC 29615-1727

TOWNES, CHARLES HARD, physics educator; b. Greenville, S.C., July 28, 1915; s. Henry Keith and Ellen Sumter (Hard) T.; m. Frances H. Brown, May 4, 1941; children: Linda Lewis, Ellen Screven, Carla Keith, Holly Robinson. B.A., B.S., Furman U., 1935; M.A., Duke U., 1937; Ph.D., Calif. Inst. Tech., 1939. Mem. tech. staff Bell Telephone Lab., 1939-47; assoc. prof. physics Columbia U., 1948-50, prof. physics, 1950-61; exec. dir. Columbia Radiation Lab., 1950-52, chmn. physics dept., 1952-55; provost and prof. physics MIT, 1961-66, Inst. prof., 1966-67; v.p., dir. research Inst. Def. Analyses, Washington, 1959-61; prof. physics U. Calif., Berkeley, 1967-86, 94, prof. physics emeritus, 1986-94, prof. grad. sch., 1994—; Guggenheim fellow, 1955-56; Fulbright lectr. U. Paris, 1955-56, U. Tokyo, 1956; lectr., 1955, 60; dir. Enrico Fermi Internat. Sch. Physics, 1963; Richtmeyer lectr. Am. Phys. Soc., 1959; Scott lectr. U. Cambridge, 1963; Centennial lectr. U. Toronto, 1967; Lincoln lectr., 1972-73, Halley lectr., 1976, Krishnan lectr., 1992, Nishina lectr., 1992, Rajiv Gandhi lectr., 1997; dir. Gen. Motors Corp., 1973-86, Perkin-Elmer Corp., 1966-85; mem. Pres.'s Sci. Adv. Com., 1966-69, vice chmn., 1967-69; chmn. sci. and tech. adv. com. for manned space flight NASA, 1964-69; mem. Pres.'s Com. on Sci. and Tech., 1976; researcher on nuclear and molecular structure, quantum electronics, interstellar molecules, radio and infrared astrophysics. Author: Making Waves, 1996, (with A.L. Schawlow) Microwave Spectroscopy, 1955; author, coeditor: Quantum Electronics, 1960, Quantum Electronics and Coherent Light, 1964; editorial bd. Rev. Sci. Instruments, 1950-52, Phys. Rev., 1951-53, Jour. Molecular Spectroscopy, 1957-60, Procs. Nat. Acad. Scis., 1978-84, Can. Jour. Physics, 1995—; contbr. articles to sci. publs.; patentee masers and lasers. Trustee Calif. Inst. Tech., Carnegie Instn. of Washington, Grad. Theol. Union, Calif. Acad. Scis.; mem. corp. Woods Hole Oceanographic Instn. Decorated officier Légion d'Honneur (France); recipient numerous hon. degrees and awards including Nobel prize for physics, 1964; Stuart Ballantine medal Franklin Inst., 1959, 62; Thomas Young medal and prize Inst. Physics and Phys. Soc., Eng., 1963; Disting. Public Service medal NASA, 1969; Wilhelm Exner award Austria, 1970; Niels Bohr Internat. Gold medal, 1979; Nat. Sci. medal, 1983, Berkeley citation U. Calif., 1986; named to Nat. Inventors Hall of Fame, 1976, Engring. and Sci. Hall of Fame, 1983; recipient Common Wealth award, 1993, ADION medal Observatory Nice, 1995. Fellow IEEE (life, Medal of Honor 1967), Am. Phys. Soc. (pres. 1967, Plyler prize 1977), Optical Soc. Am. (hon., Mees medal 1968, Frederick Ives medal 1996), Indian Nat. Sci. Acad., Calif. Acad. Scis.; mem. NAS (coun. 1968-72, 78-81, chmn. space sci. bd. 1970-73, Comstock award 1959, Carty medal 1962), Am. Philos. Soc., Am. Astron. Soc., Am. Acad. Arts and Scis., Royal Soc. (fgn. mem.), Russian Acad. Scis. (fgn. mem.), Pontifical Acad. Scis., Max-Planck Inst. for Physics and Astrophysics (fgn. mem.), N.Y. Acad. Scis. (hon. life). Office: U Calif Dept Physics Berkeley CA 94720

TOWNES, PHILIP LEONARD, pediatrician, educator; b. Salem, Mass., Feb. 18, 1927; s. Saul and Lillian (Kravetsky) T.; m. Marjorie Joan Greenstone, Aug. 27, 1956; children: Elizabeth Ann, Susan Jane, David Andrew. A.B., Harvard, 1948; Ph.D., U. Rochester, 1952, M.D., 1959. Diplomate: Am. Bd. Pediatrics, Am. Bd. Med. Genetics. Intern Strong Meml. Hosp., Rochester, 1959-60; asst. resident Strong Meml. Hosp., 1963, chief resident pediatrics, 1965; mem. faculty U. Rochester Sch. Medicine, 1952-79, prof. pediatrics, 1969-79; prof. anatomy (genetics), chmn. div.

genetics, dir. Genetic Clinic, 1966-79; prof. pediatrics U. Mass. Sch. Medicine, 1979-95, dir. Genetic Clinic, 1979-95, dir. Cytogenetics Lab., 1981-95, prof. pediatrics/ob-gyn. emeritus, 1995—; pediatrician Strong Meml. Hosp.; cons. attending Newark State Hosp., Genesee Hosp.; hon. research asst. Univ. Coll., London, Eng., 1965-66; mem. adv. com. for genetics services Mass. Dept. Pub. Health, 1979—, chmn. com., 1982—; mem. steering com. New Eng. Regional Genetics Group, 1981—. Contbr. articles to med. jours. Mem. com. qualifications cytogenetics N.Y. State Dept. Health, 1968-74; bd. dirs. Monroe County chpt. Nat. Found., 1965-79, chmn. med. adv. com., 1967-79, hon. bd. dirs., 1979—, also cons.; trustee Seven Hills Found., 1996—. USPHS predoctoral fellow, 1951-52; sr. research fellow, 1960-61; research career devel. award, 1961-66. Mem. Am. Acad. Pediatrics, Am. Assn. Anatomists, Soc. Pediatric Research, Am. Soc. Human Genetics, Am. Pediatric Soc., Teratology Soc., Sigma Xi, Alpha Omega Alpha. Home: 14 Spring Valley Rd Worcester MA 01609-1151

TOWNLEY, ROBERT GORDON, medical educator; b. Omaha, Nebr., July 27, 1928. MD, Creighton U., 1955. Pvt. practice in internal medicine and allerty Physicians Clinic, Omaha, 1960-62; attending staff mem. Douglas County Hosp., Omaha, 1960-62; instr. dept. medicine and allergy Creighton U., Omaha, 1960-62; asst. prof. medicine Creighton U., 1966-69, assoc. prof. medicine and microbiology, 1969-74, chief allergy sect., 1969—, prof. medicine, prof. microbiology, 1974—; instr. dept. medicine and allergy U. Colo. Med. Sch., 1962-66; asst. chief dept. asthma-allergy Nat. Jewish Hosp., Denver, 1962-66; mem. presdl. task NHLI, 1973-74. Editor three books on allergic diseases; contbr. numerous articles to profl. publs. Recipient Disting. Rsch. Career award Best Doctors in Am., Creighton U., 1993-96. Fellow Am. Acad. Asthma, Allergy and Immunology; mem. Am. Thoracic Soc., Nebr. Thoracic Soc. (pres. 1970). Office: Creighton U Allergic Disease Ctr Dept Medicine Omaha NE 68178

TOWNS, EDOLPHUS, congressman; b. Chadbourn, N.C., July 21, 1934; m. Gwendolyn Forbes, 1960; children: Darryl, Deidra. B.S., N.C. A & T State U., Greensboro, 1956; M.S.W., Adelphi U., Garden City, N.Y., 1973; PhD (hon.), N.C. A&T, Shaw U. Tchr. Medgar Evers Coll., Bklyn., N.Y.C. Pub. Schs.; dep. hosp. adminstr., 1965-71; dep. pres. Borough of Bklyn., 1976-82; mem. 98th-105th Congresses from 11th (now 10th) N.Y. dist., Washington, D.C., 1982—; ranking minority mem. subcom. Human Resources and Intergovtl. Affairs; mem. Commerce com. Mem. adv. council Boy Scouts Am.; active Salvation Army. Served with U.S. Army, 1956-58. Named to Acad. of Distinction Adelphi U. Mem. Kiwanis, Phi Beta Sigma. Democrat. Office: US Ho of Reps 2232 Rayburn Ho Office Bldg Washington DC 20515*

TOWNSEND, ALAIR ANE, municipal official; b. Rochester, N.Y., Feb. 15, 1942; d. Harold Eugene and Dorothy (Sharpe) T.; m. Robert Harris, Dec. 31, 1970 (div. 1994). BS, Elmira Coll., 1962; MS, U. Wis., 1964; postgrad. Columbia U., 1970-71. Assoc. dir. budget priorities Com. on Budget, U.S. Ho. of Reps., Washington, 1975-79; dep. asst. sec. for budget HEW, Washington, 1979-80, asst. sec. for mgmt. and budget, 1980-81; dir. N.Y.C. Office Mgmt. and Budget, 1981-85; dep. mayor for fin. and econ. devel. City of N.Y., 1985-89; pub. Crain's N.Y. Bus., N.Y.C., 1989—; former vice chmn., trustee Elmira Coll.; former mem. Coun. on Fgn. Rels.; bd. govs. Am. Stock Exchange; chmn. Am. Woman's Econ. Devel. Corp.; bd. dir. Armor Holdings Inc.; former chmn. N.Y.C. Sports Commn.; bd. dirs. Lincoln Ctr.; chmn. Consol. Corp. Fund of Lincoln Ctr. Mem. Women's Forum, Advt. Women N.Y., N.Y.C. Partnership, N.Y.C. of C. and Industry (bd. dir),. N.Y. State Bus. Coun. (vice chmn.). Office: Crain's NY Bus 220 E 42nd St New York NY 10017-5806

TOWNSEND, ANN VAN DEVANTER, foundation administrator, art historian; b. Washington, June 20, 1936; d. John Ward and Ellen Keys (Ramsey) Cutler; m. Willis Van Devanter, Dec. 27, 1958 (div. May 1974); 1 child, Susan Earling Van Devanter (Mrs. John Philip Newell); m. Lewis Raynham Townsend, Dec. 10, 1983. BA, Brown U., 1958; MA, George Washington U., 1975. Grantsmanship ctr. cert. Guest curator Balt. Mus. Art, 1971-77; dir. cultural affairs Chevy Chase (Md.) Savs. & Loan, Inc., 1978-81; dir. spl. partnership projects NEA, Washington, 1982-83; founding pres. The Trust for Mus. Exhbns., Washington, 1984—; organizer over 60 nat. and internat. mus. exhbns. for more than 240 mus. Co-author: Self-Portraits of American Artists, 1670-1973, 1974; author: Anywhere So Long As There Be Freedom, 1975, Two Hundred Years of American Painting, 1976; contbr. articles to mags. U.S. commr. Cagnes-Sur-Mer Internat. Afts Festival, France, 1977, 78; mem. women's com. Washington Opera, 1993—; bd. dirs. Friends of Corcoran Gallery of Art, Washington, 1975-76, Strathmore Hall Arts Ctr., Rockville, Md., 1978-80, Am. Swedish Hist. Mus., Phila., 1987-89, U.S. Com. World Fedn. Friends of Mus., 1995—. Acad. grad. fellow Johns Hopkins Sch. Advanced Internat. Studies, 1958. Mem. Nat. Soc. Arts & Letters, Am. News Women's Club, Soc. Women Goegraphers, Sulgrave Club. Episcopalian. Avocations: backgammon, gourmet cooking, ballroom dancing. Office: The Trust for Mus Exhbns 1424 16th St Ste 600 Washington DC 20036-2211

TOWNSEND, CHARLES EDWARD, Slavic languages educator; b. New Rochelle, N.Y., Sept. 29, 1932; s. Charles Edward and Lois (Fukushima) T.; m. Janet Linner, Sept. 18, 1957; children: Erica, Sylvia, Louise. B.A., Yale U., 1954; M.A., Harvard U., 1960, Ph.D., 1962. Instr., then asst. prof. Harvard U., 1962-66; mem. faculty Princeton U., 1966—, dir. Critical Langs. Program, 1968-70, prof. Slavic langs., 1971—, chmn. dept., 1970—. Author: Russian Word Formation, 1968, Continuing With Russian, 1970, Memoirs of Princess Natalja Borisovna Dolgorukaja, 1977, Czech Through Russian, 1981, A Description of Spoken Prague Czech, 1990, Russian Readings for Close Analysis, 1993, Common and Comparative Slavic, 1996. Served with U.S. Army, 1955-58. IREX grantee, 1968, 89; Fulbright grantee, 1954-55, 71, 83, 88; Ford Found. fellow, 1958-60; NDEA fellow, 1960-62. Mem. Am. Coun. Tchrs. Russian, Am. Assn. Tchrs. Slavic and East European Langs. (Disting. Contbn. to Profession award), N.Am. Assn. Tchrs. Czech (pres. 1992-94), Am. Assn. Advancement Slavic Studies, Linguistic Soc. Czech Republic (hon.), Czechoslovak Soc. Arts. and Scis., Phi Beta Kappa. Home: 145 Hickory Ct Princeton NJ 08540-3434 Office: Princeton U Dept Slavic Langs 28 Pine St Princeton NJ 08542-3810

TOWNSEND, CHARLES H., publishing executive. Pub. Glamour, Conde Nast Pub. Inc., N.Y.C.; exec. v.p. Conde Nast Pub. Inc., N.Y.C. Office: Conde Nast Publications Inc 350 Madison Ave New York NY 10017-3704*

TOWNSEND, EARL C., JR., lawyer, writer; b. Indpls., Nov. 9, 1914; s. Earl Cunningham and Besse (Kuhn) T.; m. Emily Macnab, Apr. 3, 1947 (dec. Mar. 1988); children: Starr, Vicki M. (Mrs. Christopher Katterjohn), Julia E. (Mrs. Edward Goodrich Dunn Jr.), Earl Cunningham III, Clyde G. Student, De Pauw U., 1932-34; AB, U. Mich., 1936, JD, 1939. Bar: Ind. 1939, Mich. 1973, U.S. Supreme Ct. 1973, U.S. Ct. Appeals (4th, 5th, 6th, 7th cirs.), U.S. Dist. Ct. (no. and so. dists.) Ind., U.S. Dist. Ct. (ea. dist.) Va., U.S. Dist. Ct. (ea. dist.) Mich. Sr. ptnr. Townsend & Townsend, Indpls., 1941-64, Townsend, Hovde & Townsend, Indpls., 1964-84, Townsend & Townsend, Indpls., 1984—; dep. prosecutor, Marion County, Ind., 1942-44; radio-TV announcer WIRE, WFBM, WFBM-TV, Indpls., 1940-53, 1st TV announcer Indpls. 500 mile race, 1949, 50; Big Ten basketball referee, 1940-47; lectr. trial tactics U. Notre Dame, Ind. U., U. Mich., 1968-79; chmn. faculty seminar on personal injury trials Ind. U. Sch. Law, U. Notre Dame Sch. Law, Valparaiso Sch. Law, 1981; mem. Com. to Revise Ind. Supreme Ct. Pattern Jury Instrns., 1975-83; lectr. Trial Lawyers 30 Yrs. Inst., 1986; counsel atty gen., 1988-92. Author: Birdstones of the North American Indian, 1959; editor: Am. Assn. Trial Lawyers Am. Jour., 1964-88; contbr. articles to legal and archeol. jours.; composer (waltz) Moon of Halloween. Trustee Cathedral High Sch., Indpls., Eiteljorg Mus. Am. Indian and Western Art, Cale J. Holder Scholarship Found. Ind. U. Law Sch.; life trustee, bd. dirs., mem. fin. and bldg. coms. Indpls. Mus. Art; life trustee Ind. State Mus.; founder, dir. Meridian St. Found.; mem. dean's coun. Ind. U.; founder, life fellow Roscoe Pound/Am. Trial Lawyers Found., Harvard U.; fellow Meth. Hosp. Found. Recipient Ind. Univ. Writers Conf. award, 1960, Hanson H. Anderson medal of honor Arsenal Tech. Schs., Indpls., 1971; named to Coun. Sagamores of Wabash, 1969; Rector scholar, 1934, Ind. Basketball Hall of Fame; hon. chief Black River-Swan Creek Saginaw-Chippewa Indian tribe. Fellow Internat. Acad. Trial Lawyers, Internat. Soc. Barristers, Ind. Bar Found. (life trustee, disting. fellow award); mem. ASCAP, ABA (com. on trial techniques 1964-76, aviation and space 1977—), Assn. Trial Lawyers Am. (v.p.), Ind. State Bar Assn. (Golden Career award 1989), Indpls. Bar Found. (disting. charter 1986), Ind. Trial Lawyers Assn. (pres. 1965, pres. Coll. Fellows 1984-90, Lifetime Achievement award 1992), Am. Bd. Trial Advs. (diplomate, pres. Ind. chpt. 1980-86), Am. Arbitration Assn. (nat. arbitrators panel), Am. Judicature Soc., State Bar of Mich. (Champion of Justice award 1989), Roscommon County Bar Assn., 34th Jud. Cir. Bar Assn., Bar Assn. 7th Fed. Cir. (bd. govs. 1966-68), Mich. Trial Lawyers Assn., Soc. Mayflower Descendants (gov. 1947-49), Ind. Hist. Soc., Marion County/Indpls. Hist. Soc. (bd. dirs.), Key Biscayne C. of C. (founder, charter mem.), U. Mich. Pres. Club, U. Mich. Victors Club (founder, charter mem.), Trowel and Brush Soc. (hon)., Genuine Indian Relic Soc. (founder, pres., chmn. frauds com.), The Players Club, Key Biscayne Yacht Club, Columbia Club, Indpls. Athletic Club, Masons (33 degree), Shriners, Delta Kappa Epsilon, Phi Kappa Phi. Republican. Methodist. Avocations: art, Indian relics. Home: 5008 N Meridian St Indianapolis IN 46208-2624

TOWNSEND, FRANK MARION, pathology educator; b. Stamford, Tex., Oct. 29, 1914; s. Frank M. and Beatrice (House) T.; m. Gerda Eberlein, 1940 (dec. div. 1944); 1 son, Frank M.; m. Ann Graf, Aug. 25, 1951; 1 son, Robert N. Student, San Antonio Coll., 1931-32, U. Tex., 1932-34; MD, Tulane U., 1938. Diplomate: Am. Bd. Pathology. Intern Polyclinic Hosp., N.Y.C., 1939-40; commd. 1st lt. M.C., U.S. Army, 1940, advanced through grades to lt. col., 1946; resident instr. pathology Washington U., 1945-47; trans. to USAF, 1949, advanced through grades to col., 1956; instr. pathology Coll. Medicine, U. Nebr., 1947-48; asso. pathologist Scott and White Clinic, Temple, Tex., 1948-49; asso. prof. pathology Med. Br. U. Tex., Galveston, 1949-59; flight surgeon USAF, 1950-65; dir. labs. USAF Hosp. (now Wilford Hall USAF Hosp.), Lackland AFB, Tex., 1950-54; cons. pathology Office of Surgeon Gen. Hdqrs. USAF, Washington, 1954-63, chief cons. group Office of Surgeon Gen. Hdqrs., 1954-55; dep. dir. Armed Forces Inst. Pathology, Washington, 1955-59; dir. Armed Forces Inst. Pathology, 1959-63; vice comdr. aerospace med. divsn. Air Force Systems Command, 1963-65; ret., 1965; practice medicine specializing in pathology San Antonio, 1965—; dir. labs. San Antonio State Chest Hosp.; consulting pathologist Tex. Dept. Health hosps., 1965-72; clin. prof. pathology U. Tex. Med. Sch., San Antonio, 1969-72; prof., chmn. dept. pathology Health Sci. Ctr. U. Tex. Med. Sch., 1972-86, emeritus chmn., prof., 1986—; cons. U. Tex. Cancer Ctr.-M.D. Anderson Hosp., 1966-80, NASA, 1967-75; mem. adv. bd. cancer WHO, 1958-75; mem. Armed Forces Epidemiology Bd., 1983-91; bd. govs. Armed Forces Inst. Pathology, 1984-95. Mem. editorial bd. Tex. Med. Jour., 1978-86; contbr. articles to med. jours. Mem. adv. coun. Civil War Centennial Commn., 1960-65; bd. dirs. Alamo Area Sci. Fair, 1967-73. Decorated D.S.M., Legion of Merit; recipient Founders medal Assn. Mil. Surgeons, 1961, medal of honor DAR, 1997; recipient Comdr.'s award Armed Forces Epidemiol. Bd., 1990; F.M. Townsend Chair of Pathology endowed in his honor by faculty of Dept. Pathology, U. Tex. Health Sci. Ctr., 1987. Fellow ACP, Coll. Am. Pathologists (edn. advisor on accreditation, commr. lab. accreditation South Ctrl. States region 1971-84), Am. Soc. Clin. Pathologists (Ward Burdick award 1983), Aerospace Med. Assn. (H.G. Mosely award 1962); mem. AMA, AAAS, Tex. Med. Assn., Internat. Acad. Aviation and Space Medicine, Tex. Soc. Pathologists (Caldwell award 1971), Am. Assn. Pathologists, Internat. Acad. Pathology, Acad. Clin. Lab. Physicians and Scientists, Soc. Med. Cons. to Armed Forces, Torch Club. Home: PO Box 77 Harwood TX 78632-0077 Office: U Tex Health Sci Ctr Dept Pathology 7703 Floyd Curl Dr San Antonio TX 78284-6200

TOWNSEND, HAROLD GUYON, JR., publishing company executive; b. Chgo., Apr. 11, 1924; s. Harold Guyon and Anne Louise (Robb) T.; AB, Cornell U., 1948; m. Margaret Jeanne Keller, July 28, 1951; children: Jessica, Julie, Harold Guyon III. Advt. salesman Chgo. Tribune, 1948-51; gen. mgr. Keller-Heartt Co., Clarendon Hills, Ill., 1951-62; pub. Santa Clara (Calif.) Jour., 1962-64; chmn. bd. dirs., pub. Dispatch-Tribune newspaper Townsend Communications, Inc., Kansas City, Mo., 1964—. Chmn., Suburban Newspaper Research Commn., 1974—; dir. Certified Audit Bur. of Circulation, 1968-72. del. Rep. Nat. Conv., 1960; chmn. Mission Hills Rep. Com., 1966-77; bd. dirs. Kansas City Jr. Achievement, 1966-68, Kansas City council Girl Scouts U.S.A., 1969-71, Kansas City council Boy Scouts Am., 1974, Kansas City chpt. ARC, 1973-79, Kansas City Starlight Theater, Clay County (Mo.) Indsl. Commn.; treas., trustee Park Coll., Parkville, Mo., 1970-78. Mem. adv. com. North Kansas City Hosp.; bd. dirs. Taxpayers Research of Mo., 1978—, Nelson Gallery Friends of Art, 1980-85. Served with inf. AUS, World War II. Mem. Kansas City Advt. and Sales Club, Kansas City Press Club, Suburban Press Found. (pres. 1969-71), Suburban Newspapers Am. (pres. 1976-77), Kansas City Printing Industries Assn. (pres., dir.), Printing Industries of Am. (pres. non-heatset web sect. 1980-82), North Kansas City C. of C. (dir., pres. 1964-70), Univ. Assocs. (treas. 1977-80), Sigma Delta Chi, Pi Delta Epsilon, Phi Kappa Psi. Clubs: University (treas. 1977); Indian Hills Country; Hinsdale (Ill.) Golf; Field (Sarasota, Fla.). Home: 23 Compton Ct Prairie Village KS 66208-5205 Office: 7007 NE Parvin Rd Kansas City MO 64117-1532

TOWNSEND, JAMES WILLIS, computer scientist; b. Evansville, Ind., Sept. 9, 1936; s. James Franklin and Elma Elizabeth (Galloway) T.; m. Leona Jean York, Apr. 20, 1958; 1 child, Eric Wayne. BS in Arts and Scis., Ball State U., 1962; PhD, Iowa State U., 1970. Rsch. technologist Neuromuscular div. Mead Johnson, Evansville, 1957-60; chief instr. Zoology dept. Iowa State U., Ames, 1965-67; asst. prof. Ind. State U., Evansville, 1967-72; cons. electron microscopy Mead Johnson Rsch. Ctr., Evansville, 1971-73; mgr. neurosci. Neurosci. Lab., Kans. State U., Manhattan, 1974-76; head electron microscopy Nat. Ctr. for Toxicology Rsch., Jefferson, Ark., 1976-82; dir. electron microscopy U. Ark. Med. Sci., Little Rock, 1982-87; dir. computer ops. pathology dept. Univ. Hosp., Little Rock, 1987—; workshop presenter Am. Soc. Clin. Pathology, 1980-81, Nat. Soc. Histotechnologists, 1984-88. With USAF, 1957. Contbr. articles to profl. jours.; reviewer Scanning Electron Microscopy, 1977-78. Nat. Def. fellowship NDEA, Iowa State U., 1962-65; recipient Chgo. Tribune award Chicago Tribune, 1955. Mem. Sigma Xi, Sigma Zeta. Baptist. Avocations: genealogy, American Civil War. Home: 4 Breeds Hill Ct Little Rock AR 72211-2514 Office: Univ Ark for Med Sci Dept Pathology Slot 517 4301 W Markham St Little Rock AR 72205-7101

TOWNSEND, JANE KALTENBACH, zoologist, educator; b. Chgo., Dec. 21, 1922; B.S., Beloit Coll., 1944; M.A., U. Wis., 1946; Ph.D., U. Iowa, 1950; m. 1966. Asst. in zoology U. Wis., 1944-47; asst., instr. U. Iowa, 1948-50; asst., project assoc. in pathology U. Wis., 1950-53; Am. Cancer Soc. research fellow Wenner-Grens Inst., Stockholm, 1953-56; asst. prof. zoology Northwestern U., 1956-58; asst. prof. to assoc. prof. zoology Mt. Holyoke Coll., South Hadley, Mass., 1958-70, prof., 1970-93, chmn. biol. scis., 1980-86, prof. emeritus, 1993—. Fellow AAAS (sec. sect. biol. sci. 1974-78); mem. Am. Assn. Anatomists, Am. Inst. Biol. Scis., Am. Soc. Zoologists, Soc. Experimental Biology and Medicine, Soc. Devel. Biology, Corp. of Marine Biol. Lab., Sigma Xi, Phi Beta Kappa. Office: Mount Holyoke Coll Dept Biology South Hadley MA 01075

TOWNSEND, JERRIE LYNNE, environmental services administrator; b. Pine Bluff, Ark., July 19, 1951; d. Charles Ray Sr. and Billie Jean (Morgan) Jones; m. Dennis Ewell Townsend, June 15, 1975 (dec. June 1980). BS, Ark. State U., 1973; MLIS, U. Okla., 1987. Cert. profl. sec. Sec. divsn. art Ark. State U., Jonesboro, 1973-74; adminstrv. sec. Steelship Corp., Pine Bluff, Ark., 1974; tchr. 5th grade Coleman Middle Sch., Pine Bluff, Ark., 1974-75; sec. I Mgmt. Devel. Ctr. U. Tulsa, Okla., 1975-76; sec. II City of Tulsa, 1976-78, adminstrv. sec., 1978-80; exec. sec. Hilti, Inc., Tulsa, 1980, statis. asst., 1980-82, sales promotion, mktg. analyst, 1982-87, mngr. sales planning, 1987-96; owner Townsend Environ. Solutions, Broken Arrow, Okla., 1996—. Mem. Citizen's Com. MTTA/City of Broken Arrow (Okla.) Bus. Svc., 1977-79, Office Sci. Adv. Com. Tulsa Jr. Coll., 1980-83, Civic Ctr. Com., Broken Arrow, 1988-90, Broken Arrow City Coun., 1990-97, Spl. Transp. Adv. Com., Tulsa, 1995-96; pres. Friends of Broken Arrow Libr., 1984-85; bd. dirs. Indian Nation Coun. Govts., Tulsa, 1992-97; sec. bd. trustees Broken Arrow Comty. Playhouse, 1992-94; vice mayor Broken Arrow, 1992-97; v.p. Broken Arrow Hist. Soc., 1992-93, pres., 1994-95; libr. Broken Arrow Geneal. Soc., 1985, sec., 1992-94. Named Competent Toastmaster, Out-to-Lunch Toastmasters, Tulsa, 1985; elected to Broken Arrow Hall of Fame, 1996. Mem. Profl. Secs. Internat. (rec. sec. Tulsa chpt. 1979-80, pres. 1980-81, Outstanding Mem. of Yr. 1983). Democrat. Southern Baptist. Avocations: genealogy, historical research.

TOWNSEND, JOHN MICHAEL, lawyer; b. West Point, N.Y., Mar. 21, 1947; s. John D. and Vera (Nachman) T.; m. Frances M. Fragos, Oct. 8, 1994; 1 child, James E. BA, Yale U., 1968, JD, 1971. Bar: N.Y. 1972, U.S. Dist. Ct. (so. and ea. dists.) N.Y. 1975, U.S. Ct. Appeals (2nd cir.) 1975, U.S. Supreme Ct. 1975, U.S. Ct. Appeals (8th cir.) 1982, U.S. Ct. Appeals (7th and 10th cirs.) 1986, D.C. 1990, U.S. Dist. Ct. D.C. 1990, U.S. Ct. Appeals (D.C. cir.) 1990, U.S. Ct. Appeals (4th cir.) 1991. Assoc. Hughes Hubbard & Reed, N.Y.C., 1971-73, 1975-80, ptnr., 1980; assoc. Hughes Hubbard & Reed, Paris, 1973-74; arbitrator U.S. Dist. Ct. (ea. dist.) N.Y., Am. Arbitration Assn., bd. dirs., exec. com.; trustee U.S. Coun. Internat. Bus. 1st lt. USAR, 1971-75. Mem. ABA, Am. Law Inst., Internat. Bar Assn., Assn. of Bar of City of N.Y., N.Y. Lawyers for Pub. Interest, D.C. Bar Assn., Union Internat. des Advs., Univ. Club (Washington), Yale Club (N.Y.C.). Democrat. Episcopalian. Office: Hughes Hubbard & Reed 1300 I St NW Washington DC 20005-3314

TOWNSEND, JOHN WILLIAM, JR., physicist, retired federal aerospace agency executive; b. Washington, Mar. 19, 1924; s. John William and Elenore (Eby) T.; m. Mary Irene Lewis, Feb. 7, 1948; children: Bruce Alan, Nancy Dewitt, John William III, Megan Lewis; m. JoAnn C. Clayton, Sept. 17, 1997. BA, Williams Coll., 1947, MA, 1949, ScD, 1961. With Naval Research Lab., 1949-55, br. head, 1955-58; with NASA, 1958-68, dep. dir. Goddard Space Flight Ctr., 1965-68; dep. adminstrn. Environmental Scis. Services Adminstrn., 1968-70; asso. adminstr. Nat. Oceanic and Atmospheric Adminstrn., 1970-77; pres. Fairchild Space and Electronics Co., 1977-82; v.p. Fairchild Industries, 1979-85; pres. Fairchild Space Co., 1983-85; sr. v.p. Fairchild Industries, 1985-87; chmn. bd. Am. Satellite Co., 1985, sr. v.p., exec. aerospace group, 1987, exec. v.p., 1987; dir. NASA Goddard Space Flight Ctr., 1987-90; ret., 1990; mem. U.S. Rocket, Satellite Rsch. Panel, 1950-60; chmn. space applications bd. NRC, 1985-87; bd. dirs., trustee Telos Corp., 1990-92; mem. adv. bd. Loral Corp., 1990-92; mem. coms. NRC, 1990—; bd. dirs CTA, Inc. Author numerous papers, reports in field. Pres. town council, Forest Heights, Md., 1951-55. Served with USAAF, 1943-46. Recipient Profl. Achievement award Engrs. and Architects Day, 1957; Meritorious Civilian Service award Navy Dept., 1957; Outstanding Leadership medal NASA, 1962; Distinguished Service medal, 1971, 90; recipient Arthur S. Fleming award Fed. Govt., 1963. Fellow AIAA, AAAS, Am. Meteorol. Soc.; mem. NAE (com. 1990—), Am. Phys. Soc., Am. Geophys. Union. (fin. com. 1991—), Internat. Astronautical Fedn. (mem., trustee internat., acad. astronautics), Sigma Xi. Home: 6532 79th St Cabin John MD 20818

TOWNSEND, KATHLEEN KENNEDY, state official; m. David Townsend; children: Meaghan, Maeve, Kate, Kerry. BA cum laude, Harvard U., 1974; JD, U. N.Mex., 1978. Instr. Dundalk C.C., 1985-86, Essex C.C., 1986-87, U. Pa., 1987-88; exec. dir. Md. Student Svcs. Alliance, 1990-93; dep. asst. atty. gen. U.S. Dept. Justice, Washington, 1993-94; lt. gov. State of Md., 1995—; chair so. region Nat. Conf. Lt. Govs., chair oversight com. Johns Hopkins U., Peabody Inst.; expert adv. bd. Export-Import Bank U.S. Editor U. N.Mex. Law Rev. Founder Robert F. Kennedy Human Rights award; chair Cabinet Coun. Criminal and Juvenile Justice, 1995—; chair Md. del. Pres.'s Summit Am.'s Future, 1997. Recipient 4 hon. degrees. Office: Lt Gov State House 100 State Cir Annapolis MD 21401-1925

TOWNSEND, KENNETH ROSS, retired priest; b. Holly Grove, Ala., Oct. 31, 1927; s. James Ernest and Mary H. (Jordan) T.; m. Irene Fogleman, Mar. 18, 1951; children; Marietta, Martha, Kenneth Ross, Elizabeth. AB, Birmingham South Coll., 1956; postgrad., Union Theol. Sem., 1960-63; MDiv, Va. Theol. Sem., 1964. Ordained priest Episcopal Ch., 1965. Pastor meth. chs. N.C. and Va. Confs., 1954-63; priest Bath Priest Parish, Dinwiddie, Va., 1964-69, St. Paul's Ch., Vanceboro, N.C., 1969-89; ret., 1989; lectr. philosophy Richard Bland Coll. of Coll. William and Mary, Williamsburg, Va., 1966-68; del. to synod Province IV, 1973; mem. liturgical com. Episcopal Diocese of East Carolina, Wilmington, N.C., 1971-82, mem. prison commn., 1984; occasional supply priest Olivet Ch., Franconia, Va. Writer, painter. With USNR, 1945-46. Mem. Delta Sigma Phi. Home: 2521 Paxton St Lake Ridge Woodbridge VA 22192 *Yearning for self fulfillment in a better world is the 'mother of the will' to be and to accomplish. By this will we define ourselves. This will identifies our goals in work and relationships. Such a self concept informs our minds as to what is right and correct. The yearning, the will, the goals and accomplishment are thinkable and obtainable. The world awaits our resolve.*

TOWNSEND, LEROY B., chemistry educator, university administrator, researcher; b. Lubbock, Tex., Dec. 20, 1933; s. L.B. and Ocie Mae (McBride) T.; m. Sammy Beames, Sept. 15, 1953; children: Lisa Loree, LeRoy Byron. BA in Chemistry and Math., N.Mex. Highlands U.-Las Vegas, 1955, MS, 1957; PhD, Ariz. State U.-Tempe, 1965; DSc. (hon.), U. Nebr. Assoc. prof. medicinal chemistry U. Utah, Salt Lake City, 1971-75, prof., 1975-78, adj. prof. chemistry, 1975-78; prof. medicinal chemistry U. Mich., Ann Arbor, 1979—, Albert B. Prescott prof. medicinal chemistry, 1985—, prof. chemistry, 1979—, chmn., 1979—, dir. interdept. grad. program in medicinal chemistry, 1979—; chmn. drug discovery and devel. program Comprehensive Cancer Ctr.; mem. cancer rsch. com. Nat. Cancer Inst., 1979—, com. on devel. treatments for rare genetic disease dept. human genetics; mem. nat. adv. com. on AIDS to NIAID; mem. steering com. on chemotherapy of malaria WHO; mem. study sect. on chemotherapy of cancer Nat. Am. Cancer Soc.; mem. Am. Cancer Soc. study sect. drug devel.. hematology and pathology; various ad hoc site visit teams Nat. Cancer Inst.; chmn. purines and pyrimidines Gordon Rsch. Conf.; chmn. Nat. Medicinal Chemistry Symposium; pres. Internat. Congress Heterocyclic Chemistry; participant symposia in field; lectr. various nat. and internat. sci. congresses. Contbr. articles to profl. jours.; assoc. editor Internat. Jour. Heterocyclic Chemistry; mem. editorial bd. Jour. Carbohydrates, Nucleosides, Nucleotides, Jour. Nucleosides and Nucleotides, Jour. Chinese Pharm. Soc., Jour. Medicinal Chemistry. Recipient Smissman-Bristol Myers-Squibb award in medicinal chemistry, Taito O. Soine Meml. award; various grants; named Disting. prof. MAGB. Fellow AAAS; mem. Am. Chem. Soc. (chmn., counsilor medicinal chemistry div.), Internat. Soc. Heterocyclic Chemistry (treas., pres. 1973-79), Nat. Am. Chem. Soc. (chmn. divsn. of medicinal chemistry), Sigma Xi, Phi Kappa Phi. Home: 3317 E Dobson Pl Ann Arbor MI 48105-2583 Office: U Mich Coll Pharmacy Coll Pharmacy 4569 Pharmacy CC Little Bldg Ann Arbor MI 48109-1065

TOWNSEND, LINDA LADD, mental health nurse; b. Louisville, Apr. 26, 1948; d. Samuel Clyde and Mary Elizabeth (Denton) Ladd; m. Stanley Allen Oliver, June 7, 1970 (div. 1978); 1 child, Aaron; m. Warren Terry Townsend Jr., Jan. 1, 1979; children: Mark, Amy, Sarah. Student, Catherine Spalding Coll., 1966-67; BSN, Murray State U., 1970; MS in Psychiat./Mental Health Nursing, Tex. Woman's U., 1976. RN, Tex., Ky.; lic. advanced nurse practitioner, profl. counselor, marriage and family therapist, Tex.; cert. group psychotherapist. Charge nurse med. and pediatric units Murray (Ky.)-Calloway County Hosp., 1970-71; team leader surg./renal transplant unit VA Hosp., Nashville, 1971-73; team leader, charge nurse gen. med.-surg. unit Providence Hosp., Waco, Tex., 1973-74; outpatient therapist Mental Hygiene Clinic, Ft. Hood, Tex., 1975-76; outpatient nurse therapist Ctrl. Counties Ctr. for Mental Health/Mental Retardation, Copperas Cove & Lampasas, Tex., 1977-80; psychiat. nurse clin. specialist, marriage/family therapist Profl. Counseling Svc., Copperas Cove, 1979—; cons. Metroplex Hosp. and Pavilion, Killeen, Tex., 1980—. Founding mem. Family Outreach of Coryell County, Copperas Cove, 1986—, also past pres. and past sec.; founding mem. Partnership for a Drug and Violence-Free Copperas Cove; vol. music therapist Windcrest Nursing Ctr.; advocate Tex. Peer Assistance Program for Nurses; active Walk to Emmaus, 1993. Recipient Mary M. Roberts Writing award Am. Jour. of Nursing, 1970; named Mem. of Yr.-Vol., Family Outreach of Coryell County. Mem. ANA (cert. clin. specialist in adult psychiat. and mental health nursing, cert. clin. specialist in child and adolescent psychiat. and mental health nursing), AAUW (v.p. for membership, past bd. dirs., sec.-treas.), Tex. Nurses Assn., Am. Group Psychotherapy Assn. (cert.), Learning Disabilities Assn., Inst. for Humanities at Salado, Sigma Theta Tau. Democrat. Methodist. Avocations: genealogy, camping, nature activiites, music, sports. Home: RR 1 Box 253-E Kempner TX 76539-9502 Office: Profl Counseling Svc 806 E Avenue D Ste F Copperas Cove TX 76522-2231

TOWNSEND, MARJORIE RHODES, aerospace engineer, business executive; b. Washington, Mar. 12, 1930; d. Lewis Boling and Marjorie Olive (Trees) Rhodes; m. Charles Eby Townsend, June 7, 1948; children: Charles Eby Jr., Lewis Rhodes, John Cunningham, Richard Leo. BEE, George Washington U., 1951. Electronic scientist Naval Rsch. Lab., Washington, 1951-59; rsch. engr. to sect. head Goddard Space Flight Ctr.-NASA, Greenbelt, Md., 1959-65, tech. asst. to chief systems divsn., 1965-66, project mgr. small astronomy satellites, 1966-75, project mgr. applications explorer missions, 1975-76, mgr. preliminary systems design group, 1976-80; aerospace and electronics cons. Washington, 1980-83; v.p. systems devel. Space Am., 1983-84; aerospace cons. Washington, 1984-90; dir. space systems engrng. BDM Internat., Inc., Washington, 1990-91; dir. space applications BDM ESC, Washington, 1991-92; sr. prin. staff mem. BDM Fed., Inc., Washington, 1992-93; aerospace cons., Washington, 1993—. Patentee digital telemetry system. Decorated Knight Italian Republic Order, 1972; recipient Fed. Women's award, 1973, EUR award for Culture, 1974, Engr. Alumni Achievement award George Washington U., 1975, Gen. Alumni Achievement award George Washington U., 1976, Exceptional Svc. medal NASA, 1971, Outstanding Leadership medal NASA, 1980, Eye-of-the-Needle award NASA, 1991. Fellow IEEE (chmn. Washington sect. 1974-75), AIAA (chmn. nat. capitol sect. 1985), AAAS (coun. del. 1985-88), Washington Acad. Sci. (pres. 1980-81); mem. Internat. Acad. Astronautics, Am. Geophys. Union, Soc. Women Engrs., Wing of Aerospace Med. Assn., Inc. (hon.), DAR, Daus. Colonial Wars, Mensa, Sigma Kappa, Sigma Delta Epsilon (hon.). Republican. Episcopalian. Home and Office: 3529 Tilden St NW Washington DC 20008-3194

TOWNSEND, MILES AVERILL, aerospace and mechanical engineering educator; b. Buffalo, N.Y., Apr. 16, 1935; s. Francis Devere and Sylvia (Wolpa) T.; children: Kathleen Townsend Hastings, Melissa, Stephen, Joel, Philip. BA, Stanford U., 1955; BS MechE, U. Mich., 1958; advanced cert., U. Ill., 1963, MS in Theoretical and Applied Mechanics, 1967; PhD, U. Wis., 1971. Registered profl. engr., Ill., Wis., Tenn., Ont. Project engr. Sundstrand, Rockford, Ill., 1959-63, Twin Disc Inc., Rockford, 1963-65, 67-68; sr. engr. Westinghouse Electric Corp., Sunnyvale, Calif., 1965-67; instr., fellow U. Wis., Madison, 1968-71; assoc. prof. U. Toronto, Ont., Can., 1971-74; prof. mech. engrng. Vanderbilt U., Nashville, 1974-81; Wilson prof. mech. and aerospace engrng. U. Va., Charlottesville, 1982—, chmn. dept., 1982-91; ptnr., v.p. Endev Ltd., Can. and U.S., 1972—; cons. in field. Contbr. numerous articles to profl. jours.; 7 patents in field. Recipient numerous research grants and contracts. Fellow ASME (mem. coun. on engrng., productivity com., tech. editor Jour. Mech. Design); mem. AAAS, N.Y. Acad. Scis., Sigma Xi, Phi Kappa Phi, Pi Tau Sigma. Avocations: running, reading, music. Home: 221 Harvest Dr Charlottesville VA 22903-4850 Office: U Va Dept Mech and Aerospace Engrng Thornton Hall Charlottesville VA 22903-2442

TOWNSEND, PALMER WILSON, chemical engineer, consultant; b. Bronx, N.Y., Aug. 1, 1926; s. Atwood Halsey and Mildred Brower (Wilson) T.; m. Helen Anne Lydecker, Feb. 6, 1949; children: Janet M., Martha L., Andrew W., Amy E., Rebecca L. AB in Chemistry, Dartmouth Coll., 1947; BSChemE, Columbia U., 1947, MSChemE, 1948, PhDChemE, 1956. Instr. chem. engrng. Columbia U., N.Y.C., 1948-53; sr. engr. pilot plant divsn. Air Reduction Co., Inc., Murray Hill, N.J. and N.Y.C., 1953-56, sect. head chem. engrng. divsn., 1957-61, asst. dir., 1961-1964, mgr. exptl. engrng., cen. engrng. dept., 1964-66, asst. to group v.p., 1966-67, dir. comml. devel. Chem. and Plastics divsn., 1967-70; dir. comml. devel. Plastics divsn. Allied Chem. Corp., 1970-72; cons. Morris Plains, N.J., 1972—. Editor phys. sci. sect. Good Reading, 1956, 60, 64; contbr. articles to profl. jours. With USNR, 1944-46. DuPont fellow, 1951. Mem. Am. Inst. Chem. Engrs., Am. Chem. Soc., Soc. Plastic Engrs., Soc. Plastics Industries, Assn. Cons. Chemists and Chem. Engrs. (pres. 1991-92), Sigma Xi, Phi Lambda Upsilon, Theta Tau. Congregationalist. Achievements include patents for processes for trifluorethyl vinyl ether, trifluoro ethanol, cryogenic composition of matter, carbon dioxide snow; development of molding approach for the plastic spacers used in superconducting magnets for ISAbelle and the Superconducting Super Collider; establishment of rigid PVC molding materials in the Bell Telephone System; invention of improved processes for production of fluorochemical intermediates to anesthetic agents; research on plastics development and processes, chemicals and monomers, energy development, polyvinyl chloride resin production and market applications. Home and Office: 93 Continental Rd Morris Plains NJ 07950-1291

TOWNSEND, PAUL BRORSTROM, editor; b. Port Washington, N.Y., Feb. 22, 1919; s. Richard Edwin and Alice (Brorstrom) T.; BA, Hobart Coll., 1940; JD, Columbia U., 1943; LHD, Hofstra U., 1971; LLD, Dowling Coll., 1984; m. Terry De Marco, Dec. 8, 1961; children: Wendy, Tobin, Kim. Bar: N.Y. 1946. Sales mgr. Creative Mailing Svc., 1946-47; sales and advt. dir. Corydon M. Johnson Co., 1947-50; pres. Townsend & Willis, pub. rels. counsel, 1951-54; ptnr. Tex McCrary Inc., 1955-57; devel. cons. North Shore Hosp., 1949-66; exec. dir. L.I. Fund, 1951-59; editor L.I. Bus. News, 1957—; ptnr. L.I. Communicating Svcs., 1959—; pres. L.I. Stage, 1984-86; comm. counsel L.I. Midsuffolk Bus. Action, 1968—. Trustee North Shore Univ. Hosp. With CIC, U.S. Army, 1943-45. Fellow Poly. Inst. N.Y., 1980. Mem. Deepdale Club. Office: 2150 Smithtown Ave Ronkonkoma NY 11779-7348

TOWNSEND, PHILIP W., JR., library director; b. Phila., Aug. 14, 1949; s. Philip Walsh and Eleanor (Clay) T.; m. Mary Rasmussen, Aug., 1973; children: Grace, Philip, Erica. BA, U. Utah, 1973; MSLS, Villanova U., 1988. Libr. dir. Valley Forge Mil. Coll., Wayne, Pa., 1985—; mem. Washington Meml. Pipe Band. Capt. U.S. Army Res., 1973-83. Office: Valley Forge Mil Coll Office of Libr 1001 Eagle Rd Wayne PA 19087-3613

TOWNSEND, P(RESTON) COLEMAN, agricultural business executive; b. Salisbury, Md., Dec. 27, 1945; s. Preston Coleman and Rachel (Morris) T.; m. Susan Marshall, Dec. 8, 1981. B.S., U. Del., 1969. Chmn., CEO Townsends, Inc., Millsboro, Del., 1969—. Bd. visitors Del. State U. Mem. Nat. Broiler Council (bd. dirs.). Republican. Office: Townsends Inc Route 24 PO Box 468 Millsboro DE 19966

TOWNSEND, ROBERT, film director; b. Chgo., Feb. 6, 1957; s. Robert and Shirley (Jenkins) T. Actor: (stage) Take It From the Top, 1979, Bones, 1980, (films) Cooley High, 1974, Willie and Phil, 1980, Streets of Fire, 1983, A Soldier's Story, 1983, American Flyers, 1984, Odd Jobs, 1984, Ratboy, 1985, The Mighty Quinn, 1989, That's Adequate, 1990, (t.v. movies) Women At West Point, 1979, Senior Trip!, 1981, In Love With an Older Woman, 1982; actor, prod., dir., co-writer: (films) Hollywood Shuffle, 1987, The Five Heartbeats, 1990, The Meteor Man, 1993; dir.: (films) Eddie Murphy Raw, 1987, B.A.P.S., 1997; stand-up comedian: (t.v. spls.) Robert Townsend and His Partners in Crime, Take No Prisoners, Robert Townsend and His Partners in Crime II.TV series: Townsend Television, 1992, The Parent 'Hood, 1995. Office: Tinsel Townsend 8033 W Sunset Blvd Ste 890 Los Angeles CA 90046-2427 also: CAA 9830 Wilshire Blvd Beverly Hills CA 90212-1804

TOWNSEND, ROBERT J., lawyer; b. Charlotte, Mich., Nov. 11, 1938; s. Robert Wright and Rhea Lucille (Jennings) T.; m. Thea E. Kolb, Aug. 1, 1964; children: Melissa, Bradley. BA, Mich. State U., 1960; LLD, Harvard U., 1963. Bar: Ohio 1964, U.S. Dist. Ct. (so. dist.) Ohio 1964, U.S. Ct. Appeals (6th cir.) 1971, U.S. Supreme Ct. 1992. Assoc. Taft, Stettinus & Hollister, Cin., 1963-72, ptnr., 1972—; dir. Employers Resource Assn., Cin., 1989—. With U.S. Army, 1963-64, 68-69. Office: 1800 Star Bank Ctr 425 Walnut St Cincinnati OH 45202

TOWNSEND, SUSAN ELAINE, social service institute administrator, hostage survival consultant; b. Phila., Sept. 5, 1946; d. William Harrison and Eleanor Irene (Fox) Rogers; m. John Holt Townsend, May 1, 1976. BS in Secondary Edn., West Chester State U., 1968; MBA, Nat. U., 1978; PhD in Human Behavior, La Jolla U., 1984. Biology tchr. Methacton Sch. Dist., Fairview Village, Pa., 1968-70; bus. mgr., analyst profl. La Jolla Research Corp., San Diego, 1977-79; pastoral asst. Christ Ctr. Bible Therapy, San Diego, 1980-82, also bd. dirs.; v.p., pub. relations World Outreach Ctr. of Faith, San Diego, 1981-82, also bd. dirs.; owner, pres., cons. Townsend Research Inst., San Diego, 1983-89; teaching assoc. La Jolla U. Continuing Edn., 1985-86, adminstr., assoc. registrar, adj. faculty, 1990. Author: Hostage Survival-Resisting the Dynamics of Captivity, 1983; contbr. articles to profl. jours. Instr. USN Advanced Survival Evasion Resistance Escape Sch., 1986-89; security officer Shield Security, San Diego, 1991-92; bd. dirs. Christ Fellowship Ch. of San Diego, 1987-96, music dir., 1992—; religious vol. Met. Correctional Ctr., San Diego, 1983-89, San Diego County Jail Ministries, 1978—, scheduling coord., 1993—. Comdr. USN, 1970-76, USNR, 1976-93. Mem. Naval Res. Assn. (life), Res. Officers Assn.(outstanding Jr. Officer of Yr. Calif. chpt. 1982), Navy League U.S. (life), West Chester U. Alumni Assn., Nat. U. Alumni Assn. (life), La Jolla U. Alumni Assn., Gen. Fedn. Women's Club (pres. Peninsula Women's Club 1983-85, 94-96, pres. Parlimentary Law Club 1984-86, 96—, rec. sec. Past Pres.' Assn. 1994-96), Calif. Fedn. Women's Clubs (v.p.-at-large San Diego dist. 25 1982-84, rec. sec. 1994-96, 1st v.p./dean of chmn. 1996—).

TOWNSEND, SUSAN LOUISE, elementary school administrator; b. Denver, Apr. 16, 1951; d. Calvin William and Roselyn Louise (Wilder) Scheidler; m. John Richard Townsend, July 28, 1973; children: Jeffrey, Kristen. BA in Elem. Edn., U. No. Colo., 1973, MA in Ednl. Adminstrn., 1990. Cert. tchr. elem. edn., adminstr., Colo. Tchr. Arlington Elem. Sch., Greeley, Colo., 1973-75, Meeker Elem. Sch., Greeley, 1975-77; adminstr. Child Devel. Ctr., Billings, Mont., 1982-84; tchr. Cameron Elem. Sch., Greeley, 1984-88; tchr. Scott Elem. Sch., Greeley, 1988-89, spl. adminstrv. assignment, 1989-91, adminstr., 1991-94; curriculum coord. Weld Sch. Dist. 6, 1994—; auditor PDK Internat. Curriculum Mgmt. Audit Ctr., 1996—; cons. Weld Sch. Dist. 6, Greeley, 1988—; presenter on edn. and classroom mgmt., Greeley, 1988—. Author: (learning programs) Jump Start, 1989—, Fast Track, 1990—, Read, Write and Launch, 1991—, Parent Power Plus, 1991 (Gov.'s Creativity Initiative award 1991). Named United Meth. Woman of Yr. United Meth. Ch., 1982; nominated for Colo. Excellence in Edn. award, 1993, Phi Delta Kappa Outstanding Educator award, 1994. Fellow Danforth Assn.; mem. NEA, ASCD, Colo. Assn. Sch. Execs., Colo. Edn. Assn., Greeley Educators Assn., Phi Delta Kappa, Alpha Delta Kappa (sec. 1976—). Avocations: reading, crafts, family activities, decorating, woodworking. Office: Weld Sch Dist 6 Ednl Svcs Bldg Greeley CO 80631-4304

TOWNSEND, TERRY, publishing executive; b. Camden, N.J., Dec. 14, 1920; d. Anthony and Rose DeMarco; BA, Duke U., 1942; LHD (hon.) Dowling Coll., 1991; m. Paul Brorstrom Townsend, Dec. 8, 1961; 1 son, Kim. Pub. rels. dir. North Shore Univ. Hosp., Manhasset, N.Y., 1955-68; pres. Theatre Soc. L.I., 1968-70; pres. Townsend Comm. Bur., Ronkonkoma, N.Y., 1970—, L.I. Communicating Service, Ronkonkoma, 1977—; columnist, writer L.I./Bus., Ronkonkoma, 1970-75; pub. L.I. Bus. News, 1978—; v.p. Parr Meadows Racetrack, Yaphank, N.Y., 1977. Assoc. trustee North Shore U. Hosp., 1968—; bd. govs. Adelphi U. Friends Fin. Edn., 1978-85; chmn. ann. archtl. awards competition N.Y. Inst. Tech., 1970-83; trustee Dowling Coll., 1984-96, hon. life trustee, 1996—; trustee L.I. Fine Arts Mus., 1984-85; pub. broadcasting Sta. WLIW TV, Garden City, L.I., N.Y., 1990-93; bd. dirs. Family Svc. Assn. Nassau County, 1982-92; dinner chmn. L.I. 400 Ball, 1987; trustee Mus. at Stony Brook, 1994—. Recipient Media award 110 Center Bus. and Profl. Women, 1977, Enterprise award Friends of Fin. Edn., 1981, L.I. Loves Bus. Showcase Salute, 1982, Community Svc. award N.Y. Diabetes Assn., 1983, Disting. Long Islander in Communications award L.I. United Epilepsy Assn., 1984, Spl. award Dowling Coll. Spring Tribute, 1989, Disting. Svc. award Episcopal Health Svcs., 1989, Disting. Citizen award Dowling Coll., 1991, Gilbert Tilles award Nat. Assn. Fundraising Execs., 1994, Hadassah Cmty. Svc. award, 1996, Golden Rule award Little Village Sch., 1997; named First Lady of L.I., L.I. Public Relations Assn., 1973, L.I. Woman of Yr. L.I. Assn. Action Com., 1989. Office: LI Bus News 2150 Smithtown Ave Ronkonkoma NY 11779-7348

TOWNSEND, THOMAS PERKINS, former mining company executive; b. Bryn Mawr, Pa., Mar. 28, 1917; s. John and Mildred (Perkins) T.; m. Laura M. Trench, Sept. 14, 1940; children: Joanne Townsend Taber, Hunter, Elizabeth Macdonald. B.S. in Econs., U. Pa., 1939; postgrad., Harvard U., 1944. C.P.A., Pa. Sr. acct. Price Waterhouse & Co., 1945-48; treas., dir. Fox Products Co., 1948-53, Wilcolator Co., 1953-55; staff acct. Tex. Gulf Sulphur Co., N.Y.C., 1955-57; asst. treas. Tex. Gulf Sulphur Co., 1958-61, v.p., controller, 1961-62, v.p., treas., 1962-64, v.p. internat. ops., 1964-68; exec. v.p. Bosco Middle East Oil Corp., Greenwich, Conn., 1968-69; pres. Conn. Real Estate Corp., Greenwich, 1969-70, also bd. dirs., 1969—; v.p. finance Rosaria Resources Corp., N.Y.C., 1970-81; treas. Unidyne Corp., 1984-85; cons. AMAX, Inc., 1981-85; bd. dirs. Thermal Exploration Corp., Carlin Gold Co. Chmn. nat. com. for employment youth Nat. Child Labor Com., 1968-70; trustee, pres. South Kent Sch.; trustee Soc. to Advance Retarded, Norwalk, Conn.; bd. dirs. United Way of Tri-State, Denison Pequotsegos Nature Ctr.; mem. New Canaan Bd. Fin., Conn., 1985-89 . Served to lt. (s.g.) Supply Corps, USNR, World War II. Mem. Am. Inst. Accts., N.Y. State Soc. CPAs, Fin. Execs. Inst., Mason's Island Yacht Club, Off Soundings Club. Episcopalian (treas., vestryman 1960-72, 87-95). Home: 9 Kensington Ct Mystic CT 06355-3116 *The principal goal in my life has been to be a straight dealer, to be honest in thought, word and deed. It has paid off for me. Crooked dealing may make more money, but it does not lead to a happier life. One must live by his God.*

TOWNSEND, WARDELL C., JR., federal agency administrator; b. Balt., Oct. 16, 1952; s. Wardell Clinton Sr. and Toyoko Yonamine; m. Diane Martin, 1979; 4 children. BS in Psychology and Social Welfare, Western Carolina U., 1975; MSW with distinction, W.Va. U., 1977. Project dir. Congressman Jamie Clarke, Washington, 1983-85, Congressman Doug Applegate, Washington, 1985-87; from legis. dir. to adminstrv. asst./chief of staff Congressman Mike Espy, Washington, 1987-93; sr. adv. Presdl. Transition Team, Washington, 1992-93; asst. sec. adminstrn. USDA, Washington, 1993—. Former group counselor Boys Club, Asheville, N.C.; former health educator, outreach coord. Assn. Sickle Cell Disease, Charlotte, N.C.; former planning and devel. mgr. Human Resource Devel. Found., Morgantown, W.Va.; former dir. Community Devel. Dept., Henderson County, N.C.; former bus. mgr. Cherokee Minority Bus. Devel. Ctr., Asheville, N.C.; bd. dirs. Shepherd's Table, Inc., 1985-88, chmn. pub. rels. com., 1986-87; sr. warden ministry Ascension Episc. Ch., Silver Spring, Md., 1986-90, vestry mem., treas., chmn. fin. com., chmn. rector search com.; mem. diocesan investment com. Episc. Diocese Washington, 1991—; active YMCA, Silver Spring, 1988—. Mem. NASW, Adminstrv. Assts. Assn. (bd. dirs. 1991, 92, v.p. 1992), Coun. African-Am. Adminstrv. Assts., Acad. Cert. Social Workers, Global Leders for the Soutn, House Adminstrv. Assts. Alumni Assn. (bd. dirs. 1994). Office: Dept Agriculture Office Asst Sec Administrn 14th & Independence Ave SW Washington DC 20250-0002*

TOWNSHEND, PETER, musician, composer, singer; b. London, England, May 19, 1945. Co-founder (with Keith Moon, Roger Daltry, John Entwhistle), guitarist, composer music and lyrics for musical group, The Who (originally called The High Numbers, The Detours), 1964-82; composer: (rock operas) Tommy, 1969 (Tony Award, Best Score - Broadway prodn., 1993), Quadrophenia, 1973, (other albums) The Who Sings My Generation, 1965, Happy Jack, 1966, The Who Sell Out, 1967, Magic Bus: The Who on Tour (U.S. only), Live At Leeds, 1970, Who's Next, 1971, The Who By Numbers, 1975, Who Are You, 1978, Face Dances, 1981, It's Hard, 1982, Join Together, 1990, solo albums include Who Came First, 1972, (with Ronnie Lane) Rough Mix, 1977, Secret Policeman's Ball, 1980, Empty Glass, 1980, All the Best Cowboys Have Chinese Eyes, 1982, Scoop, 1983, White City, 1985, Another Scoop, 1986, Deep End Live, 1987, The Iron Man, 1989, Psychoderelect, 1993, Psychoderelict, 1993, The Best of Pete Townsend, 1996; rec. 13 albums with The Who; author (short stories) Horse's Neck, 1985; musical dir. (film and soundtrack) Tommy, 1975 (Oscar award nomination 1975); Broadway musical The Who's Tommy (Tony awd., best original score), 1993. Office: Atlantic Records 75 Rockefeller Plaza New York NY 10019*

TOY, CHARLES DAVID, lawyer; b. N.Y.C., June 29, 1955; s. Frank H.F. and Louise S.K. (Louie) T.; m. Sandra Lynn Youla, Mar. 10, 1984. BA cum laude, Harvard U., 1977, JD, 1980. Bar: N.Y. 1981. Assoc. Milbank, Tweed, Hadley & McCloy, N.Y.C., 1980-84; assoc. Kaye, Scholer, Fierman, Hays & Handler, Hong Kong, 1984-88, ptnr., 1989-91; ptnr. Kaye, Scholer, Fierman, Hays & Handler, N.Y.C., 1991-93; v.p., gen. counsel Overseas Pvt. Investment Corp., Washington, 1993—, v.p., fin., 1995-96; spkr. seminars Bus. Internat., 1985, Cookson Asia Conf., 1988, Korea Fgn. Trade Assn., 1989, 90, World Trade Inst., 1992, U. Pa., 1993, 94, 95, Washington Internat. Trade Assn., 1993, Am. Conf. Inst., 1994, 95, 96, Am. Soc. Internat. Law, 1994, 96, 97, Small Bus. Exporters Assn., 1994, Inst. for Infrastructure Fin., 1995, Assn. Bar City of N.Y., 1995, Infocast, 1995, Calif. Coun. Internat. Trade, 1995, World Econ. Devel. Congress, 1995, 96, Baker & McKenzie Ann. Mtg. Client Conf., 1995, Ctr. for Bus. Intelligence, 1995, Corp. Legal Times Roundtable, 1996, Com. of 100, 1996, Asian Am. Bar Assn., 1996, Asian Bus. Assn., 1996, Asian Pacific Am. Bar Assn., 1996, 97, Forbes, 1997; profile subject Internat. Fin. Law Rev., 1996. Contbg. editor Taxes and Investment in Asia and the Pacific, 1985, Tax News Svc., 1986—, Bull. for Internat. Fiscal Documentation, 1986—; bd. editors Strategic Alliance Alert, 1994-95. Bd. trustees Lower East Side Tenement Mus., 1994—. Mem. ABA (spkr. seminar 1994, 95, 97), Am. Arbitration Assn., N.Y. State Bar Assn., Assn. Bar City of N.Y., Nat. Asian Pacific Am. Bar Assn., Asian Am. Bar Assn. N.Y., Asia Soc., Hong Kong Assn. N.Y., Harvard Law Sch. Assn., Harvard Club (N.Y.C. and Washington), Am. Club (Hong Kong), Ladies Recreation Club (Hong Kong), Phi Beta Kappa. Democrat. Roman Catholic. Office: Overseas Pvt Investment Corp 1100 New York Ave NW Washington DC 20527-0001

TOY, PEARL TAK-CHU YAU, transfusion medicine physician; b. Hong Kong, July 31, 1947; came to U.S., 1965; d. Tse-Wah Yau and Grace Liang; m. Larry Toy, Dec. 12, 1970; 1 child, Jennifer. BA, Smith Coll., 1969; MD, Stanford U., 1973. From asst. prof. to assoc. prof. dept. lab. medicine U. Calif. Sch. Medicine, San Francisco, 1980-91, prof. dept. lab. medicine, 1991—; chief blood bank and donor ctr. Moffitt-Long Hosp., U. Calif., San Francisco, 1991—; chair expert panel on autologous transfusion NIH, Bethesda, Md., 1988-94, chair rsch. tng. rev. com., 1992. Contbr. articles to profl. jours., chpts. to books. Recipient numerous grants NIH, 1983—. Mem. Phi Beta Kappa, Sigma Xi, Alpha Omega Alpha. Achievements include research in autologous blood transfusion; blood transfusions.

TOYER, RICHARD HENRY, accountant; b. Snohomish, Wash., Aug. 6, 1944; s. Henry James Toyer and Bertha Maud (Darrow) Gilmore; m. Jean Ann Moore, July 1, 1966; 1 child, David K. BS in Acctg., Cen. Wash. U., 1973. CPA. Staff acct. Moss, Adams and Co., Everett, Wash., 1973-74, sr. staff acct., 1975-77; prin. Toyer and Assocs., CPAs Inc., PS, Everett, Wash., 1977—. Mayor City of Lake Stevens, Wash., 1983-91, city councilman, 1977-83; state treas. Wash. Jaycees, 1975-76; mem. Snohomish County Estate Planning Coun.; chmn. Snohomish County Subregional Coun., 1981-82; exec. bd. Puget Sound Regional Coun.,1 981-83; chmn. City of Everett Navy Rev. Task Force, 1987-88, Snohomish County HUD policy adv. bd., 1982-91; chmn. Snohomish County Cities and Towns, 1983-84, Snohomish County Transp. Authority, 1987-89, Snohomish County Dept. Emergency Mgmt., 1981-91, Snohomish County Tomorrow Steering Com., 1989-91; treas. Lake Stevens Aquafest, 1983-84; sponsor Miss Lake Stevens Pageant, 1983-84; bd. dirs., treas. Josephine Sunset Home, 1993-94; bd. dirs. Vols. of Am., 1995—. Sgt. U.S. Army, 1965-67, Vietnam. Mem. AICPA, Wash. Soc. CPAs, Everett C. of C. (treas. 1990-94), Marysville C. of C., Lake Stevens C. of C. (charter), Rotary (charter). Lutheran. Home: 15128 76th St SE Snohomish WA 98290-6150 Office: 3705 Colby Ave Everett WA 98201-4910

TOZER, W. JAMES, JR., investment company executive; b. Salt Lake City, Feb. 9, 1941; s. W. James and Virginia (Somerville) T.; m. Elizabeth Farran, July 30, 1965; children: Farran Virginia, Katharine Coppins. B.A. cum laude, Trinity Coll., 1963; M.B.A., Harvard U., 1965. Investment officer First Nat. City Overseas Investment Corp., N.Y.C., 1965-70; v.p. corp. devel. Citicorp, N.Y.C., 1970-71; sr. v.p. and head Citicorp Subs. Group, 1971-74; sr. v.p., gen. mgr., head Merchant Banking Group, 1974-75, sr. v.p., gen. mgr. N.Y. banking div., 1975-77; sr. exec. v.p., dir. and head investment banking div. Shearson Hayden Stone, Inc., N.Y.C., 1978-79; sr. exec. v.p. Marine Midland Bank and Marine Midland Banks, Inc., 1979-80, sr. exec. v.p. ops., fin. and strategic staff units, 1980-85, mem. office of chmn., sector exec. corp., instl. and internat. banking, 1985-87; chmn. Mountain West Banking Corp., Denver, 1988-89; pres., chief operating officer Prudential-Bache Securities, Inc., N.Y.C., 1989-90; pres., CEO Lincolnshire Mgmt., Inc., N.Y.C., 1993-94; mng. dir. Vectra Mgmt. Group, 1990—; bd. dirs. Vectra Banking Corp. Chmn. bd. Fellows Trinity Coll., 1972-78; trustee, treas. Community Service Soc., 1976-87; mem. Securities Industry Assn., 1977-78 trustees The Sch. for Field Studies, 1995—; mem. Citizens Budget Commn., 1986—; adv. council Atlanta U. Sch. Bus. Adminstrn., 1985-89. Mem. N.Y. State Bankers Assn. (legis. policy com. 1981-87), Assn. Res. City Bankers (govt. rels. com. 1984-87), Am. Bankers Assn. (govt. rels. coun. 1985-87), Economic Club, University Club, Bond of N.Y. Club, Millbrook Club, Mashomack Club, River Club (N.Y.C.), Alta Club, (S.L.C). Home: 1112 Park Ave New York NY 10128-1235 Office: 65 E 55th St New York NY 10022-3219

TOZER, WILLIAM EVANS, entomologist, educator; b. Binghamton, N.Y., July 7, 1947; s. William Evans and Gertrude Genevieve (Lewis) T. BS in Natural Sci., Niagara U., 1969; MS in Biology, Ball State U., 1979; PhD in Entomology, U. Calif., Berkeley, 1986. Cert. C.C. biology and zoology tchr. Calif. Jr. H.S. sci. and English tchr. St. Patricks Sch., Corning, N.Y., 1969-71; tchg. asst. biology Ball State U., Muncie, Ind., 1974-76; pvt. practice biol. eviron. cons. Berkeley, Calif., 1976-79, 86-88; rsch. asst. U. Calif., Berkeley, 1979-86; dept. head tng. USN Disease Vector Ecology and Control Ctr., Poulsbo, Wash., 1988—; mem., acting chmn. San Francisco Bay Area Mosquito Control Coun., Alameda, 1988-96; vice chmn. com., mem. Armed Forces Pest Mgmt. Bd., Washington, 1994—. Editor (field handbook) Navy Environmental Health Center, 1994; contbr. articles to profl. jours. With U.S. Army, 1971-73. Mem. Am. Entomol. Soc., Sigma Xi. Achievements include first to publish evidence for underwater behavioral thermoregulation in adult insects. Avocations: photography, tennis, hiking, bicycling, softball. Home: 1407 NW Santa Fe Ln Apt 304 Silverdale WA 98383 Office: USN Disease Vector Ecol Control Ctr 19950 7th Ave NE Ste 201 Poulsbo WA 98370-7405

TRABITZ, EUGENE LEONARD, aerospace company executive; b. Cleve., Aug. 13, 1937; s. Emanuel and Anna (Berman) T.; m. Caryl Lee Rine, Dec. 22, 1963 (div. Aug. 1981); children: Claire Marie, Honey Caryl; m. Kathryn Lynn Bates, Sept. 24, 1983; 1 stepchild, Paul Francis Rager. BA, Ohio State U., 1965. Enlisted USAF, 1954, advanced through grades to maj.; served as crew commdr. 91st Stragetic Missile Div., Minot, S.D., 1968-70; intelligence officer Fgn. Tech. Div., Dayton, Ohio, 1970-73; dir. external affairs Aero Systems Div., Dayton, 1973-75; program mgr. Air Force Armament Div., Valparaiso, Fla., 1975-80; dir. ship ops. Air Force Ea. Test Range, Satellite Beach, Fla., 1980-83; dep. program mgr. Air Force Satellite Text Ctr., Sunnyvale, Calif., 1983-84; ret., 1984; sr. staff engr. Ultrasystems Inc., 1984-86; pres. TAWD Systems Inc., Palo Alto, Calif., 1986-92, Am. Telenetics Co., San Mateo, Calif., 1992—; cons. Space Applications Corp., Sunnyvale, 1986-87, Litton Computer Svcs., Mountain View, Calif., 1987-91, Battelle Meml. Inst. Columbus, 1993—. V.p. Bd. County Mental Health Clinic, Ft. Walton Beach, Fla., 1973-75. Decorated Bronze Star. Mem. DAV (life), World Affairs Coun., U.S. Space Found. (charter), Air Force Assn. (life), Assn. Old Crows, Nat. Sojourners, Commonwealth Club Calif., Masons (32 degree). Avocations: golf, tennis, racketball, sailing, bridge. Home: 425 Anchor Rd Apt 317 San Mateo CA 94404-1058

TRACANNA, KIM, elementary and secondary physical education educator; b. Washington, Pa., Nov. 3, 1960; d. Frank and Mary Lou (Nardi) T. BSEd in Health and PE, Slippery Rock U., 1982; MS, U. N.C., 1985. Cert. health and physical edn. tchr. K-12, Fla., CPR, Advanced First Aid, ARC. Instr. PE Young World, Inc., Greensboro, N.C.; instr. PE and Health Beth-Ctr. Elem. Sch., Fredericktown, Pa.; rsch. asst. Physical Edn. Dept. U. N.C., Greensboro; instr. phys. edn., health coord. Lakeside Elem. Sch., Orange Park, Fla., 1986—; mem. exec. bd. Fla. Striders CORE Team Curriculum Coun. Active in civic orgns., bd. dirs. Clay County Tchrs. Acad. Excellence, 1994—. Recipient World Fellowship award for Outstanding Young Scholar, 1987, cert. of Outstanding Achievment in Elem. PE, 1987, Supt.'s Cert. of Achievement Clay County Sch. Bd., 1987, Gov.'s Leadership award, 1988, Unsung Hero of Yr. award, Jacksonville Track Club, 1989; named to Young Profl. Hall of Fame, 1987: named Tchr. of Yr. Lakeside Elem. Sch., 1995; dist finalist for Tchr. of Yr., Clay County Schs., 1995. Mem. AAHPERD, Fla. Alliance for Health, Phys. Edn., Recreation and Dance (Profl. Recognition award 1995), Am. Running and Fitness Assn.,

Clay County Reading Coun., Clay County Edn. Assn., Nat. Assn. for Edn. of Young Children, Nat. Assn. for Sports and Phys. Edn., Nat. Assn. for Girls and Women in Sports, Phi Epsilon Kappa (Outstanding PE Major award 1982), Sigma Sigma Kappa.

TRACEY, EDWARD JOHN, physician, surgeon; b. Norwalk, Conn., July 26, 1931; s. Edward John and Clara (Hammond) T.; m. Ann Marie Schenk, Sept. 7, 1957; children: Sharon, Scott. BA, Yale U., 1954; MD, N.Y. Med. Coll., N.Y.C., 1958. Diplomate Am. Bd. Surgery. Intern Bellevue Hosp., N.Y.C., 1958-59; resident in surgery NYU-Bellevue Med. Ctr., N.Y.C., 1958-63; attending surgeon Norwalk (Conn.) Hosp., 1965—, asst. dir. dept. surgery, 1975-82, chief of staff, 1982-85, chief sect. gen. surgery, 1989-95, trustee, 1972, 82-85, 92—; dir., physician support svcs., 1995—. Lt. comdr. USNR, 1963-65. Mem. ACS, AMA, Conn. Med. Soc., Fairfield County Med. Soc., Norwalk Med. Soc. (pres. 1976-77). Clubs: Cath. (Norwalk, Conn., pres. 1974-75), Shore and country (Norwalk, Conn.). Home: 124 East Ave Norwalk CT 06851-5713

TRACEY, JAY WALTER, JR., retired lawyer; b. Rocky Ford, Colo., June 13, 1925; s. Jay Walter and Margaret Louise (Bish) T.; m. Elizabeth Longfellow Henry, Nov. 1, 1952 (div. July 1988); children: Jay Walter III, William H., Anne T. Landstrom, John B.; m. Elizabeth Folk Flinn, Apr. 22, 1989. BS, Yale U., 1949; LLB, Harvard U., 1952. Bar: Colo. 1952, U.S. Dist. Ct. Colo. 1952, U.S. Ct. Appeals (10th cir.) 1958. Assoc. Holland & Hart, Denver, 1952-57, ptnr., 1957-71, 72-89; pres. Von Frellick Assocs., Inc., Denver, 1971-72; dir. Ctr. for Dispute Resolution, Denver, 1984-88. Councilman, City of Cherry Hills Village (Colo.), 1965-70, mayor pro tem, 1966-70, mem. Home Rule Charter Conv., 1966; trustee Denver Country Day Sch., 1967-70. With U.S. Army, 1943-46. Decorated Purple Heart. Mem. Colo. Bar Assn., Denver Bar Assn., Colo. Yale Assn. (pres. 1971-72), Assn. Yale Alumni (del. 1975-78), Harvard Law Sch. Assn. Colo. (pres. 1962-63), Harvard Law Sch. Assn. (v.p. 1963-64), Univ. Club (pres. 1967-69) Denver Country Club, Mile High Club, Round Hill Club (Greenwich, Conn.), Denver Rotary (sec. 1979-80, bd. dirs. 1980-82, 1st v.p. 1981-82). Republican. Episcopalian. Office: 555 17th St Ste 3200 Denver CO 80202-5555

TRACEY, MARGARET, dancer; b. Pueblo, Colo.. Student, Sch. Am. Ballet, 1982. With corps de ballet N.Y.C. Ballet, 1986-88, soloist, 1989-91, prin., 1991. Featured in ballets (Balanchine) Ivesiana, Tarantella, The Nutcracker, Symphony in C, Jewels, Square Dance, Tschaikovsky Pas de Deux, Tschaikovsky Suite No. 3, Vienna Waltzes, Apollo, Ballo Della Regina, Divertimento No. 15, Donizetti Variations, Harlequinade, A Midsummer Night's Dream, Sonatine, La Source, Stars and Stripes, Symphony in Three Movements, Valse Fantaisie, Western Symphony, Who Cares?, (Robbins) Afternoon of a Faun, The Four Seasons, The Goldberg Variations, (Martins) Les Petits Riens, Mozart Serenade, Fearful Symmetries, Zakouski, Sleeping Beauty, (Anderson) Baroque Variations; also appeared in N.Y.C. Ballet's Blanchine Celebration, 1993; toured in Europe, Asia. Recipient U.S.A. award Princess Grace Found., 1985-86; scholar Atlantic Richfield Found., 1982-85. Office: NYC Ballet NY State Theater 20 Lincoln Center Plz New York NY 10023-6913*

TRACHSEL, WILLIAM HENRY, corporate lawyer; b. El Paso, Tex., Apr. 20, 1943. BS in Aerospace Engring., U. Fla., 1965; JD, U. Conn., 1971. Bar: Conn. 1971. With United Tech. Corp., Hartford, Conn., 1965-93, v.p., sec. and dep. gen. counsel, 1993—. Mem. ABA, Am. Corp. Counsel Assn. Office: United Tech Corp United Tech Bldg Hartford CT 06101

TRACHT, ALLEN ERIC, electronics executive; b. Bethesda, Md., Aug. 14, 1957; s. Myron Edward and Diane Serena (Goldberg) T.; m. Donna June Carothers, Sept. 14, 1986; children: Michael, Diane, Daniel. BS in Physics and Elec. Engring., MIT, 1979; MSEE, Calif. Inst. Tech., 1980. Biomed. researcher Case Western Res. U., Cleve., 1980-85; exec. engr. IOtech. Inc., Cleve., 1985—; cons. engring. Keithley Instruments, Cleve., 1985. Contbr. articles to profl. jours. NIH grantee Case Western Res. U., 1982. Mem. IEEE, Assn. for Computing Machinery, Sigma Xi, Tau Beta Kappa, Eta Kappa Nu. Home: 3066 Scarborough Rd Cleveland OH 44118-4065

TRACHTENBERG, MATTHEW J., bank holding company executive; b. N.Y.C., June 20, 1958; s. Mark Trachtenberg and Joanne Horne. BA magna cum laude, NYU, 1974; JD, Bklyn. Law Sch., 1977; MBA in Fin., Fordham U., 1982. Bar: N.Y. 1979. Mgmt. trainee Mfrs. Hanover Trust Co., N.Y.C., 1977-78, credit analyst, 1978-79, corp. banking rep., 1979-80, asst. sec., 1980-82, asst. v.p., 1982, v.p., 1982-86, v.p., corp. sec., 1987-92; v.p., corp. sec. Mfrs. Hanover Corp., N.Y.C., 1987-92; dir. Mfrs. Hanover Found., 1987-92; v.p., sec. regional bd. Chem. Bank, N.Y.C., 1992-96; v.p., dep. corp. sec. Chem. Banking Corp., N.Y.C., 1992-96, Chem. Bank, 1992-96; sec. Chem. Bank Regional Bd., 1992-96; v.p. Chem. Bank, 1992-96, Chem. Banking Corp., 1992-96; v.p. asst. corp. sec. Chase Manhattan Corp., N.Y.C., 1996—, Chase Manhattan Bank, N.Y.C., 1996—; sec. Chase Manhattan Regional bd., 1996—. Bd. dirs., treas. Nat. Orch. Assn.; bd. dirs., treas. N.Y. Eye and Ear Infirmary; pres. U.S.O. of Met. N.Y.; mem. adv. ttan direct svcs.com. Lighthouse for th e Blind. N.Y. State Regents scholar. Mem. N.Y. State Bar Assn., Am. Soc. Corp. Secs., Phi Beta Kappa, Pi Sigma Alpha. Avocations: music, fishing, painting, writing. Office: Chase Manhattan Corp 270 Park Ave New York NY 10017-2014

TRACHTENBERG, STEPHEN JOEL, university president; b. Bklyn., Dec. 14, 1937; s. Oscar M. and Shoshana G. (Weinstock) T.; m. Francine Zorn, June 24, 1971; children: Adam Maccabee, Ben-Lev. BA, Columbia U., 1959; JD, Yale U., 1962; M in Pub. Adminstrn., Harvard U., 1966; LHD (hon.), Trinity Coll., 1986; HHD (hon.), U. Hartford, 1989; LLD (hon.), Hanyang U., Seoul, 1990, Richmond Coll., London, 1995; DPA (hon.), Kyonggi U., Seoul, 1994; MD (hon.), Odessa State Med. U., Ukraine, 1996; LLD (hon.), Mount Vernon Coll., 1997. Bar: N.Y. 1964, U.S. Supreme Ct. 1967. Atty. AEC, 1962-65; legis. asst. to Congressman John Brademas of Ind., Washington, 1965; tutor law Harvard Coll., also; teaching fellow edn. and pub. policy J.F. Kennedy Grad. Sch. Govt., Harvard U., 1965-66; spl. asst. to U.S. edn. commr. Office of Edn., HEW, Washington, 1966-68; asso. prof. polit. sci. Boston U., 1969-77, asso. dean, 1969-70, dean, 1970-74, assoc. v.p., co-counsel, 1974-76, v.p. acad. services, 1976-77; pres., prof. pub. adminstrn. U. Hartford, Conn., 1977-88, George Washington U., Washington, 1988—; mem. adv. bd. Ednl. Record; bd. dirs. Consortium of Univs. Washington Met. Area; mem. Fed. City Coun.; bd. dirs. NationsBank, Greater Washington Bd. Trade, Nat. Edn. Telecom. Orgn., Washington Rsch. Libr. Consortium, Dist. Columbia Tax Revision Commn., Newcomen Soc. U.S.; assoc. mem. Am. Coun. Learned Soc., DC Com.to Promote Washington; mem. Nat. Captioning Inst. Consulting editor Jour. Edn.; contbr. articles to profl. jours. Bd. dirs. Urban League, Washington; mem. D.C. Mayor's Bus. Adv. Coun.; mem. exec. panel Chief Naval Ops.; bd. overseers List Coll. Jewish Theol. Sem. Am. Winston Churchill fellow Eng., 1969; named Outstanding Young Person, Boston Jr. C. of C., 1970, One of 100 Young Leaders, Acad. Am. Council Learning, 1978, Alumnus of Yr. James Madison High Sch., Bklyn., 1982, one of Fifty Outstanding Alumni Problem Solvers Harvard's John F. Kennedy Sch. Government, 1987; recipient Myrtle Wreath award Hadassah, 1982, Scopus award Am. Friends of Hebrew U., 1986, assoc. fellow Morse Coll. Yale U., 1980, Human Rels. award NCCJ, 1987, award NAACP, 1988, citation Conn. Bar Assn., 1988, Univ. medal of highest honor Kyung Hee U., Seoul, Korea, 1990, Martin Luther King, Jr. Internat. Salute award, 1992, Hannah G. Solomon award Nat. Coun. Jewish Women, 1992, Father of Yr. award Washington Urban League, 1993, Univ. Pres. medal Kyonggi U., Seoul, 1993, Am. Czech and Slovak Assn. Merit award, 1993, John Jay award Columbia U., 1995, Spirit of Democracy award Am. Jewish Congress, 1995, Newcomen Soc. award, 1995, Disting. Achievement medal Greenberg Ctr. for Judaic Studies U. Hartford, 1995. Mem. Am. Coun. Learned Soc., Am. Assn. Univ. Adminstrs. (Disting. Svc. award 1996, B'nai B'rith Humanitarian award 1996), N.Y. Acad. Scis., Internat. Assn. Univ. Pres. (N.Am. coun., Mount Vernon Adv. Coun. for 1999), Coun. Fgn. Rels., Sr. Soc. Sachems, Ind. Retail Cattleman's Assn. (adv. coun.), Masons, Scottish Rite Freemasonry (33d degree), Harvard Club (N.Y.C.), Tumblebrook Country Club (Bloomfield, Conn.), Cosmos Club (Washington), Univ. Club (Washington), 1925 F St. Club (Washington), Phi Beta Kappa. Office: George Washington U Office of President Washington DC 20052

TRACI, DONALD PHILIP, retired lawyer; b. Cleve., Mar. 13, 1927; m. Lillian Traci Calafiore; 11 children. BS cum laude, Coll. of the Holy Cross, Worcester, Mass., 1950; JD magna cum laude, Cleve. State U., 1955; LLD (hon.), U. Urbino, Italy, 1989. Bar: Ohio 1955, U.S. Dist. Ct. (no. and so. dists.) Ohio 1955, U.S. Ct. Appeals (3d, 6th and 7th cirs.), U.S. Dist. Ct. (we. and ea. dists.) Pa., U.S. Supreme Ct. 1965. Ptnr. Spangenberg, Shibley, Traci, Lancione & Liber, Cleve., 1955-95; lectr. York U., Toronto, Ont., Can., Case Western Res. U., Cleve. Marshall Law Sch., U. Mich., Akron U., U. Cin., Ohio No. U., Harvard U. Trustee Cath. Charities Diocese of Cleve., past pres. Bd. Cath. Edn.; former chmn. bd. regents St. Ignatius H.S., Cleve.; mem. pres.'s coun. Coll. of Holy Cross; Eucharist min. St. Rose of Lima Ch. With USN, 1945-46. Fellow Am. Coll. Trial Lawyers, Internat. Acad. Trial Lawyers (past pres.), Am. Bd. Trial Advocacy; mem. ABA, ATLA (trustee Lambert Chair Found., lectr. trial practice), Ohio State Bar Assn. (lectr. trial practice), Ohio Acad. Trial Lawyers (past chmn. rules seminar, lectr. trial practice), Cuyahoga County Bar Assn. (lectr. trial practice), Cleve. Acad. Trial Lawyers (lectr. trial practice), Trial Lawyers for Pub. Justice (sustaining founder), Cleve. Bar Assn. (chmn. Advocacy Inst., trustee, CLE com., jud. selection com., spl. justice ctr. com., fed. ct., common pleas ct. and ct. appeals com., pres. 1986), Jud. Conf. U.S. 6th Cir. Ct. (life), Jud. Conf. 8th Jud. Dist. Ohio life), Knights of Malta, Delta Theta Phi. Home: 10416 Lake Ave Cleveland OH 44102-1206 Office: 2400 National City Ctr Cleveland OH 44114

TRACT, MARC MITCHELL, lawyer; b. N.Y.C., Sept. 20, 1959; s. Harold Michael and Natalie Ann (Meyerowitz) T.; m. Sharon Beth Widrow; children: Melissa Hope, Harrison Michael, Sarah Michelle. BA in Biology, Ithaca Coll., 1981; JD, Pepperdine U., 1984. Bar: N.Y. 1985, N.J. 1985, D.C. 1986. Assoc. Kroll & Tract, N.Y.C., 1985-90, ptnr., 1990-94; ptnr. Rosenman & Colin LLP, N.Y.C., 1994—; bd. dirs. Sorema N.Am. Reinsurance Co., N.Y.C., Colonia Ins. Co., N.Y.C., Folksamerica Reinsurance Co., N.Y.C., Navigators Group Inc., N.Y.C., Fortress Ins. Co. Am., N.Y.C., N.Y. Surety Co., Great Neck, N.Y., Chatham Reinsurance Corp., San Francisco, C.A., Nordstern Ins. Co. Am., N.Y.C., Colonia Underwriters Ins. Co., Ft. Smith, Ark., The Mercantile & Gen. Reinsurance Co. Am., N.Y.C., 400 East 85th St. Realty Corp., N.Y.C., Oriska Corp., Oriskany, N.Y., Am. Industries Assurance (Cayman) Ltd., Grand Cayman. Mem. ABA, Assn. of Bar of City of N.Y., N.Y. State Bar Assn., N.J. State Bar Assn., N.Y. County Lawyers Assn., Am. Coun. Germany, Old Westbury Golf and Country Club, Met. Club, Econ. Club N.Y. Republican. Office: Rosenman & Colin LLP 575 Madison Ave New York NY 10022-2511

TRACY, ALAN THOMAS, government official; b. Janesville, Wis., May 3, 1947; s. Robert Elmer and Frances Dina (Daane) T.; m. Kris Cunningham; children: Chad, Paul, Sarah. B.S. in Agrl. Econs., Cornell U., Ithaca, N.Y., 1969; M.B.A., U. Wis., 1970. With Tracy & Son Farms, Inc., Janesville, Wis., 1970-81, v.p., 1973-76, pres., 1976-81; gen sales mgr., assoc. adminstr. Dept. Agr., Washington, 1981-82, dep. undersec. for internat. affairs and commodity programs, 1982-85, dep. asst. sec. dor mktg. and inspection services, 1985-86; spl. asst. to pres. for agrl. trade and food assistance The White House, 1986-89; spl. asst. to sec. for agrl. promotion Wis. Dept. Agr., Trade & Consumer Protection, Madison, 1989, sec., 1990—; dir. Heritage Bank, Beloit, Janesville, 1978-81. Trustee Beloit Coll., Wis., 1980-83; chmn. Republican party Rock County, 1972-74. Named Outstanding Young Farmer Wis. Wis. Jaycees, 1980; Nat. Merit scholar, 1965. Mem. Janesville C. of C. (chmn. agribus. com. 1978-79). Methodist. Lodge: Rotary-Janesville (dir. 1980-81). Home: 8030 Stagecoach Rd Cross Plains WI 53528-9796 Office: Wis Dept Agr, Trade & Consumer Protection 801 W Badger Rd # 8911 Madison WI 53713-2526

TRACY, ALLEN WAYNE, manufacturing company executive; b. Windsor, Vt., July 25, 1943; s. J. Wayne and Helen (Bernard) T.; m. Karla Noelte, Dec. 14, 1968; children: Tania, Tara. BA, U. Vt., 1965; MBA cum laude, Boston U., 1974. Retail salesman Exxon Corp., Boston, 1965-72; mfg. mgr. Leonard Silver Mfg. Co., Inc., Boston, 1974-78, v.p. ops., 1979-81; pres. OESM Corp., N.Y.C., 1978-81; pres. Gold Lance Inc., Houston, 1981-91, also bd. dirs.; v.p. ops. Town & Country Corp., 1989-92; sr. v.p. L.G. Balfour Co., 1990-92; asst. to pres. Syratech Corp., Boston, 1993; dir. ops. Goldman-Kolber Co., Inc., Norwood, Mass., 1994; exec. v.p., COO George H. Fuller & Son Co., Inc., Pawtucket, R.I., 1994—; bd. dirs. Verilyte Gold, Inc., L.G. Balfour Co., Inc. Mem. Bd. Selectmen, Town of Ashland, 1977-78; chmn. Ashland Study Town Govt. Com., 1976-77; vice chmn. ch. council Federated Ch. of Ashland, 1979-80, chmn., 1981; bd. dirs. Nottingham Forest Civic Assn., 1986. Served with U.S. Army, 1965-68. Mem. Nottingham Forest Club (Houston, bd. dirs. 1986), Beta Gamma Sigma. Home: 455 Prospect St Seekonk MA 02771-1503 Office: George H. Fuller & Son Co Inc 151 Exchange St Pawtucket RI 02860-2210 *The key to economic and social mobility is education. Education, however must be coupled with perseverance, diligence, hard work and a genuine appreciation of the efforts of all the people that one interacts with.*

TRACY, BARBARA MARIE, lawyer; b. Mpls., Oct. 13, 1945; d. Thomas A. and Ruth C. (Roby) T. BA, U. Minn., 1971; JD, U. Okla., 1980. Bar: Okla. 1980, U.S. Dist. Ct. (we. dist.) Okla. 1980, U.S. Dist. Ct. (no. dist.) Tex. 1991, U.S. Supreme Ct. 1988, U.S. Dist. Ct. (ea. dist.) Tex. 1995. Assoc. Pierce, Couch, Hendrickson, Johnston & Baysinger, Oklahoma City, 1980-82; ptnr. Rizley & Tracy, Sayre, Okla., 1982-84; pvt. practice Oklahoma City, 1984-90; gen. atty. U.S. Army Corps Engrs., Ft. Worth, 1991—. Mem. citizens adv. bd. O'Donoghue Rehab. Inst., Oklahoma City. Mem. ABA, Okla. Bar Assn., Fed. Bar Assn., Internat. Tng. in Commn. (pres. Ace Club chpt.). Democrat. Roman Catholic. Avocations: photography, flying, water sports. Office: 819 Taylor St Fort Worth TX 76102-6114

TRACY, CAROL COUSINS, association executive, former educator; b. N.Y.C., Jan. 31, 1943; d. James Franklin and Ruth (Hubbard) Cousins; m. William Ferber Tracy, Feb. 14, 1963; children: Lisa, Scott, Jennifer. BA, Duke U., 1965. Cert. educator, math. Tchr. Thrasher Sch., Signal Mountain, Tenn., 1967-69; tchr., math. Girls Prep. Sch., Chattanooga, 1980-91; exec. dir., founder Psi Beta, Chattanooga, 1981—; fin. officer Psi Chi, 1991—. Vol., bd. dirs. Jr. League, Chattanooga, 1973-83; tutor Inner City, Chattanooga, 1974-75, 88-90; sec., vol. Allied Arts, Chattanooga; publicity LWV; v.p., pres. Chattanooga Ballet Bd., 1991—; sec., bd. dirs. Signal Mountain Libr. Avocations: skiing, reading, roller blading. Home: 1500 Lyndhurst Dr Chattanooga TN 37405-3121 Office: Psi Beta Psi Chi 407 E 5th St Ste B Chattanooga TN 37403-1823

TRACY, DAVID, theology educator; b. Yonkers, N.Y., Jan. 6, 1939. Licentiate in Theology, Gregorian U., Rome, 1964, Doctorate in Theology, 1969; hon. doctorate, U. of the South, 1982, Cath. Theol. Union, 1990; LHD (hon.), Rosary Coll., 1992, Fairfield U., 1993, Williams Coll., 1994, Fontbonne Coll., 1995, St. Xavier U., 1996. Instr. theology Cath. U. Am., Washington, 1967-69; prof. theology Divinity Sch., U. Chgo., 1969—, prof. com. analysis of ideas and methods, 1981—, Disting. Svc. prof., 1985, Andrew Thomas Greeley and Grace McNichols Greeley Disting. Svc. prof. Cath. studies, 1987, prof. com. social thought, 1990—; lectr. Beijing Inst. Sci. Study of Religion, Trinity Coll., Dublin, Gregorian U., Rome, World Coun. Chs., Geneva, Cath. U., Leuven, Belgium, Union Theol. Sem., Princeton Theol. Sem., numerous U.S. univs. including Harvard, Yale, Fordham, Notre Dame, Vanderbilt, So. Meth., Xavier, Marquette. Author: The Achievement of Bernard Lonergan, 1970, Blessed Rage for Order: The New Pluralism in Theology, 1975, The Analogical Imagination: Christian Theology and the Context of Pluralism, 1981, Plurality and Ambiguity: Hermeneutics, Religion and Hope, 1987, Religion and the Public Realm, 1987, Dialogue with the Otter, 1990, On Naming the Present, 1994; co-author: (with John Cobb) Talking About God, 1983, (with Stephen Happel) The Catholic Vision, 1983, (with Robert M. Grant) A Short History of the Interpretation of the Bible, 1984; co-editor: (with Hans Küng and Johann Baptist Metz) Towards Vatican III: The Work That Needs to be Done, (with H. Küng) Theologie-Wohin?. German edit., 1983, English edit., 1985, (with Hans Küng) Paradigm Change in Theology, 1989; editor or co-editor various spl. vols. for Jour. Religion, Concilium jour.; co-editor Jour. Religion, Religious Studies Rev., Commonweal; past mem. editorial bd. Jour. Am. Acad. Religion, Theol. Studies jour.; current editorial bd. Theology Today, Jour. Pastoral Psychology; contbr. articles to scholarly and popular jours. including Jour. Religion, Theology Today, Critical Inquiry, Daedalus, Jour. Am. Acad. Religion, New Republic, N.Y. Times Book Rev., Christian Century. Mem. Am. Acad. Arts and Scis., Am. Acad. Religion, Am. Theol. Soc., Cath. Theol. Soc. Am. (pres. 1977-78). Office: U Chgo The Divinity Sch 1025 E 58th St Chicago IL 60637-1509

TRACY, JAMES DONALD, historian; b. St. Louis, Feb. 14, 1938; s. Leo W. and Marguerite M. (Meehan) T.; m. Nancy Ann McBride, Sept. 6, 1968 (div. 1993); children: Patrick, Samuel, Mary Ann; m. Suzanne K. Swan, May 2, 1997. BA, St. Louis U., 1959; MAS, Johns Hopkins U., 1960; MA, Notre Dame U., 1961; PhD, Princeton U., 1967. Instr. U. Mich., 1964-66; instr. to prof. history U. Minn., Mpls., 1966—, dept. chmn., 1988-91; vis. prof. U. Leiden, Netherlands, spring 1987. Author: Erasmus: The Growth of a Mind, 1972, The Politics of Erasmus: A Pacifist Intellectual and His Political Milieu, 1979, True Ocean Found; Paludanus' Letters on Dutch Voyages to the Kara Sea, 1980, A Financial Revolution in the Habsburg Netherlands: Renten and Renteniers in the County of Holland, 1515-1565, 1985, Holland under Habsburg Rule: The Formation of a Body Politic, 1506-1566, 1990, Erasmus of the Low Countries, 1996; editor: Luther and the Modern State in Germany, 1986, The Rise of Merchant Empires: Long Distance Trade in the Early Modern Era, 1350-1750, 1990, The Political Economy of Merchant Empires: Long Distance Trade and State Power in the Early Modern World, 1991, (with T.A. Brady and H.O. Oberman) Handbook of European History in the Late Middle Ages, Renaissance and Reformation, Vol. 1, 1994, Vol. 2, 1995; mem. editl. bd. Sixteenth Century Jour., 1979—; mng. editor Jour. Early Modern History, 1997—. Guggenheim fellow, 1972-73; NEH summer grantee, 1977, 85; Fulbright rsch. grantee, Belgium, 1979, Netherlands, 1980; resident fellow Netherlands Inst. for Advanced Studies, 1993-94. Mem. Am. Cath. Hist. Soc., Soc. Reformation Rsch. (pres. 1995-97), 16th Century Studies Conf. (pres. 1985-86). Republican. Roman Catholic. Home: 63 Avon St S Apt 33 Saint Paul MN 55105-3336 Office: U Minn 614 Social Sci Bldg Minneapolis MN 55455

TRACY, JAMES JARED, JR., accountant, law firm administrator; b. Cleve., Jan. 17, 1929; s. James Jared and Florence (Comey) T.; m. Elizabeth Jane Bourne, June 30, 1953 (div. 1988); children: Jane Mackintosh, Elizabeth Boyd, James Jared IV, Margaret Gardiner; m. Judith Anne Cooper, Feb. 18, 1989. AB, Harvard U., 1950, MBA, 1953. CPA, Ohio. Acct., mgr. Price Waterhouse & Co., Cleve., 1953-65; treas., CFO Clevite Corp., Cleve., 1965-69; asst. treas. Republic Steel Corp., Cleve., 1969-70, treas., 1970-75; v.p., treas. Johns-Manville Corp., Denver, 1976-81; v.p., treas., CFO I. T. Corp., L.A., 1981-82; exec. dir. Hufstedler, Miller, Carlson & Beardsley, L.A., 1983-84, Shank, Irwin & Conant, Dallas, 1984-85, Pachter, Gold & Schaffer, L.A., 1985-86; v.p., sr. cons. Right Assocs., L.A., 1987-91; dir. adminstrn. Larson & Burnham, Oakland, Calif., 1991-95; retired Larson & Burnham, 1995; adminstrv. dir. Law Offices of Thomas E. Miller, Newport Beach, Calif., 1996—; trustee and v.p. Miss Hall's Sch., Pittsfield, Mass., 1970-78; dir. Union Commerce Bank, Cleve., 1971-76; adv. bd. mem. Arkwright-Boston Ins. Co., Boston, 1976-81. Trustee and v.p. Cleve. Soc. for Blind, 1965-76; trustee Western Res. Hist. Soc., Cleve., 1972-76; treas. St. Peters by the Sea Presbyn. Ch., Palos Verdes, Calif., 1981-91. Recipient Alumni award Harvard U., Denver, 1981. Mem. AICPA, Ohio Soc. CPAs, Assn. Legal Adminstrs., Piedmont Montclair Rotary Club (pres. 1995-96), Harvard Club San Francisco, Harvard Bus. Sch. Club No. Calif. Avocations: sailing, golf, gardening, railroad layouts. Home: 2204 Fortuna Newport Beach CA 92660-4011

TRACY, JANET RUTH, legal educator, librarian; b. Denison, Iowa, July 16, 1941; d. L. M. and Grace (Harvey) T.; m. Rodd Mc Cormick Reynolds, Feb. 15, 1975 (dec. June 1993); children: Alexander, Lee. BA, U. Oreg., 1963; ML, U. Wash., 1964; JD, Harvard U., 1969. Bar: N.Y. 1970. Reference libr. Harvard Coll. Librs., Cambridge, Mass., 1964-66; assoc. Kelley Drye & Warren, N.Y.C., 1969-71; dir. data base design Mead Data Ctrl., Inc., N.Y.C., 1971-75; dir. rsch. Mvpl. Employees Legal Svc. Fund, N.Y.C., 1975-76; from asst. to assoc. prof. N.Y. Law Sch., N.Y.C., 1976-82; asst. libr. dir. Law Libr. Columbia U., N.Y.C., 1982-86; prof., law libr. dir. Fordham U., N.Y.C., 1986—; chmn. Conf. Law Librs. Jesuit Univs., 1988-89. Co-author: Professional Staffing and Job Security in Academic Law Libraries, 1989. Recipient Catalog Automation award Winston Found., 1990, 91, 92. Home: 285 Riverside Dr New York NY 10025-5276 Office: Fordham U Sch of Law 140 W 62nd St New York NY 10023-7407

TRACY, JOEL DEAN, marketing researcher; b. Wisconsin Rapids, Wis., Jan. 13, 1961; s. James E. and Betty R. (Sarver) T.; children: Joshua, Matthew. BS, U. Wis., 1985, MS, 1987. Mgr., sales rep. Kirby Co., Schofield, Wis., 1979-82; sales devel. rep. Am. Greetings, Cleve., 1985-86; market rsch. project coord. U. Wis. Hosp., Madison, 1986-87; mktg. rsch. analyst The Upjohn Co., Kalamazoo, Mich., 1987-89; sr. mktg. rsch. analyst S.C. Johnson and Sons, Racine, Wis., 1989-91; bus. intelligence planning mgr. Pharmacia & Upjohn, Kalamazoo, 1991-97; mktg. rsch. mgr. Westwood Squibb divsn. Bristol Myers-Squibb, Buffalo, N.Y., 1997—. Mem. Am. Mktg. Assn., Beta Gamma Sigma. Home: 4311 Fireside Ave Kalamazoo MI 49002-5841

TRACY, MICHAEL CAMERON, choreographer, performer; b. Florence, Italy, Feb. 1, 1952; s. Stanley B. and Elizabeth Lee (McIntosh) T. B.A. Magna cum laude, Dartmouth Coll., 1973. Adj. faculty Yale U., New Haven, Conn., 1992—. Artistic dir. Pilobolus Dance Theatre, Washington, Conn., 1974—; choreographer Die Zauberflöte, European prodn. with John Eliot Gardiner's Monteverdi Choir and English Baroque Soloists, 1995; co-choreographer: Ciona, 1974, Monkshood's Farewell, 1975, Untitled, 1976, Day Two, 1980, Pyramid of the Moon, 1996, Aeros, 1996, Eysian Fields, 1997; choreographer Curiouser and Curiouser Nat. Theatre of Deaf, 1996. Recipient Berlin Critics award, 1975, New Eng. Theatre Conf. prize, 1977, Brandeis award, 1978, Excellence in Arts award Conn. Commn. on the Arts, 1981; sr. fellow Dartmouth Coll., 1973. Office: PO Box 388 Washington Depot CT 06794-0388

TRACY, PATRICIA ANN KOOP, secondary school educator; b. Chickasaw, Ala., Sept. 28, 1947; d. Augustus Galloway Koop and Mildred (Willingham) Koop Conlon; m. Charles Gerald Tracy, Jan. 24, 1970; children: Charles Gerald Jr., William Todd, Michael Patrick. BS in Edn., U. Ala., Tuscaloosa, 1970; postgrad., Ala. State U., Montgomery, 1988, Troy State U., 1989, U. Ala., Huntsville, 1989, Ala. State U., 1995, Auburn U., Montgomery, 1994. Cert. secondary sci. tchr. Tchr. sci. St. Bede Sch., Montgomery, Ala., 1986-90, coord. Sci. Fair, head dept. sci., 1986-90; libr., media specialist Our Lady Queen Mercy Sch., 1992-93, libr., media specialist, computer tchr., 1993-94, mem. libr. and media, earth sci. tchr., 1994—; established reading program for grades K-8 involving parents of K-2 and computers in grades 3-8; developed hands on approach in media with filmstrip, book tapes, computer games, and other games involving cognitive skills; sci. fair co-coord., 1994—. Mem. Ala. Edn. Assn., Nat. Cath. Edn. Assn., Ala. Sci. Tchrs. Assn., Montgomery Cath. H.S. PTO, Ala. Conservancy, Ala. Alumni Assn., Ala. Mus. Natural History, Wetumpka H.S. PTO, Alpha Xi Delta. Roman Catholic. Avocations: crafts, water sports, reading, gardening, work for cleaner environment. Home: 2424 Trotters Trl Wetumpka AL 36092-8410 Office: 4435 Narrow Lane Rd Montgomery AL 36116-2953

TRACY, ROBERT (EDWARD), English language educator, poetry translator; b. Woburn, Mass., Nov. 23, 1928; s. Hubert William and Vera Mary (Hurley) T.; m. Rebecca Garrison, Aug. 26, 1956; children: Jessica Janes, Hugh Garrison, Dominick O'Donovan. AB in Greek with honors, Boston Coll., 1950; MA, Harvard U., 1954, PhD, 1960. Teaching fellow Harvard U., Cambridge, Mass., 1954-58; instr. Carleton Coll., Northfield, Minn., 1958-60; from asst. prof. English, to assoc. prof., then prof. U. Calif., Berkeley, 1960-89, prof. English and Celtic Studies, 1989—, assoc. dir. Dickens Project, 1994-95; vis. prof., Bruern fellow in Am. studies U. Leeds, Eng., 1965-66; vis. prof., Leverhulme fellow Trinity Coll., Dublin, 1971-72; vis. Kathryn W. Davis prof. slavic studies Wellesley (Mass.) Coll., 1979; Charles Mills Gayley lectr. U. Calif., Berkeley, 1989-90; vis. prof. Anglo-Irish lit. Trinity Coll., 1995-96. Author: Trollope's Later Novels, 1978; translator (poems by Osip Mandelstam): Stone, 1981, 2d edit., 1991; editor J.M Synge's The Aran Islands, 1962, The Way We Live Now (Anthony Trollope), 1974, The Macdermots of Ballycloran (Anthony Trollope), 1989, Nina Balatka and Linda Tressel (Anthony Trollope), 1991, In A Glass Darkly (Sheridan Le Fanu) 1993, Rhapsody in Stephen's Green (Flann O'Brien), 1994; adv. editor The Recorder, 1985—, LIT (Lit., Interpretation,

Theory), 1989—; contbr. articles and revs. to numerous jours. including Shakespeare Quarterly, So. Rev., Nineteenth-Century Fiction, Eire-Ireland, Irish Literary Supplement, others; poetry translations in New Orleans Rev., Poetry, N.Y. Rev. of Books, others. Appointed mem. cultural panel San Francisco-Cork Sister City Com. Fulbright travel grantee, 1965-66; recipient humanities research fellowships U. Calif., Berkeley, 1962, 69, 78, 81, 86 , 92; Guggenheim fellow, 1981-82. Mem. MLA, Philol. Assn. Pacific Coast, Am. Conf. for Irish Studies, Internat. Assn. for Study of Irish Lit. Avocation: exploring western Ireland and no. Calif. Office: U Calif Dept English Berkeley CA 94720

TRACY, THOMAS MILES, international health organization official; b. Great Barrington, Mass., July 8, 1936; s. Thomas Paul and Marion (Miles) T.; m. June Betts, June 17, 1967; children: Miles Christopher, Keir Thomas John. B.A., Colgate U., 1958; M.A., Stanford U., 1959; M.B.A., Columbia U., 1973. Fgn. service officer Dept. State, Washington, 1960-84; counselor Am. Embassy, Moscow, 1975-78, Bonn, Germany, 1978-79; asst. sec. Dept. State, Washington, 1979-83; chief adminstrn. Pan Am./WHO, Washington, 1983—; v.p. Pan-Am. Health and Edn. Found. Trustee, treas. Chelsea Sch.; treas. Pam Am. Health and Edn. Found. With U.S. Army, 1959-60. Recipient Superior Honor award Dept. State, 1978. Mem. Am. Fgn. Svc. Assn. (dir. 1970-72), Am. Fgn. Svc. Protective Assn. (dir. 1988—), Am. Fgn. Svc. Protective Found. (sec., treas.). Home: 5902 Devonshire Dr Bethesda MD 20816-3416 Office: Pan Am WHO 525 23rd St NW Washington DC 20037-2847

TRADER, JOSEPH EDGAR, orthopedic surgeon; b. Milw., Nov. 2, 1946; s. Edgar Joseph and Dorothy Elizabeth (Senzig) T.; m. Janet Louise Burzycki, Sept. 23, 1972 (div. Nov. 1987); children: James, Jonathan, Ann Elizabeth; m. Rhonda Sue Schultz, May 26, 1990. Student, Marquette U., 1964-67; MD, Med. Coll. Wis., 1971. Diplomate Am. Bd. Orthopaedic Surgery. Emergency rm. physician columbia, St. Joseph's Hosps., Milw., 1972-76; orthopaedic surgeon Orthopaedic Assn., Manitowoc, Wis., 1978—; mem. exec. com. Holy Family Meml. Med. Ctr., Manitowoc, 1985-96, chief-of-staff, 1994-96, ethics com., 1995—. Chmn. bd. dirs., past pres. Holy Innocents Mens Choir; county del. State Med. Soc. Charitable Sci. and Edn. Found.; mem. adv. bd. Manitowoc Area Cath. Schs. Endowment Fund. Fellow Am. Acad. Orthopaedic Surgeons (orthopaedic rsch. and edn. found. state com.), ACS; mem. AMA, Wis. State Med. Soc. (del. gov. affairs com.), Wis. Orthopaedic Soc., Midwest Orthopaedic Soc., Milw. Orthopaedic Soc., Phi Delta Epsilon, Psi Chi, Crown & Anchor. Roman Catholic. Club: Manitowoc Yacht. Avocations: singing, piano, scuba diving, tennis, skiing, sailing. Home: 1021 Memorial Dr Manitowoc WI 54220-2242 Office: Orthopaedic Assocs 501 N 10th St Manitowoc WI 54220-4039

TRAEGER, CHARLES HENRY, III, lawyer; b. Bethlehem, Pa., Sept. 30, 1942; s. Charles Henry Jr. and Dorothy Shelly (Weinberger) T.; m. Carole Lynn DeGraff, Feb. 20, 1972; children: Chad, Erin, Seth, Anna, Claire, Benjamin. AB, Coll. William and Mary, 1964; JD, Stanford U., 1967. Bar: Calif. 1967, N.Y. 1972, Mass. 1976, Ariz. 1980. Assoc. Milbank, Tweed, Hadley & McCloy, N.Y.C., 1967, 71-76; v.p., gen. counsel Shawmut Corp., Boston, 1976-80, Shawmut Bank of Boston, N.A., 1976-80; assoc. Snell & Wilmer, Phoenix, 1980-83, ptnr., 1983-91; v.p., asst. gen. counsel Bank One Ariz. N.A., Phoenix, 1991-95; assoc. gen. counsel Ariz. State U., Tempe, 1996—. Contbr. Stanford Law Rev. Lt. comdr. USNR, 1968-71. Phi Beta Kappa. Republican. Mem. LDS Ch.

TRAFFORD, ABIGAIL, editor, writer, columnist; b. N.Y.C., July 14, 1940; d. William Bradford and Abigail (Sard) T.; children from previous marriage: Abigail, Victoria, Brett; m. Donald Lloyd Neff, Nov. 25, 1989. BA cum laude, Bryn Mawr Coll., 1962. Researcher Nat. Geog. Soc., Washington, 1964-67; tchr. Hermansberg Mission, Northern Ter., Australia, 1967-68; spl. corr. Time mag., The Washington Post, Houston, 1969-74; writer, asst. mng. editor U.S. News & World Report, Washington, 1975-86; health editor The Washington Post, 1986—; syndicated columnist Universal Press Syndicate. Author: Crazy Time: Surviving Divorce and Building a New Life, 1982, revised edit., 1992. Journalism fellow Harvard Sch. Pub. Health, 1980. Mem. Nat. Press Club, Washington Press Club Found. (bd. mem. 1989—, pres. 1993-95). Home: 2600 Upton St NW Washington DC 20008-3826 Office: The Washington Post 1150 15th St NW Washington DC 20071-0001

TRAFICANT, JAMES A., JR., congressman; b. Youngstown, Ohio, May 8, 1941; s. James A. and Agnes T. Traficant; m. Patricia Coppa; children: Robin, Elizabeth. B.S., U. Pitts., 1963, M.S., 1973; M.S., Youngstown State U., 1976. Exec. dir. Mahoning County Drug Program, Ohio, 1971-81; sheriff Mahoning County, Ohio, 1981-85; mem. 99th-105th Congresses from 17th Ohio dist., Washington, D.C., 1985—; ranking minority mem. transp. and infrastructure subcom. on Coast Guard and maritime transp., mem. sci. com. Office: US House of Reps Office of House Members 2446 Rayburn Bldg Ofc Washington DC 20515-3517*

TRAFICANTE, DANIEL DOMINICK, chemist; b. Hoboken, N.J., Nov. 20, 1933; s. Paul and Mary T.; m. Doris Marilyn Poley, Aug. 20, 1955 (div. 1983); children: Daniel D., Mark S., Christopher, Dawn; m. Margaret Mary Kelly, May 19, 1984; children: Paul C., Katrina A.M. BS, Syracuse U., 1955; PhD, MIT, 1962. Commd. 2d lt. USAF, 1956, advanced through grades to capt., 1960, resigned, 1967; dir. undergrad. labs. MIT, Cambridge, 1968-70, dir. nuclear magnetic resonance lab., 1970-78; dir. nuclear magnetic resonance lab. Yale U., New Haven, 1978-81; dir. Nuclear Magnetic Resonance Inst., Cranford, N.J., 1981-83; dir. chem. instrumentation NSF, Washington, 1983-85; pres. Nuclear Advancement Corp., Kingston, R.I., 1976—; rsch. fellow, dir. life scis. nuclear magnetic resonance consortium Monsanto Co., Chesterfield, Mo., 1985-86; mem. sci. adv. bd. Inst. Clin. Applications, Boston, 1991-93; dir. Nuclear Magnetic Resonance Concepts; dir. nuclear magnetic resonance rsch. lab. and prof. chemistry U. R.I., 1986—. Author: Chemistry, 1978; editor-in-chief Concepts in Magnetic Resonance jour., 1989—; contbr. articles to profl. jours. Recipient Letter of Commendation Syracuse U., 1987; named Man of Yr. Societa Italiana, 1991. Mem. Am. Chem. Soc. Home: 26 Wood Cove Dr Coventry RI 02816-6602 Mailing Address: PO Box 1024 Coventry RI 02816-0018

TRAFTON, LAURENCE MUNRO, astronomer; b. Boston, July 31, 1938; s. Herbert Meara and Vesta Estelle Trafton. BS, Calif. Inst. Tech., 1960, MS, 1961, PhD, 1965. Assoc. scientist Jet Propulsion Lab., Pasadena, Calif., summers 1961-62; project officer Kirtland AFB, Albuquerque, 1968, project scientist, 1968-69; spl. rsch. assoc. dept. astronomy U. Tex., Austin, 1969-72, rsch. scientist dept. astronomy, 1972-93, sr. rsch. scientist McDonald Obs., 1993—; mem. instrument definition team for high resolution spectrograph Hubble Space Telescope project NASA. Mem. editl. bd. Icarus, 1976-79, assoc. editor, 1980—; contbr. articles over 135 articles to sci. jours. 1st lt. USAF, 1965-68. Fellow AAAS; mem. Am. Astron. Soc. (com. mem. div. planetary sci. 1977-80, meeting program chmn. 1976), Internat. Astron. Union. Office: Univ Tex Dept Astronomy Austin TX 78712

TRAFTON, STEPHEN J., bank executive; b. Mt. Vernon, Wash., Sept. 17, 1946; m. Diane Trafton; children: John, Roland. BS in Zoology, Wash. State U., 1968. V.p., mgr. dept. money market Seattle-First Nat. Bank, 1968-79; v.p., mgr. bank consulting group Donaldson Lufkin Jennrette, N.Y.C., 1980; exec. v.p., treas. Gibraltar Savings Bank, L.A., 1980-84; banking cons., 1984-86; v.p., treas. Hibernia Bank, San Francisco, 1986-88; sr. v.p., treas. Goldome Bank, Buffalo, N.Y., 1988-90; sr. exec. v.p., CFO Glenfed Inc., 1990-91, vice chmn., CFO, 1991—, pres., 1992—; sr. exec. v.p., CFO Glendale Fed. Bank, 1990-91, vice chmn., CFO, 1991, pres., COO, 1991-92, chmn. bd., pres., CEO, 1992—, also bd. dirs. Mem. Phi Eta Sigma. Office: Glendale Fed Bank 414 N Central Ave Glendale CA 91203-2002

TRAGER, DAVID G., federal judge; b. Mt. Vernon, N.Y., Dec. 23, 1937; s. Sol and Clara (Friedman) T.; m. Roberta E. Weisbrod, May 2, 1972; children: Mara Emet, Josiah Samuel, Naomi Gabrielle. B.A., Columbia Coll., 1959; LL.B., Harvard U., 1962. Bar: N.Y. Assoc. Berman & Frost, 1963-65, Butler, Jablow & Geller, 1965-67; asst. corp. counsel Appeals Div. City of N.Y., 1967; law clk. Judge Kenneth B. Keating, N.Y. State Ct. Appeals, 1968-69; asst. U.S. atty. chief, appeals div., 1970-72; U.S. atty. Ea. Dist. N.Y., Bklyn., 1974-78; prof. Bklyn. Law Sch., 1972-94, dean, 1983-94; judge U.S. Dist. Ct. (ea. dist.) N.Y., Bklyn., 1994—; chmn. Mayor's Com. on Judiciary, 1982-89, N.Y. State Temp. Commn. on Investigation, 1983-90. Mem. N.Y.C. Charter Rev. Commn., 1986-89. With USAR, 1962-65, USNR, 1965-69. Mem. ABA, N.Y. State Bar Assn., Assn. Bar City N.Y., Fed. Bar Council (pres. 1986-88), Am. Law Inst., Am. Judicature Soc. Office: US Courthouse 225 Cadman Plz E Brooklyn NY 11201-1818

TRAGER, MICHAEL DAVID, lawyer; b. N.Y.C., Feb. 15, 1959; s. Philip and Ina (Shulkin) T.; m. Mariella Gonzalez, Sept. 12, 1987; children: Nicholas, Alexander. BA, Wesleyan U., Middletown, Conn., 1981; JD, Boston U., 1985. Bar: Mass. 1985, Conn. 1986, Fla. 1988, D.C. 1989. Staff atty. enforcement divsn. Securities & Exchange Com., Washington, 1985-87; assoc. Morgan, Lewis & Bockius, Miami, Fla., 1987-88; participating assoc. Fulbright & Jaworski, Washington, 1989-92; ptnr. Trager & Trager, Washington, 1992-93; of counsel Fulbright & Jaworski, Washington, 1993-94, ptnr., 1995—. Bd. dirs. Jewish Nat. Fund-Mid-Atlantic Region, 1993—. Mem. ABA (bus. law sect. fed. regulation securities com. and civil litigation and SEC enforcement matters subcom., litigation sect. securities litigation com. and SEC enforcement subcom., class action and derivative litigation com. and securities litigation subcom.), D.C. Bar (corp., fin. and securities law sect. corp. counsel and planning group for broker-dealer programs 1992-94, broker-dealer regulation com.), Mass. Bar, Fla. Bar, Conn. Bar. Office: Fulbright & Jaworski 801 Pennsylvania Ave NW Washington DC 20004-2615

TRAGER, PHILIP, photographer, lawyer; b. Bridgeport, Conn., Feb. 27, 1935; s. Bernard Harold and Mina (Rubenstein) T.; m. Ina Louise Shulkin, Sept. 2, 1957; children: Michael, Julie. B.A., Wesleyan U., Middletown, Conn., 1956; J.D., Columbia U., 1960. Bar: Conn. 1960, N.Y. 1981, U.S. Supreme Ct. 1963. With Trager & Trager, P.C., Fairfield, Conn., 1960—. One-man shows Wesleyan U. Davison Art Ctr., 1970, 74, 81, 87, 92, Balt. Mus. Art, 1977, Mus. City of N.Y., 1980, Witkin Gallery, 1973, 80, 86, Jacobs Pillow, 1992, 93, Drew U., 1993, Recontres Internationales de Photographie, Arles, France, 1994, Mus. Photog. Arts, 1994, Photog. Resource Ctr., Boston, 1995; exhibited in group shows, including Yale U. Art Gallery, 1979, Santa Barbara (Calif.) Mus. Art, 1979, Internat. Ctr. Photography, 1987, N.Y. State Mus., Albany, 1982, Bklyn. Mus., 1989, Bibliothèque Nationale, Paris, 1982, NYU, 1985; represented in permanent collections Balt. Mus. Art, Corcoran Gallery Art, Met. Mus. Art, Mus. Modern Art, New Orleans Mus. Art, Yale U. Gallery Art; author: Echoes of Silence, 1972, Photographs of Architecture, 1980 (Book of Yr., Am. Inst. Graphic Arts), Wesleyan Photographs, 9182, The Villas Palladio, 1986, Dancers, 1992, Persen Lone, 1995. Bd. dirs. Bridgeport Hosp., 1985-95, Bridgeport Hosp. Found., 1993-95, New Eng. Found. for Arts, 1988-95. Recipient Lay Person award Conn. Soc. Architects, 1980; recipient Disting. Alumnus award Wesleyan U., 1981. Mem. ABA, Conn. Bar Assn. Home: 20 Rolling Ridge Rd Fairfield CT 06430-2254 Office: Trager and Trager PC 1305 Post Rd Fairfield CT 06430-6016

TRAGER, WILLIAM, biology educator; b. Newark, Mar. 20, 1910; s. Leon and Anna (Emilfork) T.; m. Ida Sosnow, June 16, 1935; children—Leslie, Carolyn, Lillian. B.S., Rutgers U., 1930, Sc.D. (hon.), 1965; M.A., Harvard U., 1931, Ph.D., 1933; Sc.D. (hon.), Rockefeller U., 1987. Fellow Rockefeller U., N.Y.C., 1934-35, mem. faculty, 1935—, assoc. prof., 1950-64, prof. biology, 1964-81, prof. emeritus, 1981—; guest investigator West African Inst. Trypanosomiasis Research, 1958-59, Nigerian Inst. Trypanosomiasis Research, 1973-74; vis. prof. Fla. State U., 1962, U. P.R. Med. Sch., 1963, U. Mex. Med. Sch., 1965; mem. study sect. parasitology and tropical medicine Nat. Inst. Allergy and Infectious Diseases, 1954-58, 67-70, mem. tng. grant com., 1961-64, mem. microbiology and infectious diseases adv. com., 1978-79; mem. malaria commn. Armed Forces Epidemiol. Bd., 1965-73; mem. study group parasitic diseases Walter Reed Army Inst. Research, 1977-79; chmn. sci. adv. council Liberian Inst. Tropical Medicine, 1965-66; rapporteur 6th, 7th Congresses Tropical Medicine; pres. Am. Found. for Tropical Medicine, 1966-69; mem. steering com. Malaria Immunology Group, WHO, 1977-80; cons. WHO, Bangkok, 1978, Panama, 1979, Shanghai, 1979; hon. pres. Asia and Pacific Conf. on Malaria, 1985. Author: Symbiosis, 1970, Living Together: The Biology of Animal Parasitism, 1986; editor Jour. Protozoology, 1954-65; contbr. articles on insect physiology and exptl. parasitology to profl. jours. Served to capt. AUS, 1943-45. Recipient Leuckart medal Deutsche Gesellschaft fur Parasitologie, 1982, First Rameshwardas Birla Internat. award in Medicine, 1982, Darling medal WHO, Manson medal Royal Soc. Tropical Medicine and Hygiene, 1986, Prince Mahidol award in Med. Sci., 1994; fellow NRC, 1933-34, Guggenheim Found., 1973-74, Avivah Zuckerman fellow Kuvin Ctr. Infections and Tropical Diseases, Hebrew U., 1982. Fellow AAAS, N.Y. Acad. Scis.; mem. Nat. Acad. Scis., Am. Soc. Parasitologist (council 1956-57, v.p. 1973, pres. 1974), Soc. Protozoologists (pres. 1960-61), Am. Soc. Tropical Medicine and Hygiene (pres. 1978-79, Le Prince medal 1991). Office: Rockefeller U York Ave At 66th St New York NY 10021

TRAGOS, GEORGE EURIPEDES, lawyer; b. Chgo., July 15, 1949; s. Euripedes G. and Eugene G. (Gatziolis) T.; m. Donna Marie Thalassites, Nov. 18, 1978; children: Louise, Gina, Peter. BA, Fla. State U., 1971, JD, 1974; Bar: Fla., U.S. Dist. Ct. (mid., so. dists.) Fla., U.S. Dist. Ct. (we. dist.) Tenn., U.S. Ct. Appeals (5th, 11th cirs.). Legis. aide Fla. Ho. of Reps., 1972-73, tax analyst tax and fin. com., 1973-74; chief, felony asst. states atty. State of Fla., Clearwater, 1974-78; partner firm Case, Kimpton, Tragos & Burke, P.A., Clearwater Beach, 1978-83; chief criminal div. U.S. Atty.'s Office for Middle Dist. Fla., Tampa, 1983-85; lead trial asst. Pres. Organized Crime Task Force, Tampa, 1985; sole practice, Clearwater, 1985—. Contbr. articles to profl. jours. and frequent lectr. Mem. Clearwater Bar (pres. 1994), Fla. Bar Assn. (chmn. fed. practice com. 1986, treas. exec. coun. criminal law sect., chmn. bar evidence com. 1990), Fla. Assn. Criminal Def. Lawyers (pres. 1991), Fla. Acad. Trial Lawyers, Am. Trail Lawyers Assn., Fla. State U. Alumni Assn. Law Sch., (bd. dirs.), Tampa Bay Fed. Bar Assn. (v.p. 1989), Clearwater Beach Jaycees (pres. 1979), Fla. U. Gold Key Club (pres. 1972), Ahepa. Democrat. Mem. Greek Orthodox Ch. Avocations: boating, tennis. Office: 600 Cleveland St Ste 700 Clearwater FL 33755-4158

TRAICOFF, GEORGE, college president; b. Elyria, Ohio, May 16, 1932; s. George and Lena (Szaroff) T.; m. Diane C. Schneider, Dec. 28, 1965; children: George Scott, Paula Jane, Amy Jo. BS, Miami U., Oxford, Ohio, 1954; MEd, Kent State U., 1959; EdD, Ind. U., 1967. Tchr. bus. LaGrange (Ohio) High Sch., 1956-57, Elyria High Sch., 1956-57; instr., coord. Ind. U., 1959-60, Ohio State U., 1960-63; prof., head dept. No. Mich. U., Marquette, 1963-66, dir. program gen. studies, 1966-67; dean community svcs. Cuyahoga Community Coll., Cleve., 1967-73; pres. North Shore Community Coll., Danvers, Mass., 1973—; pres. New Eng. Jr. Community and Tech. Coll. Coun.; vice chmn. regional employment bd. Pvt. Industry Coun.; bd. dirs. Century Bank and Trust Co. With U.S. Army, 1954-56. Mem. Am. Assn. Community and Jr. Colls., Nat. Coun. Community Svcs. (past pres.), Mass. Adminstrs. Community Colls., Mass. Community Coll. Assn. (treas.). Episcopalian. Office: North Shore Community Coll 1 Ferncroft Rd Danvers MA 01923-4017

TRAIN, HARRY DEPUE, II, retired naval officer; b. Washington, Nov. 5, 1927; s. Harold Cecil and May (Philipps) T.; m. Catharine Peck Kinnear, July 8, 1950; children: Louise Lucas, Catharine Philipps, Elizabeth Langdon, Cecilia Spencer. B.S., U.S. Naval Acad., 1949. Commd. ensign U.S. Navy, 1949, advanced through grades to adm., 1978; comdr. Cruiser-Destroyer Flotilla 8, 1971-72; dir. internat. security affairs East Asia and Pacific Region Office Asst. Sec. Def., 1972-73; dir. Systems Analysis Div., Office Chief Naval Ops., 1973-74; dir. joint staff Orgn. Joint Chiefs of Staff, 1974-76; comdr. U.S. 6th Fleet, 1976-78; comdr.-in-chief U.S. Atlantic Fleet and supreme allied comdr. Atlantic, 1978-82, ret., 1982; mgr. Hampton Rds. Ops., Sci. Applications Internat. Corp.; bd. dirs. Aydin Corp.; bd. trustees Inst. for Def. Analyses. Bd. dirs. Am. Cancer Soc., Inc. Decorated D.S.M. with 3 gold stars, Def. Disting. Svc. medal, Legion of Merit with 3 gold stars, Meritorious Svc. medal, Joint Svcs. Commendation medal, Navy Commendation medal; comdr. Order Republic of Tunisia; Order Naval Merit Brazil; Pedro Campbell medal Uruguay; Order of Pres. of Republic Chile; decorated Portuguese Mil. Order Christ; Netherlands Order Orange-Nassau; German Order Merit; French Legion of Honor; Colombian Naval Order Admiral Padilla; Mex. Order Spl. Merit; sr. fellow Flag and Gen. Officers Course, Nat. Def. U. Mem. U.S. Naval Inst., Coun. on Fgn. Rels., Def. Sci. Study Group (sr. mentor). Clubs: Columbia Country (Chevy Chase, Md.), Town Point (chmn. bd. govs.). Home: # 10 401 College Pl Norfolk VA 23510

TRAIN, JOHN, investment counselor, writer, government official; b. N.Y.C., May 25, 1928; s. Arthur Cheney and Helen (Coster) T.; m. Maria Teresa Cini di Pianzano, 1961 (div. 1976); children: Helen, Nina, Lisa; m. Frances Cheston, July 23, 1977. BA magna cum laude, Harvard U., 1950, MA, 1951. Founder, mng. editor Paris Rev., 1952-54; staff Asst. Sec. Army, Washington, 1954-56; assoc. de Vegh & Co., 1956-58; chmn. Train, Smith Counsel (and predecessor firms), N.Y.C., 1958-94, chmn. emeritus, 1995—; co-chmn., then dir. ICAP, S.A., Athens, 1964—; chmn. Montrose Advisors, N.Y.C., 1992—; pres. Chateau Malescasse, Lamarque-Margaux, Bordeaux, France, 1970-81; columnist Forbes mag., 1977-83, Harvard mag., 1983-95, Wall St. Jour., 1984—, Worth Mag., Boston, 1991-93, Town and Country mag., 1994-95, Fin. Times, London, 1994—; bd. dirs. African Devel. Found., Washington, 1988-94; bd. dirs. Bulgarian-Am. Enterprise Fund, Washington, Genesis Funds, London, Internat. Rescue Com., N.Y.C.; bd. govs. East-West Ctr., Hawaii, 1993-96; overseer Nat. Endowment for Democracy Internat. Forum for Democratic Studies, 1995—. Author: Dance of the Money Bees, 1973, Remarkable Names, 1977, Even More Remarkable Names, 1979, Remarkable Occurrences, 1978, Remarkable Words, 1980, The Money Masters, 1980, Remarkable Relatives, 1971, Preserving Capital and Making it Grow, 1983, Famous Financial Fiascos, 1984, John Train's Most Remarkable Names, 1985, The Midas Touch, 1987, The New Money Masters, 1989, Valsalva's Maneuver, 1989, John Train's Most Remarkable Occurences, 1990, Wit, 1991, Love, 1993, The Craft of Investing, 1994, Crazy Quilt, 1996; contbr. articles to profl. publs. Chmn. Italian Emergency Relief Com., 1976-77; pres. Afghanistan Relief Com., 1986-95; trustee Harvard Lampoon, Cambridge, Mass., 1974-90, World Monuments Fund, 1988-92; chmn. Free Elections Project, 1990, Brit. Mus. Nat. Hist. Internat. Trust, 1990—; trustee Am. U. Bulgaria, 1996—. With U.S. Army, 1954-56. Decorated commendatore Ordine del Merito della Repubblica, commendatore Ordine Della Solidarieta, medal Provincia di Udine (Italy); recipient Disting. Grotonian award, 1996. Mem. Order Colonial Lords of Manors, The Pilgrims, Century Club, Racquet and Tennis Club, Met. Club (Washington), Brooks's Club (London), Beefsteak Club (London), Travellers Club (Paris). Office: 667 Madison Ave New York NY 10021-8029

TRAINA, ALBERT SALVATORE, publishing executive; b. Bklyn., Apr. 30, 1927; s. Salvatore and Guilia (LeBarbara) T.; m. Vail Devereux, June 27, 1957; children—Caroline Vail, Robert Brooks. B.S. (N.Y. State War Service scholar), Seton Hall U., 1950; postgrad., Columbia U., 1950-51; M.B.A., NYU, 1954. Circulation promotion advt. space salesman Fairchild Publs., N.Y.C., 1951-53; Eastern advt. mgr. Modern Bride mag. Ziff-Davis, N.Y.C., 1953-58; advt. mgr. Bride and Home mag. Hearst Mags., N.Y.C., 1958-60; pub. Bride and Home mag. Hearst Mags., 1960-64; pub. Sports Afield mag., 1964-65, Town and Country mag., 1965-67, Harpers Bazaar mag., 1967-70; pres., chief exec. officer Bartell Media Corp., 1970-74; pres. Ziff-Davis Mag. Network, 1974-76, group v.p., 1976-78; sr. v.p. Ziff-Davis Pub. Co., 1978-81; pres. Ziff-Davis Consumer Mag., 1981-85; exec. v.p. mags. CBS, N.Y.C., 1985; pres. Traina Assocs., N.Y.C., 1985—. Mem. Scarsdale Bi-Partisan Com., 1975-78; bd. dirs. Crane Berkeley Assn., 1978-88, pres., 1983-84; mem. nat. bd. dirs., chmn. comms. com., treas. Goodwill Industries of Am., 1979—, chmn. bd., 1988-92; bd. dirs. Goodwill Industries of N.Y., 1983—. With USNR, 1945-46. Mem. NYU Grad. Sch. Bus. Adminstrn. Alumni Assn., NYU Alumni Fedn. (comms. com. 1970-73), Fox Meadow Tennis Club (Scarsdale), Union League Club (N.Y.C.). Home: RR 1 Box 201 Chebeague Island ME 04017-9723

TRAINA, JEFFREY FRANCIS, orthopedic surgeon; b. Nagoya, Japan, Apr. 17, 1956; s. Vincent L. and Carol A. (Anselmo) T.; m. Kathy Traina, Oct. 7, 1981; children: Kristin, Kourtney. B in Gen. Studies, U. Mich., 1975; MD, So. Ill. U., 1978. Intern Emory U./Grady Meml. Hosp., Atlanta, 1978-79; resident Wake Forest U./N.C. Bapt. Hosp., Winston-Salem, N.C., 1979-83; orthopedic instr. Bowman-Gray Med. Sch., Salem, N.C., 1979-83; rsch. fellow Med. Sch. Harvard U., Boston, 1983-84; asst. prof. U. Tex. Med. Sch., Houston, 1984-86; clin. asst. prof. Coll. Medicine U. Ill., Peoria, 1987—; orthopedic surgeon U. Tex. Med. Sch., Houston, 1984-86, Orthopaedic Assocs., Peoria, 1986-89, Heartland Orthopedic Inst., Peoria, 1989-91, Assoc. Orthopaedic Surgeons, Ltd., Peoria, 1992—. Contbr. articles to profl. jours. Recipient Nat. Rsch. Svc. award, 1983; biomed. rsch. support grantee U. Tex., 1985. Mem. AMA, AAAS, N.Y. Acad. Scis., Orthopaedic Rsch. Soc., Peoria Med. Soc., Ill. State Med. Soc., Am. Acad. Orthopaedic Surgeons, Ill. Orthopaedic Soc., Assn. for Arthritic Hip and Knee Surgery, Bowman-Gray Orthopaedic Alumni Assn. Home: 5618 N Prospect Rd Peoria IL 61614-4324 Office: Assoc Orthopaedic Surgeons 2805 N Knoxville Ave Peoria IL 61604-2869

TRAINA, RICHARD PAUL, academic administrator; b. San Francisco, June 3, 1937; s. Frank Ignatius and Isabelle (Thomas) T.; m. Margaret Bradley Warner, June 6, 1959; children: Cristina Traina Hutchison, Michelle Traina Riecke, Matthew Warner, Michael Derek. B.A., U. Santa Clara, 1958; M.A., U. Calif.-Berkeley, 1960, Ph.D., 1964. Instr. history Wabash Coll., Crawfordsville, Ind., 1963-64, asst. prof., 1964-68, assoc. prof., 1968-74, dean, 1969-74; dean, prof. Franklin & Marshall Coll., Lancaster, Pa., 1974-81, acad. v.p., dean, 1981-84; pres. Clark U., Worcester, Mass., 1984—. Author: American Diplomacy and the Spanish Civil War, 1968; co-editor: (with A. Rappaport) Present in the Past, 1972. Mem. Orgns. of Am. Historians, Soc. for Values in Higher Edn. Democrat. Roman Catholic. Home: 130 Woodland St Worcester MA 01610-1370 Office: Clark U 950 Main St Worcester MA 01610-1400

TRAINA, VINCENT MICHAEL, pharmaceutical company executive; b. L.I., N.Y., May 8, 1943; s. John Joseph and Anne (Copertino) T.; m. Lynn R. Miko, Aug. 20, 1978; children: Allison, Kimberly, Brent. BA in Biology, Rutgers U., 1965, MS in Biology, 1970, PhD in Physiology, 1973. Diplomate Am. Bd. Toxicology. Research investigator in toxicology Squibb Inst., New Brunswick, N.J., 1966-74; mgr. toxicology Ciba-Geigy Corp., Summit, N.J., 1974-79, assoc. dir. toxicology and pathology, 1979-82, dir. toxicology, 1982-84, exec. dir. toxicology and pathology, 1984-88, v.p. toxicology/pathology, 1988-92; v.p. toxicology/pathology/metabolism Ciba-Geigy Corp., Summit, 1992; v.p. and head preclinical safety worldwide Ciba-Geigy Pharm. Div., Summit, 1992-96, Novantis Pharms., East Hanover, N.J., 1997—; mem. indsl. rels. and negotiation com. Ciba-Geigy Corp., Summit, 1986-92; faculty Residential Sch. of Medicinal Chemistry, Drew U., 1989—. Mem. Am. Coll. Toxicology, Soc. Toxicology, Environ. Mutagen Soc., Am. Inst. Biol. Scis., Soc. Sigma Xi. Republican. Roman Catholic. Avocations: finances, team sports. Office: Novantis Pharm Rte 10 East Hanover NJ 07936-1080

TRAINOR, BERNARD EDMUND, retired military officer; b. N.Y.C., Sept. 2, 1928; s. Joseph Patrick and Ann Veronica (Whelan) T.; m. Margaret Ann Hamilton, June 13, 1959; children: Kathleen Marie, Theresa Ann, Eileen Cecile, Claire Hamilton. BS, Coll. of Holy Cross, 1951; MA, U. Colo., 1963, postgrad., 1970—; ed., Air War Coll., Montgomery, Ala., 1969-70. Commd. 2nd lt. USMC, 1951, advanced through grades to lt. gen., 1983; inf. comdr. USMC, Korea, 1952; assigned to USS Columbus USMC, 1953-55, mem. staff Marine Corps Hdqrs., 1955-58, with exch. office Royal Marine Commandos, 1958-59, inf. comdr. 1st Marine divsn., 1959-61; asst. prof. naval sci. U. Colo., Boulder, 1961-64; assigned to Marine Corps Command and Staff Coll., 1964-65; adv. Republic of Vietnam, 1965-66; instr. Marine Corps Command and Staff Coll., 1966-69; bn. comdr. Vietnam, 1970-71; staff officer Hdqrs. Marine Corps, Washington, 1970-71; dir. First Marine Corps Dist., N.Y.C., 1974-76; asst. depot comdr. Marine Corps Recruit Depot, Parris Island, S.C., 1976-78; dir. Edn. Ctr., Quantico, Va., 1978-81; dep. chief of staff for plans, policies and ops. Hdqrs. Marine Corps, 1981-85; cons., 1985—; mil. corr. N.Y. Times, 1986-90; dir. nat. security program Kennedy Sch. Govt. Harvard U., Cambridge, Mass., 1990-96, assoc. Ctr. Sci. and Internat. Affairs, 1996—; retired USMC, 1985. Author: History of the U.S. Marine Corps, 1968, The Generals' War, 1995; contbg. author: American Defense Annual, 1990, 2d edit., 1996, Defense Beat, 1991, After the Storm, 1992, The Almanac of Seapower, 1993, Newsmen and National Defense, 1991, Perspectives on Warfighting, 1992; mem. editl. adv. bd. Naval War Coll. Rev.; mem. editl. bd. Amphibious Warfare Rev.; contbr. articles to profl. jours. Mil. analyst NBC News; rsch. bd. dirs. Inst. for Fgn. Policy Analysis. Decorated D.S.M., Legion of Merit with combat V and two stars,

Bronze Star with combat V, Navy Commendation medal with two gold stars, others; recipient Anderson Meml. award Air War Coll., 1970. Mem. Naval Inst., Internat. Inst. Strategic Studies, Marine Corps Assn., Coun. Fgn. Rels., World Affairs Coun., Army-Navy Club. Roman Catholic. Home: 80 Potter Pond Lexington MA 02173-8250 Office: Harvard U Kennedy Sch Govt 79 JFK St Cambridge MA 02138-5801

TRAINOR, JOHN FELIX, retired economics educator; b. Mpls., Dec. 1, 1921; s. James Patrick and Myra Catherine (Pauly) T.; m. Margaret Dolores Pudenz, July 3, 1965 (dec. 1977); children: John Anthony, Patrick James. BA cum laude, Coll. St. Thomas, 1943; MA, U. Minn., 1950; PhD, Wash. State U., 1970. Instr. high sch. Mpls., 1946-47; instr. Coll. St. Thomas, 1949-50; v.p. Trainor Candy Co., Mpls., 1949-56; instr., asst. prof. econs. Rockhurst Coll., Kansas City, Mo., 1956-62; instr. Wash. State U., Pullman, 1966-67; asst. prof. Moorhead (Minn.) State U., 1967-70, assoc. prof. econs., 1971-87, prof. econ., 1988-89, chmn. dept. econs., 1981-89; prof. emeritus, 1989—. Author: (with Frank J. Kottke) The Nursing Home Industry in the State of Washington, 1968. Ensign to Lt. (j.g.) USNR, 1943-46, ETO. Mem. Minn. Econs. Assn. (pres. 1976-77), Assn. Social Econs., Omicron Delta Epsilon. Roman Catholic. Home: 1333 4th Ave S Moorhead MN 56560-2971

TRAISMAN, HOWARD SEVIN, pediatrician; b. Chgo., Mar. 18, 1923; s. Alfred Stanley and Sara (Sevin) T.; m. Regina Gallagher, Feb. 29, 1956; children—Barry D. Lifschultz, Edward S., Kenneth N. B.S. in Chemistry, Northwestern U., 1943, M.B., 1946, M.D., 1947. Intern Cook County Hosp., Chgo., 1946-47; resident in pediatrics Children's Meml. Hosp., Chgo., 1949-51; attending physician div. endocrinology Children's Meml. Hosp., 1951—; mem. faculty Northwestern U. Med. Sch., 1951—, prof. pediatrics, 1973—. Author articles in field, chpts. in books. Served to capt. M.C. AUS, 1943-46, 47-49. Recipient Northwestern U. Alumni Merit award, 1995. Mem. Am. Diabetes Assn. (Disting. Service award 1976), Am. Pediatric Soc., Am. Acad. Pediatrics, Endocrine Soc., Lawson Wilkins Pediatric Endocrine Soc., AMA, Midwest Soc. Pediatric Research, Ill. Med. Soc., Chgo. Pediatric Soc., Chgo. Med. Soc., Inst. Medicine Chgo. Democrat. Jewish. Office: 1325 Howard St Evanston IL 60202-3766

TRAISTER, ROBERT EDWIN, naval officer, engineer; b. Haverhill, Mass., Sept. 15, 1937; s. Frank and Anne (Schlafman) T.; m. Janet Weinberger; children: James, Jeffrey. Student, Bowdoin Coll., 1955-56; BS, U.S. Naval Acad., Annapolis, Md., 1960; MSME, U.S. Naval Postgrad. Sch., Monterey, Calif., 1967. Commd. ensign USN, 1960, advanced through grades to rear adm., 1988; surface warfare officer, chief engr. USS William R. Rush, 1962-64; ship supt. Puget Sound Naval Shipyard, Bremerton, Wash., 1969-72, shipbuilding/repair/prodns. officer, 1982-86; chief engr. USS Springfield, USS Little Rock, 1972-75; trials officer Office Comdr. Naval Sea Systems, DD963 PRGM, Washington, 1975-78; comdg. officer Pearl Harbor (Hawaii) Naval Shipyard, 1986-88; maintenance officer Office Comdr. in Chief Pacific Fleet, Pearl Harbor, 1988-90; dep. comdr. surface ships Naval Sea Systems Command, Washington, 1990-94; dir. projects and site svcs. Westinghouse Hanford Corp., Richland, Wash., 1994-96; mgr. def. and space group Boeing, 1996—. Decorated Legion of Merit. Mem. Am. Soc. Naval Engrs. Assn., Am. Def. Preparedness Assn. (bd. dirs. 1990-92), U.S. Naval Acad. Alumni Assn. (pres. 1989-90), Bowdoin Coll. Alumni Assn. Address: 2786 142d Pl NE Bellevue WA 98007

TRAKAS, GEORGE, sculptor; b. Quebec, Canada, May 11, 1944. Attended, Brookly Mus. Art Sch., N.Y.; BS, Hunter Coll, NYU. Speaker in field. Commissioned works Omaha Opportunities Industln. Ctr., Nat. Oceanic and Atmospheric Admin., Seattle; group exhibitions include Pier 18, N.Y.C., Mus. Mod. Art, N.Y.C., 1971, Guggenheim Mus. (Theodoron awards), N.Y.C., 1971, Walker Art Ctr., Minpls., Minn., 1977. Biennial, Whitney Mus. Art, N.Y.C., 1979, San Diego Mus. Contemporary Art, La Jolla, Calif, 1989, La Mus. Humlebaek, Denmark, 1989, Le Pont d'Epee au Cruex de l'Enfer, Thiers, France, 1989, Todd Terr., Wash. State U., Pullman, 1990, Quint Krichman Projects, San Diego, Calif., 1992, others. Recipient NEA fellowship, 1979, Guggenheim, 1983, Amer. Acad. Arts and Letters merit award, 1996. Address: PO Box 395 Canal St Station New York NY 10013-0395*

TRAMMELL, HERBERT EUGENE, physicist, laboratory executive; b. Laurel, Miss., Apr. 19, 1927; s. Homer Lee and Evie Louisa (Breazeale) T.; m. Jane Walker, Dec. 28, 1948; children—Carmen, Bert, Lisa, Brian. B.A. in Physics, U. Miss., 1947, M.A., 1948. With Nuclear div. Union Carbide, Oak Ridge, 1949-89, mgr. barrier devel. programs, 1967-69, dir. gaseous diffusion devel. div., 1969-77; dir. engring. tech. div. Oak Ridge Nat. Lab., 1977-89, ret., 1989; with Martin Marietta Energy Systems, 1983-89. Bd. dirs. Emory Valley Sch. for Retarded Children, 1962-68, v.p., 1966-68; mem. Tenn. Med. Malpractice Rev. Bd., 1974-80; active PTA. Served with U.S. Navy, 1944-45. Methodist. Club: Rotary (pres. 1980-81). Home: 901 Johnson St Key West FL 33040-4745

TRAMONTE, MICHAEL ROBERT, school psychologist. AB in Sociology, Boston Coll., 1960; EdM, Boston State Coll., 1963; Cert. Advanced Edn. Specialization, Boston Coll., 1971; Comprehensive Cert. in Paralegal Studies, Bentley Coll., 1982; EdD in Human Devel. and Edn., Boston U., 1986. Lic. psychologist; cert. health svc. provider, Mass.; lic. ednl. psychologist, Mass.; lic. cert. social worker, Mass.; cert. secondary sch. social studies tchr., moderate spl. needs tchr., sch. psychologist, supt., asst. supt., guidance counselor, supr., dir., secondary sch. prin., Mass.; nat. cert. sch. psychologist; cert. sch. psychologist, N.H. Substitute tchr. Medford (Mass.) Pub. Schs., 1960-61, jr. H.S. tchr. social studies, 1961-68; instr. psychology and edn. Anna Maria Coll., 1968-69; adj. instr. psychology Mass. Bay C.C., 1972-80, Middlesex C.C., 1977—; sch. psychologist Lowell (Mass.) Pub. Schs., 1970—; lectr. edn. Rivier Coll., 1983, 87—; spkr. in field. Chmn. Medford chpt. Greater Boston Assn. Retarded Children, 1969-70; vol. spkr. support groups Mass. chpt. Nat. Multiple Sclerosis Soc., 1971-88. Recipient awards Medford Mental Health Assn., 1968, Medford chpt. Greater Boston Assn. Retarded Children, 1970, Mass. chpt. Nat. Multiple Sclerosis Soc., 1979, Faculty award for Secondary Edn., Rivier Coll., 1994. Home: 24 Erie St Woburn MA 01801

TRAMONTINE, JOHN ORLANDO, lawyer; b. Iron Mountain, Mich., Sept. 21, 1932; s. Orlando F. and Susan M. (Hollar) T.; m. Nancy A. McCabe, July 14, 1956; 1 child, Margaret A. BSChemE, U. Notre Dame, 1955; postgrad., Georgetown U., 1956-58; LLB, NYU, 1960. Bar: N.Y. 1960, U.S. Dist. Ct. (no. dist.) Ill. 1963, U.S. Dist. Ct. (so. and ea. dists.) N.Y. 1965, U.S. Ct. Appeals (2d and 5th cirs.) 1967, U.S. Supreme Ct. 1970, U.S. Ct. Appeals (8th cir.) 1970, (3d cir.) 1973, (7th cir.) 1976, (fed. cir.) 1979, U.S. Dist. Ct. (we. dist.) N.Y. 1981. Examiner U.S. Patent Office, 1956-58; patent agt. Arthur, Dry & Dole, N.Y.C., 1958-60; assoc. Arthur, Dry, Kalish, Taylor & Wood, N.Y.C., 1960-62, Wolfe, Hubbard, Voit & Osann, Chgo., 1962-63; assoc. Fish & Neave, N.Y.C., 1963-70, ptnr., 1970—. 2nd lt. USMCR, 1955. Fellow Am. Coll. Trial Lawyers, Am. Bar Found.; mem. ABA, Assn. of Bar of City of N.Y. (chmn. patent com. 1974-77), Fed. Cir. Bar Assn., N.Y. Intellectual Property Law Assn. (pres. 1985-86), St. Andrews Golf Club (sec. 1981-83). Office: Fish & Neave 1251 Avenue Of The Americas New York NY 10020-1104

TRAMUTOLA, JOSEPH LOUIS, lawyer, educator; b. Union City, N.J., Mar. 6, 1931; s. Joseph Emil and Elda (Brioli) T.; m. Mary Ann Banull, Sept. 4, 1965; children Karen, Kim, Karla. BA, St. Peter's Coll., Jersey City, 1953; JD, Fordham U., 1959. Bar: N.J. 1961. Atty. Toolan, Haney, Romand, Perth Amboy, N.J., 1959-65; prof. law Fairleigh Dickinson U., Madison, N.J., 1965—, creator, dir. ednl. program for older persons, 1972—; cons. Thomas Edison Coll., Trenton, N.J., 1976—, Chartered Pub. Underwriters, East Orange, N.J., 1976-81; adj. faculty U. Mich., 1976-77; dir. Fairleigh Dickinson U. Patent Inst., 1965-71; seminar dir. student law, Calif., Ill., Mass., N.Y., Ga. Author: Guided Book for Student Rights, 1976, Legal Perspective for Student Personal Administration, 1977, Legal Rights of the New Student, 1978; dir. CPA Law Rev., 1966-82. With U.S. Army, 1955-57. Named Outstanding Educator Outstanding Educators Inc., 1973, 1974, Commendation for Civic Contb. N.J. Legis., 1993. Roman Catholic. Avocations: photography, clock making, gardening, zymology, music. Home: 12 Brownings Ct Mendham NJ 07945-3301 Office: Fairleigh Dickinson U 285 Madison Ave Madison NJ 07940-1006

TRAN, HENRY BANG Q., social work case manager; b. Binh Dinh, Vietnam, Dec. 28, 1952; came to U.S., 1975; s. Mau Dinh and Ho Thi Tran; m. Thuhong T. Ngo; children: John, Michael, Robert, Richard, Jennifer. BA, Northeastern Ill. U., 1977, MA, 1978. Cert. social worker, real estate broker. Social worker Tex. Dept. Human Svcs., Houston, 1980-96; founder, pres. Texo Properties, Inc., Houston, 1984-85; pres. N.E.W.S. Properties, Houston, 1985—; case mgr. Tex. Workforce Commn., 1996—; instr. math. City Colls. Chgo., 1977, Vietnamese lang. U. Houston, 1985. V.p. Buddhist Assn. for Services of Humanity in Am., Houston, 1985—; pres. Quang Trung Mut. Assistance Assn., Houston, 1984—. Fellow U. Miami, 1979. Mem. Nat. Assn. Realtors, Tex. Pub. Employee Assn., Dalat U. Alumni Assn., Asia Soc., Houston Vietnam Lions Club (pres. 1991). Avocations: tennis, soccer, jogging.

TRAN, LONG TRIEU, industrial engineer; b. Saigon, Vietnam, Oct. 10, 1956; came to U.S., 1973; s. Nguyen Dinh and Thiet Thi (Nguyen) T.; m. Khanh Thi-Hong Phan, Aug. 3, 1988. BS in Mech. Engring. with honors, U. Kans., 1976; MS in Mech. Engring., MIT, 1980; MBA in Bus. Adminstrn. with honors, U. Louisville, 1993. Cert. quality engr.; cert. mfg. engr.; cert. project mgmt. profl. Tchg. asst. U. Kans., 1975-76, U. Calif., Berkeley, 1977; rsch. asst. Lawrence Berkeley Labs., 1977, MIT, 1977-80; libr. staff Harvard U. Med. Sch. Libr., 1977-78; mem. staff New England Deaconess Hosp., Boston, 1978-80; prodn. programming engr. GE, Cleve., 1980-81; advanced mfg. engr. GE, Louisville, 1981-82, quality sys. engr., 1982-84, quality control engr., 1984-86, sr. quality info. equipment engr., 1986-89, sr. quality indsl. engr., 1990-94, sr. supplier tech. assistance engr., 1995-96, sr. advanced supplier quality engr., 1996—; exec. advisor Jr. Achievement Inc., Louisville, 1983-84; monitor/reader Rec. for the Blind, 1994—; fundraiser The Dream Factory Inc., 1994—. Vol. NCCJ, 1994—, Clothe-A-Child, 1993—, Dare-To-Care, 1994—, Ronald McDonald House, 1994—. Mem. AAAS, ASME, Am. Soc. Quality Control, Computer and Automated Sys. Assn. (charter), Am. Prodn. and Inventory Control Soc., Robot Inst. Am., Robotics Internat. (charter), Soc. Mfg. Engrs. (sr.), Instrument Soc. Am. (sr.), Am. Mgmt. Assn., N.Y. Acad. Scis., Internat. Platform Assn., Indsl. Computing Soc. (founding), Project Mgmt. Inst., Nat. Pks. Conservation Assn., U.S. Libr. Congress Assocs. (founding), Sigma Xi, Pi Tau Sigma, Tau Beta Pi, Phi Kappa Phi, Beta Gamma Sigma. Republican. Achievements include research on grinding processes and material surface analysis, also manufacturing project management. Home: 3423 Brookhollow Dr Louisville KY 40220-5009 Office: GE AP2-117 Louisville KY 40225

TRAN, TOAN VU, electronics engineer; b. Saigon, Vietnam, June 18, 1956; came to U.S., 1981; s. Kham The Tran and Bac Thi Vu; m. Mong Huyen Vu Nguyen, Oct. 27, 1992; 1 child, Alexander Phiet The. AA, Fla. Community Coll., 1983; BS in Elec. Engring. with honors, U. Fla., 1986. Quality control technician Medfusion System, Inc., Duluth, Ga., 1988; instrumentation specialist Emory U., Atlanta, 1988-89; electronics engr. Dept. Def., Security Operational Test Site, Ft. McClellan, Ala., 1989-95, Nav. Air Warfare Ctr. Tng. Sys. Divsn., Orlando, Fla., 1995—. Avocations: travel, tennis, guitar. Home: 123 Blue Creek Dr Winter Springs FL 32708-5501

TRANI, EUGENE PAUL, academic administrator, educator; b. Bklyn., Nov. 2, 1939; s. Frank Joseph and Rose Gertrude (Kelly) T.; m. Lois Elizabeth Quigley, June 2, 1962; children: Anne Chapman, Frank. BA in History with honors, U. Notre Dame, 1961; MA, Ind. U., 1963, PhD, 1966. Instr. history Ohio State U., Columbus, 1965-67; asst. prof. So. Ill. U., Carbondale, 1967-71, assoc. prof., 1971-75, prof., 1975-76; asst. v.p. acad. affairs, prof. U. Nebr., 1976-80; prof., vice chancellor acad. affairs U. Mo. Kansas City, 1980-86; prof., v.p. acad. affairs U. Wis. System, 1986-90; pres. Va. Commonwealth U., 1990—; pres., bd. dirs. Va. Biotechnology Rsch. Park, 1992—; vis. asst. prof. U. Wis. Milw., 1969; bd. dirs. Crestar Bank Richmond Met. Bd., Crestar Fin. Corp., Lawyers Title Corp., Innovative Tech. Authority; cons. various univ. presses, jours., govtl. agys.; advisor gov. La., Okla. State Regents Higher Edn.; mem. commn. Internat. Edn. Am. Coun. Higher Ed., 1991—; bd. gov. Ctr. Russian Am. Bus., Washington, 1993—; bd. advisors Inst. for U.S. Studies, I. London, 1993—; adv. coun. mem. Coun. on Grad. Studies and Rsch., U. Notre Dame, 1994—. Author, editor: Concerns of a Conservative Democrat, 1968, The Treaty of Portsmouth: An Adventure in American Diplomacy, 1969, The Secretaries of the Department of the Interior, 1849-69, 1975, (with David Wilson) The Presidency of Warren G. Harding, 3d edit., 1989; contbr. articles to profl. jours., newspapers; book reviewer. Permanent mem. Coun. Fgn. Rels., N.Y.C., 1979—; bd. dirs. Richmond Ballet, 1991—, NCCJ, Richmond, 1991—, Va. Spl. Olympics, 1991—, YMCA of Greater Richmond, 19926, Richmond Renaissance, 1992—, Met. Found., 1992-95; mem. U.S. Savs. Bond Vol. Com., chmn. higher edn. area, 1992, 93; adv. bd. Greater Richmond chpt. ARC, 1992—. Fellow Russian and East European Inst., 1964-65, Nat. Hist. Publs. Commn., 1969-70, Woodrow Wilson Internat. Ctr. Scholars, 1972-73, So. Ill. U. Sabbatical Leave, 1975-76, Coun. Internat. Exchange Scholars, 1981, U. Mo. Faculty, 1981; grantee U.S. Dept. Interior Rsch., 1965, 66, So. Ill. U. Office Rsch. and Projects, 1967-74, Am. Philos. Soc., 1968, 72, So. Ill U. Summer Rsch. 1970, 72, 75, Lilly Endowment, 1975-76, Sloan Commn. Govt. and Higher Edn., 1978, U.S. Info. Agy. Am. Participants Program, 1984, 85, 86, 88, 90; recipient Younger Humanist award NEH, 1972-73, Leadership and Achievement award Ctrl. Richmond Assn., 1992. Mem. Internat. Inst. Strategic Studies, Am. Assn. Advancement Slavic Studies, Orgn. Am. Historians, Soc. Historians Am. Fgn. Rels., Met. Richmond C. of C. (bd. dirs. 1991—), Va. Ctr. for Innovative Tech., Ctrl. Richmond Assn. (leadership award, 1992), Phi Kappa Phi. Roman Catholic. Avocations: reading, travel, basketball, golf. Office: Va Commonwealth U Box 842512 910 W Franklin St Richmond VA 23284-2512*

TRANK, DOUGLAS MONTY, rhetoric and speech communications educator; b. Lincoln, Nebr., Sept. 8, 1944; s. Walter John and Hazel Elaine (Stegeman) T.; children: Heather Nicole, Jessica Celeste; m. Christine Marie Quinn, 1992. BA in English, U. Nebr., Kearney, 1967, MS in Comm., 1970; PhD in Comm., U. Utah, 1973. Tchr. Ogallala (Nebr.) High Sch., 1967-70; teaching fellow in communications U. Utah, Salt Lake City, 1970-72; prof. communications Old Dominion U., Norfolk, Va., 1972-74; prof. rhetoric and edn. U. Iowa, Iowa City, 1974—, chmn. rhetoric dept., 1984-89; chmn. bd. control athletics, faculty senate, mem. ednl. policy com., faculty adv. com., faculty assembly, exec. com. U. Iowa. Author book, chpts. books, monographs; editor Communication Edn., 1993-96; assoc. editor Communication Studies; contbr. articles to profl. jours. Recipient Admiral award Ace Adventures, Inc., Iowa, 1987, Hemingway prize, 1992. Mem. Speech Communication Assn., Iowa Communication Assn. (pres. 1980-82, editor 1977-81, mem. jour. editorial bd.), Cen. States Communication Assn. (pres. 1990-91), Fedn. Iowa Speech Orgns. (pres. 1977-79), Iowa City Optimist Club (dir. 1982-89, pres. 1987-88). Democrat. Avocations: ice sailing, hunting, fishing, canoeing. Office: U Iowa Dept Rhetoric Iowa City IA 52242

TRANQUADA, ROBERT ERNEST, medical educator, physician; b. Los Angeles, Aug. 27, 1930; s. Ernest Alvro and Katharine (Jacobus) T.; m. Janet Martin, Aug. 31, 1951; children: John Martin, James Robert, Katherine Anne. B.A., Pomona Coll., 1951; M.D., Stanford U., 1955; D.Sc. (hon.), Worcester Poly. Inst., 1985. Diplomate Am. Bd. Internal Medicine. Intern in medicine UCLA Med. Center, 1955-56, resident in medicine, 1956-57; resident Los Angeles VA Hosp., 1957-58; fellow in diabetes and metabolic diseases UCLA, 1958-59; fellow in diabetes U. So. Calif., 1959-60, asst. prof. medicine, 1960-63, assoc. prof., 1964-68, chmn. dept. community medicine, 1967-70; med. dir. Los Angeles County/U. So. Calif. Med. Center, 1969-74; regional dir. Central Region, Los Angeles County Dept. Health Services, 1974-76; assoc. dean UCLA Sch. Medicine, 1976-79; chancellor and dean U. Mass. Med. Sch., 1979-86; dean U. So. Calif. Sch. Medicine, 1986-91; prof. medicine U. So. Calif., L.A., 1986-92, Norman Topping/Nat. Med. Enterprises prof. med./pub. policy, 1992-97; prof. emeritus, 1997—. mem., chair L.A. County Task Force on Health Care Access, 1992-94. Trustee Pomona Coll., 1969—, vice chmn., 1987-91, chmn., 1991—; mem. bd. fellow Claremont U. Ctr., 1971-79, 91—; bd. trustees Grad. Inst. Applied Life Scis., Claremont U., 1997—, vice-chmn., 1997—; corporator Worcester Art Mus., 1980-86; bd. dirs. Nat. Med. Fellowships, Inc., 1973—, chmn., 1980-85; trustee Charles Drew U. Med. and Sci., 1968-79, 86-95, Orthopaedic Hosp., 1986-91, Barlow Hosp., 1987-89; bd. dirs. Worcester Acad., 1984-86, U. So. Calif. Univ. Hosp., 1988-91, Alliance for Childrens Rights, 1991-95; bd. dirs. Good Hope Med. Found., 1994—; mem. Ind. Commn. on L.A. Police Dept., 1991-92; mem. governing bd. L.A. County Local Initiative Health Authority, 1994—. Milbank faculty fellow, 1967-72. Fellow AAAS, Am. Antiquarian Soc.; mem. AMA, Am. Diabetes Assn., Western Soc. Clin. Investigation, Los Angeles County Med. Assn., Los Angeles Acad. Medicine, Calif. Med. Assn., Inst. Medicine of Nat. Acad. Scis., Phi Beta Kappa, Sigma Xi, Alpha Omega Alpha. Office: U So Calif VKC # 368A Los Angeles CA 90089-0041

TRANSOU, LYNDA LEW, advertising art administrator; b. Atlanta, Dec. 11, 1949; d. Lewis Cole Transou and Ann Lynette (Taylor) Putnam; m. Lue Gregg Loso, Oct. 25, 1991. B.F.A. cum laude, U. Tex.-Austin, 1971. Art dir., The Pitluk Group, San Antonio, 1971, Campbell, McQuien & Lawson, Dallas, 1973-74, Bozell & Jacobs, Dallas, 1974-75; art dir., ptnr. The Assocs., Dallas, 1975-77; art dir. Belo Broadcasting, Dallas, 1977-80; creative dir., v.p. Allday & Assocs., Dallas, 1980-85; owner Lynda Transou Advt. & Design, 1986—. Recipient Merit award N.Y. Art Dirs. Show, 1980; Gold award Dallas Ad League, 1980, Silver award, 1980, Bronze award, 1981, 82, 2 Merit awards Houston Art Dirs. Club, 1978-86; Merit award Broadcast Designers Assn., 1980, 82; Merit awards Dallas Ad League, 1978, 87; Silver award Houston Art Dirs. Show; Gold award Tex. Pub. Relations Assn., 1982, 85; Gold award N.Y. One Show, 1982, Creativity award Art Direction mag., 1986, Print award Regional Design Annual, 1988, Telly Finalist, 1987. Mem. Am. Inst. Graphic Arts, Dallas Soc. Visual Communications (Bronze award 1980, Merit awards, 1978-86), Delta Gamma (historian 1969-70).

TRAPOLIN, FRANK WINTER, retired insurance executive; b. New Orleans, Jan. 29, 1913; s. John Baptiste and Florence Bertha (Winter) T.; BS in Econs., Loyola U. of South, New Orleans, 1935; cert. official U.S.A. Track & Field. m. Thelma Mae Mouledoux, Oct. 27, 1937; children: Timothy, Patricia Couret, Jane Oaksmith, Anne Britt. Agt., Godchaux & Mayer, New Orleans, 1935-42, 46-51; pres. Trapolin-Couret Ins. Agy., Inc., New Orleans, 1953-92, 92-93; v.p. Gillis, Ellis & Baker, Inc., New Orleans, 1993-94, ret., 1994; mem. faculty Loyola U.; TV lectr., seamanship instr. Coast Guard Aux., New Orleans Former pres. Cath. Human Rels. Commn. Greater New Orleans, Associated Cath. Charities New Orleans, Maryland Dr. Homeowners Assn., Loyola U. Alumni Assn.; former chmn. adv. bd. Ursuline Nuns New Orleans, New Orleans Juvenile Cts.; former scoutmaster Boy Scouts Am., former chmn. Boy Scout troop com.; former v.p. Cmty. Rels. Coun. Greater New Orleans, New Orleans Jr. C.of C., La. Interch. Conf.; former trustee United Fund Greater New Orleans Area; treas. emeritus La. Interchurch Conference, dir. emeritus Catholic Book Store Found., tng. officer 8th Coast Guard Dist. Aux.; former mem. adv. bd. Coll. Bus. Adminstrn., Loyola U., Mother-house of Sisters of Holy Family, Immaculate Conception Cath. Ch.; group captain Manresa Retreats, 1947—; former bd. dirs. St. John Berchman Orphanage, New Orleans Interfaith Conf., St. Elizabeth's Home for Girls, Cath. Book Store Found., Manresa Retreat House; adv. bd. New Orleans Track Club; founder, Serra Run for Vocations; bd. dirs. Audubon Blvd. Assn. Served with USN, 1942-46, 51-53, capt. Res. ret. Recipient Merit cert. City of New Orleans, 1972; Order of St. Louis, 1976; winner 80 and over category La. Sr. Olympics 5000 meter walk, 1995, 96; lector Catholic Ch., 1964-87; eucharistic min., 1986—. Mem. La. Assn. Ins. Agts., Nat. Assn. Ins. Agts., New Orleans Ins. Exch., Navy League, Mil. Order World Wars, Greater New Orleans Exec. Assn. (pres. 1985, named Exec. of the Year 1985, lifetime hon. mem.), New Orleans Photog. Soc., Sierra Club, Blue Key. Democrat. Roman Catholic. Clubs: Sertoma (pres. New Orleans 1955-56), Serra (pres. New Orleans 1973-74), Internat. House, New Orleans Track, Greater New Orleans Runners Assn., New Orleans Yacht, Pass Christian Yacht. Lodge: KC (4 deg.). Patentee gunnery, tng. and machinery devices for USN. Home: 119 Audubon Blvd New Orleans LA 70118-5538

TRAPP, FRANK ANDERSON, art educator; b. Pitts., June 13, 1922; s. Frank Louis and Mary (Anderson) T. BA, Carnegie Inst. Tech., 1943; AM, Harvard, 1947, Ph.D., 1952; AM (hon.), Amherst Coll., 1963. Teaching fellow Harvard (also resident tutor Adams House), 1948-51; mem. faculty Williams Coll., 1951-56; mem. faculty Amherst (Mass.) Coll., 1956-92, prof. art, 1963-92, William R. Mead prof., 1976-89, Arms prof., 1989-92, dir. Mead Art Mus., 1969-89; rsch. assoc. fine arts U. Pitts., 1994—; vis. Mellon prof. dept. fine arts U. Pitts., 1979-80. Author: The Attainment of Delacroix, 1970, Peter Blume, 1987, The Grand Tradition: British Art in the Amherst College Collection, 1988 (with others) Clarence Holbrook Carter, 1989; contbg. author and editor Mead Mus. Publs.; contbr. articles to profl. jours. Served with AUS, 1943-46, PTO. Fulbright grantee, 1949-50; Belgian-Am. Ednl. Found. fellow, 1954; Nat. Endowment for the Humanities sr. fellow, 1971-72. Home: 4609 Bayard St Apt 51 Pittsburgh PA 15213-2735

TRAPP, JAMES MCCREERY, lawyer; b. Macomb, Ill., Aug. 11, 1934. BA, Knox Coll., 1956; JD, U. Mich., 1961. Bar: Ill. 1961. Ptnr. McDermott, Will & Emery, Chgo. Chmn. Ill. Inst. Continuing Legal Edn., 1978-79, bd. dirs., 1980-86, pres., 1984-85. Fellow Am. Coll. Trust and Estate Coun. (Ill. chmn. 1980-83, nat. regent 1983—, treas. 1989-90, sec. 1990-91, v.p. 1991-92, pres.-elect 1992-93, pres. 1993-94, exec. com. 1986-94), Am. Bar Found., Ill. Bar Found.; mem. ABA, Ill. State Bar Assn., Chgo. Bar Assn. (chair trust law com. 1972-73, com. on coms. 1972-74), Internat. Acad. Estate and Trust Law, Am. Law Inst. (pres.), Chgo. Estate Planning Coun. Office: McDermott Will & Emery 227 W Monroe St Chicago IL 60606-5016

TRAPPE, JAMES MARTIN, mycologist; b. Spokane, Wash., Aug. 16, 1931; s. Martin Carl and Esther Louise (Koss) T.; m. Beverly Joan Reller, Dec. 27, 1963; children: Matthew, Erica, John, Angela. B.S., U. Wash., 1953, Ph.D., 1962; M.F., SUNY, Syracuse, 1955. With U.S. Forest Service, 1954-85; prin. mycologist, project leader Pacific N.W. Forest and Range Experiment Sta., Corvallis, Oreg., 1965-85; mem. faculty Oreg. State U., Corvallis, 1965—; prof. botany-plant pathology and forest sci. Oreg. State U., 1977—; co-chmn. Corvallis FISH, 1971-73. Contbr. articles to profl. jours. Recipient Civil Rights Accomplishment award U.S. Forest Svc., 1979, Civil Liberties award ACLU, 1990, Barrington Moore Meml. award Soc. Am. Foresters, 1995; grantee NSF, 1971—, Am. Philos. Soc., 1968-72, Sigma Xi, 1968-72, U.S. Spain Joint Com. Sci. and Tech. Cooperation, 1985-87, Indo-Am. Sci. and Tech. Initiative, 1984-91. Fellow AAAS; mem. Mycological Soc. Am. (council 1976-77, program chmn. 1976-77, v.p. 1984-85, pres. 1986-87), N.W. Sci. Assn. (past pres., Outstanding Scientist award 1991), Oreg. Acad. Sci., Oreg. Mycological Soc. (hon. life), Soc. Mex. de Micologia, Japanese Mycological Soc., Brit. Mycological Soc., N.Am. Truffling Soc. (hon. life). Home: 2165 NW Maser Pl Corvallis OR 97330-2223 Office: Oreg State U Dept Forest Sci Corvallis OR 97331-7501

TRASK, THOMAS EDWARD, religious organization administrator; b. Brainard, Minn., Mar. 23, 1936; m. Shirley Burkhart; children: Kimberly, Bradley, Todd, Tom. BA, North Ctrl. Bible Coll., 1956, DDiv (hon.), 1994. Ordained min. Assemblies of God, 1958. Pastor First Assembly of God, Hibbing, Minn., 1956-60; pastor First Assembly of God, Vicksburg, Mich., 1960-64; Mich. dist. A/G youth leader First Assembly of God, 1964-68; sr. pastor Saginaw (Mich.) First Assembly of God, 1968-73, Brightmoor Tabernacle, Southfield, Mich., 1976-88; supt. Mich. Dist. Coun., Dearborn, 1973-76; gen. treas. The Gen. Coun. Assemblies of God, Springfield, Mo., 1988-93; gen. supt. The Gen. Coun. Assemblies of God, Springfield, Mich., 1993—. Co-author: Back to the Altar: A Call to Spiritual Awakening, 1994, Back to the Word, A Call to Biblical Authority, 1996, The Battle, Defeating the Enemies of Your Soul, 1997. Office: Assemblies of God 1445 N Boonville Ave Springfield MO 65802-1894

TRAUB, J(OSEPH) F(REDERICK), computer scientist, educator; b. June 24, 1932; m. Pamela Ann McCorduck, Dec. 6, 1969; children: Claudia Renee, Hillary Anne. B.S., CCNY, 1954; Ph.D., Columbia U., 1959. Mem. tech. staff Bell Labs., Murray Hill, N.J., 1959-70; prof. computer sci. and math., head dept. computer sci. Carnegie-Mellon U., Pitts., 1971-79; Edwin Howard Armstrong prof. computer sci., chmn. dept., prof. math. Columbia U., 1979-86; prof. computer sci. Princeton (N.J.) U., 1986-87; pres. John Von Neumann Nat. Supercomputer Ctr., Consortium for Sci. Computing, Princeton, 1986-87; Edwin Howard Armstrong prof., chmn. dept. computer sci., prof. math. Columbia U., N.Y.C., 1987-89, Edwin Howard Armstrong prof. computer sci., math., 1989—; dir. N.Y. State Ctr. Computers and Info. Systems, 1982-88; disting. lectr. MIT, 1977; vis. Mackay prof. U. Calif., Berkeley, 1978-79; cons. Hewlett-Packard, 1982, IBM, 1984, Schlumberger, 1986; mem. pres.'s adv. com. computer sci. Stanford U., 1972-75, chmn.,

1975-76; mem. adv. com. Fed. Jud. Center; mem. sci. council I.R.I.A., Paris, 1976-80; mem. central steering com., computing sci. and engring. research study NSF, also liaison to panel on theoretical computer sci. and panel on numerical comp., 1974-80; mem. adv. com. Carnegie-Mellon Inst. Research, 1978-79; mem. applied math. div. rev. com. Argonne Nat. Lab., 1973-75; mem. adv. com. math. and computer sci. NSF, 1978-80; chmn. computer sci. and tech. bd. NRC, 1986-90; chmn. computer sci. and telecommunications bd. NRC, 1990-92; trustee Columbia U. Press, 1983-85; founding chair Spl. Interest Group on Numerical Math., 1965-71. Author: Iterative Methods for the Solution of Equations, 1964, Russian edit., 1985; (with H. Wozniakowski) A General Theory of Optimal Algorithms, 1980, Russian edit., 1983; (with G. Wasilkowski and H. Wozniakowski) Information, Uncertainty, Complexity, 1983, Information-Based Complexity, 1988; editor: Complexity of Sequential and Parallel Numerical Algorithms, 1973, Analytical Computational Complexity, 1976, Algorithms and Complexity: New Directions and Recent Results, 1976, Jour. Assn. Computing Machinery, 1970-76, Transactions on Math. Software, 1974-76, Jour. Computer and Sys. Scis., 1973-86, Internat. Jour. on Computers and Math. with Applications, 1974—, Cohabiting With Computers, 1985; founding editor Jour. Complexity, 1985—, Ann. Rev. Computer Sci., 1986-92; assoc. editor Complexity, 1995—. Sherman Fairchild Disting. scholar Calif. Inst. Tech., 1991, 92; recipient Award for Disting. Svc. to Computing Rsch. Computer Rsch. Assn., 1992, Lezione Lincee Acad. Nazionale dei Lincei, 1993, Sr. Scientist award Alexander Von Humboldt Found., 1992—. Fellow AAAS (coun. 1971-74), ACM (chmn. award com. 1974-76); mem. IEEE (Emanuel R. Piore Gold medal 1991), NAE (membership com. for computer sci., elec. engring. and control 1986-87, membership com. for computer sci. and engring. 1987-91, presdl. search com. 1993-94), Conf. Bd. Math. Scis. (coun. 1971-74), Soc. Indsl. and Applied Math., Am. Math. Soc., N.Y. Acad. Sci. (exec. com., bd. govs. 1987-89), Nat. Acad. Sci. (mem. study on high performance computing and comm. 1994-95). Office: Columbia University Dept Computer Sci New York NY 10027

TRAUB, RICHARD KENNETH, lawyer; b. Lakewood, N.J., Aug. 4, 1950; s. Harold W. and Muriel N. (Zurlin) T.; m. Barbara Lynn Wright, July 9, 1972; children: Russell S., Melissa L. BBA, U. Miami, Coral Gables, Fla., 1972, JD cum laude, 1975. Bar: Fla. 1975, N.Y. 1976, N.J. 1976, U.S. Dist. Ct. N.J. 1976, U.S. Supreme Ct. 1979, U.S. Dist. Ct. (ea. & so. dists.) N.Y. 1981. Ptnr. Wilson, Elser, Moskowitz, Edelman & Dicker, N.Y.C., 1975-95, Traub Eglin Lieberman Straus, Hawthorne, N.Y., 1996—; ptnr. Time for Patty Stables, N.J., 1992—; officer, dir. X-Ray Duplications, Inc., N.J.; ptnr., founder Fractured Greetings, N.J.; mem., lectr. Fedn. Ins. and Corp. Counsel, 1993—, mem. admissions com., industry cooperation ins. coverage and ADR coms.; lectr. Inst. for Internat. Rsch., Washington, 1988, Engring. News Record Constrn. Claims Conf., 1991. Author: Legal and Professional Aspects of Construction Management, 1990; contbr. articles to profl. jours. Bd. dirs. Pop Warner Football Assn., Holmdel, N.J., 1989—. Mem. ABA (forum com. on constrn. industry 1989, tort and ins. practice sect. 1985—, computer litigation sect.), N.Y. State Bar Assn., N.J. Bar Assn., Fla. Bar Assn., Fedn. Ins. and Corp. Counsel (spkr. ins. coverage sect., mem. ins. coverage and industry coop. sects., mem. admissions com.). Office: Traub Eglin Lieberman Straus Mid-Westchester Exec Park Three Skyline Dr Hawthorne NY 10532 also: 505 Main St Hackensack NJ 07601-5900

TRAUDT, MARY B., elementary education educator; b. Chgo., Jan. 1, 1930; d. Lloyd Andrews Haldeman and Adele Eleanor (MacKinnon) Haldeman-Oliver; m. Eugene Peter Traudt, Dec. 6, 1952 (dec.); 1 child, Victoria Jean. BS, Cen. Mich. U., 1951; MA, Roosevelt U., 1978; postgrad., U. Ill., 1982. Asst. editor Commerce Clearing House, Chgo., 1951-53; tchr. Cleve. Elem. Sch., 1954-56, Chgo. Sch. System, 1956-57, Community Consolidated # 54, Hoffman Estates, Ill., 1957-64, Avoca Elem. Sch., Wilmette, Ill., 1964—; ret., 1995. Recipient Computer award Apple Computer Co. Mem. Avoca Edn. Assn. (v.p. 1986-91), Alpha Psi Omega. Presbyterian. Avocations: reading, sewing, music, travel, gardening. Home: 107 Lincoln St Glenview IL 60025-4916 Office: Avoca Elem Sch 235 Beech Dr Glenview IL 60025-3274

TRAUGER, ALETA ARTHUR, judge. BA in English magna cum laude, Cornell Coll., Iowa, 1968; MAT, Vanderbilt U., 1972, JD, 1976. Tchr. Tenn., Eng., 1970-73; assoc., law clk. Barrett, Brandt & Barrett, P.C., Nashville, 1974-77; asst. U.S. atty., first asst., chief of criminal divsn. No. Dist. Ill. and Mid. Dist. Tenn., 1977-82; assoc. Hollins, Wagster & Yarbrough, P.C., Nashville, 1983-84; legal counsel Coll. of Charleston, S.C., 1984-85; counsel, ptnr. Wyatt, Tarrant, Combs, Gilbert & Milom, Nashville, 1985-91; judge Tenn. Ct. of the Judiciary, 1987-93; chief of staff Mayor's Office, Nashville, 1991-92; bankruptcy judge U.S. Bankruptcy Ct. (mid. dist.) Tenn., Nashville, 1993—; mem. hearing panel bd. profl. responsibility Tenn. Supreme Ct., 1983-84, mem. adv. com. on rules of civil and appellate procedure, 1989—; lectr. Vanderbilt U. Sch. Law, 1986-88, mem. alumni bd., 1989-92; master of bench Harry Phillips Am. Inn of Ct., 1990-94; mem. Internat. Women's Forum, 1993—, v.p. Tenn. chpt., 1996—; mem. Nat. Conf. Bankruptcy Judges, 1994—, chmn. ethics com., 1994—. Bd. dirs. Nashville Inst. for Arts, 1992—, Miriam's Promise (adoption agy.), 1995—; bd. dirs. Renewal House, 1996—. Fellow Am. Bar Found., Tenn. Bar Found., Nashville Bar Found.; mem. ABA (vice chmn. com. on bankrupcty judges jud. adminstrn. divsn), FBA (v.p. 1983-84, 85-86), Nashville Bar Assn. (bd. dirs. 1984, 89-91), Lawyers Assn. for Women (bd. dirs. 1983-84, 86-88), Tenn. Lawyers Assn. for Women (v.p. 1988-89, bd. dirs. 1990-91), Nat. Assn. Women Judges. Office: Customs House 701 Broadway Fl 2 Nashville TN 37203-3944

TRAUGER, DONALD BYRON, nuclear engineering laboratory administrator; b. Exeter, Nebr., June 29, 1920; s. Charles C. and Ethel L. (Downey) T.; m. Elaine Causey, Sept. 2, 1945; children: Byron Roscoe, Thomas Charles. A.B., Nebr. Wesleyan U., 1942, D.Sc. (hon.), 1974; postgrad., Columbia U., 1942-46, U. Tenn., 1946-49; D.Sc. (hon.), Tenn. Wesleyan Coll., 1977. Supr. test equipment devel. Manhattan Dist. Project, 1942-46; supr. Devel. Lab., Oak Ridge Gaseous Diffusion Plant, 1946-54; with Oak Ridge Nat. Lab., 1954-93, assoc. dir. nuclear and engring. technologies, 1970-84, sr. staff asst. to dir., 1984-93; cons. in energy tech., 1993—. Editorial advisor Anns. Nuclear Engring, 1973—; design features editor sect. IV Nuclear Safety Jour., 1989—. Mem. Oak Ridge Bd. Edn., 1961-67; pres. Oak Ridge PTA Coun., 1969-70, Oak Ridge Parents Adv. Coun., 1958-59; chmn. exec. com., trustee Tenn. Wesleyan Coll., 1976-81, chmn. bd. govs., 1986-90, chmn. bd. trustees, 1990-93. Recipient Alumni Achievement award Nebr. Wesleyan U., 1962. Fellow Am. Nuclear Soc. (chmn. planning com. 1981-83); mem. AAAS, Am. Phys. Soc., Sigma Xi (pres. Oak Ridge chpt. 1987-88), Sigma Pi Sigma. Methodist. Club: Rotary. Office: PO Box 2008 Oak Ridge TN 37831-2008

TRAUGH, DONALD GEORGE, III, secondary education educator; b. Tucson, Aug. 5, 1950; s. Donald G. Jr. and Leatrice (Rhodes) Traugh-Long; m. Brenda Kay Kreischer, June 14, 1975; children: Jonathan P., Brandon M. AB in Edn., Fairmont (W.Va.) State U., 1974; MEd in Social Studies, Bloomsburg (Pa.) State U., 1980. Cert. tchr., Pa. Tchr. social studies Bloomsburg Area Sch. Dist., 1974—, chmn. dept. social studies, 1978—; cochair social studies curriculum staff Bloomsburg Area Sch. Dist., 1984—. Vol. firefighter Catawissa (Pa.) Hose Co. 1, 1969—, chief dept., 1987—; mem. Catawissa Borough Coun., 1977-89, v.p., 1987-89. Mem. NEA, Pa. Edn. Assn., Bloomsburg Area Edn. Assn., Nat. Coun. Social Studies, Mid. States Assn. Social Studies, Pa. Coun. Social Studies, Nat. Fire Protection Assn., Keystone State Fire Chiefs Assn., Pi Gamma Mu, Delta Sigma Phi. Democrat. Lutheran. Avocations: coaching football, hunting, fishing, scouting, gardening. Home: 503 E Main St Catawissa PA 17820-1030 Office: Bloomsburg HS 1200 Railroad St Bloomsburg PA 17815-3613

TRAUGOTT, ELIZABETH CLOSS, linguistics educator and researcher; b. Bristol, Eng., Apr. 9, 1939; d. August and Hannah M.M. (Priebsch) Closs; m. John L. Traugott, Sept. 26, 1967; 1 dau., Isabel. BA in English, Oxford U., Eng., 1960; PhD in English lang., U. Calif., Berkeley, 1964. Asst. prof. English U. Calif., Berkeley, 1964-70; lectr. U. East Africa, Tanzania, 1965-66, U. York, Eng., 1966-67; lectr., then assoc. prof. linguistics and English Stanford U., Calif., 1970-77, prof., 1977—, chmn. linguistics dept., 1980-85; vice provost, dean grad. studies Stanford U., 1985-91, mem. grad. record examinations bd., 1989-93, mem. test of English as a fgn. lang. bd., 1989-91, chmn. test of English as a fgn. lang. bd., 1991-92; mem. higher edn. funding coun. Eng. Assessment Panel, 1996. Author: A History of English Syntax, 1972, (with Mary Pratt) Linguistics for Students of Literature, 1980, (with Paul Hopper) Grammaticalization, 1993; editor: (with ter Meulen, Reilly, Ferguson) On Conditionals, 1986, (with Heine) Approaches to Grammaticalization, 2 vols., 1991; contbr. numerous articles to profl. jours. Am. Coun. Learned Socs. fellow, 1975-76, Guggenheim fellow, 1983-84, Ctr. Advanced Study of Behavioral Scis. fellow, 1983-84. Mem. MLA, AAUP, AAUW, Linguistics Soc. Am. (pres. 1987, sec.-treas. 1994—), Internat. Soc. Hist. Linguistic (pres. 1979-81). Office: Stanford Univ Dept Linguistics Bldg 460 Stanford CA 94305-2150

TRAUM, JEROME S., lawyer; b. Newark, Sept. 26, 1935; s. Max and Evelyn (Fein) T.; m. Lynda Sturner, Apr. 16, 1972; children: David, Norman, Daniel, Edward. A.B., U. Mich., 1956, J.D. with distinction, 1959. Bar: N.Y. 1960, U.S. Supreme Ct. 1976. Assoc. Chadbourne, Parke, Whiteside & Wolff, N.Y.C., 1959-62; assoc. to ptnr. Spear and Hill, N.Y.C., 1962-67; ptnr. Janklow and Traum, N.Y.C., 1967-89; v.p., then pres. Morton L. Janklow Assocs., Inc., lit. agy., 1977-89; gen. ptnr. investment bankers The Blackstone Group, N.Y.C., 1989-91; of counsel Proskauer, Rose, Goetz & Mendelsohn, N.Y.C., 1991-95; ptnr. Moses & Singer, N.Y.C., 1995—; adj. prof. fed. securities regulation Syracuse U. Coll. Law, 1975; bd. dirs. Interep Nat. Radio Sales, Inc. Bd. dirs. McCaffery & McCall, Inc., 1987-90, Open Channel, 1971-77, Call for Action, 1978-83, Playwright's Forum, Inc., 1981—, Penny McCall Found., Inc., 1987—; trustee Jose Limon Dance Found., 1968. Mem. Assn. of Bar of City of N.Y., ABA (com. fed. regulation securities), Order of Coif. Home: 111 W 67th St Apt 30C New York NY 10023 Office: Moses & Singer 1301 Avenue Of The Americas New York NY 10019-6022

TRAUTH, JOSEPH LOUIS, JR., lawyer; b. Cin., Apr. 22, 1945; s. Joseph L. and Margaret (Walter) T.; m. Barbara Widmeyer, July 4, 1970; children: Jennifer, Joseph III, Jonathan, Braden, Maria. BS in Econs., Xavier U., 1967; JD, U. Cin., 1973. Bar: Ohio 1973, U.S. Dist. Ct. (so. dist.) Ohio 1973, U.S. Ct. Appeals (6th cir.) 1973, U.S. Supreme Ct. 1988. Assoc. Keating, Muething & Klekamp, Cin., 1973-80, ptnr., 1980—; speaker real estate law, 1974—. Contbr. articles to real estate publs. Mem. Rep. Leadership Coun., Cin., 1987—, Parish Coun., Cin., 1990. Mem. Cin. Bar Assn. (grievance com., real estate com., negligence com.). Roman Catholic. Avocations: running, tennis, reading. Office: Keating Muething & Klekamp 1800 Provident Tower 1 E 4th St Cincinnati OH 45202-3717

TRAUTMAN, DONALD W., bishop; b. Buffalo, June 24, 1936. Ed., Our Lady of Angels Sem., Niagara Falls, N.Y., Theology Faculty, Innsbruck, Austria, Pontifical Biblical Inst., Rome, Cath. U., St. Thomas Aquinas U., Rome. Ordained priest Roman Cath. Ch., 1962, consecrated bishop, 1985. Titular bishop of Sassura and aux. bishop Diocese of Buffalo, 1985; bishop Erie, Pa., 1990—; Episc. moderator Diocesan Fiscal Mgmt. Conf.; mem. com. for review of scripture translations on doctrine and migration Nat. Conf. Cath. Bishops; chmn. Bishops' Liturgy Com. Home: 205 W 9th St Erie PA 16501-1304 Address: St Mark's Ctr PO Box 10397 Erie PA 16514-0397

TRAUTMAN, HERMAN LOUIS, lawyer, educator; b. Columbus, Ind., Sept. 26, 1911; s. Theodore H. and Emma (Guckenberger) T.; m. Marian Lucille Green, Sept. 1, 1940; children: Stephen M., Pamela C.; LLB with distinction Ind. U., 1937, BA, 1946, JD with distinction, 1946; postgrad., NYU, 1953, Ford Found. faculty fellow, Harvard U., 1954-55. Bar: Ind. 1937, U.S. Tax Ct., U.S. Ct. Appeals (6th cir.) Tenn. Sole practice, Evansville, Ind., 1937-43; pres. Crescent Coal Co., Evansville, 1941-43; prof. law U. Ala. Tuscaloosa, 1946-49; prof. law Vanderbilt U., 1949—, prof. law emeritus, 1977; NYU vis. prof., 1955, U. Mich., Ann Arbor, 1963-64; ptnr. Trautman & Trautman, Nashville, 1976-85; sole practice, Nashville, 1986—. Served to lt. comdr. USN, 1943-46. Mem. ABA, Am. Law Inst., Tenn. Bar Assn., Nashville Bar Assn., Nat. Conf. Jud. Adminstrs., Estate Planning Coun., Order of Coif, Phi Gamma Delta, Belle Meade Club, Univ. Club, Kiwanis. Methodist. Address: PO Box 150862 Nashville TN 37215-0862

TRAUTMAN, WILLIAM ELLSWORTH, lawyer; b. San Francisco, Nov. 27, 1940; s. Gerald H. and Doris Joy (Tucker) T.; m. Dorothy Williamson, June 17, 1962; children: Darcey, Torey. AB, U. Calif., Berkeley, 1962, LLB, 1965. Bar: Calif. U.S. Supreme Ct., Calif. Dist. Ct., U.S. Ct. Appeals (9th and fed. cirs.). Assoc. Chickering & Gregory, San Francisco, 1965-71, ptnr., 1972-81; ptnr. Brobeck, Phleger & Harrison, San Francisco, 1981—, mng. ptnr., 1992-96, litigation dept. chair, 1984-91. Pres. Oakland (Calif.) Mus. Assn., 1981-83; mem. profl. ethics com. State Bar Calif., 1974-77. Fellow Am. Coll. Trial Lawyers; mem. Legal Aid Soc. (bd. dirs. 1982-93, pres. 1985-88), Bar Assn. San Francisco (bd. dirs. 1972-73), Calif. Barristers (bd. dirs., v.p.), Barrister's Club of San Francisco (v.p. 1973), Boalt Hall Alumni Assn. (bd. dirs. 1993—, pres.-elect 1996—). Office: Brobeck Phleger & Harrison 1 Market San Francisco CA 94105

TRAUTMANN, PATRICIA ANN, communications educator, storyteller; b. Hot Springs, S.D., Jan. 6, 1932; d.. Forest Houston and Clara Ruth (Allen) Doling; m. Robert D. Trautmann, Aug. 11, 1954; children: Kurt, Elaine, Sarah, Cynthia, Gretchen. BA, Jamestown Coll., 1954; MA, U. Northern Colo., 1962; PhD, Vanderbilt U., 1984; postgrad., Ga. Southern U., 1992-93. Tchr. various schs., Colo., N.D., Mich., 1954-67; part-time instr. English Kans. State Coll., Pittsburg, 1967-70; part-time instr. English, children's lit. Baldwin-Wallace Coll., Berea, Parma, Ohio, 1970-73; part-time instr. children's lit., reading, lang. arts U. Tenn., Nashville, 1973-78; English instr. Valdosta (Ga.) H.S., 1978-82; assoc. prof. English, Speech, Langs.; asst. dir. programs Ga. Mil. Coll., Milledgeville, 1982-86; assoc. prof. English, art, humanities, langs. South Ga. Coll., Douglas, 1986-94; chairperson humanities, 1988-94; assoc. prof. English, comm. skills Isothermal C.C., Spindale, N.C., 1995—; cons. for reading, children's books in schs. and other instns., Kans., Ohio, Tenn., Ga., N.C., 1964—. Storyteller, spkr., internat. lore, poetry, children's lit., world mythology, 1967—. Recipient Humanities award South Ga. Coll., 1993. Mem. AAUW, Music Club. Democrat. Avocations: drawing, painting, singing, gardening, hiking. Home: 611 N Washington St Rutherfordton NC 28139 Office: Isothermal Cmty Coll Spindale NC 28139

TRAUTMANN, THOMAS ROGER, history and anthropology educator; b. Madison, Wis., May 27, 1940; s. Milton and Esther Florence (Trachte) T.; m. Marcella Hauolilani Choy, Sept. 25, 1962; children: Theodore William, Robert Arthur. BA, Beloit Coll., 1962; PhD, U. London, 1968. Lectr. in history Sch. Oriental and African Studies, U. London, 1965-68; asst. prof. history U. Mich., Ann Arbor, 1968-71, assoc. prof., 1971-77, prof., 1977—, Richard Hudson rsch. prof., 1979, prof. history and anthropology, 1984—, chmn. dept. history, 1987-90, Steelcase rsch. prof., 1993-94. Author: Kautilya and the Arthasastra, 1971, Dravidian Kinship, 1981, Lewis Henry Morgan and the Invention of Kinship, 1987, (with K.S. Kabelac) The Library of Lewis Henry Morgan, 1994 (with Diane Owen Hughes) Time: Histories and Ethnologies, 1995; mem. editl. bd. Comparative Studies in Soc. and History; contbr. various articles on India, kinship and history of anthropology. Sr. Humanist fellow NEH, 1984. Fellow Royal Asiatic Soc.; mem. Am. Anthrop. Assn., Assn. Asian Studies, Am. Oriental Soc., Am. Inst. Indian Studies (trustee, sr. rsch. fellow in India 1985), Phi Beta Kappa. Office: U Mich Dept History Ann Arbor MI 48109-1045

TRAUTWEIN, GEORGE WILLIAM, conductor; b. Chgo., Aug. 5, 1927; s. William Jacob and Hilda (Martin) T.; m. Barbara Wilson, Jan. 20, 1955; children: Paul Martin, Matthew Richard. MusB, Oberlin Conservatory, Ohio, 1951; MusM, Cleve. Inst. Music, 1955; MusD, Ind. U., 1961. mem. faculty U. Minn., U. Tex., Austin, Armstrong (Ga.) State Coll.; arts cons. Nat. Endowment Arts; dir. internat. study program for Wake Forest U. at Tokai U., Japan, 1995. Violinist Indpls. Symphony Orch., 1947-48, Balt. Symphony Orch., 1951-52, Nat. Symphony Orch., Washington, 1952-53, Cleve. Orch., 1953-57, Chautauqua Symphony Orch., N.Y., 1953-59, Camerata Acad., Salzburg, 1957-58, Mozarteum Orch., Salzburg, 1958 (Fulbright grantee 1958), assoc. condr. Dallas Symphony Orch., 1962-66, Mpls. Symphony, 1966-73; music dir. S.D. Symphony, 1971-75, Internat. Congress Strings, Ohio, 1973-75; music dir., condr. Savannah (Ga.) Symphony Orch., 1974-77; music adv., prin. guest condr. Evansville (Ind.) Philharm., 1979-80; music dir., condr. RIAS Edn. Network, Berlin, 1979, Tucson Symphony Orch., 1977-81; artistic dir., condr. Piedmont Chamber Orch.; prin. condr. Internat. Music program; dir. orchestral programs, N.C. Sch. of Arts, 1981-83; dir. instrumental ensembles, Wake Forest U., 1983-96, dir. Artists series, 1985—; guest appearances with orchs., U.S., Germany, Sweden, France, Rumania, Jugoslavia, Portugal, Hong Kong, India, P.R., Mex. Adv. bd. Avery Fisher Found., N.Y.C. Served with USN, 1948-49. Recipient Orpheus award Phi Mu Alpha, 1971, ASCAP award, 1979, 82, World Peace award Ministry of World Harmony, 1983; Fulbright grantee Mozarteum, Salzburg, 1958; Sr. Fulbright lectr., India, 1989-90. Mem. Am. Fedn. Musicians, Chamber Music Soc. Am., Sir Thomas Beecham Soc., Erich Wolfgang Korngold Soc., Wilhelm Furtwaengler Soc., Literacy Initiative Assn. Avocations: string quartet, art reproduction, Wordsworth, Scandinavian cuisine, William Wordsworth. Office: Wake Forest U PO Box 7411 Winston Salem NC 27109-7411

TRAVAGLINI, RAYMOND DOMINIC, corporate executive; b. Greenville, Pa., May 3, 1928; s. Perugino and Mary Ann (DiFalco) T.; children: Alan, Lynne, Debbie, Kimberly, Kristine. LHD (hon.), Youngstown State U., 1993. Mgr. Kroger Co., Meadville, Pa., 1949-62; owner Suburban Water Conditioning, Warren, Ohio, 1962-65; ptnr. Sanray Corp., Meadville, 1965—; bd. dirs. Bank One, Youngstown, Ohio. Bd. dirs. Butler Inst. Am. Art, Youngstown, Mahoning Valley Econ. Devel. Corp.; mem. Base Comty. Coun. Dept. Air Force. Named Man of Yr. Boys' Towns of Italy, 1979, Italian Scholarship League, 1984, Mahoning Valley County Econ. Devel. Corp., 1985, Nat. Italian-Am. Sports Hall of Fame, 1992, Outstanding Citizen of Yr., Niles, Ohio, 1997; recipient Disting. Citizen award Youngstown State U. Alumni Assn., 1993. Office: Sanray Corp 1323 Youngstown Warren Rd Niles OH 44446-4616

TRAVANTI, DANIEL JOHN, actor; b. Kenosha, Wis., Mar. 7, 1940; s. John and Elvira (DeAngelis) T. BA, U. Wis.; MA, Loyola Marymount, L.A. Performances include: (TV movies) The Love War, 1970, Adam, 1983, Aurora, 1984, Murrow, 1986, Adam: His Song Continues, 1986, I Never Sang for My Father, 1988, A Case of Libel, Howard Beach: Making the Case for Murder, 1989, Fellow Traveler, 1990, Tagget, 1991, Eyes of a Witness, 1991; (TV series) appeared as Capt. Frank Furillo in Hill Street Blues, 1981-87, Missing Persons, 1993-94; (films) St Ives, 1976, Midnight Crossing, 1988, Millenium, 1989, Megaville, 1991, Weep No More My Lady, 1993, Siao Yu, 1994, Who Killed Teddy Bear, 1994, Just Cause, 1995; (stage) Othello, Who's Afraid of Virginia Woolf?, The Taming of the Shrew, I Never Sang for My Father, Only Kidding, Les Liaisons Dangereuses, A Touch of the Poet. Gen. Motors fellow U. Wis., 1958-61; Woodrow Wilson fellow, 1961; Yale U. Sch. Drama, 1961-62; recipient Emmy award for role as Capt. Frank Furillo in Hill Street Blues, 1981, 82; Golden Globe award, 1981. *

TRAVELSTEAD, CHESTER COLEMAN, former educational administrator; b. Franklin, Ky., Sept. 25, 1911; s. Conley and Nelle (Gooch) T.; m. Marita Hawley, Aug. 1, 1936; children—Coleman, Jimmie. A.B., Western Ky. State Coll., Bowling Green, 1933; M.Music, Northwestern U., 1947; Ph.D., U. Ky., 1950; D.Hum., Morehead (Ky.) State U., 1975; Ph.D., John F. Kennedy U., Buenos Aires, 1975; LHD, U. N.Mex., 1980. Tchr., prin. rural and consol. schs. Mecklenberg County, Va., 1931-32, 33-35; tchr. gen. sci., math., music Picadome High Sch., Lexington, Ky., 1935-37; dir. music Henry Clay High Sch., Lexington, 1937-42; personnel supr. Lexington Signal Dept., Dept. War, 1942-43; supr. music Lexington pub. schs., 1945-47; rep. Investors Diversified Services, Inc., 1947-48; coordinator in-service tchr. edn. Ky. Dept. Edn., 1950-51; asst. prof. edn., asst. dean Coll. Edn., U. Ga., Athens, 1951-53; dean Sch. Edn., U. S.C., Columbia, 1953-56; dean Coll. Edn. U. N.Mex., Albuquerque, 1956-68; v.p. acad. affairs U. N.Mex., 1968-76, provost, 1976-77; Mem. Nat. Council Accreditation Tchr. Edn., 1960-66, chmn., 1963-65. Author books; contbr. articles in field to profl. jours. Pres. bd. dirs. N.Mex. Symphony Orch., 1977-78, 84-85; treas. U.S. Senator Jeff Bingaman's re-election campaign, 1988-93. With USNR, 1943-45; PTO. Mem. NEA, Nat. Soc. Study Edn., Soc. Advancement Edn., AAUP, Phi Kappa Phi, Phi Delta Kappa., Kappa Delta Pi. Home: 320 Fontana Pl NE Albuquerque NM 87108-1167

TRAVER, COURTLAND LEE, lawyer; b. New Haven, Sept. 20, 1935; s. Courtland L. Sr. and Bertha (Wilmot) T.; (div.); children: Lee, Kim, Amy. BA, U. Conn., 1957; LLB, Georgetown U., 1966. Bar: D.C. 1966, Va. 1967. Law clk. to presiding justice Ct. of Gen. Sessions, Washington, Va., 1965-66; clk. U.S. Ct. Appeals (D.C. cir.), Washington, 1966-67; ptnr. McGuire, Woods, Battle & Boothe, McLean, 1967—. Contbr. articles on real estate law to jours. Lt., pilot USN, 1957-63. Mem. ABA (various coms.), Va. State Bar Assn. (chmn. real estate com.). D.C. Bar Assn., Va. Bar Assn. (chmn. real estate sect.). Home: 4755 40th St N Arlington VA 22207 Office: McGuire Woods Battle & Boothe 8280 Greensboro Dr Ste 900 Mc Lean VA 22102-3807

TRAVER, ROBERT WILLIAM, SR., management consultant, author, lecturer, engineer; b. Waterbury, Conn., Oct. 13, 1930; s. Alfred Matthew Sr. and Dorothy Viola (Thomson) T.; m. Eleanor Jean Finnemore (div. Feb. 1963); children: Robert William Jr., Jeffrey Matthew, Elizabeth; m. Valarie Jane Mason. B in Mech. Engring., Clarkson U., 1955; MBA, U. Mass., 1963. Registered profl. engr., N.Y. Quality control engr. Gen. Electric Co., Pittsfield, Mass., 1955-62; mgr. reliability and quality assurance Tansitor Electronics, Inc., Bennington, Vt., 1962-65; sr. cons. Rath & Strong, Inc., Lexington, Mass., 1965-70; regional mgr. TAC, Inc., Albany, N.Y., 1970-72; dist. mgr. IDS, Inc., Albany, 1972-81; v.p. Reddy, Traver & Woods, Inc., Lexington, 1981-96; owner Traver Assocs., Averill Pk., N.Y., 1996—; participant in edn1. exch. with Peoples Republic of China, 1985, Australia and New Zealand, 1986. Author: Manufacturing Solutions for Consistent Quality and Reliability; contbr. articles to profl. jours. Chmn. lake com. Crooked Lake Improvement Assn., Averill Park, N.Y., 1973-74; v.p. Sand Lake (N.Y.) Businessmen's Assn., 1974-76. With U.S. Army, 1950. Fellow Am. Soc. for Quality Control; mem. Inst. Mgmt. Cons., Trout Unltd. Republican. Congregationalist. Avocations: fishing, gardening, hockey. Home and Office: Twin Lions On Crooked Lk Averill Park NY 12018

TRAVERS, ROSE ELAINE, nursing supervisor; b. Aberdeen Proving Grounds, Md., July 30, 1956; d. Calvin Mace and Margaret Rose (Duncan) T. AA, Harford Community Coll., Bel Air, Md., 1976; BS magna cum laude, Towson State U., 1985; MSA, Cen. Mich. U., 1992. Nursing asst. Brevin Nursing Home, Havre de Grace, Md., 1973, Citizen's Nursing Home, Havre de Grace, 1974; staff nurse Harford Meml. Hosp., Havre de Grace, 1976-84; RN supr. Keswick Home, Balt., 1985—.

TRAVERSE, ALFRED, palynology educator, clergyman; b. Port Hill, P.E.I., Can., Sept. 7, 1925; s. Alfred Freeman and Pearle (Akerley) T.; m. Elizabeth Jane Insley, June 30, 1951; children: Paul, Martha, John, Celia. SB, Harvard U., 1946, AM, 1948, PhD, 1951; cert. in botany, Kings Coll., Cambridge, Eng., 1947; MDiv, Episcopal Theol. Sem. S.W., 1965. Tchg. fellow Harvard U., 1947-51; coal technologist U.S. Bur. Mines, Grand Forks, N.D., 1951-55; head Fuels Microscopy Lab., Denver, 1955; palynologist Shell Devel. Co., Houston, 1955-62; cons. palynologist Austin, Tex., 1962-65; asst. prof. geology U. Tex., Austin, 1965-66; assoc. prof. geology and biology Pa. State U., University Park, 1966-70, prof. palynology, 1970-96, prof. emeritus, 1996—; ordained to ministry Episcopal Ch., 1965; asst. priest St. Matthew's Ch., Austin, 1965-66, St. Paul's Ch., Philipsburg, Pa., 1966-75, Christuskirche (Old Cath.), Zurich, Switzerland, 1980-81; vicar St. John's Ch., Huntingdon, Pa., 1975-80; adj. prof. geobiology Juniata Coll., 1977-82; guest prof. Geol. Inst., Swiss Fed. Tech. Inst., Zurich, 1980-81; councillor Internat. Commn. Palynology, 1973-77, 80—, pres., 1977-80, archivist, historian, 1986—; on-bd. scientist Glomar Challenger, 1975; Fulbright prof. Senckenberg Rsch. Inst., Frankfurt, 1992. Author: Paleopalynology, 1988, Sedimentation of Organic Particles, 1994; mem. editl. bd. Catalog Fossil Spores and Pollen, 1957-66, editor-in-chief, 1966-76; palynological editor: Palaeontographica, 1989-95. Recipient Best Paper award Internat. prize Palaeobot. Soc. India, 1990-91, Korrespondierendes Mitglied, Senckenbergische Naturforschende Gesellschaft, 1992—; NSF rsch. grantee, 1966-87. Fellow AAAS, Geol. Soc. Am.; mem. Bot. Soc. Am. (sec.-treas. paleobot. sect. 1957-60, chmn. sect. 1960-61), Internat. Assn. Plant Taxonomists (sec. com. fossil plants 1969-93), Am. Assn. Stratigraphic Palynologists (sec.-treas. 1967-70, pres. 1970-71, chmn. type collections com. 1989-91, Best Paper award 1973), Internat. Fedn. Palynol. Soc. (pres. 1976-80, archivist 1980—). Home: RR 2 Box 390 Huntingdon PA 16652-9209 Office: 435 Deike Bldg University Park PA 16802-2713

TRAVIS, ANDREW DAVID, lawyer; b. Washington, Mar. 23, 1944; s. Don Carlos Jr. and Nevenna (Tsanoff) T. BA, Rice U., 1966; JD, U. Tex., 1969. Bar: Tex. 1969. Sole practice Houston, 1971-75; atty. Allright Corp. (formerly Allright Auto Parks Inc.), Houston, 1975-82, v.p., legal counsel, 1982—. Mem. ABA, Tex. Bar Assn., Houston Bar Assn. Home: 307 Timber Terrace Rd Houston TX 77024-5602 Office: Allright Corp 1111 Fannin St Ste 1300 Houston TX 77002-6923

TRAVIS, DEMPSEY JEROME, real estate executive, mortgage banker; b. Chgo., Feb. 25, 1920; s. Louis and Mittie (Strickland) T.; m. Moselynne Hardwick, Sept. 17, 1949. B.A., Roosevelt U., 1949; grad., Sch. Mortgage Banking, Northwestern U., 1969; D.Econs., Olive Harvey Coll., 1974; D.B.A. (hon.), Daniel Hale Williams U., Chgo., 1976; PhD (hon.), Kennedy-King Coll., 1982. Cert. property mgr.; cert. real estate counselor. Pres. Travis Realty Co., Chgo., 1949—, Urban Rsch. Press, 1969—. Author: Don't Stop Me Now, 1970, An Autobiography of Black Chicago, 1981, An Autobiography of Black Jazz, 1983, An Autobiography of Black Politics, 1987, Real Estate is the Gold in Your Future, 1988, Harold: The People's Mayor, 1989, Racism: American Style a Corporate Gift, 1990, I Refuse to Learn to Fail, 1992, Views From the Back of the Bus During World War II and Beyond, 1995, The Duke Ellington Primer, 1996, The Louis Armstrong Odessey: From Jazz Alley to America's Jazz Ambassador, 1997; Racism: Goes Around and Around, 1998. Trustee Northwestern Meml. Hosp., Chgo., Chgo. Hist. Soc., Auditorium Theater, Chgo., Roosevelt U. With AUS, 1942-46. Recipient award Soc. Midland Authors, 1982, Chgo. Art Deco Soc., 1985, The Human Rights award The Gustavus Myers Ctr. for Study of Human Rights in N.Am., 1995, Humanitarian award Kennedy-King Coll., 1997; named to Jr. Achievement Chgo. Bus. Hall of FAme, 1995; named embedded in sidewalk of Brunizeville Walk of Fame, Chgo. Mem. United Mortgage Bankers Assn. Am. (pres. 1961-74), Dearborn Real Estate Bd. (pres. 1957-59, 70-71), Nat. Assn. Real Estate Brokers (1st v.p. 1959-60), Inst. Real Estate Mgmt., Soc. Profl. Journalists, Soc. Midland Authors (pres. 1988-90), NAACP (pres. Chgo. 1959-60), Beta Gamma Sigma, Lambda Alpha. Clubs: Economics, Forty of Chgo., Assembly (Chgo.), Cliff Dwellers. Office: Travis Realty Co 840 E 87th St Chicago IL 60619-6248 *I refuse to learn to fail.*

TRAVIS, FREDERICK FRANCIS, academic administrator, historian; b. Brookhaven, Miss., Nov. 10, 1942; s. John Alice and Katharine (Brennan) T.; m. Alix Gregory Hallman Travis, May 15, 1971; children: Brennan Nunn, Rachel Frances. BS in Math., U. Miss., Oxford, 1965, MA in History, 1967; PhD in History, Emory U., Atlanta, 1974. Asst. prof. history Fordham U., N.Y.C., 1977-84, assoc. prof. history, 1984-88; assoc. prof. history John Carroll U., Cleve., 1988-92, prof. history, 1992—; dean Coll. of Arts and Scis., 1988-94, acting pres., 1995-96, acad. v.p., 1994—. Author: George Kennan and the American-Russian Relationship, 1865-1924, 1990; contbr. articles to profl. jours. Trustee, pres. Heights Cmty. Congress, Cleveland Heights, Ohio, 1993—, 1996-97. Named Univ. fellow U. Miss., Oxford, 1965-66, Emory U., Atlanta, 1968-69, vis. scholar Kennan Inst. for Advanced Russian Studies, Washington, 1980; recipient Rsch. Grant Travel to Collections, Nat. Endowment for Humanities, Washington, 1988. Mem. Am. Hist. Assn., Am. Assn. for Advancement of Slavic Studies, Soc. for Historians of Am. Fgn. Rels., Ohio Acad. History, Am. Conf. of Acad. Deans. Avocations: hiking, tennis, swimming, contract bridge, chess. Home: 2318 Coventry Rd Cleveland Heights OH 44118 Office: John Carroll Univ 20700 N Park Blvd Cleveland Heights OH 44118

TRAVIS, J(AMES) FRANK, manufacturing company executive; b. Atlanta, Mar. 12, 1936; s. L. Earl and Willene E. (Brisendine) T.; m. Eleanor Jackson, Aug. 26, 1961; children: T. Eric, J. Gregory. BSME, Auburn U., 1959; postgrad., So. Tex. Coll. Law, 1964-66. Various engring. and managerial positions Ingersoll-Rand Co., Woodcliff Lake, N.J., 1959-89, corp. v.p., 1990-94, exec. v.p., 1994-96, vice chmn., 1996—; pres. Ingersoll Air Co. Group, 1989-90, Ingersoll-Torrington Group, 1990-94; bd. dirs. Nat. Assn. Mfrs., Washington, N.Am. Com., Washington. Home: 21 Brezzy Knls Avon CT 06001-2842 Office: Ingersoll-Rand Co 200 Chestnut Ridge Rd Woodcliff Lk NJ 07675-7703

TRAVIS, LAWRENCE ALLAN, accountant; b. Bloomington, Ill., Sept. 17, 1942; s. Willard Burns and Florence May (Harvey) T.; m. Katy Quinones, Apr. 16, 1965 (div. Feb. 1978); children: Lawrence Allan Jr., Matthew B.; m. Kathleen Lucas, May 20, 1995. BS in Bus. Edn., Ill. State U., 1968; MA in Pub. Adminstrn., U. Ill., Springfield, 1976. CPA, Ill. Staff acct. Alexander Grant & Co., Chgo., 1969; internal auditor State Farm Ins., Bloomington, 1969-73; dep. dir. Ill. Dept. Ins., Springfield, 1973-74; audit mgr. Ill. Auditor Gen., Springfield, 1974-81; pres. Lawrence Travis & Co., P.C., CPAs, Virden, Normal, Springfield, Ill., 1979—; also bd. dirs. Lawrence Travis & Co., P.C., CPAs, Virden, Normal, Springfield; v.p., bd. dirs. Virden Broadcasting Corp., 1986-95; registered rep. Terra Securities, 1994—; pres., bd. dirs. Travco, Inc., Virden, Ka-Lar Enterprises, Inc., Springfield; v.p., bd. dirs. Carlinville Broadcasting Corp., Miller Comm., Inc. Mem. Ill. Common Cause, Springfield. Mem. AICPA, Assn. Govt. Accts., Ill. CPA Soc., Internat. Platform Assn., Nat. Space Soc., Smithsonian Assocs., World Future Soc., Internat. Traders. Democrat. Roman Catholic. Avocation: sports. Home: 2409 Idlewild Dr Springfield IL 62704-5403 Office: Lawrence Travis & Co 1700 S 1st St Springfield IL 62704-3902

TRAVIS, MARLENE O., healthcare management executive; b. Edmonton, Alta., Can.; Came to U.S. 1959.; d. LeRoy David and Della Jessie (Campbell) T.; m. Gary T. McIlroy, Aug. 20, 1962; children: Jennifer Renee, Montgomery Travis. Student (mass comms.), St. Cloud State U., 1974-76; exec. edn., U. Pa., Stanford U., 1989-92. Cert. exec. edn. Owner Travis Communications, Brainerd, Minn., 1975-77; co-founder, operating officer Midwest Lab. Assoc., Mpls., 1977-80; dir., corp. v.p. Meidinger-HRM (MHRM), Mpls., 1981-83; co-founder, exec. v.p., bd. dirs. Health Risk Mgmt. Inc., Mpls., 1977—, dir., pres., COO, 1986—; chair of bd., CEO HRM Ltd. (Can.), 1989—; founder, chair CEO Inst. Healthcare Quality, Mpls., 1991—; vice-chair Med. Alley, 1994—, bd. dirs. Co-author Self Health Guide to Laboratory Tests, 1982. Chmn. Minn. Task Force on Battered Women, 1977-79; bd. dirs., exec. com. Minn. Task Force on Sexual Assault, 1974-76; co-founder, chair Mid Minn. Women's Ctr. Brainerd, 1975; founder, chair Crow Wing County Task Force on Sexual Assault, Brainerd, 1974-77; founder Crow Wing County Task Force to Support Battered Women, 1974; mem. Minn. Commr. of Edn.'s Task Force to Eliminate Sexism in Edn., 1973-74; mem. leadership group Amnesty Internat., 1990—, com. of 200, 1991—. Named Cornerstone Leader in Giving United Way Mpls., 1992—. Mem. AAUW, NOW (convenor Marshfield, Wis. chpt. 1972, Brainerd area chpt. 1974), C-200 Found. (mentor contbr.), Nat. Assn. Corp. Dirs., Toastmasters (sponsor 1988), Phi Beta Gamma. Avocations: skiing, photography, travel, women's studies, piano. Office: Health Risk Mgmt Inc 8000 W 78th St Minneapolis MN 55439-2534

TRAVIS, MARTIN BICE, political scientist, educator; b. Iron Mountain, Mich., Sept. 22, 1917; s. Martin Bice and Helen (Carrett) T.; m. Olivia Brewster Taylor, Nov. 29, 1942; children: Elizabeth Nichols (Mrs. Usama Mugharbil), Helen Willard. A.B., Amherst Coll., 1939; student, Heidelberg (Germany) U., 1937; M.A., Fletcher Sch. Law and Diplomacy, 1940; Ph.D., U. Chgo., 1948. Asst. prof. internat. relations Syracuse U., 1948-49; asst. prof. polit. sci. Duke U., 1949-52; asst. prof., then assoc. prof. polit. sci. Stanford U., 1953-61; prof. polit. sci. SUNY-Stony Brook, 1961-92; coordinator SUNY Program Am. U., Beirut, Lebanon, 1972-73; chmn. dept., 1961-68; dir. Inst. Am. Studies SUNY-Stony Brook, 1965-93; vis. prof. Sch. Internat. Affairs, Columbia, 1956-57; vis. summer prof. U. Guadalajara, Mex., 1959, 62, U. Wash., 1961; Bd. dirs. State U N.Y. Inst. Am. Studies in France, 1966-77; cons. to industry. Author: (with E.E. Robinson) Powers of the President in Foreign Affairs, 1966; Co-editor, contbr.: (with Philip W. Buck) Control of Foreign Relations in Modern Nations, 1957; bd. editors: Western Polit. Quar, 1956-58; adv. bd.: Almanac of Current World Leaders, 1957—; editorial critic for book pubs. Mem. sch. bd., Cold Spring Harbor, N.Y., 1965-71, v.p. 1967-68, pres. 1968-69; trustee Village of Laurel Hollow, 1983-95, police com., 1983-85, mayor, 1985-95; established Martin B. Travis Scholarship fund for pre-law majors at SUNY, Stonybrook, 1995. Grantee Ford Found. 1960-61. Mem. Coun. Fgn. Rels., Phi Delta Theta, Phi Delta Kappa. Home: 533 Cold Spring Rd Syosset NY 11791-1206 Office: Dept Polit Science Suny Stony Brook NY 11794

TRAVIS, NANCY, actress; b. New York, NY, Sept. 21, 1961. BA, NYU. stage appearances include: Brighton Beach Memoirs (touring prodn.), It's Hard to Be a Jew, 1984, I'm Not Rappaport, 1986, The Signal Season of Dummy Hoy, 1987-88; television appearances include: High School Narc, 1985, Malice in Wonderland, 1985, Harem, 1986, I'll Be Home for Christmas, 1988, Almost Perfect, 1995-96, (voice) Duckman, 1994; films include: Three Men and a Baby, 1987, Eight Men Out, 1988, Married to the Mob, 1988, Air America, 1990, Internal Affairs, 1990, Loose Cannons, 1990, Three Men and a Little Lady, 1990, Passed Away, 1992, Chaplin, 1992, The Vanishing, 1993, So I Married an Ax Murderer, 1993, Greedy, 1994, Fluke, 1995, Destiny Turns On the Radio, 1995, Lieberman in Love, 1995, Bogus, 1996. Office: CAA 9830 Wilshire Blvd Beverly Hills CA 90212-1804

TRAVIS, NEIL, film editor. Editor: (TV movies) Roots, 1977 (Emmy award outstanding film editing of drama series for Part 1 1977), The Atlanta Child Murders, 1985, Shannon's Deal, 1989, (films) Jaws II, 1978, The Idolmaker, 1980, Second Thoughts, 1983, The Philadelphia Experiment, 1984, Cujo, 1984, Marie, 1985, No Way Out, 1987, Cocktail, 1988, Dances with Wolves, 1990 (Academy award best film editing 1990), Patriot Games, 1992, Bopha!, 1993, Clear and Present Danger, 1994, Outbreak, 1995, Moll Flanders, 1996.

TRAVIS, RANDY BRUCE, musician; b. Monroe, N.C., 1959; married. Musician Country City U.S.A., 1977-82, Nashville Palace, 1982-85. Rec. artist Warner Bros. Records, 1985—; albums include debut Storms of Life, 1986 (Album of Yr., Acad. Country Music 1987, Album of Yr., Music City News 1987), Always & Forever, 1987 (Album of Yr., Country Music Assn. 1987), Old 8x10, 1988, No Holdin' Back, 1989, An Old Time Christmas, 1989, Heroes and Friends, 1990, High Lonesome, 1991, Greatest Hits, 1992, Wind in the Wire, 1993, This is Me, 1994; songs include On the Other Hand (Best Song, Acad. Country Music 1987, Best Single, Acad. Country Music 1987, Single of Yr., Music City News 1987), Diggin' Up Bones, No Place Like Home, Forever and Ever, Amen (Single of Yr., Song of Yr.,Country Music Assn. 1987, Best Country Record, AMOA Jukebox 1987), I Won't Need You Anymore, No Holding Back, 1989; film appearances include: Frank and Jesse, 1994, The Legend of O.B. Taggart, 1995, Edie & Pen, 1996; (TV mini series) Texas, 1994, (TV movie) Dead Man's Revenge, 1994. Named Top Male Vocalist, Acad. Country Music, 1987, Male Vocalist of Yr., Music City News, 1987, Star of Tomorrow, Music City News, 1987, Male Vocalist of Yr., Country Music Assn., 1987, Entertainer of Yr. Music City News, 1988, Male Artist of Yr., 1988, Favorite Entertainer, Favorite Entertainer, Nashville Network Viewers Choice Awards, 1988; recipient Horizon award Country Music Assn., 1986, Grammy award, 1987, Am. Music award, best country album, 1988, Am. Music award, best country single, 1988, Country Music Assn. best male vocalist, 1988. Mem. Grand Ole Opry. Office: Warner Bros Rec 20 Music Square E Nashville TN 37203*

TRAVIS, SHIRLEY LOUISE, nursing administrator; b. Falls City, Nebr., July 16, 1950; d. Vernon J. and Gladys E. (Veach) Gerweck; children: Stacy, Kimberly. Diploma, Clarkson Coll. Nursing, Omaha, 1971; BS, Coll. St. Francis, Joliet, Ill., 1982; MSA, Ctrl. Mich. U., 1992. RN. Staff nurse Lincoln (Nebr.) Gen. Hosp., 1971-73, head nurse, 1973-74, staff asst., 1974-76, dir. nursing, 1976-87, v.p., 1987—; chair ADN, LPN S.E. Cmty. Coll. Bd., Lincoln, 1976—. Alumni Leadership Lincoln, 1992—. Mem. ANA (cert. nurse adminstr. 1985, 90), Am. Orgn. Nurse Execs., Nebr. Nurses Assn. (conv. del. 1992—), Nebr. Orgn. Nurse Execs. (pres., Nurse Exec. Leadership award 1994). Avocations: reading, walking, swimming. Home: 6900 Pike Pl Lincoln NE 68516-1571

TRAVIS, VANCE KENNETH, petroleum business executive; b. Coriander, Sask., Can., Jan. 30, 1926; s. Roy Hazen and Etta Orilla (Anderson) T.; m. Louise Mary, Nov. 30, 1948 (div. 1979); children: Stuart, Shirley, Gordon, Donald, Marian; m. Mildred Elaine, June 29, 1979; stepchildren: Susan, Nancy, Gordon, Sandra, Karen. Chmn. bd. Turbo Resources Ltd., 1970-83, Challenger Internat., 1977-83, Bankeno Mines Ltd., 1977-83, Queenston Gold Mines Ltd., Toronto, Ont., Can., 1977-84, Health Risk Mgmt. Inc., Mpls., 1984-86, Triad Internat. Inc., 1985—; dir. Health Resource Mgmt. Ltd., Edmonton, 1990—; bd. dirs. Vencap Equities Alta. Ltd., Edmonton, 1981-86, L.K. Resources Ltd., Calgary, 1973-84. Mem. Young. Pres.'s Orgn., Calgary, 1964-76, World Pres. Orgn. Recipient Presdl. pin Jr. Achievement, 1963, Best Pitcher award Petroleum Fastball League, 1955. Clubs: Calgary Petroleum, Ranchmen's. Office: Triad Internat Inc, 150-6 Ave SW Ste 3200, Calgary, AB Canada T2P 3Y7 also: Health Resource Mgmt Ltd, 10104-103rd Ave Ste 800, Edmonton, AB Canada T5J 4R5 also: Med Tech Corp, 100 Med Tech Plz, 6005-11 St SE, Calgary, Canada T2H 2Z3

TRAVISANO, FRANK PETER, professional management consultant, business broker; b. Newark, Feb. 5, 1921; s. Peter Fountain and Carmela Elizabeth (Tellone) T.; m. Nancy Jean Drees; children: Peter, Thomas, James, Theresa, Patricia. BS in Bus., Rutgers U., 1943, postgrad. in mktg., 1945, postgrad. in real estate, 1946; Cert. Computers, morris C.C., Morris County, Randolph, 1985. Cert. profl. mgmt. cons. Various to pres. Rochester Lubricator Co., Newark, 1943-71, Franklin Hosp. Equipment Co., Newark, 1955-71, Acme Plating Works, Newark, 1961-72, Micro Machine Co., Union, N.J., 1962-72, Darwin Phoenix Co., Cranbury, N.J., 1972—, Darwin Safety Packaging Co., Cranbury, 1986—; exec. v.p. Logos Group, Chester, N.J., 1987—; bd dirs., mktg. mgr. Artisan Controls Corp., Parsippany, N.J., 1991—; mktg. cons., bd. dirs. 1st Occupl. Ctr. of N.J.; cons. dir. TPI Inc., Lodi, N.J., 1991—; sr. cons. Solutions Group, Madison, N.J., 1991—; cons. OM Internat., 1982—, Man-Roland PPI, 1985—, Superior MPM Plastics, 1990—; mgmt. cons. First Occupl. Ctr. N.J., 1996—, Guidon Inc., Reliance Internat. Inventor in field of hosp. products and saftety packaging materials. Co-founder Essexfields Youthful Offenders Program, pres. 1965; sr. assoc. First Occupl. Ctr. of N.J. Recipient various svc. awards Rutgers U. Mem. Inst. Chem. Physics (chmn. bd. dirs. 1993—), Rutgers U. Alumni Assn. (bd. dirs., pres. 1966-67), Kiwanis (bd. dirs.), Newark Execs. Assn. (pres. 1960). Avocations: inventions in field.

TRAVOLTA, JOHN, actor; b. Englewood, N.J., Feb. 18, 1954; s. Salvatore and Helen (Burke) T.; m. Kelly Preston; one child, Jett. Appeared in TV series Welcome Back Kotter, 1975-77; TV movies: The Boy in the Plastic Bubble, 1976; films: Carrie, 1976, Saturday Night Fever, 1977 (Best Actor award Nat. Bd. Rev., 1977, Best Actor Acad. award nominee 1977, Best Actor 1st runner up Nat. Soc. Film Critics 1977, Best Actor 2nd runner up N.Y. Film Critics Circle 1977), Grease, 1978 (Golden Globe World Film Favorite 1978), Moment-By-Moment, 1979, Urban Cowboy, 1980, Blow Out, 1981, Staying Alive, 1983 (Male/Box Office Star of Yr., Nat. Assn. Theatre Owners ShowEast 1983), Two of a Kind, 1983, Perfect, 1985, The Dumb Waiter, 1987, The Experts, 1989, Chains of Gold, 1980, Look Who's Talking, 1989 (Male/Box Office Star of Yr., Nat. Assn. Theatre Owners ShowEast 1989), Look Who's Talking Too, 1990, The Tender, 1991, Shout, 1991, Look Who's Talking Now, 1993, Pulp Fiction, 1994 (Best Actor Acad. award nominee 1994, Best Actor award nominee Brit. Acad. Film and TV Arts 1994, Golden Globe Best Actor award nominee 1994, Best Actor award nominee SAG 1994, Best Actor award nominee Chgo. Film Critics 1994, Best Actor award nominee Comedy awards 1994, Best Actor award L.A. Film Critics 1994, Best Actor award Stockholm Film Festival 1993, Best Actor award London Film Critics Cir. 1994), Get Shorty, 1995, White Man's Burden, 1995, Broken Arrow, 1995, Phenomenon, 1996, Michael, 1996, Face Off, 1997; author: Staying Fit, 1984; rec. artist album, 1976, 77. Recipient Best Male Vocalist Billboard award, 1976, Best Male Vocalist award Record World and Music Retail mag., 1976, Best Actor Golden Apple award Cue mag., Juno award Can. Acad. Rec. Arts and Scis., 1978; nominated Best New Male Star Women's Press Club, 1976; named Man of Yr., Hasty Pudding Club, Harvard U., 1981.

TRAWICK, LEONARD MOSES, English educator; b. Decatur, Ala., July 4, 1933; s. Leonard M. and Frances (Earle) T.; m. Kerstin Ekfelt, July 16, 1960; children: Eleanor, Matthew. BA, U. of South, 1955; MA in English, U. Chgo., 1956; PhD in English, Harvard U., 1961. Asst. prof. Columbia U., N.Y.C., 1961-69; from assoc. prof. to prof. English Cleve. State U., 1969—; editor Poetry Ctr., Cleve. State U., 1971—, dir., 1990-92. Editor: Backgrounds of Romanticism, 1968, World, Self, Poem, 1990, (poems) Beastmorfs, 1994; editor, prin. translator: German Literature of the Romantic Era and Age of Goethe, 1993; author (opera libretto) Mary Stuart: A Queen Betrayed, 1991; founding editor mag. The Gamut, 1980-92 (Ohioana award for Editl. Excellence 1991). Recipient Individual Artist award Ohio Arts Coun., 1980; Ohioana Poetry award, 1994. Office: Cleve State U Dept English Cleveland OH 44115

TRAXLER, WILLIAM BYRD, retired lawyer; b. Greenville, S.C., July 10, 1912; s. David Byrd and Mary Willey (Gatling) T. Student The Citadel, 1929-30, U. Tex., 1930-32; JD, George Washington U., 1940. Bar: D.C. 1940, S.C. 1940, U.S. Ct. Appeals (4th cir.) 1960. Ptnr. Hinson, Traxler and Hamer, Greenville, 1950-58, Rainey, Fant, Traxler and Horton, 1958-60; sole practice, Greenville, 1960-94; ret., 1994. Bd. dirs. Phyllis Wheatly Assn., 1954, Vis. Nurse Assn., Greenville, 1957-59, United Way, Greenville, 1976; vice-chmn. bd. health City of Greenville, 1960-68; life mem. The Citadel Endowment Fund; prosecutor So. Bavaria Mil. Govt., asst. in reopening German civil cts. Capt. U.S. Army, 1942-46. Recipient Alumni Achievement award George Washington U., 1946. Fellow S.C. Bar Found.; mem. S.C. State Bar Assn., Greenville County Bar Assn. (pres. 1976), Greenville C. of C. (Chmn. of Yr. 1967, chmn. taxation com.), Law Sci. Acad., George Washington U. Law Assn. (life), Phi Alpha Delta (justice 1939), Beta Theta Pi, Torch Club (pres. 1956), Greenville Country Club (bd. govs. 1982-85). Author: Military Government in Germany, 1960, Political Third Parties, 1968, History of the Fourteenth Amendment, 1974, The Jury Numbers Game, 1976, Medieval Harmony, 1982, Presumptions of Life and Death, 1989. Home: 100 Trails End Greenville SC 29607-1741

TRAXLER, WILLIAM BYRD, JR., federal judge; b. Greenville, S.C., May 1, 1948; s. William Byrd and Bettie (Wooten) T.; m. Patricia Alford, Aug. 21, 1971; children: William Byrd III, James McCall. BA, Davidson Coll., 1970; JD, U. S.C., 1973. Assoc. William Byrd Traxler, Greenville, 1973-75; asst. solicitor 13th Jud. Ct., Greenville, 1975-78, dep. solicitor, 1978-81, solicitor, 1981-85, resident crct. judge, 1985-92; U.S. Dist. judge Dist. of S.C., Greenville, 1992—. Recipient Outstanding Svc. award Solicitors Assn., S.C., 1987, Leadership award Probation, Parole & Pardon Svcs., S.C., 1990. Office: US Dist Ct 300 E Washington St Greenville SC 29601-2800

TRAYLOR, ANGELIKA, stained glass artist; b. Munich, Bavaria, Germany, Aug. 24, 1942; Came to U.S., 1959; d. Walther Artur Ferdinand and Berta Kreszentia (Boeck) Klau; m. Lindsay Montgomery Donaldson, June 10, 1959 (div. 1970); 1 child, Cameron Maria Greta; m. Samuel William Traylor III, June 12, 1970. Student, Pvt. Handelsschule Morawetz Jr. Coll., Munich, 1958. Freelance artist, 1980—. Works featured in profl. jours. including the Daylily Jour., 1987, Design Jour., South Korea, 1989, The Traveler's Guide to American Crafts, 1990, Florida Mag., 1991, Florida Today, 1993, Melbourne Times, 1994, The Orbiter, 1996, The Glass Collector's Digest, 1996. Recipient Fragile Art award Glass Art mag., 1982, 1st Yr. Exhibitor award Stained Glass Assn. Am., 1984, 2d pl. Non-figurative Composition award Vitraux des USA, 1985, Best of Show Stained Glass Assn. Am., 1989, 3d pl., 1989, Merit award George Plimpton All-Star Space Coast Art Open, 1994; named Hist. Woman of Brevard, Brevard Cultural Alliance, 1991, one of 200 Best Am. Craftsmen Early Am. Life mag., 1994, 95, 97. Home and Office: 100 Poinciana Dr Indian Harbor Beach FL 32937

TRAYLOR, JOAN SADLER, interior design educator; b. Pique, Ohio; d. Carl E. and Mary E. (Bond) Sadler; children: Douglas Traylor, Michelle Traylor. BS in Interior Design and Art, Western Ky. U., 1981, MS in Interior Design, 1984. Interior designer Interiors By Biggers, Glasgow, Ky., 1981-83; teaching fellow Western Ky. U., Bowling Green, 1983-84, instr. interior design, 1985; asst. prof. interior design U. So. Miss., Hattiesburg, 1985-91, assoc. prof. interior design, 1991—, interior design program coord., 1990—; prof. Brit. studies abroad program, 1989—; presenter profl. assn. meetings. Contbr. articles and abstracts to profl. publs. Mem., officer Warren County Arts Alliance, Bowling Green, 1977-85; mem. Jr. Woman's Club, Bowling Green, 1970-76. Mem. Interior Design Educators Coun., Am. Soc. Interior Design Educators Coun., Am. Soc. Interior Designers (La. chpt. presdl. citation 1991), Inst. Bus. Designers (officer Delta chpt. 1992-94), Nat. Trust for Hist. Preservation, New Orleans Preservation Resource Ctr., Hattiesburg Hist. Soc., Designed Comm. Assn., Internat. Interior Design Assn. (Miss. dir. 1994—), Phi Upsilon Omicron, Phi Delta Kappa, Delta Kappa Gamma. Avocations: travel, drawing and painting, textile design. Home: 315 Woodshire Dr Hattiesburg MS 39402 Office: U So Miss SS Box 5035 Hattiesburg MS 39406-5035

TRAYLOR, ORBA FOREST, economist, lawyer, educator; b. Providence, Ky., June 16, 1910; s. Eddie Ewing and Dillie (Stuart) T.; m. Josephine Zananiri, Nov. 17, 1945; children—Joseph Marion, Robert Forest, John Christopher. B.A., Western Ky. U., 1930; M.A., U. Ky., 1932, Ph.D., 1948; J.D., Northwestern U., 1936. Bar: Ky. 1941. Head dept. econs. Ashland Coll., 1935-36; legal asst. trust dept. 1st Nat. Bank, Chgo., 1936-37; assoc. prof. econs., sociology Western Ky. U., 1938-40; research asst. Bur. Bus. Research, U. Ky., 1939; research dir. Ky. Legislative Council, 1939-41; dir. research and statistics Ky. Dept. Welfare, 1941; assoc. econ. analyst div. tax research U.S. Treasury Dept., 1942; acting chief acctg. UNRRA, Balkan Mission, 1944-45; asst. prof. econs. and bus. U. Denver, 1946-47, U. Mo., 1947-50; tax specialist, asst. econ. commr. ECA, Greece, 1950-53; coordinator exec. devel. programs Ordnance Corps, Dept. Army, 1954; pub. fin. expert UN; lectr. fin. adminstrn. Inst. Pub. Adminstrn., Egypt, 1954-56; exec. asst. to lt. gov. Ky. Legislative Research Commn., Frankfort, 1956-58; commr. fin. State of Ky., Frankfort, 1958-59; dir. finance Office High Commr., Ryukyu Islands, 1960-64; dir. econ. affairs Office High Commr., 1964-65; prof. econs. and pub. adminstrn. U. Ala., Huntsville, 1965-75; chmn. dept. bus. and pub. adminstrn. U. Ala., 1966-68, chmn. econs., 1968-70; vis. prof. pub. adminstrn. San Diego State U., 1975-76, Western Ky. U., 1976-77; fin. economist AID, U.S. State Dept., 1977-78; adj. prof. Ala. A&M U., 1978-81, N.Y. U. and Rider Coll., 1981-82, Columbia Coll., 1982—; cons. economist Am. Tech. Services, Inc., 1982-91; cons. ops. research Johns Hopkins U., 1957-61; fiscal cons. various orgns.; vis. lectr. econs. various univs. and colls.; lectr. U. Md. Far East Div., 1960-65, Ala. A&M U., 1976-77, Fla. Inst. Tech., 1977; sr. adv. Bank of Ryukyus, 1960-65, Joint Fgn. Investment Bd., 1964-65; chmn. bd. Ryukyuan Devel. Loan Corp., 1960-65, Joint Petroleum Bd., 1960-65; counsellor Oak Ridge Asso. Univs., 1966-67. Mem. editorial bd.: Public Adminstrn. Rev, 1973-79; contbr. articles to profl. publs. Mem. Ala. Edn. Study Commn. Fin. Task Force, 1968-69; chmn. fin. com. Top of Ala. Health Planning Agy., 1974-75; mem. adv. com. Ala. Legislature, 1981-94. With AUS, 1942-46; lt. col. Res. (ret.). Mem. Am., So. econs. assns., Am. Soc. for Pub. Adminstrn. (council 1973-75), Am., Ky. bar assns., Nat. Tax Assn. (dir. 1971-74), local C. of C., Res. Officers Assn., Mil. Order World Wars, Beta Gamma Sigma, Delta Sigma Pi. Democrat. Baptist. Club: Rotary. Address: 216 Westmoreland Ave SE Huntsville AL 35801-2726

TRAYLOR, ROBERT ARTHUR, lawyer; b. Syracuse, N.Y., Jan. 15, 1949; s. Robert Arthur and Julia Elizabeth (McNulty) T.; m. Bonita Lynn Schmidt, Nov. 26, 1977. BS, LeMoyne Coll., 1970; JD cum laude, Syracuse U., 1975. Bar: N.Y., U.S. Dist. Ct. (no. dist.) N.Y., U.S. Tax Ct. Atty. Love, Balducci & Scaccia, Syracuse, N.Y., 1976-77; estate tax atty. IRS, Syracuse, 1977-81; atty. Scaccia Law Firm, Syracuse, 1981—. Contbr. articles to profl. jours. Of counsel The Saint Ann Sch., Syracuse, 1981—, mem. coordinating com. Vision 2000 1994—). With U.S. Army, 1970-72. Recipient Outstanding Acctg. award Fin. Execs. Inst.-Syracuse Chpt., 1972, Cert. Achievement, Commanding Gen.-VII Corps., U.S. Army, 1972, Am. Jurisprudence award Adminstrv. Law, 1975. Mem. ABA, Onondaga County Bar Assn. (vol. lawyer program 1993—, Vol. Lawyer of Month 1994), World Wildlife Fedn. Republican. Roman Catholic. Avocations: motorsports, military history, Catholic education. Home: 112 Knowland Dr Liverpool NY 13090-3130 Office: Scaccia Law Firm Ste 402 State Tower Bldg Syracuse NY 13202

TRAYNHAM, JAMES GIBSON, chemist, educator; b. Broxton, Ga., Aug. 5, 1925; s. James G. and Eddie Louise (Greer) T.; m. Margaret A. Egert, 1948; children: David F., Peter C.; m. Gresdna A. Doty, 1980. Student, South Ga. Coll., 1942-43; B.S., U. N.C., 1946; Ph.D., Northwestern U., 1950. Instr. Northwestern U., 1949-50; asst. prof. Denison U., 1950-53; mem. faculty La. State U., Baton Rouge, 1953—; prof. chemistry La. State U., 1963-88, prof. emeritus, 1988—, chmn. dept. chemistry, 1968-73, vice chancellor for advanced studies and rsch., dean Grad. Sch., 1973-81;

postdoctoral research fellow Ohio State U., 1951-53. Author: Organic Nomenclature: A Programmed Introduction, 1966, 5th edit., 1997; editor: Essays on the History of Organic Chemistry, 1987; contbr. articles to profl. jours. Bd. dirs. Council Grad. Schs. in U.S., 1981. Recipient Petroleum Research Fund-Am. Chem. Soc. Type D award Eidg. Technische Hochschule, Zurich, Switzerland, 1959-60; Charles E. Coates award Baton Rouge sects. Am. Chem. Soc. and Am. Inst. Chem. Engrs., 1965; NATO sr. fellow in sci. Universität des Saarlandes, Saarbrücken, Fed. Republic Germany, 1972. Mem. Am. Chem. Soc. (councilor, past chmn. Baton Rouge sect., chmn. divsn. history of chemistry 1988), La. Acad. Sci., Internat. Union Pure and Applied Chemistry (titular mem. commn. on nomenclature of organic chemistry, sec. 1994—), Phi Beta Kappa, Sigma Xi, Phi Lambda Upsilon, Phi Kappa Phi (past pres. La. State U. chpt.). Home: 628 Polytech Dr Baton Rouge LA 70808-4755

TRAYNOR, J. MICHAEL, lawyer; b. Oakland, Calif., Oct. 25, 1934; s. Roger J. and Madeleine (Lackmann) T.; m. Shirley Williams, Feb. 11, 1956; children: Kathleen Traynor Millard, Elizabeth Traynor Fowler, Thomas. B.A., U. Calif., Berkeley, 1955; J.D., Harvard U., 1960. Bar: Calif. 1961, U.S. Supreme Ct. 1966. Dep. atty. gen. State of Calif., San Francisco, 1961-63; spl. counsel Calif. Senate Com. on Local Govt., Sacramento, 1963; assoc. firm Cooley Godward, LLP, San Francisco, 1963-69, ptnr., 1969—; adviser 3d Restatement of Unfair Competition, 1988-95, 3d Restatement of Torts; Products Liability, 1992—, Apportionment, 1994—, 1988 Revs. 2d Restatement of Conflict of Laws, 2d Restatement of Restitution, 1981-85; lectr. U. Calif. Boalt Hall Sch. Law, Berkeley, 1982-89, 1996—; chmn. Sierra Club Legal Defense Fund, 1989-91, pres. 1991-92, adv. bd., 1996—, Trust for Pub. Land, 1997—. Mem. bd. overseers Inst. for Civil Justice The RAND Corp., 1991-97; bd. dirs. Environ. Law Inst., 1992—, Sierra Legal Defence Fund, 1990-96. Served to 1st lt. USMC, 1955-57. Fellow AAAS, Am. Bar Found. (life); mem. Am. Law Inst. (coun. 1985—, 2d v.p. 1993—), Bar Assn. San Francisco (pres. 1973). Home: 3131 Eton Ave Berkeley CA 94705-2713 Office: Cooley Godward LLP 1 Maritime Plz Ste 2000 San Francisco CA 94111-3510

TRAYNOR, SEAN GABRIAL, manufacturing executive; b. Waterford, Ireland, Jan. 6, 1950; came to U.S., 1974; s. Sean Gerard and Norah Mary (Gower) T.; m. Geraldine Margaret Turner, Aug. 21, 1974; children: Kevin, Patrick, Tara. BA in Chemistry magna cum laude, Trinity Coll., 1971, PhD in Chemistry, 1974. Rsch. chemist SCM Glidco Organics, 1975, mgr. devel., 1980, dir. devel. and engring., 1984, dir. mktg., 1986, v.p. sales and mktg., 1986-93; chmn., CEO Garden State Tanning Inc., King of Prussia, Pa., 1993—; bd. dirs. Leather Industries Am. Co-author: (chpt.) Chemistry of Turpentine, 1989; contbr. over 30 articles to profl. jours. Pres. Irish Cultural Assn., Jacksonville, Fla., 1980. Recipient Exec. Achievement award Hanson Industries, 1990. Fellow Am. Inst. Chemists, Am. Chem. Soc.; mem. Anethole Task Force (co-chmn. 1989-92), Rotary (bd. dirs. Jacksonville chpt. 1991-92). Achievements include 12 patents in field organic chemistry. Office: Garden State Tanning Inc 630 Freedom Bus Ctr King Of Prussia PA 19406

TREACY, GERALD BERNARD, lawyer; b. Newark, July 29, 1951; s. Gerald B. Sr. and Mabel L. (Nesbitt) T.; m. Joyce M. Biazzo, Apr. 6, 1974. BA summa cum laude, Rider Coll., 1973; JD, UCLA, 1981. Bar: Calif. 1981, Wash. 1982, D.C. 1995. Tchr. English Arthur L. Johnson Regional High Sch., Clark, N.J., 1973-77; assoc. Gibson, Dunn & Crutcher, L.A., 1981-82; ptnr. Perkins Coie, Bellevue, Wash., 1982-94, McGuire Woods Battle & Boothe, McLean, Va., 1994-96; McGuire Woods Battle & Boothe, Bellevue, Wash.; ptnr. Egger, Betts, Austin, Treacy & Bellingham, Bellevue, Wash., 1996-97, Ahrens, Egger, Treacy & DeAngelis, Boise, Idaho, 1997—; chmn. bd. dirs. estate planning adv. bd. U. Wash., Seattle, 1990-92; presenter TV Seminar, Where There's a Will, PBS affiliate. Author: Washington Guardianship Law, Administration and Litigation, 1988, supplemented, 1991, 2d edit., 1992, supplemented, 1993, Supporting Organizations, 1996. Mem. endowment fund com. United Way, Seattle, 1987-89, exec. com. Washington Planned Giving Coun., 1993-94, 96—; bd. dirs., mem. adv. bd. ARC, Seattle, 1985-89, Arthritis Gift, 1987-89, Seattle Symphony, 1992—, Seattle U., 1996—. Mem. Eastside King County Estate Planning Coun., Order of Coif. Avocations: photography, hiking, ethnic and classical music, poetry, host/writer Gilbert & Sullivan radio show. Office: Egger Betts Austin Treacy 500 108th Ave NE Ste 2300 Bellevue WA 98004-5500

TREACY, VINCENT EDWARD, lawyer; b. Mass., Jan. 30, 1942; m. Edith Barnett. AB, Boston Coll., 1964; JD with honors, George Washington U., 1971. Bar: Va. 1972, D.C. 1973. Atty. Fed. Labor Rels. Coun., Washington, 1971-73; legis. atty. Am. law divsn. Congrl. Rsch. Svc., Libr. Congress, Washington, 1973—; cons. Romanian Legal Analysis and Legis. Drafting Conf., Senate and Chamber Duputies Romania, Bucharest, 1996. Mem. law rev. staff George Washington Law Rev., 1970. Cons. Romanian legal analysis and legis. drafting conf. Senate and Chamber of Deps. of Romania, Bucharest, 1996. Mem. ABA, Fed. Bar Assn., U.S. Supreme Ct. Bar, George Washington Law Alumni Assn. (pres. Capitol Hill chpt. 1986-87), Order of the Coif.

TREACY, WILLIAM JOSEPH, electrical and environmental engineer; b. N.Y.C., Jan. 16, 1959; s. William Joseph and Angela Bridget (Keane) T.; m. Tamra Jeanne Ackerman, Dec. 7, 1985; 1 child, Denise Marie. BSEE, Manhattan Coll., 1981; M in Aero. Sci., Embry-Riddle U., 1987. Commd. 2d lt. USAF, 1981, advanced through grades to capt.; project mgr. USAF, Victorville, Calif., 1981-84; dept. chief Netherlands GLCM program office USAF, Ramstein, Germany, 1984-88; chief engr. USAF, Soesterberg, The Netherlands, 1988-91; heavy repair supt. USAF, Plattsburgh, 1991-92; CFO USAF, Plattsburgh, N.Y., 1992-94, chief environ. engr., 1994-95; bldg. systems supr. Plattsburgh Airbase Redevel. Corp., 1995—; computer technician, Plattsburgh, 1992—. Active Red Cross, Plattsburgh, 1992. Decorated Meritorious Svc. medal, Air Force Commendation medal with one oak leaf cluster, others; USAF ROTC Program Acad. scholar, 1978. Mem. IEEE, Aircraft Owners and Pilots Assn., Friends of Fort Ticonderoga, Am. Legion. Republican. Roman Catholic. Avocations: flying, star trek memorabilia, cross-country skiing. Home: 60 Leonard Ave Plattsburgh NY 12901 Office: Plattsburgh Airbase Redevel Corp 426 Us Oval Ste 1000 Plattsburgh NY 12903-3333

TREADWAY, JAMES CURRAN, investment company executive, lawyer, former government official; b. Anderson, S.C., May 21, 1943; s. James C. and Maxine (Hall) T.; m. Susan Pepper Davis, Sept. 6, 1969; children: Elizabeth Pepper Hall, Caroline Worrell Harper. A.B., U. Ga., 1964; JD summa cum laude, Washington and Lee U., 1967. Bar: Ga. 1967, Mass. 1968, D.C. 1970. Assoc. Candler, Cox, McClain & Andrews, Atlanta, 1967-68, Gadsby & Hannah, Boston and Washington, 1968-72; ptnr. Dickstein, Shapiro & Morin, Washington, 1972-82; commr. SEC, Washington, 1982-85; ptnr. Baker & Botts, Washington, 1985-87; exec. v.p. PaineWebber Group Inc., N.Y.C., 1987—; chmn. Nat. Commn. on Fraudulent Fin. Reporting, 1985-87. Mem. Mass. Bar Assn., Ga. Bar Assn., D.C. Bar Assn., Chevy Chase (Md.) Club, Bedford (N.Y.) Golf and Tennis Club, City Tavern Club, Met. Club, Univ. Club (Washignton), Verbank Hunting and Fishing Club (Uniondale N.Y.; dir. 1995—), Order of Coif, Phi Beta Kapap, Omicron Delta Kappa. Republican. Roman Catholic. Home: Laurel Ledge RD 4 Croton Lake Rd Bedford Corners NY 10549 Office: PaineWebber Group Inc 1285 Ave Of The Americas New York NY 10019-6028

TREADWAY, JOHN DAVID, history educator; b. San Bernardino, Calif., June 30, 1950; s. Emery Russell and Mabel A. (Batchelor) T.; m. Sandra Gioia, Sept. 4, 1976; 1 child, Robyn. BA summa cum laude, Fla. State U., 1972; PhD, U. Va., 1980. Prof. History U. Richmond, Va., 1980—; vis. prof. U. Belgrade, 1990; hist. cons. Fgn. Svc. Inst. Author: The Falcon and the Eagle, 1983; co-editor: The Soviet Union under Gorbachev, 1987; contbg. author: Crises in the Balkans, 1997, Ency. of Modern East Europe, 1997; editor Ind. Slavic Studies/Balkanistica, 1991-92; book reviewer Am. Hist. Rev., Historian, Choice, Slavic Rev., Serbian Studies, Austrian History Yearbook, others; contbr. articles to profl. jours. Recipient Disting. Educator award U. Richmond, 1985, 88, 91, 95, Outstanding faculty award Va., 1993; fellow ITT Internat., 1975-76, Fulbright, 1985, 90, Woodrow Wilson Ctr., 1989, Va. Found. for the Humanities, 1997; grantee NDFL, 1976-77, ACLS, 1981, Internat. Rsch. and Exch. Bd., 1981. Mem. Am. Hist. Assn., Southern Hist. Assn. (Snell prize 1985-87), Va. Hist. Soc., Am. Assn. for Advancement Slavic Studies, Am. Assn. Southeast European Studies (pres. 1987-89), North Am. Soc. Serbian Studies (exec. com. 1985-88), Library Svc. and Construction Act Adv. Coun., Va. Social Sci. Assn. (exec. bd. 1987-89), Soc. for Austrian and Habsburg History. Lutheran. Home: 8201 Gaylord Rd Richmond VA 23229-4121 Office: U Richmond Dept History Richmond VA 23173

TREADWAY-DILLMON, LINDA LEE, athletic trainer, actress; b. Woodbury, N.J., June 4, 1950; d. Leo Elmer and Ona Lee (Wyckoff) Treadway; m. Randall Kenneth Dillmon, June 19, 1982. BS in Health, Phys. Edn. & Recreation, West Chester State Coll., 1972, MS in Health and Phys. Edn., 1975; postgrad., Ctrl. Mich. U., 1978; Police Officer Stds. Tng. cert. complaint dispatcher, Goldenwest Coll., 1982. Cert. in safety edn. West Chester State Coll.; cert. EMT, Am. Acad. Orthopaedic Surgeons. Grad. asst., instr., asst. athletic trainer West Chester (Pa.) State Coll., 1972-76; asst. prof., program dir., asst. athletic trainer Ctrl. Mich. U., Mt. Pleasant, 1976-80; police dispatcher City of Westminster, Calif., 1980-89; oncology unit sec. Children's Hosp. Orange County, Orange, Calif., 1989-96; control clk. food & beverage Marriott Hotel, Anaheim, Calif., 1996—. Stuntwoman, actress United Stunt Artists, SAG, L.A., 1982—; dancer Disneyland, Anaheim, Calif., 1988—; contbr. articles to profl. jours. Athletic trainer U.S. Olympic Women's Track and Field Trials, Frederick, Md., 1972, AAU Jr. World Wrestling Championships, Mt. Pleasant, Mich., 1977, Mich. Spl. Olympics, Mt. Pleasant, 1977, 78, 79. Named Outstanding Phys. Educator, Delta Psi Kappa, Ctrl. Mich. U., 1980, Outstanding Young Woman of Am., 1984; named to Disneyland Entertainment Hall of Fame, 1995. Mem. SAG, Nat. Athletic Trainers Assn. (cert., women and athletic tng. ad hoc com. 1974-75, placement com. 1974-79, program dirs. coun. 1976-80, ethics com. 1977-80, visitation team 1978-80, 25 Yr. award 1997), U.S. Field Hockey Assn. (player), Pacific S.W. Field Hockey Assn. (player, Nat. Champion 1980, 81, 82), L.A. Field Hockey Assn. (player), Swing Shift Dance Team (dancer). Presbyterian. Avocations: flying, piano, athletics, stitchery, travel. Home: 15400 Belgrade St Apt 152 Westminster CA 92683-6962

TREADWELL, ALEXANDER F., state official; b. London, Mar. 25, 1946; m. Libby, 1970; children: Carrie, Zach. BA, U. N.C. Former chmn. Essex Cty. Rep. Committee; vice chmn. NY St. Rep. Party, 1989; sec. of state State of N.Y., 1995—; Reporter & freelance journalist, Sports Illustrated, writer, Classic Magazine, NY Magazine. Author: The World of Marathons, Stewart, Tabori & Chang, 1987. NY Army Natl. Guard, 1968-74. Office: Ofc of Sec State 162 Washington Ave Albany NY 12210-2304*

TREADWELL, HUGH WILSON, publishing executive; b. Waurika, Okla., Nov. 21, 1921; s. Hugh and Jessie Ellen (Cogdell) T.; m. Edith Albena Doolittle, June 20, 1959; children—Pamela, Hugh, Cynthia. B.A., U. Okla., 1949, M.A., 1952; diploma in French Studies (Rotary Found. fellow), Institut de Touraine, U. Poitiers, France, 1950. Asst. editor internat. lit. quar. Books Abroad, U. Okla., 1952-53; field rep. coll. dept. The Macmillan Co., 1953-60, Holt, Rinehart & Winston, Inc., Okla. and Tex., 1960-62; mgr. coll. programs in fgn. lang. dept. Holt, Rinehart & Winston, Inc., N.Y.C., 1962-67; sr. editor coll. dept. Random House-Knopf, N.Y.C., 1967-72; dir. U. N.Mex. Press, Albuquerque, 1973-80, Tex. Western Press, U. Tex., El Paso, 1981-85; pvt. practice cons., 1985—; field rep. coll. dept. W. W. Norton & Co., Tex., N.Mex., Okla., 1988-93; instr. ESL El Paso C.C., 1994—; instr. French U. Okla., 1952-53; Industry rep. Nat. Com. Support of Fgn. Langs., 1971. Pres. El Paso Council for Internat. Visitors, 1987-88. Served with USAAF, 1943-46. Decorated Air medal. Mem. Phi Beta Kappa. Democrat. Club: Alliance Francaise (El Paso). Home: 6832 La Cadena Dr El Paso TX 79912-2810 *In my mind, the pursuit of happiness has always been bound up with the pursuit of knowledge—knowledge not in a purely abstract sense, but purposeful knowledge humanely applied. The professions of teaching and publishing, if practiced in the light of the highest ethical standards associated with each, make this pursuit possible and offer the greatest satisfaction to those who view life as I do. I consider myself fortunate to have served in both of these professions.*

TREANOR, CHARLES EDWARD, scientist; b. Buffalo, Oct. 22, 1924; s. William Michael and Margaret Mary (Powers) T.; m. Ruth Ziegelmaier, Jan. 28, 1950; children: Timothy, John, Peter, Michael, Melissa. B.A., U. Minn., 1947; Ph.D., U. Buffalo, 1956. Instr. physics U. Buffalo, 1952-53; physicist Cornell Aero. Lab., Buffalo, 1954-68, head aerodynamic research dept., 1968-78; v.p. phys. sci. group Calspan Corp., Buffalo, 1978-83, v.p., chief scientist, 1983-90; pres. CTSA, Inc., 1990—. Contbr. articles to profl. jours. Patentee in field. Served to lt. U.S. Army, 1943-46. Recipient C.C. Furnas award SUNY, Buffalo, 1989. Fellow Am. Phys. Soc. (div. chmn. 1977), AIAA (com. chmn. 1975-76, 87-89, Fluid and Plasma Dynamics award 1978); mem. NAE. Home: 140 Segsbury Rd Buffalo NY 14221-3425

TREANOR, GERARD FRANCIS, JR., lawyer; b. Medford, Mass., July 1, 1943. AB, Holy Cross Coll., Worcester, Mass.; 1965; JD, Cath. U., Washington, 1968. Bar: D.C. 1969. Law clk. to chief judge U.S. Dist. Ct. D.C., Washington, 1968-69; spl. counsel U.S. Ho. of Reps., Washington, 1972-73; asst. U.S. atty. U.S. Dept. Justice, Washington, 1973-77; ptnr. Dolan & Treanor, Arlington, Va., 1977-86, Venable, Baetjer, Howard & Civiletti, Washington, 1986-92, Cacheris & Treanor, Washington, 1993—. Lt. USNR, 1969-72, Australia. Fellow Am. Bar Found., Am. Coll. of Trial Lawyers. Home: 1213 Aldebaran Dr Mc Lean VA 22101-2304 Address: 1100 Conn Ave NW Ste 730 Washington DC 20036

TREANOR, HELEN JUNE, nursing administrator, geriatrics professional; b. Battle Creek, Mich., Dec. 22, 1931; d. Antoine Joseph and Helen June (Jevnem) Hudon; m. Richard Clifford Treanor, Aug. 8, 1953; children: Kathleen, Theresa, Peggy, Michael, John, Sharon, Thomas. Diploma, U. Ill./Cook Co. Sch. Nursing, 1953; BS, Barat Coll., 1986; MBA, Lake Forest Grad. Sch., 1990. RN, CNA, Ill.; cert. nursing home adminstr., Ill., 1992. Staff nurse McNeal Meml. Hosp., Berwyn, Ill., 1953-55, Lake Forest (Ill.) Hosp., 1977-79; staff nurse, head nurse Good Shepherd Hosp., Barrington, Ill., 1979-87; pres., CEO N.W. Suburban Microfilm, Inc., Arlington Heights, Ill., 1987-91; dir. nursing and aux. svcs. Libertyville (Ill.) Manor Rehab. and Healthcare Ctr., 1991—; adv. bd. Lake County Vocat. Sch., Grayslake, Ill., 1992—. Pres. Friends of the Ela Area Libr., Lake Zurich, 1976-77, St. Frances de Sales Women's Orgn., Lake Zurich, Ill., 1970's. Mem. Nat. Assn. Dirs. Nursing Adminstrn. Avocations: aerobics, walking, gardening, reading, writing. Home: 21539 W Boschome Dr Kildeer IL 60047-7826 Office: Libertyville Manor Rehab and Healthcare Ctr 610 Peterson Rd Libertyville IL 60048-1014

TREASTER, JOSEPH B. (BLAND), journalist; b. Mt. Union, Pa., May 19, 1941; s. Ellsworth F. and Anna Katherine (Chalupka) T.; m. Barbara A. Gluck, June 6, 1970 (div. Aug. 1976); m. .Barbara J. Dill, Feb. 24, 1990; 1 child, Chloe Qiao Xing. BA, U. Miami, 1965; student, Sorbonne, Paris, 1971, San Francisco de Marroquin, Guatemala, 1988; MS, Columbia U., 1996. Reporter Miami (Fla.) Herald, 1963; staff asst. Saigon bur. N.Y. Times, 1965-67, Vietnam corr., 1968-69, 72-74; reporter N.Y. Times, N.Y.C., 1969-70; chief Conn. bur. N.Y. Times, 1970-72, investigative reporter N.J. bur., 1974-75, crime/youth violence writer, 1975-76, rewrite desk and spl. assignments to Washington, L.Am. and Mid. East, 1976-84, chief Caribbean bur., 1984-90, drug policy corr. with spl. assignments to the Mid-East, 1990-95, fin. writer, 1996—; freelance corr. Atlantic Monthly, Rolling Stone, The Nation, others; fellow Poynter Inst., St. Petersburg, Fla., 1993, U. Nev. Bus. Journalism, 1995; Knight-Bagehot fellow in econs. and bus. Columbia U., 1995-96; Poynter fellow Yale U., 1975. Co-author: No Hiding Place: Inside Report on the Hostage Crisis (in Iran), 1981; contbg. author: Encyclopedia Britannica, Insight Guide to Caribbean, Youth Violence, 1992. Served with U.S. Army, 1963-65, Vietnam. Recipient Page One award N.Y. Newspaper Guild, 1977, 79; Tom Wallace award Inter-Am. Press Assn., 1980, citation and awards Overseas Press Club Am., 1977, 80, 85, News Analysis award Soc. of Silurians, 1993, Casey medal for meritorious journalism U. Md., 1995, others. Mem. Mystery Writers Am. Avocations: skiing, sport fishing, running, bicycling. Office: NY Times 229 W 43rd St New York NY 10036-3913

TREASURE, JOHN ALBERT PENBERTHY, advertising executive; b. Usk, Monmouthshire, Eng., June 20, 1924; s. Harold Paul and Constance (Shapl) T.; m. Valerie Bell, Apr. 1954; children—Jonathan, Julian, Simon. Ph.D., Cambridge U., 1956. Research officer Brit. Market Research Bur., Ltd., London, 1952-56; mng. dir. Brit. Market Research Bur., Ltd., 1957-60; dir. research and mktg. J. Walter Thompson Co., Ltd., London, 1960-66; chmn. J. Walter Thompson Co., Ltd., 1967-77, John Treasure and Partners, London, 1981-83; dean City U. Bus. Sch., London, 1978-81; vice chmn. Saatchi & Saatchi Advt. Ltd., 1983-89; chmn. Taylor Nelson AGB plc, 1992—. Contbr. articles to profl. jours. Friend Royal Coll. Physicians; trustee Found. for Bus. Responsibilities. Fellow Inst. Practitioners in Advt. (past pres.); mem. Market Research Soc. (past pres.). Home: 20 Queensberry House, Friars Ln, Richmond, Surrey TW9 1NT, England Office: Taylor Nelson AGB, AGB House, West Gate, Hanger Ln, London W5 1UA, England

TREAT, JOHN ELTING, management consultant; b. Evanston, Ill., June 20, 1946; s. Carlin Alexander and Marjorie Ann (Mayland) T.; adopted s. Howard Elting Jr.; m. Barbara Laflin, May 27, 1984; children: Charles, Luli, Tyler. BA, Princeton U., 1967; MA, Johns Hopkins U., 1969. Legis. asst. U.S. Senate, 1966; assoc. ops. officer Office of Sec., U.S. Dept. State, 1971-73; research coordinator Presdl.-Congressional Commn. on Orgn. of Govt. for Conduct of Fgn. Policy, Washington, 1973-74; dir. research trade U.S. Fed. Energy Adminstrn., Washington, 1974-78; dep. asst. sec. U.S. Dept. Energy, Washington, 1979-80; staff mem. Nat. Security Council, 1980-81; sr. v.p. N.Y. Merc. Exchange, N.Y.C., 1981-82, pres., 1982-84; ptnr. Bear Stearns & Co., Los Angeles, 1984-85; exec. pub. Petroleum Intelligence Weekly, N.Y.C., 1985-87; pres. Regent Internat., Washington and The Hague, 1987-89; v.p., ptnr. Booz, Allen & Hamilton, Inc., San Francisco, 1989—. Chmn. spl. gifts Am. Cancer Soc., 1983; chmn. bd. dirs. Mirror Repertory Co., 1987—; trustee, mem. exec. com., chmn. corp. rels. com. No. Calif. World Affairs Coun.; mem. San Francisco Fgn. Rels. com.; bd. trustees Am. U. of Cairo. With USNR, 1969-71. Decorated AF Commendation medal; Ford Found. European Area Travel grantee, 1972; Woodrow Wilson fellow, 1967; McConnell fellow, 1966. Mem. Coun. Fgn. Rels., Internat. Assn. for Energy Econs. Democrat. Unitarian. Clubs: Colonial (Princeton, N.J.), St. Francis Yacht Club, Bankers (San Francisco). Home: 42 San Carlos Ave Sausalito CA 94965-2048

TREAT, LAWRENCE, author; b. N.Y.C., Dec. 21, 1903; s. Henry and Daisy (Stein) Goldstone; m. Rose Ehrenfreund, 1943. BA, Dartmouth Coll., 1924; LLB, Columbia U., 1927. Author: fiction Run Far, Run Fast, 1937, B as in Banshee, 1940, D as in Dead, 1941, H as in Hangman, 1942, O as in Omen, 1943, The Leatherman, 1944, V as in Victim, 1945, H as in Hunted, 1946, Q as in Quicksand, 1947, Over the Edge, 1948, F as in Flight, 1948, Trial and Terror, 1949, Big Shot, 1951, Weep for a Wanton, 1956, Lady, Drop Dead, 1960, Venus Unarmed, 1961, P as in Police, 1970, True Crime With Judge Norbert Ehrenfreund: You're the Jury, 1992; originator of police procedurals and pictorial mysteries, Bringing Sherlock Home, 1931, Crime and Puzzlement, 1981, Crime and Puzzlement 2, 1982, You're the Detective, 1983, The Clue Armchair Detective, 1983, Crime and Puzzlement 3, 1988, Cherchez le Coupable, 1 and 2, 1989, Crime and Puzzlement, My Cousin Phoebe, 1991, Crime and Puzzlement on Martha's Vineyard, 1993; editor: Murder in Mind, 1967, The Mystery Writer's Handbook, 1976, A Special Kind of Crime, 1982; contbr. short stories to mags. including Alfred Hitchcock's Mystery Mag., Ellery Queen's Mystery Mag., Red Book, others. Recipient Ceremonial sword Mystery Writers Japan, 1961, Edgar Allan Poe award Mystery Writers of Am., 1965, 78, Spl. Edgar Allan Poe award for story in Alfred Hitchcock TV Hour, 1986; prize Internat. Crime Writer's Conv., Stockholm, 1981. Mem. Mystery Writers Am. (founder, past pres.), Phi Beta Kappa. Office: RFD Box 475A Edgartown MA 02539 also: care Vicky Bijur 333 W End Ave New York NY 10023-8128

TREBEK, ALEX, television game show host; b. Sudbury, Ont., Can., July 22, 1940; came to U.S., 1973; s. George Edward and Lucille (Lagace) T.; m. Elaine Callei (div. 1981); m. Jean Currivan, Apr. 30, 1990; 2 children. BA and PhB, U. Ottawa, Ont., 1961. Staff announcer CBC, Toronto, Ont., 1961-73; game show host Wizard of Odds for NBC, Calif., 1973-74, High Rollers for NBC, Calif., 1974-79, Stars on Ice for Can. TV, 1974-77, $128,000 Question for Global TV, Can., 1976-77, Double Dare for CBS, Calif., 1977-78, Battle Stars for NBC, Calif., 1981-82; game show host, producer Jeopardy!, Calif., 1984-87, game show host, 1987—; game show host Classic Concentration, Calif., 1987-90, To Tell the Truth, 1991. film appearances include: Short Cuts, 1993. Mem. Screen Actors Guild, AFTRA, Assn. Can. TV and Radio Artists. Roman Catholic. Avocations: golf, hockey, tennis, water skiing. Office: Jeopardy! 1020 W Washington Blvd Culver City CA 90232

TREBING, DAVID MARTIN, corporate finance manager; b. Lincoln, Nebr., June 2, 1961; s. Harry Martin and Joyce Alice (Christie) T. BA in Mktg., Mich. State U., 1984; MBA in Finance, Wake Forest U., 1986. Project mgr. mktg./sales Gilbarco div. Exxon Corp., Greensboro, N.C., 1984-86; cash mgmt. analyst Chrysler Fin. Corp., Troy, Mich., 1986-87; sr. corp. fin. specialist Chrysler Corp., Highland Park, Mich., 1987-92; mgr. activity-based costing implementation Chrysler Corp., Detroit, Mich., 1993-96, mgr. Europe Sales Fin., 1996—. Mem. Internat. Armed Forces Coun., Detroit, 1987-92, Detroit Hist. Soc., Jr. Coun./Detroit Inst. Arts, St. George's Soc. N.Y., N.Y.C.; mem. exec. com. Meadow Brook Theatre and Festival; mem. Detroit com. Coun. on Fgn. Rels.; bd. dirs. devel. fund Mich. State U. Lt. (j.g.) USNR, 1987-90. Inst. fellow Inst. Pub. Utilities, 1983. Mem. Econ. Club Detroit, Detroit Athletic Club (intermediate coun. 1985-90), Univ. Club, Army and Navy Club, Detroit Club, Ch. Club of N.Y., Vet. Corps Arty. State N.Y., SAR (pres. Detroit chpt. 1987-89, 1st v.p. Mich. Soc. 1996—), Soc. War 1812 (1st v.p. Mich. Soc. 1989-91), Soc. Colonial Wars (chmn. grants and awards com., gov., treas. Mich. Soc.), English-Speaking Union (1st v.p.), Pres. Club Mich. State U. Avocations: skiing, tennis, travel, skeet/trap shooting. Home: 3463 Wendover Rd Troy MI 48084-1261 Office: Chrysler Corp 800 Chrysler Dr Auburn Hills MI 48326-2757

TRECKELO, RICHARD M., lawyer; b. Elkhart, Ind., Oct. 22, 1926; s. Frank J. and Mary T.; m. Anne Kosick, June 25, 1955; children: Marla Treckelo Buck, Mary Treckelo Lucchesi. AB, U. Mich., 1951, JD, 1953. Bar: Ind. 1953, U.S. Dist. Ct. (no. and so. dists.) Ind. Pvt. practice, Elkhart, 1953-70; ptnr. Barnes and Thornburg Elkhart, South Bend, Indpls., Ft. Wayne, Washington, Elkhart, South Bend, Indpls., Ft. Wayne, 1971-91; of counsel Barnes and Thornburg Elkhart, South Bend, Indpls., Ft. Wayne, Chgo., Washington, Elkhart, South Bend, Indpls., Ft. Wayne, Chgo., 1992—; sec. Skyline Corp., Elkhart, 1959-94, bd. dirs., 1961-91. Bd. dirs. Elkhart Gen. Hosp. Found., Elkhart Park Found.; co-chmn. Elkhart Constl. Bicentennial Commn. Served with USAF, 1945-46. Mem. ABA, Elkhart City Bar Assn. (pres. 1975), Ind. Bar Assn., Elkhart County Bar Assn., Pres.'s Club (U. Mich.), Christiana Country Club, Rotary. Republican. Office: Barnes & Thornburg 121 W Franklin St Ste 200 Elkhart IN 46516-3200

TREDINNICK, ARTHUR FRED, private detective; b. Darby, Pa., Apr. 7, 1944; s. Albert Fred and Agnes (Hunter) T.; m. Marcia Jane Campbell, Jan. 27, 1968; 1 child, Megan Elizabeth. AA, Lehigh County C.C., Schnecksville, Pa., 1973; BA, Alvernia Coll., Reading, Pa., 1976; AAS, Delaware County C.C., Media, Pa., 1982; MS, St. Joseph's U., Phila., 1987. Cert. fire and explosion investigator, fraud examiner. Patrol trooper Pa. State Police, Fogelsville, 1968-75; crime trooper Pa. State Police, Bethlehem, 1975-85, Fogelsville, 1985-90; from patrol cpl. to crime sgt. Pa. State Police, Bethlehem, 1990-95; dir. Associated Investigative Svcs., Inc., Allentown, Pa., 1995—; bd. dirs. Hidden Harbour III Condominium Assn., Ocean City, Md., 1995; disaster assistance employee, security specialist FEMA, Washington, 1995—; adj. faculty Lehigh County C.C., 1997. Author: Fire Protection Master Plan-Lower Macungie Township, Lehigh County, Pa., 1979. Mem. Pub. Safety Commn., Lower Macungie Township, 1989-95; dep. dir. Emergency Mgmt., Lower Macungie Township, 1991-95. With U.S. Army Res., 1971-95. Mem. Am. Soc. Indsl. Security, Internat. Assn. Arson Investigators, Pa. Assn. Arson Investigators (charter), Nat. Assn. Fire Investigators, Nat. Assn. Investigative Specialist, Assn. Cert. Fraud Examiners. Avocations: golf, fishing. Office: Associated Investigative Svcs Inc 3140-B Tilghman St Ste 175 Allentown PA 18104

TREDWAY, THOMAS, college president; b. North Tonawanda, N.Y., Sept. 4, 1935; s. Harold and Melanya (Scorby) T.; m. Catherine Craft, Jan. 12, 1991; children: Daniel John, Rebecca Elizabeth. BA, Augustana Coll.,

1957; MA, U. Ill., 1958; BD, Garrett Theol. Sem., 1961; PhD, Northwestern U., 1964. Instr. history Augustana Coll., Rock Island, Ill., 1964-65, asst. prof., 1965-69, assoc. prof., 1969-71, prof., 1971—, v.p. acad affairs, 1970-75, pres., 1975—; vis. prof. ch. history Waterloo Lutheran Sem., 1967-68. Mem. Am. Hist. Assn., Am. Soc. Ch. History, Phi Beta Kappa, Omicron Delta Kappa. Lutheran. Office: Augustana Coll Office of President 639 38th St Rock Island IL 61201-2210

TREE, DAVID L., advertising agency executive. Formerly sr. v.p., creative dir. D'Arcy Masius Benton & Bowles, Inc., N.Y.C.; vice chmn., chief creative officer Campbell Mithun Esty, Mpls., 1989—. Office: Campbell Mithun Esty 222 S 9th St Minneapolis MN 55402-3389

TREE, MICHAEL, violinist, violist, educator; b. Newark, Feb. 19, 1934; s. Samuel and Sada (Rothman) Applebaum; m. Johanna Kreck, Sept. 8, 1966; children: Konrad Efrem, Anna Louise. Diploma, Curtis Inst. Music, Phila., 1955; DFA (hon.), U. South Fla., 1975, SUNY, Binghamton, 1983. Faculty Harpur Coll., Binghamton, 1965-70, Curtis Inst. Music, 1970—, U. Md., College Park, 1981—, St. Louis Conservatory Music, 1982-88, Rutgers U., 1988—, Manhattan Sch. Music, 1993—; co-artistic dir. Phila. Chamber Orch., 1985-88; Misha Elman chair Manhattan Sch. Music, 1991. Violin recital debut at Carnegie Hall, 1954; soloist with major orchs. and at maj. internat. festivals, 1958—; founding mem. Guarneri String Quartet, 1964—, rec. artist for Philips, RCA, Columbia, Nonesuch, Vanguard, Sony Classics, Arabesque records. Recipient Seal of Recognition City of N.Y., 1982. Avocations: hiking, tennis. Home: 45 E 89th St New York NY 10128-1251 Office: care Herbert Barrett Mgmt Inc 1776 Broadway New York NY 10019-2002

TREECE, JAMES LYLE, lawyer; b. Colorado Springs, Colo., Feb. 6, 1925; s. Lee Oren and Ruth Ida (Smith) T.; m. Ruth Julie Treece, Aug. 7, 1949 (div. 1984); children—James (dec.), Karen Treece, Teryl Wait, Jamilyn Smyser, Carol Crowder. Student Colo. State U., 1943, Colo. U., 1943, U.S. Naval Acad., 1944-46; B.S., Mesa Coll., 1946; J.D., U. Colo., 1950; post-grad. U. N.C., 1976-77. Bar: Colo. 1952, U.S. Dist. Ct. Colo. 1952, U.S. Ct. Appeals (10th cir.) 1952, U.S. Supreme Ct. 1967. Assoc., Yegge, Hall, Treece & Evans and predecessors, 1951-59, ptnr., 1959-69; U.S. atty., Colo., 1969-77; pres. Treece & Bahr and predecessor firms, Littleton, Colo., 1977-91; mcpl. judge, 1967-68; mem. faculty Nat. Trial Advocacy Inst., 1973-76, Law-Sci. Acad., 1964. Chmn. Colo. Dept. Pub. Welfare, 1963-68; chmn. Colo. Dept. Social Services, 1968-69; mem. Littleton Bd. Edn., 1977-81. Served with USNR, 1944-46. Recipient awards Colo. Assn. Sch. Bds., 1981, IRS, 1977, FBI, 1977, DEA, 1977, Fed. Exec. Bd., 1977. Mem. Fed. Bar Assn. (pres. Colo. 1975, award 1975), Colo. Bar Assn. (bd. govs.), Denver Bar Assn. (v.p., trustee). Republican. Episcopalian. Home: 12651 N Pebble Beach Dr Sun City AZ 85351-3327

TREECE, JOSEPH CHARLES, insurance broker; b. Loma Linda, Calif., Sept. 1, 1934; s. Roy G. and Jeane L. (Reade) T.; m. Sandra Treece; children: Debbie, Mike, David. BA, Chapman Coll., 1956. Cert. Ins. Counselor, Assoc. in Risk Mgmt. Comml. banker Security Pacific Nat. Bank, Hemet, Calif., 1959-72; ins. broker H.I.S./Kent & Hamilton, Hemet, 1972-89, Russell & Kaufmann, Hemet, 1989-96, Sawyer, Cook & Co., Redlands, Calif., 1996—. Dir. YMCA, Hemet. Lt. USN, 1956-59. Recipient Associate Achievement award Am. Assn. Mng. Gen. Agts., 1991, Disting. Svc. award Cert. Profl. Ins. Agents Soc., 1995. Mem. Ramona Pageant Assn. (life, chmn.-supr. 1962—), Profl. Ins. Assn. (state dir. 1988-91), Profl. Ins. Agts. (pres. Riverside and San Bernardino, Calif. 1989-90), Joint Ins. Assn. (pres. Riverside and San Bernardino 1991), Ind. Ins. Agts. (pres.), Cert. Profl. Ins. Agts. (nat. pres. 1992, Disting. Svc. award 1995), Hemet C. of C. (pres. 1970), Kiwanis Club (life, Hemet chpt. pres. 1971, lt. gov. divsn. 6 Cal-Na-Ha 1972). Avocations: golf, camping, fishing, canoeing. Home: 39049 Don Dr Hemet CA 92543 Office: Sawyer Cook & Co 1 E State St Redlands CA 92373-4729

TREFFERT, DAROLD ALLEN, psychiatrist, author, hospital director; b. Fond du Lac, Wis., Mar. 12, 1933; s. Walter O. and Emma (Leu) T.; m. Dorothy Marie Sorgatz, June 11, 1955; children: Jon, Joni, Jill, Jay. B.S., U. Wis., 1955, M.D., 1958. Diplomate: Am. Bd. Psychiatry and Neurology. Resident in psychiatry U. Wis. Med. Sch., 1959-62, assoc. clin. prof. psychiatry, 1965—; chief children's unit Winnebago (Wis.) Mental Health Inst., 1962-64, supt., 1964-79; supt. Central State Hosp., Waupun, Wis., 1977-78; dir. Dodge County Mental Health Center, Juneau, Wis., 1964-74; mem. staff St. Agnes Hosp., Fond du Lac, 1963—; exec. dir. Fond du Lac County Mental Health Center, 1979-92; chmn. Controlled Substances Bd. Wis.; mem. critical health problems com. Wis. Dept. Pub. Instrn., med. examining bd. State of Wis. Author: Extraordinary People: Understanding Savant Syndrome, 1989, edits. in U.S., U.K., Italy, Japan, The Netherlands, Sweden; autism cons. (movie) Rainman, 1988. Fellow Am. Coll. Psychiatrists; mem. AMA, Wis. Med. Soc. (pres. 1979-80), Wis. Psychiat. Assn. (pres.), Am. Assn. Psychiat. Adminstrs. (pres.), Alpha Omega Alpha. Home: W 4065 Maplewood Ln Fond Du Lac WI 54935-9562 Office: 481 E Division St Fond Du Lac WI 54935-3748 *People often spend too much time regretting what they are not and far too little time savoring that which they are.*

TREFFINGER, KARL EDWARD, architectural firm executive; b. Columbus, Ohio, Oct. 21, 1927; s. Raymond Hartman and Eldred (Ruffner) T.; m. Beverly Jean Beck, Mar. 21, 1957 (dec. 1994); children: Kathy Anne, Julia Frances Wirth, Karl Raymond, Frederick Charles. BA, Yale U., 1948, MArch, 1952. Registered arch. Calif., Oreg. Wash., Nev., Ohio, Ill., Fla., Okla.; cert. Nat. Coun. Archtl. Registration Bds. Draftsman Stanley Morse, Denver, 1955-56; pvt. practice Columbus, Ohio, 1956-57; apprentice Edward Durrell Stone, Palo Alto, Calif., 1957-58; designer Wurster, Bernardi and Emmons, San Francisco, 1959-60; arch. Karl Treffinger & Assoc., San Francisco, 1960-78; prin. Treffinger, Walz and MacLeod, San Francisco and San Rafael, Calif., 1978-92. Prin. works include Harbor Point Beach Club, Strawberry Peninsula, Calif., Telegraph Hill Apts., San Francisco, Peninsula Squash Club, San Mateo, Calif., Sheraton Inn-Walden, Schaumburg, Ill., Court of Flags Complex, Orlando, Fla., Growers Sq., Walnut Creek, Calif. Walden Office Sq., Schaumburg, Wescot Internat., San Rafael, Treffinger, Walz & MacLeod Offices, San Rafael, Remillard Brick Yard, Larkspur, Calif., Walden Market Sq. Project, Schaumburg, Walden, Schaumburg, Walden Lakes, Bensenville, Ill., Smith Ranch Master Plan, San Rafael, Bon Air Project, Greenbrae, Calif., Ridgeland Devel. Project, Marin City, Calif., condominiums, townhouses, apts.; contbr. articles to profl. jours. Lt. USN, 1952-55, Korea. Recipient civic awards for design excellence. Fellow AIA (corp., pres. No. Calif. chpt. 1974, sec. Calif. coun., awards design excellence). Home: 700 SW Schaeffer Rd West Linn OR 97068-9644

TREFRY, ROBERT J., healthcare administrator; b. Springfield, Vt., Mar. 29, 1947; married. Bachelors' degree, Ga. Inst. Tech., 1970; Masters' degree, George Washington U., 1974. With Greater Southeast Community Hosp., Washington, 1973, adminstrv. asst., 1973-74, asst. adminstr., 1974-79; sr. v.p. North Kansas City (Mo.) Community Hosp., 1979-83; exec. v.p., chief exec. officer St. Agnes Hosp., White Plains, N.Y., 1983-88; exec. v.p., chief operating officer Carle Found. Hosp., Urbana, Ill., 1988-91; exec. v.p., chief oper. officer Bridgeport (Conn.) Hosp., 1991-94, pres., CEO, 1994—. With U.S. mil. 1970-71. Office: Bridgeport Hosp 267 Grant St Bridgeport CT 06610-2805

TREGELLAS, PATRICIA, musical director, composer; b. Kans., Feb. 22, 1936; d. Clarence and Lena T.; BMus in Edn., U. Denver, 1959; scholar, Trossingen, Germany, 1960-61; MA in Teaching Music, CUNY, 1985. Concert artist, chamber musician, condr.; music supr. Prowers County (Colo.) High Sch. Band and Chorus, 1962-65; accordionist and orch. leader USO tours abroad, 1966-69; mem. orch., asst. condr. Hal Prince musicals on nat. tours, 1969-71; freelance musician, N.Y.C., 1972—; mus. dir., condr. N.Y. Concerto Orch., 1979—; condr. workshops, Tokyo, London, N.Y.C.; performed in premier performances of new music; subs. accordionist Broadway musical Victor Victoria, 1996. Bd. dirs. The Music Educators Assn. of N.Y.C., 1990—, Am. Accordionists Assn., 1994—. Recipient cert. appreciation Gen. Westmoreland and others for work in Vietnam with USO; fellow Conducting Inst. S.C., 1994. Home: 817 W End Ave Apt 3aa New York NY 10025-5323 also: 2372 S Clayton St Denver CO 80210-5418

TREGLE, LINDA MARIE, dance educator; b. Fort Sill, Okla., Sept. 8, 1947; d. Franklin and Helen Marie (Diggs) T. BA, Mills Coll., Stockton, Calif., 1970, MA, 1974; life credential, U. Calif., 1974. founder, dir., choreographer Internat. Studios, Inc., Stockton, 1970—; dance instr. San Joaquin Delta Coll., Stockton, 1970—; program cons., choreographer Alpha Kappa Alpha, Stockton, 1984—, choreographer SDW Motion Pictures, Stockton, 1983—; advisor Internat. Dance Club San Joaquin, 1970—; founder, dir. Tregles Internat. Dance Co., 1970—; mem. Ruth Beckford's Dance Studio. Directed and choreographed numerous dance prodn. videos. Mem. NAACP, Black Employment Trends (community rep. 1988—), Calif. Tchrs. Assn., Alpha Kappa Alpha. Avocations: creative writing, table sports, drama, arts, dance. Home: 2411 Arden Ln Stockton CA 95210-3256 Office: San Joaquin Delta Coll 5151 Pacific Ave Stockton CA 95207-6304

TREGURTHA, PAUL RICHARD, marine transportation and construction materials company executive; b. Orange, N.J., 1935; married. BSME, Cornell U., 1958; MBA, Harvard U., 1963. V.p., contr. Brown & Sharpe Mfg. Co., 1969-71; v.p. fin. Moore McCormack Resources, Inc., Stamford, Conn., 1971-73, exec. v.p. fin., 1973-78, pres., COO, from 1978, pres., CEO, chmn., 1987-88; chmn., co-owner Mormac Marine Group, Inc., Stamford, 1988—; vice chmn., co-owner The Interlake Steamship Co., 1988—; chmn. Meridian Aggregates Acquisitions, Inc., 1991, Moran Transp. Co., 1994—; bd. dirs. Fleet Fin. Group, Brown & Sharpe Mfg., FPL Group, Inc. Trustee emeritus Cornell U., Ithaca, N.Y.; trustee Tchrs. Ins. and Annuity Assn. 1st lt. USAF, 1958-61. Named Baker Scholar, Harvard U., 1963. Office: Mormac Marine Group Inc Three Landmark Sq Stamford CT 06901

TREIBL, HANS GEORGE, industrial chemist; b. Vienna, Austria, Aug. 7, 1914; came to U.S., 1950; s. Robert and Ida (Salzer) T.; m. Gertrude Schacherl, Nov. 22, 1951. PhD in Engring., States Rsch. Inst. Organic Ind, Vienna, 1935; Culturate Doctorate in Chemistry (hon.), World U., 1984. Analytical chemist United Labs. of Austrian Health Dept., Vienna, 1937-38; petrochemist Cathay Oil Co., Shanghai, 1939-49; assayer, supr. Luscar (Alta., Can.) Oil Co., 1949-50; chief chemist Hydrocarbon Chems., Newark, 1951-57; rsch. chemist Diamond Alkali, Newark, 1957-58; dir. rsch., chief chemist Std. Chlorine Chem. Co., Inc., Kearney, N.J., 1958-83, rsch. dir., 1979—; mem. product rsch. panel Chem. Engring. Mag., 1970-71. Contbr. articles to Encyclopedia of Industrial Chemical Analysis, 1972. Recipient Cert. of Merit Dictionary of Internat. Biography, 1979. Fellow AIChE (emeritus), Am. Chem. Soc. Achievements include research on chlorination of aromatic hydrocarbons and naphthalene, kinetics of catalysts in halogenations of aromatic hydrocarbons. Home: Century Village 1002 Newport G Deerfield Beach FL 33442

TREIBLE, KIRK, college president; b. Newton, N.J., Mar. 29, 1941; s. William Bryan and Grace Almond T.; BS, W.Va. Wesleyan Coll.; MBA, W.Va. U.; LLD, La Grange Coll.; m. Carol Ann Mosher, June 20, 1964; 1 son, Todd. Bus. mgr. Parkersburg (W.Va.) Community Coll., 1969-71; devel. officer W.Va. Wesleyan Coll., 1972-75, acting treas., 1975-77; v.p. fin. Southwestern U., Georgetown, Tex., 1977-88; pres. Andrew Coll. Cuthbert, Ga., 1988—; bd. dirs. Citizen Bank, Geogetown, Tex., 1978-88; chair bd. dirs. 1st State Bank and Trust Co., Cuthbert, Ga., 1989—; cons. Nebr. Wesleyan U.; cons. So. Assn. Schs. and Colls. Bd. dirs. Georgetown Airport Authority, 1981-83; chmn. adminstrv. bd. First United Methodist Ch., 1983-85, univ. senate; mem. W.I.H. and Lula E. Pitts Found., Peed Scholarship Trust, United Meth. Ch. Served with USAF, 1966-69. Mem. Assn. Pvt. Colls. and Univs. Ga. (pres., dir.), Nat. Assn. Schs. and Colls. United Meth. Ch. Home: 408 N Lumpkin St Cuthbert GA 31740-1115 Office: Andrew Coll 413 College St Cuthbert GA 31740-1313

TREIGER, IRWIN LOUIS, lawyer; b. Seattle, Sept. 10, 1934; s. Sam S. and Rose (Steinberg) T.; m. Betty Lou Friedlander, Aug. 18, 1957; children: Louis H., Karen I., Kenneth B. BA, U. Wash., 1955, JD, 1957; LLM in Taxation, NYU, 1958. Bar: Wash. 1958, D.C. 1982, U.S. Dist. Ct. (we. dist.) Wash., U.S. Ct. Appeals (9th cir.), U.S. Supreme Ct. Assoc. Bogle & Gates, Seattle, 1958-63, ptnr., 1964—; chmn., 1986-94. Pres. Jewish Fedn. Greater Seattle, 1993-95; chmn. Mayor's Symphony Panel, 1986, Corp. Coun. for the Arts, 1987-88; pres. Seattle Symphony Found., 1986—; trustee, co-chmn. Cornish Coll. of the Arts, 1990—; trustee The Seattle Found., 1992—, Samis Found., 1989—; chmn. King County Baseball Pk. Commn., 1995. Fellow Am. Coll. Tax Counsel; mem. ABA (chmn. taxation sect. 1988-89, sect. del. 1990-96), Wash. State Bar Assn. (chmn. taxation sect. 1975), Greater Seattle C. of C. (chmn. 1993-94), Seattle Rotary Svc. Found. (v.p. 1995-96, pres. 1996—). Jewish. Office: Bogle & Gates 601 Union St Seattle WA 98101-2327

TREIMAN, SAM BARD, physics educator; b. Chgo., May 27, 1925; s. Abraham and Sarah (Bard) T.; m. Joan Little, Dec. 27, 1952; children—Rebecca, Katherine, Thomas. Student, Northwestern U., 1942-44; S.B., U. Chgo., 1948, S.M., 1949, Ph.D., 1952. Mem. faculty Princeton U., 1952—, instr., 1952-54, asst. prof., 1954-58, assoc. prof., 1958-63, prof. physics, 1963—, Eugene Higgins prof., 1976—, chmn. dept., 1981-87, chmn. univ. rsch. bd., 1988—. Author: (with M. Grossjean) Formal Scattering Theory, 1960, (with R. Jackiw and D.J. Gross) Current Algebra and Its Applications, 1972; Contbr. articles to profl. jours. Served with USNR, 1944-46. Recipient Oersted medal Am. Assn. Physics Tchrs. Mem. NAS, Am. Phys. Soc., Am. Acad. Arts and Scis. Home: 60 Mccosh Cir Princeton NJ 08540-5627

TREISTER, GEORGE MARVIN, lawyer; b. Oxnard, Calif., Sept. 5, 1923; s. Isadore Harry and Augusta Lee (Bloom) T.; m. Jane Goldberg, Jan. 24, 1946; children: Laura, Neil, Adam, Dana. B.S., UCLA, 1943; LL.B., Yale U., 1949. Bar: Calif. 1950. Law clk. to chief justice Calif. Supreme Ct., 1949-50; law clk. to Assoc. Justice Hugo L. Black U.S. Supreme Ct., 1950-51; asst. U.S. atty. So. Dist. Calif., 1951-53; dep. atty. gen. Calif., 1953; practiced in Los Angeles, 1953—; mem. Stutman, Treister and Glatt, 1953—; instr. U. So. Calif. Law Sch., 1954—, Stanford U. Law Sch., 1977-81; mem., former vice chmn. Nat. Bankruptcy Conf.; former mem. adv. com. on bankruptcy rules Jud. Conf. U.S. Contbr. articles to profl. jours. Served with USNR, 1943-46. Mem. Am. Law Inst., Am. Judicature Soc. Home: 1201 Neil Creek Rd Ashland OR 97520-9778 Office: 3699 Wilshire Blvd Los Angeles CA 90010-2719

TREITEL, DAVID HENRY, financial consultant; b. Lynn, Mass., Apr. 22, 1954; s. Henry David and Lotte (Elkeses) T.; m. Madelynn Drimmer, Sept. 1982 (div. Oct. 1988); m. Amy Gail Granowitz, Apr. 18, 1990. BA in Econs. with honors, Middlebury Coll., 1976; MBA, Columbia U., 1978. Sr. assoc. Simat Helliesen & Eichner, Inc., N.Y.C., 1980-84, 1980-84, v.p., 1984-88, sr. v.p., 1988-90, exec. v.p., 1990-95; pres. Simat Hellliesen & Eichner, Inc., N.Y.C., 1995—, CEO, chmn., 1996—; bd. dirs. Midwest Express Airlines, Milw., TransDign, Cleve. Contbr. articles to profl. jours. Bd. dirs. Am. Friends of Rambam Med. Ctr., N.Y. Mem. The Wings Club (bd. dirs.). Republican. Avocations: golf, tournament bridge, travel. Home: 190 E Seventy Second St New York NY 10021 Office: Simat Helliesen & Eichner 90 Park Ave New York NY 10016

TREJO, JOANN, medical researcher; b. Stockton, Calif., Jan. 23, 1964. BS, U. Calif., Davis, 1986; PhD, U. Calif., San Diego, 1992. Postdoctoral fellow Cardiovascular Rsch. Inst., U. Calif., San Francisco, 1992—; undergrad. rsch. asst. Lawrence Berkeley Lab. Divsn. Biology and Medicine, 1983-86; teaching asst. dept. environ. toxicology U. Calif., Davis, 1986, dept. pharmacology, San Diego, 1988-91, dept. biology, 1989. Contbr. articles to profl. jours. Katherine Larcara, Jack O'Keefe and Kiwanis Club Undergrad scholar, 1982; San Diego and Grad. Opportunity fellow, 1986-88, Dissertation fellow Nat. Rsch. Coun. Ford Found., 1991-92, Pres.'s Postdoctoral fellow U. Calif., 1993-95; recipient Nat. Hispanic Scholarship Fund award, 1990-91, Minority Scientist Career Devel. award Am. Heart Assn., 1995; Tng. grantee NIH/NHLBI Cardiovascular Rsch. Inst., 1992-93. Mem. AAAS, LWV, Am. Soc. Cell Biology, Soc. Advancement of Chicanos and Native Americans in Sci. Home: 215 Upper Ter Apt B San Francisco CA 94117-4515 Office: U Calif Cardiovascular Rsch Inst 505 Parnassus Ave San Francisco CA 94122-2722

TRELEASE, ALLEN WILLIAM, historian, educator; b. Boulder, Colo., Jan. 31, 1928; s. William, Jr. and Helen (Waldo) T.; children—William C. (dec. 1990), Mary E., John A. A.B., U. Ill., 1950, M.A., 1951; Ph.D., Harvard U., 1955. Mem. faculty Wells Coll., Aurora, N.Y., 1955-67; prof. history Wells Coll., 1965-67, chmn. dept. history and govt., 1963-67; prof. history U. N.C., Greensboro, 1967-94, head dept., 1984-92, prof. emeritus, 1994—. Author: Indian Affairs in Colonial New York: The Seventeenth Century, 1960, White Terror: The Ku Klux Klan Conspiracy and Southern Reconstruction, 1971, Reconstruction: The Great Experiment, 1971, The North Carolina Railroad, 1849-1871, and the Modernization of North Carolina, 1991, Changing Assignments: A Pictorial History of the U. of N.C. at Greensboro, 1991. Mem. Am., So. Hist. assns., Orgn. Am. Historians, Hist. Soc. N.C. (pres. 1986-87), AAUP, Phi Beta Kappa, Phi Kappa Phi, Phi Eta Sigma, Phi Kappa Psi.

TRELEAVEN, PHILLIPS ALBERT, retired publishing company executive; b. Oak Park, Ill., July 20, 1928; s. Harry William and Mary Elizabeth (Gregory) T. BA, Duke U., 1950; AM, Boston U., 1959; DBA (hon.), Unity Coll., 1988; graduate gemologist, Gemological Inst. Am., 1994. With G. K. Hall & Co., Boston, 1956-60, 61-67, 69-79; pres. G. K. Hall & Co., 1969-78, chmn. bd., 1970-78; underwriter mcpl. bonds Scharff & Jones, New Orleans, 1959-61; instr. in polit. economy Boston U., 1967-69; vis. lectr. econs. Unity Coll., 1979-90; owner Odyssey Hill Farms, Thorndike, Maine, 1971-75; pres., pub. Thorndike Press, 1977-87, chmn. bd. dirs., 1988-89; pres. pubs./info. group Sr. Svc. Corp., 1987-89; bd. dirs. Marco Polo Pasta House, Inc., 1989-92, pres., 1991-92; mng. dir. Lanna Gem Products, Chiangmai, Thailand, 1992—. Selectman, Thorndike, 1979-81; trustee Unity Coll., 1985-90, 92—, chmn., 1988-90. Served with AUS, 1950-53. Mem. Phi Beta Kappa. Home: PO Box 40 Thorndike ME 04986-0040 *The biggest blunders I have made in my life have usually resulted from taking myself or my circumstances too seriously.*

TRELFA, RICHARD THOMAS, paper company executive; b. Alpena, Mich., July 5, 1918; s. Fred R. and Mable (Hagen) T.; m. Heidi Brigitte Ruckstuhl, Dec. 3, 1965;(dec. Oct. 31, 1996); children: Thomas W., Barbara E., Jeffrey C., Michael F. BS, U. Mich., 1940. With Hercules Powder Co., 1941-52, Watervliet Paper Co., Mich., 1952-58; exec. v.p., treas., dir. Perkins-Goodwin Co., Inc., N.Y.C., 1958-70; v.p., treas., CFO Perkins-Goodwin Co., Inc., 1970, sr. v.p., 1974-82; chmn. bd. Elcon, Inc., Houston, 1983-91; vice chmn. bd. B.S. & W Whiteley Ltd., Eng., 1983-88; bd. dirs. B.S. & W Whiteley Ltd.; treas., dir. Kennebec River Pulp & Paper Co., Madison, Maine, 1967-69, chmn. bd., treas., 1969-72, chmn. bd., mem. exec. com., 1972-73, dir., mem. exec. com., 1973-75; pres. Castle & Overton (Can.) Ltd., 1971-82; chmn. bd. EHV Weidmann Industries, Inc., St. Johnsbury, Vt., 1974-84, Franconia Paper Co. Inc., Lincoln, N.H., 1978-80; N.H. State rep. to Gen. Ctr., 1990—; water commr. Lisbon, N.H., 1990-97, selectman, Lisbon, 1995—. Fellow Am. Soc. Quality Control, TAPPI (past divsn. chmn., dir.); mem. Paper Industry Mgmt. Assn. (past divsn. chmn.), Am. Inst. Chem. Engrs., Am. Chem. Soc., Soc. Rheology, Masons, Univ. Mich. Club. Republican. Home: 245 Northey Rd Lisbon NH 03585-0245

TREMAIN, ALAN, hotel executive; b. Kent, England, Aug. 18, 1935; came to U.S., 1966; s. Archibalt and Elizabeth (Morris) T.; divorced; 1 child, Warren. Grad., Westminster Hotel Sch., 1952, Canterbury Sch. Econs., 1962; LL.B., La Salle Sch., Chgo., 1971. Chef de Pertie Grosvenor House, London, 1954-55; food and beverage mgr. Peninsula, Hong Kong, 1956-57; gen. mgr. Warners Hotel, also The Russley, Christchurch, New Zealand, 1958-64, Menzies, Sydney, Australia, 1964-65, Empress Hotel, Vancouver, B.C., Can., 1966-69; pres. Planned Food Facilities (Internat.) Ltd., Toronto, 1970-72; resident mgr. Sheraton Boston, 1972; mng. dir. Copley Plaza Hotel, Boston, 1972—; chmn. Hotels of Distinction, Inc., Boston. Author: A Guide to the Fine Art of Living, 1963, A Meal for To-Night, 1965. Decorated officer Order Brit. Empire (U.K.); recipient Culinary Merit award from Cercle Epicurien Mondel, Paris, 1956. Fellow Hotel and Catering Inst. (U.K.); founding mem. Internat. Soc. Chefs de Cuisine (chmn. 1954). Clubs: Mason, Montreal Badminton and Squash, The Beach Club, Palm Beach, Les Ambs., London, Rolls Royce Owners. Address: Hotels of Distinction Inc 380 S County Rd 200 Palm Beach FL 33480

TREMAINE, SCOTT DUNCAN, astrophysicist; b. Toronto, Ont., Can., May 25, 1950; s. Vincent Joseph and Beatrice Delphine (Sharp) T. BSc, McMaster U., Hamilton, Ont., 1971; PhD, Princeton U., 1975. Postdoctoral fellow Calif. Inst. Tech., Pasadena, 1975-77; rsch. assoc. Inst. Astronomy, Cambridge, Eng., 1977-78; long-term mem. Inst. for Advanced Study, Princeton, N.J., 1978-81; assoc. prof. MIT, Cambridge, 1981-85; prof., dir. Canadian Inst. for Theoretical Astrophysics U. Toronto, 1985-96; dir. program in cosmology and gravity Can. Inst. Advanced Rsch., Toronto, 1996—. Author: Galactic Dynamics, 1987; contbr. articles to profl. jours. E.W.R. Steacie fellow Natural Scis. and Engring. Rsch. Coun., 1988; recipient H.B. Warner prize Am. Astron. Soc., 1983, Steacie prize, 1989, C.S. Beals award Canadian Astron. Soc., 1990, Rutherford medal Royal Soc. Can., 1990, Heinemann prize for Astrophysics, 1997. Fellow Royal Soc. London, Royal Soc. Can.; mem. Am. Acad. Arts and Scis. (fgn. hon.). Office: U Toronto-CITA McLennan Lab, 60 St George St, Toronto, ON Canada M5S 3H8

TREMBLAY, ANDRE GABRIEL, lawyer, educator; b. Jonquiere, Que., Can., Nov. 10, 1937; s. Jean-Charles T. and Julienne (Tremblay) Laberge; children: Jean-Francois, Frederic, Alexandre Reynold. B.A., U. Laval-Que. Can., 1959, LL.L., 1962; D.E.S. in Law, U. Ottawa-Ont. Can., 1964, LL.D., 1966. Bar: Que. 1963. Asst., law U. Ottawa, 1966-70; assoc. U. Montreal, Que., 1970-75, prof., 1972—, pres. Gen. Assn. Profs.; dir. Pub. Law Ctr., Que., 1972-76, vice dean Sch. Law, 1982-86; dir. grad. studies U. Ottawa, 1968-70; pres. Com. on Human Rights, Montreal, 1981—; legal adv. to bar, govts., law firms, cos. Can., 1972—; sr. Constl. adviser to Que. Govt., 1986-92; pres. Prof.'s Union, U. Montreal, 1995—. Author: Les competences legislatives, 1967 (1st prize Govt. Que. 1968), Precis de droit municipal, 1973, Precis de droit constitutionnel, 1982, Droit Constitutionnel-Principles, 1993, La Revision Constitutionnell, 1997, Droit Constitutionnelle-Documents, 1996; contbr. articles, chpts. to legal publs. Sec. Polit. Chmn., Que. Liberal Party, Montreal, 1977-81; mem. observer's mission, Internat. Commn. Jurists, Geneva, 1981—, mem. coun. Can. sect., Ottawa, 1981—; v.p. Can. Human Rights Found., Montreal, 1982—. Mem. Assn. Can. Law Tchrs. (pres. Ottawa Chpt. 1974-75). Christian Scientist. Office: Faculty Law U Montreal, CP 6201 succ A, Montreal, PQ Canada H3C 3T1

TREMBLAY, ANDRÉ-MARIE, physicist; b. Montreal, Que., Can., Jan. 2, 1953; m. Marié à Guylaine Séguin; children: Noémie, Rachel. BSc, U. Montreal, 1974; PhD, MIT, 1978. With Energie Atomique du Can. Limitée, 1973-74, MIT, Boston, 1974-75, Inst. de Recherche de l'Hydro-Que., 1976, Cornell U., Ithaca, N.Y., 1978-80; prof. physics U. Sherbrooke, Que., 1980—, dir. Rsch. Ctr. Physics of Solids, 1991—; cons. Cornell U., 1981, Ohio State U., 1982, IBM, 1984; vis. scientist Cornell U., 1986-87; vis. rsch. physicist Inst. for Theoretical Physics, Santa Barbara, Calif., 1989, 96; vis. scientist Brookhaven (N.Y.) Nat. Lab, 1984; assoc. prof. U. Provence, France, 1982, 83. Contbr. articles to profl. publs. Recipient Herzberg medal Can. Assn. Physics, Steacie prize Natural Scis. and Engring. Rsch. Coun., 1987; Killam fellow, 1992-94. Mem. Can. Inst. Advanced Rsch. Office: Sherbrooke U, Dept Physics, Sherbrooke, PQ Canada J1K 2R1

TREMBLAY, MARC ADÉLARD, anthropologist, educator; b. Les Eboulements, Que., Can., Apr. 24, 1922; s. Willie and Laurette (Tremblay) T.; m. Jacqueline Cyr, Dec. 27, 1949; children: Geneviève, Lorraine, Marc, Colette, Dominique, Suzanne. A.B., U. Montreal, 1944, L.S.A., 1948; M.A., Laval U., 1950; Ph.D., Cornell U., 1954; PhD (hon.), Ottawa U., 1982, Guelph U., 1983, U. N. B.C., 1994, Carleton U., 1995. Research asso. Cornell U., 1953-56; mem. faculty Laval U., 1956-93, prof. anthropology, 1963-68, 81-93, prof. emeritus, 1994, vice dean social scis., 1968-71, dean Grad. Sch., 1971-79, also mem. univ. council.; pres. Quebec Coun. Social Rsch., 1987-91; dir. Inuit and Circupolar Study Group, Laval U., 1991-93. Author 25 books and monographs in social scis., about 200 articles. Recipient Que. Lit. prize, 1965, Innis-Gerin prize Royal Soc. Can., 1979, Molson prize Can. Coun., 1987, Prix Marcel Vincent ACFAS, 1988, Contbn. exceptionnelle Societé de sociologie et d'anthropolotie, 1990, Esdras Minville award Soc. St.-Jean Baptiste, 1991; named Officer of Order of Can., 1980, Gt. Officer of Order of Que., 1995; named to Internat. Order of Merit, Internat. Biog. Inst., Cambridge, Eng., 1990. Mem. Royal Soc. Can. (pres. 1981-84), Acad. des Scis. Morales et Politiques (sec.), Royal Soc. Inst. Pub. Policy, Am. Anthrop. Assn. (past fellow), Can. Soc. Applied Anthropology,

Can. Sociology and Anthropology Assn. (founding pres.), Can. Ethnology Soc. (past pres.), Assn. Can. Univs. for Northern Studies (past pres.), Assn. Internat. Sociology, Societe des savants et sci. Can. (v.p.). Home: 835 N Orléans St, Sainte Foy, PQ Canada G1X 3J4 Office: Laval Univ, Dept Anthropology, Quebec, PQ Canada G1K 7P4

TREMBLAY, RICHARD ERNEST, psychology educator; b. Nov. 23, 1944. BA, U. Ottawa, Can., 1966; MPsed, U. Montreal, 1970; PhD, U. London, 1976. Asst. prof. U. Montreal, 1976-81, assoc. prof., 1981-86, prof., 1986—; clinician St. Charles Psychiat. Hosp., Joliette, Can., 1966-69; psychologist Boscoville, Montreal, Can., 1967-70, Phillippe Pinel Psychiat. Inst., Montreal, 1970-73; chmn. Sch. of Psycho-Edn., Faculty of Arts and Scis., U. Montreal, 1986-90; invited prof. ethology lab. U. Rennes I, 1993-94, dept. psychology U. Jyväskylä, Finland, 1991; invited scientist psychophysiology lab. U. Franche-Com., 1982-83; presenter in field. Author: (with others) Preventing Antisocial Behavior from Birth to Adolescence, 1992, Les enfants agressifs: Perspective Development Interculturelle, 1992, Famille, Inadaption et Intervention, 1991, Human Development and Criminal Behavior: New Ways of Advancing Knowledge, 1992, Les Relations Entre Enfants, 1988, Le Traitement des Adolescents Delinquants, 1985, Ethologie et Development de l'enfant, 1985, Face to Face with Giftedness, 1983; contbr. chpts. to books and numerous articles to profl. jours. Molson fellow Can. Inst. of Advanced Rsch. Fellow Royal Soc. of Can., Can. Psychol. Assn.; mem. AAAS, Internat. Soc. for the Study of Behavioral Devel. (exec. com. 1994—), Internat. Soc. for Rsch. on Agression (coun. mem. 1992-96), Am. Soc. of Criminology, Assn. Canadienne-Française pour l'Avancement des Scis., European Assn. for Psychology and Law, Internat. soc. for Human Theology, N.Y. Acad. Scis., soc. for Rsch. in Child Devel. Office: Rsch Unit on Children's Psych, 750 Gouin E / CP6128 A, Montreal, PQ Canada H2C 1A6

TREMBLAY, RODRIGUE, economics educator; b. Matane, Que., Can., Oct. 13, 1939; s. George and Germaine (St. Louis) T.; m. Carol Howard, Sept. 5, 1964; children: Jean-Paul, Alain, Joanne. BA, Laval U., Quebec City, 1961; BS in Econs., U. de Montreal (Que.), 1963; MA in Econs., Stanford U., 1965, PhD in Econs., 1968. Prof. Univ. de Montreal, 1967—; mem. nat. assembly Parliament of Que., 1976-81; min. industry and commerce Govt. of Que., 1976-79; mem. arbitrage panel Can.-U.S. Free Trade Agreement Ottawa (Can.) and Washington, 1989—. Woodrow Wilson Found. fellow, 1964-65. Mem. N.Am. Econs. and Fin. Assn. (pres. 1986-87). Office: U Montreal, Dept of Economics, Montreal, PQ Canada H3C 3J7

TREMBLY, CRISTY, television executive; b. Oakland, Md., July 11, 1958; d. Charles Dee and Mary Louise (Cassidy) T. BA in Russian, German and Linguistics cum laude, W.Va. U., 1978, BS in Journalism, 1978, MS in Broadcast Journalism, 1979; advanced cert. travel, West L.A. Coll., 1982; advanced cert. recording engring., Soundmaster Schs., North Hollywood, Calif., 1985. Videotape engr. Sta. WWVU-TV, Morgantown, W.Va., 1976-80; announcer, engr. Sta. WVVW Radio, Grafton, W.Va., 1979; tech. dir., videotape supr. Sta. KMEX-TV, L.A., 1980-85; broadcast supr. Sta. KADY-TV, Oxnard, Calif., 1988-89; news tech. dir. Sta. KVEA-TV, Glendale, Calif., 1985-89; asst. editor, videotape technician CBS TV Network, Hollywood, Calif., 1989-90; videotape supr. Sta. KCBS-TV, Hollywood, 1990-91, mgr. electronic news gathering ops., 1991-92; studio mgr., engr.-in-charge CBS TV Network, Hollywood, 1992—; radio operator KJ6BX Malibu Disaster Comm., 1987—. Prodr. (TV show) The Mountain Scene, 1976-78. Sr. orgn. pres. Children of the Am. Revolution, Malibu, Calif., 1992—; chmn. adminstrv. coun. Malibu United Meth. Ch., 1994—; sec., mem. adv. com. Tamassee (S.C.) Sch., 1992—; vol. Ch. Coun., L.A. Riot Rebldg., Homeless shelter work, VA Hosps., Mus. docent; sponsor 3 overseas foster children. Named one of Outstanding Young Women of Am., 1988; recipient Asst. editor Emmy award Young and the Restless, 1989-90, Golden Mike award Radio/TV News Assn., 1991, 92. Mem. ATAS (mem. exec. com. on electronic prodn. 1992—, mem. nat. awards com. 1994—), DAR (state chair jr. membership 1987-88, state chair scholarships 1992-94, state chmn. jr. contest 1994-96, others, Malibu chpt. regent 1991, state chair motion pictures radio and TV Calif. 1988-90, Mex. 1990—, Nat. Outstanding Jr. 1993, nat. vice-chair broadcast media 1995—), Am. Women in Radio and TV (so. Calif. bd. 1984-85, 93-95, pres.-elect 1995-96, pres. 1996-97), Soc. Profl. Journalists, Women in Comms., Travelers Century Club (program chair 1987—), Soc. Broadcast Engrs. (1995—), Mensa (life), Soc. Motion Picture/TV Engrs. (pres. 1995—), Beta Sigma Phi. Democrat. Methodist. Avocations: singing, cooking, travel, genealogy, languages. Home: 2901 Searidge St Malibu CA 90265-2969 Office: CBS TV City 7800 Beverly Blvd Los Angeles CA 90036-2165

TREMBLY, DENNIS MICHAEL, musician; b. Long Beach, Calif., Apr. 16, 1947; s. Fred Lel and Jewel Fern (Bouldin) T. Student, Juilliard Sch. Music, 1965-68. Asst. adj. prof. U. So. Calif., 1981—. Bass player, 1959—, with Los Angeles Philharmonic Orch., 1970-73, co-prin. bass, 1973—. Recipient 2d pl. Internat. Solo Bass competition, Isle of Man, 1978. Mem. Internat. Soc. Bassists. Office: L A Philharm Orch 135 N Grand Ave Los Angeles CA 90012-3013

TREML, VLADIMIR GUY, economist, educator; b. Kharkov, USSR, Mar. 27, 1929; came to U.S., 1950, naturalized, 1953; s. Guy Alexey and Lydia Vladimir (Timofeev) T.; m. Emma Miro, July 12, 1952; children—Irene Treml Cagney, Tatiana, Alexey. B.A. in Econs, Bklyn. Coll., 1955; M.A. in Econs, Columbia U., 1956; Ph.D. in Econs, U. N.C., 1963. Dept. supr. Bache & Co., N.Y.C., 1953-58; research asso. Inst. for Social Scis., U. N.C., Chapel Hill, 1958-61; asso. prof. econs. Franklin and Marshall Coll., 1961-66; research asso. Inst. Study USSR, Munich, Germany, 1966-67; prof. econs. Duke U., 1967—; dir. Ctr. for Slavic Studies U.S. Dept. Edn. of Duke U., 1991—; cons. in field; expert Dept. Commerce, other fed. agys., 1971—; vis. Ford research prof. U. Calif., Berkeley, 1984-85; vis. research prof. U. Hokkaido, Sapporo, Japan, 1985. Author: (with others) Structure of the Soviet Economy, 1972, Input-Output Analysis and the Soviet Economy, 1975; contbr. reports to publs. of Joint Econ. Com., U.S. Congress; contbr. articles to profl. publs.; editor: Soviet Economic Statistics, 1972; editor, contbg. author: Studies in Soviet Input-Output Analysis, 1977, Alcohol in the USSR, 1982; contbg. editor: Soviet Economy Jour. Trustee Nat. Council for Soviet and East European Research, Inc., Washington, 1978-84. Served with USMC, 1951-53. Ford Found. grantee, 1972-81, Dept. Def.-Advanced Rsch. Project Agy. grantee, 1975-76, Dept. State grantee, 1976-77, Dept. Def. grantee, 1985-90, Georgetown U. grantee, 1984-86, Olin Found. grantee, 1989; Fulbright fellow Moscow U., 1992. Mem. So. Econ. Assn., Am. Econ. Assn., Assn. Comparative Econ. Studies (exec. com. 1972-74), Am. Assn. Advancement Slavic Studies, So. Conf. on Slavic Studies (pres. 1977-78), Phi Beta Kappa. Democrat. Eastern Orthodox. Home: 603 Longleaf Dr Chapel Hill NC 27514-3039

TRENBERTH, KEVIN EDWARD, atmospheric scientist; b. Christchurch, New Zealand, Nov. 8, 1944; came to U.S., 1977; s. Edward Maurice and Ngaira Ivy (Eyre) T.; m. Gail Neville Thompson, Mar. 21, 1970; children: Annika Gail, Angela Dawn. BSc with honors, U. Canterbury, Christchurch, 1966; ScD, MIT, 1972. Meteorologist New Zealand Meteorol. Service, Wellington, 1966-76, supt. dynamic meteorology, 1976-77; assoc. prof. meteorology U. Ill., Urbana, 1977-82, prof., 1982-84; scientist Nat. Ctr. Atmospheric Research, Boulder, Colo., 1984-86, sr. scientist, 1986—, leader empirical studies group, 1987, head sect. climate analysis, 1987—; dep. dir. climate and global dynamics divsn. Nat. Ctr. Atmospheric Rsch., Boulder, Colo., 1991-95; mem. joint sci. com. for world climate programme, com. climate changes and the ocean Tropical Oceans Global Atmosphere Program Sci. Steering Group, 1990-94; mem. Climate Variability and Predictability Sci. Steering Group, 1995—, co-chair, 1996—. Editor: Climate System Modeling, 1992, Earth Interactions, 1996—; contbr. articles to profl. jours. Grantee NSF, NOAA, NASA. Fellow Am. Meteorol. Soc. (editor sci. jour. 1981-86, com. chmn. 1985-87, Editor's award 1989), AAAS (coun. del. sect. atmosphere and hydrosphere sci. 1993-97), Royal Soc. New Zealand (hon.); mem. NAS (earth scis. com. 1982-85, tropical oceans global atmosphere adv. panel 1984-87, polar rsch. bd. 1986-90, climate rsch. com. 1987-90, global oceans atmosphere land sys. panel 1994—), Atmosphere Obs. Panel of Globe Climate Observing Sys., Meterol. Soc. New Zealand. Home: 1445 Landis Ct Boulder CO 80303-1122 Office: Nat Ctr Atmospheric Research PO Box 3000 Boulder CO 80307-3000

TRENCH, WILLIAM FREDERICK, mathematics educator; b. Trenton, N.J., July 31, 1931; s. George Daniel and Anna Elizabeth (Taylor) T.; m. Lucille Ann Marasco, Dec. 26, 1954 (div. Dec. 1978); children: Joseph William, Randolph Clifford, John Frederick, Gina Margaret; m. Beverly Joan Busenshut, Nov. 22, 1980. BA in Math., Lehigh U., 1953; AM, U. Pa., 1955, PhD, 1958. Applied mathematician Moore Sch. Elec. Engring., U. Pa., 1953-56; with GE Corp., Phila., 1956-57, Philco Corp., Phila., 1957-59, RCA, Moorestown, N.J., 1957-64; assoc. prof. math. Drexel U., Phila., 1964-67, prof., 1967-86; Andrew G. Cowles disting. prof. math. Trinity U., San Antonio, 1986-97, prof. emeritus math., 1997—. Author: Advanced Calculus, 1971, (with Bernard Kolman) Elementary Multivariable Calculus, 1971, Multivariable Calculus with Linear Algebra and Series, 1972; contbr. rsch. articles in numerical analysis, ordinary differential equations, smoothing, prediction and spl. functions to profl. jours. Mem. Am. Math. Soc., Soc. Indsl. and Applied Math., Phi Beta Kappa, Eta Kappa Nu, Pi Mu Epsilon. Achievements include development of Trench's Algorithm for inversion of finite Toeplitz matrices, of fast algorithms for computing eigenvalues of structured matrices, of asymptotic theory of solutions of nonlinear functional differential equations under mild integral smallness conditions. Home: 413 Lake Dr W Divide CO 80814-9612

TRENERY, MARY ELLEN, librarian; b. Conran, Mo., Jan. 10, 1939; d. John Herman and Stella Cecelia (Durbin) Hulshof; m. Frank E. Trenery, June 10, 1967. BA in Classics, Coll. New Rochelle, 1962; MALS, Rosary Coll., River Forest, Ill., 1966; postgrad., Fla. Atlantic U., Boca Raton, 1986-89. Tchr. grades 6, 8 Archdiocesan Sch. System, St. Louis, 1962-64; serials and acquisition libr. U. Ill., Chgo., 1966-69; acquisitions, circulation and cataloging libr. Rosary Coll., River Forest, Ill., 1964-66, 70-72; libr. media specialist St. Coleman Cath. Sch., Pompano Beach, Fla., 1973-94; coord. for self study St. Coleman Schs., 1982, 83, 89, 90; cons. Pompano Beach City Libr. Author: Policies and Procedures for School Libraries, 1976, UICC Call Number (founding editor), 1967-68, NIUCLA Newsletter (editor 1969-72). Fed. Funding liaison with Broward County Sch. Bd., 1974-94. Mem. Ill. Libr. Assn. (rsch. and tech. svcs. div. chair 1967-69), Cath. Libr. Assn. (No. Ill. unit chair, sec. 1969-72).

TRENNEPOHL, GARY LEE, finance educator, consultant; b. Detroit, Dec. 6, 1946; s. Leo Donald and Wilma Mae (Tiensvold) T.; m. Sandra K. Yeager, June 9, 1968; children: Paige E., Adrienne A. BS, U. Tulsa, 1968; MBA, Utah State U., 1971; PhD, Tex. Tech U., 1976. Asst. prof. aero. studies Tex. Tech U., Lubbock, 1972-74; asst. prof. fin. Ariz. State U., Tempe, 1977-80, assoc. prof., 1980-82; prof. U. Mo., Columbia, 1982-86, dir. Sch. Bus., 1984-86; prof. fin., dept. head Tex. A&M U., College Station, 1986-91, assoc. dean Coll. Bus., 1991-93, Peters prof. fin., 1992—, exec. assoc. dean, 1994-95; dean Coll. Bus. Okla. State U., Stillwater, 1995—; mem. faculty Options Inst., Chgo. Bd. Options Exchange, 1987—. Author: An Introduction to Financial Management, 1984, Investment Management, 1993; assoc. editor Jour. Fin. Research, 1983-96, Rev. Bus. Studies, 1992—; contbr. chpts. Encyclopedia of Investments, oPTIONS: eSSENTIAL cONCEPTS; contbr. articles to profl. jours. Capt. USAF, 1968-72. Decorated Commendation medal with oak leaf cluster, Vietnam Svc. medal. Mem. Fin. Mgmt. Assn. (v.p. program 1993, pres. 1993-94), So. Fin. Assn., Southwestern Fin. Assn. (bd. dirs. 1983-84, pres. 1986), Midwest Fin. Assn. (bd. dirs. 1985-89). Republican. Lutheran. Office: Okla State U 201 Business Stillwater OK 74078-4013

TRENNER, NELSON RICHARDS, JR., communications executive, writer; b. Plainfield, N.J., Aug. 3, 1948; s. Nelson Richards and Kathryn Theresa (Farrell) T.; m. Annabelle Clare Radcliffe, June 24, 1988; children: Miles Richards Radcliffe, Winslow Radcliffe. AB, Princeton U., 1970; MA, Rutgers U., 1978. Mng. editor Princeton (N.J.) Packet Newspapers, 1971-72; mgr. trade sales promotion Little, Brown & Co., Boston, 1972-73; assoc. curator New England Hist. Geneal. Soc., Boston, 1974-76; mng. editor Del. Valley News, Flemington, N.J., 1976-77; pres. Advanced Communication Tng., Princeton, 1981—; cons. AT&T Labs., Murray Hill, N.J., 1981—; lectr. Woodrow Wilson Sch. Public and Internat. Affairs Princeton U., 1987-88, 91—; sr. cons. Franklin Quest Co., Salt Lake City, 1992-96. Author: The Bell Labs Writer, 1985; co-author: The Bell Labs Editor, 1986, The Bell Labs Style Guide, 1988 (internat. award for excellence 1989); co-author, editor: E. L. Doctorow, 1983; asst. editor Ontario Rev., 1980, 82-83. Campaign worker House and Senate Campaigns, N.J., Mass., 1974, 76, 78, 80, 82, 84, 92; com. chmn. Coalition for Nuclear Disarmament, N.J., 1980—; campaign staff writer Millicent Fenwick for U.S. Senate, N.J., 1981-82; admissions assoc. Princeton U., 1981-83; fellow Blue Mountain Ctr., Blue Mountain Lake, N.Y., 1983-87, 95, Millay Colony for the Arts, Austerlitz, N.Y., 1985, Va. Ctr. for the Creative Arts, Sweet Briar, 1986, 95; trustee Starfish Found. Children with AIDS, Inc., 1997—, Youth Found., Princeton, N.J., 1997—; com. chair Planned Parenthood, Mercer County, 1997—. Rutgers U. fellow, Columbia U. fellow; recipient Adirondack Fiction award Blueline Mag., 1986. Democrat. Episcopalian. Avocations: book collecting, photography, journalism, hiking. Home: 4590 Province Line Rd Princeton NJ 08540-2212 Office: Princeton U W Wilson Sch Pub & Internat Affairs Robertson Hall Princeton NJ 08544

TRENT, CLYDE NATHANIEL, legal assistant; b. Pitts., Nov. 25, 1945; s. Isaiah and Grace Sarah (Massie) T.; m. Mary Julia Kelly, Nov. 22, 1974; children: Robert, Nathaniel. BA, U. Pitts., 1979; paralegal cert., Pa. State U., 1984; AS, C.C. Allegheny, Monroeville, Pa., 1986; paralegal cert., U. Pitts., 1987. Letter carrier U.S. Postal Svc., Pitts., 1968-80; legal asst. Strassburger & McKenna, Pitts., 1980-85, Feldstein Law Office, Pitts., 1985-90, Elderly Citizens Ctr., Mt. Lebanon, Pa., 1990-91; claims examiner Office Econ. Security, Pitts., 1991—; adv. bd. mem. Legal Intellect, Inc., Monroeville, 1988—. Mem. Western Pa. Hist. Soc., Pitts., 1993—. With U.S. Army, 1965-67. Mem. Am. Criminal Justice, Pitts. Paralegal Assn. (com. 1990), Pa. State Alumni (vol. 1986-94), Lambda Alpha Epsilon (pres. 1979-80), Phi Theta Kappa. Avocations: horseback riding, student pilot, cooking, historical research.

TRENT, DARRELL M., academic and corporate executive; b. Neosho, Mo., Aug. 2, 1938; s. Clarence Melvin and Edna Ruth T.; m. Judith Mercy Turner; children: Darrell Michael, Derek Montgomery, Mercy Ruth. A.B., Stanford U., 1961; postgrad., Internat. Law Sch., The Hague, Netherlands, summer 1961, Wharton Grad. Sch. Bus., U. Pa., summer 1962; M.B.A., Columbia U., 1964. Owner, mgr. Trent Enterprises, Kans. and Mo., 1963-66; pres., chief exec. officer N.Am. Carmen, Ltd., Del., 1965-68, Assoc. Stores, Inc., Okla., 1967-69, Plaza Supermarkets, Inc., Kans., 1966-69, Food Service, Inc., Kans., 1966-69, Supermarkets, Inc., Kans., 1966-69, Acton Devel. Co., Inc., Kans., 1966-81; research/writer Nixon for Pres., 1968; staff dir. for personnel Presdl. Transition, 1968-69; commr. Property Mgmt. and Disposal Service, GSA, 1969; dep. asst. to Pres. U.S., 1969-70; exec. dir. Property Rev. Bd., Exec. Office of Pres., 1969-73; dep. dir. Office Emergency Preparedness, 1970-72, acting dir., 1973; mem. Cost of Living Council, 1973, Oil Policy Com., 1973; chmn. Joint Bd. Fuel Supply and Fuel Transp., 1973; mem. NSC, 1973; chmn. Pres.'s Adv. Council CD, 1973; U.S. mem. NATO Sr. Civil Emergency Planning Com., 1973; sr. research fellow Hoover Inst., Stanford U., 1974-81, 89—, assoc. dir., 1974-81, bd. overseers, 1985-89; dep. campaign mgr. Citizens for Reagan, 1976; dep. campaign mgr., cons. Reagan for Pres. Com., 1979-80, sr. policy advisor, 1980; dir. Office Policy Coordination, Presdl. Transition, 1980-81; U.S. alt. rep. Nato Com. Challenges of Modern Soc., 1982-83; dep. sec. U.S. Dept. Transp., 1981-82, acting sec., 1982-83; chmn. U.S. del. European Civil Aviation Com. with rank ambassador, 1983-88; chmn. Action Devel. Corp., Inc., 1988—; chmn., chief exec. officer Rollins Environ. Svcs., Inc., 1983-88, TEC Systems, Inc., 1990-91, Clean Earth Techs., Inc., 1992—; chmn. Fed. Home Loan Bank Pitts., 1983-91; cons. ACDA, 1974-81, HUD, 1974, Dept. Commerce, 1974-76; bd. advisors Chronicle Info. Svcs., Inc., 1984-87. Author: The U.S. and Transnational Terrorism, 1980, Transportation: Policy, Goals, Accomplishments, 1984; co-author: Terrorism: Threat, Reality, Response, 1979; contbr. articles to profl. publs. Bd. regents Pepperdine U., 1985—; bd. dirs. Found. Teach Econs., 1988-90; dep. chmn. Ronald Reagan Presdl. Found., 1985-88. Mem. Bohemian Club. Republican. Methodist. Office: 1325 N Pegram St Alexandria VA 22304-1931

TRENT, DONALD STEPHEN, thermo fluids engineer; b. Cloverdale, Oreg., Mar. 29, 1935; s. James Charles and Emma (Bauer) T.; (div. Jan., 1986); children: Steve, Lynn Trent Wooldridge, Greg; m. Alta Mae Brown, Aug. 20, 1994. BSAE, Oregon State U., 1962, MSME, 1964, PhD in Mech. Engring., 1972. Chief scientist (emeritus) Battelle Meml. Inst., Richland, Wash., 1965-96; retired, 1996, cons., 1996—; cons. in field, 1996—; courtesy prof. Oreg. State U., Corvallis, 1987—; rsch. affiliate MIT, Cambridge, Mass., 1990—; mem. tchg. staff Wash. State U., Richland, 1991—; vis. U. Md., College Park, 1995—. Sgt. U.S. Army, 1958-61. Recipient Fed. Lab. Consortium award, 1992. Mem. ASME, Phi Kappa Phi, Sigma Xi. Achievements include patent on a heat pipe; 2 copyrights on computational fluid dynamics software. Home: 721 Lynnwood Loop Richland WA 99352

TRENT, JAMES ALFRED, city official; b. Bklyn., May 25, 1946; s. Alfred and Helen (Vanasco) T. Assoc. deg. Applied Sci., SUNY, Farmingdale, 1966; B.Landscape Architecture, U. Ga., 1969. Jr. landscape architect Dept. Design & Constrn., N.Y.C., 1969-70, asst. landscape architect, 1970-79, chief profl. contracts, 1979-84, asst. to dir. Bur. Bldg. Design, 1984-87, dep. chief profl. contracts mgmt. sect., 1987-92; project mgr. Archtl. Specialties, 1992-94; chief profl. contracts sect., 1994—; v.p. Joint Bellerose Bus. Dist. Devel. Corp., Inc., 1997—. Art editor Civil Svc. Merit Coun. Inc., 1972-81, 86. Pres., Creedmoor Civic Assn. Inc., Bellerose, N.Y., 1970-80, v.p., 1980-84, exec. mem., 1984-94, treas., 1989—; mem. ornamental hort. adv. commn. Occupational Edn. Adv. Coun., N.Y.C. Bd. Edn., 1973-85; founder, pres. Queens County Farm Mus., 1975—; pres. Profl. Svc. Ctrs. for the Handicapped, Inc., 1980-81; 1st v.p. Eastern Queens Civic Coun., 1975—; mem. Queens County Com. Rep. Party, 1968-85; v.p. Midland Rep. Club, N.Y. 23d Assembly Dist., 1970-80, pres., 1981-93, grants disbursement judge Queens Coun. on Arts, 1982-86; chmn. bd. dirs. Queens Village Rep. club., 1993—. Named Grad. of Yr., SUNY at Farmingdale Alumni Assn., 1966; Humanitarian of 1977, 105th Police Precinct Community Coun. Mem. Met. Hist. Structures Assn. (dir. 1982—), Poppenhusen Inst. (bd. dirs. 1991-95, v.p. 1995—), Mcpl. Engrs. City of N.Y. (bd. dirs. 1995—, asst. editor jour. 1995—). Roman Catholic. Home: 24233 90th Ave Bellerose NY 11426-1115 Office: Rm 4-018 30-30 Thomson Ave Long Island City NY 11101

TRENT, ROBERT HAROLD, business educator; b. Norfolk, Va., Aug. 3, 1933; s. Floyd Murton and Myrtle Eugenia (White) T.; m. Joanne Bell, Aug. 17, 1951; 1 child, John Thomas. B.S., U. Richmond, 1963; Ph.D., U. N.C., 1968. Asst. prof. U. N.C., Chapel Hill, 1968-69; assoc. prof. commerce McIntire Sch. Commerce U. Va., Charlottesville, 1970-74, prof. commerce, 1975-84, Ralph A. Beeton prof. free enterprise, 1985-91; C. & P. Telephone Co. prof. commerce U. Va., Charlottesville, 1991—. Co-author: Marketing Decision Making, 1976, 4th edit., 1988; editor: Developments in Management Information Systems, 1974. Mem. Inst. Mgmt. Scis., Soc. Info. Mgmt., Assn. Comp. Machinery, Decision Scis. Inst., Beta Gamma Sigma, Omicron Delta Kappa. Office: U Va Monroe Hall Charlottesville VA 22903

TRENT, WARREN C., mechanical engineer; b. Boswell, Okla., Feb. 22, 1921; s. Clem and Fannie Edora (Greer) T.; m. Ruth Magdalene Potts, Apr. 2, 1948; 1 child, Paul Dudley. BSME, Okla. State U., 1943; MSME, Purdue U., 1948. Engr. Boeing Airplane Co., Seattle, 1943-45; instr. Okla. State U., Stillwater, 1946-47; rsch. engr. Kans. State U., Manhattan, 1948-51; mgr. sect. LTV Aerospace, Dallas, 1951-65; dir. engring. tech. McDonnell Douglas, St. Louis, 1965-77; owner Trent Assocs., Tyler, Tex., 1977-93; CEO Trent Techs., Inc., Tyler, 1993—; cons. Rockwell Internat., El Segundo, Calif., 1982-87; lectr. Navy Aviation Exec. Inst., Washington, 1973-76. Patentee in field. Arbitrator Better Bus. Bur., Tyler, 1985—. With USN, 1945-46. Fellow AIAA (assoc.); mem. ASHRAE, Tex. Profl. Engrs., Mo. Profl. Engrs. Republican. Baptist. Avocations: bridge, golf. Home: 1410 Woodlands Dr Tyler TX 75703-5718 Office: Trent Techs Inc 535 WSW Loop 323 Ste 301 Tyler TX 75701

TRENT, WENDELL CAMPBELL, business owner; b. Sneedville, Tenn., Nov. 1, 1940; s. William Campbell and Inez Hall (Daugherty) T.; m. Donna Lee Posey, May 31, 1964. BA, Berea Coll, 1963; MPH, UCLA, 1971; D in Pub. Adminstrn., Nova U., 1980. Asst. USPHS, UCLA, 1969; pres. Lockwood MacDonald Hosp., Petoskey, Mich., 1971-75, Allegan Gen. Hosp., Mich., 1975-79, Bethany Meth. Hosp., Chgo. 1979-84, St. Ansgar Hosp., Moorhead, Minn., 1984-85; pres. Meml. Hosp., Lawrenceville, Ill., 1985-89; midwest devel. dir. Brim Healthcare, 1989-90; prin. Larson & Trent Assocs., Dandridge, Tenn., 1990—; mem. Gov.'s Health Care Task Force; mem. Govs. Com. on Healthcare. Contbr. articles to profl. jours. Maj. USAF, 1963-69. Decorated Bronze Star. Fellow Am. Coll. Hosp. Adminstrs. (article of year com.); mem. Rotary, Kiwanis. Republican. Presbyterian. Avocations: photography, amateur radio. Home: 1837 Oakdale Dr Dandridge TN 37725-4422

TREPP, LEO, rabbi; b. Mainz, Germany, Mar. 4, 1913; s. Maier and Selma (Hirschberger) T.; m. Miriam de Haas, Apr. 26, 1938; 1 child, Susan Trepp Lachtman. PhD, U. Wurzburg, Ger., 1935; Dr.Phil, U. Oldenburg, Ger., 1989; DD, Hebrew Union Coll., 1985; postgrad., Harvard U., 1944-45; PhD (hon.), U. Wurzburg, 1985, U. Oldenburg, 1989. Ordained rabbi, 1936. Rabbi various temples, various locations, 1940-51; part-time rabbi Santa Rosa, Calif., 1951-61, Eureka, Calif., 1961-90; Jewish chaplain Vets. Home of Calif., Yountville, Calif., 1954—; prof. Judaic studies U. Mainz, 1983—. Author: Eternal Faith, Eternal People - A Journey into Judaism, 1962, Judaism, Development and Life, 1966, 2d edit. 1984, A History of the Jewish Experience, 1974, The Complete Book of Jewish Observance, 1980, Judaism and the Religions of Humanity, 1985, What if Shylock were a Marrano, 1985, The Controversy between Samson Raphael Hirsch and Seligmann Baer Bamberger—Halakhical and Societal Implications, 1991, Yamim Nora'im: The Traditional Liturgy and "Gates of Repentance", 1991; author numerous books in other langs.; major works include Die Juden, 1982, Der jüdischen Gottesdienst—Form und Entfaltung, 1991, Die Amerikamischen Juden—Profil einer Gemeinschaft, 1991, Gerchichlege der deutschen Juden, 1996; contbr. articles to profl. jours. Mem. Napa Planning Commn., 1964-69. Recipient Great Seal, City of Oldenburg, 1971, George Washington Honor medal, Freedoms Found., 1979; hon. freeman City of Oldenburg, 1990, Hon. Senator, U. Mainz, 1996, Gatenburg Plaquette, City of Mainz. Mem. Cen. Conf. Am. Rabbis, Rabbinical Assembly, Am. Philos. Assn., Am. Acad. Religion, No. Calif. Bd. Rabbis, Silverado Club. Home: 295 Montecito Blvd Napa CA 94559-2119

TREPPLER, IRENE ESTHER, retired state senator; b. St. Louis County, Mo., Oct. 13, 1926; d. Martin H. and Julia C. (Bender) Hagemann; student Meramec Community Coll., 1972; m. Walter J. Treppler, Aug. 18, 1950; children: John M., Steven A., Diane V. Anderson, Walter W. Payroll chief USAF Aero. Chart Plant, 1943-51; enumerator U.S. Census Bur., St. Louis, 1960, crew leader, 1970; mem. Mo. Ho. of Reps., Jefferson City, 1972-84; mem. Mo. Senate, Jefferson City, 1985-96; chmn. Minority Caucus, 1991-92. ActiveGravois Twp. Rep. Club, Concord Twp. Rep. Club; alt. del. Rep. Nat. Conv., 1976, 84. Recipient Spirit Enterprise award Mo. C. of C., 1992, Appreciation award Mo. State Med. Assn., Nat. Otto Nuttli Earthquake Hazard Mitigation award, 1993, Disting. Legislator award Cmty. Colls. Mo., 1995; named Concord Twp. Rep. of Yr., 1992. Mem. Nat. Order Women Legislators (rec. sec. 1981-82, pres. 1985), Nat. Fedn. Rep. Women. Mem. Evangelical Ch.

TRESCOTT, SARA LOU, water resources engineer; b. Frederick, Md., Nov. 17, 1954; d. Norton James and Mabel Elizabeth (Hall) T.; m. R. Jeffrey Franklin, Oct. 8, 1983. AA, Catonsville C.C., Balt., 1974; BA in Biol. Sci., U. Md., Balt., 1980. Sanitarian Md. Dept. Health & Mental Hygiene, Greenbelt, 1982; indsl. hygienist Md. Dept. Licensing & Regualtion, Balt., 1982-85; from water resources engr. to chief dredging div. Md. Dept. Natural Resources, Annapolis, 1985-92; chief navigation div. Md. Dept. Natural Resources, Stevensville, 1992-96, chief ops. & maintenance, 1996—; chair adv. bd. EEO, Annapolis, 1990-92; tech. com. Nat. Mgmt. Info. Systems, Balt., 1983. Contbr. articles to profl. jours. Mem. ASCE, County Engrs. Assn. Md. Democrat. Achievements include research in beneficial uses of dredged material; development of technology for hydrographic surveying, providing Md. with an improved waterway transportation network. Home: PO Box 22 Woodbine MD 21797-0022 Office: DNR Navigation Divsn 305 Marine Academy Dr Stevensville MD 21666-2859

TRESELER, KATHLEEN MORRISON, retired nursing educator; b. Tacoma, Wash., Apr. 28, 1925; d. Charles T. and Elizabeth M. (McDermott) Morrison; m. Donald K. Treseler, July, 1949; children: Michael S., C. Maureen, Patrick A. BS, Seattle Coll., 1946; MSN, U. Wash., 1966. Prof.

Seattle U. Sch. Nursing, 1968-91, prof. emeritus, 1991—. Author: Clinical Laboratory and Diagnostic Tests, 1982, 3d edit., 1995. Home: 17401 17th Pl NE Shoreline WA 98155-5201

TRESHIE, R. DAVID, newspaper publishing executive. Publ. The Orange County Register, Santa Ana, Calif. Office: The Orange County Register 625 N Grand Ave Santa Ana CA 92701-4347

TRESNOWSKI, BERNARD RICHARD, retired health insurance company executive; b. Chgo., Oct. 14, 1932; s. Al and Luella (Stewart) T.; m. Beverly Ann Gesmond, Nov. 26, 1955; children: Linda, Judy, Mark, Tom, MaryBeth, David; m. Leanne Patricia Irish, Aug. 1985; 1 child, Megan. B.S., U. Mich., 1955; M.P.H. in Hosp. Adminstrn, U. Pitts., 1958. Second asst. adminstr., then asst. adminstr. Albert Einstein Med. Center, Phila., 1958-61; research asso. U. Mich., 1961-62; assoc. adminstr. St. Joseph Mercy Hosp., Pontiac, Mich., 1963-67; sr. v.p. Blue Cross Assn., Chgo., 1967-78; exec. v.p. Blue Cross Assn., 1977-78; exec. v.p. Blue Cross and Blue Shield Assn., Chgo., 1978-81, pres., 1981-94; ret. Blue Cross and Blue Shield Assn., 1994; mem. Health Adminstrs. Study Soc. Author articles in field. Mem. Am. Hosp. Assn., Am. Coll. Health Care Execs., Am. Pub. Welfare Assn., Health Mgmt. Edn. Assn., Soc. Health Svc. Adminstrs., Internat. Found. Employee Benefit Plans, Internat. Fedn. Vol. Health Svc. Funds. (pres.), Am. Health Planning Assn., The Conf. Bd.

TRESTMAN, FRANK D., distribution company executive; b. Mpls., Sept. 3, 1934; s. Saul and Rose (Hyster) T.; m. Carol Lynn Wasserman, Apr. 3, 1960; children—Lisa Ellen, Jill Susan. B.B.A. with high distinction, U. Minn., 1955. Exec. v.p., treas. Napco Industries, Inc., Mpls., 1965-74, pres., dir., 1974-84; chmn, CEO Mass Merchandisers, Inc., Hopkins, Minn., 1984-86; pres. Trestman Enterprises, Golden Valley, Minn., 1987—; bd. dirs. Best Buy Co., Mpls., Western Container Corp., Mpls., Insignia Systems, Inc., T.C.F. Industries, Metris Cos., Inc. Mem. bd. govs. Mt. Sinai Hosp., Mpls., 1978-91, Abbott Northwestern Hosp., 1993—; chmn. bd. trustees Mpls. Fedn. Endowment Fund; bd. dirs. Harry Kay Found. With USN, 1957-58. Jewish. Clubs: Oak Ridge Country (Hopkins); Presidents Country (West Palm Beach, Fla.). Home: 4544 Woodridge Rd Minnetonka MN 55345-3936 Office: Trestman Enterprises 5500 Wayzata Blvd Ste 1045 Minneapolis MN 55416-1241

TREU, JESSE ISAIAH, venture capitalist; b. N.Y.C., Apr. 10, 1947. BS, Rensselaer Poly. Inst., 1968; MS, Princeton U., 1971, PhD, 1973. Physicist, liaison sci. components, materials group Gen. Electric Co., Schenectady, N.Y., 1973-77; tech. dir. Technicon Corp., Tarrytown, N.Y., 1977-82; v.p. Channing Weinberg-CW Ventures, N.Y.C., 1982-85; gen. ptnr. Domain Assocs., Princeton, N.J., 1986—. Office: Domain Assocs 1 Palmer Sq Princeton NJ 08542-3718

TREUHOLD, CHARLES RICHARD, retired investment banker; b. Bklyn., May 24, 1930; s. Eugene and Selma (Straus) T.; m. Kerstin Margareta Nevrell, July 28, 1956; 1 child, Robert Charles. BA, Yale U., 1952; postgrad., U. Paris, 1955-56. Syndicate assoc. Lehman Bros., N.Y.C., 1956-61; syndicate mgr. Paribas Corp., N.Y.C., 1961-66; sr. v.p., syndicate mgr. Arnhold & S. Bleichroeder, Inc., N.Y.C., 1966-95. Editor: Bawl St. Jour., 1977, 88. Lt. (j.g.) USN, 1952-55). Mem. Internat. Securities Market Assn. (bd. dirs. 1979-86, prin. del. 1969-95), Bond Club N.Y. (gov. 1988-95), Union Club. Home: 200 E 66th St New York NY 10021-6728

TREUMANN, WILLIAM BORGEN, university dean; b. Grafton, N.D., Feb. 26, 1916; s. William King and Dagny Helen (Borgen) T.; m. Mildred Elizabeth Jenkins, Aug. 14, 1948; children—Richard Roy, Robert Evan, Beverly Kay. B.S., U. N.D., 1942; M.A., U. Ill., 1944, Ph.D., 1947. Teaching asst. chemistry U. Ill., 1942-45, teaching asst. math., 1945-46, vis. prof., summers 1948-50; from asst. prof. to prof. chemistry N.D. State U., 1946-55; mem. faculty Moorhead (Minn.) State U., 1960—, prof. chemistry, 1962—, asso. dean acad. affairs, 1968-70, dean faculty math. and sci., 1970—. Contbr. to profl. jours. Research Corp. Am. grantee, 1954; Minn. U. Bd. grantee, 1967. Fellow Am. Inst. Chemists; mem. Am. Chem. Soc., Am. Assn. U. Profs., Minn. Acad. Sci., Fedn. Am. Scientists, Phi Beta Kappa, Sigma Xi. Home: One 2nd St S Apt 5-204 Fargo ND 58103-1921 Office: Math Dept Moorhead State U Moorhead MN 56560

TREUTING, EDNA GANNON, retired nursing administrator; b. New Orleans, Dec. 16, 1925; d. Alphonse Joseph and Clara Josephine (David) Gannon; m. August Raymond Treuting, Sept. 4, 1948 (dec.); children: Keith, Karen Treuting Stein, Madeline Treuting LeBlanc, Jaime Treuting Gonzales, Jay (dec.). Diploma, Charity Hosp. Sch. Nursing, New Orleans, 1946; BS in Nursing Edn., La. State U., 1953; MPH, Tulane U., 1972, DPH, 1978. RN, La.; cert. family nurse practitioner Tulane U. Head nurse premature nursery Charity Hosp., New Orleans, 1946-47, head nurse pediatrics, 1947-49; instr. pediatrics Charity Hosp. Sch. Nursing, New Orleans, 1949-52, 54, instr., LPN, 1953; pvt. duty Touro, Hotel Dieu, New Orleans, 1957-59; instr. maternal and child health La. State U. Sch. Nursing, New Orleans, 1960, 65, 69-71; from instr. to prof., sect. head Tulane Sch. Pub. Health and Tropical Medicine, New Orleans, 1972-83; dean, prof. Our Lady Holy Cross Coll. Nursing Div., New Orleans, 1983-84; chief nurse Dept. Health and Hosp., New Orleans, 1984-94; region IV nurse practitioner Baylor U., Health Edn. and Welfare, 1974-76; citizen amb. to South Am. People to People, 1979; presentor U. Hawaii Pub. Health and Nursing, 1977; planner, advisor, reviewer continuing edn. U. Tenn., Memphis, 1990-95. Author, editor: Occupation Health Nursing, 1979; sect. head, prin. investigator Practitioner Programs Family and Pediatric, 1973-83; item writer Nurse Practitioners, Community Health and Occupational Nursing, 1974-80; mem. editl. bd. to sci. jours. and Nurse Practitioner Jour. Pres. Oti-Mrs. Internat., New Orleans, 1955-68; sponsor bd. dirs. Holy Cross H.S. Treuting Scholarship, New Orleans, 1966—; hurricane and disaster nurse ARC, New Orleans, 1966-77; v.p. Pandora Carnival Club, New Orleans, 1968-78; alternate state health dept. Commn. Nursing Supply and Demand by Legislation, 1991-94; planner, presentor La. State Rsch. Day, 1990-92. Named outstanding woman in the mainstream world's fair women of achievement, 1984. Mem. New Orleans Dist. Nurses Assn. (First J.B. Hickey Meml. Community award 1985, Great 100 Nurse-First Yr. 1987), La. Pub. Health Assn. (Dr. C.B. White Merritorious Diligent Svc. 1990), La. Nurse Practitioners Assn.(Edna Treuting scholarship named in her honor), Tulane U. Alumni Assn. (past pres.), Tulane Med. Alumni Assn. (past pres.), Delta Omega (past pres. nat.,Eta chpts.), Sigma Theta Tau (Epsilon Nu chpt.). Republican. Roman Catholic. Avocations: traveling, dancing, swimming, photography, reading. Home: 1914 Marlin Dr Mandeville LA 70448-1069

TREVES, SAMUEL BLAIN, geologist, educator; b. Detroit, Sept. 11, 1925; s. Samuel and Stella (Stork) T.; m. Jane Patricia Mitoray, Nov. 24, 1960; children: John Samuel, David Samuel. BS, Mich. Tech. U., 1951; postgrad., U. Otago, New Zealand, 1953-54; MS, U. Idaho, 1953; PhD, Ohio State U., 1959. Geologist Ford Motor Co., 1951, Idaho Bur. Mines and Geology, 1952, Otago Catchment Bd., 1953-54; mem. faculty U. Nebr., Lincoln, 1958—, prof. geology, 1966—, chmn. dept., 1964-70, 74-89, assoc. dean Coll. Arts and Scis., 1989-96; curator geology Nebr. State Mus., 1964—; participant expdns. to Antarctica and Greenland, 1960-61,63, 65, 70, annually 72-76. Rsch. and publs. on geology of igneous and metamorphic rocks of Idaho, New Zealand, Mich., Antarctica, Nebr., Can., Greenland with emphasis on origin of Precambrian granite complexes and basaltic volcanic rocks. Fulbright scholar U. Otago, New Zealand, 1953-54. Fellow Geol. Soc. Am., AAAS, Explorers Club; mem. Am. Mineral Soc., Sigma Xi, Tau Beta Pi, Sigma Gamma Epsilon. Home: 1710 B St Lincoln NE 68502-1524

TREVILLIAN, WALLACE DABNEY, economics educator, retired dean; b. Charlottesville, Va., May 1, 1918; s. Robert Carr and Mary Anna (Perry) T.; m. Mary Lou McEachern Moody, Nov. 28, 1963; children: Malcolm McEachern, Edward Dabney. BS, U. Va., 1940, MA, 1947, PhD, 1954; postgrad., U. Calif., 1950-51. Mem. faculty Clemson (S.C.) U., 1947—, successively instr. econs., asst. prof., assoc. prof., 1947-55, prof. econs., head dept. indsl. mgmt., 1955-63, founding dean Coll. Commerce and Industry, 1963-80, prof., dean emeritus, 1983—; vis. scholar U. Sussex, Eng., 1980—; mem. Regional Export Expansion Council, 1965-77; sec. commn. on edn. for bus. professions Nat. Assn. State Univs. and Land-Grant Colls., 1975-77; pres. Nat. Council for Textile Edn., 1978-80. Master sgt. AUS, 1941-45. Econ. in Action fellow Case Inst. Tech., 1958. Mem. St. Andrews Soc. Upper S.C., Newcomen Soc., Thomas Jefferson Soc. of Alumni U. Va. Episcopalian. Home: PO Box 1258 Clemson SC 29633-1258

TREVIÑO, FERNANDO MANUEL, medical educator; b. Brownsville, Tex., Aug. 20, 1949; s. Manuel Emilio and Consuelo Ivern (Galindo) T.; m. Dorothy Dell Bullock, Mar. 1, 1980 (div. Mar.1990); m. Lorene Samora Treviño, Feb. 14, 1992; 1 child, Gabriela Alejandra. BS, U. Houston, 1971; MPH, U. Tex., Houston, 1975; PhD, U. Tex., Galveston, 1979. Sr. scientist AMA, Chgo., 1986-88; assoc. prof. U. Tex. Med. Br., Galveston, 1988-94, dir. Ctr. for Cross-Cultural Rsch., 1989-94; prof. and dean S.W. Tex. State U., San Marcos, 1991-93; exec. dir. APHA, Washington, 1993-96; pres. World Fedn. Pub. Health Assns., Geneva, Switzerland, 1995-97; prof., chmn. dept. pub. health and preventive medicine U. North Tex. Health Sci. Ctr. Exec. editor Am. Jour. Pub. Health, 1993-96. Mem.Interncultural Cancer Coun., 1995—. Capt. U.S. Army, 1971-79. Recipient Disting. Author award Jour. Allied Health, 1995. Fellow Royal Soc. Health (hon.); mem. Nat. Medicine/Pub. Health Initiative (co-chair 1994-96). Avocations: photography, motorcycles, camping. Home: 1213 Kelpie Ct Fort Worth TX 76111 Office: U North Tex Health Sci Ctr Dept Pub Health Preventive 3500 Camp Bowie Blvd Fort Worth TX 76107-2644

TREVINO, JERRY ROSALEZ, secondary school principal; b. Mathis, Tex., July 9, 1943; s. Geronimo R. and Hilaria (Rosalez) T.; m. Juanita Escalante, Jan. 1, 1985; 1 child, John-Michael. BA, U. Houston, 1967, MEd, 1974; PhD, Kennedy-Western U., 1988; postgrad., U. Tex., Odessa, 1988-92. Cert. tchr., adminstr., supt., Tex. Tchr. N.E. Houston Sch. Dist., 1966-70, pub. rels. officer, 1970-72, asst. prin., 1972-76; tchr. Harris County Dept. Edn., Houston, 1968-72, Austin (Tex.) Ind. Sch. Dist., 1977-87; asst. prin. Tex. Youth Commn., Pyote, 1987-91, prin., 1991-96; Title VII project dir. U.S. Dept. Edn., Pyote, 1988-96; instr. Austin C.C., 1980-84, chair, Prin. Coun. for Edn. of Lang. Minority Students, S.W. Ednl. Devel. Lab., Austin. Editor newsletter The Flyer, 1970-72; contbr. articles to profl. publs. Mem. Community Adv. Coun., Pyote, 1987-96; mem. Tex. Children's Mental Health Plan, Monahans, Tex., 1991-96; mem. planning com. Permian Basin Quality Work Force, Midland, Tex., 1992-96; mem. Supt.'s Coun., Pyote, 1987-96. Named Outstanding Adminstr. of Permian Basin (Golden Apple award) Permian Basin Private Industry Coun., 1994. Mem. ASCD, Nat. Assn. for Bilingual Edn., Am. Biog. Inst. (rsch. bd. advisors 1992—, Recognition plaque 1992, diploma of honor 1992, Commemorative Medal of Honor), Tex. Assn. Secondary Sch. Prins. Presbyterian. Avocations: flying, travel, reading, landscaping. Home: 12009 Rotherham Dr Austin TX 78753

TREVINO, LEE BUCK, professional golfer; b. Dallas, Dec. 1, 1939; s. Joe and Juanita (Barrett) T.; m. Claudia Bove; children: Richard Lee, Lesley Ann, Tony Lee, Troy Liana, Olivia Leigh, Daniel Lee. Ed. pub. schs. Head profl. Hardy's Driving Range, Dallas, 1961-65; asst. profl. Horizon Hills Country Club, El Paso, Tex., 1966-67; chmn. bd. Lee Trevino Enterprises, Inc., 1967—. Hon. chmn. Christmas Seal campaign, 1969-72, sports ambassador, 1971; mem. Pres.'s Conf. on Phys. Fitness and Sports; grand marshal Sun Carnival Parade, 1969-70, 71-72; mem. sports com. Nat. Multiple Sclerosis Soc. Served with USMCR, 1956-60. Recipient Hickok Belt award, 1971; named Golf Rookie of Yr., 1967, PGA Player of Yr., 1971, Tex. Pro Athlete of Yr., 1970, Gold Tee award, 1971, AP Pro Athlete of Yr., 1971, Player of Yr. Golf Mag., 1971, Sportsman of Yr. Sports Illustrated, 1971, PGA Sr. Tour Players of Yr., 1990, 92, 94, Internat. Sports Personality of Yr. Brit. Broadcasting Assn., 1971, Rookie and Player of Yr., Sr. PGA Tour, 1990; mem. Tex. Hall of Fame, Am. Gulf Hall of Fame, World Golf Hall of Fame. Tournament winner Tex. Open, 1965, 66, N.Mex. Open, 1966, U.S. Open, 1968, 71, Amana Open, 1968, 69, Hawaiian Open, 1968, Tucson Open, 1969, 70, World Cup, 1969, 71, Nat. Airlines Open, 1970, Brit. Open, 1971, 72, Canadian Open 1971, 77, 79, Can. PGA, 1979, Danny Thomas-Memphis Classic, 1971, 72, 80, Tallahassee Open, 1971, Sahara Invitational, 1971, St. Louis Classic, 1972, Hartford Open, 1972, Jackie Gleason Classic, 1973, Doral-Eastern Open, 1973, Mexican Open, 1973, 75, Chrysler Classic, Australia, 1973, PGA Championship, 1974, 84, World Series Golf, 1974, Greater New Orleans Open, 1974, Fla. Citrus Open, 1975, Colonial Nat. Invitational, 1976, 78, Colgate Mixed Team Matches, 1979, Brit. Masters, 1985, U.S. Sr. Open, 1990; King Hassan Moroccan trophy II, 1977; Lancome trophy Benson & Hedges, 1978, 80; 1st golfer to have scored four sub-par rounds in U.S. Open Competition, 1968; leading Money winner, 1970, 2d pl. money winner 1971, 1972; Vardon trophy winner, 1970 1972, 74, 80; Can. PGA, 1983; PGA Seniors Championship, 1994; capt. Ryder Cup Matches, 1985; first golfer to have scored 4 sub-par rounds in PGA competition. Office: 5757 Alpha Rd Ste 620 Dallas TX 75240-4668*

TREVISAN, MAURIZIO, epidemiologist, researcher; b. Naples, Italy, Jan. 31, 1952; came to U.S., 1979; s. Ilario and Bianca (Bruni) T.; m. Lisa Monagle, Dec. 22, 1983; children: Simona, Alessia, Stefan. MD magna cum laude, U. Naples, Italy, 1977; MS, SUNY, Buffalo, 1989. Cert. in medicine and surgery, Italy, 1977, diabetes and metabolic disease, Italy, 1980. Resident dept. internal medicine Med. Sch. U. Naples, 1977-79; rsch. fellow dept. community health and preventive medicine Med. Sch. Northwestern U., 1979-82; co-prin. investigator, dir. Cellular Ion Transport Lab Project Gubbio, U. Naples, 1983-85; asst. prof. dept. social and preventive medicine SUNY, Buffalo, 1985-88, clinical asst. prof. dept. family medicine, 1988-89, assoc. prof. dept. social and preventive medicine, 1988-92, clinical assoc. prof. nutrition program, 1989-94, assoc. prof. dept. family medicine, 1989-94, interim chair dept social and preventive medicine, 1991-92, prof. and chmn. dept. social and preventive medicine, 1993—, prof. dept. family medicine, 1994—; prin. investigator Women's Health Initiative WNY Vanguard Clin. Ctr., 1993—; vis. physician dept. physiology Harvard Med. Sch., 1982; cons. inst. internal medicine and metabolic disease rsch. U. Naples, 1982-85; adj. asst. prof. dept. cmty. health and preventive medicine Northwestern U. Med. Sch., 1987—; adj. prof. nutrition program SUNY, Buffalo, 1994—, dir., health in housing, SUNY, Buffalo. Fellow Am. Heart Assn. Coun. on Epidemiology. Recipient Rsch. Career Devel. award NIH, 1989-94. Fellow, Am. Coll. of Epidemiology; mem. Epidemiol. Soc. Achievements include population-based epidemiological investigation of ion transport abnormalities as risk factors for essential hypertension. Office: SUNY Buffalo Dept Social & Preventive Medicine 270 Farber Hall Buffalo NY 14214-8001

TREVOR, ALEXANDER BRUEN, computer company executive; b. N.Y.C., Apr. 12, 1945; s. John B. Jr. and Evelyn (Bruen) T.; m. Ellen Ruth Armstrong, Sept. 21, 1974; children: Anne Wood, Alexander Jay Bruen. BS, Yale U., 1967; MS, U. Ariz., 1971. Rsch. asst. U. Ariz., Tucson, 1971; systems analyst CompuServe Inc., Columbus, Ohio, 1971-73, dir. systems, 1973-74, v.p., 1974-81, exec. v.p., chief tech. officer, 1981-96, also bd. dirs., 1985-96; pres. Nuvocom, Inc., Columbus, 1996—. Author (software program) CB Simulator, 1980. Trustee Trudeau Inst., Saranac Lake, N.Y., Aviation Safety Inst., Worthington, Ohio. 1st lt. Signal Corps, U.S. Army, 1968-70, Vietnam. Decorated Bronze Star. Mem. IEEE, Assn. for Computing Machinery, SAR (N.Y.), Union Club (N.Y.), Scioto Country Club. Republican. Episcopalian. Office: 910 Clayton Dr Worthington OH 43085-3301

TREVOR, BRONSON, economist; b. N.Y.C., Nov. 12, 1910; s. John Bond and Caroline Murray (Wilmerding) T.; A.B., Columbia Coll., 1931; m. Eleanor Darlington Fisher, Nov. 8, 1946; children—Eleanor, Bronson, Caroline. Own bus., 1931—; dir., asst. sec. Northwestern Terminal R.R., 1952-58; chmn. bd. Texinia Corp., 1959-92. Former dir. chmn. fin. com. Gen. Hosp. of Saranac Lake mem. Council for Agrl. and Chemurgic Research, Am. Forestry Assn. Mem. Republican County Com. of N.Y. County, 1937-39; leader in primary election campaigns N.Y. County, 1937, 38, 39 to free local Rep. party orgn. from leftwing affiliations. Served with U.S. Army, 1942, World War II. Mem. S.A.R., Soc. Colonial Wars. Clubs: Union, Knickerbocker, Racquet and Tennis, Piping Rock, Bath and Tennis. Author: (pamphlet) The United States Gold Purchase Program, 1941; also numerous articles on econ. subjects. Home: Heron Ln Paul Smiths NY 12970 Office: PO Box 182 Oyster Bay NY 11771-0182

TREVOR, KIRK DAVID NIELL, orchestra conductor, cellist; b. London, Feb. 8, 1952. Student, Dartington Coll., 1968-69; grad. with distinction, Guildhall Sch. Music and Drama, 1974; student, N.C. Sch. Arts, 1975-77. Asst. condr. Guildhall Opera Sch., 1973-74; music dir. Youth Symphony of Carolinas, 1978-82; music dir., condr. Knoxville (Tenn.) Symphony Orch., 1984—; chief condr. Martinu Philharmonic Czech Rep., 1995—; assoc. condr. Charlotte (N.C.) Symphony Orch., 1978-82, Exxon Art Endowment and Dallas Symphony, 1982-85; former resident condr. Dallas Symphony; dir. music Indpls. Chamber Orch., 1988—; instr. U. Tenn., 1985—; guest condr. U.S., S.Am., USSR, Czech Republic, Poland, Romania, Switzerland; tchr. Condrs. Symphonic Workshop in Zlin, Czech Republic, 1991—, Artistic Dir. Recipient Libottom Meml. prize, 1972, Kappilis Condr. prize, 1974, Toussant prize, 1974; winner Am. Condrs. Program, 1990; Fulbright Exchange grantee U.K. and U.S. Dept. State, 1975, Am. Condrs. Program grantee, 1990. Mem. Condrs. Guild, Am. Symphony Orch. League. Office: Knoxville Symphony Orch 623 Market St Ste 600 Knoxville TN 37902-2243*

TREVOR, LEIGH BARRY, lawyer; b. Galesburg, Ill., Aug. 29, 1934; s. Dean Spaulding and Jean Elizabeth (Barry) T.; m. Mary Witherell, Aug. 8, 1978; children: John W. Hoffman, Ann Kete, Stephen S., Julia B. Kramer, Elizabeth P. Grad., Phillips Acad., 1952; AB magna cum laude, Harvard U., 1956, LLB, 1962. Bar: Ohio 1963, U.S. Dist. Ct. D.C. 1970. Assoc. Jones, Day, Reavis & Pogue, Cleve., 1962-68, ptnr., 1969—, ptnr.-in-charge, 1990-93; dir., sec. Dix & Eaton, Inc., Cleve.; lectr. on hostile corp. takeovers, other corp. law topics. Contbr. articles to profl. jours. Trustee, sec. State Troopers of Ohio, 1985—; pres. Stakeholders in Am., Mpls., 1987-88; trustee Cleveland State U. Found., 1990-94, Gt. Lakes Theater Festival, 1991-94. Lt. (j.g.) USN, 1956-59. Fellow Ohio State Bar Found.; mem. Ohio State Bar Assn. (mem. tender offer subcom. 1982—, corp. governance subcom. 1986—, chmn. corp. law com. 1989-91, coun. of dels. 1991—), Cleve. Bar Assn., D.C. Bar Assn., Nat. Investor Rels. Inst. (bd. dirs. local chpt. 1985-92, pres. Cleve.-Akron chpt. 1990-91), Phi Beta Kappa. Republican. Episcopalian. Home: 3 Hidden Vly Rocky River OH 44116-1143 Office: Jones Day Reavis & Pogue 901 Lakeside Ave Cleveland OH 44114-1116

TREXLER, EDGAR RAY, minister, editor; b. Salisbury, N.C., Sept. 17, 1937; s. Edgar Ray and Eula Belle (Farmer) T.; m. Emily Louise Kees, Aug. 21, 1960; children: David Ray, Mark Raymond, Karen Emily. AB, Lenoir-Rhyne Coll., 1959, LittD, 1978; MDiv, Luth. Theol. So. Sem., 1962; MA, Syracuse U., 1964; postgrad., Boston U., 1960, Luth. World Fedn. Study Project, Geneva, 1977, 81; LittD (hon.), Midland Coll., 1990; DD, Wittenberg U., 1994. Ordained to ministry United Luth. Ch. Am., 1962; pastor St. John's Luth. Ch., Lyons, N.Y., 1962-65; features editor Luth. Mag., Phila., 1965-72, assoc. editor, 1972-78, editor, 1978-87; editor Luth. Mag., Chgo., 1988—; sec. Commn. Ch. Papers, Luth. Ch. Am., 1971-72, mem. staff team comm., 1972-78; chmn. Interch. Features, 1971-76; chmn. postal affairs com. Assoc. Ch. Press, 1983-90, Work Group on New Ch. Periodical, 1985-86; Evangelical Luth. Ch. Am. Cabinet of Execs., 1988—. Author: Ways to Wake Up Your Church, 1969, Creative Congregations, 1972, The New Face of Missions, 1973, Mission in a New World, 1977, LWF/6, 1978, Anatomy of a Merger, 1991; mem. editl. adv. bd. The New World, Roman Cath. Archdiocese of Chgo., 1994—. Pres. Lyons Coun. Chs., 1964; trustee Lenoir Rhyne Coll., 1975-84, 97—. Recipient Disting. Alumnus award Lenoir-Rhyne Coll., 1991, Disting. Svc. award Newberry Coll., 1992, Bachman award for disting. leadership Luth. Theol. So. Sem., 1993, award of merit for editls. Assoc. Ch. Press, 1991, award of merit for articles in mission mags. Assoc. Ch. Press, 1974. Mem. Nat. Luth. Editors Assn. (pres. 1975-77). Home: 1401 Sequoia Rd Naperville IL 60540-6391 Office: Luth Mag 8765 W Higgins Rd Chicago IL 60631-4101

TREXLER, SUZANNE FRANCES, geriatrics nurse; b. Harrisburg, Pa., Feb. 8, 1963; d. Walter Richard and Catherine Frances (Mourawski) Markham; m. Barry Kenneth Trexler, Nov. 9, 1991; children: William Chester, Brittany Nancy, Katye Iona. LPN, Harrisburg Stelton Highs, Sch. Practical Nursing, 1984; ADN, Harrisburg (Pa.) Area C.C., 1984; BA in Long Term Care Adminstrn., St. Joseph Coll., 1994, postgrad., 1994—; BSN, York (Pa.) Coll., 1997. Nurse ICU and critical care unit Meml. Hosp., York, Pa., 1987-88; staff nurse emergency dept. Polyclinic Med. Ctr., Harrisburg, 1988-91; assoc. prof. Nat. Edn. Ctr.-Jr. Coll., Harrisburg, 1991; dir. nursing Camp Hill (Pa.) Care Ctr., 1991-92; resident assessment supr. Susquehanna Ctr., Harrisburg, 1992-94; dir. nursing Susquehanna Luth. Village, Millersburg, Pa., 1994-95; asst. adminstr. Dauphin Manor, Harrisburg, 1995—; ACLS, CPR instr. Am. Heart Assn., Harrisburg, 1989—; BCLS, CPR instr. ARC, Harrisburg, 1992—; RN, paramedic Lebanon (Pa.) County First Aide and Safety Patrol, 1992—. Sec. Little People PTA, Harrisburg, 1991-92; pres. Student Human Resource Mgmt. Club, York (Pa.) Coll., 1992—; v.p. Prince of Peace PTO, 1997-98. Recipient Nurse of Hope award Am. Cancer Soc., Dauphin County, Harrisburg, 1983-84. Mem. AACN, Pa. Nurses Assn., Pa. Dir. Nursing Assn. for Long Term Care, PANPHA (advocate), York Coll. Alumni Assn. (bd. dirs. Susquehanna Valley). Roman Catholic. Avocations: ceramics, ballet, flute. Office: Dauphen Manor Paxton St Harrisburg PA 17111

TREYNOR, JACK LAWRENCE, financial advisor, educator; b. Council Bluffs, Iowa, Feb. 21, 1930; s. Jack Vernon and Alice (Cavin) T.; m. Elizabeth Glassmeyer, Aug. 29, 1968; children: Elizabeth Childs, Wendy F.C., Thomas Pirrie, V. BA, Haverford Coll., 1951; MBA with distinction, Harvard U., 1955; postgrad., MIT, 1962-63. Jr. faculty Harvard U. Sch. Bus., Cambridge, Mass., 1955-56; ops. research staff Arthur D. Little, Cambridge, 1956-66; mgr. computer applications Merrill Lynch, N.Y.C., 1966-69; editor Fin. Analysts Jour., N.Y.C., 1969-81; chief investment officer Treynor-Arbit Assocs., Chgo., 1981-85; assoc. vis. prof. dept. of fin. and bus. econs. U. So. Calif., Los Angeles, 1985-88; pres. Treynor Capital Mgmt., Palos Verdes Estates, Calif.; gen. ptnr., trustee, dir. certain mutual funds Eaton Vance, 1970—. Author: (with Patrick Regan and William Priest) The Financial Reality of Pension Funding Under ERISA, 1976; mem. editl. bd. Fin. Analysts Jour., 1969—; co-author and contbr. numerous articles in fin. jours. (Graham and Dodd Scroll award 1968, 82, twice in 1987, Graham and Dodd Plaque for best paper in Fin. Analysts Jour. 1981). Trustee Fin. Analysts Research Found., 1970-85; mem. vis. com. Grad. Sch. Bus. Adminstrn. U. Chgo., 1984-89. Served with U.S. Army, 1951-53. Recipient James R. Vertin award Fin. Analysts Rsch. Found., 1997. Fellow Inst. for Quantitative Rsch. in Fin. (disting., bd. dirs. 1970—); mem. Fin. Analysts Fedn. (Nicholas Molodovsky award 1985), Am. Fin. Assn. (bd. dirs. 1979-81), Haverford Varsity Club, Longwood Cricket Club (Chestnut Hill, Mass.), N.Y. Athletic Club, Manursing Island Club (Rye, N.Y.), Winter Club (Lake Forest, Ill.),), Palos Verdes Tennis Club, Palos Verdes Beach and Athletic Club. Episcopalian. Avocations: jazz piano, sports cars, antique trains.

TREYZ, JOSEPH HENRY, librarian; b. Binghamton, N.Y., Nov. 23, 1926; s. Joseph Henry and Edna Belle (Leonard) T. B.A., Oberlin Coll., 1950; postgrad., Harvard U., 1951; M.L.S., Columbia U., 1952. Circulation asst. N.Y. Acad. Medicine Library, 1950-51; cataloger Columbia Libraries, N.Y.C., 1951-53, Stevens Inst. Tech., Hoboken, N.J., 1953-54; adminstrv. asst. Yale Library, 1955, asst. head catalogue dept., 1955-61; head new campuses program U. Calif., La Jolla, 1961-65; asst. dir. U. Mich. Library, Ann Arbor, 1965-71; dir. libraries U. Wis., Madison, 1971-83, asst. to chancellor, 1983-85; sec.-treas. L.D. Repos, Inc., 1985-87, pres., 1987—; univ. rep. Consumer Reaction Project for Catalog Card Reprodn. Study, 1961; condr. survey tech. services Fordham U. Libraries, 1967-69, Brandeis U. Libraries, 1970-71; mem. Wis. Gov.'s Com. on Library Devel., 1973-81, Wis. com. Library Services and Constrn. Act, 1979-81; del. U.S. Mission to China on Libraries, 1979. Author: Books for College Libraries, 1967, also articles. Bd. dirs. Wis. Center for Theatre Research. Served with AUS, 1945-46. Mem. Universal Serials and Book Exchange (v.p. 1976, pres., chmn. bd. dirs. 1977), ALA (councilor 1970-74, 77-81, chmn. various coms. 1967-69, recipient Melvil Dewey medal 1970), Assn. Research Libraries (commn. orgn. materials, dir. 1975-78), Midlnet (v.p. 1978-79, pres. 1979-80), Assn. Coll. and Research Libraries (chmn. editorial bd. Choice 1968-70), Wis. Library Consortium (pres. 1975-76), Wis. Assn. Acad. Libraries (chmn. 1973-74), Council U. Wis. Librarians (chmn. 1975-76, 79-80, 81-83), Wis. Library Assn. (bd. dirs. 1973-74, mem. White House Conf. com. 1977-78), Madison Area Library Council (v.p. 1973-74), Mich. Library Assn. (chmn. tech. services sect. 1968-69), N.Y. Tech. Services Librarians (pres. 1959-60). Methodist. Home: 801 N Venetian Dr Miami FL 33139-1007

TREZEK, GEORGE JAMES, mechanical engineer; b. Chgo., July 10, 1937; s. George A. T.; m. Joan A. Arcieri, Aug. 18, 1962; children: Wendy Marie, Keith R., Cynthia Ann. B.M.E., Gen. Motors Inst., 1960; M.S., U. Ill., 1962, Ph.D., 1965. Asst. prof. mech. engring. Northwestern U., 1965; asst. prof. U. Calif., Berkeley, 1966-70, assoc. prof., 1970-74, prof., 1974-90, prof.

emeritus, 1990—; v.p. R&D Greenfield Environ.; dir. recycling ops. BKK Corp., 1990-96; pres. Trezek Group, Inc., 1996—; tech., innovation-devel., implementation cons. to industry, state and fed. govtl. agys. Contbr. numerous articles on heat transfer, bio-engring. and environ. engring., solid waste mgmt. and hazardous waste mgmt., heavy metals treatment tech., marine sediments remediation, plastics recycling tech. to profl. jours. Mem. ASME, ASTM. Roman Catholic. Home: 2210 Canyon Oak Ln Danville CA 94506-2014

TREZISE, PHILIP HAROLD, government official; b. Calumet, Mich., May 27, 1912; s. Norman and Emma (Anderson) T.; m. Ruth Elenor Dorsey, Nov. 26, 1938; children: John Dorsey, David Philip. A.B., U. Mich., 1936, M.A., 1939; student, Nat. War Coll., 1949-50. Research asso. U. Mich., 1940-41; fellow Social Sci. Research Council, 1941-42; ofcl. Office Def. Transportation, 1942-43; with Dept. State, 1946-71; advisor U.S. delegation to U.N. Commn. on Indonesian question, 1948, cons. report to Pres. on fgn. econ. policy, 1950; dep. dir. Office Intelligence Research, intelligence activities, 1952-55, mem. policy planning staff, 1956-57; minister econ. affairs Am. embassy, Tokyo, 1957-61; dep. asst. sec. for econ. affairs Dept. State, 1961-65; U.S. ambassador to OECD, Paris, France, 1966-69; asst. sec. state econ. affairs, 1969-71; mem. Washington Policy Council Internat. Mgmt. and Devel. Inst., Trilateral Commn., 1976-83; sr. fellow Brookings Instn., 1971—; Adj. prof. dept. polit. sci. Columbia U., 1978; Dir. Bank of Tokyo Trust Co., 1976, Atlantic Council; mem. Nat. Commn. Supplies and Shortages, 1975-76. Contbg. editor: Yomiuri Shimbun, 1979-86. Pres. Japan-Am. Soc., 1973-76. Served as lt. OSS USNR, 1943-46. Decorated Order of Rising Sun (Japan); recipient Pres.'s award for disting. fed. civilian svc., 1965, Disting. Honor award Dept. State, 1971, Disting. Alumnus award U. Mich., 1980. Mem. Council Fgn. Relations, Phi Beta Kappa. Episcopalian. Club: Internat. Nat. Economists (Washington). Home: Apt 1109 9707 Old Georgetown Rd Bethesda MD 20814 Office: 1775 Massachusetts Ave NW Washington DC 20036-2188

TREZZA, ALPHONSE FIORE, librarian, educator; b. Phila., Dec. 27, 1920; s. Vincent and Amalia (Ferrara) T.; m. Mildred Di Pietro, May 19, 1945; children: Carol Ann Trezza Johnston, Alphonse Fiore. B.S., U. Pa., 1948, M.S., 1950, postgrad.; LHD (hon.), Rosary Coll., 1997. Page Free Library, Phila., 1940-41, 45-48; library asst. Free Library, 1948-49; cataloger, asst. reference librarian Villanova U., 1949-50, instr., 1956-60; head circulation dept. U. Pa. Library, 1950-56; lectr. Drexel Inst. Sch. Library Sci., 1951-60; editor Cath. Library world, 1956-60; exec. sec. Cath. Library Assn., 1956-60; assoc. exec. dir. ALA, exec. sec. library adminstrn. div., 1960-67, assoc. dir. adminstrv. services, 1967-69; dir. Ill. State Library, Springfield, 1969-74; lectr. Grad. Sch. Library and Info. Sci., Cath. U., 1975-82; exec. dir. Nat. Commn. on Libraries and Info. Scis., Washington, 1974-80; dir. intergovt. library Cooperation Project Fed. Library Com./Library of Congress, Washington, 1980-82; assoc. prof. Sch. Library and Info. Studies Fla. State U., Tallahassee, 1982-87, prof., 1987-93, emeritus prof., 1993—; mem. Ill. Library LSCA TITLE I-II Adv. Commn., 1963-69; mem. network devel. com. Library of Congress, 1977-82; bd. visitors Sch. Library and Info. Sci., U. Pitts., 1977-80; cons. Becker & Hayes, Inc., 1980-84, King Research, Inc., 1981-82; mem. planning com and steering com. Fla. Gov.'s Conf. on Library and Info. Svcs., 1988-91. Nat. chmn. Cath. Book Week, 1954-56; pres. Joliet Diocesan Bd. Edn., 1966-68; Democratic committeeman, Lombard, Ill., 1961-69; auditor Borough of Norwood (Pa.), 1958-60. Served to 1st lt. USAAF, 1942-45. Decorated Air medal; recipient Ofcl. commendation White House Conf. on Libr. and Info. Svc., 1979, citation State Libr. Agys., 1994, Silver award Commn. Libr. Info. Sci., 1996. Mem. ALA (coun. 1973-82, 88-92, mem. exec. bd. 1974-79, chmn. stats. coordinating com. 1970-74, mem. pub. com. 1975-78, 81-83, 87-89, chmn. adv. com. interface, 1979-83, chmn. membership com. 1983-84, chmn. nominating com. 1988-89, mem. legis. com. 1989-91, adv. bd. ALA Yearbook 1976-91, Assn. Specialized and Coop. Library Agys. legis. com., 1987-89, ad hoc com. White House Conf. on Libr. and Info. Svcs. 1989-91, chmn. awards com. 1990-92, Exceptional Achievement award 1981, J.B. Lippincott award 1989), Cath. Library Assn. (life, adv. coun. 1960—), Ill. Library Assn. (chmn. legis.-library devel. com. 1964-69, mem. exec. bd., libr's. citation 1974), Fla. Library Assn. (bd. dirs. 1987-93, pres. 1991-92, intellectual freedom com., chmn. com. on Fla. Librs. publ., editor, publ. com., planning com., 1991, site com.), Continuing Libr. Edn. Network and Exchange (pres. 1982-83), Internat. Fedn. Library Assns. and Institutions (statistics standing com. 1976-85, planning com.), Coun. Nat. Library Assns. (chmn. 1959-61), Assn. Coll. and Research Librarians (pres. Phila. chpt. 1953-55), Drexel Inst. Library Sch. Alumni Assn. (pres. 1955-56, exec. bd. 1956-60, chmn. chief officers State Library Agys. 1973-74), Chgo. Library Club (pres. 1969), Assn. Library and Info. Sci. Edn. (govt. relation com. 1985-87), Drexel U. Alumni Assn. (Outstanding Alumnus award 1963), Kappa Phi Kappa (chpt. pres. 1948), Beta Phi Mu (hon.). Lodge: K.C. Office: Fla State U Sch Libr and Info Studies Tallahassee FL 32306 *You can't do anything alone. You need support and you need opposition. Opposition provides you with challenge. Challenge brings out the best in you.*

TRIANDIS, HARRY CHARALAMBOS, psychology educator; b. Patras, Greece, Oct. 16, 1926; s. Christos Charalambos and Louise J. (Nikokavouras) T.; m. Pola Fotitch, Dec. 23, 1966; 1 child, Louisa. B.Engring., McGill U., 1951; M.Commerce, U. Toronto, Ont., Can., 1954; Ph.D., Cornell U., 1958; Doctorate (hon.), U. Athens, Greece, 1987. Asst. prof. U. Ill., Champaign, 1958-61; assoc. prof. U. Ill., 1961-66, prof. psychology, 1966-97; cons. USIA, 1970-75, NSF, 1968-75; prof. emeritius, 1997—. Author: Attitudes and Attitude Change, 1971, The Analysis of Subjective Culture, 1972, Varieties of Black and White Perception of the Social Environment, 1975, Interpersonal Behavior, 1977, Culture and Social Behavior, 1994, Individualism and Collectivism, 1995; editor: Handbook of Cross-Cultural Psychology, Vol. 1-6, 1980-81, Handbook of Industrial and Organizational Psychology, Vol. 4, 1994; editorial cons.; Jour. Personality and social Psychology, 1963-71, Jour. Applied Psychology, 1970-79, Sociometry, 1971-74, Jour. Cross-Cultural Psychology, 1974—, others. Chmn. fgn. grants com. Am. Psychol. Found., 1968—. Sr. fellow Ford Found., 1964-65; Guggenheim fellow, 1972-73; grantee USPHS, 1956-60, 62; grantee Office Naval Research, 1960-68, 80-85; grantee Social and Rehab. Service, HEW, 1968-73; grantee Ford Found., 1973-75; recipient award Interam. Soc. Psychology, 1981. Mem. Soc. for Psychol. Study of Social Issues (pres. 1975-76), Internat. Assn. Cross-Cultural Psychology (pres. 1974-76), Interam. Soc. Psychology (pres. 1985-87), Soc. for Exptl. Social Psychology (chmn. 1972-74), Soc. for Personality and Social Psychology (pres. 1976-77), Internat. Assn. Applied Psychology (pres. 1990-94). Home: 1 Lake Park Rd Champaign IL 61821-7101 Office: 603 E Daniel St Champaign IL 61820-6232

TRIANTAFYLLOU, MICHAEL STEFANOS, ocean engineering educator; b. Athens, Greece, Oct. 27, 1951; came to U.S., 1974; s. Stefanos M. and Penelopi I. (Koutras) T.; m. Joan L. Kimball, Sept. 22, 1985; children: Stefanos R., Kimon K. MS in Ocean Engring., MIT, 1977, MSME, 1977, ScD, 1979. Rsch. assoc. MIT, Cambridge, Mass., 1978-79, asst. prof., 1979-83, assoc. prof., 1983-86, tenured assoc. prof., 1986-90, prof., dir. ocean engring. testing tank, 1990—; vis. scientist Woods Hole (Mass.) Oceanographic Inst., 1990—. Featured cover Scientific American; contbr. articles to profl. jours. Rsch. grantee OFfice NAval Rsch., Office Naval Tech., NSF, Doherty Found. Dept. Commerce, 1979—. Mem. Internat. Soc. Offshore and Polar Engrs. (founding mem.), Soc. Naval Architects and Marine Engrs. (papers com., vice chmn. OC-2 com.), Am. Phys. Soc. Office: MIT 77 Massachusetts Ave Rm 5-323 Cambridge MA 02139-4301

TRIANTAPHYLLOU, EVANGELOS, industrial engineering educator; b. New Orestias, Greece, Nov. 17, 1959; came to U.S., 1983; s. John and Helen (Psaltopoulou) T.; m. Alexandra Moustakatou, June 4, 1988. BS in Archtl. Engring., Nat. Tech. U. Athens, 1983; MS in Ops. Rsch., MS in Environ., Pa. State U., 1985, MS in Computer Sci., 1988, PhD in Indsl. Engring. and in Ops. Rsch., 1990. Teaching asst. Pa. State U., University Park, 1983-87, systems analyst Dept. Entomology, 1986-87, computing rsch. cons. Ctr. Acad. Computing, 1987-90; asst. prof. Dept Industrial Engring. Kans. State U., Manhattan, 1990-93; assoc. prof. Dept. Industrial Engring. La. State U., Baton Rouge, 1993-97, assoc. prof., 1997—; Speaker, presenter, lectr. in field. Editl. bd. mem. Internat. Jour. Industrial Engring: Applications and Practice; contbr. articles to profl. jours. Grantee AT&T, USN, NASA, La. Mem. Am. Assn. Artificial Intelligence, Ops. Rsch. Soc. Am., Assn. Computing Machinery, Decision Scis. Inst., Inst. Industrial Engineers, N.Am. Fuzzy Info. Processing Soc. Achievements include advancements in use of artificial intelligence and operations research techniques in solving problems in engineering, business, and medicine. Office: La State U Dept Indsl Engring 3128 Cedar Ave Baton Rouge LA 70805-7877

TRIANTAPHYLLOU, H. H., plant pathologist; b. Fuerth, Bavaria, Germany, Jan. 16, 1927; came to U.S., 1954; d. Friedrich and Ferdinandine (Schonleben) Hirschmann; m. Anastasios Christos Triantaphyllou, July 9, 1960; 1 child, Christos F. PhD, U. Erlangen, Erlangen, Germany, 1951. From tech. asst. to prof. N.C. State Univ., Raleigh, N.C., 1954-92; ret. Contbr. articles to profl. jours., chpts. to books in field. Recipient rsch. award Soc. Sigma Xi, 1962, Ruth Allen award Am. Phytopathol. Soc., 1993, Soc. Nematologists fellowship, 1981. Mem. Helminthological Soc. Wash., Soc. European Nematologists, Soc. of Nematologists, Soc. Sigma Xi. Avocations: sailing, music, piano. Office: N C State U Dept Plant Pathology Box 7616 Raleigh NC 27695-7616

TRIBBLE, ALAN CHARLES, physicist; b. Little Rock, Aug. 11, 1961; s. George Alan and Barbara Jean (Stocks) T.; m. Elizabeth Ellen Gunion, July 30, 1988; children: Matthew Alan, Daniel Jay. BS, U. Ark., 1983; MS, U. Iowa, 1986, PhD, 1988. Physicist Rockwell Internat., Cedar Rapids, Iowa, 1988—; instr. U. So. Calif.; U.S. rep. to Internat. Standards Orgn.; prin. investigator space environments and effects program NASA. Author: The Space Environment: Implications for Spacecraft Design, Princeton Guide to Advanced Physics. Grad. Student Rschr. Program fellowship NASA, 1987. Mem. AIAA, Am. Geophys. Union, Am. Phys. Soc.

TRIBBLE, RICHARD WALTER, brokerage executive; b. San Diego, Oct. 19, 1948; s. Walter Perrin and Catherine Janet (Miller) T.; m. Joan Catherine Sliter, June 26, 1980. BS, U. Ala., Tuscaloosa, 1968; student, Gulf Coast Sch. Drilling Practices, U. Southwestern La., 1977. Stockbroker Shearson, Am. Express, Washington, 1971-76; ind. oil and gas investment sales, Falls Church, Va., 1976-77; pres. Monroe & Keusink, Inc., Falls Church and Columbus, Ohio, 1977-87; instnl. investment officer FCA Asset Mgmt., 1983-85; fin. cons. Merrill Lynch Pierce, Fenner & Smith, Inc., Phoenix, 1987—, cert. fin. mgr., 1989—, sr. fin. cons., 1992—, asst. v.p., 1993—. Served with USMC, 1969-70. Republican. Methodist. Office: 2525 E Camelback Rd Phoenix AZ 85016-4219

TRIBLE, PAUL SEWARD, JR., former United States senator; b. Balt., Dec. 29, 1946; s. Paul Seward and Katherine (Schilpp) T.; m. Rosemary Dunaway; children: Mary Katherine, Paul Seward III. B.A., Hampden-Sydney Coll., 1968; J.D., Washington and Lee U., Lexington, Va., 1971. Bar: Va. 1971. Law clk. to U.S. dist. judge Albert V. Bryan, Jr., 1971-72; asst. U.S. atty. Office U.S. Atty. Eastern Dist. Va., 1972-74; commonwealth's atty. Essex County, Va., 1974-76; U.S. Congressman 1st Va. Dist., Washington, 1976-82; U.S. Senator from Va., 1982-89; of counsel Shuttleworth, Ruloff & Giordano, 1989-95; pres. Jefferson Group, Washington, 1991-95, Christopher Newport U., Newport News, Va., 1996—. Mem.: Washington and Lee Law Rev. Republican. Episcopalian. Office: Christopher Newport Univ Office of President 50 Shoe Ln Newport News VA 23606-2949

TRIBUS, MYRON, quality counselor, engineer, educator; b. San Francisco, Oct. 30, 1921; s. Edward and Marie D. (Kramer) T.; m. Sue Davis, Aug. 30, 1945; children—Louanne, Kamala. B.S. in Chemistry, U. Calif. at Berkeley, 1942; Ph.D. in Engring, U. Calif. at Los Angeles, 1949; D.Sc. (hon.), Rockford (Ill.) Coll., 1965, Oakland (Mich.) U., 1971. Registered profl. engr., Mass. Instr. to prof. engring. U. Calif. at Los Angeles, 1946-61; dir. aircraft icing research U. Mich., 1951-54; dean engring. Thayer Sch. Engring., Dartmouth Coll., 1961-69; asst. sec. sci. and tech. Dept. Commerce, Washington, 1969-70; sr. v.p. tech. and engring. info. tech. group Xerox Corp., Rochester, N.Y., 1970-74; dir. Center for Advanced Engring. Study, Mass. Inst. Tech., Cambridge, 1974-86; cons. in quality mgmt., 1986—; dir. rsch., co-founder Exergy, Inc., Hayward, Calif., 1987—; cons. heat transfer Gen. Electric Co., 1950; cons. Fed. Office Saline Water; tech. adv. bd. Dept. Commerce; adviser to NATO, 1953; mem. Nat. Adv. Com. Oceans and Atmosphere, 1971-72; bd. dirs. Exergy, Inc., Hayward, Calif. Author: Thermostatics and Thermodynamics, 1961, Rational Descriptions, Decisions and Designs, 1969; Contbr. articles to profl. jours. Bd. govs. Technion, Haifa, Israel, 1973-84. Served to capt. USAAF, 1942-46. Recipient Thurman H. Bane award Inst. Aero. Scis., 1945, Wright Bros. medal Soc. Automotive Engrs., 1945; Alfred Noble prize Engring. Socs., 1952, Robert Fletcher awrd Thayer Sch. Engring., Dartmouth Coll., 1994; named UCLA Alumnus of Yr., 1972. Mem. ASME, IEEE, NSPE. Home: 350 Britto Ter Fremont CA 94539-3824 Office: Exergy Inc 22320 Foothill Blvd Hayward CA 94541-2710

TRICARICO, JOSEPH ARCHANGELO, lawyer; b. N.Y.C., May 6, 1940; s. Nicholas and Frances Tricarico; m. Mildred Grandi, Feb. 12, 1972; 1 child, Nicholas. BS, St. Johns U., 1963, JD, 1967. V.p. trust counsel U.S. Trust Co. N.Y., N.Y.C., 1973—. Author: Generation-Skipping Transfers: A Primer, 1984. Pro bono arbitrator small claims ct. Civil Ct. of City of N.Y., S.I., 1981—; trustee Eger Health Care Ctr., S.I., 1990—. Mem. ABA (com. bus. law 1990—, vice chair com. generation-skipping transfers 1993—, com. taxation 1984—), Am. Corp. Counsel Assn. (com. securities litigation 1991—, com. environ. law 1992—), N.Y. Bankers Assn. (spl. counsel trust legis. and regulatory com. 1991—), N.Y. Bar Assn., New York County Lawyers Assn. (com. on legis. 1989—), Am. Judges Assn. (hon. judge 1985—). Office: US Trust Co NY 114 W 47th St New York NY 10036-1510

TRICE, WILLIAM HENRY, paper company executive; b. Geneva, N.Y., Apr. 4, 1933; s. Clyde H. T.; m. Sandra Clayton, July 16, 1955; children—Russell, Amy. B.S. in Forestry, State U. N.Y., 1955; M.S., Inst. Paper Chemistry, Appleton, Wis., 1960, Ph.D., 1963. With Union Camp Corp., 1963—, tech. dir. bleached div., 1972-74; v.p., corp. tech. dir. research and devel. Union Camp Corp., Wayne, N.J., 1974-79; sr. v.p. tech. Union Camp Corp., 1979-85, exec. v.p., 1985-96; chmn. bd. dirs. Bush Boake Allen, Inc. Trustee, pres. Western Mich. U.-Paper Tech. Found., Syracuse Pulp and Paper Found. With USAF, 1955-57. Fellow TAAPI (bd. dirs. 1978-81), Inst. Paper Sci. and Tech. (trustee, exec. commn. alumni assn.).

TRICHEL, MARY LYDIA, middle school educator; b. Rosenberg, Tex., Feb. 2, 1957; d. Henry John and Henrietta (Jurek) Pavlicek; m. Keith Trichel, Aug. 8, 1981; children: Daniel, Nicholas. BS cum laude, Tex. A & M U., 1980. Cert. tchr., Tex. Social studies tchr. grades 6, 7 and 8 St. Francis de Sales, Houston, 1980-81; English tchr. grades 7 and 8 Dean Morgan Jr. High, Casper, Wyo., 1983-86; English and journalism tchr. grades 9 and 11 Tecumseh (Okla.) High Sch., 1987; English tchr. grade 6 Christa McAuliffe Middle Sch., Houston, 1988-92; tchr. Tex. history grade 7, journalism grade 8 Lake Olympia Middle Sch., Missouri City, Tex., 1991-92; tchr. social studies 6th grade Lake Olympia Mid. Sch. Ft. Bend Ind. Sch. Dist., 1993—. Recipient teaching awards. Mem. Nat. Coun. Tchrs. English, Nat. Coun. Tchrs. Social Studies, Am. Fedn. Tchrs. Avocations: desktop publishing, scuba diving, traveling. Home: 3707 Pin Oak Ct Missouri City TX 77459-7018

TRICHOPOULOS, DIMITRIOS VASSILIOS, epidemiologist, educator; b. Volos, Greece, Dec. 9, 1938; s. Vassilios Konstantinou and Alexandra Dimitrios (Kataropoulou) T.; m. Antonia Athanasiou Polychronopoulou, June 17, 1967. MD, Athens U., Greece, 1963, PhD, 1971; MS, Harvard Sch. Pub. Health, 1968; MD honoris causa, Uppsala (Sweden) U., 1994. Diplomate Am. Coll. Epidemiology. Lectr. preventive medicine U. Athens Med. Sch., 1965-67, prof., chair preventive medicine, 1972-89; lectr. epidemiology Harvard Sch. Pub. Health, Boston, 1969-70, prof., chair epidemiology, 1989-96; prof., dir. Harvard Ctr. Cancer Prevention, Boston, 1994—; chmn. health group Coun. European Union, Brussels, 1988. Editor: Teaching Epidemiology, 1992; contbr. numerous articles to profl. jours. Decorated officier Ordre Palmes Academiques (France). Mem. Royal Acad. Medicine Belgium (corr., fgn.), Nat. Acad. Medicine France (corr., fgn.), Harvard Club, Athens Club. Greek Orthodox. Office: Harvard Sch Pub Health 677 Huntington Ave Boston MA 02115-6028

TRICK, TIMOTHY NOEL, electrical and computer engineering educator, researcher; b. Dayton, Ohio, July 14, 1939; s. Edmund Louis and Roberta Elizabeth (Heckel) T.; m. Dorothe Lee Jacobs, Feb. 18, 1958; children: Patricia, Michael, Thomas, William, Gregory, Andrew. BSEE, U. Dayton, 1961; MSEE, Purdue U., 1962, PhD, 1966. Instr. Purdue U., West Lafayette, Ind., 1963-65; asst. prof. elec. and computer engring. U. Ill., Urbana, 1965-70, assoc. prof., 1970-75, prof., 1975—, dir. Coordinated Sci. Lab., 1984-86, head dept. elec. and computer engring., 1985-95. Author: Introduction to Circuit Analysis, 1978. Fellow IEEE (bd. dirs. 1986-89, v.p. publs. 1988-89, Guillemin-Cauer award 1976, Centennial medal 1984, Meritorious Svc. award 1987); mem. NSPE, Circuits and Sys. Soc. of IEEE (pres. 1979, Van Valkenburg award 1994), Am. Soc. Engring. Educators. Roman Catholic. Avocations: hiking, camping. Office: U Ill Dept Elec & Computer Engring 1406 W Green St Urbana IL 61801-2918

TRICOLES, GUS PETER, electromagnetics engineer, physicist, consultant; b. San Francisco, Oct. 18, 1931; s. Constantine Peter and Eugenia (Elias) T.; m. Beverly Mildred Ralsky, Dec. 20, 1953 (dec. Dec. 1974); children: Rosanne, Robin; m. Aileen Irma Aronson, Apr. 1, 1980 (div. June 1980). BA in Physics, UCLA, 1955; MS in Applied Math., San Diego State U., 1958; MS in Applied Physics, U. Calif., San Diego, 1962, PhD in Applied Physics, 1971. Engr. Convair div. Gen. Dynamics, San Diego, 1955-59, engr. Electronics div., 1962-75, engring. mgr. Electronics div., 1975-89, sr. engring. staff specialist, 1989-92; engr. Smyth Rsch. Assn., San Diego, 1959-61; rsch. asst. Scripps Instn. Oceanography, La Jolla, Calif., 1961-62; sr. engring. staff specialist G.D.E. Systems, Inc., San Diego, 1992—; cons. Ga. Inst. Tech., Atlanta, 1972, 79-80, Transco Industries, L.A., 1973, Aero Geo Industries, San Antonio, 1980-82, Vantage Assocs., San Diego, 1988; rsch. reviewer NRC, NAS, Boulder, Colo., 1986-88. Author: (with others) Radome Engineering Handbook, 1970, Antenna Handbook, 1988; contbr. articles to profl. jours.; holder 19 patents. With USN, 1952-53. Fellow IEEE (antenna standards com. 1980—, advancement com. 1988), Optical Soc. Am. (local sect. v.p. 1966); mem. N.Y. Acad. Scis., Am. Geophys. Union. Avocations: woodworking, photography. Home: 4633 Euclid Ave San Diego CA 92115-3226 Office: GDE Sys Inc PO Box 92150 San Diego CA 92150-9009

TRICOLI, JAMES VINCENT, cancer genetics educator; b. Buffalo, Aug. 29, 1953; s. Vincent Peter and Theresa Magdeline (Siuda) T.; m. Margaret Wimmer, Aug. 16, 1975; 1 child, Lucas. BA, Canisius Coll., 1975; MA, SUNY, Buffalo, 1979, PhD, 1982. Postdoctoral researcher Roswell Park Cancer Inst., Buffalo, 1982-86; instr. Harvard Med. Sch., Boston, 1986-87; asst. prof. U. Cin. Coll. of Medicine, 1987-94; assoc. mem. Fox Chase Cancer Ctr., Phila., 1994—. Contbr. articles to profl. jours. including Biochemistry, Nature, Exptl. Cell Rsch., Cancer Rsch., Genes Chromosomes and Cancer. Am. Cancer Soc. grantee, 1989, NIH Biomed. Rsch. grantee, 1989, Kidney Found. grantee, 1990, NIH/Nat. Cancer Inst. grantee, 1992. Mem. Am. Assn. Cancer Rsch., Soc. Basic Urol. Rsch., Planetary Soc., Sigma Xi. Achievements include research in purification of DNA Topoisomerase I, of mapping of the insulin-like growth factor I and II genes, of the characterization of IGF-I and -II genes in colon carcinoma, characterization of Y chromosomal gene expression in prostate carcinoma/tumor suppressor gene involvement in prostate cancer. Office: Fox Chase Cancer Ctr 7700 Burholme Ave Philadelphia PA 19111-2413

TRIECE, ANNE GALLAGHER, magazine publisher; b. Bklyn., July 1, 1955; d. Anthony J. and Mary Ann (Clines) Gallagher; m. David Mark Triece, Nov. 3, 1990. BBA cum laude, CUNY, 1978. Media planner Isidore Lefkowitz Elgort, N.Y.C., 1978-80; sr. media supr. Ted Bates Advt., N.Y.C., 1980-83; account mgr. Prevention mag., N.Y.C., 1983-85; N.Y. mgr. Home mag., N.Y.C., 1985-92; assoc. pub. Met. Home mag., N.Y.C., 1992—. Coord. Arts Program for Homeless, N.Y.C., 1994. Recipient advt. excellence award Knapp Comm., 1985. Mem. Advt. Women N.Y. (commendation 1985). Roman Catholic. Avocations: scuba diving, tennis, skiing.

TRIENENS, HOWARD JOSEPH, lawyer; b. Chgo., Sept. 13, 1923; s. Joseph Herman and Myrtle (Wilsberg) T.; m. Paula Miller, Aug. 27, 1946; children: John, Thomas, Nancy. BS, Northwestern U., 1945; JD, 1949. Bar: Ill. 1949, N.Y. 1980, U.S. Dist. Ct. (no. dist.) Ill. 1949, U.S. Dist. Ct. (so. and ea. dists.) N.Y. 1980, U.S. Ct. Appeals (2d, 3d, 7th, 9th, 10th, 11th and D.C. cirs.), U.S. Supreme Ct. 1954. Assoc. firm Sidley, Austin, Burgess & Harper, Chgo., 1949-50; law clk. to Chief Justice Vinson, 1950-52; assoc. Sidley, Austin, Burgess & Smith, Chgo., 1952-56; ptnr. Sidley & Austin, Chgo., 1956—; v.p., gen. counsel AT&T, 1980-86. Trustee Northwestern U., 1967—. With USAAF, 1943-46. Mem. ABA, Ill. Bar Assn., Chgo. Bar Assn., N.Y. State Bar Assn., Am. Coll. Trial Lawyers, Legal Club (Chgo.), Law Club (Chgo.), Chgo. Club, Casino Club (Chgo.), Mid-Day Club, Skokie Country Club, Shoreacres Club, Glen View Club (Golf, Ill.), Met. Club (Washington), Old Elm Country Club, Sigma Chi. Democrat. Home: 690 Longwood Ave Glencoe IL 60022-1761 Office: Sidley & Austin 1 First Natl Plz Chicago IL 60603-2003

TRIER, JERRY STEVEN, gastroenterologist, educator; b. Frankfurt, Germany, Apr. 12, 1933; came to U.S., 1938, naturalized, 1943; s. Kurt J. and Alice L. (Cahn) T.; m. Laurel M. Bryan, June 8, 1957; children: Stanley, Jeryl, Stephen. M.D., U. Wash., 1957; M.A. (hon.), Harvard U., 1973. Diplomate: Am. Bd. Internal Medicine. Intern U. Rochester, N.Y., 1957-58; resident in medicine U. Rochester, 1958-59; clin. asso. Nat. Cancer Inst., Bethesda, Md., 1959-61; trainee in gastroenterology U. Wash., Seattle, 1961-63; asst. prof. medicine U. Wis., Madison, 1963-67; asso. prof. U. N.Mex., Albuquerque, 1967-69, Boston U., 1969-73, Harvard U. Med. Sch., Cambridge, Mass., 1973-76; prof. Harvard U. Med. Sch., 1976—; sr. physician Brigham and Women's Hosp.; cons. Sidney Farber Cancer Ctr., Boston VA Hosp., W. Roxbury VA Hosp. Nat. Inst. Diabetes and Digestive and Kidney Disease; adv. coun. NIH, 1986-90. Editor: Internal Medicine; mem. editorial bd.; Anatomical Record, 1969—, Gastroenterology, assoc. editor, 1971-77, mem. editorial bd., 1967-71, 78-83, 93—, chmn., 1988-93, Am. Jour. Medicine, 1978-87, Current Opinion in Gastroenterology, 1990—; contbr. articles to chpts. on gastrointestinal histology, pathology, devel. and disease to med. jours. and books. Served as surgeon USPHS, 1959-61. USPHS/NIH grantee, 1963-94. Mem. Am. Soc. Clin. Investigation, Assn. Am. Physicians, Am. Gastroent. Assn. (pres. 1985-86), Am. Soc. Cell Biology, Am. Fedn. Clin. Research. Home: 119 Pine St Weston MA 02193-1178 Office: Brigham and Women's Hosp 75 Francis St Boston MA 02115-6110

TRIEWEILER, TERRY NICHOLAS, justice; b. Dubuque, Iowa, Mar. 21, 1948; s. George Nicholas and Anne Marie (Oastern) T.; m. Carol M. Jacobson, Aug. 11, 1972; children: Kathryn Anne, Christina Marie, Anna Theresa. BA, Drake U., 1970, JD, 1972. Bar: Iowa 1973, Wash. 1973, U.S. Dist. Ct. (so. dist.) Iowa 1973, U.S. Dist. Ct. (we. dist.) Wash. 1973, Mont. 1975, U.S. Dist. Ct. Mont. 1977. Staff atty. Polk County Legal Services, Des Moines, 1973; assoc. Hullin, Roberts, Mines, Fite & Riveland, Seattle, 1973-75, Morrison & Hedman, Whitefish, Mont., 1975-77; sole practice, Whitefish; justice Mont. Supreme Ct., Helena, 1991—; lectr. U. Mont. Law Sch., 1981—; mem. com. to amend civil proc. rules Mont. Supreme Ct., Helena, 1984, commn. to draft pattern jury instrns., 1985; mem. Gov.'s Adv. Com. on Amendment to Work Compensation Act, adv. com. Mont. Work Compensation Ct. Mem. ABA, Mont. Bar Assn. (pres. 1986-87), Wash. Bar Assn., Iowa Bar Assn., Assn. Trial Lawyers Am., Mont. Trial Lawyers Assn. (dir., pres.). Democrat. Roman Catholic. Home: 1615 Virginia Dale St Helena MT 59601-5823 Office: Mont Supreme Ct 414 Justice Bldg 215 N Sanders St Rm 323 Helena MT 59601-4522 also: 215 N Sanders St Helena MT 59601-4522*

TRIFFIN, NICHOLAS, law librarian, law educator; b. Boston, May 30, 1942; s. Robert and Lois (Brandt) T.; m. Mary M. Bertolet, June 1, 1965 (div. June 1975); children: Amyk (dec.), A. Robert; m. Madeleine J. Wilken, May 30, 1981. BA cum laude, Yale U., 1965, JD, 1968; MLS, Rutgers U., 1978. Bar: N.Y. 1969, Conn. 1973, U.S. Dist. Ct. Conn. 1973, U.S. Ct. Appeals (2nd cir.) 1973, U.S. Tax Ct. 1974. Assoc. Willkie Farr & Gallagher, N.Y.C., 1968-70; dean students Johnson (Vt.) State Coll., 1970-72; assoc. Di Sesa & Evans, New Haven, 1972-76; head pub. services, instr. law U. Conn., W. Hartford, 1977-81; law library dir., assoc. prof. Hamline U., St. Paul, 1982-84; dir. law library, prof. Pace U., White Plains, N.Y., 1984—; bd. dirs. Hale Found.; bd. advisors Oceana Pub., Inc., 1987-95; chief info. svcs. Inst. Internat. Comml. Law, 1993-94, dir., 1994—; adj. prof. Hartford Coll., 1978-80. Author: Law Books Published, 1984-95, Law Books in Print, 5th edit., 1987, 6th edit., 1991, 7th edit., 1995, Law Books in Review, 1984-92, Drafting History of the Federal Rules of Criminal Procedure, 1991;

columnist Law Libr. Jour., 1983-84. Justice of peace, Conn., 1976-78. Mem. Am. Assn. Law Librs. (chmn. reader svcs. spl. interest sect. 1982-83, chmn. legal history and rare books spl. interest sect. 1991-92, chmn. constn. and bylaws com. 1994-95), Westchester Acad. Libr. Dirs. Orgn., Inc. (v.p. 1990-91, pres. 1991-92, exec. bd. dirs. 1992-94), Law Libr. New Eng. (pres. 1981-82), Minn. Assn. Law Librs. (v.p. 1983-84), Westchester Libr. Assn. (exec. bd. 1990-91), Inclusion Body Myositis Assn., Mory's Club, Beta Phi Mu. Mem. Soc. of Friends. Avocations: kayaking, rare books, opera. Office: Pace U Law Sch 78 N Broadway White Plains NY 10603-3710 *Society delights in putting barriers between people. Our greatest task is to remove these barriers - to use every encounter with others as an opportunity to empathise and to expand the horizons of our understanding - and to see that fundamentally we are all one.*

TRIFOLI-CUNNIFF, LAURA CATHERINE, psychologist, consultant; b. L.I., N.Y., June 8, 1958; d. Peter Nicholas and Susan Maria (Graziano) T.; m. John Kevin Cunniff, June 6, 1992; 1 child, James Peter. BA, Hofstra U., Uniondale, N.Y., 1980, MA, 1982, PhD, 1986. Founder, prin. Quality Cons., West Islip, N.Y., 1980-87; sr. tng. officer Norstar Bank, Garden City, N.Y., 1985-87; asst. v.p. mgmt. devel. First Boston Corp., N.Y.C., 1986-90; mgr. exec. devel. Merrill Lynch, N.Y.C., 1990-91; pres. The Exec. Process, 1991—; cons. Am. Mgmt. Assn., N.Y.C., 1981-83, AT&T, Basking Ridge, N.H., 1982-83, The First Boston Corp., 1991—, Goldman Sachs, 1991—, Merrill Lynch & Co., 1991—, Union Bank of Switzerland, 1991—, Sanford C. Bernstein & Co., 1992—, Alexander & Alexander, 1993—, S.G. Warburg, 1994; instr. dept. psychology Hofstra U., 1983-85. Author: Vietnam Veterans: Post Traumatic Stress and its Effects, 1986; contbr. articles to profl. publs. Shift coord. Islip Hotline, 1976-78; eucharistic min. Hofstra U. Cath. Soc., 1980-85, Good Samaritan Hosp., West Islip, N.Y., 1988—. Scholar, Hofstra U., 1978-81, fellow, 1980, 81. Mem. Am. Psychol. Assn., Am. Soc. Tng. and Devel., Nat. Psychol. Honor Soc., Internat. Platform Soc. Roman Catholic. Avocations: equestrian sports, art, music. Office: 2906 Bree Hill Rd Oakton VA 22124-1212

TRIGERE, PAULINE, fashion designer; b. Paris, Nov. 4, 1912; came to U.S., 1937, naturalized, 1942; d. Alexandre and Cecile (Coriene) Trigere; children: Jean-Pierre, Philippe Radley. Student, Victor Hugo Coll., Paris. Began career at Martial et Armand, Paris, 1937; became asst. designer at Hattie Carnegie, N.Y.C.; started House of Trigere, N.Y.C., 1942. Recipient Coty Am. Fashion Critics award, 1994, Return award, 1951, Neiman-Marcus award, 1950, Cotton award Nat. Cotton Coun., 1959, award Filene's, 1959, Coty Hall of Fame award, 1959, Silver medal City of Paris, 1972, medal of Vermeil City of Paris, 1982, Lifetime Achievement award, 1992, Nat. Arts Club award, 1993, Coun. of Fashion Designers Lifetime Achievement award Lincoln Ctr., 1994; celebrated 50 yrs. in the bus. at Fashion Inst. Tech., 1992. Office: Trigere Inc 498 7th Ave New York NY 10018-6701

TRIGG, PAUL REGINALD, JR., lawyer; b. Lewistown, Mont., Mar. 25, 1913; s. Paul Reginald and Opal Stella (Fay) T.; m. Helen Ruth Leake, Dec. 25, 1938; children: Paul Reginald III, Mary Adra. BA, Grinnell Coll., 1935; JD, U. Mich., 1938. Bar: Mich. 1938. Practiced law in Detroit; ptnr. Dykema, Gossett (and predecessor), 1938—. Mem. ABA, Mich. Bar Assn., Detroit Bar Assn., Detroit Country Club, Yondotega Club. Clubs: Detroit, Detroit Country, Yondotega.

TRIGG, ROGER HUGH, philosophy educator; b. Pontypridd, Wales, Aug. 14, 1941; s. Ivor and Muriel Grace (Collins) T.; m. Julia Gibbs, July 12, 1972; children: Nicholas (dec.), Alison. MA, Oxford U., Eng., 1967, DPhil, 1968. From lectr. to sr. lectr. then reader U. Warwick, Coventry, Eng., 1966-87, prof. philosophy, 1987—, chmn. dept. philosophy, 1984-91, 94-95; dir. Ctr. for Rsch. in Philosophy and Lit., Coventry, 1985-91; vis. fellow St. Cross Coll., Oxford U., 1986-87, 91-92; vis. fellow Harris Manchester Coll., Oxford U., 1996; Stanton lectr. in Philosophy of Religion U. Cambridge, 1996-97. Author: Pain and Emotion, 1970, Reason and Commitment, 1973, Reality At Risk, 1980, The Shaping of Man, 1982, Understanding Social Science, 1985, Ideas of Human Nature, 1988, Rationality and Science, 1993. Justice of the Peace, Warwickshire, Eng., 1981-91. Mem. Brit. Soc. for Philosophy of Religion (pres. 1993-96), Royal Inst. Philosophy (of coun.), Mind Assn. (pres. 1997-98). Office: U Warwick, Dept Philosophy, Coventry West Midlands CV4 7AL, England

TRIGGER, BRUCE GRAHAM, anthropology educator; b. Cambridge (formerly Preston), Ont., Can., June 18, 1937; s. John Wesley and Gertrude Elizabeth (Graham) T.; m. Barbara Marian Welch, Dec. 7, 1968; children: Isabel Marian, Rosalyn Theodora. BA, U. Toronto, 1959; PhD, Yale U., 1964; DSc (hon.), U. N.B., 1987; LittD (hon.), U. Waterloo, 1990; LLD (hon.), U. Western Ont., 1995. Asst. prof. Northwestern U., 1963-64; asst. prof. McGill U., 1964-67, assoc. prof., 1967-69, prof. anthropology, 1969—, chmn. dept., 1970-75; bd. govs., 1996—; bd. govs. McGill-Queen's U. Press, 1988—; trustee McGill Inst. for the Study of Can., 1996—; V.G. Childe Meml. lectr. U. London, 1982; Harry Hawthorn Disting. lectr., 1988; Disting. lectr. in archaeology Am. Anthrop. Assn., 1990; Disting. vis. prof. Am. U. in Cairo, 1992, Newman lectr., 1995. Author: History and Settlement in Lower Nubia, 1965, Beyond History, 1968, The Huron: Farmers of the North, 1969, 2d edit., 1990, Cartier's Hochelaga, 1972, Nubia Under the Pharaohs, 1976, The Children of Aataentsic, 1976, Time and Traditions, 1978, Gordon Childe: Revolutions in Archaeology, 1980, Natives and Newcomers, 1985, A History of Archaeological Thought, 1989, Early Civilizations, 1993; vol. editor: Handbook of North American Indians, Vol. 15, 1978; editor Native and Northern Series; co-editor: Cambridge History of the Native Peoples of the Americas, North America Volume. Recipient Can. Silver Jubilee medal, 1977, Cornplanter medal, 1979, John Porter prize, 1987, Prix Victor-Barbeau Acad. Canadienne-française, 1991, Prix Leon-Gérin (prov. du Québec), 1991, James R. Wiseman Book award Archaeol. Inst. Am., 1991; Woodrow Wilson fellow, 1959-60, Woodrow Wilson dissertation fellow, 1962-63, Can. Coun. Leave fellow, 1968-69, 76-77, Killam rsch. fellow Can. Coun., 1970-71, 90, 91, leave fellow Social Scis. and Humanities Rsch. Coun. of Can., 1983. Fellow Royal Soc. Can. (Innis-Gerin medal 1985), Soc. Antiquaries of Scotland (hon.); mem. Prehistoric Soc. U.K. (hon.), Huron Great Turtle Clan (adopted), Sigma Xi. Home: Apt 603, 3495 Mountain St, Montreal, PQ Canada H3G 2A5 Office: McGill U Dept Anthropology, 855 Sherbrooke St W, Montreal, PQ Canada H3A 2T7

TRIGGER, KENNETH JAMES, manufacturing engineering educator; b. Carsonville, Mich., Sept. 6, 1910; married, 1939; 3 children. BS, Mich. State U., 1933, MS, 1935, ME, 1943. Asst. Mich. State Coll., 1933-34, instr. mech. engring., 1935-36; instr. mech. engring. Swarthmore (Pa.) Coll., 1937-38, Lehigh (Pa.) U., 1938-39; assoc. U. Ill., Urbana, 1939-45, from asst. prof. to prof., 1945-70, prof. mech. and indsl. engring.; cons. nuclear divsn. Union Carbide Corp., Continental Can Co., Aeroprojects Inc., Atlantic Richfield Co., numerous others. Fellow Soc. Mfg. Engrs. (medal 1959), Am. Soc. Mech. Engrs. (life), (Blackall award 1957, William T. Ennor Mfg. Tech. award 1992), Am. Soc. Metals (life); mem. Am. Soc. Engring. Edn. Achievements include research in metal cutting and machinability, physical metallurgy, cutting termperatures and temperature distribution in cutting of metals and mechanism of tool wear. Office: U Illinois Dept Mech Engr Indust Engr 140 1206 W Green St Urbana IL 61801-2906

TRIGGLE, DAVID JOHN, university dean, consultant; b. U.K., Apr. 5, 1935; came to U.S., 1962; s. William John and Maud F. (Henderson) T.; m. Ann. M. Jones, Sept. 22, 1959; children: Andrew B., Jocelyn A. BSc in Chemistry, U. Southampton, United Kingdom, 1956; PhD, U. Hull, United Kingdom, 1959. Research fellow U. Ottawa, Ont., Can., 1959-61, U. London, 1961-62; asst. prof. SUNY Sch. of Pharmacy, Buffalo, 1962-65, assoc. prof., 1965-69, prof., 1985-95, chmn. dept., 1971-85, dean, 1985-95, Disting. prof., 1987—, vice-provost for grad. edn., 1995—. Author: Chemical Aspects of Autonomic Nervous System, 1965, Neurotransmitter-Receptor Interactions, 1971, Chemical Pharmacology of the Synapse, 1976. Recipient Volwiler Rsch. Achievement award Am. Assn. Colls. Pharmacy, 1988, 89, George Koepf award Biomed. Rsch. Med. Found. Buffalo, 1994. Fellow AAAS; mem. Am. Chem. Soc., Am. Soc. Pharmacology and Therapeutics (Otto Krayer award 1995), Soc. Neurosci., Brit. Pharmacology Soc. Office: SUNY Grad Sch 410 Capen Buffalo NY 14260

TRIGIANO, LUCIEN LEWIS, physician; b. Easton, Pa., Feb. 9, 1926; s. Nicholas and Angeline (Lewis) T.; children: Lynn Anita, Glenn Larry, Robert Nicholas. Student Tex. Christian U., 1944-45, Ohio U., 1943-44, 46-47, Milligan Coll., 1944, Northwestern U., 1945, Temple U., 1948-52. Intern, Meml. Hosp., Johnstown, Pa., 1952-53; resident Lee Hosp., Johnstown, 1953-54; gen. practice, Johnstown, 1953-59; med. dir. Pa. Rehab. Center, Johnstown, 1959-62, chief phys. medicine and rehab., 1964-70; fellow phys. medicine and rehab. N.Y. Inst. Phys. Medicine and Rehab., 1962-64; dir. rehab. medicine Lee Hosp., 1964-71, Ralph K. Davies Med. Center, San Francisco, 1973-75, St. Joseph's Hosp., San Francisco, 1975-78, St. Francis Meml. Hosp., San Francisco, 1978-83; asst. prof. phys. medicine and rehab. Temple U. Sch. Medicine; founder Disability Alert. Served with USNR, 1944-46. Diplomate Am. Bd. Phys. Medicine and Rehab. Mem. AMA, A.C.P., Pa., San Francisco County Med. socs., Am. Acad. Phys. Medicine and Rehab., Am. Congress Phys. Medicine, Calif. Acad. Phys. Medicine, Nat. Rehab. Assn., Babcock Surg. Soc. Author various med. articles. Home: 1421 Casa del Rey Ct Las Vegas NV 89117 Office: 1150 Bush St Ste 4B San Francisco CA 94109-5920

TRILLIN, CALVIN MARSHALL, writer, columnist; b. Kansas City, Mo., Dec. 5, 1935; s. Abe and Edyth T.; m. Alice Stewart, Aug. 13, 1965; children: Abigail, Sarah Stewart. BA, Yale U., 1957; DLitt (hon.), Beloit Coll., 1987; LHD (hon.), Albertus Magnus Coll., 1990; DLitt (hon.), SUNY, 1996. Reporter, writer Time mag., 1960-63; staff writer New Yorker mag., 1963—; columnist Nation mag., 1978-85; syndicated columnist, 1986-95; columnist Time mag., 1996—; trustee N.Y. Pub. Libr. Author: An Education in Georgia, 1964, Barnett Frummer is an Unbloomed Flower, 1969, U.S. Journal, 1971, American Fried, 1974, Runestruck, 1977, Alice, Let's Eat, 1978, Floater, 1980, Uncivil Liberties, 1982, Third Helpings, 1983, Killings, 1984, With All Disrespect, 1985, If You Can't Say Something Nice, 1987, Travels With Alice, 1989, Enough's Enough, 1990, American Stories, 1991, Remembering Denny, 1993, Deadline Poet, 1994, Too Soon to Tell, 1995, Messages From My Father, 1996; author, performer one-man show Calvin Trillin's Uncle Sam, Am. Place Theatre, N.Y.C., 1988, Calvin Trillin's Words, No Music, Am. Place Theatre, 1990. Office: care New Yorker 20 W 43rd St New York NY 10036-7400

TRILLING, GEORGE HENRY, physicist, educator; b. Bialystok, Poland, Sept. 18, 1930; came to U.S., 1941; s. Max and Eugenie (Walfisz) T.; m. Madeleine Alice Monic, June 26, 1955; children: Stephen, Yvonne, David. BS, Calif. Inst. Tech., Pasadena, 1951, PhD, 1955. Research fellow Calif. Inst. Tech., Pasadena, 1955-56; Fulbright post-doctoral fellow Ecole Polytechnique, Paris, 1956-57; asst. to assoc. prof. U. Mich., Ann Arbor, 1957-60; assoc. to prof. dept. physics U. Calif., Berkeley, 1960-94, prof. emeritus, 1994—. Fellow Am. Phys. Soc., Am. Acad. Arts and Scis.; mem. NAS. Research in high energy physics. Office: Lawrence Berkeley Lab Berkeley CA 94720

TRILLING, HELEN REGINA, lawyer; b. Boston, May 13, 1950; d. Charles Alexander and A. Lillian Trilling. AB magna cum laude, Radcliffe Coll., 1973; JD, Harvard U., 1976. Bar: Mass. 1977, U.S. Dist. Ct. Mass. 1978, U.S. Supreme Ct. 1980, D.C. 1984, U.S. Ct. Appeals (10th cir.) 1984. Asst. gen. counsel Blue Cross/Blue Shield, Boston, 1976-79; sp. asst. to gen. counsel HHS, Washington, 1979-83; assoc. Hogan & Hartson, Washington, 1983-86, ptnr., 1987—. Mem. ABA (health law forum com.), Nat. Health Lawyers Assn., Women and Health Roundtable, Women's Legal Def. Fund, Wash. Council Lawyers.

TRILLING, LEON, aeronautical engineering educator; b. Bialystok, Poland, July 15, 1924; came to U.S., 1940, naturalized, 1946; s. Oswald and Regina (Zakhejm) T.; m. Edna Yuval, Feb. 17, 1946; children: Alex R., Roger S. B.S., Calif. Inst. Tech., 1944, M.S., 1946, Ph.D., 1948. Research fellow Calif. Inst. Tech., 1948- 50; Fulbright scholar U. Paris, 1950-51, vis. prof., 1963-64; mem. faculty MIT, Cambridge, 1951—, prof. aeros. and astronautics, 1962-94, prof. emeritus, 1994—, mem. coun. on primary and secondary edn., 1992—; mem. Program in Sci. Tech. and Society, Engring. Edn. Mission to Soviet Union, 1958; vis. prof. Delft Tech. U., 1974-75; vis. prof. engring. Carleton Coll., 1987;. Pres. Met. Com. Ednl. Opportunity, 1967-70, Council for Understanding of Tech. in Human Affairs, 1984—. Guggenheim fellow, 1963-64. Fellow AAAS. Home: 180 Beacon St Boston MA 02116-1401 Office: MIT 77 Massachusetts Ave Cambridge MA 02139-4301

TRIM, DONALD ROY, consulting engineer; b. Saginaw, Mich., June 23, 1937; s. Roy E. and Agnes (Kontranowski) T.; m. Dorothy Mae Franek, Aug. 11, 1962; children—Jeffrey D., Gregory S., Christopher M. B.S. in Civil Engring., U. Mich., 1959. Registered profl. engr., Mich., Ohio, Fla.; registered land surveyor, Mich. Engr., Francis Engring., Saginaw, 1959-64, Edwin M. Orr, Inc., Dearborn, Mich., 1964-66; pres. Wade-Trim Group, Plymouth, Mich., 1966-96, CEO, 1996—; pres. Wade-Trim Inc., Tampa, Fla., 1984—. Vice pres. Plymouth Canton Basketball Assn., 1980-84; bd. govs. Greater Mich. Found., Lansing, 1983-85. Mem. Nat. Soc. Profl. Engrs., Cons. Engrs. Council Mich. (dir. 1972-73, pres. 1983-84), Am. Cons. Engrs. Council (v.p. 1986-88, pres. elect 1997—), Am. Waterworks Assn. Roman Catholic. Office: Wade-Trim Group 400 Monroe St Ste 310 Detroit MI 48226-2920

TRIMBLE, EDDIE DON, television executive; b. Kansas City, Mo., Apr. 7, 1948; s. Henry Edward and Gladys (Rogers) T.; m. Coleen Ann, May 25, 1984; children: Blake, Kristina. BSBA, U. Mo., 1970. Acct. exec. WOW-TV, Omaha, 1973-78, KWGN-TV, Denver, 1978-79; gen. sales mgr. WPGH-TV, Pitts., 1979-83; v.p. sales BMA Broadcasting, Sacramento, 1983-84; v.p. gen. mgr. KDVR-TV, Denver, 1984-85, KHTV, Houston, 1985—; cons. in field. Mem. Houston Crackdown on Drugs, 1986—, Houston Econ. Devel., 1985—; bd. dirs. United Way, Houston, 1985. With Nat. Guard, 1970-76. Mem. Nat. Assn. Broadcasters, INTV, Tex. Assn. Broadcasters, NATPE, Masons, Houston Rotary. Republican. Office: Sta KHTV 7700 Westpark Dr Houston TX 77063-6414

TRIMBLE, GEORGE SIMPSON, industrial executive; b. Phila., Oct. 12, 1915; s. George Simpson and Edna Mae (Mytinger) T.; m. Janet Anna Bogue, Apr. 15, 1939 (dec. June 1995); children: Robert Bogue, Frank George; m. Betty J. Noonan, Jan. 3, 1997. S.B., Mass. Inst. Tech., 1936. With The Martin Co., Balt., 1937-67; successively draftsman, design engr., chief fluid dynamics, mgr. aerodynamics, mgr. advanced design, v.p. advanced design The Martin Co., 1937-55, v.p. engring., 1955-60, v.p. advanced programs, 1960-67; dir. Advanced Manned Missions Program, NASA, Washington, 1967; dep. dir. Johnson Spacecraft Center, Houston, 1967-69; pres., dir. Bunker Ramo Corp., Oak Brook, Ill., 1970-80; dir. Richardson Co., Des Plaines, Ill., 1978-82, Martin Marietta Corp., 1970-78; owner, pres. Carefree Engine Co. (Ariz.), 1981—; cons. Sci. Adv. Bd. Aero Vehicle Panel, 1959-61, Office Dir. Def., Research and Engring. Trustee Devereux Found., 1968—; chmn. bd. trustees, 1976-79. Fellow AIAA; mem. Tau Beta Pi. Home: PO Box 1355 Carefree AZ 85377-1355 Office: Carefree Engine Co Carefree AZ 83577

TRIMBLE, JAMES T., JR., federal judge; b. Bunkie, La., Sept. 13, 1932; s. James T. Sr. and Mabel (McNabb) T.; m. Murel Elise Biles, Aug. 18, 1956; children: Lise Ann Reed, Mary Olive Beacham, Martha McNabb Elliott, Sarah Palmer Trimble. Attended, U. Southwestern La. (formerly Southwestern La. Inst.), 1950-52; BA in Law, La. State U., 1955, JD, 1956. Bar: La. 1956. With Gist, Murchison & Gist (now Gist, Methvin, Hughes & Munsterman), 1959-78, Trimble, Percy, Smith, Wilson, Foote, Walker & Honeycutt, 1979-86; U.S. magistrate U.S. Dist. Ct. (we. dist.) La., 1986-91, judge, 1991—. Lt. USAF, 1956-59. Mem. Fed. Judges Assn., Southwest La. Bar Assn., La. Bar Assn., La. Bar Found. Avocations: jogging, gardening, tennis. Office: 611 Broad St Ste 237 Lake Charles LA 70601-4380*

TRIMBLE, PHILLIP RICHARD, law educator; b. Springfield, Ohio, Nov. 12, 1937; s. Melvin R. and Dorothy (Lang) T.; m. Stephanie Gardner, July 20, 1963 (div. 1977); children: John, William. BA, Ohio U., 1958; MA, Tufts U., 1959; JD, Harvard U., 1963. Bar: NY 1964. Legal writing instr. U. Calif., Berkeley, 1963-64; assoc. Cravath, Swaine & Moore, N.Y.C., 1964-70; staff mem. senate fgn. rels. com. Dept. State, Washington, 1971-72, asst. legal adviser, 1973-78; counsel to the mayor N.Y.C., 1978; dep. mayor N.Y.C., 1979; U.S. ambassador Nepal, 1980-81; prof. law UCLA, 1981—; mem. exec. com. Asia Soc. So. Calif. Ctr., L.A., 1981-94; vis. prof. law Stanford U., 1988-89, U. Mich., 1995-96; U.S. panelist under U.S.-Can. Free Trade Agreement; cons. ACDA, 1989-92. Mem. bd. editors Am. Jour. Internat. Law. Fellow Explorers Club; mem. Am. Soc. Internat. Law, Am. Alpine Club (bd. dirs. 1978-87). Democrat. Avocation: mountaineering. Office: UCLA Law Sch 405 Hilgard Ave Los Angeles CA 90095-9000

TRIMBLE, PRESTON ALBERT, retired judge; b. Salina, Okla., Aug. 27, 1930; s. James Albert and Winnie Louella (Walker) T.; m. Patricia Ann Beadle; children: Todd, Beth, Amy. B.A., U. Okla., 1956, LL.B., 1960. Bar: Okla. 1960. Practice law, 1960; asst. county atty. Cleveland County, Okla., 1960-62; county atty., 1962-67, dist. atty., 1967-79, dist. judge, 1979-91; spl. instr. S.W. Center Law Enforcement Edn.; cons. prosecution mgmt. Mem. Jud. Council Okla.; chmn. Okla. Corrections Workshop; mem. planning com. Nat. Inst. Crime and Delinquency; mem. com. on multi-agy. problems in criminal justice Appellate Judges Conf. Bd. dirs. Okla. U. Crisis Ctr., 1970—, ARC, Lake Murray Conservation Assn.; trustee Nat. Assn. Pretrial Svc. Agys. Resource Ctr., Sarkeys Found., 1994—. With USNR, 1948-52; col. USAFR. Mem. Okla., Cleveland County bar assns., Nat. Dist. Attys. Assn. (past pres.), Okla. Dist. Attys. Assn. (past pres.), Nat. Coll. Dist. Attys. (bd. regents), Am. Legion. Democrat. Methodist. Club: Lion. Home: 1886 Trailview Dr Norman OK 73072-6655 Office: 231 S Peters Ave Norman OK 73069-6035 *An elected public official must remember that the people own his position and he only holds it in trust for them.*

TRIMBLE, STANLEY WAYNE, hydrology and geography educator; b. Columbia, Tenn., Dec. 8, 1940; s. Stanley Drake and Clara Faye (Smith) T.; m. Alice Erle Gunn, Aug. 16, 1964; children: Alicia Anne, Jennifer Lusanne. BS, U. North Ala., 1964; MA, U. Ga., 1970, PhD, 1973. Asst. prof. hydrology and geography U. Wis., Milw., 1972-75; from assoc. prof. to prof. UCLA, 1975—; vis. asst. prof. U. Chgo., 1978, vis. assoc. prof., 1981, vis. prof. environ. geography, 1990—; vis. lectr. U. London, 1985; hydrologist U.S. Geol. Survey, 1974-84; vis. prof. U. Vienna, 1994; Frost lectr. Brit. Geomorphological Rsch. Group, Durham, Eng., 1994; vis. rsch. lectr. Oxford U., 1995; Fulbright scholar in U.K., 1995; vis. fellow Keble Coll., Oxford U., 1995. Author: Culturally Accelerated Sedimentation on the Middle Georgia Piedmont, 1971, Man-Induced Erosion on the Southern Piedmont, 1700-1970, 1974, Soil Conservation and the Reduction, 1982, Sediment Characteristics of Tennessee Streams, 1984; joint editor: Catena, 1995—; contbr. articles to profl. jours. Served to 1st lt. U.S. Army, 1963-65. Grantee U.S. Geol. Survey, Washington, 1974-79, Wis. Dept. Natural Resources, Madison, 1978, 82, 93, 94, 95, NSF, Washington, 1976, Agrl. Rsch. Svc. of USDA, Washington, 1972, Nat. Geographic Soc., 1993. Mem. NAS (com. on watershed mgmt. 1996—), Assn. Am. Geographers, Am. Geophys. Union, Soil Conservation Soc. Am., Brit. Geomorphol. Rsch. Group, Sigma Xi. Republican. Avocations: historic houses, documentation and restoration. Office: UCLA Dept Geography 405 Hilgard Ave Los Angeles CA 90095-9000

TRIMBLE, THOMAS JAMES, retired utility company executive, lawyer; b. Carters Creek, Tenn., Sept. 3, 1931; s. John Elijah and Mittie (Rountree) T.; m. Glenna Kay Jones, Sept. 3, 1957; children: James Jefferson, Julie Kay. BA, David Lipscomb U., 1953; JD, Vanderbilt U., 1956; LLM, NYU, 1959. Bar: Tenn. 1956, Ariz. 1961, U.S. Dist. Ct. Ariz. 1961, U.S. Dist. Ct. D.C. 1963, U.S. Ct. Appeals (10th cir.) 1971, U.S. Supreme Ct. 1972, U.S. Ct. Appeals (9th cir.) 1975. From assoc. to ptnr. Jennings, Strouss & Salmon, Phoenix, 1960-85, mng. ptnr., 1985-87; sr. v.p., gen. counsel, corp. sec. S.W. Gas Corp., Las Vegas, Nev., 1987-96, gen. counsel, 1987-92; corp. sec. Primerit Bank, 1990-92, pres., 1994-96; exec. v.p. Energy Ins. (Bermuda) Ltd., 1992-94, bd. dirs., 1992-97; bd. dirs. Energy Ins. Mut. Ltd., 1988-97, vice chmn., 1992-94, chmn., 1994-96. Mem. editorial bd. Vanderbilt U. Law Rev., 1954-56. Mem. Pepperdine U. Bd. Regents, Malibu, Calif., 1981—, sec., 1982—, mem. exec. com., 1982-89; bd. visitors Pepperdine Sch. Law, Malibu; pres. Big Sisters Ariz., Phoenix, 1975, bd. dirs., 1970-76; chmn. Sunnydale Children's Home, Phoenix, 1966-69, bd. dirs., 1965-75; pres. Clearwater Hills Improvement Assn., Phoenix, 1977-79, bd. dirs., 1975-80; trustee Nev. Sch. of Arts, 1988-92, chmn., 1989-90. 1st lt. JAGC, USAF, 1957-60. Fellow Ariz. Bar Assn. (editorial bd. Jour. 1975-80), Am. Gas Assn. (legal sect. mng. com. 1987-96), Order of Coif, Spanish Trail Country Club (Las Vegas), Southshore Golf Club (Las Vegas), Kiwanis (pres. Phoenix 1972-73), Phi Delta Phi. Republican. Mem. Ch. Christ. Home: 5104 Turnberry Ln Las Vegas NV 89113-1394

TRIMBLE, VANCE HENRY, retired newspaper editor; b. Harrison, Ark., July 6, 1913; s. Guy L. and Josephine (Crump) T.; m. Elzene Miller, Jan. 9, 1932; 1 dau., Carol Ann. Student pub. schs., Wewoka, Okla. Cub reporter Okemah (Okla.) Daily Leader, 1928; worked various newspapers in Okmulgee, Muskogee, Tulsa and, Okla.; successively reporter, rewrite man, city editor Houston Press, 1939-50, mng. editor, 1950-55; news editor Scripps-Howard Newspaper Alliance, Washington, 1955-63; editor Ky. Post and Times-Star, Covington, 1963-79. Author: The Uncertain Miracle, 1974, Sam M. Walton, 1990, (biography) E.W. Scripps, 1992, Frederick Smith of Federal Express, 1993, An Empire Undone: Rise and Fall of Chris Whittle, 1995; co-author: Happy Chandler Autobiography, 1989; editor: Scripps-Howard Handbook, 1981. Trustee Scripps-Howard Found., 1974-79. Recipient Pulitzer prize for nat. reporting, 1960, Raymond Clapper award, 1960, Sigma Delta Chi award for disting. Washington correspondence, 1960, Frank Luther Mott award for journalism book rsch. U. Mo., 1993; named to Okla. Journalism Hall of Fame, 1974. Mem. Am. Soc. Newspaper Editors. Baptist. Clubs: Nat. Press (Washington); Press (Houston); Cincinnati, Ft. Mitchell Country. Home: 1013 Sunset Rd Covington KY 41011-1168

TRIMBLE, WILLIAM CATTELL, JR., lawyer; b. Buenos Aires, Argentina, Feb. 7, 1935; s. William Cattell and Nancy Gordon (Carroll), T.; m. Barbara Janney, June 19, 1960; children: William C., Margery M. Kennelly. A.B., Princeton U., 1958; LL.B., U. Md., 1964. Bar: Md. 1965. With firm Ober, Grimes & Shriver, Balt., 1965-87, ptnr., 1970-87, mng. ptnr., 1973-77; counsel Semmes, Bowen & Semmes, Balt., 1987—; mem. Gov.'s Commn. to Revise Annotated Code of Md., 1975-83. Pres. bd. trustees Valley Sch., 1968-73; trustee Garrison Forest Sch., 1975-95, Gilman Sch. 1980-84; hon. consul of The Netherlands, 1986—. Lt. USNR, 1958-61. Mem. Am., Md., Balt. bar assns. Episcopalian. Clubs: Colonial (Princeton); Md, Greenspring Valley Hunt, Soc. of Cin. Office: Semmes Bowen Semmes PC 16th Fl 250 W Pratt St Fl 16 Baltimore MD 21201-2423

TRIMMER, HAROLD SHARP, JR., lawyer, international telecommunications consultant; b. Somerville, N.J., July 27, 1938; s. Harold Sharp and Mary Elizabeth (Knox) T. B.A., Wesleyan U., 1960; J.D., Harvard U., 1963. Instr. law UCLA, 1963-64; Congl. fellow Am. Polit. Sci. Assn., Washington, 1964-65; assoc. Royall, Koegel & Rogers, Washington and N.Y.C., 1965-66, McCutchen, Doyle, Brown & Enersen, San Francisco, 1966-69; with GSA, Washington, 1969-75; exec. asst. to adminstr. GSA, 1969-70, asst. adminstr., 1970-72, commr. automated data and telecommunications, 1972-73, assoc. adminstr. fed. mgmt. policy, 1973, gen. counsel, 1974-75; sec., gen. counsel Garfinckel, Brooks Bros., Miller & Rhoads, Inc., Washington, 1976-82, v.p., 1979-82; v.p. internat. MCI Communications Corp., Washington, 1982-83, v.p. regulatory policy, 1983-84, v.p. fin. and adminstrn. M.A. div., 1984-86, v.p. govt. systems, 1986-87; pres. Pacific div. MCI Communications Corp., San Francisco, 1987-89, sr. v.p. internat. devel., 1990-91; cons. internat. telecom., 1991—. Trustee World Affairs Council No. Calif., 1969-70, Wesleyan U., 1971-74; dir. Am. Friends Edinburgh Internat. Festival, 1996—. George F. Baker scholar. Mem. State Bar Calif., Phi Beta Kappa. Home: 169 Filbert Ave Sausalito CA 94965-1846

TRIMMIER, ROSCOE, JR., lawyer; b. Charlotte, N.C., July 22, 1944; s. Roscoe and Susie Elizabeth (Stitt) T.; divorced; 1 child, Leigh Snowden. AB, Harvard U., 1971, JD, 1974. Bar: Mass. 1974, U.S. Dist. Ct. Mass. 1975, U.S. Ct. Appeals (1st cir.) 1975, U.S. Supreme Ct. 1979, U.S. Claims Ct. 1983. Assoc. Ropes & Gray, Boston, 1974-83, ptnr., 1983—; mem. hearing com. Bd. Bar Overseers, 1983-89; bd. dirs., v.p. Family Counseling & Guidance Ctr., Inc., Boston, 1980-93; overseer Mus. of Sci., 1981-93; mem. exec. com. Jud. Nominating Commn., 1991-96; corp. mem. Mass. Gen. Hosp., 1992—; overseer N.E Med. Ctr. Hosps., 1992—. Served to 1st lt. U.S. Army, 1965-68. Fellow Am. Bar Found. (life), Mass. Bar Found. (life), Am. Coll. Trial Lawyers; mem. ABA (standing com. on fed. judiciary),

Mass. Bar Assn., Boston Bar Assn., Am. Law Inst., Mass. Soc. for Prevention of Cruelty to Children, Mass. Black Lawyers Assn. (life). Home: 1265 Beacon St Brookline MA 02146-5243 Office: Ropes & Gray 1 International Pl Boston MA 02110-2602

TRIMPIN, artist. M in Music and Art, U. Berlin. co-chair electronic music dept. Sweelinck Conservatory, Amsterdam, 1985-87; composer Composer Conf., Telluride, Colo., Bklyn. Acad. Music, 1989, Mus. Technorama, Switzerland, Walter Reade Theatre Gallery, N.Y., 1994, Sound Culture, San Francisco, 1996. Co-creator Rain Wall at Seattle Ctr.; inventor numerous instruments which utilize the latest technology and the natural elements to produce acoustical sounds. Guggenheim Found. fellow, 1997, MacArthur fellow, 1997. Address: 1131 36th Ave Seattle WA 98122*

TRINGALI, JOSEPH, financial planner, accountant; b. Balt., May 8, 1960; s. Dominic J. Sr. and MaryJane (DiPaolo) T.; m. Tina L. Shifflett, Oct. 24, 1987; children: Alex R., Eric M., Crystal N. BS in Acctg., U. Balt., 1982. CFP; CPA, Md.; lic. Nat. Assn. Securities Dealers. Asst. legis. auditor Md. State Div. of Audits Dept. of Fiscal Svcs., Balt., 1983-84; sr. acct. Jay Leikin, CPA, Columbia, Md., 1984-88; ptnr. Friedman & Assocs., PA, Balt., 1988—. Scholarship Comml. Credit Corp., 1981. Mem. AICPA, Md. Assn. of CPAs (chmn. CFP Pub. Awareness com. 1990-92), Internat. Bd. of Standards and Practices for CFP, Inc., Delta Mu Delta. Republican. Roman Catholic. Avocations: scuba diver, skiing, dancing, computers, reading. Office: Friedman & Assocs PA 1700 Reisterstown Rd Ste 222 Baltimore MD 21208-2934

TRINIDAD, FELIX, professional boxer; b. Cupey Alto, P.R., Jan. 10, 1973. IBF Welterweight champion, 1993. Office: Internat Boxing Fedn 134 Evergreen Pl Ste 9 East Orange NJ 07018-2012

TRINKAUS, JOHN PHILIP, cell and developmental biologist; b. Rockville Centre, N.Y., May 23, 1918; s. Charles Edward and Fransiska Magdalena (Krueger) T.; m. Madeleine Francine Marguerite Bazin, Oct. 6, 1963; children: Gregor, Tanya, Erik. B.A. with honors and high distinction in Biology, Wesleyan U., Middletown, Conn., 1940; M.A. (Cramer fellow in genetics), Columbia U., 1941; Ph.D., Johns Hopkins U., 1948. Mem. faculty Yale U., New Haven, 1948—; prof. cell. and devel. biology Yale U., 1964—, dir. grad. studies in biology, 1965, master of Branford Coll., 1966-73, also dir. undergrad. studies in biology, prof. emeritus biology, 1988—, sr. rsch. scientist, 1988—; chmn. Gordon Rsch. Conf. on Cell Contact and Movement, 1979; mem. staff embryology course Woods Hole (Mass.) Marine Biol. Lab., 1953-57, 78, trustee, 1991—; mem. space biology adv. panel NASA, 1976-79; lectr. internat. symposia, including Internat. Inst. Embryology, Moscow, 1969, Ciba, London, 1972, Devl. Biol Fishes, Tampa, 1979, 500th anniversary U. Uppsala, Sweden, 1977, Conf. on Malignancy, Keystone, Colo., 1979, Conf. on Cell Behaviour, London, 1982 and Oxford, 1987, Gastrulation, Louisville, 1982, Biol. Fundulus, Phila., 1983, Conf. Cell Traffic, Zurich, 1984, Cellular Basis of Morphogenesis, Woods Hole, 1988, Experimental Embryology of Aquatic Plants and Animals, Banyuls-sur-Mer, 1989, Gastrulation: Movements, Patterns and Molecules, Bodega Bay, 1990, Cytoskeleton. in Devel. Biology, Kingston, Ont., 1991, Gastrulation, Brighton, U.K., 1992, Devl. and Genetics of Zebrafish, Cold Spring Harbor, 1994, Soc. Devel. Biology, La Jolla, 1995; Streisinger lectr. Zebrafish Devel. and Genetics, Cold Spring Harbor, 1996. Author: Cells into Organs-The Forces that Shape the Embryo, 1969, 2d rev. edit., 1984, On the Mechanism of Metazoan Cell Movements, 1976; also articles on cell motility, invasiveness, morphogenesis, gastrulation and differentiation; assoc. editor: Jour. Exptl. Zoology, 1964-68. Served to capt. USAAF, 1942-46. Recipient citation for distinction in scholarship and teaching Wesleyan U., 1960; John Simon Guggenheim fellow Coll. de France, 1959-60; NSF grantee, 1952-76; NIH grantee, 1974—; MERIT award NIH, 1987-96. Mem. Am. Soc. Zoologists, Am. Soc. Cell Biology, Am. Soc. Developmental Biology (Edwin Grant Conklin medal 1995), Internat. Inst. Embryology, ACLU, Phi Beta Kappa, Sigma Xi. Clubs: Yale (N.Y.C.); Mory's. Home: Moose Hill Rd Guilford CT 06437-2356 Office: Yale Univ Osborn Meml Lab Dept Biology New Haven CT 06520

TRINKUS, LAIMA MARY, special education educator; b. Chgo., Mar. 6, 1950; d. Steven and Antonia (Ambrasas) Trinkus. BS in Sociology, Daemen Coll., Buffalo, 1974; MS in Behavioral Sci. Spl. Edn., SUNY, Buffalo, 1987. Cert. spl. edn. tchr., N.Y. Tchr. aide Cantalician Ctr. for Learning, Buffalo, 1975-78, tchr. spl. edn., 1978-85; tchr. spl. edn. Erie I Bd. Coop. Edn. Svcs., Lancaster, N.Y., 1985—. Vol. Spl. Olympics, Buffalo, 1976—. Home: 9821 Greiner Rd Clarence NY 14031

TRIOLO, PETER, advertising agency executive, marketing educator, consultant; b. N.Y.C., Feb. 20, 1927; s. Antonino and Cira T.; m. Audrey Sullivan, Aug. 7, 1954; children—Stuart, Bruce, Ellen, Leslie. A.B., Adelphi U., Garden City, N.Y., 1952; exec. program, Columbia U. Grad. Sch. Bus., 1966. Vice pres. Ogilvy & Mather, Inc., N.Y.C., 1958-64; sr. v.p. Ketchum, MacLeod & Grove Inc., Pitts. and N.Y.C., 1964-68; founder, exec. v.p. Marketronics Inc., N.Y.C., 1968-72; chief adminstrv. officer Rosenfeld, Sirowitz & Lawson Inc., N.Y.C., 1972-76; sr. v.p., media dir. William Esty Co., Inc., N.Y.C., 1976-87; cons. Internat. Exec. Svc. Corps, Stamford, Conn., 1987—; adj. prof. mktg. Baruch Coll., City U. N.Y., 1980-86, Fordham U., N.Y.C., 1987—. Guest editor: Mktg. and Media Decisions, 1967. Served with USAAF, 1945-47. Mem. Assn. Nat. Advertisers (TV workshops), Advt. Age Media Workshops Faculty, Mktg. and Media Decisions Faculty.

TRIPATHY, SUKANT KISHORE, chemistry educator; b. Chakradharpur, Bihar, India, Aug. 4, 1952; came to U.S., 1976; s. Jyotish C. and Usha (Pani) T.; m. Susan Thomson, Sept. 5, 1981; children: Sheila, Aneil. MS, I.I.T. Kharagpur, 1974; PhD, Case Western Res. U., 1981. Tech. staff mem. GTE Labs., Waltham, Mass., 1981-83; rsch. mgr. GTE Labs., Waltham, 1983-86; assoc. prof. chemistry U. Lowell, Mass., 1986-87; prof. chemistry U. Lowell, 1987—; dir. ctr. advanced materials U. Mass., Lowell, 1992—; dir. Molecular Technologies, Inc., Lowell, 1987—; vice chancellor acad. affairs U. Mass., Lowell, 1994-96. Contbr. over 250 articles to profl. jours. Mem. AAAS, Am. Chem. Soc. (Carl S. Marvel Creative Polymer Chemistry award 1993), Am. Phys. Soc., Sigma Xi, MRS, SPE. Achievements include 20 patents. Home: 8 Northbriar Rd Acton MA 01720-5826 Office: U Mass Ctr for Advanced Materials 1 University Ave Lowell MA 01854-2827

TRIPLEHORN, CHARLES A., entomology educator, insects curator; b. Bluffton, Ohio, Oct. 27, 1927; s. Murray E. and Alice Irene (Lora) T.; m. Wanda Elaine Neiswander, June 12, 1949 (dec. Nov. 1985); children: Bradley Alyn, Bruce Wayne; m. Linda Sue Parsons, July 11, 1987. B.Sc., Ohio State U., 1949, M.S., 1952; Ph.D., Cornell U., 1957. Asst. prof. entomology U. Del., Newark, 1952-54; teaching asst. entomology Cornell U., Ithaca, N.Y., 1954-57; asst. prof. entomology Ohio Agrl. Research and Devel. Ctr., Wooster, Ohio, 1957-61; asst. prof. entomology Ohio State U., Columbus, 1961-62, assoc. prof. entomology, 1962-66, prof. entomology, 1966-92, prof. emeritus, 1992—; econ. entomologist U.S. AID/Brazil, Piracicaba, Sao Paulo, 1964-66; vis. curator Can. Nat. Collection, Ottawa, Ont., 1977. Co-author: Introduction to the Study of Insects, 6th edit., 1989. Cubmaster Boy Scouts Am., Wooster, Ohio, 1959-60, scoutmaster, Columbus, 1971-72; football coach Upper Arlington Football Assn., Ohio, 1968-71. Grantee Am. Philos. Soc., 1963, NSF, 1979, 85. Mem. Entomol. Soc. Am. (pres. 1985), Coleopterists Soc. (pres. 1976), Royal Entomol. Soc. London, Entomol. Soc. Washington, Sigma Xi, Gamma Sigma Delta. Republican. Methodist. Club: Wheaton (pres.). Avocations: sports; music; reading; writing. Home: 3943 Medford Sq Hilliard OH 43026-2219 Office: Mus Biol Diversity Div Insects The Ohio State University 1315 Kinnear Rd Columbus OH 43212-1157

TRIPLETT, E. EUGENE, editor; b. LaJolla, Calif., Mar. 12, 1949; s. Erbin Eugene Triplett and Marjorie Ann (Aldrich) Heath; m. Vannie Carol Crow, July 19, 1968; 1 child, Aaron Eugene. BA in Journalism, Ctrl. State U., 1975. Reporter, columnist The Okla. Jour., Oklahoma City, 1976-80; entertainment editor The Daily Oklahoman, Oklahoma City, 1981-85, asst. city editor, 1985-89, city editor, 1989—. Comm. com. Okla. Heart Assn., 1989-92. With U.S. Army, 1969-71, Vietnam. Recipient 1st. Place Feature Writing award Soc. Profl. Journalist, 1987, 2d. Place Feature Writing award AP/One, 1988. Mem. AP/Okla. News Exec. (pres.-elect 1994-95, pres. 1995-96). Democrat. Avocations: collecting recorded music, feature films, vintage TV shows. Home: 2821 Tealwood Dr Oklahoma City OK 73120-1777 Office: The Daily Oklahoman 9000 Broadway Ext Oklahoma City OK 73114-3708

TRIPLETT, KELLY B., chemist; b. Cin.. BA, Northwestern U., 1968; PhD in Chemistry, U. Mich., 1974. Rsch. assoc. Mich. State U., 1974-76; rsch. chemist Stauffer Chem. Co., Dobbs Ferry, N.Y., 1976-78, supr., 1978-82, tech. mgr., 1982-84, bus. mgr., 1984-87; program mgr., bus. mgr. Akzo Chem. Inc., Dobbs Ferry, N.Y., 1987-90, mgr. rsch. ctr., 1990—, dir. rsch., 1992—; v.p. Akzo Nobel Ctrl. Rsch., 1994. Mem. Am. Chem. Soc., Indsl. Rsch. Inst. Achievements include development of new research and development methodologies; research in new polymerization products and process, organometallics and transition metal chemistries; investigation of chemical routes to advanced ceramics. Office: Akzo Nobel Chems Inc 1 Livingstone Ave Dobbs Ferry NY 10522-3401

TRIPLETT, LOREN O., religious organization administrator; b. San Jose, Calif., July 5, 1926; m. Mildred Triplett; children: Donald, Debora, Marcus, Timothy. Grad., Bethany Bible Coll., 1946; student, Ctrl. Bible Coll., Evangel Coll., Dade Jr. Coll. Ordained min. Assemblies of God, 1950. Pastor various orgns., Oreg. and Nebr., 1947-54; missionary Life Pubs., Nicaragua, 1954-73; field dir. Divsn. Fgn. Missions, Springfield, Mo., 1973-89; exec. dir. Divsn. Fgn. Ministries, Springfield, Mo., 1990—. Contbr. articles to profl. jours. Office: Assemblies of God 1445 N Boonville Ave Springfield MO 65802-1894*

TRIPODI, LOUIS ANTHONY, advertising agency executive; b. N.Y.C., July 7, 1931; m. Mary Gail Ennis; children: Pascal, William, Louis, James, Stephen, Michela, Gian, Christian, Blanid, Theresa, Michael. B.A., Bklyn. Coll., 1952. Dir. corp. pub. relations Kenyon & Eckhardt, N.Y.C., 1965-68; sr. v.p., corp. dir. pub. relations Needham Harper Worldwide, N.Y.C., 1968-87; exec. v.p., corp. dir. pub. affairs DDB Needham Worldwide, N.Y.C., 1987—. Mem. ASCAP, Am. Assn. Advt. Agys. (chmn. pub. relations com. 1982-83), Am. Advt. Fedn. (chmn. pub. relations com.). Home: 565 Kiowa Dr Franklin Lakes NJ 07417-1208 Office: DDB Needham Worldwide Inc 437 Madison Ave New York NY 10022-7001

TRIPOLI, MASUMI HIROYASU, financial consultant and diplomat; b. Fukuyama, Japan, Apr. 23, 1956; d. Yoshimi and Suzuko Hiroyasu; 1 child, Mona Lisa Tripoli. BA cum laude, U. Wash., 1978; MA, Sophia U., Tokyo, 1981; MBA, Ecole des Hautes Etudes Comml, Jouy-en-Josas, France, 1983. Cert. fin. planner, chartered fin. cons. Corp. planning mgr. Kowa Corp., Osaka, Japan, 1983-85; internat. bond trader Banque Baribas, Tokyo, 1985-86, Westpac Bank, Tokyo, 1987-88; fin. cons. CIGNA Fin. Advisors, Glendale, Calif., 1989Ô, Masumi Tripoli & Assocs., Glendale, Calif., 1989Ô; anchor newscaster United TV, L.A., 1989-92; condr. seminars in field. Contbr. articles to profl. jours. Grantee Sophia U., 1979, H.E.C., 1983. Mem. Internat. Bd. Cert. Fin. Planners, Ritz-Carlton Fitness Club. Avocations: child education, horseback riding, sailing. Office: Masumi Tripoli and Assocs 330 N Brand Blvd Ste 400 Glendale CA 91203-2308

TRIPP, FREDERICK GERALD, investment advisor; b. Chgo., Oct. 1, 1936; s. Gerald F. and Kathryn Ann (Siebold) T.; m. Terry Anne Shull, Aug. 26, 1967; children: Mark A., Karin M., Tracy L. Clark, Tricia L., Patrick G. BS in Econs., Purdue U., 1958; MBA, Lehigh U., 1964; PhD, The Am. U., 1972. Sr. v.p. CRI, Inc., Rockville, Md., 1979-82, Security Pacific, Inc., Seattle, 1982-83; pres. Frederick G. Tripp & Assocs., Inc., Rockville, 1983—; instr. Troy State U., 1965-67, Am. U., 1975-77, Indsl. Coll. Armed Forces, 1975-80; mem. pres.'s coun. Investment Mgmt. and Rsch., Inc., 1985—. Pres. Doctoral Assn., The Am. U., 1973. Maj. U.S. Army, 1958-67, Vietnam. Mem. Internat. Assn. Fin. Planning, Investment Mgmt. Cons. Assn., Sigma Pi. Methodist. Avocations: skiing, boating, racquetball, flying. Office: Frederick G Tripp & Assocs 3200 Tower Oaks Blvd # 300 Rockville MD 20852-4216

TRIPP, KAREN BRYANT, lawyer; b. Rocky Mount, N.C., Sept. 2, 1955; d. Bryant and Katherine Rebecca (Watkins) Tripp; m. Robert Mark Burleson, June 25, 1977 (div. 1997); 1 child, Hamilton Chase Barnett. BA, U. N.C., 1976; JD, U. Ala., 1981. Bar: Tex. 1981, U.S. Dist. Ct. (so. dist.) Tex. 1982, U.S. Dist. Ct. (ea. dist.) Tex. 1991, U.S. Ct. Appeals (fed. cir.) 1983, U.S. Supreme Ct. 1994. Law clk. Tucker, Gray & Espy, Tuscaloosa, Ala., 1978-81, to presiding justice Ala. Supreme Ct., Montgomery, summer 1980; atty. Exxon Prodn. Rsch. Co., Houston, 1981-86, coord. tech. transfer, 1986-87; assoc. Arnold, White and Durkee, Attys. at Law, Houston, 1988-93, shareholder, 1994—; pres. Blake Barnett & Co., 1996—. Editor: Intellectual Property Law Review, 1995, 96, 97; contbr. articles to profl. jours. Recipient Am. Jurisprudence award U. Ala., 1980, Dean's award, 1981. Mem. ABA (intellectual property law section, ethics com. 1992-95), Houston Bar Assn. (interprofl. rels. com. 1988-90), Houston Intellectual Property Lawyers Assn. (mem. outstanding inventor com. 1982-84, chmn. 1994-95, chmn. student edn. com. 1986, sec. 1987-88, chmn. awards com. 1988-89, chmn. program com. 1988-91, 95-96, treas. 1991-92, bd. dirs. 1992-94, nominations com. 1993, 96), Tex. Bar Assn. (antitrust law com. 1984-85, chmn. Internat. Law com. of Intellectual Property Law Sect. 1987-88, internat. transfer tech. com. 1983-84), Am. Intellectual Property Lawyers Assn. (mem. patent law com. 1995), Women in Tech. (founder), Phi Alpha Delta (clk. 1980). Democrat. Episcopalian. Office: Arnold White & Durkee PO Box 4433 Houston TX 77210-4433

TRIPP, LUKE SAMUEL, educator; b. Atoka, Tenn., Feb. 6, 1941; s. Luke Samuel and Dorothy Mae (Watson) T.; m. Hedwidge Mary Bruyns, Aug. 21, 1989; children: Ruth, Azania, Comrade. BS, Wayne State U., 1966; MA, U. Mich., 1974, PhD, 1980. Computer programmer No. Elec. Co., Montreal, Que., Can., 1966-68; tchr. elem. sch. math. Santa Maria Edn. Ctr., Detroit, 1969-70; instr. black studies Wayne County C.C., Detroit, 1971-72; tchr. secondary sch. sci. Cmty. Skills Ctr., Ann Arbor, Mich., 1971-73; dir. grad. rsch. U. Mich., Ann Arbor, 1977-80; asst. prof. U. Ill., Champaign, 1981-82, So. Ill. U., Carbondale, 1982-89; from asst. prof. to prof. social sci. St. Cloud (Minn.) State U., 1989-95, prof., 1995—; co-founder, coord. Faculty/Staff Color Caucus, St. Cloud, 1989—; founder, dir. Human Rights Coputhon, St. Cloud, 1989-91, So. Ill. Anti-Aparthied Coalition, Carbondale, 1984-87. Dir. polit. edn. Nat. Black Ind. Polit. Party, Ann Arbor, 1980-81; co-founder, mem. exec. bd. Labor Defense League, Detroit, 1970-71, League Revolutionary Black Workers, Detroit, 1968-70; coord. Nat. Black Econ. Devel. Conf., Detroit, 1969-70; student activist SNCC, Detroit, 1960-65. Mem. Nat. Coun. Black Studies, Assn. Study Afro-Am. Life and History. Office: St Cloud State U 720 4th Ave S Saint Cloud MN 56301-4442

TRIPP, MARIAN BARLOW LOOFE, retired public relations company executive; b. Lodge Pole, Nebr., July 26; d. Lewis Rockwell and Cora Dee (Davis) Barlow; m. James Edward Tripp, Feb. 9, 1957; children: Brendan Michael, Kevin Mark. BS, Iowa State U., 1944. Writer Dairy Record, St. Paul, 1944-45; head, product promotion div., pub. rels. dept. Swift & Co., Chgo., 1945-55; mgmt. supr., v.p. pub. rels. J. Walter Thompson Co., N.Y.C. and Chgo., 1956-74; v.p. consumer affairs, Chgo., 1974-76; pres. Marian Tripp Communications Inc., Chgo., 1976-94. Mem. Pub. Rels. Soc. Am., Am. Inst. Wine and Food, Les Dames d'Escoffier, Chgo. Network, Fortnightly Club, Confriere de la Chaine des Rotisseriers (officer Chgo. chpt.) Episcopalian. Office: 100 E Bellevue Pl Chicago IL 60611

TRIPP, MICHAEL WINDSOR, accountant; b. Fall River, Mass.; s. Frederick and Elizabeth (Azevedo) T.; m. Ella Charlene Middlebrooks, May 24, 1966; children: Sandra Lee, Wendy Ann. Cert. computer programming with honors, Plus Sch. Bus., Providence, 1971; BSBA in Acctg. cum laude, Bryant Coll., 1975. CPA, R.I. Fin. mgr. trainee I.T.T. Aetna Fin., Pawtucket, R.I., 1969-70; computer programmer B.A. Ballou & Co., Inc., East Providence, R.I., 1970-72; adminstrv. asst. Manasett Corp., Providence, 1972-74; profl. staff Peat, Marwick & Mitchell, Providence, 1974-76; ptnr. Turosz, Maccarone, Keenan & Tripp, East Providence, 1976-88; adminstr. Licht & Semonoff, Providence, 1988-89; pvt. practice East Providence, 1989—; dir. A New Leaf, Providence, 1988-96. Vice-chmn., clk. Barrington (R.I.) Sch. Com., 1980-88; active Rep. Town Com., Barrington, 1980—; treas. Hampden Meadows PTA, Barrington, 1976-80, Rhode Islanders for Chafee, Providence, 1976. With USMC, 1965-69, Vietnam. Decorated Purple Heart, Air medal, Navy Commendation medal with combat V. Fellow AICPA; mem. R.I. Soc. CPAs, Manny Moniz Meml. Hockey League (treas. 1992—), Barrington Yacht Club (treas. 1992-93), Narragansett Bay Yachting Assn., Bryant Coll. Alumni Assn. (exec. dir., treas. 1977-80), La Salle Acad. Alumni Assn. (phonathon chmn. 1992-93), Appalachian Mountain Club, U.S. Sailing Assn. Republican. Roman Catholic. Avocations: sailing, hockey, mountain climbing. Home: 40 Lamson Rd Barrington RI 02806-2643 Office: 589 Warren Ave Ste 3 East Providence RI 02914-2800

TRIPP, SUSAN GERWE, museum director; b. Balt., Dec. 28, 1945; d. Earl Joseph and Maria Elizabeth (Wise) Gerwe; m. David Enders Tripp, June 9, 1977. BS, U. Md., 1967. Home econs. tchr. Balt. County Pub. Sch. Sys., 1967-74; curator of art Johns Hopkins U., Balt., 1974-76; curator of art, archivist Johns Hopkins U., 1976-78, instr. evening coll., 1978-84, dir. univ. collections, 1979-91; supr., instr. art history Goucher Coll., Notre Dame U., Balt., 1977-86; dir. docent tng. Homewood Mus., Balt., 1987-89; exec. dir. Old Westbury (N.Y.) Gardens, 1992-96; writer Stuyvesant, N.Y., 1996—; dir. Homewood Restoration Adv. Com., 1983-92, Evergreen Restoration Adv. Com., 1988-92; lectr. in field. Co-author: The Garrett Collection of Japanese Art, 1993 (NEA Grant 1980), Contbr. articles to profl. jours. Trustee Columbia County Hist. Soc., 1996—. Recipient Hist. Preservation award Balt. Heritage, Inc., 1988, 91, Rsch. award Am. Soc. Interior Designers, 1991. Mem. Am. Assn. Bot. Gardens and Arboreta, Brit. Mus. Soc., Oriental Ceramic Soc., Balt. Mus. Art, Oriental Ceramic Soc. Hong Kong, Assn. of Frick Art Ref. Libr. So. Garden Hist. Soc., Furniture History Soc., N.Y. Zool. Soc., Am. Assn. Mus. John Hopkins U. Falcuty Club., Omicron Nu. Avocations: architecture, archaeology, Chinese ceramics, historical restoration. Office: PO Box G Stuyvesant NY 12173

TRIPPE, KENNETH ALVIN BATTERSHILL, shipping industry executive; b. Kansas City, Mo., Jan. 3, 1933; s. Alvin C. and Blanche (Battershill) T.; m. Jane Muir Mitchell, June 11, 1955 (dec. Jan. 1988); children: Kenneth, Tracy, Robert; m. Josphine M. Kling, May 12, 1990. B.S. in Bus. Adminstrn, Kans. U., 1955; LL.B., U. Mo., 1958; postdoctoral mgmt. program, MIT, 1972. Bar: Mo. 1958. With Miss. River Corp., St. Louis, 1958-68, asst. sec., 1958-64, sec., 1964-65, asst. to pres., 1965-68; asst. treas. Internat. Utilities Corp. (name IU Internat. Corp. 1973), Phila., 1968-69; asst. treas. corporate and internat. fin. Internat. Utilities Corp. (name IU Internat. Corp. 1973), 1970-72, v.p., treas., 1972-75; exec. v.p., dir. subs. Gotaas-Larsen Shipping Corp., 1975-77, pres., chief exec. officer, dir., 1977-82; founder, chmn. Cruiseship Info. Systems Inc., Coral Gables, Fla., 1982-91, Cruise Brokers Inc., 1990—, Trippe & Co., 1990—; dir. The Herzfeld Caribbean Basin Fund; v.p. fin. Kans. Gas & Electric Co., Wichita, 1969-70. Patentee cruise info. and booking data processing system. Mem. Fisher Island Club, Union League N.Y.C., Phi Delta Phi, Sigma Chi. Republican. Episcopalian. Home and Office: 2134 Fisher Island Dr Fisher Island FL 33109

TRIPPENSEE, GARY ALAN, aerospace executive; b. Jefferson City, Mo., May 23, 1940; s. Walter Anton and Juanita (Schneider) T.; m. Concha Elvira Perez, Aug. 18, 1981; children: Jena, Darin. BSME, U. Mo., Rolla, 1962; AA in Bus., Antelope Valley Coll., Lancaster, Calif., 1974. Lic. airframe and powerplant mechanic, FAA; single/multi-engine comml. aircraft lic. land & sea. Aircraft flight test engr. McDonnell Douglas, St. Louis, 1965-79; project mgr. NASA/Dryden Flight Rsch. Ctr., Edwards, Calif., 1979—, project mgr. F14, 1983-84, project mgr. F15, 1984-85, project mgr. X-29, 1985-91, project mgr. X-31, 1991-92; internat. test. orgn. dir. X-31, 1993-95, project mgr. X-33, 1996—. Capt. U.S. Army C.E., 1962-65. Recipient Laurels award for aeronautics/propulsion Aviation Week & Space Tech., 1990, 93. Mem. AIAA. Avocations: flying, fishing, R/C models. Home: 3773 Knox Ave Rosamond CA 93560-6413

TRIPPET, SUSAN ELAINE, nursing educator; b. Princeton, Ind., Nov. 3, 1946; d. Charles Kightly and Isabel (Key) T. AA, Ind. U., Indpls., 1971, MS in Nursing, 1983; DS in Nursing, U. Ala., Birmingham, 1988. Lectr. Ind. U., Indpls., 1976-83, asst. prof., 1983-84; CNS perinatal div. U. Hosps., Birmingham, 1984-85; assoc. prof. U. So. Miss., Hattiesurg, 1988-94; pres. D.J.S. Resources P.A., 1995—; pres. D.J.S. Resources P.A.; various presentations on older women, relationship issues, mothers & daughters, and therapeutic use of music. Mem. Am. Nursing Assn., So. Nursing Rsch. Soc., Internat. Coun. Women's Health Issues, Sigma Theta Tau, Sigma Tau Delta.

TRISCO, ROBERT FREDERICK, church historian, educator; b. Chgo., Nov. 11, 1929; s. Richard E. and Harriet Rose (Hardt) T. B.A., St. Mary of Lake Sem., Mundelein, Ill., 1951; S.T.L., Pontifical Gregorian U., Rome, 1955, Hist. Eccl.D., 1962; LHD (hon.), Belmont Abbey Coll., 1992. Ordained priest Roman Catholic Ch., 1954. Mem. faculty Cath. U. Am., Washington, 1959—; prof. ch. history Cath. U. Am., 1975—; expert 2d Vatican Coun., 1962-65; pres. Am. subcom. Internat. Commn. Comparative Ch. History, 1978-80, assesseur, 1980—; mem. subcoms. Nat. Conf. Cath. Bishops, 1966-76, 87-92; mem. Pontifical Com. Hist. Scis., 1982—; hon. mem. Accademia di San Carlo (Milan), 1986—; hon. prelate (monsignor), 1992. Author: The Holy See and Nascent Church in the Middle Western U.S., 1826-1850, 1962, Bishops and Their Priests in the United States, 1988; co-author: A Guide to American Catholic History, 2d edit., 1982; editor: Catholics in America, 1976; editor CAth. Hist. Rev., 1963—; co-editor, contbr.: Studies in Catholic History in Honor of John Tracy Ellis, 1985; contbr. articles to profl. publs. Named Knight, Equestrian Order of the Holy Sepulchre of Jerusalem, 1993. Mem. Am. Soc. Ch. History (coun. 1980-82), Am. Cath. Hist. Assn. (exec. sec. 1961—, sec., treas. 1983—). Office: Cath U Am Mullen Library Rm 318 Washington DC 20064

TRISKA, JAN FRANCIS, retired political science educator; b. Prague, Czechoslovakia, Jan. 26, 1922; came to U.S., 1948, naturalized, 1955; s. Jan and Bozena (Kubiznak) T.; m. Carmel Lena Burastero, Aug. 26, 1951; children: Mark Lawrence, John William. J.U.D., Charles U., Prague, 1948; LL.M., Yale U., 1950, J.S.D., 1952; Ph.D., Harvard U., 1957. Co-dir. Soviet treaties Hoover Instn., Stanford, Calif., 1956-58; lectr. dept. polit. sci. U. Calif.-Berkeley, 1957-58; asst. prof. Cornell U., Ithaca, N.Y., 1958-60; assoc. prof. Stanford U., Calif., 1960-65, prof. polit. sci., 1965-89, assoc. chmn. dept., 1965-66, 68-69, 71-72, 74-75, emeritus prof. polit. sci., 1990—; cons. Inst. State and Law, Czech Acad. Scis., Prague, 1995—. Co-author: (with Slusser) The Theory, Law and Policy of Soviet Treaties, 1962, (with Finley) Soviet Foreign Policy, 1968, (with Cocks) Political Development and Political Change in Eastern Europe, 1977, (with Ike, North) The World of Superpowers, 1981, (with Gati) Blue Collar Workers in Eastern Europe, 1981, Dominant Powers and Subordinate States, 1986; bd. editors: East European Quar. Comparative Politics, Internat. Jour. Sociology, Jour. Comparative Politics, Studies in Comparative Communism, Soviet Statutes and Decisions, Documents in Communist Affairs. Recipient Rsch. award Ford Found., 1963-68, Josef Hlavka Commemorative medal Czechoslovak Acad. Scis., 1992, M.A. Comenius 1592-1992 Meml. medal Czechoslovak Pedagogical Mus., Prague, 1991; fellow NSF, 1971-72, Sen. Fulbright fellow, 1973-74, Woodrow Wilson fellow Internat. Ctr. for Scholars, 1980-81. Mem. Am. Polit. Sci. Assn. (sec. pres. conf. on communist studies 1970-76), Assn. Advancement Slavic Studies (bd. dirs. 1975-83), Am. Soc. Internat. Law (exec. coun. 1964-67), Czechoslovak Soc. Arts and Scis. (pres. 1978-80, 90-92), Inst. for Human Scis. Vienna (acting for Commn. European Communities, Brussels, com. experts on transformation of nat. higher edn. and rsch. system in Ctrl. Europe, Brussels 1991—). Democrat. Club: Fly Fishers (Palo Alto, Calif.). Home: 720 Vine St Menlo Park CA 94025-6154 Office: Stanford U Dept Polit Sci Stanford CA 94305

TRITES, DONALD GEORGE, human service consultant; b. Boston, Sept. 26, 1941; s. George Herman and Ada Christena (Patten) T.; m. Ruth Ann Lewis, June 15, 1963 (div. 1987); children: Sarah Jeanne, Amy Bray; m. Beverly Jean Baker, Apr. 8, 1989; children: Erica Christena, Philip Jameson Granville. AB, Colgate U., 1963; EdM, Tufts U., 1964; PhD, Syracuse U., 1976. Thcr., then chair history dept. Hamilton (Mass.)-Wenham Regional H.S., 1964-70; instr. divsn. ednl. studies Emory U., Atlanta, 1973-76, asst. prof. edn l. studies, 1976-81, vis. faculty, 1981-36; exec. dir. Ga. Advocacy Office, Inc., Atlanta, 1981-86, Devel. Svcs. Strafford County, Inc., Dover, N.H., 1986-95; founder, pres. Jebdas Consulting, Eliot, Maine, 1995—; program mgr. Mental Retardation Svcs. State of Maine, Augusta, 1996—; cons. in human svc. mgmt. and evaluation, U.S. and Europe, 1978—. Editor, author: The College and A Human Future, 1986; contbr. articles to profl.publs. Bd. dirs. New England Assn. for Persons with Severe Handicaps; deacon, First Bapt. Ch., Melrose, Mass., 1968-69, Syracuse, N.Y., 1972-73; deacon, Ctrl. Congl. Ch., Atlanta, 1984-86. Mem. Assn. for Persons with Severe Handicaps, Delta Upsilon. Democrat. Mem. United Ch. of Christ. Avocations: reading, gardening. Home: 351 Gardiner Rd Jefferson ME 04348-9785 Office: Dept Mental Health & Mental Retardation 40 State House Sta Augusta ME 04333-0040

TRITT, TRAVIS, country music singer, songwriter; b. Marietta, Ga., 1963; m. Theresa Nelson, Apr. 12, 1997. Recording artist Warner Bros., 1990—. Albums include Country Club, 1990 (platinum), It's All About to Change, 1991 (platinum), T-R-O-U-B-L-E, 1992 (platinum), A Travis Tritt Christmas: Loving Time of the Year, 1992 (with Marty Stuart, Hank Williams Jr., Waylon Jennings) Ten Feet Tall and Bulletproof, 1994; #1 singles The Whiskey Ain't Workin' (Grammy award with Marty Stuart 1993), Here's a Quarter (Call Someone Who Cares), Anymore, Can I Trust You with my Heart; author: (with Michael Bane) 10 Foot Tall and Bullet Proof, 1994. Named Billboard's Top New Male Country Artist, 1990; recipient Horizon award Country Music Assn., 1991, (with Marty Stuart) Vocal Event of Yr. award Country Music Assn., 1992; inductee Grand Ole Opry, 1992. Office: Warner Bros Records 3300 Warner Blvd Burbank CA 91505-4632*

TRITTEN, JAMES JOHN, national security educator; b. Yonkers, N.Y., Oct. 3, 1945; s. James Hanley and Jennie (Szucs) T.; m. Kathleen Tritten, (div. 1983); children: Kimberly, James John Jr.; m. Jasmine Clark, Dec. 29, 1990. BA in Internat. Studies, Am. U., 1971; MA in Internat. Affairs, Fla. State U., 1978; AM in Internat. Rels., U. So. Calif., L.A., 1982, PhD in Internat. Rels., 1984. Commd. officer USN, 1967, advanced through grades to commdr., 1981; joint strategic plans officer Office of the Chief of Naval Ops., Washington, 1984-85; asst. dir. net assessment Office of the Sec. of Def., Washington, 1985-86; chmn. dept. nat. security affairs Naval Postgrad. Sch., Monterey, Calif., 1986-89; ret. USN, 1989; assoc. prof. nat. security affairs Naval Postgrad. Sch., Monterey, 1989-93; spl. asst. to comdr. Naval Doctrine Command, Norfolk, Va., 1993-96; exercise and tng. dir. U.S. Atlantic Command Joint Tng., Analysis, Simulation Ctr., Suffolk, Va., 1996—; cons. Rand Corp., Santa Monica, Calif., 1982-84; with Nat. Security Rsch., Fairfax, Va., 1992, AmerInd, Alexandria, Va., 1996. Author: Soviet Naval Forces and Nuclear Warfare, 1986, Our New National Security Strategy, 1992 (George Washington Honor medal 1991), A Doctrine Reader, 1996; contbr. chpts. to books and articles to profl. jours. Mem. Adv. Bd. on Alcohol Related Problems, Monterey County, Calif., 1987-90; bd., officer Leadership Monterey (Calif.) Peninsula, 1989-92, Carmel Valley (Calif.) Property Owners Assn., 1989-91; commr. Airport Land Use Commn., Monterey County, 1990-93, mem. Nat Eagle Scout Assn. Decorated Def. Superior Svc. medal Sec. Def., Washington, 1986, Meritorious Svc. medal Sec. Navy, Monterey, 1989, Navy Civilian Supr. Svc. medal, 1996; recipient Alfred Thayer Mahan award for literary achievement Navy League of U.S., Arlington, Va., 1986. Mem. Mil. Ops. Rsch. Soc. (v.p. 1990-91), U.S. Naval Inst. (Silver and Bronze medals), Pi Sigma Alpha, Pi Gamma Mu. Republican. Presbyterian. Avocations: hiking, camping. Office: US Atlantic Command Joint Tng Analysis Simulation Ctr 116 Lake View Pkwy Ste 2170 Suffolk VA 23435-2663

TRITTER, RICHARD PAUL, strategic planning consulting executive; b. Boston, Sept. 30, 1945; s. Herman Louis and Rose (Greenblatt) T.; 1 child, Melissa Rosanne; m. Marcy Lynn Kroll, June 17, 1984; children: Matthew Alexander, Rachel Danielle, Adam Levi. AB, Columbia Coll., N.Y.C., 1967; JD, Northeastern U., 1976. Bar: Mass. 1977, U.S. Supreme Ct. 1980. Mktg. mgr./cons. Digital Equipment Corp., Merrimack, N.H., 1979-81, 83-86; nat. dir. high-tech. industry program Coopers & Lybrand, Boston, 1981-83; pres. Video/Demo Ctrs., Inc., Burlington, Mass., 1986-88; v.p. bus. devel. Info. Resources, Inc., Boston, 1988-91; dir. facilitation consulting svcs. Arthur Andersen LLP, Boston, Chgo., 1991-96; dir. control self-assessment svcs. Deloitte & Touche LLP, Boston, 1996—; panelist MIT Enterprise Forum, Cambridge, 1983-89; pres. Somali Lobster Exports Co., 1995. Author: Control Self-Assessment: Experienced Current Thinking & Best Practices, 1996; creator software application Compliance Testing and Verification, 1981. UN rep. Jubaland Relief and Rehab. Soc., Somalia; dir. Save Somalia Livestock Campaign, 1993. Recipient Better Govt. award Pioneer Inst. for Pub. Policy Rsch., Boston. Facilitated meetings between opposing clans in the Juba region of southern Somali; initiated lobster export project with cooperation of Gen. Omar Jess, Col. Ahmed Hashi and other Somali leaders. Home: 20 Cambridge Ter # 3 Cambridge MA 02140 Office: CSA/Facilitation Svcs 40 Dana St Cambridge MA 02138-4204

TRIVEDI, SUDHIR K., computer science educator, researcher; b. Agra, India, Dec. 5, 1959; came to U.S., 1987; s. Sewa Ram and Sarala Dewi (Misra) T. MS in Math., Agra U., India, 1981, MPhil in Math., 1982, PhD in Math., 1985; PhD in Computer Sci., La. State U., 1993. Rsch. fellow Coun. Scientific and Indsl. Rsch., India, 1982-87; teaching asst. in computer sci. dept. La. State U., 1988-93; asst. prof. in computer sci. Southern U., Baton Rouge, 1993—; rsch. asst. Robotics Rsch. Lab., La. State U., 1993; rsch. project dir. NASA AMES Rsch. Ctr. Mem. IEEE, IEEE Computer Soc., Assn. Computing Machinery (reviewer 32d, 33d, 34th S.E. Conf.), Soc. Indsl. and Applied Math. (session chmn. 7th conf. on discrete math.), Indian Math. Soc., Upsilon Pi Epsilon. Home: 3000 July St Apt 140 Baton Rouge LA 70808-2045 Office: Southern U. PO Box 9221 Baton Rouge LA 70813

TRIVELPIECE, ALVIN WILLIAM, physicist, corporate executive; b. Stockton, Calif., Mar. 15, 1931; s. Alvin Stevens and Mae (Hughes) T.; m. Shirley Ann Ross, Mar. 23, 1953; children: Craig Evan, Steve Edward, Keith Eric. B.S., Calif. Poly. Coll., San Luis Obispo, 1953; M.S., Calif. Inst. Tech., 1955, Ph.D., 1958. Fulbright scholar Delft (Netherlands) U., 1958-59; asst. prof., then asso. prof. U. Calif. at Berkeley, 1959-66; prof. physics U. Md., 1966-76; on leave as asst. dir. for research div. controlled thermonuclear research AEC, Washington, 1973-75; v.p. Maxwell Labs. Inc., San Diego, 1976-78; corp. v.p. Sci. Applications, Inc., La Jolla, Calif., 1978-81; dir. Office of Energy Research, U.S. Dept. Energy, Washington, 1981-87; exec. officer AAAS, Washington, 1987-88; dir. Oak Ridge (Tenn.) Nat. Lab., 1989—; v.p. Martin Marietta Energy Systems, 1989-95, Lockheed Martin Energy Systems, 1995; pres. Lockheed Martin Energy Rsch. Corp., 1996—; head del. joint NAS and Soviet Acad. Scis. mtg. and conf. on energy and global ecol. problems, USSR, 1989; chmn. math. scis. ednl. bd. NAS, 1990-93; chmn. coordinating coun. for edn. NRC, 1991-93, mem. Commn. on Phys. Scis., Math. and Applications, 1993-96; bd. dirs. Bausch & Lomb, Inc., Rochester, N.Y.; mem. Tenn. Sci. and Tech. Adv. Commn., 1993-96, chmn., 1996—; adv. com. Federal Networking Coun., 1992-96. Author: Slow Wave Propagation in Plasma Wave Guides, 1966, Principles of Plasma Physics, 1973; also articles. Named Disting. Alumnus, Calif. Poly. State U., 1978, Calif. Inst. Tech., Pasadena, Calif., 1987; recipient U.S. Sec. of Energy's Gold medal for Disting. Svc., 1986; Guggenheim fellow, 1966. Fellow AAAS, IEEE (Outstanding Engr. award region 3 1995), Am. Phys. Soc.; mem. AAUP, NAE, Am. Nuclear Soc., Am. Assn. Physics Tchrs., Capital Hill Club, Nat. Press Club, Sigma Xi. Achievements include patents in field. Home: 8 Rivers Run Way Oak Ridge TN 37830-9004 Office: Oak Ridge Nat Lab Office of Dir PO Box 2008 Oak Ridge TN 37831-6255

TRIVELPIECE, CRAIG EVAN, computer electronics executive; b. Pasadena, Calif., Apr. 23, 1957; s. Alvin William and Shirley Ann T. Student, Calif. Inst. Tech., 1974-75; BA in Physics, U. Md., 1979. Scientist Maxwell Labs, San Diego, 1979-81; design engr. Rockwell Internat., Costa Mesa, Calif., 1981-83; mgr. engring. Tex. Instruments, Irvine, Calif., 1983-84; owner, pres. CST Engings Inc., Irvine, 1984-91, Circuit Plus, Inc., 1990—, 4 Every Wall, Inc., 1990-92, Transnational Telecom Inc., 1995—; cons. Payview Ltd., Hong Kong, 1985-88, Airmedia, Inc., 1996—. Coinventor: Video Scrambling System, 1985, home video product with Smart Card Access, 1992. Republican. Avocations: karate, judo, running, skiing, Japanese. Home: 3715 W Balboa Blvd Newport Beach CA 92663-3003 Office: Circuit Plus Inc 3345 Newport Blvd Newport Beach CA 92663-3826

TRIVISONNO, NICHOLAS LOUIS, communications company executive, accountant; b. Bklyn., Apr. 10, 1947; s. Nicholas John and Anne (Mucciardi) T.; m. Doris Frances Conaty; children: Drew Michael, Danielle Marie. BBA in Acctg., St. Francis Coll., Bklyn., 1968. CPA, N.Y., Conn., La. Ptnr. Arthur Andersen & Co., N.Y.C., 1979-85, mng. ptnr, Stamford, Conn., 1985-88; sr. v.p. fin. GTE Corp., Stamford, 1988—. Bd. dirs. St. Joseph Med. Ctr., Stamford, 1986—, Jr. Achievement, Stamford, 1986—; mem. Gov.'s Task Force Am. Shakespeare Theatre, Conn., 1987-88. Mem. Am. Inst. CPA's, N.Y. State Soc. CPA's. Conn. Soc. CPA's, La. Soc. CPA's, Conn. Golf Club (Easton) (treas. 1986—). Republican. Roman Catholic. Avocation: Golf. Office: GTE 1 Stamford Forum Stamford CT 06901-3516

TROCANO, RUSSELL PETER, lawyer; b. Hackensack, N.J., Sept. 7, 1963; s. Rosario Mario and Barbara Ann (Costa) T. BA, Seton Hall U., 1984; JD, Fordham U., 1987, LLM, 1992. Bar: N.J. 1987, N.Y. 1988. Law clk. to presiding justice County of Middlesex, New Brunswick, N.J., 1987-88; assoc. Sellar Richardson Law Firm, Newark and Roseland, N.J., 1988, Morgan Melhuish Monaghan Law Firm, Livingston, N.J., 1988-89; prin., owner Russell P. Trocano, Ridgewood, N.J., 1989—. Mem. San Guisseppe Societa de Santa Croce de Camerina, Paterson, N.J., 1989—. Fordham U. scholar, 1987. Mem. ABA, N.J. Bar Assn., N.Y. State Bar Assn., Bergen County Bar Assn., Passaic County Bar Assn., Brehon Law Soc., Arthur T. Vanderbilt Inn of Cts., Phi Alpha Theta. Roman Catholic. Avocations: mineral collecting, travel, reading. Home: 60 S Maple Ave Ridgewood NJ 07450-4542 Office: 7 E Ridgewood Ave Ridgewood NJ 07450-3807

TRODDEN, STEPHEN ANTHONY, federal agency administrator; b. Washington, D.C., Dec. 13, 1939; s. Stephen Albertson and Margaret Mary (Myers) T.; m. Regina Lee Miller, Dec. 26, 1962; children: Mark Andrew, Sharon Ruth. BS in Engring., U. Mich., 1962; JD, Georgetown U., 1965. Bar: Va. 1965. Indsl. engr. U.S. Army Materiel Command, 1962-66; staff officer missile systems U.S. Army Missile Command, 1966-69; tech. advisor, budget analyst Directorate for Procurement, Office of Sec. Def., 1969-73; dep. dir. R & D Office Asst. Sec. Defense, 1973-75, dep. dir., 1975-81, dir. procurement, 1981-83; dir. major acquisition programs Dept. Defense, 1983-86; asst. insp. gen. auditing Office of Insp. Gen., 1986-90; insp. gen. Dept. Vets. Affairs, 1990-96; ret., 1996; chmn. inspection com. Pres. Coun. Integrity and Efficiency, Washington, 1990-94. Lay dir. No. Va. Cursillo Movement, 1988-91. Recipient Meritorious Civilian Svc. award Sec. Defense, Washington, 1983, Disting. Civilian Svc. award, 1990, Meritorious Exec. Pres. rank award U.S. Govt., 1990. Mem. Va. State Bar. Avocations: basketball, jogging, beach, reading, bicycling. *

TROEN, PHILIP, physician, educator; b. Portland, Maine, Nov. 24, 1925; s. Ben and Gertrude (Cope) T.; m. Betty Ann Zelig, Mar. 22, 1953 (dec.); children: Mark Lawrence, Bruce Robert, Gail Sheri. A.B., Harvard U., 1944, M.D., 1948. Diplomate: Nat. Bd. Med. Examiners, Am. Bd. Internal Medicine. Intern Boston City Hosp., 1948-49, asst. resident in medicine, 1949-50; resident in medicine Beth Israel Hosp., Boston, 1950, 52-53; chief resident Beth Israel Hosp., 1953-54, asst. in medicine, 1955-56, USPHS research fellow, 1955-56, assoc. in med. research, 1956-64, assoc. in medicine, 1956-58, asst. vis. physician, 1959-64; teaching fellow Harvard Med. Sch., 1952-53, asst. in medicine, 1953-54, research fellow, 1955-56, instr. medicine, 1956-59, asso. in medicine, 1959-60, asst. prof., 1960-64; prof. medicine U. Pitts. Sch. Medicine, 1964—, assoc. chmn. dept. medicine, 1969-79, vice chmn. dept. medicine, 1979-90, interim chief divsn. of endocrinology and metabolism, 1995—, physician in chief Montefiore Univ. Hosp., 1964-90, physician in chief emeritus, 1990—; sci. counselor NIH, key cons. contraceptive devel. br., 1980; sci. counselor rev. Intramural Reproductive Biology Program, Nat. Inst. Child Health and Human Devel., 1977; cons. male fertility and infertility Nat. Inst. Occupational Safety and Health, 1977; mem. med. res. service merit rev. bd. in endocrinology VA, 1979-82; mem. contract rev. com. Nat. Inst. Child Health and Human Devel., 1975-84, chmn., 1976-89, reviewer intramural site visit devel. endocrinology br., 1983, 87; mem. endocrinologic and metabolic drugs adv. com. FDA, 1984-88, chmn. 1987-88; mem. expert advisor panel on occupational health, WHO, 1987-96. Mem. editorial bd. Jour. Andrology, Jour. Clin. Endocrinology and Metabolism, Internat. Jour. Andrology, Andrologia; contbr. articles to profl. jours. Served to capt. M.C., AUS, 1950-52. Fellow in endocrinology and metabolism Mayo Clinic, Rochester, Minn., 1954-55; Kendall-Hench research fellow, 1955; Ziskind teaching fellow, 1956-59; Med. Found. Greater Boston research fellow, 1959-63; Guggenheim fellow Stockholm, 1960-61. Mem. AAAS, Assn. Am. Physicians, Am. Soc. Clin. Investigation, Am. Soc. for Biochemistry and Molecular Biology, Am. Fedn. Clin. Rsch., Am. Soc. Andrology (program and publs. com., exec. coun., 1977-79, v.p. 1979-80, pres. 1980-81, chmn. publ. com. 1990-93, Disting. Andrologist award 1991, Disting. Svc. award 1996), Internat. Soc. Andrology (sec. 1981-89, pres. 1989-93), Endocrine Soc. (publ. com. 1984-90, chmn. 1987-90), N.Y. Acad. Scis., Ctrl. Soc. Clin. Rsch., Soc. Study of Reproduction. Office: U Pitts Med Ctr 200 Lothrop St Rm 548 Falk Pittsburgh PA 15213-2546

TROGANI, MONICA, ballet mistress; b. Newark, Sept. 2, 1963; m. Jay Brooker, July 3, 1993. Grad. high sch., 1980. Ballet dancer N.J. Ballet, West Orange, 1980-83; field asst., coder Reichman Rsch., Inc., N.Y.C., 1984-86; ballet mistress, prin. dancer Dance Theatre of L.I., Port Washington, N.Y., 1984-88; exec. sec. programming dept. The First N.Y. Internat. Festival of the Arts, N.Y.C., 1987-89; guest regisseur Alta. Ballet, Edmonton, Can., 1988-89, ballet mistress, asst. to artistic dir., 1989-93; guest regisseur Ballet du Nord, Roubaix, France, 1991, Dance Theatre of Harlem, N.Y.C., 1993-94; ballet mistress Les Grands Ballets Canadiens, Montreal, 1994—. Avocation: singing. Office: Les Grands Ballets Canadien, 4816 Rue Rivard, Montreal, PQ Canada H2J 2N6*

TROIDL, RICHARD JOHN, banker; b. Buffalo, July 2, 1944; s. Henry Albert and Lola Julian (Davern) T.; m. Diane Budney, Nov. 20, 1982; children: Nicholas, Holly. AAS, SUNY, Buffalo, 1973. Sr. v.p. Empire Am. Fed. Savs. Bank, Buffalo, 1969-93; pres. Express Svcs. of Am., Inc., Las Vegas, Nev., 1993—. With U.S. Army, 1965-71. Home: 6120 W Tropicana #A16 Las Vegas NV 89103-4694 Office: Express Svcs Am Inc 6120 W Tropicana Ave Ste A-16 Las Vegas NV 89103-4694

TROISPOUX, CHRISTIANNE VALERIE ANN, psychologist; b. Pasadena, Calif., June 10, 1968; d. Claude and Georgette (Guestault) T. BA in Psychology, Mt. St. Mary's Coll., 1990; MA in Psychology, Calif. State U, Northridge, 1993. Cert. sch. psychologist. Ednl. therapist Hillside Devel. Learning Ctr., La Canada, Calif., 1990-93; sch. psychologist L.A. Unified Sch. Dist., 1993—. Mem. Calif. Assn. Sch. Psychologists, NOW. Democrat. Roman Catholic. Avocations: arts and crafts, biking, hiking, reading. Office: LAUSD Spl Edn 450 N Grand Ave Los Angeles CA 90012-2123

TROLANDER, HARDY WILCOX, engineering executive, consultant; b. Chgo., June 2, 1921; s. Elmer Wilcox and Freda Marie (Zobel) T.; m. Imogen Davenport, July 3, 1946; children: Megan, Patricia. BS in Engring., Antioch Coll., 1947. Instr. Antioch Coll., Yellow Springs, Ohio, 1947-48; co-founder, CEO Yellow Springs Instrument Co., Inc., 1948-86; dir., co-founder Cook Design Ctr., Dartmouth Coll., Hanover, N.H., 1975-88; bd. dirs. Deban Inc., Yellow Springs, Camax Tool co., Arvada, Colo. Contbr. articles to profl. jours.; patentee in field. Co-founder, trustee Yellow Springs Community Found., 1974-83; trustee Autioch Coll., 1968-74, chmn. bd., 1972-74; trustee Engring. and Sci. Found., Dayton, 1982-96, Engrs. Club Dayton Found., 1994—, Engring. and Sci. Hall of Fame, 1994—; mem. adv. bd. Coll. Engring. and Computer Sci. Wright State U., 1993—; bd. dirs. united Way Greater Dayton Area, 1984-92. 1st lt. U.S. Army Air Corps., 1943-46. Named Outstanding Engr., Dayton Affiliate Socs., 1967, 89. Fellow Dayton Engrs. Club; mem. ACLU, Nat. Acad. Engring., Amnesty Internat. Democrat. Avocations: restoring antique radios and automobiles. Home and Office: 1475 President St Yellow Springs OH 45387-1326

TROLINGER, JAMES DAVIS, laser scientist; b. Shelbyville, Tenn., Mar. 2, 1940; s. Winston Perry and Euna Mae (Davis) T.; children: James D. Jr., Kristina Lin, Jonathan P. BS, U. Tenn., 1963; MS, La. State U., 1964; PhD, U. Tenn., 1967. Scientist Sverdrup Tech., Tullahoma, Tenn., 1967-73, Sci. Applications, Tullahoma, 1973-75; chief scientist, founder Spectron, Costa Mesa, Calif., 1975-88; gen. ptnr., founder MetroLaser, Irvine, Calif., 1988—; cons. Adv. Group for Aerospace R & D, NATO, Chatillon, France, 1985-88. Recipient George W. Goddard award Internat. Soc. Optical Engring., 1992. Home: 3417 Wimbledon Way Costa Mesa CA 92626-1645 Office: MetroLaser 18006 Sky Park Cir Irvine CA 92614-6406

TROLLER, FRED, graphic designer, painter, visual consultant, educator; b. Zurich, Switzerland, Dec. 12, 1930; came to U.S., 1961; s. Albert and Katherina (Iseli) T.; m. Beatrice Stocklin, Nov. 22, 1952; children—Simon, Meret. B.A. in Graphic Design, Kunstgewerbeschule, Zurich, 1950. Art dir. Geigy Corp., Ardsley, N.Y., 1961-66; pres. Fred Troller Assoc., Visual Communications Cons., Rye, N.Y., 1966—; chmn., prof. design div. design Sch. Art and Design N.Y. State Coll. Ceramics at Alfred U., 1991—. Author and illustrator articles. Served to pvt. 1st class Inf. Swiss Army, 1949-60. Mem. Am. Inst. Graphic Arts, Alliance Graphique Internationale. Home & Office: Fred Troller Assocs 12 Harbor Ln Rye NY 10580-2213

TROMBINO, ROGER A., food products executive; b. Kenosha, Wis., Sept. 23, 1939; s. Paul and Lena T.; m. Joann M. Buchholtz, 1961; children: Tracey, Suzanne, Steven. BS, U. Wis., 1962. CPA, Fla. Audit mgr. Ernst & Young, Chgo., 1962-73; sr. v.p., exec. officer Norin Corp./Norris Cos., Miami, Fla., 1973-85; executor, trustee Norris Group, Miami, 1986-92; exec. v.p. West Indies Sugar Corp. Chmn. bd. Bon Secours Hosp., Miami, 1979-94. Mem. Riviera Country Club.

TRONE, DONALD BURNELL, investment company executive; b. Gettysburg, Pa., Jan. 22, 1954; s. Donald Burnell and Mary Ann (Moreau) T.; children:from previous marriage Tara C., Donald Timothy. BS in Govt., USCG Acad., 1977; MS in Fin. Svcs., Am. Coll., Bryn Mawr, Pa., 1989. Registered investment adviser. Commd. ensign USCG, 1977, advanced through ranks to lt. comdr., 1988, aviator, 1977-87; resigned, 1987; sr v.p. Investment Adv. Svcs. of Raymond James, St. Petersburg, Fla., 1987-89, USF&G, Cin., 1989; v.p. mktg. SEI Wealth Mgmt., 1989-91; dir. investment mgmt. coun. divsn. div. Callan Assocs. Inc., San Francisco, 1991—. Pilot (film) Cocoon, 1985; co-author: Procedural Prudence, 1991, The Management of Investment Decisions, 1995. Recipient Sikorsky Heroism award United Techs., 1981. Republican. Episcopalian. Home: 3 Rose Ct Sausalito CA 94965-2065 Office: Callan Assocs Inc 71 Stevenson St Ste 1300 San Francisco CA 94105-2960

TROOBOFF, PETER DENNIS, lawyer; b. Balt., June 22, 1942; s. Benjamin M. and Rebecca C. (Cohen) T.; m. Rhoda Morss, Aug. 10, 1969; children: Hannah, Abigail. BA cum laude, Columbia U., 1964; LLB cum laude, Harvard U., 1967; LLM, London Sch. Econs., 1968; diploma cum laude, Hague (Netherlands) Acad. Internat. Law, 1968. Bar: N.Y. 1968, D.C. 1970. Rsch. assoc., Harvard U. Law Sch., 1968-69; asst. to exec. editor for The Advocates, Sta. WGBH-TV, Boston, 1969; assoc. Covington & Burling, Washington, 1969-75, ptnr., 1975—; lectr., dir. seminars The Hague Acad. Internat. Law, 1972, 82, lectr., 1986, mem. curatorium, 1991—; lectr. The Hague Acad. External Programn Beijing, 1987, Harare, 1993, internat. orgns. U. Va. Sch. Law, 1973; head U.S. del. 3d Inter-Am. Specialized Conf. Pvt. Internat. Law, La Paz, Bolivia, 1984; mem. U.S. del. Hague Conf. private internat. law, 1993, 96; mem. sec. of state adv. com. private internat. law, 1990—. Frank Knox Meml. fellow. Mem. Coun. Fgn. Rels., Am. Soc. Internat. Law (pres. 1990-92, bd. editors Am. Jour. of Internat. Law 1980-92, 94—), Internat. Law Assn., Washington Inst. Fgn. Affairs. Club: Cosmos, City (Washington). Contbr. chpts., articles to profl. publs.; editor: Law and Responsibility in Warfare-The Vietnam Experience, 1975. Office: Covington & Burling PO Box 7566 1201 Pennsylvania Ave NW Washington DC 20044

TROOST, BRADLEY TODD, neurologist, educator; b. Mankato, Minn., July 5, 1937; s. Henry Bradley and Elizabeth (Todd) T.; m. Elizabeth Gail Godet, Apr. 17, 1976; children: Elizabeth Claire, Laurie Anne. BS with honors in Biophysics, Yale U., 1959; MD, Harvard U., 1963. Diplomate Am. Bd. Psychiatry and Neurology. Intern, Colo. Gen. Hosp., Denver, 1963-64; resident in neurology U. Colo., Denver, 1966-69; NIH fellow in neuro-ophthalmology U. Calif.-San Francisco, 1969-70; asst. prof. U. Miami (Fla.), 1970-76; assoc. prof. U. Pitts., 1976-80; prof. Case Western Res. U., Cleve., 1980-83; prof., chmn. dept. neurology Bowman Gray Sch. Medicine, Winston-Salem, N.C., 1983—; chief dept. neurology VA med. ctrs., Pitts., Cleve. Bd. dirs. Greater Miami Epilepsy Found., 1973-76. Served to capt. U.S. Army, 1964-66. Fellow Am. Acad. Neurology; mem. Am. Neurol. Assn., Am. Assn. Univ. Profs. Neurology (pres.-elect), Barany Soc. Republican. Episcopalian. Contbr. numerous articles to profl. publs.*

TROST, BARRY MARTIN, chemist, educator; b. Phila., June 13, 1941; s. Joseph and Esther T.; m. Susan Paula Shapiro, Nov. 25, 1967; children: Aaron David, Carey Daniel. B.A. cum laude, U. Pa., 1962; Ph.D., MIT, 1965; D (hon.), U Claude Bernard, Lyons, France, 1994, Technion, Israel, 1997. Mem. faculty U. Wis., Madison, 1965—, prof., chemistry, 1969—, Evan P. and Marion Helfaer prof. chemistry, from 1976; Vilas rsch. prof. chemistry U. Wis.; prof. chemistry Stanford U., 1987—, Tamaki prof. humanities and scis., 1990, chmn. dept., 1996—; cons. Merck, Sharp & Dohme, E.I. duPont de Nemours.; Chem. Soc. centenary lectr., 1982. Author: Problems in Spectroscopy, 1967, Sulfur Ylides, 1975; editor-in-chief Comprehensive Organic Synthesis, 1991—, ChemTracts/Organic Chemistry, 1993—; editor: Structure and Reactivity Concepts in Organic Chemistry series, 1972—; assoc. editor Jour. Am. Chem. Soc., 1974-80; mem. editl. bd. Organic Reactions Series, 1971—, Chemistry A European Jour., 1995—, Sci. of Synthesis, Houben-Weyl Methods of Molecular Transformations, 1995—; contbr. numerous articles to profl. jours. Recipient Dreyfus Found. Tech.-Scholar award, 1970, 77, Creative Work in Synthetic Organic Chemistry award, 1981, Baekland medal, 1981, Alexander von Humboldt award, 1984, Guenther award, 1990, Janssen prize, 1990, Roger Adams award Am. Chem. Soc. 1995; named Chem. Pioneer, Am. Inst. Chemists, 1983; NSF fellow, 1963-65, Sloan Found. fellow, 1967-69, Am. Swiss Found. fellow, 1975—, Zencca fellow, 1997; Cope scholar, 1989. Mem. AAAS, Am. Chem. Soc. (award in pure chemistry 1977, Roger Adams award 1995), Nat. Acad. Scis., Am. Acad. Arts and Scis., Chem. Soc. London. Office: Stanford U Dept Chemistry Stanford CA 94305

TROST, CARLISLE ALBERT HERMAN, retired naval officer; b. Valmeyer, Ill., Apr. 24, 1930; s. Elmer Herman and Luella Caroline (Hoffman) T.; m. Pauline Louise Haley, May 1, 1954; children—Carl, Laura Lee, Steven, Kathleen. Student, Washington U., St. Louis, 1948-49; B.S., U.S. Naval Acad., 1953; Olmsted scholar, U. Freiburg, W. Ger., 1960-62. Commd. ensign U.S. Navy, 1953, advanced through grades to adm., 1985; exec. officer U.S.S. Scorpion, 1962-63, U.S.S. Von Steuben, 1963-65; mil. asst. to Dep. Sec. Def., 1965-68; comdg. officer U.S.S. Sam Rayburn, 1968-69; staff Comdr. Sub Force Atlantic, 1969-70; exec. asst. to Sec. Navy, 1970-73; comdr. Submarine Group Five, 1973-74; asst. chief Bur. Naval Personnel, 1974-76; dir. systems analysis div. Office Chief Naval Ops., Washington, 1976-78; dep. comdr.-in-chief U.S. Pacific Fleet, 1978-80; comdr. U.S. Seventh Fleet, 1980-81; dir. Navy program planning Office Chief Naval Ops., 1981-85; comdr.-in-chief U.S. Atlantic Fleet, 1985-86, chief naval ops., 1986-90; bd. dirs. Lockheed Martin Corp., La. Land and Exploration, Gen. Pub. Utility Corp., GPU Nuclear Corp., Bird-Johnson Co., Gen. Dynamics Corp., Precision Components Corp. Trustee U.S. Naval Acad. Found. Decorated Def. D.S.M. with cluster, Navy D.S.M. with 2 clusters, Army D.S.M., Air Force D.S.M., Legion of Merit with 2 oak leaf clusters, Navy Achievement medal, Def. Disting. Svc. medal; named Outstanding Young Man of Am. Nat. Jr. C. of C., 1964. Mem. U.S. Naval Inst., U.S. Naval Alumni Assn. (trustee). Episcopalian. Home: 10405 Windsor View Dr Rockville MD 20854-4025

TROST, EILEEN BANNON, lawyer; b. Teaneck, N.J., Jan. 9, 1951; d. William Eugene and Marie Thelma (Finlayson) Bannon; m. Lawrence Peter Trost Jr., Aug. 27, 1977; children: Lawrence Peter III, William Patrick, Timothy Alexander. BA with great distinction, Shimer Coll., 1972; JD cum laude, U. Minn., 1976. Bar: Ill. 1976, U.S. Dist. Ct. (no. dist.) Ill. 1976, Minn. 1978, U.S. Tax Ct. 1978, U.S. Supreme Ct. 1981. Assoc. McDermott, Will & Emery, Chgo., 1976-82, ptnr., 1982-93; v.p. No. Trust Bank Ariz. N.A., Phoenix, 1993-95; ptnr. Sonninachein Nath & Rosenthal, Chgo., 1995—. Mem. Am. Coll. Trust and Estate Coun., Minn. Bar Assn., Internat. Acad. Estate and Trust Law. Roman Catholic. Office: Sonnenschein Nath & Rosenthal 8000 Sears Tower Chicago IL 60606

TROST, J. RONALD, lawyer; b. Fresno, Calif., Nov. 27, 1932; s. David Trost and Betty (Shapiro) Buno; m. Florence Stern; children: Gregory, Larry, Leslie, Jacqueline. BA, Rice U., 1954; JD, U. Tex., 1957. Bar: Tex. 1957, D.C. 1960, Calif. 1963, N.Y. 1994. With U.S. Dept. Justice, Washington, 1957-59; pvt. practice law Washington, 1959-62; pvt. practice L.A., 1963—; ptnr. Sidley & Austin, L.A., 1980—; adj. prof. law UCLA; instr. law U. So. Calif., Los Angeles. Contbr. articles to law revs. and jours.; contbg. editor Collier on Bankruptcy. Served with U.S. Army, 1957-63. Mem.

ABA, Am. Law Inst., Nat. Bankruptcy Conf. Office: Sidley & Austin 875 3rd Ave New York NY 10022-6225

TROSTEL, MICHAEL FREDERICK, architect; b. Balt., May 19, 1931; s. Louis Jacob and Katharine (Fisher) T. BArch, U. Pa., 1954, MArch, 1957; diploma, Ecole des Beaux Arts, Fontainebleau, France, 1957. Registered architect, Md., D.C., Va. Draftsman Taylor & Fisher, Balt., 1958-59, Fisher, Nes, Campbell & Ptnrs., Balt., 1959-60; assoc. James R. Edmunds, Jr., Balt., 1960-73; v.p. Edmunds & Hyde, Balt., 1973-81; prin. Michael F. Trostel, FAIA, Balt., 1981-94, Trostel & Pearre, 1995—; mem. adv. bd. Md. House and Garden Pilgrimage, 1982—; archtl. advisor Hammond-Harwood House Assn., 1988-94. Author: Mount Clare, 1981, Domestic Maryland Architecture, 1984, Wines and Other Potables in Maryland, 1987, Mondawmin: Baltimore's Last Country Estate, 1991, The Maryland Orangeries, 1996; editor Architect's Report mag., 1963-65. Bd. dirs. Balt. Heritage, Inc., 1970-73, Am. Wing Balt. Mus. Art, 1994—; mem. art commn. City of Balt., 1972-80, chmn., 1978-80; mem. gov.'s com. for Nat. Register Hist. Places, State of Md., 1984—, vice-chmn., 1987-92, chmn., 1993, 95. Recipient Award of Excellence, Balt. Bldg. Congress, 1980, 83, 87, Honor award Balt. Heritage, 1986, 90, Commendation award Preservation Md., 1986, 90, Preservation award Md. Hist. Trust, 1991, 92, 96. Fellow AIA (mem. com. on hist. preservation); mem. Soc. for Preservation of Md. Antiques (bd. dirs. 1965-68, 81-84, sec. 1968-79), Nat. Trust for Hist. Preservation (mem. bd. advisors 1990—, Honor award 1992), Assn. for Preservation of Tech., Soc. Archtl. Historians, Vernacular Architecture Form, Soc. Colonial Wars, Md. Club. Home and Office: 1307 Bolton St Baltimore MD 21217-4102

TROSTEN, LEONARD MORSE, lawyer; b. Bklyn., Jan. 25, 1932; s. David and Anne Bertha (Belkin) T.; m. Arthea Howell Dickson, Aug. 21, 1954 (dec. Jan. 1978); children: Amanda Trosten-Bloom, Jessica Howell Trosten Forrest; m. Addie Jane Tyner Harris, Jan. 12, 1979; children: Hope Harris Pampillonia, Arthur F.M. Harris. A.B., Columbia U., 1953, LL.B., 1955. Bar: N.Y. 1955, D.C. 1965. Assoc. Dwight, Royall, Harris, Koegel & Caskey, N.Y.C., 1955-58; with Office of Gen. Counsel AEC, Washington, 1958-64; staff counsel Joint Congrl. Com. on Atomic Energy, Washington, 1964-67; ptnr. LeBoeuf, Lamb, Leiby & MacRae, Washington, 1968-90, of counsel, 1991—. Contbr. articles to profl. jours.; editor Columbia Law Rev., 1953-55. Mem. Columbia Country Club (Chevy Chase, Md.), The Landings Club (Savannah, Ga.), Rotary, The Oglethorpe Club (Savannah, Ga.), Phi Beta Kappa. Republican. Episcopalian. Avocations: bridge, walking. Home: 3 Mainsail Crossing Savannah GA 31411-2723 Office: LeBoeuf Lamb Greene MacRae 1875 Connecticut Ave NW Washington DC 20009-5728

TRÖSTER, ALEXANDER I., neuropsychologist, educator; b. Vienna, Austria, Oct. 16, 1960; came to U.S., 1984; s. Guy W. and Christine U. (Rieder) T.; m. Kristy A. Straits. BSc in Psychology with honors, U. Zimbabwe, Harare, 1983; MS, N.D. State U., 1986; PhD, San Diego State U. & U. Calif., San Diego, 1991. Lic. psychologist, Kans., Mo. Asst. prof. psychology Wash. State U., Pullman, 1991-93; asst. prof. neurology U. Kans. Med. Ctr., Kansas City, 1993—; external grant reviewer Dept. Vets. Affairs Rsch. Svc., Md., 1995—; ad hoc reviewer Jour. Neuropsychiatry and Clin. Neurosci., Washington, 1995—, Brain and Cognition, San Diego, 1995—, Jour. Clin. and Exptl. Neuropsychology, The Netherlands, 1994—; presenter in field. Contbr. numerous articles to profl. jours., chpts. to books. Fellow Epilepsy Found. Am., 1988, 89; recipient Butters award for rsch. contbns. to clin. neuropsychology Nat. Acad. Neuropsychology, 1993. Mem. APA, Internat. Neuropsychol. Assn., Am. Neuropsychiat. Assn., Behavioral Neurology Soc., Am. Epilepsy Soc., Movement Disorder Soc. Avocations: travel, cooking. Office: U Kans Med Ctr Neurology Dept 3901 Rainbow Blvd Kansas City KS 66160-0001

TROSTORFF, ALEXANDER PETER, lawyer; b. Queens, N.Y., Apr. 6, 1951; s. Peter W. and Cecilia (Rott) T.; m. Danielle Lombardo, June 30, 1984. BA, Davidson Coll., 1973; JD, Washington U., 1976; LLM in Taxation, Georgetown U., 1981. Bar: N.Y. 1978, La. 1981. Tax law specialist IRS, Washington, 1978-80; assoc. Jones, Walker, Waechter, Poitevant, Carrere & Denegre, New Orleans, 1980-84, ptnr., 1984—. Lutheran. Avocations: tennis, basketball, golf. Home: 1414 Eleonore St New Orleans LA 70115-4318 Office: Jones Walker Waechter Poitevant Carrere & Denegre 201 Saint Charles Ave New Orleans LA 70170-1000

TROTMAN, ALEXANDER J., automobile manufacturing company executive; b. 1933; married. MBA, Mich. State U., 1972. Various positions Ford Motor Co., Europe, 1955-69, Dearborn, Mich., 1969-71, dir. sales and mktg. planning, 1971-72, exec. dir. product planning and research, 1972-75, chief car planning mgr. Car Product Devel. Group, 1975-77, exec. dir. ops. planning, 1977-78, asst. gen. mgr. truck and recreational products ops., 1978-79, corp. v.p., from 1979, v.p. truck ops. Ford of Europe, Inc., then pres. Ford Asia-Pacific Inc., 1983-84, pres., chmn. Ford of Europe, Inc., from 1984, then exec. v.p. No. Am. auto ops., 1989, now chmn. bd., pres., CEO, dir. Ford Motor Co., 1993—; bd. dirs. IBM Corp., Armonk, N.Y., NYSE, Imperial Chem. Industries, London. Served with RAF, 1951-55. Office: Ford Motor Co The American Rd Dearborn MI 48121

TROTT, SABERT SCOTT, II, marketing professional; b. Concord, N.C., Nov. 21, 1941; s. Sabert Scott and Mary Welker (Crooks) T.; m. Brenda Lee Bost, Nov. 27, 1964; children—Sabert Scott III, David Lee. B.S. in Textile Tech., N.C. State U., 1964; M.B.A., U. N.C., 1969. Mgr. trainee Cannon Mills Co., Kannapolis, N.C., 1969-70, mktg. mgr., 1970-75, v.p. mktg., 1975-82, sr. v.p. mktg., 1982-86, dir. telemktg. and premium sales, 1987-89; mgr. spl. markets, mktg. & sales Fieldcrest Cannon Inc., mktg. mgr., telemarketing sales mgr., 1989-92; v.p. mktg. and sales Spencer's Inc., Mt. Airy, N.C., 1992-93; v.p. mktg. Carpenter Co., Richmond, Va., 1994—. Chmn. Cabarrus-Rowan Parks and Recreation Commn., N.C., 1982-86; mem. Cabarrus County Parks and Recreation Commn., N.C., 1980-88; Rep. candidate County Commr., Cabarrus County, 1990; bd. dirs. Cabarrus Meml. Hosp., 1992, N.C. Ctr. for Applied Textile Tech.; vestryman local Episcopal ch., 1988-93. Capt. U.S. Army, 1965-70. Decorated Commendation medal (2). Republican. Lodge: Rotary. Avocations: canoeing; rafting; golf; basketball; racquetball. Home: 2607 Helmsley Ct Midlothian VA 23113 Office: Carpenter Co 5016 Monument Ave Richmond VA 23230-3620

TROTT, STEPHEN SPANGLER, federal judge, musician; b. Glen Ridge, N.J., Dec. 12, 1939; s. David Herman and Virginia (Spangler) T.; divorced; children: Christina, Shelley. B.A., Wesleyan U., 1962; LL.B., Harvard U., 1965; LLD (hon.), Santa Clara U., 1992. Bar: Calif. 1966, U.S. Dist. Ct. (cen. dist.) Calif. 1966, U.S. Ct. Appeals (9th cir.) 1983, U.S. Supreme Ct. 1984. Guitarist, mem. The Highwaymen, 1958—; dep. dist. atty. Los Angeles County Dist. Atty.'s Office, Los Angeles, 1966-75; chief dep. dist. atty. Los Angeles County Dist. Atty.'s Office, 1975-79; U.S. dist. atty. Central Dist. Calif., Los Angeles, 1981-83; asst. atty. gen. criminal div. Dept. Justice, Washington, 1983-86; mem. faculty Nat. Coll. Dist. Attys., Houston, 1973—; chmn. central dist. Calif. Law Enforcement Coordinating Com., Houston, 1981-83; coordinator Los Angeles-Nev. Drug Enforcement Task Force, 1982-83; assoc. atty. gen. Justice Dept., Washington, 1986-88; chmn. U.S. Interpol, 1986-88; judge U.S. Ct. of Appeals 9th Cir., Boise, Idaho, 1988—; chmn. U.S. Interpol. Trustee Wesleyan U., 1984-87; bd. dirs. Children's Home Soc., Idaho, 1990—, Boise Philharm. Assn., 1995—. Recipient Gold record as singer-guitarist for Michael Row the Boat Ashore, 1961, Disting. Faculty award Nat. Coll. Dist. Attys., 1977. Mem. Am. Coll. Trial Lawyers, Wilderness Fly Fishers Club (pres. 1975-77), Brentwood Racing Pigeon Club (pres. 1977-82), Magic Castle, Internat. Brotherhood Magicians, Idaho Classic Guitar Soc. (founder, pres. 1989—). Republican. Office: US Ct Appeals 9th Cir 666 US Courthouse 550 W Fort St Boise ID 83724-0101

TROTTA, FRANK PAUL, JR., lawyer; b. New Rochelle, N.Y., Jan. 19, 1955; s. Frank Anthony Trotta and Lorraine Burigo. BA, SUNY, Albany, 1975; JD, Union U., Albany, 1978; LLM, NYU, 1986; MBA, Columbia U., 1992. Bar: N.Y. 1979, U.S. Dist. Ct. (no. and we. dists.) N.Y. 1979, U.S. Ct. Mil. Appeals 1979, U.S. Dist. Ct. (so. and ea. dists.) N.Y. 1980, U.S. Ct. Internat. Trade 1980, U.S. Tax Ct. 1982, U.S. Supreme Ct. 1982, U.S. Ct. Appeals (D.C. cir.) 1983, U.S. Ct. Customs and Patent Appeals 1984, D.C. 1985, Conn. 1988, Pa. 1991. Assoc. Weil, Gotshal & Manges, N.Y.C., 1978-81; gen. counsel Lehrman for Gov., N.Y.C., 1981-82; pvt. practice Washington, N.Y.C., 1981-86, New Rochelle, 1981-92, Greenwich, Conn., 1986—; bd. dirs. Numbercrunchers Inc., New Rochelle, N.Y., Lehrman, Bell Mueller Cannon Inc., Arlington, Va.; mng. dir. N.Y. Consultancy, New Rochelle, 1981—; gen. counsel L.E. Lehrman Corp., Pa., 1982—, sec., treas., 1983—, COO, 1986—; gen. counsel Citizens for Am., Washington, 1983-87, sec., treas., 1985-87; sec., v.p., treas. Monroe Corp., Harrisburg, Pa., 1985-86, pres., 1986-90; mem. bd. govs. Fund for Justice and Edn., 1987-90, ABA, 1987-90; bd. advs. U.S. Fed. Small Bus., Schenectady, N.Y., 1985-95; mem. faculty Practicing Law Inst., 1979; governing mem. Nat. Jud. Coll., 1987-90, Am. Bar Endowment, 1987-90, ABRA Pension Fund, 1987-90; chmn. bd. advisors Columbia U. Grad. Sch. Bus., Inst. for Non-for-Profit Mgmt., 1992-95; devel. com. Greenwich Cath. Sch., 1994-96; chair fin. com. St. Mary's Parish, Greenwich, 1994-96. Author: Lois Lane's On Hold: What a Lawyer Should Do if a Reporter Calls, 1987; (with others) Federal Regulation of Consumer Credit, 1979; co-editor: Finishing First: A Campaign Manual, 1983, Starting and Organizing a Business-A Legal & Tax Guide for Small Business; legal corr. The Westchester Eagle; patentee system and method for automated shopping. Mem. nat. com. Cath. Campaign Am.; chmn. New Rochelle Rep. Party, 1982-85. Named one of Outstanding Young Men Am., 1976. Fellow Am. Bar Found. (life); mem. N.Y. State Bar Assn. (mem. assn. pub. rels. com., mem. banking law com. bus. law sect., mem. election law com., mem. task force on solo and small practices), Am. Arbitration Assn., Guild of Cath. Lawyers (mem. ethics com.), Mensa Internat., Pro-Life Athletes (mem. dinner com.), Columbian Lawyers Westchester (bd. dirs.), Knights of Malta. Avocations: computers, politics, magic. Address: 1 Fawcett Pl Ste 131 Greenwich CT 06830

TROTTER, F(REDERICK) THOMAS, retired academic administrator; b. L.A., Apr. 17, 1926; s. Fred B. and Hazel (Thomas) T.; m. Gania Demaree, June 27, 1953; children—Ruth Elizabeth, Paula Anne (dec.), Tania, Mary. AB, Occidental Coll., 1950, DD, 1968; STB, Boston U., 1953, PhD, 1958; LHD, Ill. Wesleyan U., 1974, Cornell Coll., 1985, Westmar Coll., 1987; LLD, U. Pacific, 1978, Wesleyan Coll., 1981; EdD, Columbia Coll., 1984; LittD, Alaska Pacific U., 1987. Exec. sec. Boston U. Student Christian Assn., 1951-54; ordained elder Calif.-Pacific, Methodist Ch., 1953; pastor Montclair (Calif.) Meth. Ch., 1956-59; lectr. So. Calif. Sch. Theology at Claremont, 1957-59, instr., 1959-60, asst. prof., 1960-63, assoc. prof., 1963-66, prof., 1966, dean, 1961; prof. religion and arts, dean Sch. Theology Claremont, 1961-73; mem. Bd. Higher Edn. and Ministry, United Meth. Ch., 1972-73, gen. sec., 1973-87; pres. Alaska Pacific U., Anchorage, 1988-95; ret., 1995; dir. Inst. for Antiquity and Christianity at Claremont. Author: Jesus and the Historian, 1968, Loving God with One's Mind, 1987, weekly column local newspapers; editor-at-large: Christian Century, 1969-84. Trustee Dillard U. Served with USAAF, 1944-46. Kent fellow Soc. for Values in Higher Edn., 1954; Dempster fellow Meth. Ch., 1954. Mem. Rotary Internat. (Anchorage Downtown), Commonwealth North. Home: 75-136 Kiowa Dr Indian Wells CA 92210

TROTTER, HAYNIE SEAY, lawyer; b. Clarksville, Va., Feb. 24, 1931; s. William Augustus and Frances (Seay) T.; m. Marguerite Stapleford, Feb. 6, 1958 (dec. Feb. 1981); children: Richard Haynie, Frances Patricia; m. Katrin Gunnarsdottir, May 31, 1986. AB, Coll. of William & Mary, 1952; LLB, U. Va., 1957. Bar: Va. 1957, U.S. Dist. Ct. (ea. dist.) Va. 1957, U.S. Ct. Appeals (4th cir.) 1963, U.S. Supreme Ct. 1963. Sole practice Vienna, Va., 1957-58; assoc. William C. Bauknight, Fairfax, Va., 1958-59; ptnr. Bauknight, Williams, Swann & Trotter, Fairfax, 1959-61, Bauknight, Prichard, McCandlish & Williams, Fairfax, 1961-71, Boothe, Prichard & Dudley, McLean, Va., 1971-87, McGuire, Woods, Battle & Boothe, 1987—; ret.; bd. trustees Nat. Hosp. Orthopaedics and rehab., Alexandria, Va., 1981-93; bd. dirs. Network Health Plan, Alexandria. Mem. ABA, Va. Bar Assn., Fairfax Bar Assn., Assn. Trial Lawyers Am. Republican. Episcopalian. Avocations: tennis, fishing. Home: 9185 Old Dominion Dr Mc Lean VA 22102-1018 Office: McGuire Woods Battle & Boothe 8280 Greensboro Dr Ste 900 Mc Lean VA 22102-3807

TROTTER, HERMAN EAGER, JR. (HERMAN TROTTER), music critic; b. Providence, Sept. 25, 1925; s. Herman Eager, Sr. and Shelley Fern (Jones) T.; m. Johanne Marguerite Haberstro, Sept. 22, 1956 (div. Apr. 1996); children: Kim Avery. Holly Anne. Joy Caroline; m. Rosa Spillane Whetzle, July 22, 1996. BA, Yale U., 1946. Pub. utility sec. analyst Mass. Mut. Life Ins. Co., Springfield, 1947-51; sales engr. B-I-F Industries, Providence, 1951-56; asst. sec. Buffalo Batt and Felt Co, Depew, N.Y., 1956-68; account exec. Harold Warner Advt., Buffalo, N.Y., 1968-77; freelance music critic Buffalo News, 1968-77, staff music critic, 1977—. Contbr. articles to profl. and popular jours. Program annotator Buffalo Philharm., 1964-70. Lt. (j.g.) USN, 1943-46, PTO. Mem. Music Critics Assn. (v.p. 1988-93). Avocations: travel, skiing, record collecting. Home: 125 Edward St No 1 J Buffalo NY 14201 Office: The Buffalo News PO Box 100 Buffalo NY 14240-0100

TROTTER, LESLIE EARL, operations research educator, consultant; b. Muskogee, Okla., Nov. 17, 1943; s. Leslie Earl and Sylvia Helene (Freeze) T.; m. Jomi Tuggle, July 19, 1968 (div. Dec. 1995); children: Colleen Nicole, Eamonn Scott. AB in Math., Princeton U., 1965; MS in Indsl. and Systems Engring., Ga. Inst. Tech., 1971; PhD in Ops. Rsch., Cornell U., 1973. Sci. computer programmer Lockheed-Ga. Co., Marietta, 1965-68; computer applications analyst Control Data Corp., Atlanta, 1968-70; postdoctoral rsch. assoc. Math. Rsch. Ctr., U. Wis., Madison, 1973; asst. prof. Yale U. Sch. Orgn. and Mgmt., New Haven, 1974-75; assoc. prof. ops. rsch. Cornell U. Sch. Ops. Rsch. and Indsl. Engring., Ithaca, N.Y., 1975-84, dir. of Sch., 1983-87, prof., 1984—; dir. Advanced Computational Optimization Lab. Cornell Theory Ctr., 1995—; vis. prof. Bonn (Germany) U., 1977-79, math. dept. E.P.F.L., Lausanne, Switzerland, 1984-85, 91-92, Math. Inst., Augsburg (Germany) U., 1987-88; vis. cons. Bell Labs., Holmdel, N.J., 1981. Editor optimization area Jour. Ops. Rsch., 1982-87; contbr. numerous articles to profl. jours. Recipient tchg. excellence awards Cornell U., 1977, 81, 93, 94, sr. U.S. scientist award Alexander von Humboldt Found., Germany, 1988; numerous rsch. grants NSF, 1974—, including High Performance Computing and Comms. Grand Challenge award, 1995—. Mem. Ops. Rsch. Soc. Am., Math. Programming Soc. (treas. 1988-94), Soc. for Indsl. and Applied Math. Avocations: running, skiing, music. Home: 161 Highgate Rd Ithaca NY 14850-1469 Office: Cornell U Sch Ops Rsch Engring Rhodes Hall Ithaca NY 14853

TROTTER, THOMAS ROBERT, lawyer; b. Akron, Ohio, Apr. 11, 1949; s. Fred and Josephine (Daley) T. BA, Ohio U., 1971; JD, Tulane U., 1975. Bar: Ohio 1975, U.S. Dist. Ct. (no. dist.) Ohio 1975. Assoc. Squire, Sanders & Dempsey, Cleve., 1975-80; mem. Buckingham, Doolittle & Burroughs, Akron, 1980—; chair taxation and legis. com. Akron Regional Devel. Bd., 1988-95. Trustee Akron Symphony Orch., 1984-93, Cascade CDC, Inc., Akron, 1983—, Akron/Summit Solid Waste Mgmt. Authority, 1994—, Weathervane Cmty. Playhouse, 1996—. Mem. ABA, Ohio Bar Assn. (chair local govt. law com.), Akron Bar Assn., Nat. Assn. Bond Lawyers, Sigma Alpha Epsilon. Democrat. Home: 589 Avalon Akron OH 44320-2048 Office: Buckingham Doolittle & Burroughs PO Box 1500 50 S Main St Akron OH 44308-1828

TROTTIER, BRYAN JOHN, professional sports team coach, former professional hockey player; b. Val Marie, Sask., Can., July 17, 1956; s. Eldon J. and Mary (Gardner) T.; m. Laura Lynn Theis, July 14, 1976; children-:Bryan John, Lindsay Ann. Student public schs., Val Marie; student, Swift Current Comprehensive High Sch. Mem. N.Y. Islanders Hockey Club, Farmingdale, 1975-90; owner, operator Bryan Trottier Skating Acad., Port Washington, N.Y.; player Pitts. Penguins, 1990-93; asst. coach Pittsburgh Penguins, 1993—; hockey cons. Right Guard Corp., Phila; spokesman 1980 Winter Olympics, Lake Placid, N.Y.; pres. NHL Player's Assn. Recipient Calder Meml. trophy as Rookie of Yr. Nat. Hockey League, 1976; Hart Meml. trophy as Most Valuable Player, 1979; Art Ross trophy as Leading Scorer; Conn Smythe trophy as Most Valuable Player in Nat. Hockey League Playoffs, 1979-80. Office: Pitts Penguins Civic Arena Gate 9 Pittsburgh PA 15219*

TROUBETZKOY, ALEXIS SERGE, foundation administrator, educator; b. Paris, Mar. 6, 1934; came to U.S., 1936; s. Serge G. and Luba A. (Obolensky) T.; m. Helene de Klebnikoff, July 8, 1967; children: Anne, Andrew. BA, Sir George William U., 1958; grad. diploma in Edn., Bishop's U., 1960. Tchr. Stanstead Coll., 1959-60, Bishop's Coll. Sch., Lennoxville, Que., Can., 1960-66; registrar St. Stephen's Sch., Rome, 1966-68; asst. headmaster Appleby Coll., Oakville, Ont., Can., 1968-71, headmaster, 1981-87; headmaster Selwyn House Sch., Montreal, Que., 1971-81, Toronto (Ont.) French Sch., 1987-92; exec. dir. Tolstoy Found., N.Y.C., 1992-95; county rep. I.O.C.C., Moscow, 1995—. Author: The Road to Balaklava, 1986. Regent Cathedral St. John the Divine, N.Y.C.; mem. lt.-gov.'s conservation award selection com., Ont.; active Sir Edmund Hillary Found. Mem. Can. Assn. Internat. Affairs (pres. Sherbrooke br. 1964-66), Assn. Russian-Am. Scholars, Can. Assn. Ind. Schs. (pres. 1980-81), European Coun. Internat. Schs., Quebec Assn. Ind. Schs. (pres. 1979-81), Amities Internat. Napoleoniennes. Mem. Orthodox Ch. in Am. Avocations: hist. reading and writing, music. Home: 50 Rosehill Ave #1611, Toronto, ON Canada M4T 1G6

TROUNSTINE, PHILIP J., editor, journalist; b. Cin., July 30, 1949; s. Henry P. and Amy May (Joseph) Trounstine; children: Jessica, David; m. Deborah Williams, May 1, 1993; children: Amy, Ryan, Patrick Wilkes. Student, U. Vt., 1967-68, Stanford U., 1968-70; BA in Journalism, San Jose State U., 1975. Graphic artist Eric Printing, San Jose, Calif., 1972-75; reporter Indpls. Star, Ind., 1975-78; reporter San Jose Mercury News, Calif., 1978-83, editl. writer, 1983-86, polit. editor, 1986—; ednl. cons. Teen Recovery Strategies, 1995—. Co-author: Movers & Shakers: The Study of Community Power, 1981. Creator, writer SPJ Gridiron Show, San Jose, 1981-91. Pulliam fellow, 1975, Duke U., 1991, J.S. Knight Stanford U., 1993-94. Mem. Soc. Profl. Journalist (mem. nat. ethics com. 1993—). Jewish. Avocations: golf, fishing. Home: 960 Asbury St San Jose CA 95126-1805 Office: San Jose Mercury News 750 Ridder Park Dr San Jose CA 95131-2432

TROUPE, BONNIE LEE, college program coordinator, teacher; b. Quincy, Mass., Mar. 22, 1966; d. Stanley G. and Penelope J. (Erikson) T.; 1 child, Emma Elizabeth. BA in English and Secondary Edn., Salve Regina Coll., Newport, R.I., 1988; MA in English, Bridgewater State Coll., 1992. Cert. secondary tchr., R.I. ESL tchr. Hampton Sch. English, Tokyo, 1988-89; grad. asst. Bridgewater (Mass.) State Coll., 1990-92; staff assoc. office of grants and sponsored projects Bridgewater State Coll., 1992-95, coord. office of grants and sponsored projects, 1995—; journalism tchr. Project Contemporary Competitiveness, Bridgewater, 1986—; proposal reviewer U.S. Dept. Edn., Washington, 1994; instr. Bridgewater State Coll., 1995—; mem. Russian-Am. Spl. Edn. Collaborative, 1992—. Mem. bd. Mass. Soc. Prevention of Cruelty to Children, S.E. region, Brockton, 1992—. O'Donnell scholar, Trinity and All Saints Coll., Leeds, Eng., 1986-87, grad. scholar Wadham Coll., Oxford (Eng.) U., 1991; recipient Sarah Brown Sullivan award, Salve Regina Coll., 1988. Mem. AAUW, Nat. Coun. Univ. Rsch. Adminstrs., Profl. and Orgnl. Devel., Rsch. Adminstrs. Discussion Group, Soc. Rsch. Adminstrs., Mass. Women in Pub. Higher Edn. Avocations: art appreciation, travel. Home: 195 Twin Lakes Dr Halifax MA 02338-2213 Office: Office Grants and Sponsored Projects Bridgewater State Coll Bridgewater MA 02325

TROUPE, MARILYN KAY, education educator; b. Tulsa, Sept. 30, 1945; d. Ernest Robinson and Lucille (Andrew) Troupe. BA in Social Sci., Langston U., Okla., 1967; MA in History, Okla. State U., 1976; EdD Okla. State U., 1993; Lic. in Cosmetology, Troupe's Beauty Sch., 1970. Cert. tchr. Okla., Tenn. Tchr. social studies Margaret Hudson Program, Tulsa, 1969-81, tutor Tulsa Indian Youth, 1971-72; instr. cosmetology McLain-Tulsa Pub. Schs., 1982-94; instrnl. devel. specialist Okla. Dept. Vocat. and Tech. Edn., Stillwater, 1987-94; asst. prof., coord. tchr. preparation program, chair divsn. liberal studies and edn. Lane Coll., Jackson, Tenn., 1995—; vis. lectr. Okla. State U., 1980-81; cons., lectr. cosmetology; bd. dirs., adv. bd. Stillwater Park & Recreation, Stillwater Community Relations and Fair Housing, 1991-94; bd. dirs Adult Day Care Center, 1990-94; v.p. Okla. Recreation and Park Soc., 1994; judge Okla. Sch. Sci. and Math., 1994; mem. Leadership Stillwater, 1990; vol. Special Olympics State Games, Meals on Wheels, United Way; mem. women's adv. coun. Jackson Regional Hosp. Roman Catholic Ch., Tulsa, 1985-86. Recipient numerous awards for profl. and civic contbns. including Woman of Yr., Zeta Phi Beta, 1985; Salute award Gov. Okla., 1985; Outstanding Community Service Cert., WomenFest, 1985. Mem. ASCD, Okla. Assn. Advancement of Black Ams. in Vocat. Edn. (Golden Torch award 1994), Vocat. Indsl. Clubs Am. (dist. advisor 1985-86, Appreciation award 1985), Am. Vocat. Assn., Okla. Vocat. Assn., Okla. State Beauty Culturalists League (pres. 1979-85, Outstanding Service award 1985), Nat. Assn. Bus. and Profl. Women's Club (charter mem., past pres.), Stillwater C. of C. (bd. dirs.), Langston Alumni Assn., Phi Alpha Theta, Theta Nu Sigma, Alpha Kappa Alpha (Soror of Yr. 1993), Iota Lambda Sigma, Phi Delta Kappa. Democrat. Roman Catholic. Clubs: Jackson Links, Cath. Daus. Am. Avocations: travel, reading, collecting antiques, volunteer work, shopping. Home: 18 Rachel Dr Apt 10 Jackson TN 38305-8605

TROUSDALE, STEPHEN RICHARD, newspaper editor; b. L.A., May 29, 1963; s. Richard Gardner Trousdale and Geraldine Barbara Wisdom. AB, Stanford U., 1985. News editor L.A. Daily Commerce, 1986-87; edit. page editor L.A. Daily Jour., 1987-89, mng. editor, 1989-96; bus. editor Copley L.A. Newspapers, 1996—. Mem. Soc. Profl. Journalists (past pres. L.A. chpt.), AP Mng. Editors, Calif. Soc. Newspaper Editors, Soc. Newspaper Design, Soc. Am. Bus. Editors and Writers, Toastmasters Internat. Avocations: skiing, karate. Home: 10933 Huston St Apt 203 North Hollywood CA 91601-5135 Office: Copley LA Newspapers 5215 Torrance Blvd Torrance CA 90503-4009

TROUT, CHARLES HATHAWAY, historian, educator; b. Seattle, Nov. 3, 1935; s. Charles Whyron and Elizabeth (Hathaway) T.; m. Margot Stevens, Dec. 30, 1961 (div. 1983); children: Nicholas H., Benjamin C.; m. Katherine Taylor Griffiths, Oct. 6, 1984. B.A., Amherst Coll., 1957; M.A., Columbia U., 1961, Ph.D., 1972. History instr. Hill Sch., Pottstown, Pa., 1958-59, Philips Exeter Acad., (N.H.), 1960-69; prof. history Mt. Holyoke Coll., South Hadley, Mass., 1969-80; provost, dean faculty Colgate U., Hamilton, N.Y., 1980-90; pres. Washington Coll., Chestertown, Md., 1990-95; prof. history U. Nairobi, 1996—; vis. prof. U. Mass. Labor Rels. and Rsch. Ctr., 1974-80. Author: Boston, The Great Depression, and the New Deal. Trustee Md. Citizens for the Arts, Chesapeake Bay Maritime Mus., Pickering Creek Environ. Ctr. Columbia U. Pres.'s scholar, 1959-60; NEH rsch. fellow, 1975-76; Charles Warren fellow Harvard U., 1978-79. Democrat. Episcopalian. Home: 109 S Mill St Chestertown MD 21620 Office: Washington Coll Office of President Chestertown MD 21620-1197*

TROUT, LINDA COPPLE, judge; b. Tokyo, Sept. 1, 1951. BA, U. Idaho, 1973, JD, 1977. Bar: Idaho 1977. Judge magistrate divsn. Idaho Dist. Ct. (2d jud. divsn.), 1983-90; dist. judge Idaho Dist. Ct. (2d jud. divsn.), Lewiston, 1991-92; acting trial ct. adminstr. Idaho Dist. Ct. (2d jud. divsn.), 1987-91; justice Idaho Supreme Ct., 1992—, chief justice, 1997—; instr. coll. law U. Idaho, 1983, 88. Mem. Idaho State Bar Assn., Clearwater Bar Assn. (pres. 1980-81).

TROUT, MAURICE ELMORE, foreign service officer; b. Clifton Hill, Mo., Sept. 17, 1917; s. David McCamel and Charlotte Temple (Woods) T.; m. Margie Marie Mueller, Aug. 24, 1943; children—Richard Willis, Babette Yvonne. B.A., Hillsdale Coll., 1939; M.A. in Pub. Adminstrn, St. Louis U., 1948, Ph.D. in Polit. Sci, 1950. Joined U.S. Fgn. Service, 1950; assigned Paris, France, 1950-52, Vienna, Austria, 1952-55, London, Eng., 1955-59, Vientiane, Laos, 1959-61; with Office Exec. Dir. Bur. Far Eastern Affairs, Dept. State, Washington, 1961-65; Am. consulate gen. Munich, Germany, 1965-69; 1st sec., consul Am. embassy, Bangkok, Thailand, 1969-72; dep. office dir. Bur. Politico-Mil. Affairs, Dept. State, Washington, 1972-75; Dept. State advisor Armed Forces Staff Coll., Norfolk, Va., 1975-77. Bd. dirs. Internat. Sch., Bangkok, 1970-72. Served with USCG, 1939-45; capt. USAFR, 1951-55. Recipient Achievement award diplomacy and internat. affairs Hillsdale Coll., 1962. Mem. Am. Fgn. Service Assn., Diplomatic and Consular Officer, Delta Tau Delta, Delta Theta Phi, Pi Gamma Mu. Home: 6203 Hardy Dr Mc Lean VA 22101

TROUT, MONROE EUGENE, hospital systems executive; b. Harrisburg, Pa., Apr. 5, 1931; s. David Michael and Florence Margaret (Kashner) T.; m. Sandra Louise Lemke, June 11, 1960; children: Monroe Eugene, Timothy William. AB, U. Pa., 1953, MD, 1957; LLB, Dickinson Sch. of Law, 1964, JD, 1969; LLD (hon.), Dickinson Sch. Law, 1996, Bloomfield Coll., 1994. Intern Great Lakes (Ill.) Naval Hosp., 1957-58; resident in internal medicine

Portsmouth (Va.) Naval Hosp., 1959-61; chief med. dept. Harrisburg State Hosp., 1961-64; dir. drug regulatory affairs Pfizer, Inc., N.Y.C., 1964-68; v.p., med. dir. Winthrop Labs., N.Y.C., 1968-70; med. dir. Sterling Drug, Inc., N.Y.C., 1970-74, v.p., dir. med. affairs, 1974-78, sr. v.p., dir. med. affairs, bd. dirs., mem. exec. com., 1978-86; pres., CEO Am. Healthcare Sys., Inc., 1986-95, chmn., 1987-95; also bd. dirs. Am. Healthcare Systems, Inc.; chmn. emeritus Am. Healthcare Sys., Inc., 1995—; interim CEO Cytran Inc., 1996; bd. dirs. Baxter Internat., SAIC, West Co., Inc., Cytyc, Inc.; chmn. bd. dirs. Am. Excess Ins. ltd., 1990-95; adj. assoc. prof. Bklyn. Coll. Pharmacy; spl. lectr. legal medicine, trustee Dickinson Sch. Law, 1970-93; trustee Ariz. State U. Sch. Health Adminstrn., 1988-91; mem. Sterling Winthrop Rsch. Bd., 1977-86, Joint Commn. Prescription Drug Use, 1976-80; sec. Commn. on Med. Malpractice, HEW, 1971-73, cons., 1974; co-chmn. San Diego County Health Commn., 1992-94; past dir. Biotransplantation, Inc., Gensia, Inc., Criticare Inc., 1991-95. Mem. editl. bd. Hosp. Formulary Mgmt., 1969-79, Forensic Sci., 1971—, Jour. Legal Medicine, 1973-79, Reg. Tox. and Pharmac, 1981-87, Med. Malpractice Prevention, 1985—; editl. reviewer Annals of Internal Medicine; contbr. articles to profl. jours. Exec. com. White House Mini Conf. on Aging, 1980; Rep. dist. leader, New Canaan, Conn., 1966-68; mem. Nat. Health Adv. Bd. AAA, N.Y. State Commn. Substance Abuse, 1978-80, Town Coun., New Canaan, 1978-86, vice chmn., 1985-86; bd. dirs. New Canaan Interchurch Svc. Com., 1965-69, Athletes Kidney Found., Circle in Sq. Theatre Inc., 1984-86; trustee U. Calif.-San Diego Thornton Hosp. and Med. Ctr., 1990-97, Albany Med. Coll., 1977-86, St. Vincent DePaul Ctr. for the Homeless, 1987-90, Cleve. Clinic, 1971-87; trustee, vice chmn. Morehouse Med. Sch., 1980-89; assoc. trustee U. Pa.; bd. visitors U. Pa. Sch. Nursing, 1988-92; pres. bd. trustees U. Calif. San Diego Found., 1994-97; vice chmn. Med. Commn. for Food and Shelter, Inc.; chmn. bd. Am. Coll. Legal Medicine Found., 1983-87; chmn. Internat. B'nai B'rith Dinner, 1989, 94. Recipient Alumni award of merit U. Pa., 1953, Disting. Alumni award Dickinson Sch. Law, 1989, Nat. Healthcare award Internat. B'nai B'rith, 1991, Entrepreneur of Yr. award San Diego, 1994, Horatio Alger award, 1995, Salvation Army Tradition of Caring award, 1996; named to Hon. Order Ky. Cols., Tenn. Cols. Fellow Am. Coll. Legal Medicine (v.p., pres., bd. govs.); mem. AMA (Physician's Recognition awards 1969, 72, 76, 82, 85, 88, 92), Med. Execs. (pres. 1975-76), Delta Tau Delta (Alumni Achievement award 1996). Lutheran. Office: PO Box 8052 Rancho Santa Fe CA 92067-8052

TROUTMAN, E. MAC, federal judge; b. Greenwood Township, Pa., Jan. 7, 1915; s. Emmett Theodore and Kathryn (Holman) T.; m. Margaret Petrick, Nov. 23, 1944; children—Jane A., Jean K. A.B., Dickinson Coll., 1934, LL.B., 1936. Bar: Pa. 1937. With Phila. and Reading Coal and Iron Co., 1937-58, gen. counsel, 1954-58; gen. atty. Phila. and Reading Corp., 1958-67; gen. counsel Reading Anthracite Co., 1958-61, Reserve Carbon Corp., 1961-66, So. Carbon Corp., 1966-67; solicitor Blue Mountain Sch. Dist., 1963-67, Blue Mountain Area Sch. Authority, 1963-67, Orwigsburg Municipal Authority, 1966-67, Am. Bank and Trust Co., Reading and Pottsville, Pa., 1957-67; exec. sec., gen. counsel Pa. Self-Insurers Assn., 1962-67; U.S. judge Eastern Dist. Pa., from 1967, now sr. judge. Bd. dirs. Greater Pottsville Indsl. Devel. Corp., 1963-67, Pa. C. of C., 1955-65, Greater Pottsville Area C. of C., 1961-64, Orwigsburg Community Meml. Assn., 1950-66, Schuylkill County Soc. Crippled Children, 1945-67; v.p., dir. Pottsville Hosp. and Warne Clinic, 1960-67. Served with AUS, World War II. Mem. ABA, Pa. Bar Assn., Schuylkill County Bar Assn. (vice chancellor 1955-57, chmn. jud. vacancies and unauthorized practice coms. 1960, chmn. medico-legal com. 1963-65). Lutheran (pres. coun. 1961—). Club: Lion (bd. dirs. Orwigsburg 1964). Home: Kimmel's Rd Orwigsburg PA 17961 Office: US District Ct The Madison Bldg 400 Washington St Rm 400 Reading PA 19601-3915*

TROUTMAN, GEORGE GLENN, retired aerospace executive, retired military officer; b. Albany, Ga., Feb. 11, 1925; s. Baldwin Littleton and Helen Albaugh (Fulwood) T.; m. Dorothy Mae Beavers, Oct. 19, 1946; children: George Glenn Troutman Jr., Sandra Mae Troutman Wiseman, Diane Elaine Troutman Hickok. Attended, U. Ill., Urbana, 1950; BSEE, USAF Inst. Tech., Dayton, Ohio, 1953. Pilot B-24 U.S. Army Air Corps., 1943-47; pilot B-29 USAF, 1947-52, staff officer R&D missiles and space programs, 1953-65; asst. gen. mgr. Gen Dynamics Corp., Washington, 1965-75; gen. mgr. Gen. Elec. Corp., Washington, 1975-81; v.p. Washington Operation Bell Helicopter-TEXTRON, Washington, 1981-91; ptnr. Sullivan, Taylor & McLeary, Washington, 1995—; pres. Profl. Recruitment On-Line Svcs. Pres. nation's capitol chpt. Air Force Assn., Washington, 1972-74, Auth. Road Citizen's Assn., Prince Georges County, Md., 1968-71. Recipient Air medal, U.S. Army Air Corps., Army Commendation medal, Disting. Flying Cross award, USAF Commendation medal. Methodist. Avocations: farming, investing. Home: 6406 S Osborne Rd Upper Marlboro MD 20772 Office: Profl Recruitment On-Line Svcs 1717 K St NW Ste 1112 Washington DC 20006-1501

TROUTMAN, GEORGE WILLIAM, geologist, geological consulting firm executive; b. Brandenburg, Ky., Aug. 8, 1949; s. George I. and Ellen G. T.; m. Marcia Lyn Roseman, Aug. 14, 1971; children—Nancy, Anthony, Janet, David, Barbara, Jonathan. Student Murray State U., 1967-68; B.S. in Geology, Western Ky. U., 1974. Geophys. engr. Birdwell div. Seismograph Service Corp., Ohio, Pa., W.Va., 1974-77; geologist Consolidated Natural Gas, Clarksburg, W.Va., 1977-79; exploration geologist Mountain Fuel Supply Corp., Denver, 1979-80; regional exploration geologist Al-Aquitaine Exploration, Ltd., Denver, 1980-81; sr. staff geologist Resources Investment Corp., Denver, 1981-82; geol. mgr. Petro-Lewis Corp., MCR, Oklahoma City, 1982-84; pres., geologist Troutman Geol. & Assocs., Edmond, Okla., 1984—. Served with USN, 1968-70. Mem. Am. Assn. Petroleum Geologists (cert.), Soc. Profl. Well Log Analysts, Oklahoma City Geol. Soc. (exec. com. 1985-86, editor Shale Shaker Digest XI 1982-85, treas. 1987-88, v.p. 1988-89, pres.-elect 1996-97, pres. 1997—), Ardmore Geol. Soc., New Orleans Geol. Soc., Computer Oriented Geol. Soc., Geophysical Soc. of Oklahoma City. Republican. Mem. Ch. of Jesus Christ of Latter-day Saints. Office: Troutman Geological & Assocs 4406 Karen Dr Ste 100 Edmond OK 73013-8124

TROUTMAN, RONALD R., electrical engineer; b. Lewisburg, Pa., Oct. 4, 1940; m. Roy Marlin and Dorothy Irene (Savidge) T.; m. Gail McCarthy Owen, July 30, 1966; children: Kelby Scott, Ramsay Owen. BS, MIT, 1962; PhD, NYU, 1966. Staff engr. gen. tech. div. IBM, Essex Junction, Vt., 1969-73, adv. engr., 1973-81, sr. engr., 1981-87; sr. engr. IBM T.J. Watson Rsch. Ctr., Yorktown Heights, N.Y., 1987-91, engring. staff mem., 1991—; Fellow MIT Ctr. for Advanced Engring. Studies, Cambridge, 1983-84. Author: Latchup in CMOS Technology: The Problem and Its Cure, 1966; contbr. over 60 articles to profl. jours. Lt. USN, 1966-68. Fellow IEEE; mem. IBM Acad. of Tech. Achievements include patents on random access memory design, semiconductor technology development, others; analysis and characterization of short channel effects, subthreshold behavior and hot electron phenomena in field-effect transistors, modeling and control of latchup in CMOS technology, management of TFT/LCD materials and devices research and of TFT/LCD array tester development, research onb flat panel displays. Home: 38 Deer Hill Dr Ridgefield CT 06877-5308 Office: IBM TJ Watson Rsch Ctr PO Box 218 Yorktown Heights NY 10598-0218

TROUTWINE, GAYLE LEONE, lawyer; b. Kansas City, Mo., Feb. 26, 1952. BS, N.W. Mo. State U., 1973; JD with honors, U. Mo., 1978. Bar: Mo. 1978, Oreg. 1983, U.S. Dist. Ct. (we. dist.) Mo., Wash. 1984, U.S. Ct. Appeals (9th cir.), U.S. Dist. Ct. (we. dist.) Wash., U.S. Supreme Ct., Hawaii 1995. Ptnr. Williams & Troutwine, P.C., Portland, Oreg., 1986—; speaker in field. Contbr. articles to profl. jours. Steering com. mem. Breast Implant Litigation, 1992—, Tobacco Litigation; bd. mem. Portland Area Women's Polit. Caucus, 1992-95, Oreg. Women's Polit. Caucus, 1996—; mem. Jud. Steering com., 1994. Named Queen of Torts Wall St. Jour., 1996. Mem. ATLA (bd. govs.), Hawaii State Bar, Mo. Bar, Oreg. State Bar (exec. bd. litigation sect. 1984-88, chmn. 1987-88, procedure and practice com. 1985-88, bd. govs. 1990-93), Wash. State Bar, Oreg. Trial Lawyers Assn. (bd. govs. 1987-91), Calif. Trial Lawyers Assn., Hawaii Trial Lawyers Assn., Wash. Trial Lawyers Assn., Women Lawyers Assn., Greater Kansas City (sec. 1981-82), Western Trial Lawyers Assn. (bd. govs. 1992—). Democrat. Office: Williams and Troutwine PC 1001 SW 5th Ave Ste 1900 Portland OR 97204-1135

TROVATO, E. RAMONA, government official. Chemist U.S. EPA, Washington, region III inorganic chemistry lab. mgr., quality assurance officer Chesapeake Bay Program, hdqs. liaison environ. svcs. divsns., dir. ground water protection divsn., dir. water enforcement divsn., dir. Office Radiation and Indoor Air; co-chair Interagy. Steering Com. on Radiation Stds.; mem. adv. com. on external regulation of Dept. of Energy nuclear safety; co-chair Human Resources Coun., EPA, mem. sci. and tech. careers adv. com., exec. resources bd., sci. policy coun., environ. monitoring mgmt. coun.; co-chair Superfund Analytical Svcs. Adv. Com.; exec. dir. Nat. Environ. Lab. Accreditation Program; bd. mem. Nat. Environ. Lab. Accreditation Conf.; co-chair Environ. Lab. Adv. Bd.; mem. Com. on Nat. Accrediation of Environ. Labs. Office: US EPA Radiation & Indoor Air 401 M St SW # 6601J Washington DC 20460-0001

TROW, JO ANNE JOHNSON, retired university official; b. Youngstown, Ohio, Feb. 10, 1931; d. Raymond Leonard Johnson and Mary Belle Beede; m. Clifford W. Trow, Oct. 10, 1969. BA, Denison U., 1953; MA, Ind. U., 1956; PhD, Mich. State U., 1965. Case worker Office Pub. Assistance, Cleve., 1953-54; asst. dean women Denison U., Granville, Ohio, 1956-59, Wash. State U., Pullman, 1959-63; asst. dir. resident program Mich. State U., East Lansing, 1964; dean women Oreg. State U., Corvallis, 1965-69, assoc. dean students, 1969-83, v.p. student affairs, 1983-95, program dir., 1983-95; presenter, speaker in field. Contbr. articles to profl. jours. Bd. dirs. Benton County Mental Health Assn., 1975-79, United Way Benton County, 1977—, United Way Oreg., 1977-80; mem. adv. bd. Old Mill Sch., 1979-95, chmn., 1983, 94-95; mem. Oreg. Cmty. Corrections Adv. Bd., 1988-95; moderator 1st Congl. Ch., 1977, trustee, 1979-83, 91-95; mem. Oreg. Gov.'s Com. on Status of Women, 1972-78, vice chmn., 1976-77; mem. fund campaign Good Samaritan Hosp. Found. Cancer Care Ctr., 1982-83. Recipient Corvallis Woman of Achievement award, 1974, Boss of Yr. award Oreg. State U. Office Personnel Assn., 1979, White Rose award March of Dimes, 1987, Elizabeth A Greenleaf Disting. Alumna award Ind. U., 1987, Scott Goodnight award, 1989, Disting. Alumni Citation, Denison U., 1993, Coun. Woman of Distinction award Oreg. State U. Meml. Union Program, 1993. Mem. Nat. Assn. Women Deans, Adminstrs. and Counselors (pres. 1981-82), Am. Coll. Personnel Assn. (sec. 1969-70), Nat. Assn. Student Personnel Adminstrs., Am. Coun. on Edn., N.W. Assn. Schs. and Colls. (comn. on colls. 1989-95), Am. Assn. for Higher Edn., N.W. Coll. Personnel Assn. (life, pres. 1969-70), Assn. Oreg. Faculties, AAUW (state and local bd. dirs.), LWV (bd. dirs., v.p. Corvallis 1966-69, 79-80), Corvallis Area C. of C. (bd. dirs. 1972-74, 78-80), Mortar Bd., Phi Delta Kappa, Phi Kappa Phi, Alpha Lambda Delta. Democrat.

TROWBRIDGE, ALEXANDER BUEL, JR., business consultant; b. Englewood, N.J., Dec. 12, 1929; s. Alexander Buel and Julie (Chamberlain) T.; m. Eleanor Hutzler, Apr. 18, 1981; children by previous marriage: Stephen C., Corrin S., Kimberly. Grad., Phillips Acad., Andover, Mass., 1947; AB cum laude, Princeton U., 1951; LLD (hon.), D'Youville Coll., 1967, Hofstra U., 1968, Hobart Coll., William Smith Coll., 1975. With Calif. Tex. Oil Co., 1954-59; ops. mgr. Esso Standard Oil S.A. Ltd., Panama C.Z., 1959-61; div. mgr. Esso Standard Oil S.A. Ltd., El Salvador, 1961-63; pres. Esso Standard Oil Co., P.R., 1963-65; asst. sec. commerce for domestic and internat. bus. U.S., 1965-67; sec. of commerce, 1967-68; pres. Am. Mgmt. Assn., N.Y.C., 1968-70, The Conf. Bd., Inc., N.Y.C., 1970-76; vice chmn. bd. Allied Chem. Corp., 1976-80; bd. dirs. NAM, Washington, 1978—, pres., 1980-90; bd. dirs. New Eng. Life Ins. Co., Warburg Pincus Funds, Sun Co. Inc., ICOS Corp., Rouse Co., Harris Corp., Gillette Co., Waste Mgmt., Inc. Trustee Phillips Acad., Andover, Mass.; mem. Pres.'s Task Force on Pvt. Sector Initiatives, Nat. Commn. on Social Security Reform, 1982; mem. Nat. Commn. on Exec., Legis. and Jud. Salaries, 1985, Nat. Commn. on Pub. Svcs.; mem. Competitiveness Policy Coun., 1991. With USMCR, 1951-53, maj. Res. Decorated Bronze Star with combat V; recipient Arthur Flemming award, 1966, Pres.'s E cert. for export service, 1968, Bryce Harlow award for Bus.-Govt. Rels., 1988. Mem. Coun. Fgn. Rels., Met. Club, Georgetown Club, Univ. Club. Home: 1823 23rd St NW Washington DC 20008-4030 Office: 1317 F St NW Ste 500 Washington DC 20004-1105

TROWBRIDGE, DALE BRIAN, educator; b. Glendale, Calif., May 17, 1940; s. Dale Beverly and Alison Amelia (Goldsborough) T.; m. Helen Elaine Turner, July 2, 1966; children: Katelin Elizabeth, David Brian. BA, Whittier Coll., 1961; MS, U. Calif., Berkeley, 1964, PhD, 1970. Chemist Aerojet Gen., Azusa, Calif., 1961-62; chemistry tchr. Berkeley (Calif.) High Sch., 1964-66; prof., chemistry dept. chmn. Sonoma State U., Rohnert Park, Calif., 1969—; vis. prof. chemistry U. Calif., Berkeley, 1970-74, 88; rsch. assoc. Cambridge U., 1978. Contbr. articles to profl. jours. Mem. Am. Chem. Soc., AAAS, Internat. Platform Assn., Sigma Xi. Home: 6039 Elsa Ave Rohnert Park CA 94928-2246 Office: Sonoma State U 1801 E Cotati Ave Rohnert Park CA 94928-3613

TROWBRIDGE, JOHN PARKS, physician; b. Dinuba, Calif., Mar. 24, 1947; s. John Parks Sr. and Claire Dovie (Noroian) T.; m. Evelyn Anne Parker, Apr. 20, 1996; children: Sharla Tyann, Lyndi Kendyll. AB in Biol. Scis., Stanford U., 1970; MD, Case Western Res. U., 1976; postgrad., Fla. Inst. Tech., 1983-85. Diplomate in Preventive Medicine, Am. Bd. Chelation Therapy (examiner for bd. 1987—), Am. Bd. Biologic Reconstructive Therapy (examiner for bd. 1994—, protocol coun. 1996—), Nat. Bd. Med. Examiners. Intern in gen. surgery Mt. Zion Hosp. & Med. Ctr., San Francisco, 1976-77; resident in urol. surgery U. Tex. Health Sci. Ctr., Houston, 1977-78; pvt. med. practice health recovery unit, pain relief unit Life Ctr. Houston, Humble, Tex., 1978—; chief corp. med. cons. Tex. Internat. Airlines, Houston, 1981-83; indsl. med. cons. to several heavy and light mfg. and svc. cos., Houston, 1979-84; immunology research asst. Stanford U. Med. Ctr., Stanford, Calif., 1967-70; night lab. supr. Kaiser Found. Hosp., Redwood City, Calif., 1971-72; advisor to bd. dirs. Am. Inst. Med. Preventics, Laguna Hills, Calif., 1988-90; featured lectr. profl. and civic orgns., U.S., 1983—; sr. aviation med. examiner FAA, 1983-96, rep. to Chelation Protocol Coun., 1996—, Am. Bd. Chelation Therapy. Co-author: The Yeast Syndrome, 1986, Chelation Therapy, 1985, 2d edit., 1990, Yeast Related Illnesses, 1987, Do What You Want to Do, 1996; contbr. Challenging Orthodoxy: America's Top Medical Preventives Speak Out, 1991; edit. adv. bd. mem. nat. health and wellness newsletters, and jours., 1990—; contbr. articles to profl. jours. Adv. bd. mem. Tex. Chamber Orchestra, Houston, 1979-80; med. dir. Humble unit Am. Cancer Soc., 1980-81; med. cons. personal fitness program Lake Houston YMCA, 1981-83. Nat. Merit scholar, 1965-69, Calif. State scholar, 1967-69; recipient Resolution of Commendation house of dels., 1974 Am. Podiatry Assn., Spl. Profl. Svc. Citation bd. trustees, 1976, Am. Podiatry Students Assn. Fellow Am. Acad. Neurol. and Orthopaedic Surgery, Am. Soc. for Laser Medicine and Surgery, Am. Coll. Advancement in Medicine (v.p. 1987-89, pres.-elect 1989-91); mem. AMA, Am. Coll. Preventive Medicine, Am. Preventive Med. Assn. (charter, bd. dirs. 1992—), Legal and Edn. Found. Am. Preventive Med. Assn. (charter, bd. dirs. 1996—), Am. Acad. Environ. Medicine, Am. Soc. Gen. Laser Surgery, Nat. Health Fedn. (chmn. bd. govs. 1989), Am. Acad. Thermology, Am. Assn. Nutritional Cons., Am. Soc. Life Extension Physicians (founding), Am. Assn. Physicians and Surgeons, Am. Acad. Anti-Aging Medicine, Tex. Med. Assn., Harris County Med. Soc., Houston Acad. Medicine, Aerospace Med. Assn., N.Y. Acad. Scis., Internat. Acad. Bariatric Medicine, The Arthritis Trust Am. (med. adv. bd. 1995—), Inst. Health Freedom (bd. dirs. 1997—), Huxley Inst. for Biosocial Rsch., Great Lakes Coll. Clin. Medicine (med. rsch. instnl. rev. bd., v.p. 1993-94, pres. 1994-95, program chair Advanced Tng. Seminar in Heavy Metal Toxicology 1996—), Soc. for Orthomolecular Medicine, The Royal Soc. Medicine (London; sect. orthopaedics), N.Am. Cervicogenic Headache Soc. Avocations: private piloting, computer applications, personal watercraft. Office: LIFE CTR HOUSTON 9816 Memorial Blvd Ste 205 Humble TX 77338-4206

TROWBRIDGE, PHILLIP EDMUND, surgeon, educator; b. Hartford, Conn., Oct. 17, 1930; s. John Henry and Isabelle Story (Warner) T.; m. Fay Elaine Russell, June 23, 1956; children: Kimberly, Heather, Allison, John, David. BA, Trinity Coll., 1952; postgrad., Harvard U., 1955; MD, Tufts Med. Sch., 1959. Diplomate Am. Bd. Surgery. Intern Hartford Hosp., 1959-60, resident in gen. surgery, 1960-65, from mem. surg. staff to sr. surgeon, 1965—; clin. asst. prof. Surgery U. Conn. Med. Sch., Farmington, 1986—; adj. asst. prof. Surgery Dartmouth Med. Sch., Hanover, N.H., 1986—. Contbr. 17 articles to profl. jours. Corporator Hartford Sem., Hartford, 1975-77, 86—, trustee, 1977-86; dir. West Hartford Street Ministry, 1974-79. With USAF, 1952-54. Mem. ACS, Hartford Med. Soc. (pres. 1988, trustee 1989-93, Loving Cup award 1994), Am. Soc. Gen. Surgeons (chmn. Conn. chpt. 1993—), New Eng. Surg. Soc., New Eng. Cancer Soc., Internat. Surg. Soc., Soc. for Surgery Alimentary Tract. Republican. American Baptist. Avocations: golf, tennis, skiing, photography, painting. Home: 11 Lucy Way Simsbury CT 06070-2534 Office: 85 Seymour St Hartford CT 06106-5501

TROWBRIDGE, RONALD LEE, college admininstrator; b. Ft. Wayne, Ind., Dec. 4, 1937; s. Perry and Arola May (Erb) T.; m. Pamela Gay Chapman, Aug. 11, 1962; children: Andrew Lee, Stephen Scott, Elizabeth Chapman. BA, U. Mich., 1960, MA, 1962, PhD in English Lang. and Lit., 1967. Prof. English Ea. Mich. U., Ypsilanti, 1965-78; v.p. Hillsdale (Mich.) Coll., 1978-81, 90—; assoc. dir. U.S. Info. Agy., Washington, 1981-86; dir. fed. and internat. programs Commn. on Bicentennial of U.S. Constitution, Washington, 1986-88, staff dir., 1988-90. Contbr. articles to profl. jours. Mem. Ann Arbor (Mich.) City Coun., 1975-79. Recipient George Washington Honor medal Freedoms Found. Valley Forge, 1979. Mem. Mont Pelerin Soc., Phila. Soc. Republican. Presbyterian. Avocations: politics, writing, speaking. Home: 1500 Lake Pleasant Rd S Osseo MI 49266-9636 Office: Hillsdale Coll Office of the Vice Pres Hillsdale MI 49242

TROWBRIDGE, THOMAS, JR., mortgage banking company executive; b. Troy, N.Y., June 28, 1938; s. of Thomas and Elberta (Wood) T.; m. Delinda Bryan, July 3, 1965; children: Elisabeth Tacy, Wendy Bryan. BA, Yale U., 1960; MBA, Harvard U., 1965. V.p. James W. Rouse & Co., Balt., 1965-66, Washington, 1966-68, San Francisco, 1968-73, 76-78; pres. Rouse Investing Co., Columbia, Md., 1973-76; pres., CEO Trowbridge, Kieselhorst & Co., San Francisco, 1978—, chmn., 1997—. Bd. dirs. Columbia Assn., 1975-76; trustee, treas. The Head-Royce Sch., Oakland, Calif., 1980-84; trustee, pres. Gen. Alumni Assn. Phillips Exeter Acad., 1984-90. Lt. USNR, 1960-63. Mem. Urban Land Inst., Calif. Mortgage Bankers Assn. (bd. dirs. 1991—, pres. 1996—), Mortgage Bankers Assn. Am. (bd. govs. 1993—), Olympic Club, Pacific Union Club, Lambda Alpha Internat. Republican. Presbyterian. Avocations: running, golf. Home: 4 Ridge Ln Orinda CA 94563-1318 Office: Trowbridge Kieselhorst & Co 555 California St Ste 2850 San Francisco CA 94104-1604

TROXEL, DONALD EUGENE, electrical engineering educator; b. Trenton, N.J., Mar. 11, 1934; s. Shirley Monroe and Emma Ruth (Marvel) T.; m. Eileen Millicent Cronk, Aug. 23, 1963; children: Gregory, Jocelyn, Andrea. BS, Rutgers U., 1956; SM, MIT, 1960, PhD, 1962. Ford Found. postdoctoral fellow, asst. prof. MIT, Cambridge, Mass., 1962-64, asst. prof. dept. elec. engring., 1964-67, assoc. prof., 1967-85, prof. elec. engring., 1985—; asst. prof. Tufts U., Medford, Mass., 1963; bd. dirs. ECRM, Inc., Tewksbury, Mass. 1st lt. U.S. Army, 1956-58. Mem. IEEE (sr. mem., Leonard G. Abraham Prize Paper award 1971), Assn. for Computing Machinery, Sigma Xi, Tau Beta Pi, Eta Kappa Nu, Pi Mu Epsilon. Home: 4 Madison St Belmont MA 02178-3536 Office: MIT 77 Massachusetts Ave # 36-287 Cambridge MA 02139-4301

TROY, ANTHONY FRANCIS, lawyer; b. Hartford, Conn., Apr. 16, 1941; children: Anthony John, Francis Gerard II. BA in Govt., St. Michael's Coll., Vt., 1963; LLB, T.C. Williams, U. Richmond, Richmond, Va., 1966. Bar: Va. 1966, D.C. 1972, U.S. Dist. Ct. (ea. dist.) Va. 1966, U.S. Dist. Ct. (we. dist.) Va. 1967, U.S. Ct. Appeals (4th cir.) 1967, U.S. Supreme Ct. 1969. Asst. atty. gen. Commonwealth of Va., Richmond, 1966-72, dep. atty. gen., 1974-75, chief dep. atty. gen., 1975-76, atty. gen., 1977-78; assoc. Colson & Shapiro, Washington, 1972-74; ptnr. Mays & Valentine, Richmond, 1978—. Contbr. articles to profl. jours. Trustee Sci. Mus. Va. Fellow Am. Law Found., Va. Law Found. Home: 1814 Park Ave Richmond VA 23220-2832 Office: Mays & Valentine 1111 East Main St PO Box 1122 Richmond VA 23218-1122

TROY, FREDERIC ARTHUR, II, medical biochemistry educator; b. Evanston, Ill., Feb. 16, 1937; s. Charles McGregor and Virginia Lane (Minto) T.; m. Linda Ann Price, Mar. 23, 1959; children: Karen M., Janet R. BS, Washington U., St. Louis, 1961; PhD, Purdue U., 1966; postdoctoral, Johns Hopkins U., 1968. Asst. prof. U. Calif. Sch. Medicine, Davis, 1968-74, assoc. prof., 1974-80, prof., 1980—, chmn., 1991-94; vis. prof. Karolinska Inst. Med. Sch., Stockholm, 1976-77; cons. NIH, Bethesda, Md., 1974—, NSF, Washington, 1975—, Damon Runyon Cancer Found., N.Y.C., 1980-81, VA, Washington, 1984-88. Mem. editl. bd. Jour. Biol. Chem., 1988—, Glycobiol., 1990—; contbr. articles to profl. jours. Recipient Research Cancer Devel. award Nat. Cancer Inst., 1975-80; Eleanor Roosevelt Internat. Cancer fellow Am. Cancer Soc., 1976-77. Mem. AAAS, Am. Soc. Biol. Chemistry and Molecular Biology, Am. Assn. Cancer Rsch., Am. Chem. Soc., Am. Soc. Enologists, Biochemistry Soc., Biophysics Soc., Am. Fedn. for Clin. Rsch., N.Y. Acad. Scis., Soc. for Glycobiol. (pres. 1991-92), Am. Med. and Grad. Sch. Dept. Biochem. (pres.-elect 1995—), Sigma Xi. Office: U Calif Sch Medicine Davis CA 95616

TROY, J. EDWARD, bishop; b. Chatham, N.B., Can., Sept. 2, 1931; s. J. Thomas and Lilian Mary (Barry) T. BA, St. Francis Xavier U., Antigonish, N.S., 1951; lic. philosophy, Louvain (Belgium) U., 1953, PhD, 1962; BD, Holy Heart Sem., Halifax, N.S., 1959; LLD (hons), St. Thomas U., Fredericton, N.B., 1985. Ordained priest Roman Cath. Ch., 1959. Prof. philosophy St. Thomas U., Chatham, N.B., 1959-63; commd. Canadian Armed Forces, 1963, advanced through grades to col., 1979, ret., 1984, chaplain, 1963-84; dir. personnel adminstrn. Can. Forces Chaplaincy, Ottowa, Ont., 1981-84; bishop Roman Cath. Ch., St. John, N.B., 1984—; episcopal promoter Apostleship of the Sea, Can., 1985—. Columnist New Freeman newpaper, 1984—. Chancellor St. Thomas U., 1986—. Mem. Canadian Conf. Cath. Bishops, Anglican/Roman Cath. Dialogue. Avocations: reading, bird watching. Office: Diocese St John, 1 Bayard Dr, Saint Johns, NF Canada E2L 3L5*

TROY, JOSEPH FREED, lawyer; b. Wilkes-Barre, Pa., Aug. 16, 1938; s. Sergei and Shirley Jean T.; m. Brigitta Ann Balos, June 9, 1962; children: Darcy Kendall, Austin Remy. BA, Yale U., 1960; LLB, Harvard U., 1963. Bar: Calif. 1964, D.C. 1979. Assoc. Hindin, McKittrick & Marsh, Beverly Hills, Calif., 1964-68, ptnr., 1968-70; pres. Troy & Gould, Los Angeles, 1970—; lectr. Calif. Continuing Edn. of Bar, 1972-80, 94; dir. Amerigon Inc., 1993-96, Movie Gallery, Inc., 1994—, Digital Video Systems, Inc., 1996—. Author: Let's Go: A Student Guide to Europe, 1962, Accountability of Corporate Management; co-author: Protecting Corporate Officers and Directors from Liability, 1994. Pres. L.A. Chamber Orch. Soc., 1968-75, chmn. bd. dirs., 1975-78, vice chmn. bd. dirs., 1978-81; bd. dirs. Music Ctr. Opera Assn., 1972—, v.p., mem. exec. com., 1987—; hon. consul of Tunisia, L.A., 1984-88; pres. Internat. Festival Soc.; bd. dirs. Brentwood Pk. Property Owners Assn., 1988-93. Reid Hall fellow U. Paris, 1958. Mem. ABA, Calif. State Bar Assn. (chmn. bus. ct. com.), D.C. Bar Assn., L.A. County Bar Assn. (chmn. bus. and corp. law sect. 1977-78), French Am. C. of C. U.S. (exec. v.p. 1983-85), French Am. C. of C. L.A. (pres. 1982-84), Wine and Food Soc. So. Calif. Inc. (bd. dirs.), Beach Club, Calif. Club. Office: 1801 Century Park E Ste 1600 Los Angeles CA 90067-2318

TROYER, ALVAH FORREST, seed corn company executive, plant breeder; b. LaFontaine, Ind., May 30, 1929; s. Alvah Forrest and Lottie (Waggoner) T.; m. Joyce Ann Wigner, Sept. 22, 1950; children: Anne, Barbara, Catherine, Daniel. B.S., Purdue U., 1954; M.S., U. Ill., 1956; Ph.D., U. Minn., 1964. Research assoc. U. Ill., Urbana, 1955-56; research fellow U. Minn., St. Paul, 1956-58; research sta. mgr. Pioneer Hi-Bred Internat., Inc., Mankato, Minn., 1958-65, research coordinator, 1965-77; dir. research and devel. Pfizer Genetics, St. Louis, 1977-81, v.p. and dir. research and devel., 1981-82; v.p. research and devel. DEKALB Plant Genetics, Ill., 1982-93; cons.Hybrid Seed Divsn. Cargill, Mpls., 1993—; researcher corn breeding, econ. botany, crop physiology, increasing genetic diversity, recent corn evolution. Contbr. articles to numerous publs.; developer of popular corn inbred lines and hybrids. Master sgt. U.S. Army, 1951-53, Korean War. Decorated Battle Star U.S. Army; recipient Nat. Coun. Comml. Plant Breeders Genetics and Plant Breeding award, 1992. Fellow AAAS, Am. Soc. Agronomy, Crop Sci. Soc. Am.; mem. Am. Genetic Assn., Genetic Soc. Am., N.Y. Acad. Sci., CAST, Sigma Xi, Gamma Sigma Delta, Alpha Zeta, Lambda Chi Alpha, Gamma Alpha, VFW. Methodist. Lodge: Masons. Home: 611 Joanne Ln De Kalb IL 60115-1862

TROYER, LEROY SETH, architect; b. Middlebury, Ind., Nov. 23, 1937; s. Seth and Nancy (Miller) T.; m. Phyllis Eigsti, May 24, 1958; children: Terry,

Ronald, Donald. BArch, U. Notre Dame, 1971. Prin. LeRoy Troyer and Assocs., South Bend, 1971; sr. ptnr. LeRoy Troyer and Assocs., Mishawaka, Ind., 1977; pres. Southfield, Inc., 1988, The Troyer Group, Inc., Mishawaka, 1988—; bd. dirs. Lead Devel., Inc. dD. Past pres. Environic Found. Internat., Inc.; bd. dirs. Habitat for Humanity Internat. Americus, 1987-93, Coalition for Christian Colls. and Univs., 1991-96, Habitat for Humanity St. Joseph County, Ind., 1992—; bd. dirs. Bethel Coll., 1988-97, Mishawaka, Housing Devel. Corp., South Bend, CONNECT, South Bend. Recipient numerous local, state and nat. awards and honors. Fellow AIA (practice mgmt. com., chmn. 1983-84), Ind. Soc. Architects, Mennonite Econ. Devel. Assn. Internat. (chmn. bd. 1987-91). Avocations: photography, travel, reading, art, woodworking. Home: 1442 Deerfield Ct South Bend IN 46614-6429 Office: The Troyer Group Inc 415 Lincoln Way E Mishawaka IN 46544-2213

TROYER, THOMAS ALFRED, lawyer; b. Omaha, Aug. 15, 1933; s. Robert Raymond and Dorothy (Darlow) T.; m. Sally Jean Brown, June 28, 1958; children: Kenneth D., Robert C., Virginia D., Thomas C. BA, Harvard U., 1955; JD, U. Mich., 1958. Bar: Colo. 1958, U.S. Ct. Appeals (D.C. cir.) 1967. Assoc. Holme, Roberts, More & Owen, Denver, 1958-61; USAF, Denver, 1961-62; trial atty. U.S. Dept. Justice, Washington, 1962-64; mem. legal staff Asst. Sec. Treasury for Tax Policy, Washington, 1964-66; assoc. tax legis. counsel U.S. Dept. Treasury, Washington, 1966-67; mem. Caplin & Drysdale, Washington, 1967—; pres. Stern Fund, N.Y.C., 1985-86; bd. dirs., Children's Def. Fund, Washington, Mineral Policy Ctr., Washington, Am. Tax Policy Inst., Washington; mem. bd. trustees Natural Resources Def. Coun., N.Y.C., 1977—, Carnegie Corp., N.Y.C., 1983-91, Found. Nat. Capital Region, 1992—. Contbr. numerous articles to profl. jours. Bd. dirs. Common Cause, Washington, 1980-83; mem. Treasury Adv. Commn. on Pvt. Philanthropy and Pub. Needs, Washington, 1976-77; mem. adv. group to Commr. Internal Rev., Washington, 1978-80; mem. com. of visitors U. Mich. Law Sch., Ann Arbor, 1982—; mem. IRS Commr.'s Exempt Orgn. Adv. Group, Washington, 1987-90. Fellow Am. Bar Found., Am. Coll. Tax Counsel; mem. ABA (vice chmn. govt. rels. tax sect. 1989-91, commn. on homelessness and poverty 1992-94), Coun. for Excellence in Govt., Am. Law Inst. Democrat. Home: 16 Primrose St Chevy Chase MD 20815-4229 Office: Caplin & Drysdale Chartered 1 Thomas Cir NW Washington DC 20005-5802

TROZZOLO, ANTHONY MARION, chemistry educator; b. Chgo., Jan. 11, 1930; s. Pasquale and Francesca (Vercillo) T.; m. Doris C. Stoffregen, Oct. 8, 1955; children: Thomas, Susan, Patricia, Michael, Lisa, Laura. BS, Ill. Inst. Tech., 1950; MS, U. Chgo., 1957, PhD, 1960. Asst. chemist Chgo. Midway Labs., 1952-53; assoc. chemist Armour Rsch. Found., Chgo., 1953-56; mem. tech. staff Bell Labs., Murray Hill, N.J., 1959-75; Charles L. Huisking prof. chemistry U. Notre Dame, 1975-92, Charles L. Huisking prof. emeritus, 1992—, asst. dean Coll. Sci., 1993—, P.C. Reilly lectr., 1972, Hesburgh Alumni lectr., 1986, Disting. lectr. sci., 1986; vis. prof. Columbia U., N.Y.C., 1971, U. Colo., 1981, Katholieke U. Leuven, Belgium, 1983, Max Planck Inst. für Strahlenchemie, Mülheim/Ruhr, Fed. Republic Germany, 1990; vis. lectr. Academia Sinica, 1984, 85; Phillips lectr. U. Okla., 1971; C.L. Brown lectr. Rutgers U., 1975; Sigma Xi lectr. Bowling Green U., 1976, Abbott Labs., 1978; M. Faraday lectr. No. Ill. U., 1976; F.O. Butler lectr. S.D. State U., 1978; Chevron lectr. U. Nev., Reno, 1983; plenary lectr. various internat. confs.; founder, chmn. Gordon Conf. on Organic Photochemistry, 1964; trustee Gordon Rsch. Confs., 1988-92; cons. various chem. cos. Assoc. editor Jour. Am. Chem. Soc., 1975-76; editor Chem. Revs., 1977-84; editorial adv. bd. Accounts of Chem. Rsch., 1977-85; cons. editor Encyclopedia of Science and Technology, 1982-92; contbr. articles to profl. jours.; patentee in field. Fellow AEC, 1951, NSF, 1957-59; named Hon. Citizen of Castolibero, Italy, 1997; recipient Pietro Bucci prize U. Calabria/Italian Chem. Soc., 1997. Fellow AAAS, Am. Inst. Chemists (Student award 1950), N.Y. Acad. Scis. (chmn. chem. scis. sect. 1969-70, Halpern award in photochemistry 1980); mem. AAUP, Am. Chem. Soc. (Disting. Svc. award St. Joseph Valley sect. 1979, Coronado lectr. 1980, 93, N.Y. state lectr. 1993, Hoosier lectr. 1995, Ozark lectr. 1995, Rocky Mountain lectr. 1996, Tex. Coast lectr. 1996), Sigma Xi. Roman Catholic. Home: 1329 E Washington St South Bend IN 46617-3340 Office: U Notre Dame Dept Chemistry-Biochemistry Notre Dame IN 46556

TRPIS, MILAN, vector biologist, scientist, educator; b. Mojsova Lucka, Slovakia, Dec. 20, 1930; came to U.S., 1971, naturalized, 1977; s. Gaspar and Anna (Sevcikova) T.; m. Ludmila Tonkovic, Dec. 15, 1956; children: Martin, Peter, Katarina. M.S., Comenius U., Bratislava, 1956; Ph.D., Charles U., Prague, 1960. Research asst. Slovak Acad. Sci., Bratislava, 1953-56; sci. asst. Slovak Acad. Sci., 1956-60, scientist, 1960-62, ind. scientist, 1962-69; ecologist-entomologist East Africa-Aedes Rsch. Unit WHO, Dar es Salaam, Tanzania, 1969-71; asst. faculty fellow dept. biology U. Notre Dame, 1971-73, assoc. faculty fellow, 1973-74; assoc. prof. med. entomology Johns Hopkins U. Sch. Hygiene and Pub. Health, 1974-78, prof., 1978—, dir. labs. med. entomology; med. entomology; rsch. assoc. U. Ill., Urbana, 1966-67, Can. Dept. Agr., Lethbridge, Alta., 1967-68; dir. Biol. Rsch. Inst. Am., 1971-79; external dir. rsch. Liberiran Inst. Biomed. Rsch., 1981-89; dir. AID project on transmission of river blindness in areas of Liberia, Sierra Leone, and Cote d'Ivoire; dir. WHO rsch. grant; tech. adv. com. AID Vector Biology and Control Project, 1986-91; dir. Johns Hopkins U./Fed. U. Tech. Akure Onchocerciasis Project in Nigeria, 1991-94, Johns Hopkins U./Organisation de Coordination et de Cooperation pour la Lutte les Grandes Endemies-Pierre Richet Inst. Onchocerciasis Project, Bouakè, Ivory Coast, 1993-96; dir. Johns Hopkins U./Pierre Richet Inst./ORSTOM onchocerciasis project in Ivory Coast, 1993-96; prof.-advisor doctoral students, Africa, Asia, Cen. Am., 1979—. Editor: Jour. Biologia, 1956-71, Jour. Entomol. Problems, 1960-72; zool. sect.: Jour. Biol. Works, 1960-71; Contbr. articles to profl. jours. Dir. WHO project on prophylactic drugs for river blindness, Liberia, 1985-87. Recipient Slovak Acad. Sci., 1st prize for research project. Mem. AAUP, AAAS, Am. Inst. Biol. Soci., Am. Mosquito Control Assn., Am. Soc. Parasitologists, Helminthol. Soc. Washington, Am. Soc. Tropical Medicine and Hygiene, Entomol. Soc. Am., Am. Genetic Assn., Soc. of Vector Ecology, N.Y. Acad. Scis., Johns Hopkins U. Tropical Medicine Club, Smithsonian Assocs., Royal Soc. Tropical Medicine and Hygiene, Royal Entomol. Soc. of London, Sigma Xi, Delta Omega (Alpha chpt.). Home: 1504 Ivy Hill Rd Cockeysville MD 21030-1418 Office: Johns Hopkins U 615 N Wolfe St Baltimore MD 21205-2103

TRUBIN, JOHN, lawyer; b. East Orange, N.J., Aug. 1, 1917; s. Albert J. and Fanny (Babetch) T.; m. Edna Glassman, June 24, 1945; children—Priscilla Jo, Andrew James. Student, Johns Hopkins U., 1935-36, Coll. City N.Y., 1936-39; J.D., N.Y.U., 1943. Bar: N.Y. 1943. Asso. firm Strauss, Reich & Boyer, N.Y.C., 1943-46; pvt. practice N.Y.C., 1946-48; asst. atty. gen. N.Y. State, 1948-50; law sec. to Surrogate George Frankenthaler, 1950-53; chief counsel to Moreland Act Commn. on Workmen's Compensation, N.Y.C., 1953-54; first asst. atty. gen. N.Y. State, 1955-57; partner firm Trubin Sillcocks Edelman and Knapp, N.Y.C., 1958-84; counsel firm Parker Chapin Flattau & Klimpl., 1984-86; pvt. practice N.Y.C., 1986-90; mem. chief investigative counsel N.Y. State Senate Com. on Investigation, 1986-90; mem. N.Y.C. Housing Authority, 1990-94; commr. N.Y.C. Tax Appeals Tribunal, 1994—; mem. com. on character and fitness First Jud. Dept., 1976—. Trustee-at-large Fedn. Jewish Philanthropies; trustee N.Y.C. Police Found., Inc.; bd. dirs. Citizen's Com. for N.Y.C., Inc.; bd. overseers Center for N.Y.C. Affairs, New Sch. for Social Research; bd. dirs. United Jewish Appeal Greater N.Y. Mem. N.Y. County Lawyers Assn. (dir. 1967-73), Assn. Bar City N.Y., N.Y. State, Am. bar assns., Am. Judicature Soc. Home: 26 E 10th St New York NY 10003-5945 Office: 1 Centre St Rm 2400 New York NY 10007-1602

TRUBY, JOHN LOUIS, computer, management and trucking consultant; b. New Kensington, Pa., Nov. 28, 1933; s. George N. Sr. and Bertha (Deyber) T.; m. Mary Ann Holmes, Dec. 10, 1952 (dec.); children: Leslie Ann, Jacque Lee, Barbara Holmes. BBA cum laude, U. Pitts., 1959. Fin. analyst Union R.R., East Pittsburgh, Pa., 1959-64; adminstrn. mgr. Westvaco, Luke, Md., 1964-70; controller Lehigh Portland Cement Co., Allentown, Pa., 1970-72; v.p. finance Lehigh Portland Cement Co., 1972-74; pres. J. Truby Co., Zanesville, Ohio, 1974—, Truby Enterprises, Inc., Zanesville, 1981—, TruCom Inc., 1989—. Past pres. Keyser Jaycees, Mineral County Sch. Bd. Levy; class of 1959 agt. U. Pitts.; v.p., treas. Zanesville Habitat for Humanity; elder Cen. Presbyn. Ch. 1st lt. AUS, 1953-56. Named Outstanding Personality of the South, 1967. Mem. Am. Inst. Individual Investors, Fin. Execs. Inst., Zanesville Country Club. Home: 225 W Willow Dr Zanesville OH 43701-1252 Office: PO Box 2519 Zanesville OH 43702-2519

TRUCANO, MICHAEL, lawyer; b. Washington, May 28, 1945; s. Peter Joseph and Fern Margaret (Bauer) T.; m. Doreen E. Struck, 1969; children: Michael, David. BA, Carleton Coll., 1967; JD, NYU, 1970. Assoc. Dorsey & Whitney, Mpls., 1970-75, ptnr., 1976—. Office: Dorsey & Whitney 220 S 6th St Minneapolis MN 55402-4502

TRUCE, WILLIAM EVERETT, chemist, educator; b. Chgo., Sept. 30, 1917; s. Stanley C. and Frances (Novak) T.; m. Eloise Joyce McBroom, June 16, 1940; children—Nancy Jane, Roger William. B.S., U. Ill., 1939; Ph.D., Northwestern U., 1943. Mem. faculty Purdue U., 1946-88, prof. chemistry, 1956-88, prof. chemistry emeritus, 1988—, asst. dean Grad. Sch., 1963-66; Mem. numerous univ. dept. and profl. coms.; chmn. various profl. meetings. Co-author book; contbr. articles to profl. jours., chpts. to books. Guggenheim fellow Oxford U., 1957. Mem. Am. Chem. Soc., Phi Beta Kappa. Research in new methods of synthesis, devel. new kinds of compounds and reactions. Home: 220 Hopi Pl Boulder CO 80303 Office: Purdue U Dept Chemistry Lafayette IN 47907

TRUCKSIS, THERESA A., retired library director; b. Hubbard, Ohio, Sept. 1, 1924; d. Peter and Carmella (DiSilverio) Pagliasotti; m. Robert C. Trucksis, May 29, 1948 (dec. May 1980); children: M. Laura, Anne, Michele, Patricia, David, Robert, Claire, Peter; m. Philip P. Hickey, Oct. 19, 1985 (dec. May 1993). BS in Edn., Youngstown Coll., 1945; postgrad., Youngstown State U., 1968-71; MLS, Kent State U., 1972. Psychometrist Youngstown (Ohio) Coll., 1946-49; instr. ltd. svc. Youngstown State U., 1968-71; libr. Pub. Libr. Youngstown & Mahoning County, Youngstown, 1972-73, asst. dept. head, 1973-74, asst. dir., 1985-89, dir., 1989-97; dir. NOLA Regional Libr. System, Youngstown, 1974-85. Contbr. articles to profl. jours. Mem. bd. Hubbard Sch. Dist., 1980-85. Mem. ALA, Ohio Libr. Assn. (bd. dirs. 1979-81), Pub. Libr. Assn. Office: Pub Libr Youngstown & Mahoning County 305 Wick Ave Youngstown OH 44503-1003

TRUDEAU, GARRETSON BEEKMAN (GARRY TRUDEAU), cartoonist; b. N.Y.C., 1948; m. Jane Pauley, June 14, 1980; children: 1 son, Ross, 1 dau., Rachel (twins). M.F.A., Yale U., 1970, D.H.L., 1976. Artist graphics studio, New Haven, CT; syndicated cartoonist, writer. Creator: comic strip Doonesbury; syndicated nationwide comic strip; author: Still a Few Bugs in the System, 1972, The President is a Lot Smarter Than You Think, 1973, But This War Had Such Promise, 1973, Call Me When You Find America, 1973, Guilty, Guilty, Guilty, 1974, Joanie, 1974, The Doonesbury Chronicles, 1975, What Do We Have for the Witnesses, Johnnie?, 1975, Dare to Be Great, Ms. Caucus, 1975, Wouldn't A Gremlin Have Been More Sensible?, 1975, We'll Take it From Here, Sarge, 1975, Speaking of Inalienable Rights, Amy..., 1976, You're Never Too Old for Nuts and Berries, 1976, An Especially Tricky People, 1977, As the Kid Goes For Broke, 1977, Stalking the Perfect Tan, 1978, Any Grooming Hints for Your Fans, Rollie?, 1978, Doonesbury's Greatest Hits, 1978, But The Pension Fund was Just Sitting There, 1979, We're Not Out of the Woods Yet, 1979, A Tad Overweight, but Violet Eyes to Die For, 1980, And That's My Final Offer!, 1980, The People's Doonesbury, 1981, He's Never Heard of You, Either, 1981, In Search of Reagan's Brain, 1981, Ask for May, Settle for June, 1982, Unfortunately, She Was Also Wired for Sound, 1982, Adjectives Will Cost You Extra, 1982, Gotta Run, My Government is Collapsing, 1982, The Wreck of the Rusty Nail, 1983, You Give Great Meeting, Sid, 1983, Guess Who Fish Face, 1983, It's Supposed to be Yellow Pinhead: Selected Cartoons From Ask For May, Settle For June, Vol. I, 1983, Do All Birders Have Bedrooms, 1983, Farewell to Alms, 1984, Doonesbury Dossier: The Reagan Years, 1984, Doonesbury: A Musical Comedy, 1984, Check Your Egos at the Door, 1985, That's Doctor Sinatra, You Little Bimbo, 1986, Death of a Party Animal, 1986, Doonesbury Deluxe: Selected Glances Askance, 1987, Downtown Doonesbury, 1987, Calling Dr. Whoopee, 1987, The Doonesbury Desk Diary 1988, 1987, Talking Bout My G-G-Generation, 1988, We're Eating More Beets, 1988, Read My Lips, Make My Day, Eat Quiche & Die! A Doonesbury Collection, 1989, Small Collection, 1989, The Doonesbury Stamp Album, 1990, 1990, Recycled Doonesbury: Second Thoughts on a Gilded Age, 1990, You're Smokin' Now, Mr. Butts! A Doonesbury Book, 1990, Welcome to Club Scud: A Doonesbury Book, 1991, The Portable Doonesbury, 1993, In Search of Cigarette Holder Man: A Doonesbury Book, 1994, Doonesbury Nation, 1995; co-author: Talks From the Margaret Mead Taproom, 1979; contbr.: (with Nicholas von Hoffman) publs. including The People's Doonesbury; many others (recipient Pulitzer prize 1975); plays include: Doonesbury, 1983, Rapmaster Ronnie, A Partisan Review (with Elizabeth Swados), 1984. Pulitzer Prize for Editorial Cartooning, 1975. *

TRUDEAU, GARRY See TRUDEAU, GARRETSON BEEKMAN

TRUDEAU, PIERRE ELLIOTT, lawyer, former Canadian prime minister; b. Montreal, Que., Can., Oct. 18, 1919; s. Charles-Emile and Grace (Elliott) T.; m. Margaret Sinclair, Mar. 4, 1971 (div.); children: Justin Pierre, Alexandre Emmanuel, Michel Charles-Emile. B.A., Jean de Brebeuf Coll., Montreal, 1940; LL.L., U. Montreal, 1943; M.A., Harvard U., 1946; student, Ecole des Sciences Politiques, Paris, London Sch. Econs.; LLD (hon.), U. Alta., 1968, Queen's U., Kingston, 1968, U. Ottawa, 1974, Duke U., 1974, U. Keio, Japan, 1976, St. Xavier U., N.S., 1982, Notre Dame U., 1982, Dalhousie U., 1983, McGill U., 1985, U. B.C., 1986, U. Montreal, 1987, U. East Asia, Macau, 1987, Mt. Allison U., 1989, U. Toronto, 1991; LittD (hon.), U. Moncton, 1969. Bar: Que. 1944, Ont. 1967; created Queen's counsel 1969. Lawyer Montreal, 1952—; jr. economist staff Privy Coun., Ottawa, Ont., Can., 1949; assoc. prof. law, mem. Inst. Pub. Law U. Montreal, 1961-65; former mem. Ho. of Commons, from 1965; parliamentary sec. to prime minister, 1966-67; minister justice, atty. gen. Can., 1967-68; leader Liberal party, from 1968; prime minister Can., 1968-79, 80-84; leader of opposition in parliament, 1979-80, mem. Privy Council,, from 1979; lawyer Heenan Blaikie and predecessor firms, 1984—; co-founder Cité Libre (monthly rev.); del. France-Can. Interparliamentary Assn., 1966, UN, 1966. Author: Towards a Just Society: The Trudeau Years, 1990, Memoirs, 1993, The Canadian Way: Shaping Canada's Foreign Policy, 1968-84, Ivan Head and Pierre Trudeau, 1995, Against the Current, 1996. Decorated Order of Companions of Honor (Gt. Britain). Recipient Order of Merit U. Montreal, 1975, Berkeley citation U. Calif., 1977, Family of Man award N.Y.C. Council Chs., 1981, Ralston prize Faculty of Law Stanford U., Calif., 1990; Albert Einstein Internat. Peace prize, 1984; named Freeman of City of London, 1975, Companion of Honour, 1984, Companion of the Order of Can., 1985, hon. dean Faculty of Law U. Poitiers, France, 1975; hon. fellow London Sch. Econs., 1968. Mem. Canadian Bar Assn., Montreal Civil Liberties Union, Royal Soc. Can. Liberal. Roman Catholic. Office: Heenan Blaikie y Assocs Bur 2500, 1250 boul René-Lévesque Ouest, Montreal, PQ Canada H3B 4Y1

TRUDEL, MARC J., botanist. PhD, Cornell U. Prof. plant physiology and horticulture Laval U., former dean sch. agrl. and food scis., dir. gen. continuing edn. Office: Universite Laval, Ctr Continuing Edn, Quebec, PQ Canada G1K 7P4

TRUDNAK, STEPHEN JOSEPH, landscape architect; b. Nanticoke, Pa., Feb. 25, 1947; s. Stephen Adam and Marcella (Levulis) T.; m. Arden Batchelder Weill, Sept. 6, 1980. BS in Landscape Architecture, Pa. State U., 1970. Jr. landscape architect Kling Partnership, Phila., 1970-72; landscape architect firm Keith French Assocs., Washington, 1972-73; head dept. landscape architecture Linganore Center Design, Frederick, Md., 1973-74; head dept. landscape architecture Toups and Loiederman, Rockville, Md., 1974-76; project landscape architect Dade County Transit Improvement Program, Kaiser Transit Group, So. Calif. Rapid Transit Dist., Metro Rail Transit Cons.; v.p. Harry Weese & Assocs., Ltd., Miami, Fla., 1976-84; v.p. landscape architecture Canin Assocs., Orlando, Fla., 1984-87; dir. planning and design Bonita Bay Properties Inc., Bonita Springs, Fla., 1987-91; prin. Stephen J. Trudnak, P.A., Landscape Architecture and Land Planning, 1991—. V.p. bd. dirs. Koreshan State Hist. Site, 1989-94; mem. 'not for profit' com. Bonita Springs Cmty. Redevel. Agy., 1994-97; v.p. Bonita Springs Mainstreet Program, 1996, pres., 1997. Fellow Am. Soc. Landscape Architects (pres. Fla. chpt. 1983, chpt. adv. bd. 1984-85, elections task force 1986, publs. task force 1987, trustee 1987-89, membership task force, chmn. 1989-90, nat. v.p. chpt. and mem. svcs. 1992-94, non-dues revenue task force 1994-95, Landnet task force 1997—), Nat. Xeriscape Coun. (Fla. steering com.), Nat. Speleol. Soc. SCARAB; mem. Bonita Springs C. of C. (chair beautification com. 1991-92, 1994-95, bd. dirs. 1995—, v.p. edn. divsn. 1996—). Home: 554 104th Ave N Naples FL 33963-3225 Office: 3461 Bonita Bay Blvd Bonita Springs FL 34134-4384

TRUE, EDWARD KEENE, architectural engineer; b. Boston, July 12, 1915; s. Edward Payson and Laura Keene (Darling) T.; m. Mildred Louise Richenburg, Aug. 31, 1940; children: Edward Bartlett, Robert Payson, Peter Keene, James Duncan. B.S., MIT, 1939. Engr. Concrete Steel Co., Boston, 1939-40; instr. architecture U. Oreg., 1940-42; sr. engr. Raytheon Mfg. Co., Waltham, Mass., 1943-45; mem. faculty Grad. Sch. Design, Harvard U., 1945-76, prof. architecture, 1958-76; trustee, mem. bd. investment Middlesex Savs. Banks, Natick, Mass., 1954-88; cons. engr. and architect, 1947-59; ptnr. Souza and True, engrs., Cambridge, 1959—; engr. Souza and True Inc., 1970, pres., 1970-86; chmn. bd. Souza, True and Ptnrs. Inc., 1986—. Mem. Concord Planning Bd., 1948-58, chmn., 1954-58; mem. Concord Bd. Appeals, 1959-66, chmn., 1959-61; mem. Concord Bd. Selectmen, 1970-76, chmn., 1972-73; mem. exec. com. Mass. League of Cities and Towns, 1974-76, Searsport Yacht Club; pres. Hist. Soc./Hope, Maine, 1994-95. Home: PO Box 483 Searsport ME 04974-0483 Office: 653 Mount Auburn St Watertown MA 02172-2017

TRUE, JEAN DURLAND, Entrepreneur, oil company executive; b. Olney, Ill., Nov. 27, 1915; d. Clyde Earl and Harriet Louise (Brayton) Durland; m. Henry Alfonso True, Jr., Mar. 20, 1938; children: Tamma Jean (Mrs. Donald G. Hatten), Henry Alfonso III, Diemer Durland, David Lanmon. Student, Mont. State U., 1935-36. Ptnr. True Drilling Co., Casper, Wyo., 1951—, True Oil Co., Casper, 1951-94, Eighty-Eight Oil Co., 1955-94, True Geothermal Energy Co., 1980—, True Ranches, 1981-94; officer, dir. White Stallion Ranch, Inc., Tucson, Smokey Oil Co., Casper. Mem. steering com. YMCA, Casper, 1954-55, bd. dirs., 1956-58; mem. bd. dirs. Gottsche Rehab. Ctr., Thermopolis, Wyo., 1966-93, mem. exec. bd. 1966-93, v.p., 1973-90; mem. adv. bd. for adult edn. U. Wyo., 1966-68; mem. Ft. Casper Commn., Casper, 1973-79; bd. dirs. Mus. of Rockies, Bozeman, Mont., 1983-87, mem. Nat. Adv. Bd., 1997—; bd. dirs. Nicolaysen Art Mus., 1988-93; mem. Nat. Fedn. Rep. Women's Clubs; del. Rep. nat. conv., 1972; trustee Trooper Found., 1995—. Mem. Rocky Mountain Oil and Gas Assn., Casper Area C. of C., Alpha Gamma Delta, Casper Country Club, Petroleum Club (Casper). Episcopalian. Office: Rivercross Rd PO Box 2360 Casper WY 82602-2360

TRUE, RICHARD BROWNELL, electrical engineer; b. Framingham, Mass., Apr. 4, 1943; s. Charles Richard and Marjorie Brownell (Clapp) T.; m. Sarah Jellison, Feb. 5, 1966; children: Christopher Edmund, Jonathan Richard. BSEE, Brown U., 1966; MS in Microwave Engring., U. Conn., 1968, PhD in Electrophysics, 1972. Elec. engr. Raytheon Co., Inc., Portsmouth, R.I., 1966; lectr., rschr. U. Conn., Storrs, 1966-72; tech. cons., elec. engr. Microwave Assocs., Inc., Burlington, Mass., 1972-73; sr. engr., dept. analyst Litton Systems, Inc., San Carlos, Calif., 1973-78, sr. scientist, 1978-90, chief scientist, 1990—; cons. True Sci., Sunnyvale, 1985—; bd. dirs. AFTER Program U. Utah, 1980-85, chmn. recruiting brochure, 1981, organizer spl. topics course, 1982, 83, lectr. spl. topics course, 1982-86, indsl. thesis advisor, 1982-87; bd. dirs. AFTER Program Stanford U., 1979-81, organizer spl. topics course, 1980, 81, lectr. spl. topics course, 1978-81, indsl. thesis advisor, 1978-81. Patentee in field; contbr. articles to profl. jours. and papers to meetings. Recipient Paul Rappaport award for best paper of yr. in IEEE Electron Devices Soc. publ., 1987, Litton Industries Corp. Advanced Tech. award for electron beam dynamics software, 1992; NDEA fellow, 1967-70, NSF fellow, 1970-71. Fellow IEEE (mem. advminstrv. com. electron devices soc. 1988-94, assoc. editor IEEE Transactions on Electron Devices 1986-90, Paul Rappaport award electron devices soc. 1987); mem. Sigma Xi. Home: 1760 Karameos Dr Sunnyvale CA 94087-5226 Office: Litton Systems Inc 960 Industrial Rd San Carlos CA 94070-4116 *Focus is everything.*

TRUE, ROY JOE, lawyer; b. Shreveport, La., Feb. 20, 1938; s. Collins B. and Lula Mae (Cady) T.; m. Patsy Jean Hudsmith, Aug. 29, 1959; children: Andrea Alane, Alyssa Anne, Ashley Alisbeth. Student, Centenary Coll., 1957; BS, Tex. Christian U., 1961; LLB, So. Meth. U., 1963, postgrad., 1968-69. Bar: Tex. 1963. Pvt. practice Dallas, 1963—; pres. Invesco Internat. Corp., 1969-70, True & Sewell and predecessor firms, 1975—; bus. adviser, counselor Mickey Mantle, 1969-95; dir. The Mickey Mantle Found. Editorial bd.: Southwestern Law Jour, 1962-63. Served with AUS, 1956. Mem. Am., Dallas bar assns., Tex. Assn. Bank Counsel, Phi Alpha Delta. Home: 5601 Ursula Ln Dallas TX 75229-6429 Office: 8080 N Central Expy Ste 9 Dallas TX 75206-1806

TRUEBA, FERNANDO, film director and producer, screenwriter; b. Madrid, Jan. 18, 1955; s. Maximo Rodriguez and Palmira Trueba; m. Cristina Huete, Oct. 8, 1982; 1 child, Jonas-Groucho. Film critic El Pais, newspaper, Madrid, 1976-79; editor, dir. Casablanca, film mag., Madrid, 1981-83. Dir., screenwriter Opera Prima, 1980 (Silver Hugo award Chgo. Film Festival 1980), Mientras el Cuerpo Aguante, 1982, Sal Gorda, 1983, Se Infiel y No Mires con Quien, 1985, El Año de Las Luces, 1986 (Silver Bear award Berlin Film Festival 1987), The Mad Monkey, 1989, Belle époque, 1992 (Academy Award, Best Foreign Language Film, 1993), Two Much, 1996; producer, screenwriter A Contratiempo, 1981, De Tripas Corazon, 1984, La Mujer de tu Vida, 1988-89; producer Lulu de Noche, 1985, El Juego Mas Divertido, 1987, Earth Magicians, 1989—, Amo tu cama rica, 1991, Alas de mariposa, 1991 (Concha of Gold award San Sebastian Film Festival 1991), Sublet, 1992; also dir. short films. Mem. Acad. Motion Pictures Spain (pres. 1988). Home: Bueso Pineda 29, 28043 Madrid Spain Office: Antonio Caver0 37, 28043 Madrid Spain also: The Gersh Agy 232 N Canon Dr Beverly Hills CA 90210*

TRUEBLOOD, ALAN STUBBS, former modern language educator; b. Haverford, Pa., May 3, 1917; s. Howard M. and Louise (Nyitray) T. B.A., Harvard U., 1938, M.A., 1941, Ph.D., 1951; M.A. (hon.), Brown U., 1957. Ednl. dir. Chile-U.S. Cultural Inst., Santiago, 1942-43; mem. faculty Brown U., 1947—, prof. Spanish, 1963-82, prof. comparative lit., 1972-82, adj. prof., 1982-87, prof. emeritus, 1987—, chmn. dept. Hispanic and Italian studies, 1967-72, chmn. dept. comparative lit., 1973-77; Fulbright lectr. Am. studies, Colombia, 1972; Sr. Resident scholar Merton Coll., Oxford (Eng.) U., 1973. Author: Experience and Artistic Expression in Lope de Vega, 1974, Antonio Machado, Selected Poems, 1982, (with E. Honig) Lope de Vega, La Dorotea, 1985, Letter and Spirit in Hispanic Writers: Selected Essays, 1986, A Sor Juana Anthology, 1988; transl. Gongora (Picasso), 1985, Garcia Lorca, Complete Poems, 1991, Selected Poems, 1995, Songs, Lament for Ignacio Sanchez Mejias, Villegas, Colombia from the Air, 1993, Villegas, The Route of Humboldt: Colombia and Venezuela, 2 vols., 1994. Served to lt. USNR, 1943-46. Fulbright research scholar Chile, 1958; Guggenheim fellow, 1965-66; Nat. Endowment for Humanities grantee, 1977-81; recipient Spanish Govt. award Order of Isabel la Catolica, 1990. Home: 54 Willow Ave Little Compton RI 02837-1532 Office: Brown U PO Box 1961 Providence RI 02912-1961

TRUEBLOOD, HARRY ALBERT, JR., oil company executive; b. Wichita Falls, Tex., Aug. 28, 1925; s. Harry A. and Marguerite (Barnhart) T.; m. Lucile Bernard, Jan. 22, 1953; children: Katherine T. Astin, John B. Student, Tex. A&M Coll., 1942-43; BS in Petroleum Engring., U. Tex., 1948. Petroleum engr. Cal. Co., 1948-51; chief engr. McDermott & Barnhart Co., Colo., Tex., 1951-52; cons. petroleum and geol. engr. Denver, 1952-55; pres. Colo. Western Exploration Inc., Denver, 1955-58; pres. Consol. Oil and Gas., Inc., 1958-88, chmn. bd., chief exec. officer, 1969-88; chmn. bd., chief exec. officer Princeville Devel. Corp., 1979-87, pres., 1984-86; chmn. bd., chief exec. officer Columbus Energy Corp., 1983—; chmn. bd., CEO, Princeville Airways, Inc., 1979-87; pres. CEC Resources, Ltd., 1984—. With USNR, 1944-46, ensign, 1949-52. Mem. Soc. Petroleum Engrs., Am. Petroleum Inst., World Pres. Orgn., Chief Execs. Orgn. (bd. dirs.), Ind. Petroleum Assn. Am. (exec. com.), Natural Gas Supply Assn. (exec. com.), Denver Petroleum Club, Cherry Hills Country Club, Univ. Club, One Hundred Club. Roman Catholic. Home: 2800 S University Blvd Apt 82 Denver CO 80210-6056 Office: Columbus Energy Corp 1660 Lincoln St Ste 2400 Denver CO 80264-2401

TRUEBLOOD, KENNETH NYITRAY, retired chemist, educator; b. Dobbs Ferry, N.Y., Apr. 24, 1920; s. Howard Moffit and Louise (Nyitray) T.; m. Jean Turner, Mar. 7, 1970. A.B., Harvard, 1941; Ph.D., Calif. Inst. Tech., 1947. Postdoctoral fellow chemistry dept. Calif. Inst. Tech., Pasadena, 1947-49; faculty UCLA, 1949-89, prof. chemistry, 1960-89, ret., chmn. dept. chemistry, 1965-70, 90-91, dean Coll. Letters and Sci., 1971-74, chmn. acad. senate, 1983-84; vis. prof. chemistry U. Ibadan, Nigeria, 1964-65; Mem. U.S. Nat. Com. on Crystallography, 1960-65, vice chmn., 1963-65; exchange visitor to USSR, 1965. Co-author Crystal Structure Analysis: A Primer, 1972; editor: Dorothy Hodgkin and Linus Pauling - A Tribute, 1995. Recipient Fulbright award Oxford (Eng.) U., 1956-57, UCLA Disting. Teaching award, 1961, award for excellence in teaching Mfg. Chemists Assn., 1978, Coll. prize Coll. Letters and Scis., UCLA, 1982; Guggenheim fellow Eidgenössiche Technische Hochschule Zurich, Switzerland, 1976-77, Recipient Fankuchen Memorial awardAm. Crystallographic Assn., 1995. Mem. Am. Chem. Soc., Am. Crystallographic Assn. (Fankuchen award 1995), Phi Beta Kappa, Sigma Xi, Alpha Chi Sigma. Research and publs. on theory of chromatography, chem. crystallography including high speed computer applications; analysis of molecule motion in crystals. Home: 1089 Moraga Dr Los Angeles CA 90049-1620

TRUEBLOOD, PAUL GRAHAM, retired English educator, author, editor; b. Macksburg, Iowa, Oct. 21, 1905; s. Charles E. and Adele (Graham) T.; m. Helen Churchill, Aug. 19, 1931; children—Anne Williams, Susan Stuart. BA, Willamette U., 1928; MA, Duke U., 1930, Ph.D., 1935; Litt.D. (hon.), Willamette U., 1984. Instr. Friends U., 1931-34; English master Mohonk Sch. Boys, Lake Mohonk, N.Y., 1935-37; instr. U. Idaho, 1937-40; asso. prof. Stockton Coll., 1940-46; asst. prof. U. Wash., 1947-52; vis. prof. U. Oreg., 1954-55; prof. English, head dept. Willamette U., 1955-70, prof. emeritus, 1971—; vis. lectr. U. B.C., summer 1963. Author: The Flowering of Byron's Genius, 2d edit, 1962, Lord Byron, 2d edit, 1977; Editor: Byron's Political and Cultural Influence in Nineteeth-Century Europe: A Symposium, 1981; Contbr. to charter issues Keats-Shelley Jour, 1952, Byron Jour, 1973. Pendle Hill fellow, 1934-35; fellow Am. Council Learned Socs., 1952-53; recipient Disting. Alumni citation Willamette U., 1975. Mem. MLA, Keats-Shelley Assn. Am., Philol. Assn. Pacific Coast (exec. com. 1964-65), Byron Soc. (founding mem. Am. com. 1973, bd. dirs. 1975, delivered lecture to Byron Soc. in Ho. of Lords 1975). Home: Capitol Manor 1955 Dallas Hwy NW Apt 903 Salem OR 97304-4496

TRUEHEART, HARRY PARKER, III, lawyer; b. Rochester, N.Y., Mar. 27, 1944; s. Harry Parker and Bertha (Hendryx) T.; m. Karen Ellingson, June 26, 1965; children: Eric Parker, Kathryn Marie. BA, Harvard U., also JD. Bar: N.Y. 1970, Fla. 1975. Assoc. Nixon, Hargrave, Devans & Doyle LLP, Rochester, 1969-77, ptnr., 1977—; spkr. fed. ct. practice, 1979-83; mng. ptnr., 1995—; arbitrator, mediator Ctr. Pub. Resources, Inst. Dispute Resolution, Am. Arbitration Assn. Trustee Sta WXXI Broadcasting, The Greater Rochester Metro C. of C.; bd. dirs. Rochester Downtown Devel. Corp., High Tech. of Rochester, Inc., Park Ridge Found. Fellow N.Y. Bar Found.; mem. ABA, N.Y. State Bar Assn. (chair comml. and fed. litigation sect. 1992-93, house of del.), Monroe County Bar Assn., Fed. Bar Coun (v.p.), Am. Arbitration Assn. Co-author: Federal Civil Practice; contbr. chpt. to book; contbr. articles on fed. ct. litigation, microfilm records, profl. liability in connection with use of computers to profl. jours. Office: Nixon Hargrave Devans & Doyle LLP Clinton Sq Rochester NY 14604 also: Nixon Hargrave Devans & Doyle 437 Madison Ave New York NY 10022

TRUEHILL, MARSHALL, JR., minister; b. New Orleans, Sept. 5, 1948; s. Marshall Truehill and Inez Gray Williams; adopted s. Elizabeth (May) T.; m. Mary Ola Williams, Dec. 20, 1969 (div. 1972); m. Valli Maria Dobard, July 22, 1972; children: Briana Traci, Marshall III, Jessica, Quentin. B in Music Edn., Xavier U., 1973; BTh, Christian Bible Coll., 1979; MDiv, Orleans Bapt. Theol. Sem., 1986; D Ministry, New Orleans Bapt. Theol. Seminary, 1990; postgrad., U. New Orleans. Ordained to ministry Bapt. Ch., 1980; cert. tchr., La. Tchr. Orleans Parish Sch. Bd., New Orleans, 1973-78, Delgado Community Coll., New Orleans, 1975-78; pastor Faith in Action Bapt. Ch., New Orleans, 1982—; founder, dir. Faith in Action Evangel. Team, New Orleans, 1977—; lectr. Nat. Bapt. Conv. on Congl. Evangelism, New Orleans, 1977-79; cons. So. Bapt. Conv. Home Mission Bd., La., 1986—. Bd. dirs. Project New Orleans, 1983—. Democrat. Avocations: computers, aquariums, interior decorating, aerobics. Office: Faith in Action Evang Team 2544 Onzaga St New Orleans LA 70119-2344 *The greatest investment one can make in this life is an investment in the life of another person. That is the only investment with eternal value.*

TRUEMAN, WILLIAM PETER MAIN, broadcaster, newspaper columnist; b. Sackville, N.B., Can., Dec. 25, 1934; s. Albert William and Jean Alberta (Miller) T.; m. Eleanor Joy Wark, Dec. 22, 1956; children: Anne, Mark, Victoria. Student, U. N.B., 1951-54. UN corr. Montreal Star, 1957-62, Washington corr., 1962-65; Parliamentary corr. Toronto Star, Ottawa, Ont., 1965-67; nat. dir. UN Assn. in Can., 1967-68; nat. news writer CBC, Toronto, 1968-69; exec. producer news, head network news CBC, 1969-72; freelance reporter, 1972-73; anchorman Global TV News, Don Mills, Ont., 1974-88; free lance broadcaster, 1988—; media critic Toronto Star's Starweek mag., 1988-96; Kingston Whig-Std., 1989-96. Host, writer Canadian Discovery Channel TV series Great Canadian Parks, 1995—. Recipient Bowater award for journalism, 1962, Sam Ross award, 1983.

TRUEMPER, JOHN JAMES, JR., retired architect; b. Helena, Ark., June 18, 1924; s. John James and Mary Ann (Jacob) T.; m. Julia Clare Wood, Nov. 21, 1956; children: Zachary Wood, John James III, Ann Rutland Penick. BS in Arch., U. Ill., 1950; DHL (hon.), Lyon Coll., 1995. With archtl. firm Cromwell, Truemper, Levy, Thompson, Woodsmall Inc. (and predecessors), Little Rock, 1950-94; v.p. Cromwell, Truemper, Levy, Thompson, Woodsmall Inc. (and predecessors), 1972-74, pres., 1974-81, chmn. bd., 1980-89; ret., 1994; mem. Ark. Bd. Architects, 1974-82. Prin. works include Ark. system for edn. and tng. mentally retarded, 1956-78, Winrock Farm, Morrilton, Ark., 1953-58, Ark. State Parks, 1955-75, Ark. Power & Light Co., 1961-89, Lyon Coll., Batesville, 1983-94; author: A Century of Service, 1885-1985, 1985. Pres. Ark. Arts Ctr., 1979, chmn. bd., 1980; mem. Little Rock Bldg. Code Bd. Appeals, 1961-86, chmn., 1971-86; mem. Ark. Hist. Preservtion Rev. Bd.; bd. dirs. Little Rock Met. YMCA, 1975-84; mem. Friends of Libr. Bd., U. Ark., Little Rock, 1989, pres. 1995. With USAAF, 1943-46. Recipient Winthrop Rockefeller Meml. award Ark. Arts Center, 1980. Fellow AIA, Greater Little Rock C. of C. (dir. 1979-88). Roman Catholic. Home: 5216 Crestwood Dr Little Rock AR 72207-5404

TRUESDALE, JOHN CUSHMAN, government executive; b. Grand Rapids, Mich., July 17, 1921; s. John Cushman and Hazel (Christianson) T.; m. Karin A. Nelson, Feb. 10, 1957; children—John Cushman, Charles N., Margaret E., Andrew C. A.B., Grinnell Coll., 1942; M.S., Cornell U., 1948; J.D., Georgetown U., 1972. Bar: Md. bar 1972, D.C. bar 1973. Field examiner NLRB, Buffalo and New Orleans, 1948-52; adminstrv. analyst NLRB, Washington, 1952-57, assoc. exec. sec., 1963-68; dep. exec. sec. NLRB, 1968-72, exec. sec., 1972-77, 81-94, mem., 1977-81, 94, 95; labor arbitrator, 1996—; dir. info., dir. World Data Center/Rockets and Satellites, IGY, Nat. Acad. Scis., Washington, 1957-63. Editor-in-chief: How to Take a Case Before the NLRB, 1997—. Served with USCG, 1942-46. Recipient Presdl. award Pres. of U.S., 1988. Mem. ABA, D.C. Bar Assn., Assn. Labor Rels. Agys. (pres. 1992-93). Democrat. Congregationalist. Office: Nat Labor Rels Bd 1099 14th St NW Washington DC 20570-0001

TRUESDELL, TIMOTHY LEE, research director, consultant, real estate investor; b. Niles, Mich., Oct. 8, 1951; s. Patrick Daniel and LaVonne Marie (Fries) T. BA, U. Notre Dame, 1974. Asst. to exec. dir. Notre Dame U. Alumni Assn., 1974-77, asst. dir., 1977-79; alumni editor Notre Dame mag., 1979-83; v.p. Truesdell Real Estate Investment, Sacramento, 1983-85; dir. devel. rsch. U. Notre Dame, 1985—; devel. cons. Am. Acad. Neurology, 1991-92, Hospice of St. Joseph County, South Bend, Ind., 1992-93, U. St. Thomas, Mpls., Xavier U., Cin.,1993-94, Niles Comty. Libr., 1993—, St. Joseph Mishawaka (Ind.) Health Svcs., 1995-96, Berrien County ARC, 1996, Advancement Ptnrs., Inc., Columbus, 1996—, Little Flower Cath. Ch., South Bend, Ind., 1997—. Councilman City of Niles, 1983-91; pres. St. Mary's Sch Bd. Edn., Niles, 1981-82; chmn. S.W. Mich. Comty. Ambulance, Niles, 1985-89; mem. Berrien County (Mich.) Reps.; pres. Fernwood Botanic Gardens, Niles, 1993—. Mem. Coun. for Advancement and Support of Edn., Assn. Profl. Rschrs. for Advancement (bd. dirs. Ind. Chpt.), Optimists (sec. 1983-84), Knights of Malta. Republican. Roman Catholic. Avocations: golf, investments, antique collecting, fishing. Home: 37 N Lincoln Ave Niles MI 49120-1501 Office: U Notre Dame 100 Grace Hall Notre Dame IN 46556-5612

TRUESDELL, WALTER GEORGE, minister, librarian; b. N.Y.C., Oct. 22, 1919; s. George Anson and Hattie (Evans) T.; m. Mary Schurok, June 10, 1944; children: Walter George, Susan Hattie. AB, Columbia U., 1941, MA, 1975; MDiv, Phila. Theol. Sem., 1944; BLS, Pratt Inst., 1950. Ordained to ministry Ref. Episcopal Ch., 1944. Asst. min. 1st Ref. Episcopal Ch., N.Y.C., 1944-54, sr. assoc. min., 1989—; lectr. apologetics and English Bible Theol. Sem. Ref. Episcopal Ch., Phila., 1945-48, libr., 1964-93; libr. Shelton Coll., 1951-69; libr. Cummins Meml. Theol. Sem. Reformed Episcopal, Summerville, S.C., 1996—; rector Ch. of the Redemption, Bklyn., 1956—; chmn. com. on state of ch. Ref. Episcopal Ch., 1960-87, mem., 1987—, mem. gen. com. 1978—. Editor Episcopal Recorder, 1980—. Mem. ALA (life), Pa. Libr. Assn., Assn. Statisticians Am. Religious Bodies. Home and Office: 306 E 90th St New York NY 10128-5144 Office: Cummins Meml Theol Sem 705 S Main St Summerville SC 29483-5911 *Out of the privilege of a broad educational background and living in the astonishing technology of the 20th century, and yet to be, in the turbulence of war, crime, starvation, and distress of mind and spirit, I am convicted anew of the need to know Christ, who said, "I am the way, the truth, and the life."*

TRUESDELL, WESLEY EDWIN, public relations and investor relations consultant; b. Bklyn., Dec. 16, 1927; s. Wesley Edwin and Anna Josephine (Gippert) R.; m. Mabel Johnsen, Oct. 4, 1957. BBA, St. John's U., Jamaica, N.Y., 1956. With Doremus & Co. (advt. and pub. rels.), N.Y.C., 1953-88; v.p. Doremus & Co., 1969-74; dir. Doremus & Co. (advt. and pub. rels.), 1970-88, sr. v.p., mgr. public relations dept., 1974-81, exec. v.p., 1981-88, mem. exec. com., 1978-88, chmn. profit sharing com., 1975-81; dir. Creamer, Dickson, Basford (subs. EuroRSCG, Paris), N.Y.C., 1988-91, exec. v.p., gen. mgr., 1988-89, dep. chmn., 1989-91, also bd. dirs.; pres. The W.E. Truesdell Co., 1991—. Contbg. author: Dealing With The Business and Financial Media, 1989, Dartnell's Public Relations Handbook, 1996; contbr. articles profl. jours. V.p. S.I. Citizens Planning Com., 1965-72; trustee S.I. Inst. Arts and Scis., 1970-88; chmn. High Rock Park Conservation Ctr., 1970-75. Master sgt. USAR, 1950-52, Korea. Mem. Pub. Rels. Soc. Am. (editor newsletter Fin. Communications Report 1990-95), Nat. Investor Rels. Inst. (pres. N.Y.C. chpt. 1979-80), Women Execs. in Pub. Rels. (bd. dirs. 1993—), Downtown-Lower Manhattan Assn. (dir. 1975-88), Profl. Communicators N.Y., Bklyn. Tech. Rsch. Found. Inc. (bd. dirs. 1988—). Republican. Home: Silver Ct Staten Island NY 10301-3420 Office: The W E Truesdell Co 200 Park Ave Fl 26 New York NY 10166-0005

TRUETT, HAROLD JOSEPH, III (TIM TRUETT), lawyer; b. Alameda, Calif., Feb. 13, 1946; s. Harold Joseph and Lois Lucille (Mellin) T.; 1 child, Harold Joseph IV; m. Anna V. Billante, Oct. 1, 1983; 1 child, James S. Carstensen. BA, U. San Francisco, 1968, JD, 1975. Bar: Calif. 1975, Hawaii 1987, U.S. Dist. Ct. (ea., so., no., and cen. dists.) Calif. 1976, Hawaii 1987, U.S. Ct. Appeals (9th cir.) 1980, U.S. Supreme Ct. 1988, U.S. Ct. Fed. Claims, 1995. Assoc. Hoberg, Finger et al, San Francisco, 1975-78, Bledsoe, Smith et al, San Francisco, 1979-80, Abramson & Bianco, San Francisco, 1980-83; mem. Ingram & Truett, San Rafael, 1983-90; prin. Law Office of H.J. Tim Truett, San Francisco, 1991-93, Winchell & Truett, San Francisco, 1994—; lectr. trial practice Am. Coll. Legal Medicine, 1989, 90, Calif. Continuing Edn. of the Bar. Bd. dirs. Shining Star Found. 1991—, Marin County, Calif.; mem. Marin Dem. Coun., San Rafael, 1983-90. Lt., aviator USN, 1967-74. Mem. ABA, Hawaii Bar Assn., Assn. Trial Lawyers Am., Calif. Bar Assn. (com. for adminstrn. of justice, conf. of dels.), San Francisco Bar Assn., Calif. Trial Lawyers Assn., Lawyers Pilots Assn. Roman Catholic. Home: 2622 Leavenworth St San Francisco CA 94133-1614

TRUEX, DOROTHY ADINE, retired university administrator; b. Sedalia, Mo., Oct. 6, 1915; d. Chester Morrison and Madge (Nicholson) T. AB, William Jewell Coll., 1936; MA, U. Mo., 1937; EdD, Columbia U., 1956. Asst. dean women N.W. Mo. State U., Maryville, 1939-43; dean women N.W. Mo. State U., 1943-45, Mercer U., Macon, Ga., 1945-47, U. Okla., Norman, 1947-69; assoc. prof. U. Okla., 1969-72, dir. rsch. and program devel., 1969-74, prof. edn., 1972-74, dir. grad. program in student pers. svcs., 1969-74; vice chancellor for student affairs U. Ark., Little Rock, 1974-83; alumni specialist U. Ark., 1983-84, acad. adviser, 1984-87; exec. bd. N. Cen. Assn. Schs. and Colls., 1977-83. Mem. Nat. Assn. Women Deans, Adminstrs. and Counselors (pres. 1973-74), So. Coll. Pers. Assn. (pres. 1970), Okla. Coll. Pers. Assn. (pres. 1972-73), William Jewell Coll. Alumni Assn. (pres. 1970-73), Pi Beta Phi, Alpha Lambda Delta, Mortar Bd., Sigma Tau Delta, Cardinal Key, Gamma Alpha Chi, Kappa Delta Pi, Pi Lambda Theta, Alpha Psi Omega, Pi Gamma Mu, Delta Kappa Gamma, Phi Delta Kappa, Phi Kappa Phi. (nat. v.p. 1986-89). Avocation: novelist. Home: 14300 Chenal Pky Apt 7422 Little Rock AR 72211-5819

TRUHLAR, DONALD GENE, chemist, educator; b. Chgo., Feb. 27, 1944; s. John Joseph and Lucille Marie (Vancura) T.; m. Jane Teresa Gust, Aug. 28, 1965; children: Sara Elizabeth, Stephanie Marie. BA in Chemistry summa cum laude, St. Mary's Coll., Winona, Minn., 1965; PhD in Chemistry, Calif. Inst. Tech., 1970. Asst. prof. chemistry and chem. physics U. Minn., Mpls, 1969-72; assoc. prof. U. Minn., Mpls., 1972-76, prof., 1976-93, Inst. of Tech. prof., 1993—; cons. Los Alamos Sci. Lab.; vis. fellow Joint Inst. for Lab. Astrophysics, 1975-76; sci. dir. Minn. Supercomputer Inst., 1987-88, dir., 1988-96. Editor Theoretica Chimica Acta, 1985-96, Computer Physics Comms., 1986—, Topics Phys. Chemistry, 1992—, Understanding Chem. Reactivity, 1990-92, Internat. Jour. Modern Physics C, 1994—; mem. editorial bd. Jour. Chem. Physics, 1978-80, Chem. Physics Letters, 1982—, Jour. Phys. Chemistry, 1985-87, Advances in Chem. Physics, 1993—, IEEE Computational Sci. and Engring., 1994—, Internat. Jour. Quantum Chemistry, 1996—, Theoretical Chemistry Accounts, 1997—. Ruhland Walzer Meml. scholar, 1961-62; John Stauffer fellow, 1965-66, NDEA fellow, 1966-68, Alfred P. Sloan Found. fellow, 1973-77; grantee NSF, 1971—, NASA, 1987-95, U.S. Dept. Energy, 1979—, NIST, 1995—. Fellow AAAS, Am. Phys. Soc.; mem. Am. Chem. Soc. (sec.-treas. theoretical chemistry subdivsn. 1980-89, councilor 1985-87, editor jour. 1984—). Achievements include research, numerous publications in field. Home: 5033 Thomas Ave S Minneapolis MN 55410-2240 Office: U Minn Minn Supercomputer Inst 1200 Washington Ave S Minneapolis MN 55415-1227

TRUHLAR, DORIS BROADDUS, lawyer; b. Oklahoma City, Sept. 18, 1946; d. Elbridge Sidney and Doris Mary (Prock) Broaddus; divs.; chlidren: Samara Taryle, Brett Taryle (dec.); m. Robert John Truhlar, June 24, 1978; children: Ivy, Holly. B in journalism, U. Mo., 1967; MA, U. Denver, 1976, JD with honors, 1980. Bar: Colo. 1981, U.S. Dist. Ct. Colo. 1981, U.S. Ct. Appeals (10th cir.) 1981. Law clk. to Hon. Robert H. McWilliams, Jr. U.S. Ct. Appeals (10th cir.), Denver, 1980-81; assoc. Holme, Roberts & Owen, Denver; corp. sec., gen. counsel Hart Exploration and Prodn. Co., Englewood, Colo.; ptnr. Truhlar & Truhlar, Littleton, Colo., 1985—; adj. prof. U. Denver Coll. Law, 1986-88, 90-91, mem. adv. com. advocacy skills program, 1990; spkr. CLE Programs; expert witness regarding attys. fees; mem. Thursday Night Bar Adv. Bd., 1995—, chair, 1996-97. Trainer attys. and vols. who work with abused and neglected children; active various vol. programs; vestry bd. Good Shepherd Episcopal Ch., 1992-95; mem. adv. com. Metro Parenting and Divorce Ctr., 1995—. Recipient Woman of Achievement, Entreprneur of Yr. award Met. YWCA of Denver, 1993, Denver Gridiron award, 1st pl. Editorial Writing award Nat. Edn. Writers Assn., also several Mo. Press Assn. awards and newspaper writing awards. Mem: ABA, Am. Trial Lawyers Assn., Denver Bar Assn. (Vol. Atty. of Yr. award), Colo. Bar Assn. (organizer, tchr. pro se div. clinics, ethics com. 1984-91, calling com.), Colo. Trial Lawyers Assn. (chmn. Torts Involving Children 1990), Colo. Women's Bar Assn. (mem. jud. com. 1995—), Arapahoe County Bar Assn. (Community Svc. award, Pro Bono Atty. 1992). Office: 1901 W Littleton Blvd Littleton CO 80120-2022

TRUHLSEN, STANLEY MARSHALL, physician, educator; b. Herman, Nebr., Nov. 13, 1920; s. Henry and Lola Mollie (Marshall) T.; m. Ruth Haney, June 2, 1943 (dec. Dec. 1976); children: William, Nancy, Stanley M., Barbara; m. Dorothy D. Johnson, Jan 10, 1981. AB, U. Nebr., 1941, MD, 1944. Diplomate Am. Bd. Ophthalmology. Intern Albany (N.Y.) Hosp., 1944-45; resident Barnes Hosp., St. Louis, 1948-51; practice medicine specializing in ophthalmology Omaha, 1951—; mem. staff U. Nebr., Clarkson, Immanuel; pres. med. staff Immanuel Hosp., 1961, Clarkson Hosp., 1972-73; prof. ophthalmology U. Nebr. Coll. Medicine, 1974-81, clin. prof., 1981-93, interim chmn. dept. ophthalmology, 1989-90; dir. Nebr. Blue Cross and Blue Shield, 1971-95, vice chmn. bd., 1986-96; dir. Health Planning Council Midlands, 1972-75, Clarkson Hosp., 1974-76, Nebr. Soc. Prevention Blindness., Lions Eye Bank of Nebr., 1983-91. Trustee Omaha Home of Boys, 1966—, Brownell Talbot Sch., 1966-69, Omaha Citizens Assbmely, 1972—, U. Nebr. Found., 1985—, Action Internat., Inc., 1994-96. With AUS, 1946-48. Recipient Alumni Achievement award U. Nebr., 1986, Disting. Alumnus Achievement award U. Nebr. Med. Ctr., 1989, Ann. Hon. awards for civic and community contbns.; named Omaha Health Citizen of Yr., 1989; named King Aksarben XCI for outstanding contbns. to Nebr. community, 1985. Fellow ACS (bd. govs. 1985-91); mem. Am. Ophthal. Soc. (asst. editor transactions 1973-79, editor 1979-84, coun. 1987-92, v.p. 1994, pres. 1995), Am. Acad. Ophthalmology and Otolaryngology (assoc. editor transactions 1968-75, editor 1975-80), Am. Acad. Ophthamology (1st v.p. 1981, pres. 1983, vice chmn. AAO Found. 1992—), Nebr. Acad. Ophthalmology (pres. 1975), Am. Eye Study Club (pres. 1962), Omaha Med. Soc. (pres. 1973), Omaha Country Club (pres. 1977-78), U. Nebr. Med. Ctr. Alumni Assn. (pres. 1958), Masons, Rotary (pres. local club 1981-82), Sigma Xi, Alpha Omega Alpha, Sigma Nu, Phi Rho Sigma. Republican. Home: 10086 Fieldcrest Dr Omaha NE 68114-4939

TRUITT, ANNE DEAN, artist; b. Balt., Mar. 16, 1921; d. Duncan Witt and Louisa Folsom (Williams) Dean; m. James McConnell Truitt, Sept. 19, 1947 (div.); children—Alexandra, Mary McConnell, Samuel Rogers. BA, Bryn Mawr Coll., 1943; postgrad., Inst. Contemporary Art, Washington, 1948-50. Exhibited in one woman shows at Andre Emmerich Gallery, N.Y.C., 1963, 65, 69, 75, 80, 86, 91, Minami Gallery, Tokyo, 1964, 67, Balt. Mus. Art, 1969, 75, 92, Pyramid Galleries, Washington, 1971, 73, 75, 77, Whitney Mus. Am. Art, N.Y.C., 1973-74, Corcoran Gallery, Washington, 1974, Osuna Gallery, Washington, 1979, 81, 86, 89, 91-92, Neuberger Mus., Purchase N.Y., 1986; exhibited in group shows at Balt. Mus. Art, 1970, 72-73, 82, Whitney Mus. Am. Art, 1970-71, 72, 77, Phillips Collection, Washington, 1971-72, Pyramid Galleries, 1972, 73, Mus. Contemporary Art, Chgo., 1974, 77, Indpls. Mus. Art, 1974, Nat. Gallery Art, Washington, 1974, Corcoran Gallery Art, Washington, 1975, numerous others; translator: (with C.J. Hill) Marcel Proust and Deliverance from Time (Germaine Brée), 1955; author: Daybook: The Journal of an Artist, 1982, Turn: The Journal of an Artist, 1986, Prospect: The Journal of an Artist, 1996. Guggenheim fellow, 1970; Nat. Endowment for Arts fellow, 1971, 77; Australia Council for Arts fellow, 1981. Home: 3506 35th St NW Washington DC 20016-3114

TRUITT, CHARLOTTE FRANCES, clergywoman; b. Newark, Feb. 8, 1922; d. Frank Wilson and Charlotte (Hook) T.; m. Robert Kennedy Carter, Mar. 17, 1946 (div. 1972); children: Mary Elizabeth Carter O'Brien, Robert Truitt Carter; m. Robert Harold Bonthius Sr., Apr. 29, 1977. Student, Ohio State U., 1941-46; MA in Christian Edn., Meth. Theol. Sch., Delaware, Ohio, 1976, MDiv, 1977. Ordained to ministry United Ch. of Christ, 1979. Asst. dir. youth program YWCA, Columbus, Ohio, 1965-68, dir. youth program, 1968-70, dir. family life and racial justice programs, 1970-72; mission coord. and youth minister First Cmty. Ch., Columbus, 1972-75; min. Christian edn. Broad St. United Meth. Ch., Columbus, 1975-76; cons., trainer Action Tng. Network, Ohio and Maine, 1976-90; pres. bd. Family Life and Sex Edn. Coun., Columbus, 1971-72; bd. dirs. Ohio Coun. Chs., Columbus, 1973-74; del. United Ch. of Christ, Nicaragua, 1983, and co-founder Nat. Witness for Peace, 1983. Contbr. articles to religious jours. and publs. Pres. bd. dirs. North Ctrl. Mental Health Ctr., Columbus, 1973-74; mem. Columbus Urban League Edn. Commn., 1965-67, Hancock Comprehensive Plan Commn., Hancock, Maine, 1990; chair scholarship bd. Thorsen Scholarship Fund, Hancock, 1988-89; bd. dirs., fin. chair The Next Step Domestic Violence Project, Ellsworth, Maine, 1993-94; bd. dirs. Witness for Peace, pers. chair, 1983-85, chair, 1994-95. Recipient Martin Luther King Jr. award NAACP, Portland, Maine, 1989, Disting. Svc. award The Next Step Domestic Violence Project, Ellsworth, 1994. Mem. AAUW, Hancock-Waldo Clergy Assn., Friends Taunton Bay, Natural Resources Coun. of Maine, Peace Action, Religious Coalition for Reproductive Choice, United Ch. of Christ Christians for Justice Action, Witness for Peace. Mem. United Ch. of Christ. Avocations: flower gardening, bird watching, reading, nature walks, drawing. Home and Office: RR 1 Box 422A Hancock ME 04640-9802

TRUITT, WILLIAM HARVEY, private school educator; b. Alton, Ill., May 27, 1935; s. Howard Earl and Mary Margaret (Haper) T.; m. Janetha Mitchell, Aug. 5, 1961; children: Joy Elizabeth, Janita Ann. BA, Principia Coll., 1957; MA, So. Ill. U., 1964. Headmaster Forman Schs., Litchfield, Conn.; prin. upper and lower sch. The Principia, St. Louis, headmaster. Mem. NASSP, Mo. Assn. Secondary Prins., St. Louis Ind. Sch. Heads, Mo. Ind. Schs. (pres. 1983-84), Am. Coun. for Am. Pvt. Edn. (v.p. 1983-84), North Cen. Accrediting Assn. (exec. bd. dirs. 1988-91). Home: 13201 Clayton Rd Saint Louis MO 63131-1002

TRUJILLO, ANGELINA, endocrinologist; b. Long Beach, Calif.. BA in Psychology, Chapman Coll., 1974; postgrad., U. Colo., 1974-75, MD, 1979. Resident in internal medicine Kern Med. Ctr., Bakersfield, Calif., 1979-82; fellow in endocrinology UCLA, Sepulveda, Calif., 1982-84, chief resident dept. internal medicine, 1985-86; chief diabetes clinic Sepulveda (Calif.) VA Med. Ctr., 1986-89; physician specialist Olive View Med. Ctr., Sylmar, Calif., 1989; chief divsn. endocrinology U. S.D. Sch. Medicine, Sioux Falls, 1990—; coord. R&D Royal C. Johnson VA Med. Ctr., Sioux Falls, 1993—; adj. instr. UCLA, 1982-84, adj. asst. prof. medicine, 1985-89, clin. asst. prof. family medicine, 1994—; asst. prof. U. S.D. Sch. Medicine, 1990-94, assoc. prof., 1994—, assoc. dir. internal medicine residency program, 1992-95; spkr. in field. Mental health vol. Counselor/Lompoc Mental Health, Lompoc, Calif., 1971; bd. dirs. Lompoc (Calif.) Assn. Retarded Citizens, 1973-74, Santa Barbara Health Planning Com., Lompoc, 1974; vol. counselor Pike's Peak Mental Health Assn., 1974-75; hot line counselor Terros, Colorado Springs, Colo., 1974-75; 5th grade catechist tchr. Our Lady of Perpetual Help, Valencia, Calif., 1984-89; pub. spkr. in diabetes, women and heart disease. Grantee NIH, 1986-89, 91-92, Am. Diabetes Assn., 1985-87, Pfizer, Inc., 1990-91, Nat. Heart, Lung, and Blood Inst., 1994—, Bristol-Myers Squibb, 1994. Mem. ACP, Am. Fedn. Clin. Rsch. (med. sch. rep., endo/metabolism subspecialty coun.), Am. Soc. Hypertension, Am. Diabetes Assn., Assn. Program Dirs. in Internal Medicine, Assn. Clerkship Dirs. in Internal Medicine, S.D. State Med. Assn., Seventh Dist. Med. Soc., Wilderness Med. Soc. (mem. environ. coun.). Office: U SD Sch Med 1400 W 22d St Sioux Falls SD 57105-1305

TRUJILLO, LORENZO A., lawyer, educator; b. Denver, Aug. 10, 1951; s. Filbert G. and Marie O. Trujillo; children: Javier Antonio, Lorenzo Feliciano. BA, U. Colo., 1972, MA, 1974, postgrad.; EdD, U. San Francisco, 1979; JD, U. Colo., 1993. Bar: Colo. 1994, U.S. Dist. Ct. Colo. 1994, U.S. Ct. Appeals (10th cir.) 1994; cert. edn. tchr., prin., supt., Colo., Calif. Exec. assoc. Inter-Am. Rsch. Assocs., Rosslyn, Va., 1980-82; exec. dir. humanities Jefferson County Pub. Schs., Golden, Colo., 1982-89; pvt. practice edn. cons. Lakewood, Colo., 1989-93; gen. corp. counsel Am. Achievement Schs., Inc., Lakewood, Colo., 1994-96; atty. Frie, Arndt & Trujillo Law Firm, Arvada, Colo., 1994-96, ptnr., 1995-97; in-house counsel/hearing officer, dir. of instrn. Adams County Sch. Dist. 14, 1997—; co-chair Mellon fellowships The Coll. Bd., N.Y.C., 1987-93; cons. U.S.I.A. Fulbright Tchr. Exch. Program, Washington, 1987-93; editorial advisor Harcourt, Brace, Jovanovich Pub., Orlando, Fla., 1988-93. Contbr. numerous articles to profl. jours. Mem. panel of arbitrators Am. Arbitration Assn., 1994. Recipient Legal Aid Clinic Acad. award Colo. Bar Assn., 1993, Pro Bono award, 1993, Loyola U. Acad. award, 1993, Gov.'s award for excellence in the arts State of Colo., 1996. Mem. Colo. chpt. Am. Assn. Tchrs. of Spanish and Portuguese (pres. 1985-88), Am. Immigration Lawyers Assn., Nat. Sch. Bds. Coun. Sch. Attys., Nat. Assn. Judiciary Interpreters and Translators, Colo. Bar Assn. (family law sect., probate and trust sect., grievance policy com. 1995—, ethics com. 1995-96), Soc. Security Benefits Panel, U. San Francisco Alumni Assn. (founder, pres. 1987-90), Phi Delta Kappa (chair internat. edn. com. 1988-89), Phi Alpha Delta. Avocation: violinist. Home: 1556 S Van Dyke Way Lakewood CO 80228 Office: Adams County Sch Dist 14 Divsn Ednl Svcs 4720 E 69th Ave Commerce City CO 80022-2358

TRUJILLO, SANDRA SUE, nurse; b. Circle, Mont., July 5, 1945; d. Theodore Ward and Ethel Marie (Wilhelm) Keeland; children: Nichola, Helena, Jodi, Kevin. ADN, Mont. State U., 1966; BSN, U. N.Mex., 1991; MSN, Tex. A&M U., 1996. Staff psychiat. nurse Mont. State Hosp., Warm Springs, 1966-81; critical care staff nurse Betsy Johnson Hosp., Dunn, N.C., 1981-82, Calais (Maine) Regional Hosp., 1982-83, Rumford (Maine) Cmty. Hosp., 1983-84, Albemarle Hosp., Elizabeth City, N.C., 1984-86; charge nurse, nurse mgr. St. Vincent Hosp., Santa Fe, 1986-91; nurse mgr. McAllen (Tex.) Med. Ctr., 1991-93, Scott & White Hosp., Temple, Tex., 1993—. Mem. Oncology Nurse Soc., Sigma Theta Tau. Home: PO Box 5255 Temple TX 76505-5255 Office: Scott & White Meml Hosp 2401 S 31st Temple TX 76505

TRULUCK, JAMES PAUL, JR., dentist, vintner; b. Florence, S.C., Feb. 6, 1933; s. James Paul and Catherine Lydia (Nesmith) TruL.; m. Kay Bowen (dec. Oct. 1981); children: James Paul III, David Bowen, Catherine Ann; m. Amelia Nickels Calhoun, Apr. 26, 1983; 1 child, George Calhoun. BS, Clemson (S.C.) U., 1954; DMD, U. Louisville, 1958. Pvt. practice Lake City, S.C., 1960—; founder, pres. TruLuck Vineyards & Winery, Lake City, 1976, Chateau TruLuck Natural Water Co., Lake City, 1990. Member bd. advisors Clemson U., 1978-84; mem. bd. visitors Coker Coll., Hartsville, S.C., 1978-84; pres., bd. dirs. Lions, Lake City, 1960-73; chmn. Greater Lake City Lake Commn., 1967-84. Capt. USAF, 1958-67. Recipient S.C. Bus. and Arts Partnership award S.C. State Arts Commn., 1988. Mem. ADA, Am. Assn. Vinters (bd. dirs. 1982-86), Am. Wine Soc. (nat. judge 1982-88), Am. Soc. Clin. Hypnosis (emeritus), Internat. Acad. Laser Dentistry (chartered), S.C. Dental Assn., Florence County Dental Assn., Soc. First Families of S.C. (exec. sec. 1991—), Descs. Colonial Govs. of Am., Descs. Magna Carta Barons Runnymede, Soc. Gem Cutters Am., Soc. of the Decendants of the Knight of the Gaster, Soc. of the St. George, Windsor Castle (Eng.). Episcopalian. Avocations: genealogy, gemealogy, tennis, sailing, writing. Home: 1036 Mccutcheon Rd Lake City SC 29560-5616 Office: 125 Epp St Lake City SC 29560-2449

TRULY, RICHARD H., academic administrator, former federal agency administrator; b. Fayette, Miss., Nov. 12, 1937; s. James B. Truly; m. Colleen Hanner; children: Richard Michael, Daniel Bennett, Lee Margaret. B.Aero. Engring., Ga. Inst. Tech., 1959. Commd. ensign U.S. Navy, 1959; advanced through grades to vice adm., assigned Fighter Squadron 33, served in U.S.S. Intrepid, served in U.S.S. Enterprise; astronaut Manned Orbiting Lab. Program USAF, 1965-69; astronaut NASA, from 1969, comdr. Columbia Flight 2, 1981; comdr. Columbia Flight 2 Challenger Flight 3, 1983; dir. Space Shuttle program, 1986-89; adminstr. NASA, 1989-92; now v.p., dir. Georgia Tech Rsch. Inst., Atlanta, Ga. Recipient Robert H. Goddard Astronautics award AIAA, 1990. Office: Georgia Inst Tech Georgia Tech Rsch Inst 400 Tenth St Atlanta GA 30332

TRUMAN, EDWARD CRANE, real estate manager, consultant, composer; b. Des Moines, Dec. 28, 1915; s. Wright Edward and Annie Louise (Cate) T.; m. Maxine LeVon Hemping, June 28, 1947 (dec. Apr. 1983); 1 child, Robert E.C. Student, UCLA, 1966, 72; BA in English, Immaculate Heart Coll., 1978; MA in Psychology, U. Redlands, 1980. Asst. program dir. Cowles Broadcasting, Des Moines, 1938-44; pub. rels. writer Armed Forces Radio Svcs., Hollywood, Calif., 1944-46; staff musician Don Lee Mut. Radio, Hollywood, Calif., 1946-48, ABC-TV, Hollywood, Calif., 1948-53; music dir., composer TV series NBC-TV, Burbank, Calif., 1955-60; freelance organist, composer Hollywood, 1960—, real estate property mgr., owner, 1974—; bd. dirs. Gen. Affiliates U. Calif., Santa Barbara, chair scholarship com., 1988—; co-founder Artasia Seminars, L.A., 1972-75. Composer: Matinee, 1956, Broadcast Mood Music, Bowie Knife, 1958, Songs for Builders, 1960. Endowment grantor in religious studies U. Calif., Santa Barbara, 1984—, mem. pres.'s ctr., 1993—; endowment grantor in humanities Drake U., Des Moines, 1994, mem. pres.'s cir., 1995—; mem. judging panels acad. advancement program UCLA, 1994—. Recipient citation Dept. Edn., 1976, commendation City Atty. Office, L.A., 1993. Mem. Nat. Acad. TV Arts and Scis. (Emmy panels, music br.), Pacific Pioneer Broadcasters (bd. dirs. 1988-91, Golden Circle award 1991), Musician's Union (asst. to pres. Local 47 1969-77). Democrat. Episcopalian. Avocations: stamp and coin collecting, biking. Home: 1826 Jewett Dr Los Angeles CA 90046-7702 Office: Compass-Am Group 1826 Jewett Dr Los Angeles CA 90046-7702

TRUMAN, MARGARET, author; b. Independence, Mo., Feb. 17, 1924; d. Harry S. (32nd Pres. U.S.) and Bess (Wallace) T.; m. E. Clifton Daniel Jr., Apr. 21, 1956; children: Clifton T., William, Harrison, Thomas. LHD, Wake Forest U., 1972; HHD, Rockhurst Coll., 1976. Concert singer, 1947-54, actess, broadcaster, author, 1954—; author: Souvenir, 1956, White House Pets, 1969, Harry S. Truman, 1973, Women of Courage, 1976, Murder in the White House, 1980, Murder on Capitol Hill, 1981, Letters from Father, 1981, Murder in the Supreme Ct., 1982, Murder in the Smithsonian, 1983, Murder on Embassy Row, 1985, Murder at the FBI, 1985, Muder in Georgetown, 1986, Bess W. Truman, 1986, Murder in the CIA, 1987, Muder at the Kennedy Center, 1989, Murder in the National Cathedral, 1990, Murder at the Pentagon, 1992, Murder on the Potomac, 1994, First Ladies, 1995, Murder in the National Gallery, 1996; editor: Where the Buck Stops: The Personal and Private Writings of Harry S. Truman, 1989. Trustee and v.p. Harry S. Truman Inst.; sec. bd. trustees Harry S. Truman Found.

TRUMBLE, ROBERT ROY, business educator; b. Wabeno, Wis., Mar. 21, 1940; s. Clarence Lincoln and Celia (Ward) T.; children: Eric, Monica. BA, Hamline U., 1962; MA, U. Minn., 1963, PhD, 1971. Vol. Peace Corps., Lima, Peru, 1963-65; mgr. Latin Am. programs U. Minn., Mpls., 1965-67; asst. dir. internat. programs Cooperative League USA, Washington, 1967-69; program dir. Ops. Research Inc., Washington, 1969-71; chief party Ohio State U., Caracas, Venezuela, 1971-72; div. dir. NIH, Bethesda, Md., 1972-76; sect. head NSF, Washington, 1976-84; dean grad. sch. mgmt. Kent (Ohio) State U., 1984-88; dean sch. bus. Va. Commonwealth U., Richmond, 1988-93; dir. Va. Labor Studies Ctr., 1993—; adj. faculty George Washington U., Washington, 1976-84; pres. Ctr. for Applied Studies, Kent, 1971—; CEO Trumble Investments, St. Croix, V.I., 1987—; bd. dirs. Cen. Allied Ent., Willmar, Minn. Contbr. articles to profl. jours. U.S. State Dept. grantee, 1971-72, State of Ohio grantee, 1986-87. Mem. Am. Assembly Collegiate Schs. Bus., Indsl. Relations Research Assn., Ohio Bus. Deans, Fgn. Policy Assn. (Outstanding Young Person 1968), Mensa, LWV (fin. com. 1987), Delta Sigma Pi, Beta Gamma Sigma, Phi Gamma Mu, Tau Kappa Epsilon (trustee 1960—). Presbyterian. Avocations: Spanish lang., sports, music, painting. Home: 8101 Spencely Pl Richmond VA 23229-8426 Office: VCU Sch of Bus 1015 Floyd Ave Richmond VA 23284-9000

TRUMBULL, DOUGLAS, film director, writer, creator special effects; b. Apr. 8, 1942. Created spl. effects for films including: 2001: A Space Odyssey, 1968, Silent Running, 1971 (also dir.), Close Encounters of the Third Kind, 1977, Star Trek, 1979, Blade Runner, 1982, Brainstorm, 1983 (also prodr., dir.), Spaced Invaders, 1990; inventor Showscan process. Address: The Gersh Agy 232 N Canon Dr Beverly Hills CA 90210*

TRUMBULL, RICHARD, psychologist; b. Johnstown, N.Y., Apr. 6, 1916; s. Milton Elmer and Hazel (Busse) T.; m. Alice Esther McDaniel, June 17, 1939; children—Judith Trumbull Townsend, Joanne Trumbull Titus, Janice Trumbull Smith, Joyce Ellen Trumbull Setzer. A.B., Union Coll., 1937; M.S., Union U., 1939; Ph.D., Syracuse U., 1951. Asst. prof. psychology Green Mountain Jr. Coll., Poultney, Vt., 1939-41; chmn. dept. psychology, 46-49; lectr. Syracuse U., 1941-43; chmn. undergrad. program psychology, 49-51; mem. research staff Sch. Aviation Medicine, U.S. Navy, 1951-53, asst. head physiol. psychology br., Office of Naval Research, 1953-54, head, 1954-61, dir. psychol. scis., 1961-67; dir. research Office Naval Research, Washington, 1967-70; dep. exec. officer AAAS, 1970-74; exec. dir. Am. Inst. Biol. Scis., Arlington, Va., 1974-79, Renewable Natural Resources Found., Bethesda, Md., 1979-80; chmn. adv. group on human factors NATO; research advisory com. NASA; surgeon gen. advisory com. FAA. Author: Research and Its Management, 1984; joint editor: Sensory Deprivation, 1961, Psychological Stress: Issues in Research, 1966, The Dynamics of Stress, 1986, Scientific Freedom and Responsibility in Psychology, Science and Human Affairs, 1994; contbr. articles to profl. jours. Trustee Green Mountain Jr. Coll., Biol. Scis. Info. Service. Served with USNR, 1943-46, 51-53. Recipient Navy Distinguished Civilian Service award, 1961, Longacre award in aerospace medicine, 1966; Sustained Super Accomplishment award, 1966. Mem. AAAS, Aerospace Med. Assn., Natural Resources Council Am. (sec. 1977), Sigma Xi. Home: 4708 N Chelsea Ln Bethesda MD 20814-3714

TRUMKA, RICHARD LOUIS, labor leader, lawyer; b. Nemacolin, Pa., July 24, 1949; s. Frank Richard and Eola Elizabeth (Bertugli) T.; m. Barbara Vidovich, Nov. 27, 1982; 1 child, Richard L. BS, Pa. State U., 1971; JD, Villanova U., 1974. Bar: U.S. Dist. Ct. (D.C.) 1974, U.S. Ct. Appeals (3d, 4th and D.C. cirs.) 1975, U.S. Supreme Ct. 1979. Atty. United Mine Workers Am., Washington, 1974-77, 78-79, internat. pres., 1982-95; miner, operator Jones & Laughlin Steel, Nemacolin, Pa., 1977-78, 79-81; internat. exec. bd. Dist. 4 United Mine Workers Am., Masontown, Pa., 1981-82; sec. treas. AFL-CIO, Washington, 1995—; pres. emeritus United Mine Workers Assn., 1995—; bd. dirs. Am. Coal Found.; mem. Nat. Coal Council, 1985. Trustee Pa. State U. Recipient Labor Responsibility Award, Martin Luther King Ctr. for Nonviolent Social Change, 1990. Democrat. Roman Catholic. Office: AFL-CIO 815 16th St NW Washington DC 20006-4104

TRUMP, DONALD JOHN, real estate developer; b. N.Y.C., 1946; s. Fred C. and Mary Trump; m. Ivana Zelnicek, 1977 (div. 1991); children: Donald Jr., Ivanka, Eric; m. Marla Maples, Dec. 20, 1993; 1 child, Tiffany. Student, Fordham U.; BA, U. Pa., 1968. Pres. Trump Orgn., N.Y.C.; owner Trump Enterprises Inc., N.Y.C., The Trump Corp., N.Y.C., Trump Devel. Co., N.Y.C., Wembly Realty Inc., Park South Co., Land Corp. of Calif., Trump Tower, Trump Parc, Trump Palace, 40 Wall St., N.Y.C., Empire State Bldg., Trump Internat. Hotel and Tower, N.Y.C., Trump Pla., Trump Castle, Trump Taj Mahal, Trump's World Fair, Atlantic City, Trump Casino Riverboat, Buffington Harbor, Ind., West Side Rail Yards to be devel. as Riverside South, N.Y.C., Seven Springs Mansion, Bedford, N.Y., Mar-a-Lago Club, Palm Beach, Fla.; owner 40 Wall St., N.Y.C., Seven Springs Mansion, Bedford, N.Y.C., Briar Hall Country Club, Briarcliff Manor, N.Y.; pres. Trump Pageants LP, includes Miss Universe, Miss USA and Miss Teen USA. Author: The Art of the Deal, 1987, Surviving at the Top, 1990. Co-chmn. N.Y. Vietnam Vets. Meml. Fund; founding mem. constrn. com. Cathedral of St. John the Divine; mem. N.Y. Citizens Tax Coun., Fifth Ave Assn., Realty Found. of N.Y., Met. Mus. of Art's Real Estate Coun.; bd. dirs. Police Athletic League; mem. adv. bd. Lenox Hill Hosp., United Cerebral Palsy; spl. advisor to Pres.'s Coun. on Phys. Fitness and Sports; mem. N.Y. Sportsplex Commn.; bd. of overseers Wharton Sch.; mem. adv. bd. Wharton Real Estate Ctr.; bd. dirs. Fred C. Trump Found.; chmn. N.Y. citizens com. 78th Ann. NAACP Conv., 1987; grand marshall Nation's Parade, 1995. Recipient Entrepreneur of Yr. award Wharton Entrepreneurial Club, 1984, Ellis Island Medal of Honor, 1986; inducted Wharton Hall of Fame.

TRUNDLE, W(INFIELD) SCOTT, publishing executive newspaper; b. Maryville, Tenn., Mar. 24, 1939; s. Winfield Scott and Alice (Smith) T.; m. Elizabeth Latshaw, Oct. 14, 1989; children: Stephen, Allison. B.A., Vanderbilt U., 1961, J.D., 1967. Bar: Tenn. 1967. Spl. agt. U.S. Secret Service, 1963-66; asso. to partner firm Hunter, Smith, Davis & Norris, Kingsport, Tenn., 1967-72; pub. Kingsport (Tenn.) Times-News, 1972-78; pres. Greensboro (N.C.) Daily News, 1978-80; exec. v.p. Jefferson Pilot Publs., Inc., Greensboro and Clearwater, Fla., 1980-82; v.p., bus. mgr. Tampa Tribune (Fla.), 1982-91; sr. v.p. Hillsborough Community Coll., 1991-93; publisher Ogden (Utah) Standard Examiner, 1993—; assoc. prof. E. Tenn. State U., 1973-77. Bd. dirs. Downtown Ogden, Inc. Mem. Tenn. Bar Assn., Utah Press Assn. (pres., bd. dirs.), Weber Ogden C. of C. (bd. dirs.). Methodist. Home: 1580 Maule Dr Ogden UT 84403-0413 Office: Ogden Publ Corp 455 23d St PO Box 951 Ogden UT 84402

TRUOG, DEAN-DANIEL WESLEY, educator, consultant; b. Denver, Apr. 1, 1938; s. George Calvin and Zelma Elizabeth (Bennett) T.; m. Dorothy Anne Harding, May 31, 1961; children: David Robert, Denise Dawne. Student, Bethel Coll., 1960-61, L'Abri Fellowship Found., Switzerland, 1967-68; diploma in Bible and Leadership Devel., The Navigators Internat. Tng. Inst., 1968; BA in European History, U. Colo., 1971; Diploma in Gen. Univ. Studies in French Civilization, U. Strasbourg, France, 1977; MA in Liberal Edn., St. John's Coll., 1986; M of Liberal Arts in History of Sci., Harvard U., 1987; postgrad., Boston U., 1987-93. Sr. resident adv. U. Colo., Boulder, 1964-65; rep., tutor, lectr. biblical studies and practical christianity The Navigators, 1965-93; rep. for greater Washington area, 1965-67; training asst. The Navigators, Colorado Springs, Colo., 1968; rep. at U. Colo. The Navigators, Boulder, 1968-70, No. Colo. dir., 1970-71; spl. adv. The Navigators, Birmingham, Eng., 1971-72; rep. at large The Navigators, Boulder, Colo., 1979-80; founding dir., pres. Les Navigateurs, France, 1972-84; v.p. Les Navigateurs, France, 1984-85, rep. to U. Strasbourg, 1973-79, rep. to U. Grenoble, 1980-85; sr. teaching fellow in non-deptmental studies Harvard U., Cambridge, Mass., 1987-90; founding pres., life mgmt. cons./counselor Cornerstone Inst. for Values and Relationships, 1990—; v.p. U.S.-Bulgaria Inst., Cambridge, 1991—; spl. cons. to mems. U.S. Congress, 1993—; tutor North House, Harvard U., 1987-91; founding chmn. Harvard Christian Assocs., 1987-92; spkr., tchr. profl. confs.; designer, dir. leadership devel. programs, Boston, Washington, Colo., Austria, France, Switzerland. With USN, 1958-59. Mem. AAAS, History of Sci. Soc., Am. Sci. Affiliation, Soc. Christian Philosophers, Assn. for Religion and Intellectual Llife, Inst. on Religion in Age of Sci., Ctr. for Theology and Natural Scis., Nat. Assn. Scholars, Rotary. Presbyterian. Avocations: cycling, gardening, skiing, tennis, reading. Home and Office: 15 Sheridan Rd Swampscott MA 01907-2046

TRUPO, FRANK J., plastic surgeon; b. N.Y.C., Oct. 15, 1957; s. Frank and Rose T.; m. Gail Stringer, May 22, 1987; children: Stephanie, Thomas. BS, Bethany Coll., 1979; MD, W.Va. U., 1984. Diplomate Nat. Bd. Med. Examiners, Am. Bd. Plastic Surgery. Resident gen. surgery Charleston (W.Va.) Area Med. Ctr., 1984-87; resident plastuc, reconstructive, cosmetic, maxillofacial and head and neck surgery Kans. U. Med. Ctr., Kansas City, 1987-89; pvt. practice plastic surgery Charleston, W.Va., 1990—; chief sect. plastic surgery St. Francis Hosp., Charleston, 1993—, chmn. credentials com., 1997—, med. adv., peer reviewer, 1994—; med. advisor, peer reviewer W.Va. Med. Inst., Mountain State BC/BS, Primary One, Inc. Fellow ACS, Am. Soc. Lasers in Medicine and Surgery; mem. Am. Soc. Aesthetic Plastic Surgery, So. Med. Assn., Kanawha Med. Soc. (pres. 1997), Am. Soc. Plastic and Reconstructive Surgeons. Office: 331 Laidley St Ste 510 Charleston WV 25301-1605

TRURAN, JAMES WELLINGTON, JR., astrophysicist; b. Brewster, N.Y., July 12, 1940; s. James Wellington and Suzanne (Foglesong) T.; m. Carol Kay Dell'Acy, June 26, 1965; children—Elaina Michelle, Diana Lee, Anastasia Elizabeth. B.A. in Physics, Cornell U., 1961; M.S. in Physics, Yale U., 1963, Ph.D. in Physics, 1966. Postdoctoral rsch. assoc. NAS-NRC Goddard Inst. Space Studies, NASA, N.Y.C., 1965-67; asst. prof. physics Belfer Grad. Sch. Sci., Yeshiva U., 1967-70; rsch. fellow in physics Calif. Inst. Tech., 1968-69; assoc. prof. Belfer Grad. Sch. Sci., Yeshiva U., 1970-72, prof., 1972-73; prof. astronomy U. Ill., Urbana, 1973-91; sr. vis. fellow, Guggenheim Meml. Found. fellow Inst. Astronomy, U. Cambridge, Eng., 1979-80; trustee Aspen Ctr. Physics, 1979-85, 91-93, v.p., 1985-88; assoc. U. Ill. Center for Advanced Study, 1979-80, 86-87; prof. astronomy astrophysics U. Chgo., 1991—; Alexander von Humboldt-Stiftung sr. scientist Max-Plank Inst., Munich, Germany, 1986-87, 94. Contbr. articles to profl. jours.; co-editor: Nucleosynthesis, 1968, Nucleosynthesis— Challenges and New Developments, 1985, Nuclear Astrophysics, 1987; editor: Physics Letters B, 1974-80. Co-recipient Yale Sci. and Engring. Assn. annual award for advancement basic or applied sci., 1980. Fellow AAAS, Am. Phys. Soc.; mem. Am. Astron. Soc., Am. Phys. Soc., Internat. Astron. Union. Home: 210 Wysteria Dr Olympia Fields IL 60461-1202 Office: U Chgo Dept Astronomy Astrophysics 5640 S Ellis Ave Chicago IL 60637-1433

TRURAN, WILLIAM RICHARD, electrical engineer; b. Franklin, N.J., Feb. 14, 1951; s. Wilfred Hardy and Stella Eva (Hall) T.; m. Virginia Lynn Johnson, Aug. 18, 1979; children: Michael, Wendy. BSEE, U. Tenn., 1972; MBA, Fairleigh Dickinson U., 1981; MS in Indsl. Engring., Columbia U., 1994; postgrad. studies, Stevens Inst. Tech., 1994—; Columbia U. Registered profl. engr., N.J., N.Y., Pa., Calif.; registered profl. planner, N.J. Design engr. Gordos Corp., Bloomfield, N.J., 1972-73; project engr. Edwards Engring., Pompton Plains, N.J., 1973-78; sr. engr. Apollo Tech., Whippany, N.J., 1978-81; elec. product mgr. Dodge-Newark, Fairfield, N.J., 1981—; pres. Trupower Engring., Sparta, N.J., 1984—; pres. T.E.C. Corp. of N.J., Sparta; cons. in field. Contbr. articles to profl. jours. Active foster child orgn. Christian Children's Fund. Mem. Nat. Soc. Profl. Engrs. (legis. action network, minuteman), Nat. Assn. Environ. Profls., Wilderness Soc., Sierra Club. Episcopalian. Avocations: skiing, water skiing, triathlons, marathons, antique Corvettes. Home and Office: 37 Rainbow Trl Sparta NJ 07871-1724

TRUS, BENES LOUIS, structural chemist; b. Tyler, Tex., May 9, 1946; s. Joseph N. and Ruthie (Mosier) T.; m. Susan Gale Evans, Apr. 23, 1972; children—Aaron Baram, Anthony Phillip. BS cum laude with honors, Tulane U., 1968; PhD, Calif. Inst. Tech., 1972. Jane Coffin Childs postdoctoral fellow Calif. Inst. Tech., Pasadena, 1972-75; research fellow NIH, Bethesda, Md., 1975-77, sr. research fellow, 1977-80, research chemist, 1980-93; chief image processing rsch. sect., computational biosci. and engring. lab., computer rsch. and tech. divsn. NIH, 1993—; mem. steering com. NIH wide image processing group, Bethesda, 1984— (NIH Dirs. award, 1987, 94). Contbr. articles to profl. jours., chpt. to book. Tulane U. scholar and fellow 1965-68. Mem. Am. Crystallographic Assn., Chesapeake Soc. for Microscopy, Microscope Soc. Am., N.Y. Acad. Scis., Montgomery County Rd. Runners Club, NIH Health's Angels Running Club, Phi Beta Kappa, Sigma Xi. Mem. NIH 1986-88 Marathon Team (1st Place Marine Corps Marathon, Govt. Team Competition 1986, 3d place 1987, 88, 2d place Masters Team, 1993). Avocations: music, running, carpentry. Office: NIH Rm 2033 Bethesda MD 20892-5624

TRUSCHEL, JACK HENRY, II, university official, consultant; b. Neubruke, Germany, Apr. 25, 1957; came to U.S., 1967; s. Jack Henry and Geraldine (Ezzo) T.; m. Sharon Lewandowski, July 31, 1978; children: Jack Henry III, Caitlin. BA in Psychology, King's Coll., 1981; MA in Psychology, Marywood Coll., 1983, MPA, 1986; EdD, Temple U., 1995. Exec. dir. Family Svcs., Pottsville, Pa., 1985-88; dir. instl. giving East Stroudsburg (Pa.) U., 1989—; cons. Regional Lit. Consortium, Towanda, Pa., 1993—, Lackawanna Jr. Coll., Scranton, 1989-93, Serve Inc., Towanda, 1994—. Author: (books) The ABC's of Computing, 1992, Get Funded, 1993. 2nd Lt. U.S. Army, 1984-89. Grantee Pa. Office Vocat. Rehab., 1993. Mem. Masons, Phi Delta Kappa. Republican. Roman Catholic. Office: East Stroudsburg U Rosenkrans W East Stroudsburg PA 18301

TRUSKOWSKI, JOHN BUDD, lawyer; b. Chgo., Dec. 3, 1945; s. Casimer T. and Jewell S. (Kirk) T.; m. Karen Lee Sloss, Mar. 21, 1970; children: Philip K., Jennifer B. BS, U. Ill., 1967; JD, U. Chgo., 1970. Bar: Ill. 1970, U.S. Dist. Ct. (no. dist.) Ill. 1970, U.S. Tax Ct. 1977. Assoc. Keck, Mahin & Cate, Chgo., 1970-71, 74-78, ptnr., 1978—. Author, editor Callaghan's Federal Tax Guide, 1987. Served to lt, USNR, 1971-74. Mem. ABA, Ill. State Bar Assn., Chgo. Bar Assn. Republican. Presbyterian. Avocations: model railroading, stamp collecting. Home: 251 Kimberly Ln Lake Forest IL 60045-3862 Office: Keck Mahin & Cate 77 W Wacker Dr Fl 49 Chicago IL 60601-1635

TRUSSELL, CHARLES TAIT, columnist; b. Balt., May 9, 1925; s. Charles Prescott and Beatrice (Tait) T.; m. Woodley Grizzard, Dec. 27, 1953 (div. 1990); children: Galen Tait, Thomas Marshall; m. Nancy Rathbun Billington, Dec. 19, 1990. B.A. in Journalism, Washington and Lee U., 1949. Reporter St. Petersburg (Fla.) Times, also; writer Congl. Quar. News Features, 1951-54; reporter Wall St. Jour., 1954-56, Washington Evening Star, 1956; asso. editor Nation's Business mag., 1956-64, mng. editor, 1964-69; sr. editor Congressional Quar., Inc., 1969-70; dir. pub. relations and advt. Investment Co. Inst., Washington, 1970-72; free-lance writer, real estate investor, 1972-74; v.p. Am. Forest Inst., Washington, 1974-79, sr. v.p., 1980-81; v.p. Am. Enterprise Inst., 1981-86; dir. communications Constitution Bicentennial Commn., 1986-88; freelance writer, columnist, 1988—. Producer: documentary record album The Best of Washington Humor, 1963; author: Beating the Competition, 1992; editor: (with others) Successful Management, 1964, (with Paul Hencke) Dear NASA Please Send Me a Rocket, 1964. Served with USNR, 1944-46. Recipient Loeb Spl. Achievement award for mags. U. Conn., 1961, Benjamin Fine Journalism award, 1992. Mem. Washington Assembly (exec. com. 1961-65, chmn. 1965), Country Club of Mt. Dora, Beta Theta Pi. Home: 6014 Spring Creek Ct Mount Dora FL 32757-6952

TRUSSELL, JAMES, dean; b. Columbus, Ga., Oct. 17, 1949; m. Claire Roberts, Sept. 3, 1988. BS summa cum laude in Maths., Davidson Coll., 1971; BPhil, Oxford U., 1973; PhD in Econs., Princeton U., 1975. From asst. prof. econs. to prof., dean Princeton (N.J.) U., 1975—. Co-author: The Loving Book, 1972, Contraceptive Technology, 1994; contbr. articles to profl. jours. Mem. Am. Statis. Assn., Am. Pub. Health Assn., Population Assn. Am., Australia Population Assn., Phi Beta Kappa., Assn. Reproductive Health Profls., Internat. Union for the Scientific Study of Population. Office: Princeton U Office of Population Rsch 21 Prospect Ave Princeton NJ 08544

TRUSSELL, R(OBERT) RHODES, environmental engineer; b. National City, Calif; s. Robert L. and Margaret (Kessing) T.; m. Elizabeth Shane, Nov. 26, 1969; children: Robert Shane, Charles Bryan. BSCE, U. Calif.-Berkeley, 1966, MS, 1967, PhD, 1972. With Montgomery Watson, Inc. (formerly J.M. Montgomery Cons. Engrs.), Pasadena, Calif., 1972—, v.p., 1977, sr. v.p., 1986, dir. applied tech., 1988-92, sr. v.p., dir. of corp. devel., 1992— Mem. com. on water treatment chems. Nat. Acad. Sci., 1980-82, mem. com. 3d part cert., 1982-83, com. on irrigation-induced water quality problems, 1985-88, indirect potable pense, 96—, Am. Water Work Commn. on mixing of water treatment chems., 1988-90; mem. U.S./German rsch. com. on corrosion of water systems, 1984-85; mem. U.S./Dutch rsch. com. on organics in water, 1982-83; mem. U.S./USSR rsch. com. on water treatment, 1985-88, U.S./E.C. Com. Corrosion in Water, 1992-94. Mem. joint editl. bd. Standards Methods for Examination of Water and Wastewater, 1980-89; mem. editl. adv. bd. Environ. and Sci. and Tech., 1977-83; contbr. articles to profl. publs. Mem. AIChE, NAE, Water Works Assn. (mem. editl. adv. bd. jour. 1987-94, EPA sci. adv. bd. com. on drinking water 1988-91, 94—, cons. radon disinfectant by products 1993, cons. on disinfection and disinfection byproducts 1994, ad hoc sci. adv. com. on arsenic 1995-96), Internat. Water Supply Assn. (U.S. rep. to standing com. on water quality and treatment 1990-94, chmn. com. on disinfection and mem. sci. and tech. coun. 1994—), Water Pollution Control Fedn., Internat. Water Pollution Rsch. Assn., Am. Chem. Soc., Nat. Assn. Corrosion Engrs., Sigma Xi. Office: Montgomery Watson 300 N Lake Ave Ste 1200 Pasadena CA 91101-4109

TRUTA, MARIANNE PATRICIA, oral and maxillofacial surgeon, educator, author; b. N.Y.C., Apr. 28, 1951; d. John J. and Helen Patricia (Donnelly) T.; m. William Christopher Donlon, May 28, 1983; 1 child Sean Liam Riobard Donlon. BS, St. John's U., 1974; DMD, SUNY, Stonybrook, 1977. Intern The Mt. Sinai Med. Ctr., N.Y.C., 1977-78, resident, 1978-80, chief resident, 1980-81; asst. prof. U. of the Pacific, San Francisco, 1983-85, clin. asst. prof., 1985-94; asst. dir. Facial Pain Rsch. Ctr., San Francisco, 1986-92; pvt. practice oral and maxillofacial surgery Peninsula Maxillofacial Surgery, South San Francisco, Calif., 1985—, Burlingame, Calif., 1988—, Redwood City, Calif., 1990-95, San Carlos, Calif., 1995—. Contbr. articles to profl. jours., chpts. to textbooks. Mem. Am. Assn. Oral Maxillofacial Surgeons, Am. Dental Soc. Anesthesiology, Am. Soc. Cosmetic Surgery, Am. Assn. Women Dentists, Western Soc. Oral Maxillofacial Surgeons, No. Calif. Soc. Oral Maxillofacial Surgeons, San Mateo County Dental Soc. (bd. dirs. 1995). Office: Peninsula Maxillofacial Surgery 1860 El Camino Real Ste 300 Burlingame CA 94010-3114

TRUTTER, JOHN THOMAS, consulting company executive; b. Springfield, Ill., Apr. 18, 1920; s. Frank Louis and Frances (Mischler) T.; m. Edith English Woods II, June 17, 1950; children: Edith English II, Jonathan Woods. BA, U. Ill., 1942; postgrad., Northwestern U., 1947-50, U. Chgo., 1947-50; LHD (hon.), Lincoln Coll., 1986. Various positions Ill. Bell, Chgo., 1946-58, gen. traffic mgr., from asst. v.p. pub. rels. to gen. mgr., 1958-69, v.p. pub. rels., 1969-71, v.p. operator svcs., 1971-80, v.p. community affairs, 1980-85; mem. hdqs. staff AT&T, N.Y.C., 1955-57; pres. John T. Trutter Co., Inc., Chgo., 1985—; pres., CEO Chgo. Conv. and Visitors Bur., 1985-88; pres. Chgo. Tourism Coun., 1988-90; mem. adv. bd. The Alford Group, Chgo., 1984—, Bozell-Worldwide, Chgo., 1994-96; chancellor Lincoln Acad. of Ill., 1985—. Co-author: Handling Barriers in Communication, 1957, The

Governor Takes a Bride, 1977. Past chmn., life trustee Jane Addams Hull House Assn.; chmn. United Cerebral Palsy Assn. Greater Chgo., 1967-95, hon. chmn., 1995—, chmn. Canal Corridor Assn., 1991—; bd. dirs. Chgo. Crime Commn., Abraham Lincoln Assn., Lyric Opera Chgo.; v.p. English Speaking Union, 1989-91, bd. govs., 1980—; chmn. bd. City Colls. Chgo. Found., 1987-91; past chmn. Children's Home and Aid Soc. Ill.; v.p. City Club Chgo.; treas. Chgo. United, 1970-85; mem. Ill. Econ. Devel. Commn., 1985; past presiding co-chmn. NCCJ; v.p., bd. dirs. Ill. Humane Soc. Found.; numerous others; bd. govs. Northwestern U. Libr. Coun., 1984—; trustee Lincoln (Ill.) Coll., 1987-90, Mundelein Coll., 1988-91; mem. sch. problems coun. State Ill. Assembly, 1985-91, spl. commn. on adminstrn. of justice in Cook County, 1986-92. Lt. col. U.S. Army, 1945. Decorated Legion of Merit; recipient Laureate award State of Ill., 1980, Outstanding Exec. Leader award Am. Soc. Fundraisers, Humanitarian of Yr. award, Jane Addams award The Hull House Assn., 1991, Nat. Infinitec award for individual leadership in assistive technology for disabled people, 1997. Mem. Pub. Rels. Soc. Am., Sangamon County Hist. Soc. (founder, past pres.), Ill. State Hist. Soc. (pres. 1985-87), Coun. on Ill. History (chmn. 1991—), U. Ill. Alumni Assn. (bd. dirs. 1990-94), Tavern Club, Econ. Club, Mid-Am. Club, Alpha Sigma Phi (Nat. Merit Achievement award 1994), Phi Delta Phi, founding chm. Evanston Historical Soc. advisory council 1995—.

TRUXAL, JOHN GROFF, electrical engineering educator; b. Lancaster, Pa., Feb. 19, 1924; s. Andrew Gehr and Leah Deldee (Groff) T.; m. Doris Teresa Mastrangelo, June 11, 1949; children—Brian Andrew, Carol Jean. A.B., Dartmouth, 1944; B.S., Mass. Inst. Tech., 1947, Sc.D., 1950; D.Eng. (hon.), Purdue U., 1964, Ind. Inst. Tech., 1971. Asso. prof. elec. engring. Purdue U., 1950-54; asso. prof. elec. engring. Poly. Inst. Bklyn., 1954- 57, prof., head dept., 1957-72, v.p. ednl. devel., 1961-72, dean engring., 1964-66, provost, 1966-68, acad. v.p., 1969-72; dean engring. State U. N.Y., Stony Brook, 1972-76; prof. engring. SUNY, 1976-91, Disting. Teaching prof. emeritus, 1991—; Cons. control engring. Author: Automatic Feedback Control System Synthesis, 1955, Introductory System Engineering, 1972, (with W.A. Lynch) Signals and Systems in Electrical Engineering, 1962; co-author: (with W.A. Lynch) The Man Made World, 1969, Man and His Technology, 1973, Technology: Handle With Care, 1975, The Age of Electronic Messages, 1991; editor: Control Engineers' Handbook, 1958. Recipient Rufus Oldenburger medal ASME, 1991. Fellow IEEE, AAAS; mem. NAE, Instrument Soc. Am. (pres. 1965), Am. Soc. Engring. Edn., Phi Beta Kappa, Sigma Xi, Tau Beta Pi, Eta Kappa Nu, Phi Kappa Psi. Home: 8 Avon Ct Dix Hills NY 11746-4921 Office: SUNY Coll Engring Stony Brook NY 11794

TRYBUL, THEODORE NICHOLAN, education educator; b. Chgo., Apr. 12, 1935; s. Theodore and Sophie T.; m. (dec.); children: Adreienne, Barbie, Cathy, Diane, Elizabeth, Teddy. BS, U. Ill., 1957; MS, U. N.Mex., 1963; DSc, George Washington U., 1976. Registered profl. engr., D.C. Dir. Sr. Exec. Svc., ES-IV Fed. Govt., Washington, 1966-83; prof. George Washington U., Washington, 1983-94, Tex. Grad. Sch., Corpus Christi, Tex., 1994—; adv. bd. NSF, Nat. Acad. Engring., NIH, Surgeon Gens. Office. Contbr. articles to profl. jours. Officer Corpus Christi C. of C., Neuces Club, Millionaires Club, CC Town Club. Col. U.S. Army, 1957. Fellow ASME, Soc. for Computer Simulation, Health Care Execs., Sir Isaac Walton, Audubon Soc., Sierra Club; mem. Pi Tau Sigma, Phi Betta Kappa, Kappa Mu Epsilon, Sigma Xi. Avocations: golf, tennis, fishing, mountain climbing. Office: Tex Grad Sch 14514 E Cabana St Corpus Christi TX 78418-5900

TRYBUS, RAYMOND J., higher education executive, psychologist; b. Chgo., Jan. 9, 1944; s. Fred and Cecilia (Liszka) T.; m. Sandra A. Noone, Aug. 19, 1967; children: David, Nicole. BS, St. Louis U., 1965, MS, 1970, PhD, 1971. Lic. psychologist, Md., D.C., Calif. Clin. psychologist Jewish Vocat. Svc., St. Louis, 1968-71; clin. psychologist Gallaudet U., Washington, 1971-72, rsch. psychologist, 1972-74, dir. demographic studies, 1974-78, dean grad. studies and rsch., 1978-88; provost, prof. psychology Calif. Sch. of Profl. Psychology, 1988—, chancellor, 1992—; dir. Rehab. Rsch. and Tng. Ctr., 1994—; pres. CSPP Rsch. and Svc. Found., 1996—; mem. Sci. Rev. Bd. Dept. Vets. Affairs Rehab. Rsch. and Devel. Program, 1991—; cons. Mental Health Ctr. for Deaf, Lanham, Md., 1982-88, Congl. Rsch. Svc., 1982-84, McGill U. Nat. Study Hearing Impairment in Can., 1984-88. Contbg. author: The Future of Mental Health Services for the Deaf, 1978, Hearing-impaired Children and Youth with Devel. Disabilities, 1985; editor Jour. Am. Deafness and Rehab. Assn., 1988-91. Grantee NIMH, Nat. Inst. Disability and Rehab. Rsch., Spencer Found., Tex. Edn. Agy., W.K. Kellogg Found. Mem. APA, Am. Assn. Univ. Adminstrs., Calif. Psychol. Assn. (pres. div. edn. and tng. 1990-92), San Diego Psychol. Assn., Am. Coun. Edn., Am. Deafness and Rehab. Assn., Am. Assn. Higher Edn., Am. Psychol. Soc. Roman Catholic. Home: 6342 Cibola Rd San Diego CA 92120-2124 Office: 6160 Cornerstone Ct E San Diego CA 92121-3710

TRYGSTAD, LAWRENCE BENSON, lawyer; b. Holton, Mich., Mar. 22, 1937. BA, U. Mich., 1959; JD, U. So. Calif., 1967. Bar: Calif. 1968, U.S. Supreme Ct. 1974. Legal counsel Calif. Tchrs. Assn., United Tchrs. L.A., L.A., 1968-71; ptnr. Trygstad & Odell, L.A., 1971-80; pres. Trygstad Law Corp., L.A., 1980—; instr., tchr. negotiation U. Calif.-Northridge; panelist TV shows Law and the Teacher. Bd. dirs. George Washington Carver Found., L.A. Mem. ABA, Calif. Bar Assn., L.A. County Bar Assn., Calif. Trial Lawyers Assn., L.A. Trial Lawyers Assn., Nat. Orgn. Lawyers for Edn. Assns., Am. Trial Lawyers Assn., Phi Alpha Delta. Home: 4209 Aleman Dr Tarzana CA 91356-5405 Office: 1880 Century Park E Bldg 404 Los Angeles CA 90067-1604

TRYTEK, DAVID DOUGLAS, insurance company executive; b. Cleve., Jan. 18, 1955; s. Edmund Trytek and Mary Elaine Salzwedel Blech; m. Lorie Ann Stone, Apr. 10, 1982; children: Dane, Douglas. BS in BA, Bowling Green (Ohio) State U., 1977. Claims adjuster Liberty Mus. Ins. Co., Toledo, 1977-80; claims supr. Liberty Mus. Ins. Co., Milw., 1980-85; spl. claims examiner Liberty Mus. Ins. Co., Boston, 1986-89; claims mgr. Liberty Mus. Ins. Co., Green Bay, Wis., 1989-93; tech. svcs. mgr. Liberty Mut. Ins. Co., Milw., 1993-95; regional field investigations supr. Liberty Mutual Ins. Co., Milw., 1996—; arbitrator Inter-Co. Arbitration Com., Milw., 1984-85. Coach Toledo Optimists Youth Hockey Assn., 1979-80, Wauwatosa (Wis.) Recreation Dept., 1980-85, YMCA Youth Baseball, 1994; alt. Worker's Compensation divsn. Ins. Adv. Com., Madison, Wis., 19941 youth baseball and football coach, Sussex, Wis., 1994-96. Mem. Exptl. Aircraft Assn., Air Force Assn., Warbirds of Am., USA Hockey Inc., Internat. Assn. of Spl. Investigation Units. Avocations: camping, ice hockey, golf, military aircraft. Office: Liberty Mutual Ins PO Box 0915 15700 W Bluemound Rd Brookfield WI 53008

TRYTHALL, HARRY GILBERT, music educator, composer; b. Knoxville, Tenn., Oct. 28, 1930; s. Harry Gilbert and Clara Hannah (Akre) T.; m. Jean Marie Slater, Dec. 28, 1951 (div. 1976); children: Linda Marie, Karen Elizabeth; m. Carol King, Sept. 19, 1985. BA, U. Tenn., 1951; MusM, Northwestern U., 1952; DMA, Cornell U., 1960. Asst. prof. music Knox Coll., Galesburg, Ill., 1960-64; prof. music theory and composition George Peabody Coll. Tchrs., Nashville, 1964-75; dean Creative Arts Ctr., 1975-81; prof. music W.Va. U., Morgantown, 1975-96; ret., 1997; pres. Luxikon Music, Pandora-Synthe Records, Westover, W.Va., 1983—. Author: Principles and Practice of Electronic Music, 1974, Eighteenth Century Counterpoint, 1993, Sixteenth Century Counterpoint, 1994; past mem. editorial bd. Music Educators Jour.; composer orchestral music, chamber and electronic music. With USAF, 1953-57. Home: 41 W Main St Morgantown WV 26505-4561 Office: KBA Software PO Box 2281 Westover WV 26502-2281

TRZEBIATOWSKI, GREGORY L., education educator; b. Buena Vista, Wis., May 19, 1937; s. Bert Bernard and Amelia O. (Brychell) T.; m. Maxine Eder, June 18, 1960 (dec. Sept. 1991); children: Peggy, Heidi, Molly; m. Ana Virginia Mangili Godoy, June 5, 1992; children: Gregory L., Jr., Thomas John. BS, U. Wis., Stout, 1959; PhD, Mich. State U., 1967. Tchr. Madison (Wis.) Pub. Schs., 1959-62; asst. prof. U. So. Calif., Los Angeles, 1965-67; from asst. to assoc. prof. Coll. Edn. Ohio State U., Columbus, 1967-74, prof. edn. Coll. Edn., 1974-92, asst. dean, 1970-77, assoc. dean med. and grad. edn., Coll. Medicine, 1978-87, prof. emeritus, 1992; rector, pres., chief exec. officer The Thomas Jefferson Sch., Concepción, Chile; dir. Office Geriatrics and Gerontology, 1985-92, Alzheimer's Disease Rsch. Ctr., 1987-92, Ohio State U.; cons. U. Concepcion, Chile, 1979—, Meml. Hosp. Union County, Marysville, Ohio, 1978-87; mem. peer rev. com. Nat. Cancer Inst., Bethesda, Md., 1979-84; cons., sci. rev. com. Pan Am. Health Orgn., Rio de Janeiro, 1978-82; pres., CEO Inmobiliaria Monticello S.A., Talcahauno, Chile. Author: Medical Education for the 21st Century, 1985; contbr. articles to profl. jours. V.p. Friends of Upper Arlington (Ohio) Library, 1987, pres. 1988-91; bd. dirs. Ohio State U. Friends of Library, 1987-92. Recipient Stout Medallion, U. Wis., 1959, Outstanding Alumni award Mich State U., 1979, Disting. Alumni award U. Wis. Stout, 1980; named hon. prof. U. Concepcion, Chile, 1981. Mem. Am. Assn. Sch. Adminstrs., Alzheimer's Assn. (trustee Columbus chpt. 1988-92), Am. Fedn. Aging Research (bd. dirs. Ohio affiliate 1988-92), Phi Beta Delta (pres. Hon. Soc. for Internat. Scholars Ohio State U. 1989-90, nat. pres. 1990-91). Roman Catholic. Avocations: bicycling, jogging, woodworking, collecting books. Home: Casilla #2532, Concepcion Chile Office: Thomas Jefferson Sch, Avenida Jorge Alessandri #26, Casilla 2532 Concepcion Chile

TRZETRZELEWSKA, BASIA See BASIA

TSAI, BOR-SHENG, educator; b. Kaohsiung, Taiwan, China, Apr. 8, 1950; came to U.S., 1978; s. Yu-shiu and Huo-chu T.; m. Shiu-hwa Yu; 1 child, Shengdar. BA in Libr. Sci., Fu-jen Cath. U., 1974; MS in Info. Sci., Case Western Reserve U., 1979, PhD in Info. Sci., 1987. Intern Libr. Plastics Techs., Kaohsiung, 1973; acquisitions libr. Nat. Cen. Libr., Taiwan, 1976-77; reference libr. Case Western Reserve U., Cleve., 1981; instr., designer CATS, bilingual/multicultural program Cleve. Pub. Schs., 1985-86; asst. prof. libr. and info. sci. program Wayne State U., Detroit, 1987—; cons. in field. Mem. ALA, AAUP, Am. Soc. Info. Sci. (chpt. rep. 1992-93, info. sci. commn., Continuing Edn. Commn. 1993-95), Chinese-Am. Librs. Assn. (coord., chmn. E-Mail com. 1991-94, chmn. E-Pub. com. 1994-95, editor Jour. Libr. Info. Sci., pub. com. 1990-93, 94, scholarship com. 1996-97, editor E-Jour. 1992-95), Mich. Libr. Assn., Assn. Libr. and Info. Sci. Edn., Internat. Soc. Scientometrics & Infometrics. Avocations: painting, soccer, chess, writing, sightseeing. Office: Wayne State U Libr and Info Sci Program 315 Kresge Libr Detroit MI 48202

TSAI, STEPHEN WEI-LUN, aeronautical educator; b. Beijing, July 6, 1929; U.S. citizen; married; two children. BE, Yale U., 1952, D Mech. Engring., 1961. Project engr. Foster Wheeler Corp., 1952-58; dept. mgr. material rsch. aeronutronic divsn. Philco Corp., 1961-66; prof. engring. Washington U., St. Louis, 1966-68, affiliate prof., 1968—; chief scientist Air Force Material Lab., Wright-Patterson AFB, Ohio, 1968-72, scientist, 1972—; rsch. prof. dept. aeronautics and astronautics Stanford (Calif.) U., 1990—; lectr. UCLA, 1965-66; Battelle vis. prof. Ohio State U., Columbus, Ohio, 1969. Editor-in-chief Jour. Composite Materials, 1966-95. Mem. NAE, Sigma Xi. Office: Stanford U Dept Aeros-Astronautics Stanford CA 94305

TSAI, TOM CHUNGHU, chemical engineer; b. Kaohsiung, Taiwan, Oct. 24, 1948; came to U.S., 1971, naturalized, 1984; s. Shu and Kwei (Kao) T.; m. Joyce Chionhwa Pai, Dec. 17, 1974; children: Wayne, Jimmy Payne. BS in Chem. Engring., Nat. Taiwan U., Taipei, 1970; MS in Chem. Engring., Purdue U., 1973, PhD in Chem. Engring., 1975. Registered profl. engr., Tex. Sr. process engr. CE-Lummus Co., Bloomfield, N.J., 1975-80; sr. engr. Bechtel Petroleum Inc., Houston, 1980-83; cons. engr. TDS Assocs., Houston, 1983-88; process engring. assoc. Dow Chem. Co., Freeport, Tex., 1988—; mem. internat. adv. bd. Ency. Chem. Processing and Design, 1995—. Co-author, contbr.: Ethylene-Keystone to the Petrochemical Industry, 1980, Kirk-Othmer Encyclopedia of Chemical Technology, 1980, Pyrolysis: Theory and Industrial Practice, 1983, Encyclopedia of Chemical Processing and Design, 1990, 94, 95, Unit Operations Handbook, 1992; contbr. articles to profl. jours. Bd. dirs. H.S. for Performing and Visual Arts PTO, Houston, 1993-95. 2d lt. Republic of China Army, 1970-71. Mem. Am. Inst. Chem. Engrs., Assn. Am. Chinese Profls. (div. chmn. 1988-89). Achievements include patent for liquid removal from natural gas; research in flare system design by microcomputer, yield correlations for AGO cracking, sizing a vertical separator by microcomputer, surface reactions in pyrolysis units, technical improvement in heater design for olefins production, hydrodechlorination of chlorinated hydrocarbons, liquid removal of fuel gas, inspired polycarbonate polymers and monomers, gasoline additives by reductive amination, and propylene oxide/styrene process development. Home: 1503 Ashford Hollow Ln Houston TX 77077-3903 Office: The Dow Chem Co 2301 N Brazosport Blvd Freeport TX 77541-3203

TSAI, TSU-MIN, surgeon; b. Taipei, Taiwan, Dec. 15, 1936; arrived in U.S., 1976; m. Fu-Mei Tsai; children: Yi-Yi Tsai Chen, Ring-Ring Tsai Tien, Berlin Tsai. MD, Taiwan U., 1961. Diplomate Am. Bd. Orthopedic Surgeons with added qualifications in surgery of the hand. Intern Nat. Taiwan U. Hosp., China, 1961-62, resident in urology, surgery and orthopedics, 1964-70; intern U. Louisville, 1976-77, resident in orthopedics, 1977-79; Christine Kleinert fellow in hand surgery U. Louisville Affiliated Hosps., 1976; clin. prof. orthopaedic surg. Louisville Sch. Medicine, 1980—; presenter in field, including Oxmoor Ctr., Louisville, Shanghai, China, Dublin, Ireland, U. Ky., Lexington, Nara, Japan, Med. Coll. Ohio, Toledo, ASSH Ann. Meeting, Cin. (all 1994), Internat. Congress European Soc. Biomechs., Cologne, Germany, Chang Gung Meml. Hosp., Taipei, Taiwan, Shriner's Hosps. for Crippled Children, Lexington, Ky., IFSSH, Helsinki, Finland, French Surg. Soc., Paris, Harkess Soc., Nashville, Tenn., Hand Forum, Sea Island, Ga., 1st Internat. Workshop for Reconstructive Microsurgery, Inst. Plastic Surgery, Mexico City (all 1995), Mini symposium on Pediatric Hand and Microsurgery, Taipei, Taiwan, Internat. Soc. Reconstructive Microsurgery, Singapore, JSSH/ASSH Combined Meeting, Maui, Hawaii, European Congress Hand Surgery, Paris, Japanese Soc. Surgery of the Hand, Okinawa, Hiroshima (Japan) U. Hand Club, Keio U., Tokyo, Internat. Microsurg. Soc., Montreal, Que., Can., Christine M. Kleinert Inst., Louisville, Hand Forum, Sedona, Ariz., ASSH Ann. Meeting, Nashville, Assn. Argentina Orthopedia y Traumatologia, Buenos Aires (all 1996); Disting. Vis. Prof. Divsn. Plastic and Reconstructive Surgery, Washington Hosp. Ctr., 1990, others. Contbr. articles to profl. jours. and publs. Fellow Am. Coll. Surgeons, Am. Acad. Orthopedic Surgeons; mem. Jefferson Count Med. Soc., Jefferson County Orthopaedic Soc., Ky. Orthopaedic Soc., Ky. Med. Soc., Ky. Pediat. Soc., AMA, Internat. Soc. Reconstructive Microsurgery, Am. Soc. Reconstructive Microsurgery, Western Pacific Orthopedic Assn., Am. Soc. Surgery of the Hand, Hand Forum, Clin. Orthopedic Soc., Japanese Orthopaedic Assn. SICOT Soc. Avocations: fishing, tennis. Office: Kleinert Kutz & Assocs 225 Abraham Flexner Way Louisville KY 40202-1846

TSAI, WEN-YING, sculptor, painter, engineer; b. Xiamen, Fujian, China, Oct. 13, 1928; came to U.S., 1950, naturalized, 1962; s. Chen-Dak and Ching-Miau (Chen) T.; m. Pei-De Chang, Aug. 7, 1968; children: Lun-Yi and Ming Yi (twins). Student, Ta Tung U., 1947-49; BSME, U. Mich., 1953; postgrad., Art Students League N.Y., 1953-57, New Sch. Polit. and Social Sci., New Sch., 1956-58. cons. engr., 1953-63; project mgr. Cosentini Assocs., 1962-63; project engr. Guy B. Panero, Engrs., 1956-60. Creator cybernetic sculpture based on prin. harmonic motion, stroboscopic effects; one-man shows include, Ruth Sherman Gallery, N.Y.C., 1961, Amel Gallery, N.Y.C., 1964, 65, Howard Wise Gallery, N.Y.C., 1968, Kaiser Wilhelm Mus. Haus Lange, Krefeld, Germany, 1970, Hayden Gallery of MIT, Cambridge, Ont. Sci. Centre, Toronto, Can., 1971, Corcoran Gallery Art, 1972, Denise René Gallery, 1972, 73, Musée d'Art Contemporain, Montreal, 1973, Museo de Arte Contemporáneo, Caracas, 1975, Wildenstein Art Center, Houston, 1978, Museo de Bellas Artes, Caracas, 1978, Hong Kong Mus. Art, 1979, Isetan Mus. Art, Tokyo, 1980, Galerie Denise René, Paris, 1983, Nat. Mus. History, Taipei, Taiwan, 1989, Taiwan Mus. of Art, Taichung, 1990, China Nat. Mus. Fine Arts, Beijing, 1997; represented maj. internat. exhbns., also numerous group exhbns., in permanent collections, Centre Georges Pompidou, Paris; Tate Gallery, London, Albright-Knox Gallery, Buffalo Mus., Addison Gallery Am. Art, Andover, Mass., Museo de Arte Contemporáneo, Caracas, Museo de Bellas Artes, Caracas, Whitney Mus., Chrysler Art Mus., Orlando Sci. Ctr., MIT, Hayden Gallery, Kaiser Wilhelm Mus., Mus. Modern Art, Israel Mus., Jerusalem, Artware, Kunst und Elektronik, Honnover-Messe, Great Exploration-The Hands on Mus., Taiwan Mus. Art, Saibu Gas Mus., Nagoya City Mus., Mus. fü Holographie, Kanagawa Sci. Pk., Hong Kong Sci. Mus., others; commd. works include: fountain at Land Mark, Hong Kong, 1980, , water sculpture at Shell Tower, Singapore, 1982, cybernetic upward falling fountains (2), Paris; creator spatial dynamic hydro-cybernetic systems for 42d Internat. Exhbn. Art-La Biennale di Venezia, 1986, Digital Visions-Computers and Art, Everson Mus. of Art, 1987, Contemporary Arts Ctr. Cin., 1987, IBM Gallery of Sci. and Art, N.Y.C., 1988, Phenomena Art Expo, Fukuoka, Japan, 1989, Artec '91, Wonderland of Sci.-Art Kanagawa Internat. Art Sci. Exhbn., Kawasaki, Japan, 1989, Vienna Messe-Wiener Festwochen, 1989, Kanagawa Internat. Art & Sci. Exhbn., Kawasaki, Japan, 1989, Artec 91, Internat. Biennale in Nagoya, Japan, 1991 (Artec Grand Prix winner); creator first CD-ROM version of cybernetic sculpture, 1995, Info-Art Kwang Ju Internat. Biennale Korea, Osaka Triennale, 1995—, Internet Graphics Gallery, 1995; featured: Art for Tomorrow-The 21st Century, CBS-TV, 1969, Video Variation, WGBH-TV, 1971, Science and Art, Japan TV Man Union, 1982, Art and Sci.-Innovation, Sta. WNET-TV, 1988, The World of Wen-Ying Tsai, Taiwan Pub. TV, 1991. John Hay Whitney fellow, 1963; MacDowell fellow, 1965; fellow Center Advanced Visual Studies, MIT, 1969, 70. Inventor upward falling fountain, computer mural, multiple light computer array, utilizing environ. feedback control system.

TSALIKIAN, EVA, physician, educator; b. Piraeus, Greece, June 22, 1949; came to U.S., 1974; d. Vartan and Arousiak (Kasparian) T. M.D., U. Athens, 1973. Research fellow U. Calif.-San Francisco, 1974-76; resident pediatrics Children's Hosp., Pitts., 1976-78, fellow endocrinology, 1978-80; research fellow Mayo Clinic, Rochester, Minn., 1980-83; from asst. prof. dept. pediatrics to assoc. prof. U. Iowa, Iowa City, 1983—. Fellow Juvenile Diabetes Found., 1978-80, Heinz Nutrition Found., 1980-81; recipient Young Physician award AMA, 1977. Mem. Am. Diabetes Assn. Home: 1217 Dolen Pl Iowa City IA 52246-4524 Office: U Iowa Dept Pediatrics 2856 JCP Iowa City IA 52242*

TSAMBASSIS, NICHOLAS ALEXANDER, pediatrician; b. Evanston, Ill., Sept. 3, 1956; s. Alexander Nicholas and Katharine (Voulelis) T. BS, Calif. U. Pa., 1979; MD, Ross U., 1985. Diplomate Am. Bd. Pediatrics. Intern Trenton (N.J.) Affiliated Hosps., 1985-86; resident Lincoln Med. and Mental Health Ctr., Bronx, N.Y., 1986-89; pvt. practice Gardner Healthcare Initiative, Portland, Tenn., 1990, Centerville (Pa.) Clinics, Inc., 1991—; med. dir. South Fayette Nursing Ctr., Markleysburg, Pa., 1993-95. Active Rock Out Censorship, Jewett, Ohio, 1992, ACLU, N.Y.C., 1994, People for the Am. Way, Washington, 1994, Ams. United, Washington, 1995. Mem. Pa. Med. Soc., Assn. Am. Physicians and Surgeons. Avocations: writing, reading, pool, travel, photography. Home: 237 Charlemagne Blvd Clarksville TN 37042 Office: Dover Rd Med Ctr 363 Dover Rd Clarksville TN 37042

TSAO, GEORGE T., chemical engineer, educator; b. Nanking, China, Dec. 4, 1931; married; 3 children. BSc, Nat. Taiwan U., 1953; MSc, U. Fla., 1956; PhD in Chem. Engring., U. Mich., 1960. Asst. prof. physics Olivet Coll., 1959-60; chem. engr. Merck & Co., Inc., 1960-61; rsch. chemist TVA, 1961-62; sect. leader hydrolisys and fermentation, rsch. dept. Union Starch & Refining Co. divsn. Miles Labs., Inc., 1962-65, asst. rsch. dir., 1965-66; from assoc. prof. to prof. chem. engring. Iowa State U., 1966-77; prof. chem. engring. Purdue U., West Lafayette, Ind., 1977—, dir. Lab. Renewable Resources Engring. Recipient John Ericsson award Dept. Energy, 1989. Mem. AIChE, Am. Chem. Soc., Am. Soc. Engring. Edn. Office: Purdue U Lab Renewable Resources Engring 1295 Potter Dr West Lafayette IN 47906-1333*

TSCHANTZ, BRUCE ALLEN, civil engineer, educator; b. Akron, Ohio, Sept. 15, 1938; s. Miles Emerson and Gladys Marcella (Krichbaum) T.; m. Penelope Ann Ford, Dec. 20, 1962; children: Peter Allen, Michael Ford. BS, Ohio No. U., 1960; MS, N.Mex. State U., 1962, ScD, 1965. Registered profl. engr., Ohio, Tenn., Va. San. engr. Bur. Indian Affairs, Albuquerque, 1962-63; civil engr. White Sands (N.Mex.) Missile Range, 1965; asst. prof. civil engring. U. Tenn., Knoxville, 1965-69; asso. prof. U. Tenn., 1969-74, prof., 1974—, M. E. Brooks Disting. prof., 1978, R.N. Condra Disting. prof.; acting dir. Tenn. Water Resources Rsch. Ctr., 1991-94; cons. hydrologist U.S. Geol. Survey, Noxville, 1973-76; cons. Exec. Office of Pres., Office Sci. Tech. POlicy, Washington, 1977-80, Tenn. Dept. Transp., 1976—, Tenn. Dept. Conservation, 1978; chief fed. dam safety FEd. Emergency Mgmt. Agy., Washington, 1979-80; mem. Tenn. Gov.'s Adv. Com. on Dams, 1972; adviser, cons. Coun. of State Govts., Lexington, Ky.; mem. U.S. Com. on Large Dams; mem. bd. on radioactive waste mgmt. NAS/NRC; mem. Ward Valley, Calif. Commn. on Low Level Radioactive Waste. Contbr. articles on dam safety, flood control, hydrologic impacts of strip mining to profl. jours., chpts. to books. Recipient Robert Fulton Engring. Prof. award, 1980, Outstanding Tchr. award, 1985, 89, 91, 92, 93, 94, President's award Assn. State Dam Safety Ofcls., 1986, Centennial Outstanding Alumnis award N.Mex. State U., 1988, Engring. Coll. Leon and Nancy Cole Outstanding Tchg. award, 1995. Mem. ASCE (Faculty of Year award Student chpt. 1968), Am. Soc. Engring. Edn. (civil engr. chmn. S.E. sect. 1972, Dow Chem. award 1969, Western Electric award 1980), Nat. Soc. Profl. Engrs., Tenn. Soc. Profl. Engrs. (v.p., pres. Knoxville br. 1973-75), U.S. Com. on Large Dams, Knoxville Tech. Soc. (Knoxville Young Engr. award 1970), N.Mex. Acad. Civil Engring., Sigma Xi, Tau Beta Pi, Chi Epsilon. Home: 1508 Meeting House Rd Knoxville TN 37931-4427 Office: U Tenn 63 Perkins Hall Knoxville TN 37996

TSCHERNY, GEORGE, graphic designer; b. Budapest, Hungary, July 12, 1924; s. Mendel and Bella (Heimann) T.; m. Sonia Katz, July 7, 1950; children—Nadia, Carla. Student, Pratt Inst., Bklyn., 1947-50. Staff designer Donald Deskey & Assocs., N.Y.C., 1950-53; designer, assoc. George Nelson & Assocs., N.Y.C., 1953-55; pres. George Tscherny, Inc., N.Y.C., 1955—; instr. Pratt Inst., Bklyn., 1956, bd. advisors, 1979; instr. Sch. Visual Arts, N.Y.C., 1955-64; curriculum cons. Phila. Coll. Art, 1967; Mellon vis. prof. Cooper Union, N.Y., 1978. Retrospective exhbn. Visual Art Mus., N.Y.C., 1992; exhibited in group shows, Germany, 1962-67, Italy, 1974, U.S., 1975; represented in permanent collections Mus. Modern Art, N.Y.C., Cooper Hewitt Mus., N.Y.C., Libr. of Congress, Washington, Kunstgewerbeschule der Stadt Zurich. Contbr. design svcs. to UN Assn., Sta. WNET Pub. TV, Am. Lung Assn., Peace Corps, Cystic Fibrosis Found., L.I. State Park Commn. With U.S. Army, 1943-46, ETO. Recipient numerous awards, Am. Inst. Graphic Arts medal, 1988, Art Dirs. Club N.Y., N.Y. Type Dirs. Club, Silver medal Warsaw Biennale, 1976; inducted into Art Dirs. Club Hall of Fame, 1997. Mem. Am. Inst. Graphic Arts (pres. 1966-68), Alliance Graphique Internationale. Office: 238 E 72nd St New York NY 10021-4503

TSCHINKEL, ANDREW JOSEPH, JR., law librarian; b. Catskill, N.Y., Aug. 8, 1952; s. Andrew Joseph and Marie Frances (O'Connor) T.; m. Frances K. Quigley, Nov. 4, 1989. BA summa cum laude, St. John's Coll., Jamaica, N.Y., 1975, MLS, 1977; MBA, Fordham U., 1983. Grad. asst. div. libr. sci. St. John's Coll., Jamaica, 1975-77, asst. law libr., 1977-79, adj. law librarian, 1983-87; head librarian Christ the King High Sch., Middle Village, N.Y., 1979-80; sr. law librarian Bklyn. Supreme Ct., 1980-81; prin. law librarian N.Y. Supreme Ct., Jamaica, 1981—. Recipient Pub. Svc. award Queens Borough Pres. and N.Y. Tel. Co., 1986; named Alumnus of Yr. Grad. Sch. Arts & Scis. Divsn. Libr. & Info. Sci. St. John's U., 1993. Mem. Am. Assn. Law Librs., Law Libr. Assn. Greater N.Y., Elks, Beta Phi Mu. Republican. Office: NY Supreme Ct Libr 88-11 Sutphin Blvd Jamaica NY 11435-3716

TSCHOEPE, THOMAS, bishop; b. Pilot Point, Tex., Dec. 17, 1915; s. Louis and Catherine (Sloan) T. Student, St. Thomas Sch. Pilot Point, 1930, Pontifical Coll. Josephinum, Worthington, Ohio, 1943. Ordained priest Roman Cath. Ch., 1943; asst. pastor in Ft. Worth, 1943-46, Sherman, Tex., 1946-48, Dallas, 1948-53; adminstr. St. Patrick Ch., Dallas, 1953-56; pastor St. Augustine Ch., Dallas, 1956-62, Sacred Heart Cathedral, Dallas, 1962-65; bishop San Angelo, Tex., 1966-69; bishop Dallas, 1969-90, ret. bishop, 1990; asst. pastor St. Joseph Parish, Waxahachie, Tex., 1990—. Home and Office: St Joseph Ch 504 E Marvin St Waxahachie TX 75165-3406

TSCHUMI, BERNARD, dean; b. Lausanne, Switzerland, Jan. 25, 1944. BArch, Fed. Inst. Tech., Zurich, Switzerland, 1969. Tchr. Archtl. Assn., London, 1970-80, Inst. Architecture and Urban Studies, N.Y.C., 1976, Princeton U. Sch. Architecture, 1980-81, Cooper Union, 1980-83; dean Columbia U. Grad. Sch. Architecture, Planning & Preservation, N.Y.C.; head firm Bernard Tschumi Architects, N.Y.C. and Paris; Davenport vis. prof. architecture. Contbr.: The Manhattan Transcripts, 1981, Architecture and Disjunction, 1994, Event Cities, 1994, Bernard Tschumi: Architecture and Event, 1994. Recipient 1st prize for design of new Sch. of Architecture, Paris, 1994. Office: Col University Planning & Preservation 116 St & Broadway New York NY 10027*

TSE, EDMUND SZE-WING, insurance company executive; b. Hong Kong, Jan. 2, 1938; s. Kai-Sum and Chao-Sui (Tsui) T.; m. Peggy Pik-Kin Wai, Dec. 18, 1965; children: Ada Koon-Hang, Elaine Koon-Ming. BA, U. Hong Kong, 1960; diploma, Life Ins. Agy. Mgmt. Assn., 1972, Stanford U., 1980. Mng. supr. Nan Shan Life Ins. Co., Ltd., Taipei, Taiwan, 1970-74, pres., mng. dir., 1975-83; chmn. Nan Shan Life Ins. Co., Ltd., 1990; various positions Am. Internat. Assurance Co., Ltd., Hong Kong, 1961-70, pres., CEO, 1983—, also bd. dirs.; exec. v.p. Am. Internat. Group, Inc., 1996—; vice chmn. Am. Life Ins. Co., Wilmington, Del., 1992—, Am. Internat. Assurance Life Co. Ltd., Can., 1994—, Philippine Am. Life Ins. Co., 1992—; v.p. C.V. Starr & Co., Inc., 1994—, P.T. Asuransi AIU Indonesia, 1991—; pres. Am. Internat. Assurance Co. (Bermuda) Ltd., 1983—; pres., CEO Am. Internat. Assurance Co. Ltd., 1983—; mng. dir. Met. Land Co. Ltd., Hong Kong, 1987—, Realty Investment Ltd., Hong Kong, 1987—; chmn. AIG Taiwan Fund Ltd., 1992—, Asia Pacific Assistance Svcs., Ltd., 1991—, Universal Fin. Co., Taiwan, 1991—; chmn., pres. Green Heights, Inc., Panama, 1986—; mng. dir., chmn. Nan Shan Life Ins. Co., Ltd., Taiwan, 1979—; dep. chmn. Am. Internat. Assurance Co. (Australia) Ltd., 1985—, AIA Superannuation Co. Ltd., 1986—; dir. China Am. Holding Co., AIA Capital Corp. (Holdings) Ltd., Bermuda, AIG Asian Infrastructure Mgmt. Ltd., AIG Investment Corp. (Asia) Ltd., Am. Internat. Reins. Co. Ltd., AIA Capital Corp. Ltd., Am. Internat. Assurance Co. (Trustee) Ltd., Am. Internat. Data Ctr. Ltd., China Am. Ins. Co. (Hong Kong) Ltd., Seacliff Ltd., SPC Credit Ltd., AIA Capital Corp. (BVI) Ltd., Am. Internat. Trustee Ltd., Equitable Investment Co. (Hong Kong) Ltd., Shanghai Jin Jiang-Universal Devel. Co. Ltd., UGC Singapore Ltd., P.T. Asuransi AIA Indonesia, Dana Pensiun Lembaga Keuangan AIA Indonesia, Australian Am. Assurance Co. Ltd. Fiji, SEA Ins. Co. Pty. Ltd. Founding mem. adv. bd. for Asia Project HOPE, U.S.A.; pres., dir. AIA Found. Ltd.; trustee The Harvard Club of Hong Kong. Mem. Gen. Ins. Coun. Hong Kong (chmn. 1989-90, chmn. legis. subcom. 1988-89), Hong Kong Fedn. Insurers (dep. chmn. 1991-92, chmn. 1992-93), Chief Execs. Orgn. (U.S.), Pacific Ins. Conf. (nat. area chmn. 1985—), Bus. and Profls. Fedn. Hong Kong (mem. exec. com., fin. specialist group 1993—), Pres. Orgn. (U.S.), Life Ins. Mktg. and Rsch. Assn. (bd. dirs.). Home: 10C Headland Rd, Repulse Bay Hong Kong Office: Am Internat Assurance Co Ltd, No 1 Stubbs Rd, Hong Kong Hong Kong

TSE, HARLEY Y., immunologist, educator; b. China, July 17, 1947; s. Ton-cheuk and Hou-Ying (Choy) T.; m. Kwai-Fong Chui, Jan. 13, 1979; children—Kevin Y., Alan C., Leslie W. B.S. with honors, Calif. Inst. Tech., 1972; Ph.D., U. Calif.-San Diego, 1977; M.B.A., Rutgers U., 1986. Fellow Arthritis Found., NIH, Bethesda, Md., 1977-80; sr. research immunologist Merck Sharp & Dohme Research Lab., Rahway, N.J., 1980-83, research fellow, 1983-86; adj. asst. prof. Columbia U., 1981-84 ; assoc. prof. Wayne State U. Sch. Medicine, 1986—. Contbr. articles to profl. jours. Bd. dirs. Chinese Social Service Center, San Diego, 1975. Recipient NIH Rsch. Career Devel. award, 1992-97; Calif. Biochem. Research fellow, 1975, Arthritis Found. fellow, 1977-80; NIH grantee, Nat. Multiple Sclerosis Soc. grantee, 1988—. Mem. Am. Assn. Immunologists,, NIH Immunological Sci. Study Sec., 1995-99, Chinese Student Assn. (pres. 1974-76)., Soc. Chinese Bioscientist in Am., Detroit Immunological Soc. (pres. 1989-91). Roman Catholic. Home: 5393 Tequesta Dr West Bloomfield MI 48323-2351 Office: Wayne State U Sch Medicine 540 E Canfield St Detroit MI 48201-1928

TSE, MAN-CHUN MARINA, special education educator; b. Kai-Ping, China, Dec. 14, 1948; came to U.S., 1972; d. Sun-Poo and Su-ling Cheung. BA in English, U. Chinese Culture, Taipei, Taiwan, 1970; MS in Spl. Edn., U. So. Calif., 1974. Cert. tchr., spl. edn. tchr., Calif. Rsch. asst. lit. U. Chinese Culture, 1970-72; English tchr. Tang-Suede Mid. Sch., Taiwan, 1970-72; instr. Willing Workers, Adult Handicapped Program L.A. Sch. Dist., 1976-77; instr. ESL Evans Adult Sch., L.A., 1977-82; instr. ESL, polit. sci. Lincoln Adult Sch., L.A., 1986-94; spl. edn. tchr. Duarte (Calif.) Unified Sch. Dist., 1977—; commr., program co-chair Calif. Spl. Edn. Adv. Commn., Sacramento, 1994-96; coun. mem. L.A. County Children Planning Coun., 1995—; com. mem. L.A. County Sci. & Engring. Fair Com., 1993—; bd. dirs. Asian Youth Ctr., Alhambra, Calif., 1992—; mem. Calif. State Bd. Edn., 1996—. Appeared on numerous TV and radio programs. Bd. pres. Bruggemeyer Libr., Monterey Park, Calif., 1993—; pres. L.A. County Coun. Reps., 1994—; com. mem. United Way Diversity Com., Acadia, Calif., 1995—, Calif. Statewide Focus Group Diversity, Sacramento, 1995—; chair Chinese Am. Edn. Assn., 1993—; co-chair, co-founder Multi-Cultural Cmty. Assn., 1992—; bd. dirs. Rosemead-Taipei Sister City, 1993—, San Gabriel Valley Charity Night Com., 1992—; chair L.A. County/Taipei County Friendship Com., 1996—. Recipient Recognition cert. Duarte Edn. Found., 1990, cert. Valley View Sch., 1991, award State Calif., 1991, Appreciation award City Rosemead, 1992, Commendation cert. Alhambra Sch. Dist., 1992-93, Edn. award Asian Youth Ctr., 1992, 1992, Commendation cert. City L.A., 1992, commendation County L.A., 1992, award U.S. Congress, 1993, Recognition cert. Calif. Legis. Assembly, 1993, Proclamation City Alhambra, 1993, Chinese Am. PTA award, 1993, John Anson Ford award L.A. County Human Rels. Com., 1993, Appreciation cert. Chinese Consolidated Benevolent Assn., 1994, Recognition cert. Calif. State Senate, 1994, Appreciation cert. City Monterey Park, 1995, Spl. Achievement award Calif. Spl. Edn. Adv. Commn., 1997, Outstanding Comm. Svc. award City of Duarte, Calif., 1997, Spl. Achievement award Duarte United Edn. Ctr., 1997, Disting. Woman of Yr. award Calif. 24th Dist. Sen.'s Office, 1997. Mem. Calif. Tchr. Assn., Chinese Edn. Assn. Office: Duarte Unified Sch Dist 1620 Huntington Dr Duarte CA 91010-2534

TSENG, FELIX HING-FAI, accountant; b. Kowloon, Hong Kong, May 11, 1964; s. Hin-Pei and Selena Suk-Ching Tseng; m. Rachel Wai-Chu, Feb. 16, 1992; children: Walter Fan-Kong, Riley Fan-Wei. BS, Pepperdine U., 1985, MBA, 1989. CPA. Acct. Ronald A. Stein CPA, Woodland Hills, Calif., 1989-93; contr. Benebase Investment Inc., Monterey Park, Calif., 1991—; also bd. dirs. Benebase Investment Inc., Monterey Park, Calif., Hong Kong; ptnr. Lilly Property Mgmt., L.A., 1995—; bd. dirs. YTT Corp., Monterey Park. Editor (newsletter) El Toro, 1993-96. Mem. AICPA, Inst. Mgmt. Accts. (v.p. comm. 1994-95, pres. 1995-96), Calif. Soc. CPA, So. Calif. Soc. CMAs, Assn. MBA Execs. Avocations: sports, fishing, bridge, good foods. Office: Benebase Investment Inc 108 N Ynez Ave Ste 209 Monterey Park CA 91754-1680

TSIEN, RICHARD WINYU, biology educator; b. Tating, Kweichow, People's Republic China, Mar. 3, 1945; s. Hsue-Chu and Yi-Ying (Li) T.; m. Julia Shiang Aug. 29, 1971; children: Sara Shiang-Ming, Gregory Shiang-An, Alexa Tsien-Shiang. BS, MIT, 1965, MS, 1966; DPhil, Oxford U., Eng., 1970. Rsch. student Eaton Peabody Lab. Auditory, Physiology, Mass. Eye and Ear Infirmary, 1966; asst. prof. dept. physiology, Yale U. Sch. Medicine, New Haven, 1970-74, assoc. prof., 1974-79, prof., 1979-88; George D. Smith prof. molecular and cellular physiology Stanford (Calif.) U., 1988—, chmn. dept., 1988-94; established investigator Am. Heart Assn., 1974-79. Author: Electric Current Flow in Excitable Cells, 1975. Recipient Otsuka award Internat. Soc. Heart Rsch., 1985; Rhodes Scholar, 1966; Weir Rsch. fellow, 1966-70 Univ. Coll., Oxford, 1966-70, lecturing fellow Balliol Coll., Oxford, 1969-70. Mem. Soc. Gen. Physiologists (pres. 1988), Biophys. Soc. (Kenneth S. Cole award 1985), Soc. for Neurosci. Democrat. Home: 866 Tolman Dr Palo Alto CA 94305-1026 Office: Stanford U Dept Molecular and Cellular Physiology 300 Pasteur Dr Palo Alto CA 94305

TSINA, RICHARD VASIL, chemistry educator; b. Boston, Aug. 13, 1941; s. Vasil Anastas and Theodora (Kasuli) T.; m. Irene Wang, Nov. 28, 1970; children: Lesley, Katherine. BA, Boston U., 1963; MA, Duke U., 1965; PhD, Tufts U., 1968. Asst. prof. chemistry Rutgers U., New Brunswick, N.J., 1970-73; v.p. Sultra Corp., N.Y.C., 1973-76; dean continuing edn. Cogswell Coll., San Francisco, 1976-79; asst. dean U. Calif., Berkeley, 1990-95, vice chmn. engring. ext., 1982-85, chmn., 1995—, dir. tech. programs, 1995—. Contbr. articles to profl. jours. Mem. IEEE (chmn. San Francisco sect. 1984-85, chmn. fin. coun. 1985-86, meritorious achievement award in continuing edn. 1995, chair continuing edn. adv. com. 1995—, chair profl. devel. com. 1997—, ednl. activities bd. 1997—), Sigma Xi, Tau Beta Pi (eminent engr. com.). Home: 1424 Dana Ave Palo Alto CA 94301-3149 Office: U Calif Continuing Edn Engring 1995 University Ave # 7010 Berkeley CA 94704-1058

TSINIGINE, ALLEN, educator; b. Tuba City, Ariz., Feb. 25, 1952; s. Claw and Desbah (Martin) T.; 1 child, Ryan Allen. BS in Elem. Edn., No. Ariz. U., 1974. Cert. tchr., Ariz. Tchr. Page (Ariz.) Unified Sch. Dist. # 8, 1974-85; asst. dir., instr. LeChee Vocat. Tech. Ctr., Page, 1987-93; instr. pre-algebra, algebra Coconino County C.C., Page, 1992—; instr. math. Coconino C.C., Page, 1992—; presdl. appointee, exec. staff asst. Navajo Dept. Edn., 1993-95; mem. Nat. Indian Policy Ctr., George Washington U., 1995-96; edn. com. co-chair Nat. Congress Am. Indians, 1995-96. Mem. gov. bd. dirs. Page Unified Sch. Dist. #8, 1987-93, pres., 1988-90, 91-92, clk., 1990-91, 92-93; sec.-treas. LeChee chpt. Navajo Nation, 1979-87; mem. Navajo Way, Inc., Window Rock, Ariz., 1987-92. Mem. Nat. Sch. Bds. Assn., Native Am. Caucus, Nat. Ind. Edn. Assn. (pres.). Avocations: ranching, livestock. Home: PO Box 292 Page AZ 86040-0292 Office: LeChee Vocat Tech Ctr Coppermine Rd-LeChee Page AZ 86040

TSIROS, JOHN ANDREAS, accountant; b. Boston, Oct. 2, 1963; s. Constantine Louis and Martha Sophia (Pappas) T. BA, Boston U., 1985; MBA, U. So. Calif., 1990. CPA, Calif. Acct. Golden/Goldberg Acctg. Corp., L.A., 1990-94, Kellogg & Andelson Acctg. Corp., Sherman Oaks, Calif., 1994—. Greek Orthodox. Office: Kellogg & Andelson Acctg Corp 14724 Ventura Blvd Sherman Oaks CA 91403-3501

TSIRPANLIS, CONSTANTINE N., theology, philosophy, classic and history educator; b. Kos, Greece, Mar. 18, 1935; came to U.S., 1957; m. Sophia Pappas, July 12, 1975; children: Kalliope-Chrysoula, Nike. BA, STM, lic. in theology magna cum laude, Halke Theol. Sem., Istanbul, Turkey, 1957; ThM, Harvard U., 1962; ThD, Union Theol. Sem., 1963; MA, Columbia U., 1966, PhD, 1970; PhD, Fordham U., 1973. Instr., organizer Greek-Am. communities, 1958-63; founder, chmn., prof. modern Greek studies NYU, 1963-70; prof. world history N.Y. Inst. Tech. N.Y.C. and Delaware County Coll., Media, Pa., 1967-75; disting. prof. theology, history, ecumenism, Greek studies Union Theol. Sem., Barrytown, N.Y., 1976—; chmn., prof. classics Collegiate Sch., N.Y.C., 1967-69; prof. modern Greek lang. and lit. New Sch. for Social Rsch., N.Y.C., 1968-70; prof. classical mythology Hunter Coll. CUNY, 1968-70. Author numerous books including A Short History of the Greek Language, 1966, rev. edit., 1970, A Modern Greek Reader for Americans, 1967, rev. edit., 1968, A Modern Greek Idiom and Phrase Book, 1978, Mark Eugenicus, 1979, N. Cabasilas, 1979, Greek Patristic Theology, 9 vols.; editor The Patristic and Byzantine Rev., 1981—; pub., editor-in-chief Hellenism In Am., 1969—; contbr. articles to profl. jours. Decorated Medal of Nat. Rebirth 1821 (Greece), medals of Byzantine nobility, including count, baron, G. chevalier, Gt. Prior of N.Am., medal of Accademia Ferdinandea, medals of Diethnés Hetereia Hellenōn Logotechnōn, also hon. pres. Mem. Am. Soc. Neohellenic Studies (founder, v.p.), Pan Dodecanisian Fedn. U.S., Am. Hist. Assn., Am. Philog. Assn., Am. Acad. Medieval Studies, Internat. Assn. Byzantine Studies, Am. Philos. Assn., N.Am. Patristic Soc., Hellenic Philog. Assn., Am. Soc. Papyrologists, Am. Inst. Patristic-Byzantine Studies (pres., founder), Justinianum Oikoumenikon R.C. (pres., founder), World Acad. Arts and Culture (hon. mem., hon. DLitt. 1993). Home: 12 Minuet Ln Kingston NY 12401-9801 Office: Union Theol Sem 10 Dock Rd Barrytown NY 12507-5000

TSIVIDIS, YANNIS P., electrical engineering educator; b. Piraeus, Greece, Dec. 22, 1946; came to U.S., 1970; s. Pelopidas I. and Maria (Filippa) T. BS, U. Minn., 1972; MS, U. Calif., Berkeley, 1973, PhD, 1976. Asst. prof. elec. engring. Columbia U., N.Y.C., 1976-81, assoc. prof., 1981-84, prof., 1984—; prof. Nat. Tech. U., Athens, Greece, 1992-95; cons. AT&T Bell Labs., Murray Hill, N.J., 1977-88. Author: Operation and Modeling of the Mos Transistor, 1987, Mixed Analog-Digital VLSI Devices and Technology, 1996; co-editor: Design of Mos VLSI Circuits for Telecommunications, 1985, Integrated Continuous-Time Filters, 1993, Design of Analog-Digital VLSI Circuits for Telecommunications and Signal Processing, 1994; contbr. over 100 articles to profl. jours.; patentee in field. Recipient best paper award European Solid State Cirs. Conf., 1986, Great Tchr. award Columbia U., 1991. Fellow IEEE (Baker best paper award 1984, Darlington award 1987). Office: Columbia Univ Dept Elec Engring New York NY 10027

TSO, TIEN CHIOH, federal agency official, plant physiologist; b. Hupeh, China, July 25, 1917; came to U.S., 1947, naturalized, 1961; s. Ya Fu and Suhwa (Wang) T.; m. Margaret Lu, Aug. 28, 1949; children: Elizabeth, Paul. B.S., Nanking U., China, 1941, M.S., 1944; Ph.D., Pa. State U., 1950; postgrad., Oak Ridge Inst. Nuclear Studies. Supt. exptl. farm Ministry Social Affairs, China, 1944-46; exec. sec. Tobacco Improvement Bur., 1946-47; research chemist Gen. Cigar Research Lab., 1950-51; with U.S. Dept. Agr., 1952—; prin. plant physiologist crop research div. Agrl. Research Service, Beltsville, Md., 1964-66; leader tobacco quality investigations, tobacco and sugar crops research br. Agrl. Research Service, 1966-71, chief tobacco lab., 1972-83, sr. exec. service, 1974-83, collaborator, 1984—; exec. dir. Internat. Devel. and Edn. in Agr. and Life Scis., 1984—; cons. World Bank, Nat. Cancer Inst., Ky. Tobacco Health Rsch. Inst., China Nat. Tobacco Corp., Philippine Tobacco Rsch. Ctr., Philip Morris Tobacco Corp. Author: Physiology and Biochemistry of Tobacco Plants, 1972, Production, Physiology and Biochemistry of Tobacco Plants, 1991; contbg. author: Ann. Rev. Plant Physiology, Vol. 9, 1958, The Chemistry of Tobacco and Tobacco Smoke, 1972, Toward Less Harmful Cigarettes, 1968, 71, 75, 80; editor: Structural and Functional Aspects of Phytochemistry, 1972, Recent Advances in Tobacco Science, vol. 1, 1975. Fellow AAAS, Am. Soc. Agronomy (chmn. colloquium on agr. and life scis. in China 1983, 84, 85, 86, 87, 88-89), Am. Inst. Chemists; mem. Am. Chem. Soc., Am. Soc. Plant Physiologists, Phytochem. Soc. N.Am. (pres. 1971, life mem.), Tobacco Chemists Rsch. Conf. (symposium chmn. 1965, 79, chmn. 1975, 83), World Conf. Smoking and Health (sect. chmn. 1967, 71, 75), Tobacco Workers Conf., N.Y. Acad. Scis., Interagy. Smoking and Health Forum (chmn. 1979-83), Nat. Coordinating Com. on Tobacco-Related Rsch., Sigma Xi, Gamma Sigma Delta. Research publs. on establishment of loci of alkaloid formation, biosynthetic pathway, interconversion and fate of alkaloids in tobacco plants, chem. composition as affected by macro and micro elements, homogenized leaf curing, health-related factors including mycotoxins and phenolics. Home: 4306 Yates Rd Beltsville MD 20705-2758 Office: Beltsville Agr Rsch Ctr Bldg 005 Beltsville MD 20705 also: Ideals Inc 5010 Sunnyside Ave Beltsville MD 20705-2320 *We are thankful to those fools. They are the only ones who dare to dream of something new and seemingly impossible.*

TSOI, EDWARD TZE MING, architect, interior designer, urban planner; b. New Orleans, Aug. 7, 1943; s. Edward Mong Yok and Ruby Liu Wei (Hsia) T.; m. Louise Smoyer, June 15, 1968; children: Laura Li Ling, Alison Li Mei. BArch, MIT, 1966; MArch, U. Pa., 1968, M in City Planning, 1968, cert. in urban design, 1969. Registered architect, Mass., La. Assoc. Sert/Jackson & Assocs., Cambridge, Mass., 1969-76; assoc. prin. Skidmore Owings & Merrill, Boston, 1976-83; prin. Tsoi/Kobus & Assocs., Inc., Cambridge, 1983—, pres., 1985-89, 93—; instr. Sch. Design, Harvard U., Cambridge, 1980-84. Designer Marine Resource Ctr., 1994. Chmn. Arlington (Mass.) Redevel. Bd., 1972—; chmn. 1st parish Unitarian Universalist Ch., Arlington, 1990; pres. bd. dirs. Cambridge Salvation Army, 1990—; mem. Boston Civic Design Commn., 1993—. Recipient Best New Med. Facility award Symposium on Healthcare, 1993, Grand Honor award Assn. Gen. Contractors, 1993, award Lotus Devel. Corp. landscape award Urban Design, 1991, nat. award for renovation Ford Model T plant Urban Land Inst., 1995. Fellow AIA; mem. Boston Soc. Architects (pres. 1993-94). Democrat. Avocations: windsurfing, boating, woodworking, carpentry. Home: 16 Devereaux St Arlington MA 02174-8114 Office: Tsoi/Kobus & Assocs Inc PO Box 9114 Cambridge MA 02238-9114

TSOU, TANG, political science educator, researcher; b. Canton, Guangdong, China, Dec. 10, 1918; came to U.S., 1941; s. Lu and Chien-yun (Hsu) T.; m. Yi-chuang Lu. BA, Nat. Southwest Associated U., Kunming, Yunnan, China, 1940; PhD, U. Chgo., 1951. Rsch. assoc. Ctr. for Study Am. Fgn. Policy, U. Chgo., 1955-62, asst. prof. dept. polit. sci., 1959-62, assoc. prof., 1962-66, prof., 1966-84, Homer J. Livingston prof., 1984-88, Homer J. Livingston prof. emeritus, 1989—; bd. dirs. Nat. Com. on U.S.-China Rels., N.Y.C., 1971-87, emeritus, 1987—; mem. Joint Com. on Contemporary China, Social Sci. Rsch. Coun. and Am. Coun. Learned Socs., 1972-74. Author: America's Failure in China, 1963 (Gordon J. Laing prize 1965), The Cultural Revolution and Post-Mao Reforms, 1986, Chinese Politics in the Twentieth-Century: Macrohistory and Micro-mechanisms, 1994; co-editor, co-author: China in Crisis, 1968; mem. editorial bd. World Politics, China Quarterly, Asian Survey, Modern China; contbr. articles to profl. jours. Named Hon. Prof. Peking U., Beijing, 1986; rsch. grantee Joint Com. on Contemporary China, Social Sci. Rsch. Coun. and Am. Coun. Learned Socs., 1962-63, 68-69, 75-76; fellow Rockefeller Found., 1966-67, Luce Found., 1982-83. Mem. Am. Polit. Sci. Assn. Office: U Chgo Dept Polit Sci 5828 S University Ave Chicago IL 60637-1515

TSOU, WALTER HAI-TZE, physician; b. Boston, Nov. 1, 1952; s. Kwan Chung and Teresa (Lee) T. BA, U. Pa., 1974, MD, 1978; MPH, Johns Hopkins U., 1988. Diplomate Am. Bd. Internal Medicine. Resident in internal medicine Presbyn. U. Pa. Med. Ctr., Phila., 1978-81; clinician Phila. Dept. Pub. Health, 1981-84, clin. dir., 1984-91; med. dir. Montgomery County Health Dept., Norristown, Pa., 1991—, dep. dir. personal health svcs., 1991—; asst. prof. Med. Coll. Pa., Phila., 1990—; mem. Phila. AIDS Consortium, 1991-93. Contbg. editor Physicians News Digest, Narberth, Pa., 1989—. Mem. fund distbn. com. United Way of S.E. Pa., Phila., 1994—; co-chair Physicians for a Nat. Health Program, Phila., 1991—. Recipient John C. Hume award Johns Hopkins Sch. Pub. Health, 1988. Fellow Coll. Physicians of Phila. (chair com. pub. health 1994—); mem. APHA, ACP, Pa. Pub. Health Assn. (bd. dirs. 1995—), Chinese-Am. Med. Soc., Delta Omega. Avocations: computers, photography, travel. Office: Montgomery County Hlth Dept 1 Lafayette Pl Ste 325 Norristown PA 19401

TSOUCALAS, NICHOLAS, federal judge; b. N.Y.C., Aug. 24, 1926; s. George Michael and Maria (Monogenis) T.; m. Catherine Aravantinos, Nov. 21, 1954; children: Stephanie, Georgia. BSBA, Kent State U., 1949; LLB, N.Y. Law Sch., 1951. Bar: N.Y. 1953. Sole practice, N.Y.C., 1953-55, 59-68; asst. U.S. atty. So. Dist. N.Y., 1955-59; judge Criminal Ct., City of N.Y., 1968-86; acting supreme ct. judge State of N.Y., N.Y.C., 1975-82; judge U.S. Ct. Internat. Trade, N.Y.C., 1986—; now sr. judge. Dist. leader Republican Party N.Y. County, N.Y.C., 1961-68; mem. Rep. Exec. Com., N.Y.C., 1961-68. Served with USN, 1944-46, 51-52. Recipient Proficiency in Constl. Law award N.Y. Law Sch., N.Y.C., 1951, Man of Yr. award St. Paul Soc., N.Y.C., 1971. Mem. ABA, N.Y. County Lawyers Assn., Queens County Bar Assn., Fed. Bar Assn., Greek Am. Lawyers Assn., Am. Hellenic Ednl. Prog. Assn. Republican. Greek Orthodox. Lodges: Parthenon, Masons. Avocations: basketball, racquetball, stamp collecting, walking, dancing. Office: US Ct Internat Trade 1 Federal Plz New York NY 10278-0001*

TSOULFANIDIS, NICHOLAS, nuclear engineering educator, university official; b. Ioannina, Greece, May 6, 1938; came to U.S., 1963; s. Stephen and Aristea (Ganiou) T.; m. Zizeta Koutsombidou, June 21, 1964; children: Stephen, Lena. BS in Physics, U. Athens, Greece, 1960; MS in Nuclear Engring., U. Ill., 1965, PhD in Nuclear Engring., 1968. Registered profl. engr., Mo. Prof. nuclear engring. U. Mo., Rolla, 1968—, vice chancellor acad. affairs, 1985-86, asst. dean Sch. Mines and Metallurgy, 1989—; sr. engr. Gen. Atomic Co., San Diego, 1974-75; engr. Ark. Power and Light Co., 1976-80; researcher Cadarache France, 1986-87. Author: Measurement and Detection of Radiation, 1984, 2d edit. 1995; co-author: Nuclear Fuel Analysis and Management, 1990; editor: Nuclear Technology, 1997. Electric Power Research Inst. grantee, 1980-84. Mem. Am. Nuclear Soc. (chmn. radiation protection shielding div. 1987-88), Health Physics Soc., Nat. Soc. Profl. Engring., Rotary. Office: U of Mo Rolla Dept Nuc Engring 1870 Miner Cir Rolla MO 65409-0001

TSUANG, MING TSO, psychiatrist, educator; b. Tainan, Taiwan, Nov. 16, 1931; came to U.S., 1971; s. Ping Tang and Chhun Kuei (Lin) T.; m. Snow Huei S. Ko, Nov. 24, 1958; children—John, Debby, Grace. M.D., Nat. Taiwan U., Taipei, 1957; Ph.D. in Psychiatry, Ph.D. (Sino-Brit. Fellowship Trust scholar); certs. in epidemiology and stats., population genetics, psychiat. genetics, U. London, 1965; D.Sc. in Psychiat. Genetics and Epidemiology, Faculty of Sci., U. London, 1981. Intern Nat. Taiwan U. Hosp., 1956-57, resident in psychiatry, 1957-61, assoc. prof. psychiatry, staff psychiatrist, 1968-71; collaborating investigator Internat. Pilot Study of Schizophrenia, WHO, 1966-71; vis. assoc. prof. psychiatry Washington U. Sch. Medicine, St. Louis, 1971-72; assoc. prof., staff psychiatrist U. Iowa Coll. Medicine, Iowa City, 1972-75; prof. psychiatry U. Iowa Coll. Medicine, 1975-82, prof. psychiat. epidemiology, 1978-82; clin. tchr., lectr. to residents, med. students; cons. psychiatrist VA Hosp., Iowa City, 1972-82; prof., vice chmn. sect. of psychiatry and human behavior Brown U., Providence, 1982-85; assoc. med. dir. Butler Hosp., Providence, 1982-85, dir. psychiat. epidemiology research unit, 1982-85; prof. psychiatry Harvard Inst. Psychiat. Epid. and Genetics Harvard U. Med. Sch. and Harvard Sch. Pub. Health; dir. psychiat. epidemiology and genetics Mass. Mental Health Ctr., Boston; chief psychiatry, chmn. Ctr. for Mental Health Brockton-West Roxbury VA Med. Ctr., 1985-94; head and supt. dept. psychiatry Harvard U. at Mass. Mental Health Ctr., 1992—; Stanley Cobb prof. Psychiatry Harvard U., 1993—; mem. epidemiol. studies rev. com. NIMH, 1976-79, mem., chmn. rsch. scientist devel. rev. com. NIMH, 1982-86, chmn. epidemiologic studies rev. com., 1989-90; mem. extramural sci. adv. bd. NIMH, 1990—; mem. med. rsch. svc. planning coun. Vets. Health Svcs. and Rsch. Adminstrn., VA Cen. Office, 1990—; vis. prof. psychiatry (Josiah Macy faculty scholar award) Oxford U., Eng., Warneford Hosp., 1979-80; chmn. mental health policy working group, div. health and policy research and edn. Harvard U., 1986—. Author: (with R. Vandermey) Genes and The Mind: Inheritance of Mental Illness, 1980, Schizophrenia: The Facts, 2d edit., 1997, (with S.V. Faraone) The Genetics of Mood Disorders, 1990; co-editor: Schizoaffective Psychoses, 1986, Handbook of Schizophrenia, vol. 3, 1988, Affective and Schizoaffective Disorders, Similarities and Differences, 1990, also monographs.; contbr. chpts. to books, numerous articles to profl. jours. Recipient Clin. Rsch. award Am. Acad. Clin. Psychiatrists, 1983, Rema Lapous award APHA, 1984, Stanley Dean award for rsch. on schizophrenia Am. Coll. Psychiatrists, 1989, Lifetime Achievement award Internat. Soc. Psychiat. Genetics, 1995, Taiwanese-Am. award for Achievement in Sci. and Engring., 1995. Mem. Psychiat. Rsch. Soc., Am. Psychopathol. Assn., Soc. for Life History Rsch. in Psychopathology (steering com. 1989—, Inst. of Medicine/NAAS, Academia Sinica Taiwan, Sigma Xi. Home: 354 Dudley Rd Newton MA 02159-2829 Office: MMHC 74 Fenwood Rd Boston MA 02115 *My constant goal is to do the best work I can, to eschew anxiety about the result, to learn from failure, and to build upon success, not for personal honor but for the good of mankind, as God's servant within a serving profession. Helping others is not possible without self-discipline, self-sufficience, and self-sacrifice; at the same time, helping others strengthens the self for its tasks.*

TSUBAKI, ANDREW TAKAHISA, theater director, educator; b. Chiyoda-ku, Tokyo, Japan, Nov. 29, 1931; s. Ken and Yasu (Oyama) T.; m. Lilly Yuri, Aug. 3, 1963; children: Arthur Yuichi, Philip Takeshi. BA in English, Tokyo Gakugei U., Tokyo, Japan, 1954; postgrad. in Drama, U. Saskatchewan, Saskatoon, Canada, 1958-59; MFA in Theatre Arts, Tex. Christian U., 1961; PhD in Speech & Drama, U. Ill., 1967. Tchr. Bunkyo-ku 4th Jr. High Sch., Tokyo, Japan, 1954-58; instr., scene designer Bowling Green (Ohio) State U., 1964-68; asst. prof. speech & drama U. Kans., Lawrence, 1968-73, assoc. prof., 1973-79; visiting assoc. prof. Carleton Coll., Northfield, Minn., 1974; lectr. Tsuda U., Tokyo, Japan, 1975; visiting assoc. prof. theatre Tel-Aviv (Israel) U., 1975-76; visiting prof. theatre Mo. Repertory Theatre, Kansas City, Mo., 1976, Nat. Sch. Drama, New Delhi, India, 1983; prof. theatre, film, east Asian Languages and Cultures U. Kans., Lawrence, 1979—; dir. Internat. Theatre Studies Ctr., U. Kans., Lawrence, 1971—, Operation Internat. Classical Theatre, 1988—; Benedict disting. vis. prof. Asian studies Carleton Coll., 1993; area editor Asian Theatre Jour., U. Hawaii, Honolulu, 1982-94; chmn. East Asian Langs. and Cultures, U. Kans., Lawrence, 1983-90; mem. editl. bd. Studies in Am. Drama, Oxford, Miss., 1985—. Dir. plays Kanjincho, 1973, Rashomon, 1976, 96, King Lear, 1985, Fujito and Shimizu, 1985, Hippolytus, 1990, Busu and the Missing Lamb (Japan) 1992, Suehirogari and Sumidagawa, 1992, 93, Tea, 1995; choreographed Antigone (Greece), 1987, Hamlet (Germany), 1989, The Resistible Rise of Arturo Ui, 1991, Man and the Masses (Germany), 1993, The Children of Fate (Hungary), 1994, The Great Theatre of the World (Germany); editor Theatre Companies of the World, 1986; contbg. author to Indian Theatre: Traditions of Performance, 1990; contbr. 7 entries in

Japanese Traditional plays to the Internat. Dictionary of Theatre, vol. 1, 1992, vol. 2, 1994. Recipient World Univ. Svc. Scholarship U. Saskatchewan, 1958-59, University fellow U. Ill., 1961-62, Rsch. fellow The Japan Found., 1974-75, 90, Rsch. Fulbright grantee, 1983. Mem. Am. Theatre Assn., Asian Theatre Program (chair 1976-79), Assn. for Asian Studies, Assn. Kans. Theatres., Assn. Kans. Theatres U/C Div. (chmn. 1980-82), Assn. for Theatre in Higher Edn., Assn. for Asian Performance. Democrat. Buddhist. Avocations: Ki-Aikido (3d Dan), photography, travel. Home: 924 Holiday Dr Lawrence KS 66049-3005 Office: U Kans Theatre And Film Lawrence KS 66045

TSUBOUCHI, DAVID H., Canadian provincial official. BA in English, York U.; LLB, Osgoode Hall Law Sch. Ward 5 councillor Town of Markham, 1988-94; sr. ptnr. Tsubouchi & Nichols & Assocs., 1994-95; apptd. Min. of Cmty. and Social Svcs. Ont. Progressive Conservative Govt., 1995—; chmn. planning and devel. com., econ. alliance com., indsl. and corp. devel. com. Markham Hist. Mus. Named Optimist of Yr., 1985-86; recipient Air Can. Heart of Gold award, 1988; granted Coat of Arms, Gov. Gen.'s Office, 1993. Office: Hepburn Block, Queens Park, Toronto, ON Canada M7A 1E9

TSUI, LAP-CHEE, molecular genetics educator; b. Shanghai, Dec. 21, 1950; arrived in Can., 1981; s. Jing Lue Hsue and Hui Ching Wang; m. Ellen Lan Fong, Feb. 11, 1977; children: Eugene, Felix. BS, Chinese U. Hong Kong, 1972, MPhil, 1974, DSc (hon.), 1991; PhD, U. Pitts., 1979; DCL (hon.), U. King's Coll., Halifax, N.S., Can., 1991; DSc (hon.), U. N.B., Can., 1991; DLL (hon.), U. St. Francis Xavier, Antigonish, N.S., Can., 1994. Postdoctoral investigator Oak Ridge (Tenn.) Nat. Lab., 1979-80; postdoctoral fellow Hosp. for Sick Children, Toronto, Ont., Can., 1981-83, geneticist-in-chief, 1996—, Sellers chair cystic fibrosis rsch., 1990—; asst. prof. depts. genetics and med. genetics U. Toronto, Ont., Can., 1983-88, assoc. prof., 1988-90, prof., 1990—, univ. prof., 1994—; chmn. chromosome 7 subcom. Human Gene Mapping Workshop, 1986—; mem. mammalian genetics study sect. NIH, Bethesda, Md., 1988-93; dir. Cystic Fibrosis Rsch. Ctr., Hosp. for Sick Children Spl. Rsch. Ctr., 1994—; scientist Med. Rsch. Coun. Can., 1989—; advisor European Jour. Human Genetics, 1992—, Molecular Medicine Today, 1995—. Editor Cytogenetics and Cell Genetics, 1988-92, Internat. Jour. Genome Rsch., 1990—; assoc. editor Am. Jour. Human Genetics, 1990-93, Genomics, 1994—; mem. editl. bd. Mammalian Genome, 1990, Clin. Genetics, 1991—, Human Molecular Genetics, 1991—; communicating editor Human Mutation, 1995—, Molec. Medicine Today; contbr. over 200 articles to sci. jours.; co-discoverer cystic firbrosis gene, 1989. Trustee Edn. Found., Fedn. Chinese Canadian Profls., Toronto, 1987—. Recipient Paul di Sant Agnese Disting. Achievement award Cystic Firbosis Found., 1989, Gold medal of honor Pharm. Mfrs. Assn. Can., 1989, award of excellence Genetics Soc. Can., 1990, Gairdner Internat. award 1990, Cresson medal Franklin Inst., 1992, E. Mead Johnson award, 1992, Disting. Scientist award The Canadian Soc. Clin. Investigators, 1992, Canadian Conf. medal 1992, Sarstedt Rsch. prize, 1993, Sanremo Internat. award for Genetic Rsch., 1993, J.P. Lecocq prize Inst. de France, 1994, Henry Friesen award The Canadian Soc. for Clin. Investigation and the Royal Coll. of Physicians and Surgeons of Can., 1995, CMA award of honour, 1996; named scholar Can. Cystic Fibrosis Found., 1984-86. Fellow Royal Soc. Can., Royal Soc. London, Academia Sinica; mem. Human Genome Orgn., Am. Soc. Human Genetics. Office: Hosp for Sick Children, 555 University Ave, Toronto, ON Canada M5G 1XG

TSUI, SOO HING, educational research consultant; b. Hong Kong, Aug. 2, 1959; came to U.S., 1985; d. Sik Tin and Yuk Kam (Cheung) T. BSW cum laude, Nat. Taiwan U., 1983; MSW cum laude, Columbua U., 1987, postgrad., 1992—. Cert. social worker, N.Y. Dir. cmty. handicapped ctr. Taipei, Taiwan, 1983-85; dir. youth recreational program N.Y., 1986; social work dept. supr. St. Margaret's House, N.Y.C., 1987-89; chief bilingual sch. social work N.Y.C. Bd. Edn., 1990—, rsch. cons., 1993—; rschr. Columbia U., N.Y.C., 1991-95; chief rsch. cons. N.Y.C. Dept. Transp., 1993-96; cheif rschr. immigrant social svcs. N.Y.C. Bd. Edn., 1996—. Bilingual social worker Nat. Assn. Asian/Am. Edn., 1989—; union social work regional rep. N.Y.C. Bd. Edn., 1990-93, citywide bilingual social work rep., 1991-93, citywide social work budget allocation comms. rep., 1992-93; mem. conf. planning com. bd. Amb. For Christ, Boston, 1991-93; coord. doctoral colloquial com. bd., 1991-93, Scholarships Coun. Social Work Edn., Columbia U., N.Y.C., 1992-94; mem. planning com. social work bd. Asian Am. Comms., N.Y.C., 1991-95; exec. dir. alumni bd. Columbia U. Sch. Social Work, 1995—, Chinese for Christ, 1993-95. Recipient Nat. Acad. award, 1979-83; Nat. Acad. scholar, 1987-88; Nat. Rsch. fellow Sch. Coun. on Social Work Edn., 1992-94. Home: 507 W 113th St Apt 22 New York NY 10025-8070

TSZTOO, DAVID FONG, civil engineer; b. Hollister, Calif., Oct. 13, 1952; s. John and Jean (Woo) T.; m. Evelyn Yang, July 31, 1982; children: Michaela Gabrielle, Shawn Michael. BS, Calif. Poly. State U., 1974; MS in Engring., U. Calif., 1976. Registered profl. civil engr., Calif. Engr., dispatcher Conlec Corp., Hollister, Calif., 1972-73; rsch. asst. U. Calif. Engring. Dept., Berkeley, 1975-76; jr. civil engr. Contra Costa County Pub. Works, Martinez, Calif., 1977-78, asst. civil engr., 1978-81, civil engr. III, 1981-83; assoc. civil engr. East Bay Mucpl. Util. Dist., Oakland, Calif., 1983-88; sr. civil engr. East Bay Mucpl. Util. Distbr., Oakland, Calif., 1988—; chpt. chmn. We. Coun. Engrs., Martinez, Calif., 1977-82; mem. Nat. Soc. Profl. Engrs., Martinez, Calif., 1977-82. Co-author: Energy Absorbing Devices in Structures, 1977, EQ Testing of Stepping Frame with Devices, 1977, Development of Energy-Absorbing Devices, 1978. Sponsor Sing & Bring Children's Club, Oakland, San Lorenzo, Calif., 1982-90; v.p. Sun Country Homeowners, Martinez, Calif., 1977-82. Recipient Presdl. Design Achievement award Nat. Endowment for the Arts, Washington, 1984. Mem. Am. Soc. Civil Engrs., Tau Beta Pi, Phi Kappa Phi. Republican. Baptist. Achievements include patent for application work, Conlec Corp., Hollister, Calif., 1973. Office: E Bay Mcpl Util Dist 375-11th St Oakland CA 94607

TU, JOHN, engineering executive; b. 1941. With Motorola Co., Wiesbaden, Germany, 1966-74; pres. Tu Devel., L.A., 1975-82, Camintonn Corp., Santa Ana, Calif., 1982-85; v.p., gen. mgr. AST Rsch., Irvine, Calif., 1985-87; pres. Newgen Systems Corp., Fountain Valley, Calif., 1987—; CEO Kingston Tech., Fountain Valley, 1988—. Office: Kingston Tech Co 17600 Newhope St Fountain Vly CA 92708-4220*

TU, WEI-MING, historian, philosopher, writer; b. Kunming, Yunnan, China, Feb. 26, 1940; came to U.S., 1962, naturalized, 1976; s. Shou-tsin (Wellington) and Shu-li (Sonia Ou-yang) T.; m. Helen I-yu Hsiao, Aug. 24, 1963 (div.); 1 son, Eugene L.; m. Rosanne V. Hall, Mar. 17, 1982; children: A. Yalun, Mariana Mei-ling B., Rosa Wen-yun. B.A., Tunghai U., 1961; M.A., Harvard U., 1963; Ph.D., 1968. Vis lectr. humanities Tunghai (Taiwan) U., 1966-67; vis. lectr. East Asian studies Princeton U., 1967-68, asst. prof., 1968-71; asst. prof. history U. Calif., Berkeley, 1971-73, assoc. prof., 1973-77, prof., from 1977; vis. prof. Chinese history and philosophy Harvard U., 1981-82, prof. Chinese history and philosophy, 1982—, chmn. com. on study of religion, 1984-87, chmn. dept. East Asian langs. and civilizations, 1991-92, coord. Dialogue of Civilizations, 1990-93; dir. Inst. Culture and Communication, East-West Ctr., Honolulu, 1990-91; vis. prof. dept. philosophy Peking U., 1985; disting. vis. prof. depts. philosophy and history Taiwan U., 1988; 10th Ch'ien Mu lectr. New Asia Coll., The Chinese U. of Hong Kong, 1989; 1st Henry Chai lectr. Hong Kong U., 1989; vis. prof. Ecole Pratique des Hautes Etudes, U. Paris, 1991; bd. dirs. Inst. Advanced Rsch. in Asian Sci. and Medicine, 1993—; trustee Adironack Work-Study Project, Inc., 1990—; chmn. adv. bd. Inst. Literature and Philosophy, Academia Sinica, 1993—; gov. Inst. East Asian Political Economy, Singapore, 1983-93; pres. Contemporary Mag., Taiwan, 1986-96; acad. adviser Chinese Culture Acad., Beijing; vice-chmn. Internat. Confician Assn., Beijing, 1994, Annual Freeman Lectr. Wesleyan U., 1982; assembly speaker Grinnell Coll., 1983; commencement speaker Grad. Theol. Union at Berkeley, 1990; keynote speaker alumni conf. East-West Ctr., Bangkok, 1990; GET lectr. Bal State U., 1991; panelist 1st World Chinese Enterprises Conv., Singapore, 1991; Paul Desjardins Meml. lectr. Haverford Coll., 1992; baccalaureate speaker Swarthmore Coll., 1993; co-moderator seminar, the Chineses in the Global Community, Aspen Inst., 1994—; guest prof. Wuhan U., Peking U., 1996—; Foester lectr. U. Calif. Berkeley, 1996; Green lectr. U. B.C., 1997; Burke lectr. U. Calif. San Diego, 1997; dir. Harvard Yenchnig Inst., 1996—. Author: Neo-Confucian Thought in Action—Wang Yangming's Youth, 1976, Centrality and Commonality—An Essay on Chung-Yung, 1976, Humanity and Self-Cultivation—Essays in Confucian Thought, 1980, Confucian Ethics Today: The Singapore Challenge, 1984, Confucian Thought: Selfhood as Creative Transformation, 1985, The Way, Learning, and Politics: Perspective on the Confucian Intellectual, 1988, Toward the "Third Epoch" of Confucian Humanism: Problems and Prospects (in Chinese), 1989, A Reflection on Confucian Self-Consciousness (in Chinese), 1990, The Modern Spirit and the Confucian Tradition (in Chinese), 1993; editor: The Triadic Tension: Confucian Ethics, Max Weber and Industrial East Asia, 1991, The Confucian World Observed, 1992, The Living Tree: Changing Meaning of Being Chinese, 1993, China in Transformation, 1994, Confucian Traditions in East Asian Modernity, 1996; mem. editorial bd. Asian Thought and Soc., 1976—, Harvard Jour. Asiatic Studies, 1983, Philosophy East and West, 1984—, The Twenty-First Century (Chinese); contbr. articles Philosophy East and West, Jour. Asian Studies, Daedalus, The Monist, Chinese lang. jours. and newspapers. Am. Council Learned Socs. fellow, 1968-69; research grantee Center East Asian Studies, Harvard U., 1968-69; research grantee Humanities Council Princeton U., 1970-71; research grantee U. Calif., 1973-74; sr. scholar Com. on Scholarly Communication with People's Republic of China Nat. Acad. Scis., 1980-81; Fulbright-Hays research scholar Peking U., 1985; interviewed by Bill Moyer in World of Ideas, 1991. Fellow Am. Acad. Arts and Scis. (exec com. fundamentalism project 1988-96), Soc. for Study of Value in Higher Edn.; mem. Am. Soc. for the Study Religion, Assn. Asian Studies (dir. 1971-75), Am. Hist. Assn., Soc. Asian and Comparative Philosophy, Am. Acad. Religion, AAAS, Asia Soc. N.Y. Office: Harvard U Dept East Asian Langs and Civilizations Cambridge MA 02138 *As an all-embracing humanist tradition, Confucianism seeks to find integrated and holistic solutions to socio-political problems. One of its core ideas is self-cultivation, signifying that the way to universal peace takes personal knowledge as the point of departure. Learning to be human, in the Confucian perspective, entails an unceasing spiritual transformation. This quest for self-realization involves an ever-expanding circle of human-relatedness. It is not simply a search for one's own inner spirituality but a concern for the establishment of a fiduciary community for humankind as a whole.*

TUAN, DEBBIE FU-TAI, chemistry educator; b. Kiangsu, China, Feb. 2, 1930; came to U.S., 1958; d. Shiau-gien and Chen (Lee) T.; m. John W. Reed, Aug. 15, 1987. BS in Chemistry, Nat. Taiwan U., Taipei, 1954, MS in Chemistry, 1958; MS in Chemistry, Yale U., 1960, PhD in Chemistry, 1961. Rsch. fellow Yale U., New Haven, 1961-64; rsch. assoc. U. Wis., Madison, 1964-65; asst. prof. Kent (Ohio) State U., 1965-70, assoc. prof., 1970-73, prof., 1973—; rsch. fellow Harvard U., Cambridge, 1969-70; vis. scientist SRI Internat., Menlo Park, Calif., 1981; rsch. assoc. Cornell U., Ithica, N.Y., 1983; vis. prof. Yeshiva U., N.Y.C., 1966, Academia Sinica of China, Nat. Taiwan U. and Nat. Tsing-Hwa U., summer 1967, Ohio State U., 1993, 95. Contbr. articles to profl. jours. Recipient NSF Career Advanced award, 1994—; U. Grad. fellow Nat. Taiwan U., 1955-58, F.W. Heyl-Anon F fellow Yale U., 1960-61, U. Faculty Rsch. fellow Kent State U., 1966, 68, 71, 85; Pres. Chiang's scholar Chinese Women Assn., 1954, 58, Grad. scholar in humanity and scis. China Found., 1955. Mem. Am. Chem. Soc., Am. Phys. Soc., Sigma Xi. Office: Kent State U Chemistry Dept Williams Hall Kent OH 44242

TUAZON, JESUS OCAMPO, electrical engineer, educator, consultant; b. Manila, Jan. 2, 1940; came to U.S., 1963; s. Filomeno and Patrocino (Ocampo) T.; m. Norma Mamangun, Oct. 12, 1963; children: Maria, Noel, Norman, Mary, Michelle. BSEE, Mapua Inst., Manila, 1962; MSEE, Iowa State U., 1965, PhD, 1969. Elec. prof. Calif. State U., Fullerton, Calif., 1969—; scientist Jet Propulsion Lab., Pasadena, Calif., 1984—; computer cons. Hughes Aircraft, Fullerton, 1977, Gen. Dynamic, Pomona, Calif., 1983, U.S. Naval Weapon Sta., Seal Beach, Calif., 1978-83. Author of papers for profl. confs. Mem. IEEE, Am. Assn. Engring Educators. Democrat. Roman Catholic. Avocations: jogging, swimming, chess. Home: 816 S Verona St Anaheim CA 92804-4035 Office: Calif State Univ 800 N State College Blvd Fullerton CA 92831-3547 also: Jet Propulsion Lab 4800 Oak Grove Dr Pasadena CA 91109-8001

TUBB, JAMES CLARENCE, lawyer; b. Corsicana, Tex.; s. Cullen Louis and Sarah Elmore (Chapman) T.; m. Suzanne Alice Smith, Nov. 22, 1954; children: James Richard, Sara Elizabeth, Daniel Chapman. BA, So. Meth. U., 1951, JD, 1954. Bar: Tex. 1954, U.S. Dist. Ct. (no. dist.) Tex. 1955, U.S. Ct. Appeals (5th cir.) 1959, U.S. Supreme Ct. 1978; cert. comml. real estate specialist; lic. Tex. real estate broker; cert. mediator Dallas Bar Assn. With legal dept. Schlumberger Well Surveying Corp., Houston, 1954-55; claims atty. Franklin Am. Ins. Co., Dallas, 1957-58; ptnr. Vial, Hamilton, Koch, Tubb & Knox and predecessor firm Akin, Vial, Hamilton, Koch & Tubb, Dallas, 1958-84; dir., ptnr. Winstead, McGuire, Sechrest & Minick, Dallas, 1984-90; pvt. practice Dallas, 1990—; guest lectr. on real estate broker liability Real Estate Ctr., Tex. A&M U., 1987. Bd. dirs. Christian Concern Found., 1965-71, bd. deacons, 1972-78; ruling elder Highland Park Presbyn. Ch., Dallas, 1978-84, 88-91; mem. permanent jud. commn. Grace Presbytery, 1984-90; bd. dirs. Am. Diabetes Assn. Dallas County affiliate, 1991-95. 1st lt. JAGC, SAC, USAF, 1955-57, 1st lt. USAFR, ret. Recipient Outstanding Student award Student Bar Assn., 1954. Fellow Tex. Bar Found.; mem. ABA (chmn. comml. law com. gen. practice sect. 1982-84, real estate probate and trust law sect.), Tex. Bus. Law Found., Tex. Bar Assn., Am. Arbitration Assn. (comml. arbitration panelist), Soc. Profls. in Dispute Resolution, Dallas Country Club, Dallas County Rep. Men's Club (sec. 1978-79). Home: 3407 Haynie Ave Dallas TX 75205-1842 Office: 8325 Douglas Ste 805 Ste 805 Lock Box 21 8235 Douglas Dallas TX 75225

TUBBS, DAVID EUGENE, mechanical engineer, marketing professional; b. Springfield, Ill., Jan. 12, 1948; s. Eugene Lewellyn and Jacqueline Flo (Jones) T.; m. Linda Alyson Smith, Aug. 2, 1970; children: Corbin David, Cavan Scott. BSME, Ill. Inst. Tech., 1970; postgrad., Okla. State U., 1992. Registered profl. engr., Ill., Okla. Project engr. Sargent & Lundy, Chgo., 1970-82, bus. devel. mgr., 1982-83; mgr. power sales Yuba Heat Transfer Corp., Tulsa, 1983-85; with press products mktg. Nordam, Tulsa, 1985-86; dir. mktg. Brooks Aero. Svc. div. Nordam, Tulsa, 1986-91; mech. dept. mgr. The Benham Group, Tulsa, 1991-93; chief mech. engr. EDECO Engrs./Cons., Tulsa, 1993-94; mktg. support mgr. AGC Tech. Svcs. Inc., Tulsa, 1994—. Mem. ASME, Am. Welding Soc., Ill. Inst. Tech. Alumni Assn. (bd. dirs. 1977-80), Delta Tau Delta, Pi Tau Sigma. Republican. Club: Toastmasters. Avocations: bridge, racquetball, USSF soccer referee. Home: 8313 E 60th St Apt 2322 Tulsa OK 74145 Office: AGC Tech Svcs Inc 10810 E 45th St Ste 103 Tulsa OK 74146-3802

TUBESING, RICHARD LEE, library director; b. Kansas City, Mo., Nov. 25, 1937; s. Clarence and Letha (Thacker) T. BA, Yale U., 1959; MA, U. Chgo., 1969; MSL, Western Mich. U., 1972. Asst. to dir. U. Louisville, 1972-73; reference libr. Ga. Tech. Libr., Atlanta, 1973-76; head bus. and sci. Atlanta Pub. Libr., 1976-79; libr. dir. Lewis U., Romeoville, Ill., 1979-81; collection devel. coord. U. Toledo Libr., 1981-86; libr. dir. Coll. of the Southwest, Hobbs, N.Mex., 1986-89; libr. dir., dir. libr. sci. program Glenville (W.Va.) State Coll., 1989—. Author: Architectural Preservation, 1978, Architectural Preservation and Urban Renovation, 1982. Program coord. Lea County Archaeol. Soc., Hobbs, 1987-89. Lt. j.g. USNR, 1960-63. Mem. W.Va. Libr. Assn., Lea County Libr. Assn. (v.p. 1987-88, pres. 1988-89). Avocation: collecting primitive and peasant art. Home: Rte 76 Box 17 Glenville WV 26351 Office: Glenville State Coll Robert F Kidd Libr Glenville WV 26351

TUBMAN, WILLIAM CHARLES, lawyer; b. N.Y.C., Mar. 16, 1932; s. William Thomas and Ellen Veronica (Griffin) T.; m. Dorothy Rita Krug, Aug. 15, 1964; children: William Charles Jr., Thomas Davison, Matthew Griffin. BS, Fordham U., 1953, JD, 1960; postdoctoral, NYU Sch. Law, 1960-61. Bar: N.Y. 1960, U.S. Ct. Appeals (2d cir.) 1966, U.S. Supreme Ct. 1967, U.S. Ct. Customs and Patent Appeals 1971. Auditor Peat, Marwick Mitchell & Co., N.Y.C., 1956-60; sr. counsel Kennecott Corp., N.Y.C., 1960-82; sr. counsel Phelps Dodge Corp., N.Y.C., 1982-85, sec., 1985-95, v.p., 1987-95; pres. Phelps Dodge Found., Phoenix, 1988-95. Author: Legal Status of Minerals Beyond the Continental Shelf, 1966. Mem. scholarship adv. coun. U. Ariz., 1990-92; active Big Bros., Inc., N.Y.C., 1963-73; trustee Phoenix Art Mus., 1989-94; bd. dirs. St. Joseph Hosp. Found., 1994—, chmn., 1994-95; bd. dirs. The Phoenix Symphony, 1994-95. Recipient Disting. Svc. cert. Big Brothers Inc., 1968. Mem. ABA, N.Y. State Bar Assn., Maricopa County Bar Assn. Democrat. Roman Catholic.

TUCCI, GERALD FRANK, manufacturing company executive; b. N.Y.C., Sept. 9, 1926; s. Frank and Mary (Fattizzi) T.; student Dartmouth Coll., 1944; Sc.B. in Naval Sci., Brown U., 1946; Sc.B. In Mech. Engring., 1948; M.B.A. with distinction, Harvard U., 1950; m. Eva G. Gyllander, May 14, 1968; children—Francis Henrik, Michael Fredrik, Amy Christina. Mfg. trainee Am. Can Co., Jersey City, 1950-51; asst. v.p., plant mgr. Artcraft Hosiery Mills, Inc., Darby, Pa., 1951-53; v.p. Leach & Garner Co., Attleboro, Mass., 1953-63, Gen. Findings, Inc., Attleboro, 1953-63; pres. Micro Contacts Inc., Hicksville, N.Y., 1963—; v.p. Mold-A-Matic Corp., Oneota, N.Y., 1965—; pres. Micro Pneumatic Logic, Inc., Ft. Lauderdale, Fla., 1975—. Served to lt. (s.g.) USNR, 1944-47. Mem. ASME, Am. Soc. Mfrs., Beta Theta Pi. Republican. Roman Catholic. Clubs: North Hempstead Country, Metropolitan (N.Y.), Harvard Bus. Sch. N.Y., Frenchman's Creek Country (Palm Beach Gardens, Fla.). Office: 62 Alpha Plz Hicksville NY 11801-2618

TUCCI, MARK A., state agency administrator; b. Trenton, N.J., Dec. 14, 1950; s. William F. and Theresa M. (Miccio) T.; m. Carolyn J. Bilecki, July 10, 1971; children: Nicholas A., Anthony M., Vincent J. BS, Trenton State Coll., 1972, MEd, 1978; cert. pub. mgr., Rutgers U. Cert. N.J. chief sch. adminstr., prin., supr., tchr. of deaf, tchr. of handicapped, N.J. Tchr. Katzenbach Sch. for the Deaf, West Trenton, N.J., 1972-82; spl. asst. to supt. Katzenbach Sch. for the Deaf, West Trenton, 1982-85; exec. asst. to asst. commr. edn. N.J. Dept. Edn., Trenton, 1985-87; chief of enterprise license bur. N.J. Casino Control Commn., Atlantic City, 1987-91, dir. organizational devel., 1991—, dir. adminstrn., 1992-93; examiner N.J. Quality Achievement Award Program, 1993-94, 96, sr. examiner, 1994; judge N.J. Exemplary State and Local Awards Program, 1994—; chmn. N.J. Quality Achievement Award Focus Group, 1994-96. Mem. editorial bd. periodical for Trenton chpt. Phi Delta Kappa, 1986-88; columnist Total Quality Management, 1994; contbr. articles to profl. pubs. Chmn. bd. trustees AIDS Support Found., Inc., 1995; cub scout leader Trenton chpt. Boy Scouts Am., 1981-84, dist. com. Jersey Shore Coun., 1995-96; pres. Katzenbach chpt. N.J. State Employees' Assn., 1979; co-chmn. adv. coun. Mercer County Spl. Edn. Assn., 1984; mem. bus. adv. coun. Atlantic C.C., 1990—. Mem. Am. Soc. for Quality Control (cert.), Cert. Pub. Mgrs. Soc. N.J. (fellow trustee), Phi Delta Kappa, Kappa Delta Pi. Roman Catholic. Avocations: reading, journalism, martial arts, photography, songwriting. Home: 273 Neptune Dr Manahawkin NJ 08050-5026 Office: NJ Casino Control Commn Tennessee Ave Atlantic City NJ 08401-4602

TUCCI, STANLEY, actor; b. N.Y.C., 1960. Appeared in films Fear Anxiety and Depression, 1990, Men of Respect, 1991, In The Soup, 1992, Beethoven, 1992, Prelude to A Kiss, 1992, Undercover Blues, 1993, The Pelican Brief, 1993, Mrs. Parker and the Vicious Circle, 1994, Jury Duty, 1995, Kiss of Death, 1995; actor, co-dir., co-prodr. Big Night, 1996. Office: William Morris Agy 151 El Camino Beverly Hills CA 90212*

TUCCI, STEVEN MICHAEL, health facility administrator, physician, recording industry executive; b. N.Y.C., Oct. 5, 1949; s. Louis Alexander and Nina Ida (Cerone) T.; m. Mari E. Koerner, Nov., 1974; children: Alexander, Michael, Lara. BS, Manhattan Coll., 1971; MS, SUNY, Brockport, 1977; PhD, Albany Med. Coll., 1978, MD, 1981. Diplomate Am. Coll. Phys. Medicine and Rehab., Am. Coll. Pain Mgmt.; cert. Nat. Bd. Med. Examiners. Rsch. fellow Birth Defects Inst. N.Y. State Dept. Health, 1976-81; instr. anatomy Albany (N.Y) Med. Coll., 1977-78, rsch. assoc. divns. endocrinology, 1978-81, asst. prof. anatomy, 1978-79, rsch. assoc. dept. anatomy, 1979-81; commd. officer student trainee, extern Nat. Inst. Neurol. and Communicative Disorders and Stroke/NIH, 1981; from intern to resident divsn. phys. medicine and rehabilitation George Washington Univ., 1981-84; staff fellowclin. ctr. dept. phys. medicine and rehabilitation NIH, 1983-84; mem. staff dept. medicine Commonwealth Hosp., Fairfax, Va., 1983-84; mem. med. staff Doctor's Hosp., Sarastota, Fla., 1984, med. dir. phys. medicine and rehab., 1989, med. dir., 1994—; founding med. dir. The Ctr. at Manatee Springs, Bradenton, Fla., 1985-86, The Rehab. Inst. Sarasota, Fla., 1986-88; med. dir. Fawcett Meml. Hosp., Port Charlotte, Fla., 1988—; med. dir. phys. medicine and rehab. Charlotte Community Rehab. Ctr., Port Charlotte, 1988; co-founder Sports, Pain and Rehab. Medicine Assocs., Sarasota and Port Charlotte, 1992; med. dir. Manatee Meml. Hosp., Bradenton, 1993—; pres., CEO Groove Tone Records, Sarasota, 1994—. Writer: (music) Take Me Down to the Ballgame, 1994, Spell on Me, 1994, On the Road to Nowhere, 1994; contbr. articles, papers to profl. jours. Mem. AMA, USTA, Am. Acad. Phys. Medicine and Rehab., Am. Coll. Sprots Medicine, Am. Congress Rehabilitative Medicine, Am. Soc. Pain Mgmt., Fla. Med. Assn., Fla. Soc. Phys. Medicine and Rehab., Major League Baseball Players Alumni Assn., Rep. Presdl. Task Force, Rep. Senatorial Inner Circle. Republican. Roman Catholic. Avocations: musician, tennis, fishing. Office: Sports and Rehab Medicine 3920 Bee Ridge Rd Sarasota FL 34233-1207

TUCHMAN, AVRAHAM, physicist, researcher; b. N.Y.C., July 1, 1935; s. Max and Rebecca (Brick) T.; m. Sylvia Crystal, Dec. 26, 1957; children: Davida, Ari, Sima, Pnina. BA, Yeshiva U., 1956; PhD, MIT, 1963. Scientist, group leader to sect. chief Avco Rsch. and Advanced Devel., Wilmington, Mass., 1963; prin. scientist, staff scientist to prin. staff scientist Avco Systems Div., Wilmington; chief scientist Textron Def. Systems, Wilmington, 1988-93; owner, sr. cons. physicist Added Value Innovations (AVI), Brookline, Mass., 1994—; vis. prof. Weizmann Inst. Sci., Rehovot, Israel, 1974, 78, 82. Contbr. numerous articles to profl. jours. Founder, pres. Kehilla Day Camp of Jewish Community Ctrs., Westwood, Mass., 1975-86; chmn. Brookline (Mass.) Traffic Commn., 1975-81; pres. Mikvah Rescue Svc., Brighton, Mass., 1969-77; pres. Temple Beth Avraham, Brookline, 1969—. Recpient award for outstanding cantorial artistry Am. Soc. Forktwangers, Detroit, 1970. Fellow AIAA (sr.). Avocations: computers, gardening, softball, homecraft. Office: AVI 138 Tappan St Brookline MA 02146-5818

TUCHMAN, GARY ROBERT, television news correspondent; b. Chgo., Oct. 2, 1960; s. Ronald E. and Louise R. (Lyon) T.; m. Kathy M. Stark, Dec. 1, 1990; children: Lindsay, Daniel. BS in Broadcast Journalism, Boston U., 1982. News anchor, reporter Sta. WBOC-TV, Salisbury, Md., 1982-85, Sta. WPEC-TV, West Palm Beach, Fla., 1985-90; corr. CNN-TV, N.Y.C., 1990—. Emmy nominee series on West Bank and Gaza Strip, 1990. Host United Cerebral Palsy TV Telethons. Recipient Emmy award and ACE award for coverage Okla. City bombing, 1995. Avocations: sports, rollerblading, public speaking, traveling. Office: CNN 5 Penn Plz New York NY 10001-1810

TUCHMAN, MAURICE SIMON, library director; b. Bklyn., Sept. 14, 1936; s. William and Rose (Luria) T.; m. Helene Lillian Bodner, Aug. 30, 1959; children: Joel Aron, Miriam Auri. BA, CUNY, 1958; MLS, Columbia U., 1959; B Hebrew Lit., Jewish Theol. Sem., N.Y.C., 1964; D of Arts in LS, Simmons Coll., 1979. Cataloger. svcs. Buffalo and Erie County, 1959-60; asst. libr. N.Y. State Maritime Coll., Ft. Schuyler, 1962-64; libr. cons. Mid-Hudson Librs., Poughkeepsie, N.Y., 1964-66; libr. dir. Hebrew Coll., Brookline, Mass., 1966—; book appraiser, Auburndale, Mass., 1980—; book reviewer Libr. Jour., 1970—. With U.S. Army, 1960-62. N.Y. Regents scholar, 1959. Mem. ALA, Assn. Jewish Librs., Coun. Archives and Rsch. Librs. Jewish Studies, Ch. and Synagogue Libr. Assn. (pres. 1974-75), Fenway Libr. Consortium (coord. 1980-82, treas. 1990—). Home: 16 Duffield Rd Newton MA 02166-1004 Office: Hebrew Coll 43 Hawes St Brookline MA 02146-5412 *It is our most difficult task and our greatest accomplishment to reach our potential as a thinking and ethical human being.*

TUCHMAN, PHYLLIS, critic; b. Passaic, N.J., Jan. 4, 1947; d. Jack and Evelyn (Sugarman) T. BA, Boston U., 1968; MA, NYU, 1973. Independent critic N.Y.C., 1968—; adj. lectr. Hunter Coll., CUNY, N.Y.C., 1976-79; vis. prof. Williams Coll., Williamstown, Mass., 1981-83; curator Six in Bronze Williams Coll. Mus. Art & Tour, 1985, Big Litte Sculpture, 1988, Drawing Redux San Jose Mus. Art & Tour, 1992; contbr. N.Y. Newsday, 1985-94, Town & Country, 1995—. Author: George Segal, 1983; contbr. articles to profl. jours. Art Critics grantee NEA, 1978-79; vis. fellow Princeton U., NEH, 1980. Mem. Internat. Assn. Art Critics (Am. sect. pres. 1986-89), Art

Table (bd. dirs. 1984-87, v.p. 1986-87). Home: 340 E 80th St New York NY 10021

TUCHMANN, ROBERT, lawyer; b. N.Y.C., July 7, 1946; s. Frederick C. and Hildegard (Jung) T.; m. Naomi R. Walfish, June 1, 1969; children; David, Paul. AB, Oberlin Coll., 1967; JD, Harvard U., 1971. Bar: Mass. 1971, U.S. Dist. Ct. Mass. 1971. Assoc. Hale and Dorr, Boston, 1971-76, jr. ptnr., 1976-80, sr. ptnr., 1980—; lectr. Mass. Continuing Legal Edn., 1976—. Pres. Project Bread-The Walk for Hunger, Boston, 1990—; mem. com. Oberlin Coll., 1990; chair Ctrl. Artery Environ. Oversight Com., 1992—; mem. New Fed. Courthouse Task Force, 1993—. Mem. Boston Bar Assn. (com. chairperson 1977-81), Mass. Conveyancers Assn. (com. chairperson 1984-89), Boston Transp. Mgmt. Assn. (chairperson 1996—), Abstract Club. Office: Hale and Dorr 60 State St Boston MA 02109-1800

TUCK, EDWARD HALLAM, lawyer; b. Brussels, June 27, 1927; s. William Hallam and Hilda (Bunge) T.; m. Liliane Solmsen, June 8, 1978; children by previous marriage—Edward, Jessica, Matthew. B.A., Princeton U., 1950; LL.B., Harvard Law Sch., 1953. Bar: N.Y. Assoc. Shearman & Sterling, N.Y.C., 1953-62, ptnr., 1962-86, of counsel, 1986—; bd. dirs. The French-Am. Found.; bd. dirs. Lafarge Corp., Comml. Bank. Bd. dirs. Belgian Am. Ednl. Found., The Drawing Ctr., Am. Assn. for Internat. Commn. of Jurists; trustee French Inst. Alliance Francaise; chmn. bd. North Country Sch., Inc., 1974-78, The Drawing Ctr., Gateway Citizens Com., 1972-74; pres. The Parks Council, 1970-74; chmn. N.Y. State Parks and Recreation Commn., City of N.Y., 1971-76. Served with USN, 1945-46. Mem. Assn. Bar City N.Y., Coun. on Fgn. Rels., Racquet and Tennis Club, The Brook Club, The Ivy Club, Pilgrims, Soc. of the Cin. Episcopalian. Office: Shearman & Sterling 599 Lexington Ave New York NY 10022-6030

TUCK, GRAYSON EDWIN, real estate agent, former natural gas transmission executive; b. Richmond, Va., May 11, 1927; s. Bernard Okly and Erma (Wiltshire) T.; m. Rosalie Scroggs, June 6, 1947; children—Janice Lorrain, Kenneth Edwin, Carol Lynn. B.S., U. Richmond, 1950. Payroll clk., cost clk. Gen. Baking Co., Richmond, 1948-51; jr. accountant Commonwealth Natural Gas Corp., Richmond, 1951-55; sr. accountant Commonwealth Natural Gas Corp., 1956-57, accounting supr., 1957-58, asst. treas., 1959-62, asst. sec., asst. treas., 1963-64, treas., asst. sec., 1965-77; treas. Commonwealth Natural Resources, Inc., 1977-81, CNG Transmission Co. subs., 1977-79; sec.-treas. Air Pollution Control Products, Inc., Richmond, 1970-73; asst. treas., asst. sec. Commonwealth Gas Distbn. Corp., Richmond, 1969-79; mgr. taxes and cash mgmt. Commonwealth Gas Pipeline Corp., subs. Columbia Gas System Inc., 1981-86; investor, realtor Bill Eudailey & Co., 1986—. Active Boy Scouts Am., 1965-69; bd. dirs. Henrico Area Mental Health Retardation Services, 1983-85. Served with USNR, 1945-46. Mem. Nat. Assn. Accts. (assoc. dir. 1963-64). Presbyn. (deacon 1958-86, elder 1986—, treas. 1968-70). Home: 2923 Oakland Ave Richmond VA 23228-5827 Office: 6401 Mallory Dr Richmond VA 23226-2911

TUCK, JOHN CHATFIELD, former federal agency administrator, public policy advisor; b. Dayton, Ohio, May 28, 1945; m. Jane McDonough; 3 children. BS, Georgetown U., 1967. Various positions as asst. to Rep. leaders Ho. of Reps., Washington, 1974-77, chief Rep. floor ops., 1977-81; asst. sec. to majority U.S. Senate, 1981-86, spl. asst. then dep. asst. to pres. for legis. affairs, 1986-87; dep. asst. to Pres. of U.S. and exec. asst. to chief of staff Office Chief of Staff, The White Ho., 1987-88; asst. to Pres. and dir. Office Chief of Staff, 1988-89; under sec. Dept. Energy, Washington, 1989-92; sr. pub. policy advisor Baker, Donelson, Bearman & Caldwell, Washington, 1992—. With USN, 1968-73, ret. capt. USNR, 1973-94. Office: Baker Donelson Bearman & Caldwell 801 Pennsylvania Ave NW Washington DC 20004-2615

TUCK, MARY BETH, nutritionist, educator; b. Point, Tex., Dec. 9, 1930; d. Basil Barney and Daisy (Morris) Rabb; children: Karen, Kenny (dec.). BS, East Tex. State U., 1952, MEd, 1966; PhD, Tex. Woman's U., 1970. Lic. dietitian, Tex. Tchr. Longview (Tex.) Pub. Schs., 1952-64; instr. nutrition Stephen F. Austin U., Nacogdoches, Tex., 1966-69; assoc. prof. East Tex. State U., Commerce, Tex., 1970-96; ret., 1996; cons. Women, Infants and Children Program, Hunt County, Tex., 1989, East Tex. State U. Wellness Program, Commerce, 1989—, Selvaggi Med. Clinic, Commerce, 1989—; nutrition del. People to People Citizen Amb. Program, USSR, 1990; lectr. in field. Reviewer, editor textbooks; contbr. articles to profl. jours. Bd. dirs. Commerce div. Am. Heart Assn., 1994—; mem. Meth. Mission Work/Study Team, Israel, Palestine, Egypt, 1996, Ch. of Commerce Leadership Inst., 1997; mem. missions com., SPRC com., choir, chmn. assoc. pastor parsonage com., First United Meth. Ch., 1996—. Recipient Gold Blazer award East Tex. State U. Alumni Assn., 1995. Mem. Am. Dietetic Assn., Tex. Dietetic Assn., Northeast Tex. Ret. Tchrs. Assn. (v.p. 1996—), Afflatus Culture Club (pres. 1988-91), Louise Drake Garden Club (v.p. 1991-92, pres. 1997—), Commerce Area Alumni Assn. (1st v.p. 1993-94), Delta Kappa (sec. 1988-92, 94-96).

TUCK, RUSSELL R., JR., former college president; b. June 9, 1934; m. Marjorie Gay Tuck; children: Russell R. III, Catherine Elizabeth. BS in Chemistry, Union U., 1956; MS in Biology, Vanderbilt U., 1957, PhD in Curriculum and Instrn., 1971; study, Wash. U., 1960-61. Instr. biology, asst. coordinator Korean Tchr. Edn. Program George Peabody Coll. Vanderbilt U., Nashville, 1957-59; tchr. biology, chmn. sci. dept. University City (Mo.) Sr. High Sch., 1960-63, from asst. prin. to prin., 1963-70; prin. Parkway North Sr. High Sch., St. Louis County, Mo., 1971-78; asst. supt. Parkway Sch. Dist., St. Louis County, 1979-81, assoc. supt., 1981-84; pres. Calif. Bapt. Coll., Riverside, 1984-95, pres. emeritus, 1995—. Contbr. articles to profl. jours. Bd. dirs. Opera Assn.; pres. Riverside County chpt. ARC, 1989-90; active Bapt. Ch., local hosp. assn. bd., local edn. com.; World Affairs Coun. Mem. Calif. Bapt. Hist. Soc. (bd. dirs.), Calif. Bapt. Devel. Found. (bd. dirs.), Am. Assn. Sch. Adminstrs., Inland Empire Higher Edn. Coun. (pres. 1987-88), Kappa Delta Pi, Phi Delta Kappa. Lodge: Rotary.

TUCKER, ALAN CURTISS, mathematics educator; b. Princeton, N.J., July 6, 1943; s. Albert William and Alice Judson (Curtiss) W.; m. Amanda Almira Zeisler, Aug. 31, 1968 (div. 1997); children: Lisa, Kathryn; m. Ann K. Hong, Feb. 16, 1997. BA, Harvard U., 1965; MS, Stanford U., 1967, PhD, 1969. Asst. prof. applied math. SUNY, Stony Brook, 1970-73, assoc. prof. applied math., 1973-78, prof. applied math., chmn., 1978-89, SUNY Disting. Teaching prof., 1989—; vis. asst. prof. math. U. Wis., Madison, 1969-70; vis. assoc. prof. computer sci. U. Calif., San Diego, 1976-77; vis. prof. ops. research Stanford U., 1983-84; cons. Sloan Found., 1981-85; acad. cons. 40 colls. and univs. Author: Applied Combinatorics, 1980, Unified Introduction to Linear Algebra, 1987, Linear Algebra, 1993; assoc. editor Math. Monthly, 1996—, Applied Maths. Letters, 1986—; contbr. 45 rsch. articles to profl. jours. Ga. U. Consortium Disting. Visitor, 1982; NSF grantee, 1972-86. Mem. Math. Assn. Am. (chmn. publs. 1982-86, editor Studies in Math. series 1979-86, v.p. 1988-90, chmn. ednl. coun. 1990-96, Disting. Tchr. award 1994, Trevor Evans award 1996), U.S. Commn. Math. Instrn., Am. Math. Soc., Ops. Rsch. Soc. Am., Soc. Indsl. Applied Maths., Sigma Xi (chpt. pres. 1987—). Home: 14 Salt Meadow Ln Stony Brook NY 11790-1110 Office: SUNY At Stony Brook Dept of Applied Math Stony Brook NY 11794

TUCKER, ALAN DAVID, publisher; b. Erie, Pa., Mar. 9, 1936; s. Meredith LaDue and Monica (Klocko) T.; m. Kiyoko Iizuka, Feb. 8, 1963; 1 child, Kumi Tucker. A.B., Princeton U., 1957. Assoc. editor Hawthorn Books, N.Y.C., 1964-66; editor John Day Co., Inc., N.Y.C., 1966-72; mng. editor David McKay Co., Inc., N.Y.C., 1972-75, v.p., 1975-78, exec. v.p., editorial dir., 1978-84; editorial dir. Fodor's Travel Guides, Inc., N.Y.C., 1978-84; producer, Penguin Travel Guides and other publs. N.Y.C., 1984-91; gen. editor Berlitz Travellers Guides, N.Y.C., 1991-95; sr. analyst Genesis Group Assocs., Montclair, N.J., 1995—; mktg. cons. The Benjamin Group, N.Y.C., 1996—. Served to USNR, 1957-60. Mem. Soc. Am. Travel Writers, N.Y. Travel Writers Assn. (v.p.). Office: 186 Riverside Dr New York NY 10024-1007

TUCKER, ALLEN BROWN, JR., computer science educator; b. Worcester, Mass., Feb. 19, 1942; s. Allen Brown and Louise (Woodberry) T.; m. Maida Somerville, Dec. 18, 1965; children: Jennifer, Brian. BA, Wesleyan U., Middletown, Conn., 1963; MS, Northwestern U., 1969, PhD, 1970. Asst. prof. computer sci. U. Mo., Rolla, 1970-71; asst. prof. computer sci. Georgetown U., Washington, 1971-76, assoc. prof., chmn., 1976-83; MacArthur prof., chmn. Colgate U., Hamilton, N.Y., 1983-88, assoc. dean faculty, 1986-88; prof. Bowdoin Coll., Brunswick, Maine, 1988—; dir. acad. computing Georgetown U., 1976-83; cons. in field, 1976—. Author: Programming Languages, 1977, 2d rev. edit., 1986, Text Processing, 1979, Computer Science: A Second Course, 1988, Fundamentals of Computing I, 1992, 2d edit., 1995, Fundamentals of Computing II, 1993, 2d edit., 1995; assoc. editor Jour. of Computer Langs., 1979—, Jour. of Machine Translation, 1986—; contbr. articles to profl. jours.; editor-in-chief Handbook of COmputer Science and Engineering, 1997. NSF fellow, 1984-86, ACM fellow, 1994—, Fulbright lectureship, 1986, 92. Fellow Assn. for Computing Machinery (Outstanding Contbn. award 1991); mem. Computer Soc. of IEEE, N.Y. Acad. Scis., Sigma Xi. Democrat. Episcopalian. Avocations: squash, golf, jogging, music, travel. Home: 1 Boody St Brunswick ME 04011-3005 Office: Bowdoin Coll Dept of Computer Sci Brunswick ME 04011

TUCKER, ALVIN LEROY, government official; b. Bklyn., Sept. 7, 1938; s. Alvin Leroy and Alveria (Klune) T.; m. Jacqueline Twiggs, Aug. 27, 1966; children: Hazel, Pluma, Jacqueline, Alvin. BS, U. Md., 1965. CPA, Md.; cert. internal auditor, govt. fin. mgr. Auditor Dept. Army, Washington, 1965-67; dep. insp. gen. HUD, Washington, 1986-89; auditor Dept. Def., Washington, 1967-72, budget analyst, 1972-79, dir. tng. and edn., 1979-83, dep. asst. insp. gen., 1983-86, dep. comptr., 1989-94, dep. CFO, 1991—, chmn. concessions com., 1989—; mem. steering com. Joint Fin. Mgmt. Improvement Program, 1990-93; mem. CFO's Coun., 1989—, chmn. fin. sys. com., 1989—; mem. Fed. Acctg. Stds. Adv. Bd., 1991—. With U.S. Army, 1958-61. Mem. AICPA, Am. Soc. Mil. Comptrs., Assn. Govt. Accts. (nat. exec. com. 1993-94), Kiwanis (club pres. 1981-82, 86-87). Avocation: genealogy. Office: Pentagon Undersec of Defense/Comptr Rm 3E831 Washington DC 20301

TUCKER, BOWEN HAYWARD, lawyer; b. Providence, Apr. 13, 1938; s. Stuart Hayward and Ardelle Chase (Drabble) T.; m. Jan Louise Brown, Aug. 26, 1961; children: Stefan Kendric Slade, Catherine Kendra Gordon. AB in Math., Brown U., 1959; JD, U. Mich., 1962. Bar: R.I. 1963, Ill. 1967, U.S. Supreme Ct. 1970. Assoc. Hinckley & Allen, Providence, 1962-66; sr. atty. Caterpillar, Inc., Peoria, Ill., 1966-72; counsel FMC Corp., Chgo., 1972-82, sr. litigation counsel, 1982—. Chmn. legal process task force Chgo. Residential Sch. Study Com., 1973-74, mem. Commn. on Children, 1983-85, Ill. Com. on Rights of Minors, 1974-77, Com. on Youth and the Law, 1977-79; mem. White House Conf. on Children, ednl. svcs. subcom., 1979-80; chairperson Youth Employment Task Force, 1982-83; mem. citizens com. on Juvenile Ct. (Cook County), 1978-94, chmn. detention subcom., 1982-94; mem. econ. effects adv. com. Rand Inst. Civil Justice, 1990-92. 1st lt. U.S. Army, 1962-69. Mem. ABA, Am. Law Inst., Ill. State Bar Assn., R.I. Bar Assn., Chgo. (chmn. com. on juvenile law, 1976-77), Engine Mfrs. Assn. (chmn. legal com. 1972), Constrn. Industry Mfrs. Assn. (exec. com. of Lawyers' Coun. 1972, 1975-79, vice chmn. 1977, chmn. 1978-79), Mfrs. Alliance (products liability coun. 1974-95, vice chmn. 1981-83, chmn. 1983-85), Product Liability Adv. Coun. (bd. dirs. 1986—, exec. com. 1990—, vice chmn. 1991-93, chmn. 1993-95), ACLU (bd. dirs. Ill. div. 1970-79, exec. com. 1973-79, sec. 1975-77), Am. Arbitration Assn. (mem panel of arbitrators 1985-96), Phi Alph Delta. Club: Brown Univ. of Chgo. (nat. alumni schs. program 1973-85, v.p. 1980-81, pres. 1981-86). Home: 107 W Noyes St Arlington Heights IL 60005-3747 Office: 200 E Randolph St Ste 6700 Chicago IL 60601-6436

TUCKER, CYNTHIA ANNE, journalist; b. Monroeville, Ala., Mar. 13, 1955; m. Michael Pierce, Dec. 26, 1987 (div. 1989). BA, Auburn U., 1976. Reporter The Atlanta Jour., 1976-80, editorial writer, columnist, 1983-86; reporter The Phila. Inquirer, 1980-82; assoc. editorial page editor The Atlanta Constitution, 1986-91, editorial page editor, 1992—. Bd. dirs. ARC, 1989-93, Families First, 1988—, Internat. Women's Media Found., 1994—. Nieman fellow Harvard U., 1988-89. Mem. Am. Soc. Newspaper Editors. Mem. United Ch. Christ. Office: Atlanta Jounal Constitution 72 Marietta St NW Atlanta GA 30303-2804

TUCKER, CYNTHIA DELORES NOTTAGE (MRS. WILLIAM M. TUCKER), political party official, former state official; b. Phila., Oct. 4, 1927; d. Whitfield and Captilda (Gardiner) Nottage; m. William M. Tucker, July 21, 1951. Student, Temple U., Pa. State U., U. Pa.; student hon. degrees, Villa Maria Coll., Erie, Pa., 1972, Morris Coll., Sumter, S.C., 1976. Sec. of state Commonwealth of Pa., Harrisburg, 1971-77; nat. pres. Fedn. Democratic Women, 1979-81; v.p. Pa. chpt. NAACP, nat. v.p. bd. trustees; mem. nat. adv. bd. Nat. Women's Polit. Caucus; now chair Black Caucus Nat. Dem. Com.; mem., vice chair Pa. Black Dem. Com., 1966—; chair Women for Dem. Action, 1967—; founding vice chair Nat. Polit. Congress of Black Women, Inc., 1984-92, nat. chair, 1992—; sec., mem. Phila. Zoning Bd. Adjustment, 1968-70; vice chair Pa. Dem. State Com., 1970-76; mem. exec. com. Dem. Nat. Com., 1972-76; Dem. candidate lt. gov., Pa., 1978; v.p. Phila. Tribune Newspaper. Del. to White Ho. Conf. on Civil Rights; bd. dirs. Phila. YWCA, New Sch. Music, Martin Luther King Ctr. for Social Change; pres., founder Phila. Martin Luther King Assn.; mem. Commonwealth bd. Med. Coll. Pa.; bd. assocs. Messiah Coll.; founder, pres. Bethune-DuBois Fund. Recipient Svc. and Achievement award NAACP, 1964, Phila. Tribune Charities Ann. award, Cmty. Svc. award Opportunities Industrialization Ctr., Emma V. Kelley Achievement award Nat. Elks, 1971, Lincoln U. Nat. Leadership award, 1993, Cmty. Svc. award Quaker City chpt. B'nai B'rith; named Best Dressed Woman of Yr., Ebony mag., One of 100 Most Influential Black Ams., 1973-77; included in 1996 People mag.'s list of Twenty-Five Most Intriguing People. Mem. Nat. Assn. Secs. State (v.p.), Bus. and Profl. Women's Club, Links (dir.), Alpha Kappa Alpha (hon.). Home: 6700 Lincoln Dr Philadelphia PA 19119-3155

TUCKER, DEWEY DUANE, systems analyst; b. Burns, Oreg., Nov. 6, 1947; s. Dewey and Evelyn Evadine (Stewart) T.; m. Bertha Lorene Beach, Mar. 22, 1971; children: Tamera Reneé, Nicole Marie, Natasha Lynn. AS, Ricks Coll., Rexburg, Idaho, 1967; BS, Oreg. State U., 1971; MS, Naval Postgrad. Sch., Monterey, Calif., 1985. Distributor Oreg. Jour., Burns, 1959-63; clk. Richey's Supper Market, Burns, 1964-65; mailman U.S. Post Office, Burns, 1966-67; sawmill worker Hines (Oreg.) Lumber Co., 1965-67; mem. staff Sta. KOAC-AM/FM-TV, Corvallis, Oreg., 1969-71; commd. 2d lt. USMC, Washington, 1971; advanced through grades to lt. col. USMC, 1972-92; sr. systems analyst Potomac Systems Engring., Annandale, Va., 1992-95, Computing Technologies, Inc., Fairfax, Va., 1995—. Mem. Mil. Ops. Rsch. Soc., Marine Corps Assn. Republican. Avocations: hunting, fishing, dancing, hiking. Home: 7879 Blue Gray Cir Manassas VA 20109-2825 Office: Computing Technologies Inc 3028 Javier Rd Ste 400 Fairfax VA 22031-4622

TUCKER, DON EUGENE, retired lawyer; b. Rockbridge, Ohio, Feb. 3, 1928; s. Beryl Hollis and Ruth (Primmer) T.; m. Elizabeth Jane Parke, Aug. 2, 1950; children: Janet Elizabeth, Kerry Jane, Richard Parke. B.A., Aurora Coll., 1951; LL.B., Yale, 1956. Bar: Ohio 1956. Since practiced in Youngstown, Ohio; asso. Manchester, Bennett, Powers & Ullman, 1956-62, ptnr., 1962-73, of counsel, 1973-87; gen. counsel Comml. Intertech Corp., Youngstown, 1973-75, v.p., gen. counsel, 1975-83, also dir., sr. v.p., gen. counsel, 1983-87, sr. v.p., 1987-93; ret., 1993. Solicitor Village of Poland, Ohio, 1961-63; former chmn. bd., pres., trustee United Cerebral Palsy Assn., Youngstown and Mahoning County; trustee Mahoning County Tb and Health Assn.; former trustee, pres. Indsl. Info. Inst.; former pres., trustee Ea. Ohio Lung Assn.; trustee, former chmn. Cmty. Corp.; trustee, former pres. Butler Inst. Am. Art. With USMCR, 1946-48, 51-53. Mem. Ohio Bar Assn., Mahoning County Bar Assn. (pres. 1972, trustee 1970-73), Youngstown Area C. of C. (chmn. bd. dirs. 1979). Methodist. Home: 322 N Bayshore Dr Columbiana OH 44408 Office: Comml Intertech Corp PO Box 239 Youngstown OH 44501-0239

TUCKER, EDWIN WALLACE, law educator; b. N.Y.C., Feb. 25, 1927; s. Benjamin and May Tucker; m. Gladys Lipschutz, Sept. 14, 1952; children: Sherwin M., Pamela A. BA, NYU, 1948; LLB, Harvard U., 1951; LLM, N.Y. Law Sch., 1963, JSD, 1964; MA, Trinity Coll., Hartford, Conn., 1967. Bar: N.Y. 1955, U.S. Dist. Ct. (ea. and so. dists.) N.Y. 1958, U.S. Ct. Appeals (2d cir.) 1958, U.S. Supreme Ct. 1960. Pvt. practice, N.Y.C., 1955-63; Disting. Alumni prof. and prof. bus. law U. Conn., Storrs, 1963—, mem. bd. editors occasional paper and monograph series, 1966-70. Author: Adjudication of Social Issues, 1971, 2d edit., 1977, Legal Regulation of the Environment, 1972, Administrative Agencies, Regulation of Enterprise, and Individual Liberties, 1975, CPA Law Review, 1985; co-author: The Legal and Ethical Environment of Business, 1992; book rev. editor Am. Bus. Law Jour., 1964-65, adv. editor, 1974—; co-editor Am. Bus. Jour., 1965-73; mem. editl. bd. Am. Jour. Small Bus., 1979-86; editor Jour. Legal Studies Edn., 1983-85, editor-in-chief, 1985-87, adv. editor, 1987—; mem. bd. editors North Atlantic Regional Bus. Law Rev., 1984—. With USAF, 1951-55. Recipient medal of excellence Am. Bus. Law Assn., 1979. Mem. Acad. Legal Studies in Bus., North Atlantic Regional Bus. Law Assn. Home: 11 Eastwood Rd Storrs Mansfield CT 06268-2401

TUCKER, FRANCES LAUGHRIDGE, civic worker; b. Anderson, S.C., Dec. 4, 1916; d. John Franklin and Sallie V. (Cowart) Laughridge; m. Russell Hatch Tucker, Aug. 30, 1946 (dec. Aug. 1977); children—Russell Hatch, Pamela Tucker (dec.). Student U. Conn., 1970, Sacred Heart U., Fairfield, Conn., 1977, 79, Fairfield U., 1978, U. S.C., 1984. Sec. to atty., Asheville, N.C., 1935-37; sec. to gen. mgr. Ga. Talc Mining & Mfg., Asheville, 1937-42; sec. engring. dept. E.I. duPont de Nemours, Wilmington, Del., 1942-46. Chmn. radio com. D.C. chpt. ARC, 1947-48, bd. dirs., chmn. pub. rels. Westport-Weston Ct. chpt., 1968-73, mem. adv. coun. ARC Ct. Divsn., 1973-80, chmn. pub. rels., Hilton Head Island, S.C., 1981-84, 89-92, chmn. pub. rels. bloodmobile, Hilton Head Island, 1984-89; bd. dirs., mem. pub. relations com. United Fund, Westport-Weston, Conn., 1968-69, bd. dirs. Beaufort County chpt. ARC, 1982-87, 89-92; mem. media communications St. Luke's Episcopal Ch., Hilton Head Island, 1980-94, office vol., 1995—; with Hilton Head Hosp. Aux., 1984-89. Mem. Sea Pines Country Club. Home: 13 Willow Oak Rd Hilton Head Island SC 29928-5926

TUCKER, FREDERICK THOMAS, electronics company executive; b. Herkimer, N.Y., May 27, 1940; s. Edmond and Martha R. (Rich) T.; m. Mary McDonald; children: Michael, Lisa. BSEE, Rochester Inst. Tech., 1963. Coop. student designer Delco Products div. Gen. Motors, Rochester, N.Y., 1960-65; salesman Motorola, N.Y., N.J., Conn., 1965-70; prodn. engr. Motorola, Phoenix, 1970-73, prodn. mgr., 1973-78, from ops. mgr. to v.p., div. ops., 1978-79, v.p., gen. mgr. power products div., 1981-84; v.p., gen. mgr. bipolar i.c. div. Motorola, 1984-87; corp. v.p., asst. gen. mgr. automotive and indsl. electronics group Motorola, Schaumburg, Ill., 1987-88; sr. v.p., gen. mgr. Motorola, Northbrook, Ill., 1988-92, exec. v.p., gen. mgr. automotive and inds. electronics group, 1992-93; exec. v.p., gen. mgr. automotive, energy and controls group, 1993-97, exec. v.p., pres., gen. mgr. automotive, energy, components, 1997—. Patentee in field. Bd. dirs. Jr. Achievement Chgo.; trustee Rochester Inst. Tech., 1986. Named Disting. Alumnus Coll. Engring., Rochester Inst. Tech., 1983, Disting. Alumnus Rochester Inst. Tech., 1997; Alumni Honor Roll of Excellence, Rochester Inst. Tech., 1986. Mem. Intelligent Transp. Soc. Am. (chmn. bd. 1993). Republican. Lutheran. Office: Motorola Inc 4000 Commercial Ave Northbrook IL 60062-1829

TUCKER, GARLAND SCOTT, III, investment banker; b. Raleigh, N.C., June 17, 1947; s. Garland Scott Jr. and Jean Smith (Barnes) T.; m. Greyson Conrad Shuff, Jan. 15, 1972; children—Greyson Carrington, Elizabeth Bradford. B.S. magna cum laude, Washington and Lee U., 1969; M.B.A., Harvard U., 1972. V.p. Tucker Furniture Co., Wilson, N.C., 1972-76; corp. fin. assoc. Investment Corp. of Va., Norfolk, 1976-78; v.p., to pres., chief exec. officer Carolina Securities Corp., Raleigh, N.C., 1978-88; v.p. corp. banking and fin. Chem. Bank, N.Y.C., 1988-90; pres. First Travelcorp., Inc., Raleigh, 1990—; ptnr. Chatham Ptnrs., Inc., 1996—. Mem. N.Y. Stock Exchange, 1983-88; mem. regional firms adv. com. N.Y. Stock Exchange, 1984-87. Dir. Raleigh Rescue Mission, 1980-83; vestry Christ Episcopal Ch., Raleigh, 1981-84; bd. advisors NCO Investors, N.Y.C, 1991—; trustee N.C. Mus. Art Found., 1990—, Chatham Hall Sch., 1990-96, Penick Episcopal Home for Aging, 1992-94, Trinity Episc. Sem., Pitts., FOCUS, N.Y.C. Mem. Carolina Securities Corp. (bd. dirs. 1979-88), Securities Industry Assn. (bd. dirs. Mid-Atlantic region 1981-82, 84-88, regional firms com. 1983-86), Raleigh C. of C. (bd. dirs. 1984-86), Phi Beta Kappa. Republican. Clubs: Capital City, Carolina Country (Raleigh); Harvard of N.Y.C., Roaring Gap Club. Home: 2327 Lake Dr Raleigh NC 27609-7667 Office: First Travelcorp Inc 4513 Creedmoor Rd Raleigh NC 27612-3811

TUCKER, GARY JAY, physician, educator; b. Cleve., Mar. 6, 1934; s. Isadore Martin and Blanche Hanna (Luftig) T.; m. Sharon Ruth Pobby, June 10, 1956; children: Adam, Clare. AB, Oberlin Coll., 1956; MD, Case Western Res. U., 1960; postdoctoral fellow, Yale U., 1961-64; MA (hon.), Dartmouth Coll., 1977. Diplomate Am. Bd. Psychiatry and Neurology. Asst. prof. psychiatry Sch. Medicine Yale U., New Haven, 1967-70, assoc. prof. psychiatry, 1970-71; with Dartmouth Med. Sch., Hanover, N.H., 1971-85, prof. psychiatry, 1974-85, chmn. dept., 1978-85; prof., chmn. psychiatry and behavioral scis. Sch. Med. U. Wash., Seattle, 1985—; bd. dirs. Am. Bd. Psychiatry and Neurology. Co-author: Rational Hospital Psychiatry, 1974, Behavioral Neurology, 1985; contbr. articles to profl. jours. Lt. Commdr. USN, 1964-67. Fellow Am. Psychiat. Assn.; mem. W. Coast Coll. Biol. Psychiatry, Sigma Xi, Alpha Omega Alpha. Democrat. Jewish. Avocations: photography, motorcycles. Office: Univ of Washington Dept Psychiatry Box 356560 Seattle WA 98195

TUCKER, GARY WILSON, nurse educator; b. Oct. 2, 1956; s. Clayton Wilson Jr. and Jewell (Shelton) T. ADN, Cleveland (Tenn.) State Community Coll., 1980; BSW, Lamar U., Beaumont, Tex., 1991; MPH, U. Tex. Sch. Pub. Health, 1996. CCRN, ACLS. Nurse, relief shift supr. Moccasin Bend Mental Health Inst., Chattanooga, 1980-81; staff nurse pediat. ICU Thompson Childrens', Chattanooga, 1981-83; nurse, cons. King Fahad Hosp., Riyadh, Saudi Arabia, 1983; staff nurse ICU/ CCU Beaumont (Tex.) Med.-Surg. Hosp., 1984-88; charge nurse CCU Bapt. Hosp., Beaumont, 1988-93, staff nurse, hemodialysis, 1988-93, cardio-vascular nurse educator, 1993-96, staff devel. and continuing edn. nurse, 1996—. Mem. AACN, Tex. Nurses Assn. Home: 601 22nd St Beaumont TX 77706-4915 Office: Bapt Hosp PO Drawer 1591 Beaumont TX 77704

TUCKER, GEORGE MAXWELL, SR., interactive distribution company executive, business and political consultant; b. Bainbridge, Ga., Jan. 17, 1950; s. John Pierce, Sr., and Isabel (Slade) T.; BA in Polit. Sci. and Christianity, Mercer U., 1972, postgrad. Sch. Theology, 1972-74; m. Janet Almand, July 18, 1981; children: George Jr., Michael Almand, Kelly Marie, Jennifer Rose. Mem. high sch. ministry team and exec. staff Internat. Devel. Campaign and spl. field rep. for pres. Campus Crusade for Christ Internat., San Bernardino, Calif., 1972-77; dir. pub. rels., acting adminstr., Shepherd Prodns., Inc., Denver, 1977-78; personnel mgr. Riverside Mfg. Co., Moultrie, Ga., 1978; sales mgr. Western U.S., Plains Mfg. Co., Sidney, Nebr., 1978-79; asst. to pres. for spl. projects Campus Crusade for Christ, Internat., San Bernardino, Calif., 1979-80, assoc. staff exec. ministries, 1980-86; owner, gen. mgr. Environ. Control Bldg. Maintenance Co., Chamblee, Ga., 1980-92, also Environment Control of Cobb County, Ga., 1983-85; pres., COO Environment Control of Atlanta, Inc., Bldg. Maintenance Cos., 1984-94; sr. assoc. McNair Assocs., Inc. Mgmt. Cons., 1992-94; prin. Tucker Enterprises, 1992—. Elder Presbyn. Ch.; chmn. Gwinnett County Ga. Rep. Party, 1989-91 (recipient Clean Sweep award 1991); mem. adv. bd. Ga. Railroad Preservation League, Inc., 1990—; campaign mgr. McNair for Gov. Ga., 1994. Recipient Youth Leadership award, Elks Club, 1968. Mem. Christian Conciliation Svcs. of Atlanta, Inc. (bd. dirs. 1983-87), East Coast Mgmt. Assn. Environment Control Bldg. Maintenance Cos. (sec./treas. 1987-91), Exec. Leadership Found. (bd. dirs. 1991-93), Alpha Tau Omega. Co-author: A Resource Manual for Church Youth Workers, 1976. Office: 3875 Waterford Dr Suwanee GA 30024-1479

TUCKER, H. RICHARD, oil company executive; b. Streator, Ill., Oct. 2, 1936; s. H.L. and Dorothy A. (Miller) T.; children by previous marriage: Randall R., Brian A.; m. Cheryl L. Kirk, Jan. 14, 1984. BS in Chem. Engring., Purdue U., 1958; MBA, Northwestern U., 1962. Project engr. crude oil supply Amoco Corp., Chgo., 1958-64, specialist product supply, 1965-66, coord. fgn. crude oil supply, 1967-68; coord. orgn. planning Amoco Internat. Corp., Chgo., 1969-70; coord. orgn. planning Amoco Corp., Chgo., 1970-72, mgr. adminstrv. svcs., 1972-84, mgr. real estate svcs., 1984-86, coord. spl. studies, 1986-89, dir. quality mgmt., 1989-92; mgr. cost mgmt.,

1992-94; v.p. Amoco Realty Co., 1984-91, Amoco Devel. Co., 1984-91. Mem. adv. com. Sch. Bd. Wheaton, Ill., 1966; mem. Citizen's Nominating Com., Wheaton, 1972; leader Boy Scouts Am., Wheaton, 1979-82; dir. Oak Brook Colony Condominium Assn., 1992-94. Mem. Westhaven Home Owners Assn. (pres. 1965-67), Phi Eta Sigma, Omega Chi Epsilon, Beta Gamma Sigma, Tau Beta Pi. Avocations: tennis, bridge, hiking.

TUCKER, HOWARD MCKELDIN, investment banker, consultant; b. Washington, Apr. 1, 1930; s. Howard Newell and Bessie Draper (McKeldin) T.; m. Julia Spencer Merrell, Feb. 1, 1952; children: Deborah, Mark, Alexander, H. David; m. Megan Evans, Aug. 17, 1979. BA, U. Va., 1954; MBA, NYU, 1956. CFA. Pension investment dept. J.P. Morgan & Co., N.Y.C., 1954-61; registered rep.-analyst Mackall & Coe, Washington, 1962-69; dir. internat. dept., analyst Legg Mason Wood Walker & Co., Washington, 1969-79; with Govt. Rsch. Corp./Nat. Jour., 1979-82, Potomac Asset Mgmt., 1982-91; ptnr., mng. dir. Capital Insights Group, Washington, 1992—; cons. County Natwest (Washington Analysis Corp.), 1985-90; bd. dirs. Monarch Enterprises, Inc., Uniflight, Inc., Sci. Mgmt. Assocs., Inc., Jeffrey Bigelow Assocs.; mem. task force on balance-of-payments U.S. Dept. Treasury, 1967-70; co-organizer U.S.-Ger. Parliamentary Exchange, 1980-82; observer OECD, 1980-82; spl. overseas visitor Australian Govt., 1982. Author: Literature in Medicine; writer London Investment Jour.; contbr. articles to fin. jours. Trustee Nat. Cathedral Sch. for Girls, 1972-78; chmn. Missionary Devel. Fund Episcopal Diocese of D.C., 1974; vestryman Christ Episcopal Ch., Georgetown, 1962-65; mem. chpt. Washington Nat. Cathedral, 1966-72; del. Va. Republican Conv., 1968; dir. Washington Area Coun. Chs., 1962-65; co-dir. Andover-Exeter Washington Intern Program, 1976-86; patron West Europe program Woodrow Wilson Ctr., 1985-86. Served with USNR, 1950-56. Mem. Washington Soc. Investment Analysts, Nat. Economists Club, Cogswell Soc. Clubs: Naval and Mil. (London), Nat. Press, Georgetown Visitation Tennis, Saints and Sinners, Dumplings Yacht Club, Beta Theta Pi. Home: 4 Potomac Ct Alexandria VA 22314-3821 Office: Capital Insights Group 1700 K St NW Ste 1200 Washington DC 20006-3821

TUCKER, JACK WILLIAM ANDREW, writer, film editor; b. Portland, Oreg., May 1, 1944; s. Admyrl Foster and Aileen Eloise (McDaniels) T. BA in English, Portland State U., 1964. Film editor MGM TV, Culver City, Calif., 1984-86, Cannon Film Group, Beverly Hills, Calif., 1988, Columbia TV, Burbank, Calif., 1988, Paramount Pictures, Hollywood, Calif., 1990—. Editor: (TV) Winds of War, 1982 (Emmy award nominee 1983), The Fifth Missile, 1986, 240-Robert, 1979, Flatbed Annie and Sweetpie, 1979, (films) Shogun, 1980, Salsa, 1988, They're Playing With Fire, 1983, Viper, 1988, Nightmare on Elm Street IV, 1988, Distortions, 1987, Diplomatic Immunity, 1991, Illusions, 1992, Double-O-Kid, 1993, A Million to Juan, 1994, To the Ends of Time, 1996, Cinemeditor mag. Sgt. USAF, 1964-68, Vietnam. Mem. NATAS, Am. Cinema Editors (treas. 1993—, editor CONEMEDITOR mag. 1994—).

TUCKER, JAMES RAYMOND, primary education educator; b. Pueblo, Colo., Apr. 18, 1944; s. James George and Pauline F. (Sena) T.; m. Kathie Owens; 1 child, Brittany. BA, U. So. Colo., 1966; MA, U. No. Colo., 1990, postgrad., 1991. Tchr. Sinclair Mid. Sch., Englewood, Colo., 1971-93, Denver Pub. Schs., 1993—; co-dir. Nick Bolleteri Tennis Acad., Boulder, Colo., 1986; head tennis coach Englewood High Sch., 1971—. Sgt. U.S. Army, 1967-70. Mem. NEA, U.S. Profl. Tennis Assn., U.S. Profl. Tennis Registry, Internat. Platform Assn., Colo. Edn. Assn., Meadow Creek Tennis and Fitness, Colo. H.S. Coaches Assn. (Achievement award 1989, 92, Tchr. of Yr. 1973, 78, 86, Coach of Yr. 1986, 87, 90, 96, 97, Franklin award 1988, 89). Home: 2316 S Harlan Ct Denver CO 80227-3962

TUCKER, JOHN MARK, librarian, educator; b. Natchez, Miss., Oct. 25, 1945; s. Paul Marlin and Edith (Upton) T.; m. Barbara Ann Wilson, Mar. 22, 1968. BA, David Lipscomb Coll., 1967; MLS, George Peabody Coll. Tchrs., 1968, specialist in edn., 1972; PhD, U. Ill., 1983. Head libr. Freed-Hardeman Coll., Henderson, Tenn., 1968-71; reference libr. Wabash Coll., Crawfordsville, Ind., 1973-79; reference libr. Purdue U., West Lafayette, Ind., 1979-82, asst. prof. libr. sci., 1979-85, assoc. prof. libr. sci., 1985-89, sr. reference libr. Humanities, Social Sci. and Edn. Libr., 1982-90, prof. libr. sci., 1989—, libr. Humanities, Social Sci. and Edn. Libr., 1990—; grantee com. on instnl. coop. NEH, 1991-94. Co-editor: Reference Services and Library Education, 1983, User Instruction in Academic Libraries, 1986, American Library History, 1989; editor: Civil Rights, Libraries and Black Librarianship, 1997contbr. articles to profl. publs. Thomas S. Wilmeth grantee for innovative excellence, 1988, Frederick B. Artz rsch. grantee Oberlin Coll. Archives, 1991; Coun. on Libr. Resources rsch. fellow, 1990. Mem. ALA (chair Libr. History Round Table 1993-94), SCV, Assn. for Bibliography of History, Assn. Coll. and Rsch. Librs., Disciples of Christ Hist. Soc., Soc. for Historians of the Gilded Age and Prog. Era, So. Hist. Assn., Friends of Univ. Ill. Libr., Phi Kappa Phi, Beta Phi Mu. Democrat. Mem. Chs. of Christ. Home: 1055 Southernview Dr S Lafayette IN 47905-3797 Office: Purdue U Humanities Social Sci & Edn Libr 1530 Stewart Ctr West Lafayette IN 47907-1530

TUCKER, JOHN ROBERT, financial executive; b. West Palm Beach, Fla., Jan. 27, 1931; s. William Herman Tucker Sr. and Jessie Brasselle Tucker Massingale; m. Charlotte Ann Kause, Oct. 10, 1959; children: Helene Ann, Thomas Kenneth. BA in Arts and Humanities, U. Md., 1951; M Internat. and Pub. Affairs, Columbia U., 1955, cert. East Asian Inst., 1955; diploma, Indsl. Coll. Armed Forces, 1957. Asst. to pres. Govt. Employees Ins. Co., Washington, 1956-62; pres., CEO Tucker Corp., Potomac, Md., 1963-80, Icon Corp., Washington, 1985—; sr. fellow Pres.'s Pvt. Sector Survey on Cost Control, Washington, 1981-84. Author: The Bicentennial Tragedy, 1975, The Megapower, 1995. Capt. USAF, 1951-53. Recipient Gov.'s Cup from Gov. of Md., 1951. Mem. U. Md. College Park Alumni Assn., Harvard U. Grad. Sch. Arts and Scis. Alumni Assn., George Washington U. Gen. Alumni Assn., Harvard Club of Washington, Nat. Economists Club, Pres. Club U. Md. Republican. Episcopalian. Avocations: photography, gardening, travel. Home: 4701 Kenmore Ave Apt # 303 Alexandria VA 22304-1206

TUCKER, L. DAN, lawyer; b. El Dorado, Ark., Oct. 23, 1936; s. Floyd A. and Harriet Kathleen (Graves) T.; m. Katherine Washburn, June 21, 1958; children: Laurie Tucker Diaz, Dana Tucker Kleine. BS in Chem. Engring., U. Okla., 1959, LLB, 1962. Bar: Okla. 1962, Tex. 1972. Patent atty. Phillips Petroleum Co., Bartlesville, Okla., 1964-67, Monsanto Co., St. Louis, 1967-70; patent mgr. Monsanto Co., Texas City, Tex., 1970-74; ptnr. Hubbard, Tucker & Harris, Dallas, 1974-94, Harris, Tucker & Hardin, Dallas, 1994—. 1st lt. U.S. Army, 1962-64. Republican. Episcopalian. Avocations: fishing, hunting, traveling. Office: Harris Tucker & Hardin PC 2100 Galleria Tower I Dallas TX 75240

TUCKER, LOUIS LEONARD, historical society administrator; b. Rockville, Conn., Dec. 6, 1927; s. Joseph and Dora (Conn) T.; m. Beverley Jones, Mar. 27, 1953; children: Mark T., Lance K.; m. Carolyn woollen, Sept. 14, 1996. B.A., U. Wash., 1952, M.A., 1954, Ph.D., 1957. Instr. history U. Calif., Davis, 1958; fellow Inst. Early Am. History and Culture, Williamsburg, Va., 1958-60; instr. history Coll. William and Mary, 1958-60; dir. Cin. Hist. Soc., 1960-66; asst. commr., state historian of N.Y., N.Y State Edn. Dept., 1966-76; also dir. N.Y. State Bicentennial Commn., 1969-76; dir. Mass. Hist. Soc., Boston, 1977—. Author: Puritan Protagonist, 1962, Cincinnati During Civil War, 1962, Cincinnati's Citizen Crusaders, 1967, Our Travels, 1968, Cincinnati: Students Guide to Local History, 1969, James Allen, Jr.: From Elkins to Washington, 1969, Connecticut's Seminary of Sedition, Yale College, 1974, Clio's Consort: Jeremy Belknap and the Founding of the Massachusetts Historical Society, 1990, The Massachusetts Historical Society: A Bicentennial History, 1791-1971, 1996. Dir. Shaker Mus., 1967-74; Am. Heritage Co., 1973-75, Ft. Ticonderoga Assn., 1990-97. Served with AUS, 1946-47. Winston Churchill fellow, 1969. Mem. Am. Assn. State and Local History (pres. 1972-74). Home: 6 Lawrence St Boston MA 02116 Office: Massachusetts Historical Society 1154 Boylston St Boston MA 02215-3631

TUCKER, MARCUS OTHELLO, judge; b. Santa Monica, Calif., Nov. 12, 1934; s. Marcus Othello Sr. and Essie Louvonia (McLendon) T.; m. Indira Hale, May 29, 1965; 1 child, Angelique. BA, U. So. Calif., 1956; JD, Howard U., 1960. Bar: Calif. 1962, U.S. Dist. Ct. (cen. dist.) Calif. 1962, U.S. Ct. Appeals (9th cir.) 1965, U.S. Ct. Internat. Trade 1970, U.S. Supreme Ct. 1971. Pvt. practice, Santa Monica, 1962-63, 67-74; dep. atty. City of Santa Monica, 1963-65; asst. atty. U.S. Dist. Ct. (Cen. Dist.) Calif., 1965-67; commr. L.A. Superior Ct., 1974-76; judge mcpl. ct. Long Beach (Calif.) Jud. Dist., 1976-85; judge superior ct. L.A. Jud. Dist., 1985—; supervising judge L.A. County Dependency Ct. L.A. Superior Ct., 1991-92, presiding judge Juvenile divsn., 1993-94; asst. prof. law Pacific U., Long Beach, 1984, 86; justice pro tem U.S. Ct. Appeals (2nd cir.), 1981; mem. exec. com. Superior Ct. of L.A. County, 1995-96. Mem. editl. staff Howard U. Law Sch. Jour., 1959-60. Pres. Community Rehab. Industries Found., Long Beach, 1983-86, Legal Aid Found., L.A., 1976-77; bd. dirs. Long Beach coun. Boy Scouts Am., 1978-92. With U.S. Army, 1960-66. Named Judge of Yr. Juvenile Cts. Bar Assn., 1986, Disting. Jurist Long Beach Trial Trauma Coun., 1987, Honoree in Law Handy Community Ctr., L.A., 1987, Bernard S. Jefferson Jurist of Yr. John M. Langston Bar Assn. Black Lawyers, 1990, Judge of Yr. Long Beach Bar Assn., 1993; recipient award for Law-Related Edn. Constl. Rights Found./L.A. County Bar Assn., 1992, commendation L.A. County Bd. Suprs., 1994. Fellow Internat. Acad. Trial Judges; mem. ABA, Calif. Judges Assn. (chmn. juvenile law com. 1986-87), Langston Bar Assn. (pres. bd. dirs. 1972, 73), Calif. Assn. Black Lawyers, Santa Monica Bay Dist. Bar Assn. (treas. 1969-71), Am. Inns of Ct., Selden Soc. Avocations: comparative law, traveling. Office: 7281 Quill Dr Dept 250 Downey CA 90242-2001

TUCKER, MICHAEL, elementary school principal. Prin. Grace Abbott Elem. Sch., Omaha. Recipient Elem. Sch. Recognition award U.S. Dept. Edn., 1989-90. Office: Grace Abbott Elem Sch 1313 N 156th St Omaha NE 68118-2371*

TUCKER, NINA ANGELLA, hospital administrator; b. Miami, Fla., June 6, 1965; d. Joseph John and Diane (Accolla) A.; 1 child, Ryan. BA, Emory U., Atlanta, Ga., 1987; MA in Health Adminstrn., U. Fla., Gainesville, 1990, MBA, 1990. Asst. adminstr. Med. City Dallas, 1990-92, Meml. Hosp. West, Pembroke Pines, Fla., 1992-95; adminstr. JDCH/WS at Meml. Regional Hosp., Hollywood, Fla., 1995—; pres. Meml. Employees Fedl. Credit Union, 1993—. Recipient Regents award Am. Coll. Healthcare Execs., 1996. Roman Catholic. Avocations: walking, water skiing. Office: Meml Regional Hosp 3501 Johnson St Hollywood FL 33021-5421

TUCKER, PHYLLIS ANITA, sales representative, guidance counselor; b. Arkadelphia, Ark., July 26, 1952; d. Charles Wilson and Mary Katherine (Carter) T.; divorced. BS in Edn., Henderson State Coll., 1974, MEd, 1976. Teaching cert. for secondary social studies and guidance counseling. Social studies tchr. Monroe Acad., Wheatley, Ark., 1974-75; peer tutor Henderson State U., Arkadelphia, 1975-76; career orientation tchr. Heber Springs (Ark.) Mid. Sch., 1976-77; counselor Augusta (Ark.) Mid. Sch., 1977-78, Augusta H.S., 1978-86; vocat. special needs counselor White River Vocat.-Tech., Newport, Ark., 1986-87; guidance supr. Ark. Dept. Edn., Little Rock, 1987-89, ednl. supr., 1989-90; sales rep. Holt, Rinehart & Winston, Irving, Tex., 1990—. Chmn. Augusta Heart Fund Drive, 1979; bd. dirs. Saline County Chpt. Am. Cancer Soc., 1991. Named Young Career Woman of Yr. Augusta Bus. and Profl. Women, 1979. Mem. NAFE, Phi Delta Kappa. Republican. Methodist. Avocations: needlework, reading. Office: Holt Rinehart & Winston/HB 8551 Esters Blvd Irving TX 75063-2206

TUCKER, RANDOLPH WADSWORTH, engineering executive; b. Highland Pk., Ill., Dec. 3, 1949; s. Thomas Keith and Nancy Ellen (Jung) T.; m. Jean Marjorie Zenk, June 30, 1973 (div. 1991); 1 child, Nicholas Randolph; m. Lori Kaye Hicks, June 21, 1991. BS in Fire Protection Engring., Ill. Inst. Tech., 1972; M in Mgmt., Northwestern U., 1979. Registered profl. engr., Ill., Tex., Fla., La., Ga. With Ins. Svcs. Office of Ill., Chgo., 1972-74, bldg. insp., fire protection cons., 1972-74; with Rolf Jensen & Assocs., Inc., Deerfield, Ill., 1974—, cons. engr., 1974-77, mktg. mgr., 1977-81, mgr. Houston office, 1981-83, v.p. engring., mgr. Houston, 1983-89, v.p., tech. officer for Atlanta, Houston, N.Y.C., and Washington offices, 1989-90, sr. v.p., 1990-94, sr. v.p. internat. devel., 1994—; mem. adv. coun. Tex. State Fire Marshal, Austin, 1983-91; Dept. of Justice/Nat. Inst. Corrections cons. to Tex. Commn. on Jail Stds., 1993—. Editorial advisor Rusting Publs., N.Y.C., 1981—, Cahners Pub., 1993—; author articles in field. V.p. Juvenile Fire Setters Program, Houston, 1982-84; assoc. mem. Internat. Devel. Rsch. Coun., Urban Land Inst. Named one of Outstanding Young Men Am., U.S. Jaycees, 1981. Mem. AIA (profl. affiliate), Soc. Fire Protection Engrs. (chmn. nat. qualifications bd. 1985, pres. Houston chpt. 1983-84), Soc. Mktg. Profl. Svcs. (pres. Houston chpt. 1985, nat. pres. 1989-90), Nat. Fire Protection Assn., Internat. Conf. Bldg. Ofcls., Soc. Bldg. Code Cong. Internat., Inc., Bldg. Ofcls. Assn. Tex., Tex. Soc. Architects (profl. affiliate), Internat. Devel. Rsch. Coun., Houston C. of C. (vice chmn. fire protection com. 1983, govt. rels. com. 1984—), Aircraft Owners and Pilots Assn., Waller County Club. Republican. Episcopalian. Avocations: flying, golf. Office: Rolf Jensen & Assoc Inc 13831 Northwest Fwy Ste 330 Houston TX 77040-5205

TUCKER, RICHARD BLACKBURN, III, lawyer; b. Pitts., Oct. 28, 1943; s. Richard B. Jr. and Alice (Reed) T.; m. Dorothy Dohoney, Aug. 24, 1974; 1 child, R. Wade. BA, U. Va., 1965; JD, Columbia U., 1968. Bar: Pa. 1970, R.I. 1971, U.S. Supreme Ct. 1984. Vista vol. Greater Kansas City (Mo.) Legal Aid & Defender Soc., 1968-69; atty. R.I. Legal Svcs., Providence, 1970-76, Tucker Arensberg, P.C., Pitts., 1976—. Active western Pa. chpt. Nat. Hemophilia Found., Pitts., 1976-82. Mem. Pa. Bar Assn., Allegheny County Bar Assn. (vice-chmn. appellate practice com. 1994-95, chmn., 1996—). Democrat. Episcopalian. Avocations: tennis, skiing. Home: 217 Edgeworth Ln Sewickley PA 15143 Office: Tucker Arensberg PC 1500 One PPG Pl Pittsburgh PA 15222

TUCKER, RICHARD LEE, civil engineer, educator; b. Wichita Falls, Tex., July 19, 1935; s. Floyd Alfred and Zula Florence (Morris) T.; m. Shirley Sue Tucker, Sept. 1, 1956; children: Brian Alfred, Karen Leigh. BCE, U. Tex., 1958, MCE, 1960, PhD in Civil Engring., 1963. Registered profl. engr., Tex. Instr. civil engring. U. Tex., 1960-62; from asst. prof. to prof. U. Tex., Arlington, 1962-74, assoc. dean engring., 1963-74; v.p Luther Hill & Assoc., Inc., Dallas, 1974-76; C.T. Wells prof. project mgmt. U. Tex., Austin, from 1976, dir. Constrn. Industry Inst., from 1983, dir. Constrn. Engring. and Project Mgmt. Program, 1976—; pres. Tucker and Tucker Cons., Inc., Austin, 1976—. Contbr. numerous articles and papers to profl. jours. Recipient Erwin C. Perry award, Coll. Engring., U. Tex., 1978, Faculty Excellence award, 1986, Joe J. King Profl. Engring. Achievement award, 1990, Disting. Engring. Grad., 1994; Ronald Reagan award for Individual Initiative, Constrn. Industry Inst., 1991; named Outstanding Young Engr., Tex. Soc. Profl. Engrs., 1965, Outstanding Young Man, City of Arlington, 1967; Michael Scott Endowed Rsch. fellow Inst. for Constructive Capitalism, 1990-91. Fellow ASCE (R.L. Peurifoy award 1986, Thomas Fitch Rowland prize 1987, Tex. sect. award of honor 1990); mem. NSPE (Constrn. Engring. Educator award of the Profl. Engrs. in Constrn. 1993), Nat. Acad. Engring., NRC, Soc. Am. Mil. Engrs., The Moles (hon.). Baptist. Office: Univ Tex Coll Engring Constrn Industry Inst 3208 Red River St Ste 300 Austin TX 78705-2650

TUCKER, RICHARD LEE, financial executive; b. Boston, Jan. 16, 1940; s. Frank Lee and Dorothy (Mansell) T.; m. Melinda Nichols, 1970 (div. 1987); children: Anne P., John M.; m. Elizabeth M. Lyne, 1988; children: Christopher B., William M. AB, Harvard U., 1962. CFA. Portfolio mgr. Scudder Stevens & Clark, Boston, 1963-72, v.p. investments, 1972-80; sr. v.p., mgr. trust div. The Boston Co., 1980-86; supervising portfolio mgr., v.p. Trinity Investment Mgmt. Corp., Boston, 1986—, mng. dir., 1992—; dir. Data Gen. Corp., 1994—. Trustee Phillips Exeter (N.H.) Acad., 1975-86. Served with U.S. Army, 1962-63. Mem. Inst. Chartered Fin. Analysts, Somerset Club (pres.), The Country Club (Brookline). Home: 23 Woodman Rd Chestnut Hill MA 02167-1221 Office: Trinity Investment Mgmt 75 Park Plz Boston MA 02116-3934

TUCKER, ROBERT ARNOLD, electrical engineer; b. Atlanta, Jan. 30, 1941; s. Hugh Dorsey and Mary Ella (Dobbs) T.; m. Judy Elizabeth Henley, Sept. 18, 1964 (div. Sept. 13, 1979); children: Paige Elizabeth, Priscilla Elaine, Matthew Arnold; m. Joan Janet Ashton, Nov. 18, 1983; children: Beth Bennett, Russell E. McKenna III. BEE, Ga. Inst. Tech., 1964. Registered profl. engr., Ala., Fla., Ga., Tenn. Engr. in tng. Patterson & Dewar Engrs. Inc., 1964; substation design engr. Ga. Power Co., 1964-65, comml. sales engr., sr. engr., 1965-67, 72-73; dist. sales engr. Sylvania Elec. Products, Inc., 1967-71; regional sales mgr. The J.H. Spaulding Co., 1971-72; gen. sales mgr. Perimeter Lighting, Inc., 1973-74; utility mgmt. engr. Colonial Stores, Inc., 1975-76; prin. R. Arnold Tucker & Assocs., P.C., 1977-82; dist. sales engr. GTE Products Corp., 1982-86, mgr. tech. programs, 1986-90, engr. regional lighting/energy mgmt., 1990-93; comml. engr. Osram Sylvania Inc., Atlanta, 1993—. Contbr. articles to profl. jours. Mem. Kiwanis. Mem. NSPE, Illuminating Engring. Soc., Assn. Energy Engrs. Republican. Baptist. Home: 2130 Wynfield Point Dr Buford GA 30519-6740 Office: Osram Sylvania Inc 5169 Pelican Dr Atlanta GA 30349-5979

TUCKER, ROBERT DENNARD, health care products executive; b. Tifton, Ga., July 18, 1933; s. Robert Buck and Ethel Margaret (Dennard) T.; m. Peggy Angelyn Smith, June 23, 1957; children: Robert Barron, Jennifer Lee. BBA, Ga. State U., 1958. With sales and sales mgmt. Johnson & Johnson Inc., New Brunswick, N.J., 1958-68; v.p., gen. mgr. ASR Med. Industries, N.Y.C., 1968-72, Howmedica Suture div. Pfizer Inc., N.Y.C., 1972-75; exec. v.p., chief operating officer R. P. Scherer Corp., Detroit, 1976-79; pres., chief operating officer Scherer Sci. Inc., Atlanta, 1980-95, also bd. dirs; chmn., chief exec. officer Scherer Health Care Inc., Atlanta, 1980-95, also bd. dirs.; bd. dirs. Nat. Travel Mgmt., Atlanta Biofor Inc., Waverly, Pa., Clean Air Corp. Am., Atlanta, U.S. Environ. Compliance Corp., Atlanta, Body Care Inc., Atlanta; chmn., CEO Throwleigh Techs., LLC, 1995—. Pub: Tuckers of Devon, 1983; author, pub.: Descendants of William Tucker of Throwleigh, Devon. Chmn. bd. Health Industries Mfrs. Assn. polit. action com., Washington, 1983-85; trustee, past pres. Ga. Horse Found., Atlanta; trustee Brenau Coll., Gainesville, Ga., 1985—. Served with USN, 1951-54, Korea. Decorated Knight of Malta, Imperial Russian Order of St. John; recipient Disting. Service award Brenau Coll., 1987. Mem. Nat. Assn. Mfrs., Health Industries Mfrs. Assn. (bd. dirs. 1979-86, disting. service recognition 1981, 86), Pharm. Mfrs. Assn., Thoroughbred Owners and Breeders Assn. Ky. and Ga. (Man of Yr. 1984). Republican. Methodist. Clubs: Cherokee (Atlanta); Big Canoe (Ga.). Avocations: scuba diving, tennis, genealogical research. Home: 405 Townsend Pl NW Atlanta GA 30327-3037 Office: Throwleigh Techs PO Box 767655 Roswell GA 30076-7655

TUCKER, ROBERT KEITH, environmental sciences educator, researcher; b. Santa Ana, Calif., Feb. 22, 1936; s. Lloyd Levi and Margaret Corinne (Skiles) T.; m. Sharon Penney Langs, 1961 (div. 1974); children: Katherine Penney, Lee Ann; m. Joan Cook Luckhardt, Oct. 9, 1977. BA in Biochemistry, U. Calif., Berkeley, 1963; MA in Marine Biology, Humbolt State U., 1967; PhD in Zoology, Physiological Ecology, Duke U., 1971. Rsch. biologist Sandy Hook Lab. NOAA Nat. Marine Fisheries Svc., Highlands, N.J., 1971-77; rsch. scientist N.J. Dept. Environ. Protection and Energy, Trenton, 1977-95, dir. Divsn. Sci. and Rsch., 1986-95; prof. human ecology/ecology, evolution, natural resources Rutgers U., 1995—, dir. Ecopolicy Ctr., 1995—; chmn. environ. task force Gov.'s Coun. Prevention Mental Retardation and Devel. Disabilities, 1984-86, Interagy. Task Force Prevention Lead Poisoning, 1986-95; mem. bd. trustees N.J. Marine Scis. Consortium, 1987-95; mem. N.J. Commn. Cancer Rsch., 1984-95; mem. adv. bd. Environ. and Occupational Health Scis. Inst. U. Medicine and Dentistry N.J., 1987-95, trustee N.J. Environ. Fedn., 1996—, Stonybrook-Millstone Watershed Assn., 1996—, N.J. Comprehensive Cancer Ctr., 1991-95, Greater N.Y. Bight Marine Rsch., 1992-94; mem. external adv. bd. Nat. Inst. Occupational Safety and Health, 1990-92; mem. review panel estuarine rsch. northeast ctr. NOAA, Nat. Marine Fisheries Svc., 1989; organizer, dir. session 100th anniversary meeting Am. Soc. Testing and Materials, 1984; external com. mem. for PhD candidates Ruthers U., CUNY, Hunter Coll., U. Medicine and Dentistry N.J., 1972—. Contbr. over 50 articles to profl. jours. Fellow USPHS, 1967-70; recipient Merit citation NOAA, 1975, Outstanding Scientist award N.J. DEP, 1980. Mem. AAAS, Am. Chem. Soc. (organizer, dir. sessions on environ. chemistry Mid-Atlantic regional meeting 1979), Internat. Soc. Environ. Epidemiology, Soc. Occupational and Environ. Health, Crustacean Soc. Democrat. Unitarian. Achievements include reasearch in lead poisoning, problems dealing with petroleum contaminated soils, toxics in drinking water and groundwater, effects of toxic contaminants on marine resources.

TUCKER, ROY NELSON, mathematics educator, minister; b. LaGrange, Ga., Aug. 12, 1941; s. Henry Patrick Jr. and Katherine Irene (Irwin) T.; m. Sharon Elizabeth Knapp, May 10, 1974; children: Cheryl, Tina, David. PhD in Clin. Psychology, Ohio Christian U., 1967; MDiv, Southeastern Bapt. Theol. Sem., 1970; PhD in Psychology of Religion, Baylor U., 1978; MS in Math., Prairie View A&M U., 1983; MEd, Pan Am. U., 1987. Salesman, divsn. mgr. Sears, Roebuck & Co., Macon, Ga., 1962-66; learning lab coord. W.W. Holding Tech Inst., Raleigh, N.C., 1968-70; teaching asst. Baylor U., Waco, Tex., 1970-73; instr. Tex. State Tech. Inst., Waco, 1976-80, Blinn Coll., Bryan-College Sta., Tex., 1982-84, Tex. Southmost Coll., Brownsville, 1984-87, Embry-Riddle Aero. U., Beeville, Tex., 1988-89; assoc. prof. math./psychology Palo Alto Coll., San Antonio, 1988—. Author: Social Structures, 1978, Human Relations in Industry, 1979, A Time to Laugh, A Time to Cry, 1992, (play) The Innkeeper's Christmas, 1991. Pastor First Bapt. Ch., Jewell, Ga., 1965-67, Cmty. Bapt. Ch., Wake Forest, N.C., 1967-70, Marquez (Tex.) Bapt. Ch., 1975-79, Evang. U. C.C., Lyons, Tex., 1980-84, First Christian Ch., Aransas Pass, Tex., 1988-91, First Christian Ch., Devine, Tex., 1994—; pres. Boosters Assn., Waco, 1978-79; v.p. Family Abuse Ctr., Waco, 1978-79; pres. Faculty Senate Palo Alto Coll., 1995—; city councilman City of Hewitt, Tex., 1980. Maj. USAR, 1962-69. Mem. Tex. Faculty Assn., Tex. C.C. Tchrs. Assn., Masons. Republican. Avocations: travel, sports. Home: 6208 Sawyer Rd San Antonio TX 78238-2205 Office: Palo Alto Coll 1400 W Villaret Blvd San Antonio TX 78224-2417

TUCKER, SHIRLEY LOIS COTTER, botany educator, researcher; b. St. Paul, Apr. 4, 1927; d. Ralph U. and Myra C. (Knutson) Cotter; m. Kenneth W. Tucker, Aug. 22, 1953. BA, U. Minn., 1949, MS, 1951; PhD, U. Calif., Davis, 1956. Asst. prof. botany La. State U., Baton Rouge, 1967-71, assoc. prof., 1971-76, prof., 1976-82, Boyd prof., 1982-95, prof. emerita, 1995—; adj. prof. dept. biology U. Calif., Santa Barbara, 1995—. Co-editor: Aspects of Floral Development, 1988, Advances in Legume Systematics, Vol. 6, 1994; contbr. numerous articles on plant devel. to profl. jours. Fellow Linnean Soc., London, 1975—; Fulbright fellow Eng., 1952-53. Mem. Bot. Soc. Am. (v.p. 1979, program chmn. 1975-78, pres.-elect 1986-87, pres. 1987-88, Merit award 1989), Am. Bryological and Lichenological Soc., Brit. Lichenological Soc., Am. Inst. Biol. Scis., Am. Soc. Plant Taxonomists (pres.-elect 1994-95, pres. 1995-96), Phi Beta Kappa, Sigma Xi. Home: 3987 Primavera Rd Santa Barbara CA 93110-1467 Office: Univ Calif Dept Biology EEMB U Calif Santa Barbara CA 93106

TUCKER, STANLEY R., headmaster. Headmaster Girls Prep. Sch., Chattanooga. Office: Girls Prep Sch 200 Barton Ave PO Box 4736 Chattanooga TN 37405*

TUCKER, STEFAN FRANKLIN, lawyer; b. Detroit, Dec. 31, 1938. Assoc. in Bus., Flint Jr. Community Coll., 1958; BBA, U. Mich., 1960, JD, 1963. Bar: U.S. Dist. Ct. D.C. 1964, U.S. Ct. Appeals (D.C. cir.) 1964, U.S. Ct. Claims 1964, U.S. Tax Ct. 1964. Clk. to judge U.S. Tax Ct., Washington, 1963-64; assoc. Arent, Fox, Kintner, Plotkin & Kahn, Washington, 1964-69, ptnr., 1970-74; ptnr. Tucker, Flyer & Lewis, Washington, 1975—; profl. lectr. law George Washignton U. Nat. Law Ctr., 1970—; adj. prof. law Georgetown U. Law Ctr., 1990—; adj. profl. lectr. law U. Miami Law Ctr., 1975-78; mem. adv. com. Ann. Inst. Estate Planning, U. Miami, 1978-91; trustee Mass. Sch. Law, Andover, 1989—, mhg. bd. trustees, 1989-95; mem. visitors com. U. Mich. Law Sch., 1989—. Author: Tax Planning for Real Estate Transactions, 1989; mem. editl. bd. Taxation for Lawyers, 1972—; mem. adv. bd. Bur. Nat. Affairs Housing and Devel. Reporter, 1973-76, Mertens on Federal Income Taxation, 1985—, The Tax Times, 1986-87; mem. editl. adv. bd. Jour. Real Estate Taxation, 1975—, Practical Real Estate Lawyer, 1984—. Mem. nat. com. U. Mich. Law Sch. Fund, 1972-78. Mem. ABA (tax sect., chmn. real estate tax problems com. 1977-79, chmn. continuing legal edn. com. 1984-86, coun. mem. 1987-91, vice chmn. com. ops. 1991-93, chairperson-elect 1997—), FBA, D.C. Bar Assn. (taxation divsn., mem. steering com. 1980-82), Nat. Trust Hist. Preservation (mem. com. on legal svcs. 1978-85). Office: 1615 L St NW Ste 400 Washington DC 20036-5619 *I believe that each person has an obligation to share with others,* *whether through teaching, lecturing or writing, the knowledge and experience gained through his life's work. Such sharing provides a greater reward than monetary gain can ever provide.*

TUCKER, STEPHEN LAWRENCE, health administration educator, consultant; b. Cin., Oct. 18, 1940; s. Lawrence Henry and Blanche Virginia (Greenwood) T.; m. Lucille Frances Dinda, June 15, 1968; children: Gregory Lawrence, David John. BA, Dartmouth Coll., 1962; MBA, Xavier U., Cin., 1966; D Bus. Adminstrn., George Washington U., 1970. Adminstrv. asst. Presbyn.-U. Pa. Med. Ctr., Phila., 1966-67; assoc. adminstr. Harrisburg (Pa.) Hosp., 1970-73; assoc. prof. Xavier U., 1973-76; dept. chmn. Trinity U., San Antonio, 1976-81, prof. healthcare adminstrn., 1981-87, 94—, dean, 1987-94; cons. on healthcare adminstrn., San Antonio, 1976—. Co-author: Analysis Manual for Hospital Information Systems, 1980; contbr. articles to profl. jours., chpts. to books. Bd. dirs. Bexar County Mental Health and Mental Retardation Ctr., San Antonio, 1979-85; bd. dirs., chmn. S.W. Neuropsychiat. Inst., San Antonio, 1986-92. 1st lt. U.S. Army, 1962-64. Recipient Disting. Alumni Svc. award Xavier U., 1984; fellow Accrediting Commn. Grad. Edn. in Hosp. Adminstrn., 1974, WHO, Eng., 1975. Fellow Am. Coll. Healthcare Execs. (various coms. 1966—); mem. Soc. for Healthcare Planning and Mktg. (bd. dirs. 1983-86). Home: 347 Tophill Rd San Antonio OH 78209 Office: Trinity U Dept of Hlth Adm 715 Stadium Dr San Antonio TX 78212-3104

TUCKER, TANYA DENISE, singer; b. Seminole, Tex., Oct. 10, 1958; d. Beau and Juanita Tucker; children: Presley, Beau Grayson. Regular on Lew King Show; rec. artist formerly with Columbia Records, MCA Records, Capital Records; albums include Tear Me Apart, Chagnes, Delta Dawn, Dreamlovers, Here's Some Love, TNT, Girls Like Me, Greatest Hits, 1989, Greatest Hits (1972-75), Greatest Hits Encore, 1990, Greatest Country Hits, 1991, Greatest Hits 1990-92, 1993, Love Me Like You Use To, 1987, Strong Enough to Bend, 1988, Tanya Tucker Live, Tennesee Woman, 1990, What Do I Do With Me, 1991, (with Delbert McClinton) Can't Run From Youself, 1992, Soon, 1993, Fire to Fire, 1994, (with T. Graham Brown, Delbert McClinton) Tanya, 1995; TV appearances include A Country Christmas, 1979, The Georgia Peaches, 1980; actress: (mini-series) The Rebels, 1979, (film) Jeremiah Johnson, 1968. Recipient: Country Music Assn. award, 1991, female vocalist of the year; 2 Grammy nominations, 1994. Office: Tanya Tucker Inc 5200 Maryland Way Ste 202 Brentwood TN 37027-5018 also: Capitol 3322 West End Ave Nashville TN 37203*

TUCKER, THOMAS JAMES, investment manager; b. Atlanta, Sept. 5, 1929; s. Thomas Tudor and Carol (Govan) T.; m. Margaret Guerard. B.A., U. of the South, 1952. With CIT Corp, N.Y.C., 1957-72; pres., chief exec. officer AmSouth Fin. Corp., Birmingham, Ala., 1972-82; chmn. bd. Am-South Fin. Corp., 1982, also dir., 1972-93; exec. v.p. AmSouth Bank N.A., Birmingham, 1982-93, chief credit officer, 1992; ret. Tucker Investments, Birmingham, 1993, prin., 1994—; exec. v.p. AmSouth Bankcorp, Birmingham, 1982-93; bd. dirs. Alabanc Properties Corp., Birmingham, chmn., 1991-93; bd. dirs. Birmingham Broadway Series Inc., treas., 1996—. Contbr. articles on credit and leasing to trade jours.; photographer gen. interest mags., 1970—. Bd. dirs. Birmingham Community Devel. Corp.; chmn. bd., 1990-93. 1st lt. USAF, 1952-56. Mem. Vulcan Trail Assn., Birmingham Art Mus. Assn., Birmingham Canoe Club (bd. dirs. 1990—), Photography Guild, Shades Valley Camera Club, Cahaba River Soc. (adv. bd. 1991-92, bd. dirs. 1993, v.p. orgnl. devel. 1995—), Ala. Growth Strategies Task Force, Regional Open Space and Trails Alliance, The Club, Jefferson Club, Summit Club. Episcopalian. Avocations: photography, high altitude hiking, white water canoeing. Home and Office: Tucker Investments 4132 Old Leeds Rd Birmingham AL 35213-3210

TUCKER, THOMAS RANDALL, public relations executive; b. Indpls., Aug. 6, 1931; s. Ovie Allen and Oris Aleen (Robertson) T.; A.B., Franklin Coll., 1953; m. Evelyn Marie Armuth, Aug. 9, 1953; children—Grant, Roger, Richard. Grad. asst. U. Minn., 1953-54; dir. admissions, registrar Franklin Coll., 1954-57; with Cummins Engine Co., Inc., Columbus, Ind., 1957; dir. pub. relations, 1968-88; pub. rels. cons. Mem. Bd. Sch. Trustees Bartholomew County, Ind., 1966-72, pres., 1968-69; mem. Ind. State Bd. Edn., 1977-89; treas. Bartholomew County Rep. Cen. Com., 1960-80; mem. Columbus Visitors Ctr.; chmn. Columbus 2000; hon. trustee, Franklin Coll. Mem. Pub. Relations Soc. Am., Columbus (Ind.) C. of C. (Community Service award 1986), Rotary, Kappa Tau Alpha, Phi Delta Theta, Sigma Delta Chi. Lutheran. Home: 4380 N Riverside Dr Columbus IN 47203-1123 Office: PO Box 3005 Columbus IN 47202-3005

TUCKER, THOMAS WILLIAM, mathematics professor; b. Princeton, N.J., July 15, 1945; s. Albert William Tucker and Alice Judson (Curtiss) Beckenbach; m. Mollie Dalton; children: Thomas John, Emily McDonnell. AB magna cum laude, Harvard U., 1967; PhD, Dartmouth Coll., 1971. Instr. Princeton U., 1971-73; from asst. prof. to prof. math. Colgate U., Hamilton, N.Y., 1973-83, prof., 1983—, Charles G. Hetherington prof. math., 1994—, chmn. math. dept., 1982-86, acting dean coll., 1991-92, dir. divsn. nat. sci., 1993—; vis. assoc. prof. Dartmouth Coll., Hanover, N.H., 1978-79; cons. Ednl. Testing Svc., 1973—, Inst. for Def. Analyses, Princeton, (summers) 1974, 75, 78, 79, 84, 85; chmn. advanced placement calculus com. Coll. Bd., N.Y.C., 1983-87. Co-author: Topological Graph Theory, 1987; editor: Priming the Calculus Pump, 1990; contbr. numerous articles to profl. jours. NSF grantee, 1976-77, 80-82, 86-88, 89, 90—. Mem. Math. Assn. Am. (mem., chmn. many coms., v.p. 1990-92), Am. Math. Soc. Home: 21 Hamilton St Hamilton NY 13346-1329 Office: Colgate U Dept Math Hamilton NY 13346

TUCKER, WATSON BILLOPP, lawyer; b. Dobbs Ferry, N.Y., Nov. 16, 1940; s. Watson Billopp and Mary (Prema) T.; m. Ann Bryant Cramer, June 19, 1981; children: Robin, Craig, Christopher, Alexander, John. BS, Northwestern U., Evanston, Ill., 1962; JD, Northwestern U., 1965. Bar: Ill. 1965, U.S. Dist. Ct. (no. dist.) Ill. 1966, U.S. Supreme Ct. 1971, U.S. Dist. Ct. (no. dist.) N.Y. 1976, U.S. Ct. Appeals (7th cir.) 1970, U.S. Ct. Appeals (2d cir.) 1976, U.S. Ct. Appeals (3d cir.) 1981. Ptnr. Mayer, Brown & Platt, Chgo., 1965—. Fellow Am. Coll. Trial Lawyers. Office: Mayer Brown & Platt 190 S La Salle St Chicago IL 60603-3410

TUCKER, WILLIAM EDWARD, academic administrator, minister; b. Charlotte, N.C., June 22, 1932; s. Cecil Edward and Ethel Elizabeth (Godley) T.; m. Ruby Jean Jones, Apr. 8, 1955; children: Janet Sue, William Edward, Gordon Vance. BA, Barton Coll., Wilson, N.C., 1953, LLD (hon.), 1978; BD, Tex. Christian U., 1956; MA, Yale U., 1958, PhD, 1960; LHD (hon.), Chapman Coll., 1981; DH (hon.), Bethany Coll., 1982; DD (hon.), Austin Coll., 1985; LHD (hon.), Kentucky Wesleyan Coll., 1989. Ordained to ministry Disciples of Christ Ch., 1956; prof. Barton Coll., 1959-66, chmn. dept. religion and philosophy, 1961-66; mem. faculty Brite Div. Sch., Tex. Christian U., 1966-76, prof. ch. history, 1969-76, dean, 1971-76, chancellor, 1979—; pres. Bethany (W.Va.) Coll., 1976-79; dir. Justin Industries, Inc., Tandy Corp., Brown and Lupton Found.; mem. gen. bd. Christian Ch. (Disciples of Christ), 1971-74, 75-87, adminstrv. com., 1975-81, chmn. theol. edn. commn., 1972-73, mem. exec. com., chmn. bd. higher edn., 1975-77; dir. Christian Ch. Found., 1980-83; moderator Christian Ch. (Disciples of Christ), 1983-85. Author: J.H. Garrison and Disciples of Christ, 1964, (with others) Journey in Faith: A History of the Christian Church (Disciples of Christ), 1975; also articles. Bd. dirs. Ft. Worth Symphony Orch. Assn., 1980—, Van Cliburn Internat. Piano Competition, 1981—. Mem. Newcomen Soc. N.Am. Coll. Football Assn. (chmn. bd. 1993-96), Exch. Club, Phi Beta Kappa. Home: 2900 Simondale Dr Fort Worth TX 76109-1250 Office: Tex Christian U Office of Chancellor Fort Worth TX 76129

TUCKER, WILLIAM P., lawyer, writer; b. Kingston, N.Y., Jan. 26, 1932; s. Philip and Mary (McGowan) T.; m. Dolores F. Beaudoin, June 10, 1961; children: Andrew M., Thomas B., Mary A. BA with honors, Hunter Coll., 1958; JD with honors, St. John's U., 1962. Bar: N.Y. 1962, U.S. Dist. Ct. (ea. dist.) N.Y. 1962, Fla. 1980. Assoc. Mendes & Mount, N.Y.C., 1962-63; ptnr. Cullen and Dykman, Bklyn. and Garden City, N.Y., 1963—; gen. counsel Broadway Nat. Bank, Roosevelt Savs. Bank, Olympian Bank, GreenPoint Bank, Ridgewood Savs. Bank, Atlantic Liberty Savs., F.A., Bethpage Fed. Credit Union, Mcpl. Credit Union, Episcopal Health Svcs., Inc., St. John's Episcopal Hosp., Smithtown, St. John's Home for the Aged and Blind, St. John's Episcopal Nursing Home, Wartburg Luth. Svcs., Luth. Ctr. for the Aging, Martin Luther Ter. Apartments, Inc., Interfaith Med. Ctr.; spl. counsel OCI Mortgage Corp., Wilshire Mortgage Corp., C-BASS Mortgage Corp., Bklyn. C. of C., Downtown Bklyn. Bus. Assn., Bank of N.Y., Chase Manhattan Bank, Fleet Bank, Kraft Credit Union, Apple Bank for Savs., Barclays Bank of N.Y. Mem. Selective Svc. Bd.; past pres. St. Vincent Ferrer Home Sch. Assn.; del. Diocesan Union Holy Name Socs.; mem. coun. St. Johns's U.; mem. coun. of regents St. Francis Coll., Bklyn.; bd. dirs. Faith Home Found. Mem. N.Y. State Bar Assn., Fla. Bar Assn., Savs. Banks Lawyers Assn. Bklyn., N.Y. Land Title Assn., Suffolk County Bar Assn., Savs. Bank Assn. N.Y. State (law com.), Bklyn. Mcpl. Club, Knight of Malta. Avocations: co-owner Salem Keizer Volcanoes N.W. League baseball team. Home: 23 Bunker Hill Dr Huntington NY 11743-5705 Office: Cullen and Dykman 100 Quentin Roosevelt Blvd Garden City NY 11530-4843 Office: One Gateway Ctr Newark NJ 07102 also: 177 Montague St Brooklyn NY 11201-3633

TUCKER, WILLIAM THOMAS, III, computer software company executive; b. Milw., June 26, 1942; s. William Thomas and Shirley Audrey (Holmes) T.; m. Barbara Ann Granof, Sept. 8, 1965 (dec. Sept. 1982); children: Pamela Ann, Penelope Lynn, Matthew Louis. BS cum laude, U. Wis., 1969. Lic. real estate broker, Wis. Dir. pub. rels. Jr. Achievement S.E. Wis., Milw., 1969-71; exec. dir. Jr. Achievement Fox Valley, Appleton, Wis., 1971-74; mktg. dir. Southridge Mall, Milw., 1974-81; asst. mall mgr. Southridge and Northridge Malls, Milw., 1981-83; pres. Buyer Publs., Inc., San Diego, 1983-86; mall mgr. Mayfair Mall, Milw., 1987-89; pres. CompSys Inc., Milw., 1989—; cons. House Trader mag. Home Buyer Inc., San Diego, 1986—; instr. Waukesha County Tech. Coll. Design engr. computer software Home Search System, 1989. Dep. state dir. Naval Acad. Info. Program, Milw., 1981—; mem. nominating com. Sanator Kasten Acad., Milw., 1990-93, Congressman Kleczka Acad., Milw., 1990-93, Senator Kohn Acad., Milw., 1991—; mem. Naval Recruiting Dist. Coun., 1977—. Capt. USNR. Lutheran. Avocations: desktop publishing, genealogy, history, psychology, salesmanship. Home: 6065 Doyle St Greendale WI 53129-2215 Office: ML-Asst Inc 6065 Doyle St Greendale WI 53129-2215

TUCKER, WILLIAM VINCENT, vocational evaluator, former college president; b. Beatrice, Nebr., May 23, 1934; s. Casimir Augustine and Mary Margaret (Carmichael) T.; m. Marian Elizabeth Cooper, Aug. 9, 1958; children: Catherine, Jean, Rose Marie, Alan. B.A., Benedictine Coll., 1955; M.S., Emporia State U., 1963; Ed.D., U. S.D., 1968. Tchr. Kelly (Kans.) High Sch., 1958-61; grad. asst. Emporia State U., 1960-61, instr., 1961-63; instr. Briar Cliff Coll., 1963-65, asst. prof. ednl. psychology, assoc. prof., 1968-70, prof., 1970-71, acad. v.p., 1967-71; pres., prof. St. Mary of the Plains Coll., 1971-75; pres. Mt. Marty Coll., 1975-83; sr. devel. rep. State of S.D., 1983-84; pres. Greater Huron Devel. Corp., 1984-87; owner Career Devel., Inc., 1987—; cons. Social Security Adminstrn., 1962—; vocat. evaluator Goodwill Rehab., 1992—. Contbr. articles on ednl. rehab., placement of physically handicapped to profl. jours. Trustee Dodge City Area Hosp. Assn., Kans.; chmn. bd. Colls. of Mid Am.; pres. S.D. Found. Private Colls. Served with U.S. Army, 1955-57. Mem. Am. Econ. Devel. Council, Yankton C. of C. (dir.), Phi Delta Kappa. Roman Catholic. Clubs: Elks, Rotary. Home: 2605 W 37th St Sioux Falls SD 57105-5201

TUCKMAN, BRUCE WAYNE, educational psychologist, educator, researcher; b. N.Y.C., Nov. 24, 1938; s. Jack Stanley and Sophie Sylvia (Goldberg) T.; children: Blair Z., Bret A. BS, Rensselaer Poly. Inst., 1960; MA, Princeton U., 1962, PhD, 1963. Rsch. assoc. Princeton (N.J.) U., 1963; rsch. psychologist Naval Med. Rsch. Inst., Bethesda, Md., 1963-65; assoc. prof. edn. Rutgers U., New Brunswick, N.J., 1965-78; dir. Bur. Research and Devel.-Rutgers U., New Brunswick, 1975-78; dean Coll. Edn. Baruch Coll., CUNY, 1978-82; sr. rsch. fellow CUNY, 1982-83; dean Coll. Edn. Fla. State U., Tallahassee, 1983-85, prof., 1985—. Author: Preparing to Teach the Disadvantaged, 1969 (N.J. Assn. Tchrs. of English Author's award 1969), Conducting Educational Research, 1972, 4th rev. edit., 1994 (Phi Delta Kappa Rsch. award 1973), Evaluating Instructional Programs, 1979, 2d rev. edit., 1985, Analyzing and Designing Educational Research, 1979, Effective College Management, 1987, Testing for Teachers, 1988; (novel) Long Road to Boston, 1988, Educational Psychology: From Theory to Application, 1992. Rsch. dir. Task Force on Competency Standards, Trenton, N.J., 1976. N.Y. State Regents scholar, 1956; Kappa Nu grad. scholar, 1960; NIMH predoctoral fellow, 1961, 62; Rutgers U. faculty study fellow, 1974-75;. Fellow APA, Am. Psychol. Soc.; mem. Am. Ednl. Rsch. Assn., Phi Delta Kappa. Office: Fla State Univ Dept Edn Rsch 307 Stone House Rd Tallahassee FL 32301-3355

TUCKMAN, HOWARD PAUL, economics educator, consultant; b. Bklyn., Dec. 23, 1941; s. Louis A. and Beatrice (Eisen) T.; m. Barbara Hauben, Dec. 25, 1966; children: Alec, Andrew. B.S., Cornell U., 1963; M.A., U. Wis., 1967, Ph.D., 1970. Analyst U.S. Bur. Budget, Washington, 1963-65; research assoc. Tech. U., Lyngby, Denmark, 1967-68; asst. prof. econs. Fla. State U., 1970-73, assoc. prof., 1973-78, prof., 1978-79, disting. prof. econs., 1979—, dir. ctr. econ. edn., 1986-87; interim dean Fogelman Coll. Bus. and Econs., Memphis State U., 1992—; dir. Ctr. for Study of Edn. and Tax Policy, 1976-79; Brookings policy fellow Office of Sec. HEW, Washington, 1979—; v.p. Human Resources Policy Corp., Los Angeles, 1980—; mem.oversight bd. John P. Minter & Assocs., Denver, 1981-85; bd. dirs. Brooks Photo Circle. Author: The Demand for Higher Education, 1972, Part Time Faculty Personnel Management Policies, 1986, Educational Technology Developing Countries, 1987, On Time To the Doctorate, 1990, Publication, Teaching and The Reward Structure in Academe, 1976; contbr. numerous articles to profl. jours.; editor: Subsidies to Higher Education, 1981. Bd. dirs. Charter Lakesid; trustee Levi Hosp. Ford Found. fellow, 1968-70; grantee Joint Council on Econ. Edn., 1973-74, AID, 1977, AAUP, 1977-80; NSF grantee, 1977-81; NEH grantee, 1982-83, NIMH grantee, 1989-92. Mem. Eastern Econ. Assn. (exec. bd. 1976—, v.p. 1979-80), Am. Econ. Assn., Am. Assn. Higher Edn., Nat. Assn. Bus. Economists, So. Econ. Assn., Leadership Memphis. Office: Memphis State U Coll Bus Memphis TN 38152

TUCK-RICHMOND, DOLETTA SUE, prosecutor; b. Hugo, Okla., June 18, 1966; d. Benny Doyle and Tommie Marie (Cousins) T.; m. Lyle Richmond, Sept. 30, 1995. AS, Murray State Coll., Tishomingo, Okla., 1986; BS magna cum laude, S.E. Okla. State U., 1988; JD with highest honors, U. Okla., 1991. Bar: Okla. 1991, U.S. Dist. Ct. (we., ea., and no. dists.), U.S. Ct. Appeals (10th cir.). Summer assoc. Andrews Davis, Oklahoma City, 1989-90; instr. in legal rsch, writing and oral advocacy U. Okla., Norman, 1989-91; assoc. Crowe & Dunlevy, Oklahoma City, 1991-93, Tulsa, Okla., 1993-94; pvt. practice Antlers, Okla., 1994; exempt orgn. specialist IRS, Oklahoma City, Okla., 1994-95; asst. atty. gen. State of Okla., Oklahoma City, 1995—; with U.S. Atty's. Office (we. dist.) Okla. Contbg. author, editor: Oklahoma Environmental Law Practitioner's Handbook, 1992. Firm com. mem., participant Harvest Food Dr., Oklahoma City, 1991; chairperson Okla. Young Lawyers Rape Victims Assistance Com., 1992-94; bd. dirs. Okla. County Young Lawyers Divsn., 1993; participant, vol. Legal Aide of Western Okla., 1991. Named Miss Murray State Coll., Student Senate Pres., Tishomingo, Okla., 1986-86, Order of Coif U. Okla., Norman, Okla., 1991, Okla. Law Review U. Okla., Norman, 1991. Mem. Fed. Bar Assn., Okla. Bar Assn. (bd. dirs., young lawyers divsn. 1993-95, mock trial com. 1994-95, liaison mental health com. 1994-95), Am. Agrl. Law Assn., Phi Delta Phi, Phi Kappa Phi (Spl. Act award for U.S. Atty. 1996). Democrat. Baptist. Avocations: tennis, reading, writing, knitting, sports events. Home: 1624 SW 128th Pl Oklahoma City OK 73170 Office: US Atty's Office Western Dist of Okla 210 Park Ave Ste 400 Oklahoma City OK 73102-5602

TUCKSON, REED V., university president. Pres. Charles R. Drew U., L.A. Office: Charles R Drew U Office of President 1730 E 118th St Los Angeles CA 90059-2518*

TUCKWELL, BARRY EMMANUEL, musician, music educator; b. Melbourne, Australia, Mar. 5, 1931; s. Charles Robert and Elizabeth (Hill) T.; children: David Michael, Jane Madeleine, Thomas James; m. Susan Levitan, June 21, 1992. Grad., Sydney (Australia) State Conservatorium; DMus (hon.), Sydney U., Australia, 1994. Prof. French horn Royal Acad. Music, 1962-74; mem. mgmt. com. London Symphony Orch. Trust, 1963-68; mem. faculty congregation arts Dartmouth Coll., 1968-69; guest prof. Harvard U., Yale U., others. With Melbourne, Sydney, Halle, Scottish Nat. and Bournemouth symphony orchs., 1947-55; solo French horn, London Symphony Orch., 1955-68; tchr., soloist and chamber music player, 1968—, mem. Chamber Music Soc. of Lincoln Ctr., N.Y.C., 1974-81, dir. London Symphony Orch. Ltd., 1957-68, chmn., 1961-68, mem. Tuckwell Wind Ensemble, Tuckwell Wind Quintet, Tuckwell Horn Quartet, chief condr. Tasmanian Symphony Orch., 1980, condr., music dir. Md. Symphony Orch., 1982—, rec. artist for RCA, CRI, Angel, London, Argo.; author: Playing the Horn, 1978, The Horn, 1983; editor: Horn Lit. for G. Schirmer, Inc; leader ann. French horn workshop, Fla. State U., Claremont Music Festival, 1970-71. Decorated Order Brit. Empire; companion Order of Australia; recipient Harriet Cohen Meml. medal for soloists, 1968. Fellow Royal Coll. Music, Royal Soc. arts; mem. Internat. Horn Soc. (hon., pres. 1969-77, 92-94), Royal Acad. Music (hon.), Guildhall Sch. Music (hon.). Address: 13140 Fountain Head Rd Hagerstown MD 21742-2839 Office: Maryland Sym Orch 13 S Potomac St Hagerstown MD 21740-5512*

TUDOR, JIM PATRICK, law enforcement officer, photographer; b. Ft. Smith, Ark., Nov. 20, 1946; s. W.A. and Geraldine (Batchelor) T.; m. Darlena Michelle Davis; children: Scott Patrick, James David Panetti. Student, U. Ark., Fayetteville, 1964-68. Lic. pvt. investigator, 1997. Dir. comm. Ark. State Police, Little Rock, 1966-71, spl. asst. to dir., 1976-78, asst. comdr. records, 1978-80, comdr. records, 1980—; spl. asst. to dir. Ark. Crime Info. Ctr., Little Rock, 1971-76; owner Thru the Lens, Little Rock, 1982-94, Dynamic Publs., Bryant, Ark.; designer Ark. State Police Automated Fingerprint Identification System, 1994—, Mobile Data Workstation Network, 1997; user exec. bd. Printrak Internat. Inc., 1997. Author: Research Methods, History of Arkansas State Police; contbr. numerous articles and photographs to mags. Chief staff Gov.'s Nat. Resources Bd., Little Rock, 1977; mem. Gov.'s Commn. on Sci. and Tech., 1978-80; mem. Water Safety Adv. Com., Little Rock, 1982-83. Fellow British Fingerprint Soc.; mem. Profl. Photographers Am., Internat. Fire Photographers Assn., Ark. Law Enforcement Assn., Internat. Assn. for Identification (bd. dirs. Ark. divsn. 1997), Exch. Club (Police Officer of Yr. 1971). Avocations: writing, photography, metal detecting, recreational gold/gem mining. Home: PO Box 329 Bryant AR 72089-0329 Office: Ark State Police 1 State Police Plz Little Rock AR 72209-4822 also: Dynamic Publs PO Box 329 Bryant AR 72039-0329

TUDRYN, JOYCE MARIE, professional society administrator; b. Holyoke, Mass., July 27, 1959; d. Edward William and Frances Katherine (Bajor) T.; m. William Wallace Friberger III, Sept. 18, 1982; 1 child, Kristen. BS in Comm., Syracuse U., 1981. Asst. editor Nat. Assn. Broadcasters, Washington, 1981-83; dir. programs Internat. Radio and TV Soc. Found., N.Y.C., 1983-87; assoc. exec. dir. Internat. Radio and TV Soc., N.Y.C., 1988-94, exec. dir., 1994-97, pres., 1997—; spkr. in field; nat. adv. bd. Alpha Epsilon Rho Broadcasting Soc., 1988-91, 93-94, hon. trustee, 1994—; v.p. Corp. for Ednl. Radio and TV, 1988-94. Editor-in-chief IRTS News, 1983—; columnist TV Facts, Figures and Film mag., 1983-88. Recipient Mass. Kodak Photography award, 1977; S.I. Newhouse scholar Syracuse U., 1980-81. Mem. N.Y. Media Roundtable, Gamma Phi Beta. Avocations: photography. Home: 602 Bennington Dr Union NJ 07083-9104 Office: Internat Radio and TV Soc Found Ste 1714 420 Lexington Ave Rm 1714 New York NY 10170-1799

TUELL, JACK MARVIN, retired bishop; b. Tacoma, Nov. 14, 1923; s. Frank Harry and Anne Helen (Bertelson) T.; m. Marjorie Ida Beadles, June 17, 1946; children—Jacqueline, Cynthia, James. B.S., U. Wash., 1947, LL.B., 1948; S.T.B., Boston U., 1955; M.A., U. Puget Sound, 1961, DHS, 1990; D.D., Pacific Sch. Religion, 1966; LLD, Alaska Pacific U., 1980. Bar: Wash. 1948; ordained to ministry Meth. Ch., 1955. Practice law with firm Holte & Tuell, Edmonds, Wash., 1948-50; pastor Grace Meth. Ch., Everett, Wash., 1950-52, South Tewksbury Meth. Ch., Tewksbury, Mass., 1952-55, Lakewood Meth. Ch., Tacoma, 1955-61; dist. supt. Puget Sound dist. Meth. Ch., Everett, 1961-67; pastor 1st United Meth. Ch., Vancouver, Wash., 1967-72; bishop United Meth. Ch., Portland, Oreg., 1972-80, Calif.-Pacific Conf., United Meth. Ch., L.A., 1980-92; interim sr. pastor First United Meth. Ch., Boise, Idaho, 1995; Mem. gen. conf. United Meth. Ch., 1964, 66, 68, 70, 72; pres. coun. of Bishops United Meth. Ch., 1989-90. Author: The Organization of the United Methodist Church, 1970, 7th edit. 1993. Pres. Tacoma U.S.O., 1959-61, Vancouver YMCA, 1968; v.p. Ft. Vancouver Seamens Cnt., 1969-72; vice chmn. Vancouver Human Rels. Commn., 1970-72; pres. Oreg. Coun. Alcohol Problems, 1972-76; trustee U. Puget Sound, 1961-73, Vancouver Meml. Hosp., 1967-72, Alaska Meth. U., Anchorage, 1972-80, Willamette U., Salem, Oreg., 1972-80, Willamette View Manor, Portland, 1972-80, Rogue Valley Manor, Medford, Oreg., 1972-76, Sch. Theology at Claremont, Calif., 1980-92, Methodist Hosp., Arcadia, Calif., 1983-92; pres. nat. div. bd. global ministries United Meth. Ch., 1972-76, pres. ecumenical and interreligious concerns div., 1976-80, Commn. on Christian Unity and intereligious concerns, 1980-84, Gen. Bd. of Pensions,1984-92, Calif. Coun. Alcohol Problems, 1985-88. Jacob Sleeper fellow, 1955. Mem. Lions. Home and Office: 2697 S North Bluff Rd Greenbank WA 98253-9713

TUFARO, RICHARD CHASE, lawyer; b. N.Y.C., July 9, 1944; s. Frank P. and Stephania A. (Maida) T.; m. Helen M. Tufaro, June 25, 1977; children: Mary C., Edward F., Paul R., Cynthia M. AB magna cum laude, Dartmouth Coll., 1965; LLB cum laude, Harvard U., 1968. Bar: N.Y. 1969, D.C. 1992, Md. 1994; U.S. Dist. Ct. (so. dist.) N.Y. 1973, U.S. Dist. Ct. (ea. dist.) N.Y. 1978, U.S. Dist Ct. (D.C. dist.), 1994; U.S. Dist. Ct. (Md. dist.), 1996, U.S. Ct. Apls. (2d cir.) 1973, (5th cir.) 1976, (9th cir.) 1979, (6th cir.) 1980, (4th cir.), 1995; U.S. Ct. Claims, 1985, U.S. Ct. Appeals (3d cir.) 1990, U.S. Ct. Appeals (D.C. cir.) 1992; U.S. Sup. Ct., 1975. Law clk. Appellate-Div. N.Y. State, N.Y.C., 1970-71, assoc. Milbank, Tweed, Hadley & McCloy, N.Y.C., 1971-72, adminstrv. asst. White House Domestic Coun., Washington, 1972-73, assoc. Milbank, Tweed, Hadley & McCloy, N.Y.C., 1973-77, ptnr. 1978—. Served to capt. U.S. Army, 1968-70. Decorated Bronze Star with oak leaf cluster. Mem. ABA, Am. Mgmt. Assn., Phi Beta Kappa. Home: 7109 Heathwood Ct Bethesda MD 20817-2915 Office: 1825 I St NW Ste 1100 Washington DC 20006-5417

TUFT, MARY ANN, executive search firm executive; b. Easton, Pa., Oct. 11, 1934; d. Ben and Elizabeth (Reibman) T. BS, West Chester (Pa.) State Coll., 1956; MA, Lehigh U., 1960. Cert. assn. exec. Nat. trainer Girl Scouts U.S.A., N.Y.C., 1965-68; cons. Nat. League for Nursing, N.Y.C., 1968-69; exec. dir. Nat. Student Nurses Assn., N.Y.C., 1970-85; mem. Commn. on Dietetic Registration, Am. Dietetic Assn., 1981-85; pres. Specialized Cons. Ltd., 1983-85; exec. dir. Radiol. Soc. N.Am., Oak Brook, Ill., 1985-88; pres. Tuft & Assocs., Inc., 1989—. Bd. dirs. Nurses House, Inc., 1981-85; bd. dirs. Chgo. Sinai Cong., 1987-91, v.p., 1988. Mary Ann Tuft Scholarship Fund named in her honor Found. Nat. Student Nurses Assn.; Kepner-Tregoe scholar, 1966. Mem. ALA (pub. mem. com. on accreditation 1993-95), Am. Soc. AAssn. Execs. (bd. dirs. 1980-83, trustee for cert. 1980-83, vice chmn. 1983-84), N.Y. Soc. Assn. Execs. (pres. 1978-79, bd. dirs. 1975-78, 1st Outstanding Exec. award 1982), Continuing Care Accreditation Assn. (bd. dirs. 1983-85), Specialized Cons. in Nursing (faculty).

TUFTE, EDWARD ROLF, statistics educator, publisher; b. Kansas City, Mo., Mar. 14, 1942; s. Edward E. and Virginia (James) T.; m. Inge Druckrey. BS, Stanford U., 1963, MS, 1964; PhD, Yale U., 1968; HHD (hon.), Cooper Union, 1992, Conn. Coll., 1995. Asst. prof. pub. policy Princeton U., 1967-71, assoc. prof., 1971-74, prof., 1974-77; prof. polit. sci., stats., computer sci. and graphic design Yale U., New Haven, 1977—; pres. Graphics Press, Cheshire, 1983—; cons. in field; mem. com. on nat. stats. NRC, 1979-84. Author: Quantitative Analysis of Social Problems, 1970, Size and Democracy, 1973, Data Analysis, 1974, Political Control of the Economy, 1978 (Kammerer award 1979, Citation Classic 1989), The Visual Display of Quantitative Information, 1983 (Citation Classic 1992), Envisioning Information, 1990. Pres. Cheshire Neighborhood Assn., 1984-87. Recipient Best Graphic Design award Internat. Design, 1990, Wittenborn award, 1991, Best Book Design award Assn. Ind. Publs., Computer Press Assn. award, 1991, Sci. award Phi Beta Kappa, 1991; Ctr. for Advanced Study in Behavioral Scis. fellow, 1973-74; Guggenheim fellow, 1977. Fellow Am. Acad. Arts and Scis., Am. Statis. Assn. Office: Yale U PO Box 208301 New Haven CT 06520-8301

TUFTE, OBERT NORMAN, retired research executive; b. Northfield, Minn., May 30, 1932; s. Ole Nels and Stella Josephine (Lundene) T.; m. Doris Helen Wisbroecker, Dec. 29, 1956; children: Keith, Brian, Stephen, Jon. BA in Physics, St. Olaf Coll., 1954; PhD in Physics, Northwestern U. 1960. Rsch. scientist Honeywell Inc., Hopkins, Minn., 1960-69; rsch. mgr. Honeywell Inc., Bloomington, Minn., 1969-84; rsch. fellow Honeywell Inc., Bloomington, 1984-87, chief scientist, 1987-93; ret., 1994, pvt. cons. in field, 1994—. Contbr. articles to profl. jours., 1960-88; inventor 7 U.S. patents, 1962-89. Mem. IEEE (sr.), Am. Phys. Soc., Sigma Xi. Home: 14937 Manitou Rd NE Prior Lake MN 55372-1114

TUFTS, DONALD WINSTON, electrical engineering educator; b. Yonkers, N.Y., Mar. 5, 1933; s. Fletcher Gorham Tufts and Myrtle (Ayers) Gordon; m. Barbara Michelsen, Mar. 24, 1956; children: Cynthia Tufts Anderson, David Jost, John Lawrence. MS; Diploma, The Hotchkiss Sch., Lakeville, Conn., 1951; BA, Williams Coll., 1955; BS, MS, MIT, 1957, DSc, 1960. Engr. Sanders Assocs., Nashua, N.H., summer 1960; cons. Sanders Assocs., Nashua, 1960—; asst. prof. applied math. Harvard U., Cambridge, Mass., 1960-67; prof. elec. engring. and computer sci. U. R.I., 1967—; cons. NASA, AT&T, others, 1966-75. Contbg. author books, papers in field. Chmn. East Greenwich (R.I.) Sch. Commn., 1976, 77; bd. dirs. East Greenwich Acad. Found., 1989-91. Recipient Bell Fellowship AT&T, 1957-60, Rsch. award URI, 1987, 90. Fellow IEEE (chmn. providence sect. 1985-87, 93—, CNEC div. 1990-91); mem. Assn. Computer Mach., Tau Beta Pi, Sigma Si, Eta Kappa Nu. Democrat. Unitarian. Achievements include four patents and one patents pending. Home: 490 Carrs Pond Rd East Greenwich RI 02818-1007 Office: Univ RI 199 Kelly Hall Kingston RI 02881

TUFTS, ROBERT B., academic administrator; b. Cleve., Nov. 5, 1940; s. Robert L. and Dora Mae (Yingling) T.; m. Nancy Intihar, June 22, 1968 (div. Feb. 1990); children: Therese, Kevin R. BA cum laude, Cleve. State U., 1967; MA, Case Western Res. U., 1972; postgrad., U. Akron, 1973-76. Admissions counselor Cleve. State U., 1967-69, asst. registrar, 1969-70; asst. registrar Youngstown (Ohio) State U., 1970-73; asst. registrar U. Akron (Ohio), 1973-75, assoc. registrar, 1975-78; registrar Portland (Oreg.) State U., 1978—; com. mem. Park Recreation Adv. Bd., W. Linn., Oreg., 1981-84; presenter on fraudulent credentials, 1987—. Contbr. articles to profl. jours. With U.S. Army, 1959-62, Korea. Mem. Oreg. Assn. Registrars and Admissions Officers (sec.-treas. 1988-90), Pacific Assn. Collegiate Registrars and Admissions Officers (mem. program com. 1986-87, exec. bd., chair local arrangement 64th Ann. Mtg., Portland 1990), Am. Assn. Collegiate Registrars and Admissions Officers (local arrangements com., chair pub. com. 82nd Ann. Mtg., Reno, 1996, mem. facilities planning mgmt. com. 1975-78, chmn. of com. 1977-78), Nat. Assn. Coll. and Univ. Bus. Officers, Theta Rho. Democrat. Mem. Unitarian Ch. Avocations: mountaineering, camping, home projects. Home: 4981 Prospect St West Linn OR 97068-3116 Office: Portland State U PO Box 751 Portland OR 97207-0751

TUFTY, HAROLD GUILFORD, editor, publisher; b. Chgo., Sept. 1, 1922; s. Harold and Esther (Van Wagoner) T.; m. Barbara Jean Taeusch, Dec. 29, 1948; children: Christopher, Karen, Steven. BME, U. Va., 1949; postgrad., Sorbonne/Alliance Franciase, 1949-50. Corr. Tufty News Svc., Washington, 1946—; reporter Denver Post, 1949-51; European corr. Denver Post, Paris, 1951-52; pub. rels. Grant Advt., N.Y.C., 1953-55; info. officer U.S. Info. Agy., Madras, India, 1955-58, Bombay, India, 1958-59; pub. affairs officer, press attache U.S. Info. Agy., Conakry, Guinea, 1960, Abidjan, Ivory Coast, 1961-62; dir. French speaking African programs Peace Corps, Washington, 1963-64; pres. Tufty & Assoc., Washington, 1964—; bureau chief Tufty News Svc., Washington, 1984—; comml. pilot, single engine, land and sea, 1947—; mem. media staff conf. on civil rights White House, Washington, 1964; cons. U.S. Senate Com. Pub. Works, Washington, 1966-80; dir. The Ad Agy., Inc., Washington, 1970-78; pres. The Value Found., Washington, 1979—; congl. value engring. witness, testimony rschr., 1967—; presenter value engring. workshops in Bombay, Madras, Delhi, Hyderabad, Bangalore, and Calcutta; mem. U.S. Senate Press Gallery, 1980—, White House Corrs. Ann's, 1980—. Author: Compendium on Value Engineering, 1983, rev. 2d edit., 1989; editor, pub. Value Engring. and Mgmt. Digest, 1972—; columnist Interactions, 1988—. Nat. v.p. Soc. Am. Value Engrs., Washington, 1970-72; bd. dirs. SAVE Nat. Capital, Washington, 1964—, chmn., 1973—, congl. receptions; founding dir., asst. sec. Lower Cacapon River Com., 1995. Lt. USN, 1944-46. Recipient Capital Honor award SAVE, 1971, Disting. Svc. award SAVE, 1977-78, Fallon Value-In-Life award SAVE, 1994. Fellow Soc. Am. Value Engrs. (nat. pres. 1990-92); mem. Nat. Dem. Club. Avocations: reading, understanding my computer, haiku, chess, instructing sailing using aerodynamic principles. Home: 3812 Livingston St NW Washington DC 20015-2803 Office: Tufty Comm Co 2107 National Press Bldg Washington DC 20045

TUGGLE, FRANCIS DOUGLAS, management educator; b. Portsmouth, Va., Jan. 19, 1943; s. Francis Joyner and Florence Eleanor (Dahlgren) T.; m. Mary Ann Tredway, June 3, 1967; children: Wendy Elizabeth, Laura Michelle. SB, MIT, 1964; MS, Carnegie-Mellon U., 1967, PhD, 1971. Prof. bus. adminstrn. and computer sci. U. Kans., Lawrence, 1968-78; Jesse H. Jones prof. mgmt. Rice U., Houston, 1978-90; dean Kogod Coll. Bus. Adminstrn., Am. U., Washington, 1990-96, prof. info. systems, 1996—; bd. dirs. Equus II, Inc., Houston, Internat. Expert Sys. Inc., Houston, v.p. mktg. devel.; mem. coun. acad. advisors Bryce Harlow Found., 1994-96; dir.-at-large Inst. for Ops. Rsch. and Mgmt. Scis., 1995. Author: How to Program a Computer, 1975, Organizational Processes, 1978. Com. chmn. United Way Tex. Gulf Coast, Houston, 1985-88. Ford Found. fellowship, 1966. Mem. AAAS, Inst. for Ops. Rsch. and Mgmt. Scis. (bd. dirs. 1995, v.p. 1992-94), Am. Assn. Artificial Intelligence, Assn. for Computing Machinery, Acad. of Mgmt., Sigma Xi, Beta Gamma Sigma, Alpha Kappa Psi. Episcopalian. Avocations: golf, bicycling, jogging. Home: 4709 Ft Sumner Dr Bethesda MD 20816-2466 Office: Am U Kogod Coll Bus Adminstrn 4400 Massachusetts Ave NW Washington DC 20016-8001

TUGGLE, JESSIE LLOYD, professional football player; b. Spalding County, Ga., Feb. 14, 1965. Student, Valdosta State Coll. Linebacker Atlanta Falcons, 1987—. Selected to Pro Bowl, 1992, 94. Office: Atlanta Falcons Complex One Falcon Pl Suwanee GA 30174*

TUINEI, MARK PULEMAU, professional football player; b. Nanakuli, Hawaii, Mar. 31, 1960. Student, Univ. Calif., Univ. Hawaii. Offensive tackle Dalls Cowboys, 1983—. Selected to Pro Bowl, 1984-95; Dalls Cowboys Super Bowl Champions, 1992, 93. Office: One Cowboys Pkwy Irving TX 75063*

TUKE, ROBERT DUDLEY, lawyer, educator; b. Rochester, N.Y., Dec. 5, 1947; s. Theodore Robert and Doris Jean (Smith) T.; m. Susan Devereux Cummins, June 21, 1969; children: Andrew, Sarah. BA with distinction, U. Va., 1969; JD, Vanderbilt U., 1976. Bar: Tenn. 1976, U.S. Dist. Ct. (mid. dist.) Tenn. 1976, U.S. Ct. Appeals (6th cir.) 1976, U.S. Ct. Appeals (4th cir.) 1978, U.S. Ct. Appeals (fed. cir.) 1993, U.S. Supreme Ct. 1986, U.S. Ct. Internat. Trade 1993. Assoc. Farris, Warfield & Kanaday, Nashville, 1976-79, ptnr., 1980-94; ptnr. Tuke Yopp & Sweeney, Nashville, 1994—; lectr. law Vanderbilt U. Law Sch., Nashville; faculty PLI, 1995—; mem. AMA Drs.' Adv. Network. Author: (with others) Tennessee Practice, 1992; contbr. articles to profl. jours. Mem. Tenn. Adoption Law Study Commn., 1993-96, Metro CATV Com. Capt. USMC, 1969-73. Decorated Cross of Gallantry; Patrick Wilson Merit scholar. Mem. ABA, Nat. Health Law Assn., Nat. Assn. Bond Lawyers, Am. Acad. Adoption Attys., Tenn. Bar Assn., Nashville Bar Assn., Nashville C. of C. (mem. bd. govs.), Order of Coif. Democrat. Episcopalian. Avocations: rowing, running, cycling, hiking, travel. Office: NationsBank Plz 414 Union St Ste 1100 Nashville TN 37219-1758

TUKEY, HAROLD BRADFORD, JR., horticulture educator; b. Geneva, N.Y., May 29, 1934; s. Harold Bradford and Ruth (Schweigert) T.; m. Helen Dunbar Parker, June 25, 1955; children: Ruth Thurbon, Carol Tukey Schwartz, Harold Bradford. B.S., Mich. State U., 1955, M.S., 1956, Ph.D., 1958. Research asst. South Haven Expt. Sta., Mich., 1955; AEC grad. research asst. Mich. State U., 1955-58; NSF fellow Calif. Inst. Tech, 1958-59; asst. prof. dept. floriculture and ornamental horticulture Cornell U., Ithaca, N.Y., 1959-64, assoc. prof., 1964-70, prof., 1970-80; prof. urban horticulture U. Wash., Seattle, 1980—, dir. Arboreta, 1980-92, dir. Ctr. Urban Horticulture, 1980-92; cons. Internat. Bonsai mag., Electric Power Rsch. Inst., P.R. Nuclear Ctr., 1965-66; mem. adv. com. Seattle-U. Wash. Arboretum and Bot. Garden, 1980-92, vice chmn., 1982, chmn., 1986-87; vis. scholar U. Nebr., 1982; vis. prof. U. Calif., Davis, 1973; lectr. U. Western Sydney-Hawkesburg U. Melbourne, Victoria Coll. Agrl. and Horticulture, 1995, Massey U., 1996; Hill prof. U. Minn., 1996; mem. various coms. Nat. Acad. Scis.-NRC; bd. dirs. Arbor Fund Bloedel Res., 1980-92, pres., 1983-84. Mem. editorial bd. Jour. Environ. Horticulture, Arboretum Bull. Mem. nat. adv. com. USDA, 1990—; pres. Ithaca PTA; troop advisor Boy Scouts Am., Ithaca. Lt. U.S. Army, 1958. Recipient B.Y. Morrison award USDA, 1987; NSF fellow, 1958-59; named to Lansing (Mich.) Sports Hall of Fame, 1987; grantee NSF, 1962, 75, Bot. Soc. Am., 1964; hon. dr. Portuguese Soc. Hort., 1985. Fellow Am. Soc. Hort. Sci. (dir. 1970-71); mem. Internat. Soc. Hort. Sci. (U.S. del. to coun. 1971-90, chmn. commn. for amateur horiticulture 1974-83, exec. com. 1974-90, v.p. 1978-82, pres. 1982-86, past pres. 1986-90, chmn. comm. Urban Horticulture 1990-94, hon. mem. 1994), Wash. State Nursery and Landscape Assn. (hon. mem. 1995), Internat. Plant Propagators Soc. (hon., ea. region dir. 1969-71, v.p. 1972, pres. 1973, internat. pres. 1976), Am. Hort. Soc. (dir. 1972-81, exec. com. 1974-81, v.p. 1978-80, citation of merit 1981), Royal Hort. Soc. (London) (v.p. hon. 1993—), Bot. Soc. Am., N.W. Horticulture Soc. (dir. 1980-92), Arboretum Found. (dir. 1980-92), Rotary, Sigma Xi, Alpha Zeta, Phi Kappa Phi, Pi Alpha Xi, Xi Sigma Pi. Presbyterian. Home: 3300 E St Andrews Way Seattle WA 98112-3750 Office: U Wash Ctr Urban Horticulture Box 354115 Seattle WA 98195

TUKEY, LOREN DAVENPORT, pomology educator, researcher; b. Geneva, N.Y., Dec. 4, 1921; s. Harold Bradford and Margaret (Davenport) T.; m. Louise Arleyne Young, Feb. 2, 1952; children: David Davenport, Barbara Ann Tukey Shea. B.S., Mich. State U., 1943, M.S., 1947; Ph.D., Ohio State U., 1952. Asst. prof. pomology Pa. State U., University Park, 1950-57, assoc. prof., 1957-66, prof., 1966-91, prof. emeritus pomology, 1992—; fruit rsch. cons. Nat. Inst. Agrl. Tech., Argentina, 1965-70; rsch. cons. Instituto Interamericano Cooperacion Agricultura, Argentina, 1988; rsch. cons. cocoa Malaysian Agr. Rsch. and Devel. Inst., Malaysia, 1993. Editor: Pa. State Hort. Revs., 1962-91; assoc. editor: Jour. Hort. Sci. (Eng.), 1978-92; researcher numerous publs. in field. Bd. dirs. State College chpt. ARC, 1963-82; mem. Borough of State College Traffic Commn., 1976-80. Served to capt. Q.M.C., U.S. Army, 1943-46, ETO. Named Outstanding Horticulturist State Hort. Assn. Pa., 1986; recipient Milo Gibson award N.Am. Fruit Explorers, 1989. Fellow Am. Soc. Hort. Sci., AAAS; mem. Internat. Soc. Hort. Sci., Am. Soc. Plant Physiologists, Plant Growth Regulator Soc. Am., Am. Pomological Soc. (sec. 1968-74, Paul Howe Shepard award 1964, treas. and bus. mgr. 1968-89), Internat. Dwarf Fruit Tree Assn. (Svc. and Leadership award 1988), Academie d'Agriculture de France (corr.), Brit. Soc. for Plant Growth Regulation, Sigma Xi, Gamma Sigma Delta (pres. chpt. 1967-68), Phi Epsilon Phi, Theta Chi, Rotary (pres. State Coll. 1971-72, Paul Harris fellow). Republican. Presbyterian. Growth and development of tree fruits: growth regulating chemicals, environ. factors in fruit sizing, orchard productivity, intensive orchard systems and rootstocks. Developer of Penn State low-trellis hedgerow system for apple culture. Home: 549 Glenn Rd State College PA 16803-3473 Office: 103 Tyson Bldg University Park PA 16802-4200

TULAFONO, TOGIOLA T.A., senator; b. Aunu'u Island, American Samoa, Feb. 28, 1947; s. Aitu and Silika (Vaatu'itu'i) T.; m. Maryann Taufaasau Mauga, Sept. 17, 1984; children: Puataunofo, Olita, Cherianne, Emema, Timoteo, Rosie. Grad., Honolulu Police Acad., 1967; BA, Chadron State Coll., 1970; JD, Washburn U., 1975. Bar: Kans., Am. Samoa. Police instr. Am. Samoa Police Dept., Pago Pago, 1967; adminstrv. asst. Sec. of Samoan Affairs, Pago Pago, 1970-71; legal asst. Atty. Gen., Pago Pago, 1971-72; assoc. Law Offices of George A. Wray, Pago Pago, 1975-77; v.p. South Pacific Island Airways, Pago Pago, 1977-79; judge Dist. Ct. of Am. Samoa, Pago Pago, 1979-80; chmn. bd. dirs. Am. Samoa Power Authority, Pago Pago, 1978-80; mem. Am. Samoa Senate, Pago Pago, 1981-85, 89—; pres. Nayram Samoa, Ltd., Pago Pago, 1985-88; chmn. Senate Investigation Com., 1993—. Chmn. Bd. Higher Edn., Am. Samoa, 1993—; bd. dirs. Am. Samoa Jr. Golfers' Assn.; deacon Sailele Congrl. Ch. Mem. ATLA, Am. Samoa Bar Assn., Kans. Bar Assn., Samoa Profl. Golfer's Assn. (pres. 1985-87), Am. Samoa Golf Assn. (pres.). Democrat. Congregationalist. Home: PO Box Ppe Pago Pago AS 96799-9733

TULCHIN, DAVID BRUCE, lawyer; b. N.Y.C., Dec. 2, 1947; s. Philip Tulchin and Mary (Weiner) Black; m. Nora Barrett, Aug. 20, 1972; children: Rachel, Daniel, Laura. BA, U. Rochester, 1970; JD, Harvard U., 1973. Bar: N.Y. 1974, U.S. Dist. Ct. (so. & ea. dists.) N.Y. 1975, U.S. Ct. Appeals (2d cir.) 1975, U.S. Supreme Ct. 1977, U.S. Ct. Appeals (5th cir.) 1978, U.S. Ct. Appeals (1st & 6th cirs.) 1984, U.S. Dist. Ct. (no. dist.) Ohio 1984, U.S. Ct. Appeals (3d, 4th & Fed. cirs.) 1988, U.S. Ct. Appeals (7th cir.) 1991, U.S. Dist. Ct. (we. dist.) N.Y., 1996. Law clk. to Judge Frederick V.P. Bryan U.S. Dist. Ct. So. Dist. N.Y., N.Y.C., 1973-75; assoc. Sullivan & Cromwell, N.Y.C., 1975-82, ptnr., 1982—. Mem. ABA, Assn. Bar of City of N.Y., Fed. Bar Coun., N.Y. State Bar Assn., Fed. Cir. Bar Assn. Office: Sullivan & Cromwell 125 Broad St New York NY 10004-2400

TULCHIN, STANLEY, banker, lecturer, author, business reorganization consultant. Founder, chmn. bd. Stanley Tulchin Assocs., Westbury, N.Y., 1955-95; bd. dirs. N.Y. Inst. Credit, Topps Corp., PCA Internat.; founder, chmn. Reprise Capital Corp. Recipient Leadership in Credit Edn. award N.Y. Inst. Credit, 1990. Mem. Comml. Law League Am. (Pres'. Cup award 1975, past bd. govs., vice-chmn. bd. editors Comml. Law Jour., bd. dirs. Fund for Pub. Edn.), Nat. Assn. Credit Mgmt. Office: Stanley Tulchin Assocs 400 Post Ave PO Box 185 Westbury NY 11590

TULL, JOHN E., JR., federal agency administrator; b. Lonoke, Ark., Mar. 15, 1925; s. John E. and Nettie (Frohlich) T.; m. Mary Ybarrondo, Sept. 7, 1952; children: John E. Tull, III, Elizabeth Tull Landers, Mary Tull Eldridge. BS in Commerce, U. N.C. Apptd. commr. by presdl. nom. Commodity Futures Trading Commn., 1993—; mem., chmn. Ark. State Planning Bd.; pres. Ark. Rice Coun., Nat. Rice Coun.; chmn. bd. dirs. European subcom. Nat. Rice Coun.; chmn. Govs. Rail Safety Com.; mem. adv. bd. agr. Cattleman's Found.; mem. bd. dirs. Bayou Metro Irrigation Dist., U.S. Rice Found.; mem. adv. bd. First Comml. Bank Cabot, Ark. Lt. U.S. Navy. Mem. Ark. Seed Growers Assn. (pres.), Ark. Cattlemen's Assn. (pres.), Ark. Soybean Assn. (pres.), Trade's Rice Working Group (mem. chgo. bd.), Gamma Sigma Delta (hon.). Presbyterian. Office: Commodity Futures Trading Commn 3 Lafayette Ctr 1155 21st St NW Washington DC 20036-3302

TULL, THERESA ANNE, retired ambassador; b. Runnemede, N.J., Oct. 2, 1936; d. John James and Anna Cecelia (Paull) T. B.A., U. Md., 1972; M.A., U. Mich., 1973; postgrad., Nat. War Coll., Washington, 1980. Fgn. svc. officer Dept. State, Washington, 1963, Brussels, 1965-67, Saigon, 1968-70; dep. prin. officer Am. Consulate General, Danang, Vietnam, 1973-75; prin. officer Cebu, Philippines, 1977-79; dir. office human rights, 1980-83; charge d'affaires Am. Embassy, Vientiane, Laos, 1983-86; Dept. State Senior Seminar, 1986-87; ambassador to Guyana, 1987-90; diplomat-in-residence Lincoln U., Pa., 1990-91; dir. office regional affairs, bur. East Asian & Pacific affairs Dept. State, Washington, 1991-93; amb. to Brunei Bandar Seri Begawan, 1993-96. Recipient Civilian Service award Dept. of State, 1970, Superior Honor award, 1977. Mem. Am. Fgn. Svc. Assn. Address: #204 4400 Pleasure Ave Sea Isle City NJ 08243

TULL, WILLIS CLAYTON, JR., librarian; b. Crisfield, Md., Feb. 22, 1931; s. Willis Clayton and Agnes Virginia (Milbourne) T.; m. Taeko Itoi, Dec. 18, 1952. Student, U. Balt., 1948, Johns Hopkins U., 1956; BS, Towson (Md.) State Coll., 1957; MLS, Rutgers U., 1962; postgrad., Miami U., Oxford, Ohio, 1979. Editorial clk. 500th Mil. Intelligence Svc. Group, Tokyo, 1952-53; tchr. Hereford Jr.-Sr. High Sch., Parkton, Md., 1957-59; aide Enoch Pratt Free Libr., Balt., 1959-61, prof. asst., 1962-64; coord. adult svcs. Washington County Free Libr., Hagerstown, Md., 1964-67; asst. area libr. Eastern Shore Area Libr., Salisbury, Md., 1967; br. libr. Balt. County Pub. Libr., Pikesville, Md., 1968-71; asst. area br. libr. Balt. County Pub. Libr., Essex, Md., 1971-72; sr. info. specialist Balt. County Pub. Libr., Catonsville, Md., 1972-87; on-line supr. Balt. County Pub. Libr., Towson, Md., 1988-89; sr. info. specialist Balt. County Pub. Libr., Reisterstown, Md., 1989-90; exec. dir. Milbourne and Tull Rsch. Ctr., 1991—. Contbr. to profl. and geneal. jours. Mem. Rep. Cen. Com. Balt. County, 1971-72. With U.S. Army, 1949-52. Mem. Asia Soc., Japan Soc., Nat. Congress Patriotic Orgns. (founding fellow), Internat. Rescue Com., Heritage Found., Freedom to Read Foun., Friends of Johns Hopkins U. Librs., Freedom House, Nat. Assn. Scholars, Assn. of Lit. Scholars and Critics, Md. Libr. Assn. (chmn. intellectual freedom com. 1969-70), Md. Assn. Adult Edn. (coord. Western Md. region 1965-67), Nat. Alumni Forum, Unitarian and Universalist Geneal. Soc. (founder, bd. dirs. 1971-87), Md. Geneal. Soc., Royal Soc. St. George, Sons and Daus. of the Pilgrims, Descendants of Early Quakers, Soc. War of 1812, SAR, Ea. Shore Soc. Balt. City, Balt. Coun. Fgn. Affairs, Star Spangled Banner Flag House Assn., Md. Coalition Against Crime, Empower Am., Woodrow Wilson Internat. Ctr. Scholars, Ancient and Hon. Mech. Co. Balt., Nature Conservancy, Ctr. Study Popular Culture, Media Rsch. Ctr., World Future Soc., U.S. Holocaust Meml. Mus., Kappa Delta Pi. Home and Office: 10605 Lakespring Way Hunt Valley MD 21030-2818

TULLER, HARRY LOUIS, materials science and engineering educator. BS, Columbia U., 1966, MS, 1967, DSc in Engring., 1973. Rsch. assoc. physics Technion, Haifa, Israel, 1974-75; from asst. to assoc. prof. materials sci. and engring. MIT, Cambridge, 1975-81, prof. materials sci. and engring., 1981—; dir. Crystal Physics and Electroceramics Lab., Cambridge, 1985—; vis. prof. U. Pierre et Marie Curie, Paris, 1990; faculty chair Sumitomo Electric Industries, 1992. Co-editor: High Temperature Superconductors, 1988, Electroceramics and Solid State Ionics, 1988, Science and Technology of Fast Ion Conductors, 1989, Sold State Ionics, 1992; series editor: Electronic Materials: Science and Technology; editor-in-chief Jour. Electroceramics. Fulbright travel grantee, 1990, Alexander von Humboldt, 1996; Humboldt fellow, 1997. Fellow Am. Ceramic Soc. (N.E. chair 1983); mem. IEEE, Electrochem. Soc. (co-organizer 1st and 2d internat. symposium ionic and mixed conducting ceramics 1991, 94, co-organizer 1997 NATO/ASI Oxygen Ion & Mixed Conductors Summer Sch.), Materials Rsch. Soc. Jewish. Avocations: photography, gardening. Office: MIT 77 Massachusetts Ave Rm 13-3126 Cambridge MA 02139-4301

TULLIS, EDWARD LEWIS, retired bishop; b. Cin., Mar. 9, 1917; s. Ashar Spence and Priscilla (Daugherty) T.; m. Mary Jane Talley, Sept. 25, 1937; children: Frank Loyd, Jane Allen (Mrs. William Nelson Offutt IV). AB, Ky. Wesleyan Coll., 1939, LHD, 1975; BD, Louisville Presbyn. Theol. Sem., 1947; DD, Union Coll., Barbourville, Ky., 1954, Wofford Coll., 1976; LHD, Claflin Coll., 1976, Lambuth Coll., 1984. Ordained to ministry Methodist Ch., 1941; service in chs. Frenchburg, Ky., 1937-39, Lawrenceburg, Ky., 1939-44; asso. pastor 4th Ave. Meth. Ch., Louisville, 1944-47, Irvine, Ky., 1947-49; asso. sec. ch. extension sect. Bd. Missions, Meth. Ch., Louisville, 1949-52; pastor First Meth. Ch., Frankfort, Ky., 1952-61, Ashland, Ky., 1961-72; resident bishop United Meth. Ch., Columbia, S.C., 1972-80, Nashville area, 1980-84; ret. United Meth. Ch., 1984; instr. Bible Ky. Wesleyan Coll., 1947-48; instr. Louisville Presbyn. Theol. Sem., 1949-52; mem. Meth. Gen. Conf., 1956, 60, 64, 66, 68, 70, 72, Southeastern Jurisdictional Conf., 1952, 56, 60, 64, 68, 72, bd. mgrs. Bd. Missions, 1962-72, mem. bd. discipleship, 1972-80, v.p. Gen. Council on Fin. and Adminstrn., 1980-84; Chaplain Ky. Gen. Assembly, 1952-61; chmn. Frankfort Com. Human Rights, 1956-61, Mayor's Advisory Com. Human Relations, Ashland, 1968-72. Author: Shaping the Church from the Mind of Christ, 1984. Contbr. articles to religious jours. Sec., bd. dirs. Magee Christian Edn. Found.; trustee Emory U., 1973-80, Alaska Meth. U., 1965-70, Ky. Wesleyan Coll., Martin Coll., Lambuth Coll., McKendree Manor, Meth. Hosps., Memphis, Lake Junaluska Assembly, 1966-88; chair adv. bd. Found. for Evangelism, United Meth. Ch., 1991—. Recipient Outstanding Citizen award Frankfort VFW, 1961, Mayor's award for outstanding service, Ashland, 1971. Club: Kiwanis. Home: PO Box 754 Lake Junaluska NC 28745-0754

TULLIS, JOHN LEDBETTER, retired wholesale distributing company executive; b. Quanah, Tex., May 9, 1911; s. John Ledbetter and Coral (Horton) T.; m. Bettye Bishop Winston, Mar. 22, 1980; children—Tom, Jeff, Alan Winston. B.S. in Elec. Engring, U. Tex., Austin, 1933. With AMF, Inc. and predecessors, 1947-74, pres., chief oper. officer, 1967-74; gen. mgr. Interstate Electric Co., Inc., Shreveport, La., 1974-83, ret., 1983; cons. in field. Chmn. devel. council Schumpert Med. Center, Shreveport, 1974-82; mem. chancellor's council U. Tex., Austin, 1974—. Recipient Disting. Engring. Grad. award U. Tex., Austin, 1963. Mem. Tex. Hist. Assn. Methodist. Clubs: Shreveport Country, Shreveport. Home: 1806 Hunter Cir Shreveport LA 71119-4104

TULLOCH, BRIAN ROBERT, endocrinologist; b. Chunya, Tanzania, May 30, 1938; came to U.S., 1977; s. Robert Graeme and Audrey Madelein (Bremner) T.; m. Elizabeth Watkins Rogg, Jan. 26, 1980; children: Nathaniel, Genevieve. BSc, Natal U., S. Africa, 1959, MSc, 1961; BM, BCh, Oxford (Eng.) U., 1966. House physician to specialists in gen., plastic, thoracic surgery, Univ. Coll. Hosp., London, 1965-66; house physician to specialist in gen. and renal medicine Radcliffe Infirmary, Oxford, Eng., 1966-67; house physician to cardiologist Hammersmith Hosp., London, 1967; house physician Brompton Chest Hosp., London, 1967-68; med. registrar Nat. Heart Hosp., London, 1968-69; clin. rsch. fellow, sr. registrar, clin. tutor, cons. Med. Rsch. Coun. endocrine unit Royal Postgrad. Med. Sch., London, 1969-72; Wellcome sr. rsch. fellow dept. medicine Royal Postgrad. Med. Sch., London, 1972-74; sessional cons. in endocrinology and diabetes St. Charles Hosp., London, 1973-74; hon. lectr. in medicine Hammersmith Hosp., London, 1972-74; sr. lectr. in medicine, hon. cons. physician Manchester (Eng. Royal Infirmary), 1974-77; endocrinologist Diagnostic Clinic, Houston, 1977—; clin. assoc. prof. internal medicine and ophthalmology U. Tex. Med. Sch., Houston, 1977—, M.D. Anderson Hosp. and Tumor Inst., Houston, 1977—; attending physician, Diagnostic Ctr. Hosp., Houston, Hermann Hosp., Houston, Park Plaza Hosp., Houston; mem. student promotions com. U. Tex.. tissue com. Hermann Hosp.; NIH site visitor, Diabetes Rsch and Tng. Ctr., NIH advisor Diabetes Epidemiology in Egypt; invited participant NIH Conf. on flushing, markers for Type II Diabetes Mellitus, 1980, Conf. on Lipoprotein Physiology, San Diego, 1981, Lipid Metabolism, N.Y., 1985; reviewer Diabetologia, Hormone and Metabolic Rsch., Clin. Sci., Cardiovascular Rsch., Biochem. Pharmacology, Artery, Metabolism: Clin. and Exptl.; advisor Ministry of Health, Kuwait, 1976-78, ICI Internat., 1976-78; for rev. lectures given to Univs. Cairo, Ain Shams, Assyut, Mansoura and Alexandria in Egypt; invited disting. guest lectr. Sudan Assn. Physicians, Khartoum, 1978. Contbr. numerous articles and abstracts to profl. jours.; speaker to nat. and internat. sci. confs. as well as lay groups on diabetes and related health care topics. Recipient Caltex scholarship, 1955-59, Coun. for Sci. and Indsl. Rsch. scholarship, 1960-61, Charelick Salemon scholarship, 1960-61, Rhodes scholarship, St. Johns Coll. Oxford U., 1961-64, Croxon fellowship, 1964-65, Convenators Trust, 1964-65, Preventive Cardiology Acad. award; grantee: MRC (heavy equipment grant), Manchester Regional Rsch. Fund, 1975, U. Tex., 1977, Am. Diabetes Assn., Warner Lambert-Parke Davis, 1979-81, CO-PI, 1979-82, 1983-86. Fellow ACP, Am. Endocrine Soc., Am. Diabetes Assn. (pres. Houston chpt. 1982-83, pres. Tex. affiliate 1984-86), Royal Coll. Physicians; mem. Brain-Pituitary Soc. (treas. 1981-86), Houston-Galveston Endocrine Assn., Am. Heart Assn., The Endocrine Soc., Harris County Med. Soc., Harveian Soc. London, Manchester Med. Soc., Med. Rsch. Soc., Soc. for Endocrinology, European Assn. for Study of Diabetes, Brit. Diabetic Soc., Royal Soc. Medicine London (com. mem. endocrine sect.), Royal Ocean Racing Club London, Hellenic Travelers Club London, Egypt Exploration Soc. London, Houston Yacht Club (fleet surgeon 1983-84), Tex. Offshore Racing Club, Galveston Bay Cruising Assn. Republican. Episcopalian. Avocations: sailboat racing, scuba diving, duck hunting, bird watching, fishing. Office: Diagnostic Clinic 6448 Fannin St Houston TX 77030-1511

TULLOS, HUGH SIMPSON, orthopedic surgeon, educator; b. Waco, Tex., Aug. 7, 1935; s. Hugh Simpson and Roberta (Thomas) T.; m. Marcelle Gaye Unger; children: Paul R., Hugh S. III. Student, Vanderbilt U., 1952-55; MD, MS in Cancer Biology, Baylor U., 1960. Diplomate Am. Bd. Orthopaedic Surgeons (examiner 1974—). Intern Jefferson Davis Hosp., Houston, 1960-61; gen. surgery resident Baylor Coll. Medicine, Houston, 1961-62, orthopedic surgery resident, 1964-67; successively asst. instr., instr., asst. prof. to assoc. prof. div. Orthopedic Surgery, Baylor Coll. Medicine, 1967-75; pvt. practice Fonden Orthopedic Group, Houston, 1967-88; head div. orthopedic surgery Tex. Med. Ctr., Houston, 1989—, Wilhemina Barnhart chmn., prof. dept. orthopedic surgery, 1991—; chief orthopedic svc. Meth. Hosp., Houston, 1974, Ben Taub Gen. Hosp., Houston, 1974; clin.

assoc. prof. dept. surgery U. Tex. Med. Sch. Health Sci. Ctr., Houston, 1975; vis. lectr. sports medicine symposium Hosp. for Joint Diseases, N.Y.C., 1982; vis. prof. Peruvian Orthopaedic Soc., 1978, U. Miami Sch. Medicine, 1979, Health Sci. Ctr., Tex. Tech U., 1983, Rex Dively Lecturship, Kansas City, Mo., 1985; presenter numerous instructional courses, profl. symposia, meetings; Murray S. Danforth surgeon-in-chief pro tempore Brown U., R.I. Hosp., Providence, Nov., 1988. Author: (with others) Principles of Sport Medicine, 1984, The Elbow, 1985, Injuries to the Throwing Arm, 1985, Art of Total Hip Arthoplasty, 1987, other books, also Instructional Course Lectures Am. Acad. Orthopaedic Surgeons, vols. 25, 33, 1984, 86; editorial bd. Jour. of Arthroplasty, 1988; bd. assoc. editors Clin. Orthopaedics and Related Rsch., 1986—; cons. to editor Tex. Medicine; contbr. numerous articles, abstracts to profl. jours.; presenter exhibits, films med. meetings. Patentee orthopedic devices. Capt. U.S. Army, 1961-63. Fellow Am. Acad. Orthopaedic Surgeons (bd. dirs. 1976, sec. com. sports medicinew 1974-81, com. instructional courses 1987—, chmn. 1988; mem. AMA, Am. Orthopaedic Assn., Am. Orthopaedic Soc. Sports Medicine (founding, chmn. nominating com. 1980, chmn. ann. meeteing 1982), Assn. Bone and Joint Surgeons, Assn. Orthopaedic Chmn., Clin. Orthopaedic Soc., Harris County Med. Soc., Houston Orthopaedic Assn., Houston Surg. Soc., Internat. Congress Knee Surgeons, Internat. Soc. of the Knee (founding, bd. dirs. 1983-88, sec.-treas. 1989), Mid-Am. Orthopaedic Assn., Orthopaedic Rsch. Soc., Pan Am. Med. Assn., Soc. Am. Shoulder and Elbow Surgeons, 20th Century Orthopaedic Soc. (chmn. ann. meeting 1987), Tex. Soc. Athletic Team Physicians (pres. 1978), Tex. Med. Assn., Tex. Orthopaedic Assn., Tex. Rheumatism Soc., The Knee Soc., Baylor Orthopaedic Alumni Assn. (pres. 1970—). Office: Tex Med Ctr Bay Coll of Med Div Orthopedic Surgery 6550 Fannin St Ste 2525 Houston TX 77030-2709*

TULLOS, JOHN BAXTER, banker; b. Morton, Miss., Dec. 3, 1915; s. William Baxter and Mell (Roberts) T.; m. Maxine Stone, Sept. 20, 1941. Student, Miss. Coll., 1934, Am. Inst. Bank, Jackson, Miss., 1936-40, Sch. Banking South, La. State U., 1955-57. With Trustmark Nat. Bank, Jackson, 1935-88; exec. agt. Trustmark Corp. (formerly 1st Capital Corp.); faculty Sch. Banking South La. State U.; 1st pres. Miss. Young Bankers Assn.; mem. Miss. Valley World Trade Council, 1965—; mem. La.-Miss. Regional Export Expansion Council div. U.S. Dept. Commerce, 1967-74; vice-chmn. Ala.-Miss. Dist. Export Council, 1975-80; chmn. Miss. Dist. Export Council, 1980-85. Former chmn. budget com. United Givers Fund. Served with AUS, World War II. Mem. Miss. Bankers Assn. (past chmn. operations/automation com.). Methodist. Clubs: Lion, Capitol City Petroleum. Home: 8 Eastbrooke St Jackson MS 39216-4714 Office: PO Box 2343 Jackson MS 39225-2343

TULLY, DANIEL PATRICK, financial services executive; b. 1932; married. BBA, St. Johns U., 1953. With Merrill Lynch, Pierce, Fenner & Smith, N.Y.C., 1955—, mem. acctg. dept., 1955-59, acct. exec. trainee, 1959-63, asst. to mgr. Stamford, Conn. office, 1963-70, mgr., 1970-71, v.p., 1971-79, dir. individual sales, 1976-79, exec. v.p., 1979-82, pres. individual services group, 1982-84, pres. consumer mktg., from 1984; pres., COO Merrill Lynch & Co., Inc., N.Y.C., 1985; former exec. v.p. Merrill Lynch & Co. (parent), N.Y.C., 1979, CEO, 1992—, chmn., 1993—. Served U.S. Army, 1953-55. Office: Merrill Lynch & Co Inc World Fin Ctr No Tower 250 Vesey St New York NY 10281-1332

TULLY, DARROW, newspaper publisher; b. Charleston, W.Va., Feb. 27, 1932; s. William Albert and Dora (McCann) T.; m. Victoria Lynn Werner; children: Bonnie Tully Paul, Michael Andrew. Student, Purdue U., 1951; BA in Journalism, St. Joseph's Coll., 1972; PhD in Journalism (hon.), Calumet (Ind.) Coll., 1975. V.p., gen. mgr. Stas. WDSM-AM-FM and WDSM-TV, Duluth, Minn., 1956-59; bus. mgr. Duluth Herald & News Tribune, 1960-62; gen. mgr. St. Paul Dispatch & Pioneer Press, 1962-66; pub. Gary (Ind.) Post-Tribune, 1966-73; v.p., pub. Wichita (Kans.) Eagle & Beacon, 1973-75; pres. San Francisco Newspaper Agy., 1975-78; exec. v.p., pub. Ariz. Republic & Phoenix Gazette, 1978-85; editor., pub., chief exec. officer Ojai (Calif.) Valley News, 1987-90; pres., pub., CEO Beacon Comms., Acton, Mass., 1990-92; asst. to pres. newspaper divsn. Chronicle Pub. Co., 1992-94. Author: Minority Representation in the Media, 1968. Trustee Calumet Coll. Recipient Disting. Achievement award Ariz. State U., 1982, Disting. Journalist award No. Ariz. U./AP, 1983, 1st Pl. Editorial Writing award Ariz. Planned Parenthood, 1983. Mem. Am. Soc. Newspaper Editors, Soc. Profl. Journalists. Office: 9862 Bridgeton Dr Tampa FL 33626-1802

TULLY, JOHN CHARLES, research chemical physicist; b. N.Y.C., May 17, 1942; s. Harry V. and Pauline (Fischer) T.; m. Mary Ellen Thomsen, Jan. 23, 1971; children: John Thomsen, Elizabeth Anne, Stephen Thomsen. BS, Yale U., 1964; PhD, U. Chgo., 1968. NSF postdoctoral fellow U. Colo. and Yale U., 1968-70; mem. tech. staff AT&T Bell Labs., Murray Hill, N.J., 1970-82, disting. mem. tech. staff, 1982-85, head phys. chemistry rsch. dept., 1985-90, head materials chem. rsch. dept., 1990-96; prof. dept. chemistry, physics and applied physics Yale U., New Haven, Conn., 1996—; vis. prof. Princeton (N.J.) U., 1981-82, Harvard U., Cambridge, Mass., 1991. Contbr. articles to sci. jours.; author, prodr. movie Dynamics of Gas-Surface Interactions, 1979. NSF predoctoral fellow, 1965-68. Fellow AAAS, Am. Phys. Soc. (chem. physics exec. com. 1983-86), Am. Acad. Arts & Scis.; mem. Am. Chem. Soc. (chmn. theoretical chemistry subdiv. 1991-92, phys. chemistry div. 1993-94, Peter Debye award 1995), Nat. Acad. Sci., Sigma Xi. Achievements include patent on Method and Apparatus for Surface Characterization Utilizing Radiation from Desorbed Particles; fundamental theoretical contributions towards atomic level understanding of chemical reaction dynamics. Office: Yale Univ Dept Chemistry 225 Prospect St New Haven CT 06511-8499

TULLY, MICHAEL J., JR., state senator; b. N.Y.C., June 23, 1933; s. Michael and Elizabeth (Carpenter) T.; children: Michael, Christpher, Maura, Brian. JD, St. John's U.; DHL (hon.) N.Y. Inst. Tech., 1994. Asst. dist. atty. Nassau County; town councilman Town of North Hempstead, Manhasset, N.Y., 1967-71, town supr., 1971-82; senator State of N.Y., Roslyn, 1982—; chmn. senate water resources com.; mem. coun. healthcare fin.; mem. health com. Nat. Conf. State Legislators; mem. coun. state Govts.' Health Policy Task Force. Bd. dirs. NCCJ, Am. Com. on Italian Migration; adv. bd. Assn. for Help of Retarded Children; mem. Am. Legis. Exchange Coun. Served with U.S. Army, USAR. Recipient Hon. Law Enforcement Man of Year award, Nassau County Police Dept. Detectives Assn., 1984, Outstanding Cmty. Svc. award, United Jewish Y's L.I., Frank A. Gulotta Criminal Justice award, Former Asst. Dist. Atty.'s Assn., 1980 award, 1976, 1975, medal for assistance Displaced Homemakers, 1988, Pres.' medal N.Y. Inst. Tech., 1988, Leadership award N/S Health Systems Agy., 1988, Health Care Leader Yr. award N.C. Health Facilities Assn., 1992, plaque Am. Acad. Pediatrics, Med. Soc. N.Y. State, Am. Coll. Obstetrics and Gynecologists, 1992, Legislator of Yr. award, Legislative Leadership award Am. Coll. Emergency Physicians, 1994. Lodge: K.C., Ancient Order of Hibernians, Order Sons of Italy, Elks (New Hyde Park past exalted ruler). Republican. Roman Catholic. Avocations: golf; reading. Office: NY State Senate 201 Expressway Plz 1 Roslyn Heights NY 11577

TULLY, SUSAN BALSLEY, pediatrician, educator; b. San Francisco, July 12, 1941; d. Gerard E. Balsley Sr. and Norma Lilla (Hand) Carey; m. William P. Tully, June 19, 1965; children: Michael William, Stephen Gerard. BA in Premed. Studies, UCLA, 1963, MD, 1966. Diplomate Am. Bd. Pediatrics, Am. Bd. Pediatric Emergency Medicine. Intern L.A. County-U. So. Calif. Med. Ctr., 1966-67, jr. resident pediatrics, 1967-68; staff pediatrician, part-time Permanente Med. Group, Oakland, Calif., 1968; sr. resident pediatrics Kaiser Found. Hosp., Oakland, 1968-69; sr. resident pediatrics Bernalillo County Med. Ctr., Albuquerque, 1969-70, chief resident pediatric outpatient dept., 1970; instr. pediatrics, asst. dir. outpatient dept. U. N.Mex. Sch. Medicine, 1971-72; asst. prof. pediatrics, dir. (ambulatory pediatrics) U. Calif., Irvine, 1972-76, asst. prof. clin. pediatrics, vice chair med. edn., 1977-79; staff pediatrician Ross-Loos Med. Group, Buena Park, Calif., 1976-77; assoc. prof. clin. pediatrics and emergency medicine U. So. Calif. Sch. Medicine, 1979-86; dir. pediatric emergency dept. L.A. County/U. So. Calif. Med. Ctr., 1979-87; prof. clin. pediatrics and emergency medicine U. So. Calif. Sch. Medicine, 1986-89; dir. ambulatory pediatrics L.A. County/U. So. Calif. Med. Ctr., 1987-89, L.A. County-Olive View/UCLA Med. Ctr., 1989—; clin. prof. pediatrics UCLA, 1989-93, prof. clin. pediats., 1993-97; prof. emeritus, 1997—; dir. ambulatory pediatrics UCLA, 1989-96, chief pediatrics, 1996-97; pediatric toxicology cons. L.A. County Regional Poison Control Ctr. Med. Adv. Bd., 1981-97; clin. faculty rep. UCLA Sch. Medicine, 1992-93; pediatric liaison dept. emergency medicine Olive View/UCLA Med. Ctr., 1989-96, dir. lead poisoning clinic, 1993—; mem. quality assurance com. Los Angeles County Cmty. Health Plan, 1986-89; mem. survey team pediatric emergency svcs. L.A. Pediatric Soc., 1984-86; mem. adv. bd. preventive health project univ. affiliated program Children's Hosp. L.A., 1981-83; active numerous coms. Author: (with K.E. Zenk) Pediatric Nurse Practitioner Formulary, 1979; (book chpt. with W.A. Wingert) Pediatric Emergency Medicine: Concepts and Clinical Practice, 1992, 2d edit., 1996; (with others) Educational Guidelines for Ambulatory/General Pediatrics Fellowship Training, 1992, Physician's Resource Guide for Water Safety Education, 1994; reviewer Pediatrics, 1985-89; editl. cons. Advanced Pediatric Life Support Course and Manual, 1988-89, Am. Jour. of Childhood, 1996—; dept. editor Pediatric Pearls Jour. Am. Acad. Physician Assts., 1989-94; tech. cons., reviewer Healthlink TV Am. Acad. Pediatrics, 1991; reviewer Pediatric Emergency Care, 1992—, Archives of Pediatrics and Adolescent Medicine, 1995—; question writer sub-bd. pediatric emergency medicine Am. Bd. Pediatrics, 1993—; assoc. editor: Curriculum for the Training of General Pediatricians, 1996; cons. to lay media NBC Nightly News, Woman's Day, Sesame Street Parents, Parenting, Los Angeles Times; author numerous abstracts; contbr. articles to profl. jours. cons. spl. edn. programs Orange County Bd. Edn., 1972-79; mem. Orange County Child Health Planning Coun., 1973-79; co-chairperson Orange County Child Health and Disability Prevention Program Bd., 1975-76; mem. Orange County Child Abuse Consultation Team, 1977-79; mem. project adv. bd. Family Focussed "Buckle Up" Project, Safety Belt Safe, U.S.A., 1989—;. Fellow Am. Acad. Pediatrics (life, active numerous sects. and coms., active Calif. chpt.); mem. APHA, Ambulatory Pediatric Assn., L.A. Pediatric Soc. (life), L.A. Area Child Passenger Safety Assn. Democrat. Avocations: art needlework, reading. Office: Olive View UCLA Med Ctr Pediatrics 3A108 14445 Olive View Dr Sylmar CA 91342-1437

TULLY, THOMAS ALOIS, building materials executive, consultant, educator; b. Dubuque, Iowa, Nov. 11, 1940; s. Thomas Aloysius and Marjorie Mae (Fosselman) T.; m. Joan Vonnetta Dubay, Nov. 30, 1963; children: Thomas Paul, Maureen Elizabeth. BA, Loras Coll., 1962; postgrad., Georgetown U., 1963-66; MPA, Harvard U., 1968. Mgmt. trainee Office of Sec. Def., Washington, 1962-63, fgn. affairs officer, 1963-70; v.p. Dubuque Lumber Co., 1970-84, pres., 1984-91; pres. Tully's, 1991-92, LBM Mktg. Assocs., Inc., 1992—; adj. instr. Divine Word Coll., 1971, Loras Coll., 1972; adj. instr. Clarke Coll., 1987-89, instr., 1989-91, asst. prof., 1992-97, chmn. dept. acctg. and bus., 1993-97, dir. small bus. inst., 1994-97; pres. Hills and Dales Child Devel. Ctr., Inc., 1992-96; trustee Alverno Apts., 1995—; dir. domestic MBA program U. Dubuque, 1997—. Mem. Dubuque Human Rights Commn., 1974-75, chmn., 1975, Iowa State Com. for Employer Support of Guard and Res. Forces, 1988—; city councilman, Dubuque, 1975-79; bd. dirs. League Iowa Municipalites, 1977-79; mayor City of Dubuque, 1978; vice chmn. Iowa Temporary State Land Pres. Policy Com., 1978-79; pres. N.E. Iowa Regional Coordinating Council, 1985-93, East Cen. Intergovtl. Assn. Bus. Growth, Inc., 1987—, chmn., 1993—; bd. dirs. Pvt. Industry Council of Dubuque and Delaware Counties, Inc., 1983-86; trustee Divine Word Coll., 1986—; pres. Barn Community Theatre, 1988-89; chmn. bd. trustees United Way Svcs. of Dubuque, 1990, campaign chmn., 1991, bd. mem., 1980-94. Recipient Meritorious Civilian Svc. award Sec. of Def., 1970, Gov.'s Vol. award, 1989. Mem. Nat. Lumber and Bldg. Material Dealers Assn. (exec. com. 1988-90), Iowa Lumbermen's Assn. (pres. 1984, chmn. legis. com. 1985-90), Northwestern Lumbermen Assn. (bd. dirs. 1984-87, 2d v.p. 1988, 1st v.p. 1989-90, pres. 1990-91). Democrat. Roman Catholic. Home: 838 Stone Ridge Pl Dubuque IA 52001-1362 Office: LBM Mktg Assocs PO Box 771 Dubuque IA 52004-0771

TULSKY, ALEX SOL, physician; b. Chgo., Aug. 10, 1911; s. Solomon and Clara (Tarnipolsky) T.; m. Klara Glottmann, July 20, 1948; children—Shayne Lee, Steven Henry, Asher Arthur, James Aaron. B.S., U. Ill., 1932, M.D., 1934. Intern Michael Reese Hosp., Chgo., 1934-36; attending obstetrician and gynecologist Michael Reese Hosp., 1938—, pres. med. staff, 1962-64; house officer Bklyn. Jewish Hosp., 1937-38; pvt. practice Chgo., 1938—; clin. prof. obstetrics and gynecology Abraham Lincoln Sch. Medicine, U. Ill., 1980—. Served to lt. col. M.C. AUS, 1941-45. Decorated Bronze Star. Mem. A.M.A., Chgo., Ill. med. socs., Chgo. Gynecol. Soc., Chgo. Inst. Medicine, Chgo. Oriental Inst., Pan Am. Med. Assn., Chgo. Soc. History Medicine. Home: 442 W Wellington Ave Chicago IL 60657-5804 Office: 111 N Wabash Ave Chicago IL 60602

TULSKY, FREDRIC NEAL, journalist; b. Chgo., Sept. 30, 1950; s. George and Helen (Mailick) T.; m. Kim Rennard, June 20, 1971; children: Eric George, Elizabeth Rose. B.J., U. Mo., 1972; J.D. cum laude, Temple U., Phila., 1984. Bar: Pa. 1984. Reporter Saginaw News, Mich., 1973-74, Port Huron Times Herald, Mich., 1974-75, Jackson Clarion-Ledger, Miss., 1975-78, Los Angeles Herald Examiner, 1978-79, Phila. Inquirer, 1979-93; mng. editor Ctr. for Investigative Reporting, San Francisco, 1993-94, exec. dir., 1994; reporter L.A. Times, 1995—; adj. prof. urban studies U. Pa., 1990-93. Recipient nat. awards including Robert F. Kennedy Found. award, 1979, Heywood Broun award Newspaper Guild, 1978, Disting. Svc. medal Sigma Delta Chi, 1978, Pub. Svc. award AP Mng. Editors, 1978, Silver Gavel award ABA, 1979, 87, Pulitzer prize for investigative reporting, 1987, Pub. Svc. award Nat. Headliners Club, 1987; Nieman fellow Harvard U., 1989, Investigative Reporters and Editors medal, 1997. Mem. Investigative Reporters and Editors (pres. 1988-91, chair 1991-93), Reporters Com. for Freedom of Press, Kappa Tau Alpha. Office: LA Times 388 Market St Ste 1550 San Francisco CA 94111-5316

TULVING, ENDEL, psychologist, educator; b. Estonia, May 26, 1927; s. Johannes and Linda T.; m. Ruth Mikkelsaar, June 24, 1950; children: Elo Ann, Linda. BA, U. Toronto, Ont., Can., 1953, MA, 1954; PhD, Harvard U., 1957; MA (hon.), Yale U., 1969; FD (hon.), U. Umea (Sweden), 1982; DLitt (hon.), U. Waterloo, 1987, Laurentian U., 1988; D Psychology (hon.), U. Tartu, Estonia, 1991. Lectr. U. Toronto, 1956-59, asst. prof., 1959-62, asso. prof., 1962-65; prof., 1965-70; prof. psychology Yale U., New Haven, 1970-75; prof. psychology U. Toronto, 1972-85, chmn. dept., 1974-80, univ. prof., 1985-92, Univ. prof. emeritus psychology, 1992—; vis. scholar U. Calif., Berkeley, 1964-65; fellow Ctr. Advanced Study in Behavioral Scis., Stanford, Calif., 1972-73; Commonwealth vis. prof. Oxford (Eng.) U., 1977-78; Tanenbaum chair in cognitive neurosci. Rotman Rsch. Inst. of Baycrest Ctr., Can., 1992—; disting. prof. neurosci., disting. prof. psychology U. Calif., Davis, 1993—. Author: Elements of Episodic Memory, 1983; editor Jour. Verbal Leaning and Verbal Behavior, 1969-72, Psychol. Rsch., 1976-88; co-editor: Organization of Memory, 1972, Memory Systems 1994, 1994; mem. editl. bd. Oxford Psychology Series, 1979-95; contbr. numerous articles on memory to sci. jours. Recipient Izaak Walton Killam Meml. prize Can. Coun., 1994, Meml. scholar, 1976-77, Gold medal award for life achievemnt in psychol. sci. Am. Psychol. Found., 1994; Guggenheim fellow, 1987-88. Fellow Can. Psychol. Assn. (disting. sci. contbn. award 1983), APA (disting. sci. contbn. award 1983, William James fellow), Royal Soc. Can., AAAS (fgn. hon.), Soc. Exptl. Psychologists (Warren medal 1982), Royal Soc. London; mem. NAS (fgn. assoc.), Soc. for Neurosics., Psychonomic Soc. (governing bd. 1974-80), Royal Swedish Acad. Scis. (fgn.), Cognitive Neurosci. Soc. Home: 45 Baby Point Crescent, Toronto, ON Canada M6S 2B7 Office: Rotman Rsch Inst of Baycrest Ctr, Bathurst St, North York, ON Canada M6A 2E1

TULY, CHARLES A., mathematics and computer science educator; b. N.Y.C., Feb. 17, 1947; s. Bernard and Ruth (Rimler) T.; m. Eileen Aida, Nov. 22, 1969; children: Beth, Benay. BS in Edn., Buffalo State, 1967; MS, Yeshiva U., 1971. Perm. cert., N.Y. Tchr. Yonkers (N.Y.) High Sch., 1967-85, Rockland C.C., Suffern, N.Y., 1980-83, Charles E. Gorton High Sch., Yonkers, 1985—; mgr. H. & R. Block, Pearl River, N.Y., 1975-83. Mem. Nat. Coun. Tchrs. Math., Assn. Math. Tchrs. N.Y., Yonkers Fedn. Tchrs. (rep. to edn. 2000 steering com.). Avocations: fantasy baseball, telecommunications. Home: 19 Oakwood Terr New Hempstead NY 10977 Office: Shonnard Pl Yonkers NY 10703

TUMAN, WALTER VLADIMIR, Russian language educator, researcher; b. Heidelberg, Germany, Jan. 21, 1946; came to U.S., 1949; s. Val Alexander Tuman and Valida (Zedins) Grasis; m. Helena Eugenia Makarowsky, June 6, 1970; children: Gregory Vladimir, Larissa Alexandra. BA, Fordham U., 1967; MS in Russian, Linguistics, Georgetown U., 1970, PhD in Russian, 1975. Supr. Russian dept. Def. Lang. Inst., Washington, 1972-75; developer course-curriculum Def. Lang. Inst., Monterey, Calif., 1975-78; asst. prof. Russian Hollins (Va.) Coll., 1978-84; dir. fgn. lang. lab. La. State U., Baton Rouge, 1984-90; assoc. prof., coord. Russian program Thunderbird Campus Am. Grad. Sch. Internat. Mgmt., Glendale, Ariz., 1990-95, prof., 1995—; cons. various univs.; grant participant, cons. US AID Consortia Am. Buss., NIS, 1993—, U.S. Commerce Dept., Nizhny Novgorod, Volgograd, Am. Bus. Ctrs., 1994—. Author: Think Russian: Level I, 1993; editor: A Bibliography of Computer-Aided Language Learning, 1986; contbg. editor Jour. Ednl. Techniques and Techs., 1987—; mem. editl. bd.: Jour. Lang. in Internat. Bus.; author book revs., computer programs, conf. presentations; contbr. articles to profl. jours. Georgetown U. fellow, 1969; recipient Prof.'s Exch. award Internat. Rsch. and Exchs. Bd. (USSR), 1979; Mednick Meml. Fund grantee Va. Found. for Ind. Colls. (Australia), 1983, Apple Computer grantee, 1989, U.S. Dept. Edn. grantee Ctr. Internat. Bus. Edn. and Rsch., 1993—. Mem. Am. Assn. Tchrs. Slavic and East European Langs. (v.p. 1981-84, founder Monterey, Calif. chpt.), Am. Coun. on the Teaching Fgn. Langs., Am. Coun. Tchrs. Russian (bd. dirs. 1992—), Internat. Assn. Learning Lab. Dirs., Assn. Internat. Linguistique Appliquée. Russian Orthodox. Office: Am Grad Sch Internat Mgmt 59th and Greenway Glendale AZ 85306

TUMAY, MEHMET TANER, geotechnical consultant, educator, research director; b. Ankara, Turkey, Feb. 2, 1937; came to U.S., 1959; s. Bedrettin and Muhterem (Uybadin) T.; m. Karen Nuttycombe, June 15, 1962; children: Peri, Suna. BS in Civil Engring., Robert Coll. Sch. Engring. (Turkey), 1959; MCE, U. Va., 1961; postgrad. UCLA, 1963-64; PhD, Tech. U. Istanbul (Turkey), 1971; Fugro-Cesco postdoctoral research fellow U. Fla., Gainesville, 1975-76. Instr. civil engring. U. Va., Charlottesville, 1961-62; asst. prof. civil engring. U. Louisville, 1962-63; teaching fellow UCLA, 1963-64; asst. prof. civil engring. Robert Coll. Sch. Engring., Istanbul, 1966-71; assoc. prof. dept. civil engring. Bogazici U., Istanbul, 1971-75; assoc. prof. then prof. civil engring., coord. geotech. engring. La. State U., Baton Rouge, 1976—; adv. prof. U. Vicosa, Minas Gerais, Brazil, 1991—, Tongji U., Shanghai, China, 1991—; dir. Geomechanics Program NSF, Washington, 1990-94; dir. rsch. Louisiana Transp. Rsch. Ctr., Baton Rouge, 1994—; maitre de conferences Ecole Nationale des Ponts et Chaussees, Paris, 1980—; geotech. cons. Sauti, Spa, Cons. Engrs., Italy, 1969-72, SOFRETU-RATP, Paris, 1972-73, D.E.A., Cons. Engrs., Istanbul, 1974-75, BOTEK, Ltd., Istanbul, 1975—, Senler-Campbell Assos., Louisville, 1979—, Fugro Gulf-Geogulf, Houston, 1980—; cons. UN Devel. Program, 1982-84, 87; cons. in field. Contbr. articles to profl. jours. AID scholar, 1975-76; lic. civil engr., La., Ga., S.C., Turkish Chamber of Civil Engring; French Ministry External Relations scholar, 1982. Fellow ASCE; mem. Am. Soc. Engring. Edn., ASTM, La. Engring. Soc., Turkish Soil Mechanics Group (charter), Turkish Chamber Civil Engrs., Internat. Soc. Soil Mechanics and Found. Engring., Sigma Xi, Chi Epsilon, Tau Beta Pi. Home: 1915 W Magna Carta Pl Baton Rouge LA 70815-5521 Office: La State U La Transp Rsch Ctr Dept Civil Engring Baton Rouge LA 70808

TUMMINELLO, STEPHEN CHARLES, consumer electronics manufacturing executive; b. Paterson, N.J., Nov. 7, 1936. Grad., Fairleigh Dickinson U., 1958. Former pres. N.Am. Philips Lighting Corp.; exec. v.p., former v.p., group exec. Philips Electronics N.Am. Corp. (formerly N.Am. Philips Corp.), 1984-90; pres., chief exec. officer Philips Electronics N.Am. Corp. (formerly N.Am. Philips Corp.), N.Y.C., 1990—. Office: Philips Electronics N Am Corp 100 E 42nd St New York NY 10017-5613

TUMPOWSKY, IRA BRUCE, advertising agency executive; b. N.Y.C., Sept. 24, 1938; s. Mortimer Herbert and Pearl (Weissberger) T.; m. Audrey Francine Klieger, Jan. 13, 1963; children: Jeffrey Lon, Andrew Keith, Brian Peter. BS in Mktg., NYU, 1961. Media buyer Lennen & Newell, N.Y.C., 1962-65; media supr. Young & Rubicam, N.Y.C., 1965-71; v.p., media dir. Young & Rubicam, Houston, 1971-79, sr. v.p., group supr., 1980-86; sr. v.p., group media dir. Young & Rubicam, N.Y.C., 1988-90; sr. v.p. dir. Local Broadcast, 1990-93; media cons., 1993-94; exec. v.p., dir. media svcs. Ferrell Calvillo Comm., Inc., 1994—; sr. v.p., media dir. Wunderman, Ricotta & Kline, N.Y.C., 1979-80. Writer, speaker: (cable TV conv.) The Love Triangle, 1982-88, pres. 1984-88). V.p. bd. trustees Temple Israel, Westport, Conn., 1982-88. With U.S. Army, 1961-67. Named to NYU Student Hall of Fame, 1961. Mem. Bus. Pubis. Audit (Edward Bill award 1980), Alpha Delta Sigma. Democrat. Jewish. Avocations: tennis, gardening, golf, travel. Home: 25 Colony Rd Westport CT 06880-3703 Office: Ferrell Calvillo Comm Inc 250 Park Ave South New York NY 10003

TUMPSON, JOAN BERNA, lawyer. BA with highest distinction, Northwestern U., 1969; JD, Yale U., 1973. Bar: N.Y. 1974, U.S. Dist. Ct. (so. and ea. dists.) N.Y. 1974, U.S. Ct. Appeals (2d cir.) 1975, U.S. Dist. Ct. (no. dist.) Ohio 1977,. U.S. Supreme Ct., 1977, Ohio 1980, Fla. 1980, U.S. Dist. Ct. (so. dist.) Fla. 1981. Gen. assignment reporter, rewriteman AP, N.Y. Bur., A.P. Stringer, Yale U., 1970-72; assoc. Debevoise Plimpton Lyons & Gates (now Debevoise & Plimpton), N.Y.C., 1973-77; staff atty., lectr. law Cleve. Marshall Law Sch., Cleve. State U., 1977-78; vis. asst. prof. law Case Western Res. U., Cleve., 1978-79; assoc. Sage Gray Todd & Sims, Miami, Fla., 1980-82; ptnr. Tumpson & Astbury, Miami, 1982-92, Tumpson & Charchat, Miami, 1993—. Class of 73 sec. Yale Law Sch.; bd. dirs. Greater Miami Jewish Fedn. Cable TV, Inc., 1988-92, long term planning com.; trustee Dade County Art in Pub. Places Trust, 1989-93; host south Fla. talk show One to One Sta. WAXY-AM, 1994—; active Dem. Bus. Coun., 1996—. Mem. Fla. Bar, Yale Club Miami. Office: Tumpson & Charchat 848 Brickell Ave Ste 400 Miami FL 33131-2915

TUNE, BRUCE MALCOLM, pediatrics educator, renal toxicologist; b. N.Y.C., Aug. 26, 1939; s. Buford M. and Sylvia (Newman) T.; m. Nancy Carter Doolittle, Sept. 13, 1969; children: Sara E., Steven M. AB, Stanford U., 1963, MD, 1965. Diplomate Am. Bd. Pediatrics, Am. Bd. Pediatric Neöhrology, Nat. Bd. Med. Examiners. Intern in medicine and pediatrics Strong Meml. Hosp., Rochester, N.Y., 1965-66; rsch. assoc. Lab. Kidney and Electrolyte Metabolism, Nat. Heart Inst., NIH, Bethesda, Md., 1967-69, clin. assoc., 1968-69; resident in pediatrics Stanford (Calif.) U. Sch. Medicine, 1966-67, chief resident, 1969-70, fellow in pediatric renal and metabolic disease, 1970-71, asst. prof., 1971-77, assoc. prof., 1977-83, prof., 1983—, acting chmn. dept., 1991-93, dir. pediatric nephrology, 1971—; attending physician, chief pediatric renal svcs. Stanford U. Hosp., Palo Alto, Calif., 1971-91, Children's Hosp. at Stanford, Palo Alto, 1971-91; cons. physician Santa Clara Valley Med. Ctr., San Jose, Calif., 1973—; attending physician, chief pediatric renal svcs. Lucile Salter Packard Children's Hosp. at Stanford, 1991—, acting chief pediatric medicine, 1991-93; mem. rev. panel internat. study kidney diseases in children NIH, N.Y.C., 1973, 74, polycystic kidney disease study group, Albuquerque, 1984; mem. spl. study sect. on genetics and kidney maturation, Bethesd, Md., 1992; cons. Lilly Rsch. Labs., Indpls., 1980, Merck Sharp and Dohme Labs., Rahway, N.J., 1980, Bristol Labs., Syracuse, N.Y., 1982, ICI Pharms., Cheshire, Eng., 1992, Gilead Scis., Foster City, Calif., 1993, Zeneca Pharms., Mereside, Eng., 1994—; organizing mem., chmn. session on antibiotics NIH and EPA Conf. on Nephrotoxicity of Drygs and Environ. Toxicants, Pinehurst, N.C., 1981; co-dir. Coop. Study Therapy of Steroid-Resistant Focal Glomerulosclerosis in Children, 1988—; mem. rsch. grant rev. panel Ont. (Can.) Ministry Health, 1992—, Wellcome Trust, London, 1994—; reviewer bd. environ. studies and toxicology NRC, 1994. Mem. editl. bd. Am. Jour. Kidney Diseases, 1981-94; guest editor Contemporary Issues in Nephrology, 1984, Jour. Am. Soc. Nephrology, 1991; contbr. articles to med. jours. Grantee NIH, 1985-89, 90-95. Mem. Am. Soc. Nephrology, Internat. Soc. Nephrology, Am. Soc. Pediatric Nephrology (coun. 1978-82, rsch. subcom. 1993—), Internat. Pediatric Nephrology Assn., Western Soc. for Pediatric Rsch., Soc. for Pediatric Rsch., Am. Pediatric Soc., Am. Heart Assn. (coun. on kidney diseases, grantee 1985-88, 89-92), Am. Soc. for Pharmacology and Exptl. Therapeutics, Am. Soc. Renal Biochemistry and Metabolism, Phi Beta Kappa, Alpha Omega Alpha. Office: Stanford U Sch Medicine Dept Pediatrics 300 Pasteur Dr Palo Alto CA 94304-2203

TUNE, TOMMY (THOMAS JAMES TUNE), musical theater director, dancer, choreographer, actor; b. Wichita Falls, Tex., Feb. 28, 1939; s. Jim P. and Eva Mae (Clark) T. Student, Lon Morris Jr. Coll., 1958-59; BFA, U.

Tex., 1962; postgrad., U. Houston, 1962-63. Dancer, choreographer, dir. various prodns., N.Y.C., 1963—. Dancer (Broadway prodns.): Baker Street, 1965, A Joyful Noise, 1966, How Now Dow Jones, 1967, Seesaw, 1973 (Tony award Best Featured Actor musical 1974), (films): Hello Dolly, 1968, The Boyfriend, 1971; dir., choreographer Broadway prodns.: The Best Little Whorehouse in Texas, 1978 (Tony award nominations Best Dir. musical 1979, Best Choreography 1979, Drama Desk award Best Dir. musical 1979), A Day in Hollywood/A Night in the Ukraine, 1980 (Tony award Best Choreography 1980, Tony award nomination Best Dir. musical 1980, Drama Desk awards Best Musical Staging, 1980, Best Choreography 1980), Nine, 1982 (Drama Desk award Best Dir. musical 1982, Tony award Best Dir. musical 1982, Tony award nomination Best Choreography 1982), Grand Hotel, 1989 (Tony awards Best Choreography 1990, Best Dir. 1990, Drama Desk awards Best Choreography 1990, Best Dir. musical 1990); dir., actor, choreographer My One and Only, 1983 (Tony awards Best Actor musical 1983, Best Choreography 1983, Tony award nomination Best Dir. musical 1983, Drama Desk award Outstanding Choreography 1983), The Will Rogers Follies, 1990 (Tony awards Best Choreography 1991, Best Dir. 1991, Drama Desk award Best Choreography 1991); tour Bye, Bye Birdie, 1991-92; dir. Broadway prodn.: Stepping Out, 1987; dir. Off-Broadway prodns.: The Club, 1976 (Obie award 1977), Sunset, 1977, Cloud 9, 1981 (Drama Desk award Best Dir. 1982, Obie award Disting. Direction 1982); performed in the USSR, 1988. Recipient Drama League Musical Achievement award, 1990. Mem. Dirs. Guild Am., Stage Soc. Dirs. and Choreographers, Actors Equity Assn. Office: care Internat Creative Mgmt 40 W 57th St New York NY 10019-4001*

TUNG, FRANK YAO-TSUNG, microbiologist educator; b. Tainan, Taiwan, Republic of China, Feb. 6, 1958; came to U.S., 1984; m. Man-Hwa Do, July 10, 1982; children: Kuang-Tsung, Jack. BS, Tunghai U., Taichung, Taiwan, Republic of China, 1980; MS, Nat. Yangming U., Taipei, Taiwan, 1984; PhD, U. Tenn., 1987. Postdoctoral fellow Harvard U., Boston, 1988-90; asst. prof. U. Fla., Gainesville, 1990-94, U. Pitts., 1994—. Contbr. articles to profl. jours. Recipient Rsch. awards NIH, 1991—, Am. Cancer Soc., 1994-95. Mem. Am. Soc. Microbiology. Office: U Pittsburgh 130 Desoto St Rm 439 Pittsburgh PA 15213-2535

TUNG, KO-YUNG, lawyer; b. Peking, Peoples Republic China, Feb. 20, 1947; came to U.S., 1964; s. Tien-chung and Hung-Fang (Wong) T.; m. Alison Heydt, Feb. 2, 1975; children: Vanessa, Adrian, Cameron, Gregory. BA, Harvard U., 1969; JD, U. Tokyo, 1971. Bar: N.Y., 1973. Assoc. Debevoise & Plimpton, N.Y.C., 1973-76; ptnr. Tung, Drabkin & Boynton, N.Y.C., 1976-84, O'Melveny & Myers, N.Y.C., 1985—; adj. assoc. prof. sch. law NYU, 1974-88. mem. Coun. on Fgn. Rels., N.Y.C., 1986—, The Brookings Inst., 1990, Overseas Devel. Coun., Washington, 1990—, The Japan Soc., 1990, Asia Soc., 1994—, Presl. Commn. U.S. Pacific Trade Investment Policy, 1996-97, Trilateral Commn., N.Y.C., 1990-97; chmn., bd. govs. East West Ctr., Honolulu, 1990—; U.S. Nat. Commn. for Pacific Econ. Cooperation, 1991—; bd. dirs. Asian Am. Legal Def. and Edn. Fund, 1990—; mem. adv. coun. Human Rights Watch/Asia, 1997—, Am. Law Inst., 1997—. Law Faculty fellow Harvard U., 1993. Mem. Phi Beta Kappa. Office: O'Melveny & Myers Citicorp Ctr 153 E 53rd St New York NY 10022-4611

TUNG, PHOEBUS CHE-SE, biomedical educator; b. Nanking, China, Nov. 19, 1948; s. Cheng and Nai-Tsai (Ku) T.; m. Chang-Chu Fu, Aug. 3, 1975; children: Chen-Wen, Chen-Li. MD, Nat. Def. Med. Ctr., Taipei, Taiwan, 1975; PhD in Pharmacology, Vanderbilt U., 1983. Diplomate in medicine. Tchg. asst. Dept. Physiol. and Biophysics, Taipei, 1975-78; tchg. asst. dept. pharmacology Nat. Def. Med. Ctr., Taipei, 1978-79, assoc. prof. dept. pharmacology, 1984-88, prof. dept. pharmacology, 1988-89, prof. dept. physiology and biophysics, 1989-91, prof., chmn. dept. physiology and biophysics, 1991-96; prof. dept. physiology and biophysics, dean acad. affairs Nat. Def. Med. Ctr., 1996—; rsch. assoc. Dept. Medicine and Pharmacology, Nashville, 1983-84; vis. scientist dept. pharmacology Karolinska Inst., Sweden, 1988-89; jointed prof. dept. biomed. engring Chung-Yuan Christian U., Taipei, 1990-91; trustee Chinese Soc. Pharmacology, Taiwan, 1984—, Chinese Soc. Neurosci., Taiwan, 1991—; cons. Bur. of Drug, Dept. Agr., Taiwan, 1986—. Col. Chinese Army, 1969—. Hrafn Sveinbjarnarson Postdoctoral fellow, Nashville, 1983-84; Rsch. grantee Nat. Sci. Coun., Taiwan, 1984—. Mem. Am. Autonomic Soc., Am. Soc. for Pharmacology and Exptl. Therapeutics, Am. Fedn. Clin. Rsch., Chinese Physiol. Soc., The Planetary Soc. Avocations: traveling, reading, mountain hiking, watching movies. Office: Nat Def Med Ctr Dean Acad Affairs, PO Box 90024, Taipei Taiwan

TUNG, ROSALIE LAM, business educator, consultant; b. Shanghai, China, Dec. 2, 1948; came to U.S., 1975; d. Andrew Yan-Fu and Pauline Wai-Kam (Cheung) Lam. BA (Univ. scholar), York U., 1972; MBA, U. B.C., 1974, PhD in Bus. Adminstrn. (Univ. fellow, Seagram Bus. fellow, H.R. MacMillan Family fellow), 1977; m. Byron Poon-Yan Tung, June 17, 1972; 1 child, Michele Christine. Lectr. diploma div. U. B.C., 1975, lectr. exec. devel. program, 1975; asst. prof. mgmt. grad. sch. mgmt. U. Oreg., Eugene, 1977-80; assoc. prof. U. Pa. , Phila. 1981-86; prof., dir. internat. bus. ctr. U. Wis., Milw., 1986-90; endowed chaired prof. Simon Fraser U., 1991—; vis. scholar U. Manchester (Eng.) Inst. Sci. and Tech., 1980; vis. prof. UCLA, 1981, Harvard U., 1988, Copenhagen Bus. Sch., 1995, Chinese U. Hong Kong, 1996; Wis. disting. prof. U. Wis. System, 1988-90, Ming and Stella Wong chair in internat. bus., 1991—. Mem. Acad. Internat. Bus. (mem. exec. bd., treas. 1985-86), Acad. Mgmt. (bd. govs. 1987-89), Internat. Assn. Applied Psychology, Am. Arbitration Assn. (comml. panel arbitrators). Author: Management Practices in China, 1980, U.S.-China Trade Negotiations, 1982, Chinese Industrial Society After Mao, 1982, Business Negotiations with the Japanese, 1984, Key to Japan's Economic Strength: Human Power, 1984, The New Expatriates: Managing Human Resources Abroad, 1988; editor: Strategic Management in the U.S. and Japan, 1987, International Management in International Library of Business and Management Series, 1994, Internat. Encyclopedia Bus. & Mgmt., 1996. Oppehheimer Bros. Found. fellow, 1973-74, U. B.C. fellow, 1974-75, H.R. MacMillan Found. fellow, 1975-77; named Wis. Disting. Prof., 1988, Ming and Stella Wong Prof., 1991. Roman Catholic; recipient Leonore Rowe Williams award U. Pa., 1990, U. B.C. Alumni 75th Anniversary award, 1990. Avocation: creative writing. Office: Simon Fraser U, Faculty Bus Adminstrn, Burnaby, BC Canada V5A 1S6

TUNG, SHIH-MING SAMUEL, medical physicist; b. Taipei, Aug. 18, 1954; came to U.S., 1983; s. Yao-Ching and Chen-Ping (Yen) T.; m. Hilda Tung, Oct. 16, 1983; children: Margaret, David. BS in Nuclear Engring., Nat. Tsing Hua U., Hsinchu, Taiwan, 1976, MS in Nuclear Engring., 1980; MS in Radiol. Sci., U. Colo. Health Sci. Ctr., Denver, 1985. Cert. Am. Bd. Radiology, Taiwan Nat. Bd. Health Physics; lic. med. physicist, Tex. Med. physicist Chung Gung Meml. Hosp., Taipei, 1980-81; health physicist Atomic Energy Coun., Taipei, 1981-83; physicist, radiation safety officer Bishop Clarkson Meml. Hosp., Omaha, 1986-89; med. physicist U. Tes. MD Anderson Cancer Ctr., Houston, 1989—. Contbr. articles to profl. jours. Mem. Am. Assn. Physicists in Medicine, Health Physics Soc. Baptist. Achievements include patents for Tungsten shields for electron beam treatment, computer-controlled miniature multileaf collimator device. Avocations: church choir, reading. Home: 12710 Water Oak Dr Missouri City TX 77489-3902 Office: U Tex MD Anderson Cancer Ctr 1515 Holcombe Blvd # 94 Houston TX 77030-4009

TUNHEIM, JERALD ARDEN, academic administrator, physics educator; b. Claremont, S.D., Sept. 3, 1940; s. Johannes and Annie (Ness) T.; m. Patricia Ann Witham, June 7, 1963; children: Jon, Angie, Alec. BS in Engring. Physics, S.D. State U., 1962, MS in Physics, 1964; PhD in Physics, Okla. State U., 1968. Vis. scientist Sandia Corp., Albuquerque, 1970-71, Ames (Iowa) AEC Labs., 1972; asst. prof. S.D. State U., Brookings, 1968-73, assoc. prof., 1973-78, prof., 1978-80, prof., head physics dept., 1980-85; dean Ea. Wash. U., Cheney, 1985-87; pres. Dakota State U., Madison, S.D., 1987—; bd. dirs. NSF Systemic Initiative. Co-author: Elementary Particles and Unitary Symmetry, 1966, Quantum Field Theory, 1966; contbr. articles to profl. jours. Bd. dirs. Madison Devel. Corp., 1988—. Grantee USDA, 1987-88, S.D. Govt. Office Edn. Devel., 1988-89, U.S. Dept. Edn., Eisenhower Program, 1985-86, 87-90, 92-93, 95-96, U.S. Dept. Edn. Math. and Sci. Program, 1989-92; named Tchr. of Yr. S.D. State U., 1972. Mem. NSPE, Am. Phys. Soc., Am. Assn. Physics Tchrs., Madison C. of C. (bd. dirs. 1990—), Rotary. Republican. Lutheran. Office: Dakota State U Office of President 820 N Washington Ave Madison SD 57042-1735

TUNISON, ELIZABETH LAMB, education educator; b. Portadown, Northern Ireland, Jan. 7, 1922; came to U.S., 1923; d. Richard Ernest and Ruby (Hill) Lamb; m. Ralph W. Tunison, Jan. 24, 1947 (dec. Apr. 1984); children: Eric Arthur, Christine Wait, Dana Paul. BA, Whittier Coll., 1943, MEd, 1963. Tchr. East Whittier (Calif.) Schs., 1943-59; tchr. T.V. TV Channels 13 and 28, So. Calif. Counties, 1960-75; dir. curriculum Bassett (Calif.) Schs., 1962-65; elem. sch. prin. Rowland Unified Schs., Rowland Heights, Calif., 1965-68; assoc. prof. edn. Calif. State Poly. U., Pomona, 1968-71; prof. Whittier Coll., 1968-88, prof. emerita, 1988—; bd. dirs. Restless Legs Syndrome Found., facilitator for So. Calif. Orgn. Bd. dirs. Presbyn. Intercmty. Hosp. Found.; founder Restless Legs Support Group (chmn. 1995—). Recipient Whittier Coll. Alumni Achievement award 1975; Helen Hefernan scholar 1963. Mem. AAUP, Assn. Calif. Sch. Adminstrs. (state bd., chmn. higher edn. com. 1983-86, region pres. 1981-83, Wilson Grace award 1983), PEO (pres. 1990-92), Assistance League of Whittier (v.p. 1994-96), Delta Kappa Gamma (v.p. 1996-97). Home: 5636 Ben Alder Ave Whittier CA 90601-2111

TUNLEY, NAOMI LOUISE, retired nurse administrator; b. Henryretta, Okla., Jan. 10, 1936; d. Alexander and Ludia Bell (Franklin) T. BSN, Dillard U., 1958; MA, U. Mo., Kansas City, 1974. RN, Okla. Staff nurse, assoc. chief nursing svc. Oklahoma City VA Med. Ctr., 1958-65; instr. Iowa Luth. Hosp. Sch. Nursing, Des Moines, 1965-66; charge nurse emergency rm. Mercy Hosp., Iowa City, Iowa, 1966-67; charge nurse, assoc. chief nursing svc. Kansas City (Mo.) VA Med. Ctr., 1967-76, charge nurse neurol. unit, 1976-79, nurse mgr. orthopedic unit, 1979-80, nurse mgr. substance abuse unit, 1980-94; ret., 1994; equal employment opportunity counselor Kansas City (Mo.) VA Med. Ctr., 1976-86; trustee Nat. Coun. Alcohol and Other Drugs, Kansas City, 1986-90. Vol. Am. Cancer Soc., Kansas City, 1971-79, March of Dimes, Kansas City, 1971-79; big sister Big Bros.-Sisters Am., Kansas City, 1974-84. Mem. ARC, Sigma Theta Tau. Avocations: fishing, golf, tennis. Home: 3120 Poplar Ave Kansas City MO 64128-1803

TUNLEY, ROUL, author; b. Chgo., May 12, 1912; s. Joseph Hartley and Lillian (Boyd) T. BA, Yale, 1934. Reporter N.Y. Herald Tribune, 1934-37; asst. circulation mgr. Look mag., 1937-39; syndicated columnist, 1939-41; mem. English faculty Yale, 1946-47; fellow Jonathan Edwards Coll., 1946—; dir. editorial promotion Look mag., 1948-50; staff writer, assoc. editor Am. mag., 1951-56; asst. mng. editor Woman's Home Companion, 1956; assoc. editor Sat. Eve. Post, 1961-63. Author: Kids, Crime and Chaos, 1962, The American Health Scandal, 1966, (with Anne Wahle) Ordeal by Fire, 1966; frequent contbr. to nat. mags. including Reader's Digest, 1951—. Lt. comdr. USNR, 1942-45. Mem. Authors Guild (coun.), Elizabethan Club (adjoining chmn.). Address: PO Box T Stockton NJ 08559-0993

TUNNER, WILLIAM SAMS, urological surgeon; b. San Antonio, Nov. 14, 1933; s. William Henry and Sarah Margaret (Sams) T.; m. Sallie Berry Woodul, Dec. 4, 1965; children: William Woodul, Jonathan Sams. Student Washington and Lee U., 1952-55; MD, U. Va., 1960. Diplomate Am. Bd. Urology. Intern in surgery, then asst. surg. resident Duke Hosp., 1960-62; fellow cancer surgery Cancer Inst. NIH, Bethesda, Md., 1962-64; resident in urol. surgery Cornell-N.Y. Hosp., 1964-68, fellow transplantation, dialysis and biochemistry, instr. surgery, 1968-70; asst. prof. urol. surgery U. Tex. Med. Sch., San Antonio, 1970-72; pvt. practice medicine specializing in pediatric and adult urology, Richmond, Va., 1972—; mem. staff Henrico County St. Marys Hosp., Chippenham, Johnston-Willis hosps.; asst. clin. prof. urology Med. Coll. Va., 1972—. Fellow ACS, (past pres. Va. chpt., gov.-at-large), Am. Acad. Pediatrics (affiliate); mem. AMA, SocietéInternationalde Urologié, Transplantation Soc., Soc. Pediatric Urology, Am. Urol. Assn., Am. Nephrology Assn., SR, Country Club of Va., Deep Runt Hunt Club, Alpha Epsilon Delta, Beta Theta Pi. Episcopalian. Contbr. articles to med. jours., films. Home: Braedon Farm 1240 Shallow Well Rd Manakin Sabot VA 23103-2300 Office: St Mary's Hosp Profl Bldg 5855 Bremo Rd Richmond VA 23226-1926

TUNNESSEN, WALTER WILLIAM, JR., pediatrician; b. Hazleton, Pa., July 25, 1939; s. Walter William and Grace Louise (Schaller) T.; m. Nancy Louise Layton, Aug. 24, 1963; children: Walter William III, Anne L. BA, Lafayette Coll., Easton, Pa., 1961; MD, U. Pa., 1965. Diplomate Am. Bd. Pediatrics (bd. dirs. 1986—). Resident Children's Hosp. of Phila., 1965-67; chief resident in pediatrics Hosp. U. Pa., Phila., 1967-68; isntr., dir. newborn nurseries Hosp. U. Pa./U. Pa. Sch. Medicine, Phila., 1970-72; from asst. prof. to assoc. prof. pediatrics SUNY Health Sci. Ctr., Syracuse, 1972-81, prof. pediat., 1981, acting chair dept., 1985-86; assoc. prof. pediatrics and dermatology Johns Hopkins U. Sch. Medicine, Balt., 1986-90, dir. pediatric dermatology, dir. pediatric diagnostic clinic, 1986-90; assoc. chmn. for med. edn. Children's Hosp. of Phila., 1990-95; prof. pediatrics U. Pa. Sch. Medicine, Phila., 1990-95; sr. v.p. Am. Bd. Pediatrics, Chapel Hill, N.C., 1995—; Robert Wood Johnson clin. Scholar Yale U. Sch. Medicine, New Haven, 1978-79; mem. Nat. Bd. Med. Examiners, 1989-91; mem. sci. bd. Nat. Found. for Ectodermal Dysplasia, 1989-93. Author: Signs and Symptons in Pediatrics, 1983, 2d edit., 1988; editor monthly jour. sects. Capt. USAF, 1968-70. Mem. Am. Acad. Pediats. (sect. on dermatology exec. com. 1993-95), Soc. for Peidat. Dermatology (pres. 1988-89, bd. dirs.), Am. Pediat. Soc. Avocation: furniture refinishing. Office: Am Bd Pediatrics 111 Silver Cedar Ct Chapel Hill NC 27514-1512

TUNNICLIFF, DAVID GEORGE, civil engineer; b. Ord, Nebr., Sept. 18, 1931; s. George Thomas and Ada Ellen (Ward) T.; m. Elaine Jean Interrante, Oct. 17, 1959 (div.); children: Martha Allison Tunnicliff Loeb, Vivian Jean Tunnicliff; m. Joan Elizabeth Duchesneau, Oct. 25, 1975. BS, U. Nebr., 1954; MS, Cornell U., 1958; PhD, U. Mich., 1972. Registered profl. engr., Nebr., Mass. Engr. Nebr. Dept. Rds., Lincoln, 1954-60; asst. prof., then assoc. prof. Wayne State U., Detroit, 1960-67; chief tech. svcs. Warren Bros. Co., Cambridge, Mass., 1967-79; prin., cons. engr. D.G. Tunnicliff, Cons. Engr., Omaha, 1979—. Contbr. to profl. publs. Rep. precinct del., Detroit, 1965-66. With U.S. Army, 1955-56. Mem. ASTM (chair subcom. 1973-94), ASCE, Assn. Asphalt Paving Tech. (bd. dirs. 1976-78), Transp. Rsch. Bd. (com. chair 1983-89). Mem. Evangel. Covenant Ch. Home and Office: DG Tunnicliff Cons Engr 9624 Larimore Ave Omaha NE 68134-3038

TUOHEY, MARK HENRY, III, lawyer; b. Rochester, N.Y., Sept. 27, 1946; s. Mark Henry T.; m. Martha; children—Brendan, Sean, Devin. B.A. in History, St. Bonaventure U., 1968; J.D., Fordham U., 1973. Bar: D.C. 1973, U.S. Supreme Ct. 1980, U.S. Ct. Appeals (D.C. cir.) 1974, U.S. Dist. Ct. D.C. 1974, N.Y. 1984. Asst. U.S. atty. U.S. Atty.'s Office, Washington, 1973-77; spl. trial counsel U.S. Dept. Justice, Washington, 1977-79; spl. counsel to U.S. Atty. Gen., Washington, 1979; ptnr. Vinson & Elkins, Washington; dep. ind. counsel Whitewater Investigation, 1994-95. Served to 1st lt. U.S. Army, 1970-71. Fellow Am. Law Inst., Am. Bar Found. (bd. dirs. 1980-85), Am. Coll. Trial Lawyers; mem. ABA (litigation sect. coun. 1980-90, chair standing com. on continuing edn. of bar, chair 1980-85, Am. Law Inst./ABA com. on continuing profl. edn. 1983—), D.C. Bar (pres. 1993-94, bd. govs. 1988-94), Jud. Conf. U.S. Ct. Appeals (D.C. cir.), Wm. Bryant Inn of Ct. (master). Home: 1655 Kalmia Rd NW Washington DC 20012-1125 Office: Vinson & Elkins The Willard Office Bldg 1455 Pennsylvania Ave NW Washington DC 20004-1008

TUOHY, WILLIAM, correspondent; b. Chgo., Oct. 1, 1926; s. John Marshall and Lolita (Klaus) T.; m. Mary Ellyn Dufek, 1955 (div.); m. Johanna Iselin 1964 (div.); 1 child, Cyril Iselin. BS, Northwestern U., 1951. Reporter, night city editor San Francisco Chronicle, 1952-59; assoc. editor, nat. polit. corr., fgn. corr. Newsweek mag., 1959-66; Vietnam corr. L.A. Times, 1966-68; Middle East corr. L.A. Times, Beirut, 1969-71; bur. chief L.A. Times, Rome, 1971-77, London, 1977-85, Bonn, Fed. Republic Germany, 1985-90; European security corr. L.A. Times, London, 1990—. Author: Dangerous Company, 1987. Served with USNR, 1944-46. Recipient Nat. Headliner award for Vietnam bur. coverage, 1965, Pulitzer prize internat. reporting (Vietnam), 1969, Overseas Press Club award for best internat. reporting (Middle East), 1970, various others.

TUPPER, CHARLES JOHN, physician, educator; b. Miami, Ariz., Mar. 7, 1920; s. Charles Ralph and Grace (Alexander) T.; m. Mary Hewes, Aug. 4, 1942; children: Mary Elizabeth, Charles John. B.A. in Zoology, San Diego State Coll., 1943; M.D., U. Nebr., 1948. Diplomate: Am. Bd. Internal Medicine. Intern U. Mich. Hosp., Ann Arbor, 1948-49; asst. resident U. Mich. Hosp., 1949-50, resident, 1950-51, jr. clin. instr., 1951-52; pvt. practice specializing in internal medicine Ann Arbor, 1954-66; practice medicine specializing internal medicine Davis, Calif., 1966—; rsch. asst. Inst. Indsl. Health, U. Mich., 1951-52, rsch. assoc., 1954-56, instr. internal medicine, 1954-56, asst. prof., 1956-59, assoc. prof., 1959-66, sec. Med. Sch., 1957-59, asst. dean, 1959-61, assoc. dean, 1961-66, dir. periodic health appraisal program univ. faculty, 1956-66; prof. internal medicine Sch. Medicine U. Calif., Davis, 1966-90, prof. emeritus cmty. health & family medicine, 1990—, dean, 1966-80, prof. cmty. health, 1980-90, prof. family practice, 1981-90, acting chair cmty. health, 1989-91, 94-95; mem. adv. bd. Golden State Svcs. Dir. consultation services U. Mich. Health Service, 1956-66, 73-76; pres. Calif. Med. Assn., 1979-80; vice chmn. U. Calif. Davis Found., 1993—, Sacramento Regional Found., 1993-97. Served from 1st lt. to capt. USAF, 1952-54. Fellow ACP; mem. AMA (trustee 1985-89, pres. elect 1989-90, pres. 1990-91, immediate past pres. 1991-92, chmn. coun. sci. affairs 1977-79, coun. sect. med. schs. 1977-78), Internat., Am., Calif. socs. internal medicine, Am. Coll. Health Assn., Assn. Am. Med. Colls., Am. Assn. Automotive Medicine, Yolo County Med. soc., Calif. Med. Assn. (pres. 1979-80, chmn. sci. bd. 1970-78, chmn. liaison to state bar com., chmn. com. on state legislation 1975-85, del. to AMA 1975-85), Sci. Rsch. Club. Club: El Macero Country (dir.). Home: PO Box 2007 El Macero CA 95618-0007 Office: U Calif Med Sch Dept Epidemiology Davis CA 95616

TURAJ, FRANK, university dean, literature and film educator; b. Derby, Conn., May 31, 1934; children: Kristyn, Julie. B.A., U. Conn., 1959, M.A., 1960; Ph.D., Brown U., 1968. Instr. George Washington U., 1962-65; asst. prof. lit. Am. U., Washington, 1965-68, assoc. prof., 1969-74, prof., 1975—, chmn. dept. lit., 1974-76, acting dean Coll. Arts and Scis., 1976-77, dean, 1977-85, founder Am. studies program, 1970, cinema studies program, 1975; Polish exchange and Italian study program Am. U. Author: H.L. Mencken and American Literature, 1968, The Modern Cinema of Poland, 1988; (with others) Post New Wave Cinema in the Soviet Union and Eastern Europe, 1988; co-writer and co-producer: USIA documentary The Impact of Film, 1973. Served with USAF, 1951-55. Recipient Disting. Teaching award Am. U., 1968, Media Achievement award Perspectives mag., Washington, 1980, medal for svc. to Polish culture Govt. of Poland, 1981, Spl. award Polish Filmmakers Assn., 1983, Presdl. citation Am. U., 1985; Disting. Svc. medal Adam Mickiewicz U., Poznan, Poland, 1986, Spl. 70th Ann. of Univ. award, 1989. Mem. Am. Assn. Higher Edn., Am. Assn. Slavic Studies, Assn. Am. Colls., Polish Inst. Arts and Scis. (bd. dirs.). Office: Am Univ Dept of Literature 4400 Massachusetts Ave NW Washington DC 20016-8001

TURANCHIK, MICHAEL, research and development director. Dir. R&D Editek, Inc., Burlington, N.C. Office: 1238 Anthony Rd Burlington NC 27215-8936

TURANO, DAVID A., lawyer; b. Ashtabula, Ohio, Sept. 9, 1946; s. Egidio A. and Mary Agnes (Bartko) T.; m. Karen J. Emmel, Aug. 29, 1970; children: Aaron, Thad, Bethen, Kyle. BS, Kent State U., 1968; JD, Ohio State U., 1971. Bar: Ohio 1971. Staff atty. The Pub. Utilities Commn. Ohio, Columbus, 1971-72; assoc., then ptnr. George, Greek, King, McMahon and Mcconnaughey, Columbus, 1972-79; ptnr. Baker & Hostetler, Columbus, 1979-96, Harris, Carter, Mahota, Turano & Mazza, Columbus, 1996—. Mem. ABA, Ohio State Bar Assn., Columbus Bar Assn., Transp. Lawyers Assn. Roman Catholic. Office: Harris Carter Mahota Turano & Mazza 500 S Front St Ste 1010 Columbus OH 43215-7619

TURANO, EMANUEL NICOLAS, architect; b. Bklyn., Mar. 1, 1917; s. Dominick and Ann (Girordi) T.; m. Sybyl Rosmarin, July 1, 1951; children: Lisa, Laurie, Leslie. Cert. in architecture, Cooper Union, 1941, Profl. Achievement citation (hon. Ph.D.), 1964; BArch, Harvard, 1947, MArch, 1963. Designer Skidmore, Owings & Merrill, 1947-50; chief design Kelly & Gruzen, N.Y.C., 1950-52; prin. E.N. Turano (architects and planners), N.Y.C., 1952—; dir. T-4 Studios, N.Y.C., 1965; tchr. 3d, 4th, 5th and master studios Pratt Inst., Bklyn., 1959-62; archtl. instr. 4th yr. studio Columbia, N.Y.C., 1959-60; Cons. HUD, 1963-67, Sussex Woodlands, Inc., N.J., 1963-66. Mem. Boca Raton (Fla.) Bd. Adjustments and Appeals, 1979—; chmn. Boca Raton Code Enforcement Bd. Served with USAAF, 1941-45, PTO. Decorated D.F.C., Air medal. Recipient several awards including Pub. Housing Authority awards, Archtl. award excellence for Pan Am. Passenger Terminal Bldg., Archtl. award excellence for Am. Inst. Steel Constrn., 1961; Fulbright fellow, 1950. Fellow AIA (exec. com. N.Y.C. 1962-66); mem. N.Y. State Assn. Architects, Nat. Inst. Archtl. Edn. (past sec. treas.), N.Y. Soc. Architects, Municipal Art Soc., Cooper Union Alumni Assn. (gov. 1964-67), Cooper Union Adv. Council (chmn. edn. com. 1957-59). Home and Office: 1900 Isabel Rd Este Boca Raton FL 33486-6734

TURBEVILLE, ROBERT MORRIS, engineering executive; b. Cleve., May 2, 1951; s. Wilfred and Patricia Alice (Lamb) T.; m. Lisa Edelman, Apr. 2, 1977; children: Adam, Dennis, Diana. Student, Drew U., London, 1971-72; BA in History, W. Va. Wesleyan, 1973. Mgmt. trainee U.S. Steel, Pitts., 1973-74, foreman, 1975-79; mgr. standard products Heyl & Patterson, Inc., Pitts., 1979-83, sales mgr. to gen. mgr., 1983-88, v.p., 1988-91, pres., CEO, 1991—; dir. Heyl & Patterson, Inc., Pitts., 1988—; chmn. Bridge & Crane Inspection, Inc., Pitts., 1990—. Asst. leader Cub Scouts Am., Pitts., 1991—; coach Mt. Lebanon Soccer Assn., Pitts., 1990—. Mem. AIME, Coal Prep. Adv. Bd. (co-chmn. 1985-89), Process Equipment Mfrs. Assn., Young Pres. Orgn. Republican. Methodist. Avocations: car restoration, travel, music. Office: Heyl & Patterson Inc PO Box 36 Pittsburgh PA 15230-0036*

TURBIDY, JOHN BERRY, investor, management consultant; b. Rome, Ga., Oct. 18, 1928; s. Joseph Leo and Louyse (Berry) T.; m. Joan Marsales, Dec. 19, 1958 (dec.); children: John Berry, Trevor Martin; m. Jaquelin Lamond Schulter, June 8, 1995. Grad., Darlington Sch., 1945; B.A., Duke U., 1950; postgrad., NYU, 1952, Emory U., 1954-56. 84259 positions Lockheed Aircraft, Marietta, Ga., 1951-56; gen. mgmt. cons. McKinsey & Co., N.Y.C. and London, 1956-63; v.p. adminstrn. ITT Europe, Inc., Brussels, 1963, v.p., group exec. European consumer products, 1964-65, v.p., group exec. for No. Europe, 1965-67; corp. v.p. adminstrn. Celanese Corp., N.Y.C., 1967-68; pres., mng. dir. SIACE, SP.A. subs., Milan, Italy, 1968-69; chmn. bd., pres. Vecta Group, Kalamazoo, Mich., 1970-74; v.p. corp. devel. IU Internat. Corp., Phila., 1974-76, sr. v.p., 1976-77, exec. v.p., 1978-83; exec. v.p. Pitcairn Inc., Jenkintown, Pa., 1984-85; pres., chief exec. officer Pitcairn Fin. Mgmt. Group, 1986-89; chmn. Office John Turbidy, 1990-95; mng. dir. Friedman, Turbidy & Co., Inc., N.Y.C., 1995—. Bd. dirs. Statute of Liberty Ellis Island Found. Served with USNR, 1952. Club: Merion Cricket. Address: 10 Stonehedge Ln Little Silver NJ

TURBIN, RICHARD, lawyer; b. N.Y.C., Dec. 25, 1944; s. William and Ruth (Fiedler) T.; m. Rai Saint Chu-Turbin, June 12, 1976; children—Laurel Mei, Derek Andrew. B.A. magna cum laude, Cornell U., 1966; J.D., Harvard U., 1969. Bar: Hawaii 1971, U.S. Dist. Ct. Hawaii 1971. Asst. atty. gen. Western Samoa, Apia, 1969-70; dep. pub. defender Pub. Defender's Office, Honolulu, 1970-74; dir. Legal Aid Soc. Hawaii, Kaneohe, 1974-75; sr. atty., pres. Law Offices Richard Turbin, Honolulu, 1975—; legal counsel Hawaii Crime Commn., 1980-81. Co-author: Pacific; author: Medical Malpractice, Handling Emergency Medical Cases, 1991; editor Harvard Civil Rights-Civil Liberties Law Rev., 1969. Legal counsel Democratic Party, Honolulu County, 1981-82; elected Neighborhood Bd., 1985, elected chair, 1990-97; bd. dirs. Hawaii chpt. ACLU, 1974-78. East-West Ctr. grantee, 1971, 72. Mem. Hawaii Bar Assn., ABA (chair internat. torts and ins. law and practice com., mem. governing coun.), Am. Trial Lawyers Assn., Hawaii Trial Lawyers Assn. (bd. govs.), Hawaii Jaycees (legal counsel 1981-82), Chinese Jaycees Honolulu (legal counsel 1980-81), Honolulu Tennis League (undefeated player 1983). Jewish. Club: Hawaii Harlequin Rugby (sec., legal counsel 1978-82). Lodge: Elks. Home: 4557 Kolohala St Honolulu HI 96816-4953 Office: 737 Bishop St Ste 1850 Honolulu HI 96813-3202

TURCHI, PETER JOHN, aerospace and electrical engineer, educator, scientist; b. N.Y.C., Dec. 30, 1946; s. Charles Orlando and Fay Florence (Breglia) T.; m. Judith Ann Radogna, June 13, 1967; children: Janita Nicole,

Rebecca Lenore. BSE in Aerospace and Mech. Sci./Physics, Princeton U., 1967, MA, 1969, PhD, 1970. Rsch. assoc. Plasma Propulsion Lab., Princeton U. (N.J.), 1963-70; plasma physicist Air Force Weapons Lab., Kirtland AFB, N.Mex., 1970-72; rsch. physicist Naval Research Lab., Washington, 1972-77, chief Plasma Tech. br., 1977-80; scientist R&D Assocs., Arlington, Va., 1980-81; dir. RDA Washington Rsch. Lab., Alexandria, Va., 1981-89; prof. Aerospace Engring. Ohio State U., Columbus, 1989—; chmn. Megagauss Inst., Inc., Alexandria, 1979-89, bd. dirs., 1989—; chmn. mech. and aero. engring. adv. coun. Princeton U., 1988-92, mem. engring sch. adv. coun., 1988-92, dean's leadership coun., 1992-93; resident/collateral faculty Ohio Aerospace Inst., 1989—; lab cons. Los Alamos (N.Mex.) Nat. Lab., 1989—; intergovtl. sr. rsch. scientist USAF Phillips Lab., Kirtland AFB, N.Mex, 1990—, vis. chief scientist Advanced Weapons & Survivability, 1996-97; lectr. George Washington U., 1987-89, Air Force Pulsed Power Lecture Program, 1979-81; cons. on pulsed power tech.; chmn. 2d Internat. Conf. on Megagauss Fields, Arlington, 1979; chmn. Spl. Conf. on Prime-Power for High Energy Space Systems, Norfolk, Va., 1982; mem. internat. organizing com. Megagauss Magnetic Field Confs., 1979—. Pres. Collingwood Civic Assn. (Va.), 1980-81; rep. Mt. Vernon Council, Mt. Vernon Dist., Fairfax County, Va.; pres. Pulsed Power Conf. Inc., Albuquerque, 1985-87, bd. dirs., 1983—. Served to 1st lt. USAF, 1970-72. Recipient AIAA Nat. Student award, 1967, Invention award U.S. Air Force, 1972; Research Publ. award Naval Rsch. Lab., 1976, U.S. Navy and Air Force invention awards, 1978-83; NSF grad. fellow, 1967-70. Fellow AIAA (assoc., internat. chmn. 18th, 19th, 21st and 22d electric propulsion confs. 1985-91, mem. tech. com. plasmadynamics and lasers, 1983-86, mem. elec. propulsion com. 1987-93, chmn., 1991-93); mem. IEEE (sr. tech. chmn. 5th and gen. chmn. 6th pulsed power confs. 1985-87, mem. plasma sci. and applications exec. com. 1987-89, mem. pulsed power sci. and tech. standing com. 1995—), Am. Phys. Soc., Am. Soc. Engring. Edn., Electric Rocket Propulsion Soc. (pres. 1994—), Planetary Soc., Sigma Xi, Tau Beta Pi. Clubs: Princeton Campus, Va. Ki Soc., Albuquerque Aikido Soc. Editor: Space Propulsion, Vol. I, Propulsion Techniques: Action and Reaction, 1997, Megagauss Physics and Tech., 1980; assoc. editor Jour. Propulsion and Power, 1990-93; contbr. numerous articles in field to profl. jours. and chpts. to books; patentee in field; research on electromagnetic implosion soft x-ray source, high energy x-ray generation by ultrahigh speed plasma flows, plasma flow switch for magnetic energy delivery above 10 megamperes; stabilized liner implosion system for controlled thermonuclear fusion. Office: Ohio State U 328 Bolz Hall 2036 Neil Ave Columbus OH 43210

TURCO, LEWIS PUTNAM, English educator; b. Buffalo, N.Y., May 2, 1934; s. Luigi and May Laura (Putnam) T.; m. Jean Cate Houdlette, May 29, 1934; children: Melora Ann, Christopher Cameron. BA, U. Conn., 1959; MA, U. Iowa, 1962. Instr. Cleve. State U., 1960-64; asst. prof. Hillsdale (Mich.) Coll., 1964-65; asst. prof. to full prof. SUNY, Oswego, 1965-96, poet-in-residence, 1995, prof. emeritus, 1996; grad. asst. English, U. Conn., 1959; editorial asst. Writer's Workshop, U. Iowa, 1959-60; vis. prof. SUNY, Potsdam, 1968-69; Bingham Poet in Residence, U. Louisville, 1982; Writer in Residence, Ashland U., 1991; founding dir. Cleve. State U. Poetry Ctr., 1962, program in writing arts, SUNY Oswego, 1968. Author: First Poems, 1960, Awaken, Bells Falling: Poems 1959-67, 1968, The Inhabitant, 1970, Pocoangelini: A Fantography and Other Poems, 1971, American Still Lifes, 1981, numerous other poetry books including The Shifting Web: New and Selected Poems, 1989; author numerous non-fiction books including The Book of Forms: A Handbook of Poetics, 1968, The New Book of Forms, 1986, Visions and Revisions of American Poetry, 1986, Dialogue, 1989, Emily Dickinson, Woman of Letters, 1993, others; articles. Sec. City of Oswego Charter Revision Commn., 1990-91; active Oswego Opera Theater Chorus, Oswego Festival Chorus, 1986—. With USN, 1952-56. Recipient scholarship Meriden Record-Jour. Pub. Co., U. Conn., 1957-58, 58-59, Disting. Alumnus award, 1992, Melville Cane award Poetry Soc. Am., 1986, others; resident fellowships Yaddo Found., 1959, 77, Faculty fellowships Rsch. Found. of SUNY, 1966-67, 69, 71, 73, 78; grant-in-aid, 1969; inducted into Meriden Hall of Fame, 1993. Home: PO Box 161 Dresden ME 04342-0161

TURCO, RICHARD PETER, atmospheric scientist; b. N.Y.C., Mar. 9, 1943; s. Salvatore Joseph and Mary Louise (Cuocolo) T.; m. Barbara Marie Bren, July 1, 1967 (div. Sept. 1990); 1 child, Richard Cameron; m. Linda Kay Stevenson, July 27, 1991. BSEE, Rutgers U., 1965; PhDEE and Physics, U. Ill., 1971. Research fellow Ames Research Ctr., NASA, Moffett Field, Calif., 1971; research scientist R&D Assocs., Los Angeles, 1971-88; prof. UCLA, 1988—, Disting. Faculty Rsch. lectr., 1992—, dept. chair, 1993—; founding dir. Inst. of the Environment, 1995—. Author: Environmental Consequences of Nuclear War, 1986, (with Carl Sagan) A Path Where No Man Thought: Nuclear Winter and the End of the Arms Race, 1990, Earth Under Seige: From Air Pollution to Global Change, 1997; proposed nuclear winter theory, 1983. Recipient H. Julian Allen award NASA, 1983, 88, Peace Garden award U. N.D., 1984, Leo Szilard award Am. Phys. Soc., 1985; MacArthur Found. fellow, 1986. Mem. Am. Geophys. Union (pres. atmospheric scis. sect. 1992-94, assoc. editor Jour. Geophys. Rsch. 1982-91, fellow 1993), Sigma Xi. Avocations: hiking, handball.

TURCOTTE, DONALD LAWSON, geophysical sciences educator; b. Bellingham, Wash., Apr. 22, 1932; s. Lawson Phillip and Eva (Pearson) T.; m. Joan Meredith Luecke, May 17, 1957; children: Phillip Lawson, Stephen Bradford. BS, Calif. Inst. Tech., 1954, PhD, 1958; M in Aero. Engring., Cornell U., 1955. Asst. prof. aero. engring. U.S. Naval Postgrad. Sch., Monterey, Calif., 1958-59; asst. prof. aero. engring. Cornell U., Ithaca, N.Y., 1959-63; assoc. prof. Cornell U., 1963-67, prof., 1967-73, prof. geol. scis., 1973-85, Maxwell Upson prof., 1985—, chmn., 1981-90. Author: (with others) Statistical Thermodynamics, 1963, Space Propulsion, 1965, Geodynamics, 1982, Fractals and Chaos in Geology and Geophysics, 1992. Trustee U. Space Research Assn., 1975-79. NSF sr. postdoctoral research fellow, 1965-66; Guggenheim fellow, 1972-73; Recipient Charles A. Whitten award Am. Geophysical Union, 1995. Mem. Am. Geophys. Union (Charles A. Whitten Medal, 1995), Geol. Soc. Am. (Day medal 1982), Seismol. Soc. Am., Nat. Acad. Scis., Am. Acad. Arts and Scis. Club: Ithaca Country. Home: 703 Cayuga Heights Rd Ithaca NY 14850-1463 Office: Cornell U Snee Hall Ithaca NY 14853

TURCOTTE, JEAN-CLAUDE CARDINAL, archbishop; b. Montreal, Que., Can., June 26, 1936; s. Paul-Émile and Rita (Gravel) T. Attended, U. Catholique de Lille, France; DD (hon.), McGill U. Grand Seminaire of Montreal Lic. Theology, ordained priest Roman Catholic Ch., consecrated bishop. Aux. bishop Diocese of Montreal, Que., Can., 1982-90, archbishop, 1990—; cardinal Diocese of Montreal, Que., Can., 1994. Home: 1071 de la Cathedrale St, Montreal QC Canada H3B 2V4 Office: Diocese de Montreal, 2000 rue Sherbrooke ouest, Montreal, PQ Canada H3H 1G4

TURCOTTE, JEREMIAH GEORGE, physician, surgery educator; b. Detroit, Jan. 20, 1933; s. Vincent Joseph and Margaret Campau (Meldrum) T.; m. Claire Mary Lenz, July 5, 1958; children: Elizabeth Margaret, Sarah Russell, John Jeremiah, Claire Meldrum. BS with high distinction, U. Mich., 1955, MD cum laude, 1957. Diplomate Am. Bd. Surgery (dir. 1982-88); added qualification in surg. critical care, 1986. Intern U. Mich. Med. Ctr., Ann Arbor, 1957-58, resident in surgery, 1958-60, 61-63, research asst. USPHS grant surgery dept., 1960-61; mem. faculty U. Mich. Med. Sch., Ann Arbor, 1963—, prof. surgery, 1971—, Frederick A Collre prof. surgery, 1977-87, chmn. dept., 1974-87, head sect. gen. surgery, 1974-81, dir. Transplant and Health Policy Ctr., 1985-95, dir. Organ Transplant Ctr., 1984-96, dir. liver transplant program, 1984—; mem. residency rev. com. for surgery Am. Coun. for Grad. Med. Edn., 1980-86; chmn. ethics com. United Network for Organ Sharing, 1987-91. Author 8 books, 51 book chpts. contbr. some 185 articles to profl. jours. Recipient Henry Russell award U. Mich., 1970, Mich. State Med. Soc. award, 1991, Nat. Kidney Found. Mich. Champion of Hope award, 1996. Fellow ACS (gov. 1982-92, pres. Mich. chpt. 1979-80); mem. Transplantation Soc. Mich. (pres. 1973-75), Assn. Acad. Surgeons, Am. Surg. Assn., Soc. Univ. Surgeons, Internat. Transplantation Soc., Ctrl. Surg. Assn. (pres. 1990-91), Midwest Surg. Assn., Am. Gastroenterol. Assn., Western Surg. Assn., Soc. Surgery Alimentary Tract, Am. Soc. Transplant Surgeons (pres. 1979-80, chmn. ethics com. 1991-94), Frederick A. Coller Soc. (pres. 1982-83), Am. Trauma Soc. (founder), Halsted Soc., Mich. State Med. Soc. (Pres.'s award 1991), Am. Liver Found., Am. Coun. on Transplantation (bd. dirs. 1987-90), Ctrl. Surg. Assn. Found. (executor and sec. 1992—), Internat. Liver Transplantation Soc. Roman Catholic. Home: One Regent Dr Ann Arbor MI 48104-1738

TURE, NORMAN BERNARD, public policy research organization executive; b. Cleve., Sept. 8, 1923; s. Albert Abel and Anne T.; m. Donna Jeanne Cramer, Oct. 23, 1979; children: Martha Elizabeth, Peter Douglas, Heather, Julianne, Keli, Anne Claire. Student, Ohio State U., 1941-43; M.A., U. Chgo., 1947, Ph.D. in Econs., 1968. Mem. staff Treasury Dept., 1951-55, Joint Econ. Com., 1955-61, Nat. Bur. Econ. Research, 1961-68, Planning Research Corp., 1968-71; pres. Norman B. Ture, Inc., Washington, 1971-80, Inst. Research Econs. Taxation, Washington, 1977-80; undersec. tax and econ. affairs Treasury Dept., 1981-82; pres. Inst. Research on Econs. of Taxation, 1983—. Author: Accelerated Depreciation in the United States 1954-60, 1967, Tax Policy, Capital Formation, and Productivity, 1973, The Future of Private Pension Plans, 1976, The Effects of Tax Policy on Capital Formation, 1977, Wealth Redistribution and the Income Tax, 1978, The Value Added Tax: Facts and Fancies, 1979, Measuring the Benefits and Costs of Section 936. Served with AUS, 1943-44. Republican. Roman Catholic. Club: Capitol Hill. Office: 1300 19th St NW Ste 240 Washington DC 20036-1629

TURECK, ROSALYN, concert performer, author, editor, educator; b. Chgo., Dec. 14, 1914; d. Samuel and Mary (Lipson) T.; (w. 1964). Piano studies with Sophia Brilliant-Liven, Chgo., 1925-29; with Jan Chiapusso, 1929-31; harpsichord studies with Gavin Williamson, Chgo., 1931-32; piano studies with Olga Samaroff, N.Y.C., 1931-35, studies with Leon Theremin with 2 electronic instruments, 1931-32; BA cum laude, The Juilliard Sch. Music, 1935; MusD (hon.), Colby Coll., 1964, Roosevelt U., 1968, Wilson Coll., 1968, Oxford U., Eng., 1977, Music and Arts Inst., San Francisco, 1987. Mem. faculty Phila. Conservatory Music, 1935-42, Mannes Sch., N.Y.C., 1940-44, Juilliard Sch. Music, N.Y.C., 1943-55, Columbia U., N.Y.C., 1953-55; prof. music, lectr.; regents prof. U. Calif., San Diego, 1966, prof. music, 1966-74; vis. prof. Washington U., St. Louis, 1963-64, U. Md., 1981-85, Yale U., 1991-93; vis. fellow St. Hilda's Coll., Oxford (Eng.) U., 1974, hon. life fellow, 1974—; vis. fellow Wolfson Coll., Oxford, 1975—; lectr. numerous ednl. instns., U.S., Eng., Spain, Denmark, Holland, Can., Israel, Brazil, Argentina, Chile; lectr. Royal Inst. Great Britain, 1993, 96, Boston U., 1993, 94, Smithsonian Instn., 1994, Rockefeller U., 1994, U. Calif., Santa Barbara, 1995, Hebrew U., Israel, Royal Inst. Gt. Britain, London, U. Southampton, Oxford U., 1993, 96, 97, Internat. Piano Found., Lake Como, Italy, 1993, 94, 95, 97, 97; 10th Internat. Congress Logic, Methodology and Philosophy Sci., 1995; founder Composers of Today, 1949-53; soc. for performance internat. contemporary music, founder, dir. Tureck Bach Players, London, 1957, N.Y.C., 1981; founder, dir. Internat. Bach Soc., Inst. for Bach Studies, 1968; founder, dir. Tureck Bach Inst., Inc., 1981, Symposia 1968-86, Tureck Bach Rsch. Found., Oxford, U.K., 1994; Second Ann. Symposium, Structure: Principles and Applications in the Sciences and Music, 1997; Accademia Bartolomeo Cristofori, Florence, 1993-97; Regents prof. UCLA, Santa Barbara, 1995; lectr. Royal Instn., London, 1996, Oxford U., 1996, 97, internat. Piano Found., Lake Como, Italy, 1993-97; with Second Internat. Symposium: Structure, Principles, and Applications in the Scis. and Music: The Notion of Authenticity, 1997. Debut solo recital, Chgo., 1924; soloist Ravinia Park, Chgo., 1926, 2 all-Bachrecitals; Chgo., 1930; N.Y.C. debut Carnegie Hall with Phila. Orch., 1936; series 6 all-Bach recitals, Town Hall, N.Y.C., 1937, ann. series 3 all-Bach recitals, N.Y.C., 1944-54, 59—, ann. U.S.-Can. tours, 1937—; European debut Copenhagen, 1947; extensive ann. European tours; continuing ann. concert tours, recitals, master classes in Spain, Italy, Russia, Eng., Germany, U.S., 1995; world tours in Far East, India, Australia, Europe, 1971, S.Am., 1986, 87, 88, 89, 91, 92, Europe, Israel, Turkey, Spain, 1986-90, Argentina, Chile, 1989, 90, 91, 92, Casals Festival, 1991; N.Y.C. series Met. Mus. Art and Carnegie Hall, 1969—; numerous solo recitals including N.Y.C., 1992, Mostly Mozart Festival, Lincoln Ctr., N.Y.C. , 1994; appeared with leading orchs. U.S., Can., Europe, South Africa, S.Am., Israeli; condr., soloist Collegium Musicum, Copenhagen, 1957, London Philharm. Orch., 1959, N.Y. Philharm., 1960, Glyndebourne Festival Tureck Bach Players, London, 1960-72, San Antonio Symphony, Okla. Symphony, 1962, Scottis Nat. Symphony, Edinburg, Glasgow, 1963, Israel Philharm., Tel Aviv, Haifa and Kol Israel orchs., 1963, Glyndebourne series: Tureck Bach Players, Carnegie Hall, N.Y.C., 1967—, Kans. City Philharm., 1968, Washington Nat. Symphony, 1970, Madrid Chamber Orch., 1970, Israel Festival, Internat. Bach Soc. Orchs., 1967, 69, 70, Tureck Bach Players, Wales, 1976, Carnegie Hall, N.Y., 1975-86, St. Louis Symphony Orch., 1981; Bach festivals cities, Eng., Ireland, Spain, 1959—, Carnegie Hall Ann. Series, N.Y.C., 1975—; TV series Well-Tempered Clavier, Book I, Granada TV, Eng., 1961; BBC series Well-Tempered Clavier, Books 1 and 2, 1976; numerous TV appearances, U.S., 1961—, including Wm. F. Buckley's Firing Line, 1970, 85, 87, 89, Today Show, Camera Three, Bach recitals on piano, harpsichord, clavichord, antique and electronic instruments, 1963—; video concert Teatro Colon, Buenos Aires, 1992; recs. for HMV, Odeon, Decca, Columbia Masterworks, Everest, Allegro, Sony, Video Artists Internat., 1993—, R. Tureck Plays Bach, Goldberg Variations, Great Solo Works Vol. 1 and 2, Live at the Teatro Colon, Rosalyn Tureck: Live in St. Petersburg Videos: Live at the Teatro Colon Live in St. Petersburg, The R. Tureck Collection, vol. 1 The Young Firebrand, vol. 2 The Young Visionary, Tribute to a Keyboard Legend, vol. 3 Tribute to a Keyboard Legend, vol. 4 Rosalyn Tureck: Premiere Performances, vol. 5 Harpsichord Recital; author: Introduction to the Performance of Bach, 3 vols., 1960, Authenticity, 1994, J.S. Bach and Number, Symmetries and Other Relationships, Music and Mathematics, 1995, Cells, Functions and Relationships in Musical Structure and Performance-Proceedings of the Royal Instn., London, 1996; contbr. articles to various mags.; editor Bach-Sarabande, C minor, 1960, Tureck Bach Urtext Series: Italian Concerto, 1983, 2d edit., 1991, Lute Suite, E minor, 1984, C minor, 1985, Schirmer Music, Inc., Carl Fischer Paginini-Tureck: Moto Perpetuo, A. Scarlatti: Air and Gavotte; films: Fantasy and Fugue: Rosalyn Tureck Plays Bach, 1972, Rosalyn Tureck plays on Harpsichord and Organ, 1977, Joy of Bach, 1978, Camera 3: Bach on the Frontier of the Future, CBS film, Ephesus, Turkey, 1985. Decorated Officers Cross of the Order of Merit, Fed. Republic Germany, 1979; recipient 1st prize Greater Chgo. Piano Playing Tournament, 1928, 1st Town Hall Endowment award, 1937, Phi Beta award, 1946, 1st prize and Schubert Meml. Contest winner, 1935, Nat. Fedn. Music Clubs Competition winner, 1935, Musician of Yr., Music Tchrs. Nat. Assn., 1987; NEH grantee. Fellow Guildhall Sch. Music and Drama (hon.); mem. Royal Mus. Assn. London, Am. Musicological Soc., Inc. Soc. Musicians (London), Royal Philharmonic Soc. London, Sebastian Bach de Belgique (hon.), Am. Bach Soc., Oxford Soc. Clubs: Century (N.Y.C., Oxford and Cambridge, London), Bohemians (N.Y.C.) (hon.). Office: Windrush House Davenant Rd, Oxford OX2 8BX, England also: Tureck Bach Rsch Found, Windrush House Davenant Rd, Oxford OX2 8BX, England *My work in Bach is not a narrow specialization, although concentration on a single composer may seemingly give that impression. It spreads to performance on antique instruments, harpsichord, clavichord, fortepiano, to the contemporary piano and electronic Moog, to the organ, to conducting. My work embraces scholarly research in original sources of manuscript notetexts, period treatises, studies in concepts of form and structure ranging from the ancient Far East to medieval, renaissance and baroque culture as well as those concepts which emerge from the 19th and 20th centuries. The years of concertizing in compositions of all periods—pre-Bach, romantic, contemporary, and electronic music and scholarly studies in these fields—have all brought a rich tapestry of understanding to the magisterial requirements for interpreting music of a past era authentically and significantly as a contemporary artist.*

TUREK, SONIA FAY, journalist; b. N.Y.C., Aug. 2, 1949; d. Louis and Julia (Liebson) T.; m. Gilbert Curtis, June 18, 1995. BA in English, CCNY, 1970; MSLS, Drexel U., 1972; MS in Journalism, Boston U., 1979. Children's libr. Wissahickon Valley Pub. Libr., Ambler, Pa., 1973; supr. children's svcs. Somerville Pub. Libr., 1973-78; stringer The Watertown (Mass.) Sun, 1979, The Bedford (Mass.) Minuteman, 1979; reporter The Middlesex News, Framingham, Mass., 1979-82, county bur. chief, 1982-83; reporter The Boston Herald, 1983, asst. city editor, city editor, 1983-86, asst. mng. editor features, 1986-89, asst. mng. editor Sunday, 1989-93, dep. mng. editor, arts and features, 1993—; tchr. Cambridge (Mass.) Ctr. for Adult Edn., 1982, 83; adj. prof. Boston U., 1986; travel writer The Boston Herald, 1984-88, wine columnist, 1984—. Avocations: wine and food, travel, sailing. Office: The Boston Herald One Herald Sq Boston MA 02106

TUREKIAN, KARL KAREKIN, geochemistry educator; b. N.Y.C., Oct. 25, 1927; s. Vaughan Thomas and Victoria (Guleserian) T.; m. Arax Roxanne Hagopian, Apr. 22, 1962; children: Karla Ann, Vaughan Charles. A.B., Wheaton (Ill.) Coll., 1949; M.A., Columbia U., 1951, Ph.D., 1955; DSc (hon.), SUNY, Stony Brook, 1989. Lectr. geology Columbia U., 1953-54, rsch. assoc. Lamont-Doherty Earth Obs., 1954-56; faculty, asst. prof. Yale U., 1956-61, assoc. prof., 1961-65, prof. geology and geophysics, 1965-72, Henry Barnard Davis prof. geology and geophysics, 1972-85, Benjamin Silliman prof., 1985—, chmn. dept., 1982-88, curator meteorites, archaeology coun., dir. Ctr. for the Study of Global Change; chmn. studies in the environment, 1992-93; cons. Pres.'s Commn. Marine Sci. Engring. and Resources, 1967-68; oceanography panel NSF, 1968-70; NASA exobiology panel Am. Inst. Biol. Scientists, 1966-69; mem. NAS-NRC climate rsch. bd., 1977-80, ocean sci. bd., 1979-82, ocean studies bd., 1989-92, bd. on global change, 1992-95, Commn. Phys. Scis., Math. Resources, 1986-90, Commn. Geoscis., Environment, Resources, 1990-92, Com. Global Change Rsch., 1994—; mem. group experts sci. aspects Marine Pollution UN, 1971-73. Author: Oceans, 1968, 2d edit., 1976, Chemistry of the Earth, 1972, (with B.J. Skinner) Man and the Ocean, 1973, (with C.K. Drake, J. Imbrie and J.A. Knauss) Oceanography, 1978, Global Environmental Change, 1996; editor: Jour. Geophys. Resource, 1969-75, Earth and Planetary Sci. Letters, 1975-89, Global Biogeochemical Cycles, 1990-95, Geochim. Cosmochim. Acta, 1997—. Served with USNR, 1945-46. Guggenheim fellow Cambridge U., 1962-63; Fairchild Disting. scholar Calif. Inst. Tech., 1988. Fellow AAAS, Geol. Soc. Am., Meteoritical Soc., Am. Geophys. Union (Maurice Ewing medal 1997), Am. Acad. Arts and Scis.; mem. NAS, Am. Chem. Soc., Geochem. Soc. (pres. 1975-76, V.M. Goldschmidt medal 1989), Sigma Xi (pres. Yale chpt. 1961-62). Home: 555 Skiff St North Haven CT 06473-3013 Office: Yale U Dept Geology and Geophysics PO Box 208109 New Haven CT 06520-8109

TUREN, BARBARA ELLEN, lawyer; b. Newark, Nov. 4, 1951; d. Samuel and Elaine (Goldfarb) T.; m. Leonard Paul Caplan, May 22, 1982 (div. June 1987); 1 child, Andrew. BA with distinction, George Washington U., Washington, 1973; MA with honors, London U., 1974; JD magna cum laude, Seton Hall U., 1990. Bar: N.J. 1990, U.S. Dist. Ct. N.J. 1990, U.S. Ct. Appeals (3d cir.) 1991, U.S. Supreme Ct. 1995. Fundraiser Am. Pl. Theatre, N.Y.C., 1978-79; lit. scout Warner Theatre Prodns., N.Y.C., 1979-80; lit. cons. Theatre Now, Inc., N.Y.C., 1980-82; lit. and talent agt. Don Buchwald & Assocs., N.Y.C., 1982-85; assoc. Hannoch Weisman, Roseland, N.J., 1990-92, Vogel, Chait, Schwartz and Collins, Morristown, N.J., 1992-93; dep. atty. gen. Divsn. Law and Pub. Safety, State of N.J., Newark, 1994—; adj. prof. law Seton Hall U. Sch. Law, Newark, 1994—. Pre-sch. vol. Head Start, Washington, 1970-73; lit. vol. N.Y.C. Sch. System, 1978-85. Recipient Cert. of Membership Seton Hall Constl. Law Jour., Newark, 1989-90. Mem. ABA, N.J. Bar Assn., Essex County Bar Assn., Morris County Bar Assn., Phi Alpha Delta. Jewish. Avocations: travel, theatre, reading, collecting rare books.

TURGEON, EDGAR LYNN, economics educator; b. Mitchell, S.D., Aug. 26, 1920; s. Edgar Franklin and Margie (Fellows) T.; m. Livia Racko, Oct. 13, 1950 (div. 1988); 1 child, Danielle Kim. AB, U. Calif., Berkeley, 1942, MA, 1948; PhD, Columbia U., 1959. With Rand Corp., Santa Monica, Calif., 1950-57; prof. econs. Hofstra U., Hempstead, N.Y., 1957-90, prof. emeritus, 1991—; Fulbright lectr. Moscow State U., 1978, Acad. for Fgn. Trade, Moscow, 1991. Author: The Contrasting Economies, 1963, The Advanced Capitalist System, 1980, State and Discrimination, 1989, Bastard Keynesianism, 1996. Lt. USN, 1942-46, PTO. Home: 30 Duncan Rd Hempstead NY 11550-4616 Office: Hofstra U Dept Econs Hempstead NY 11550

TURGEON, PIERRE, professional hockey player; b. Rouyn, Quebec, Aug. 29, 1969. With N.Y. Islanders, 1992-95, Montreal Canadiens, 1995—; played in NHL All-Star Game, 1990, 93, 94. Recipient Michel Bergeron Trophy, 1985-86, Michael Bossy Trophy, 1986-87, Lady Byng Meml. Trophy, 1992-93. Office: care Montreal Canadiens, 1260 rue de la Gauchetiere, Montreal, PQ Canada H3B 5E8

TURILLO, MICHAEL JOSEPH, JR., management consultant; b. Hartford, Conn., Aug. 22, 1947; s. Michael Joseph and Alice (Vargas) T.; m. Deborah Sherburne; children: Stephanie, Christopher. BS, Providence Coll., 1969; MBA, Syracuse U., 1972; MS, U. Mass., 1973. Cons. Peat, Marwick, Mitchell & Co. (name changed to KPMG Peat Marwick), Boston, 1974-77, mgr., 1977-82, ptnr., 1982—, nat. cons. practice dir. for fin. svc. cos., 1985-91; chmn. Internat. Mgmt. Cons. Practice Com. on Banking and Fin., 1986—; nat. ptnr.-in-charge Fin. Svcs.-Specialized Cons., 1990-93, Capital Strategies, 1995—, nat. lead ptnr. in charge Global Capital Group, 1993-94. Com. mem. United Way, Boston, 1981-83; trustee Elliot Montessori, South Natick, Mass., 1984-85; dir. Greater Boston coun. Boy Scouts Am., 1988—. Capt. U.S. Army, 1969-71, Vietnam. Decorated Bronze Star. Mem. Bank Mktg. Assn., Assn. Planning Execs., Assn. Corp. Planners, Beta Gamma Sigma. Roman Catholic. Avocations: tennis, photography, travel, golf. Home: 47 South St Natick MA 01760-5526 Office: KPMG Peat Marwick 99 High St Boston MA 02110-2320 also: 345 Park Ave New York NY 10154-0004

TURINO, GERARD MICHAEL, physician, medical scientist, educator; b. N.Y.C., May 16, 1924; s. Michael and Lucy (Arciero) T.; m. Dorothy Estes, Aug. 25, 1951; children: Peter, Phillip, James. A.B., Princeton U., 1945; M.D., Columbia U., 1948. Diplomate: Am. Bd. Internal Medicine. Intern Columbia U., Bellevue Hosp., 1948-49, asst. resident in medicine, 1949-50; resident in medicine New Haven Hosp., 1950-51; chief resident in medicine Columbia U. div. Bellevue Hosp., 1953-54; sr. fellow N.Y. Heart Assn., 1956-60; career investigator Health Research Council City of N.Y., 1961-71; asst. prof. medicine Columbia U., 1960-67, assoc. prof., 1967-72, prof. medicine, 1973-83, John H. Keating prof. medicine, 1983—; mem. staff Presbyn. Hosp., N.Y.C., 1960—; attending physician Presbyn. Hosp., 1983—; dir. med. svcs. St. Lukes-Roosevelt Hosp., N.Y.C., 1983-92; cons. on sci. affairs Am. Thoracic Soc., 1992—; mem. sci. adv. com. Nat. Heart, Lung, and Blood Inst., Am. Lung Assn., Am. Heart Assn., N.Y. Lung Assn., N.Y. Heart Assn.; mem. staff divsn. med. sci. Nat. Rsch. Coun., Washington; cons. VA Hosp., East Orange, N.J., 1962-67; cons. in medicine Englewood (N.J.) Hosp., Hackensack (N.J.) Hosp., pres.-elect Am. Bur. Med. Advancement in China, 1994, pres., 1994—. Contbr. articles to med. jours. Mem. Bd. Edn., Alpine, N.J., 1960-67. Served to capt. USAF, 1951-53. Recipient Joseph Mather Smith prize Columbia U., 1965, Alumni medal, 1983; Silver medal Alumni Assn. Coll. Physicians and Surgeons Columbia U., 1979, gold medal, 1986. Fellow AAAS; mem. Assn. Am. Physicians, Am. Soc. Clin. Investigation, Harvey Soc., Am. Thoracic Soc. (pres. 1987-88), Am. Fedn. Clin. Rsch., Am. Physiol. Soc. (chmn. steering com. respiration sect.), Am. Heart Assn. (award of merit 1980, Disting. Achievement award 1989, bd. dirs.), N.Y. Heart Assn. (pres. 1981-83, dir.), N.Y. Lung Assn. (dir.), N.Y. Med.-Surg. Soc. (pres. 1995), N.Y. Clin. Soc., Princeton Club (N.Y.C.), Maidstone Club, Devon Yacht Club, Century Assn. Club. Home: 66 E 79th St New York NY 10021-0217 Office: St Lukes-Roosevelt Hosp W 114th St and Amsterdam Ave New York NY 10025

TURINSKY, PAUL JOSEF, nuclear engineer, educator; b. Hoboken, N.J., Oct. 20, 1944; s. Paul J. and Wilma A. (Budig) T.; m. Karen Ann DeLuca, Aug. 29, 1966; children: Grant Dean, Beth Noelle. BS, U. R.I., 1966; MSE, U. Mich., 1967, PhD, 1970; MBA, U. Pitts., 1979. Asst. prof. Rensselaer Poly. Inst., Troy, N.Y., 1971-73; engr., mgr. nuclear design Westinghouse Elec. Corp., Pitts., 1973-78, mgr. core devel., 1978-80; head dept. nuclear engring. N.C. State U., Raleigh, 1980-88, prof., 1980—, dir. Electric Power Rsch. Ctr., 1989—; pres. Nuclear Fuel Mgmt. Assocs., 1994—; bd. dirs. Quantum Rsch. Svcs.; cons. Electric Power Rsch. Inst., Palo Alto, Calif., 1980—, Sci. Applications Internat. Corp., 1990-92, U.S. Dept. of Energy, 1993; tech. specialist Internat. Atomic Energy Agy., Vienna, Austria, 1982—; mem. nuclear safety rev. bd. Duke Power Co., Charlotte, N.C., 1986—. Author: (with others) CRC Handbook of Nuclear Reactor Calculations, 1986; contbr. more than 100 articles to tech. jours. Recipient Oustanding Tchr. award N.C. State U., 1985, Alcoa Disting. Rsch. award, 1993, Supercomputer award IBM, 1991. Fellow Am. Nuc. Soc. (chmn. reactor physics divsn. 1987-88, chmn. math. and computer divsn. 1995-96, Mark Mills award 1971, bd. dirs. 1990-93); mem. AAAS (mem. math. com.), IEEE Computer Soc., Am. Soc. Engring. Educators (chmn. nuc. engring.

divsn. 1984-85, Glenn Murphy award 1990), Edison Electric Inst. (Power Engring. Educator award 1992), Soc. Indsl. and Applied Math. Office: NC State U Dept Nuclear Engring PO Box 7909 Raleigh NC 27695-7909

TURK, AUSTIN THEODORE, sociology educator; b. Gainesville, Ga., May 28, 1934; s. Hollis Theodore and Ruth (Vandiver) T.; m. Janet Stuart Irving, Oct. 4, 1957 (div. 1977); children: Catherine, Jennifer; m. Ruth-Ellen Marie Grimes, July 27, 1985. BA cum laude, U. Ga., 1956; MA, U. Ky., 1959; PhD, U. Wis., 1962. Acting instr. sociology U. Wis., Madison, 1961-62; from instr. to prof. sociology Ind. U., Bloomington, 1962-74; prof. U. Toronto, Can., 1974-88; prof. U. Calif., Riverside, 1988—, chmn. dept. sociology, 1989-94; interim dir. Robert B. Presley Ctr. for Crime and Justice Studies, 1994-95. Author: Criminality and Legal Order, 1969, Political Criminality, 1982; gen. editor crime and justice series SUNY Press, Albany, 1990—; contbr. articles to jours. in field. Mem. Calif. Mus. Photography, 1988—, Citizens Univ. Com., 1990—. Recipient Paul Tappan award Western Soc. Criminology, 1989. Fellow Am. Soc. Criminology (pres. 1984-85); mem. Am. Sociol. Assn. (chair criminology sect. 1975-76), Law and Soc. Assn. (trustee 1982-85), Acad. Criminal Justice Scis. Democrat. Avocations: gardening, reading, swimming, tennis. Office: Dept Sociology U Calif Riverside Riverside CA 92521

TURK, JAMES CLINTON, federal judge; b. Roanoke, Va., May 3, 1923; s. James Alexander and Geneva (Richardson) T.; m. Barbara Duncan, Aug. 21, 1954; children—Ramona Leah, James Clinton, Robert Malcolm Duncan, Mary Elizabeth, David Michael. A.B., Roanoke Coll., 1949; L.L.B., Washington and Lee U., 1952. Bar: Va. bar 1952. Assoc. Dalton & Poff, Radford, Va., 1952-53; ptnr. Dalton, Poff & Turk, Radford, 1953-72; U.S. senator from Va., 1959-72; judge U.S. Dist. Ct. (we. dist.) Va., Roanoke, 1972-73, chief judge, 1973—; dir. 1st & Mchts. Nat. Bank of Radford. Mem. Va. Senate, from 1959, minority leader.; Trustee Radford Community Hosp., 1959—. Served with AUS, 1943-46. Mem. Order of Coif, Phi Beta Kappa, Omicron Delta Kappa. Baptist (deacon). Home: 1002 Walker Dr Radford VA 24141-3018 Office: US Dist Ct 246 Franklin Rd SW # 220 Roanoke VA 24011-2204

TURK, MATT, football player; b. Greenfield, Wis., June 16, 1968. Student, U. Wis. Punter Washington Redskins, 1995—. Named to Pro Bowl, 1996. Office: care Washington Redskins PO Box 17247 Dulles Internat Airport Washington DC 20041*

TURK, MILAN JOSEPH, chemical company executive; b. Baton Rouge, Nov. 25, 1938; s. Frank P. and Zdenka (Cop) T.; m. Margot Genre, Sept. 10, 1937; children: Milan J. Jr., Margot C., Richard P. BS in Chem. Engring., La. State U., 1960, MBA, 1962; grad. advanced mgmt. program, Harvard U., 1985. Process engring. and bus. analyst Exxon Corp., Baton Rouge, 1960-64; with Stauffer Chem. Co., 1965-85; asst. to v.p. mfg. Consol. Chem. Div. Houston, 1965-67; with Stauffer Chem. Co., 1967-85; asst. to v.p. corp. planning Stauffer Chem. Co., N.Y.C., 1967-69; fin. adminstr. ind. chem. div. Stauffer Chem. Co., 1969-72; dir. corp. devel. Stauffer Chem. Co., N.Y.C., 1972-73; dir. ops. Latin Am. div. Stauffer Chem. Co., Westport, Conn., 1972-3; gen. mgr. Latin Am. div. Stauffer Chem. Co., 1973-75; dep. gen. mgr. Europe div. Stauffer Chem. Co., Geneva, 1975-76, corp. v.p., gen. mgr. Europe div., 1976-80; corp. v.p. spl. projects Stauffer Chem. Co., Westport, Conn., 1980-81; corp. v.p., gen. mgr. food ingredients div. Stauffer Chem. Co., 1981-82, corp. group v.p. agr./food products, 1982-85; pres. agr. products div., corp. v.p. Chesebrough-Pond's Inc., Westport, Conn., 1985-88; exec. v.p., mem. exec. com., bd. dirs. Mobay Corp., Pitts., 1988-90; corp. v.p., group exec. Internat. Paper Co., Purchase, N.Y., 1990-92; sr. v.p. Internat. Paper Co., 1992-96, exec. v.p., 1996—. Mem. Am. Inst. Chem. Engring., Soc. Chem. Ind., Nat. Agrl. Chem. Assn. (bd. dirs. 1986-88, exec. com. 1986-88). Republican. Roman Catholic. Club: Patterson (Fairfield, Conn.). Home: 553 Silvermine Rd New Canaan CT 06840-4322 Office: Internat Paper Co 2 Manhattanville Rd Purchase NY 10577-2118

TURK, PATRICIA AVEDON, dance company executive. Gen. mgr. N.Y.C. Ballet. Office: NYC Ballet New York State Theatre 20 Lincoln Center Plz New York NY 10023-6913*

TURK, RICHARD ERRINGTON, retired psychiatrist; b. Staten Island, N.Y., Oct. 6, 1925; s. Richard Jason and Marian (Errington) T.; m. Dec. 30, 1948 (widowed Dec. 23, 1978); children: Stephanie, Jeffrey, Alan. BS, Dartmouth Coll., 1945; MD, Johns Hopkins Med. Sch., 1948. Diplomate Am. Bd. Psychiatry. Intern Highland-Alameda County Hosp., Oakland, Calif., 1948-49; resident Herrick Meml. Hosp., Berkeley, Calif., 1949-50; fellow psychiatry Harvard Med. Sch., Boston, 1950-51, 53-54; clin. instr. UCLA Med. Sch., 1954-70; pvt. practice psychiatry Berkeley, 1954-85; pvt. practice, Walnut Creek, Calif., 1972-88; staff Herrick Meml. Hosp., 1954-85, Walnut Creek Hosp., 1972-88, John Muir Meml. Hosp., Walnut Creek, 1980-88. Capt. USAF, 1951-53, Korea. Mem. AMA, Am. Psychiat. Assn., No. Calif. Psychiat. Assn., Calif. Med. Assn., Alameda-Contra Costa County Med. Assn. Avocations: travel, bicycling, boating, car camping.

TURK, ROBERT LOUIS, radiologist; b. Lima, Ohio, Oct. 30, 1940; s. Herman Matthew and Daphne Carol (Stout) T.; m. Penelope Bryant, Mar. 25, 1964; children: Marjorie Carol Turk Desmond, Susan Elizabeth Turk Charles. BA, Stanford U., 1962; MD, UCLA, 1966. Diplomate Am. Bd. Radiology, Am. Bd. Nuclear Medicine. Rotating intern U. Iowa, Iowa City, 1966-67; resident in radiology Harbor Gen.-UCLA Hosp., Torrance, Calif., 1967-70; radiologist, chief staff, vice chief, head radiology El Cajon (Calif.) Valley Hosp., 1972-83; pvt. practice, El Cajon, 1983—. Elder Presbyn. Ch., 1966—. Maj. M.C., USAR, 1970-72, Vietnam. Mem. Am. Coll. Radiology, Radiol. Soc. N.Am., Calif. Radiol. Soc., San Diego Radiol. Soc. (pres. 1990-91, past treas., rep.), Calif. Med. Soc., San Diego Med. Soc. Democrat. Avocations: tennis, sailing, plays. Home: 1760 Key Ln El Cajon CA 92021-1507 Office: El Cajon X-Ray Imaging 1663 Greenfield Dr El Cajon CA 92021-3520

TURK, RUDY HENRY, artist, retired museum director; b. Sheboygan, Wis., June 24, 1927; s. Rudolph Anton and Mary Gertrude (Stanisha) T.; m. Wanda Lee Borders, Aug. 4, 1956; children: Tracy Lynn, Maria Teresa, Andrew Borders, Jennifer Wells. BS in Edn., U. Wis., 1949; MA in History, U. Tenn., 1951; postgrad., Ind. U., 1952-56. Instr. art history, gallery dir. U. Mont., Missoula, 1957-60; dir. Richmond (Calif.) Art Ctr., 1960-65; asst. dir. San Diego Mus. Art, 1965-67; dir. Ariz. State U. Art Mus., 1967-92; from assoc. prof. to prof. art Ariz. State U., 1967-77. Painter, paintings exhibited in solo and group exhbns. including Stable of Udinotti Gallery, Scottsdale, 1970—; mus. cons., juror, art cons., art lectr.; author: (with Cross and Lamm) The Search for Personal Freedom, 2 vols., 1972, 76, 80, 85, Merrill Mahaffey: Monumental Landscapes, 1979, (with others) Scholder, 1983, also commentaries and critiques. Bd. dirs. Chandler Arts Com., 1987-89, Friends of Mex. Art, Ariz., 1986-96, pres. 1988-90; mem. Tempe Arts Com., 1987-89, Ariz. Living Treasures Com., 1988-93; bd. dirs. Ariz. Mus. for Youth, 1993—; mem. adv. bd. Tempe Hist. Mus., 1995—. Recipient merit award Calif. Coll. Arts and Crafts, 1965, Senator's Cultural award State of Ariz., 1987, Golden Crate award Western Assn. Art Mus., 1974, Ariz. Gov.'s Art award, 1992; named Hon. Ariz. Designer Craftsman, 1975; named dir. emeritus Ariz. State U. Art Mus., 1992, Rudy Turk Gallery at Ariz. State U. Art Mus. named in his honor, 1992; Fulbright scholar U. Paris, 1956-57; hon. fellow Am. Craft Coun., 1988. Mem. Nat. Coun. Edn. Ceramic Arts (hon. mem. coun. 1991), Phi Alpha Theta, Phi Kappa Phi. Democrat. Home: 760 E Courtney Ln Tempe AZ 85284-4003

TURK, S. MAYNARD, lawyer; b. Roanoke County, Va., Oct. 14, 1925; s. James Alexander and Geneva (Richardson) T.; m. Patricia A. Tucker, June 1, 1957; children—Heather F., William A., Thomas M.T. B.A. in Econs., Roanoke Coll., 1949; LL.B., Washington and Lee U., 1952. Bar: Va. 1951, Del. 1961, U.S. Patent and Trademark Office 1975. With Hercules Inc., 1954-90; sr. counsel Hercules Inc., Wilmington, Del., 1966-70, sr. patent counsel, 1972, dir. patent dept., 1972-76, gen. counsel, 1976-90, sec., 1980-82, v.p., 1982—, also bd. dirs.; of counsel Morris, Nichols, Arsht & Tunnel, Wilmington, 1990—; bar examiner State of Del. Bd. Examiners, 1987-91. Mem. Assn. Gen. Counsel, ABA, Phila. Patent Law Assn., Mfg. Chemists Assn. (legal adv. com.), Atlantic Legal Found. (bd. dirs.), Southwestern Legal Found. (adv. bd.), Licensing Execs. Soc., N.A.M., Assn. Corp. Patent Counsel (emeritus), Nat. Security Indsl. Assn. Home: PO Box 3958 Wilmington DE 19807-0958 Office: Morris Nichols Arsht & Tunnell 1201 N Market St Wilmington DE 19801-1147

TURK, STANLEY MARTIN, advertising agency executive; b. Newark, N.J., June 4, 1934; s. Jack and Sylvia (Rachmiel) T.; m. Helga Louise Haberle, Dec. 1, 1962; children: Russell, Laura. BS, Purdue U., 1956; MBS, UCLA, 1989. Sr. account exec. Cunningham & Walsh Advt. Agy., N.Y.C., 1964-68; mgr., v.p. Meltzer Aaron & Lemon, N.Y.C. and San Francisco, 1968-70; pres. Promotion Devel. Specialists, N.Y.C., 1970-75; sr. v.p., ptnr. Chalek & Dreyer, N.Y.C., 1975-80; exec. v.p. Korhausen & Calene, N.Y.C., 1980-88; pres. The Turk Group, N.Y.C., 1991—; tchr. N.Y. Inst. Advt., N.Y.C., 1968-75. Capt. U.S. Army, 1958-60. Recipient Jesse Neal award Am. Bus. Publs. Assn., 1963. Mem. Nat. Assn. Chain Drug Stores, Am. Mktg. Assn. (Effie award 1982). Office: The Turk Group 200 Clearbrook Rd Elmsford NY 10523-1314

TURKEL, STANLEY, hotel consultant, management executive; b. N.Y.C., Sept. 2, 1925; s. Nathan and Mollie (Kurtzman) Turkeltaub; m. Barbara Bell, June 12, 1955 (div. Apr. 1971); children: Marc Alexander, Allison Lee; m. Rima Sokoloff, Apr. 26, 1971; stepchildren: Joshua Bernard Forrest, Benay Debra Forrest. BS, NYU, 1947; MBA, St. Johns U., Jamaica, N.Y., 1980. Laundry cons. Victor Kramer Co. Inc., N.Y.C., 1952-59; v.p., space planner Michael Saphier Assocs., N.Y.C., 1959-62; with spl. hotel svcs. Loews Hotel Corp., N.Y.C., 1962-63; res. mgr. Americana Hotel, N.Y.C., 1963-64; gen. mgr. Drake Hotel, N.Y.C., 1964-66; mng. dir. Summit Hotel, N.Y.C., 1966-67; product line mgr. hotels ITT, N.Y.C., 1968-73; pres. Stanley Turkel Co., Hotel Cons., N.Y.C., 1973—; mem. faculty NYU Ctr. Hospitality, Tourism and Travel Adminstrn. Contbr. articles to N.Y. Times, Wall St. Jour., N.Y. NEwsday, Washington Post, Crain's N.Y. Bus., N.Y. Observer, Smithsonian Mag., N.Y. Mag., N.Y. Post, N.Y. Daily News, Hotel and Motel Mgmt., World's-Eye View, Cornell Quar., Lodging Hospitality, Lodging Mag., Hotel & Resort Industry, The Bottomline, Ariz. Hospitality Trends, FIU Hospitality Rev. Mem. ACLU. With USAAF, 1943-45. Mem. Am. Hotel and Motel Assn. (MHS cert.), Internat. Soc. Hospitality Cons. (ISHC cert.), Civic Affairs Forum (chmn. 1987-93), City Club N.Y. (trustee 1964-97, pres. 1966-68, chmn. 1977-88, chmn. exec. com. 1988-91). Avocations: Reconstruction period of Am. history, civic affairs, autograph collecting, tennis. Office: 10 Rockefeller Plz Ste 1250 New York NY 10020-1903 *As a lifelong civil libertarian, I have learned to cherish the first amendment which provides protection for unpopular speech. We should not carve out exceptions to the first amendment because we are disgusted by vile language or racist epithets.*

TURKEVICH, ANTHONY LEONID, chemist, educator; b. N.Y.C., July 23, 1916; s. Leonid Jerome and Anna (Chervinsky) T.; m. Ireene Podlesak, Sept. 20, 1948; children: Leonid, Darya. B.A., Dartmouth Coll., 1937, D.Sc., 1971; Ph.D., Princeton U., 1940. Research assoc. spectroscopy physics dept. U. Chgo., 1940-41; asst. prof., research on nuclear transformations Enrico Fermi Inst. and chemistry dept., 1946-48, assoc. prof., 1948-53, prof., 1953-86, James Franck prof. chemistry, 1965-70, Distinguished Ser. prof., 1970-86, prof. emeritus, 1986; war research Manhattan Project, Columbia U., 1942-43, U. Chgo., 1943-45, Los Alamos Sci. Lab., 1945-46; Participant test first nuclear bomb, Alamogordo, N.Mex., 1945, in theoretical work on and test of thermonuclear reactions, 1945—, chem. analysis of moon, 1967—; cons. to AEC Labs.; fellow Los Alamos Sci. Lab., 1972—. Del. Geneva Conf. on Nuclear Test Suspension, 1958, 59. Recipient E.O. Lawrence Meml. award AEC, 1962; Atoms for Peace award, 1969. Fellow Am. Phys. Soc.; mem. N.Y. Acad. Sci. (Pregel award 1988), AAAS, Am. Chem. Soc. (nuclear applications award 1972), Am. Acad. Arts and Scis. Mem. Russian Orthodox Greek Cath. Ch. Clubs: Quadrangle, Cosmos. Home: 175 Briarwood Loop Oak Brook IL 60521-8713 Office: U Chicago Dept Chemistry 5640 S Ellis Ave Chicago IL 60637-1433

TURKIN, MARSHALL WILLIAM, symphony orchestra, festival and opera administrator, arranger, composer; b. Chgo., Apr. 1, 1926; 4 children. Student, U. Kans., 1946-48; Mus. B. in Music Composition, Northwestern U., 1950, Mus. M., 1951; postgrad., Juilliard Sch. Music, Columbia U., U. Ind. instr. Fla. Atlantic U. Record rev. columnist, classical music commentator, gen. mgr., Honolulu Symphony and Opera Co., 1959-66; orch. festival mgr.; Ravinia Festival for Chgo. Symphony, 1966-68; founding mgr.; Blossom Festival for Cleve. Orch., 1968-70; gen. mgr. Detroit Symphony, 1970-73, exec. dir., 1973-79, mng. dir., Pitts. Symphony Orch., 1979-88; gen. dir. Hawaii Opera Theatre, Honolulu, 1988-91. Served with USN, World War II. Avocations: jazz musician, newspaper music critic, teaching.

TURKISH, LANCE, physician, ophthalmologist; b. Jersey City, Aug. 6, 1949; s. Solomon and Rosalyn (Lieb) T.; m. Karen Rose Stern, Mar. 10, 1984; children: Hallie Greer, Lainie Brett, Evan Spencer. AB, Case Western Res. U., 1970, MD, 1973. Diplomate Am. Bd. Ophthalmology. Intern Charity Hosp.-Tulane U., New Orleans, 1973-74; resident in ophthalmology 5th Ave. Hosp.-N.Y. Med. Coll., 1974-77; fellow in diseases and surgery of the vitreous and retina Vitreoretinal Rsch. Found., Memphis, 1977; pvt. practice New Orleans, 1978—; co-investigator Early Treatment Diabetic Retinopathy Study, NEI-NIH, 1983-89. Contbr. articles to profl. jours. Chmn. bd. Communal Hebrew Sch., New Orleans, 1993-96; mem. bd. dirs. Juvenile Diabetes Found., La., 1985—, Am. Diabetes Assn., New Orleans, 1980-93, Anti-Defamation League of B'nai B'rith, New Orleans, 1990-96. Recipient scholarship Omicron Delta Kappa. Fellow Am. Acad. Ophthalmology, ACS, Internat. Coll. Surgeons. Jewish. Avocations: swimming, softball. Home: 3700 Edenborn Metairie LA 70002 Office: 3434 Prytania St Ste 305 New Orleans LA 70115-3532

TURKO, ALEXANDER ANTHONY, biology educator; b. Bridgeport, Conn., Aug. 19, 1943; s. Alexander I. and Elizabeth K. (Kulcsar) T.; m. Nancy Bally Hoinacky, Dec. 30, 1967; children: Michelle Lynn, Mark A. BA, So. Conn. State U., 1965, MS, 1967, postgrad., 1976. Assoc. prof. So. Conn. State U., New Haven, 1965—. Mem. AAUP. Home: 11 Birchwood Ln Monroe CT 06468-1025

TURKOT, DOROTHY REGESTER FELTON, writer, illustrator; b. Knoxville, Jan. 31, 1927; d. John William and Dorothy Ester (Regester) Felton; divorced; children: Lynda Anne, Karl Wayne, Terry Nolan, Paul Allison. Student, Chgo. Inst. Fine Arts, 1945. Art tchr. Haddonfield (N.J.) Friends, 1962-86; builder Progress Photos, Haddonfield, 1972; model, actress Phila. and N.Y.C., 1985—. Author, illustrator: (children's books) Mother Cat, 1989, Greta Goose, 1990, (cookbook) Star-lit Kitchens, 1996; designer toy Study Buddy, 1995; paintings exhibited in shows in N.J., Pa. (awards); solo shows include Beach Haven Yacht Club, 1984, High Bar Harbor Yacht Club, 1985; group shows include Phila. Bank, 1986-96, Pine Shore Art Assn., Manahawkin, N.J., 1988-96, Old New Castle, Del., 1991—; appeared in various stage prodns., including Arsenic and Old Lace, Fort Carats, Dear Me, The Sky is Falling, Second Time Around, The Man, The Children's Hour, Guys 'N Dolls, also various indsl. films and commls. Recipient award Nat. Libr. of Poetry, 1994. Mem. Long Beach Island Hist. Assn., Ship Bottom Civic Assn., N.Y. Theater Guild, Friends of Surf-light Theater. Avocations: biking, swimming, boating, boat refurbishing, travel. Home: 353 W 12th St Ship Bottom NJ 08008-4525

TURKUS-WORKMAN, CAROL ANN, educator; b. Balt., Nov. 12, 1946; d. Stanley Phillip and Catherine Anna (Koppleman) Turkus; m. William Thomas Workman, Apr. 23, 1973 (div. 1983); children: Devin Thomas, Timothy Michael. BA in History, Calif. State U., Long Beach, 1969; spl. cert. classroom mgmt., Centralia Sch. Dist., 1980, crosscultural devel. and acad. devel. cert., 1994; M in Adminstrn. Mgmt., U. La Verne, 1997. Cert. crosscultural lang. and acad. devel.; cert. adminstrv. credential. Educator Centralia Sch. Dist., Buena Park, Calif., 1970—; ednl. tech. Centralia Sch. Dist., Buena Park, 1986—; cons. U. Sch.-Space Sci. Acad., Cleve., 1991. Unit commr. Boy Scouts Am., Orange County Coun., 1989-96; co. systems officer Starfleet Bulletin Bd. System, Long Beach, 1990-94; life mem. PTA, Buena Park. Recipient Gold Leaf, PTA Nat., 1991, Woodbadge Beads, Boy Scouts Am., 1991. Mem. Computer Using Educators, Order of Arrow, Kappa Delta Pi. Republican. Roman Catholic. Avocations: sailing, camping, reading, writing, gamer. Office: Centralia Sch Dist 6215 San Rolando Way Buena Park CA 90620-3635 Address: 11762 Argyle Dr Los Alamitos CA 90720-4226

TURLEY, LINDA, lawyer; b. Altus, Okla., July 16, 1958; d. Windle and Shirley (Lacey) Turley; m. Thomas J. Stutz, Mar. 30, 1985; 1 child, Lacey. BS, Georgetown U., 1980; JD with honors, U. Tex., 1983. Bar: Tex. 1983; bd. cert. in personal injury trial law. Atty., head product liability dept. Law Offices of Windle Turley, P.C., Dallas, 1986-95; sole practitioner Dallas, 1995—; mem. task force on Tex. rules of civil procedure Tex. Supreme Ct., 1992-93. Mem. ATLA (bd. govs. 1993—, chair women trial lawyers' caucus 1989-90, chair product liability sect. 1996-97), Tex. Trial Lawyers Assn. (bd. dirs. 1989—). Office: 6440 N Central Expy Ste 610 Dallas TX 75206-4135

TURLEY, MICHAEL ROY, lawyer; b. St. Louis, Mar. 7, 1945; s. W. Richard and Mary Jeanne (Ogle) T.; m. Patricia Ederle, Aug. 21, 1968; children: James, Alisyn. AB, Princeton U., 1967; JD, Mo. U., 1970. Bar: Mo. 1970, U.S. Dist. Ct. (ea. dist.) Mo. 1975. Assoc. Lewis, Rice & Fingersh (formerly Lewis & Rice), St. Louis, 1970-71, 74-80, ptnr., 1980—. Mem. Jefferson County Planning and Zoning Commn., 1987—; bd. dirs. Ctr. for Emerging Techs. Mem. ABA, Mo. Bar Assn., St. Louis Met. Bar Assn., Princeton Club. Episcopalian. Office: Lewis Rice & Fingersh 500 N Broadway Ste 2000 Saint Louis MO 63102-2130

TURLEY, STEWART, retired retail company executive; b. Mt. Sterling, Ky., July 20, 1934; s. R. Joe and Mavis S. Turley; children from previous marriage: Carol Cohen, Karen Shockley; m. Linda A. Mulholland; stepchildren: Kathleen Smiley, Kristine Johnson. Student, Rollins Coll., 1952-53, U. Ky., 1953-55. Plant mgr. Crown Cork & Seal Co., Orlando (Fla.), Phila., 1955-66; mgr. non-drug ops., dir. corporate employee rels. and spl. svcs. Eckerd Corp. (formerly Jack Eckerd Corp.), Clearwater, Fla., 1966-68; v.p. Eckerd Corp., Clearwater, Fla., 1968-71, sr. v.p., 1971-74, dir., 1971-97, pres., chief exec. officer, 1974-96, chmn. bd., 1975-97; bd. dirs. Sprint Corp., Barnett Banks, Inc., Springs Industries, Inc. Trustee emeritus Eckerd Coll., St. Petersburg, chmn. US Ski Team Found.; vice chmn. U.S. Ski Assn. Mem. Fla. Coun. Econ. Ed. (bd. dirs.), Nat. Assn. Chain Drug Stores (bd. dirs., chmn. bd. 1978-79, 88-89), Fla. Coun. 100 (chmn.), World Pres.'s Orgn., Chief Execs. Orgn., Carlouel Yacht Club, Belleair Country Club, Eagle Springs Golf Club, Kappa Alpha. Office: 1465 S Fort Harrison Ave Clearwater FL 33756-2504

TURMEL, JEAN BERNARD, banker; b. Lac Etchemin, Que., Can., Dec. 17, 1944; s. Joseph N. and Rose Marie (Chabot) T.; m. Lorraine Louise Langevin, June 4, 1966; children—Andree, Elaine, Johanne. B.Commerce, Laval U., Quebec, Can., 1966, M.C.S., 1967. Salesman Macmillan Bloedel, Montreal and Vancouver, Can., 1967-68; money market trader Dominion Securities, Montreal, Que., 1968-78, Merrill Lynch Can., Montreal and Toronto, Can., 1978-81; v.p. treasury Nat. Bank Can., Montreal, 1981-83, sr. v.p. treasury and exchange, 1983-86, exec. v.p. treasury, 1986-89, sr. exec. v.p., 1989—; chmn. bd., NBC Clearing, Levesque Beaubien & Co.; d. dirs. Cirano, Levesque Beaubien, Natcan Investment Mgmt., Inc., Cartons St.-Laurent; outside advisor investment com. Assn. Bienfaisance et Retraite de communauté urbaine de Montreal; City of Montreal Pension Plan. Liberal. Roman Catholic. Avoations: music, golf, fishing. Office: Nat Bank Can, 1155 Metcalfe, Montreal, PQ Canada H3B 5G2

TURNAGE, FRED DOUGLAS, lawyer; b. Ayden, N.C., Sept. 24, 1920; s. Fred C. and Lou (Johnson) T.; m. Margaret Futrell, Aug. 21, 1943 (div. Nov. 1980); children: Betty Lou Griffith, Douglas C.; m. Elizabeth Louisa Turnage, Jan. 23, 1981. Grad. Naval Sch. on Far Eastern Civil Affairs, Princeton U., 1945; LLB, Wake Forest U., 1948, LLD, 1970. Bar: N.C. 1948, U.S. Supreme Ct. 1953, U.S. Dist. Ct. D.C. 1965, U.S. Ct. Appeals (D.C. cir.) 1967, U.S. Ct. Appeals (4th and 7th cirs.) 1979. Trial atty. antitrust div. U.S. Dept. Justice, Kansas City, Mo., 1948-51; sr. trial atty. antitrust div. U.S. Dept. Justice, Washington, 1951-65, spl. asst. to atty. gen., 1965; sr. ptnr. Cleary, Gottlieb, Steen & Hamilton, Washington, 1968—; lectr. continuing legal edn. courses, 1973-77. Contbr. articles to profl. jours. Bd. Visitors Wake Forest U. Sch. Law, Winston-Salem, N.C., 1980—. Served to 1st lt. AUS, 1942-46. Recipient Disting. Service in Law citation Wake Forest U., 1979. Mem. ABA (antitrust and litigation sects.), Fed. Bar Assn., Adv. Bd. Antitrust Bulletin, Wake Forest U. Alumni Assn. (pres. 1977), Nat. Lawyers Clubs. Methodist. Avocations: fishing, golf, writing. Home: 209 N Liberty St Arlington VA 22203-1050 Office: 1752 N St NW Washington DC 20036-2907

TURNAGE, JEAN A., state supreme court chief justice; b. St. Ignatius, Mont., Mar. 10, 1926. JD, Mont. State U., 1951; D Laws and Letters (non.), U. Mont., 1995. Bar: Mont. 1951, U.S. Supreme Ct. 1963. Formerly ptnr. Turnage, McNeil & Mercer, Polson, Mont.; formerly Mont. State senator from 13th Dist.; pres. Mont. State Senate, 1981-83; chief justice Supreme Ct. Mont., 1985—. Mem. Mont. State Bar Assn., Nat. Conf. Chief Justices (past pres.), Nat. Ctr. State Courts (past chair). Office: Mont Supreme Ct 215 N Sanders St Helena MT 59601-4522

TURNAGE, LARRY, military career officer; b. Bainbridge, Ga., Dec. 20, 1944; s. Curtiss and Susie Bell (Calhoun) T.; m. Barbara Ann Rich, Apr. 14, 1965; children: Tina, Stanley, Jeffrey, Ronald. BS, U. Tampa, 1973; MA, Webster U., 1980; postgrad., U.S. Army War Coll., 1990. Commd. officer U.S. Army, 1967, advanced through grades to col.; battalion comdr. 269t Aviation Battalion, Ft. Bragg, N.C., 1985-87, U.S. Army Recruiting Battalion, Lansing, Mich., 1987-89; brigade comdr. 2nd Armor Divsn. Aviation Brigade, Ft. Hood, Tex., 1990-91, 17th Aviation Brigade, South Korea, 1991-93; garrison comdr. U.S. Army, Ft. Rucker, Ala., 1993-95; sr. army advisor 99th U.S. Army Regional Supt., Oakdale, Pa., 1995—. Decorated 3 Legion of Merit medals, Def. Meritorious Svc. medal, 4 Meritorious Svc. medals, Bronze Star, 2 Purple Hearts, 4 Air medals. Mem. Army Aviation Assn. Am. (nat. exec. bd. 1991-93, nat. awards bd. 1993—), Asn. U.S. Army. Avocation: aviation. Office: 99th Regional Support Command 5 Lobaugh St Oakdale PA 15071-5005

TURNBAUGH, ROY CARROLL, archivist; b. Peoria, Ill., Oct. 16, 1945; s. Roy Carroll and Zora (Alexander) T.; m. Donna Marie Chase, Mar. 28, 1970; children: Andrew, Peter. BA, Aurora Coll., 1969; AM, U. Ill., 1973, PhD, 1977. Asst. prof. U. Ill., Urbana, 1977-78; archivist Ill. State Archives, Springfield, 1978-85; dir. Oreg. State Archives, Salem, 1985—. Office: Oreg State Archives 800 Summer St NE Salem OR 97310-1347

TURNBULL, ADAM MICHAEL GORDON, financial executive, accountant; b. Dumfries, Scotland, Dec. 29, 1935; emigrated to Canada, 1977; s. Robert Wilson and Catherine Russell (Strang) T.; m. Karen Margaret Walker, June 12, 1965; children: Candida Louise, Andrew Robert. M.A., Edinburgh U., 1956, LL.B., 1958. Chartered acct., Scotland, 1960. With Price Waterhouse, Paris, 1960-62, U.S. Time Corp., France and U.S., 1962-64; group chief acct. Formica Internat. Ltd., London, 1965-70; group fin. dir. Donald Macpherson Group Ltd., London, 1970-77; controller, asst. treas. Indal Ltd., Weston, Ont., Can., 1978-81; controller Indal Inc., Weston, 1978-81; v.p., treas. Indal Ltd., Weston, Ont., Can., 1981-90; v.p. fin., CFO, Hawker Siddeley Can. Inc., Mississauga, Ont., Can., 1990-94, sr. v.p. fin., CFO, 1994—. Mem. Inst. Chartered Accts. Scotland. Home: 2610 Hammond Rd, Mississauga, ON Canada L5K 2M3 Office: Hawker Siddeley Can Inc, 3 Robert Speck Pkwy, Mississauga, ON Canada L4Z 2G5

TURNBULL, ANN PATTERSON, special education educator, consultant; b. Tuscaloosa, Ala., Oct. 19, 1947; d. H. F. and Mary (Boone) Patterson; m. H. Rutherford Turnbull III, Mar. 23, 1974; children: Jay, Amy, Kate. BS in Edn., U. Ga., 1968; MEd, Auburn U., 1971; EdD, U. Ala., 1972. Asst. prof. U. N.C., Chapel Hill, 1972-80; prof., co-dir. Beach Ctr. U. Kans., Lawrence, 1980—; cons. Dept. Edn., Washington, 1987—, Australian Soc. for Study of Intellectual Disability, Adelaide and Washington, 1990. Author: Disability and the Family, 1989, Exceptional Lives: Special Education in Today's Schools, 1995, Families, Professionals and Exceptionality, 1996. Recipient Rose Kennedy Internat. Leadership award, Kennedy Found., 1990; Joseph P. Kennedy Jr. Found. fellow, 1987-88. Mem. Am. Assn. on Mental Retardation (bd. dirs. 1986-88), Assn. for Retarded Citizens (named Educator of Yr. 1982), Zero to Three: Nat. Ctr. for Infants and Toddlers (bd. dirs. 1993-96), Internat. League Socs. for Persons with Mental Handicap (com. chair 1986-90). Democrat. Avocations: travel, exercise. Home: 1636 Alvamar Dr Lawrence KS 66047-1714 Office: Univ Kans Beach Ctr 3111 Haworth Hall Lawrence KS 66044-7516

TURNBULL, CHARLES VINCENT, real estate broker; b. Mpls., May 13, 1933; s. Charles Vivien and Lucille Frances (Dallas) T.; m. Gloria Marlene Tilley, July 21, 1956; children—Charlene Kay, Charles Vincent II, Terry Lucille, Mary Marlene. B.A., U. Minn., 1960, M.S.W., 1962. Unit dir. Mental Health Treatment Service, Cambridge (Minn.) State Hosp., 1962-67, dir. rehab. therapies, 1967-68, program dir., 1973-74; program dir. Minn. Valley Social Adaptation Center, St. Peter, Minn., 1968-73; chief exec. officer Faribault (Minn.) State Hosp., 1974-84; owner Turnbull's Shady Acres Resort, 1979-85; adminstr. Minn. Vets. Homes, Mpls. and Hastings, 1984-85; owner, broker Turnbull Realty, Faribault, Minn., 1986-96; realtor Turnbull Bedker Real Estate Co., 1997—; program cons. Rochester (Minn.) Social Adaptation Center, 1970-71; cons. St. Louis State Sch. and Hosp., 1973-74. Chmn. United Fund Drive, St. Peter, 1971; scoutmaster Twin Valley council Boy Scouts Am., 1973-75; co-chmn. Faribault Bi-Centennial Horizons Subcom., 1975-76; pres. River Bend Nature Center, 1981-84, bd. dirs. 1976-87; mem. Minn. Developmental Disabilities Planning Council, 1975-79, Chmn. comprehensive plan subcom., 1977-78; mem. Cannon River Adv. Council, 1978-79; Mayor, Village of Lexington, Minn., 1962-64; candidate for U.S. rep. 2d Dist. Minn., 1972, 74. Served with USMC, 1953-56. Mem. Democratic Farmer Labor party. Lutheran. Home: Box 38 Rte 3 Saint Peter MN 56082

TURNBULL, DAVID JOHN (CHIEF PIERCING EYES-PENN), cultural association executive; b. Hornell, N.Y., May 18, 1930; s. Gerald and Dorothy Esther (Badgley) T.; m. Martha Lillian Crouse, Aug. 12, 1949 (div. 1960); children: Garry David, Mary Jane Stuhr, Dorothy Grace Houde; m. Frances Early Spring Vickery, May 4, 1985. Degree in ministry, Elim Bible Coll., 1964. Dir. pub. rels. Elim Bible Inst., Lima, N.Y., 1960-61; pastor Eagle Harbor (N.Y.) Ch., 1962-65, South Lima (N.Y.) Gospel Ch., 1962-66; ind. ins. agent, 1965-82; chief, counselor, performer weddings and funerals Pan-Am. Indian Assn., Nocatee, Fla., 1980—, pub. Pan.-Am. Indian Assn. News, 1984—; pastor Cherokee Bapt. Ch., Arcadia, Fla., 1994. Mem. Ministerial Assn. Libertarian. Mem. LDS Ch. Avocation: experimental gardening. Home and Office: 2596 SE Durrance Rd Arcadia FL 34266-1029

TURNBULL, H. RUTHERFORD, III, law educator, lawyer; b. N.Y.C., Sept. 22, 1937; s. Henry R. and Ruth (White) T.; m. Mary M. Slingluff, Apr. 4, 1964 (div. 1972); m. Ann Patterson, Mar. 23, 1974; children: Jay, Amy, Katherine. BA, Johns Hopkins U., 1959; LLB with hon., U. Md., 1964; LLM, Harvard U., 1969. Bar: Md., N.C. Law clerk to Hon. Emory H. Niles Supreme Bench Balt. City, 1959-60; law clerk to Hon. Roszel C. Thomsen U.S. Dist. Ct. Md., 1962-63; assoc. Piper & Marbury, Balt., 1964-67; prof. Inst. Govt. U. N.C., Chapel Hill, 1969-80, U. Kans., Lawrence, 1980—. Editor-in-chief Md. Law Review. Cons., author, lectr., co-dir. Beach Ctr. on Families and Disability, U. Kans.; pres. Full Citizenship Inc., Lawrence, 1987-93; spl. staff-fellow U.S. Senate subcom. on disability policy, Washington, 1987-88; bd. dirs. Camphill Assn. N.Am., Inc., 1985-87; trustee Judge David L. Bazelon Ctr. Mental Health Law, 1993-97. With U.S. Army, 1960-65. Recipient Nat. Leadership award Nat. Assn. Pvt. Residential Resources, 1988, Nat. Leadership award Internat. Coun. for Exceptional Children, 1996; Public Policy fellow Joseph P. Kennedy, Jr. Found., 1987-88. Fellow Am. Assn. on Mental Retardation (pres. 1985-86, bd. dirs. 1980-86, Nat. Leadership award 1997); mem. ABA (chmn. disability law commn. 1991-95), U.S.A. Assn. for Retarded Citizens (sec. and dir. 1981-83), Assn. for Persons with Severe Handicaps (treas. 1988, bd. dirs. 1987-90), Nat. Assn. Rehab. Rsch. and Tng. Ctrs. (chair govt. affairs com. 1990-93), Internat. Assn. Scientific Study of Mental Deficiency, Internat. League of Assns. for Persons with Mental Handicaps, Johns Hopkins U. Alumni Assn. Democrat. Episcopalian. Home: 1636 Alvamar Dr Lawrence KS 66047-1714 Office: U Kans 3111 Haworth Hall Lawrence KS 66044-7516

TURNBULL, JOHN CAMERON, pharmacist, consultant; b. Regina, Sask., Can., Sept. 5, 1923; s. Cameron Joseph and Lillian Irene (Pentz) T.; m. Hazel Evelyn Rockwell, July 31, 1948; children—Lillian Elizabeth, John Rockwell, Jocelyn Hazel. B.S. in Pharmacy, U. Sask., 1949. Pharmacist with village and city pharmacies, 1945-50; supr. pharm. services Dept. Pub. Health, Province of Sask., Regina, 1950-52; ops. mgr. Nat. Drugs, Ltd., Winnipeg, and Saskatoon, 1953; exec. dir. Can. Pharm. Assn., Toronto, Ont., 1953-78; sec.-treas., mng. dir. Canadian Pharm. Realty Co. Ltd.; mem. provisional bd. Pharmacare Ltd.; registrar-treas. Pharmacy Examining Bd. of Can., 1963-68, mem. bd., 1963-78; pharmacy cons., dir. drug service Ministry of Health, Barbados, 1979-84; staff assoc. Mgmt. Scis. for Health, Boston, 1984-85; cons. logistics and pharms. USAID, East Caribbean, PanAm. Health Orgn./WHO (Belize, Cen. Am.), 1985—. Chmn. Govt.'s Spl. Com. on Acetylsalicylic Poisonings, 1967; mem. Emergency Health Services Advisory Com. Served to squadron leader RCAF, 1941-45. Decorated D.F.C., Order of Can., 1975; recipient Can. Centennial medal, 1967, Queen's Jubilee medal, 1977, Can. 125th Anniversary medal, 1992, John C. Turnbull rsch. ann. award in socio-econs. pharmacy established in his honor Can. Pharm. Assn., 1990. Mem. Fedn. Internationale Pharmaceutique (v.p.), Inst. of Assn. Execs. (hon. life), Conf. on Pharmacy Registrars of Can. (sec.), Commonwealth Pharm. Assn. (coun. 1969-78); hon. mem. Am., Canadian, Saskatchewan, B.C., Alta., Ont., Man., N.S. Pharm. Assns., Sask. Pharm. Assn., Ont. Pharmacists Assn., Canadian Soc. Hosp. Pharmacists, Rho Pi Phi. Mem. United Ch. of Canada. Club: Bayview Country (past dir.). Home: 40 Banstock Dr, North York, ON Canada M2K 2H6

TURNBULL, JOHN NEIL, retired chemical company executive; b. South Shields, U.K., Feb. 13, 1940; s. John Smith and Kathleen Bernadette (Higgins) T.; m. Aloysia Lindemann, Feb. 9, 1966; children: John Michael, David Stephen. BSChemE with honors, Kings Coll./Univ. Durham, Eng., 1961. Chartered engr., U.K. Process engr. Brit. Petroleum PLC, Sunbury, Eng., 1961-64; engr. Deutsche B.P., Dinslaken, Fed. Republic Germany, 1964-66; rsch. project mgr. Brit. Petroleum PLC, Sunbury, 1967-70; prodn. mgr. BP Chems., Port Talbot, Eng., 1975-80; pres. BP Chems. Suisse, Geneva, 1982-84; dir. BP Chems., London, 1984-89, dep. chief exec. officer, 1991-93; pres. BP Chems., Cleve., 1989-91; cons. in field. Patentee in field; contbr. articles to profl. jours. Bd. dirs. Playhouse Square Found., Cleve., 1990, The Internat. Forum, Phila., 1995—. Fellow Instn. Chem. Engrs., Royal Acad. Engring. Avocations: skiing, theatre, reading, walking, music.

TURNBULL, RENALDO, professional football player; b. St. Thomas, V.I., Jan. 5, 1966. Degree in Comm., W.Va. U. Linebacker New Orleans Saints, 1990-97, defensive lineman, 1997—. Named to Pro Bowl Team, 1993. Office: New Orleans Saints 7800 Airline Hwy Metairie LA 70003-5151*

TURNBULL, ROBERT SCOTT, manufacturing company executive; b. North Dumfries, Ont., Can., Dec. 19, 1929; s. Leslie William and Marjorie Clara (Scott) T.; m. Dawna Rose Sinclair, Feb. 17, 1956. Sr. Matriculation, Galt U., Ont., 1950; M.T.C., U. Western Ont., 1975. Cert. mgmt. acct. Credit mgr Can. Gen. Tower, Cambridge, Ont., 1951-53, gen. acct., 1953-62, comptroller, 1962-68, v.p. mktg., 1968-78, v.p., gen. mgr., 1978-80, pres., 1980—, also bd. dirs. Mem. Chem. Fabrics and Films Assn. (bd. dirs.), Soc. Plastics Industry (bd. dirs.), Japan Soc. (bd. dirs.), Soc. Mgmt. Accts. Home: 26 Lansdowne Rd S, Cambridge, ON Canada N1S 2T3 Office: Can Gen Tower, 52 Middleton St, Cambridge, ON Canada N1R 5T6

TURNBULL, WILLIAM, JR., architect; b. N.Y.C., Apr. 1, 1935; s. William and Elizabeth (Howe) T. A.B., Princeton U., 1956, M.F.A. in Architecture, 1959; student, Ecole des Beaux Arts Fontainebleau, France, 1956. With Skidmore, Owings & Merrill, San Francisco, 1960-63; founding ptnr. Moore, Lyndon, Turnbull, Whitaker, 1962; partner-in-charge Moore, Turnbull (San Francisco office), 1965-69; mem. design group Pres.'s Adv. Coun. Pennsylvania Ave., 1963; lectr. U. Calif.-Berkeley, Berkeley, 1965-69; vis. prof. U. Oreg., 1966-68; dir. MLTW/Turnbull Assocs., 1970-83; dir. William Turnbull Assocs. William Turnbull Assocs., 1983—; lectr. Stanford U., 1974-77, vis. design critic MIT, 1975, U. Calif., Berkeley, 1977-81, 95; Mobil vis. design critic Yale U., 1982, Bishop vis. prof. archtl. design, 1986; Hyde prof. excellence U. Nebr., 1994; design cons. Formica Corp., 1977-84, World Savs. and Loan, 1976-95; mem. design rev. bd. U. Calif., San Diego, 1988-93, City of Sausalito, Calif., 1976-77; mem. fgn. bldgs. adv. bd. Dept. of State, 1991—; design critic Calif. Coll. Arts & Crafts, 1997. Author: Global Architecture Series: Moore, Lyndon, Turnbull & Whitaker: The Sea Ranch, The Sea Ranch Details, The Poetics of Gardens, 1988; illustrator: The Place of Houses; prin. works include Sea Ranch Condominium I, 1965, Sea Ranch Swim Tennis Club, 1966, Lovejoy Fountain Plaza, Portland (assoc. architect), Faculty Club at U. Calif.-Santa Barbara, Kresge Coll. at U. Calif.-Santa Cruz, Biloxi (Miss.) Library, Am. Club, Hong Kong, Ariz. State U. Sonora Ctr., Tempe, Foothill Student Housing, U. Calif., Berkeley, Mountain View City Hall and Community Theater, Calif., Grace Cathedral Close, San Francisco, St. Andrews Ch., Sonoma, Calif.; mem. editl. adv. bd. Architecture California, 1986-92. Mem. tech. adv. com. Calif. Legislature Joint Com. Open Space Lands, 1968-71; mem. regional honor awards (90) jury AIA, 1968—, nat. honor awards jury, 1969, chmn. jury, 1977, 1988; chmn. jury C.E. honor award, 1973, 79; mem. Progressive Architecture Honor Awards Jury, 1975, Pres.'s Jury for Nat. Design Excellence, 1984; bd. dirs. Pub. Sculpture Pub. Places, 1981-85. Served with AUS, 1959-60. Recipient Calif. Gov. award Planned Communities, 1966, citation Progressive Architecture Design awards, 1962-66, 68-70, 81, 1st honor award, 1971, 74, 1st honor award Homes for Better Living, 1963, Merit award, 1966; Honor award Western Home awards, 1961-62, 62, 63, 66-67, 88, 89, 93, 95; Merit award, 1966-67; House of Yr. award Archtl. Record, 1961, 67, 69, 70, 72, 83; award of Honor San Francisco Art Commn., 1982; Am. Wood Coun. Design award, 1984, Honor award, 1985, 89, 92, 93, 94; Firm of Yr. award Calif. Coun. AIA, 1986, Maybeck award, 1993, cited for continuous distinctive practice of architecture in Calif. by an individual; Am. Wood Coun. Merit award, 1991; Honor award San Francisco AIA, 1988, 91, 93. Fellow AIA (dir. chpt. 1981, Nat. Honor award 1967, 68, 73, 79, 90, 91, 95, award of merit Bay Region honor awards 1963, 67, 7, 78, 82, Nat. 25 Yr. Honor award 1991), Am. Acad. in Rome. Office: William Turnbull Assocs Pier 1 1/2 The Embarcadero San Francisco CA 94111

TURNDORF, HERMAN, anesthesiologist, educator; b. Paterson, N.J., Dec. 22, 1930; s. Charles R. and Ruth (Blumberg) T.; m. Sietske Huisman, Nov. 24, 1957; children: David, Michael Pieter. AB, Oberlin Coll., 1952; MD, U. Pa., 1956. Diplomate Am. Bd. Anesthesiology. Instr. anesthesiology U. Pa. Hosp., 1957-59; asst. anesthetist med. sch. Harvard U., Mass. Gen. Hosp., Boston, 1961-63; assoc. attending anesthesiologist, asst. dir. dept. anesthesiology Mt. Sinai Hosp., N.Y.C., 1963-70; clin. prof. anesthesiology Mt. Sinai Hosp., 1966-70; prof., chmn. dept. anesthesiology W.Va. U. Sch. Medicine and Med. Ctr., Morgantown, 1970-74, NYU Sch. Medicine, 1974—; dir. anesthesiology NYU Tisch Hosp., 1974—; pres. med. bd., med. dir. Bellevue Hosp. Med. Ctr., 1990-91; cons. in anesthesiology Manhattan VA Hosp., Armed Forces Sch. Medicine, 1974-77. Co-author: Anesthesia and Neurosurgery, 2nd edit., 1986, Trauma, Anesthesia and Intensive Care, 1990; contbr. over 150 articles to profl. jours. Lt. M.C., USNR, 1959-61. Fellow Am. Coll. Chest Physicians, Am. Coll. Anesthesiologists (mem. bd. govs. 1977-85, chmn. bd. govs. 1984), N.Y. Acad. Medicine; mem. AMA, Am. Soc. Anesthesiologists, Assn. Univ. Anesthetists, Internat. Soc. Study of Pain, Soc. Acad. Anesthesia Chairmen, Soc. Critical Care Medicine, Soc. Neurosurg. Anesthesia and Neurologic Supportive Care, N.Y. Acad. Scis., N.Y. State Soc. Anesthesiologists. Home: 2 Beekman Pl New York NY 10022 Office: NY Univ Dept Anesthesiology 550 1st Ave New York NY 10016-6481

TURNDORF, JAMIE, clinical psychologist; b. Boston, July 12, 1958; d. Gary Owen and Sharon (Sandow) T.; m. Emile Jean Pin, Jan. 2, 1988. AB in Am. Culture, Vassar Coll., 1980; MSW, Adelphi U., 1983; PhD, Calif. Coast U., 1994. Lic. social worker, N.Y. Pvt. practice psychology N.Y.C. and Millbrook, N.Y., 1981—; lead creative movement and psychodrama program Lincoln Farms Work Camp, Roscoe, N.Y., 1976; with Astor Child Guidance Clinic, Poughkeepsie, N.Y., 1982-83; leader various groups Braig House Hosp., Beacon, N.Y., 1982-87, developer, dir. eating disorders program, 1984-86; founder, dir. INC.TIMACY, 1990—, J.T. Developers, Inc., Poughkeepsie, 1983-91; dir. Hudson Valley br. Ctr. for Advancement Group Studies, Ctr. for Emotional Comm., Millbrook, 1990—. Author: (with Emile Jean Pin) The Pleasure of Your Company: A Socio-Psychological Analysis of Modern Sociability, 1985; columnist Dr. Love various newspapers; love and relationship advice on internet; host Ask Dr. Love, Sta. WEVD, N.Y.C., 1992; creator, inventor LoveQuest: The Game of Finding Mr. Right, 1990 (one of best new games award Fun and Games mag. 1991). Mem. NASW, N.Y. State Soc. Clin. Social Work Psychotherapists. Avocations: house restoration, opera singing, antiques. Home and Office: PO Box 475 Millbrook NY 12545-0475

TURNER, ALMON RICHARD, art historian, educator; b. New Bedford, Mass., July 28, 1932; s. Louis Alexander and Margaret (Mather) T.; m. Jane Beebe; children: Louis Hamilton, David Alexander. AB, Princeton U., 1955, MFA, 1958, PhD, 1959. Instr. in fine arts U. Mich., Ann Arbor, 1959-60; from instr. to prof. art and archaeology Princeton (N.J.) U., 1960-68; prof. fine arts Middlebury (Vt.) Coll., 1968-74, dean faculty, 1970-74; prof. fine arts, pres. Grinnell (Iowa) Coll., 1975-79; prof., dir. Inst. Fine Arts NYU, N.Y.C., 1979-82, dean faculty arts and scis., 1982-85, prof. dept. fine arts, 1985—, dir. N.Y. Inst. Humanities, 1986-93, Paulette Goddard prof. in arts and humanities, 1994—. Author: Vision of Landscape in Renaissance Italy, 1966, 73, (With G. Andres and J. Hunisak) Art of Florence (L'Art de Florence), 1988 (prix 1989), Inventing Leonardo, 1993, Renaissance Florence: The Invention of a New Art, 1997. Mem. Coll. Art Assn., Century Assn., N.J. Aubudon Soc. (1st v.p. 1990-93, pres. 1993-96), Phi Beta Kappa. Democrat. Unitarian Universalist. Avocations: birding, photography. Home: PO Box 2322 Cape May NJ 08204-7322 Office: NYU Dept Of Fine Arts New York NY 10003

TURNER, ARTHUR CAMPBELL, political science educator, author; b. Glasgow, Scotland, May 19, 1918; naturalized, 1958; s. Malcolm and Robina Arthur (Miller) T.; m. Anne Gordzialkowska, Jan. 21, 1950; 1 child, Nadine (Mrs. M.J. O'Sullivan). M.A. with 1st class honors, U. Glasgow, 1941; B.A. with 1st class honors in Modern History, Queen's Coll., Oxford U., 1943, M.A., 1947, B.Litt., 1948, M.Litt., 1979; Ph.D., U. Calif., Berkeley, 1951. Lectr. history U. Glasgow, 1945-51; asst. prof. history U. Toronto, 1951-53; Commonwealth Fund fellow U. Calif., Berkeley, 1948-50, vis. prof., summers 1950, 66, 71, 78; assoc. prof. polit. sci. U. Calif., Riverside, 1953-58, prof., 1958—, chmn. div. social scis., 1953-61, dean grad. div., 1960-61, chmn. dept. polit. sci., 1961-66; prof. internat. relations, govt. Claremont Grad. Sch., part-time 1962-72; vis. prof. UCLA, 1967, Pomona Coll., 1977; Exec. com. Inst. World Affairs, 1960—, dir., 1965. Author: The Post-War House of Commons, 1942, Free Speech and Broadcasting, 1944, Mr. Buchan, Writer: A Life of the First Lord Tweedsmuir, 1949, Scottish Home Rule, 1952, Bulwark of the West: Implications and Problems of NATO, 1953, Towards European Integration, 1953, Pakistan: The Impossible Made Real, 1957, The Unique Partnership: Britain and the United States, 1971; co-author: Control of Foreign Relations, 1957, (with L. Freedman) Tension Areas in World Affairs, 1964, The Regionalization of Warfare, 1985, Power and Ideology in the Middle East, 1988, Fights of Fancy: Armed Conflict in Science Fiction, 1993; contbr.: Ency. Americana Annual, 1957—; mem. editorial com. U. Calif. Press, 1959-65, 80-83, 90, chmn., U. Calif. Press, 1962-65. Recipient Cecil prize, 1939, Blackwell prize U. Aberdeen, 1943, 51; Wilton Park fellow, 1966, 76, Santa Barbara Seminar on Arms Control fellow, 1983; Rockefeller rsch. grantee Cambridge, Eng., 1959-60, NSF travel grantee Geneva, Switzerland, 1964. Mem. Am. Soc. Internat. Law, Am., Canadian hist. assns., Am. Polit. Sci. Assn., Hist. Assn. (Eng.)., Phi Beta Kappa. Republican. Home: 1992 Rincon Ave Riverside CA 92506-1628 Office: U Calif Dept Polit Sci Riverside CA 92521 *It is now popular to say that we are nothing but the playthings of large, impersonal forces. Actually people, and peoples, bring most of their troubles on themselves. Our success and happiness are, to a large extent, in our own hands.*

TURNER, ARTHUR EDWARD, college administrator; b. Hemlock, Mich., Jan. 31, 1931; s. Alvin S. and Grace E. (Champlain) T.; m. Johann M. Jordan, May 10, 1953; children: Steven Arthur, Michael Scott, Kathryn Jo. BS, Alma (Mich.) Coll., 1952; MEd, Wayne State U., 1954; postgrad., Cen. Mich. U., U. Mich.; LLD, Ashland Coll., 1968; HUD, Colegio Americano de Quito, Ecuador, 1968; LLD, Northwood U., Cedar Hill, Tex., 1984. Admissions counselor Alma Coll., 1952-53, dir. admissions, alumni relations, 1953-59; co-founder Northwood U., Midland, Mich., 1959, 1st pres., 1959-74, chmn. bd., chief exec. officer, trustee, 1974-78, chmn. bd. trustees, 1978-82. Founder, lay minister Presbyn. Ch., Alma, 1956-59; trustee Epilepsy Found., Palm Beach, Fla., 1982; bd. dirs. Margaret Chase Smith Libr., Skowhegan, Maine, 1978, Salvation Army, 1989. Recipient People of Peru award, 1966, Horatio Alger award Horatio Alger Assn., 1981, Great Ams. award Internat. City of Care Fund, 1989, Internat. Freedom of Mobility award Nat. Automobile Dealers Assn., 1986; named one of Outstanding Young Americans, U.S. Jaycees, 1965. Mem. Palm Beach Round Table (chmn. bd.), Midland Country Club, Beach Club, Gov.'s Club (Palm Beach, Fla.), Masons (33 deg.), Shriners, Rotary, Alpha Psi Omega, Phi Phi Alpha. Home: 340 S Ocean Blvd Palm Beach FL 33480 Office: Northwood U Office of Trustees West Palm Beach FL 33409

TURNER, BERT S., construction executive; b. 1921. Grad., La. State U., 1943, Harvard U., 1949. With Esso Standard Oil Co., 1946-57, Nichols Constrn. Inc., Baton Rouge, 1957-61, Nichols Constrn. Corp., Baton Rouge, 1961—; chief exec. officer Turner Industries Ltd., Baton Rouge. Office: Turner Inds Ltd PO Box 2750 Baton Rouge LA 70821*

TURNER, BILLIE LEE, botanist, educator; b. Yoakum, Tex., Feb. 22, 1925; s. James Madison and Julia Irene (Harper) T.; m. Virginia Ruth Mathis, Sept. 27, 1944 (div. Feb. 1968); children: Billie Lee, Matt Warnock; m. Pauline Henderson, Oct. 22, 1969 (div. Jan. 1975); m. Gayle Langford, Apr. 18, 1980; children (adopted)—Roy P., Robert L. B.S., Sul Ross State Coll., 1949; M.S., So. Meth. U., 1950; Ph.D., Wash. State U., 1953. Teaching asst. botany dept. Wash. State U., 1951-53; instr. botany dept. U. Tex., Austin, 1953; asst. prof. U. Tex., 1954-58, asso. prof., 1958-61, prof., 1961—, now S.F. Blake prof. botany, chmn., 1967-75, dir. Plant Resources Ctr., 1957—; Asso. investigator ecol. study vegetation of, Africa, U. Ariz., Office Naval Research, 1956-57; vis. prof. U. Mont., summers 1971, 73, U. Mass., 1974. Author: Vegetational Changes in Africa Over a Third of a Century, 1959, Leguminosae of Texas, 1960, Biochemical Systematics, 1963, Chemotaxonomy of Leguminosae, 1972, Biology and Chemistry of Compositae, 1977, Plant Chemosystematics, 1984; Asso. editor: Southwestern Naturalist, 1959—. Served to 1st lt. USAAF, 1943-47. NSF postdoctoral fellow U. Liverpool, 1965-66. Mem. Bot. Soc. Am. (sec. 1958-59, 60-64, v.p. 1969), Tex. Acad. Sci., Southwestern Assn. Naturalists (pres. 1967, gov.), Am. Soc. Plant Taxonomists (Asa Gray award 1991), Internat. Assn. Plant Taxonomists, Soc. Study Evolution, Phi Beta Kappa, Sigma Xi. Office: U Tex Plant Resources Ctr Main Bldg 228 Austin TX 78712

TURNER, BILLIE LEE, II, geography educator; b. Texas City, Tex., Dec. 22, 1945; s. Billie Lee and Virginia Ruth (Mathis) T.; m. Linda Lee Van Zandt, June 6, 1968; children: Billie Lee III, Victoria Kelly. BA in Geography, U. Tex., 1968, MA in Geography, 1969; PhD, U. Wis., Madison, 1974. Asst. prof. geography U. Md., Catonsville, 1974-76, U. Okla., Norman, 1976-79; asst. prof. geography Clark U., Worcester, Mass., 1980-81, assoc. prof., 1981-85, prof., 1985—, dir. grad. sch., 1983-88, 97—; dir. George Perkins Marsh Inst., 1991-97; The Higgins chair environment and soc., 1996—. Author: Once Beneath the Forest, 1983; editor Pre-Hispanic Maya Agriculture, 1978, Pulltrouser Swamp, 1983, Comparative Farming Systems, 1987, The Earth as Transformed By Human Action, 1990, Population Growth and Agriculture of Change in Africa, 1993, Changes in Land Use and Land Cover: A Global Perspective, 1994, Global Land-Use Change: A Perspective From the Columbian Encounter, 1995, Regions at Risk: Comparisons of Threatened Environments, 1995; contbr. articles to profl. publs. Served with U.S. Army, 1969-71. Rsch. grantee NSF, 1978-82, 84-85, 89-90, 93-96, Nat. Geog. Soc., 1984-85, NEH, 1987-89, A.W. Mellon, 1987-90, Rockefeller Bros., 1988, NASA, 1992-94, 97—, SSRC, 1993, Centenany medal Royal Scottish Geog. Soc., 1996; Guggenheim fellow, 1981-82; sr. fellow Green Ctr. for Sci. and Soc., 1994; fellow Ctr. for Advanced Studies in the Behavioral Scis., 1994-95. Mem. NAS, AAAS, Assn. Am. Geographers (rsch. honors 1995), Soc. Am. Archeology. Home: 19 Farnum St Worcester MA 01602-2101 Office: Grad Sch Geography Clark U Worcester MA 01610

TURNER, BONESE COLLINS, artist, educator; b. Abilene, Kans.; d. Paul Edwin and Ruby (Seybold) Collins; m. Glenn E. Turner; 1 child, Craig Collins. BS in Edn., U. Idaho, MEd; MA, Calif. State U., Northridge, 1974. Instr. art L.A. Pierce Coll., Woodland Hills, Calif., 1964—; prof. art Calif. State U., Northridge, 1986-87; art instr. L.A. Valley Coll., Van Nuys, 1987-89, Moorpark (Calif.) Coll., 1988—, Arrowmont Coll. Arts & Crafts, Gatlinburg, Tenn., 1995-96; advisor Coll. Art and Arch. U. Idaho, 1988—; juror for numerous art exhbns. including Nat. Watercolor Soc., 1980, 91, San Diego Art Inst., Brand Nat. Watermedia Exhbn., 1980, 96-97, prin. gallery Orlando Gallery, Sherman Oaks, Calif. Prin. works exhibited in The White House, 1984, 85, Smithsonian Inst., 1984, 85, Olympic Arts Festival, L.A., 1984, Royal Birmingham Soc. of Artists Gallery, Birmingham, Eng., 1996; one-woman shows include Angel's Gate Gallery, San Pedro, Calif., 1989, Art Store Gallery, Studio City, Calif., 1988, L.A. Pierce Coll. Gallery, 1988, Brand Art Gallery, Glendale, Calif., 1988, 93, Coos (Oreg.) Art Mus., 1988, U. Nev., 1987, Orlando Gallery, Sherman Oaks, Calif., 1993, others; prin. works represented in pub. collections including Smithsonian Inst., Hartung Performing Arts Ctr., Moscow, Idaho, Home Savs. and Loan, San Bernardino Sun Telegram Newspapers, Oreg. Coun. for the Arts, Newport, Nebr. Pub. Librs., Lincoln (Nebr.) Indsl. Tile Corp. Recipient awards Springfield (Mo.) Art Mus., 1989, Butler Art Inst., 1989, Nat. award Acrylic Painters Assn. Eng. and U.S.A., 1996. Mem. Nat. Acrylic Painters Assn. of Eng. (award 1996), Nat. Mortar Bd. Soc., Nat. Watercolor Soc. (life, past pres., Purchase prize 1979), Watercolor U.S.A. Honor Soc. (award), Watercolor West. Avocations: tennis, bicycling, music, singing.

TURNER, CATHY, Olympic athlete; b. Apr. 10, 1962. BS in Computer Sys., No. Mich. U., 1991. Gold medal 500 meter short-track speedskating Albertville Olympic Games, 1992, also silver medal 3000 meters relay, 1992; Star made in Am. tour Ice Capades, 1992-93; Gold medalist 500 meter speedskating Winter Olympics, Lillehammer, Norway, 1994, Bronze medalist 3000 meter relay, 1994; owner, pres. Cathy Turner's Empire Fitness; motivational spkr. Profl. singer, songwriter, actress. Olympic recordholder 500 meter speedskate: 45.98. Address: US Olympic Committee 1750 E Boulder St Colorado Springs CO 80909-5724

TURNER, CHRISTOPHER EDWARD, cell biology educator; b. Birmingham, Eng., Sept. 17, 1961; came to U.S., 1987; s. Frank and Brenda Turner; m. Susan Benoit, Sept. 2, 1989. BSc, Sheffield (Eng.) U., 1983; DPhil, Oxford (Eng.) U., 1986. Postdoctoral fellow U. N.C., Chapel Hill, 1987-91; asst. prof. cell biology SUNY Health Sci. Ctr., Syracuse, 1991—. Contbr. articles to Jour. Cell Biology, Jour. Cell Sci., Jour. Biol. Chemistry. Rsch. grantee NIH, 1991—, Muscular Dystrophy Assn., 1992—; established investigator Am. Heart Assn., 1995-2000. Mem. AAAS, Am. Soc. for Cell Biology, Brit. Soc. for Cell Biology. Avocations: hiking, biking, golf. Office: SUNY Health Sci Ctr 750 E Adams St Syracuse NY 13210-2306

TURNER, CRAIG, journalist; b. Pasadena, Calif., May 24, 1949; s. Donald Leslie and Dorothy A. (Kupseck) T.; m. Ellen Bevier, Oct. 10, 1973 (div. Dec. 1983); m. Joyce Huyett, Sept. 10, 1988. BS in Journalism, San Jose State U., 1971. Reporter L.A. Times, Orange County, Calif., 1971-79; asst. city editor L.A. Times, San Diego, 1979-83; asst. met. editor L.A. Times, L.A., 1983-89, met. editor, 1989-93; fgn. corr. L.A. Times, Toronto, Ont., 1994-95; bur. chief UN, 1997—. Co-recipient Pulitzer Prize for journalism, 1993, George Polk award Long Island U., 1993. Mem. Soc. Profl. Journalists. Episcopalian. Avocations: outdoor activities, travel, theatre. Office: Los Angeles Times 780 3rd Ave Rm 3801 New York NY 10017-2024

TURNER, CRISTINA BENITEZ, advertising professional; b. Easton, Md., July 20, 1946; d. Rafael Celestino Benitez and Nancy Shannon Critchlow; divorced; 1 child, Todd Turner. BA, Furman U., 1971, MA, 1972. Spanish tchr. Greenville (S.C.) County Schs., 1971-80; account exec. Multimedia Comms., Greenville, 1980-85; account supr. Atwood Internat., N.Y.C., 1987-89; cons. Gannett Pub., N.Y.C., 1989; v.p., account svc. Grey Advt., N.Y.C., 1989-95; sr. v.p., Hispanic mktg. dir. Draft Direct Worldwide, Chgo., 1995—. Tutor Greenville Literacy Program, 1980-85; vol. St. Mary's Soup Kitchen, N.Y.C., 1990-95; mem. inaugural opening com. Chgo. Mus. Contemporary Art. Mem. Direct Mktg. Assn., Directo (operating com.), Women in Direct Mktg. (program com.), Hispanic Alliance for Career Enhancement, Chgo. Coun. on Fgn. Rels., Latin Am. C. of C. Avocations: running (N.Y.C. Marathon 1991, 92), Latin music, dancing. Office: Draft Direct Worldwide 633 N Saint Clair St Chicago IL 60611-2818

TURNER, DAVID REUBEN, publisher, author; b. N.Y.C., Dec. 9, 1915; s. Charles and Eva (Turner) Moskowitz; m. Ann Louise Perkins, Apr. 29, 1946 (div. 1976); children—Eve (Mrs. William Watters), Ruth. B.S., Coll. City N.Y., 1936, M.S. in Edn, 1937. Co-founder Arco Pub. Co., N.Y.C., 1937; pub., dir. Arco Pub. Co., 1937-78; v.p. parent co. Prentice-Hall, Inc., 1979-

80; pres. Turner Pub., 1980-92; pub. cons. under Ford Found. contract Burma Translation Soc., Rangoon, 1959-60. Author: more than 300 books on tests and testing, including High School Equivalency Diploma Tests, 1951, 75, How to Win a Scholarship, 1955, Scoring High On College Entrance Tests, 1969, 71, Food Service Supervisor, 1968, Bank Examiner, 1968, Accountant-Auditor, 1960, 77, Officer Candidate Tests, 1978, Professional-Administrative Career Exams, 1979, English Grammar and Usage for Test-Takers, 1976, College Level Examination Program, 1979. Adviser bd. publs. Union Am. Hebrew Congregations. Home and Office: 13 Glengary Rd Croton On Hudson NY 10520-2139

TURNER, DOUGLAS LAIRD, writer, editor, columnist; b. Buffalo, N.Y., Jan. 5, 1932; s. Henry Albert and Effie Donna (McIndoo) T.; m. Mary Joan Hassett, July 7, 1962; children: Christopher Henry, Mary Julia, Albert William. BA, Brown U., 1954; postgrad., Stanford U., 1968. Reporter Buffalo (N.Y.) Courier-Express, 1957-60, state capital corr., 1960-64, fin. editor, 1964, city editor, 1964-70, exec. editor, 1971-80, Washington bur. chief, 1981-82; Washington corr. Buffalo (N.Y.) Evening News, 1982, Washington columnist, 1983, Washington bur. chief, 1989—; adj. assoc. prof. faculty social scis. State Univ. at Buffalo, 1995; founders' com. Niagara Frontier Chpt. Profl. Journalism Soc., N.Y. State Commn. on Pub. Access to Records, 1976-81; founder, dir. Friends of Williamsburg Rowing Inc., 1993—. Mem. U.S. Olympic Rowing Team, 1956; founder Erie County Forensic Psychiatry Svc., Buffalo, 1975, Area Leadership Group, Buffalo, 1977-79. Spl. agt. U.S. Army Counter Intelligence Corps, 1956-57. Nation champion four-oared shell with cox, 1956; winner Hanlan Trophy, Royal Can. Henley Regatta, 1956; recipient numerous awards Am. Newspaper Guild, N.Y. State Associated Press Assn., personal citations Erie County Legislature, N.Y. State Assembly, Buffalo Common Coun. Mem. Nat. Press Club (former gov. 1988), Potomac Boat Club, Gridiron Club (Wash.). Roman Catholic. Avocations: classical guitar, piano, voice, rowing, sailing. Home: 7923 Saint George Ct Springfield VA 22153-2741 Office: Buffalo News Washington Bur 1141 National Press Building Washington DC 20045-2101

TURNER, E. DEANE, lawyer; b. Auburn, N.Y., Aug. 4, 1928; s. Alfred Edward and Bertha (Deane) T.; A.B. summa cum laude, Princeton U., 1950; LL.B. cum laude, Harvard U., 1953. Bar: N.Y. 1953. Assoc., Dewey Ballantine and predecessor firms, N.Y.C., 1953-63, ptnr., 1963—, of counsel, 1991-93; treas. Harvard Law Sch. Assn. N.Y.C., 1964-83. Elder, trustee Brick Presbyn. Ch., N.Y.C., 1976—, pres. bd. trustees, 1988-90; trustee Presbytery N.Y.C., 1993—, pres. bd. trustees, 1995—; mem. com. to adminstr. James N. Jarvie Endowment, 1993—. Fellow Am. Coll. Investment Counsel; mem. Union Club, John's Island Club, Phi Beta Kappa. Republican. Home: 1120 5th Ave New York NY 10128-0144 also: 381 Llwyds Ln Johns Island Vero Beach FL 32963 Office: Dewey Ballantine 1301 Avenue Of The Americas New York NY 10019-6022

TURNER, ED SIMS, broadcast executive, writer; b. Bartlesville, Okla., Sept. 25, 1935; s. Ed and Dee (Sims) T.; m. Beth Coburn, June 25, 1964; 1 child, Christopher. BA in Journalism, U. Okla., 1957. Producer, dir. documentary films Okla U., Norman, 1957-59; reporter Sta. KWTV, Oklahoma City, 1959-64; v.p. news Sta. WTTG, Washington, 1966-68; v.p. news and pub. affairs Metromedia, N.Y.C., 1968-74; v.p. news United Press Internat. TV News, N.Y.C., 1975; news producer CBS. N.Y.C., 1975-78; news dir. Sta. KWTV, Oklahoma City, 1978-79; managing editor Cable News Network, Atlanta, 1979-81, exec. producer, 1982, chief Wash. bur., 1983, exec. v.p., 1984—; spl. instr. Okla. U., 1968, Mary Mount Coll., N.Y.C., 1978. Dir. ednl. documentary (Best Documentary award Cannes Film Festival 1958); creative producer (TV spl.) Crossfire; creator, engr. (TV spl.) Novak Reports. Press sec. Bud Wilkinson for U.S. Senate campaign, 1964-65. Recipient Best Reporting award UPI, 1959-64, 8 Emmys, 1966-72, Channels mag. Award of Excellence, 1987, Peabody awards, 1983, 87, 89, 91, 6 Ace awards for cable excellence; named Producer of Yr. Millmeter mag., 1984, Outstanding Alumni, Okla. U. Sch. Journalism, 1985, One of 25 Who Count in TV/Motion Picture Industry, View mag., 1986. Mem. Radio TV News Dirs. Assn., Sigma Delta Chi (nat. reporting awards 1963), Phi Gamma Delta. Republican. Office: CNN One CNN Ctr 1 Cnn Ctr NW Atlanta GA 30303-2705*

TURNER, EDWIN LEWIS, astronomy educator, researcher; b. Knoxville, Tenn., May 3, 1949; s. George Lewis and Gladys Love (Gregory) T.; m. Joyce Beldon, Aug. 15, 1971; children: Alexander, Daniel. SB in Physics, MIT, 1971; PhD in Astronomy, Calif. Inst. Tech., 1975. Fellow Inst. for Advance Study, Princeton, N.J., 1975-76; asst. prof. dept. astronomy Harvard U., Cambridge, Mass., 1977-78; asst. prof. dept. astrophysics Princeton U., 1978-81, Alfred P. Sloan Found. Rsch. fellow, 1980-84, assoc. prof., 1981-86, prof., 1986—, assoc. chmn., 1988-95, acting chmn. dept. astrophysics, 1995-96; counselor Space Telescope Inst. Counsel, Balt., 1989—; dir. Apache Point Obs. 3.5 meter telescope, 1995—. Contbr. over 100 articles to astron. publs. Bd. dirs. Assn. Univs. for Rsch. in Astronomy, Inc., Tucson, 1980-89. Mem. Internat. Astron. Union, Am. Astron. Assn. Achievements include research in galaxy masses, cosmic structure formation, quasars, gravitational lenses, and cosmology. Office: Princeton U Obs Ivy Ln Princeton NJ 08544-0001

TURNER, ELAINE S., allergist, immunologist; b. Glen Cove, N.Y., 1947. MD, Med. Coll. Pa., 1974. Diplomate Am. Bd. Allergy & Immunology, Am. Bd. Internal Medicine. Intern Michael Reese Hosp., Chgo., 1974-75; resident in internal medicine Cleve. Clinic, 1976-78; fellow in allergy & immunology Northwestern U., Chgo., 1975-76, 78-80; with St. Mary's Hosp., Va., Henrco Doctors, Va., Health South Hosp., Va.; asst. prof. medicine Med. Coll. Va., McGuire Med. Group, Richmond, Va. Mem. ACP, Am. Acad. Allergy, Asthma and Immunology, Richmond Acad. Medicine. Office: McGuire Med Group 7702 E Parham Rd Richmond VA 23294-4301

TURNER, ELIZABETH ADAMS NOBLE (BETTY TURNER), healthcare executive, former mayor; b. Yonkers, N.Y., May 18, 1931; d. James Kendrick and Orrel (Baldwin) Noble; m. Jack Rice Turner, July 11, 1953; children: Jay Kendrick, Randall Ray. BA, Vassar Coll., 1953; MA, Tex. A&I U., 1964. Ednl. cons. Noble & Noble Pub. Co., N.Y.C., 1956-67; psychometrist Corpus Christi Guidance Ctr., 1967-70; psychologist Corpus Christi State Sch., 1970-72, dir. programs, asst. supt., 1972, dir. devel. and vol. svc., 1972-76, dir. rsch. and tng., 1977-79, psychologist Tex. Mental Health and Mental Retardation, 1970-79; pres. Turner Co., 1979—; program cons. Tex. Dept. Mental Health and Mental Retardation, 1979-85; mayor pro tem. Corpus Christi, 1981-85, mayor, 1987-91; CEO, pres. Corpus Christi C. of C., 1991-94; v.p. bus. and govt. rels. ctrl. and south Tex. divsns. Columbia Healthcare Corp., 1994—. Dir. alumni Corpus Christi State U., 1976-77; coord. vols. Summer Head Start Program, Corpus Christi, 1967; chmn. spl. gifts coml United Way, Corpus Christi, 1970; mem. Corpus Christi City Coun., 1979-91; family founded Barnes and Noble, N.Y.C.; with Leadership Corpus Christi II; founder Com. of 100 and Goals for Corpus Christi; pres. USO; bd. dirs. Coastal Bends Coun. Govts., Corpus Christi Mus., Harbor Playhouse, Communities in Schs., Del Mar Coll. Found., Pres.' Coun., Food Bank, Salvation Army, Jr. League; bd. govs. Southside Community Hosp., 1987-93, Gulfway Nat. Bank, 1985-92, Bayview Hosp., 1992—, strategic planning com. Meml. Hosp., 1992, Tex. Capital Network Bd., 1992—, Humana Hosp., Rehab. Hosp. South Tex., Admiral Tex. Navy; apptd. Gov.'s Commn. for Women, 1984-85, Leadership Tex. Class I; founder Goals for Corpus Christi, Bay Area Sports Assn., Assn. Coastal Bend Mayor's Alliance; founder Mayor's Commn. on the Disabled, Mayor's Task Force on the Homeless; active Port Aransas Cmty. Ch. Recipient Love award YWCA, 1970, Y's Women and Men in Careers award, 1988, Commander's Award for Pub. Svc. U.S. Army, Scroll of Honor award Navy League, award Tex. Hwy. Dept., Road Hand award Tex. Hwy. Commn., 1989; named Corpus Christi Newsmaker of Yr., 1987. Mem. Tex. Psychol. Assn. (pres., mem. exec. bd.), Psychol. Assn. (pres., founder), Tex. Mcpl. League (bd. dir.), Corpus Christi C. of C. (pres., CEO), Jr. League Corpus Christi, Tex. Bookman's Assn., Tex. Assn. Realtors, Kappa Kappa Gamma, Corpus Christi Town Club, Corpus Christi Yacht Club, Jr. Cotillion Club. Home: 4600 Ocean Dr Apt 801 Corpus Christi TX 78412-2543

TURNER, ELVIN L., retired educational administrator; b. Springfield, Ohio, Jan. 9, 1938; s. Willie and Jinada (Lawson) T.; m. Betty Jo Breckinridge, June 11, 1966 (div. Jan. 1972); 1 child, Anthony; m. Carrie Johnson, Aug. 3, 1972; 1 child, Brenetta Bell. BS in Biology and Chemistry, Knoxville (Tenn.) Coll., 1962; MEd, U. Cin., 1968; postgrad., Nova U., Ft. Lauderdale, Fla., 1973, Kensington U., Glendale, Calif., 1993—. Cert. secondary prin., tchr., Ohio. Spl. edn. tchr. Cin. Pub. Schs., 1965-69, coord. spl. edn., 1969-72, asst. prin., 1972-78, prin., 1978-90, asst. prin., 1990-93; part-time adj. prof. Mt. St. Joseph (Ohio) Coll., 1987-88; mem. adv. com. Millcreek Psychiat. Ctr. for Children, Cin., 1988-89; bus driver Bristol Village Retirement Cmty., 1997—; ombudsman Pro-Srs., Cin., 1993-96, Waverly, Ohio, 1997—. Bd. dirs. Big Bros./Big Sisters, Cin., 1973; mem. bd. deacons New Hope Bapt. Ch., Hamilton, Ohio, 1993; Sunday sch. tchr. Bethel AME Ch., Lebanon, Ohio, 1996; elected sec. exec. adv. coun. Bristol Village Nat. Ch. Residencies, Waverly, Columbus, Ohio, 1997. Recipient plaques and grants. Mem. Nat. Assn. for Secondary Sch. Prins., Ohio Assn. for Secondary Sch. Prins., Knoxville Coll. Alumni Assn., Phi Delta Kappa, Alpha Phi Alpha. Avocations: bowling, golf, reading, travel. Home: 320 Valerie Dr Waverly OH 45690-1525

TURNER, ERIC RAY, professional football player. Safety Cleveland Browns, 1991—. Selected to Pro Bowl, 1994; tied for lead in interceptions (9), 1994. Office: c/o Cleveland Browns 11001 Owings Mills Blvd Owings Mills MD 21117-2857*

TURNER, EUGENE ANDREW, manufacturing executive; b. Bridgeton, N.J., Aug. 7, 1928; s. Benjamin Homer and Pearl Irene (Wolbert) T.; m. Paula Ann Webb, 1987; children: Mary Ann, John-Reed. BA, Rutgers U., 1966; student, Columbia U., 1980. With Owens Ill., 1950-73, regional mgr. West Coast, 1970-73; v.p. adminstrn. Midland Glass Co., Cliffwood, N.J., 1973-76, pres., chief operating officer, 1981-82, also bd. dirs.; v.p., gen. mgr. Anchor Hocking Corp., Lancaster, Ohio, 1976-81; dir. ops. Theo Chem. Labs., Tampa, Fla., 1988-90, Profit Counselors Inc, Sarasota, Fla., 1990-94; pres. Profit Sys. Inc., Oklahoma City, 1994—; mng. cons. 1987-88. Mem. Harbor Island Club, Seaview Country Club, Navesink Country Club. Home: 1103 Tedford Way Oklahoma City OK 73116-6006 *Take time to learn the chosen business then develop credibility by doing what you say you will do.*

TURNER, EVAN HOPKINS, retired art museum director; b. Orono, Maine, Nov. 8, 1927; s. Albert Morton and Percie Trowbridge (Hopkins) T.; m. Brenda Winthrop Bowman, May 12, 1956; children: John, Jennifer. A.B. cum laude, Harvard U., 1949, M.A., 1950, Ph.D., 1954. Head docent svc. Fogg Mus., Cambridge, Mass., 1950-51; curator Robbins Art Collection of Prints, Arlington, Mass., 1951; teaching fellow fine arts Harvard U., 1951-52; lectr., research asst. Frick Collection, N.Y.C., 1953-56; gen. curator, asst. dir. Wadsworth Atheneum, Hartford, Conn., 1956-59; dir. Montreal Mus. Fine Arts, Que., Can., 1959-64, Phila. Mus. Art, 1964-77, Ackland Art Mus., 1978-83, Cleve. Mus. Art, 1983-93; adj. prof. art history U. Pa., U. N.C., Chapel Hill, 1978-83; disting. vis. prof. Oberlin Coll., 1993-95. Mem. Assn. Art Mus. Dirs., Coll. Art Assn. Am., Am. Mus. Assn., Century Assn. Club. Home: 3071 N Park Blvd Cleveland OH 44118-4114

TURNER, FLORENCE FRANCES, ceramist; b. Detroit, Mar. 9, 1926; d. Paul Pokrywka and Catherine Gagal; m. Dwight Robert Turner, Oct. 23, 1948; children: Thomas Michael, Nancy Louise, Richard Scott, Garry Robert. Student, Oakland C.C., Royal Oak, Mich., 1975-85, U. Ariz., Yuma, 1985, U. Las Vegas, 1989—. Pres., founder Nev. Clay Guild, Henderson, 1990-94, mem. adv. bd., 1994—; workshop leader Greenfield Village, Dearborn, Mich., 1977-78, Plymouth (Mich.) Hist. Soc., 1979, Las Vegas Sch. System, 1989-90, Detroit Met. area, 1977-85. Bd. dirs. Las Vegas Art Mus., 1987-91; corr. sec. So. Nev. Creative Art Ctr., Las Vegas, 1990-94. Mem. So. Nev. Rock Art Enthusiasts, Las Vegas Gem Club, Nev. Camera Club, Golden Key, Phi Kappa Phi. Avocations: photography, collecting gems, travel. Office: Nev Clay Guild PO Box 50004 Henderson NV 89016-0004

TURNER, FRANK MILLER, historian, educator; b. Springfield, Ohio, Oct. 31, 1944; s. Ronald O. and Mary Elizabeth (Miller) T.; m. Margaret Good, Aug. 26, 1967 (div. 1981); m. Nancy Rash, July 29, 1984 (dec. Mar. 1995). BA, Coll. of William and Mary, 1966; MPhil, Yale U., 1970, PhD, 1971; LHD (hon.), Coll. William and Mary, 1991. Asst. prof. Yale U., New Haven, Conn., 1972-77, assoc. prof., 1977-82, prof., 1982—, provost, 1988-92, John Hay prof. history, 1992—. Author: Between Science and Religion, 1974, The Greek Heritage in Victorian Britain, 1981, Contesting Cultural Authority: Essays in Victorial Intellectual Life, 1993; co-author: The Western Heritage, 1979, 83, 87, 91, 94, 97, Heritage of World Civilizations, 1985, 90, 93, 96; editor: John Henry Newman, The Idea of a University, 1996. Trustee Conn. Coll., New London, 1996—. Guggenheim fellowship, 1983; recipient Brit. Coun. prize Conf. on Brit. Studies, 1982, Yale Press Gov.'s award, 1983. Office: Yale U History Dept PO Box 208324 New Haven CT 06520-8324

TURNER, FRANKLIN DELTON, bishop; b. Norwood, N.C., July 19, 1933; s. James T. and Dora (Streeter) T.; m. Barbara Dickerson, July 6, 1963; children: Jennifer, Kimberly, Franklin. AB, Livingstone Coll., 1956; DD (hon.), 1993; MDiv, Yale U., 1965; DD (hon.), Berkeley Div. Sch., Yale U., 1977. Ordained deacon and priest Episcopal Ch., 1965, consecrated bishop, 1988. Vicar Epighany Ch., Diocese of Dallas, 1965-66; rector St. George's Ch., Diocese of Washington, 1966-72; officer nat. staff Episcopal Ch. Ctr., N.Y.C., 1972-83; mem. bishop's staff for congl. devel. Episcopal Diocese of Pa., Phila., 1983-86, suffragan bishop, 1988—. Author: Black Leaders in the Episcopal Church, 1975. 1st It. U.S. Army, 1966-72. Office: Diocese of Pa 240 S 4th St Philadelphia PA 19106-3722*

TURNER, GEORGE PEARCE, consulting company executive; b. Dallas, Aug. 22, 1915; s. Fred Horatio and Florence (Phillips) T.; m. June Lori Haney, Feb. 4, 1943 (div. 1976); children: Bruce Haney, Brian Phillips, Mark Richardson; m. Kathryn Blank Hauf, June 1976. Student, U. Tex., 1932-33, 35-36, 40-41, So. Methodist U., 1934; BA in Internat. Rels. cum laude, U. So. Calif., 1962, MS in Internat. Pub. Adminstrn. summa cum laude, 1966; PhD in Econs. and Internat. Rels., Columbia Pacific U., 1982, PhD in Pub. Adminstrn. and Internat. Rels., 1985. Archtl. designer L.A., 1946-48; prin. Lieburg & Turner (cons. engrs.), Pasadena, Calif., 1947-48; pres. Radiant Heat Engring., Inc., Pasadena, 1948-53; exec. asst. to dir. fgn. subsidiaries S.Am. Fluor Corp. Ltd., L.A., 1953-54; mem. exec. staff Coast Fed. Savs. & Loan Assn., 1954-55; exec. staff Holmes & Narver, Inc., L.A., 1955-61; mgr. project devel. S.Am. ops. Southwestern Engring. Co., L.A., 1962; pres. Haney Devel. Corp., 1964-90, Fomento e Inversiones Quisqueyanos C. por A., Santo Domingo de Guzman, Dominican Republic, 1967—; gen. mgr. for Venezuelan ops. Hale Internat. Inc., Caracas, 1970-71; dir., mgr. Consortium Lomas de La Lagunita, Caracas, 1970, Consortium Desarrollos Urbanos, Valencia, Venezuela, 1970; pres. Haney Investment Corp. (HANCO), 1974-90, Casa FOMIQ, 1978—, Caribbean Vagabond Ltd., Grand Cayman Island, B.W.I., 1981-90, Kay Pearce & Turner, Ltd., Newtown Square, Pa., 1981—; sec. Integrated Industries of Atlantic County, N.J.; gen. ptnr. N.Y. Ave. Parking Assocs., Atlantic City, 1980-91; adviser, provisional pres., Dominican Republic, 1965-66, constl. pres. of republic, 1966-68; projects programmer Nat. Planning Inst. Peru Tri-Partite Mission, 1962-65; ofcl. OAS adviser Nat. Office Tourism Dominican Republic, 1966-67, Nat. Office Cultural Patrimony, Liga Mcpl. Dominicana, 1967-68; cons., dir. projects, programming, tech. matters Mission Recovery and Rehab., Dominican Republic, 1965-67; dep. dir. Tech. Assistance Mission Dominican Republic, 1967-68; cons. assignments for program assistance Inter-Am. Tng. Ctr., Fed. U. Ceara, Brazil; OAS adviser on tech. assistance to Chile, Argentina, Uruguay, Peru, Brazil, 1962-68; cons. Wildwood Ocean Towers, N.J., 1969-70, Capital Investment Devel. Corp., Downing Ctr., Downingtown, Pa., 1971-77; dir. for Project Monitor and owners agt., hosp. tower Hahnemann Med. U. and Hosp., Phila., 1975-78; pres. Urban Planning and Devel. Corp., Exton, Pa., 1978-79; cons., corp. sec., v.p. Constrn. Devel. and Properties Mgmt. Group, Integrated Industries Inc., Exton, 1978-80; ltd. ptnr. Marsh Creek Assocs. Two, 1985—; apptd. to faculty Columbia Pacific U., 1987; cons. internat. consortium for multi-billion dollar econ. devel. program with projects in countries of Pacific Rim and Ea. Europe, 1993-95; established Casa FOMIQ awards program, 1995. Author: An Analysis of the Economy of El Salvador, 1961, The Alliance for Progress: Concept Versus Structure, 1966, Some Observations on the Decade of the 1960s - U.S. vis-a-vis Latin America, 1982, Latin American Odyssey, 1985, Third Generation, 1990, Growing Up Male in America: With the Prince Charming Mystique, 1993; pub., editor Fountain of Age, The Jour. of Casa FOMIQ, 1995; contbr. articles to profl. publs. With USAF, 1941-45. Decorated OAS Medal of Honor; recipient Citation for Valiant Svc. in Dominican Republic, 1965-66, Ofcl. OAS Commendation for Program Contbns., Peru, Dominican Republic, Brazil, Venezuela, 1969. Mem. Delta Phi Epsilon, Alpha Sigma Lambda. Home: 8 Fox Run Ln Newtown Square PA 19073-1004 Office: Kay Pearce & Turner Ltd PO Box 419 Newtown Square PA 19073-0419

TURNER, GERALD PHILLIP, hospital administrator; b. Winnipeg, Man., Can., May 13, 1930; s. Lorry and Shirley (Litman) Turbovsky; m. Clare Henteleff, June 12, 1955 (dec.); children: Robin Joy, Neil Lindsay, Daryl Lyon; m. Donna Ireland, May 22, 1994. B.Sc. in Pharmacy, U. Man., Winnipeg, 1953; Diploma in Hosp. Adminstrn., U. Toronto, Ont., Can., 1955. Asst. adminstr. Mt. Sinai Hosp., Toronto, 1955-62; assoc. adminstr. Mt. Sinai Hosp., 1962-66, adminstr., 1966-74, exec. dir., 1974-84, pres., chief exec. officer, 1984-93, pres. emeritus, 1993—; exec. v.p. Mt. Sinai Inst., Toronto, 1976-86; pres. Mt. Sinai Hosp. Found. (formerly Inst.), Toronto, 1987-88, vice chmn., 1988—; assoc. prof. health adminstrn. U. Toronto, 1971-90, prof., 1990—; chmn. rsch. bd. Samuel Lunenfeld Rsch. Inst. Author: (with Joseph Mapa) The Choice is Yours: Making Canada's Medical System Work for You, 1981; co-editor: (with Joseph Mapa) Humanizing Hospital Care, 1979; Humanistic Health Care: Issues for Caregivers, 1988. Recipient Queen's Silver Jubilee medal, Pres.'s Achievement award, Extendicare award, Toronto Chpt. award for Disting. Svcs., Can. Coll. Health Svc. Execs., 1993. Fellow Am. Coll. Healthcare Execs., Can. Coll. Health Service Execs. (founder mem., cert. mem.), Ont. Hosp. Assn. (chmn. elect 1986-87, chmn. 1987-88). Office: Mt Sinai Hospital, 600 University Ave, Toronto, ON Canada M5G 1X5

TURNER, GLORIA TOWNSEND BURKE, social services association executive; b. Lumberton, N.C., Nov. 16, 1938; d. John B. and Alice (Haite) Townsend; m. James Rae Burke, June 3, 1957 (dec. 1974); children: William H., Sonya Kyle; m. Robert R. Turner,June 23, 1977. Student, U. S.C., 1974; degree in nursing, York Tech. Coll./U. S.C., 1976. RN, S.C. Staff nurse, head nurse York Gen. Hosp., Rock Hill, S.C., 1976-78; head med. dept., indsl. nursing J.P. Stevens Plant, Rock Hill, 1976-78; hsop., nursing home auditor S.C. Med. Found., Columbia, 1978-79; exec. dir. Kershaw County Coun. on Aging, Camden, S.C., 1979-93; dir. med.-surg. units Conway (S.C.) Hosp., 1993—; bd. dirs. S.C. Fedn. Older Ams., 1988-95; mem. state adv. com. on Alzheimers, Columbia, 1984—; trustee Kershaw County Meml. Hosp., Camden, 1989-93. Mem. Camden C. of C., Rotary. Methodist. Avocations: reading, watching football and basketball, travel. Home: 147 Dusty Trail Ln Surfside Beach SC 29575

TURNER, HAL WESLEY, state agency administrator; b. Winchester, Mass., Nov. 18, 1932; s. Wesley Francis and Anna Louise (Hodgkins) T.; m. Jean Marie Turner; children: Julie, Karen. BA, U. Sioux Falls, S.D., 1955. Cert. Govtl. Fin. Mgr. Mem. tech. and mgmt. staff Boeing Computer Svcs., Seattle, 1958-69; mgr. prodn. systems Kennecott Copper Corp., Salt Lake City, 1970-71; dir. MIS State of Idaho, Boise, 1971-74, adminstr. of budget, 1974-77; sales assoc. White Riedel Realtors, Boise, 1978-81; chief dep. Idaho State Controller's Office, Boise, 1981—; pres., Student Loan Fund Idaho, Inc., Fruitland, 1978—. Mem. Boise Samaritan Village Health Facility Adv. Bd.; region 4 chmn. Idaho Com. for Employer Support of Guard and Res. With U.S. Army, 1955-57. Mem. Nat. Assn. State Auditor's Comptr. and Treas., Nat. Assn. Govtl. Accts., Elks, Broadmore Country Club. Democrat. Methodist. Avocations: golf, racquetball. Home: 3512 S Brookshore Pl Boise ID 83706-5582 Office: State Contrs Office PO Box 83720 Boise ID 83720-0011

TURNER, HAROLD EDWARD, education educator; b. Hamilton, Ill., Nov. 22, 1921; s. Edward Jesse and Beulah May (White) T.; m. Catherine Skeeters, Apr. 5, 1946; children: Michele Turner Nimerick, Thomas, Barbara Turner McMahon, Krista Turner Landgraf. A.B., Carthage Coll., 1950; M.S., U. Ill. - Urbana, 1951, Ed.D. (George Peabody fellow), 1956. Tchr. Taylorville (Ill.) Jr. H.S., 1951-52, Moline (Ill.) Jr. H.S., 1952-54; dir. elem. edn. Jefferson County, Colo., 1955-57; prin. Jefferson County H.S., 1957-60; asst. prof. edn. North Tex. State U., Denton, 1960-63; asst. supt. curriculum Sacramento City Schs., 1963-66; assoc. prof., chmn. dept. curriculum and instrn. U. Mo., St. Louis, 1966-69, prof., 1971-85, prof. emeritus, 1985—, chmn. dept. adminstrn., founds., secondary edn., 1977-78, dept. chmn., 1983-85; vis. prof. Adams State Coll., Alamosa, Colo., 1959, U. Ga., Athens, 1981-82; adj. prof. NYU, 1965, U. Ill., 1980; cons. various sch. dists., Tex., Mo.; spl. cons. Mo. State Dept. Edn., 1973. Author: (with Adolph Unruh) Supervision for Change and Innovation, 1970; contbr. articles to profl. jours. Served with USNR, 1942-46. Mem. Profs. Supervision. Presbyterian (elder). Home: 3155 S Calle Pueblo Green Valley AZ 85614-1058 Office: U Mo St Louis Sch Edn 8001 Natural Bridge Rd Saint Louis MO 63121-4401

TURNER, HARRY EDWARD, lawyer; b. Mt. Vernon, Ohio, Dec. 25, 1927; s. Paul Hamilton and Harriett (Krafft) T.; m. Shirley Marilyn Eggert, July 8, 1950; children: Harry Edward, Thomas Frederick (dec. Mar. 1995). B.A., Baldwin Wallace Coll., 1951; J.D., Ohio No. U., 1954. Bar: Ohio 1954, U.S. Supreme Ct. 1966. Practice in Mt. Vernon, 1954—; state rep. Ohio Gen. Assembly, 1973-85; solicitor Mt. Vernon, 1958-62; Prosecutor Mt. Vernon Municipal Ct., 1955-58. Mem. Mt. Vernon City Sch. Bd., 1964-70, pres., 1965-70; trustee Ohio Sch. Bd. Assn., 1968-70, Hannah Browning Home, 1987—, Sta. Break/Commn. on Planning Svcs., 1989-95; mem. Knox County Pub. Defender Commn., 1987-91. With USN, 1946-47. Mem. Ohio State Bar Assn., Knox County Bar Assn. (pres. 1970), Alpha Sigma Phi, Sigma Delta Kappa. Republican. Lutheran. Home: 400 E Vine St Mount Vernon OH 43050-3442 Office: 118 E High St Mount Vernon OH 43050-3402

TURNER, H(ARRY) SPENCER, preventive medicine physician, educator; b. Dayton, Ohio, July 25, 1938; s. Eli and Daphne (Cunagin) T.; children: Michael, Mary, Daniel. BA, Manchester Coll., North Manchester, Ind., 1960; MD summa cum laude, Ohio State U., 1963, MS in Preventive Medicine, 1968. Diplomate Am. Bd. Preventive Medicine. Resident in preventive (aerospace) medicine Ohio State U., Columbus, 1966-69, chief resident, 1968-69, clin. asst. prof. dept. preventive medicine, 1969-80, dir. Univ. Health Svc., 1970-80; pvt. practice Dayton, 1980-90; head team physician U. Ky., Lexington, 1991—, prof. preventive medicine and environ. health, 1991—. Contbr. articles and papers to profl. jours. and meetings. Bd. dirs. Blue Shield, 1981-86; mem. Cin. Internat. Chorale, 1989-94; mem. Lexington Singers, 1992—. Capt. U.S. Army, 1964-66. Fellow Am. Coll. Preventive Medicine, Am. Coll. Health Assn. (pres. 1980, Ruth Boynton award 1982, Edw. Hitchcock award 1996), Alpha Omega Alpha. Lutheran. Avocation: music. Office: U Ky Coll Medicine Univ Health Svc Lexington KY 40536

TURNER, HARRY WOODRUFF, lawyer; b. Blairsville, Pa., May 2, 1939; s. James McKinnie and Dorothy Elizabeth (Tittle) T.; m. Mary Elizabeth Phelan, Dec. 30, 1972; children: James William, David Woodruff. AB, U. Pitts., 1961; JD, Harvard U., 1964. Bar: Pa., 1965, U.S. Supreme Ct., 1979. Assoc. Kirkpatrick & Lockhart, Pitts., 1964-71, ptnr., 1971—; mem. Fed. Jud. Selection Commn. Pa., 1995—, chair, 1997—. Trustee Hist. Soc. Western Pa. 1996—, U. Pitts., 1995—, Wilson Coll., Chambersburg, Pa., 1978-89, Aspinwall Baseball Assn., 1985-97; trustee, sec. Adoptive Rights Coun., Pitts. Opera, 1993—; pres. U. Pitts. Nat. Alumni Assn., 1990-91; alt. del. Rep. Nat. Conv., Miami, 1968, Houston, 1992, Rep. State Com., 1996—; trustee, v.p. Torrance (Pa.) State Hosp., 1969-73; trustee ann. giving fund U. Pitts. 1982-95; chair distbn. com. William L. Benz Found., 1985-97; bd. dirs. Pitts. divsn. Am. Heart Assn., 1993—; bd. vis. U. Pitts. Med. Sch., 1995—, U. Pitts. Coll. Arts & Scis., 1988—, chair bd. vis. Sch. Info. Scis. Mem. ABA, Pa. Bar Assn., Am. Law Inst., Internat. Acad. Trial Lawyers, Allegheny County Bar Assn., Allegheny County Acad. Trial Lawyers, SAR (pres. 1995-96), Fox Chapel Golf Club, Duquesne Club, Harvard-Yale-Princeton Club, Univ. Club, Allegheny Club. Presbyterian. Office: Kirkpatrick & Lockhart 1500 Oliver Bldg Pittsburgh PA 15222-2404

TURNER, HAZEL M., educator; b. Birmingham, Ala., Mar. 1, 1926; d. Will and Georgia Ann (Beard) McCarter; m. Victor Caesar Turner Jr., Nov. 28, 1957; children: Victor C. III, Michael David. BS in Elem. Edn., Tuskegee U., 1950; MA in Guidance and Counseling, NYU, 1952, EdD in

Student Pers. Adminstrn., 1960. Dean of women Alcorn Coll., Lorman, Miss., 1950-53; dir. student svcs. Tuskegee (Ala.) U., 1955-58; dir. youth programs Lansing (Mich.) YWCA, 1960-61; dir. spl. edn. Lansing Pub. Schs., 1961-66; dir. student pers. svcs. Ann Arbor (Mich.) Pub. Schs., 1966-85; vis. lectr. Ea. Mich. U., Ypsilanti, 1985—; mem. from Mich. State Dept. Pub. Instrn. to seminar Harvard U., 1968. Co-chair fundraising Ann Arbor Cmty. Ctr., 1972-74; vol. United Way, Lansing and Ann Arbor, 1970-74; mem. divsnl. bd. Catherine McAuley Health Ctr., Mission Health, Ann Arbor, 1980-85; chair Ret. Sr. Vol. Program, Ann Arbor, 1988—, mem. adv. com. 1993-95; co-chair pers. com. Housing Bur. for Srs., 1990-94. Named Outstanding Female Educator, Delta Kappa Gamma, 1978; recipient Founder's Day award NYU, 1971. Mem. AAUW, Mich. Assn. Tchr. Educators, the Links, Inc. (v.p., pres. 1985-87, rep. to UN Decade of Women Conf., Nairobi, Kenya 1985), Alpha Kappa Alpha. Avocations: computers, reading, travel, spectator sports, bridge. Home: 1219 Ardmoor Ave Ann Arbor MI 48103-5345

TURNER, HENRY A., retired political science educator, author; b. King City, Mo., Jan. 2, 1919; s. Henry A. and Bessie Marie (Claxton) T.; m. Mary Margaret Tilton, May 23, 1943; children—John Andrew, Nancy Ellen, Stephen Heald. B.S., N.W. Mo. State U., 1939; M.A., Mo. U., 1941; Ph.D., U. Chgo., 1950. Jr. coll. instr., 1940-42; instr. Iowa State U., 1945-46; from instr. to assoc. prof. U. Calif.-Santa Barbara, 1948-62, prof., 1962-87; prof. emeritus, 1987—; chmn. dept. polit. sci. U. Calif.-Santa Barbara, 1960-65, acad. vice chancellor, 1971-73; mem. summer faculty U. Mo., 1951, U. Nebr, 1956, U. Calif.-Berkeley, 1958; vis. prof. polit. sci. U. Khartoum, Sudan, 1962-63; Fulbright lectr. U. Witwatersrand, Republic South Africa, 1968, U. Teheran, Iran, 1974; cons. Bur. Budget, 1953; mem. staff White House, 1953. Author: (with J.A. Vieg) The Government and Politics of California, 4th edit., 1971, American Democracy: State and Local Government, 1968, 2d edit., 1970; co-author: American Democracy in World Perspective, 1967, 5th edit., 1980, The Wilson Influence on Public Administration, 1990; editor: Politics in the United States, 1955; contbr. articles to profl. jours. Staff mem. Democratic Nat. Com., 1952. Served from ensign to lt. USNR, 1942-45. Mem. Am. Polit. Sci. Assn., Western Polit. Sci. Assn. Home: 703 Foxen Dr Santa Barbara CA 93105-2516

TURNER, HENRY BROWN, finance executive; b. N.Y.C., Sept. 3, 1936; s. Henry Brown III and Gertrude (Adams) T.; m. Sarah Jean Thomas, June 7, 1958 (div.); children: Laura Eleanor, Steven Bristow, Nancy Carolyn. A.B., Duke U., 1958; M.B.A., Harvard U., 1962. Controller Fin. Corp. of Ariz., Phoenix, 1962-64; treas., dir. corporate planning Star-Kist Foods, Terminal Island, Calif., 1964-67; dir., 1st v.p. Mitchum, Jones & Templeton, Los Angeles, 1967-73; asst. sec. Dept. Commerce, Washington, 1973-74; v.p. fin. N-Ren Corp., Cin., 1975-76; v.p. Oppenheimer & Co., N.Y.C., 1976-78; exec. v.p., mng. dir. corporate fin. Shearson Hayden Stone Inc., N.Y.C., 1978-79; sr. mng. dir. Ardshiel Inc., 1980-81, pres., 1981-93, chmn. emeritus, 1994—; vis. lectr. U. Va. Sch. of Bus.; bd. dirs. MacDonald & Co., Pembrook Mgmt., Inc., Golden State Vitners, Inc., Cellu-Tissue Corp., Wrangler Stewart Ranch, Cave Creek, Ariz. Sponsor Jr. Achievement, 1964-67. Served to lt. USNR, 1958-60. Coll. Men's Club scholar Westfield, N.J., 1954-55. Mem. Fed. Govt. Accountants Assn. (hon.), Duke Washington Club, Omicron Delta Kappa.

TURNER, HESTER HILL, management consultant; b. San Antonio, Jan. 31, 1917; d. Orvin A. and Edna Lee (Guerguin) Hill; m. William Hoag Turner, Mar. 7, 1939 (div. Aug. 1957); children: William Hoag, John Daniel, Mary Lee, Jane Livingston (Mrs. S. Thomas Toleno). B.S., Our Lady of Lake U., 1938; M.A., S.W. Tex. State Coll., 1940; J.D., U. Ariz., 1945; Ed.D., Oreg. State U., 1956; L.H.D. (hon.), Drury Coll., Our Lady of the Lake, Salem Coll. Faculty Lewis and Clark Coll., Portland, 1947-66, dean students, 1961-66; nat. exec. dir. Camp Fire Girls, Inc., Kansas City, Mo., 1966-79; vis. instr. Oreg. State U., Western Wash. Coll., Portland State Coll.; dir. profl. services Oreg. Edn. Assn., Portland, 1959-61. Contbr. articles and chpts. to profl. publs. Mem. Oreg. Commn. on Status of Women, 1964-66; del. White House Conf. on Status of Women, 1965; mem. Portland met. steering com. OEO, 1965-66, Nat. Citizens Adv. Com. Vocat. Rehab., 1966-68; mem. Def. Adv. Com. Women in Svcs., 1966-69, chmn., 1968-69; mem. N.Y. State Vocat. Rehab. Planning Coun., 1967-68; trustee Coun. for Advancement and Support of Edn.; chmn. Accreditation Commn., Nat. Home Study Coun., 1983-89; mem. Army Adv. Coun. on ROTC Affairs, 1974-75; bd. dirs. Nat. Wildlife Fedn., 1982-88, Yosemite Inst., 1983-90; bd. dirs. Lincoln Found. and Lincoln Inst. Land Planning, 1983-89, New Century Conservation Trust, Inc., 1992-96. Recipient Dept. Def. medal for disting. pub. service, 1970; named Disting. Citizen U. Ariz. Mem. NEA, Oreg. Assn. Health and Phys. Edn. (pres. 1959-60), Oreg. Bar Assn., Ariz. Bar Assn., Am. Forestry Assn. (v.p. 1977-79, pres. 1980-82), Forest History Soc. (pres. 1991-93), Gemological Inst. Am. (bd. dirs. 1989-92), Phi Kappa Phi, Delta Kappa Gamma. Home and Office: 601 E 20th St New York NY 10010-7622 *One learns to make decisions only by making them. All adults who care about young people are presented with a special challenge: If we want to help them become responsible adults, we must have both the courage to stand for our own beliefs, and the faith to allow them to discover their own.*

TURNER, HUGH JOSEPH, JR., lawyer; b. Paterson, N.J., Oct. 5, 1945; s. Hugh Joseph and Louise (Sullivan) T.; m. Charlene Chiappetta, Feb. 11, 1983. BS, Boston U., 1967; JD, U. Miami, Coral Gables, Fla., 1975. Bar: Fla. 1975, U.S. Dist. Ct. (so. & mid. dists.) Fla. 1975, U.S. Ct. Appeals (11th cir.) 1981, U.S. Supreme Ct. 1984. Tchr. Browne & Nichols, Cambridge, Mass., 1968-72; ptnr. Smathers & Thompson, Miami, Fla., 1981-87, Kelley Drye & Warren, Miami, 1987-93, English, McCaughan & O'Bryan, Ft. Lauderdale, 1993—; chmn. Fla. Bar internat. law sect., 1988-89. Contbg. author book on internat. dispute resolution Fla. Bar, 1989; contbr. articles to profl. jours. Bd. dirs. Japan Soc. South Fla., Miami, 1989—; mem. Sea Ranch Lakes Village Coun. Mem. ABA, Def. Rsch. Inst. Avocation: running. Office: English McCaughan O'Bryan 100 NE 3rd Ave Fort Lauderdale FL 33301-1176

TURNER, JAMES THOMAS, judge; b. Clifton Forge, Va., Mar. 12, 1938; s. James Thomas and Ruth (Greene) T.; m. Patricia Sue Renfrow, July 8, 1962; 1 child, James Thomas. BA, Wake Forest Coll., 1960; JD, U. Va., 1965. Bars: Va. 1965, U.S. Ct. Appeals (4th and fed. cirs.), U.S. Supreme Ct. Assoc. firm Williams, Worrell, Kelly & Greer, Norfolk, Va., 1965, ptnr., 1971-79; U.S. magistrate U.S. Dist. Ct., Eastern Dist. Va., Norfolk, 1979-87; judge, U.S. Ct. Fed. Claims, 1987—. Mem. ABA, FBA, Va. Bar Assn., Norfolk and Portsmouth Bar Assn. (sec. 1975-79). Office: US Ct Fed Claims 717 Madison Pl NW Washington DC 20005-1011

TURNER, JAMES WESLEY, minister, former church administrator; b. Hampton, Va., May 30, 1914; s. James Hugh Turner and Lizzie Emma Moger; m. Ruth Clark Brown, Sept. 28, 1940; children: James Wedford, Susan Clark. BA, Randolph-Macon Coll., 1937, DD, 1961; MDiv, Emory U., 1940. Ordained to ministry Meth. Ch., 1940. Pastor Meth. Ch., Richmond, Va., 1940-82; dir. program coun. United Meth. Ch., Richmond, 1976-82; dist. supt. United Meth. Ch., Arlington, Va., 1971-76; chmn. fin. Va. Conf. Credit Union, Inc., 1954-97; pres. Chaplain Svc. Va., Richmond, 1994-97; mem. bd. ordained ministry, Richmond, 1989-96. Vice pres. Robert E. Lee coun. Boy Scouts Am., 1978—; mem. allocation panel United Way Greater Richmond, 1987-95. Recipient Gold medal Freedom Found., 1967, Silver Beaver award Boy Scouts Am., 1980, Algernon Sydney Sullivan award Randolph-Macon Coll., 1997. Mem. Masons. Avocations: photography, golf, travel. Home and Office: 10201 Glendye Rd Richmond VA 23235-2122

TURNER, JANE ANN, federal agent; b. Rapid City, S.D., Aug. 26, 1951; d. John Owen and Wilma Veona (Thompson) T.; 1 child, Victoria Thompson. BA, Carroll Coll., 1973; student forensic psychology, John Jay Sch. Criminal Justice, N.Y.C., 1985-87. Spl. agt. FBI, Seattle and N.Y.C., 1978-87; sr. resident spl. agt. FBI, Minot, N.D., 1987—; spkr., instr. FBI, Seattle, N.Y.C. and Minot, 1978—, Psychol. Profiler, 1983—. Mem. Minot Commn. on the Status of Women, 1991-93; mem. domestic violence bd. Minot Housing Authority. Mem. Gen. Fedn. Women's Clubs (v.p. 1992-93), Women in Law Enforcement, N.D. Peace Officer Assn., Optimists. Office: FBI PO Box 968 Fed Bldg Minot ND 58701

TURNER, JANET SULLIVAN, painter; b. Gardiner, Maine, Nov. 15, 1935; d. Clayton Jefferson and Frances (Leighton) Sullivan; m. Terry Turner, Oct. 6, 1956; children: Lisa Turner Reid, Michael Ross, Jonathan Brett. BA cum laude, Mich. State U., 1956. rep. Am. Women in Art, UN World Conf. on Women, Nairobi, Kenya, 1985. One-artist shows include San Diego Art Inst., 1971, Villanova (Pa.) U. Gallery, 1982, Pa. State U., Middletown (Pa.), 1985, Temple U. (Pa.), 1986, Widener U. Art Mus., Chester, Pa., 1987, 94, Rosemont Coll., Pa., 1995; group shows include Del. Art Mus., Wilmington, 1978, Woodmere Art Mus., Phila., 1980, Port of History Mus., Phila., 1984, Allentown Art Mus., 1984, Trenton (N.J.) City Mus. Ellarslie Open VIII, 1989, Ammo Gallery, Bklyn., 1989, Pa. State Mus., Harrisburg, 1990-94, Galeria Mesa, Ariz., 1991, Del. Ctr. for Contemporary Arts, Wilmington, 1992, Holter Mus., Helena, Mont., 1992, S.w. Tex. State U., San Marcos, 1993, Fla. State U. Mus., Tallahassee, 1993, Newark Mus., 1993, U. Del., 1994, 1st St. Gallery, N.Y.C., 1994, Noyes Mus., N.J., 1995, Sande Webster Gallery, Phila. 1995, 96, Phil. Art Mus., 1997; represented in permanent collections Nat. Mus. Women in Arts, Washington, Mich. State U., East Lansing, ARA Svcs. Inc., Phila., Blue Cross/Blue Shield, Phila., am. Nat. Bank and Trust co., Rockford, Ill., Burroughs Corp., Lisle, Ill., State Mus. Pa., Harrisburg, Bryn Mawr (Pa.) Coll., Rosemont Coll., Villanova (Pa.) Coll.; contbg. writer and art critic Art Matters, Phila., 1987. Bd. dirs. Rittenhouse Sq. Fine Arts Ann., Phila., 1984-86. Recipient 2d pl. award San Diego Art Inst. 19th Ann. Exhbn., 1971, award of merit Pavilion Gallery, Mt. Holly, N.J., 1991, 3d pl. Katonah Mus. of Art, N.Y., 1992, purchase award State Mus. of Pa., Harrisburg, 1992. Mem. Artists Equity (bd. dirs. 1985-86, 1st v.p. Phila. 1986-87, newsletter editor 1985-86, pres. 1987-88), Phila. Watercolor Club, Delta Phi Delta. Republican. Roman Catholic. Home and Studio: 88 Cambridge Dr Glen Mills PA 19342-1545

TURNER, JEAN-LOUISE, public relations executive; b. Washington, Sept. 29, 1942; d. Fletcher Wood and Mary Louise (Gant) T.; student Howard U., 1959-62; B.A., Fed. City Coll., 1970; M.A., 1972; children—Nathaniel Anthony Landry, Mark Andrew Landry. Coordinator public relations Sta. WRC-TV, Washington, 1969; adminstr. prodn., 1970-72; mgmt. trainee NBC, Washington, 1972; producer spls. Sta. WRC-TV, 1972-76, asso. producer documentaries, 1972-76; mgr. community affairs and public affairs, host Sta. WRC/WKYS, Washington, 1976-78, producer WRC 1978-79; media rep. PEPCO, Washington, 1979-81; press aide D.C. City Council, 1981-82; dir. pub. relations LaMancha, Inc., 1983-84; v.p. Talisman Assocs., 1984—; mgr. Jafra Skin Care, 1994; judge Gabriel awards; mem. media panel D.C. Arts and Humanities Commn.; bd. dirs. Epilepsy Found. Am.; pres. parish coun. St. Francis de Sales Roman Cath. Ch., 1993, 94—; career role model St. Anthony's High Sch. Recipient Hallmark award Jr. Achievement, 1976, Public Service award Washington Area Council Alcoholism and Drug Abuse, 1977; Public Interest award Council Better Bus. Burs. Inc., 1977. Mem. Capital Press Club, Washington Assn. Black Journalists, Nat. Acad. TV Arts and Scis., Nat. Assn. Public Continuing Adult Edn., Anchor Mental Health Assn. (bd. dirs., chmn. 1992-94, Award of Appreciation 1994), Washington Women's Forum (charter), Alpha Kappa Alpha. Roman Catholic. Editorial bd. NAPCAE Exchange, 1979-81. Home: 2715 31st Pl NE Washington DC 20018-1601 Office: 4005 20th St NE Washington DC 20018-3255

TURNER, JEROME, federal judge; b. Memphis, Feb. 18, 1942; s. Cooper and Eugenia (Morrison) T.; m. Shirley Broadhead, Oct. 18, 1969 (div. July 1986); children: Alexandra Cox, Christian Annette; m. Kay Farese, Aug. 22, 1987. BA, Washington and Lee U., 1964, LLB cum laude, 1966. Bar: Tenn. 1966. Law clk. to judge U.S. Dist. Ct., Memphis, 1966-67; assoc. Canada, Russell & Turner, Memphis, 1967-73, ptnr., 1974-78; ptnr. Wildman, Harrold, Allen, Dixon & McDonnell, Memphis, 1978-87; judge U.S. Dist. Ct. (we. Dist.) Tenn., Memphis, 1988—. Author: Law Rev. Comment, Washington and Lee Law Rev., 1964, 65; editor: Law Rev., 1966. Treas. Elect Don Sundquist to Congress Com., 1981-82, Reelect Don Sundquist to Congress Com., 1983-86. Fellow Tenn. Bar Found.; mem. ABA, Memphis and Shelby County Bar Found. (bd. dirs. 1982-83, 87, 96-97), Memphis and Shelby County Bar Assn. (pres. 1988, treas. 1984, bd. dirs. 1978-79), Fed. Bar Assn., Tenn. Bar Assn., Leo Bearman Sr. Am. Inn of Ct. (pres. 1995-96, 97), Order of Coif, Omicron Delta Kappa. Roman Catholic. Avocations: hunting, tennis, reading, gardening. Office: Clifford Davis Fed Bldg 167 N Main St Ste 1111 Memphis TN 38103-1830

TURNER, JIM, congressman; m. Ginny Turner; children: John, Susan. BA in Bus., U. Tex., Austin, MBA, JD. Mem. Tex. Ho. Reps., Tex. Senate, U.S. Ho. Reps. from 2d Tex. dist., 1996—. Mayor City of Crockett, Tex.; deacon, Sunday sch. tchr. First Bapt. Ch. Crockett. Capt. U.S. Army. Democrat. Office: Ho Reps 1508 Longworth H O B Washington DC 20515

TURNER, JOHN FREELAND, non-profit administrator, former federal agency administrator, former state senator; b. Jackson, Wyo., Mar. 3, 1942; s. John Charles and Mary Louise (Mapes) T.; m. Mary Kay Brady, 1969; children: John Francis, Kathy Mapes, Mark Freeland. BS in Biology, U. Notre Dame, 1964; postgrad., U. Innsbruck, 1964-65, U. Utah, 1965-66; MS in Ecology, U. Mich., 1968. Rancher, outfitter Triangle X Ranch, Moose, Wyo.; chmn. bd. dirs. Bank of Jackson Hole; photo-journalist; state senator from Sublette State of Wyo., Teton County, 1974-89; mem. Wyo. Ho. of Reps. Teton County, 1970-74; pres. Wyo. Senate, 1987-89; chmn. legis., minerals bus. and econ. devel. com. Teton County, Wyo., 1987-89; dir. Fish and Wildlife Svc. Dept. Interior, Washington, 1989-93; pres. Conservation Fund, Arlington, Va., 1993—; sr. cons. Sch. Environ. and Natural Resources, U. Wyo., Laramie, 1993—; exec. adv. Hancock Timber Resource Group, 1993—; bd. dirs. Land Trust Alliance, 1994—, N.E. Utilities, Nat. Assn. Chem. Distbn. Found.; mem. Nat. Coal Coun., 1995—, Teton Sci. Sch. Bd., Nat. Wetland Forum, 1983, 87; mem. exec. com. Coun. of State Govts.; chmn. Pride in Jackson Hole Campaign, 1986; bd. dirs. Wyo. Waterfowl Trust; chmn. steering com. of UN conv. on Wetlands of Internat. Importance, 1990—; head U.S. delegation to Conv. on Internat. Trade Endangered Species. Author: The Magnificent Bald Eagle: Our National Bird, 1971. Named Citizen of Yr. County of Teton, 1984; recipient Nat. Conservation Achievement award Nat. Wildlife Fedn., 1984, Sheldon Coleman Great Outdoors award, 1990, Pres.'s Pub. Svc. award The Nature Conservatory, 1990, Stewardship award Audobon Soc., 1992, Nat. Wetland Achievement award Ducks Unlimited, 1993, Chevron/Times-Mirror Nat. Conservation Leadership award, 1995. Republican. Roman Catholic.

TURNER, JOHN NAPIER, former prime minister of Canada, legislator; b. Richmond, Eng., June 7, 1929; s. Leonard and Phyllis (Gregory) T.; m. Geills McCrae Kilgour, May 11, 1963; children: Elizabeth, Michael, David, Andrew. BA with honors in Polit. Sci., U. B.C., Can., 1949; BA, Oxford U., Eng., 1951, BCL, 1952; MA, Oxford U., 1957; postgrad., U. Paris, 1952-53; LLD, U. N.B., 1968, York U., Toronto, 1969, U. B.C., 1994, U. Toronto, 1996; D. of Civil Law (hon.), Mt. Allison U., N.B., 1980. Bar: Eng. 1953, Que. 1954, Ont. 1968, B.C. 1969, Y.T. 1969, N.W.T. 1969, Barbados 1969, Trinidad 1969. With Stikeman, Elliot, Tamaki, Mercier and Turner, Montreal, Que., 1953-65, McMillan Binch, Toronto, 1976-84; M.P. for St. Lawrence-St. George Montreal, 1962-68, Ottawa-Carleton, 1968-75; parliamentary sec. to Minister of Northern Affairs and Nat. Resources, 1963-65; minister without portfolio, 1965-67; registrar-gen. Govt. of Can., 1967-68, minister of consumer and corp. affairs, 1968, solicitor-gen., 1968, minister of justice and atty.-gen. of Can., 1968-72, minister of fin., 1972-75, prime minister of Can., 1984; leader Liberal Party Can., 1984-90; mem. parliament Vancouver Quadra, 1984-93; with Miller Thomson, Toronto, 1990—; created Queen's Counsel, Ontario and Quebec, 1968; former positions include minister without portfolio, registrar gen., minister consumer and corp. affairs, solicitor gen., minister justice and atty. gen., minister fin. Author: Senate of Canada, 1961, Politics of Purpose, 1968. Can. Track Field Champion, 1948; mem. English Track and Field Team, 1950-51. Appointed Companion of Order of Can., 1995. Mem. Eng. Bar Assn., Grey's Inn London, Bar. Assns. of Ont., Que., B.C., Barbados, Trinidad, Mt. Royal Club, Montreal Racquet Club, Cercle Universitaire d'Ottawa Club, Aylmer (Que.) Country Club, Queen's Club, Badminton and Racquet Club, York Club, The Vancouver Club. Liberal. Roman Catholic. Avocations: tennis, canoeing, skiing. Home: 27 Dunloe Rd, Toronto, ON Canada M4V 2W4 Office: Miller Thomson, 20 Queen St Box 27 Ste 2500, Toronto, ON Canada M5H 3S1

TURNER, JOHN SIDNEY, JR., otolaryngologist, educator; b. Bainbridgw, Ga., July 25, 1930; s. John Sidney and Rose Lee (Rogers) T.; m. Betty Jane Tigner, June 5, 1955; children: Elizabeth, Rebecca, Jan Marie. BS, Emory U., 1952, MD, 1955. Diplomate Am. Bd. Otolaryngology. Intern U. Va. Hosp., 1955-56; resident in otolaryngology Duke U. Med. Ctr., 1958-61; prof. otolaryngology Emory U., Atlanta, 1961-95, chmn. dept., 1961-95; cons. Healthcare Partnership Cons., Atlanta, 1995—; ear specialist, chief otolaryngology Emory Clinic, 1961-95; area cons. in field U.S. 3d Army, 1962-69; assoc. dir. heart disease control program Fla. Bd. Health, 1956-58; Ga. state chmn. Deafness Rsch. Found., 1968—; v.p. Clifton Casualty Ins. Co., Atlanta, 1975-95. Mem. internat. editl. bd. Drugs Jour., 1982—, Ethicals in Med. Progress, 1982—, Dialogue Jour., 1988-95; mem. editl. bd. Otolaryngology—Head and Neck Surgery, 1991; contbr. chpts. to books, articles to profl. jours. With USPHS, 1956-58. Recipient Appreciation award Children of Fulton County and Fulton County Health Dept., 1975, Citation for Disting. Svc., Fla. divsn. Am. Cancer Soc., 1957, Lester A. Brown award Ga. Soc. Otolaryngology—Head and Neck Surgery, 1995. Mem. AMA, So. Med. Assn. (chmn. otolaryngology sect. 1974, cert. of appreciation 1974), Am. Acad. Otolaryngology--Head and Neck Surgery (Honor award 1994), Triological Soc. (v.p., chmn. so. sect. 1991—), Am. Acad. Otolaryngic Allergy, Ga. Soc. Otolaryngology (pres. 1973), Med. Assn. Ga., Med. Assn. Atlanta, Assn. Acad. Depts. Otolaryngology, Optimists (pres. Atlanta 1975), Alpha Omega Alpha. Democrat. Methodist. Home: 1388 Council Bluff Dr NE Atlanta GA 30345-4132

TURNER, KATHLEEN J., communication educator, consultant; b. Canton, Ohio, Jan. 8, 1952; d. Josiah Shelden Turner and Anne Alexander; m. Raymond Sprague, May 30, 1981. BA in Speech Comm., English summa cum laude, U. Kans., 1974; MA in Comm., Purdue U., 1976, PhD in Comm., 1978. Teaching asst. Purdue U., West Lafayette, Ind., 1976-78; asst. prof. Denison U., Granville, Ohio, 1978-79, U. Notre Dame, South Bend, Ind., 1979-85; vis. assoc. prof. U. Tulsa, 1985-86; assoc. prof. Tulane U., New Orleans, La., 1986—; also chair dept. comm., 1992-95; mem. comm. course and curriculum com. U. Tulsa, 1985-86; mem. com. comm. program curriculum U. Notre Dame, 1979-80, com. for redesigned comm. curriculum, 1983-84; mem. jr. yr. abroad com. Tulane U., 1987-88, Am. studies com., 1987-88, Univ. Coll. com. on bus. studies, 1988-91, univ. senate, 1989-91, search com. for v.p. devel., 1989, juror 5th yr. architecture student thesis reviews, 1987, 88, 89, 90, 93, 96, chair univ. senate com. on devel., 1991-94, women's studies com., 1986-91, chair com. Newcomb ctr. for Rsch. on Women, 1988-90, mem., 1990-94, 95-96; lectr. numerous seminars; presenter numerous workshops. Author: Lyndon Johnson's Dual War: Vietnam and the Press, 1985, paperback, 1986; contbr. chpts. and articles numerous books; book and jour. reviewer; contbr. articles to profl. jours. Invited to 16th Air Force Acad. Assembly, 1974; recipient Paul B. Lawson award U. Kans., 1973, Allen Crafton scholarship U. Kans., 1972-73, 73-74, fellowship Purdue U., 1974-75, 75-76; Residential fellow Tulane U., 1992-96, Newcomb fellow Tulane U., 1989—. Mem. Speech Comm. Assn. (life, rsch. bd. 1990-93, short course selection com. 1992-93, assoc. editor Quar. Jour. Speech 1986-89, assoc. editor Comm. Edn. 1980-81), Ctrl. States Comm. Assn. (life, chair fin. com. 1984-85, assoc. editor Ctrl. States Speech Jor. 1982-86), So. States Comm. Assn. (chair rhetoric and pub. address div. 1992-93), Popular Culture Assn., Am. Culture Assn. Home: 2412 Jay St New Orleans LA 70122-4310 Office: Tulane Univ Dept Comm New Orleans LA 70118

TURNER, LEE, travel company executive; b. 1952. BS, Worcester Polytechnic Inst., 1974; MBA, Dartmouth, 1976. With Baxter Healthcare, Deerfield, Ill., 1976-79, 82-87, Southeastern Pub. Svc. Co., Miami Beach, Fla., 1979-82; exec. v.p. BTI Ams., Inc., Northbrook, Ill., 1987—. Office: BTI Ams Inc 400 Skokie Blvd Fl 8 Northbrook IL 60062-2816

TURNER, LEE S., JR., civil engineer, consultant, former utilities executive; b. Dallas, Nov. 5, 1926; s. James A. and Fay Sims; m. Donetta Mae Johnson, Jan. 17, 1947. BCE, Tex. A&M U., 1948; JD, So. Meth. U., 1957. Engr. Dallas Power & Light Co., 1948, various exec. positions, pres., chief exec., 1967-76; dir. Tex. Utilities Co., 1967-82; exec. v.p. Tex. Utilities Co., Dallas, 1976-84; cons., 1989—. Trustee Com. for Econ. Devel., Southwestern Med. Found.; past pres., bd. dirs. Dallas Citizens Coun.; bd. dirs. So. Meth. U. Found. for Sci. and Engring.; past chmn. Children's Med. Ctr.; past chmn. United Way, YMCA, Community Coun. of Greater Dallas; past pres. Greater Dallas Ahead, Inc., Dallas Assembly. With U.S. Army, 1945-46. Mem. ABA, Am. Arbitration Assn. Presbyterian.

TURNER, LISA PHILLIPS, human resources executive; b. Waltham, Mass., Apr. 10, 1951; d. James Sinclair and Virginia Turner. BA in Edn. and Philosophy magna cum laude, Washington Coll., Chestertown, Md., 1974; AS in Electronics Tech., AA in Engring., Palm Beach Jr. Coll., 1982; MBA, Nova U., 1986, DSc, 1989; PhD, Kennedy Western U., 1990. Cert. Sr. Profl. in Human Resources, quality engr.; lic. USCG capt.; lic. pvt. pilot FAA. Founder, pres. Turner's Bicycle Svc., Inc., Delray Beach, Fla., 1975-80; electronics engr., quality engr. Audio Engring. and Video Arts, Boca Raton, 1980-81; tech. writing instr. Palm Beach Jr. Coll., Lake Worth, Fla., 1981-82; adminstr. tng. and devel. Mitel Inc., Boca Raton, 1982-88; mgr. communications and employee rels. Modular Computer Systems, Inc., Ft. Lauderdale, Fla., 1988-89; U.S. mktg. project mgr. Mitel, Inc., Boca Raton, Fla., 1990-91; v.p. human resources Connectronics, Inc., Ft. Lauderdale, Fla., 1991-93; sr. mgr. human resources Sensormatic Electronics Corp., Boca Raton, Fla., 1993—. With USCG Aux. Mem. Soc. for Human Resource Mgmt., Internat. Assn. Quality Cirs., Am. Soc. Quality Control, Fla. Employment Mgmt. Assn., Am. Acad. Mgmt., Employment Assn. Fla., Am. Capts. Assn., Citizens Police Acad., Aircraft Owners and Pilot's Assn., Exptl. Aircraft Assn., Fla. Aero. Club. Home: 1358 Farifax Cir E Lantana FL 33462-7412 Office: Sensormatic Electronics Corp 6600 Congress Ave Boca Raton FL 33487-1213

TURNER, LOYD LEONARD, advertising executive, public relations executive; b. Grady, N.Mex., Nov. 5, 1917; s. James R. and Maude (Brown) T.; m. Lee Madeleine Barr, Apr. 13, 1944; children: Terry Lee, Loyd Lee. Student, Tex. Tech. U., 1935-36, Okla. Bapt. U., 1936-37; BA, Baylor U., 1939, MA, 1940; postgrad., U. Pa., 1940-42. Instr. dept. English U. Pa., Phila., 1940-42; pub. relations coordinator Consol. Vultee Aircraft Corp., San Diego, 1946-48; dir. pub. relations Consol. Vultee Aircraft Corp., Fort Worth, 1948-53; asst. to pres. Fort Worth div. Gen. Dynamics Corp., 1953-72; exec. asst. to pres. and chmn. bd. Tandy Corp., Fort Worth, 1972-76; v.p. Tandy Corp., 1976-85; sr. v.p. Witherspoon and Assocs., Inc., Fort Worth, 1986—, also bd. dirs.; mem. Gov.'s Com. on Public Sch. Edn., Tex., 1966-69; pres. Tex. Council Major Sch. Dists., 1968-69. Author: The ABC of Clear Writing, 1954. Bd. dirs. Tarrant County chpt. ARC, 1956-59; bd. dirs. Pub. Communication Found. for North Tex., 1970-76, Tex. Com. Pub. Edn., 1961-69; bd. dirs. Ft. Worth Child Study Ctr., 1974-81, 85-88, v.p., 1986-88; bd. dirs. Parenting Guidance Ctr., 1976-78, Longhorn coun. Boy Scouts Am., 1976-91, One Broadway Plaza, 1978-88; planning and research coun. United Way, Tarrant County, 1976-80; bd. dirs. Casa Manana Musicals, 1978—, pres., 1978-80; bd. dirs. Fort Worth Citizens Organized Against Crime, 1976-90, vice chmn., 1978-89; bd. dirs. Jr. Achievement Tarrant County, 1982-87, North Central chpt. March of Dimes, 1983-84; mem. Christian edn. coordinating bd. Bapt. Gen. Conv., Tex., 1976-80; trustee Ft. Worth Pub. Libr. Bd., 1953-63, pres., 1958-63; trustee Ft. Worth Bd. Edn., 1959-71, pres., 1965-71; trustee Baylor U., Waco, Tex., 1980-89. Served with USAAF, 1942-46. Named Library Trustee of Yr. Tex. Library Assn., 1961; Paul Harris fellow Rotary Internat., 1983; recipient Silver Beaver award Boy Scouts Am., 1986. Mem. Pub. Relations Soc. Am. (pres. N.Tex. chpt. 1977), Pub. Rel. Soc. Am. (Paul M. Lund Pub. Service award 1980), Nat. Mgmt. Assn., Tex. Congress of Parents and Tchrs. (hon. life mem.), West Tex. C. of C. (bd. dirs. 1982-87, v.p. 1985-87, Leadership award 1966, 69), NEA (pres. Best Bd. of Large Sch. Systems in U.S. 1968), Tex. Assn. of Sch. Bds. (bd. dirs. 1966-71, Outstanding Service award 1971), Advt. Club of Fort Worth (pres. 1977-78), Air Force Assn. (Spl. citation 1962), Assn. for Higher Edn. of N. Tex. (vice chmn. 1979-82), Fort Worth C. of C. (bd. dirs. 1974-76, 78-81, 83-87, vice chmn. 1985-87), Arts Council of Fort Worth (dir. 1973-75, 80-89), Tex. Assn. Bus. (bd. dirs. 1977-82, 83-86), Tex. Research League (bd. dirs. 1979-87), Baylor U. Devel. Council (pres. 1975-77), Baylor U. Alumni Assn. (bd. dirs. 1958-61), Fort Worth Safety Council (bd. dirs. 1980-83), Am. Advt. Fedn. (Silver Medal award 1981), Soc. Profl. Journalists (pres. Fort Worth chpt. 1961-62). Baptist. Clubs: Admirals, Bear, Frog. Lodge: Rotary (pres. 1974-75; William B. Todd Service Above Self award 1987).

Home: 3717 Echo Trl Fort Worth TX 76109-3432 Office: Witherspoon and Assocs Inc 1000 W Weatherford St Fort Worth TX 76102-1842

TURNER, LULA MAE MANSUR, retail executive; b. Denver, Feb. 12, 1917; d. Daniel Isaiah and Elizabeth Wilhelmina (Bellin) Mansur; m. Gordon Eugene Turner, June 12, 1938; 1 child, Daniel Gordon. Grad. high sch., Creston, Iowa. With steongraphic and acctg. dept. Iowa So. Utilities, Creston, 1935-38; sales and acctg. Kunath's, Creston, 1944; stenographic clk. Union County Draft Office, Creston, 1941-44; asst. mgr. Turner Appliance & Gifts, Creston, 1945-83, mgr., 1983—. Mem. DAR (regent 1954-56, state conv. chmn. 1974-76), Creston Womens Club (pres. 1945-46), Creston C. of C. (chmn. women's bur. 1966-67). Republican. Christian Scientist. Avocations: reading, classical music, art. Office: Turner Appliances & Gifts 200 N Elm St Creston IA 50801-2304

TURNER, LYNNE ALISON (MRS. PAUL H. SINGER), harpist; b. St. Louis, July 31, 1941; d. Sol and Evelyn (Klein) T.; m. Paul H. Singer, June 2, 1963; children: Bennett Lloyd, Rachel E. Singer Sullivan. Degree with high honors, Paris Conservatory Music (Premier Prix Hors Concours-Harp), 1959-60; studied with Pierre Jamet. lectr. in field. Harpist Chgo. Symphony Orch., 1962—, acting prin. harpist, 1994—; soloist Chgo. Symphony Orch., Israel Philharm. Orch., other maj. orchs. in U.S. and Europe, also chamber groups; founding mem. L'Ensemble Recamier, The Chgo. Duo (harp and violin); instr. harp Sch. Music, DePaul U., Chgo., 1976-86; instr. harp Lake Forest Coll., 1988-90; instr. pvt. students. Recipient 1st prize 2d Internat. Harp Competition, Israel, 1962. Mem. Am. Harp Soc., Chgo. Hist. Soc. (costume com.), Women's Assn. Chgo. Symphony Orch., Antiquarian Soc. Art Inst. Chgo., Internat. Visitors Ctr. Chgo., Chgo. Arts Club, The Casino Club. Avocations: gardening, decorating, collecting antiques. Office: Orch Hall 220 S Michigan Ave Chicago IL 60604-2501

TURNER, MALCOLM ELIJAH, biomathematician, educator; b. Atlanta, May 27, 1929; s. Malcolm Elijah and Margaret (Parker) T.; m. Ann Clay Bowers, Sept. 16, 1948; children: Malcolm Elijah IV, Allison Ann, Clay Shumate, Margaret Jean; m. Rachel Patricia Farmer, Feb. 1, 1968; children: Aleta van Riper, Leila Samantha, Alexis St. John, Walter McCamy. Student, Emory U., 1947-48; B.A., Duke U., 1952; M.Exptl. Stats., N.C. State U., 1955, Ph.D., 1959. Analytical statistician Communicable Disease Center, USPHS, Atlanta, 1953; rsch. assoc. U. Cin., 1955, asst. prof., 1955-58; asst. statistician N.C. State U., Raleigh, 1957-58; assoc. prof. Med. Coll. Va., Richmond, 1958-63, chmn. div. biometry, 1959-63; prof., chmn. dept. statistics and biometry Emory U., Atlanta, 1963-69; chmn. dept. biomath., prof. biostats. and biomath. U. Ala., Birmingham, 1970-82, prof. biostats. and biomath., 1982—; instr. summers Yale U., 1966, U. Calif. at Berkeley, 1971, Vanderbilt U., 1975; prof. U. Kans., 1968-69; vis. prof. Atlanta U., 1969; cons. to industry. Mem. editorial bd. So. Med. Jour., 1990—; contbr. articles to profl. jours. Fellow Ala. Acad. Sci., Am. Statis. Assn. (hon.), AAAS (hon.); mem. AAUP, AMA (affiliate), Biometrics Soc. (mng. editor Biometrics 1962-69), Soc. for Indsl. and Applied Math., Mensa, Sigma Xi, Phi Kappa Phi, Phi Delta Theta, Phi Sigma. Home: 1734 Tecumseh Trl Pelham AL 35124-1012 *The logic of induction is the quest.*

TURNER, MARSHALL CHITTENDEN, JR., venture capitalist, consultant; b. Santa Monica, Calif., 1941; s. Marshall C. and Winifred H. Turner; m. Ann Curran, 1965; children: Erin, Benjamin, Brian. BSME, Stanford U., 1964, MS in Product Design, 1965; MBA with distinction, Harvard U., 1970. Indsl. designer Mattel Toy Co., Hawthorne, Calif., 1965; rsch. engr. GM Def. Rsch. Lab., Santa Barbara, Calif., 1965-66; med. engr. NIH, Bethesda, Md., 1966-68; White House fellow Washington, 1970-71; asst. to dep. adminstr. EPA, Washington, 1971-73; venture analyst Crocker Assocs., L.P., San Francisco, 1973-75; v.p. fin., COO Sierra R.R., 1973-75; pres., CEO Liquid Crystal Tech., Inc., San Leandro, Calif., 1975-80, chmn. bd. dirs., 1975-82; gen. ptnr. Taylor & Turner Assocs., Ltd., San Francisco, 1981—; bd. dirs. DuPont Photomasks, Inc., Alliance Tech. Fund, N.Y., Remanco Internat., Inc., Wilmington, Mass., Virtual Ass., Inc. Purchase, N.Y.; chmn. bd. dirs. Corp. Pub. Broadcasting, Washington, 1990-92; chmn. bd. dirs. KQED, Inc., San Francisco, 1985-87, acting CEO, 1993. Contbr. articles to profl. jours. Trustee Reed Union Sch. dist., Tiburon, Calif., 1977-81, chmn., 1979-81; bd. dirs. George Lucas Ednl. Found., San Rafael, Calif., 1992—, PBS, Alexandria, Va., 1993—, PBS Enterprises, Inc., 1992—; trustee Mus. TV and Radio, N.Y.C., 1991-92. Lt. USPHS, 1966-68; mem. adv. bd. Nat. Mus. Natural History, Washington, 1997—. Recipient Creative design award Machinery Inst., 1965. Avocations: fly fishing, theatrical set design. Office: Penthouse 10 220 Montgomery St San Francisco CA 94104-3402

TURNER, MARTA DAWN, youth program specialist; b. Morgantown, W.V., Oct. 7, 1954; d. Trubie Lenard and Dorothy Genevieve (Helmick) T.; m. David Michael Dunning, Mar. 1, 1980. Student, Royal Acad. Dramatic Art, London, 1975; BA with honors, Chatham Coll., 1976; grad. cert. in arts adminstrn., Adelphi U., 1982; MA Devel. Drama, Hunter Coll., 1988. Cert. video prodn. specialist. Asst. dir. Riverside Communications, N.Y.C., 1985-88; dir. drama, video youth environ. group Water Proof, Cornell Coop. Extension, 1989-91; playwright, dir. Awareness Players, The Disabled Theatre of Maine, 1993-95. Exec. prodr. video projects including Hispanic City Sounds, Time for Peace, Home, Home in Inwood, 1985—; asst. dir., dir. video series Riverside at Worship, 1985-88. Bd. dirs. Trinity Presbyn. Ch., N.Y.C., 1980-90, Am. Diabetes Assn., 1986-87. Avocations: swimming, Scrabble, karate, Marilyn Monroe fan/memoribilia collection. Home and Office: 134 Phillip St Bangor ME 04401

TURNER, MARY JANE, educational administrator; b. Colorado Springs, Colo., June 1, 1923; d. David Edward and Ina Mabel (Campbell) Nickelson; m. Harold Adair Turner, Feb. 15, 1945 (dec.); children: Mary Ann, Harold Adair III. BA in Polit. Sci., U. Colo., 1947, MPA in Pub. Adminstrn., 1968, PhD in Polit. Sci., 1978. Secondary tchr. Canon City (Colo.) Sch. Dist., 1950-53; tchr. assoc. in polit. sci. U. Colo., Denver, 1968-70, Boulder, 1970-71; rsch. asst. Social Sci. Edn. Consortium, Boulder, 1971, staff assoc., 1972-77; dir. Colo. Legal Edn. Program, Boulder, 1977-84; assoc. dir. Ctr. for Civic Edn., Calabasas, Calif., 1984-88; dir. Close Up Found., Alexandria, Va., 1988-92; sr. edn. advisor Close Up Found., Arlington, Va., 1992—. Author: Political Science in the New Social Studies, 1972; co-author: American Government: Principles and Practices, 1983, 4th edit., 1996; Civics: Citizens in Action, 1986, 2d edit., 1991, U.S. Government Resource Book, 1989; contbg. author: Internat. Ency. Dictionary of Edn. Mem. Nat. Coun. for Social Studies (chair nominations 1983-84, chair bicentennial com. 1986), Social Sci. Edn. Consortium (pres. 1986-87, bd. dirs. 1984-87), Pi Lambda Theta, Pi Sigma Alpha. Democrat. Presbyterian. Office: Close Up Found 44 Canal Center Plz Alexandria VA 22314-1592

TURNER, MICHAEL GRISWOLD, advertising executive, writer; b. Pitts., Mar. 2, 1925; s. James Jewett and Madelaine Eunice (Griswold) T.; m. Elizabeth Anne Tufel, Sept. 8, 1951; children: Jason A., Michael G., Nanci S. Turner Steveson, James A., Craig C., Ashley S. BA cum laude, Princeton U., 1949. Rsch. asst. to mgmt. supr. Benton & Bowles, N.Y.C., 1950-60; dir. Benton & Bowles, London, 1960-63; mgmt. supr. Benton & Bowles, N.Y.C., 1963-66; exec. v.p., dir. Ogilvy & Mather, N.Y.C., 1966-70, Houston, 1970-85; creative dir. Ogilvy & Mather, Washington, 1985-86; vice chmn. Earle Palmer Brown, Bethesda, Md., 1986-91, Atlanta, 1986-91; chmn. Turner & Turner Comm., Inc., Atlanta, 1992—; cons. and lectr. in field. Contbr. articles to trade jours. With USNR, 1943-46, PTO. Mem. Bay Head Yacht Club (N.J.). Home: 750 Olde Clubs Dr Alpharetta GA 30202-6890 Office: Turner & Turner Comm Inc 1168 14th Pl Atlanta GA 30309

TURNER, MICHAEL STANLEY, physics educator; b. L.A., July 29, 1949; s. Paul Joseph and Janet Mary (Lindholm) T.; m. Terri Lee Shields, Aug. 1978 (div. Sept. 1980); m. Barbara Lynn Ahlberg, Sept. 10, 1988; children: Rachel Mary, Joseph Lucien. BS in Physics, Calif. Inst. Tech., 1971; MS in Physics, Stanford U., 1973, PhD in Physics, 1978. Enrico Fermi fellow U. Chgo., 1978-80, from asst. to assoc. prof., 1980-85, prof., 1985—; scientist Fermi Nat. Accelerator Lab, Batavia, Ill., 1983—; trustee Aspen (Colo.) Ctr. Physics, 1984—, pres., 1989-93; Halley lectr. Oxford U., 1994. Author: (with E.W. Kolb) The Early Universe, 1990; contbr. over 150 articles to profl. jours. Sloan fellow A.P. Sloan Found., 1983-88. Fellow Am. Acad. Arts and Scis., Am. Phys. Soc. (mem. exec. bd. 1992-94, chmn. publ. oversight com. 1993-94, Lilienfeld prize 1997); mem. NAS, Am. Astron. Soc. (Helen B. Warner prize 1984), Internat. Astron. Union, Sigma Xi. Office: U Chgo Enrico Fermi Inst 5640 S Ellis Ave Chicago IL 60637-1433

TURNER, MILDRED EDITH, day care owner; b. Winnebago, Wis., Jan. 11, 1926; d. Jewett Candfield and Angeline Mary (Long) T. BS, State Tchrs. Coll., 1949; MS of Edn., U. Wis., Milw., 1962; postgrad., U. Wis., Oshkosh, 1965-70. Cert. tchr., Wis. Tchr. Winnebago County, Omro, Wis., 1945-47, Plymouth (Wis.) Pub. Schs., 1949-51, Ripon (Wis.) Pub. Schs., 1951-53, Omro Pub. Schs., 1953-88; instr. U. Wis., Oshkosh, 1971, supervising tchr. of student tchrs., 1970-91; owner, operator Wee Care Children's Ctr., Omro, 1974—. Contbr. articles to newspapers, profl. publs., children's books. Acolyte coord. Algoma Blvd. United Meth. Ch.; supt. Sunday sch., pianist, choir dir., ch. music dir. Eureka/Waukau United Meth. Ch.; sub-dist. children's dir. Watertown sub-dist. United Meth. Ch. Mem. Ret. Tchrs. Assn. Winnebago County, Ret. Tchrs. Assn. Omro, Fox Valley Assn. for Edn. of Young Children, Word and Pen Christian Writers (sec.-treas.), Alumni Assn. U. Wis. Oshkosh), Alumni Assn. Omro (treas.), Odd Fellows (past noble grand Rebekah lodge), Omro Study Club (past pres.). Avocation: collecting nativity sets. Home and Office: 305 E Scott St Omro WI 54963-1707

TURNER, NORV, professional football coach. Head coach Washington Redskins, 1994—. Office: Washington Redskins PO Box 17247 Washington DC 20041-0247

TURNER, PETER MERRICK, retired manufacturing company executive; b. Toronto, Ont., Can., July 4, 1931; s. William Ian MacKenzie and Marjorie (Merrick) T.; m. Beverley Brophey, Sept. 13, 1958 (dec.); children: Peter Merrick, Christopher Harold, David MacKenzie; m. Alix Johanna Houston, Aug. 17, 1991. BASc, U. Toronto, 1954; MBA, Harvard U., 1956. Staff asst. controllers dept. Bridgeport Brass Co., Conn., 1956-57; sec. treas. Perkins Paper Products Co., Montreal, Que., Can., 1957-58; with Texaco Can. Ltd., Montreal, 1958-63, treas., 1966-68; dir. budgeting and planning, corp. devel. Molson Breweries Ltd., Montreal, 1968—; v.p. planning Molson Breweries Can. Ltd., 1968-70; v.p. corp. devel. Molson Industries Ltd., Toronto, 1970-72; exec. v.p. Bennett Pump Inc., Muskegon, Mich., 1972-73, pres., chief exec. officer, 1973-78; v.p. corp. planning and devel. Sealed Power Corp., Muskegon, 1978-83, group v.p. internat., 1981-83, group v.p. Gen. Products Group, 1984-89; v.p. bus. devel. SPX Corp., Muskegon, 1989-91, v.p. ops., 1991-92, v.p. corp. planning and devel., 1992-94; ret., 1994; bd. dirs. Grand Trunk Corp., Grand Trunk Western Ry., Domestic Four Leasing Corp.; lectr. extension dept. McGill U., 1960-67, Grand Valley State Coll., 1979. Gen. chmn. red shield appeal Montreal Salvation Army, 1969-70; chmn. McGill Assocs., Montreal, 1969-70; bd. dirs. Hackley Hosp., 1975-94, West Shore Symphony Orch., 1976-94; bd. dirs. Muskegon C.C. Found., 1976-94. Mem. Mount Royal Club, Granite Club, Lake O'Hara Trail Club, Zeta Psi. Episcopalian. Home: 45 Heath St W, Toronto, ON Canada M4V 1T2

TURNER, PHILIP MICHAEL, university official and dean, author; b. West Acton, Mass., Nov. 26, 1948; s. William Albert and Evelyn Olena (Peterson) T.; m. Lis Jane VanderBeke, Aug. 16, 1969; children: Gabrielle, Adrienne. BS in Edn., Boston State Coll., 1970; MS, U. Wis. at La Crosse, 1972; MSLS, East Tex. State U., 1977, EdD, 1977. Tchr. math. Edgewood Jr. High Sch., Merritt Island, Fla., 1969-71; ptnr. Video Guide Prodn. Co., Denver, 1973; libr. media specialist Edison Jr. High Sch., Green Bay, Wis., 1973-76; prof. libr. sci. U. Ala., Tuscaloosa, 1977-88; dean Sch. Libr. and Info. Studies U. North Tex., Denton, 1996—; asst. vice chancellor acad. affairs U. Ala. System, 1991-96; assoc. v.p. for acad. affairs for distance edn. U. North Tex., Denton, 1996—. Author: Handbook for In-School Media Personnel, 1980, Helping Teachers Teach, 1985, 2d edit., 1993, Casebook for Helping Teachers Teach, 1988. Vol. Meals on Wheels, Tuscaloosa, 1987-96. Recipient Outstanding Commitment To Teaching award U. Ala. Alumni Assn., 1979, Outstanding Svc. award Ala. Libr. and Media Prodrs., 1987, publ. award Div. Sch. Libr. Media Specialist, 1987, award for mng. info. tech., 1994, Ala. Libr. Assn. Disting. Svc. award, 1996; named Libr. of Yr., Beta Phi Mu, 1991. Mem. ALA, Assn. Sch. Librs. (chair rsch. com. 1987-90, bd. dirs. 1990-94), Assn. for Ednl. Comm. and Tech. (chair evaluation com. 1979). Unitarian. Office: U North Tex Sch Libr and Info Scis PO Box 13796 Denton TX 76203-6796

TURNER, RALPH HERBERT, sociologist, educator; b. Effingham, Ill., Dec. 15, 1919; s. Herbert Turner and Hilda Pearl (Bohn) T.; m. Christine Elizabeth Hanks, Nov. 2, 1943; children: Lowell Ralph, Cheryl Christine. B.A., U So. Calif., 1941, M.A., 1942; postgrad., U. Wis., 1942-43; Ph.D., U. Chgo., 1948. Rsch. assoc. Am. Coun. Race Relations, 1947-48; faculty UCLA, 1948—, prof. sociology and anthropology, 1959-90, prof. emeritus, 1990—, chmn. dept. sociology, 1963-68; chmn. Acad. Senate U. Calif. System, 1983-84; bd. dirs. Founds. Fund for Rsch. in Psychiatry; vis. summer prof. U. Wash., 1960, U. Hawaii, 1962; vis. scholar Australian Nat. U., 1972; vis. prof. U. Ga., 1975, Ben Gurion U., Israel, 1983; vis. fellow Nuffield Coll. Oxford U., 1980; disting. vis. prof. Am. U., Cairo, Egypt, 1983; adj. prof. China Acad. Social Scis., Beijing, People's Republic China, 1986. Author: (with L. Killian) Collective Behavior, 1957, 2d edit., 1972, 3d edit., 1987, The Social Context of Ambition, 1964, Robert Park on Social Control and Collective Behavior, 1967, Family Interaction, 1970, Earthquake Prediction and Public Policy, 1975, (with J. Nigg, D. Paz, B. Young) Community Response to Earthquake Threat in So. Calif., 1980, (with J. Nigg and D. Paz) Waiting for Disaster, 1986; editl. cons., 1959-62; editor: Sociometry, 1962-64; acting editor: Ann. Rev. of Sociology, 1977-78; assoc. editor, 1978-79, editor, 1980-86; adv. editor: Am. Jour. Sociology, 1954-56, Sociology and Social Rsch., 1961-74; editl. staff: Am. Sociol. Rev., 1955-56; assoc. editor: Social Problems, 1959-62, 67-69; cons. editor: Social. Inquiry, 1968-73, Western Sociol. Rev., 1975-79; mem. editl. bd. Mass Emergencies, 1975-79, Internat. Jour. Crit. Sociology, 1974-76, Symbolic Interaction, 1977-90, 95—, Mobilization, 1996—. Mem. behavioral scis. study sect. NIH, 1961-66, chmn., 1963-64; dir.-at-large Social Sci. Rsch. Coun., 1965-66; chmn. panel on pub. policy implications of earthquake predictions Nat. Acad. Scis., 1974-75, also mem. earthquake study del. to Peoples Republic of China, 1976; mem. policy adv. bd. So. Calif. Earthquake Preparedness program, 1987-92, mem. com. social edn. and action L.A. Presbytery, 1954-56. Served to lt. (j.g.) USNR, 1943-46. Recipient Faculty prize Coll. Letters and Scis. UCLA, 1985; Faculty Rsch. fellow Social Sci. Rsch. Coun., 1953-56; Sr. Fulbright scholar U.K., 1956-57; Guggenheim fellow, U.K., 1964-65; Faculty Rsch. lectr. UCLA, UCLA Emeritus of Yr., 1997. Mem. AAAS (exch. del. to China 1988), AAUP, Am. Sociol. Assn. (coun. 1959-64, chmn. social psychology sect. 1960-61, pres. 1968-69, chmn. sect. theoretical sociology 1973-74, chmn. collective behavior and social movements sect. 1983-84, Cooley-Mead award 1987), Pacific Sociol. Assn. (pres. 1957), Internat. Sociol. Assn. (coun. 1974-82, v.p. 1978-82), Soc. Study Social Problems (exec. com. 1962-63), Soc. for Study Symbolic Interaction (pres. 1982-83, Charles Horton Cooley award 1978, George Herbert Mead award 1990), Sociol. Rsch. Assn. (pres. 1989-90), Am. Coun. of Learned Soc. (exec. com. of coun. 1990-93), UCLA Emeriti Assn. (pres. 1992-93, chair-elect 1996-97, chair 1997—). Home: 1126 Chautauqua Blvd Pacific Palisades CA 90272-3808 Office: UCLA 405 Hilgard Ave Los Angeles CA 90095-9000

TURNER, RAYMOND EDWARD, science educator, researcher, administrator; b. Portsmouth, Va., Dec. 13, 1948; s. Vernon and Kate Alicia (Ely) T.; m. Merlene Jeanette Blackett, Aug. 12, 1972 (div. June 1982); 1 child, Ebony Elysia; m. Margaret Elizabeth Alleyne, May 25, 1985. BS in Chemistry, Bklyn. Coll., 1974; MS, Fordham U., 1982; MS, PhD, Polytech U., Bklyn., 1986. Postdoctoral fellow Sch. of Pub. Health Harvard U., Boston, 1987-88; prof. maths. & chemistry Roxbury C.C., Boston, 1987-94, assoc. dean Math., Sci. and Tech., 1995—; rsch. assoc. in anatomy and cellular biology Tufts U., Boston, 1989-94; cons. U.S. Army Med. Rsch. Inst. Chem. Def., Aberdeen Proving Grounds, Md. Author: (textbook) Developing Concepts in Science, 1991, rev. 2d edit., 1994. Major MSC, USAR, 1984—, Vietnam. Mem. Am. Chem. Soc., Sigma Xi. Methodist. Achievements include research on the solution properties of hyaluronic acid oligosaccharides. Office: Roxbury Cmty Coll Divsn Math, Sci and Tech 1234 Columbus Ave Boston MA 02120-5300

TURNER, ROBERT COMRIE, composer; b. Montreal, Que., Can., June 6, 1920; s. William Thomson and Myrtle Wellsteed (Snowdon) T.; m. Sara Nan Scott, June 30, 1949; children: Alden, Martin, Carolyn. BM, McGill U., 1943, MusD, 1953; student, Royal Coll. Music, 1947-48; MusM, George Peabody Coll. Tchrs., 1950. Sr. music producer Canadian Broadcasting Corp., Vancouver, B.C., 1952-68; lectr. in music U. B.C., Vancouver, 1955-57; asst. prof. music Acadia U., Wolfville, N.S., Can., 1968-69; prof. composition U. Manitoba, Winnipeg, 1969-85; prof. emeritus U. Manitoba, 1985—; composer-in-residence MacDowell Colony, Peterborough, N.Y., 1987. Over 70 compositions including Opening Night: A Theatre Overture, 1955, The Third Day (Easter Cantata), 1962, Symphony for Strings, 1960, Capriccio Concertante, 1975, Third String Quartet, 1975, opera The Brideship, 1967, Trio Transition for Violin Cello and Piano, 1969, The Phoenix and the Turtle, 1964, Concerto for Two Pianos and Orchestra, 1971, Johann's Gift to Christmas, 1972, Eidolons, 1972, Variations on the Prairie Settler's Song, 1974, From a Different Country, 1976, Lament for Linos, 1978, Amoroso Canto, 1978, Shadow Pieces I (after Joseph Cornell), 1981, opera Vile Shadows, 1983, Symphony in One Movement, 1983, Encounters I-IX, 1984, Time for Three, 1985, Playhouse Music, 1986, Concerto for Viola and Orchestra, 1987, Shades of Autumn, 1987, Manitoba Memoir, 1989, Third Symphony, 1990, a Group of Seven, 1991, The River of Time, 1994, House of Shadows, 1994, Four "Last Songs", 1995; All-Turner concert, 1989, Canada House, London; com. mem. Vancouver Internat. Festival; adjudicator Met. and San Francisco Opera auditions; Brawell Tovey and The Winnipeg Symphony Orch. premiered The River of Time for SATB chorus and orch. in celebration of Robert Turner's 75th yr., 1996. Served with Royal Can. Air Force, 1943-45. Recipient Commemorative medal for 125th Anniversary of Confedn. of Can., 1993; overseas scholar Royal Coll. Music, 1947-48; fellow Can. Coun., 1966-67; grantee Man. Arts Coun., 1982-83, 85, Can. Coun. Artists, 1990-92. Mem. Soc. Composers, Authors and Music Pubrs. of Can., Can. League Composers, Can. Music Ctr., MacDowell Colony. Home: 126 Handsart Blvd, Winnipeg, MB Canada R3P 0C5

TURNER, ROBERT EDWARD, psychiatrist, educator; b. Hamilton, Ont., Can., June 8, 1926; s. Robert William and Alice May (Johnson) T.; m. Gene Anne Stewart, Sept. 27, 1952; children: Margaret, John, Robert, Richard. B.A. with honors in Zoology and Chemistry, McMaster U., 1948; M.D., U. Toronto, 1952. Intern Hamilton Gen. Hosp., 1952-53; resident Bristol (Eng.) Mental Hosps. Group, 1953-55; practice medicine specializing in psychiatry Toronto, Ont.; dir. Forensic Clinic Toronto Psychiat. Hosp., 1958-66; sr. psychiatrist forensic service Clarke Inst. Psychiatry, Toronto, 1966; chief forensic service Clarke Inst. Psychiatry, 1967-69, med. dir., 1969-76; asst. prof. dept. psychiatry U. Toronto, 1964-68, prof., 1973-77, prof. forensic psychiatry, 1977-91, prof. emeritus, 1991—; cons. in psychiatry Law Reform Commn. Can., 1972-85; staff psychiatrist, 1987—; dir. Met. Toronto Forensic Service, 1977-87; hon. cons. Clarke Inst. Psychiatry, 1991—. Author: Pedophilia and Exhibitionism, 1964; contbr. articles on psychiatry and law to profl. jours. Pres. Kenneth G. Gray Found., 1971—; mem. legal task force Com. on Mental Health Svcs. for Ont., Ont. Coun. Health, 1978-79; dep. warden Cathedral Ch. of St. James, Toronto, 1978-79, 92-94, rector's warden, 1994-96; bd. dirs. Clin. Inst. Addiction Rsch. foun. Ont., 1973-86, chmn., 1985-86; bd. dirs. Addiction Rsch. Found., 1982-86. Fellow Royal Coll. Physicians and Surgeons Can., Am. Psychiat. Assn. (life), Can. Psychiat. Assn. (life, bd. dirs. 1974-77), Ont. Psychiat. Assn. (life, pres. 1975-76), Can. Med. Assn., Ont. Med. Assn., Med.-Legal Soc. Toronto (coun. 1979-82). Home: 18 Rolph Rd, Toronto, ON Canada M4G 3M6 Office: U Toronto Dept Psychiatry, 250 College St, Toronto, ON Canada M5T 1R8

TURNER, ROBERT FOSTER, law educator, former government official, writer; b. Atlanta, Feb. 14, 1944; s. Edwin Witcher and Martha Frances (Williams) T. AB, Ind. U., Bloomington, 1968; postgrad., Stanford U., 1972-73; JD, U. Va., 1981, SJD, 1996. Bar: Va. 1982, U.S. Supreme Ct. 1986. Rsch. assoc., pub. affairs fellow Hoover Instn. on War, Revolution and Peace, Stanford U., 1971-74; spl. asst., legis. asst. U.S. Sen. Robert P. Griffin, 1974-79; assoc. dir. Ctr. for Nat. Security Law U. Va., Charlottesville, 1981, 87—; sr. fellow, 1985-86; spl. asst. undersec. for policy Dept. Def., 1981-82; counsel Pres.'s Intelligence Oversight Bd., White House, 1982-84; prin. dep. asst. sec. for legis. and intergovtl. affairs Dept. State, 1984-85; pres. U.S. Inst. Peace, Washington, 1986-87; lectr. in law and in govt. and fgn. affairs U. Va., Charlottesville, 1988-93, assoc. prof., 1993-97, prof., 1997—; Charles H. Stockton prof. internat. law Naval War Coll., 1994-95; disting. lectr. U.S. Mil. Acad., West Point, 1995. Author: Myths of the Vietnam War: The Pentagon Papers Reconsidered, 1972, Vietnamese Communism: Its Origins and Development, 1975, The War Powers Resolution: Its Implementation in Theory and Practice, 1983, Nicaragua v. United States: A Look at the Facts, 1987, Repealing the War Powers Resolution: Restoring the Rule of Law in U.S. Foreign Policy, 1991, (with John Norton Moore) The Legal Structure of Defense Organization, 1986, International Law and the Brezhnev Doctrine, 1987, Readings on International Law, 1995, (with John Norton Moore and Frederick Tipson) National Security Law, 1990, (with John Norton Moore and Guy B. Roberts) National Security Law Documents, 1995; contbr. articles to profl. jours. and newspapers. Pres. Endowment of U.S. Inst. Peace, 1986-87; trustee Intercollegiate Studies Inst., 1986-92; bd. dirs. Thomas Jefferson Inst. for Public Policy, 1997—. Capt. U.S. Army, 1968-71, Vietnam. Grantee Hoover Press, 1972, Earhart Found., 1980, 1989-90, Inst. Ednl. Affairs, 1980, Carthage Found., 1980. Mem. ABA (chmn. com. on exec.-congl. rels., sec. internat. law and practice 1983-86, adv. com. on law and nat. security 1984-86, standing com. on law and nat. security 1986-92, chmn. 1989-92, editor ABA Nat. Security Law Report 1992—), Bd. Rsch. Cons., Inst. Fgn. Policy Analysis, Mensa, Am. Soc. Internat. Law, Nat. Eagle Scout Assn., Coun. on Fgn. Rels., Acad. of Polit. Sci. Home: 3671 Pritchett Ln Charlottesville VA 22911-9819 Office: Univ Va Sch of Law Ctr for Nat Security Law Charlottesville VA 22903-1789

TURNER, ROBERT GERALD, university president; b. Atlanta, Tex., Nov. 25, 1945; s. Robert B. and Oreta Lois (Porter) T.; m. Gail Oliver, Dec. 21, 1968; children: Angela Jan, Jessica Diane. AA, Lubbock Christian Coll., 1966, LLD (hon.), 1985; LLD (hon.), Pepperdine U., 1989; BS, Abilene Christian U., 1968; MA, U. Tex., 1970, PhD, 1975. Tchr. Weatherford High Sch., Tex., 1968-69; tchr. Lanier High Sch., Austin, Tex., 1969-70; instr. psychology San Antonio Coll., 1970-72; instr. Prairie View A & M U., Tex., 1973-75; asst. prof. psychology Pepperdine U., Malibu, Calif., 1975-78, assoc. prof. psychology, 1978-79, dir. testing, 1975-76, chmn. social sci. div., 1976-78, assoc. v.p. univ. affairs, 1979; assoc. prof. psychology U. Okla., Norman, 1979-84, exec. asst. to pres., 1979-81, acting provost, 1982, v.p. exec. affairs, 1981-84; chancellor U. Miss., University, 1984-95; pres. So. Meth. U., Dallas, 1995—; pres. Southeastern Conf., 1985-87; rsch. asst. Tex. Adoption Study, 1973-75; mem. Pepperdine U., 1994-95; mem. Commn. on Telecomm., Nat. Assn. State Univs. and Land-Grant Colls., 1985-86, chmn. Commn. on Edn. for Tchg. Profession, 1990-91; mem. Pres.'s Commn., NCAA, 1989-92, chmn., 1991-92; mem. Knight Commn. on Intercollegiate Athletics, 1991-95; chmn. pres. coun. Miss. Assn. Colls., 1985-86; mem. def. adv. com. Svc. Acad. Athletic Programs, 1992—; bd. dirs. ChemFirst, J.C. Penney, Mobil Techs., River Oaks Furniture. Author: (with L. Willerman) Readings About Individual and Group Differences, 1979. Contbr. articles to profl. jours. Recipient Outstanding Alumni award Abilene Christian U., 1989; inducted New Boston H.S. Athletic Hall of Fame, 1993. Mem. Young Pres. Orgn., Coun. on Competitiveness, Am. Inst. Pub. Svc. (bd. nominators 1989), Sigma Xi, Beta Alpha Psi, Phi Theta Kappa, Alpha Chi, Phi Kappa Phi. Mem. Ch. of Christ. Avocations: tennis; golf; reading; traveling. Office: So Meth Univ Office of the Pres Dallas TX 75275

TURNER, ROBERT J., health facility administrator; married; two children. BBA cum laude, Cleve. State U., 1972; MPH, U. Pitts., 1974. Methods engr. Allison Divsn. GM, Cleve., 1965-70; from adminstrv. asst. to COO North Hills Passavant Hosp., 1974-87; pres., CEO Weirton Med. Ctr. Corp., Weirton Med. Ctr. Found., 1987-92, Weirton Med. Ctr., 1987-92, Ctrl. Fla. Healthcare Devel. Corp., 1992-94, Leesburg Regional Med. Ctr., Inc., 1992-94; exec. dir., CEO The Bossier Med. Ctr., 1994-96. Pres. Main Street Weirton, 1991, 92; chmn. United Way Campaign, 1991; active Bossier City Arts Coun., 1995-96. Paul Harris fellow Rotary Internat. Mem. Am. Coll. Healthcare Execs. (regents adv. com. 1991, 92), Am. Hosp. Assn., Alpha Chi. Avocations: golf, photography, bicycling, fishing. Home: 5222 Rue Royale Haughton LA 71037

TURNER, ROBERT LLOYD, state legislator; b. Columbus, Miss., Sept. 14, 1947; s. Roosevelt and Beatrice (Hargrove) T.; m. Gloria Harrell; children: Roosevelt, Robert, Ryan. BS, U. Wis., Racine, 1976. Mgr. French Quarter Restaurant, Racine, 1989; legislator Wis. State Assembly, Madison, 1990—, chmn. transp. com. bldg. commn., mem. ways and means com., hwy. com., elections, correction & constitution com., excise fees and license com.; br. sales mgr. ETG Temporaries, Inc., Racine, 1989—; pub. Communicator News, Racine, 1989—; v.p. Racine Raider Football Team. State chmn. Dem. Black Polit. Caucus, Madison; pres. Bd. Health, Racine; chmn. Wis. State Elections Bd., Madison, 1990; alderman Racine City Coun., 1976—; chair Econ. Devel. Com., Racine; regional dir. Badger State Games, Racine; active Pvt. Industry Coun. Southeastern Wis., 1988-89, bd. dirs. Racine County Youth Sports Assn.; active Racine Juneteenth Day Com., bd. advisors Big Bros./Big Sisters. Sgt. USAF, 1967-71, Vietnam. Decorated Commendation medal; named Man of Yr. 2d Missionary Bapt. Ch., 1983. Mem. Urban League (pres. bd. dirs.), NAACP (2d v.p.), VFW, Am. Legion, Masons, Shriners. Home: 36 Mckinley Ave Racine WI 53404-3414 Office: Wis Assembly PO Box 8953 Madison WI 53708-8953

TURNER, ROSS JAMES, investment corporation executive; b. Winnipeg, Man., Can., May 1, 1930; permanent U.S. resident, 1980; s. James Valentine and Gretta H. (Ross) T.; children: Ralph, Rick, Tracy. U. Man. Extension, 1951, Banff Sch. Advanced Mgmt., 1956. Various sr. operating and mgmt. positions Genstar Corp., San Francisco, 1961-76, chmn./pres., CEO, 1976-86, also bd. dirs.; chmn. Genstar Investment Corp., San Francisco, 1987—; bd. dirs. Rio Algom Ltd., Blue Shield of Calif., Guy F. Atkinson Co. of Calif. Fellow Soc. Mgmt. Accts. Can.; mem. Toronto Club, Pacific Union Club, Rancho Santa Fe Golf Club, Peninsula Golf and Country Club. Office: Genstar Investment Corp 950 Tower Ln Foster City CA 94404-2121

TURNER, SCOTT MACNEELY, lawyer; b. Clinton, N.Y., Nov. 8, 1948; s. Frederick George and Ruth Alys (Thomas) T.; m. Susan Lynn Funkhouser, June 20, 1970; children: Katherine, Benjamin, Robert. AB with honors, Colgate Univ., N.Y., 1970; JD magna cum laude, Washington & Lee, Va., 1973. Bar: N.Y. 1974, D.C. 1996, U.S. Dist. Ct. (we. dist.) N.Y. 1974, U.S. Ct. Appeals (2d cir.) N.Y. 1987, (3d cir.) N.Y. 1988. Assoc. Nixon Hargrave Devans & Doyle, Rochester, N.Y., 1973-80, ptnr., 1981—; chmn. environ. practice group Nixon Hargrove Devans & Doyle, 1984—; chmn. legis. regulatory affairs com. Internat. Gas Turbine Inst. Atlanta, 1993-95. Editor: (Book) N.Y. Environmental Law Handbook, 1996. Bd. dirs. Park Ridge Hosp., Rochester, N.Y., 1992—, Park Ridge Found., Rochester, 1987-92, Monroe County Cmty. Svcs. Bd., Rochester, 1992-95; town leader Ogden Rep. Party, Spencerport, N.Y., 1981-86. Capt. USAR, 1972-73. Mem. Air & Waste Mgmt. Assn. (chmn. legal com. 1984-88), N.Y. State Bar Assn. (environ. sect., co-chmn. solid and hazardous waste com. 1982-94). Republican. Congregationalist. Home: 408 Dewey St Churchville NY 14428-9103 Office: Nixon Hargrave Devans & Doyle Clinton Sq PO Box 1051 Rochester NY 14603-1051

TURNER, STANSFIELD, former government official, lecturer, writer, teacher; b. Chgo., Dec. 1, 1923; s. Oliver Stansfield and Wilhelmina Josephine (Wagner) T.; m. Eli Karin Gilbert, Mar. 16. 1985. Student, Amherst Coll., 1941-43, DCL, 1975; BS, U.S. Naval Acad., 1946; MA (Rhodes scholar), Oxford U., 1950; LHD, Sierra Nev. Coll., 1984; HumD, Roger Williams Coll., 1975; DSc in Edn, Bryant Coll., 1977; LLD, Salve Regina Coll., 1977, The Citadel, 1980, Pace U., 1980. Ensign USN, 1946, advanced through grades to adm., 1975, ret., 1979; served primarily in destroyers; commd. U.S.S. Horne, guided missile cruiser, 1967-68; aide to Sec. Navy; comdr. carrier task group 6th Fleet, 1970-71; dir. systems analysis div. Office Chief Naval Ops., Navy Dept., Washington, 1971-72; pres. Naval War Coll., Newport, R.I., 1972-74; comdr. U.S. Second Fleet, 1974-75; comdr.-in-chief Allied Forces So. Europe, NATO, 1975-77; dir. CIA, Washington, 1977-81; John M. Olin Disting. prof. nat. security U.S. Mil. Acad., West Point, 1989-90; prof. U. Md. Grad. Sch. Pub. Affairs, 1991—; sr. rsch. fellow Norwegian Nobel Inst., Oslo, Norway, 1995-96; mem. bd. visitors U.S. Naval Acad., 1996—. Author: Secrecy and Democracy, 1985, Terrorism and Democracy, 1991, America's Challenge: Caging the Nuclear Genie, 1997. Decorated Nat. Security medal, Legion of Merit, Bronze Star. Home and Office: 1320 Skipwith Rd Mc Lean VA 22101-1834

TURNER, SYLVESTER, state legislator, lawyer; b. Houston, Sept. 27, 1954; 1 child, Ashley Paige. BA in Polit. Sci., U. Houston; JD, Harvard U. Assoc. Fulbright & Jaworski, Houston, 1980-83; owner firm Barnes & Turner, Houston, 1983—; mem. Tex. Ho. of Reps., Austin, 1988—; mem. appropriations and calendars coms.; vice-chair state affairs. Candidate for mayor City of Houston, 1991; active Negro Coll. Fund, Houston Met. Ministries, Houston-Galveston Area Food Bank, Acres Homes War on Drugs Com., Brookhollow Bapt. Ch.. Named Rookie of Yr., Tex. Monthly, Legislator of Yr. and One of the Ten Best Legislators, Houston Police Patrolman's Union, Rising Star, Harris County Dems., Outstanding Houstonian, Houston Jaycees, 1990. Office: Texas House Reps PO Box 2910 Austin TX 78768-2910 also: PO Box 2910 Austin TX 78768-2910

TURNER, TED (ROBERT EDWARD TURNER), television executive; b. Cin., Nov. 19, 1938; s. Robert Edward and Florence (Rooney) T.; m. Judy Nye (div.), m. Jane Shirley Smith, June 1965 (div. 1988); children: Beau, Rhett, Jennie; children by previous marriage: Laura Lee, Robert Edward IV; m. Jane Fonda, Dec. 21, 1991. Grad. in classics, Brown U.; DSc in Commerce (hon.), Drexel U., 1982; LLD (hon.), Samford U., 1982, Atlanta U., 1984; D Entrepreneurial Sci. (hon.), Cen. New Eng. Coll. Tech., 1983; D in Pub. Adminstrn. (hon.), Mass. Maritime Acad., 1984; D in Bus. Adminstrn. (hon.), U. Charleston, 1985. Account exec. Turner Advt. Co., Atlanta, 1961-63, pres., chief oper. officer, 1963-70; pres., chmn. bd. Turner Broadcasting System, Inc., Atlanta, 1970-96; vice chmn. Time Warner Inc. (merger Turner Broadcasting System), 1996—; bd. dirs. Atlanta Hawks; owner Atlanta Braves. Bd. dirs. Martin Luther King Ctr., Atlanta. Won America's Cup in his yacht Courageous, 1977; named Yachtsman of Yr. 4 times.Recipient Outstanding Entrepreneur of Yr. award Sales Mktg. and Mgmt. Mag., 1979, Salesman of Yr. award Sales and Mktg. Execs., 1980, Pvt. Enterprise Exemplar medal, Freedoms Found. at Valley Forge, 1980, Communicator of Yr. award Pub. Rels. Soc. Am., 1981, Communicator of Yr. award N.Y. Broadcasters, 1981, Internat. Communicator of Yr. award Sales and Mktg. Execs., 1981, Nat. News Media award VFW, 1981, Disting. Svc. in Telecommunications award Ohio U. Coll. Communication, 1982, Carr Van Anda award Ohio U. Sch. Journalism, 1982, Spl. award Edinburgh Internat. TV Festival, Scotland, 1982, Media Awareness award United Vietnam Vets. Orgn., 1983, Bd. Govs. award Atlanta chpt. NATAS, 1982, Spl. Olympics award Spl. Olympics Com., 1983, Dinner of Champions award Ga. chpt., Multiple Sclerosis Soc., 1983, Praca Spl. Merit award N.Y. Puerto Rican Assn. for Community Affairs, 1983, World Telecommunications Pioneer award, N.Y. State Broadcasters Assn., 1984, Golden Plate award Am. Acad. Achievement, 1984, Outstanding Supporter Boy Scouting award Nat. Boy Scout Coun., 1984, Silver Satellite award Am. Women in Radio and TV, Lifetime Achievement award N.Y. Internat. Film and TV Festival, 1984, Corp. Star of Yr. award Nat. Leukemia Soc., 1985, Disting. Achievement award U. Georgia, 1985, Tree of Life award Jewish Nat. Fund, 1985, Bus. Exec. of Yr. award Ga. Security Dealers Assn., 1985, Life Achievement award Popular Culture Assn., 1986, George Washingtonn Disting. Patriot award S.R., 1986, Mo. Honor medal Sch. Journalism, U. Mo., 1987, Golden Ace award Nat. Cable TV Acad., 1987 Sol Taishoff award Nat. Press Found., 1988, Citizen Diplomat award Ctr. for Soviet-Am. Dialogue, 1988, Chmn.'s award Cable Advt. Bur., 1988, Directorate award NATAS, 1989, Paul White award Radio and TV News Dirs. Assn., 1989 Bus. Marketer of Yr. Am. Mktg. Assn., 1989, Disting. Svc. award Simon Wiesenthal Ctr., 1990, Glasnost award Vols. Am. and Soviet Life mag., 1990, numerous others; inducted into Hall of Fame, Promotion and Mktg. Assn., 1980, Dubuque (Iowa) Bus. Hall of Fame, 1983, Nat. Assn. for Sport and Phys. Edn. Hall of Fame, 1986. Mem. Nat. Cable TV Assn. (Pres.'s award 1979, 89, Ace Spl. Recognition award 1980), NAACP (life, bd. dirs. Atlanta chpt., Regional Employer of Yr. award 1976), Nat. Audubon Soc., Cousteau Soc., Bay Area Cable Club (hon.). Avocations: sailing, fishing. Office: Turner Broadcasting 1 CNN Ctr PO Box 105366 Atlanta GA 30348-5366

TURNER, TERRY MADISON, architect; b. Bastrop, La., Apr. 5, 1938; s. Eugene Campbell and Anna Pauline (Terry) T.; m. Mary Alice Fischer, June 20, 1964; children: Mat Madison, Paul Alison, William Terry. BBA, Memphis State U., 1958; BS in Archtl. Scis., Washington U., St. Louis, 1961, BArch, 1963. Registered architect, Mo., N.C.A.R.B. Asst. prof. Sch. Architecture Auburn (Ala.) U., 1965-66, U. Va., Charlottesville, 1966-69; chief architect HUD-FHA, St. Louis, 1969-79; prin. Terry M. Turner, Architect, Clayton, Mo., 1979—; CEO Westminster Apts., Inc., St. Louis, 1993—. Regent Harris-Stowe State Coll., St. Louis, 1992-97. 1st lt. USAR, 1963-70. Republican. Episcopalian. Home and Office: 50 Hillvale Dr Clayton MO 63105

TURNER, THOMAS MARSHALL, telecommunications executive, consultant; b. Cumberland, Md., Aug. 17, 1951; s. James Richard and Laura Roselie (Durst) T. BS in Indsl. Tech. and Mgmt., U. Md., 1973, MA in Indsl. Tech. and Mgmt., 1980. Grad. asst U. Md., College Park, 1975-76; sales assoc., gen. mgr. Equity Trades Reality, Riverdale, Md., 1976-83; account exec. RCA Corp., Greenbelt, Md., 1983; sr. telecommunications cons. CMC, Inc., Washington, 1984-86, ORS Assoc., McLean, Va., 1986-87; owner, pres. T-1 Communications, Boca Raton, Fla., 1987—; cons. Marriott Corp., Bethesda, Md., 1990—, Group Health, Inc., N.Y.C., 1991-92, Colgate-Palmolive Co., 1993-94, State of Md., 1993, Trump Corp., 1993, Martin-Marietta, 1994, Matsushita, 1994, Montgomery Wards, 1994, Nabisco Foods, 1994, Harris Corp., 1995, Urban League, 1995, EDS, 1995—, Chem. Bank, 1996—; grad. asst. instr. Dale Carnegie Inst., 1992. Contbr. articles to profl. jours. Vol. ARC, Riverdale, Md., 1977-80; instr. Jr. Achievement Bus. Co-op, Rockville, Md., 1979-82. Recipient Highest Achievment award Dale Carnegie Inst., 1989. Mem. Am. Soc. Tng. and Devel., Telecommunications Mgrs. Assn. of Capital Area, Toastmasters, Sigma Alpha Epsilon Alumni Assn.

TURNER, THOMAS PATRICK, architect; b. Gaffney, S.C., May 13, 1926; s. Thomas Patrick and Lily Mae (Clarke) T.; m. Lola Ann Love, Aug. 17, 1950; children: Sheryl A., Thomas P. III, A. Bryan. BS in Archtl. Engring., Clemson U., 1951, postgrad., 1952. Registered architect; lic. real estate broker; lic. contractor. Draftsman John H. Truluck, Walterboro, S.C., 1951-52, M.R. Marsh, Charlotte, N.C., 1953-55; architect in tng. Holroyd, Folk and Gray, Charlotte, 1955-57; architect A.G. Odell & Assocs., Charlotte, 1957-77; pres., owner ADEP Architects, Charlotte, 1977—. Precinct chmn. Dem. Party, 1993-94; elder Myers Park Presbyn. Ch. With U.S. Navy, 1943-45. Fellow AIA (nat. bd. dirs. 1987—, v.p. 1990, pres. Charlotte sect. 1966), N.C. Inst. Architects (bd. dirs. 1970, 71, 76, 77, v.p. 1972-73, pres. 1985), Rotary. Office: ADEP Architects 401 S Independence Blvd Ste 72 Charlotte NC 28204-2623

TURNER, THOMAS WILLIAM, lawyer; b. Indpls., Nov. 17, 1946; s. Tal Andy and Mary Etta (Eddleman) T.; m. Judith Ann Stewart, Mar. 14, 1970; children: Laura Marie, Brian Christopher. AB, Ball State U., 1969; JD cum laude, Wayne State U., 1974. Bar: Mich. 1974, Ind. 1975, Fla. 1985. Trial atty. criminal div. fraud sect. U.S. Dept. Justice, Washington, 1974-78; 1st asst. atty. U.S. Dept. Justice, Springfield, 1978-81; asst. atty. U.S. Dept. Justice, Indpls., 1981-83; managing asst. atty. U.S. Dept. Justice, Orlando, Fla., 1983-86; sole practice Orlando, 1986-91, pvt. practice, 1991—; asst. U.S. atty. U. S. Dept. Justice, Orlando. Mem. Orange County bar Assn., Am. Inns of Ct., Delta Theta Phi. Republican. Methodist. Office: 201 Federal Bldg 80 N Hughey Ave Orlando FL 32801-2231

TURNER, TINA (ANNA MAE BULLOCK), singer; b. Brownsville, Tenn., Nov. 26, 1939; m. Ike Turner, 1956 (div. 1978); children: Craig, Ike Jr., Michael, Ronald. Singer with Ike Turner Kings of Rhythm, and Ike and Tina Turner Revue; appeared in films: Gimme Shelter, 1970, Soul to Soul, 1971, Tommy, 1975, Sgt. Pepper's lonely Hearts Club Band, 1978, Mad Max Beyond Thunderdome, 1985, Break Every Rule, 1986, Last Action Hero, 1993; concert tours of Europe, 1966, Japan and Africa, 1971; Showtime TV concert of Wildest Dreams; albums with Ike Turner include Hunter, 1970, Ike and Tina Show II, Ike and Tina Show, 1966, Ike and Tina Turner, Bad Dreams, 1973, Ike and Tina Turner Greatest Hits, vol. 1.2 and 3, 1989, Greatest Hits, 1990, Proud Mary, 1991, The Ike and Tina Turner Collection, 1993; solo albums include Let Me Touch Your Mind, 1972, Tina Turns the Country On, 1974, Acid Queen, 1975, Love Explosion, 1977, Rough, 1978, Airwaves, 1979, Private Dancer, 1984, Break Every Rule, 1986, Tina Live In Europe, 1988, Foreign Affair, 1989, Simply the Best, 1991, What's Love Got to Do With It? (soundtrack), 1993, The Collected Recordings: Sixties to Nine Ties, with others, 1994, Wildest Dreams, 1996; performed with USA for Africa on song We are The World, 1985; author (autobiography) I, Tina, 1985 (filmed as What's Love Got To Do With It?, 1993). Recipient Grammy award, 1972, 85 (three), 86, Grammy nomination (Best Pop Female Vocal) for "I Don't Wanna Fight", 1994; inducted into Rock and Roll Hall of Fame, 1991. Address: care CAA 9830 Wilshire Blvd Beverly Hills CA 90212-1804*

TURNER, WADE SLOVER, biochemist, pilot; b. Terre Haute, Ind., Dec. 21, 1965; s. Howard Royce and Euleta (Slover) T. BS, Ind. State U., 1987, MS, 1990. Registered environ. profl., Ind.; cert. PADI advanced and night scuba diver. Lab. mgr., biochemist Foxfire Environ., Inc., Jasonville, Ind., 1990-92; gen. mgr. Turner Farms, Inc., Shelburn, Ind., 1992-94; biochemist, flight instr. NASA-Marshall & U.S. Space Ctrs., Huntsville, Ala., 1993-95; pilot Am. Trans Air, Inc., Terre Haute, 1992-94; spl. ops. analyst, USNR, Wright Patterson AFB, 1995—; instr. NRA, Shelburn, 1994—; chemistry instr. Ind. State U., 1989, 90; physics instr. Indiana State U., 1995—. Contbr. articles to profl. publs. including Protein Kinase C Signal Transduction in Microgravity. Lt., USNR. Collegiate Scholar Ind. State U., 1985, 86, 92, 93, Nat. Deans List scholar, 1984-88, Disting. Alumni award 1996. Fellow Phi Kappa Phi; mem. Am. Assn. Airport Execs., Am. Legion, Raritan Club, Sigma Xi, Phi Mu Epsilon, Alpha Eta Rho, Alpha Sigma Lambda, Golden Key, Blue Key. Achievements include Protein Kinase C research in Nb2 lymphocytes; presentations to EPA on multi-million dollar environmental projects; laboratory work for Space Station Freedom project at NASA, special operations in USNR. Avocations: shooting, flying, jogging, golf, tennis. Home: 1502 E Mill St Shelburn IN 47879-8206 Office: Office of Naval Intelligence Unit 1905 NAIC/RI 4180 Watson Way Wright Pat OH 45433-5648

TURNER, WALLACE L., reporter; b. Titusville, Fla., Mar. 15, 1921; s. Clyde H. and Ina B. (Wallace) T.; m. Pearl Burk, June 12, 1943; children: Kathleen Turner, Elizabeth Turner Everett. B.J., U. Mo., 1943; postgrad. (Nieman fellow), Harvard U., 1958-59. Reporter Springfield (Mo.) Daily News, 1943, Portland Oregonian, 1943-59; news dir. Sta. KPTV, Portland, 1959-61; asst. sec. HEW, Washington, 1961-62; reporter N.Y. Times, San Francisco, 1962—; bur. chief N.Y. Times, 1970-85, Seattle bur. chief, 1985-88. Author: Gamblers Money, 1965, The Morman Establishment, 1967. Recipient Heywood Broun award for reporting, 1952, 56; Pulitzer Prize for reporting, 1957. Office: Box 99269 Magnolia Sta Seattle WA 98199-4260

TURNER, WARREN AUSTIN, state legislator; b. Berkeley, Calif., Dec. 21, 1926; s. Warren Mortimer and Rebecca Oline (Noer) T.; m. Beverly Daune Mackay, Mar. 29, 1952; children: Daune Scott, Warren Adair, Alan Corey. BA, U. Calif., Berkeley, 1950, BS, 1952, MPH, 1958. Pub. acct. Price Waterhouse, San Francisco, 1951-52, AW Blackman, Las Vegas, Nev., 1952-56; asst. adminstr. Marin Gen. Hosp., San Rafael, Calif., 1958-60; assoc. dir. UCLA Hosp., 1960-68; founding adminstr. Walter O. Boswell Meml. Hosp., Sun City, Ariz., 1968-81; pres. Sun Health Corp., 1981-89; mem. Ariz. Senate, Phoenix, 1993-97, chmn. rules com., vice chair health com., mem. appropriations, family svcs. and transp. com., 1995-97; chmn. appropriation subcom. K-12, C.C.'s and natural resources. With USN, 1944-46. Mem Ariz. Acad., Rotary Internat. Republican. Avocations: breeding and showing Siamese cats, fishing, mining. Home: 18432 W Glendale Ave Waddell AZ 85355-9737

TURNER, WILLIAM BENJAMIN, electrical engineer; b. Bklyn., Sept. 23, 1929; s. Jacob Joshua and Mollie (Klein) T. BEE, CCNY, 1955; MBA, NYU, 1964; DD (hon.), UCLA, 1978. Cert. tchr., N.Y. Chief engr. Esan Electronic Labs., Fla. and N.Y., 1969—; cons. in field, 1965—. Author: Theology—The Quintessence of Science, 1981, Nothing and Non-Existence, 1986, Hyper Light Speed Technology, 1992, Outer Space Communications, 1994, Eulogy for Our Dying World, 1994, Advanced Concepts and Limitations in Science, 1994, Reincarnation—The Concept Involving Memory, 1996, The Soul, The Reference of Life, 1997, The Soul-Identifying the Scientific Counterpart of that which Religion Calls the "Soul", 1997. Sgt. U.S. Army, 1951-53, Korea. Decorated Bronze Star. Mem. Mensa, Boynton Beach C. of C. Achievements include invention of the world's fastest computers, advanced concepts in time theory, development of multi-dimensional geometry theory of the universe, development new physics method that exceeds speed of light, research into hyper light speed communications equipment to probe far off regions of outer space, research into the physics of the human thinking process. Home and Office: 429 Seaview Ave Palm Beach FL 33480-4109

TURNER, WILLIAM COCHRANE, international management consultant; b. Red Oak, Iowa, May 27, 1929; s. James Lyman and Josephine (Cochrane) T.; m. Cynthia Dunbar, July 16, 1955; children: Scott Christopher, Craig Dunbar, Douglas Gordon. BS, Northwestern U., 1952, LLD (hon.), Am. Grad. Sch. Internat. Mgmt., 1993. Pres., chmn. bd. dirs. Western Mgmt. Cons., Inc., Phoenix, 1955-74, Western Mgmt. Cons. Europe, S.A., Brussels, 1968-74; U.S. amb., permanent rep. OECD, Paris, 1974-77, vice chmn. exec. com., 1976-77, U.S. rep. Energy Policy Com., 1976-77, mem. U.S. dels. internat. meetings, 1974-77; mem. western internat. trade group U.S. Dept. Commerce, 1972-74; chmn., CEO Argyle Atlantic Corp., Phoenix, 1977—; chmn. European adv. coun., 1981-88, Asia Pacific adv. coun. AT&T Internat., 1981-88; founding mem. Pacific Coun. Internat. Policy, L.A., 1995—; mem. U.S.-Japan Bus. Coun., Washington, 1987-93, European adv. coun. IBM World Trade Europe/Mid. East/Africa Corp., 1977-80; mem. Asia Pacific adv. coun. Am. Can Co., Greenwich, Conn., 1981-85, GE of Brazil adv. coun. GE Co., Coral Gables, Fla., 1979-81, Caterpillar of Brazil adv. coun. Caterpillar Tractor Co., Peoria, Ill., 1979-84, Caterpillar Asia Pacific Adv. Coun., 1984-90, U.S. adv. com. Trade Negotiations, 1982-84; bd. dirs. Goodyear Tire & Rubber Co., Akron, Ohio, Rural/Metro Corp., Microtest, Inc., Phoenix; chmn. bd. dirs. GO Wireless Internat. Ltd., Melbourne, Fla., 1995—; chmn. internat. adv. coun. Avon Products, Inc., N.Y.C., 1985—; mem. Spencer Stuart adv. coun. Spencer Stuart and Assocs., N.Y.C., 1984-90; chmn., mem. internat. adv. coun. Advanced Semiconductor Materials Internat. NV., Bilthoven, The Netherlands, 1985-88; bd. dirs. The Atlantic Coun. of U.S., Washington, 1977-92; co-chmn. internat. adv. bd. Univ. of Nations, Kona, Hawaii, 1985—; bd. dirs. World Wildlife Fund/U.S., 1983-85, World Wildlife Fund/The Conservation Found., 1985-89, Nat. Coun., 1989-95, 1996—; bd. govs. Joseph H. Lauder Inst. Mgmt. and Internat. Studies, U. Pa., 1983—; trustee Heard Mus., Phoenix, 1983-86, mem. nat. adv. bd., 1986-93; trustee Am. Grad. Sch. Internat. Mgmt., 1972—, chmn. bd. trustees, 1987-89; bd. govs. Atlantic Inst. Internat. Affairs, Paris, 1977-88; adv. bd. Ctr. Strategic and Internat. Studies, Georgetown U., 1977-81; dir. Pullman, Inc., Chgo., 1977-80, Nabisco Brands, Inc., Parsippany, N.J., 1977-85, Salomon Inc., N.Y.C., 1980-93, AT&T Internat., Inc., Basking Ridge, N.J., 1980-84, Atlantic Inst. Found., Inc., N.Y.C., 1984-90; mem. European Cmty.-U.S. Businessmen's Coun., 1978-79; bd. govs. Am. Hosp. of Paris, 1974-77; trustee Nat. Symphony Orch. Assn., Washington, 1973-83, Am. Sch., Paris, 1976-77, Orme Sch., Mayer, Ariz., 1970-74, Phoenix Country Day Sch., 1971-74; mem. nat. coun. Salk Inst., 1978-82; mem. U.S. Adv. Com. Internat. Edn. and Cultural Affairs, 1969-74; nat. rev. bd. Ctr. Cultural and Tech. Interchange between East and West, 1970-74; mem. vestry Am. Cathedral, Paris, 1976-77; pres., bd. dirs. Phoenix Symphony Assn., 1969-70; chmn. Ariz. Joint Econ. Devel. Com., 1967-68; exec. com., bd. dirs. Ariz. Dept. Econ. Planning and Devel., 1968-70; chmn. bd. Ariz. Crippled Children's Services, 1964-65; treas. Ariz. Rep. Com., 1956-57; chmn. Ariz. Young Rep. League, 1955-56; chmn. bd. Mercy Ships Internat., Inc., A Ministry of Youth With A Mission, Lindale, Tex., 1985—; mem. trade and environment com. Nat. Adv. Coun. for Environ. Policy and Tech.-U.S. EPA, Washington, 1991-95; dir. exec. com., chmn. internat. com. Ariz. Econ. Coun., Phoenix, 1989-93; dir. exec. com. Orgn. for Free Trade and Devel., Phoenix, 1991-93; chmn. Internat. Adv. Coun. Plasma Tech., Inc., Sante Fe, 1992—. Recipient East-West Ctr. Disting. Svc. award, 1977. Mem. U.S. Coun. Internat. Bus. (trustee, exec. com.), Coun. Fgn. Rels., Coun. of Am. Ambs. (vice chmn. bd.), Nat. Adv. Coun. on Bus. Edn., Coun. Internat. Edn. Exchange, Greater Phoenix Leadership, Govs. Strategic Partnership Econ. Devel., Phoenix, 1992-95, Met. Club, Links Club (N.Y.C.), Plaza Club (Phoenix), Paradise Valley (Ariz.) Country Club, Bohemian Club. Episcopalian. Office: 4350 E Camelback Rd Ste 240B Phoenix AZ 85018-2722

TURNER, WILLIAM JOSEPH, retired psychiatrist; b. Wilkinsburg, Pa., Sept. 22, 1907; s. William Moore and Phoebe Emma (Smith) T.; m. Kathryn Morrow, Aug. 12, 1925 (div. May 1959); children: William Morrow, James Quigly. BS, Pa. State Coll., 1927; MA, Johns Hopkins U., 1933. Cert. in medicine. Rotating intern Harrisburg Hosp., Harrisburg, Pa., 1933-34; asst. resident pathology Balt. City Hosp., 1934-35; asst. resident medicine Billings Hosp., U. Chgo., 1935-36; staff physician Cresson The Hosp., Cresson, Pa., 1936-37; staff psychiatrist VA Hosp., N. Little Rock, Ark., 1937-40; psychiatrist VA Hosp., L.A., 1940-41, Northport, N.Y., 1941-50; rsch. psychiatrist Cen. Islip State Hosp., Cen. Islip, N.Y., 1954-76, SUNY, Stony Brook, 1976-82; prof. emeritus psychiatry, 1982-90, ret.; med. dir. Dreyfus Med. Found., N.Y.C., 1964-68, cons., 1966—. Author papers on subjects in field including evidence of genetic foundation of gender variants, 1995. Pres., various positions Suffolk County Dist. br. Am. Psychiat. Assn., 1960-92; chmn. com. for liaison with lay groups S.C.D.P. Lt. col. U.S. Army, 1943-46. Fellow Am. Psychiat. Assn. (life); mem. AMA (life), Am. Coll. Neuropsychopharmacology (life), AAAS, N.Y. Acad. Sci., Am. Chem. Soc., Soc. Biol. Psychiatry.

TURNER, WILLIAM W., JR., surgeon, educator; b. Miami, Fla., Aug. 30, 1947; s. William W. and Melba A. (Wilson) T.; m. Rosemary C. MD, Tuland U., 1972. Prof. surgery Ind. U., Indpls., U. Tex. Southwestern, Dallas, 1979-92; dir. surgery Clarian Helath Ptnrs., Indpls., 1992—; dir. surgery Meth. Hosp., Indpls., 1992—. Bd. dirs. Indpls. Symphonic Choir, 1994—. Maj. USAF, 1979. Fellow ACS (pres. Ind. chpt. 1996—); mem. Western Surg. Assn., Southwestern Surg. Assn., Am. Soc. Parenteral Enteral Nutritiion. Republican. Episcopalian. Avocations: auto racing, audiovideo, computing. Office: Clarian Health Ptnrs 1633 N Capitol Ave Ste 650 Indianapolis IN 46202-1281

TURNER, WILLIAM WEYAND, author; b. Buffalo, N.Y., Apr. 14, 1927; s. William Peter and Magdalen (Weyand) T.; m. Margaret Peiffer, Sept. 12, 1964; children: Mark Peter, Lori Ann. BS, Canisius Coll., 1949. Spl. agt. in various field offices FBI, 1951-61; free-lance writer Calif., 1963—; sr. editor Ramparts Mag., San Francisco, 1967—; investigator and cons. Nat. Wiretap Commn., 1975; U.S. del. J.F.K. Internat. Seminar, Rio de Janeiro, 1995. Author: The Police Establishment, 1968, Invisible Witness: The Use and Abuse of the New Technology of Crime Investigation, 1968, Hoover's F.B.I.: The Men and the Myth, 1970, Power on the Right, 1971, (with Warren Hinckle and Eliot Asinof) The Ten Second Jailbreak, 1973, (with John Christian) The Assassination of Robert F. Kennedy, 1978, (with Warren Hinckle) The Fish is Red: The Story of the Secret War Against Castro, 1981, updated, expanded, retitled as Deadly Secrets: The CIA-Mafia War Against Castro and the Assassination of JFK, 1992; contbg. author: Investigating the FBI, 1973; contbr. articles to popular mags. Dem. candidate for U.S. Congress, 1968. Served with USN, 1945-46. Mem. Authors Guild, Internat. Platform Assn., Press Club of San Francisco. Roman Catholic. Avocation: tennis. Home and Office: 163 Mark Twain Ave San Rafael CA 94903-2820

TURNER, WILLIAM WILSON, hospital administrator; b. Valley Mills, Tex., Apr. 21, 1916; s. Will S. and Nettie A. (Vickrey) T.; m. Wilma David, Feb. 22, 1945; 1 child, Elizabeth Ann. B.B.A., Baylor U., 1938; postgrad., Grad. Sch. Bus., Northwestern U., 1939. Bus. mgr. Hillcrest Meml. Hosp., Waco, Tex., 1941-47; asst. adminstr. Meml. Bapt. Hosp. (name changed to Meml. Hosp. System), Houston, 1947-50; adminstr. Meml. Bapt. Hosp. (name changed to Meml. Hosp. System), 1955-63, exec. dir. hosp. system, 1963-71, pres. system, 1971-81, pres. emeritus, cons., 1981—; adminstr. Bapt. Hosp., Alexandria, La., 1950-54, Miss. Bapt. Hosp., Jackson, 1954-55; hon. life dir. Blue Cross-Blue Shield Tex., Group Life and Health Ins. Co.; mem. Council on Manpower and Edn., 1974-77. Served to lt. USNR, 1942-45, PTO, ATO. Recipient Collier award for distinguished hosp. adminstrn., 1974, Tex. Assn. Hosp. Governing Bds. Founders award, 1980, Meml. Stewardship award, 1992. Fellow Am. Coll. Hosp. Adminstrs.; mem. Am. Protestant Hosp. Assn. (del. 1970—, council ch.-hosp. relations 1962-66, council on edn. 1972-75, Hosp. Adminstrn. award 1979), Am. Hosp. Assn. (del. 1969-75), Tex. Hosp. Assn. (trustee 1961-68, treas. 1969, pres. 1971-72), Bapt. Hosp. Assn. (past pres., trustee), Houston Area Hosp. Assn. (past pres.), Mental Health Assn. Houston (profl. adv. com.), Tex. Assn. Hosp. Accountants (past pres., disting. life mem.), Houston Area Hosp. Council (past pres.), Houston C. of C., Tex. League Nursing (dir. 1961-63), Delta Sigma Pi. Baptist (deacon). Lodge: Masons. Developer satellite hosp. concept. Home: 7480 Beechnut St Apt 303 Houston TX 77074-4507 Office: 7480 Beechnut St Apt 303 Houston TX 77074-4507

TURNEY, JAMES EDWARD, computer scientist; b. Greensburg, Pa., May 14, 1933; s. James Edward and Mary Elizabeth (Koch) T.; m. Joan Lois Sweeney, Sept. 1, 1957 (dec. Jan. 1982); m. Audra Varnagy, Mar. 27, 1982; children: Audrey, Jennifer, Jill, Joy. BS in Indsl. Engring., Northeastern U., 1961; MS in Indsl. Mgmt., MIT, 1964; PhD in Mgmt., Calif. Coast U., 1993. Sr. cons. Peat Marwick Mitchell Co., L.A., 1965-68; gen. mgr. Technicolor, Inc., Hollywood, Calif., 1968-70; dir. Intercontinental Computing, Inc., Kansas City, Mo., 1970-72; v.p. Insight Systems, Ltd., Des Moines, 1972-76; pres. Pro Data Sys., Inc., Austin, Tex., 1976—. Bd. dirs. Luth. Ch., Wayland, Mass., 1964-66, Palos Verdes, Calif., 1967-71, Overland Pk., Kans., 1973-76, San Jose, Calif., 1991-92, Corpus Christi, Tex., 1993-95; pres. Tex. Jazz Festival Soc., 1995—. Sgt. U.S. Army, 1953-56. Mem. Am. Inst. Indsl. Engrs. (pres. 1966-67), Mensa (local sec. 1994—), Tex. Jazz Festival Soc. (pres. 1995—). Republican. Avocations: sailing, music, photography, writing, running. Home and Office: Pro Data Systems Inc 5219 Summerset Trail Austin TX 78749-1357

TURNHEIM, PALMER, banker; b. S.I., N.Y., June 30, 1921; s. Gustav and Helga (Hansen) T.; m. Gloria Freer, June 1948 (dec.); 1 child, Joy Karen. BS magna cum laude, NYU, 1960; Am. Inst. Banking, 1947; grad., Stonier Grad. Sch. Banking, Rutgers U., 1958, Advanced Mgmt. Program, Harvard, 1962. Asst. mgr. credit dept. Chase Nat. Bank, 1951-55, asst. treas., 1955; asst. v.p. Chase Manhattan Bank, N.Y.C., 1956-61; v.p. Chase Manhattan Bank, 1961-71, sr. v.p., 1971-86; sr. v.p. Chase Manhattan Capital Markets Corp.; exec. v.p. 1st Fidelity Bank, Newark, 1990-95, First Union Bank, Newark, 1996—; instr. mgmt. decision lab. Stern Grad. Sch. Bus. NYU, 1986-90; pres. Chasex Assocs., Inc. Author: International Finance Corporation, 1958. Nat. pres. United Cerebral Palsy Assns., Inc., 1967-70; dir. United Cerebral Palsy Research and Ednl. Found.; Mem. U.S. govt. com. on cash mgmt. Gen. Services Adminstrn., Washington, Am. Bankers Assn. task force advising Dept. Energy on gasoline rationing, 1979-81; Bd. dirs. Fund for Theol. Edn., 1957-84, N.Y. Inst. Credit, 1971-84. Served with USAAF, 1942-46. Mem. N.Y. State Bankers Assn. (dir. 1972-75), N.Y.U. Stern Sch. Bus. Alumni Assn. (pres. 1982-83, v.p. 1986—), NYU Alumni Assn. (v.p., dir.), Am. Legion, Beta Gamma Sigma, Phi Alpha Kappa. Lutheran. Clubs: Harvard Bus. Sch., Union League. Home: 23 Oak Ln Mountain Lakes NJ 07046-1311

TURNIPSEED, BARNWELL RHETT, III, journalist, public relations consultant, government official; b. Gainesville, Ga., Apr. 6, 1929; s. Barnwell Rhett and Leone (Rogers) T.; m. Jane Whitley, June 12, 1982. BA in Journalism, U. Ga., 1950, MA in Journalism, 1960. Program dir., ops. cons. Ga. broadcasting stas., 1953-60; sr. corr., sci. editor Voice of Am. Worldwide English, 1960-72; coordinator rado-TV pub. affairs HEW, 1972-73; mem. staff Ga. congressman Phil Landrum, 1974-75; dir. tech. info. dissemination Solar Energy Program, ERDA and Dept. Energy, 1975-77; spl. asst. Office of Asst. Sec. for Conservation and Solar Energy, Dept. Energy, Washington, 1977-81; cons. energy devel., advt., pub. relations, Atlanta, 1981-88; instr. West Ga. Coll., Carrollton, 1988-89, 90-94; asst. prof. journalism Brenau Coll., Gainesville, Ga., 1989-90; mgr. Sta. WBCX-FM, Gainesville, 1989-90, Sta. WWGC-FM, Carrollton, 1990-94; free-lance writer; promoter aviation and aerospace devel.; comml. pilot. Symphony Guild rep. for Louisville and Columbus, Ga. Jaycees; active community symphony and arts devel. Served to sgt., U.S. Army, 1950-52; Korea. Recipient 2 meritorious service awards USIA. Mem. Nat. Assn. Sci. Writers (life), Aircraft Owners and Pilots Assn., Sigma Delta Chi. Democrat. Methodist. Author: History of Georgia Broadcasting, 1972; prin. corr. Voice of Am. Peabody award-winning space exploration broadcasts, 1969. Home: 4297 Doublegate Dr Douglasville GA 30135-4247

TURNLEY, DAVID CARL, photojournalist; b. Fort Wayne, Ind., June 22, 1955; s. William Loyd and Elizabeth Ann (Protsman) T.; m. Karin Nicolette, Apr. 15, 1989. BA in French, U. Mich., 1977; student, Sorbonne, Paris, 1975; DMus (hon.), Keele (Eng.) U., 1991. Staff photogapher Sliger Home Newspapers, Northville, Mich., 1978-80, Detroit Free Press, 1980—; European based photographic corr. Detroit Free Press/Black Star Paris, 1988—. Author: Why Are They Weeping? South Africans under Aparthied, 1988, Beijing Spring, 1989, Moments of Revolution: Eastern Europe, 1990; artist London Decca Records. Recipient Canon essay award for S. African coverage, 1985, World Press Picture of Yr. award for Earthquake in Armenia, 1988, Robert Capa Gold medal for China, Romania coverage, 1990, Pulitzer prize for China, E. Europe coverage, 1990. Office: Detroit Free Press 321 W Lafayette Blvd Detroit MI 48226*

TURNLUND, JUDITH RAE, nutrition scientist; b. St. Paul, Sept. 28, 1936; d. Victor Emanuel and Vida Mae (Priddy) Hanson; m. Richard Wayne Turnlund, Nov. 9, 1957; children: Michael Wayne, Mark Richard, Todd Hanson. BS in Chemistry and Psychology, Gustavus Adolphus Coll., 1958; PhD in Nutrition, U. Calif., Berkeley, 1978. Registered dietitian. Postdoctoral fellow U. Calif., Berkeley, 1978-80, lectr., 1984-92, adj. assoc. prof., 1989—; rsch. nutrition scientist Western Regional Rsch. Ctr./Western Human Nutrition Ctr., USDA, San Francisco and Albany, Calif., 1980—, rsch. leader, 1993-96; vis. asst. prof. Am. U. Beirut, Lebanon, 1979, 80. Editor: Stable Isotopes in Nutrition, 1984; contbr. articles to profl. jours. Recipient Cert. of Merit, USDA/ARS, 1984, 1993, Disting. Alumni citation Gustavus Adolphus Coll., 1988, Am. Inst. Nutrition's Lederle award in Human Nutrition, 1996; USDA grantee, 1982-90, Nat. Dairy Coun. grantee, 1986. Mem. Am. Inst. Nutrition (Lederle award in human nutrition 1996), Am. Soc. Clin. Nutrition, Am. Dietetic Assn. Home: 2276 Great Hwy San Francisco CA 94116-1555 Office: USDA/ARS PO Box 29997 San Francisco CA 94129-0997

TURNOFF, WILLIAM CHARLES, judge; b. Phila., Nov. 19, 1948; s. David and Frieda (Kleiman) T.; m. Joy Rahinsky, Aug., 1971; children: Wendy, Dana. A.B. cum laude, Franklin and Marshall Coll., 1970; J.D., Cornell U., 1973. Bar: Pa. 1973, Fla. 1977, U.S. Dist. Ct. (ea. dist.) Pa. 1973, U.S. Dist. Ct. (so. dist.) Fla. 1980; U.S. Ct. Appeals (5th cir.) 1980, U.S. Ct. Appeals (11th cir.) 1981. Asst. dist. atty., Phila., 1973-80; asst. U.S. atty. office of U.S. Atty., Miami, Fla., 1980-86, chief maj. crimes sect., 1982-86; apptd. magistrate judge U.S. Dist. Ct. (so. dist.) Fla., 1986—, chief magistrate judge, 1994-97. Chmn. Fla. Bar Grievance Com., 1985-86. Recipient Judicial Distinction award Miami chpt. Fla. Assn. Criminal Defense Lawyers, 1992. Mem. B'nai B'rith (pres. bench-bar unit 1991-92), Phi Beta Kappa.

TURNOVSKY, STEPHEN JOHN, economics educator; b. Wellington, New Zealand, Apr. 5, 1941; came to U.S., 1981; s. Frederick and Liselotte Felicitas (Wodak) T.; m. Michelle Henriette Louise Roos, Jan. 21, 1967; children: Geoffrey George, Jacqueline Liselotte. BA, Victoria U., Wellington, 1962, MA with honors, 1963; PhD, Harvard U., 1968. Asst. prof. econs. U. Pa., Phila., 1968-71; assoc. prof. U. Toronto, Ont., Can., 1971-72; prof. Australian Nat. U., Canberra, 1972-82; IBE disting. prof. econs. U. Ill., Champaign, 1982-87; prof. econs. U. Wash., Seattle, 1987—, chmn. dept., 1990-95; Castor prof., 1993—; rsch. assoc. Nat. Bur. Econ. Rsch., Cambridge, Mass., 1983-93. Author: Macroeconomic Analysis and Stabilization Policy, 1977, International Macroeconomic Stabilization Policy, 1990, Methods of Macroeconomic Dynamics, 1995, International Macroeconomics Dynamics, 1997; mem. editl. bd. several jours.; contbr. numerous articles to profl. jours. Fellow Econometric Soc., Acad. Social Scis. in Australia; mem. Soc. Econ. Dynamics and Control (pres. 1982-84, editor Jour. Econ. Dynamics and Control 1981-87, 95—). Avocations: skiing, hiking, music. Home: 6053 NE Kelden Pl Seattle WA 98105-2045 Office: U Wash Coll Arts and Scis Dept Econs 301 Savery Hall Seattle WA 98195

TURNQUIST, PAUL KENNETH, agricultural engineer, educator; b. Lindsborg, Kans., Jan. 3, 1935; s. Leonard Otto and Myrtle Edith (Ryding) T.; m. Peggy Ann James, Dec. 22, 1962; children: Todd, Scott, Greg. BS Agrl. Engring., Kans. State U., 1957; MS in agrl. engring., Okla. State U., 1961, PhD agrl. engring., 1965. Registered profl. engr., Okla. Rsch. engr. Caterpillar Tractor Co., Peoria, Ill., 1957; instr., asst. prof. Okla. State U., Stillwater, 1958-62; assoc. prof., prof. S.D. State U., Brookings, 1964-76; prof., dept. head Auburn (Ala.) U., 1977—; mem. ABET Engring. Accreditation Commn., 1992-97. Co-author: Tractors & Their Power Units, 1989; contbr. articles to profl. jours. Fellow Am. Soc. Agrl. Engrs. (life, trustee found. 1990-93, bd. dirs. edn. com. 1992-94); mem. NSPE, Am. Soc. for Engring. Edn., Coun. Forest Engrs., Sigma Xi. Methodist. Home: 1216 Nixon Dr Auburn AL 36830-6302

TURO, JOANN K., psychoanalyst, psychotherapist, consultant; b. Westerly, R.I., Feb. 13, 1938; d. Angelo and Anna Josephine (Drew) T. BS in Biology and Chemistry, U. R.I., 1959; MA in Human Rels. and Psychology, Ohio U., 1964; postgrad., NYU, 1966-71, N.Y. Freudian Inst., N.Y.C., 1977-85, Mental Health Inst., N.Y.C., 1977-80. Rsch. asst. biochemistry studies on schizophrenia Harvard U. Med. Sch., Boston, 1959-60; indsl. psychology asst. studies on managerial success N.Y. Telephone Co., N.Y.C., 1964-66; staff psychologist Testing and Advisement Ctr. NYU, 1966-70; psychology intern Kings County Hosp., Bklyn., 1970-71; staff psychologist M.D.C. Psychol. Svcs., N.Y.C., 1971-72; clin. dir. Greenwich House Substance Abuse Clinic, N.Y.C., 1973-76; cons. psychotherapist Mental Health Consultation Ctr., N.Y.C., 1977-82; pvt. practice psychoanlysis and psychotherapy N.Y.C., 1981—; mental health cons. Bklyn. Ctr. for Psychotherapy, 1976-78; with Psychoanaltyic Consultation Svcs., 1994—; presenter in field. Mem. Itnernat. Psychoanalytic Assn. (cert., presenter fall meeting 1995), Soc. for Personality Assessment (cert.), N.Y. Freudian Soc. (cert., co-chmn. grad. com. 1985-86, mem. continuing edn. com. 1986—, pub. rels. com. 1992-93, psychoanalytic consult svc. 1994—, tng. and supr. psychoanalyst 1995—), N.Y. Coun. Psychoanalytic Psychotherapists (cert.), Met. Assn. for Coll. Mental Health Practitoners (cert.). Office: 175 W 12th St Apt 9H New York NY 10011-8211

TURO, RON, lawyer; b. Fort Wayne, Ind., Apr. 2, 1955; s. John B. and Joan L. (Gluntz) T.; m. Claire Teresa Fetterman T., May 24, 1980; children: Andrew Jacob, Patricia Erin, Dominic Earl. BA in History with honors, Pa. State U., 1978; JD, Dickinson Sch. Law, 1981. Bar: Pa. 1981, U.S. Dist. (mid. dist.) Pa. 1982, U.S. Supreme Ct. 1987, U.S. Ct. Appeals (3d cir.) 1989. Ast. pub. defender Cumberland County, Carlisle, Pa., 1981-84; ptnr. Griffie & Turo, Carlisle, 1984-89; pvt. practice Carlisle, 1989—. Founder West Shore Police Recognition Dinner, Camp Hill, Pa., 1985—; mem. Pa. Assn. Retarded Citizens, 1996—; mem. Nat. Cath. Com. on Scouting, 1988-92; chmn. Region III, Pa., N.J., 1993-95, parliamentarian and legal coun., 1991—; mem. Big Bros./Big Sisters Carlisle select com., 1993—; bd. dirs. AHEDD, Inc., 1993-94, vice chmn. 1994-95, chmn., 1995—. Recipient St. George Emblem Boy Scouts Am., Harrisburg, Pa., 1983, Golden AAD Emblem, 1989. Mem. Nat. Lawyer's Assn., Nat. Assn. Criminal Def. Lawyers, Pa. Bar Assn., Pa. Assn. Criminal Def. Lawyers, Cumberland County Bar Assn. (social chmn. 1985—), Dickinson Sch. Law Alumni Orgn. (bd. dirs. 1987—), Trinity H.S. Alumni Orgn. (pres. 1988-90), Mensa (local sec. 1990-92, editor 1992-95), KC (pres. Capital area chpt. 1989, Knight of Yr. 1981, Grand Knight 1985-87, 93-95). Republican. Roman Catholic. Avocations: politics, scouting, scuba diving, travel. Home: 539 Baltimore Pike Mount Holly Springs PA 17065 Office: 32 S Bedford St Carlisle PA 17013-3302

TUROCK, BETTY JANE, library and information science educator; b. Scranton, Pa., June 12; d. David and Ruth Carolyn (Sweetser) Argust; BA magna cum laude (Charles Weston scholar), Syracuse U., 1955; postgrad. (scholar) U. Pa., 1956; MLS, Rutgers U., 1970, PhD, 1981; m. Frank M. Turock, June 16, 1956; children: David L., B. Drew. Library and materials coordinator Holmdel (N.J.) Public Schs., 1963-65; story-teller Wheaton (Ill.) Public Library, 1965-67; ednl. media specialist Alhambra Public Sch., Phoenix, 1967-70; br. librarian, area librarian, head extension service Forsyth County Public Library System, Winston-Salem, N.C., 1970-73; asst. dir. Montclair (N.J.) Public Library, 1973-75, dir., 1975-77; asst. dir. Monroe County Library System, Rochester, N.Y., 1978-81; asst. prof. Rutgers U. Grad. Sch. Communications, Info. and Library Studies, 1981-87, assoc. prof. 1987-93, prof. 1994—, dept. chair, 1989-95, dir. MLS program, 1990-95; vis. prof. Rutgers U. Grad. Sch. Library and Info. Studies, 1980-81; adviser U.S. Dept. Edn. Office of Libr. Programs, 1988-89. Trustee, Raritan Twp. (N.J.) Public Library, 1961-62, Keystone Coll., 1991—, Freedom to Read Found., 1994—, Libs. for the Future, 1994—, Fund for Am.'s Libs., 1995; mem. Bd. Edn. Raritan Twp., 1962-66; ALA coord. Task Force on Women, 1978-80, mem. action coun.; treas. Social Responsibilities Round Table, 1978-82. Recipient N.J. Libr. Leadership award, 1994; named Woman of Yr., Raritan-Holmdel Woman's Club, 1975. Mem. AAUP, Am. Soc. Info. Sci., Assn. Libr. and Info. Sci. Edn., Am. Libr. Assn. (pres. 1995—, pres.-elect 1994-95, exec. bd. 1991—, coun. 1988—), Rutgers U. Grad. Sch. Library and Info. Studies Alumni Assn. (pres. 1977-78, Disting. Alumni award 1994, pres. award for Pub. Svc., 1997), Phi Theta Kappa, Psi Chi, Beta Phi Mu, Pi Beta Phi. Unitarian. Author: Serving Older Adults, 1983, Creating a Financial Plan, 1992; editor: The Bottom Line, 1984—; contbr. articles to profl. jours. Home: 39 Highwood Rd Somerset NJ 08873-1834 Office: Rutgers U 4 Huntington St New Brunswick NJ 08901-1071

TUROFSKY, CHARLES SHELDON, landscape architect; b. Chgo., Oct. 1, 1942; s. Joseph and Lillian R. (Brownstein) T.; m. Diane Adrienne Haber, Aug. 22, 1971; children: Benjamin, Alexi, Nicole. BFA, U. Ill., 1964; M Landscape Architecture, U. Mich., 1966; student, Harvard Grad. Sch. Design, 1971. Registered landscape architect, N.Y., Conn., N.J., Mass., N.C. Assoc. landscape architect Sasaki Office, Watertown, Mass., 1966-71; prin. landscape architect Charles Turofsky, P.C., Great Neck, N.Y., 1971—; pres. Turlab Constrn. Corp., Great Neck, N.Y., 1984—; prof. Rutgers U., 1975-76, Westchester Community Coll., Valhalla, N.Y., 1971-75, N.Y. Bot. Garden, Bronx, N.Y., 1975-81; tchr. Yonkers (N.Y.) Pub. Schs., 1973-85; teaching fellow U. Mich., Ann Arbor, 1965. Prin. works include Tarry Town Corp. Ctr., GE World Hdqrs., Fairfield, Conn., Rosecliff Condominiums, Briarcliff, N.Y., Tarry Elm Bus. Ctr., Elmsford, N.Y., Woodmere (N.Y.) Country Club, Hampshire Country Club, Mamaroneck, N.Y., adult handicapped playground Young Adult Inst., Tarrytown, N.Y., Hebrew Hosp., Valhalla, N.Y., Mita Copy Star, Fairfield, N.J., AT&T Switching Ctr., Rego Park, Horizon Ho., Great Neck, N.Y., 104 Corporate Dr., Purchase, N.Y., Ophir Farms, Purchase, N.Y., Eastchester (N.Y.) Glen, others. Recipient award Garden Clubs of Am., 1982, award N.Y. State Nurserymen Assn., 1987, 88. Mem. Am. Soc. Landscape Architects, N.Y. State United Tchrs. (rep. 1983-85), Westchester-Putnam Builders Inst. (Excellence in Landscaping award 1986). Jewish. Avocations: painting, fishing, gardening, travel, theatre, museums. Office: 6 Bly Ct Great Neck NY 11023-1706

TUROK, PAUL HARRIS, composer, music reviewer; b. N.Y.C., Dec. 3, 1929; s. Joseph and Esther (Pashman) T.; m. Susan Kay Frucht, Mar. 24, 1967. BA, Queens Coll., N.Y.C., 1950; MA, U. Calif., Berkeley, 1951; MS, Baruch Coll., 1986. Music dir. Sta. KPFA, Berkeley, 1955-56; lectr. CCNY, 1959-63; vis. prof. Williams Coll., Williamstown, Mass., 1963-64; music critic New York Herald-Tribune, 1964-65; critic, columnist Music Jour., New York, 1964-79, Ovation mag., New York, 1980—; critic, contbr. New York Times, 1984—, Sta. WQXR, First Hearing, New York, 1985—; pub. Turok's Choice, 1990—. Composer musical compositions, premiered Indpls. Symphony, 1971, Louisville Orch., 1973, Cleve. Orch., 1973, Phila Orch., 1976; opera Richard III, 1975, Sousa Overture, 1976, Lanier Songs, 1978, English Horn Quintet, 1982, Cello Sonata, 1984, Organ Toccata, 1984, Tourist Music, 1985, String Quartet No. 4, 1986, Rhapsody for Band, 1987, Piano Dance, 1988, Violin Sonata, 1989, From Sholem Aleichem, 1990, Abac for trumpet and organ, 1990, Partita for three winds, 1991, Concerto for two violins and orchestra, 1991, Piano Trio, 1992, C.C. 6 for bassoon and orchestra, 1992, Fantasy for 4 flutes and piano, 4 hands, 1994, Clap, Cluck, Count: Three Interactive Proverbs for Chidren and Orchestra, 1995, Sonata No. 2 for Cello and Piano, 1996, Concerto for Piano and Orch., 1997. Served with U.S. Army, 1953-55. Hertz travelling scholar, U. Calif., 1956-58; Grammy nominee 1992, 93. Jewish. Avocations: world travel, computing.

TUROV, DANIEL, financial writer, investment executive; b. Bklyn., Jan. 15, 1947; s. Bernard and Mildred (Stevelman) T.; B.A. in Econs., CCNY, 1969; m. Rosalyn B. Kalishock, Aug. 25, 1968 (dec.); children: Joshua Nathaniel, Steven Russell. Registered investment advisor. Account exec. Walston & Co., 1969-72, Thomson McKinnon Securities, 1972-75; sr. v.p. Faulkner Dawkins & Sullivan, 1975-77, Cowen & Co., N.Y.C., 1977-80; dir. Turov Investment Group div. Moore & Schley, Cameron & Co., N.Y.C., 1980-82; v.p. Dean Witter Reynolds, Inc., 1982-83, sr. v.p., 1983-84; pres. Just Right Comm., 1992—; chmn. Philtrum Advt. Corp., 1982-84. Author: (monthly) Turov on Investments and Hedging, 1972-80, monthly; investment column Best Buys Mag., 1982-83; editor New Innovations Pub. Corp., 1979-86, Turov on Timing, 1993—; contbr. articles to profl. jours. and newspapers. Mem. faculty N.Y. Inst. Fin., New Sch. Social Research; mem. panel The Wall St. Transcript's Option Roundtable; speaker in field. Office: Just Right Comm 154 Whippoorwill Ln Oak Ridge TN 37830-8645

TUROW, JOSEPH GREGORY, communication educator; b. Bklyn., Apr. 5, 1950; s. Abraham and Danuta (Chaikin) T.; m. Judith Anne Forrest, June 17, 1979; children: Jonathan, Marissa, Rebecca. BA, U. Pa., 1971, MA, 1973, PhD, 1976. From asst. prof. to prof. Purdue U., West Lafayette, Ind., 1976-86; from assoc. prof. to prof. comms. U. Pa., 1986—. Author: Getting Books to Children, 1979, Entertainment, Education and the Hard Sell, 1981, Media Industries, 1984, Playing Doctor, 1989, Media Systems in Society, 1992, 2d edit., 1994, Breaking Up America, 1997. Recipient Russell Nye award Popular Culture Assn., 1982; NEH grantee, 1986, 94; FCC grantee, 1978. Mem. Speech Comm. Assn. (divsn. head 1987), Internat. Comm. Assn. (divsn. chair 1995—), Phi Beta Kappa. Avocation: viewing residential architecture. Office: U Pa Annenberg Sch 3620 Walnut St Philadelphia PA 19104-6220

TUROW, SCOTT F., lawyer, author; b. Chgo., Apr. 12, 1949; s. David D. and Rita (Pastron) T.; m. Annette Weisberg, Apr. 4, 1971; 3 children. BA magna cum laude, Amherst Coll., 1970; MA, Stanford U., 1974; JD cum laude, Harvard U., 1978. Bar: Ill. 1978, U.S. Dist. Ct. (no. dist.) Ill. 1978, U.S. Ct. Appeals (7th cir.) 1979. Asst. U.S. atty. U.S. Ct. Appeals (7th dist.), Chgo., 1978-86; ptnr. Sonnenschein Nath & Rosenthal, Chgo., 1986—; E. H. Jones lectr. Stanford U., 1972-75. Author: One L.: An Inside Account of Life in the First Year at Harvard Law School, 1977, Presumed Innocent, 1987, The Burden of Proof, 1990, Pleading Guilty, 1993, The Laws of Our Fathers, 1996; contbr. articles to profl. jours. Mem. Chgo. Bar Assn., Chgo. Coun. of Lawyers. Office: Sonnenschein Nath Rosenthal 233 S Wacker Dr Chicago IL 60606-6306

TURPEN, LOUIS A., airport terminal executive. Pres., CEO Greater Toronto Airports Authority (formerly Lester B. Pearson Internat. Airport), Ont., Can., 1996—; dir., San Francisco Airports Commn. Office: Greater Toronto Airports Authority, PO Box 6031, Toronto, ON Canada*

TURPEN, MICHAEL CRAIG, lawyer; b. Tulsa, Nov. 10, 1949; s. Wallace Kendall and Marjorie Allyce (Kinkaid) T.; m. Susan Lynn Haugen; children: Sean Michael, Patrick Michael, Sarah Allyce. BS in History Edn., U. Tulsa, 1972, JD, 1974. Bar: Okla. 1975. Legal advisor Muskogee Police Dept., Okla., 1975-76; asst. dist. atty. City of Muskogee, 1976, dist. atty., 1977-82; atty. gen. State of Okla., 1983-87; ptnr. Riggs, Abney, Neal & Turpen, Oklahoma City, 1987—; conf. speaker; mem. Okla. Spl. Legis. Com. on Criminal Justice System, 1978-79; adj. prof. bus. law N.E. Okla. State U.-Tahlequah, 1977; adj. prof. criminal law Connors State Coll., 1977-79. Author: Police-Prosecutor Training Manual, 1975; contbr. articles to profl. jours. Mem. Gov.'s Alts. to Incarceration Com., 1980-81; bd. dirs. Call Rape, Inc., Okla. Acad. State Goods; apptd. by Pres. Clinton JFK Performing Arts Ctr. Adv. Bd.; vice chmn. Okla. Crime Commn., 1980-81; commr. Okla. State Bur. Investigation, 1978-79; bd. dirs., coach Muskogee Green Country Girls Softball Assn.; mem. Muskogee H.S. Booster Club; mem., coach Muskogee Knothole League Boys Baseball Assn.; mem. Muskogee County Human Soc., Muskogee County Women's Dem. Club; hon. mem. Okla. Hwy. Patrol, 1980; co-chmn. Clinton/Gore Okla., 1992, 96, Al Gore for Pres., 1988; chmn. State Dem. Party Okla., 1992-94; active Westminster Presbyn. Ch., Okla. City. Recipient Maurice Merrill Golden Quill award Okla. Bar Jour., 1981, Donald Santarelli award Nat. Orgn. Victim Assistance, Toronto, 1981, Mayor's commendation City of Muskogee, 1976, Mayor's commendation City of Owasso, 1975, $10,000 Cash award Found. for Improvement Justice, Inc., Achievement award Found. for Improvement Justice, Inc., 1986; named Outstanding Young Oklahoman, Okla. Jayees, 1979, Outstanding Young Lawyer, Okla. Bar Assn., 1975, Outstanding Young Man, Muskogee Jaycees, 1979, One of Ten Outstanding Nat. Leaders in field of victim rights, Nat. Orgn. for Victim Assistance, 1986, One of Men and Women Under 40 Who are Changing Nation, Esquire Mag., 1985. Mem. ABA, Okla. Bar Assn., Muskogee County Bar Assn. (past sec.), Okla. Dist. Attys. Assn. (pres. 1980-81, bd. dirs.), Tulsa U. Alumni Assn., Rotary, Tulsa U. Hurricane Club, Fraternal Order of Police. Office: Riggs Abney Neal & Turpen Ste 101 5801 Broadway Ext Oklahoma City OK 73118-7489 also: 502 W 6th St Tulsa OK 74119-1016

TURPIN, DAVID HOWARD, biologist, educator; b. Duncan, B.C., Can., July 14, 1956; s. George Howard and Marilyn Elizabeth (Jones) T.; m. S. Laurene Clark, Oct. 4, 1985; children: Chantal, Joshua. BSc in Biology, U. B.C., 1977, PhD in Botany, Oceanography, 1980. Post-doctoral rsch. fellow Natural Sci. & Engring. Coun., 1980-81; rsch. assoc. Simon Fraser U., 1980; v.p. Sigma Resource Cons., Vancouver, B.C., 1980-81; from asst. prof. to assoc. prof. Queen's U., Kingston, Ont., Can., 1981-90; prof. biology Queen's U., Kingston, Ont., 1990-91, dean arts & sci., 1993-95, vice prin. acad., 1993—; prof., head botany U. B.C., 1991-93; invited speaker profl. meetings, univs. worldwide. Co-editor: Plant Physiology, Biochemistry and Molecular Biology, 1990, 2nd edit., 1996; mem. editl. bd. Jour. Phycology, 1992-96, Plant Physiology, 1988-92, Plant Cell and Environment, 1994—, Jour., Exptl. Botany, 1995—; contbr. chpts. to books; author numerous articles, conf. procs. V.p. Great Lakes Tomorrow, 1986-90; mem. program com. Great Lakes Course-Ont. Sci. Ctr., 1988; Kingston City rep. Cataraqui Regional Conservation Authority, 1984-86. Recipient Excellence in Teaching Alumni award Queen's U., 1989, Outstanding Alumni award U. B.C., 1990, Darbaker prize in phycology Am. Bot. Assn., 1991; Natural Sci. and Engring. Rsch. Can. E.W.R. Stacie Meml. fellow, 1989-90; Capt. T.S. Byrne Meml. scholar U. B.C., 1980; postgrad. scholar Natural Scis. and Engring. Rsch. Coun., 1979-81, Edith Ashton Meml. scholar U. B.C., 1979, Nat. Rsch. Coun. scholar, 1978-79; Natural Scis. and Engring. Rsch. Coun. grantee, 1982—. Mem. Phycological Soc. Am., Am. Soc. Limnology & Oceanography, Can. Soc. Plant Physiologists (C.D. Nelson award 1989), Am. Soc. Plant Physiologists (cert. recognition 1992). Office: Queen's U Office of Vice Prin Acad, 239 Richardson Hall, Kingston, ON Canada K7L 3N6

TURPIN, JOSEPH OVILA, counselor, educator; b. Rockford, Ill., July 11, 1943; s. D. John and Mona Belle (Albright) T.; m. Hester R. Thompson, June 26, 1969; children: Matthew, Michael. AB in Sociology, Ind. U., 1965, MS in Mental Retardation, 1966, postgrad., 1966-67; PhD in Rehab. Psychology, U. Wis., 1986. Rsch. assoc. Ind. U., Bloomington, 1966-67; instr. U. Wis. Parkside Extension, Kenosha, 1967-71; tchr. Kenosha Unified Sch. Dist., 1967-71; coord. Racine area Gov.'s Com. on Spl. Learning State of Wis. Dept. Adminstrn., 1971-73; dir. Racine County Comprehensive Mental Health, Mental Retardation, Alcohol and Other Drug Abuse Svcs. Bd, 1973-78; vocat. cons., counselor supr. Industrial Injury Clinic, Neenah, Wis., 1978-83; owner, vocat. expert Vocat. Counseling Svc., Inc., Madison, Wis., 1983-88; teaching intern, counseling supr., student tchr. supr. U. Wis., Madison, 1983-86; asst. prof. rehab. counselor edn. Ohio U., Athens, 1986-89; assoc. prof. rehab. counseling program Calif. State U., San Bernardino, 1989-94, prof. rehab. counseling program, 1994—, coord. rehab. counseling program, 1990-94; mem. sch. psychologist exam. com. Dept. Edn. State of Ohio, 1989; rschr., presenter, cons. in field. Contbr. articles to profl. publs. Bd. dirs. United Cerebral Palsy of Racine County, 1969-73, Children's House, Inc., Racine, 1971-73, Ctrl. Ohio Regional Coun. on Alcoholism, 1987-89, Inland Caregivers Resource Ctr., 1993—, Health and Hosp. Planning Com. of Racine County, 1976; treas. Cub Scout Pack # 68, Boy Scouts Am., Neenah, 1981-83, Whitcomb Village Assn., Inc., 1984; bd. dirs. Aquinas H.S., 1992-94, pres. 1994; H.S. liaison West Point Parents Club of Inland Empire, 1992-94; budget rev. com. United Fund Racine County, 1975. Grantee Rehab. Svcs. Adminstrn., 1985-88, Ohio U., 1987-88, Ohio U. Coll. Osteo. Medicine and Coll. Edn., 1989, Office Spl. Edn. and Rehab., 1989-92. Mem. ACA (pub. policy and legis. com. 1992-94, various subcoms.), APA, Assn. Counselor Educators and Suprs. (we. region legis. chair 1996—), Am. Rehab. Counseling Assn. (exec. coun. 1992-94, ethics com. 1990-91, chair coun. on profl. preparation and stds. 1992-94), Nat. Rehab. Counseling Assn. (bd. dirs. 1993-94, chmn. grievance com., pres. 1997). Office: Calif State U 5500 University Pky San Bernardino CA 92407-2318

TURRELL, RICHARD HORTON, SR., retired banker; b. Kingston, Pa., Apr. 9, 1925; s. George Henry and Margaret (Clark) T.; m. Sally Wolfe, May

28, 1955; children: Richard H. Jr., David C., Douglas W. (dec.). Student, Cornell U., 1943; BS in Commerce, Washington and Lee U., 1949. Rep. sales Del. Lackawanna and Western Coal Co., Phila., 1949-51; asst. to pres. N.Y.C., 1951-58; broker Auchincloss Parker & Redpath, N.Y.C., 1958-61; mgr. investments Fiduciary Trust Co. Internat., N.Y.C., 1961-94, v.p., 1968-94, sr. v.p., 1968-94, sec., 1971-84; asst. sec. Blue Coal Corp., N.Y.C., 1953-58; v.p., bd. dirs. Pine Raleigh (N.C.) Corp., 1966-93. Trustee, overseer Simon's Rock of Bard Coll., Gt. Barrington, Mass., 1968-93; trustee Monmouth Univ., West Long Branch, N.J., 1980—, chmn. bd. trustees, 1989-92; chmn. Millburn-Short Hills (N.J.) Rep. Com., 1973-78; trustee Children's Specialized Hosp. Found., Mountainside, N.J., 1989-95. With Signal Corps, U.S. Army, 1943-46, PTO. Named Disting. Alumnus, Washington and Lee U., 1986. Mem. Baltusrol Golf Club (Springfield, N.J., gov. 1977), Capitol Hill Club (Washington), Turtle Creek Club (Tequesta, Fla.), Masons, Irem Temple Aaonms, Phi Beta Kappa, Phi Eta Sigma, Alpha Kappa Psi, Omicron Delta Kappa (hon.), Beta Gamma Sigma, Phi Delta Theta. Presbyterian. Avocations: golf, history, education. Home: 114 Turtle Creek Dr Tequesta FL 33469-1547

TURRENTINE, HOWARD BOYD, federal judge; b. Escondido, Calif., Jan. 22, 1914; s. Howard and Veda Lillian (Maxfield) T.; m. Virginia Jacobsen, May 13, 1965 (dec.); children: Howard Robert, Terry Beverly; m. Marlene Lipsey, Nov. 1, 1992. AB, San Diego State Coll., 1936; LLB, U. So. Calif., 1939. Bar: Calif. 1939. Practiced in San Diego, 1939-68; judge Superior Ct. County of San Diego, 1968-70, U.S. Dist. Ct. (so. dist.) Calif., Calif.; sr. judge U.S. Dist. Ct. (so. dist.) Calif., San Diego, 1970—. Served with USNR, 1941-45. Mem. ABA, Fed. Bar Assn., Am. Judicature Soc. Office: US Dist Ct 940 Front St San Diego CA 92101-8994

TURRENTINE, STANLEY WILLIAM, musician; b. Pitts., Apr. 5, 1934; m. Shirley Scott. Plays tenor saxophone; played with, Ray Charles, 1952, Earl Bostic, 1953, Max Roach, 1959-60; led group with wife, organist Shirley Scott, 1960-71; solo artist thereafter; rec. numerous albums including: Straight Ahead, 1985, Turrentine Again, Tender Togetherness!, Betcha Use the Stairs, What About You?, West Side Highway, Night Wings, The Man with the Sad Face, Everybody Come on Out, Have You Ever Seen the Rain?, In the Pocket, Pieces of Dreams, Salt Song, Cherry, Don't Mess with Mr. T., The Sugar Man, Sugar, Another Story, Common Touch, Always Something There, Easy Walker, The Spoiler, Rough'n Tumble, Joyride, Hustlin', A Chip Off the Old Block, Never Let Me Go, Jubelee Shouts, That's Where It's At, Dearly Beloved, Up at Minton's, Blue Hour, Ain't No Way, Mr. Natural, In Memory Of, New Time Shuffle, Straight Ahead, Wonderland, The Best of Stanley Turrentine, 1989, More Than A Mood, 1993, (with others) If I Could, 1993, Up at Minton's, 1995, (with others) T Time, 19995, (with others) Pieces of Dreams, 1995. Office: care Associated Booking Corp 1955 Broadway New York NY 10023-6504 also: Fantasy Inc 10th and Parker Berkeley CA 94710*

TURRI, JOSEPH A., lawyer; b. Seneca Falls, N.Y., July 24, 1943; s. Louis Arthur and Assunta (Faiola) T.; m. Susan Ruth Testa, Dec. 29, 1975; 1 child, Michael James. BA, SUNY, Buffalo, 1965; JD, Cornell U., 1970. Bar: N.Y. 1971, U.S. Dist Ct. (we. dist.) N.Y. 1971, U.S. Supreme Ct. 1974, U.S. Dist. Ct. (so. dist.) N.Y. 1996, U.S. Ct. Appeals (2d cir.) 1996. Ptnr. Harris, Beach & Wilcox, Rochester, N.Y., 1970—; mgmt. ptnrs. com. Harris, Beach & Wilcox, Rochester, 1991—, chmn. constrn. law dept., 1992—, chmn. litigation dept., 1994-96; bd. dirs. Thousand Island Park Corp., N.Y., Castle Bay Ltd., Rochester, N.Y.; arbitrator Am. Arbitration Assn., Syracuse, 1985—. Bd. dirs. Rochester Downtown Devel. Corp., 1992—. Mem. N.Y. Bar Assn., Monroe County Bar Assn., Assn. Gen. Contractors, Met. Forum (trustee). Avocations: horseback riding, antique wooden boats. Home: 110 Merriman St Rochester NY 14607-1506 Office: Harris Beach & Wilcox 130 Main St E Rochester NY 14604-1620

TURRILL, FRED LOVEJOY, surgeon; b. Redlands, Calif., Sept. 14, 1922; s. Gardner Stilson and Virginia Marie (Johnson) T.; m. Edith Mae Brown, Mar. 17, 1951; children: Brian Casey, Kevin Michael, Ann Louise, Mark. AS, Glendale Coll., 1942; BSE, U. Mich., 1944; MD, U. So. Calif., 1950. Diplomate Am. Bd. Surgery. Intern L.A. County/U. So. Calif. Med. Ctr., 1950-52, resident surgery, 1952-56; surgeon Turrill, Shader & Myles, Glendale, Calif., 1956—; prof. surgery U. So. Calif., L.A., 1974—. Contbr. articles to profl. jours. With U.S. Army, 1942-46. Grantee USPS, 1956-57. Mem. ACS (gov. 1977-84), Collegium Internat. Chirurgiae, Pacific Coast Surg. Assn. (councillor 1980-83), We. Surg. Assn., Soc. Grad. Surgeons (life hon., pres. 1970-71), L.A. Surg. Soc. (pres. 1975). Republican. Avocations: fishing, boating, hunting, travel.

TURRO, NICHOLAS JOHN, chemistry educator; b. Middletown, Conn., May 18, 1938; s. Nicholas John and Philomena (Russo) T.; m. Sandra Jean Misenti, Aug. 6, 1960; children: Cynthia Suzanne, Claire Melinda. BA, Wesleyan U., 1960, DSc (hon.), 1984; PhD, Calif. Inst. Tech., 1963. Instr. chemistry Columbia U., N.Y.C., 1964-65, asst. prof., 1965-67, assoc. prof., 1967-69, prof. chemistry, 1969—, William P. Schweitzer prof. chemistry, 1982—, chmn. chemistry dept., 1981-84; Cons. E.I. duPont de Nemours and Co., Inc. Author: Molecular Photochemistry, 1965, Vol. 2, 1970, Vol. 3, 1971, (with A.A. Lamola) Energy Transfer and Organic Photochemistry, 1971, Modern Molecular Photochemistry, 1978; mem. editl. bd. Langmuir Ency. Phys. Sci. and Tech., Jour. Reactive Intermediates. Fellow NSF, Alfred P. Sloan Found., Guggenheim fellow, Oxford U., 1985; recipient Eastman Kodak award for excellence in grad. rsch. pure chemistry, 1973, E.O. Lawrence U.S. Dept. Energy, 1983, Porter medal European Photochem. Soc., Inter-Am. Photochem Soc., 1994, Havinga medal Leiden, The Netherlands, 1994, Disting. Alumni award Calif. Inst. Tech., 1996. Mem. NAS, Am. Chem. Soc. (mem. editl. bd. jour. 1984—, Harrison Howe award Rochester, N.Y. sect. 1986, Arthur C. Cope award 1986, Fresenius award 1973, award for pure chemistry 1974, James Flack Norris award 1987), Am. Acad. Arts and Scis., Chem. Soc. (London), N.Y. Acad. Scis. (Freda and Gregory Halpern award in photochemistry 1977), Inter-Am. Photochemistry Soc. (award 1991, 94), European Photo-Chem. Assn. (Porter medal), Phi Beta Kappa, Sigma Xi. Office: Columbia U 3030 Broadway New York NY 10027-6902

TURSI, FRANK VINCENT, journalist; b. Bklyn., Apr. 30, 1951; s. Dominick and Grace (Berardi) T.; m. Doris Ann Foster, Nov. 12, 1973; 1 child, Diana. BA in English, East Carolina U., 1973. Reporter Clemmons (N.C.) Courier, 1973-74, Key Biscayne (Fla.) Island News, 1974-75; news editor Coral Gables (Fla.) Times-Guide, 1975-77; sports writer, copy editor Miami (Fla.) Herald, 1977-79; sports writer, copy editor Winston-Salem (N.C.) Jour., 1979-81, copy editor, layout editor, 1981-85, med./sci. reporter, 1985-88, spl. projects reporter, 1988—. Author: Where the Land Meets the Sea, 1990, Winston-Salem: A History, 1994, The Winston-Salem Journal: Magnolia Trees and Pulitzer Prizes, 1996. Pres. Old Meadowbrook Homeowners Assn., 1991-92; mem. Winston-Salem Mayor's Com. for Handicapped, 1989-90; vol. camp counselor Muscular Dystrophy Assn. Recipient Media award N.C. chpt. Am. Planning Assn., 1987, Environ. Media award for Excellence N.C. Sierra Club, 1987, Conservation Communicator award N.C. Wildlife Fedn., 1988. Roman Catholic. Home: 3851 Willowood Dr Clemmons NC 27012 Office: Winston Salem Journal 418 N Marshall St Winston Salem NC 27101-2815

TURSO, VITO ANTHONY, public relations executive; b. N.Y.C., Jan. 3, 1948; s. Vito Anthony and Helen (Smanko) T.; m. MaryAnn Ponzo, July 12, 1980; children: Lisa Lynn, Laura Mae, Nicole Vita. Student, Queens Coll., Flushing, N.Y., 1965-69. Reporter L.I. Press, Jamaica, N.Y., 1966-77; asst. editor The Trib, N.Y.C., 1977-78; dir. pub. affairs N.Y.C. Dept. Sanitation, 1978-90; dep. commr. for pub. affairs N.Y.C. Dept. Correction, 1990-94; dep. commr. for pub. affairs and community svcs. N.Y.C. Dept. of Environ. Protection, 1994-95; sr. v.p. Dan Klores Assoc. Pub. Rels., 1995—; guest lectr. New Sch. for Social Rsch., N.Y.C., 1988, Pace U., 1990. Host pub. affairs shows on TV and radio, 1981, 88; contbr. articles to pop. mags. Bd. dirs. Ozone Tudor Civic Assn., Ozone Park, N.Y., 1982-90. Recipient Bronze medal Internat. Film and TV Festival N.Y., 1985, Page One award N.Y. Newspaper Guild, 1976. Mem. Pub. Rels. Officers Soc. N.Y. (pres. 1983-85), Pub. Rels. Soc. Am. (bd. dirs. 1987-88), Am. Diabetes Assn. (bd. dirs. N.Y. chpt. 1989-91), Bklyn. Tech. H.S. Alumni Assn. (bd. dirs. 1984—), N.Y. Press Club, Inc. (bd. dirs. 1978), Old Pucks Old Timers Ice Hockey Club, KC. Roman Catholic. Avocations: ice hockey, softball, music. Home: 133-33 84th St Ozone Park NY 11417 Office: 386 Park Ave S New York NY 10016-8804

TURTELL, NEAL TIMOTHY, librarian; b. N.Y.C., Nov. 1, 1949; s. Richard Roland and Ann Grace (Glover) T. AB, Fordham U., 1971; MLS, Pratt Inst., 1975. Cataloger-libr. Ford Found., N.Y.C., 1972-75, U.S. Dept. Transp., Washington, 1975-77; spl. projects libr. Smithsonian Instn., Washington, 1977-81, chief catalogue records, 1981-82; asst. dir. tech. svcs. U. Wis., Oshkosh, 1982-83, asst. prof. libr. sci., 1982-83; asst. chief libr. Nat. Gallery of Art, Washington, 1983-87, exec. libr., 1987—. Contbr. to book revs. Libr. Jour., 1972-75, exhbn. catalogue. Bd. trustees Pyramid Atlantic Ctr. for Printmaking and the Art of the Book, Riverdale, Md., 1988—, v.p. bd. trustees, 1991—. Mem. Art Librs. Soc. N.Am., Rsch. Librs. Group (steering com. for art and architecture 1988-89), Grolier Club. Home: 1631-B S Hayes Arlington VA 22202 Office: Nat Gallery of Art 4th & Constitution Ave NW Washington DC 20565-0001

TURTELTAUB, JON, film director. Dir. films Think Big, 1990, Driving Me Crazy: Trabbi Goes to Hollywood, 1991, 3 Ninjas, 1992, Cool Runnings, 1993, While You Were Sleeping, 1995, Phenomenon, 1996. Office: Endeavor Agy 9701 Wilshire Blvd 10th Fl Beverly Hills CA 90212*

TURTURRO, JOHN, actor; b. Brooklyn, Feb. 28, 1957; s. Nicholas and Katherine Turturro; m. Katherine Borowitz; 1 child, Amadeo. Grad., SUNY (New Paltz), 1978; student, Yale Drama Sch. Worked in regional theater and off-Broadway in Danny and the Deep Blue Sea (Obie award 1985), Men Without Dates, Tooth of the Crime, La Puta Vida, Chaos and Hard Times, The Bald Soprano, Of Mice and Men, The Resistable Rise of Arturo Ui, 1991; appeared in Broadway prodn. Death of a Salesman, 1984; appeared in films Raging Bull, 1980, The Flamingo Kid, 1984, To Live and Die in L.A., 1985, Desperately Seeking Susan, 1985, Hannah and Her Sisters, 1986, Gung Ho, 1986, Offbeat, 1986, The Color of Money, 1986, The Sicilian, 1987, Five Corners, 1988, Do the Right Thing, 1989, Miller's Crossing, 1990, Men of Respect, Mo Better Blues, 1990, Jungle Fever, 1991, Barton Fink, 1991 (winner best actor award, Cannes Film Festival, 1991, David Donatello award Montreal Film Festival-Best Actor), Backtrack, 1991, Brain Donors, 1992, Fearless, 1993, Being Human, 1994, Quiz Show, 1994, Grace of My Heart, 1994, Search and Destroy, 1995, Unstrung Heroes, 1995, Clockers, 1995, Box of Moonlight, 1996, Girl 6, 1996, The Big Lebowski, 1997, Animals, 1997; film dir. (debut) Mac (Camera d'Or award Cannes Film Festival, 1992). Office: care ICM 8942 Wilshire Blvd Beverly Hills CA 90211-1934 also: 16 N Oak St # 2 A Ventura CA 93001-2631*

TUSCHMAN, JAMES MARSHALL, lawyer; b. Toledo, Nov. 28, 1941; s. Chester and Harriet (Harris) T.; m. Ina S. Cheloff, Sept. 2, 1967; children: Chad Michael, Jon Stephen, Sari Anne. BS in Bus., Miami U., Oxford, Ohio, 1963; JD, Ohio State U., 1966. Bar: Ohio 1966, U.S. Ct. Appeals (6th and 7th cirs.), U.S. Supreme Ct. Assoc. Shumaker, Loop & Kendrick, Toledo, 1966-84, ptnr. 1970-84; co-founder, chmn. ops. com. Jacobson Maynard Tuschman & Kalur, Toledo, 1985—; chmn. bd., sec. Tuschman Steel Co., Toledo, 1969-76; vice-chmn. bd. Kripke Tuschman Industries, Inc., 1977-85, dir. 1977-86; chmn. bd., sec. Toledo Steel Supply Co., 1969-86; ptnr. Starr Ave. Co., Toledo, 1969-86; bd. dirs. Capital Holdings Inc., Toledo, Capital Bank, Toledo, Fetal Devel. Eval., Ltd., Toledo. Mem. bd. trustees U. Toledo; past trustee, chmn. fin. com., past treas. Maumee Valley Country Day Sch.; past trustee, v.p., treas. Temple B'nai Israel, 1984-88. Fellow Internat. Soc. Barristers; mem. Am. Bd. Trial Advocates, Ohio Bar Assn., Toledo Bar Assn., Def. Rsch. and Trial Lawyers Assn., Ohio Civil Trial Lawyers Assn., Toledo Club, Inverness Country Club, Zeta Beta Tau, Phi Delta Phi. Home: 2579 Olde Brookside Rd Toledo OH 43615-2233 Office: 333 N Summit St Toledo OH 43604-2617

TUSEO, NORBERT JOSEPH JOHN, marketing executive, consultant; b. N.Y.C., Apr. 9, 1950; s. Joseph R. and Lorraine (Babcock) T.; 1 child, Christine. AAS in Hotel and Restaurant Mgmt., N.Y. C.C., 1969, AA in Real Estate Mgmt., 1978; B degree. Lic. real estate broker, Fla.; lic. mortgage broker; lic. securities series 63, 22; cert. radon measurement technician, Fla. Mgr. Steak & Brew, N.Y.C., 1971-75; pres. Howard Beach (N.Y.) Racquet Club, 1978-80; dir. sales mktg. and tng. Vacation Interval Mktg., Ponta Gorda, Fla., 1980-83; v.p. sales mktg. and tng. Treco/Sunstate, Jacksonville, Fla., 1984-86; pres. Sunstate Mktg., Inc., St. Augustine and Jacksonville, Fla., 1986—; pres. Sunstate Radon Cons., 1986—; mortgage broker Sunstate Fin. Svcs.; real estate broker Interval Sunstate Mktg. and Sunstate Realty & Devel., Inc.; mgr. Sunstate Travel Agy.; developer Frank B. Butler Cert. 1906 Historic Bldg.; pub., founder St. John's County edit. The Real Estate Book, Jacksonville edit. The Real Estate Book. Appeared in TV commercials; pub. (periodicals) Real Estate Books; contbr. 30 articles to profl. jours. Leader Boy Scouts Am., Queens, N.Y., 1963-70, vol. campaign to elect Neil Perry sheriff St. John's County, Robert Vogal sheriff Volusia County. Recipient Capitol award Nat. Leadership Coun., 1991. Fellow World Literary Acad. (Cambridge, Eng.); mem. Am. Resort and Residential Devel. Assn. (registered resort profl., Nat. Silver award Mktg., 1991, Silver award Sales, 1991, Silver award Tng., 1991, 92, 93, Capitol award 1992), Kiwanis (pub. rels. com. 1980). Avocation: bicycling, investments, economics, bible study, walking. Home: 101 LaQuinta Pl Saint Augustine FL 32084-4372 Office: Sunstate Mktg 101 La Quinta Pl Saint Augustine FL 32084-4318

TUSHER, THOMAS WILLIAM, retired apparel company executive; b. Oakland, Calif., Apr. 5, 1941; s. William C. and Betty J. (Brown) T.; m. Pauline B. Kensett, Jan. 1, 1967; children: Gregory Malcolm, Michael Scott. B.A., U. Calif., Berkeley, 1963; M.B.A., Stanford U., 1965. Asst. to v.p. internat. Colgate Palmolive Co., N.Y.C., 1965-67; product mgr. Colgate-Palmolive P.R., 1967-68; supt. corp. planning Levi Strauss & Co., San Francisco, 1969; pres. Levi Strauss Internat., 1977-84; sr. v.p. Levi Strauss & Co., before 1984, exec. v.p., chief operating officer, dir., from 1984, pres., chief oper. officer; now ret.; regional gen. mgr., Australia/N.Z., Levi Strauss Australia, 1970-74; area gen. mgr. Levi Strauss No. Europe, London, 1974-75; pres. European div. Levi Strauss Internat., San Francisco, 1976; dir. various subs's. Levi Strauss Internat.; dir. Gt. Western Garment Co., Can. Bd. dirs. Calif. Council Internat. Trade, 1977—, U. Calif. Grad. Bus. Sch. Served with Intelligence Corps. USAR, 1966-67. Mem. San Francisco C. of C. (dir.). Republican. Presbyterian. Clubs: World Trade, Bay. Office: Levi Strauss & Co 1155 Battery St San Francisco CA 94111-1230

TUSHINGHAM, (ARLOTTE) DOUGLAS, museum administrator; b. Toronto, Ont., Can., Jan. 19, 1914; s. Arthur Douglas and Lottie Elizabeth (Betts) T.; m. Margaret McAndrew Thomson, Apr. 9, 1948; children: Margaret Elizabeth, Ian Douglas. B.A., U. Toronto, 1936; B.D., U. Chgo., 1941, Ph.D., 1948, LL.D., 1982. Instr. U. Chgo., 1948-51; ann. prof. Am. Sch. Oriental Research, Jerusalem, 1951-52; dir. Am. Sch. Oriental Research, 1952-53; assoc. prof. Queen's U., 1953-55; head art and archaeology div. Royal Ont. Mus., Toronto, 1955-64; chief archaeologist Royal Ont. Mus., 1964-79, head Jerusalem project, 1979—, trustee, 1984-90; prof. emeritus dept. Nr. Eastern studies U. Toronto, Ont., 1955-79; Asst. dir. Jericho Excavations, 1952, 53, 56; dir. Dhiban Excavations, 1952-53; assoc. dir. Jerusalem Excavations, 1962-67; mem. Toronto Hist. Bd., 1960—, chmn., 1967-73. Author: (with V.B. Meen) Crown Jewels of Iran, 1968, (with Denis Baly) Atlas of the Biblical World, 1971, The Excavations at Dibon (Dhībân) in Moab, 1952-53, 1972, Gold for the Gods, 1976, Ancient Peruvian Metalworking, 1979, Excavations in Jerusalem, I, 1985. Served as lt. Royal Canadian Navy, 1942-45. Fellow Soc. Antiquaries of London, Royal Soc. Can., Canadian Museums Assn. (pres. 1964, 65), Archaeol. Inst. Am. Home: Apt 501, 20 Baif Blvd, Richmond Hill, ON Canada L4C 8T1

TUSHMAN, J. LAWRENCE, wholesale distribution executive. CEO Sherwood Food Distbrs., Detroit. Office: Sherwood Food Distributors 18615 Sherwood St Detroit MI 48234-2813*

TUSHNET, MARK VICTOR, law educator; b. Newark, N.J., Nov. 18, 1945; s. Leonard and Fannie (Brandchaft) T.; m. Elizabeth Alexander, Aug. 23, 1969; children: Rebecca, Laura. BA magna cum laude, Harvard U., 1967; JD, MA in History, Yale U., 1971. Law clk. Judge George Edwards, Detroit, 1971-72, Justice Thurgood Marshall, Washington, 1972-73; prof. U. Wis. Law Sch., 1973-81; prof. Georgetown U. Law Ctr., Washington, 1981—, assoc. dean rsch. and scholarship, 1992-96, Carmack Waterhouse prof. constl. law, 1996—; vis. prof. U. Tex., 1977-78, U. So. Calif., 1989, U. Chgo., 1994. Author: (with Stone, Seidman and Sunstein) Constitutional Law, 1986, ed edit., 1996, (with Fink) Federal Jurisdiction: Policy and Practice, 1984, 2nd ed., 1987, (with Fink, Mullenix and Rowe) Federal Courts in the 21st Century, 1996, The American Law of Slavery, 1981, The NAACP's Legal Strategy Against Segregated Education 1925-1950, 1987 (Littleton-Griswold prize Am. Hist. Assn.), Red, White, and Blue: A Critical Analysis of Constitutional Law, 1988; editor: Comparative Constitutional Federalism: Europe and America, 1990, Making Civil Rights Law: Thurgood Marshall and the Supreme Court, 1936-61, 1994, Making Constitutional Law: Thurgood Marshall and the Supreme Court, 1961-1991, 1997; contbr. articles to profl. jours. Jewish. Office: Georgetown U Law Ctr 600 New Jersey Ave NW Washington DC 20001-2075

TUSIANI, JOSEPH, foreign language educator, author; b. Foggia, Italy, Jan. 14, 1924; came to U.S., 1947, naturalized, 1956; s. Michael and Maria (Pisone) T. Dottore in Lettere summa cum laude, U. Naples, 1947, Litt.D., 1971. Lectr. in Italian lit. Hunter Coll., 1950-62; chmn. Italian dept. Coll. Mt. St. Vincent, 1948-71; vis. assoc. prof. NYU, 1956-64, CUNY, 1971-83; prof. Herbert H. Lehman Coll., 1971-83; NDEA vis. prof. Italian Conn. State Coll., 1962. Author: Dante in Licenza, 1952, Two Critical Essays on Emily Dickinson, 1952, Poesia Missionaria in Inghilterra Ed America, 1953, Sonettisti Americani, 1954, Melos Cordis; poems in Latin, 1955, Lo Speco Celeste, 1956, Odi Sacre; poems, 1958, The Complete Poems of Michelangelo, 1960, Rind and All, 1962, Lust and Liberty (The Poems of Machiavelli), 1963, The Fifth Season, 1963, Dante's Inferno (Introduced to Young People), 1964, Envoy from Heaven, 1965, Dante's Purgatorio (Introduced to Young People), 1969, Dante's Paradise (Introduced to Young People), 1970, Tasso's Jerusalem Delivered; verse transl., 1970, Boccaccio's Nymphs of Fiesole, 1971, Italian Poets of the Renaissance, 1971, From Marino to Marinetti, 1973, The Age of Dante, 1973, America the Free, 1976, Tireca Tàreca, 1978, Tasso's Creation of the World, 1982, Rosa Rosarum, poems in Latin, 1984, In Exilio Rerum, poems in Latin, 1985; poems, 1978, Gente Mia and Other Poems, 1978; (autobiography) La Parola Difficile, vol. I, 1988, (poems in Latin) Confinia Lucis et Umbrae; La Parola Nuova, vol. II, 1991, La parola antica, vol. III, 1992, (poems in Italian) Il Ritorno, 1992, Bronx America, 1992, Annemale Parlante, 1994, Carmina Latina, 1994, Le Poesie Inglesi di G.A. Borgese, 1995, La Poceide, 1996. Recipient Greenwood prize for poetry in England, 1956, outstanding tchr. award, 1969, cavaliere ufficiale Italian Republic, 1973, Leonardo Covello's educator award, 1980, Leone di San Marco award, 1982, Avis award, 1983, Joseph Tusiani scholarship fund established in his honor at Lehman Coll., 1983, Congl. medal merit, 1984, Progresso medal liberty, 1986, gold plaque City Hall San Marco, 1986, outstanding tchr. award Am. Assn. Tchrs. Italian, 1986, Renoir literary award, 1988; Joseph Tusiani, Poet, Translator, Humanist (An Internat. Homage), 1995, Enrico Fermi award, 1995, Melvin Jones fellow, 1995. Mem. Poetry Soc. Am. (v.p.), Cath. Poetry Soc. Am. (dir. 1958, Spirit gold medal 1968). Home: 308 E 72d St New York NY 10021 *Strange how this continually re-edited Who's Who forces one to work and achieve.*

TUSSING, MARILEE APPLEBY, music educator; b. Decatur, Ill., Feb. 6, 1953; d. Robert William and Dorothymaie (Mallory) Appleby; m. Donald Tussing, April 17, 1976; 1 child, Torrance Ashley. B in Music Edn., Ill. State U., 1975; M in Music Edn., U. Okla., 1985. Music tchr. Shannon Elem., Shannon, Ill., 1976-80, Thompson Schs., Thompson, Ill., 1980-82; Kodaly music specialist Southgate Elem., Moore, Okla., 1982—; riding instr. Shenandoah Riding Ctr., Galena, Ill. 1977-81, freelance Norman, Okla., 1982—. Dist. Commr. Sooner Pony Club, 1985—; judge Okla. Kids Talent Search, 1993-96; mem. Moore Assn. Classroom Tchrs. 1982—; pres. Moore Elem. Music Orgn., 1990-91; founder Southgate Entertainer's Club; dir. Am. Kids Celebrity Chorus, 1996-97. Recipient Equestrian Event Silver medal Sooner (Okla.) State Games, 1989. Mem. Midwest Kodaly Music Educators (bd. dirs. 1983-85), U.S. Pony Club (knowdown judge, 1990-95), U.S. Combined Tng. Assn. (cert. of achievement, 1985, 89, area V adult team mem. award, 1993), Nat. Edn. Assn., Okla. Edn. Assn., Am. Quarter Horse Assn. Republican. Mem. Christian Ch. (Disciples of Christ). Avocations: skiing, needlepoint, violin, guitar, collecting and reading horse books. Home: 11850 E Rock Creek Rd Norman OK 73071-8155

TUTEN, RICHARD LAMAR, professional football player; b. Perry, Fla., Jan. 5, 1965. BS in Econs., Fla. State U., 1986. Mem. Phila. Eagles, 1989, Buffalo Bills, 1990; punter Seattle Seahawks, 1991—. Named to NFL Pro Bowl, 1994. Office: Seattle Seahawks 11220 NE 53rd St Kirkland WA 98033-7505*

TUTHILL, JOHN WILLS, former diplomat, educator; b. Montclair, N.J., Nov. 10, 1910; s. Oliver Bailey and Louise Jerolomen (Wills) T.; m. Erna Lueders, July 3, 1937; children: Carol Anne (dec.), David. SB, Coll. William and Mary, 1932, LLD, 1978; MBA, NYU, 1936; AM, Harvard U., 1943; LLD, MacMurray Coll., 1967. Teller First Nat. Bank, Paterson, N.J., 1932-34; corporate trust adminstr. Bankers Trust Co. N.Y., 1934-36; investment counsel Fiduciary Counsel, N.Y.C., 1936-37; instr. Northeastern U., 1937-39, asst. prof. banking and finance, 1939-40; apptd. fgn. service officer Dept. State, 1940; served as vice counsul Windsor, Ont., Can., 1940-41, Mazatlan, Mexico, 1942; 3d sec. embassy Ottawa, Ont., 1942-44; sec. mission Office U.S. Polit. Adviser SHAEF, 1944-45; sec. mission and Am. Mil. Govt. for Germany, 1945-47, Am. consul, 1947; asst. chief shipping div. Dept. State, 1948, adviser, 1949; counselor of embassy Stockholm, 1949-51; spl. asst. ambassador London, 1952; dep. dir. Office Econ. Affairs, Bonn, W. Ger., 1952-54, USOM, Bonn, 1954; dir. USOM, 1954-56, counselor of embassy for econ. affairs, 1955-56; counselor embassy for econ. affairs with personal rank of minister Paris, 1956-59; dir. Office European Regional Affairs, Dept. State, 1959; minister-counselor econ. affairs U.S. Mission to NATO, European Regional Orgns., U.S.; rep. prep. com. for OECD; also dep. U.S. rep. OEEC, 1960; U.S. rep. OECD with personal rank of ambassador, 1960-62; U.S. ambassador to European Communities, 1962-66, Brazil, 1966-69; prof. internat. politics Johns Hopkins U., Bologna Center, Italy, 1969; pres. Salzburg Seminar in Am. Studies, Cambridge, Mass., 1977-85; vis. fellow Woodrow Wilson Nat. Fellowship Found., Princeton, 1978-80; exec. dir., trustee The Am.-Austrian Found., 1985-88. Author: Some Things to Some Men: Serving in the Foreign Service, 1995. Gov. Atlantic Inst. for Internat. Affairs, Paris, 1969-86, dir. gen. 1969-76. Recipient All Am. Silver Anniversary award Sports Illustrated, 1956; named to Athletic Hall of Fame Coll. William and Mary, 1979; Dir. Gen.'s Cup Dept. State, 1983. Mem. N.Y. Coun. Fgn. Rels., Washington Inst. Fgn. Policy, Am. Acad. Diplomacy (bd. dirs.), Jean Monnet Coun. (bd. dirs. 1985-95), Harvard Club (N.Y.C.), Cosmos Club (Washington), Flat Hat of William and Mary, Omicron Delta Kappa, Theta Delta Chi. Home: 2801 New Mexico Ave NW Washington DC 20007-3921

TUTHILL, WALTER WARREN, retail executive; b. Madison, N.J., Nov. 28, 1941; s. Walter Warren and Elizabeth Emma (Kniskern) T.; m. Barbara Ann Stephens, Apr. 22, 1967. BSBA, U. N.C., 1964. CPA, N.Y., N.J., N.C.; cert. info systems auditor, cert. internal auditor. Sr. mgr. Price Waterhouse, N.Y.C., 1964-77; dir. internal audit Carter Hawley Hale Stores Inc., L.A., 1977-82, gen. auditor, 1982-85, v.p., 1985-93; v.p. retail control Broadway Stores, Inc., L.A., 1993-96, Federated Dept. Stores, Inc., L.A., 1996-97; coo Gelfand, Renners & Feldman, CPA's (divsn. Coopers & Lybrand), E. Los Angeles, 1997—; lectr. in field. Contbr. articles to profl. jours. Pres. Twin W Rescue Squad, Princeton Junction, N.J., 1976-77. Mem. AICPA, N.Y. Soc. CPA's, Am. Statis. Assn., Am. Acctg. Assn., Inst. Internal Auditors, Nat. Retail Mchts. Assn. (chmn. bd. internal audit group 1982-84, bd. dirs.), EDP Auditors Assn. Avocations: travel, computers, classical music, photography. Office: Gelfand Rennert & Feldman CPAs 1880 Century Park East Los Angeles CA 90067 *Life is what happens when we're planning something else.*

TUTKO, ROBERT JOSEPH, radiology administrator, educator; b. Buffalo, Nov. 18, 1955; s. Robert Edward and Agatha (Pagliaccio) T.; m. Susan Joy Biddle, Oct. 29, 1976; children: Suzan Denise, Nicola Marie. Student, SUNY, Brockport, 1973-74; AAS, Trocaire Coll., 1982; BS, Pacific Western U., 1992, MS, PhD, 1995; postgrad. in nursing, SUNY, 1997—. Dir. X-ray svcs. Fla. Ctr. for Knee Surgery, Clearwater, 1985-86; surgery X-ray technologist St. Joseph's Hosp., Tampa, Fla., 1986-90; dir. radiology Met. Gen. Hosp., Pinellas Park, Fla., 1990-91; dir. med. imaging Univ. Gen. Hosp. and Women's Med. Ctr., Seminole, Fla., 1991-92; program dir. Sch.

Radiology St. Joseph Hosp., Memphis, 1992-94; physician asst. DeSoto Family Practice, Olive Branch, Miss., 1995-96; mem. med. staff Klein Internal Medicine, Germantown, Tenn., 1996—; founder, dir. continuing edn. TCB Med. Edn., Palm Harbor, Fla., 1985-91, pres., CEO, Germantown, Tenn., 1992—; tchr. Hillsborough County Schs., Tampa, 1989-92; lectr. profl. confs.; nat. radiology specialist Concorde Career Colls., Inc., Kansas City, Mo., 1994-95. Author: (curriculum) Limited X-Ray, 1995, Limited Basic Medical Assistant, 1996, Occupational Burnout in Healthcare Workers, 1996; contbr. articles to profl. jours. County chmn. radiology group Pinellas County Non-Profit Hosp. Venture Group, 1990-91; lectr. Pinellas County Sch. System, 1984-91. Sgt. U.S. Army, 1974-75. Recipient commendation letter Pinellas Park Police Dept., 1991. Mem. Am. Legion, Am. Educators Radiol. Scis., Am. Soc. Radiol. Technologists, Tenn. Soc. Radiol. Technologists, Fla. Soc. Radiol. Technologists, Ga. Soc. Radiol. Technologists, Colo. Soc. Radiol. Technologists, Am. Healthcare Radiology Adminstrs., KC (treas. 1989-91, Knight of Month Dec. 1989). Democrat. Roman Catholic. Avocations: cooking, sports, cars, golf, music. Home and Office: 4701 Falling Oak Cv Germantown TN 38125-4723

TUTTLE, ARTHUR NORMAN, JR., architect, university administrator; b. Balt., May 14, 1929; s. Arthur Norman and Georgia Pauline (Roberts) T.; m. Betty Gray Finney, Aug. 9, 1952 (dec. 1979); children: Arthur Norman III, George Gray; m. Barbara Jean Hassler, Apr. 15, 1983; 1 child, Katherine Elizabeth James Olsen. BS, Va. Poly. Inst. and State U., 1952; MFA, Princeton U., 1956; M in Regional Planning, U. N.C., 1962. Registered architect, N.C., Va., S.C., Okla.; cert. planner. Urban planner City of Charlestown, S.C., 1957; rsch. fellow U. N.C., Chapel Hill, 1958, dir. planning, 1959-70; architect-planner U. Health Scis. Ctr., Oklahoma City, 1970-73; univ. architect U. Okla., Norman, 1973-95, spl. asst. to v.p., 1995; cons. architect Norman, 1996—; hosp. planning cons. U. N.C., 1962-66, lectr. in planning, 1965-69; assoc. prof. health U. Okla., Oklahoma City, 1970-95, prof. architecture, 1970-95. Chmn. Town Planning Bd., Chapel Hill, 1964-69; sec. Capitol-Med. Ctr. Planning Commn., Oklahoma City, 1974-81. Fellow Assn. Univ. Architects (pres. 1990-91); mem. AIA, Am. Inst. Cert. Planners, Acad. Architecture for Health (v.p. 1970—). Presbyterian. Avocations: travel, photography. Home and Office: 1813 Cedar Hill Rd Norman OK 73072-3161

TUTTLE, CLIFFORD HORACE, JR., electronics manufacturing company executive; b. Teaneck, N.J., Aug. 3, 1930; s. Clifford Horace Sr. and Mary (Rodman) T.; m. Martha M. Greene, Apr. 23, 1952; children: Deborah Tuttle Fox, Michael R., Sandra, Mary Tuttle Faucher. BA in Psychology, Amherst, 1952. V.p. mktg. Vitramon, Inc., Monroe, Conn., 1957-63; pres. Mktg. Assistance, Inc., Weston, Mass., 1963-70; v.p. mktg. AVX Corp., New Bedford, Mass., 1970-72; chmn. Aerovox, Inc., New Bedford, 1973-96; mem. exec. com., bd. govs. Electronic Industries Assn., Washington, 1994-95. Trustee Southcoast Hosp., New Bedford, 1984—. Served to lt. USCG, 1953-55. Mem. IEEE, C. of C. (v.p. New Bedford chpt. 1982-89). Republican. Avocation: boating. Office: Aerovox Inc 370 Faunce Corner Rd North Dartmouth MA 02747-1257

TUTTLE, DAVID BAUMAN, data processing executive; b. N.Y.C., Oct. 25, 1948; s. John Bauman and Charlotte (Root) T.; m. Mildred Suzanne Lamb, May 5, 1973 (div. May 1978); m. Nancy Viola Caraber, Mar. 14, 1981; children: Jason David, John Paul. Student, MIT, 1966-69. Assoc., sr. assoc. programer IBM Cambridge (Mass.) Sci. Ctr., 1968-71; staff programmer IBM VM/370 Devel., Burlington, Mass., 1971-76; sr. prin. S/W engr. Digital Equipment Corp., Maynard, Mass., 1976-78; mgr. Cambridge Telecom/GTE Telenet, Burlington, 1978-81; sr. scientist GTE Telenet, Burlington, 1981-84, chief scientist, 1984-85; sr. tech. cons. Prime Computer, Inc., Framingham, Mass., 1985-86; prin. tech. cons. Prime Computer, Inc., Framingham, 1986-89; sr. rsch. engr. Ungermann-Bass Inc., Andover, Mass., 1990-91; chief engr. Ungermann-Bass, Inc., Andover, Mass., 1991-93; cons. engr. Augment Sys., Inc., Bedford, Mass., 1993-95; chief tech. officer Augment Systems Inc., Westford, Mass., 1995—; strategy forum del. Corp. for Open Systems, McLean, Va., 1986-89, architecture com. mem., 1989, strategy forum nominating com., 1986-87; patent rev. com. Prime Computer, Inc., 1985-89. Co-author and editor: 3270 Display System Protocol, 1981, 83, Hotline BSC Access Method, 1970. Donor mem. Smithsonian Inst., Washington, 1980—. Mem. IEEE, IEEE Computer Soc., Nat. Space Soc. (life mem.), The Cousteau Soc., USS Constitution Mus. Assn., Black and Blues of Killington (treas. 1986-89), Mandala Folk Dance Ensemble (dancer 1970-73). Republican. Presbyterian. Avocations: Duplicate Bridge (life master, Am. Contract Bridge League, 1983), alpine skiing. Home: 27 Heather Dr Reading MA 01867-3961 Office: Augment Sys Inc 2 Robbins Rd Westford MA 01886-4113

TUTTLE, GEORGE D., lawyer; b. Detroit, Nov. 20, 1940. BA magna cum laude, Yale U., 1963, LLB, 1967. Bar: Calif. 1967. Ptnr. Brobeck, Phleger & Harrison, San Francisco. Mem. Phi Beta Kappa. Office: Brobeck Phleger & Harrison Spear St Tower 1 Market Plz San Francisco CA 94105

TUTTLE, JEREMY BALLOU, neurobiologist; b. N.Y.C., Oct. 9, 1947; s. John Bauman and Charlotte Marion (Root) T.; m. Sara Jane Stasko, Mar. 23, 1971. AB, U. Rochester, 1969; PhD, Johns Hopkins U., 1977. Postdoctoral fellow U. Conn., Storrs, 1976-79, vis. asst. prof., 1980, asst. prof. in residence, 1981-84; asst. prof. physiology U. Va., Charlottesville, 1984-87, asst. prof. neuroscience, 1987-90, rsch. asst. prof., 1990-93, assoc. prof. urology neuroscience, 1993—. Contbr. articles to Devel. Biology, Science, Jour. Neuroscience, others. Chmn. mem. Common Area Planning Commn., 1984-87; pres. bd. Earlysville Forest Homeowner's Assn., 1986-89, Earlysville, Va. U. Rochester Hon. scholar, 1965-69, Regent's scholar for Medicine, 1969, NIH predoctoral fellow, 1971-75, Nat. Rsch. Svc. fellow, 1976-79, Nat. Spinal Cord Injury Found. rsch. fellow, 1979-80; recipient Rsch. Career Devel. award NINCDS/NIH, Muscular Dystrophy Assn. Rsch. award, 1990—; Am. Heart Assn. grantee, 1987-89, 90—, fellowship, Fogarty Internat. Ctr. for Rsch. NIH, Japan, 1997. Achievements include research on NGF dynamics in hypertrophic disease, carbon dioxide transport and chemosensitivity, molecular mechanisms of quantal synaptic transmission, nerve growth factor synthesis by vascular smooth muscle, trophic regulation of motor neurons, neurodegenerative diseases. Home: 900 Stillwater Ln Earlysville VA 22936-9538 Office: U Va Med Sch PO Box 230 Charlottesville VA 22902-0230

TUTTLE, JERRY OWEN, retired naval officer, business executive; b. Hatfield, Ind., Dec. 18, 1934; s. Charles Merritt and Wenonah Hathaway (Parker) T.; m. Barbara Ann Bonifay, Dec. 31, 1956; children—Michael Charles, Vicky Ann, Mark Gerrald, Stephen Scott, Monique Therese. Grad., Devry Tech. Inst., 1953; B.S., Naval Postgrad. Sch., 1963; M.A. in Internat. Relations, George Washington U., 1969; postgrad., Naval War Coll., 1968-69. Enlisted U.S. Navy, 1955, commd. ensign, 1956, advanced through grades to vice adm., 1987; aide and flag lt. to comdr-in-chief Pacific Fleet, 1969-70; exec. officer Attack Squadron 174, 1970-71; exec. officer Attack Squadron 81, comdg. officer, 1972-73; mem. staff comdr. U.S. Naval Air Forces, Atlantic Fleet, 1973-74; comdr. Attack Carrier Air Win 3, 1974-75; comdg. officer USS Kalamazoo, 1975-76, USS John F. Kennedy, 1977-78; spl. asst. to chief of naval ops. Washington, 1979; dir. for plans and policy div. Def. Intelligence Agy., Washington, 1979; dep. dir. for def. intelligence and external affairs Def. Intelligence Agy., 1979-81, asst. vice dir. for collection mgmt., 1981—; comdr. Carrier Group 8, Norfolk, Va., 1981-83, Carrier Group 2/Battle Force 6th Fleet, Naples, Italy, 1983-84; naval insp. gen. Washington, 1984-85; dep., chief of staff U.S. Atlantic Fleet/Chief of Staff, U.S. Atlantic Command, 1985-86; dir. for command, control, communication systems Office of Joint Chiefs of Staff, 1987-89; ret. USN, 1993; v.p. bus. devel. Oracle Corp., 1994-96; pres. ManTech Sys. Engring. Corp., 1996—; sr. v.p. ManTech Internat. Corp., 1996—. Decorated Def. Superior Svc. medal, Legion of Merit (4), Meritorious Svc. medal (2), D.F.C. (3), Air medal (23), Def. Disting. Svc. medal, Disting. Svc. medal, Commandeur de L'Ordre Nat. du Mérite (France); recipient John Paul Jones award for inspirational leadership Navy League, 1978; listed in Fed. Computer Week's 1991, 92 Federal 100 for his impact on govt. computer systems. Mem. AIAA (Control, Com. and Intelligence award for contbn. to overall effectiveness of C3I Systems 1991), AFCEA (contbn. award 1989, Jon Boyce award 1992), Assn. Naval Aviators. *Drive yourself to lead others; to think only of the best; to work only for the best and expect only the best; to be just as enthusiastic about the success of others as you are about your own.*

TUTTLE, MARTHA BENEDICT, artist; b. Cin., Feb. 4, 1916; d. Harris Miller and Florence Stevens (McCrea) Benedict; m. Richard Salway Tuttle, June 3, 1939; children: Richard, Jr., McCrea Benedict (dec.), Martha (dec.), Elisabeth Hall. Grad. high sch., Cin.; student, Art Acad. Cin., 1934-38. V.p. Barg Bottling Co., Inc., Cin., 1948-80. One-woman shows include KKAE Gallery, 1963, Univ. Club, 1967, Miller Gallery, 1971, St. Clements, N.Y., 1973, Livingston Lodge, 1974, Holly Hill Antiques, 1979, Peterson Gallery, 1983, Art Acad. Cin., 1984, Closson Gallery, 1986, Camargo Gallery, 1992; represented in permanent collection Cin. Art Mus. Tchr. Sunday sch. Grace Episcopal Ch. and Indian Hill Ch., Cin., 1953-75; shareholder Cin. Art Mus.; founder partnership to save the William and Phebe Betts House; donor with partnership to The Nat. Soc. Colonial Dames of Am. the William and Phebe Betts House for establishing a Rsch. Ctr. Mem. Soc. Colonial Dames Am. (bd. dirs. 1976-89), Camargo Club, Univ. Club. Republican. Home: 5825 Drewry Farm Ln Cincinnati OH 45243-3441

TUTTLE, TONI BRODAX, swimming pool company executive; b. Bklyn., July 19, 1952; d. Abraham Paul and Marilyn (Monte) Brodax; m. Roy Lee, May 21, 1978; 1 child, Sean Monte. student Lesley Coll., 1972; B.A. in Journalism, U. R.I., 1974. Reporter Mexico City Daily News, 1972; freelance photographer, writer N.Y. Yankees, Comm. Group, Ft. Lauderdale, Fla., 1974-78; editl. asst. Boating Mag., N.Y.C., 1974-76; pub. rels. cons. B. Altmans Dept. Store, N.Y.C., 1975-76; dir. pub. rels. Windjammer Barefoot Cruises, Miami, Fla., 1976-78; acct. exec. Art Jacobson Advt., Miami, 1978-79; v.p. Tuttle's Pool Co., Inc., Miami, 1979—. Mem. Dramatists Guild, Inc. Jewish. Home: 6740 SW 94th St Miami FL 33156-1735

TUTTLE, WILLIAM G(ILBERT) T(OWNSEND), JR., research executive; b. Portsmouth, Va., Nov. 26, 1935; s. William Gilbert and Edith Inez (Ritter) T.; m. Helen Lynn Warren, Dec. 27, 1959; children: Lynn, Robert, Jonathan. B.S., U.S. Mil. Acad., 1958; M.B.A., Harvard U., 1963. Commd. 2d lt. U.S. Army, 1958, advanced through grades to gen., 1989; dir. combat service support (Office Combat Devels., Hdqrs. Tng. and Doctrine Command), Ft. Monroe, Va., 1976-77; comdr. 3d Armored Div. Support Command Frankfurt, W. Ger., 1977-79; comdr. Mil. Traffic Mgmt. Command Eastern Area Bayonne, N.J., 1979-81; dir. force mgmt. Hdqrs. Dept. Army, Washington, 1981-82; chief policy and programs br. Supreme Hdqrs. Allied Powers Europe, 1982-84; comdr. U.S. Army Operational Test and Evaluation Agy., 1984-86; dep. comdg. gen. Logistics, Tng. and Doctrine Command and comdg. gen. U.S. Army Logistics Ctr., Ft. Lee, Va., 1986-89; comdg. gen. U.S. Army Materiel Command, Alexandria, Va., 1989-92; ret., 1992; pres., CEO, bd. trustees Logistics Mgmt. Inst., McLean, Va., 1993—; U.S. Army Kermit Roosevelt lectr., 1991; bd. dirs. Procurement Round Table; mem. bd. advisors Nat. Contract Mgmt. Assn.; cons. to Def. Sci. Bd. Prin., Coun. on Excellence in Govt.; nat. councillor Atlantic Coun. Decorated Def., USAF, USN, USA, D.S.M. (3), Bronze Star (3), Legion of Merit, Def. Superior Service medal. Mem. Nat. Def. Transp. Assn., Assn. U.S. Army (Pres.'s award 1992). Lutheran. Office: Logistics Mgmt Inst 2000 Corporate Rdg Mc Lean VA 22102-7805

TUTTLE, WILLIAM MCCULLOUGH, JR., history educator; b. Detroit, Oct. 7, 1937; s. William McCullough and Geneva (Duvall) T.; m. Linda Lee Stumpp, Dec. 12, 1959 (div.); children: William McCullough III, Catharine D., Andrew S.; m. Kathryn Nemeth, May 6, 1995. BA, Denison U., 1959; MA, U. Wis., 1964, PhD, 1967. Faculty mem. U. Kans., Lawrence, 1967—, prof. history, 1975—, intra-univ. prof., 1982-83; sr. fellow in So. and Negro history Johns Hopkins U., 1969-70; Charles Warren fellow Harvard U., Cambridge, Mass., 1972-73; vis. prof. U. Sc., Columbia, 1980; assoc. fellow Stanford Humanities Ctr., 1983-84; research assoc. U. Calif., Berkeley, 1986-88; vis. scholar Radcliffe Coll., 1993-94. Author: Race Riot: Chicago in the Red Summer of 1919, 1970, 2d edit., 1996, W.E.B. Du Bois, 1973, (with David M. Katzman) Plain Folk, 1982, (with others) A People and A Nation, 1982, 4th edit., 1994, "Daddy's Gone to War": The Second World War in the Lives of America's Children, 1993; contbr. chpts. to books, numerous articles to profl. jours. Dem. precinct committeeman, Lawrence, 1980-90. Lt. USAF, 1959-62. Recipient Merit award Am. Assn. for State and Local History, 1972; Younger Humanist fellow NEH, 1972-73, Guggenheim fellow, 1975-76, NEH fellow, 1983-84, rsch. fellow Hall Ctr., 1990; grantee Evans, 1975-76, Beveridge, 1982, NEH, 1986-89. Mem. Soc. Am. Historians (elected), Am. Hist. Assn., Orgn. Am. Historians, Am. Studies Assn., Assn. for Study of Afro-Am. Life and History, So. Hist. Assn., Lawrence Trout Club, Golden Key (hon.), Omicron Delta Kappa, Phi Beta Delta, Phi Gamma Delta. Home: 713 Louisiana St Lawrence KS 66044-2339 Office: U Kans Dept History Lawrence KS 66045

TUTTLETON, JAMES WESLEY, English educator; b. St. Louis, Aug. 19, 1934; s. Clarence M. and Nora Belle (Sutt) T. B.A., Harding U., Searcy, Ark., 1955; M.A., U. N.C., 1957, Ph.D., 1963. Instr. Clemson U., S.C., 1956-59, U. N.C., Chapel Hill, 1962-63; asst. prof. U. Wis., Madison, 1963-68; assoc. prof. English NYU, N.Y.C., 1968-74, prof., 1974—, chmn. dept., 1974-83; assoc. dean Grad Sch. Arts & Scis. NYU, 1988-89. Author: The Novel of Manners in America, 1972, Thomas Wentworth Higginson, 1978; editor: The American (Henry James), 1978, Washington Irving: History, Tales and Sketches, 1983, Voyages and Discoveries of the Companions of Columbus (Washington Irving), 1986, The Sweetest Impression of Life: The James Family and Italy, 1990, Edith Wharton: The Contemporary Reviews, 1992, Washington Irving: The Critical Reaction, 1993, Vital Signs: Essays on American Literature and Criticism, 1996. Served with USAFR, 1956-63. Mem. Century Assn. Home: 37 Washington Square W 11-D New York NY 10011 Office: NYU Dept English New York NY 10003

TUTUN, EDWARD H., retired retail executive; b. Boston, Jan. 26, 1924; s. J.J. and Esther L. T.; m. Joan M. Bocoffer, Oct. 23, 1953. B.S. in chem. Engring., Northeastern U., 1947. V.p. W.R. Grace & Co., N.Y.C., 1978-82, sr. v.p., 1982-83, exec. v.p., 1983-87, ret., 1987; vice chmn. Herman's Sporting Goods, Inc., Cartaret, N.J., 1983. Served with USAAF, 1942-45, ETO. Mem. Nat. Retail Mchts. Assn. (dir. 1983), DIY Inst. (dir. 1983). Club: N.Y. Yacht (N.Y.C.). Home: 544 Pinellas Bayway S Tierra Verde FL 33715-1966 also: 237 Guinea Rd Stamford CT 06903-3722 Office: WR Grace & Co 1114 Avenue Of The Americas New York NY 10036-7703

TUTWILER, CHARLES RICHARD (DICK TUTWILER), insurance company executive; b. Charleston, W.Va., Dec. 26, 1946; s. Jacob Oliver and Mary Helen (Nisbet) T.; m. Linda Ann Julia, Oct. 6, 1979; 1 child, Richard Patrick. BBA, Marshall U., 1973. Various positions Travelers Ins. Co., Tampa, Fla., 1973-83; property ops. pres. Charles R. Tutwiler & Assocs., Inc., Tampa, 1983—. Editor/pub. (newsletter) Jour. for Ins. Loss Adjusting, 1989, Quar. Update F.A.P.I.A., 1993. Mem. Clara Barton Soc. Red Cross, Tampa, 1993. With USAF, 1965-69. Mem. Am. Arbitration Assn., Soc. of Claim Law Assn., Nat. and State Assn. of Pub. Ins. Adjustors, Tampa Bay Exec. Assn. (bd. dirs. 1990—), Fla. Assn. of Pub. Ins. Adjustors (com. chmn. 1993, pres. 1996-97), Community Assn. Inst., The John Marshall Soc. (Marshall U.). Avocations: boating, jogging, scuba diving, family. Office: 2203 N Lois Ave Ste 720 Tampa FL 33607-2387 Home: 51 N Pine Cir Belleair FL 34616

TUYAKBAEV, ZHARMAKHAN AITBAJEVICH, prosecutor; b. Kazgurt District, South Kazakhstan Region, Kazakhstan, Nov. 22, 1947; s. Aitbaj and Tynym (Kenshymbaeva) T.; m. Bagila Nagometovna Aptaeva, May 19, 1972; children: Aziza, Tchingiz, Adilzhan. Degree, Kazakh State U., Almaty, Kazakhstan, 1971. Cert. lawyer. Asst. to prosecutor, head investigative sect. Shymkent oblast, 1971-78; dep. prosecutor, prosecutor Manghyshlak and Guriev oblasts Kazak Soviet Socialist Republic, 1981-90; gen. prosecutor Republic of Kazakhstan, 1990-95, chmn. State Com. Investigation, 1995—. Hon. prosecutor officer USSR, 1982; state counselor justice Republic Kazakhstan, 1982, col.-gen. justice, 1996; dep. People's Supreme Council Kazakstan, 1990-94; mem. Legis., Legality, and Law and Order Com. Recipient For Labour Promess medal, 1980. Avocation: tennis. Home: Internationalnaya Street 120-16, Almaty Kazakhstan Office: Embassy of Kazakhstan 3421 Massachusetts Ave NW Washington DC 20007-1446

TUZLA, KEMAL, mechanical engineer, scientist; b. Adapazari, Sakarya, Turkey, Feb. 23, 1943; came to U.S., 1974; s. Hayrettin and Muberra (Horozlu) T.; m. Asuman Fatma Cokmez. MME, Istanbul (Turkey) Tech. U., 1966, PhD in Mech. Engring., 1972. Instr. Istanbul Tech. U., 1966-72, asst. prof., 1974, assoc. prof., 1978-81; instr. Air Force Coll., Istanbul, 1973-74; rsch. asst. prof. U. Wash., Seattle, 1974-78; sr. rsch. scientist Lehigh U., Bethlehem, Pa., 1981—; mem. organizing com. 2d Thermal Sci. Conf., Istanbul; 1979, 3d Conf., Trabzon, Turkey, 1981; cons. Goodyear Tire & Rubber Co., Akron, Ohio, 1984-86, Exxon Nuclear, Richland, Wash., 1985-88. Editor Proc. 2d Thermal Sci. Conf., 1979; contbr. articles in area of thermal scis. to profl. jours. Co-founder Turkish Am. Cultural Assn., Seattle, 1977. Rsch. grantee Goodyear Tire & Rubber Co., 1985-86, Los Alamos (N.Mex.) Nat. Lab., 1989-91, Ben Franklin Tech. Ctr., Bethlehem, 1989-96, Gas Rsch. Inst., 1987-91, Elec. Power Rsch. Inst., 1991-94. Mem. ASHRAE, AIChE. Achievements include research in heat transfer in two-phase flows, boiling, fluidized beds, electronic components and nuclear safety. Avocations: skiing, tennis, chess, bridge. Home: 96 Valley Park S Bethelehem PA 18018-1360 Office: Lehigh U Chem Engring Iacocca Hall 111 Research Dr Bethlehem PA 18015-4732

TWACHTMAN-CULLEN, DIANE, communication disorders and autism specialist; b. Hartford, Conn.; d. Peter and Olga Margaret (DeSarro) DeMaio; m. Walter A. Twachtman Jr., June 4, 1966; children: Jennifer Leigh, Erich Todd; m. James T. Cullen. BA, U. Conn., 1965, MA in Speech-Lang. Pathology, 1968, diploma in early childhood spl. edn., PhD, 1991—. Lic. speech lang. pathologist, Conn. Pvt. practice speech-lang. pathology cons.; exec. dir. Autism and Devel. Disabilities Consultation Ctr., Cromwell, Conn., 1991—; former instr., clin. supr. U. Conn.; adj. faculty mem. Cen. Conn. State U. Author: A Passion to Believe. Mem. Am. Speech-Lang.-Hearing Assn., Conn. Speech-Lang.-Hearing Assn., Autism Soc. Am. (bd. profl. advisors), Autism Soc. Ohio, Internat. Soc. for Augmentative and Alternative Communication, Assn. for Persons With Severe Handicaps, Conn. Down Syndrome Congress, Neurodevel. Treatment Assn., Autism Soc. Conn. (pres.), Sensory Integration Internat., Asperger's Assn. New Eng., Autism Nat. Com., Greater Hartford Autism Soc. (founding), NAMI CAN. Home: 22 S Side Blf Haddam CT 06438-1359

TWADDLE, ANDREW CHRISTIAN, sociology educator; b. Hartford, Conn., Apr. 21, 1938; s. Paul Holmes and Ruth Bridenbaugh (Christian) T.; m. Sarah A. Wolcott, June 15, 1963; children: Lisa, Kristin. AB, Bucknell U., 1961; MA, U. Conn., 1963; PhD, Brown U., 1968. Instr. sociology Coll. of Holy Cross, Worcester, Mass., 1966-67; instr. preventive medicine Harvard U. Med. Sch., Boston, 1967-69; asst. prof. sociology and community medicine U. Pa., Phila., 1969-71; assoc. prof. sociology and family and community medicine U. Mo., Columbia, 1971-74, prof. sociology, 1974—, chmn. dept., 1988-93; guest prof. U. Göteborg, Sweden, 1978-79; Fulbright rsch. fellow Linköping U., Sweden, 1993; guest rschr. Uppsala U., Sweden, 1993. Author: Sickness Behavior and the Sick Role, 1979; co-author: A Sociology of Health, 1987, Disease, Illness and Sickness, 1994, Salvaging Medical Care, 1994. Chair Columbia Bd. Health, 1980-83. Recipient John Kosa Meml. prize Pergamon Press, Eng., 1974. Mem. Internat. Sociol. Assn., Am. Sociol. Assn., Midwest Sociol. Soc., Muleskinners Club (v.p. 1985-87, 94—). Democrat. Unitarian-Universalist. Avocations: genealogy, sailing. Home: 919 Edgewood Ave Columbia MO 65203-2823 Office: U Mo Dept Sociology 109 Sociology Columbia MO 65211

TWAIN, SHANIA, country musician; b. Windsor, Can.. Recs. include Shania Twain, The Woman in Me (Album of Yr. Canadian Country Music Awards, 1995, Female Video Artist of Yr. ABC Radio Networks Country Music Awards, 1995, Album of Yr. Acad. Country Music Awards, 1996, Grammy award for Best Country Album 1996). Recipient Rising Star award Country Music TV/Europe, 1993, Favorite New Country Artist Am. Music Awards, 1995, Female Vocalist award Canadian Country Music Awards, 1995, Outstanding New Artist award RPM's Big Country Awards, 1995, Top New Female Vocalist award Acad. of Country Music Awards, 1996, Favorite New Country Artist award Blockbuster Entertainment Awards, 1996, Female Artist of Yr. Country Music TV/Europe, 1996, Internat. Rising Star award Gt. British Country Music Awards, 1996, Country Female Vocalist award Juno, 1996, Entertainer of Yr. award Juno, 1996, others. Office: Mercury Nashville 66 Music Sq W Nashville TN 37203-3208 also: Fan Club, PO Box 1150, Timmins, ON Canada P4N 7H9*

TWARDOWICZ, STANLEY JAN, artist, photographer; b. Detroit, July 8, 1917; s. Joseph and Anna Ligenski; m. Lillian Dodson, Mar. 15, 1971. Student, Meinzinger Art Sch., Detroit, 1940-44, Skowhegan (Maine) Sch. Painting and Sculpture, summer 1946. Instr. Ohio State U., 1946-51; prof. Hofstra U., 1965-87. Exhibited paintings Mus. Modern Art, Guggenheim Mus., Whitney Mus., Art Inst. Chgo., Carnegie Internat., Pa. Acad. Fine Arts, Am. Acad. Arts and Letters, Houston Mus., Milw. Art Ctr., Peridot Gallery, N.Y.C., others; retrospective exhbns. Hecksher Mus., Huntington, N.Y., 1974, Emily Lowe Gallery, Hempstead, N.Y., 1979, 40 Yr. Retrospective of Paintings Firehouse Gallery, Garden City, N.Y.; exhibited photographs Images Gallery, N.Y.C., one man show: Odeon Gallery, Sag Harbor, N.Y., 1993, Ursala Lanning Gallery, Columbus, Ohio, 1995, Mitchell Algus Gallery, N.Y.C., 1996-97; represented in permanent collections Mus. Modern Art, L.A. County Mus., Newark Mus., Milw. Art Ctr., Ball State Tchrs. Coll., Harvard U., Vassar Coll., Hirshhorn Mus. and Sculpture Garden, others. Guggenheim fellow, 1956. Home: 133 Crooked Hill Rd Huntington NY 11743-3811

TWARDY, STANLEY ALBERT, JR., lawyer; b. Trenton, N.J., Sept. 13, 1951; s. Stanley Albert Twardy and Dorothy M. Stonaker. BS with honors, Trinity Coll., 1973; JD, U. Va., 1976; LLM, Georgetown U., 1980. Bar: Conn. 1976, D.C. 1978, U.S. Supreme Ct. 1979, U.S. Ct. Appeals (2d cir.) 1984. Assoc. Whitman & Ransom, Greenwich, Conn., 1976-77; counsel com. on small bus. U.S. Senate, 1977-79, counsel to Senator Lowell Weicker Jr., 1979-80; ptnr. Silver, Golub & Sandak, Stamford, Conn., 1980-85; U.S. atty. Dist. of Conn., New Haven, 1985-91; chief of staff Office of Gov. Lowell Weicker, Conn., 1991-93; ptnr. Day, Berry & Howard, Stamford, Conn., 1993—. Mem. vestry St. John's Episcopal Ch., Stamford, 1983-86; bd. dirs. Drugs Don't Work!, 1989-93, 94—, chmn. program com., 1989-91; mem. nat. alumni exec. com. Trinity Coll., 1985-90, mem. athletic adv. com., 1992—, bd. trustees, 1996—; bd. dirs. Spl. Olympics World Summer Games Organizing Com., Inc., 1993-95, Easter Seals Rehab. Ctr. S.W. Conn., Inc., 1993—; chmn. City of Stamford Police Chief Selection Panel, 1993-94; mem. area adv. com. U. Conn. at Stamford, 1993—; mem. strategic planning mgmt. com. U. Conn., 1993-95; bd. dirs. Stamford Hosp. Health Found.; trustee Trinity Coll. Mem. ABA, Conn. Bar Assn., Assn. Trial Lawyers Am., Conn. Trial Lawyers Assn., Phi Beta Kappa. Office: One Canterbury Green Stamford CT 06901

TWAROG, SOPHIA NORA, international association administrator; b. Columbus, Ohio, Nov. 29, 1964; d. Leon I. and Katherine (Foster) T.; m. Alberto Klaas, July 2, 1993; 1 child, Kevin Leon Twarog Klaas. BA in Econs. magna cum laude, U. Notre Dame, Ind., 1987; MA in Economics, Ohio State U., 1989, PhD in Economics, 1993. Intern Ctr. of Concern, Washington; vol. in Ctr. America Sisters of the Assumption, Phila., 1987-88; vol. in India Christian Found. for Children & Aging, Kansas City, Mo., 1988; rsch. cons. Nat. Bur. Econ. Rsch., Cambridge, Mass., 1990; grad. teaching assoc. Ohio State U., Columbus, 1989-91; econ. affairs officer UN Conf. on Trade and Devel., Geneva, 1993—; contbd. to preparation of UN Internat. Symposium on Trade Efficiency, Columbus, 1994. Contbr. articles to books and mags. Founder, pres. Overseas Devel. Network-U. Notre Dame, 1986-87; chmn. First Ann. Great Hunger Clean-up, South Bend, Ind., 1987; chmn., co-chmn. Third World Awareness Week, U. Notre Dame, 1986, 87. Recipient Glenna R. Joyce scholar Joyce Found., 1983-87, John W. Gardner Leadership award U. Notre Dame, 1987; U. Multi-Yr. fellow Ohio State U., 1988, 92, rsch. fellow Rheinische Friedrich-Wilhelms U., Bonn, 1990-91, Dice fellow Ohio State U., 1993. Mem. Am. Econ. Assn., Phi Beta Kappa, Phi Kappa Phi. Avocations: traveling, hiking, stained glass artwork, silk painting, salsa dancing, reading. Home: 182 Oakland Park Ave Columbus OH 43214-4122 Office: UN Conf on Trade & Devel, Palais Des Nations, Ch 1211 Geneva 10, Switzerland

TWAY, BOB, professional golfer; m. Tammie Tway. Professional golfer, 1974—; winner Andy Williams Open, 1986, Westchester Classic, 1986, Atlanta Classic, 1986, PGA, 1986. Office: care PGA Tours 112 Tpc Blvd Ponte Vedra Beach FL 32082-3046*

TWEED, JOHN LOUIS, consultant, association executive, lecturer, small business owner; b. Neptune, N.J., Sept. 27, 1947; s. Harry Scullion and Mary Jane (Manniello) T.; m. Joan Marie Parente, Sept. 12, 1970 (div. Apr. 1989); children: Jennifer F., Christin A., Jonathan M.; m. Carolyn G. Joos, June 21, 1992; stepchildren: Jennifer G. Joos, Kimberly K. Joos, Edward S. Joos. AA in Bus. Adminstrn., Ocean County Coll., Toms River, N.J., 1978. Notary pub.; lic. life ins. prodr.; registered legis. agt. Br. mgr. Retail Delivery Service, Paterson, N.J., 1969-75; pres., chief exec. officer Ambicab, Inc., Toms River, 1975 85; proprietor Bob's Auto Wax Shop, Asbury Park, N.J., 1985-87; mng. ptnr. Investment Enterprises, Toms River, N.J., 1984-86; founder John L. Tweed & Assocs., 1984—; v.p. strategic planning Multi-Care Emergency Med. Service, Matawan, 1986-89; founder Formal Limousine Service Inc., Toms River, 1988-90; ptnr. Ultimate Achievement, Toms River, 1994—; v.p. On the Double Messenger Svc., Inc., Aberdeen, N.J., 1988-91; chmn. bd. Performax Inc., Toms River, 1995—; neutral chmn. labor-mgmt. com. N.J. Dept. Labor, 1991. Sec. Toms River Soccer Assn., 1987-89; coach divsn. I girls and divsn. III boys N.J. Youth Soccer Assn., 1981-89; coach Toms River Basketball Assn., 1989-97; pres. Dover Twp. Dem. Club, 1990-91; committeeman Dover Twp., 1990; mem. Cities in Schs. Pre-Implementation Com.; mem. adv. coun. Ocean County Human Svcs.; mem. adv. bd. Toms River Alt. Learning Ctr., Family Life Bur., Diocese of Trenton; mem. Ocean County Planning Bd., 1990-94; gov. rels. dir. Coalition for Responsible Day Care; usher St. Joseph's Ch.; transp./access com. Bldg. a Healthier Ocean County. Sgt. USAF, 1965-69; mem. N.G. Mem. Am. Ambulance Assn. (dir.-at-large 1982-87), Nat. Med. Transp. Assn. (bd. dirs. 1995—), N.J. Assn. Execs., Med. Transp. Assn. N.J. (pres. 1978-84, exec. dir. 1985—), Assn. Residential Care Homes (exec. dir. 1995—), Am. Entrepreneur's Assn., Am. Soc. Assn. Execs., 200 Club Ocean County, Kiwanis Daybreak (bd. dirs. Toms River club 1982-83), Optimist Club (pres. 1992-93, v.p. 1991), Facilitator Divorced and Separated Groups, St. Joseph's Holy Name Soc. (pres. 1996—), Ocean County Coll. Alumni Assn. (sec. 1996—). Roman Catholic. Home and Office: 1587 Country Club Ln Toms River NJ 08753-2789

TWEEDIE, RICHARD LEWIS, statistics educator, consultant; b. Leeton, NSW, Australia, Aug. 22, 1947; came to U.S., 1991; s. Lewis Chabaud and Nel (Dahlenburg) T.; m. Catherine Robertson, Sept. 13, 1971; 1 child, Marianne Louise Robertson. BA, Australian Nat. U., Canberra, 1968, MA, 1969, DSc, 1986; PhD, Cambridge (Eng.) U., 1972. Sr. rsch. scientist Commonwealth Sci. and Indsl. Rsch. Orgn., Canberra, 1974-77; prin. rsch. scientist Commonwealth Sci. and Indsl. Rsch. Orgn., Melbourne, Australia, 1979-81; assoc. prof. U. Western Australia, Perth, 1978; gen. mgr. Siromath Pty. Ltd., Sydney, Australia, 1981-83, mng. dir., 1983-87; prof., dean Bond U., Gold Coast, Australia, 1987-91; prof. stats. Colo. State U., Ft. Collins, 1991—, chair dept. stats., 1992-97. Author: Markov Chains and Stochastic Stability, 1993; also over 100 articles. Fellow Inst. Math. Stats., Internat. Statis. Inst.; mem. Statis. Soc. Australia (pres. 1984-85). Avocations: squash, science fiction. Office: Colo State U Dept Stats Fort Collins CO 80523-1877

TWEEDT, ANNE ELIZABETH, lawyer, legislative policy analyst; b. Hartford, Conn., May 29, 1966; d. William Patrick and Irene Fallon (Kelley) Murray; m. Darin Edward Tweedt, Sept. 11, 1993; children: Madeleine Clare, Samuel Edward. BA, Conn. State U., 1988; JD, Willamette U. Coll. Law, 1993. Bar: Oreg. 1993. Legis. asst. to Spkr. of Ho. Conn. Gen. Assembly, Hartford, 1987-89, fin. com. clk., 1989-90; atty. pvt. practice, Salem, Oreg., 1993-95; health and human svcs. policy analyst Legis. Policy and Rsch., Salem, Oreg., 1995—. Roman Catholic. Office: Policy and Rsch Office State Capitol Salem OR 97310

TWEEDY, ROBERT HUGH, equipment company executive; b. Mt. Pleasant, Iowa, Mar. 24, 1928; s. Robert and Olatha (Miller) T.; B.S. in Agrl. Engring., Iowa State U., 1952; m. Genevieve Strauss, Aug. 15, 1969; children—Bruce, Mark; 1 stepdau., Mary Ellen Francis. Sr. engr. John Deere Waterloo Tractor Works, Waterloo, Iowa, 1953-64; mktg. rep. U.S. Steel Corp., Pitts., 1964-68; mgr. product planning agrl. equipment div. Allis-Chalmers Corp., Milw., 1969-76, mgr. strategic bus. planning Agrl. Equipment Co., 1976-85; mgr. strategic bus. planning Deutz-Allis Corp., 1985-89; project mgr. AGCO Corp., Batavia, Ill., 1989-94; retired, 1994; chmn. agrl. research com. Farm and Indsl. Equipment Inst., Chgo., 1974-76, mem. safety policy adv. com., 1972-89; mem. farm conf. Nat. Safety Council, Chgo., 1973-89; mem. industry sector adv. com. No. 16, U.S. Dept. Commerce, 1982-85; bd. dirs. C.V. Riley Meml. Found. Recipient citation in engring. Iowa State U., 1983. Fellow Am. Soc. Agrl. Engrs. (v.p. 1974-78, pres. 1981-82, gen. chmn. hdqrs. bldg. project 1968-70; chmn. Found. Trustees 1983-88, Wis. Engr. of Year award 1980, McCormick-Case Gold medal 1989); mem. Soc. Automotive Engrs., Masons. Patentee in field. Home: 3301 Alt 19N # 172 Dunedin FL 34698-1524

TWENTYMAN, LEE, foreign service officer, economist; b. Cortland, N.Y., June 12, 1947; s. Gerald L. and Esther (Forbes) T. BS, Cornell U., 1969; MS, U. Md., 1973. Mktg. specialist Export Mktg. Svc., USDA, Washington, 1973; internat. devel. intern U.S. AID, Asuncion, Paraguay, 1973-75; capital projects officer U.S. AID, Santiago, Chile, 1975-76; dir. devel. resources U.S. AID, Lima, Peru, 1976-81; dir. Food for Peace U.S. AID, Washington, 1981-83; dir. for Lebanon U.S. AID, Beirut, 1983-84; dep. dir. for Thailand U.S. AID, Bangkok, 1984-88; dep. dir. for Indonesia U.S. AID, Jakarta, 1988-91; AID dir. to Cambodia U.S. AID, Phnom Penh, 1991—. Mem. Royal Bangkok Sports Club. Address: PO Box 1418 Sarasota FL 34230-1418

TWERSKY, VICTOR, mathematical physicist, educator; b. Lublin, Poland, Aug. 10, 1923; came to U.S., 1928, naturalized, 1940; s. Israel and Gertrude (Levinson) T.; m. Shirley Fine, Feb. 26, 1950; children: Lori, Mark, Nina. B.S., CCNY, 1947; A.M., Columbia U., 1948; Ph.D., N.Y. U., 1950. Assoc. guidance project, biology dept. CCNY, 1946-49; teaching asst. physics N.Y. U., 1949; research assoc. electromagnetic theory Courant Inst. Math. Scis., 1950-53; assoc. Nuclear Devel. Assos., 1951-53; with Sylvania Electric-Gen. Telephone Electronics, 1953-66; head research Electronic Def. Labs., 1958-66, Electronics Systems-West, 1964-66; prof. math. U. Ill. at Chgo., 1966-90, prof. emeritus, 1991; lectr. Stanford U., 1956-58; vis. prof. Technion-Israel Inst. Tech., Haifa, 1962-63, Hebrew U., Jerusalem, summer 1972, Tel Aviv U., summer 1972, Weizmann Inst. Sci., Rehovoth, 1979, Ben-Gurion U., Beersheva, 1979, Stanford U., 1972, 73, 79-80, summers 1967-89, vis. scholar, 1991-97, others; summer mem. Courant Inst. Math. Scis., 1963; assoc. Ctr. for Advanced Study, U. Ill., 1969-70; cons. in field. Editor jours. in field.; contbr. articles to profl. jours. Mem. tech. research com. Am. Found. for Blind, 1947-49; mem. Sch. Math. Study Group, 1964-66, U.S. com. B, Internat. Sci. Radio Union; mem.-at-large Conf. Bd. Math. Scis., 1975-77. Served with AUS, 1943-46. Guggenheim fellow, 1972-73, 79-80. Fellow AAAS, Am. Phys. Soc., Acoustical Soc. Am., Optical Soc. Am. (dir.-at-large 1961), IEEE; mem. Am. Math Soc., Soc. Indsl. and Applied Math., Sci. Research So. Am. (pres. Sequoia br. 1958). Address: 14848 Manuella Rd Los Altos CA 94022-2026

TWICHELL, CHASE, poet; b. New Haven, Conn., Aug. 20, 1950; d. Charles P. and Ann (Chase) T. BA, Trinity Coll., Hartford, 1973; MFA, U. Iowa, 1976. Editor Pennyroyal Pr., W. Hatfield, Mass., 1976-84; assoc. prof. English U. Ala., 1984-88; asst. prof. Hampshire Coll., 1983-84; co-editor Alabama Poetry Series, 1984-88; lectr. Princeton U., 1990—. Author: (poetry) Northern Spy, 1981, The Odds, 1986, Perdido, 1991, The Ghost of Eden, 1995; editor: The Practice of Poetry, 1992, Borderlands, 1993. Recipient Acad. award in lit. Am. Acad. Arts and Letters, 1994; Nat. Endowment for Arts fellow, 1987, 93, Guggenheim fellow, 1990. Office: Princeton U Creative Writing Program 185 Nassau St Princeton NJ 08540

TWIGG-SMITH, THURSTON, newspaper publisher; b. Honolulu, Aug. 17, 1921; s. William and Margaret Carter (Thurston) Twigg-S.; m. Bessie Bell, June 9, 1942 (div. Feb. 1983); children: Elizabeth, Thurston, William, Margaret, Evelyn; m. Laila Roster, Feb. 22, 1983 (div. Dec. 1994); m. Sharon Smith, Feb. 28, 1996. B.Engring., Yale U., 1942. With Honolulu Advertiser, 1946—, mng. editor, 1954-60, asst. bus. mgr., 1960-61, pub., 1961-86; pres., dir., chief exec. officer Honolulu Advertiser, Inc., 1962-93, chmn., 1993—; chmn., dir., CEO Persis Corp.; bd. dirs. Atalanta/Sosnoff Capital Corp., N.Y. Trustee Punahou Sch., Old Sturbridge Inc., Honolulu Acad. Arts, The Contemporary Mus., Hawaii, Mus. Contemporary Art, L.A., The Skowhegan Sch., Maine, Yale Art Gallery, New Haven, Philatelic Found., N.Y., Whitney Mus. Am. Art, N.Y. Maj. AUS, 1942-46. Mem. Honolulu C. of C., Waialae Country Club, Pacific Club, Oahu Country Club, Outrigger Canoe Club. Office: Persis Corp PO Box 3110 96802 605 Kapiolani Blvd Honolulu HI 96813

TWINAME, JOHN DEAN, minister, health care executive; b. Mt. Kisco, N.Y., Dec. 27, 1931; s. C.G. and Constance Jean (Ulmer) T.; m. Carolyn Anderson, Aug. 6, 1955; children: Karen, Jeanne, Julia. A.B., Cornell U., 1953; M.B.A., Harvard U., 1957; M.Div., Union Theol. Sem., 1983. Ordained to ministry Presbyn. Ch. 1983. Sales rep. Am. Hosp. Supply Corp., Evanston, Ill., 1957-60; dir. product research Am. Hosp. Supply Corp., 1961, sales mgr., 1962, asst. to div. pres., 1963, product mgr., 1964, mktg. mgr., 1965-67, mktg. v.p., 1968-69; dep. adminstr. Social and Rehab. Service, HEW, Washington, 1969-70; adminstr. Social and Rehab. Service, HEW, 1970-73; adminstr. Office Health Office Health, Cost of Living Coun., 1973-74; pvt. cons. Mott-McDonald Assocs., Inc., Washington, 1974-76, pres., 1976-78; exec. v.p. Am. Health Found., N.Y.C., 1978-81; co-pres. HealthCare Chaplaincy, Inc., N.Y.C., 1983-93, co-chair exec. com., 1993-94, life trustee, 1995—; cons. exec. Coll. Chaplains, 1997—. Chmn. bd. Chgo. Bus.-Indsl. Project, 1967-68, People to People Com. for Handicapped, 1976-78, Bauman Bible Telecasts, Inc., 1976-80; treas. U.S. com. Internat. Council Social Welfare, 1977-80; sec. bd. dirs. U.S. Council Internat. Year of Disabled Persons, 1979-81; founding bd. mem. Am. Paralysis Assn. (formerly Paralysis Cure Research), 1976-83; bd. dirs. Epilepsy Found. Am., 1978-85, N.Y. Regional Transplant Program, 1988-92; mem. pres. coun. United Hosp. Fund, 1991—; voting mem. Empire Blue Cross/Blue Shield, 1994. 1st lt. AUS, 1953-55. Recipient Disting. Svc. award Coll. Chaplains, 1992, Baker scholar, Harvard U. Home: 163 Harbor Rd Southport CT 06490-1378 Office: HealthCare Chaplaincy Inc 307 E 60th St New York NY 10022-1505

TWINING, CHARLES HAILE, ambassador; b. Balt., Nov. 1, 1940; s. Charles Haile and Martha R. (Caples) T.; m. Irene Verann Metz, May 30, 1995; children: Daniel, Steven. BA, U. Va., 1962; MA, Johns Hopkins U., 1964; postgrad., Cornell U., 1977-78. Joined Fgn. Svc., Dept. State, Washington, 1964; former dep. chief of mission Am. Embassy, Cotonou; former prin. officer Am. Embassy, Douala; former dep. chief of mission Am. Embassy, Ouagadougou, Burkina Faso; former dir. Office of Vietnam, Laos and Cambodia Dept. State, Washington; amb. to Cambodia Phnom Penh, 1993-95; amb. to Cameroon Dept. State, Yasunde, 1996—; Contbr.: Cambodia: 1975-78, 1990. Office: US Ambassador Yaounde Pouch American Embassy DOS Washington DC 20521-2520*

TWINING, HENRIETTA STOVER, retired English language educator; b. Pawnee, Okla., Feb. 25, 1931; d. Leonard E. and Olga (Wolf) Stover; children: Patricia T. Rioux, Donald E. BS in Edn. summa cum laude, Ctrl. State U. (now called U. Ctrl. Okla.), Edmond, Okla., 1962, M in Teaching cum laude, 1967; postgrad., Old Dominion U., 1970, Ala. A&M U., 1980-82. Cert. elem. sch. tchr., secondary sch. tchr., post secondary, Ala. Secondary tchr. Huntsville (Ala.) City Pub. Schs.; elem. and secondary tchr. Okla. City Pub. Schs., Okla.; prof. English Ala. A&M U., Huntsville, 1969-93; also chmn. textbook selection com. Ala. A&M U., Huntsville, Ala., 1981-93; ret., 1993; chair, co-chair sessions Conf. Coll. Composition & Comm. Internat. Orgn., 1988-93; co-chair Nat. Coun. Accreditation of Tchr. Edn., Ala. A&M U., 1988-89; chair English dept., editorial com. instl. self-study reaffirmation accreditation So. Assn. Colls. & Schs., Ala. A&M U., 1992-93. Author: Instructor's Quiz Book to accompany Prentice Hall Reader, 2d edit.; mem. editorial adv. bd. Collegiate Press, 1988-92; textbook reviewer Prentice Hall, Harcourt Brace, Collegiate Press, Allyn & Bacon, Wadsworth, et al., 1982-92; reviewer, editor Ala. A&M Univ. Ofcl. Pubs., 1982-92. Sr. staff mem. Cmty. Action Agy. of Huntsville-Madison/Limestone Counties, Inc., 1978-92. Named Most Outststanding Female Instr., Ala. A&M U. Student Govt. Assn., 1979-80; recipient Recognitions for Cmty. Svc. Mem. NEA, MLA, Ala. Edn. Assn., Nat. Coun. Tchrs. English, Nat. Coun. Accreditation Tchr. Edn., Ala. Coun. Tchrs. English, Assn. Coll. English Tchrs. Ala., Ctrl. State Coll.-U. Ctrl. Okla. Alumni Assn. (life), Alpha Chi, Kappa Delta Pi. Home: 2524 Leeshire Rd Tucker GA 30084-3026

TWINING, LYNNE DIANNE, psychotherapist, writer; b. Midland, Mich., Aug. 14, 1951; d. James and Dorothy Twining; m. Alan Howard Mass. BA in Psychology, Oakland U., 1974; MSW, Wayne State U., 1977; MA in Psychology, Yeshiva U., 1993, D in Psychology, 1995. Diplomate Am. Bd. Clin. Social Work; cert. Bklyn. Inst. Psychotherapy and Psychoanalysis. Social work supr. non-profit orgn., Detroit, 1977-83; co-founder, co-dir. Women Psychotherapists Bklyn., 1986-95, dir., 1995—; pvt. practice Bklyn. and N.Y.C., 1987-95; psychotherapy rschr. Beth Israel Med. Ctr., N.Y.C., 1992-94. Author: (with other) Metro Detroit Guide, 1975; contbg. editor: Detroit Guide, 1983; asst. prodr. docudrama Home; columnist Bklyn. Woman; contbr. articles to profl. jours., papers to profl. confs. Bd. dirs. Progressive Artists and Educators Coalition, Detroit, 1977-79. Fellow Am. Orthopsychiat. Assn.; mem. NASW (diplomate), ACLU (sec. exec. bd. Mich. chpt. 1982-83), APA, Am. Mehtl Health Alliance (charter), Internat. Fedn. Psychoanalytical Edn., N.Y. State Psychol. Assn., N.Y. Acad. Scis., Soc. for Psychotherapy Rsch., Nat. Trust for Hist. Preservation, Tng. Inst. Mental Health Practitioners, Nat. Assn. Advancement Psychoanalysis (affiliate), Women Psychotherapists Bklyn. (founding mem.), Amnesty Internat. (freedom writer), Acad. Cert. Social Workers, Bklyn. Inst. Psychotherapy and Psychoanalysis Grad. Assn (mem. steering com.). Avocations: comparative literature, contemporary dance, jazz. Office: 55 Eastern Pky Apt 3A Brooklyn NY 11238-5913

TWISDALE, HAROLD WINFRED, dentist; b. Roanoke Rapids, N.C., Apr. 28, 1933; s. James Robert and Elma (Smith) T.; m. Barbara Ann Edmonds, Aug. 2, 1958 (div. Apr. 1974); children: Harold Winfred, Leigh Ann.; m. Frances Jean Winstead, July 1983. B.S. in Dentistry, U. N.C., 1955, D.D.S., 1958. Individual practice dentistry Charlotte, N.C., 1961—; head, dept. dental prosthetics Meml. Hosp., 1964-66; lectr. dental subjects.; pres., gen. mgr. WCTU-TV, Charlotte Telecasters, Inc., 1967-69, WATU-TV, Augusta, Ga., Augusta Telecasters, Inc., 1968-69, Television Presentations, Inc., Charlotte, 1967-69; partner Twisdale and Steel Assos., Charlotte, 1965-70; propr. Twisdale Enterprises, Charlotte, 1965-70; Pres. Memphis Telecasters, Inc., 1966-76, Va. Telecasters, Inc., Richmond, 1966—, Durham-Raleigh Telecasters, Inc., Durham, N.C., 1966-70, Gentil Elite, Inc., 1979—. Transp. chmn. Miss N.C. Pageant, 1965; v.p. N.C. Jaycees, 1963-64; Trustee Boys Home, Lake Waccomaw, N.C., 1966-67. Served to capt. USAF, 1958-60. Recipient various awards Charlotte Jaycees, 1962-66. Mem. ADA, N.C. Dental Found., N.C. Dental Soc., Charlotte Dental Soc. (chmn. various coms. 1961—), Am. Analgesia Soc., Internat. Analgesic Soc. (dir. 1980-85), N.C. Dental Soc. Anesthesiology (v.p. 1983-84), Charlotte Analgesia Study Club (co-founder 1970), N.C. 2d Dist. Dental Soc., Metrolina Dental Soc. (founder 1994, pres. 1994-95), U. N.C. Dental Alumni Assn., Southeastern Analgesia Soc. (founder 1972, pres. 1972-74), Lambda Chi Alpha, Delta Sigma Delta. Republican. Methodist. Home: 2221 Streatley Ln Matthews NC 28105-6648 Office: 6623 Executive Circle #110 PO Box 25528 Charlotte NC 28212 *I must give the full credit for any achievement I might have accomplished in life to my mother and father. They not only provided me the means and direction one needs to make even the slightest accomplishment in our mortal life, but most of all, they gave me love, understanding, and a sense of values. These values have never deserted me, nor have they been compromised, even in the darkest hours of depression or during the brightest times of accomplishment. They have been my steady companions.*

TWISS, JOHN RUSSELL, JR., federal government agency executive; b. N.Y.C., Sept. 16, 1938; s. John R. and Edith Jordan (Liddell) T.; m. Mary Hawthorne Sheldon, Jan. 20, 1973; children: John Stewart, Alison McIntosh, Emily Ellsworth. BA, Yale U., 1961. Polar rschr. U.S. Govt., 1961-63; NSF rep. in charge U.S. Sci. Programs in Antarctica, 1964-65; mem. staff internat. divsn. Smith Kline & French Labs., 1966-67; v.p. EPC Labs., 1967-68; sci. leader So. Ocean expdn. NSF, 1968-69, spl. asst. to head Internat. Decade Ocean Exploration, 1970-74; exec. dir. Marine Mammal Commn., Washington, 1974—; mem. strategic adv. coun. Sch. Forestry and Environ. Studies Yale U., 1990-94, assoc. fellow Branford Coll., 1990—; mem. adminstrv. bd. Michael C. Rockefeller Meml. fellowship Harvard U., 1991-97; chmn. bd. dirs. Kokrobitey Sch., Ghana, 1992-95; bd. overseers Leadership Decisions Inst., 1992—; lectr., cons. in field; mem. numerous adv. coms. and U.S. dels. Mem. Met. Club Washington, Army and Navy Club, Squadron A Club, Ends of the Earth Club. Office: Marine Mammal Commn Rm 905 4340 E West Hwy Ste 905 Bethesda MD 20814-4411

TWISS, PAGE CHARLES, geology educator; b. Columbus, Ohio, Jan. 2, 1929; s. George Ransom and Blanche (Olin) T.; m. Nancy Homer Hubbard, Aug. 29, 1954; children—Stephen Ransom, Catherine Grace, Thomas Stuart. B.S. in Geology, Kans. State U., 1950, M.S., 1955; Ph.D., U. Tex. at Austin, 1959. Mem. faculty dept. geology Kans. State U., Manhattan, 1959-95, prof. emeritus, 1995—; assoc. prof. Kans. State U., 1964-69, prof., 1969-95; prof. emeritus Kans. State U., Manhattan, 1995—; also head dept. Kans. State U., 1968-77; geologist agrl. research service U.S. Dept. Agr., 1966-68; research scientist U. Tex., Austin, 1966-67. Contbr. articles to profl. jours. Chmn. Manhattan Council Human Relations, 1960-61; vice pres. Riley County Democratic Club, 1970-71; mem. Dem. Precinct Com., Manhattan, 1970-72, 74-80. Served with USAAF, 1951-53. Fellow Pan Am. Petroleum Found., 1957-58; Shell Found. fellow, 1958-59. Fellow Geol. Soc. Am. (chmn. south cen. sect. 1972-73, 95, sec.-treas. 1980-89, vice-chmn. 1994-95, chmn. 1995-96); mem. Am. Assn. Petroleum Geologists (geologic maps com. 1968-70), Soc. Econ. Paleontologists and Minerologists, Kans. Acad. Sci. (mem. rsch. awards com. 1966-70, assoc. editor 1977-92), AAAS, Am. Soc. Archaeology, Clay Minerals Soc., Kans. Geol. Soc., W. Tex. Geol. Soc., Am. Soc. Agronomy, Soil Sci. Soc. Am., Internat. Soc. Soil Sci., Internat. Assn. Sedimentologists, Assn. Internationale pour l'Etude des Argiles, Am. Quaternary Assn., AAUP (chpt. v.p. 1971-72, chpt. pres. 1972-73), Nat. Assn. Geology Tchrs., Mineral. Soc. Am., Soc. Phytolith Rsch. (organizing com. 1990-92, mem.-at-large, exec. com. 1992-93, pres.-elect 1993-94, pres. 1994-95, past pres. 1995-96), Sigma Xi, Sigma Gamma Epsilon, Gamma Sigma Delta. Home: 2327 Bailey Dr Manhattan KS 66502-2733

TWISS, ROBERT MANNING, prosecutor; b. Worcester, Mass., Aug. 2, 1948; s. Robert Sullivan Jr. and Marion (Manning) T.; m. Joan Marie Callahan, Aug. 4, 1979. BA, U. Mass., 1970; JD, U. San Francisco, 1975; MA in Criminal Justice, Wichita State U., 1979; LLM, Georgetown U., 1981. Bar: Mass. 1976, U.S. Ct. Mil. Appeals 1976, U.S. Dist. Ct. Mass. 1976, Calif. 1989, U.S. Ct. Appeals (1st cir.) 1976, U.S. Ct. Appeals (5th cir.) 1986, U.S. Dist. Ct. (ea. and cen. dist.) Calif. 1989. Atty. office chief counsel IRS, Washington, 1980-86; trial atty. criminal div. U.S. Dept. Justice, Washington, 1986-87; asst. U.S. atty. U.S. Dept. Justice, Sacramento, 1987-93, 94—, chief narcotics and dangerous drugs, 1991-92, 1st asst. U.S. atty., 1992-93, U.S. atty., 1993, exec. assst. U.S. atty., 1994. Contbr. articles to profl. jours. Capt. JAGC, U.S. Army, 1976-80. Named to McAuliffe Honor Soc. U. San Francisco, 1975; recipient Markham award Office Chief Counsel IRS, Washington, 1985. Avocation: athletics. Office: Office US Atty Fed Courthouse 650 Capitol Mall Sacramento CA 95814

TWITCHELL, E. EUGENE, lawyer; b. Salt Lake City, Mar. 4, 1932; s. Irvin A. and E. Alberta (Davis) T.; m. Joyce A. Newey, Aug. 9, 1957 (div. May 1989); children: Robert R., Lauren E., David J., Michael S.; m. Linda Sue Wilson, 1991; children: Bonnie Wilson, Jimmy Wilson, Benjamin Wilson, Stefanie Wilson. Student, Brigham Young U., 1954-55; BA, Calif. State U., Long Beach, 1959; JD, UCLA, 1966. Bar: Mich. 1977, U.S. Dist. Ct. (ea. dist.) Mich., U.S. Supreme Ct. 1987. Contract adminstr. Rockwell No. Am. Aviation, Seal Beach, Calif., 1966-68; sr. contracts adminstr. McDonnell Douglas Corp., Long Beach, Calif., 1968-73; in-house counsel Albert C. Martin & Assocs., L.A., 1973-77; instr. bus. law Golden West Coll., Huntington Beach, 1973-74; corp. counsel, corp. sec. Barton Malow Co., Southfield, Mich., 1977-97, ret., 1997; mem. Detroit EEO Forum, 1983-87; arbitrating cons., 1997—. Pres. Corona (Calif.) Musical Theater, 1975-76; dist. chmn. Boy Scouts of Am.-North Trails, Oakland County, Mich., 1978-80; treas. Barton Malow PAC, Southfield, 1983-97. Sgt. USAF, 1950-52. Mem. ABA, Mich. Bar Assn., Am. Arbitration Assn. (arbitrator Detroit area 1985—), Am. Corp. Counsel Assn. (v.p., dir. 1983-97). Republican. LDS. Avocations: cartooning, painting, karate, music, theatre, writing.

TWITCHELL, KENT, mural artist; b. Lansing, Mich., Aug. 17, 1942; s. Robert E. and Wilma Doris (Berry) T.; m. Susan Catherine Fessler, Dec. 27, 1975 (div. 1986); m. Pandora Seaton, Feb. 23, 1990; children: Rory, Artie. AA, East L.A. Coll., 1969; BA, Calif. State U., 1972; MFA, Otis Art Inst., 1977; DA (hon.), Biola U., 1989; DFA (hon.), Otis Coll. Art and Design, 1996. Illustrator USAF, 1960-65; display artist J.C. Penney Co., Atlanta, 1965-66; abstract artist, painter L.A., 1968-70, mural artist, 1971—; instr. L.A. County High Sch. for the Arts, L.A., 1987-90, Otis/Parsons Art Inst., L.A., 1980-83; cons. Olympic Murals Program, L.A., 1983-84. Executed exterior murals at Union at 12th St. (Steve McQueen monument), L.A., 1971, Hollywood Fwy. (The Freeway Lady), L.A., 1974, Hill St. at Olympic (Edward Ruscha monument), 1987, 405 Fwy. (La Marathon mural), Inglewood, Calif., 1987, 1420 Locust St. (Dr J monument), Phila., 1989, Harbor Fwy. (La Chamber Orch.), L.A., 1991-93, Calif. Theater, San Bernardino, Calif., 1997; one-man shows include: L.A. Mcpl. Art Gallery, 1980, Loyola Marymount U., L.A., 1985, Thinking Eye Gallery, L.A., 1986, Valparaiso (Ind.) U. Art Mus., 1987, Westmont Coll. Art Gallery, Santa Barbara, Calif., 1987, Biola U. Art Gallery, La Mirada, Calif., 1987, Vincent Price Gallery-East L.A. Coll., 1990, Lizardi-Harp Gallery, Pasadena, Calif., 1991, U. Redlands Art Gallery, 1997; exhibited in group shows at L.A. Mcpl. Art Gallery, 1977, 81, 94, 96, Calif. Polytech. U., Pomona, 1978, Santa Monica Coll., 1978, L.A.C.E. Gallery, L.A., 1981, Otis/Parsons Art Inst., L.A., 1987, Mayer Schwarz Gallery, Beverly Hills, 1988, 90, Principia Coll., Elsah, Ill., 1989, Koplin Gallery, Santa Monica, 1992, 95, L.A. County Mus. Art, 1992, Robert Berman Gallery, Santa Monica, 1995, Art Ctr./Coll. Design, Pasadena, 1996, Riverside (Calif.) Art Mus., 1996. Mem. adv. bd. Artists Equity Assn., 1980—, Mural Conservancy of L.A., 1988—. Grantee Calif. Arts Coun., 1978, Nat. Endowment for Arts, 1986. Avocations: theology, classical and bluegrass music. Studio: 9429 Main St PO Box 145 Upper Lake CA 95485-0145

TWOMEY, ELIZABETH MOLLOY, education commissioner; b. Lynn, Mass.; d. Hugh E. and Theresa A. (Callahan) Molloy; children: Ann, Paula, Charles. AB, Emmanuel Coll., 1959; MEd, Mass. State Coll., 1964; EdD, Boston Coll., 1982; LLB (hon.), Notre Dame, Manchester, N.H., 1984. Elem. sch. tchr. Lynn (Mass.) Pub. Schs., 1959-63; English tchr. Reading (Mass.) Pub. Schs., 1973-75, prin., 1975-81, vice prin., 1981-82; supt. Lincoln (Mass.) Pub. Schs., 1982-88; assoc. commr. Dept. Edn., Quincy, Mass., 1988-92; dep. commr. Dept. Edn., Concord, N.H., 1992-94, commr., 1994—. Trustee Emmanuel Coll., Boston, 1975-85, U. N.H., Durham, 1994—. Recipient Disting. Alumni award Emmanuel Coll., 1984. Avocations: walking, reading, gardening. Office: Dept Edn 101 Pleasant St Concord NH 03301-3852

TWOMLEY, BRUCE CLARKE, commissioner, lawyer; b. Selma, Ala., Jan. 23, 1945; s. Robert Clarke and Eleanor Jane (Wood) Anderson T.; m. Sara Jane Minton, June 13, 1979; children: Christopher Mario, Jonathan Marion. BA in Philosophy, Northwestern U., 1967; LLM, U. Calif., San Francisco, 1970; postgrad. Nat. Jud. Coll., Reno, Nev., 1983, 88. Bar: Calif. 1972, Alaska 1973, U.S. Dist. Ct. Alaska, 1973, U.S. Ct. Appeals (9th cir.) 1982. VISTA vol., Anchorage, 1972-73; lawyer Alaska Legal Services Corp., Anchorage, 1973-82; commr. Alaska Comml. Fisheries Entry Commn., Juneau, 1982-83, chmn., 1983—; mem. Gov.'s Fisheries Cabinet, 1983—, Child Support Enforcement Divsn. Rural Task Force, 1985—, Alaska Fedn. of Natives Task Force on IRS and Alaska Native Fishermen, 1994; cons. IRS, Sta. WNED-TV, Buffalo, 1988; mem. Bristol Bay Native Assn. Blue Ribbon Commn. on Ltd. Entry, 1994—; presenter in field. Contbr.: Limited Access Management: A Guidebook to Conservation, 1993. Recipient Alaska Legal Services Disting. Service award, 1983, 92. Mem. Juneau Racquet Club (adv. bd. 1989—), Kappa Sigma (pres. interfraternity council 1966-67). Home: PO Box 20972 Juneau AK 99802-0972 Office: Alaska Comml Fisheries Entry Commn 8800 Glacier Hwy Ste 109 Juneau AK 99801-8079

TYER, TRAVIS EARL, library consultant; b. Lorenzo, Tex., Oct. 23, 1930; s. Charlie Earl and Juanita (Travis) T.; m. Alma Lois Davis, Nov. 6, 1951; children: Alan Ross, Juanita Linn. BS, Abilene Christian U., 1952; BLS, U. North Tex., 1959; AdM in LS, Fla. State U., 1969, postgrad., 1969-71. Librarian, tchr. pub. schs. Gail, Lubbock, and Seminole, Tex., 1952-61; with Dallas Pub. Library, 1961-66, coordinator young adult services, 1962-66; library dir. Lubbock Pub. Library, 1966, Lubbock City-County Libraries, 1967-68; grad. library sch. faculty-state personnel coordinator Emporia (Kans.) State U., 1971-72; sr. cons. profl. devel. Ill. State Library,

Springfield, 1972-80; exec. dir. Great River Libr. Sys., Quincy, Ill., 1980-94; cons. pub. rels. and comm. Alliance Libr. Sys., Quincy, 1994-97; ind. libr. cons., 1997—; lectr. summer workshops Tex. Woman's U., U. Okla., U. Utah, Fla. State U., U. North Tex.; adj. faculty U. Mo., 1986-89; cons. in field; mem. adv. com. Ill. State Libr., 1984-87, 93-96; pres. Resource Sharing Alliance West Ctrl. Ill., Inc., 1981-94, sec., 1994-97; pres. Ill. Libr. System Dirs. Orgn., 1992-94. Contbr. articles to library jours. Inductee U. North Tex. Libr. and Info. Sci. Hall of Fame, 1990. Mem. ALA, Ill. Libr. Assn., Med. Libr. Assn., Ill. Ctr. for the Book, Friends of Librs. U.S.A., U. North Tex. Sch. Libr. and Info. Sci. (life), Friends Lubbock City-County Librs. (life), Assn. Ednl. Comm. and Tech., Ill. Assn. for Ednl. Comm. and Tech., Ill. Sch. Libr. MEdia Assn. Democrat. Mem. Ch. of Christ. Home and Office: 2008 Arrowood Ct Quincy IL 62301-8961

TYERS, GEDDES FRANK OWEN, surgeon; b. Giroux, Man., Can., Nov. 6, 1935; s. William Frederick and Catherine Marguerite (Stoddart) T.; m. Phyllis Amelia Randall, May 14, 1960; children: Randall Geddes, Owen Frank. M.D., U. B.C., 1962. Research and teaching fellow pharmacology U. B.C. Faculty Medicine, 1959-60; intern Vancouver Gen. Hosp., Vancouver, B.C., 1962-63; from asst. instr. to instr. surgery U. Pa. Med. Sch., 1963-68; asst. prof., then assoc. prof. surgery Pa. State U. Coll. Medicine, Hershey, 1970-77; prof., chief div. cardiovascular and thoracic surgery U. Tex. Med. Br., Galveston, 1977-79; prof., head div. cardiovascular and thoracic surgery U. B.C. Faculty Medicine, 1979-97, head divsn. cardiovasc. surgery, 1997—; cons. pacemaker power sources, telemetry monitoring cardiac pacemakers, med. device reliability; dir. tng. program cardiovasc. and thoracic surgery, chmn. residency tng. com.; mem. adv. com. on med. devices Health and Welfare Can., 1993-94. Mem. editorial bd. Jour. Investigative Surgery, 1995—, assoc. editor, 1996—. Recipient 1st prize essay contest Phila. Acad. Surgery, 1966, 1st prize essay contest Pa. Assn. Thoracic Surgery, 1977; Hamish Haney MacIntosh Meml. prize Dr. W.A. Whitelaw scholarship, 1962. Fellow ACS, Royal Coll. Surgeons Can. (nucleus com. cardiovascular surgery), Am. Heart Assn. (coun. cardiovascular surgery); mem. Am. Surg. Assn., N.Am. Soc. Pacing and Electrophysiology (founder), Am. Assn. Thoracic Surgery (reviewer JTCS), Can. Cardiovascular Soc. (med. devices com., mem. working group cardiac pacing, chairperson registry, database subcom.), Soc. Univ Surgeons, Can Med. Assn., Soc. Vascular Surgery, Assn. Acad. Surgery, Western Thoracic Surg. Soc., Internat. Cardiac Pacing and Electrophysiology Soc. (bd. dirs.), Soc. Thoracic Surgeons. Patentee in field. Office: Vancouver Hosp, 700 W 10th Ave Fl C-314, Vancouver, BC Canada V5Z 4E5

TYGRETT, HOWARD VOLNEY, JR., lawyer; b. Lake Charles, La., Jan. 12, 1940; s. Howard Volney and Hazel (Wheeler) T.; m. Linda Lee; children: Carroll Diane, Howard V. III. BA, Williams Coll., 1961; LLB, So. Methodist U., 1964. Bar: Tex. 1964. Gen. atty. SEC, 1964-65; law clk. to chief judge U.S. Dist. Ct. No. Dist. Tex., 1965-67; ptnr. Tygrett & Walker and predecessors, Dallas, 1968—. Bd. dirs. Routh St. Center, 1976-83, Theatre Three, 1974-75, Shakespeare Festival, 1978-81, Suicide and Crisis Ctr., 1983-86. Mem. Tex. Bar Assn., Civitan (lt. gov. Tex. dist. 1976-77, gov. 1979-80), Delta Phi, Delta Theta Phi. Episcopalian. Home: 8530 Jourdan Way Dallas TX 75225-3214 Office: Tygrett & Walker 8111 Preston Rd Ste 600 Dallas TX 75225-6300

TYKESON, DONALD ERWIN, broadcasting executive; b. Portland, Oreg., Apr. 11, 1927; s. O. Ansel and Hillie Martha (Haveman) T.; m. Rilda Margaret Steigleder, July 1, 1950; children: Ellen, Amy, Eric. BS, U. Oreg., 1951. V.p., dir. Liberty Communications, Inc., Eugene, Oreg., 1963-67, pres., chief exec. officer, dir., 1967-83; chmn. bd. Bend Cable Communications, Inc., 1983—, Telecomm Systems, Inc., 1983—; pres. Telecomm Svcs. Inc., 1988—; chmn. bd. Ctrl. Oreg. Cable Advt., Inc., 1992—; chmn., CEO Bend Cable Comm. Inc., 1983—. Bd. dirs. Nat. Coalition Rsch. in Neurol. and Communicative Disorders, 1984-89, Sacred Heart Med. Ctr. Found., 1995—; chmn. Nat. Coalition in Rsch. pub. and govt. info. com., 1986-89, C-SPAN, 1980-89; mem. bus. adv. coun. U. Oreg. Coll. Bus. Adminstrn., 1973—; trustee U. Oreg. Found., 1996—; vice-chmn. we. area Nat. Multiple Sclerosis Soc., 1983—, dir., mem. rsch. and med. programs com., 1986—; trustee Eugene Art Found., 1980-85, Oreg. Health Scis. U. Found., 1988-91, mem. investment com., 1992—; mem. Oreg. Investment Coun. State of Oreg., vice chmn., 1988-92. Mem. Nat. Assn. Broadcasters, Nat. Cable TV Assn. (dir. 1976-83), Chief Execs. Orgn., Vintage Club (bd. dirs. 1996—, chmn. fin. com., treas. 1996—, pres. Custom Lot Assn. 1992—), Country Club Eugene (dir. 1975-77, sec. 1976, v.p. 1977), Multnomah Athletic Club, Arlington Club, Rotary, Elks. Home: 447 Spyglass Dr Eugene OR 97401-2091 Office: Bend Cable Comm Inc PO Box 70006 Eugene OR 97401-0101

TYL, NOEL JAN, baritone, astrologer; b. West Chester, Pa., Dec. 31, 1936. BA, Harvard U., 1958. Bus. mgr. Houston Grand Opera Assn., 1958-60; account exec. Ruder and Finn Pub. Rels., N.Y.C., 1960-62; profl. astrologer, 1970—; editor Astrology Now mag., 1974-79; pres. Tyl Assocs., Inc. pub. rels. and advt., 1980-89; media spokesman; internat. lectr., locations including U.S., Moscow, London, Oslo, Copenhagen, Berlin, Amsterdam, The Netherlands, Toronto, Ont., Tel Aviv, Bologna. Winner Am. Opera Auditions, 1964; opera singer U.S. and Europe, 1964-80; Wagner specialist; appearances include Vienna State Opera, Düsseldorf, Rome, Milan, Barcelona, N.Y.C. Opera, also throughout U.S.; author: Principles and Practice of Astrology, 12 vols., 1973-75, Teaching and Study Guide, 1976, The Horoscope as Identity, 1974, Holistic Astrology, 1980, Prediction in Astrology, 1991, Synthesis and Counseling in Astrology, 1994. Home: 17005 E Player Ct Fountain Hills AZ 85268

TYLER, ANNE (MRS. TAGHI M. MODARRESSI), author; b. Mpls., Oct. 25, 1941; d. Lloyd Parry and Phyllis (Mahon) T.; m. Taghi M. Modarressi, May 3, 1963; children: Tezh, Mitra. B.A., Duke U., 1961; postgrad., Columbia U., 1962. Author: If Morning Ever Comes, 1964, The Tin Can Tree, 1965, A Slipping-Down Life, 1970, The Clock Winder, 1972, Celestial Navigation, 1974, Searching for Caleb, 1976, Earthly Possessions, 1977, Morgan's Passing, 1980, Dinner at the Homesick Restaurant, 1982, The Accidental Tourist, 1985, Breathing Lessons, 1988 (Pulitzer Prize for fiction 1989), Saint Maybe, 1991, (juvenile) Tumble Tower, 1993, Ladder of Years, 1995; contbr. short stories to nat. mags. Home: 222 Tunbridge Rd Baltimore MD 21212-3422

TYLER, BARBARA A., museum director. Exec. dir., CEO McMichael Can. Art Collection, Kleinburg, Ont. Office: McMichael Can Art Collect, Islington Ave, Kleinburg, ON Canada L0J 1C0*

TYLER, CARL WALTER, JR., physician, health research administrator; b. Washington, Aug. 22, 1933; s. Carl Walter and Elva Louise (Harlan) T.; m. Elma Hermione Matthias, June 23, 1956 (dec. Dec. 1991); children: Virginia Louise, Laureen, Jeffrey Alan, Cynthia T. Crenshaw. A.B., Oberlin Coll., 1955; M.D., Case-Western Res. U., 1959. Diplomate Am. Bd. Ob-Gyn. Rotating intern Univ. Hosps. of Cleve., 1959-60, resident in ob-gyn, 1960-64; med. officer USPHS, 1964; obstetrician-gynecologist USPHS Indian Health Service, Tahlequah, Okla., 1964-66; epidemic intelligence service officer Bur. Epidemiology, Ctrs. for Disease Control, Atlanta, 1966-67; dir. family planning evaluation div. Bur. Epidemiology, Ctrs. for Disease Control, 1967-80, asst. dir. for sci., 1980-82, acting dir. Ctr. for Health Promotion and Edn., 1982, dir. epidemiology program office, 1982-88, med. epidemiologist Office of Dir., 1988-90, asst. dir. for acad. programs, pub. health practice program office, 1990—; clin. assoc. prof. ob.-gyn. Emory U. Sch. Medicine, Atlanta; clin. asst. prof. ob-gyn Emory U. Sch. Medicine, Atlanta, 1966-80, clin. assoc. prof., 1980—, also clin. assoc. prof. preventive medicine and community health, adj. assoc. prof. sociology Coll. Arts and Scis., 1977-90; adj. assoc. prof. pub. health Sch. Pub. Health, 1990—; clin. prof. pub. health and community medicine Morehouse Sch. Medicine, Atlanta, 1990—; mem. Nat. Sleep Disorders Rsch. Commn., 1990—; mem. adv. com. on oral contraception WHO, Geneva, 1974-77, mem. adv. com. maternal and child health, 1982-88; lectr. in field. Editor: (monograph) Venereal Infections; assoc. editor: Maxcy-Rosenau Textbook of Public Health and Preventive Medicine, 13th edit., 1992; contbr. articles to profl. jours. Chmn. Dekalb County Schs. com. on instruction programs, subcom. on health, phys. edn. and safety, (Ga.), 1967-68; active Ga. State Soccer Coaches Assn., Atlanta, 1973-79, DeKalb County YMCA. Josiah Macy Found. fellow, 1956-58; NIH grantee, 1961-64; recipient Superior Service award, 1974, Meritorious Service medal USPHS, 1984, Disting. Service medal, 1988; Carl S. Shultz Population award APHA, 1976, medal of Excellence Ctrs. for Disease Control, 1984. Fellow Am. Coll. Ob-Gyn (chmn. community health com. 1974-77), Am. Coll. Preventive Medicine, Am. Coll. Epidemiol.; mem. Am. Epidemiologic Soc., Internat. Epidemiologic Assn., Assn. Tchrs, Preventive Medicine (bd. dirs. 1988-89), Am. Pub. Health Assn. (governing council 1976-78), Assn. Planned Parenthood Profls., Population Assn. Am., Sierra Club. Avocations: photography; camping. Office: HHS Ctrs for Disease Control Mailstop E-42 1600 E Clifton Rd NE Atlanta GA 30307-1276

TYLER, DAVID EARL, veterinary medical educator; b. Carlisle, Iowa, July 12, 1928; s. Guy Earl and Beatrice Virginia (Slack) T.; m. Alice LaVon Smith, Sept. 6, 1952; children: John William, Anne Elizabeth. B.S., Iowa State U., 1953, D.V.M., 1957, Ph.D., 1963; M.S., Purdue U., 1960. Instr. dept. vet. sci. Purdue U., 1957-60; asst. prof. dept. pathology Coll. Vet. Medicine, Iowa State U., 1960-63, asso. prof., 1963-66; prof., head dept. pathology and parasitology Coll. Vet. Medicine, U. Ga., 1966-71, head dept. pathology, 1971-79, prof., 1971-91, prof. emeritus, 1991—, ret., 1991; co-founder internat. vet. pathology slide bank, 1984, co-dir., 1984—; apptd. discussant Charles L. Davis Found. for Advancement Vet. Pathology, 1977-91. Cub Scout master, 1967-69, scout com. chmn., 1970-72; elder Disciples of Christ Ch., 1968—, chmn. ch. bd., 1973-74, 92-94; mem. citizens com. to County Bd. Edn., 1968-70; bd. dirs. Christian Coll., Ga., 1974-77. With AUS, 1946-48. Recipient Borden award Gail Borden Co., 1956, Norden Disting. Teaching award Norden Labs., 1964, 69, 81, 85, 91, Prof. of Yr. award Coll. Vet. Medicine, Iowa State U., 1965, Outstanding Prof. award Coll. Vet. Medicine, U. Ga., 1970, 76, 80-81, 83, 86, 87-88, 90, Joshia Meigs Teaching award, 1985, Stange award Coll. Vet. Med., Iowa State U., 1987, Phi Zeta Teaching award, 1985, N.Am. Outstanding Tchr. award, 1991, Omicron Delta Kappa Outstanding Prof. award U. Ga., 1981, Harold W. Casey award C.L. Davis Found., 1995. Mem. AVMA, Farm House, Am. Coll. Vet. Pathologists (mem. council 1975-77, exam. com. 1982-85), Am. Assn. Vet. Med. Colls. (chmn. com. teaching-learning materials 1975-77), Nat. Program for Instructional Devel. in Vet. Pathology (adv. com. 1976-77), Aghon, Sigma Xi, Phi Eta Sigma, Alpha Zeta, Gamma Sigma Delta, Phi Kappa Phi, Phi Zeta (chpt. sec.-treas. 1982-84), Omega Tau Sigma. Home: 160 Sunnybrook Dr Athens GA 30605-3348

TYLER, DONALD EARL, urologist; b. Ontario, Oreg., Oct. 3, 1926; s. Charles Maurice and Iva (Hess) T.; 1 child, Paul Donald. MD, U. Oreg. Med. Sch., 1950; JD, U. Denver Coll. Law, 1967. Diplomate Am. Bd. Urology, Am. Coll. Legal Medicine. Fellow in gen. surgery, urology The Mayo Found., Rochester, Minn., 1952, 55-58; clin. instr. in urology U. Utah Med. Sch., Salt Lake City, 1959-64. Author: A New and Simple Theory of Gravity, 1970, Originations of Life from Volcanoes and Petroleum, 1983, Earliest Man of America in Oregon, USA: With Photographs of Paleolithic Artifacts, 1986, The Other Guy's Sperm: The Cause of Cancer and Other Diseases, 1994. Served to lt. USNR, 1944-45, 52-55, WWII, Korea. Mem. Alpha Omega Alpha, Phi Eta Sigma. Avocations: archaeology, anthropology, geology, skiing, swimming. Home: 1092 SW 2nd Ave Ontario OR 97914-2121

TYLER, GAIL MADELEINE, nurse; b. Dhahran, Saudi Arabia, Nov. 21, 1953 (parents Am. citizens); d. Louis Rogers and Nona Jean (Henderson) Tyler; m. Alan J. Moore, Sept. 29, 1990; 1 child, Sean James. AS, Front Range C.C., Westminster, Colo., 1979; BS in Nursing, U. Wyo., 1989. RN. Ward sec. Valley View Hosp., Thornton, Colo., 1975-79; nurse Scott and White Hosp., Temple, Tex., 1979-83, Meml. Hosp. Laramie County, Cheyenne, Wyo., 1983-89; dir. DePaul Home Health, 1989-91; field staff nurse Poudre Valley Hosp. Home Care, 1991—; parish nurse Cornerstone Evangelical Free Ch., 1996—. Avocations: collecting internat. dolls, sewing, reading, travel.

TYLER, H. RICHARD, physician; b. Bklyn., Oct. 16, 1927; s. Max M. and Beatrice F. T.; m. Joyce Colby, June 17, 1951; children—Kenneth, Karen, Douglas, Lori. AB, Syracuse U., 1947; BS in Medicine, Washington U., 1951, MD, 1951; MA (hon.), Harvard U., 1989. Diplomate Am. Bd. Neurology and Psychiatry. Intern Peter Bent Brigham Hosp., Boston, 1951-52; resident in neurology Boston City Hosp., 1952-54; public health fellow Neurol. Inst., Queen's Sq., London, Salpêtrière, Paris, 1954-55; asst. in pediatrics and neurology Johns Hopkins Hosp., Balt., 1955-56; neurologist Peter Bent Brigham Hosp., Boston, 1956-74; asst. in neurology Harvard Med. Sch., Boston, 1956-59; assoc. in neurology Harvard Med. Sch., 1959-61, instr., 1961-64, asst. prof., 1964-68, assoc. prof., 1968-73, prof., 1974—; sr. physician Brigham and Women's Hosp., Boston, 1974—, dir. neurol. svc., 1979-88. Co-editor: Current Neurology I and II, 1979, 80; mem. editorial bd.: Jour. Neurology, 1979-84, Classics on Neurology and Neurosurgery Libr., 1983—; contbr. articles in field to profl. jours. Trustee Brookline Pub. Library, 1970—, chmn. bd. trustees, 1985-86, 90-91. Served with U.S. Army, 1946-47. Mem. Am. Neurol. Assn., Am. Acad. Neurology, Mass. Med. Soc. Office: 1 Brookline Pl Brookline MA 02146-7224

TYLER, HAROLD RUSSELL, JR., lawyer, former government official; b. Utica, N.Y., May 14, 1922; s. Harold Russell and Elizabeth (Glenn) T.; m. Barbara L. Eaton, Sept. 10, 1949; children: Bradley E., John R., Sheila B. Grad., Philips Exeter Acad., 1939; AB, Princeton U., 1943; LLB, Columbia U., 1949. Bar: N.Y. 1950. Pvt. practice N.Y.C., 1950-53, 55-60; mem. firm Gilbert & Segall, 1957-60, 61-62; asst. U.S. atty., 1953-55, asst. atty. gen. U.S. charge civil rights div., 1960-61; commr. N.Y.-N.J. Waterfront Commn., 1961-62; U.S. dist. judge So. Dist., N.Y., 1962-75; dep. atty. gen. U.S., 1975-77; mem. firm Patterson, Belknap, Webb & Tyler, N.Y.C., 1977—; adj. prof. NYU Law Sch., 1966-75, Albany (N.Y.) Law Sch., 1991—; vis. lectr. Inst. Criminology, Cambridge, 1968; vice chmn. Adminstrv. Conf. USA, 1975-77. Bd. dirs. Fed. Jud. Center, Washington, 1968-72; trustee Practising Law Inst., N.Y.C.; chmn. William Nelson Cromwell Found., Law Center Found. Home: 2 Beekman Pl New York NY 10022-8058 Office: Patterson Belknap Webb & Tyler 1133 Avenue Of The Americas New York NY 10036-6710

TYLER, JOHN RANDOLPH, lawyer; b. Canandaigua, N.Y., Aug. 3, 1934; s. John Randolph and Helen McGregor (Tewinkle) T.; m. Carroll Smith, Apr. 1, 1962 (div. Sept. 28, 1981); children: John R. III, Carroll Barrett; m. Janet MacAdam, June 5, 1982. BA cum laude, Amherst Coll., 1956; JD, Harvard U., 1963. Bar: N.Y. 1983. Assoc. Nixon, Hargrave, Devans & Doyle, Rochester, N.Y., 1963-70, ptnr., 1971—. Contbr. articles to profl. jours. Bd. dirs. Geva Theater, 1990—, treas., 1993-96, Flower City Habitat, 1992—. Lt. USNR, 1956-59. Mem. ABA, N.Y. State Bar Assn. (chmn. exec. com. bus. corp. banking sect. 1981-82, ho. of dels. 1984-87, 95-97, opinion com. 1986—), Chi Psi. Republican. Epicopalian. Clubs: Genesee Valley (Rochester), Adirondack League. Avocations: sailing, skiing, environ. matters. Home: 25 Oak Ln Rochester NY 14610-3133 Office: Nixon Hargrave Devans & Doyle PO Box 1951 Clinton Sq Rochester NY 14604-1729

TYLER, LLOYD JOHN, lawyer; b. Aurora, Ill., May 28, 1924; s. Lloyd J. and Dorothy M. (Curtis) T.; m. Inez Chappell Busener, Feb. 25, 1970; children by previous marriage: Barbara Tyler Miller, John R., Benjamin C., Robert B., Amy C. B.A., Beloit Coll., 1948; J.D., U. Mich., 1951. Bar: Ill., Mich. bars 1951. Mem. firm Sears, Streit, Tyler and Dreyer and (predecessors), Aurora, Ill., 1951-62, Tyler and Hughes (P.A.), Aurora, 1962—; lectr., speaker on profl. subjects, 1964—. Contbr. chpts. to profl. books, articles to profl. jours. Democratic precinct committeeman, 1954-59; mem. Batavia (Ill.) Sch. Bd., 1959-62. Served with USAAF, 1943-46. Fellow Am. Bar Found.; mem. Am. Bar Assn. (Ho. of Dels. 1975-79), Ill. Bar Assn. (gov. 1970-78, pres. 1978-79, chmn. legislative com. 1980, task force on alternative forms of legal service 1981-82, long range planning com. 1982-88, fed. judiciary appointment com. 1984-90, spl. com. on merit selection 1987—), Ill. Bar Found. (pres. 1972-75), Ill. Inst. Continuing Legal Edn. (dir. 1971-75, 77-79), Ill. Lawyers Polit. Action Com. (trustee 1982—, chmn. 1987-88), Soc. Trial Lawyers Ill., Appellate Lawyers Assn., Phi Beta Kappa, Omicron Delta Kappa. Presbyterian. Home: 701 Fargo Blvd Geneva IL 60134-3227 Office: Tyler and Hughes PO Box 4425 Aurora IL 60507-4425

TYLER, NOEL, geological researcher and educator; b. Johannesburg, South Africa, Dec. 6, 1950; came to U.S., 1978; s. Paul and Lorna (Timms) T.; m. Erica E. Forster, Jan. 27, 1976; children: Kristin, Caroline. BSc, U. Witwatersrand, South Africa, 1975, BSc with honours, 1976, MSc in Geology cum laude, 1978; PhD, Colo. State U., 1981. Rsch. officer Econ. Geology rsch. unit U. Witwatersrand, 1976-78; rsch. assoc. Bur. Econ. Geology, U. Tex., Austin, 1981-85, rsch. scientist, 1985-91, lectr. dept. geol. scis., 1988—, assoc. dir. oil resources, 1991-94, dir., Tex. state geologist, 1994—; cons. BP, Mobil, Texaco, Chevron, Dept. Energy, Petrobras, So. Oil Exploration Corp., others, 1986—; adj. prof. Curtin U. Tech., Perth, Australia, 1995—. Author reports, monographs, brochures, pamphlets and bulls.; contbr. chpts. to books, articles to profl. jours. Colo. Fellowship Fund fellow, 1980, Jim and Gladys Taylor Edn. Trust scholar, 1978-80; grantee Coun. for Sci. and Indsl. Rsch. Bursary, 1975, Johannesburg Consol. Investment Corp., 1976-77; named Disting. Alumnus for 1994 Coll. of Forestry and Natural Resources, Colo. State U. Fellow Geol. Soc. Am.; mem. Am. Assn. Petroleum Geologists, Soc. Petroleum Engrs., Soc. Econ. Paleontologists and Mineralogists. Avocations: boating, hiking, squash, tennis. Office: Bur Econ Geology University Sta Box X Austin TX 78713

TYLER, PAYNE BOUKNIGHT, museum executive; b. Johnston, S.C., Mar. 11, 1933; d. William Miller and Frances Payne (Turner) B.; m. Harrison Ruffin Tyler, July 17, 1958; children, Harrison Ruffin Tyler Jr., Julia Gardiner Tyler Samaniego, William Bouknight. BA, U. S.C., 1955; post-grad., N.Y. Sch. Interior Design, 1956. Pres. Historic Sherwood Forest Corp., Charles City, Va., 1975—. Author: James River Plantations Cookbook, 1983, Virginia Presidents Cookbook, 1989. Active Colonial Dames Am., Richmond, 1959, Jr. League Richmond, Va., 1959—; Jr. League vol. Valentine Mus. Docent, Richmond, 1959-60; bd. mem., pres. Hist. Richmond Found., 1960-61; regional worker Rep. Party, Charles City, 1989-96; sec. Planning Commn., Charles City, 1990—; coun. Va. Mus. Fine Arts; others. Mem. U.S. Polo Assn., Nat. Soc. Colonial Dames of Am., Jamestowne Soc., Jr. League Richmond, Deep Run Hunt Club (Richmond), Princess Anne Hunt Club (Charles City), Santa Fe Hunt Club (Rancho Santa Fe, Calif.), Whiskey Road Hounds (Aiken, S.C.), Rancho Santa Fe Polo Club, Country Club Va. (Richmond), Richmond Cotillion and Va. Creepers (Richmond), Garden Club Am. (Richmond). Episcopalian. Avocations: fox hunting, polo, painting, writing. Home: PO Drawer 8 5416 Tuckahoe Ave Richmond VA 23226 Office: Historic Sherwood Forest Corp PO Drawer 8 Sherwood Forest Plantation Charles City VA 23030

TYLER, PRISCILLA, retired English language and education educator; b. Cleve., Oct. 23, 1908; d. Ralph Sargent and Alice Lorraine (Campbell) T. BA in Latin and Greek, Radcliffe Coll., 1932; MA in Edn., Case Western Res. U., 1934, PhD in English, 1953; LLD (hon.), Carleton U., Ottawa, Ont., Can., 1993. Parole officer, case worker Cleve. Sch. for Girls, 1934-35; tchr. English, Latin and French Cleveland Heights (Ohio) Pub. Schs., 1935-45; instr. to asst. prof. English Flora Stone Mather Coll., Cleve., 1945-59; asst. dean Flora Stone Mather Coll. Western Reserve U., Cleve., 1957-59; asst. prof. edn., head dept. English Sch. of Edn. Harvard U., Cambridge, Mass., 1959-63; assoc. prof. English, U. Ill., Champaign-Urbana, 1963-67, dir. freshman rhetoric, 1966-67; prof. English and edn. U. Mo., Kansas City, 1967-78, prof. emeritus, 1978—; instr. N.S. (Can.) Dept. Edn., Halifax, summers 1972-73; condr. numerous seminars; former lectr. U. Calif., Berkeley, U. Chgo., Purdue U., U. Mo., Columbia, U. Nebr., Emory U., Fresno State U., Calif. State U., Hayward, San Jose State Coll., Mills Coll., Ala., Tift Coll., Ga., Va. Poly. Inst. and Midwestern U., Tex. Editor: Harpers Modern Classics, 19 vols., 1963, Writers the Other Side of the Horizon, 1964, (with Maree Brooks) Inupiat Paitot, 1974; co-author introduction and co-editor: (with Maree Brooks) Sevukakmet, Ways of Life on St. Lawrence Island (Helen Slwooko Carius), 1979, (with Maree Brooks) The Epic of Qayaq, 1995 (Lela Kiana Oman), World Literature Written in English, 1965-69; interviewed authors, Jan Carew, Wilson Harris, Guyana, George Lamming, Barbados, Christopher Okigbo and Chinua Achebe, Nigeria, Derek Wolcott, St. Lucia, Andrew Salkey, Jamaica; also articles. Mem. Ohio Gov.'s Com. on Employment of Physically Handicapped, 1957; mem. Friends of Art of Carleton U., Nelson Atkins Mus. Art, Kansas City, Ottawa (Kans.) Art Gallery, Friends of Libr., Ottawa, Kansas. Recipient Outstanding Achievement and Contbns. in Field of Edn. award Western Res. U., 1962, Disting. Alumna award Laurel Sch., Cleve., 1994; Priscilla Tyler Endowment Fund named in her honor Case Western Res. U., 1980. Mem. MLA, NEA, Archaeol. Inst. Am., Nat. Coun. Tchrs. English (v.p. 1963, mem. com. on history of the profession 1965-68, Commn. on Composition 1968-71, trustee Rsch. Found. 1970-78, Disting. Svc. award 1978), Conf. on Coll. Composition and Comm. (pres. 1963), Arctic Inst. N.Am., Inuit Art Found., Franklin County (Kansas) Hist. Assn., Calif. Assn. Tchrs. English (hon.. Curriculum Commn. Ctrl. Calif.), Delta Kappa Gamma (pres. Upsilon chpt. 1950-52). Democrat. Presbyterian. Avocations: collecting rare books of American and English grammar, Inuit art, history and culture, travel. Home: 4213 Kentucky Ter Ottawa KS 66067-8715

TYLER, RICHARD, fashion designer; b. Sunshine, Australia, Sept. 22, 1950; m. Doris Taylor (div.); 1 child, Sheridan; m. Lisa Trafficante, 1989; 1 child, Edward Charles. Prin. Zippity-doo-dah, Melbourne, Australia, 1968-80, Tyler-Trafficante, L.A., 1988—; design dir. Anne Klein Collection, N.Y.C., 1993-94. Designer Richard Tyler Couture introduced for Women, 1989, Richard Tyler Collection debut for Men, April 1997, Richard Tyler Shoes for Women, 1996, Richard Tyler Collection for Women, 1997, Richard Tyler Shoes for Men, 1997. Recipient New Fashion Talent Perry Ellis award Coun. Fashion Designers Am., 1993, Womenswear Designer of Yr. award, 1994, Perry Ellis award for new fashion talent in menswear, 1995. Office: 1617 E 7th St Los Angeles CA 90021-1207

TYLER, RICHARD JAMES, personal and professional development educator; b. Warwick, R.I., June 16, 1957; s. Virginia (Campanella) Tyler. Gen. mgr. Gem Exch., Charlotte, N.C., 1977; nat. sales mgr. So. Merchandising, Charlotte, 1978; pres. Direct Import Distributing, New Orleans, 1981; nat. territorty dir. TV Fanfare Pub., 1982; v.p. ARC Pub., New Orleans, 1983; exec. v.p., gen. mgr. Superior Bedrooms, Inc., 1984; CEO Shopportunities, Inc., Houston, Richard Tyler Internat., Inc., Houston, Tyler Internat. Rsch. Inst., Inc., Houston, Internat. Bus. Inst., Inc., Houston; mem. adv. bd. Sales and Mktg. Mag., N.Y.C., 1991—; founder Leadership of Tomorrow program; speaker, cons. in field. Author: Creating Excellence in Quality and Service, 1991, The Science and Art of Excellent Selling, 1993, Richard Tyler's Guide to Entrepreneurial Excellence, 1993, Richard Tyler's Smart Business Strategies. The Guide to Small Business Marketing Excellence, 1995; pub. newsletter Richard Tyler's Excellence Edge, 1992; contbr. articles to profl. pubis. Mem. Rep.-Senatorial Inner Cir., Washington, 1991. Mem. ASTD, Internat. Platform Assn., Nat. Speakers Assn. Avocations: sports, theater, deep sea fishing, amateur wrestling.

TYLER, RONNIE CURTIS, historian; b. Temple, Tex., Dec. 29, 1941; s. Jasper J. and Melba Curtis (James) T.; m. Paula Eyrich, Aug. 24, 1974. BSE, Abilene (Tex.) Christian Coll., 1964; MA, Tex. Christian U., 1966, PhD (Univ. fellow), 1968; DHL, Austin Coll., 1986. Instr. history Austin Coll., Sherman, Tex., 1967-68; asst. prof. Austin Coll., 1968-69; asst. dir. collections and programs Amon Carter Mus., Ft. Worth, 1969-86; dir. Tex. State Hist. Assn., 1986—; prof. history U. Tex., Austin, 1986—; adj. prof. history Tex. Christian U., 1971-72; cons. visual materials Western. Am. art. Author: Santiago Vidaurri and the Confederacy, 1973, The Big Bend: The Last Texas Frontier, 1975, The Image of America in Caricature and Cartoon, 1975, The Cowboy, 1975, The Mexican War: A Lithographic Record, 1974, The Rodeo Photographs of John Addison Stryker, 1978, Visions of America: Pioneer Artists in a New Land, 1983, Views of Texas: The Watercolors of Sarah Ann Hardinge, 1852-56, 1988, Nature's Classics: John James Audubon's Birds and Animals, 1992, Audubon's Great National Work: The Royal Octavo Edition of the Birds of America, 1993, Prints of the West, 1994; (with Paula Eyrich Tyler) Texas Museums: A Guidebook, 1983; editor: (with Lawrence R. Murphy) The Slave Narratives of Texas, 1974, Posada's Mexico, 1979, Alfred Jacob Miller: Artist on the Oregon, 1982, Wanderings in the Southwest in 1855 (J.D.B. Stillman), 1990. Pres. Tarrant County (Tex.) Hist. Soc., 1975-77. Good Neighbor Commn. scholar Instituto Tecnologico Monterrey, Mex., 1967; Am. Philos. Soc. grantee, 1970-71; recipient H. Bailey Carroll award, 1974; Coral H. Tullis award, 1976. Mem. Am. Antiquarian Soc., Tex. Inst. Letters (Friends of Dallas Pub. Libr. award), Philos. Soc. Tex. (sec. 1990—), Phi Beta Kappa. Home: 4400 Balcones Dr Austin TX 78731-5710 Office: Ctr Studies Tex Hist 2/306 Richardson Hall University Station Austin TX 78712

TYLER, STEVEN, singer; b. Yonkers, N.Y., Mar. 26, 1948; children: Liv, Mia. Lead singer Aerosmith, 1970—. Albums include Aerosmith, 1973,

Get Your Wings, 1974, Toys in the Attic, 1975, Rocks, 1976, Pure Gold, 1976, Draw the Line, 1977, Live Bootleg, 1978, A Night in the Ruts, 1979, Greatest Hits, 1980, Rock in a Hard Place, 1982, Done with Mirrors, 1986, Classics Live, 1986, Permanent Vacation, 1987, Gems, 1989, Pump, 1989, Pandora's Box, 1991, Get a Grip, 1993, Big Ones, 1994, Box of Fire, 1994, Nine Lives, 1997. recipient w/Aerosmith: MTV Video of the Year for "Cryin'", 1994, Grammy award Best Rock Group. Office: c/o Aerosmith Geffen/GDC Records 9130 W Sunset Blvd Los Angeles CA 90069-3110

TYLER, W(ILLIAM) ED, printing company executive; b. Cleve., Nov. 3, 1952; s. Ralph Tyler and Edith (Green) Kauer; m. Vickie Sue Boggs, Feb. 7, 1976; children: Stacia Leigh, Adam William. BS in Elec. Engring., Ind. Inst. Tech., 1974; MBA, Ind. U., 1977; postgrad., Harvard U., 1981; postgrad. in bus., Baruch U., 1988. Electronic engr. to various mgmt. positions R.R. Donnelley & Sons Co., Warsaw, Ind., 1974-89; group pres. R.R. Donnelley & Sons Co., N.Y.C., 1989—, sector pres., 1993—, exec. v.p., 1995—. Office: R R Donnelley & Sons Co 77 W Wacker Dr Chicago IL 60601

TYLER, WILLIAM HOWARD, JR., advertising executive, educator; b. Elizabethtown, Tenn., May 21, 1932; s. William Howard and Ethel Margaret (Schueler) T.; m. Margery Moss, Aug. 31, 1957; children: William James, Daniel Moss. Student, Iowa State U., 1950-52, U. Iowa, 1952; AB in Lit., BJ in Advt., U. Mo., 1958, MA in Journalism, 1966. Advt. mgr. Rolla (Mo.) Daily News, 1958-59; instr. sch. journalism U. Mo., Columbia, 1959-61; copy writer, then v.p. copy dir. D'Arcy Advt. Agy., St. Louis, 1961-67; writer, producer, creative supr. Gardner Advt. Co., St. Louis, 1967-69; sr. v.p., creative dir. D'Arcy, McManus, Masius, St. Louis, 1969-77; exec. v.p., creative dir. Larson Bateman Advt. Agy., Santa Barbara, Calif., 1977-80; v.p. advt. Pizza Hut, Inc., Wichita, Kans., 1980-82; v.p., creative dir. Frye-Sills/Y&R, Denver, 1980; exec. v.p., creative dir. Gardner Advt. Co., St. Louis, 1982-88; exec. v.p., ptnr., creative dir. Parker Group, St. Louis, 1988-91; pres. TYLERtoo Advt./Communications, St. Louis, 1991—; assoc. prof. St. Louis U., 1993—. Mng. editor St. Louis Advt. Mag., 1992-95. Trustee Blackburn Coll., Carlinville, Ill., 1983-84; bd. advisors U. Mo. Journalism Sch., 1986-91. 1st lt. USMC, 1952-55, Korea. Mem. St. Louis Advt. and Mktg. Assn. (bd. dirs. 1987-90), U. Mo. Alumni Assn. (bd. dirs. 1969-70), St. Louis Ind. Prodn. Profls., St. Louis Radio Profls. Episcopalian. Office: Saint Louis U Dept Comm 3733 W Pine Saint Louis MO 63108

TYNDALL, DAVID GORDON, business educator; b. Bangalore, India, Nov. 19, 1919; s. Joseph and Gladys E. (Pickering) T.; m. Margaret Patricia Davies, Apr. 4, 1942; children: Caroline Lee, David Gordon, Benjamin. B.Comm., U. Toronto, 1940, M.A., 1941; Ph.D., U. Calif., 1948. Asst. prof. bus. adminstrn. Cornell U., Ithaca, N.Y., 1947-49; assoc. prof. Carnegie-Mellon U., Pitts., 1949-53; assoc. prof., dir. analytical studies U. Calif., Berkeley, 1955-67; lectr. U. Calif., 1979-82; v.p. fin. and adminstrn., investment officer U. Alta., Edmonton, 1967-74; prof. fin., 1974-79; investment adv. Berkeley, 1979-96. Served with Royal Can. Air Force, 1942-45. Fulbright fellow, 1952. Unitarian-Buddhist. Home: 88 Clarewood Ln Oakland CA 94618-2243

TYNDALL, RICHARD LAWRENCE, microbiologist, researcher; b. Mt. Joy, Pa., Mar. 29, 1933; s. William Leroy and Reba May (Ream) T.; m. Thelma Mae Sherk, June 19, 1955; children: Sharon Tyndall Headley, Michael L., Sandra Tyndall Holland. BS in Microbiology, Pa. State U., 1955, MS in Microbiology, 1959, PhD in Microbiology, 1961. Rsch. staff biology div. Oak Ridge (Tenn.) Nat. Lab., 1961-73; rsch. staff med. div. Oak Ridge Assoc. Univs., 1973-76; assoc. prof. rsch. zoology dept. U. Tenn., Knoxville, 1976-87; adj. rsch. assoc. Biology and Environ. Scis. div. Oak Ridge Nat. Lab., 1976-87; rsch. staff mem. Health and Safety Rsch. div. Oak Ridge Nat. Lab., 1988—; founder, CEO Microbial Monitoring, Clinton, Tenn., 1985—; co-founder Reprotech Inc., Knoxville, 1981; cons. in field. Contbr. numerous articles to profl. jours.; patentee in field. Mem. com. for control of Legionella, State of Wis. With U.S. Army, 1955-57. AEC postdoctoral fellow. Fellow Am. Acad. Microbiology; mem. AAAS, ASHRAE (subcom. on Legionella), Am. Soc. Microbiology, Phi Sigma, Gamma Sigma Delta (awards). Methodist. Avocations: travel, humor, jazz, the Arts. Home: 209 Woodland View Rd Clinton TN 37716

TYNER, HOWARD A., publishing executive, newspaper editor, journalist; b. Milw., May 30, 1943; s. Howard Arthur and Katharine Elizabeth Tyner; m. Elizabeth Jane Adams, May 3, 1969; children: Sophie Elizabeth, Ian Adams. BA, Carleton Coll., 1965; MSJ, Northwestern U., 1967. Sports editor Chippewa Herald-Telegram, Chippewa Falls, Wis., 1965-66; fgn. corr. UPI, Europe, 1967-77; with Chgo. Tribune, 1977—; fgn. corr. Chgo. Tribune, Moscow, 1982-85; fgn. editor Chgo. Tribune, Chgo., 1985-88, asst. mng. editor, 1988-90, dep. mng. editor, 1990-92, assoc. editor, 1992-93, v.p., editor, 1993—; mem. adv. bd. Alfred Friendly Press Fellowships, Washington, 1988—; mem. exec. bd. World Press Inst., 1994—. Home: 2700 Park Pl Evanston IL 60201-1337 Office: Chgo Tribune Co 435 N Michigan Ave Chicago IL 60611*

TYNER, LEE REICHELDERFER, lawyer; b. Annapolis, Md., Mar. 12, 1946; d. Thomas Elmer and Eleanor Frances (Leland) Reichelderfer; m. Carl Frederick Tyner, Aug. 31, 1968; children: Michael Frederick, Rachel Christine, Elizabeth Frances. BA, St. John's Coll., 1968; MS, U. Wash., 1970; JD, George Washington U., 1975. Bar: Wash., D.C., U.S. Dist. Ct. (D.C.), U.S. Ct. Appeals (4th cir., 1st cir., 9th cir., D.C. cir., 5th cir., 8th cir., 11th cir., 10th cir.), U.S. Ct. Claims, U.S. Supreme Ct. Profl. staff U.S. Senate Commerce Com., Washington, 1970-72; trial atty. Land and Natural Resources div. U.S. Dept. Justice, Washington, 1975-85; atty. Office of Gen. Counsel U.S. EPA, Washington, 1985—. Bd. dirs. Grace Episcopal Day Sch., Silver Spring, Md., 1987-89; den leader, cubmaster Boy Scouts Am., Silver Spring, 1987-91. Recipient Bronze medals, U.S. EPA, 1988, 92. Mem. Order of the Coif. Episcopalian. Home: 1416 Geranium St NW Washington DC 20012-1518 Office: US EPA 401 M St SW Washington DC 20460-0001

TYNER, MCCOY, jazz pianist, composer; b. Phila., 1938. Mem. Art Farmer and Benny Golson's Jazztet, 1959, John Coltrane Quartet, 1960-65; ind. pianist, 1965—. Rec. artist: (with John Coltrane) A Love Supreme, Live at the Village Vanguard, Coltrane, Meditations, (solo albums) Reaching Fourth, The Real McCoy, Time for Tyner, Extensions, Asante, Tender Moments, (with Jackie McLean) It's About Time, Echoes of a Friend, Enlightenment, Atlantis, Passion Dance, Together, 4 x 4, 13th House, Dimensions. Recipient Best Jazz Instrumental Performance, Individual or Group Grammy award, 1996. Office: care Abby Hoffer Enterprises 223 1/2 E 48th St New York NY 10017-1538*

TYNER, NEAL EDWARD, retired insurance company executive; b. Grand Island, Nebr., Jan. 30, 1930; s. Edward Raymond and Lydia Dorothea (Kruse) T.; children: Karen Tyner Redrow, Morgan. BBA, U. Nebr., 1956. Jr. analyst Bankers Life Nebr., Lincoln, 1956-62, asst. v.p. securities, 1962-67, v.p. securities, treas., 1967-69, fin. v.p., treas., 1970-72, sr. v.p. fin., treas., 1972-83, pres., chief exec. officer, 1983-87, chmn., pres., chief exec. officer, 1987-88, chmn., CEO, 1988-95; bd. dirs. Union Bank & Trust Co., Union Bank of Ariz., N.A.; chmn. emeritus Ameritas Life Ins. Corp. Trustee U. Nebr. Found., Lincoln Found., Investment Banking Inst., NYU; bd. govs. Nebr. Wesleyan U. Capt. USMC, 1950-54, Korea. Fellow CFAs; mem. Omaha/Lincoln Soc. Fin. Analysts, Paradise Valley Country Club. Lutheran. Avocations: tennis, computers. Office: 8225 N Golf Dr Paradise Vly AZ 85253-2716

TYNER, WALLACE EDWARD, economics educator; b. Orange, Tex., Mar. 21, 1945; s. Richard D. and Jeanne (Gullahorn) T.; m. Jean M. Young, May 2, 1970; children: Davis, Jeffrey. BS in Chemistry, Tex. Christian U., 1966; MA in Econs., U. Md., 1972, PhD in Econs., 1977. Vol. Peace Corps., India, 1966-68; math, sci., ednl. skill desk chief Peace Corps., Washington, 1968-70; grad. teacher asst. U. Md., Balt., 1971-73; assoc. scientist Earth Satellite Corp., Washington, 1973-74; rsch. assoc. Cornell U., Ithaca, N.Y., 1974-77; asst. prof., assoc. prof. natural resource econs. and policy Purdue U., West Lafayette, Ind., 1977-84, prof., asst. dept. head, 1983-88, dept. head, 1989—; cons. UN Food and Agrl. Orgn., Rome, Office Tech. Assessment, Washington, U.S. Dept. Interior, Washington, OECD, Paris, World Bank, Washington, USDA, Washington. Author: Energy Resources and Economic Development in India, 1978, A Perspective on U.S. Farm Problems and Agricultural Policy, 1987. Mem. Am. Assn. Agrl. Economists, Am. Econs. Assn., Internat. Assn. Energy Economists, Assn. Environmental and Resource Economists, Sigma Xi, Gamma Sigma Delta. Home: 116 Arrowhead Dr West Lafayette IN 47906-2105 Office: Purdue U Krannert Bldg West Lafayette IN 47907-1145

TYNES, THEODORE ARCHIBALD, educational administrator; b. Portsmouth, Va., Sept. 24, 1932; s. Theodore Archibald and Mildred Antonette (Lee) T.; m. Bettye Clayton, June, 1955 (div. June 1970); children: Karen A. Culbert, David Lee, Tammy Alecia Simpers; m. Cassandra Washington, Nov. 17, 1989; 1 child, Jordan Alexandria. BS in Edn., W.Va. State Coll., 1954; postgrad., Calif. State U., L.A., 1959, Mt. San Antonio Coll, 1962, Chaffey Coll., 1962, Azusa Pacific Coll., 1967; MA in Ednl. Adminstrn., U. Calif., Berkeley, 1969; PhD in Adminstrn. and Mgmt., Columbia Pacific U., 1989. Tchr., athletic dir., coach Walker Grant High Sch., Fredericksburg, Va., 1958-59; dir. programs and aquatics L.A. Times Boys Club, L.A., 1959-62; tchr., dir. recreation, acting edn. supr. youth tng. sch. Calif. Youth Authority, Chino, 1962-68; tchr., dir. drug abuse program Benjamin Franklin Jr. High Sch., San Francisco, 1968-70; asst. prin. Pomona (Calif.) High Sch., 1970-72; prin. Garey High Sch., Pomona, 1972-75; adminstrv. asst. to supt. Bd. Edn., East Orange, N.J.; asst. to commr. U.S. Dept. Edn., Washington; Rockefeller fellow, supt. adminstrv. intern Rockefeller Found., N.Y.C., 1975-76; supervising state coord. sch. programs Office Essex County Supt. N.J. State Dept. Edn., East Orange, 1976-77; rsch. asst., dir. tech. assistance career info. system U. Oreg., Eugene, 1977-79; dir. ednl. placement U. Calif., Irvine, 1979; prin. edn. svcs. Woodrow Wilson Rehab. Ctr., Fisherville, Va., 1980-87; med. courier Urology Inc., Richmond, Va., 1988-90; vice prin. Ithaca (N.Y.) H.S., 1991-94; asst. prin. Wyandanch (N.Y.) Meml. High Sch., 1996-97; cons. Fielder and Assocs., Berkeley, 1969-80, Jefferson High Sch., Portland, Oreg., 1970, U. Calif., Berkeley, 1972, U. Calif., Riverside, 1972, Calif. Luth. Coll., 1972, Compton Unified Sch. Dist., 1973, Goleta Unified Schs., 1973, Rialto Sch. Dist., 1973, Grant Union Sch. Dist., Sacramento, Calif., 1973-75, San Mateo Sch. Dist., Tri Dist. Drug Abuse project, 1973, North Ward Cultural Ctr., Newark, N.J., 1976, Nat. Career Conf., Denver, 1978, Opportunities Indulstrialization Ctrs. Am., Phila., Bklyn., Detroit, Poughkeepsie, N.Y., 1980, Tynes & Assocs., 1988; lectr. seminar San Francisco City Coll., 1968-69. Author various curricula, monitoring procedures, grants. 1965—. City commr. Human Rels., Pomona, Calif., 1972-74; pres. San Antonio League, Calif., 1972-75. With USAF, 1954-57. Named Coach of Yr. L.A. Times Boys Club, 1959; fellow Rockefeller Found., 1975; recipient Administrv. award for Excellence Woodrow Wilson Rehab., 1987. Mem. NAACP, Am. Assn. Sch. Adminstrs., Nat. Assn. Secondary Sch. Prins., Nat Alliance Black Sch. Adminstrs., Assn. Supervision and Career Devel., Assn. Ednl. Data Systems., Assn. Calif. Sch. Adminstrs., Va. Govtl. Employees Assn., Va. Rehab. Assn., South Bay Pers. Guidance Assn., Pomona Adminstrs. Assn., Ithaca Prins. Assn., Fisherville Ruritan, Phi Delta Kappa, Omega Psi Phi (Basilius Pi Rho chpt. 1965). Democrat. Episcopalian. Avocations: video and still photogrpahy, music, art, sports. Home: 102 Sherwood Dr Waynesboro VA 22980-9286

TYNG, ANNE GRISWOLD, architect; b. Kuling, Kiangsi, China, July 14, 1920; d. Walworth and Ethel Atkinson (Arens) T. (parents Am. citizens); 1 child, Alexandra Stevens. AB, Radcliffe Coll., 1942; M of Architecture, Harvard U., 1944; PhD, U. Pa., 1975. Assoc. Stonorov & Kahn, Architects, 1945-47; assoc. Louis I. Kahn Architect, 1947-73; pvt. practice architecture Phila., 1973—; adj. assoc. prof. architecture U. Pa. Grad. Sch. Fine Arts, 1968—; assoc. cons. architect Phila. Planning Commn. and Phila. Redevel. Plan, 1954; vis. disting. prof. Pratt Inst., 1979-81, vis. critic architecture, 1969; vis. critic architecture Rensselaer Poly. Inst., 1969, 78, Carnegie Mellon U., 1970, Drexel U., 1972-73, Cooper Union, 1974-75, U. Tex., Austin, 1976; lectr. Archtl. Assn., London, Xian U., China, Bath U., Eng., Mexico City, Hong Kong U., 1989, Baltic Summer Sch., Architecture and Planning, Tallinn, Estonia, Parnu, Estonia, 1993; panel spkr. Nat. Conv. Am. Inst. Architects, N.Y.C., 1988, also numerous univs., throughout U.S. and Can.; asst. leader People to People Archtl. del. to China, 1983; vis. artist Am. Acad., Rome, 1995. Subject of films Anne G. Tyng at Parsons Sch. of Design, 1972, Anne G. Tyng at U. of Minn., 1974, Connecting, 1976, Forming the Future, 1977; work included in Smithsonian Travelling Exhbn., 1979-81, 82, Louis I. Kahn: In the Realm of Architecture, 1990-94; contbr. articles to profl. publs.; prin. works include Walworth Tyng Farmhouse (Hon. mention award Phila. chpt. AIA 1953); builder (with G. Yanchenko) Probability Pyramid. Fellow Graham Found. for Advanced Study in Fine Arts, 1965, 79-81. Fellow AIA (Brunner grantee N.Y. chpt. 1964, 83, dir., mem. exec. bd. dirs. Phila. chpt. 1976-78, John Harbeson Disting. Svc. award Phila. chpt. 1991); mem. Nat. Acad. Design (nat. academician), C.G. Jung Ctr. Phila. (planning com. 1979—), Form Forum (co-founder, planning com. 1978—). Democrat. Episcopalian. Home: 2511 Waverly St Philadelphia PA 19146-1049 Office: Univ Pa Dept Architecture Grad Sch Fine Arts Philadelphia PA 19107

TYRAN, GARRY KEITH, banker; b. Washington, D.C., Feb. 25, 1953; s. Benjamin and Jeanne Marie (Deckman) T.; children: Keith West, Charlotte Lyles. BA, Stanford U., 1975; MBA, UCLA, 1982. Rep. Fahran Overseas, Ltd., Burlingame, Calif., 1976-77; with Tarfa Comml. and Indsl. Co., Riyadh, Saudi Arabia, 1977-79; mgmt. asst. Fahran Overseas, Ltd., Ashland, Ore., 1979-80; economist Dept. Energy, Washington, 1980; v.p. Bank Am., Houston, 1982-90; v.p., mgr. Bank Am., Pleasant Hill, Calif., 1990-97; v.p., mgr. Bank Am., San Francisco, 1996-97, mng. dir., 1997—. Mem. Kappa Sigma, Stanford Alumni Assn. Methodist. Avocations: tennis, golf, political biography. Home: 1846 Shirley Dr Benicia CA 94510-2668 Office: Bank Am 1455 Market St Fl 12 San Francisco CA 94103-1308

TYREE, ALAN DEAN, clergyman; b. Kansas City, Mo., Dec. 14, 1929; s. Clarence Tillman and Avis Ora (Gross) T.; m. Gladys Louise Omohundro, Nov. 23, 1951; children: Lawrence Wayne, Jonathan Tama, Sharon Avis. B.A., U. Iowa, 1950; postgrad., U. Mo.-Columbia, 1956-58, U. Mo.-Kansas City, 1961-62. Ordained min. Reorganized Ch. of Jesus Christ of Latter Day Saints, 1947; appointee min. Lawrence, Kans., 1950-52; mission adminstr. (Mission Sanito), French Polynesia, 1953-64; regional adminstr. Denver, 1964-66; mem. Council Twelve Apostles, Independence, Mo., 1966-82; sec. Council Twelve Apostles, 1980-82, mem. First Presidency, 1982-92; ret. First Presidency, 1992; mem. Joint Coun. and Bd. Appropriations, 1966-92; originator music appreciation broadcasts Radio Tahiti, 1962-64, Mission Sanito Radio Ministry, 1960-64; instr. Music/Arts Inst., 1992—, Met. C.C.'s, 1994—. Editor: Cantiques des Saints French-Tahitian hymnal, 1965, Exploring the Faith: A Study of Basic Christian Beliefs, 1987; mem. editing com.: Hymns of the Saints, 1981; author: The Gospel Graced by a People: A Biography of Persons in Tahiti, 1993, Evan Fry: Proclaimer of Good News, 1995, Priesthood: For Other's Sake, 1996. Bd. dirs. Outreach Internat. Found., 1979-82, mem. corp. body, 1982-92; mem. corp. body Independence Regional Health Ctr., 1982-92, v.p., 1983-92, bd. dirs., 1984-93; mem. bd. publs. Herald House, 1984-92; mem. corp. body restoration Trail Found., 1982-92; chmn. Temple Art Com., 1988-94; bd. dirs. Independence Symphony Orch., 1992-96, pres., 1995-96; mem. human rels. commn. city of Independence, 1995—, chmn., 1996—. Recipient Elbert A. Smith Meml. award for publ. articles, 1968, 72. Mem. Phi Beta Kappa, Phi Eta Sigma. Home and Office: 3408 S Trail Ridge Dr Independence MO 64055-1984

TYREE, LEWIS, JR., retired compressed gas company executive, inventor, technical consultant; b. Lexington, Va., July 25, 1922; s. Lewis Sr. and Winifred (West) T.; m. Dorothy A. Hinchcliff, Aug. 21, 1948; children: Elizabeth Hinchcliff, Lewis III, Dorothy Scott. Student, Washington & Lee U., 1939-40; BS, MIT, 1947. Cryogenic engr. Joy Mfg. Co., Michigan City, Ind., 1947-49; v.p. Hinchcliff Motor Service, Chgo., 1949-53; cons. engr. Cryogenic Products, Chgo., 1953-76, Liquid Carbonic Corp., Chgo., 1960-76; exec. v.p. Liquid Carbonic Industries, Chgo., 1976-87; bd. dirs. Liquid Carbonic Industries, Chgo., Worldwide Cryogenics (MVE), New Prague, Minn. Patentee in cryogenics. Served to 1st lt. U.S. Army, 1943-46, PTO. Mem. Soc. Cin., ASME, Am. Soc. Heating, Refrigeration, and Air Conditioning Engring., Hinsdale Golf Club, Lexington Golf and Country Club. Republican. Episcopalian. Home: Mulberry Hill Liberty Hall Rd Lexington VA 24450-1703

TYRELL, LORNE S., dean. Dean U. Alberta. Office: U Alberta Faculty Medicine, 8440 112th St, Edmonton, AB Canada T6G 2B7*

TYRER, JOHN LLOYD, retired headmaster; b. Brockton, Mass., Jan. 16, 1928; s. Lloyd Perkins and Dorothy (Nicholson) T.; m. Jeanne Irene Dunning, June 7, 1952; children: Alison Jane, John Lloyd, David Dunning, Jill Anne. A.B., Bowdoin Coll., 1949; M.A., Middlebury (Vt.) Coll., 1959. Tchr. Wilbraham (Mass.) Acad., 1949-53; tchr., adminstr. Hill Sch., Pottstown, Pa., 1953-64; headmaster Asheville (N.C.) Sch., 1964-92; headmaster emeritus, 1994—; cons. Ind. Ednl. Svcs., 1994—; mem. adv. bd. Warren Wilson Coll., 1972-87. Bd. dirs. Asheville Cmty. Concert Assn., 1970-93, chmn., 1988-90; bd. dirs. Asheville Country Day Sch., 1965-68, A Better Chance, 1988-92, St. Genevieve/Gibbons Hall Sch., 1970-77, Webb Sch., Tenn., 1986-89, Ind. Ednl. Svcs., 1970-75, Coun. Religion in Ind. Schs., 1969-78, ASSIST, 1991—, chmn., 1996—; bd. dirs. Ft. Myers Cmty. Concert Assn., 1993—, Lit. Vols. of Am., Lee County, Fla., 1995—. With U.S. Army, 1946-47. Mem. Nat. Assn. Ind. Schs. (bd. dirs., chmn. com. on boarding schs., chmn. membership com.), So. Assn. Ind. Schs. (pres., bd. dirs.), Mid.-South Assn. Ind. Schs. (bd. dirs.), N.C. Assn. Ind. Schs. (pres., bd. dirs.), Headmasters Assn., So. Headmasters Assn., English-Speaking Union (bd. dirs., pres. Asheville br., chmn. secondary sch. exchange com.), Theta Delta Chi. Episcopalian. Home: 1353 Kingswood Ct Fort Myers FL 33919-1927

TYRRELL, GERALD GETTYS, banker; b. Canton, China, Dec. 27, 1938; came to U.S., 1940.; s. Gerald Fraser and Virginia Lee (Gettys) T.; m. Jane Haldeman, June 1961 (div. Aug. 1975); children: Gerald F., Jane N., Robert M.; m. Elizabeth Ann Drautman, Mar. 31, 1978. BA, Yale U., 1960; MA, Rutgers U., 1971. Cert. real estate financier. With 1st Nat. Bank of Louisville, 1961-89, sr. v.p., 1975-81, exec. v.p., 1981-89; pres., chmn. Churchill Mortgage Corp., 1975-77; chief fin. cons. City of Louisville Office of Downtown Devel., 1989—. Author: A Positive Approach to Financing Black Business, 1972. Trustee, treas. Patton Mus., Ft. Knox, Ky., 1970; treas. Soc. Colonial Wars in Commonwealth of Ky., 1970; mem. exec. bd. Boy Scouts Am., 1983; bd. dirs. The Louisville Orch., 1984. Served to capt. U.S. Army, 1960-68. Recipient Disting. Service Ribbon Ky. Nat. Guard, 1966. Mem. Robert Morris Assocs., Nat. Soc. Real Estate Fin. (bd. govs). Democrat. Clubs: Louisville Country, Pendennis. Avocations: fine wines, tennis. Office: City of Louisville Office Downtown Devel 600 W Main St Ste 300 Louisville KY 40202-4235

TYRRELL, ROBERT EMMETT, JR., editor-in-chief, writer; b. Chgo., Dec. 14, 1943; s. R. Emmett and Patricia (Rogers) T.; m. Judy Mathews Tyrrell, Feb. 12, 1972 (div. Dec. 1989); children: Patrick, Kathryn, Anne. BA, Ind. U., 1965, MA, 1967. Editor-in-chief The Am. Spectator, Arlington, Va., 1967—; pres. Am. Spectator Ednl. Found., Arlington, Va., 1967—. Editor: Network News Treatment of the 1972 Democratic Presidential Candidates, 1972, The Future That Doesn't Work, 1977, Orthodoxy, 1987; author: Public Nuisances, 1979, The Liberal Crack-Up, 1984, The Conservative Crack-Up, 1992, Boy Clinton: The Biography, 1996; writer nationally syndicated polit. column. Recipient Am. Eagle award Invest in Am. Coun., 1977; named Greatest Pub. Svc. Performed by an American 35 Years or Under award Am. Inst. for Pub. Svc., 1977, Ten Most Outstanding Young Men in Am., Jaycees, 1978. Roman Catholic. Avocations: handball, fishing, listening to classical music, reading. Office: The American Spectator 2020 14th St N Ste 750 Arlington VA 22201-2515

TYSON, CICELY, actress; b. N.Y.C., Dec. 19, 1933; d. William and Theodosia Tyson; m. Miles Davis, 1981 (div.). Student, N.Y. U., Actors Studio; hon. doctorates, Atlanta U., Loyola U., Lincoln U. Former sec., model; co-founder Dance Theatre of Harlem; bd. dirs. Urban Gateways. Stage appearances include: The Blacks, 1961-63, off-Broadway, Moon on a Rainbow Shawl, 1962-63, Tiger, Tiger, Burning Bright, Broadway; films include: Twelve Angry Men, 1957, Odds Against Tomorrow, 1959, The Last Angry Man, 1959, A Man Called Adam, 1966, The Comedians, 1967, The Heart is a Lonely Hunter, 1968, Sounder, 1972 (Best Actress, Atlanta Film Festival, Nat. Soc. Film Critics, Acad. award nominee, Best Actress, Emmy award, Best Actress in a spl., 1973), The Blue Bird, 1976, The River Niger, 1976, A Hero Ain't Nothin' but a Sandwich, 1978, The Concorde-Airport 79, 1979, Bustin' Loose, 1981, Fried Green Tomatoes, 1991, Jefferson in Paris, 1995; TV appearances include: (series) East Side, West Side, 1963, Sweet Justice, 1994-95, Road to Galveston, 1996; (films) Marriage: Year One, 1971, The Autobiography of Miss Jane Pittman, 1974, Just an Old Sweet Song, 1976, Wilma, 1977, Roots, 1977, A Woman Called Moses, 1978, King, 1978, The Marva Collins Story, 1981, Benny's Place, 1982, Playing With Fire, 1985, Samaritan: The Mitch Snyder Story, 1986, Acceptable Risks, 1986, Intimate Encounters, 1986, The Women of Brewster Place, 1989, Heat Wave, 1990, Winner Takes All, 1990, The Kid Who Loved Christmas, 1990, When No One Would Listen, 1992, Duplicates, 1993, House of Secrets, 1993, Oldest Living Confederate Widow Tells All, 1994 (Emmy Awd., Best Supporting Actress - Miniseries); other appearances include: Wednesday Night Out, 1972, Marlo Thomas and Friends in Free to Be...You and Me, 1974, CBS: On the Air, 1978, Liberty Weekend, 1986, The Blessings of Liberty, 1987, Without Borders, 1989, Visions of Freedom: A Time Television Special, 1990, Clippers, 1991, A Century of Women, 1994. Trustee Human Family Inst.; trustee Am. Film Inst. Recipient Vernon Price award, 1962; also awards NAACP Nat. Council Negro Women; Capitol Press award. Address: care CAA 9830 Wilshire Blvd Beverly Hills CA 90212-1804

TYSON, CYNTHIA HALDENBY, academic administrator; b. Scunthorpe, Lincolnshire, Eng., July 2, 1937; came to U.S., 1959; d. Frederick and Florence Edna (Stacey) Haldenby; children: Marcus James, Alexandra Elizabeth. BA, U. Leeds, Eng., 1958, MA, 1959, PhD, 1971. Lectr. Brit. Council, Leeds, 1959; faculty U. Tenn., Knoxville, 1959-60, Seton Hall U., South Orange, N.J., 1963-69; faculty, v.p. Queens Coll., Charlotte, N.C., 1969-85; pres. Mary Baldwin Coll., Staunton, Va., 1985—; bd. dirs. Am. Coun. on Edn./Commn. on Higher Edn. and Adult Learning, Washington, 1981-85. Contbr. articles to profl. jours. Mem. Va. Internat. Trade Commn., Richmond, 1987; bd. dirs. Am. Frontier Culture Mus., Va., United Way, Staunton, 1986—; mem. Va. Lottery Bd.; trustee Woodrow Wilson Birthplace Found., Staunton, 1985—; ruling elder Presbyn. Ch.; mem. gov's. adv. coun. on self determination & federalism, 1995—. Fulbright scholar, 1959; Ford Found. grantee Harvard U., 1981; Shell Oil scholar Harvard U., 1982. Fellow Soc. for Values in Higher Edn.; mem. Operation Enterprise Coun. of Am. Mgmt. Assn., So. Assn. Colls. for Women (pres. 1980-81). Republican. Office: Mary Baldwin Coll Office of the President Staunton VA 24401

TYSON, DONALD JOHN, food company executive; b. Olathe, Kans., Apr. 21, 1930; s. John W. and Mildred (Ernst) T.; m. Twilla Jean Womochil, Aug. 24, 1952; children: John H., Cheryl J., Carla A. Student, U. Ark. Plant mgr. Tyson Foods, Inc., Springdale, Ark., 1951-55, pres., 1955-67, chmn., chief exec. officer, 1967-95, sr. chmn., 1995—; chief exec. officer Eagle Distbg. Inc., Tyson Export Sales Inc., Poultry Growers Inc., Tyson Carolina Inc., Spring Valley Farms Inc., Lane Processing Inc., Lane Farms Inc. Lodge: Elks. Home: 2210 W Oaklawn Dr Springdale AR 72762-6900 Office: Tyson Foods Inc PO Box 2020 Springdale AR 72765-2020*

TYSON, GAIL L., health federation administrator; b. Havre de Grace, Md., Dec. 28, 1954; d. William Alva Way and Virginia Lorena Tyson; m. Joseph Matthew Pease, May 17, 1986; 1 child, Loren Juliette Tyson Pease. BA, Dickinson Coll., 1976. Dir. edn. Harrisburg (Pa.) Area Rape Crisis Ctr., 1976-77; community response specialist CONTACT Harrisburg, 1978-81, asst. dir., 1981-85; pub. info. coord. Dauphin County Human Svcs., Harrisburg, 1985-87; unit exec. dir. Am. Cancer Soc., Harrisburg, 1988-92; exec. dir. Nat. Voluntary Health Agys. Pa. Com., Harrisburg, 1992—; v.p. Human Svcs. Program, 1987; chmn. Nat. Voluntary Health Agys. Coun. State Affiliates, 1997. Mem. adv. com. Harrisburg Area C.C., 1985-87; mem. adv. bd. Ret. Sr. Vol. Program, Harrisburg, 1986-88, sec., 1987; lifetime mem. Girl Scouts U.S., bd. dirs. Hemlock coun., 1977-91, v.p., 1982-88, pres., 1988-91, chmn. diversity task force, 1992. Recipient Thanks badge Hemlock coun. Girl Scouts U.S., 1991. Mem. Wheel and Chain Hon. Soc. Methodist. Office: Nat Voluntary Health Agy Pa 2213 Forest Hills Dr Ste 3 Harrisburg PA 17112-1090

TYSON, H. MICHAEL, retired bank executive; b. Houston, Aug. 16, 1938; s. Howard Ellis and Myrle (Daunoy) T.; m. Judith O. Gilbert, June 24, 1960; children: H. Michael II, Michelle Lee. B.B.A. cum laude, U. Tex., 1962; postgrad., Stonier Grad Sch. Banking, Rutgers U., 1974. Personnel mgr.

Foods div. Anderson Clayton Co., Dallas, 1962-70; exec. v.p. adminstrn. Tex. Commerce Bancshares, Houston, 1970-79; v.p. fin. and adminstrn., chief fin. officer, dir. Houston Chronicle Pub. Co., 1979-87; vice chmn., dir. Tex. Commerce Bank-Houston; exec. v.p., exec. trust officer Tex. Commerce Bancshares, 1987-95; dir. Paranet Inc., Assoc. Bldg. Svcs. Bd. dirs. Harris County Heritage Soc., Houston Symphony, Tax Rsch. Assn., Sam Houston coun. Boy Scouts Am., Houston Festival Found., Lighthouse for the Blind, Goodwill Industries; trustee Gulf Coast United Way, McCullough Found.; chmn. The Houston Parks Bd. Served with USMCR, 1961-67. Mem. Houston C. of C. (com. chmn.), Pers. Round Table, Am. Newspaper Pub. Assn., Houston Indsl. Rels. Group, Fin. Execs. Inst. (bd. dirs.), Internat. Newspaper Fin. Execs., Houston Club (dir., pres.), River Oaks Country Club (dir.), Inns of Ct. Methodist.

TYSON, HARRY JAMES, investment banker; b. Bklyn., Aug. 17, 1945; s. George William and Eileen Regina (Dunphy) T.; m. Sarah Lorretta Halloran, Mar. 9, 1969; children: Kelly J., Stacey L., Harry D. BS in Math., St. Francis Coll., Brooklyn Heights, N.Y., 1968. Analyst Smith Barney, Harris Upham & Co., N.Y.C., 1968, 2d v.p., 1974-76, v.p., 1976-78, 1st v.p., 1978-83, sr. v.p., 1983-90, mem. bd. dirs., 1987-90, exec. v.p., 1990-92; mng. dir. Dillon Read & Co. Inc., N.Y.C., 1992—, also bd. dirs., 1992—. Author: Harah's Universal Bond Basis Converter, 1970. Mem. Assn. for Help Retarded Children, Nassau, N.Y., 1987—, N.Y. Zool. Soc., 1978—, St. Christopher Ottille Guardian Club, Nassau, 1987—. Trans. named Deal of the Yr., Inst. Investor, 1984, 85. Mem. Govt. Fin. Officers Assn., P.R. C. of C. (bd. dirs. 1990-92), N.Y. Athletic Club, North Hempstead Country Club. Republican. Roman Catholic. Avocations: skiing, tennis, golf. Office: Dillon Read & Co Inc 535 Madison Ave New York NY 10022-4212

TYSON, KENNETH ROBERT THOMAS, surgeon, educator; b. Houston, July 30, 1936; s. Howard Ellis and Myrle Henrietta (Daunoy) T.; m. Sue Ann Delahoussaye, Nov. 20, 1971; children: Deborah, Kenneth, Michael, Jill. B.A., U. Tex., 1956; M.D., U. Tex. Med. Br., 1960. Diplomate: Am. Bd. Surgery, Am. Bd. Thoracic Surgery. Intern Ind. U. Med. Ctr., Indpls., 1960-61; resident in gen. and thoracic surgery Ind. U. Med. Center, 1961-66; resident in pediatric surgery Children's Hosp. Med. Center, Boston, 1966-67; chief pediatric gen., thoracic surgery U. Tex. Med. Br., Galveston, 1967-80; asst. prof. surgery U. Tex. Med. Br., 1967-71, asso. prof., 1971-75, prof., 1975-80; surgeon-in-chief Child Health Center, 1974-80; clin. prof. surgery U. Calif., Davis, 1980-91, U. Tex. Med. Br., Galveston, 1991—. Contbr. articles to profl. jours. Fellow A.C.S., Am. Acad. Pediatrics, Am. Coll. Cardiology; mem. Am. Assn. Thoracic Surgery, Soc. Surgery Alimentary Tract, So. Thoracic Surg. Assn., Am. Pediatric Surg. Assn., Soc. Univ. Surgeons, So. Surg. Assn., Pacific Coast Surg. Assn., Sigma Xi, Alpha Omega Alpha, Delta Kappa Epsilon, Alpha Kappa Kappa. Episcopalian. Home: 7126 Las Ventanas Dr Austin TX 78731-1814 Office: U Tex Med Br Dept Pediatric Surgery Galveston TX 77550

TYSON, KIRK W. M., business consultant; b. Jackson, Mich., July 2, 1952; s. George Carlton and Wilma Marion (Barnes) T.; m. Janice Lynn Lorimer, Aug. 25, 1979 (div. Dec. 1984); m. Kathryn Margit Kennell, June 24, 1986; 1 child, Robert. BBA, Western Mich. U., 1974; MBA, DePaul U., Chgo., 1982. CPA, Ill.; cert. mgmt. cons., 1985. Bus. cons. Arthur Andersen & Co., Chgo., 1974-84; v.p. cons. First Chgo. Corp., 1984; chmn. Kirk Tyson Internat., Lisle, Ill., 1984—. Author: Business Intelligence: Putting It All Together, 1986, Competitor Intelligence: Manual and Guide, 1990, Competition in the 21st Century, 1996. Pres., Chgo. Jr. Assn. Commerce and Industry Found., 1977-79; active Easter Seals Soc., 1977, Am. Blind Skiing Found., 1977-78, Jr. Achievement, 1976-77, United Way Met. Chgo., 1979-80, Urban Gateways, 1975; Rep. Precinct Committeeman Downers Grove township, precinct 114, 1985-88; treas. St. Charles H.S. Football Booster Club, 1994-95. Fellow Soc. Competitive Intelligence Profls.; mem. The Strategic Leadership Forum, Assn. Global Strategic Info., Inst. Mgmt. Cons., Am. Mktg. Assn., Assn. for Corp. Growth, Global Bus. Devel. Alliance, Alpha Kappa Psi (Disting. Alumni Svc. award 1974-86). Office: Kirk Tyson International Ltd 4343 Commerce Ct Ste 615 Lisle IL 60532-3619

TYSON, MIKE G., professional boxer; b. N.Y.C., June 30, 1966; s. John Kilpatrick and Lorna Tyson; m. Robin Givens, Feb. 7, 1988 (div. Feb. 1989);. Defeated Trevor Berbick to win World Boxing Coun. Heavyweight Title, Nov. 1986, defeated James Smith to win World Boxing Assn. Heavyweight Title, 1987, defeated Tony Tucker to win Internat. Boxing Fedn. Heavyweight Title, Aug. 1987, defeated Michael Spinks to win Internat. Boxing Fedn. Heavyweight Title, June 1988, undisputed heavyweight champion 1988-90 (defeated by James "Buster" Douglas), defeated Frank Bruno to win WBC Heavyweight Title, 1996, defeated by Evander Holyfield, 1996; commentator for Showtime. Hon. sports chmn. Cystic Fibrosis Assn. N.Y., 1987—, Young Adult Inst., N.Y.C., 1987—. Youngest heavyweight champion in history. Office: Don King Prodns 871 W Oakland Park Blvd Fort Lauderdale FL 33311-1731*

TYSON, ROSENDO FELICITO, JR., urban planner; b. Araunustadt, Aruba, May 27, 1951; came to the U.S., 1952; s. Rosendo Felicito and Marie Albertine (Gumbs) T.; m. Lora Lea Trail, Aug. 14, 1976; children: Ian Scott, Brent Marshall. BA in Sociology, Wheaton Coll., 1973; MS in Higher Mil. Strategic Studies, U.S.A. Command/Gen. Staff Coll, 1984; MS in Urban Planning, U. Louisville, 1989; postgrad. diploma, Nat. Def. U., 1991. Commd. 2d lt. U.S. Army, 1973, advanced through grades to maj., 1984, ret., 1986; cons., trainer U.S. Postal Mgmt. Acad., Potomac, Md., 1986-88; cons., trainer, faculty U. Louisville, 1988—; chief planner bd. adjustment Lexington-Fayette (Ky.) Urban County Govt., 1989-94, sr. planner, 1994—; commr. Planning Commn., Vine Grove, Ky., 1987-89; mem. adv. bd. Ctrl. Ky. Regional Planning Coun., Lexington, 1995-96. Author: Tank Platoon Leader's Notebook, 1985, Cavalry Platoon Leader's Notebook, 1985; contbr. articles to profl. jours. Area facilitator dialogue group Christian Unity Task Force on Race Rels., Lexington, 1995, 96; dist. dir. Dem. Ctrl. Com. Ky., Lexington, 1995. Decorated Army Commendation medal, Medallion of Freedom, Regiment du March de Chad; named Ky. Col., 1986—. Mem. Civil Svc. (bd. dirs., v.p. 1995, pres. 1996), Govt. Adv. Bd. on Tng. Facilities and Instrn. (chair 1995). Presbyterian. Avocations: military war gaming, sports, reading, writing, public speaking. Home: 2980 Candlelight Way Lexington KY 40502-2826 Office: Lexington-Fayette Urban County Govt 200 E Main St Lexington KY 40507-1315

TYSON-AUTRY, CARRIE EULA, legislative consultant, researcher, small business owner; b. Fayetteville, N.C., July 13, 1943; d. Henry McMillan II and Adeline Amelia (Williams) Tyson. BA in Social Studies and Lang. Edn., U. N.C., 1974, MA in Adminstrn., 1992; postgrad., U. Sterling, Scotland, 1978, Coll. Charleston, 1986-87; postgrad., doctoral candidate, Fayetteville State U., 1995—. Cert. tchr., N.C., S.C. Legislative aide, cons. N.C. Gen. Assembley, Raleigh, 1957-86; tchr. various states, 1963-88; postgrad. S.C. U., 1995—; rschr. U. N.C., Chapel Hill, 1991—; columnist Orkney, Scotland, 1992—; instr. Pope Air Force Base (CIC), Pope AFB (CTC), 1995—; mem. N.C. joint legis. com. edn., 1976-80; mem. N.C. gov. adv. com. exceptional children, 1977-78; gov. state coord. task force on reading, 1977; U.S. del. to world congr. edn., Scotland, 1978; mem. gov. conf. rural edn., Hilton Head, S.C., 1987. Author: Marlboro County Handbook, 1982-86; developer various curricula, 1977-88. Mem. adminstrv. campaign staff numerous nat. and state candidates; active St. John's Episc. Ch. With U.S. Army, 1973-77. Grantee GED, 1974-75. Mem. ASCD, Am. Heritage Assn., Scotland's Land Trust Soc., Scottish-Am. Geneol. Soc., Nat. Trust Hist. Preservation, Smithsonian Soc., Mus. Cape Fear (docent), Mensa, Phi Delta Kappa. Republican. Avocations: furniture restoration, reading. Home: Grays Creek Gray's Creek RR7 Box 284 Fayetteville NC 28306-9535

TYTELL, JOHN, humanities educator, writer; b. Antwerp, Belgium, May 17, 1939; came to U.S., 1941; s. Charles and Lena (Gano) T.; m. Mellon Gregori, May 28, 1967. BA, CCNY, 1961; MA, NYU, 1963, PhD, 1968. Grad. reader NYU, 1963-67; lectr. Queens Coll., N.Y.C., 1963-68, assoc. prof., 1968-73, 1973-76, prof. English, 1977—; exec. editor Am. Book Rev., 1979—; vis. prof. Rutgers U., 1980, U. Paris, 1983; cons. Nat. Humanities Faculty, Ga., 1978—. Author: The American Experience, 1970, Naked Angels, 1976, Ezra Pound: The Solitary Volcano, 1987, Passionate Lives, 1991, The Living Theatre: Art, Exile and Outrage, 1995; contbr. articles to mags. including Am. Scholar, Partisan Rev., Vanity Fair, Fame. NEH fellow, 1974. Home: 69 Perry St New York NY 10014-3297 Office: Queens College Flushing NY 11367

TYTLER, LINDA JEAN, communications and public affairs executive; b. Rochester, N.Y., Aug. 31, 1947; d. Frederick Easton and Marian Elizabeth (Allen) T.; m. George Stephen Dragnich, May 2, 1970 (div. July 1976); m. James Douglas Fisher, Oct. 7, 1994. AS, So. Sem., Buena Vista, Va., 1967; student U. Va., 1973; student in pub. adminstrn. U. N. Mex., 1981-82. Spl. asst. to Congressman John Buchanan, Washington, 1971-75; legis. analyst U.S. Senator Robert Griffin, Washington, 1975-77; ops. supr. Pres. Ford Com., Washington, 1976; office mgr. U.S. Senator Pete Domenici Re-election, Albuquerque, 1977; pub. info. officer S.W. Community Health Service, Albuquerque, 1978-83; cons. pub. relations and mktg., Albuquerque, 1983-84; account exec. Rick Johnson & Co., Inc., Albuquerque, 1983-84; dir. mktg. and communications St. Joseph Healthcare Corp., 1984-88; mktg. and bus. devel. cons., 1987-90; mgr. communications and pub. affairs Def. Avionics Systems div., Honeywell Inc., 1990—; sgt. N.Mex. Mounted Patrol, 1993—; bd. dirs. Jobs for N.Mex.; mem. N.Mex. Ho. of Reps., Santa Fe, 1983-95, ret. 1995, vice chmn. appropriations and fin. com., 1985-86, interim com. on children and youth, 1985-86, mem. consumer and pub. affairs com., transp. com., 1992-95; chmn. Rep. Caucus, 1985-88; chmn. legis. campaign com. Rep. Com.; del. to Republic of China, Am. Council of Young Polit. Leaders, 1988. Bd. dirs. N. Mex. chpt. ARC, Albuquerque, 1984. Recipient award N.Mex. Advt. Fedn., Albuquerque, 1981, 82, 85, 86, 87. Mem. Am. Soc. Hosp. Pub. Rels. (cert.), Nat. Advt. Fedn., Soc. Hosp. Planning and Mktg., Am. Mktg. Assn., N.Mex. Assn. Commerce and Industry (bd. dirs., exec. com. 1996—). Republican. Baptist.

TYUNAITIS, PATRICIA ANN, elementary school educator; b. Kenosha, Wis., Feb. 15, 1942; d. John Anton and Antoinette (Tunkieicz) T. BS, Alverno U., 1966; MAT, Webster U., 1982; postgrad., Walden U., 1994—. Cert. elem., secondary tchr., Wis. Tchr. St. John the Bapt. Sch., Johnsburg, Wis., 1964-67, St. Matthew's Sch., Campbellsport, Wis., 1967-68, St. Monica's Sch., Whitefish Bay, Wis., 1968-71; math. tchr. New Holstein (Wis.) Elem. Sch., 1971—, mem. sch. restructuring com., 1994; adj. prof. Silver Lake Coll., Manitowoc, Wic., 1993—, Marian Coll., Fond du Lac, Wis., 1993—. Mem. performance assessment tng. team Dept. Pub. Instrn., Madison, Wis., 1992—. Recipient Herb Kohl award for excellence in teaching State of Wis., 1991, Wis. Presdl. award for excellence in tchg. math. Mem. ASCD, Nat. Coun. Tchrs. Math., Math. Assn. Am., Nat. Assn. Tchrs. Am., New Holstein Edn. Assn., Wis. Math. Coun., Optimist Club (coord. local forensic contest 1991—, sch. coach Odyssey of the Mind 1986—, sch. coord. Odyssey of the Mind 1992, regional dir. Stevens Point chpt. 1992—). Home: N 10335 Hwy 151 Malone WI 53049 Office: New Holstein Elem Sch 2226 Park Ave New Holstein WI 53061-1008

TZAGOURNIS, MANUEL, physician, educator, university administrator; b. Youngstown, Ohio; came to Oct. 20, 1934,; s. Adam and Argiro T.; m. Madeline Jean Kalos, Aug. 30, 1958; children: Adam, Alice, Ellen, Jack George. B.S., Ohio State U., 1956, M.D., 1960, M.S., 1967. Intern Phila. Gen. Hosp., 1960-61; resident Ohio State U., Columbus, 1961-63, chief med. resident, 1966-67, instr., 1967-68, asst. prof., 1968-70, assoc. prof., 1970-74, prof., 1974—, asst. dean Sch. Medicine, 1973-75, assoc. dean, med. dirs. hosps., 1975-80, v.p. health svcs., dean of medicine, 1981-95, v.p. health scis., 1995—; gen. practice medicine Columbus, 1967—; mem. staff Ohio State U. Hosps./James Cancer Hosp. & Rsch. Ctr.; mem. Coalition for Cost Effective Health Services Edn. and Research Group State of Ohio, 1983. Contbg. author: textbook Endocrinology, 1974, Clinical Diabetes: Modern Management, 1980; co-author: Diabetes Mellitus, 1983, 88. Citation Ohio State Senate Resolution No. 984, 1989. Capt. U.S. Army, 1962-64; bd. trustees Hellenic Coll./Holy Cross. Recipient Homeric Order of Ahepa Cleve. chpt., 1976, Phys. of Yr. award Hellenic Med. Soc. N.Y., 1989; citations Ohio State Senate and Ho. of Reps., 1975, 83. Mem. AMA (med. edn. coun. 1993—), Am. Red Cross (chair ctrl. Ohio 1996—), Assn. Am. Med. Colls., Ohio State Med. Assn., Assn. of Acad. Health Ctrs., Columbus Med. Assn., Deans' Council. Mem. Greek Orthodox Ch. Home: 4335 Sawmill Rd Columbus OH 43220-2243 Office: Ohio State U Coll Medicine 200 Meiling Hall 370 W 9th Ave Columbus OH 43210-1238

TZIMAS, NICHOLAS ACHILLES, orthopedic surgeon, educator; b. Greece, Apr. 18, 1928; came to U.S., 1955, naturalized, 1960; s. Archilles Nicholas and Evanthia B. (Exarchou) T.; m. Helen J. Papastylopoulos, Apr. 22, 1958; children: Yvonne, Christina. M.D., U. Athens, Greece, 1952. Intern St. Mary's Hosp., Hoboken, N.J., 1955-56; resident in gen. surgery Misericordia Hosp., N.Y.C.; resident in orthopedic surgery Bellevue Hosp., N.Y.C., 1957-60; instr. orthopedic surgery N.Y. U. Sch. Medicine, 1961-63, asst. clin. prof., 1963-65, asso. clin. prof., 1965-71; clin. prof., 1971—; mem. staff Univ. and Bellevue Hosps.; chief children's orthopedics, 1966—; orthopedic cons. Inst. Rehab. Medicine, N.Y. U., 1966—, St. Agnes Hosp., White Plains, N.Y., 1972—; advisory com. Bur. Handicapped Children, N.Y.C., 1975—; spl. invitations for teaching, Osaka, Japan, 1970, Jerusalem, 1974, São Paolo, Brazil, 1976, Taranto, Italy, 1977, Bari, Italy, 1978, Barquisimeto, Venezuela, 1979, Bogotá, Colombia, 1983, Buenos Aires, Argentina, 1983. Author articles on spina bifida child mgmt. Served with M.C. Greek Army, 1952-55. Named ofcl. Knight of Italian Republic, 1979. Fellow Am., Internat. colls. surgeons; mem. N.Y. Acad. Medicine, N.Y. State, N.Y. County med. socs., Am. Acad. Orthopedic Surgeons, Am. Congress Rehab. Medicine, Am. Acad. Cerebral Palsy. Mem. Greek Orthodox Ch., Archon of the Ecumenical Patriarchate of Constantinople. Home: 33 Edgewood St Tenafly NJ 07670-2909 Office: 530 1st Ave New York NY 10016-6451

TZIMOPOULOS, NICHOLAS D., science and mathematics education specialist; b. Eptachorion, Greece, Feb. 19, 1941; came to U.S., 1956; s. Demetrius and Soultana (Davos) T. BA in Chemistry and Math., U. N.H., 1965; MS in Analytical Chemistry, Boston Coll., 1967, PhD in Phys. Chemistry, 1971. Dir. research So. N.H. Services, Manchester, 1978-80; prof. phys. chemistry U. Northern Fla., Jacksonville, 1981-82; chmn. math and sci. The Bartram Sch., Jacksonville, Fla., 1980-83; prof. chemistry Valencia Community Coll., Orlando, Fla., 1983-84; dir. sci. edn. Schs. of the Tarrytowns, North Tarrytown, N.Y., 1984-91; dir. sci., math. and tech. Lexington (Mass.) Pub. Schs., 1989—. Author: Modified Null-Point Potentiometry, 1967, Irreversible Processes, 1971, mathematics-Science Curricula, 1982, Modern Chemistry, 1990, 93, Life, Earth, Physical Sciences, 1987, 90, General Sciences Books 1 and 2, 1987, 90, The Next Generation: Teachers Resources Curriculum Guide, 1993, The Stuff of Dreams: Teachers Resource Curriculum Guide, 1993. N.H. rep. N.E. Metric Action Council, 1978-80; Tufts U. del. New Eng. Energy Congress, 1978; liaison Kiwanis Regional Sci. and Engring. Fair, Jacksonville, 1983; founder N.H. Legis. Acad. Sci. and Tech., Concord, 1980. Recipient Outstanding commendations in sci. achievement Internat. Sci. and Engring. Fair, 1986, CMA Catalyst award, 1987, N.Y. State Presdl. award for excellence in sci. and math., 1989. Fellow Sigma Xi; mem. AAAS, ASCD, Am. Chem. Soc. (Fla. congl. del. 1984, treas. Fla. sect. 1983, 84, chmn. Jacksonville sect. 1982-83, dir. Westchester County, N.Y. sub-sect. 1986—, high sch. exams. com. 1982-86, Outstanding Chemistry Tchr. Fla. 1982, S.E. U.S. 1983, Nichols award 1986), N.Y. Acad. Sci., Fla. Acad. Sci., Nat. Sci. Tchrs. Assn., Greek Orthodox Youth Assn. (pres. Manchester, N.H. 1963-65). Democrat. Avocations: photography, classical music, guitar, travel, soccer.

UBELL, EARL, magazine health editor; b. Bklyn., June 21, 1926; s. Charles and Hilda (Kramer) U.; m. Shirley Leitman, Feb. 12, 1949; children—Lori Ellen, Michael Charles. B.S., CCNY, 1948. With N.Y. Herald Tribune, 1943-66, successively messenger, asst. sec. to mng. editor, reporter, 1943-53, sci. editor, 1953-66, syndicated columnist, 1956-66; sci. commentator MBS, 1958-59; spl. sci. editor WNEW, N.Y., 1962; health and sci. editor WCBS-TV, N.Y.C., 1966-72, 78-95; health editor PARADE mag., 1983—. Dir. TV news NBC News, N.Y.C., 1972-76; producer spl. broadcasts TV news, 1976-78; producer documentaries Medicine in America, 1977, Escape from Madness, 1977; author: The World of Push and Pull, 1964, The World of The Living, 1965, The World of Candle and Color, 1969, How to Save Your Life, 1972, (with Carol C. Flax) Mother/Father/You, 1980, (with Randi Londer) Parade Family Health Companion, 1996. Pres. Council Advancement Sci. Writing, Inc., 1960-66, bd. dirs., 1960-96, founder, 1996—; chmn. Center Modern Dance Edn., Inc., 1962-82; pres. North Jersey Cultural Council, 1966-72; bd. dirs. Dance Notation Bur., 1968—, chmn. bd., 1975-94; bd. dirs. Sex Info. and Edn. Council U.S., 1967-69, YMHA, Bergen County, 1968-73, Nat. Center Health Edn., 1977. Served as aviation radioman USNR, 1944-46. Recipient Mental Health Bell award N.Y. State Soc. Mental Health, 1957, Albert Lasker med. journalism award, 1958, Nat. Assn. Mental Health award for radio program, 1962, Sci. Writers award Am. Psychol. Found., 1965, Westinghouse award AAAS, 1960, Empire State award, 1963, TV Reporting award N.Y. Assoc. Press, 1969, 71, N.Y. Emmy award, 1971, Samuelson award N.Y. League for Hard of Hearing, Legal-Med. award Milton Helpern Library of Legal Medicine, Spl. Achievement award Deadline Club, 1982, Disting. Contbn. award, 1983, Nat. Media award Am. Diabetes Assn., 1985, N.Y. State Mental Health Council award, 1987, Ann. Svc. award Dance Notation Bur., 1990. Mem. Nat. Assn. Sci. Writers (pres. 1960-61), Nuclear Energy Writers Assn. (pres. 1965-66), Phi Beta Kappa (pres. Gamma chpt. 1976-77). *I learn something new, in depth, every 5 years—x-ray crystallography, French, statistics, polling, stock market—I am refreshed.*

UBELL, ROBERT NEIL, editor, publisher, consultant, literary agent; b. Bklyn., Sept. 14, 1938; s. Charles and Hilda (Kramer) U.; m. Rosalyn Deutsche, Sept. 24, 1976; children: Jennifer Hayslett-Ubell, Elizabeth Miller. BA, Bklyn. Coll., 1961; postgrad., Acad. Fine Arts, Rome, Italy, 1959-60, CUNY, 1961-62, Pratt Graphic Arts Workshop, N.Y.C., 1972-73. Assoc. editor Nuclear Industry, Atomic Industrial Forum, 1962-64; from editor to sr. editor Plenum Pub. Corp., N.Y.C., 1965-70; v.p., editor in chief Plenum Pub. Corp., 1970-76; editor The Sciences, N.Y. Acad. Scis., N.Y.C., 1976-79; Am. pub. Nature, N.Y.C., 1979-83; founding pub. Nature Biotechnology, 1983; pres. Robert Ubell Assocs., N.Y.C., 1983—, BioMedNet, Ltd., 1996—; bd. dirs. Marcel Dekker, Inc. Author: (with Marvin Leiner) Children Are the Revolution, 1974; (with Mark Tesoriero) Negotiating Networked Licensing Agreements, 1995, Cost Centers and Measures in the Networked Information Value Chain, 1997; editor Nature Directory of Biologicals, 1981, Physics Today Buyer's Guide, 1984-89; exec. editor: Linguistics: The Cambridge Survey, 1987-88, Pre-Med Handbook, 1986, International Encyclopedia of the Social Sciences, Vol. 19, 1991, Encyclopedia of Astronomy and Astrophysics, 1991, Sci. Am. Triumph of Discovery, 1995, Oxford Encyclopedia of Climate and Weather, 1996; cons. editor ISI Press, 1985-87, Am. Inst. of Physics Book Program, 1986-96; Am. Chem. Soc. Book Program, 1989; cons. pub. Computers in Physics, 1987-91; series editor Masters of Modern Physics, 1991-96, Creators of Modern Chemistry, 1994-95, Sci. Am. Focus, 1995-96; contbr. articles to profl. jours. Mem. AAAS, N.Y. Acad. Scis., Nat. Assn. Sci. Writers. Office: BioMedNet 111 8th Ave New York NY 10011-5201

UBERALL, HERBERT MICHAEL STEFAN, physicist, educator; b. Neunkirchen, Austria, Oct. 14, 1931; came to U.S., 1953, naturalized, 1963; s. Michael and Stefanie (Hacker) U.; m. Reyna Tosta, 1981; children by previous marriage: Bernadette Chauvallon, Bertrand. Ph.D., U. Vienna, Austria, 1953, Cornell U., 1956; PhD (honoris causa), U. Le Havre, France, 1987. Staff mem. Signal Corps. Labs., Ft. Monmouth, N.J., 1953-54; research asst. Cornell U., 1954-56; research fellow Nuclear Physics Research Lab., U. Liverpool, Eng., 1956-57; Ford Found. fellow CERN, Geneva, Switzerland, 1957-58; research physicist Carnegie Inst. Tech., Pitts., 1958-60; asst. prof. U. Mich., Ann Arbor, 1960-64; assoc. prof. Cath. U. Am., Washington, 1964-65, prof. physics, 1965-84, prof. emeritus, 1984—; vis. prof. U. Paris VII Jussieu, 1984-85, U. Le Havre, 1990, 92, 94, 96, U. Bordeaux, 1993, 95, U. Aix-Marseille II and Lab. Mech. Acoustics, 1995, Ecole Centrale de Lille, 1997; cons. Naval Rsch. Lab., Washington, 1966-96. Author: Electron Scattering from Complex Nuclei, 1971; co-author: Giant Resonance Phenomena, 1980, Nuclear Pion Photoproduction, 1991; editor: Acoustic Resonance Scattering, 1992; co-editor: Long Distance Neutrino Detection, 1979, Classical and Quantum Dynamics, 1991, Coherent Radiation Sources, 1985, Coherent Radiation Processes in Strong Fields, 1991, Radar Target Imaging, 1994; contbr. 300 articles to profl. jours. Recipient Fgn. medal French Soc. Acoustics, 1996. Fellow IEEE, Am. Phys. Soc., Acoustical Soc. Am., Washington Acad. Scis. (Achievement award 1984); mem. AAUP, Am. Acad. Mech., Electromagnetics Acad., Internat. Union Radio Sci. Home: 5101 River Rd Apt 1417 Bethesda MD 20816-1571 Office: Catholic U Dept Physics Washington DC 20064

UBEROI, MAHINDER SINGH, aerospace engineering educator; b. Delhi, India, Mar. 13, 1924; came to U.S., 1945, naturalized, 1960; s. Kirpal Singh and Sulaksha (Kosher) U. B.S., Punjab U., Lahore, India, 1944; M.S., Calif. Inst. Tech., 1946; D.Eng., Johns Hopkins U., 1952. Registered profl. engr. Mem. faculty U. Mich., Ann Arbor, 1953-63, prof. aeros., 1959-63, vis. prof., 1963-64; prof. aerospace engring. U. Colo., Boulder, 1963—, chmn. dept. aerospace engring., 1963-75; fellow F. Joint Inst. for Lab. Astrophysics, Boulder, 1963-74; hon. rsch. fellow Harvard U., 1975-76; invited prof. U. Que., Can., 1972-74; vis. scientist Max Planck Inst. for Astrophysics, Munich, 1974. Author numerous rsch. publs. on dynamics of ionized and neutral gases and liquids with and without chem. reactions, gravity and electromagnetic fields; editor Cosmic Gas Dynamics, 1974. Council mem. Ednl. TV Channel 6, Inc., Denver, 1963-66. Guggenheim fellow Royal Inst. Tech., Stockholm, Sweden, 1958; exchange scientist U.S. Nat. Acad. Scis.; exchange scientist Soviet Acad. Scis., 1966. Mem. Am. Phys. Soc., Tau Beta Pi. Home: 819 6th St Boulder CO 80302-7418

UBINGER, JOHN W., JR., lawyer; b. Pitts., Jan. 31, 1949. BBA, Ohio U., 1970; JD, U. Notre Dame, 1973. Bar: Pa. 1973. Ptnr. Jones, Day, Reavis & Pogue, Pitts.; instr. environ. dispute resolution Duquesne U. Sec. Pa. Environ. Coun., chmn. task force on reuse of indsl. sites, 1994-95; bd. dirs., treas. Allegheny Land Trust; adv. com. Allegheny County Dept. Air Pollution Control, Allegheny County Contaminated Sites Redevel. Study, 1994-95. Mem. ABA (natural resources, energy and environ. law sect.) Pa. Bar Assn. (chmn. environ., mineral and natural resources law sect. 1990-91), Allegheny County Bar Assn. (chmn. environ. law sect. 1991), Air and Waste Mgmt. Assn. (chmn. We. Pa. Sect. 1989-90), Environ. Law Inst. (assoc.). Office: Jones Day Reavis & Pogue 1 Mellon Bank Ct 500 Grant St Pittsburgh PA 15219-2502

UBUKA, TOSHIHIKO, biochemistry educator, dean; b. Kagaminocho, Okayama, Japan, Jan. 31, 1934; s. Yoshio and Shigeko (Hashimoto) U.; m. Satoko Iwamiya, Oct. 18, 1960; children: Takayoshi, Hiromi, Atsue. MD, Okayama U., 1959, PhD, 1964. With Okayama U., 1964-73, asst. prof., 1973-80, assoc. prof. Med. Sch., 1980-81, prof. Med. Sch., 1981—, dean Med. Sch., 1997—; rsch. assoc. Med. Coll. Cornell U., N.Y.C., 1968-71. Coauthor: Methods in Enzymology, vol. 143, 1987; editor Acta Med Okayama, 1980—, Physiol Chem Phys and Med NMR, 1982—, Amino Acids, 1991—; chief editor Acta Med Okayama, 1987-90. Fellow Japanese Biochem. Soc., Japanese Soc. Nutrition and Food Sci.; mem. AAAS, N.Y. Acad. Scis., Internat. Soc. Amino Acid Rsch., Soc. Study Inborn Errors Metabolism, The Protein Soc. Achievements include research in sulfur biochemistry, sulfur nutrition, cysteine metabolism in mammals, protein modification with mixed disulfides, inborn errors of cysteine metabolism. Home: 527-1 Nishikarakawa, Okayama 701-12, Japan Office: Okayama U Med Sch Dept Biochemistry, 2-5-1 Shikatacho, Okayama 700, Japan

UCCELLO, VINCENZA AGATHA, artist, director, educator emerita; b. Hartford, Conn., May 11, 1921; d. Salvatore and Josephine (Bordonaro) U. B.S., St. Joseph Coll., West Hartford, Conn., 1956; M.A. in Liberal Studies, Wesleyan U., 1961; M.F.A., Villa Schifanoia, Florence, Italy, 1963. Tchr. art Glastonbury High Sch., Conn., 1957-61, East Hartford Pub. Schs., Conn., 1963-64; prof. fine arts St. Joseph Coll., 1964—, chmn. dept. fine arts, 1967-85, acting curator, dir. coll. art collections, 1978—. One-woman shows Villa Schifanoia, Florence, 1963, St. Joseph Coll., 1965, 81, Pump House Gallery, Hartford, Conn., 1986; group shows Am. Painters in Paris Exhbn., Nat. Print and Drawing Exhbn., Ohio U., Athens, Ball State U., Muncie, Ind., Austin Art Ctr., Trinity Coll., Hartford, Munson Gallery, New Haven; represented in permanent collections St. Joseph Coll., N.Y. Pub. Libr., Ctr. for Book Arts, Conn. Nat. Bank, Hartford; pvt. collections. Trustee West Hartford Art League. Recipient Harper Meml. award in painting, 1969; fellow Venice Artists Workshop, 1965; Yale U. fellow Andrew U. Mellon Found., 1980; second prize Atria Gallery Blues Show, Disting. Alumnae award St. Joseph Coll. Mem. Coll. Art Assn. Am. Conn. Women Artists (pres. 1974-76), Canton Artists Guild, Am. Assn. Mus. Home: 51 Hilltop Dr West Hartford CT 06107-1434

UCHIDA, IRENE AYAKO, cytogenetics educator, researcher; b. Vancouver, B.C., Can., Apr. 8, 1917; d. Sentaro and Shizuko (Takano) U. BA, U. Toronto, 1946, PhD, 1951; DSc honoris causa, U. Western Ont., 1996. Rsch. assoc. Hosp. Sick Children, Toronto, 1951-59; dir. med. genetics Children's Hosp., Winnipeg, Man., Can., 1960-69; asst. prof. U. Man., 1963-67, assoc. prof., 1967-69; dir. cytogenetics lab. McMaster U. Med. Ctr., Hamilton, Ont., 1969-91; prof. pediatrics, pathology McMaster U., 1969-85, prof. emeritus, 1985—; dir. cytogenetics Oshawa (Ont.) Gen. Hosp., 1991-95; mem. sci. adv. com. Inst. for Basic Research, Staten Island, N.Y., 1984—; vis. scientist Med. Research Council Can., U. London and Harwell Radiobiol. Research Unit, 1969; vis. prof. Med. Research Council Can., U. Western Ont., 1973. Author medcom slide tape series, 1987; contbr. articles to profl. jours. and chpts. to books. Mem. Sci. Council Can., Ottawa, 1970-73; mem. adv. com. Ont. Ministry Health, Toronto, 1979-85. Decorated officer Order of Can.; recipient Woman of Yr. award Women's Advt. Sales Club, 1963, Woman of Century award Nat. Coun. Jewish Women, 1967, achievement award Altrusa Club, 1969; named One of 25 Outstanding Women, Ont. Govt., 1975; Ramsay Wright scholar, 1947; fellow Rockefeller Found., 1959; grantee Nat. Found. March of Dimes, 1962-69, 71-77, NIH, 1962-69, 89-91, Nat. Heart, Lung and Blood Inst., 1977-79. Fellow Can. Coll. Med. Geneticists (emeritus 1992, Founder's award 1995), Am. Coll. Med. Genetics (emeritus 1993); mem. Am. Soc. Human Genetics (pres. 1968), Peruvian Soc. Med. Genetics (hon.). Office: McMaster U, 1200 Main St W, Hamilton, ON Canada L8N 3Z5

UCHITELLE, LOUIS, journalist; b. N.Y.C., Mar. 21, 1932; s. Abraham and Alice Lee (Cronbach) U.; m. Joan Eva Shapiro, Oct. 7, 1966; children: Isabel Anne, Jennifer Emily. B.A., U. Mich., 1954. Reporter Mt. Vernon (N.Y.) Daily Argus, 1955-57; with AP, 1957-80; fgn. corr. and bur. chief AP, San Juan, P.R., 1964-67, Buenos Aires, 1967-73; supervising editor AP Newsfeatures, N.Y.C., 1974-76; bus. news editor AP, 1977-80; asst. bus. and fin. editor N.Y. Times, 1980-87, econ. writer, 1987—; instr. journalism Sch. Gen. Studies, Columbia U., 1976-89. Home: 11 Ridgecrest W Scarsdale NY 10583-2046 Office: NY Times 229 W 43rd St New York NY 10036-3913

UCHRIN, CHRISTOPHER GEORGE, environmental scientist; b. South Amboy, N.J., Oct. 27, 1950; s. George Christopher and Annette Rose Marie (Skokan) U. B in Civil Engring., Manhattan Coll., 1972, M. in Environ. Engring., 1974; PhD in Environ. Engring., U. Mich., 1980. Registered profl. engring. N.Y. Environ. engr. U.S. EPA, N.Y.C., 1972-77; Rackham fellow U. Mich., Ann Arbor, Mich., 1977-78, rsch. asst., 1978-80; asst. prof. Rutgers U., New Brunswick, N.J., 1980-86, assoc. prof., 1986-90, prof. environ. sci., 1990—; chair dept. environ. sci. Rutgers U., New Brunswick, 1991-94, dir. grad. program in environ. sci., 1986-91; co-dir. Joint PhD Program in Exposure Assessment, Rutgers U. & UMDNJ/Robert Wood Johnson Med. Sch., 1991—. Mem. ASCE, Am. Chem. Soc., Water Environment Fedn., Am. Soc. for Materials, Soc. Environ. Toxicology and Chemistry, N.J. Acad. Sci. (pres. 1991-92), Sigma Xi. Office: Rutgers U Dept Environ Sci PO Box 231 New Brunswick NJ 08903

UCHUPI, ELAZAR, geologist, researcher; b. N.Y.C., Oct. 31, 1928; parents Alfonso and Carmen (Urbizu) U. BS, CCNY, 1952; MS, U. So. Calif., 1954, PhD, 1962. Rsch. asst. U. So. Calif., L.A., 1955-62; rsch. asst. Woods Hole (Mass.) Oceanographic Inst., 1962-64, assoc. scientist, 1964-79; sr. scientist Woods Hole (Mass.) Oceanog. Inst., 1979-93, sr. scientist emeritus, 1993—, J. Seward Johnson chmn. oceanography, 1989-93; mem. Gulf of Mexico panel Joint Oceanog. Instns. Deep Earth Sampling, 1972-74; mem. Sci. Com. for Oceanic Rsch. Working Group 41, 1973-74; mem. steering com. U.S. Oceanog. Office Relief Map Worlds' Oceans; mem. site survey panel Joint Oceanog. Instns., 1978-85; compiler geol. maps on ocean margin drilling. Mem. editl. staff Offshore Mag., 1972-74, Marine Geology, 1971-75; co-author 3 books North Atlantic, geology of Atlantic Ocean, and morphology of rocky mems. of Solar Sys. Recipient cert. of recognition Nat. Assn. Geology Tchrs., Inc., and its Crustal evolution Edn. project, 1979, medal editl. adv. bd. Offshore Mag., 1974, Frances P. Shepard award, 1991. Mem. Am. Geophys. Union, Archeol. Inst. Am., Sociedad Geologica de España. Achievements include research in seismic reflection, magnetic and gravity profiles of the eastern Atlantic continental margin and adjacent deep seafloor, Caribbean, Bahamas, Iberian Margins, New England margin, Branefield Trough, South Scotia Ridge, Canary Islands, Red Sea, Persian Gulf, Gulf of Oman, Black Sea, Egyptian Margin, Western Mediterranean, East Pacific Rise, Mohns Ridge, suspended matter and other properities of surface waters of the northeastern Atlantic Ocean, the continental margin off western Africa: Angola to Sierra Leone, Senegal to Portugal, sediments of 3 bays of Baja, Calif.: Sebastian Viscaino, San Cristobal and Todos Santos, characteristics of sediments of the mainland shelf of southern Calif., submarine geology of the Santa Rosa-Cortes Ridge, sediments on the continental margin off eastern U.S., the continental slope between San Francisco and Cedrow Island, Mex., sediments of the Palos Verdes shelf, sediments and topography of Kane Basin, statistical parameters of Cape Cod Beach and eolian sands, basins of Gulf of Mex., structure of Georges Bank, and the continental margin of the Atlantic coast of the U.S., topography and structure of Northeast Channel, Gulf of Mex., and Cashes Ledge, Gulf of Maine, distribution and geologic structure of Triassic rocks in the Bay of Fundy and the northeastern part of the Gulf of Maine, microrelief of the continental margin south of Cape Lookout, N.C., shallow structure of the Straits of Fla., sub-surface morphology of L.I., Block Island, Rhode Island sounds, and Buzzards Bay, bathymetry of the Gulf of Mex., slumping on the continental margin southeast of L.I., N.Y., woody debris on the mainland shelf off Ventura, southern Calif., the continental margin south of Cape Hatteras, N.C., the Atlantic continental shelf and slope of the U.S., geological structure of the continental margin off Gulf Coast of the U.S., and more. Office: Woods Hole Oceanographic Inst Dept Geology Geophysic Woods Hole MA 02543

UCKO, DAVID ALAN, museum director; b. N.Y.C., July 9, 1948; s. Lawrence L. and Helen H. U.; m. Barbara Alice Clark, Aug. 13, 1977; 1 child, Aaron. BA, Columbia Coll., N.Y.C., 1969; PhD, MIT, 1972. Asst. prof. chemistry Hostos Community Coll., CUNY, Bronx, 1972-76; asst. prof. chemistry Antioch Coll., Yellow Springs, Ohio, 1976-79, assoc. prof. chemistry, 1979; rsch. coord. Mus. Sci. and Industry, Chgo., 1979-80, dir. sci., 1981-87, v.p., 1986-87; dep. dir. Calif. Mus. Sci. and Industry, L.A., 1987-90; pres. Kansas City (Mo.) Mus., 1990—; rsch. assoc. chemistry dept. Columbia U., 1973-76; rsch. assoc., assoc. prof. dept. edn. U. Chgo., 1982-87; adj. staff scientist C.F. Kettering Rsch. Lab., Yellow Springs, 1977-79. Author: (book) Basics for Chemistry, 1982, Living Chemistry, 2d edit., 1986; contbr. articles to profl. jours.; host, producer (radio program) Science Alive!, 1983-87; developer numerous mus. exhibits. V.p., bd. dirs. Heritage League, Greater Kansas City, 1991-92; mem. Mid. Am. Regional Coun., Regional Amenities Task Force, Kansas City, 1990-96; bd. dirs. Cultural Alliance Greater Kansas City, 1995—, Appointed to Nat. Mus. Svcs. Bd. 1996; bd. trustees Mus. Without Walls, 1996—. Woodrow Wilson fellow, 1969, NIH postdoctoral fellow, 1972; grantee NSF, NEH, U.S. Dept. Edn., Ill. Humanities Coun., 1976-88; recipient Up and Comers award Jr. Achievement of Mid.-Am., 1992. Fellow AAAS (at large sect. Y 1987-93) mem. Assn Sci. Tech. Ctrs. (publs. com. 1984-94, chmn. 1988-94, ethics com., 1994-95, legis. com., chmn. 1996—, Greater Kansas City C. of C. (edn. com. 1993-96), Alpha Sigma Nu (hon.), Phi Lambda Upsilon, Sigma Xi. Home: 1007 W 66th St Kansas City MO 64113-1815 Office: Kansas City Mus 3218 Gladstone Blvd Kansas City MO 64123-1111

UDALL, CALVIN HUNT, lawyer; b. St. Johns, Ariz., Oct. 23, 1923; s. Grover C. and Dora (Sherwood) U.; m. Doris Fuss, Dec. 11, 1943; children: Fredric, Margaret Udall Moses, Julie (Mrs. Blair M. Nash), Lucinda (Mrs. Douglas Johnson), Tina Udall Rodriguez. LL.B., U. Ariz., 1948. Bar: Ariz. 1948. Ptnr. Fennemore Craig, 1953—; Ariz. spl. counsel Arizona v. California, 1954-62; mem. Coun. on Legal Edn. Opportunity, 1983-93. Mem. cast Phoenix Mus. Theatre, 1959-65. Fellow Am. Bar Found. (bd. dirs. 1986-89, fellows chmn. 1988-89), Ariz. Bar Found. (Disting. Svc. award 1993), Am. Coll. Trial Lawyers; mem. ABA (ho. dels. 1962-92, bd. govs. 1981-84, exec. com. 1983-84, chmn. task force on minorities 1984-86), Maricopa County Bar Assn. (pres. 1957, Disting. Pub. Svc. award 1986), State Bar Ariz. (bd. govs. 1960-65), Ariz. Law Coll. Assn. (founding bd. dirs. 1967-80, pres. 1978-79, U. Ariz. Disting. Citizen award 1984, bd. visitors 1991—). Office: Fennemore Craig One Renaissance Sq 2 N Central Ave Ste 2200 Phoenix AZ 85004-4406

UDALL, THOMAS, state attorney general; b. Tucson, May 18, 1948; s. Stewart and Lee Udall; m. Jill Z. Cooper; 1 child, Amanda Cooper. BA, Prescott Coll., 1970; LLB, Cambridge U., Eng., 1975; JD, U. N.Mex., 1977. Law clk. to Hon. Oliver Seth U.S. Ct. Appeals (10th cir.), Santa Fe, 1977-78; asst. U.S. atty. U.S. Atty.'s Office, 1978-81; pvt. practice Santa Fe, 1981-83; chief counsel N.Mex. Health & Environ. Dept., 1983-84; ptnr. Miller, Stratvert, Togerson & Schlenker, P.A., Albuquerque, 1985-90; atty. gen. State of N.Mex., 1990—. Dem. candidate U.S. Ho. Reps., 1988; past pres. Rio Chama Preservation Trust; mem. N.Mex. Environ. Improvement Bd., 1986-87; bd. dirs. La Compania de Teatro de Albuquerque, Santa Fe Chamber Music Festival, Law Fund. Mem. Nat. Assn. Attys. Gen. (pres. 1996), Kiwanis. Office: Atty Gen Office PO Box 1508 Galisteo St Santa Fe NM 87504-1508

UDASHEN, ROBERT N., lawyer; b. Amarillo, Tex., June 10, 1953; s. Leo Joe and Esther K. (Klugsberg) U.; m. Dale Lynn Sandgarten, Aug. 15, 1976. BA with high honors, U. Tex., 1974, JD, 1977. Bar: Tex. 1977, U.S. Ct. Appeals (5th cir.) 1978, U.S. Dist. Ct. (no. and so. dists.) Tex. 1978, U.S. Ct. Appeals (11th cir.) 1981, U.S. Supreme Ct. 1981, U.S. Dist. Ct. (ea. dist.) Tex. 1989, U.S. Dist. Ct. (we. dist.) Tex. 1991. Staff atty. Staff Counsel for Inmates, Huntsville, Tex., 1977-79; assoc., ptnr. Crowder, Mattox & Udashen, Dallas, 1979-85; ptnr. Udashen & Goldstucker, Dallas, 1985-87; pvt. practice, 1987-94; ptnr. Milner, Lobel, Goranson, Sorrels, Udashen & Wells, Dallas, 1995—; bd. dirs. Open, Inc., Dallas; instr. trial advocacy Sch. Law So. Meth. U., 1993-95. Contbr. articles to profl. publs. Adv. bd. Coalition for Safer Dallas, 1994. Mem. State Bar Tex. (penal code com. 1992-93), Nat. Assn. Criminal Def. Lawyers, Tex. Criminal Def. Lawyers Assn., Dallas Criminal Def. Lawyers Assn. Office: Milner Lobel Goranson Sorrels Udashen & Wells 2515 Mckinney Ave # 21 Dallas TX 75201-1978

UDDIN, WAHEED, civil engineer, educator; b. Karachi, Pakistan, Feb. 8, 1949; came to U.S., 1981; s. Hameed and Amjadi (Begum) U.; m. Rukhsana Tayyab, July 1, 1978; children: Omar W., Usman W., Asad W. BSCE, U. Karachi, 1970; MS in Geotech. Engring., Asian Inst. Tech., Bangkok, 1975; PhD in Transp. Engring., U. Tex., 1984. Registered profl. engr., Tex. Lab. engr. Airport Devel. Agy., Ltd., Pakistan, 1971-73; materials engr. Netherlands Airport cons., Jeddah, Saudi Arabia, 1975-78; asst. rsch. engr. U. Petroleum and Minerals Rsch. Inst., Dhahran, Saudi Arabia, 1978-81; rsc. engr. Austin (Tex.) Rsch. Engrs., Inc., 1984-87; pavement/materials engr. Tex. R&D Found., Riverdale, Md., 1987-89; UN pavement expert UNCHS/Dubai Municipality, Dubai, 1989-91; asst. prof. U. Miss., University, 1993—; founder, infrastructure cons. Engring. Mgmt. Applications, Inc., Silver Spring, Md., 1992—; liaison officer for Saudi Arabia and UAE Asian Geotech. Info. Ctr., Bangkok, 1976-81; numerous conf. presentations in field. Co-author: Infrastructure Management; contbr. over 60 articles to profl. jours. M Engring. scholar Govt. of U.K., 1973-75. Mem. ASCE, ASTM, Internat. Soc. Asphalt Pavements (founder), Chi Epsilon. Achievements include patent for highway pavement nondestructive testing and analysis methodology, infrastructure maintenance methodology, road user cost and benefit analysis software. Office: U Miss Dept Civil Engring University MS 38677

UDELL, RICHARD, lawyer; b. Bklyn., Dec. 27, 1932; s. Alvin and Gertrude (Langsam) U.; BA, Reed Coll., 1955; LLB, U. Pa., 1958; m. Marguerite Hartshorne, July 3, 1955; children: Benjamin Alan, Edward H. Bar: N.Y. 1958, Fla. 1984. Pvt. practice, N.Y.C., 1959-65; counsel RCA Records, N.Y.C., 1965-69; assoc. firm Machat & Kronfeld, N.Y.C., 1969-71; counsel Famous Music Corp., N.Y.C., 1971-72, Random House, Inc. subs. RCA, N.Y.C., 1972-75; gen. counsel Simon & Schuster, Inc., subs. Gulf & Western Industries, Inc., N.Y.C., 1975-77; adminstrv. v.p., chief counsel Harcourt Brace Jovanovich, Inc., N.Y.C., 1977-92; v.p. gen. coun. McGraw Hill Sch. Pub. Co., 1992—. Mem. Bar Assn. City N.Y., Orange County Bar Assn., Fla. Bar Ass. Jewish. Office: McGraw-Hill Sch Pub Co 1221 Avenue Of The Americas New York NY 10020-1001

UDELL TURSHEN, ROCHELLE MARCIA, publishing executive; b. N.Y.C., Nov. 29, 1944; d. Julius David and Beatrice Kafka; m. James Edward Udell, Oct. 12, 1969 (div. 1976); m. Doug Edward Turshen, Mar. 9, 1980; children: Ben, Julia. BA, Bklyn. Coll., 1966; MA, Pratt Inst., 1967. Tchr. Sheepshead Bay High Sch., Bklyn., 1967-70; asst. art dir. N.Y. Mag., N.Y.C., 1970-71; art dir. MS. Mag., N.Y.C., 1970-71, Vogue, N.Y.C., 1971-77; creative dir. Calvin Klein Advt., N.Y.C., 1975-84; art dir. House & Garden, Self, GQ, N.Y.C., 1982-84; agy. pres. Della Femina Travisano & Ptnrs., N.Y.C., 1984-88; assoc. editorial dir. Conde Nast Pubs., N.Y.C., 1988—; lectr. Fashion Group, Women in Communications, Advt. Women in N.Y. and Radcliffe Pub Course. Author: How to Eat an Artichoke. Bd. dirs. Bklyn. Coll., Am. Mus. of the Moving Image. Mem. Am. Soc. Mag. Editors, Women in Need, Japan Soc., Fashion Group. Democrat. Jewish. Avocations: reading, running, tennis. Office: Conde Nast Pubs 350 Madison Ave New York NY 10017-3704

UDEN, DAVID ELLIOTT, cardiologist, educator; b. Montreal, Sept. 7, 1936; s. Reginald and Elsie Ada (Elliott) U.; children: Thomas Elliott, Linda Ann, Christopher Elliott. BSc, McGill U., 1958; MD, McGill U., Quebec, Can., 1962. Diplomate Am. Bd. Internal Medicine; cert. cardiovascular disease. Attending cardiologist Toronto Western Hosp., 1972-93, The Wellesley Hosp., Toronto, 1990-93; asst. prof. medicine U. Toronto, 1975-93; chief of cardiology Oconee Meml. Hosp., Seneca, S.C., 1993—, chief of medicine, 1994-96; elected mem. S.C. Med. Discipline Commn., 1996—. Contbr. articles to sci. and profl. jours. With RCAF, 1963-66. Fellow Am. Coll. Cardiology, Am. Heart Assn. Coun. on Clin. Cardiology. Avocations: travel, photography. Office: 103 Omni Dr # B Seneca SC 29672-9448

UDENFRIEND, SIDNEY, biochemist; b. N.Y.C., Apr. 5, 1918; s. Max and Esther (Tabak) U.; m. Shirley Frances Reidel, June 20, 1943; children: Aliza, Elliot. B.S., Coll. City N.Y., 1939; M.S., N.Y. U., 1942, Ph.D., 1948; D.Sc. honoris causa, N.Y. Med. Coll., 1974, Coll. Medicine and Dentistry of N.J., 1979, Mt. Sinai Sch. Medicine, City U. N.Y., 1981. Lab. asst. N.Y.C. Dept. Health, 1940-42; jr. chemist NYU Rsch. Svc., 1942-43, asst. chemist, 1943-44, research chemist, 1944-46; research asst. Med. Sch., 1946-47, instr., 1947-48; instr. Washington U. Med. Sch., 1948-50; biochemist Nat. Heart Inst., Bethesda, Md., 1950-53; head sect. cellular pharmacology lab. chem. pharmacology Nat. Heart Inst., 1953-56, chief lab. clin. biochemistry, 1956-68; dir. Roche Inst. Molecular Biology, N.J., 1968-83, head lab. molecular neurobiology, 1983-96, dir. emeritus, 1996—; dir. Dana Inst., Drew U., Madison, N.J., 1996—; professorial lectr. George Washington U., 1962-69; adj. prof. human genetics and devel. dept. Columbia U., 1969-74; adj. prof. dept. biochemistry City U. N.Y., 1968-95; dept. pharmacology Emory U., 1976-78; adj. prof. biochemistry Cornell U. Med. Sch., 1982-95; mem. sci. adv. bd. Scripps Clinic and Research Found., 1974-78; mem. adv. com. to dir. NIH, 1976-78; mem. Sci. Adv. Com. for Cystic Fibrosis; mem. adv. council of sci. and engring. City U. N.Y., 1980—; mem. sci. adv. com. Mass. Gen. Hosp., 1980-84. Trustee Wistar Inst., 1968-71; mem. adv. bd. Weizmann Inst. Sci., 1978-79, bd. govs., 1979—. Recipient Cert. of Merit for studies on malignant carcinoid A.M.A., 1956, Arthur S. Flemming award, 1958; City of Hope research award, 1975; NIH fellow St. Mary's Hosp. Med. Sch., London, Eng., 1957; Harvey lectr., 1964; recipient Superior Service award Dept. HEW, 1965, Distinguished Service award, 1966; Gairdner Found. award, 1967; Heinrich Waelsch lectr. in neurosci., 1978; recipient Townsend Harris medal CCNY Alumni Assn., 1979; Rudolph Virchow gold medal, 1979; Chauncey Leake lectr. U. Calif., 1980. Fellow N.Y. Acad. Scis. (trustee 1978—); mem. NAS, AAAS, Am. Soc. Biol. Chemists, Am. Soc. Pharmacology and Exptl. Therapeutics (sec.), Soc. Exptl. Biology and Medicine, Am. Assn. Clin. Chemists (Van Slyke award 1967, Ames award 1969), Am. Chem. Soc. (Hillebrand award 1962, Torald Sollmann award 1975), Am. Acad. Arts and Scis., Japanese Pharmacol. Soc. (hon.), Japanese Biochem. Soc. (hon.), Czechoslovak Pharmacology Soc. (hon.), Congress Internat. Neuropsychopharmacologists (hon.), Instituto de Investigaciones Citológicas (corr.) (Spain), Phi Beta Kappa, Sigma Xi. Office: Dana Inst Drew U Madison NJ 07940

UDEVITZ, NORMAN, publishing executive; b. Cheyenne, Wyo., Jan. 22, 1929; s. Jay and Edith (Stienberg) U.; m. Marsha Rae Dinner, Dec. 17, 1960; children: Jane, Kathryn, Andrew. Student, U. Colo., 1946-49. With Cheyenne Newspapers Inc. Cheyenne, 1949-54; editor-pub. Wyo. Buffalo, Cheyenne, 1954-63; account supr. Tilds & Cantz Advt. Agy., L.A., 1963-66; exec. v.p. Fitzgerald, Maahs & Miller, L.A., 1966-71; staff writer The Denver Post, 1971-88; dir. pubs. Am. Water Works Assn., Denver, 1988-97; ret., 1997. Sgt. USNG, 1950-53. Named Colo.'s Outstanding Journalist, U. Colo., 1977; recipient Pulitzer Prize Gold medal Columbia U., 1986. Mem. Investigative Reporters and Editors Inc., (bd. dirs. 1978-80, 81-83), The Newspaper Guild (McWilliams award 1976, 77). Jewish. Home: 4677 E Euclid Ave Littleton CO 80121-3224

UDICK, ROBERT ALAN, political science and media educator; b. Bellvue, Nebr., Nov. 27, 1957; s. Earl Walter Udick and Rosemarie (Hicks) Richards. BA in History, La. State U., 1980, MA in Polit. Sci., 1983; PhD in Social Scis., Syracuse U., 1994. Rsch. asst. Inst. Govt. Rsch. La. State U., Baton Rouge, 1981-83; Blueprint editor and labor studies coord. Inst. Human Rels. Loyola U., New Orleans, 1983-87; rsch. asst., program coord. Ctr. for Study of Citizenship Syracuse (N.Y.) U., 1987-89, rsch. assoc. social sci. program Maxwell Sch. Citizenship, 1988-91; univ. senator, univ. senate hon. degrees com. Syracuse (N.Y.) U., N.Y., 1992-93; univ. senate affirmative action grievance handling com. Syracuse (N.Y.) U., 1992-93, grad. study ad hoc parking and transit com., 1992-93, grad. student rep. to bd. trustees, 1991-92; vis. prof. polit. sci. Colgate U., Hamilton, N.Y., 1994, La. State U., 1994; mgr. front office Prytania Pk. Hotel, New Orleans, 1995-96; presented papers at Assn. for Edn. in Journalism and Mass. Comm., Ga. State U., Atlanta, 1993, Nat. Social Sci. Assn., Memphis, 1991, Orlando, Fla., 1992, New Orleans, 1994, N.Y. State Polit. Sci. Assn., Buffalo, 1992. Founding editor The Pulse, 1989-91, Maxwell Progress, 1989-91; contbr. articles to profl. jours. Bd. dirs. New Orleans Progressive Alliance, 1985-87. Mem. Assn. for Edn. in Journalism and Mass Comm., Nat. Social Sci. Assn., Educators for Social Responsibilty (nat. bd. dirs. 1987-89).

UDLER, RUBIN YAKOVLEVITCH, linguist; b. Braila, Muntenia, Romania, Sept. 27, 1925; came to U.S., 1992; s. Yakov Aronovitch and Dina Vladimirovna (Gleizer) U.; m. Malka Il'initchna Alexenberg, July 8, 1956; children: Arthur, Angela. B Philol. Sci., U. Chernovtsy, Ukrainian S.S.R., 1951; M Philol. Sci., USSR Acad. Scis., Moscow, 1961; D Philol. Sci., USSR Acad. Scis., Leningrad, 1974. Dep. chmn. fgn. langs. dept. Chernovtsy State Pedagogical Inst., 1951-56; jr. sci. researcher dialectology sect. Moldavian br. USSR Acad. Scis., Kishinev, Moldavian S.S.R., 1956-61; chief dialectology and exptl. phonetics sect. Moldavian Acad. Scis., Kishinev, Moldavian S.S.R., 1961-80, chief dialectology and history of lang. sect., 1980-86, chief dialectology and linguistic geography dept., 1986-92, dep. of academician-sec. of social studies dept., 1989-92; ctr. assoc. U. Ctr. for Internat. Studies U. Pitts., 1994—; translator Soviet Bucovina newspaper, Chernovtsy, 1951-52; mem. editl. bd. Moldavian Lang. and Lit., 1961-91, Jour. of Linguistics and Study of Lit., 1991-92; sr. sci. rschr. All-Union Cert. Com., Moscow, 1963. Author: Moldavian Dialects of the Chernovtsy Area Consonantism, 1964, Dialectological Division of the Moldavian Language, Parts 1 and 2, 1976; co-author: The Moldavian Linguistic Atlas, 4 parts, 1968-73, Dialectological Dictionary, 5 vols., 1985-86, Dialectological Texts, 6 parts, 1969-87, The Historical Grammar of the Moldavian Language, 1964, Notes on Modern Moldavian Literary Language, 1967, Moldavian Dialectology, 1976, The Carpathian Dialectological Atlas, 5 vols., 1987-93; author more than 230 pub. works with total volume of more than 420 editl. sheets; mng. editor, co-editor approximately 60 monographs, dictionaries, atlases, collection of dialectological texts, collections of articles, theses, brochures with total volume of more than 1235 editl. sheets. Corr. mem. Moldavian Acad. Scis. Presidium of Moldavian Acad. Scis.; mem. MLA, Am. Assn. Tchrs. Slavic and East European Langs., Am. Soc. Romanian Studies, Holocaust Ctr. United Jewish Fedn. Greater Pitts. Jewish. Avocations: collecting old books, coins, travel. Home: 1535 Shady Ave Pittsburgh PA 15217-1455 Office: Univ Ctr Internat Studies U Pitts 41 G40 Forbes Quadrangle Pittsburgh PA 15260

UDOFF, ERIC JOEL, diagnostic radiologist; b. Balt., Oct. 8, 1948; s. Melvin Jerome and Esther (Fisher) U.; m. Ronni Ann Chapin, June 7, 1980; children: Brian Evan, Jonathan Andrew. AB, Washington U., 1969; MD, U. Rochester, 1973. Intern, resident in diagnostic radiology U. Chgo., 1973-77; instr. in cardiovasc. radiology Johns Hopkins U., Balt., 1977-79; radiologist Sinai Hosp., Balt., 1979-86, Mt. Sinai Med. Ctr., Milw., 1986-88, Sinai Hosp., Balt., 1988-90; asst. prof. radiology Johns Hopkins U. Hosp., 1990-91; radiologist North Fulton Regional Hosp., Roswell, Ga., 1991—. Mem. AMA, Am. Roentgen Ray Soc., Am. Coll. Radiology, Radiol. Soc. N.Am., Soc. Cardiovasc. and Interventional Radiology, Ga. Radiol. Soc., Phi Beta Kappa. Avocation: reading, tennis. Office: North Fulton Regional Hosp 3000 Hospital Blvd Roswell GA 30076-4917

UDRY, J. RICHARD, sociology educator; b. Covington, Ky., Oct. 12, 1928. BS in Sociology, Northwestern U., 1950; MA in Social Sci., Long Beach State Coll., 1956; PhD in Sociology, U. So. Calif., 1960. Instr. Chaffey Coll., 1960-62; asst. prof. Calif. State Poly. Coll., 1962-65; assoc. prof. maternal and child health and sociology U. N.C., Chapel Hill, 1965-69, prof., 1969—, dir. demographic rsch. unit Carolina Population Ctr., 1973-77, dir. Carolina Popluation Ctr., 1977-92, Kenan prof., 1992—. Author: The Social Context of Marriage, 1966, 3d edit., 1974, The Media and Family Planning, 1974; editor: (with Earl Huyck) The Demographic Evaluation of Domestic Family Planning Programs, 1975; contbr. numerous articles and reports to profl. publs. Mem. AAAS, APHA, Am. Sociol. Assn., Population Assn. Am., Nat. Coun. on Family Rels., Sociol. Rsch. Assn. Office: U NC Carolina Population Ctr Univ Sq CB 8120 Chapel Hill NC 27516-3997

UDVAR-HAZY, STEVEN F., leasing company financial executive; b. Budapest, Hungary, Feb. 23, 1946; came to U.S., 1958; m. Christine L. Henneman, June 7, 1980; 3 children. BA, UCLA, 1968; HHD (hon.), U. Utah (Dixie Coll.), 1990. Cert. airline transp. jet pilot. Pres. Internat. Lease Fin. Corp., Beverly Hills, Calif., 1973—; bd. dirs. Sky West Inc., St. George, Utah. Mem. Wings Club (Achievement to Aviation award 1989).

UDVARHELYI, GEORGE BELA, neurosurgery educator emeritus, cultural affairs administrator; b. Budapest, Hungary, May 14, 1920; came to U.S., 1955; s. Bela and Margaret (Bakacs) U.; m. Elspeth Mary Campbell, July 24, 1956; children: Ian Steven, Susan Margaret, Jane Elizabeth. BS, St. Stephen Coll., 1938; MD, U. Budapest, 1944, U. Buenos Aires, 1952; D honoris causa, Semmelweis Med. Sch., Budapest, 1988, Western Md. Coll., 1997. Diplomate Am. Bd. Neurol. Surgery. Intern resident in surgery Red Cross Hosp./11th Mil. Hosp., Budapest, 1942-44; asst. resident Neurol. Univ. Clinic, Budapest, 1944-46; postdoctoral fellow U. Vienna, Austria, 1946-47; fgn. asst. Psychiat. Clinic, U. Berne, Switzerland, 1947-48; asst. resident in neurosurgery Hosp. Espanol, Cordoba, Argentina, 1948-50; resident neurosurgeon Inst. Neurosurgery, U. Buenos Aires, 1950-53; asst. Neurolsurgical Clinic, U. Cologne, Fed. Republic Germany, 1953-54; registrar Royal Infirmary, Edinburgh, Scotland, 1954-55; from fellow to full prof. Johns Hopkins U., Balt., 1955-84, prof. emeritus, dir. cultural affairs, 1984-92, assoc. prof. radiology, 1963-84, Phi Beta Kappa lectr., 1980; neurosurg. cons. Social Security Adminstrn., Balt., 1962-89, Disability Determination Svc., Balt., 1991-93; vis. prof., guest lectr. U. Va., Charlottesville, 1977, Children's Hosp. Ea. Ont., Ottawa, Can., 1977, U. Salzburg, Austria, 1981, U. Vienna, Austria, 1983, Mayo Clinic, Rochester, Minn., 1983, U. Cape Town, Republic of South Africa, 1984, U. Porto, Portugal, 1985; vis. prof. Temple U., Phila., 1979, U. Vt., Burlington, 1980, Aukland (New Zealand) Gen. Hosp., 1989, George Washington U., 1991, U. Mainz, Fed. Republic Germany, 1991, numerous others; lectr. in field. Contbr. numerous articles to profl. jours., book chpts. Mem. program com. Balt. Symphony Orch., 1972-80, edn. com. Walters Art Gallery, Balt., 1985-88. Recipient Lincoln award Am. Hungarian Found., 1980, Eisenberg award Humanities, 1996; Humanities grantee NEH, 1984-91. Fellow ACS; mem. AAUP, Am. Assn. Neurol. Surgeons (life, Humanitarian award 1991), Congress Neurol. Surgeons (sr.), Am. Assn. Neuropathologists, Pan-Am. Med. Assn., Soc. Brit. Neurol. Surgeons (corr.), Pavlovian Soc. N.Am., German Neurol. Soc. (corr.), Internat. Soc. Pediatric Neurosurgery (founding), Hungarian Neurosurg. Soc. (corr.), Argentine Acad. Sci. (corr.), Am. Soc. for Laser Medicine and Surgery (charter), Johns Hopkins Med. Assn., Johns Hopkins Faculty Club, 14 West Hamilton Club (chair steering com. 1977-83), Cosmos Club (chair program subcom. 1991—), Landsdowne Club (London), Alpha Omega Alpha. Roman Catholic. Avocations: music, literature, travel, chess. Home and Office: 111 Hamlet Hill Rd # 1414 Baltimore MD 21210-9999

UEBERROTH, PETER VICTOR, former baseball commissioner; b. Evanston, Ill., Sept. 2, 1937; s. Victor and Laura (Larson) U.; m. Virginia Nicolaus, Sept. 1959; children—Vicky, Heidi, Keri, Joe. B.S. in Bus., San Jose State Coll., 1959. Ops. mgr. then v.p. Trans Internat., 1959-62; founder, chmn. Transp. Cons. Internat., 1963-79; pres., mng. dir. Los Angeles Olympic Organizing Com., 1979-84; commr., chief exec. officer of major league baseball N.Y.C., 1984-89; co-chmn. Doubletree Hotels Corp., Phoenix, 1993—; former chmn. Ask Mr. Foster Travel Service; chmn. Colony Hotels, Intercontinental Tours, Inc., First Travel Corp; mem. bd. dirs. California Angels. Author: Made in America, 1985. Named Man of Yr., Time mag. and Sporting News, 1984; recipient Scopus award Am. Friends of Hebrew U., Jerusalem, 1985. Office: Doubletree Hotels Corp 410 N 44th St Ste 700 Phoenix AZ 85008*

UEHLEIN, E(DWARD) CARL, JR., lawyer; b. Boston, May 7, 1941; s. Edward Carl and Elizabeth (Thatcher) U.; m. Judith Taylor, June 16, 1962; children: Christine, Sara. Student, Bowdoin Coll., Brunswick, Maine, 1958-59; BA, Swarthmore Coll., 1962; LLB, Boston Coll., 1965. Bar: Mass. 1965, D.C. 1968. Atty. Nat. Labor Relations Bd., Atlanta, 1965-68; assoc. Morgan, Lewis & Bockius, Washington, 1968-71; exec. asst. to sec. U.S. Dept. Labor, Washington, 1971-73; ptnr. Morgan Lewis & Bockius, Washington, 1973—; sec.-treas. Carlou Corp., Wilmington, Del., 1969-71. Fellow Ford Found., 1961. Mem. ABA, FBA, D.C. Bar Assn., Belle Haven Country Club, Ballybunion Golf Club, Royal Dornoch Golf Club. Republican. Avocations: travel, golf, reading. Office: Morgan Lewis & Bockius 1800 M St NW Washington DC 20036-5802

UEHLING, BARBARA STANER, educational administrator; b. Wichita, Kans., June 12, 1932; d. Roy W. and Mary Elizabeth (Hilt) Staner; children: Jeffrey Steven, David Edward. B.A., U. Wichita, 1954; M.A., Northwestern U., 1956, Ph.D., 1958; hon. degree, Drury Coll., 1978; LLD (hon.), Ohio State U., 1980. Mem. psychology faculty Oglethorpe U., Atlanta, 1959-64, Emory U., Atlanta, 1966-69; adj. prof. U. R.I., Kingston, 1970-72; dean Roger Williams Coll., Bristol, R.I., 1972-74; dean arts scis. Ill. State U., Normal, 1974-76; provost U. Okla., Norman, 1976-78; chancellor U. Mo.-Columbia, 1978-86, U. Calif., Santa Barbara, 1987-94; sr. vis. fellow Am. Council Edn., 1987; mem. Pacific Rim Pub. U. Pres. Conf., 1990-92; exec. dir. Bus. and Higher Edn. Forum, Washington, 1995—; cons. North Ctr. Accreditation Assn., 1974-86; mem. nat. educator adv. com. to Compt. Gen. of U.S., 1978-79; mem. Commn. on Mil.-Higher Edn. Rels., 1978-79, Am.Coun. on Edn., bd. dirs. 1979-83, treas., 1982-83, mem. Bus.-Higher Edn. Forum, 1980-94, exec. com. 1991-94; Commn. on Internat. Edn., 1992-94, vice chair 1993; bd. dirs. Coun. of Postsecondary Edn., 1986-87, 90-93, Meredith Corp., 1980—; mem. Transatlantic Dialogue, PEW Found., 1991-93. Author: Women in Academe: Steps to Greater Equality, 1979; editorial bd. Jour. Higher Edn. Mgmt., 1986—; contbr. articles to profl. jours. Bd. dirs., chmn. Nat. Ctr. Higher Edn. Mgmt. Sys., 1977-80; trustee Carnegie Found. for Advancement of Teaching, 1980-86, Santa Barbara Med. Found. Clinic, 1989-94; bd. dirs. Resources for the Future, 1985-94; mem. select com. on athletics NCAA, 1983-84, also mem. presdl. commn.; mem. Nat. Coun. on Edn. Rsch., 1980-82. Social Sci. Research Council fellow, 1954-55; NSF fellow, 1956-57; NIMH postdoctoral research fellow, 1964-67; named one of 100 Young Leaders of Acad. Change Mag. and ACE, 1978; recipient Alumni Achievement award Wichita State U., 1978, Alumnae award Northwestern U., 1985, Excellence in Edn. award Pi Lambda Theta, 1989. Mem. Am. Assn. Higher Edn. (bd. dirs. 1974-77, pres. 1977-78), Western Coll. Assn. (pres.-elect 1988-89,k pres. 1990-92), Golden Key, Sigma Xi. Office: Bus-Higher Edn Forum One Dupont Cir Ste 800 Washington DC 20036

UELAND, SIGURD, JR., lawyer; b. Mpls., June 1, 1937; s. Sigurd and Harriet (Scofield) U.; m. Harriet Moulton, Dec. 27, 1963; children: Scott, Leif, Tora, Sigurd III. B.A., Yale U., 1959; LL.B., U. Minn., 1962. Bar: Minn. 1963. Asso. firm Neville, Johnson & Thompson, Mpls., 1963-67; corp. atty. Whirlpool Corp., Benton Harbor, Mich., 1968-69, Honeywell Inc., Mpls., 1969—; sec. Honeywell Inc., 1977—, asst. gen. counsel, 1980—, v.p., 1983—. Mem. ABA, Am. Soc. Corp. Secs. (chmn. 1996-97), Minn. Bar Assn., Hennepin County Bar Assn. Congregationalist. Home: 8206 Norman Creek Trl Bloomington MN 55437-3814 Office: Honeywell Plz Minneapolis MN 55408

UEMURA, TERUKI, child brain developmentalist; b. Tokyo, Mar. 25, 1944; came to U.S., 1973; s. Kiichi and Teru (Koizumi) U. BA, Keio U., Tokyo, 1967, diploma in bus. adminstr., 1972; M Mgmt., Northwestern U., 1975; postgrad., U. Pa., 1976-81. Mem. staff Aichi Steel Works, Ltd., Nagoya, Japan, 1967-81; coord. Insts. for Achievement Human Potential, Phila., 1984—; vice dir. intellectual growth at The Children's Ctr. The Children's Ctr., Phila., 1984-91; vice dir. The Children's Ctr. Insts. for Achievement Human Potential, Phila., 1991-94; vice dir. Insts. Achievement of Intellectual Excellence, Phila., 1994—; rsch. asst. Harvard U., Cambridge, Mass., 1972-74, U. Pa., Phila., 1979-81; translator U.S. State Dept., Washington, 1980—. Program coordinator Coun. Internat. Visitors, Phila., 1978-81. Recipient Brazilian Gold medal of Humanities, World Orgn. for Human Potential, 1984, 88, Sakura Koro Sho award, 1986, Leonardo da Vinci award, 1993. Fellow Internat. Acad. Child Brain Devel., Japan Group II. Avocations: reading, tennis, travel, history, science. Office: Inst for the Achievement Human Potential 8801 Stenton Ave Wyndmoor PA 19038-8319

UENO, EDWARD ISAO, environmental science educator; b. Numazu-shi, Japan, Nov. 28, 1938; s. Hirokichi and Sei (Sajiki) Saito; m. Taeko Ueno, Apr. 8, 1970; children: Mikako, Masanobu. BSc, Tokai U., 1961; MSc, Meiji U., 1963, PhD, 1966. Ednl. official Ministry of Edn., Tokyo, 1966—; vis. prof. Tech. U., Braunschweig, Germany, 1975-78, Tex. Tech. U., Lubbock, 1980; res. R&D group of intense neutron source U. Tokyo, 1980-89, rep. of fusion sci. group, 1989—; vis. prof. FM Tokyo Broadcasting Sta., 1981; adviser policy planning com. Japanese Govt., 1994, Hitoyoshi City, 1994. Author: Energy and Resources, 1992, 93, Waste and Resource, 1994, 95, 96, 97, Ekoshisutemu Noho no Kiseki (The Miracle based on Agricultural Method of Microbiological Ecosystems), 1995, Twentieth Century Achievement Award of Five Hundred Leaders of Influence, 1996; contbr. numerous articles to profl. jours. Dozenten fellow Alexander von Humboldt Found., 1975; spl. rsch. grant Ministry of Edn., 1980, grants-in-aid for scientific rsch., 1981. Mem. AAAS, Inst. for Ecosystem Agr. (chief sec. 1992—), Soc. for the Study to Design Water (dir. 1993—), Soc. of Waste and Resource Rsch. (mgr. 1994—), The Inst. for Eco and Economy System (pres. 1995—), Order Internat. Fellowship, Internat. Order Merit (Eng.), Club of Fusion Sci. (chief dir. 1983—), Vereinigung der Humboldtlaner in Japan. Avocations: go, karate, traveling, reading, writing. Office: The Club of Fusion Sci, 3-1-17-903 Sendagi, Bunkyo-ku Tokyo 113, Japan

UENO, HIROSHI, biochemist; b. Sakai, Osaka, Japan, Dec. 9, 1950; s. Haruko (Hachihama) U.; m. Yumiko Matsuzaki, Feb. 11, 1978; 1 child, Leo Dale. BE, Kyoto U., 1974; MA, Brandeis U., 1976; PhD in Biochemistry, Iowa State U., 1982. Rsch. assoc. Rockefeller U., N.Y.C., 1982-83, Rockefeller Found. fellow, 1984-85, asst. prof. biochemistry, 1986—; assoc. prof. dept. agrl. chemistry Kyoto (Japan) U., 1993—; summer investigator Woods Hole Marine Biology Lab., 1984—; vis. scientist Population Coun., 1984—; mem. ad hoc com. Nat. Heart, Lung and Blood Inst., NIH, Bethesda, Md., 1987—; mem. organizing com. 8th Internat. Congress on Vitamin B6 and Carbonyl Catalysis, Osaka, 1990; vis. prof. Kumamoto U., Japan, 1990. Recipient Molly Berns Meml. Investigator, Am. Heart Assn., 1989—. Mem. Am. Soc. Biochemistry and Molecular Biology, Am. Chem. Soc., Harvey Soc., N.Y. Acad. Scis. Research in chemistry of Gossypol, transaminases, hemoglobins. Office: Kyoto U Faculty Agr, Dept Agrl Chemistry, Sakyo 606-01, Japan

UENO, TOMIKO F., forestry company executive; b. Mie, Japan, May 26, 1930; d. Fusataro and Masuye (Higashi) U.; m. Kohei Ueno, Nov. 20, 1953; children: Fusako, Takuro, Toyotsugu. AB, Tokyo Kaseigakuin U., 1952. Pres., chief exec. officer Ueno Corp., Tokyo, 1975—; bd. dirs. Ueno Ringyo Ltd., Tokyo. Mem. Forestland Owners Assn. Japan. Avocations: travel, cooking. Office: Ueno Ringyo Ltd, 5-17 Fuyuki, Koto-ku, Tokyo 135, Japan

UFFELMAN, MALCOLM RUCJ, electronics company executive, electrical engineer; b. Clarksville, Tenn., Oct. 22, 1935; s. Malcolm C. and Margaret Lillian (Davidson) U.; m. Sarah White Barksdale, June 11, 1957; children: Malcolm Rucj Jr., Katharina White, Davidson Barksdale, Jefferson Churchill. BS, Vanderbilt U., 1957; MS, George Washington U., 1963. Engr. Melpar, Inc., Falls Church, Va., 1957-60; v.p. Scope, Inc., Reston, Va., 1960-73; sr. cons. MRI, Inc., McLean, Va., 1973-78; v.p. Racal Communications Inc., Rockville, Md., 1978-80; sr. cons. MRJ, Inc., Fairfax, Va., 1980-82; v.p., gen. mgr., Ctr. Advanced Planning and Analysis E-Systems Inc., Fairfax, 1982-96; v.p. Constellation Comm., Inc., Fairfax, 1996—; pvt. practice patent agt., Vienna, Va., 1975—. Contbr. numerous articles to profl. jours.; holder 7 patents in field. Scoutmaster Troop 183 Boy Scouts Am., Oakton, Va., 1973-79. Capt. USAR, 1957-69. Fellow IEEE, AIAA (assoc.); mem. N.Y. Acad. Scis., Assn. Old Crows, Navy League, Cosmos Club (Washington). Republican. Episcopalian. Avocations: tennis, sailing, fishing, reading, travel. Office: Constellation Comm 11911 Freedom Dr Ste 500 Reston VA 20190-5602

UFFORD, CHARLES WILBUR, JR., lawyer; b. Princeton, N.J., July 8, 1931; m. Isabel Letitia Wheeler, May 20, 1961; children: Eleanor Morris Ufford Léger, Catherine Latourette Ufford-Chase, Alison Wistar Ufford Salem. BA cum laude (Francis H. Burr scholar), Harvard U., 1953, LLB, 1959; postgrad. (Lionel de Jersey Harvard studentship), Cambridge U., Eng., 1953-54. Bar: N.Y. 1961, U.S. Tax Ct. 1963. Assoc. Riggs, Ferris & Geer, N.Y.C., 1959-61; from assoc. to ptnr. Jackson, Nash, Brophy, Barringer & Brooks, 1961-78; ptnr. Skadden, Arps, Slate, Meagher & Flom, N.Y.C., 1978-92, of counsel, 1993-96. Contbr. articles to legal jours. Trustee Nat. Squash Racquets Ednl. Found., N.Y.C., 1972-81; mem. Princeton monthly meeting Soc. of Friends, clk., 1986-88; exec. com. Friends Com. on Nat. Legislation, 1997—. Nat. Intercollegiate Squash Racquets champion, 1952-53; mem. NCAA All-Am. Soccer 1st team, 1952. Fellow Am. Coll. Trust and Estate Counsel (transfer tax study com. 1990-93); mem. ABA, N.Y. Bar Assn. (chmn. trusts and estates law sect. 1984), Assn. Bar City N.Y., N.Y. State Office of Ct. Adminstrn. (Surrogates Ct. Adv. Com., 1994-96), Internat. Acad. Trusts and Estates Law, U.S. Squash Racquets Assn. (hon. life; trustee endowment fund 1984-96), Internat. Lawn Tennis club U.S.A. (dir. 1982—). Home: 150 Mercer St Princeton NJ 08540-6827 Office: Skadden Arps Slate Meagher & Flom 919 3rd Ave New York NY 10022 *Integrity, perseverance, compassion and humor are all very well--but the key is to be blessed by a Divine Improvidence.*

UFIMTSEV, PYOTR YAKOVLEVICH, physicist, electrical engineer, educator; b. Ust'-Charyshskaya Pristan', Altai Region, Russia, July 8, 1931; s. Yakov Fedorovich and Vasilisa Vasil'evna (Toropchina) U.; m. Tatiana Vladimirovna Sinelschikova; children: Ivan, Vladimir. Grad., Odessa State U., USSR, 1954; PhD, Cen. Rsch. Inst. of Radio Industry, Moscow, 1959; DSc, St. Petersburg State U., Russia, 1970. Engr., sr. engr., sr. scientist Cen. Rsch. Inst. of Radio Industry, Moscow, 1954-73; sr. scientist Inst. Radio Engring. & Electronics Acad. Scis., Moscow, 1973-90; vis. prof., adj. prof. UCLA, 1990—; mem. Sci. Bd. of Radio Waves, Acad. Scis., Moscow, 1960-90. Author: Method of Edge Waves in the Physical Theory of Diffraction, 1962; contbr. articles to profl. jours. Recipient USSR State Prize, Moscow, 1990, Leroy Randle Grumman medal for outstanding sci. achievement, N.Y.C., 1991. Mem. AIAA, IEEE, Electromagnetics Acad. (U.S.), A.S. Popov Sci. Tech. Soc. Radio Engring., Electronics & Telecommunication (Russia). Achievements include origination of the Physical Theory of Diffraction, used for design of American stealth aircrafts and ships; for radar-cross-section calculation, and antenna design. Office: UCLA Dept Elec Engring 405 Hilgard Ave Los Angeles CA 90095-9000

UGHETTA, WILLIAM CASPER, lawyer, manufacturing company executive; b. N.Y.C., Feb. 8, 1933; s. Casper and Frieda (Bohland) U.; m. Mary L. Lusk, Aug. 10, 1957; children: William C., Robert L., Edward F., Mark R. A.B., Princeton U, 1954; LL.B, Harvard U., 1959. Bar: N.Y. 1959. Assoc. Shearman & Sterling, N.Y.C., 1959-67; asst. sec. Corning Glass Works, N.Y., 1968-70, sec., counsel, 1971-72, v.p., gen. counsel, 1972-82, sr. v.p., gen. counsel, 1983—; bd. dirs. Corning Internat. Corp., Siecor Corp., Corning Europe Inc., Corning France, Chemung Canal Trust Co. Bd. dirs. Steuben Area coun. Boy Scouts Am.; officer Corning Mus. Glass, Corning Glass Works Found.; trustee Corning Community Coll. Served to lt. (j.g.) U.S. Navy, 1954-56. Mem. Assn. Bar. City N.Y., ABA, N.Y. State Bar Assn., Am. Corp. Counsel Assn. (trustee 1982-85). Clubs: Princeton (N.Y.C.), Univ. (N.Y.C.); Corning Country. Home: 13 North Rd Corning NY 14830-3235 Office: Corning Inc 1 Riverfront Plz Corning NY 14831-0001

UGWU, MARTIN CORNELIUS, pharmacist; b. Enugu, Anambra, Nigeria, Aug. 22, 1956; came to U.S., 1978; s. Nneji and Maria Uchenwa (Igwesi) U.; m. Renee Mashell Momon, June 30, 1990; children: Martin Cornelius Jr., Kyla Chikanya. AA/AS in Civil Engring. and Gen. Studies, Brevard Community Coll., 1980; BS in chemistry, Grambling State U., 1982; PharmD, Fla. A&M U., 1986. Registered clin. pharmacist Dept. Profl. Regulation, Fla. Pharmacist Rite Aid Pharmacy, Miami, Fla., 1986-87, mgr., 1989-93; clin. pharmacist Mercy Hosp., Miami, 1987-88, Miami Heart Inst., Miami Beach, Fla., 1995—; mem. pharmacy and therapeutic com. Palmetto Gen. Hosp., Miami, 1986. Named one of Outstanding Young Men of Am., 1986. Mem. Am. Pharm. Assn., Am. Soc. Hosp. Pharmacists, Am. Soc. Parenteral and Enteral Nutrition, Fla. Pharmacy Assn., Fla. Soc. Hosp. Pharmacists. Roman Catholic. Home: PO Box 600651 North Miami Beach FL 33160 Office: Miami Heart Inst 4701 N Meridian Ave Miami FL 33140-2910 Mailing: PO Box 600651 North Miami Beach FL 33160

UHDE, GEORGE IRVIN, physician; b. Richmond, Ind., Mar. 20, 1912; s. Walter Richard and Anna Margaret (Hoopes) U.; m. Maurine Elizabeth Whitley, July 27, 1935; children—Saundra Uhde Seelig, Thomas Whitley, Michael, Janice. M.D., Duke U., 1936. Diplomate: Am. Bd. Otolaryngology. Intern Reading (Pa.) Hosp., 1936-37, resident in medicine, 1937-38; resident in otolaryngology Balt. Eye, Ear, Nose and Throat Hosp., 1938-40, U. Oreg. Med. Sch., Portland, 1945-47; practice medicine specializing in otolaryngology Louisville, 1948—; asst. prof. otolaryngology U. Louisville Med. Sch., 1945-62, prof. surgery (otolaryngology), head dept., 1963-92, prof. emeritus, 1992—, dir. otolaryngology services, 1963—; mem. staffs Meth., Norton's-Children's, Jewish, St. Joseph's, St. Anthony's, St. Mary and Elizabeth's hosps.; cons. Ky. Surg. Tb Hosp., Hazlewood, VA Hosp., Louisville, U. Louisville Speech and Hearing Center. Author 4 books.; Contbr. articles to profl. jours. Bd. dirs. Easter Seal Speech and Hearing Ctr. Lt. col. M.C. U.S. Army, 1940-45, ETO, Gen. Eisenhower staff, 1943-45. Recipient Disting. Service award U. Louisville, 1972. Fellow A.C.S., Am. Acad. Ophthalmology and Otolaryngology, So. Med. Soc.; mem. N.Y. Acad. Scis., Am. Coll. Allergists, Am. Acad. Facial Plastic and Reconstructive Surgery, AAAS, Assn. U. Otolaryngologists, AAUP, Assn. Mil. Surgeons U.S., Am. Laryngol., Rhinol. and Otol. Soc., Am. Audiology Soc., Soc. Clin. Ecology, Am. Soc. Otolaryngology Allergy, Centurian Otol. Research Soc. (Ky. rep.), Am. Council Otolaryngology (Ky. rep. 1968—), Hoopes Quaker Found., SAR (life), Gen. Soc. Colonial Wars (hereditary mem.), Alpha Kappa Kappa. Democrat. Methodist. Clubs: Filson, Big Spring Country, Jefferson. Home: 708 Circle Hill Rd Louisville KY 40207-3627 Office: Med Towers Louisville KY 40202

UHDE, THOMAS WHITLEY, psychiatry educator, psychiatrist; b. Louisville, Jan. 6, 1948; s. George Irwin and Maurine U.; m. Marlene Ann Kraus, Oct. 22, 1977; children: Miles August, Katherine Kraus. BS, Duke U., 1971; MD, U. Louisville, 1975. Postdoctoral fellow Yale U., New Haven, 1975-79, chief resident clin. rsch. unit, 1979; rsch. fellow NIMH, 1979-81; pvt. practice in psychiatry Bethesda, Md., 1979-93; clin. adminstr. sect. psychobiology BPB, NIMH, ADAMHA, Bethesda, Md., 1979-80, chief unit on anxiety and affective disorders, 1982-89, chief 3-West clin. rsch. unit, 1980-90, chief sect. on anxiety and affective disorders, 1989-93; asst. clin. prof. Uniformed Svcs. U. Health Scis., Bethesda, Md., 1982-85, assoc. clin. prof. uniformed svcs., 1985-91, clin. prof. psychiatry, 1991—; attending staff Clin. Ctr. NIH, Bethesda, Md., 1982-93; chmn. dept. psychiatry Detroit Receiving Hosp. and Harper Hosp., 1994—; psychiatrist in chief Detroit Med. Ctr., 1993—; clin. prof. Uniformed Svcs. U. Health Scis. Sch. Medicine, Bethesda, 1991—; prof., chmn. of psych. dept. Wayne State U. Sch. of Medicine, Detroit, 1993—; mem. sci. adv. com. Bethesda, Md., 1990—; cons. Rsch. Scientist Devel. Rev. Com., HHS, ADAMHA, 1983—, Career Devel. Program Awards Com., VA, Washington, 1986—, Primary Care Rsch. Program, ADAMHA, 1988—, Assessment (DATTA) program AMA, Chgo., 1991—; exec. bd. ADDA, chair ADDA sci. adv. bd., Rockville, Md., 1991-93. Editor-in-chief (jour.) Anxiety; co-editor-in-chief Depression and Anxiety; mem. editl. bd. Actualities Medicales Internationales en Psychiatrie, 1983, Jour. Affective Disorders, 1986, Jour. Anxiety Disorders, 1987-95; contbr. over 225 sci. articles to profl. jours. Capt. USPHS, 1979-93. Recipient The Ackerly award, 1975, Nat. Rsch. Svc. award, 1979, A.E. Bennet Neuropsychiat. Rsch. Found. award, Brain, Body & Mind award USPHS, Recognition award ADAA; Am. Coll. Neuropsychopharmacology travel fellow. Mem. Am. Assn. Chmn. Depts. Psychiatry, Am. Coll. Psychiatry, Soc. of Clin. Psychopharmomcology, Internat. Brain Rsch. Orgn., Sleep Rsch. Soc., ACNP. Office: Wayne State Sch Medicine 42011 St Antoine St 9B UHC Detroit MI 48201-2153

UHL, SCOTT MARK, state agency administrator; b. Balt., July 6, 1950; s. Edward George and Maurine Barbara (Keleher) U.; m. Charlene Hughins, Feb. 29, 1988. BA, Lehigh U., 1972. Cmty. systems developer Md. Mental Hygiene Adminstrn., Balt., 1979-82, chief, housing and cmty. support, 1982-89; adminstr., cmty. programs, dep. secretariat pub. health Md. Health and Mental Hygiene, Balt., 1989-95; dep. dir. Md. Devel. Disabilities Adminstrn., Balt., 1995—; cons. in field, 1983-85; pres. Waterfields Press, Inc., 1994—; mem. adv. bd. C.A.R.E., Md. Dept. Human Resources, Balt., 1987-94; prin. staff Md. Gov.'s Task Force on Long Term Fin. Planning for Individuals with Disabilities, 1991-92. Gov.'s appointee State Adv. Coun. on Adminstrv. Hearings, 1993—. Recipient Govs. citation, 1992. Republican. Home: 4594 Kingscup Ct Ellicott City MD 21042-5986 Office: Md Health & Mental Hygiene 201 W Preston St Baltimore MD 21201-2323

UHLENBECK, KAREN KESKULLA, mathematician, educator; b. Cleve., Aug. 24, 1942; d. Arnold Edward and Carolyn Elizabeth (Windeler) Keskulla; m. Olke Cornelis, June 12, 1965 (div.). BS in Math., U. Mich., 1964; PhD in Math., Brandeis U., 1968. Instr. math. MIT, Cambridge, 1968-69; lectr. U. Calif., Berkeley, 1969-71; asst. prof., then assoc. prof. U. Ill., Urbana, 1971-76; assoc. prof., then prof. U. Ill., Chgo., 1977-83; prof. U. Chgo., 1983-88; Sid W. Richardson Found. Regents' Chair in Math. U. Tex., 1988—; spkr. plenary address Internat. Conress Maths., 1990; mem. com. women on sci. and engring. NRC, 1992-94; mem. steering com., dir. mentoring program for women Inst. for Advanced Study/Park City Math. Inst. Author: Instantons and Four Manifolds, 1984. Contbr. articles to profl. jours. Recipient Common Wealth award for Sci. and Invention, PNC Bank, 1995; NSF grad. fellow, 1964-68, Sloan Found. fellow, 1974-76, MacArthur Found. fellow, 1983-88. Mem. AAAS, NAS, Alumni Assn. U. Mich. (Alumnae of Yr. 1984), Am. Math. Soc., Assn. Women in Math., Phi Beta Kappa. Avocations: gardening, canoeing, hiking. Office: U Tex Dept Math Austin TX 78712

UHLENHUTH, EBERHARD HENRY, psychiatrist, educator; b. Balt., Sept. 15, 1927; s. Eduard Carl Adolph and Elisabeth (Baier) U.; m. Helen Virginia Lyman, June 20, 1952; children: Kim Lyman, Karen Jane, Eric Rolf. BS in Chemistry, Yale U., 1947; MD, Johns Hopkins U., 1951. Intern Harborview Hosp., Seattle, 1951-52; resident in psychiatry Johns Hopkins Hosp., Balt., 1952-56; asst. psychiatrist in charge outpatient dept. Johns Hopkins Hosp., 1956-61, psychiatrist in charge, 1961-62; chief adult psychiatry clinic U. Chgo. Hosps. Clinics, 1968-76; instr. psychiatry Johns Hopkins U., 1956-59, asst. prof., 1959-67, assoc. prof., 1967-68; assoc. prof. U. Chgo., 1968-73, prof., 1973-85, acting chmn., 1983-85; prof. psychiatry U. N.Mex., Albuquerque, 1985—, vice chmn. for edn., 1991-94; cons. in field; mem. clin. psychopharmacology rsch. rev. com. NIMH, 1968-72, treatment devel. and assessment rev. com., 1987; mem. psychopharmacology adv. com. FDA, 1974-78; mem. adv. group to Treatment of Depression Collaborative Rsch. Program, NIMH, 1978-92; study rev. com. Xanax Discontinuation Program, The UpJohn Co., 1988-92, Nat. Adv. Coun. on Drug Abuse, NIDA, 1989-92, Coop. Studies Evaluation Com., VA, 1989-92. Mem. editl. bd. Jour. Affective Disorders, 1978—, Psychiatry Rsch., 1979-96, Behavioral Medicine, 1982—, Neuropsychopharmacology, 1992-94, Exptl. and Clin. Psychopharmacology, 1992—, Anxiety, 1993—; contbr. articles to profl. jours. Recipient Research Career Devel. award USPHS, 1962-68, Research Scientist award, 1976-81. Fellow Am. Coll. Neuropsychopharmacology (pres. 1986), Am. Psychiat. Assn., Am. Psychopath. Assn.; mem. Balt.-Washington Soc. for Psychoanalysis, Collegium Internat. Neuro-Psychopharmacologicum, Psychiat. Rsch. Soc. Office: U NMex Dept Psychiatry 2400 Tucker NE Albuquerque NM 87131

UHLER, WALTER CHARLES, government official, writer, reviewer; b. Lebanon, Pa., Feb. 23, 1948; s. Victor Cornelius and Barbara Jean (Malin) U.; m. Judy Ann Sherk, Aug. 7, 1967 (div. 1984); children: Terry Allen, Matthew David. Life partner: Carol A. DePrisco. BA in Polit. Sci. cum laude, Pa. State U., 1973, BA in Russian cum laude, 1973, cert. Russian area, 1973, MPA, 1992. Tchg. asst. Pa. State U., University Park, 1975-76; procurement agt. Naval Aviation Supply Office, Phila., 1976-80; contracts adminstr. GSA, Phila., 1980-81; contracting officer Def. Logistics Agy., Phila., 1981-86, corp. contracting officer, 1986-94; chief fin. svcs., 1993—; regional cons. Def. Logistics Agy., L.A., 1985-86; nat. cons. Def. Logistics Agy., Cameron Station, Va., 1989-90; leader Testing Labs. Privatization Assessment Team Def. Logistics Agy., Ft. Belvoir, Va., 1997—; participant Air Force Intelligence Conf. on Soviet Affairs, Arlington, Va., 1988, Venona Conf., Washington, 1996; spkr. on contracts DOD Conf., Cleve., 1988, on restructuring costs, Memphis, 1994; chmn. Ann. Nat. Conf. Contracting Officers and Auditors, 1987-93; mem. Citizen Amb. Archivists' Del. to Russia and Poland, 1995, Citizen Amb. Del. to China, 1996. Contbr. articles to profl. jours. Baseball coach Valley Athletic Assn., Bensalem, Pa., 1979-88, basketball coach, 1980-85, coord., 1981; tutor Ctr. for Literacy, Phila., 1991-93, Project GIVE, Phila., 1995—; citizen amb. del. to China, 1996. Recipient Comdrs. Excellence award Defense Contract Mgmt. Area Ops., 1993. Mem. Am. Assn. for Advancement Slavic Studies, Am. Def. Preparedness Assn., Acad. Polit. Sci., Phila. Writers Orgn., Am. Acad. of Polit. and Social Scis., Friends of the Free Libr. of Phila. Democrat. Avocations: history, literature, Pa. State U. football. Office: DCMC Phila DCMDE-GDTC PO Box 7699 Philadelphia PA 19101-7699

UHLIR, ARTHUR, JR., electrical engineer, university administrator; b. Chgo., Feb. 2, 1926; s. Arthur and Helene (Houghteling) U.; m. Ingeborg Williams, July 24, 1954; children: Steven, Donald, David. BS, Ill. Inst. Tech., 1945, MSChemE, 1948; SM in Physics, U. Chgo., 1950, PhD in Physics, 1952. Process analyst Douglas Aircraft, Chgo., 1945; asst. engr. Armour Rsch. Found., Chgo., 1945-48; tech. staff Bell Telephone Labs., Murray Hill, N.J., 1951-58; dir. semi- condr. research and devel., mgr. semicondr. div., group v.p. engring. Microwave Assos., Inc., Burlington, Mass., 1958-69; dir. rsch. Computer Metrics, Rochelle Park, N.J., 1969-73; prof. elec. engring. Tufts U., Medford, Mass., 1970-94; chmn. dept. elec. engring. Tufts U., 1970-75, dean of engring., 1973-80. AEC fellow, 1949-51. Fellow IEEE, AAAS; mem. Am. Phys. Soc., Sigma Xi. Home: 45 Kendal Common Rd Weston MA 02193-2159 Office: Tufts Univ Elec Engring Dept Elec Engring & Computer Sci Medford MA 02155

UHLMANN, FREDERICK GODFREY, commodity and securities broker; b. Chgo., Dec. 31, 1929; s. Richard F. and Rosamond G. (Goldman) U.; m. Virginia Lee Strauss, July 24, 1951; children: Richard, Thomas, Virginia, Karen, Elizabeth. B.A., Washington and Lee U., 1951. Ptnr. Uhlmann Grain Co., Chgo., 1951-61; v.p. Uhlmann & Co., Inc., Chgo., 1961-65; sr. v.p. H. Hentz & Co., Chgo., 1965-73, Drexel Burnham Lambert Inc., Chgo., 1973-84; exec. v.p., dir. bus. futures Dean Witter Reynolds Inc., Chgo., 1984-85; sr. v.p., mgr. commodity dept. Bear, Stearns & Co., Inc., Chgo., 1985-88; exec. v.p. Rodman & Renshaw, Inc., 1988-95; sr. v.p. LIT-Divsn. of First Options Inc., Chgo., 1995—; chmn. Chgo Bd. Trade, 1973-74. Trustee Highland Park Hosp., Ill.; bd. dirs. Dist. 113 H.S. Found., 1990—. Mem. Nat. Futures Assn. (dir. 1981—), Futures Industry Assn. (bd. dirs., chmn. 1975-76). Clubs: Lake Shore Country (Glencoe, Ill.) (dir.); Standard (Chgo.). Home: 783 Whiteoaks Ln Highland Park IL 60035-3656

UHRICH, RICHARD BECKLEY, hospital executive, physician; b. Pitts., June 11, 1932; s. Leroy Earl and Mabel Hoffer (Beckley) U.; m. Susan Kay Manning, May 25, 1985; children by previous marriage—Mark, Karen, Kimberly. BS, Allegheny Coll., 1954; MD, U. Pa., 1958; MPH, U. Calif.-Berkeley, 1966. Diplomate: Am. Bd. Preventive Medicine. Intern Lancaster Gen. Hosp., (Pa.), 1958-59; commd. asst. surg. USPHS, 1959, advanced through grades to med. dir., 1967; resident U. Calif., 1965-66; various adminstrv. positions regional and service unit levels Indian Health Services, until 1971; dir. div. programs ops. Indian Health Service, Health Services Adminstrn. USPHS, Washington, 1971-73; assoc. dir. div. profl. resources Office Internat. Health, Office Asst. Sec. for Health, HEW, Washington, 1973-74; assoc. dir. for program devel. and coordination Office Internat. Health, 1974-78; dir. Phoenix Indian Med. Ctr. and Phoenix Services Unit, 1978-81, ret., 1982; sr. adminstr. Good Samaritan Med Ctr., Phoenix, 1981-82, chief exec. officer, 1982-89; v.p. for managed care programs Samaritan Health Svcs., Phoenix, 1989-90; cons. health care systems Phoenix, 1990-93; dir. S.E. Asia, internat. dir. Med. Ambs. Internat., Modesto, Calif., 1993-95, ret., 1995; mem. Phoenix Regional Hosp. Coun., 1981-88, pres., 1982-83; bd. dirs. Med. Ctr. Redevel. Corp., Phoenix, Med. Ambs. Internat.; v.p. Samaritan Redevel. Corp., 1983-88. Bd. dirs. Phoenix Symphony Orch., 1984-89, Ariz. Sr. Olympics Bd., 1985-89, Med. Ambs. Internat., 1995—. Recipient Meritorious Service medal USPHS, 1973; recipient citation USPHS, 1973, Commd. Officers award, 1981. Mem. Ariz. Hosp. Assn. (bd. dirs. 1980-86, chmn. council on planning 1980-81, council on human resources 1982-83, council on patient care 1983-84, fin. com. 1984-86), Am. Coll. Health Care Adminstrs., Am. Pub. Health Assn., Christian Med. Soc.

UHRIG, ROBERT EUGENE, nuclear engineer, educator; b. Raymond, Ill., Aug. 6, 1928; s. John Matthew and Anna LaDonna (Fireman) U.; m. Paula Margaret Schnepf, Nov. 27, 1954; children: Robert John, Joseph Charles, Mary Catherine, Charles William, Jean Marie, Thomas Paul, Fredrick James. B.S. with honors, U. Ill., 1948; M.S. Iowa State U, 1950, Ph.D., 1954; grad. Advanced Mgmt. Program, Harvard U., 1976. Registered profl. engr., Iowa, Fla. Instr. engring. mechanics Iowa State U., 1948-51; assoc. engr., research asst. Inst. Atomic Research (at univ.), 1951-54, assoc. prof. engring. mechanics and nuclear engring., also group leader, 1956-60; prof. nuclear engring., chmn. dept. U. Fla., Gainesville, 1960-68; on leave U. Fla., 1967-68, dean Coll. Engring., 1968-73; dean emeritus, 1989—; dep. asst. dir. research Dept. Def., Washington, 1967-68; dir. nuclear affairs Fla. Power & Light Co., Miami, 1973-74; v.p. for nuclear affairs Fla. Power & Light Co., 1974-75, v.p. nuclear and gen. engring., 1976-78, v.p. advanced systems and tech., 1978-86; disting. prof. engring. U. Tenn., Knoxville, 1986—; disting. scientist Oak Ridge Nat. Lab., 1986—; Rep. Dept. Def. to com. on acad. sci. and engring. Fed. Council Sci. and Tech., 1967; chmn. engring. adv. com. NSF, 1972-73; bd. dirs. Engring. Council Profl. Devel., 1968-72; mem. commn. edn. for engring. profession Nat. Assn. State Univs. and Land Grant Colls., 1969-72. Author: Random Noise Techniques in Nuclear Reactor Systems, 1970, trans. into Russian, 1974; co-author: (with Lefteri H. Tsoukalas) Fuzzy and Neural Approaches in Engineering, 1997. Served to 1st lt. USAF; instr. engring. mechanics U.S. Mil. Acad. 1954-56. Recipient Sec. of Def. Civilian Service award, 1968, Outstanding Alumni award U. Ill. Coll. Engring., 1970, Alumni Profl. Achievement award Iowa State U., 1972, President's medallion U. Fla., 1973; Disting. Achievement citation Iowa State U. Alumni Assn., 1980, Glenn Murphy awd., Am. Soc. for Engineering Education, 1992. Fellow ASME (life, Richards Meml. award 1969), AAAS, Am. Nuclear Soc. (chmn. edn. com. 1962-64, chmn. tech. group for edn. 1964-66, dir. 1965-68, exec. com. bd. 1966-68); mem. Am. Soc. Engring. Edn. (pres. S.E. sect. 1972-73, chmn. nuclear engring. divsn. 1966-67, 88-89, rsch. award S.E. sect. 1962, Glenn Murphy award as Outstanding Educator 1992), John Henry Newman Honor Soc., Sigma Xi, Tau Beta Pi, Phi Mu Epsilon, Pi Tau Sigma, Phi Kappa Phi (Disting. Mem. award 1997). Home: 113 Connors Dr Oak Ridge TN 37830-7662 Office: U Tenn Pasqua Nuclear Engring Bldg Knoxville TN 37996-2300

UHRY, ALFRED FOX, playwright; b. Atlanta, Dec. 3, 1936; s. Ralph Kahn and Alene (Fox) U.; m. Joanna Kellogg; children: Emily Uhry Rhea, Elizabeth Uhry MacCurrach, Katharine, Nell. BA, Brown U., 1958. worked with composer Frank Loesser, 1960-63; instr. Eng., drama Calhoun High Sch., 1963-80; instr. lyric writing NYU, 1985-88. Author: (play) Driving Miss Daisy, 1987 (Drama Desk award nomination for best play 1987, Pulitzer Prize for drama 1988, L.A. Drama Critics Circle award for best play 1989); (musicals) Chapeau, 1977, (adapter) Little Johnny Jones, 1982, (adapter) Follow Thru, 1984; (lyrics) Here's Where I Belong, 1968, Swing, 1980; (lyrics, libretto) The Robber Bridegroom, 1978 (Drama Desk award nomination for best play 1975, Tony award nomination for best book of a musical 1976), America's Sweetheart, 1985; (screenplays) Mystic Pizza, 1988, Driving Miss Daisy, 1989 (Academy award for best adapted screenplay 1989, WGA award 1989), Rich in Love, 1993, Last Night Of Ballyhoo, 1996 (Tony award for Best Play, 1997). Mem. Dramatists Guild (coun. 1989—, Elizabeth Martow prize 1987). Office: care Flora Roberts 157 W 57th St Ph A New York NY 10019-2210*

UICKER, JOSEPH BERNARD, engineering company executive; b. State College, Pa., Mar. 29, 1940; s. John Joseph and Elizabeth Josephine (Flint) U.; m. Mary Catherine Howze, June 5, 1965 (div. Oct. 1971); children: Patricia, Suzanne; m. Janet Ann Ballman, Sept. 22, 1973. B.S.M.E., U. Detroit, 1963, M.S., 1965. Registered profl. engr., Mich. Engr., Smith Hinchman & Grylls, Detroit, 1964-72, chief mech. engr. health facilities, 1972-73, asst. dir. health facilities, 1973-75, v.p., dir. mech. engring., 1975-82, v.p., dir. profl. staff, 1983—, also dir.; dir. Smith Group, Detroit, 1984—. Served to capt. U.S. Army, 1966-67. Mem. Nat. Soc. Profl. Engrs., ASME, ASHRAE, Soc. Am. Mil. Engrs. Clubs: Engring. Soc., Athletic (Detroit). Avocations: golf; photography; gardening. Home: 15250 Knolson St Livonia MI 48154-4736 Office: Smith Group Inc 150 W Jefferson Ave Detroit MI 48226-4415

UILKEMA, GAYLE BURNS, mayor, councilwoman, business educator; b. Detroit, Sept. 2, 1938; d. Joseph A. and Pearl (Rasmussen) Burns; children: Lynn, Sharon. BS in Edn., U. Mich., 1959; MPA, Calif. State U., Hayward, 1987. Instr. bus. edn. and mgmt. subjects Heald Coll., Oakland, Calif., 1961-62; tchr. bus. edn. dept. Oakland High Sch., 1962-66; lectr. Calif. State U. Grad. Sch. Pub. Adminstrn., Hayward; mem. coun. City of Lafayette, 1978-97, mayor, 1981-84, 90-91, 94-95; lectr. in field; cons. U. Calif. Ext., Berkeley; adj. prof. John F. Kennedy U. Sch. of Mgmt., Walnut Creek, Calif., 1989-96; v.p. Dimensional Resources, Inc., Telecomms. Cons.; bd. suprs. Contra Costa, 1996; commr. BCDC, 1997—, Bay Area Quality Mgmt. Dist., 1997—. Mem. Contra Costa Local Agy. Formation Commn., 1986—, commr., former chair, 1986, 95; mem. exec. bd. dirs. state bd. Calif. Assn. Local Agy. Formation Commn.; Lafayette dir., former chair, bd. dirs. Cen. Contra Costa Transit Authority, 1980—, chmn. fin. com., 1981-85, 94, chmn. ops. and scheduling, 1986, dir. ops. and scheduling com., 1987, chmn., 1989, bd. dirs., 1990—. Recipient award Met. Transp. Commn. Bay Area, 1981, Am. Leadership award Nat. Assn. Towns and Twps., Washington, 1996; named Alumnae of Year Calif. State U., 1997. Mem. AAUW (bd. dirs. 1971-78, pres. 1972-73, state bd. dirs. 1974-76, nat. rep. 1977-78, Disting. Woman award 1978), Soroptimists Internat. Republican. Roman Catholic. Avocations: tennis, gardening, interior decorating, piano, sewing. Home: 670 Sky Hy Cir Lafayette CA 94549-5228 Office: 651 Pine St Rm 108A Martinez CA 94553-1229

UITTI, KARL DAVID, language educator; b. Calumet, Mich., Dec. 10, 1933; s. Karl Abram and Joy (Weidelman) U.; m. Maria Esther Clark, Feb. 15, 1953 (div. Feb. 1973); children: Maria Elisabeth, Karl Gerard (dec.); m. Michelle Alice Freeman, Mar. 13, 1974; children: David Charles, Jacob Christian. AB, U. Calif., Berkeley, 1952; AM, U. Calif., Berkley, 1952, PhD, 1959; postgrad., Nancy and Bordeaux U., 1952-54. From instr. to assoc. prof. Princeton U., 1959-68, class of 1936 preceptor, 1963-66, prof., 1968—, John N. Woodhull prof. modern langs., 1978—, chmn. dept. Romance langs., 1972-78; vis. prof. Universidad de P.R., U. Pa., Queens Coll., U. Iowa, U. Wash., Rutgers U., UCLA, Johns Hopkins U., Ecole Normale Superieure de Saint-Cloud, Paris, U. Warwick, England; corr. Romance Philology, 1970-85; NEH dir. summer seminars for coll. tchrs., 1983, 87, 94, cons., 1976-78, bd. dirs.; bd. dirs. Alumni Coll. Princeton U., Paris, Fontevraud, France. Author: The Concept of Self in the Symbolist Novel, 1961, La Passion Littéraire de Remy de Gourmont, 1962, Linguistics and Literary Theory, 1969, Story, Myth and Celebration in Old French Narrative Poetry (1050-1200), 1973, (with A. Foulet) Chrétien de Troyes, Le Chevalier de la Charrette, 1989, Letteratura europea: dalle origini a Dante, 1993, Chrétien de Troyes, Le Chevalier au Lion, 1994, Chrétien de Troyes Revisited, 1995; contbr. numerous articles and revs. to scholarly jours.; editor: Edward C. Armstrong Monographs on Medieval Literature; mem. edit. bd. Romance Philology, French Forum; mem. adv. coun. Dictionary of the Middle Ages. Chmn. bd. elders Luth. Ch. of Messiah, Princeton, N.J., 1978-81. With AUS, 1954-56. Decorated officier des Palmes Académiques, France; Guggenheim fellow, 1964-65, sr. fellow Nat. Endowment for Humanities, 1974-75, vis. fellow All Souls Coll., Oxford (Eng.) U., 1975. Mem. MLA, Linguistic Soc. Am., Medieval Acad. Am. Société de linguistique romane, Phi Beta Kappa. Club: Codrington (Oxford, Eng.). Home: 50 Grover Ave Princeton NJ 08540-3654 Office: Dept Romance Langs and Lits Princeton U 309 E Pyne Princeton NJ 08544-5264

UKROP, JAMES E., retail executive; b. 1937. Vice chmn., CEO Ukrop's Super Markets Inc., 1958—. Office: Udrop's Super Markets Inc 600 Southlake Blvd Richmond VA 23236-3922 Office: Ukrop's Supermarkets Inc 600 Southlake Blvd Richmond VA 23236-3922*

UKROPINA, JAMES R., lawyer; b. Fresno, Calif., Sept. 10, 1937; s. Robert J. and Persida (Angelich) U.; m. Priscilla Lois Brandenburg, June 16, 1962. A.B., Stanford U., 1959, M.B.A., 1961; LL.B., U. So. Calif., 1965. Bar: Calif. 1966, D.C. 1980. Assoc. firm O'Melveny & Myers, Los Angeles, 1965-72, ptnr., 1972-80, 92—; exec. v.p., gen. counsel Santa Fe Internat. Corp., Alhambra, Calif., 1980-84, dir., 1981-86; exec. v.p., gen. counsel Pacific Enterprises, Los Angeles, 1984-86, pres. and dir., 1986-89, chmn. bd. and chief exec. officer, 1989-91; bd. dirs. Lockheed Martin Corp., Pacific Mut. Life Ins. Co., Calif. Club. Editor in chief So. Calif. Law Rev, 1964-65. Trustee Stanford U. Mem. ABA, Calif. Bar Assn., Los Angeles County Bar Assn., Annandale Golf Club, Calif. Club, Beta Theta Pi. Office: O'Melveny & Myers 400 S Hope St Los Angeles CA 90071-2801

ULABY, FAWWAZ TAYSSIR, electrical engineering and computer science educator, research center administrator; b. Damascus, Syria, Feb. 4, 1943; came to U.S. 1964; s. Tayssir Kamel and Makram (Ard) U.; m. Mary Ann Hammond, Aug. 28, 1968; children: Neda, Aziza, Laith. BS in Physics, Am. U. Beirut, 1964; MSEE, U. Tex., 1966, PhDEE, 1968. Asst. prof. elec. and computer engring. U. Kans., Lawrence, 1968-71, assoc. prof., 1971-76, prof., 1976-84; prof. elec. engring. and computer sci. U. Mich., Ann Arbor, 1984—, dir. NASA Ctr. for Space Terahertz Tech., 1988—, Williams Disting. prof., 1993—. Author: Microwave Remote Sensing, Vol. 1, 1981, Vol. 2, 1982, Vol. 3, 1986, Radar Polarimetry, 1990. Recipient Kuwait prize in applied scis. Govt. of Kuwait, 1987, NASA Group Achievement award, 1990. Fellow IEEE (gen. chmn. internat. symposium 1981, Disting. Achievement award 1983, Centennial medal 1984); mem. IEEE Geosci. and Remote Sensing Soc. (exec. editor jour., pres. 1979-81), Internat. Union Radio Sci., Nat. Acad. Engring. Avocations: flying kites, racketball. Office: U Mich 3228 EECS 1301 Beal Ave Ann Arbor MI 48109-2122

ULAM, ADAM B., history and political science educator; b. Lwow, Poland, Apr. 8, 1922; came to U.S., 1939, naturalized, 1949; s. Jozef and Anna (Auerbach) U.; children—Alexander Stanislaw, Joseph Howard. A.B., Brown U., 1943, LL.D.(hon.), 1983; Ph.D., Harvard U., 1947. Mem. Harvard U., Cambridge, Mass., 1947—; prof. govt. Harvard U., 1959-92, Gurney prof. history and polit. sci., 1979-92, prof. emeritus, 1992—, rsch. assoc. Russian Rsch. Ctr., 1948—, ctr. dir., 1973-76, 80-92, mem. exec. com. Russian research ctr., 1968—. Author numerous books including: The Bolsheviks and Lenin, 1965, Stalin, 1972, 2nd edit., 1987, Expansion and Coexistence, 1973, The Unfinished Revolution, rev. edit., 1979, The Kirov Affair, 1988, Dangerous Relations: The Soviet Union in World Politics, 1970-1982, 1983, The Communists: The Story of Power and Lost Illusions, 1948-91, 1992. Guggenheim fellow, 1956, 69, Rockefeller fellow, 1957, 60. Mem. Am. Acad. Arts and Scis., Am. Philos. Soc. Clubs: The Signet, Harvard U. Eliot House (assoc.) (Cambridge). Avocation: tennis. Office: Harvard U Russian Rsch Ctr 1727 Cambridge St Cambridge MA 02138-3016

ULANOFF, STANLEY M., communications executive; b. Bklyn., May 30, 1922; s. Samuel H. and Minnie (Druss) U.; m. Bernice Mayer, June 15, 1947; children: Roger, Amy Ulanoff Christie, Lisa M. Ulanoff Peddie, Dory Ulanoff Kennedy. BA in Journalism, U. Iowa, 1943; MBA in Mktg., Hofstra U., 1955; PhD in Comm., NYU, 1968. Asst. to pres. SUNY, Stony Brook, 1962-64; prof. mktg., head advt., sales promotion & pub. rels. divsn. Baruch Coll. (CUNY), N.Y., 1964-86; pres. Viewmark Prodns. Inc. d.b.a. Advisions, 1986—; cons. U.S. Dept. Def., Grosset & Dunlap pubs., Siebel/Mohr, U.S. Postal Svc.; cons, asst. to pres. Compton Advt.; arbitrator N.Y. Stock Exch., Nat. Assn. Securities Dealers. Author or editor 28 books including Handbook of Sales Promotion, also mags., newspaper articles, rsch. papers; prodr. over 50 video documentaries. 2nd lt. U.S. Army, 1945; Brig. gen. USAR, 1942-84. Decorated Chevalier dans l'Ordre des Palmes Academique, Republic of France, Legion of Merit, Meritorious Svc. medal, Army Commendation medal, Army Achievement medal, Silver Conspicuous Svc. Cross, State of N.Y.; named VIP (Very Important Prof.) Splty. Adv. Assn. Internat. (2); Am. Advt. Assn. fellow, Eastman-Kodak fellow in film prodn.; Lewis Kleid Direct Mail Advt. scholar. Mem. Mil. Intelligence Res. Soc. (pres.), Res. Officers Assn. (pres.). Office: 17 The Serpentine Roslyn NY 11576-1736

ULBRECHT, JAROMIR JOSEF, chemical engineer; b. Ostrava, Czechoslovakia, Dec. 16, 1928; s. Josef and Leopolda U.; m. Vera Krafneter, July 10, 1952; children: Jan Stanislav, Magdalena Vera. Ing., Czech Inst. Tech., Prague, 1952, Ph.D., 1958. Dept. head Research div. synthetic rubber co. Zlin, Czechoslovakia, 1958-63; head lab. engring. rheology Czechoslovak Acad. Scis., Prague, 1963-68; prof. chem. engring. U. Salford, Eng., 1968-78; prof., chmn. dept. chem. engring. SUNY, Buffalo, 1978-83; chief div. chem. process metrology Nat. Bur. Standards, Washington, 1984-88; dep. dir. office tech. evaluation and assessment Nat. Inst. Standards and Tech. (formerly Nat. Bur. Standards), Washington, 1989-90, dir. tech. programs, tech. svcs., 1991-94; pres. OFI Tech Svcs., Rockville, Md., 1994—. Author: Non-Newtonian Liquids, 1967, Mixing of Liquids by Mechanical Agitation, 1985, Process Sensing and Diagnostics, 1983, Competitiveness of the U.S. Chemical Industry in International Markets, 1990; editor: Chemical Engineering Communications, 1976-86; contbr. numerous articles to profl. jours. Recipient Outstanding Scholarship award Czech Acad. Scis., 1965, 67; Alexander von Humboldt fellow, 1967. Fellow Am. Inst. Chem. Engrs.; mem. Soc. Rheology, Am. Chem. Soc., Czech Acad. Engring. (hon. fgn.), Sigma Xi. Office: OFI Tech Svcs Inc 2407 Mccormick Rd Rockville MD 20850-3072

ULE, GUY MAXWELL, JR., stockbroker; b. Chgo., Jan. 2, 1940; s. Guy Maxwell and Margaret (Karahuta) U.; m. Angela Joanne Genelli, Nov. 17, 1975. BA, Harvard U., 1961, MBA, 1967. Analyst, phys. distbn. specialist TWA, N.Y.C. and Phila., 1967-69; supr. comml. passenger sales TWA, N.Y.C., 1969-71; pvt. practice cons. N.Y.C., 1971-72; mgr. sales mktg. Source Equities, N.Y.C., 1972; ptnr., N.Y.C. office mgr. Daley, Coolidge & Co., 1972-77; v.p., divsn. mgr. Rosenkrantz, Ehrenkrantz, Lyon & Ross Inc., 1977-85, Ingham Becker & Co., Inc., 1985-87; v.p., asst. sec. Meyers, Pollock, Robbins Inc., 1987-89; v.p., Max Ule divsn. Herzog Heine Geduld Inc., 1989—; pres. Max Ule & Co., Inc., N.Y.C., 1977—, Max Ule Advt. & Mktg., Inc., N.Y.C., 1980—; brokerage info. cons. Internet World Wide Web, 1995. Creator first discount brokerage system on computer, 1980. Chmn., pres. Assn. in Manhattan for Autistic Children, 1985-86. Lt. USN, 1962-65. Mem. Racquet & Tennis Club, Knickerbocker Club. Republican. Episcopalian. Avocations: photography, court tennis, overseas travel. Home: 8 Gramercy Park # 5B New York NY 10003 Office: Herzog Heine Geduld Inc 26 Broadway New York NY 10004-1703

ULERICH, WILLIAM KEENER, publishing company executive; b. Latrobe, Pa., Apr. 18, 1910; s. William Wesley and Anna (Keener) U.; m. Edith O. Orton, May 26, 1934 (dec. 1950); 1 dau., Constance K.; m. Alethea M. Jones, Aug. 23, 1950 (dec.). A.B., Pa. State U., 1931; LL.D., Dickinson Sch. Law, 1977. Editor Daily Times, State College, Pa., 1931-45; assoc. prof. journalism Pa. State U., 1934-45; pub. Clearfield (Pa.) Daily Progress, 1946; chmn. bd. dirs., chief exec. officer Prog. Pub. Co., Inc., Clearfield, Pa.; dir. emeritus County Nat. Bank, Clearfield. Bd. dirs., past pres. Clearfield Meml. Hosp.; trustee Pa. State U., 1952-57, 64-85, v.p. bd. trustees, 1973-76, pres. bd. trustees, 1976-79, pres. emeritus, 1985. Served with AUS, World War II. Mem. Pa. Newspaper Pubs. Assn. (pres. 1952). Methodist. Home: 724 S 2nd St Clearfield PA 16830-1904 Office: 206 E Locust St Clearfield PA 16830-2423

ULERY, SHARI LEE, lawyer; b. Marshalltown, Iowa, July 13, 1953; d. Kenneth Eugene and Edith Viola (Harding) U.; m. Steven Bernard Nelson (div. 1987); children: Benjamin, Christopher. BS, Iowa State U., 1975; JD, Drake U., 1980. Bar: Iowa 1980, Colo. 1981. Staff atty. Geico Fin. Svcs., Denver, 1985-87, asst. gen. counsel, 1987-89, v.p., gen. counsel, 1989—. Mem. Am. Assn. Corp. Counsel, Colo. Bar Assn., Colo. Womens Bar Assn., Colo. Chpt. Am. Corp. Coun. Assn. (pres. elect). Office: Geico Fin Svcs Inc 10403 W Colfax Ave Lakewood CO 80215-3811

ULETT, GEORGE ANDREW, psychiatrist; b. Needham, Mass., Jan. 10, 1918; s. George Andrew and Mabel Elizabeth (Caswell) U.; m. Pearl Carolyn Lawrence; children: Richard Carlton, Judith Anne, Carol Lynn. BA in Psychology, Stanford U., 1940; MS in Anatomy, U. Oreg., 1943, PhD in Anatomy, 1944, MD, 1944. Diplomate Am. Bd. Psychiatry and Neurology. Asst. psychiatrist Barnes Hosp., St. Louis, 1950-64; med. dir. Malcolm Bliss Hosp., St. Louis, 1951-61; dir. Mo. Dept. Mental Health, Jefferson City, Mo., 1962-72; prof., chair Mo. Inst. Psychiatry, St. Louis, 1964-73; dir. psychiatry Deaconess Hosp., St. Louis, 1973-94; interim dir. Mo. Inst. of Mental Health, St. Louis, 1990-91; assoc. dir. for policy and ethics Mo. Inst. of Mental Health, 1991-94; clin. prof. dept. family and cmty. medicine St. Louis U. Sch. Medicine, 1995—; mem. adv. coun. Mental Health Assn. St. Louis, 1965-66, 69-70, mem. profl. adv. com., 1965; chair health and hosp. com. Health & Welfare Coun. St. Louis, 1960; mem. alcohol rev. com., psychopharmacology study sect., alcoholism study sect., 1993, grants rev. com. for alternative medicine NIMH, Rockville, Md.; prof. psychiatry Washington U. Sch. Medicine, St. Louis, 1956-61; clin. prof. cmty. and family medicine St. Louis U. Sch. Medicine, 1981-89, U. Mo. Sch. Medicine, 1990—. Author 10 books; contbr. 225 articles to profl jours. Capt. U.S. Air Force, 1946-47. Recipient Ann. award Mo. Assn. for Mental Health, 1966, Recognition award, 1970, AMA Honorable Mention award Foster Com. Exhibit, 1974, Pax Mundi Fellowship award for profl. excellence, 1989; named hon. mem. Turkish Coll. Neuropharmacology, 1969. Fellow Am. Psychiat. Assn.; mem. Am. Soc. Acupuncture (past pres.), Am. Soc. of Med. Psychiatry (past pres.), Mo. Acad. Psychiatry (past pres.). Office: Mo Inst Mental Health 5247 Fyler Ave Saint Louis MO 63139-1300

ULEVICH, NEAL HIRSH, photojournalist; b. Milw., June 18, 1946; s. Ben and Lea Jean (Klitsner) U.; m. Maureen Ann Vaughan, Sept. 25, 1974; children: Jacob Vaughan, Sarah Beatrice. B.A. in Journalism, U. Wis., 1968. Reporter A.P., 1968-69, photographer, photo editor, 1971-78, Asia photo editor, 1978-83; freelance writer, Vietnam, Hong Kong, 1969-71; fellow in journalism U. Wis.-Madison, 1971-72. Recipient Pulitzer prize for news photography, 1977. Jewish. Home: 2841 Perry St Denver CO 80212-1442

ULLBERG, KENT JEAN, sculptor; b. Gothenburg, Sweden, July 15, 1945; came to U.S., 1974; s. Jean Wilgot and Kerstin Aina (Axelson) U.; m. Veerle Rufina Vermeir, May 5, 1978; children: Robert, Gerald. Diploma in sculpture, Swedish State Sch. Art, 1966. Cert. conservator German Assn. Museology. Curator Nat. Mus. and Art Gallery, Botswana, Africa, 1971-74; curator III Mus. Natural History, Denver, 1974-75. Sculptor: monument Lincoln Ctr. Eagle, Dallas, 1981, Wind in the Sails, Corpus Christi, Tex., 1983, Genesee Eagle, Mumford, N.Y., 1984, Deinonychus Dinosaurs, Phila., 1987, Whooping Cranes Fountain, Washington, 1989, Broward Conv. Ctr., Fountain, Ft. Lauderdale, Fla., Rudor Monument bronze, Stockholm, 1991, Monumental Triptych Art Mus. South Tex., 1993, Bird Mountain Telecom. Hdqs., Stockholm, 1994, Christ Monument, Corpus Christi, 1995, Grizzly Bear monument Nat. Mus. Wildlife Art, Jackson, Wyo., 1994. Recipient Gold medal Tex. Rangers Hall of Fame, 1980, Rungius award Nat. Mus. Wildlife Art, 1996; named Master Wildlife Artist, 1987. Fellow Nat. Sculpture Soc. (Percival Dietsch award 1979, gold medal 1983, Hering award 1993), NAD (academician 1990, Barnett prize 1975, Speyer prize 1995), Nat. Acad. Western Art (gold medal 1981, 82, 88, 90, 95), Am. Soc. Marine Artists; mem. Soc. Animal Artists (medal of merit 1979, 80, 82, 87, 96), Allied Artists of Am. (N.Y. Silver medal 1989), Soc. for Wildlife Art of the Nations. Home: 14337 Aquarius St Corpus Christi TX 78418-6003

ULLESTAD, MERWIN ALLAN, tax services executive; b. Hampton, Iowa, June 29, 1949; s. Alan L. and Georgene E. (Simms) U.; m. Crystal R. (Kleppinger), Sept. 17, 1977. BS, Iowa State U., 1971. CPA, PFS, Iowa, Tenn.; lic. capt. inland waters USCG. Ptnr. Coopers and Lybrand, Des Moines, 1971-83; ptnr. in charge, tax svcs. Touche Ross and Co., Nashville, 1983-89; ptnr. in tax svcs. Deloitte & Touche, Nashville, 1989—. Editor: Abingdon Clergy Income Tax Guide, 1989-96. Bd. dirs., mem. exec. com., treas. United Way Mid. Tenn., 1990-96, mem. allocations panel, 1983-89; bd. dirs., mem. exec. com. Am. Cancer Soc., Des Moines, 1977-83, Nashville City Ballet, 1983-85; bd. dirs., chmn. fin. com. Watkins Inst., 1996—; sustaining membership capt. Mid. Tenn. Coun. Boy Scouts Am., 1985-88; mem. Econ. Devel. Com., 1988-90. Mem. AICPA (cert. Pers. Fin. Specialist), Tenn. Soc. CPAs, Iowa Soc. CPAs, Am. Mgmt. Assn., Internat. Assn. for Fin. Planning (pres., bd. dirs. Nashville chpt. 1987-90), Nashville Estate Planning Coun. (pres., dir.), Nashville Songwriters Assn. Internat. (fin. cons. to bd. dirs. 1990—), Nashville C. of C., Kiwanis (treas. Nashville 1990-91), Nashville City Club, Old Hickory Country Club, Gildas Club Nashville (bd. dirs. 1996). Avocations: sailing, hiking, music. Office: Deloitte and Touche LLP 424 Church St Nashville TN 37219

ULLIAN, JOSEPH SILBERT, philosophy educator; b. Ann Arbor, Mich., Nov. 9, 1930; s. Hyman Benjamin and Frieda G. (Silbert) U. AB, Harvard U., 1952, AM, 1953, PhD, 1957. Instr. philosophy Stanford U., Calif., 1957-58; asst. prof. philosophy Johns Hopkins U., Balt., 1958-60; vis. asst. prof. philosophy U. Pa., Phila., 1959-60, rsch. assoc. in linguistics, 1961-62; vis. asst. prof. philosophy U. Chgo., 1962-63; asst. prof. U. Calif., Santa Barbara, 1964-66; assoc. prof. Washington U., St. Louis, 1965-70, prof., 1970—; lectr. U. Calif., Berkeley, 1961; cons. Rsch. Directorate System Devel. Corp., Santa Monica, Calif., 1962-70. Co-author: The Web of Belief, 1970, 2d edit., 1978; contbr. articles to profl. jours. Mem. Am. Philos. Assn., Assn. for Symbolic Logic (exec. com. 1974-77), Am. Soc. for Aesthetics, Phi Beta Kappa. Democrat. Avocations: sports, theatre, music. Home: 984 Tornoe Rd Santa Barbara CA 93105-2229 Office: Washington U Dept Philosophy 1 Brookings Dr Saint Louis MO 63130-4862

ULLMAN, EDWIN FISHER, research chemist; b. Chgo., July 19, 1930; s. Harold P. and Jane F. Ullman; m. Elizabeth J. Finlay, June 26, 1954; children—Becky L., Linda J. BA, Reed Coll., 1952; MA, Harvard U., 1954, PhD, 1956. Research chemist Lederle Labs., Am. Cyanamid, Pearl River, N.Y., 1955-60; group leader central research div. Am. Cyanamid, Stamford, Conn., 1960-66; sci. dir. Synvar Research Inst., Palo Alto, Calif., 1966-70; v.p., dir. research Syva Co., Palo Alto, 1970-95; v.p., dir. rsch. Behring Diagnostics Inc., San Jose, Calif., 1995-97; scientific cons., 1997—; mem. various sci. adv. bds.; mem. adv. bd. San Francisco State U. Coll. of Sci. and Engring., 1994-96. Edit. bd.: Jour. Organic Chemistry, 1969-74, Jour. Immunoassay, 1979—, Jour. Clin. Lab., Analysis, 1986-87; contbr. articles to sci. jours. Patentee in field. NSF predoctoral fellow, 1952-53; U.S. Rubber Co. fellow, 1954-55. Recipient Clin. Ligand Assay Soc. Mallinckrodt award, 1981, Can. Soc. Clin. Chemists Health Group award, 1982, Inventor of Yr. award Peninsula Patent Law Assn., 1987. Fellow AAAS; mem. Am. Chem. Soc., Am. Assn. Clin. Chemistry (Van Slyke award N.Y. sect. 1984, No. Calif. sect. award 1991, Outstanding Contbns. to Clin. Chemistry in Selected Area of Rsch. award 1997), Am. Soc. Biol. Chemists, Clin. Ligand Assay Soc., Phi Beta Kappa.

ULLMAN, FRANK GORDON, electrical engineering educator; b. N.Y.C., Dec. 14, 1926; s. Samuel Robert and Ella (Fischl) U.; m. Deborah Halpern, July 15, 1951; children: Diane Ella, Marian Ruth, Eileen Jane. BA, NYU, 1949; MS, Poly. Inst. Bklyn., 1951, PhD, 1958. Rsch. fellow Poly. Inst. Bklyn., N.Y.C., 1949-51; jr. engr. Sylvania Electric Products, Inc., Mineola, N.Y., 1951-54; rsch. asst. Poly. Inst. Bklyn., N.Y.C., 1954-57, rsch. assoc., 1957-58; sr. rsch. physicist Nat. Cash Register Co., Dayton, Ohio, 1958-66; prof. elec. engring. and physics U. Nebr., Lincoln, 1966-96, prof. emeritus, 1996—, assoc. chmn. dept. elec. engring., 1987-91; instr. U. Dayton, 1960-62; vis. prof. Hebrew U., Jerusalem, 1982; co-dir. Ctr. Laser-Analytical Studies of Trace Gas Dynamics, 1988-96. Mem. editorial bd. Ferroelectrics, Ferroelectrics Letters; contbr. articles in field to profl. jours. With U.S. Army, 1945-46. Mem. AAUP, IEEE (sr. mem.), Am. Phys. Soc., Sigma Xi. Democrat. Jewish. Avocations: handball, tennis. Office: U Nebr Dept Elec Engring Lincoln NE 68588-0511

ULLMAN, JEFFREY DAVID, computer science educator; b. N.Y.C., Nov. 22, 1942; s. Seymour and Nedra L. (Hart) U.; m. Holly E., Nov. 19, 1967; children: Peter, Scott, Jonathan. B.S., Columbia U., 1963; Ph.D., Princeton

U., 1966; Ph.D. hon., U. Brussels, 1975, U. Paris-Dauphine, 1992. Mem. tech. staff Bell Labs., Murray Hill, N.J., 1966-69; cons. Bell Labs., 1969-89; prof. elec. engring., computer sci. Princeton U., 1969-79; prof. computer sci. Stanford (Calif.) U., 1979—, chmn. dep., 1990-94, Stanford W. Ascherman prof. computer sci., 1994—; cons. Bell Labs., 1969-79; mem. computer sci. adv. panel NSF, 1974-77, mem. info., robotics and intelligent sys. adv. panel, 1986-88; mem. exam. com. for computer sci. grad. record exam. Ednl. Testing Svc., 1978-86; cons. editor Computer Sci. Press, 1982-95; chmn. doctoral rating com. for computer sci. N.Y. State Regents, 1989-93; bd. dirs. Junglee Corp. Author: Principles of Database and Knowledge-Base Systems, 1988, 89, (2 vols.), (with A.V. Aho and J.E. Hopcroft) Data Structures and Algorithms, 1983, (with J.E. Hopcroft) Introduction to Automata Theory, Languages and Computation, 1979, (with A.V. Aho, R. Sethi) Compilers: Principles, Techniques and Tools, 1986, (with A.V. Aho) Foundations of Computer Science, 1992, Elements of ML Programming, 1994. Guggenheim fellow, 1989. Fellow Assn. Computing Machinery (coun. 1978-80); mem. NAE, Spl. Interest Group on Automata and Computability Theory (sec.-treas. 1973-77), Spl. Interest Group on Mgmt. Data (vice chn. 1983-95), Computing Rsch. Assn. (bd. dirs. 1994—). Home: 1023 Cathcart Way Palo Alto CA 94305-1048 Office: Stanford U 332 Margaret Jacks Hall Stanford CA 94305

ULLMAN, LEO SOLOMON, lawyer; b. Amsterdam, The Netherlands, July 14, 1939; s. Frank Leo and Emily (Konyn) U.; m. Katharine Laura Marbut, Aug. 27, 1960; children: Laura, Susan, Valerie, Frank. AB, Harvard U., 1961, JD, Columbia U. Sch. of Law, 1964, MBA, Columbia U. Grad. Sch. Bus., 1964. Bar: N.Y. 1966, U.S. Ct. Claims 1966, U.S. Tax Ct. 1969, U.S. Customs Ct. 1970. Assoc. Sullivan & Cromwell, N.Y.C., 1965-68; pres. and mem. Ullman, Miller & Wrubel and predecessors, N.Y.C., 1970-81; mem. Reid & Priest, 1984-91, of counsel, 1991-92; of counsel Schnader, Harrison, Segal & Lewis, N.Y.C., 1993—; adj. prof. internat. bus. NYU, 1972-77; lectr., panelist profl. organs. programs; chmn. Amvest Properties, Inc., SKR Mgmt., Inc., Brentway Mgmt., Inc. Mem. Port Washington (N.Y.) Bd. Edn., 1970-73, pres. 1972-73; dir. Found. for Jewish Hist. Mus. in Amsterdam, Inc.; chmn. bd. dirs. Anne Frank Ctr., U.S.A. Served with USMCR, 1959-65. Co-recipient Community Service Award, Port Washington, 1981; Harlan Fiske Stone scholar, Columbia Law Sch., 1963. Mem. ABA (tax sect. com. U.S. taxation of fgn. persons), N.Y. State Bar Assn. (tax sect. com. internat. trade and investment). Clubs: Harvard, Netherlands. Editor: European Taxation, Internat. Bur. Fiscal Documentation, Amsterdam, 1964-65; founding editor: Taxation of Private Investment Income in Europe; co-author Investeringen in Onroerend Goed in de Verenigde Staten, 1982; contbr. articles to profl. publs. Home: Seacoast Ln Sands Point NY 11050-1230 Office: Schnader Harrison Segal & Lewis 330 Madison Ave New York NY 10017-5001

ULLMAN, MYRON EDWARD, III, retail executive; b. Youngstown, Ohio, Nov. 26, 1946; s. Myron Edward Jr. and June (Cunningham) U.; m. Cathy Emmons, June 20, 1969; children: Myron Cayce, Denver Tryan, Peter Brynt, Benjamin Kyrk, Kathryn Kwynn. BS in Indsl. Mgmt., U. Cin., 1969; postgrad. Inst. Ednl. Mgmt., Harvard U., 1977. Internat. account mgr. IBM Corp., Cin., 1969-76; v.p. bus. affairs U. Cin., 1976-81; White House fellow The White House, Washington, 1981-82; exec. v.p. Sanger Harris div. Federated Stores, Dallas, 1982-86; mgr. dir., chief oper. officer Wharf Holdings Ltd., Hong Kong, 1986-88; chmn., CEO, dir. R.H. Macy & Co. Inc., N.Y.C., 1986-95; dir. Federated Dept. Stores, Inc.; chmn., CEO, dir. DFS Group Ltd., San Francisco, 1995—; mng. dir. Lane Crawford Ltd., Hong Kong, 1986-88; bd. advisors Gt. Traditions Corp., Cin.; dep. chmn. Omni Hotels, Hampton, N.H., 1988; vice chmn. bd. dirs. Mercy Ships Internat. Internat. v.p. U. Cin. Alumni Assn., 1980—; bd. dirs. Nat. Multiple Sclerosis Soc., N.Y.C.; bd. dirs. Brunswick Sch., Greenwich, Conn., U. Cin. Found., Lincoln Ctr. Devel. Mem. White House Fellow Alumni Assn., Econ. Club N.Y.C. (bd. dirs., exec. com. 1993—), Nat. Retail Fedn. (vice chmn., bd. dirs., exec. com. 1993—), Delta Tau Delta (treas. 1967-68). Republican. Office: DFS Group Ltd 655 Montgomery St San Francisco CA 94111-2635

ULLMAN, NELLY SZABO, statistician, educator; b. Vienna, Austria, Aug. 11, 1925; came to U.S., 1939; d. Viktor and Elizabeth (Rosenberg) Szabo; m. Robert Ullman, Mar. 20, 1947 (dec.); children: Buddy, William John, Martha Ann, Daniel Howard. BA, Hunter Coll., 1945; MA, Columbia U., 1948; PhD, U. Mich., 1969. Rsch. assoc. MIT Radiation Lab, Cambridge, Mass., 1945; instr. Polytechnic Inst. of Bklyn., 1945-63; asst. prof. to prof. Ea. Mich. U., Ypsilanti, 1963—. Author: Study Guide To Actuarial Exam, 1978; contbr. articles to profl. jours. Mem. Am. Math. Assn., Am. Stat. Assn., Biometric Soc., Am. Assn. Univ. Profs. Office: Ea Mich Univ Dept Math Ypsilanti MI 48197

ULLMAN, RICHARD HENRY, political science educator; b. Balt., Dec. 12, 1933; s. Jerome E. and Frances (Oppenheimer) U.; m. Margaret Yoma Crosfield, July 4, 1959 (div.); children: Claire Frances, Jennifer Margaret; m. Susan Sorrell, May 6, 1977 (div.); m. Gail Marie Morgan, Dec. 24, 1983. AB, Harvard U., 1955; BPhil, Oxford (Eng.) U., 1957, DPhil, 1960. Rsch. fellow European history and politics St. Antony's Coll., Oxford U., 1958-59; from instr. govt. to asst. prof. Harvard U., 1960-65; assoc. prof. politics and internat. affairs Princeton (N.J.) U., 1965-69, prof., 1969-77, 79—, David K.E. Bruce prof. internat. affairs, 1988—; George Eastman vis. prof. Oxford U., 1991-92; mem. policy planning staff Office Asst. Sec. Def., 1967-68; mem. staff Nat. Security Coun., Exec. Office Pres., 1967; dir. studies Coun. Fgn. Rels., 1973-76, dir. 1980's project, 1974-77, editor fgn. policy, 1978-80. Author: Intervention and the War, 1961, Britain and the Russian Civil War, November 1918-January 1920, 1968, The Anglo-Soviet Accord, 1972, vols. I, II and III Anglo-Soviet Relations, 1917-21, Securing Europe, 1991; editor, contbr. Fgn. Policy Jour., 1978-80, Western Europe and the Crisis in U.S.-Soviet Relations, 1987, The World and Yugoslavia's Wars, 1996, (with others) Theory and Policy in International Relations, 1972; mem. editorial bd. N.Y. Times, 1977-78; contbr. articles to profl. jours. Chmn. bd. trustees World Peace Found., Boston, 1980-84, 95—. Rhodes scholar, 1955-58; recipient George Louis Beer prize Am. Hist. Assn., 1969. Fellow Am. Acad. Arts and Scis.; mem. Coun. Fgn. Rels., Internat. Inst. Strategic Studies. Home: 12 Maple St Princeton NJ 08542-3852 Office: Ctr Internat Studies Bendheim Hall Princeton Univ Princeton NJ 08544-1022

ULLMAN, TRACEY, actress, singer; b. Slough, Eng., Dec. 30, 1959; m. Allan McKeown, 1984; children: Mabel Ellen, John Albert Victor. Student, Itaia Conti Stage Sch., London. Appeared in plays Gigi, Elvis, Grease, The Rocky Horror Show, Four in a Million, 1981 (London Theatre Critics award), The Taming of the Shrew, 1990, The Big Love, (one-woman stage show) 1991; films include The Young Visitors, 1984, Give My Regards to Broad Street, 1984, Plenty, 1985, Jumpin' Jack Flash, 1986, I Love You To Death, 1990, Household Saints, 1993, I'll Do Anything, 1994, Bullets over Broadway, 1994, Ready to Wear (Prêt-à-Porter), 1994, Everybody Says I Love You, 1996; Brit. TV shows include Three of a Kind, A Kick Up the Eighties, Girls on Top; actress TV series: The Tracey Ullman Show, from 1987-90 (Emmy award Best Performance, Outstanding Writing, 1990, Golden Globe award Best Actress, 1987), Tracey Takes On, 1996; album You Broke My Heart in Seventeen Places (Gold album). Recipient Brit. Acad. award, 1983, Am. Comedy award, 1988, 90, 91, Emmy award for Best Performance in a Variety/Music Series for "Tracey Ullman Takes on New York", 1994.

ULLOA, JUSTO CELSO, Spanish educator; b. Havana, Cuba, Oct. 20, 1942; came to U.S., 1960; s. Derby Celso Ulloa and Margo (Hernandez) Usame; m. Leonor Rosario Alvarez, July 17, 1971; children: Sandra Leonor, Justin Alfonso. BS, Fla. State U., 1966; MA, U. Ga., 1969; PhD, U. Ky., 1973. With Va. Poly. Inst. and State U., Blacksburg, 1972-74, asst. prof., 1974-79, prof., 1987—; vis. prof. U. Ky., Lexington, Spring 1989. Author: Graded Spanish Reader, 1981, 2d edit., 1987, Lezama Lima y sus Lectores: guia y compendio bibliografico, 1987; assoc. editor, book rev. editor Critica Hispanica, 1979—; editor-in-chief Cuban Literary Studies, 1990. Recipient Acad. Teaching Excellence, Va. Tech., 1992, Alumni Teaching award, 1992. Mem. South Atlantic MLA (exec. com. 1996-99), Mountain Interstate Fgn. Lang. Conf. (v.p. 1975-76, 82-83, 90-91, 97—, pres. 1976-77, 83-84, 92-93), Order of the Discoverers, Phi Kappa Phi, Sigma Delta Pi (state dir. 1976-86, 96-99, v.p. 1986-90). Office: Va Poly Inst and State U Dept Fgn Lang Lit Blacksburg VA 24061-0225

ULLRICH, LINDA J., medical technologist; b. Rockford, Ill., May 10, 1944; d. Glenn H. and R. Catherine (Mathews) Person; m. John R. Brody, June 11, 1966 (div. July 1978); children: Kevin R. Brody, Keith A. Brody; m. Sterling O. Ullrich Sr., Mar. 10, 1979; stepchildren: Sterling O. Jr., Eugene, Lee Anna, Michelle. BA, Thiel Coll., 1966; MPA, Kent State U., 1993, postgrad., 1996—. Cert. med. tech., specialist in hematology. Staff med. tech. Sharon (Pa.) Gen. Hosp., 1966-76; supervisor hematology, coagulation, urinalysis sects. Sharon Regional Health Sys. (formerly Sharon Gen. Hosp.), 1976-96, lab. mgr., 1996—; edn. coord. Beaver County C.C., Pa., 1976-80; tech. supr. lab. Cancer Care Ctr., Hermitage, Pa., 1993—; adj. prof. Thiel Coll., Greenville, Pa., 1994-95; com. mem. Sharon Regional Health Sys., 1990—. Merit badge counselor, com. mem. Troop 67 Boy Scouts Am., Newton Falls, Ohio, 1982-95. Lutheran. Avocations: bicycling, hiking, knitting, reading. Home: 1577 Wilson Ave Newton Falls OH 44444-9754 Office: Sharon Regional Health Sys 740 E State St Sharon PA 16146-3328

ULLRICH, ROBERT ALBERT, business management educator; b. Port Jefferson, N.Y., Mar. 25, 1939; s. Albert Herman and Marie Kathryn (Miller) U.; divorced; children: Karl Albert, Eleanor Marie. BS, U.S. Mcht. Marine Acad., 1960; MBA, Tulane U., 1964; D in Bus. Adminstrn., Washington U., 1968. Marine engr. Lykes Bros. Steamship Co., New Orleans, 1960-62; trainee IBM Corp., New Orleans, 1964-65; sr. rsch. officer London Sch. Econs., 1968-69; prof. Vanderbilt U., Nashville, 1969-88; dean Clark U., Worcester, Mass., 1988-96, prof., 1996—. Author: Motivation Methods, 1981, Robotics Primer, 1983; co-author: Organization Theory and Design, 1980; editor: The American Work Force, 1984. Lt. j.g. USNR, 1960-66. Mem. Beta Gamma Sigma. Office: Grad School Management Clark University 950 Main St Worcester MA 01610-1400

ULLRICH, ROXIE ANN, special education educator; b. Ft. Dodge, Iowa, Nov. 10, 1951; d. Rocco William and Mary Veronica (Casady) Jackowell; m. Thomas Earl Ullrich, Aug. 10, 1974; children: Holly Ann, Anthony Joseph. BA, Creighton U., 1973; MA in Teaching, Morningside Coll., 1991. Cert. tchr., Iowa. Tchr. Corpus Christi Sch., Ft. Dodge, Iowa, 1973-74, Westwood Community Schs., Sloan, Iowa, 1974-80, Sioux City Community Schs., 1987—. Cert. judge Iowa High Sch. Speech Assn., Des Moines, 1975—. Mem. Am. Paint Horse Assn., Am. Quarter Horse Assn., Sioux City Hist. Assn., M.I. Hummel Club, Phi Delta Kappa. Avocations: doll collector, plate collector, horse-back riding. Home: 819 Brown St Sloan IA 51055

ULMAN, LOUIS JAY, lawyer; b. Balt., Mar. 24, 1946; s. Erwin Ira And Rose (Clayman) U.; m. Diana Lynn Milford, Aug. 17, 1969; children: Kenneth, Douglas. BA, Dickinson Coll., 1967; JD, Am. U., 1970. Bar: Md. 1970. Assoc. Ulman & Cohan, Balt., 1970-75; ptnr. Ulman & Ulman, Balt., 1975-80, Weinberg & Green, Columbia, Md., 1980-92; prin. Hodes, Ulman, Pessin & Katz, Columbia, 1992—; adj. prof. law Washington Coll. of Law, Am. U. Pres. Santa Claus Anonymous, Balt., 1975; mem. Howard County Bd. Social Svc., Ellicott City, Md., 1990. Mem. Md. State Bar Assn. (com. on rels. with fin. profls. 1985-92), Howard County Bar Assn., Internat. Assn. for Fin. Planning. Democrat. Jewish. Office: 10500 Little Patuxent Pkwy Columbia MD 21044-3585

ULMER, FRANCES ANN, state official; b. Madison, Wis., Feb. 1, 1947; m. Bill Council; children: Amy, Louis. BA in Econs. and Polit. Sci., U. Wis.; JD with honors, Wis. Sch. Law. Polit. advisor Gov. Jay Hammond, Alaska, 1973-83; former mayor City of Juneau, Alaska; mem. 4 terms, minority leader Alaska Ho. Reps.; lt. gov. State of Alaska, 1995—. Home: 1700 Angus Way Juneau AK 99801-1411 Office: State Capitol PO Box 110015 Juneau AK 99811

ULMER, MELVILLE JACK, economist, educator; b. N.Y.C., May 17, 1911; s. Saul and Lillian (Ulmer) U.; m. Naomi Zinken, June 1, 1937; children: Melville Paul, Stephanie Marie. BS, NYU, 1937, MA, 1938; Ph.D., Columbia, 1948. Writer N.Y. Am., 1930-37; chief, price research sect. Bur. Labor Statistics, 1940-45; sr. economist Smaller War Plants Corp., 1945; chief financial analysis sect. Dept. Commerce, 1946-48; editor Survey of Current Bus., 1948-50; asso. prof. econs. Am. U., 1950-52, prof., 1952-61, chmn. dept., 1953-61; prof. econs. U. Md., 1961-86, emeritus prof., 1986—; vis. prof. econs. Netherlands Sch. Econ., Rotterdam, 1958-59, 65-66; research asso. Nat. Bur. Econ. Research, 1950-60; cons. OAS, 1954, Dept. Commerce, 1955, Gen. Services Adminstrn., 1957, Dept. State, 1962, Bur. Budget, 1967-69. Author: numerous books including The Economic Theory of Cost of Living Index Numbers, 1949, Trends and Cycles in Capital Formation by U.S. Railroads, 1870-1950, 1954, Economics: Theory and Practice, 2d edit., 1965, Capital in Transportation, Communications and Pub. Utilities, 1960, The Welfare State: U.S.A. 1969, The Theory and Measurement of International Price Competitiveness, 1969; co-author: (with John M. Blair) Wartime Prices, 1944, (with C. Wright Mills) Small Business and Civic Welfare, 1946; contbg. editor: The New Republic, 1970-80; contbr. articles in Am. Econ. Rev., Jour. Am. Statis. Assn., Commentary, Atlantic Monthly, Challenge, Am. Spectator, Pub. Interest, Jour. of Econ. Issues, also others. Recipient Sr. Fulbright award, 1958, 65, Medal of Honor Free U. of Brussels, 1986; Merrill Found. fellow, 1957; Wilton Park fellow Gt. Britain, 1966; Peoples Coll. fellow Denmark, 1966; Nuffield fellow Can., 1971; Nat. Endowment for Humanities sr. fellow, 1973; NSF grantee, 1973; State Dept. econ. specialist grantee, 1977, 78. Fellow AAAS; mem. Am. Econ. Assn., Am. Statis. Assn., Econometric Soc., Assn. Evolutionary Econs. (exec. bd.), Atlantic Econ. Soc. (disting assoc.), Artus Soc., Pi Gamma Mu. Club: Cosmos (Washington). Home: 10401 River Rd Potomac MD 20854-4912 Office: U Md Dept Econs College Park MD 20742 *Failure must be taken as an instructive experience that aids in exposing the pitfalls to achievement.*

ULMER, MELVILLE PAUL, physics and astronomy educator; b. Washington, Mar. 12, 1943; s. Melville Jack and Naomi Louise (Zinkin) U.; m. Patricia Elifson, Dec. 28, 1968; children: Andrew Todd, Jeremy John, Rachel Ann. BA, Johns Hopkins U., 1965; PhD, U. Wis., 1970. Asst. research U. Calif., San Diego, 1970-74; astrophysicist Harvard Smithsonian Ctr. for Astrophysics, Cambridge, Mass., 1974-76; asst. prof. Dept. Physics and Astoronomy, Northwestern U., Evanston, Ill., 1976-82, assoc. prof., 1982-87, dir. astrophysics program, 1982—, prof., 1987—; dir. Lindheimer and Dearborn Obs. Northwestern U., 1982—; co-investigator on Gamma Ray Ob. experiment and Orbiting Solar Ob. 7. Contbr. articles to profl. jours. Fellow Am. Phys. Soc.; mem. Am. Astron. Soc., Soc. Photo-optical Instrumentation Engrs., Internat. Astron. Union. Home: 2021 Noyes St Evanston IL 60201-2556 Office: Northwestern U Dearborn Obs 2145 Sheridan Rd Evanston IL 60208-0834

ULMER, SHIRLEY SIDNEY, political science educator, researcher, consultant; b. North, S.C., Apr. 15, 1923; s. Shirley S. and Anna R. (Reed) U.; m. Margaret Anel Lipscomb, Mar. 18, 1946; children: Margaret, William, Susan, John, Mary. BA cum laude, Furman U., 1952, LLD (hon.), 1981; MA, Duke U., 1954, PhD, 1956. Rockefeller fellow Duke U., 1952-53, instr. polit. sci., 1954-55, Ottis Greene fellow, 1955-56; instr. U. Houston, summer 1956; mem. faculty Mich. State U., 1956-63, asst. prof., 1956-59, assoc. prof. polit. sci., 1960-63, chmn. dept., 1961-62; prof. polit. sci., chmn. dept. U. Ky., Lexington, 1963-69, Disting. prof. arts and scis., 1975-76, Alumni prof., 1978-88, alumni prof. emeritus, 1988—; mem. polit. sci. panel NSF, 1968-70; chmn. bd. overseers NSF Supreme Ct. data base project, 1984-87; vis. prof. SUNY, Buffalo, summer 1969, U. Wis.-Milw., summer, 1974, Ariz. State U., 1980; lectr. in field. Author: Military Justice and the Right to Counsel, 1971, Courts as Small and Not so Small Groups, 1971, Supreme Court Policy Making and Constitutional Law, 1986; editor, contbr.: Introductory Readings in Political Behavior, 1961, Political Decision Making, 1969, Courts, Law and Judicial Processes, 1981; Contbr. articles to profl. jours. Served with USAAF, 1942-45, PTO. Decorated Air medal with 4 oak leaf clusters, Phila. Liberation medal; recipient Sang award for outstanding contbns. to grad. edn., 1973-74, Outstanding Polit. Sci. Tchr. award Pi Sigma Alpha, 1983, 87; Social Sci. Rsch. Coun. fellow, summers 1958, 67; NSF grantee, 1969-71, 78-82, 87-90. Mem. Am. Polit. Sci. Assn. (editorial assoc. rev. 1963-67), So. Polit. Sci. Assn. (exec. council 1965-68, v.p. 1966-67, pres. 1971-72), editorial bd. jour. (1965-72), Midwest Polit. Sci. Assn. (editorial bd. jour. 1963-64, 84-85), Ky. Polit. Sci. Assn. (v.p. 1966-67), Inter-Univ. Consortium Polit. Research (exec. council 1966-67, council chmn. 1967-68), Omicron Delta Kappa, Phi Beta Kappa. Home: 1701 Williamsburg Rd Lexington KY 40504-2013

ULMER, WALTER FRANCIS, JR., consultant, former army officer; b. Bangor, Maine, Apr. 2, 1929; married; 3 children. BS in Engring., U.S. Mil. Acad., 1952; M of Regional Planning, Pa. State U., 1973. Commd. 2d lt. U.S. Army, 1952, advanced through grades to lt. gen., 1982; dep. comdr. U.S. Army Armor Ctr., Ft. Knox, Ky., 1974-75; commandant-of cadets U.S. Mil. Acad., West Point, N.Y., 1975-77; dir. human resources devel. U.S. Army, Washington, 1978-79; comdr. 3d Armored Div., Frankfurt, Germany, 1979-82; comdg. gen. III Corps and Ft. Hood, Tex., 1982-85, ret., 1985; pres., CEO Ctr. for Creative Leadership, Greensboro, N.C., 1985-94; ind. cons., 1995—; lectr. in field. Contbr. articles to profl. jours. Home: 250 Riverbay Dr Moneta VA 24121-3138

ULRICH, JOHN AUGUST, microbiology educator; b. St. Paul, May 15, 1915; s. Robert Ernst and Mary Agnes (Farrell) U.; m. Mary Margaret Nash, June 6, 1940 (dec. May 1985); children: Jean Anne, John Joseph, Robert Charles, Karl James, Mary Ellen, Lenore Alice; m. Mary Matkovich, July 19, 1986. BS, St. Thomas Coll., 1938; PhD, U. Minn., 1947. Instr. De La Salle High Sch., Mpls., 1938-41; rsch. asst. U. Minn., Mpls., 1941-45, 49, Hormel Inst., U. Minn., Austin, 1945-49; instr. Mayo Clinic, U. Minn., Rochester, 1949-55; asst. prof. Mayo Found., U. Minn., Rochester, 1955-66; assoc. prof. U. Minn., Mpls., 1966-69; prof. U. N.Mex., Albuquerque, 1969-82, prof. emeritus, 1982—; chmn. Bacteriology & Mycology Study Sect., NIH, Washington, 1961-64, Communicable Diseases Study Sect., Atlanta, 1968-69; cons. VA Hosp., Albuquerque, 1970—, Sandia Labs., Albuquerque, 1971—, U.S. Hosp. Supply, 1978, Internat. Chem. Industries, U.S., 1979—, Minn. Mining and Mfg. Co., 1980—, Johnson and Johnson, 1981; mem. com. on surface sampling APHA, 1974; mem. FDA-Over the Counter Drugs Panel, 1975-77, FDA-Hosp. and Personal Use Device Panel, 1978-80; mem. internat. working group on air handling in hosps. and energy conservation U. Minn., 1978-79; rsch. chmn. in field; others. Chmn. Zumbo Valley exec. bd. Boy Scouts Am., Rochester, 1953-55; mem. Gamehaven exec. bd. Boy Scouts Am., Rochester, 1952-62, Dem. Com., Olmsted County, Minn., 1964-69. Recipient Silver Beaver award Boy Scouts Am., 1962, Bishop's award Winona Diocese, 1962, Katahli award U. N.Mex., 1980. Mem. Am. Soc. Microbiology (coun. mem. 1978-80), Am. Chem. Soc., Am. Bd. Med. Mycology, Am. Acad. Microbiology, Am. Acad. Dermatology (affiliate) Elks. Democrat. Roman Catholic. Achievements include discoveries in food preservation; survival of microorganisms at low temperatures; urinary amino acid excretions in variety of disease states; post-operative wound infections; bacterial skin populations; hospital epidemiology. Home: 3807 Columbia Dr Longmont CO 80503-2122

ULRICH, JOHN ROSS GERALD, aerospace engineer; b. Kalispell, Mont., Nov. 25, 1929; s. Alva Austin and Hattie Lenora (Kingston) U.; m. Virginia Jean Breinholt, June 19, 1954; children: Virginia, John, Annette, Lenora, James. BS in Engring., Northrup U., 1952. Registered profl. engr., Colo. Engr. Lockheed Aircraft, Burbank, Calif., 1952-54, Radioplane, Van Nuys, Calif., 1956-57; sect. head Aerojet-Gen., Sacramento, 1957-65; chmn. of SCUT Martin Marietta, Denver, 1965-92. Lectr. Arapahoe County Pub. Schs. With U.S. Army, 1954-56. Mem. AIAA. Achievements include invention of skyline technique for the solution to simultaneous equations, Photographic Strain Measurement Technique; buoyant suspension of gun launched space rockets. Home: 3435 E Arapahoe Littleton CO 80122

ULRICH, LARS, drummer. Drummer Metallica, 1981—. Albums include Kill 'em All, 1983, Ride the Lightning, 1984, Master of Puppets, 1986, ...And Justice for All, 1988, Metallica, 1991, Live Sh*t: Binge and Purge, 1993, Garage Days Re-visited, Load, 1996, Kill 'Em All, 1995. Recipient Grammy award, 1990, 91. Office: c/o Metallica Elektra Records 75 Rockefeller Plz New York NY 10019-6908*

ULRICH, LAUREL THATCHER, historian, educator; b. Sugar City, Idaho, July 11, 1938; d. John Kenneth and Alice (Siddoway) Thatcher; m. Gael Dennis Ulrich, Sept. 22, 1958; children: Karl, Melinda, Nathan, Thatcher, Amy. BA in English, U. Utah, 1960; MA in English, Simmons Coll., 1971; PhD in History, U. N.H., 1980. Asst. prof. humanities U. N.H., Durham, 1980-84, asst. prof. history, 1985-88, assoc. prof. history, 1988-91, prof. history, 1991-95; prof. history and women's studies Harvard U., Cambridge, Mass., 1995—; audiocourse cons. Annenberg Found.; cons., participating humanist numerous exhibits, pub. programs, other projects; project humanist Warner (N.H.) Women's Oral History Project; bd. editors William & Mary Quar., 1989-91, Winterthur Portfolio, 1991—. Author: Good Wives: Image and Reality in the Lives of Women in Northern New England, 1650-1750, 1982, A Midwife's Tale: The Life of Martha Ballard Based on Her Diary, 1785-1812, 1990 (Pulitzer Prize for history 1991); contbr. articles, abstracts, essays and revs. to profl. publs. Coun. mem. Inst. Early Am. History and Culture, 1989-91; trustee Strawberry Banke Mus., 1987-93. John Simon Guggenheim fellow, 1991-92, NEH fellow, 1982, 84-85; women's studies rsch. grantee Woodrow Wilson Fellowship Found., 1979; co-recipient Best Book award Berkshire Conf. Women's Historians, 1990; recipient Best Book award Soc. for History of Early Republic, 1990, John S. Dunning prize and Joan Kelly Meml. prize Am. Hist. Assn., 1990, Bancroft Prize for Am. History, 1991. Mem. Orgn. Am. Historians (nominating com. 1992—, ABC-Clio award com. 1989), Am. Hist. Assn. (rsch. coun. 1993-96). Office: Harvard U Dept History Robinson Hall Cambridge MA 02138*

ULRICH, MAX MARSH, executive search consultant; b. Kokomo, Ind., Mar. 21, 1925; s. Max Dan and Esther Stone (Marsh) U.; m. Mary Ellen Fisher, Sept. 12, 1950; children—Max Dwight, Jeanne Nanette; m. Geraldine A. Kidd, Jan. 25, 1973; 1 child, Amanda Marsh. B.S., U.S. Mil. Acad., 1946; M.S. in Civil Engring, Mass. Inst. Tech., 1951. Comd. 2d lt. C.E. U.S. Army, 1946, advanced through grades to capt., 1950; resigned, 1954; asst. to mng. dir. Edison Electric Inst., 1954-58; with Consol. Edison Co., N.Y.C., 1958-71; asst. v.p. Consol. Edison Co., 1962-63, v.p. charge advt. and pub. relations, 1963-67, v.p. customer service, 1968-69, v.p. Bklyn. div., 1969-71; prin., dir. Ward Howell Internat. Inc., N.Y.C., 1971-74; pres., chief exec. officer Ward Howell Internat. Inc., 1974-84, chmn., chief exec. officer, 1984-88; pres. Ward Howell Internat. Group, Inc., 1988-92, cons., 1992—. Mem. Sigma Xi. Home: 2 Kingswood Dr Orangeburg NY 10962-1806 Office: Ward Howell Internat Inc 99 Park Ave New York NY 10016-1601

ULRICH, PAUL GRAHAM, lawyer, author, publisher, editor; b. Spokane, Wash., Nov. 29, 1938; s. Donald Gunn and Kathryn (Vandercook) U.; m. Kathleen Nelson Smith, July 30, 1982; children—Kathleen Elizabeth, Marilee Rae, Michael Graham. BA with high honors, U. Mont., 1961; JD, Stanford U., 1964. Bar: Calif. 1965, Ariz. 1966, U.S. Supreme Ct. 1969, U.S. Ct. Appeals (9th cir.) 1965, U.S. Ct. Appeals (5th cir.) 1981. Law clk. judge U.S. Ct. Appeals, 9th Circuit, San Francisco, 1964-65; assoc. firm Lewis and Roca, Phoenix, 1965-70; ptnr. Lewis and Roca, 1970-85; pres. Paul G. Ulrich P.C., Phoenix, 1985-92, Ulrich, Thompson & Kessler, P.C., 1992-94, Ulrich & Kessler, P.C., Phoenix, 1994-95, Ulrich, Kessler & Anger, P.C., Phoenix, 1995—; owner Pathway Enterprises, 1985-91; judge pro tem Divsn. 1, Ariz. Ct. Appeals, Phoenix, 1986; instr. Thunderbird Grad. Sch. Internat. Mgmt., 1968-69, Ariz. State U. Coll. Law, 1970-73, 78, Scottsdale C.C., 1975-77, also continuing legal edn. seminars. Author and pub.: Applying Management and Motivation Concepts to Law Offices, 1985; editor, contbr.: Arizona Appellate Handbook, 1978—, Working With Legal Assistants, 1980, 81, Future Directions for Law Office Management, 1982, People in the Law Office, 1985-86; co-author, pub.: Arizona Healthcare Professional Liability Handbook, 1992, supplement, 1994, Arizona Healthcare Professional Liability Defense Manual, 1995, Arizona Healthcare Professional Liability Update Newsletter, 1992—; co-author: Federal Appellate Practice Guide: Ninth Circuit, 1994, supplement, 1997; contbg. editor Law Office Econs. and Mgmt., 1984—, Life, Law and the Pursuit of Balance, 1996, 2d edit., 1997. Mem. Ariz. Supreme Ct. Task Force on Ct. Orgn. and Adminstrn., 1988-89; mem. com. on appellate cts. Ariz. Supreme Ct., 1990-91; bd. visitors Stanford U. Law Sch., 1974-77; adv. com. legal assisting program Phoenix Coll., 1985-95. With U.S. Army, 1956. Recipient continuing legal edn. award State Bar Ariz., 1978, 86, 90, Harrison Tweed spl. merit award Am. Law Inst./ABA, 1987. Fellow Ariz. Bar Found. (founding 1985—); mem. ABA (chmn. selection and utilization of staff pers. com., econs. of law sect. 1979-81, mem. standing com. legal assts. 1982-86, co-chmn. joint project on appellate handbooks 1983-85, co-chmn. fed. appellate handbook project 1985-88, chmn. com. on liaison with non-lawyers orgns. Econs. of Law Practice sect. 1985-86), Am. Acad. Appellate Lawyers, Am.

Law Inst., Am. Judicature Soc. (Spl. Merit citation 1987), Ariz. Bar Assn. (chmn. econs. of law practice com. 1980-81, co-chmn. lower ct. improvement com. 1982-85, co-chmn. Ariz. appellate handbook project 1976—), Coll. Law Practice Mgmt., Maricopa County Bar Assn. (bd. dirs. 1994-96), Calif. Bar Assn., Phi Kappa Phi, Phi Alpha Delta, Sigma Phi Epsilon. Democrat. Home: 2529 E Lupine Ave Phoenix AZ 85028 Office: 3030 N Central Ave Ste 1000 Phoenix AZ 85012-2717

ULRICH, PETER HENRY, banker; b. Munich, Germany, Nov. 24, 1922; s. Hans George and Hella (Muschweck) U.; m. Carol A. Peek, Oct. 21, 1944; children: Carol Jean (Mrs. D. Scott Hewes), Patricia Diane (Mrs. Damon Eberhart), Peter James. Student, Northwestern U., 1941-42, U. Iowa, 1943, Sch. Mortgage Banking, 1954-56. Lic. real estate broker, cert. mortgage banker; cert. rev. appraiser; cert. mortgage underwriter. Escrow officer Security Title Ins. Co., Riverside, Calif., 1946-53; asst. cashier Citizens Nat. Trust & Savs., Riverside, 1953-57; v.p. Security First Nat. Bank, Riverside, 1957-63; sr. v.p. Bank of Calif. (N.A.), Los Angeles, 1963-72; pres. Ban Cal Mortgage Co., 1972-74, Ban Cal Tri-State Mortgage Co., 1974-75; cons., 1975-76; pres., dir. Beneficial Standard Mortgage Co., 1976-88; real estate cons., 1988—; instr. real estate and bus. San Bernardino Valley Coll., Riverside City Coll., Pasadena City Coll. Pres. Residential Rsch. Com. So. Calif., 1965, Riverside Opera Assn., 1956-59, Riverside Symphony Soc., 1959-61; trustee Idyllwild Arts Found., 1957—, pres., 1970-73, sec., 1986-87; mem. adv. bd. Salvation Army, 1959—, vice chmn., 1971-74, chmn., 1975; chmn. Harbor Light Com., 1965-68; convocator Calif. Luth. U., 1976-80, 81-83, regent, 1981-90; bd. dirs. Guild Opera Co., 1983—, v.p., 1991—; bd. dirs. Lark Ellen Lions Charities, 1976—, pres., 1987-90, 94—; treas. Opera Buffs, 1983—; mem. Arcadia Beautiful Commn., 1989-95, vice chair, 1991-92, chmn., 1992-93; trustee Calif. Luth. Edn. Found., 1989—; bd. dirs. Arcadia Tournament Roses Assn., 1994—, v.p. 1997, Arcadia Heart Assn., 1995-96, vice chair, 1996; mem. Arcadia City Coun., 1995-96. Served with AUS, 1943-46. Recipient Resolution of Commendation Riverside City Council, 1963; Resolution of Appreciation Los Angeles City Council, 1968, 1973, Arcadia Vol. of Yr., 1997. Mem. Nat. Mortgage Bankers Assn. (chmn. Life Ins. Co. com. 1986-87), Calif. Mortgage Bankers Assn. (sec. 1965, dir. 1972-75), So. Calif. Mortgage Bankers Assn. (dir. 1975, 80-81, v.p. 1982, pres. 1983), Indland Empire Mortgage Bankers Assn. (pres. 1962, hon. dir.), Assn. Real Estate Execs. (sec. 1967-71, pres. 1974-75, v.p. 1995—). Lutheran. Home: 447 Fairview Ave Unit 2 Arcadia CA 91007-6877 Office: 201 S Lake Ave Ste 409 Pasadena CA 91101-3016 *Being of foreign birth, I particularly appreciate and cherish the American way of life. I am grateful for the opportunities which it has afforded me. I also feel strongly that we who have had the benefit of these opportunities owe something in return to our communities and to our country. I have tried to the best of my abilities to conduct myself and my business affairs in an honorable and forthright manner, thus helping to preserve what I feel is still the best life style in the world.*

ULRICH, RICHARD WILLIAM, finance executive; b. Toledo, Oct. 30, 1950; s. Richard William Josef and Vera (Bender) U.; m. Pamela Ann Momenee, Apr. 19, 1974; 1 child, Nathanial Richard James. BBA, U. Toledo, 1973; postgrad., Stanford U., 1987. CPA, Ill. Sr. acct. Assocs. Mgmt. Co., South Bend, Ind., 1973-76; acquisition analyst Assocs. Fin. Svcs., South Bend, 1975-76; sr. v.p., contr. Assocs. Comml. Corp., Chgo., 1976-87; sr. v.p. corp. fin. Assocs. Corp. N.Am., Dallas, 1987—. Mem. AICPA, Ill. CPA Soc.

ULRICH, ROBERT GARDNER, retail food chain executive, lawyer; b. Evanston, Ill., May 6, 1935; s. Charles Clemens and Nell Clare (Stanley) U.; m. Diane Mary Granzin, June 6, 1964; children—Robert Jeffrey, Laura Elizabeth, Meredith Christine. LL.B. (Law Rev. key), Marquette U., Milw., 1960. Bar: Wis. 1960, Ill. 1960, N.Y. 1981. Law clk. to fed. dist. judge Milw., 1961-62; atty. S.C. Johnson & Son, Inc., Racine, Wis., 1962-65, Motorola, Inc., Franklin Park, Ill., 1965-68; atty., then asst. gen. counsel Jewel Cos., Inc., Melrose Park, Ill., 1968-75; v.p., gen. counsel Gt. Atlantic & Pacific Tea Co., Inc., Montvale, N.J., 1975—; sr. v.p., gen. counsel Gt. Atlantic & Pacific Tea Co., Inc., 1981—. Mem. Am. Bar Assn., N.Y. State Bar Assn. Home: 500 Weymouth Dr Wyckoff NJ 07481-1217 Office: Gt Atlantic & Pacific Tea Co Box 418 2 Paragon Dr Montvale NJ 07645-1718

ULRICH, ROBERT GENE, judge; b. St. Louis, Nov. 23, 1941; s. Henry George Ulrich and Wanda Ruth (Engram) Webb; m. JoAnn Demark, July 3, 1965; children—Jill Elizabeth, Jane Ashley. B.A., William Jewell Coll., 1963; J.D., U. Mo.-Kansas City, 1969; LLM, U. Mo., 1972. Bar: Mo. 1969. Assoc. Von Erdmannsdorff, Voigts & Kuhlman, North Kansas City, Mo., 1969-72; pvt. practice Raytown, Mo., 1972; asst. U.S. atty. Dept. Justice, Kansas City and Springfield, Mo., 1973-76, 78-81; ptnr. Pine & Ulrich, Warrensburg, Mo., 1976-77; litigation atty. Shifran, Treiman, et al., Clayton, Mo., 1977-78; U.S. atty. We. Dist. Mo., Kansas City, 1981-89; judge Mo. Ct. Appeals (we. dist.), Kansas City, 1989-96, chief judge, 1996—; mem. U.S. Atty. Gen.'s Econ. Crime Council, 1983-89 , Atty. Gen.'s Adv. Com. of U.S. Attys., chmn. 1986-89, adv. com. U.S. Ct. Appeals (8th cir.), 1983-86. Appointed mem. steering com. Protect our Children Campaign, Gov. of Mo., chmn. legis. subcom., 1985; mem. resource bd., personnel mgmt. bd. Dept. Justice, 1985-89; trustee Liberty Meml. Assn., 1989—; vice chmn. Orgn. Crime Drug Enforcement Task Force Nat. Program, Dept. Justice, 1987-89. Col. USMC, 1963-66. Mem. Am. Judicature Soc., Inst. Jud. Adminstrn., Mo. Bar Assn., Kansas City Met. Bar Assn., Marine Corps Res. Officers' Assn. (exec. councillor 1986-87), U. Mo.-Kansas City Law Sch. Alumni Assn. (v.p. 1994-95, pres. 1995—). Office: Missouri Ct Appeals 1300 Oak St Kansas City MO 64106-2904

ULRICH, ROBERT J., retail discount chain stores executive; b. 1944. Grad., U. Minn., 1967, Stanford U., 1978. Chmn., chief exec. officer, dir. Dayton Hudson Corp.; with Dayton Hudson Corp., Mpls., 1967—, exec. v.p. dept. stores divsn., 1981-84, pres. dept. stores divsn., 1984-87, chmn., CEO Target stores divsn., 1987-93, dir., 1993—, chmn, CEO, 1994—. Office: Dayton Hudson Corp 777 Nicollet Mall Minneapolis MN 55402-2004*

ULRICH, RUSSELL DEAN, osteopathic physician; b. LaPorte, Ind., Apr. 15, 1947; s. Russell Denzel and Betty Faye (Higgins) U.; m. Evelyn Kay Gove, July 14, 1967; children—Tonya Kay, Nolan Dean, Bryce Alan. B.A. in Religion, Wesleyan Holiness Coll., Phoenix, 1970; B.A. in Psychology, U. Ariz., 1974; D.O., Coll. Osteo. Medicine and Surgery, Des Moines, 1978. Diplomate Am. Osteo. Bd. Family Physicians with qualification in geriatrics. Tchr., Montezuma Schs., Cottonwood, Ariz., 1970-72; intern William Beaumont Army Med. Ctr., 1978-79; gen. practice medicine Piedmont Med. Clinic, Ala., 1982-85, Piedmont Family Practice Ctr., 1985—; asst. chief of staff Piedmont Hosp., 1983-84, chief of staff, 1984-92. Med. adviser Piedmont Rescue Squad, 1982—; mem. Calhoun County Disaster Preparedness Com., Anniston, Ala., 1984—; bd. dirs. Hobe Sound Bible Coll., Dayspring Ministries. Served to capt. U.S. Army, 1978-82. Mem. AMA (Physician's Recognition award 1982, 85, 89, 92, 95), Am. Osteo. Assn., Ala. Osteopathic Med. Assn. (sec.- treas. 1988—). Republican. Methodist. Home: 932 Maple Ln Jacksonville AL 36265-6845 Office: Piedmont Family Practice Ctr PO Box 450 800 W Memorial Dr Piedmont AL 36272-1930

ULRICH, THEODORE ALBERT, lawyer; b. Spokane, Wash., Jan. 1, 1943; s. Herbert Roy and Martha (Hoffman) Ulrich; m. Nancy Allison, May 30, 1966; children: Donald Wayne, Frederick Albert. BS cum laude, U.S. Mcht. Marine Acad., 1965; JD cum laude, Fordham U., 1970; LLM, NYU, 1974. Bar: N.Y. 1971, U.S. Ct. Appeals (2nd cir.) 1971, U.S. Supreme Ct. 1974, U.S. Ct. Claims 1977, U.S. Customs Ct. 1978, U.S. Ct. Internat. Trade 1981, U.S. Ct. Appeals (5th cir.) 1988, U.S. Ct. Appeals (D.C. cir.) 1992, Colo. 1993, U.S. Ct. Appeals (10 cir.) 1994. Mng. clk. U.S. Dept. Justice, N.Y.C., 1968-69, law clk. to federal dist. judge, 1969-70; assoc. Cadwalader, Wickersham & Taft, N.Y.C., 1970-80, ptnr., 1980-94; ptnr. Popham, Haik, Schnobrich & Kaufman, Ltd., Denver, 1994-96. Co-author: Encyclopedia of International Commercial Litigation, 1991, Arbitration of Construction Contracts, V, 1991; contbg. author: Mainre Engineering Economics and Cost Analysis, 1995; author, editor Fordham Law Rev., 1969. Leader Boy Scouts Am., Nassau County, N.Y., 1984-94, Denver, 1994—. Lt. comdr. USCGR, 1965-86. Mem. ABA, Colo. Bar, Denver Bar, Maritime Law Assn., Am. Soc. Internat. Law, Soc. Naval Architects and Marine Engrs., U.S. Naval Inst., Am. Arbitration Assn. Home and Office: 4300 E 6th Ave Denver CO 80220

ULRICH, WERNER, patent lawyer; b. Munich, Germany, Mar. 12, 1931; came to U.S., 1940, naturalized, 1945; s. Karl Justus and Grete (Rosenthal) U.; m. Ursula Wolff, June 28, 1959; children—Greta, Kenneth. B.S., Columbia U., 1952, M.S. (NSF fellow 1952-53), 1953, Dr.Engring. Sci., 1957; M.B.A., U. Chgo., 1975; J.D., Loyola U., Chgo, 1985. Bar: Ill., 1985. With AT&T Bell Labs, Naperville, Ill., 1953-95; head electronics switching dept. AT&T Bell Labs., Naperville, Ill., 1964-68; dir. Advanced Switching Tech., Naperville, 1968-77, head maintenance architecture dept., 1977-81; sr. atty. Intellectual Property Law Orgn., Naperville, 1981-95; vis. lectr. U. Calif., Berkeley, 1966-67. Inventor of over 20 telecommunications inventions; patentee electronic switching systems. Fellow IEEE; mem. ABA, Ill. State Bar Assn., Am. Intellectual Property Law Assn., Tau Beta Pi, Beta Gamma Sigma. Office: 434 Maple St Glen Ellyn IL 60137-3826

ULRICH, WERNER RICHARD, union education administrator; b. N.Y.C., Sept. 26, 1941; s. Werner and Erna (Schreiner) U.; m. Marie Sciacca, July 18, 1965; children: Kenneth, Clifford, Richard. AAS, Voorhees Tech. Inst., 1969; BA, SUNY, Old Westbury, 1985; MS, N.Y. Inst. Tech., 1990. Mechanic "A" Con Edison of N.Y., N.Y.C., 1963-68; apprentice steamfitter Steamfitters', Local Union # 638, Long Island City, N.Y., 1968-73, journeyman steamfitter, 1973-85; dir. edn. Steamfitters' Edn. Fund, N.Y.C., 1985—. Blood dr. coord. Steamfitters', Local Union # 638, Long Island City, 1987—; usher, capt. Holy Name of Mary Roman Cath. Ch., 1984—; mem. steering coun. L.I. Women's Coun., 1992—; skilled worker emeritus N.Y. State Tng. Partnership Coun., 1993—; mem. S.I. Job Svc. Employer Com., 1993—. With U.S. Army, 1959-62. Recipient John J. Theobald award N.Y. Inst. Tech., 1989, Commr.'s award N.Y. State Dept. Labor, 1991, L.I. Women's award L.I. Women's Coun., 1991, N.Y. State Gov.'s cert. of Appreciation, 1994. Mem. ASME, Nat. Fire Protection Assn., U.S. Apprenticeship Assn., Am. Legion, KC. Avocations: horticulture.

ULTAN, LLOYD, historian; b. Bronx, N.Y., Feb. 16, 1938; s. Louis and Sophie U. BA cum laude, Hunter Coll., 1959; MA, Columbia U., 1960. Assoc. Edward Williams Coll. Fairleigh Dickinson U., Hackensack, N.J., 1964-74; asst. prof. history Edward Williams Coll. Fairleigh Dickinson U., Hackensack, 1974-75, assoc. prof. Edward Williams Coll., 1975-83, prof. Edward Williams Coll., 1983—; cons. in field. Editor Bronx County Hist. Soc. Pres., 1981—; author: The Beautiful Bronx, 1920-50, 1979, Legacy of the Revolution: The Valentine-Varian House, 1983, The Bronx in the Innocent Years, 1890-1925, 1985, The Presidents of the United States, 1989, The Bronx in the Frontier Era: From the Beginning to 1696, 1993, The Bronx: It Was Only Yesterday, 1935-65, 1993; contbr. Ency. N.Y. City, 1995, Roots of the Republic, Vol. VI, 1996; editor Bronx County Hist. Soc. Jour., 1964—. Gen. sec. Bronx Civic League, 1964-67; v.p. bd. trustees Bronx County Hist. Soc., 1965-67, 77-84, curator, 1968-71, pres., 1971-76, historian, 1986—; founding mem., bd. dir. Bronx Coun. on Arts, 1968-71; chmn. Bronx County Bicentennial Commn., 1973-76, Bronx Borough Pres.'s Bicentennial Adv. Com., 1974-76; vice chmn. Commn. Celebrating 350 Yr. of the Bronx, 1989; program guidelines com. N.Y.C. Dept. Cultural Affairs, 1976-77; bd. dirs. Nat. Shrine Bill of Rights, Mt. Vernon, N.Y., 1983—; mem. N.Y.C. Com. on Cultural Concerns, 1982-88; bd. sponsors Historic Preservation com. St. Ann's Ch. Morrisania, 1987—; bd. dirs. 91 Van Cortlandt Owners Corp., 1986—; official historian Bronx Borough, N.Y., 1996—. Recipient Fairleigh Dickinson U. 15-Yr. award, 1979, 20-Yr. award, 1984, 25-Yr. award, 1989, 30-Yr. award, 1994, Outstanding Tchr. of Yr. award, 1994; named to Hunter Coll. Alumni Hall of Fame, 1974; N.Y. State Regents Coll. Teaching fellow, 1959. Mem. AAUP (v.p. Teaneck chpt. 1992-93, sec. coun. of FDU chpts. 1992-93), Am. Hist. Assn., N.Y. Hist. Soc., Phi Alpha Theta, Alpha Chi Alpha, Sigma Lambda. Home and Office: 91 Van Cortlandt Ave W Bronx NY 10463-2712 *Transmitting the heritage of the past to the youth and to the mature adult, either through the spoken or written word, not only ensures that the civilization we inherited will be passed on, it will also warn people about earlier mistakes that should now be shunned and will, hopefully, inspire them to add their own positive contribution. I believe I am continuing to perform this service.*

ULTES, ELIZABETH CUMMINGS BRUCE, artist, retired art historian and librarian; b. Urbana, Ohio, Mar. 27, 1909; d. William Mansfield and Helen Finnette (Cummings) B.; m. William Ultes, Jr., May 2, 1934 (dec. Oct. 1973); 1 child, Elizabeth Cummings Ultes Hoffman. BA in Econs., Hollins Coll., 1930; BFA in History of Art, Wittenberg U., 1979; student painting, Positano, Italy, 1960, San Miguel Allende, Mex., 1980. Instr. art history continuing edn. dept. Wittenberg U., Springfield, Ohio, 1959-80; warder, art libr. Springfield Pub. Libr., 1959-70; ret., 1970; former writer art critiques Springfield Daily News-Sun. Exhibited in 2 one-woman shows, Springfield, group shows in Dayton Art Mus., Springfield Fair, Springfield Mus.; 3 paintings in permanent collection Clark County Hist. Mus. Included in The Library and Rsch. Ctr., Nat. Mus. Women in the Arts, 1997. Avocations: painting, genealogy, reading, cooking. Home: 5155 N High St Columbus OH 43214-1525

ULTMANN, JOHN ERNEST, physician, educator; b. Vienna, Austria, Jan. 6, 1925; came to U.S., 1938, naturalized, 1943; s. Oskar and Hedwig (Schechter) U.; m. Ruth E. Layton, May 25, 1952; children: Monica, Michelle, Barry. Student, Bklyn. Coll., 1946, Oberlin Coll., 1946-48; M.D., Columbia U., 1952; Dr honoris causa, Heidelberg U., Fed. Republic Germany, 1986, Vienna U., Austria, 1991. Diplomate Nat. Bd. Med. Examiners, Am. Bd. Internal Medicine. Intern N.Y. Hosp.-Cornell Med. Center, N.Y.C., 1952-53; resident N.Y. Hosp., 1953-55; Am. Cancer Soc. fellow in hematology Columbia, 1955-56; practice medicine specializing in internal medicine N.Y.C., 1956-68, Chgo., 1968—; mem. staff Francis Delafield Hosp., 1955-68, Presbyn. Hosp., 1956-68, Bellevue Hosp., 1961-68; career scientist Health Research Council City N.Y., 1959-68; cons. Harlem Hosp., N.Y.C., 1966-68; dir. clin. oncology Franklin McLean Meml. Research Inst., 1968-91; prof. medicine Sch. Medicine U. Chgo., 1970—, dir. Cancer Rsch. Ctr., 1973-91, assoc. dir., 1991-94, dir. emeritus, 1994—, dean for rsch. and devel., 1978-88; hon. prof. Cancer Inst. Chinese Acad. Med. Scis., People's Republic of China, 1988; chmn. bd. sci. counselors div. cancer treatment Nat. Cancer Inst., 1976-80, mem. bd. sci. counselors div. cancer prevention and control, 1985-88; mem. adv. bd. Cancer Control to Gov. of Ill., 1976-93, chmn., 1985-93. Assoc. editor: Cancer Research, 1974-78; editorial bd.: Annals Internal Medicine, 1974-81, Blood, 1975-77; cons. editor: Am. Jour. Medicine, 1975—; Contbr. articles to profl. jours. Bd. dirs. Assn. Am. Cancer Insts., 1974-75, pres.-elect, 1983-84, pres., 1984-85, chmn. bd., 1985-86; bd. dirs. at-large Ill. div. Am. Cancer Soc., 1976-79; trustee Ill. Cancer Coun., 1976-93; chmn. Nat. Coalition for Cancer Rsch., 1985-90. With AUS, 1943-46. Fellow A.C.P., Inst. Medicine Chgo.; mem. Am. Fedn. Clin. Investigation, Soc. Study Blood, Am. Assn. Cancer Rsch., Am. Socs. Hematology, AAUP, AAAS, Harvey Soc., Am. Soc. Clin. Oncology (dir. 1978-83, pres.-elect 1980-81, pres. 1981-82, past pres. 1982-83), Chgo. Soc. Internal Medicine, Central Soc. Clin. Rsch., Sociedad Chilena de Cancerologia, Sociedad Chilena de Hematologia, Phi Beta Kappa, Alpha Omega Alpha. Home: 5632 S Harper Ave Chicago IL 60637-1872 Office: U Chgo Cancer Rsch Ctr 5841 S Maryland Ave Chicago IL 60637-1463

ULVESTAD, ANNE ELIZABETH, art director; b. Yonkers, N.Y., Oct. 19, 1953; d. William George and Rita Agnes (Schug) Bachop; m. Odd Inge Ulvestad, July 1, 1982; 1 child, Kjersti Anita. BS, RN, Hunter/Bellevue Sch. Nursing, N.Y.C., 1974; postgrad., Unification Theol. Sem., Barrytown, N.Y., 1979-80. Missionary Unification Ch., N.Y.C., 1974-79; comms. dir. Assn. for Edn. and Devel., Kenya, 1980-82; high sch. art tchr. Muslim High Sch., The Gambia, 1982-84; dir. The Heart-Parent Scholarship Found., Banjul, The Gambia, 1982-84; graphic designer Trinity Corp., N.Y.C., 1985; sect. designer The World & I Mag., Washington, 1986-91, art dir., 1991—; founder Graphics for the World, Washington, 1993—. Founding mem. Unification Ednl. Found., Landover Hills, Md., 1990; sec. PTA New Hope Acad., Landover Hills, 1990-92. Recipient Cert. of Distinction for design Creativity '92, 1992, Cert. of Distinction for illustration Creativity '92, 1992, Annual Exhbn. award Illustrator's Club, 1993, 94. Mem. Am. Inst. Graphic Arts, Nat. Assn. Desk Top Pubs., Nat. Trust Hist. Preservation, Women's Fedn. for World Peace, Nat. Parks and Conservation Assn. Christian Appalachian Project. Office: The World and I Mag 3600 New York Ave NE Washington DC 20002-1947

UMAKANTHA, KAGGAL V., physiatrist; b. Bellary, India, 1943. BS, MD, MS (orthop.), Karnatak Med. Coll., Hubli, India, 1965. Diplomate Am. Bd. Phys. Medicine and Rehab. Intern Karnatak Med. Coll. Hosp., Hubli, 1965-66; house surgeon Miraj (India) Med. Ctr., 1966-67; resident in orthopedic surgery King George's Med. Hosp., Lucknow, India, 1967-69; lectr. in orthopaedic surgery Govt. Med. Coll. and Hosp., Bellary, India, 1969-71; registrar orthopaedic surgery Govt. Hosp., Port-of-Spain, Trinidad and Tobago, 1971-74; resident in phys. medicine and rehab. Rehab. Inst. Chgo., 1975-78; chief, phys. medicine and rehab. VA Med. Ctr., Tuscaloosa, Ala.; clin. asst. prof. Coll. Community Health Scis. Lt. col. USAFR. Fellow Am. Bd. Electrodiagnostic Medicine. Office: VA Hosp 117 Tuscaloosa AL 35404

UMAN, MARTIN ALLAN, electrical engineering educator, researcher, consultant; b. Tampa, Fla., July 3, 1936; s. Morrice S. and Edith G. (Brown) U.; m. Dorit Brigitta Kalbas, Mar. 6, 1962; children: Jon, Mara, Derek. BS in Engring., Princeton U., 1957, MA, 1959, PhD, 1961. Assoc. prof. elec. engring. U. Ariz., Tucson, 1961-65; fellow physicist Westinghouse Rsch. Labs., Pitts., 1965-71; prof. dept. elec. and computer engring. U. Fla., Gainesville, 1971-91, prof., chmn. dept., 1991—; pres. Lightning Location & Protection, Inc., Tucson, 1975-83; mem. Internat. Commn. on Atmospheric Electricity, 1975-92; cons. Boeing Aircraft, Patrick AFB, Mobil Oil Corp., McDonnell Douglas, United Techs., IBM, Flamex Corp., NOAA, NASA, No. Telecom Can., Tampa Cable TV, Bonneville Power Adminstrn., Martin Marietta, Sandia Nat. Labs., Walt Disney World, SRI, other cos. Author: Introduction to Plasma Physics, 1964, Lightning, 1969, rev. edit., 1984, Understanding Lightning, 1971, All About Lightning, 1986, The Lightning Discharge, 1987; also over 130 articles; assoc. editor Jour. Geophys. Rsch., 1980-83; patentee in field. Mem. senate U. Fla., 1988-90, 93—, bd. dirs. div. sponsored rsch., 1989-91. Recipient Editor's Citation, Jour. Geophys. Rsch., 1989, Outstanding Fla. Scientist award Fla. Acad. Scis., 1991, Group Achievement award for Galileo Spacecraft NASA, 1992, 96; rsch. grantee various orgns. Fellow IEEE (com. mem. working group on lightning performance distbn. ins. 1979—, working group on estimating performance transmission ins. 1985—, Heinrich Hertz medal 1996), Am. Geophys. Union, Am. Meteorol. Soc.

UMAN, SARAH DUNGEY, editor; b. Dayton, Ohio, July 22, 1942; d. Arthur Bertram and Lucretia M. (Nash) Dungey; child from previous marriage: Michael Uman; m. Marshall B. Allen; 1 child, Sebastian. Student, New Sch. for Social Rsch., 1962-64. Editl. assoc., publicity dir. Grove Press, Inc., N.Y.C., 1970-79; sr. editor Playboy Paperbacks, N.Y.C., 1979-81, Berkley Pub., N.Y.C., 1982-85; exec. editor Consumer Reports Books, Yonkers, N.Y., 1985-94, Rights Unltd., N.Y.C., 1994-96; editor Red Bear Editl. Svcs., Bronx, N.Y., 1996—.

UMANS, ALVIN ROBERT, manufacturing company executive; b. N.Y.C., Mar. 11, 1927; s. Louis and Ethel (Banner) U.; m. Nancy Jo Zadek, June 28, 1953 (div.); children: Kathi Lee Umans Lind, Craig Joseph; m. Madeleine Sayer, Sept. 21, 1985; 1 child, Valentine Brett. Student, U. Rochester, 1945. Sales mgr. Textile Mills Co., Chgo., 1954-56; regional sales mgr. Reflector Hardware Corp., Melrose Park, Ill., 1956-58; nat. sales mgr. Reflector Hardware Corp., 1959-62, v.p., 1962-65, pres., treas., dir., 1965-92; pres., CEO RHC/Spacemaster Corp., 1992—; chmn. bd. dirs., Garcy Corp., Ala.; v.p., bd. dirs. Goer Mfg. Co., Inc., Charleston, S.C.; chmn. Discovery Plastics, Oreg.; pres., treas., dir. Spacemaster Corp., Del.; chmn. Morgan Marshall Industries, Inc., Ill., Capitol Hardware, Inc., Ill.; dir., v.p. Spartan Showcase Inc., Mo.; dir. Adams Comm., Chgo.; bd. dirs. Monroe Comm., Chgo. Trustee Mt. Sinai Hosp. Med. Ctr., Chgo., chmn. bd., 1987-89; trustee Schwab Rehab. Hosp., Chgo., chmn. bd., 1987-89; dir., chmn. Sinai Health Sys., Chgo., 1995—; mem. Cook County Bur. Adv. Com., 1994—; trustee Driehaus Mutual Funds, 1996—; bd. dirs. Milton & Rose Zadek Fund, 1965-78; governing bd. mem. Cinema/Chgo., 1988-89. Served with AUS, 1943-46. Mem. Nat. Assn. Store Fixture Mfrs. (dir. 1969-70), Chgo. Pres.'s Orgn. Club: Standard (Chgo.). Home: 132 E Delaware Pl Chicago IL 60611-1445 Office: RHC/Spacemaster Corp 1400 N 25th Ave Melrose Park IL 60160-3001

UMBEHOCKER, KENNETH SHELDON, priest; b. Mpls., Sept. 23, 1934; s. Kenneth and Mildred Adeline (Johnson) U. BA, Vanderbilt U., 1956; Licentiate in Theology, Seabury-Western, Evanston, Ill., 1959; M in Mgmt., U. Ga., 1974. Ordained to ministry Episcopal Ch., 1959. Priest-in-charge St. John's Ch., Hallock, Minn., 1959-62; rector St. Paul's Ch., Virginia, Minn., 1962-67; priest-in-charge Emmanuel Ch., Rushford, Minn., 1968-74; asst. to dean Gethsemane Cathedral, Fargo, N.D., 1974-86; priest-in-charge St. Peter's Ch., Warroad, Minn., 1986-90; rector Ch. of the Good Shepherd, Windom, Minn., 1990-94, St. John's by the Lake, Worthington, Minn., 1990-94, Holy Trinity, Luverne, Minn., 1990-94, Episcopal Parish of St. Mark and St. John, Jim Thorpe, Pa., 1995—; community developer, 1968-86; trustee Episcopal Diocese of Minn., Mpls., 1987-90, coun. mem., 1980-94. Field rep. Am. Cancer Soc., Mpls., 1965-67; dept. mgr. Rochester (Minn.) Area C. of C., 1967-74; exec. dir. Fargo Parking Authority and Downtown Assn., 1974-86. Seabury fellow Seabury-Western Sem., 1980; named Young Man of Yr. Rochester Jaycees, 1970; recipient Order of Purple Cross, York Rite Coll. North Am., 1988; Canterbury scholar Canterbury Cathedral of Kent, Eng., 1996. Mem. Am. Acad. Parish Clergy, Am. C. of C. Execs., Nat. Parking Assn. (v.p. 1983-86, Disting. Svc. award 1985), Knights Templar (grand comdr. N.D. club 1985-86), Masons (grand chaplain Minn. club 1994), Seven Continents Club. Home: 32 Race St Jim Thorpe PA 18229-2004 *Working in the secular world as well as in the sacred makes a person more attuned to the needs and wants of the people in the pew and I find that that has enhanced my life tremendously.*

UMBREIT, WAYNE WILLIAM, bacteriologist, educator; b. Markesan, Wis., May 1, 1913; s. William Traugott and Augusta (Abendroth) U.; m. Doris McQuade, July 31, 1937; children: Dorayne Loreda, Jay Nicholas, Thomas Hayden. B.A., U. Wis., 1934, M.S., 1936, Ph.D., 1939. Instr. soil microbiology Rutgers U., 1937-38; faculty U. Wis., Madison, 1938-44; asst. prof. bacteriology and chemistry U. Wis., 1941-44; faculty Cornell U., 1944-47, prof. bacteriology, 1946-47; head dept. enzyme chemistry Merck Inst., Rahway, N.J., 1947-58; asso. dir., 1958; chmn. dept. bacteriology Rutgers U., New Brunswick, N.J., 1958-75; prof. microbiology, dir. grad. programs Rutgers U., 1969-83, prof. emeritus microbiology, 1983—; dir. labs. So. Br. Watershed Assn., 1983-89. Author: (with Burris, Stauffer) Manometric Techniques, 1945, 5th edit., 1972, (with Oginsky) An Introduction to Bacterial Physiology, 1954, Metabolic Maps, 1960, Modern Microbiology, 1962, Essentials of Bacterial Physiology, 1976; Editor: Advances in Applied Microbiology, vols. 1-10, 1959-68; Contbr. articles to profl. jours. Recipient Biochem. Congress Symposium medal Paris, France, 1952. Fellow Am. Acad. Microbiology, N.Y. Acad. Sci., A.A.A.S.; mem. Am. Soc. for Microbiology (Eli Lilly award in bacteriology 1947, Carski Found. award for distinguished teaching 1968), Soc. Biol. Chemists, Am. Chem. Soc., Theobald Smith Soc. (Waksman award in microbiology 1957, past pres.), AAUP, Sigma Xi. Home: 826 Covered Bridge Rd Holland PA 18966

UMEBAYASHI, CLYDE SATORU, lawyer; b. Honolulu, Sept. 2, 1947; s. Robert S. and Dorothy C. Umebayashi; m. Cheryl J. Much, June 27, 1975. BBA in Travel Industry Mgmt., U. Hawaii, 1969, JD, 1980. Spl. dept. atty. gen. Labor and Indsl. Rels. Appeals Bd., Honolulu, 1980-81; atty., dir., shareholder Kessner Duca Umebayashi Bain & Matsunaga, Honolulu, 1981—; commr. Hawaii Criminal Justice Commn. Bd. dirs. Wesley Found., Honolulu, 1993-97. Mem. Hawaii State Bar Assn. Office: Kessner Duca Umebayashi 220 S King St Fl 19 Honolulu HI 96813-4526

UMFLEET, LLOYD TRUMAN, electrical engineering technology educator; b. Grangeville, Idaho, June 2, 1944; s. Lloyd Truman Sr. and Bessie Viola (MacKay) U.; m. Ruth Ann Strickland, Oct. 26, 1968. BSEE, U. Mo., 1966; MSIM, Poly. Inst. Bklyn., 1971; M in Engring., U. Colo., 1988. Registered profl. engr., Tex. Asst. engr. Union Electric, St. Louis, 1966; elec. engr. Power Authority State of N.Y., N.Y.C., 1967-68, Consol. Edison, N.Y.C., 1968-71; ind. engring. cons. Toledo, 1971-76; chief elec. engr. Goldston Engring., Inc., Corpus Christi, Tex., 1976-80; mgr. elec. engring. Berry Engring., Inc., Corpus Christi, 1980-84; instr. elec. tech. Bee County Coll., Beeville, Tex., 1984-86; asst. prof. Del Mar Coll., Corpus Christi, 1988—; cons. engring. Ctrl. Power and Light, Corpus Christi, 1991, 92, INDTECH, Inc., Corpus Christi, 1994, 95, Schneider Engring. Inc., Boerne, Tex., 1996.

Mem. IEEE (sr.), Am. Soc. Engring. Edn., Instrument Soc. Am., Rockport Sailing Club (commodore 1982). Achievements include development of universal power circle for educational purposes. Office: Del Mar Coll 101 Baldwin Blvd Corpus Christi TX 78404-3805

UMMER, JAMES WALTER, lawyer; b. Pitts., July 16, 1945; s. Walter B. and Rose P. (Gerhardt) U.; m. Janet Sue Young, Dec. 21, 1968; children: James Bradley, Benjamin F. BA, Thiel Coll., 1967; JD, Duke U., 1972. Bar: Pa. 1972. Trust officer Pitts. Nat. Bank, 1972-75; tax atty., shareholder Buchanan Ingersoll P.C., Pitts., 1975-92; prin. Hirtle, Callaghan & Co., Pitts., 1992-93; with Babst, Calland, Clements and Zomnir, Pitts., 1993—, SPEC Conss., Inc., Trafford, Pa.; mng. dir. Morgan Franklin & Co., Pitts., Golf Course Cons., Orlando, Fla. Trustee Thiel Coll., Greenville, Pa., 1984—, The Rehab. Inst. Pitts., 1984—, Snee-Reinhardt Charitable Found., Pitts., 1987—. Fellow Am. Coll. Probate Counsel; mem. Estate Planning Coun. Western Pa. (pres. 1986-87), Tax Club (Pitts.), Duquesne Club, Rolling Rock Club, Oakmont Country Club. Republican. Presbyterian. Home: 200 Woodland Farms Rd Pittsburgh PA 15238-2024 Office: Babst, Calland, Clements & Zomnir 2 Gateway Ctr Fl 8 Pittsburgh PA 15222-1402

UMMINGER, BRUCE LYNN, government official, scientist, educator; b. Dayton, Ohio, Apr. 10, 1941; s. Frederick William and Elnora Mae (Waltemathe) U.; m. Judith Lackey Bryant, Dec. 17, 1966; children: Alison Grace, April Lynn. BS magna cum laude with honors in biology, Yale U., 1963, MS, 1966, MPhil, 1968, PhD, 1969; postgrad., U. Calif., Berkeley, 1963-64; cert. univ. adminstrv./mgmt. tng. program, U. Cin., 1975; cert., Fed. Exec. Inst., 1984. Asst. prof. dept. biol. scis. U. Cin., 1969-73, assoc. prof. dept. biol. scis., 1973-75, acting head dept. biol. scis., 1973-75, prof. dept. biol. scis., 1975-81, dir. grad. affairs, 1978-79; program dir. regulatory biology program NSF, Washington, 1979-84, dept. dir. cellular bioscis. divsn., 1984-89, mem. sr. exec. svc., 1984—, acting divsn. dir., 1985-87, 88-89, divsn. dir. cellular bioscis. divsn., 1989-91, divsn. dir. integrative biology and neurosci. divsn., 1991—; sr. advisor on health policy Office of Internat. Health Policy Dept. State, Washington, 1988; sr. advisor on biodiversity Smithsonian Instn., 1993-94; exec. sec. Nat. Sci. Bd. Com. on Ctrs. and Individual Investigator Awards, 1986-88; mem. NSF rev. panel Exptl. Program to Stimulate Competitive Rsch., 1989, Rsch. Improvement in Minority Instns., 1986, 87, U.S.-India Coop. Rsch. Program, 1981-82, U.S.-India Exchange of Scholars Program, 1979-81; vice chmn. biotech. rsch. subcom. Fed. Coord. Coun. on Sci. Engring. and Tech., Office Sci. and Tech. Policy, 1991-94; exec. sec. subcom. biodiversity and ecosystem dynamics, com. on environment and natural resources Nat. Sci. and Tech. Coun., 1994; mem. group nat. experts on safety in biotech., OECD, 1988-89; mem. sr. exec. panel Exec. Potential Program, Office Pers. Mgmt., 1988-89; mem. space shuttle proposal rev. panel in life scis. NASA, 1978, rsch. assocs. in space biology award com., 1985-91, chmn. cell and devel. biology discipline working group, space biology program, 1990-91, chmn. gravitational biology panel, NASA Specialized Ctrs. Rsch. and Tng., 1990, chmn. NASA specialized ctrs. rsch. and tng. peer rev. panel, 1995, mem. exec. steering com. in life scis., 1991, mem. gravitational biology facility sci. working group, 1992-95, mem. space sta. biol. rsch. project sci. working group, 1995-96, mem. NASA neurolab. steering com., 1993; mem. panel study biol. diversity, Bd. Sci. and Tech. Internat. Devel. NRC, 1989; exec. sec. adv. planning bd. Nat. Biodiversity Info. Ctr., Smithsonian Instn., 1993-94; mem. adv. screening com. in life scis. Coun. for Internat. Exchange of Scholars, 1978-81; liaison rep. nat. heart, lung and blood adv. coun. NIH, 1979-87, nat. adv. child health and human devel. coun., 1990—; recombinant DNA adv. com., 1988; laison represenative agrl. biotechnology Rsrch. Adv. com., USDA, 1989-94; mem. InteragencyRsch. animal com., 1984-88; Interagency working group on Internat. Biotechnology, 1988-94. Author book chpts. and contbr. articles to profl. jours.; assoc. editor Jour. Exptl. Zoology, 1977-79; editorial adv. bd. Gen. and Comparative Endocrinology, 1982. Mem. world mission com. Ch. of the Redeemer, New Haven, 1967-68; Sunday Sch. steering com. Calvary Episcopal Ch., Cin., 1972-73; sr. acolyte, 1972-77, adult edn. com., 1975-76; deacon Faith Presbyn. Ch., Springfield, Va., 1996—; adv. com. mem. Wakefield H.S., 1991-92, PTA exec. bd., 1991-92; sci. adv. com. Arlington Pub. Schs., 1987-92, adv. coun. on instrn., 1991-92; adv. bd. mem. Campbell Comml. Coll., Cin., 1977-79. Recipient George Rieveschl, Jr. Rsch. award U. Cin., 1973, Presdl. Rank Meritorious Exec. award NSF, 1992; U. Cin. Grad. Sch. fellow 1977—, NSF fellow 1964; rsch. grantee NSF 1971-79. Fellow AAAS (coun. 1980-83, 89-90, mem. program com. for 1989 ann. meeting 1988, chairperson-elect sect. G-Biol. Scis. 1987-88, chairperson 1988-89, ret. 1989-90), N.Y. Acad. Scis.; mem. Am. Soc. Zoologists (sec., mem. exec. com. 1979-81, chmn. nominating com. 1981, sec. divsn. of comparative physiology and biochemistry 1976-77, chmn. Congl. Sci. Fellow Program com. 1986-89, mem. 1991-93), Am. Physiol. Soc. (program adv. com. 1978-81, program exec. com., 1983-86, mem. steering com., comparative pysiology sect. 1978-81, sec. Am. Physiol. Soc.-Am. Soc. Zoologists Task Force on Comparative Physiology 1977-78), Am. Inst. Biol. Scis. (chmn. selection com. congl. fellow liaisons com. 1991), Am. Soc. for Gravitational and Space Biology, Sr. Execs. Assn., Assn. of Yale Alumni (del. 1990-93), Mory's Assn., Yale Club (Washington), Masons (32 degree), Knights Templar, Shriners, Sigma Xi (Disting. Rsch. award U. Cin. chpt. 1973, pres. U. Cin. chpt. 1977-79), Mensa, Promise Keepers. Presbyterian. Achievements include development of science policy in biodiversity, space biology, integrative biology, neuroscience, and biotechnology; research in low temperature biology, in comparative physiology, endocrinology and biochemistry of fish, and in visual orientation of crustacea. Home: 4087B S Four Mile Run Dr Arlington VA 22204-5604 Office: NSF Divsn Integrative Biology and Neuroscience 4201 Wilson Blvd Arlington VA 22230-0001

UNAKAR, NALIN JAYANTILAL, biological sciences educator; b. Karachi, Sindh, Pakistan, Mar. 26, 1935; came to U.S., 1961; s. Jayantilal Virshankar and Malati Jaswantrai (Buch) U.; m. Nita Shantilal Mankad; children: Rita, Rupa. BS, Gujerat U., Bhavnagar, India, 1955; MSc, Bombay U., 1961; PhD, Brown U., 1965. Research asst. Indian Cancer Research Ctr., Bombay, 1955-61; USPHS trainee in biology Brown U., Providence, 1961-65; research assoc. in pathology U. Toronto, Ont., Can., 1965-66; asst. prof. biology Oakland U., Rochester, Mich., 1966-69, assoc. prof., 1969-74, prof., chmn. biology dept., 1974-87; prof., 1974—; adj. prof. biomed. scis. Oakland U., Rochester, Mich., 1984—; mem. coop. cataract research group Nat. Eye Inst., Bethesda, Md., 1977—; mem. visual scis. study sect. NIH, Bethesda, 1982-86, mem. cataract panel, 1980—. Mem. vis. bd. Lehigh U., Bethlehem, Pa., 1986-89. Grantee Nat. Cancer Inst., NIH, 1967-70, Nat. Eye Inst., NIH, 1976—. Mem. AAAS, Am. Soc. Cell Biology, Assn. Rsch. in Vision and Ophthalmology, Sigma Xi. Home: 2822 Rhineberry Rd Rochester Hls MI 48309-1912 Office: Oakland U Dept Of Biol Scis Rochester MI 48309

UNANUE, JOSEPH, food products executive. Chmn., CEO Goya Foods, Secaucus, NJ. Office: Goya Foods Inc 100 Seaview Dr Secaucus NJ 07094-1800*

UNDE, MADHAVJI ANANT (MARK UNDE), welding specialist; b. Pune, India, June 28, 1934; came to U.S., 1974; s. Anant Narasinh Unde and Laxmibal A. Unde; m. Dhanawanti B. Joshi, June 11, 1982 (div. Oct. 1983); 1 child, Abhijeet, 2 adopted daughters: Swati, Bhagyashree. M.I.E., Instn. Engrs., Calcutta, India, 1973; M.I.Prod.E., Instn. Prodn. Engrs., London, 1972; MS in Welding, Ohio State U., 1978. Chartered engr. Divsn. welding engr. Fruehauf Corp.; tool engr. Danly Machine/Ingersoll Milling Machines, Inc.; mechanical engr. Sacramento Army Depot; pres. Calif. Consulting Engrs., Sacramento. Inventor In Process Stress Relief, Equivalent Heat Sink Process for welding; patents in mechanisms, welding, casting and non-destructive testing. Recipient Presdl. award Advanced Rsch. Project Agy., 1994. Office: Calif Consulting Engrs 1980 Watt Ave Sacramento CA 95825-2151

UNDERBERG, ALAN JACK, lawyer; b. Rochester, N.Y., Oct. 12, 1929; s. Henry and Anne (Landau) U.; m. Joyce Wisbaum, Oct. 19, 1952; children: Mark A., Amy Allen, Lisa Hamburg, Kathryn Zimmerman. BS, Cornell U., 1951; JD, Harvard U., 1956. Bar: N.Y. 1956, U.S. Dist. Ct. (we. dist.) N.Y. 1957, U.S. Supreme Ct. 1961. Ptnr. Underberg & Kessler, Rochester, 1963—; cons. to Commn. on Govt. Procurement, Washington,. 1970-71. Commr., co-founder Monroe County Human Rels. Commn., Rochester, 1961-64; trustee The Harley Sch., Rochester, 1972-75; mem. bd. mgrs. Meml. Art Gallery, Rochester, 1978-94, pres. 1990-92; mem. N.Y. State Bd. Equalization and Assessment, Albany, 1976-84; mem. Nat. Pk Sys. Adv. Bd., Dept. Interior, 1981-85, chmn. 1983-84; bd. govs. the Genesee Hosp., Rochester, 1984—, chmn. 1987-89; chmn. The Genesee Hosp. Health Sys., Inc., 1989-94; vice chmn. Greater Rochester Health Sys., Inc., 1994-96, chmn. 1996—; bd. dirs. Managerial Econs. Rsch. Ctr., William E. Simon Grad. Sch. Bus. Adminstrn.; bd. trustees U. Rochester, 1986-96, mem. exec. com.; chmn. U. Rochester Assocs., 1976-77; bd. dirs. YMCA Greater Rochester, 1980-86, mem. exec. com. 1982-86. 1st lt. USAF, 1951-53. Mem. ABA, Monroe County Bar Assn. (bd. dirs. Found. 1985-88), N.Y. Bar Assn. (lectr. continuing legal edn. program 1962-69, com. corp. law, banking, corp. and bus. law sect. 1963-93), Genesee Valley Club (pres. 1985-87), Country Club Rochester, Cornell Club N.Y.C., Harvard Club N.Y.C. Avocations: golf, tennis, skiing. Office: Underberg & Kessler 1800 Chase Sq Rochester NY 14604-1910

UNDERBERG, MARK ALAN, lawyer; b. Niagara Falls, N.Y., July 9, 1955; s. Alan Jack and Joyce Love (Wisbaum) U.; m. Diane Englander, Mar. 22, 1986; children: Andrew Englander, James Englander. BA, Cornell U., 1977, JD, 1981. Bar: N.Y. 1981. Law clk. to chief judge U.S. Ct. Appeals (3d cir.), Wilmington, Del., 1981-82; assoc. Debevoise & Plimpton, N.Y.C., 1982-87; mng. dir., dep. gen. counsel Henley Group, Inc., N.Y.C., 1987-90, mng. dir., gen. counsel, 1990-92; v.p., gen. counsel Abex Inc., Hampton, N.H., 1992-95; v.p., gen. counsel Fisher Sci. Internat. Inc., Hampton, N.H., 1991—. Editor-in-chief Cornell Law Rev., 1980-81. Mem. ABA, Assn. of Bar of City of N.Y., Genesee Valley Club, University Club. Office: Fisher Scientific Internat 375 Park Ave Ste 2001 New York NY 10152-2099

UNDERDOWN, DAVID EDWARD, historian, educator; b. Wells, Eng., Aug. 19, 1925; s. John Percival and Ethel Mary (Gell) U. B.A., U. Oxford, 1950, M.A., 1951; M.A., Yale U., 1952; B.Litt., U. Oxford, 1953; D.Litt. hon., U. of South, 1981. Asst. prof. U. of South, Sewanee, Tenn., 1953-58, assoc. prof., 1958-62; then assoc. prof. U. Va., Charlottesville, 1962-68; prof. Brown U., Providence, 1968-85, Munro-Goodwin Wilkinson prof., 1978-85; vis. prof. Yale U., New Haven, 1979; prof. Yale U., 1986-94, George Burton Adams prof., 1994-96, emeritus, 1996—; dir. Yale Ctr. Parliamentary History, 1985-96; vis. Mellon prof. Inst. for Advanced Study, 1988-89; vis. fellow All Souls Coll., Oxford, 1992; Ford's lectr. Oxford U., 1992. Author: Royalist Conspiracy in England, 1960, Pride's Purge, 1971, Somerset in the Civil War and Interregnum, 1973, Revel, Riot and Rebellion, 1985, Fire from Heaven, 1992, A Freeborn People, 1996. Guggenheim fellow, 1964-65, 91-92, fellow Am. Coun. Learned Socs., 1973-74, NEH fellow, 1980-81. Fellow Royal Hist. Soc., Brit. Acad. (corrs.); mem. Am. Hist. Assn., Conf. Brit. Studies. Office: Yale U Dept History New Haven CT 06520

UNDERHILL, ANNE BARBARA, astrophysicist; b. Vancouver, B.C., Can., June 12, 1920; d. Frederic Clare and Irene Anna (Creery) U. BA, U. B.C., 1942, MA, 1944, DSc (hon.), 1992; PhD, U. Chgo., 1948; DSc (hon.), York U., Toronto, Ont., 1969. Sci. officer Dominion Astrophys. Obs., Victoria, B.C., 1949-62; prof. astrophysics U. Utrecht, The Netherlands, 1962-70; lab chief Goddard Space Flight Ctr./NASA, Greenbelt, Md., 1970-77, sr. scientist, 1978-85; hon. prof. U. B.C., Vancouver, 1985—. Author: The Early-type Stars, 1966; author/editor: B Stars with and without Emission Lines, 1982, O, Of and Wolf-Rayet Stars, 1988; contbr. articles to profl. jours. Fellow NRC, 1948, Can. Fedn. Univ. Women, 1944, 47. Fellow Royal Soc. Can., Royal Astron. Soc.; mem. Internat. Astron. Union (pres. commn. #36 1963-66), Am. Astron. Soc., Can. Astron. Soc. Anglican. Avocation: church choir singing. Office: U BC, Dept Physics & Astronomy, Vancouver, BC Canada V6T 1Z4

UNDERHILL, JACOB BERRY, III, retired insurance company executive; b. N.Y.C., Oct. 25, 1926; s. Jacob Berry, Jr. and Dorothy Louise (Quinn) U.; m. Cynthia Jane Lovejoy, Sept. 9, 1950 (div. Sept. 1962); children: David Lovejoy, Kate Howell Underhill Kerwin, Benedict Quinn; m. Lois Beachy, Nov. 2, 1963 (div. July 1987); m. Betsy F. Ashton, Oct. 17, 1987. Grad., Phillips Exeter Acad., 1944; A.B., Princeton U., 1950. Editor Courier & Freeman, Potsdam, N.Y., 1950-53; reporter Democrat & Chronicle, Rochester, N.Y., 1953-56; chief editorial writer St. Petersburg (Fla.) Times, 1956-59; asso. editor McGraw Hill Publ. Co., N.Y.C., 1959-61, Newsweek, N.Y.C., 1961-63; asst. press sec. to Gov. N.Y., 1963-67; dep. supt., 1st dep. supt. State N.Y. Ins. Dept., 1967-72; v.p., sr. v.p., exec. v.p., dir., vice chmn. bd., pres. N.Y. Life Ins. Co., N.Y.C., 1972-86. Hon. chmn. bd. dirs. Manhattan Eye, Ear and Throat Hosp.; trustee emeritus Nat. Trust for Hist. Preservation. With USNR, 1944-46. Mem. Players Club, Links Club, Piping Rock Club (Locust Valley, N.Y.). Home: 410 E 57th St New York NY 10022-3059

UNDERHILL, ROBERT ALAN, consumer products company executive; b. Columbus, Ohio, June 9, 1944; s. Robert Alan and Grace Ruth (Smith) U.; m. Lynn Louise Stentz, Oct. 18, 1963; children: Robert Alan III, Richard Louis. Student, Case Western Res. U., 1962-64, Ohio State U., 1965. With tech. svc. dept. Gen. Tire & Rubber Co., Akron, Ohio, 1966-69; quality control engr. Edmont-Wilson Co., Canton, Ohio, 1969-70; mgr. quality assurance Pharmaseal Labs., Massillon, Ohio, 1970-72; mgr. R & D Internat. Playtex Corp., Paramus, N.J., 1972-78; from mgr. to dir. R & D Kimberly-Clark Corp., Neenah, Wis., 1978-83, v.p. R & D, 1983-93, sr. v.p. R & D, sr. tech. officer, 1994—; trustee United Health Group, 1994—, exec. com., vice-chmn., 1997—, chmn. compensation com., 1994—; trustee Novus Health Group, 1993-94; bd. dirs. Appleton (Wis.) Med. Ctr., 1993-96. Patentee (U.S. and fgn.) med. device. Mem. exec. bd. Bay Lakes Coun. Boy Scouts Am., 1988-92; bd. dirs. Outagamie County (Wis.) chpt. ARC, 1993—, chmn. nominations com., 1993—, mem. exec. com., 1994—, sec., 1994—; bd. dirs. Cmty. Blood Ctr., Appleton, Wis., 1996—, vice-chmn., 1997—. Mem. N.Y. Acad. Scis., Am. Assn. Blood Banks (stds. com. 1997—), Riverview Country Club, Pi Delta Epsilon. Republican. Avocations: stock market investment analysis, travel. Home: 1225 W Cedar St Appleton WI 54914-5567 Office: Kimberly-Clark Corp 2100 Winchester Rd Neenah WI 54956-9317 also: 1400 Holcomb Bridge Rd Roswell GA 30076-2190

UNDERWEISER, IRWIN PHILIP, mining company executive, lawyer; b. N.Y.C., Jan. 3, 1929; s. Harry and Edith (Gladstein) U.; m. Beatrice J. Kortchmar, Aug. 17, 1959; children: Rosanne, Marian, Jeffrey. B.A., CCNY, 1950; LL.D., Fordham U., 1954; LL.M., NYU, 1961. Bar: N.Y. 1954. With firm Scribner & Miller, N.Y.C., 1951-54, 56-62; partner firm Feuerstein & Underweiser, 1962-73, Underweiser & Fuchs, 1973-77, Underweiser & Underweiser, 1977—; v.p., sec. Sunshine Mining Co., Kellogg, Idaho, 1965-70, chmn. bd., 1970-78, pres., 1971-74, 77, v.p., 1977-83; vice chmn., dir. Underwriters Bank and Trust Co., N.Y.C., 1969-73; sec., dir. Bus. Consortium Fund, 1994—, Triad Capital Corp. N.Y.; dir. Anchor Post Products, Inc. Bd. dirs. Silver Inst. Inc., Bronx Mus. Arts, 1993—, Sheltering the Homeless is Our Responsibility, 1993—; gen. counsel, mem. bus. council Friends City Center Music and Drama, N.Y.C., 1966-67; pres. W. Quaker Ridge Assn., 1969-70; treas. Scarsdale Neighborhood Assn. Presidents, 1970-71. Served with AUS, 1954-56. Mem. Am., N.Y. State bar assns., Bar Assn. City N.Y., Phi Beta Kappa, Phi Alpha Theta. Home: 7 Rural Dr Scarsdale NY 10583-7701 Office: 405 Park Ave New York NY 10022-4405

UNDERWOOD, BERNARD EDWARD, religious organization administrator; b. Bluefield, W.Va., Oct. 26, 1925; s. W. B. and Annie Theresa (Bain) U.; m. Esther Parramore, Dec. 22, 1947; children: Paul, Karen, Pam. BA, Emmanuel Coll., Franklin Springs, Ga., 1947; MA, Marshall U., 1954. Lic. to ministry Pentecostal Holiness Ch., 1942; ordained, 1944. Mem. Pentecostal Holiness Youth Soc. bd. Va. conf. Pentecostal Holiness Ch., Kingsport, Tenn., 1946-53; Christian edn. dir. Pentecostal Holiness Ch., Va. Conf., 1951-60, asst. supt., 1958-64; supt. Va. conf. Pentecostal Holiness Ch., Roanoke, 1964-69, 74-78; exec. dir. world missions Pentecostal Holiness Ch., Oklahoma City, 1969-73, 77-89, vice chmn., 1981-89, gen. supt., 1989—. Author: Gifts of the Spirit, 1967, Spiritual Gifts: Ministries and Manifestations, 1984, 16 New Testament Principles for World Evangelization, 1988; contbr. numerous articles to profl. jours. Phi Alpha Theta scholar, 1954. Mem. Nat. Assn. Evangelicals (mem. exec. com. 1989—), Pentecostal Fellowship N.Am. (pres. 1991—), Pentecostal Renewal Svcs. (chmn. 1987—), Evang. Fgn. Missions Assn. (bd. adminstrn. 1981—). Republican. Avocation: reading. Office: Pentecostal Holiness Ch PO Box 12609 Oklahoma City OK 73157-2609*

UNDERWOOD, BRENDA S., microbiologist, grants administrator; b. Oak Ridge, Tenn., Mar. 19, 1948; d. William Henry Hensley and Maudell (Walker) Townsend; m. Thomas L. Janiszewski, Feb. 14, 1984; 1 child, Thomas Zachary Janiszewski. BS, U. Tenn., 1970; MS, Hood Coll., 1980; MBA, Mt. St. Mary's Coll., 1993. Scientist I chem. carcinogenesis Frederick (Md.) Cancer Rsch. Ctr., 1977-84; microbiologist NCI/NIH, Bethesda, Md., 1984-86; sci. tech. writer Engring. and Econs. Rsch., Germantown, Md., 1987-88; spl. asst. to dir., program dir. grants div. Cancer Biology Diagnosis Ctrs., NCI/NIH, Bethesda, 1988-91; indexer, div. extramural activities Rsch. Analysis and Evaluation br. NCI/NIH, Bethesda, 1991—. Vol. Riding for the Handicapped, Frederick, 1990-96; mem., recreational sec. Capital Hill Equestrian Soc., Washington, 1988. Mem. AAAS, Am. Soc. for Microbiology, Am. Assn. for Cancer Rsch., Women in Cancer Rsch., Federally Employed Women. Avocations: English riding, hiking, swimming, biking, gardening. Office: NCI-NIH RAEB Divsn Extramural Activ Bethesda MD 20892

UNDERWOOD, CECIL H., governor, company executive; b. Josephs Mills, W.Va., Nov. 5, 1922; s. Silas and Della (Forrester) U.; m. Hovah Hall, July 25, 1948; children: Cecilia A., Craig Hall, Sharon. AB, Salem (W.Va.) Coll., 1943; AM, W.Va. U., 1952; AM research fellow, Amelia Earhart Found., Ann Arbor, Mich., 1954-56; LLD, Marietta (Ohio) Coll., 1957, Bethany (W.Va.) Coll., 1957, W.Va. U., 1957, W.Va. Inst. Tech., 1957, W.Va. State Coll., 1961, Concord Coll., 1960; D of Humanics, Salem Coll., 1957; Dr. Pub. Adminstrn., W.Va. Wesleyan Coll., 1958; LHD (hon.), Shepherd Coll., 1964; LittD, Western New Eng. Coll., 1969. Tchr. high sch., 1943-46; mem. staff Marietta Coll., 1946-50; v.p. Salem Coll., 1950-56; gov. State of W.Va., 1957-61, 1997—; v.p. Island Creek Coal Co., 1961-64; dir. civic affairs Monsanto Co., 1965-67, v.p., 1967; pres. Cecil H. Underwood Assocs., 1965-80, Franswood Corp., 1968-75, Bethany (W.Va.) Coll., 1972-75, Princess Coals, Inc., Huntington, 1978-81, Morgantown (W.Va.) Indsl. Park, Inc., 1983-96, Software Valley, 1989-92, Mon View Heights of W.Va., 1993-96; field underwriter N.Y. Life Ins. Co., 1976-78;, 1994; chmn. bd. Princess Coals, Inc., Huntington, 1981-83; sec. bd. dirs. Huntington Fed. Savs. and Loan Assn.; bd. dirs. Huntington Found. Mem. W.Va. Ho. Dels., 1944-56, minority floor leader, 1949, 51, 53, 55; Mem. exec. com. Gov.'s Conf., 1959; chmn. So. Regional Edn. Bd., 1959-60; Pres. Young Republican League of W.Va., 1946-50; parliamentarian Young Rep. Nat. Conv., Boston, 1951; del.-at-large Rep. Nat. Conv., 1960, 64, 72, 76, 80, 84, 88, temporary chmn., 1960; Chmn. bd. dirs. W.Va. Found. Ind. Colls., Appalachian Regional Hosps.; chmn. bd. dirs. W.Va. div. Am. Cancer Soc., nat. bd. dirs., chmn. nat. crusade com., 1976-77, chmn. com. on legacies and planned giving, 1979; chmn. bd. dirs. Salem Coll., 1978-89, Salem Teikyo U., 1989—; bd. dirs. Higher Edn. Loan Program of W.Va., 1980-94; chair W.Va. Coun. on Vocat. Edn., 1982-96; chair W.Va. State Coll. System, 1991; regional vice chmn. Boy Scouts Am., 1961-67. Mem. Nat. Assn. State Coun. Vocat. Edn. (pres. 1994-96), Masons, Shriners, Elks, Rotary, Sigma Phi Epsilon, Pi Kappa Delta. Methodist. Home: Governors Mansion 1716 Kanawha Blvd E Charleston WV 25311 Office: Office of the Gov State Capitol Bldg 1900 Kanawha Blvd E Charleston WV 25305-0370

UNDERWOOD, JANE HAINLINE HAMMONS, anthropologist, educator; b. Ft. Bliss, Tex., Oct. 30, 1931; d. Frank and Lydia (Williams) Hammons; m. Van K. Hainline, Oct. 20, 1947 (div. 1966); children: Michael K., Susan J.; m. John W. Underwood, July 4, 1968; 1 dau., Anne K. A.A., Imperial Valley Coll., 1957; B.A., U. Calif., Riverside, 1960; M.A., UCLA, 1962, Ph.D., 1964. Asst. prof. U. Calif., Riverside, 1963-68; research anthropology Yap Islands, 1964, 65-66; prof. anthropology U. Ariz., Tucson, 1968—; assoc. dean Grad. Coll. U. Ariz., 1979-80, asst. provost for grad. studies, 1980-82, acting dir. Sch. Health Related Professions, 1980-82, asst. v.p. research, assoc. dean Grad. Coll., 1982-87; assoc. Micronesian Area Research Ctr., 1987—. Contbr. articles to profl. jours. Woodrow Wilson fellow, 1960-61; UCR Jr. Faculty fellow, 1968. Fellow AAAS; mem. Am. Assns. Phys. Anthropologists (v.p. 1980-82), Assn. Study Human Biology, Pacific Sci. Assn. (life), Assn. for Study Social Biology (bd. dirs. 1996—), Sigma Xi (pres. U. Ariz. chpt. 1991-92). Home: 2228 E 4th St Tucson AZ 85719-5118 Office: Dept Anthropology U Ariz Tucson AZ 85721

UNDERWOOD, JOANNA DEHAVEN, environmental research and education organizations president; b. N.Y.C., May 25, 1940; d. Louis Ivan and Helen (Guiterman) U.; m. Saul Lambert, July 31, 1982; stepchildren: Jonathan Whitty, Katherine Aviva. BA, Bryn Mawr Coll., 1962; Diplome d'etudes de Civilisation francaise with honors, Sorbonne U., Paris, 1965. Audio-visual dir. Planned Parenthood World Population, N.Y.C., 1968-70; co-dir. Council on Econ. Priorities, N.Y.C., 1970-73; founder, pres. INFORM, Inc., N.Y.C., 1973—; bd. dirs. N.Y. State Energy R&D Authority, Albany, Hampshire Rsch. Inst., Clean Sites, Rocky Mtn. Inst., Keystone Ctr.; mem. Dow Environ. Adv. Coun., 1992-96; awards com. Pres.'s Coun. on Environ. Quality, 1991; mem. eco-efficiency task force Pres.'s Coun. on Sustainable Devel., 1995-96. Author (with others) Voices from the Environmental Movement: Perspectives for a New Era, 1991; co-author: Paper Profits, 1971; editor: The Price of Power, 1972; contbr. articles to profl. jours. Circle of dirs. Planned Parenthood of N.Y.C. Recipient U.S. EPA Environ. Achievement award, 1987, 92. Home: 138 E 13th St New York NY 10003-5306 Office: Inform Inc 120 Wall St Fl 16 New York NY 10005-3904

UNDERWOOD, MARTHA JANE MENKE, artist, educator; b. Quincy, Ill., Nov. 28, 1934; d. Francis Norman Menke and Ruth Rosemary (Wells) Zoller; divorced; children: Leslie, Stephen. BA, Scripps Coll., 1956; MFA, Otis Art Inst., 1958. Cert. adult edn. and post secondary tchr. Designer staineglass windows Wallis-Wiley Studio, Pasadena, Calif., 1959-60; mural asst., designer Millard Sheets Murals, Inc., Claremont, Calif., 1960-68; art instr. adult edn. Monrovia, Pomona and Claremont Sch. Dists., Calif., 1967-69; prof. art Chaffey C.C., Alta Loma, Calif., 1970-96; ret., 1996; free lance illustrator Claremont, 1975—, watercolorist, 1970—; lectr. and demonstrator in field. Contbr. photographs to: How to Create Your Own Designs, 1968, Weaving Without Loom, 1969; illustrator: Opening a Can of Words, 1994, coloring books about baseball team mascots, 1995, 96; contbr. illustrations to Wayfarers Jour. Co-chmn. Recording for the Blind annual fundraiser, Upland, Calif., 1995, 96, 97. Mem. Scripps Fine Arts Found. Recipient Strathmore award, 1985, Grumbacher award Assoc. Artists of Upland, Calif., 1990, 92, 95, 96 Associated Artists of Inland Empire; Faculty Initiated Projects Program grantee, 1991-92. Mem. Associated Artists, Soc. Children's Book Writers and Illustrators, Pomona Valley Art Assn. Avocations: travel, bicycle touring, languages, history, golf.

UNDERWOOD, PAUL BENJAMIN, obstetrician, educator; b. Greer, S.C., Aug. 8, 1934; s. Paul Benjamin and Gladys (Guest) U.; m. Peggy Joyce Outen, July 7, 1957; children: Paul Benjamin III, Mary Barton. MD, Med. U. S.C., 1959. Diplomate Am. Bd. Ob-Gyn, Am. Bd. Gynecol. Oncology. Intern Med. U. S.C., Charleston, 1959-60, resident, 1960-64; fellow M.D. Anderson Hosp. and Tumor Inst., Houston, 1966-67; asst. prof. U. S.C., 1967-70, assoc. prof., 1970-74, prof., 1974-79; chmn. dept. ob-gyn U. Va. Sch. Medicine, Charlottesville, 1979—. Contbr. numerous articles to med. jours. With USN, 1964-66. Recipient Alumni of Yr. award Med. U. S.C., 1989. Mem. Am. Coll. Ob-Gyn., Soc. Gynecol. Oncologists (coun. 1972-75, v.p. 1977-78, pres. 1983), Am. Assn. Ob-Gyn. (sec. 1992-95), Felix Rutledge Soc. (pres. 1977), Am. Gynecol. Club (pres. 1996), So. Med. Soc., Charlottesville Med. Soc., S.C. Ob-Gyn Soc., Thegos Soc., Alpha Omega Alpha. Office: U Va School Medicine Med Ctr PO Box 387 Charlottesville VA 22908

UNDERWOOD, ROBERT ANACLETUS, congressional delegate, university official; b. Tamuning, Guam, July 13, 1948; m. Lorraine Aguilar; 5 children. BA with honors in History, Calif. State U., 1969, MA in History, 1971; cert. edn. adminstrn., U. Guam, 1976; DEd, U. So. Calif., 1987. Loader, sorter United Parcel Svc., L.A., 1966-72; tchr. George Washington High Sch., 1972-74, asst. prin. for bus. and student pers., 1974-76; asst. and acting prin. Inarajan Jr. High Sch., 1976; instr., dir. bilingual bicultural tng. program U. Guam, 1976-81, asst. prof., 1981-83, dir. bilingual edn. assistance for Micronesia project, 1983-88, dean Coll. Edn., 1988-90, acad. v.p., 1990—; del. 104th Congress from Guam, 1993—; part-time curriculum writer Guam Bilingual Edn. Project, 1973-76; chair Chamorro Lang. Commn., 1979-90. Named citizen of yr. Nat. Assn. Bilingual Edn., 1996.

Roman Catholic. Office: US Ho Reps 424 Cannon Ho Office Bldg Washington DC 20515-5301

UNDERWOOD, ROBERT LEIGH, venture capitalist; b. Paducah, Ky., Dec. 31, 1944; s. Robert Humphreys and Nancy Wells (Jessup) U.; BS with gt. distinction (Alcoa scholar), Stanford U., 1965, MS (NASA fellow), 1966, PhD (NSF fellow), 1968; MBA, Santa Clara U., 1970; m. Susan Lynn Doscher, May 22, 1976; children: Elizabeth Leigh, Dana Whitney, George Gregory. Rsch. scientist, project leader Lockheed Missiles & Space Co., Sunnyvale, Calif., 1967-71; spl. asst. for engring. scis. Office Sec., Dept. Transp., Washington, 1971-73; sr. mgmt. assoc. Office Mgmt. and Budget, Exec. Office Pres., 1973; with TRW Inc., L.A., 1973-79, dir. retail nat. accounts, 1977-78, dir. product planning and devel., 1978-79; pres., CEO OMEX, Santa Clara, Calif., 1980-82; v.p. Heizer Corp., Chgo., 1979-85; v.p. No. Trust Co., pres. No. Capital Corp., Chgo., 1985-86; mng. ptnr. ISSS Ventures, 1986-88; exec. v.p. N.Am. Bus. Devel. Co., Chgo., 1988—; dir. various pvt. and pub. portfolio cos., MECC 1991-96; trustee Burridge Mut. Funds, 1996—; mem. adv. com. indsl. innovation NSF, 1982-96; mem. sch. bd. Avoca Dist. 37, 1990—, v.p., 1996—; mem. adv. bd. Leavey Sch. Bus. and Adminstrn. Santa Clara U., 1995—. Mem. IEEE, Sigma Xi, Phi Beta Kappa, Tau Beta Pi, Beta Gamma Sigma. Elder, Presbyterian Ch., 1978-79. Clubs: Union League Chgo., Chgo. Club; Manasquan River Yacht (Brielle, N.J.); Indian Hill (Winnetka, Ill.). Contbr. articles to profl. jours. Home: 59 Woodley Rd Winnetka IL 60093-3748 Office: 135 S La Salle St Chicago IL 60603-4105

UNDERWOOD, STEVEN CLARK, publishing executive; b. Arlington Heights, Ill., Dec. 1, 1960; s. Donald William and Mary Frances (Clark) U. BBA, U. Tex., 1982, MBA, 1987; JD, So. Meth. U., 1985. Bar: Tex. 1985. Sr. fin. analyst CBS, Inc., N.Y.C., 1987-89; assoc. bus. mgr. Supplementary Edn. Group Simon & Schuster, Englewood Cliffs, N.J., 1989-90; bus. mgr. Fearon/Janus/Quercus divsn. Simon & Schuster, Belmont, Calif., 1990-92, pres. Fearon/Janus/Quercus divsn., 1992-93; pres. Globe Fearon divsn. Simon & Schuster, Upper Saddle River, N.J., 1993-96; dir. of bus. devel. Secondary Edn. Group, Simon and Schuster, Upper Saddle River, N.J., 1996—. Mem. ABA, Am. Mgmt. Assn. (pres.'s assn.), Assn. Am. Pubs., Nat. Eagle Scout Assn., Coll. Bus. Adminstrn. Found., Tex. Bar Assn., Tex. Alumni Assn., U. Tex. Century Club, Alpha Phi Omega, Beta Gamma Sigma, Phi Kappa Phi, Phi Eta Sigma, Golden Key. Republican. Methodist. Avocations: sailing, scuba diving, camping, rafting. Home: 123 Magnolia Rd Ramsey NJ 07446-1145

UNDERWOOD, VERNON O., JR., grocery stores executive; b. 1940. With Youngs Market Co., L.A., pres., from 1976, chmn. bd., 1989—, also chief exec. officer. Office: Young's Market Co 2164 N Batavia St Orange CA 92865-3104

UNDLIN, CHARLES THOMAS, banker; b. Madison, Minn., Mar. 4, 1928; s. Jennings C. and Alice M. (Berg) U.; m. Lois M. Anderson, June 23, 1953; children: Sarah, Mary Lee, Margaret, Thomas. BA, St. Olaf Coll., 1950. Asst. cashier Northwestern State Bank, Osseo, Minn., 1950-55, N.W. Bancorp., Mpls., 1955-57, Security Bank & Trust Co., Owatonna, Minn., 1957-59, Norwest Bank Black Hills, Rapid City, S.D., 1959-67; pres. and chief exec. officer Norwest Bank S.D., Rapid City, 1967-84, vice-chmn., 1984-85; pres. Norwest Bank Nebr., Omaha, 1985-88, also bd. dirs.; vice-chmn. Rushmore State Bank, Rapid City, 1988—. Past bd. dirs. Children's Hosp., Omaha, 1986. Sgt. U.S. Army, 1951-52. Mem. S.D. Bankers Assn. (past pres.), Arrowhead Country Club. Republican. Lutheran. Avocations: golf, skiing, fishing. Office: Rushmore State Bank PO Box 2290 Rapid City SD 57709-2290

UNGACTA, MALISSA SUMAGAYSAY, software engineer; b. Agana, Guam, July 3, 1967; d. Renerio Ong and Irene Acfalle (Salas) S. BS in Info. Sci., U. Hawaii, 1989; MS in Info. Tech. Mgmt., Johns Hopkins U., 1992. Cert. power builder developer assoc. Programmer, analyst Facilities Mgmt. Office, Honolulu, 1987-89, Data House Inc., Honolulu, 1989-90, ANSTEC Inc., Fairfax, Md., 1990-93; software specialist, project leader HJ Ford Assocs. Inc., Crystal City, Va., 1993-94; software cons. McDonnell Douglas Tech. Svcs., 1994—. Mem. NAFE. Avocations: tennis, running, computers. Home: PO Box 1546 Agana GU 96932-1546 Office: McDonnell Douglas 1807 Park 270 Ste 500 Saint Louis MO 63146-4021 also: 4554 Laclede Ave Apt 107 Saint Louis MO 63108-2145

UNGAR, ERIC EDWARD, mechanical engineer; b. Vienna, Austria, Nov. 12, 1926; came to U.S. 1939; s. Irwin Isidor and Sabina (Schlesinger) U.; m. Goldie Edna Becker, July 1, 1951; children: Judith Fishman, Susan Green, Ellen Borgenicht, Sharon Ungar Lane. BSME, Washington U., St. Louis, 1951; MS, U. N.Mex., 1954; Eng.Sc.D., NYU, 1957. Aero-ordnance engr. Sandia Corp., Albuquerque, 1951-53; research scientist/asst. prof. NYU, 1953-58; chief cons. engr. Bolt Beranek & Newman, Inc., Cambridge, Mass., 1958-97; chief engring. scientist Acentech Inc., Cambridge, 1993—. Co-author: Structure-Borne Sound, 1973, 2nd edit. 1988; contbr. articles to profl. jours., chpts. to books. 1st lt. U.S. Army, 1945-48; ETO. Recipient Per Bruel Gold Medal for Noise Control and Acoustics, Am. Soc. of Mechanicl Engineers, 1994. Fellow ASME (life; chmn. design engring. divsn. 1978-80, Centennial medallion 1981, Per Bruel Gold medal for noise control and acoustics 1994), AIAA (assoc.), Acoustical Soc. Am. (pres. 1991-92, Trent-Crede Silver medal 1983); mem. Inst. for Noise Control and Engring. (bd. cert., pres. 1985). Home: 15 Considine Rd Newton MA 02159-3603 Office: Acentech Inc 33 Moulton St Cambridge MA 02138-1118

UNGAR, IRWIN ALLAN, botany educator; b. N.Y.C., Jan. 21, 1934; s. Isador and Gertrude (Fageles) U.; m. Ana Celia Del Cid, Aug. 10, 1959; children: Steven, Sandra, Sharon. BS, CCNY, 1955; MA, U. Kans., Lawrence, 1957, PhD, 1961. Instr., U. R.I., Kingston, 1961-62; asst. prof. Quincy Coll., Ill., 1962-66; asst. prof. Ohio U., Athens, 1966-69, assoc. prof., 1969-74, prof. botany, 1974—, chmn. dept., 1984-89—, dir. Dysart Woods Lab., 1985—, dir. Environ. Studies Program, 1991-95; vis. prof. dept. plant scis. and vis. fellow Wolfson Coll., Oxford U., Eng., 1990-91; panelist Nat. Sea Grant Program, 1984; grant proposal reviewer NSF, 1980-95; manuscript reviewer Am. Jour. Botany, 1972-96, Bot. Gazette, 1976-96; contbr. articles to profl. jours. NSF grantee, 1974-76, 76-78, 80-83, 94-95, rsch. grantee Petroleum Environ. Rsch. Forum, 1992-96. Fellow Ohio Acad. Sci.; mem. AAAS, Am. Inst. Biol. Scis., Bot. Soc. Am., Ecol. Soc. Am., Sigma Xi. Home: 44 Walker St Athens OH 45701-2252 Office: Ohio Univ Dept Of Botany Athens OH 45701

UNGAR, MANYA SHAYON, volunteer, education consultant; b. N.Y.C., May 30, 1928; d. Samuel and Ethel M. (Liese) Shayon; m. Harry Fireman Ungar, June 25, 1950; children: Paul Benedict, Michael Shayon. BA, Mills Coll., 1950. Actress TV and radio NBC, CBS, N.Y.C., 1950-58; founder chpt. AFS, Scotch Plains-Fanwood, N.J., 1963; vol. project dir. handicapped cub scouts Boy Scouts Am., Plainfield, N.J., 1958-61; founder, co-dir. Summer Theater Workshop, Scotch Plains, 1967-78; legis. v.p. N.J. State PTA, 1977-79, pres., 1979-81; legis. v.p. Nat. PTA, Chgo., 1981-85, 1st v.p., 1985-87, pres., 1987-89; mem. arts edn. adv. panel Nat. Endowment Arts, Washington, 1988-91, panel Nat. Inst. Work and Learning, 1988-91; adv. coun. Nat. Panel Drug Free Schs., Washington, 1989-91, edn. adv. bd. NBC, 1988-92, PBS, 1988-91, Scholastic, Inc., 1990-94; bd. dirs. Math. Sci. Edn. Bd., 1988-92. Trustee N.J. Children's Specialized Hosp., 1990—, N.J. Pub. Edn. Inst., 1987—; mem. adv. coun. Natural Resources Def. Coun., Mothers and Others, 1990—; mem. geography assessment adv. coun. Nat. Assessment Edn. Progress, 1991-92, mem. nat. oversite commn. on geog. stds., 1992-94; mem. N.J. Basic Skills Coun., 1990-94; chmn. N.J. Math. Coalition, 1994—; mem. accreditation com. APA, 1992—; mem. tchr. programs adv. panel Ednl. Testing Svc., 1990-94; mem. external rev. com. Ctr. Disease Control Preventing Risk Behaviors in Adolescents, 1993; voters svc. dir. N.J. LWV, 1995-96; bd. dirs. Washington Rock Girl Scout Coun., 1995—. Manya Shayon Ungar Scholarship and Auditorium named in her honor, 1989; named Outstanding Citizen N.J. Jaycees, 1979, Scotch Plains Twp., 1989, 92, State of N.J., 1987, Bd. of Freeholders, 1987; named life mem. nat. PTA, 45 state PTAs. Mem. LWV (chmn. voters svc. Westfield area 1991-95). Avocations: piano, acting, singing, recording talking books. Home: 10 Brandywine Ct Scotch Plains NJ 07076-2550

UNGAR, ROSELVA MAY, primary and elementary educator; b. Detroit, Oct. 31, 1926; d. John and Elva (Mutchler) Rushton; m. Kenneth Sawyer Goodman, Dec. 26, 1946 (div. 1950); m. Fred Ungar, June 22, 1952 (div. 1977); children: Daniel Brian, Carol Leslie, Lisa Maya. Student, U. Mich., 1946-48; BA, UCLA; postgrad., Pacific Oaks Coll. Cert. elem. tchr., early childhood tchr., bilingual cert. of competency in Spanish. Recreation dir. Detroit City Parks and Recreation, 1946-50; recreation dir. L.A. Unified Sch. Dist., 1950-52, tchr., 1953-84; mentor tchr. elem. edn. L.A. Unified Sch. Dist., L.A., 1988-94; tchr. head start Found. Early Childhood Edn., L.A., 1965-73; staff organizer Early Childhood Fedn. Local 1475 AFT, L.A., 1973-79; staff rep. Calif. Fedn. Tchrs., L.A. contbr. articles to profl. jours. Com. mem. Gov.'s Adv. Com. Child Care, L.A., 1980-83; mem. Nat. Parks and Conservation Assn., Washington, 1988—, Sierra Club, 1978—; vol. So. Calif. Libr. Social Studies, L.A., 1989—; charter mem. Mus. Am. Indian Smithsonian Inst., 1994—; Nat. Ctr. Early Childhood Workforce, Children's Def. Fund, S.W. Mus., Ctr. Sci. in Pub. Interest, Internat. League for Peace and Freedom, ACLU, So. Poverty Law Ctr., Food First, Meiklejohn Civil Liberties Inst.; bd. dirs. Found. for Early Childhood Edn., 1997—. Mem. Calif. Assn. Bilingual Edn., So. Calif. Assn., Assn. Edn. Young Children, Early Childhood Fedn. (pres. emeritus 1979—), United Tchrs. L.A. (chpt. chair 1984-96, east area dir. and UTLA bd. dirs. 1996—), Coalition Labor Union Women (bd. mem. 1980-86). Avocations: guitar, folk songs, hiking. Home: 3131 Hamilton Way Los Angeles CA 90026-2107 Office: Glen Alta Sch LA Unified Sch Dist 3410 Sierra St Los Angeles CA 90031-2137

UNGARETTI, RICHARD ANTHONY, lawyer; b. Chgo., May 25, 1942; s. Dino Carl and Antoinette (Calvetti) U.; children: Joy A., Paul R. BS, DePaul U., 1964, JD, 1970. Bar: Ill. 1970, U.S. Dist. Ct. (no. dist.) Ill. 1970, U.S. Supreme Ct. 1980. Assoc. Kirkland & Ellis, Chgo., 1970-74; ptnr. Ungaretti & Harris, Chgo., 1974—. Mem. adv. coun. DePaul Coll. Law, Chgo., 1988. Mem. ABA, Chgo. Bar Assn., Ill. State Bar Assn., Internat. Coun. Shopping Ctrs., Am. Coll. Real Estate Lawyers, Justinian Soc., Urban Land Inst. (assoc.), Lamda Alpha. Avocations: golf, fishing, hunting. Office: Ungaretti & Harris 3500 Three First Nat Plz Chicago IL 60602

UNGARO, EMANUEL MATTEOTTI, fashion designer; b. Aix-en-Provence, France, Feb. 13, 1933; s. Cosimo and Concetta (Casalino) U.; m. Laura; 1 dau. Student, Lycée, Aix-en-Provence, 1943-50. Worked with father as tailor Aix-en-Provence, 1951-54; then for Camps Paris, 1955-57; with Cristobal Balenciaga, Paris, 1957-64, dir. Balenciaga br., Madrid, 1958-60; worked for André Courréges, Paris, 1964; ind. couturier, Paris, 1965. Designer of both couture and ready-to-wear men's and women's fashions; also fragrance designer since 1977. Office: 2 Ave Montaigne, F 75008 Paris France also: 650 Fifth Ave Fl 20 New York NY 10019-6108

UNGARO, JOSEPH MICHAEL, newspaper publishing executive, consultant; b. Providence, Nov. 4, 1930; s. Rocco and Lucy (Mott) U.; m. Evelyn Short, Apr. 15, 1961; children: Elizabeth Anne, Joseph Michael, Ellen Lucia. B.A., Providence Coll., 1952; M.S. in Journalism, Columbia, 1953. With Providence Jour.-Bull., 1951-73, mng. editor Evening Bull., 1967-72; mng. editor Eve. Bull., also dir. planning and devel. Providence Jour. and Bull., 1972-73; mng. editor Westchester-Rockland Newspapers, White Plains, N.Y., 1974-75, v.p., exec. editor, 1975-84, pres., gen. mgr., 1984-86, pres., publisher, 1986-90; pres., chief exec. officer Detroit Newspaper Agy., 1990-91; cons., 1991—. Mem. Am. Newspaper Pubs. Assn. (past chmn. research inst., conv. program com.), Am. Soc. Newspaper Editors, AP Mng. Editors Assn. (past pres.). Home: 379 Pond Shore Dr Charlestown RI 02813-2031

UNGARO, SUSAN KELLIHER, magazine editor. Editor-in-chief Family Circle mag., N.Y.C. Office: Family Circle 110 5th Ave New York NY 10011-5601*

UNGARO-BENAGES, URSULA MANCUSI, federal judge; b. Miami Beach, Fla., Jan. 29, 1951; d. Ludivico Mancusi-Ungaro and Ursula Berliner; m. Michael A. Benages, Mar., 1988. Student, Smith Coll., 1968-70; BA in English Lit., U. Miami, 1973; JD, U. Fla., 1975. Bar: Fla. 1975. Assoc. Frates, Floyd, Pearson et al, Miami, 1976-78, Blackwell, Walker, Gray et al, Miami, 1978-80, Finley, Kumble, Heine et al, Miami, 1980-85, Sparber, Shevin, Shapo et al, Miami, 1985-87; cir. judge State of Fla., Miami, 1987-92; U.S. dist. judge Miami, 1992—; mem. Fla. Supreme Ct. Race & Ethnic & Racial Bias Study Commn., Fla., 1989-92, St. Thomas U. Inns of Ct., Miami, 1991-92. Bd. dirs. United Family & Children's Svcs., Miami, 1981-82; mem. City of Miami Task Force, 1991-92. Mem. ABA, Fed. Judges Assn., Fla. Assn. Women Lawyers, Dade County Bar Assn., Eugene Spellman Inns of Ct. U. Miami. Office: US Dist Ct 301 N Miami Ave Fl 11 Miami FL 33128-7702

UNGER, ALBERT HOWARD, allergist, immunologist; b. Chgo., June 24, 1923. MD, Northwestern U., 1947. Diplomate Am. Bd. Allergy and Immunology. Rotating intern Wesley Meml. Hosp., Chgo., 1946-47; resident in Internal Medicine Cook County Hosp., Chgo., 1947-49; with Sierra Med. Ctr., El Paso, Tex.; ret. Fellow AMA, Am. Assn. Allergy and Immunology; mem. Am. Assn. Clin. Immunology and Allergy, Am. Coll. Chest Physicians.

UNGER, BARBARA, poet, educator; b. N.Y.C., Oct. 2, 1932; d. David and Florence (Schuchalter) Frankel; m. Bernard Unger, 1954 (div. 1976); m. Theodore Sakano, 1987. B.A., CCNY, 1955, M.A., 1957; advanced cert. NYU, 1970; children: Deborah, Suzanne. Grad. asst. Yeshiva U., 1962-63; edn. editor County Citizen, Rockland County, N.Y., 1960-63; tchr. English, N.Y.C. Pub. Schs., 1955-58, Nyack (N.Y.) High Sch., 1963-67; guidance counselor Ardsley (N.Y.) High Sch., 1967-69; prof. English, Rockland Community Coll., Suffern, N.Y., 1969—; poetry fellow Squaw Valley Community of Writers, 1980; writer-in-residence Rockland Ctr. for Arts, 1986. Author: (poetry) Basement, 1975, Learning to Fox Trot, 1989, The Man Who Burned Money, 1980, Inside the Wind, 1986, Blue Depression Glass in Troika One, 1991; (fiction) Dying for Uncle Ray, 1990; contbr. poetry to over 50 lit. mags., including: Kans. Quar., Carolina Quar., Beloit Poetry Jour., Minn. Rev., Poet and Critic, The Nation, Poetry Now, Invisible City, Thirteenth Moon, So. Poetry Rev., Mass. Rev., Nebr. Rev., Wis. Rev., So. Humanities Rev., Denver Quarterly, Mississippi Valley REv., The G.W. Rev. Wordsmith; contbr. to Anthology Mag. Verse, Yearbook Am. Poetry, 1984, 89; contbr. poetry (anthologies) Two Worlds Walking, Life on the Line, Looking for Home, 80 on the Eighties, Disenchantments, Women and Work, If I Had a Hammer, Sexual Harassment: Women Speak Out; contbr. fiction to True to Life Adventure Stories, Midstream, Esprit, Beloit Fiction Jour., Am. Fiction '89 and numerous others; poetry reading in colls. and libraries throught N.Y. and elsewhere; critical reviewer Contact II. Ragdale Found. fellow, 1985, 86, 89, SUNY Creative Writing fellow, 1981-82, Edna St. Vincent Millay Colony fellow, 1984, Djerassi Found. fellow, 1991, Hambidge Ctr. for Creative Arts and Scis. fellow, 1988; NEH grantee, 1975. Recipient Goodman Poetry award, 1989, Anna Davidson Rosenberg award Judah Magnes Mus., 1989, Roberts Writing award, 1990, New Letters Literary awards, 1990; finalist Am. Fiction Competition, 1989, W.Va. Writing Competition, 1982, John Williams Narrative Poetry Competition, 1992; honorable mention Chester Jones Nat. Poetry Contest. Mem. Poets and Writers, Poetry Soc. Am., Writers' Community. Office: Rockland Community Coll 145 College Rd Suffern NY 10901-3611

UNGER, GARY A., recording industry executive, singer, lyricist; b. Clinton, Iowa, Aug. 14, 1947; s. Charles Elmer Unger and Lois Grace Brothers. G-rad. h.s., Ill. Internat. import-export mgr. G & U Enterprises, Clinton, 1968—; mgr., pres. Groove Song Music, Clinton, 1968—, Narrow Rd. Music, Clinton, 1968—; mgr., v.p. AGI Internat. Records, Clinton, 1978-79; mgr., pres. ECI Internat. Records, Clinton, 1980-96, GTM, Clinton, 1973, Music Wave Dist., Nashville, 1981; guest Art Bell Radio Talk Show, CBC Radio Network, 1996, 97. Lyricist: Home, I Will Always Love You, Southern Rain, I Like It, I Love It, I Write the Songs, Thinkin About You, Give Them All to Jesus, Heart to Heart, 1968, Fool for Your Love (co-writer: Gary Russen), 1968, God Bless You Jesus, 1967, Born in the U.S.A., 1967, Iv'e Never been to England, God Knows, If You're Not in it for Love, Real Love, Hey June and Darline, I Got Jesus on My Mind, Oh! Baby Doll, You Win My Love, Oh! Sweet Honey, Sweet Baby Doll!, Girl I Love You, Goodnight Jackie, Love is Like a Butterfly, Let Us Pray Together, My Coloring Book, Lost in the 50's Tonight, Southern Kentucky Rain, Blue I'm so Blue, All I Want Is A Life With You Jesus, On the 4th of July, Boot Scootin Boogie, Love Is and others. Mem. ASCAP, BMI, AFM, CMA, AGAC, RIAA, Continental Record Club. Home: PO Box 13 Camanche IA 52730 Office: Ste 217 38 Music Square East Nashville TN 37202

UNGER, GERE NATHAN, physician, lawyer; b. Monticello, N.Y., May 15, 1949; s. Jessie Aaron and Shirley (Rosenstein) U.; m. Alicen J. McGowan, July 21, 1990; children: Elijah, Breena, Ari, Sasha, Arlen. JD, Bernadean U., 1979; MD, Inst. Polytecnico, Mexico City, 1986; D Phys. Medicine, Met. U., Mexico City, 1987; postgrad., Boston U., 1993, Harvard Law Sch., 1994-96. Dipomate Am. Bd. Forensic Examiners, Am. Bd. Med. Legal Analysis in Medicine and Surgery, Am. Bd. Forensic Medicine, Am. Bd. Risk Mgmt. Med. dir. Vietnam Vets. Post-Traumatic Stress Disorder Program, 1988-90; emergency rm. physician, cons. in medicaid fraud Bronx (N.Y.)-Lebanon Hosp., 1990—; clin. legal medicine Paladin Profl. Group, P.A., Palm Beach, Fla., 1992—; mediator, arbitrator, negotiator World Intellectual Property Orgn., 1994; mem. peer rev. com. Nat. Inst. on Disability and Rehab. Rsch., Office Spl. Edn., U.S. Dept. Edn., 1993; mem. clin. ethics com. Inst. Medecine Legale et de Medecine Sociale, Strasbourg, France, 1994; mem. surg. critical care com. Am. Soc. Critical Care Medicine, 1992; N.Y. state capt. Am. Trial Lawyers Exch., 1992. Editl. rev. bd. Am. Bd. Forensic Examiners, 1993, Jour. Neurol. and Orthopaedic Medicine and Surgery, 1993. Commandant Broward County Marine Corps League, 1995—. With USMC, 1968-72. Fellow Internat. Coll. Surgeons (mem. ethics com. 1994, mem. emergency response program Ea. region 1994), Am. Acad. Neurol. and Orthopaedic Surgeons, Am. Coll. Legal Medicine, Am. Coll. Forensic Examiners; mem. ABA, ATLA, FBA (mem. health com., rep. ABA 1994, chmn. med. malpractice/tort com. and FBA liaison to AMA), Nat. Coll. Advocacy, Internat. Bar Assn., Am. Coll. Physician Execs. (chair forum on law and med. mgmt. 1995), Kennedy Inst. Ethics, Nat. Health Lawyers Assn., Am. Soc. of Laser Medicine and Surgery, Nat. Assn. of Forensic Econs., Nat. Lawyers Assn. Avocations: flying, boating. Office: 235 S County Rd Ste 9 Palm Beach FL 33480-4292

UNGER, IRWIN, historian, educator; b. Bklyn., May 2, 1927; s. Elias C. and Mary (Roth) U.; m. Bernate Myra Spaet, Feb. 1956 (div.); children—Brooke David, Miles Jeremy, Paul Joshua; m. Debi Irene Weisstein, May 11, 1970; stepchildren—Anthony Allen, Elizabeth Sarah. B.Social Scis., City Coll. N.Y., 1948; M.A., Columbia, 1949, Ph.D., 1958; student, U. Wash., 1949-51. Instr. Columbia, 1956-58; vis. lectr. U. P.R., 1958-59; asst. prof. Long Beach (Calif.) State Coll., 1959-62; assoc. prof. U. Calif., Davis, 1962-66; prof. history NYU, NYC, 1966—. Author: The Greenback Era: A Social and Political History of American Finance: 1865-1879, 1964, The Movement: A History of the American New Left, 1974, (with Debi Unger) The Vulnerable Years: The United States, 1896-1917, Turning Point: 1968, 1988, The Best of Intentions: The Rise and Fall of the Great Society Programs, 1996. Served with AUS, 1952-54. Recipient Pulitzer prize for history, 1965; Guggenheim fellow, 1972-73, Rockefeller humanities fellow, 1980-81, Harry Frank Guggenheim fellow, 1987-88. Home: 473 W End Ave New York NY 10024-4934

UNGER, LAURA S., lawyer; b. N.Y.C., Jan. 8, 1961; d. Raymond and Susan Marie (Vopata) Simone; m. Peter Van Buren Unger, June 29, 1991. BA in Rhetoric, U. Calif., Berkeley, 1983; JD, N.Y. Law Sch., 1987. Bar: Conn. 1987, N.Y. 1988. Staff atty. divsn. enforcement SEC, 1988-90; legis. counsel to Sen. Alfonse M. D'Amato, 1990-91; minority counsel Senate com. banking, housing and urban affairs, 1991-95, counsel, 1995—. Recipient Performance award SEC, N.Y., 1988, D.C., 1989. Mem. ABA (subcom. on civil litigation and SEC enforcement matters and subcom. on SEC adminstrn., budget and legislation of the ABA bus. law sect. com. on federal regulation of securities), Fed. Bar Assn., Jr. League Washington, Decade Soc., Women in Housing and Fin. Roman Catholic. Avocations: tennis, jogging, movies, concerts, music. Office: Banking Housing & Urban Affairs 534 Sen Dirksen Office Bldg Washington DC 20510

UNGER, PAUL WALTER, soil scientist; b. Winchester, Tex., Sept. 10, 1931; s. Edwin Herman and Elsie Anna (Schmidt) U.; m. Barbara Charlene Dutton, Sept. 13, 1960; children: Gary Robert, Paula Dianne. BS, Tex. A&M U., 1961; MS, Colo. State U., 1963, PhD, 1966. Soil scientist USDA Agrl. Rsch. Svc., Bushland, Tex., 1965-81, soil scientist/rsch. leader, 1981-87, supervisory soil scientist/rsch. leader, 1987-93, soil scientist, 1993—; cons. Food and Agrl. Orgn. UN, Rome, 1986. Author or co-author bulls. and articles; co-editor conf. proc.; editor book. With U.S. Army, 1952-55. Recipient Disting. Svc. award Great Plains Agrl. Coun., 1984; named Scientist of Yr., USDA-Agrl. Rsch. Svc., So. Plains Area, 1987. Fellow Am. Soc. Agronomy (selection com. 1988-89), Soil Sci. Soc. Am. (assoc. editor 1977-82, divsn. chmn. 1986, mem. selection com. 1994-95, Applied Rsch. award 1991), Soil and Water Conservation Soc. (various local and state offices, photography awards 1990-92); mem. Internat. Soil Tillage Rsch. Orgn., Internat. Soil Sci. Soc., World Assn. Soil and Water Conservation, Coun. Agrl. Sci. and Tech. Lutheran. Avocations: photography, gardening, woodworking. Office: USDA Agrl Rsch Svc PO Box 10 Bushland TX 79012-0010

UNGER, PETER KENNETH, philosophy educator; b. N.Y.C., Apr. 25, 1942; s. Sidney and Naomi (Fein) U.; m. Susan Gill, June 2, 1977; 1 child, Andrew. BA, Swarthmore Coll., 1962 DPhil, Oxford U., Eng., 1966. Instr. U. Wis., Madison, 1965-66, asst. prof., 1966-70, assoc. prof., 1970-72; assoc. prof. NYU, N.Y.C., 1972-75, prof., 1975—. Author: Ignorance, 1975, Philosophical Relativity, 1984, Identity, Consciousness and Value, 1990, Living High and Letting Die, 1996; contbr. articles to profl. jours. Guggenheim fellow, 1974, NEH fellow, 1993. Mem. Am. Philos. Assn. Democrat. Home: 100 Bleecker St New York NY 10012-2201 Office: Dept Philosophy NYU 503 Main Bldg Washington Sq New York NY 10003

UNGER, PETER VAN BUREN, lawyer; b. Cin., Nov. 15, 1957; s. Sherman Edward and Polly Van Buren (Taylor) U.; m. Laura Meth Simone, June 29, 1991; 1 child, Simone Taylor. BA in History, Polit. Sci., Miami U., Oxford, Ohio, 1980; JD, U. Cin., 1983; LLM in Securities, Georgetown U., 1987. Bar: Ohio 1984, D.C. 1985, U.S. Supreme Ct. 1991. Law clk. chief judge U.S. Dist. Ct. (so. dist.) Fla., Ft. Lauderdale, 1983-85; trail atty. enforcement div. SEC, N.Y.C., 1986-88; assoc. Fulbright & Jaworski, Washington, 1988-89, participating assoc., 1990-94, ptnr., 1995—. Mem. ABA (bus. law sect., com. fed. regulation of securities, sub-com. on civil litigation and SEC enforcement matters 1989—, litigation sect. com. on securities litigation sub-com. on SEC enforcement practice 1990—), Securities Industry Assn. (compliance and legal divsn.). Home: 3308 N St NW Washington DC 20007-2807 Office: Fulbright & Jaworski 801 Pennsylvania Ave NW Washington DC 20004-2615

UNGER, RICHARD WATSON, history educator; b. Huntington, W.Va., Dec. 23, 1942; s. Abraham I. and Marion Patterson (Simons) U.; m. Katharine Lawrence, June 4, 1966; 1 child, Emily Patterson. BA, Haverford Coll., Pa., 1963; AM, U. Chgo., 1965; MA, Yale U., 1967, MPhil, 1969, Ph.D., 1971. Prof. dept. history U. B.C., Vancouver, Can., 1969—. Author: Dutch Shipbuilding Before 1800, 1978; The Ship in the Medieval Economy, 600-1600, 1980; The Art of Medieval Technology: The Image of Noah the Shipbuilder, 1991; editor: Cogs, Caravels and Galleons, 1994; co-editor: Nautical Archaeology: Progress and Public Responsibility, 1984; co-editor Studies in Medieval and Renaissance History, 1978-95; contbr. articles to profl. jours. Trustee Vancouver Maritime Mus., 1979-83. Mem. Medieval Assn. Pacific (pres. 1994-96), Econ. History Soc., Soc. Nautical Rsch., Soc. Hort. Tech. Office: U BC Dept History, 1297-1873 East Mall, Vancouver, BC Canada V6T 1Z1

UNGER, ROBERTA MARIE, special education educator; b. Oakland, Calif., Apr. 22, 1944; d. Lowber and Roberta June (Hedrick) Randolph; m. William Mitchell Unger, Jr., June 29, 1970; 1 child by previous marriage, Diana Marie Holt; 1 child, William Mitchell III. BA in Edn., San Francisco State U., 1965; postgrad., Utah State U., 1967, 73, Frostburg (Md.) State U., 1973, 84, Lamar U., 1991; MA in Ednl. Adminstrn., W.Va. U., 1984. Cert. tchr., Calif., Utah, Md., W.Va.; cert. elem. tchr., supervising tchr., tchr. edn. assoc. elem. edn./mentally retarded, English tchr., gifted edn., learning disabilities, behavior disorders, pre-sch. tchr., mentally retarded, W.Va. Tchr. 2d grade North Park Elem. Sch., Box Elder County, Utah, 1965-67; tchr. spl. edn. emotionally disturbed grades 5-8 Centre St. Sch., Allegany County, Md., 1967-68; tchr. 3rd grade Dennett Rd. Elem. Sch., Garrett

County, Md., 1968-69; tchr. 2d & 3rd grades Grantsville Elem. Sch., Garrett County, Md., 1969-70; tchr. 1-high sch. grades spl. and regular edn. Short Gap Elem. Sch., Mineral County, W.Va., 1970-77; supervising tchr. W.Va. U., Morgantown, 1973-76; tchr. summer satellite program gifted edn. Frostburg State U., 1985; tchr. spl. edn. Frankfort H.S., Ridgeley, W.Va., 1977—, collaborative and consulting spl. edn. tchr., 1983—, mentor tchr., 1991-92, 96-97. Former vol. San Francisco Hosp.; past usher Oakland Civic Light Opera Assn.; mem. Cmty. Concert Assn., Allied Arts Coun., St. Thomas Woman's Study Group, No. Maidu Tribe Calif. Native Ams., Frostburg Cmty. Orch., 1968; dir. youth programs grades 7-12 Emmanuel Episcopal Ch., Cumberland (Md.) Sunday Sch. tchr.; coach Odyssey of the Mind, 1987—; club sponsor Ski Club, AFS, Classic Club. Grantee W.Va. Dept. Edn., 1986, 87, 89-91; Match Free Competitive grantee W.Va. Dept. Edn., 1990-91. Mem. NEA, W.Va. Edn. Assn., Mineral County Edn. Assn. (past bldg. rep., past dept. chair spl. edn., past county chair mentally impaired, past chair county secondary integrative collaboration com., county chair integrative collaboration spl. edn. svc. ages 6-12), Nat. Coun. for Exceptional Children (nat. conv. presenter 1989, 92, 93, 95, 97), W.Va. State Coun. for Exceptional Children (Mem. of Yr. award 1991, state conf. presenter 1984—, sec. 1990, 91, 92, v.p. 1993, pres.-elect 1994, pres. 1995-96, newsletter editor 1992—, subdivsn. mental retardation developmental disabilities organizing chair 1992-93, pres. divsn. mental retardation 1994-95, pres., chair state conv. 1993—, coun. exceptional children Nat. MRDD membership com. 1995—, coun. exceptional children Nat. DLD multicultural com., 1995—), Coun. for Exceptional Children (v.p. W.Va. divsn. learning disabilities 1988, membership chmn. 1988-89, pres. 1990, newsletter editor divsn. learning disabilities 1991—, sec. Coun. Exceptional Children Am. Indian caucus 1989—, del. nat. conv. 1990—), Am. Indian Soc. Washington, Allegany County Hist. Soc., Mineral County Hist. Soc., Mooretown Maidu Rancheria. Episcopalian. Avocations: playing piano and cello, skiing, painting and sewing, operating farmette, collecting antiques. Office: Frankfort High Sch RR 3 Box 169 Ridgeley WV 26753-9510

UNGER, ROGER HAROLD, physician, scientist; b. N.Y.C., Mar. 7, 1924; s. Lester and Beatrice (Raphael) U.; m. Barbara Latz, June 28, 1946; children: Christine, Craig, Jimmy; m. Marlise Mantel, Dec. 16, 1981; 1 child, Romy-Michelle. BS, Yale U., 1944; MD, Columbia U., 1947; MD (hon.), U. Geneva, 1976, U. Liège, Belgium, 1980. Diplomate Am. Bd. Internal Medicine. Asst. prof. internal medicine U. Tex. Med. Sch., Dallas, 1959-64, assoc. prof., 1964-69, prof., 1969—; dir. Ctr. for Diabetes Research, U. Tex. Health Sci. Ctr., Dallas, 1985—; Disting. chair diabetes rsch. Touchstone/West, 1989—; sr. med. investigator VA Med. Ctr., Dallas, 1979—; mem. Nat. Diabetes Adv. Bd., Bethesda, Md., 1985—. Editor: Glucagon, 1972, Glucagon Physiology etc., 1981; assoc. editor (jour.) Diabetes, 1979-84, mem. editorial bd., 1975-79; mem. editorial bd. (jour.) Endocrinology, 1976-81; author 50 chpts. in textbooks, 300 papers for scientific jours. Served with USPHS, 1950-52. Recipient Lilly award Am. Diabetes Assn., 1964, Banting medal Am. Diabetes Assn., 1975, David Rumbough award Juvenile Diabetes Assn., 1975, Joslin medal Harvard U., 1979, Claude Bernard award European Assn. for Study Diabetes, 1979, Fred Conrad Koch award Endocrine Soc., 1983. Mem. NAS, Am. Acad. Arts and Scis., Am. Assn. Physicians, Am. Soc. for Clin. Investigation (emeritus). Office: Ctr for Diabetes Research 5323 Harry Hines Blvd Dallas TX 75235-7208

UNGER, SONJA FRANZ, package company executive, travel consultant, ceramist; b. Zagreb, Croatia, former Yugoslavia, Oct. 28, 1921; came to U.S., 1947; d. Karl Dragutin and Elisabeth (Bihler) Franz; m. Paul A. Unger, Jan. 2, 1947; children: Alan, Gerald, Tamara. BS in Engring., U. Zagreb, 1944, MS in Architecture, 1945. City planner Ministry of Constrn., Zagreb, 1945-47; architect John Graham, Washington, 1947-53; corp. sec., designer The Unger Co., Cleve., 1953-94; travel cons. Kollander World Travel, Cleve., 1985—; vis. com. mem. Case Western Res. U., Cleve. Mem. citizens adv. com. Juvenile Ct. Cuyahoga County, Ohio; asst. sec. Glenville Neighborhood Ctr., Cleve.; vice chmn., sec. Cuyahoga County Dem. Exec. Com., Cleve.; ward leader Shaker Heights Dem. Party, 1958-78; forelady Grand Jury Cuyahoga County; v.p. Nationalities Svcs. Ctr., Cleve.; mem. Cercle/Confs. Francaises. Recipient Golden Door award Nationalities Svcs. Ctr., 1975, Community Svc. award Cuyahoga County Commrs., 1975; Sonja F. Unger Day proclaimed by Mayor of Cleve., 1975. Mme. Il Cenacolo Italiano (pres.), Croatian Found. of Am. (v.p.), Am. Croating Acad. Club (v.p.), Print Club of Cleve., Cleve. Skating Club, Cleve. Playhouse Club, City Club of Cleve., Cleve. Blue Book.

UNGER, STEPHEN HERBERT, electrical engineer, computer scientist; b. N.Y.C., July 7, 1931; s. Julius I. and Rebecca (Cooper) U.; m. Marion Ruth Baker, Apr. 8, 1960 (div. July 1978); children—Donald N., Debra Susan; m. Shirley Aronson, July 5, 1986. B.E.E., Poly. Inst. Bklyn., 1952; S.M., MIT, 1953, Sc.D., 1957. Research asst. MIT Rsch. Lab. of Electronics, 1954-57; mem. tech. staff Bell Telephone Labs., Whippany, N.J., 1957-61; assoc. prof. elec. engring. and computer sci. Columbia U., 1961-68, prof., 1968—, prof. computer sci., 1980—; vis. prof. U. Calif.-Berkeley, 1967; vis. prof. computer sci. Danish Tech. U., Lyngby, 1974-75; sr. research assoc. Center for Policy Research, N.Y.C., 1970-74; cons. in field. Author: Asynchronous Sequential Switching Circuits, 1969, Controlling Technology: Ethics and the Responsible Engineer, 1982, 2d edit., 1994, The Essence of Logic Circuits, 1989, 2d edit., 1997; rschr., contbr. numerous articles on computer sci. Bd. dirs. Morris County Urban League, N.J., 1959-60. Guggenheim fellow,1967, IEEE fellow, 1975, AAAS fellow, 1989; NSF grantee, 1966-70, 71-74, 79-81. zem. IEEE (chmn. Com. on Social Implications Tech. working group on ethics and employment practices 1971-78, 81—, chmn. 1979-80, ethics com. 1995—, chmn. 1996, U.S. Activities Bd. ethics com. 1987-92, bd. dirs. 1995-96, editl. bd. Spectrum 1995—, publs. bd. 1996, Centennial medal 1984, Disting. Contbns. Engring. Professionalism award 1987), AAAS (mem. com. on sci. freedom and responsibility 1981-84), IEEE Soc. on Social Implications Tech. (adminstrv. com. 1983-91, 93-96, pres. 1985-86), AAUP, Assn. Computing Machinery, Sigma Xi, Eta Kappa Nu, Tau Beta Pi. Patentee parallel data processing apparatus. Home: 135 Van Houten Flds West Nyack NY 10994-2525 Office: Columbia U Dept Computer Sci New York NY 10027 *Unless, in doubtful situations, we act as though good may triumph, it surely won't.*

UNGERER, WALTER JOHN, minister; b. Bklyn., Nov. 11, 1936; s. Walter and Alice Elizabeth (Fleischmann) U.; m. Janet M. Hagmann, Aug. 25, 1962; children: Cheryl Lyn, Walter J., Brian Alan. BS, Nyack Coll., 1961; DivB, New Brunswick Theol. Sem., 1964; M of Theology, Princeton Theol. Sem., 1965, D of Ministry, 1983. Ordained to ministry, Presbyn. Ch., 1965. Student pastor Olivet Presbyn. Ch., Bklyn., 1958-62; student supply Fairfield (N.J.) Presbyn. Ch., 1964-65; asst. pastor Webster (N.Y.) Presbyn. Ch., 1965-66, assoc. pastor, 1967-71; sr. pastor Northfield (Ohio) Presbyn. Ch., 1972-77, 1st Presbyn. Ch., Kokomo, Ind., 1977—; co-founder, chmn. bd. dirs. Man to Man Internat.; moderator Presbytery Wabash Valley, Ind., 1983; mem. gen. assembly coun. Presbyn. Ch., Louisville, 1991-97; pres. bd. dirs. Synod Lincoln Trails, Indpls., 1989-91; bd. dirs. Kokomo Rescue Mission, 1992—, v.p. 1995—. Author: Habakkuk, The Man with Honest Questions, 1976, A Look Up, 1992; co-author: Miltenberg Germany to Brooklyn, 1988. Pres. Presbyns. United for Biblical Concerns, 1986-88. Recipient Leadership award Man to Man Assn. Ohio, Columbus, 1977. Mem. Midwest Tool Collectors Assn., Early Am. Indsl. Soc., Elks, Rotary. Democrat. Avocations: 18th and 19th century antiques, antique tools, fly fishing, golf, genealogy. Home: 2808 Locust Ct E Kokomo IN 46902-2952 Office: 1st Presbyn Ch 2000 W Jefferson St Kokomo IN 46901-4126

UNGERS, OSWALD M., architect, educator; b. Kaisersesch, Germany, July 12, 1926; came to U.S., 1969; s. Anton and Maria (Michels) U.; m. Liselotte Gabler, July 4, 1956; children: Simon, Sibylle, Sophia. Diploma Tng., Tech. U., Karlsruhe, Germany, 1950. Archtl. practice Cologne, Germany, 1950-62, Berlin, 1962-69, Itahaca, N.Y., 1969—; prof. architecture Tech. U. Berlin, 1963-73, dean faculty architecture, 1965-67; prof. architecture emeritus Cornell U., Ithaca, 1968—; chmn. dept. Cornell U., 1968-74; vis. prof. Harvard U., 1972, 77, UCLA, 1973; prof. emeritus Kunstakademie Dusseldorf, 1986-90; organizer 1st and 2d Berlin Summer Acads. for Architecture. Author: (with wife) Megastructure in Habitation; also numerous articles on architecture to internat. mags., numerous chpts. in books; subject of O.M. Ungers 1951-94, Bauten und Projekte; exhibited in biennale, Venice, Italy, 1976, also Berlin, London, N.Y.C.; prin. works include Mus. Architecture, Frankfurt, high rise bldg. and gallery, Frankfurt, Alfred-Wegener-Institut für Polarforschung, Bremerhaven, Badische Landesbibliôthek, Karlsruhe, Supreme Ct., Karlsruhe, family court Berlin-Kreuzberg, art mus. Hamburg, Bayerische Hypotheken-und Wechselbank Düsseldorf, thermae mus. Trier, German Embassy Residential Washington, Friedrichstadt-Passagen Berlin, new fair building, Berlin. Recipient prizes in several urban design competitions, BDA Prize, GroBer, 1987, Prix Rhénan d'Architecture, 1989. Mem. AIA, Acad. di San Luca (Rome), BDA Berlin (hon.), Moscow Br. Internat. Acad. Architecture. Research on cast optimisation in large-scale housing, urban pattern devel. in N.Y. State, subsystems of cities. Designer large-scale pub. housing projects in Germany. Office: 60 Belvederestrasse, 50933 Cologne Germany also: Marienstrasse 10, 10117 Berlin Germany also: 17 Jay St New York NY 10013-2855

UNIS, RICHARD L., state supreme court justice; b. Portland, Oreg., June 11, 1928. Grad., U. Va., U. Oreg. Bar: Oreg. 1954, U.S. Dist. Ct. Oreg. 1957, U.S. Ct. Appeals (9th cir.) 1960, U.S. Supreme Ct. 1965. Judge Portland Mcpl. Ct., 1968-71; judge Multnomah County Dist. Ct., 1972-76, presiding judge, 1972-74; former judge Oreg. Cir. Ct. 4th Judicial Dist., 1977; former sr. dep. city atty. City of Portland; adj. prof. of local govt. law and evidence Lewis & Clark Coll. Northwestern Sch. Law, 1969-76, 77—; faculty mem. The Nat. Judicial Coll., 1971—; former faculty mem. Am. Acad. Judicial Edn. Author: Procedure and Instructions in Traffic Court Cases, 1970, 101 Questions and Answers on Preliminary Hearings, 1974. Bd. dirs. Oreg. Free from Drug Abuse; mem. Oreg. Adv. Com. on Evidence Law Revision, chmn. subcom., 1974-79. Maj. USAFR, JAGC, ret. Recipient Meritorius Svc. award U. Oregon sch. Law, 1988; named Legal Citizen of Yr. Oreg. Law Related Edn., 1987; inducted into The Nat. Judicial Coll. Hall of Honor, 1988. Mem. Am. Judicature Soc. (bd. dirs. 1975), Am. Judges Assn., Multnomah Bar Found., Oregon Judicial Conf. (chmn. Oreg. Judicial Coll. 1973-80, legis. com. 1976—, exec. com. of judicial edn. com., judicial conduct com.), N.Am. Judges Assn. (tenure, selection and compensation judges com.), Dist. Ct. Judges of Oreg. (v.p., chmn. edn. com.), Nat. Conf. Spl. Ct. Judges (exec. com.), Oreg. State Bar (judicial adminstrn. com., sec. local govt. com., com. on continuing certification, uniform jury instrn. com., exec. com. criminal law sect., trial practice sect. standards and certification com., past chmn., among others), Oreg. Trial Lawyers Assn. (named Judge of Yr. 1984). Office: US Dist Ct House 620 SW Main St Portland OR 97205-3037

UNITHAN, DOLLY, visual artist; came to U.S., 1976; BFA, Hornsey Coll. Art, 1975; MFA, Pratt Inst., 1978; postgrad., Brit. Coun. Fine Arts Exch., 1974, Ecole Nationale des Beaux Arts de Nancy, France, 1974. Summer intern Guggenheim Mus., N.Y.C., 1976; panelist, artist in residence Asian Am. Arts Ctr., N.Y.C., 1993; lectr. in field. One-person shows include Internat. Art Ctr., London, 1975, Am. Assn. State Colls. and Univs., Orlando, Fla., 1977, Sloan Gallery, Lock Haven State Coll., Pa., 1978, Permanent Mission of Malaysia to UN, N.Y.C., 1987, Kerr Gallery, N.Y.C., 1987, Lyman Allyn Art Mus., New London, Conn., 1990, U.N. Secretariat, N.Y.C., 1991, Gracie Mansion, N.Y.C., 1994, Angel Orensanz Found., N.Y.C., 1995, Cathedral of St. John the Divine, N.Y.C. St. Boniface Chapel Gallery, 1996; exhibited in group shows including Palace of Westminster, Hos. of Parliament, London, 1978, City Mus. and Art Gallery, Gloucester, Eng., 1978, Mus. Art, Hove, Eng., 1978, Contemporary Gallery, Warsaw, Poland, 1978, Arts Coun. Gallery, Belfast, No. Ireland, 1978, BWA Gallery, Wroclaw, Poland, 1978, Parrish Art Mus., Southampton, N.Y., 1979, Modern Art Ctr., Guadalajara, Mex., 1979, Alternative Mus., N.Y.C., 1981, Nat. Mus. Fine Arts, Havana, Cuba, 1986, Hillwood Art Mus., Brookville, N.Y., 1988, PS 1 Mus., N.Y.C., 1990, Nat. Art Gallery, Kuala Lumpur, 1991-92, League of Nations Archives, Palais des Nations, Geneva, 1993, Jewish Mus., Vienna, Austria, 1993, Peace Mus., Remagen, Germany, Westbeth Galleries, N.Y.C., Tweed Courthouse Gallery, N.Y.C., 1994, China Art Mus., Beijing, 1995, Ulrich bei Steyr Peace parish, Austria, 1996, Ctrl. Children's and Youth Art Palace, Samarkand, Uzbekistan, 1997; represented in permanent collections including Lock Haven State Coll., Pa., Alternative Mus., N.Y.C., Am. Assn. State Colls. and Univs., Washington, Permanent Mission of Malaysia to UN, Wilfredo Lam Ctr., Havana, Malaysian Embassy, Washington, Spirit Found., N.Y.C., Asian Am. Arts Ctr., N.Y.C.; artwork included in (jours.) Multicultural Edn., 1994, Artspiral, 1994, (book) Sculpture. Technique, Form, Content. Recipient Artist award Rainbow Art Found., N.Y.C., 1985, Art award ArtQuest '88 Internat. Art Competition, Calif., 1988; named to Archives of Contemporary Arts Venice Biennale, 1990; grantee Lee Found., Singapore, 1972, 76, Pollock-Krasner Found., 1991-92; grad. scholar Mara, Malaysia, 1976-78. Avocation: collecting antiques.

UNKLESBAY, ATHEL GLYDE, geologist, educator; b. Byesville, Ohio, Feb. 11, 1914; s. Howard Ray and Madaline (Archer) U.; m. Wanda Eileen Strauch, Sept. 14, 1940 (dec. 1971); children: Kenneth, Marjorie, Carolyn, Allen; m. Mary Wheeler Myhre, June 8, 1973 (dec. 1980). A.B., Marietta Coll., 1938, D.Sc. (hon.), 1977; M.A., State U. Iowa, 1940, Ph.D., 1942. Geologist U.S. Geol. Survey, 1942-45, Iowa Geol. Survey, 1945-46; asst. prof. Colgate, 1946-47; mem. faculty U. Mo., Columbia, 1947—; prof. geology U. Mo., 1954—, chmn. dept., 1959-67, v.p. adminstrn., 1967-79; exec. dir. Am. Geol. Inst., 1979-85; cons. in field. Author: Geology of Boone County, 1952, Common Fossils of Missouri, 1955, Pennsylvanian Cephalopods of Oklahoma, 1962, Missouri Geology, 1992; also articles. Mem. Columbia Bd. Edn., 1954-70, Columbia Parks and Recreation Commn., 1954-57. Wilton Park fellow, 1968, 72, 76. Mem. Am. Assn. Petroleum Geologists, Paleontol. Soc. Am., Geol. Soc. Am., Nat. Assn. Geology Tchrs., Kiwanis. Methodist. Home: 37 Broadway Village Dr Apt G Columbia MO 65201-8662

UNNI, CHANDRA SHEILA, psychiatrist; b. India, July 28, 1940; came to U.S., 1972; d. Deshraj and Satyawati (Arora) Deshraj; m. K. Krishnan Unni, June 16, 1968; children: Akhil, Aditya, Adosh. Premed. Edn., Delhi U., India, 1958; MB, BS, All India Inst. Medical Scis., New Delhi, India, 1964. Diplomate Am. Bd. Psychiatry and Neurology. Intern All Indian Inst. Med. Scis., New Delhi, 1964; resident Irwin Hosp., New Delhi, 1964-65; pvt. practice New Delhi, 1967-68, 70-72, Rochester, Minn., 1983—; staff physician Rochester State Hosp., 1968-70, sr. staff physician and psychiatrist, 1973, 78-81; pres., exec. dir. Aiimsonion Clinic, Rochester, 1984—; acting med. dir. mental health unit Health Cen. Owatonna, Minn., 1987-88; cons. psychiatris The Gables, Rochester, 1984-88, psychiatric dir., 1988-89; cons. psychiatrist Rice County Family Svcs., Faribault, Minn., 1980-81, 83—; Hiawatha Valley Mental Health Ctr., Winona, Minn., 1984—; asst. clin. prof. U. Minn., St. Paul, 1990—. Office: Aiimsonion Clinic 300 3rd Ave SE Ste 206 Rochester MN 55904-4632

UNPINGCO, JOHN WALTER SABLAN, federal judge; b. 1950. BA, St. Louis U., 1972; MBA, JD, NYU, 1976; LLM, Georgetown U., 1983. Bar: Guam 1977, D.C. 1983, Calif. 1992. Atty. Ferenz, Bramhall, Williams & Gruskin, Guam, 1976-77; atty. Office Staff Judge Advocate USAF, 1977-85, 85-87; counsel Office U.S. Naval Air Warfare Ctr., China Lake, Calif., 1987-92; fed. judge U.S. Dist. Ct. (Guam dist.), 1992—; part-time instr. U. Md. Far East divsn., Yokota Air Base, Tokyo, 1983-87, European divsn., RAF Mildenhall, Suffolk, U.K., 1979-82, U. Gnam, 1994—. Mem. ABA, State Bar Calif., Guam Bar Assn., Internat. Legal Soc. Japan, D.C. Bar Assn., NWC Community Fed. Credit Union (bd. dirs. 1991-92). Office: Pacific News Bldg 238 Archbishop FC Flores St 6th Fl Agana GU 96910

UNRUH, JAMES ARLEN, business machines company executive; b. Goodrich, N.D., Mar. 22, 1941; m. Candice Leigh Voight, Apr. 28, 1984. BSBA, Jamestown Coll., 1963; MBA, U. Denver, 1964. Dir. corp. planning and analysis Fairchild Camera & Instrument, Calif., 1974-76, v.p. treasury and corp. devel., 1976-79, v.p. fin., 1979-80; v.p. fin. Memorex Corp., Santa Clara, Calif., 1980-82; v.p. fin. Burroughs Corp. (now known as Unisys Corp.), Detroit, 1982-84, sr. v.p. fin., 1984-86, exec. v.p. fin., 1986, exec. v.p., 1986-89, pres., chief oper. officer, 1989-90, pres., chief exec. officer, 1990-91, chmn. bd. dirs., chief exec. officer, 1991—; mem. exec. com. Computer Systems Policy Project; mem. Pres.'s Nat. Telecomms. Security Adv. Com.; bd. dirs. Ameritech Corp., Prudential Ins. Co. Am. Vice chmn. Greater Phila. First Found.; bd. trustees Jamestown Coll., N.D.; chmn. Franklin Inst.; bd. overseers Wharton Sch. Bus., U. Pa. Mem. Greater Phila. C. of C. (exec. com.). Office: Unisys Corp Township Line & Union Mtg Blue Bell PA 19424

UNSELD, WESTLEY SISSEL, professional sports team executive, former professional basketball coach, former professional basketball player; b. Louisville, Mar. 14, 1946; m. Connie Martin; children: Kimberly, Westley. Student, U. Louisville, 1964-68. Basketball player Balt. Bullets (name changed to Washington Bullets), 1968-81; v.p. Washington Bullets, 1981-94, head coach, 1988-94, exec. v.p., gen. mgr., 1994—. Office: Washington Bullets USAir Arena Landover MD 20785*

UNSELL, LLOYD NEAL, energy organization executive, former journalist; b. Henryetta, Okla., May 12, 1922; s. John William and Rhoda Elizabeth (Martinez) U.; m. Nettie Marie Rogers, Sept. 24, 1944 (dec.); children: Lloyd Neal, Jonna Kay Unsell Wilhelm, James Allan (dec.). Student, U. Ill., Kalamazoo Coll., 1942-43. Mem. editorial staff Tulsa Daily World, 1947-48; successively staff writer, dir. communications, v.p. pub. affairs, exec. v.p., pres. and chief exec. officer Ind. Petroleum Assn. Am., Washington, 1948-87; chmn. selection com. for Milburn Petty award Am. Petroleum Inst.-Assn. Petroleum Writers, 1972-86. Author reports and articles in field. Co-chmn. corp. adv. com. Vietnam Vets. Meml., 1981-82. Served with U.S. Army, 1942-46, ETO, PTO. Recipient Spl. award as outstanding petroleum industry communicator Assn. Petroleum Writers, 1960, Russell B. Brown Meml. award, 1981, Robert J. Enright award Am. Petroleum Inst./Assn. Petroleum Writers, 1986, Disting. Service award Nat. Energy Resources Orgn., 1987; named Hon. Chief Roughneck U.S. petroleum industry, 1986. Mem. Nat. Press Club, Rocky Mountain Oil and Gas Assn. (hon. life), The Jefferson Energy Found. (co-founder 1987). Republican. Baptist. Club: Washington Golf and Country. Home: 38335 Point Breeze Rd Coltons Point MD 20626 Office: 1101 16th St NW Washington DC 20036

UNSER, AL, professional auto racer; b. Albuquerque, May 29, 1939; s. Jerry H. and Mary C. (Craven) U.; m. Wanda Jesperson, Apr. 22, 1958 (div.); children: Mary Linda, Debra Ann, Alfred; m. Karen Barnes, Nov. 22, 1977 (div.). Auto racer U.S. Auto Club, Speedway, Ind., 1964-94. Placed 3d in nat. standings, 1968, 2d in 1969, 77, 78, 1st in 1970, 4th in 1976; winner Indpls. 500, 1970, 71, 78, 87, Pocono 500, 1976, 78, Ont. 500, 1977, 78; placed 3d in U.S. Auto Club Sports Car Club Am. Formula 5000, 1975, 2d place, 1976; Internat. Race of Champions champion, 1978; 2d pl. Indpls. Motor Speedway, 1983; CART/PPG Indy Car champion, 1983, 85. Home: 7625 Central Ave NW Albuquerque NM 87121-2115

UNSER, ALFRED, JR., professional race car driver; b. Apr. 19, 1962; s. Al Sr. U.; m. Shelley Unser; children: Al, Cody, Shannon. Runner-up Indpls. 500, 1989. Winner Indianpolis 500 1992, 94, Indy Car Champion 1990, 94; 1981 SCCA Super Vee Champion, 1986 24 Hours of Daytona winner and IROC champion, 1987 24 Hours of Daytona winner, 1988 IROC champion, 1990 Driver of Yr.; named ABC's Wide World of Sports, 1994 Athlete of Yr.; recipient ESPN's ESPY award for Auto Racing Performer of the Yr., 1994; winner 8 out of 16 Indy car races, 1994, 31 car career victories and 7 career poles. Office: c/o US Auto Club 4910 W 16th St Speedway IN 46224-5703*

UNSWORTH, RICHARD PRESTON, minister, school administrator; b. Vineland, N.J., Feb. 7, 1927; s. Joseph Lewis and Laura (MacMillan) U.; m. Joy Merritt, Aug. 20, 1949; children: Sarah, John, Mary, Lucy. BA, Princeton U., 1948; BD, Yale U., 1954; ThM, Harvard U., 1963; STD, Dickinson Coll., 1971; LHD, Washington and Jefferson Coll., 1971; LLD, Smith Coll., 1992. Ordained to ministry Presbyn. Ch., 1953. Tchr. Bible and English Mt. Hermon Sch., 1948-50; asst. chaplain Yale U., New Haven, Conn., 1950-54; chaplain, assoc. prof. Smith Coll., Northampton, Mass., 1954-64, chaplain, prof. religion, 1967-80; dean William Jewett Tucker Found. and prof. religion Dartmouth (N.H.) Coll., 1963-67; headmaster Northfield (Mass.) Mt. Hermon Sch., 1980-88, pres., 1989-91, headmaster emeritus, 1991—; headmaster Berkshire Sch., Sheffield, Mass., 1991-96; interim dean of the chapel Smith Coll., 1996-98; pres. Critical Langs. and Area Studies Consortium, 1987-97; bd. dirs. Bank of New Eng.-West, 1984-90; cons. Ednl. Assocs., Inc., 1967-69, U.S. Office Edn., 1969-77. Author: Sexuality and the Human Community, 1970, Dignity and Exploitation: Christian Reflections on Images of Sex in the 1970s, 1974, A Century of Religion at Smith College, 1975, (with Arnold Kenseth) Prayers for Worship Leaders, 1978; contbg. author; Sex Edn. and the Schs., 1967. Leader Operation Crossroads Africa unit, Nigeria, 1961, mem. adv. bd., 1961-66; mem. adminstrv. com. Student Christian Movement New Eng., 1964; mem. Mass. unit So. Christian Leadership conf., 1968; trustee Conf. on Religion in Ind. Schs., 1961-63; pres. Am. Friends of Coll. Cevenol, France, 1957-63, 90-94, Am. rep., 1958-82; trustee Mt. Holyoke Coll., 1982-89, chair, 1984-89, chmn. emeritus, 1989—, Am. Sch. Tangier, Morocco, 1982-87, Eaglebrook Sch., 1992—, Mus. Sci., Boston, 1993-95; bd. dirs. Family Planning Coun. Western Mass., 1972-81; bd. dirs. Ind. Schs. Assn. Mass., 1992-96. Mem. AAUP, Nat. Assn. Coll. and Univ. Chaplains, Am. Acad. Religion, Assn. Ind. Schs. New Eng. (pres. 1993-96), Headmasters Assn. Home: 197 Elm St Northampton MA 01060-2915 Office: Chapel Smith Coll Northampton MA 01063

UNTENER, KENNETH E., bishop; b. Detroit, Aug. 3, 1937. Ed., Sacred Heart Sem., Detroit, St. John's Provincial Sem., Plymouth, Mich., Gregorian U., Rome. Ordained priest Roman Cath. Ch., 1963, ordained bishop, 1980. Bishop Diocese of Saginaw, Mich., 1980—. Office: Chancery Office 5800 Weiss St Saginaw MI 48603-2762*

UNTERBERGER, BETTY MILLER, history educator, writer; b. Glasgow, Scotland, Dec. 27, 1923; d. Joseph C. and Leah Miller; m. Robert Ruppe, July 29, 1944; children: Glen, Gail, Gregg. B.A., Syracuse U., N.Y., 1943; M.A., Harvard U., 1946; Ph.D., Duke U., 1950. Asst. prof. E. Carolina U., Greenville, 1948-50; assoc. prof., dir. liberal arts ctr. Whittier Coll., Calif., 1954-61; assoc. prof. Calif. State U.-Fullerton, 1961-65, prof., chmn. grad. studies, 1965-68; prof. history Tex. A&M U., College Station, 1968—; vis. prof. U. Hawaii, Honolulu, summer 1967, Peking U., Beijing, 1988; vis. disting. prof. U. Calif., Irvine, 1987—, Patricia and Bookman Peters prof. history, 1991—; vis. prof. Charles U., Prague, Czechoslovakia, summer 1992; mem. adv. com. fgn. rels. U.S. Dept. State, 1977-81, chair, 1981; mem. hist. adv. com. U.S. Dept. Army, 1980-82, USN, 1991—; mem. Nat. Hist. Publs. and Records Commn., 1980-84. Author: America's Siberian Expedition 1918-1920: A Study of National Policy, 1956, 69 (Pacific Coast award Am. Hist. Assn. 1956); editor: American Intervention in the Russian Civil War, 1969, Intervention Against Communism: Did the U.S. Try to Overthrow the Soviet Government, 1918-20, 1986, The United States, Revolutionary Russia and the Rise of Czechoslovakia, 1989; contbr.: Woodrow Wilson and Revolutionary World, 1982; editorial adv. bd.: The Papers of Woodrow Wilson, Princeton U., 1982-92; bd. editors: Diplomatic History, 1981-84, Red River Valley Hist. Rev., 1975-84. Trustee Am. Inst. Pakistan Studies, Villanova U., Pa., 1981—, sec., 1989-92; mem. League of Women Voters. Woodrow Wilson Found. fellow, 1979; recipient Disting. Univ. Tchr. award State of Calif. Legislature, 1966. Mem. LWV, NOW, AAUW, Am. Hist. Assn. (chair 1982-83, nominating com. 1980-83), Orgn. Am. Historians (govt. relations com.), Soc. Historians of Am. Fgn. Relations (exec. council 1978-81, 86-89, govt. relations com. 1982-84, v.p. 1985, pres. 1986, co-winner Myrna F. Bernath prize 1991), Am. Soc. for Advancement Slavic Studies, Coordinating Com. on Women in Hist. Profession, Rocky Mountain Assn. Slavic Studies (program chair 1973, v.p. 1973-74), So. Hist. Assn., Asian Studies Assn., Assn. Third World Studies, Czechoslovak Soc. Arts and Scis., Czechoslovak History Conf., Women's Fgn. Policy Coun., Beyond War, Peace History Soc., Sierra Club, Phi Beta Kappa, Phi Beta Delta. Office: Tex A&M U Dept History College Station TX 77843

UNTERMAN, THOMAS E., newspaper publishing company executie, lawyer; b. Newport, R.I., Oct. 23, 1944; s. Martin D. and Ruth (Marcus) U.; m. Janet M. Mead, Sept. 27, 1980; children: Rebecca, Amy. AB, Princeton U., 1966; JD, U. Chgo., 1969. Bar: Calif. 1970. Assoc. Orrick, Herrington & Sutcliffe, San Francisco, 1969-75, ptnr., 1975-86; ptnr. Morrison & Foerster, San Francisco, 1986-92; sr. v.p., gen. counsel The Times Mirror Co., L.A., 1992-95, sr. v.p., CFO, 1995—. Democrat. Jewish. Office: The Times Mirror Co Times Mirror Sq Los Angeles CA 90053

UNTHANK, G. WIX, federal judge; b. Tway, Ky., June 14, 1923; s. Green Ward and Estell (Howard) U.; m. Marilyn Elizabeth Ward, Feb. 28, 1953. J.D., U. Miami, Fla., 1950. Bar: Ky. 1950. Judge Harlan County, 1950-57; asst. U.S. atty., Lexington, Ky., 1966-69; commonwealth atty.

Harlan, 1970-80; judge U.S. Dist. Ct. (ea. dist.) Ky., Pikeville, 1980-88; sr. judge U.S. Dist. Ct. (ea. dist.) Ky., London, 1988—. Served with AUS, 1940-45, ETO. Decorated Purple Heart, Bronze Star, Combat Inf. badge. Mem. ABA, Am. Judicature Soc., Ky. Bar Assn., Fla. Bar Assn. Democrat. Presbyterian. Office: Sr Judge's Chambers PO Box 5112 London KY 40745-5112

UNTHANK, TESSA See **NELSON-HUMPHRIES, TESSA**

UNTRACHT, STEVEN HARRIS, surgeon; b. Bklyn., Jan. 30, 1955; s. Harry and Lillian (Barshatzky) U. BA summa cum laude, Boston U., 1975; PhD in Biophysics & Theoretical Biology, U. Chgo., 1980, MD, 1981. Diplomate Am. Bd. Surgery, Nat. Bd. Med. Examiners, Am. Bd. Forensic Examiners. Resident in surgery Mass. Gen. Hosp., Boston, 1981-86, clin. and rsch. fellow, 1986; hon. sr. registrar in thoracic surgery Wessex Cardiothoracic Ctr., Southampton, Eng., 1987; clin. fellow in surgery Harvard Med. Sch., Boston, 1981-87; asst. attending physician Morristown (N.J.) Meml. Hosp., 1987-88; active staff dept. of surgery West Jersey Health Sys., Camden, N.J., 1988-92; assoc. in gen. surgery Guthrie Med. Group, P.A., Corning, N.Y., 1992-94; attending surgeon Lee Hosp. and Conemaugh Meml. Med. Ctr., Johnstown, Pa., 1994—; tchg. attending, surg. residency Conemaugh Meml. Med. Ctr., Johnstown, 1994—; mem. profl. adv. bd. Lee Regional Hospice, Johnstown, 1995—; mem. Drs. Without Borders, 1996—, med. missionary Batticaloa, Sri Lanka, 1996; clin. asst. prof. surgery Temple U., Phila., 1997—. Contbr. articles to profl. jours. Recipient Med. Alumni award U. Chgo., 1981. Fellow ACS (liaison physician commn. on cancer Lee Hosp. 1997—), Am. Coll. Forensic Examiners; mem. Soc. Critical Care Medicine, Phi Beta Kappa. Office: 321 Main St Ste 3B Johnstown PA 15901-1632

UOTILA, URHO ANTTI KALEVI, geodesist, educator; b. Pöytyä, Finland, Feb. 22, 1923; came to U.S., 1951, naturalized, 1957; s. Antti Samuli and Vera Justina (Kyto) U.; m. Helena Vanhakartano, Aug. 6, 1949; children: Heidi, Kirsi, Elizabeth, Julie, Trina, Caroline. B.S., Finland's Inst. Tech., 1946, M.S., 1949; Ph.D., Ohio State U., 1959. Surveyor, geodesist Finnish Govt., 1944-46, 46-51; geodesist Swedish Govt., 1946; research asst. Ohio State U., 1952-53, research assoc., 1953-58, research supr., 1959-88, lectr. in geodesy, 1955-57, asst. prof., 1959-62, assoc. prof., 1962-65, chmn. dept. geodetic sci., 1964-84, prof., 1965-89, chmn., prof. emeritus, 1989—; mem. Solar Eclipse Expdn. to Greenland, 1954; Mem. adv. panel on geodesy U.S. Coast and Geodetic Survey, Nat. Acad. Sci., 1964-66; mem. geodesy and cartography working group, space sci. steering com. NASA, 1965-67, mem. geodesy/cartography working group, summer conf. lunar exploration and sci., 1965, mem. geodesy and cartography adv. subcom., 1967-72; mem. ad hoc com. on N.Am. datum div. earth scis. Nat. Acad. Scis.-N.A.E., 1968-70; bd. dirs. Internat. Gravity Bur., France, 1975-83; mem. com. on geodesy Nat. Acad. Scis., 1975-78. Mem. editorial adv. com.: Advances in Geophysics, 1968-77; Contbr. articles to profl. jours., encys. Served with Finnish Army, 1942-44. Recipient Kaarina and W.A. Heiskanen award, 1962, Apollo Achievement award NASA, 1969, Disting. Svc. award Surveyor's Inst. Sri Lanka, Earle J. Fennell award Am. Congress on Surveying and Mapping, 1989. Fellow Am. Geophys. Union (v.p. geodesy sect. 1964-68, pres. 1968-70), Am. Congress Surveying and Mapping (nat. dir. 1970-73, 2d v.p. 1977-78, pres.-elect 1978-79, pres. 1979-80), Internat. Assn. Geodesy (pres. spl. study group 5.30 1967-71, pres. sect. V 1971-75, exec. com. 1971-79); mem. Am. Assn. Geodetic Surveying (pres. 1984-86), Am. Soc. Photogrammetry, Can. Inst. Surveying, Univs. Space Research Assn. (trustee 1973-75), Finnish Nat. Acad. Scis. (fgn.), Profl. Land Surveyors Ohio (hon.), Ala. Soc. Profl. Land Surveyors (hon.), Tenn. Assn. Profl. Surveyors (hon.). Research in geometric geodesy, phys. geodesy and statis. analysis of data. Home: 4329 Shelbourne Ln Columbus OH 43220-4243 Office: Ohio State U 2070 Neil Ave Columbus OH 43210-1226

UPADHYAY, YOGENDRA NATH, physician, educator; b. Gorakhpur, India, Dec. 21, 1938; came to U.S., 1963; s. Murlidhar and Vansraji (Pande) U.; m. Cecile R. Yonish; children: Asha, Sameer, Sanjay. MB, BS, All India Inst. Med. Scis., New Delhi, 1962. Diplomate Am. Bd. Psychiatry and Neurology, Am. Bd. Pediatrics. Instr. in pediatrics Johns Hopkins U. Sch. Medicine, Balt., 1969-71; fellow in child psychiatry Johns Hopkins Hosp./Johns Hopkins U., Balt., 1971-72; resident, then sr. resident in psychiatry Albert Einstein Coll. Medicine/Bronx Mcpl. Hosp. Ctr., 1972-74, fellow in child psychiatry, 1974-75; chief, partial hosp. program for children, dept. psychiatry Brookdale Hosp., Bklyn., 1976-77; med. dir. West Nassau Mental Health Ctr., Franklin Sq., N.Y., 1977-80; asst. prof. clin. psychiatry SUNY, Stony Brook, 1978-92; dir. child and adolescent psychiatry Nassau County Med. Ctr., East Meadow, N.Y., 1980-92; sr. psychiatrist South Oaks Hosp., Amityville, N.Y., 1992—, pres. med. staff, 1995-97. Fellow Am. Psychiat. Assn. 9cons. task force treatments psychiat. disorders 1989—), Am. Acad. Child and Adolescent Psychiatry, Allmsonians of Am. (founding pres. 1982-86). Office: S Oaks Hosp 400 Sunrise Hwy Amityville NY 11701-2508

UPATNIEKS, JURIS, optical engineer, researcher, educator; b. Riga, Latvia, May 7, 1936; came to U.S., 1951; s. Karlis and Eleonora (Jegers) U.; m. Ilze Induss, July 13, 1968; children: Ivars, Ansis. BSEE, U. Akron, Ohio, 1960; MSEE, U. Mich., 1965. Rsch. asst., then rsch. assoc. Willow Run Labs. U. Mich., Ann Arbor, 1960-69; rsch. engr. Inst. Sci. and Tech., U. Mich., Ann Arbor, 1969-72, Environ. Rsch. Inst. Mich., Ann Arbor, 1973-93; sr. engr. Applied Optics, Ann Arbor, 1993—; lectr. elec. engring. dept. U. Mich., 1971-73, adj. assoc. prof. elec. engring. and computer sci. dept., 1974—. Contbr. articles to profl. jours.; patentee in field. 2d lt. U.S. Army, 1961-62. Recipient Holley medal ASME, 1976, Inventor of Yr. award Assn. for Advancement Invention and Innovation, 1976. Fellow Optical Soc. Am. (R.W. Wood prize 1975), Soc. Photographic Instrumentation Engrs. (Robert Gordon award 1965), Am. Latvian Assn., Acad. Soc. Austrums, Latvian Acad. Sci. (elected 1991). Avocations: camping, gardening, hiking. Office: Applied Optics 2662 Valley Dr Ann Arbor MI 48103-2748

UPBIN, HAL JAY, consumer products executive; b. Bronx, N.Y., Jan. 15, 1939; s. David and Evelyn (Sloan) U.; m. Shari Kiesler, May 29, 1960; children: Edward, Elyse, Danielle. BBA, Pace Coll., 1961. CPA, N.Y. Tax sr. Peat, Marwick, Mitchell & Co., N.Y.C., 1961-65; tax mgr. Price Waterhouse & Co., N.Y.C., 1965-71; dir. taxes Wheelabrator-Frye Inc., N.Y.C., 1971-72, treas., 1972-74; pres. Wheelabrator Fin. Corp., N.Y.C., 1974-75; v.p., chief fin. officer Chase Manhattan Mortgage and Realty Trust (became Triton Group Ltd. 1980), N.Y.C., 1975-76, pres., 1976-78, pres., chmn., 1978-83, also dir.; chmn., pres., dir. Isomedics, 1983-85; chmn., pres. Fifth Ave. Cards, Inc., Fifth Retail Corp., Ashby's Stores, Ashby's Outlet Stores, 1984-88; bd. dirs. Stacy Industries, 1984-88; vice chmn. Am. Recreation Products, St. Louis, 1985-88, vice chmn., pres., 1988—, chmn., 1992—; v.p. corp. devel., chmn. acquistion com: Kellwood Co., Chesterfield, Mo., 1990—, exec. v.p. corp. devel., chmn. acquisition com., 1992—, pres., COO, 1994—; pres., COO, dir. Kellwood Co., Chesterfield, 1995—. Alumni advisor to bd. trustees Pace U.; past pres. Jewish Temple. Mem. AICPA, N.Y. State Soc. CPA's, Franklin Jaycees (v.p.). Home: 625 S Skinker Blvd Saint Louis MO 63105-2301 Office: Kellwood Co PO Box 14374 Saint Louis MO 63178

UPBIN, SHARI, theatrical producer, director, agent, educator; b. N.Y.C.; children: Edward, Elyse, Danielle. Master tap instr. Talent mgr. Goldstar Talent Mgmt., Inc., N.Y.C., 1989-91; guest tchr. Total Theatre Lab., N.Y.C.; faculty Nat. Shakespeare Conservatory, N.Y.; bd. dirs. The Barrow Group, N.Y.C. Asst. dir. 1st Black-Hispanic Shakespeare prodn. Julius Ceasar, Coriolanus at Pub. Theatre, N.Y., 1979; dir., choreographer Matter of Opinion, Players Theatre, N.Y., 1980, Side by Side, Sondheim Forum Theatre, N.J., 1981 (Nominated Best Dir. of Season N.J. Theatre Critics); prodr., dir. Vincent, The Passions of Van Gogh, N.Y., 1981; prodr. Bojangles, The Life of Bill Robinson, Broadway, 1984, Captain America, nat. Am. tour, Virtual Theatre, 1996, The Story of My Father, 1997; dir. Fiddler on the Roof, Cabaret, Life with Father, Roar of the Grease Paint, regional theatre, 1979-82, Feminist Movements, Off Broadway, 1997, The Story of My Father, Broadway; co-prodr. One Mo' Time, Village Gate, N.Y., nat. and internat. tour.; prodr./dir. off-Broadway musical Flypaper, 1991-92, Women on Their Own, Things My Mother Never Told Me, Theatre East, N.Y., Virtual Theatre, N.Y. Founded Queens Playhouse, N.Y., Children's Theatre, Flushing, N.Y.; mem. Willy Mays' Found. Drug Abused Children. Recipient Jaycees Svc. award Jr. Miss Pageants Franklin Twp., N.J., 1976. Mem. League Profl. Theatre Women (pres.), Soc. Stage Dirs. and Choreographers, Actors Equity Assn., Villagers Barn Theatre (1st woman pres.), N.Y. Womens Agenda (bd. dirs.). Address: The Bristol 300 E 56th St New York NY 10022

UPCHURCH, GARLAND RUDOLPH, JR., paleontologist, researcher; b. Ft. Worth, Nov. 1, 1952; s. Garland Rudolph and Nancy Block (Corneille) U.;children: Garland Michael, Lauren Elise. BS in Botany, U. Nebr., 1975; MS in Botany, U. Mich., 1978, PhD in Botany, 1981. Postdoctoral fellow Smithsonian Institution, Washington, 1981-83; rsch. assoc. Ind. U., Bloomington, 1983-84; postdoctoral rsch. assoc. U.S. Geol. Survey, Denver, 1984-86; rsch. assoc. U. Colo. Mus., Boulder, 1986—; postdoctoral fellow Nat. Ctr. for Atmospheric Rsch., Boulder, 1988-91; rsch. assoc. Denver Mus. Natural History, 1990—; asst. prof. dept. biology Southwest Tex. State U., San Marcos, 1991—; cons. Denver Mus. Natural History, 1989, Colo. Dept. Hwys., Denver, 1990, Amoco Prodn. Co., Houston, 1990; external advisor exhibits Denver Mus., 1990-95; rsch. assoc. Nebr. State Mus., Lincoln, 1990-95. Contbr. numerous articles to profl. jours. NSF grantee, 1986-88, 88, 90, 91-94; numerous other grants; recipient Excellence in Presentation award Soc. Econ. Paleontologists and Mineralogists, 1986. Mem. AAAS, Internat. Orgn. Palaeobotany. Episcopalian. Avocations: music appreciation, public lectures on paleontology. Home: 6801 Mount Sharp Rd #G Wimberley TX 78676

UPCHURCH, PAUL, principal. Prin. Centerfield Elem. Sch., Crestwood, Ky. Recipient DOW Elem. Sch. Recognition award, 1989-90. Office: Centerfield Elem Sch 4512 S Highway 393 Crestwood KY 40014-9288*

UPCHURCH, SALLY ANN, school counselor; b. Owensboro, Ky., July 16, 1951; d. Ezekiel Thomas and Anna Myrl (Duncan) Allen; m. Gary Allen Upchurch, Aug. 5, 1972; children: Jeffrey Allen, Gregory Wayne, Michael Shane. BA in English Lang. and Lit. Edn., Ky. Wesleyan Coll., 1974; MA in Guidance and Counseling Edn., Western Ky. U., 1979, postgrad., 1984—. Cert. English tchr., guidance and counseling, Ky. English tchr. Fordsville (Ky.) High Sch., 1974-76; lang. arts tchr. Ohio County Mid. Sch., Hartford, Ky., 1976-90; guidance counselor Ohio County Schs., Hartford, 1990—. Pres. Central City Bus. and Profl. Women, 1989-91, del. nat. conv., 1989, del. Ky. conv., 1988-90, bd. dirs. S.W. region, 1991, bd. dirs. Ky., 1989-91. Named Woman of Yr., Central City Bus. and Profl. Women, 1988, Appreciation award, Central City Bus. and Profl. Women, 1990; named Ky. Col., State of Ky., 1990. Mem. Ky. Counseling Assn., Ky. Sch. Counselors Assn., Am. Counseling Assn., Daviess/McLean Bapt. Assn. (child care com. 1989-93). Baptist. Avocations: church librarian, reading, singing, music, cooking. Home: 1644 Hamlin Chapel Rd Hartford KY 42347-9712 Office: Fordsville Sch 359 W Main St Fordsville KY 42343-9763

UPDEGRAFF SPLETH, ANN L., church executive, pastor; b. Newark, Ohio, Sept. 15, 1949; d. John C. and Lela V. (Mervine) Updegraff; m. Randall Alan Spleth; children: Andrew Alan, Claire Campbell. BA, Transylvania Coll., 1971; MDiv, Vanderbilt U., 1974; DMin, Claremont Sch. Theology, 1985. Ordained min. Christian Ch. (Disciples of Christ), 1973. Assoc. min. First Christian Ch., New Castle, Ind., 1974-75, Sacramento, 1975-78; sr. assoc. regional min. Pacific S.W. region Christian Ch., L.A., 1978-85; exec. v.p. Divsn. Homeland Ministries, Indpls., 1985-89, pres., 1990—. Author: Youth Ministry Manual, 1980; co-author: Congregation: Sign of Hope, 1989, Worship and Spiritual Life, 1992; editor Vanguard, 1990—; contbr. articles to profl. jours. Founding mem. Profl. Women's Forum, L.A., 1978-85. Mem. Ind. Soc. of Washington. Democrat. Home: 8961 Sawmill Ct Indianapolis IN 46236-9171 Office: United Christian Missionary Society 130 E Washington St Indianapolis IN 46204-3615*

UPDIKE, HELEN HILL, economist, investment manager, financial planner; b. N.Y.C., Mar. 27, 1941; d. Benjamin Harvey and Helen (Gray) Hill; m. Charles Bruce Updike, Sept. 7, 1963 (div. 1989); children: Edith Hill, Nancy Lamar. B.A., Hood Coll., 1962; Ph.D., SUNY, Stony Brook, 1978; postgrad., Harvard U., 1986. Asst. prof. Suffolk U., Boston, 1965-67; lectr. SUNY-Stony Brook, 1969-75, vis. asst. prof., 1977-78; asst. prof. U. Mass., Boston, 1975-77; asst. prof. Hofstra U., Hempstead, N.Y., 1978-85, assoc. prof., 1985-90, chmn. dept. econs. and geography, 1981-84; assoc. dean Hofstra Coll. Hofstra U., 1984-87; pres. Interfid Capital Corp., 1987—; dir. McCrory Corp., 1987—; cons. on econ. policy, 1973—. Author: The National Banks and American Economic Development, 1870-1900, 1985. Trustee, v.p. L.I. Forum for Tech., 1979-85; trustee Madeira Sch., Greenway, Va., 1984-88, N.Y. Outward Bound, 1988—; mem. nat. adv. bd. Outward Bound USA, 1984-92. Mem. AAAS, Cosmopolitan Club, Cold Spring Harbor Beach Club. Office: Interfid Capital Corp 27th Fl 150 E 58th St Fl 27 New York NY 10155-0099

UPDIKE, JOHN HOYER, writer; b. Shillington, Pa., Mar. 18, 1932; s. Wesley R. and Linda G. (Hoyer) U.; m. Mary E. Pennington, June 26, 1953 (div. 1976); children: Elizabeth, David, Michael, Miranda; m. Martha Bernhard, Sept. 30, 1977. AB, Harvard U., 1954; student, Ruskin Sch. Drawing and Fine Art, 1954-55. With New Yorker mag., N.Y.C., 1955-57. Author: (fiction) The Poorhouse Fair, 1959 (Richard and Hinda Rosenthal Found. award Am. Acad. and Nat. Inst. Arts and Letters 1960), The Same Door, 1959, Rabbit, Run, 1960, Pigeon Feathers, 1962, The Centaur, 1963 (Nat. Book award 1963, Prix Medicis Etranger 1966), Olinger Stories, 1964, Of the Farm, 1965, The Music School, 1966, Couples, 1968, Bech: A Book, 1970, Rabbit Redux, 1971, Museums and Women, 1972, Warm Wine, 1973, A Month of Sundays, 1975, Marry Me, 1976, Couples, 1976, The Coup, 1978, From the Journal of a Leper, 1978, Problems, 1979, Too Far to Go: The Maples Stories, 1979 (Am. Book award nomination 1980), Three Illuminations in the Life of an American Author, 1979, Your Lover Just Called: Stories of Joan and Richard Maple, 1980, The Chaste Planet, 1980, Rabbit Is Rich, 1981 (Pulitzer prize for fiction 1982, Nat. Book Critics Circle award 1982, Am. Book award 1982), Invasion of the Book Envelopes, 1981, Bech Is Back, 1982, The Beloved, 1982, The Witches of Eastwick, 1984, Confessions of a Wild Bore, 1984, Roger's Version, 1986 (Nat. Book Critics Circle award nomination 1986), Trust Me, 1987, More Stately Mansions, 1987, S., 1988, Rabbit at Rest, 1990 (Pulitzer prize for fiction 1991, Nat. Book Critics Circle award 1991), Memories of the Ford Administration, 1992, Brazil, 1994, The Afterlife, 1994, In the Beauty of the Lilies, 1996, Toward the End of Time, 1997, (poetry) The Carpentered Hen and Other Tame Creatures, 1958, Telephone Poles, 1963, A Child's Calendar, 1965, The Angels, 1968, Bath after Sailing, 1968, Midpoint, 1969, Seventy Poems, 1972, Six Poems, 1973, Tossing and Turning, 1977, Sixteen Sonnets, 1979, Five Poems, 1980, Spring Trio, 1982, Jester's Dozen, 1984, Facing Nature, 1985, Collected Poems 1953-1993, 1993, A Helpful Alphabet of Friendly Objects, 1995, In the Cemetery High Above Shillington, 1996, (plays) Three Texts from Early Ipswich, 1968, Buchanan Dying, 1974, (non-fiction) Assorted Prose, 1965, On Meeting Authors, 1968, A Good Place, 1973, Picked-Up Pieces, 1975, Hub Fans Bid Kid Adieu, 1977, Talk from the Fifties, 1979, Ego and Art in Walt Whitman, 1980, Hawthorne's Creed, 1981, Hugging the Shore, 1983 (Nat. Book Critics Circle award 1984), Emersonianism, 1984, Just Looking, 1989, Self-Consciousness, 1989, Odd Jobs, 1991, Golf Dreams, 1996; adapter: (librettos) The Magic Flute, 1962, The Ring, 1964, (plays) Bottom's Dream, 1969; author words and music: (with Gunther Schuller) The Fisherman and His Wife, 1970; editor: Pens and Needles, 1970, (with S. Ravenel) The Best American Short Stories 1984, 1984. Recipient O. Henry First Short Story award, 1966, 91, MacDowell medal for literature, 1981, Medal of Honor for literature Nat. Arts Club, 1984, PEN/Malamud Meml. prize PEN/Faulker award Found., 1988, Nat. Medal of Arts, 1989; Guggenheim fellow, 1959. Mem. AAAL, Am. Acad. Arts. and Scis. Democrat. Episcopalian.

UPGREN, ARTHUR REINHOLD, JR., astronomer, educator, outdoor lighting consultant; b. Mpls., Feb. 21, 1933; s. Arthur Reinhold and Marion (Andrews) U.; m. Joan Koswoski, Jan. 7, 1967; 1 child, Amy Joan. BA, U. Minn., 1955; MS, U. Mich., 1958; PhD, Case Western Res. U., 1961. Research assoc. Swarthmore Coll., Pa., 1961-63; astronomer U.S. Naval Obs., Washington, 1963-66; asst. prof. Wesleyan U., Middletown, Conn., 1966-73, assoc. prof., 1973-81, dir. Van Vleck Obs., 1973-93, John Monroe Van Vleck prof., 1981—, chmn. dept. astronomy, 1968-86, 90-93; v.p. Fund Astrophys. Research, N.Y.C., 1973—, chmn. grants com., 1985—; vis. lectr. U. Md., 1964-66, George Washington U., 1965-66, Thames Sci. Ctr., New London, Conn., 1990, 92; vis. prof. Yale U., 1979-80, sr. rsch. scientist, 1997—; adj. prof. U. Fla., 1984—; outdoor lighting cons. Wesleyan U., 1991—, Vt. State Agy. Natural Resources, 1993-94; dir. Internat. Dark-Sky Assn., 1997—; reviewer books in astronomy, meteorology, classical music and urban demographics. Editor: The Nearby Stars and the Stellar Luminosity Function, 1983, Mapping the Sky-Past Heritage and Future Directions, 1988, Star Catalogues: A Centennial Tribute to A.N. Vyssotsky, 1989, Fundamentals of Astronomy, 1990, Precision Photometry: Astrophysics of the Galaxy, 1991, Objective Prism and Other Surveys, 1991, Databases for Galactic Structure, 1993, Hot Stars in the Halo, 1994, New Developments in Array Technology and Applications, 1995. Conn. state chair New Eng. Light Pollution Adv. Group, 1994—. Grantee NSF, 1967—; fellow Wesleyan Ctr. for Humanities, 1996. Fellow Royal Astron. Soc.; mem. Internat. Astron. Union (commn. v.p. 1982-85, pres. commn. 24 1985-88), Am. Astron. Soc. (Harlow Shapley lectr. 1977—, vice-chmn. dynamical astronomy div. 1988-89, chmn. 1989-90), Astron. Soc. Pacific, Illuminating Engring. Soc. N.Am., Internat. Dark Sky Assn., Sigma Xi. Office: Wesleyan U 349 Sci Ctr Middletown CT 06459

UPHOFF, JAMES KENT, education educator; b. Hebron, Nebr., Sept. 1, 1937; s. Ernest John and Alice Marie (Dutcher) U.; m. Harriet Lucille Martin, Aug. 6, 1962; 1 child, Nicholas James. BA, Hastings Coll., 1959; MEd, U. Nebr., 1962, EdD, 1967. Tchr., Walnut Jr. High Sch., Grand Island, Nebr., 1959-65, dept. chmn., 1962-65; instr. dept. edn. U. Nebr., Lincoln, 1965-66; curriculum intern Bellevue (Nebr.) Pub. Schs., 1966-67; asst. prof. edn. Wright State U., Dayton, Ohio, 1967-70, assoc. prof., 1970-75, prof. edn., 1975—, co-dir. pub. edn. religion studies ctr., 1972-75, dean br. campuses, 1974-79, dir. lab. experiences, 1982-91, chmn. dept. tchr. edn., 1994—, dir. coll. student svcs., 1994—, dir. profl. field experiences, 1995—; vis. prof. U. Dayton, 1968-69. Author: (with others) Summer Children: Ready or Not For School, 4th edit., 1986; School Readiness and Transition Programs: Real Facts from Real Schools, 1990, 2nd edit., 1995; editor: Dialogues on Develop. Curriculum K and I, 1987, Changing to a Developmentally Appropriate Curriculum-Successfully: 4 Case Studies, 1989; weekly columnist Oakwood Register newspaper, monthly columnist Dayton Parent newspaper. Recipient Disting. Rsch. award Coll. Edn. and Human Svcs. Wright State U., 1988, 91, Deans' award, 1991; Phi Delta Kappa scholar, 1969; Malone fellow in Arab Islamic studies, 1989. Bd. dirs. pub. edn. fund Dayton Found., 1985—; mem. Luth. Ch. coun., 1987-90, chair 1988-90; mem. Oakwood City Schs. Bd. Edn., 1989—, v.p., 1994-95, pres., 1996—. Mem. Am. Ednl. Rsch. Assn., Nat. Coun. Tchrs. English, Western Ohio Edn. Assn. (pres. 1974-75, exec. com. 1979-85), Assn. Supervision and Curriculum Devel. (dir. 1974-79, editor early childhood network 1989—, editor pub. edn. and religion network 1992—), Assn. Tchr. Educators, Assn. Childhood Edn. Internat., Ohio Assn. Supervision and Curriculum Devel. (v.p. 1972-73), Nat. Coun. Social Studies, Ohio Coun. Social Studies, Am. Edn. Rsch. Assn., Ohio Sch. Bds. Assn. (chair rules com. 1993-94, mem. policy and legislation com. 1994—, Achievement award 1995, bd. trustees 1996—), Nat. Assn. Edn. Young Children, Dayton Area Coun. Social Studies (pres. (1970-71, 85-87), Ohio Assn. Edn. Young Children (com. chair 1992-95), Dayton Assn. for Young Children (exec. bd. 1988-94), LWV Greater Dayton (edn. dir. 1981-85), Ohio Council Chs. (edn. com. 1973-75), Optimists Club (pres. 1983-85, sec./treas. 1988—), Golden Key (chpt. advisor 1991—), Phi Delta Kappa (chpt. pres. 1983-84, chpt. advisor 1988-94), Kappa Delta Pi. Republican. Home: 150 Spirea Dr Dayton OH 45419-3409 Office: Wright State U 322 Millett Edn Dayton OH 45435

UPLEDGER, JOHN EDWIN, osteopath, physician; b. Detroit, Feb. 10, 1932; s. Edwin Chauncey and Eleanor Bernice (Cave) U.; m. divorced; children from previous marriage: Leslie, John, Mark, Michael; m. Dianne Lucille Dennison, Nov. 23, 1970 (div. 1994); m. Lisa Kraftsow, Oct. 5, 1996. BA, Wayne State U, 1953; DO, Kirkville Coll. Osteo. Surgery; DSc, Medicine Alternativa, Sri Lanka, 1987. Pvt. practice Clearwater, Fla., 1964-75; prof. biomechs. Mich. State U., East Lansing, 1975-82; med.dir., clin. researcher Unity Ctr. for Health, Edn. and Rsch., West Palm Beach, Fla., 1982-85; clin.dir. Upledger Inst., Upledger Found., Palm Beach Gardens, Fla., 1985—; mem. adv. coun. NIH Office of Alt. Medicine, 1993-95. Author: Craniosacral Therapy, Vol. I-II, 1982, 85, Somato Emotional Release and Beyond, 1990, A Brain is Born, 1995; contbr. articles to profl. jours. Bd. dirs. Cleatwater/St. Petersburg Free Clinics, Fla., 1968-75. Fellow Am. Acad. Osteopathy; mem. Soc. Osteopathes (acad. fellow 1978). Achievements include craniosacral therapy; somato emotional release; therapist-patient electrocircuitry; neurocircuitry redevel.; therapeutic work with dolphins concurrently with human therapists. Office: Upledger Inst 11211 Prosperity Farms Rd West Palm Beach FL 33410-3446

UPPMAN, THEODOR, concert and opera singer, voice educator; b. San Jose, Calif., Jan. 12, 1920; s. John August and Hulda Maria (Thörnström) U.; m. Jean Seward, Jan. 31, 1943; children: Margot, Michael. Student, Coll. of Pacific, 1938-39, Curtis Inst. Music, 1939-41, Stanford U., 1941-42, U. So. Calif., 1948-50. mem. profl. com. regional auditions Met. Opera; voice faculty Mannes Coll. Music, 1977—, Manhattan Sch. Music, 1988—; tchr. master classes Britten-Pears Sch. Advanced Mus. Studies, 1985—, Glimmerglass Opera, Cooperstown, N.Y., 1990, 93, Opera Theatre of St. Louis, 1993, Steans Inst. at Ravinia Festival, 1995; dir. vocal dept. Music Acad. of the West, Santa Barbara, Calif., 1988. Profl. debut as baritone, No. Calif. Symphony, 1941, appeared with, San Francisco Symphony, 1947; performed in: Pelleas et Melisande, City Ctr. Opera Co., N.Y., 1948; debut, San Francisco Opera Co., 1948, N.Y. recital, Times Hall, 1950; appeared: title role Billy Budd opera premiere, Royal Opera House, London, Eng., 1951, Theatre des Champs Elysees, Paris, France, 1952; performed in: Billy Budd, NBC-TV Opera Theatre, 1952, Pelleas et Melisande, Met. Opera Co., 1953-62, Britten's Gloriana, Cin. May Festival, 1956 (U.S. premiere), Magic Flute, 1956-77, La Perichole, 1956-71, Don Giovanni, 1957-73, Madam Butterfly, 1961-78, Cosi fan Tutte, 1962-71, L'Italiana in Algeri, 1973-75; world premieres of Floyd's The Passion of Jonathan Wade, N.Y.C. Opera, 1962, Villa Lobos' Yerma, Santa Fe Opera, 1971, Pasatieri's Black Widow, Seattle Opera, 1972, Barab's Philip Marshall, Chautauqua, 1974; Aix en Provence Festival, summer 1964, Aldeburgh Festival, summer 1975, Chgo. Lyric Opera debut, 1964, War Requiem by Britten, Dallas, Cleve., Cin. orchs., 1965, Damnation of Faust, N.Y. Philharmonic, 1966; Am. premiere: Billy Budd, Chgo. Lyric Opera, 1970, Death in Venice (Britten), Geneva Opera, 1983; World premiere: A Quiet Place (Bernstein), Houston Opera, 1983, A Quiet Place, LaScala, 1984, A Quiet Place, Vienna Staatsoper, 1986; recordings include world premiere broadcast Billy Budd, 1951; concert opera symphony appearances throughout, U.S., also radio, TV. Hon. dir. Britten-Pears Sch. for Advanced Mus. Studies, 1987—. With U.S. Army, 1943-46, World War II. Recipient 1st prize Atwater Kent Found. Auditions, Gainsborough Found. award, 1947. Address: 201 W 86th St New York NY 10024-3328

UPPOOR, RAJENDRA, pharmaceutical scientist, educator, researcher; b. Ripponpete, Karnataka, India, Feb. 11, 1960; came to U.S., 1989; s. Vittal Kamath and Suvarna Vittal U.; m. VenKata Ramana K. Sista, Oct. 31, 1995. B in Pharmacy, Govt. Coll. of Pharmacy, Bangalore, India, 1981, M in Pharmacy, 1984; diploma in pharmaceutical tech., State U. Ghent, Belgium, 1986; PhD, Med. U. of S.C., Charleston, 1995. Registered pharmacist Karnataka State Pharmacy Coun., India. Prodn. mgr. Gururaj Micropulverizers, Bangalore, India, 1979-85; student trainee Burroughs Wellcome (India), Bombay, 1981; trainee supr. Eskaylab India, Bangalore, 1982; asst. prof. St. John's Pharmacy Coll., Bangalore, 1984-85; mktg. officer Associated Capsules, Bombay, 1985-87; devel. officer Sci. Tech. Ctr., Bombay, 1986-87; pharmacist Ministry of Health, Riyadh, Saudi Arabia, 1987-88; rsch. asst. Med. U. of S.C., Charleston, 1989-94; cons. Ohmeda PPD, Inc., Murray Hill, N.J., 1994; sr. scientist Ohmeda PPD, Inc., Murray Hill, 1994-96, lead scientist, 1996—; review chemist Divsn. of Anti-Inflammatory, Analgesics and Ophthalmic Drug Products, Ctr. for Drugs. Pres. Internat. Student Orgn. Med. Univ. S.C., Charleston, 1991-92; gen. sec. Pharm. Soc. The Gov. Coll. of Pharmacy, Bangalore, India. 1983-84; student rep. in Indian schs. and colls., 1966-84. Grantee Univ. Grants Commn. scholarship Govt. of India, 1982-84; Recipient Nat. Merit scholarship Govt. of India, 1975-81, Internat. fellowship WHO, Geneva, State U. Ghent, Belgium, 1986; Ohmeda Pres'. award, 1995. Mem. Am. Assn. Pharm. Scientists, Vivekananda Kendra Yoga Therapy and Rsch. Ctr.(instr. 1981-82, life mem.), National Cadet Corps (Naval Wing), India, 1972-77; Sigma Xi, Rho Chi. Achievements include concentric coating technique/application for sustained release of drugs; application of glucose oxidase-catalase as an anti-oxidant system in pharmaceutical solutions; formulation, product development, scale-up and manufacturing of lipid emulsions for intravenous use, freeze drying of pharmaceuticals. Avocations: philately, travel, religions, history, photography. Home: Apt 104 1646 E Jefferson St Rockville MD 20852-4019 Office: HFD-830/550 Rm N333 CDER FDA 9201 Corporate Blvd Rockville MD 20850-3202

UPRIGHT, DIANE WARNER, art dealer; b. Cleve.; d. Rodney Upright and Shirley (Warner) Lavine. Student, Wellesley Coll., 1965-67; BA, U. Pitts., 1969; MA, U. Mich., 1973, PhD, 1976. Asst. prof. U. Va., Charlottesville, 1976-78; assoc. prof. Harvard U., Cambridge, Mass., 1978-83; sr. curator Ft. Worth Art Mus., 1984-86; dir. Jan Krugier Gallery, N.Y.C., 1986-90; sr. v.p., head contemporary art dept. Christie's, N.Y.C., 1990-95; pres. Diane Upright Fine Arts, N.Y.C., 1995—; trustee Aldrich Mus. Contemporary Art, Ridgefield, Conn. Author: Morris Louis: The Complete Paintings, 1979, Ellsworth Kelly: Works on Paper, 1987, various exhbn. catalogues; contbr. articles to art jours. Mem. Art Table, Inc. Office: Diane Upright Fine Arts 20 E 68th St New York NY 10021-5844

UPSHAW, DAWN, soprano; b. Nashville, Tenn., July 17, 1960. BA, Ill. Wesleyan Univ., 1982; MA, Manhattan Sch. Music, 1984; studied with Jan DeGaetani at Aspen, Colo., Music Sch. Recitalist, opera singer; sang in 1983 premiere performance, Sancta Susanna (Hindemith); with Met. Opera, 1985—; other appearances include Salzburg Festival, 1987, Aix-en-Provence, 1988-89; recordings include Ariadne auf. Naxos, Mass in G (Schubert), Knoxville Summer of 1915, The Girl With Orange Lips (songs for solo voice and chamber ensemble). Winner Young Concert Artist auditions; co-winner, Naumburg Competition, N.Y.C., 1985. Office: CAMI ARBIB Div 165 W 57th St New York NY 10019-2201 also: Electra Nonesuch 75 Rockefeller Plz New York NY 10019*

UPSHAW, GENE, sports association executive; b. Robstown, Tex., Aug. 15, 1945; s. Eugene and Cora (Riley) U.; 1 son, Eugene; m. Teresa Buich, 1986; children: Justin, Daniel. B.S., Tex. A&I U., 1968; postgrad., Calif. State U., 1969, Golden Gate U., 1980. Player Los Angeles (formerly Oakland) Raiders, 1967-82; player rep.-alt. NFL Players Assn., Oakland, Calif., 1970-76, mem. exec. com., 1976-80, pres., 1980-83, exec. dir., 1983—; ptnr. Gene Upshaw & Assocs., Mgmt. Cons. Firm, Oakland, Calif., 1970-78. Mem. Calif. Gov.'s Council Wellness and Phys. Fitness; mem. Calif. Bd. Govs. for Community Colls.; former planning commr. Alameda County, Calif., coordinator voter registration and fund raising. Served with U.S. Army, 1967-73. Named Offensive Lineman of Yr., Am. Football Conf., 1973, 74, 77, Lineman of Yr., NFL, 1977, Pro Bowl selection 6 times, All Pro selection Sporting News, 1967-77, All Pro selection UPI, 1967-77, All Pro selection AP, 1967-77, All Pro selection TV Guide, 1967-77, All Pro selection Profl. Football Writers, 1967-77; mem. NFL Championship Team, 1976, 1980; recipient Byron (Whizzer) White Humanitarian award NFL Players Assn., 1980, A. Philip Randolph A. Philip Randolph Inst., 1982; listed 13th in Top 100 Most Powerful People in Sports, Sporting News, 1993. Mem. Alpha Phi Alpha. Democrat. Baptist. Office: Fedn Professional Athletes 2021 L St NW Fl 6 Washington DC 20036-4909

UPSHAW, HARRY STEPHAN, psychology educator; b. Birmingham, Ala., July 10, 1926; s. N.H. and Florence (Arnold) U.; m. Paula Binyon, June 18, 1950; children: Alan Binyon, Phyllis, David Arnold, Stephan Lipner. Student, U. Ala., 1946-47; A.B., U. Chgo., 1949; M.A., Northwestern U., 1951; Ph.D., U. N.C., 1956. Asst prof. psychology U. Ala., 1954-57; spl. instr. psychology Simmons Coll., Boston, 1957-58; research asso. Ednl. Research Corp., Cambridge, Mass., 1957-58; asst. prof., then assoc. prof. pub. health U. N.C., 1958-61, lectr., assoc. prof. psychology, 1958-64, rsch. prof. psychology, 1991—; assoc. prof. Bryn Mawr (Pa.) Coll., 1964-65; assoc. prof., then prof. emeritus psychology U. Ill., Chgo., 1965-91, prof. emeritus, 1991—, dept. head, 1968-72; assoc. dir. Office of Social Sci. Rsch., 1981-87; guest prof. U. Mannheim, Germany, 1975, Fulbright scholar Technische Universitaet Berlin, 1978-79; vis. scholar Inst. for Rsch. in Social Sci., U. N.C., 1991-92. Editorial cons., Jour. Exptl. Social Psychology, Research in Personality, Jour. Applied Social Psychology, Jour. Personality Social Psychology; Contbr. articles to profl. jours. Served with AUS, 1944-46. Fellow Am. Psychol. Assn., Soc. Exptl. Social Psychol. Home: 209 Kirkwood Dr Chapel Hill NC 27514-5136

UPSHUR, CAROLE CHRISTOFK, psychologist, educator; b. Des Moines, Oct. 18, 1948; d. Robert Richard and Margaret (Davis) Christofk; 1 child, Emily. AB, U. So. Calif., 1969; EdM, Harvard U., 1970, EdD (NIMH fellow), 1975. Lic. psychologist, Mass. Planner, Mass. Com. on Criminal Justice, Boston, 1970-73; licensing specialist, planner, policy specialist Mass. Office for Children, Boston, 1973-76; asst. prof. Coll. Public and Cmty. Svc., U. Mass., Boston, 1976-81, assoc. prof., 1982-93, prof., 1993—, chmn. Ctr. for Cmty. Planning, 1979-81, 84-86, 1995-96, sr. rsch. fellow Maurice Gaston Inst. Latino Pub. Policy, 1993—, Ctr. Social Devel. & Edn., 1991—, sr. rsch. fellow Gerontology Inst., 1996—, dir. PhD in Pub. Policy program, 1995—; cons. to govt. and cmty. agys. on mental health and social svc. policy and mgmt., 1970—; cons. Harvard Family Rsch. Project, 1983-93; assoc. in pediatrics, sr. rsch. assoc. U. Mass. Med. Sch., 1983-94; adj. prof. Heller Sch. Social Welfare, Brandeis U., 1985—. Commr. Brookline Human Rels.-Youth Resources Commn., 1988-91, Gov's. Commn. on Facility Consolidation, 1991-92, Mass. Healthcare Adv. Com., 1993—. Fellow Mass. Psychol. Assn.; mem. APA, Am. Assn. on Mental Retardation (cons. editor Mental Retardation, Amer. Jour. on Mental Retardation 1981—, AJMR Monographs. Office: PhD Program in Public Policy U Mass Boston MA 02125

UPSON, DONALD V., financial executive; b. Hutchinson, Kans., Feb. 8, 1934; s. William Ernest and Luella Beatrice (Hutchinson) U.; m. Janis Carol Anderson, Sept. 16, 1956; children: Mark Steven, Brent William. B.S., Kans. State U., 1956. C.P.A. With Peat, Marwick, Mitchell & Co., 1956, 60-81, ptnr., 1974-81; exec. v.p., dir. internal audit Del E. Webb Corp., Phoenix, 1981-85; mgr. info. systems Tiernay Turbines Inc., Phoenix, 1986; chief fin. officer Schomac Corp., Tucson, 1986-88; adminstr. U. Ariz., Tucson, 1988-90; pres., chief exec. officer Ariz. Commerce Bank, Tucson, 1990-91; chief fin. officer O'Connor, Cavanagh, Anderson, Westover, Killingsworth & Beshears, P.A., Phoenix, 1991-94; fin. cons., 1995—. Pres. Community Orgn. for Drug Abuse, Alcohol and Mental Health Services, Inc., 1977-78; bd. dis. Phoenix council Boy Scouts Am., elder Presbyterian Ch. Served to lt. USAF, 1956-59. Mem. Am. Inst. C.P.A.s, Ariz. Soc. C.P.A.s, Beta Theta Pi (pres. 1955-56). Republican. Home and Office: 407 W Stacey Ln Tempe AZ 85284-3956

UPSON, STUART BARNARD, advertising agency executive; b. Cin., Apr. 14, 1925; s. Mark and Alice (Barnard) U.; m. Barbara Jussen, Nov. 2, 1946; children: Marguerite Nichols, Anne Marcus, Stuart Barnard. BS, Yale U., 1945. With Dancer, Fitzgerald, Sample, Inc., N.Y.C., 1946—, sr. v.p., 1963-66, exec. v.p., 1966-67, pres., 1967-74, chmn., 1974-86; chmn. DFS-Dorland, N.Y.C., 1986-87, Saatchi & Saatchi Advt. Inc., N.Y.C., 1987—; bd. dirs. Manhattan Life Ins. Co. Bd. dirs. Fresh Air Fund, N.Y., Advt. Coun. With USNR, 1943-46. Mem. St. Elmo Soc. Clubs: Wee Burn Country (Darien); Sky (N.Y.C.); Blind Brook, Pine Valley Golf. Home: 16 Wrenfield Ln Darien CT 06820-2201 Office: Saatchi & Saatchi Advt Inc 375 Hudson St New York NY 10014-3658

UPSON, THOMAS FISHER, state legislator, lawyer; b. Waterbury, Conn., Sept. 30, 1941; s. J. Warren and Grace (Fisher) U.; m. Barbara Secor (div. Jan. 1979); children: Secor, Chauncey Julius; m. Katherine Wolff, June 1, 1996. BA in History, Washington and Jefferson Coll., 1963; LLB, U. Conn., 1968; postgrad., Trinity Coll., 1969-72, Georgetown U., 1969-72. Bar: Conn., 1969, U.S. Dist. Ct. (2d dist.), 1969. Lawyer Upson & Secor, Waterbury, 1969-70, 74-76; lawyer, spl. asst. U.S. Dept. Commerce, Washington, 1970-72; lawyer, spl. asst. to adminstr. GSA, Washington, 1973-74; dir. admissions St. Margaret's McTernan Sch., Waterbury, 1977-78; with div. spl. revenue State of Conn., Hartford, 1978-82; assoc. Moynahan & Ruskin, Waterbury, 1979-8l; pvt. practice Upson & Daly, Waterbury, 1981—; mem. Conn. Senate, Hartford, 1985—, dep. majority leader, chmn. jud. com., 1995—, dep. minority leader, ranking mem. jud. com., 1996—. Moderator 1st Congl. Ch., Waterbury, 1986-91; bd. dirs. Easter Seals-United Way, Waterbury, 1984-88; mem. Conn. Rep. Ctrl. com., 1983-91; dir. Mattatuck Mus., 1993—; former dir. Waterbury Symphony Orch. Mem. ABA, Conn. Bar Assn., Waterbury Bar Assn., SAR, Soc. Colonial Wars, Phi Gamma Delta, Univ. Club (Waterbury. Republican. Congregationalist. Lodge: Kiwanis (former pres., lt. gov. SW New Eng. dist.), Elks. Avocations: hiking, music, history. Home: 10-1 827 Oronoke Rd Waterbury CT 06708-3940 Office: Conn Senate Capitol Bldg Hartford CT 06106 also: 52 Holmes Ave Waterbury CT 06710-2412

UPTON, ARTHUR CANFIELD, experimental pathologist, educator; b. Ann Arbor, Mich., Feb. 27, 1923; s. Herbert Hawkes and Ellen (Canfield) U.; m. Elizabeth Bache Perry, Mar. 1, 1946; children: Rebecca A., Melissa P., Bradley C. Grad., Phillips Acad., Andover, Mass., 1941; BA, U. Mich., 1944, MD, 1946. Intern Univ. Hosp., Ann Arbor, 1947; resident Univ. Hosp., 1948-49; instr. pathology U. Mich. Med. Sch., 1950-51; pathologist Oak Ridge (Tenn.) Nat. Lab., 1951-54, chief pathology-physiology sect., 1954-69; prof. pathology SUNY Med. Sch. at Stony Brook, 1969-77, chmn. dept. pathology, 1969-70, dean Sch. Basic Health Scis., 1970-75; dir. Nat. Cancer Inst., Bethesda, Md., 1977-79; prof., chmn. dept. environ. medicine NYU Med. Sch., N.Y.C., 1980-92, prof. emeritus, 1993—; clin. prof. radiology U. N.Mex. Sch. Medicine, 1993—, clin. prof. pathology, 1992-95; clin. prof. environ. and cmty. medicine U. Medicine and Dentistry N.J.-Robert Wood Johnson Med. Sch., 1995—; attending pathologist Brookhaven Nat. Lab., 1969-77; dir. Inst. Environ. Medicine, Med. Sch., NYU, 1980-91; mem. various coms. nat. and internat. orgns.; lectr. in field. Assoc. editor: Cancer Research; mem. editorial bd.: Internat. Union Against Cancer. Served with AUS, 1943-46. Recipient Ernest Orlando Lawrence award for atomic field, 1965, Comfort-Crookshank award for cancer rsch. Inst. Med., NAS, 1979, Claude M. Fuess award 1980, Sarah L. Poilley award for pub. health, 1983, CHUMS Physician of Yr. award 1985, Basic Cell Rsch. in Cytology Lectureship award 1985, Fred W. Stewart award, 1986, Ramazzini award, 1986, Lovelace Med. Found. award, 1993; Sigma Xi nat. lectr., 1989-91. Fellow Soc. Risk Analysis, N.Y. Acad. Sci.; mem. Am. Assn. Pathologists and Bacteriologists, Internat. Acad. Pathology, Inst. Medicine NAS, Radiation Rsch. Soc. (councilor 1963-64, pres. 1965-66), Internat. Assn. Radiation Rsch. (pres. 1983-87), Am. Assn. Cancer Rsch. (pres. 1963-64), Am. Soc. Exptl. Pathology (pres. 1967-68), AAAS, Gerontol. Soc., Sci. Rsch. Soc. Am., Soc. Exptl. Biology and Medicine, Peruvian Oncology Soc. (hon.), Japan Cancer Assn. (hon.), N.Y. State Health Rsch. Coun. (chmn. 1982-90), Internat. Assn. Radiation Rsch. (pres. 1983-87), Assn. Univ. Environ. Health Sci. Ctrs. (pres. 1982-90), Ramazzini Inst. (pres. 1992—), Phi Beta Kappa, Phi Gamma Delta, Alpha Omega Alpha, Nu Sigma Nu, Sigma Xi. Achievements include research on pathology of radiation injury and endocrine glands, on cancer, on carcinogenesis, on experimental leukemia, on aging. Home: Apt 12B 401 E 86th St New York NY 10028 Office: 681 Freylinghuysen Rd Piscataway NJ 08855-1179

UPTON, FREDERICK STEPHEN, congressman; b. St. Joseph, Mich., Apr. 23, 1953; s. Stephen E. and Elizabeth Brooks (Vial) U.; m. Amey Richmond Rulon-Miller, Nov. 5, 1983; 2 children. BA in Journalism, U. Mich., 1975. Staff asst. to Congressman David A. Stockman, Washington, 1976-81; legis. asst. Office Mgmt. and Budget, Washington, 1981-83, dep. dir. legis. affairs, 1983-84, dir. legis. affairs, 1984-85; mem. 100th-105th Congresses from 4th (now 6th) Mich. dist., Washington, 1986—; mem. commerce com. Field mgr. Stockman for Congress, St. Joseph, 1975; campaign mgr. Globensky for Congress, St. Joseph, 1981. Republican. Office: US House of Reps 2333 Rayburn Bldg Washington DC 20515-2206*

UPTON, HOWARD B., JR., management writer, lawyer; b. Tahlequah, Okla., May 17, 1922; s. Howard B. and Marjorie (Ross) U.; m. Jean Devereaux, June 14, 1945; children—Pamela, Barbara, Martha, Brian. BA, U. Okla., 1943, LLB, 1948. Cert. assn. exec. Dir. indsl. relations Western Petroleum Refiners Assn., Tulsa, 1948-51; exec. v.p. Petroleum Equipment Inst., Tulsa, 1951-87; dir. Telex Corp., Tulsa, 1972-88; mgmt. columnist Inflight Mag. of Southwest Airlines, 1988-93; lectr. dept. engrng. profl. devel. U. Wis., 1988—, U. Alaska, Fairbanks, 1991-93. Frequent contbr. to Wall St. Jour. Dir. Tulsa Zoo Friends, Inc., 1993—. Mem. Am. Soc. Assn. Execs. (bd. dirs. 1964-68, Gold Circle award 1977, 82), Okla. Bar Assn., Mens Forum of Tulsa. Republican. Home: 5133 E 25th Ct Tulsa OK 74114-3749 Office: Upton Comm PO Box 4634 Tulsa OK 74159-0634

UPTON, LARRY DEWAYNE, refrigeration engineer; b. Walnut Ridge, Ark., Dec. 29, 1949; s. Avon Ernest and Arizina Elizabeth (Evans) U.; m. Rhonda d. Frazier, Sept. 27, 1967 (div. Mar. 1976); children: Melony April Upton-Lewis, Alesha Raquel Upton-Rogers; m. Elizabeth Irene Garner, Mar. 27, 1976; 1 child, Jason Dewayne. Cert. refrigeration tech., Pulaski Vocat. Tech. Inst., 1985; student, Worcester Polytech., 1988, Am. Internat. Coll., 1989; M in Mgmt., Cambridge Coll., 1996. Cert. hypnotist; registered hypnotherapist. Owner, operator North Shore Maintenance, Inc., North Little Rock, Ark., 1979-83; owner 12th St. Laundry & Cleaners, Little Rock, 1979-83; owner, real estate broker Larco Realty & Investments, North Little Rock, 1979-83; chief engr. Holiday Inn, Inc., Little Rock, 1983-86; plant engr. Arctic Ice & Cold Storage, Little Rock, 1986-87, Rathbone Precision Metals, Palmer, Mass., 1987-89; cen. engrng. Monsanto Chem. Co., Indian Orchard, Mass., 1989—; engr. The Upton Group, East Longmeadow, Mass., 1996—. Active North Little Rock Jaycees, 1977; pres. Benton (Ark.) Jaycees, 1982; head coach Suburban League Football, East Longmeadow, Mass., 1989-92; commn. mem. East Longmeadow Recreation Com., 1990-92; coach Suburban League Baseball, East Longmeadow, 1991. Recipient Ark. award for pub. svc. State Ark., Benton, 1982, Cert. Appreciation East Longmeadow Recreation Com., 1989-91. Fellow Nat. Youth Sports Coaches Assn., Nat. Guild Hypnotists, Pioneer Valley Ycht Club, Elks, Masons (bd. dirs., steward East Longmeadow 1990-91), Shriners. Avocations: sailing, hiking, fishing, woodworking. Home: PO Box 331 East Longmeadow MA 01028-0331

UPTON, LORRAINE FRANCES, elementary education educator; b. Balt., Dec. 26, 1947; d. Meyer and Adeline (Kanstor) Cohen; m. Michael K. Upton, Sept. 25, 1970; 1 child, Matthew Colin. BS, Boston U., 1969; MEd, Temple U., 1974. Cert. elem. tchr., reading specialist, Pa. VISTA employee Brighton, Mass., 1968; tchr. Boston Pub. Sch. Dist., 1969-70, tchr. 3d grade, 1971-94; tchr. 4th grade Neshaminy Sch. Dist., Langhorne, Pa., 1995—; instr. The Learning Mag., The Reading Teaching. Contbr. articles to profl. jours. Active social outreach programs; minority inspector during polit. elections, Yardley, Pa.; instr. Learning Mag., The Reading Tchr. Recipient Gift of Time tribute Am. Family Inst. Pa., 1992; Harold C. Case scholar Boston U., 1969. Mem. Internat. Reading Assn., Internat. Platform Assn. Home: 5 Beechwood Ln Yardley PA 19067 Office: Samuel Everett Elem Sch Forsythia Dr Levittown PA 19056

UPTON, RICHARD THOMAS, artist; b. Hartford, Conn., May 26, 1931; s. Ray Granville and Helen Marie (Colla) U.; 1 son, Richard Thomas, II. BFA, U. Conn., 1960; MFA, Ind. U., 1963. Artist-in-residence Artists for the Environ., Del. Water Gap, 1972, UGA Program Abroad, Corona, Italy, 1982-85. Exhbns. include E'stampe Contemporaine, Galerie Mansart, Bibliot Nat., France, 1969, 74, L'estampe aujourd'hui, 1973-78, Sala Internat., Palacio de Bellas Artes, Mexico City, 1969, Sept. Graveures un Sculpteur de Medailles, Mus. Deonon, Chalon-Sur Saone, France, 1973, Brit. Internat. Print Biennale, U.S. sect. touring Eng., 1973, Del. Water Gap, Corcoran Gallery Art, Washington, 1975, Everson Mus. Art, Syracuse, N.Y., 1975, Nat. Collection Prints and Poetry, Library of Congress, 1976-77, U. Ga., Palazzo Vignoti, Cortona, Italy, retrospective prints from, Atelier 17, Paris, 1977, Okla. Art Center, Oklahoma City, 1977, Tweed Mus. Art, Duluth, Minn., 1977, Weatherspoon Art Gallery, Greensboro, N.C., 1977, Chiesadi San Stae, Venice, Italy, 1989, Grey Gallery, N.Y.C., 1990, Everson Mus. of Art, Krannert Mus. Art, 1990—, Paysage Demoralise: Landscape at the End of the Century, Grey Art Gallery and Study Ctr., N.Y.C., 1990, Tuscany Rediscovered: Richard Upton at Cortona, Everson Mus. Art, Syracuse, 1991, Richard Upton: Italian Landscapes, Krannert Art Mus., Champaign, Ill., 1992, The Italian Landscapes: Richard Upton at Cortona, Mus. Am. Art, New Britain, Conn., 1992, Richard Upton: Ten Years of Italian Landscapes, James Michener Art Mus., Pa., 1994, Phila. Art Alliance, 1994, Condeso/Lawler Gallery, N.Y.C., 1995, Nat. Acad. of Design, 1996, Sordoni Art Gallery, 1997; represented in permanent collections Nat. Zimmerli Art Mus. of Am. Art at Smithsonian Instn., Mus. Modern Art, N.Y.C., Victoria and Albert Mus., London, Bibliot Nat., Paris, Montreal Mus. Fine Arts; commns. include Eros Thanatos Suite (German poem and woodcuts), Interlaken Corp., Providence, 1967, Salamovka Poster, Okla. Art Ctr., 1974, (with poems by Stanley Kunitz) River Road Suite, 1976; suite of drawing Robert Lowell at 66, 1977; suite of drawings Salmagundi mag. for humanities; The Anxious Landscape, paintings, drawings Bellarmine Coll., Louisville, 1989. With USNR, 1950-54. Recipient designer award Interlaken Corp., 1967; subject of monographs: Richard Upton and the Rhetoric of Landscape, Paul Hayes Tucker, U. Mass., U. Wash. Press, 1991, The Tuscan Landscapes of Richard Upton, Stanley C. Grand Sordoni Art Gallery & Fred Licht, curator, Collezione Peggy Guggenheim, Venice, Wilkes U., 1997, The Drawings of Richard Upton David Shapiro, 1997, List Gallery, Ben Shahn Galleries; fellow Fulbright Found., 1964, Ballinglen Arts Found., Ireland, 1994; grantee Nat. Endowment for Arts Artists for Environ., 1972, Richard Florsheim Fund, 1992; elected to Nat. Acad. of Design, 1995. Home: 113 Regent St Saratoga Springs NY 12866-4323

UPTON, THOMAS VERNON, medical educator; b. Antigo, Wis., Apr. 27, 1948; s. Laverne Leo and Mildred Helen (Burmeister) U.; m. Teresa Anne Ugis, June 11, 1977; children: Mark, Paul, Catherine, Marie. BA, Cath. U. Am., MA, 1972, PhD, 1977. Assoc. prof. Gannon U., Erie, Pa., 1977-83, 84—; vis. prof. Cath. U. Am., Washington, 1983-84; cons. in field. Contbr. articles to profl. jours. Basselin Found. scholar, 1968-71; J.K. Ryan Found. fellow, 1974-77, NEH fellow, 1980, 83, 86, 88. Mem. Am. Philos. Assn., Cath. Philos. Assn. (bd. dirs. 1984-86), Soc. Ancien. Republican. Roman Catholic. Avocations: jogging, fishing, reading, exercising, golf. Office: Gannon U Box 209 Erie PA 16541

URAKAMI, AKIO, manufacturing company executive; b. Tokyo, Apr. 17, 1942; came to U.S., 1991; s. Yutaka and Tomiko (Nagai) U.; m. Keiko Tanaka, Feb. 7, 1971; children: Yuji, Masako, Kota. BS, Tokyo Inst. Tech., 1965; MS, Northwestern U., 1967, PhD, 1970. Rsch. engr. Ryobi Ltd., Hiroshima, Japan, 1970-72, corp. planning mgr., 1972-76, v.p. internat., 1976-84, exec. v.p., 1984-91; chmn., pres. Ryobi N.Am., Inc., Easley, S.C., 1991—; mem. pres.'s adv. coun. Clemson (S.C.) u., 1992—. Trustee The Urakami Found., Hiroshima, 1978—; bd. dirs. Japan Am. Assn. of We. S.C., Greenville, 1992—. Mem. Keizai Doyu Kai. Office: Ryobi NAm Inc PO Box 1947 101 Grace Dr Easley SC 29641-1947

URAL, OKTAY, civil engineering educator. BA in Math., Trinity U., 1956; BS in Civil Engrng., Tex. A&M U.; MSCE, U. Tenn., 1959; PhD in Civil Engrng., N.C. State U., 1964; BSCE, 1958. Asst. prof. U. Mo., Rolla, 1967-69, assoc. prof., 1969-73, prof., 1973, founding dir. Inst. for Interdisciplinary Housing Studies; prof. Fla. Internat. U., Miami, 1973—, founding dir. constrn. div. Coll. Engrng. and Applied Scis., dir. Inst. Housing and Bldg.; lectr. various univs.; chmn., dir., 30 nat. and internat. confs.; bd. dirs. Internat. Found. Earth Constrn., Internat. Coun. Bldg. Rsch. Studies and Documentation, Rotterdam, The Netherlands, 1978-80; mem. sci. adv. panel UN Disaster Relief Orgn.; pres. Turkish Housing Authorit, advisor to prime min. Turkish Republic, 1990-92. Author: Matrix Operations and Use of Computers in Structural Engineering, 1971, Finite Element Method: Basic Concepts and Applications, 1973, A Systematic Approach to Basic Utilities in Developing Countries, 1974, Construction of Lower-Cost Housing, 1980; editor-in-chief Internat. Jour. Housing Sci. and Its Applications, 1977—; editor 22 vols. of sci. congress procs.; contbr. articles to profl. jours. Grantee HUD, Washington, Com. on Banking and Currency, U.S. Ho. of Reps., NSF, Fla. Power and Light Co., Fla. Internat. U. Found., Inc., Dept. Edn., State Fla.; recipient Medail de Vermeil for Experts, Govt. France. Fellow ASCE (chmn. structures com. on electronic computation edn. com., urban planning and devel. div. housing com., control group, Harland Bartholomew award); mem. Internat. Assn. Housing Sci. (pres.), Am. Soc. Engrng. Edn. (internat. com.), Sigma Xi, Tau Beta Pi, Phi Kappa Phi, Chi Epsilon. Home: 3608 Anderson Rd Coral Gables FL 33134-7053 Office: Fla Internat U Internat Inst Housing & Bldg Civil Engrng Dept Miami FL 33199

URAM, GERALD ROBERT, lawyer; b. Newark, July 11, 1941; s. Arthur George and Mildred (Stein) U.; m. Melissa Gordon, May 27, 1995; children: Michael, Alison, Carolyn Gordon Lewis. BA, Dartmouth Coll., 1963; LLB, Yale U., 1967. Bar: N.Y. 1967. Assoc. Paul, Weiss, Rifkind, Wharton & Garrison, N.Y.C., 1967-74; v.p., corp. counsel Prudential Bldg. Maintenance Corp., N.Y.C., 1974; ptnr. Davis & Gilbert, N.Y.C., 1974—; lectr. N.Y. Law Sch. Bd. dirs. St. Francis Friends of Poor, Inc. Mem. ABA, N.Y. State Bar Assn., Assn. Bar City of N.Y. Contbr. to profl. publs. Office: 1740 Broadway Fl 3 New York NY 10019-4315

URATO, BARBRA CASALE, entrepreneur; b. Newark, Oct. 10, 1941; d. Dominick Anthony and Concetta (Castrichini) Casale; m. John Joseph Urato, June 20, 1965; children: Concetta U. Graves, Gina E., Joseph D. Student, Seton Hall U., 1961-63. File clk. Martin Gelber Esquire, Newark, 1956-58; policy typist Aetna Casualty Ins., Newark, 1959-61; sec. to dean Seton Hall U., South Orange, N.J., 1961-63; paralegal sec. Judge Robert A. McKinley, Newark, 1963-65, Joseph Garrubbo, Esquire, Newark, 1965-66; office mgr. Valiant I.M.C., Hackensack, N.J., 1971-73; asst. pers. mgr. Degussa Inc., Teterboro, N.J., 1975-78; night mgr. The Ferryboat Restaurant, River Edge, N.J., 1976-78; mgr. Fratello's and Ventilini's, Hilton Head, S.C., 1978-80; day mgr. Ramada Inn Restaurant, Paramus, N.J., 1980-81; mgr. Gottlieb's Bakery, Hilton Head, 1982-83; asst. mgr. closing dept. Hilton Head Mortgage Co., 1983-84; owner, mgr. All Cleaning Svc., Hilton Head, 1984—; owner Hilton Head Investigations, 1990-93, Hilton Head Island, 1990-92; owner Aaction Investigators, 1992-94. Mem. NAFE, Profl. Women of Hilton Head, Assn. for Rsch. and Enlightenment, Rosicrucian Order. Roman Catholic. Avocations: metaphysics, music, gardening, dancing. Office: PO Box 4953 Hilton Head Island SC 29938-4953

URBACH, FREDERICK, physician, educator; b. Vienna, Austria, Sept. 6, 1922; s. Erich and Josepha (Kronstein) U.; m. Nancy Ann Phillips, Dec. 20, 1952; children: Erich J., Gregory M., Andrew D. AB cum laude, U. Pa., 1943; MD, Jefferson Med. Coll., 1946; MD (hon.), U. Göttingen, Fed. Republic Germany, 1987. Diplomate: Am. Bd. Dermatology. Intern Jefferson Hosp., 1946-47; fellow in dermatology U. Pa. Hosp., 1949-52; fellow pediatric dermatology Children's Hosp., Phila., 1950-52; asst. vis. physician Phila. Gen. Hosp., Skin and Cancer Hosp., U. Pa. Hosp., 1952-54; assoc. chief cancer research (dermatology) Roswell Park Meml. Inst., Buffalo, 1954-55, chief cancer research (dermatology), 1955-58; asst. med. dir. Skin and Cancer Hosp. Phila., 1958-67, med. dir., 1967-88; research prof. physiology U. Buffalo Grad. Sch., 1955-58; assoc. prof. dermatology Temple U. Sch. Medicine, 1958-60, prof. research dermatology, 1960-67, chmn. dept. dermatology, 1967-88; dir. Ctr. for Photobiology, 1977-89, prof. dermatology emeritus, 1989—; dep. dir. Health Rsch. Inc., Buffalo, 1954-58; mem. U.S. nat. com. photo-biology Nat. Acad. Sci., 1973-80. Author: The Biology of Cutaneous Cancer, 1963, The Biologic Effects of Ultraviolet Radiation, 1969, (with Parrish, Anderson and Pitts) UVA, 1978; (with Gange) Biologic Effects of UVA Radiation, 1985, Responses to UVA Radiation, 1992; contbr. articles to profl. jours. Served with AUS, 1943-46; with USAAF, 1947-49. Recipient Ritter Meml. medal German Dermatology Soc., 1980. Fellow AAAS, N.Y. Acad. Sci.; mem. AMA, ACP, FACP, Am. Soc. Photobiology (councilor 1973-76, pres. 1977), Am. Assn. Cancer Rsch. Soc. Exptl. Biology and Medicine, Internat. Soc. Tropical Dermatology, Internat. Assn. Photobiology (v.p. 1976-79, pres. 1980-84, Finsen medal 1992); hon. mem. Danish Soc. Dermatology, Swedish Soc. Dermatology (Hellerstoöm medal 1977), Polish Soc. Dermatology, Austrian Soc. Dermatology, German Soc. Dermatology, Philippine Soc. Dermatology. Research epidemiology of cancer, photobiology, phototherapy. Home: 438 Clairemont Rd Villanova PA 19085-1706 Office: Temple Med Practices 220 Commerce Dr Fort Washington PA 19034-2402

URBAN, CARLYLE WOODROW, retired lawyer; b. Beverly, Kans., Dec. 14, 1914; s. Joseph William and Anna Bell (Murphy) U.; m. Lois Ball, June 10, 1946 (dec. Mar. 1987); children: Elizabeth Anne Urban Alexander, Michael Joseph; m. Zara Walker, Feb. 11, 1989. Student, Kans. Wesleyan U., 1931-33; LL.B., U. Tex., Austin, 1941. Bar: Tex. 1941. Practiced in Austin, 1941-42, Houston, 1944-86; assoc. firm Powell, Wirtz, Rauhut & Gideon, Austin, 1941-42; partner firms Elledge, Urban & Bruce, Houston, 1944-62, Urban & Coolidge, Houston, 1963-85. Scoutmaster Sam Houston Area council Boy Scouts Am., 1959-61; Precinct committeeman Harris County (Tex.) Democratic Exec. Com., 1957-63. Served with USAAF, 1942-44. Mem. Order of Coif, Delta Theta Phi. Methodist (trustee, chmn. bd. trustees dist. conf.). Lodge: Lion. Home: 1610 Stonegate Dr Cleburne TX 76031-4554 *Have we done our children any favor by making life easier for* *them than for us as parents? I think not. I fear we have done our children a disservice by depriving them of the "right to struggle". We have created an environment of leniency. Being required to suffer the consequences of failure has gone out of fashion. Even our courts have pursued a policy of leniency. If our system is to be preserved, I sincerely believe that greater respect must be given to personal self-discipline, pride in personal achievement and excellence of performance.*

URBAN, GARY ROSS, computer and information processing consultant; b. Corpus Christi, Tex., May 17, 1947; s. Ross. O. and Nell (Hall) U.; m. Jeanette Corbitt, Dec. 14, 1968 (div. 1979); children: Kimberly, Bryan, Sheryl. Pvt. practice computer and info. processing cons. GRU Enterprises, Houston, 1972—. Recipient Achievement cert. U.S. Army, 1971. Mem. Mensa.

URBAN, GLEN L., management educator; b. Wausau, Wis., Apr. 15, 1940. BSME, U. Wis., 1963, MBA, 1964; PhD, Northwestern U., 1966. Asst. prof. MIT, Cambridge, Mass., 1966-70, assoc. prof., 1970-77, prof. mktg. and mgmt. sci., 1977—, Dai-Ichi Kangyo Bank prof. mgmt., 1987-93, dep. dean Sloan Sch. Mgmt., 1987-91, co-dir. Internat. Ctr. for Rsch. on Mgmt. of Tech., 1992-93, dean Sloan Sch. Mgmt., 1993—; co-founder Mgmt. Decision Systems, Inc., 1970, Mgmt. Sci. for Health, Inc., 1972, Mktg. Tech. Interface, Inc., 1991. Author: (with D.B. Montgomery) Management Science in Marketing, 1969, (with J.R. Hauser and N. Dholakia) Essentials of New Product Development, 1987, (with Steven H. Star) Advanced Marketing Stragety: Phenomena, Analysis and Decisions, 1991, Design and Marketing of New Products, 2d edit., 1993; mem. editl. bd. Mktg. Sci.; reviewer for Mgmt. Sci. (Best Paper award 1986), Jour. Mktg. Rsch. (O'Dell award 1983, 88), Ops. Rsch., Jour. Mktg. (Best Paper award 1996); contbr. over 30 articles to profl. jours. Recipient Best Paper award Jour. of Mktg., 1996. Mem. Inst. Mgmt. Sci., Ops. Rsch. Soc. Am., Am. Mktg. Assn. (Converse award for Lifetime Achievements in Mktg. 1996). Office: MIT Sloan Sch Mgmt 50 Memorial Dr # E52 473 Cambridge MA 02142-1347

URBAN, HENRY ZELLER, newspaperman; b. Buffalo, July 11, 1920; s. George Pennock and Florence Lenhard (Zeller) U.; m. Ruth deMoss Wickwire, Apr. 28, 1948; children: Ruth Robinson Urban Smith, Florence de Moss Urban Hunn, Henry Zeller, Ward Wickwire. Grad., Hotchkiss Sch., 1939; B.S., Yale U., 1943. Treas. George Urban Milling Co., 1946-53; with Buffalo Eve. News, 1953—, asst. bus. mgr., 1957-62, bus. mgr., 1962-71, treas., dir., 1971-74, pres., pub., 1974-83; dir. G. F. Zellers Sons, Inc., 1948-53. Bd. dirs. Travelers Aid Soc., 1953-59, Buffalo Fine Arts Acad., 1960-63, 73-76, 82-85, 86-89, YMCA, 1955-68; trustee Elmwood-Franklin Sch., 1967-70; trustee Canisius Coll., 1977-83, bd. regents, 1972-78; adv. bd. Medaille Coll., 1968-83; chmn. parents council Hamilton Coll., 1977. Served to lt. USNR, 1942-46. Mem. Buffalo C. of C., N.Y. State Pubs. Assn. (dir. 1970-73, 76-79). Clubs: Mid-day (Buffalo), Tennis and Squash (Buffalo), Buffalo (Buffalo), Buffalo Country (Buffalo), Saturn (Buffalo), Pack (Buffalo); Sankaty Head (Nantucket); Nantucket Yacht. Home: 57 Tudor Pl Buffalo NY 14222-1615 Office: 1 News Plz Buffalo NY 14203-2930

URBAN, JAMES ARTHUR, lawyer; b. West Palm Beach, Fla., Feb. 18, 1927; s. Arthur Joseph and Elsie Elizabeth (Wespeaker) U.; m. Alice Burmah Steed, June 21, 1952; children: James Arthur, Katherine Elizabeth. A.B., Duke U., 1950; J.D. with high honors, U. Fla., 1953. Bar: Fla. 1953. Of counsel Carlton, Fields, Ward, Emmanuel, Smith, & Cutler (P.A.), Orlando, Fla.; dir. Fla. Legal Services, Inc., 1975-76. Bd. visitors Coll. Law Fla. State U., Tallahassee, 1973-79, mem. council advisers, 1975-79; mem. pres.'s council U. Fla., Gainesville, 1976-77; charter mem. Indsl. Devel. Commn. Mid-Fla., 1977—. Served with U.S. Army, 1945-47. Recipient Outstanding Alumnus award U. Fla. Law Rev. Alumni Assn., 1975. Fellow Am. Coll. Trust and Estate Counsel, Am. Coll. Real Estate Lawyers, Am. Bar Found.; mem. ABA (Ho. of Dels. 1976-80), Am. Law Inst., Fla. Bar Assn. (bd. dirs. 1975-84, pres. 1977-79), Nat. Conf. Bar Founds. (bd. dirs. 1979-90), Orlando C. of C. (bd. dirs. 1971-73), Phi Kappa Phi, Theta Chi. Episcopalian. Clubs: Rotary (Orlando), Citrus (Orlando), Univ., Country (Orlando). Home: 931 Ventura Ave Orlando FL 32804 Office: Carlton Fields Ward Emmanuel Smith & Cutler PA PO Box 1171 Orlando FL 32802-1171 also: 1601 CNA Tower Orlando FL 32801

URBAN, JOHN S., engineering company executive; b. Newark, July 1, 1933; s. John Urban and Julia (Ostenski) Cahoon; m. Janet Ann Scott, June 23, 1956; children: Debra Sue Urban Doolittle, John Stanley, Gregg Scott, Jeffrey Scott. BS in Civil Engring., N.J. Inst. Tech., 1956. Registered profl. engr., N.Y., N.J., Mass., Pa., Del., Ga. Jr. engr. Edwards & Kelcey, 1956-59, engr., 1959-61, sr. engr., 1961-65, prin. engr., 1965-69, with, 1969-71, asst. v.p., 1971-74, v.p., 1974-84, sr. v.p., 1984-88, exec. v.p., 1988-90, pres., CEO, 1990-94, chmn., 1994—. Mem. bd. overseers N.J. Inst. Tech. With Army, 1957. Named Businesswoman of Yr. Meadowlands Regional C. of C., 1997, Bridge Engr. of Yr. ABCD N.E. Region, Inc., 1997; recipient Edward E. Weston medal Disting. Profl. Achievement by NJIT Alumnus, 1997. Fellow ASCE (mem. hwy. divsn. rsch. com., Robert Ridgeway award), Am. Consulting Engrs. Coun.; mem. Am. Rd. & Transp. Builders Assn. (planning and design divsn. dir.), Soc. Am. Mil. Engrs., N.Y. Assn. Consulting Engrs. (mem. transp. com.), N.J. Soc. Profl. Engrs., N.J. Alliance Action (bd. dirs.), N.J. C. of C. (mem. transp. com.), Consulting Engrs. Coun. N.J. (past pres.), Regional Plan Assn. (mem. N.J. com.), Internat. Bridge, Tunnel and Turnpike Assn. (mem. engring. design com.), Scotch Ball Assn., Basking Ridge Golf Club (pres.), Highlander Club (N.J. Inst. Tech., chmn.). Avocations: gardening, photography, golfing. Office: Edwards and Kelcey Inc Box 1936 299 Madison Ave Morristown NJ 07962

URBAN, JOSEPH JAROSLAV, engineer, consultant; b. Chocen, Czechoslovakia, Mar. 11, 1922; came to U.S., 1955; s. Josef and Ludmila (Moravcova) U.; children: H.U. Heinicke, R. Bruce. Diploma in engring., U. Prague, Czechoslovakia, 1948; postgrad., U. Toronto, 1952-55. Registered profl. engr. Mgr. Urban Mfg., Chocen, 1942-48; prof. Masaryk U., Nuernberg, Fed. Republic Germany, 1950; designer C.A. Meadows Cons. Engrs., Toronto, 1952-55, Rondo Devel. Corp., Stamford, Conn., 1955-58; designer, chief engr., v.p. Huck Co. Inc. Engrs., Montvale, N.J., 1958-72, also bd. dirs.; pvt. practive cons. engr. Pleasantville, N.Y., 1972—; exec. cons. Crown Cork and Seal Co. Inc., Phila., 1972=94. Designer various types of machines for U.S. govt. and U.S. industries-printing presses, book binding, dinsetters and can mfg. equipment, pinsetter, computers, glass machines; patentee in field. Recipient World War II decoration Field Marshall Alexander, 1945. Mem. Acad. Art and Sci. (Czech Republic), Moose, Sir Knight Columbus. Roman Catholic. Avocations: protection of wildlife, naturalist, painting, classical music, fine art collector.

URBAN, LEE DONALD, lawyer; b. Portland, Maine, July 12, 1946; s. Donald Franklin and Mirriam Gertrude (Percy) U.; m. Anna Sanger Kirkpatrick, Feb. 15, 1975; children: Anna, Reid, Seth, Christopher. BA, Colby Coll., 1968; JD, Georgetown U., 1974. Bar: Maine 1974, D.C. 1975. Atty. FTC, Washington, 1974-75; assoc. then ptnr. Perkins, Thompson, Hinckley & Keddy, Portland, 1975-84; ptnr. Pierce, Atwood, Scribner, Allen, Smith & Lancaster, Portland, 1985-94, mediator, facilitator, 1994—; pvt. practice law Portland, 1994—; instr. real estate U. So. Maine, Portland, 1980-86, instr. negotiation skills, 1997—; cons. nonprofit orgns., 1994—. Co-founder, bd. dirs. Inst. for Civic Leadership, 1993-95; bd. dirs. Maine Consensus Project, 1993-95; officer, bd. dirs., mem. adv. bd. Greater Portland Landmarks, Inc., 1975—; bd. advisors Nat. Trust for Historic Preservation, Washington, 1984-90; officer, bd. dirs. Intown Portland Exch., 1982-88, Maine Real Estate Devel. Assn., 1985-94, Cumberland County Affordable Housing Venture, 1988-90, The Maine Alliance, 1992-94, Portland Concert Assn., 1997—, Portland West Neighborhood Planning Coun., 1997—; chmn. Portland Hist. Preservation Com., 1990-93, Downtown Bus. Adv. Com., 1990—. Lt. (j.g.) USN, 1968-71. Democrat. Avocations: bicycling, music, harmonica playing.

URBAN, PATRICIA A., former elementary school educator; b. Chgo., Oct. 15, 1932; d. Clifford and Caroline (Viegi) Brocken; m. Francis C. Urban, Oct. 20, 1956; children: Jim, David, Anthony, Mary Joan, Barbara, Margaret, Judy, Sharon, Jennifer. BA, Rosary Coll., River Forest, Ill., 1954; MS in Edn., Chgo. State U., 1979; MEd, Loyola U., Chgo., 1986. Cert. tchr., reading tchr., Ill. Tchr. St. Joseph Ch. Sch., Summit, Ill., 1954-56; profl. reading tutor Loyola U., 1987-90; tchr. social studies and reading Dist. 104 Schs., Summit, 1974-94; ret., 1994. Named. Dist. 104 Tchr. of Yr., 1987. Mem. ASCD, Internat. Reading Assn., Am. Fedn. Tchrs., West Suburban Tchrs. Union, Alpha Upsilon Alpha. Home: 1019 Walter St Lemont IL 60439-3920

URBANAS, ALBAN WILLIAM, financial planner; b. Balt., Jan. 5, 1952; s. William Peter and Anna Mary (Danaitis) U.; m. Elizabeth Iza Davis, Nov. 18, 1995. BA, U. Paris-Sorbonne, 1976, PhD, 1982; MBA, George Mason U., 1994. Instr. ESL The Paris-Am. Acad., Paris, 1977-78; coord. French & English programs Marubeni-France, Paris, 1978-81; adj. asst. prof. English U. Paris, 1978-81; coord. French & English programs CACI Lang. Ctr., Arlington, Va., 1983-85; adj. asst. prof. philosophy Georgetown U., Washington, 1983-84; vis. asst. prof. French George Washington U., Washington, 1985, adj. asst. prof. philosophy, 1985-86; asst. prof. philosophy & French Franklin Coll., Lugano, Switzerland, 1986-89; vis. asst. prof. philosophy Colby Coll., Waterville, Maine, 1989-90; vis. asst. prof. French N.Y.U., Paris, 1990; assoc. prof. philosophy & French Wesley Coll., Dover, Del., 1990-97; vis. assoc. prof. philosophy Washington Coll., Chestertown, Md., 1997—. Author: La notion d'accident chez Aristote, 1988; contbr. articles to profl. jours. Bd. dirs. Dover Arts Coun., 1993-96, Del. Ballet, 1994-95, Alliance Française of Wilmington, Del., 1993-96, v.p. Recipient Lithuanian Lang. Inst. Title grant U.S.S.R. Ministry Culture, 1986, grant NEH, 1991, scholarship French Cultural Svcs., Strasbourg, France, 1992, fellowship Jesse Ball duPont Found., 1992. Avocations: skiing, running, hiking, computer, international travel. Office: CIGNA Fin Advs 570 Taxter Rd Elmsford NY 10523-2311

URBANETTI, JOHN SUTHERLAND, internist, consultant; b. Mineola, N.Y., Aug. 14, 1943; s. Anthony Joseph and MIldred S. U.; m. LInda J. Sample, July 16, 1978; children: Andrew, Alexis. AB, Johns Hopkins U., 1964, MD, 1967. Diplomate Am. Bd. Internal Medicine and Pulmonary Diseases. Internal medicine intern Johns Hopkins Hosp., Balt., 1967-68, internal medicine resident, 1968-69; fellow in pulmonary cardiology McGill U., Montreal, Can., 1971-74; asst. prof. medicine and dir. pulmonary lab. Tufts New Eng. Med. Ctr. Hosp., Boston, 1974-80; asst. prof. clin. medicine and pulmonary diseases Yale U., New Haven, Conn., 1980—; cons. toxic inhalation US Surgeon Gen., U.S. Army, USN, USAF, 1974—. Author: (books) Carbon Monoxide Poisoning, 1980, Pulmonary Management of Surgical Patients, 1982, Battlefield Chemical Inhalation, 1988; contbr. articles to profl. jours. Capt. USAF, 1969-71. Recipient Commdr's award for pub. svc. U.S. Army, 1990. Fellow Royal Coll. Physicians and Surgeons (Can.), Am. Coll. Physicians, Am. Coll. Chest Physicians; mem. Am. Thoracic Soc., Aerospace Medicine Soc. Avocation: swimming. Office: Southeastern Pulmonary Assocs 155 Montauk Ave New London CT 06320-4842

URBANIK, THOMAS, II, research civil engineer; b. Oceanside, N.Y., Feb. 15, 1946; s. John George and Helen Rita (Waterhouse) U.; m. Cynthia Ellen Myers, Feb. 23, 1948; children: Michael T., Steven J. BS, N.Y. State Coll. Forestry, 1968; BSCE, Syracuse U., 1969; MSCE, Purdue U., 1971; PhD, Tex. A&M U., 1982. Registered profl. engr., Mich., Tex. Traffic engr. City of Ann Arbor (Mich.), 1971-76; rsch. engr. Tex. A&M U., College Station, 1977—; cons. Battelle Pacific N.W. Labs., Richland, Wash., 1987—, Fed. Hwy. Adminstrn., Washington; mem. steering com. on advanced traffic mgmt. sys. Intelligent Transp. Soc. Am. Mem. ASCE, Inst. Transp. Engrs., Transp. Rsch. Bd. (assoc.). Republican. Lutheran. Office: Tex A&M U Tex Transp Inst College Station TX 77843

URBANOWSKI, FRANK, publishing company executive; b. Balt., Mar. 5, 1936; s. Frank and Tofilla (Jakubik) U.; m. Julia Blocksma; children: Alexandra, Tasha. B.S. in Ceramic Engring., Va. Poly. Inst.; postgrad., Columbia U. Rep. Ronald Press, 1960-61; editor coll. dept. Macmillan Co., 1961-66; editorial dir. Glencoe Press, 1966-68, v.p., 1968-72, pub., 1972-73; dir. market planning Ednl. Testing Service, 1973-75; dir. Mass. Inst. Tech. Press, Cambridge, 1975—; chmn. exec. council Profl. Scholarly Publs. div., 1979-81; bd. dirs. Cambridge Insight Meditation Ctr., 1985—. Mem. Am. Assn. Pubs. (dir. 1979-81), Assn. Am. Univ. Press (dir. 1979-81, pres. 1990-91), Cambridge Boat Club. Home: 129 Franklin St Cambridge MA 02139 also: Mountain Rd Cornwall VT 05753 Office: MIT Press 5 Cambridge Ctr Cambridge MA 02142-1407

URBIK, JEROME ANTHONY, financial consultant; b. Chgo., Oct. 30, 1929; s. Anthony Frank and Sophie Elizabeth (Stripeikis) U.; m. Barbara Jean Chamernik, Sept. 1956; children: Laura M. Kern, Michael A., Anthony J., Mary L. King, John T., Maria M. BA in Philosophy, St. Mary's Coll., Techny, Ill., 1953; CLU degree, Am. Coll., 1970, ChFC degree, 1979. CLU, Chartered Fin. Cons. Field underwriter MONY Fin. Svcs., Chgo., 1955-59; merchandising specialist Mut. of N.Y., N.Y.C., 1959; pvt. practice brokerage cons. Northfield, Ill., 1960-64; CEO Hinsdale (Ill.) Assocs. Fin. Svcs. Corp., 1964—; v.p. Interstate Coll. Personology, San Diego, 1982-87; pres. Gen. Agts. Mgrs. Conf., 1967-68. Mem. publ. com. Crisis mag., Washington, 1989—; contbr. articles on industry to profl. jours.; mem. editl. bd. Leaders mag., 1981-90. Mem. adv. coun. Congressman Henry Hyde, Nat. Rep. Com., Washington; mem. Small Bus. Devel. Ctr. exec. bd. advisors Lewis U., Lockport, Ill., 1987-90; exec. coord. Legatus (Cath. CEO) Bd. dirs. United Rep. Fund, 1987-92; bd. advisors Am. Life League, Washington; bd. dirs. Nat. Coalition Reps. for Life. Named Small Bus. Acct. of Yr. for State of Ill. SBA, 1987. Mem. Am. Soc. CLUs, Am. Life League (bd. advisers), Chgo. Orchestral Assn., Chgo. Lyric Opera. Roman Catholic. Avocations: reading, writing, power boating, classical music. Home: 474 South St Elmhurst IL 60126-4120 Office: Hinsdale Assoc Fin Svc Corp 15 Spinning Wheel Rd Ste 414 Hinsdale IL 60521-2987

URBINA, MANUEL, II, legal research historian, history educator; b. Rodriguez, Nuevo Leon, Mex., Sept. 23, 1939; came to U.S., 1947; s. Manuel and Irene (Salce) de Urbina. BA, Howard Payne Coll., 1962; postgrad., Nat. Autonoma U. Mex., Mexico City, 1963-64; MA, U. Tex., 1967, PhD, 1976; postgrad., Cambridge (Eng.) U., 1982; JD, U. Houston, 1983. Prof. Latin Am. history Coll. of the Mainland, Texas City, Tex., 1967—; founder, curator Urbina Mus. History of Mex., Houston, 1990—; chmn., legal counsel Urbina Found., Houston, 1985—; chmn., CEO Urbina Pub. Co. Inc., Houston and Mexico City, 1985—. Editor, interviewer history videos, oral history interviews with participants in the Mexican Revolution. Founder Cinco de Mayo Assn., Galveston County, Tex., 1976; founder, faculty sponsor Mex. Am. Student Assn., Coll. of Mainlan, 1974—. Named Hispanic of Yr. Galveston County League of United Latin Am. Citizens, 1982; NEH grantee, 1971-72; U.S. Dept. State scholar diplomat, 1979. Mem. League of United Latin Am. Citizens, Tex. State Hist. Assn., Howard Payne U. Alumni Assn., U. Houston Law Alumni Assn., Interam. C. of C. Democrat. Baptist. Avocations: reading, research, travel, trumpet playing, volunteer work. Home: 889 Old Genoa Red Bluff Rd Houston TX 77034-4010 Office: Museo Urbina de Historia de Mexico 889 Old Genoa Red Bluff Rd Houston TX 77034-4010

URBOM, WARREN KEITH, federal judge; b. Atlanta, Nebr., Dec. 17, 1925; s. Clarence Andrew and Anna Myrl (Irelan) U.; m. Joyce Marie Crawford, Aug. 19, 1951; children: Kim Marie, Randall Crawford, Allison Lee, Joy Renee. AB with highest distinction, Nebr. Wesleyan U., 1950, LLD (hon.), 1984; JD with distinction, U. Mich., 1953. Bar: Nebr. 1953. Mem. firm Baylor, Evnen, Baylor, Urbom, & Curtiss, Lincoln, Nebr., 1953-70; judge U.S. Dist. Ct. Nebr., 1970—; chief judge U.S. Dist. Ct. Dist. Nebr., 1972-86, sr. judge, 1991—; mem. com. on practice and procedure Nebr. Supreme Ct., 1965-95; mem. subcom. on fed. jurisdiction Jud. Conf. U.S., 1975-83; adj. instr. trial advocacy U. Nebr. Coll. Law, 1979-90; bd. dirs. Fed. Jud. Ctr., 1982-86; chmn. com. on orientation newly apptd. dist. judges Fed. Jud. Ctr., 1986-89; mem. 8th Cir. Com. on Model Criminal and Civil Jury Instrns., 1983—; mem. adv. com. on alternative sentences U.S. Sentencing Com., 1989-91. Contbr. articles to profl. jours. Trustee St. Paul Sch. Theology, Kansas City, Mo., 1986-89; active United Methodist Ch. (bd. mgrs., bd. global ministries 1972-76, gen. com. on status and role of women, 1988-96, gen. conf. 1972, 76, 80, 88, 92, 96); pres. Lincoln YMCA, 1965-67; bd. govs. Nebr. Wesleyan U., chmn. 1975-80. With AUS, 1944-46. Recipient Medal of Honor, Nebr. Wesleyan U. Alumni Assn., 1983. Fellow Am. Coll. Trial Lawyers; mem. ABA, Nebr. Bar Assn. (ho. of dels. 1966-70, Outstanding Legal Educator award 1990), Lincoln Bar Assn. (Liberty Bell award 1993, pres. 1968-69), Kiwanis (Disting. Svc. award 1993), Masons (33 deg.), Am. Inns of Ct. (Lewis F. Powell Jr. award for Professionalism and Ethics 1995). Methodist. Home: 4421 Ridgeview Dr Lincoln NE 68516-1516 Office: US Dist Ct 586 Fed Bldg 100 Centennial Mall N Lincoln NE 68508-3804

URCH, DIANE SHERMAN, librarian; b. Woodbury, N.J., Nov. 17, 1936; d. Arthur T. and Elizabeth V. (Haines) Sherman; m. Juergen K. Schoeler, Mar. 20, 1959 (div. June 1975); children: Jodi L. Schoeler Hecht, Susan E. Schoeler Anderson, Ellen Nell Schoeler; m. Wesley V. Urch, Apr. 18, 1991. BA in History, U. Del., 1958; MA in Librarianship, U. Denver, 1970. Circulation and acquisitions libr. Emporia (Kans.) State U., 1970-79; acquisitions libr. U. Tex., El Paso, 1979-84; asst. dir. libr. U. Wis., Oshkosh, 1984—. Mem., mem. Oshkosh adv. bd. Children's Svcs. Soc. Wis., 1991—. Mem. ALA, AAUW (pres. Oshkosh br. 1996-98), Wis. Libr. Assn. Office: U Wis Librs and Learning Resource 800 Algoma Blvd Oshkosh WI 54901-3551

URCIUOLI, J. ARTHUR, investment executive; b. Syracuse, N.Y., Nov. 13, 1937; s. Joseph R. and Nicoletta Anne (Phillips) U.; m. Margaret Jane Forelli, Aug. 13, 1966; children: Karen Sloan, Christian J.A. B.S., St. Lawrence U., 1959; J.D., Georgetown U., 1966; grad. Advanced Mgmt. Program, Harvard Bus. Sch., 1982. Bar: N.Y. 1966. Atty. Brown, Wood, Fuller, Caldwell & Ivey, N.Y.C., 1966-69; internat. investment banker, dir. internat. fin. Merrill Lynch, N.Y.C., Paris, 1970-78; pres. Merrill Lynch Internat., 1978-82; chmn. Merrill Lynch Internat. Bank, London; dir. banking div. Merrill Lynch Capital Markets, 1980-84; dir. Merrill Lynch Bus. Fin. Services, Merrill Lynch Co., 1984-93; dir. mktg. group Merrill Lynch Pvt. Client, 1993-97; chmn. Internat. Pvt. Client Group, 1997—. Contbr. articles to profl. jours. Trustee St. Lawrence U., 1976-89, Bruce Mus., Greenwich, Conn., 1990-94; bd. dirs. United Way, Greenwich, 1978-81. Capt. USMC, 1959-63. Mem. Securities Assn. (chmn. sales and mktg. com. 1987-89), Forum for Investor Advice (chmn. 1996—), River Club (N.Y.C.), N.Y. Yacht Club, Riverside (Conn.) Yacht Club, Rocky Point Club (Old Greenwich, Conn.). Republican. Congregationalist. Clubs: River (N.Y.C.); N.Y. Yacht, Riverside (Conn.) Yacht; Rocky Point (Old Greenwich, Conn.). Office: Merrill Lynch 800 Scudders Mill Rd Plainsboro NJ 08536-1606

URDANG, ALEXANDRA, book publishing executive; b. N.Y.C., June 29, 1956; d. Laurence Urdang and Irena (Ehrlich) Urdang de Tour. BA in English Lit., U. Conn., 1977. Customer svc. and fulfillment mgr. Universe Books, N.Y.C., 1978-79, sales mgr., assoc. mktg. mgr., 1980-82; asst. v.p., dir. spl. sales Macmillan Pub. Co., N.Y.C., 1982-88; v.p. new markets Warner Books, Inc., N.Y.C., 1988—. Avocations: architecture, art, antiques. Office: Warner Books Inc Time and Life Bldg 1271 Avenue Of The Americas New York NY 10020-1300

URDANG, LAURENCE, lexicographer, publisher; b. N.Y.C., Mar. 21, 1927; s. Harry Rudman and Annabel (Schafran) U.; m. Irena B. Ehrlich vel Sluszny, May 23, 1952 (div.); children: Nicole Severyn, Alexandra Stefanie. B.S., Columbia U., 1954, postgrad., 1954-58. Lectr. gen. linguistics NYU, 1956-61; assoc. editor dictionary dept. Funk & Wagnalls, Inc., N.Y.C., 1957; reference editor Random House, Inc., N.Y.C., 1957-61, dir. reference dept., 1962-69; pres. Laurence Urdang, Inc., Old Lyme, Conn. and Aylesbury, Eng., 1969—; chmn. bd. Laurence Urdang Assocs., Ltd., Aylesbury, 1969-78; editor Verbatim, Old Lyme and Aylesbury, 1974—. Compiler, editor, author numerous books; mng. editor: Random House Unabridged Dictionary, 1966; editor in chief: Random House College Dictionary, 1968, Random House Dictionary of Synonyms and Antonyms, 1960, N.Y. Times Everyday Reader's Dictionary of Misunderstood, Misused, Mispronounced Words, 1972, 2d edit., 1985, Editor, Verbatim, The Language Quar., 1974, Dictionary of Advertising Terms, 1977, Official Associated Press Almanac, 1976, Hammond Almanac, 1977, Picturesque Expressions, 1980, 2d edit., 1985, Illustrated Children's Dictionary, 1979, Basic Dictionary of Synonyms and Antonyms, 1979, 2d edit., 1986, The Synonym Finder, 1979, Collins English Dictionary, 1979, Verbatim: Vols. I, II, 1978, Vols. III, IV, V, VI and Index, 1981, -Ologies & -Isms, 1978, 81, 86, Twentieth Century American Nicknames, 1979, A Treasury of Biblical Quotations, 1980, The Timetables of American History, 1981, Mosby's Medical and Nursing Dictionary, 1983, Allusions, 1982, 86, Modifiers, 1982, Suffixes, 1982, Prefixes, 1984, Holidays and Anniversaries, 1985, Slogans, 1985, Mottoes, 1986, Numerical Allusions, 1986, Names and Nicknames of Places and Things, 1987, Loanwords Dictionary, 1987, The Whole Ball of Wax, 1988, The Dictionary of Confusable Words, 1988, A Fine Kettle of Fish, 1990, The Oxford Thesaurus, 1992, 2nd edit., 1997, The Oxford Desk Dictionary, 1995, The Oxford Desk Thesaurus, 1995, The New Century Dictionary, 1996, The New Century Thesaurus, 1996, The Compact Oxford Thesaurus, 1997. Served with USNR, 1944-45. Mem. Linguistic Soc. Am., Am. Name Soc., Am. Dialect Soc., Dictionary Soc. N.Am., Soc. Indexers, Euralex. Clubs: Athenaeum, Naval (London); Century Assn.

URDEA, JOHN, electromechanical engineer; b. Sercaia, Romania, Feb. 15, 1946; s. Nicolae and Maria U.; m. Elena Greserink, Oct. 27, 1979; 1 child, Alex. MSEE, Polytech. Inst., Romania, 1968. Jr. engr. TLHS/Constrn. Site, Bucharest, Romania, 1968-69; elec. engr. TLHS/Elec. Constrn., Bucharest, 1969-71; design engr. TLHS/Design Dept., Bucharest, 1971-75; chief energetical engr. TLHS Hdqtrs., Bucharest, 1975-82; v.p. electromech. Romagrimex, Raqqa, Syria, 1982-83; maintenance mgr. Aqua Spa, Oklahoma City, 1984-85, plant mgr., 1985-86; project mgr. Econowatt Corp., Pelham, N.Y., 1986-88; systems engr., project mgr. Con Edison, N.Y.C., 1988—; cons. Fin. Square, Inc., N.Y.C., 1986-88. Mem. Rep. Nat. Com., Washington, 1990. Mem. IEEE, N.Y. Acad. Scis. Republican. Greek Orthodox. Avocations: music, skiing, soccer, auto repair. Home: 6 W Oak Hill Dr Oyster Bay NY 11771

URHAUSEN, JAMES NICHOLAS, real estate developer, construction executive; b. Berwyn, Ill., Oct. 6, 1943; s. Jack Nicholas and Florence Frances (Stalzer) U.; m. Philomena Anne Malizia, July 16, 1966 (div. 1980); children: Kristen Anne, James Nicholas III; m. Anne Siegert, July 22, 1983; children: Bradley James, Samantha Elise. BA, St. Procopius Coll., Lisle, Ill., 1965. High sch. tchr. Nazareth Acad., LaGrange Park, Ill., 1965-66; asst. village mgr. Village of Hinsdale, Ill., 1966-69; village mgr. Village of Oak Brook, Ill., 1969-73; v.p., sec.-treas. Collins Devel. Corp., St. Charles, Ill., 1973-80; exec. v.p. Westway Constrn. Corp., St. Charles, Ill., 1980-84, pres., chief exec. officer, 1984—; guest lectr. No. Ill. U., Dekalb, 1976—; expert witness Ill. Dept. of Transp., Chgo., 1976—; dir. Harris Bank/St. Charles, Ill., 1992—. Chmn. Hotel Baker Bd. Gov.'s St. Charles, 1982-84, Bd. of Fire and Police Commmrs., St. Charles, 1986—; mem. 708 Comty. Mental Health Bd., St. Charles, 1986—, Kane County Selective Svc. Sys. Bd., St. Charles, 1981—, Kane County Solid Waste Adv. Com., Geneva, 1990—, Metra Citizen's Adv. Bd., 1993—; bd. dirs. Neighborhood Improvement Assn., St. Charles Twp., 1992—, pres., 1996—; bd. dirs. Delnor Comty. Hosp. Found., 1993—, Glenwood Sch. for Boys, 1996—; chair tech. adv. com. Kane County Stormwater Mgmt. Com., 1996—. Mem. Home Bldrs. Assn. Greater Chgo. (dir. 1989—), Nat. Assn. Home Bldrs., No. Ill. Home Bldrs. Assn., Fox Valley Polit. Action Group, St. Charles C. of C. (amb. 1988, Community Devel. award 1989, Charlemagne award 1993, Sam Walton Bus. Leadership award 1996). Republican. Roman Catholic. Avocations: golf, rail photography, power boating, model trains. Home: 3103 Greenwood Ln Saint Charles IL 60175-5627 Office: Westway Constrn Corp 440 S 3rd St Saint Charles IL 60174-2825

URI, GEORGE WOLFSOHN, accountant; b. San Francisco, Dec. 8, 1920; s. George Washington and Ruby Uri; m. Pamela O'Keefe, May 15, 1961. AB, Stanford U., 1941, IA, 1943, MBA, 1946; postgrad., U. Leeds, Eng., 1945. CPA, Calif.; CFP. CMA, ChFC; Accredited Estate Planner. Mem. acctg., econs. and stats. depts. Shell Oil Co., Inc., San Francisco, 1946-48; ptnr. Irelan, Uri, Mayer & Sheppie, San Francisco; pres. F. Uri & Co., Inc.; instr. acctg. and econs. Golden Gate Univ., 1949-50. Contbr. articles to profl. jours. Chmn. San Rafael Redevel. Adv. Com., 1977-78, mem., 1978-91, mem. emeritus, 1991— ; bd. dirs. San Francisco Planning and Urban Renewal Assn., 1958-60. Served with AUS, 1942-46, to col. Res. (ret.). Recipient Key Man award San Francisco Jr. C. of C.; Meritorious Service medal Sec. of Army, 1978. Mem. AICPA (hon., cert. personal fin. specialist), INFORMS (treas. No. Calif. chpt. 1961-62), Calif. Soc. CPAs (hon.; sec.-treas. San Francisco chpt. 1956-57, dir. 1961-63, state dir. 1964-

66, mem. Forbes medal com. 1968-69, chmn. 1969-71), Am. Econs. Assn., Inst. Mgmt. Accts., San Francisco Estate Planning Coun. (dir. 1965-68, Am. Soc. Mil. Comptrollers, Execs. Assn. San Francisco (pres. 1965-66), Inst. Cert. Mgmt. Accts. (Disting. Performance cert. 1978), Inst. Cert. Fin. Planners, Am. Soc. CLUs and ChFC, World Trade Club (San Francisco), Commonwealth Club (quar. chmn. 1971), Stanford (San Francisco; dir. 1990-97), Army and Navy (Washington). Home: 11 McNear Dr San Rafael CA 94901-1545 Office: 100 Pine St Ste 2300 San Francisco CA 94111-5209

URIE, JOHN JAMES, lawyer, retired Canadian federal judge; b. Guelph, Ont., Can., Jan. 2, 1920; s. G. Norman and Jane A. U.; m. Dorothy Elizabeth James.; children: David, Janet, Alison. B.Commerce, Queen's U.; LL.B., Osgoode Hall Law Sch. Bar: Ont. 1948. Ptnr. firm Burke-Robertson, Urie, Weller & Chadwick, Ottawa, Ont., 1948-73; judge Fed. Ct. Can., Ottawa, 1973-90; counsel Scott and Aylen, Ottawa, 1991—; gen. counsel to Joint Com. of Senate and House of Commons on Consumer Credit; chmn. planning com. First Nat. Conf. on Law, Ottawa, 1972; judge Ct. Martial Appeal Ct., 1973-90. Past pres. County of Carleton Law Assn.; past v.p. Children's Aid Soc.; past pres. Eastern Profl. Hockey League. Served with Cameron Highlanders of Ottawa Can. Army, 1942-45. Mem. Royal Can. Mil. Inst., Phi Delta Phi. Mem. United Ch. of Canada. Clubs: Cameron Highlanders of Ottawa Assoc. (Ottawa), Ottawa Hunt and Golf (Ottawa), Rideau (Ottawa). Office: Scott and Aylen, 60 Queen St, Ottawa, ON Canada K1P 5Y7

URIOSTE, FRANK J., film editor. Cert. Am. Cinema Editors. Films include Whatever Happened to Aunt Alice, The Grissom Gang, Boys in Company C, Fast Break, Loving Couples, Jazz Singer, The Entity, Trenchcoat, Amityville 3-D, Conan II, The Destroyer, Red Sonja, The Hitcher, Robocop (Acad. award nomination), Total Recall, Basic Instinct, Cliffhanger, (co-editor) Midway, Hoosiers, Die Hard (Acad. award nomination). Office: care Lawrence Mirisch The Mirisch Agency 10100 Santa Monica Blvd Ste 700 Los Angeles CA 90067-4011 also: 1610 Highland Ave Glendale CA 91202-1260*

URIS, LEON MARCUS, author; b. Balt., Aug. 3, 1924; s. Wolf William and Anna (Blumberg) U.; m. Betty Katherine Beck, Jan. 5, 1945 (div. 1968); children: Karen Lynn, Mark Jay, Michael Cady; m. Margery Edwards, 1968 (dec. 1969); m. Jill Peabody, Feb. 15, 1970; 1 child, Rachael Jackson. Ed., Balt. City Coll.; hon. doctorate, U. Colo., 1976, Santa Clara U., 1977, Wittenberg U., 1980, Lincoln Coll., 1985. Author: Battle Cry, 1953, The Angry Hills, 1955, Exodus, 1957, Exodus Revisited,1959, Mila 18, 1960 (Calif. Literature Silver Medal award 1962), Armageddon, 1964 (Calif. Literature Gold Medal award 1965), Topaz, 1967, The Third Temple, 1967, QB VII, 1970, Ireland: A Terrible Beauty, 1975, Trinity, 1976, (with Jill Uris) Jerusalem, Song of Songs, 1981, The Haj, 1984, Mitla Pass, 1988, Redemption, 1995; screenwriter: (films) Battle Cry, 1954, Gunfight at the O.K. Corral, 1957; adaptor: (musical play) Ari, 1971. Served with USMCR, 1942-46. Recipient Daroff Meml. award, 1959, John F. Kennedy medal Irish/Am. Soc. of N.Y., 1977, Eire Soc. of Boston Gold medal, 1978, Jobotinsky medal State of Israel, 1980, Scopus award Hebrew U. of Jerusalem, 1981; Nat. Inst. Arts and Letters grantee, 1959; Hall fellow (with Jill Uris) Concord Academy, 1980. Office: 1540 Broadway New York NY 10036-4039*

URIST, MARSHALL RAYMOND, orthopedic surgeon, educator, researcher; b. Chgo., June 11, 1914; s. Irwin and Minna (Vision) U.; m. Alice Elizabeth Pfund, Aug. 16, 1941; children—Marshall McLean, Nancy Scott Urist Miller, John Baxter. B.A., U. Mich., 1936; M.S., U. Chgo., 1937; M.D., Johns Hopkins U., 1941; M.D. (hon.), U. Lund, Malmo, Sweden, 1977. Diplomate Am. Bd. Orthopedic Surgery. Practice medicine specializing in orthopedic surgery Los Angeles, 1948—; mem. staff U.S. VA Hosp. Wadsworth, Los Angeles, 1948-69; adj. assoc. prof. surgery Sch. Medicine, UCLA Med. Ctr., 1954-69, prof. orthopedic surgery, 1969—; dir. bone research lab. UCLA Med. Ctr., 1950—; cons. to surgeon gen. U.S. Army Com. on Trauma, D.C., 1963-71, U.S. Navy, D.C., 1964; keynote speaker Gordon Conf. Bone Growth and Regulation, 1988. Author: Bone: Fundamentals of Physiology of Bone, 1968, Fundamental & Clinical Bone Physiology, 1980; editor-in-chief Clin. Orthopedics and Related Research; contbr. 325 articles to med. jours. Served to lt. col. U.S. Army, 1943-46, ETO. Recipient Sir Henry Wellcome award Assn. Mil. Surgeons of U.S., 1947, Kappa Delta awards Am. Acad. Orthopedic Surgeons, Chgo., 1950, 81, Claude Bernard medal U. Montreal, Que., Can., 1962, Disting. Service medal Am. Assn. Tissue Banks, 1988, Gold medal for sci. achievement Orthopedic Soc. Spain, 1988, Outstanding Rsch. award U.S. Army R&D Command, 1989, 91, Bristol Meyers Squibb Zimmer award, 1993, J. B. Lippincott award, 1994; Guggenheim Found. fellow, N.Y.C., 1972; Dallas Phemister lectureship U. Chgo., 1978, Annual Assn. Bone and Joint Surg. Urist lectureship, 1994; honoree Conf. on Bioactive Factors, U. Tex., San Antonio, 1988, honoree Internat. Conf. Bone Morphogenetic Proteins, Johns Hopkins U. Sch. Medicine, 1994. Fellow ACS, Royal Coll. Surgeons (Edinburgh); mem. AAAS, Assn. Bone and Joint Surgeons (pres. 1967-68, editor-in-chief Jour. Clin. Orthopedic Rsch. 1966-93, Marshall R. Urist Young Investigators award 1995, emeritus 1993—), Hip Soc. (founding, pres. 1978-79), Am. Orthopedic Assn. (hon.), UCLA Medical Alumni Assn. (1995 Medical Scis. award). Republican. Avocation: agriculture; achievement include discovery of bone morphogenetic protein (BMP) in 1965. Home: 796 Amalfi Dr Pacific Palisades CA 90272-4508 Office: 1033 Gayley Ave Los Angeles CA 90024-3417

URKOWITZ, MICHAEL, banker; b. Bronx, N.Y., June 18, 1943; s. David and Esther (Levy) U.; m. Eleanor Naomi Dreazen, July 2, 1966; children—Brian, Denise. B.Engring., CCNY, 1965, M.M.E., 1967. Project engr. Lunar Module program Grumman Corp., Bethpage, N.Y., 1964-72; asst. to dep. commr. for housing code compliance, project mgr. City of N.Y., 1972-74; 2d v.p. Chase Manhattan Bank, N.Y.C., 1974-77, v.p. group exec. ops. dept., money transfer group, 1977-80, sr. v.p., 1980—, group exec. internat. bank services, 1981-82, product and prodn. risk mgmt. exec., 1982-85, exec. v.p., corp. ops. and systems exec., 1985-87; sector exec. Chase InfoServ Internat., 1987-95; exec. consumer products integration and tech. Chase InfoServ Internat., N.Y.C., 1995-96, Chase credit card bus. exec., 1996—; bd. mem. Depository Trust Co., N.Y.C., 1992-95; bd. dirs. CEDEL, Luxembourg, 1992—; lectr. CCNY, 1967-68. Contbg. author: Thermal Control and Radiation, 1972. Mem. adv. bd. N.Y.C. chpt. Salvation Army, 1989—. Mem. Tau Beta Pi, Pi Tau Sigma. Office: Chase Manhattan Corp 1 Chase Manhattan Plz Fl 17 New York NY 10081-1000 *Working against my own standards as opposed to the standards set by others, provides the greater challenge but yields greater satisfaction.*

URMER, DIANE HEDDA, management firm executive, financial officer; b. Bklyn., Dec. 15, 1934; d. Leo and Helen Sarah (Perlman) Leverant; m. Albert Heinz Urmer, Sept. 2, 1952; children: Michelle, Cynthia, Carl. Student U. Tex., 1951-52, Washington U., St. Louis, 1962-63; BA in Psychology, Calif. State U.-Northridge, 1969. Asst. auditor Tex. State Bank, Austin, 1952-55; v.p., contr. Enki Corp., Sepulveda, Calif., 1966-70, also dir., 1987—; v.p., fin. Cambia Way Hosp., Walnut Creek, Calif., 1973-78; v.p., contr. Enki Health & Rsch. Sys., Inc., Reseda, Calif., 1978—, sr. v.p., 1993—; also dir. Contbr. articles to profl. jours. Pres. Northridge PTA, 1971; chmn. Northridge Citizens Adv. Council, 1972-73. Mem. Women in Mgmt. Club: Tex. Execs. Avocations: bowling, sailing, handcrafts, golf. Office: Enki Health and Rsch Systems Inc 21601 Devonshire St Chatsworth CA 91311-2946

UROFSKY, MELVIN IRVING, historian, educator, director; b. N.Y.C., Feb. 7, 1939; s. Philip and Sylvia (Passow) U.; m. Susan Linda Miller, Aug. 27, 1961; children: Philip Eric, Robert Ian. AB, Columbia U., 1961, MA, 1962, PhD, 1968; JD, U. Va., 1983. Instr. history Ohio State U., 1964-67; asst. prof. history and edn., then asst. dean SUNY, Albany, 1967-74; prof. history Va. Commonwealth U., Richmond, 1974—, dir. doctoral program pub. policy, 1996—; Harrison vis. prof. Coll. William and Mary, 1990-91; adj. prof. law U. Richmond, 1989—. Author: Big Steel and Wilson Adminstration, 1969, Why Teachers Strike, 1970, A Mindo of One Piece, 1971, American Zionizm from Herzl to The Holocaust, 1976, We Are One!, 1978, Louis D. Brandeis and the Progressive Tradition, 1980, A Voice that Spoke for Justice: The Life and Times of Stephen S. Wise, 1981, The Supreme Court, the Bill of Rights and the Law, 1986, A March of Liberty, 1987, The Douglas Letters, 1987; A Continuity of Change, 1990, A Conflict of Rights, 1991, Felix Frankfurter, 1991, Letting Go, 1993, Division and Discord, 1997, Commonwealth and Community, 1997; co-editor: Brandeis Letters, 5 vols., 1971-78, Half Brother, Half Son, 1991. Chmn. exec. com. Zionist Academic Council, 1976-79; mem. nat. bd. Am. Zionist Fedn., 1976-79; co-chmn. Am. Zionist Ideological Commn., 1976-78; nat. bd. Assn. Reform Zionists Am., 1978-84. Mershon Found. fellow, 1965, sr. rsch. fellow NEH, 1976-77; recipient Kaplun award Jewish Book Coun., 1976; grantee NEH, Am. Coun. Learned Socs.; NEH scholar-in-residence, 1994-95, univ. award for excellence, 1995. Mem. Am. Jewish Hist. Soc. (chmn. acad. coun. 1979-83), Am. Legal History Soc. (bd. dirs., exec. com. 1991—), Orgn. Am. Historians, Va. Hist. Soc. (trustee 1992—). Office: Va Commonwealth U Ctr Pub Policy Richmond VA 23284-2001

UROWSKY, RICHARD J., lawyer; b. N.Y.C., June 28, 1946; s. Jacob and Anne (Granick) U. BA, Yale U., 1967, JD, 1972; BPhil, Oxford U., Eng., 1970. Bar: N.Y. 1973, U.S. Dist. Ct. (so. dist.) N.Y. 1973, U.S. Ct. Appeals (2d cir.) 1973, U.S. Supreme Ct. 1977. Law clk. to Justice Reed U.S. Supreme Ct., Washington, 1972-73; assoc. Sullivan & Cromwell, N.Y.C., 1973-80, ptnr., 1980—. Mem. ABA, Assn. of the Bar of the City of N.Y., Fed. Bar Coun., N.Y. County Lawyers Assn., Yale Club. Office: Sullivan & Cromwell 125 Broad St New York NY 10004-2400

URQUHART, ANDREW WILLARD, engineering and business executive; b. Burlington, Vt., Aug. 24, 1939; s. John Wardrop and Dorothy Helen (Hefflon) U.; m. Carolyn Fay Powell, Mar. 9, 1963; children: Marion, Dorothy. AB, Dartmouth Coll., 1961, MS, 1964, PhD, 1971. Engr. Div. of Naval Reactors, AEC, 1962-67, Creare, Inc., Hanover, N.H., 1967-68; metallurgist Gen. Electric Corp Rsch. and Devel., Schenectady, 1971-75, br. mgr., 1975-84; v.p. rsch., devel. and engring. Lanxide Corp., Newark, Del., 1984-89, sr. v.p. tech., 1989-93; pres., CEO Lanxide Electronic Components, Inc., 1993—. Contbr. articles to profl. jours.; more than 30 patents in the field. Lt. USN, 1962-67. Mem. ASM Internat. (chmn. Ea. N.Y. sect. 1978-79), Am. Ceramic Soc., Internat. Microelectronics and Packaging Soc., Phi Beta Kappa, Sigma Xi. Avocations: outdoor and family activities. Home: 48 Bridleshire Rd Newark DE 19711-2454 Office: Lanxide Electronic Components Inc 1300 Marrows Rd PO Box 6077 Newark DE 19714-6077

URQUHART, GLEN TAYLOR, investment and development executive; b. Pitts., Nov. 10, 1948; s. George Taylor and Bernice (Wasserman) U.; m. Angela Margaret Boleyn, Dec. 3, 1977; children: Robert, Yates, Kim, Lisa, Caroline. B.S., U. Va., 1971. Fin. mgr. Victor Wilburn & Assocs., Washington, 1972-74; v.p. Chantilly Devel. Corp., Va., 1976-79; pres. Urquhart & Co., Inc., Washington, 1979—; chmn. Nat. Capital Planning Commn., Washington, 1983—; dir. Pennsylvania Ave. Devel. Corp., Washington, 1983—; mem. Council Govts., Washington, 1983—; trustee Fed. City Council, Washington, 1983—. Mem. Com. for Dulles, Dulles Internat. Airport, Washington, 1983—; active, founding mem. Ctr. Internat. Security Studies, Washington, 1984—, World Strategy Network, Washington, 1984—; mem. U.S. Global Strategy Coun., Washington, 1984—; bd. dirs. Am. Def. Found., Washington, 1984—; mem. bd. endowment Cmty. Leadership, 1989—, Campus Crusade for Christ, Young Life, Fellowship Christian Athletes. Republican. Office: Urquhart & Co 7601 Lewinsville Rd Mc Lean VA 22102-2815

URQUHART, JOHN, medical researcher, educator; b. Pitts., Apr. 24, 1934; s. John and Wilma Nelda (Martin) U.; m. Joan Cooley, Dec. 28, 1957; children: Elizabeth Urquhart Vdovjak, John Christopher (dec. 1965), Robert Malcolm, Thomas Jubal. BA with honors, Rice U., 1955; MD with honors, Harvard U., 1959; PhD (honoris causa) U. Utrecht, 1997. Lic. physician, Calif. Walter B. Cannon fellow in physiology Harvard Med. Sch., Boston, 1956, Josiah Macy, Jr. fellow, 1956-58, 59-61; intern in surgery Mass. Gen. Hosp., Boston, 1959-60, asst. resident, 1960-61; investigator Nat. Heart Inst., NIH, Bethesda, Md., 1961-63; asst. prof. physiology U. Pitts. Sch. Medicine, 1963-66, assoc. prof., 1966-68, prof., 1968-70; prof. biomed. engring. U. So. Calif., L.A., 1970-71; prin. scientist ALZA Corp., Palo Alto, Calif., 1970-86, dir. biol. scis., 1971-74, pres. research div., 1974-78, dir., 1976-78, chief scientist, 1978-82, sr. v.p., 1978-85; co-founder APREX Corp., Fremont, Calif., pres., 1986-88, dir. 1986-95, chmn., 1988-91, chief scientist, 1988-95; co-founder, chief scientist AARDEX Ltd., Zug, Switzerland, 1995—; vis. prof. pharmacology U. Limburg Sch. Medicine, Maastricht, The Netherlands, 1984-85, vis. prof. pharmaco-epidemiology, 1986-91; prof. pharmaco-epidemiology, 1992—; adj. prof. biopharm. scis. U. Calif.-San Francisco, 1984—; mem. dir.'s adv. com. NIH, 1986-88; Boerhaave lectr. U. Leiden, The Netherlands, 1991, 94, 95. Co-author: Risk Watch, 1984; contbr. numerous articles to sci. jours.; patentee therapeutic systems for controlled drug delivery and regimen compliance monitoring (43). Trustee GMI Engring. and Mgmt. Inst., Flint, Mich., 1983—. Served with USPHS, 1961-63. NIH grantee, 1963-70; Bowditch lectr. Am. Physiol. Soc., 1969. Mem. Biomed. Engring. Soc. (pres. 1976), Boyleston Med. Soc., Internat. Soc. Pharmaco-epidemiology, Am. Soc. Clinical Pharmacology and Therapeutics, Soc. for Clinical Trials, Endocrine Soc., Saturday Morning club Palo Alto., Am. Physiol. Soc., Soc. Risk Analysis. Home and Office: 975 Hamilton Ave Palo Alto CA 94301-2213

URQUHART, JOHN ALEXANDER, management consultant; b. Savannah, Ga., Aug. 26, 1928; s. George Walter and Helen Catherine (Ruwe) U.; m. Mary Anne Harvey, Apr. 23, 1954; children: Jane Harvey Urquhart Lowe, John Alexander. B.S. in Ind. Engring., Va. Poly. Inst. and State U., 1948. Registered profl. engr., Mass. With GE, 1949-90, sr. v.p. Indsl. & Power Systems, exec. v.p. Power Systems Sector, exec. v.p. Internat. Sector; vice chmn. Enron Corp., 1991—; bd. dirs. Aquarion Co., Enron Corp., Hubbell, Inc., TECO Energy Inc., The Weir Group, PLC. Mem. Brit.-N.Am. com. Fgn. Policy Assn.; trustee Am. U. of Cairo, ASME Found., Inc. 1st lt. C.E., U.S. Army, 1952-54. Mem. ASME, Country Club of Fairfield, Black Rock Yacht Club (Bridgeport, Conn.), Peguot Yacht Club (Southport, Conn.), Philanthropic Lodge (Marblehead, Mass.). Office: 111 Beach Rd Fairfield CT 06430-6668

URQUHART, SALLY ANN, environmental scientist, chemist; b. Omaha, June 8, 1946; d. Howard E. and Mary Josephine (Johnson) Lee; m. Henry O. Urquhart, July 31, 1968; children: Mary L. Urquhart Kelly, Andrew L. BS in Chemistry, U. Tex., Arlington, 1968; MS in Environ. Scis., U. Tex., Dallas, 1986. Registered environ. mgr.; lic. asbestos mgmt. planner, Tex.; Asbestos Hazard Emergency Response Act accredited inspector, mgmt. planner, project designer. Rsch. asst. U. Tex. Dallas, Richardson, 1980-82; high sch. sci. tchr. Allen (Tex.) Ind. Sch. Dist., 1983-87; hazardous materials specialist Dallas Area Rapid Transit, 1987-90, environ. compliance officer, 1990-94, environmental compliance coordination officer, 1994-95; pres. Comprehensive Environ. Svcs. Inc., Dallas, 1995—. Pres. Beacon Sunday Sch. Spring Valley United Meth. Ch., Dallas, 1987, adminstrv. bd. dirs., 1989, com. status and role of women, 1992; vol. Tex. Natural Resource Conservation commn. EnviroMentor Program, 1997—. Scholar Richardson (Tex.) Br. AAUW, 1980. Mem. Am. Inst. Chemists, Am. Chem. Soc., Am. Soc. Safety Engrs., Am. Indsl. Hygiene Assn., Am. Conf. Govtl. Indsl. Hygienists (affiliate), Nat. Registry Environ. Profls., Soc. Tex. Environ. Profls. (sec.-treas. Dallas chpt. 1994, v.p. Dallas chpt., 1996, pres. Dallas chpt. 1997), U. Tex.-Dallas Alumnae Assn. (com. 199294), Soc. of Environ. Mgmt. and Tech. Avocations: jewelry design, counted cross stitching. Home: 310 Sallie Cir Richardson TX 75081-4229

URQUHART, TONY, artist, educator; b. Niagara Falls, Ont., Can., Apr. 9, 1934; s. Archer Marsh and Maryon Louise (Morse) U.; m. Madeline Mary Jennings, July 1958 (div. 1976); children: Allyson, Robin, Marsh, Aidan; m. Mary Jane Carter Keele, May 1976; 1 dau., Emily. B.F.A., U. Buffalo, 1958. Artist-in-residence U. Western Ont., London, 1960-63, 64-65, asst. prof. fine arts, 1967-70, assoc. prof., 1970-72; prof. fine art U. Waterloo, Ont., 1972—, chmn. dept., 1977-79, 82-85, 94-96; lectr. McMaster U., Hamilton, Ont., 1966-67. One-man shows Winnipeg Art Gallery, 1959, Walker Art Gallery, Mpls., 1960, Richard Demarco Gallery, Edinburgh, Scotland, 1975, group shows, Pitts. Biennial, 1958, Guggenheim Internat., N.Y.C., 1958, Art of the Ams. and Spain, Madrid, Barcelona, Rome, Paris, 1964, Nat. Gallery Can., Toronto, 1972, Mus. Modern Art, Paris, 1976; represented permanent collections, Nat. Gallery Can., Art Gallery, Ont., Fed. Art Bank of Ottawa, Montreal Mus., Vancouver Art Gallery, Mus. Modern Art, Victoria and Albert Mus., London, Museo Civico, Lugano, Switzerland; chmn., Jack Chambers Meml. Found., 1978-85; resident artist, Kitchener-Waterloo Art Gallery, Kitchener, Ont., 1981-83; illustrator: The Broken Ark: A Book of Beasts, 1969, I Am Walking in the Garden of His Imaginary Palace by Jane Urquhart, 1982, False Shuffles by Jane Urquhart, 1982, (50 drawings) Cells of Ourselves (text G.M. Dault), 1989, Memories of a Governor General's Daughter, 1990, Warbrain: poems by Stuart MacKinnon, 1994. Recipient Edits, I Arts Coun., Ont., 1974, Kilchener Waterloo Visual Arts award, 1994; winner Nat. Outdoor Sculpture Competition MacDonald Stewart Art Ctr., 1987; appointed mem. Order of Can., 1995; grantee Can. Coun. award, 1963, 79, travel trantee, 1967, 69, 70, 74, 75, 76, 88, 91, project cost grantee, 1981, 82, short-term grantee, 1991, All Can. Coun. Mem. Can. Artists Representation (founding, sec. 1968-71). Office: Dept Fine Arts U Waterloo, Waterloo, ON Canada N2L 3G1

URRY, GRANT WAYNE, chemistry educator; b. Salt Lake City, Mar. 12, 1926; s. Herbert William and Emma (Swanner) U.; m. Lillian Alibertini, Sept. 4, 1946; children—Lisa, Claudia, Serena, Anthony. S.B., U. Chgo., 1947, Ph.D., 1953. Research asst., then research assoc. U. Chgo., 1949-53, research assoc., asst. prof., 1954-55; asst. prof. Washington U., St. Louis, 1955-58; assoc. prof. Purdue U., Lafayette, Ind., 1958-64, prof., 1964-68; prof. chemistry Tufts U., Medford, Mass., 1968-92, Robinson prof. chemistry, 1970-92, chmn. dept., 1968-73, Robinson prof. emeritus chemistry, 1992—. Alfred P. Sloan fellow, 1956-58. Fellow N.Y. Acad. Scis., Am. Inst. Chemists, AAAS; mem. Am. Chem. Soc., Am. Soc. Sci. Glassblowers, Fedn. Am. Scientists, Sigma Xi, Phi Lambda Upsilon. Office: Tufts U Dept Chemistry Medford MA 02155

URSACHE, VICTORIN (HIS EMINENCE THE MOST REVEREND ARCHBISHOP VICTORIN), archbishop; b. Manastioara-Siret, Dist. of Suceava, Romania, 1912. Grad., State Lyceum of Siret; L.Th., U. Cernauti, Romania; postgrad., Bibl. Inst. Jerusalem. Ordained deacon Romanian Orthodox Ch., 1937, ordained priest, 1937. Consecrated bishop Romanian Orthodox Ch., 1966, elevated to archbishop, 1973; prof. religion Orthodox Lyceum of the Romanian Orthodox Metropolis of Cernautsi, 1936-37; prof. theology Seminary of Neamtzu Monastery, 1937-46, asst. dir. sem., 1937-40, dir. sem., superior of monastery, 1940-44; rep. Romanian Orthodox Ch. at Holy Places in, Jerusalem, 1946-56; bishop Romanian Orthodox Missionary Episcopate in Am., 1966-73; archbishop Romanian Orthodox Archdiocese in Am., 1973—; Mem. Holy Synod, Romanian Orthodox Ch. of Romania; bd. dirs. U.S. Conf., World Council Chs.; mem. central com.; mem. Standing Conf. Canonical Orthodox Bishops in, Ams. Editor: Locurile Sfinte. Address: Romanian Orthodox Ch in Am 19959 Riopelle St Detroit MI 48203-1249

URSANO, ROBERT JOSEPH, psychiatrist; b. Heidelberg, Ger., May 26, 1947; s. James Joseph and Neoma Faye (Summers) U.; m. Diane T. Ursano; children: Amy, Anna. BS magna cum laude, U. Notre Dame, 1969; MD, Yale U., 1973; grad., Washington Psychoanalystic Ins, 1986. Diplomate Nat. Bd. Med. Examiners, Am. Bd. Psychiatry and Neurology; lic. physician N.Y., Tex., Md. Resident in psychiatry Wilford Hall USALF Med. Ctr., 1973-75; postdoctoral fellow in psychiatry Yale U./Yale Psychiat. Inst., 1975-77; staff psychiatrist USAF Sch. Aerospace Medicine, Brooks AFB, Tex., 1977-79; clin. asst. prof. U. Tex. Health Sci. Ctr., San Antonio, 1977-79; asst. prof. and dir. third yr. clerkships Dept. psychiatry, Uniformed Svcs. U. Health Scis., Bethesda, Md., 1979-81; assoc prof. and dir. 3rd yr. clerkships Dept. psychiatry, Uniformed Svcs. U. Health Scis., 1981-83, assoc. prof. and assoc. chmn. dept. psychiatry, 1983-86, prof. and assoc. chmn. dept. psychiatry, 1987-82; prof., chair dept. psychiatry Uniformed Svcs. U. Health Scis., Bethesda, Md., 1992—; examiner Am. Bd. Psychiatry and Neurology, 1984—; asst. prof. Nat. Naval Med. Ctr Dept. Psychiatry, Georgetown U. Sch. Medicine, Washington, 1980-84, assoc. prof., 1984-88, prof., 1988—. Author: Concise Guide to Psychodynamic Psychotherapy, 1990, Concise Guide to Principles and Practice of Psychodynamic Psychotherapy in the Era of Managed Care, 1997; editor: Individual and Community Responses to Trauma and Disaster: The Structure of Human Chaos, 1994, Emotional Aftermath of The Persian Gulf War: Veterans, Families, Communities and Nations, 1996, Acute and Chronic PTSD, 1997; reviewer Am. Jour. Psychiatry, Jour. Nervous and Mental Disease, Psychosomatics, Psychiatry, Jour. Applied Social Psychology, Archives of Gen. Psychiatry, Hosp. and Community Psychiatry, all 1986—, Jour. Neuropsychiatry and Clin. Neurosci., 1988—, Jour. Traumatic Stress, 1989—; contbr. numerous articles to profl. jours., chpts. to books. Decorated Air Force Commendation medal, Dept. Def. Humanitarian Svc. medal; recipient William C. Porter award Assn. Mil. Surgeons of U.S. Fellow Am. Psychiat. Assn., Am. Coll. Psychiatrists, Am. Coll. Psychoanalysts; mem. Am. Psychoanalytic Assn., Internat. Psychoanalytic Assn., Am. Psychosomatic Soc., Washington Psychiat. Soc., Washington Psychoanalytic Soc., Soc. of USAF Psychiatrists (v.p. 1981-82), Assn. for Acad. Psychiatry, Alpha Epsilon Delta, Phi Beta Kappa. Home: 3900 Cleveland St Kensington MD 20895-3804 Office: Uniformed Svcs U Health Sci 4301 Jones Bridge Rd Bethesda MD 20814-4712

URSHAN, NATHANIEL ANDREW, minister, church administrator; b. St. Paul, Aug. 29, 1920; s. Andrew David and Mildred (Hammergren) U.; m. Jean Louise Habig, Oct. 1, 1941; children: Sharon, Annette, Nathaniel, Andrew. Student, Columbia U., 1936-39; DTh (hon.), Gateway Coll. Evangelism, 1976. Ordained to ministry United Pentecostal Ch. Internat. Evangelist, 1941-44; assoc. pastor Royal Oak, Mich., 1944-46, N.Y.C., 1947-48, Indpls., 1948-49; pastor Calvary Tabernacle, Indpls., 1949-78; presbyter Ind. Dist. United Pentecostal Chs., 1950-77; asst. gen. supt. United Pentecostal Ch. Internat., 1971-77; gen. supt. United Pentecostal Ch. Internat., Hazelwood, Mo., 1977—; host radio show Harvestime, 1961-78, 81—; chaplain Ind. Ho. of Reps., 1972. Author: Consider Him, 1962, These Men Are Not Drunk, 1964, Book of Sermons of the Baptism of the Holy Spirit, 1968, Major Bible Prophecy, 1971. Mem. internat. com. YMCA, 1958-79, bd. dirs. Indpls. chpt. 1961-79, world service chmn. Region L., 1969-71; chmn. Heart Fund Campaign, 1968-69; mem. screening com. Marion County Reps., Ind., 1973-74; chmn. Ministerial Com. of Richard Lugar for May of Indpls., 1968, William Hudnut for Mayor, 1975; bd. dirs. Little Red Door, Cancer Soc. Indpls., 1974-77. Recipient gold and brass medallion Heart Fund., Indpls., 1968-69; Nathaniel A. Urshan Day named in his honor, Nov. 3, 1979, Mayor Hudnut, Indpls. Mem. Indpls. Ministerial Assn. Office: United Pentecostal Ch Internat 8855 Dunn Rd Hazelwood MO 63042-2212*

URSPRUNG, DEBORAH LYNN, special education educator; b. Liberty, Tex., Sept. 10, 1952; d. Norman Arnold and Roberta Starr (Gay) U.; m. Ernest Fredrick Fritzsching, July 14, 1979 (div. Dec. 1982). Grad., Sam Houston State U., Huntsville, Tex., 1975. Cert. tchr., Tex.; cert. diagnostician. Elem. tchr. psychology, tchr. spl. edn. Aldine Ind. Sch. Dist., Houston, 1976-79; secondary tchr. spl. edn. Tarkington (Tex.) Ind. Sch. Dist., 1982-85, Vidor (Tex.) Ind. Sch. Dist., 1985-93; secondary tchr. spl. edn., dir., mem. attendance bd. Hull Daisetta (Tex.) Ind. Sch. Dist., 1994—. Mem. ASCD, AAUW, Tex. Assn. Classroom Tchrs., Archaeol. Inst. Am., Alpha Delta Kappa (sec. 1996—). Republican. Roman Catholic. Avocations: southwest art and jewelry, needlework, travel, archaeology, natural history. Home: PO Box 725 Rye TX 77369-0725 Office: Hull Daisetta Ind Sch Dist PO Box 477 Daisetta TX 77533-0477

URSTADT, CHARLES J., real estate executive; b. N.Y.C., Oct. 27, 1928; s. Charles G. and Claire C. (Jordan) U.; m. Elinor McClure Funk, Mar. 23, 1957; children: Charles Deane, Catherine Urstadt Biddle. BA, Dartmouth Coll., 1949, MBA, 1951; LLB, Cornell U., 1953; LLD honors. Pace U., 1990. Bar: N.Y. Assoc., Nevius Brett & Kellogg, N.Y.C., 1953-58; asst. sec. Webb & Knapp, Inc., N.Y.C., 1958-63; v.p., sec., counsel Alcoa Residences, Inc., N.Y.C., 1963-67; commr. N.Y. State Div. Housing and Community Renewal, N.Y.C., 1967-73 ; chmn., Battery Park City Authority, N.Y.C., 1968-78; chmn. bd., pres., dir. Urstadt Property Co. Inc., N.Y.C., 1979—; trustee HRE Properties (formerly Hubbard Real Estate Investments), N.Y.C., 1975—, chmn., 1986—, chief exec. officer, 1989—; trustee Tchrs. Ins. and Annuity Corp., 1985—; N.Y. Trustee, Pace U., 1973—; mem. fin. com. N.Y. Rep. State Com., 1981—, del. Rep. Nat. Conv., 1988; mem. Gov.'s Task Force on N.Y. Housing, 1988-90; bd. dirs. N.Y.C Partnership, Inc., 1984-93, chmn. Realty Found. of N.Y., 1989-95; chmn. N.Y. State Statue of Liberty Celebration Found., 1983-84, N.Y. State Housing Fin. Agy., 1969, Tri-State Regional Planning Commn., 1969-70; mem. Pres.'s Commn. on Housing, 1981-82, others. Lt. USNR, 1954-56. Recipient Man of Yr. award Realty Found. N.Y., 1979. Exec. v.p. Assoc. Builders and Owners Greater N.Y., dir. 1979—. Mem. Nat. Soc. Real Estate Fin. Mem. Reformed Church. Clubs: Links, Union League (N.Y.C.); Siwanoy Country (Bronxville); Bohemian (San Francisco). Office: HRE Properties 321 Railroad Ave Greenwich CT 06830-6306

URSU, JOHN JOSEPH, lawyer; b. 1939. BA, U. Mich., 1962, JD, 1965. Bar: Mich. 1966, Ky. 1970, Minn. 1972. Trial atty. FTC, 1965-67; staff mem. Pres.'s Commn. on Civil Disorders, 1967; advisor to commr. FTC, 1968-69; legal counsel GE, 1969-72; divsn. atty. 3M, 1972-74, sr. atty., 1974-76, assoc. counsel, 1976-81, asst. gen. counsel, 1981-86, assoc. gen. counsel, 1986-90, dep. gen. counsel, 1990-92, gen. counsel, 1992-93; v.p. legal affairs & gen. counsel 3M, St. Paul, 1993-96, sr. v.p. legal affairs and gen. counsel, 1997—; adj. faculty William Mitchell Coll. Law, 1978-82. Office: 3M Exec Offices 3M Center # 07 Saint Paul MN 55144-0001

URVAL, KRISHNA RAJ, health facility administrator, educator; b. Mangalore, India, July 3, 1955; came to U.S., 1984; s. Rajgopal Rao and Bhoomi Devi (Kanemar) U.; m. Purnima K. Hebbar, May 23, 1985; children: Nikita, Nikhil. MBBS, MD, Govt. Med. Coll., Mysore City, India, 1979; DCH, U. West Indies, Kingston, Jamaica, 1985. Bd. cert. pediatrics, allergy/immunology. Resident pediatrics U. West Indies, Jamaica, 1980-85; resident pediatrics Interfaith Med. Ctr., Bklyn., 1985-88, chief resident, 1987-88; fellow immunology U. South Fla., St. Petersburg, 1988-90; assoc. Wyo. Chest and Allergy Clinic, Casper, 1990-91; med. dir. Ohio Valley Allergy Inst., Wheeling, W.Va., 1991—; clin. asst. prof. W.Va. U., Morgantown, 1991—; bd. dirs. W.Va. Am. Lung Assn., Charleston. Bd. dirs. Child Care Resource Ctr., Wheeling, 1992—; med. dir. Asthma Support Group, Wheeling, 1992—. Fellow Am. Acad. Pediatrics; mem. AMA, Am. Coll. Allergy/Immunology, Am. Acad. Allergy/Immunology. Democrat. Hindu. Avocations: tennis, ping pong, shuttle badmitton. Office: Ohio Valley Allergy Inst 2101 Jacob St Ste 601 Wheeling WV 26003-3800

USCHEEK, DAVID PETROVICH, chemist; b. University Heights, Ohio, July 9, 1937; s. Peter Ivanovich and Marie (Ocasek) U. BS, Case Western Res. U., 1959. Chemist The Glidden Co., Cleve., 1963-67, Mobil Chem. Co., Cleve., 1967-71, Limbacher Coatings, Cleve., 1971-72, Continental Products, Euclid, Ohio, 1972-80, Body Bros. Paint Corp., Bedford, Ohio, 1980-83, Harrison Paint Corp., Canton, Ohio, 1983-88, Akron (Ohio) Paint and Varnish, 1988-95; with Ritrama Duramark, 1995—; cons. The Analyst, Chardon, Ohio, 1991—. Mem. Am. Chem. Soc., Internat. Union of Pure and Applied Chemists, N.Y. Acad. Scis. Achievements include rsch. on EPA compliant waterborne and high solids coatings with abnormally low volatile organic compound content, high performance corrosion inhibitive water-based primers and topcoats for industrial applications. Home: 8602 Auburn Rd Chardon OH 44024-8711 Office: Ritrama Duramark 341 Eddy Rd Cleveland OH 44108-1601

USDIN, GENE LEONARD, physician, psychiatrist; b. N.Y.C., Jan. 31, 1922; s. I. L. and Eva (Miller) U.; m. Cecile Weil, Nov. 8, 1947; children: Cecile Catherine Burka, Linda Ann, Steven William, Thomas Michael. Student, U. N.C., 1939-40, U. Fla., 1940-41; B.S., Tulane U., 1943; M.D., 1946. Diplomate: Am. Bd. Psychiatry and Neurology (asst. examiner, 1956-80), Am. Bd. Legal Medicine. Intern Touro Infirmary, New Orleans, 1946-47; resident psychiatry Cin. Gen. Hosp., 1949-51; fellow psychiatry Tulane Sch. Medicine, 1951-52; pvt. practice psychiatry New Orleans, 1952-86, 96—; asst. prof. clin. psychiatry Tulane U., 1959-62, assoc. clin. prof., 1962-67; assoc. clin. prof. La. State U., 1967-71, clin. prof., 1971—; sr. psychiatrist Ochsner Clinic, 1986-96; prof. Notre Dame Sem., 1969-75; chief div. neurology and psychiatry Touro Infirmary, New Orleans, 1962-66; dir. psychiat. services Touro Infirmary, 1966-71; McLaughlin-Gallie vis. prof. Royal Coll. Physicians and Surgeons of Can., 1983; Robert O. Jones lectr. Atlantic Maritime Provinces Psychiat. Assn. (Can.), 1976; sr. psychiatrist DePaul and Charity Hosps.; sr. psychiat. cons. Oshsner Med. Found., New Orleans, 1980-85, Timberlawn Psychiat. Hosp., Dallas, 1979-93; chmn. psychiat. cons. com. Am. Bar Found., 1970-73; mem. nat. psychiatric adv. bd. Achievement and Guidance Ctrs. Am., Inc., 1991-92. Editor in chief Psychiatry Digest, 1964-71, 75-79, Psychiatry Digest (Europe), 1981-92, ACP-Psychiatric Update, 1980-94, co-editor, 1994-95, editor 1995-96; editor Medilex Digest of Psychiatry, 1980—; mem. editorial bd. Academic Psychiatry, 1989-92, Mental Hygiene, 1969-76, Clin. Medicine, 1965-71, 75-88, Med. Digest, 1965-71, Jour. Hosp. and Community Psychiatry, 1975, chmn., 1980-81, Jour. Psychiat. Edn., 1975-89, Am. Jour. Family Therapy, 1978—, Am. Jour. Social Psychiatry, 1981-87, Swiss Med. Digest, Psychiatry, 1981—, Extracta Medica Practica Psychiatrie, 1981—, Behavioral Scis. and the Law, 1982-92, Dynamic Psychotherapy, 1982-90, Psychiat. Medicine, 1982-88, Advances in Therapy, 1983-96, Clin. Psychiatry News, 1983-92, Contemporary Psychiatry, 1984-93, Health Disease, 1986—, The Psychiat. Times, 1985—, Clinical Advances in the Treatment of Psychiatric Disorders, 1987—, Jour. Ottawa Med. Sch, 1976-90, Psychiatry Bookshelf, 1976-78, Women's Psychiat. Health, 1992—; mem. internat. adv. bd. Jour. Psicopatologia, Madrid, 1989-94; editor: Psychoneurosis and Schizophrenia, 1966, Practical Lectures in Psychiatry for the Medical Practitioner, 1966, Adolescence: Care and Counseling, 1967, Perspectives on Violence, 1972, (with Peter A. Martin and A.W. Swipe) A Physician in the General Practice of Psychiatry, 1970, The Psychiatric Forum, 1973, Sleep Research and Clinical Practice, 1973, Psychiatry: Education and Image, 1973, Overview of the Psychotherapies, 1975, Schizophrenia: Biological and Psychological Perspective, 1976, Depression: Clinical, Biological and Psychological Perspectives, 1977, Psychiatric Medicine, 1977, (with Charles K. Hofling) Aging: The Process and the People, 1978, (with Jerry M. Lewis, II) Psychiatry in General Medical Practice, 1979, (with David R. Hawkins) The Office Guide to Sleep Disorders, 1980, (with Jerry M. Lewis) Treatment Planning in Psychiatry, 1982; Contbr. articles to profl. jours. Bd. trustees United Fund Greater New Orleans, 1966-70. Served to lt. (j.g.) USNR, 1947-49. Recipient Physician of Yr. award Orleans Parish Med. Soc., 1984, Outstanding Alumni Lectr. award Tulane U. Sch. Medicine, 1986, Seymour Pollack Disting. Svc. award Am. Acad. Psychiatry and the Law, 1988, Outstanding Contbrn. to Social Psychiatry award Am. Assn. for Social Psychiatry, 1993, Lifetime Achievement awards Tulane Med. Alumni Assn., 1996, Fla. Hosp. Ctr. for Psychiatry, 1996; named Psychiatrist of Yr., La. Psychiat. Med. Assn., 1994. Fellow Am. Psychiat. Assn. (chmn. com. on psychiatry and law 1964-68, mem. com. on ethics 1970-74, com. on membership 1970-74, com. on evaluation svcs. bd. 1974-77, com. on pub. affairs 1976-78, chmn. ad hoc com. on election procedures, 1980-81, trustee at large 1978-81, coun. on internat. affairs 1986-91, sec. gen. Interamerican Coun. of Psychiatric Orgns. 1988-91, recipient 3d ann. Certificate of Recognition for Excellence in Med. Student Edn. 1993, Warren Williams award, 1995), So. Psychiat. Assn. (bd. regents 1969-72, chmn. 1971-72, pres. 1973-74), La. Psychiat. Assn. (past pres.), Am. Coll. Psychiatrists (bd. regents 1967-70, pres. 1978-79, E.B. Bowis award for Outstanding Contbns. 1973, Disting. Service award for Oustanding Contbns. in Am. Psychiatry 1980), Acad. Psychosomatic Medicine (mem. exec. council 1974-76), New Orleans Soc. Psychiatry and Neurology (past pres.), Group Advancement Psychiatry (bd. dirs. 1970-77, treas. 1973-77), Am. Assn. Social Psychiatry (pres. 1986-88), World Assn. for Social Psychiatry (exec. coun. 1988-90); mem. La. Med. Soc. (chmn. com. on mental health 1966-70), Orleans Parish Med. Soc., Nat. Assn. Mental Health (mem. profl. advisory counc. 1968-75), Inst. of Mental Hygiene (pres. 1978-79). Home and Office: 3 Newcomb Blvd New Orleans LA 70118-5527

USEEM, JOHN HEARLD, sociologist, anthropologist; b. Buffalo, N.Y., Oct. 15, 1910; s. Abram and Sema (Ross) Usem; m. Ruth Marie Hill, June 6, 1940; children: Michael, Howard, Bert. B.A., UCLA, 1934; student, Harvard U., 1934-36; Ph.D., U. Wis., 1939. Prof. U. S.D., 1939-42; vis. lectr. Barnard Coll., Columbia U., 1946; assoc. prof. U. Wis., 1946-49; prof. sociology and anthropology Mich. State U., 1949-81, prof. emeritus, 1981—, head dept., 1958-65; lectr., cons. Fgn. Svc. Inst., U.S. Dept. State, 1950—; cons. Nat. Inst. Growth and Devel.; mem. adv. com. Edward W. Hazen Found., Social Sci. Rsch. Coun., NIMH, Conf. Bd. Assoc. Rsch. Coun.; sr. fellow East-West Ctr., 1972, mem. internat. adv. panel, 1978-79; rsch. on transnat. roles of higher educated in periods of internat. conflict and change. Author: The Western-Educated Man in India, 1955; contbg. author: Human Problems in Technological Change, 1952, Cultural Patterns and Technical Change, 1953, Reconstituting the Human Community, 1972, Bonds Without Bondage, 1979, Study Abroad: The Experiences of American Undergraduates in Western Europe and in the United States, 1990; contbr. articles to profl. jours. Bd. govs. Arctic Inst. Served as lt. USNR, World War II; mil. gov. in South Pacific. Recipient Mich. State U. Disting. Faculty award, 1962, Disting. Scholar award in internat., cultural and sci. affairs Internat. Soc. Ednl., Cultural and Sci. Interchange, 1979, Disting. Profl. Service award North Central Sociol. Assn., 1982, Research in Internat. Ednl. Exchange, Council on Internat. Ednl. Exchange, 1986. Mem. Am. Sociol. Assn., Am. Anthrop. Assn., North Central Sociol. Assn. (pres. 1971), Soc. Applied Anthropology, Social. Research Assn., Soc. Study Social Problems (chmn. internat. div., Lee Founders' award for disting. career 1987), Central States Anthrop. Soc., Phi Beta Kappa, Phi Kappa Phi, Alpha Kappa Delta, Pi Gamma Mu, Pi Sigma Alpha. Home: 227 Chesterfield Pky East Lansing MI 48823-4110

USEEM, RUTH HILL, sociology educator; b. Hamilton, Ohio, May 31, 1915; d. William E. and Anna E. (Starlin) Hill; m. John Hearld Useem, June 6, 1940; children: Michael, Howard Sheldon, Bert. B.A., Miami U., Oxford, Ohio, 1936; Ph.D., U. Wis., 1947. Asst. prof. Queens Coll., N.Y.C., 1942-43, 1944-45; research cons. Mich. State U., East Lansing, 1951-52; instr. Mich. State U., 1952-58, asst. prof., 1958-60, asso. prof., 1960-70, prof. sociology and edn., 1970-85; Sr. fellow East-West Center, 1970. Author: (with J. Useem) The Western-Educated Man in India, 1955, (with F. Kempf) Psychology: Dynamics of Behavior in Nursing; contbr. articles to profl. jours. Disting. scholar Internat. Soc. Ednl., Cultural and Sci. Interchanges, 1979; recipient Excellence award Mich. State U. Faculty Women's Assn., 1979, award for Research in Internat. Ednl. Exchange, Council Internat. Ednl. Exchange, 1986; Edward W. Hazen Found. grantee India, 1952-53, 58; Edward W. Hazen Found. grantee Philippines, 1968-75; recipient Lee Founders' award for disting. career Soc. for Study of Social Problems, 1987, Pioneering Rsch. on Third Culture Kids award Global Nomads Internat., 1988. Mem. Am. Sociol. Assn. (council 1973-75, com. on coms. 1975-76, com. world sociology 1975-77, com. nominations 1979-81, liaison AAAS com. 1986-87), North Cen. Sociol. Assn. (council 1976-77, v.p./program chmn. 1977-78, pres. 1979-80, Disting. Profl. Service award 1984), Sociologists for Women in Soc., Soc. Internat. Edn., Tng. and Research (council 1978-81), Internat. Soc. Ednl., Cultural and Sci. Interchanges, Sociol. Research Assn., Mortar Bd.; fellow Am. Anthrop. Assn. Home: 227 Chesterfield Pky East Lansing MI 48823-4110

USELMANN, CATHERINE ROSE (KIT USELMANN), small business owner, network marketer, behavioral researcher, financial independence consultant; b. Madison, Wis., Sept. 17, 1960; d. Richard Lewis and Evelyn Mae (Parr) U. AA, Madison Area Tech. Coll., 1982; BA in Sociology, U. Wis., 1984, MA in Rsch. and Analysis, 1985; DD (hon.), Charter Ecumenical Ministries Internat., 1994. Pub. utility rate analyst Pub. Svc. Commn. Wis., Madison, 1986-89; rsch. mgr. Wis. Lottery, Madison, 1989-90; energy cons., tech. analyst II HBRS, Inc., Madison, 1990-91; sr. cons., project mgr. XENERGY, Inc., Burlington, Mass., 1991-93; pres. CRU Prodns., Madison, 1993-97; Platinum exec. Nutrition For Life Internat., Houston, 1995—; exec. Trudeau Mktg. Group, Chgo., 1995—; team coord. I-Team, Cyberspace, 1996—; speaker Nat. Assn. Regulatory Utility Commrs., 1987-89; contbg. mem., speaker Assn. for Demand-Side Mgmt. Profls., 1991-93. Univ. rep. operating com. Mall/Concourse, Madison, 1982-84; lobbyist Inst. for Rsch. Poverty, Madison, 1984; activist, mem. People for Ethical Treatment Animals, Washington, 1989—. Mem. Fin. Independence Assn., U. Wis. Alumni Assn., Badger Quarter Horse Assn. (life). Lakota and Lutheran. Avocations: gourmet cooking, health, wealth. Home and Office: 3753 Robin Hood Way Madison WI 53704-6243

USELTON, JAMES CLAYTON, engineering executive; b. Tullahoma, Tenn., Oct. 2, 1939; s. Hubert and Edna Mae (Fagg) U.; m. Janice Marie Widner, Oct. 30, 1959; children: Debra Leigh, Clayton Seth, Arnold Jay. BS, U. Tenn., 1962; MS, U. Tenn. Space Inst., Tullahoma, 1966, postgrad., 1966-70. Registered profl. engr. Tenn., Mo., Fla., Mich., Tex., Mass., Ohio. Project engr. Sverdrup Tech., Inc., Tullahoma, 1962-70, lead engr., 1971-74, asst. br. mgr., 1974-77, br. mgr., 1978-79, dir., 1979-81, v.p., 1981-85, sr. v.p., 1985-86, exec. v.p., 1986-88; exec. v.p., dir. Sverdrup Corp., Maryland Heights, Mo., 1989-95, pres., 1996—; pres., CEO Sverdrup Investments, Inc., Maryland Heights, Mo., 1992—; chmn. Sverdrup Tech., Inc., Tullahoma, Tenn., 1993—; bd. dirs. Trans Fin. Bank, Tullahoma. Contbr. articles to profl. jours. Fellow AIAA (assoc.); mem. Nat. Mgmt. Assn. Methodist. Avocations: golf, skiing. Home: 16333 Wilson Farm Dr Chesterfield MO 63005-4542 Office: Sverdrup Corp 13723 Riverport Dr Maryland Hts MO 63043-4819

USHER, ELIZABETH REUTER (MRS. WILLIAM A. SCAR), retired librarian; b. Seward, Nebr.; d. Paul and Elizabeth (Meyer) Reuter; m. Harry Thomas Usher, Feb. 25, 1950; m. William Arthur Scar, Mar. 28, 1992. Diploma, Concordia Tchrs. Coll., Seward, Litt.D. (hon.), 1981; B.S. in Edn., U. Nebr., 1942; B.S. in library Sci., U. Ill., 1944. Tchr. Zion Luth. Sch., Platte Center, Nebr. and; St. Paul's Luth. Sch., Paterson, N.J.; library asst. charge res. book reading room U. Nebr., 1942-43; asst. circulation librarian Mich. State U., 1944-45; librarian Cranbrook Acad. Art, Bloomfield Hills, Mich., 1945-48; catalog and reference librarian Met. Mus. Art, N.Y.C., 1948-53; head cataloger and reference librarian Met. Mus. Art, 1953-54, asst. librarian, 1954-61, chief of art reference library, 1961-68, chief librarian, Thomas J. Watson Library, 1968-80, chief librarian emeritus, 1980—, acting librarian, 1954-57. Contbr. articles to profl. periodicals, library publs. Trustee N.Y. Met. Reference and Research Library Agy., 1968-80, sec. to bd., 1971-77, v.p., 1977-80; 1st v.p. Heritage Village Library, 1982-88, 91-92, pres., 1988-91, 95—. Mem. Spl. Libraries Assn. (pres. 1967-68, dir. 1960-63, 66-69, Hall of Fame 1980—), Coll. Art Assn. (chmn. libraries session 1972-73), N.Y. Library Club, Archons of Colophon (convener 1980-82), Heritage Village Rep. Club (pres. 1992-95, 97—), Philanthropic Ednl. Orgn. (v.p. chpt. Q 1994-97, pres. 1997—). Lutheran. Home: 711B Heritage Vlg Southbury CT 06488-1606

USHER, SIR LEONARD GRAY, retired news association executive; b. Paeroa, New Zealand, May 29, 1907; s. Robert and Mary Elizabeth (Johnston) U.; m. Mary Gertrude Lockie, Nov. 30, 1940 (div. 1962); children: Lala Athene Frazer, Miles Gray; m. Jane Hammond Derne, July 11, 1962 (dec. 1984). Tchrs. certificate, Auckland Tng. Coll., 1926-27; B.A., Auckland U., 1934. Headmaster schs. Fiji, 1930-43; pub. relations officer Govt. of Fiji, 1943-56; exec. dir. Fiji Times & Herald, Suva, 1956-73; dir. Fiji Times & Herald, 1973-77; editor Fiji Times, 1958-73; organizing dir. Pacific Islands News Assn., 1974-85, councillor, life mem., 1985—; chmn. bd. Fiji Devel. Bank, 1978-82, Suva Stock Exch., 1979-92, Island Lottlers Ltd., Fiji, 1980-86; dep. chmn. Nat. Bank Fiji, 1974-82; bd. dirs. Connoisseur Products (Pacific) Ltd., Bus. Mgmt. Group Ltd., Mt. Pleasant Ltd. Mem. Fiji Broadcasting Commn., 1954-56, Fiji Visitors Bur., 1953-56; pres. Fiji Bd. Fire Commrs., 1967-70, 75-76; councillor Suva, 1962-71, 75-77, mayor, 1967-70, 75-76; mem. council U. South Pacific, 1975-78; trustee Fiji Crippled Children Soc., 1965—, pres., 1971-74; sec. Fiji Press Council, 1986-94; chmn. Fiji Coll. Honour, 1995—. Served with inf. Fiji Army, 1942-45. Decorated comdr. and knight comdr. Order Brit. Empire, Companion Order Fiji. Mem. Royal Commonwealth Soc. (sec. Fiji), Fiji Arts Club (pres.), Royal Suva Yacht Club, 1961. Methodist. Clubs: Masons (master Fiji 1949-50, 74-75), United Grand Lodge Eng. (past grand, dir. ceremonies 1991), Defence (life mem., trustee), Fiji Arts (pres., life mem., trustee), United (life mem., trustee) (Suva), Royal Automobile (Sydney). Home: GPO Box 13250, Suva Fiji Office: 24 Des Voeux Rd, GPO Box 13250, Suva Fiji *I would like to be worthy of C.E. Montague's tribute to three friends: "They were not ruled by fear or desire, and you could believe what they said".*

USHER, PHYLLIS LAND, state official; b. Winona, Miss., Aug. 29, 1944; d. Sandy Kenneth and Ruth (Cottingham) L.; m. William A. Usher (dec. Dec. 1993). B.S., U. So. Miss., Hattiesburg, 1967; M.S. (Title II-B fellow 1968-69), U. Tenn., Knoxville, 1969; postgrad. Purdue U., Ind. U., Utah State U. Librarian, Natchez (Miss.)-Adams County schs., 1967-68; materials specialist Fulton County Bd. Edn., Atlanta, 1969-71; cons. div. instructional media Ind. Dept. Public Instrn., Indpls., 1971-74, dir. div., 1974-82, dir. fed. resources and sch. improvement, 1982-85; acting assoc. supt. Ind. Dept. Edn., 1985; sr. officer Ctr. for Sch. Improvement, Ind. Dept. Edn., 1985-96, asst. supt., 1996—; pres. bd. dirs. INCOLSA, mcpl. corp., 1980-82; pres., owner Usher Funeral Home, Inc.; pres. NU Realty Corp.; mem. task force sch. Libraries Nat. Commn. Libraries and Info. Sci.; dir., pres. NURC; cons. in field. Bd. dirs. Hawthorne Cmty. Ctr.; mem. Gov. Inst. Conf. Children and Youth Task Force. Recipient citation Internat. Reading Assn., 1975. Mem. ALA, Nat. Assn. State Ednl. Media Profls., West Deanery Bd. Edn., Indpls. Archdioces, Delta Kappa Gamma. Adv. bd. Booklist. Office: State House Rm 229 Indianapolis IN 46204-2728

USHER, THOMAS JAMES, steel executive, energy executive; b. Reading, Pa., Sept. 11, 1942; s. Paul T. and Mary (Leonard) U.; m. Sandra L. Mort, Aug. 14, 1965; children—Leanne, Jimmy, Lauren. B.S. in Indsl. Engring., U. Pitts., 1964, M.S. in Ops. and Research, 1965, Ph.D. in Systems Engring., 1971. Indsl. engr. U. S. Steel Corp., Pitts., 1966-76, asst. gen. supt., 1975-78; asst. div. supt. U. S. Steel Corp., Gary, Ind., 1978-81; asst. to pres., mng. dir. facility planning and engring. U. S. Steel Corp., Pitts., 1982-83, v.p. engring., 1982-83, pres., 1991; pres. U.S. Steel Mining Co., Inc., Pitts., 1983-84, v.p. engring. steel, 1984—, sr. v.p. steel ops., 1984—, exec. v.p. heavy products steel divsn., 1986-89, pres. steel divsn., 1990; pres., COO USX Corp., Pitts., 1994—, chmn., CEO, 1995—. Mem. Leadership Pitts., 1984; trustee Multiple Sclerosis, Pitts., 1985; chmn. Allegheny Trails council Boy Scouts Am., Pitts., 1985, United Way, Pitts., 1985; chmn. U.S.-Korea Bus. Coun., 1993—, U.S.-Japan Bus. Coun.; trustee U. Pitts., 1994—; The Bus. Roundtable Nat. Flag Found., 1995; vice chmn. Bus. Coun. Internat. Iron and Steel Inst., 1997. Mem. Am. Iron and Steel Engrs. (bd. dirs. 1984-85), Am. Iron and Steel Inst., Dinamo/Ovia (bd. dirs. 1985). Clubs: Rolling Rock, Duquesne, Laurel Valley, Double Eagle, Oakmont, Burning Tree. Avocations: golf; tennis; racquetball; scuba diving; swimming. Home: 840 12th St Oakmont PA 15139-1151 Office: USX Corp Room 6170 600 Grant St Ste 6170 Pittsburgh PA 15219-2801

USHIJIMA, JOHN TAKEJI, state senator, lawyer; b. Hilo, Hawaii, Mar. 13, 1924; s. Buhachi and Sano (Nitahara) U.; m. Margaret Kunishige, June 6, 1954. B.A., Grinnell Coll., 1950; J.D., George Washington U., 1952. Bar: Hawaii, 1953. Ptnr. Pence & Ushijima, Hilo, 1953-61, Ushijima & Nakamoto, Hilo, 1961-69; mem. Hawaii Senate, 1959—, pres. pro tem, 1974—; bd. dirs. Cyanotech Corp., Woodinville, Wash. Bd. dirs. Waiakea Settlement YMCA. With AUS, 1943-46, ETO. Mem. Am. Bar Assn., Phi Delta Phi. Democrat. Home: 114 Melani St Hilo HI 96720-2766 Office: 192 Kapiolani St Hilo HI 96720-2687

USSERY, LUANNE, communications consultant; b. Kershaw, S.C., Feb. 20, 1938; d. Ralph Thurston and Mary Elizabeth (Haile) U. B.A., Winthrop Coll., 1959. Assoc. editor Kershaw News-Era, 1959-61; advt. saleswoman Nonpareil newspaper, Coun. Bluffs, Iowa, 1961-67; mag. editor Mutual of Omaha-United of Omaha Ins. Co., 1968-78, asst. v.p., 1978-82, 2d v.p., 1982-87. Editor: The Presbyterian, Presbytery of Missouri River Valley, Omaha, 1984-88, Presbyterian Times, Providence Presbytery, Rock Hill, S.C., 1990-93, 96—, co-editor 1993-96; weekly columnist Kershaw News Era, 1988-92. Elder, clk. of session First Presbyn. Ch. U.S.A., Coun. Bluffs, 1974-88, Beaver Creek Presbyn. Ch., Kershaw, 1990-92, 97—; chair communications com. Presbytery of Missouri River Valley, 1985-87, moderator, 1988; trustee Christian Home Assn./Children's Sq. U.S.A., Coun. Bluffs, 1985-88, Internat. Assn. Bus. Communicators (pres. Omaha chpt. 1972, Communicator of Yr. award Omaha chpt. 1973).

USTINOV, SIR PETER ALEXANDER, actor, director, writer; b. London, Apr. 16, 1921; s. Iona and Nadia (Benois) U.; m. Isolda Denham, 1940 (div.); 1 child, Tamara; m. Suzanne Cloutier, Feb. 15, 1954 (div. 1971); children: Pavla, Igor, Andrea; m. Hélène du Lau d'Allemans, 1972. Student, Westminster Sch., London, Mr. Gibbs Prep. Sch., London, London Theatre Sch.; D.Mus. (hon.), Cleve. Inst. Music, 1967; LL.D. (hon.), U. Dundee, 1969, LaSalle Coll. of Phila., 1971, U. Ottawa, 1991; Litt.D. (hon.), U. Lancaster, 1972; Doctorate (hon.), U. Toronto, 1984, 95; LHD (hon.), Georgetown U., 1988; Doctorate (hon.), Free U. Brussels, 1995. Stage appearances include The Wood Demon, 1938, The Bishop of Limpopoland, 1939, Madame Liselotte Beethoven-Fink, 1939, White Cargo, Rookery Nook, Laburnum Grove, Pygmalion, 1939, First Night, 1940, Swinging the Gate, 1940, Fishing For Shadows, 1940, Hermione Gingold Revue, 1940, Diversion No. 1 Revue, 1940, Squaring the Circle, 1941, Crime and Punishment, 1946, Frenzy, 1948, Love in Albania, 1949, The Love of Four Colonels, 1951-52 (N.Y. Critics award, Donaldson award), Romanoff and Juliet, 1956 (Evening Standard drama award), Photo Finish, 1962, 63, The Unknown Soldier and His Wife, 1968, 73, Who's Who in Hell, 1974, King Lear, 1979, 80, Beethoven's Tenth, 1983, 83-84, 87-88; currently appearing worldwide in An Evening with Peter Ustinov; film appearances include One of Our Aircraft Is Missing, 1941, The Way Ahead, 1944, Private Angelo, 1949, Odette, 1950, Quo Vadis (Acad. award nomination for Best Supporting Actor), 1950, Hotel Sahara, 1952, Beau Brummel, 1953-54, The Egyptian, 1954, We're No Angels, 1955, Lola Montez, 1955, The Spies, 1955, An Angel Flew Over Brooklyn, 1955, I Girovaghi, 1955, The Sundowners, 1960, Spartacus, 1960-61 (Acad. award for Best Supporting Actor), Romanoff and Juliet, 1961, Billy Budd, 1962, Topkapi, 1963, John Goldfarb, Please Come Home!, 1964, Blackbeard's Ghost, 1967, The Comedians, 1967, Hot Millions, 1968, Viva Max, 1969, Hammersmith Is Out, 1971, Big Truck and Poor Clare, 1971, One of Our Dinosaurs Is Missing, 1974, Logan's Run, 1975, Treasure of Matecumba, 1975, The Last Remake of Beau Geste, 1976, Purple Taxi, 1977, Death on the Nile, 1977, The Thief of Baghdad, 1978, Ashanti, 1979, Charlie Chan and the Curse of the Dragon Queen, 1980, Evil Under the Sun, 1981, Memed, My Hawk, 1982, Appointment With Death, 1988, The French Revolution, 1989, Lorenzo's Oil, 1992, The Phoenix and The Magic Carpet, 1993; dir.: (plays) Squaring the Circle, 1941, Love in Albania, 1949, No Sign of the Dove, 1952, A Fiddle at the Wedding, 1952, Romanoff and Juliet, 1956, Photo Finish, 1962, 64, Half Way Up the Tree, 1967, The Unknown Soldier and His Wife, 1968, 73, (operas) L'Heure Espagnole (Ravel), Covent Garden, 1962, Gianni Schicchi (Puccini), Covent Garden, 1962, Erwartung (Schoenberg), Covent Garden, 1962, The Magic Flute (Mozart), Hamburg Opera, 1968; dir., scenery and costume designer: Don Giovanni (Mozart), Edinburgh Festival, 1973; dir., producer, set and costume designer: Don Quichotte (Massenet), Paris Opera, 1973; dir., producer: The Brigands (Offenbach), The German Opera, Berlin, 1978; dir., writer libretto: The Marriage (Moussorgsky), Piccola Scala, 1981; dir.: Mavra and The Flood (Stravinsky), Piccola Scala, 1982, Katja Kabanowa (Janacek), Hamburg Opera, 1985, The Marriage of Figaro, Mozarteum and the Hamburg Opera, 1987, Jolanthe (Tchaikovsky) and Francesca da Rimini (Rachmaninoff), Dresden Opera, 1993; appeared on radio, London (BBC), Germany, Belgium, Rome, Paris, N.Y.C., Hollywood; TV appearances include In All Directions (host, producer, co-star), BBC, History of Europe, BBC, Einstein's Universe, PBS and BBC, 1979, Barefoot in Athens (Emmy award), Storm in Summer (Emmy award), The American Revolution, CBS (George Peabody award), Omnibus (Emmy award), The Well Tempered Bach (Emmy award nomination), PBS, 1984, 13 at Dinner, CBS, 1985, Deadman's Folly, CBS, 1985, Peter Ustinov's Russia, 1985, Appointment with Death, 1987, Around the World in Eighty Days, NBC, 1988-89, Secret Identity of Jack the Ripper, 1989-90, Monet: Legacy of Light, 1990, Ustinov Aboard the Orient Express, 1991-92, Ustinov Meets Pavarotti, 1993, Inside the Vatican, 1994, The Old Curiosity Shop, 1995, Haydn Gala, 1995, documentaries on Thailand and Hong Kong, 1995, an Evening with Sir Peter Ustinov, 1995, Russia Now, 1995, Paths of the Gods, 1996, occasional political commentaries, BBC; recordings include Mock Mozart, The Grand Prix of Gibraltar, Peter and the Wolf (directed by Herbert Von Karajan), Nutcracker Suite, The Soldier's Tale (Stravinsky) (with Jean Cocteau), Hary Janos (Kodaly), London Symphony Orch., The Little Prince (St. Exupéry), (narration) Grandpa, Babar and Father Christmas, The Old Man of Lochnagar, Grandpa, Peter Ustinov Reads the Orchestra; author: (plays) Fishing for Shadows, 1940, House of Regrets, 1942, Blow Your Own Trumpet, 1943, Beyond, 1943, The Banbury Nose, 1944, The Tragedy of Good Intentions, 1945, The Indifferent Shepherd, 1948, Frenzy, 1948, The Man in the Raincoat, 1949, The Moment of Truth, 1951, The Love of Four Colonels, 1951, High Balcony, 1952, No Sign of the Dove, 1953, Romanoff and Juliet, 1956, The Empty Chair, 1956, Paris Not So Gay, 1958, Photo Finish, 1962, The Life in My Hands, 1964, The Unknown Soldier and His Wife, 1967, Halfway Up the Tree, 1967, Who's Who in Hell, 1974, Overheard, 1981, Beethoven's Tenth, 1983, 87-88, others, (films) The Way Ahead (with Eric Ambler), 1942-43, School for Secrets, 1946, Vice Versa, 1947, Private Angelo, 1949, Romanoff and Juliet, 1961, Billy Budd (with DeWitt Bodeen), 1962-63, The Lady L (with Ira Wallach), 1964, Hot Millions (with Ira Wallach), 1968, Memed, My Hawk, 1982, (cartoon) We Were Only Human, 1960, (short stories) Add a Dash of Pity, 1960, Frontiers of the Sea, 1966, (novels) The Loser, 1961, Krumnagel, 1971, The Disinformer, 1989, The Old Man and Mr. Smith, 1991, (autobiography) Dear Me, 1977,

My Russia, 1983, Ustinov in Russia, 1987, Ustinov at Large, 1991, Still at Large, 1993, Quotable Ustinov, 1995. Chancellor U. Durham, 1992; pres. World Federalist Movement, 1992. With Brit. Army, 1942-46. Decorated Comdr. Order of Brit. Empire, 1975, Commandeur des Arts et Lettres, 1985, Knight of the Realm, 1990; recipient Disting. Svc. award UNICEF, 1978, Prix de la Butte, 1978, Best Actor award Variety Club Gt. Britain, 1979, medal of Honor Charles U. (Prague), 1991, Britannia award, 1992, Critic's Circle award, 1993, German Cultural award, 1994, German Bambi, 1994, Internat. Child Survival award, 1995, Rudolph Valentino award, 1995, Norman Cousins Global Governance award, 1995; named rector U. Dundee, 1971-73; elected to Acad. Fine Arts Paris, 1988.

UTELL, MARK JEFFREY, medical educator; b. N.Y.C., July 25, 1946; m. Lois Brooks; 1 child, Michael Jon. BA cum laude, Dartmouth Coll., 1968; MD, Tufts U., 1972. Diplomate Am. Bd. Internal Medicine. Intern St. Elizabeth's Hosp., Boston, 1972-73, resident in internal medicine, 1973-75; from instr. to prof. sch. medicine U. Rochester, N.Y., 1975-92; prof. Sch. Medicine U. Rochester, 1992—, prof. medicine and environ. medicine Sch. Medicine; dir. respiratory and med. ICUs Strong Meml. Hosp., Rochester, 1977-89, mem. intensive care com., 1977-87; co-dir. pulmonary and CCU sch. medicine U. Rochester, 1984-91, occupl. medicine program, 1988—, assoc. chmn. clin. affairs dept. environ. medicine, 1992—, dir. occupl. and environ. medicine divsn., 1992—; cons. VA, 1977—, EPA, 1980—, mem. clean air sci. adv. com., 1988-94; reviewer site visit com. NIH, 1982, outside reviewer respiratory and applied physiology sect. NHLBI, 1982; mem. rev. study sect. Nat. Inst. Environ. Health Scis., 1990-94, mem. task force for rsch. planning; mem. health rsch. com. Health Effects Inst., 1985-94; mem. N.Y. State Commr.'s Panel on Tuberculosis, Syracuse, 1988; mem. commn. life scis. NRC, NAS, 1989; mem. panel airborne particulate matter in spacecraft NASA, 1987, mem. environ. health scis. working group, 1993-94. Co-author: Inhalation Toxicology of Air Pollution: Clinical Research Considerations, 1985, Susceptibility to Inhaled Pollutants, 1989; co-editor: Advances in Controlled Clinical Inhalation Studies, 1993; mem. editl. bd. Jour. Aerosol Medicine, Annals of Internal Medicine, Inhalation Technology; guest reviewer various jours.; contbr. over 100 articles to profl. jours. Bd. dirs. Am. Lung Assn. N.Y. State, 1986-88. Grantee NASA, Nat. Inst. Environ. Health Scis., Nat. Heart Lung and Blood Inst., Elec. Power Rsch. Inst., Ctr. Indoor Air Rsch., Dow Corning Corp., Allied Signal, Inc. Fellow AAAS, ACP, Am. Coll. Chest Physicians (mem. steering com. sect. environ. occupl. health 1983-87, assessment asthma in workplace com. 1994); mem. Am. Physiol. Soc., Am. Thoracic Soc. (chmn. scientific assembly on environ. and occupl. health 1987, mem. planning com., 1992-94, respiratory protective guidelines com., 1993-95, other coms.), Am. Coll. Occupl. Environ. Medicine, N.Y. Trudeau Soc. (pres. 1986). Home: 16 Framingham Ln Pittsford NY 14534 Office: U Rochester Sch Medicine Dept Medicine Pulmonary 601 Elmwood Ave Rochester NY 14642-8692*

UTER, CARMENLITA, secondary education language educator, translator; b. Sea Islands coast, Oct. 25, 1949; d. Charles and Helena (Uter) Cook; m. Gottfried Lehmann, Apr. 10, 1968; children: Michael Lehmann, Sharon Lehmann. BA, Hunter Coll., 1974, MA, 1979; postgrad., Coll. New Rochelle, N.Y., 1994. Cert. tchr. Spanish and English, N.Y. Tchr. fgn. langs. N.Y.C. Bd. Edn., 1974—; founder, dir. Creole-Am. Geneal. Soc., Inc., N.Y.C., 1983—; propr. Tignon Typing Translation Svcs. Author: The Mulatto's Lament, 1989 (under the pen name of Miss Utera). Mem. Assn. Am. Tchrs. Spanish and Portuguese, Archivist Round Table of Met. N.Y., Assn. Profl. Genealogists. Roman Catholic. Avocations: translation, genealogy, writing. Home: PO Box 740501 Rego Park NY 11374

UTHMAN, BASIM MOHAMMAD, neurologist, epileptologist, consultant; b. Tripoli, Lebanon, Sept. 25, 1958; came to the U.S., 1984; s. Mohammad Assa'ad and Mariam Mohammad (Moukalled) U. BSc, Am. U. Beirut, 1978, MD, 1984. Diplomate Am. Bd. Psychiatry and Neurology, Am. Bd. Clin. Neurophysiology. Intern Am. Univ. Beirut Med Ctr., Lebanon, 1983-84; resident in neurologyDept. Neurology U. Cin., 1984-87, clin. fellow in neurophysiology, epilepsy, preceptor, 1987-88; clin. rsch. fellow in epilepsy, neurophysiology and neuropharmacology U. Fla., Gainesville, 1988-90, clin. instr., 1990-91; vis. assoc. prof. dept. neurology U. Fla., 1991-92; asst. prof. dept. neurology, brain inst. U. Fla., Gainesville, 1992-96, assoc. prof. dept. neurology, brain inst., 1996—; staff neurologist VA Med. Ctr., Gainesville, 1990—, asst. chief neurology svc., 1992—, dir. status epilepticus team, 1990-95, contracting officers tech. rep., 1990-92, acting chief neurology svc., 1993, dir. clin. neurophysiology lab. EEG/EP, 1991—; chmn. med. record rev. com. VA, 1995—; chmn. Adminstrv. Bd. Investigation VA Med. Ctr., Gainesville, 1993; attending epideptologist Shands Hosp., 1993—; mem. U. Fla. Instnl. Rev. Bd. Health Sci. Ctr., 1994-96. Ad hoc referee U.S. Pharmacopeial Conv., 1988-89, Drug Evaluations, 1990, Epilepsia, 1990, Jour. Neuroimaging, 1990, Drugs, 1993—; contbr. articles to profl. jours., chpts. to books. Active emergency blood donation campaign, Beirut, 1982-83, worker war disaster plan, 1982-83; vol. Lebanese Red Cross, Beirut, 1982-83; organizer children's med. ednl. presentations, 1984; profl. adv. bd. Epilspsy Found. Fla., 1992-93, chmn., 1993. A.S. Khalidi scholar Am. U. Beirut, 1978, Azeez B. Ajloini scholar, 1979, Tamari-Saab scholar, 1979, Dr. Haddad, 1980; fellow Bowman Gray Med. Sch., Winston-Salem, N.C., 1987; grantee Epilepsy Rsch. Found. Fla., 1988-90, Cyberonics, 1989—, Marion Merryl Dow and Hoechst, Marion, Roussel, Inc., 1994—, Coop. Studies Program Coordinating Ctr., 1990-95, 96—, VA Affairs Med. Ctr. Allotment, 1991-92, Abbott Labs., 1991—, U. Fla., 1991-92, Ceiba-Geigy, 1991-94, U. Fla. Brain Inst., 1992, Parke-Davis 1993—. Mem. AMA, Am. Acad. Neurology, Am. Epilepsy Soc., Am. Sleep Disorders Assn., Am. Electroencephalographic Soc., Am. Soc. Neurophysiological Monitoring, Am. Coll. Internat. Physicians, Nat. Stroke Assn., Am. Neuromodulation Soc. (bd. dirs. 1996—), So. Clin. Neurol. Soc., So. Electroencephalographic Soc., Fla. Med. Assn., Alachua County Med. Soc., Nat. and Internat. Spkrs. Bur. (Parke-Davis, Marion Merryl Dow, Burroughs Wellcome, Abbott Labs., Ciba-Geigy, Cyberonics 1993—), Internat. Neuromodulation Soc. (bd. dirs. 1996—). Moslem. Avocations: tennis, cooking, traveling, jogging, music. Office: VA Med Ctr-Neurology Svc 127 1601 SW Archer Rd Gainesville FL 32608-1135

UTHOFF, MICHAEL, dancer, choreographer, artistic director; b. Santiago, Chile, Nov. 5, 1943; came to U.S., 1962; s. Ernst and Lola (Botka) U.; m. dau., Michelle. Grad. biology, high sch., Chile; dance tng. with Juilliard Sch., 1962-65, Martha Graham, 1962-63, Joffrey Ballet, 1965-68, Sch. Am. Ballet, 1962-64; Laureate in Humanities, St. Joseph Coll., Hartford, Conn. Leading dancer Jose Limon Dance Co., 1964-65, City Center Joffrey Ballet, 1965-68, N.Y.C. Opera, 1968-69; leading dancer, asst. dir. First Chamber Dance Co. N.Y., from 1969; artistic dir. Hartford Ballet Co., 1972-92, Ballet Ariz., 1992—; mem. faculty Juilliard Sch. Music, N.Y.C., from 1969; guest artist, tchr. Princeton Ballet Soc.; prof. dance SUNY, Purchase, 1972-74; instr. dance and drama movement, Yale U.; works premiered by Compania Nacional de Danzas, Mexico City, 1989; guest choreographer Shanghai Ballet, Republic of China, 1986; led Hartford Ballet on 3-week 11-city tour of Peoples Republic of China by invitation of Shanghai Internat. Culture Assn., 1988, 5-week 9-country tour Latin Am., 1991. Choreographer, dancer-actor film Seafall, 1968; opera prodns. Aida and La Cenerentola, Honolulu, 1972, Conn. Opera Romeo et Juliette, 1989, Pitts. Opera Aida, 1988; choreographer Quartet, City Center Joffrey Ballet, 1968, The Pleasure of Merely Circulating, Juilliard Sch. Music, 1969, Windsong, Reflections, Dusk, Promenade, First Chamber Dance Co., 1969-70, Mozart's Idomeneo for Caramoor Music Festival, 1970, Concerto Grosso for Ballet Clasico 70 of Mexico, also restaged Dusk, 1972, Aves Mirabiles, 1973, Danza a Quattro, 1973, Marosszek Dances, 1973, Duo, 1974, Pastorale, 1974, Brahms Variations, 1974, Autumalal, 1975, Mir Ken Geharget Veren, 1976, Tom Dula, 1976, Unstill Life, 1977, Songs of a Wayfarer, 1977, Ask Not..., 1977, White Mountains Suite, 1978, Bach Cantata, 1978, The Nutcracker, 1979, Romeo and Juliet, 1981, Cachivaches, 1981, Reflections on the Water, 1981, Weeping Willow, 1982, Carmencita Variations, 1982, Hansel and Gretel, 1983, Coppelia, 1986, Speak Easy, 1986, New England Triptych, 1986, Los Copihues, 1988, Petrouchka, 1988, RFD #1, 1989, Classical Symphoniette, 1990, Alice in Wonderland, 1991, Nocturnes, 1991, Sinfonia Danzante, 1991; Nat. Endowment Arts commns. for choreography: Primavera, Minn. Dance Theatre, 1975, Panvezitos, Greater Houston Civic Ballet, 1976, Sonata, The Prodigal Son, Hartford Ballet, 1977, 79. Recipient award for best choreography for Murmurs of the Stream, Chilean Nat. Press, 1983, Critic's Circle Best of Yr. in Arts award, Chile, 1984, Milagno en la Alameda award for Chilean Nat. Women, 1995; grantee various founds. Office: Ballet Ariz 3645 E Indian School Rd Phoenix AZ 85018-5126

UTIAN, WULF HESSEL, gynecologist, endocrinologist; b. Johannesburg, South Africa, Sept. 28, 1939; came to U.S., 1976; s. Harry and Ethel (Nay) U.; m. Moira Mervis, Oct. 4, 1964; children: Brett David, Lara Peta. MBBCh, Witwatersrand U., Johannesburg, S.Africa, 1962; PhD, U. Cape Town, S. Africa, 1970. Cons. ob-gyn Groote Schuur Hosp., Cape Town, 1967-76; dir. reprodn. endocrinology Univ. Hosps., Cleve., 1976-80; dir. ob-gyn Mt. Sinai Med. Ctr., Cleve., 1980-89; dir. Cleve. Menopause Clinic, 1986—; prof., chmn. dept. reproductive biology Case Western Reserve U., Cleve., 1989—; dir. ob-gyn. U. Hosps. of Cleve., 1989—; cons. Internat. Health Found., Geneva, Switzerland, 1976-92; assoc. prof. Case Western Res. U., Cleve., 1976-89, prof. reproductive biology, 1989—; exec. com. Internat. Menopause Soc., pres., 1993-96; exec. dir., hon. founding pres. N.Am. Menopause Soc.; pres. Rapid Med. Rsch., 1996—. Author: Menopause in Modern Perspective, 1980, Your Middle Years, 1980, The Menopause and Hormonal Rplacement Therapy--Facts and Controversies, 1991, Managing Your Menopause, 1992; editor: Maturitas, 1980-93, Premenstrual Syndrome, 1981, Menopause Management, 1988—, Menopause, 1993—. Fellow Royal Coll. Ob-Gyn, Am. Coll. Ob-Gyn, Internat. Coll. Surgeons (v.p. 1983-89). Avocations: sailing, hiking. Home: 9725 Lake Shore Blvd Cleveland OH 44108-1048 Office: Univ Hosps 1110 Euclid Ave Cleveland OH 44115-1603

UTIGARD, PHILIP RICHARD, real estate executive; b. Indpls., July 18, 1952; s. Richard Charles and Maedell (Hazen) U.; m. Becki A. Elliott, Sept. 27, 1975; children: Emilie, Benjamin, Kevin. BS, Miami U., Oxford, Ohio, 1974. Mktg. rep. IBM Corp., West Lafayette, Ind., 1974-80; regional mktg. rep. IBM Corp., Detroit, 1981; mktg. mgr. IBM Corp., Ft. Wayne, Ind., 1981-85; adminstr. asst. to chmn. IBM Corp., Armonk, N.Y., 1985-86; br. mgr. IBM Corp., N.Y.C., 1986-89; v.p. LaSalle Ptnrs. Ltd., Chgo., 1989-93; v.p. John Buck Co., Chgo., 1993, mng. dir., 1994, prin., 1995—; mng. dir. Mesinow Stein Real Estate Co., Chgo., 1996; bd. dirs. Heartland Alliance for Human Rights and Needs. Fellow Leadership Greater Chgo. Mem. Internat. Devel. Rsch. Coun., Met. Club. Avocations: family, skiing, travel, boating. Home: 601 N Elm St Hinsdale IL 60521-3540 Office: Mesinow Stein Real Estate Co Mesinow Stein Realty Co 227 W Monroe Chicago IL 60606

UTIGER, ROBERT DAVID, medical editor; b. Bridgeport, Conn., July 14, 1931; s. David Alfred and Aldine (Frey) U.; m. Sally Baldwin, Nov. 27, 1953; children: Jane, David, Nancy. A.B., Williams Coll., 1953; M.D., Washington U., 1957. Intern, resident in medicine Barnes Hosp., St. Louis, 1957-61; investigator Nat. Cancer Inst., Bethesda, Md., 1961-63; asst. prof. medicine Washington U. Sch. Medicine, 1963-69; assoc. prof. U. Pa. Sch. Medicine, Phila., 1969-73; prof. U. Pa. Sch. Medicine, 1973-79; prof. medicine U. N.C. Sch. Medicine, Chapel Hill, 1979-89; clin. prof. medicine Harvard Med. Sch., Boston, 1989—; dep. editor New Eng. Jour. Medicine, Boston, 1989—. Editor-in-chief: Jour. Clin. Endocrinology and Metabolism, 1983-89. Mem. Am. Soc. Clin. Investigation, Assn. Am. Physicians, Nat. Bd. Med. Examiners, Endocrine Soc., Phi Beta Kappa, Alpha Omega Alpha. Office: New Eng Jour Medicine 10 Shattuck St Boston MA 02115-6011

UTKU, SENOL, civil engineer, computer science educator; b. Suruc, Turkey, Nov. 23, 1931; s. Sukru and Sukufe (Gumus) U.; m. Bisulay Bereket, May 9, 1964; children: Ayda, Sinan. Dipl. Ing., Istanbul Tech. U., 1954; M.S., MIT, 1959, Sc.D., 1960. Civil engr., Istanbul, Turkey. Research engr. IBM, 1959-60; asst. prof. structural engring MIT, 1960-62; assoc. prof. Middle East Tech U., Ankara, Turkey, 1962-63; exec. dir. Computation Ctr., Istanbul Tech. U., 1963-65; mem. tech. staff Jet Propulsion Lab., Pasadena, Calif., 1965-70; assoc. prof. civil engring Duke U., Durham, N.C., 1970-72, prof., 1972-79, prof. civil engring., prof. computer sci., 1979—, dir. undergrad. studies, 1980-87, dir. grad. studies, 1987-89; sr. lectr. to Turkey, 1998. Author: Linear Analysis of Discrete Structures, 1991, Theory of Adaptive Structures (Static Part), 1995; co-author: Dynamics of Offshore Structures, 1984, Finite Element Handbook, 1987, Elementary Structural Analysis, 4th edit., 1991, Parallel Processing in Computational Mechanics, 1993, Intelligent Structural Systems, 1992; contbr. articles to profl. jours. Fulbright scholar, 1957 (Turkey); recipient Pres.'s fund Calif. Inst. Tech., 1981, award NASA, 1969, 71, 77, 84, 86, 87, Internat. Joint Rsch. award NSF, 1991-92. Fellow ASCE; mem. Acad. Mechanics, Fulbright Assn., Am. Soc. for Engring. Edn., Sigma Xi, Chi Epsilon. Home: 1843 Woodburn Rd Durham NC 27705-5754 Office: Duke U 134 Hudson Hall Durham NC 27708

UTLAUT, WILLIAM FREDERICK, electrical engineer; b. Sterling, Colo., July 26, 1922; s. Frederick Ernst and Francis Ruth Hanna U.; m. Jeanne Elizabeth Pomeroy, Aug. 4, 1946; children—Mark William, Niles Frederick, Paige Elizabeth. Utlaut Moore. B.S.E.E., U. Colo., 1944, M.S.E.E., 1950, Ph.D. in Elec. Engring, 1966; diploma, Naval Radar Sch., 1945. Engr. Gen. Electric Co., Schenectady, 1946-48, Nat. Bur. Standards, Boulder, Colo., 1952-53; instr. U. Colo., 1948-52, 53-54; dir. Inst. for Telecommunications Scis., U.S. Dept. Commerce, Boulder, 1954—; assoc. adminstr. Nat. Telecom and Info. Adminstrn., Boulder, 1980—; chmn. U.S. study group 1, Internat. Radio Consultative Com., 1975—, mem. U.S. nat. com., 1970-81; mem. electromagnetic wave propagation panel, adv. group aerospace research and devel. NATO, 1978-81, adv. com. Nat. Research Council, 1986—; chmn. ANSI-ECSA tech. com. on Integrated Services Digital Network, 1984—, U.S. nat. com. Internat. Consultative Com. on Telegraph and Telephone Joint Working Party, 1986—. Guest co-editor spl. joint issue: IEEE Trans. on Spectrum Mgmt, 1981, IEEE Trans. on Communications, 1975; guest editor spl. issue: Radio Sci, 1974; contbr. numerous articles to profl. jours. Bd. dirs. YMCA, 1955—; memb. bd. mgmt. 1st Congl. Ch., 1960-66, 78—; mem. engring. devel. council U. Colo., 1969-81. Served in USN, 1943-46. Recipient Gold medal U.S. Dept. Commerce, 1971, 95, Disting. Engring. Alumnus award U. Colo., 1973. Fellow IEEE (Harry Dimond Meml. award leadership radio sci. and engring. 1989, Presdl. Rank award 1990, 96, policy bd. Comm. Soc.), Internat. Sci. Radio Union, Am. Nat. Stds. Inst., Exch. Carriers Stds. Assn. Office: Inst for Telecom Scis US Dept Commerce 325 Broadway St Boulder CO 80303-3337*

UTLEY, F. KNOWLTON, library director, educator; b. Northampton, Mass., May 4, 1935; s. Frederick K. and Florence E. (Moore) U.; m. Faith E. Green, July 2, 1960; children: Richard F., Stephen R., David E. BS, Castleton State Coll., 1960; MA, U. Conn., 1967; EdD, Boston U., 1979; MLS, U. Ala., 1983. Tchr. indsl. arts Montpelier (Vt.) High Sch., 1960-61, Southwick (Mass.) High Sch., 1961-63; tchr., drafting instr. Putnam (Conn.) High Sch., 1963-68; media specialist Cen. Conn. State U., New Britain, 1968-69, dir. media svcs., 1969-72; doctoral teaching fellow Boston U., 1972-73; dir. libr., media svcs. Manchester (Mass.) Pub. Schs., 1973-79; assoc. prof. libr. scis. U. Maine, Farmington, 1979-80; dir. grad. program libr. media Livingston (Ala.) U., 1980-83; dir. libr. media svcs. Am. Internat. Coll., Springfield, Mass., 1983—; pres. C/W Mars-Cen. and Western Mass. Auto Res., 1987-88; chmn. bd. dirs. Cooperating Librs. of Great Springfield, 1988-89, Western Mass. Media Coun., 1991-93; founder, headmaster Hampshire Christian Acad., South Hadley, Mass., 1996—. Mem. ALA, Am. Christian Schs. Internat., Assn./Edn. Comm. and Tech. New Eng. Edn. Media Assn., New Eng. Libr. Assn., Mass. Sch. Libr. Media Assn., Mass. Libr. Assn., Phi Delta Kappa. Home: 11 Canal Dr Belchertown MA 01007-9224 Office: Am Internat Coll 1000 State St Springfield MA 01109-3151

UTNIK, DAVID ALAN, newspaper editor, journalist; b. June 17, 1960; s. Valentine Peter and Jessie Lenora (Land) U.; m. Pamela Annette Clyburn, May 11, 1991. BS in Journalism, Radford U., 1983. Sports reporter Md. Ind., Waldorf, 1983-84, Potomac News, Woodbridge, Va., 1984-85; sports info. dir. Radford (Va.) U., 1985-87; feature contbr. Radford U. Mag., 1986; sports editor Culpeper (Va.) Star Exponent, 1987-94, news editor, 1994-96, sports editor, 1987-94, 96—; guest lectr. AP seminar series, 1991; freelance writer Balls and Strikes Mag., 1992, Carolina League Beat, 1993; guest features writer AP, 1993-95. Coach Culpeper Little League, 1988—, fast pitch softball team Culpeper Recreation Dept., 1988-89, NCAA Div. I Women's Softball, Radford U., 1986-87; chmn. comm. Culpeper United Meth. Ch., 1993—. Recipient 1st place award Page Design and Column Writing Worrell Pub. Co., 1989, Layout and Sports Writing award Chesapeake Pub., 1984. Mem. Md.-Del.-D.C. Press Assn. (1st pl. feature photography award 1983), Coll. Sports Info. Dirs., Radford U. Sports Info., Va. Press Assn. (1st pl. column writing award 1988, 89, feature writing award 1987, 90, 1st pl. for page design 1989, 1st pl. sports event writing 1993, 1st pl. lifestyle writing 1993, sports page design award 1994, feature writing award 1994, sports news writing award 1994, 1st pl. editl. writing 1995, sports event writing award 1996, sports column writing award 1996, feature series writing award 1996), Soc. Collegiate Journalists (v.p. 1982). Avocations: baseball card collector, Wizard of Oz collector, softball player. Home: 124 W Mason St Culpeper VA 22701-3239 Office: Culpeper Star Exponent 122 W Spencer St Culpeper VA 22701-2628

UTROSKA, WILLIAM ROBERT, veterinarian; b. Greenwood, Miss., Oct. 21, 1946; s. Robert Julius and Ruth (McNeal) U.; m. Dian Anderson, Aug. 3, 1968; 1 child, Amy Elizabeth. BS, Miss. State U., 1968; DVM, Auburn U., 1971. Diplomate Am. Bd. Vet. Practitioners. Staff veterinarian Animal Hosp.-Brooks Rd., Memphis, 1971-73, Whitehaven Animal Hosp., Memphis, 1973-75; owner, operator Stateline Animal Clin., Southaven, Miss., 1975—; cons. VIP Products/Pet Chems., Memphis, 1984. Contbr. articles to profl. jours. Alderman City of Southaven, 1989—, mem. planning commn., 1980-89. Mem. Exchange Club (pres. 1978). Republican. Methodist. Avocations: flight instructor, golf. Home: 577 Litchfield Pl Southaven MS 38671-5926 Office: Stateline Animal Clin 100 Guthrie Dr Southaven MS 38671-5828

UTT, GLENN S., JR., motel investments and biotech industry company executive; b. Neodesha, Kans., Aug. 7, 1926; s. Glenn S. and Reba Pauline (White) U.; m. Mary Lou Ford, Aug. 8, 1948; 1 child, Jan A. B.S.E.E., BSBA, Kans. State U., 1949; M.B.A., Harvard U., 1951. Salesman Drexel Furniture Co., N.C., 1951-55; v.p. Booz Allen & Hamilton, Chgo. and Zurich, Switzerland, 1955-62; exec. v.p. Abbott Labs., North Chicago, Ill., 1962-83, also dir., ret., 1983; chmn. bd. Glendon Enterprises, Iron Mountain, Mich., Janmar Enterprises, Minocqua, Wis., Marjan Inc., Houghton, Mich., U.P. Hotel Group Inc., Houghton; bd. dirs. Sugen, Inc., Redwood City, Calif. Co-author: Lalique Perfume Bottles, 1990. Alderman City of Lake Forest, Ill., 1972-76, chmn. recreational bd., 1975-78; mem. exec. com. Lake County Republican Fedn., Waukegan, Ill., 1974-83. With USN, 1944-46. Mem. Beta Theta Pi. Avocations: antiques; objects of art. Home: PO Box 292 Palm Desert CA 92261-0292 Office: Janmar Enterprises PO Box 575 Minocqua WI 54548-0575

UTTAL, WILLIAM R(EICHENSTEIN), psychology and engineering educator, research scientist; b. Mineola, N.Y., Mar. 24, 1931; s. Joseph and Claire (Reichenstein) U.; m. Michiye Nishimura, Dec. 20, 1954; children: Taneil, Lynet, Lisa. Student, Miami U. Oxford, Ohio, 1947-48; B.S. in Physics, U. Cin., 1951; Ph.D. in Exptl. Psychology and Biophysics, Ohio State U., 1957. Staff Psychologist, mgr. behavioral sci. group IBM Research Center, Yorktown Heights, N.Y., 1957-63; assoc. prof. U. Mich., Ann Arbor, 1963-68, prof. psychology, 1968-86, research scientist, 1963-86, prof. emeritus, 1986—; grad. affiliate faculty dept. psychology U. Hawaii, 1986-88; research scientist Naval Ocean Systems Ctr.-Hawaii Lab., Kailua, 1985-88; prof., chmn. dept. psychology Ariz. State U., Tempe, 1988-92, prof. dept. indsl. and mgmt. systems engring., 1992—, affiliated prof., Dept. of Computer Sci. and Engring., 1993—; vis. prof. Kyoto (Japan) Prefectural Med. U., 1965-66, Sensory Sci. Lab., U. Hawaii, 1968, 73, U. Western Australia, 1970-71, U. Hawaii, 1978-79, 80-81, U. Auckland, 1996, U. Freiburg, 1997; pres. Nat. Conf. on On-Line Uses Computers in Psychology, 1974. Author: Real Time Computers: Techniques and Applications in the Psychological Sciences, 1968, Generative Computer Assisted Instruction in Analytic Geometry, 1972, The Psychobiology of Sensory Coding, 1973, Cellular Neurophysiology and Integration: An Interpretive Introductin, 1975, An Autocorrelation Theory of Visual Form Detection, 1975, The Psychobiology of Mind, 1978, A Taxonomy of Visual Processes, 1981, Visual Form Detection in Three Dimensional Space, 1983, Principles of Psychobiology, 1983, The Detection of Nonplanar Surfaces in Visual Space, 1985, The Perception of Dotted Forms, 1987, On Seeing Forms, 1988, The Swimmer: A Computational Model of a Perceptual Motor System, 1992, Toward a New Behaviorism: The Case Against Perceptual Reductionism, 1997; also numerous articles; editor: Readings in Sensory Coding, 1972; assoc. editor Behavioral Research Method and Instrn., 1968-90, Computing: Archives for Electronic Computing, 1963-75, Jour. Exptl. Psychology: Perception and Performance, 1974-79; cons. editor Jour. Exptl. Psychology: Applied, 1994—. Served to 2d lt. USAF, 1951-53. USPHS spl. postdoctoral fellow, 1965-66; NIMH research scientist award, 1971-76. Fellow AAAS, Am. Psychol. Soc. (charter), Soc. Exptl. Psychologists (chmn. 1994-95); mem. Psychonomics Soc. Patentee in field. Office: Ariz State U Dept Indsl and Mgmt Systems Engring Tempe AZ 85287-1104

UTTER, ROBERT FRENCH, retired state supreme court justice; b. Seattle, June 19, 1930; s. John and Besse (French) U.; m. Elizabeth J. Stevenson, Dec. 28, 1953; children: Kimberly, Kirk, John. BS, U. Wash., 1952; LLB, 1954. Bar: Wash. 1954. Pros. atty. King County, Wash., 1955-57; individual practice law Seattle, 1957-59; ct. commr. King County Superior Ct., 1959-64, judge, 1964-69; judge Wash. State Ct. Appeals, 1969-71; judge Wash. State Supreme Ct., 1971-95, chief justice, 1979-81; ret., 1995; lectr. in field, leader comparative law tour People's Republic of China, 1986, 87, 88, 91, USSR, 1989; adj. prof. constl. law U. Puget Sound, 1987, 88, 89, 90, 91, 92, 93, 94; cons. CEELI, 1991, 93—, USIA, 1992; visitor to Kazakhstand and Kyrgystan Judiciary, 1993, 94, 95, 96; lectr. to Albanian Judiciary, 1994, 95. Editor books on real property and appellate practice. Pres., founder Big Brother Assn., Seattle, 1955-67; pres., founder Job Therapy Inc., 1963-71; mem. exec. com. Conf. of Chief Justices, 1979-80, 81-86; pres. Thurston County Big Bros./Big Sisters, 1984; lectr. Soviet Acad. Moscow, 1991; USIA visitor to comment on jud. system, Latvia, 1992, Kazakstan, 1993-94; trustee Linfield Coll. Named Alumnus of Yr., Linfield Coll., 1973, Disting. Jud. Scholar, U. Ind., 1987, Judge of Yr., Wash. State Trial Lawyers, 1989, Outstanding Judge, Wash. State Bar Assn., 1990, Outstanding Judge, Seattle-King County Bar Assn., 1992, Conder-Faulkner lectr. U. Wash. Sch. Law, 1995, Disting. Alumnus Sch. Law U. Wash., 1995. Mem. ABA (commentator on proposed constns. of Albania, Bulgaria, Romania, Russia, Lithuania, Azerbaijan, Uzbekistan, Byelarus, Kazakhstan & Ukraine), Am. Judicature Soc. (Herbert Harley award 1983, sec. 1987—, chmn. bd. dirs., mem. exec. com.), Order of Coif. Baptist.

UUKAS, RONALD, publishing executive. Pres. Jour. Porperty Mgmt., Chgo. Office: Jour Property Mgmt 430 N Michigan Ave Chicago IL 60611-4002

UVENA, FRANK JOHN, retired printing company executive, lawyer; b. Ernest, Pa., Feb. 2, 1934. AB, Ohio U., Athens, 1959; LLB, Ohio State U., Columbus, 1963. Bar: Ill. 1963. Assoc. firm McDermott, Will & Emery, Chgo., 1963-68; atty. R.R. Donnelley & Sons, Chgo., 1968-75, v.p., gen. counsel, 1975-84, sr. v.p. law and corp. staffs, 1984-95. Bd. dirs. Infant Welfare League Chgo., 1995, Am. Liver Soc., Chgo., 1996, Parents/Friends Elizabeth Ludeman Devel. Ctr., 1996. With AUS, 1954-56. Mem. AMA, Ill. Bar Assn., Chgo. Bar Assn.

UY, PHILIP M., aeronautical engineer; b. Catanduanes, Philippines, July 10, 1956; came to U.S., 1980; s. Mariano J. and Roqueta (Madrid) U.; m. Lisa G. Kelly, Jan. 1, 1982; children: Andre, Ethan, Randi Jo, Melanie, Meagan, Morgan. BS in Aero. Engring., Feati U., Manila, 1977. Video technician IBYC, Chgo., 1982; test technician Tandy Home Computer, Ft. Worth, 1982-83; test supr. Deutsch Relays, Inc., East Northport, N.Y., 1983-86; program mgr. Optronic Devices, Inc., Hauppauge, N.Y., 1986-96; mgr. Coherent Comm. Sys. Corp., Hauppauge, 1996—. Avocation: camping. Home: 19 Willow Pl Lake Ronkonkoma NY 11779-2246 Office: Coherent Comm Sys Corp 60 Commerce Dr Hauppauge NY 11788-3929

UYEDA, SEIYA, geophysics educator; b. Tokyo, Nov. 28, 1929; s. Seiichi and Hatsuo (Okino) U.; m. Mutsuko Kosaka, July 6, 1952; children: Taro, Makiko, Naoko. BS, U. Tokyo, 1952, DSc, 1958; DSc (hon.), U. Athens, Greece, 1996. Rsch. assoc. Earthquake Rsch. Inst. U. Tokyo, 1957-64, assoc. prof. Geophys. Inst., 1964-69, prof. Earthquake Rsch. Inst., 1969-90; prof. dept. marine sci. and tech. Tokai U., Shimizu, Japan, 1990-94, dir. earthquake prediction rsch. ctr., 1995-96; prof. Tex. A&M U., College Station, 1990-95; rsch. leader Internat. Frontier Program on Earthquake Rsch. Riken, 1996—. Author: Debate About the Earth, 1966, Island Arcs, 1973, The New View of the Earth, 1978. Recipient Tanakadte prize Soc. Terrestial

Magnetism and Electricity, 1955, G.P. Woollard award Geol. Soc. Am., 1989, Matsumae Prize for Academic Accomplishment, Tokai Univ., 1992. Fellow AAAS (hon.), Nat. Acad. Sci. (fgn. assoc., A Agassiz medal 1972), Russian Acad. Scis. (fgn.), Geol. Soc. London (hon.), European Union Geoscis. (hon.), Am. Geophys. Union (Walter Bucher medal 1991); mem. Am. Acad. Arts and Scis. (fgn.), Soc. Geology France (assoc.), Japan Acad. (Acad. prize 1987). Home: 2-39-6 Daizawa, Setagaya-ku, Tokyo 155, Japan Office: Tokai U, 3-20-1, Orido, Shimizu 424, Japan

UYEHARA, CATHERINE FAY TAKAKO (YAMAUCHI), physiologist, educator, pharmacologist; b. Honolulu, Dec. 20, 1959; d. Thomas Takashi and Eiko (Haraguchi) Uyehara; m. Alan Hisao Yamauchi, Feb. 17, 1990. BS, Yale U., 1981; PhD in Physiology, U. Hawaii, Honolulu, 1987. Postdoctoral fellow SmithKline Beecham Pharms., King of Prussia, Pa., 1987-89; asst. prof. in pediatrics U. Hawaii John Burns Sch. Medicine, Honolulu, 1991—; rsch. pharmacologist Kapiolani Med. Ctr. for Women and Children, Honolulu, 1990—; statis. cons. Tripler Army Med. Ctr., Honolulu, 1984-87, 89—, chief rsch. pharmacology , 1991—, dir. coop. rsch. and devel. projects, 1995—; asst. prof. pharmacology U. Hawaii John A. Burns Sch. Medicine, 1993—; grad. faculty Interdisciplinary Biomed. Sci. program, 1995—. Contbr. articles to profl. jours. Mem. Am. Fedn. Clin. Rsch., Am. Physiol. Soc., Soc. Uniformed Endocrinologists, Endocrine Soc., We. Soc. Pediatric Rsch., N.Y. Acad. Scis. Democrat. Mem. Christian Ch. Avocations: swimming, diving, crafts, horticulture, music. Office: Tripler Army Med Ctr Dept Clin Investigation MCHK-CI 1 Jarrett White Rd Rm 131 Tripler Army HI 96859-5000

UYEHARA, HARRY YOSHIMI, library educator; b. Honolulu, Jan. 6, 1934; s. Saburo and Uto (Yamashiro) U. BEd, U. Hawaii, 1958; AMLS, U. Mich., 1965; MA, Columbia U., 1970, EdD, 1978. Cert. sch. libr., media specialist. Tchr., libr. Waiakea-Kai Elem. & Intermediate Sch., Hilo, Hawaii, 1960-61; libr. Wahiawa (Hawaii) Intermediate Sch., 1961-66; program specialist Hawaii State Dept. of Edn., Honolulu, 1966-76; asst. prof. library studies U. Hawaii, Honolulu, 1976-83; dean U. Guam, Mangilao, 1983-89; assoc. prof. libr. and info. studies U. Hawaii, Honolulu, 1989-91; assoc. prof. Edn. U. Guam, Mangilao, 1991-93; prof. libr. faculty Guam C.C., Mangilao, 1994-96, ret., 1997; mem. in-svc. adv. coun. Hawaii State Dept. of Edn., Honolulu, 1977-80, adv. coun. of librs. Guam Pub. Libr., Agana, 1983-89. Editor (jours.) HLA Jour., 1978, The Golden Key, 1981, 82. With U.S. Army, 1958-60. Mem. Hawaii Libr. Assn. (pres. 1977-78), Hawaii Assn. Sch. Librs. (pres. 1982-83), Guam Libr. Assn. (pres. 1984-85), Phi Delta Kappa, Kappa Delta Pi. Home: 710 Lunalio St Apt 1208 Honolulu HI 96813

UYEHARA, OTTO ARTHUR, mechanical engineering educator emeritus, consultant; b. Hanford, Calif., Sept. 9, 1916; s. Rikichi and Umi (Nakayama) U.; m. Chisako Suda, Aug. 12, 1945; children: Otto Kenneth, Susan Joy Uyehara Schultheiss, Emi Ryu Uyehara-Stewart. BS, U. Wis., 1942, MS, 1943, PhD, 1946. Postdoctoral fellow U. Wis., Madison, 1945-46, rsch. assoc., 1946-47, asst. prof., then assoc. prof., 1949-57, prof., 1957-82, prof. emeritus, 1982—; pvt. practice cons. Anaheim, Calif., 1985—; mem. sci. adv. com. Eclin Corp., Branford, Conn., 1980—. Recipient Sci. Achievement award Japan Soc. Automotive Engrs, Internal Combustion Engine award ASME, 1994. FEllow Soc. Automotive Engrs.; mem. ASME (internal combustion divsn., Internal Combustion award 1994), Japan Soc. Mech. Engrs. (hon.). Home: 544 S Bond St Anaheim CA 92805-4823

UYEMOTO, JERRY KAZUMITSU, plant pathologist, educator; b. Fresno, Calif., May 27, 1939; married, 1965; 1 child. BS in Agronomy, U. Calif., Davis, 1962, MS in Plant Pathology, 1964, PhD in Plant Pathology, 1968. Lab. tech. U. Calif., Davis, 1964-66; from asst. to assoc. prof. virology N.Y. State Agrl. Expt. Sta., Cornell U., 1968-77; prof. Kansas State U., Manhattan, 1977-81; sr. staff scientist Advanced Genetic Scis., 1982-84; vis. scientist U. Calif., Davis, 1984-86, rsch. plant pathology, USDA Agrl. Rsch. Svc., 1986—. Recipient Lee M. Hutchins award Am. Phytopath. Soc., 1993. Mem. Assn. Applied Biologists, Am. Phytopath Soc.. Achievements include research on a variety of crop plants; research contributions were also made on virus diseases of pome, stone fruit, and annual crop plants; ELISA protocols tested and/or established for serological indexing of ilarviruses in all Prunus tree sources used for scion buds and seeds. Office: UC-Davis Dept Plant Path USDA ARS Davis CA 95616

UYGUR, MUSTAFA ETI, materials and mechanical engineering educator; b. Kayseri, Turkey, Jan. 22, 1941; s. Ali and Mumine (Oktay) U.; m. Selime Kobakci, Dec. 16, 1971; children: Ayse, Esra, Zeynep, Ali. BSME, Mid. East Tech. U., Ankara, Turkey, 1963, MSc in Mech. Engring., 1964; MSc in Engring., Purdue U., 1967; PhD in Materials Sci. & Engring., Mid. East Tech. U., Ankara, Turkey, 1971. Rsch. assoc. Am. Oil Co. Rsch. Labs., Whiting, Ind., 1967; instr. Mid. East Tech. U., Ankara, Turkey, 1967-71, asst. prof., 1971-77, assoc. prof., 1977-84; prof. Gazi U., Ankara, Turkey, 1984-90; prof. mech. engring. dept. King Saud U., Riyadh, Saudi Arabia, 1990—; asst. chmn. materials sci. and engring. dept. Mid. East Tech. U., Ankara, 1977-80; dep. dean faculty tech. edn. Gazi U., Ankara, 1984-86, mem. coll. coun., grad. coll. coun., univ. senate, 1984-90; tech. & sci. advisor to dep. Min. of Nat. Def., Def. Industries Devel. Adminstrn., Ankara, 1987-90. Author: Dynamic NDT of Materials, 1976, 83, Glossary of Powder Metallurgy Terms, 1982, X-Ray Crystallography, 1983, CD-Materials Sci & Engring, 1997; editor-in-chief: Science-Research-Technology Five-Year Main Plan, 1988; contbr. over 90 articles to profl. jours. and conf. procs.; supr. for devel. of many ednl. computer programs. Mem. specialization com. on nonferrous materials State Planning Orgn., Ankara, 1982, chmn. specialization com. on transfer of high tech. and employment, 1987-88, mem. specialization com. on sci. rsch., tech., 1987-88, chmn. editl. com. on sci., rsch., tech., 1988. Lt. (engr.) Turkish Army Tech. Svc.-Weapons Dept., 1973-74. Scholar Turkish Iron-Steel Works, 1963-64; rsch. grantee Turkish Sci. Rsch. Coun., 1971-73. Mem. Internat. Plansee Soc. Powder Metallurgy, Internat. Soc. Crystallographers, Am. Powder Metallurgy Inst. Internat., Am. Soc. for Metals Internat., Am. Soc. for Metals Internat.-Metall. Soc. Avocations: reading in all areas, listening to music, computers and programming, swimming, bowling. Office: King Saud U Coll Engring, PO Box 800, 11421 Riyadh Saudi Arabia

UYTERHOEVEN, HUGO EMIL ROBERT, business educator and consultant; b. Eindhoven, The Netherlands, Aug. 6, 1931; came to U.S., 1955, naturalized, 1967; s. Willem and An (Von der Nahmer) U.; children: Monique, An, Sonia, Laura. D Iur, U. Zurich, 1955; D in law, U. Ghent, 1955; MBA, Harvard U., 1957, DBA, 1963. Mem. faculty Grad. Sch. Bus. Adminstrn. Harvard U., 1960—, Timken prof. bus. adminstrn. Grad. Sch. Bus. Adminstrn., 1974—, sr. assoc. dean Grad. Sch. Bus. Adminstrn., 1980-89; bd. dirs. The Stanley Works, Harcourt Gen., Inc., Bombardier, Inc., Ecolab, Inc.. Author: (with others) Strategy and Organization: Text and Cases in General Management, 1973, 2d edit., 1977, Business Policy, 8th edit., 1995. Mem. Planning Bd. Weston (Mass.), 1969-72, Conservation Commn., 1972-76; pres. Weston Forest and Trail Assn., 1970-77; trustee Concord Acad., 1982-88. Belgian-Am. Ednl. Found. fellow, 1955-57. Office: Harvard U Sch Bus Boston MA 02163

UZAN, BERNARD, general and artistic director; b. Tunis, Tunisia, Dec. 5, 1944; arrived in Can., 1988; s. Henri and Elise Gabrielle (Pansieri) U.; m. Diana Soviero, Nov. 9, 1984. PhD, Paris U., 1968. Gen. & artistic dir. Théâtre français d'Amérique, Boston, 1973-83, Tulsa Opera, 1987-88, L'Opéra de Montreal, Que., Can., 1988—; adminstr., exec. dir. Alliance français de Boston, 1974-83; stage dir.: U.S.: San Francisco, Fla., Phila., New Orleans, Portland, Dallas, others; Can.: Montreal, Toronto, Vancouver, Ottawa, Quebec City, Edmonton, Calgary, Winnipeg; Europe: Monte-Carlo, Zurich, Palermo, Turin, others. Office: L'Opéra de Montréal, 260 de Maisonneuve W, Montreal, PQ Canada H2X 1Y9

UZENDA, JARA CARLOW, technical writer; b. Brookline, Mass., May 24, 1946; d. Roscoe William and Gloria Pauline (St. Jacques) Carlow; m. William Anthony Perry, June 1, 1963 (dec. Dec. 1971); children: Troy Anthony, William Lance, Richard A. Student, R.I. Jr. Coll., 1965-67, U. R.I., 1967-68; BS in Journalism, U. Colo., 1975, MS in Telecommunications, 1978. Mktg. mgr. Humidor Smoke Shoppes, Warwick, R.I., 1965-69; telecommunication cons. Arthur D. Little, Inc., Boston, 1976-78; dir. research Horizon House Internat., Boston, 1978-80; market analyst Internat. Telecommunications, Boulder, Colo., 1980-81; field service engr. Allied Info. Systems, Boulder, 1981-83; gen. ptnr. Kentucky Gold Ltd., San Jose, Calif., 1984; sr. tech. writer Paradyne Corp., Largo, Fla., 1984-86; sales and mktg. Piedmont Airlines Golf Resort Directory, Myrtle Beach, S.C., 1986-87; cons. Data Security, Little River, S.C., 1987—; v.p. mktg. So. Golfer, 1989—; pres. 110% Inc., Myrtle Beach, 1994—; vis. prof. Prescott Coll., Flagstaff, Ariz., 1972; film dir. Niel Minority News, Estes Park, Colo., 1973-74; featured artist Denver Post, 1973; spl. expert Latin Am. Telecommunications, Washington, 1980. Author: Electronic Fund Transfer, 1978; contbr. articles to jours. Grantee Nat. Endowment Arts, 1973. Mem. Coun. Internat. Rels. and UN Affairs, Internat. Rels. Club, Soc. Women Engrs., U. Colo. Alumni Assn., Mortar Bd., Optimists, Civitans. Lodge: Optimists. Avocations: golf, computer programming, flying, boating. Home: Lyons Cove III 407 Chesterfield Ct Myrtle Beach SC 29577-8025

UZMAN, BETTY GEREN, pathologist, retired educator; b. Fort Smith, Ark., Nov. 17, 1922; d. Benton Asbury and Myra Estelle (Petty) Geren; m. L. Lahut Uzman, Dec. 17, 1955 (dec.); 1 dau., Betty Tuba. Student, Fort Smith Jr. Coll., 1939-40; B.S., U. Ark., 1942; M.D., Washington U., 1945; postgrad., M.I.T., 1948-50; M.A. (hon.), Harvard U., 1967. Intern Childrens Hosp., Boston, 1945-46; resident in pathology Barnes Hosp., St. Louis, 1946-48; Am. Cancer Soc. research fellow MIT, Cambridge, Mass., 1948-50; chief biol. ultrastructure and exptl. pathology Children's Cancer Research Found., Boston, 1950-71; instr. Harvard Med. Sch., Boston, 1949-53, assoc., 1953-56, research assoc., 1956-67, assoc. prof., 1967-71, prof., 1971-72; head research dept. Sparks Regional Med. Center, Fort Smith, 1972-74; prof. pathology La. State U., Shreveport, 1974-77, U. Tenn., Memphis, 1978-89; assoc. chief staff rsch. VA, Shreveport, 1974-77; staff pathologist VA, Memphis, 1978-89, chief lab. svc., 1986-87; chief field ops., spl. asst. to dir. VA Central Office, Washington, 1978-79, dir. med. rsch. svcs., 1979-80; chmn. pathology A Study sect. NIH, 1973-76; cons. to sci. dir. Children's Cancer Rsch. Found., Boston, 1971-73; mem. adv. com. on prevention, diagnosis and treatment Am. Cancer Soc., 1970-73, 77-80; mem. adv. bd. Office Regeneration Rsch., VA, 1985-89; disting. vis. investigator Inst. Venezolano Investigation Cientificas, Caracas, 1972-74. Decorated Order of Andres Bello 1st class Venezuela; recipient Weinstein award United Cerebral Palsy, 1964; Am. Cancer Soc. research fellow, 1948-50. Mem. AAAS, Am. Soc. Cell Biology, Soc. Devel. Biology, Am. Acad. Neurology (assoc.), Am. Soc. Neurochemistry, Microscopy Soc. Am. (Diatome poster award 1985), Internat. Acad. Pathology, Am. Assn. Neuropathology (assoc.), Soc. Neurosci., Am. Assn. Cancer Rsch. Home and Office: Geren Farm 16048 E State Highway 197 Scranton AR 72863-9271

UZSOY, PATRICIA J., nursing educator and administrator; b. Corning, Ark.; m. Namik K. Diploma, Mo. Bapt. Hosp. Sch. Nursing, St. Louis, 1960; BSN, Washington U., St. Louis, 1962; MEd, Lynchburg Coll., 1977, EdS, 1981; MS in Nursing, U. Va., 1987. RN, Va. Dean Schs. of Nursing Lynchburg (Va.) Gen. Hosp. Mem. ANA, NLN, Va. Nurses Assn. (Nurse of Yr. dist. III 1987).

UZZELL-BAGGETT, KARON LYNETTE, career officer; b. Goldsboro, N.C., Apr. 28, 1964; d. Jesse Lee and Ernestine Smith (Merriweathers) Uzzell; m. Ronald Walter Baggett, July 26, 1990; stepchildren: Christina, Brian, Adam. BS, U. N.C., 1986; postgrad., U. Md., 1993-96. Commd. 2d lt. USAF, 1986, advanced through grades to capt., 1990; exec. officer 6ACCS USAF, Langley AFB, Va., 1986-88; ops. tng. officer 7393MUNSS USAF, Murted AFD, Turkey, 1988-89; command and control officer 52FW USAF, Spangdahlem AB, Germany, 1989-92; SENEX mission dir. 89AW USAF, Andrews AFB, Md., 1992-95, dep. chief classified control Office Sec. Def., 1995—. Emergency med. technician Orange County Rescue Squad, Hillsborough, N.C., 1985-86; treas. Melwood PTA, Upper Marlboro, Md., 1994-97; meml. vol. Women in Mil. Svc., Washington, 1993—; entitlements vol. Whitman Walker Clinic, Washington, 1993—. Mem. Women in Mil. Svc. for Am., So. Poverty Law Ctr. Democrat. Baptist. Avocations: running, weightlifting, sewing, cross stitching, gardening. Home: 10704 Tyrone Dr Upper Marlboro MD 20772-4631

VAADIA, BOAZ, sculptor; b. Petah-Tiqva, Israel, Nov. 13, 1951; s. Nissim and Rivka Vaadia; m. Kim Turner, Sept. 10, 1989; children: Rebecca Danielle, Sara Madeline. Student, Avni Inst. Fine Art, Tel Aviv, 1971. vis. artist Appalachian State U., Boone, N.C., 1982; resident Internat. Tel-Hai '80 Internat. Meeting, Israel, 1980. One-person shows include O.K. Harris Works of Art, N.Y.C., 1986, 88, 89, 94, Helander Gallery, Palm Beach, Fla., 1988, Jewish Mus., N.Y.C., 1988-89, Hokin Kaufman Gallery, Chgo., 1989, 90, Fay Gold Gallery, 1993, Allene Lapides Gallery, Santa Fe, 1995, Jaffe Baker Gallery, Fla., 1996, 97, Imago Gallery, Calif., 1997, others; exhibited group shows at Helander Gallery, 1989-90, Utsukushi-ga-hara Open Air Mus., Japan, 1994, First Lady's Sculpture Garden, White House, 1995, Buschlen Mowatt Fine Arts, Vancouver, B.C., 1996, Philharm. Ctr. for the Arts, Naples, Fla., 1996, 97, among others. Grantee NEA, 1988, Ariana Found. for Arts, 1986, Artists Space, 1983, Am.-Israel Cultural Found., 1975-76, Am. the Beautiful Fund, Palisades Internstate Park, 1977; Beeckman scholar, 1976-77. Home: 475 Broadway # 7flr New York NY 10013-5905 Studio: 104 Berry St Brooklyn NY 11211-2806

VACANO, JOST, cinematographer. Cinematographer: (films) Soldier of Orange, 1977, Spetters, 1980, Das Boot, 1981, The Neverending Story, 1984, 52 Pick-up, 1986, Robocop, 1987, Rocket Gibraltar, 1988, Total Recall, 1990, Untamed Heart, 1993, Showgirls, 1995. Office: The Skouras Agy 725 Arizona Ave Ste 406 Santa Monica CA 90401*

VACCA, JOHN JOSEPH, JR., television executive; b. Chgo., Apr. 7, 1922; s. John Joseph and Caroline (Bain) V.; m. Alice Isabel Ure, May 2, 1944; children: John Joseph, Dawn Susan, Kim Frances. Student, Northwestern U., 1940-42, Internat. Corr. Schs., 1950-54, Harvard U., 1966. Editor, Midwest Times, Chgo., 1940-41; with prodn. dept. NBC Radio, 1946-47; news dir. sta. KECK, Odessa, Tex., 1947-49; chief announcer sta. KECK, 1948-49; program mgr. KOSA-Radio, Odessa, 1949-55; sta. mgr. KOSA-TV, 1955-61, gen. mgr., 1962-72; v.p., dir. Trigg Vaughn Stas., Inc., Odessa, 1962-67; sec. Odessa Broadcasting Co., 1950-72; asst. sec. Doubleday Broadcasting Co., 1967-77, v.p., 1967-75, sr. v.p., 1975-77; gen. mgr. KDTV, Dallas, 1972-73; TV cons. Dallas, 1978—; v.p., dir., gen. mgr. Heart O'Texas Broadcasting, Waco, Tex., 1978-83; v.p. Dunn Prodns., Inc., Dallas, 1984-88, pres., 1989-92; ind. TV producer Dallas, 1992—. Author: Seven Keys to Success, 1981. Bd. dirs. Odessa Community Chest, 1964-72, Better Bus. Bur., 1956-72; campaign maj. ARC, 1951-72; publicity adviser Ector County chpt. Nat. Found. for Infantile Paralysis, 1949-72; campaign coordinator Civic Music Assn., 1950-72; sponsor, adviser Permian Playhouse, 1959-72, v.p., bd. dirs., 1971-72, City councilman, Odessa, 1962-64; Bd. dirs. Am. Cancer Soc. Served with USAAF, 1942-46. Recipient Zeus award Epsilon Sigma Alpha, 1971. Mem. Nat., Tex. assns. broadcasters, Tex. AP Broadcasters Assn., Advt. Club Odessa (pres. 1960-61, dir. 1960-63), C. of C. (publicity adviser 1950-72), Holy Name Soc. Roman Catholic. Club: K.C. (sec. Odessa 1950-51). Home and Office: 646 Harvest Hill Ln Lewisville TX 75067-3588 *A philosophy of service, personal and through broadcasting, coupled with a sincere approach to excellent Human Relations have formed the keystone of my career. Consistent honesty and a constant effort to give and produce much more than required have always been guiding principles. My goals have been set with flexible policies to implement them, ever mindful that 'change' is an integral part of life and progress.*

VACCARO, LOUIS CHARLES, college president; b. L. A., July 25, 1930; s. Louis Charles and Louise (Vinciguerra) V.; m. Jean Hudak, Jan. 29, 1955 (div. Aug. 1983); children: Mary Lou, Theresa, Victoria, Frances, Michelle, Justin; m. Linda Lasher, July, 1987. A.B., U. So. Calif., 1957, M.Ed., 1961; M.A., Calif. State U.-Northridge, 1960; Ph.D., Mich. State U., 1963; Litt.D. (hon.), St. Martin's Coll., Olympia, Wash., 1969; L.H.D. (hon.), Vt. Coll. of Norwich U., Montpelier, 1978; LLD (hon.), Coll. of St. Rose, Albany, N.Y., 1996. Asst. to v.p. acad. affairs Marquette U., Milw., 1963-67; v.p. acad. affairs U. Portland, Oreg., 1967-70; pres. Marycrest Coll., Davenport, Iowa, 1970-72, Colby-Sawyer Coll., New London, N.H., 1972-77, Siena Heights Coll., Adrian, Mich., 1977-83, Coll. of St. Rose, 1983—; bd. dirs. Inst. Internat. Edn., N.Y.C., 1977, First Albany Asset Mgmt. Corp. Author: Notes from a College President, 1976, Planning in Small Colleges, 1979, In Search of Wisdom, 1994; editor: Student Freedom in American Higher Education, 1969, Reshaping American Higher Education, 1969. Bd. dirs. Albany Strategic Planning, 1983—, Albany Symphony Orch., 1984—; mem. Tricentennial Commn. City of Albany, 1986—; chmn. Bicentennial Commn. U.S. Constn. City of Albany, 1987. Served with USAF, 1951-52. W. K. Kellogg Found. fellow Mich. State U., East Lansing, 1961-63; Exxon Found. grantee, 1975. Mem. Nat. Cath. Edn. Assn. (exec. com., chair bd. dirs.), Hudson-Mohawk Consortium Colls., Ft. Orange Club, Univ. Club. Roman Catholic. Avocations: reading; walking; Italian cooking; travel; racquet sports. Home: 47 Mordella Rd Albany NY 12205

VACCARO, RALPH FRANCIS, marine biologist; b. West Somerville, Mass., Apr. 30, 1919; s. Angelo Ralph and Adelaide (Alberlini) V.; m. Martha Ann Walsh, Apr. 19, 1955; children: Christopher Ralph, Adelaide Marie, John Michael, Mark Joseph, Thomas James (dec.), Peter Anthony. B.S., Tufts U., 1941; M.P.H., MIT, 1943. Sanitary engring. aide Commonwealth of Mass., Boston, 1946-47; pub. health bacteriologist Assn. Am. Railroads, Balt., 1947-48; sr. rsch. scientist Woods Hole Oceanographic Inst. (Mass.), 1948-86, chmn. dept. biol., 1984-85; cons. environ. quality; assoc. math.-sci. staff Falmouth (Mass.) High Sch., 1989—. Patentee in field. Served with USPHS, 1956—; served with U.S. Army, 1943-46. Mem. Am. Soc. Limnology and Oceanography, AAAS. Republican. Roman Catholic. Home: PO Box 245 West Falmouth MA 02574-0245

VACCO, DENNIS C., state attorney general; b. Buffalo, Aug. 16, 1952; s. Carmen A. and Mildred V.; m. Adrienne Venczel (div.). BA, Colgate U., 1974; JD, SUNY, Buffalo, 1978. Bar: N.Y. 1978, Fed. Ct. 1978, 82. Asst. dist. atty. Office of Erie County Dist. Atty., Buffalo, 1978-82, chief G.J. bureau, 1982-88; U.S. Atty. We. Dist. N.Y. Buffalo, 1988—; now Atty. Gen. State of New York, Albany; chmn. Atty. Gen.'s Environ. Subcom., Atty. Gen.'s Subcom. on Organized Crime and Violent Crime; mem. Nat. Environ. Enforcement Coun. Co-chair Erie County Community Commn. on Alcohol and Substance Abuse; bd. dirs. United Way of Erie County. Recipient Environ. Enforcement Leadership award Atty. Gen. Dept. of Justice, Washington, 1991. Mem. N.Y. State Bar Assn., Erie County Bar Assn., Nat. Dist. Attys. Assn., N.Y. State Dist. Attys. Assn., NCCJ, Hamburg Devel. Corp., 100 Club of Buffalo, U. Buuffalo Law Alumni Assn. (bd. dirs.). Republican. Roman Catholic. Avocations: travel, sports. Office: Off of Atty Gen State Capitol Rm 220 Albany NY 12224*

VACHHER, PREHLAD SINGH, psychiatrist; b. Rawalpindi, Punjab, Pakistan, Nov. 30, 1933; came to U.S., 1960; s. Thakar Singh and Harbans Kaur (Ghai) V.; m. Margaret Mary Begley, Oct. 9, 1963; children: Paul, Sheila, Mary Ann, Eileen, Mark. Grad., Khalsa Coll., India, 1950; MD, Panjab U., Amritsar, India, 1956. Diplomate Am. Bd. Psychiatry. Staff N.J. State Hosp., Trenton, 1965-66, Wayne County Gen. Hosp., Eloise, Mich., 1966-68; pvt. practice Livonia, Mich., 1966-75, Woodstock, Va., 1991—; pres. Vachher Psychiat. Ctr., P.C., Livonia, 1975-91; dir. community psychiatry Northville (Mich.) State Hosp., 1968-71; cons. staff Kingswood Hosp., Ferndale, Mich., 1967-72, Annapolis Hosp., Wayne, 1967-88, St. Joseph Mercy Hosp., Ann Arbor, 1970-89; westland staff Margaret Montgomery Hosp., 1988-91; bd. dirs. Oakland Rental Housing Assn., 1990-91; med. dir. mental health unit Shenandoah County Meml. Hosp., Woodstock, Va., 1991-94. Mem. Am. Psychiat. Assn., Va. Psychiat. Soc., Sikh Physicians in Mich. (bd. dirs. 1987), Canton C. of C. (pres. 1975), Sikh Bus. Profl. Coun. (pres. 1988—), Rotary (Canton and Plymouth, Mich., Woodstock), Prince William County C. of C. Office: 14573 Potomac Mills Rd Woodbridge VA 22192-6808

VACHHER, SHEILA ANN, information systems analyst; b. Trenton, N.J., May 27, 1966; d. Prehlad Singh and Margaret Mary (Begley) V. BA magna cum laude, U. Mich., 1988; MBA, Tex. A&M U., 1993. Retirement accounts rep. Gt. Lakes Bancorp., Ann Arbor, Mich., 1988-89, 91; strategic planning and fin. analyst Ricoh Corp., West Caldwell, N.J., 1993-95, sr. tech. planning and control analyst, 1996-97; sr. systems analyst Ricoh Corp., West Caldwell, 1997—; career ctr. adv. coun. Tex. A&M U., College Station, 1993. Recipient Regents Alumni scholarship, 1984, Women's Club of Plymouth scholarship, 1984, James B. Angell scholar U. Mich., 1986-87, Otto Graf scholarship U. Mich., 1987-88, Lechner fellowship Tex. A&M U., 1991-92, scholarship Tex. A&M U. Coll. Bus. Adminstrn., 1992, Washington Campus scholarship Tex. A&M U., 1992. Mem. NAFE, Tex. A&M Club ofN.Y.C. (v.p. 1994—), U. Mich. Club No. N.J. (bd. dirs. 1996—), N.Y. Metro Bus. Objects User Group (steering com. 1996—). Avocations: photography, travel, arts, computers. Home: 42 Legion Pl Whippany NJ 07981-1404 Office: Ricoh Corp 5 Dedrick Pl West Caldwell NJ 07006-6304

VACHON, LOUIS, psychiatrist, educator; b. Montreal, June 15, 1932; m. Monique Blain, June 25, 1960; children: Philip, Dominique. BA, U. Montreal, 1952, MD, 1958. Diplomate Am. Bd. Psychiatry and Neurology. Intern Hotel Dieu de Montreal, Que., 1957-58, resident in psychiatry, 1958-61; intern Hotel Dieu de Montreal, 1957-58; psychiat. resident Instiut Albert Prevost, Montreal, 1958-61; sr. physician Medfield (Mass.) State Hosp., 1961-62; rsch. assoc., then instr. Boston U. Med. Sch., 1962-68, asst. prof., then assoc. prof., 1968-87, interim chmn. div. psychiatry, 1985-87, prof., chmn. div. psychiatry, 1987-96; dir. psychiatry outpatient svc. Univ. Hosp., Boston, 1978-85, interim psychiatrist-in-chief, 1985-87, psychiatrist-in-chief, 1987-96, vis. physician in psychiatry, 1987—. Contbg. author: Comprehensive Textbook of Psychiatry, 1989. Fellow Am. Psychiat. Assn.; mem. Boston Psychoanalytic Soc. Inst., Am. Psychoanalytic Assn., Internat. Psychoanalytic Assn., Mass. Psychiat. Soc., Am. Psychosomatic Soc., Mass. Med. Soc., Boston. Office: Boston U Sch Medicine 720 Harrison Ave Rm 914 Boston MA 02118-2334

VACHON, LOUIS-ALBERT CARDINAL, archbishop; b. St. Frederic, Que., Can., Feb. 4, 1912; s. Napoleon and Alexandrine (Gilbert) V. D.Ph., Laval U., 1947, hon. degree, 1982; D.Th., St. Thomas Aquinas U., Rome, 1949; hon. degrees, U. Montreal, McGill and Victoria, 1964, Guelph U., 1966, Moncton U., 1967, Bishop's, Queen's and Strasbourg U., 1968, U. Notre Dame, 1971, Carleton U., 1972, Laval U., 1982. Superior Grand Seminaire Québec, 1955-59; superior gen. Le Séminaire de Qué., 1960-77; prof. philosophy Laval U., 1941-47, prof. theology, 1949-55, vice-rector, 1959-60, rector, 1960-72; protonotary apostolic, 1963-77, aux. bishop of Que., 1977-81, archbishop of Que. and primate of Can., 1981-90, apptd. Cardinal with title St. Paul of the Cross, 1985; Past pres. Corp. Laval U. Med. Centre; mem. Sacred Congregation for Clergy, Vatican, 1986—; adminstrv. bd. Nat. Order of Qué., 1985—, Can. Conf. Cath. Bishops, 1981—. Author: Espérance et Présomption, 1958, Verité et Liberte, 1962, Unité de l'universite, 1962, Apostolat de l'universitaire catholique, 1963, Memorial, 1963, Communauté universitaire, 1963, Progres de l'universite et consentement populaire, 1964, Responsabilite collective des universitaires, 1964, Les humanites aujourd'hui, 1966, Excellence et loyauté des universitaires, 1969, Pastoral Letters, 1981—. Hon. pres. La Société des etudes grecques et latines du Québec; assoc. mem. bd. Quebec Symphony Orch.; bd. govs. Laval U. Found. Decorated officier de l'Ordre de la Fidelité française, companion Order of Can., du Conseil de langue française, Ordre nat. du Qué., officier de la Légion d'honneur, France. Fellow Royal Soc. Can.; mem. Canadian Assn. French Lang. Educators (pres. 1970-72), Assn. Univs. and Colls. Can. (pres. 1965-66), Conf. Rectors and Prins. Que. Univs. (pres. 1965-68), Internat. Assn. Univs. (dep. mem. adminstrv. bd. 1965-70), Assn. des universites partiellement ou entierement de langue française (adminstrv. bd. 1961-69), Internat. Fedn. Cath. Univs. (adminstrv. bd. 1963-70), Ordre des francophones d'Amérique.

VACHON, MARILYN ANN, retired insurance company executive; b. Fort Wayne, Ind., Dec. 12, 1924; d. Robert J. and Maude (Shaffer) V. Asst. treas Lincoln Nat. Life Ins. Co., Fort Wayne, Ind., 1961-87, asst. v.p., 1973-87; sec. Lincoln Nat. Life Ins. Co., Fort Wayne, 1980-87; asst. sec. Lincoln Nat. Corp., Fort Wayne, 1977-80, asst. treas., 1977-87, sec., 1980-87. Home: 1825 Cortland Ave Fort Wayne IN 46808-2446

VACHON, SERGE JEAN, bank executive; b. Montreal, Que., Can., May 15, 1939; s. Adrien Joseph and Helene Marie (Contre) V. M.Econ. Sci., U. Montreal, 1963; diploma, Inst. IMF, Washington, 1966. Asst. prof. U. Montreal, Que., Can., 1962-63; adviser to gov. Bank of Can., Ottawa, Ont., 1980—, officer, 1981-83; chmn. Can. Payments Assn., Ottawa, Ont., 1981—. Recipient 1st prize Best Thesis in Econs. and Fin. Montreal Stock Exchange, 1963; recipient medal Lt. Gov. Que., 1963; Can. Council fellow,

1964. Mem. Societe Canadienne de Science Economique (dir. 1975-77). Roman Catholic. Club: Cercle Universitaire (Ottawa, Ont., Can.).

VACIK, JAMES PAUL, university administrator; b. North Judson, Ind., Nov. 30, 1931; s. George J. and Elsie E. (Paulsen) V.; m. Dorothy M. Nobles, Dec. 27, 1967; children: Deborah, Pamella, James, Stephen, Joshua, Jonathan. BS in Pharmacy, Purdue U., 1955, MS in Medicinal Chemistry, 1957, PhD in Bionucleonics, 1959. Cert. hazard control mgr.; registered biosafety profl., registered pharmacist, Ind., N.D., Ala. Asst. prof. bionucleonics dept. Purdue U., Lafayette, Ind., 1959-60; assoc. prof., dept. chmn. pharm. chemistry & bionucleonics N.D. State U., Fargo, 1960-63; prof., dept. chmn. pharm. chemistry & bionucleonics N.D. State U., 1963-76; assoc. prof. pharmacology Univ. S. Ala., Mobile, 1976-82; adj. prof., dir. environ. safety Univ. S. Ala., 1982—; Pub. Health Svc. grant dir. N.D. State U., Fargo, 1963-71; VA Hosp. cons. VA Hosp. System, Washington, 1966; vis. prof. Nat. Reactor Testing Sta., Idaho Falls, Idaho, 1968; pvt. cons. to various indsl. firms, 1970—. Contbr. articles to profl. Mem., first dir. "Showboat on the Red," Jaycees, Fargo, 1965. With U.S. Army, 1949-52, ETO. Named Outstanding Educator Am., Fuller & Dees, Washington, 1975. Mem. Am. Chem. Soc., Am. Pharm. Assn., Health Physics Soc. (chmn. com.), Am. Biol. Safety Assn. (bd. dirs. 1985-87), Health Physics Soc. (pres., treas., bd. dirs. Ala chpt. 1977—, pres., bd. dirs. N. Ctrl. chpt. 1969—), Masons. Baptist. Avocations: camping, fishing, woodworking. Home: 1220 Vendome Dr W Mobile AL 36609-3326 Office: U South Ala CC CB 307 University Blvd N Mobile AL 36688-3053

VACKETTA, CARL LEE, lawyer; b. Danville, Ill., Aug. 3, 1941; s. Peter G. and Julia M. (Columbus) V. BS, U. Ill., 1963, JD, 1965. Bar: Ill. 1965, D.C. 1968, U.S. Dist. Ct. D.C. 1968, U.S. Ct. Fed. Claims 1968, U.S. Supreme Ct. 1970. Tax lawyer GM, Detroit, 1965-66; ptnr. Sellers, Conner & Cuneo, Washington, 1968-74, Pettit & Martin, Washington, 1974-95, Piper & Marbury, Washington, 1995—; adj. prof. law Georgetown U., 1971—. Capt. U.S. Army, 1966-68. Fellow ABA (sec. pub. contract law sect. 1978-79, coun. 1979-82, contract law sect., editor-in-chief Public Contract Law Jour. 1994—), Nat. Contract Mgmt. Assn.; mem. Fed. Bar Assn., D.C. Bar Assn., Nat. Assn. Purchasing Mgrs. Roman Catholic. Club: University (Washington). Co-author: Government Contract Default Termination, 1991, 93, 95, 97; co-editor Extraordinary Contractual Relief Reporter, 1974—. Office: Piper & Marbury 7th Fl 1200 19th St NW Fl 7 Washington DC 20036-2430 also: Piper & Marbury 11th Fl 36 S Charles St Baltimore MD 21201

VACQUIER, VICTOR DIMITRI, biology educator; b. Pitts., July 20, 1940; s. Victor and Vera (Vinogradoff) V.; m. Judith Ellen Payne, July 1, 1973; children: Paul Andre, Marc Christian. AB, San Diego State U., 1963; PhD, U. Calif.-Berkeley, 1968. Rsch. asst. U. Calif.-Berkeley, 1963-68; rschr. Internat. Lab. Genetics and Biophysics, Naples, Italy, 1968-69; postdoctoral rschr. Hopkins Marine Sta., Stanford U., Pacific Grove, Calif., 1970-71; asst. rsch. biologist Scripps Inst. Oceanography, U. Calif.-San Diego, La Jolla, 1971-73, assoc. prof. biology, 1978-80, prof., 1980—; asst. prof. zoology U. Calif.-Davis, 1973-75, assoc. prof., 1975-78. Assoc. editor Gamete Rsch., 1980—, Devel. Biology, 1983—. Mem. Am. Soc. Cell Biology, Soc. Developmental Biology, Internat. Soc. Devel. Biology. Office: U Calif Scripps Instn Oceanography Marine Biology Rsch Divsn La Jolla CA 92093-0202

VADEN, FRANK SAMUEL, III, lawyer, engineer; b. San Antonio, Nov. 13, 1934; s. Frank Samuel Jr. and Helen Alyne (Roberts) V.; m. Caroline Chittenden Gerdes, Feb. 20, 1960; children; Christina Louise (Mrs. Eugene Linton), Olivia Anne (Mrs. Warren Augenstein), Cecilia Claire (Mrs. Scott Johnson). BSEE and BS in Indsl. Engring., Tex. A&M U., 1957; JD, So. Meth. U., 1963. Bar: Tex. 1963, U.S. Dist. Ct. (we. and so. dists.) Tex. 1963, U.S. Ct. Appeals (5th, 9th, 11th and Fed. cirs.) 1963, U.S. Supreme Ct. 1986; registered U.S. Patent and Trademark Office 1964. Assoc. Arnold & Roylance, Houston, 1963-66; ptnr. Arnold, White & Durkee, Houston, 1966-73, mng. ptnr., 1973-78; prin. Frank S. Vaden III, P.C., Houston, 1978-80; sr. ptnr. Vaden, Eickenroht & Thompson, L.L.P., Houston, 1980—; bd. dirs. Phoenix Annydrous, Inc., Houston; lectr. in field. Author: Invention Protection for Practicing Engineers, 1971; contbr. numerous articles to profl. jours. Capt. S.C., U.S. Army, 1957-67. Fellow Tex. Bar Found. (sustaining), Houston Bar Found. (sustaining); mem. ABA (mem. standing com. on spcecilization), Tex. Bar Assn. (chair intellectual property law sec. 1984-85), Houston Bar Assn., Am. Intellectual Property Law Assn., Houston Intellectual Property Law Assn. (pres. 1985-86), U.S. Trademark Assn., Licensing Exec. Soc. (chmn. Houston chpt. 1987-88). Republican. Episcopalian. Office: Vaden Eickenroht & Thompson 1 Riverway Ste 1100 Houston TX 77056-1903

VADUS, GLORIA A., scientific document examiner; b. Forrestville, Pa.. Diploma, Cole Sch. Graphology, Calif., 1978; BA in Psychology Counseling, Columbia Pacific U., 1981, MA in Psychology, 1982; diploma handwriting expert, Edith Eisenberg, Bethesda, Md., 1991. Cert. Am. Acad. Graphology, Washington, 1978, tchr. Coun. Graphological Socs., 1980; ct. qualified document examiner; registered graphologist; cert. behavioral profiling and cert. questioned documents, diplomate Am. Bd. Forensic Examiners, 1993/94. Pres., owner Graphinc, Inc., 1976—; accredited instr. graphology Montgomery County Schs., Md., 1978; instr. Psychogram Centre, 1978-85; testifier superior and probate cts. Author numerous studies, papers, and environ. articles in field. Chmn. Letter of Hope for POW's; vol. Montgomery County, 1987-88. Recipient Gold Nib Analyst of Yr. award, 1982, Dancing Fan award IEEE, Japan chpt., 1991, Spl. award U.S./Japan Marine Facilities Panel, 1978-94, Valuable Contbns. Japanese Panel UJNR/MFP, 1994; named Woman of Yr. ABI, 1990, 93-96, IBC, 1991992-93, 95-96. Fellow Am. Bd. Forensic Examiners (Meritorious award 1994, Outstanding Contbrn. cert.); mem. Am. Handwriting Analysis Found. (cert., pres. 1982-84, chmn. rsch. com., adv. bd. 1981-86, chmn. nominations com. 1985-86, officiator 1986, mem. policy planning and ethics com. 1986-91, ethics chmn. 1989-91, chmn., past pres. adv. bd. 1989-91), Nat. Forensic Ctr., Nat. Assn. Document Examiners (ethics hearing bd. 1986, chmn. nominations com. 1987-88, elections chmn. 1988, parliamentarian 1988-92), Internat. Platform Assn., Soc. Francaise de Graphologie for Am. Handwriting Analysis Found., Nat. Writers Club, Menninger Found., Soroptomist Internat. (v.p., judge, chmn. flower shows), Sierra Club. Home: 8500 Timber Hill Ln Potomac MD 20854-4237

VADZEMNIEKS, MICHAEL LESTER, plastics company executive; b. Buffalo, Oct. 31, 1955; s. Olgerts and Linda Lou (Evans) V. Assoc. Archtl. Tech., Williamsport (Pa.) Cmty. Coll., 1975. Plant mgr. Engineered Plastics, Inc., Lake City, Pa., 1977-83; prodn. supr. Hoover Universal, Erie, Pa., 1983-84; engring. mgr. OEM/Erie, Inc., 1984-88; plant mgr. PHB-Molding Divsn., Fairview, Pa., 1988-93; gen. mgr. Springfield Plastics, Inc., East Springfield, Pa., 1993—. Founding trustee Old Lake Rd. Summer, East Springfield, Pa., 1986; pres., trustee City Trust, 1987-89, 95-97; dir. Lake Erie Cmty. Fed. Credit Union, pres. 1989—; organist, pianist Federated Ch., 1988—. Mem. Northwestern Sportsmen's Club (treas. 1990-95). Republican. Avocations: music performance-piano, downhill skiing, gourmet cooking, carpentry, gardening. Home: 13478 Old Lake Rd East Springfield PA 16411 Office: Springfield Plastics Inc 3247 Route 215 East Springfield PA 16411-9707

VAETH, AGATHA MIN-CHUN FANG, clinical nurse; b. Beijing, Feb. 19, 1935; d. Yung-Cheng and Wen-Pu (Cheng) Fang; m. Randy H. Vaeth, July 20, 1971; children: David Sun, Elizabeth Cheng, Philip Cheng. Diploma, Mary View Hosp. Sch. Nursing, Portsmouth, Va., 1959; student, Okla. State U., 1969-73; BS, St. Joseph's Coll., North Windham, Maine, 1986, postgrad., 1989—; postgrad., La. State U., 1986. Staff nurse, charge nurse Stillwater (Okla.) Mcpl. Hosp., 1969-74; clin. nurse USIHH Hosp., Pawnee, Okla., 1974-75; clin. nurse, relief supr. Gillis W. Long Hansen's Disease Ctr., Carville, La., 1975-91, supervisory clin. nurse, 1991—; wellness cons.; part-time home health nurse, 1993—. Translator video cassettes on Hansens Disease; illustrator herpetology lab manuel; art exhbns. at Barton Rouge Art & Artist Guild, 1976-77. Recipient Outstanding Performance award GWLHD, PHS, DHHS, 1991, 1993, High Quality Performance award, 1978, Dedicated Svc. to Clin. Br. award, 1981, Outstanding Nurses award Baton Rouge Dist. Nurses' Assn., 1994. Fellow Internat. Biog. Assn. (life); mem. ANA, AAUW, La. Nurses Assn. (nominating com. 1990-94), Baton Rouge Nurses Assn., Baton Rouge Chinese Culture Club (officer-sec. 1993—). Avocations: ballroom dancing, swimming, travel, painting, writing. Home: 1274 Marilyn Dr Baton Rouge LA 70815-4928

VAGELOS, PINDAROS ROY, pharmaceutical company executive; b. Westfield, N.J., Oct. 8, 1929; s. Roy John and Marianthi (Lambrinides) V.; m. Diana Touliatos, July 10, 1955; children: Randall, Cynthia, Andrew, Ellen. AB, U. Pa., 1950; MD, Columbia U., 1954; DSc (hon.), Washington U., 1980, Brown U., 1982, U. Medicine and Dentistry of N.J., 1984, NYU, 1989, Columbia U., 1990; LLD (hon.), Princeton U., 1990; LHD (hon.), Rutgers U., 1991; DSc (hon.), N.J. Inst. Tech., 1992, SUNY, 1994. Intern medicine Mass. Gen. Hosp., 1954-55, asst. resident medicine, 1955-56; surgeon Lab. Cellular Physiology, NIH, 1956-59; surgeon Lab. Biochemistry, 1959-64, head sect. comparative biochemistry, 1964-66; prof. biochemistry, chmn. dept. biol. chemistry Washington U. Sch. Medicine, St. Louis, 1966-75; dir. divsn. biology and biomed. scis. Washington U. Sch. Medicine, 1973-75; sr. v.p. research Merck, Sharp & Dohme Research Labs., Rahway, N.J., 1975-76, pres., 1976-84; corp. sr. v.p. Merck & Co., Inc., Rahway, N.J., 1982-84, exec. v.p., 1984-85, CEO, 1985-86, chmn., CEO,, 1986-94, also bd. dirs.; chmn. Regeneron Pharms., Inc., Tarrytown, N.Y., 1995—; mem. Inst. Medicine, NAS, 1974—; chmn. sci. adv. bd. Ctr. for Advanced Biotech. and Medicine, 1985-94; bd. dirs. Estee Lauder, Prudential Ins. Co., PepsiCo, Inc., McDonnell Douglas Corp. Trustee U. Pa., 1988—, chmn. bd., 1994—; trustee Rockefeller U., 1976-94, Danforth Found., 1978—; mem. President's Commn. on Environ. Quality, 1991-93, Adv. Com. Trade Policy and Negotiations, 1992-94, Bus. Coun., 1987—; bd. mng. dirs. Met. Opera Assn., Inc., 1989-95; bd. dirs. N.J. Performing Arts Ctr., 1989—, co-chmn , 1992. Recipient award for chemistry in svc. to soc., NAS, 1995, Pupin medal, 1995. Mem. Am. Chem. Soc. (Enzyme Chemistry award 1967), Am. Soc. Biol. Chemists, Nat. Acad. Scis., Am. Acad. Arts and Scis., Am. Philosophical Soc., Bus. Roundtable (policy com. 1987-94). Avocations: jogging, tennis. Discoverer of acyl-carrier protein. Home: 82 Mosle Rd Far Hills NJ 07931-2228 Office: Regeneron Pharms Inc 777 Old Saw Mill River Rd Tarrytown NY 10591-6700

VAGET, HANS RUDOLF, language professional, educator; b. Marienbad, Czekoslovakia, Feb. 2, 1938; came to U.S., 1964; s. Hans Ernst and Berta (Isop) V.; m. Ann Leone; children: Melanie Claudine, Erec Alexander. MA, U. Tübingen, Fed. Republic Germany, 1964; PhD, Columbia U., 1969. Instr. Columbia U., N.Y.C., 1964-67; from instr. to prof. Smith Coll., Northampton, Mass., 1967—; vis. prof. U. Calif., Irvine, 1979, Columbia U., 1985, Princeton U., 1986-87, Yale U., 1991, U. Hamburg, 1992. Author: Dilettantismus bei Goethe, 1971, Goethe. Der Mann von 60 Jahren, 1982, Thomas-Mann Kommentar, 1984; author, editor: Briefwechsel T. Mann-Agnes Meyer, 1992, J.W. Goethe: Erotic Poems, 1996; contbr. articles to profl. and ednl. publs. Recipient Thomas Mann-Medaille, 1994; grantee NEH, 1985, Am. Coun. Learned Socs., 1986. Mem. MLA, Assn. Tchrs. of German, Deutsche Schillergesellschaft, Thomas-Mann-Gesellschaft, Goethe Soc. N.Am. (co-founder), Wagner Soc., Am. Musicol. Soc. Office: Smith Coll Dept German Northampton MA 01063-0001

VAGLIANO, ALEXANDER MARINO, banker; b. Paris, France, Mar. 15, 1927; came to U.S., 1940, naturalized, 1945; s. Andre M. and Barbara (Allen) V.; children: Barbara A., Andre M., Justin C. Grad., St. Paul's Sch., Concord, N.H., 1944; B.A., Harvard, 1949, LL.B. cum laude, 1952. Bar: N.Y. bar 1952. Assoc. firm White & Case, N.Y.C., 1952-58; asst. treas. J.P. Morgan & Co., Inc., N.Y.C., 1959; v.p. Morgan Guaranty Trust Co., N.Y.C., 1959-62, 65-66; sr. v.p. Morgan Guaranty Trust Co., 1968-76, exec. v.p., 1976-81; chief exec. officer Banca Vonwiller, Milan, Italy, 1967-68; chmn. Morgan Guaranty Internat. Finance Corp., 1976-81, J.P. Morgan Overseas Capital Corp., 1976-81; ptnr. Price Waterhouse and Ptnrs., 1983-85; chmn. Sunset Ridge Farm, Inc., 1983—, Michelin Fin. Corp., Greenville, S.C., 1985—; chmn. bd. advisors Equity Linked Investors, N.Y.C., 1985—; pres. The N.Y. Farmers, 1992-94; bd. dirs. Holographics, Inc., N.Y.; dir. office of capital devel. and fin. Near East and South Asia, AID, 1963-65; adviser Yale Econ. Growth Ctr., 1973—, NYU Inst. French Studies, 1979—; trustee Coun. for Excellence in Govt., 1990—. Pres. Parks Council N.Y.C., 1971-73; bd. dirs. French Am. Found. , N.Y.C., 1986—; gov. The Atlantic Inst. Internt. Affairs, 1986-90. Served with AUS, 1945-47. Mem. Council Fgn. Relations. Clubs: Brook (N.Y.C.); Travellers (Paris). Home and Office: Sunset Ridge Farm Inc Norfolk CT 06058

VAGTS, DETLEV FREDERICK, lawyer, educator; b. Washington, Feb. 13, 1929; s. Alfred and Miriam (Beard) V.; m. Dorothy Larkin, Dec. 11, 1954; children: Karen, Lydia. Grad., Taft Sch., 1945; AB, Harvard U., 1948, LLB, 1951. Bar: Mass. 1961. Assoc. Cahill, Gordon, Reindel & Ohl, N.Y.C., 1951-53, 56-59; asst. prof. law Harvard Law Sch., 1959-62, prof., 1962—, Eli Goldston prof., 1981-84, Bemis prof., 1984—; counselor internat. law Dept. State, 1976-77. Author: (with others) Transnational Legal Problems, 1968, 4th edit., 1994, Basic Corporation Law, 1973, 3d edit., 1989; editor: (with others) Secured Transactions Under the Uniform Commercial Code, 1963-64; assoc. reporter: (with others) Restatement of Foreign Relations Law; book rev. editor Am. Jour. Internat. Law, 1986-93, co-editor-in-chief, 1993—. 1st lt. USAF, 1953-56. Recipient Max Planck Rsch. award, 1991. Mem. ABA, Am. Soc. Internat. Law, Coun. Fgn. Rels., Phi Beta Kappa. Home: 29 Follen St Cambridge MA 02138-3502 Office: Sch Law Harvard U Cambridge MA 02138

VAGUE, JEAN MARIE, physician; b. Draguignan, France, Nov. 25, 1911; s. Victor Francois and Marie (Voiron) V.; m. Denise Marie Jouve, Sept. 3, 1936; children: Philippe, Thierry, Irene (Mrs. Claude Juhan), Maurice. Baccalaureat, Cath. Coll., Aix en Provence, France, 1928; MD, Marseilles (France) U., 1935. Intern, Hotel Dieu Conception, Marseilles, 1930, resident, 1932-39; practice medicine specializing in endocrinology, Marseilles, 1943—; assoc. prof. Marseilles U., 1946-57, prof., clinic endocrinology, 1957—. Dir. Ctr. Alimentary Hygiene and Prophylaxis Nutrition Diseases Nat. Rys. Mediterranean region, 1958—; expert chronic degenerative diseases (diabetes) WHO, 1962—. Served to lt. French Army, 1939-40. Decorated Cross Legion Honor, Acad. Palms, knight pub. health, knight mil. merit, War Cross; recipient Willendorf Internat. award, 1990. Mem. Endocrine Soc. U.S., Am. Diabetes Assn., Royal Soc. Medicine (London), European Assn. for Study Diabetes, Spanish, Italian, French (past pres.) socs. endocrinology, French Acad. Medicine, Spanish Acad. Medicine, Italian Acad. Medicine, Belgian Acad. Medicine, French Lang. Diabetes Assn. (past pres.). Author: Human Sexual Differentiation, 1953, Notions of Endocrinology, 1965, Obesities, 1991, Dawn on Iaboc's Ford, History of Man, History of Men, 1993, others. Achievements include first identification of the metabolic and vascular complications of android obesity and their mechanism; research in demonstration of diabetogenic and atherogenic power of obesity with topographic distbn. fat in upper and deep part of body, evolution of android diabetogenic obesity from 1st stage of efficacious hyperinsulinism to less efficacious hyperinsulinism and hypoinsulinism-neuro-germinal degeneration, degenerative lesions of germinal epithelium and nervous system. Home: 6 Prado Parc, 411 Ave du Prado, 13008 Marseille France Office: Hopital U Timone Clin Endocrinologique, Blvd Jean-Moulin, 13385 Marseilles France

VAHAVIOLOS, SOTIRIOS JOHN, electrical engineer, scientist, corporate executive; b. Mistra, Greece, Apr. 16, 1946; s. John Apostolos and Athanasia (Pavlakos) V.; m. Aspasia Felice Nessas, June 1, 1969; children: Athanasia, Athena, Kristy. BSEE, Fairleigh Dickinson U., 1970; MSEE, Columbia U., 1972, M in Philosophy, 1975, PhDEE, 1976. Mem. tech. staff Bell Telephone Labs., Princeton, N.J., 1970-75, supr., 1975-76, dept. head, 1976-78; founder, pres., CEO Phys. Acoustics Corp., Princeton, 1978—, MISTRAS Holdings Corp., Princeton, 1984—; adviser Greece Ministry Def., Athens, 1986-88; bd. dirs. Orthosonics, Inc., N.Y.C.; chmn. policy com. Internat. Com. of Nondestructive Testing. Contbr. more than 100 papers to profl. publs. 13 U.S. patents, 7 fgn. patentsin field. Bd. dirs. Holy Cross Greek Orthodox Sch. Theology, Boston, 1989—; pres. bd of trustees St. George Greek Orthodox Cmty., Trenton, N.J.; adv. bd. Trenton State Coll., N.J., 1983—; chmn. Princeton sect. United Fund, 1976-78. Recipient Spartan Merit award Spartan World Soc., 1987, Entrepreneur of Yr. award Arthur Young/Inc. Mag., N.J., 1989. Fellow IEEE (Centennial medal award 1984, Dr. Ing Eugene Mittlemen Achievement award 1993), Am. Soc. Nondestructive Testing (bus. and fin. com. 1984-87, 88—, bd. dirs. 1985, sec. 1989, treas. 1990, v.p. 1991, pres. 1992, chmn. bd. 1993, chmn. internat. com. nondestructive testing 1994—, chmn. internat. com. on nondestructive testing, editor handbook on Acoustic Emission 1988), Acoustic Emission Working Group; mem. ASTM, IEEE Indsl. Electronics Soc. (sr. mem. adminstrv. com. 1988, founder, v.p. conf. 1974-78, 2d prize Student Paper Contest 1970, Outstanding Young Engr. award 1984, editor Trans. on Indsl. Electronics 1976-82), N.Y. Acad. Scis. Independent. Greek Orthodox. Avocations: bird hunting, soccer, technical writing, gardening. Home: 7 Ridgeview Rd Princeton NJ 08540-7601 Office: Phys Acoustics Corp PO Box 3135 Princeton NJ 08543-3135

VAI, STEVE, guitarist; b. Carle Place, NY, June 6, 1960; married; 1 child. Student, Berklee Coll. of Music. Transcriber & stunt guitarist for Frank Zappa, 1979-83; guitarist Alcatrazz, 1984, David Lee Roth, 1986-89, Whitesnake, 1990; solo artist, 1991—. albums include Flex-able, 1984, Passion & Warfare, 1990, Sex & Religion, 1994; (with Frank Zappa) Tinsel Town Rebellion, 1980, You Are What You Is, 1981, The Man From Utopia, 1982, Ship Arriving Too Late to Save a Drowning Witch, 1983, Them or Us, 1984, Flexable, 1984, Passion and Warfare, 1990, Hey Stoopid, 1991, Sex & Religion, 1993, Alien Love Secrets, 1995, Fire Garden, 1996; (with Alcatrazz) Disturbing the Peace, 1984; (with David Lee Roth) Eat 'Em and Smile, 1986, Skyscraper, 1988; (with Whitesnake) Slip of the Tongue, 1990, (with Frank Zappa) Shut Up N' Play Yer Guitar, 1986, (with Shanker) The Epidemics; film appearances include: Crossroads, 1986; film soundtracks include Less Than Zero, 1987, Bill and Ted's Bogus Journey, 1991; comoser for film PCU, 1994. Recipient Rock Instrumental Grammy Award for "Sofa" from Zappa's Universe, 1993. Office: Sony Records 550 Madison Ave New York NY 10022*

VAIL, CHARLES DANIEL, veterinarian, consultant; b. Denver, June 11, 1936; s. Allan Paden and Katherine Marie (Phillips) V.; m. Jean Williams Ebsen, June 15, 1963; children: Ellen Marie, David Elston. BS, Colorado A&M, 1958; DVM, Colo. State. U., 1960. Asst. veterinarian Colo. Racing Commn., Littleton, 1958-60; equine practitioner Littleton Large Animal Clinic, 1960—; track veterinarian Centennial Race Track, Littleton, 1962-63. Editor in chief Equine Practice, 1986—; contbr. articles to profl. jours. Mem. selection com. Outstanding Biology Tchr. award Colo., 1978-80, 88—, Arapahoe Fair Assn., Littleton, 1965-84, gallery disting. grads. Colo. State U. Coll. Vet. Medicine, 1989; chmn. Littleton Rotary Western Heritage Art Fair; bd. dirs. Animal Assistance Found. Denver, 1991—, v.p., 1995-96; pres. Animal Assistance Found., 1996—; active Colo. State U. Alumni Found., 1997—. Recipient Honor Alumni award Coll. Vet. Medicine, Colo. State U., 1991. Mem. AVMA (publs. com. 1981-87), Am. Assn. Equine Practitioners (pres. 1985), Colo. Vet. Medicine Assn. (pres. 1980, Veterinarian of Yr. award 1987), Denver Area Vet. Medicine Soc. (pres. 1975), Arapahoe Town and Gown Soc., Nottingham Club, Rotary (pres. Littleton 1992-93), Sigma Alpha Epsilon, Omicron Delta Kappa. Home: 5921 S Cherrywood Cir Littleton CO 80121-2465 Office: Littleton Large Animal Clinic PC 8025 S Santa Fe Dr Littleton CO 80120-4305

VAIL, IRIS JENNINGS, civic worker; b. N.Y.C., July 2, 1928; d. Lawrence K. and Beatrice (Black) Jennings; grad. Miss Porters Sch., Farmington, Conn.; m. Thomas V.H. Vail, Sept. 15, 1951; children: Siri J., Thomas V.H. Jr., Lawrence J.W. Exec. com. Garden Club Cleve., 1962-93; mem. women's coun. Western Res. Hist. Soc., 1960—, Cleve. Mus. Art, 1953—; chmn. Childrens Garden Fair, 1966-75, Public Square Dinner, 1975; bd. dirs. Garden Center Greater Cleve., 1963-77; trustee Cleve. Zool. Soc., 1971—; mem. Ohio Arts Coun., 1974-76, pub. sq. com. Greater Cleve. Growth Assn., 1976-93, pub. sq. preservation and maintenance com. Cleve. Found., 1989-93, chmn. pub. sq. planting com., 1993. Recipient Amy Angell Collier Montague medal Garden Club Am., 1976, Ohio Gov.'s award, 1977. Chagrin Valley Hunt Club, Cypress Point Club, Kirtland Country Club, Colony Club, Women's City of Cleve. Club (Margaret A. Ireland award). Home: 14950 County Line Rd Chagrin Falls OH 44022-6800

VAIL, THOMAS VAN HUSEN, retired newspaper publisher and editor; b. Cleve., June 23, 1926; s. Herman Lansing and Delia (White) V.; m. Iris W. Jennings, Sept. 15, 1951; children: Siri Jennings, Thomas Van Husen, Jr. A.B. in Politics cum laude, Princeton U., 1948; H.H.D. (hon.), Wilberforce U., 1964; L.H.D., Kenyon Coll., 1969, Cleve. State U., 1973. Reporter Cleve. News, 1949-53, polit. editor, 1953-57; with Cleve. Plain Dealer, 1957-91, v.p., 1961-63, pub., editor, 1963-91, pres., 1970-91; dir. AP, 1968-74; ret., 1991. Bd. dirs. Greater Cleve. Growth Assn.; bd. dirs., past pres. Cleve. Conv. and Visitors Bur.; mem. Nat. Adv. Commn. on Health Manpower; presdl. apptd. to U.S. Adv. Commn. on Info., Pres.'s Commn. for Observance 25th Anniversary UN; trustee No. Ohio region NCCJ, Nat. Brotherhood Week chmn., 1969; trustee Cleve. Coun. World Affairs; fellow Cleve. Clinic Found.; former mem. Downtown Cleve. Corp.; former mem. distbn. com. Cleve. Found.; chmn., founder New Cleve. Campaign; trustee, founder Cleve. Tomorrow; former trustee Com. Econ. Devel.; former mem. Pres.'s Adv. Coun. on Pvt. Sector Initiatives; participant Nat. Conf. Christians and Jews. Lt. (j.g.) USNR, 1944-46. Recipient Nat. Human Relations award, 1970, Cleve. Man of Year award Sales and Mktg. Execs. Cleve., 1976, Ohio Gov.'s award, 1982, Downtown Bus. Council recognition award Greater Cleve. Growth Assn., 1983. Mem. Nat. Assn. Profl. Journalists (Lifetime Hall of Fame), Am. Newspaper Pubs. Assn., Am. Soc. Newspaper Editors, Soc. Profl. Journalists, Kirtland Country Club (Willoughby, Ohio), Cypress Point Club (Pebble Beach, Calif.), Bohemian Club (San Francisco), Chagrin Valley Hunt Club (Gates Mills, Ohio), Links Club (N.Y.C.). Episcopalian. Home: 14950 County Line Rd Hunting Valley Chagrin Falls OH 44022 Office: 29225 Chagrin Blvd Ste 200 Pepper Pike OH 44122-4629

VAIL, VAN HORN, German language educator; b. Buffalo, Dec. 23, 1934; s. Curtis Churchill and Faith Newbrook (Ely) V.; m. Michele Juliette Edelstein, May 5, 1969; 1 son, Mark Curtis. B.A., U. Wash., 1956; M.A., Princeton U., 1961, Ph.D., 1964. Instr. Princeton U., 1962-65, asst. prof., 1965-66; asst. prof. German Middlebury (Vt.) Coll., 1966-69, assoc. prof., 1969-75, prof., 1975—; chmn. dept. Middlebury Coll., Vt., 1970-73, 87-88; dir. studies Middlebury Sch. in Germany Middlebury Coll., 1967-68, 70-71, 74-75, 85-86, 88-89, 92-93, 95-96; mem. nat. screening com. Fulbright Scholarships, 1979-81. Author: German in Review, 1967, 2d edit., 1986, Der Weg zum Lesen, 1967, 2d edit., 1974, 3d edit., 1986, Modern German, 1971, 2d edit., 1978, 3d edit., 1992, Tonio Kröger als Weg zur Literatur, 1974, Workbook for Modern German, 1992. Served to 1st lt. M.I., U.S. Army, 1956-58. Fulbright scholar U. Heidelberg, 1958-59. Mem. MLA. Home: RD 2 Box 614 Cider Mill Rd Middlebury VT 05753 Office: Middlebury Coll Dept of Interdisciplinary Studies Middlebury VT 05753

VAILLANCOURT, JEAN-GUY, sociology educator; b. Chelmsford, Ont., Can., May 24, 1937; s. Royal A. and Marie (Lavallée) V.; m. Pauline Hansen, June 6, 1966 (div. 1983); 1 child, Véronique. BA magna cum laude, Laurentian U., Sudbury, Ont., 1957; licenciate in philosophy, Faculté des Jésuites, Montreal, Que., Can., 1961; licentiate in sociology, Gregorian U., Rome, 1964; PhD in Sociology, U. Calif., Berkeley, 1975. Lectr. St. Boniface (Man.) Coll., Can., 1964-65; asst. prof. U. de Montréal, Que., Can., 1969-76, assoc. prof., 1976-83, prof. sociology, 1983—, chmn. dept., 1984-87; mem. consultative com. Can. ambassador for disarmament, Ottawa, Ont., 1984-91, consultative com. on environ. Hydro-Que., 1984-90. Author: Papal Power, 1980, Essais d'écosociologie, 1982; co-editor: Le processus électoral au Québec, 1976, Roots of Peace, 1986, Environnement et développement Problèmes socio-politiques, 1991, Gestion de l'environnement, éthique et société, 1992, Instituer le développement durable, 1994, Aspects sociaux des prècipitations acides au Québec, 1994, La recherche sociale en environnement Nouveaux paradigmes, 1996; editor-in-chief Sociologie et Sociétés, 1978-87. Mem. coun. City of Dunham, Que., 1976-80; bd. dirs. Oxfam-Que., 1976-79, Can. Inst. Internat. Peace and Security, Ottawa, Ont., 1986-89, European Univ. Ctr. for Peace Studies, Burg Schlaining, Burgenland, Austria, 1989-93, Groupement forestier du Haut-Yamaska, 1993—, Club 2/3, 1995—. Grantee Conseil de Recherche en science sociale du Québec, 1982, FCAR, 1989-95, 96—, Social Sci. Rsch. Coun., 1983-86, 90—, Can. Inst. Internat. Peace and Security, 1985, 91; fellow Can. Coun., 1965-68. Mem. Internat. Sociol. Assn., Assn. Can. des sociologues et anthropologues de langue française, Sci. for Peace, Pugwash, Group 78. Roman Catholic. Avocations: tree farming, travelling. Home: 953 Cherrier # 2, Montréal, PQ Canada H2L 1J2 Office: U Montréal, Dept Sociology, Montreal, PQ Canada H3C 3J7

VAILLANT, GEORGE EMAN, psychiatrist; b. N.Y.C., June 16, 1934; s. George Clapp and Mary Suzannah (Beck) V.; m. Leigh McCullough, Dec. 4,

1993; children: George Emery, John Holden, Henry Greenough, Anne Liberty, Caroline Joanna. A.B., Harvard U., 1955, M.D., 1959; postgrad., Boston Psychoanalytic Inst., 1967-76. Resident in psychiatry Mass. Mental Health Center, Boston, 1960-63; from asst. prof. to asso. prof. psychiatry Tufts U. Sch. Medicine, 1966-71; asso. prof. psychiatry Harvard Med. Sch., 1971-77, prof., 1977-82, 93—; dir. tng. Cambridge (Mass.) Hosp., 1976-81, Mass. Mental Health Center, Boston, 1981-83; prof. Dartmouth Sch. Medicine, 1983-92; dir. study of adult devel. Harvard U. Health Services, 1972—. Author: Adaptation to Life, 1977, Natural History of Alcoholism, 1983, Wisdom of the Ego, 1993; contbr. articles to profl. jours. Served with USPHS, 1963-65. Fellow Center for Advanced Study in Behavioral Scis., 1978-79. Fellow Am. Psychiat. Assn.; mem. Boston Psychoanalytic Soc. Episcopalian. Home: 943 High St Dedham MA 02026-4220 Office: Brigham Women's Hosp 75 Francis St Boston MA 02115-6110

VAINSTEIN, ROSE, librarian, educator; b. Edmonton, Alta., Can., Jan. 7, 1920; d. Rabbi Nathan and Jane (Simenstein) V. AB, Miami U., Oxford, Ohio, 1941; BLS, Western Res. U., 1942; MS, U. Ill., 1952. Jr. librarian Cuyahoga County Libr., Cleve., 1942-43; young people's librarian Bklyn. Public Libr., 1943-44; br. librarian Contra Costa County Libr., Martinez, Calif., 1948-51; cons. Calif. State Libr., Sacramento, 1953-55; head extension dept. Gary (Ind.) Public and Lake County Libr., 1955-57; public libr. specialist U.S. Office Edn., Washington, 1957-61; asso. prof. Sch. Librarianship, U. B.C., Vancouver, 1961-64; dir. Bloomfield Twp. Pub. Libr., Bloomfield Hills, Mich., 1964-68; prof. libr. sci. U. Mich., Ann Arbor, 1968-82, Margaret Mann prof. emeritus, 1982—; dir. Middle Mgmt. Inst. for Pub. Librs., 1969, 1st Margaret Mann Disting. prof. libr. sci., 1974—; libr. U.S. Armed Forces U.S., Hawaii, Japan, 1944-48; dir. B.C. (Can.) Pub. Librs. Rsch. Study, 1963-64; mem. steering com. Kendal Corp. Strategic Planning and Orgnl. Devel. Project Phase II, 1993. Contbr. articles to profl. jours. Mem. Jewish Community Coun. of Washtenaw County, Mich., 1981-84; bd. dirs. Jewish Community Ctr., 1986-89; mem. geriatric svcs. steering com. U. Mich. Med. Ctr., 1988-89. Fulbright Research scholar Eng., 1952-53; Council on Library Resources fellow, 1974-75; scholar-in-residence Sch. Librarianship, U. B.C., 1981. Mem. ALA (chmn. public libr. stds. com. 1969-73, chmn. public libr. activities com. 1974-76, mem. coun. 1975-79, mem. coun. budget assembly 1977-79, chmn. nominating com. 1976-77), Mich., Canadian library assns., U. Mich. Women's Rsch. Club (treas. 1971-72, chmn. loan fund com. 1976-79, Spl. 75th Anniversary award 1978), LWV, Hadassah (life, co-chmn. study group Ann Arbor chpt. 1982-83), Crossland Residents Assn. (bd. dirs. 1992-94, chair genealogy study group 1990-95, forum com. 1990-93, treas. 1992-93, long range planning group 1993-94, pres. 1995-96), Phi Beta Kappa (Alumnus mem. Iota of Ohio chpt. 1976), Beta Phi Mu (dir. 1974-77). Home: Apt 179 179 Crosslands Dr Kennett Square PA 19348-2019

VAIRA, PETER FRANCIS, lawyer; b. McKeesport, Pa., Mar. 5, 1937; s. Peter Francis and Mary Louise (Bedogne) V.; m. Mary Hohler, 1981. B.A., Duquesne U., 1959, J.D., 1962. Bar: Pa. 1963, D.C. 1968, Ill. 1984, U.S. Ct. Appeals (D.C. cir.) 1964, Ill. Supreme Ct. Ill. 1984, U.S. Dist. Ct. (no. dist.) Ill., U.S. Dist. Ct. (ea. dist.) Pa. Atty. Chgo. Strike Force, Justice Dept., 1968-72; atty. in charge Phila. Strike Force, 1972-73, Chgo. Strike Force on Organized Crime, 1973-78; U.S. atty. Phila., 1978-83; ptnr. firm Lord Bissel & Brook, Chgo., 1983-86; ptnr. Fox, Rothschild, O'Brien & Frankel, Phila., 1986-90, Buchanan Ingersoll, Phila., 1990-92, Vaira & Assocs., Phila., 1992-93, Vaira, Backstrom & Riley, Phila., 1993—; exec. dir. Pres.'s Commn. on Organized Crime, 1983; ind. hearing officer Laborers Internat. Union N.Am., 1995—; Chgo. crime com. and better govt. assn. ind. panel to rev. Palatine murder investigation, 1996-97; panelist, seminar, controlling internat. organized crime, Rome, Sorrento, Italy, June 1994; panelist, Internat. Conf. on Trial by Jury, Buenos Aires, Oct. 1996. Author: Corporate Responses to Grant Jury Investigation, 1984, Pennsylvania Federal Practice Rules, 1996; contbr. articles to profl. jours. Mem. Mayor's Search Com. for Police Commr., Phila., 1992; corruption task force Phila. Police, 1997. Served with USNR, 1963-68. Recipient Spl. Commendation award Justice Dept., 1976. Fellow Am. Coll. Trial Lawyers (chmn. criminal procedure com.); mem. ABA (mem. criminal justice coun. 1986), Am. Law Inst., Union League, Phila. Country Club. Office: Vaira Backstrom & Riley 1600 Market St Ste 2650 Philadelphia PA 19103-7226

VAIRO, ROBERT JOHN, insurance company executive; b. Bklyn., Sept. 27, 1930; s. John and Antonietta (DeRose) V.; m. Carol P. Andross, Apr. 8, 1951 (div. Feb. 1979); children: Robert J., Gregory J.; m. Inge R. Buhlbecker, Feb. 20, 1979. Student, Coll. Ins., N.Y.C., 1953-62; Exec. Program in Bus. Adminstrn., Columbia U., 1973. CPCU. Under asst. mgr. Atlantic Cos., N.Y.C., 1952-62; underwriter mgr., v.p. Fireman's Fund Ins. Co., N.Y.C., 1962-75; v.p., sr. v.p. underwriting C & F Ins. Cos., Morristown, N.J., 1975-79; exec. v.p., pres. U.S. Ins. Group, Morristown, N.J., 1979-82; chmn., chief exec. officer C & F Underwriters Group and The North River Ins. Co., Morristown, N.J., 1982-86; pres., chief oper. officer Crum and Forster, Inc., Morristown, 1987-88, pres., chief exec. officer, 1988-90, chmn., pres., chief exec. officer, 1990-92, also bd. dirs.; chmn. Ins. Services Office, N.Y.C., 1983, Am. Ins. Assn., Washington, 1990. Pres. Lincoln Park City Council, N.J., 1971-76. Served with USMC, 1951-53. Mem. Soc. CPCUs, Am. Inst. for Chartered Property Casualty Underwriters (dir., chmn. 1991-92), Desert Highlands Golf Club (pres. 1997). Roman Catholic. Home: # 451 10040 E Happy Valley Rd Scottsdale AZ 85255-2388

VAISHNAVI, VIJAY KUMAR, computer science educator, researcher; b. Srinagar, Kashmir, India, Mar. 25, 1948; came to U.S., 1980; s. Nand Lal and Prabhawati (Hakhu) V.; m. Kirti Ganju, July 17, 1972; children: Sandeep, Neil. BEE, Regional Engring. Coll., Srinagar, 1969; MEE, Indian Inst. Tech., India, 1972, PhD, 1976. Asst. prof. IIT Kanpur, 1973-77; postdoctoral fellow McMaster U., Hamilton, Ont., Can., 1977-79; vis. asst. prof. Concordia U., Montreal, 1979-80; asst. prof. Ohio U., Athens, 1980-81; assoc. prof. Ga. State U., Atlanta, 1981-87, prof., 1987—; vis. scientist U. Dortmund, Fed. Republic Germany, 1980; cons. AT&T, others, 1990—; rsch. dir. COMSOFT, 1990—. Contbr. articles to profl. jours. Recipient rsch. grants; collegiate faculty recognition, Coll. of Bus. Adminstrn., Ga. State U., Atlanta, 1989, 93. Mem. Assn. for Computing Machinery, Computer Soc. of IEEE (software engring. tech. com.), IEEE (sr.). Avocations: reading, gardening, table-tennis. Office: Ga State U Computer Info Systems Dept PO Box 4015 Atlanta GA 30302-4015

VAITKEVICIUS, VAINUTIS KAZYS, foundation administrator, medical educator; b. Kaunas, Lithuania, Jan. 12, 1927; came to U.S., 1951; s. Henrikas and Camille Vaitkevicius; m. Ingeborg Jausen; children: Eva, Henri, Peter, Camille, Walter, Martin. Diploma, Lithuanian Coll., Eichstett, Germany, 1946; MD, J.W. Goethe U., Frankfurt, Germany, 1951. Diplomate Am. Bd. Internal Medicine, Am. Bd. Med. Oncology. Intern Grace Hosp., Detroit, 1951-52, resident, 1955-56; resident Detroit Receiving Hosp., 1956-58; fellow in cancer rsch. Detroit Inst. Cancer Rsch., 1958-59; from asst. to assoc. prof. medicine sch. medicine Wayne State U., Detroit, 1962-72, prof., 1972—, dir. divsn. conjoint svcs. and curricula oncology, 1966-72, chmn. dept. oncology, 1972-82, chmn. dept. internal medicine, 1982-89; clin. dir. Detroit Inst. Cancer Rsch., 1962-66; acting chief medicine Detroit Gen. Hosp., 1970-71; chief divsn. medicine Grace Hosp., 1973-76; chief oncology Harper-Grace Hosps., Detroit, 1977-82, chief medicine, 1982-89; assoc. dir. clin. activities Comprehensive Cancer Ctr. Met. Detroit, 1978-82; physician-in-chief Detroit Med. Ctr., 1982-89; pres. Mich. Cancer Found., Detroit, 1991-95; pres. emeritus, bd. dirs. B.A. Karmanos Cancer Ctr., 1995—; mem. com. human and animal experimentation Wayne State U., 1968-73, chmn., 1971-73, mem. presdl. selection adv. com., 1981, mem. univ. coun., 1981-83, mem. budget com. of univ. coun., 1981-83, mem. presdl. com. cancer programs, 1981—; mem. Nat. Colorectal Cancer Adv. Com., 1971-73, Com. Evaluate Cancer Curricula Am. Med. Schs., 1971-79; mem. exec. com. S.W. Cancer Chemotherapy Study Group, 1972-73; mem. evaluation adv. coun. Southeastern Regional Cancer Programs, 1972-74; chmn. gastrointestinal com. S.W. Oncology Group, 1974-79; mem. exec. bd. Wayne State U./U. Mich. Inst. Gerontology, 1975-86; mem. oper. com. Comprehensive Cancer Ctr. Met. Detroit, 1978—; mem. commd. jury Saint-Vincent Internat. Prize Med. Scis., Rome, 1979, 83; chmn. coun. dept. chairmen sch. medicine Wayne State U., 1979-81, mem. dean's coun. grad. med. edn. program, 1983-89, mem. dean's rev. com., 1986, mem. pharmacy and medicine task force, 1986, chmn. radiation oncology search com., 1987; mem. med. staff fin. and budget com. Harper-Grace Hosps., 1983-84, mem. gerontology svcs. planning com., 1984-87, chmn. NMR adv. com., 1984—; mem. transplantation com. Detroit Med. Ctr., 1985-86, mem. med. bd., 1985-89, chmn. task force cancer programs, 1987; presenter in field. Contbr. chpts. to books and articles to profl. jours.; mem. adv. bd. Cancer Treatment Reports, 1980-82. Mem. exec. com. bd. trustees Mich. Cancer Found., 1975-85; mem. blood svc. ops. com. ARC Southeastern Mich., 1981-84; bd. dirs. Wayne County unit Am. Cancer Soc., 1976-79; trustee Hospice Southeastern Mich., 1991—; mem. Nat. Cancer Adv. Bd., 1994—. Capt. U.S. Army, 1953-55. Recipient Life award Am. Cancer Soc. Met. Detroit, 1981, Mercy Medallion, 1983, Tree-of-Life award Nat. Jewish Fedn., 1987, Michiganian-of-Yr. award The Detroit News, 1987, Hospice Humanitarian award, 1989; inductee Internat. Heritage Hall of Fame, Inst. Met. Detroit, 1989; honored by Am. Cancer Soc., 1989, Weizmann Inst. Sci., 1992. Mem. AAAS, ACP, Am. Assn. Cancer Rsch., Am. Fedn. Clin. Rsch., Am. Soc. Hematology, Am. Soc. Clin. Oncology (mem. program com. 1981), Am. Assn. Cancer Edn. (mem. exec. coun. 1971—, pres. 1976-77), Mich. State Med. Soc. (mem. cancer com. 1965-73, Flag award 1992), N.Y. Acad. Scis., Mich. Soc. Internal Medicine, Wayne County Med. Soc. (mem. del. body 1981-87, mem. task force referral edn. 1986, mem. physician tech. svcs. 1986—), Detroit Physiol. Soc., Detroit Acad. Medicine, Ctrl. Soc. Clin. Rsch., James Ewing Soc., Aesculapian Soc. (hon.), Alpha Omega Alpha, Phi Lambda Kappa (hon.). Office: Harper Hosp 3990 John R St Detroit MI 48201-2018*

VAITUKAITIS, JUDITH LOUISE, medical research administrator; b. Hartford, Conn., Aug. 29, 1940; d. Albert George and Julia Joan (Vaznikaitis) V. BS, Tufts U., 1962; MD, Boston U., 1966. Investigator, med. officer reproductive rsch. Nat. Inst. Child Health and Human Devel., NIH, Bethesda, Md., 1971-74; assoc. dir. clin. rsch. Nat. Ctr. Rsch. Resources NIH, Bethesda, Md., 1986-91, dir. gen. clin. rsch. ctr., 1986-91, dep. dir. extramural rsch., 1991; acting dir. Nat. Ctr. Rsch. Resources NIH, Bethesda, 1991-92, dir., 1993—; from assoc. prof. to prof. medicine Sch. Medicine Boston U., 1974-86, assoc. prof. physiology, 1975-80, assoc. prof. ob-gyn., 1977-80, program. dir. gen. clin. rsch. ctr., 1977-86, prof. physiology, 1980-86; head sect. endocrinology and metabolism Boston City Hosp., 1974-86. Mem. editorial bd. Jour. Clin. Endocrin. and Metabolism, 1973-80, Proc. Soc. Exptl. Biol. and Medicine, 1978-87, Endocrine Rsch., 1984-88. Author: Clinical Reproductive Neuroendocrinology, 1982; contbr. articles to profl. jours. Recipient Disting. Alumna award Sch. Medicine, Boston U., 1983, Mallincrodt award for Inv. Rsch. Clin. Radiossay Soc., 1980. Mem. Am. Fedn. Clin. Rsch., Endocrine Soc., Am. Soc. Clin. Rsch., Inst. Medicine-NAS. Office: Nat Ctr Rsch Resources NIH Bldg 31 Rm 3B11 31B Center Dr MSC 2128 Bethesda MD 20892-2128

VAJK, HUGO, manufacturing executive; b. Ljubljana, Slovenia, Mar. 26, 1928; emigrated to Can., 1947, naturalized, 1953; s. Hugo and Magda (Slatnar) V.; m. Barbara Lois Hallin, June 13, 1953; children: Tanja Astrid, Hugo Anthony, Madeleine Louise, Anita Marie, Nicolette Cecile, Moira Suzanne. Student, Institut Polytechnique, Grenoble, France, 1947; B.Eng. with honors, McGill U., Montreal, 1951; M.S., Carnegie Mellon U., Pitts., 1953. Product mgr. Joy Mfg. Co., Buffalo, 1957-59; dir. gen. Joy Mfg. Co., Paris, 1960-63; with Massey-Ferguson, Ltd., 1964-78; pres. Moteurs Perkins S.A., Paris, 1964-65, Massey-Ferguson Ltd., Paris, 1966-69; v.p. logistics parent co. Massey-Ferguson Ltd., Toronto, 1970-72, exec. v.p., 1973-78; dir. GEC Inc., subs. Gen. Electric Co., Eng., 1979; chmn. English Electric Corp., Elmsford, N.Y., 1979; with Garret Corp. div. Signal Cos., 1980-84; v.p. Garrett Automotive Products; pres. Garrett Automotive Group, Allied-Signal, Inc., 1985-87; chmn. Inovatek Advisors, Inc., Tarpon Springs, Fla., 1988—; pres. ATM Communications Internat., Inc., Wilmington, Del., 1991—. Mem. ASME, Soc. Automotive Engrs., Assn. Profl. Engrs. Ont., Inst. Mgmt. Sci., Inst. Dirs., Inst. Mgmt. Cons., Nat. Assn. Corp. Dirs., Univ. Club (Toronto), Royal Can. Yacht Club (Toronto), Union Interaliée (Paris), Yacht Club de France (Paris), Royal Thames Yacht Club (London). Office: Inovatek Advisors Inc Ste 200 905 E Martin Luther King Jr Dr Tarpon Springs FL 34689-4864

VAJTAY, STEPHEN MICHAEL, JR., lawyer; b. New Brunswick, N.J., Mar. 18, 1958; s. Stephen Michael and Veronica Gizella (Fehèr) V.; m. Gabriella Katherine Soltèsz, Aug. 5, 1989; children: Stephen, Andrew, Gregory. BA, Rutgers U., 1980; JD, Georgetown U., 1983; LLM, NYU, 1989. Bar: N.J. 1984, U.S. Tax Ct. 1985. Assoc. McCarter and English, Newark, N.J., 1983-91, ptnr., 1991—; chmn. bd. trustees Hungarian Scout Assn. in Exteris, Garfield, N.J., 1985—; trustee Partnership for a Drug-Free N.J., Inc., Montclair, 1993—; adj. prof. law Seton Hall U. Sch. Law, Newark, 1995—; spkr. at lectrs. and seminars, 1992—. Contbr. articles to profl. jours. Mem. Bd. of Adjustment, New Brunswick, N.J., 1993—. Mem. ABA, N.J. Bar Assn., Tax sect. N.J. Bar Assn., Essex County Bar Assn., Phi Beta Kappa. Roman Catholic. Office: McCarter and English Four Gateway Ctr 100 Mulberry St Newark NJ 07102

VAKALO, EMMANUEL-GEORGE, architecture and planning educator, researcher; b. Athens, Greece, May 10, 1946; came to U.S., 1965; s. George Constantine and Eleni (Stavrinou) V.; m. Kathleen Leitgabel, July 20, 1974. BArch, Cornell U., 1969, MArch, 1972, M in Regional Planning, 1977; PhD, U. Mich., 1985. Instr. U. Mich., Ann Arbor, 1975-79, asst. prof., 1979-91, assoc. prof., 1991—, chmn. doctoral program in arch. coll. arch. urban planning, 1994—; cons. JP Industries, Ann Arbor, 1987-88; guest prof. Tech. U. Wien, U. Okla., Carnegie-Mellon U., La. State U., U. Notre Dame, Ryerson Poly. Inst., Calif. State Poly. U., Pomona. Author: Visual Studies, 1983, Visual Syntax: Function and Production of Forms, 1988. Mem. Am. Planning Assn., Environ, Design Rsch. Assn., Nat. Inst. Archtl. Edn., Inst. Math. Geography. Avocations: photography, drawing, reading, sailing. Office: U Mich Coll Arch and Urban Planning 2000 Bonisteel Dr Ann Arbor MI 48109-2021

VALADE, ALAN MICHAEL, lawyer; b. Berwyn, Ill., Jan. 26, 1952; s. Merle F. and Vera M. (Gildersleave) V.; m. June 17, 1978. BA, U. Mich., 1974; JD, Wayne State U., 1977; LLM in Taxation, NYU, 1978. Bar: Mich. 1978, Fla. 1987. Assoc. Kemp, Klein, Endelman & Beer, Birmingham, Mich., 1978-79; shareholder Valade, MacKinnon & Higgins, P.C., Detroit, 1979-84, Schwendener & Valade, P.C., Mason, Mich., 1985-91; ptnr. Honigman Miller Schwartz and Cohn, Lansing, Mich., 1991—. Co-author: The Michigan Single Business Tax, 1991; contbr. articles to profl. jours. Mem. ABA, State Bar Mich. (chmn. state and local tax com. 1991, tax. coun. 1989-92), State Bar Fla., Oak Pointe Country Club. Avocations: reading, traveling, running, skiing. Office: Honigman Miller Schwartz & Cohn 222 N Washington Sq Ste 400 Lansing MI 48933-1800

VALADE, ROBERT CHARLES, apparel company executive; b. Detroit, Apr. 19, 1926; s. Cyril K. and Marion I. (Anderson) V.; m. Gretchen Carhartt, Sept. 18, 1948; children: Gretchen Garth, Mark R. Degree in bus. adminstrn., Mich. State U., 1947. Salesman Royal Typewriter, Detroit, 1947-50; v.p. Carhartt Inc., Detroit, 1950-59; pres., CEO Carhartt Inc., Dearborn, Mich., 1959-95, chmn. bd., CEO, 1995—. with USN, 1944-46, PTO. Mem. World Pres.'s Orgn. (bd. dirs. 1980-82), Detroit Racquet Club (pres. 1950-54), Country Club Detroit, Fiddle Sticks Country Club (Ft. Myers, Fla.). Republican. Roman Catholic. Avocations: golf, hunting, fishing.

VALASKAKIS, KIMON P., ambassador, economics educator; b. Sept. 29, 1941; s. Platon and Marie-Claire V.; m. Gail Guthrie (div.); children: Ion, Paris; m. Iris Fitzpatrick, May 21, 1983; 1 stepson, Andrew. B.A., Am. U. Cairo; B. Law, U. St. Joseph; Ph.D., Cornell U., 1966. Asst. prof. U. Montreal, 1966-72, assoc. prof., 1972-77, assoc. dir. Centre de Recherches en Devel. Economique, 1971-72, prof., 1977—; pres. GAMMA Inst., Montreal, 1977—; cons. UN, MIT, UNESCO, NATO; amb. of Can. to OECD Paris, 1995—. Author: Conserver Society, 1980, Le Quebec International, 1980, Le Quéébec au Conditionnel, 1982. Donner Found. grantee; Can. Council fellow; Social Scis. and Humanities Council fellow. Mem. Am. Econ. Assn.

VALASQUEZ, JOSEPH LOUIS, industrial engineer; b. Balt., Apr. 15, 1955; s. Jose Louis and Edith Rosabel (Saunders) V.; m. Nicole Diane Feldser, Sept. 4, 1983; children: Alexandra Nicole, Joseph Jr. AA, Essex Coll., 1977; BS in Indsl. Engring., U. Ariz., 1982; MBA in Fin., So. Ill. U., 1985. Registered profl. engr., Fla.; cert. quality engr.; cert. quality auditor; cert. quality mgr.; pvt. pilots license. Machinist Bausch & Lomb, Balt., 1974-77; indsl. engr. IBM Corp., Tucson, 1980-81; sr. indsl. engr. Gen. Dynamics, San Diego, 1981-83; supr. engring. Avco Corp., Nashville, 1983-84; mgr. engring. Burroughs Corp., Coral Springs, Fla., 1984-85; dir. total quality mgmt. Lambda Novatronics, Inc., Pompano Beach, Fla., 1985—; pres. Woodland Properties; corp. mgt. continuous improvement Sensormatic Corp.; computer cons., Margate, Fla., 1987; founder, owner E.P.I. Cons., Pompano Beach. Mem. Am. Inst. Indsl. Engrs., Fla. Engring. Soc. Republican. Roman Catholic. Avocations: real estate management, computer programming, mountain climbing, canoeing, private pilot. Home: PO Box 9821 Coral Springs FL 33075-0821

VALBERG, LESLIE STEPHEN, medical educator, physician, researcher; b. Churchbridge, Sask., Can., June 3, 1930; s. John Stephen and Rose (Vikfusson) V.; m. Barbara Tolhurst, Sept. 14, 1954; children: John, Stephanie, Bill. M.D., C.M., Queens U., 1954, M.S.C., 1958. Cert. internal medicine specialist Royal Coll. Physicians and Surgeons of Can. Asst. prof. Queens U. Kingston, Ont., Can., from 1960—, prof., until 1975; prof. medicine U. Western Ont., London, 1975-95, chmn. dept., 1975-85; dean faculty of medicine U. Western Ont., 1985-92; prof., 1995—; cons. Univ. Hosp., 1975-95; prof. emeritus U. We. Ont., London, Can., 1995—. Rsch. Assoc. Med. Council of Can., 1960-65. Fellow Royal Coll. Physicians and Surgeons; mem. Am. Gastroent. Assn., Med. Rsch. Coun. Can. (v.p. 1980-82). Home: 1496 Stoneybrook Crescent, London, ON Canada N5X 1C5 Office: U Western Ont, London, ON Canada N6A 5C1

VALBUENA-BRIONES, ANGEL JULIAN, language educator, author; b. Madrid, Jan. 11, 1928; naturalized, 1963; s. Angel Valbuena-Prat and Francisca Briones; m. Barbara Northrup Hobart, Nov. 9, 1957; children: Teresa, Vivian. Licenciado summa cum laude, Murcia (Spain) U., 1949; Ph.D. with honors, Madrid U., 1952. Prof. Ayudante Murcia U., 1949-51; lectr. Oxford (Eng.) U., 1953-55; prof. Ayudante Madrid U., 1955-56; vis. lectr. U. Wis., 1956-58; asst. prof. Yale U., 1958-60; Elias Ahuja prof. Spanish lit. U. Del., 1960—; lecture tour, S.Am., summer 1957; vis. prof. NYU, summers 1960, 61, U. Madrid, 1970-71, summers 1965, 77, U. Mex. at Aragon, summer 1979, Inst. Caro y Cuervo, Bogota, Colombia, summer 1980; mem. Fulbright-Hays nat. screening com., 1981-83, 89-90; mem. edit. com. for CD-ROM edit. Spanish Golden Age Theatre, Chadwyck-Healey/Spain and Consejo Superior Investigacione Cientificas, 1995-97; bd. dirs. publs. U. Barcelona, Spain, Bull. Comediantes, U. Calif., Riverside, Hispanic Jour., Pa., Juan de la Cuesta Edits., Del.; profl. cons. NEH. Author: Neuva Poesia de Puerto Rico, 1952, Comedias de Capa y Espada de Calderon, 1954, Dramas de Honor de Calderon, 2 vols., 1956, Obras Completas de Calderon, vol. I, 1959, 3d reprinting, 1991, vol. II, 1956, 6th edit. 2 vols., 1988, Literatura Hispanoamericana, 1962, Perspectiva critica de los dramas de Calderon, 1965, Ideas y Palabras, 1968, El alcalde de Zalamea de Calderon, 1971, rev. 13th edit., 1995, Primera Parte de Comedias de Pedro Calderon de la Barca, Vol. 1, 1974, Vol. 2, 1981, 12th reprinting, 1995, Calderon y la comedia nueva, 1977, La vida es sueno. Antes que todo es mi dama. Pedro Calderon de la Barca, 1988, El mayor monstruo del mundo. de Calderon, 1995; contbr. articles to profl. jours., chpts. to books. Founder, pres. Valbuena Inst. Spanish Lit., Inc., 1986. Consejo Superior de Investigaciones Cientificas fellw, 1951, 70-71, Instituto de Cultura Hispánica fellow, 1951-52; recipient Excellence in Teaching award U. Del., 1988, Outstanding Scholar award U. Del. Coll. Arts and Sci., 1996. Mem. MLA, AAUP, Am. Assn. Tchrs. Spanish and Portuguese, Inst. Iberoam. Lit., Internat. Fedn. Modern Langs. and Lits., Assn. Lit. Scholars and Critics, Internat. Assn. Hispanists, Am. Comparative Lit. Assn., Assn. for Hispanic Classic Theatre, Philol. Assn. Pacific Coast, Greenville Country Club, Sigma Delta Pi (hon.), Phi Kappa Phi. Home: 203 Nottingham Rd Newark DE 19711-7402

VALCIC, SUSAN JOAN, lawyer; b. N.Y.C., Mar. 23, 1956; d. Joseph and Eve Manderville; m. Alexander C. Valcic, July 28, 1979. BA magna cum laude, Columbia U., 1983; JD, Cardozo Sch. Law, 1986. Assoc. attorney Bailey, Marshall & Hoeniger, N.Y.C., 1986-87, Zalkin, Rodin & Goodman, N.Y.C., 1987-89; pvt. practice N.Y.C., 1989—. Apptd. adminstrv. law judge, N.Y., 1990. Mem. Assn. Bar City N.Y., N.Y. County Lawyers Assn., N.Y. State Bar. Assn., Fed. Bar. Assn., Columbia Club, Phi Beta Kappa.

VALDES, JACQUELINE C., neuropsychologist, consultant, researcher; b. Bklyn., Sept. 17, 1962; d. Gabriel and Rosy (Mosseri) Chehebar; m. Manuel Valdes, June 3, 1990. BA, U. Conn., 1983; cert. in substance abuse studies, Nova U., 1987, MS, 1988; PhD, Nova U., Ft. Lauderdale, 1992. Diplomate Am. Coll. Forensic Examiners. Children's outpatient coord. Jewish Family Svc., Miami Beach, Fla., 1988-89; neuropsychology apprentice Robert A. Levitt, Ph.D., PA, Miami Beach, Fla., 1989-90; intern Columbia Presbyn. Med. Ctr., N.Y.C., 1990-91; fellow and resident Robert A. Levitt, PhD, PA, Ft. Lauderdale, 1991-93; pvt. practice, 1993—; dir. neuropsychology svcs. Hollywood (Fla.) Meml. Med. Ctr., Rehab. Unit, 1995—; psychology supr., educator Sunrise (Fla.) Rehab. Hosp., 1992—; rschr., asst. dir. internship North Broward Med. Ctr., Memory Disorders Ctr. Neurolog. Inst., Pompona, Fla., 1993—, dir., 1994—; neuropsychologist Neurologic Cons., Fort Lauderdale, Fla., 1992—, Hollywood, Fla., 1992—, Memory Disorder Ctr., 1992—; neuropsychology cons. Sunrise (Fla.) Rehab. Hosp., 1992-94; chairperson minority affairs Broward County Psych. Assn., 1997—. Contbr. articles to profl. jours. Sec. Spanish Speaking Neuropsychology Interest Group, L.A., 1993-94; apptd. Child Sexual Abuse Svc. Provider Task Force, 1989. Mem. APA, Internat. Neuropsychol. Soc., Nat. Acad. Neuropsychologists, Am. Acad. Neurology, Brain Injury Assn., Fla. Psychol. Assn. Democrat. Jewish. Home: 520 E Mt Vernon Dr Plantation FL 33325 Office: No Broward Med Ctr Neurol Inst and Memory Disorder Ctr 201 E Sample Rd Pompano Beach FL 33064-3502

VALDES, MAXIMIANO, conductor. Student, Conservatory of Music, Santiago, Chile, Accademia Santa Cecilia, Rome. Asst. condr. Teatro Fenice, Venice, Italy, 1976; worked as conducting fellow with Leonard Bernstein and Seiji Ozawa, 1977; condr. Buffalo Philharm. Orch., 1989—. Operatic debut with La Traviata, Nice Opera, France; Paris Opera debut with Romeo and Juliet, 1986; London debut with English Chamber Orch., 1987; other opera appearances include The Barber of Seville in Lausanne, Le Nozze di Figaro and Werther in Barcelona, Agnese di Hohenstaufen and The Barber of Seville at Rome Opera, Eugene Onegin at Bonn Opera, Faust in Copenhagen; condr. orchs. of Spain, Denmark, Italy, S.Am.; leader London Philharm. Orch. on tour to Spain, Monte Carlo Philharm. on tour to Italy; prin. condr. Nat. Orch. of Spain, 1986-87; recs. with Monte Carlo Philharm., London Symphony, Nice Philharm., New Zealand Symphony; N.Am. debut with Buffalo Philharm., 1987; appointed music dir. Buffalo Philharm. Orch., 1989, asst. conductor at the Teatro Fenice in Venice, 1976. Recipient 2d prize Rupert Found. Conducting Competition, London, 1978, 1st prize Nicolai Malko Competition, Copenhagen, 1980, 1st prize Vittorio Gui Competition, Florence, Italy; awarded the Del Carlo Tanglewood fellowship, 1977. Office: Buffalo Philharm Orch 71 Symphony Circle PO Box 905 Buffalo NY 14213*

VALDES, ROLANDO HECTOR, library director, law librarian; b. Havana, Cuba, Jan. 13, 1939; came to U.S., 1966; s. Juan Manuel Valdes-Anciano and Sylvia (Nunez) Marasco. BA, Sancti-Spiritus Coll., Las Villas, Cuba, 1961; MLS, Havana (Cuba) U., 1963, postgrad. in tchr. edn., 1963-65. Libr. asst. The Newberry Libr., Chgo., 1966-68; reference libr. Sandard and Poor's Corp., N.Y.C., 1968-72; evening supr. Hunter Coll. Libr., N.Y.C., 1970-72; med. social worker Flower and Fifth Ave. Hosps., N.Y.C., 1973-76; social worker Mt. Carmel Guild, Union City, N.J., 1976-79, Queensborough Soc. for Prevention of Cruelty to Children, 1979-82, State of Fla. Dept. Health and Rehab. Svcs., 1982-84; libr. specialist, law libr., libr. dir. Dade Correction Instn. Librs., Florida City, Fla., 1984—. Contbr. articles to profl. jours. Mem. Dade County Libr. Assn., Reforma. Avocations: opera studies, audio-visual collector, chess, baseball, art films. Home: 38277 SW 192nd Ave Lot 28 Florida City FL 33034-6606 Office: Dade Correctional Libr 19000 SW 377th St Florida City FL 33034-6407

VALDES-DAPENA, MARIE AGNES, pediatric pathologist, educator; b. Pottsville, Pa., July 14, 1921; d. Edgar Daniel and Marie Agnes (Rettig) Brown; m. Antonio M. Valdes-Dapena, Apr. 6, 1945 (div. Oct. 1980); children: Victoria Maria Valdes-Dapena Dead, Deborah Anne Valdes-Dapena Malle, Maria Cristina, Andres Antonio, Antonio Edgardo, Carlos Roberto, Marcos Antonio, Ricardo Daniel, Carmen Patricia Valdés-Dapena Fater, Catalina Inez Valdés-Dapena Amram, Pedro Pablo. BS, Immaculata Coll., 1941; MD, Temple U., 1944. Diplomate: Am. Bd. Pathology (spl. qualification-pediatric pathology 1990). Intern Phila. Gen. Hosp., 1944-45, resident in pathology, 1945-49; asst. pathologist Fitzgerald Mercy Hosp., Darby, Pa., 1949-51; dir. labs. Woman's Med. Coll. Pa., Phila., 1951-55; instr. pathology Woman's Med. Coll. Pa., 1947-51, asst. prof., 1951-55, assoc. prof., 1955-59; assoc. pathologist St. Christopher's Hosp. for Children, Phila., 1959-76; dir. sect. pediatric pathology U. Miami (Fla.)-Jackson Meml. Hosp., 1976-81, pediatric pathologist, dir. div. edn. in pathology, 1981-93, co.-dir. edn. in pathology, 1993—; cons., lectr. U.S. Naval Hosp., Phila., 1972-76; instr. pathology Sch. Medicine U. Pa., 1945-49; instr. Sch. Medicine U. Pa. (Sch. Dentistry), 1947, Sch. Medicine U. Pa. (Grad. Sch. Medicine), 1948-55, vis. lectr., 1960-62; asst. prof. Temple U. Med. Sch., 1959-63, assoc. prof., 1963-67, prof. pathology and pediatrics, 1967-76; prof. pathology and pediatrics U., Miami, 1976-93, prof. emeritus pathology and pediatrics, 1993—; cons. pediatric pathology div. med. examiner Dept. Pub. Health Phila., 1967-70; mem. perinatal biology and infant mortality research and tng. com. Nat. Inst. Child Health and Human Devel., NIH, 1971-73; mem. sci. adv. bd. Armed Forces Inst. Pathology, 1976-82; assoc. med. examiner, Dade County, Fla., 1976-97; chmn. med. bd. Nat. Sudden Infant Death Syndrome Found., 1961-81, 87-91, pres., 1984-87, chmn. bd., 1985-88; mem. med. and sci. adv. coun. The SIDS Alliance, 1990-95. Contbr. articles to profl. jours. NIH grantee. Mem. U.S. and Can. Acad. Pathology, Coll. Physicians Phila., Internat. Assn. Pediatric Pathology, Soc. for Pediatric Pathology (pres. 1980-81), Alpha Omega Alpha. Roman Catholic. Home: 729 N Jackson St Media PA 19063 Office: Dept Pathology U Miami Sch Medicine PO Box 016960 Miami FL 33101-6960

VALDIVIA, HECTOR HORACIO, medical educator; b. Loreto, Mex., Aug. 23, 1958; married. MD, Nat U. Mex., 1982, PhD, 1987. Teaching asst. Nat. U. Mex. Sch. Medicine, Mexico City, 1980-86; rsch. assoc. Baylor Coll. Medicine, Houston, 1986-89; assoc. scientist U. Wis. Sch. Medicine, Madison, 1989-92; rsch. asst. prof. U. Md. Med. Sch., Bapt., 1992-94; asst. prof. dept. physiology U. Wis. Med. Sch., Madison, 1994—; lectr. and researcher in field. Contbr. articles to profl. jours., chpts. to books. Cystic Fibrosis Found. fellow, 1989-91. Mem. Am. Heart Assn. (scintific coun. 1995—), Biophys. Soc. U.S.A. Office: U Wis Med Sch Dept Physiology 1300 University Ave Madison WI 53706-1510

VALE, MARGO ROSE, physician; b. Balt., June 16, 1950; d. Henry and Pauline Esther (Koplow) Hausdorff; m. Michael Allen Vale, Aug. 22, 1971; children: Edward, Judith. BA magna cum laude, Brandeis U., 1971; MD, Albert Einstein Coll. Medicine, 1975. Diplomate Am. Bd. Dermatology. Resident in internal medicine and dermatology NYU, N.Y.C., 1975-79, Bellevue Hosp., N.Y.C., 1975-79, VA Hosp., N.Y.C., 1975-79; staff physician HIP Greater N.Y., Bay Shore, 1979-81; pvt. practice medicine Huntington, N.Y., 1981—; cons. in dermatology Huntington Hosp., 1981—, Gurwin Jewish Geriatric Ctr., Commack, N.Y., 1990—. Contbr. articles to profl. jours. Mem. Am. Acad. Dermatology, Med. Soc. State N.Y., Long Island Dermatology Soc., Suffolk County Med. Soc., Suffolk Dermatology Soc. (pres. 1990-92), Phi Beta Kappa. Avocations: cooking, photography, sketching, music. Office: 205 E Main St Huntington NY 11743-2923

VALEK, BERNARD MICHAEL, accounting executive; b. Joliet, Ill., Nov. 19, 1945; s. Peter Anthony and Ann Monica (Hertko) V.; m. Kathleen Mary Clarke, Aug. 16, 1969; 1 child, Emily Ann. BS, No. Ill. U., 1968, MBA, 1969. CPA, Calif., Ill. Asst. prof. Ferris State U., Big Rapids, Mich., 1969-72; staff mgr. Arthur Andersen & Co., Chgo., 1972-78; dir. Calif. CPA Fedn., Palo Alto, 1979-84; pres. Alliance of Practicing CPAs, Long Beach, Calif., 1985—; cons. ANA, L.A., 1984-86. Author: ANA Practice Management Manuals, 1985; pub. (newsletter) The CPAdvocate, 1990—. Bd. dirs. Am. Heart Assn., Long Beach, 1993-94; bd. dirs., treas. Cities in Schs. Long Beach, 1988—, Long Beach Phone Friend, 1988-93. Named One of 100 Most Influential People in Acctg., Acctg. Today newspaper, 1996. Mem. AICPA (bd. dirs. 1982-84), Calif. CPA Soc. (bd. dirs. 1979-84). Roman Catholic. Avocations: exercising, hiking, travel, health. Office: Alliance of Practicing CPAs 3909 California Ave Long Beach CA 90807-3511

VALENTA, ZDENEK, chemistry educator; b. Havlickuv Brod, Czechoslovakia, June 14, 1927; came to Can., 1950; s. Karel Valenta and Jindra (Komers) Valentova; m. Noreen Elizabeth Donahoe, July 29, 1957; children—Katherine Elizabeth, Richard Karel, Michael Francis. Dipl. Ing. Chem., E.T.H., Zurich, Switzerland, 1950; M.S., U. N.B., 1952, Ph.D., 1953. Spl. lectr. dept. chemistry U. N.B., Fredericton, Can., 1953-54, lectr., 1954-56, asst. prof., 1957-58, assoc. prof., 1958-63, prof., 1963-90; rsch. prof. U. N.B., Fredericton, 1990—; head chemistry dept. U. N.B., Fredericton, Can., 1963-72; cons. Delmar Chems., LaSalle, Que., Can., 1970—, Ayerst Research Labs., Montreal, Que., Can., 1980-85, Torcan Chem., Toronto, Ont., Can., 1980—. Contbr. articles to profl. jours. Recipient Excellence in Teaching award U. N.B., 1974, Sci. Teaching award Atlantic Provinces Coun. on Scis./Northern Telecom 1987, award for chem. edn. Union Carbide, 1989. Fellow Chem. Inst. Can. (Merck, Sharp and Dohme award 1967), Royal Soc. Can. Home: 872 Windsor St, Fredericton, NB Canada E3B 4G5 Office: U NB Dept Chemistry, Bag Service 45222, Fredericton, NB Canada E3B 6E2

VALENTE, LOUIS PATRICK (DAN VALENTE), business and financial consultant; b. Somerville, Mass., July 26, 1930; s. Luigi and Mary Constance (Fedele) V.; m. Jeanne Barbara Peters, Oct. 3, 1992; children: Louis, Marianne, Steven, Diane, Richard, Carol, Susan. Cert., Bentley Coll., Boston, 1955. Cost acct. Cambridge Corp., Lowell, Mass., 1953-55; sr. acct. Flaherty, Bliss & Co., CPAs, Boston, 1956-61; fin. analyst Sanders Assocs., Nashua, N.H., 1961-62; fin. cons. Burlington, Mass., 1961-68; contract audit adminstr. Dept. Def. Audit Agy., Boston, 1962-66, DOE, Las Vegas, 1966-68; asst. controller EG&G, Inc., Wellesley, Mass., 1968-71, asst. v.p., treas., 1971-74, dir. fin., 1974-79, officer, corp. treas., 1979-83, v.p. bus. devel., 1985-91, sr. v.p. mergers, acquisitons and investments, 1991-95; bus. and fin. cons., 1995—; bd. dirs. Meditech Inc., Westwood, Mass., Micrion Corp., Peabody, Mass., Ga. Patient Care Tech., Atlanta, MKS Instruments, Inc., Andover, Mass., Palomar Med. Tech. Inc., Beverly, Mass., Tytronics, Inc. Bedford, Mass. Selectman Town of Burlington, 1970-73, 76-79, chmn., 1972-79; trustee, mem. fin. com. Choate-Symmes Hosp., Woburn, Mass., 1972-80; pres.'s adv. coun. Bentley Coll. With USAF, 1951-53. Mem. AICPA, Fin. Execs. Inst., Mass. Soc. CPAs, Bentley Coll. Alumni Assn., New Eng. Council. Roman Catholic. Lodge: K.C. Home: 44 Concord Rd Weston MA 02193-1223 *Creativeness and its benefit to the business world is important. Credit to, and exposure of the creator is trivial.*

VALENTE, PETER CHARLES, lawyer; b. N.Y.C., July 3, 1940; s. Francis Louis and Aurelia Emily (Cella) V.; m. Judith Kay Nemeroff, Feb. 19, 1966; children: Susan Lynn, David Marc. BA, Bowdoin Coll., 1962; LLB, Columbia U., 1966; LLM, N.Y.U., 1971. Bar: N.Y. 1967. Assoc. Tenzer Greenblatt LLP, N.Y.C., 1967-73, ptnr., 1973—, ptnr. in charge trusts and estates dept. Co-author column on wills, estates and surrogate's practice N.Y. Law Jour. Fellow Am. Coll. Trust and Estate Counsel; mem. ABA, N.Y. State Bar Assn. (lectr. on wills, trusts and estates), Assn. of Bar of City of N.Y., N.Y. County Lawyers' Assn. (former bd. dirs. and chmn. com. on surrogates' ct., lectr. on wills, trusts and estates), Phi Beta Kappa. Office: Tenzer Greenblatt LLP 405 Lexington Ave New York NY 10174-0002

VALENTI, CARL M., newspaper publisher. Pres., pub.-info. svc. Wall St. Jour., N.Y.C.; also sr. v.p. Dow Jones & Co., N.Y.C. Office: The Wall Street Journal Dow Jones & Co Inc 200 Liberty St New York NY 10281-1003*

VALENTI, JACK JOSEPH, motion picture executive; b. Houston, Sept. 5, 1921; m. Mary Margaret Wiley, June 1, 1962; children: Courtenay Lynda, John Lyndon, Alexandra Alice. BA, U. Houston, 1946; MBA, Harvard U., 1948. Co-founder, formerly exec. v.p. Weekley and Valenti, Inc. (advt.), 1952-63; spl. asst. to Pres. Johnson, 1963-66; pres., chief exec. officer Motion Picture Assn. Am., Inc., 1966—; chmn. Alliance Motion Picture and TV Producers, Inc., 1966—; chmn., chief exec. officer Motion Picture Export Assn. Am.; adj. prof. govt. and pub. adminstrn. Am. U., 1977; bd. dirs. Riggs Nat. Corp. Washington. Author: Bitter Taste of Glory, 1971, A Very Human President, 1976, Speak Up With Confidence: How To Prepare, Learn and Deliver an Effective Speech, 1982, Protect and Defend, 1992; contbr. articles to mags. Trustee, bd. dirs. Am. Film Inst. Served with USAAF, 1942-45. Decorated D.F.C., Air medal with five oak leaf clusters, Disting. Unit Citation with cluster, European Theater Ribbon with 4 battle stars, Chevalier de la Legion d'honneur (France). Address: Motion Picture Assoc 1600 I St NW Washington DC 20006-4010 also: MPAA 15503 Ventura Blvd Encino CA 91436

VALENTIN, JOHN WILLIAM, professional baseball player; b. Mineola, N.Y., Feb. 18, 1967. Ed., Seton Hall U. Shortstop Boston Red Sox, 1992—. Named to Sporting News Am. League Silver Slugger Team, 1995. Achievements include completion of unassisted triple play (10th player in MLB history to do so). Office: Boston Red Sox 4 Yawkey Way Boston MA 02215-3409*

VALENTINE, ALAN DARRELL, symphony orchestra executive; b. San Antonio, July 18, 1958; s. Lonnie Darrell Jr. and Marjorie (Childs) V.; m. Jari Ann Ruhl, Aug. 10, 1979 (div. 1987); children: Brandon Darrell, Chelsea Michelle; m. Karen Kay Bingham, Oct. 21, 1989; 1 child, Nathan Lee. MusB, U. Houston, 1981. Orch. mgr. U. Houston Symphony, 1977-81; gen. mgr. Mid-Columbia Symphony Soc., Richland, Wash., 1981-83, Greensboro (N.C.) Symphony Soc., 1983-85; orch. mgr. Symphony Soc. San Antonio, 1985-87; mng. dir. Chattanooga Symphony and Opera, 1987-88; exec. dir. Okla. Philharm. Soc., Oklahoma City, 1988-; mem. adj. faculty Arts Administrn., Oklahoma City U., 1992—. Recs. include Best of Greensboro Symphony Orchestra Silver Season, 1983, A Christmas Festival-San Antonio Symphony, 1986, A Time of Healing-Oklahoma City Philharmonic, 1995; TV prodns. include Music of the Americas-Placido Domingo with San Antonio Symphony, 1986, Perry Como Christmas Special-San Antonio Symphony, 1986, Sagebrush Symphony-Oklahoma City Philharmonic with Michael Martin Murphey, 1996, Kathie Lee: Just In Time for Christmas-Okla. City Philharmonic & Guests, 1996. Bd. dirs. Classen Sch. for Artistically and Academically Gifted, Arts Festival Okla. Mem. Am. Symphony Orch. League (bd. dirs. Community and Urban Symphony Orch. divsn. 1981-83, mem. policy com. A 1995—, chmn. group III mgrs. 1996—), Rotary, Phi Mu Alpha. Presbyterian. Avocations: computers, racquetball, reading. Office: Okla City Philharm 428 W California Ave Ste 210 Oklahoma City OK 73102-2454

VALENTINE, FOY DAN, clergyman; b. Edgewood, Tex., July 3, 1923; s. John Hardy and Josie (Johnson) V.; m. Mary Louise Valentine, May 6, 1947; children: Mary Jean, Carol Elizabeth, Susan Foy. BA, Baylor U., 1944, LLD (hon.), 1979; ThM, Southwestern Baptist Theol. Sem., 1947, ThD, 1949; DD, William Jewell Coll., 1966, Louisiana Coll., 1989. Ordained to ministry Bapt. Ch., 1942. Dir. Bapt. student activities colls. in Houston, 1949-50; pastor First Bapt. Ch., Gonzales, Tex., 1950-53; dir. Christian life commn. Bapt. Gen. Conv. Tex., 1953-60; exec. dir., treas. Christian life commn. So. Bapt. Conv., 1960-87, exec. officer for devel., 1987-88; chmn. So. Bapt. inter-agy. council, 1965-67; Willson lectr. applied Christianity Wayland Bapt. Coll., 1963; Christian ethics lectr. Bapt. Theol. Sem., Ruschlikon-Zurich, Switzerland, 1966; Layne lectr. New Orleans Bapt. Theol. Sem., 1974; Jones lectr. Union U., 1976; Staley Disting. Christian scholar/lectr. La. Coll., 1981; Simpson lectr. Acadia Divinity Coll., Nova Scotia, 1982; H.I. Hester lectr. on preaching Midwestern Bapt. Theol. Sem., 1984; Belote lectr. Christian ethics Hong Kong Bapt. Theol. Sem., 1990; co-chmn. commn. religious liberty and human rights Bapt. World Alliance, 1966-75, chmn. commn. Christian ethics, 1976-80, mem. gen. coun., 1976-80; mem. Nashville Met. Human Rels. Commn., 1966-78, Pres.'s Commn. for Nat. Agenda for the Eighties, 1980; guest columnist USA Today; lectr. on Christian ethics Bible Inst. for Evangelism and Missions, St. Petersburg, USSR, 1991. Author: Believe and Behave, 1964, Citizenship for Christians, 1965, The Cross in the Marketplace, 1966, Where the Action Is, 1969, A Historical Study of Southern Baptists and Race Relations 1917-1947, 1980, What Do You Do After You Say Amen?, 1980, Hebrews, James, 1 and 2 Peter: Layman's Bible Book Commentary, 1981; editor: Christian Faith in Action, 1956, Peace, Peace, 1967, Christian Ethics Today, 1995—; contbr. to numerous anthologies, articles to profl. jours. Pres. Ctr. for Christian Ethics, 1990—; trustee Interfaith Alliance, 1994—, Ams. United for Separation of Ch. and State, 1960-93, pres., 1989-93; bd. dirs. Bapt. Joint Com. Pub. Affairs, 1960-87, Chs. Ctr. Theology and Pub. Policy, 1976-87, T.B. Maston Found., Texans Against Gambling; mem. bd. fellows Interpreter's House, 1967-78, Ctr. for Dialogue and Devel., 1987-96. Recipient Disting. Alumnus award Southwestern Bapt. Theol. Sem., 1970, Brooks Hays Meml. Christian Citizenship award, 1983, Disting. Alumni award Baylor U., 1987. Mem. Am. Soc. Christian Ethics. Democrat. Home and Office: 12527 Matisse Ln Dallas TX 75230-1741

VALENTINE, GENE C., securities dealer; b. Washington, Pa., June 19, 1950; s. John N. and Jane S. Valentine. BS in Psychology, Bethany Coll., 1972; student, U. Vienna, Austria, 1971-72. Commd. ensign USN, 1972, advanced through grades to lt., 1987, hon. discharged, 1978; owner Horizon Realty, San Francisco, 1978-82; dir. land acquisitions Windfarms Ltd. subs. Chevron, U.S.A., San Francisco, 1980-82; v.p. mktg. Christopher Weil & Co., Sherman Oaks, Calif., 1982-85; co-chmn., CEO Pacific Asset Group Inc. (name now Fin. West Group, Inc.), Pasadena, Calif., 1985—; bd. dirs. Fin. West Group, Inc., Paradox Holdings, Kennsington Holdings; founder, chmn., dir. Second Byte Found. Chmn., founder Second Byte Found.; mem. Rep. Party, L.A. Mem. NASD, Internat. Assn. Fin. Planning (bd. dirs. L.A. chpt. 1982—). Episcopalian. Avocations: equestrian, sailing, tennis, golf, running. Office: Fin West Group Inc 600 Hampshire Rd Ste 200 Westlake Vlg CA 91361-2500

VALENTINE, H. JEFFREY, legal association executive; b. Phila., Sept. 28, 1945; s. Joshua Morton and Olga W. (Wilson) V.; 1 child, Karyn. BS, St. Louis U., 1964, postgrad., 1966-68. Programmer, systems analyst Honeywell Electronic Data Processing, Wellesley Hills, Mass., 1964-66; account exec. Semiconductor div. Tex. Instruments, New Eng., 1966-68; New Eng. sales exec., Mid-Atlantic regional mgr. Electronic Instrumentation Co., 1968-70; pres. Nat. Free Lance Photographers Assn., Doylestown, Pa., 1970-89; pres., dir. Towne Print & Copy Ctrs. Inc.; v.p., exec. dir. Nat. Paralegal Assn., 1982—; pres. Paralegal Assocs., Inc., 1982—; chief operating officer Doylestown Parking Corp., 1977-88; bd. dirs. Law Enforcement Supply Co., Solebury, Valtronics Supply Co., Towne Print & Copy Centers Inc., Solebury, Doylestown Stationery and Office Supply, Energy Mktg. Assocs., Inc., Solebury, Paralegal Placement Network; pres. Paralegal Pub. Corp., 1983-90; pub. Paralegal Jour.; pres. Valco Enterprises Inc., 1986—, Paralegal Employment Sys., Inc., 1988, Solebury Press, Inc., 1989—; ptnr. J&S Gen. Contractors, 1993—, J&S Landscaping Tree Svc., 1993—; owner Specialized Computer Consulting, 1992—. Author: Photographers Bookkeeping System, 1973, rev. edit., 1978, Photographers Pricing Guides, 1971, 72, 74, 75, Available Markets Director's - 4 Vols., 1973-77, National Model Sources Directory, Nat. Paralegal Salary and Employment Survey, 1985-86, 88, 90-92, 93-94; also articles, bulls. and pamphlets. Exec. sec. Doylestown Bus. Assn., 1972-78, pres., 1979, 83, v.p., 1981. Recipient Internat. Men of Achievement award, 1988; named Personalities of the Am., 1988. Mem. London Coll. Applied Scis., Nat. Fedn. Paralegal Assns., Photog. Industry Coun., Nat. Assn. Legal Assts., Am. Soc Assn. Execs., Soc. Assn. Mgrs., Nat. Fedn. Ind. Business (mem. action com. com.), Nat. Parking Assn., Nat. Office Products Assn., Graphic Arts Assn. Delaware Valley, Nat. Assn. Federally Licensed Firearms Dealers, Nat. Compostition Assn., Internat. Platform Assn. Office: PO Box 406 Solebury PA 18963-0406

VALENTINE, HERMAN EDWARD, computer company executive; b. Norfolk, Va., June 26, 1937; s. Frank and Alice Mae (Heigh) V.; m. Dorothy Jones, Nov. 27, 1958; children: Herman Edward, Bryce Thomas. BS in Bus. Adminstrn., Norfolk State Coll., 1967; postgrad., Am. U., 1968; grad. student, Coll. William and Mary. Asst. bus. mgr. grad. sch. Dept. Agr., 1967, exec. officer grad. sch., 1967-68; bus. mgr. Norfolk State Coll., 1968; chmn., pres. Systems Mgmt. Am. Corp., Norfolk, 1969—, chmn., CEO, 1995—; chmn. Century Capitol Holders, Inc. Bd. dirs. PUSH Internat. Trade Bur., Cooperating Hampton Roads Orgn. for Minorities in Engring., Operation Smile, Greater Norfolk Corp.; mem. president's coun. Old Dominion U.; mem. adv. bd. Tidewater Vets. Meml. Project; mem. adv. coun. Va. Stage Co. Named Entrepreneur of Yr. Dept. Commerce Minority Bus. Devel. Agy., 1984, one of 10 Top Minority Owned Fed. Govt. Contractors Govt. Computer News, 1988, Outstanding Business Person of Yr. Va. Black Pres.'s Roundtable Assn., 1987, Amb. City of Norfolk, Va., 1986, Citizen of Yr. William A. Hunton YMCA, 1986, Pres.'s Coun. Am. Inst. Mgmt.; recipient Cert. of Merit City of Chg., 1985, McDonald's Hampton Roads Black Achievement award United Negro Coll. Fund., 1986, Colgate Whitehead Darden award, U. Va., 1987, cert. recognition Lt. Gov. Commonwealth of Va., 1987, Class III Supplier of Yr. award Nat. Minority Supplier Devel. Coun., 1987, Regional Minority Mfr. of Yr. award Minority Bus. Devel. Agy., 1988, Patriotic Svc. award U.S. Treasury Dept., 1989, Black Diamond award Operation Push, 1989; recognized by Upscale Mag., 1993. Mem. Armed Forces Communications and Electronics Assn., Tidewater Regional Minority Purchasing Coun., Downtown Norfolk Devel. Corp., Air Traffic Control Assn., Soc. Logistics Engrs., U.S. Navy League, Hampton Roads C. of C. Office: Systems Mgmt Am Corp 5 Koger Ctr Ste 217 Norfolk VA 23502-4107

VALENTINE, I. T., JR. (TIM VALENTINE), former congressman; b. Nashville, N.C., Mar. 15, 1926; s. I.T. and Hazel (Armstrong) V.; m. Elizabeth Salyer Carr, Sept. 6, 1953 (dec. 1981); children: Stephen, Mark, Philip, Beth; m. Barbara Reynolds, June 27, 1987; stepchildren: Mark, Vaughn, Bryan. A.B. in Polit. Sci., The Citadel, Charleston, S.C., 1948; LL.B., U. N.C., 1952. Pvt. practice law Nashville, N.C., 1952-82; mem. 98th-103rd Congresses from 2nd N.C. dist., Washington, D.C., 1982-94; zone whip N.C., Tenn., S.C. 98th-102d Congresses, Washington, 1986, 88, 90; mem. Pub. Works and Transp. com., subcoms. Aviation, Surface Transp., Sci., Space and Tech. com., subcoms. Water Resources, Tech., Environ., Aviation; mem. N.C. Gen. Assembly, Raleigh, N.C., 1955-60, chmn. house judiciary com., 1959; legal advisor to gov., Raleigh, 1965; legis. counsel to gov. 1967. Chmn. N.C. Dem. Exec. Com., Raleigh, 1966-68. Served to sgt. USAF, 1944-46; PTO. Mem. Nash-Edgecombe Bar Assn., N.C. Bar Assn., ABA, N.C. Acad. Trial Lawyers, Nashville C. of C., Morning Star Lodge. Democrat. Baptist.

VALENTINE, JAMES WILLIAM, paleobiology, educator, author; b. Los Angeles, Nov. 10, 1926; s. Adelbert Cuthbert and Isabel (Davis) V.; m. Grace Evelyn Whysner, Dec. 21, 1957 (div. 1972); children—Anita, Ian; m. Cathryn Alice Campbell, Sept. 10, 1978 (div. 1986); 1 child, Geoffrey; m. Diane Mondragon, Mar. 16, 1987. B.A., Phillips U., 1951; M.A., UCLA, 1954, Ph.D., 1958. From asst. prof. to assoc. prof. U. Mo., Columbia, 1958-64; from assoc. prof. to prof. U. Calif., Davis, 1964-77; prof. geol. scis. U. Calif., Santa Barbara, 1977-90; prof. integrative biology U. Calif., Berkeley, 1990—. Author: Evolutionary Paleoecology of the Marine Biosphere, 1973; editor: Phanerozoic Diversity, 1985; co-author: Evolution, 1977, Evolving, 1979; also numerous articles, 1954—. Served with USNR, 1944-46; PTO. Fulbright research scholar, Australia, 1962-63; Guggenheim fellow Yale U., Oxford U., Eng., 1968-69; Rockefeller Found. scholar in residence, Bellagio, Italy, summer 1974; grantee NSF, NASA. Fellow AAAS, Am. Acad. Arts and Scis., Geol. Soc. Am.; mem. NAS, Paleontol. Soc. (pres. 1974-75, medal 1996). Avocation: collecting works of Charles Darwin. Home: 1351 Glendale Ave Berkeley CA 94708-2025 Office: U Calif Dept Integrative Biolo Berkeley CA 94720

VALENTINE, JOHN LESTER, state legislator, lawyer; b. Fullerton, Calif., Apr. 26, 1949; s. Robert Lester and Pauline C. (Glood) V.; m. Karen Marie Thorpe, June 1, 1972; children: John Robert, Jeremy Reid, Staci Marie, Jeffrey Mark., David Emerson, Patricia Ann. BS in Acctg. and Econs., Brigham Young U., 1973, JD, 1976. Bar: Utah 1976, U.S. Dist. Ct. Utah, U.S. Ct. Appeals (10th cir.), U.S. Tax Ct.; CPA. Atty. Howard, Lewis & Petersen, Provo, Utah, 1976—; mem. Utah Ho. Reps., 1988—; instr. probate and estates Utah Valley State Coll.; instr. fin. planning., adj. prof. law Brigham Young U.; mem. exec offices, cts., corrections and legis. appropriations subcom., 1988-90, capital facilities subcom., 1988-90, retirement com., 1988-90, judiciary com., 1988-92, strategic planning steering com., 1988-90, interim appropriations com., 1988-94, tax. review commn., 1988-96, ethics com., 1990-92, human svcs. and health appropriations subcom., 1990-92, revenue and taxation com., 1988—, vice chmn. 1990-92; vice chmn. exec. appropriations., 1990-92; chmn. exec. appropriations com., 1992-94, chmn. rules com., 1994-96, higher edn. appropriations com. 1994-96, asst. majority whip, 1996—; bd. dirs. Utah Corrections Industries. Mem. adv. bd. Internat. Sr. Games, 1988—; active Blue Ribbon Task Force on Local Govt. Funding, Utah League Cities and Towns, 1990-94, Criminal Sentencing Guidelines Task Force, Utah Judicial Coun., 1990-92, Access to Health Care Task Force, 1990-92, Utah County Sheriff Search and Rescue, Orem Met. Water Bd., Alpine Sch. Dist. Boundary Line Com., Boy Scouts Am.; bd. regents Legis. Adv. Com. UVCC.; mem. exec. bd. Utah Nat. Parks Coun.; mem. adv. coun. Orchard Elem. Sch., Mountainlands Com. an Aging; bd. trustees Utah Opera Co.; judge nat. and local competitions Moot Ct.; voting dist. chmn.; state, county del.; lt. incident command sys. Utah County Sheriff. Recipient Silver Beaver award Boy Scouts Am., Taxpayer Advocate award Utah Taxpayer Assn. Mem. ABA (tax sect.), Utah State Bar, CPA Com., Tax Sect. Specialization Com., Bicentennial Com. Republican. Mormon. Avocation: mountain climbing. Office: Howard Lewis & Petersen 120 E 300 N Provo UT 84606-2907

VALENTINE, MARK CONRAD, dermatologist; b. Parkersburg, W.Va., Sept. 26, 1948; s. Sestel and Margaret Elaine (Sabolo) V.; m. Elizabeth Michelle Monezis, Apr. 21, 1975; children: Perry Martin, Owen Mark. BA, W.Va. U., 1970; MD, Johns Hopkins U., 1974. Intern, resident U. Hosps. Cleve., 1974-76, resident, 1976-79; dermatologist pvt. practice, Everett, Wash., 1979—; clin. assoc. prof. U. Wash., Seattle, 1979—; active med. staff Providence Gen. Med. Ctr., Everett, 1979—. Bd. dirs., sec. City Libr. Bd., Mukilteo, Wash., 1994—; bd. dirs., v.p. Everett Symphony Bd., 1982-85; bd. dirs. Book Arts Guild, Seattle, 1988-90. Nat. Merit scholar, 1966. Mem. AMA, Am. Acad. Dermatology (adv. coun. 1983-86), Wash. State Dermatological Assn. (pres.-elect 1996, pres. 1996—), Seattle Dermatology Soc. (pres. 1985-86), Combined Med. Staff Everett (sec./treas. 1986-87), Soc. Dermatologic Surgery, Rotary (Everett), Phi Beta Kappa. Avocations: book collecting, book binding, guitar, piano. Office: 3327 Colby Ave Everett WA 98201-4308

VALENTINE, RALPH SCHUYLER, chemical engineer, research director; b. Seattle, Nov. 3, 1932; s. John Campbell and Elizabeth Florence (Patterson) V.; m. Jeanne Marie Belanger, June 15, 1957; children: Susan Diana, Jacqueline Leigh, John Campbell. BSChemE, U. Wash., 1955, PhDChemE, 1963; MSChemE, U. Ill., 1956. Registered profl. engr., Calif., Va., Wash. Rsch. engr. Chevron Rsch. Corp., Richmond, Calif., 1956-61; instr. U. Wash., Seattle, 1961-63; mgr. fluid dynamics Aerojet-Gen., Sacramento, 1963-69; mgr. chem. tech. Atlantic Rsch. Corp., Alexandria, Va., 1969-79; mgr. rsch. United Techs. Chem. Systems, San Jose, Calif., 1979-91; lectr. U.S. Naval Postgrad. Sch., Monterey, Calif., 1968, UCLA Modern Devels. in Propulsion, L.A., 1967-68, USAF Astronautics Labs., Lancaster, Calif., 1967, U.S. Army R & D Unit, Sacramento, 1966. Contbr. 23 tech. articles to profl. jours.; patentee in field. Recipient NASA commendation for Apollo work, Houston, 1969, 1st prize Ceramographic Exhbn. Am. Ceramics Soc., 1974. Mem. Am. Inst. Chem. Engrs. (life). Republican. Home: 7242 Via Mimosa San Jose CA 95135-1413

VALENTINE, STEVEN RICHARDS, lawyer; b. Memphis, Jan. 30, 1956; s. William Robert and Lenita Joanne (Nelms) V.; m. Susan Marie Burke, Jan. 14, 1984; children: Christina Michele, William Robert II, Steven Richards Jr., Thomas Burke. Student, Earlham Coll., 1974-77; B of Gen. Studies with distinction, Ind. U., 1979, JD, 1982. Bar: Ill. 1983, D.C. 1985, U.S. Ct. Appeals (D.C. cir.) 1986, U.S. Supreme Ct. 1986, U.S. Ct. Appeals (9th cir.) 1989. Chief investigator consumer protection divsn. Office Atty. Gen., State of Ind., 1980-82; exec. dir. Ams. United for Life Legal Def. Fund, Chgo., 1982-83; chief counsel subcom. on separation of powers U.S. Senate, Washington, 1983-85, chief counsel subcom. on cts., 1985; adminstrv. asst. U.S. Senator John P. East, Washington, 1985-86; dir. Office of Policy Devel. and Comm. Legal Svcs. Corp., 1986-87; counselor to asst. atty. gen. civil divsn. U.S. Dept. Justice, 1987-88; dep. asst. atty. gen. civil divsn. U.S. Justice Dept., 1988-93, legis. dir., 1996—; gen. counsel U.S. Senator Robert C. Smith, 1993—; mem. exec. com., bd. dirs. Deluxe West, Inc.; vice chmn. bd. dirs. D. Elton Trueblood Yokefellow Acad. Endowment, Inc. Author: Each Time A Man, 1978, All Shall Live, 1980, (with others) Abortion and the Constitution, 1987; contbr. articles to profl. jours. Recipient spl. commendation U.S. Atty. Gen., 1993; John C. Stennis Congl. staff fellow, 1995-96. Mem. SAR, Wider Quaker Fellowship, Capitol Hill Club. Republican. Roman Catholic. Avocations: history, baseball. Home: 6513 Old Coach Ct Alexandria VA 22315-5045 Office: 307 Dirksen Ofc Bldg Washington DC 20510-2903

VALENTINE, WILLIAM EDSON, architect; b. Winston-Salem, N.C., Sept. 3, 1937; s. Howard Leon and Sally (Cunningham) V.; m. Jane Dorward, Aug. 13, 1939; children: Anne, Karen, William. BArch, N.C. State U., 1960; MArch, Harvard U., 1962. Co-chmn. Hellmuth, Obata and Kassabaum Inc., San Francisco, 1962—; chmn. Hellmuth, Obata & Kassabaum Design Bd., also bd. dirs. Served to 1st lt. U.S. Army, 1960-61. Fellow AIA. Club: Harvard. Office: Hellmuth Obata & Kassabaum Inc 71 Stevenson St Ste 2200 San Francisco CA 94105-2979

VALENTINE, WILLIAM NEWTON, physician, educator; b. Kansas City, Mo., Sept. 29, 1917; s. Herbert S. and Mabel W. (Watson) V.; m. Martha Hickman Winfree; children: William, James, Edward. Student, U. Mich., Ann Arbor, 1934-36, U. Mo., Columbia, 1936-37; MD, Tulane U., New Orleans, 1942. Diplomate: Am. Bd. Internal Medicine. Intern Strong Meml. Hosp., Rochester, N.Y., 1942-43, asst. resident in medicine, 1943, chief resident in medicine, 1943-44; specialist, attending physician in internal medicine Wadsworth Hosp., L.A., 1949-88, VA Ctr., L.A., 1949-88; specialist, attending physician in internal medicine Ctr. Health Scis. UCLA, 1949—, prof. medicine, 1957-88, chmn. dept., 1963-71; prof. emeritus medicine UCLA, Los Angeles, 1988—. Contbr. articles to profl. jours. Served to capt. MC, AUS, 1944-47. Recipient Mayo Soley award for excellence in research Western Soc. Clin. Research, 1978; 53d Annual UCLA faculty research lectr., 1978; Henry Stratton lectr. Am. Soc. Hematology, 1978; John Phillips Meml. award for Disting. Achievements in Internal Medicine, ACP, 1979. Fellow Am. Soc. Hematology, Internat. Soc. Hematology (v.p. U.S. 1976-80); mem. Am. Bd. Internal Medicine, ACP (master), Am. Soc. Clin. Investigation (v.p. 1962), Assn. Am. Physicians, Nat. Acad. Scis., Western Assn. Physicians (pres. 1969-70), Western Soc. Clin. Research, Am. Acad. Arts and Scis. Republican.

VALERIANI, RICHARD GERARD, news broadcaster; b. Camden, N.J., Aug. 29, 1932; s. Nicholas and Christine (Camerota) V.; m. Kathie Berlin, Apr. 20, 1980; 1 child, Kimberly. BA, Yale U., 1953; postgrad., U. Pavia, Italy, 1953-54, U. Barcelona, Spain, 1954. Reporter The Trentonian, Trenton, 1957; with AP, 1957-61; corr. AP, Havana, Cuba, 1959-61; with NBC-TV News, 1961—; corr. NBC-TV News, Washington, 1964-83; nat. corr. NBC-TV News, N.Y.C., 1983-88; free-lance journalist and media cons., 1988—; participant 2d Carter-Ford debate, 1976. Author: Travels With Henry, 1979; actor: (feature film) Crimson Tide, 1995. With AUS, 1955-56. Recipient Overseas Press Club award for best radio reporting, 1965. Mem. Elihu Soc. Home: 23 Island View Dr Sherman CT 06784-2036

VALERIO, JOSEPH M., architectural firm executive, educator; b. Dec. 26, 1947; m. Linda A. Searl; children: Joseph Jr., Anthony. BArch, U. Mich., 1970; MArch, UCLA, 1972. Registered architect, Wis., Ill., Ind., Mo., Calif., Tex., Ariz., Minn., Ala., Iowa, Ind.; cert. Nat. Coun. Archtl. Registration Bds. Pres. Chrysalis Corp. Architects, 1970-85; assoc. prof. U. Wis., 1973-86; design dir. Swanke Hayden Connell Architects, 1985-86; v.p. architecture A. Epstein and Sons, Inc., 1986-88; pres. Valerio-Assocs. Inc., 1988-94; prin. Valerio Dewalt Train Assocs., Inc., Chgo., 1994—; speaker Ariz. State U., UCLA, U. Ariz., U. Cin., others; cons. USG Interiors, Formica Corp., AAAS, NAS, NEA: vis. critic and lectr. in field. Prin. works include corp., high-tech. indsl., retail, health and residential bldgs.; author: Movie Palaces, 1983; editor: Architectural Fabric Structures, 1985. Mem. exec. bd. men's coun. Mus. Contemporary Art, 1989-91; mem. exec. bd. Contemporary Arts Coun., 1994. Recipient Honor awards Wis. Soc. Architects, 1975, 81, 84, 85, Gov.'s Award for Design Excellence, State of Mich., 1979, Gold medal Inst. Bus. Designers, 1988, Design award Progressive Architecture, 1991, Disting. Interior award Inst. Bus. Designers, Chgo., 1993; honored by Emerging Voices series Archtl. League N.Y., Met. Home mag., Interiors mag. Fellow AIA (programs chmn. design com. Chgo. chpt. 1990, mem. long range planning com. 1992, chair nat. com. on design 1997, Nat. Honor award 1981, 93, 96, Interiors award Chgo. chpt. 1988, 90, 92, 95, Disting. Bldg. award 1991, 93, Nat. Interior award 1993, 96), Chgo. Architecture Club (pres. 1994). Office: Valerio Dewalt Train Assocs 200 N La Salle St Ste 2400 Chicago IL 60601-1021

VALERIO, MICHAEL ANTHONY, financial executive; b. Detroit, Sept. 20, 1953; s. Anthony Rudolph and Victoria (Popoff) V.; m. Barbara Ann Nabozny, Oct. 8, 1983. BA, U. Mich, Dearborn, 1975. CPA, Mich. Jr. acct. Carabell, Bocknek CPA's, Southfield, Mich., 1975-76; sr. acct. Purdy, Donovan & Beal, CPA's, Detroit, 1976-77; mgr. Buctynck & Co., CPA's, Southfield, 1978-79; controller Transcontinental Travel, Harper Woods, Mich., 1979-80; exec. v.p. Holland Cons., Inc., Detroit, 1980-85; controller, CFO SLC Recycling Industries, Inc., Warren, Mich., 1985—; owner Pinnacle Fin. Consulting, 1994—. Mem. AICPA, Mich. Soc. CPAs, Acctg. Rsch. Found. Roman Catholic. Office: SLC Recycling Industries Inc 21000 Hoover Rd Warren MI 48089-3153

VALERO, RENÉ ARNOLD, clergyman; b. N.Y.C., Aug. 15, 1930; s. Caesar J. and Maria Luisa (Cordova) Valero; B.A. in Liberal Arts, Immaculate Conception-Cathedral Coll., 1952; M.S.W., Fordham U., 1962. Ordained to ministry Roman Cath. Ch., 1956; asso. pastor St. Michael-St. Edward, Bklyn., 1956-57, St. Agatha, Bklyn., 1957-60; dir. Bklyn. Cath. Charities Family Service, 1960-69; dir. Bklyn. Diocesan Office for Aging, 1969-74; coordinator Bklyn. Diocesan Hispanic Apostolate, 1974-79; pastor Blessed Sacrament, Jackson Heights, N.Y., 1979-82; aux. bishop Diocese of Bklyn., 1980—; vicar for immigrants and refugees Diocese of Bklyn., 1983-90; regional bishop Queens, 1990-94, Queens North, 1994—. Home: 34-43 93rd St Jackson Hts NY 11372-3743 Office: Immaculate Conception Ctr 7200 Douglaston Pky Douglaston NY 11362-1941

VALETTE, REBECCA MARIANNE, Romance languages educator; b. N.Y.C., Dec. 21, 1938; d. Gerhard and Ruth Adelgunde (Bischoff) Loose; m. Jean-Paul Valette, Aug. 6, 1959; children: Jean-Michel, Nathalie, Pierre. BA, Mt. Holyoke Coll., 1959, LHD (hon.), 1974; PhD, U. Colo., 1963. Instr., examiner in French and German U. So. Fla., 1961-63; instr. NATO Def. Coll., Paris, 1963-64, Wellesley Coll., 1964-65; asst. prof. Romance Langs. Boston Coll., 1965-68, assoc., 1968-73, prof., 1973—; lectr., cons. fgn. lang. pedagogy; Fulbright sr. lectr., Germany, 1974; Am. Council on Edn. fellow in acad. adminstrn., 1976-77. Author: Modern Language Testing, 1967, rev. edit., 1977, French for Mastery, 1975, rev. edit., 1988, Contacts, 1976, rev. edit., 1993, 97, C'est Comme Ça, 1978, rev. edit., 1986, Spanish for Mastery, 1980, rev. edit., 1989, 94, Album: Cuentos del Mundo Hispanico, 1984, rev. edit., 1992, French for Fluency, 1985, Situations, 1988, rev. edit., 1994, Discovering French, 1994, 97, A votre tour, 1995; contbr. articles to fgn. lang. pedagogy and lit. publs. Decorated officer Palmes académiques (France). Mem. Modern Lang. Assn. (chmn. div. on teaching of lang. 1980-81), Am. Coun. on Teaching Fgn. Langs., Am. Assn. Tchrs. French (v.p. 1980-86, pres. 1992-94), Am. Assn. Tchrs. German, Phi Beta Kappa, Alpha Sigma Nu, Palmes Academiques. Home: 16 Mt Alvernia Rd Chestnut Hill MA 02167-1019 Office: Boston Coll Lyons 311 Chestnut Hill MA 02167

VALIANT, LESLIE GABRIEL, computer scientist; b. Mar. 28, 1949; s. Leslie and Eva Julia (Ujlaki) V.; m. Gayle Lynne Dyckoff, 1977; children—Paul A., Gregory J. MA, Kings Coll., Cambridge, U.K., 1970; DIC, Imperial Coll., London, 1973; PhD, U. Warwick, U.K., 1974. Vis. asst. prof. Carnegie-Mellon U., Pitts., 1973-74; lectr. U. Leeds, Eng., 1974-76; lectr., reader U. Edinburgh, Scotland, 1977-82; vis. prof. Harvard U., 1982, Gordon McKay prof. computer sci. and applied math., 1982—. Guggenheim fellow, 1985-86; recipient Nevanlinna prize Internat. Math. Union, 1986. Fellow Royal Soc., Am. Assn. for Artificial Intelligence. Office: Harvard U 33 Oxford St Cambridge MA 02138-2901

VALK, HENRY SNOWDEN, physicist, educator; b. Washington, Jan. 26, 1929; s. Henry Snowden and Dorothy (Blencowe) V.; m. Gillian Wedderburn, June 20, 1968; children—Alison, Diana, Robert, Richard. B.S., George Washington U., 1953, M.S. (Agnes and Eugene Meyer scholar), 1954; postgrad., Johns Hopkins, 1953-54; Ph.D. (Shell fellow), Washington U., St. Louis, 1957. Profl. asst. NSF, 1957, asst. program dir. physics, 1959-60; asst. prof. physics U. Oreg., 1957-59; mem. faculty U. Nebr., 1960-70, prof. physics, 1964-70, chmn. dept., 1966-70; prof. physics Coll. Scis. and Liberal Studies, Ga. Inst. Tech., Atlanta, 1970—, acting dir. physics, 1991-96, dean, 1970-82; cons. physics sect. NSF, 1961-62, program dir. theoretical physics, 1965-66; chmn. Gordon Rsch. Conf. Photonuclear Reactions, 1969; vis. prof. U. Frankfurt/Main, Germany, 1970, Rensselaer Poly. Inst., 1982, 88, Cath. U. Am., 1982-83, 88-89; chmn. SE regional Marshall scholarship com., 1974-92. Author: (with M. Alonso) Quantum Mechanics: Principles and Applications, 1973; contbr. articles to profl. jours. Decorated Most Excellent Order Brit. Empire. Fellow Am. Phys. Soc.; mem. Am. Math. Soc., Am. Assn. Physics Tchrs., Math. Assn. Am., Cosmos Club (Washington), Phi Beta Kappa, Sigma Xi. Home: 3032 St Helena Dr Tucker GA 30084-2227

VALK, ROBERT EARL, corporate executive; b. Muskegon, Mich., Aug. 21, 1914; s. Allen and Lulu (Schuler) V.; m. Ann Parker, August 9, 1941 (div. July 1959); children: James A., Sara C.; m. Alice Melick, Dec. 29, 1960; children: Marie, Susan. B.S. in Mech. Engring, U. Mich., 1938. With Nat. Supply Co., 1938-55; plant mgr. Nat. Supply Co., Houston, 1945-48; works mgr. Nat. Supply Co., Toledo, Houston and Gainesville, Tex., 1949-55; asst. v.p. prodn. Electric Auto-Lite Co., Toledo, 1956, v.p., group exec. gen. products, 1956-60; gen. mgr. mfg. automotive div. Essex Internat., Inc., 1960-66, v.p. corp., gen. mgr. automotive div., 1966-74; pres. ITT Automotive Elec. Products Div., 1974-80; v.p. ITT N.Am. Automotive Ops. Worldwide, 1980-86; chmn. Chamberlin, Davis, Rutan & Valk, 1986—; trustee Henry Ford Health Care Sys., Detroit. Bd. dirs. Ecumenical Theological Ctr. Mem. Am. Soc. Naval Engrs., Soc. Automotive Engrs., Am. Ordnance Assn., Am. Mgmt. Assn., Air Force Assn., Am. Mfrs. Assn., Wire Assn., Nat. Elec. Mfrs. Assn., Engring. Soc. Detroit. Republican. Episcopalian. Clubs: Country (Detroit), Renaissance Club, Yondotega, Economics (Detroit); Grosse Pointe, Bay View Yacht; Little Harbor (Harbor Springs, Mich., Question Club. Home: 80 Renaud Rd Grosse Pointe MI 48236-1742 Office: 21 Kercheval Ave Ste 270 Grosse Pointe MI 48236-3634

VALLANCE, JAMES, church administrator, religious publication editor. Dir. Master's Men Dept. of the Nat. Assn. of Free Will Baptists, Antioch, Tenn.; pub. Attack, A Magazine for Christian Men. Office: Natl Assn of Free Will Baptists PO Box 5002 Antioch TN 37011-5002*

VALLBONA, CARLOS, physician; b. Granollers, Barcelona, Spain, July 29, 1927; came to U.S., 1953, naturalized, 1967; s. José and Dolores (Calbó) V.; m. Rima Gretel Rothe, Dec. 26, 1956; children—Rima Nuria, Carlos Fernando, María Teresa, Marisa. B.A., B.S., U. de Barcelona, 1944, M.D., 1950. Diplomate Am. Bd. Pediatrics. Child health physician Escuela de Puericultura, Barcelona, 1952, Stagier Etranger Hôpital des Enfants Malades, Paris, 1952-53; intern, resident U. Louisville, 1953-55; resident Baylor Coll. of Medicine, 1955-56; prof. rehab. medicine Baylor Coll. Medicine, 1967—; assoc. prof. physiology and pediatrics Baylor U. Coll. Medicine, 1962-69, prof., chmn. dept. community medicine, 1969—, prof. family medicine, 1980—; adj. prof. U. Tex. Sch. Pub. Health, U. Tex. Health Sci. Ctr., Houston; chief community medicine service Harris County Hosp. Dist.; staff gen. med. service Tex. Children's Hosp.; staff The Inst. Rehab. and Research; staff St. Luke's Episcopal Hosp., con. staff VA Med. Ctr., Houston; Fulbright vis. prof., 1967; cons. WHO, NIH, Nat. Center Health Stats. Pan Am. Health Orgn., Nat. Center Health Service Research; advisor Conseller Sanitat, Catalunya. Author numerous articles in field; editorial bd. several Sci. jours. French Ministry of Edn. fellow, 1952; Children's Internat. Center fellow, 1953; co-recipient Gold medal 6th Internat. Congress Phys. Medicine, 1972; Public Citizen of Yr. San Jacinto chpt. Nat. Assn. Social Workers, 1974; Outstanding Tchr. award Baylor Coll. Medicine Class of 1980, 83, 85, 87, 88; decorated officer Order of Civil Merit (Spain), Medalla Narcis Monturiol (Catalunya). Mem. Am. Acad. Family Physicians, Am. Coll. Med. Informatics (founding mem. 1984), Nat. Acad. Practice (disting. practitioner 1984), Soc. Pediatric Research (emeritus), AMA, Tex. Med. Assn., Am. Coll. Chest Physicians, Am. Pub. Health Assn. (chmn. elect med. care sect. 1989-90), Am. Coll. Preventive Medicine, U.S.-Mex. Border Health Assn., AAAS, Am. Congress Rehab. Medicine, Catalan Soc. Pediatrics (hon.), Argentinian Soc. Internal Medicine (hon. 1986), Argentinian Med. Soc. (hon. 1986), Spanish Acad. Pediatrics (ambulatory pediatrics sect. hon. 1987), Assn. Tchrs. Preventive Medicine, Spanish Profls. Am. (pres. 1988), Soc. Catalana Hipertensio (hon. pres.), Sigma Xi, Alpha Omega Alpha. Roman Catholic. Home: 2001 Holcombe Blvd Houston TX 77030-4222 Office: Baylor Coll Medicine One Baylor Pla Houston TX 77030*

VALLBONA, MARISA, public relations counselor; b. Houston, Jan. 2, 1964; d. Carlos and Rima (Rothe) Vallbona; m. Don R. Rayner Jr., July 12, 1986 (div.); children: Donald R. Rayner III, Timothy Carlos Rayner. Student, U. Colo., U. de Dijon, France; BS in Journalism, U. Tex. Account exec. Jae Stefan & Assocs., Austin, Tex., 1987-88; media rels. asst. America's Cup XXVII, 1988; sr. account exec. pub. rels. Berkman & Daniels, 1988-90; prin. Rayner & Vallbona Inc. Advt. & Pub. Rels., San Diego, 1990-97; pres. CIM, Inc., San Diego, 1997—. Editor: Flowering Inferno, 1994, Soldiers Cry By Night, 1994, Assumed Name, 1994, People on the Prowl, 1995; contbr. articles to profl. jours. Pub. rels. chair, bd. dirs. Women of St. James Episc. Ch., 1994, 1st v.p., 1995; mem. pub. affairs disaster task force ARC, 1993—; pub. rels. chair Sunkist Am. Cancer Soc. Cup Regatta, 1989; mem. elections mktg. task force City of San Diego, 1989. Mem. Pub. Rels Soc. Am. (accredited, San Diego chpt. chair accreditation com. 1994, dir.-at-large 1995, bd. dirs. 1996—, sec. 1997), Am. Soc. Health Care Mktg. and Pub. Rels., Health Care Communicators San Diego (v.p., bd. dirs. 1994, sec. 1993, numerous awards), Pub. Rels. Club San Diego (exec. bd. dirs. 1991-92, various awards), Jr. League San Diego. Avocations: snow skiing, tennis, sailing. Office: CIM Inc 6961 Petit St San Diego CA 92111-3303

VALLBONA, RIMA-GRETEL ROTHE, foreign language educator, writer; b. San Jose, Costa Rica, Mar. 15, 1931; d. Ferdinand Hermann and Emilia (Strassburger) Rothe; m. Carlos Vallbona, Dec. 26, 1956; children: Rima-Nuri, Carlos-Fernando, Maria-Teresa, Maria-Luisa. BA/BS, Colegio Superior de Senoritas, San Jose, 1948; diploma, U. Paris, 1953; diploma in Spanish Philology, U. Salamanca, Spain, 1954; MA, U. Costa Rica, 1962; D in Modern Langs., Middlebury Coll., 1981. Tchr. Liceo J.J. Vargas Calvo, Costa Rica, 1955-56; faculty U. St. Thomas, Houston, 1964-95, prof. Spanish, 1978-95, Cullen Found. prof. Spanish, 1989, head dept. Spanish, 1966-71, chmn. dept. modern fgn. langs., 1978-80, prof. emeritus, 1995—; vis. prof. U. Houston, 1975-76, Rice U., 1980-83, 95, U. St. Thomas, Argentina, 1972, vis. prof. U. St. Thomas Merida program, 1987-95; vis. prof. Rice U. program in Spain, 1974. Author: Noche en Vela, 1968, Yolanda Oreamuno, 1972, La Obra en Prosa de Eunice Odio, 1981, Baraja de Soledades, Las Sombras que Perseguimos, 1983, Polvo del Camino, 1972, La Salamandra Rosada, 1979, Mujeres y Agonias, 1982, Cosecha de Pecadores, 1988, El arcangel del perdon, 1990, Mundo, demonio y mujer, 1991, Los infiernos de la mujer y algo mas, 1992, Vida i sucesos de la Monja Alférez, critical edition, 1992, Flowering Inferno-Tales of Sinking Hearts, 1994, La narrativa de Yolanda Oremuno, 1996, Tormy, la Prodigiosa Gata de Donaldito, 1997; mem. editorial bd. Letras Femeninas, Alba de America, U.S.; co-dir. Foro Literario, Uruguay, 1987-89; contbg. editor The Americas Review, 1989—; contbr. numerous articles and short stories to lit. mags. Mem. scholarship com. Inst. Hispanic Culture, 1978-79, 88, 91, chmn., 1979, bd. dirs., 1974-76, 88-89, 91-92, chmn. cultural activities, 1979, 80, 85, 88-89; bd. dirs. Houston Pub. Libr., 1984-86; bd. dirs. Cultural Arts Coun. of Houston, 1991-92. Recipient Aquileo J. Echeverria Novel prize, 1968, Agripina Montes del Valle Novel prize, 1978, Jorge Luis Borges Short Story prize, Argentina, 1977, Lit. award S.W. Conf. Latin Am. Studies, 1982; Constantin Found. grantee for rsch. U. St. Thomas, 1981; Ancora Lit. award, Costa Rica, 1984, Civil Merit award King Juan Carlos I of Spain, 1989. Mem. MLA, Am. Assn. Tchrs. Spanish and Portuguese, Houston Area Tchrs. of Fgn. Langs., South Cen. MLA, S.W. conf. Orgn. Latin Am. Studies, Latin Am. Studies Assn., Inst. Internat. de Lit. Iberoam., Latin Am. Writers Assn. of Costa Rica, Inst. Hispanic Culture of Houston, Casa Argentina de Houston, Inst. Lit. y Cultural Hispanico, Phi Sigma Iota, Sigma Delta Pi (hon.), Nat. Writers Assn. Roman Catholic. Home: 3706 Lake St Houston TX 77098-5522

VALLE, LAURENCE FRANCIS, lawyer; b. N.Y.C., Feb. 16, 1943; s. Mario John and Marian Josephine (Longinotti) V.; m. Joan Strachan, June 11, 1966 (dec.); children: Christopher John, Stacia Lyn. BS, U. Miami, 1966, JD, 1969. Bar: Fla. 1969, U.S. Ct. Mil. Appeals 1970, U.S. Dist. Ct. (so. and mid. dists.) Fla. 1975, U.S. Ct. Appeals (D.C. cir.) 1975, U.S. Ct. Appeals (5th and 11th cirs.) 1981, U.S. Dist. Ct. (we. dist.) Tex. 1989. Assoc. Underwood, Gillis & Karcher PA, Miami, Fla., 1973-77; ptnr. Underwood, Gillis, Karcher & Valle PA, Miami, 1977-87, Dixon, Dixon, Nicklaus & Valle, Miami, 1987-90, Nicklaus, Valle, Craig & Wicks, Miami, 1990-95, Valle & Craig, P.A., Miami, 1995—; of counsel Greater Miami Marine Assn., 1983—. Contbr. articles to profl. jours. Served to capt. U.S. Army, 1970-74. Mem. ABA, Fla. Bar Assn. (chmn. grievance com., 1982-85), Assn. Trial Lawyers Am., SE Admiralty Law Inst., Maritime Law Assn. of U.S., Bankers Club Miami. Republican. Roman Catholic. Avocations: tennis, running, water skiing, snow skiing. Office: Valle & Craig PA 80 SW 8th St Miami FL 33130-3003

VALLEE, BERT LESTER, biochemist, physician, educator; b. Hemer, Westphalia, Germany, June 1, 1919; came to U.S., 1938, naturalized, 1948; s. Joseph and Rosa (Kronenberger) V.; m. Natalie T. Kugris, May 29, 1947. ScB, U. Berne, Switzerland, 1938; MD, NYU, 1943; AM (hon.), Harvard, 1960; MD (honoris causa), Karolinska Institutet, Stockholm, Sweden, 1987; prof. (hon.), Tsinghua U., Beijing, 1987; DSC honoris causa, Naples, Italy, 1991; PhD in Chemistry (honoris causa), Ludwig-Maximilians U., Munich, 1995. Rsch. fellow Harvard Med. Sch., Boston, 1946-49; rsch. assoc. Harvard Med. Sch., 1949-51, assoc., 1951-56, asst. prof. medicine, 1956-60, assoc. prof., 1960-64, prof. biol. chemistry, 1964-65, Paul C. Cabot prof. biol. chemistry, 1965-80, Paul C. Cabot prof. emeritus, biochem. scis., 1980—, Disting. Sr. prof. biochem. scis., 1989-90, Edgar M. Bronfman Disting. sr. prof., 1990—; rsch. assoc. dept. biology MIT, Cambridge, 1948—; physician Peter Bent Brigham Hosp., Boston, 1961-80; biochemist-in-chief Brigham & Women's Hosp., Boston, 1980-89, emeritus, 1989—; sci. dir. Biophysics Rsch. Lab., Harvard Med. Sch., Peter Bent Brigham Hosp., 1954-80; head Ctr. for Biochem. and Biophys. Scis. and Medicine, Harvard Med. Sch. and Brigham & Women's Hosp., 1980—; Messenger lectr. Cornell U., 1988. Author 9 books; contbr. articles and chpts. to sci. publs. Founder, trustee Boston Biophysics Research Found., 1957—; founder, pres. Endowment for Research in Human Biology, Inc., 1980—. Recipient Warner-Chilcott award, 1969, Buchman Meml. award Calif. Inst. Tech., 1976; Linderstøm-Lang award and gold medal, 1980; Willard Gibbs Medal award, 1981, William C. Rose award in biochemistry, 1982, Order Andres Bello First Class of Republic of Venezuela. Fellow NAS, AAAS, Am. Acad. Arts and Scis., N.Y. Acad. Scis.; mem. Am. Soc. Biol. Chemists, Am. Chem. Soc. (Willard Gibbs gold medal 1981), Optical Soc. Am., Biophys. Soc., Swiss Biochem. Soc. (hon. fgn. mem.), Royal Danish Acad. Scis. and Letters, Japan Soc. for Analytical Chemistry (hon.), Alpha Omega Alpha. Home: 56 Browne St Brookline MA 02146-3445

VALLEE, JUDITH DELANEY, environmentalist, writer, fundraiser; b. N.Y.C., Mar. 14, 1948; d. Victor and Sally Hammer; m. John Delaney, Apr. 9, 1974 (div. 1978); m. Henry Richard Vallee, May 15, 1987. BA, CUNY, 1976. Exec. dir. Save the Manatee Club, Maitland, Fla., 1985—; apptd. U.S. Manatee Recovery Plan Team, Jacksonville, Fla., 1988-97, Fla. Manatee Tech. Adv. Coun., Tallahassee, 1989—, Save the Manatee Com., Orlando, Fla., 1985-92, World Conservation Union/Sirenia Specialist Group, Switzerland, 1996; advisor Save the Wildlife Inc., Chuluota, Fla., 1992-93; bd. dirs. Environ. Fund for Fla. Lobbyist Save the Manatee Club, 1989; vol. Broward County Audubon Soc., Ft. Lauderdale, 1983, 84, Wild Bird Care Ctr., Ft. Lauderdale, 1984. Recipient Refuge Support award Chassahowitzka Nat. Wildlife Refuge, 1989. Mem. Fla. Coalition for Peace and Justice, People for Ethical Treatment of Animals, Friends of the Wekiva River. Democrat. Avocations: creative writing, antiques, wildlife observation, canoeing. Office: Save the Manatee Club Inc 500 N Maitland Ave Maitland FL 32751-4482

VALLERAND, PHILIPPE GEORGES, sales executive; b. Montreal, Que., Can., June 12, 1954; came to U.S., 1982; s. Louis Philippe and Beatrice (Goupil) V.; m. Laura Jean Frombach, Sept. 25, 1979; children: Harmonie May, Jeremy Thomas, Emilie Rose. Student, U. Montreal, 1974, U. Sherbrooke, 1975, U. Que., 1976, White Mgmt. Sch., London, 1981. Dir. resort Club Mediterranee Inc., Bahamas, Switzerland,, Africa,, Guadelupe, West Indies, 1978-80; v.p. Franglo/Sunsaver Inc., London and Hyeres, France, 1980-82; v.p. sales Source Northwest, Inc., Woodinville, Wash., 1982-93; pres. Prime Resource Group. Sr. comdr. Royal Rangers Boys Club, Monroe, Wash., 1988—; bd. mem. Christian Faith Ctr., Monroe, 1988-94; mem. Rep. Nat. Com. Named to 500 Inc. Mag., 1983, 89; recipient Disting. Sales & Mktg. Exec. award Internat. Orgn. Sales & Mktg. Execs., 1993, 96. Mem. Am. Mktg. Assn. (new mem. adv. bd.). Avocations: skiing, archery.

VALLERY, JANET ALANE, industrial hygienist; b. Lincoln, Nebr., Apr. 4, 1948; d. Gerald William and Lois Florence (Robertson) V.; BS, U. Nebr., Lincoln, 1970; diploma Bryan Meml. Sch. Med. Tech., Lincoln, 1971. Med. technologist Lincoln Gen. Hosp., 1971-72; congressional sec., 1973; lab. scientist Nebr. Dept. Health, 1973-79; sr. indsl. hygienist Nebr. Dept. Labor, 1979-85; indsl. hygienist U.S. Dept. Labor OSHA, 1985-89; indsl. hygienist VA Med. Ctr., Omaha, Nebr., 1989—. Mem. Am. Conf. Govt. Indsl. Hygienists, Am. Soc. Clin. Pathologists (assoc.), Arabian Horse Assn. Nebr., Nebr. Dressage Assn., Am. Indsl. Hygiene Assn., Am. Legion Aux. Republican. Methodist. Home: 4900 S 30th St Lincoln NE 68516-1603 Office: VA Med Ctr 4101 Woolworth Ave Omaha NE 68105-1850

VALLES, JEAN-PAUL, finance company executive; b. Paris, Oct. 17, 1936; came to U.S., 1963; s. Jacques Pierre and Simone (Bourlinski) V.; m. Carol Ann Bennett, Dec. 28, 1935; children: Alain, Suzanne, Sandra. BA, Lycee Corneille, Rouen, France, 1956; Diplome D'enseignement Comml. Superieur, Ecole Supérieure de Commerce de Paris, 1960; MBA, NYU, 1961, PhD, 1967. Bus. economist W.R. Grace, N.Y.C., 1963-68; asst. to chmn. Pfizer Inc., N.Y.C., 1968-70, dir. corp. planning, 1970-72, controller, 1972-80, v.p. fin., 1980-89; sr. v.p. Pfizer, Inc., N.Y.C., 1989-91, exec. v.p., 1991-92, chmn., 1992; also bd. dirs. Pfizer Inc., N.Y.C.; bd. dirs. Pfizer, Inc., N.Y.C., Nat. Assn. Mfrs.; chmn., CEO Minerals Technologies, Inc.. Author: The World Market For Bananas, 1968. Dir. Jr. Achievement N.Y., 1986. Served to sgt. French USAF, 1960-61. Mem. Fin. Execs. Inst., Am. Econ. Assn., French Am. C. of C., Jr. Achievement of N.Y. Club: Econ. of N.Y. Home: 78 East Middle Patent Rd Bedford NY 10506-9775 Office: Minerals Technologies Inc 405 Lexington Ave New York NY 10174-0002

VALLET, JEAN-MARIE P., health care company executive; b. Laval, France, Oct. 21, 1955; s. Jacques Vallet and Françoise Daussy; m. Evelyne P. Gouilloud, Apr. 28, 1987; children: Marine, Cyril. PhD, U. Geneva, 1986, MBA, 1989. Tchg. asst. U. Geneva, Switzerland, 1981-85; project leader genetic engring. Battelle Inst., Geneva, 1985-88; dir. export Jouan SA, Nantes, France, 1989-90; from asst. to sr. vice dir. Pierre Fabre SA, Toulouse, France, 1990-92; dir. adm. & fin. clin. dept. Parke Davis GmbH, Freiburg, Germany, 1992-94; sr. dir. planning investment dept. Warner-Lambert & Co., Morris Plains, N.J., 1994-96; v.p. bus. devel. Europe Bristol-Myers-Squibb, Princeton, N.J., 1996—. Avocations: forestry, bicycling, skiing. Home: 37 Bouvant Dr Princeton NJ 08540-1208

VALLEY, GEORGE EDWARD, JR., physicist, educator; b. N.Y.C., Sept. 5, 1913; s. George Edward and Edith Ringgold (Cummins) V.; m. Louisa King Williams, July 19, 1941 (div. Dec. 1960); children: George Cummins, John Williams, Katharine; m. Alice Shea LaBronté, 1960. S.B., Mass. Inst. Tech., 1935; Ph.D., U. Rochester, 1939. Optical engr. with Bausch & Lomb Optical Co., 1935-36; teaching asst. U. Rochester, 1936-39; research asso. Harvard, 1939-41, NRC fellow nuclear physics, 1940-41; project supr., sr. staff Radiation Lab., Mass. Inst. Tech., 1941-45; editorial bd. Radiation Lab. Tech. Series, 1945; successively asst. prof., asso. prof. Mass. Inst. Tech., 1946-57, prof. physics, 1957-78; prof. emeritus, founder Lincoln Lab. Lincoln Lab., 1949, assoc. dir., 1953-57, undergrad. planning prof., 1965-68; mem. Air Force Sci. Adv. Bd., 1946-64; chmn. Air Def. Systems Engring. Com. for Chief Staff USAF, 1950-51, chief scientist, 1957-58. Author and editor books and monographs. Recipient U.S. Army certificate of appreciation; President's certificate of merit; Air Force Assn. Sci. award; exceptional civilian service medal USAF, 1956, 58, 64. Fellow Am. Phys. Soc., Inst. Elec. and Electronics Engrs.; mem. Sigma Xi. Address: 607 Main St Concord MA 01742-3303

VALLONE, JOHN CHARLES, motion picture production designer; b. Phila., June 23, 1953; s. Louis Phillip and Laura Anne (Gagilone) V.; divorced; children: Gabriella, Lilli. BFA, NYU, 1975. Prodn. designer: (feature films) Southern Comfort, 1981, 48 Hours, 1982, Brainstorm, 1983, Streets of Fire, 1984, Brewster's Millions, 1985, Commando, 1985, Predator, 1987, Red Heat, 1988, The Adventures of Ford Fairlane, 1990, Die Hard 2,

1990, Rambling Rose, 1991, Cliffhanger, 1993, Bad Boys, 1995, 3 Wishes, 1995, (TV pilots) Private Eye, 1987, Sweet Justice, 1994, (TV movies) Shannon's Deal, 1989, Angel City, 1990; art dir.: (film) Star Trek: The Motion Picture, 1979 (Academy award nomination best art direction 1979). Mem. AOPA, SMPTVAD, Acad. Motion Picture Arts and Scis. (Best Art Direction award nomination 1981). Republican. Avocations: restoration of wooden yacht, pilot, sailing, woodworking, skiing.

VALOIS, CHARLES, bishop; b. Montreal, Apr. 24, 1924. Ordained priest Roman Cath. Ch., 1950; ordained bishop St. Jerome, Que., Can., 1977—. Office: 355 St George St, Saint Jerome, PQ Canada J7Z 5V3*

VALOIS, ROBERT ARTHUR, lawyer; b. N.Y.C., May 13, 1938; s. Frank Jacob and Harriet Frances (LaCroix) V.; m. Ruth Emilie Skacil, Dec. 23, 1961; children: Marguerite Jeannette, Robert Arthur Jr. BBA, U. Miami, 1962; JD, Wake Forest U., 1972. Bar: N.C. 1972, Fla. 1972, U.S. Ct. Appeals (4th cir.) 1973, U.S. Dist. Ct. (ea. and mid. dists.) 1974, U.S. Supreme Ct. 1975, U.S. Ct. Appeals (6th cir.) 1986. Field examiner NLRB, Winston-Salem, N.C., 1962-70; from assoc. to ptnr. Maupin. Taylor, Ellis & Adams P.A., Raleigh, N.C., 1972—; chmn. labor and employment sect. Maupin, Taylor, Ellis & Adams P.A., Raleigh, N.C., 1972—; vice chmn. Legal Svcs. Corp., Washington, 1984-90, bd. dirs. Served with USN, 1956-59. Mem. Greater Raleigh C. of C. (chmn. fed. govt. com. 1991—), Capitol City Club. Democrat. Presbyterian.

VALSARAJ, KALLIAT THAZHATHUVEETIL, chemical engineering educator; b. Tellichery, Kerala, India, Oct. 2, 1957; came to U.S., 1980; s. Mundayat B. Nambiar and Kalliat T. Bhanumathy; m. Nisha Valsaraj, Dec. 24, 1990; 1 child, Viveca. MS, Indian Inst. Tech., Madras, India, 1980; PhD, Vanderbilt U., 1983. Affiliate faculty U. Ark., Fayetteville, 1983-86; sr. rsch. assoc. Hazardous Waste Rsch. Ctr. La. State U., Baton Rouge, 1986-90, asst. prof., 1990-93, assoc. prof., 1994—, dept. chem. engring.; mem. panel directions in separations NSF, 1989-90; cons. Balsam Engr. Cons., Salem, N.H., 1990-91; presenter in field. Author: Elements of Environmental Engineering: Thermodynamics and Kinetics, 1995; contbr. over 70 articles to profl. jours. Grantee Dept. Def., 1986-89, NSF, 1989, 92-95, EPA, 1989-92, 93-97. Mem. Am. Chem. Soc., Am. Inst. Chem. Engrs., Nat. Geographic Soc., Indian Chem. Soc. Achievements include patent for innovative groundwater treatment. Home: 1924 Hobbiton Rd Baton Rouge LA 70810-3414 Office: La State U Dept Chem Engring Baton Rouge LA 70803

VALUKAS, ANTON RONALD, lawyer, former federal official; b. Chgo., June 21, 1943; s. Anton J. and Mary Ann (Giusto) V.; m. Janice C. (div.); children: Amy Paige, Beth Catherine; m. Maria Finitzo; children: Catherine Sara, Paul Alexander. B.A. in Polit. Sci., Art History, Lawrence U., 1965; J.D., Northwestern U., 1968. Bars: Ill. 1968, U.S. Dist. Ct. (no. dist.) Ill. 1968, U.S. Ct. Appeals (7th cir.) 1969, U.S. Ct. Appeals (10th cir.) 1977, U.S. Ct. Appeals (3d cir.) 1982. Dir. Nat. Defender Project, Chgo., 1968-70; asst. U.S. atty. U.S. Atty.'s Office, Chgo., 1970-76; ptnr. Jenner & Block, Chgo., 1976-85, 1989—; U.S. atty. No. Dist. Ill., Dept. Justice, Chgo., 1985-89; dir., treas. Met. Fair and Exposition Authority, Chgo., 1985; chmn. Ill. Task Force crime and corrections, 1992-93. Mem. several commns. and coms. Evanston Housing Commn., Ill.; chmn. Ill. Task Force on Crime and Corrections, 1992-93. Recipient Spl. Commendation award Dept. Justice, Chgo., 1975, Disting. Grad. award Palatine High Sch., Ill., 1984, John Marshall Law Sch. Freedom award, Chgo., 1985, Citizen of Yr. award Constnl. Rights Found., 1987; named one of Ten Outstanding Young Citizens of Chgo., Jr. C. of C., 1976. Fellow Am. Coll. Trial Lawyers; mem. Chgo. Bar Assn. Club: Law of Chgo. Home: 1601 Wesley Ave Evanston IL 60201-4105 Office: Jenner & Block 1 E Ibm Plz Chicago IL 60611-3586

VALVO, BARBARA-ANN, lawyer, surgeon; b. Elizabeth, N.J., June 7, 1949; d. Robert Richad and Vera (Kovach) V. BA in Biology, Hofsta U., 1971; MD, Pa. State U., 1975; JD, Loyola Sch. Law, 1993. Diplomate Am. Bd. Surgery; Bar: La. 1993. Surg. intern Nassau County Med. Ctr., East Meadow, N.Y., 1975-76; resident gen. surgery Allentown-Sacred Heart Med. Ctr., Allentown, Pa., 1976-80; asst. chief surgery USPHS, New Orleans, 1980-81; pvt. practice gen. surgery New Orleans, 1981-89, pvt. practice law, 1995—. Upjohn scholar, 1975. Fellow ACS; mem. ABA, FBA, La. Bar Assn., La. Trial Lawyers Assn. Republican. Avocations: computers, raising animals. Home and Office: PO Box 640217 Kenner LA 70064-0217

VAMVAKETIS, CAROLE, health services administrator; b. Bklyn., Mar. 1, 1943; d. William and Helen (Calacanis) Vamvaketis; 1 child, William. AA, Packer Collegiate Inst., Bklyn., 1962; BS, Columbia U., 1964; MA, Columbia Tchrs. Coll., 1969; AAS in Nursing, Rockland C.C., Suffern, N.Y., 1981; BSN, Dominican Coll., 1991. Tchr. elem. sch. A. Fantis Parochial Sch., 1964-67; tchr. Adelphi Acad., 1967-72, girls dean, 1968-72; nurse Nyack (N.Y.) Hosp., 1981-91; nurse mgr. Kings Harbor Care Ctr., 1991-93; assoc. dir. nursing Port Chester Nursing Home, 1993-94; CQI/edn. coord. Highbridge Woodycrest Ctr., 1994-95; profl. svcs. cons. Multicare Cos., Inc., Nanuet, N.Y., 1995-96, personal svcs. cons., 1995-96, divsn. dir. clin. svcs., 1996—; asst. dir. nursing, dir. staff devel. Beth Abraham Health Svcs., Bronx, N.Y., 1996—; dir. of nursing Ridgewood Nursing and Rehab. Ctr., Multicare Cos., Inc., 1997—. Home: 102 Poplar St Nanuet NY 10954-2007

VAN, GEORGE PAUL, international money management consultant; b. Isle Maligne, Que., Can., Feb. 12, 1940; s. Raymond Murdoch and Germaine Marie (Brassard) V.; m. Janine Marie Irene Therese Yvette Boily, Sept. 15, 1962; children: John, Robert, Caroline. BA, McGill U., 1961; DHA, U. Toronto, 1963. Sr. cons. Agnew Peckham and Assos., Toronto, Ont., Can., 1963-65; chief exec. officer, exec. dir. Misericordia Corp., Edmonton, Alta., Can., 1965-68; chief operating officer, exec. v.p. Texpack, Ltd., Brantford, Ont., 1968-70, also bd. dirs.; group v.p. Will Ross, Inc., Milw., 1970-73; exec. v.p. Nortek, Inc., Cranston, R.I., 1973-77, also bd. dirs.; pres., chief operating officer Hosp. Affiliates Internat. Inc. subs. INA Corp., Nashville, 1977-80, also bd. dirs.; chmn., pres., chief exec. officer Health Group Inc., Nashville, 1980-84; chmn., chief exec. officer Columbia Corp. (formerly Franklin Corp.), Nashville, 1984-88; pres. Grinders Switch Farms, Grinders Switch Shooting Club, Centerville, Tenn., 1990—; chmn. Van Hedge Fund Advisors, Inc., Nashville, 1992—. Bd. dirs. Tulane U. Med. Ctr., 1977-80, Nashville Inst. for the Arts, 1987-88, Nashville Symphony, 1987-88, Fedn. Internat. de Tir aux Armes Sportives de Chasse, Paris, 1990-92; mem. Internat. Tech. Commn. for Sporting Clays, Paris, 1990; bd. overseers U. Pa. Sch. of Nursing, 1979-82, 84-88, assoc. trustee U. Pa., 1979-82, 84-88; chmn. internat. com. U.S. Sporting Clays Assn., 1989-92; active pres.'s coun. Andrew Jackson Inst., 1993-94; adv. bd. Fin. Mktg. Rsch. Ctr. Vanderbilt U. Recipient several scholarships. Mem. Westside Club, Grinders Switch Club. Contbr. articles to profl. jours. Home and Office: 1608 Chickering Rd Nashville TN 37215-4906

VAN, PETER, lawyer; b. Boston, Sept. 7, 1936; s. Frank Lewis and Ruth (Spevack) V.; m. Faye Anne Zinck, 1991; children: Jami Lynne, Robert Charles. BA, Dartmouth, 1958; LLD, Boston Coll., 1961. Bar: Mass. 1962. Assoc. Brown, Rudnick, Freed and Gesmer, Boston, 1961-63; assoc. Fine and Ambrogne, Boston, 1963-65, ptnr., 1966-73, sr. ptnr., 1973—, mng. ptnr., chmn. exec. com., 1988-90; ptnr., mem. exec. com. Mintz, Levin, Cohn, Ferris, Glovsky and Popeo, P.C., Boston, 1990-97; ptnr. Bingham, dana & Gould, Boston, 1997—. Mem. fin. com., overseer Beth Israel Hosp. Boston. Mem. Masons. Office: 150 Federal St Boston MA 02110

VAN ACKEREN, MAURICE EDWARD, college administrator; b. Cedar Rapids, Nebr., Aug. 21, 1911; s. Edward M. and Frances (O'Leary) Van A. B.A. in Chemistry, Creighton U., 1932; M.A. in Edn., St. Louis U., 1946; LL.D. (hon.), Benedictine Coll., 1976. Ordained Jesuit priest Roman Cath. Ch., 1943. Tchr. Campion High Sch., Prairie du Chien, Wis., 1937-40; prin. St. Louis U. High Sch., 1946-51; pres. Rockhurst Coll., Kansas City, Mo., 1951-77, chancellor, 1977—. Recipient Knight of Holy Sepulchre award Catholic Ch., Chgo., 1968, Chancellor's medal U. Mo.-Kansas City, 1981, Mr. Kansas City award Greater Kansas City C. of C., 1983; named to Creighton U. Athletic Hall of Fame, Omaha, 1971; named Mktg. Exec. of Yr., Sales and Mktg. Club Kansas City, 1979. Mem. C. of C. of Greater Kansas City. Lodge: Rotary (Paul Harris fellow 1983). Avocations: fishing; golf; baseball; football. Home and Office: 1100 Rockhurst Rd Kansas City MO 64110-2508*

VAN ALLEN, JAMES ALFRED, physicist, educator; b. Mt. Pleasant, Iowa, Sept. 7, 1914; s. Alfred Morris and Alma E. (Olney) Van A.; m. Abigail Fithian Halsey, Oct. 13, 1945; children: Cynthia Schaffner, Margot Cairns, Sarah Trimble, Thomas, Peter. BS, Iowa Wesleyan Coll., 1935; MS, U. Iowa, 1936, PhD, 1939; ScD (hon.), Iowa Wesleyan Coll., 1951, Grinnell Coll., 1957, Coe Coll., 1958, Cornell Coll., Mt. Vernon, Iowa, 1959, U. Dubuque, 1960, U. Mich., 1961, Northwestern U., 1961, Ill. Coll., 1963, Butler U., 1966, Boston Coll., 1966, Southampton Coll., 1967, Augustana Coll., 1969, St. Ambrose Coll., 1982, U. Bridgeport, 1987. Research fellow, physicist dept. terrestial magnetism Carnegie Instn., Washington, 1939-42; physicist, group and unit supr. applied physics lab. Johns Hopkins U., 1942, 46-50; organizer, leader sci. expdns. study cosmic radiation Peru, 1949, Gulf of Alaska, 1950, Arctic, 1952, 57, Antarctic, 1957; prof. physics, head dept. U. Iowa, Iowa City, 1951-85, Carver prof. physics, 1989-92, Regent disting. prof., 1992—; Regents fellow Smithsonian Instn., 1981; rsch. assoc. Princeton U., 1953-54; mem. devel. group radio proximity fuze Nat. Def. Rsch. Coun., OSRD; pioneer high attitude rsch. with rockets, satellites and space probes. Author: Origins of Magnetospheric Physics, 1983, First to Jupiter, Saturn and Beyond, 1981; 924 Elementary Problems and Answers in Solar System Astronomy, 1993; contbg. author: Physics and Medicine of Upper Atmosphere, 1952, Rocket Exploration of the Upper Atmosphere; editor: Scientific Uses of Earth Satellites, 1956, Cosmic Rays, the Sun, and Geomagnetism: The Works of Scott E. Forbush, 1993; acting editor Jour. Geophys. Rsch.-Space Physics, 1991-92; contbr. numerous articles to profl. jours. *. Lt. comdr. USNR, 1942-46, ordnance and gunnery specialist, combat observer. Recipient Physics award Washington Acad. Sci., 1949, Space Flight award Am. Astronautical Soc., 1958, Louis W. Hill Space Transp. award Inst. Aero. Scis., 1959, Elliot Cresson medal Franklin Inst., 1961, Golden Omega award Elec. Insulation Conf., 1963, Iowa Broadcasters Assn. award, 1964, Fellows award of merit Am. Cons. Engrs. Coun., 1978, Nat. Medal of Sci., 1987, Vannevar Bush award NSF, 1991, Gerard P. Kuiper prize Am. Astron. Soc. 1994; named comdr. Order du Merit Pour la Recherche et l'Invention, 1964; Guggenheim Found. rsch. fellow, 1951. Fellow Am. Rocket Soc. (C.N. Hickman medal devel. Aerobee rocket 1949), IEEE, Am. Phys. Soc., Am. Geophys. Union (pres. 1982-84, John A. Fleming award 1963, William Bowie medal 1977); mem. NAS, AAAS (Abelson prize 1986), Iowa Acad. Sci., Internat. Acad. Astronautics (founding), Am. Philos. Soc., Am. Astron. Soc., Royal Astron. Soc. U.K. (gold medal 1978), Royal Swedish Acad. Sci. (Crafoord prize 1989), Am. Acad. Arts and Scis., Cosmos Club, Sigma Xi (Procter prize 1987), Gamma Alpha. Presbyterian. Achievements include discovery of radiation belts around earth. Office: Univ Iowa 701 Van Allen Hall Iowa City IA 52242-1403*

VAN ALLEN, KATRINA FRANCES, painter; b. Phoenix, Feb. 18, 1933; d. Benjamin Cecile Sherrill and Magdalen Mary (Thomas) Adams; m. Ray C. Bennett II, Dec. 31, 1950 (div. 1955); m. William Allen Van Allen, Mar. 15, 1963 (dec. Mar. 1971); m. Donovan Wyatt Jacobs, Apr. 22, 1972; children: Ray Crawford Bennett III, Sherri Lou Bennett Maraney. Student, Stanford U., 1950, 51, 52, Torrance C.C., 1962, 63; MA, U. Tabriz, Iran, 1978; studied with Martin Lubner, Jerold Burchman, John Lepper, L.A.; student, Otis Art Inst., Immaculate Heart Coll.; studied with Russa Graeme, 1968, 69, 70. Office mgr. H.P. Adams Constrn. Co., Yuma, Ariz., 1952-59; nurse Moss-Hathaway Med. Clin., Torrance, Calif., 1962-63; interviewer for various assns. N.Y.C., 1964-70. Solo shows include: Zella 9 Gallery, London, 1972, Hambleton Gallery, Maiden Newton, Eng., 1974, Intercontinental Gallery, Teheran, Iran, 1976, USIA Gallery, Teheran, 1977, 78, Coos Art Mus., Coos Bay, Oreg., 1993; exhibited in group shows at La Cienega Gallery, L.A., 1970, 80, 81, 82, Design Ctr. Gallery, Tucson, 1985, Coos Art Mus., 1992-97; represented in permanent collections at Bankers Trust Bd. Room, London, Mfrs. Hanover Bank, London, U. Iowa Med. Sch., Iowa City, Bank of Am., Leonard E. Blakesley Internat. Law Offices, Marina del Rey, Calif., and numerous pvt. collections. Bd. dirs. Inst. for Cancer and Leukemia Rsch., 1966-67, 68. Recipient Five City Tour and Honorarium, Iran Am. Soc., 1977, Most Improved player C.C.C. Ladies Golf Assn., 1995. Mem. Nat. Women in the Arts, L.A. Art Assn., Coos Bay Art Assn., Coos Bay Power Squadron, Lower Umpqu Flycasters. Avocations: fly-fishing, hiking, bridge, golf, the Arts. Home and Studio: 3693 Cape Arago Hwy Coos Bay OR 97420-9604

VAN ALLEN, WILLIAM KENT, lawyer; b. Albion, N.Y., July 30, 1914; s. Everett Kent and Georgia (Roberts) Van A.; m. Sally Schall, Nov. 11, 1944; children: William Kent, Jr., George Humphrey, Peter Cushing. A.B., Hamilton Coll., 1935; LL.B., Harvard U., 1938. Bar: N.Y. 1938, D.C. 1939, N.C. 1951, U.S. Dist. Ct. (we. dist.) N.C. 1951, U.S. Dist. Ct. (mid. dist.) N.C. 1953, U.S. Ct. Appeals (4th cir.) 1951, U.S. Ct. Claims 1946, U.S. Tax Ct. 1940, FCC 1939, ICC 1940, U.S. Supreme Ct. 1946. With Hanson, Lovett & Dale, Washington, 1938-41, 46-50; ptnr. Lassiter, Moore and Van Allen and Moore and Van Allen, Charlotte, N.C., 1951-87; of counsel Moore & Van Allen, Charlotte, 1988—; permanent mem. Jud. Conf. 4th Jud. Circuit. Vestryman Episc. Ch., 1957-60, 66-69; mem. Mecklenburg County Bd. Public Welfare, 1954-59, chmn. 1957-59; bd. dirs. N.C. Found. Commerce and Industry, 1965-73, Found. U. N.C. at Charlotte, 1979-89, Charlotte Symphony Orch., 1981-82, Mercy Health Svcs., 1983-88; chmn. Charlotte Area adv. coun. Am. Arbitration Assn., 1967-76; bd. dirs. United Community Svcs., 1972-77, v.p., 1972; bd. mgrs. Charlotte Country Day Sch., 1956-61, chmn., 1959-61, bd. visitors, 1978—, chmn., 1987-88; bd. advisers U. N.C.-Charlotte, 1983-84; trustee Spastics Hosp., 1951-60, Mint Mus. Art, 1976-79, Surtman Found., 1955-90, Mercy Hosp. Found., 1979-84; bd. visitors Johnson C. Smith U., 1978-89; pres. Charlotte Symphony League, 1980-81, Friends of U. N.C. at Charlotte, 1990-91. Served with USNR, 1941-45, commdg. officer destroyer escort ATO and PTO; released to inactive duty as lt. comdr. Mem. ABA, Charlotte C. of C. (bd. dirs. 1971-75, v.p. 1972-75). Mil. Order of Carabao, Holland Soc. N.Y., Charlotte Country Club, Charlotte City Club, Chevy Chase Club (Md.), Mullett Lake Country Club (Mich.), Phi Beta Kappa, Chi Psi. Office: Moore & Van Allen 4700 NationsBank Corp Ctr Charlotte NC 28202-4003

VAN ALLSBURG, CHRIS, author, artist; b. Grand Rapids, Mich., June 18, 1949; s. Richard Allen and Doris Marie (Christiansen) Van A.; m. Lisa Carol Morrison, Aug. 17, 1976. BFA, U. Mich., 1972; MFA, R.I. Sch. Design, 1975. Tchr. R.I. Sch. Design, Providence. Author, illustrator: The Garden of Abdul Gasazi, 1979 (Caldecott Honor Book 1980, Irma Simonton Black award Bank St. Coll. Edn. 1980, Boston Globe/Horn Book award 1980), Jumanji, 1981 (Caldecott medal 1982, Boston Globe/Horn Book award 1982, Children's Choice award Internat. Reading Assn. 1982, Am. Book award, 1982, Ky. Bluegrass award No. Ky. U. 1983, Buckeye Children's Book award Ohio State Libr. 1983, Wash. Children's Choice Picture Book award Wash. Libr. Media Assn. 1984, W. Va. Children's Book award 1985), Ben's Dream, 1982 (Parents Choice award for illustration Parents' Choice Found. 1982), Wreck of the Zephyr, 1983 (Silver medal Soc. Illustrators 1983), The Mysteries of Harris Burdick, 1984 (Parents Choice award for illustration Parents' Choice Found. 1984, Irma Simonton Black award Bank St. Coll. Edn. 1985, Boston Globe/Horn Book award 1985, World Fantasy award 1985), The Polar Express, 1985 (Parents Choice award for illustration Parents' Choice Found. 1985, Caldecott medal 1986, Boston Globe/Horn Book award 1986, Ky. Bluegrass award No. Ky. U. 1987), The Stranger, 1986 (Parents Choice award for illustration Parents' Choice Found. 1986), The Z Was Zapped: A Play in Twenty-Six Acts, 1987, Two Bad Ants, 1988, Just A Dream, 1990, The Wretched Stone, 1991, The Widow's Broom, 1992, The Sweetest Fig, 1993, The Two Figs, 1993, Bad Day at River Bend, 1995; illustrator: Swan Lake, 1989; exhibited works at Whitney Mus. Art, N.Y.C., Mus. Modern Art, N.Y.C., Alan Stone Gallery, N.Y.C., Grand Rapids (Mich.) Art Mus., Port Washington (N.Y.) Pub. Libr.; permanent collections include Kerlan Collection at U. Minn. Recipient Hans Christian Andersen award nomination, 1985. Jewish. Office: Houghton Mifflin Co 222 Berkeley St Boston MA 02116-3748*

VAN ALSTYNE, JUDITH STURGES, English language educator, writer; b. Columbus, Ohio, June 9, 1934; d. Rexford Leland and Wilma Irene (Styan) Van A.; m. Dan C. Duckham (div. 1964); children: Kenton Leland, Jeffrey Clarke. BA, Miami U., Oxford, Ohio, 1956; MEd, Fla. Atlantic U., 1967. Sr. prof. Broward C.C., Ft. Lauderdale, Fla., 1967-88; ret., 1988; spl. asst. for women's affairs Broward C.C., 1972-88, dir. cmty. svcs., 1973-74, dir. cultural affairs, 1974-75; spkr., cons. Malaysian Coll., 1984; ednl. travel group tour guide, 1984-88; v.p., ptnr. Downtown Travel Ctr., Ft. Lauderdale, Fla., 1993—. Author: Write It Right, 1980, Professional and Technical Writing Strategies, 3d edit., 1994; freelance writer travel articles; contbr. articles and poetry to profl. jours. Bd. dirs. Broward C.C. Found., Inc., 1973-89, Broward Friends of the Libr., 1994—, Broward Friends of Miami City Ballet, 1994—; active Sister Cities/People to People, Ft. Lauderdale, 1988—; docent Ft. Lauderdale Mus. Art, 1988—; officer Friends of Mus., Ft. Lauderdale, 1992—. Recipient award of achievement Soc. for Tech. Comm., 1986, award of distinction Fla. Soc. for Tech. Comm., 1986. Mem. English-Speaking Union (bd. dirs. 1984-89). Democrat. Episcopalian. Avocations: writing, reading, travel. Home and Office: # 265 1688 S Ocean Ln Fort Lauderdale FL 33316-3346

VAN ALSTYNE, VANCE BROWNELL, arbitration management consultant; b. Rochester, N.Y., Feb. 3, 1924; s. Guy Brownell and Jessie Cary Van A.; B.A., U. Rochester, 1948; LL.B., Blackstone Coll. Law, 1964; m. Jane Kotary, Aug. 12, 1950; children—Cary B., Stacey E. Rsch. asst. Gilbert Assos., Inc., N.Y.C., 1950-56; corp. sec., v.p., dir. R.C. Simpson & Staff, Inc., Newark and Ridgewood, N.J., 1956-74, pres., dir. R.C. Simpson, Inc., Ridgewood, 1975—. 2d lt. USAF, 1943-45. Decorated Air medal. Mem. Am. Mgmt. Assn., Indsl. Rels. Rsch. Assn., Am. Arbitration Assn., Internat. Atlantic Salmon Fedn., Swiss-Icelandic Salmon Assns., Trout Unltd. Republican. Home: 6853 N Baltusrol Ln Charlotte NC 28210-7365 Office: RC Simpson Inc 5950 Fairview Rd Ste 604 Charlotte NC 28210-3104

VAN ALSTYNE, W. SCOTT, JR., lawyer, educator; b. East Syracuse, N.Y., Sept. 21, 1922; s. Walter Scott and Cecil Edna (Folmsbee) Van A.; m. Margaret Reed Hudson, June 23, 1949 (div.); children: Gretchen Anne, Hunter Scott; m. Marion Graham Walker, May 3, 1980. B.A., U. Buffalo, 1948; M.A., U. Wis., 1950, LL.B., 1953, S.J.D., 1954. Bar: Wis. 1953. Assoc. Shea & Hoyt, Milw., 1954-56; asst. prof. law U. Nebr., 1956-58; pvt. practice Madison, Wis., 1958-72; prof. law U. Fla., 1973-90, prof. emeritus, 1990—; lectr. law U. Wis., 1958-72; lectr. Cambridge-Warsaw Trade Program Cambridge U. (Eng.), 1976; vis. prof. law Cornell U., 1977, U. Leiden, The Netherlands, 1988, 91; spl. lectr. U. Utrecht, The Netherlands, 1991; vis. prof. Wake Forest U., 1997; spl. counsel Gov. of Wis., 1966-70; bd. dirs. non-resident divsn. State Bar Wis., 1981-96, pres., 1988-90, bd. govs. 1988-90. Prin. author: Goals and Missions of Law Schools, 1990; contbr. articles to profl. jours. Mem. Gov.'s Commn. on edn., Wis., 1969-71; cons. Wis. Commn. on Legal Edn., 1995-96. Served with AUS, 1942-45, 61-62; col. Res., ret. Decorated Legion of Merit. Mem. SR (N.Y.), Holland Soc. (N.Y.), Madison (Wis.) Club, Ft. Rennselaer (N.Y.) Club, Netherland Club (N.Y.C.), Order of Coif, Phi Beta Kappa, Omicron Delta Kappa, Phi Delta Phi. Republican. Presbyterian. Office: U Fla Holland Law Ctr Gainesville FL 32611

VAN ALTENA, ALICIA MORA, language educator; b. San Juan, Argentina, May 31, 1945; came to U.S., 1986; d. Francisco and Pilar (Garcia) Mora; m. William Foster van Altena, June 2, 1986. MA in Edn., Nat. U., San Juan, 1978. Prof. 2d lang. state colls. and high schs., San Juan, 1971-80; asst. prof. State U., San Juan, 1981-86; teaching asst. So. Conn. State U., New Haven, 1987-88; lectr. Yale U., New Haven, 1987-91, dir .beginners, 1992-94, lang. coord., 1993-94, sr. lectr., 1993—; bd. dirs. Fedn. of Tchrs. of English, Argentina, 1983-86. Roman Catholic. Avocations: travel, photography, gardening. Home: 105 Swarthmore St Hamden CT 06517-1916 Office: Yale U Yale Spanish Dept 82-90 Wall St New Haven CT 06520

VANALTENBURG, BETTY MARIE, lumber company executive; b. Tulsa, Dec. 27, 1963; d. Floyd Albert and Charolette Virginia (Quinton) V. BA in Comm., U. Tulsa, 1986. Adminstrv. supr. All Wood Products Co., Tulsa, 1986—. Bd. mem. Tulsa Oklahomans for Human Rights, 1987-89, interim pres., 1989; mem. host com. Names Project, 1990, 93, 95, 97, co-chair ctrl. region logistics, Washington, 1996, quilt display coord., 1997—; bd. mem. Follies Revue, Inc., Tulsa, 1993-97, v.p., 1994-97; vol. acctg. Children's Med. Ctr.-Children's Miracle Network Telethon, 1994, 95, 96, 97. Mem. Order of Eastern Star (worthy matron Tulsa chpt. # 133 1995-96), Daughters of The Nile Zibiah Temple #102 (Princess Tirzah 1995-96, Princess Royal 1996-97, Queen 1997—). Republican. Presbyterian. Avocations: model trains, reading, travel, fundraising.

VAN AMRINGE, JOHN HOWARD, retired oil industry executive, geologist; b. L.A., Oct. 11, 1932; s. Edwin Verne and Viola (Hail) Van A.; m. Mary Jane Lothras, Jan. 29, 1955; children: Kathryn Jean Van Amringe Ball, Kenneth Edwin. AA, Pasadena City Coll., 1954; BA, UCLA, 1956, MA, 1957. Geologist Unocal Corp., Santa Maria, Calif., 1957-58, Santa Fe Springs, Calif., 1958-64, New Orleans, 1964-66; dist. geologist Unocal Corp., Lafayette, La., 1966-68, dist. exploration mgr., 1968-79; exploration mgr. western region Unocal Corp., Pasadena, Calif., 1979-88; v.p. exploration Unocal Corp., L.A., 1988-92. Editor: Typical Offshore Oil and Gas Fields, 1973; author profl. paper. Bd. dirs. Pasadena City Coll. Found., 1986—, treas., 1992-95; pres. Pasadena Cmty. Orch., 1990-94. With U.S. Army, 1949-52, Korea. Named Geologist of Yr., Lafayette chpt. Am. Inst. Profl. Geologists, 1972. Mem. Am. Assn. Petroleum Geologists (del. 1972-73), Pacific Sect. of Am. Assn. Petroleum Geologists (editor 1961-63), Lafayette Geol. Soc. (pres. 1971-72). Republican. Avocations: tennis, travel, sailing, collecting, photography. Home: 1455 Old House Rd Pasadena CA 91107-1518

VAN ANDEL, JAY, direct selling company executive; b. Grand Rapids, Mich., June 3, 1924; s. James and Nella (Vanderwoude) Van A.; m. Betty J. Hoekstra, Aug. 16, 1952; children: Nan, Stephen, David, Barbara. Student, Pratt Jr. Coll., 1945, Calvin Coll., 1942, 46, Yale, 1943-44; DBA (hon.), No. Mich. U., 1976, Western Mich. U., 1979, Grand Valley State U., 1992; LLD (hon.), Ferris State Coll., 1977, Mich. State U., 1997. Co-founder, sr. chmn. Amway Corp., Ada, Mich.; founder Van Andel Edn. and Med. Rsch., Grand Rapids, Mich.; U.S. amb., commr. gen. Genoa Expo '92, 1992 World's Fair marking 500th Anniversary of Columbus Journey to Am.; chmn. bd. Amway Internat., Amway Hotel Corp., Amway Environ. Found., Nutrilite Products, Inc.; chmn. Ja-Ri Corp., Ada, Mich.; mem. adv. coun. Am. Private Edn. Participant White Ho. Conf. Indsl. World Ahead, 1972; chmn. Mich. Rep. fin. com., 1975-81; Founding chmn. Right Place Com., Grand Rapids, Mich.; mem. adv. council Nat. 4H Found.; trustee Hillsdale (Mich.) Coll., Citizens Rsch. Coun. Mich., Hudson Inst., Indpls. and Washington; dir. Jamestown Found., Gerald R. Ford Found.; bd. dirs., trustee, treas. Washington, Heritage Found., Washington; pres. Van Andel Found.; co-chmn. Mich. Botanic Garden Capital Campaign; founding chmn. Citizen's Choice, Washington; former bd. dirs. BIPAC, Washington, former chmn. Netherlands-Am. Bicentennial Commn; former mem. bd. govs. USO World. Served to 1st lt. USAAF, 1943-46. Knighted Grand Officer of Orange-Nassau, The Netherlands; recipient Disting. Alumni award Calvin Coll., 1976, Golden Plate award Am. Acad. Achievement, Gt. Living Am. award and Bus. and Profl. Leader of the Yr. award Religious Heritage Am., George Washington medal of Honor Freedom Found., Gold medals Netherland Soc. of Phila. and N.Y.C., Disting. Citizen award Northwood Inst., Patron award Mich. Found. for Arts, 1982, Achievement award UN Environment Programme, 1989, UN Environment Programme Achievement award Amway, 1989, Adam Smith Free Enterprise award Am. Legis. Exchange Coun., 1993, Disting. Svc. award Rotary Grand Rapids, Gold Medal Netherlands Soc. N.Y., Edison Achievement award Am. Mktg. Assn., 1994; named Bus. Person Yr. Econ. Club Grand Rapids, 1990; named to Grand Rapids Bus. Hall of Fame; World fellow Duke of Edinburgh's award. Mem. Sales and Mktg. Execs. Internat. Acad. Achievement (charter), Direct Selling Assn. (bd. dirs., hall of fame), U.S. C. of C. (past chmn. bd.), Right Place Com. (founding chmn.), de Tocqueville Soc. (former chmn.), Nat. Chamber Found. (dir.), Mensa Soc. USA, Peninsular Club, Cascade Hills Country Club, Lotus Club, Capitol Hill Club (Washington), Macatawa Bay Yacht Club (Holland, Mich., Le Mirador Country Club (Switzerland), Econ. Club (Grand Rapids), Omicron Delta Kappa (hon.). Mem. Christian Reformed Ch. (elder). Home: 7186 Windy Hill Dr SE Grand Rapids MI 49546-9745 Office: Amway Corp 7575 Fulton St E Ada MI 49355-0001

VAN ANDEL, STEVE ALAN, business executive; b. Ada, Mich., Oct. 9, 1955. BLS in Econs. and Bus., Hillsdale Coll., 1978; MBA in MKtg., Miami U., Oxford, Ohio, 1979. V.p. mktg. Amway Corp., Worldwide; chmn. exec. com. policy bd. Amway Corp., Ada; vice chmn. Amway Japan Ltd.; chmn. Amway Asia Pacific Ltd.; chmn. Amway Corp., Ada, now CEO; bd. dirs. Met. Hosp., Mich. Nat. Bank Corp.; mem. dean's adv. bd. Seidman Sch. of Bus. Bd. dirs. Grand Rapids John Ball Soc., Amway Environmental

Found. Mem. U.S. C. of C. (bd. dirs.). Office: Amway Corp 7575 Fulton St E Ada MI 49355-0001

VAN ANTWERPEN, FRANKLIN STUART, federal judge; b. Passaic, N.J., Oct. 23, 1941; s. Franklin John and Dorothy (Hoedemaker) Van A.; m. Kathleen Veronica O'Brien, Sept. 12, 1970; children: Joy, Franklin W., Virginia. BS in Engring. Physics, U. Maine, 1964; JD, Temple U., 1967; postgrad., Nat. Jud. Coll., 1980. Bar: Pa. 1969, U.S. Dist. Ct. (ea. dist.) Pa. 1971, U.S. Ct. Appeals (3d cir.) 1971, U.S. Supreme Ct. 1972. Corp. counsel Hazeltine, Corp., N.Y.C., 1967-70; chief counsel Northampton County Legal Aid Soc., Easton, Pa., 1970-71; assoc. Hemstreet & Smith, Easton, 1971-73; ptnr. Hemstreet & VanAntwerpen, Easton, 1973-79; judge Ct. Common Pleas of Northampton County (Pa.), 1979-87, U.S. Dist. Ct. (ea. dist.) Pa., Phila., 1987—; appointed to U.S. Sentencing Commn. Judicial Working Group, 1992-93; trial judge U.S. vs. Scarfo, 1988-89; adj. prof. Northampton County Area Community Coll., 1976-81; solicitor Palmer Twp., 1971-79; gen. counsel Fairview Savs. and Loan Assn., Easton, 1973-79. Recipient Booster award Bus. Indsl. and Profl. Assn., 1979, George Palmer award Palmer Twp., 1980, Man of Yr. award, 1981, Law Enforcement Commendation medal Nat. Soc. SAR, 1990; named an Alumnus Who Has Made a Difference in the World, U. Maine, 1991. Mem. ABA (com. on jud. edn.), Fed. Bar Assn. (hon.), Pa. Bar Assn., Northampton County Bar Assn., Am. Judicature Soc., Fed. Judges Assn., Pomfret Club, Nat. Lawyers Club Washington, Union League Club, Pa. Soc. Club, Sigma Pi Sigma. Office: US Dist Ct Holmes Bldg 2nd and Ferry St Easton PA 18042

VAN ANTWERPEN, REGINA LANE, underwriter, insurance company executive; b. Milw., Aug. 16, 1939; d. Joseph F. Gagliano and Sophia B. (Johannik) Wolfe; widowed; children: Thomas II, Victoria. Student, U. Wis., Milw., 1954-57. Office mgr. Gardner Bender Inc., Milw., 1972-80; mfg. rep. Rosenbloom & Co., Chgo., 1980-81; spl. agt. Northwestern Mut. Life Equities Inc., Milw., 1981-88, registered rep., 1985-88; account rep. Fin. Instn. Mktg. Co., Milw., 1988-93; investment specialist Fimco Securities Group, Inc., Milw., 1993—; pres. Anvers Ltd., 1990—, 1990—. Author: (poetry) One More Time Its Christmas, 1978, True Friendship, 1979, Beautiful Brown Eyes, 1990 (award 1992). Mgr. Sch. Bd. Elections, Fox Point, 1969; v.p. Suburban Rep. Women's CLub, Milw., 1968-72; vol. tchr. St. Eugene Sch., Milw., 1968-72. Mem. AAUW, Milw. Life Underwriters, Women's Life Underwriters (v.p. 1982-83), Legis. Orgn. Life Underwriters, Nat. Assn. Securities Dealers (lic.), Investment Club (sec. 1989-90, pres. 1990—). Republican. Roman Catholic. Avocations: writing, service work, gardening. Office: Fin Instn Mktg Co 111 E Kilbourn Ave Ste 1850 Milwaukee WI 53202-6611

VAN ARK, JOAN, actress; d. Carroll and Dorothy Jean (Hemenway) Van A.; m. John Marshall, Feb. 1, 1966; 1 child, Vanessa Jeanne. Student, Yale Sch. Drama. Appeared at Tyrone Guthrie Theatre, Washington Arena Stage, in London, on Broadway; performances include: (stage) Barefoot in the Park, 1965, School for Wives, 1971, Rules of the Game, 1974, Cyrano de Bergerac, Ring Round the Moon, A Little Night Music, 1994, Three Tall Women, 1995; (TV series) Temperatures Rising, 1972-73, We've Got Each Other, 1977-78, Dallas, 1978-81, Knots Landing, 1979-92 (also dir. episodes Letting Go, Hints and Evasions); (TV movies) The Judge and Jake Wyler, 1972, Big Rose, 1974, Shell Game, 1975, The Last Dinosaur, 1977, Red Flag, 1981, Shakedown on the Sunset Strip, 1988, My First Love, 1989, Murder at the PTA, 1990, To Cast a Shadow, 1990, Always Remember I Love You, 1990, Grand Central Murders, 1992, Tainted Blood, 1992, Someone's Watching, 1993, When the Darkman Calls, 1994; (TV miniseries) Testimony of Two Men, 1978; dir., star ABC-TV Afterschool Spl. Boys Will Be Boys, 1993. Recipient Theatre World award, 1970-71, L.A. Drama Critics Circle award, 1973, Outstanding Actress award Soap Opera Digest, 1986, 89. Mem. AFTRA, SAG, Actors Equity Assn., San Fernando Valley Track Club. Address: care William Morris Agy Inc 151 S El Camino Dr Beverly Hills CA 90212-2704 also: 1325 Avenue Of The Americas New York NY 10019-6026*

VAN ARNEM, HAROLD LOUIS, marketing professional; b. Cin., Dec. 19, 1940; s. Harold Louis and Elizabeth (Smith) Van A.; m. Karen Schram, Aug. 31, 1963 (div. 1980); children: Aleise, Heidi, Heather, Harold Louis IV; m. Bridget Elizabeth Sahlin, Feb. 17, 1990; children: Adam, Maxwell, Sean. BBA, U. Cin., 1964; postgrad., U. Detroit, 1968, 69, 71. With fin. and mktg. depts. GE Computers, Phoenix, 1964-67; chief exec. officer Acts Computing Corp., Southfield, Mich., 1967-74; contractor Illiac IV Arpa/DOD Arpanet, 1969-75; chief exec. officer Van Arnem, Birmingham, Mich., 1974—, Finalco Group, Inc., Boca Raton, Fla., 1988—; gen. ptnr. Finalco Ltd., Birmingham, 1988—, Gemini Equities Ltd., Boca Raton, 1989—; chmn., chief exec. officer Gemini Group, Inc., Boca Raton, 1989—; CEO Libra Technologies, Inc., Deerfield Beach, Fla., 1994—; gen. ptnr. Detroit Express, profl. soccer team, Pontiac, Mich., 1978-84; commr. Am. Soccer League, Pontiac, 1980; chmn. Decision Systems Internat., Paris, 1997—, Thomainfor, Paris, 1997—, Location Informatique, Paris, 1995—. Co-producer feature film Love at First Bite, 1979; assoc. producer feature film Quick and the Dead, 1978. Co-chmn. Mich. Rep. Legis. Com., 1977-81. Mem. CEO Orgn., Young Pres. Orgn., World Bus. Coun., Oakland Hills Country Club (Birmingham), Adios Golf Club (Deerfield Beach), Ocean Reef Yacht Club (Key Largo, Fla.). Avocations: jump rope, aerobics, spear fishing, golf. Office: Libra Tech Svcs 1301 W Newport Center Dr Deerfield Beach FL 33442-7734

VAN ARSDALE, DICK, professional basketball team executive; b. Indpls., Feb. 22, 1943; m. Barbara V.; children: Jill, Jason. AB in economics, Indiana U., 1965. Player New York Knicks (Nat. Basketball Assn.), N.Y.C., 1965-68; with Phoenix Suns, Phoenix, Ariz., 1968-77; color commentator, TV broadcasts Phoenix Suns, from 1977, interim mgr., 1987, v.p., player personnel, dir. player personnel. Named "Mr. Basketball" of Indiana during high school, NCAA All-American, Indiana U. Office: care Phoenix Suns 201 E Jefferson St Phoenix AZ 85004-2412*

VAN ARSDALE, STEPHANIE KAY LORENZ, cardiovascular clinical specialist, nursing educator, researcher; b. Butte, Mont., June 20, 1952; d. Hubert Nelson and Pauline Anna (Tebo) Lorenz; m. Roy Burbank Van Arsdale, June 18, 1978; children: Christopher, Erica. Diploma, St. Johns McNamara, Sch. Nursing, 1973; BSN cum laude, U. Utah, 1978, MSN, 1979; EdD, U. Ark., 1993. RN, Ark.; cert. ACLS instr., Am. Heart Assn.; cert. BLS instr.-trainer, Am. Heart Assn. Staff nurse cardiovascular surg. ICU Presbyn. Hosp. Ctr., Albuquerque, 1975-76; staff nurse surg. ICU and CCU U. Utah Med. Ctr., Salt Lake City, 1976-78; clin. specialist residency LDS Hosp., Salt Lake City, 1979; asst. prof. dept. Baccalaureate Nursing Ea. Ky. U., Richmond, 1980-84; staff nurse critical care unit Pattie A. Clay Hosp., Richmond, 1981-83; med. clinician Washington Regional Med. Ctr., Fayetteville, Ark., 1985; cardiovascular clin. specialist VA Med. Ctr., Fayetteville, 1985-93; assoc. prof. U. Memphis, 1993-96; asst. prof. U. Ark. for Med. Scis., Little Rock, 1996—; CPR instr. in cmty., Fayetteville and Richmond, 1980-93; mem. adj. faculty div. nursing Northeastern State U., Tahlequah, Okla., 1986-93, U. Ark., Fayetteville, 1989-93; mem. adj. clin. faculty U. Ark. for Med. Scis. Coll. Nursing, Little Rock, 1988-93; charter mem., spkr. N.W. Ark. Critical Care Consortium, Area Health Edn. Ctr., Fayetteville, 1989-93; presenter in field. Contbr. articles to profl. jours. Coord., vol. Home Meals Delivery Program, Richmond, Ky., 1981-84; adminstrv. bd., Sunday sch. tchr., sec. adult forum Ctrl. United Meth. Ch., Fayetteville, 1986-87; troop leader Girl Scouts Am. NOARK Coun., Fayetteville, 1987-90; sound sys. operator Christ United Meth. Ch., 1993—. Recipient Nurse of Yr. award for excellence in nursing practice Dist. 9, Ark. State Nurses Assn., 1987; grantee Ctrl. U.S. Earthquake Consortium, 1993, U.S. Geologic Survey, 1994, Miss. Emergency Mgmt. Agy., 1996. Mem. ANA (v.p. Dist. 9 1985-86, pres. 1987-88, mem. image com. 1990-93, chmn. program com. 1986-87, state 2d v.p. 1988-90, clin. nurse specialist coun. 1991—), AACN (CCRN; bd. dirs., chpt. sec. program com. 1994—), Nat. League for Nursing (mem. nominating com. Ky. 1984-85), Sigma Theta Tau. Methodist. Avocations: basketball coaching, skiing, tennis. Home: 8872 Farmoor Rd Germantown TN 38139-6517 Office: U Ark for Med Scis Coll Nursing Slot 529 4301 W Markham St Little Rock AR 72205-7101

VAN ARSDALL, ROBERT ARMES, engineer, retired air force officer; b. Omaha, Oct. 5, 1925; s. Samuel Peter and Althea (Armes) Van A.; m. Margaret Cooper Kiersted, June 9, 1948; children—Robert Armes, Janet Althea, Susan DeBaun, Kathryn Ann. BS, U.S. Mil. Acad., 1948; postgrad., U. Colo., spring 1961; MS, George Washington U., 1968. Commd. 2d lt. USAF, 1948, advanced through grades to col., 1968; grad. Randolph AFB, Tex., 1949; assigned 5th Air Rescue Group, Westover AFB, Mass., 1949-51; student USAF Squadron Officer Sch., Maxwell AFB, Ala., 1950; pilot, ops. officer 9th Air Rescue Group, Burton-Wood, Manston and Bushy Park, Eng., 1951-55; ops. officer Hdqrs. Air Rescue Service, Orlando AFB, Fla., 1955-57; plans officer Hdqrs. Air R & D Command, Balt., also Andrews AFB, Md., 1957-60; grad. USAF jet qualification course, Randolph AFB, 1959; tng.-with-industry Air Force Inst. Tech., Martin Co., Denver, 1960-61; chief plans div. Hdqrs. Space Systems Div., L.A., 1961-63; exec. officer Office Space Systems, Office Sec. Air Force, 1963-67; assoc. Air War Coll. program, Washington, 1964-66; student Naval War Coll., 1967-68; dep. dir. Dept. Def. Manned Space Flight Support Office, Patrick AFB, Fla., 1968-69; dir. range engring., 1969-70; dir. range ops. Air Force Eastern Test Range, 1970-72; comdr. USAF Satellite Test Ctr., Sunnyvale, Calif., 1972-73; vice comdr. USAF Satellite Control Facility, L.A., 1973-74; comdr. USAF Satellite Control Facility, 1974-76; staff engr. Pan Am. World Airways, Cocoa Beach, Fla., 1976-78; project dir. Pan Am. World Airways, 1978-79, program mgr., 1980-85, dir. internat. projects, 1985-88; program dir. Diego Garcia, 1989, ret., 1989. Decorated Air Force Commendation medal with two oak leaf clusters, Legion of Merit with oak leaf cluster. Life mem. Assn. Grads. U.S. Mil. Acad.; charter mem. Nat. Soujourners, USAF Acad. Athletic Assn. Republican. Methodist. Clubs: Mason, Burtonwood Air Force (gov.), Bushy Park Air Force (gov.), Orlando Air Force (gov.), Andrews Air Force (gov.), Space Systems Division Air Force (gov.). Home: 660 Cinnamon Ct Satellite Beach FL 32937-4391

VANARSDALL, ROBERT LEE, JR., orthodontist, educator; b. Crewe, Va., Feb. 7, 1940; s. Robert Lee Sr. and Margie Mae (Jenkins) V.; m. Sandra E. Hoffman, Aug. 11, 1962; children: Robert Lee III, Lesley, Ashley. BA in Econs., Coll. William and Mary, 1962; DDS, Med. Coll. Va., 1970; cert. Orthodontics and Periodontics, U. Pa., 1973. Diplomate Am. Acad. Periodontology, Am. Bd. Orthodontics. Staff Children's Hosp., Phila., 1973—; prof. orthodontics, chmn. dept. orthodontics U. Pa., Phila., 1981—; prof. dentistry, chmn. Med. Coll. Pa., Phila., 1989—; bd. dirs. Nat. Dental Ins. Co., Denver. Editor: Internat. Jour. Adult Orthodontics and Orthognathic Surgery, 1986—, Orthodontoics: Current Principles and Techniques, 2d edit., 1994; editorial bd. profl. jours.; contbr. articles to profl. jours. Bd. dirs. Phila. Soc. William and Mary Alumni Assn. Lt. USNR, 1962-65. Fellow Coll. Physicians of Phila. 1978, Am. Coll. Dentistry 1980. Mem. ADA, Am. Assn. Orthodontists, Stomatological Club Phila., Angle Soc. Orthodontists, Phila. Soc. Orthodontists (pres. 1989, chmn. sci. affairs coun. 1990—). Roman Catholic. Avocations: antiques, architecture. Home: 208 Ashwood Rd Villanova PA 19085-1504 Office: Sinkler Bldg 588 E Lancaster Ave Radnor PA 19087-5235

VAN ARSDEL, EUGENE PARR, tree pathologist, consultant meteorologist; b. Emaus, Pa., Dec. 4, 1925; s. William Campbell and Mabel Elizabeth (Hedde) Van A.; m. Rose Price, Aug. 23, 1948 (div. Aug. 1991); children: Jonathan Eugene, Elizabeth Rose. BS in Forestry, Purdue U., 1947; MS, U. Wis., 1952, PhD, 1954. Plant pathologist Lake States Forest Expt. Sta. U. Wis., Madison, 1956-59, plant pathologist, 1959-62; prin. plant pathologist, project leader No. Conifer Disease Rsch., No. Ctrl. Forest Expt. Sta. U. Minn., St. Paul, 1962-68, prof. plant pathology, 1967-68; assoc. prof. plant sci. Tex. A&M U., College Station, 1968-80; plant pathologist, forester Profl. Tree Svc., Inc., Bryan, Tex., 1981-96, Van Arsdel Tree Svc., Inc., 1996—; vol. U.S. Forest Svc., 1994—; vis. prof. Yale U., New Haven, 1965-66. Assoc. editor Ecol. Soc. Am. Jour., 1968-71; contbr. chpts. to books, articles to Am. Meteorol. Soc., Am. Soc. Foresters, Am. Phytopath. Soc., others. An organizer, mem. Brazos Chorale, Bryan, Tex., 1970—. Grantee NSF, 1962-63, Tex. Peanut Producers Bd., 1972, USDA Forest Svc., 1973-77, Mrs. Lyndon B. Johnson, 1977-82, I.S.A. Rsch. Trust, 1986. Fellow AAAS; mem. Soc. Am. Foresters, Internat. Soc. Arboriculture, Am. Phytopath Soc. (emeritus). Achievements include development of effective treatment for wilt diseases in oaks of Texas; study of climatic.microclimatic relationship of the spread of white pine blister rust; research in long-distance transport of fungous spores. Office: Van Arsdel Tree Svc Inc PO Box 1870 Tijeras NM 87059-1870

VAN ARTSDALEN, DONALD WEST, federal judge; b. Doylestown, Pa., Oct. 21, 1919; s. Isaac Jeans and May Mable (Danenhower) Van A.; m. Marie Catherine Auerbach, June 20, 1953. Student, Williams Coll., 1937-40; LL.B., U. Pa., 1948. Bar: Pa. 1948, U.S. Supreme Ct. 1956. Practiced in Doylestown, 1948-70; dist. atty. Bucks County (Pa.), 1954-58; judge U.S. Dist. Ct. Pa. (ea. dist.), Phila., from 1970, now sr. judge, 1987. Served with Canadian Army, 1940-42; Served with AUS, 1942-45. Mem. Orde of the Coif. Office: US District Court 14614 US Courthouse Ind Mall W 601 Market St Philadelphia PA 19106-1713*

VAN ARTSDALEN, ERVIN ROBERT, physical chemist, educator; b. Doylestown, Pa., Nov. 13, 1913; s. Isaac J. and May M. (Danenhower) Van A.; m. Mary Louise Naylor, June 14, 1945. B.S. in Chemistry cum laude, Lafayette Coll., 1935; Internat. Exchange fellow U. Munich, Germany, 1935-36; A.M., Harvard, 1939, Ph.D. in Phys. Chemistry, 1941. Instr., then asst. prof. chemistry Lafayette Coll., 1941-45; on leave to Nat. Def. Research Com., Johns Hopkins Med. Sch., 1943-45; group leader Los Alamos Atomic Bomb Lab., 1945-46; asst. prof. chemistry Cornell U., 1946-51; adminstrv. group leader Oak Ridge Nat. Lab., 1951-56; asst. dir. research, basic lab. Union Carbide Corp., Cleve., 1956-63; John W. Mallet prof. chemistry, chmn. dept. U. Va., 1963-68; prof. chemistry U. Ala., 1968-84, prof. emeritus, 1984—, head dept., 1968-72; with Inst. Energy Analysis, Oak Ridge, 1975-76; cons. to govt. and industry; mem. chemistry adv. com. USAF Office Sci. Rsch., 1958-72, chmn., 1963-70; mem. Radiation Safety Bd. of Health, State of Ala., 1980—. Contbr. to profl. jours., govt. reports.; Mem. editorial bd.: Jour. Phys. Chemistry, 1958-62. Dir. High Sch. Students and Tchrs. Sci. Workshops and Seminars, Cleve., 1957-60; bd. dirs. Oak Ridge Sch. Music, 1953-56, Oak Ridge Asso. Univs., 1969-75; mem. 1st Presbyn. Ch., Tuscaloosa. Recipient Distinguished Alumni Sci. Tchr. citation Lafayette Coll., 1966. Fellow Am. Inst. Chemists; mem. AAAS, Am. Chem. Soc., Am. Phys. Soc., Va. Acad. Sci., Oak Ridge Country Club, Indian Hills Country Club (Tuscaloosa, Ala.), Exch. Club, Phi Beta Kappa, Alpha Chi Sigma, Gamma Alpha, Gamma Sigma Epsilon, Kappa Delta Rho. Clubs: Oak Ridge Country; Indian Hills Country (Tuscaloosa, Ala.). Spl. research reaction kinetics and photochemistry, thermodynamics, fused salts, nuclear energy, energy analysis. Home: 1512 Bellingrath Dr Reston Pl Tuscaloosa AL 35406

VANASKIE, THOMAS IGNATIUS, judge; b. Shamokin, Pa., Nov. 11, 1953; s. John Anthony and Delores (Wesoloski) V.; m. Dorothy Grace Williams, Aug. 12, 1978; children: Diane, Laura, Thomas. BA magna cum laude, Lycoming Coll., 1975; JD cum laude, Dickinson U., 1978. Bar: Pa. 1978, U.S. Dist. Ct. (mid. dist.) Pa. 1980, U.S. Ct. Appeals (3rd cir.) 1982, U.S. Supreme Ct. 1983. Law clk. to chief judge U.S. Dist. Ct. (mid. dist.) Pa., Scranton, 1978-80; assoc. Dilworth, Paxson, Kalish & Kauffman, Scranton, 1980-85, ptnr., 1986-92; prin. mem. Elliott, Vanaskie & Riley, 1992-94; judge U.S. Dist. Ct. (mid. dist.) Pa., Scranton; counsel Gov. Robert P. Casey Com., Harrisburg, Pa., 1987-92. Contbr. articles to profl. jours. Mem. Scranton Waste Mgmt. Com., 1989. Recipient James A. Finnegan award Finnegan Found. Mem. ABA, Judicature, Assn. Trial Lawyers Am., Pa. Bar Assn., Pa. Trial Lawyers Assn. Democrat. Avocations: golf, reading. Office: US Dist Ct Fed Courthouse 4th Fl Washington Ave & Linden St Scranton PA 18501

VAN ASPEREN, MORRIS EARL, banker; b. Wessington, S.D., Oct. 5, 1943; s. Andrew and Alyce May (Flagg) Van A.; m. Anne Virginia Merritt, July 2, 1966; 1 child, David Eric. BS in Math., U. Okla., 1966; MBA, Pepperdine U., 1979. Mgr. western dist. Svc. Rev. Inc., Northbrook, Ill., 1970-77; v.p. Hooper Info. Systems Inc., Tustin, Calif., 1977-78; v.p., chief fin. officer ATE Assocs. Inc., Westlake Village, Calif., 1978-84; mgmt. cons. Thousand Oaks, Calif., 1984-94; sr. v.p. Nat. Bank Calif., L.A., 1986—; chmn. liaison com. region IX SBA, 1990-94; adj. faculty U. Phoenix, 1997—. Nat. advocate fin. svcs. SBA, 1989. Lt. USN, 1966-70. Mem. Nat. Assn. Govt. Guaranteed Lenders (bd. dirs. 1990-93), Robert Morris Assocs., Nat. Assn. Credit Mgmt., Am. Legion (bd. dirs. Post 339 1995). Avocations: art, music. Office: Nat Bank Calif 145 S Fairfax Ave Los Angeles CA 90036-2166

VAN ASSENDELFT, ONNO WILLEM, hematologist; b. Brummen, The Netherlands, Aug. 23, 1932; came to U.S. 1976; s. Frederik and Anna Maria (Veenbaas) Van A.; m. Theodora Henriette Teunissen, July 15, 1960; children: Anne C.E., Frederik H.B., Albert H.P., Diederik A.A., Catharina E.E. MD, U. Groningen, 1959, PhD, 1970. Rsch. scientist, assoc. prof. Lab. Regulatory Physiology, Groningen, 1961-76; sec., dean Groningen Med. Sch., 1973-75; supervisory med. rsch. officer Ctrs. for Disease Control and Prevention, Atlanta, 1976—; cons. FDA, 1979—; bd. secretariat Internat. Coun. Standardization in Hematology, 1978—, chmn. secretariat, 1994—; bd., exec. com. Nat. Comm. Clin. Lab. Stds., Villanova, Pa., 1982-94, pres., 1990-92; chmn. U.S. delegation to ISO/TC 212 on clin. lab. testing and in vitro diagnostic test sys., 1995—. Author: Spectrophotometry of Hemoglobin Derivatives, 1970; editl. bd. ECRI Healthcare Product Comparison System, Lab. Hematology; contbr. articles to profl. jours., chpts. to books. Capt. Royal Netherlands Army, 1959-61. Recipient Sec. Group award USPHS, 1986, Bronze plaque Ministry of Health, Chile, 1983, Russel J. Eilers award Nat. Com. for Clin. Lab. Stds., Villanova, 1988, Spl. award Nat. Hemophilia Found., 1992. Mem. AAAS, Am. Soc. Hematology, Internat. Soc. Lab. Hematology, N.Y. Acad. Scis. Achievements include research on hematology and clinical laboratory testing. Office: Ctrs Disease Control Prevention 1600 Clifton Rd NE Atlanta GA 30329-4018

VANATTA, BOB, athletic administrator; b. Columbia, Mo., July 7, 1918; s. Claude W. and Viola (Toler) V.; m. Lois A. Williams; children: Robert, Thomas, Timothy. BA, Ctrl. Meth. Coll., 1942; MEd, U. Mo., 1949. Tchr., coach Boonville (Mo.) High Sch., 1942-43, Kemper Mil. Sch., Boonville, 1943-44, Springfield (Mo.) High Sch., 1944-47; tchr., dir. athletics, coach Ctrl. Meth. Coll., Fayette, Mo., 1947-50, S.W. Mo. State U., Springfield, 1950-53; coach U.S. Mil. Acad., West Point, N.Y., 1953-54; dir. athletics, coach Bardley U., Peoria, Ill., 1954-56; tchr., coach Memphis State U., 1956-62, U. Mo., Columbia, 1962-68; bank mktg. officer Empire Bank, Springfield, 1968-71; profl. basketball exec. dir. Memphis Pros, 1971-72; tchr., coach Delta State U., Cleve., 1972-73; dir. athletics Oral Roberts U., Tulsa, 1973-77; commr. Ohio Valley Athletic Conf., Nashville, 1977-80, Trans Am. Athletic Conf., Shreveport, La., 1980-83; dir. athletics La. Tech. U., Rustin, 1983-86; commr. Sunshine State Athletic Conf., Jupiter, Fla., 1986-94; cons., speaker in field. Author: Coaching Pattern Play Basketball, 1959; contbr. articles to profl. jours. Chpt. mem. Nat. Football Found. Hall of Fame. Named to Ctrl. Meth. Coll. Hall of Fame, S.W. Mo. State U. Hall of Fame, Nat. Athletic Intercollegiate Assn. Hall of Fame, Greater Springfield Hall of Fame, John Q. Hammons Mo. Sports Hall of Fame, U. Memphis Hall of Fame, Nat. Assn. Collegiate Dir. of Athletics. Mem. Nat. Assn. Basketball Coaches, Am. Football Coaches Assn., Nat. Assn. Collegiate Dirs. Athletics.

VANATTA, CHESTER B., business executive, educator; b. Bartlesville, Okla., Sept. 3, 1935; s. Benjamin Franklin and Iona Ruth (Hayes) V.; m. Patsy Lou Straub, May 29, 1958; children—Tracy Ann, Christopher B., John Scott. B.S. in Mktg., U. Kans., Lawrence, 1959, M.S. in Acctg., 1962; Advanced Mgmt. Program, Harvard U., Cambridge, 1972. Mem. staff Arthur Young & Co., Kansas City, Mo., 1962-69; regional dir, Arthur Young & Co., Dallas, 1969-72, ptnr., 1969-85; mng. ptnr. Arthur Young & Co., Chgo., 1972-76, dir., 1973-85; mng. ptnr., vice chmn. ops. Arthur Young & Co., N.Y.C., 1976-81; mng. ptnr., vice chmn. S.W. Region Arthur Young & Co., Dallas, 1981-85; pres. Exec. Cons. Group, Lawrence, Kans., 1985-96; exec. in residence, Paul J. Adam Disting. lectr. U. Kans. Sch. Bus., Lawrence, 1985-90; bd. dirs. Atlantis Group Inc., Miami, Fla., Arcadian Corp., Memphis, Adams Bus. Forms, Topeka. Trustee, exec. com., fin. com. Kans. U. Endowment Fund, 1983—; bd. dirs. Kans. Alumni Assn., 1984-91, pres., 1986-87. Mem. Am. Inst. CPA's, Kans. Soc. CPA's (Gold Key 1962), Alvamar Country Club, Elkhorn Golf Club, Skyline Country Club. Republican. Avocations: golf, travel, photography. Home: 5140 Ed Mission Hill Dr Tucson AZ 85718-6768

VAN ATTA, DAVID MURRAY, lawyer; b. Berkeley, Calif., Oct. 20, 1944; s. Chester Murray and Rosalind (Eisenstein) Van A.; m. Jo Ann Masaoka; 1 child, Lauren Rachel. BA, U. Calif., Berkeley, 1966; JD, U. Calif., Hastings, 1969. Bar: Calif. 1970. Asst. gen. counsel Boise Cascade Corp., Palo Alto, Calif., 1970-73; ptnr. Miller, Starr & Regalia, San Francisco, 1973-87, Graham & James, San Francisco, 1987-93, Hanna & Van Atta, Palo Alto, 1993—; instr. Golden Gate U., San Francisco, 1984-85; U. Calif., Berkeley, 1976-84. Mem. ABA, Am. Coll. Real Estate Lawyers, Calif. Bar Assn. (vice chmn. exec. com. real property law sect. 1982-85, chmn. condominium and subdivsn. com. real property law sect. 1981-83), Cmty. Assn. Inst., Urban Land Inst., Lambda Alpha Internat. Soc. Avocations: skiing, tennis, painting. Office: Hanna & Van Atta 525 University Ave Ste 705 Palo Alto CA 94301-1921

VANATTA, JOHN CROTHERS, III, physiologist, physician, educator; b. Lafayette, Ind., Apr. 22, 1919; s. John Crothers and Ida Lahr (Raub) V.; m. Carol Lee Geisler, July 30, 1944; children: Lynn Ellen, Paul Richard. B.A., Ind. U., 1941, M.D., 1944. Intern Wayne County Gen. Hosp., Eloise, Mich., 1944-45, resident in internal medicine, 1946-47; fellow in physiology, pharmacology Southwestern Med. Coll., Dallas, 1947-48, fellow in exptl. and internal medicine, 1948-49; instr. physiology U. Tex. Southwestern Med. Sch., 1949-50, asst. prof., 1950-53, assoc. prof., 1953-57, prof. physiology, 1957—, Robert W. Lackey prof. physiology, 1987-89; prof. physiology So. Meth. U. Dallas, Dallas, 1969-80, Baylor Coll. Dentistry, Dallas, 1992—; mem. staff Parkland Meml. Hosp., Dallas, 1953-57, VA Hosp., Dallas, McKinney, Tex., 1956-58; cons. div. nuclear edn. tng. AEC, 1964-67. Author: Oxygen Transport, Hypoxia and Cyanosis, 1974, Fluid Balance - A Clinical Manual, 1988; contbr. articles to profl. jours. Scouter, Circle 10 council Boy Scouts Am., Dallas, 1963-78; v.p. Luth. Health Care Council N. Tex., 1975-80, pres., 1980-81. Served as lt. (j.g.) M.C., USNR, 1945-46, PTO. Mem. AMA, AAAS, Am. Physiol. Soc., Soc. Exptl. Biology and Medicine, Phi Beta Pi, Sigma Xi, Delta Tau Delta. Lutheran (councilman 1951-91, v.p. 1974-75). Home: 10416 Remington Ln Dallas TX 75229-5262

VAN AUKEN, ROBERT DANFORTH, business administration educator, management consultant; b. Chgo., Oct. 31, 1915; s. Howard Robert and Mable (Hanlon) Van A.; student Guilford Coll., 1933-35, Gen. Motors Inst. Tech., 1936-38, U. Pitts., 1953-54; BS, U. Dayton, 1958; MA, U. Okla., 1967; m. Ruth Bowen Cutler, Nov. 24, 1939 (dec.); children: Robert Hanlon, Joseph Marshall, David Danforth, Howard Evans, Jonathan Lewis; m. Vernia Maurine Long, July 9, 1993. Commd. aviation cadet U.S. Air Force, 1938; advanced through grades to lt. col., 1961; fighter pilot, squadron comdr., ops. officer, 1939-45; asst. air attaché, Paris, 1946-49; staff officer, Pentagon 1950-53; procurement-prodn. staff officer Wright-Patterson AFB, 1954-58, Tinker AFB, 1958-60, Holloman AFB, 1960-61, ret., 1961; personnel officer U. Okla., Norman, 1962-65, mem. faculty, 1965—, asst. prof. mgmt., 1979-83, prof. emeritus bus. adminstrn., 1983—, dir. student programs and career devel. Coll. Bus. Adminstrn., 1975-79; cons. seminars mgmt. amd compensation, 1963—; adj. instr. Park Coll., 1991—; instr. Park Coll., 1991—; cattle rancher, 1970—; owner VA Farms. Mem. Oklahomans for Improvement in Nursing Care Homes; active Heritage Found.; Decorated Silver Star, Purple Heart. Mem. NRA, Newcomen Soc. U.S., Oklahoma City Human Resources Assn., Acad. Mgmt., Internat. Platform Assn., Nat. Cattlemen's Beef Assn., Okla. Cattlemans Assn., Okla. Alliance Aging, Air Force Assn., Am. Legion, Ret. Officers Assn., Mil. Order of World Wars, (life. mem.), Order of Deadalians, 5th Air Force Meml. Found., 49th Fighter Group Assn., 31st Fighter Officers Assn., (life mem.), Disabled Am. Vets. (life mem.), Masons, Beta Gamma Sigma, Delta Sigma Pi. Republican. Contbr. monographs in field. Home: 420 S Highland Rd Oklahoma City OK 73110-2138 Office: U Okla 307 W Brooks St Norman OK 73069-8822 *A person's success in life is often measured by the accumulation of wealth or influence. But a better measure might be that person's progress toward predetermined personal goals, whatever they may be.*

VANAUKER, LANA LEE, recreational therapist, educator; b. Youngstown, Ohio, Sept. 19, 1949; d. William Marshall and Joanne Norma (Kimmel) Speece; m. Dwight Edward VanAuker, Mar. 16, 1969 (div. 1976); 1 child, Heidi. BS in Edn. cum laude, Kent (Ohio) State U., 1974; MS in Edn., Youngstown (Ohio) U., 1989. Cert. tchr., Ohio; nat. cert. activity cons. Phys. edn. instr. St. Joseph Sch., Campbell, Ohio, 1973-75; program dir.

YWCA, Youngstown, 1975-85; exercise technician Youngstown State U., 1985-86; health educator Park Vista Retirement Ctr., Youngstown, 1986-87; sch. tchr. Salem (Ohio) City Sch., 1987-88; recreational therapist Trumbull Meml. Hosp., Warren, Ohio, 1988—; activity cons. Mahoning/Trumbull Nursing Homes, Warren, 1990-92; adv. bd. rep. Ohio State Bur. Health Promotion Phys. Fitness, 1996—; mem. adv. bd. Ohio State Executive Physical Fitness Dept. Health, 1996. Producer chair exercise sr. video Excercise is the Fountain of Youth, 1993; photographer, choreographer. Vol. Am. Cancer Soc., 1980—, Am. Heart Assn., 1986—, Dance for Heart, 1980-86; mem. State of Ohio Phys. Fitness Adv. Bd., 1996-97. Youngstown State U. scholar, 1986-89. Mem. AAHPERD, Youngstown Camera Club (social chair 1989-90, pres. 1993-95), Resident Activity Profl. Assn. (pres. 1994, 95, 96), Pa. Activity Profl. Assn., Kappa Delta Pi. Democrat. Presbyterian. Avocations: photography, international dance, volleyball, aerobics, travel. Home: 385 N Broad St Canfield OH 44406-1256 Office: Trumbull Meml Hosp 1350 E Market St Warren OH 44483-6608

VAN BEBBER, GEORGE THOMAS, federal judge; b. Troy, Kans., Oct. 21, 1931; s. Roy Vest and Anne (Wenner) V.; m. Alleen Sara Castellani. AB, U. Kans., 1953, LLB, 1955. Bar: Kans. 1955, U.S. Dist. Ct. Kans. 1955, U.S. Ct. Appeals (10th cir.) 1961. Pvt. practice, Troy, 1955-58, 1961-82; asst. U.S. atty. Topeka, Kansas City, Kans., 1958-61; county atty. Doniphan County, Troy, 1963-69; mem. Kans. House of Reps., 1973-75; chmn. Kans. Corp. Commn., Topeka, 1975-79; U.S. magistrate Topeka, 1982-89; judge U.S. Dist. Ct., Kansas City, Kan., 1989—, chief judge, 1995—. Mem. ABA, Kas. Bar Assn. Episcopalian. Home: 6701 W 66th Ter Shawnee Mission KS 66202-4146 Office: US Dist Ct 529 US Courthouse 500 State Ave Kansas City KS 66101-2403

VAN BEEK, GUS WILLARD, archaeologist; b. Tulsa, Mar. 21, 1922; s. Gus Willard and Dovie Lucille (Crupper) Van B.; children: John Phillip, Christopher Hicks, Stephen Dart; m. Ora Braunstein, Sept. 25, 1972. BA with honors, U. Tulsa, 1943; BD, McCormick Theol. Sem., Chgo., 1945; PhD, Johns Hopkins U., 1953. Fellow Hebrew Union Coll., Cin., 1947-49, Am. Schs. Oriental Research, Jerusalem, 1952; research assoc. Johns Hopkins U., Balt., 1954-59; assoc. curator Smithsonian Instn., Washington, 1959-67, curator, 1967—; dir. archeol. expdn. Hadhramaut, Arabia, 1961-62, Nejran, Saudi Arabia, 1968, Tell Jemmeh, Israel, 1970—; trustee Am. Schs. Oriental Rsch., 1988-93, mem. adv. bd., 1993—. Author: Hajar Bin Humeid, 1969; editor: The Scholarship of William Foxwell Albright: An Appraisal, 1989; also 150 articles on archeology, history; producer/curator exhibits: Dead Sea Scrolls of Jordan, 1965, Arabia Felix, 1972. Recipient Disting. Alumnus award U. Tulsa Coll. Arts. Scis., 1971. Mem. Archeol. Inst. Am., Am. Inst. Yemeni Studies, Am. Schs. Oriental Rsch., Phi Beta Kappa. Democrat. Presbyterian. Office: Smithsonian Inst Mus Natural History 112 Michigan Ave NE Washington DC 20017-1032

VANBIESBROUCK, JOHN, professional hockey player; b. Detroit, Sept. 4, 1963; m. Rosalinde V. With N.Y. Rangers, 1981-93, Vancouver Canucks, 1993, Florida Panthers, 1993—; mem. NHL All-Star team, 1985-86; player NHL All-Star game, 1994. Recipient Vezina Trophy (NHL outstanding goaltender), 1985, 86, (with Ron Scott) Terry Sawchuk trophy, 1983-89, (with Marc D'Amour) F.W. Dinty Moore trophy, (with D. Bruce Affleck) Tommy Ivan trophy, 1983-84; named NHL All-Star, 1985-86, Sporting News NHL All-Star, 1985-86, 93-94. Office: Florida Panthers 100 NE 3rd Ave Fl 10 Fort Lauderdale FL 33301-1155*

VAN BLARICUM, AMY JOAN, perioperative nurse; b. Englewood, N.J., Sept. 23, 1963; d. Julius Herbert Jr. and Mildred Doris Van Blaricum. BSN, Widener U., Chester, Pa., 1987. RN, Pa.; cert. in chemotherapy adminstrn., venipuncture, 1987. Nurse med.-surg. unit Mercy Cath. Med. Ctr., Darby, Pa., 1987, nurse oncology unit, 1988, nurse operating room, 1989. Mem. Assn. Oper. Rm. Nurses (cert. oper. rm. nurse, 1992).

VANBRODE, DERRICK BRENT, IV, trade association administrator; b. Elgin, Ill., Sept. 3, 1940. Grad., N.Y. Inst. Criminology, 1963. Sr. v.p. Am. Fraternal Programmers, Inc., North Miami, Fla., 1977—; mgmt. cons. Am. Fedn. Police, Am. Law Enforcement Officers Assn., Nat. Assn. Chiefs of Police, Am. Police Acad. Editor: Who's Who in American Law Enforcement, 1976-93, Crime Watch mag, 1981—, Police Times/Command, 1975—. Pres. Greater Miami Assn. Licensed Beverage Owners, 1973—. Decorated Grand Cross Knights of St. Michael; comdr. Royal Knights of Justice. Mem. Greater North Port Fla. C. of C. (founder, pres.). Clubs: Miami Millionaires (founder, past pres.), Millionaires Internat. (pres. 1983—), Miami Shores Country, Racquet. Office: 3801 Biscayne Blvd Miami FL 33137-3732

VAN BRUNT, ALBERT DANIEL, advertising agency executive; b. N.Y.C., Nov. 13, 1920; s. Ernest Robert and Helen (Rothschild) Isaacs. B.S. in Mktg., NYU, 1942. Dir. advt. Air France, N.Y.C., 1947-50; v.p. Buchanan Advt. Agy., N.Y.C., 1951-57; pres. Van Brunt & Co., Advt.-Mktg., Inc., N.Y.C., 1958-88, chmn. bd., 1989-90; pres. IMAA, Inc., N.Y.C., 1965-70; sr. v.p. IMAA, Inc., 1970-89; exec. v.p. Van Brunt & Co., Chgo., Inc., 1969-76, Van Brunt/Schaeffer, 1979-89; v.p. HBC/Van Brunt, Chgo., 1976-77; pres., chief exec. officer WDB Advt., Inc., N.Y.C., 1990—. Trustee N.Y. chpt. Leukemia Soc. Am., 1979-80; bd. dirs. Leukemia program Coll. Physicians and Surgeons, Columbia U. Served to lt. USNR, 1942-46. Mem. Am. Assn. Advt. Agys. (dir. N.Y. council 1969-74), Internat. Advt. Assn., SAR. Clubs: Wings (N.Y.C.), Lotos (N.Y.C.) (dir. 1966-72, 76-87, dir. emeritus 1987—, sec. 1972-75, treas. 1975-76). Home: 315 E 68th St New York NY 10021-5692 also: Jason's Ln East Hampton NY 11937 Office: WDB Prodns Inc 419 E 57th St New York NY 10022-3060

VAN BRUNT, EDMUND EWING, physician; b. Oakland, Calif., Apr. 28, 1926; s. Adrian W. and Kathryn Anne (Shattuck) Van B.; m. Claire Monod, Feb. 28, 1949; children: Karin, Deryk, Jahn. BA in Biophysics, U. Calif., Berkeley, 1952; MD, U. Calif., San Francisco, 1959; ScD, U. Toulouse, France, 1978. Postdoctoral fellow NIH, 1961-63; rsch. assoc. U. Calif., San Francisco, 1963-67; staff physician Kaiser Permanente Med. Ctr., San Francisco, 1964-91; dir. div. rsch. Kaiser Permanente Med. Program, Oakland, Calif., 1979-91; assoc. dir. Kaiser Found. Rsch. Inst., Oakland, 1985-91, sr. cons., 1991—; adj. prof. U. Calif., San Francisco, 1975-92; chmn. instnl. rev. bd. Kaiser Found. Rsch. Inst., 1986—; pres. bd. trustees French Found. Med. Rsch. and Edn., San Francisco, 1992—. Contbr. articles to profl. books and jours. With U.S. Army, 1944-46. Fellow ACP, Am. Coll. Med. Informatics; mem. AAAS, Calif. Med. Assn., U. Calif. Emeritus Faculty Assn., Sigma Xi. Avocations: flying, photography, swimming.

VAN BUREN, ABIGAIL (PAULINE FRIEDMAN PHILLIPS), columnist, author, writer, lecturer; b. Sioux City, Iowa, July 4, 1918; d. Abraham and Rebecca (Rushall) Friedman; m. Morton Phillips, July 2, 1939; children: Edward Jay, Jeanne. Student, Morningside Coll., Sioux City, 1936-39; Litt.D. (hon.), Morningside Coll., 1965; L.H.D. (hon.), U. Jacksonville, Fla., 1984. Vol. worker for causes of better mental health Nat. Found. Infantile Paralysis; tng. Gray Ladies, ARC, 1939-56; pres. Minn.-Wis. council B'nai B'rith Aux., 1945-49; columnist Dear Abby San Francisco Chronicle, 1956, McNaught Syndicate, 1956-74, Chgo. Tribune Syndicate, 1974-80, Universal Press Syndicate, 1980—; syndicated U.S., Brazil, Mex., Japan, Philippines, Fed. Republic Germany, India, Holland, Denmark, Can., Korea, Thailand, Italy, Hong Kong, Taiwan, Ireland, Saudi Arabia, Greece, France, Dominican Republic, P.R., Costa Rica, U.S. Virgin Islands, Bermuda, Guam; host radio program The Dear Abby Show, CBS, 1963-75; life-time cons. Group for Advancement Psychiatry, 1985—. Author: Dear Abby, 1957 (also translated into Japanese, Dutch, German, Spanish, Danish, Italian, Finnish), Dear Teen Ager, 1959, Dear Abby on Marriage, 1962, The Best of Dear Abby, 1981, reissued, 1989, Dear Abby on Planning Your Wedding, 1988, Where Were You When President Kennedy Was Shot?: Memories and Tributes to a Slain President as Told to Dear Abby, 1993. Mem. nat. adv. council on aging NIH, HEW, 1978-81; hon. chairwoman 1st Nat. Women's Conf. on Cancer, Am. Cancer Soc., Los Angeles, 1979; mem. public adv. council Center for Study Multiple Gestation, 1981; trustee, mem. adv. bd. Westside Community for Ind. Living, 1981; bd. dirs. Guthrie Theatre, Mpls., 1970-74; charter mem. Franz Alexander Research Found., Los Angeles; charter trustee Armand Hammer United World Coll. of Am. West; bd. dirs. Am. Fedn. for Aging Research Inc.; mem. nat. bd. Goodwill Industries, 1968-75; nat. chmn. Crippled Children Soc., 1962; founding mem. The Amazing Blue Ribbon 400; hon. chmn. Easter Seal campaign Nat. Soc. Crippled Children and Adults, Washington, 1963; del. to Democratic Nat. Conf. from Calif., 1964; Calif. del. White House Conf. on Children and Youth, 1974; non. life mem. Concern for Dying-Am. Ednl. Council; mem. White House Conf. on Physically Handicapped, 1976, NIH, 1976; mem. adv. council Suicide Prevention Ctr., Los Angeles, 1977; mem. com. on aging HHS, 1977-82; council sponsor Assn. Vol. Sterilization, 1981; mem. Women's Trusteeship, 1980; sponsor Mayo Found., Rochester, 1982; bd. dirs. Lupus Found. Am., 1983; mem. adv. com. Ams. for Substance Abuse Prevention, 1984; participant XIII Internat. Congress Gerontology, N.Y.C., 1985; mem. adv. bd. Young Writer's Contest Found., 1985; bd. dirs. Am. Found. for AIDS Research, 1985—; mem. adv. bd. Nat. Council for Children's Rights, Washington, 1988; mem. adv. bd. San Diego Hospice, 1990; mem. adv. bd. Rhonda Fleming Mann Clinic for Women's Comprehensive Care, 1991; mem. Scripps Rsch. Coun. Recipient Times Mother of Yr. award, L.A., 1958; Golden Kidney award, L.A., 1960; Sarah Coventry award, Miami, 1961; Woman of Yr. award Internat. Rotary Club, Rome, 1965; award NCCJ, St. Louis, 1968; award for disting. svc. to sightless Internat. Lions Club, Dallas, 1972; Disting. Svc. award Suicide Prevention Ctr., San Mateo, Calif., 1975; Good Samaritan award Salvation Army, San Francisco, 1970; Margaret Sanger award for outstanding svcs. in mental health So. Psychiat. Assn., 1974; Robert T. Morse writer's award Am. Psychiat. Assn., 1977; Tex. Gov.'s award in recognition of exceptional svc. to youth of Am. for Ops. Peace of Mind, 1979; Humanitarian award Gay Acad. Union, L.A., 1979, Braille Inst. So. Calif., 1981, Gay and Lesbian Cmty. Svcs. Ctr., 1984; pub. Awareness trophy for Living Will, Soc. for Right to Die, 1983; citation of commentation Simon Weisenthal Found., 1984; Internat. Image in Media award Gay Fathers Coalition, 1985; 1st ann. Woman of Yr. Humanitarian award Rainbow Guild of Amy Karen Children's Cancer Clinic, Cedars-Sinai Med. Ctr., L.A. 1985; Pub. Svc. award Nat. Kidney Found., 1985, John Rock award Ctr. Population Options, 1986, Genesis award Fund for Animals, 1986, Disting. Svc. award Inst. Studies Destructive Behavior and Suicide Prevention Ctr., 1986, Citizen of Yr. award Beverly Hills, Calif. C. of C., 1988, Humanitarian award Nat. Coun. on Alcoholism, 1988, Helen B. Taussig medal Internat. Socs. for the Right to Die with Dignity, 1988, Media award So. Psychiat. Soc., 1988; named Hon. Dir. Found. for Carniofacial Deformities, 1988; Disting. Achieve. Mem. Women in Communications (hon.), Am. Coll. Psychiatrists (hon. life mem.), Newspapers Features Council, Soc. Profl. Journalists, Nat. Orgn. Women, "Women For", Nat. Com. Preserve Social Security and Medicare, Korean War Vets. Assn. (hon.), L.A. World Affairs Coun., Sigma Delta Chi. Office: Phillips-Van Buren Inc Ste 2710 1900 Avenue Of The Stars Los Angeles CA 90067-4301 *"If a man loves the labor of his trade, apart from any question of success of fame, the gods have called him." (Robert Louis Stevenson.) The same holds true for women and I am one of them.*

VANBUREN, DENISE DORING, media relations executive; b. Troy, N.Y., May 15, 1961; d. James L. and Eunice A. (Myers) Doring; m. Steven Paul VanBuren, Apr. 1, 1989; children: Schuyler Paul, Troy James Doring, Brett Steven VanBuren. BA in Mass Comm. magna cum laude, St. Bonaventure U., 1983; MBA, Mount St. Mary Coll., 1997. Reporter, news anchor Sta. WGNY-AM-FM, Newburgh, N.Y., 1984; news dir., anchor NewsCtr. 6, Dutchess County, N.Y., 1985-90; dir. media rels. Ctrl. Hudson Gas & Electric, Poughkeepsie, 1993—; bd. dirs. Gateway Industries, Beacon, N.Y., Craig House Hosp. City councilwoman City of Beacon, 1992-93; pres. Beacon Hist. Soc., 1989-94. Recipient Salute to Women in Bus. & Industry award D.C. YWCA, 1990, 97. Mem. Nat. Soc. DAR (Melzingah chpt., vice-regent 1990—). Republican. Roman Catholic. Avocations: genealogy, needlework. Home: 37 Deerfield Pl Beacon NY 12508-1514 Office: Ctrl Hudson Gas & Electric Corp 284 South Ave Poughkeepsie NY 12601-4838

VAN BUREN, WILLIAM BENJAMIN, III, retired pharmaceutical company executive; b. Bklyn., Mar. 25, 1922; s. William Benjamin and Dorothy Marjorie (Way) Van B.; m. Joan Cottrell Whitford, Sept. 11, 1948; children—Susan (dec.), Patricia, William S., Richard W. B.A., Washington and Lee U., 1944; LL.B., Yale U., 1949. Bar: N.Y. 1950. V.p., sec. Merck & Co., Inc., 1976-86; pres. Merck & Co. Found., 1982-86. Served with USNR, 1943-46. Mem. Phi Beta Kappa. Home: 8 Point North Dr Salem SC 29676-4113

VAN BURKLEO, BILL BEN, osteopath, emergency physician; b. Tulsa, Nov. 21, 1942; s. Walter Russell and Joan Vera (Brimm) Van B.; m. Paula Mae Brinkley, Mar. 5, 1965 (div. Feb. 1974); children: Baron, Kristy and Kelly (twins); m. Robin Jay, Nov., 1995; children: Laci, Hailey. BS, U. Tulsa, 1965; DO, Okla. State U., 1981. Diplomate Nat. Bd. Osteo. Examiners. Defensive back, quarterback, punter Can. Football League, Ottawa, Calgary, 1966-73; dir. sports and spl. events Tulsa Cable TV, 1974-78; rotating intern Corpus Christi (Tex.) Osteo. Hosp., 1981-82; family physician Antlers (Okla.) Med. Clinic, 1982-90, Colbert (Okla.) Med. Clinic, 1989-90; dir. dept. emergency Valley View Regional Hosp., Ada, Okla., 1990-94; regional med. dir. Okla., N.Mex., Ariz., Calif. Okla. Spectrum Emergency Care, Inc., 1994—; mem. clin. faculty Coll. Osteo. Medicine, Okla. State U. Author newspaper column, several computer programs. Mem. Rep. Senatorial Inner Ctr., Washington, 1990-91 (medal of Freedom 1994); affiliate faculty Am. Heart Assn. Named to Alltime Greats of Okla., Jim Thorpe Award Com., 1975. Fellow Assn. Emergency Physicians; mem. Am. Assn. Physician Specialists, Am. Osteo. Assn., Am. Coll. Gen. Practitioners, Okla. Osteo. Assn., S.W. Okla. Osteo. Assn. (pres. 1990-91). Avocations: tennis, flying, sailing. Home: PO Box 2740 Ada OK 74821-2740

VANBUTSEL, MICHAEL R., real estate developer, healthcare consultant; b. Alma, Nebr., Dec. 7, 1952; s. Julius and Margaret (McCorkle) VanB.; m. Jené Hendley; children: Vanessa, Stephanie, Jamie. BArch, U. Nebr., 1975. Lic. real estate broker, Fla. Asst. to v.p. constrn. cen. adminstrn. U. Nebr., Lincoln, 1975-76; architect Consol. Architects Engrs., Omaha, 1976-77; archtl. project mgr. Dana, Larson, Roubal Architects, Phoenix, 1977-79; mktg. dir. Dick, Fritsche Architects, Phoenix, 1979-81; mktg. mgr. Lendrum Design Group, Phoenix, San Diego, 1982-85; owner Developers Mgmt. Group, Phoenix, 1985-86; contracts mgr. Turner Constrn., Phoenix, 1986-87; v.p. devel. The Bay Plaza Co., St. Petersburg, Fla., 1987-96; COO, exec. v.p. Internat. Care, St. Petersburg, 1996—; bd. dirs. Cen. Ariz. Health Systems Agy. Commr. Housing Commn., City of Phoenix; mem. Paradise Valley Planning Com.; pres. The Mariners for Senator John McCain, Ariz.; surrogate spkr. for Congressman Eldon Rudd; mem. Senate roundtable Senator Connie Mack, Fla.; bd. dirs. Am. Stage Theater; campus adv. bd. U. South Fla., St. Petersburg, chmn. facilities and strategic planning com., chmn. acad. planning com.; bd. dirs. Pinellas Econ. Devel. Coun.; chmn. Environ. Com., Transp. Com.; bd. dirs. St Petersburg C. of C.; mem. environ. adv. com. S.W. Fla. Water Mgmt. Dist.; mem. Pinellas adv. bd. ARC. Mem. Fla. Gulfcoast Comml. Assn. Realtors, Leadership Tampa Bay, Urban Land Inst., Valley Leadership (Phoenix). Republican. Avocations: gourmet cooking, body building, geo-political books.

VAN CAMP, BRIAN RALPH, lawyer; b. Halstead, Kans., Aug. 23, 1940; s. Ralph A. and Mary Margaret (Bragg) Van C.; m. Diane D. Miller, 1992; children: Megan M., Laurie E. AB, U. Calif., Berkeley, 1962, LLB, 1965. Bar: Calif. 1966. Dep. atty. gen. State Calif., 1965-67; agy. atty. Redevel. Agy., City of Sacramento, 1967-70; asst./acting sec. Bus. and Transp. Agy., State Calif., 1970-71; commr. of corps. State of Calif., Sacramento, 1971-74; partner firm Diepenbrock, Wulff, Plant & Hannegan, Sacramento, 1975-77, Van Camp & Johnson, Sacramento, 1978-90; sr. ptnr. Downey, Brand, Seymour & Rohwer, 1990-97; judge Superior Ct., Sacramento County, 1997—; lectr. Continuing Edn. Bar, Practicing Law Inst., Calif. CPA Soc., others; mem. adv. bd. UCLA Securities Law Inst., 1978. Contbr. articles to profl. jours. Mem. Rep. State Ctrl. Com. Calif., 1974-78; pres. Sacramento Area Commerce and Trade Orgn., 1986-87; mem. electoral coll. Presdl. Elector for State of Calif., 1976; mem. Calif. Health Facilities Fin. Authority, 1985-89; mem. Capital Area Devel. Authority, 1989-97, chmn., 1990-97; bd. dirs. Sacramento Symphony Assn., 1973-85, 92-94, Sacramento Symphony Found., 1993—, Rep. Assocs. Sacramento County, 1975-79, Sacramento Valley Venture Capital Forum, 1986-90, League to Save Lake Tahoe, 1988-95, Valley Vision, Inc., 1993-97; elder Fremont Presbyn. Ch., 1967—. Recipient Sumner-Mering Meml. award Sacramento U. of Calif. Alumni Assn., 1962, Thos. Jefferson award Am. Inst. Pub. Svc., 1994; Paul Harris fellow, 1995; named Outstanding Young Man of Yr., Sacramento Jaycees, 1970, Internat. Young Man of Yr., Active 20-30 Club Internat., 1973. Mem. ABA, Calif. State Bar (mem.com. on corps. 1977-80, partnerships and unincorporated bus. assns. 1983-87), Sacramento County Bar Assn., Calif. C. of C. (chmn. statewide energy task force 1979-85, bd. dirs. 1982-97, chmn. edn. com. 1988-90), Sacramento Met. C. of C. (co-chmn. econ. devel. com. 1979, bd. dirs. 1986-88), Boalt Hall Alumni Assn. (bd. dirs. 1991-94), Lincoln Club Sacramento Valley (bd. dirs., pres. 1984-86), U. Calif. Men's Club (pres. 1968), Sutter Club, Kanadhar Ski Club, Rotary Club Sacramento (pres. 1993-94, Paul Harris Fellow award 1995). Republican. Presbyterian. Office: 720 9th St Sacramento CA 95814-1311

VAN CASPEL, VENITA WALKER, retired financial planner; b. Sweetwater, Okla.; d. Leonard Rankin and Ella Belle (Jarnagin) Walker; m. Lyttleton T. Harris IV, Dec. 26, 1987. Student, Duke, 1944-46; BA, U. Colo., 1948, postgrad., 1949-51; postgrad., N.Y. Inst. Fin., 1962. CFP. Stockbroker Rauscher Pierce & Co., Houston, 1962-65, A.G. Edwards & Sons, Houston, 1965-68; founder, pres., owner Van Caspel & Co., Inc., Houston, 1968—, Van Caspel Wealth Mgmt.; owner, mgr. Van Caspel Planning Svc., Van Caspel Advt. Agy.; sr. v.p. investments Raymond James and Assocs., 1987-95; ret., 1995; owner Diamond V Ranch; moderator PBS TV show The Money Makers and Profiles of Success, 1980; 1st women mem. Pacific Stock Exchange. Author: Money Dynamics, 1978, Money Dynamics of the 1980's, 1980, The Power of Money Dynamics, Money Dynamics for the 1990's, 1988; editor: Money Dynamics Letter. Bd. dirs. Horatio Alger Assn., Robert Schuller Ministries. Recipient Matrix award Theta Sigma Phi, 1969, Horatio Alger award for Disting. Americans, 1982, Disting. Woman's medal, Northwood Univ., 1988, Georgia Norlin award U. Colo. Alumni Assn., 1987. Mem. Internat. Assn. Fin. Planners, Inst. Cert. Fin. Planners, Phi Gamma Mu, Phi Beta Kappa. Methodist. Home: 4 Saddlewood Estates Dr Houston TX 77024 Office: 6524 San Felipe St Ste 102 Houston TX 77057-2611

VANCE, ANDREW PETER, lawyer; b. Detroit, Jan. 23, 1925; s. Peter Andrew and Anna (Maktos) V.; m. Olvia Cambourelis, Nov. 23, 1952; children: Peter, Cathy, Penny, Dorothy. BA, Harvard Coll., 1948; LLB, Harvard Law Sch., 1952. Trial atty. U.S. Dept. Justice, Washington, 1953-62; chief customs sect. U.S. Dept. Justice, N.Y.C., 1962-76; sr. ptnr. Barnes, Richardson & Colburn, N.Y.C., 1976-93, of counsel, 1994—; mem. adv. com. U.S. Ct. Appeals (fed. cir.), Washington, 1983-96, chmn., 1992-96; mem. adv. com. Ct. Internat. Trade, N.Y.C., 1987-93. Contbr. articles to profl. jours. Trustee Greenwood Union Cemetary, Rye, N.Y., 1984—, St. Photios Found., St. Augustine, Fla., 1990—, Juanita Coll., Huntingdon, Pa., 1990—. Recipient St. Paul's medal Greek Orthodox Archdiocese N. Am. and S. Am., 1976. Mem. ABA (chmn. Standing Com. on Customs Law 1991-93), Customs and Internat. Trade Bar Assn. (pres. 1990-92), Fed. Cir. Bar Assn. (pres. 1989-90), Order of St. Andrew. Greek Orthodox. Office: Barnes Richardson & Colburn 475 Park Ave S New York NY 10016-6901

VANCE, BERNARD WAYNE, lawyer, government official; b. Meridian, Miss., May 31, 1947; s. Jack Bernard and Marjorie Opal (Ezell) V. BBA, U. Miss., 1969, JD, 1975. Bar: Miss. 1975, D.C. 1975. Trial atty. admiralty sect. Dept. Justice, Washington, 1975-77, dep. asst. atty. gen., 1982-85; chief of staff Sec. Transp., Washington, 1985-87; general counsel Dept. of Transp., Washington, 1987-89; atty. pvt. practice Washington, 1989—. Editor-in-chief Miss. Law Jour., 1975, articles editor, 1974. Lt. USN, 1969-72. Mem. ABA, D.C. Bar Assn., Phi Delta Phi, Phi Delta Theta, Phi Kappa Phi, Omicron Delta Kappa. Republican. Episcopalian. Office: 1203 Essex Manor Ct Alexandria VA 22308-1000

VANCE, CAROL STONER, lawyer; b. Beaumont, Tex., July 26, 1933; s. Carol Stoner and Fanelle (Philp) V.; m. Carolyn Ruth Kongabel, Dec. 6, 1954; children: Lynnell, Carroll III, Karen, Harold, Cheryl. BBA, U. Tex., 1955, LLB, 1958. Bar: Tex. 1957, U.S. Dist. Ct. (so. dist.) Tex. 1960, U.S. Dist. Ct. (no. dist.) Tex. 1964, U.S. Ct. Appeals (5th cir.) 1964, U.S. Supreme Ct. 1964. Asst. dist. atty. Harris County Dist. Atty.'s Office, Houston, 1958-66, dist. atty., 1966-79; sr. ptnr. Bracewell & Patterson, Houston, 1979—; adj. prof. law U. Houston Sch. Law, 1972-79; chmn. Tex. Dept. Criminal Justice, 1992-95. Recipient Outstanding Young Man of Houston award Houston Jr. C. of C., 1967. Mem. ABA (spl. com. on criminal justice standards 1975-77, coun. sect. criminal justice 1972-79), Am. Coll. Trial Lawyers, Tex. Bar Assn. (chmn. criminal law sect. 1969-70), Houston Bar Assn. (appellate judiciary com.), Houston Bar Found., Nat. Coll. Dist. Attys. (bd. regents), Tex. Bar Found. (life), Tex. Assn. Def. Counsel, Tex. Young Lawyers Assn. (bd. dirs. 1963-66, Outstanding Young Lawyer of Tex. award 1970), Tex. Dist. Atty.'s Assn. (pres. 1969-70), Nat. Dist. Atty.'s Assn. (pres. 1972-73, Outstanding Dist. Atty. award 1972), Houston Young Lawyers' Assn. (pres. 1964), Nat. Coll. Dist. Attys. (chmn. bd. regents 1979-80, mem. bd. 1973—), Houston C. of C. (crime control com., chmn. legis. com.), Phi Alpha Delta. Avocations: tennis, golf. Office: Bracewell & Patterson South Tower Pennzoil Pl 711 Louisiana St Ste 2900 Houston TX 77002-2721

VANCE, CHARLES FOGLE, JR., lawyer; b. Winston-Salem, N.C., Oct. 4, 1924; s. Charles Fogle and Margaret (Vaughn) V.; m. Eleanor James, May 10, 1952; children: Lucy, Charles, Burton, Margaret. BA in Physics, U. N.C., 1946, JD, 1949. Bar: N.C. 1949, U.S. Dist. Ct. (mid. dist.) N.C. 1949, U.S. Ct. Appeals (4th cir.) 1949. Pvt. practice Winston-Salem, 1949-52; assoc. Womble Carlyle Sandridge & Rice, Winston-Salem, 1952-57, ptnr., 1957—; asst. solicitor Mcpl. Ct. Winston-Salem, 1951-52. Trustee Moravian Coll., Bethlehem, Pa., 1953-59, Salem Coll., Winston-Salem, 1974-80, chmn., 1977-80. With U.S. Army, 1944-45. Recipient Whitney North Seymour medal Am. Arbitration Assn., 1984. Fellow Am. Coll. Trial Lawyers; mem. ABA, Am. Bar Found., nat. Assn. R.R. Trial Counsel, N.C. Bar Assn., N.C. State Bar Coun. (councilor 1986-95), Forsyth County Bar Assn. (pres. 1966), 4th Cir. Jud. Conf. Democrat. Avocations: coastal fishing, piano. Office: Womble Carlyle Sandridge & Rice So Nat Fin Ctr PO Box 84 200 W 2d St Winston Salem NC 27102-0084

VANCE, CYNTHIA LYNN, psychology educator; b. Norwalk, Calif., Mar. 31, 1960; d. Dennis Keith and Donna Kay (Harryman) V. BS, U. Oreg., 1982; MS, U. Wis., Milw., 1987, PhD, 1991. Tchg. asst. U. Wis., Milw., 1983-89; computer graphics mgr. Montgomery Media, Inc., Milw., 1987-92; asst. prof. Cardinal Stritch Coll., Milw., 1992-93, Piedmont Coll., Demorest, Ga., 1993—. Contbr. articles to profl. jours. Mem. bd. advisors North Ga. Tech. Inst., 1997—; vol. Dunwoody (Ga.)-DeKalb Kiwanis Club, 1993—. Mem. AAUP, APA, Assn. Women in Psychology, S.E. Psychol. Assn., Am. Psychol. Soc., Am. Assn. Higher Edn. Office: Piedmont Coll PO Box 10 Demorest GA 30535-0010

VANCE, CYRUS ROBERTS, lawyer, former government official; b. Clarksburg, W.Va., Mar. 27, 1917; s. John Carl and Amy (Roberts) V.; m. Grace Elsie Sloane, Feb. 15, 1947; children: Elsie Nicoll, Amy Sloane, Grace, Camilla, Cyrus Roberts. Student, Kent Sch.; B.A., Yale U., 1939, LL.B., 1942, LL.D. (hon.), 1968; LL.D. (hon.), Marshall U., 1963, Trinity Coll., 1968, W.Va. U., 1969, Bowling Green U., 1969, Salem Coll., 1970, Brandeis U., 1971, Amherst Coll., 1974, W.Va. Wesleyan U., 1974, Harvard U., 1981, Colgate U., 1981, Gen. Theol. Sem., 1981, Williams Coll., 1981, Notre Dame U., 1982, Mt. Holyoke Coll., 1982, Brown U., Davidson Coll., U. Haifa, Fairfield U., NYU, Northwestern U. Bar: N.Y. State 1947, U.S. Supreme Ct. 1970. Asst. to pres. Mead Corp., 1946-47; assoc. Simpson Thacher & Bartlett, N.Y.C., 1947-56; ptnr. Simpson Thacher & Bartlett, 1956-61, 67-77, 80—; spl. counsel preparedness investigating subcom. Senate Armed Services Com., 1957-60; gen. counsel Dept. Def., 1961-62; sec. of army, 1962-63, dep. sec. def., 1964-67; spl. rep. of Pres. Johnson in Cyprus crisis, 1967, Korea, 1968; U.S. negotiator Paris Peace Conf. on Vietnam, 1968-69; sec. state, 1977-80, personal envoy UN Sec. Gen. on Yugoslavia crisis, 1991-92, personal envoy UN Sec. Gen. on South Africa and Nagorno-Karabakh, 1992; co-chmn. UN-EC Internat. Conf. on Former Yugoslavia, 1992-93; spl. envoy UN Sec.-Gen. Greece-FYROM Negotiations, 1993—; cons. counsel Spl. Com. on Space and Astronautics, U.S. Senate, 1958; chmn. com. on adjudication of claims Adminstrv. Conf. U.S.; mem. Com. To Investigate Alleged Police Corruption in N.Y.C., 1970-72; chmn. UN Devel. Corp., 1976; mem. Ind. Com. on Disarmament and Security Issues, N.Y. State Commn. on Govt. Integrity, N.Y. State Jud. Commn. on Minorities in the Ct.; bd. dirs. N.Y. Times; bd. dirs. Fed. Res. Bank of N.Y., 1989-93, chmn., 1989-91; chmn. Internat. Commn. on Missing Persons in the Former Yugoslavia, 1995—. Trustee Yale Corp., 1968-78, 80-87; trustee Rockefeller Found., 1970-77, 80-82, chmn., 1975-77; chmn. Am. Ditchley Found., 1981-94. Lt.

USNR, 1942-46. Recipient Medal of Freedom, 1969, Grand Cordon of Order of Rising Sun Govt. of Japan, 1990, Legion of Honor French Rep., 1993; apptd. Hon. Knight Comdr. in Civil div. of Most Excellent Order of British Empire, 1994. Fellow Am. Coll. Trial Lawyers; mem. ABA, Assn. of Bar of City of N.Y. (pres. 1974-76), Council on Fgn. Relations (dir., vice chmn. 1985-87), Japan Soc. (chmn. 1985-93). Office: Simpson Thacher & Bartlett 425 Lexington Ave New York NY 10017-3903

VANCE, DAVID ALVIN, management educator; b. Anchorage, Oct. 5, 1948; s. Alvin Victor and Mary V.; m. Nancy Louise Neimann; children: John Michael, Emily Suzanne. AA, Grossmont Coll., 1976; BBA, Nat. U., 1982, MBA, 1984, postgrad., 1985; postgrad., So. Ill. U., 1994—. Tech. supr. USN, San Diego, 1970-74; engr., project mgr. Wavetek Data Communications, San Diego, 1975-79; v.p. ops. Specialized Systems, Inc., San Diego, 1979-81; prin. Sunhill R&D, San Diego, 1981-84; exec. dir. Brunswick Inst. Tech., San Diego, 1985; tech. staff mem. Veda, Inc., Orlando, Fla. and San Diego, 1985-88; tng. analyst Eagle Tech., Inc., Winter Park, Fla., 1988-89; prof. mgmt. Fla. So. Coll., Orlando, 1988-94; tchr., student mgmt. doctoral program So. Ill. U., Carbondale, 1994—; prin. DA Vance & Assocs., Winter Park, 1986-94; adj. prof. mgmt. Webster U., 1991-94; vis. assoc. prof. So. Ill. U., 1991-94. Author, lectr. on mgmt. and tech. Rep. precinct committeeman, Orange County, Fla., 1988, del. state conv., 1988; chmn. svc. com. CSO, Inc., 1991. Recipient Achievement award ACCESS, San Diego, 1980; Worthy scholar Woodrow Wilson Found., 1966, Leadership scholar Nat. U., San Diego, 1984. Mem. Am. MENSA, Ltd., Internat. Platform Assn., Acad. of Mgmt., Info. Resources Mgmt. Assn., Computer Profls. for Social Responsibility. Avocations: outdoor sports, music. Office: So Ill U Dept Mgmt Rehn Hall Rm 214 Carbondale IL 62901

VANCE, DENNIS EDWARD, biochemistry educator; b. St. Anthony, Idaho, July 14, 1942; s. Russell Ernest and Josephine (Renner) V.; m. Jean Stuart Eaton, June 10, 1967; children: Russell Eaton, Fiona Natalie. BS, Dickinson Coll., 1964; PhD, U. Pitts., 1968. Postdoctoral fellow U. Pitts., 1968-70; postdoctoral fellow Harvard U., Cambridge, Mass., 1970-72, U. Warwick, Coventry, Eng., 1972-73; asst. prof. biochemistry U. B.C., Vancouver, Can., 1973-77, assoc. prof., 1977-82, prof., 1982-86, assoc. dean medicine, 1978-81, head dept., 1982-86; prof. biochemistry U. Alta., Edmonton, 1986—, dir. Lipid/Lipoprotein Group, 1986—. Author: (with others) Principles of Biochemistry, 1995; editor: Phosphatidylcholine Metabolism, 1989, Biochemistry of Lipids, Lipoproteins and Membranes, 1991, 1996, Phospholipid Biosynthesis, 1992. Grantee Med. Rsch. Coun., 1973—, Heart and Stroke Found. Can., 1974—. Fellow Royal Soc. Can.; mem. Am. Soc. Biochem. and Molecular Biology, Can. Soc. Biochemistry, Molecular and Cellular Biology (Boeringer Mannheim Can. prize 1989), Biochem. Soc. U.K. (Heinrich Wieland prize, Munich, 1995). Avocations: fishing, skiing, golf. Office: Univ Alta Faculty of Medicine, Lipid/Lipoprotein Rsch Group, Edmonton, AB Canada T6G 2S2

VANCE, ELBRIDGE PUTNAM, mathematics educator; b. Cin., Feb. 7, 1915; s. Selby Frame and Jeannie (Putnam) V.; m. Margaret Gertrude Stoffel, Aug. 5, 1939 (div. 1975); children: Susan (Mrs. Timothy Griffin), Peter Selby, Douglas Putnam, Emily (Mrs. Charles Harold Beynon III); m. Jean Haigh, Jan. 1975. Student, Haverford Coll., 1932-33; A.B., Coll. Wooster, 1936; M.A., U. Mich., 1937, Ph.D., 1939. Asst. U. Mich., 1937-39; instr. U. Nev., 1939-41, asst. prof., 1941-43; vis. lectr. Oberlin (Ohio) Coll., 1943-46, asst. prof., 1946-50, asso. prof., 1950-54, prof., 1954-83, prof. emeritus, 1983—, chmn. dept., 1948-77, acting dean Coll. Arts and Scis., 2d semester, 1965-66, 1st semester, 1970-71; chmn. advanced placement com. Coll. Entrance Exam. Bd., 1961-65, chief reader, 1956-61; chmn. com. examiners math. Comprehensive Coll. Tests, Ednl. Testing Service, 1965-67. Author: Trigonometry, 2d edit, 1969, Unified Algebra and Trigonometry, 1955, Fundamentals of Mathematics, 1960, Modern College Algebra, 3d edit, 1973, Modern Algebra and Trigonometry, 3d edit, 1973, An Introduction to Modern Mathematics, 2d edit, 1968, Mathematics 12, 1968, Solution Manual for Mathematics 12, 1968; Book review editor: Am. Math. Monthly, 1949-57; asso. editor, 1964-67. Mem. Oberlin Sch. Bd., 1952-60, pres., 1957-60. NSF Faculty fellow, 1960-61. Mem. Math. Assn. Am., Nat. Council Tchrs. of Math., Am. Math. Soc., Phi Beta Kappa, Sigma Xi, Phi Kappa Phi. Home: 5035 Strafford Oaks Dr Sebring FL 33872

VANCE, RALPH BROOKS, oncologist and educator; b. Jackson, Miss., Dec. 4, 1945; s. Brooks C. and Chrystine G. (Gober) V.; m. Mary Douglas Allen, June 18, 1979; children: Brooks, Barrett. BA in Biology and German, U. Miss., 1968, MD, 1972. Asst. prof. medicine U. Miss., Jackson, 1978-86, assoc. prof. medicine, 1986-93, prof. medicine, 1993—; chief of staff U. Miss. Hosp. and Clinics, Jackson, 1989-90; pres. faculty senate Univ. Med. Ctr., Jackson, 1986-87, univ. clin. assoc., pres., 1987-89. Author (with others) Development in Molecular Virology: Herpes Virus DNA, 1982; contbr. numerous articles and abstracts to profl. jours. Bd dirs. Am. Cancer Soc., Atlanta, nat. bd. dirs., exec. com.; bd. dirs. ARC, Jackson; med. adv. bd. Blue Cross/Blue Shield, Jackson, 1989-92. Named to Hall of Fame, U. Miss., 1968. Mem. Am. Assn. for Cancer Edn., Am. Fedn. for Clin. Rsch., Am. Soc. Clin. Oncology, Am. Assn. for Cancer Rsch., Miss. Acad. Scis., S.W. Oncology Group, Sigma Xi. Episcopalian. Office: Univ of Miss Sch Medicine 2500 N State St Jackson MS 39216-4500

VANCE, ROBERT MERCER, textile manufacturing company executive, banker; b. Clinton, S.C., July 9, 1916; s. Robert Berly and Mary Ellen (Bailey) V.; m. Virginia Sexton Gray, Dec. 27, 1949; children: Mary Bailey Vance Suitt, Robert Mercer, Russell Gray. BSBA, Davidson Coll., 1937; postgrad., Northwestern U., 1942; postgrad. Carolina Bankers Conf., U. N.C., 1948-57; HHD (hon.), Presbyn. Coll., 1968. Trainee Clinton Cotton Mills, summers, 1931-36; paymaster Lydia Cotton Mills, Clinton, 1937-41; dir., asst. treas. Clinton Cotton Mills Inc. and Lydia Cotton Mills, 1948-53, v.p., 1953-58, pres., treas., 1958-75; pres., treas. Clinton Mills, Inc. (now known as CMI, Industries, Inc.), 1975; chmn. bd. Clinton Mills, Inc. (merger Clinton Cotton Mills and Lydia Cotton Mills), 1975-86, chmn. emeritus, 1986—; with M.S. Bailey & Son, Bankers, Clinton, S.C., 1946—; pres. M.S. Bailey & Son, Bankers, Clinton, 1948, chmn. bd., 1975—; dir. Clinton Mills Sales Corp., N.Y.C., 1948, v.p., asst. treas., 1953, treas., 1958-86; bd. dirs. Palmetto Expo. Ctr., Greenville, S.C.; trustee J.E. Sirrine Textile Found., Inst. Textile Tech., 1959-93, mem., advisor nat. Cotton Coun., 1970—; mem. N.Y. Cotton Exch., 1965—. Mem. orgn. com., dir., treas Community Chest Greater Clinton, 1952-55, pres., 1958; former mem. nom. com. for S.C. Carolinas United Community Svcs.; trustee exec. com. Edn. Resources Found., 1965; sec. bd. trustees Thornwell Orphanage, Clinton, 1959-67; mem. state adv. com. Commn. on Higher Edn., Clinton, 1965-67; mem. S.C. Commn. on Higher Edn., 1967-71, chmn., 1968-71; trustee S.C. Found. Ind. Colls.; trustee Presbyn. Coll., Clinton, 1953-76, chmn., 56-67, 73-93; bd. visitors Davidson (N.C.) Coll., 1959-62, 77—; mem. S.C. Water Resources Commn., 1981-83; deacon, elder First Presbyn. Ch., Clinton, 1950—, treas., 1950-58, past pres. Men's Sunday Sch. Class, other coms. With U.S. Army, 1941; lt. USN, 1942-46; lt. comdr. USNR, 1946-54. Decorated 17 battle stars; Named Clinton Man of Yr. Lions Club, 1955, Textile Man of Yr. N.Y. Bd. Trade, 1978. Mem. S.C. Bankers Assn. (v.p. 1953-55, pres. 1963-64), S.C. Textile Mfrs. Assn. (dir., v.p. 1966-67, pres. 1967-68), S.C. C. of C. (dir. 1959-60), Laurens County C. of C. (dir. 1982-86), Am. Legion, Poinsett Club (Greenville, S.C.), Lakeside Club (Clinton), Litchfield Club (Pawleys Island, S.C.), Musgrove Mill Golf Club, Moose. Masons, Kiwanis (former dir., pres. 1955), Shriners, Kappa Alpha. Presbyterian. Home: 311 S Broad St Clinton SC 29325-2506 Office: MS Bailey & Son Bankers 211 N Broad St Clinton SC 29325-2303 also: Clinton Mills Inc 600 Academy St Clinton SC 29325

VANCE, ROBERT PATRICK, lawyer; b. Birmingham, Ala., Feb. 12, 1948; s. James Robert and Lucy Juanita (McMath) V.; m. Sarah Elizabeth Savoia, June 11, 1971; 1 son, Robert Patrick, Jr. B.A. with honors, La. State U., 1970, J.D., 1975. Bar: La. 1975, U.S. Dist. Ct. (ea. dist.) La. 1975, U.S. Dist. Ct. (mid. dist.) La. 1978, U.S. Dist. Ct. (we. dist.) La. 1979, U.S. Ct. Appeals (5th cir.) 1975, U.S. Ct. Appeals (11th cir.) 1981, U.S. Supreme Ct. 1981. Assoc. Jones, Walker, Waechter, Poitevent, Carrere & Denegre, New Orleans, 1975-80, ptnr., 1980—, exec. com. 1991-95, mng. ptnr., 1994-95. Contbr. La. Law Rev.; author, editor: Bankruptcy Rules: Parts I, II, VII, VIII and IX, 1983; Overview of the Bankruptcy Code and the Court, 1983. Co-author: Bankruptcy-Current Developments, 1983, Current Developments in Commercial Law, 1984, Basic Bankruptcy of Louisiana, 1989, Fundamentals of Bankruptcy Law & Procedure in La., 1993; contbr. articles to profl. jours. Fellow Am. Coll. Bankruptcy, Nat. Bankruptcy Conf.; mem. ABA (chair bankruptcy litigation com.), Am. Law Inst., Am. Bankruptcy Inst., Fed. Bar Assn. (mem. bankruptcy law com., polit. campaign and election law com., editorial bd. Bankruptcy Briefs), La. State Bar Assn. (pres. consumer and bankruptcy law sect., chmn. CLE com.), New Orleans Bar Assn., La. Bankers Assn. (chmn. bank counsel com. 1992-93), Pi Sigma Alpha, Phi Beta Kappa (Faculty Group award), Phi Kappa Phi. Democrat. Roman Catholic. Home: 1821 State St New Orleans LA 70118-6219 Office: Jones Walker Waechter Poitevent Carrere & Denegre 201 Saint Charles Ave New Orleans LA 70170-1000

VANCE, SARAH S., federal judge; b. 1950. BA, La. State Univ., 1971; JD, Tulane Univ., 1978. With Stone, Pigman, Walther, Wittmann & Hutchinson, New Orleans, 1978-94; dist. judge U.S. Dist. Ct. (La. ea. dist.), 5th cir., New Orleans, 1994—. Recipient Phi Beta Kappa Faculty Group award. Mem. ABA, Am. Law Inst., Fed. Judges Assn., Nat. Assn. Women Judges, La. State Bar Assn., Fed. Bar Assn., New Orleans Bar Assn., Bar Assn. of the Fed. Fifth Circuit, Order of Coif. Address: US Courthouse 500 Camp St Rm C-255 New Orleans LA 70130-3313

VANCE, STANLEY CHARLES, management educator; b. Minersville, Pa., May 5, 1915; s. Stanley and Margaret (Zelin) V.; m. Regina Dober, Mar. 4, 1946. A.B., St. Charles Sem., 1937; M.A., U. Pa., 1944, Ph.D., 1951. Instr. U. Pa., 1945-47; asst. prof. U. Conn., 1947-52; prof. U. Mass., 1952-56; dean Coll. Bus. Adminstrn., Kent State U., 1956-60; H.T. Miner prof. bus. adminstrn. U. Oreg., Eugene, 1960-75; head dept. personnel and indsl. mgmt. U. Oreg., 1963-71; also acting dean Coll. Bus. Adminstrn.; William B. Stokely prof. mgmt. U. Tenn., Knoxville, 1975—; Mem. nat. council Nat. Planning Assn.; bd. dirs., pres. Inst. Adminstrv. Research. Author: American Industries, 1955, Industrial Administration, 1959, Management Decision Simulation, 1960, Industrial Structure and Policy, 1961, Quantitative Techniques for Operations Management, 1962, Board of Directors Structure and Performance, 1964, The Corporate Director, 1968, Managers and Mergers, 1971, Corporate Leadership: Boards, Directors and Strategy, 1983; Editor book revs.; scanning editor: Dirs. and Bds. Fellow Nat. Acad. Mgmt. (dean of fellows, pres. Western div., editor Jour. 1966-70, newsletter, 1971—, pres. 1975—), Internat. Acad. Mgmt. (vice chancellor); mem. AIM, C. of C., Am. Soc. Personnel Adminstrn., N.Am. Simulation and Gaming Assn. (dir.), Assn. Bus. Simulation and Exptl. Learning (pres.), N.Am. Simulation and Gaming Assn. (gov.), Dirs. Coun. Corp. Bds., Nat. Assn. Corp. Dirs., N.Am. Mgmt. Coun. (pres.), Rotary. Home: 1701 Cherokee Blvd Knoxville TN 37919-8335

VANCE, THOMAS RAY, engineer; b. Charleston, W.Va., Sept. 24, 1938; s. Bethel Raymond and Madolyn Elizabeth (Fisher) V.; m. Janice Lee Jordan, Dec. 23, 1958; children: Barbara Vance, Jeffrey Ross, Deborah. BSME, W.Va. U., 1960, MSTAM, 1966, PhD, 1968. Registered profl. engr., W.Va., Ohio. Devel. engr. The Babcock and Wilcox Co., Alliance, Ohio, 1960-63; staff engr. Los Alamos (N.Mex.) Scientific Lab., 1964-66; program mgr. Tech. divsn. IBM Corp., Hopewell Junction, N.Y., 1968-92; dir. W.Va. State Farm Mus., Point Pleasant, W.Va., 1994-97; prin. Vance & Assocs., Point Pleasant, 1992—; instr. coll. engring. W.Va. U., Morgantown, 1966-68; instr. evening dirsn. Dutchess C.C., Poughkeepsie, N.Y., 1962-68; chmn. adv. com. Dept. Engring. Ohio State U., 1988-91; mem. Stevens Inst. of Tech., Alliance for Tech. Mgmt., Hoboken, N.J.. Contbr. articles to profl. jours. Vice chmn. Point Pleasant River Mus. Com., 1993-94; mem. Point Pleasant Hist. Dist. Com., 1993-94. Scholarship NASA. Mem. W.Va. Assn. of Profl. Engrs., Nat. Assn. of Profl. Engrs. Republican. Lutheran. Achievements include patent in repair of thin film lines. Home: 4 Main St Point Pleasant WV 25550-1026 Office: Vance and Assocs 329 Main St Point Pleasant WV 25550

VANCE, VERNE WIDNEY, JR., lawyer; b. Omaha, Mar. 10, 1932; s. Verne Widney and June Caroline (Henckler) V.; m. Anita Paine, June 27, 1970; children: Lisa Joy, Charles Hebard Paine, Virginia Caroline. AB, Harvard U., 1954, JD, 1957. Bar: D.C. 1957, Mass. 1964. Law clk. U.S. Dist. Judge, Mass., 1957-58; assoc. Covington & Burling, Washington, 1958-60; atty. adv. Devel. Loan Fund, Washington, 1960-61; legal counsel U.S. AID, Washington, 1961-63; assoc. Foley, Hoag & Eliot, Boston, 1963-67, ptnr., 1967—; lectr. law Boston U., 1964-66; corp. clk. S.S. Pierce Co., 1971-72. Pres. UN Assn. Greater Boston, 1964-66, 77-78, treas., 1974-77; mem. Mass. Adv. Council on Edn., 1969-75, chmn., 1975; mem. Dem. City Com., Newton, Mass., 1972—, Gov.'s Local Govt. Adv. Commn., 1986-90; alderman City of Newton, 1982-91; pres. Newton Bd. of Aldermen, 1988-91; mem. Newton Sch. Com., 1994—; trustee Judge Baker Children's Ctr., 1994—; trustee Mass. Bay C.C., 1987—, vice chmn., 1989-91, chmn. 1991-97; pres. Mass. C.C. Assn., 1996-97. Mem. Boston Bar Assn. (mem. bd. of editors bar jour. 1986-90) bd. dirs. Boston Archtl. Ctr., 1991-92. Unitarian. Club: Longwood Cricket (Chestnut Hill, Mass.). Editor Harvard Law Rev., 1955-57; contbr. articles to profl. jours. Home: 101 Old Orchard Rd Chestnut Hill MA 02167-1202 Office: Foley Hoag & Eliot 1 Post Office Sq Boston MA 02109

VANCE, ZINNA BARTH, artist, writer; b. Phila., Sept. 28, 1917; d. Carl Paul Rudolph Barth and Dorothy Ellice (Wilson) Hart; m. Nathan E. Curry (div. 1959); m. Samuel Therrel Vance, Dec. 2, 1960; children: Barry, Scott Hart. BS in Edn. summa cum laude, Southwestern U., Georgetown, Tex., 1965; MA in Communications, U. Tex., 1969. Cert. in teaching langs., Tex. Freelance writer various publs., 1946-56; assoc. editor, newspaper Canacao Clipper, Philippines, 1956-58; dir. Region One Tex. Fine Arts Assn., Austin, 1962-63; curricular cons. U. Tex. Curricular Conf., 1966; sec. Tex. Fgn. Langs. Assn., 1967; publicity dir. Burnet (Tex.) Creative Arts, 1983—; freelance portrait artist, Liberty Hill, Tex.; owner Gallery Zinna Portrait Studio, Liberty Hill, Tex., 1978—; artist registry Hill Country Arts Found., Ingram, Tex., 1984—; art columnist two newspapers Burnet, 1983—. Contbr. numerous articles to profl. jours.; exhibited in pvt. and corp. collections; illustrator children's books; numerous one-woman shows. Active Hill Country Arts Found., 1978—, Burnet Creative Arts, 1980—, Hill Country Council of Arts, 1986—. Named one of Tex. Emerging Artists, Hill Country Arts Found., 1985; featured as Cover Story Philippines Internat. mag., 1957, featured in book Artists of Texas, 1989, 94. Mem. Nat. Mus. Women in Arts (charter mem.), Nat. Portrait Inst., Alpha Chi, Phi Kappa Phi. Republican. Episcopalian. Avocations: ranching, figure skating, Chinese brush painting. Home: 937CR323 Liberty Hill TX 78642-9501

VANCE SIEBRASSE, KATHY ANN, newspaper publishing executive; b. Kansas City, Kans., Oct. 28, 1954; d. Donald Herbert Vance and Barbara June (Boris) Vance-Young; m. Charles Richard Siebrasse, Mar. 8, 1980; 1 stepson, Michael; 1 son, Bradley. BS in Journalism, No. Ill. U., 1976. Reporter Des Plaines (Ill.) Suburban Times and Park Ridge Herald, 1974-75, DeKalb (Ill.) Daily Chronicle, 1976-78; stringer Rockford (Ill.) Register Star, 1978; editor The MidWeek Newspaper, DeKalb, 1978-81, owner and pub., 1982—. Active No. Ill. U. Found., 1992—, mem. exec. bd., 1994—, chair bus. and industry for No. Ill. U. campaign, 1993-94; pres. DeKalb Athletic Barb Boosters, 1995-97; chair Kishwaukee Hosp. Health Coun., Comm. Com., 1984-92, DeKalb County Partnership for a Substance Abuse Free Environment, 1990—; bd. dirs. DeKalb Edn. Found., sec., 1987-89, pres., 1989-93, active, 1987-94; sponsor Big Bros./Big Sisters Bowl-a-Thon. Recipient Comty. Svc. award Nat. Assn. of Advt. Pubs., 1980, Athena award Oldsmobile, DeKalb C. of C., 1990, Bus. of Yr., 1994. Mem. Ill. Press Assn., No. Ill. Newspaper Assn., Ind. Free Papers Am. (Cmty. Svc. award 1992-93, 2d pl. nat. gen. excellence award 1996), DeKalb County Farm Bur., DeKalb and Sycamore C. of C. (editor Sycamore newsletter 1994-96, mem. DeKalb Athena award com., bd. dirs., v.p. DeKalb 1996, chair 1997). Avocations: photography, reading, swimming, skiing, sailing. Office: The MidWeek Newspaper 121 Industrial Dr De Kalb IL 60115-3931

VAN CITTERS, ROBERT LEE, medical educator, physician; b. Alton, Iowa, Jan. 20, 1926; s. Charles and Wilhemina (Heemstra) Van C.; m. Mary E. Barker, Apr. 9, 1949; children: Robert, Mary, David, Sara. A.B., U. Kans., 1949; M.D., U. Kans. Med. Ctr., Kansas City, 1953; Sc.D. hon., Northwestern Coll., Orange City, Iowa, 1977. Intern U. Kans. Med. Ctr., Kansas City, 1953-54, resident, 1955-57, fellow, 1957-58; research fellow Sch. Medicine, U. Wash., Seattle, 1958-61, asst. prof. physiology and biophysics, 1962-65, assoc. prof., 1965-70, prof., 1970—; prof. medicine Sch. Medicine, U. Wash., 1970—, assoc. dean Sch. Medicine, 1968-70, dean Sch. Medicine, 1970-81; mem. staff Scripps Clinic and Research Found., La Jolla, Calif., 1961-62; exchange scientist joint U.S.-U.S.S.R. Sci. Exchange, 1962; mem. Liason Commn. on Med. Edn., Washington, 1981-85; mem. various coms., nat. adv. research council NIH, Bethesda, Md., 1980-83; mem. Va. Spl. Med. Adv. Commn., 1974-78, chmn., 1976-78; chmn. working group on mech. circulatory support systems Nat. Heart, Lung and Blood Inst. NIH, 1985—, mem. adv. coun. clin. applications and prevention, 1985-89. Contbr. numerous articles to profl. jours. Served to 1st lt. U.S. Army, 1943-46, PTO; to capt. M.C., USAF, 1953-55. Recipient research career devel. USPHS. Fellow AAAS; mem. Assn. Am. Med. Colls. (adminstrv. bd. and exec. council 1972-78, Disting. Service mem.), Am. Coll. Cardiology (Cummings medal 1970), Nat. Acad. Sci. Inst. Medicine, Am. Heart Assn., Wash. State Med. Assn. (hon. life). Office: U Wash Sch Medicine Seattle WA 98195

VAN CLEAVE, WILLIAM ROBERT, international relations educator; b. Kansas City, Mo., Aug. 27, 1935; s. Earl Jr. and Georgiana (Offutt) Van C.; children: William Robert II, Cynthia Kay. B.A. in Polit. Sci. summa cum laude, Calif. State U., Long Beach, 1962; M.A. in Govt. and Internat. Relations, Claremont (Calif.) Grad. Sch., 1964, Ph.D., 1966. Mem. faculty U. So. Calif., 1967-87, prof. internat. rels., 1974-87, dir. def. and strategic studies ctr., 1971-87; prof., dept. head, dir. Ctr. for Def. and Strategic Studies Southwest Mo. State U., 1987—; sr. rsch. fellow Hoover Instn. Stanford U., 1981—; chmn. Strategic Alternatives Team, 1977-90; acting chmn. Pres.'s Gen. Adv. Com. on Arms Control, 1981-82; spl. asst. Office Sec. Def., mem. Strategic Arms Limitation Talks (SALT) delegation, 1969-71; mem. B team on Nat. Intelligence Estimates, 1976; mem. exec. panel, bd. dirs. Com. Present Danger, 1980-93; dir. transition team Dept. Def., 1980-81; sr. nat. security advisor to Ronald Reagan, 1979-80; mem. nat. security affairs adv. council Republican Nat. Com., 1979—; research council Fgn. Policy Research Inst., Inst. Fgn. Policy Analysis; co-dir. Ann. Internat. Security Summer Seminar, Fed. Republic Germany; trustee Am. com. Internat. Inst. Strategic Studies, 1980—; vis. prof. U.S. Army Advanced Russian Inst., Garmisch, Fed. Republic Germany, 1978-79; chmn. adv. bd. Internat. Security Coun., 1991—; cons. in field, mem. numerous govt. adv. coms. Co-author: Strategic Options for the Early Eighties: What Can Be Done?, 1979, Tactical Nuclear Weapons, 1978, Nuclear Weapons, Policies, and the Test Ban Issue, 1987; author: Fortress USSR, 1986; bd. editors: Global Affairs. Co-chmn. Scholars for Reagan, 1984; mem. exec. coun., dir. NCAA rels. Haka Bowl, NCAA Postseason Football Bowl. With USMC, 1953-61. Recipient Freedom Found. award, 1976, Outstanding Contbn. award Air War Coll., 1979, award teaching excellence U. So. Calif., 1980, 86; named Outstanding Prof. U. So. Calif., 1977, Disting. Alumnus Claremont Colls., 1978; Woodrow Wilson fellow, 1962, NDEA fellow, 1963-65. Mem. Internat. Inst. Strategic Studies (U.S. com.). Home: 8226 E Panther Hollow Ln Rogersville MO 65742-8386 Office: Ctr for Def and Strategic Studies Southwest Mo State U Springfield MO 65804-0095

VAN CLEVE, JOHN VICKREY, history educator, university official; b. Evanston, Ill., Apr. 8, 1947; s. John William and Mildred Madelane (Vickrey) Van C. Student, U. Ill., 1965-67; BA, Western State Coll. Colo., 1970; MA, PhD, U. Calif., Irvine, 1976. Instr. history Gallaudet U., Washington, 1976-77, asst. to assoc. prof. history, 1977-84, chmn. dept. history, 1983-95, prof. history, 1984—, asst. to v.p. for acad. affairs, 1995—; dir. Gallaudet Univ. Press, Washington, 1997—. Author: (with Barry A. Crouch) A Place of Their Own: Creating the Deaf Community in America, 1989; chmn. editorial bd. Gallaudet U. Press, 1985-96; editor in chief Gallaudet Encyclopedia of Deaf People and Deafness, 1987 (Pres.' award); editor Deaf History Unveiled: Selections from the new Scholarship, 1993; contbr. articles to profl. jours. Mem. Orgn. Am. Historians, Hist. of Edn. Soc., Conv. Am. Instrs. of Deaf. Office: Gallaudet Univ Dept of History 800 Florida Ave NE Washington DC 20002-3660

VAN CLEVE, RUTH GILL, retired lawyer, government official; b. Mpls., July 28, 1925; d. Raymond S. and Ruth (Sevon) Gill; m. Harry R. Van Cleve, Jr., May 16, 1952; children: John Gill, Elizabeth Webster, David Hamilton Livingston. Student, U. Minn., 1943; A.B. magna cum laude, Mt. Holyoke Coll., 1946, LL.D., 1976; LL.B., Yale, 1950. Bar: D.C. 1950, Minn. 1950. Intern Nat. Inst. Pub. Affairs, 1946-47; atty. Dept. Interior, 1950-54, asst. solicitor, 1954-64; dir. Office Territorial Affairs, 1964-69, 1977-80, dep. asst. sec., 1980-81, acting asst. sec., 1993; atty. Solicitor's Office, 1981-93; atty. FPC, 1969-75, asst. gen. counsel, 1975-77. Author: The Office of Territorial Affairs, 1974, The Application of Federal Laws to the Territories, 1993. Recipient Fed. Woman's award, 1966, Disting. Service award Dept. Interior, 1968, Presdl. Rank award, Pres. U.S., 1989. Mem. Phi Beta Kappa. Unitarian. Home: 4400 Emory St Alexandria VA 22312-1321

VAN CLEVE, WILLIAM MOORE, lawyer; b. Mar. 17, 1929; s. William T Van Cleve and Catherine (Baldwin) Moore Van Cleve; m. Georgia Hess Dunbar, June 27, 1953; children: Peter Dunbar, Robert Baldwin, Sarah Van Cleve Van Doren, Emory Basford. Grad., Phillips Acad., 1946; AB in Econs., Princeton U., 1950; JD, Washington U., St. Louis, 1953. Bar: Mo. 1953. Assoc. Dunbar and Gaddy, St. Louis, 1955-58; ptnr. Bryan Cave (and predecessor firm), St. Louis, 1958—, chmn., 1973-94; bd. dirs. Emerson Electric Co. Trustee Washington U., 1983—, vice chmn. bd. trustees, 1988-93, 95—, chmn., 1993-95, mem. exec. com., 1985—; pres. Eliot Soc., 1982-86; chmn. Law Sch. Nat. Coun., 1986-93; commr. St. Louis Sci. Ctr., 1993—; bd. dirs., v.p. Parents As Tchrs. Nat. Ctr., 1991—. Mem. ABA, Bar Assn. Met. St. Louis, Mound City Bar Assn., St. Louis County Bar Assn., Order of Coif (hon.). Democrat. Episcopalian. Clubs: Princeton (pres. 1974-75), Noonday (pres. 1985), St. Louis Country, Bogey (pres. 1990-91), Round Table (St. Louis). Home: 8 Dromara Rd Saint Louis MO 63124-1816 Office: Bryan Cave 211 N Broadway Fl 36 Saint Louis MO 63102-2733

VANCO, JOHN L., art museum director; b. Erie, Pa., Aug. 21, 1945; s. John Jr. and Alice (Crozier) V.; m. Kathleen Merski, 1971; children: John H., Jesse L. BA, Allegheny Coll., 1967. Dir. Erie (Pa.) Art Mus., 1968—; mem. adv. panels Pa. Coun. on the Arts, Harrisburg, 1974—, Mid Atlantic Arts Found., Balt., 1992. Photographer miscellaneous exhbns.; curator miscellaneous exhbns. including Teco: Art Pottery of the Prairie Sch., In Harmony with the Earth; author: A Roycroft Desktop: Musings on Elbert Hubbard and the Roycroft Shops, 1994. Chief adminstrv. officer Discovery Square, Erie, 1991-92. Office: Erie Art Mus 411 State St Erie PA 16501-1106

VANCRUM, ROBERT JAMES, retired state senator, lawyer; b. ElDorado, Kans., Dec. 2, 1946; s. Merle Benjamin and Lucille Mabel (Mosteller) C.; m. Joyce Lynn Lynch, Jan. 31, 1968; children: Brian Christopher, Melissa Lynn. AB in Polit. Sci. and English, U. Kans., 1968; JD, U. Chgo., 1971; LLM in Taxation, U. Mo., Kansas City, 1980. Bar: Mo. 1971, Kans. 1981, U.S. Tax Ct., U.S. Ct. Appeals (8th cir.), U.S. Ct. Appeals (10th cir.). Assoc. Watson, Ess, Marshall & Enggas, Kansas City, Mo., 1971-75; ptnr. Brown, Koralchik & Fingersh, Kansas City, 1975-84, Gage & Tucker, Overland Park, Kans., 1984-94, Morrison & Hecker, Overland Park, 1994—; state rep. State of Kans., Topeka, 1981-93, state senator, 1993-96. Contbr. articles to profl. jours. Mem. ABA (mem. tax sect., mem. tax com. 1978—), Kans. Bar Assn. (corp. tax com. 1981—), Mo. Bar Assn. (mem. corp. tax com. 1971—), Rotary Internat., Coll. Blvd. Breakfast Club (founder 1988). Republican. Methodist. Avocations: skiing, running, golf.

VAN CULIN, SAMUEL, religious organization administrator; b. Honolulu, Sept. 30, 1930; s. Samuel and Susie (Mossman) Van C. A.B., Princeton U., 1952; B.D., Va. Theol. Sem., 1955, D.D. (hon.), 1955. Curate St. Andrew's Cathedral, Honolulu, 1955-56; Canon precentor, rector Hawaiian Congregation, Honolulu, 1956-58; asst. rector St. John's Ch., Washington, 1958-60; gen. sec. Lyman Internat., Washington, 1960-61; asst. sec. overseas Exec. Council of Episcopal Ch., N.Y.C., 1962-68, sec. for Africa, Middle East, 1968-76; exec. for world mission Episcopal Ch. U.S.A., N.Y.C., 1976-83; sec. gen. Anglican Consultative Council Eng., London, 1983-95; asst. priest All Hallows Ch., London, 1995—. Named Hon. Canon Canterbury, 1983, Jerusalem, 1983, Ibadan, 1984, Ch. Province of So. Africa, 1989, St. Andrew's Cathedral, Honolulu, 1994. Clubs: Atheneum (London); Princeton (N.Y.). Avocations: Music; travelling. Home: 16a Burgate, Canterbury 2HG, England Office: All Hallows Ch, 43 Trinity Sq, London EC3N 4DJ, England

VAN CURA, JOYCE BENNETT, librarian; b. Madison, Wis., Mar. 25, 1944; d. Ralph Eugene and Florence Marie (Cramer) Bennett; m. E. Jay Van Cura, July 5, 1986. BA in Liberal Arts (scholar), Bradley U., 1966; MLS, U. Ill., 1971. Library asst. rsch. library Caterpillar Tractor Co., Peoria, Ill., 1966-67; reference librarian, instr. library tech. Ill. Central Coll., East Peoria, 1967-73; asst. prof. Sangamon State U. (U. Ill.-Springfield), Springfield, Ill., 1973-80, assoc. prof., 1980-86; head library ref. and info. svcs. dept. Ill. Inst. Tech., 1987-90; dir. Learning Resources Ctr. Morton Coll., 1990—; convenor Coun. II, Ill. Clearinghouse for Acad. Library Instrn., 1978; presentor 7th Ann. Conf. Acad. Library Instrn., 1977, Nat. Women's Studies Assn., 1983, others; participant Gt. Lakes Women's Studies Summer Inst., 1981, Nat. Inst. Leadership Devel. seminar, 1995. Dem. precinct Committeewoman, 1982-85. Pres., Springfield chpt. NOW, 1978-79. Ill. state scholar, 1962-66; recipient Am. Legion citizenship award, 1962; cert. of recognition Ill. Bicentennial Commn., 1974; invited Susan B. Anthony luncheon, 1978, 79, vice-moderator Fourth Presbyn. Women, 1989-90; elder Riverside (Ill.) Presbyn. Ch., 1992—; mem. adv. bd. Suburban Libr. System, 1992-94, Nat. Commn. Learning Resources; bd. dirs. Berwyn-Cicero Coun. on Aging; v.p. membership Riverside chpt. Lyric Opera Chgo., 1994-96; active Riverside (Ill.) Arts Ctr. Mem. ALA, Assn. Coll. and Rsch. Librs., Libr. Adminstrn. and Mgmt. Assn. (mem. reference and adult svcs. divsn.), Libr. Info. and Tech. Assn., Nat. Assn. Women in C.C., Ill. Library Assn. (presentor 1984) Ill. Assn. Coll. and Rsch. Libraries (bibliog. instrn. com.), Spl. Libraries Assn., No. Ill. Learning Resources Consortium Bd., Am. Mgmt. Assn., Women in Mgmt., AAUW (chmn. standing com. on women Springfield br., mem. com. on women Ill. state divsn., bd. dirs. Riverside br., 1992-94), Nat. Women's Studies Assn. (presentor 1983, 84, 85), No. Ill. Learning Resources Coop. (del. 1990—, steering com. w. suburban post secondary consortium 1996—, bd. dirs. Berwgn-Cicero coun. on aging 1996—), Springfield Art Assn., Nat. Trust Historic Preservation, Beta Phi Mu. Reviewer Libr. Jour., Am. Reference Books Ann. Contbr. article in field to publ. Home: 181 Scottswood Rd Riverside IL 60546-2221 Office: Morton Coll Learning Resources Ctr 3801 S Central Ave Chicago IL 60804-4306

VANCURA, STEPHEN JOSEPH, radiologist; b. Norton, Kans., June 26, 1951; s. Cyril William J. and Clara Mae (Ruthstrom) V.; BA in Chemistry magna cum laude, Kans. State U., 1972; MD, Kans. U., 1976; m. Lydia Acker, Dec. 10, 1976. Intern in medicine Letterman Army Med. Center, San Francisco, 1976-77, resident in radiology, 1977-80; practice medicine specializing in radiology, 1980—; chief dept. radiology Darnall Army Hosp., Ft. Hood, Tex., 1980-82; pvt. practice diagnostic radiology, 1982—; chief of staff Metroplex Hosp., 1985-86, 88-90. Served to maj. M.C., U.S. Army, 1976-82 Recipient Ollie O. Mustala award in clin. pharmacology Kans. U. Med. Center, 1974; A. Morris Ginsberg award in phys. diagnosis Kans. U. Med. Center, 1975; Resident Tchr. of Yr. award Letterman Army Med. Center, 1979; Staff Tchr. of Yr. award Darnall Army Hosp., 1982. Trembly Meml. scholar, 1972. Diplomate Am. Bd. Radiology. Mem. Am. Coll. Radiology, Radiologic Soc. N. Am., AMA, Tex. Med. Assn., Tex. Radiol. Soc., Ind. Med. Practitioners Assn. Ctrl. Tex. (pres.), Clinical Magnetic Resonance Soc., Sigma Xi, Alpha Chi Sigma, Alpha Omega Alpha. Home: 3302 Walnut Cir Harker Heights TX 76548 Office: Metroplex Hosp Dept Radiology 2201 Clear Creek Rd Killeen TX 76542

VAN DAM, HEIMAN, psychoanalyst; b. Leiden, The Netherlands, Feb. 5, 1920; s. Machiel and Rika (Knorringa) van D.; m. Barbara C. Strona, Oct. 6, 1945; children: Machiel, Claire Ilena, Rika Rosemary. AB, U. So. Calif., 1942, MD, 1945. Fellowship child psychiatry Pasadena (Calif.) Child Guidance Clinic, 1950; gen. practice psychiatry and psychoanalysis L.A., 1951—; instr. L.A. Psychoanalytic Inst., 1959—, co-chmn. com. on child psychoanalysis, 1960-67, tng. and supervising psychoanalyst, 1972—; supr. child and adolescent psychoanalysis So. Calif. Psychoanalytic Inst., 1986—; cons. Reiss Davis Child Study Center, 1955-76, Neighborhood Youth Assn., Los Angeles, 1964-69; asso. clin. prof. psychiatry and pediats. UCLA Sch. Medicine, 1960-96, clin. prof. psychiatry and pediats., 1996—; vis. supr. child psychoanalysis San Francisco Psychoanalytic Inst., 1969-79, Denver Psychoanalytic Inst., 1972-74; mem. adv. bd. Western State U. Coll. Law, Fullerton, Calif., 1965-83. Corr. editor Arbeits Hefte Kinderanalyse, 1985—; contbr. articles to profl. jours. Trustee, mem. edn. com. Center for Early Edn., 1964-92, v.p., 1978-79; bd. dirs. Child Devel. and Psychotherapy Tng. Program, Los Angeles, 1975-80, pres., 1975-77; bd. dirs. Los Angeles Child Devel. Center, 1977-86, treas., 1978-80; mem. cult clinic Jewish Family Service, Los Angeles, 1978-86; bd. dirs. Lake Arrowhead Crest Estates, 1990—. Served to capt. M.C. AUS, 1946-48. Mem. Am. Psychoanalytic Assn. (com. on ethics 1977-80), Assn. Child Psychoanalysis (councillor 1966-69, sec. 1972-74, mem. nominating com. 1978-84, membership com. 1988—, Marianne Kris lectr. 1995), Internat. Assn. Infant Psychiatry (co-chmn. program com. 1980-83), Internat. Soc. Adolescent Psychiatry (sci. adv. com. 1988—), Phi Beta Kappa. Office: 1100 Glendon Ave Ste 941 Los Angeles CA 90024-3513

VANDAMENT, WILLIAM EUGENE, academic administrator, educator; b. Hannibal, Mo., Sept. 6, 1931; s. Alva E. and Ruth Alice (Mahood) V.; m. Margery Vandament, Feb. 2, 1952; children: Jane Louise, Lisa Ann. BA, Quincy Coll., 1952; MS, So. Ill. U., 1953; MS in Psychology, U. Mass., 1963, PhD, 1964. Psychologist Bacon Clinic, Racine, Wis., 1954-61; NDEA fellow U. Mass., Amherst, 1961-64; asst. prof. SUNY, Binghamton, 1964-69, univ. examiner and dir. instl. research, 1969-73, asst. v.p. planning, instl. research, 1972-76; exec. asst. to pres., dir. budget and resources Ohio State U., Columbus, 1976-79, v.p. fin. and planning, 1979-81; sr. v.p. adminstrn. NYU, N.Y.C., 1981-83; provost, vice chancellor acad. affairs Calif. State U. System, Long Beach, 1983-87; Trustees prof. Calif. State U., Fullerton, 1987-92; pres. No. Mich. U., 1991—. Contbr. articles to psychol. jours. and books on higher edn. Home: 1440 Center St Marquette MI 49855-1625 Office: Northern Michigan U 1401 Presque Isle Ave Marquette MI 49855-5305

VAN DECKER, WILLIAM ARTHUR, cardiologist; b. Passaic, N.J., May 27, 1957; s. William and Louise Adelaide (Meli) Van D.; m. Generosa Grana; children: Stephanie, William, Christopher. BS in Biology summa cum laude, Fairfield (Conn.) U., 1979; MD, Georgetown U., 1983. Diplomate am. Bd. Internal Medicine, Cert. Coun. Nuclear Cardiology; Am. Soc. Echocardiography spl. competency testing. Intern Temple U. Hosp., Phila., 1983-84, resident internal medicine, 1984-86, cardiology fellow, 1986-88, non-invasive cardiology imaging tng./rsch. fellow, 1988-89; assoc. dir. Non-Invasive Imaging, dir. Cardiology Clinic Med. Coll. Pa., Phila., 1989-95, asst. prof. medicine and cardiology, 1989—, dir. Heart Sta., 1990—; mem. com. on radiation safety Med. Coll. Pa., Phila., 1990—, chmn. com. on radiation safety, 1993—, mem. pharmacy and therapeutics com., 1992—, chmn. pharmacy and therapeutics com. 1993—, mem. continuing med. edn. com., 1992-96, vice-chmn. quality assurance com., 1993—, group leader freshman bioethics, 1992-95, med. student advisor, 1992—; presenter in field. Manuscript Peer reviewer Annals of Internal Medicine, 1993—; contbr. articles to profl. jours. Fellow Am. Heart Assn., Am. Coll. Cardiology, Am. Coll. Chest Physicians; mem. AMA, ACP, Am. Soc. for Echocardiography, Am. Fedn. for Clin. Rsch., Pa. Med. Soc., Soc. Nuclear Medicine, Am. Assn. for Nuclear Cardiology (founding mem.), Am. Soc. Nuclear Cardiology (founding mem.), Soc. Cardiovascular Magnetic Resonance (founding mem.), Philadelphia County Med. Soc. (ho. of dels. 1996—), Alpha Epsilon Delta, Alpha Omega Alpha. Office: Med Coll Pa 3300 Henry Ave Philadelphia PA 19129-1121

VANDE HEY, JAMES MICHAEL, corporate executive, former air force officer; b. Maribel, Wis., Mar. 15, 1916; s. William Henry and Anna (Zimmerman) VandeH.; m. Jean Margretta Schilleman, June 23, 1944; children: James Todd, Dale Michael, Dean Clark. Student, U. Wis., 1947-49; BA, U. Philippines, 1955; postgrad., Air War Coll., Maxwell AFB, Montgomery, Ala., 1956-57. Commd. 2d lt. USAAF, 1941; advanced through grades to brig. gen. USAF, 1967; fighter pilot PTO, 1941-45; including Hawaii, Dec. 7, 1941; duty in command and USAF level including duty in Europe (NATO) and Philippines, 1945-69; dep. chief of staff Hdqrs. USMACV, Saigon, Vietnam, 1969-71; assigned Hdqrs. Tactical Air Command, 1971—; mem. faculty Air War Coll., 1957-59, dep. for acads., dean of faculty, 1959-61; ret., 1971; pres. Vanson Inc., 1971—, Vande Hey Inc., 1976—. Decorated D.S.M., Legion of Merit with two oak leaf cluster, D.F.C. with two oak leaf cluster, Bronze Star, Air medal with 7 oak leaf clusters, decorations from Philippine, Vietnamese and Korean govts. Mem. USAF Hist. Found., Air Force Assn. Roman Catholic. Home: 3374 S El Dorado Austin TX 78734-5232

VAN DE KAMP, JOHN KALAR, lawyer; b. Pasadena, Calif., Feb. 7, 1936; s. Harry and Georgie (Kalar) Van de K.; m. Andrea Fisher, Mar. 11, 1978; 1 child, Diana. BA, Dartmouth Coll., 1956; JD, Stanford U., 1959. Bar: Calif. 1960. Asst. U.S. atty. L.A., 1960-66, U.S. atty., 1966-67; dep. dir. Exec. Office for U.S. Attys., Washington, 1967-68, dir., 1968-69; spl. asst. Pres.'s Commn. on Campus Unrest, 1970; fed. pub. defender L.A., 1971-75; dist. atty. Los Angeles County, 1975-83; atty. gen. State of Calif., 1983-91; with Dewey Ballantine, L.A., 1991-96, of counsel, 1996—; pres. Thoroughbred Owners, Calif., 1996—; bd. dirs. United Airlines. Mem. Calif. Dist. Attys. Assn. (pres. 1975-83), Nat. Dist. Attys. Assn. (v.p. 1975-83), Peace Officers Assn. L.A. County (past pres.), Nat. Assn. Attys. Gen. (exec. com. 1983-91), Conf. Western Attys. Gen. (pres. 1986). Office: Dewey Ballantine 333 S Hope St Ste 3000 Los Angeles CA 90071-3039

VANDE KROL, JERRY LEE, architect; b. Oskaloosa, Iowa, Oct. 5, 1949; s. Glen Vande Krol and Nola Fern (Monsma) Emmert; m. Constance Louise Wood, May 30, 1970; children: Sarah Lynn, Rachel Ann, Molly Jayne. BArch, Iowa State U., 1972. Registered architect, Iowa. Designer City of Akron, Ohio, 1972-76; architect Brooks Borg and Skiles, Des Moines, 1976-90; founder VOV Architecture and Design, P.C., Des Moines, 1990—. Recipient Merit Desigh award Ohio Chpt. Soc. Landscape Architects, 1977. Mem. AIA (Iowa chpt., Design award 1984, 90, regional chpt. Design award 1985, 91), Des Moines Architects Coun. Republican. Mem. Brethren Ch. Avocations: music, classical guitar, reading, golf. Office: Vov Architecture Design 108 3rd St Ste 200 Des Moines IA 50309-4758

VANDELL, DEBORAH LOWE, educational psychology educator; b. Bryan, Tex., June 5, 1949; d. Charles Ray and Janice (Durrett) Lowe; m. Kerry Dean Vandell, May 16, 1970; children: Colin Buckner, Ashley Elizabeth. AB, Rice U., 1971; EdM, Harvard U., 1972; PhD, Boston U., 1977. Tchr. Walpole (Mass.) Pub. Schs., 1972-73; rschr. Ralph Nader Congress Project, Washington, 1972; asst. prof. U. Tex., Dallas, 1976-81, assoc. prof., 1981-89; prof. ednl. psychology U. Wis., Madison, 1989—; vis. scholar MacArthur Rsch. Network, Cambridge, Mass., 1985-86, U. Calif., Berkeley, 1988-89; mem. steering com. NICHD Study of Early Child Care. Assoc. editor Child Devel., 1993-95; mem. editl. bd. Child Devel., 1980-93, Jour. Family Issues, 1983-89, Devel. Psychology, 1989-93; co-author books; contbr. articles to profl. jours. Bd. dirs. Infant Mental Health Assn., 1988-89; bd. dirs. Cmty. Coord. Child Care, Madison, Wis., chair, 1991-93; mem. Day Care Adv. Bd., State of Wis.; mem. altar guild and vestry St. Andrew's Ch., 1992-95. Named Outstanding Young Scholar, Found. for Child Devel., 1982. Mem. Am. Psychol. Assn. (exec. com. div. 7 1985-88), Southwestern Soc. Rsch. in Human Devel. (pres. 1988-90), Am. Psychol. Soc., Soc. for Rsch. in Child Devel., Phi Beta Kappa. Episcopalian. Office: U Wis Dept Ednl Psychology 1025 W Johnson St Madison WI 53706-1706

VANDELL, KERRY DEAN, real estate and urban economics educator; b. Biloxi, Miss., Jan. 8, 1947; s. Benedict Sandy and Eleanor Ruby (Lenhart) V.; m. Deborah Ann Lowe, May 16, 1970; children: Colin Buckner, Ashley Elizabeth. BA, MME, Rice U., 1970; M City Planning, Harvard U., 1973; PhD, MIT, 1977. Assoc. engr. Exxon Co., USA, Houston, 1970-71; asst. prof. So. Meth. U., Dallas, 1976-80, assoc. prof., 1980-86, prof., chmn. dept., 1986-89; prof. real estate and urban land econs., chm. dept. U. Wis., Madison, 1989-93, dir. Ctr. for Urban Land Econs. rsch., 1989—, Tiefenthaler chairholder, 1996; vis. assoc. prof. Harvard U., Cambridge, Mass., 1985-86; vis. prof. U. Calif., Berkeley, 1988-89; bd. dirs. Park Bank, Madison, U. Rsch. Pk.; chmn. bd. dirs. Domus Equity Corp. Mem. editl. bd. Jour. Real Estate Fin. and Econs., 1989—, Land Econs., 1989—, Jour. Property Rsch., 1989-94; contbr. numerous articles on mortgage default risk, neighborhood dynamics, econs. of architecture, and appraisal theory to profl. jours. Fellow Homer Hoyt Advanced Studies Inst. (faculty 1989—, bd. dirs.), Urban Land Inst.; mem. Am. Real Estate and Urban Econs. Assn. 92d v.p. 1989, 1st v.p. 1990, pres. 1991, co-editor jour. 1991-96). Episcopalian. Home: 3301 Topping Rd Madison WI 53705-1436 Office: U Wis Sch Bus 975 University Ave Madison WI 53706-1324

VANDEMARK, MICHELLE VOLIN, critical care, neuroscience nurse; b. Sioux Falls, S.D., Feb. 14, 1962; d. Verlynne V. and Suzanne (Cronin) Volin; m. Richard E. VanDemark, June 5, 1982; children: Andrew Porter, Hannah Elizabeth. BA in Biology, Lake Forest (Ill.) Coll., 1984; BSN, Northwestern U., Chgo., 1986; MS in Nursing, Loyola U., Chgo., 1990. RN, Ill., S.D.; cert. neurosci. nursing, CNRN, ACLS. Staff nurse neurosci. unit Evanston Hosp., Ill., 1986-90, staff nurse intensive care unit, 1990-93; neurosci. clin. nurse specialist Sioux Valley Hosp., Sioux Falls, S.D., 1995—. Mem. Am. Assn. Neurosci. Nurses (pres. Gt. Plains chpt. 1995-96), Sigma Theta Tau, Alpha Sigma Nu.

VANDEMARK, ROBERT GOODYEAR, retired retail company executive; b. Youngstown, Ohio, Sept. 1, 1921; s. Arthur Glenn and Lola (Goodyear) V.; m. Jean Chapman, Sept. 19, 1943; children: Ann (Mrs. William K. Butler), Peggy Lynn (Mrs. Michael Murray). B.Sc., Ohio U., 1943. Dept. mgr. F. & R. Lazarus, Columbus, Ohio, 1947-54; asst. controller Boston Store, Milw., 1954-57; v.p., treas. Cleland Simpson Co., Scranton, Pa., 1957-65; asst. to exec. v.p. Bergdorf Goodman, N.Y.C., 1965-68; treas. Garfinckel, Brooks Bros., Miller & Rhoads, Inc., Washington, 1968-69; v.p. Garfinckel, Brooks Bros., Miller & Rhoads, Inc., 1969-73, exec. v.p., 1973-79, vice chmn., 1979-83; chmn., chief exec. officer Garfinckel's, 1983-87. Head dept. and specialty stores div. United Fund, Scranton, Pa., 1960-65; bd. dirs. Goodwill Industries, 1964-65; treas. Washington Nat. Cathedral. Served to 1st lt. AUS, 1943-46; col. Res. Decorated Bronze Star with V and cluster, Mil. Order of Wilheim. Mem. Fin. Execs. Inst., Nat. Retail Mchts. Assn. (sec., treas., 1st v.p., pres., dir., mem. exec. com. fin. exec. divsn.), Delta Tau Delta, City Club Washington, Washington Golf and Country Club, Army-Navy Club, Burning Tree Golf Club, Laurel Oak Country Club (Fla.), Masons (32d degree), Kiwanis (Fla.). Home: 670 Potomac River Rd Mc Lean VA 22102

VAN DEMARK, RUTH ELAINE, lawyer; b. Santa Fe, N. Mex., May 16, 1944; d. Robert Eugene and Bertha Marie (Thompson) Van D.; m. Leland Wilkinson, June 23, 1967; children: Anne Marie, Caroline Cook. AB, Vassar Coll., 1966; MTS, Harvard U., 1969; JD with honors, U. Conn., 1976. Bar: Conn. 1976, U.S. Dist. Ct. Conn. 1976, Ill. 1977, U.S. Dist. Ct. (no. dist.) Ill. 1977, U.S. Supreme Ct. 1983, U.S. Ct. Appeals (7th cir.) 1984. Instr. legal research and writing Loyola U. Sch. Law, Chgo., 1976-79; assoc. Wildman, Harrold, Allen & Dixon, Chgo., 1977-84, ptnr., 1985-94; prin. Law Offices of Ruth E. Van Demark, Chgo., 1995—; bd. dirs., sec. Systat, Inc., Evanston, Ill., 1984-94; mem. Ill. Supreme Ct. Rules com., 1996—, dist. ct. fund adv. com. U.S. Dist. Ct. (no. dist.) Ill., 1997—. Assoc. editor Conn. Law Rev., 1975-76. Mem. adv. bd. Horizon Hospice, Chgo., 1978—; del.-at-large White House Conf. on Families, Los Angeles, 1980; mem. adv. bd. YWCA Battered Women's Shelter, Evanston, Ill., 1982-86; mem. alumni coun. Harvard Divinity Sch., 1988-91; vol. atty. Pro Bono Advocates, Chgo., 1982-92, bd. dirs. 1993—, chair devel. com., 1993; bd. dirs. Friends of Pro Bono Advocates Orgn., 1987-89, New Voice Prodns., 1984-86, Byrne Piven Theater Workshop, 1987-90; founder, bd. dirs. Friends of Battered Women and their Children, 1986-87; chair 175th Reunion Fund Harvard U. Div. Sch., 1992. Mem. ABA, Ill. Bar Assn., Conn. Bar Assn., Chgo. Bar Assn., Appellate Lawyers Assn. Ill. (bd. dirs. 1985-87, treas. 1989-90, sec. 1990-91, v.p. 1991-92, pres. 1992-93), Women's Bar Assn. Ill., Jr. League Evanston (chair State Pub. Affairs Com. 1987-88, Vol. of Yr. 1983-84). Clubs: Chgo. Vassar (pres. 1979-81), Cosmopolitan (N.Y.C.). Home: 1127 Asbury Ave Evanston IL 60202-1136 Office: Law Offices of Ruth E VanDemark 225 W Washington St Ste 2200 Chicago IL 60606-3418

VAN DEN AKKER, JOHANNES ARCHIBALD, physicist; b. L.A., Dec. 5, 1904; s. John and Mabel (Freebairn) Van den A.; m. Adelaide H. Carrier, June 20, 1930 (dec. Jan. 1955); 1 child, Valerie; m. Carmen L. Haberman, June 9, 1958 (dec. Mar. 1989); m. Margaret Koller, Jan. 20, 1990. BS in Physics/Engring., Calif. Inst. Tech., 1926, PhD in Physics, 1931. Instr. Washington U., St. Louis, 1930-34; prof. physics Inst. Paper Chemistry, Appleton, Wis., 1935-70; cons. Am. Can Co., Neenah, Wis., 1971-82, James River Corp., Neenah, 1982-85, Appleton, Wis., 1985—; lectr. short courses TAPPI, Atlanta. Co-author 10 books; contbr. Encyclopedia of Physics, 1st and 2d edit. and articles to physics and tech. jours. Named to Paper Industry Hall of Fame, 1995; sr. Fulbright scholar U. Manchester, Eng., 1961-62. Fellow AAAS, TAPPI (gold medal 1968), Am. Phys. Soc.; mem. Am. Inst. Physics, Optical Soc. Am., Am. Assn. Physics Tchrs., Sigma Xi, Tau Beta Pi, Phi Gamma Delta. Achievements include research on spatial distribution of x-ray photo-electrons, ultraviolet spectrophotometers, analog computers, methods for measuring centroid wavelengths of broad band/filter spectrophotometers, methods of measuring absolute reflectance of diffuse surfaces, designs of special instrumentation for study of optical, physical and mechanical properties of paper, and development of theories for these properties. Home: 1101 E Glendale Ave Appleton WI 54911-3144

VANDENBERG, EDWIN JAMES, chemist, educator; b. Hawthorne, N.J., Sept. 13, 1918; s. Albert J. and Alida C. (Westerhoff) V.; m. Mildred Elizabeth Wright, Sept. 9, 1950; children: David James, Jean Elizabeth. M.E. with distinction, Stevens Inst. Tech., 1939, Dr.Engring. (hon.), 1965. Rsch. chemist Hercules Inc. Rsch. Ctr., Wilmington, Del., 1939-44, asst. shift supr. Sunflower Ordnance Works, Kans., 1944-45, rsch. chemist Research Ctr., Wilmington, 1945-57, sr. research chemist, 1958-64, rsch.assoc., 1965-77, sr. rsch. assoc., 1978-82; adj. prof. chemistry Ariz. State U., Tempe, 1983-91, rsch. prof. chemistry, 1992—. Author: Polyethers, 1975; Coordination Polymerization, 1983; Contemporary Topics in Polymer Science V, 1984, Catalysis in Polymer Synthesis, 1992. Patentee in field. Mem. adv. bd. Jour. Polymer Sci., 1967-93, Macromolecules, 1979-81; chmn. Gordon Rsch. Conf. on Polymers, 1978. Recipient Indsl. Rsch. 100 award, 1965, Internat. award Soc. Plastics Engrs., 1994. Mem. Am. Chem. Soc. (councillor Del. sect. 1974-81, chmn. 1976, chmn. div. polychemistry 1979, coord. indsl. sponsors 1982—, Del. sect. award 1965, 79, Polymer Chemistry award 1981, Exceptional Svc. award 1983, 95, Applied Polymer Sci. award 1991, Charles Goodyear medal, 1991, Herman F. Mark award 1992). Home: 16223 E Inca Ave Fountain Hls AZ 85268-4518 Office: Ariz State U Dept Chemistry and Biochemistry Tempe AZ 85287-1604

VANDENBERG, JOHN DONALD, entomologist; b. Benton Harbor, Mich., Jan. 24, 1954; s. Robert Landis and Madelaine Louise (Westendorf) V.; m. Alice C. L. Churchill, Oct. 8, 1983. B.S. with Honors, U. Mich., 1975; M.S., U. Maine, 1977; Ph.D., Oreg. State U., 1982. Grad. rsch. asst. U. Maine, Orono, 1975-77; grad. teaching asst. Oreg. State U., Corvallis, 1977-78, grad. rsch. asst., 1978-82; postdoctoral assoc. Boyce Thompson Inst., Ithaca, N.Y., 1982-83; rsch. entomologist Agrl. Rsch. Svc., U.S. Dept. Agr., Beltsville, Md., 1983-87, rsch. leader Agrl. Rsch. Svc., Logan, Utah, 1987-93; lead scientist Agrl. Rsch. Svc., Ithaca, N.Y., 1993—; acting asst. dir. Midwest area Agrl. Rsch Svc., Peoria, Ill., 1991; equal employment opportunity counsellor, 1985-87. Contbr. articles to profl. jours. Mem. AAAS, Soc. for Invertebrate Pathology (chair elect microbial control divsn. 1995—, sec./treas. 1993-95), Entomol. Soc. Am., Am. Soc. for Microbiology, Sigma Xi. Avocations: singing, guitar, softball, gardening. Office: USDA-ARS Plant Protection US Plant Soil & Nutrition Lab Tower Rd Ithaca NY 14853

VANDENBERG, PETER RAY, magazine publisher; b. Geneva, Ill., Sept. 8, 1939; s. Don George and Isabel (Frank) V.; m. Kathryn Stock, June 1973 (div. Apr. 1977). BBA, Miami U., 1962. Creative adminstr. E.F. McDonald Incentive Co., Dayton, Ohio, 1966-73; mfrs.' rep. Denver, 1974-75; mgr. Homestake Condominiums, Vail, Colo., 1975-76; desk clk. Vail Run Resort, 1976-77; sales rep. Colo. West Advt., Vail, 1977-79, pres., 1980-83; pres. Colo. West Publ., Vail, 1983—. With U.S. Army, 1963-66. Mem. Sigma Chi. Avocations: sports, music, reading.

VAN DEN BERGH, SIDNEY, astronomer; b. Wassenaar, Netherlands, May 20, 1929; emigrated to U.S., 1948; s. Sidney J. and Mieke (van den Berg) vandenB.; m. Paulette Brown; children by previous marriage: Peter, Mieke, Sabine. Student, Leiden (The Netherlands) U., 1947-48; A.B., Princeton U., 1950; M.Sc., Ohio State U., 1952; Dr. rer. nat., Goettingen U., 1956, DSc (honoris causa), 1995. Asst. prof. Perkins Obs., Ohio State U., Columbus, 1956-58; research assoc. Mt. Wilson Obs., Palomar Obs., Pasadena, Calif., 1968-69; prof. astronomy David Dunlap Obs., U. Toronto, Ont., Can., 1958-77; dir. Dominion Astrophys. Obs., Victoria, B.C., 1977-86; prin. rsch. officer NRC Can., 1977—; adj. prof. U. Victoria, 1977—. Decorated officer Order of Can. Fellow Royal Soc. London, Royal Soc. Can.; mem. Am., Royal Astron. Soc. (assoc.), Canadian Astronomy Soc. (sr. v.p. 1988-90, pres. 1990-92). Home: 418 Lands End Rd, Sidney, BC Canada V8L 5L9

VAN DEN BERGHE, PIERRE LOUIS, sociologist, anthropologist; b. Lubumbashi, Zaire, Jan. 30, 1933; s. Louis and Denise (Caullery) van den B.; m. Irmgard C. Niehuis, Jan. 21, 1956; children—Eric, Oliver, Marc. B.A., Stanford U., 1952, M.A., 1953; Ph.D., Harvard U., 1960. Asst. prof. sociology Wesleyan U., Middletown, Conn., 1962-63; asso. prof. sociology SUNY, Buffalo, 1963-65; prof. sociology and anthropology U. Wash., Seattle, 1965—; vis. prof. U. Natal, South Africa, 1960-61, Sorbonne, Paris, 1962, U. Nairobi, Kenya, 1967-68, U. Ibadan, Nigeria, 1968-69, U. Haifa, Israel, 1976, U. New South Wales, Australia, 1982, U. Strasbourg, France, 1985, U. Tuebingen, Fed. Republic Germany, 1986, Tel Aviv U., 1988, U. Cape Town, South Africa, 1989; fellow Advanced Study in Behavioral Scis., Stanford, Calif., 1984-85. Author: 22 books including South Africa, A Study in Conflict, 1965, Race and Racism, 1967, Academic Gamesmanship, 1970, Man in Society, 1978, Human Family Systems, 1979, The Ethnic Phenomenon, 1981, Stranger in Their Midst, 1989, State Violence and Ethnicity, 1990, The Quest for the Other, 1994. Served with M.C. U.S. Army, 1954-56. Mem. Am. Sociol. Assn., Am. Anthrop. Assn., Sociol. Research Assn., Human Behavior and Evolution Soc. Home: 2006 19th Ave E Seattle WA 98112-2902 Office: U Wash Dept Sociology DK-40 Seattle WA 98195

VANDENBOS, GARY ROGER, psychologist, publisher; b. Grand Rapids, Mich., Dec. 16, 1943; s. Paul Martin and Irene (Dorenbos) V.; m. Jane Annunziata, Dec. 16, 1983; 1 child, Bret. BS, Mich. State U., 1967, MA, 1969; PhD, U. Detroit, 1973. Dir. Howell (Mich.) Area Community Mental Health Ctr., 1973-77; dir. nat. policy studies Am. Psychol. Assn., Washington, 1977-82, exec. dir. for publs., 1984—; prof. U. Bergen, Norway, 1982-84; project cons. Rand Corp., Santa Monica, Calif., 1984-89; bd. dirs. Am. Biodyne Found., San Francisco; newspaper pub. APA Monitor, 1985—. Author: Psychotherapy with Schizophrenic, 1981; editor Psychology and National Health Insurance, 1979; assoc. editor Am. Psychologist Jour. Office: Am Psychol Assn 750 1st St NE Washington DC 20002-4241

VANDEN BOUT, PAUL ADRIAN, astronomer, physicist, educator; b. Grand Rapids, Mich., June 16, 1939; s. Adrian and Cornelia (Peterson) Vanden B.; m. Rachel Ann Eggebeen, Sept. 1, 1961; children—Thomas Adrian, David Anton. A.B., Calvin Coll., 1961; Ph.D., U. Calif.-Berkeley, 1966. Postdoctoral fellow U. Calif., Berkeley, 1966-67; postdoctoral fellow Columbia U., N.Y.C., 1967-68; instr. Columbia U., 1968-69, asst. prof., 1969-70; asst. prof. U. Tex., Austin, 1970-74; assoc. prof. U. Tex., 1974-79, prof., 1979-84; dir. Nat. Radio Astronomy Obs., Charlottesville, Va., 1985—; cons. NSF, NASA. Fellow Fulbright Found., Heidelberg, Fed. Republic Germany, 1961-62, Leiden, Netherlands, 1977. Fellow AAAS, Am. Phys. Soc.; mem. Am. Astron. Soc., Internat. Astron. Union, Internat. Radio Sci. Union. Office: Nat Radio Astronomy Obs 520 Edgemont Rd Charlottesville VA 22903-2454

VANDENBROUCKE, RUSSELL JAMES, theatre director; b. Chgo., Aug. 16, 1948; s. Arthur C. Sr. and Ardelle (Barker) V.; m. Mary Allison Dilg, Sept. 7, 1974; children: Aynsley Louise, Justin Arthur. BA, U. Ill., 1970; MA, U. Warwick, Coventry, Eng., 1975; MFA in Drama, Yale U., 1977, DFA in Drama, 1978. Asst. literary mgr. Yale Repertory Theatre, New Haven, 1977-78; lit. mgr., dramaturg Mark Taper Forum, Los Angeles, 1978-85; assoc. producing dir. Repertory Theatre St. Louis, 1985-87; artistic dir. Northlight Theatre, Evanston, Ill., 1987—; vis. prof. Yale U., 1978, La. State U., 1981, U. Calif.-San Diego, 1983, Middlebury Coll., 1985, Washington U., 1986; adj. assoc. prof. Northwestern U., 1987—. Author: Truths the Hand Can Tough: The Theatre of Athol Fugard, 1985; adapted play Eleanor: In Her Own Words (for TV), 1985 (Emmy award 1986) (dir. for stage 1990), Los Alamos Revisted (for stage and radio), 1984, 87, Holiday Memories (from Truman Capote), 1991, Atomic Bombers, 1997; adapted, stage dir. Feiffer's America, 1988, Eleanor: In Her Own Words, 1990; adapted An Enemy of the People, 1991; stage dir. Lucky Lindy, Love Letters on Blue Paper, 84 Charing Cross Road, Three Women Talking (also radio),

Smoke on the Mountain, The White Rose, Betrayal, My Other Heart, Later Life, Hedda Gabler, Bubbe Meises, Valley Song, Fires in the Mirror; contbr. articles to mags. and newspapers. Recipient L.A. Drama Critics Cir. award, 1984, Spl. Actors Equity Assn. award, 1990; Fulbright sr. scholar, Australia, 1996. Avocation: basketball. Office: Northlight Theatre 9501 Skokie Blvd Skokie IL 60076

VAN DEN HENDE, FRED J(OSEPH), human resources executive; b. Chgo., Sept. 28, 1953; s. Maurice Everett and Alice Helen (Davey) Van Den H.; m. Sharon Joyce Kucharski, Oct. 4, 1975; children: John Michael, Karen Michelle. BA, DePaul U., 1975; cert. of grad., U. Wash., 1981; postgrad., Nat. Louis U. Cert. sr. profl. human resources. Asst. v.p. human resources Land of Lincoln Savs. and Loan, Berwyn, Ill., 1977-84; v.p. human resources Uptown Fed. Bank FSB, Niles, Ill., 1984-88; dir. human resources Archdiocese of Chgo., 1988—; mem. Savs. Assn. Pers. Adminstrn., Berwyn, 1977-84; part-time instr. Inst. Fin. Edn., Chgo., 1984—, Moraine Valley C.C., Palos Hills, Ill., 1984—. Sch. bd. treas. St. Rene Sch., Chgo., 1981; sch. bd. mem. St. Daniel the Prophet Sch., Chgo., 1986-88, 93-95, sch. bd. chmn., 1988-89; boy scout leader St. Daniel Parish, Chgo., 1987-94. Recipient Oustanding Achievement in the Field of Athletics award St. Rita H.S. Alumni Assn., Chgo., 1991; Athletic scholar DePaul U., Chgo., 1971-75. Mem. Nat. Assn. Ch. Pers. Adminstrs., Soc. for Human Resource Mgmt., Ill. State C. of C. (human resources com. 1979—), Inst. Internat. Human Resources. Roman Catholic. Avocations: camping, fishing, coaching youth sports teams. Home: 5130 S Mulligan Ave Chicago IL 60638-1316 Office: Archdiocese of Chgo 155 E Superior St Chicago IL 60611-2911

VANDEN HEUVEL, KATRINA, magazine editor; b. N.Y.C., Oct. 7, 1959; d. William Jacobus and Jean Babette (Stein) Vanden H.; m. Stephen F. Cohen, Dec. 4, 1988; 1 child, Nicola Anna. BA summa cum laude in Politics, Princeton U., 1982. Prodn. assoc. ABC Closeup Documentaries, 1982-83; asst. editor The Nation, N.Y.C., 1984-89, editor-at-large, 1989-93, acting editor-in-chief, 1994-95, editor-in-chief, 1995—; vis. journalist Moscow News, 1989; Moscow coord. Conf. Investigative Journalism After the Cold War, 1992; co-founder, co-editor Vyi i Myi, 1990—. Editor: The Nation, 1865-1990: Selections from the Independent Magazine of Politics and Culture, 1990; co-editor: Voices of Glasnost: Interviews with Gorbachev's Reformers, 1989; contbr. articles to newspapers. Recipient Maggie award Planned Parenthood Fedn. Am., 1994. Mem. Correctional Assn. N.Y. (dir.), Coun. Fgn. Rels., Inst. Policy Studies (trustee), Network of East-West Women (bd. advisors), Franklin and Eleanor Roosevelt Inst. (trustee), Moscow Ctr. for Gender Studies (mem. adv. com.), MSNBC (contbr.). Office: The Nation 72 5th Ave New York NY 10011-8004*

VAN-DEN-NOORT, STANLEY, physician, educator; b. Lynn, Mass., Sept. 8, 1930; s. Judokus and Hazel G. (Van Blarcom) van den N.; m. June Le Clere, Apr. 17, 1954; children: Susanne, Eric, Peter, Katherine, Elizabeth. A.B., Dartmouth, 1951; M.D., Harvard, 1954. Intern then resident Boston City Hosp., 1954-56, resident neurology, 1958-60; research fellow neurochemistry Harvard, 1960-62; instr. medicine Case Western Res. U., Cleve., 1962-66; asst. prof. Case Western Res. U., 1966-69, assoc. prof., 1969-70; prof. neurology U. Calif., Irvine, 1970—; chair dept. neurology U. Calif., 1970-72, 86—, assoc. dean Coll. Medicine, 1972-73, dean, 1973-85; mem. cons. staff U. Calif., Irvine Med. Center; mem. Long Beach (Calif.) Meml. Hosp., Long Beach VA Hosp.; mem. com. of revision U.S. Pharmacopoeial Conv., 1990-95. Mem. med. adv. bds., Nat. Multiple Sclerosis Soc./Myasthenia Gravis, 1971—, Orange County chpt. Nat. Multiple Sclerosis Soc., 1971—, Orange County Health Planning Coun., 1971-85, Nat. Com. Rsch. in Neurol. Disease, 1982-87. Lt. M.C. USNR, 1956-58. Fellow ACP, Am. Acad. Neurol.; mem. AAUP, AMA, Am. Neurol. Assn., Orange County Med. assn., Calif. Med. Assn., Am. Heart Assn. Home: 17592 Orange Tree Ln Tustin CA 92780-2353 Office: U Calif Dept Neurology 100 Irvine Hall Irvine CA 92697-4275

VANDER AARDE, STANLEY BERNARD, retired otolaryngologist; b. Orange City, Iowa, Sept. 26, 1931; s. Bernard John and Christina (Luchtenberg) Vander A.; m. Agnes Darlene De Beer, June 19, 1956; children: Paul, David, Debra, Mary. BA, Hope Coll., 1953; MD, Northwestern U., 1957. Diplomate Am. Bd. Otolaryngology. Intern Cook County Hosp., Chgo., 1957-59; resident in otolaryngology Northwestern U. Hosp., Chgo., 1966-70; mem. staff Mary Lott Lyles Hosp., Madanapalle, India, 1961-66, 71-87; mem. staff Affiliated Med. Clinic, Willmar, Minn., 1987-95, ret., 1995. Served to capt., USAF, 1959-60. Fellow ACS, Am. Bd. Otolaryngology, Am. Acad. Otolaryngology. Republican. Mem. Reformed Church in America. Home: 708 2nd St SE Apt 112 Orange City IA 51041-2165 Office: Affiliated Med Clinic 101 Willmar Ave SW Willmar MN 56201-3556

VANDERBEKE, PATRICIA K., architect; b. Detroit, Apr. 3, 1963; d. B. H. and Dolores I. VanderBeke. BS in Architecture, U. Mich., 1985, MArch, 1987. Registered architect, Ill. Archtl. intern Hobbs & Black, Assocs., Ann Arbor, Mich., 1984-86, Fry Assocs., Ann Arbor, 1988; architect Decker & Kemp Architecture/Urban Design, Chgo., 1989-92; prin., founder P. K. VanderBeke, Architect, Chgo., 1992—. Contbr. photographs and articles to Inland Architect mag.; contbr. photographs to AIA calendar. Chair recycling com. Lake Point Tower Condo. Assn., Chgo., 1990T, chair. ops. com., 1993. George S. Booth travelling fellow, 1992. Mem. AIA (participant 1st ann. leadership inst. 1997, 1st place nat. photog. contest award 1992, hon. mention 1994), Chgo. Archtl. Club. Office: 505 N Lake Shore Dr Ste 808 Chicago IL 60611-3413

VANDERBILT, ARTHUR T., II, lawyer; b. Summit, N.J., Feb. 20, 1950; s. William Runyon and Jean (White) V. BA, Wesleyan U., Middletown, Conn., 1972; JD, U. Va., 1975. Bar: N.J. 1975, U.S. Dist. Ct. N.J. 1975, U.S. Supreme Ct. 1978. Jud. clk. to presiding justice N.J. Superior Ct., 1975-76, dep. atty. gen., 1976-78, asst. counsel to gov., 1978-79; ptnr. Carella, Byrne, Bain & Gilfillan, Roseland, N.J., 1979—; chmn. Supreme Ct. Ethics Com.; mem. Supreme Ct. Adv. Com. Profl. Ethics. Author: Changing Law 1976, Jersey Justice, 1978, Law School, 1981, Treasure Wreck, 1986, Fortune's Children, 1989 (Book of the Month Club, Readers Digest and fgn. edits.), New Jersey's Judicial Revolution, 1997. Mem. ABA (Scribes award 1976), N.J. Bar Assn., Am. Judicature Soc., Nat. Assn. Bond Lawyers, The Authors Guild, Inc., Nat. Writers Union. Republican. Presbyterian. Avocation: writing. Office: Carella Byrne Bain & Gilfillan 6 Becker Farm Rd Roseland NJ 07068-1735

VANDERBILT, HUGH BEDFORD, SR., mineral and chemical company executive; b. N.Y.C., Apr. 23, 1921; s. Robert Thurlow and Mildred (Bedford) V.; m. Claire Frances McKiernan, Apr. 27, 1946; children: Laura V. Ernst, Linda V. Allen, Hugh B. Jr. Student, Trinity Coll., Hartford, Conn., 1940-42. With News Syndicate Corp., N.Y.C., 1946-54; chmn. bd. R.T. Vanderbilt Co., Inc., Norwalk, Conn., 1954—. Hon. trustee Greenwich (Conn.) Hist. Soc., 1957—; trustee hist. Deerfield (Mass.) Inc., 1976-93. 1st lt. U.S. Army, 1942-46. Mem. Chem. Mfrs. Assn. (bd. dirs. 1975-79), Blind Brook Club, Greenwich Country Club, Lyford Country Club, Everglades Club, Round Hill Club. Republican. Avocations: golf, skiing. Office: R T Vanderbilt Co Inc 30 Winfield St Norwalk CT 06855-1329

VANDERBILT, KERMIT, English language educator; b. Decorah, Iowa, Sept. 1, 1925; s. Lester and Ella (Qualley) V.; m. Vivian Osmundson, Nov. 15, 1947; 1 dau., Karen Paige. B.A., Luther Coll., Decorah, 1947, Litt. D. (hon.), 1977; M.A., U. Minn., 1949, Ph.D., 1956. Instr. English U. Minn., 1954-57; instr. U. Wash., 1958-60, asst. prof. English, 1960-62; asst. prof. San Diego State U., 1962-65, assoc. prof., 1965-68, prof., 1968-90, prof. emeritus, 1990—; vis. prof. Am. lit. U. B.C., Can., Vancouver, summer 1963; vis. prof. U. Oreg., summer 1968. Author: Charles Eliot Norton: Apostle of Culture in a Democracy, 1959, The Achievement of William Dean Howells: A Reinterpretation, 1968, American Literature and the Academy: The Roots, Growth and Maturity of a Profession, 1986 (Choice award for outstanding acad. books), Theodore Roethke in A Literary History of the American West, 1987; editor: (with others) American Social Thought, 1972, April Hopes (W.D. Howells), 1975, The Rise of Silas Lapham, 1983, spl. issue Am. Literary Realism, winter 1989, La Litterature Americaine, 1991, 2nd edit., 1994; mem. edit. bd. U. Wash. Press, 1960-62, Twentieth Century Lit., 1969—; contbr. numerous articles to profl. jours. Served with USNR, 1943-46. Outstanding Prof. San Diego State U., 1976; Guggenheim fellow, 1978-79; Huntington Library fellow, 1980; Am. Philos. Soc. grantee, 1964, Am. Council Learned Socs. grantee, 1972, Nat. Endowment for Humanities grantee, 1986. Mem. Am. Studies Assn. (exec. council 1968-69), So. Calif. Am. Studies Assn. (pres. 1968-69), Philol. Assn. Pacific Coast (chmn. sect. Am. lit. 1968), MLA, Internat. Mark Twain Soc. (hon.), United Profs. of Calif. (Disting. prof. 1978). Home: 6937 Coleshill Dr San Diego CA 92119-1920

VANDERBILT, OLIVER DEGRAY, financier; b. N.Y.C., Oct. 25, 1914; s. Oliver Degray Jr. and Madelon (Weir) V.; m. Frances Philips, Nov. 11, 1939; children: Oliver Degray IV, Madelon V. Peck. AB, Princeton U., 1937. With Tenn. Coal Iron & R.R. Co., Birmingham, Ala., 1939-40; v.p. Weir Kilby Corp., Cin., 1940-49; exec. v.p. Taylor Wharton Iron & Steel Co., Cin., 1949; pres. Taylor Wharton Iron & Steel Co., 1950-54; v.p. Harrisburg Steel Corp., 1954; pres. Twisco Corp., 1954-55; v.p., dir. Baldwin-Lima-Hamilton Corp., 1955-56; exec. v.p., dir. Blair & Co. Inc., Phila., 1957-62; chmn. Blair & Co. Inc., 1963-70; founder, pres. Vanderbilt Corp., Phila., 1963-68, Capitol Mgmt. Corp., 1968—, Innovest Group Inc., 1970—; pres., chief exec. officer Ecolaire Inc., 1971-74; founder, pres. Dorsey Corp., 1959, Standard Computers Inc., 1965, Systems Capital Corp., 1967, Marina City Corp., 1968; founder, chmn. bd. Tierra Corp., San Francisco, 1977—, Vanderbilt Energy Corp., N.Y.C., 1978—; founder, chmn. Seaborad Savs. Bank, Stuart, Fla., 1983—. Maj. AUS, 1942-45, ETO, NATOUSA. Decorated Croix de Guerre (France); Bronze Star (U.S.). Mem. Commonwealth Club, Jupiter Island Club, Ivy Club, Nassau Club, Seminole Club, Maidstone Club. Republican. Episcopalian. Avocation: golf. Home: 111 Gomez Rd Hobe Sound FL 33455-2427

VANDER CLUTE, NORMAN ROLAND, lawyer; b. N.Y.C., Nov. 14, 1932; s. Carl Frederick and Agnes (Hansen) Vander C.; m. Sandra Sheffey, Dec. 30, 1978; children: William Bowditch, Edward Carl, Jeffrey. BA, Amherst Coll., 1954; LLB, Harvard U., 1957. Bar: N.Y. 1958, D.C. 1967. Law clk. 1st Cir. Ct. Appeals, Boston, 1957-58; atty. Standard Vacuum Oil Co., Hartsdale, N.Y., 1958-60; sr. atty. Am. Airlines, Inc., N.Y.C., 1960-63; asst. gen. counsel Agy. for Internat. Devel., Washington, 1963-65, office dir., 1965-67; ptnr. Surrey & Morse, Washington, 1967-85, Jones, Day, Reavis & Pogue, Washington, 1986-93, Winston & Strawn, 1993—. Mem. ABA. Presbyterian. Avocations: boating. Office: Winston & Strawn 1400 L St NW Washington DC 20005-3509

VANDERET, ROBERT CHARLES, lawyer; b. Bklyn., Apr. 12, 1947; s. James Gustav and Bernadette Cecelia (Heaney) V.; m. Sharon Kay Brewster, Oct 3, 1970; children: Erin Anne Brewster, Aidan McKenzie Brewster. AB, UCLA, 1969; JD, Stanford U., 1973. Bar: Calif. 1973, U.S. Dist. Ct. (cen. and so. dists.) Calif. 1974, U.S. Ct. Appeals (9th cir.) 1976, N.Y. 1978, U.S. Supreme Ct. 1978, U.S. Dist. Ct. (no. dist.) Calif. 1980, U.S. Dist. Ct. (ea. dist.) Calif. 1981. Extern law clk. to Justice Tobriner Calif. Supreme Ct., 1972-73; assoc. O'Melveny & Myers, Los Angeles, 1973-80, ptnr., 1980—; transition aide Chief Justice Rose Bird, Calif. Supreme Ct., 1976. Del. Dem. Nat. Conv., 1968; bd. dirs. Legal Aid Found. L.A., 1978-90, Constn. Rights Found., 1990, Inner City Law Ctr., 1994—; trustee Lawyers Commn. for Civil Rights Under Law, 1993—; vice chancellor Episcopal Diocese of L.A. Mem. ABA (chair media law and defamation torts com. 1991-92), Calif. State Bar (chair, com. on adminstrn. of justice 1996-97), L.A. Bar Assn. (pro bono coun. chair 1993-95). Democrat. Home: 834 Greentree Rd Pacific Palisades CA 90272-3911 Office: O'Melveny & Myers 400 S Hope St Los Angeles CA 90071-2801 *Notable cases include: Galloway vs. CBS, 14 Media L. Rep. 1161, 1987, in which he represented Dan Rather and CBS in celebrated libel case; Martha Raye vs. David Letterman, 14 Media L. Rep. 2047, 1987, in which he represented David Letterman and NBC; Robert Mahev vs. CBS, 201 Calif. App. 3d 662, 1988, in which he represented CBS, Playboy and other pubs.; Crane vs. The Ariz. Republic, 729 F. Supp. 698 Ct. Dist. Calif., 1989, in which he represented The Ariz. Republic; Kruse vs. Bank of Am., 202 Calif. App. 3d 38, 1988, in which he represented Bank of Am. in successful appeal of leading lender liability case; CHH vs. The Limited, 587 F. Supp. 246, Ct. Dist. Calif., 1984, in which he represented Carter Hawley Hale Stores, Inc. in major takeover battle.*

VANDERGRIFF, CHRISTINA RAI, controller; b. Prineville, Oreg., Nov. 13, 1964; d. Marvin Ronald and Virginia Lucille (Warren) Craig; m. Kenneth Wayne Vandergriff, Aug. 23, 1987. Cert. legal adminstrn. with honors, Trend Coll., Eugene, Oreg., 1989; BA in Acctg., Morrison Coll., Reno, Nev., 1996; Assoc. Bus. Adminstrn. in Bus. Mgmt., B of Bus. Adminstr. in Acctg. Shipper, asst. loan processor Centennial Mortgage Co., Inc., Eugene, 1989-90; asst. acct. Kimwood Corp., Cottage Grove, Oreg., 1990-91; sec., asst. Bill Vollendorff Appraisal, Walla Walla, Wash., 1991-92; inventory supr., purchaser Sierra Office Concepts/Nev. Copy Systems, Reno, 1992-95, mem. employee adv. com., 1993-94; with Tahoe Office Sys. Nev. Copy Sys., Tahoe City, Calif., 1995-96; asst. adminstrn., asst. contr. Interstate Safety and Supply, Inc., Sparks, Nev., 1996-97; asst. controller Water Safety Corp., Sparks, 1997—. Active Adopt-A-Sch. Program, Reno, 1992;-co-sponsor Nev. Women's Fund, Reno, 1993. Democrat. Baptist. Avocations: reading, baking, fishing, nature hikes. Office: Water Safety Corp 320 Coney Island Dr Sparks NV 89431-6315

VANDERGRIFF, JERRY DODSON, retired computer store executive; b. Ft. Leonard Wood, Mo., Nov. 6, 1943; s. Oliver Wyatt Vandergriff and Mary Ella (Perkins) Myers; m. Donna Jean Niehof, Aug. 14, 1976 (div. Nov. 1987); children: Robert Lee II, William Oliver; m. Lisa Ann Marrett, Aug. 10, 1996. BS in Bus., Emporia State U., 1974. Customer svc. mgr. Pictures, Inc., Anchorage, 1975-83, v.p., gen. mgr., 1983-87; gen. mgr. Pictures-The Computer Store, Anchorage, 1987-96; ret., 1996. Bd. dirs. Community Schs. Coun., Anchorage, 1986-87; mem. Gov.'s Coun. on Edn., 1989-90; bd. dirs. Romig Jr. High Sch., 1989-90, pres. PTSA, 1990-92; mem. exec. bd. Alaska's Youth Ready for Work, 1989-92. Mem. VFW. Republican. Avocations: movies, reading, pool, fishing, scuba diving. Home: 3831 Balchen Dr Anchorage AK 99517-2446

VANDERHEYDEN, MIRNA-MAR, resort management and services executive; b. Freeport, Ill., Oct. 8, 1932; d. Orville Ray and Frances Elmira (Miller) Van Brocklin; m. Roger Eugene Vanderheyden, Dec. 23, 1950 (div. 1983); children: Romayne Lee, Adana Dawn, Grayling Dwayne, Willow B., Tiffany LaMarr. Cert., Brown's Bus. Coll., Freeport, Ill., 1949; BA, Milliken U., 1953. Paralegal various locations, 1953-93; pres. Carlin Bay Corp., Coeur d'Alene, Idaho, 1981—. Lobbyist PTA, Springfield, Ill., 1972. Avocations: painting, water sports, reading, gardening, skiing. Home and Office: 609 W Apple Dr Delta CO 81416-3062

VANDERHOEF, LARRY NEIL, academic administrator; b. Perham, Minn., Mar. 20, 1941; s. Wilmar James and Ida Lucille (Wothe) V.; m. Rosalie Suzanne Slifka, Aug. 31, 1963; children: Susan Marie, Jonathan Lee. B.S., U. Wis., Milw., 1964, M.S., 1965; Ph.D., Purdue U., 1969. Postdoctorate U. Wis., Madison, 1969-70; research assoc. U. Wis., summers 1970-72; asst. prof. biology U. Ill., Urbana, 1970-74; assoc. prof. U. Ill., 1974-77, prof., 1977—, head dept. plant biology, 1977-80; provost Agrl. and Life Scis., U. Md., College Park, 1980-84; exec. vice chancellor U. Calif., Davis, 1984-91, exec. vice chancellor, provost, 1991-94; chancellor, 1994—; vis. investigator Carnegie Inst., 1976-77, Edinburgh (Scotland) U., 1978; cons. in field. NRC postdoctoral fellow, 1969-70, Eisenhower fellow, 1987; Dimond travel grantee, 1975, NSF grantee, 1972, 74, 76, 77, 78, 79, NATO grantee, 1980. Mem. AAAS, Am. Soc. Plant Physiology (bd. editors Plant Physiology 1977-82, trustee, mem. exec. com., treas. 1982-88, chmn. bd. trustees 1994—), Nat. Assn. State Univ. and Land Grant Colls. Home: 615 Francisco Pl Davis CA 95616-0210 Office: U Calif Davis Office Chancellor Davis CA 95616

VANDERHOOF, IRWIN THOMAS, life insurance company executive; b. Newark, Dec. 4, 1927; s. Irwin and Dora (Blanchard) V.; m. Ruth Elizabeth Green, Feb. 18, 1949; children: Thomas Arthur Irwin, Karen McNeill Brundage. B.S., Worcester (Mass.) Poly. Inst., 1948; PhD in Fin., NYU, 1987. C.L.U.; chartered fin. analyst. Asst. actuarial supr. Met. Life Ins. Co., 1951-55; assoc. actuary U.S. Life Ins. Co., 1955-59; exec. v.p., treas. Standard Security Life Ins. Co., 1959-73; sr. v.p. Equitable Life Assurance Soc. U.S., N.Y.C., 1973-87; pres. Actuarial Investment Cons. Inc., Towaco, N.J., 1987—; prof. Stern Sch. Bus., NYU; bd. dirs. Analytic Risk Mgmt., Louisville. Author papers in field. Pres. Montville (N.J.) Twp. Bd. Edn., 1962. Fellow Soc. Actuaries, Life Officer Mgmt. Inst.; assoc. Casualty Actuarial Soc., Inst. Actuaries; mem. N.Y. Soc. Security Analysts, Am. Acad. Actuaries. Republican. Episcopalian.

VANDER HORST, KATHLEEN PURCELL, nonprofit association administrator; b. Glen Rock, N.J., Jan. 15, 1945; d. Thomas Ralph and Elizabeth Jeanne (Burnett) Purcell; m. John Vander Horst Jr., Feb. 12, 1972 (div. Oct. 1993). Dir. devel. svcs. Johns Hopkins U., Balt., 1968-71; dir. devel. Union of Colls. of Art, Kansas City, Mo., 1971-72; dir. pub. rels. Md. Ballet and Ctr. Stage, Balt., 1973-76; dir. program devel. Joint Ctr. for Polit. and Econ. Studies, Washington, 1976-90, v.p. for program devel., 1990—. Dir., chmn. fin. com. Roland Park Community Found., Balt., 1990—. Office: Joint Ctr for Polit & Econ 1090 Vermont Ave NW Washington DC 20005-4905

VAN DER KROEF, JUSTUS MARIA, political science educator; b. Djakarta, Indonesia, Oct. 30, 1925; came to U.S., 1942, naturalized, 1952; s. Hendrikus Leonardus and Maria Wilhelmina (van Lokven) van der K.; m. Orell Joan Ellison, Mar. 25, 1955 (dec.); children: Adrian Hendrick, Sri Orell. B.A., Millsaps Coll., 1944; M.A., U. N.C., 1947; Ph.D., Columbia U., 1953. Asst. prof. fgn. studies Mich. State U., 1948-55; Charles Dana prof., chair dept. polit. sci. and sociology U. Bridgeport, Conn., 1956-92, prof. emeritus, 1992—; vis. prof. Nanyang U., Singapore, U. Philippines, Quezon City, Vidyodaya U., Sri Lanka Colombo; dir. Am.-Asian Ednl. Exchange, 1969—; chmn. editorial bd. Communications Research Services, Inc., Greenwich, Conn., 1971-80; mem. internat. adv. bd. Union Trust Bank, Stamford, Conn., 1974-88, adv. bd., 1988-94; mem. nat. acad. adv. council Charles Edison Meml. Youth Fund; bd. dirs. WUBC-TV, Bridgeport, Conn., 1978-80. Author: Indonesia in the Modern World, 2 vols., 1954-56, Indonesian Social Evolution. Some Psychological Considerations, 1958, The Communist Party of Indonesia: Its History, Program and Tactics, 1965, Communism in Malaysia and Singapore, 1967, Indonesia Since Sukarno, 1971, The Lives of SEATO, 1976, Communism in Southeast Asia, 1980, Kampuchea: The Endless Tug of War, 1982, Aquino's Philippines. The Deepening Security Crisis, 1988, Territorial Claims in the South China Sea, 1992, The South China Sea Problem: Some Alternative Scenarios, 1994; mem. editorial bd. World Affairs, 1975—, Jour. Asian Affairs, 1975—, Asian Affairs, 1980—, Asian Profile, 1983—, Jour. of Govt. and Adminstrn., 1985—, Jour. of Econ. and Internat. Relations, 1987—, Asian Affairs Jour. (Karachi), 1992—; mng. editor: Asian Thought and Society, 1986-96; book rev. editor: Asian Thought and Soc, 1976-85. Mem. City Charter Revision Com. City of Bridgeport, 1983-86, 90-92. Served with Royal Netherlands Marine Corps, 1944-45. Sr. fellow Research Inst. Communist Affairs, Columbia U., 1965-66, Rockefeller Found.; fellow U. Queensland, Brisbane, Australia, 1968-69; research fellow Inst. Strategic Studies, Islamabad, Pakistan, 1982—; research fellow Mellon Research Found., 1983, 90; research fellow Internat. Ctr. Asian Studies, Hong Kong, 1983—. Mem. Univ. Profs. Acad. Order (nat. pres. 1970-71), Pi Gamma Mu, Phi Alpha Theta, Lambda Chi Alpha, Alpha Sigma Lambda Phi Sigma Iota. Home: 165 Linden Ave Bridgeport CT 06604-5730

VANDER LAAN, MARK ALAN, lawyer; b. Akron, Ohio, Sept. 14, 1948; s. Robert H. and Isabel R. (Bishop) Vander L.; m. Barbara Ann Ryzenga, Aug. 25, 1970; children: Aaron, Matthew. AB, Hope Coll., 1970; JD, U. Mich., 1972. Bar: Ohio 1973, U.S. Dist. Ct. (so. dist.) Ohio 1973, U.S. Ct. Appeals (6th cir.) 1978, U.S. Supreme Ct. 1981. Assoc. Dinsmore, Shohl, Coates & Deupree, Cin., 1972-79; ptnr. Dinsmore & Shohl, Cin., 1979—; spl. counsel Ohio Atty. Gen.'s Office, 1983—; spl. prosecutor State of Ohio, 1985-94; city solicitor City of Blue Ash, Ohio, 1987—; trustee Cin. So. Railway, 1994—. Mme. Cin. Human Rels. Commn., 1980-86; mem. Leadership Cin. Class XIII, 1989-90; trustee Legal Aid Soc. of Cin., 1981-94, pres., 1988-90. Mem. ABA, Ohio Bar Assn., Cin. Bar Assn. (ethics com. 1983—), Sixth Cir. Jud. Conf. (life), Potter Stewart Inn of Ct. (master), Queen City Club. Office: Dinsmore & Shohl 1900 Chemed Ct 255 E 5th St Cincinnati OH 45202-4700

VANDERLAAN, RICHARD B., marketing company executive; b. Grand Rapids, Mich., Sept. 2, 1931; s. Sieger B. and Helen (Kerr) V.; cert. liberal arts Grand Rapids Jr. Coll., 1952; cert. mech. engring. U. Mich., 1955; cert. indsl. engring. Mich. State U., 1960; cert. Harvard Bus. Sch., 1970; m. Sally E. Conroy, Mar. 26, 1982; children: Sheryl Vanderlaan, Pamella Vanderlaan DeVos, Brenda Vanderlaan Thompson. Tool engr. Four Square Mfg. Co., Grand Rapids, 1950-60; sales engr. Ametek, Lansdale, Pa., 1960-63; br. mgr. J.N. Fauver Co., Grand Rapids, 1964-68; v.p. Fauver Co. subs. Sun Oil Co., Grand Rapids 1968-76, exec. v.p., 1976-80; pres. House of Printers, Inc., 1980-82, also dir.; pres. Richard Vanderlaan Assocs., 1982—. Named eagle scout Boy Scouts Am. Mem. Mfrs. Agts. Nat. Assn., Soc. Automotive Engrs. Republican. Clubs: Birmingham Country, Oakland Hills Country, Economic of Detroit, Detroit Athletic. Avocations: golf, tennis. Office: 22157 Metamora Ln Franklin MI 48025-3609

VANDERLINDE, RAYMOND EDWARD, clinical chemist; b. Newark, N.Y., Feb. 28, 1924; s. Isaac Edward and Hazel Effie (Robinson) V.; m. Ruth Louise Hansen, June 19, 1948; children: Susan Kay, Jeanne, William Edward. AB magna cum laude, Syracuse U., 1944, MS, 1945, PhD in Med. Biochemistry, 1950. Diplomate: Am. Bd. Clin. Chemistry. Asst. prof. biochemistry U. Md. Sch. Medicine, 1950-53, assoc. prof., 1953-57; lab. dir., asst. prof. Syracuse Meml. Hosp.-Upstate Med. Center, Syracuse, 1957-62; clin. chemist Meml. Hosp., Cumberland, Md., 1962-65; dir. labs. for clin. chemistry N.Y. State Dept. Health, Albany, 1965-76; prof. pathology and lab. medicine Hahnemann U., Phila., 1977-90, prof. emeritus, 1990; mem. lab. tech. adv. com. Pa. Dept. Health, 1981-85; mem. Coun. Nat. Reference Sys. in Clin. Chemistry, 1978—, vice chair holder, 1987, 91-93, chair holder, 1988-90; mem. Commn. on Accreditation in Clin. Chemistry, 1980-93; mem. enzyme subcom. Commn. on World Standardization, World Assn. Socs. of Pathology, 1978-90. Editor: Selected Methods of Clinical Chemistry, 1977-83, Annals of Clinical and Laboratory Science, 1981-93, Clinical Chemistry, 1983-92. Chmn. council on ministries, lay del. to annl. conf. Berwyn United Methodist Ch., 1979-82. Nat. Inst. Arthritis, Metabolism and Digestive Diseases grantee, 1977-81; NIH Lab. Standardization Panel for Lipids, 1986-90. Fellow Am. Assn. for Clin. Chemistry (bd. dirs. 1979-81, Fisher award 1985, Rheinhold award 1992); mem. Am. Chem. Soc., Am. Soc. Clin. Pathologists (assoc.), Acad. Clin. Lab. Physicians and Scientists, Assn. of Clin. Scientists, Soc. Mayflower Descs. of Am., Masons, Rotary (past pres. Delmar, N.Y.), Phi Beta Kappa, Sigma Xi. Democrat. Methodist. Home: Brookside #636 719 Maiden Choice Ln Catonsville MD 21228-6117

VANDERLINDEN, CAMILLA DENICE DUNN, telecommunications industry manager; b. Dayton, July 21, 1950; d. Joseph Stanley and Virginia Danley (Martin) Dunn; m. David Henry VanderLinden; Oct. 10, 1980; 1 child, Michael Christopher. Student, U. de Valencia, Spain, 1969; BA in Spanish and Secondary Edn. cum laude, U. Utah, 1972, MS in Human Resource Econs., 1985. Asst. dir. Davis County Community Action Program, Farmington, Utah, 1973-76; dir. South County Community Action, Midvale, Utah, 1976-79; supr. customer service Ideal Nat. Life Ins. Co., Salt Lake City, 1979-80; mgr. customer service Utah Farm Bur. Mutual Ins., Salt Lake City, 1980-82; quality assurance analyst Am. Express Co., Salt Lake City, 1983-86, quality assurance and human resource specialist, 1986-88; mgr. quality assurance and engring. Am. Express Co., Denver, 1988-91; mgr. customer svc. Tel. Express Co., Colorado Springs, Colo., 1991-97; mem. adj. faculty Westminster Coll., Salt Lake City, 1987-88. mem. adj. faculty, mem. quality adv. bd. Red Rocks Community Coll., 1990-91. Vol. translator Latin Am. community; vol. naturalist Roxborough State Park; internat. exch. coord. EF Fgn. Exch. Program. Mem. Internat. Customer Svc. Orgn. (officer call ctr. chpt.), Colo. Springs Customer Svc. Assn. (officer). Christian. Avocations: swimming, hosting fgn. exchange students. Home: 10857 W Snow Cloud Trl Littleton CO 80125-9210

VAN DER MARCK, JAN, art historian; b. Roermond, The Netherlands, Aug. 19, 1929; s. Everard and Anny (Finken) van der M.; m. Ingeborg Lachmann, Apr. 27, 1961 (dec. 1988); m. Sheila Stamell, May 24, 1990. BA, U. Nijmegen, The Netherlands, 1952, MA, 1954, PhD in Art History, 1956; postgrad., U. Utrecht, The Netherlands, 1956-57, Columbia U., 1957-59. Curator Gemeentemuseum, Arnhem, The Netherlands, 1959-61; asst. dir. fine arts Seattle World's Fair, 1961-62; curator Walker Art Center, Mpls., 1963-67; dir. Mus. Contemporary Art, Chgo., 1967-70; assoc. prof. art history U. Wash., 1972-74; dir. Dartmouth Coll. Mus. and Galleries, 1974-80, Center for Fine Arts, Miami, 1980-85; curator 20th century art, chief curator

Detroit Inst. Arts, 1986-95. Author: Romantische Boekillustratie in Belgie, 1956, George Segal, 1975, Arman, 1984, Bernar Venet, 1988, The Art of Contemporary Bookbinding, 1997; contbr. articles to art jours., essays to catalogues. Decorated chevalier Order Arts and Letters; Netherlands Orgn. Pure Rsch. fellow, 1954-55, Rockefeller Found. fellow, 1957-59, Aspen Inst. fellow, 1974, 94; vis. sr. fellow Ctr. for Advanced Study in Visual Arts, Washington, 1986. Mem. Internat. Art Critics Assn., Internat. Coun. Museums, Grolier Club, Assn. Internat. de Bibliophilie. Office: 15 E Kirby St Detroit MI 48202

VAN DER MERWE, NIKOLAAS JOHANNES, archaeologist; b. Riviersonderend, Republic of South Africa, Aug. 11, 1940; came to U.S., 1958; s. Johannes Abraham and Rachel Maria (Burger) van der M.; m. Julia Ann Feeny, Nov. 11, 1962 (div. 1969); 1 child, Kerstin; m. Karen Elaine Bardou, Feb. 19, 1973; 1 child, Nicolina Thandiwe. BA cum laude, Yale U., 1962, MA, 1965, PhD, 1966; MA (hon.), Harvard U., 1988; DSc (hon.), U. Port Elizabeth, 1995. Curatorial asst. Yale Peabody Mus., New Haven, 1962-64; rsch. asst. Yale Radiocarbon Lab., New Haven, 1963-66; asst. prof. anthropology SUNY, Binghamton, 1966-69, assoc. prof., 1969-74; prof. archaeology U. Cape Town, Republic of South Africa, 1974-88; Landon Clay prof. sci. archaeology, earth and planetary scis. Harvard U., Cambridge, Mass., 1988—; dir. Ctr. African Studies, U. Cape Town, 1976-80. Author: The Carbon 14 Dating of Iron, 1969; co-editor: (collection of essays) Perspectives on South Africa's Future, 1979, Iron Age in Southern Africa, 1979; contbr. numerous articles to profl. jours. Fellow U. Cape Town, 1986; Ford Found. Fgn. Area fellow, 1964-66. Fellow AAAS, Royal Soc. South Africa (John F.W. Herschel medal 1994),, Am. Anthrop. Assn., Explorers Club, Soc. Antiquaries (London); mem. South African Archaeol. Soc. (life), Soc. Am. Archaeology, Hist. Metallurgy Group, South African Assn. Archaeologists (founder), West African Assn. Archaeology (founder), Soc. Archaeol. Sci. (life), Owl Club (Cape Town), Concord (Mass.) Rod and Gun, Sigma Xi. Avocations: flying, diving, shooting, hiking, cooking. Home: 475 River Rd Carlisle MA 01741-1873 Office: Harvard Univ Peabody Mus/Dept Anthropology 11 Divinity Ave Cambridge MA 02138-2019

VAN DER MEULEN, JOSEPH PIERRE, neurologist; b. Boston, Aug. 22, 1929; s. Edward Lawrence and Sarah Jane (Robertson) VanDer M.; m. Ann Irene Yadeno, June 18, 1960; children—Elisabeth, Suzanne, Janet. A.B., Boston Coll., 1950; M.D., Boston U., 1954. Diplomate: Am. Bd. Psychiatry and Neurology. Intern Cornell Med. div. Bellevue Hosp., N.Y.C., 1954-55; resident Cornell Med. div. Bellevue Hosp., 1955-56; resident Harvard U., Boston City Hosp., 1958-60, instr., fellow, 1962-66; assoc. Case Western Res. U., Cleve., 1966-67; asst. prof. Case Western Res. U., 1967-69, assoc. prof. neurology and biomed. engring., 1969-71; prof. neurology U. So. Calif., L.A., 1971—; also dir. dept. neurology Los Angeles County/U. So. Calif. Med. Center; chmn. dept. U. So. Calif., 1971-78, v.p. for health affairs, 1977—, dean Sch. Medicine, 1985-86, 95—, vice dean med. affairs, 1995—; vis. prof. Autonomous U. Guadalajara, Mex., 1974; pres. Norris Cancer Hosp. and Research Inst., 1983—. Contbr. articles to profl. jours. Mem. med. adv. bd. Calif. chpt. Myasthenia Gravis Found., 1971-75, chmn., 1974-75, 77-78; med. adv. bd. Amyotrophic Lateral Sclerosis Found., Calif., 1973-75, chmn., 1974-75; mem. Com. to Combat Huntington's Disease, 1973—; bd. dirs. Calif. Hosp. Med. Ctr., Good Hope Med. Found., Doheny Eye Hosp., House Ear Inst., L.A. Hosp. Good Samaritan, Children's Hosp. of L.A., Barlow Respiratory Hosp., USC U. Hosp., chmn., 1991—; bd. govs. Thomas Aquinas Coll.; bd. dirs. Assn. Acad. Health Ctrs., chmn., 1991-92; pres. Scott Newman Ctr., 1987-89; pres., bd. dirs. Kenneth Norris Cancer Hosp & Rsch. Inst. Served to lt. M.C. USNR, 1956-58. Nobel Inst. fellow Karolinska Inst., Stockholm, 1960-62; NIH grantee, 1968-71. Mem. AMA, Am. Neurol. Assn., Am. Acad. Neurology, L.A. Soc. Neurology and Psychiatry (pres. 1977-78), L.A. Med. Assn., Mass. Med. Soc., Ohio Med. Soc., Calif. Med. Soc., L.A. Acad. Medicine, Alpha Omega Alpha (councillor 1992—), Phi Kappa Phi. Home: 39 Club View Ln Palos Verdes Peninsula CA 90274-4208 Office: U So Calif 1540 Alcazar St Los Angeles CA 90033-4500

VANDER MOLEN, THOMAS DALE, lawyer; b. Ann Arbor, Mich., Oct. 30, 1950; s. John and Eleanor Ruth (Driesens) Vander M.; m. Marlese Kay Alden, June 29, 1974; children: Laura, David, Eric. BA, Calvin Coll., 1972; JD magna cum laude, Harvard U., 1975. Bar: Minn. 1976, U.S. Dist. Ct. Minn. 1981, U.S. Claims Ct. 1983, U.S. Tax Ct. 1977, U.S. Ct. Appeals 1988. Law clk. to judge U.S. Ct. Appeals-First Cir., Boston, 1975-76; assoc. Dorsey & Whitney, Mpls., 1976-81; ptnr. Dorsey & Whitney LLP, Mpls., 1982—, gen. counsel, 1993—. Mem. editorial bd. Harvard Law Rev., 1973-75. Presbyterian. Office: Dorsey & Whitney LLP 2100 Pillsbury Ctr S 220 S 6th St Minneapolis MN 55402-4502

VANDER MYDE, PAUL ARTHUR, technology and engineering services executive; b. Estherville, Iowa, Feb. 9, 1937; s. Louis John and Anna Marie (Pals) Vander M.; m. Jeanne Elizabeth Russell, Sept. 8, 1973. BA, U. Minn., 1959; MA, U. Iowa, 1966. Staff asst. Nat. Security Agy., Ft. Meade, Md., 1962-68; congressional fellow U.S. Rep. George Bush/U.S. Senator Bob Packwood, Washington, 1968-69; legis. asst. U.S. Senator Bob Packwood, Washington, 1969-71; exec. asst. Office of Vice-Pres., White House, Washington, 1971-73; staff mem. domestic council White House, Washington, 1973; dep. asst. sec. for conservation, research and edn. U.S. Dept. Agr., Washington, 1973-77; Rep. staff dir. Sci. and Tech. Com., Ho. of Reps., 1977-81; asst. sec. for congressional and inter-govtl. affairs U.S. Dept. Commerce, Washington, 1981-87; v.p. corp. affairs VSE Corp., Alexandria, Va., 1987—; guest speaker numerous profl. confs. and seminars. Contbr. articles to profl. jours. Bd. dirs. Profl. Svcs. Coun., Washington, U.S. Naval Aviation Mus., Pensacola, Fla; vice chmn. Adminstrv. Conf. of U.S., Washington. With USN, 1959-61; capt. USNR (ret.). Decorated Meritorious Svc. medal. Mem. Naval Res. Assn., U.S. Navy League, Alexandria C. of C. (chmn.-elect), Sovereign Mil. Order Knights Templar of Jerusalem, Belle Haven Country Club, Rotary Club Alexandria. Episcopalian. Office: VSE Corp 2550 Huntington Ave Alexandria VA 22303-1400

VANDER MYDE, PHILIP LOUIS, architectural design firm executive; b. Whiteside County, Ill., Apr. 4, 1931; s. Louis John and Ann Marie (Pals) Vander M.; m. Martha T. Grier, Mar. 15, 1969; children: Jane Gray, John Philip, Martha Maslin. Student Cen. Coll., 1949-50; BA in Arch., U. Minn., 1958. Registered architect, Va., Md., D.C., N.C., Tenn., Pa., Mich., N.J., Ill., W.Va., Del. Architect Vosbeck-Ward & Assocs., Alexandria, Va., 1962-64; assoc. ptnr. Vosbeck Vosbeck & Assos., Alexandria, 1966; ptnr. VVKR Partnership, Alexandria, 1967-70, mng. ptnr. Md. Office, University Park, 1970-80; prin. VVKR Inc., Alexandria, Va., 1980-83; mng. ptnr. for architecture Dewberry & Davis, Fairfax, Va., 1983-87; ptnr. Senseman/VanderMyde, Alexandria, 1987-89; prin. ADD, Inc., Washington, 1989-92; pres. Additions Inc., Va., 1992—. Prin works include Prince Georges Hosp. Ctr., 1977, U. Md. Law Libr., 1978, Frederick County Courthouse, 1979, Md. Dept. Agr. Hdqrs., 1980, Inglewood Office Complex, 1981, Wolf Trap Ctr. Performing Arts, 1984, First Am. Bank Va., North Tower, 1989, Internat. Gateway Office Complex, 1990, City of America, Yokohama, Japan, 1992. Mem. Inova Alexandria Hosp. Found., 1981—; Capt. USNR , 1959-91 ret. Paul Harris fellow, 1992; recipient Honor award Bicentennial Design awards, AIA; 17 design awards, 1970-86. Mem. AIA (pres. Potomac Valley chpt. 1977-78, Fed. Liaison Task Force, 1991—), Nat. Coun. Archtl. Registration Bds., Vauxcleuse Citizens Assn. (past pres.), Minn. Alumni Assn., Belle Haven Country Club, Potomac Soc., Holland Soc., Club Alexandria, Rotary (pres. 1994-95), The Priory of St. King Charles the Martyr, Sovereign Military Order of the Temple of Jerusalem, Knight of the Order, Grand Officier, Sigma Alpha Epsilon (past pres.). Republican. Presbyterian. Home and Office: Additions Inc 1100 N Howard St Alexandria VA 22304-1628

VANDERPLOEG, JAMES M., preventive medicine physician; b. Upland, Calif., Nov. 22, 1950. BA, U. Iowa, 1975. Intern U. Hosp./U. Calif., San Diego, 1975-76; resident in otolaryngoloty U. Iowa Hosps., Iowa City, 1978-79; resident in occupational medicine U. Tex. Sch. Pub. Health, Houston, 1980-82, assoc. prof. occupational health; mem. staff St. John Hosp., Nassau Bay, Tex.; pvt. practice, ptnr. group practice; part-time med. adminstr. Mem. Am. Coll. Occupational Medicine, ACPrM-AerosMA. Office: Ctr for Aerospace &Occupational Medicine 700 Gemini St Ste 110 Houston TX 77058-2735

VANDERPOEL, JAMES ROBERT, lawyer; b. Harvey, Ill., Sept. 27, 1955; s. Waid Richard and Ruth (Silberman) V.; m. Deanne Czabaranek, May 1987; children: Jacqueline, Robert, Jennifer. BS in Fin., Ind. U., 1978; JD, Santa Clara U., 1982. Bar: Calif. 1982, U.S. Dist. Ct. (no. dist.) Calif. 1982. Group contracts mgr. Motorola Computer Group, Tempe, Ariz., 1984—. Avocations: basketball, hiking, golf, snorkeling, gardening. Office: Motorola Computer Group 2900 S Diablo Way Tempe AZ 85282-3214

VANDERPOOL, WARD MELVIN, management and marketing consultant; b. Oakland, Mo., Jan. 20, 1919; s. Oscar B. and Clara (McGuire) V.; m. Lee Kendall, July 7, 1935. MEE, Tulane U. V.p. charge sales Van Lang Brokerage, Los Angeles, 1934-38; mgr. agrl. div. Dayton Rubber Co., Chgo., 1939-48; pres., gen. mgr. Vee Mac Co., Rockford, Ill., 1948—; pres., dir. Zipout, Inc., Rockford, 1951—, Wife Saver Products, Inc., 1959—; chmn. bd. Zipout Internat., Kenvan Inc., 1952—, Shevan Corp., 1951—, Atlas Internat. Corp.; pres. Global Enterprises Ltd., Global Assos. Ltd.; chmn. bd. dirs. Am. Atlas Corp., Atlas Chem. Corp., Merzat Industries Ltd.; trustee Ice Crafter Trust, 1949—; bd. dirs. Atlas Chem. Internat. Ltd., Kenlee Internat., Ltd., Shrimp Tool Internat. Ltd.; mem. Toronto Bd. Trade; chmn. bd. dirs. Am. Atlas Corp., Am. Packaging Corp. Mem. adv. bd. Nat. Security Council, congl. adv. com. Heritage Found.; mem. Rep. Nat. Com., Presdl. Task Force, Congrl. Adv. Com. Hon. mem. Internat. Swimming Hall of Fame. Mem. Nat. (dir. at large), Rock River (past pres.) sales execs., Sales and Mktg. Execs. Internat. (dir.), Am. Mgmt. Assn., Rockford Engring. Soc., Am. Tool Engrs., Internat. Acad. Aquatic Art (dir.), Am. Inst. Mgmt. (pres. council), Am. Ordnance Assn., Internat. Platform Assn., Heritage Found., Ill. C. of C. Clubs: Jesters, Elks, IAA Swim, Exec., Elmcrest Country, Pyramid, Dolphin, Marlin, Univ., Univ. Athletic, Oxford. Lodges: Masons (consistory), Shriners, Elks. Home: 374 Parkland Dr SE Cedar Rapids IA 52403-2031 also: 40 Richview Rd # 308, Toronto, ON Canada M9A 5C1 also: 704 Park Center Dr Santa Ana CA 92705-3563 Office: PO Box 1972 Cedar Rapids IA 52406-1972 also: 111 Richmond St W Ste 318, Toronto, ON Canada M5H 1T1

VANDER PUTTEN, LEROY ANDREW, insurance company executive; b. Appleton, Wis., Aug. 20, 1934; s. Theo S. and Lorraine M. (Quella) Vander P.; m. Evon Marie Schumacher, July 3, 1956; children: Suzanna, Dale, Lisa, Carole, Kim. BS in Math. and Psychology, Wis. State U., 1961; Advanced Mgmt. Program, Harvard U., 1983-84. Asst. sec. EDP research Aetna Life & Casualty, Hartford, Conn., 1968-69, asst. cashier, 1969-74, dir. investment planning, 1974-79, asst. v.p. investment planning, 1979-81, v.p. investment planning, 1981-82, v.p. corp. fin., 1982-86, v.p. and deputy treas., 1986-87, chmn., pres., chief exec. officer Exec. Re Idemnity Inc., Simsbury, Conn., 1987-93; chmn., chief exec. officer Exec. Risk, Inc., Simsbury, Conn., 1994—, also bd. dirs., 1986—; adv. bd. Fleet Bank 1988—; Chmn. South Windsor Econ. Devel. Com., Conn., 1977; trustee Hartford Rensselear Grad. Ctr., The Conf. Bd.; bd. dirs. Ultimate Software Group, Ins. Ctr. Inc.; chancellors adv. coun. U. Wis., Oshkosh. Recipient Distinguished Alumni award U. Wis., 1987—. With USCG, 1952-56. Mem. AMP 91 Assocs. of Boston (treas. 1982—). Republican. Roman Catholic. Avocations: sailing, sports car restoration, canoeing. Office: Exec Risk Inc 82 Hopmeadow St PO Box 2002 Simsbury CT 06070

VANDERRYN, JACK, philanthropic foundation administrator; b. Groningen, The Netherlands, Apr. 14, 1930; came to U.S., 1939; s. Herman Gabriel and Henrietta S.E. (Hartog) V.; m. Margrit Wolfes, Mar. 18, 1956; children: David, Judith, Amy, Daniel. BA, Lehigh U., 1951, MS, 1952, PhD, 1955. Rsch. and grad. teaching asst. Lehigh U., Bethlehem, Pa., 1952-55; asst. prof. chemistry Va. Poly. Inst., Blacksburg, 1955-58; rsch. participant Oak Ridge (Tenn.) Nat. Lab., 1957; chemist AEC, Oak Ridge, 1958-62, tech. adviser to asst. gen. mgr. R & D, Washington, 1962-67, asst. to gen. mgr., 1971-72, tech. asst. to dir. div. applied tech., 1972-73, chief energy tech. br., div. applied tech., 1973-75; acting dir. div. energy storage Energy Rsch. and Devel. Adminstrn., Washington, 1975, dir. Office Internat. R & D Programs, 1975-77; dir. Office Internat. Programs Dept. Energy, Washington, 1977-82; dir. energy and natural resources AID, Washington, 1982-91; program dir. environment Moriah Fund, Chevy Chase, Md., 1991—; sr. sci. adviser U.S. Mission to Internat. Atomic Energy Agy., Dept. State, Vienna, Austria, 1967-71; lectr. Brookings Instn., 1965-66. Mem., dep. pres., exec. bd. Am. Internat. Sch., Vienna, 1968-71; v.p. Oak Ridge Civic Music Assn., 1959-60; pres. Washington Print Club, 1986-91. Fellow AAAS. Home: 8112 Whittier Blvd Bethesda MD 20817-3123 Office: Moriah Fund Ste 1000 1634 I St NW Washington DC 20006-4003

VANDERSALL, JOHN HENRY, dairy science educator; b. Helena, Ohio, July 20, 1928; s. Clarence C. and Ida M. (Barnhope) V.; m. Patricia L. King, May 11, 1963; children: Eric John, Karen Susan. B.S., Ohio State U., 1950, M.S., 1954, Ph.D., 1959. Farm researcher Ralston Purina Co., 1950; from research asst. to instr. Ohio State U. Agrl. Expt. Sta., 1953-59; mem. faculty U. Md., 1959—, prof. dairy sci., 1971-93, prof. emeritus, 1993—. Contbr. articles to profl. jours. Served with AUS, 1950-52. Mem. Am. Dairy Sci. Assn., Am. Soc. Animal Sci., AAAS, Sigma Xi. Home: 10906 Ashfield Rd Hyattsville MD 20783-1003 Office: Dept Animal Sci Univ Md College Park MD 20742

VANDERSLICE, JOSEPH THOMAS, chemist; b. Phila., Dec. 21, 1927; s. Joseph R. and Mae (Daly) V.; m. Patricia Mary Horstmann, Nov. 20, 1954; children: Sharon, Joseph, Julie, Peter, John, Polly, Jeffrey, Amy. BS in Chemistry magna cum laude, Boston Coll., 1949; Ph.D. in Phys. Chemistry (Allied Chem. and Dye fellow), Mass. Inst. Tech., 1953. Faculty Cath. U. Am., 1952-56, asst. prof., 1955-56; faculty U. Md., College Park, 1956-79, prof. emeritus, 1978—; prof. chem. physics U. Md., 1963-79; dir. U. Md. Inst. Molecular Physics, 1967-69, chmn. chemistry dept., 1968-76; rsch. chemist Nutrition Inst., U.S. Dept. Agr., Beltsville, Md., 1978-94. Author: (with Schamp and Mason) Thermodynamics, 1966; mem. editl. bd. Jour. Micronutrient Analysis, 1985-91, Food Chemistry, 1992, Food Rsch. Internat., 1992—, Jour. Food Composition, 1994—; contbr. articles to profl. jours. Inducted into Boston Latin Sch. Athletic Hall of Fame, 1992; recipient Outstanding Alumni award Boston Coll., 1979. Fellow Washington Acad. Scis., Am. Phys. Soc.; mem. AAAS, Am. Inst. Food Technologists, Cosmos Club, Sigma Xi (award for sci. achievement 1971). Home: PO Box 350 Cobb Island MD 20625-0350

VANDERSLICE, THOMAS AQUINAS, electronics executive; b. Phila., Jan. 8, 1932; s. Joseph R. and Mae (Daly) V.; m. Margaret Hurley, June 9, 1956; children: Thomas Aquinas, Paul Thomas Aquinas, John Thomas Aquinas, Peter Thomas Aquinas. BS in Chemistry and Philosophy, Boston Coll., 1953; PhD in Chemistry and Physics, Cath. U. Am., 1956. With GE, Fairfield, Conn., from 1956, gen. mgr. electronic components bus. div., 1970-72, v.p., 1970, group exec. spl. systems and products group, 1972-77, sr. v.p., sector exec. Power System Sector, 1977-79, exec. v.p., sector exec. Power System Sector, 1979-84; chief oper. officer, dir. Gen. Tel. & Electronics Corp., Stamford, Conn., 1979-83; chmn., CEO, Apollo Computer, Inc., Chelmsford, Mass., 1984-89, M/A COM, Inc., Lowell, Mass., 1989-95; bd. dirs. Texaco, Inc. Patentee low pressure gas measurements and analysis, gas surface interactions and elec. discharges; co-author: Ultra High Vacuum and Its Applications, 1963; reviser: Scientific Foundations of Vacuum Technique, 1960; contbr. to profl. jours. Trustee Boston Coll., past chmn., past trustee Comm. Econ. Devel. Recipient Bicentennial medal Boston Coll., 1976; Fulbright scholar, 1953-56. Mem. NAE, ASTM, Am. Vacuum Soc., Am. Chem. Soc., Am. Inst. Physics, Royal Poinciana Golf Club (Naples, Fla.), Oyster Harbors Club, Sigma Xi, Tau Beta Pi, Alpha Sigma Nu, Sigma Pi Sigma. Office: TAV Associates Ste 3001 Two International Pl Boston MA 02110

VAN DER SMISSEN, M. E. BETTY, physical education educator; b. Great Bend, Kans., Dec. 27, 1927; d. Theodor Alwin and Margaret (Dirks) van der S. AB, U. Kans., 1949, JD, 1952; MS, Ind. U., 1954, D. Recreation, 1955. cons. in sport law, personal injury and negligence. Asst. prof. U. Iowa, Iowa City, 1956-65; prof. Pa. State U., University Park, 1965-79; dir. sch. health physical edn./prof. recreation Bowling Green (Ohio) State U., 1979-90; prof., chmn. park, recreation and tourism resources Mich. State U., East Lansing, 1990—. Author: Legal Liability and Risk Management of Public & Private Entities, 1990. Mem. Nat. Commn. for Accreditation of Park and Recreation Agys., 1st chair, 1994—. Recipient Disting. Fellow award Soc. Park and Recreation Educators, 1974, W.W. Patty Disting. Alumni award Ind. U. Sch. Health, Phys. Edn. and Recreation, 1993. Fellow Acad. Leisure Scis. (founder), Am. Leisure Acad. (founder); mem. AAHPERD (R. Tait McKenzie award 1991), Nat. Recreation and Park Assn. (trustee 1988-90), Am. Acad. Park and Recreation Adminstrn. (bd. dirs. 1990-93), Am. Assn. Leisure and Recreation (Jay B. Nash award 1987), Am. Camping Assn. (nat. pres. 1980-82), Assn. for Experiential Edn. (Kurt Hahn award 1987), Nat. Coun. Accreditation Adventure Programs. Home: 1920 Opaline Dr Lansing MI 48917-8639 Office: Mich State U 131 Natural Resources East Lansing MI 48824-1222

VAN DER SPIEGEL, JAN, engineering educator; b. Aalst, Belgium, Apr. 12, 1951; came to U.S., 1980; s. Robert and Celestine Van der Spiegel. BSEE, U. Leuven, 1971, MSEE, 1974, PhD in Elec. Engring., 1979; M of Arts and Sci., U. Pa., 1988. 2d lt. Belgian Air Force, 1979-90; asst. prof. elec. engring. U. Pa., Phila., 1981-87, assoc. prof., 1987-95, prof. elec. engring., 1995—, dir. Ctr. Sensor Tech., 1989—. Patentee integ. ambient sensing, radiation sens. retina sens., gen prupost neural comp., novel ferroelectric sensors; editor Sensors and Actuators, 1986—. Postdoctoral fellow U. Pa., 1980-81; named Presdl. Young Investigator The White House, 1984. Mem. IEEE (sr.), Neural Network Soc., Tau Beta Pi. Office: U Pa Ctr Sensor Techs Moore Sch 200 S 33d St Rm 308 Philadelphia PA 19104-6314

VANDERSTAPPEN, HARRIE ALBERT, Far Eastern art educator; b. Heesch, The Netherlands, Jan. 21, 1921; came to U.S., 1959; s. Johannes and Johanna (van de Poel) V. Student, Theol. Sch., Helvoirt and Teteringen, The Netherlands, 1939-45, Chinese Lang. Sch., Peking, People's Republic of China, 1946-48; Ph.D. in Far Eastern Art, U. Chgo., 1955. Ordained priest Roman Catholic Ch., 1945. Student lang., also tchr., writer Tokyo, 1955-57; tchr. Nansan U., Nagoya, Japan, 1957-59; prof. Far Eastern art U. Chgo., 1959-92, chmn. dept. art, 1964-69. Author: The T.L. Yuan Bibliography of Chinese Art and Archaeology, 1975; author, editor: Ritual and Reverence, 1989; assoc. editor Monumenta Serica, 1955—; contbr. articles to profl. jours. Recipient Teaching of Art History award Nat. Coll. Art Assn. Am., 1985. Mem. Asia Soc., Assn. Asian Arts. Home: 2147 Bennett Ave Evanston IL 60201-2158

VANDERSTAR, JOHN, lawyer; b. Jersey City, Sept. 17, 1933; s. John Vanderstar and Rosemarie (Torraco) Legette; m. Beth S. Vanderstar, Nov. 7, 1956 (div. Oct. 1984); children: Pippa, Alexandra, Thankful, Eliza; m. M. Elizabeth Culbreth, Mar. 16, 1985. BSE, Princeton U., 1954; LLB cum laude, Harvard U., 1961. Bar: D.C. 1961, U.S. Dist. Ct. (D.C. dist.) 1961, U.S. Dist. Ct. Md. 1985, U.S. Ct. Claims 1976, U.S. Ct. Appeals (8th cir.) 1966, U.S. Ct. Appeals (5th cir.) 1969, U.S. Ct. Appeals (1st cir.) 1971, U.S. Ct. Appeals (4th cir.) 1974, U.S. Ct. Appeals (3d cir.) 1979, U.S. Ct. Appeals 11th cir.) 1981, U.S. Ct. Appeals (Fed. cir.) 1983, U.S. Supreme Ct. 1966. Assoc. Covington & Burling, Washington, 1961-70, ptnr., 1970—. Pres. ACLU Nat. Capital Area, Washington, 1976-78, bd. dirs., 1971-78; bd. dirs. NOW Legal Def. and Edn. Fund, N.Y.C., 1979-94. Lt. USNR, 1954-58. Recipient Alan Barth award, ACLU Nat. Capital Area, 1984. Mem. ABA, D.C. Bar (bd. govs. 1985-88). Episcopalian. Home: 3642 N Monroe St Arlington VA 22207-5317 Office: Covington & Burling 1201 Pennsylvania Ave NW PO Box 7566 Washington DC 20044

VANDERVEEN, JOHN E., federal agency administrator; b. Prospect Park, N.J., May 13, 1934; m. Ernestine Neuhardt, June 3, 1967; children: Keith Bradley, Kimetha Leigh. BS, Rutgers U., 1956; PhD, U. N.H., 1961. Nutritionist USAF, 1961-75; dir. divsn. nutrition FDA, Washington, 1975-92, dir. office plant & dairy foods and beverages, 1992—. Served to 1st lt. USAF, 1961-64. Office: FDA Ctr Food Safety and Applied Nutrition 200 C St SW Washington DC 20204-0001

VANDER VEER, SUZANNE, aupair business executive; b. Phila., Sept. 21, 1936; d. Joseph Bedford Vander Veer and Ethel K. Short; m. James Robb Ledwith, Nov. 29, 1958 (div. Sept. 1978); children: Cheryl Day, James Robb Jr., Scott Wiley; m. Herbert Keyser Zearfoss, Nov. 14, 1992. AA, Colby Sawyer Coll., 1957; postgrad., State U. Iowa, 1957-58. Tchr. Booth Sch., Bryn Mawr, Pa., 1958; profl. tour guide Cities of Phila., N.Y.C. and Washington, D.C., 1976-89; regional dir. Transdesigns, Woodstock, Ga., 1979-87; area rep. Welcome Wagon Internat., Tenn., 1987-93; mem. local bd. Welcome Wagon Internat., 1987-93; condo. complex mgr. St. Davids, Pa., 1990-93; area dir. E.F. Aupair, Cambridge, Mass., 1993—; art cons., 1979—. Chair host family program Internat. House of Phila., 1966-74; mem. women's com. Pa. Hosp., 1966-71; mem. com. Phila. Antique Show, 1995—; docent Phila. Mus. of Art, 1974-80; bd. dirs. Plays for Living, Phila., 1966-84; chair congl. care coun. Office of Deacon Bryn Mawr Presbyn. Ch., 1997—. Mem. PEO (officer), Jr. League of Phila. (bd. dirs., sustainer chair 1993-95, Pres.' Cup 1995, sustainer bd. 1985—), Merion Cricket Club. Home: 532 Candace Ln Villanova PA 19085

VAN DERVEER, TARA, university athletic coach; b. Niagara Falls, N.Y., 1954. Grad., Indiana U., 1975. Coach women's basketball Stanford U. Cardinals, 1985—, U.S. Nat. Women's Team, 1995—; coach gold medalist Women's Olympic Team, 1996. Champions NCAA Divsn. 1 A, 1990, 92. Office: Stanford U Dept of Athletics Stanford CA 94305-6150*

VANDERVELD, JOHN, JR., waste disposal company executive; b. Chgo., Oct. 24, 1926; s. John J. and Rose (Renkema) V. Pres. Nat. Disposal Contractors, Barrington, Ill., 1952-71; sr. v.p., dir. Browning Ferris Industries, Houston, 1971-78; pres. Pioneer Equities, Inc., 1975-90, C.J.V. Corp., Dallas, 1990-92; sr. corp. advisor Vector Environmental Techs., Inc., 1993—; dir. Am. Far East, Inc., Dallas and Tokyo; adv. bd. Southwestern Legal Found. Bd. dirs., exec. com. Internat. Bible Soc. Mem. Nat. Solid Waste Mgmt. Assn. (former chmn. govt. industry coordinating council, mem. environ. research com.). Home: 7031 Brookshire Dr Dallas TX 75230-4248

VANDER VELDE, WALLACE EARL, aeronautical and astronautical educator; b. Jamestown, Mich., June 4, 1929; s. Peter Nelson and Janet (Keizer) Vander V.; m. Winifred Helen Bunai, Aug. 29, 1954; children—Susan Jane, Peter Russell. B.S. in Aero Engring, Purdue U., 1951; Sc.D., Mass. Inst. Tech., 1956. Dir. applications engring. GPS Instrument Co., Inc., Newton, Mass., 1956-57; mem. faculty Mass. Inst. Tech., 1957—, prof. aero. and astronautics, 1965—; Cons. to industry, 1958—. Author: Flight Vehicle Control Systems, Part VII of Space Navigation, Guidance and Control, 1966, (with Arthur Gelb) Multiple-Input Describing Functions, 1968; also papers. Served to 1st lt. USAF, 1951-53. Recipient Edn. award Am. Automatic Control Coun., 1988. Fellow AIAA; mem. IEEE. Home: 50 High St Winchester MA 01890-3314 Office: MIT Rm 9-467 Dept Aero and Astronautics Cambridge MA 02139

VANDERVER, TIMOTHY ARTHUR, JR., lawyer; b. Birmingham, Ala., Jan. 25, 1944; s. Timothy Arthur and Jeanette (Grimes) V.; m. Virginia Cassandra Nye, Oct. 1, 1966; children: Timothy A. III, Glenn Bruce, Benjamin Richard. BA, Washington and Lee U., 1965; BA in Law, Oxford (Eng.) U., 1967, MA, 1983; JD, Harvard U., 1969. Bar: D.C., U.S. Ct. Appeals (D.C. cir.) 1969, U.S. Ct. Appeals (5th cir.) 1984, U.S. Ct. Appeals (3d and 11th cirs.) 1989, U.S. Supreme Ct. 1978. Assoc. Covington & Burling, Washington, 1969-72, Dept. of Interior, Washington, 1972-76; ptnr. Patton Boggs L.L.P., Washington, 1976—. Editor: Clean Air Law and Regulation, 1992, Environmental Law Handbook, 1994. Capt. U.S. Army, 1970-71. Presbyterian. Home: 9000 Congressional Ct Potomac MD 20854-4608 Office: Patton Boggs LLP 2550 M St NW Washington DC 20037-1301

VAN DER VOO, ROB, geophysicist; b. Zeist, The Netherlands, Aug. 4, 1940; came to U.S., 1970; s. Maximiliaan and Johanna Hendrika (Baggerman) Van der V.; m. Tatiana M. C. Graafland, Mar. 26, 1966; children—Serge Nicholas, Bjorn Alexander. B.S., U. Utrecht, Netherlands, 1961, M.S., 1965, Ph.D., 1969. Research asst. U. Utrecht, 1964-65, research asso., 1965-69, sr. research asso., 1969-70; vis. asst. prof. U. Mich., Ann Arbor, 1970-72; asst. prof. U. Mich., 1972-75, asso. prof., 1975-79, prof. geophysics, 1979—, chmn., 1981-88, 91-95, Arthur F. Thurnau prof., 1994—; guest prof. ETH, Zurich, Switzerland, 1978, Kuwait U., 1979. Author: Paleomagnetism of the Atlantic, Tethys and Iapetus Oceans, 1993; contbr. articles to profl. jours. Recipient Russel award U. Mich., 1976, Disting. Faculty Achievement award U.Mich., 1990. Mem. Geol. Soc. Am., Am. Geophys. Union, Geologische Vereinigung (W.Ger.), Royal Dutch

Geol. and Mining Soc., Royal Acad. Scis. (Netherlands), Sigma Xi, Phi Kappa Phi. Home: 2305 Devonshire Rd Ann Arbor MI 48104-2703 Office: U Mich 4528 CC Little Bldg Ann Arbor MI 48109

VANDER VOORT, DALE GILBERT, textile company executive; b. Paterson, N.J., Feb. 7, 1924; s. Gilbert H. and Lillian (Hatton) Vander V.; m. Florine E. Storey, Aug. 6, 1944; children: Lydia Ann, Dale Gilbert, Roy Lee. B.M.E., Clemson U., 1944. Gen. mgr., dir. Stevens Line Assos., Webster, Mass., 1954-56; gen. mgr. Montreal Cottons Ltd., Valleyfield, Que., Can., 1951-54; supt. Mill 4 Dan River Mills, Danville, Va., 1946-51; sr. v.p. United Merchants & Mfrs. Inc., N.Y.C., 1972-77; chmn. bd. Asso. Textiles Can. Ltd., 1969-77; pres., chief exec. officer Arnold Print Works, Inc., Adams, Mass., 1977-83, Alton Fabrics, Allentown, Pa., 1983-85; pres. Asheville Dye & Finishing, Swannanoa, N.C., 1985-87; pres., chief exec. officer River Dyeing and Finishing Co., Asheville, N.C., 1988—; dir. Northwestern Bank, Asheville, N.C., Western Carolina Industries Inc., Brit. Silk Dyeing Co., Valchem Australia, Profile Sports Corp., West Lebanon, N.H. Mem. coun. Luth. Ch., 1962—. Lt. AUS, 1943-46. Decorated Bronze Star, Purple Heart. Mem. ASME, Am. Assn. Textile Chemists and Colorists, Can. Textile Inst. (dir.), Soc. Advancement of Mgmt. (nat. gov. 1961-62), Can. Club (N.Y.), Asheville Country Club. Home: 214 Stratford Rd Asheville NC 28804-1440 also: 131 Riverside Dr Asheville NC 28801-3136

VANDERWALKER, DIANE MARY, materials scientist; b. Springfield, Mass., Nov. 1, 1955. BS, Boston Coll., 1977; PhD, MIT, 1981. NATO fellow U. Oxford, Eng., 1981-82; asst. prof. SUNY, Stony Brook, 1983-85; materials rsch. engr. Army Rsch. Lab. (formerly U.S. Army Materials Tech. Lab.), Watertown, Mass., 1986-94; cons. IBM, Yorktown Heights, N.Y. Contbr. articles to profl. publs. Mem. N.Y. Acad. Scis. Roman Catholic.

VANDER WEIDE, BOB, professional sports team executive; m. Cherl Vander Weide; 3 children. V.p. basketball ops. Orlando (Fla.) Magic, 1992-94, pres., CEO, 1994—; CEO RDV Sports, 1994—; pres., CEO Orlando Solar Bears, 1996—. Office: Orlando Magic 1 Magic Pl Orlando FL 32801-1116

VANDER WEIDE, CHERI DEVOS, sports team executive, marketing professional; b. Grand Rapids, Mich., Feb. 3, 1961; m. Robert A. Vander Weide. BA in Bus. Adminstrn., Hope Coll. Dir. health and beauty mktg. Amway Corp., Ada, Mich., v.p. corp. affairs, mem. policy bd.; exec. vice-chmn. gov. bd. Orlando Magic Basketball. Trustee United Arts of Ctrl. Fla.; chmn. children's hosp. com. Butterworth Hosp. Office: Amway Corp 7575 Fulton St E Ada MI 49355-0001

VANDERWERF, MARY ANN, elementary school educator, consultant; b. Buffalo, N.Y., Aug. 18, 1938; d. Richard and Petronella Gertruida (Hell) V.; m. Malcolm Donald Brutman, Apr. 30, 1989; 1 child, Susan Still. BS in Edn., SUNY, Buffalo, 1970, MA in English, 1971, PhD in Rsch. and Evaluation in Edn., 1981. Cert. tchr., N.Y. Legal sec. Hetzelt & Watson, Buffalo, 1957-64; exec. sec. Bell Aerospace Corp., Wheatfield, N.Y., 1964-69; tchr. Amherst (N.Y.) Ctrl. Schs., 1972-94; instr. SUNY, Buffalo, 1979, 85-86, children's lit. cons., 1980-92; pres., cons., facilitator The Synergy Advantage, Inc., Amherst, 1994—; collaborator U.S. Space and Rocket Ctr./U.S. Space Acad., Huntsville, Ala., 1995—; presenter Williamsville Ctrl. Schs., Internat. Reading Assn., Ireland, 1982, Anaheim, Calif., 1983, New Orleans, 1985, 89, Toronto, Ont., Can., 1988, N.Y. State English Coun., Amherst, 1984, St. Bonaventure U., 1984, Amherst Ctrl. Sch. Dist., 1986, 92, 94, Creative Problem Solving Inst., Buffalo, 1986—, Early Childhood Edn. Conf., 1988, Early Childhood Edn. Coun. Western N.Y., Buffalo, 1990, U. Nev., Las Vegas, 1991; book reviewer Harper Collins Children's Books, 1991. Author: (with others) Science and Technology in Fact and Fiction/Children's, 1989, Science and Technology in Fact and Fiction: Young Adult, 1990, Teacher to Teacher: Strategies for the Elementary Classroom, 1993; contbr. articles to profl. jours. Advisor child life dept. Children's Hosp., Buffalo, 1984-85. Mem. Am. Fedn. Tchrs., Internat. Reading Assn. (cons. Niagara Frontier Reading Coun.), Creative Edn. Found., N.Y. State Coun. Tchrs. English (presenter), Children's Lit. Assn., Hans Christian Andersen Soc., Pi Lambda Theta (Alpha Nu chpt.). Avocations: sailing, reading, grandparenting, traveling. Home: 1860 N Forest Rd Williamsville NY 14221-1321 Office: The Synergy Advantage Inc 2495 Kensington Ave Amherst NY 14226-4929

VANDER WILT, CARL EUGENE, banker; b. Ottumwa, Iowa, Aug. 17, 1942; s. John Adrian and Wilma (Hulsbos) V W.; m. Carol Anne Szymanski, Jan. 29, 1977; children—Dirk Francis, Neal Adrian. BS, Iowa State U., 1964, PhD, 1968; grad. Advanced Mgmt. Program, Harvard U., 1986. Research economist Fed. Res. Bank, Chgo., 1970-73, asst. v.p., 1973-74, v.p., 1974-79, sr. v.p., 1979-84, sr. v.p., chief fin. officer, 1984—. Mem., bd. dirs. Goodwill Industries Met. Chgo., Roosevelt U. Served to capt. U.S. Army, 1968-70. Mem. Execs. Club Chgo. (dir., chmn. reception com.), Banker's Club Chgo., Econ. Club Chgo. Home: 656 Locust St Winnetka IL 60093-2012 Office: Fed Res Bank 230 S La Salle St Chicago IL 60604-1496

VANDEUSEN, BRUCE DUDLEY, company executive; b. Lorain, Ohio, Aug. 20, 1931; s. Clarence Elmer and Margaret (Richards) VanD.; m. Ann Marie Groves, Aug. 17, 1957; children: David Bruce, Elizabeth Ann. Janet Marie. B.A., Ohio Wesleyan U., 1952; M.S., U. Mich., 1958, Ph.D., 1971; M.A.E., Chrysler Inst. Engring., Highland Park, Mich., 1958. Registered profl. engr., Mich. Fellow Ohio State U., Columbus, 1953-54; student engr. Chrysler Corp., Highland Park, 1956-58, sr. research scientist, 1958-67; chief engr. Chrysler Def., Inc., Center Line, Mich., 1967-79, mgr. advanced devel., 1979-82; dir. advanced devel. Gen. Dynamics, Warren, Mich., 1982-87, program dir., 1987-93; pres. Edn. Svcs., Birmingham, Mich., 1994—. Contbr. numerous articles to profl. publs.; patentee electronic cirs. Trustee Birmingham Bd. Edn., Mich., 1976-88, pres., 1979-84, 87-88; trustee Birmingham Community House, 1981-87. Mem. Soc. Automotive Engrs. (chmn. sci. engring. activity 1967-69, Arch T. Colwell award 1968), Am. Def. Preparedness Assn., Assn. U.S. Army. Republican. Methodist. Home: 1492 W Lincoln St Birmingham MI 48009-1830 Office: Edn Svcs PO Box 170 Birmingham MI 48012-0170 *Accept, embrace and instigate change, not for the sake of change but for the sake of improvement.*

VANDEVENDER, BARBARA JEWELL, elementary education educator, farmer; b. Trenton, Mo., Dec. 4, 1929; d. Raleigh Leon and Rose Rea (Dryer) S.; m. Delbert Lyle Vandevender, Aug. 15, 1948; children: Lyle Gail, James R. BS, N.E. Mo. State U., 1971, MA, 1973. Elem. tchr. Williams Sch., Spickard, Mo., 1948-49; reading specialist Spikard R-2 Sch., 1971-74, Princeton (Mo.) R-5 Sch., 1974-89; mem. ad hoc com. State Dept. Edn., Jefferson City, Mo., 1994-95; speaker in field. Pres. Spickard PTA, 1963-64, Women's Ext. Club, Galt, Mo.; foster mother Family Svcs., Trenton, Mi., 1972-79; mem. ad hoc com. State Dept. of Edn., Jefferson City, Mo., 1994-95. Pres. Spickard PTA, 1963-64, Women's Ext. Club, Galt, Mo.; foster mother Family Svcs., Trenton, Mo., 1972-79; mem. ad hoc com. State Dept. Edn., Jefferson City, Mo., 1994-95. Recipient Mo. State Conservation award Goodyear Tire Co., Akron, Ohio, 1972, Balanced Farming award Gulf Oil Co., N.Y.C., 1972, Mo. State Farming award Kansas City C. of C., 1974, FHA State Farming award, Jefferson City, Mo., 1974, Outstanding Leadership Mo. U., Columbia, 1976, Ednl. Leadership award MSTA, Columbia, 1984, Outstanding Contbn. to Internat. Reading Assn., Newark, Del., 1988. Mem. Internat. Reading Assn. (pres. North Ctrl. coun. 1985-86). Republican. Baptist.

VAN DEVENDER, J. PACE, physical scientist, management consultant; b. Jackson, Miss., Sept. 12, 1947; m. Nancy Jane Manning, 1971; 3 children. BA in Physics, Vanderbilt U., 1969; MA in Physics, Dartmouth Coll., 1971; PhD in Physics, U. London, 1974. Physicist diagnostics devel. Lawrence Livermore Lab., 1969; mem. tech. staff pulsed power rsch. and devel. Sandia Nat. Labs., 1974-78, divsn. supr. pulsed power rsch. divsn., 1978-82, dept. mgr. fusion rsch., 1982-84; dir. pulsed power scis. Sandia Nat. Labs., Albuquerque, 1984-93, dir. corp. comm., 1993, dir. Nat. Indsl. Alliances Ctr., 1993-95; pres. Prosperity Inst., 1995—; mem. rev. bd. Adv. Photon Source Project, Argonne Nat. Lab. Mem. editorial bd. Laser and Particle Beams, 1987-90. Mem. bd. trust Vanderbilt U., 1969-73. With U.S. Army, 1969-71. Recipient Ernest Orlando Lawrence Meml. award U.S. Dept. Energy, 1991; named one of 100 Most Promising Scientists Under 40, Sci. Digest, 1984; Marshal scholar U. London, 1971-74. Fellow Am. Phys. Soc.; mem. Naval Studies Bd., Phi Beta Kappa, Omicron Delta Kappa, Sigma Xi. Office: Prosperity Inst 7604 Lamplighter Ln NE Albuquerque NM 87109-3217

VAN DEVENTER, ARIE PIETER, agricultural engineer; b. Hardinxveld-Giessendam, The Netherlands, June 11, 1963; m. Corine Margreet Geljon, Aug. 25, 1989; 1 child, Raisa Céline. BS, MS in Soil and Water Engring., Agrl. U. Wageningen, The Netherlands, 1981-88; PhD in Agrl. Engring., Ohio State U., 1992. Rsch. assoc. Ohio State U., Columbus, 1989-92, postdoctoral rschr. dept. agrl. engring., 1992-93; cons. dept. remote sensing and digital photogrammetry Grontmij Geogroep, Roosendaal, The Netherlands, 1993-95, head dept. geodata, 1995-96, head geodata svcs., 1996—; chmn. Interest Group on Global Understanding, 1991-93; treas. Stichting Auto Reizen Indonesia, 1993—. Contbr. articles to profl. jours. Mem. Am. Soc. Agrl. Engrs. (Robert E. Stewart Engring. Humanities award 1993), Am. Soc. Photogrammetry and Remote Sensing, Gamma Sigma Delta, Alpha Epsilon, Phi Kappa Phi, Phi Beta Delta. Home: Van Wassenaerlaan 19, 4797 CS Willemstad The Netherlands Office: Grontmij Geogroep, Postbus 1747, 4700 BS Roosendaal The Netherlands

VANDEVER, WILLIAM DIRK, lawyer; b. Chgo., Aug. 1, 1949; s. Lester J. and Elizabeth J. V.; m. Kathi J. Zellmer, Aug. 26, 1983; children: Barton Dirk, Brooke Shelby. BS, U. Mo., Kansas City, 1971, JD with distinction, 1974. Bar: Mo. 1975, U.S. Dist. Ct. (we. dist.) Mo. 1975. Dir. Popham Law Firm, Kansas City, Mo., 1975—; lectr. medicine, engring. and multiple CLE various hosps. and colls., Kansas City Mo., 1979—. Issue editor U. Mo.-Kansas City Law Rev., 1974. Mem. ABA, Am. Trial Lawyers Assn., Mo. Assn. Trial Attys., Kansas City Met. Bar Assn. (treas., sec., pres., exec. com. 1986—, elected to 16th Jud. Commn. 1988—), Kansas City Bar Found. (treas. 1992, sec. 1994, pres. 1996-97), Interest on Lawyer Trust Accts. of Mo. (bd. govs.), Kansas City Mem. Svcs. (pres. 1988—, commr. 16th jud. cir. selection com.), Phi Delta Phi, Beta Theta Pi. Avocations: tennis, skiing, running, reading. Home: 11380 W 121st Ter Shawnee Mission KS 66213-1978 Office: Popham Law Firm 1300 Commerce Trust Bldg Kansas City MO 64106

VAN DE VYVER, SISTER MARY FRANCILENE, academic administrator; b. Detroit, Sept. 6, 1941; d. Hector Joseph and Irene Cecilia (Zygailo) V. BA, Madonna Coll., 1965; MEd, Wayne State U., 1970, PhD, 1977. Joined Sisters of St. Felix of Cantalice, Roman Cath. Ch., 1967. Tchr. Ladywood High Sch., 1965-74; adminstrv. asst. to pres. Madonna Coll., Livonia, Mich., 1974-75, acad. dean, 1975-76; now pres. Madonna U., Livonia, Mich. Office: Madonna U Office of President 36600 Schoolcraft Rd Livonia MI 48150-1176*

VAN DE WALLE, ETIENNE, demographer; b. Namur, Belgium, Apr. 29, 1932; came to U.S., 1961; s. Arnould and Yolande (Blommaert) Van De W.; m. Francine Robyns de Schneidauer, Aug. 24, 1955; children: Dominique, Nicolas, Jean-Francois, Patrice. Dr. in Law, U. Louvain, Belgium, 1956, MA in Econs., 1957, PhD in Demography, 1973. Researcher Irsac, Rwanda, Burundi, 1957-61; rsch. assoc. Princeton (N.J.) U., 1962-64, rsch. staff, 1964-67, rsch. demographer, 1967-72; vis. lectr. U. Calif., Berkeley, 1971-72; prof. U. Pa., Phila., 1972—; dir. Population Studies Ctr., U. Pa., 1976-82; sr. assoc. The Population Coun., Bamako, Mali, 1982. Author: The Female Population of France, 1974; co-author: The Demography of Tropical Africa, 1968. Fellowship Woodrow Wilson Ctr. for Scholars, 1976. Mem. Internat. Union for Scientific Study of Population, Population Assn. of Am. (pres. 1992). Home: 261 Sycamore Ave Merion Station PA 19066-1545 Office: Population Studies Ctr 3718 Locust Walk Philadelphia PA 19104-6209

VANDEWALLE, GERALD WAYNE, state supreme court chief justice; b. Noonan, N.D., Aug. 15, 1933; s. Jules C. and Blanche Marie (Gits) VandeW. B.Sc., U. N.D., 1955, J.D., 1958. Bar: N.D., U.S. Dist. Ct. N.D. 1959. Spl. asst. atty. gen. State of N.D., Bismarck, 1958-75, 1st asst. atty. gen., 1975-78; justice N.D. Supreme Ct., 1978-92, chief justice, 1993—; mem. faculty Bismarck Jr. Coll., 1972-76. Editor-in-chief N.D. Law Rev, 1957-58. Active Bismarck Meals on Wheels. Recipient Sioux award U. N.D., 1992, Ednl. Law award N.D. Coun. Sch. Attys., 1987, Love Without Fear award Abused Adult Resource Ctr., 1995. Mem. ABA (co-chair bar admissions com., mem. coun. sect. legal edn. and admissions), State Bar Assn. N.D., Burleigh County Bar Assn., Conf. of Chief Justices (bd. dirs., chair fed.-state tribal rels. com.), Am. Contract Bridge League, Order of Coif, N.D. Jud. Conf. (exec. com.), Phi Eta Sigma, Beta Alpha Psi (Outstanding Alumnus award Zeta chpt. 1995), Beta Gamma Sigma, Phi Alpha Delta. Roman Catholic. Clubs: Elks, K.C. Office: ND Supreme Ct State Capitol 600 E Boulevard Ave Bismarck ND 58505-0660

VAN DE WETERING, JOHN E(DWARD), academic administrator; b. Bellingham, Wash., Jan. 20, 1927; s. John and Jessie Van De W.; m. Maxine Schorr, Mar. 7, 1961; 1 son, Josh. B.A. in History, U. Wash., 1950, M.A. in History, 1953, Ph.D. in History, 1959. Instr. U. Idaho, 1959; instr. U. Wash., 1959-61, vis. asst. prof. history, 1963; asst. prof. U. Mont., 1961-64, asso. prof., 1964-69, prof., chmn. dept. history, 1969-76; acting pres. Eastern Mont. Coll., 1976-77, pres., 1977-81; pres. SUNY, Coll. at Brockport, 1981—; mem. Mont. Com. for Humanities, 1972-74; Danforth asso. Author: (with Jack Bumsted) What Must I Do to Be Saved?: The Great Awakening in Colonial America, 1976; contbr. articles to profl. jours. Bd. dirs. Park Ridge Long Term Care Bd., Rochester, N.Y., George Eastman House Mus. Photography, Rochester, Rochester Area Ednl. TV Assn. With C.E. U.S. Army, 1955-57. Home: 230 Holley St Brockport NY 14420-2124 Office: SUNY Coll at Brockport Office of Pres Brockport NY 14420

VAN DINE, HAROLD FORSTER, JR., architect; b. New Haven, Aug. 28, 1930; s. Harold Forster and Marguerite Anna (Eichstedt) Van D.; m. Maureen Kallick, Mar. 1, 1983; children by previous marriage: Rebecca Van Dine, Stephanie Van Dine Natale, Gretchen Van Dine Natale. BA, Yale Coll., 1952; MArch, Yale Sch. Arch., 1958. Registered architect. Designer Minoru Yamasaki & Assocs., Detroit, 1958-60; chief designer Gunnar Birkerts & Assocs., Detroit, 1960-67; prin. Straub, Van Dine & Assocs., Troy, Mich., 1967-80; chief architecture and design officer Harley Ellington Design, Southfield, Mich., 1980-95; archtl. design cons. Birmingham, Mich., 1995—; v.p. Fields, Devereaux, HEPY, L.A., 1984-95. Prin. works include Mcpl. Libr., Troy, Mich., campuses for Oakland (Mich.) Community Coll., North Hills Ch., Troy, First Ctr. Office Plaza, chemistry bldgs at. U. Mich. and Ind. U., G.M.F. Robotics Hdqrs., Flint Ink Rsch. and Devel. Ctr., Comerica Bank Ops. Ctr., Christ the King Mausoleum, Chgo., Resurrection Mausoleum, Staten Island, Mich. Biotech Inst., Ford Sci. Rsch. Labs, Fetzer Inst. Hdqrs. and Retreat Ctr., Cen. Mich. U. Music Sch., Oakland U. Sci. Techs. Bldg., Corning (N.Y.) Credit Union. Bd. dirs. Cultural Coun. Birmingham/Bloomfield, 1990—. Served to lt. (j.g.) USN, 1952-55. Recipient Book award AIA, 1958, Excellence in Architecture Silver medal AIA, 1958, Gold medal Detroit chpt. AIA, 1987, Mich. Soc. of Architects gold medal, 1991, over 50 major design awards; William Wirt Winchester travelling fellowship Yale U. Sch. Architecture, 1958; elect. to AIA Coll. Fellows, 1979. Mem. Pewabic Soc. (bd. dirs. 1983—). Home and Office: 544 S Bates St Birmingham MI 48009-1423

VAN DINE, PAUL EDWIN, clergyman; b. Bluffton, Ind., June 19, 1939; s. Charles W. and Nellie Ruth (Maupin) Van D.; m. Carolyn Ann Shimp, June 12, 1960; children: Vicki Linn, Mark David, Karen Joan. BA magna cum laude, U. Miami, 1960; MDiv cum laude, Drew U., 1964. Ordained to ministry Meth. Ch., 1961. Student pastor Stockholm (N.J.) Meth. Ch., 1961-64; pastor Sylvan Abbey Meth. Ch., Clearwater, Fla., 1964-67, Union Park United Meth. Ch., Orlando, Fla., 1967-69, Port Orange (Fla.) United Meth. Ch., 1969-75; sr. pastor Cypress Lake United Meth. Ch., Ft. Myers, Fla., 1980-92, First United Meth. Ch., Clearwater, Fla., 1992—; assoc. pastor Pasadena Community Ch., St. Petersburg, Fla., 1975-80; sec. bd. missions and ch. extension Fla. Conf. United Meth. Ch., 1972-75, chmn. com. on communications, 1980-84; chmn. St. Petersburg Dist. Council on Ministries, 1977-80; bd. dirs., mem. exec. com. United Meth. Reporter newspaper, 1980-86. Contbr. prayers and sermons to religious publs. Democrat. Home: 305 Eastleigh Dr Clearwater FL 33756-2503 Office: First United Meth Ch 411 Turner St Clearwater FL 33756-5328

VAN DINE, VANCE, investment banker; b. San Francisco, July 2, 1925; s. Melvin Everett and Grace Winifred (Harris) Van D.; m. Isabel Erskine Brewster, Sept. 8, 1956; 1 dau., Rose M. (dec.). BA, Yale U., 1949; LLB, NYU, 1955. Assoc. Morgan Stanley & Co., N.Y.C., 1953-59, 61-63; ptnr. Morgan Stanley & Co., 1963-75; mng. dir. Morgan Stanley & Co., Inc., N.Y.C., 1970-83; adv. dir. Morgan Stanley & Co., N.Y.C., 1983—; cons. Internat. Bank for Reconstn. and Devel., 1959-61; chmn. Doane Western Co. Author: The Role of the Investment Banker in International Transactions, 1970, The U.S. Market After Controls, 1974. Bd. dirs. Yale U. Alumni Fund, Combined Health Appeal of Greater N.Y., Rec. for Blind, Inc., N.Y.C., 1979-89; trustee Cancer Rsch. Inst., N.Y.C., Nassau County Art Mus., L.I. U., 1979-91; gov. dir. Fgn. Policy Assn., 1980-89. With USN, 1943-46. Recipient Yale Class of 1949 Disting. Service award, 1983. Mem. The Pilgrims of the U.S., Union Club, Piping Rock Club, N.Y. Yacht Club, Seawanhaka Corinthian Yacht Club, Church Club, Yale Club (N.Y.C.), Met. Opera Club. Republican. Episcopalian. Office: Morgan Stanley & Co 1251 Avenue Of The Americas New York NY 10020-1104

VANDIVER, FRANK EVERSON, institute administrator, former university president, author, educator; b. Austin, Tex., Dec. 9, 1925; s. Harry Shultz and Maude Folmsbee (Everson) V.; m. Carol Sue Smith, Apr. 19, 1952 (dec. 1979); children: Nita, Nancy, Frank Alexander; m. Renée Aubry, Mar. 21, 1980. Rockefeller fellow in humanities, U. Tex., 1946-47, Rockefeller fellow in Am. Studies, 1947-48, MA, 1949; PhD, Tulane U., 1951; MA (by decree), Oxford (Eng.) U., 1963; HHD (hon.), Austin Coll., 1977; DHL (hon.), Lincoln Coll., 1989, BA (hon.), 1994. Apptd. historian Army Service Forces Depot, Civil Service, San Antonio, 1944-45, Air U., 1951; prof. history La. State U., summers 1953-57; asst. prof. history Washington U., St. Louis, 1952-55; asst. prof. history Rice U., Houston, 1955-56, assoc. prof., 1956-58, prof., 1958-65, Harris Masterson Jr. prof. history, 1965-79, chmn. dept. history and polit. sci., 1962-63, dept. history, 1968-69, acting pres., 1969-70, provost, 1970-79, v.p., 1975-79; pres., chancellor N. Tex. State U., Denton and Tex. Coll. Osteo. Medicine, 1979-81; pres. Tex. A&M U., College Station, 1981-88, pres. emeritus, disting. U. prof., 1988—; founding pres. Acad. Marshall Plan, 1992; Sara and John Lindsey chair in humanities, 1988; Harmsworth prof. Am. history Oxford U., 1963-64; vis. prof. history U. Ariz., summer 1961; master Margarett Root Brown Coll., Rice U., 1964-66; Harman lectr. Air Force Acad., 1963; Keese lectr. U. Chattanooga, 1967; Fortenbaugh lectr. Gettysburg Coll., 1974; Phi Beta Kappa assoc. lectr., 1970—; vis. prof. mil. history U.S. Mil. Acad., 1973-74; hon. pres. Occidental U., St. Louis, 1975-80; chmn. bd. Am. U. Cairo, 1992—. Editor: The Civil War Diary of General Josiah Gorgas, 1947, Confederate Blockade Running Through Bermuda, 1981-65: Letters and Cargo Manifests, 1947, Proceedings of First Confederate Congress, 4th Session, 1953, Proceedings of Second Confederate Congress, 1959, A Collection of Louisiana Confederate Letters; new edit., J.E. Johnston's Narrative of Military Operations; new edit., J.A. Early's Civil War Memoirs, The Idea of the South, 1964, Battlefields and Landmarks of the Civil War, 1996; author: Ploughshares Into Swords: Josiah Gorgas and the Confederate Command System, 1956, Mighty Stonewall, 1957, Fields of Glory, (with W.H. Nelson), 1960, Jubal's Raid, 1960, Basic History of the Confederacy, 1962, Jefferson Davis and the Confederate State, 1964, Their Tattered Flags: The Epic of the Confederacy, 1970, The Southwest: South or West?, 1975, Black Jack: The Life and Times of John J. Pershing, 1977 (Nat. Book Award finalist 1978), (address) The Long Loom of Lincoln, 1986, Blood Brothers: A Short History of the Civil War, 1992, Shadows of Vietnam: Lyndon Johnson's Wars, 1997; also hist. articles, mem. bd. editors: U.S. Grant Papers, 1973—. Mem. bd. trustees Am. U. in Cairo, 1988, chmn., 1992—. Recipient Laureate Lincoln Acad., Ill., 1973, Carr P. Collins prize Tex. Inst. Letters, 1958, Harry S. Truman award Kansas City Civil War Round Table, Jefferson Davis award Confederate Meml. Lit. Soc., 1970, Fletcher Pratt award N.Y. Civil War Round Table, 1970, Outstanding Civilian Svc. medal Dept. Army, 1974, Nevins-Freeman award Chgo. Civil War Round Table, 1982, T. Harry Williams Meml. award, 1985; named Hon. Knight San Jacinto, 1993, Hon. Mem. Sons of Republic of Tex., 1986; rsch. grantee Am. Philos. Soc., 1953, 54, 60, Huntington Libr. rsch. grantee, 1961; Guggenheim fellow, 1955-56. Fellow Tex. Hist. Assn.; mem. Am. Hist. Assn., So. Hist. Assn. (assoc. editor jour. 1959-62, pres. 1975-76), Tex. Inst. Letters (past pres.), Jefferson Davis Assn. (pres., chmn. adv. bd. editors of papers), Soc. Am. Historians (councillor), Tex. Philos. Soc. (pres. 1978), Civil War Round Table (Houston), Orgn. Am. Historians, Phi Beta Kappa, SAR of Tex. (hon., Knight San Jacinto 1993). Clubs: Cosmos, Army and Navy (Washington); Briarcrest Country (College Station). Office: Tex A&M U Mosher Inst Internat Policy Studies College Station TX 77843-2400

VANDIVER, PAMELA BOWREN, research scientist; b. Santa Monica, Calif., Jan. 12, 1946; d. Roy King and Patricia (Woolard) Evans; m. J. Kim Vandiver, Aug., 1968 (div. 1984); 1 child, Amy. BA in Humanities and Asian Studies, Scripps Coll., 1967; postgrad., U. Calif., Berkeley, 1968; MA in Art, Pacific Luth. U., 1971; MS in Ceramic Sci., MIT, 1983, PhD in Materials Sci. and Near Eastern Archeology, 1985. Instr. in glass and ceramics Mass. Coll. of Art, Boston, 1972; lectr. MIT, Cambridge, 1973-78, rsch. assoc., 1978-85; rsch. phys. scientist Conservation Analytical Lab., Washington, 1985-89; sr. scientist in ceramics C.A.L. Smithsonian Instn., Washington, 1989—; instr. semester-at-sea U. Pitts., spring 1995; vis. prof. Northwest Inst. Light Industry, Xianyang, China, 1996; bd. dirs. Rolatape Corp., Spokane, Wash.; guest rschr. Nat. Inst. Stds. and Tech., Gaithersburg, Md., 1989-91. Co-author: Ceramic Masterpieces, 1986; co-editor: Materials Issues in Art and Archaeology, vol 1 1988, vol. 5, 1997; bd. editors Archeomaterials, 1986-93; contbr. numerous articles to profl. jours. Sponsor mentorship program Thomas Jefferson H.S. of Sci. and Tech., Alexandria, 1992. Recipient Disting. Alumna Achievement award Scripps Coll., 1993. Fellow Am. Anthrop. Assn.; mem. AAAS, Am. Inst. Archeology, Soc. Am. Archeology, Internat. Inst. of Conservation, Soc. for History of Tech., Am. Ceramics Soc. (ancient ceramics com. 1978—), Materials Rsch. Soc. (guest editor bull. 1992), Am. Chem. Soc., Cosmos Club, Sigma Xi. Avocations: sailing, diving, photography. Office: Smithsonian Inst Conservation Analytical Lab Washington DC 20560

VANDIVIER, BLAIR ROBERT, lawyer; b. Rapid City, S.D., Dec. 24, 1955; s. Robert Eugene and Barbara Jean (Kidd) V.; m. Elizabeth Louise Watson, July 26, 1980; children: Jessica Elizabeth, Jennifer Louise. BS magna cum laude, Butler U., 1978; JD cum laude, Ind. U., 1981. Bar: Ind. 1981, U.S. Dist. Ct. (so. dist.) Ind. 1981, U.S. Tax Ct. 1985. Assoc. Henderson, Daily, Withrow, Johnson & Gross, Indpls., 1981-83; assoc., ptnr. Johnson, Gross, Densborn & Wright, Indpls., 1983-85, of counsel, 1985-87; v.p., sec. Benchmark Products, Inc. (formerly Benchmark Chem. Corp.), Indpls., 1985-91, pres., 1991—, also bd. dirs.; ptnr. Gross & Vandivier, Indpls., 1987-89; of counsel Riley, Bennett & Egloff, Indpls., 1990—; mgmt. rep. Pro Com, L.L.C., 1991—; v.p. Seleco Inc., Indpls., 1988-93, pres., 1993—. Mem. com. Conner Prairie Settlement Fund Dr., Indpls., 1983-85, Riley Run, 1987—; mem. regulatory study com. City of Indpls., 1993—. Mem. ABA, Ind. Bar Assn., Indpls. Bar Assn (bd. dirs. young lawyers divsn. 1982-85), Am. Electroplaters & Surface Finisher's Soc. (chmn. nat. law com. 1986—, pres. Indpls. br. 1989, tech. conf. bd. 1991—, chmn. surface finishers ann. tech. conf. and exhbn. 1994, chmn. surface finishers focus group 1994—, Tech. Conf. Bd. Recognition award 1996), Metal Finishing Suppliers Assn. (spl. projects svcs. com., 1988-93, chmn. 1993—, chmn. hazardous materials br. 1991-93, trustee 1992-95, v.p. 1995-97), Highland Golf Club, Highland Country Club (chmn. ins. com. 1989-94, golf. com. 1992-94, bd. dirs. 1995—, chmn. fin. com. 1996—) Surface Finishing Industry Coun. (bd. dirs., sec. 1997—), Econ. Club Indpls., Delta Tau Delta (chmn. 1987—, bd. dirs. Beta Zeta Found. 1986, Outstanding Alumnus Beta Zeta chpt. 1986). Republican. Episcopalian. Avocations: golf, reading. Home: 8927 Woodacre Ln Indianapolis IN 46234-2848 Office: Benchmark Products Inc PO Box 68809 Indianapolis IN 46268-0809

VAN DOMELEN, JOHN FRANCIS, academic administrator; b. Havana, Cuba, Oct. 19, 1942; s. Floyd and Sara (Molina) Van D.; m. Naomi Ruth Kittlesen. BS in Applied Physics, Mich. Tech. U., 1964; MS in Water Res. Mgmt., U. Wis., Madison, 1972; PhD in Civil Engring., U. Wis., 1974. Commd. 2nd lt. USAF, 1964, advanced through grades to col., 1988; mgr. engring. Charmin Paper Products Co., Green Bay, Wis., 1969-70; asst. prof. Norwich U., Northfield, Vt., 1974-79, head engring. and tech. dept., 1979-83, head engring. and tech. div., 1983-85, v.p. acad. affairs, dean of faculty, 1985-90; pres. Wentworth Inst. Tech., Boston, 1990—; mem. Engring. Workforce Commn. Contbr. articles to profl. jours. Mem. MassPep, Boston, 1990—. Decorated Cross of Gallantry (Vietnam); recipient Centennial medal IEEE, 1984. Mem. ASCE, Am. Soc. Engring. Edn., Sci. Rsch.

Soc. N.Am., New Eng. Assn. Schs. and Colls. (commr. for inst. higher edn. 1994—). Avocations: racquetball, golf, science fiction. Office: Wentworth Inst Tech 550 Huntington Ave Boston MA 02115-5901

VAN DOMMELEN, DAVID B., artist, educator; b. Grand Rapids, Mich., Aug. 21, 1929; s. Henry and Thelma (Brown) Van D.; m. Michal Bohnstedt; children: Erica, Dorn. Diploma in interior design, Harrington Inst., Chgo., 1951; BA, Mich. State U., 1956, MA, 1957. Art cons. Warren (Mich.) Schs., 1957-59; instr. home art Pa. State U., State College, 1959-62; assoc. prof. interiors Pa. State U., 1964-73, prof. art edn., 1973-87, prof. emeritus, 1987—; asst. prof. design, U. Maine, Orono, 1962-64; instr., Haystack Mountain Crafts Schs., Deer Isle, Maine, 1963, 64, 74, Arrowmont Arts and Crafts, Gatlinburg, Tenn., 1971-82; vis. prof., U. Iowa, Iowa City, 1967, 68, 70. Author: Decorative Wall Hangings: Art with Fabric, 1962, Walls: Enrichment & Ornamentation, 1965, Designing & Decorating Interiors, 1965, New Uses for Old Cannonballs, 1966, Doughboy Letters, 1977; contbr. articles to various publications; represented in numerous art exhbns. Cpl. U.S. Army, 1952-54. Grantee for craft rsch., Ford Found., 1972, OAS, 1976, Pa. State U., 1986; recipient Eleanor Fishborn award, Ednl. Press. Am., 1973. Mem. Am. Craft Coun., Am. Home Econs. Assn. (bd. dirs. 1966-71), Pa. Home Econs. Assn. (pres. 1970), Am.-Scandinavian Found., Internat. Fedn. Home Econs., Lions. Avocation: stamp collecting. Home: RR 1 Box 631 Petersburg PA 16669-9248 Office: Pa State U 207 Arts Coll University Park PA 16802

VAN DOREN, EMERSON BARCLAY, administrative judge; b. Rahway, N.J., Dec. 30, 1940; s. Emerson Maynard and Jaqueline Pendleton (Hicks) Van D.; m. Janet Elisabeth Bumbarger, Dec. 28, 1963; children: Pendleton Barclay, Virginia Cary. BA, Harvard U., 1962; JD, U. Mich., 1965; postgrad. degree (hon.), Air War Coll., Maxwell AF Base, Ala., 1985. Bar: Ky. 1965, N.H. 1971, U.S. Dist. Ct. (we. dist.) Ky. 1966, U.S. Dist. Ct. N.H. 1972. Assoc. Brown, Ardery, Todd & Dudley, Louisville, 1965-66; judge adv. USAF, 1966-71, 72-76; pvt. practice N. Conway, N.H., 1971-72; sr. procurement atty. U.S. Dept. Energy, Washington, 1976-81, dep. asst. gen. counsel for procurement, 1981-85; adminstrv. judge, mediator U.S. Energy Bd. Contract Appeals, Arlington, Va., 1985, chmn., chief adminstrv. judge, 1985—; chmn. U.S. Energy Fin. Assistance Appeals Bd., U.S. Energy Invention Licensing Appeals Bd., U.S. Energy Patent Compensation Bd. Co-chair Randolph-Macon Woman's Coll. Adv. Coun. Admissions. Capt. USAF, 1966-76, col. USAFR, command mobilization asst. to staff judge adv., 1988-90, ret., 1990. Decorated Meritorious Svc. medal with one oak leaf cluster, Commendation medal with one oak leaf cluster, Legion of Merit award; Leckie fellow, Resident fellow U. Mich.; named Outstanding Young Judge Adv., AF Systems Command, 1975. Mem. ABA, Sr. Execs. Assn. (chpt. pres. 1993-96), Bd. Contract Appeals Judges Assn. (bd. govs.), Fed. Bar Assn., N.H. Bar Assn., Ky. Bar Assn. Avocation: surf and fly fishing. Office: Energy Contract Appeals Bd 4040 Fairfax Dr Arlington VA 22203-1613

VAN DOVER, KAREN, middle and elementary school educator, curriculum consultant, language arts specialist; b. Astoria, N.Y.; d. Frederick A. and Frances L. (Thomas) Van D. BA, CUNY; MALS, SUNY, Stony Brook; postgrad., St. John's U., Jamaica, N.Y., 1992. Cert. permanent N-6 tchr., art tchr. K-12, sch. adminstr., supr., N.Y. Tchr., sch. dist. adminstr. St. James (N.Y.) Elem. Sch.; tchr. Nesaquake Intermediate Sch., St. James, lead tchr. English, 1984-92; lead tchr. English Smithtown Mid Sch., St. James, 1992-93, curriculum specialist, 1993—; leader staff devel. and curriculum devel. workshops Smithtown Sch. Dist., 1984—, mem. supt.'s adv. com. for gifted and talented, mem. supt. adv. com. for lang. arts assessment, mem. textbook selection coms. site-based mgmt. team, 1994—; mem. master tchr. bd. Prentice Hall, Englewood Cliffs, N.J., 1990—. Contbg. author: Prentice Hall Literature Copper, 1991, 94. Corr. sec. Yaphank Taxpayers and Civic Assn., 1984-86, Nesaquake Sch. PTA, 1990-91, mem., 1977-92; mem. Smithtown Mid. Sch. PTA, 1992—. Mem. ASCD, Am. Ednl. Rsch. Assn., Nat. Assn. Secondary Sch. Prins., Nat. Coun. Tchrs. English, Internat. Reading Assn., Nat. Middle Schs. Assn., N.Y. State English Coun., Nat. Assn. of Elem. Sch. Prins., Phi Delta Kappa. Home: 8 Penn Commons Yaphank NY 11980-2025 Office: Smithtown Middle Sch 10 School St Saint James NY 11780-1833

VAN DOVER, ROBERT BRUCE, physicist; b. Eatontown, N.J., Apr. 30, 1952. BS, Princeton U., 1974; MS, Stanford U., 1975, PhD, 1980. Mem. tech. staff Bell Labs., Lucent Techs., Murray Hill, N.J., 1980—. Mem. IEEE, Am. Phys. Soc., Materials Rsch. Soc. Office: Bell Labs, Lucent Techs 700 Mountain Ave Rm 1t-106 New Providence NJ 07974-1208

VAN DRESER, MERTON LAWRENCE, ceramic engineer; b. Des Moines, June 5, 1929; s. Joseph Jerome and Victoria (Love) Van D.; m. Evelyn Lenore Manny, July 12, 1952; children: Peter, Jennifer Sue. BS in Ceramic Engring., Iowa State U., 1951. Tech. supt. Owens-Corning Fiberglas Corp., Kansas City, Mo., 1954-57; rsch. engr. Kaiser Aluminum & Chem. Corp., Milpitas, Calif., 1957-60, rsch. sect. head, 1960-63, lab. mgr., 1963-65, assoc. dir. rsch., 1965-69; dir. refractories rsch. Kaiser Aluminum & Chem. Corp., Pleasanton, Calif., 1969-72; dir. non-metallic materials rsch. Kaiser Aluminum & Chem. Corp., 1972-83; v.p., dir. rsch. Indsl. Chem. div. and Harshaw/Filtrol Partnership Kaiser Aluminum & Chem. Corp., Cleve., 1983-85; dir. bus. devel. Kaiser Aluminum & Chem. Corp., Pleasanton, 1985-88, cons., 1988—; mem. adv. bd. dept. ceramic engring. U. Ill., 1974-78; chmn. tech. adv. com. Refractories Inst., 1980-84; mem. nat. materials adv. bd. Nat. Acad. Sci.; mem. Indsl. Rsch. Inst. Contbr. articles to sci. jours. Sustaining membership chmn. local dist. Boy Scouts Am., 1980; pres. PTA, 1967-68; vol. exec. Pakistan Internat. Exec. Svc. Corps, 1990-91. Aviator C.E., U.S. Army, 1951-54. Recipient Profl. Achievement citation Iowa State U., 1978; named to Lambda Chi Alpha hall of fame, 1996. Fellow Am. Ceramic Soc. (v.p. 1973-74); mem. ASTM (hon.; com.), Brit. Ceramic Soc., Nat. Inst. Ceramic Engrs., Keramos (pres. 1976-78, herald 1980-84, Greaves Walker Roll of Honor award), Metall. Soc., AIME. Lodges: Rotary (Paul Harris fellow), Masons. Patentee in field. Avocation: comml. pilot.

VANDROSS, LUTHER, singer; s. Mary Ida Vandross. Albums include The Best of Luther Vandross...The Best of Love, Busy Body, Forever, For Always, For Love, Give Me The Reason, 1986, Never Too Much, The Night I Fell In Love, Any Love, 1989, The Power of Love, 1991, Never Let Me Go, 1993 (Grammy nomination: Best Rhythym & Blues Male Vocal for "How Deep Is Your Love"), Luther, 1993. Office: Epic Records 550 Madison Ave New York NY 10022-3211*

VAN DUSEN, ALBERT CLARENCE, university official; b. Tampa, Fla., Aug. 30, 1915; s. Charles H. and Maude E. (Green) Van D.; m. Margaret Davis, Jan. 3, 1943; children: Margaret Van Dusen Pysh, Jane Katherine, Sally Elizabeth (Mrs. Frank J. Matyskiela). BS, U. Fla., 1937, AM, 1938; PhD, Northwestern, 1942; LittD, U. Tampa, 1959; L.H.D., Duquesne U., 1967. Instr., asst. prof. dept. psychology U. Fla., 1938-41; asso. prof. psychology Northwestern U., 1946, dir. summer session, 1948-52, v.p. pub. relations, 1952-56; prof. psychology, bus. adminstrn. and edn. U. Pitts., 1956-85, asst. chancellor for planning and devel., 1956-59, vice chancellor the professions, 1959-67, vice chancellor program devel. and pub. affairs, 1967-71, vice chancellor, sec. univ., 1971-80, vice chancellor emeritus, spl. asst. for pub. affairs, 1980-85, vice chancellor emeritus, prof. emeritus psychology, bus. adminstrn. and edn., 1985—, ctr. assoc. univ. ctr. for internat. studies, 1986—; bd. dirs. Dollar Bank, Pitts. Editor: Proc. Am. Coll. Personnel Assn; contbr. articles to profl. jours. Bd. govs. Pinchot Inst. Conservation Studies; vice chmn., bd. dirs. The Buhl Found., World Affairs Coun. Pitts., vice chmn. bd. dirs. Duquesne U., acting chmn., 1987-88; bd. dirs. Pitts. YMCA, ACTION Housing, Inc., Assn. Am.'s Pub. TV Stas., QED Communications Inc., chmn. 1981-88; bd. dirs. Japan-Am. Soc. Pa.; mem. Pa. Pub. TV Network Commn.; chmn., bd. trustees Pitts. History and Landmarks Found.; pres. bd. trustees H.C. Frick Ednl. Commn., United Way Pa.; dir. South Hills Child Guidance Ctr.; chmn. selfcare study Health Edn. Ctr., Pitts., 1979-80; mem. Walter Reed Hovey Fellowship com. Pitts. Found. Lt. USNR, 1942-46. Fulbright sr. scholar Australian-Am. Ednl. Found., 1980. Fellow Am. Psychol. Assn., Am. Psychol. Soc., Pa. Psychol. Assn., Internat. Found. Social Econ. Deve.; mem. Internat. Assn. Schs. Insts. Adminstrn., C. of C. (dir. 1953-55), Am. Coll. Pub. Rels. Assn. (v.p. 1956-58), Assn. Deans and Dirs. Summer Sessions (sec. 1950-51), Profl. Schs. and World Affairs Com. (chmn. edn. and world affairs 1965-67), Am. Pers. and Guidance Assn., Midwest Psychol. Assn., Ea. Psychol. Assn., Pitts. Psychol. Assn., Internat. Assn. Applied Psychology, Western Pa. Coun. Econ. Edn., Internat. Assn. Schs. and Insts. Adminstrn., Friends of Art for Pitts. Schs. (charter mem.), Phi Beta Kappa, Sigma Xi, Beta Theta Pi, Beta Gamma Sigma. Clubs: Univ. (Pitts.), Duquesne (Pitts.). Home: 108 Blue Spruce Cir Pittsburgh PA 15243-1026

VANDUSEN, BLANCHE BAKER, actress, sculptor; b. N.Y.C., Dec. 20, 1956; d. Jack and Carroll (Baker) Garfein; m. R. Bruce Vandusen; children: Zane, Dara, Wynn. Student, Wellesley Coll. Appeared in films The Handmaid's Tale, Shakedown, Raw Deal, Sixteen Candles, Cold Feet, The Seduction of Joe Tynan, TV program Holocaust (Emmy award for Best Supporting Actress); sculpture exhibited in shows at Nat. Arts Club, N.Y.C., Pent Brush Club, N.Y.C., Salmagundi Club, N.Y.C., Cropsey-Newington Found., N.Y., Perry House Galleries, Alexandria, Va., Balch Inst., Phila. Named Anti-defamation League Woman of Achievement, 1979; recipient Philip Isenberg award, Manhattan Artist Showcase award, Beaux Arts Exhibit award, H.A. Fahdli award, Pietro Montana award.

VAN DUSEN, DONNA BAYNE, communication consultant, educator, researcher; b. Phila., Apr. 21, 1949; d. John Culbertson and Evelyn Gertrude (Godfrey) Bayne; m. David William Van Dusen, Nov. 30, 1968 (div. Dec. 1989); children: Heather, James; m. L. John Maki, Dec. 27, 1996. BA, Temple U., 1984, MA, 1986, PhD, 1993. Instr. Kutztown (Pa.) U., 1986-87, Ursinus Coll., Collegeville, Pa., 1987-96; cons., rschr. Comm. Rsch. Assoc., Valley Forge, Pa., 1993-96; asst. prof. Beaver Coll., Glenside, Pa., 1995-96; researcher Fox Chase Cancer Ctr., Phila., 1985-86; adj. faculty Temple U. Law Sch., 1994—, LaSalle U., 1994-96, Wharton Sch., U. Pa., 1994-95; faculty Internat. U., 1996—, Metro State U., Denver, 1997—. Mem. NOW, AAUP, Speech Comm. Assn., Ea. Comm. Assn. Avocations: oil painting, creative writing, sailing, gardening, reading. Home: 15 Shirley Rd Narberth PA 19072

VAN DUSEN, LANI MARIE, psychologist; b. Alexandria, Va., July 23, 1960; d. Arthur Ellsworth and Ann Marie (Brennan) Van D. BS magna cum laude, U. Ga., 1982, MS, 1985, PhD, 1988. Cert. secondary tchr., Ga. Tchr. Henry County Sch. System, McDonough, Ga., 1982-83; rsch. psychologist Metrica Inc., Bryan, Tex., 1988; asst. prof. psychology U. Ga., Athens, 1988-89, chmn. Conf. for Behavioral Scis., 1987; assoc. prof. psychology Utah State U., Logan, 1989—; cons. Western Inst. for rsch. and Evaluation, Logan, 1990—; bd. dirs. Human Learrning Clinic, Logan, 1990—, Ctr. for Sch. of Future; reviewer William C. Brown Pubs., 1990, Dushkin Pub. Group Inc., 1990-91. Contbr. articles to profl. jours. Fellow Menninger Found.; mem. APA, Psychonomic Soc., Am. Ednl. Rsch. Assn., AAUP, ASCD. Republican. Avocations: hiking, tennis, skiing, knitting, swimming. Home: 1633 North 1200 East North Logan UT 84341 Office: Utah State U Dept Psychology UMC 2810 Logan UT 84322-2810

VAN DUYN, MONA JANE, poet; b. Waterloo, Iowa, May 9, 1921; d. Earl George and Lora G. (Kramer) Van D.; m. Jarvis A. Thurston, Aug. 31, 1943. B.A., U. No. Iowa, 1942; M.A., U. Iowa, 1943; D.Litt. (hon.), Washington U., St. Louis, 1971, Cornell Coll., Iowa, 1972, U. No. Iowa, 1991, U. of the South, Sewanee, Tenn., 1993, George Wash. U., 1993; LHD, Georgetown U., 1993. Instr. in English U. Iowa, Iowa City, 1943-46; instr. in English U. Louisville, 1946-50; lectr. English Univ. Coll., Washington U., 1950-67; poetry editor, co-pub. Perspective, A Quar. of Lit., 1947-67; lectr. Salzburg (Austria) Seminar Am. Studies, 1973; adj. prof. poetry workshop Washington U., Spring 1983; vis. Hurst prof., 1987; poet-in-residence Sewanee Writers Conf., 1990, Breadloaf Writing Conf., Mass., 1974. Author: Valentines to the Wide World, 1959, A Time of Bees, 1964, To See, To Take, 1970, Bedtime Stories, 1972, Merciful Disguises, 1973, Letters from a Father and Other Poems, 1983, Near Changes, 1990 (Pulitzer Prize for poetry 1991), Firefall, 1993, If It Be Not I, 1993. Recipient Eunice Tietjens award, 1956, Helen Bullis prize, 1964, 76, Harriet Monroe award, 1968, Hart Crane Meml. award, 1968, Borestone Mountains 1st prize, 1968, Bollingen prize, 1970, Nat. Book award, 1971, Sandburg prize Cornell Coll., 1982, Shelley Meml. prize Poetry Soc. Am., 1987, Lilly prize for poetry, 1989, Mo. Arts award, 1990, Golden Plate award Am. Acad. Achievement, 1992, Arts and Edn. Coun. St. Louis award, 1994; named U.S. Poet Laureate, 1992-93; grantee Nat. Coun. Arts, 1967, NEA, 1985; Guggenheim fellow, 1972. Fellow Acad. Am. Poets (chancellor 1985); mem. NAAS, Nat. Acad. Arts and Letters (Loines prize 1976), Acad. Arts Scis.

VAN DUYNE, RICHARD PALMER, analytical chemistry and chemical physics educator; b. Orange, N.J., Oct. 28, 1945; s. John Palmer and Lorraine Montgomery (Stoller) Van D.; m. Jerilyn Elise Miripol. B.A., Rensselear Poly. Inst., 1967; Ph.D., U. N.C., 1971. Asst. prof. analytical chemistry and chem. physics Northwestern U., Evanston, Ill., 1971-76, assoc. prof., 1976-79, prof., 1979-87, Charles E. and Emma H. Morrison prof. chemistry, 1987—; cons. Beckman Instrument Co., Fullerton, Calif., 1982-90, Eastman Kodak Co., Rochester, N.Y., 1978-91; disting. vis. prof. U. Tex., Austin, 1979; chmn. Vibrational Spectroscopy Gordon Conf., 1982; Camille and Henry Dreyfus lectr. U. Colo., Boulder, 1981; Kilpatrick lectr. Ill. Inst. Tech., 1982; O.K. Rice lectr. U. N.C., 1984; Henry Werner lectr. U. Kans., 1986; Arthur A. Vernon lectr. Northeastern U., 1992. Mem. adv. bd. Jour. Phys. Chemistry, 1983-88; contbr. chpts. to books, articles to profl. jours. Recipient Coblentz award, 1980, Fresenius award, 1981, Excellence in Surface Sci. award, 1996, Pitts. Spectroscopy award, 1991. Fellow AAAS, Am. Phys. Soc.; mem. Am. Chem. Soc. Home: 1520 Washington Ave Wilmette IL 60091-2417 Office: Northwestern Univ 2145 Sheridan Rd Evanston IL 60201-2926

VAN DYCK, NICHOLAS BOORAEM, minister, foundation official; b. Pasadena, Calif., Aug. 10, 1933; s. David Bevier and Anna Booraem (Richardson) van D.; m. Marcia Perera, June 14, 1958; children: Karen Rhoads, Jennifer Bevier, Sarah Paxson, Rebecca Booraem. BA, Rutgers U., 1959; BD, Union Theol. Sem., N.Y.C., 1962; PhD, U. St. Andrews, 1965. Ordained to ministry Presbyn. Ch., 1962. Pastor Palisades (N.Y.) Presbyn. Ch., 1964-68; tchr., adminstr. Princeton (N.J.) Theol. Sem., 1968-76; exec. dir. Action Research Corp., Princeton, 1976-77; exec. dir., founder Nat. Council for Children & TV, Princeton, N.Y.C. and Los Angeles, 1977-82; pres. Nat. Council for Families and TV, Princeton, N.Y.C. and Los Angeles, 1982-87; pres., chief exec. officer Religion In Am. Life, Princeton, Phila, N.Y.C., 1988—; chmn. bd. Action Research Corp., Princeton, 1987—; chmn. Assn. for Theol. Field Edn., U.S. and Can., 1975-76. Pub., editor TV and Families, 1982-87; contbr. articles to profl. jours. Bd. dirs. ARC, Princeton, 1984-89, Princeton Youth Fund, 1983-89, YMCA, Princeton, 1986-89, George H. Gallup Internat. Inst., 1990—. Lt. USNR, 1954-58. Scholar-in-residence Aspen (Colo.) Inst. for Humanistic Studies, 1985. Mem. Soc. for Psychol. Study Social Issues, Ind. Sector. Clubs: Princeton (N.Y.C.); Nassau (Princeton). Lodge: Rotary (pres. Princeton club 1981-82, bd. dirs. found. 1985—). Avocation: collecting antique autos.

VAN DYCK, WENDY, dancer; b. Tokyo. Student, San Francisco Ballet Sch. With San Francisco Ballet, 1979—, prin. dancer, 1987—. Performances include Forgotten Land, The Sons of Horus, The Wanderer Fantasy, Romeo and Juliet, The Sleeping Beauty, Swan Lake, Concerto in d: Poulenc, Handel-a Celebration, Menuetto, Intimate Voices, Hamlet and Ophelia pas de deux, Connotations, Sunset, Rodin, In the Night, The Dream: pas de deux, La Sylphide, Beauty and the Beast, Variations de Ballet, Nutcracker, The Comfort Zone, Dreams of Harmony, Rodeo, Duo Concertant, Who Cares; performed at Reykjavik Arts Festival, Iceland, 1990, The 88th Conf. of the Internat. Olympic Com., L.A., 1984, with Kozlov and Co. Concord Pavilion; guest artist performing role Swan Lake (Act II), San Antonio Ballet, 1985, Giselle, Shreveport Met. Ballet, 1994; featured in the TV broadcast of Suite by Smuin. Office: San Francisco Ballet 455 Franklin St San Francisco CA 94102-4438

VAN DYK, FREDERICK THEODORE, writer, consultant; b. Bellingham, Wash., Oct. 6, 1934; s. Ted and June Ellen (Williams) Van D.; m. Julia Jean Covacevich, Nov. 22, 1957(dec. 1996); children: Theodore, Robert, Terry Jean, Sue Ellen. B.A., U. Wash., 1955; M.S., Columbia U., 1956. Reporter, editor Seattle Times, 1956-57; advt. public relations exec. Boston and N.Y.C., 1958-62; acting dir. European Community Info. Service, Washington, 1962-64; asst. to Hubert Humphrey, Vice Pres. of U.S., 1964-68; v.p. Columbia U., N.Y.C., 1968-69; pres. Van Dyk Assocs., Washington, 1969-76; asst. adminstr. AID, Washington, 1977; v.p. Weyerhaeuser Co., Tacoma, 1978-80; pres. Center for Nat. Policy, Washington, 1981-85, Van Dyk Assocs., 1985—. Contbr. essays on govt. and politics to gen. publs. including L.A. Times, N.Y. Times, Wall St. Jour., Washington Post. Bd. dirs. Com. for Study of Am. Electorate, Franklin and Eleanor Roosevelt Inst., Jean Monnet Coun.; mem. Coun. on Fgn. Rels., Presdl. Commn. on Fgn. Assistance. Served with M.I. AUS, 1957, 61-62. Mem. Delta Upsilon (nat. trustee). Clubs: Fed. City, Army Navy (Washington), Rainier (Seattle). Home: 7500 Masters Dr Potomac MD 20854-3854 Office: Van Dyk Assocs 1250-24th St NW Washington DC 20037

VAN DYKE, CLIFFORD CRAIG, retired banker; b. Ft. Madison, Iowa, June 23, 1929; s. Charles Clifford and Frances Mary (Butterwick) Van D.; m. Edith Ellicott Powers, Aug. 4, 1951 (dec. Oct. 1980); children: Carol Elizabeth, Deborah Ellicott, Jill Anne, Lisa Ellicott. BA, Knox Coll., 1951; MBA, Harvard U., 1955. Asst. v.p. Nat. Bank of Detroit, 1962-65, v.p., 1965-76; pres. Peoples Nat. Bank & Trust Co. of Bay City, Mich., 1976-78, chmn. bd., pres., 1979-86; chmn. bd., pres., chief exec. officer New Ctr. Bank Corp., Bay City, Mich., 1986; chmn. First of Am. Bank-Bay City, N.A., 1987-89; sr. v.p. First of Am. Bank-Mid Mich. N.A., 1990-94; ret., 1994. Trustee Kantzler Found., Bay City, 1979—; bd. dirs., pres. Bay County Growth Alliance, 1987—. 1st lt. U.S. Army, 1951-53, Korea. Mem. Bay City Country Club, Saginaw Valley Torch Club, Rotary. Republican. Unitarian. Office: Bay County Growth Alliance PO Box 369 Bay City MI 48707-0369

VAN DYKE, CRAIG, psychiatrist; b. Detroit, Oct. 4, 1941; married; two children. BS, U. Wash., 1963, MD, 1967. Asst. prof. psychiatry Yale U., New Haven, Conn., 1974-78; from assoc. to prof. psychiatry U. Calif., San Francisco, 1979-86, prof., chmn. dept. psychiatry, 1994—. Mem. Am. Psychosom. Soc., Internat. Coll. Psychosom. Medicine, Soc. Neurosci., Internat. Neuropsychol. Soc. Office: U Cal San Francisco Langley Porter Psychiatric Inst 401 Parnassus Ave San Francisco CA 94122-2720

VAN DYKE, JOSEPH GARY OWEN, computer consulting executive; b. N.Y.C., Dec. 21, 1939; s. Donald Wood and Gladys Ann (Tague) Van D.; m. Lynne Diane Lammers; June 25, 1966; children: Alison Baird, Jeremy Wood, Matthew Kerr. BA, Rutgers U., 1961; postgrad., R.I. Sch. of Design, 1962, Am. U., 1964-67. Computer programmer System Devel. Corp., Paramus, N.J., 1962-64; sect. head computer tech. div. System Devel. Corp., Falls Church, Va., 1964-67; project mgr. Informatics Inc., Bethesda, Md., 1967-70; dept. dir. Informatics Inc., Rockville, Md., 1970-74, v.p., gen. mgr., 1974-78; owner, pres. J G Van Dyke and Assoc., Inc., Bethesda, 1978—; chmn. bd., chief exec. officer The Outreach Group, Inc., 1987—. Bd. dirs. Westbrook Sch., Bethesda, 1981-82, St. Columba's Ch., Washington, 1980-84; founder Computer Edn. Workshop, Bethesda, 1981; coach MSI soccer, Bethesda, 1979-89. Mem. Inst. Elec. Engring. Democrat. Episcopalian. Avocations: coaching soccer, sailing, graphic designing. Home: 5117 Dalecarlia Dr Bethesda MD 20816-1801 Office: JG Van Dyke & Assocs Inc 6550 Rock Spring Dr Ste 360 Bethesda MD 20817-1132

VAN DYKE, MILTON DENMAN, aeronautical engineering educator; b. Chgo., Aug. 1, 1922; s. James Richard and Ruth (Barr) Van D.; m. Sylvia Jean Agard Adams, June 16, 1962; children: Russell B., Eric J., Nina A., Brooke A. and Byron J. and Christopher M. (triplets). B.S., Harvard U., 1943; M.S., Calif. Inst. Tech., 1947, Ph.D., 1949. Research engr. NACA, 1943-46, 50-54, 55-58; vis. prof. U. Paris, France, 1958- 59; prof. aero. Stanford, 1959—; prof. emeritus, 1992—; pres. Parabolic Press. Author: Perturbation Methods in Fluid Mechanics, 1964, An Album of Fluid Motion, 1982; editor: Ann. Rev. Fluid Mechanics, 1969—. Trustee Soc. For Promotion of Sci. and Scholarship, Inc. Served with USNR, 1944-46. Guggenheim and Fulbright fellow, 1954-55. Mem. Am. Acad. Arts and Scis., Nat. Acad. Engring., Am. Phys. Soc., Phi Beta Kappa, Sigma Xi, Sierra Club. Office: Stanford U Div Mechs & Computation Stanford CA 94305-4040

VAN DYKE, THOMAS WESLEY, lawyer; b. Kansas City, Mo., May 12, 1938; s. Harold Thomas and Elizabeth Louise (Barritt) Van D.; m. Sharon Edgar, Jan. 30, 1960; children: Jennifer Van Dyke Winters, Jeffrey. BA, U. Kans., 1960; JD, U. Mich., 1963. Bar: Mo. 1963, Kans. 1983. Atty. SEC, Washington, 1963-64; legal asst. to commr. Hamer E. Budge, Washington, 1964-65; from assoc. to ptnr. Linde Thomson Langworthy Kohn & Van Dyke, P.C., Overland Park, Kans., 1965-91; co-chmn. ALI-ABA Tax and Bus. Planning Seminar, 1987-96; mem. securities adv. panel Sec. of State of Mo., 1984-89. Mem. ABA (fed. regulation securities com bus. law sect. 1982-95, negotatiated acquisitions com. 1989-95), Kans. Bar Assn., Mo. Bar Assn. (corp. banking and bus. law com., chmn. full com. 1983-84, past chmn. securities law subcom.), Carriage Club (bd. dirs. 1986-89). Republican. Avocations: tennis, reading. Office: Bryan Cave LLP 7500 College Blvd Ste 1100 Overland Park KS 66210-4035

VAN DYKE, WILLIAM GRANT, manufacturing company executive; b. Mpls., June 30, 1945; s. Russell Lawrence and Carolyn (Grant) Van D.; m. Karin Van Dyke; children: Carolyn Julie, Colin Grant, Alexander Grant, Stephanie Joyce. BA in Econs., U. Minn., 1967, MBA, 1972. V.p., CFO Northland Aluminum Co., Mpls., 1977-78; controller Donaldson Co., Inc., Mpls., 1978-80, v.p. controller, 1980-82, v.p., CFO, 1982-84, v.p., gen. mgr. indsl. group, 1984-94, pres., COO, 1994-96, chmn., pres., CEO, 1996—, also bd. dirs.; bd. dirs. Graco Inc. Served to lt. U.S. Army, 1968-70, Vietnam. Mem. Kappa Sigma Alumni Assn. Avocations: running; bicycling. Office: Donaldson Co Inc 1400 W 94th St Minneapolis MN 55431-2301

VAN DYKE-COOPER, ANNY MARION, retired financial company executive; b. Howard, Ont., Can., Sept. 30, 1928; d. Anthony and Anna (Koolen) Van D.; m. John Arnold Cooper, Apr. 9, 1983. BA, Concordia U., 1959. Chartered fin. analyst. Tchr. Lanoraie Sch. Bd., 1946-47; sec. Can. Nat. Rys., Montreal, Que., Can., 1947-51; sec. Sorel Industries Ltd., Sorel, Que., Can., 1952-53; with Bell Investment Mgmt. Corp. and BIMCOR, Inc. subs. Bell Canada, Montreal, 1953-83; portfolio mgr. U.S. Equities, 1971-83; chmn., dir. Cooper, Van Dyke Assocs. Inc., Bloomfield Hills, Mich., 1983-96; ret. Mem. Inst. Chartered Fin. Analysts (trustee 1979-80), Fin. Analysts Soc. Detroit, Montreal Soc. Fin. Analysts (program chmn., pres. 1974-75), Can. Coun. Fin. Analysts (vice-chmn. 1976-77), Assn. for Investment Mgmt. and Rsch. (treas. 1977-78, vice chmn. 1978-79, chmn. 1979-80). Home: Apt C228 1111 N Woodward Ave Birmingham MI 48009-5423

VAN DYKEN, AMY, swimmer, Olympic athlete; b. Engelwood, Colo., Feb. 15, 1973; m. Alan McDaniel, Oct. 1995. Attending, Colo. State U. Swimmer U.S. Nat. Resident Team, Colorado Springs, Colo., 1994, U.S. Olympic Team, Atlanta, Ga., 1996. Named Female NCAA Swimmer of the Year, 1994, Am. Record Holder 50 meter and 50 meter freestyle; recipient Bronze medal World Championships, 1994, Triple Gold medals Pan Am. Games, 1995, Silver medal Pan Am. Games, 1995, Gold medals: 50 meter freestyle, 100 meter butterfly, 4x100 meter freestyle relay, 4x100 meter medley relay Olympic Games, Atlanta, 1996. First Am. woman athlete to win 4 gold medals in any event during single Olympic game. Office: US Swimming Inc 1 Olympic Plz Colorado Springs CO 80909-5780

VANE, DENA, magazine editor-in-chief. Editor-in-chief First for Women, Englewood Cliffs, N.J. Office: First for Women Bauer Pub Co 270 Sylvan Ave Englewd Clfs NJ 07632-2521*

VANE, TERENCE G., JR., finance and insurance company executive, lawyer; b. Elgin, Ill., Jan. 17, 1942; s. Terence Gregory and Velma Mary (Mersman) V.; m. Patricia Bryant, Aug. 29, 1964; children: Terence Gregory III, Lourdene DeLynne, Christopher Theodore. BA, Ind. U., 1964, JD, 1967. Bar: Ind. 1967, Tex. 1977, N.C. 1992; cert. house counsel Fla. 1996. Staff atty. Assocs. Discount Corp., South Bend, Ind., 1967-69; asst. gen. counsel Assocs. Mgmt. Corp., South Bend, 1969-74, Assocs. Comml. Corp., South Bend, 1974-76, Assocs. Ins. Group, Inc., Dallas, 1976-77; gen. counsel, v.p. ins. ops. Assocs. Corp. N.Am., Dallas, 1977-80, gen. counsel, sr. v.p. ins. ops., 1981-82, gen. counsel, sr. v.p. consumer fin. and ins. ops., 1982-86, gen. counsel, sr. v.p. diversified consumer fin. services and credit card ops., 1986-88; exec. v.p., gen. counsel, sec., dir. Barclays Am. Corp., Charlotte, N.C., 1988-91; pres. Vector Fin. Svcs., Inc., Charlotte, 1991-95, bd. dirs.; sr. v.p., assoc. gen. counsel EquiCredit Corp., Jacksonville, Fla., 1996—. Chmn. bd. dirs., sec. Youth Concert Found. for Promotion Creative Arts, 1981—; bd. dirs. N.C. Bus. Com. Edn., 1988-91. Mem. ABA, Fla. Bar Assn., Ind. Bar Assn., Tex. Bar Assn., N.C. Bar Assn., Mecklenburg County Bar Assn., Nat. Assn. Ind. Insurers (laws com. 1978-86), Consumer Credit Ins. Assn. (chmn. property ins. legis. com. 1979-85), Am. Fin. Svcs. Assn. (law com., chmn. environ. law subcom.), Conf. Consumer Fin. Law (gen. com.). Home: 13802 Fidders Point Dr Jacksonville FL 32225 Office: PO Box 53077 Jacksonville FL 32201-3077 also: 10401 Deerwood Park Blvd Jacksonville FL 32256-0505

VANECKO, ROBERT MICHAEL, surgeon, educator; b. Chgo., Aug. 15, 1935; s. Michael and Raphael Regina (Burns) V.; m. Mary Carol Daley; children: Robert G., Mark G., Richard J., Mary Clare. BS, Georgetown U., 1957; MS, Northwestern U., 1960, MD, 1961. Diplomate Am. Bd. Surgery, Am. Bd. Thoracic Surgery. Intern Cook County Hosp., Chgo., 1961-62, resident in gen. surgery, 1962-66; instr. surgery U. Ill., 1964-66; resident in cardiothoracic surgery Cook County Hosp., Chgo., 1966-67, Hines (Ill.) VA Hosp., 1969-70; attending surgeon VA Rsch. Hosp., Chgo., 1970—; attending surgeon Cook County Hosp., Chgo., 1972—, chief sect. thoracic trauma, 1972-78; assoc. attending Northwestern Meml. Hosp., Chgo., 1970-77, attending, 1977—; assoc. in surgery Northwestern U. Med. Sch., Chgo., 1970-71, asst. prof. surgery, 1971-75, assoc. prof. surgery, 1975-88, prof. clin. surgery, 1988-93, prof. surgery, 1993—, asst. dean, then assoc. dean grad. med. edn., 1988—; mem. numerous hosp. coms. Creator, writer numerous surgical movies, 1963-84; contbr. articles to profl. jours. Bd. govs. Chgo. Heart Assn., 1980-86, 88-92, mem. phys. fitness com., 1973-80, mem. pub. policy and govt. rels. com., 1980-90; mem. alumni coun. Northwestern U. Med. Sch., mem. instl. rev. bd.; mem. adv. com. Ill. Dept. Pub. Health, 1990-94; bd. gov. Chgo. Access Corp., 1984-90, Crescent County Med. Found., 1984-87. Mem. AAAS, ACS (mem. motion picture com. 1974-80, mem. credentials com. 1978-86, chmn. met. credentials com. 1986-93), AMA (alt. del. to ho. of dels. 1984-86, del. to ho. of dels. 1986—, mem. sect. med. schs. 1987—), Am. Assn. Thoracic Surgery, Am. Coll. Chest Physicians (chmn. motion picture com. 1977-80, treas. 1980-85, pres. Ill.-Great Lakes chpt. 1981-82, dir. edn. found. 1985-96), Am. Hosp. Assn. (mem. nat. congress hosp. gov. bd. 1984-93, mem. coordinating com. med. edn. 1989—), Am. Med. Writers Assn., Am. Trauma Soc., Ctrl. Surg. Assn., Chgo. Med. Soc. (mem. health planning com., mem. health care delivery com. 1982-86, mem. health system agy. com. 1978-84, bd. trustees 1984-89, sec. 1984-86, pres. 1987-88, chmn. bd. trustees 1986-87), Chgo. Surg. Soc. (rep. to Ill. State Med. Soc. 1984-86), Ill. Med. Soc., Ill. Surg. Soc., Ill. Hosp. Assn. (bd. trustees 1986—), Inst. Medicine Chgo. (bd. govs. 1984—, mem. grad. and undergrad. med. edn. com. 1975-79, treas. 1986-89), Soc. Med. History Chgo., Soc. Thoracic Surgeons, Western Surg. Assn. Office: Northwestern Med Sch 303 E Chicago Ave Chicago IL 60611-3008

VANEGAS, JORGE ALBERTO, civil engineering educator; b. Bogota, Colombia, Oct. 17, 1956; came to U.S., 1983; s. Carlos Enrique and Cecilia (Pabon) V.; m. Adriana Martinez, Dec. 18, 1987 (div. Dec. 1992); m. Loretta Sanders, Dec. 22, 1992). BS in Architecture, U. de los Andes, Bogota, 1979; MSCE, Stanford U., 1985, PhD in Civil Engring., 1988. Rsch. and teaching asst. Stanford (Calif.) U., 1984-87, acting asst. prof., 1988; asst. prof. Purdue U., West Lafayette, Ind., 1988-93; assoc. profl. civil engring. Ga. Inst. Tech., Atlanta, 1993—; cons. U.S. and Colombia, 1982—. Mem. ASCE (assoc.), Am. Soc. Engrs. in Edn. (assoc.). Roman Catholic. Home: 4205 Newpond Trl Kennesaw GA 30144-1667 Office: Sch Civil Engring Dept Civil Engring Ga Inst Tech Atlanta GA 30332-0355

VAN ENGEN, THOMAS LEE, state legislator; b. Sioux Center, Iowa, Mar. 28, 1953; s. Leo Herman and Dolores (Nelma) Van E.; m. Rosalyn Faye Vander Plaats, 1979; children: Matthew Thomas, David James, Jeremy Lee. BA, Dordt Coll., Sioux Center, 1979. Lic. social worker, Minn. State cen., 1989-94; exec. com. chair Minn. Ho. of Reps., St. Paul, 1990-93, chair dist. 15, 1992-94, mem., 1994—. Del. Rep. dist. and state convs., 1984—, Minn. Rep. Ctrl. Com., 1989—; chmn. Pipestone County Com., Minn., 1988-89, Kandiyohi County Com., 1991-93; co-chmn. dist. 15 Minn. Senate, 1990-92, chmn., 1992—; candidate for Minn. Ho. of Reps., 1992; chmn. edn. com. Cmty. Christian Sch. Bd., 1990-94; elder Christian Reformed Ch., 1985-88, 96—; vol. handicapped children and adults, 1978-82; chem. dependency counselor, 1982. Spec 4 officer U.S. Army, 1972-74, hon. discharge, 1978. Mem. CAP, Am. Legion. Republican.

VAN ESELTINE, WILLIAM PARKER, microbiologist, educator; b. Syracuse, N.Y., Aug. 21, 1924; s. Glen Parker and Florence Marie (Lamb) Van E.; m. Marian Louise Vanderburgh, Aug. 25, 1948; children—Kenneth Leslie, Karen Elaine. A.B., Oberlin Coll., 1944; M.S., Cornell U., 1947, Ph.D., 1949. Asst. in bacteriology N.Y. State Agrl. Expt. Sta., Geneva, 1944-45, summer 1946; Asst. in bacteriology N.Y. State Coll. Agr., Cornell U., Ithaca, 1946-48; asso. prof. bacteriology Clemson (S.C.) Agrl. Coll., 1948-52; asst. prof. vet. hygiene U. Ga., Athens, 1952-59, asso. prof. microbiology and preventive medicine, 1959-67, prof. med. microbiology, 1967-87, prof. emeritus, 1987—. Contbr. articles on microbiology to profl. jours. Mem. Am. Soc. Microbiology, N.Y. Acad. Sci., Ga. Acad. Sci., Am. Leptospirosis Research Conf. (pres. 1987), AAAS, Sigma Xi, Phi Kappa Phi. Home: 237 Woodlawn Ave Athens GA 30606-4353

VANESS, CAROL, soprano; b. L.A., July 27, 1952; d. William Anthony and Dorotha Jean (Whitsun) V. BA, Calif. Poly. U., 1974; MA, Calif. State U., Northridge, 1976; student, Merola and Affiliate Artist programs, San Francisco, 1976-78. Made debut N.Y.C. Opera as Vitellia in La Clemenza di Tito, 1979; prodns. include Don Giovanni, 1980, Merry Wives of Windsor, 1981, La Boheme, Rigoletto, Pearl Fishers, Traviata and Alcina, 1983; revivals San Francisco Opera Don Giovanni, 1981, Dialogues of the Carmelites, 1982, La Traviata, 1991, Don Carlo, 1992; European debut Clemenza, Bordeaux, France, 1981, Buffalo Philharm., Rossini Stabat Mater, 1981; debut Phila. Opera as Countess in Figaro, 1982, N.Y.C. Opera in Figaro, Covent Garden debut as Mimi in La Boheme, 1982, Glyndebourne Festival Don Giovanni, 1982, Idomeneo, 1983, Cosi, 1984, Boccanegra, 1986; Paris Opera debut as Nedda in Pagliacci, 1982, Idomeneo & Clemenza, 1986, Berlin, Munich and Vienna debut in Don Giovanni, Met. Opera debut as Armida in Rinaldo, 1984, Australian debut in a Masked Ball, 1985, Rome debut in Faust, 1987, Barcelona, Spain debut in Tito, 1988, Salzburg Festival debut as Vitellia, Austria, 1988, Tito, 1988-89, Donna Elvira, 1990, Lyric Opera of Chbo. debut, 1988, Don Giovanni, 1989, N.Y. Philharm. debut, 1991, La Scala (Milan) debut Idomeneo, 1990; Met. Opera Figaro, 1985, Samson, 1986, Faust, 1990, Don Giovanni, 1990; recital debut, Liberty, Mo., 1986, Carnegie Hall debut Strauss 4 Last Songs, 1987, Live from Lincoln Ctr. Pavarotti Plus, 1986, 90, numerous recs. with EMI; rec. complete Giovanni and Cosi with Glyndebourne/Haitink; N.Y. recital debut Alice Tully Hall, 1987, , Carol Vaness Mozart An'as, Don Giovanni-Muti Mozart Duets with Placido Domingo, Rossini Stabat Matev Tosca-Muti, Verdi Requiem Iphigenie en Tauride, 1992. Winner San Francisco Opera Audition, 1976. Office: IMG Artists Europe Medin House, 3 Burlington Lane, London W4 2TH, England*

VAN ETTEN, PETER WALBRIDGE, hospital administrator; b. Boston, May 10, 1946; s. Royal Cornelius Van Etten and Peggy June (Walbridge) Hutchins; m. Mary Peters French, Sept. 5, 1968; children: Molly, Clarissa, Ellen. BA, Columbia U., 1968; MBA, Harvard U., 1973. Br. mgr. BayBanks, Brookline, Mass., 1968-71; loan officer Bank of Boston, 1973-76; CFO Univ. Hosp., Boston, 1976-79; exec. v.p., CFO New Eng. Med. Ctr., Boston, 1979-89; pres., CEO Transitions Systems, Boston, 1986-89; dep. chancellor U. Mass. Med. Ctr., Worcester, 1989-91; CFO Stanford (Calif.) U., 1991-94; pres., CEO Stanford Univ. Hosp., 1994-97, Univ. Calif. San Francisco-Stanford Health Care, 1997—; dir. Transition Sys., Inc., 1996—. Office: Stanford Health Care Pasteur Dr Stanford CA 94305

VAN EXEL, NICKEY MAXWELL, professional basketball player; b. Kenosha, Wis., Nov. 27, 1971; s. Nickey Maxwell and Joyce Van Exel; 1 child, Nickey Maxwell III. Attended, Trinity Valley C.C., 1989-91, U. Cin., 1993. Profl. basketball player L.A. Lakers, 1993—. Named to NBA All-Rookie 2d team, 1994. Office: LA Lakers Great Western Forum PO Box 10 3900 W Manchester Inglewood CA 90306*

VAN EYS, JAN, retired pediatrician, educator, administrator; b. Hilversum, The Netherlands, Jan. 25, 1929; came to U.S., 1951; s. Jan and Geertruida (Floor) van E.; m. Catherine Travis; children: Jan Peter, D. Catherine. PhD in Biochemistry, Vanderbilt U., 1955; MD, U. Wash., 1966. Diplomate Nat. Bd. Med. Examiners, Am. Bd. Pediatrics, Am. Bd. Pediatric Hematology/Oncology. Postdoctoral fellow McCollum Pratt Inst., Johns Hopkins U., Balt., 1955-57; asst. prof. biochemistry Vanderbilt U., Nashville, 1957-62, assoc. prof., 1962-71, prof., 1971-73; intern, resident in pediatrics Vanderbilt U. Hosps., Nashville, 1966-69; pediatrician M.D. Anderson Hosp. U. Tex., Houston, 1973-94, prof. pediatrics, 1973-94, Mosbacher prof. pediatrics, 1979-87, Mosbacher chair, 1988-90, chmn. dept., 1983-88, head div., 1983-90, chmn. dept. exptl. pediatrics, 1983-90; David R. Park prof. pediatrics U. Tex. Med. Sch., Houston, 1990-94, chmn. dept., 1987-94; clin. prof. pediat. Sch. Medicine, Vanderbilt U., Nashville, 1994—; cons. Cancer Info. Svcs. for Code Ethics and Pediatric Cancers, 1986-89. Author: (with T.S. Carter and C. Jordan) The Howell Kindred, 1979, Humanity and Personhood: Personal Reactions to a World in Which Children Can Die, 1981, (with M. Weiner) Nicotinic Acid, Drug, Nutrient and Cofactor, 1983; contbr. numerous articles, abstracts, papers, book chpts., and revs. to profl. publs.; editor: (with J.T. Truman and C. Pochedly) Human Values in Pediatric Hematology/Oncology, 1986, (with R.A. Dowell and D. Copeland) The Child With Cancer in the Community, 1988, Cancer in the Very Young, 1989; chief editor pediatric sect. Year Book of Cancer, 1978-87, cons. editor, 1974-78; assoc. editor Nutrition and Cancer, 1978—, Jour. Pediatric Hematology/Oncology, 1982-92, Houston Med. Jour., 1986-93, Cancer Prevention Internat., 1993—, The Pharos, 1994—; also editor/co-editor proc. of workshops, clin. and mental health confs., ann. symposiums, etc. Pres. bd. trustees Inst. Religion, Houston, 1989-94; mem. adminstrv. bd. Westbury United Meth. Ch., Houston, 1989-94. Fellow Am. Acad. Pediatrics, Am. Coll. Nutrition; mem. Am. Pediatric Soc., Am. Soc. Hematology, Am. Soc. Clin. Oncology, Am. Med. Writers Assn., Am. Soc. for Parental and Enteral Nutrition, So. Med. Assn., World Fedn. for Hemophilia, Tex. Pediatric Soc., Houston Pediatric Soc. (pres. 1981-82), Houston Acad. Medicine, Harris County Med. Assn., U. Tex. M.D. Anderson Cancer Ctr. Assocs., Sigma Xi, Alpha Omega Alpha. Home and Office: 3504 Ruland Pl Nashville TN 37215-1812

VAN FLEET, GEORGE ALLAN, lawyer; b. Monterey, Calif., Jan. 20, 1953; s. George Lawson and Wilma Ruth (Williams) Van F.; m. Laurie Elise Koch, July 20, 1975; children: Katia Elaine, Alexander Lawson. BA summa cum laude, Rice U., 1976; JD, Columbia U., 1977. Bar: Tex. 1978, U.S. Dist. Ct. (so. dist.) Tex. 1978, U.S. Dist. Ct. (we. dist.) Tex. 1987, U.S. Dist. Ct. (no. dist.) Tex, 1988, U.S. Dist. Ct. (ea. dist.) Tex. 1991, U.S. Tax Ct., 1984, U.S. Ct. Appeals (5th cir.) 1978, U.S. Ct. Appeals (11th cir.) 1981, U.S. Ct. Appeals (D.C. cir.) 1982, U.S. Ct. Appeals (fed. cir.) 1993, U.S. Supreme Ct. 1981. Law clk. U.S. Ct. Appeals (2d cir.), N.Y.C., 1977; assoc. Vinson & Elkins, Houston, 1977-84, ptnr., 1984—; mem. NAFTA Tri-Nat. Task Force. Editor: Compliance Manuals for the New Antitrust Era, 1989, quarterly rev. Litigation News, 1983-86; contbr. articles to profl. jour. Regional dir. Anti-Defamation League, 1990-94; bd. visitors Columbia U., 1992—; mem. City of Houston Ethics Com., 1992—, chmn. 1995—. Recipient Ordroneaux prize Columbia U., 1977; James Kent scholar Columbia U., 1974-77. Fellow Tex. Bar Assn.; mem. ABA (com. chmn. 1987-95, mem. coun. 1996—), Houston Bar Assn. (sec. chair 1991-93), Tex.-Mex. Bar Assn. (vice chmn. 1996—), Phi Beta Kappa. Democrat. Jewish. Home: 3430 S Parkwood Dr Houston TX 77021 Office: Vinson & Elkins 1001 Fannin St Ste 2500 Houston TX 77002-6709

VAN FLEET, WILLIAM MABRY, architect; b. Point Richmond, Calif., Jan. 22, 1915; s. Harvey Lorenz and Allie O'Dell (Taylor) Van F.; m. Colette Sims, Apr. 26, 1940; children: Christine, Ellen, Peter. AB, U. Calif., Berkeley, 1938. Pvt. practice architecture, Eureka, Calif., 1951—; lectr. design Humboldt (Calif.) State U., 1965-66; ptnr. William & Colette Van Fleet, 1954—. Prin. works include Del Norte County Courthouse and Library, Crescent City, Calif., 1957, Freshwater (Calif.) Elem. Sch., 1954, Lee residence, Sunnybrae, Calif., 1962, Zane Jr. H.S., Eureka, 1965, offices for Brooks-Scanlon Lumber Co., Bend, Oreg., 1967. Chmn., No. Humboldt Vocat. Coun., 1964-65, Humboldt County Scenic Resources Com., 1965; pres. Humboldt-Del Norte Mental Health Soc., 1970-71; mem. Humboldt County Cmty. Svcs. Ctr. 1970, Humboldt Arts Council, 1970, Humboldt County Energy Adv. Com., 1979; chmn. Eureka Beautification Com., 1969, Humboldt Sr. Retirement Homes Com., 1979-96, ret., 1996; bd. dirs. Humboldt County Assn. Retarded Children, 1960-68, Humboldt Family Svc. Ctr., 1970, Redwoods United Workshop, 1973, Open Door Clinic, 1973, Coordinating Coun. Human Svcs. Humboldt County, 1976, Calif.-Oreg. Cmty. Devel. Soc., 1980—; mem. Humboldt Energy Adv. Com., 1980—, Eureka City Housing Adv. Bd., 1982; hon. chmn. Am. Cancer Soc. 24 Hour Fun Run, 1992. Recipient Merit award HHFA, 1964, 1st Honor award Pub. Housing Adminstrn., 1964, Gov. Calif. Design award, 1966, Outstanding Svc. award Far West Indian Hist. Soc., 1973, Man of Yr. award Redwood region Nat. Audubon Soc., 1976, resolutions of commendation Calif. State Senate and Assembly, 1982, Gold medal for 10k cross-country run, 1989, Cmty. award Am. Cancer Soc., 1991, Calif. Divsn. Courage award Am. Cancer Soc., 1993; Humboldt Unitarian Universalist fellow. Mem. AIA, Net Energy Assn. (bd. dir.), Humboldt Native Plant Soc., Redwood Art Assn. (pres. 1970), Sierra Club (bd. dir. 1972), Fifty-Plus Runners Assn. (1st place in age group Nat. Fifty-Plus Runners Meet 1981). Unitarian. Club: Six Rivers Running (bd. dirs., All-Am. awards 1987, Hall of Fame, 1992). Lodge: Kiwanis (pres. Eureka 1976-77, Disting. Svc. award 1968). Participant in various marathons and races, including Internat. Marathon, Sacramento, 1983 (1st in 65-69 age group), World Vet. Championships Marathon, Rome, Italy, 1984 (1st in U.S., 8th in World, 70-74 age group), Fifty-Plus 5 mile run, Stanford, Calif., 1985 (1st in 70-74 age group, 2d all-time nationally), course records (70-74 age group) 300-meters and 5-kilometer runs Masters Hayward Classic Track & Field Meet, Eugene, Oreg., 1988, others, course record and Calif. state record (70-74 age group) in Nike Half-Marathon, San Francisco, 1988, Gold medal for 10K cross-country as a member of the U.S. team (70-74 age group), 1989, World Vets. Championships, Eugene, Oreg. (1st in 70-74 age group), 1990, All-Am. certs. 2nd nationally in 800 and 1500 meter run Pacific Assn./TAC Championship, Los Gatos, Calif., 1st half marathon, Calif., 1990, Four Generation Half Marathon (Am. Cancer Soc. award), 1993. Home: 71 Old Forest Ln Eureka CA 95503-9554

VAN FOSSAN, KATHRYN RUTH, library director; b. Elmhurst, Ill., Feb. 24, 1948; d. Norman Harvey and Ruth Marion (Shoger) Zurbrigg; m. Randy Eugene Van Fossan, Feb. 15, 1969; children: Karen Irene, David Bryan. BA in Music, U. Ill., 1969; MA in Musicology, Ill. State U., 1979; MLS, U. Ill., 1983. Interlibr. loan libr. Garrett Theol. Sem., Evanston, Ill., 1970-71; acquisitions asst. Olivet Nazarene U., Kankakee, Ill., 1978-80, cataloger, 1980-83, head tech. svcs., 1983-92, libr. dir., 1992—. Bd. dirs. Bur Oak Libr. Sys., Shorewood, Ill., 1990-93. Mem. ALA, Ill. Libr. Assn., Assn. Coll. and Rsch. Librs., Assn. Libr. Collections and Tech. Svcs. Avocations: church organist, choir director. Office: Olivet Nazarene U Benner Libr and Resource Ctr PO Box 592 Kankakee IL 60901

VANG, TIMOTHY TENG, church executive; b. Xieng Khouang, Laos, May 10, 1956; came to U.S., 1976; s. Nao Chai and Mai (Yang) V.; m. Chee Yang, Jan. 1, 1974 (dec. June 1975); m. Lydia Joua Vang, July 7, 1979; children: Jennifer P., Nathan K., Victor K., Richard M. BS in Missions, Cin. Bible Coll., 1984; MDiv in Ch. Ministries, Can. Theol. Sem., Regina, Sask., 1991; postgrad., Fuller Theol. Sem., Pasadena, Calif., 1993—. Ordained to ministry Ch. of Christ, 1984, Christian and Missionary Alliance, 1986. Machine operator Pellet Co., Green Bay, Wis., 1977-78; mental health worker Inst. Human Design, Oshkosh, Wis., 1978-80; ch. planter Ch. of Christ, Eau Claire, Wis., 1984-86; pastor Boulder (Colo.) Hmong Alliance Ch., 1986-87; dir. Christian edn. Hmong dist. Christian and Missionary Alliance, Brighton, Colo., 1986-87, dist. supt., 1991-96; Mem. bd. mgrs. Christian and Missionary Alliance, 1994-97; trustee Crown Coll., 1992-96. Organizer Fox Valley Lao/Hmong Assn., Appleton, Wis., 1979. Lt. U.S./Hmong Allied Army, 1971-75. Avocations: reading, writing, walking. Office: Sacramento Hmong Alliance Ch 9131 Locust St Elk Grove CA 95624

VANGER, MILTON ISADORE, history educator; b. N.Y.C., Apr. 11, 1925; s. Max Manuel and Rose (Rothstein) V.; m. Elsa M. Oribe, Sept. 10, 1956; children: John, Mark, Rachel. A.B., Princeton U., 1948; M.A., Harvard U., 1950, Ph.D., 1958. Teaching fellow history Harvard U., 1952-56; instr. Okla. State U., 1956-58; asst. prof. history Sacramento State Coll., 1958-62; mem. faculty Brandeis U., Waltham, Mass., 1962—; prof. history Brandeis U., 1973-84, prof. emeritus, 1984—; chmn. com. Latin Am. studies, 1971-81; invited lectr. 50th anniversary conf. commemorating death of Batlle y Ordoñez of Uruguay, 1979; invitee to inauguration of pres. Sanguinetti, Uruguay, 1985; Barnette Miller vis. prof. history, Wellesley Coll., 1990. Author: José Batlle y Ordoñez of Uruguay: The Creator of His Times, 1902-1907, 1963, 2d edit., 1980, Spanish transl., 1968, 2d edit., 1992, The Model Country: José Batlle y Ordoñez of Uruguay, 1907-1915, 1980, Spanish transl., 1983, 2d edit., 1991, Reforma o Revolución La Polémica Batlle-Mibelli, 1917, 1989; outside reviewer NEH, Radcliffe Inst.; contbr. articles to profl. jours. Juror for Lindahl Prize, Inst. Latin Am. Studies, Stockholm. With AUS, 1943-45. Doherty Found. fellow, 1950-52; grantee Am. Philos. Soc., 1966; recipient Hermes prize for best history pub. in Uruguay, 1983. Mem. New Eng. Council Latin Am. Studies (sec.-treas. 1970-72), Am. Hist. Assn., Conf. on Latin Am. History, Amnesty Internat., Phi Beta Kappa. Democrat. Jewish. Address: 931 Massachusetts Ave Ste 503 Cambridge MA 02139

VAN GESTEL, ALLAN, judge; b. Boston, Dec. 3, 1935. BA, Colby Coll., 1957; LLB, Boston U., 1961. Bar: Mass. 1961, U.S. Dist. Ct. Mass. 1963, U.S. Ct. Appeals (1st cir.) 1969, U.S. Supreme Ct. 1972, U.S. Ct. Claims 1979, U.S. Ct. Appeals (2d cir.) 1980, U.S. Dist. Ct. (no. dist.) N.Y. 1980, U.S. Dist. Ct. (we. dist.) N.Y. 1993, U.S. Ct. Appeals (3d cir.) 1993, U.S. Ct. Appeals (5th cir.) 1995. Assoc. firm Goodwin, Procter & Hoar, Boston, 1961-70; ptnr. Goodwin, Procter & Hoar, 1970-96; assoc. justice Superior Ct. Mass., 1996—; spl. counsel Boston Fin. Commn., 1974; spl. counsel to Mass. Commn. on Jud. Conduct, 1986; mem. Scituate (Mass.) Bd. Zoning Appeals, 1970, Scituate Planning Bd., 1972; spl. counsel Gov. of N.Y. on Indian Land Claims, 1985-96; spl. counsel to Gov. and Atty. Gen. of Vt. on Indian Claims, 1987-90; chmn. standing adv. com. Mass. Rules Civil Procedure, 1986-93 ; overseer Colby Coll., 1990—. Contbr. numerous articles on Eastern Indian land claims, ct. administrn., capital punishment to profl. jours. Fellow Am. Coll. Trial Lawyers; mem. ABA, Mass. Bar Assn., Boston Bar Assn. (chmn., task force on drugs and the cts.), Supreme Jud. Ct. Hist. Soc. (chmn. bd. overseers 1993-96), Mass. Hist. Soc.

VAN GILDER, JOHN CORLEY, neurosurgeon, educator; b. Huntington, W.Va., Aug. 14, 1935; s. John Ray and Sarah Pool (Corley) Van G.; m. Kerstin Margarita Olesson, Mar., 1965; children: Sarah, John, Rachel, David. BA, W.Va. U., 1957, BS, 1959; MD, U. Pitts., 1961. Diplomate Am. Bd. Neurol. Surgery. (examiner 1976, 79, 84). Intern Pa. Hosp., Phila., 1961, asst. resident in surgery, 1964-65; asst. resident in surgery Wilkes-Barre (Pa.) Hosp., 1962; asst. resident neurosurgery Barnes Hosp., St. Louis, 1966-68, sr. resident, 1968-69; instr. neurosurgery Yale U. Sch. Medicine, New Haven, 1970, asst. prof., 1970-73, assoc. prof., 1973-76; prof. neurosurgery U. Iowa, Iowa City, 1976—, chmn. div. neurosurgery, 1976—, exec. com. dept. surgery, 1978-81; fellow neurosurgery Wash. U. Sch. Medicine, St. Louis, 1965 -66, instr., 1966; attending neurosurgeon VA Hosp., New Haven, 1970-73, cons. 1973-76; assoc. to attending neurosurgeon Yale-New Haven Med. Ctr., 1970-76; cons. VA Hosp., Iowa City, 1976—; mem. clin. coordinating com. U. Iowa Cancer Ctr., 1979—; presenter numerous papers at profl. meetings., confs., symposia; vis. prof. U. Tenn., 1984, Tufts U. Med. Ctr., Boston, 1986, U. Tex., San Antonio, 1987, U. Mich., Ann Arbor, 1988, People's Republic China at Hunan Med. Coll., Beijing Neurol. Inst., Tianjin Med. Coll. Hosp., Tiantan Xili, Xian Gen. Hosp., 2d Mil. Coll., Shanghai, Suzhou Med. Coll. Shanghai, 1985, USSR at Burdenk Inst., Kiev Neurol. Inst., Leningrad Neurol. Soc., 1989, Western Reserve U., Cleve., 1993, Yale U., New Haven, Conn., 1994, U. Wash., Seattle, 1997. Author: (with others): Principles of Surgery, 2d edit., 1973, Brief Textbook of Surgery, 1976, Aneurysmal Subarachnoid Hemorrhage, 1981, Operative Meurosurgical Techniques, Indications, Methods, and Results, 1982, Sports Medicine, 1982, Neurosurgery, 1982, Clinical Neurosurgery, 1982, Operative Neurosurgical Technique, Vol. II, 1982, 88, Vol. III, 1995, Current Therapy in Neurosurgical Surgery, 1985, 2d edit. , 1987, Craniovertebral Junction Abnormalities, 1987, Decision Making in Neurological Surgery, 1987, Neurological Surgery, 3d edit., 1988, Anterior Cervical Spine Surgery, 1993, Brain Surgery: Complication Avoidance and Management, 1993, Neurosurgical Emergencies, 1994, Techniques of Spinal Fusion and Instrumation, 1995, Somatic Gene Therapy, 1995; contbr. numerous articles and abstracts to profl. jours.; co-author teaching films; mem. editorial bd. Neurosurgery jour., 1978-84. Capt. USAF, 1962-64. Grantee NIH, 1973-78, Nat. Cancer Inst., 1980-88. Fellow ACS (membership com. Iowa dist. #1 1983—); mem. AMA (Physicians Recogniton award), Am. Physiol. Soc., Congress Neurol. Surgeons (resident placement com. 1970), Am. Assn. Neurol. Surgeons (bd. dirs. 1986-90, awards com. 1986-87, chmn. 1987-88), Rsch. Soc. Neurol. Surgeons, Neurol. Soc. Am. (long range planning com. 1984—, v.p. 1985, pres.-elect 1997), Iowa Med. Soc., Johnson County Med. Soc. (program com. 1984-88, chmn. 1985-86), Iowa-Midwest Neurosurg. Soc. (pres. 1978-79), Soc. Neurol. Surgeons (chmn. membership com. 1986-87, treas. 1991—, pres. elect 1996), Midwest Surg. Assn., Am. Acad. Neurol. Surgery (v.p. 1995—), Ga. Neurosurg. Soc. (hon. life), Am. Bd. Neurol. Surgery (dir. 1992—, chmn. 1997—, residency rev. com.-neurol. surgery 1995—), Sigma Xi. Home: 330 S Summit St Iowa City IA 52240-3220 Office: U Iowa Hosps & Clinics Dept Neurosurgery 200 Hawkins Dr Iowa City IA 52242-1009

VAN GINKEL, BLANCHE LEMCO, architect, educator; b. London, Dec. 14, 1923; d. Myer and Claire Lemco; m. H. P. Daniel van Ginkel, 1956; children: Brenda Renee, Marc Ian. B.Arch., McGill U., 1945; M.C.P., Harvard U., 1950. Tech. asst. Nat. Film Bd. Can., 1943-44; mgr. City Planning Office, Regina, Sask., Can., 1946; architect Atelier Le Corbusier, Paris, 1948; asst. prof. architecture U. Pa., 1951-57; ptnr. van Ginkel Assocs., Montreal, Que., Can., also Toronto, Ont., Can., 1957—; prof. architecture U. Toronto, 1977—, dir. Sch. Architecture, 1977-80, dean faculty architecture and landscape architecture, 1980-82; vis. critic Harvard U., 1958, 70; adj. prof. U. Montreal, McGill U., others; curator exhbns. RCA, U. Toronto, others. Contbr. articles to profl. jours. Mem. adv. com. Nat. Capital Planning Com., Ottawa; mem. adv. com. Nat. Mus.'s Corp.; mem. Que. Provincial Planning Commn. Recipient Internat. Fedn. Housing and Planning Grand Prix award, 1956, Massey medal for arch., 1962, Mademoiselle Mag. award, 1957, Queen's Silver Jubilee medal, 1977, Citizenship citation Can. Govt., 1991. Fellow Royal Archtl. Inst. Can. (exec. com. 1971-74), AIA (hon.); mem. Can. Inst. Planners (bd. dirs. 1961-64), Assn. Collegiate Schs. Architecture (bd. dirs. 1981-84, v.p. 1985-86, pres. 1986-87, Disting. Prof. award 1989), Assn. Royal Inst. Brit. Archs. (assoc.), Royal Can. Acad. Art (bd. dirs. 1992—). Office: 38 Summerhill Gardens, Toronto, ON Canada M4T 1B4

VAN GORKOM, JEROME WILLIAM, financial executive; b. Denver, Aug. 6, 1917; s. A.G. and Elizabeth (Laux) Van G.; m. Betty Jean Alexander, June 27, 1942; children: Gayle, Lynne. BS, U. Ill., 1939, JD, 1941. Bar: Ill. 1941; C.P.A., 1950. Law assoc. Kix Miller, Baar & Morris, Chgo., 1945-47; accountant Arthur Andersen & Co., 1947-54, ptnr., 1954-56; treas., contr. Trans Union Corp., Chgo., 1956—; dir. Trans Union Corp., 1957—, v.p., 1958-60, exec. v.p., 1960-63, pres., 1963-78, chmn. bd., 1978-82; under sec. Dept. State, 1982-83; mng. dir. Chgo. Housing Authority, 1987-88. Chmn. bd. Lyric Opera of Chgo.; chmn. Chgo. Sch. Fin. Authority, 1980-89. With USNR, 1941-45. Clubs: Chicago, Mid America, Comml, Onwentsia, Pauma Valley Country. Home: 245 W Westminster Rd Lake Forest IL 60045-2126

VAN GRAAFEILAND, ELLSWORTH ALFRED, federal judge; b. Rochester, N.Y., May 11, 1915; s. Ivan and Elsie (Gohr) VanG.; m. Rosemary Vaeth, May 26, 1945; children—Gary, Suzanne, Joan, John, Anne. A.B., U. Rochester, 1937; LL.B., Cornell U., 1940. Bar: N.Y. 1940. Practiced in Rochester; now sr. judge U.S. Ct. Appeals for 2d Cir. Fellow Am. Bar Found., N.Y. Bar Found.; mem. ABA (ho. dels. 1973-75), N.Y. State Bar Assn. (v.p. 1972-73, pres. 1973-74, chmn. negligence compensation and ins. sect. 1968-69), Monroe County Bar Assn. (past pres.), Am. Coll. Trial Lawyers., Masons, Kent Club, Oak Hill Country Club. Home: 76 Ramsey Park Rochester NY 14610-1333 Office: Fed Bldg 100 State St Ste 423 Rochester NY 14614-1309

VAN GUNDY, GREGORY FRANK, lawyer; b. Columbus, Ohio, Oct. 24, 1945; s. Paul Arden and Edna Marie (Sanders) Van G.; m. Lisa Tamara

Langer. B.A., Ohio State U., Columbus, 1966, J.D., 1969. Bar: N.Y. bar 1971. Asso. atty. firm Willkie Farr & Gallagher, N.Y.C., 1970-74; v.p. legal, sec. Marsh & McLennan Cos., Inc., N.Y.C., 1974-79; v.p., sec., gen. counsel Marsh & McLennan Cos., Inc., 1979—. Mem. ABA, Phi Beta Kappa. Roman Catholic. Club: University (N.Y.C.). Home: 232 Fox Meadow Rd Scarsdale NY 10583-1640 Office: Marsh & McLennan Cos Inc 1166 Avenue Of The Americas New York NY 10036-2708

VAN GUNDY, JEFF, coach; b. Hernet, Calif., Jan. 19, 1962; married. Graduate cum laude, Nazareth Coll. Head coach McQuaid Jesuit H.S., Rochester, N.Y., 1985-86; grad. asst., asst. coach Providence Coll., 1986-88; asst. coach Rutgers U., N.J., 1988-89; asst. coach N.Y. Knicks, N.Y.C., 1989-96, head coach, 1996—. Office: care NY Knicks Two Pennsylvania Plz New York NY 10121*

VAN GUNDY, SEYMOUR DEAN, nematologist, plant pathologist, educator; b. Toledo, Feb. 24, 1931; s. Robert C. and Margaret (Holloway) Van G.; m. Wilma C. Fanning, June 12, 1954; children: Sue Ann, Richard L. BA, Bowling Green State U., 1953; PhD, U. Wis., 1957. Asst. nematologist U. Calif., Riverside, 1957-63, assoc. prof., 1963-68, prof. nematology and plant pathology, 1968-73, assoc. dean rsch., 1968-70, vice chancellor rsch., 1970-72, chmn. dept. nematology, 1972-84, prof. nematology and plant pathology, assoc. dean rsch. Coll. Natural and Agrl. Scis., 1985-88, acting dean, 1986, interim dean, 1988-90, dean, 1990-93, emeritus dean and prof, 1993—. Former mem. editorial bd. Rev. de Nematologie, Jour. Nematology and Plant Disease; contbr. numerous articles to profl. jours. NSF fellow, Australia, 1965-66; grantee Rockefeller Found., Cancer Res., NSF, USDA. Fellow AAAS, Am. Phytopathol. Soc., Soc. Nematologists (editor-in-chief 1968-72, v.p. 1972-73, pres. 1973-74). Home: 1188 Pastern Rd Riverside CA 92506-5619 Office: U Calif Dept Nematology Riverside CA 92521

VAN HALEN, EDDIE, guitarist, rock musician; b. Nijmegan, The Netherlands, Jan. 26, 1957; came to U.S., 1967; s. Jan and Eugenia Van Halen; m. Valerie Bertinelli, Apr. 1981. Student, Pasadena City Coll.; studied piano. Formed group Broken Combs, name later Mammoth, with bro. Alex.; leader group Van Halen, 1974—; albums include Van Halen, 1978, Van Halen II, 1979, Women and Children First, 1980, Fair Warning, 1981, Diver Down, 1982, 1984, (1984), 5150, 1986, OU812, 1988, For Unlawful Carnal Knowledge, 1991, Van Halen Live: Right Here Right Now, 1993, Balance, 1995. Office: Warner Bros Records 75 Rockefeller Plz New York NY 10019-6908*

VANHANDEL, RALPH ANTHONY, librarian; b. Appleton, Wis., Jan. 17, 1919; s. Frank Henry and Gertrude Mary (Schmidt) Van H.; m. Alice Catherine Hogan, Oct. 27, 1945; children: William Patrick, Karen Jean, Mary Jo. BA, U. Wis., 1946; AB in Libr. Sci., U. Mich., 1947. Head libr. Lawrence (Kans.) Free Pub. Libr., 1947-51, Hibbing (Minn.) Pub. Libr., 1951-54; libr. dir. Gary (Ind.) Pub. Libr., 1954-74; libr. dir. Wells Meml. Pub. Libr., Lafayette, Ind. (name now Tippecanoe County Pub. Libr.), 1974-84, libr. cons., 1963—; mem. Ind. Library Cert. Bd., 1969-84, Ind. State Library and Hist. Bldg. Expansion Commn., 1973-81. Named Ind. Librarian of Year, 1971, Sagamore of Wabash, 1984. Mem. ALA, KC, Anselm Forum (sec. 1964, v.p. 1965), Ind. Libr. Assn. (pres. 1963-64), Kans. Libr. Assn. (v.p. 1951). Home: 3624 Winter St Lafayette IN 47905-3838

VAN HAREN, W(ILLIAM) MICHAEL, lawyer; b. Grand Rapids, Mich., Feb. 15, 1948; s. Adrian William and Donna Bell (Burkett) Van H.; m. Kathryn Mary Desmet, Aug. 7, 1971; children: Ryan C., Amy K., Andrew M., Megan E. BS, U. Mich., 1970; JD magna cum laude, U. Detroit, 1975. Bar: Mich. 1975, U.S. Dist. Ct. (we. dist.) Mich. 1975. Assoc. Warner, Norcross & Judd, Grand Rapids, 1975-81, ptnr., 1981—; adj. prof. taxation Seidman Sch. Bus., Grand Valley State U., Grand Rapids, 1983-85. Assoc. editor U. Detroit Sch. Law Jour. Urban Law, 1974-75; co-editor (handbook) Probate Practice in Decedents Estates, 1985. Co-chmn. profl. divsn. Kent County United Way, Grand Rapids, 1983, 84; pres. Garfield Pk. Nature Ctr., Grand Rapids, 1977, Garfield Pk. Neighborhood Assn., Grand Rapids, 1979; bd. dirs. Western Mich. Estate Planning Coun., 1986-89, Cath. Social Svcs., 1997—. Fellow Am. Coll. Trust and Estate Coun.; mem. Mich. Bar Assn. (probate and estate planning coun. 1981—, treas. 1987-88, sec. 1989-90, vice chmn. 1990-91, chair 1992-93), Mich. Bar Found., University Club. Republican. Roman Catholic. Avocations: squash, golf, hunting. Home: 9007 Conservation St NE Ada MI 49301-9797 Office: Warner Norcross & Judd 900 Old Kent Bldg 111 Lyon St NW Grand Rapids MI 49503-2487

VANHARN, GORDON LEE, college administrator and provost; b. Grand Rapids, Mich., Dec. 30, 1935; s. Henry and Edna (Riemersma) VanH.; m. Mary Kool, June 12, 1958; children—Pamela L., Mark L., Barbara A. B.A., Calvin Coll., 1957; M.S., U. Ill., 1959, Ph.D., 1961. Asst. prof. biology Calvin Coll., Grand Rapids, Mich. 1961-68, prof., 1970-82, acad. dean, 1982-85, provost, 1985-94, sr. v.p., provost, 1994-96, prof. interdisciplinary studies, 1996—; assoc. prof. biology Oberlin Coll., Ohio, 1968-70; assoc. physiologist Blodgett Meml. Med. Ctr., Grand Rapids, 1970-76; research assoc. U. Va., Charlotteville, 1975-76. Contbr. articles to profl. jours. Mem. sci. adv. com. Gerald R. Ford, 1972-73, Blodgett Hosp. research and review com., 1978-84; pres. bd. Grand Rapids Christian Sch. Assn., 1982-85; v.p. Christian Schs. Internat., 1987-93; mem. Grand Rapids Pub. Sch. Bd., 1996—. Grass Found. fellow, 1969. Mem. AAAS, Am. Assn. Higher Edn., Phi Kappa Phi. Mem. Christian Reformed Ch. Home: 1403 Cornell Dr SE Grand Rapids MI 49506-4103 Office: Calvin Coll Dept of Interdisciplinary Studies Grand Rapids MI 49546

VAN HASSEL, HENRY JOHN, dentist, educator, university dean; b. Paterson, N.J., May 2, 1933; s. William Cornelius and Ina (Sturr) Van H.; m. Ann Newell Wiley, Dec. 28, 1960. BA, Maryville Coll., Tenn., 1954; DDS, U. Md., 1963; MSD, U. Wash., 1967, PhD, 1969. Diplomate Am.Bd. Endodontics. Dental dir. USPHS, Seattle, 1965-81; prof., chmn. dept. endodontics U. Md., Balt., 1981-84; dean dental sch. Oreg. Health Scis. U., Portland, 1984—, v.p. instl. affairs, 1989-91. Recipient Schlack award Assn. Mil. Surgeons U.S., 1976, Borrish award Acad. Gen. Dentistry, 1989. Mem. Am. Assn. Endodontists (pres. 1981-82, Grossman Gold medal 1984), Oreg. Dental Assn. (pres. 1990). Office: Oreg Health Scis U Dental Sch 611 SW Campus Dr Portland OR 97201-3001

VAN HAUER, ROBERT, former health care company executive; b. Chgo., June 9, 1910; s. Francis Anthony and Della Agnes (Mulhern) Van H.; m. Elaine Greenwood, July 24, 1944 (dec. Nov. 1961); children: Peter, Jan, Mary, Christopher, Gretchen, Juliana; m. Margaret Ann St. Pierre Viehman, May 4, 1968; stepchildren: Gayle, Edwin, Thomas, John, Michael, Daniel. B.A. in Econs; B.B.A. in Accounting (Reiman scholar), U. Mont., Missoula, 1938; M.A. in Econs, U. Minn., Mpls., 1940. Jr. Auditor Peat Marwick Mitchell, C.P.A.'s, Mpls., 1938-40; asst. sales mgr. North Star Woolen Mill, Mpls., 1940-42; dir. contracts Mpls. regional office VA, 1946-51; with Health Central, Inc., Mpls., 1951-78; exec. v.p. Health Central, Inc., 1965, pres., chief exec. officer, 1970-78; exec. dir. Health Found., Mpls., 1979-81. Mem. planning commn. Golden Valley, Minn., 1959-66; past trustee St. Margaret's Acad., Benilde-St. Margaret's High Sch. Served to maj. AUS, 1941-46. Decorated Commendation ribbon; Rieman fellow, 1938-40. Mem. Am. Hosp. Assn., Minn. Hosp. Assn. (trustee, com. chmn. 1974-79), War Meml. Blood Bank (pres., dir. 1967), Physicians Health Plan Mpls. (dir., exec. com.), Am. Legion. Republican. Roman Catholic. Clubs: Mpls. Athletic, Minn. Valley Country, Elks; Union Hills Country (Sun City, Ariz.). Home: 6837 Olson Memorial Hwy Golden Valley MN 55427-4951

VAN HENGEL, MAARTEN, banker; b. Amsterdam, The Netherlands, Mar. 29, 1927; came to U.S., 1950, naturalized, 1957; s. Adrianus J. and Helena (Gips) van H.; m. Drusilla Drake Riley, Dec. 1, 1951; children: Maarten, Virginia, Hugh, Drusilla. Student, Kennemer Lyceum, Bloemendaal, Holland, 1939-45. With tng. programs of Amsterdamsche Bank, N.V., Amsterdam, Lazard Bros. & Co. Ltd., London and Canadian Bank of Commerce, Montreal, Que., Can., 1945-49; with Brown Bros. Harriman & Co., 1950—, ptnr., 1968—; chmn. Brown Bros. Harriman Trust Co. Bd. dirs. Netherlands-Am. Found., Phelps Meml. Hosp. Served with AUS, 1951-53. Clubs: India House, Netherland (N.Y.C.); Fishers Island Country, Hay Harbor (Fishers Island); Sleepy Hollow Country (Scarborough, N.Y.). Home: 350 River Rd Briarcliff Manor NY 10510-2418 Office: Brown Bros Harriman & Co 59 Wall St New York NY 10005-2808

VAN HENGEL, MAARTEN R., financial executive; b. Montreal, Que., Can., Jan. 3, 1953; s. Maarten and Drusilla van H.; m. Claudia Bressan, May 13, 1979; children: Peter, Christina. BA, Wagner Coll., 1977. Formerly v.p. Prometheus Group, N.Y.C., 1972-81; pres. Carret Securities, N.Y.C., 1987-90; sr. v.p. Carret & Co., N.Y.C., 1981-90; exec. v.p. Clifford/Russell, Inc., N.Y.C., 1990-92; v.p. Swiss Bank Corp., N.Y.C., 1992-93, Bankers Trust Co., N.Y.C., 1993—; dir. Metallized Carbon Corp., Ossing, N.Y. Mem. Assn. Investment Mgmt. Sales Execs., Hay Harbor Club, Sleepy Hollow Country Club, Fishers Island Yacht Club.

VAN HOESEN, BETH MARIE, artist, printmaker; b. Boise, Idaho, June 27, 1926; d. Enderse G. and Freda Marie (Soulen) Van H.; m. Mark Adams, Sept. 12, 1953. Student, Escuela Esmaralda, Mexico City, 1945, San Francisco Art Inst., 1946, 47, 51, 52, Fontainbleau (France) Ecole des Arts, Acad. Julian and Acad., 5Grande Chaumier, Paris, 1948-51; B.A., Stanford U., 1948; postgrad., San Francisco State U., 1957-58. One-Woman shows include, De Young Mus., San Francisco, 1959, Achenbach Found., Calif. Palace Legion of Honor, San Francisco, 1961, 74, Santa Barbara (Calif.) Mus., 1963, 74, 76, Oakland (Calif.) Mus., 1980, John Berggruen Gallery, San Francisco, 1981, 83, 85, 88, 91; traveling exhibit Am. Mus. Assn., 1983-85; group shows include, Calif. State Fair, Sacramento, 1951 (award), Library of Congress, Washington, 1956, 57, San Francisco Mus. Modern Art, 70 (award), Boston Mus. Fine Arts, 1959, 60, 62, Pa. Acad. Fine Arts, Phila., 1959, 61, 63, 65, Achenbach Found., 1961 (award), Bklyn. Mus., 1962, 66, 68, 77, Continuing Am. Graphics, Osaka, Japan, 1970, Hawaii Nat. Print. Exhbn., Honolulu, 1980 (award), Oakland Mus., 1975 (award); represented in permanent collections, including, Achenbach Found., San Francisco, Fine Arts Mus., Bklyn. Mus., Mus. Modern Art, N.Y.C., Oakland Mus., San Francisco Mus. Modern Art, Victoria and Albert Mus., (London), Chgo. Art Inst., Cin. Mus., Portland (Oreg.) Art Mus. (Recipient award of Honor, San Francisco Art Commn. 1981); author: Collection of Wonderful Things, 1972, Beth Van Hoesen Creatures, 1987, Beth Van Hoesen Works on Paper, 1995. Mem. Calif. Soc. Printmakers (award 1993), San Francisco Women Artists. Office: care John Berggruen 228 Grant Ave Fl 3D San Francisco CA 94108-4612

VAN HOFTEN, JAMES DOUGAL ADRIANUS, business executive, former astronaut; b. Fresno, Calif., June 11, 1944; s. Adriaan and Beverly (McCurdy) van H.; m. Vallarie Davis, May 31, 1975; children—Jennifer Lyn, Jamie Juliana, Victoria Jane. B.S., U. Calif.-Berkeley, 1966; M.S., Colo. State U., 1968, Ph.D., 1976. Asst. prof. U. Houston, 1976-78; astronaut NASA, Houston, 1978-86; sr. v.p., mgr. advanced systems line Bechtel Nat., Inc., San Francisco, 1986-93; project mgr. Hong Kong New Airport projects, 1993-96; sr. v.p., mgr. N.E. Asia, gen. mgr. Bechtel Civil Co., Hong Kong, 1996—. Served with USN, 1969-74; lt. col. Air N.G. 1984—. Recipient Disting. Service award Colo. State U., 1984; Disting. Citizen award Fresno Council Boy Scouts Am., 1984; Disting. Achievement award Pi Kappa Alpha, 1984. Assoc. fellow AIAA; mem. ASCE (Aerospace Sci. and Tech. Application award 1984). Republican. Home: 10B The Harborview, 11 Magazine Gap Rd, Hong Kong Hong Kong Office: Pacific Bechtel Corp, Li Po Chun Chambers, Hong Kong Hong Kong

VAN HOLDE, KENSAL EDWARD, biochemistry educator; b. Eau Claire, Wis., May 14, 1928; s. Leonard John and Nettie (Hart) Van H.; m. Barbara Jean Watson, Apr. 11, 1950; children: Patricia, Mary, Stephen, David. B.S., U. Wis., 1949, Ph.D., 1952. Research chemist E.I. du Pont de Nemours & Co., 1952-55; research assoc. U. Wis., 1955-56; asst. prof. U. Wis. at Milw., 1956-57; mem. faculty U. Ill., Urbana, 1957-67; prof. dept. biochemistry and biophysics Oreg. State U., Corvallis, 1967; Am. Cancer Soc. rsch. prof., 1977-93, disting. prof., 1988-93, disting. prof. emeritus, 1993—; instr.-in-charge physiology course Marine Biol. Lab., Woods Hole, Mass., 1977-80; mem. research staff Centre des Recherches sur les Macromolecules, Strasbourg, France, 1964-65; mem. study sect. USPHS, 1966-69, 91—; staff Weizmann Inst., Israel, 1981, Lab. Léon Brillouin, Saclay, France, 1989-90. Author: Physical Biochemistry, 1971, Chromatin, 1988; (with C. Mathews) Biochemistry, 1989, 2nd edit., 1995; editor: Biochmica Biophysica Acta, 1966-68; mem. editl. bd. jours. Biol. Chemistry, 1968-75, 81-87, 91-92, assoc. editor, 1992—, Biochemistry, 1973-76, 82-89; contbr. profl. jours. Trustee Marine Biol. Lab., Woods Hole, 1979-82, 84-92. NSF sr. postdoctoral fellow, 1964-65; Guggenheim fellow, 1973-74; European Molecular Biology Orgn. fellow, 1975. Mem. NAS, Am. Soc. Biochemistry and Molecular Biology, Biophys. Soc., Am. Acad. Arts and Scis. Home: 229 NW 32nd St Corvallis OR 97330-5020 Office: Oreg State U Dept Biochemistry Corvallis OR 97331

VANHOLE, WILLIAM REMI, lawyer; b. Denver, June 25, 1948; s. Joseph L. and Mildred M. VanHole; m. Gemma VanHole, Feb. 7, 1971; 3 children. BS, Colo. State U., 1970; JD, U. Idaho, 1976. Bar: Idaho 1976, U.S. Dist. Ct. Idaho 1976, U.S. Ct. Appeals (9th cir.) 1983. Law clk. to judge U.S. Dist. Ct. Idaho, Boise, 1976-78; assoc. Quane, Smith, Howard & Hull, Boise, 1978-81, Langroise, Sullivan & Smylie, Boise, 1981-83; asst. U.S. atty. U.S. Dept. of Justice, Boise, 1983-87; U.S. atty. Dist. of Idaho, 1984-85; assoc. gen. counsel Boise Cascade Corp., 1987—. Served with U.S. Army, 1970-72. Mem. ABA, Fed. Bar Assn., Idaho Bar Assn., Idaho Assn. Def. Counsel, Def. Rsch. Inst., Am. Corp. Counsel Assn. Republican. Avocations: skiing, fishing, tennis. Office: Boise Cascade Corp PO Box 50 Boise ID 83728

VAN HOOMISSEN, GEORGE ALBERT, state supreme court justice; b. Portland, Oreg., Mar. 7, 1930; s. Fred J. and Helen F. (Flanagan) Van H.; m. Ruth Madeleine Niedermeyer, June 4, 1960; children: Geroge T., Ruth Anne, Madeleine, Matthew. BBA, U. Portland, 1951; JD, Georgetown U., 1955, LLM in Labor Law, 1957; LLM in Jud. Adminstrn., U. Va., 1986. Bar: D.C. 1955, Oreg. 1956, Tex. 1971, U.S. Dist. Ct. Oreg. 1956, U.S. Ct. Mil. Appeals 1955, U.S. Ct. Customs and Patent Appeals 1955, U.S. Ct. Claims 1955, U.S. Ct. Appeals (9th cir.) 1956, U.S. Ct. Appeals (D.C. cir.) 1955, U.S. Supreme Ct. 1960. Law clk. for Chief Justice Harold J. Warner Oreg. Supreme Ct., 1955-56; Keigwin teaching fellow Georgetown Law Sch., 1956-57; dep. dist. atty. Multnomah County, Portland, 1957-59; pvt. practice Portland, 1959-62; dist. atty. Multnomah County, 1962-71; dean nat. coll. dist. attys., prof. law U. Houston, 1971-73; judge Cir. Ct., Portland, 1973-81, Oreg. Ct. Appeals, Salem, 1981-88; assoc. justice Oreg. Supreme Ct., Salem, 1988—; adj. prof. Northwestern Sch. Law, Portland, Willamette U. Sch. Law, Portland State U.; mem. faculty Am. Acad. Judicial Edn., Nat. Judicial Coll.; Keigwin Teaching fellow Georgetown U. Law Sch. Mem. Oreg. Ho. of Reps., Salem, 1959-62, chmn. house jud. com. With USMC, 1951-53; col. USMCR (ret.). Recipient Disting. Alumnus award U. Portland, 1972. Master Owen M. Panner Am. Inn of Ct.; mem. ABA, Oreg. State Bar, Tex. Bar Assn., Oreg. Law Inst. (bd. dirs.), Arlington Club, Multnomah Athletic Club, Univ. Club. Roman Catholic. Office: Oreg Supreme Ct 1163 State St Salem OR 97310-1331

VAN HORN, HUGH, physicist, astronomer; b. Williamsport, Pa., Mar. 5, 1938; s. Robert Dix and Virginia Elizabeth (Moody) Van H.; m. Mary Susan Boon, Sept. 17, 1960; children: Kathleen Susan, Mary Margaret, Michael Hugh George. BSc, Case Inst. Tech., 1960; PhD, Cornell U., 1965. NASA predoctoral trainee Cornell U., Ithaca, 1963-65; rsch. assoc. U. Rochester, 1965-67, asst. prof., 1967-73, assoc. prof., 1973-77, prof., 1977-96, chmn. dept. physics and astronomy, 1980-86, acting assoc. dean Coll. Arts and Scis., 1987-89, acting chmn. dept. physics and astronomy, 1992-93; Shapley lectr. Am. Astron. Soc., 1981-95; dir. divsn. astron. sci. NSF, Arlington, Va., 1993—; vis. fellow Joint Inst. for Lab. Astrophysics, 1973-74; sr. scientist Lab. Laser Energetics, 1985-96; vis. prof. U. Tex., 1987; prin. investigator NASA and NSF grants; adj. prof. U. Rochester, 1996—. Editor: (with V. Weidemann) White Dwarfs and Variable Degenerate Stars, 1979, (with S. Ichimaru) Strongly Coupled Plasma Physics, 1983; contbr. articles on white dwarfs, neutron stars and dense matter to profl. jours. Fellow AAAS; mem. Am. Astron. Soc., Internat. Astron. Union. Office: NSF Divsn Astron Sci 4201 Wilson Blvd Arlington VA 22230-0001

VAN HORN, JOHN KENNETH, health physicist, consultant; b. St. Louis, June 22, 1948; s. Harold E. and Norma L. (Klobe) Van H.; m. Christine A. Lump, Oct. 20, 1995; children: Shawn R., Mark R., Janina. AB in Physics and Math. Edn., Drury Coll., 1971; MS in Instrnl. Tech., No. Ill. U., 1988. Physics, math. tchr. Perryville (Mo.) Pub. Schs., 1971-76; math. dept. head Alden-Hebron (Ill.) Community Schs., 1976-84; program developer prodn. tng. Commonwealth Edison, Braidwood, Ill., 1984-87, health physics instr. prodn. tng., 1987-91; health physicist LaSalle Nuclear Sta. Commonwealth Edison, Marseilles, Ill., 1991—; unit health physicist Commonwealth Edison, Marseilles, Ill., 1993; lead radiation protection instr. LaSalle Nuclear Sta. Commonwealth Edison, Marseilles, Ill., 1995-96, instr. devel. specialist, 1996—, total quality mgmt. team facilitator, 1996—, tng. and devel. auditor, 1997—; presenter Midwest Nuclear Tng. Assn., 1994. Co-author: New 10CFR20 for HP Technicians, 1992. Mem. Zoning and Planning Bd., Mazon, Ill, 1990-95; First Aid instr. ARC, Morris, Ill., 1986—; merit badge counselor Boy Scouts Am., Morris, 1989-95; elder First Christian Ch., Wilmington, Ill., 1992-95. Mem. Nat. Soc. Performance and Instrn., Health Physics Soc. (co-chmn. exam group 1991—, bd. dirs. 1991-96, pres.-elect Midwest chpt. 1993, pres. 1994, 95, mem. nat. pub. edn. com. 1996—), Kappa Delta Pi. Avocations: photography, chess, karate. Office: Commonwealth Edison Tng Dpt RR1 Box 220 2601 N 21st Rd Marseilles IL 61341

VAN HORN, LECIA JOSEPH, newswriter; b. L.A., Jan. 19, 1963; d. McKinley Joe and Opal Geneva (Ivie) Joseph; m. Philip Dale Van Horn, Apr. 19, 1986; children: Kari Christine, Brandon Joseph. BA in Journalism, U. Southern Calif., 1984. News reporter Sta. KSCR Radio, L.A., 1983; consumer news researcher Sta. KCBS-TV, L.A., 1983, Sta. KABC-TV, L.A., 1983-84; newswriter Headline News, Atlanta, 1984-85; editorial asst., newswriter, field producer Sta. KNBC-TV, Burbank, Calif., 1985-86; newswriter, assoc. producer Sta. WYFF-TV, Greenville, S.C., 1986; freelance newswriter, assoc. producer Sta. WSB-TV, Atlanta, 1987-88; newswriter CNN, Atlanta, 1987-94; freelance newswriter, assoc. producer Sta. KSTP-TV, St. Paul, 1995-96; freelance newswriter and field prodr. Sta. KABC-TV, L.A., 1996-97; freelance newswriter KNBC-TV, Burbank, Calif., 1997—; freelance prodr. E News Daily, L.A., 1997—. Author: Thoughts and Inspirational Sayings, 1985; contbr. poetry and articles to newspapers. Mem. U. So. Calif. Alumni. Mem. Science of Mind. Avocations: reading, music, dancing, gymnastics (Class III Calif. State Champion 1977), Taekwondo.

VAN HORN, O. FRANK, retired counselor, consultant; b. Grand Junction, Colo., Apr. 16, 1926; s. Oertel F. and Alta Maude (Lynch) Van H.; m. Dixie Jeanne MacGregor, Feb. 1, 1947 (dec. Nov. 1994); children: Evelyn, Dorothy. AA, Mesa Coll., 1961; BA, Western State Colo., 1963; MEd, Oreg. State U., 1969. Counselor, mgr. State of Oreg.-Employment, Portland and St. Helens, 1964-88; pvt. practice counselor and cons. St. Helens, 1988-96; chair Task Force on Aging, Columbia County, 1977-79; advisor Western Interstate Commn. on Higher Edn., Portland, 1971, Concentrated Employment and Tng., St. Helens, 1977, County Planning Bd., Columbia County, Oreg., 1977-80, City Planning Bd., St. Helens, 1978, Youth Employment Coun., St. Helens, 1978, Task Force on Disadvantaged Youth, St. Helens, 1980; counselor Career Mgmt. Specialists Internat.; instr. Portland C.C. Mem. ACA, Oreg. Counseling Assn., Internat. Assn. Pers. in Employment Svc. (Outstanding Achievement award 1975), Nat. Employment Counselors Assn. Democrat. Home: 1111 St Helens St Saint Helens OR 97051

VAN HORN, RICHARD LINLEY, academic administrator; b. Chgo., Nov. 2, 1932; s. Richard Linley and Mildred Dorothy (Wright) Van H.; m. Susan Householder, May 29, 1954 (dec.); children: Susan Elizabeth, Patricia Suzanne, Lynda Sue; m. Betty Pfefferbaum, May 29, 1988. BS with highest honors, Yale U., 1954; MS, MIT, 1956; PhD, Carnegie-Mellon U., 1976; D of Bus. (hon.), Reitsumeikan U., Kyoto, Japan, 1991. Asst. dir. Army EDP Project, MIT, Cambridge, 1956-57; research staff Rand Corp., Santa Monica, Calif., 1957-60; head mgmt. systems group Rand Corp., 1960-67; dir., prof. mgmt. systems European Inst. Advanced Studies in Mgmt., Brussels, Belgium, 1971-73; asso. dean Grad. Sch. Indsl. Adminstrn., Carnegie-Mellon U., Pitts., 1967-71, dir. budget and planning, 1973-74, v.p. for bus. affairs, 1974-77, v.p. for mgmt., 1977-80, provost and prof. mgmt., 1980-83; chancellor U. Houston, 1983-86, pres., 1986-89; pres. U. Okla., 1989-94; pres. emeritus and regent's prof. Coll. of Bus. U. Okla., Norman, 1994—; Clarence E. Page prof. aviation U. Okla., Norman, 1995—. Author: (with Robert H. Gregory) Automatic Data Processing Systems, 1960, 2nd edit. 1963, (with R.H. Gregory) Business Data Processing and Programming, 1963, (with C.H. Kriebel and J.T. Heames) Management Information Systems: Progress and Perspectives, 1971; contbr. articles to profl. jours.; asso. editor: Jour. Inst. Mgmt. Scis, 1964-78. Bd. dirs. Last Frontier coun. Boy Scouts Am., Kirkpatrick Ctr., Nelson-Atkins Art Mus., Truman Libr. Inst., State Fair Okla., Okla. Futures Commn., Okla. Health Scis. Ctr. Found., Inc., Okla. Ednl. TV Authority. Mem. Inst. Mgmt. Sci. (nat. council mem. 1963-65, sec.-treas. 1964), Assn. for Computing Machinery (nat. lectr. 1969-70), Council on Govt. Relations (bd. dirs. 1981-83). Avocation: commercial pilot. Home: 701 NW 14th St Oklahoma City OK 73103-2211 Office: U Okla Coll of Bus Norman OK 73019

VAN HORNE, JAMES CARTER, economist, educator; b. South Bend, Ind., Aug. 6, 1935; s. Ralph and Helen (McCarter) Van H.; m. Mary A. Roth, Aug. 27, 1960; children: Drew, Stuart, Stephen. AB, De Pauw U., 1957, DSc (hon.), 1986; MBA, Northwestern U., 1961, PhD, 1964. Comml. lending rep. Continental Ill. Nat. Bank, Chgo., 1958-62; prof. fin. Stanford U. Grad. Sch. Bus., 1965-75, A.P. Giannini prof. fin., 1976—, assoc. dean, 1973-75, 76-80; dep. asst. sec. Dept. Treasury, 1975-76; bd. dirs. Sanwa Bank Calif., BB&K Internat. Fund, BB&K Fund Group; chmn. Montgomery St. Income Securities; commr. workers compensation Rate Making Study Commn., State of Calif., 1990-92. Author: Function and Analysis of Capital Market Rates, 1970, Financial Market Rates and Flows, 1994, Financial Management and Policy, 1995; co-author: Fundamentals of Financial Management, 1995; assoc. editor Jour. fin. and Quantitative Analysis, 1969-85, Jour. Fin., 1971-73, Jour. Fixed Income, 1990—. Mem. bd. trustees DePauw U., 1989-96. With AUS, 1957. Mem. Am. Econ. Assn., Am. Fin. Assn. (past pres., dir.), Western Fin. Assn. (past pres., dir.), Fin. Mgmt. Assn. Home: 2000 Webster St Palo Alto CA 94301-4049 Office: Stanford U Grad Sch Bus Stanford CA 94305

VAN HORNE, R. RICHARD, oil company executive; b. Milw., June 7, 1931; s. Ralph Rupert and Edna (Benson) Van H.; m. Elizabeth Whitaker Dixon, July 3, 1954; children—Ann Van Horne Arms, R. Ross, Margaret Van Horne Shuya. B.B.A., U. Wis., 1953. Various positions Anaconda Am. Brass Co., Milw. and Kenosha, Wis., 1955-72; pres., chief exec. officer Anaconda Am. Brass Co., Waterbury, Conn., 1972-74, Anaconda Aluminum Co., Louisville, 1974-82; sr. v.p. pub. affairs Atlantic Richfield Co., Los Angeles, 1982-85; bd. dirs. Citizens Fidelity Corp. Bd. visitors Sch. Bus., U. Wis., Madison; mem. U. Wis. Found.; trustee Brooklawn, Louisville Community Found. Served to 1st lt. U.S. Army, 1953-55. Sr. fellow Bellarmine Coll. Mem. Mchts. and Mfrs. Assn. (bd. dirs. 1983-85), Am. Petroleum Inst., Nat. Planning Assn. (com. on new Am. realities 1982-84), Bascom Hill Soc., Minocqua Country Club. Republican. Episcopalian. Avocations: golf; reading; gardening. Home: 5520 Tecumseh Cir Louisville KY 40207-1692 Office: Atlantic Richfield Co 515 S Flower St Los Angeles CA 90071-2201

VAN HOUSEN, THOMAS CORWIN, III, architect, designer, builder; b. Oak Park, Ill., Jan. 2, 1927; s. Thomas Corwin and Dorothea (Saunders) Van H.; children: Deborah, Victoria, Constance. BA, Lawrence U., 1951; BArch, U. Minn., Mpls., 1954; MArch in Urban Design, Harvard U., 1962. Registered architect, Minn., Wis. With Ellerbe Assocs., Inc., St. Paul, 1951-61; architect, prin. Progressive Design Assocs., Inc., St. Paul, 1961-71; architect, developer, v.p. Landmark Devel. Corp./Appletree Enterprises, Inc., Bloomington, Minn., 1971-85; architect, developer Mortenson Devel. Co., Mpls., 1985-88; architect, design, bldg. dir. D&B Collaborative, Inc., Mpls., 1989—. Bldg. official City of North Oaks, Minn., 1964-78; mem. Minn. League of Municipalities-Metro, St. Paul, 1970-72, Gov.'s Open Space Adv. Com., St. Paul, 1972-74. With U.S. Air Force, 1945-47, ETO. Recipient Outstanding House award St. Paul Jaycees, 1958, 62; named finalist (team mem.) Archtl. competition Boston City Hall, 1962. Fellow AIA (nat. bd. dirs. 1985-88, v.p., pres.-elect Minn. chpt. 1994-95, pres. 1995, spl. award 1981, Presdl. citation 1988, 90); mem. N.W. YMCA. Republican. Lutheran. Avocations: tennis, swimming, music. Home: 6322 45th Place N Minneapolis MN 55428-5152

VAN HOUTEN, ELIZABETH ANN, corporate communications executive; b. Washington, Feb. 22, 1945; d. Raymond R. and Marian Edna (Hovemann) Van H. BA, Mary Washington Coll., 1966. Analyst U.S. Gov., Washington, 1966-68; dep. chief of publs. Found. for Coop. Housing,

Washington, 1968-72; editor Nat. League of Savs. Inst., Washington, 1972-76; dir. pub. relations Fed. Nat. Mortgage Assn., Washington, 1976-83; v.p. communications & investor relations Sallie Mae (Student Loan Mktg. Assn.), Washington, 1983-93; v.p. corp. and investor rels. Sallie Mae, Washington, 1993-95; ret., 1995. Apptd. by city coun. to Master Plan Task Force, Alexandria, Va., 1987-92; chmn. emeritus Liz Lerman Dance Exch.; mem. campaign com. for Del Pepper, Alexandria, 1987; bd. dirs. Watergate of Alexandria, 1984-89, pres., 1988-89, Washington Studio Sch., 1995—. Mem. Nat. Assn. Real Estate Editors (bd. dirs. 1980-82). Avocations: music, visual arts, reading. Home: 105 S Water St Chestertown MD 21620

VAN HOUTEN, FRANKLYN BOSWORTH, geologist, educator; b. N.Y.C., July 14, 1914; s. Charles Nicholas and Hessie Osborne (Bosworth) Van H.; m. Jean Oliver Sholes, Feb. 18, 1943; children: Jean S., F. Bosworth, David Gordon. B.S., Rutgers U., 1936; Ph.D., Princeton U., 1941. Instr. dept. geology Williams Coll., 1939-42; asst. prof. Princeton U., 1946-51, assoc. prof., 1951-55, prof., 1955-85, prof. emeritus, 1985—; vis. prof. geology UCLA, 1964, State U. N.Y. at Binghamton, 1971; geologist U.S. Geol. Survey, 1948-67; temporary geologist Geol. Survey Can., 1953, Yukon Expdn., geol. expdns. to Morocco, Tunisia, Libya, Egypt, Madagascar. Author reports and articles on geology. Served as lt. USN, 1942-46. Fellow Geol. Soc. Am.; mem. Am. Assn. Petroleum Geologists, Soc. Econ. Paleontologists and Mineralogists (hon. mem., Twenhofel medal), Internat. Assn. Sedimentologists, Colombia Geol. Soc. (hon.), Delta Upsilon. Home: 168 Fitzrandolph Rd Princeton NJ 08540-7224

VAN HOUTEN, JAMES FORESTER, insurance company executive; b. Fullerton, Calif., Jan. 13, 1942; s. James Forester and Lois Evangeline (Trout) V.H. children: Kimberly Evangeline, Lori Lynn. BA in English Lit., St. Mary's U.; MBA, Ill. State U. CPCU, CLU. Sales mgr. for Can. Motors Ins. Corp. divsn. GM, Detroit, 1963-74; v.p. sales Volkswagen Group, St. Louis, 1974-78; v.p. personal lines mktg. Wausau Ins. Cos., St. Louis, 1978-80; v.p., chief mktg. officer life and health Wausau Ins. Cos., 1980-84; v.p., chief mktg. and strategic planning officer Country Cos., Bloomington, Ill., 1984-89; pres., CEO Mut. Svc. Ins. Cos., St. Paul, 1989—; adj. prof. strategic mgmt. MBA program U. Minn., 1990—. Lectr., program leader Youth Black Achievers, St. Paul; mem. exec. bd. arrowhead coun. Boy Scouts of Am.; mem. bd. advisors CARE, Minn. Assn. Scholars. Mem. Ins. Fedn. Minn. (chmn. bd.), Nat. Coop. Bus. Assn. (bd. dirs. and exec. com., chair fin. com.), Coop. Devel. Found. (bd. dirs., ex com.), Minn. Bus. Partnership (bd. dirs., Minn. K-12 edn. com.), Ctr. Am. Experiment Think Tank (bd. dirs.). Office: Mut Svc Ins Cos 2 Pine Tree Dr Arden Hills MN 55112-3715

VAN HOUTEN, STEPHEN H., manufacturing company executive; b. Toronto. BA Honours, U. Western Ont., 1974; LLB, U. Ottawa, 1977; LLM, Osgoode Hall, Toronto, 1984. Bar: Ont. 1979. Legal counsel Gen. Motors, Can., 1980-84, mgr. bus. planning, 1984-87, dir. govt. rels., trade policy, 1987-88, dir. pub. rels., 1988-89; pres. Automotive Parts Mfrs'. Assn., Can., 1989-91, Alliance of Mfrs. and Exporters, 1991—; mem., bd. dirs. numerous mfg. assns. Contbr. numerous articles to profl. jours. Chmn. Traffic Injury Rsch. Found. Can. Office: Alliance of Mfrs and Exporters, 75 Internat Blvd Ste 400, Toronto, ON Canada M9W 6L9

VAN HOUTTE, RAYMOND A., financial executive; b. Detroit, Aug. 1, 1924; s. Maurice and Gabrielle (Hoorelbeke) Van H.; m. Margaret Graves, June 17, 1950; children—Raymond C., Jonathan P., Nancy J. B.B.A., U. Mich., 1949; J.D., U. Conn., 1955. Bar: N.Y. 1963; CPA, Conn. Sole practice Hartford, Conn., 1955-58; mem. new product devel. staff Nestle Co., White Plains, N.Y., 1958-60; pres. Ithaca Gun Co., N.Y., 1960-68; v.p. Tompkins County Trust Co., Ithaca, 1968-73, pres., chief exec. officer, 1973-89, pres. emeritus, counselor, 1990—; pres. Tompkins County Area Devel., Ithaca, 1985; trustee Mut. Funds for Bank Trust Depts., Boston; bd. dirs. Evaporated Metal Product, Inc. Author: Responsibilities of Bank Directors, 1974. Bd. dirs. Ithaca City Sch. Dist., 1965-66, Tompkins Comty. Hosp.; trustee Paleontol. Rsch. Instn., Kendal at Ithaca. With USAF, 1944-45. Mem. AICPA, N.Y. State Bankers Assn. (2d v.p. 1985-86, pres. 1987-88), Chi Phi (treas.). Lodge: Rotary (chmn.). Home: 1 Strawberry Ln Ithaca NY 14850-1413

VAN HOUWELING, DOUGLAS EDWARD, university administrator, educator; b. Kansas City, Mo., Sept. 20, 1943; s. Cornelius Donald and Roberta Irene (Olson) Van H.; m. Andrea Taylor Parks, Aug. 28, 1965; children: Robert Parks, Benjamin Parks. BS, Iowa State U., Ames, 1965; PhD, Ind. U., 1974. Asst. prof. Cornell U., Ithaca, N.Y., 1970-81; dir. acad. computing Cornell U., 1978-81; vice provost Carnegie-Mellon U., Pitts., 1981-84; adj. assoc. prof. Carnegie-Mellon U., 1981-84; vice provost, dean, prof. U. Mich., Ann Arbor, 1984—; mem. research adv. com. Online Coll. Library Consortium, Dublin, Ohio, 1984-87; trustee EDUCOM, vice chmn. bd. dirs., 1987-91; Princeton, vice chmn., 1987, council chmn., 1986-87; cofounder Interuniv. Corsortium for Ednl. Computing, 1984; chmn. bd. MERIT computer network, 1986-90, Advanced Network and Svcs., 1990—; state of Mich. del. Midwest Tech. Inst., 1986-87. Contbr. chpts. in books, articles to profl. publs. NSF fellow, 1968; Indiana U. fellow, 1969; CAUSE nat. leadership award, 1986. Mem. Simulation Symposiums (pres. 1971; grants chmn. 1972-75), N.Am. Simulation and Gaming Assn. Home: 920 Lincoln Ave Ann Arbor MI 48104-3508 Office: U Mich 503 Thompson St Ann Arbor MI 48109-1340

VAN HOWE, ANNETTE EVELYN, retired real estate agent; b. Chgo., Feb. 16, 1921; d. Frank and Susan (Linstra) Van Howe; m. Edward L. Nezelek, Apr. 3, 1961. BA in History magna cum laude, Hofstra U., 1952; MA in Am. History, SUNY-Binghamton, 1966. Editorial asst. Salute Mag., N.Y.C., 1946-48; assoc. editor Med. Econs., Oradell, N.J., 1952-56; nat. mag. publicist Nat. Mental Health Assn., N.Y.C., 1956-60; exec. dir. Diabetes Assn. So. Calif., L.A., 1960-61; corp. sec., v.p., editor, pub. rels. dir. Edward L. Nezelek, Inc., Johnson City, N.Y., 1961-82; realtor, broker, Ft. Lauderdale, 1980-96, ret., 1996; mgr. condominium, Fort Lauderdale, Fla., 1982-83; dir. Sky Harbour East Condo, 1983-88; substitute tchr. high schs., Binghamton, N.Y., 1961-63. Editor newsletters Mental Health Assn., 1965-68, Unitarian-Universalist Ch. Weekly Newsletter, 1967-71. Bd. dirs. Broome County Mental Health Assn., 1961-65, Fine Arts Soc., Roberson Ctr. for Arts and Scis., 1968-70, Found. Wilson Meml. Hosp., Johnson City, 1972-81, White-Willis Theatre, 1988—, Found. SUNY, Binghamton, mem., 1991-95; mem. Fla. Women's Alliance, 1989—; v.p. Fla. Women's Polit. Caucus, 1989-92; chair Women's History Coalition, Broward County, 1986—; pres. Fla. Women's Consortium, 1989-92; trustee Broome C.C., 1973-78; v.p. Broward County Commn. on Status of Women, 1982-93; bd. dirs. Ft. Lauderdale Women's Coun. of Realtors, 1986-88, Broward Arts Guild, 1986; grad. Leadership Broward Class III, 1985, Leadership Am., 1988; trustee Unitarian-Universalist Ch. of Ft. Lauderdale, 1982-89; mem. adv. bd. Planned Parenthood, 1991-93; pres. Broward Alliance of Planned Parenthood, 1993-94; sec. Nat. Women's Conf. Com., 1994-96; bd. dirs. Nat. Women's Party, 1987-93. Named Feminist of Yr., Broward County, 1987; Women's Hall of Fame, Broward County, 1992, Feminist Heroine Nat. Am. Humanist Assn., 1996. Mem. AAUW (legis. chair Fla. divsn. 1986-87, chair women's issues 1989-94, v.p. Ft. Lauderdale br. 1993—), NAFE, Am. Med. Writers Assn., LWV (bd. dir. Broome County 1969-70), Alumni Assn. SUNY Binghamton (bd. dir. 1970-73), Fla. Bar Assn. (grievance com. 1991-94), Am. Acad. Polit. and Social Sci. Broward Women's Alliance, Broward County Voice for Choice (pres. 1995—), Navy League (newsletter editor Ft. Lauderdale chpt. 1997—), Am. Heritage Soc., Nature Conservancy, Nat. Hist. Soc., Symphony Soc., Pacers, Zonta, Alpha Theta Beta, Phi Alpha Theta, Phi Gamma Mu, Binghamton Garden Club, Binghamton Monday Afternoon Club, Acacia Garden Club (pres.), 110 Tower Club, Tower Forum Club (bd. dirs. 1989—), Downtown Coun., Ft. Lauderdale Woman's Club. Home: 2100 S Ocean Dr Fort Lauderdale FL 33316-3806

VANÍČEK, PETR, geodesist; b. Sušice, Czechoslovakia, July 18, 1935; emigrated to Can., 1969, naturalized, 1975; s. Ivan and Irena (Blahovcová) V.; m. Valeria Vášáriová, 1991; children from previous marriage: Filip, Štěpán, Naninka. Degree in Engring., Czech Tech. U., Prague, 1959; PhD in Math. Physics, Czechoslovak Acad. Scis., Prague, 1968; DrSc in Math. and Phys. Scis., Czech Acad. Scis., 1993. Lic. profl. engr. Geodesist Inst. Surveying, Prague, 1959-63; computer cons. Czech Tech. U., 1963-67; Natural Environ. Research Council sr. research fellow Tidal Inst., U. Liverpool, Eng., 1967-68; sr. sci. officer Natural Environ. Research Council, U.K., 1968-69; NRC Can. postdoctoral fellow Fed. Govt., Ottawa, 1969-71; prof. geodesy U. N.B., Fredericton, 1971—; prof. geodesy Erindale Coll., U. Toronto, 1980-83, adj. prof., 1983-89; vis. prof. U. Parana, Brazil, summers 1975-76, 79, 87, U. Stuttgart, Germany, 1981, 82, U. São Paulo, Brazil, 1981, 84, 87; vis. scientist U.S. Geol. Survey, Menlo Park, Calif., 1977; sr. vis. scientist NAS, 1978; pres. Can. Geophys. Union, 1987-89; v.p. internat. adv. bd. tech. aspects law of sea ABLOS, 1997—; v.p. IAG Commn. on Recent Crustal Movements, 1991—; sr. vis. scientist Royal Inst. Tech., Stockholm, 1986; sr. vis. fellow Council of Sci. and Indsl. Research, South Africa, 1986. Author: (with V. Pleskot and others) Základy Programování Pro Ural, vol. I, 1964, (with J. Čulík, T. Hrušková), vol. II, 1965, (with E.J. Krakiwsky) Geodesy: The Concepts, 1982, rev. edit., 1986, (with others) Guide to GPS Positioning, 1986; editor: Proc. Internat. Symposium on N.Am. Geodetic Networks, 1974, Proc. Can. Geophys. Union Symposium on Satellite Geodesy and Geodynamics, 1975, (with S. Cohen) Slow Deformation and Transmission of Stress in the Earth, 1989, (with N. Christou) Geoid and its Geophysical Interpretations, 1993; mem. internat. editl. bd. Studia Geofisica et Geodetica; contbr. articles to profl. jours. Recipient Humboldt sr. rsch. award Federal Republic of Germany; Am. Geophys. Union fellow. Fellow Geol. Assn. Can., Internat. Assn. Geodesy, Explorers Club; mem. Can. Geophys. Union (J. Tuzo Wilson medal 1996), Czechoslovak Soc. Arts and Scis. Am., Sigma Xi. Home: 667 Golf Club Rd, Fredericton, NB Canada E3B 7S5 *As one coming from communist central Europe, I cannot stop marveling at the opportunities this society offers to anyone willing to work earnestly. One must feel sorry for those who do not conduct their lives to take an advantage of this offer.*

VANIER, JACQUES, physicist; b. Dorion, Que., Can., Jan. 4, 1934; s. Henri and Emma (Boileau) V.; m. Lucie Beaudet, July 8, 1961; children: Lyne, Pierre. BA, U. Montreal, 1955, BSc, 1958; MSc, McGill U., 1960, PhD, 1963. Lectr. U. Montreal, 1961-63, McGill U., 1960-63; physicist Varian Assocs., Beverly, Mass., 1963-67, Hewlett Packard Co., Beverly, 1967; prof. elec. engring. U. Laval, Que., 1967-83; physicist Nat. Rsch. Coun., Ottawa, 1983-94, head elec. and time standards, 1984-86, dir. Lab. Basic Standards, 1986-90, dir. gen. Inst. for Nat. Measurement Standards, 1990-93; prof. physics U. de Montreal, 1995—; cons. Comm. Components Corp., Costa Mesa, Calif., 1974-76, EGG Co., Salem, Mass., 1979-82, Kernco, Danvers, Mass., 1995—; chmn. com. A URSI, 1990-93; chmn. exec. com. CPEM, 1990-94; mem. Internat. Com. Weights and Measures, 1992-96. Author: Basic Theory of Lasers and Masers, 1971, (with C. Audoin) The Quantum Physics of Atomic Frequency Standards, 1989; contbr. articles to profl. jours.; inventor nuclear quadrupole resonance thermometer. Recipient I.I. Rabi Prize, Am. Physical Soc., 1994. Fellow IEEE (Centennial medal 1984, Rabi award 1994), Royal Soc. Can., Am. Phys. Soc.

VANIER, KIERAN FRANCIS, business forms printing company executive; b. Alliance, Ohio, May 10, 1914; s. Joseph A. and Johanna Mary (McCarthy) V.; m. Marjory S. Kitchen, 1937 (dec.); children: Denis K., Annette Vanier Fritzenkotter; m. June Day, 1975 (dec. 1995). B.S., Loyola U., 1937. Salesman Moore Bus. Forms, to 1946; founder Vanier Graphics Corp., 1946, ret. chmn. bd.; ret. vice chmn. Am. Bus. Products, Inc., Atlanta; founder, chmn. Kieran Label Corp. Founder Amoyotrophic Lateral Sclerosis Found. San Diego; past chmn. San Diego chpt. Muscular Dystrophy; past pres. San Diego Employers Assn. Knight Order of Holy Sepulcher, Pope John Paul II. Mem. San Diego Yacht Club, San Diego Country Club, De Anza Country Club. Office: 8765 Olive Ln Santee CA 92071-4165

VAN INWAGEN, PETER JAN, philosophy educator; b. Rochester, N.Y., Sept. 21, 1942; s. George Butler and Mildred Gloria (Knudson) van I; m. Margery Bedford Naylor, Mar. 31, 1967 (div. Apr. 1988); 1 child, Elizabeth Core; m. Elisabeth Marie Bolduc, June 3, 1989. B.S., Rensselaer Poly. Inst., 1965; Ph.D., U. Rochester, 1969. Vis. asst. prof. U. Rochester, N.Y., 1971-72; asst. prof. Syracuse U., N.Y., 1972-74, assoc. prof., 1974-80, prof. philosophy, 1980-95; John Cardinal O'Hara prof. of philosophy U. Notre Dame, South Bend, Ind., 1995—; vis. prof. U. Ariz., Tucson, 1981. Author: An Essay on Free Will, 1983, Material Beings, 1990, Metaphysics, 1993, God, Knowledge and Mystery, 1995; editor: Time and Cause, 1980, Alvin Plantinga, 1985; mem. editl. bd. Jour. Faith and Philosophy, Philos. Perspectives, Nous, Philos. Studies, Philosophy and Phenomenological Rsch.; contbr. articles to profl. jours. Served to capt. U.S. Army, 1969-71. NEH grantee, 1983-84, 89-90. Mem. Am. Philos. Assn., Soc. Christian Philosophers. Democrat. Episcopalian. Home: 52145 Farmington Square Rd Granger IN 46530-6403 Office: U Notre Dame Dept Philosophy South Bend IN 46556

VAN ITALLIE, JEAN-CLAUDE, playwright; b. Brussels, May 25, 1936; came to U.S., 1940; s. Hughes Ferdinand and Marthe Mathilde Caroline (Levy) van I. BA, Harvard U., 1958; PhD (hon.), Kent State U., 1977. Tchr. theater, playwriting New Sch. for Social Research, N.Y.C., 1966, Yale U. Sch. Drama, New Haven, 1969, 84, Naropa Inst., Boulder, Colo., 1976-83, 87-88, Princeton U., N.J., 1976-88, NYU, 1982-88, U. Colo., Boulder, 1985, 89, 91, Columbia U., 1986, Am. Repertory Theatre, Cambridge, Mass., 1990; vis. Mellon prof. Amherst Coll., Mass., fall 1976. Playwright for Open Theatre ensemble, N.Y.C., 1963-68; playwright War, 1963, Almost Like Being, 1965, I'm Really Here, 1965, America Hurrah, 1966 (Drama Desk award, Outer Cir. Critics award 1967), The Serpent, 1968 (Obie award 1969), A Fable, 1975, King of the United States, 1972, Mystery Play, 1973, Medea, 1979, Bag Lady, 1979, Tibetan Book of the Dead, 1983, Early Warnings, 1983, The Traveler, 1986, new English versions Chekhov's The Seagull, 1973, Cherry Orchard, 1977, Three Sisters, 1982, Uncle Vanya, 1983, Paradise Ghetto, 1981, Struck Dumb, (with Joseph Chaiken), 1987, Ancient Boys, 1989; transl.: Genet's The Balcony, 1986, The Odyssey (mus.), 1991, Bulgakhov's Master & Margarita, 1993, Tibetan Book of the Dead (opera libretto), 1996; performer, writer Guys Dreamin, 1996. Grantee Rockefeller Found., 1973, Ford Found., 1979, Creative Artists Pub. Service, 1975; recipient Playwrights award NEA, 1986, Creative Artists Pub. Service award, 1975; Guggenheim fellow, 1963, 83. Buddhist.

VANITALLIE, THEODORE BERTUS, physician; b. Hackensack, N.J., Nov. 8, 1919; s. Dorus Christian and Lucy M. (Pohle) VanI.; m. Barbara Cox, Sept. 25, 1948 (div. Mar. 1992); children: Lucy M., Theodore Bertus, Christina M., Elizabeth B., Katharine R.; m. Sallie Newton Calhoun, Mar. 11, 1992. B.S., Harvard U., 1941; M.D., Columbia U., 1945. Diplomate: Am. Bd. Internal Medicine. Intern in medicine St. Luke's Hosp., N.Y.C., 1945-46, asst. resident in internal medicine, 1948-49, resident, 1949-50, dir. nutrition and metabolism rsch. lab., 1952-55; assoc. Peter Bent Brigham Hosp., Boston, 1955-57; dir. medicine St. Luke's Hosp. Center, N.Y.C., 1957-75; dir. Obesity Rsch. Ctr., 1974-85, co-dir., 1986-88; asst. prof. Sch. Pub. Health, Harvard U., 1955-57; assoc. clin. prof. medicine Columbia, N.Y.C., 1957-65, clin. prof., 1965-71, prof., 1971-88, prof. emeritus, 1988—; vis. prof. internal medicine Am. U. Beirut, 1968-69, trustee, 1976-93; spl. advisor on human nutrition Surgeon Gen., 1980-81; mem. sci. adv. bd. Nutrition Found., 1967-71; pres. Am. Bd. Nutrition, 1968-71; mem. food and nutrition bd. NRC, 1970-76; med. adv. com. on cyclamates HEW, 1969-70; mem. gastrointestinal and nutrition tng. com. NIH, 1969-73, mem. adv. coun. Nat. Arthritis, Diabetes, Digestive and Kidney Diseases, NIH, 1978-81; mem. joint nutrition monitoring evaluation com. USDA and HHS, 1982-86; dir. Miles Labs., 1976-84; vis. physician Rockefeller U. Hosp., 1986-89; adj. prof. Rockefeller U., 1986-89; vis. prof. medicine in psychiatry, U. Pa., 1990-94. Mem. editorial bd.: Diabetes, 1960-71; editor-in-chief: Am. Jour. Clin. Nutrition, 1979-81. Mem. Englewood (N.J.) Bd. Edn., 1960-65, v.p., 1964-65; trustee St. Luke's-Roosevelt Hosp. Ctr., 1988-94. Lt. (j.g.) USNR, 1946-68. Recipient citation FDA, 1983. Fellow ACP (disting. physicians award 1987), AAAS, Am. Inst. Nutrition; mem. AMA (mem. coun. on foods and nutrition 1967-74, vice chmn. 1974, Joseph B. Goldberger award 1985), Am. Soc. Clin. Investigation, Soc. Exptl. Biology and Medicine, Am. Clin. and Climatol. Assn., Am. Soc. Clin. Nutrition (coun. 1970-73, pres. 1976-77, Elmer V. McCollum award 1985), Soc. Study of Ingestive Behavior (disting. sci. award 1994), Order of Malta (knight comdr. Quebec priory 1990—), Century Assn., Fla. Hist. Soc. (bd. dirs. 1995—). Research and contbr. numerous publs. on obesity, body composition, pancreatic hormone, glucagon, mechanism of energy balance regulation, treatment of pruritus and hypercholesteremia in biliary cirrhosis, physiology and clin. use of medium chain triglyceride. Address: PO Box 775 1678 Jose Gaspar Dr Boca Grande FL 33921

VAN KILSDONK, CECELIA ANN, retired nursing administrator, volunteer; b. Beaver Dam, Wis., Sept. 28, 1930; d. Walter and Pauline (Yagodzinski) Klapinski; (div.); children: Dan, Greg, Paula, Steve. Diploma, Mercy Hosp. Sch. Nursing, 1951; BS, Coll. of St. Frances, Peoria, Ill., 1983. Clin. nurse Divsn. of Ambulatory Care, Phoenix, 1965-70, clin. charge nurse, 1970-82, regional nursing supr., 1982-87, nurse adminstr., 1987-92; mgr. nursing svc. Maricopa County Health Dept. Svcs., Phoenix. Mem. Continuing Edn. review Com., 1989—; vol. Primary Care Ctr.; disaster nurse ARC. Mem. ANA, Ariz. Nurse's Assn., Nat. League for Nursing, Phi Theta Kappa. Home: 2502 E Minnezona Ave Phoenix AZ 85016-4927

VAN KIRK, JOHN ELLSWORTH, cardiologist; b. Dayton, Ohio, Jan. 13, 1942; s. Herman Corwin and Dorothy Louise (Shafer) Van K.; m. Patricia L. Davis, June 19, 1966 (div. Dec. 1982); 1 child, Linnea Gray. BA cum laude, DePauw U., Greencastle, Ind., 1963; BS, Northwestern U., Chgo., 1964, MD with distinction, 1967. Diplomate Am. Bd. Internal Medicine, Am. Bd. Internal Medicine subspecialty in cardiovasc. disease; cert. Nat. Bd. Med. Examiners. Intern Evanston (Ill.) Hosp., 1967-68; staff assoc. Nat. Inst. of Allergy & Infectious Diseases., Bethesda, Md., 1968-70; resident internal medicine U. Mich. Med. Ctr., Ann Arbor, 1970-72, fellow in cardiology, 1972-74, instr. internal medicine, 1973-74; staff cardiologist Mills Meml. Hosp., San Mateo, Calif., 1974—, vice-chief medicine, 1977-78, dir. critical care, 1978-96, critical care utilizaton rev., 1988—, dir. pacemaker clinic, 1976—; dir. transitional care, mem. courtesy staff Sequoia Hosp., 1996—; mem. courtesy staff Sequoia Hosp., 1996—. Contbr. rsch. articles to profl. jours. Recipient 1st prize in landscaping Residential Estates, State of Calif., 1977. Fellow Am. Coll. Cardiology; mem. AMA (Physician's Recognition award 1968, 72, 75, 77, 80, 82, 85, 87, 89, 93), Calif. Med. Assn., San Mateo County Med. Soc., Am. Heart Assn., San Mateo County Heart Assn. (bd. dirs. 1975-78, mem. Bay area rsch. com. 1975-76, mem. edn. com. 1975-77, pres.-elect 1976-77, pres. 1977-79), Alpha Omegaa Alpha. Republican. Mem. United Brethren Ch. Avocations: gardening, computer science, tennis, woodworking, electronics, ham radio. Office: Unified Med Clinics of Peninsula 50 S San Mateo Dr Ste 270 San Mateo CA 94401-3859

VAN KIRK, ROBERT JOHN, nursing case manager, educator; b. Jersey City, N.J., Sept. 18, 1944; s. Robert and Doris V.; m. Marjorie Ann Carroll, Mar. 23, 1968 (div. Nov. 30, 1993); children: Walter, Michael, Robert Jr., Peggy; m. Nancy A. Fix, Aug. 31, 1996. BA cum laude, U. Conn., 1974; MEd, Kent State U., 1983; D of Nursing, Case Western Reserve U., 1986. RN. Sales mgr. Nutmeg Home Protection, Middlebury, Conn., 1972-74; theater mgr. SBC Mgmt. Corp., Boston, 1974; dist. supr. Selected Theatres Mgmt. Corp., Lyndhurst, Ohio, 1974-86; nat. sales mgr. ZBS Video, Inc., Lyndhurst, 1981-82; staff nurse Cleve. Clinic Found., 1986-87, clin. instr., 1987-88, head nurse, 1988-93, case mgr., 1993—; asst. clin. prof. Case Western Reserve U., Frances Payne Bolton Sch. Nursing, Cleve., 1990—; case mgr. Cleve. Clin. Home Care, 1993—. Health officer Lake County (Ohio) Bd. Alcohol, Drug Addiction and Mental Health Svcs., 1991—; co-chmn. United Way, Cleve., 1991-93. Staff sgt. U.S. Army, 1964-71, Vietnam. Recipient Achievement award Greater Cleve. Nurses Assn., 1986. Mem. AACN, Am. Assn. Tchrs. German, Am. Assn. Tchrs. Portuguese and Spanish, Assn. Specialists in Aging, Frances Payne Bolton Sch. Nursing Alumni Assn. (pres. 1992-93), Kappa Delta Pi, Sigma Theta Tau. Avocations: pocket billards, furniture making. Home: 5011 Nob Hill Dr Apt 9C Chagrin Falls OH 44022-3346 Office: Cleve Clinic Found 9555 Rockside Rd Valley View OH 44125-6231

VAN KIRK, THOMAS L., lawyer; b. Pa., June 25, 1945; s. Theodore and Mary Jane (Young) Van K.; children: Thomas Jr., Christopher. BA, Bucknell U., 1967; JD cum laude, Dickinson U., 1970. Bar: Pa., U.S. Dist. Ct. (we. and ea. dists.) Pa. 1971, U.S. Ct. Appeals (3d cir.) 1972, U.S. Supreme Ct. 1976. Clk. Pa. Superior Ct., 1970-71; assoc. Buchanan Ingersoll, Pitts., 1971-77, ptnr., 1978—, chief oper. officer, 1985—; bd. dirs. Buchanan Ingersoll P.C.; v.p. State Pa. Economy League; vice chair Western Pa. Economy League. Chmn. Allegheny County Heart Assn. Walk, 1992; chair Pitts. Downtown Partnership; bd. dirs. Rivers Club Pitts.; sec., treas., bd. dirs. Capital Divsn. Pa. Economy League. Fellow Am. Bar Found.; mem. ABA, Allegheny County Bar Assn., Duquesne Club, Rivers Club, Racquet Club Phila., The Club at Nevillewood. Democrat. Lutheran. Home: 1010 Osage Rd Pittsburgh PA 15243-1014 Office: Buchanan Ingersoll PC 301 Grant St Ste 20 Pittsburgh PA 15219-1408

VAN LANDINGHAM, LEANDER SHELTON, JR., lawyer; b. Memphis, July 15, 1925; s. Leander Shelton and Bertha (Shumaker) Van L.; m. Henrietta Adena Stapf, July 5, 1959; children: Ann Henrietta, Leander Shelton III. BS in Chemistry, U. N.C., 1948, MA in Organic Chemistry, 1949; JD, Georgetown U., 1955. Bar: D.C. 1955, Md. 1963, Va. 1976. Patent adviser Dept. Navy, Washington, 1953-55; sole practice comml. law and patent, trademark and copyright law, Washington met. area, 1955—. Served to lt. USNR, 1943-46, 51-53. Mem. Am. Chem. Soc., Sci. Assn., Fed. Bar Assn., ABA, D.C. Bar Assn., Va. Bar Assn., Md. Bar Assn., Am. Intellectual Property Law Assn., Am. Judicature Soc., Sigma Xi, Phi Alpha Delta. Home: 10726 Stanmore Dr Potomac MD 20854-1518 Office: 2001 Jefferson Davis Hwy Arlington VA 22202-3603

VAN LARE, WENDELL JOHN, lawyer; b. Newark, N.Y., Mar. 1, 1945; s. Julian J. and Doris Elizabeth (Lacknor) Van L.; m. Sheila Gilbert, Aug. 20, 1967 (div. Apr. 1987); children: Jonathan S., Allison R.; m. L. Karen Stack, May 7, 1987. BS, SUNY, New Paltz, 1967; JD, Union U., 1972. Bar: N.Y. 1973, U.S. Supreme Ct., 1980. Assoc. Harter, Secrest & Emery, Rochester, N.Y., 1972-77; asst. dir. labor rels. Gannett Co., Inc., Rochester, 1977-80; dir. labor rels. Gannett Co., Inc., Rochester and Arlington, 1980-93; v.p., labor counsel Gannett Co., Inc., Arlington, 1993-94, v.p., sr. labor counsel, 1994—. Comments editor Albany Law Rev., 1971-72. Pres. Opera Theatre of Rochester, N.Y., 1983-85. Lt. (j.g.) USNR, 1968-70. Mem. ABA, N.Y. Bar Assn., River Bend Golf and Country Club. Avocation: genealogy. Office: Gannett Co Inc 1100 Wilson Blvd Arlington VA 22209-2297

VAN LEER, JERILYN MOSHER, library media specialist; b. Franklin, N.H., July 15, 1954; d. Bruce Rodney and Beverly Colleen (Remick) Mosher; m. Eric Preston Van Leer, June 5, 1976; children: Meredith Lynn, Justin Curtis. BS, So. Conn. State U., 1976, MLS, 1982, diploma in adminstrn. and supervision, 1989. Libr. media specialist, intermediate adminstr., Conn. Libr. media specialist Har-Bur Mid. Sch., Regional Sch. Dist. # 10, Burlington, Conn., 1977-85; dir. libr. media svcs. Litchfield (Conn.) Pub Schs., 1985-88; asst. instrnl. leader libr. media svcs. West Hartford (Conn.) Pub. Schs., 1988-90; libr. media specialist Sedgwick Mid. Sch., West Hartford, 1990-92; libr. media svcs. coord. West Hartford Pub. Schs., 1993—; bd. dirs. region 1 Coop. Libr. Svc. Unit, Waterbury, Conn., 1985, Capitol Region Libr. Coun., 1997; co-chair Sch. Libr. Media Specialist Roundtable, 1986, mem. planning com. Capitol Region Libr. Coun., 1989; mem. Com. Revising Libr. Media and Computer Guidelines, Dept. Edn., 1988; learning resources and tech. facilitator West Hartford Pub. Schs., 1990—. Libr. sci. and instrnl. tech. scholar So. Conn. State U., New Haven, 1982; recipient Outstanding Libr. award Conn. Libr. Assn., 1984. Mem. NEA, ALA, Assn. for Ednl. Comms. and Tech., Am. Assn. Sch. Librs., Conn. Edn. Assn., Conn. Ednl. Media Assn. (bd. dirs. 1996), New Eng. Ednl. Media Assn., Beta Phi Mu. Avocations: horseback riding, snowshoeing. Home: 213 Cotton Hill Rd New Hartford CT 06057-3417 Office: West Hartford Pub Schs 28 S Main St Hartford CT 06107-2406

VANLEEUWEN, LIZ SUSAN (ELIZABETH VANLEEUWEN), state legislator, farmer; b. Lakeview, Oreg., Nov. 5, 1925; d. Charles Arthur and Mary Delphia (Hartzog) Nelson; B.S., Oreg. State U., 1947; m. George VanLeeuwen, June 15, 1947; children—Charles, Mary, James, Timothy. Secondary sch. and adult tchr., 1947-70; news reporter, feature writer The Times, Brownsville, Oreg., 1949—; co-mgr. VanLeeuwen Farm, Halsey, Oreg.; mem. Oreg. Ho. of Reps., 1981—; mem. Western States Forestry Legis. Task Force, Pacific Northwest Econ. Region; weekly radio commentator, 1973-81. Mem. E.R. Jackman Found., PTA, sch. adv. com.; precinct committeewoman; founder, Ct. Apptd. Spl. Advocates (CASA) Linn County Ct.; mem. regional strategies bd. Linn County Commn. on Children and Families. Recipient Outstanding Service award Oreg. Farm Bur., 1975, Oreg. Farm Family of Yr. award, 1983; Chevron Agrl. Spokesman of Yr. award, 1975, Oreg. Ag Star award, 1997. Mem. Oreg. Women for Agr. (pres.), Oreg. Women for Timber, Linn-Benton Women for Agr. (pres.), Linn

County Farm Bur., Am. Legion (aux.), Linn County Econ. Devel. Com., Grange, Am. Agri-Women. Republican. Office: H-291 Capitol Bldg Salem OR 97310

VAN LEUVEN, ROBERT JOSEPH, lawyer; b. Detroit, Apr. 17, 1931; s. Joseph Francis and Olive (Stowell) Van L.;m. Merri Lee Van Leuven; children: Joseph Michael, Douglas Robert, Julie Margaret. student Albion Coll., 1949-51; BA with distinction Wayne State U., 1953; JD, U. Mich., 1957. Bar: Mich. 1957. Since practiced in Muskegon, Mich.; ptnr. Hathaway, Latimer, Clink & Robb, 1957-68, ptnr. McCroskey, Libner & Van Leuven, 1968-81, ptnr. Libner-Van Leuven, 1982—; past mem. council negligence law sect. State Bar Mich. Bd. dirs. Muskegon Children's Home, 1965-75. Served with AUS 1953-55. Fellow Mich. Bar Found., Mich. Trial Lawyers Assn., Am. Coll. Trial Lawyers; mem. Assn. Trial Lawyers Am., Delta Sigma Phi. Club: Muskegon Country. Home: 1309 Randolph Muskegon MI 49441 Office: Libner-Van Leuven Muskegon Mall 400 Comerica Muskegon MI 49443

VAN LINT, VICTOR ANTON JACOBUS, physicist; b. Samarinda, Indonesia, May 10, 1928; came to U.S., 1937; s. Victor J. and Margaret (DeJager) Van L.; m. M. June Woolhouse, June 10, 1950; children: Lawrence, Kenneth, Linda, Karen. BS, Calif. Inst. Tech., Pasadena, 1950, PhD, 1954. Instr. Princeton (N.J.) U., 1954-55; staff mem. Gen. Atomic, San Diego, 1957-74; physics cons. San Diego, 1974-75; staff mem. Mission Research Corp., San Diego, 1975-82, 83-91; cons., 1991—; spl. asst. to dep. dir. sci. and tech. Def. Nuclear Agy., Washington, 1982-83. Author, editor: Radiation Effects in Electronic Materials, 1976; contbr. articles to profl. jours. Served with U.S. Army, 1955-57. Recipient Pub. Service award NASA, 1981. Fellow IEEE. Republican. Mem. United Ch. of Christ. Home and Office: 1032 Skylark Dr La Jolla CA 92037-7733

VAN LOBEN SELS, JAMES W., transportation executive; b. Oakland, Calif.. Dir. Caltrans; dir. transp. State of Calif., Sacramento, 1991—; vice chmn. Transp. Rsch. Bd. Bd. dirs. Assn. State Hwy. & Transp. Ofcls., U.S. Transp. Rsch. Bd., Intelligent Transp. Soc. Am. Office: 1120 N St Sacramento CA 95814-5605

VAN LOPIK, JACK RICHARD, geologist, educator; b. Holland, Mich., Feb. 25, 1929; s. Guy M. and Minnie (Grunst) Van L.; 1 son, Charles Robert (dec.). B.S., Mich. State U., 1950; M.S., La. State U., 1953, Ph.D., 1955. Geologist, sect. chief, asst. chief, chief geology br. U.S. Army C.E., Waterways Expt. Sta., Vicksburg, Miss., 1954-61; chief engrs. environ. adv. bd. U.S. Army C.E., 1988-92; chief area evaluation sect., tech. dir., mgr. Space and Environ. Sci. Programs, tech. requirements dir. geosciences ops. Tex. Instruments, Inc., Dallas, 1961-68; chmn. dept. marine sci. La. State U., Baton Rouge, 1968-74; prof. dept. marine sci., dir. sea grant devel., dean Center for Wetland Resources, La. State U., Baton Rouge, 1968-91; prof. dept. oceanography and coastal scis. La. State U., Baton Rouge, 1991—; exec. dir. sea grant devel., La. State U., 1991—; chmn. Coastal Resources Directorate of U.S. Nat. Com. for Man and Biosphere, U.S. Nat. Commn. for UNESCO, 1975-82; dir. Gulf South Rsch. Inst., 1974-89; mem. Nat. Adv. Com. Oceans and Atmosphere, 1978-84; mem. Lower Miss. River Waterway Safety Com. USCG 8th dist., 1983-94; mem. adv. coun. Nat. Coastal Resources Rsch. and Devel. Inst., 1985—; ofcl. del. XX Congreso Internacional, Mexico City, 1956, XII Gen. Assembly Internat. Union Geodesy and Geophysics, Helsinki, 1960; chmn. panel on geography and land use Nat. Acad. Scis.-NRC, com. on remote sensing programs for earth resources surveys, 1969-77. Fellow Geol. Soc. Am., AAAS; mem. Am. Astronautical Soc. (dir. S.W. sect. 1967-68), Am. Soc. Photogrammetry (dir. 1969-72, chmn. photo interpretation com. 1960, 65, rep. earth scis. divsn. NRC 1968-71), Am. Geophys. Union, Am. Assn. Petroleum Geologists (acad. adv. com. 1973-78), Assn. Am. Geographers, Soc. Econ. Paleontologists and Mineralogists (rsch. com. 1962-65), Am. Mgmt. Assn., Soc. Rsch. Adminstrs., Marine Tech. Soc., Am. Water Resources Assn., Soc. Am. Mil. Engrs., Sea Grant Assn. (exec. bd. dirs. 1972-74, 80-82, 88-91, pres.-elect 1988-89, pres. 1989-90), Nat. Ocean Industries Assn. (adv. coun. 1973-83), Nat. Conf. Advancement Rsch. (exec. com. 1988-92), La. Partnership for Tech. and Innovation (bd. dirs. 1989—), Sigma Xi. Home: 9 Rue Sorbonne Baton Rouge LA 70808-4682 Office: La State U Office Sea Grant Devel Baton Rouge LA 70803

VAN LOUCKS, MARK LOUIS, venture capitalist, business advisor; b. Tampa, Fla., June 19, 1946; s. Charles Perry and Lenn (Bragg) Van L.; m. Eva Marianne Forsell, June 10, 1986; children: Brandon, Charlie. BA in Comm. and Pub. Policy, U. Calif., Berkeley, 1969. Sr. v.p. mktg., programming and corp. devel. United Cable TV Corp., Denver, Colo., 1970-81, advisor, 1983-89; sr. v.p., office of chmn. Rockefeller Ctr. TV Corp., N.Y.C., 1981-83; advisor United Artists Commun. Corp., Englewood, 1989-91; investor, business advisor in pvt. practice Englewood, 1983—; founder, prin. owner Glory Hole Saloon & Gaming Hall, Central City, Colo., 1990—, Harrah's Casino, Black Hawk, Colo., 1990—; chmn., CEO Bask Internat., Englewood, 1990—; bd. dirs. Wild West Devel. Corp., Denver; sr. v.p., bd. dirs. GSI Cable TV Assocs., Inc., San Francisco, 1984-90; guest lectr. on cable TV bus., 1985-91; cons. Telecommunications, Inc., Denver, 1989-93. Producer HBO spl. Green Chili Showdown, 1985; producer TV spl. 3 Days for Earth, 1987; producer, commd. artist nuclear war armament pieces; contbr. articles to profl. jours. Chmn. Cops in Crisis, Denver, 1990—; bd. dirs. The NOAH Found., Denver, 1976—; founding dir. Project for Responsible Advt., Denver, 1991-92; chmn. mayor's mktg. adv. bd., Central City, Colo. Named hon. capt. Denver Police Dept., 1991—, fin. advisor L. Rose Co., 1995—. Mem. Casino Owners Assn. (founding dir. 1989—), Colo. Gaming Assn. (dir. 1990—), recipient S'nnaeel Evol award, 1995), Glenmoor Country Club, The Village Club. Republican. Jewish. Avocations: music, woodworking, philanthropy, vintage autos. Office: MLVL Inc 333 W Hampden Ave Ste 1005 Englewood CO 80110-2340

VANMARCKE, ERIK HECTOR, civil engineering educator; b. Menen, Belgium, Aug. 6, 1941; came to U.S., 1965, naturalized, 1976; m. Louis Eugene and Rachel Louisa (van Hollebeke) V.; m. Margaret Maria Delesie, May 25, 1965; children: Lieven, Ann, Kristien. BS, U. Louvain, Belgium, 1965; MS, U. Del., 1967; PhD in Civil Engring, MIT, 1970. From instr. to prof. civil engring. MIT, Cambridge, 1969-85; Gilbert W. Winslow Career Devel. prof. MIT, 1974-77, dir. civil engring. systems group, 1976-80; prof. civil engring. and ops. rsch. Princeton U., 1985—, dir. grad. studies civil engring. and ops. rsch., 1990—; cons. Office Sci. and Tech. Policy, 1978-80; vis. scholar in engring. Harvard U., 1984-85; Shimizu Corp. vis. prof. Stanford U., 1991; cons. various govt. agys. and engring. firms; mem. exec. com. Princeton Materials Inst., 1991-93; mem. Princeton Environ. Inst., 1996—. Author: Random Fields: Analysis and Synthesis, 1983, Quantum Origins of Cosmic Structure, 1997; editor: Internat. Jour. Structural Safety, 1981-91. Recipient Sr. Scientist award for study in Japan, Japan Soc. for Promotion of Sci., 1991. Mem. ASCE (Raymond C. Reese rsch. award 1975, Walter L. Huber rsch. prize 1984, chair com. on safety and reliability in geotech. engring. 1993—), Am. Geophys. Union, Seismol. Soc. Am., Internat. Soc. Soil Mechanics and Found. Engring., Sigma Xi. Home: 50 Brooks Bnd Princeton NJ 08540-7500 Office: Room E311 Engring Quadrangle Princeton U Princeton NJ 08544

VAN MASON, RAYMOND, dancer, choreographer. Prin. dancer Ballet West, Salt Lake City. Dance performances include Swan Lake, Gisells, Sleeping Beauty, Romeo & Juliet, Anna Karenina, The Nutcracker, Carmina Burana, White Mourning, Ophelia; choreographer: Requiem: A Liturgical Ballet, 1990, A Pilgrimage: A Liturgical Ballet, 1992, Lady Guinevere, Chameleon, Carmina Burana, Symphony # 7, 1992, others. Office: Ballet West 50 W 200 S Salt Lake City UT 84101-1642*

VAN MATRE, JOYCE DIANNE, rehabilitation nurse; b. Bklyn., June 1, 1943; d. Gerard Thibault and Helene Clara (Wright) Hair; m. Richard Givens Van Matre, Aug. 27, 1965; children: Kimberly, Karyn, Richard. Diploma in Nursing, Gordon Keller Sch. Nursing, 1964; BS in Health Arts, Coll. of St. Francis, 1990. Cert. disability mgmt. specialist; Fla. rehab. svc. provider; cert. case mgr. Case supr. rehab. Vocat. Placement Svcs., Tampa, Fla., 1980-81; RN mgr. Always Care Nursing Svc., Tampa, 1981-82; staff nurse Vis. Nurse's Assn., Tampa, 1983-84; rehab. coord. Underwriter's Adjusting Co., Tampa, 1984-85; pres. of corp., case mgr., supr., bus. owner Ind. Group Consultants, Inc., Brandon, Fla., 1985-90; case mgr. Sullivan Health & Rehab. Mgmt., Inc., St. Petersburg, Fla., 1991-92; rehab. nurse Liberty Mut. Ins. Co., Tampa, 1992—. Recipient Disting. Acad. Achievement award Coll. of St. Francis, 1991. Mem. Assn. Rehab. Nurses, West Coast Regional Case Mgr. Assn. Office: Liberty Mut Ins Co 3350 Buschwood Park Dr Tampa FL 33618-4314

VANMEER, MARY ANN, publisher, writer, researcher; b. Mt. Clemens, Mich., Nov. 22; d. Leo Harold and Rose Emma (Gulden) VanM. Student Mich. State U., 1965-66, 67-68, U. Sorbonne, Paris, 1968; BA in Edn., U. Fla., 1970. Pres. VanMeer Tutoring and Translating, N.Y.C., 1970-72; freelance writer, 1973-79; pres. VanMeer Publs., Inc., Clearwater, Fla., 1980-88, VanMeer Media Advt., Inc., Clearwater, 1980-88; exec. dir., founder Nat. Ctrs. for Health and Med. Info., Inc., Clearwater, 1987-88, Nat. Health and Med. Info. Ctr., Palm Beach, Fla., 1990-93; pres., CEO The Thrifty Traveler, Inc. (formerly Traveling Free Publs., Inc.), 1993—. Author: Traveling with Your Dog, U.S.A., 1976, How to Set Up A Home Typing Business, 1978, Freelance Photographer's Handbook, 1979; See America Free, 1981, Free Campgrounds, U.S.A., 1982, Free Attractions, U.S.A., 1982, VanMeer's Guide to Free Attractions, U.S.A., 1984, VanMeer's Guide to Free Campgrounds, 1984, The How to Get Publicity for Your Business Handbook, 1987, Asthma: The Ultimate Treatment Guide, 1991, Allergies: The Ultimate Treatment Guide, 1992, Cancer: The Ultimate Treatment Guide, 1993, Thrifty Traveling, 1995; pub. Nat. Health and Med. Trends Mag., 1986-88, The Thrifty Traveler Newsletter, 1993—. The Over-50 Thrifty Traveler Newsletter, 1997—, Net News for The Thrifty Traveler Newsletter, 1997—. Pub. info. chairperson, bd. dirs. Pinellas County chpt. Am. Cancer Soc., Clearwater, 1983-84, 86-88; mem. fin. devel. com. ARC, Palm Beach County, 1990-92. Mem. Am. Booksellers Assn., PACT (Performing Arts, Concert, and Theatre), Author's Guild. Office: The Thrifty Traveler, Inc PO Box 8168 Clearwater FL 34618

VAN METER, ABRAM DEBOIS, lawyer, retired banker; b. Springfield, Ill., May 16, 1922; s. A.D. and Edith (Graham) Van M.; m. Margaret Schlipf, Dec. 1, 1956; children: Andy, Alice, Ann. BS, Kings Point Coll., 1946; JD, Northwestern U., 1948. Bar: Ill. 1949. Ptnr. Van Meter, Oxtoby & Funk, Springfield, 1949—; adminstrv. asst. to treas. State of Ill., Springfield, 1963; v.p. Ill. Nat. Bank, Springfield, 1964-65, pres., 1965-88, chmn. bd. dirs., 1988-90, also bd. dirs.; chmn. bd. dirs. First of Am.-Springfield, N.A., 1990-93, dir. emeritus, 1993—. Chmn. bd. dirs. Ill. Housing Devel. Authority, 1977—; chmn. bd. trustees So. Ill. U., 1989—; bd. dirs., mem. exec. com. Meml. Med. Ctr. (emeritus). Mem. ABA, Ill. Bar Assn., Sangamon Bar Assn., Chgo. Club, Chgo. Athletic Club, Sangamo Club, Island Bay Yacht Club,. Home: 6 Fair Oaks St Springfield IL 62704-3222 Office: First of Am Springfield NA 1 N Old State Capitol Plz Springfield IL 62701-1323

VAN METER, JOHN DAVID, lawyer; b. Owensboro, Ky., Oct. 30, 1951; s. Leslie Evan and Agnes Regina (Gropp) Van M.; m. Laura Ann Isbell, May 19, 1984; children: Katherine Leigh, Elizabeth Grace, Jennifer Marie. BA in Journalism, U. Ky., 1973, JD, 1978. Bar: Ky. 1978. Atty. Ashland (Ky.) Oil Inc., 1978-83, exec. asst. to chmn., 1983-88; adminstrv. v.p. Valvoline Oil Co. div. Ashland Oil, Inc., Lexington, Ky., 1988-90; pres. Ashland Internat. Ltd. subs. Ashland, Inc., London, 1990—. Mem. ABA, Ky. Bar Assn., Boyd County Bar Assn., Fayette County Bar Assn., Am. C. of C. (bd. dirs.), Ends of the Earth Club (bd. dirs.), Carlton Club, Buck's Club, Pilgrim's Club. Republican. Roman Catholic. Home: 8 Reston Pl Hyde Park Gate, London SW7 5DY, England Office: 110 Jermyn St, London SW1Y 6EE, England

VANMETER, VANDELIA L., library director; b. Seibert, Colo., July 17, 1934; d. G.W. and A. Pearl Klockenteger; m. Victor M. VanMeter, Jan. 21, 1954; children: Allison C., Kristopher C. BA, Kansas Wesleyan U., 1957; MLS, Emporia State U., 1970; PhD, Tex. Woman's U., 1986. Cert. libr. media specialist. Tchr. Ottawa County Rural Sch., Kans., 1954-55; social scis. tchr. McClave (Colo.) High Sch., 1957-58, Ellsworth (Kans.) Jr. High Sch., 1959-68; libr., media specialist Ellsworth (Kans.) High Sch., 1968-84; asst. prof. libr. sci. U. So. Miss., Hattiesburg, 1986-90; chair dept. libr./info. sci. Spalding U., Louisville, 1990-96, libr. dir., 1991—; cons. to sch., pub. and spl. librs., Kans., Miss., Ky., 1970—; mem. Ky. NCATE Bd. Examiners. Author: American History for Children and Young Adults, 1990, World History for Children and Young Adults, 1992, America in Historical Fiction, 1997; editor: Mississippi Library Media Specialist Staff Development Modules, 1988, Library Lane Newsletter, 1991—; contbr. chpts. to books; contbr. articles to profl. jours. Active City Coun., Ellsworth, Kans., 1975-79, Park Bd., Ellsworth, 1975-79; bd. dirs. Robbins Meml. Libr., 1977-79. Grantee Kans. Demonstration Sch. Libr., 1970-72, Miss. Power Found., 1989, Project Technology Enhances Curriculur Instrn., 1996-97; named Women of Yr. Bus. and Profl. Women of Ellsworth, Kans., 1976. Mem. ALA, Am. Assn. Sch. Librs., Nat. Assn. State Ednl. Media Profls., Assn. Coll. & Rsch. Librs., Ky. Libr. Assn., Ky. Sch. Media Assn., Ky. Assn. Tchr. Educators, Assn. for Libr. and Info. Sci. Educators. Office: Spalding U Libr 851 S 4th St Louisville KY 40203-2115

VAN METRE, MARGARET CHERYL, artistic director, dance educator; b. Maryville, Tenn., Nov. 24, 1938; d. Robert Fillers and Margaret Elizabeth (Goddard) Raulston; m. Mitchell Robert Van Metre II, Aug. 25, 1956; 1 child, Mitchell Robert. Elem., intermediate and advanced teaching certs. Dir. Van Metre Sch. of Dance, Maryville, 1958-96 ; artistic dir. Appalachian Ballet Co., Maryville Coll., 1972-96 ; founding dir. Appalachian Ballet Co., 1972; dir. Van Metre Arts Mgmt., S.C., 1996—; chmn. dance panel Tenn. Arts Commn.; 1973-74; chmn. Bicentennial Ballet Project, Tenn., 1975-76. Choreographer ballets: DeLusion, 1965; Hill Heritage Suite, 1972; Dancing Princesses, 1983. Mem. Tenn. Assn. of Dance (pres. 1972). Democrat. Episcopalian. Home: 2103 Myrtle St Edisto Island SC 29438

VAN MILLIGEN, JAMES M., health care administrator; b. Chgo., Feb. 12, 1949; s. Alferd C. and H. Patricia Van M.; m. Jane Van Milligen, May 5, 1971. B of Health Sci., Wichita State U., 1977, M of Health Sci., 1984. Physician asst. Wichita Osteo. Clinic, 1977-84; data mgr. Preferred Health Care, 1984-85; dir. network devel. Equicor, 1986-87; chief oper officer WPAA, Inc., 1987—, WPPA-HMO, Inc., 1995—. Mem. Wichita Traffic Commn., 1980-86, pres. 1985; pres. Wichita Ind. Neighborhoods, 1994-95, Fairmount Neighborhood Assn., Wichita, 1984-96; advisor United Sch. Dist. #249 Bus. & Tech. Com., Wichita, 1993-94, Mayor's Adv. Coun., Wichita, 1989-92. With U.S. Army, 1970-73, Vietnam. Mem. Nat. Assn. Health Underwriters (Journalism award 1991), Kans. Assn. Health Underwriters, Ctrl. Kans. Assn. Health Underwriters, Med. Soc. Sedgewick County (assoc. exec. dir. 1987—), Wichita Area C. of C. Avocations: historic restoration, farming. Home: 1717 Fairmount St Wichita KS 67208-1919 Office: WPPA Inc 1102 S Hillside St Wichita KS 67211-4004

VAN MOL, LOUIS JOHN, JR., public relations executive; b. Knoxville, Tenn., Oct. 7, 1943; s. Louis John and Evelyn (Ramsay) Van M.; m. Deborah Ruth Boyd, Nov. 1, 1969; children: Derek, Millicent. BS, U. Tenn., 1966. Staff writer, editor AP, Knoxville and Nashville, 1963-66, 69; account exec. to exec. v.p. Holder, Kennedy & Co., Nashville, 1970-74, exec. v.p., 1978-79; dir. info. TVA, Knoxville, 1974-78; co-founder, ptnr. Dye, Van Mol & Lawrence, Nashville, 1980—; bd. dirs. Fogel & Assocs., Columbia, Tenn.; chmn. bd. Goodwill Industries Mid. Tenn., 1996—. Bd. dirs. East Tenn. Children's Hosp., Knoxville, 1977-78, Martha O'Bryan Ctr., Nashville, 1985-87, United Way Comm. Com., 1987-91, Am. Heart Assn. Mid. Tenn., Nashville, 1991-92, Leadership Nashville, 1992-93, Crime Stoppers Nashville, 1986-92, Alcohol and Drug Coun. Mid. Tenn., Nashville, 1991-93. Lt. U.S. Army, 1966-68. Decorated Bronze Star. Mem. Richland Country Club (bd. dirs. 1997—), Cumberland Club, Sigma Delta Chi. Presbyterian. Home: 712 Bowling Ave Nashville TN 37215-1049 Office: Dye Van Mol & Lawrence Pub Rels 209 7th Ave N Nashville TN 37219-1802

VAN MOLS, BRIAN, publishing executive; b. L.A., July 1, 1931; s. Pierre Matthias and Frieda Carthyll (MacArthur) M.; m. Barbara Jane Rose, Oct. 1, 1953 (dec. 1968); children—Cynthia Lee, Matthew Howard, Brian; m. Nancy Joan Martell, June 11, 1977; children—Thomas Bentley, Cynthia Bentley, Kristi. A.B. in English, Miami U., Oxford, Ohio, 1953. Media supr. McCann-Erickson Inc., 1955-58; salesman Kelly Smith Co., 1959; with sales Million Market Newspaper Inc., 1959-63; sales mgr. Autoproducts Mag., 1964; sr. salesman True Mag., 1965-68, Look Mag., 1969-70; regional advt. dir. Petersen Pub. Co., Los Angeles, 1971-74; pub. Motor Trend, 1982-84; nat. automotive mktg. mgr. Playboy Enterprises, Inc., N.Y.C., 1984-85, nat. sales mgr., 1985—; western advt. dir. Playboy mag., 1985-86; assoc. pub., advt. dir. Cycle World CBS, Inc., Newport Beach, Calif., 1974-81, pub., 1981; v.p., advt. dir. Four Wheeler Mag., Canoga Pk., Calif., 1986-88; v.p., dir. advt. western div. Gen. Media, Inc., 1988-91; v.p., dir. new bus. devel. Paisano Pub., Inc., Agoura Hills, Calif., 1991-92; dir. mktg. Crown Publs., 1993-94; exec. v.p. Voice Mktg. Inc., Thousand Oaks, Calif., 1994, DMR The Reis Co., Tustin, Calif., 1995-96; COO Mesa Exhaust Prodn., Inc., Costa Mesa, Calif., 1996—. Served with U.S. Army, 1953-55. Mem. Los Angeles Advt. Club, Adcraft Club Detroit, Advt. Sportsmen of N.Y. Republican. Episcopalian. Home: 5 Odyssey Ct Newport Beach CA 92663-2349

VANN, JOHN DANIEL, III, university dean, historian; b. Raleigh, N.C., July 14, 1935; s. John Daniel Jr. and Sybil Dean (Wilson) V.; m. Ellen Jane Rogers, June 21, 1969; children: John Daniel IV, Justin Fitz Patrick. BA with honors, U. N.C., 1957; MA, Yale U., 1959, PhD, 1965; M in Librarianship, Emory U., 1971; postgrad., Columbia U., 1962-63, Stanford U., 1977-78. Ordained deacon, elder Presbyn. Ch. Assoc. prof. history Campbell Coll., Buie's Creek, N.C., 1961-63; bibliographer European history and lit. Newberry Libr., Chgo., 1963-65, asst. reference librarian, 1963-65; prof. history Calif. Bapt. Coll., Riverside, 1965-66; dir. libr., prof. history Bapt. Coll. at Charleston, S.C., 1966-69; libr. Keuka Coll., Keuka Park, N.Y., 1969-71; chief libr., prof. libr., chmn. libr. dept. S.I. Community Coll. CUNY, 1971-76; prof. libr. Coll. S.I. CUNY, 1976-79; head libr. Lockwood Libr./SUNY, Buffalo, 1979-80; asst. dir. for planning, univ. librs. SUNY, Buffalo, 1980-81; exec. dir. librs. and learning resources, prof. U. Wis., Oshkosh, 1981-87; dir. libr. svcs. Bloomsburg U. Pa., 1987-89, dean libr. svcs., 1989—; resident planner, cons. on libr. bldgs. and collection devel.; bd. dirs. Coun. Wis. Librs., 1983-86, Susquehanna Libr. Coop., 1987—, sec./treas., 1993-95. Contbr. chpts. to books, articles to profl. jours. Trustee Maplewood (N.J.) Meml. Libr., 1977-79, v.p., 1979; bd. dirs. Coun. Wis. Librs., 1983-86, Midwest Rotary Multi-Dist. Short Term Internat. Youth Exch., 1987, Oshkosh (Wis.) Symphony Assn., 1986-87, United Cerebral Palsy of Winnebagoland, Oshkosh, 1986-87; active coms. Winnebago Presbytery, Presbyn. Ch., 1984-87; com. on min. Northumberland Prsbytery, Presbyn. Ch., 1992-96, com. on preparation for ministry, 1996—. Acad. Libr. Mgmt. intern Coun. on Libr. Resources Stanford U., 1977-78. Mem. ALA (com. mem.), Am. Hist. Assn., Archons of Colophon, Assn. for Libr. Collections and Tech. Svcs., Assn. Coll. and Rsch. Librs. (com. chmn., sec. chmn. 1977-78, editl. bd., bd. dirs. 1976-78), Bibliog. Soc. Am., Libr. Adminstrn. and Mgmt. Assn. (com. mem.), Libr. and Info. Tech. Assn., Medieval Acad. Am., Pa. Libr. Assn. (sect. dir.), Bloomsburg Rotary Club, Beta Phi Mu, Phi Alpha Theta. Republican. Home: 810 E 2nd St Bloomsburg PA 17815-2011 also: 1216 Rennie Ave Richmond VA 23227 Office: Bloomsburg U Pa Harvey A Andruss Libr Bloomsburg PA 17815

VAN NELSON, NICHOLAS LLOYD, business council executive; b. Milw., Feb. 28, 1942. BS, Jacksonville U., 1963, MA, 1967; MA, Am. U., Washington, 1970; postgrad., Harvard U. Kennedy Sch. Govt., 1980. Adminstrv. asst. to Congressman Charles E. Bennett Washington, 1967-74; dir. Owens Ill. Corp., Washington, 1974-77; v.p., gen. mgr. Am. Paper Inst., Washington, 1977-80; v.p. govt. Champion Internat. Corp., Washington, 1980-89; pres. U.S.-Korea Bus. Coun., 1990—; bd. dirs., founder, mem. exec. com. Tysons Nat. Bank, 1990-92. State chmn. Fla. Jaycees, Jacksonville, 1966; scoutmaster Boy Scouts Am. Named Outstanding Civic Leader in Am., 1967; Jacksonville U. pres.'s scholar, 1961-63. Mem. Pub. Affairs Coun. (bd. dirs.), Washington Golf and Country Club, Dem. Club, Georgetown Club. Democrat. Roman Catholic. Home: 6539 Oakwood Dr Falls Church VA 22041

VANNEMAN, EDGAR, JR., lawyer; b. El Paso, Ill., Aug. 24, 1919; s. Edgar and Fern (Huffington) V.; m. Shirli Thomas, Apr. 28, 1951 (dec.); children: Jill, Thomas. BS, BA, Northwestern U., 1941, J.D., 1947. Bar: Ill. 1947. Mem. firm Campbell, Clark & Miller, 1947-48; gen. atty. Chgo. and NorthWestern R.R. Co., 1949-62; gen. atty., asst. sec. Brunswick Corp., Skokie, Ill., 1962-89, ret.; sec. Sherwood Med. Industries, Inc., 1976-82. Pres. Northeastern Ill. Planning Commn., 1978-82; dir. Suburban Health Systems Agy., 1976-82; mayor City of Evanston (Ill.), 1970-77; alt. del. Republican Nat. Conv., 1952, 56. Served with USAF, 1942-46. Decorated Bronze Star. Mem. ABA, Ill. Bar Assn. (past bd. govs.), Chgo. Bar Assn., Soc. Trial Lawyers. Presbyterian. Club: Law (Chgo.). Home: 715 Monticello St Evanston IL 60201-1745

VAN NESS, JAMES EDWARD, electrical engineering educator; b. Omaha, June 24, 1926; s. Hubert James and Jean (Woodruff) Van N.; m. Mary Ellen Dolvin, Dec. 28, 1948; children: Rebecca Ellen, Barbara Jean, Margaret Ann, Julie Lynn. B.S., Iowa State U., 1949; M.S., Northwestern U., 1951, Ph.D., 1954. Faculty elec. engring. dept. Northwestern U., 1952—, prof. emeritus, chmn. dept., 1969-72; dir. Computer Center, 1962-65; vis. assoc. prof. U. Calif., Berkeley, 1958-59; vis. prof. MIT, 1973-74, Ariz. State U., winter 1984. Contbr. Articles to profl. jours. Served with USNR, 1944-46. Fellow IEEE; mem. AAUP. Home: 2601 Noyes St Evanston IL 60201-2170

VAN NESS, JOHN RALPH, university administrator, educator; b. Columbus, Ohio, Oct. 22, 1939; s. Ralph Taylor and Norma Gertrude (Thorp) Van N.; children: Heather Thorpe, Hilary Clark. BA, The Colo. Coll., Colo. Springs, 1965, MA, U. Pa., 1969, PhD, 1979. Instr. West Chester (Pa.) U., 1969-70, Knox Coll., Galesburg, Ill., 1970-73, Fort Lewis Coll., Durango, Colo., 1974-76; cons. fund raising pvt. practice Phila., 1977-79; capital campaign con. John F. Rich Co., Phila., 1979-84; v.p. for coll. rels., adj. prof. anthropology Ursinus Coll., Collegeville, Pa., 1984-89; exec. v.p., prof. Moore Coll. Art and Design, Phila., 1989-90, pres., 1990-92; pres. Mus. N.Mex. Found., Santa Fe, 1992-93, N.Mex. State U. Found., 1995—; bd. dirs. Ctr. for Land Grant Studies, Santa Fe, 1978-94; editl. bd. Jour. of the West, Manhattan, Kans., 1980-88. Co-author: Cañones: Values, Crisis and Survival in a Northern New Mexico Village, 1981; author: Hispanos in Northern New Mexico, 1991; co-editor: Spanish and Mexican Land Grants in New Mexico and Colorado, 1980, Land, Water and Culture, 1987; editor: New Mexico Land Grant Series, vols. 1-5, 1983, 84, 87, 89, 94. Recipient Teaching Fellowship U. Pa.; grantee Ford Found., Nat. Sci. Found. Mem. Am. Anthrop. Assn., Am. Assn. Museums, Coun. for Advance and Support Edn., Nat. Soc. Fund Raising Execs., Pi Gamma Mu. Democrat. Avocations: architecture, art, running.

VAN NESS, PATRICIA CATHELINE, composer, violinist; b. Seattle, June 25, 1951; d. C. Charles and Marjorie Mae (Dexter) Van N.; m. Adam Sherman, June 26, 1983. Student in music, Wheaton (Ill.) Coll., 1969-70; student, Gordon Coll., 1972. Composer: ballet score for Beth Soll, 1985, 87, 94, for Monica Levy, 1988, for Boston Ballet, 1988, 90, for Charleston Ballet Theatre, 1994; text and music for voices and early instruments with text translated into Latin for Evensong, 1991, Five Meditations, 1993, Cor Mei Cordis, 1994, Arcanae, 1995, Ego sum Custos Angels, 1995, Tu Risa, 1996, The Nine Orders of the Angels, 1996; various scores, 1985, 86, 87, 88, 96, 97; rec. violinist A&M Records, Private Lightning, 1996, Telarc Internat. Arcanae and Ego sum Custos Angela, 1996; composer-in-residence Coro Allegro, 1997—, First Church in Cambridge (Mass.), Congregational, 1996—. Grantee Mass. Cultural Coun., 1993, 96, New Eng. Biolabs. Founds., 1989, Mass. Arts Lottery Coun., 1988; recipient Spl. Recognition award Barlow Internat. Composition for Evensong, 1993. Mem. ASCAP (Spl. award 1996), Chamber Music America, Am. Music Ctr., Alliance of Women in Music. Avocation: major league baseball.

VAN NESS, PATRICIA WOOD, religious studies educator, consultant; b. Peterborough, N.H., Sept. 12, 1925; d. Leslie Townsend and Bernice E. (Coburn) Wood; m. John Hasbrouck Van Ness, June 13, 1953; children: Peter Wood, Stephen Hasbrouck, Timothy Coburn. BA, U. Wash., 1947; MA, Inst. Transpersonal Psychology, Palo Alto, Calif., 1993. Leader various workshops and retreats, 1979—; records mgr. dept. pub. rels. Standard Oil Co., N.Y.C., 1948-50, sec. pub. rels. dept., 1951; sec. law dept. Johnson & Johnson, New Brunswick, N.J., 1953-54; reporter Hudson Valley Newspapers, Highland, N.Y., 1972-74; acting assoc. dir. office of pub. rels. SUNY, New Paltz, 1974-76; ednl. cons. Ulster County Assn. for Mental Health, Kingston, N.Y., 1973-76; coord. pub. rels., adminstrv. asst. Calif. Inst. Transpersonal Psychology, Menlo Park, 1981-83; adminstrv. asst. Ctr. for

Cont. Edn. Calif. Economy, Palo Alto, 1983-84; profl. rep. pvt. practice Palo Alto, 1984; adminstrv. asst. Inventory Transfer Systems Inc., Palo Alto, 1984-85; ednl. cons. Bedford (N.H.) Presbyn. Ch., 1986-88; ednl. cons. Meth. ch., New Paltz, N.Y., 1976-78, White Plains (N.Y.) Presbyn. Ch., 1978-81. author: Transforming Bible Study with Children, 1991; assoc. editor Bible Workbench, 1993—; contbr. numerous articles to profl. jours. Mem. Assn. Presbyn. Ch. Educators. Democrat. Avocations: swimming, reading, skiing. Home: 11 Jaquith Rd Jaffrey NH 03452-6406

VANNICE, M. ALBERT, chemical engineering educator, researcher; b. Broken Bow, Nebr., Jan. 11, 1943; s. Duane M. and Eugenia R. (Farmer) V.; m. Bette Ann Clark, Jan. 2, 1971. BSChemE, Mich. State Univ., 1964; MS, Stanford Univ., 1966, PhD, 1970. Engr. Dow Chemical Co., Midland, Mich., 1966, Sun Oil Co., Marcus Hook, Pa., 1970; sr. rsch. engr. Esso Rsch. & Engr. Co., Linden, N.J., 1971-76; assoc. prof. Pa. State Univ., State Coll., 1976-80, prof., 1980—, disting. prof., 1991—; M.R. Fenske prof. chem. engring., 1996—; cons. Eastman Chem. Co., Kingsport, Tenn., 1980—; mem. adv. bd. Adsorption Sci. & Tech., 1982-95. Mem. editorial bd. Jour. of Catalysis, 1988-94, assoc. editor, 1994—; contbr. articles to profl. jours. Recipient N.Y. Catalysis Soc. award, 1985, P.H. Emmett award, 1987, Pa.-Cleve. Catalysis Soc., 1988, Humboldt Rsch. award, 1990, Fulbright award, 1996. Mem. AICHE (profl. Progress award 1986), Am. Chem. Soc., N.Am. Catalysis Soc. (pres. 1997—). Achievements include 9 patents; effects of strong metal-support interactions on catalytic behavior; studies of CO hydrogenation, NOx reduction, catalyst characterization. Office: Pa State Univ 107 Fenske Lab University Park PA 16802-4400

VAN NORMAN, WILLIS ROGER, computer systems researcher; b. Windom, Minn., June 17, 1938; s. Ralph Peter and Thelma Pearl (Bare) Van N.; m. Irene Anna Penner, Sept. 7, 1959; children: Eric Jon, Brian Mathew, Karin Ruth. AA, Worthington Jr. Coll., 1958; BS, Mankato State Coll., 1960; MS, St. Thomas U., 1991. Tchr. chemistry, St. Peter, Minn., 1961; tchr., Byron, Minn., 1962, spl. edn., Rochester, Minn., 1963-65; instr. pilots ground sch. Rochester Jr. Coll., 1968-69; with Mayo Clinic, Rochester, 1962-88 , developer biomed. computer systems, 1974—; staff analyst Analyst Internat., 1988—; instr. Gopher Aviation, 1968-71. Named Olmsted County Conservation Farmer of Yr., 1992; recipient River Friendly Farmer award, 1997. Woodland advisor, 1995—; founding mem. Zumbro Valley Woodland Coun., 1996; treas., United Methodist Ch. Mem. Mankato State Alumni Assn. (dir.), Minn., Nat. ednl. assns., Internat. Flying Farmers (dir.), Minn Flying Farmers (v.p., pres.), Am. Radio Relay League (mgr. Minn. sect. traffic net), Rochester Amateur Radio Club (pres.). Founder, mgr. Van Norman's Flying V Ranch, 1972—, Van Norman Airport, St. Charles, 1977—. Home: 19230 26th St NE Saint Charles MN 55972-2016 Office: IBM Rochester MN 55901

VANONI, VITO AUGUST, hydraulic engineer; b. Calif., Aug. 30, 1904; s. Battista and Mariana V.; m. Edith Maria Falcinella, June 23, 1934. B.S. in Civil Engring, Calif. Inst. Tech., 1926, M.S. in Civil Engring, 1932, Ph.D., 1940. Supr. research lab. U.S. Soil Conservation Service, Pasadena, Calif., 1935-47; asst. prof. hydraulics Calif. Inst. Tech., 1942-49, asso. prof., 1949-55, prof., 1955-74, prof. emeritus, 1974—. Contbr. numerous articles on hydraulics and sedimentation to profl. jours.; editor: Sedimentation Engineering, 1975. Mem. ASCE (hon.), Internat. Assn. Hydraulic Research, Nat. Acad. Engring., Sigma Xi. Home: 3545 Lombardy Rd Pasadena CA 91107-5628 Office: 1201 E California Blvd Pasadena CA 91125-0001

VAN ORDEN, PHYLLIS JEANNE, librarian, educator; b. Adrian, Mich., July 7, 1932; d. Warren Philip and Mabel A. Nancy (Russell) Van O. BS, Ea. Mich. U., 1954; AMLS, U. Mich., 1958; EdD, Wayne State U., 1970. Sch. librarian East Detroit (Mich.) Pub. Schs., 1954-57; librarian San Diego Pub. Library, 1958-60; media specialist Royal Oak (Mich.) Pub. Schs., 1960-64; librarian Oakland U., Rochester, Mich., 1964-66; instr. Wayne State U., Detroit, 1966-70; asst. prof. Rutgers U., New Brunswick, N.J., 1970-76; prof. library science Fla. State U., Tallahassee, 1977-91, assoc. dean for instrn., 1988-91; prof. libr. sci. program Wayne State U., Detroit, 1991-93; dir. Grad. Sch. of Libr. and Info. Sci. U. Wash., Seattle, 1993-96; cons. in field, 1996—. Editor: Elementary School Library Collection, 1974-77; author: Collection Program in Schools, 1995, Library Service to Children, 1992. Fla. State Libr. grantee, 1984, 86, 88; Lillian Bradshaw scholar Tex. Woman's U., 1993. Mem. Assn. Library Svc. to Children (past pres.), ALA (library resources and tech. svcs. div. Blackwell/N.Am. Scholarship award 1983), Assn. for Library and Info. Sci. Edn. (pres. 1990, svc. award 1997), Pi Lambda Theta. Avocations: music, knitting, physical fitness, cooking, travel.

VANOVER, NEIL, advertising executive. Sr. ptnr., exec. creative dir. Tatham Euro RSCG, Chgo. Office: Tatham Euro RSCG 980 N Michigan Ave Chicago IL 60611-4501

VAN PATTEN, JAMES JEFFERS, education educator; b. North Rose, N.Y., Sept. 8, 1925; s. Earl F. and Dorothy (Jeffers) Van P.; married. BA, Syracuse U., 1949; ME, Tex. Western Coll., 1959; PhD, U. Tex., Austin, 1962. Asst. prof. philosophy and edn. Central Mo. State U., Warrensburg, 1962-64, assoc. prof., 1964-69; assoc. prof. vis. overseas U. Okla., Norman, 1969-71; prof. edn. U. Ark., Fayetteville, 1971—; visiting scholar, U. Mich., 1981, UCLA, 1987, U. Tex., Austin, 1987; vis. prof./scholar U. Fla., Gainesville, 1994. Served with inf., U.S. Army, 1944-45. Decorated Purple Heart. Mem. Am. Ednl. Studies Assn., Southern Future Soc., World Future Soc., Am. Philosophy Assn., Southwestern Philosophy of Edn. Soc. (pres. 1970), Am. Ednl. Rsch. Assn., Edn. Law Assn., Phi Delta Kappa (pres. chpt. U. Ark. 1976-77). Club: Kiwanis. Editor: Conflict, Permanency and Change in Education, 1976, Philosophy, Social Science and Education, 1989, College Teaching and Higher Education Leadership, 1990, Social-Cultural Foundations of Educational Policy in the U.S., 1991; Author: Academic Profiles In Higher Education, 1992, The Many Faces of the Culture of Higher Edn., 1993, (with John Pulliam) History of Education in America, 1995, The Culture of Higher Education: A Case Study Approach, 1996, What's Really Happening In Education: A Case Study Approach, 1997; contbr. articles to books, profl. jours.; founder Jour. of Thought. Home: 434 Hawthorne St Fayetteville AR 72701-1934

VAN PATTEN, JOYCE BENIGNIA, actress; b. Bklyn.; d. Richard Byron and Josephine (Acerno) Van P.; divorced; children: T. Casey King, Talia Balsam. Appeared in Broadway plays including Loves Old Sweet Song, 1941, Tomorrow the World, 1943, The Perfect Marriage, 1944, Wind is Ninety, 1945, Desk Set, 1956, Hole in the Head, 1957, Same Time Next Year, 1975, Murder at the Howard Johnson, 1978, The Supporting Cast, Rumors, Brighton Beach Memoirs, I Ought To Be In Pictures, Jake's Women (with daughter Talia Balsam), 1992, L.A. prodn., 1993, (off Broadway plays) Ivanov, The Seagull, All My Sons, A Fair Country, (Chgo. prodn.) Show Boat (Chgo. prodn.); (films) Trust Me, Monkey Shines, St. Elmo's Fire, Falcon and the Snowman, Billy Galvin, Mame, Blind Date, Infinity (TV shows) The Haunted, Sirens, Under The Influence, Malice In Wonderland, First Lady of the World, Show & Tell; (TV movie) Breathing Lessons, Jake's Women, Granpa's Funeral; (TV series) Unhappily Ever After; (short) Patricia Nixon Flying; writer (play) Donuts, (screenplay) Would You Show Us Your Legs Please?. Co-founder The Workshop Theatre West; fund raiser AIDS Project L.A., West Hollywood, 1989, 90. Mem. Am. Film Inst. Avocations: tennis, needlework, painting, writing.

VAN PATTEN, MARK, environmentalist; 3 children. Grad. magna cum laude, U. Mich. Founding dir. Great Lakes Natural Resource Ctr., Ann Arbor, Mich., 1982-96; pres., CEO Nat. Wildlife Fedn., Vienna, Va., 1996—. Avocations: fishing, hiking. Office: Nat Wildlife Fedn 8925 Leesburg Pike Vienna VA 22184-0001

VAN PELT, ROBERT IRVING, firefighter; b. Chgo., May 4, 1931; s. Irving Henry and Lillian Christene (Balder) Van P.; m. Donna Arlene Bengtson, Feb. 3, 1962; children: Robert Scott, Barbara Gail, James Arthur. Grad. high sch., Chgo. Fire dept. capt. Chgo. Fire Dept., 1954-89, ret., 1989. Dir. Edgebrook Cmty. Assn., Chgo., 1974-95; dist. vice chmn. programs Chgo. Area coun. Boy Scouts Am., 1985-93; scouting coord. Edgebrook Luth. Ch., Chgo., 1971—; mem. PTA Edgebrook Sch., Taft H.S. Decorated Combat Air Crew Wings, 1951; recipient Award of Merit, Boy Scouts Am., 1982, Silver Beaver award, 1987, Svc. award VFW, 1987; PTA scholar, 1956. Mem. Naval Air Mus. (founding life), Exptl. Aviation Assn., War Birds Am., E.A.A. War Bird Squadron 4, Am. Legion, Order of Arrow, Liberator (San Diego). Avocations: photography, woodworking, model making. Home: 6317 N Hiawatha Ave Chicago IL 60646-4219

VANPOOL, CYNTHIA PAULA, special education educator, special services consultant; b. San Antonio, Dec. 8, 1946; d. Walter Foye and Pauline (Karger) Phillips; m. Darrell William Vanpool, Feb. 3, 1968; children: George Karger, William Davies. AB in English, Drury Coll., 1968; MS in Spl. Edn. Tchg., Pittsburg (Kans.) State U., 1987. Cert. tchr., Kans., Mo., Okla.; cert. instr. in Quest Skills for Adolescents. Tchr. lang. arts and journalism Miami (Okla.) Pub. Schs., 1968-69; dir. Christian edn./outreach ministries First Assembly of God, Miami, 1981-83; substitute tchr. Miami Pub. Sch. Dist., 1983-85, learning disabilities specialist, journalism sponsor/advisor, 1985-93, spl. svcs. cons., 1993—; chair spl. edn. dept. Will Rogers Jr. H.S./Mid. Sch., Miami, 1988-94, nat. jr. honor soc. advisor, 1993-94; homebound instr.; cooperating educator for student tchr. practicum student supervision, supr. resident tchr.; cons., tutor, presenter in field; pvt. practice ednl. cons. Recipient Cert. of Appreciation, Miami Evening Lions Club, 1987, Disting. Svc. award Okla. Lions Clubs, 1988, Internat. Presdl. Cert. of Appreciation for Humanitarian Svc., Lions Internat., 1988; Miami Pub. Sch. Enrichment Found. grantee, 1995, 97. Mem. Coun. for Exceptional Children, Divsn. for Learning Disabilities, Coun. for Children with Behavior Disorders, Phi Kappa Phi. Mem. Assembly of God. Ch. Avocations: reading, writing, entertaining, movies, music. Home: 6996 S 590 Rd Miami OK 74354 Office: Miami Pub Schs 1930 B St NE Miami OK 74354-2117

VAN PRAAG, HERMAN MEIR, psychiatrist, educator; b. Schiedam, The Netherlands, Oct. 17, 1929; s. Marinus Maurits and Charlotte Frederigue (Leverpoll) V.P.; m. Cornelia Eikens; children: Marinus, Gido, Charlotte, Bart. MD, Leiden U., The Netherlands, 1956; PhD in Neurobiology, U. Utrecht, The Netherlands, 1962. Chief of staff dept. psychiatry Dijkzigt Hosp., Rotterdam, The Netherlands, 1963-66; founder, head dept. biol. psychiatry Psychiat. Univ. Clinic State U., Groningen, The Netherlands, 1966-77; prof., head dept. psychiatry Acad. Hosp. State U., Utrecht, 1977-82; prof., chmn. dept. psychiatry Albert Einstein Coll. Medicine, Bronx, N.Y., 1982-92, State U. Limburg, Maastricht, The Netherlands, 1992—; emeritus prof. Albert Einstein Coll. Medicine, 1992—; psychiatrist-in-chief Montefiore Med. Ctr., Bronx, 1982-92; Lady Davis vis. prof. Hebrew U. Hadassah U. Hosp., Jerusalem, 1976-77; head WHO Nat. Ref. Ctr. for Study of Psychotropic Drugs, 1969; head WHO Collaborating Ctr. for Rsch. and Tng. in Biol. Psychiatry, 1974; guest lectr. numerous univs. around the world. Editor: Psychiatria Neurologia Neurochirurgia, 1968-70, Advances in Biological Psychiatry, 1978—; editor-in-chief Psychiatria Neurologia Neurochirurgia, 1971-74, Biology of Behavior, 1975-82, Handbook of Biological Psychiatry, 1975-81, Einstein Monograph Series in Experimental and Clinical Psychiatry, 1988—; European chief-editor Progress in Neuro-Psychopharmacology, 1993—; mem. editl. bd. numerous publs. in field; reviewer Am. Jour. Psychiatry, Archives of Gen. Psychiatry, Jour. Nervous and Mental Disease; mem. internat. scientific commn. Jour. Brazilian Psychiat. Assn. Recipient numerous awards and honors. Mem. Soc. Biol. Psychiatry, Collegium Internationale Neuro-Psychopharmacologicum, Assn. for Advancement of Psychotherapy, Internat. Group for Study of Affective Disorders, Internat. Soc. Psychoneuroendocrinology, European Brain and Behavior Soc., Internat. Assn. for Suicide Prevention, Brit. Pharmacol. Soc., European Soc. for Clin. Investigation, Bataafsch Genootschap der Proefondervindelijke Wijsbegeerte, Am. Coll. Neuropharmacology, Deutsche Gesellschaft fur Psychiatrie und Nervenheilkunde, Israel Med. Assn., Psychiat. Rsch. Soc., N.Y. Acad. Medicine, Am. Psychopathol. Assn., Internat. Coll. Neurobiology, Biol. Psychiatry and Psychopharmacology, Serotonin Club, Internat. Soc. for Rsch. on Emotion, Internat. Soc. Psychoneuroendocrinology, Arbeitsgemeinschaft fur Neuropsychpharmakologie und Pharmakopsychiatrie. Office: Univ Limburg Acad Psychiat, Ctr POB 616, 6200 MD Maastricht The Netherlands

VAN RAALTE, JOHN A., research and engineering management executive; b. Copenhagen, Apr. 10, 1938; came to U.S., 1955; s. John A. and Laura W.M. (Louwerier) van R.; m. Andrée Valentine Greene, Dec. 28, 1963; children: Kirsten A., James E. BSEE, MIT, 1960, MSEE, 1960, elec. engrs. degree, 1962, PhD, 1964. Rsch. asst. MIT, Cambridge, 1960-64; mem. tech. staff RCA David Sarnoff Rsch. Ctr., Princeton, N.J., 1964-70, head display rsch., 1970-79, head videodisc record and playback, 1979-83, dir. videodisc systems rsch., 1983-84, dir. display systems rsch., 1984-87; dir. materials and process tech. lab. David Sarnoff Rsch. Ctr. subs. SRI Internat., Princeton, N.J., 1987-90; mgr. CRT engring. Thomson Consumer Electronics N.Am. Tube Div., Lancaster, Pa., 1990-92; gen. mgr. Electron Optics Lab., Thomson Tubes & Displays, Genlis, France; mem. steering com. Internat. Display Rsch. Conf., U.S., Europe, Japan, 1981-88. Author: (with others) Electronic Engineer's Reference Handbook, 4th and 5th edits. Chmn. ednl. coun. MIT, N.J., 1978-83. Fellow IEEE, Soc. for Info. Display (pres., v.p., treas., sec. 1981-88, chmn. and program chmn. Internat. Symposium 1973-78); mem. MIT Club of Princeton, Chevalier du Tastevin, Sigma Xi, Tau Beta Pi, Eta Kappa Nu (pres. Boston chpt. 1964). Home: 24 rue des Templiers, 21121 Fontaine les Dijon France Office: Thomson Tubes & Displays, Ave du Gen de Gaulle, 21110 Genlis France

VAN REENEN, JANE SMITH, speech and language pathologist; b. Baton Rouge, Sept. 16, 1949; d. William Robert and Mary Jane (Laidlaw) Smith; m. Dirk Andries van Reenen, Mar. 3, 1973; children: Andrea Lee, Erika Lynn. BS in Speech Pathology, La. State U., 1971; MEd in Speech Pathology, Ga. State U., 1984. Cert. clin. competence Am. Speech-Lang.-Hearing Assn.; lic. Ga.; cert. tchr. Ga. Speech-lang. pathologist Livingston Parish Schs., La., 1971-73, Gwinnett County (Ga.) Schs., 1973-75, 94—; pvt. practice speech-lang. pathology Norcross, Ga., 1975—; speech-lang. pathologist Nova Care, Atlanta, 1979—; grad. asst. Ga. State U., Atlanta, 1983-84, substitute clin. supr., 1988-90, interim clinic coord., 1991; speech-lang. pathologist Americana Nursing Home, Decatur, 1984; chairperson Atlanta (Ga.) Orofacial Myology Study Group, 1987-89; adv. com. Comm. Disorders Program, Atlanta, 1990-94; mem. Ga. Supervision Network, 1991—; mem. Cognitive Remediation Interest Group, Atlanta, 1993—. Mng. editor Internat. Jour. Orofacial Myology, 1989-91; contbr. articles to profl. jours. Ruling elder Northminster Presbyn. Ch., Roswell, Ga., 1981; mem. local sch. adv. com. Pinckneyville Mid. Sch., Norcross, 1987-92, co-founder sch. based drug/alchol abuse prevention program, 1988; v.p. Parent Tchr. Student Assn. Norcross H.S., 1990-91; pres. River Valley Estates Homeowners Assn., Norcross, 1991; local sch. adv. com. Norcross H.S., 1993—, AIDS rep. PTSA, 1993-96, drug/alcohol abuse rep., 1993-96, mem. care team, 1993-96. Recipient Positive Parenting awards Ga. State Supt. of Schs., Atlanta, 1987-88, 88-89; named Outstanding Sch. Vol., Gwinnet County Bd. Edn., Lawrenceville, Ga., 1989-90. Mem. Am. Speech-Lang.-Hearing Assn. (congl. action contact com. 1991—), Ga. Speech-Lang.-Hearing Assn. (honors and ethics com. 1989-91), Internat. Assn. Orofacial Myology (mng. editor 1989-91). Republican. Avocations: tennis, walking/running, yard work, cooking, working with youth. Home and Office: 3992 Gunnin Rd Norcross GA 30092-1953

VAN REES, CORNELIUS S., lawyer; b. N.Y.C., May 29, 1929; s. Cornelius Richard and Beatrice Martin (Shreve) Van R.; m. Virginia Vandewater, Mar. 15, 1953 (div. 1984); children: Pamela Millet Van Rees Lundquist, Claire Katherine; m. Alix McIvor, Jan. 2, 1985. BA, Denison U., 1951; JD, Columbia U., 1954. Bar: N.Y. 1956, U.S. Dist. Ct. (so. dist.) N.Y. 1956, Conn. 1994. Assoc. Thacher Proffitt & Wood, N.Y.C., 1956-62, ptnr., 1963-93, of counsel, 1994—; mem. exec. com., officer, bd. dirs. Graham Corp.; lectr. in field. Writer in field. Trustee, sec. Williston Northhampton Sch.; mem. senate, honors and prizes com. Columbia U. Harlem Fisk Stone scholar Columbia U., 1954. Mem. ABA (coms. on internat. fin. trans., export credits, maritime fin. and devel. in bus. fin.), Maritime Law Assn. (com. on underseas devel. and exploration), Alumni Fedn. Columbia U., Inc. (Alumni medal 1984, pres. 1979-81), N.Y. Yacht Club. Avocation: sailing. Home and Office: 35 Cove Side Ln Stonington CT 06378-2902

VAN REMOORTERE, FRANCOIS PETRUS, chemical company research and development executive; b. Haasdonk, Belgium, Dec. 16, 1943; came to U.S., 1968; s. Jozef Frederik and Celine (van de Vyver) van R.; m. Jane Louise Evans; children: Kier, Pieter, David. BS in Chemistry, U. Louvain, Belgium, 1965, PhD in Phys. Chemistry, 1968. Rsch. chemist The Dow Chem. Co., Midland, Mich., 1968-74, group leader, 1974-77, rsch. mgr., 1977-79; dir. R & D planning Am. Can Co., Greenwich, Conn., 1979-83; v.p. tech. and planning W.R. Grace & Co., Columbia, Md., 1983-86, pres. rsch. div., 1986—; mem. adv. coun. Johns Hopkins U. Whiting Sch. Engring. Bd. visitors U. Md., College Park, 1988—; trustee Howard County Gen. Hosp., 1989-93, Howard County Hosp. Found., 1993-95. Mem. AAAS, Am. Chem. Soc., Coun. for Chem. Rsch., Indsl. Rsch. Inst., N.Y. Acad. Sci., Cosmos Club (Washington). Office: W R Grace & Co Rsch Divsn Washington Rsch 7500 Grace Dr Columbia MD 21044-4053

VAN RIPER, PAUL KENT, marine corps officer; b. Brownsville, Pa., July 5, 1938; s. James Frederic and Mary Katherine (Davis) Van R.; m. Lillie Catherine Alford, Jan. 27, 1968; children: Stephen Kent, Cynthia Leigh. BA in Edn., California (Pa.) State Coll., 1963; student, Amphibious Warfare Sch., 1968. Enlisted USMCR, 1956; advanced through grades to lieut. gen. USMC, 1995, commd. 2d lt., 1963; instr. The Basic Sch., 1966-68; platoon comdr., co. exec. officer, asst. ops. officer 1st Bn. 8th Marines, Dominican Republic, 1965; Marine advisor Vietnamese Marine Corps, 1965-66; co. comdr., asst. ops. officer 3d bn. 7th Marines, 1st Marine Div., Vietnam, 1968-69; instr., staff officer JFK Inst. for Mil. Assistance, Ft. Bragg, N.C., 1969-71; spl. projects officer Office Chief of Staff, Hdqrs. Marine Corps, Washington, 1971-72; tng. specialist Tng. Div., Washington, 1972-74; ops. officer 3d bn. 8th Marines, Camp Lejeune, N.C., 1974-75, regt ops officer, 1975-76; exec. officer 1st bn. 8th Marines, 1976-77; student Naval War Coll., Newport, R.I., 1977-78; mil. observer U.S. Mil. Observer Group, UN Truce Supervision Orgn., Palestine, 1978-79; comdg. officer Marine Barracks, Naval Air Sta., Cecil Field, Fla., 1979-81; student Army War Coll., Carlisle, Pa., 1981-82; regtl. exec. officer 7th Marines, 1st Marine Div., Camp Pendleton, Calif., 1982-83, comdr. 2d bn., 1983-84; exercise, readiness and tng. officer I Marine Amphibious Force, Camp Pendleton, 1984-85; regtl. comdr. 4th Marines, 3d Marine Div., Okinawa, Japan, 1985-86; asst. chief of staff, then chief of staff 3d Marine Div., Okinawa, 1986-88; dir. Command and Staff Coll., Quantico, Va., 1988-89; pres. Marine Corps U., Quantico, 1989-90; dir. Marine Air-Ground Tng. and Edn. Ctr., Quantico, 1990-91; comdg. gen. 2d Marine Div., Camp LeJeune, N.C., 1991-93; asst. chief of staff, dir. intelligence command control, comm. and computer HQMC, Washington, 1993-95; comdg. gen. Marine Corps Combat Development Command, Quantico, 1995—. Contbr. numerous articles to profl. mil. jours. Tchr. Sunday sch. Mil. Chapels. Decorated Silver Star medal with gold star (2), Legion of Merit, Bronze Star meda with Combat V, Purple Heart, Meritorious Svc. medal, Joint Svc. Commendation medal, Army commendation medal, Navy Achievement medal, Combat Action Ribbon with gold star, Nat. Def. Svc. medal with one bronze star (2), Vietnam Svc. medal with one silver and one bronze star, others; UN medal; Gallantry Cross and Campaign medal (Republic of Vietnam); Southwest Asia Svc. meda., Kuwaiti Liberation medal. Presbyterian. Avocations: history, running, fishing. Address: USMC Quarters One MCB Quantico VA 22134

VAN RIPER, PAUL PRITCHARD, political science educator; b. Laporte, Ind., July 29, 1916; s. Paul and Margaret (Pritchard) Van R.; m. Dorothy Ann Dodd Samuelson, May 11, 1964; 1 child, Michael Scott Samuelson. A.B., DePauw U., 1938; Ph.D., U. Chgo., 1947. Instr. Northwestern U., 1947-49, asst. prof. polit. sci., 1949-51; mgmt. analyst Office Comptroller Dept. Army, 1951-52; mem. faculty Cornell U., 1952-70, prof., 1957-70; chmn. gov. bd., exec. com. Cornell Social Sci. Research Center, 1956-58; prof., head dept. polit. sci. Tex. A&M U., 1970-77, prof., 1977-81, prof. emeritus, 1981—, coordinator M.P.A. program, 1979-81, named prof. Bush Sch. Govt. and Pub. Svc., 1997—; vis. prof. U. Chgo., 1958, Ind. U., 1961, U. Strathclyde, Scotland, 1964, U. Mich., 1965, U. Okla., 1969—, U. Utah, 1979. Author: History of the United States Civil Service, 1958, Some Educational and Social Aspects of Fraternity Life, 1961, (with others) The American Federal Executive, 1963, Handbook of Practical Politics, 3d edit., 1967; editor and co-author: the Wilson Influence on Public Administration, 1990. Mem. exec. com. Civil Svc. Reform Assn., N.Y., 1960-64, hist. adv. com. NASA, 1964-66; bd. dirs. Brazos Valley Cmty. Action Agy., 1975-79, Brazos County Hist. Commn., 1976—; charter mem. Brazos Heritage Soc., pres. 1977-79. Maj. AUS, 1942-46; lt. col. USAR ret. Decorated Croix de Guerre (France). Mem. Am. Polit. Sci. Assn., So. Polit. Sci. Assn., S.W. Polit. Sci. Assn. (exec.com. 1975-77), Am. Soc. Pub. Adminstrn. (nat adv. com. 1957-60, Dimock award 1984, Waldo award 1990), Internat. Personnel Mgmt. Assn., Rotary (pres. Bryan club 1991-92), Phi Beta Kappa, Beta Theta Pi (v.p. 1962, gen. sec. 1963-65), Pi Alpha Alpha, Pi Sigma Alpha, Phi Kappa Phi, Sigma Delta Chi. Republican. Baptist. Home: 713 E 30th St Bryan TX 77803-4789 Office: Tex A and M Univ Dept Polit Sci College Station TX 77843-4348

VAN RY, GINGER LEE, school psychologist; b. Alexandria, Va., June 26, 1953; d. Ray Ellsworth Hensley and Bernice Anne (Weidel) Wolter; m. Willem Hendrik Van Ry, Aug 23, 1986; 1 child, Anika Claire. AA, U. Nev., Las Vegas, 1973; BA, U. Wash., 1983, MEd, 1985. Cert. sch. psychologist. Psychometrist The Mason Clinic, Seattle, 1980-84, supr., psychology lab., 1984-86; sch. psychologist Everett (Wash.) Sch. Dist., 1986—; mem. profl. ednl. adv. bd. U. Wash. Sch. Psychology, Seattle, 1995-98. Author: (with others) Wash. State Assn. of Sch. Psychologists Best Practice Handbook, 1993. Co-pres. Lake Cavanaugh Hghts. Assn., Seattle, 1994-95, chmn. long-range planning com., 1995—. Mem. AAUW, NEA, Nat. Assn. Sch. Psychologists (cert. sch. psychologist), Wash. State Assn. Sch. Psychologists (chair profl. devel. com. 1995—), Wash. State Edn. Assn., U. Wash. Alumni Assn. Democrat. Avocations: reading, travel, fgn. cultures, woodworking, horticulture. Office: The Everett Sch Dist 4730 Colby Ave PO Box 2098 Everett WA 98203

VAN RYSSELBERGE, CHARLES H., organization administrator; b. Evanston, Ill., Oct. 8, 1945; s. John F. Van Rysselberge and Marguerite Irene (Van Witzenburg) Van Rysselberge-Yaple; m. Joan E. Roberts, June 22, 1968; children: Denise, Michelle. ABJ, U. Ga., 1968, MA, 1971, cert. in mgmt., 1977. Membership mgr. Shreveport (La.) C. of C., 1972-74, exec. v.p., 1986-88; group mgr. Chattanooga (Tenn.) C. of C., 1974-77, gen. mgr., 1979-81; exec. v.p. Monroe (La.) C. of C., 1977-79, Dalton-Whitfield (Ga.) C. of C., 1981-86, Atlanta C. of C., 1988-93; pres. Oklahoma City C. of C., 1993—. Communications mgr. Greenville (S.C.) C. of C., 1969-70. 1st lt. Signal Corps, U.S. Army, 1970-72, USAR, 1972-73. Mem. Am. C. of C. Execs. Assn., Ga. Assn. C. of C. Execs. (bd. dirs. 1983-86), So. Assn. C. of C. Execs. (bd. dirs. 1988-90), Century Club (chmn. 1984-86), Phi Kappa Tau. Mem. Reformed Ch. Am. Avocation: jogging. Home: 5017 Misty Glen Cir Oklahoma City OK 73142-5402 Office: C of C of Oklahoma City 123 Park Ave Oklahoma City OK 73102-9031*

VAN SANT, GUS, JR., director, screenwriter; b. Louisville, 1952. BA in Filmmaking, RISD, 1975. Films include Mala Noche, 1985 (L.A. Film Critics award 1987), Drugstore Cowboy, 1989 (with Daniel Yost: Nat. Soc. Film Critics Best Dir. award 1990, Best Screenplay award 1990, N.Y. Film Critics Best Screenplay award 1990, L.A. Film Critics Best Screenplay award 1989), Internat. PEN Literary award for Screenplay Adaptation (with Daniel Yost 1989), My Own Private Idaho, 1991 (Best Screenplay 1992, Best Film 1992), Even Cowgirls Get the Blues, 1993, To Die For, 1995. Office: William Morris Agency Inc 151 S El Camino Dr Beverly Hills CA 90212-2704

VANSANT, JOANNE FRANCES, academic administrator; b. Morehead, Ky., Dec. 29, 1924; d. Lewis L. and Dorothy (Greene) VanS. BA, Denison U., Granville, Ohio; MA, The Ohio State U.; postgrad., U. Colo. and The Ohio State U.; LLD (hon.), Albright Coll., 1975. Tchr., health and phys. edn. Mayfield, Kentucky High Sch., 1946-48; instr. Denison U., Granville, Ohio, 1948; instr. women's phys. edn. Otterbein Coll., Westerville, Ohio, 1948-52, assoc. prof., 1955-62, dept. chmn., 1950-62, chmn. div. profl. studies, 1961-65, dean of women, 1952-60, 62-64, dean of students, 1964-93, v.p. student affairs, 1968-93; v.p., dean student affairs emeritus, 1993—, cons. Instnl. Advancement, 1993—. Co-pres. Directions for Youth, 1983-84, pres., 1984-85; bd. dirs. North Area Mental Health; trustee Westerville Civic Symphony at Otterbein Coll., 1983-88; active numerous other community orgns.; ordained elder Presbyn. Ch., 1967. Named to hon. Order of Ky. Cols., 1957; recipient Focus on Youth award Columbus Dispath, 1983, Vol. of the Yr. award North Area Mental Health Svcs., 1982, citation Denison U., 1996. Mem. Am. Assn. Counseling and Devel., Ohio Personnel and Guidance Assn., Ohio Assn. Women Deans, Adminstrs., Counselors (treas., exec. bd. 1972-73), Nat. Assn. Student Personnel Adminstrs., Ohio Coll.

Personnel Assn., Mortar Bd. (hon.), Zonta Internat. (pres. Columbus, Ohio club 1984-85, dist. gov. 1988-90, internat. svc. chmn. 1996—, internat. found. bd. 1997—), Vocal Arts Resource Network (chair bd. dirs. 1994-96), Cap and Dagger Club, Torch and Key Hon., Order Omega, Alpha Lambda Delta, Theta Alpha Phi, others. Avocations: musical and children's theater production, choreography. Home: 9100 Oakwood Pt Westerville OH 43082-9643 Office: Otterbein Coll Instnl Advancement Westerville OH 43081

VAN SANT, PETER RICHARD, news correspondent; b. Seattle, Feb. 21, 1953; s. Richard Murdock and Joy Marie Van Sant; m. children: Erik, Jeffrey, Stefani, Kristina; m. Sarma Anete Dindzans, Apr. 20, 1994. BS in Comm. cum laude, Washington State U., 1975. Reporter, anchor KMVT-TV, Twin Falls, Idaho, 1976; reporter KCRG-TV, Cedar Rapids, Iowa, 1976-77, KETV-TV, Omaha, 1977-78; anchor, reporter KOOL-TV, Phoenix, 1978-82; reporter WFAA-TV, Dallas, 1982-84; corr. CBS News, Atlanta, 1984-89, London, Eng., 1989-92, N.Y.C., 1992—. Recipient Emmy Investigative Reporting NATAS, 1987, Alfred I. Dupont award Columbia U., 1989-90. Avocations: hiking, fishing, travel. Office: CBS News/Street Stories 524 W 57th St New York NY 10019-2902*

VAN SCHAACK, ERIC, art historian, educator; b. Evanston, Ill., June 10, 1931; s. Cornelius Peter and Sigrid (Schold) Van S.; m. Carol Fryling, June 16, 1965; children—Elizabeth M., Leslie A. A.B., Dartmouth Coll., 1953; Ph.D., Columbia U., 1969. Lectr., rsch. asst. The Frick Collection, N.Y.C., 1960-62; asst. prof. fine arts, then full prof. visual arts Goucher Coll., Balt., 1964-77; prof. art and art history Colgate U., Hamilton, N.Y., 1977-96, chmn. dept. art and art history, 1978-83, prof. art and art history emeritus, 1996—; vis. prof. fine arts Md. Inst. Coll. Art Johns Hopkins U., Balt. Author: Master Drawings in Private Collections, 1962, Baroque Art in Italy, 1964; contbr. articles to profl. jours., encys. Served with U.S. Army, 1954-56. Grantee Fulbright/Italian Govt., 1962-63, Ford Found., 1972-73, Colgate U. faculty, 1979-80, 92-93, others. Mem. Coll. Art Assn., Am. Soc. Archtl. Historians, Nat. Trust Hist. Preservation. Club: Hamilton. Home: 28 W Pleasant St Hamilton NY 13346-1216 Office: Colgate U Dept Art & Art History Hamilton NY 13346-1398

VAN SCOY, GARY, social services administrator; b. Williamsport, Pa., Feb. 12, 1950; s. Thomas Van Scoy and Velma Lee (Coats) Valentine; m. Paula Maria Kovach, May 31, 1975; 1 child, Justin. BA in Sociology, King's Coll., 1972; MSW, Marywood Coll., 1974. Lic. social worker. Child abuse specialist Childrens Bur. Lehigh County, Allentown, Pa., 1974-76; program founder Parents Anonymous, Wilkes-Barre, Pa., 1976-78; family counselor Cath. Social Svcs., Wilkes-Barre, 1976-80, program dir., 1980-86; asst. dir. Cath. Social Svcs., Scranton, Pa., 1986-91; exec. dir. Cath. Social Svcs., Scranton, 1991-93; sr. outpatient therapist Children Svc. Ctr., Wilkes-Barre, Pa., 1993—, dir. managed care, 1994—; bd. dirs. Child Devel. Coun., Wilkes-Barre, 1978-86; bd. dirs. Child Welfare Luzerne County, Wilkes-Barre, 1976-80, pres., 1978-80. Bd. dirs. St. Michael's Sch., Tunkhannock, Pa., 1986-89; alumni mem. Leadership Wilkes-Barre, 1984. Named Outstanding Young Citizen, Scranton Jaycees, 1988; recipient award of harmony Barbershops Singers, 1980, Disting. Svc. award Wilkes-Barre Jaycees, 1980, Benjamin Rush award Luzerne County Med. Soc., 1980, 449th Daily Point of Light award Pres. of U.S., 1991. Mem. NASW (Social Worker of Yr. award 1989), KC (4 degree). Democrat. Roman Catholic. Avocations: swimming, photography. Home: 300 Chapel St Swoyersville PA 18704 Office: Children Svc Ctr 335 S Franklin St Wilkes Barre PA 18702-3808

VANSELOW, NEAL ARTHUR, university administrator, physician; b. Milw., Mar. 18, 1932; s. Arthur Frederick and Mildred (Hoffmann) V.; m. Mary Ellen McKenzie, June 20, 1958; children: Julie Ann, Richard Arthur. AB, U. Mich., 1954, MD, 1958, MS, 1963. Diplomate: Am. Bd. Internal Medicine, Am. Bd. Allergy and Immunology. Intern Mpls. Gen. Hosp., 1958-59; resident Univ. Hosp., Ann Arbor, Mich., 1959-63; instr. medicine U. Mich., 1963-64, asst. prof., 1964-68, assoc. prof., 1968-72, prof., chmn. dept. postgrad. medicine and health professions edn., 1972-74; dean Coll. Medicine U. Ariz., Tucson, 1974-77; chancellor med. ctr. U. Nebr., Omaha, 1977-82, v.p., 1977-82; v.p. health scis. U. Minn., 1982-89, prof. internal medicine, 1982-89; chancellor Tulane U. Med. Ctr., New Orleans, 1989-94; prof. internal medicine, adj. prof. health sys. mgmt. Tulane U., New Orleans, 1989—; chmn. Joint Bd. Osteo. and Med. Examiners Ariz., 1974-77; chmn. coun. on Grad. Med. Edn., Dept. Health and Human Svcs., 1986-91; mem. com. on educating dentists for future Inst. Medicine, NAS, 1993-95, chairperson com. on future of primary care, 1994-96, co-chairperson com. on the U.S. physician supply, 1995-96, scholar in residence, 1994-95. Bd. dirs. Devel. Authority for Tucson's Economy, 1975-77, Minn. Coalition for Health Care Costs, 1983-87, La. Health Care Authority, 1989-90, United Way Greater New Orleans Area, 1992-97; mem. exec. com. United Way Midlands, 1980-82, vice chmn. 1981 campaign; bd. dirs., mem. exec. com. Health Planning Coun. Midlands, Omaha, 1978-82, v.p., 1981-82; bd. dirs. Minn. High Tech. Coun., 1983-86; mem. comm. on Health Professions Pew Charitable Trusts, 1990-92, 97—; mem. Gov.'s Pan Am. Commn., La., 1991-92; mem. mktg. mgmt. governing coun. U. Hosp. Consortium, 1993-95; trustee Meharry Med. Coll., 1996—; mem. Commn. on the Future of Med. Edn. U. Calif., 1996—; mem. panel on interdisciplinary health profl. edn. Nat. League Nursing, 1996—. Fellow ACP (workgroup on physician workforce and financing med. edn. 1996—), Am. Acad. Allergy, Am. Coll. Physician Execs.; mem. Assn. Acad. Health Ctrs. (bd. dirs. 1983-89, chmn. bd. dirs. 1988), Soc. Med. Adminstrs., Phi Beta Kappa, Sigma Xi, Alpha Omega Alpha, Beta Theta Pi, Nu Sigma Nu. Home: 1828 Palmer Ave New Orleans LA 70118-6216 Office: Tulane U 1430 Tulane Ave New Orleans LA 70112-2699

VAN SETERS, JOHN, biblical literature educator; b. Hamilton, Ont., Can., May 2, 1935; s. Hugo and Anne (Hubert) Van S.; m. Elizabeth Marie Malmberg, June 11, 1960; children: Peter John, Deborah Elizabeth. B.A., U. Toronto, 1958; M.A., Yale U., 1959, Ph.D., 1965; B.D., Princeton Theol. Sem., 1962. Asst. prof. dept. Near Eastern studies Waterloo Luth. U., 1965-67; asso. prof. Old Testament Andover Newton Theol. Sch., 1967-70; asso. prof. dept. Near Eastern studies U. Toronto, 1970-76, prof., 1976-77; James A. Gray prof. Bibl. lit., dept. religion U. N.C., Chapel Hill, 1977—; chmn. dept. religious studies U. N.C., 1980-88, 93-95. Author: The Hyksos: A New Investigation, 1966, Abraham in History and Tradition, 1975, In Search of History, 1983, Der Jahwist als Historiker, 1987, Prologue to History, 1992, The Life of Moses, 1994. Recipient James Henry Breasted prize Am. Hist. Assn., 1985, Book award Am. Acad. Religion, 1986; Woodrow Wilson fellow, 1958; J.J. Obermann fellow, 1962-64; Guggenheim fellow, 1979-80; NEH fellow, 1985-86, Am. Coun. Learned Socs. fellow, 1991-92. Mem. AAUP, Soc. Bibl. Lit., Am. Schs. Oriental Rsch., Soc. Study of Egyptian Antiquities, Am. Oriental Soc., Soc. for Old Testament Study, Cath. Bibl. Assn. Home: 104 Mullin Ct Chapel Hill NC 27514-2646 Office: U NC 101 Saunders Hall CB # 3225 Chapel Hill NC 27599

VAN SICKLE, BRUCE MARION, federal judge; b. Minot, N.D., Feb. 13, 1917; s. Guy Robin and Hilda Alice (Rosenquist) Van S.; m. Dorothy Alfreda Hermann, May 26, 1943; children: Susan Van Sickle Cooper, John Allan, Craig Bruce, David Max. BSL, U. Minn., 1941, JD, 1941. Bar: Minn. 1941, N.D. 1946. Pvt. practice law, Minot, 1947-71; judge U.S. Dist. Ct. N.D., 1971-85, sr. judge, 1985—; mem. N.D. Ho. of Reps., 1957, 59. Served with USMCR, 1941-46. Mem. ABA, N.D. Bar Assn., N.W. Bar Assn., Ward County Bar Assn., Am. Trial Lawyers Assn., Am. Coll. Probate Counsel, Am. Judicature Soc., Bruce M. Van Sickle Inns of Ct., Masons, Shriners, Elks. Office: US Dist Ct 430 US Courthouse PO Box 670 Bismarck ND 58502-0670

VAN SICKLE, FREDERICK L., federal judge; b. 1943; m. Jane Bloomquist. BS, U. Wis., 1965; JD, U. Wash., 1968. Ptnr. Clark & Van Sickle, 1970-75; prosecuting atty. Douglas County, Waterville, Wash., 1971-75; judge State of Wash. Superior Ct., Grant and Douglas counties, 1975-79, Chelan and Douglas Counties, 1979-91; judge U.S. Dist. Ct. (ea. dist.) Wash., Spokane, 1991—; co-chair rural ct. com. Nat. Conf. State Trial Judges, 1987-91. 1st lt. U.S. Army, 1968-70. Mem. ABA (nat. conf. fed. judges jud. adminstrn.), Am. Adjudicature Soc., Wash. State Bar Assn., Masons (pres. Badger mountain lodge 1982-83), Scottish Rite, Spokane Rotary, Shriners. Office: US Dist Cts US Courthouse PO Box 2209 920 W Riverside Ave Rm 914 Spokane WA 99201-1008

VAN SICKLE, PAUL BRUNTON, financial executive; b. Toronto, Ont., Can., Sept. 17, 1939; came to U.S., 1967; s. Percy Orton Van Sickle and Audrey Winefred (Dandie) Palmquist; m. Christine Cornfoot, Sept. 9, 1967 (div. July 1985); children: Giles, Kirsten; m. Jeanne Marie Wetta, May 6, 1989; children: Matthew, Lauren. Grad. advanced mgmt. program, Harvard U., 1986. Canadian chartered acct. V.p. Fin. Rexcel, Ludlow, Mass., 1973-76, Specialty Products Sector, LaGrange, Ga., 1976-77; v.p. Thompson Industries, Phoenix, 1977-79, exec. v.p., 1979-81; controller Home & comml. Products Group, Northbrook, Ill., 1981-82, Duracell, Inc., Danbury, Conn., 1982-83; sr. v.p. fin. Hobart Corp., Troy, Ohio, 1983-85; v.p., controller Dart & Kraft, Inc., Northbrook, Ill., 1986; v.p., controller Premark Internat., Deerfield, Ill., 1986-88, v.p. control and info. systems, 1988-89; sr. v.p., CFO Tupperware Corp., Orlando, Fla., 1989-97, exec. v.p., 1997—. Avocations: golf, skiing. Office: Tupperware PO Box 2353 Orlando FL 32802

VAN SICKLE, SHARON, public relations executive; b. Portland, Oreg., Nov. 10, 1955. BA in Mktg. and Journalism, U. Portland, 1976, postgrad. Reporter Willamette Week, Portland, 1976-77; dir. pub. rels. Tektronix, Portland, 1977-83; prin. pub. rels. Karakas VanSickle Ouellette Advt. and Pub. Rels., Portland, 1983—. Mem. Am. Electronics Assn., Pub. Rels. Soc. Am. (pres. Portland chpt. 1994-95, chair acad. tech. com.). Office: Karakas VanSickle Oullette Advt and Pub Rels 200 SW Market St Ste 1400 Portland OR 97201-5741

VAN SINDEREN, ALFRED WHITE, former telephone company executive; b. Bklyn., June 20, 1924; s. Adrian and Jean (White) Van S.; m. Suzanne Petersen, Apr. 21, 1962; children: Alexander, David Cabot, Sylvia Van Sinderen Abbate, Jean Van Sinderen Vashaw, Katherine Van Sinderen Tucker. B.A., Yale U., 1945; M.B.A., Harvard U., 1947. With So. New Eng. Telephone Co., New Haven, 1947-85; v.p. So. New Eng. Telephone Co. (No. area), Hartford, Conn., 1962-65; v.p. ops. So. New Eng. Telephone Co., 1965-67, pres., 1967-82, chmn., chief exec. officer, 1982-84, chmn. bd., 1984-85; William H. Donaldson disting. faculty fellow Yale U. Sch. Mgmt., 1985-89. Past mem. adv. bd. Yale-U.S. Sch. Orgn. and Mgmt.; mem. Yale Libr. Assocs.; past co-chmn. Gov. Conf. Human Rights, 1967; past bd. dirs. Conn. Econ. Devel. Corp., Hartford; bd. dirs., past chmn. Shirley Frank Found.; pres Found. for New Haven Green, Inc., 1986-91. With USNR, 1943-46. Recipient Charter Oak Leadership medal Hartford, 1965; Conn. Man of Yr. New Eng. Council, 1976; Human Relations award NCCJ, 1981. Mem. Quinnipiack Club (New Haven). Home: 12 Highview Dr Woodbridge CT 06525-1934

VAN SLOOTEN, RONALD HENRY JOSEPH, dentist; b. Paterson, N.J., July 12, 1937; s. Henry and Edythe (De Marco) Van S.; m. Joyce Elenor Mandel, 1962 (div. 1969); children: Ronald Henry Jr., Timothy Jay, Lauren; m. Barbara Rose Durante, July 1, 1979; children: Jonathan Henry, Brian Joseph. DDS, Farleigh Dickinson U., 1962; FAGD, Acad. Gen. Dentistry, 1986. Dentist pvt. practice, Paterson, N.J., 1965-76, Ridgewood, N.J., 1969-78, Ho Ho Kus, N.J., 1978—; staff mem. Bainert Meml. Hosp., Paterson, 1966-75, Ridgewood Valley Hosp., 1975—; assoc. prof. Fairleigh Dickinson Dental Sch., Hackensack, N.J., 1973-90; pres. Van Slooten Harbour Marina Inc., Port Henry, N.Y., 1989—; cons. N.J. Mfrs. Ins. Co., Trenton, 1966—. Pres. Fairleigh Dickinson Sch. Dentistry Alumni Assn., 1976-77. Lt. comdr. USN, 1962-65. Fellow Acad. Gen. Dentistry, Acad. Dentistry Internat.; mem. ADA, Internat. Dental Health Found., N.J. Dental Soc., Bergen County Dental Soc. (chmn. Nat. Dental Health Week citation 1970), Moriah C. of C., Ho-Ho-Kus C. of C. Republican. Roman Catholic. Avocations: racquetball, fishing, boating. Office: Ho Ho Kus Profl Bldg 110 Warren Ave Ho Ho Kus NJ 07423-1561

VAN SOLKEMA-WAITZ, TERESE ELLEN, special education educator, consultant; b. West Palm Beach, Fla., Jan. 9, 1956; d. Richard Andrew Van Solkema and Deborah Bradshaw (Crockett) Stupey; m. John William Waitz, Oct. 4, 1986; children: Sarah Lindsay, Rebecca Elizabeth. BS, Fitchburg State Coll., 1979. Cert. tchr., spl. edn. tchr., Mass. Spl. edn. vision specialist Waltham (Mass.) Pub. Schs., 1979-80; tchr. head-injured, multi-impaired students Perkins Sch. for Blind, Watertown, Mass., 1979-83; spl. educator head-injury program Moss Rehab. Hosp., Phila., 1984-86; ind. cons., head injury home and community specialist Bensalem, Pa., 1986—; case mgr. Commonwealth of Pa. Head Injury Program, Harrisburg, 1989-96; presenter at profl. confs.; workshop leader; legal expert for Phila. law firms, 1986-87, 88. Mem. Coun. Exceptional Children, Nat. Head Injury Found., N.J. Head Injury Found., Pa. Assn. Rehab. Facilities (mem. head injury study tech. group). Mem. Soc. of Friends. Avocations: swimming, sports, photography, music, travel.

VAN STAVOREN, WILLIAM DAVID, management consultant, retired government official; b. Lunenburg, Va., Mar. 14, 1936; s. James Eugene and Marion Estelle (Boyer) Van S.; m. Rosa Kouyoundjian, Dec. 29, 1962; children: John, Christopher, Diane. B.S., Va. Poly. Inst., 1960, M.S., 1966. Budget analyst U.S. Treasury Dept., Washington, 1963-68; fin. mgr. AID, Washington, 1968-69; fin. mgr. U.S. Dept. Justice, Washington, 1969-74, dep. asst. atty. gen., 1977-84, dep. assoc. atty. gen., 1984-85; mgmt. cons., 1985—; mgmt. advisor Va. Commn. on State Govt. Mgmt., Richmond, 1974-76. Served with U.S. Army, 1954-56. Methodist. Office: 2526 E Meredith Dr Vienna VA 22181-4038

VAN STEENWYK, JOHN JOSEPH, health care plan consultant, educator; b. Mpls., July 25, 1931; s. Elmer Arnold and Marion Ione (Thompson) van S.; m. Janice Kevin Sharp, July 11, 1959; children: Jennifer Lee, Edward Arnold, Julie Ann. AB, Oberlin Coll., 1953; MBA, U. Pa., 1955. V.p., cons. The Segal Co., N.Y.C., 1957-81; pres. Health Econs., Inc., Spring House, Pa., 1982—; clin. asst. prof. cmty. and preventive medicine, N.Y. Med. Coll., Valhalla, N.Y., 1980—. With USN, 1955-57. Mem. APHA, Assn. for Health Svcs. Rsch, Am. Assn. Health Plans. Episcopalian. Avocations: gardening, woodchopping. Home: 921 E Tennis Ave Ambler PA 19002 Office: Health Economics Inc 768 N Bethlehem Pike Spring House PA 19477

VANSTROM, MARILYN JUNE, retired elementary education educator; b. Mpls., June 10, 1924; d. Harry Clifford and Myrtle Agnes (Hagland) Christensen; m. Reginald Earl Vanstrom, Mar. 20, 1948; children: Gary Alan, Kathryn June Vanstrom Marinello. AA, U. Minn., 1943, BS, 1946. Cert. elem. tchr., N.Y., Ill. Tchr. Pub. Sch., St. Louis Park, Minn., 1946-47, Deephaven, Minn., 1947-50, Chicago Heights, Ill., 1950-52, Steger, Ill., 1964; substitute tchr. Pub. Sch., Dobbs Ferry, N.Y., 1965-72, Yonkers, N.Y., 1965-92. Mem. Ch. Women, Christ Meml. Luth. Ch. Mem. AAUW (life, pres. 1988-90, Ednl. Found. award 1990, Morning Book Club, Evening Book Club Met. West br. Minn.s, So. Westchester br. N.Y.), Yonkers Fedn. Tchrs. Democrat. Avocations: painting, sketching, choir, piano, travel. Home: 12300 Marion Ln W Apt 2105 Minnetonka MN 55305-1317

VAN SWOL, NOEL WARREN, secondary education educator; b. N.Y.C., Dec. 30, 1941; s. Erwin Anton and Hildegard van S.; BA, Am. U., 1964; MA, Columbia U., 1967; MS, Syracuse U., 1972. Asst. underwriter Comml. Union Ins. Group Ltd., N.Y.C., 1964-66; tchr. social studies jr. high sch., Bklyn., 1966-67, Liberty (N.Y.) Cen. High Sch., 1967-69; instr. student personnel Sullivan County (N.Y.) C.C., 1969-70; tchr. social studies E. Syracuse-Minoa (N.Y.) H.S., 1970—, coord. social studies, 1976—; adj. prof. history & govt. Columbia Coll. Residence Edn. Ctr., 1990—; adj. instr. pub. affairs Syracuse U., 1990—, adj. instr. econ., 1992—; cons. to trainer of tchr. trainers project Syracuse U., 1971-74. Contbr. articles to profl. jours. V.p. Fremont (N.Y.) Taxpayers and Civic Assn., 1971; mem. Town of Fremont Rep. Vacancy Com., 1967, 73, 74, 78, 80, 81, 83; ; bd. dirs. Project Legal, 1983-84; candidate Teacher in Space Project. Tchr. Leadership Devel. fellow, 1971, Freedoms Found. fellow, 1986, 87. Mem. ASCD, Am. Hist. Assn., N.Y. State Hist. Assn., Am. Polit. Sci. Assn., Ind. Landholders Assn. (v.p. 1992-96, pres. 1996—), N.Y. State, Cen. N.Y. Councils Social Studies, Social Studies Suprs. Assn., Orgn. Am. Historians, Soc. for History Edn., Upper Delaware Scenic River Assn., Upper Del. Coalition Concerned Citizens, Nat. Inholders Assn., Upper Del. Citizens Alliance, Western Sullivan County Taxpayers Assn., Sch. Adminstrs. Assn. N.Y. State. Home: 91 Viaduct Rd Long Eddy NY 12760-5043

VAN TAMELEN, EUGENE EARLE, chemist, educator; b. Zeeland, Mich., July 20, 1925; s. Gerrit and Henrietta (Vanden Bosch) van T.; m. Mary Ruth Houtman, June 16, 1951; children: Jane Elizabeth, Carey Catherine, Peter Gerrit. A.B., Hope Coll., 1947, D.Sc., 1970; M.S., Harvard, 1949, Ph.D., 1950; D.Sc., Bucknell U., 1970. Instr. U. Wis., 1950-52, from asst. to asso. prof., 1952-59, prof., 1959-61, Homer Adkins prof. chemistry, 1961-62; prof. chemistry Stanford, 1962-87, prof. emeritus chemistry, 1987—, chmn. dept., 1974-78; Am.-Swiss Found. lectr., 1964. Mem. editorial adv. bd.: Chem. and Engring. News, 1968-70, Synthesis, 1969-91, Accounts of Chem. Research, 1970-73; editor: Bioorganic Chemistry, 1971-82. Recipient A.T. Godfrey award, 1947; G. Haight traveling fellow, 1957; Guggenheim fellow, 1965, 73; Leo Hendrik Baekeland award, 1965; Prof. Extraordinarius Netherlands, 1967-73. Mem. NAS, Am. Chem. Soc. (Pure Chemistry award 1961, Creative Work in Synthetic Organic Chemistry award 1970), Am. Acad. Arts and Scis., English-Speaking Union (patron 1990-92), Rolls Royce Owners Club (bd. dirs. 1996—), Churchill Club (bd. dirs. 1990-92, vice chmn. 1991-92), Los Altos Tomorrow (bd. dirs. 1991—). Home: 23570 Camino Hermosa Dr Los Altos CA 94024-6407

VAN TASSEL, JAMES HENRY, retired electronics executive; b. LaCrosse, Wis., Feb. 15, 1929; s. John Henry and Agnes Cecilia (Anderson) Van T.; m. Mary Louise Carman, Dec. 23, 1961; children: John, James. B.S., U. Wis.-LaCrosse, 1951; M.S., Tex. Tech. Coll., 1957, Ph.D., 1959. Postdoctoral fellow Princeton U., N.J., 1959-60; mem. tech. staff, mgr. Tex. Instruments Co., Dallas, 1960-80; v.p. microelectronics div. NCR Corp., Dayton, Ohio, 1980-91; ret., 1991. Contbr. articles to profl. jours.; patentee in field. Bd. dirs. Dayton Philharm. Orch., 1983-89. Recipient Florilege d'Or Am Ecia, Paris, 1976, Disting. Alumnus award U. Wis.-LaCrosse, 1979, Holley medal ASME, 1989. Episcopalian.

VAN TASSEL-BASKA, JOYCE LENORE, education educator; b. Toledo, July 28, 1944; d. Robert Rae and Eleanor Jane (Kenyon) Sloan; m. Thomas Harold Van Tassel, May 21, 1964 (div. 1975); m. Leland Karl Baska, July 25, 1980; 1 child, Ariel Sloan. BEd cum laude, U. Toledo, 1966, MA, MEd, 1969, EdD, 1981. Tchr. Toledo Pub. Schs., 1965-72, coord. gifted programs, 1973-76; dir. Ill. gifted program Ill. State Bd. Edn., Springfield, 1976-79; dir., area svc. ctr. Matteson (Ill.) Sch. Dist., 1979-82; dir. Ctr. for Talent Devel. Northwestern U., Evanston, Ill., 1982-87; Smith prof. edn. Coll. William and Mary, Williamsburg, Va., 1987—; dir. Ctr. for Gifted Edn. Coll. William and Mary, Williamsburg, 1988—; mem. Va. Adv. Bd. on Gifted and Talented, 1988—; mem. State Ohio Adv. Bd. Gifted and Talented, 1975-76; mem. edn. coun. Nat. Bus. Consortium, 1981-84. Mem. editorial bd. Roeper Rev., 1980-82; pub. Talent Devel. Quar., 1983-87; manuscript rev. editor Jour. Edn. of Gifted, 1981—; mem. editorial adv. bd. Critical Issues in Gifted Edn. series; mem. editorial bd. Gifted Child Quar., 1984—, Jour. Advanced Devel.; column editor Understanding the Gifted Newsletter author 8 books; contbr. chpts. and over 200 articles to profl. jours. Bd. trustees Lourdes High Sch., Chgo., 1985-86. Recipient Outstanding Faculty award State Coun. Higher Edn. Va., 1993; grantee U.S. Office Edn., 1977-78, 78-79, 89—, Ill. State Bd. Edn., 1979-82, 84-91, Richardson Found., 1986, 89, Fry Found., 1987-90, Va. State Coun. Higher Edn., 1987-89, 90-91, 93-95, Bur. Indian Affairs, 1989, Hughes Found., 1989-94, Va. State Libr., 1989-90, Va. State Dept. Edn., 1990-93, 93-95, Funding Agy. U.S. Dept. Edn., 1989—, 90-93, 93-95; eminent scholar Coll. William and Mary, 1987—, Nat. Ednl. policy fellow U.S. Office Edn., 1979-80, Paul Witty fellow in gifted edn., 1979, Outstanding Rsch. Paper award Mensa, 1995. Mem. ASCD, Nat. Assn. Gifted Children (bd. dirs. 1984-90), Coun. Exceptional Children, Assn. for Gifted (pres. 1980-81), World Coun. on Gifted, Am. Ednl. Rsch. Assn., Phi Beta Kappa, Phi Delta Kappa (pres. Northwestern chpt. 1986-87). Avocations: photography, tennis, writing. Home: 225 Richard Burbydge Williamsburg VA 23185-5115 Office: Coll William and Mary Jones Hall Williamsburg VA 23185

VAN'T HOF, WILLIAM KEITH, lawyer; b. N.Y.C., Feb. 18, 1930; s. William and Nell (DeValois) Van't H.; m. Barbara Marie Rogers, Oct. 6, 1961; children: Sarah Lynn, David Edward. BA, Hope Coll., 1951; LLB, U. Mich., 1954. Bar: Mich. 1954, Conn. 1955, U.S. Dist. Ct. (we. dist.) Mich. 1956, U.S. Ct. Appeals (6th cir.) 1956. Assoc. Gumbart, Corbin, Tyler & Cooper, New Haven, 1954-56; ptnr. McCobb, Heaney & Van't Hof, Grand Rapids, Mich., 1959-72, Schmidt, Howlett, Van't Hof, Smell & Vana, Grand Rapids, 1972-82, Varnum, Riddering, Schmidt & Howlett, Grand Rapids, 1983—; mem. faculty Inst. Continuing Legal Edn., Ann Arbor, Mich., 1974—. Chmn. Mich. Heart Assn., 1973-75; pres. United Way Kent County, 1979-80, hon. life mem., 1986—; chmn. Am. Heart Assn., Dallas, 1989-90. Mem. ABA, State Bar Mich. (grievance and arbitration panel 1970-91, 94—, chmn. com. on coops. and condos. 1982-86), Grand Rapids Bar Assn. (trustee 1965-67), West Mich. Hort. Soc. (pres. 1992-93), Cascade Hills Country Club, Univ. Club. Home: 3160 Hall St SE Grand Rapids MI 49506-3171 Office: Varnum Riddering Schmidt & Howlett 333 Bridge St NW Grand Rapids MI 49504-5356

VAN TIL, WILLIAM, education educator, writer; b. Corona, N.Y., Jan. 8, 1911; s. William Joseph and Florence Alberta (MacLean) Van T.; m. Beatrice Barbara Blaha, Aug. 24, 1935; children: Jon, Barbara, Roy. BA in Polit. Sci., Swarthmore Coll., 1933; MA in Sociology, U. N.C., 1935; PhD, U. Calif., Berkeley, 1946. Tchr. N.Y. State Tng. Sch. for Boys, 1933-34; instr. dept. univ. schs. Coll. Edn., Ohio State U., 1934-36, asst. prof., 1936-43, on leave, 1943-45; researchist, writer Consumer Edn. Study NEA, 1943-44; dir. learning materials Bur. Intercultural Edn., 1944-47; prof. edn. U. Ill., 1947-51; prof. edn., chmn. div. curriculum and teaching George Peabody Coll. Tchrs., Nashville, 1951-57; prof. edn., chmn. dept. secondary edn. N.Y. U., 1957-66, head div. secondary and higher edn., 1966-67; Coffman disting. prof. edn. Ind. State U., Terre Haute, 1967-77, prof. emeritus, 1977; dir. univ. workshops Writing for Profl. Publs., 1978—; founder Lake Lure Press, 1983. Author: The Danube Flows Through Fascism, Economic Roads for American Democracy, The Making of a Modern Educator, Modern Education for the Junior High School Years, The Year 2000: Teacher Education, One Way of Looking At It, Education: A Beginning, Another Way of Looking At It, Van Til on Education, Secondary Education: School and Community, Writing for Professional Publication, rev., 1986, Mapping the Third Sector: Voluntarism in a Changing Social Economy, Critical Issues in American Philanthropy; autobiography My Way of Looking At It, 1983, expanded 2d edit., 1996; Sketches, 1989; editor: Forces Affecting American Education, Curriculum: Quest for Relevance, ASCD in Retrospect, 1986; author and subject: Teachers and Mentors: Profiles of Distinguished Twentieth Century Professors of Education, 1996; co-editor: Democratic Human Relations, Intercultural Attitudes in the Making, Education in American Life; adv. editor Houghton Mifflin, 1964-70; interviewed in Social Education, 1989; editor-in-chief Nonprofit and Voluntary Sector Quar., 1979-92; contbr. to numerous other publs. including Saturday Rev., Woman's Day, Parents; author articles, reviews and editorials; columnist: Ednl. Leadership, Contemporary Edn., Kappan; adv. bd. Profl. Educator, 1984-95. Mem. Ill. Interracial Commn., 1949-51; moderator Nashville Sch. desegregation meetings, 1955-57; mem. adv. bd. Jour. Tchr. Edn., 1956-59; co-organizer Nashville Community Rels. Conf., 1956; cons. Phelps-Stokes Fund project, 1958-62; mem. staff P.R. Edn. Survey, 1958-59, Iran Tchr. Edn. Survey, 1962, V.I. Edn. Survey, 1964; lectr. abroad, 1974; mem. staff U. Ind. Phi Delta Kappa Inst., 1984-90; 1st Ann. Van Til lectr. Ind. State U., 1989. Recipient Centennial Achievement award, Ohio State U., 1970; awards N.J. Collegiate Press Assn., 1962; N.J. Assn. Tchrs. English, 1962; inducted into Edn. Hall of Fame, Ohio State U., 1989; Annual Van Til Lectr. Series, Ind. State U., est. 1989, est. Annual Van Til Writing award, 1989. Mem. John Dewey Soc. (v.p. 1957-60, acting pres. 1958-59, pres. 1964-66, award 1977, 86, Outstanding Achievement award 1991), Assn. Supervision and Curriculum Devel. (dir. 1951-54, 57-60, pres. 1961-62, chmn. res. council 1972-73, resolutions com. 1982-85), United Educators (chmn. bd. educators 1969-77), Nat. Soc. Coll. Tchrs. Edn. (pres. 1967-68), Am. Edn. Studies Assn. (editorial bd. 1970-77), Asso. Orgn. Tchr. Edn. (adv. council 1967-73, chmn. issues tchr. edn. 1972-73), Nat. Soc. Study Edn. (editor Yearbook Issues in Secondary Edn. 1976), Kappa Delta Pi (laureate 1980—, chmn. book-of-yr. com. 1984-86). Home: 1020 E Spence Ave Terre Haute IN 47803-9712 *As an educator and writer, I believe that mankind's best hope is education which meets individual needs, illuminates social realities, fosters democratic values and utilizes relevant knowledge.*

VAN TUYL, CECIL L., investment company executive. Chmn., pres., CEO VT Inc., Merriam, Kans. Office: V T Inc PO Box 795 Shawnee Mission KS 66201*

VAN TUYLE, GREGORY JAY, nuclear engineer; b. Chgo., Feb. 19, 1953; s. Willard D. and Mary E. (Kershner) Van T.; m. Frances A. Weinstein, Aug. 16, 1994; 1 child, William Steven. BSE magna cum laude, U. Mich., 1975, MSE, 1976, PhD of Nuclear Engring., 1978. From dep. divsn. head to program mgr. Brookhaven Nat. Lab., Upton, N.Y., 1978—. Contbr. articles to profl. jours. Mem. ASME, Am. Nuc. Soc. (Reactor Safety divsn. program com. sec. to vice-chmn. 1991-96, chmn. 1996-97, past pres., v.p., treas. L.I. chpt. 1979-97, founder and chair Accelerator Applications Tech. Group 1996—), Am. Phys. Soc., Brookhaven Nat. Lab. Toastmasters (pres., v.p. 1990-95, awards 91, 92, 94). Achievements include performing computer simulation of Chernobyl-4 accident based on Soviet explanation prior to release of Soviet analyses, subsequently cross-comparing analyses, confirming similarities and evaluating differences. Office: Brookhaven Nat Lab Bldg 197 D Upton NY 11973-5000

VAN TYNE, ARTHUR MORRIS, geologist; b. Syracuse, N.Y., Aug. 12, 1925; s. Roy Hanford and Isabelle Marguerite (Hoag) Van T.; m. Patricia Wilson Boyd, July 13, 1946; children: Judith, Cynthia, Mark, Peter. AB, Syracuse U., 1951, MS, 1958. Cert. petroleum geologist; lic. geologist, Pa. Field asst. Syracuse U. Rsch. Inst., 1951-53; geologist Shell Oil Co., Rockies, Gulf Coast, 1953-57; sr. geologist-in-charge N.Y. State Geol. Survey-Oil and Gas Rsch. Office, Wellsville and Alfred, N.Y., 1958-81; geol. cons. Van Tyne Cons., Wellsville, N.Y.C., 1981—; gov. appointee mem. N.Y. State Oil, Gas, and Solution Mining Adv. Bd., 1996. Contbr. articles to profl. jours. Bd. dirs. Jones Meml. Hosp., Wellsville, 1974—, bd. chmn. 1986-95, dir. Wellsville United Way, 1968-80, pres. 1974-75; dep. mayor Village of Wellsville, 1992—; committeeman Rep. Party, 1962-77. Recipient Cert. of Appreciation Am. Petroleum Inst., 1975, 80, Award of Merit Internat. Oil Scouts Assn. and Appalachian Sect., 1961, 66, 88. Mem. N.Y. Acad. Scis., Am. Assn. Petroleum Geologists (sec., dir. 1989-91, Disting. Svc. award Ea. sect. 1987, hon. mem. Ea. sect., Nat. Disting. Svc. award 1994, nat. hon. mem.), Russian Assn. Oil and Gas Geologists, N.Y. State Oil Producers Assn. (dir., exec. com. 1980, Svc. award 1981), Ind. Oil and Gas Assn. N.Y. (pres. 1985-88), No. Appalachian Geol. Soc. (pres. 1966-68), Geol. Soc. Am., Wellsville Rotary Club (pres. 1979-80, Paul Harris fellow 1994). Achievements include discoveries of gas production from queenston formation in N.Y., discovered Bass Islands thrust structure, a major oil and gas producer in N.Y. and Pa.; contributed for N.Y. State to Appalachian Gas Atlas. Home: 24 Oak St Wellsville NY 14895 Office: Van Tyne Cons 159 1/2 N Main St Wellsville NY 14895-1149

VAN UMMERSEN, CLAIRE A(NN), academic administrator, biologist, educator; b. Chelsea, Mass., July 28, 1935; d. George and Catherine (Courtovich); m. Frank Van Ummersen, June 7, 1958; children: Lynn, Scott. BS, Tufts U., 1957, MS, 1960, PhD, 1963; DSc (hon.), U. Mass., 1988, U. Maine, 1991. Rsch. asst. Tufts U., 1957-60, 60-67, grad. asst. in embryology, 1962, postdoctoral teaching asst., 1963-66, lectr. in biology, 1967-68; asst. prof. biology U. Mass., Boston, 1968-74; assoc. prof. U. Mass., 1974-86, assoc. dean acad. affairs, 1975-76, assoc. vice chancellor acad. affairs, 1976-78, chancellor, 1978-79, dir. Environ. Sci. Ctr., 1980-82; assoc. vice chancellor acad. affairs Mass. Bd. Regents for Higher Edn., 1982-85, vice chancellor for mgmt. systems and telecommunications, 1985-86; chancellor Univ. System N.H., Durham, 1986-92; sr. fellow New Eng. Bd. Higher Edn., 1992-93; sr. fellow New Eng. Resource Ctr. Higher Edn. U. Mass., 1992-93; pres. Cleve. (Ohio) State U., 1993—; cons. Mass. Bd. Regents, 1981-82, AGB, 1992—, Kuwait U., 1992-93; asst. Lancaster Course in Ophthalmology, Mass. Eye. and Ear Infirmary, 1962-69, lectr., 1970-93, also coord.; reviewer HEW; mem. rsch. team which established safety stds. for exposure to microwave radiation, 1958-65; participant Leadership Am. program, 1992-93. Mem. N.H. Ct. Systems Rev. Task Force, 1989-90; mem. New Eng. Bd. Higher Edn., 1986-92, mem. exec. com., 1989-92, N.H. adv. coun., 1990-92; chair Rhodes Scholarship Selection Com., 1986-91; bd. dirs. N.H. Bus. and Industry Assn., 1987-90, 90-93; governing bd. N.H. Math. Coalition, 1991-92; exec. com. 21st Century Learning Community, 1992-93; state panelist N.H. Women in Higher Edn., 1986-93; bd. dirs. Urban League Greater Cleve., 1993—, mem. strategic planning com., chair edn. com., 1996—, sec., exec. com., 1997—; bd. dirs. Great Lakes Sci. & Tech. Ctr., 1993—, Sci. & Tech. Coun. Cleve. Tomorrow, Ohio Aerospace Inst., 1993— (also exec. com.), Northeast Ohio Coun. Higher Edn., 1993—; mem. Leadership Cleve. Class '95; strategic planning com. United Way, 1996—; mem. Gov.'s Coun. on Sci. and Tech., 1996—. Recipient Disting. Svc. medal U. Mass., 1979, Am. Cancer Soc. grantee Tufts U., 1960. Mem. Am. Coun. on Edn. (com. on self-regulation 1987-91), State Higher Exec. Officers (fed. rels. com., cost accountability task force, exec. com. 1990-92), ACE (com. leadership devel.), Nat. Assn. Sys. Heads (exec. com. 1990-92), Nat. Ctr. for Edn. Stats. (network adv. com. 1989-92, chair accreditation teams 1988—), New Eng. Assn. Schs. and Colls. (commn. on higher edn. 1990-93), North Ctrl. Assn. Schs. and Colls. (evaluator 1993—), Soc. Devel. Biology, Greater Cleve. Round Table (bd. dirs. 1993—, exec. com. 1995), Cleve. Playhouse (trustee 1994—), United Way (bd. dirs. 1995—), Nat. Assn. State Univs. and Land Grant Colls. (exec. com. on urban agenda, state rep. AASCU, bd. dirs. AASCU 1996), Phi Beta Kappa, Sigma Xi. Office: Cleve State Univ Rhodes Tower Euclid Ave at E 24th St Cleveland OH 44115

VAN VALEN, LEIGH MAIORANA, biologist, educator; b. Albany, N.Y., Aug. 12, 1935; s. A. Donald and Eleanor (Williams) Van V.; m. Phebe May Hoff, 1959; children: Katrina, Diana; m. Virginia C. Maiorana, 1974. B.A., Miami U., Ohio, 1956; M.A., Columbia U., 1957, Ph.D., 1961. Boese postdoctoral fellow Columbia U., N.Y.C., 1961-62; NATO and NIH fellow Univ. Coll. London, 1962-63; with Am. Mus. Natural History, N.Y.C., 1963-66; asst. prof. anatomy U. Chgo., 1967-71, assoc. prof. evolutionary biology & conceptual founds. sci., 1971-73, assoc. prof. biology & conceptual founds. of sci., 1973-76, prof. biology and conceptual founds. of sci., 1976-88, prof. ecology, evolution, conceptual founds. sci., 1988—; research assoc. dept. geology Field Mus., Chgo., 1971—. Author: Deltatheridia, A New Order of Mammals, 1966, Paleocene Dinosaurs or Cretaceous Ungulates in South America?, 1988, The Origin of the Plesiadapid Primates and the Nature of Purgatorius, 1994; editor: Evolutionary Theory, 1973—, Evolutionary Monographs, 1977—; mem. editl. bd. Jour. Molecular Evolution, 1970-76, Evolución Biológica, 1988—; mem. editl. bd. commentators Behavioral and Brain Scis., 1978—; assoc. editor Evolution, 1969-71. Mem. nat. adv. bd. Voice of Reason, N.Y., 1981—. NIH Research Career Devel. awardee, 1967-72; NSF grantee, 1963-71; others. Mem. AAUP (pres. U. Chgo. chpt.), Soc. Study Evolution (v.p. 1973, 80), Am. Soc. Naturalists (v.p. 1974-75), Paleontol. Soc. (councillor 1980-82), Internat. Soc. Cryptozoology (bd. dirs.), Ecol. Soc. Am. Office: Univ Chgo Dept Ecology and Evolution 1101 E 57th St Chicago IL 60637-1503

VAN VALKENBURG, EDGAR WALTER, lawyer; b. Seattle, Jan. 8, 1953; s. Edgar Walter and Margaret Catherine (McKenna) Van V.; m. Turid L. Owren, Sept. 29, 1990; children: Ingrid Catherine, Andrew Owren. BA, U. Wash., 1975; JD summa cum laude, Willamette Coll. of Law, 1978; LLM, Columbia U., 1984. Bar: Oreg. 1978, U.S. Dist. Ct. Oreg. 1979, U.S. Ct. Appeals (9th cir.) 1980. Law clk. to assoc. justice Oreg. Supreme Ct., Salem, 1978-79; assoc. Stoel, Rives, Boley, Fraser & Wyse, Portland, Oreg., 1979-82, 84-86; ptnr. Stoel Rives LLP, Portland, Oreg., 1986—; instr. Columbia U., N.Y.C., 1982-84. Editor-in-chief: Williamette Law Jour. 1977-78. Mem. ACLU (pres. Oreg. chpt. 1991-93), Oreg. State Bar (chmn. antitrust sect. 1989-90, mem. Ho. of Dels. 1996—). Office: Stoel Rives LLP 900 SW 5th Ave Ste 2300 Portland OR 97204-1235

VAN VALKENBURG, MAC ELWYN, retired electrical engineering educator; b. Union, Utah, Oct. 5, 1921; s. Charles Mac and Nora (Walker) Van V.; m. Evelyn J. Pate, Aug. 27, 1943; children: Charles Mac II, JoLynne, Kaye, David R., Nancy J., Susan L. B.S. in Elec. Engring, U. Utah, 1943; M.S., Mass. Inst. Tech., 1946; Ph.D., Stanford, 1952. With Radiation Lab., Mass. Inst. Tech., 1943-45, Research Lab. Electronics, 1945-46; mem. faculty U. Utah, 1946-55, U. Ill., 1955-66; prof. elec. engring. Princeton, 1966-74, chmn. dept., 1966-72; prof. elec. engring. U. Ill., Urbana, 1974—, acting dean Coll. Engring., 1984-85, dean Coll. Engring., 1985-88, dean emeritus, 1988—; ret., 1988; vis. prof. Stanford, U. Colo., U. Calif., Berkeley, U. Hawaii, Manoa, 1978-79, U. Ariz., 1982-83. Author: Network Analysis, 3d edit, 1974, Introduction to Modern Network Synthesis, 1960, Introductory Signals and Circuits, 1967, Signals in Linear Circuits, 1974, Circuit Theory: Foundations and Classical Contributions, 1974, Linear Circuits, 1982, Analog Filter Design, 1982; editor-in-chief: IEEE Press, 1983-86. Recipient Disting. Alumni award U. Utah, 1991. Fellow IEEE (v.p., bd. dirs. 1969-73, editor transactions 1960-63, proc. 1966-69, Edn. medal 1972, Cirs. medal 1987), Am. Soc. Engring. Edn. (George Westinghouse award 1963, Benjamin Garver Lamme award 1978, Guillemin prize 1978, Hall of Fame 1993, Centennial Medallion 1993); mem. NAE, Sigma Xi, Tau Beta Pi, Phi Kappa Phi. Home: 2609 SW 64th Pl Portland OR 97225-3168

VAN VLACK, LAWRENCE HALL, engineering educator; b. Atlantic, Iowa, July 21, 1920; s. Claude H. and Ruth (Stone) Van V.; m. Frances E. Runnells, June 27, 1943; children: Laura R., Bruce H. B.S. in Ceramic Engring., Iowa State U., 1942; Ph.D. in Geology, U. Chgo., 1950. Registered profl. engr., Mich. With U.S. Steel Co., 1942-53; mem. faculty U. Mich., 1953—, prof. materials sci. and engring., 1958—, chmn. dept., 1967-73; cons. in field. Author: Nature and Behavior of Engineering Materials, 1956, Elements of Materials Science, 2d edit., 1964, Physical Ceramics for Engineers, 1964, Materials Science for Engineers, 1970, Textbook of Materials Technology, 1973, Materials Science and Engineering, 1975, 6th edit., 1989, Aids for Introductory Materials Courses, 1977, Nickel Oxide, 1980, Materials for Engineering, 1982, Materials for Thermal Management, 1992. Served with USNR, 1945-46. Recipient PACE award Iowa State U., 1993. Fellow AAAS, ASEE, Am. Soc. Metals (Sauveur lectr. 1979, Gold medal 1984, A.E. White Disting. Tchr. award 1985), Am. Ceramic Soc.; mem. AIME, Nat. Inst. Ceramic Engrs., N.Y. Acad. Scis., Sigma Xi, Tau Beta Pi, Alpha Chi Sigma, Alpha Sigma Mu (hon.), Phi Lambda Upsilon (Outstanding Teaching award 1963). Methodist. Address: 1700 Bronson Way Apt 322 Kalamazoo MI 49009-1084

VAN VLEET, WILLIAM BENJAMIN, retired lawyer, life insurance company executive; b. Milw., Dec. 4, 1924; s. William Benjamin and Irene (Peppey) Van V.; m. Marilyn Nilles, Dec. 26, 1946; children: Terese Van Vleet Svetich, Susan Van Vleet Waldo, William Benjamin III, Monica Van Vleet McCarthy, Mark. Student, Marquette U., 1942-43, Lawrence Coll., Appleton, Wis., 1943-44; LLB, JD, Marquette U., 1948. Bar: Wis. 1948, Ill. 1950. Gen. counsel George Rogers Clark Mut. Casualty Co., Rockford, Ill., 1948-59; gen. counsel Pioneer Life Ins. Co. Ill., Rockford, 1950-68, 81-94, v.p., 1959-91, gen. counsel, 1968-91, exec. v.p., 1981-95, also bd. dirs.; exec. v.p., gen. counsel Pioneer Fin. Svcs., Inc., Rockford, 1985-95, gen. counsel emeritus, dir., 1995-97; pres. Nat. Group Life Ins. Co., Rockford, 1992-93, exec. v.p., gen. counsel, 1993-94, also bd. dirs.; pres. Western Life Ins. Co. Am., Rockford, 1981-82, Health & Life Ins. Co. Am., Rockford, 1984-92, exec. v.p., gen. counsel, 1993-94; pres. Manhattan Nat. Life Ins. Co., Cin., 1990-92, exec. v.p., gen. counsel, 1993-94, also bd. dirs.; exec. v.p., gen. counsel Continental Life and Accident Co., Boise, Idano, 1993-94, also bd. dirs.; bd. dirs. Nat. Health Svcs. Milw. Mem. adminstrn. Boylan Ctrl. Cath. H.S., Rockford, 1965-72; pres. Diocesan Bd. Edn., Rockford, 1970-78; v.p., pres. Nat. Assn. Bds. Edn., 1972-78; v.p., pres. Nat. Assn. Bds. Edn., 1972-78; v.p., pres. Nat. Assn. Bds. Edn., 1972-78; mem. bd. advisors Marion Coll., 1976-79; mem. adv. bd. St. Anthony's Hosp., Rockford, 1978-91; bd. dirs. Crimestoppers, Rockford, 1982-90; co-chmn. United Cerebral Palsy Telethon, Rockford, 1985-95. Mem. ABA, Ill. Bar Assn., Winnebago County Bar Assn.

VAN VLIET, CAROLYNE MARINA, physicist, educator; b. Dordrecht, Netherlands, Dec. 27, 1929; emigrated to U.S., 1960, naturalized, 1967; d. Marinus and Jacoba (de Lange) Van V. BS, Free U. Amsterdam, Netherlands, 1949, MA, 1953, PhD in Physics, 1956. Rsch. fellow Free U. Amsterdam, 1950-54, rsch. assoc., 1954-56, asst. dir., 1958-60; postdoctoral fellow U. Minn., Mpls., 1956-57; faculty U. Minn., 1957-58, 60-70, prof. elec. engring. and physics, 1965-70; prof. theory physics U. Montreal, Que., Can., 1969-95; sr. rschr. math. rsch. ctr. U. Montreal, Que., 1969—; vis. prof. U. Fla., 1974, 78-88 (4 months annually); prof. elec. and computer engring. Fla. Internat. U., 1992—. Contbg. author: Fluctuation Phenomena in Solids, 1965; editor Proc. 9th Internat. Conf. Noise in Physical Systems, 1987; author numerous articles. Research grantee NSF; Research grantee Air Force OSR; Research grantee Nat. Sci. and Engring. Research Council, Ottawa. Fellow IEEE; mem. Am. Phys. Soc., Can. Phys. Soc., European Phys. Soc., N.Y. Acad. Scis., Am. Acad. Mid. Ea. Dance. Home: 9175 SW 77th Ave Apt 110 Miami FL 33156-7672 *The purpose of life is to honor God and to serve mankind.*

VAN VLIET, CLAIRE, artist; b. Ottawa, Ont., Can., Aug. 9, 1933; d. Wilbur Dennison and Audrey Ilene (Wallace) Van V. A.B., San Diego State Coll., 1952; M.F.A., Claremont Grad. Sch., 1954; DFA (hon.), U. of the Arts, Phila., 1993. Instr. printmaking Phila. Coll. Art, 1959-65; owner The Janus Press, 1954—; vis. lectr. printmaking U. Wis.-Madison, 1965-66; mem. bd. advisors Hand Papermaking. One-man exhbns. include Print Club Phila., 1963, 66, 73, 77, Wiggin Gallery, Boston Pub. Libr., 1977, Rutgers U. Art Gallery, 1978, AAA Gallery, Phila., 1980, Dolan/Maxwell Gallery, Phila., 1984, 91, Mary Ryan Gallery, N.Y.C., 1986, Mills Coll., 1986, U. of the Arts, Phila., 1989, Victoria and Albert Mus., London, 1994, Ottawa Sch. Art Gallery, Can., 1994, Bates Coll. Mus. of Art, Lewiston, Maine, 1994; group exhbns. include Bklyn. Nat., Phila. Arts Festival, Kunst zu Kafka, Germany, Paper as Medium, Smithsonian Instn., Washington, Paper Now, Cleve. Mus. Art, 1986, Boyle Arts Festival, Ireland, 1993; represented in permanent collections Nat. Gallery Art, Phila. Mus. Art, Boston Pub. Libr., Libr. of Congress, Cleve. Mus. Art, Montreal Mus. Fine Arts, Victoria and Albert Mus. London. NEA grantee, 1976-80, Ingram-Merrill Found. grantee, 1989; MacArthur fellow, 1989. Mem. Soc. Printers Boston, Nat. Acad. of Design. Address: RR 1 West Burke VT 05871-9801

VAN VOORST, ROBERT E., theology educator, minister; b. Holland, Mich., June 5, 1952; s. Robert Eugene and Donna Mae (Boeve) Van V.; m. Mary Lind Bos, June 15, 1974; children: Richard William, Nicholas John. BA, Hope Coll., 1974; MDiv, Western Sem., 1977; PhD, Union Sem., 1988. Ordained to ministry Classis of Holland Reformed Ch. in Am., 1977. Pastor Rochester Reformed Ch., Accord, N.Y., 1977-89; prof. religion Lycoming Coll., Williamsport, Pa., 1989—, dept. chair, 1997—; adj. prof. Susquehanna U., Selinsgrove, Pa., 1991, Bucknell U., Lewisburg, Pa., 1993; vis. prof. Westminster Coll., Oxford, Eng., 1997. Author: Ascents of James, 1989, Building New Testament Vocabulary, 1990, Anthology of World Scriptures, 1994, 2d edit., 1996, Readings in Christianity, 1996; co-author: Death of Jesus in Early Christianity, 1995; contbr. 6 articles Eerdmans Dictionary of the Bible, 1997; contbr. numerous articles to profl. jours. Mem. AAUP, Fairview Recreation Club, Phi Beta Kappa, Phi Kappa Phi, Eta Sigma Phi, Phi Sigma Iota. Avocations: golf, cooking. Home: 2371 Hillside Ave Williamsport PA 17701 Office: Lycoming Coll Box 3 Williamsport PA 17701

VAN VUGT, ERIC J., lawyer; b. Grand Rapids, Mich., Sept. 17, 1951; s. Ernest and Phyllis N. (Van Someren) Van V.; m. Wendy S. Yonker, June 3, 1972; children: Erin L., Heather J., Timothy D. BA, Calvin Coll., 1973; JD, Marquette Univ., 1976. Bar: Wis. 1976, U.S. Dist. Ct. (ea. and we. dist.) Wis. 1976, U.S. Dist. Ct. (we. dist.) Mich. 1993, U.S. Ct. Appeals (7th cir.) 1976, U.S. Ct. Appeals (fed. cir.) 1990, U.S. Supreme Ct. 1994. Assoc. Kluwin, Dunphy & Hankin, Milw., 1976-80; ptnr. Kluwin, Dunphy, Hankin & McNulty, Milw., 1980-85, Minahan & Peterson, Milw., 1985-91, Quarles & Brady, Milw., 1991—. Mem. ABA, State Bar Wis. Avocations: aviation, golf. Home: 14910 Hushing Brae Ct Brookfield WI 53005-2682 Office: Quarles & Brady 411 E Wisconsin Ave Milwaukee WI 53202-4409

VAN WACHEM, LODEWIJK CHRISTIAAN, petroleum company executive; b. Pangkalan Brandan, Indonesia, July 31, 1931; m. Elisabeth G. Cristofoli, June 10, 1958; 3 children. Degree Mech. Engring., Delft U., Delft, The Netherlands., 1953. With Bataafsche Petroleum Maatschappij, The Hague, The Netherlands, 1953; pres. Royal Dutch Petroleum Co., The Hague, The Netherlands, 1982-92; chmn. com. mng. dir. Royal Dutch/Shell Group, The Hague, The Netherlands, 1985-92; chmn. supr. bd. Royal Dutch Petroleum Co., The Hague, The Netherlands, 1992—; chmn. bd. dirs. Shell Oil Co. USA, 1982-92, De Nederlandsche Bank N.V., 1987-92; non-exec. dir. IBM Corp., Armonk, 1992—, Credit Suisse Holding, Zurich, 1992-96, ATCO Ltd., Calgary, 1993—, Zurich Versicherungs Gesellschaft, 1993—, AAB Brown Boveri Ltd., Zurich, 1996—; mem. supr. bd. AKZO Nobeln.v., Arnhem, 1992—, Philips Electronicsn.v., Eindhoven, 1993—, BMW A.G., Munich, 1994—, Bayer A.G., Leverkusen, 1997—; chmn. supervisory bd. Royal Dutch Petroleum Co., 1992—. Decorated C.B.E. (hon.), Knight Brit. Empire (hon.), Comdr. Order of Oranje Nassau, Knight Order Netherlands Lion. Office: Royal Dutch Petroleum Co, 30 Carel van Bylandtlaan, 2596 HR The Hague The Netherlands

VAN WAGONER, ROBERT LOUIS, lawyer; b. Lake Orion, Mich., June 4, 1936; s. Ray John and Gladys Elizabeth Van W.; m. Charlotte Robertson, June 10, 1968 (div. 1979); m. Mary Carlin Kaczor, Aug. 10, 1984. BS, Northwestern U., 1958; JD, Calif. We. U., 1966; cert., Nat. Jud. Coll., Reno, Nev., 1981. Bar: Nev. 1967, U.S. Dist. Ct. Nev. 1969, U.S. Supreme Ct. 1973. Commd. ensign USN, 1958; advanced through grades to lt., retired, 1963; asst. atty. City of Reno, 1967-69, city atty., 1971-78, 83-87; assoc. Law Offices Richard Fray, Reno, 1969-71; judge County of Washoe, Reno, 1979-82; pvt. practice Reno, 1987-88; adminstrv. law judge State of Nev. Bd. Med. Examiners, Reno, 1996—; adminstrv. atty. Pub. Svc. Commn. Nev., 1988—, adminstrv. law judge, 1989-95, adminstrv. law judge Nev. State Bd. Med. Examiners, 1996, judicial state leader Nat. Judicial Coll., 1992—. Author: Tort Liability for Firemen, 1986, (bulletin series) Reno Land Use Planning, 1983-87; editor: La Balanza Law Jour., 1963-66. Chmn. Dem. Com. County of Washoe, 1969-71; bd. dirs. Child Runaway Youth Svcs., Reno, 1987—, No. Nev. chpt. Multiple Sclerosis Soc., 1969— (citation of merit 1986); active on Nev. Crime Commn., Carson City, 1971-78; mem. Nat. Assn. of Transp. Practitioners, 1989—, Nat. Conf. State Trans. Specialists, 1990—, Nat. Assn. Administrv. Law Judges, 1992—, The Nat. Trust for Historic Preservation, 1994—; assoc. mem. Am. Mus. Nat. History, 1994—. Mem. ABA, Nev. Bar Assn., Am. Judicature Soc., U.S. Naval Inst., Elks, Masons, Prospectors, Jesters Reno Ct. (bd. dirs. 1984), Am. Legion, The Nat. Trust for Hist. Preservation, Am. Mus. of Nat. History, Nat. Assn. Transp. Practitioners, Nat. Jud. Coll. (state jud. leader 1992—), Nat. Assn. Adminstrv. Law Judges. Avocations: golf, fishing, home repair.

VAN WESTERING, JAMES FRANCIS, management consultant, educator; b. Bklyn., Dec. 7, 1940; s. Frederick Joseph and Agnes Teresa (Powell) Van W.; m. Karen Lyn Almy, Aug. 27, 1966. BA, Bklyn. Coll., 1963; MBA, Baruch Coll., 1972. Spl. asst. Fed. Res. Bank, N.Y.C., 1967-76; sr. cons. Coopers & Lybrand, N.Y.C., 1976-77; 2nd v.p. Chase Manhattan Bank, N.Y.C., 1977-78; pres. Internat. Comml. Sys., Inc., Forest Hills, N.Y., 1978—; dir. Nat. Data Corp., Atlanta, 1981-82; adj. asst. prof. Mgmt. Inst., N.Y.U., 1992—. Bd. dirs. Forest Hills (N.Y.) Gardens Corp., 1987-90; pres. N.Y. Forum on Ea. Europe, N.Y.C., 1991—; mem. exec. bd. Sister City program City of N.Y. and Budapest, Hungary, 1995. Served USMCR, 1959-60. Mem. Am. Econs. Assn., Electronic Banking Econs. Soc., Slovak-Am. C. of C. (mem. adv. bd. 1994—). Avocation: archtl. preservation. Home: 17 Ingram St Forest Hills NY 11375 Office: Internat Comml Sys Inc PO Box 4176 Parkside Sta Forest Hills NY 11375

VAN WINKLE, EDGAR WALLING, electrical engineer, computer consultant; b. Rutherford, N.J., Oct. 12, 1913; s. Winant and Jessie Walcott (Mucklow) Van W.; m. Jessie Stetler, Apr. 23, 1938 (dec. 1992); children: Barbara Van Winkle Clifton, Catrina Van Winkle Poindexter, Cornelia Van Winkle Schloss; m. Martha Polyé, May 22, 1993. B.E.E., Rutgers U., 1936; M.S. in Indsl. Engring., Columbia U., 1943, P.E. in Indsl. Engring., 1966. Registered profl. engr., N.J. Elec. engr. A.B. Dumont Labs. Passaic, N.J., 1943-48; chief engr. Facsimile Electronics, Passaic, 1948-52; cons. Bur. Ships, Washington, 1952; asst. sr. staff scientist Bendix Corp., Teterboro, N.J., 1952-67; sr. staff scientist Conrac Corp., West Caldwell, N.J., 1967-78; pres. Empac, Inc., Rutherford, N.J., 1979—. Contbr. articles, papers to profl. jours; patentee in field. Ruling elder Presbyterian Ch., Rutherford, 1984-91, chmn. endowment com., 1984—. Mem. IEEE (life, treas. artificial intelligence sect. North N.J. Chpt. 1982-84), Bendix Mgmt. Club (life), North N.J. Automatic Control Group (chmn. 1967-68), Met. Engring. Mgmt. (chmn. 1966-67), Mensa, Holland Soc., Green Pond Yacht Club (past commodore), Delta Phi. Republican. Club: Upper Montclair Country. Current work: Artificial intelligence and robotics. Subspecialty: Mathematical software. Address: 154 Lake End Rd Newfoundland NJ 07435-1207

VAN WINKLE, WESLEY ANDREW, lawyer, educator; b. Kansas City, Mo., Sept. 22, 1952; s. Willard and Cleone Verlee (O'Dell) Van W.; m. Ruth Kay Shelby, Apr. 10, 1984. B, U. Nebr., 1972; JD, San Francisco Law Sch., 1987. Bar: Calif. 1987, U.S. Dist. Ct. (no. dist.) Calif. 1987, U.S. Supreme Ct. 1994. Atty. Bagetelos & Fadem, San Francisco, 1987-91; pvt. practice Berkeley, Calif., 1991—; prof. law San Francisco Law Sch., 1990—; apptd. mem. Calif. Appellate Indigent Def. Oversight Adv. com., 1997—. Editor (legal newspaper/rev.) Res Ipsa Loquitur, 1986. Mem. Calif. Attys. for Criminal Justice, Calif. Appellate Def. Counsel (v.p., appellate indigent def. oversight adv. com.), San Francisco Law Sch. Alumni Assn., Delta Theta Phi. Democrat. Office: PO Box 5216 Berkeley CA 94705-0216

VAN WINKLE, WILLIAM, certified financial planner; b. Englewood, N.J., July 3, 1934; s. Marshall Jr. and Helen (Wescott) V.; m. Beverly Elsie Peterson, Sept. 9, 1956; children: Stuart Wilson, Ainsley Ann Hilfiger, Carrie Lee. BS in Mech. Engring. and Bus. Adminstrn., Lehigh U., 1957; MS in Fin. Svcs., The Am. Coll., Bryn Mawr, Pa., 1996. Cert. fin. planner, Coll. for Fin. Planning, 1985. Plant engr., ops. mgr. Procter and Gamble, N.Y., Ga., Kans., Calif., Ohio, 1957-67; ops. mgr. Sheffield Chem. div. Kraftco, Union, N.J., 1967-71; dir. mfg. USA C.R. Bard, Inc., Murray Hill, N.J., 1971-74; v.p. mfg. Estey Corp., Eatontown, N.J., 1974-79; pres. Van Winkle Assocs., Tinton Falls, N.J., 1979—. Host, prodr. (cable TV program) Financial Matters, 1980—; contbr. articles to profl. jours. Bd. dirs. VNA Ctrl. Jersey, Red. Bank, N.J., 1985—; trustee Greater Red Bank (N.J.) YMCA, 1986-93; past pres., trustee Brookdale C.C. Found., Lincroft, N.J. Mem. Inst. Cert. Fin. Planners, Internat. Assn. Fin. Planning (bd. dirs. ctrl. N.J. chpt. 1984-86), Am. Soc. CLU & Chartered Fin. Cons., (bd. dirs. ctr. N.J. chpt. 1986-91), Ctrl. N.J. Estate Planning Coun., Million Dollar Round Table (v.p. 1994-95), Past Commodore Shrewsbury Sailing & Yacht Club, N.J. Yacht Racing Assn., Navesink Country Club (Middletown, N.J.), Seabright (N.J.) Beach Club, Holland Soc. N.Y. (trustee 1996—), Jersey Shore Branch (pres. 1994—), others. Republican. Episcopalian. Avocations: sailing, walking, reading. Home: 41 Breezy Pt Little Silver NJ 07739-1703 Office: Van Winkle Assocs 776 Shrewsbury Ave Eatontown NJ 07724-3006

VAN WYCK, GEORGE RICHARD, insurance company executive; b. Wilmington, Vt., Feb. 6, 1928; s. Harold Wait Van Wyck and Ruth Anna Learnard; m. Jeanne Mildred Anderson, Apr. 17, 1948; children: Diana Lee Van Wyck Jenkins, Beryl Jeanne. BS in Math. cum laude, St. Lawrence U., 1953. Actuarial clk. Aetna Life Ins. Co., Hartford, Conn., 1953-55; with Am. Bankers Ins. Group, Miami, Fla., 1955-91, sec., bd. dirs., 1983-89, ret., 1991. Bd. dirs. Jr. Achievement of Greater Miami, 1966-83, pres., 1975-76; bd. dirs. Epworth Village Retirement Complex, Miami, 1966—; founding dir., pres. Brickel Children's Ctr., Miami, 1980-82; mem. pers. adv. bd., vice chmn. Dade County, Miami, 1987-89. With USAF, 1946-49. Fellow Life Office Mgmt. Inst.; mem. 1st United Meth. Ch. So. Miami, Phi Beta Kappa. Democrat. Methodist. Avocations: photography, golf, bridge. Home: 8455 SW 44th St Miami FL 33155-4126

VAN WYK, JUDSON JOHN, endocrinologist, pediatric educator; b. Maurice, Iowa, June 10, 1921; s. John Cornelius and Amelia Susan (Menning) Van W.; m. Persis Ruth Parker, June 8, 1944; children: Judith Parker, Persis Allen, Peter Menning, Judson John. AB, Hope Coll., 1943, ScD (hon.), 1979; postgrad. in biochemistry, St. Louis U., 1943-44; MD, Johns Hopkins U., 1948. Diplomate Am. Bd. Pediatrics. Intern Johns Hopkins Hosp., 1948-49, resident in pediatrics, 1949-50, fellow in pediatric endocrinology, 1953-55; resident in pediatrics Cin. Children's Hosp., 1951-52; investigator Nat. Heart Inst., 1953-55; asst. prof. pediatrics U. N.C. Sch. Medicine, 1955-59, assoc. prof., 1959-62, prof., 1962-91, prof. biology, 1987—, Kenan prof. pediatrics, 1975-91, prof. emeritus, 1992—, chief div. endocrinology, 1955-89, dir. tng. program in endocrinology and metabolism, 1962-89; mem. staff N.C. Meml. Hosp.; cons. Womack Army Hosp., Ft. Bragg, N.C., 1957-88; vis. scientist Karolinska Institutet, Stockholm, 1968-69; mem. div. cell biology Lineberger Cancer Rsch. Ctr., 1976—; vis. prof. basic med. scis. Mich. State U., 1984. Editor Progress in Growth Factor Research, 1988-94; mem. editl. bd. Jour. Clin. Endocrinology and Metabolism, 1956-71, editor, 1983-89; mem. editl. bd. Pediatrics, 1969-70; contbr. chpts. to books, articles to profl. jours. Mem. basic sci. adv. com. March Dimes, 1985-88. With USPHS, 1951-53. Recipient numerous fellowships and grants, Lauria honoris causa, U. Genoa, "To commemorate 500th Anniversary of Discovery of N. Am. by Christopher Columbus", 1992, O. Max

Gardner award Bd. Govs. U. N.C., 1980. Fellow Am. Acad. Pediatrics; mem. NIH (endocrine study sect. 1968-720, Endocrine Soc. (mem. coun. 1975-79, awards com. 1991-96, publs. com. 1996—, Fred Conrad Koch medal 1989), Soc. Pediatric Rsch., Am. Pediatric Soc., So. Soc. Clin. Investigation, Am. Fedn. Clin. Rsch., So. Soc. Pediatric Rsch., Lawson Wilkins Pediatric Endocrine Soc. (prs. 1976-77), Internat. Endocrine Soc. (ctrl. com. 1988—), La Sociedad Peruana de Pediatria (hon.), Sociedad Pediatrica de Trujillo (hon.), European Soc. for Pediatric Endocrinology (corr.), Japanese Pediatric Endocrine Soc. (hon.). Presbyterian. Home: 1020 Highland Woods Rd Chapel Hill NC 27514-4410 Office: U NC Sch Medicine Dept Pediatrics CB 7220 509 Burnett-Womack Chapel Hill NC 27599-7220

VAN WYLEN, GORDON JOHN, former college president; b. Grant, Mich., Feb. 6, 1920; s. John and Effa (Bierema) Van W.; m. Margaret E. DeWitt, Dec. 29, 1951; children—Elizabeth Ann Van Wylen Rudenga, Stephen John, Ruth Margaret Van Wylen Jasperse, David Gordon, Emily Jane Van Wylen Overway. A.B., Calvin Coll., 1942; B.S.E., U. Mich., 1942, M.S., 1947; Sc.D., MIT, 1951. Indsl. engr. duPont Co., 1942-43; instr. mech. engring. Pa. State U., 1946-48; asst. prof. mech. engring. U. Mich., 1951-55, assoc. prof., 1955-57, prof., 1957-72, chmn. dept., 1958-65, dean Coll. Engring., 1965-72; pres. Hope Coll., Holland, Mich., 1972-87, pres. emeritus, 1987—. Author: Thermodynamics, 1959, (with R.E. Sonntag) Fundamentals of Classical Thermodynamics, 1965, 4th edit., 1994, Fundamentals of Statistical Thermodynamics, 1966, Introduction to Thermodynamics, 1971, 3d edit., 1991, Encounter at Dea, 1994; contbr. articles to profl. jours. Trustee Van Andel Edn. Inst. Lt. USNR, 1943-46. Fellow ASME, AAAS; mem. Phi Beta Kappa (hon.), Sigma Xi, Tau Beta Pi, Phi Kappa Phi. Mem. Reform Ch. Am. Home: 817 Brook Village Dr Holland MI 49423-4641

VAN ZANTE, SHIRLEY M(AE), magazine editor; b. Elma, Iowa; d. Vernon E. and Georgene (Woodmansee) Borland; m. Dirk C. Van Zante. AA, Grandview Coll., 1950; BA, Drake U., 1952. Assoc. editor Mchts. Trade Jour., Des Moines, 1952-55; copywriter Meredith Pub. Co., Des Moines, 1955-60, book editor, 1960-67; home furnishings editor Better Homes and Gardens Spl. Interest Publs., Meredith Corp., 1967-74; home furnishing and design editor Better Homes and Gardens mag., 1974-89; writer, editl. cons., 1989—. Named Advt. Woman of Yr. in Des Moines, 1961; recipient Dorothy Dawe award, 1971, 73, 75, 76, 77, Dallas Market Ctr. award, 1983, So. Furniture Market Writer's award, 1984. Mem. Am. Soc. Interior Designers (press affiliate), Alpha Xi Delta. Address: 1905 74th St Des Moines IA 50322-5701

VAN ZANTEN, FRANK VELDHUYZEN, retired library system director; b. Heemstede, The Netherlands, Oct. 21, 1932; came to U.S., 1946, naturalized, 1953; s. Adrian V. and Cornelia (Van Eesteren) Van Z.; m. Lois Ruth Holkeboer, June 17, 1961; children—Kiki Maria, Lili Roxanne, Amy Suzanne. A.B., Calvin Coll., Mich., 1959; postgrad., U. Wash., 1960; M.A. in L.S, U. Mich., 1961. Cataloger, extension project asst. Mich. State Library, Lansing, 1961-62; dir. Dickinson County (Mich.) Library, 1962-65, Mid-Peninsula Library Fedn., Iron Mountain, Mich., 1963-65, St. Clair County (Mich.) Library, 1965-68, Tucson Pub. Library, 1968-73; library cons. Ill. State Library, Springfield, 1973-75; asso. dir. for library devel. Ill. State Library, 1975-78; dir. Mid-Hudson Library System, Poughkeepsie, N.Y., 1978-95; ret., 1996. Served with AUS, 1953-55. Mem. ALA, N.Y. Libr. Assn. Home: 138 Wilbur Blvd Poughkeepsie NY 12603-4635

VAN ZELST, THEODORE WILLIAM, civil engineer, natural resource exploration company executive; b. Chgo., May 11, 1923; s. Theodore Walter and Wilhelmina (Oomens) Van Z.; m. Louann Hurter, Dec. 29, 1951; children: Anne, Jean, David. B.S., U. Calif., Berkeley, 1944; BS in Naval Sci., Northwestern U., 1944, B.A.S., 1945, M.S. in Civil Engring., 1948. Registered profl. engr., Ill. Pres., Soil Testing Services, Inc., Chgo., 1948-52; pres. Soiltest, Inc., Chgo., 1948-78; chmn. bd. Soiltest, Inc., 1978-80; sec., dir. Exploration Data Cons., Inc., 1980-82; exec. v.p. Cenco Inc., Chgo., 1962-77; vice chmn. Cenco Inc., 1975-77, also dir., 1962-77; bd. dirs. Minann, Inc., Testing Sci., Inc., 26th St. Venture, Lunarè Ltd., Rsch. Park, Inc., Northwestern U., 1992-95, chmn. bd. dirs. Envirotech Svcs., Inc.1983-85; sec., bd. dirs. Van Zelst, Inc. Wadsworth, Ill., 1983—; pres., bd. dirs. Geneva-Pacific Corp., 1969-83, Geneva Resources, Inc., 1983-91. Treas. Internat. Road Fedn., 1961-64, sec., 1964-79, dir., 1973-88, vice chmn., 1980-87; pres. Internat. Road Edn. Found., 1978-80, 87-88, hon. life bd. dirs., 1988—; bd. dirs. Chgo. Acad. Scis., 1983-86, v.p., 1985-86, hon. dir., 1986—; bd. dirs. Pres.'s Assn., Chgo., 1985-86; mem. adv. bd. Mitchell Indian Mus., Kendall Coll., 1977-94. Lt. (j.g.) USNR, 1942-45. Recipient Service award Northwestern U., 1970, Merit award, 1974, Alumni medal, 1989, Svc. award U. Wis., 1971, La Sallian award, 1975. Mem. ASCE (Chgo. Civil Engr. of Yr., 1988), Nat. Soc. Profl. Engrs., Western Soc. Engrs., Evanston C. of C. (v.p. 1969-73), Ovid Esbach Soc. (pres. 1968-80), Northwestern U. Alumni Assn., Tau Beta Pi, Sigma Xi. Clubs: Economic, North Shore. Inventor engring. testing equipment for soil, rock, concrete and asphalt; co-inventor Swing-wing for supersonic aircraft. Home: 1213 Wagner Rd Glenview IL 60025-3297 Office: PO Box 126 Glenview IL 60025-0126

VARANASI, USHA, environmental scientist; b. Bassien, Burma. BS, U. Bombay, 1961; MS, Calif. Inst. Technology, 1964; PhD in Chemistry, U. Wash., 1968. Rsch. assoc. lipid biochemistry Oceanic Inst., Oahu, Hawaii, 1969-71, assoc. rsch. prof., 1971-75; supr. rsch. chemist and task mgr. Northwest Fisheries Ctr., 1975-87; dir. Environ. Conservation Divsn. Nat. Maring Fisheries Svc./Nat. Oceanic & Atmos. Adminstr., Seattle, 1987-93; rsch. prof. chemistry Seattle U., 1975—; dir. N.W. Fisheries Sci. Ctr., 1994—; vis. scientist Pioneer Rsch. Unit, Northwest Fisheries Ctr., nat. Marine Fisheries Svc., nat. oceanic & Atmospheric Adminstrn., Wash., 1969-72, rsch. chemist, 1975-80; from affil. assoc. to affil. prof. chem. U. Wash., 1980-88. Recipient Gold medal U.S. Dept. Commerce, 1993. Mem. AAAS. Office: Northwest Fisheries Sci Ctr 2725 Montlake Blvd E Seattle WA 98112-2013

VARCHETTA, FELIX R., advertising agency executive; b. Chgo., July 11, 1920; s. Vincent and Anne (Allegretti) V. BS in mktg., De Paul U., 1949; MBA, Northwestern U., 1952. Advt. & sales mgr. O-Cedar Corp., Chgo., 1951-62, Strom Becker Corp., Chgo., 1963-67; product mgr. Helene Curtis Industries, Chgo., 1962-63; account exec., owner Phil Varchetta & Assocs., Chgo., 1968—. 1st sgt. U.S. Army, 1942-46. Mem. Assn. Profl. Orchestra Leaders (bd. dirs.), Am. Philatelic Soc. Democrat. Roman Catholic. Avocations: reading, philately. Home: 5617 N Knox Ave Chicago IL 60646-6635 Office: Phil Varchetta & Assocs 5901 N Cicero Ave Ste 410 Chicago IL 60646-5711

VARCHMIN, THOMAS EDWARD, environmental health administrator; b. Chgo., Dec. 5, 1947; s. Arthur William and Laurie Eileen (Allen) V.; m. Beth Virginia Plank, Dec. 16, 1972; children: Jeffrey Thomas, Brian Arthur, Jennifer Beth, Matthew James. B.A., St. Mary's Coll., Winona, Minn., 1969; M.S., Western Ill. U., Macomb, 1977. Registered sanitarian, Wis. Virologist, microbiologist Chgo. Dept. Health, 1974-78; environ. health and safety mgr. Great Atlantic & Pacific Tea Co., Chgo., 1978-79; adminstr. occupational safety and environ. health Nat. Safety Council, Chgo., 1979-80; mgr. environ. health Lake County Health Dept., Waukegan, Ill., 1980-84, mgr. environ. health and pub. relations, 1984-87; mgr. environ. health Cook County Dept. Pub. Health, Oak Park, Ill., 1987-89, asst. dir. environ. health, mgr. intergovtl. rels., 1989—; environ. health cons. Editor: Food and Beverage Newsletter, Hospital and Health Care Newsletter, Trades and Services Newsletter, 1979-80. NSF grantee, 1968-69. Mem. Nat. Environ. Health Assn. (registered environ. health specialist), Ill. Environ. Health Assn. (registered environ. health practitioner), Nat. Safety Coun., Am. Soc. Microbiology, Anvil Club of Ill., Phi Mu Alpha, Delta Epsilon Sigma. Research on autumn food habits of game fish, behavioral and phys. devel. of barred owl nestlings in Ill. Office: Cook County Dept Pub Health 1010 Lake St Ste 300 Oak Park IL 60301-1133

VARDAMAN, JOHN WESLEY, lawyer; b. Montgomery, Ala., Apr. 22, 1940; s. John Wesley and Elizabeth (Merrill) V.; m. Marianne Fay, June 14, 1969; children: Thomas, Shannon, John Wesley III, Davis. BA, Washington & Lee U., 1962; JD, Harvard U., 1965. Bar: D.C. 1966, U.S. Dist. Ct. (D.C.) 1967, U.S. Supreme Ct. 1970. Law clk. to justice Hugo Black U.S. Supreme Ct., 1965-66; assoc. Wilmer, Cutler & Pickering, Washington, 1966-70; ptnr. Williams & Connolly, Washington, 1970—. Contbr. articles to profl. jours. Mem. ABA, Am. Coll. Trial Lawyers, William B. Bryant Am. Inn of Ct., Met. Club, Congl. Country Club (Bethesda, Md.), TPC Avenel. Baptist. Avocation: golf. Office: Williams & Connolly 725 12th St NW Washington DC 20005-3901

VARELLAS, SANDRA MOTTE, judge; b. Anderson, S.C., Oct. 17, 1946; d. James E. and Helen Lucille (Gilliam) Motte; m. James John Varellas, July 3, 1971; children: James John III, David Todd. BA, Winthrop U., 1968; MA, U. Ky., 1970, JD, 1975. Bar: Ky. 1975, Fla. 1976, U.S. Dist. Ct. (ea. dist.) Ky. 1975, U.S. Ct. Appeals (6th cir.) 1976, U.S. Supreme Ct. 1978. Instr. Midway Coll., Ky., 1970-72; adj. prof. U. Ky. Coll. Law, Lexington, 1976-78; instr. dept. bus. adminstrn. U. Ky., Lexington, 1976-78; atty. Varellas, Pratt & Cooley, Lexington, 1975-93; atty. Varellas & Pratt, Lexington, 1993—; Fayette County judge exec., Ky., 1980—; hearing officer Ky. Natural Resources and Environ. Protection Cabinet, Frankfort, 1984-88. Committeewoman Ky. Young Dems., Frankfort, 1977-80; pres. Fayette County Young Dems., Lexington, 1977; bd. dirs. Ky. Dem. Women's Club, Frankfort, 1980-84, bd. dirs., Bluegrass Estate Planning Coun., 1995—; grad. Leadership Lexington, 1981; chairwoman Profl. Women's Forum, Lexington, Ky., 1985-86, bd. dirs., 1984-87, Aequum award com, 1989-92; mem. devel. coun. Midway Coll., 1990-92; co-chair Gift Club Com., 1992. Named Outstanding Young Dem. Woman, Ky. Young Dems., Frankfort, 1977, Outstanding Former Young Dem., Ky. Young Dems., 1983. Mem. Ky. Bar Assn. (treas. young lawyers div. 1978-79, long range planning com., 1988-89), Fla. Bar, Fayette County Bar Assn. (treas. 1977-78, bd. govs. 1978-80), LWV (nominating com 1984-85), Greater Lexington C. of C. (legis. affairs com. 1994-95, bd. dirs. coun. smaller enterprises 1992-95). Club: The Lexington Forum (bd. dirs. 1996—), Lexington Philharm. Guild (bd. dirs. 1979-81, 86—), Nat. Assn. Women Bus. Owners (chmn. community liaison/govtl. affairs com. 1992-93), Lexington Network (bd. dirs. and sec. 1994—). Office: Varellas & Pratt 167 W Main St Ste 1310 Lexington KY 40507-1713

VARET, MICHAEL A., lawyer; b. N.Y.C., Mar. 9, 1942; s. Guster V. and Frances B. (Goldberg) V.; m. Elizabeth R. Varet, June 3, 1973; 3 children. BS in Econs., U. Pa., 1962; LLB, Yale U., 1965. Bar: N.Y. 1966, U.S. Supreme Ct. 1975, U.S. Dist. Ct. (ea. and so. dists.) N.Y. 1975, U.S. Tax Ct. 1975, U.S. Claims Ct. 1975, U.S. Ct. Appeals (2d cir.) 1975. Mem., chmn. Varet & Fink P.C. (formerly Milgrim Thomajan & Lee P.C.), N.Y.C., 1982-95; mem. firm Piper & Marbury LLP, N.Y.C., 1995—; dir. B. de Rothschild Found. for the Advancement of Science in Israel, 1986—; dir., sec. Am. Found. for Basic Rsch. in Israel, 1990—. Trustee Montefiore Med. Ctr., Bronx, N.Y., 1980-92, mem. exec. com., 1985-92; bd. dirs. Sem. Libr. Corp. Jewish Theol. Sem., N.Y.C., 1983-87, United Jewish Appeal-Fedn. Jewish Philanthropies of Greater N.Y., Inc., 1979-86, mem. coun. of overseers, 1986-95; bd. dirs. Mosholu Preservation Corp., Bronx, 1982-88; bd. overseers Jewish Theol. Sem., 1982-90, Jewish Publ. Soc. of Am., 1986-96, exec. com., 1989-94, 95-96; mem. exec. com. Yale Law Sch. Assn., 1990-93; bd. dirs. Piatigorsky Found., 1990—, Am. Found. Basic Rsch. Israel, 1990—. Mem. ABA, N.Y. State Bar Assn., Assn. of Bar of City of N.Y. (bd. dirs., exec. com. 1971-75), Internat. Fiscal Assn., Internat. Tax Planning Assn., Yale Club, (N.Y.C.), Lotos Club (N.Y.C.). Democrat. Office: Piper & Marbury LLP 1251 Avenue Of The Americas New York NY 10020-1104

VARGA, RICHARD STEVEN, mathematics educator; b. Cleve., Oct. 9, 1928; s. Steven and Ella (Krejcs) V.; m. Esther Marie Pfister, Sept. 22, 1951; 1 dau., Gretchen Marie. BS, Case Inst. Tech. (merged with Case Western Res. U.), 1950; AM, Harvard U., 1951, PhD, 1954; hon. doctorate, U. Karlsruhe, 1991, U. Lille, 1993. With Bettis Atomic Power Lab., Westinghouse Electric Co., 1954-60, adv. mathematician, 1959-60; full prof. math. Case Inst. Tech. (now Case We. Res. U.), 1960-69; univ. prof. Kent (Ohio) State U., 1969—, dir. rsch. Inst. for Computational Math.; Cons. to govt. and industry. Author: Matrix Iterative Analysis, 1962, Functional Analysis and Approximation Theory in Numerical Analysis, 1971, Topics in Polynomial and Rational Interpolation and Approximation, 1982, Zeros of Sections of Power Series, 1983, Scientific Computation on Mathematical Problems and Conjectures, 1990; editor: Numerical Solution of Field Problems in Continuum Physics, 1970, Padé and Rational Approximations: Theory and Applications, 1977, Rational Approximations and Interpolation, 1984, Computational Methods and Function Theory, 1990, Numerical Linear Algebra, 1993; editor-in-chief. Numerische Math., Electronic Transactions Numerical Analysis; mem. editl. bd. Linear Algebra and Applications, Constructive Approximation, Computational Mathematics (China), Utilities Mathematica, Revue Française d'Automatique, Informatique, Recherche Opérationelle, Numerical Algorithms, Analysis. Recipient Rsch. award Sigma Xi, 1965, von Humboldt prize, 1982, Pres.' medal Kent State U., 1981; Guggenheim fellow, 1963; Fairchild scholar, 1974. Home: 7065 Arcadia Dr Cleveland OH 44129-6065 Office: Kent State U Inst Computational Mat Kent OH 44242

VARGAS, PATTIE LEE, author, editor; b. Spencer, S.D., Feb. 4, 1941; d. Gilbert Helmuth and Carol Maxine (Winans) Bohlman; m. Richard D. Gulling Sr., July 17, 1960 (div. 1977); children: Richard D. Jr., David M., Toni C.; m. Allen H. Vargas, May 9, 1979 (dec. 1993). BS in Secondary Edn. cum laude, Miami U., 1969; MA in English, U. Dayton, 1972. Tchr. Kettering (Ohio) City Schs., 1972-83; editor Gurney's Gardening News, Yankton, S.D., 1984-88; dir. pub. relations Gurney Seed and Nursery Co., Yankton, 1985-89; creative supr. catalogs Dakota Advt. div. Gurney Seed and Nursery Co., Yankton, 1986-89; v.p. A.H. Vargas Assocs., Vermillion, S.D., 1987-93; editl. project mgr. Mazer Corp., Dayton, Ohio, 1993—; v.p. A.H. Vargas Assocs. Mktg. and Comm. Cons., Vermillion, S.D., 1987-93; pub. rels. cons. Cath. Conf. of Ohio, Columbus, 1975-76. Author: Country Wines, 1991, Stay Well Without Going Broke, 1993, Cordials From Your Kitchen, 1997; writer (movie): Planning Cath. Schs. Week, 1975, (multimedia show) Tribute to the Bicentennial, 1976. Mem. Miamisburg (Ohio) Sch. Bond Steering Com., 1980. Mem. Nat. Fedn. of Press Women (recipient Editorial Writing award, 1986, 87, 88), S.D. Press Women (recipient Sweepstakes award 1987, 1988, Catalog award 1988), Nat. Garden Writing Assn. Avocations: painting, boating, bicycling.

VARGHESE, MARY, secondary education educator; b. Mavelikara, Kerala, India, May 30, 1952; d. Joshua Puthenmadhom Zachariah and Kunjamma Joshua; m. Manalel Varghese, May 24, 1976; children: Renju Annu, Roger. BS, U. Kerala, 1973, BEd, 1975. Cert. secondary tchr. Tchr. St. John's High Sch., Kerala, 1977-81, Leulu Moega Fou Coll., Apia, AS, 1981-84, Leone (AS) High Sch., 1984—; sponsor, advisor Sci. Club, 1984—; chair com. judging Sci. Fair, 1989-90. Recipient Commendation award Internat. Sci. and Engring. Fair, Washington, 1990, recipient Excellence in Teaching Sci. award (U.S. Ter.), 1993. Mem. ASCD, Nat. Assn. Biology Tchrs. (Outstanding Tchr. 1990), Sci. Tchrs. Assn. AS., (recipient Presdl. award), 1992. Avocation: gardening. Home: PO Box 4740 Pago Pago AS 96799-4740 Office: Leone High Sch Pago Pago AS 96799

VARGO, RICHARD JOSEPH, accounting educator, writer. BS, Marietta Coll., 1963; MBA, Ohio U., 1965; PhD, U. Wash., 1969. CPA, Calif. Asst. prof. acctg. Sch. Bus. Adminstrn. U. So. Calif., 1968-71; assoc. prof. acctg., chair dept. acctg. Sch. Bus. Adminstrn. Coll. William and Mary, 1971-73; assoc. prof. Coll. Bus. Adminstrn. U. Tex., Arlington, 1973-74, assoc. dean for grad. studies Coll. Bus. Adminstrn., 1974-76, prof. acctg. Coll. Bus. Adminstrn., 1976-81; prof. acctg. Eberhardt Sch. Bus. U. of Pacific, 1981—; adj. prof. Family Practice and Cmty. Medicine, U. Tex. Southwestern Med. Sch., Dallas, 1977-81; adj. prof. acctg. McGeorge Sch. Law, U. of Pacific, 1982-93; spkr. in field. Author: Effective Church Accounting, 1989; co-author: (with Paul Dierks) Readings in Governmental and Nonprofit Accounting, 1982, (with Lanny Solomon and Larry Walther) Principles of Accounting, 1983, 5th edit., 1996, (with Lanny Solomon and Larry Walther) Financial Accounting, 1985, 4th edit., 1996; contbr. articles to profl. jours. Recipient grant U. Tex. Sys. Organized Rsch. Funds, 1973-74, 75-76, grant U. of Pacific and Kosciuszko Found., 1987, grant Kemper Found., 1989, grant U.S. Dept. Edn. and Rockefeller Bros. Found., 1991. Mem. Beta Alpha Psi (pres. Ohio U. chpt. 1964-65), Beta Gamma Sigma, Phi Kappa Phi. Office: Univ of Pacific Eberhardt School of Bus Stockton CA 95211

VARGUS, IONE DUGGER, university administrator; b. Medford, Mass., July 19, 1930; d. Edward and Madeline (Kountze) Dugger-Kelley; m. William Vargus, Mar. 27, 1954 (div. 1964); children: Suzanne Holoman, William; m. 2d, William H. Adams, Aug. 26, 1978 (dec. May 1988). A.B., Tufts U., 1952; M.S.S., U. Chgo., 1954; Ph.D., Brandeis U., 1971. Family worker Boston Housing Authority, 1961-64; project dir. Camp Fire Girls, Boston, 1964-67; asst. prof. Brandeis U., Waltham, Mass., 1968-71, U. Ill., Urbana, 1971-74; assoc. dean Temple U., Phila., 1974-78, dean, prof., 1978-91, acting vice provost, 1991-93, presdl. fellow, 1993-95, ret. 1995. Author: Revival of Ideology, The Afro-American Social Movement, 1977; contbr. articles to profl. jours. Trustee, Tufts U., 1981-91, emeritus, 1991—: chair Phila. Found., 1983-88; chair Family Reunion Inst., 1990—; bd. dirs. Pa. Public Policy Inst, 1989-91, Multicultural Inst., 1989—, Juvenile Law Ctr., 1991—, Valentine Found., 1994—; v.p. bd. dirs. Tucker House, 1989-95. Mem. Nat. Assn. Social Workers, Alpha Kappa Alpha. Home: 429 E Durham St Philadelphia PA 19119-1223 Office: Temple U Ritter Hall Annex Philadelphia PA 19122

VARIAN, HAL RONALD, economics educator; b. Wooster, Ohio, Mar. 18, 1947; s. Max Ronald and Elaine Catherine (Shultzman) V.; m. Carol Johnston, Nov. 1986. SB, MIT, 1969; M.A., U. Calif.-Berkeley, 1973, Ph.D. (NSF fellow), 1973. Asst. prof. econs. MIT, 1973-77; prof. U. Mich., 1977-95, prof. fin., 1983-95, Reuben Kempf prof. econs., 1984-95; prof. sch. bus., dean sch. info. mgmt. and sys. U. Calif., Berkeley, 1995—, Class of 1944 prof., 1996—; Siena chair in econs., U. Siena, Italy, 1990. Author: Microeconomic Analysis, 1978, Intermediate Microeconomics, 1987; co-editor Am. Econ. Rev., 1987-90. Guggenheim fellow, 1979-80; Fulbright scholar, 1990. Fellow AAAS, Econometric Soc.; mem. Am. Econ. Soc. Home: 1198 Estates Dr Lafayette CA 94549-2749 Office: U Calif SIMS 102 South Hall Berkeley CA 94720

VARIN, ROGER ROBERT, textile executive; b. Bern, Switzerland, Feb. 15, 1925; came to U.S., 1951; s. Robert Francois and Anna (Martz) V.; m. Annemarie Louis, May 24, 1951; children: Roger R.R., Edward C.H., Viviane A.H. BBA, Mcpl. Coll., Bern, 1944; PhD in Chemistry, U. Bern, 1951. Rsch. fellow Harvard U., Cambridge, Mass., 1951-52; rsch. assoc. E.I. DuPont De Nemours, Wilmington, Del., 1952-62; dir. rsch. Riegel Textile Corp., Ware Shoals, S.C., 1962-71; founder, chief exec. officer Varinit Corp., Greenville, S.C., 1971—; founder, chief exec. officer Varinit S.A., Geneva, 1974—. Pres. Greenville Sister City Internat., 1993. Mem. Am. Chem. Soc., Fiber Soc., Soc. Advanced Materials and Process Engring., Rotary (pres. Greenville chpt. 1979-80), Sigma Xi. Office: Varinit Corp PO Box 6602 Greenville SC 29606-6602

VARLEY, HERBERT PAUL, Japanese language and cultural history educator; b. Paterson, N.J., Feb. 8, 1931; s. Herbert Paul and Katharine L. (Norcross) V.; m. Betty Jane Geiskopf, Dec. 24, 1960. B.S., Lehigh U., 1952; M.A., Columbia U., 1961, Ph.D., 1964; DHL (hon.), Lehigh U., 1988. Asst. prof. U. Hawaii, Honolulu, 1964-65; asst. prof. dept. East Asian Langs. and Cultures Columbia U., N.Y.C., 1965-69, assoc. prof., 1969-75, prof., 1975-94, chmn. dept. East Asian Langs. and Cultures, 1983-89; Sen Soshitsu XV prof. Japanese Cultural History U. Hawaii, spring 1991-93, 94—. Author: The Onin War, 1967, The Samurai, 1970, Imperial Restoration in Medieval Japan, 1971, Japanese Culture, 1973, A Chronicle of Gods and Sovereigns, 1980, Tea in Japan: Essays on the History of Chanoyu, 1989, Warriors of Japan, As Portrayed in the War Tales, 1994. Bd. govs. Japanese Cultural Ctr. of Hawaii. Served with U.S. Army, 1952-54, Japan. Recipient Imperial Decoration Govt. Japan, Order of Rising Sun, Gold Rays With Rosette. Mem. Assn. Asian Studies, Japan Soc., Soc. Am. Magicians (pres. local chpt. 1983-84). Avocations: sleight of hand magic; piano. Home: 38 S Judd St Apt 15B Honolulu HI 96817-2607 Office: U Hawaii History Dept Sakamaki Hall A 203 2530 Dole St Honolulu HI 96822-2303

VARMA, ARVIND, chemical engineering educator, researcher; b. Ferozabad, India, Oct. 13, 1947; s. Hans Raj and Vijay L. (Jhanjhee) V.; m. Karen K. Guse, Aug. 7, 1971; children: Anita, Sophia. BS ChemE, Panjab U., 1966; MS ChemE, U. N.B., Fredericton, Can., 1968; PhD ChemE, U. Minn., 1972. Asst. prof. U. Minn., Mpls., 1972-73; sr. research engr. Union Carbide Corp., Tarrytown, N.Y., 1973-75; asst. prof. chem. engring. U. Notre Dame, Ind., 1975-77, assoc. prof., 1977-80, prof., 1980-88, Arthur J. Schmitt prof., 1988—, chmn. dept., 1983-88; vis. prof. U. Wis., Madison, fall 1981; Chevron vis. prof. Calif. Inst. Tech., Pasadena, spring 1982; vis. prof. Ind. Inst. Tech.-Kanpur, spring 1989, U. Cagliari, Italy, summer, 1989, 92; vis. fellow Princeton U., spring 1996. Co-author: Mathematical Methods in Chemical Engineering, 1997; editor: (with others) The Mathematical Understanding of Chemical Engineering Sytstems, 1980, Chemical Reaction and Reactor Engineering, 1987; series editor: Cambridge Series in Chemical Engineering, 1996—; contbr. numerous articles to profl. jours. Recipient Tchr. of Yr. award Coll. Engring. U. Notre Dame, 1991, Spl. Presdl. award 1992, R.H. Wilhelm award AIChE, 1993; Fulbright scholar; Indo-Am. fellow, 1988-89. Home: 52121 N Lakeshore Dr Granger IN 46530-7848 Office: Dept Chem Engring U Notre Dame Notre Dame IN 46556

VARMA, BAIDYA NATH, sociologist, broadcaster, poet; m. Savitri Devi. PhD, Columbia U., 1958. Radio broadcaster to India UN; Asian News Moderator Nat. Edn. TV Network, N.Y.C.; prof. emeritus sociology CUNY; prodr. radio dramas Voice of Am.; wrote, narrated over 200 documentary films, News of the Day; lectr. numerous univs. U.S., Can., Eng., India; chair Plenary Sessions World Congress of Sociology, Internat. Congress Anthrop. and Enthnological Scis; cons. Nat. Endowment Humanities, Ctr. Migration Studies, Dept. Energy, Wenner-Gren Found. Anthrop. Rsch. in U.S., Can. Coun., Indian Law Inst.; chair faculty seminars Columbia U.; presided Centenary Celebrations Indian Writers, N.Y.C.; vis. prof. Columbia U., other U.S., Indian Univs.; chair panel on religions and sexuality Parliament of World's Religions, 1993. Author: The Sociology and Politics of Development: A Theoretical Study, 1980, Social Science and Indian Society, 1985, New Directions in Theory and Methodology, 1993, Contemporary India (cert. of merit German Govt.), Love Feast, 1995, Spring of Civilization, 1995; author, editor others; contbr. articles Ency. Americana, profl. jours.; edit. adv. nat., internat. sociol. jours.; author numerous poems. Assoc. trustee Wordsworth Trust; trustee Taraknath Das Found.; bd. scholars Buddhist Cultural Inst., U.S.; judge Permanent People's Tribunal Indsl. and Environ. Hazards and Human Rights, Rome; established Varma Found.; chmn. Sravi Found.; founding mems. Lincoln Ctr. for Performing Arts, N.Y.C.; chmn. bd. trustees Soc. for Restoration of Ancient Vidyadhams of India; trustee Internat. Found. for Vedic Edn., U.S., U.S. Capitol Hist. Soc. Sr. faculty fellow Am. Inst. Indian Studies, 1964-65, 84-85; elected to Am. Film Inst.; guest fellow Oxford U., The Sorbonne, Inst. Advanced Study; named Hon. Citizen, Colonial Williamsburg; recipient Cert. of Merit, City Coun. Pres. Yonkers; named Disting. Poet of 1996, Internat. Soc. Poets; elected patron of Am. Acad. Poetry, 1996; inducted Internat. Poetry Hall of Fame, 1996. Mem. N.Y. Acad. Scis., South Asian Sociols. (1st pres.), Soc. Indian Acads. in Am. (exec. com.), Global Orgn. People of Indian Origin (life), U.S. Capitol Hist. Soc. (trustee). Home: 62 Belvedere Dr Yonkers NY 10705-2814

VARMUS, HAROLD ELIOT, government health institutes administrator, educator; b. Oceanside, N.Y., Dec. 18, 1939; s. Frank and Beatrice (Barasch) V.; m. Constance Louise Casey, Oct. 25, 1969; children: Jacob Carey, Christopher Isaac. AB, Amherst Coll., 1961, DSc (hon.), 1984; MA, Literature, Harvard U., 1962; MD, Columbia U. Med. Sch., 1966. Lic. physician, Calif. Intern, resident Presbyn. Hosp., N.Y.C., 1966-68; clin. assoc. NIH, Bethesda, Md., 1968-70; lectr. dept. microbiology U. Calif., San Francisco, 1970-72, asst. prof., depts. microbiology and immunology, biochemistry and biophysics, 1972-74, assoc. prof., 1974-79, prof., 1979-83, Am. Cancer Soc. research prof., 1984-93; dir. NIH, Bethesda, Md., 1993—; chmn. bd. on biology NRC. Editor: Molecular Biology of Tumor Viruses, 1982, 85; Readings in Tumor Virology, 1983; assoc. editor Genes and Development Jour., Cell Jour.; mem. editorial bd. Cancer Surveys. Named Calif. Acad. Sci. Scientist of Yr., 1982; co-recipient Lasker Found. award, 1982, Passano Found. award, 1983, Armand Hammer Cancer prize, 1984, GM Alfred Sloan award 1984, Shubitz Cancer prize, 1985, Nobel Prize in Physiology or Medicine, 1989. Mem. AAAS, NAS, Inst. Medicine of NAS, Am. Soc. Virology, Am. Soc. Microbiology, Am. Acad. Arts and Scis. Democrat. Research (with J. Michael Bishop) on the replication of retroviruses. Office: National Istitutes of Health Bldg 1 Rm 126 1 Center Dr MSC 0148 Bethesda MD 20892-0148

VARNEDOE, JOHN KIRK TRAIN, museum curator; b. Savannah, Ga., Jan. 18, 1946; s. Samuel Lamartine and Lilla (Train) V.; m. Elyn Zimmerman. BA with honors, Williams Coll., 1967, DFA (hon.), 1994; MA, Stanford U., 1970, PhD, 1972. Asst. instr. art history Williams Coll., 1967-68; asst. prof. art history Stanford (Calif.) U., 1973-74; asst. prof. Columbia U., N.Y.C., 1974-80; assoc. prof. Inst. Fine Arts, NYU, N.Y.C., 1980-84; prof. fine arts Inst. Fine Arts, NYU, 1984-88; chief curator dept. painting and sculpture Mus. Modern Art, N.Y.C., 1989—; vis. lectr. in law Columbia U. Law Sch., 1980-81; adj. curator dept. painting and sculpture Mus. Modern Art, 1985-88; mem. adv. bd. J. Paul Getty Program for Art on Film, 1985-87, Ctr. for Advanced Study in Visual Arts, 1990-93; mem. selection panel J. Paul Getty Postdoctoral Fellowships, 1985-88, J. Paul Getty Sr. Fellowships, 1988-90; Slade prof. art history Oxford (Eng.) U., 1992; lectr. in field. Author: The Drawings of Auguste Rodin, 1971, Vienna 1900, 1986, Gustave Caillebotte, 1987, Northern Light, 1988 (Henry Allen Moe prize 1983), A Fine Disregard--What Makes Modern Art Modern, 1990, High and Low: Modern Art and Popular Culture, 1990, Cy Twombly: A Retrospective, 1994, Jasper Johns: A Retrospective, 1996 ed. Jasper Johns: Writings, Sketchbook Notes, Interviews, 1996; mem. editl. bd. The Art Bull., 1985-90; contbr. articles and revs. to profl. jours. Decorated knight The Royal Order of Donnebroge (Denmark); David E. Finley fellow Nat. Gallery Art, 1970-73, NEH fellow, 1977-78, MacArthur Found. fellow, 1984-89; Rsch. grantee Columbia U., 1975, Travel grantee Am. Coun. Learned Socs. Fellow Am. Acad. Arts & Scis., NYU Soc. Fellows. Office: Mus of Modern Art 11 W 53rd St New York NY 10019-5401

VARNER, BARTON DOUGLAS, lawyer; b. Ida Grove, Iowa, May 2, 1920; s. Charles R. and Mary E. (Whinery) V.; m. Frances Elaine Seaton, May 9, 1943; children: Charles R., John A. Student, U. Nebr., 1938-42; LL.B., U. Mo. at Kansas City, 1951. Bar: Mo. 1951. Since practiced in Kansas City and Lake Ozark, Mo., ret. 1985; of counsel Gage and Tucker (now Lathrop & Gage), Kansas City and Lake Ozark, 1985—; partner firm Gage and Tucker (and predecessors), 1955-85. Bd. mgrs. Kansas City YMCA, 1958-80, chmn., 1962; pres. Miller County Hist. Soc., 1991-92, 94-95. With USNR, 1942-45. Mem. ABA, Mo. Bar Assn., Nebr. U. Alumni Assn. Kansas City (pres. 1958-60, bd. dirs., counsel), Kansas City Club, USN League, Delta Sigma Pi, Delta Theta Phi. Methodist (steward 1964-66, trustee 1968-69). Home: 8 Maple Tree Cir Lake Ozark MO 65049-8672 Office: Mut Benefit Life Bldg Kansas City MO 64108 *Ralph Waldo Emerson best expressed the principle that has helped me the most in attaining what success that I have attained when he stated in his Essay on Self Reliance the following: "There is a time in every man's education when he arrives at the conviction that envy is ignorance; that imitation is suicide; that he must take himself for better or worse as his portion; that though the wide universe is full of good, no kernel of nourishing corn can come to him but through his toil bestowed on that plot of ground which is given him to till. The power which resides in him is new in nature and none but he knows what that is which he can do, nor does he know until he has tried."*

VARNER, BRUCE H., JR., fire department official, educator; b. Washington, June 21, 1946; s. Bruce H. Varner and Rose A. (Parrish) Lewis; m. Elaine L. Nelson (div. 1974); 1 child, Paul A.; m. Susan A. Nungesser, Oct. 7, 1989. AA in Fire Protection, Phoenix Coll., 1972; student, Ariz. State U., 1973-77. Firefighter Phoenix Fire Dept., 1967-72, fire engr., 1972-77, fire capt., 1977-83, div. chief, 1983-85, dep. chief, 1985-92; fire chief Carrollton (Tex.) Fire Dept., 1992—. Mem. Nat. Fire Protection Assn. (tech. corr. com. fire svc. protective clothing and equipment), Internat. Assn. Fire Chiefs, Dallas County Fire Chiefs, S.W. Fire Chiefs, North Tex. Fire Chiefs Assn. (pres. 1996), Internat. Soc. Fire Svc. Instrn., Hon. Order Ky. Cols., Nat. Exch. Club of Carrollton (chmn. svc. chair 1994-96), Wingspread IV Conf., 1996. Avocations: sailing, travel, photography, raquetball. Office: Carrollton Fire Dept 1945 Jackson PO Box 110535 Carrollton TX 75011

VARNER, CHARLEEN LAVERNE MCCLANAHAN (MRS. ROBERT B. VARNER), nutritionist, educator, administrator, dietitian; b. Alba, Mo., Aug. 28, 1931; d. Roy Calvin and Lela Ruhama (Smith) McClanahan; student Joplin (Mo.) Jr. Coll., 1949-51; BS in Edn., Kans. State Coll. Pittsburg, 1953; MS, U. Ark., 1958; PhD, Tex. Woman's U. 1966; postgrad. Mich. State U., summer, 1955, U. Mo., summer 1962; m. Robert Bernard Varner, July 4, 1953. Apprentice county home agt. U. Mo., summer 1952; tchr. Ferry Pass Sch., Escambia County, Fla., 1953-54; tchr. biology, home econs. Joplin Sr. H.S., 1954-59; instr. home econs. Kans. State Coll., Pittsburg, 1959-63; lectr. foods, nutrition Coll. Household Arts and Scis., Tex. Woman's U., 1963-64, rsch. asst. NASA grant, 1964-66; assoc. prof. home econs. Central Mo. State U., Warrensburg, 1966-70, adviser to Colhecon, 1966-70, adviser to Alpha Sigma Alpha, 1967-70, 72, mem. bd. advisers Honors Group, 1967-70; prof., head dept. home econs. Kans. State Tchrs. Coll., Emporia, 1970-73; prof., chmn. dept. home econs. Benedictine Coll., Atchison, Kans., 1973-74; prof., chmn. dept. home econs. Baker U., Baldwin City, Kans., 1974-75; owner, operator Diet-Con Dietary Cons. Enterprises, cons. dietitian, 1973—, Home-Con Cons. Enterprises. Mem. Joplin Little Theater, 1956-60. Mem. NEA, Mo., Kans. state tchrs. assns., AAUW, Am., Mo., Kans. dietetics assns., Am., Mo., Kans. home econs. assns., Mo. Acad. Scis., AAUP, U. Ark. Alumni Assn., Alumni Assn. Kans. State Coll. of Pittsburg, Am. Vocat. Assn., Assn. Edn. Young Children, Sigma Xi, Beta Sigma Phi, Beta Beta Beta, Alpha Sigma Alpha, Delta Kappa Gamma, Kappa Kappa Iota, Phi Upsilon Omicron, Theta Alpha Pi, Kappa Phi. Methodist (organist). Home: PO Box 1009 Topeka KS 66601-1009

VARNER, CHILTON DAVIS, lawyer; b. Opelika, Ala., Mar. 12, 1943; s. William Cole and Frances (Thornton) Davis; m. K. Morgan Varner III, June 19, 1965; 1 child, Ashley Elizabeth. AB with distinction, Smith Coll., 1965; JD with distinction, Emory U., 1976. Assoc. King & Spalding, Atlanta, 1976-83, ptnr., 1983—; trustee Emory U., Atlanta, 1995—. Author: Appellate Handbook for Georgia Lawyers, 1995. Mem. Leadership Atlanta, 1984-85; asst. clk., elder, bd. elders Trinity Presbyn. Ch., Atlanta, 1985-88; exec. com. Ate Arts Alliance, Atlanta, 1981-85; mem. Atlanta Symphony Chorus, 1970-74. Fellow Am. Coll. Trial Lawyers; mem. ABA, Ga. Bar Assn., Atlanta Bar Assn., Bleckley Inn of Ct. (master), Order of Coif, Phi Beta Kappa. Office: King & Spalding 191 Peachtree St NE Atlanta GA 30303-1740

VARNER, DAVID EUGENE, lawyer; b. Dallas, Oct. 9, 1937; s. E.C. and D. Evelyn (Bauguss) V.; m. Joan Paula Oransky, Aug. 13, 1962; children: Michael A., Kevin E., Cheryl L. B.A., So. Meth. U., Dallas, 1958, J.D., 1961. Bar: Tex. 1961, Fla. 1974, Okla., 1977, U.S. Supreme Ct. 1978. Assoc. Eldridge, Goggans, Davidson & Silverberg, Dallas, 1962-65; atty., asst. sec. Redman Industries, Inc., Dallas, 1965-66; assoc. gen. atty. Tex. Instruments, Inc., Dallas, 1966-73; sr. atty., asst. sec. Fla. Gas Co., Winter Park, 1973-76; v.p., gen. counsel, sec. Facet Enterprises, Inc., Tulsa, 1976-78, Summa Corp., Las Vegas, Nev., 1978-82; sr. v.p., gen. counsel, sec. Transco Energy Co., Houston, 1982-95. Mng. editor Southwestern Law Jour., 1960-61. Mem. ABA, Houston Bar Assn., Tex. Bar, Okla. Bar, Fla. Bar, Am. Soc. Corp. Secs.

VARNER, JOYCE EHRHARDT, librarian; b. Quincy, Ill., Sept. 13, 1938; d. Wilbur John and Florence Elizabeth (Mast) Ehrhardt; m. Donald Giles Varner, Sept. 12, 1959; children: Amy, Janice, Christian, Matthew, Nadine. BA, Northeastern Okla. State U., 1980; MLS, U. Okla., 1984. Lab. analyst Gardner Denver Co., Quincy, 1956-60; sales rep. Morrisonville, Ill., 1963-69; libr. clk. U. Ill., Urbana, 1973-75; libr. tech. asst. Northeastern Okla. State U., Tahlequah, 1976-86; asst. reference libr. Muskogee (Okla.) Pub. Libr., 1986-90; libr. Jess Dunn Correctional Ctr., Taft, Okla., 1990—. Editor Indian Nations Audubon Nature Notes, 1977-81, 96—; contbr. articles to newspaper. Vol. Lake-Wood coun. Girl Scouts U.S.A., 1975—, bd. dirs. 1992—, pres., 1995-96; sec.-treas. Cherokee County Rural Water Dist. 7, 1987—; edn. chmn. Indian Nations chpt. Nat. Audubon Soc., 1989—. Recipient Thanks Badge, Lake-Wood coun. Girl Scouts U.S.A., 1990. Mem. ALA, AAUW, Okla. Libr. Assn. (nominating com. 1989), Okla. Acad. Sci., Okla. Ornithol. Soc. (chmn. libr. com. 1978-88, Award of Merit 1990, pres.-elect 1994, pres. 1995-96), Am. Correctional Assn., Okla. Correctional Assn., Alpha Chi, Beta Beta Beta, Phi Delta Kappa (Found. rep. 1984-86, historian 1992—). Avocations: nature study, needlework, square dancing, genealogy. Home: RR 1 Box 1 Welling OK 74471-9701 Office: Jess Dunn Correctional Ctr Leisure Libr PO Box 316 Taft OK 74463-0316

VARNER, ROBERT EDWARD, federal judge; b. Montgomery, Ala., June 11, 1921; s. William and Georgia (Thomas) V.; children: Robert Edward, Carolyn Stuart.; m. Jane Dennis Hannah, Feb. 27, 1982. BS, Auburn U., 1946; JD, U. Ala., 1949. Bar: Ala. 1949. Atty. City of Tuskegee, 1951; asst. U.S. atty. U.S. Dist. Ct. (mid. dist.) Ala., 1954-58; pvt. practice Montgomery, 1958-71; ptnr. Jones, Murray, Stewart & Varner, 1958-71; U.S. dist. judge Montgomery, 1971—; guest lectr. bus. law Huntingdon Coll. Pres. Montgomery Rotary Charity Found.; v.p., fin. chmn. Tukabatchee Area coun. Boy Scouts Am.; mem. Macon County Bd. Edn., 1950-54. With USNR, 1942-46. Recipient Silver Beaver award Boy Scouts Am. Mem. ABA, FBA, ATLA, Montgomery Bar Assn. (pres. 1971), Macon County Bar Assn., Jud. Conf. U.S. (mem. com. on operation of jury sys.), Rotary (pres. club 1961), Phi Alpha Delta (Outstanding Alumnus award 1996), Phi Delta Theta. Republican. Methodist. Office: US Dist Ct PO Box 2046 Montgomery AL 36102-2046

VARNER, STERLING VERL, retired oil company executive; b. Ranger, Tex., Dec. 20, 1919; s. George Virgle and Christina Ellen (Shafer) V.; m. Paula Jean Kennedy, Nov. 17, 1945; children: Jane Ann, Richard Alan. Student, Murray State Sch. Agr., 1940, Wichita State U., 1949. With Kerr-McGee, Inc., 1941-45; with Koch Industries, Inc., Wichita, Kans., 1945-90, pres., chief operating officer, 1974-86, vice chmn., 1987-90, chmn. bd. dirs., 1990, now bd. dirs.; ret.; owner Shadow Valley Ranch; bd. dirs. Koch Industries Inc. Bd. dirs. YMCA, Maude Carpenter Children's Ctr. Mem. Wichita Country Club, Crestview Country Club. Mem. Ch. of Christ. Home: 1515 N Linden Ct Wichita KS 67206-3312 Office: Koch Industries Inc PO Box 2256 411 E 37th St N Wichita KS 67201-2256

VARNERIN, LAWRENCE JOHN, physicist, retired educator; b. Boston, July 10, 1923; s. Lawrence John and Josephine (Nangeroni) V.; m. Marie Elizabeth Hynes, Apr. 19, 1952; children: Melanie, Lawrence, Gregory, Sharon, Suzanne, Bruce, Carol, Jeffrey. SB in Physics, MIT, 1947, PhD in Physics, 1949. Supr. TR/ATR microwave tube, electronics divsn. Sylvania corp., Boston, 1949-52; acting mgr. physics dept. Westinghouse Rsch. Labs., Pitts., 1952-57; head heterojunction IC and materials dept. AT&T Bell Labs., Murray Hill, N.J., 1957-86; Chandler-Weaver prof. elec. engring., chmn. elec. engring. computer sci. dept. Lehigh U., Bethlehem, Pa., 1986-92, Chandler-Weaver prof. emeritus, 1992—. Assoc. editor Jour. Magnetism and Magnetic Materials, 1973-94. Served with U.S. Army, 1943-46. Fellow IEEE, Am. Phys. Soc.; mem. Magnetics Soc. Roman Catholic. Home: PO Box 1107 Wolfeboro NH 03894-1107

VARNEY, CARLETON BATES, JR., interior designer, columnist, educator; b. Lynn, Mass., Jan. 23, 1937; s. Carleton Bates and Julia (Raczkowskos) V.; divorced; children: Nicholas, Seamus, Sebastian. BA, Oberlin Coll., 1958; student, U. Madrid, 1957; MA, NYU, 1969; LHD (hon.), U. Charleston, 1987. Sch. tchr., 1958-59; asst. to pres. Dorothy Draper & Co., Inc., 1959-63, exec. v.p., 1963-66, pres., 1966—; dean Carleton Varney Sch. of Art & Design, U. Charleston, W.Va. Designer: chairs, decorative fabrics, dinnerware and china, crystal glassware, table and bed linen, ready to wear resort collection Cruzanwear, 1987, mens' wear furnishings for Rawlinson & Marking, London, 1987; interior designer: Dromoland Castle, Ireland, 1963, 88, Westbury Hotel, Belgium, 1964, N.Y. World's Fair, 1965, Clare Inn, Ireland, 1968, Greenbrier Hotel, White Sulphur Springs, W.Va., 1968, Westbury Hotel, San Francisco, 1973, Copley Plaza Hotel, Boston, 1976, Amway Grand Plaza Hotel, Grand Rapids, Mich., 1980, The Grand Hotel, Mackinac Island, Mich., 1978, Equinox House, Manchester, Vt., 1984, Brazilian Ct. Hotel, Palm Beach, Fla., 1985, Waldorf Towers, N.Y.C., 1985, Dawn Beach Hotel, St. Maarten, 1985, Christian Broadcasting Conv. Ctr., 1986, Met. Opera House boutique, N.Y.C., 1985, (cruise ship) World Discoverer, 1984, Arrowwood Conv. Ctr., Purchase, N.Y., 1987, Boca Raton Hotel and Club, Fla., 1987, Speedway Club, Charlotte, N.C., 1987, Coccoloba Plantation, Anguilla, Brit. Virgin Islands, 1987, Villa Madeleine, St. Croix, V.I., 1987, Ashford Castle, Ireland, 1988, Adare Manor, Ireland, 1988, The Breakers, Palm Beach, Fla., 1989, Jackson Lake Lodge, Wyo., 1989, The Pub. Rms., V.P.'s Residence, Washington, 1989, Cormorant Cove, St. Croix, V.I., 1990, The Buccaneer Hotel, St. Croix, 1991, Dromoland Castle, Internat. Ctr., Ireland, 1991, West Village Golf Resort, Tokyo, 1993, Half Moon Bay Club, Jamaica, The Copely Plz., Boston, 1997, The Plaza, N.Y., 1997, numerous others; designer: White House party for celebration Israel-Egypt Peace Treaty, 1979; Palm Beach Cares fashion benefit for Am. Found. for AIDS Research, 1988, log home for Pres. and Mrs. Carter, Ellijay, Ga., 1983; color cons. Carter Presdl. Library, 1986; trustee and curator: former presdl. yacht U.S.S. Sequoia, 1982; retail stores: Carleton Varney By-The Yard, Sarasota, Fla., 1990, Carleton Varney Rose Cottage, Newmarket-on-Fergus, Ireland, 1991; author: numerous books including You and Your Apartment, 1960, The Family Decorates a Home, 1962 Carleton Varney Decorates Windows, 1975, Be Your Own Decorator, 1979, There's No Place Like Home, 1980, Down Home, 1981, Carleton Varney's ABC's of Decorating, 1983, Staying in Shape: An Insider's Guide to the Great Spas, 1983, Room by Room Decorating, 1984, Color Magic, 1985, The Draper Touch, 1988, Kiss the Hibiscus Goodnight, 1992; syndicated columnist: Your Family Decorator, 1968—; contbg. editor Good Housekeeping Mag., 1993-95; style editor Men's Style mag. Recipient Shelby Williams award for design achievement, 1967, Tommy design award for Covington's Heraldry collection, 1989, Interior Design Hall of Fame award, 1990. Mem. Indsl. Designers Soc. Am., N.Y. State Bd. for Interior Design. Clubs: N.Y. Athletic; Shannon Rowing (Ireland); Millbrook Golf and Tennis (N.Y.). Office: Dorothy Draper & Co Inc 60 E 56th St New York NY 10022-3204 also: Rose Cottage, NewMarket-on-Fergus, County Clare Ireland *My success, I believe, is due to an ability to understand and use vibrant color appropriately, and to strive for perfection of detail in all my designs as details separate the excellent from the ordinary.*

VARNEY, CHRISTINE A., federal official. Honors degree in Politics, Philosophy and Econs., Trinity Coll., Dublin, Ireland, 1975; BA in Polit. Sci. and History magna cum laude, SUNY, Albany, 1977; MPA in Policy Analysis, Legislation and Rsch. magna cum laude, Syracuse U., 1978; JD cum laude, Georgetown U., 1986. Legis. asst. N.Y. Senate, Albany, 1977; econ. analyst GAO, Washington, 1978; econ. devel. dir. El Centro, Calif., 1979; dir. Neighborhood Outreach Program, San Diego, 1980-82; assoc. Surry & Morse, Washington, 1984-86, Pierson, Semmes & Finley, Washington, 1986-88; counsel Hogan & Hartson, Washington, 1990-92; chief counsel Clinton for Pres. Primary Campaign, 1992, Clinton-Gore Campaign, 1992; gen. counsel Dem. Nat. Com., 1992, Presdl. Inauguration Com., 1993; dep. asst. to President U.S., sec. to Cabinet The White House, Washington, 1993-94; commissioner FTC, Wasington, 1994—. Active Women's Legal Def. Fund. Mem. D.C. Bar Assn., N.Y. State Bar Assn., Nat. Lawyer's Coun. Office: FTC 6th & Pennsylvania Ave NWRm 326 Washington DC 20580*

VARNEY, RICHARD ALAN, medical office manager; b. Concord, N.H., July 8, 1950; s. John Berry and Hattie Elizabeth (Harrington) V.; m. Cheryl Suzanne Glaab, Dec. 31, 1983; stepchildren: Alysen Suzanne, Craig Judson. BS in Phys. Edn., U. N.H., 1972; MHA in Healthcare Adminstrn., Baylor U., 1984; diploma, Command and Gen. Staff Coll., 1986. Commd. 2d lt. U.S. Army, 1973, advanced through grades to lt. col., 1991; dep. asst. CEO Cutler Army Hosp., Ft. Devens, Mass., 1973-76; field med. asst. 38th ADA Bde.., Osan Air Base, Korea, 1977-78; dep. asst. CEO 15th Med. Battalion, Ft. Hood, Tex., 1979-81; adminstrv. resident Ireland Army Hosp., Ft. Knox, Ky., 1982-83; COO, exec. officer U.S. Army Dental Activity, Ft. Knox, 1983-86; grad. instr. Army-Baylor Healthcare Program, San Antonio, 1986-90; project mgr. Office of the Army Surgeon Gen., Washington, 1990-93; ret. U.S. Army, 1993; office mgr. Aebi, Ginty, Romaker & Sprouse MD's, Inc., Lancaster, Ohio, 1993—; mem. Source Selection Evaluation Bd.-Champus Reform, Arlington, Va., 1987. Adult leader Boy Scouts Am., Tex., Va. and Ohio, 1988—; mem. Lancaster City Bd. of Health, 1996—. Decorated Legion of Merit, Order of Mil. Med. Merit award, Expert Field Med. badge; named to Hon. Order Ky. Cols., 1989, Outstanding Young Men of Am., 1982. Fellow Am. Coll. Healthcare Execs. (examiner oral portion mem. exam); mem. Ctrl. Ohio Health Adminstrs. Assn., Ohio Med. Group Mgmt. Assn., Mid-Ohio Med. Mgmt. Assn., Profl. Assn. Med. Mgrs., Am. Assn. Procedural Coders, Lancaster Area Soc. for Human Resource Mgmt., Am. Hosp. Assn., Nat. Eagle Scout Assn., The Ret. Officers Assn., Am. Legion, Alpha Phi Omega. Avocations: home improvement, camping, hiking, music. Home: 1025 E 5th Ave Lancaster OH 43130-3276 Office: Aebi Ginty Romaker Sprouse 1800 Granville Pike Lancaster OH 43130-1087

VARNEY, SUZANNE GLAAB, health facility administrator; b. Ft. Meade, Md., Dec. 17, 1951; d. Lawrence Harold and G. Sue (Strain) Glaab; m. Richard Alan Varney, Dec. 31, 1983; children: Alysen Suzanne, Judson Dietrich. Student, Ohio U., Lancaster, 1969. Cert. med. staff coord. Transp. asst. U.S. Army, Seoul, 1979-81; pers. specialist U.S. Army Hosp., Ft. Knox, Ky., 1982-84, credentials specialist, 1984-86; adminstrv. asst. Brooke Army Med. Ctr., Ft. Sam Houston, Tex., 1987, adminstr. credentials program, 1988-90; credentials program adminstr. Walter Reed Army Med. Ctr., Washington, 1990-92; med. staff coord. Fairfield Med. Ctr., Lancaster, Ohio, 1992-97; coord. med. staff Charlotte Regional Med. Ctr., Puenta Gorda, Fla., 1997—; seminar leader office basic course Army Med. Dept., Ft. Sam Houston, 1988-90. Rep. Brookwood Neighborhood Assn., San Antonio, 1987-90; mem. N.E. Ind. Sch. Dist. PTA, San Antonio, 1986-90; den leader Cub Scouts/Boy Scouts Am., San Antonio, 1986-90. Mem. NAFE, Nat. Assn. Med. Staff Svcs., Tex. Hosp. Assn., Tex. Soc. Med. Staff Svcs., Ohio Assn. Med. Staff Svcs. Avocations: piano, gymnastics, outdoor activities, travel. Home: 419 Via Cintia Punta Gorda FL 33950 Office: Charlotte Regional Med Ctr Punta Gorda FL 33950

VARNUM, JAMES WILLIAM, hospital administrator; b. Grand Rapids, Mich., May 29, 1940; s. Robert Otto and Jeannette (Badger) V.; m. Lucinda Hotchkiss, June 6, 1964; children: Kenneth James, Susan Lucinda. A.B., Dartmouth Coll., 1962; M.Hosp. Adminstrn. with honors, U. Mich., 1964. Adminstrv. asst. U. Wis. Hosps., Madison, 1963-64; asst. supt. U. Wis. Hosps., 1964-68, asso. supt., 1968-69, supt., 1969-73; hosp. adminstr. U. Wash. Hosp., Seattle, 1973-78; pres. Mary Hitchcock Meml. Hosp., Lebanon, N.H., 1978—; prof. Med. Sch., Dartmouth Coll., 1978—. Mem. Am. Hosp. Assn. (bd. trustees 1994—), The Hitchcock Alliance (pres. 1983—). Home: 7 Woodcock Ln Etna NH 03750-4403 Office: Mary Hitchcock Meml Hosp 1 Medical Center Dr Lebanon NH 03756-0001

VARON, DAN, electrical engineer; b. Tel-Aviv, Israel, July 24, 1935; came to U.S., 1961; s. Reuven and Stephanie Varon; m. Judith Hilda Mansbach, Aug. 12, 1962; 2 children:. BSEE, The Technion, Haifa, Israel, 1957, Diplom Ingenieur, 1960; MSc, Polytechnic U., Bklyn., 1963; D of Engring. Sci., NYU, 1965. Engr. Israeli Air Force, Israel, 1957-61; rsch. fellow Polytechnic U., Bklyn., 1961-63; teaching asst. NYU, N.Y.C., 1963-65; mem. tech. staff Bell Telephone Labs., Whippany, N.J., 1965-69; mgr. Tymshare (Dial Data, Inc.), Newton, Mass., 1969-71; prin. engr. Raytheon Co., Marlborough, Mass., 1971—. Contbr. articles to Bell System Tech. Jour., IEEE, Radio Sci., Jour. Air Traffic Control Assn. Mem. IEEE (mem. tech. program com. 1970), N.Y. Acad. Scis., Assn. Computing Machinery.

VARRICCHIO, CLAUDETTE GOULET, nursing educator, researcher; b. Fall River, Mass., Apr. 13, 1940; d. Joseph Wilfred Goulet and Imelda R. Barrette; m. Frederick E. Varricchio, Dec. 28, 1962; children: Nicole, Erika. BS, Boston Coll., 1961; MS, U. Md., Balt., 1977; DSN, U. Ala., Birmingham, 1983. Asst. prof. N.W. La. State U., Shreveport, 1978-80; assoc. prof. Loyola U., Chgo., 1980-91; rsch. assoc. NIH, Nat. Cancer Inst., 1989-90, program dir., nurse cons., 1992—. Recipient Chgo. Lung Assn. grant 1989-91. Mem. ANA, Oncology Nursing Soc., Am. Acad. Nursing, Am. Pain Soc., Am. Soc. Clin. Oncology, Sigma Theta Tau. Office: NIH Nat Cancer Inst DCPC EPN300 6130 Executive Blvd MSC 7340 Bethesda MD 20892-7340

VARRO, BARBARA JOAN, editor; b. East Chicago, Ind., Jan. 25, 1938; d. Alexander R. and Lottie R. (Bess) V. B.A., Duquesne U., 1959. Feature reporter, asst. fashion editor Chgo. Sun-Times, 1959-64, fashion editor, 1964-76, feature writer, 1976-84; v.p. pub. rels. Daniel J. Edelman Inc., Chgo., 1984-85; v.p. PRB/Needham Porter Novelli, Chgo., 1985-86; editor Am. Hosp. Assn. News, Chgo., 1987-94; editor spl. sects. Chgo. Tribune, 1995—. Recipient awards for feature writing Ill. AP, 1978, 79, 80. Office: Chgo Tribune 435 N Michigan Ave Chicago IL 60611

VARSBERGS, VILIS, minister, former religious organization administrator; b. Prauliena, Latvia, June 1, 1929; s. Viktors and Marta (Barbans) V.; m. Biruta Grinbergs, July 2, 1960; children: Anita Valda, Krista Maija, Victor Andrew. BA magna cum laude, Midland Coll., 1954; MDiv, Luth. Sch. Theology, Chgo., 1957; D (hon.), U. Latvia, 1996. Ordained to ministry United Luth. Ch., 1957. Mission developer, pastor Grace Luth. Ch., Albion, Mich., 1957-63; pastor Messiah Luth. Ch., Constantine, Mich., 1963-69; adminstr., dir. Latvian Ctr. Garezers, Inc., Three Rivers, Mich., 1969-72; pastor Zion Latvian Luth. Ch., Chgo., 1973-94; pres. Latvian Evang. Luth. Ch. in Am., 1984-93; dean dept. of theology U. Latvia, Riga, 1994—; assembly del. Luth. World Fedn., Budapest, Hungary, 1984, Curitiba, Brazil, 1990. Sec. Helsinki Monitoring Com., Chgo., 1983-85; mem. adv. bd. Ill. Ethnic Cons., Chgo., 1986; bd. dirs. Luth. Immigration & Refugee Svc., N.Y.C., 1988-94. Office: U Latvia, Raina Blvd 19, Riga LV1586, Latvia

VARSHA, BOB, sports commentator; b. Northport, N.Y., Apr. 21, 1951; married; 1 child. BA in Fgn. Langs., Dartmouth Coll., 1973; JD, Emory U., 1977. Pvt. practice law Atlanta, 1977-80; commentator, news host WTBS/CNN, Atlanta, 1980-84; reporter MotorWeek Illustrated, 1985-86; host, commentator ESPN, 1986—. Office: ESPN ESPN Plaza Bristol CT 06010

VARSHNI, YATENDRA PAL, physicist; b. Allahabad, India, May 21, 1932; emigrated to Can., 1960; s. Harpal and Bhagyawati V. B.Sc., U. Allahabad, 1950, M.Sc., 1952, Ph.D., 1956. Asst. prof. U. Allahabad, 1955-60; postdoctoral fellow NRC, Ottawa, Ont., Can., 1960-62; asst. prof. U. Ottawa, 1962-65, assoc. prof., 1965-69, prof., 1969—. Contbr. numerous articles to profl. jours. Fellow Am. Phys. Soc., Indian Phys. Soc., Royal Astron. Soc. (U.K.), Inst. Physics U.K.; mem. AAAS, Royal Soc. Chemistry (U.K., assoc.), Am. Astron. Soc., Astron. Soc. of Pacific, Can. Astron. Soc., Can. Assn. Physicists, Royal Astron. Soc. Can., Astron. Soc. India, Am. Assn. Physics Tchrs. Office: Dept Physics, U Ottawa, Ottawa, ON Canada K1N 6N5

VARY, THOMAS CRISPIN, physiologist; b. Fountain Hill, Pa., Sept. 15, 1954; s. George Crispin and Clairebette (Folk) V.; m. Kathleen Ann O'Neal, May 3, 1991; 1 child, Katherine Ann; stepchildren: Jennifer Taverna, Charles Taverna. BA, Johns Hopkins U., 1976; MS, Lehigh U., 1978; PhD, Pa. State U., 1982. Postdoctoral fellow Pa. State U. Coll. Medicine, Hershey, 1982; British-Am. rsch. fellow Nuffield dept. clin. biochemistry U. Oxford, England, 1982-83; asst. prof. Md. Shock Trauma Ctr., Balt., 1983-88; asst. prof. dept. cells and molecular physiology Pa. State U., 1988-90, assoc. prof., 1995-96, prof., 1996—; vis. scientist INRA, Clermont-Ferrand, France, 1995-96; vis. scientist INRA, Clermont-Ferrand, France, 1996-97. Mem. editl. bd. Shock, Am. Jour. Physiol.; contbr. articles to profl. jours. and chpts. to books. Coach Hampden Area (Pa.) Youth Soccer, 1990—, Hampden Area Little League, 1990—. NIH grantee, 1989—, Career Devel. award, 1990-95. Mem. Shock Soc., Internat. Soc. for Heart Rsch., Am. Physiol. Soc., Am. Soc. Biol. Chemists, Hershey Country Club. Republican. Episcopalian. Avocation: golf. Office: Pa State U Coll Medicine Dept Cellular Molecular Physiology Hershey PA 17033

VASHOLZ, LOTHAR ALFRED, retired insurance company executive; b. Milw., Feb. 20, 1930; s. Alfred and Charlotte Vasholz; m. Marji Cartwright, Dec. 26, 1954; children: Julie, Ann, Eric. BS, U. Colo., 1952; M (hon.), U. Rio Grande. ChFC. Sr. cons. Life Ins. Mktg. & Rsch., Hartford, Conn., 1966-70; v.p. N.Am. Life, Chgo., 1970-73; sr. v.p. Bankers Mut., Freeport, Ill., 1973-75; sales dir. Security Life of Denver, 1975-81; v.p. Union Cen. Life Ins. Co., Cin., 1981-85, sr. v.p., 1985-86; mgr. Union Cen. Life Ins. Co., Columbus, Ohio, 1986-87; sr. v.p., chief mktg. officer Union Cen. Life Ins. Co., Cin., 1987-91, exec. v.p., corp. mktg. officer, 1991-95; chmn. Carillon Investments, 1991-95; ret., 1995; cons., owner Transitions Unltd., Cin., 1995—; bd. dirs. Carillon Investments, Manhattan Life. Trustee U. Rio Grande, Ohio; elder Presbyn. Ch. Fellow Life Mgmt. Inst.; mem. Phi Delta Theta (past internat. pres.). Republican. Office: Transitions Unltd PO Box 45432 Cincinnati OH 45242-0432

VASIL, INDRA KUMAR, botanist; b. Basti, India, Aug. 31, 1932; arrived in U.S., 1962; s. Lal Chand and Pushpa Lata (Abrol) V.; married, 1959; children: Kavita, Charu. BS, Banaras Hindu U., 1952; MS in Botany, U. Delhi, 1954, PhD in Botany, 1958. Lectr. in botany U. Delhi, 1959-63; postdoctoral rsch. assoc. U. Ill., Champaign-Urbana, 1962-63, U. Wis.,

Madison, 1963-65; scientist Coun. Sci. and Indsl. Rsch., New Delhi, 1966, Dept. Sci. and Indsl. Rsch., Palmerston North, New Zealand, 1974; assoc. prof. to prof. U. Fla., Gainesville, 1967-79, grad. rsch. prof., 1979—; vis. scientific expert Cath. U., Nijmegen, Netherlands, 1970; vis. prof. U. Hohenheim/Giessen, West Germany, 1975, 76; chmn. Biotechnology Action Coun. UNESCO, Paris, 1990—; svc. many internat. coms.; dir. numerous internat. tng. courses and workshops. Editor (20 vols.) Plant Cell Culture and Somatic Cell Genetics and Cellular and Molecular Biology of Plants, 1980—; editorial bd. six major internat. scientific jours. Fulbright fellowship U.S. Ednl. Found., 1962, Climate Lab. fellowship Govt. of New Zealand, 1974; recipient Humboldt award Alexander von Humboldt Found. Mem. Internat. Soc. Plant Morphologists (pres. 1995—), Internat. Cell Rsch. Orgn. (convenor of panel on plant cell biology and biotech.). Avocations: travel, reading, stamps, gardening. Home: 4901 NW 19th Pl Gainesville FL 32605-3498 Office: U Fla 1143 Fifield Hall Gainesville FL 32611-2092

VASILACHI, GHEORGHE VASILE, priest, vicar; b. Idrici, Romania, Jan. 29, 1909; s. Gheorghe and Aglala (Nestian) V. ThD, Universiti Iassy, Romania, 1938. Dir. Mitropolia, Iasi, 1935-39; secretar patriarchy Bucharest, 1939-42, preacher patriarchy, 1942-44; abbott Monastery Antim, Bucharest, 1943-48; igumen Pocrov, Romania, 1949-59; priest for prisons, 1959-64; priest Bobâlna, 1965-69; priest Southbridge, Mass., 1969-79, Windsor, Can., 1979-84; priest St. Nicholas Parish, N.Y.C., 1984—; vicar Romanian Archdiocese Detroit, 1973. Author: Jesus Christ through the Ages, 1973, We Belong to Christ, 1980, Another World: Memories from Communist Prisons, 1987, The Supremacy of God--All in My Theology and Collection from the Word of Life, 1991; translator Holy Bible in Romanian lang.; pub. over 50 books in Romanian lang. Recipient Recognition award Commonwealth Mass., 1975. Republican. Office: The Romanian Orthodox Ch 45-03 48th Ave Woodside NY 11377-6553

VASILE, GENNARO JAMES, health care executive; b. Auburn, N.Y., Jan. 16, 1946; s. Louis Joseph and Regina Elena (Santaniello) V.; m. Mary Ellen Dwyer, Aug. 10, 1968; children: Kevin, Colleen, Brian. B.A., St. John Fisher Coll., 1967; M.B.A., Xavier U., 1969; Ph.D., U. Iowa, 1973. Asst. adminstr. St. Elizabeth Hosp., Utica, N.Y., 1971-74; sr. cons. Booz-Allen & Hamilton, Inc., N.Y.C., 1974-75; asst. provost adminstrn. Med. Coll. Va., Va. Commonwealth U., Richmond, 1975-78; dir. hosp. and health services mgmt. consulting Booz-Allen & Hamilton, Inc., Bethesda, Md., 1978-79; exec. dir. Strong Meml. Hosp. of U. Rochester, N.Y., 1979-84; pres. United Health Services Inc., Binghamton, N.Y., 1984-93; exec. v.p. Johns Hopkins Hosp., Balt., 1993-95; v.p. Gemini Cons. Am's. Healthcare Practice, 1996—; asst. prof. U. Rochester, Med. Coll. Va.; assoc. prof. Johns Hopkins U.; vis. prof. U. Rochester Med. Ctr.; dir., pres. Med. Ctr. Ins. Co.; cons. health-related agencies. Author: Comprehensive Health Planning, 1971, 74. Bd. dirs. Rochester Soc. Prevention of Cruelty to Children, 1980, asst. treas., 1981; bd. dirs. Pittsford Vince Lombardi Youth Football, 1980, v.p., 1981; bd. dirs. St. Ann's Home, Voluntary Hosps. Am. Inc., Broome County C. of C., 1985, United Way, 1985; trustee St. John Fisher Coll. Recipient Dean's award for contbns. to Sch. Medicine Med. Coll. Va., 1978, Outstanding Contbn. to Mankind, 1993, Exec. of Yr., 1985, Preceptor of Yr. Xavier U., 1992. Fellow Am. Coll. Health Care Execs., Am. Acad. Med. Care Adminstrs. (bd. dirs. 1988); mem. Am. Coll. Hosp. Adminstrs., Am. Hosp. Assn., Council Teaching Hosps., Assn. Am. Med. Colls. Roman Catholic. Home: 204 Lambeth Rd Baltimore MD 21218-1108 *The approach I have taken to my professional and personal life has been to seek out the world as it is, formulate a vision as to how it can be improved, and strive to bridge the resultant gaps. If I have been successful in bridging any gaps, it is only because of the substantial support I have received along the way.*

VASLEF, IRENE, historian, librarian; b. Budapest, Hungary, Mar. 23, 1934; came to U.S., 1956, naturalized, 1960; d. Imre and Ilona (Selyebi-Kovats) Szabo; m. Nicholas P. Vaslef, Sept. 22, 1956; children—Suzanne, Steven. B.A., San Jose (Calif.) State U., 1960; M.S., Simmons Grad. Sch. Library Sci., Boston, 1963; postgrad., Columbia U., 1968, U. Colo., 1961-62, U. Munich, 1967-68; Ph.D., Catholic U. Am., 1984. Librarian Cambridge, Mass., 1962-64; librarian Colorado Springs (Colo.) Sch. System, 1964-67; head catalog librarian Colo. Coll., Colorado Springs, 1968-72; librarian Dumbarton Oaks Rsch. Libr., Trustees for Harvard U., 1972—. Editor/compiler Am. Byzantine Bibliography in Byzantine studies/Etudes Byzantines, 1979—, Classica et Mediaevalia, 1986, Leyden: Brill, 1986; contbr. articles to profl. jours. Mem. Spl. Libraries Assn., Art Libraries Assn. N.Am., Phi Gamma Mu. Home: 4131 N River St Mc Lean VA 22101-2512 Office: Harvard U Dumbarton Oaks Rsch Libr 1703 32nd St NW Washington DC 20007-2934

VASQUEZ, WILLIAM LEROY, marketing professional, educator; b. Austin, Tex., Mar. 9, 1944; s. Eliseo M. and Janie (Garcia) V. BS with distinction, Nova U., 1983, MBA, 1985, DBA, 1992. Cert. Inst. Cert. Profl. Mgrs., 1990, Inst. Cert. Computing Profls., 1993. Svc. mgr. Data Gen. Corp., various, Latin Am., 1972-80; product mgr. Gould, Inc., Ft. Lauderdale, Fla., 1980-84, Tektronix Inc., Portland, Oreg., 1984-86, Racal-Milgo, Ft. Lauderdale, 1988-90, Citibank Internat., Ft. Lauderdale, 1990—; instr. City U., Portland campus, 1987-88; Maryhurst Coll., 1985-88, Nova Southeastern U. (domestic and internat.), 1988—, pres. internat. alumni assn.; instr. St. Thomas U., 1989—, Fla. Atlantic U., 1993—. Mem. mktg. com. Fla. Philharm. Orch., 1994; mem. adv. com. Broward County Sch. Dist. Served on USN nuclear submarines, 1962-70. Mem. IEEE, VFW, Am. Mktg. Assn. (pres.), Nat. Mgmt. Assn., Mensa. Republican. Presbyterian. Avocations: guitar, jogging, fine arts. Home: 9788 NW 18 St Coral Springs FL 33071 Office: Citibank NA 6th Fl 899 W Cypress Creek Rd Fl 6 Fort Lauderdale FL 33309-2072

VASS, JOAN, fashion designer; b. N.Y.C., May 19, 1925; d. Max S. and Rose L.; children by previous marriage: Richard, Sara, Jason. Student Vassar Coll., 1941; BA, U. Wis., 1946. Pres., Joan Vass Inc., N.Y.C., 1977—, Vass-Ludacer, N.Y.C., 1993—. Recipient Prix de Cachet, Prince Machiabelli, 1980, Coty award, 1979, Disting. Woman in Fashion award Smithsonian Instn., 1980. Office: Joan Vass Inc 117 E 29th St New York NY 10016-8022 also: 485 7th Ave Ste 510 New York NY 10018-6804

VASSALLO, EDWARD E., lawyer; b. N.Y.C., Aug. 12, 1943. BS, Columbia U., 1965, MS, 1967; JD cum laude, Fordham U., 1973. Bar: N.Y. 1974. Ptnr. Fitzpatrick, Cella, Harper & Scinto, N.Y.C. Editor Urban Law Jour., 1972-73. Mem. ABA, Am. Intellectual Property Law Assn., U.S. Trademark Assn., Fed. Cir. Bar Assn., N.Y. Patent, Trademark and Copyright Law Assn. Office: Fitzpatrick Cella Harper & Scinto 277 Park Ave New York NY 10172

VASSAR, WILLIAM GERALD, gifted and talented education educator; b. Springfield, Mass., Oct. 5, 1925; s. William Walter and Mary Ellen (Burns) V.; m. Barbara Ellen Benhard, June 21, 1952; children: William G., James P., Richard G., Carol A. Vassar Pettit. BA in History magna cum laude, Am. Internat. Coll., Springfield, 1950; MEd, Springfield Coll., 1951; cert. of advanced grad. study, U. Mass., 1967, postgrad., 1962-70. Elem. tchr. West Springfield (Mass.) Pub. Schs., 1950-53, jr. high tchr., 1953-55, secondary sch. prin., 1955-65, dir. program for gifted, 1955-65; sr. supr. academically talented Mass. State Dept. Edn., Boston, 1965-66; state dir. programs for gifted and talented Conn. State Dept. Edn., Hartford, 1966-86; coord. gifted edn., dept. spl. edn. Cen. Conn. State U., New Britain, 1968-86, asst. to dean Sch. Edn., 1986-88; spl. cons. advanced placement program The Coll. Bd., N.Y.C., 1986—; prodr. interactive satellite confs. on Advanced Placement, 1992—; coord. White House Task Force Gifted and Talented, Washington, 1967-68, U.S. Dept. Edn. Congl. Study Gifted and Talented, Washington, 1969-71, Capitol Region Edn. Coun. Info. and Resource Ctr., Windsor, Conn., 1992—; cons. gifted and talented U.S. Dept. Edn., 1967-85, Nat. Assn. State Bds. Edn., 1978-84, George Washington U. Edn. Policy Fellowship Program, 1978-84; spl. cons. gifted and talented legislation Staff of Senate subcom. on Edn., 1967-85; vis. lectr. U. Conn., 1966-83, So. Conn. State U., 1970-84, Sacred Heart U., 1986—, others. Contbg. editor The Gifted Child Quar., Jour. Talented and Gifted; author monographs; contbr. numerous articles to profl. jours. Mem. exec. bd. Mass. Commn. on Children and Youth, Boston, 1959-65, Nat. Commn. Orgn. and Children and Youth, Washington, 1964-68; mem. Conn. Commn. on Youth Svcs., Hartford, 1966-70; mem. Mass. Hwy. Safety Commn., Boston, 1957-63; baseball scout San Francisco Giants, 1957-70. With USN, 1943-46, PTO. Named Disting. Educator U.S. Dept. Edn. Office Gifted, Washington, 1974, Disting. Educator, Conn. State Legislature, Hartford, 1986; recipient Disting. Svc. award Mass. Commn. on Children and Youth, Boston, 1966. Mem. ASCD, Internat. Coun. Exceptional Children (pres. Assn. Gifted div. 1970-71, chmn. regionals 1969-78, Disting. Svc. award 1976), Nat. Assn. Gifted Children (life, pres. 1965-68, bd. dirs. 1960-68, Disting. Svc. award 1970), Coun. State Dirs. Gifted (pres. 1977-80), Conn. Assn. Gifted, Conn. Assn. Pub. Sch. Supts. (ret.), Nat. Football Hall of Fame Found., Eastern Assn. Intercollegiate Football Ofcls., Indian Hill Country Club, Eastern Coll. Athletic Conf., Phi Delta Kappa. Democrat. Roman Catholic. Avocations: reading, golf, football. Home: 47 Dowd St Newington CT 06111-2611

VASSEL, LEE HYLTON, urbanist, social services administrator, writer; b. Port Maria, Jamaica, May 30, 1939; s. Lester L. and Isamenda (Beckford) V.; m. Daisy Mae Eaddy, July 22, 1972 (dec. Sept. 1991); 1 child, Faye Maria. Cert., U. Cambridge, 1956; BA in English magna cum laude, Queens Coll.-CUNY, 1974; MA in Creative Writing, City Coll.-CUNY, 1976; MS in Urban Affairs, Hunter Coll.-CUNY, 1979. Adj. lectr. Hunter Coll.-CUNY, 1978-80; instr., grad. asst. doctor of arts program in English SUNY, Albany, 1980-83; adj. lectr. Hostos C.C., N.Y.C., 1984-85; case worker N.Y.C. Dept. Social Svcs., 1986-87, ct. liaison, 1988-89; dist. atty. liaison Adminstrn. for Children's Svcs., Bronx, N.Y.C., 1990—, ct. liaison supr., 1995—. Author: In the Black of Us, 1976; contbr. creative writings to lit. publs. (Golden prize Queens Coll./CUNY 1973, 74). Mem. Seton Falls Neighborhood Assn., Bronx, 1989—, Bronx Dist. Atty. Multidisciplinary Team on child phys. and sexual abuse. Mem. MLA, Internat. Soc. Arts, Sci. & Tech., Urban Affairs Assn., Ea. Evaluation Rsch. Soc., Alpha Sigma Lambda. Episcopalian. Avocations: walking, reading, creative writing, reggae music, study. Home: 2029 Strang Ave Bronx NY 10466 Office: Bronx Family Ct 900 Sheridan Ave Bronx NY 10451-3306

VASSELL, GREGORY S., electric utility consultant; b. Moscow, Dec. 24, 1921; came to U.S., 1951, naturalized, 1957; s. Gregory M. and Eugenia M. Wasiljeff; m. Martha Elizabeth Williams, Apr. 26, 1957; children: Laura Kay, Thomas Gregory. Dipl. Ing. in Elec. Engring, Tech. U. Berlin, 1951; MBA in Corp. Fin., NYU, 1954. With Am. Electric Power Svc. Corp., Columbus, Ohio, 1951-88; v.p. system planning Am. Electric Power Svc. Corp., 1973-76, dir., 1973-88, sr. v.p. system planning, 1976-88; electric utility cons. Upper Arlington, Ohio, 1988—; bd. dirs. Columbus & Southern Ohio Electric Co., 1981-88, Cardinal Operating Co.; mem. tech. adv. com. transmission FPC, 1968-70, FERC Task Force on Power Pooling, 1980-81; mem. U.S. com. World Energy Coun. Contbr. articles to profl. jours. Fellow IEEE (life); mem. NAE, Internat. Conf. Large High Voltage Electric Systems, Am. Arbitration Assn., The Surf Golf and Beach Club (North Myrtle Beach, S.C.). Home and Office: 2247 Pinebrook Rd Columbus OH 43220-4327

VASSIL, PAMELA, graphic designer; b. N.Y.C., Nov. 29, 1943; d. George Peter and Lenora (Zabludofsky) Vassilopoulos; 1 child, Sadye Lee. B.S. in Art Edn., Hofstra U., 1965; M.A. in Art Edn., NYU, 1968. Designer Columbia Records, N.Y.C., 1970-72; assoc. art dir. Harper's Bazaar, N.Y.C., 1972-74; designer, mech. artist Album Graphics Inc., N.Y.C., 1974-75; free-lance designer, mech. artist; prodn. dir. Push Pin Studios, N.Y.C., 1975-77; art dir. op. editorial page N.Y. Times, N.Y.C., 1977-79, art dir. arts and leisure sect., 1982-87, art dir. living sect., 1987; free-lance designer/art dir./mech. artist, 1979-82; instr. production, graphic design and illustration Parsons Sch. Design, N.Y.C., 1974—; instr. illustration Sch. Visual Arts, 1981; features art dir. The Daily News, N.Y.C., 1987; sr. art dir. Wells, Rich, Greene Inc., N.Y.C., 1987-88; free-lance graphic designer/art dir., 1988-89; design dir. Roger Black Inc., N.Y.C., 1989-90; design dir. McCall's mag., N.Y.C., 1990-91; freelance art dir., 1991-92; dir., Continuing Edn Parson's Sch. Design, 1992—. Assoc. editor and designer: (book) Images of Labor, 1981.

VASSILOPOULOU-SELLIN, RENA, medical educator; b. Dec. 29, 1949. MD, Albert Einstein Coll. Medicine, 1974. Resident Montefiore Hosp., Bronx, 1974-77; fellow Northwestern U., Chgo., 1977-80; prof. Univ. Tex., Houston, 1980—. Fellow ACP, Am. Assn. Clin. Endocrinol.; mem. AAAS, AMA, Am. Soc. Bone and Mineral Rsch., Am. Diabetes Assn., Am. Soc. Clin. Oncology, Endo Soc. Office: Anderson Cancer Ctr 1515 Holcombe Blvd # 15 Houston TX 77030-4009

VASUDEVAN, RAMASWAMI, engineering consultant; b. Trichi, Tamil Nad, India, Nov. 28, 1947; came to U.S. 1970; s. Rajagopal and Jembakalakshmi; m. Padmini Vasudevan, mar. 20, 1980 (div. 1992). BE, Madras U., India, 1970; MS, UCLA, 1972. Registered profl. engr., Calif.; cert. plant engr., Calif. Project engr. Anco Engrs., Culver City, Calif., 1971-77; mgr. Wyle Labs., Norco, Calif., 1977-78, EDAC, Palo Alto, Calif., 1978-82; project mgr. Los Alamos (N.Mex.) Tech. Assocs., 1982-85; assoc. EQE Inc., Irvine, Calif., 1985-87; pres. Sidhi Cons., Inc., Santa Ana, Calif., 1987—. Contbr. articles to profl. jours. Mem. ASME, IEEE (stds. com. 1982-84), EERI, NFPA, EPRI-EQAG, Am. Inst. Plant Engrs., Am. Facilities Engrs., Nat. Elec. Testing Assn. Republican. Avocations: photography, sailing, bicycling. Office: Sidhi Cons Inc 4642 E Chapman Ave # 210 Orange CA 92869-4111

VATER, CHARLES J., lawyer; b. Pitts., Feb. 8, 1950; s. Joseph A. and Helen M. (Genellie) V.; m. Diane E. Vater, June 10, 1972; children: Allison D., Elizabeth A. BA, U. Notre Dame, 1971; JD, U. Pitts., 1975. Bar: Pa. 1975, U.S. Dist. Ct. (we. dist.) Pa. 1975, U.S. Ct. Appeals (3d cir.) 1979. Assoc. Tucker Arensberg, P.C., Pitts., 1975-80, ptnr., shareholder, 1980—, mng. shareholder. Contbr. articles to profl. jours. Mem. Allegheny County Bar Assn. (probate coun. 1988—), Estate Planning Coun. Pitts. (bd. dirs. 1988-90, 95—), Order of Coif, Phi Beta Kappa. Home: 1615 Trolist Dr Pittsburgh PA 15241-2650 Office: Tucker Arensberg 1500 One PPG Place Pittsburgh PA 15222

VATTER, PAUL AUGUST, business administration educator, dean; b. Boston, Sept. 14, 1924; s. August John and Elizabeth Emelia (Kunstler) V.; m. Josette Roman, July 23, 1966; children: Joel Paul, Katherine Alexandra. BA, Holy Cross Coll., 1944; MA, U. Pa., 1947, PhD, 1953; MA (hon.), Harvard U., 1970. Instr. U. Pa., Phila., 1945-53, asst. prof., 1953-58, vice dean of men, 1953-58; asst. dean Harvard U. Bus. Sch., Boston, 1958-62, assoc. prof. bus. adminstrn., 1962-70, prof., 1970-95, Lawrence E. Fouraker prof. bus. adminstrn., sr. assoc. dean, 1989-91, Lawrence E. Fouraken prof. bus. adminstrn. emeritus, 1995—; assoc. fellow Templeton Coll. Oxford (Eng.) U., 1996—; bd. dirs. Sbarro, Inc., L.I., N.Y. Author: Quantitative Methods in Management, 1978, The Structure of Retail Trade by Size of Store, 1979, also video tapes. Home: 244 Clifton St Belmont MA 02178-2647 Office: Harvard U Bus Sch Soldiers Fld Boston MA 02163

VAUDRY, J. WILLIAM, JR., lawyer; b. Jacksonsville, Fla., Jan. 18, 1941. BBA, Tulane U., 1962, LLB, 1967. Bar: La. 1967. Mem. Lemle & Kelleher, LLP, New Orleans. Bd. editors Tulane Law Rev., 1965-67. Lt. (j.g.) USN, 1962-64. Mem. ABA, La. State Bar Assn., New Orleans Bar Assn., Phi Delta Phi, Order of Coif. Address: Lemle & Kelleher LLP Pan Am Life Ctr 21st flr 601 Poydras St New Orleans LA 70130-6029

VAUGHAN, ALDEN TRUE, history educator; b. Providence, Jan. 23, 1929; s. Dana Prescott and Muriel Louise (True) V.; m. Lauraine A. Freethy, June 1, 1956 (div. 1981); children: Jeffrey Alden, Lynn Elizabeth; m. Virginia Mason Carr, July 16, 1983. BA, Amherst Coll., 1950; MEd, Columbia U., 1956, MA in History, 1958, PhD, 1964. Tchr. Hackley Sch., Tarrytown, N.Y., 1950-51, A.B. Davis High Sch., Mt. Vernon, N.Y., 1956-60; From history instr. to prof. Columbia U., N.Y.C., 1961—, prof. emeritus, 1994; editor Polit. Sci. Quar., N.Y., 1970-71; gen. editor Early Am. Indian Documents, Univ. Pubs. of Am., 1977—; assoc. editor Ency. of the N.Am. Colonies, Scribners, N.Y., 1993; vis. adj. prof. CUNY, Lehman Coll., N.Y.C., 1971; vis. prof. Clark U., Worcester, Mass., 1987. Author: New England Frontier, 1965, rev. edit., 1979, 3d edit., 1995, American Genesis, 1975, Shakespeare's Caliban, 1991, Roots of American Racism, 1995; contbr. articles to Am. Heritage, Am. Hist. Rev., New Eng. Quar., others. Lt. (j.g.) USNR, 1951-55. Recipient fellowship Guggenheim Found., 1973, Sr. fellowship Folger Shakespeare Libr., 1977, 89, Sr. fellowship Am. Antiquarian Soc., 1983. Mem. Am. Antiquarian Soc. (sr. fellowship), Am. Hist. Assn., Soc. Am. Historians (exec. sec., treas. 1965-70), Orgn. Am. Historians (program chmn. 1976), Inst. Early Am. History and Culture (coun. mem. 1985-87), Colonial Soc. Mass. Home: 50 Howland Ter Worcester MA 01602-2631

VAUGHAN, AUDREY JUDD, paralegal, musician; b. Washington, May 8, 1936; d. Deane Brewster and Elizabeth (Melamed) Judd; m. Arthur Harris Vaughan Jr., Feb. 7, 1959 (div. June 1976); 1 child, Erik Brewster. BA, Cornell U., 1958; postgrad., Eastman Sch. Music, 1959-62; cert. in paralegal studies, UCLA, 1977. Tchr. music Rochester (N.Y.) Sch. Sys., 1961-64, Gooden Sch., Sierra Madre, Calif., 1975-78; paralegal Nossaman, Kruger & Marsh, L.A., 1978-80, Latham Watkins, L.A., 1980-84, Burns Ammirato, Pasadena, Calif., 1984—; dir. Los Grillos, medieval and renaissance music performing group, Pasadena, 1965—. Organizer studies and presentations, bd. dirs., spkr. LWV, Pasadena, 1965-73. Mem. L.A. Paralegal Assn. (com. for paralegal edn., spkr. 1985—). Avocations: singing, playing renaissance instruments, hiking. Home: 2034 Glenview Ter Altadena CA 91001-2808

VAUGHAN, CLYDE VERNELSON, program director; b. Nashville, Mar. 5, 1941; s. Clearwood Vernelson and Mamie May (Patterson) V.; m. Linda Carol Bean, Dec. 5, 1977; children: Vaudi, Gary, Christopher, Patrick, Cheryl, Pamela. AA in Mgmt., Hawaii Pacific Coll., 1984; BBA in Econs., Campbell U., 1987, MBA, 1990. Printer Palm Beach Post, West Palm Beach, Fla., 1960-64; coord. VA Campbell U., Buies Creek, N.C., 1987-90; dir. Campbell U., Pope AFB, N.C., 1990—; mem. bd. transfer com. Fayetteville (N.C.) Tech. Coll., 1993—. Vice chmn. Cumberland County Bd. Adjustments, Fayetteville, 1992—. With U.S. Army, 1964-87. Mem. VFW, Am. Vets. Fgn. Wars, Am. Legion, Am. Motorcycle Assn. Baptist. Avocation: motorcycling. Home: 126 W Circle Ct Fayetteville NC 28301 Office: Campbell Univ Campus 384 Maynard St Ste A Pope AFB NC 28308-2373

VAUGHAN, DENNIS J., business executive. Dir. R&D Clark-Schwebel, Inc., Anderson, S.C. Office: Clark-Schwebel Inc 2200 S Murray Ave Anderson SC 29624-3139

VAUGHAN, EDWIN DARRACOTT, JR., urologist, surgeon; b. Richmond, Va., May 13, 1939; s. Edwin Darracott and Blanche V. (Bashaw) V.; m. Virginia Anne Lloyd, June 30, 1962; children: Edwin Darracott III, Barbara Anderson. BS, Washington and Lee U., 1961; MD, U. Va., 1965, MS, 1969; DSc, Washington and Lee U., 1982. Diplomate Am. Bd. Urology (trustee, v.p. 1988, pres. 1989). Intern Vanderbilt U., 1965-66, asst. resident, 1966-67; chief resident in urology U. Va., 1970-71, asst. prof. urology, 1973-75, assoc. prof., 1975-78, prof., 1978; clin. research fellow Columbia U., 1971-72, research assoc. dept. medicine, 1972-73; James J. Colt prof. urology, chmn. dept. urology Cornell U. Med. Coll., N.Y.C. and; attending urologist-in-chief N.Y. Hosp., N.Y.C., 1978—; sr. assoc. dean clin. affairs Cornell U. Med. Coll., N.Y.C., 1993—, chmn. dept. urology, 1993—; chief med. officer Cornell Physician Orgn., 1997—; mem. sci. adv. bd. Nat. Kidney Found., 1977-81; sec.-treas. Urology Coun., 1977-80, chmn., 1980-81; mem. med. adv. bd. Coun. High Blood Pressure, 1977. Editor: Seminars in Urology, 1983-95; assoc. editor Investigative Urology, 1977-78, mem. editorial bd., 1978-94; editor Campbell's Urology; contbr. articles on obstructive uropathy, renal hemodynamics, hypertension to profl. jours. Recipient Research Career Devel. award NIH, 1976-78; NIH tng. grantee, 1967-68; USPHS grantee, 1971-73, 74-77; Am. Heart Assn. grantee, 1976-79. Mem. ACS, AAAS, N.Y. Acad. Scis., Soc. Univ. Urologists, Am. Urol. Assn. (chmn. rsch. com. 1980-91, treas. N.Y. sect. 1985, v.p. N.Y. sect. 1986, pres. N.Y. sect. 1987, Golden Cystoscope award 1981, bd. dirs. 1992-97, Disting. Contbn. award 1992), Urol. Soc. Australasia (hon.), Soc. Exptl. Biology and Medicine, Soc. Univ. Surgeons, Soc. Internat. Urology, Am. Found. Urol. Disease (pres. 1987-92), Nat. Kidney and Urol. Disease Adv. Bd. (dep. chmn.), Intersoc. for Kidney and Urol. Disease Rsch. (chmn. 1987), Am. Assn. Genito-Urinary Surgeons (Barringen medal 1993), Am. Surg. Assn., Sigma Xi, Alpha Omega Alpha (award 1976), Omicron Delta Kappa (award 1981). Home: 1165 Park Ave Apt 6A New York NY 10128-1210 Office: 525 E 68th St New York NY 10021-4873

VAUGHAN, EMMETT JOHN, academic dean, insurance educator; b. Omaha, Dec. 1, 1934; s. Leo William and Mary (Simones) V.; m. Lonne Kay Smith, July 2, 1955; children: Therese, Timothy, Mary, Joan, Thomas, Michael, Emmett (dec.). BA in Econs., Creighton U., 1960; MA in Econs. and Ins., U. Nebr., 1962, PhD in Econs. and Ins., 1964. Asst. prof. U. Iowa, Iowa City, 1963-65, assoc. prof., 1965-68, Partington Disting. prof. ins., 1968—, dean Div. Continuing Edn., 1986—. Author: Fundamentals of Risk and Insurance, 1972, 7th edit., 1996, Risk Management, 1997; contbr. numerous articles to profl. jours. Participated in assessment of war damages in Kuwait UN Commn. on Compensation, 1992. Capt. USAR, 1955-75. Mem. Japan Risk Mgmt. Soc. (hon.). Office: U Iowa 116 Internat Ctr Inst Ins Edn & Rsch Iowa City IA 52242

VAUGHAN, HERBERT WILEY, lawyer; b. Brookline, Mass., June 1, 1920; s. David D. and Elzie G. (Wiley) V.; m. Ann Graustein, June 28, 1941. Student, U. Chgo., 1937-38; SB cum laude, Harvard U., 1941, LLB, 1948. Bar: Mass. 1948. Assoc. Hale and Dorr, Boston, 1948-54, jr. ptnr., 1954-56, sr. ptnr., 1956-82, co-mng. ptnr., 1976-80; pres. Herbert W. Vaughan, P.C., sr. ptnr. Hale and Dorr, 1982-89, of counsel, 1990-95, ret. ptnr., 1996. Sec. and mem. standing com., The Trustees of Reservations; mem. com. of Fund for Preservation of Wildlife and Natural Areas; mem. bd. trustees, Am. Friends of New Coll. (Oxford Univ.). Fellow Am. Bar Found. (life); mem. ABA, Chesterton Soc. (internat. com.), Mass. Bar Assn., Boston Bar Assn., Internat. Bar Assn., Am. Law Inst., Am. Coll. Real Estate Lawyers, Nat. Alumni Forum (mem. alumni leadership coun.), Bay Badminton and Tennis Club, Union Club (Boston), Boston Econ. Club, Longwood Cricket Club (Brookline, Mass.). Office: Hale and Dorr 60 State St Boston MA 02109-1800

VAUGHAN, JOHN CHARLES, III, horticultural products executive; b. N.Y.C., July 30, 1934; s. John Charles II and Lucille Grace (Dixon) V.; m. Ruth Darden MacLeod, Mar. 4, 1962; children: Elizabeth, John IV, George. AB in Econs., Cornell U., 1956; MBA, Northwestern U., 1962. Salesman Hall & Ellis, Chgo., 1959-62; br. mgr. Vaughan's Seed Co., Downers Grove, Ill., 1963-74, exec. v.p., 1974-76, pres., 1976-84, chmn. bd., 1985-93, ret., 1993; regional v.p. Am. Seed Trade Assn., Washington, 1985-88; pres. Atlantic Seedsmen's Assn., N.Y.C., 1968; dir. McHutchison LLC, Nat. Seed Co., Ill. & N.J., Jacklin Seed Co., Post Falls, Idaho, V.J. Growers, Inc., Apopka, Fla. Bd. dirs. George Williams Coll., Downers Grove, 1982-92. 1st Lt. USMCR, 1956-59. Mem. Downers Grove C. of C. (chmn. 1989).

VAUGHAN, JOSEPH LEE, language educator; b. Lynchburg, Va., Jan. 26, 1905; s. Ellis Lee and Anna Margaret (Worley) V.; m. Ann Cleveland Doner, Aug. 3, 1938 (dec. Aug. 1992); children: Joseph Lee, Ann Sahlman. AB, U. Va., 1926, AM, 1927, PhD, 1940. Instr. English, U. Va., Charlottesville, 1930-32; instr. English dept. engring. U. Va., 1932-35, asst. prof., 1936-40, assoc. prof., 1940-45, prof., 1945—, Joseph L. Vaughan prof. humanities, chmn. dept., 1970—, provost, 1956-60, chancellor Community Colls., 1960-66, dir. studies Humanities Inst., 1968-70; lectr., cons. Inst. Textile Tech., Charlottesville, 1947-81, pres., 1951-53; assoc. dir. sch. for tchrs. of English in engring. colls. U. Mich., 1941; mem. info. coun. NSF; cons. Va.-Md. Bankers Assn., Fieldcrest Mills, State Farm Ins. Co., Va. Employment Commn. Author: (with W.O. Birk, H. Melvin, F. Holmes) Basic Principles of Writing, 1937, rev. edit., 1943; (sect.) 19th Century America; Good Reading, 1948, Oral Communications for the Layman, (with O.A. Gianniny Jr.) Thomas Jefferson's Rotunda Restored, 1981, Rotunda Tales, 1991; editor: English Notes sect. Jour. Engring. Edn., 1936-40; contbr. articles to jours., 1940—; assoc. editor: Report on Instruction in English in Engineering Colleges in the U.S., 1940; assoc. editor and contbr.: A Guide to Good Reading, 1942-48; contbr. to prof. publs. Recipient Significant Sig award, 1969, Raven award, 1970, Disting. Prof. award, 1971, Mac Wade award, 1975, Disting. Svc. award Va. Engring. Found., 1991, Vaughan House, U. Va. named in his honor, 1992. Mem. Albemarle Art Assn., Albemarle Hist. Assn., Va. Watercolor Soc., Ctrl. Va. Watercolor Guild, Phi Beta Kappa, Omicron Delta Kappa, Pi Delta Epsilon, Sigma Chi, Raven Soc. Presbyterian. Clubs: Colonnade, Farmington Country. Specialist in communication techniques. Home: The Colonnades 2600 Barracks Rd Charlottesville VA 22901-2100

VAUGHAN, JOSEPH LEE, JR., education educator, consultant; b. Charlottesville, Va., Dec. 31, 1942; s. Joseph Lee and Ann (Doner) V.; m. Linda Marie; children: Leigh Ann, Kelley. BA, U. Va., 1964, MEd, 1968, EdD, 1974. Tchr. Madison (Va.) High Sch., 1965-67, Darlington Sch., Rome, Ga., 1967-69, Woodberry Forest (Va.) Sch., 1969-74; asst. prof. edn. U. Ariz., Tucson, 1974-80; prof. Tex. A&M U., Commerce, 1980—, dir. programs in reading edn., 1980-86, 91-02; dir. programs in reading edn. East Tex. State U., 1980-86, 91-92; dir. Tex. Ctr. Learning Styles, 1989-95; bd. dirs. Nat. Learning Styles Network, 1991-95; exec. dir. Children's Inst. of Love and Discovery, Inc., 1995—. Co-author: Reading and Learning in Content Classrooms, 1978, 2d rev. edit., 1985, Reading and Reasoning Beyond The Primary Grades, 1986. Bd. govs. Sancta Sophia Sem., 1991—. Mem. ASCD, Nat. Reading Conf., Internat. Reading Assn., Internat. Inst. Integral Human Scis., Agni Yoga Soc. Universalist. Avocations: spiritual sci. studies, golf, travel, reading. Home: 3204 Wentwood Dr Dallas TX 75225 Office: Tex A&M U at Commerce 2600 Motley Dr Mesquite TX 75150-3840 *I am most content when I find time every day to laugh, love, and learn.*

VAUGHAN, JOSEPH ROBERT, lawyer; b. Los Angeles, Jan. 28, 1916; s. Vincent B. and Lucile (Eichler) V.; m. Margaret Koetters, Jan. 20, 1940; children: Barbara (Sister Kieran, CSJ), Christine, Judith (Sister Judith Marie, CSJ). A.B., Loyola U., 1937, J.D., 1939. Bar: Calif. 1939. Mem. firm Vaughan, Brandlin, Robinson & Roemer, 1939-65; v.p. finance Knudsen Creamery Co. of Calif., Los Angeles, 1965; exec. v.p. Knudsen Creamery Co. of Calif., 1965-69; pres. Knudsen Corp., 1969-71, pres., chief exec. officer, 1971-77, chmn., pres., 1977-78, chmn. bd., 1979-80; bd. dirs. Dominguez Water Co., 1983-91, Fed. Res. Bank of San Francisco, 1973-84, chmn. L.A. br., 1974-77, Carson Estate Co., 1981-89. Bd. dirs. Los Angeles Beautiful, 1957-65, fin. chmn., 1980; trustee Pacific Legal Found., 1973-85; trustee Mt. St. Mary's Coll., 1979-83, regent, 1983—; bd. dirs. Daniel Freeman Hosp., 1955-65, sec., 1959-60, pres., 1963-65; bd. dirs. Nat. Dairy Coun., 1972-81, vice chmn., 1978-81; bd. visitors Loyola Law Sch., 1978-90, chmn., 1978-79; bd. regents Loyola Marymount U., 1973-79; bd. dirs. Tom and Valley Knudsen Found., 1954-96, pres., 1971-96; bd. dirs. Fritz B. Burns Found., 1986—, William H. Hannon Found., 1989—, Dominguez Hills Found., Calif. State U., 1990-94, Kirk Mayer, Inc., 1992-94. Mem. Calif. State Bar Assn., Inst. Corp. Counsel (gov. 1981-85), Los Angeles C. of C. (gov. 1971-73). Home: 404 Lorraine Blvd Los Angeles CA 90020-4730 Office: 1434 Omni Ctr 900 Wilshire Blvd Los Angeles CA 90017-4701

VAUGHAN, KIRK WILLIAM, banker; b. St. Louis, Oct. 16, 1943; s. William Edward and Daisy Lenore (Coates) V.; m. Barbara Jean Aaron, Mar. 7, 1986; children: William Aaron, Michael Bartlett. BA, Baker U., 1966. Field sales mgr. Ford Motor Co., Richmond, Va., 1967-73; exec. v.p. United Mo. Bank of Kansas City, 1973—. Editor: The Best of Bill Vaughan, 1979. Republican. Presbyterian. Home: 800 W 54th St Kansas City MO 64112-2330 Office: United Mo Bank Kansas City 1010 Grand Blvd Kansas City MO 64106-2225

VAUGHAN, LINDA, publishing executive. Pub. Soap Opera Digest, N.Y.C. *

VAUGHAN, MARTHA, biochemist; b. Dodgeville, Wis., Aug. 4, 1926; d. John Anthony and Luciel (Ellingen) V.; m. Jack Orloff, Aug. 4, 1951 (dec. Dec. 1988); children: Jonathan Michael, David Geoffrey, Gregory Joshua. Ph.B., U. Chgo., 1944; M.D., Yale U., 1949. Intern New Haven Hosp., Conn., 1950-51; research fellow U. Pa., Phila., 1951-52; research fellow Nat. Heart Inst., Bethesda, Md., 1952-54, mem. research staff, 1954-68; head metabolism sect. Nat. Heart and Lung Inst., Bethesda, 1968-74; acting chief molecular disease br. Nat. Heart, Lung and Blood Inst., Bethesda, 1974-76, chief cell metabolism lab., 1974-94; dep. chief pulmonary and critical care medicine br. Nat. Heart, Lung, and Blood Inst., Bethesda, 1994—; mem. metabolism study sect. NIH, 1965-68; mem. bd. sci. counselors Nat. Inst. Alcohol Abuse and Alcoholism, 1988-91. Mem. editl. bd. Jour. Biol. Chemistry, 1971-76, 80-83, 88-90, assoc. editor, 1992—; editl. adv. bd. Molecular Pharmacology, 1972-80, Biochemistry, 1989-94; editor: Biochemistry and Biophysics Rsch. Comms., 1990-91; contbr. articles to profl. jours., chpts. to books. Bd. dirs. Found. Advanced Edn. in Scis., Inc., Bethesda, 1979-92, exec. com., 1980-92, treas., 1984-86, v.p., 1986-88, pres., 1988-90; mem. Yale U. Coun. com. med. affairs, New Haven, 1974-80. Recipient Meritorious Svc. medal HEW, 1974, Disting. Svc. medal NEW, 1979, Commd. Officer award USPHS, 1982, Superior Svc. award USPHS, 1993. Mem. NAS, Am. Acad. Arts and Scis., Am. Soc. Biol. Chemists (chmn. pub. com. 1984-86), Assn. Am. Physicians, Am. Soc. Clin. Investigation. Home: 11608 W Hill Dr Rockville MD 20852-3751 Office: Nat Heart Lung & Blood Inst NIH Bldg 10 Rm 5N-307 Bethesda MD 20892

VAUGHAN, MICHAEL RICHARD, lawyer; b. Chgo., Aug. 27, 1936; s. Michael Ambrose and Loretta M. (Parks) V.; m. Therese Marie Perri, Aug. 6, 1960; children—Charles Thomas, Susan Enger. Student U. Ill., 1954-59; LL.B., U. Wis., 1962. Bar: Wis. 1962. Chief atty. bill drafting sect. Wis. Legislature, 1962-68; dir. legis. attys., Wis., 1968-72; assoc. Murphy & Desmond, and predecessor, Madison, Wis., 1972-73, ptnr., 1974—; mem. Commn. Uniform State Laws, 1966-72; cons. Nat. Commn. on Marihuana and Drug Abuse, 1971-73; dir. State Bar Govtl. and Adminstrv. Law Sect., 1971-78, State Bar Interprofl. and Bus. Relations Comm., 1976-89; lectr. continuing legal edn. seminars. Warden and vestryman St. Dunstan's Episcopal Ch., 1973-78, 80-87; mem. Wis. Episc. Conf., 1972-76. Mem. ABA, State Bar of Wis., Dane County Bar Assn., U. Wis. Law Sch. Bencher Soc., Delta Kappa Epsilon. Club: Madison. Contbr. articles to profl. jours. Home: 4714 Lafayette Dr Madison WI 53705-4865 Office: 2E E Mifflin St Madison WI 53701-2038

VAUGHAN, ODIE FRANK, oil company executive; b. Camden, Ark., Feb. 3, 1936; s. Odie Frank and Bernece (May) V.; m. Sandra Beard, Sept. 8, 1962; children: Christopher Michael, Laura Elizabeth. Student, So. State U., 1954-55; BS in Acctg., La. Tech. U., 1959. Acct. Peat, Marwick, Mitchell & Co., Dallas, 1959-61; asst. v.p., dir. tax Murphy Oil Corp., El Dorado, Ark., 1962-72, treas., 1991—; v.p., treas. Ocean Drilling and Exploration Co., New Orleans, 1973-91. Mem. AICPA, Am. Petroleum Inst. (gen. tax com.), Fin. Execs. Inst., Tax Execs. Inst. Baptist. Home: 1700 N Calion Rd El Dorado AR 71730-3420 Office: Murphy Oil Corp 200 Peach St El Dorado AR 71730

VAUGHAN, PETER HUGH, theater critic; b. Oxford, Eng., Dec. 12, 1937; children: Rachel V., Thomas Hugh, Jeremy P. BA, Yale U., 1959; LLB, London U., 1963. With Mpls. Star Tribune, 1965—, theater critic, 1974—. Mem. French-Am. Theatrical Friendship Soc. Montrichard (founding), John Falstaff Eating and Drinking Ensemble of Otisville. Avocations: travel, reading, tennis, cooking, gun control. Office: Star Tribune 425 Portland Ave Minneapolis MN 55415-1511

VAUGHAN, ROLAND, church administrator. Dir. Ch. of God World Missions. Office: Ch of God World Missions PO Box 8016 Cleveland TN 37320-8016*

VAUGHAN, SAMUEL SNELL, editor, author, publisher; b. Phila., Aug. 3, 1928; s. Joseph and Anna Catherine (Alexander) V.; m. Jo LoBiondo, Oct. 22, 1949; children: Jeffrey Marc, Leslie Jane, Dana Alexander, David Samuel. B.A., Pa. State U., 1951. Deskman King Features Syndicate, N.Y.C., 1951; asst. mgr. Doubleday Syndicate, 1952-54; advt. mgr. Doubleday & Co., Inc., N.Y.C., 1954-56; sales mgr., 1956-58, sr. editor, 1958-68; exec. editor Doubleday & Co., Inc., 1969-70, pub., pres. pub. div., 1970-82, v.p. parent co., 1970-86, editor in chief, 1982-86; sr. v.p., editor Random House, Inc., 1986-90, editor-at-large, 1990—; mem. faculty dept. English, Columbia U., 1978-88; lectr. Harvard-Radcliffe U., Libr. Congress, U. Denver, Bowker meml. lectr. Author: (juvenile) Whoever Heard of Kangaroo Eggs? 1957, New Shoes, 1961, The Two-Thirty Bird, 1965, (history) The Little Church, 1969, Medium Rare: A Look at the Book and Its People, 1977, (humor) Little Red Hood, 1979, The Accidental Profession, 1979, The Community of the Book, 1983, The State of the Heart, 1985; editor: Buckley: The Right Word, 1996; contbr. to N.Y. Times, Sunday Times of London, Daedalus, Am. Heritage, others. Served with USMC, 1946-48. Named Disting. Alumnus Pa. State U., 1977, Alumni fellow, 1981. Mem. Tenafly Tennis Club, Quantuck Beach Club (Westhampton, N.Y.), Century Assn. Episcopalian. Home: 23 Inness Rd Tenafly NJ 07670-2714 Office: c/o Random House 201 E 50th St New York NY 10022-7703

VAUGHAN, THOMAS JAMES GREGORY, historian; b. Seattle, Oct. 13, 1924; s. Daniel George and Kathryn Genevieve (Browne) V.; m. Elizabeth Ann Perpetua Crownhart, June 16, 1951; children: Meagan, Margot, Stephen, Cameron. BA, Yale U., 1948; MS, U. Wis., 1950, doctoral residence, 1951-53; LittD, Pacific U., 1969; LLD, Reed Coll., 1975. Exec. dir. Oreg. Hist. Soc., Portland, 1954-90; editor in chief Oreg. Hist. Quar., 1954-89; adj. prof. Portland State U., 1968—; chmn. bd. Salar Enterprises, Ltd.; bd. dirs. Am. Heritage Pub. Co., 1976-85; film producer, 1958-76; historian laureate State of Oreg., 1989. Author: A Century of Portland Architecture, 1967, Captain Cook, R.N, The Resolute Mariner: An International Record of Oceanic Discovery, 1974, Portland, A Historical Sketch and Guide, 1976, 2d edit., 1983, Voyage of Enlightenment: Malaspina on the Northwest Coast, 1977; editor: Space, Style and Structure: Building in Northwest America, 2 vols., 1974, The Western Shore, 1975, Ascent of the Athabasca Pass, 1978, Wheels of Fortune, High and Mighty, 1981, Soft Gold, 1982, 2d edit., 1990, To Siberia and Russian America, Vols. I, II and III, also others.; co-editor: Siberica, 1989; mem. adv. bd. Am. Heritage Mag., 1977-90; prodr. film The Crimean War, 1994. 1st chmn. Oreg. State Com. for Humanities, NEH, 1969—; 1st chmn. Gov.'s Adv. Com. on Historic Preservation Oreg., 1970-77; sec. Oreg. Geog. Names Bd., 1958-89; adviser 1000 Friends of Oreg., 1972—; lay mem. Oreg. State Bar Disciplinary Rev. Bd., 1975-82; vice chmn. adv. panel Nat. Endowment Arts, 1975—; mem. Nat. Hist. Publs. and Records Commn. Matrix, 1975-76; historian laureate State of Oreg., 1989. With USMC, 1942-45. Decorated comdr. Order Brit. Empire; recipient Aubrey Watzek award Lewis and Clark Coll., 1975;, Edith Knight Hill award, 1977, Disting. Svc. award U. Oreg.; grantee English Speaking Union, 1961; Columbia Maritime Mus. 1st rsch. fellow, 1992. Fellow Royal Geog. Soc.; mem. Am. Assn. State and Local History (bd. dirs. 1955-74, pres. 1976-78), Am. Assn. Mus. (coun., exec. com.), Nat. Trust Hist. Preservation (adv. coun.), Ctr. for Study Russian Am., Russian Acad. Scis., City Club (Portland, bd. govs.), Univ. Club (Portland, bd. govs.), The Arts Club (London). Home: 2135 SW Laurel St Portland OR 97201-2367

VAUGHAN, WILLIAM WALTON, atmospheric scientist; b. Clearwater, Fla., Sept. 7, 1930; s. William Walton and Ella Vermelle (Warr) V.; m. Wilma Geraldine Stapleton, Dec. 23, 1951; children: Stephen W., David A., William D., Robert T. BS with honors, U. Fla., 1951; grad. cert., USAF Inst. Tech./Fla. State U., 1952; PhD, U. Tenn., 1976. Sci. asst. Air Force Armament Center, Eglin AFB, Fla., 1955-58; Army Ballistic Missile Agy., Huntsville, Ala., 1958-60; chief aerospace environ. div. Marshall Space Flight Center, NASA, Huntsville, 1960-76; chief atmospheric scis. div. Marshall Space Flight Center, NASA, 1976-86; rsch. prof. atmospheric sci. U. Ala., Huntsville, 1986—, dir. Rsch. Inst., 1986-94; retired, 1994; cons. atmospheric sci.; mem. adv. com. NASA. Reviewer, contbr. articles to profl. jours. Served to capt. USAF, 1951-55. Recipient Exceptional Service medal NASA, 1971. Assoc. fellow AIAA (Losey Atmospheric Scis. award 1980); fellow Am. Meterol. Soc.; mem. AAAS, Am. Geophys. Union, Sigma Xi. Office: Univ Ala Atmospheric Sci Dept Huntsville AL 35899

VAUGHAN, WORTH EDWARD, chemistry educator; b. N.Y.C., Feb. 1, 1936; s. Royal Worth and Sylvia Marie (Fernholz) V.; m. Diane Marilyn Mayer, Aug. 9, 1969; 1 child, Wayne John. B.A., Oberlin Coll., 1957; M.A., Princeton U., 1959, Ph.D., 1960. Asst. prof. chemistry U. Wis.-Madison, 1961-66, assoc. prof., 1967-76, prof., 1977—; mem. bd. advisors Am. Exchange Bank West Br., Madison, 1983-87. Author: Dielectric Properties and Molecular Behavior, 1969; editor: Digest of Literature on Dielectrics, 1974; translation editor: Dipole Moments of Organic Compounds, 1970; contbr. articles to profl. jours. Mem. Am. Chem. Soc. (pres. Wis. sect. 1968, sec. 1968, 97), Am. Phys. Soc., AAAS, Phi Beta Kappa, Sigma Xi, Alpha Chi Sigma. Avocations: canoeing, contract bridge. Home: 501 Ozark Trl Madison WI 53705-2538 Office: Univ Wis 1101 University Ave Madison WI 53706-1322

VAUGHEN, JUSTINE L., rehabilitation hospital medical professional; b. Wilmington, Del., Apr. 21, 1930; d. John Victor and Charlotte (Leicht) V.; m. Richard M. Fry, June 26, 1955; children: Martha Hilary Morrow, Amanda Tung. BS, Stetson U., 1950; MD, Temple U., 1954. Diplomate Am. Bd. Physical Medicine and Rehab. Resident physical medicine, rehab. U. Mich., Ann Arbor, 1954-59; asst. prof. physical medicine, rehab. U. Mich. Hosp., Ann Arbor, 1959-60; private practice Gainesville, Fla., 1961—; chief rehab. med. svc. VA Med. Ctr., Gainesville, Fla., 1971—; med. dir. Upreach Rehab. Hosp., Gainesville, Fla., 1986-95; co-clin. prof. U. Fla., Gainesville, 1967—; cons. Vocat. Rehab., State Fla., 1986—; adv. coun. State Divsn. Vocat. Rehab., Tallahassee, 1980-95. Pres. D.A.R.E., Gainesville, 1992-94; bd. dirs. Altrusa House, Gainesville, 1991—. Mem. AMA, Am. Acad. Phys. Medicine and Rehab., Fla. Soc. Phys. Medicine and Rehab. (pres. 1992-94), Fla. Med. Assn., Altrusa Internat., Am. Assn. Electrodiagnostic Medicine. Avocation: gardening. Office: Rehab Medicine Assoc 4881 NW 8th Ave Ste 2 Gainesville FL 32605-4582

VAUGHN, E(LBERT) HARDY, insurance and financial company executive; b. Durham, N.C., Oct. 2, 1946; s. Elbert Harding and June Gray (Bailey) V.; m. Sara Ann Hargis, June 22, 1968; 1 child, Brandon Thomas. BSBA, U. N.C., 1968; MS in Fin. Svc., Am. Coll., Bryn Mawr, Pa., 1983. CLU; chartered fin. cons. Group ins. rep. Home Security Life, Durham, 1968-70; group ins. mgr. Home Security Life, Orlando, Fla., 1970-73; v.p. Anthony & Vaughn, Inc., Orlando, 1973-89; pres. The Vaughn Group, Inc., Orlando, 1990—. Mem. Nat. Assn. Life Underwriters (nat. quality award, nat. sales achievment award, health ins. quality award), Assn. for Advanced Life Underwriting, Am. Soc. for CLU and Chartered Fin. Cons., Cen. Fla. Estate Planning Coun. (bd. dirs. pres. 1980—), Employee Benefits Coun. Cen. Fla. (bd. dirs. 1987—), Million Dollar Round Table. Republican. Avocation: golf. Home: 2115 Alameda Ave Orlando FL 32804-6903 Office: 1407 E Robinson St Orlando FL 32801-2118

VAUGHN, GREGORY LAMONT, professional baseball player; b. Sacramento, July 3, 1965. Student, Sacramento City Coll., Miami Coll. Player Milw. Brewers, 1986-96, San Diego Padres, 1996—; mem. Am. League All-Star Team, 1993, 96. Named Midwest co-MVP, 1987, Am. Assn. MVP, 1989. Office: San Diego Padres PO Box 2000 San Diego CA 92112-2000*

VAUGHN, JACKIE, III, state legislator. BA, Hillsdale (Mich.) Coll.; MA, Oberlin (Ohio) Coll.; LittB, Oxford U.; LLD (hon.), Marygrove Coll., Detroit, Shaw Coll., Detroit; HHD (hon.), Highland Park (Mich.) Community Coll. Tchr. U. Detroit, Wayne State U., Detroit, 1963-64; mem. Mich. Ho. of Reps., Lansing, 1966-78; mem. Mich. Senate, Lansing, 1978—, asst. pres. pro tem, 1978-82, pres. pro tem, 1982-86, assoc. pres. pro tem, 1986—. Past pres. Mich. Young Dems.; chmn. Mich. Dr. Martin Luther King Jr. Holiday commn.; exec. bd. dirs. Detroit NAACP. With USN. Fulbright fellow; recipient Frank J. Wieting Meml. Service award, 1977, Focus and Impact award Cotillion Club, 1980, Outstanding Achievement award Booker T. Washington Bus. Assn., Outstanding Community Service award Charles Stewart Mott Community Coll. and Urban Coalition of Greater Flint, Mich., 1981; named Outstanding State Senator of Yr., Detroit Urban League Guild, 1983, Most Outstanding Legislator of Yr., Washburn-Ilene Block Club, 1983, numerous others. Mem. Am. Oxonian Assn., Fulbright Alumni Assn. Baptist. Home: 19930 Roslyn Rd Detroit MI 48221-1853 Office: Mich Senate PO Box 30036 Lansing MI 48909-7536

VAUGHN, JAMES ENGLISH, JR., neurobiologist; b. Kansas City, Mo., Sept. 17, 1939; s. James English and Sue Katherine (Vaughn); m. Christine Singleton, June 18, 1961; children: Stephanie, Stacey. B.A., Westminster Coll., 1961; Ph.D., UCLA, 1965. Postdoctoral rsch. fellow in brain rsch. U. Edinburgh (Scotland), 1965-66; asst. prof. Boston U. Sch. Medicine, 1966-70; head sect. of molecular neuromorphology Beckman Rsch. Inst. of City of Hope, Duarte, Calif., 1970—, pres. rsch. staff, 1986, chmn. div. neuroscience, 1987—. Fellow Neuroscience Rsch. Program, 1969; Rsch. grantee NIH, 1969—, NSF, 1983-87. Mem. AAAS, Am. Soc. Cell Biology, Am. Assn. Anatomists, Soc. for Neuroscience (chmn. short course 1977), Internat. Brain Rsch. Orgn., N.Y. Acad. Scis., Sigma Xi. Achievements include original immunoelectron microscopic demonstration of a neurotransmiter synthesizing enzyme in brain synaptic terminals; original proposal and evidence of synaptotropic modulation of dendritic development in the central nervous system; discovered that genetically-associated changes in neuronal migration correlate with altered patterns of synaptic connectivity in the brain; discovered that all neurons of a major brain relay station use GABA as their neurotransmitter; discovered previously unknown cholinergic neurons in the brain and spinal cord; discovered unique migratory patterns of preganglionic sympathetic neurons in developing spinal cord; first demonstration that there are both nitric oxide positive and negative preganglionic sympathetic neurons; first demonstration that preganglionic sympathetic motor neurons are more resistant to excitotoxins than somatic motor neurons; first immunocytochemical evidence of a role gamma aminobutyric acid (GABA) neurons in focal epilepsy; first demonstration of lesion-induced synaptic plasticity of GABA neurons; contbr. articles to profl. jours.; assoc. editor Jour. Neurocytology, 1978-86; mem. editorial bd. Synapse, 1986—; reviewer for Jour. Comparative Neurology, 1974—, Brain Research, 1976—. Office: Beckman Research Inst 1450 Duarte Rd Duarte CA 91010-3011

VAUGHN, JOHN CARROLL, minister, educator; b. Louisville, Sept. 22, 1948; s. Harold D. and Morel (Johnson) V.; m. Brenda Joyce Lyttle, June 17, 1968; children: Deborah, John, Rebecca, Daniel, Joseph. BA, Bob Jones U., 1977, MMin, 1991, DD, 1989. Ordained to ministry Bapt. Ch., 1978. Sr. pastor Faith Baptist Ch., Greenville, S.C., 1977—; founder/adminstr. Hidden Treasure Christian Sch., Greenville, S.C., 1980-84; founder Iglesia Bautista de la Fe, Greenville, S.C., 1981-93; founder/dir. Hidden Treasure Ministries, Greenville, 1985—; exec. bd. Associated Gospel Chs., Hopewell, Va., 1987-93; chaplain Greenville Police Dept., 1987—. Editor: (instrnl. video) Sufficient Grace, 1987; author: (textbook) Special Education: A Biblical Approach, 1991, (biography) More Precious Than Gold, 1994. Chmn. Greenville County Human Rels. Commn., 1986-89; lt. col., chaplain Greenville Composite Squadron CAP, 1985—; counselor Greenville County Crisis Response Team, 1987-91; co-chmn. Greenville County Sex Edn. Adv. Com., 1988-91; mem. exec. bd. dirs. Fundamental Bapt. Fellowship, 1988—, The Wilds, 1992—, Internat. Bapt. Missions, 1993—, Christians for Religious Freedom, 1993—. Mem. Internat. Conf. Police Chaplains, Am. Assn. Christian Schs. (exec. bd. dirs. 1992—), ACFT Owners and Pilots Assn., S.C. Law Enforcement Assn., S.C. Assn. Christian Schs. (pres. 1988—). Republican. Avocations: flying, golf, gardening, reading, history, writing. Home: 117 Frontline Dr Taylors SC 29687-2675 Office: Faith Bapt Ch 500 W Lee Rd Taylors SC 29687-2513

VAUGHN, JOHN ROLLAND, auditor; b. Iola, Kans., Aug. 4, 1938; s. Ralph H. and Alice (Dille) V.; m. Doris K. Black, Sept. 4, 1960; children: Lisa Ann, Brian Douglas. BS in Bus, Emporia State U., 1960. Sr. auditor Arthur Andersen & Co., Kansas City, Mo., 1961-66; gen. auditor First Nat. Bank Kansas City, 1966-69, Commerce Bancshares, Inc., 1969-73; sr. v.p. Adminstrv. Services div. Peoples Trust Bank, Ft. Wayne, Ind., 1973-77; dep. gen. auditor, v.p. Crocker Nat. Bank, San Francisco, 1978-79; v.p., gen. auditor S.W. Bancshares, Houston, 1980-83; sr. v.p., gen. auditor MCorp., Houston, 1984-87, mng. dir., 1988-89; audit dir. Banc One Corp., Dallas, 1990-92; v.p., gen. auditor St. Paul Cos., St. Paul, 1992—. Treas. Overland Park (Kans.) Jr. C. of C., 1965-66; outside dir. Overland Park Credit Union; controller Fort Wayne Bicentennial Commn., 1974-77. Mem. Mo. Air N.G., 1961-67. Mem. Inst. Internal Auditors (1st v.p. Kansas City 1969-70, pres. 1970-71, midwest regional v.p. 1971-72, Twin Cities chpt. gov. 1993—, pres. 1994-95, internat. profl. conf. com. 1995—), Fin. Execs. Inst. (dir. Ft. Wayne 1976-77), Risk and Ins. Mgmt. Soc., Hartsmen, Soc. Preservation and Encouragement Barber Shop Quartet Singing in Am., Vocal Majority Chorus, Gt. No. Union Chorus, Sigma Tau Gamma. Home: 8986 Hunters Trl Woodbury MN 55125-8667 Office: 385 Washington St Saint Paul MN 55102-1309

VAUGHN, JOHN VERNON, banker, industrialist; b. Grand Junction, Colo., June 24, 1909; s. John S. and Alice Ann (Baylis) V.; m. Dorothy May Pickrell, Oct. 12, 1934; children: Dorothy (Mrs. Richard H. Stone), John Spencer. AB, UCLA, 1932; LLD (hon.), Pepperdine U., 1974. Br. mgr. Nat. Lead Co., 1932-37; sales mgr. Sillers Paint & Varnish Co., 1937-46, pres., gen. mgr., dir., 1946-58; pres., chmn. Dartell Labs., Inc., 1959-70; vice chmn. bd. Crocker Nat. Bank and Crocker Nat. Corp., San Francisco, 1970-75; dir. Crocker Nat. Bank and Crocker Nat. Corp., 1969-85; hon. dir. Crocker Nat. Bank; cons. Coopers & Lybrand, 1975-85; chmn. bd. Recon Optical, Inc., 1979-90; bd. dirs. Trust Svcs. Am., Forest Lawn Corp., Am. Security & Fidelity Corp.; IT Corp. Chmn. San Marino Recreation Commn., 1956-58, La. Better Bus. Bur., 1959-61, Invest-in-Am., 1970-73; chmn. citizen's adv. Council Pub. Transp., 1965-67; commr. Los Angeles Coliseum Commn., 1971-74; trustee Calif. Mus. Found., 1968-79; bd. dirs. Orthopaedic Hosp., 1965-87, pres., 1974-78, chmn. bd., 1978-79; bd. dirs. YMCA, Los Angeles, 1965-77, Central City Assn., So. Calif. Visitors Council, 1970-76, NCCJ, Calif. Museum Sci. and Industry, United Way of Los Angeles, Am. Heart Assn.; mem. Los Angeles Adv. Bd., Friends of Claremont Coll., 1973-78, Los Angeles Beautiful, 1972-74; regent U. Calif., 1958-59; hon. trustee UCLA Found., 1967—, Forest Lawn Meml. Park, 1968—, Claremont Men's Coll., 1970-71, Pepperdine U., 1972—; regent, mem. bd. visitors Grad. Sch. Bus. Adminstrn. UCLA, 1971-85; mem. Chancellor's Assocs., Calif. State Univs. and Colls. mem. Assistance League, So. Calif. Adv. Bd., 1974—. Recipient Disting. Svc. award UCLA, 1965, Outstanding Community Svc. award UCLA, , 1970, Alumnus of Yr. UCLA award, 1971; Brotherhood award NCCJ, 1971; Los Angeles Jaycees award of merit, 1972; Most Disting. Citizen Los Angeles Realty Bd., 1972; other honors. Mem. Los Angeles Area C. of C. (bd. dirs. 1961, pres. 1969, chmn. 1970), World Affairs Coun. (chpt. v.p., treas. 1970-85, hon. dir. 1985—), Iranian-Am. Chamber Industry and Commerce (pres. 1971-79), Paint, Varnish and Lacquer Assn. (past nat. v.p., past chpt. pres.), Town Hall Calif. (dir. 1973-75), Young Pres.'s Orgn., Jonathan Club (pres. 1964), Los Angeles Country Club (bd. dirs. 1979-85), California Club, San Gabriel Country Club (bd. dirs. 1964-68), Valley Hunt Club, Pasadena Athletic Club, Bohemian Club of San Francisco, Internat. Order St. Hubertus, Masons, Beta Theta Pi (pres. 1960). Republican. Presbyterian. Avocations: fishing, hunting, golf. Home and Office: 454 S Orange Grove Blvd Pasadena CA 91105

VAUGHN, KAREN IVERSEN, economics educator; b. N.Y.C., July 21, 1944; d. Willy and Cecelia (Douglas) Iversen; m. Garrett Alan Vaughn, Sept. 7, 1968; 1 child, Jessica Susan. BA, Queens Coll. CUNY, 1966; MA, Duke U., 1969, PhD, 1971. Asst. prof. U. Tenn., Knoxville, 1969-75; assoc. prof. George Mason U., Fairfax, Va., 1978-84, chmn. dept. econs., 1982-89, prof. econs., 1984—; sr. rsch. asssoc. Ctr. for Study Market Processes, 1981-92; adj. scholar CATO Inst., Washington, 1982-90. Author: John Locke: Economist and Social Scientist, 1980, Austrian Economics in America: The Migration of a Tradition, 1994; editor: Perspectives on the History of Economic Thought, vol. 10, 1994; mem. editorial bd. History of Polit. Economy Jour., 1984-88, Jour. of History of Economic Thought, 1993—; editor: HES Bull., 1978-84; contbr. articles to profl. jours. NDEA fellow, 1966-69. Mem. So. Econs. Assn. (exec. com. 1978-80, v.p. 1986-87, pres.-elect 1993-94, pres. 1994-95), Am. Econs. Assn., History of Econs. Soc. (v.p. 1988-89, pres.-elect 1991-92, pres. 1992-93), Soc. for the Devel. of Australian Econs. (founding mem., 1st pres. 1996-97), Mont Pelerin Soc. Avocations: piano, voice. Office: George Mason U Dept Economics 4400 University Dr Fairfax VA 22030-4422

VAUGHN, LEWIS A., magazine editor, writer; b. Greenville, S.C., Dec. 30, 1950; s. Lewis A. Vaughn and Edith (Massengill) Arnett; m. Kathleen Ann Patrick, Aug. 25, 1973; children: Erin, Patrick. BA in English, U. Dayton, 1973; MA in English, Miami U., Oxford, Ohio, 1978. Book editor, writer TAB Books, Blue Ridge Summit, Pa., 1976-79; sr. copywriter Nat. Liberty Mktg., Valley Forge, Pa., 1979-82; assoc., sr. editor Prevention Mag., Emmaus, Pa., 1982-88, mng. editor, 1988—. Author: Chilton's Guide to Home Energy Savings, 1982; editor: Health Smarts, 1990; co-author: How to Think Aboue Weird Things, 1995. Mem. Nat. Assn. Sci. Writers. Home: 5277 Lakeview St Germansville PA 18053 Office: Prevention Mag 33 E Minor St Emmaus PA 18098-0001

VAUGHN, MAURICE SAMUEL (MO VAUGHN), professional baseball player; b. Norwalk, Conn., Dec. 15, 1967. Student, Seton Hall U., 1987-89. Infielder Boston Red Sox, 1989—. Active cmty. svc. with youth groups, Boston. Named MVP Baseball Writers' Assn., 1995; named to Sporting News Silver SLugger team, 1995, Am. League All-Star Team, 1995. Office: Boston Red Sox 4 Yawkey Way Boston MA 02215-3409*

VAUGHN, ROBERT LOCKARD, aerospace and astronautics company executive; b. Rochester, N.Y., Sept. 19, 1922; s. Henry Clifford and Belva Blanche (Lockard) V.; m. Virginia Ethel Harness, June 19, 1943; children—Sandra Sue, Roberta Jean, Larry Lockard, Virginia Gail. B.S. in M.E. Iowa State U. Sci. and Tech., 1952; MS in Tech. Adminstrv. Mgmt., Calif. State U., Northridge, 1967. Registered profl. engr., Calif. Journeyman Washington Naval Gun Factory, 1940-49; lab. technician U.S. AEC, Ames (Iowa) Lab., 1949-52; with Lockheed Corp., 1953-88; corp. dir. productivity Lockheed Missiles & Space Co., Inc., Sunnyvale, Calif., 1977-88; pres. R.L. Vaughn & Assoc., Cons. Engrs., Ramona, Calif., 1988—. Contbr. over 140 articles to tech. jours. and other publications. With AUS, World War II, ETO. Recipient Calif. State Legis. Resolution award, 1982; various other awards. Fellow ASME, Soc. Mfg. Engrs. (Internat. Gold Medal award 1969), Inst. Advancement of Engring., Instn. Prodn. Engrs.; mem. San Sernando Valley Engrs. Coun. (past pres., dir.), Calif. Soc. Profl. Engrs. (past pres., dir. San Fernando Valley chpt., Oustanding Svc. award 1972, 73, 76), Nat. Mgmt. Assn., (Internat. award for mfg. excellence 1983, McGraw-Hill Am.), Am. Soc. Metals, Am. Assn. Engring. Socs. (bd. govs., dir.), Fedn. Materials Socs. (past trustee), Soc. Mfg. Engrs. (past pres., dir.). Patentee in field. Home: 23635 Barona Mesa Rd Ramona CA 92065-4339

VAUGHN, STEPHEN ANTHONY, biochemist, physician, educator; b. Henderson, Nev., Feb. 13, 1960; s. James Allison and Marie Ann (Shea) V.; m. Deborah Lynn Fritz, July 24, 1991. BS in Chemistry, BS in Biology, MIT, 1982; MS in Biochemistry, U. Calif., Irvine, 1988, PhD in Cell Biology, 1991; MD, Boston U., 1995; postgrad., Pa. State U., 1995—. Instr., tutor Boston U. Sch. Medicine, 1992-95; cons. in bioinorganic and protein chemistry, Harrisburg, Pa., 1991—. Contbr. articles to profl. jours. NIH fellow, 1985-88. Mem. AMA, Mass. Med. Soc., Pa. Med. Soc., Alpha Omega Alpha, Sigma Xi. Home and Office: 5149 Haverford Rd Harrisburg PA 17109

VAUGHN, VICKI LYNN, education educator; b. New Castle, Ind., Nov. 10, 1947; d. Robert Allen and Geneva Aileen (Bishop) Fulton; m. Virgil Encil Vaughn, Jr., Aug. 26, 1967; children: Joshua Allen, Jordan Tanner. BS, Ball State U., Muncie, Ind., 1969, MA, 1973; PhD, Purdue U., 1991. Elem. tchr. New Castle (Ind.) Cmty. Sch. Corp., 1969-86; gifted/talented tchr. Marion (Ind.) Cmty. Sch. Corp., 1986-88, Lafayette (Ind.) Sch. Corp., 1988-93; dept. chair, asst. prof. Ball State U., Muncie, 1993-96; lectr. grad. courses Purdue U., West Lafayette, Ind., 1991—; prin. Vinton Elem. Sch., Lafayette, 1993—; Challenge coord. Lafayette Sch. Corp., 1996—; assoc. Ctr. for Gifted Studies and Talent Devel., Munice, 1993—, Ctr. for Creative Learning, Sarasota, Fla., 1994—; cons. Ind. schs., 1993—; G/T coord. Lafayette Sch. Corp., Lafayette, 1993-96. Co-editor Nat. Assn. Labs. Schs. Jour.; reviewer articles Jour. Secondary Gifted Edn., Tchr. Educator, others; contbr. articles to profl. jours. Ind. Dept. Edn. learning grantee, 1993, 4Rs grantee, 1994. Mem. ASCD (assoc.), Nat. Assn. for Gifted Children, Nat. Assn. for Lab. Schs., Ind. Assn. for Gifted (rsch. com. 1988—), Phi Delta Kappa, Phi Kappa Phi. Avocations: reading, dancing, travel. Home: 1004 N Meadow Ln Muncie IN 47304-3327 Office: Vinton Elem Sch 3101 Elmwood Ave Lafayette IN 47904-1709

VAUGHN, WILLIAM PRESTON, historian, educator; b. East Chicago, Ind., May 28, 1933; s. James Carl and Georgiana (Preston) V.; m. Virginia Lee Meyer, June 10, 1961; 1 child, Rhonda Louise. AB, U. Mo., Columbia, 1955; MA, Ohio State U., 1956, PhD, 1961. Instr. in history U. So. Calif., 1961-62; asst. prof. history U. N. Tex., Denton, 1962-65, assoc. prof., 1965-69, prof., 1969-91; instr. Tex. Project, Malaysia, 1986, 88. Author: Schools for All: The Blacks and Public Education in the South, 1865-77, 1974, The Antimasonic Party in the United States, 1826-43, 1983; editor Transactions Tex. Lodge of Rsch., 1988—; contbr. numerous articles on black edn. masonry and polit. antimasonry to profl. jours. With arty. U.S. Army, 1956-57. Mem. SAR, So. Hist. Assn. (life), Historians Early Am. Republic, Masons, Phi beta Kappa, Phi Alpha Theta (manuscript competition winner 1972), Phi Delta Kappa, Phi Beta Delta. Republican. Episcopalian. Home: 908 Hilton Pl Denton TX 76201-8606

VAUGHN, WILLIAM WEAVER, lawyer; b. Los Angeles, Aug. 29, 1930; s. William Weaver and Josephine (Sweigert) V.; m. Claire Louise M'Closkey, June 2, 1962; children: Robert, Gregory, Elizabeth, Anthony, Christina, James. B.A., Stanford U., 1952; LL.B., UCLA, 1955. Bar: Calif. 1956. Mem. O'Melveny & Myers, L.A., 1955-56, 57—, ptnr., 1964—; mem. adv. group U.S. Dist. Ct. (ctrl. dist.) Calif. 1991-93, L.A. Area alt. dispute resolution panel Ctr. for Pub. Resources, 1988—. Served with U.S. Army, 1956-57. Recipient Learned Hand award Am. Jewish Com., 1991. Fellow Am. Coll. Trial Lawyers (bd. regents 1992-95); mem. L.A. County Bar Assn. (trustee 1976-78, 80-82), L.A. County Bar Found. (bd. dirs. 1991-95), Assn. Bus. Trial Lawyers (bd. govs. 1980-82), Order of Coif. Clubs: California (Los Angeles), Chancery (Los Angeles). Office: O'Melveny & Myers 400 S Hope St Los Angeles CA 90071-2801

VAUGHT, RICHARD LOREN, urologist; b. Ind., Oct. 28, 1933; s. Loren Judson and Bernice Rose (Bridges) V.; widowed, July 1987; children: Megan, Niles, Barbara, Mary; m. Nancy Lee Gusa, Aug. 1992. AB in Anatomy and Physiology, Ind. U., 1955; MD, Ind. U., Indpls., 1958. Diplomate Am. Bd. Urology. Intern, then resident in gen. surgery U.S. Naval Hosp., St. Albans, N.Y., 1958-60, resident in urology, 1960-63; spl. fellow Sloan Kettering Meml. Hosp. for Cancer and Allied Diseases, N.Y.C., 1962; pediatric urology observer Babies Hosp., Columbia-Presbyn. Med. Ctr., N.Y.C., 1962; head urology U.S. Naval Hosp., Beaufort, S.C., 1963-65; asst. chief urology, head pediatric urology U.S. Naval Hosp., San Diego, 1965-68; pvt. practice Plaza Urol., Sioux City; med. dir. dept. hyperbaric medicine St. Luke's Regional Med. Ctr., Sioux City, 1988-95; pres., chmn. bd. dirs. Care Choices of Siouxland, Sioux City, 1987-94; med. dir. Male Impotence Clinic, Marian Health Ctr., Sioux City, 1995—. Organizer telecommunications system for deaf, Siouxland, 1983. Lt. comdr. USN, 1958-68. Fellow ACS, Internat. Soc. Cryosurgery, Am. Acad. Pediat.; mem. Am. Urol. Assn., Soc. Pediatric Urology, European Soc. Pediatric Urology (corr.), Undersea and Hyperbaric Medicine Soc., Am. Coll. Hyperbaric Medicine, Am. Soc. Laser Medicine and Surgery, Am. Lithotripsy Soc., Woodbury County Med. Soc. (pres.), Am. Confedn. Urologia, Sertoma (Sertoman of Yr. award 1983). Home: 10 Cottonwood Landing South Sioux City NE 68776 Office: Plaza Urol PC 2800 Pierce St Ste 308 Sioux City IA 51104-3759

VAUGHT, WILMA L., foundation executive, retired air force officer; b. Pontiac, Mich., Mar. 15, 1930; d. Willard L. and Margaret J. (Pierce) V. BS, U. Ill., 1952; MBA, U. Ala., 1968; postgrad., Indsl. Coll. Armed Forces, 1972-73; D Pub. Affairs (hon.), Columbia Coll., 1992. Cert. cost acct. Commd. 2d lt. USAF, 1957, advanced through grades to brig. gen., 1980; chief data services div. 306th Combat Support Group USAF, McCoy AFB, Fla., 1963-67; mgmt. analyst Office Dep. Chief of Staff, comptroller Mil. Assistance Command USAF, Saigon, Vietnam, 1968-69; chief advanced logistics systems plans and mgmt. group Air Force Logistics Command USAF, Wright-Patterson AFB, Ohio, 1969-72; chief cost factors br., chief security assistance br. USAF, Washington, 1973-75, Directorate Mgmt. Analysis, Office of Comptroller, 1973-75; dir. program and budget Office Dep. Chief of Staff, comptroller Hdqrs. Air Force Systems Command USAF, Andrews AFB, Md., 1980-82; comdr. U.S. Mil. Entrance Processing Command USAF, North Chicago, Ill., 1982-85; ret. USAF, 1985; pres. Women in Mil. Svc. Meml. Found., Arlington, Va., 1987—; pres. bd. dirs. Pentagon Fed. Credit Union, 1975-82; bd. regents Inst. Cost Analysis, 1979-83; Air Force sr. mil. rep. Def. Adv. Com. on Women in Services, 1982-85; chmn. Com. on Women in Armed Forces, NATO, Brussels, 1984-85. Bd. dirs. Air Force Retired Officer Community, 1986-90; mem. adv. bd. Jane Addams Conf.; mem. bd. trustees The Teller Found. Decorated Bronze Star medal, Def. Disting. Service medal, U.S. Air Force Disting. Service medal; recipient Ill. Achievement award U. Ill., 1983. Mem. Internat. Women's Forum. Methodist. Home: 6658 Van Winkle Dr Falls Church VA 22044-1010 Office: Women in Mil Svc Meml Found 5510 Columbia Pike Ste 302 Arlington VA 22204-3123

VAUSE, EDWIN HAMILTON, research foundation administrator; b. Chgo., Mar. 30, 1923; s. Harry Russell and Sylvia Clair (Webster) V.; m. Harriet Evelyn Oestmann, June 30, 1951; children—Karen L., Russell E., Kurt H., Dirk C., Luke E. B.S., U. Ill., 1947, M.S., 1948; M.B.A., U. Chgo., 1952; D.Sc. (hon.), U. Evansville, 1977. Registered profl. engr., Ill., Ind. Engr., research dept. Standard Oil Co., Ind., 1948-52; asst. gen. foreman mfg. dept. Standard Oil Co., 1952-57; dir. research adminstrn. Mead Johnson & Co., Evansville, Ind., 1957-60; v.p. Charles F. Kettering Found., Dayton, Ohio, 1960-66; v.p., adminstrn. dir. Charles F. Kettering Found., 1966-67, exec. v.p., 1967-71, v.p. for sci. and tech., 1971-88; trustee The Found. Center, 1967-73; mem. adv. com. Acad. Forum, Nat. Acad. Scis. Vice-pres. Washington Twp. Bd. Edn., 1963-67; mem. Centerville-Washington Twp. Joint Planning Commn., 1967-68; mem. adv. bd. Center for Students Rights, Dayton, 1966-70; active Boy Scouts Am. Mem. Am. Inst. Chem. Engrs. (past chmn. Chgo. sect.), N.Y. Acad. Scis., Agrl. Research Inst., Nat. Industry State Agrl. Research Council. Republican. Lutheran. Clubs: Elks, Kiwanis (past pres.), Masons. Home: 11834 Calle Parral San Diego CA 92128-4534

VAUX, DORA LOUISE, sperm bank official, consultant; b. White Pine, Mont., Aug. 8, 1922; d. Martin Tinus and Edna Ruth (Pyatt) Palmlund; m. Robert Glenn Vaux, Oct. 25, 1941; children: Jacqueline, Cheryl, Richard, Jeanette. Grad. high sch., Bothell, Wash. Photographer Busco-Nestor Studios, San Diego, 1961-68; owner, mgr. Vaux Floors & Interiors, San Diego, 1968-82; cons., mgr. Repository for Germinal Choice, Escondido, Calif., 1983-91; adminstr. Found. for the Continuity of Mankind, Spokane, 1991—. Republican. Home: 2727 S Skipworth Rd Spokane WA 99206-5874 Office: Found Continuity of Mankind 1209 W 1st Ave Spokane WA 99201-4101 *Personal philosophy: It does not matter what our start in life has been, we can set goals and by our own hard work, achieve them. We must find our own answers to our problems and with this will come great pride and enjoyment.*

VAVALA, DOMENIC ANTHONY, medical scientist, educator, retired air force officer; b. Providence, Feb. 1, 1925; s. Salvatore and Maria (Grenci) V. BA, Brown U., 1947; MS, U. R.I., 1950; MA, Trinity U., San Antonio, 1954; PhD in Physiology, Accademia di Studi Superiori "Minerva", Italy, 1957; MEd, U. Houston, 1958; DSc (hon.), Nobile Accademia di Santa Teodora Imperatrice, Rome, 1966, DMS (hon.), 1970, DPH (hon.), Nobile Accademia di Santa Teodora Imperatrice, 1983; D Pedagogy (hon.), Studiorum Universitas Constantiniana of Sovrano Ordine Constantiniano di San Giorgio, Rome, 1966; DEd (hon.), Imperiale Accademia di San Cirillo, Pomezia, Italy, 1977; LittD, Univ. Internazionale Sveva "Frederick II", Bergamo, Italy, 1979; D Health Scis. (hon.), Johnson & Wales U., 1993. Research asst. tumor research U. R.I., also asst. entomol. research, 1950; research asst. pharmacology Boston U. Sch. Medicine, 1950-51; commd. 2d lt. med. service USAF, 1951, advanced through grades to lt. col., 1968; physiologist cold injury research team Army Med. Research Lab., Osaka (Japan) Army Hosp., 1951-52; research aviation physiologist USAF Sch. Aviation Medicine, Randolph AFB, Tex., 1952-54, 3605th USAF Hosp., Ellington AFB, Tex., 1955-57; chief physiol. tng. 3605th USAF Hosp., 1957; cons. aviation physiology, film prodn. dept. U. Houston, 1956; research aviation physiologist, head acad. sect. dept. physiol. tng. USAF Hosp., Lackland AFB, Tex., 1957-58; vis. prof. physiology Incarnate Word Coll., San Antonio, 1958; research aviation physiologist, chief physiol. tng. comdr. 832d Physiol. Tng. Flight, 832d Tactical Hosp., Cannon AFB, N.Mex., 1958-65; adj. faculty mem. Eastern N.Mex. U., Portales, 1959-64; instr. adult edn. div. Clovis (N.Mex.) mcpl. schs., 1960; research aviation physiologist, comdr. 15th Physiol. Tng. Flight, 824th USAF Dispensary, Kadena Air Base, Okinawa, 1965-66; research scientist, directorate fgn. tech., aerospace med. div. Brooks AFB, Tex., 1966-68; chief R & D support and interface div., dep. dir. for fgn. tech., 1968-70; adj. instr. Johnson & Wales U., Providence, 1973-74; instr. humanities Johnson and Wales U., Providence, 1974-75, asst. prof. humanities, 1975-77, prof. health scis. and nutrition, 1977-93, prof. emeritus, 1993—, coord. biomed. and behavioral scis. Day Coll. div., 1973-75, psychology coord. vets. div. Coll. Continuing Edn., 1974-76, assoc. dean adj. faculty, 1975, dean faculty, 1975-77, coord. acad. devel., 1977-78, dir. musical series, 1990—, curator Chapel Empress St. Theodora, 1992—; pres. corp., chmn. bd. Sovereign Constantinian Order of St. George, Inc., R.I., 1986—; pres. corp., chmn. bd. dirs. The Noble Acad. of Empress St. Theodora of R.I., Inc., 1988—; instr. anatomy, physiology and med. terminology R.I. Hosp., Providence, R.I., 1987-90. Writer, producer: (TV Series) Your Body in Flight, Sta. KUHT, Houston, 1956; (TV series) Highway to Health, Okinawa, 1965; editor-in-chief: NADUS Jour., 1963-85; compiled and edited: Fifty Years of Progress of Soviet Medicine, 1917-67; abstractor, translator in medicine Chem. Abstracts Svc., Am. Chem., Ohio State U., 1963-74; contbr. articles to profl. jours. Trustee, Gov. Ctr. Sch., Providence, 1979-85; mem. scholarship com. St. Sahag and, St. Mesrob Armenian Apostolic Ch., Providence. Served with AUS, 1943-44. Recipient Disting. Svc. award Clovis (N.Mex.) Jaycees, 1959, Acad. Palms Gold medal Accademia di Studi Superiori "Minerva", 1960, citation from chief chaplains USAF, 1970, commendation medal USAF, 1970, chief biomed. scientist insignia, biomed. scis. corps USAF Med. Svc., 1970, spl. faculty citation Johnson and Wales U., 1981; academician divsn. scis. Accademia di Studi Superiori "Minerva", 1960; Min. Plenipotentiary for U.S. of Nobile Accademia di Santa Teodora Imperatrice, Rome, 1967, rector pro tempore, 1980; decorated knight grand officer Merit Class, Sovereign Constantinian Order St. George, Rome, 1969, Knight of Grand Cross with Constantinian neckchain, Justice Class, Sovereign Constantinian Order of St. George, 1969, Knight of Grand Cordon Justice Class, Order of Teutonic Knights, Sao Paulo, 1986, Knight of Grand Cross Justice Class, Mil. Order St. Gereon, Sao Paulo, 1986, Knight of Grand Cross Justice Class, Mil. and Hospitalier Order St Jean d'Acre and St. Thomas, Capua, Italy, 1987, Knight of Grand Cross Justice Class, Mil. and Hospitalier Order St. Mary of Bethlehem, Capua, 1987, Ednl. Professionalism award Domei Toastmasters Internat., 1965; named Magnificent Rector and Pres. of the Constantinian U. (Studiorum Universitas Constantiniana), Italy, 1970. Fellow AAAS, Tex. Acad. Sci., Royal Soc. Health (London), Am. Inst. Chemists; mem. Assn. Mil. Surgeons U.S., Nat. Assn. Doctors U.S. (founder 1958, sec.-treas. 1958-85, editor-in-chief The NADUS Jour. 1963-68), Accademia di San Cirillo Italy (hon.), N.Y. Acad. Scis., Phi Sigma, Kappa Delta Pi, Phi Kappa Phi, Alpha Beta Kappa (charter mem., pres. R.I. Alpha chpt. Johnson & Wales U. 1984-92). Home: 30 Oaklawn Ave Apt 219 Cranston RI 02920-9319

VAYNMAN, SEMYON, materials scientist; b. Odessa, USSR, Oct. 2, 1949; came to U.S., 1980; s. Kelman and Esther (Potashnik) V.; m. Dora Skladman, Nov. 18, 1977; children: Ethel, Alexander. MS in Chemistry, Odessa U., 1973; PhD in Materials Sci., Northwestern U., 1986. Rsch. scientist Rsch. Inst. Foundry Tech., Odessa, 1973-77, Rsch. Inst. Power Industry, Lvov, USSR, 1977-80, GARD, Niles, Ill., 1981-84; rsch. scientist, rsch. prof. Northwestern U., Evanston, Ill., 1986—; reviewer Jour. Electronic Packaging, 1989, IEEE publ., 1988—; mem. adv. bd. sci. com. for solder joints reliability Dept. Def., Washington, 1989-90. Contbr. sci. papers to profl. publs., chpts. to books. Mem. Am. Soc. Metals, Minerals, Metals and Materials Soc. (electronic packaging and interconnection materials com. 1989—). Achievements include 2 patents in foundry technology. Office: Northwestern U 1801 Maple Ave Evanston IL 60201-3135

VAYO, DAVID JOSEPH, composer, music educator; b. New Haven, Mar. 28, 1957; s. Harold Edward and Joan Virginia (Cassidy) V.; m. Margot Ehrlich, May 16, 1981; children; Rebecca Lynne, Gordon Francis. MusB, Ind. U., 1980, MusM, 1982; D of Musical Arts, U. Mich., 1990. Prof. Nat. U., Heredia, Costa Rica, 1982-84, Nat. Symphony Youth Sch., San Jose, Costa Rica, 1982-84; asst. prof. music Conn. Coll., New London, 1988-91; asst. prof. music Ill. Wesleyan U. Sch. Music, Bloomington, 1991-95, assoc. prof., 1995—; resident artist Banff Ctr. for Arts, 1992, 94, Va. Ctr. for Creative Arts, 1994, Centrum, Port Townsend, Wash., 1996; participating composer Internat. Soc. Contemporary Music-World Music Days, Mexico City, 1993, Internat. Double Reed Festival, Rotterdam, The Netherlands, 1995. Composer chamber composition Poem, 1990 (winner Spectri Sonori Internat. Composition competition Tulane U. 1992), Symphony: Blossoms and Awakenings, 1990 (performer St. Louis Symphony, Leonard Slatkin condr. 1993), Wind Quintet, 1991 (winner Symposium Seven for New Woodwind Quintet Music, U. Ga. 1993), Eight Poems of William Carlos Williams for solo trombonist, 1994 (commd. by St. Louis Symphony); works pub. by MMB Music, Internat. Trombone Assn. Press and A.M. Percussion Publs. Charles E. Ives scholar Am. Acad. and Inst. Arts and Letters, 1988. Mem. ASCAP (awards 1988—), Am. Music Ctr. (copying assistance grantee 1992), Coll. Music Soc. (presenter nat. conf. 1990, 94, 96), Soc. for Electro-Acoustic Music in U.S. (presenter nat. conf. 1989), Soc. Composers (membership chmn. 1990—, presenter nat. conf. 1990, 92, 95, 97), Am. Composers Forum. Avocations: athletics, Latin American culture, traveling, reading. Office: Ill Wesleyan U Sch Music PO Box 2900 Bloomington IL 61702-2900

VAZIRANI-FALES, HEEA, legislative staff member, lawyer; b. Calcutta, India, Apr. 1, 1938; d. Sunder J. Vazirani; m. John Fales Jr., 1978; children: Deepika, Reetika, Ashish, Monika, Jyotika, Denise. AB, Guilford Coll., 1959; JD, Howard U., 1979. Legis. dir. Montgomery County Del, Gen. Assembly of Md., 1981-87; legis. counsel to Congresswoman Constance A. Morella, U.S. Ho. of Reps., Washington, 1987-94, counsel subcom. on postal svc. com. govt. reform-oversight, 1995—. Mem. Phi Delta Phi. Presbyterian. Office: Subcom on Postal Svc B349C Rayburn House Off Bldg Washington DC 20515

VAZIRI, NOSRATOLA DABIR, internist, nephrologist, educator; b. Tehran, Iran, Oct. 13, 1939; came to U.S., 1969, naturalized, 1977; s. Abbas and Tahera V. M.D., Tehran U., 1966. Diplomate: Am. Bd. Internal Medicine, Am. Bd. Nephrology. Intern Cook County Hosp., Chgo., 1969-70; resident Berkshire Med. Ctr., Pittsfield, Mass., 1970-71, Wadsworth VA Med. Ctr., 1971-72, UCLA Med. Ctr., 1972-74; prof. medicine U. Calif.-Irvine, 1979—, chief nephrology div., 1977—, dir. hemodialysis unit, 1977—, vice chmn. dept. medicine, 1982-94 ; chmn. dept. medicine, 1994—; mem. sci. adv. council Nat. Kidney Found., 1977—. Contbr. numerous articles to med. jours. Recipient Golden Apple award, 1977; named outstanding tchr. U. Calif-Irvine, 1975, 78, 79, 80, 82. Fellow ACP; mem. Am. Soc. Nephrology, Am. Paraplegia Soc. (pres. 1992-94), Western Assn. Physicians, Assn. Profs. of Medicine, Alpha Omega Alpha. Home: 66 Balboa Cv Newport Beach CA 92663-3226 Office: U Calif Irvine Med Ctr Div Nephrology Dept Medicine 101 The City Dr S Orange CA 92868-3201

VAZQUEZ, MARTHA ALICIA, judge; b. Santa Barbara, Calif., Feb. 21, 1953; d. Remigio and Consuelo (Mendez) V.; m. Frank Mathew, Aug. 7, 1976; children: Cristina Vazquez Matthew, Nicholas Vazquez Matthew, Nathan Vazquez Matthew. BA in Govt., U. Notre Dame, 1975, JD, 1978. Bar: N.Mex. 1979, U.S. Dist. Ct. (we. dist.) N.Mex. 1979. Atty. Pub. Defender's Office, Santa Fe, 1979-81; ptnr. Jones, Snead, Wertheim, Rodriguez & Wentworth, Santa Fe, 1981-93; judge U.S. District Ct., 10th Circuit, Santa Fe, 1993—. Chmn. City Santa Fe Grievance Bd. Mem. N.Mex. Bar Assn. (fee arbitration com., chmn. trial practice sect. 1984-85, mem. task force on minority involvement in bar activities), Santa Fe Bar Assn. (jud. liasion com.), Nat. Assn. Criminal Def. Lawyers, Assn. Trial Lawyers Am., N.Mex. Trial Lawyers Assn. Democrat. Roman Catholic. Office: US Courthouse PO Box 2710 Santa Fe NM 87504-2710*

VAZQUEZ, SUE ELLEN, elementary education educator; b. Rome, N.Y., Aug. 2, 1951; d. Louis Frank and Eileen Louella (Hayes) Mercurio; children: Katie, Kristin; m. Kermith Vazquez, Feb. 17, 1995. AA, Mater Dei Coll., 1971; BA in Elem. Edn. and Sociology, SUNY, Potsdam, 1973, MS in Edn. and Learning Disabilities, 1987. Cert. in elem. education (nursery through grade 6), N.Y. Elem. tchr. Twin Rivers Elem. Sch., Massena, N.Y., 1973-88, Nightengale Elem. Sch., Massena, N.Y., 1988—; curriculum writer, rschr. Massena Ctrl. Schs., 1980—, AIDS adv. coun., 1987-91, student assistance program, 1994—, sci. curriculum, media coord., 1986. Co-author: (curriculum) Life Education for Children, 1980, Sexual Abuse Awareness for Educators, 1985, AIDS Awareness for Children, 1987; co-editor Immaculatan, 1970-71. Mem. NEA, Massena Tchrs. Fedn. (bldg. rep. 1978-80), Am. Fedn. Tchrs., Sci. Tchrs. Assn. of N.Y. State, North Country Colls. Internat. Reading Assn., Coll. Club of Massena, Massena Home Bur. (sec. 1975-77). Roman Catholic. Avocations: travel, music, lit., racquet sports, photography. Home: 11 Sharon Dr Massena NY 13662-1601 Office: Massena Ctrl Schs 84 Nightengale Ave Massena NY 13662

VEACO, KRISTINA, lawyer; b. Sacramento, Calif., Mar. 4, 1948; d. Robert Glenn and Lelia (McCain) V. BA, U. Calif., Davis, 1978; JD, Hastings Coll. of the Law, 1981. Legal adv. to commr. William T. Bagley Calif. Public Utilities Commn., San Francisco, Calif., 1981-86; sr. counsel Pacific Telesis Group, San Francisco, Calif., 1986-94; sr. counsel corp. and securities and pol. law AirTouch Comms., San Francisco, 1994—. Mem. ABA, Calif. Women Lawyers, San Francisco Bar Assn., Am. Soc. Corp. Secs., Phi Beta Kappa. Democrat. Episcopalian. Avocations: cooking, reading. Office: AirTouch Comms Rm 2108 1 California St San Francisco CA 94111-5401

VEALE, TINKHAM, II, former chemical company executive, engineer; b. Topeka, Dec. 26, 1914; s. George W. and Grace Elizabeth (Walworth) V.; m. Harriett Alice Ernst, Sept. 6, 1941; children: Harriett Elizabeth Veale Leedy, Tinkham III, Helen Ernst Veale Gelbach. BS in Mech. Engring., Case Inst. Tech., 1937; LLD, Kenyon Coll., 1981. Registered profl. engr. With Gen. Motors Corp., 1937-38, Avery Engring. Co., 1939, Reliance Electric Co., 1940-41; asst. to pres. Ohio Crankshaft Co., 1942-46; gen. mgr. Tocco Co., 1947-51; pres. Ric Wil Corp., 1952-53; pres. Alco Chem. Corp., 1954-56, dir., 1954-86; spl. ptnr. Ball Burge & Kraus, investment bankers, 1957-60; chmn. bd. V. and V. Cos., Inc. and subs., Cleve., 1960-65, Alco Standard Corp. and subs., Valley Forge, Pa., 1965-86, Horsehead Industries, Inc. and subs., N.Y.C., 1981—, HTV Industries Inc. and subs., Cleve., 1978—; ptnr. Fair Elm Farm, 1948—, Kennedy Veale Stable, 1954—. Trustee V. and V. Charitable Found., 1966—. Recipient Silver Bowl award Case Inst. Tech., 1980; recipient Gold Medal Case Inst. Tech., 1982. Mem. Cleve. Engring. Soc., Nat. Soc. Registered Profl. Engrs., Newcomen Soc., Phi Kappa Psi. Home: Fair Elm Gate Gates Mills OH 44040 Office: HTV Industries Inc PO Box 295 Gates Mills OH 44040

VEASEL, WALTER, minister, educator; b. Balt., Apr. 11, 1925; s. William Edward Veasel and Mary Lula (Boyd-Veasel) Ebert; m. Helen Ilene Gank; children: William, Holly, Bradley, Heide. ThB, Holmes Coll. of the Bible, 1947; BS in Elem. Edn., Towson State U., 1970; M in Ministries, Zion Sem., 1986. Ordained to ministry Pentecostal Holiness Ch., 1947; cert. tchr., Md. Tchr. Balt. City Schs., 1959-84; pastor Mid Atlantic Conf. Pentecostal Holiness Ch., 1948-54, St. Catherines and London, ON, Can., 1955-59, Mid Atlantic Conf. Pentecostal Holiness Ch., Georgetown, D.C. and Daniels, Md., 1960-70; founder, pastor Community Ch., 1970-90; pastor emeritus Woodbridge Valley Ch. of God, 1990-94; prin. Tabernacle Christian Sch., Balt., 1988-94; conf. Sunday sch. sec./treas.; conf. youth v.p.; conf. sec./treas. and bd. dirs., 1950-70; instr. Tabernacle Bible Inst., 1970-75, Faith Sch. Theology, 1993. Vol. nursing homes, reform schs. and prisons, 1948—; adv. bd. Evangel Christian Acad., Balt., 1996—. Recipient Vols. Cert., House of Correction, 1975-96. Mem. Ministerial Assn. Republican. Home: 5025 Montgomery Rd Ellicott City MD 21043-6750 also: 638 Clark Lohr Rd Swanton MD 21561

VEASEY, BYRON KEITH, information systems consultant; b. Washington, Mar. 17, 1957; s. Columbus Jr. and Joan Marie (Ingram) V. BS in Indsl. and Sys. Engring., U. So. Calif., 1979; MBA, Ball State U., 1982; M Mgmt. in Info. Sys., U. Dallas, 1989. Cert. quality analyst Quality Assurance Inst., computing profl. Inst. for Certification of Computer Profls. CIM engr. Mason & Hanger, Amarillo, Tex., 1983-87; bus. sys. analyst E-Sys., Garland, Tex., 1987-89; consulting mgr. Deloitte & Touche, Dallas, 1989-93; sr. cons. CSC, Dallas, 1993-96; solutions mgr. AT&T, Chantilly, Va., 1996-97, Information Advantage, Vienna, Va., 1997—. Mem. Dallas Heart Ball, 1991-92; mem. PM League Dallas Mus. of Art, 1992-93; bd. dirs. Dallas Wind Symphony, 1992; pres. Inst. of Indsl. Engrs., Dallas, 1992-93; v.p. programs Assn. for Sys. Mgmt., Dallas, 1991-93. Capt. USAF, 1979-82. Mem. Am. Legion. Republican. Avocations: theater, saxophone, chess, computers, travel. Home: 12010 Ridge Knoll Dr # 10 Fairfax VA 22033 Office: Info Advantage 8300 Boone Blvd Ste 500 Vienna VA 22182

VEASEY, EUGENE NORMAN, justice; b. Wilmington, Del., Jan. 9, 1933; s. Eugene E. and Elizabeth B. (Norman) V.; m. Suzanne Johnson, Aug. 4, 1956; children: Andrew Scott, Douglas Ross, E. Norman Jr., Marian Elizabeth. AB, Dartmouth Coll., 1954; LLB, U. Pa., 1957. Bar: Del. 1958, U.S. Supreme Ct. 1963. Dep. atty. gen. State of Del., 1961-62, chief dep., 1962-63; ptnr. Richards, Layton & Finger, Wilmington, Del., 1963-92, chief justice, Del. Supreme Ct., 1992—. Contbr. articles to profl. jours. Bd. advisors U. Pa. Inst. for Law and Econs. Served to Capt. Del. Air N.G., 1957-63. Fellow Am. Bar Found., Am. Coll. Trial Lawyers, Am. Intellectual Property Law Assn; mem. Del. Bd. Bar Examiners (chmn. 1973-80), Del. Bar Assn. (pres. 1982-83, chmn. corp. law com. 1969-74, chmn. rules com. of Del. Supreme Ct. 1974-80), ABA (chair bus. law sect. 1994-95, chair to spl.

com. on ethics 2000, 1997—), Am. Law Inst. (bd. dirs. conf. chief justice 1994-96, chair professionalism com. 1994—). Republican. Episcopalian. Office: Del Supreme Ct PO Box 1997 Wilmington DE 19899-1997

VEATCH, J. WILLIAM, III, lawyer; b. Altanta, Sept. 5, 1946. BA, Duke U., 1968; JD, Emory U., 1974. Bar: Ga. 1974. Lawyer Kilpatrick Stockton LLP, Atlanta. Notes and comments editor Emory Law Jour., 1973-74. Mem. ABA, State Bar Ga., Atlanta Bar Assn., Lawyers Club Atlanta, Order of Coif, Omnicron Delta Kappa, Phi Delta Phi. Address: Kilpatrick Stockton LLP 1100 Peachtree St NE Ste 2800 Atlanta GA 30309-4528

VEATCH, JEAN LOUISE CORTY, telemetry nurse; b. Farmer City, Ill., June 4, 1932; d. Eugene Louis and Mary Violette (Mounce) Corty; m. July 23, 1955 (div.); children: Irvin, Ronald, Steven, Julie, James, Jeffery. Diploma, Holy Cross Cen. Sch. Nursing, 1954; BS, Coll. St. Francis, 1984; student, Valparaiso U. Cert. ACLS, coronary, critical care trained IMCU, obstetrics. Obstetrics nurse Holy Family Hosp., LaPorte, Ind., 1954-64; office nurse Dr. McDonald, Gulfport, Miss.; office nurse Dr. Jack Cartwright, LaPorte, Ind., med./telemetry unit nurse, 1977-96; staff nurse level III LaPorte Hosp., 1988-96, charge nurse, preceptor, 1979-96, diabetic resource nurse, 1987-96. Mem. Am. Heart Assn., 1995; mem. Square Dance Club; organizer yearly square dance Toys for Tots, 1981-89; den mother Cub Scouts, Valparaiso. Mem. Am. Assn. Diabetic Educators. Home: 4409 Campbell St Valparaiso IN 46383-1303

VEATCH, JOHN WILLIAM, Reiki educator, educational administrator; b. Mitchell, S.D., Dec. 9, 1923; s. William Homer and Helen Gwendolyn (Lowther) V.; m. Doris Lavelle Guthrie (dec. 1978); children: Dean, Joan; m. Joy Sullivan, Aug. 21, 1993. BA in Speech, Wash. State U., 1946, BEd, 1951; MA in Speech, U. Wash., 1950; DEd, U. Idaho, 1970. Pvt. practice speech pathology Spokane, Wash., 1950-79; pvt. practice speech pathology and ednl. cons. Tacoma, 1980-93; dir. rsch., edn. and bus. Sullivan Ctr. & Phys. Therapy, Puyallup, Wash., 1993—; tchr., master Reiki and Mind/Body Healing; lectr. in speech pathology Gonzaga U., Spokane, Wash., 1963-70; adj. prof. Wash. State U., 1972-77, Applied Psychology, Eastern Wash. U., 1977; chief exec. officer and dir. rsch. Espial Inst., Tacoma, 1982-92; mem. home health adv. bd. Spokane County Health Dept., past. pres. Wash. State Health Dept. Crippled Children's Svc. Adv. Bd. Maxillofacial Defects; co-dir. Sullivan Ctr., 1992—; cons. in field; workshops and training in energy medicine techniques; co-developer V.E.A.T.C.H. Technique. Author: (with D. Hughes) Teacher Qualities, 1947; (test profiles) Personal Stress Balance Profile, 1982, Info. Processing Style, 1984, The Deep Screening Profile of Tongue Thrusting Activity, 1985, The Tongue Thrust Screening Test, 1986, Learning Style Profile, 1986; writer, contbr. guides, workbooks, studies and films in field. Fellow Northwest Acad. Speech Pathology (pres. 1978-82, 86-91); mem. Am. Speech-Lang.-Hearing Assn. (life, pres. bd. Oakbridge U. 1989-90). Office: 2717 E Main Ave Puyallup WA 98372-3165

VEATCH, ROBERT MARLIN, philosophy educator, medical ethics researcher; b. Utica, N.Y., Jan. 22, 1939; s. Cecil Ross and Regina (Braddock) V.; m. Laurelyn Kay Lovett, June 17, 1961 (div. Oct. 1986); children: Paul Martin, Carlton Elliot; m. Ann Bender Pastore, May 23, 1987. BS, Purdue U., 1961; MS, U. Calif. at San Francisco, 1962; BD, Harvard U., 1964, MA, 1970, Ph.D., 1971. Teaching fellow Harvard U., 1968-70; research assoc. in medicine Coll. Physicians and Surgeons, Columbia U., 1971-72; assoc. for med. ethics Inst. of Society, Ethics and Life Scis., Hastings-on-Hudson, N.Y., 1970-75; sr. assoc. Inst. of Society, Ethics and Life Scis., 1975-79; prof. med. ethics Kennedy Inst. Ethics Georgetown U., 1979—, prof. philosophy, 1981—, dir., 1989-96; adj. prof. depts. community and family medicine and ob/gyn, 1984—; mem. vis. faculty various colls. and univs.; mem. gov. bd. Washington Regional Transplant Consortium, 1988—; bd. dirs. Hospice Care D.C., 1989-96, 97—, pres., 1993-95; active United Network Organ Sharing Ethics Com., 1989-95. Author: Value-Freedom in Science and Technology, 1976, Death, Dying and the Biological Revolution, 1976, rev. edit., 1989, Case Studies in Medical Ethics, 1977, A Theory of Medical Ethics, 1981, The Foundations of Justice, 1987, The Patient as Partner, 1987; (with Sarah T. Fry) Case Studies in Nursing Ethics, 1987, The Patient-Physician Relationship: The Patient as Partner, Part 2, 1991; (with James T. Rule) Ethical Questions in Dentistry, 1993, (with Harley Flack) Case Studies in Allied Health Ethics, 1997; editor or co-editor: Bibliography of Society, Ethics and the Life Sciences, 1973, rev. edit., 1978, The Teaching of Medical Ethics, 1973, Death Inside Out, 1975, Ethics and Health Policy, 1976, Teaching of Bioethics, 1976, Population Policy and Ethics, 1977, Life Span: Values and Life Extending Technologies, 1979, Cases in Bioethics From the Hastings Center Report, 1982, Medical Ethics, 1989, 2d edit., 1997, Cross Cultural Perspectives in Medical Ethics, 1989; (with Edmund D. Pellegrino and John P. Langan) Ethics, Trust, and the Professions, 1991; (with Tom L. Beauchamp) Ethical Issues in Death and Dying, 1996; assoc. editor Encyclopedia of Bioethics; editl. bd. Jour. AMA, 1976-86, Jour. Medicine and Philosophy, 1980—, Harvard Theol. Rev., 1975—, Jour. Religious Ethics, 1981—; editl. adv. bd. Forum on Medicine, 1977-81; contbg. editor Hosp. Physician, 1975-85, Am. Jour. Hosp. Pharmacy, 1989—; sr. editor Kennedy Inst. Ethics Jour., 1991—; contbr. articles to profl. jours. Mem. Soc. Christian Ethics. Home: 11200 Richland Grove Dr Great Falls VA 22066-1104 Office: Georgetown U Kennedy Inst Of Ethics Washington DC 20057

VEATCH, SHEILA WILLIAMSON, counselor; b. Fitchburg, Mass., Jan. 10, 1950; d. William Robert Barse Jr. and Joan Jessie (Tothill) Williamson; stepfather George P. Williamson; m. Michael Alan Veatch, July 3, 1993; children: Michael and Katie Pitts. BSEd, U. Ga., 1971; MEd in Counseling, West Ga. Coll., 1991, EdS in Counseling, 1992. Nat. bd. cert. counselor; lic. profl. counselor. Tchr. Cobb County Schs., Marietta, Ga., 1971-73, 86-91, counselor, 1991—; pvt. practice, 1996—; instr. Cobb Staff Devel., Marietta, 1992-93; workshop leader Kennesaw (Ga.) State U. Assn. Student Educators, 1993; presenter Cobb Mega Conf., 1992. Co-author: Manners Mania, 1993 (rsch. grantee 1992). Active Cobb Co. Child Advocacy Ctr. Named Elem. Counselor of Yr., Cobb County, 1997; rsch. grantee social skills program Cobb County, 1991-92, 92-93, anger/aggression reduction, 1993-94, parenting edn., 1994-95. Mem. Ga. Sch. Counselors Assn. (fall conf. presenter 1992, 97), Am. Sch. Counselor Assn., Lic. Profl. Counselor Assn. Ga., Cobb Sch. Counselor Assn. (v.p. 1995-96, pres. 1996—), PTA (hon., life State of Ga. 1992). Avocations: antiques, interior decorating, bridge, travel, gardening. Home: 3146 Due West Ct Dallas GA 30132-7300 Office: Cobb County Sch Sys Glover St Marietta GA 30060

VEBLEN, JOHN ELVIDGE, lawyer; b. Seattle, Feb. 14, 1944. AB magna cum laude, Harvard U., 1965; BA, MA with first class honors, Oxford U., Eng., 1967; JD, Yale U., 1971. Bar: Wash. 1971, N.Y. 1973. Law clerk U.S. Ct. Appeals (9th cir.), 1971-72; lawyer Stoel Rives LLP, Seattle. Mem. ABA, Wash. State Bar Assn., Seattle-King County Bar Assn., Phi Beta Kappa. Office: Stoel Rives LLP One Union Sq 600 University St Ste 3600 Seattle WA 98101-4109

VEBLEN, THOMAS CLAYTON, management consultant; b. Hallock, Minn., Dec. 17, 1929; s. Edgar R. and Hattie (Lundgren) V.; m. Susan Alma Beaver, Sept. 1, 1950 (div. 1971); children: Kari Christen, Erik Rodli, Mark Andrew, Sara Catherine; m. Linda Joyce Eaton, Aug. 30, 1975; 1 child, Kristen Kirby. Student, U. Calif., Santa Barbara, 1950-51; BS, Calif. Poly. U., 1953; MS, Oreg. State U., 1955. Corp. v.p. Cargill, Inc., Wayzata, Minn., 1955-75; spl. asst. Sec. Interior, Washington, 1965; dir. food and agr. SRI Internat., Menlo Park, Calif., 1975-80; pres. Food Sys. Assocs., Inc., Washington, 1980-94; also bd. dirs. Food System Assocs., Inc., Washington; chmn. Enterprise Cons., Inc., Washington, 1990—; dir. Georgetown Cons., Inc., 1993-95; convener The Superior Bus. Firm Roundtable, 1993—; dir. Georgetown Cons., Inc., 1993-95; mem. CMC Inst. Mgmt. Cons., 1988—, pres. Washington chpt., 1991-93. Author: The U.S. Food System, 1978; (with M. Abel) Creating a Superior National Food System, 1992; editor Food System Update, 1986-95. Treas., bd. dirs. White House Fellows Assn., Washington, 1985; trustee Freedom from Hunger Found., Davis, Calif., 1980—, chmn., 1986-89; bd. dirs. Patterson Sch., U. Ky., Lexington, Pax World Svc., Am. Near East Refugee Aid. Recipient Presdl. Appointment White House Fellows Commn., Washington, 1965. Mem. Coun. for Nat. Interest, Coun. on Fgn. Rels., Cosmos Club. Episcopalian. Avocations: canoeing, ice skating. Office: Enterprise Cons Inc 2806 36th Pl NW Washington DC 20007-1417

VECCHIO, ROBERT PETER, business management educator; b. Chgo., June 29, 1950; s. Dominick C. and Angeline V.; m. Betty Ann Vecchio; Aug. 21, 1974; children: Julie, Mark. BS summa cum laude, DePaul U., 1972; MA, U. Ill., 1974, PhD, 1976. Instr. U. Ill., Urbana, 1973-76; mem. faculty dept. mgmt. U. Notre Dame, 1976-86, dept. chmn., 1983-90, Franklin D. Schurz Prof. Mgmt., 1986—. Editor Jour. of Mgmt., 1995—. Mem. Acad. Mtm., Am. Psychol. Assn., Assn. Consumer Rsch., Am. Inst. Decision Scis., Midwest Acad. Mgmt., Midwest Psychol. Assn., Phi Kappa Phi, Delta Epsilon Sigma, Phi Eta Sigma, Psi Chi. Home: 16856 Hampton Dr Granger IN 46530-6907 Office: U Notre Dame Dept Mgmt Notre Dame IN 46556

VECCHIONE, FRANK JOSEPH, lawyer; b. Newark, June 11, 1935; s. Francesco and Philomena (DiDomenico) V.; m. Polly Plaisted, June 1, 1957; children: Amy, Carrie, Jennifer, Matthew. AB, Syracuse U., 1957; LLB, Seton Hall, 1964. Bar: N.J. 1965, U.S. Ct. Appeals (3d cir.) 1972. Ptnr. Crummy Del Deo Dolan Griffinger & Vecchione, Newark, 1965—; adj. prof. law Seton Hall U. Sch. Law, 1970—; lectr. Inst. Continuing Legal Edn.; del. 3d Cir. Jud. Conf., 1982-84, 86—. Contbr. articles to profl. jours. Trustee Bloomfield (N.J.) Coll., 1978-87. 1st lt. U.S. Army, 1957-59. Named Outstanding Alumnus Seton Hall Law Sch., 1992. Fellow Am. Coll. Bankruptcy, Am. Bar Found.; mem. N.J. State Bar Assn. (chmn. debtor/creditor sect. 1978-80). Office: Crummy Del Deo Dolan Griffinger & Vecchione 1 Riverfront Plz Newark NJ 07102-5401

VECCHIONE, JANE FRANCES, school nurse; b. Phila., Jan. 25, 1946; d. Frank M. and Jane (Brophy) V. Diploma, Chestnut Hill Hosp., Phila., 1984; BSN magna cum laude, LaSalle U., 1987; M in Health Edn., St. Joseph's U., 1991. Cert. sch. nurse, Pa. Staff nurse Chestnut Hill Hosp., Abington (Pa.) Meml. Hosp.; sch. nurse Phila. Sch. Dist. Recipient Martins Sci. award, Med./Surgical Nursing award, others, LaSalle U. and Chestnut Hill Hosp. Fellow The Nightingale Soc.; mem. Phila. Pub. Sch. Nurses Assn., Nat. Sch. Nurse Assn., Sigma Theta Tau.

VECCHIOTTI, ROBERT ANTHONY, management and organizational consultant; b. N.Y.C., May 21, 1941; s. R. Lucien and Louise Victoria V.; BS, St. Peter's Coll., 1962; MA, Fordham U., 1964; PhD, St. Louis U., 1973; m. Dorothea Irene Hoban, Oct. 12, 1963; children: John Robert, Rachel Irene, Sara Christine. Psychologist Testing and Advisement Ctr.NYU, Washington Sq. campus, 1964-65; group psychologist McDonnell Douglas, St. Louis, 1967-76, sr. bus. analyst, 1976-77, mgr. bus. systems planning, 1977-79; pres. Organizational Cons. Svcs., Inc., St. Louis, 1980—; adj. assoc. prof. mgmt. Maryville Coll., St. Louis, 1975-81. Bd. dirs. Cath. Charities of St. Louis, 1981-86, Cath. Family Svc., 1986—, Mental Health Assn. St. Louis, 1989—, Sta. KWMU-FM, 1989-94. With U.S. Army, 1965-67. Lic. psychologist, Mo. Mem. Am. Psychol. Assn., Strategic Leadership Forum, Inst. Mgmt. Cons., Human Factors Soc. Club: Mo. Athletic. Lodge: Rotary (past pres.). Office: Organizational Consulting Svcs Inc 230 S Bemiston Ave Ste 1107 Clayton MO 63105-1907

VECCI, RAYMOND JOSEPH, airline industry consultant; b. N.Y.C., Jan. 22, 1943; s. Romeo John and Mary (Fabretti) V.; m. Helen Cecelia Clampett, Sept. 3, 1967; children: Brian John, Damon Jay. BBA, CCNY, 1965; MBA, NYU, 1967. Adminstrv. asst. Internat. Air Transport Assn., N.Y.C., 1961-66; econ. analyst United Airlines, Chgo., 1967-74; asst. v.p. planning and regulatory affairs Alaska Airlines Inc., Seattle, 1975-76, staff v.p. planning and regulatory affairs, 1976-79, staff v.p. planning, 1979, v.p. planning, 1979-85, exec. v.p., chief operating officer, 1986-90, pres., chief exec. officer, 1990—; chmn., dir. Alaska Airlines Inc., 1991—; also chmn., pres., chief exec. officer, dir. Alaska Air Group Inc.; pres. Carnival Airlines, Danica, Fla., 1997—. Served with U.S. Army, 1968-69, Vietnam. Decorated Bronze Star. Roman Catholic. Office: Carnival Airlines 1815 Griffin Rd Ste 205 Dania FL 33004-2252*

VECELLIO, LEO ARTHUR, JR., construction company executive; b. Beckley, W.Va., Oct. 26, 1946; s. Leo Arthur and Evelyn (Pais) V.; m. Kathryn Grace Cottrill, Nov. 29, 1975; children: Christopher Scott, Michael Andrew. BCE, Va. Poly. Inst. and State U., 1968; MCE, Ga. Inst. Tech., 1969; LLD (hon.), Northwood U. Sr. v.p. Vecellio & Grogan, Inc., Beckley, 1973-96, pres., CEO, chmn. bd. dirs., 1996—; pres. Vecellio Contracting Corp. and subs. (Ranger Constrn. Industries, West Palm Beach, PAVEX Corp., Deerfield Beach, White Rock Quarries, Miami), Fla., 1982—; mng. ptnr. Vecellio Realty Co., Deerfield Property Assocs.; bd. dirs. United Nat. Bank-South, Beckley, Barnett Bank of Palm Beach County; founder, past dir. Gulf Nat. Bank, Sophia, W.Va.; founder, past dir. Nat. Bankers Trust, Beckley. Chmn. bd. dirs. Econ. Coun. Palm Beach County, Fla., 1985—, chmn.-elect, 1987, chmn., 1989; gov. Northwood U., West Palm Beach, 1985—; organizer, trustee Beckley Area Found., 1985; v.p., trustee Vecellio Family Found., Beckley, 1972-96, pres., trustee, 1996—; active Mini-Grace Commn., Fla. Coun. 100, 1989—, vice-chmn., 1991—; commn. dir., v.p. Criminal Justice Commn.; chmn. Budget Rev. Task Force, Budget Oversight Task Force; bd. dirs. Gulfstream Coun. Boy Scouts Am., 1989-93, Palm Beach County Cultural Coun. and Art Sch. Task Force, Fla. Coun. 100, Floridians for Better Transp., exec. com.; corporator Schepens Eye Rsch. Inst./Harvard U., 1993—; engring. coun. 100 Va. Tech. Capt USAF, 1969-73. Recipient Free Enterprise medal Palm Beach Atlantic Coll., 1988. Mem. Flexible Pavements Assn. (found. bd. dirs. 1979—), Contractors Assn. W. (bd. dirs. 1975—). Republican. Roman Catholic. Clubs: Mayacoo Lakes Country (West Palm Beach), Adios Golf (Coconut Creek, Fla.), Jupiter Hills (Fla.), Lost Tree. Avocations: golf, boating, skiing. Home: 771 Village Rd No Palm Beach FL 33408-3331 Office: Vecellio Contracting Corp PO Box 15065 West Palm Beach FL 33416-5065

VECOLI, RUDOLPH JOHN, history educator; b. Wallingford, Conn., Mar. 2, 1927; s. Giovanni Battista and Settima Maria (Palmerini) V.; m. Jill Cherrington, June 27, 1959; children: Christopher, Lisa, Jeremy. BA, U. Conn., 1950; MA, U. Pa., 1951; PhD, U. Wis., 1963. Fgn. affairs officer Dept. State, 1951-54; instr. history Ohio State U., 1957-59, Pa. State U., 1960-61; asst. prof. Rutgers U., 1961-65; assoc. prof. U. Ill., Champaign, 1965-67; prof. history, dir. Immigration History Research Center, U. Minn., Mpls., 1967—; vis. prof. U. Uppsala, Sweden, 1970, U. Amsterdam, The Netherlands, 1988, Maria Curie-Sklodowsk U., Lublin, Poland, 1992. Author: The People of New Jersey, 1965, Foreword to Marie Hall Ets, Rosa: The Story of an Italian Immigrant, 1970, (with Joy Lintelman) A Century of American Immigration, 1884-1984, (with others) The Invention of Ethnicity, 1990; contbg. author: Gil italiani fuori d'Italia, 1983, They Chose Minnesota: A Survey of the State's Ethnic Groups, 1981, Pane e Lavoro: The Italian American Working Class, 1980, Perspectives in Italian Immigration and Ethnicity, 1977, Immigrants and Religion in Urban America, 1977, The State of American History, 1970, The Reinterpretation of American History and Culture, 1973, Failure of a Dream, Essays in the History of American Socialism, 1984, Italian Americans: New Perspectives, 1985, May Day Celebration, 1988, In the Shadow of the Statue of Liberty, 1988, From Melting Pot to Multiculturalism, 1990, Studi Sull' Emigrazione, 1991, The Lebanese in the World, 1992, Swedes in America: New Perspectives, 1993, The Statue of Liberty Revisited, 1994, La Riscoperta delle Americhe, 1994, The Encyclopedia of Twentieth Century America, 1996, The Cambridge Survey of World Migration, 1995; editor, contbg. author: The Other Catholics, 1978, Italian Immigrants in Rural and Small Town America, 1987, The Gale Encyclopedia of Multicultural America, 1994; mem. editl. bd. Jour. Am. Ethnic History, Studi Emigrazione, America: History and Life Mid-America, Internat. Migration Rev., Estudios Migratorios Latino Americanos, Altreitalie; co-editor (with Suzanne Sinke) A Century of European Migrations, 1830-1930, 1991; contbr. articles to profl. jours. Chair history com. Statue of Liberty-Ellis Island Centennial Commn., 1983-90. With USNR, 1945-46. Decorated Knight Officer, Order of Merit (Italy), 1992; recipient Campus Major honor City of Camaiore, Italy, 1996; Newberry Libr. fellow, 1964, Am.-Scandinavian Found. fellow, 1970, NEH fellow, 1985-86; Am. Philos. Soc. grantee, 1970, Fulbright-Hays sr. rsch. scholar Italy, 1973-74; Am. Coun. Learned Soc. grantee, 1974, 86, U.S. Dept. State Travel grantee, 1977, Acad. Specialist, U.S. Info. Agy., Brazil, 1993. Mem. Am. Italian Hist. Assn. (pres., mem. exec. council), Am. Hist. Assn., Orgn. Am. Historians, AAUP, Immigration History Soc. (pres., exec. council). Home: 610 E 58th St Minneapolis MN 55417-2426

VECSEY, GEORGE SPENCER, sports columnist; b. Jamaica, N.Y., July 4, 1939; s. George Stephen and May (Spencer) V.; m. Marianne Graham; children: Laura, Corinna, David. BA in English, Hofstra Coll., 1960; LHD (hon.), Hofstra U., 1991. Sports reporter Newsday, Garden City, N.Y., 1960-68; sports reporter N.Y. Times, N.Y.C., 1968-70, nat. corr., 1970-73, met., religion reporter, 1973-80, sports reporter, 1980-82, sports columnist, 1982—. Author: (with others) Naked Came the Stranger, 1969, Joy in Mudville: Being a Complete Account of the Unparalleled History of the New York Mets, 1970, One Sunset a Week: The Story of a Coal Miner, 1974, (with Loretta Lynn) Coal Miner's Daughter, 1976, (with Jacques Lowe) Kentucky: A Celebration of American Life, 1979, (with George C. Dade) Getting Off the Ground: The Pioneers of Aviation Speak for Themselves, 1978, (with Leonore Fleischer) Sweet Dreams, 1985, (with Martina Navratilova) Martina, 1985, (with Bob Welch) Five O'Clock Comes Early: A Young Man's Battle with Alcoholism, 1982, A Year in the Sun, 1989, (with Barbara Mandrell) Get to the Heart, 1991, (with Harry Wu) Troublemaker: One Man's Crusade Against China's Cruelty, 1996, (with Lorrie Morgan) Forever Yours, Faithfully, 1997; author 8 children's books; editor: The Way It Was: Great Sports Events from the Past, 1974. Recipient Disting. Writing award Am. Soc. Newspaper Editors, 1995; named N.Y. State Sportswriter of Yr. Nat. Sportscasters and Sportswriters Assn., 1985-97. Mem. Kentuckians (bd. dirs. 1988—). Avocations: running, swimming, music, travel, languages. Office: NY Times 229 W 43rd St New York NY 10036-3913

VEDDER, BYRON CHARLES, newspaper executive; b. Adrian, Mich., Feb. 9, 1910; s. Adelbert and Adah (Dibble) V.; m. Kathleen Fry, June 20, 1936 (dec. 1960); children: Richard Kent, Robert Allen; m. Helen Cochrane, Dec. 16, 1976. A.B., U. Mich., 1933. Grad. mgr. student publs. U. Mich., Ann Arbor, 1933-34; with Champaign-Urbana (Ill.) Courier, 1934-64, pub., 1960-64; v.p. ops. Lindsay-Schaub Newspapers, Inc., 1964-75, v.p. planning, 1975-79; v.p. Sun Coast Media Inc., 1979—; sec. Pasco Pub. Inc., 1981-86; bd. dirs. Comml. Savs. & Loan Assn., Urbana, v.p., 1975-76, chmn., 1977-83; bd. dirs. Mut. Home and Savs., 1983-86. Mem. Arrowhead council exec. bd. Boy Scouts Am., 1951—, pres., 1960-64; mem. Pres.'s Com. Traffic Safety, 1954-58. Recipient Silver Beaver award Boy Scouts Am., 1959; named Boss of Year Champaign-Urbana chpt. Nat. Secs. Assn., 1958; Disting. Service to Journalism award U. Minn., 1979, Disting. Svc. award Inland Press Assn., 1991; James E. West fellow Boy Scouts of Am. award, 1995. Mem. Inland Daily Press Assn. (bd. dirs. 1950-53, pres. 1954, chmn. 1955, Disting. Svc. award 1991), Cen. States Circulation Mgrs. Assn. (pres. 1944-46), Ill. Daily Newspaper Markets Assn. (pres. 1962-63, chmn. 1963-64), Am. Newspaper Pubs. Assn. (com. chmn.), Urbana Assn. Commerce (v.p. 1946), Campus Bus. Men's Assn. (bd. dirs.), Champaign C. of C. (bd. dirs. 1955-57, Internat. Circulation Mfrs. Assn. (hon.), U. Ill. Quarterback Club (hon. life). Presbyterian (trustee). Club: Urbana Country, Champaign Country. Lodge: Kiwanis (lt. gov. 1951, dir., Kiwanian of Year 1971, pres. 1978). Home: 3 Stanford Pl Champaign IL 61820-7620

VEDDER, EDDIE, singer; b. Evanston, Ill., Dec. 23, 1965; m. Beth Liebling, June 3, 1994. lead singer (band) Pearl Jam, 1991—; albums include Ten, 1991, Vs., 1993, Vitalogy, 1994, No Code, 1996; contbr. vocals (album) Temple of the Dog, 1991, Mother Love Bone, 1992, Bob Dylan Thirtieth-Anniversary Tribute, 1993, Sweet Reliefe: A Tribute to Victoria Williams, 1993, Shame, 1993, Judgement Night Soundtrack, 1993; film appearances include Singles, 1992, Dead Man Walking, 1995. Office: c/o Epic Records 550 Madison Ave New York NY 10022-3211*

VEDROS, NEYLAN ANTHONY, microbiologist; b. New Orleans, Oct. 6, 1929; s. Phillip John and Solange Agnes (Melancon) V.; m. Elizabeth Corbett, Apr. 9, 1955; children: Sally Ann, Philippa Jane. B.S. in Chemistry, La. State U., 1951, M.S. in Microbiology, 1957; Ph.D., U. Colo., 1960. Postdoctoral fellow Nat. Inst. Allergy and Infectious Diseases, U. Oreg., Portland, 1960-62; microbiologist Naval Med. Research Inst., Bethesda, Md., 1962-66; research microbiologist Naval Biosci. Lab., Oakland, Calif., 1966-67; assoc. prof. med. microbiology and immunology U. Calif., Berkeley, 1967-72; prof. U. Calif., 1972-91, prof. emeritus, 1991—; dir. Naval Biosci. Lab., 1968-81; mem. expert panel on bacteriology WHO, 1972-91. Bd. trustees Alameda (Calif.) Library, 1973-78. Served to comdr. M.S.C. USNR, 1952-55, 62-67. Mem. Am. Assn. Immunologists, Am. Soc. Microbiology, Internat. Assn. Human and Animal Mycology, Internat. Assn. Microbiol. Sci., Internat. Assn. Aquatic Animal Medicine, Assn. Mil. Surgeons. Home: 2610 Evelyn Ct Alameda CA 94501-6333 Office: 239 Warren Hall U Calif Berkeley CA 94725

VEEDER, PETER GREIG, lawyer; b. Pitts., Aug. 13, 1941. AB, Princeton U., 1963; JD, U. Pitts., 1966. Bar: Pa. 1966, D.C. 1976. Lawyer Thorp Reed & Armstrong, Pitts. Office: Thorp Reed & Armstrong One Riverfront Ctr Pittsburgh PA 15222

VEENKER, CLAUDE HAROLD, health education educator; b. George, Iowa, July 31, 1919; s. Ralph C. and Fannie (Casjens) V.; m. Elizabeth Louise Higgins, Jan. 1, 1944; children—Jo Lee, Vicki Susan. BA, U. No. Iowa, 1943; MA, U. No. Colo., 1953; D of Health and Safety, Ind. U., 1957. Tchr. Osage (Iowa) High Sch., 1946-47, Mason City (Iowa) Pub. Schs., 1947-55; teaching asst. Ind. U., 1955-56, vis. lectr., 1956-57; asst. prof. Purdue U., Lafayette, Ind., 1957-61, assoc. prof., 1961-66, prof., 1966-84, prof. emeritus, 1984—, chmn. health edn. sect., 1961-77; chmn. health edn. test project Ednl. Testing Svc., Princeton, 1965-74; cons. bur. rsch. coop. rsch. br. U.S. Office Edn., 1966-68; cons. healthful sch. environment AMA, NEA, Washington, 1969; mem. Ind. Coun. on Sch. Health, 1971-84, Ind. Adv. Com. on Drug Edn., 1969-74, Ind. Gov.'s Regional Com. on Mental Health, 1966-67. Editor, contbr. author: Synthesis of Research in Selected Areas of Health Instruction, 1963; mem. editorial bd.: Jour. Health, Phys. Edn. and Recreation, 1961-62, 64-66; Contbr. articles to profl. jours. Served to 1st lt. USMC, 1943-46. Decorated Purple Heart. Fellow Am. Sch. Health Assn., Am. Pub. Health Assn. (governing council 1974-76, mem. sch. health sect. council 1970-73); mem. Am. Alliance for Health, Phys. Edn. and Recreation (exec. council sch. health div. 1964-67, chmn. sch. health service sect. 1959-60), Mid-Am. Coll. Health Assn., Ind. Assn. Health Educators (pres. 1970), Phi Delta Kappa, Eta Sigma Gamma. Methodist. Club: Elks. Home: 224 Knox Dr West Lafayette IN 47906-2150 Office: Purdue U Lambert Bldg West Lafayette IN 47907 *Life as a child during the Roaring 20's, as a young teen-ager during the Great Depression of the 30's, and as a young adult during World War II, was a great adventure. But the world is no easier now than it was then. It seems that living is a continual challenge: to seek, to find, to try, to conquer. To succeed, one must live with confidence and hope, fearing neither failure nor success. To live well is to live with self-discipline in the present, using the hard-learned lessons of the past to brighten one's prospects for the future.*

VEGA, BENJAMIN URBIZO, retired judge, television producer; b. La Ceiba, Honduras, Jan. 18, 1916; m. Janie Lou Smith, Oct. 12, 1989; AB, U. So. Calif., 1938, postgrad., 1939-40; LLB, Pacific Coast U. Law, 1941. Bar: Calif. 1947, U.S. Dist. Ct. (so. dist.) Calif. 1947, U.S. Supreme Ct. 1958. Assoc. Anderson, McPharlin & Connors, L.A., 1947-48, Newman & Newman, L.A., 1948-51; dep. dist. atty. County of L.A., 1951-66; judge L.A., County Mcpl. Ct., East L.A. Jud. Dist., 1966-86, retired, 1986; leader faculty seminar Calif. Jud. Coll. at Earl Warren Legal Inst., U. Calif-Berkeley, 1978. Mem. Calif. Gov.'s Adv. Com. on Children and Youth, 1968; del. Commn. of the Califs., 1978; bd. dirs. Los Angeles-Mexico City Sister City Com.; pres. Argentine Cultural Found., 1983. Recipient award for outstanding services from Mayor of L.A., 1973, City of Commerce, City of Montebello, Calif. Assembly, Southwestern Sch. Law, Disting. Pub. Service award Dist. Atty. L.A. Mem. Conf. Calif. Judges, Mcpl. Ct. Judges' Assn. (award for Outstanding Services), Beverly Hills Bar Assn., Navy League, L.A. County, Am. Judicature Soc., World Affairs Council, Rotary (hon.), Pi Sigma Alpha. Home: 101 California Ave Apt 1207 Santa Monica CA 90403-3525

VEGA, FRANK J., newspaper publishing executive. Pres., CEO Detroit Newspapers. Office: 615 W Lafayette Blvd Detroit MI 48226-3124

VEGA, J. WILLIAM, aerospace engineering executive, consultant; b. Elizabeth, N.J., Jan. 30, 1931; s. John Charles and Margaret (Walker) V.; m. Carolyn Louise Burt, June 7, 1957 (div. 1976); children: Lynn Vega Membreño, Lore Vega Hynes, Susan; m. Pauline Anne Garner, Apr. 27, 1983. BSE, Princeton U., 1952, postgrad., 1955-56; MS, U.S. Internat. U., 1973. Sr. engr. Reaction Motors, Inc., Denville, N.J., 1956-58; sr. engr.

Convair div. Gen. Dynamics, San Diego, 1958, project engr., sr. project engr., asst. chief engr., 1970-75, dir. advanced programs, 1975-83, v.p. advanced programs, 1983-88, v.p. rsch. and engring., 1988-90; cons. aerospace mgmt., 1991—. Pres. bd. dirs. Durango (Colo.) Art Ctr. Lt. USN, 1952-55. Fellow AIAA (assoc.); mem. Phi Beta Kappa. Avocations: skiing, sailing, hiking, camping.

VEGA, MARYLOIS PURDY, journalist; b. Chgo., Nov. 4, 1914; d. William Thomas and Mary Helene (Buggy) Purdy; m. Carlos Juan Vega, Sept. 4, 1965. B.A., U. Wis., Madison, 1935. With Time mag., N.Y.C., 1942-84; chief Letters to the Editor, 1951-67, chief editl. rsch., 1967-76, assoc. editor, 1976-84. Roman Catholic. Club: Overseas Press. Home: 140 West End Ave New York NY 10023-6131 also: PO Box 266 Gardiner NY 12525

VEGA, MATIAS ALFONSO, lawyer; b. Paris, Feb. 2, 1952; s. Matias Guillermo and Colette (Lafosse) V.; m. Carmella Margarita Kurczewski, Nov. 20, 1982; 1 child, Alexandra Lafosse. AB, Yale U., 1974; JD, Harvard U., 1977. Bar: N.Y. 1978, U.S. Dist. Ct. (so. and ea. dists.) N.Y. 1979, U.S. Supreme Ct. 1984, U.S. Ct. Appeals (6th and 9th cirs.) 1985, U.S. Dist. Ct. (no. dist.) Calif. 1985. Assoc. Curtis, Mallet-Prevost, Colt & Mosle, N.Y.C., 1977-85, ptnr., 1986—. Contbr. articles to profl. jours. Mem. ABA, Am. Assn. Internat. Law, N.Y. State Bar Assn. (chmn. com. Latin Am. law, internat. law and practice sect. 1987-90), Yale Club. Republican. Roman Catholic. Home: 31 Gedney Way Chappaqua NY 10514 Office: Curtis Mallet-Prevost Colt 101 Park Ave New York NY 10178

VEGA, STEVE, poet; b. N.Y.C., Nov. 13, 1949; s. Exio Ocasio Vega; m. Veronica Gonzalez, Jan. 3, 1971; children: Katherine, James-Paul Christian, Diamond Zhane. Cert. in bus. mgmt., Marion Bus. Coll., 1973; cert., John Marshall Law Sch., 1977; cert. in corrections and probations svcs., Chgo. Loop Coll., 1986; BA, Coll. of Commr. Sci., 1995, M of Commr. Svc., 1996, postgrad., 1997. Adult probation officer Cook County, Ill.; union chief steward Cook County Adult Probation Dept., AFSCME, 1989-91; 1st v.p. AFSCME local 3486 APD officers, Chgo., 1991-92; cons. Chgo. Police Dept., FBI, U.S. Secret Svc. Contbr. poetry to over 20 anthologies worldwide, 1974—; appeared in films Only the Lonely, Music Box, Gladiator, Mo' Money, Hero, Hoffa, Natural Born Killers, others. Vol., mem. com. City of Chgo. Health Systems Agy., 1981-85; asst. coun. commn. Boy Scouts Am. Troop # 935, Chgo. 1997. With USAF, 1970. Decorated USAF Commendation medal, 1969, knight comdr. (Italy); recipient Presdl. Commendations, Pres. Ronald Reagan, George Bush, 1987, 88, 90. Mem. ASCAP (composer, writer), Fraternal Order of Police (officer 1988), Sovereign, Military and Hospitaller Order of St. George in Karinthia (titular head). Roman Catholic. Avocations: singing, composing, guitarist, motorcycle riding, playing chess. Address: PO Box 221 Morton Grove IL 60053

VEIGEL, JON MICHAEL, science administrator; b. Mankato, Minn., Nov. 10, 1938; s. Walter Thomas and Thelma Geraldine (Lein) V.; m. Carol June Bradley, Aug. 10, 1962. BS, U. Washington, 1960; PhD, UCLA, 1965. Program mgr. Office of Tech. Assessment, U.S. Congress, Washington, 1974-75; div. mgr. Calif. Energy Commn., Sacramento, 1975-78; asst. dir. Solar Energy Rsch. Inst., Golden, Colo., 1978-81; pres. Alt. Energy Corp., Rsch. Triangle Park, N.C., 1981-88, Oak Ridge (Tenn.) Associated Univs., 1988-96; bd. dirs. Am. Coun. Energy Efficient Economy, Washington, Pacific Internat. Ctr. for High Tech. Rsch., Honolulu. Contbr. articles to jours. Trustee Maryville Coll., 1990-96, Mendeleyev U., Moscow, Russia. 1st lt. USAF, 1965-68. Mem. AAAS (com. on sci. and engring. pub. policy, chair). Avocations: photography, flying. Office: SunRunner Assocs PO Box 2005 Cedar City UT 84721

VEILLE, JEAN-CLAUDE, maternal-fetal medicine physician, educator; came to U.S., 1982; m. Beatrice Buehler; children: Olivier, Xavier, Patrique. BS, McGill U., 1971; MD, U. Montpellier, France, 1977. Fellow in maternal-fetal medicine Oreg. Health Scis., Portland, 1982-84; from asst. prof. to assoc. prof. Case Western Res. U., Cleve., 1984-90; chief maternal, fetal medicine Case Western Reserve U., Cleve., 1989-90; assoc. prof., dir. maternal-fetal med. fellowship program Wake Forest U. Bowman Gray Sch. Medicine, Winston-Salem, N.C., 1990-95; prof. Wake Forest U.Bowman Gray Sch. Medicine, Winston-Salem, N.C., 1995—; chief maternal-fetal medicine sect. Wake Forest U. Bowman Gray Sch. Medicine, Winston-Salem, N.C., 1997—. Contbr. articles to med. jours. Grantee NIH, 1991—. Office: Wake Forest U Bowman Gray Sch Medicine Medical Center Blvd Winston-Salem NC 27157

VEINOTT, CYRIL GEORGE, electrical engineer, consultant; b. Somerville, Mass., Feb. 15, 1905; s. Jason A. and I. Laura (Fales) V.; m. Dorothy Helen Bassett, Nov. 28, 1936 (dec. Sept. 1988); 1 child, Richard A.; m. June Urlwin, Jan. 6, 1990. BSEE cum laude, U. Vt., 1926; EE, 1939; D in Engring. (hon.), 1951. Mgr. induction motor sect. Westinghouse, Lima, Ohio, 1926-52; chief engring. analyst Reliance Elec. Co., Cleve., 1953-70; invited prof. Laval U., Quebec City, Can., 1970-72; vol. exec. Internat. Exec. Svc. Corps, N.Y.C., 1972-79; pvt. practice as consultant in computer-aided design of electric motors, Sarasota, Fla., 1970—. Author: Fractional HP Electric Motors, 1939, 4th edit. 1986; Theory and Design Small Motors, 1959; How to Design a 1-ph Motor on a Personal Computer, 1989; How to Design a Metric 1-ph Motor on a PC, 1991; Computer-Aided Design Electric Machines, 1972. Patentee in field. Recipient Merit award Rsch. Inst. Rotating Machines Czechoslovakia, 1968; named to Hall of Fame Small Motors Mfg. Assn., 1985. Fellow IEEE (chmn. standards com. 1962-63, Tesla medal 1977, Centennial medal 1984), AIEE (v.p. 1949-51, chmn. rotating machines com. 1951-53, chmn. standards com. 1961-62); mem. Navy League U.S., Phi Beta Kappa, Eta Kappa Nu, Tau Beta Pi. Republican. Presbyterian. Club: High Twelve. Lodges: Masons, Shriners, Honorable Order Ky. Cols. Avocations: devel. of computer-aided design software for induction machines, home computers. Home: 4197 Oakhurst Cir W Sarasota FL 34233-1443

VEIT, CLAIRICE GENE TIPTON, measurement psychologist; b. Monterey Park, Calif., Feb. 20, 1939; d. Albert Vern and Gene (Bunning) Tipton; children: Steven, Barbara, Laurette, Catherine. BA, UCLA, 1969, MA, 1970, PhD, 1974. Asst. prof. psychology Calif. State U., L.A., 1975-77, assoc. prof. psychology, 1977-80; rsch. psychologist The Rand Corp., Santa Monica, Calif., 1977—; rsch. cons. NATO Tech. Ctr., The Hague, The Netherlands, 1980-81; faculty Rand Grad Sch., Santa Monica, 1993—. Developer subjective transfer function (STF) method to complex sys. analysis. Mem. LWV, NOW, Mil. Ops. Rsch. Soc. Am., Inst. Mgmt. Sci., Soc. Med. Decision-Making, Soc. for Judgement and Decision-Making, L.A. World Affairs Coun., L.A. Opera League. Avocations: mountain climbing, playing piano, travel, music, theatre. Office: The Rand Corp 1700 Main St Santa Monica CA 90401-3208

VEIT, FRITZ, librarian; b. Emmendingen, Baden, Germany, Sept. 17, 1907; came to U.S., 1935, naturalized, 1940; s. Samuel W. and Helene (Geismar) V.; m. Lucille Stearns, June 11, 1939; children: Joanne Grace, Mary Catherine (dec.). Student, U. Berlin, 1927, Heidelberg U., 1928; J.U.D., U. Freiburg, 1932; B.S. in Library Sci, Peabody Library Sch., Nashville, 1936; Ph.D., U. Chgo. Grad. Library Sch., 1941. Research asst. Inst. History Law, U. Freiburg, Germany, 1932-33; librarian U. Chgo. Grad. Library Sch., 1937-42, Social Sci. Reading Room, 1942; acting librarian Law Sch., 1943; librarian Chgo. City Jr. Coll. (Englewood evening br.), 1941-48; law librarian U.S. R.R. Retirement Bd., Chgo., 1943-49; supr. library John Marshall Law Sch., 1949-57; vis. prof. library sci. Rosary Coll., River Forest, Ill., 1950-78, Western Mich. U., summer 1959, Ariz. State U., summer 1964, 65, 67, 68, Emporia State U., summer 1977, Grad. Library Sch. U. Chgo., summer 1975, 78, fall 1977; dir. libraries Chgo. State U., 1949-73, also Kennedy-King Coll., 1949-72; chmn. adv. com. library tech. program Chgo. City Colls., 1968-74; mem. adv. council librarians U. Ill. Grad. Sch. Library Sci., 1971-74. Author: The Community College Library, 1975, Presidential Libraries and Collections, 1987; mem. editorial bd. Internat. Jour. Revs. in Libr. and Info. Sci., 1984-89, Third World Librs., 1990—; contbr. articles to profl. jours. Mem. ALA (sec., chmn. tchr. edn. libraries sect. ACRL 1959-61, assoc. editor monographs 1952-60, local chmn. ACRL 1963 Conf), Ill. Library Assn., Chgo. Library Club (pres. 1964-65), Pi Gamma Mu. Home: 5550 South Shore Dr Chicago IL 60637

VEITCH, BOYER LEWIS, printing company executive; b. Phila., Oct. 20, 1930; s. Samuel Lewis and Agnes Mae (Bell) V.; AB, Lafayette Coll., 1953; postgrad. Wharton Evening Sch. Acctg. and Fin., U. Pa., 1957-59; m. Emmeline Barbara Smith, Nov. 22, 1952; children: William S., Nancy B., Thomas C. Advt. dir. Ware Bros. Co., Phila., 1956-62, v.p., 1962-69; salesman Zabel Bros. Co., Phila., 1969-75; chmn., pres. Veitch Printing Corp., Lancaster, Pa., 1975—; trustee Printers Disability Trust. Trustee Lafayette Coll., Easton, Pa., 1981-86, 87—; vice chmn. coll. rels. com., chmn. ann. fund, 1982-86, mem. fin. com., 1987-92, chmn. athletics and student affairs comn., 1992—, mem. exec. com.; bd. dirs., Boys and Girls Club, Lancaster, 1980—, pres., 1990-92; dir. Boy's Club Lancaster Found., 1989—, pres., 1992—; dir. Gt. Valley Civic Assn., 1969-79; trustee Fulton Opera House Found., 1985-91, treas., 1987-89; bd. dirs. North Mus., 1992-94, Lancaster Airport Authority, 1994—, treas., 1994—; trustee PIA Disability Trust, 1994—; chmn. citizens for Schulze Com., Pa. 5th Congressional Dist., 1972-78; vestryman, sr. Warden St. Peter's Ch. of Gt. Valley, 1972-78. Served with CIC, U.S. Army, 1954-56. Recipient Bronze Hope Chest award Nat. Multiple Sclerosis Soc., 1982, Nat. Svc. to Youth award Boys and Girls Clubs Am., 1992; named Small Bus. Person of Yr. Lancaster Co., 1991. Mem. SAR, Printing Industries Am. (dir. 1993—), Graphic Arts Assn. (dir. 1980—, chmn. 1990-92), Lancaster C. of C. and Industry (dir. 1990-93), Aircraft Owners and Pilots Assn., Lafayette Coll. Alumni Assn. (dir. 1974-78, pres. 1978-80), Pa. Economy League, Nat. Fedn. Ind. Bus., Phi Kappa Psi (past pres. and dir. chpt. alumni assn.). Republican. Episcopalian. Lodge: Rotary (Paul Harris fellow). Clubs: Hamilton (bd. dirs. 1995—), Wash Day, Lancaster Country, Dataw Country, Avalon Yacht, Lancaster Aero., Lancaster Pirates, Susquehanna Litho (dir. 1976-80, pres. 1979-80). Home: 264 Little Creek Rd Lancaster PA 17601-5514 also: 65 17th St E Avalon NJ 08202-2234 Office: Veitch Printing Corp 1740 Hempstead Rd Lancaster PA 17601-5844

VEITCH, STEPHEN WILLIAM, investment counselor; b. Albuquerque, Aug. 19, 1927; s. Kenneth Easton and Edna (Miller) V.; B.A., U. N.Mex., 1949; LL.B., Stanford, 1957; student U. Nacional, Mex., 1949; m. Nancy Baker, June 28, 1951; children—Christopher Oxnard, Julia Blair. Bar: Calif., 1958. Probate adminstr. Wells Fargo Bank, San Francisco, 1957-59; sr. v.p. Van Strum & Towne, Inc., San Francisco, 1959-76, sr. v.p., 1976-82, pres., 1982-91, vice chmn, 1991-95, chmn., 1995. Mem. Guardsman, San Francisco, 1960—. With USNR, 1945-46; 1st lt. USAF, 1950-54. Mem. Am., San Francisco bar assns., Delta Theta Phi, Sigma Chi. Republican. Episcopalian. Clubs: Commonwealth, Pacific Union (San Francisco); Menlo Circus (Atherton, Calif.). Home: 33 Spencer Ln Atherton CA 94027-4038 Office: 505 Sansome St Ste 1001 San Francisco CA 94111-3134

VEITH, ILZA, historian of psychiatric and Oriental medicine; b. Ludwigshafen, Germany, May 13, 1915; came to U.S., 1937, naturalized, 1945; m. Hans von Valentini Veith, Oct. 20, 1935 (dec. Mar. 1991). Student med. schs., Geneva and Vienna, Austria, 1934-36; M.A., Johns Hopkins, 1944, Ph.D., 1947; Igaku hakase (M.D., D.M.S.), Sch. Medicine, Juntendo U., Tokyo, 1975. Cons. Oriental medicine Armed Forces Med. Library, Washington, 1947-57; lectr. in history medicine U. Chgo., 1949-51; editorial bd. U. Chgo. Press, 1951-53; asst. prof. history medicine U. Chgo., 1953-57, assoc. prof., 1957-63; cons. in History of Medicine Nat. Inst. Health, 1959-64; vis. prof. Menninger Sch. Psychiatry, 1963; prof. history medicine, vice chmn. dept. U. Calif. at San Francisco Med. Center, 1964-79, prof. history psychiatry, 1967-79, prof. emeritus, 1979—; D.J. Davies Meml. lectr. U. Ill. Sch. Medicine, 1958; Sloan vis. prof. Menninger Found., 1963, 66; John Shaw Billings lectr. U. Ind. Sch. Medicine, Indpls., 1970; George W. Corner lectr. history medicine U. Rochester, N.Y., 1970; Logan Clendenning lectr. history of medicine U. Kans. Sch. Medicine, 1971; spl. lectr. VI World Congress Psychiatry, 1977; Hideyo Noguchi lectr. Johns Hopkins U., 1977. Author: Leverkusen, 1961, Medizin in Tibet, 1962, Hysteria: The History of a Disease, 1965, 3d edit., 1993, Yellow Emperor's Classic of Internal Medicine, 1966, Englishman or Samurai? The Story of Will Adams, 1981, Can You Hear the Clapping of One Hand? Learning to Live With a Stroke, 1988, soft cover edit., 1997; co-author: Great Ideas in the History of Surgery, 3d edit., 1961, Acupuncture Therapy: Current Chinese Practice, 1973, 2d rev. and enlarged edit., 1976, Histoire de l' hystérie, 1974, Nei-Ching: Canone di Medicina Interna dell' Imperatore Giallo, 1976, Ishimpo The Essentials of Medicine in Ancient China and Japan, 1986; mem. editorial. bd. Ency. Britannica; contbr. articles to profl. jours. Decorated officer's Cross of Merit Fed. Republic Germany, 1971; recipient Gold-Headed Cane award U. Kans. Sch. Medicine, 1976, Disting. Service award for sci. achievement Med. Alumni Assn. of U. Chgo., 1983. Hon. fellow Am. Psychiat. Assn. (Benjamin Rush Meml. lectr. 1987); mem. Am. Assn. History of Medicine (council mem. 1958-62, 73-77), AAAS, Soc. History of Medicine Chgo. (pres. 1954-64), Soc. History Med. Scis. Los Angeles (hon.), History Sci. Soc., AMA (asso.), Marin Med. Soc. (hon.), Spanish Soc. History of Medicine (hon., corr. mem.), Bay Area Med. History Soc. (v.p. 1972), Johns Hopkins Alumni Assn. (past pres. Ill.), Royal Soc. Medicine (London), Vishwa Inst. of Oriental Medicine, Sri Lanka (hon.), German Soc. History Medicine, Sci. and Tech. (hon.), Sigma Xi. Home: 2235 Centro St E Belvedere Tiburon CA 94920-1947 Office: U Calif Med Ctr San Francisco CA 94143 also: Med Ctr, PO Box 70, Abidi Village Anambra State, Nigeria *In a long and severely handicapped life I have had to live with chronic illness and pain. Thanks to my husband's endless patience and helpfulness, I have learned to accept what cannot be changed, and to change what can be altered. I have had a successful and highly satisfactory academic career in spite of endless obstacles that lie in the way of a woman scholar. In short, I have had a difficult but eminently happy life.*

VEITH, MARY ROTH, assistant dean; b. Middletown, Conn., Feb. 7, 1931; d. John Stephen and Margaret (Healey) Roth; children: Richard, Frank, Margaret, Katherine. BS, U. Conn., 1952; MBA, Iona Coll., 1975. Registered dietitian. Asst. head dietitian St. Francis Hosp., Hartford, Conn., 1954-55; dietitian Quality Control Lab A&P Corp., N.Y.C., 1955-56; head dietitian Cabrini Hosp., N.Y.C., 1956; homemaker, 1957-75; instr. mgmt. Coll. New Rochelle, N.Y., 1975; instr. mktg. Iona Coll., New Rochelle, N.Y., 1975-78, asst. prof., 1979—, asst. dean Hagan Sch. of Bus., 1979-97; ret., 1997; treas. Advt. Club Westchester, N.Y. Mem. Am. Dietetic Assn., N.Y. Dietetic Assn., Am. Mktg. Assn., World Trade Club (Westchester). Avocations: tennis, skiing. Office: Hagan Sch Business Iona College 715 North Ave New Rochelle NY 10801-1830

VEIZER, JÁN, geology educator; b. Pobedim, Slovakia, June 22, 1941; came to Can., 1973; s. Viktor and Brigita (Brandstetter) V.; m. Elena Ondrus, July 30, 1966; children: Robert, Andrew Douglas. Prom. Geol., Comenius U., Bratislava, Slovakia, 1964; RNDr, Comenius U., Bratislava, Slovak Republic, 1968; CSc, Slovak Acad. Sci., Bratislava, Slovakia, 1968; PhD, Australian Nat. U., Canberra, 1971. Asst. lectr. Comenius U., 1963-66; research scientist Slovak Acad. Sci., 1966-71; vis. asst. prof. UCLA, Los Angeles, 1972; vis. research scientist U. Göttingen, Fed. Republic Germany, 1972-73; research scientist U. Tübingen, Fed. Republic Germany, 1973; from asst. prof. to full prof. U. Ottawa, Ont., Can., 1973—; rsch. chair NORANDA/CIAR U. Ottawa, Ont., Can., 1997—; prof. Ruhr U., Bochum, Germany, 1988—; cons. NASA, Houston, 1983-86; vis. prof. and scholar Northwestern U., Evanston, Ill., 1983-87; vis. fellow Australian Nat. U., 1979; vis. prof. U. Tübingen, 1974; Lady Davis professorship Hebrew U., Jerusalem, 1987. Contbr. articles to profl. jours., chpts. to books. Served to j.lt. Med., 1965-66, Czechoslovakia. Recipient W. Leibniz prize German Rsch. Found., 1992; named Rsch. Prof. of Yr., 1987; Humboldt fellow, 1980, Killam Rsch. fellow Can. Coun., 1986-88. Fellow Royal Soc. Can. (Willet G. Miller medal 1991), Geol. Soc. Can. (Past Pres. medal 1987, Logan medal 1995), Geol. Soc. Am.; mem. Geochem. Soc. Am., Ski Club. Roman Catholic. Avocations: reading, hiking, skiing, history. Office: Dept Geology U Ottawa, Ottawa, ON Canada K1N 6N5 also: Ruhr U Inst Geologie, Lehrstuhl Sedimentgeologie, 44780 Bochum Germany

VEJSICKY, CATHLEEN LYNN, management executive, educator; b. Columbus, Ohio, June 25, 1958; d. Eugene Joseph and Jane Ann (Thomas) V. BS, U. So. Calif., L.A., 1981, MBA, 1987, postgrad. Cert. tchr., bus. mgmt. and mktg. tchr., C.C. tchr., Calif. Sr. product mgr. Dataproducts Corp., Woodland Hills, Calif., 1980-86; product mktg. mgr. Light Signatures, Century City, Calif., 1987-88; mgr., sr. mgmt. cons. KPMG Peat Marwick, L.A., 1988-92; v.p. Stranberg & Assocs., Newport Beach, Calif., 1993—; substitute tchr. Long Beach (Calif.) Unified Sch. Dist., 1993-95; tchr. Anaheim (Calif.) City Sch. Dist., 1994-97; guest mktg. lectr. U. So. Calif., 1986—; developer, leader U. So. Calif. Western Europe's Grad. Bus. Exch. Program, 1987; dir. Platinum Interchange Tricom Mgmt., 1997. Polit. campaign vol., Long Beach, Calif., 1989—; mem. Patrick Henry Leadership Team, Anaheim Unified Sch. Dist. Ins. Com., P.Q.R. sci. Team; leader Anaheim Math. Mem. Town and Gown of U. So. Calif. Republican. Presbyterian. Avocations: golf, reading, swimming, biking, kayaking. Home: 6016 Bixby Village Dr Long Beach CA 90803-6304

VELA, FILEMON B., federal judge; b. Harlingen, Tex., May 1, 1935; s. Roberto and Maria Luisa Cardenas V.; m. Blanca Sanchez, Jan. 28, 1962; children: Filemon, Rafael Eduardo, Sylvia Adriana. Student, Tex. Southmost Coll., 1954-56, U. Tex., 1956-57; JD, St. Mary's U., San Antonio, 1962. Bar: Tex. 1962. Mem. Vela & Vela, 1962-63; atty. Mexican-Am. Legal Def. Fund, 1962-75; pvt. practice law Brownsville, 1963-75; judge dist. 107, Tex. Dist. Ct., 1975-80; judge U.S. Dist. Ct. (so. dist.) Tex., Brownsville, 1980—; instr. Law Enforcement Coll. City commr., Brownsville, 1971-73. Served with U.S. Army, 1957-59. Mem. State Bar Tex. Democrat. Office: US Courthouse 500 E 10th St Brownsville TX 78520-5121*

VELARDO, JOSEPH THOMAS, molecular biology and endocrinology educator; b. Newark, Jan. 27, 1923; s. Michael Arthur and Antoinette (Iacullo) V.; m. Forresta M. Monica Power, Aug. 12, 1948 (dec. July 1976). AB, U. No. Colo., 1948; SM, Miami U., 1949; PhD, Harvard U., 1952. Rsch. fellow in biology and endocrinology Harvard U., Cambridge, Mass., 1952-53; rsch. assoc. in pathology, ob-gyn. and surgery Sch. Medicine Harvard U., Boston, 1953-55; asst. in surgery Peter Bent Brigham and Women's Hosp., Boston, 1954-55; asst. prof. anatomy and endocrinology Sch. Medicine, Yale U., New Haven, 1955-61; prof. anatomy, chmn. dept. N.Y. Med. Coll., N.Y.C., 1961-62; cons. N.Y. Fertility Inst., 1961-62; dir. Inst. for Study Human Reprodn., Cleve., 1962-67; prof. biology John Carroll U., Cleve., 1962-67; mem. rsch. and edn. divs. St. Ann Ob-Gyn. Hosp., Cleve., 1962-67, head dept. rsch., 1964-67; prof. anatomy Stritch Sch. Medicine Loyola U., Chgo., 1967-88, chmn. dept. anatomy Stritch Sch. of Medicine, 1967-73; pres. Internat. Basic and Biol.-Biomed. Curricula, Lombard, Ill., 1979—; course moderator laparoscopy Brazil-Israel Congress on Fertility and Sterility, and Brazil Soc. of Human Reproduction, Rio de Janeiro, 1973; organizer, chmn. symposia in field. AUthor: (with others) Annual Reviews Physiology, Reproduction, 1961, Histochemistry of Enzymes in the Female Genital System, 1963, The Ovary, 1963, The Ureter, 1967, rev. edit., 1981; editor, contbr.: Endocrinology of Reproduction, 1958, The Essentials of Human Reproduction, 1958; cons. editor, co-author: The Uterus, 1959; contbr. Progestational Substances, 1958, Trophoblast and Its Tumors, 1959, The Vagina, 1959, Hormonal Steroids, Biochemistry, Pharmacology and Therapeutics, 1964, Human Reproduction, 1973; co-editor, contbr.: Biology of Reproduction, Basic and Clinical Studies, 1973; contbr. articles to profl. jours.; live broadcasts on major radio and TV networks on subjects of bioscis., biomed. careers and biomed. subjects; co-author, co-dir. med. movie on human reprodn. The Soft Anvil. Apptd. U.S. del. to Vatican, 1964; charter mem. U.S. Rep. Presdl. Task Force, 1988—; rep. U.S. Senate Inner Circle, 1988—, U.S. Rep. Senatorial Commn., 1991—. With USAAF, 1943-45. Decorated Presdl. Unit citation, 2 Bronze Stars; recipient award Lederle Med. Faculty Awards Com., 1955-58; named hon. citizen City of Sao Paulo, Brazil, 1972; U.S. del. to Vatican, 1964. Fellow AAAS, N.Y. Acad. Scis. (co-organizer, chmn., consulting editor internat. symposium The Uterus), Gerontol. Soc., Pacific Coast Fertility Soc. (hon.); mem. Am. Assn. Anatomists, Am. Soc. Zoologists (organizer symposium The Uterus 1973), Am. Physiol. Soc. (vis. prof. 1962), Endocrine Soc., Soc. Endocrinology (Gt. Britain), Soc. Exptl. Biology and Medicine, Am. Soc. Study Sterility (Rubin award 1954), Internat. Fertility Assn., Pan Am. Assn. Anatomy (co-organizer symposium Reproduction 1972), Midwestern Soc. Anatomists (pres. 1973-74), Mexican Soc. Anatomy (hon.), Harvard Club, Sigma Xi, Kappa Delta Pi, Phi Sigma, Gamma Alpha, Alpha Epsilon Delta. Roman Catholic. Achievements include extensive original research and publications on the physiology and development of decidual tissue (experimental equivalent of the maternal portion of the placenta) in the rat; biological investigation of eighteen human adenohypophyses (anterior lobes of the human pituitary glands); induction of ovulation utilizing highly purified adenohypophyseal gonadotropic hormones in mammals; the pacemaker action of ovarian sex steroid hormones in reproductive processes; and the interation of steroids in reproductive mechanisms. Office: 607 E Wilson Ave Lombard IL 60148-4062 *Personal philosophy: Success is best highlighted by the invincible instruments of truth, integrity, hard work, thinking, running the extra mile, leading or giving help where no other help seems forthcoming, recognizing the talents of our fellow man and lady, and above all, practicing of the Golden Rule.*

VELASQUEZ, ANA MARIA, languages educator; b. Callao, Lima, Peru, Nov. 18, 1947; came to U.S. 1980; d. Victor and Yolanda (Reinoso) V.; m. Scott Mathew Nakada, Mar. 19, 1981; 1 child, Victor Min Nakada. Bachelor's Degree, San Marcos U., Lima, 1969; student French Paris VI U., 1971-72, student English Prince George Coll., 1983-84, student Quechua Yachay Wasi Coll., Lima, 1986. Cert. tchr., Peru. Educator San Jose de Cluny, Lima, 1968-71; translator Aubert & Duval, Paris, 1972-76; linguistic coordinator Ser. de Maquinaria, Lima, 1977-80; educator, cons. INLINGUA, Washington, 1981-83, CACI, Inc., Arlington, Va., 1982-89; educator Diplomatic Lang. Svcs., Inc., Arlington, Va., 1990-94; dir. AKTA Internat., San Diego, 1984—. Author: Pronunciacion Basica Universal, 1974; South American Dialects, 1977; Abbreviated Telephone Communications System, 1984; Teaching Languages to Adults, 1985; Languages 365 Days, 1986. Coord. literacy campaign, Puno, Peru, 1969. Mem. Intertel, Am. Assn. Applied Linguistics, Mensa. Republican. Roman Catholic. Avocations: chess, skiing. Home and Office: PO Box 502884 San Diego CA 92150-2884

VELAZQUEZ, NYDIA M., congresswoman; b. Yabucoa, P.R.. Grad., U. P.R.; MA, NYU, 1976. Mem. 103rd-105th Congress from 12th N.Y. dist., Washington, D.C., 1992—; mem. banking and fin. svcs. Office: US Ho of Reps 1221 Longworth Washington DC 20515-2508*

VELÁZQUEZ DE CANCEL, LOURDES, religious organization executive, educator, interpreter, translator, poet; b. Santurce, P.R., Jan. 28, 1941; d. Manuel Velázquez-Conde and Ramonita Torres-Marrero; m. Eduardo Cancel-Rodriguez, June 3, 1961; children: Lourdes Isabel, Eduardo Juan, Daniel Eduardo. Grad., Inst. Children's Lit., West Redding, Conn., 1993. Pres., founder Ralvec Ministries, Carolina, 1991—. Author: A Crisis of Faith, 1986, Does Anyone Care? 1991, My Secret Garden, 1991, On Love and Power, 1991, On a Daily Basis, 1991, A Question of Integrity, 1991, Amidst Deep Waters, 1991, No One is So Great or So Small, 1994, The Tree of Life, 1994, Erotika-Poems, Proverbs and Undiluted Thoughts, 1994, His Way, 1992, Tulip Woman, 1993, Erotika, 1994, It is Not Enough Not to Beg, 1994, The Money Value of Man, 1994, Come Home, Mother Come Home, 1994, The Signet, The Shield, The Pair of Keys, 1994, Tulip Man, 1994; author numerous hymns, psalms, poems and short stories; editor Resurrection Life Mag., 1991; radio broadcaster Sta. WIPR-AM, 1994, 95, 96. Translator ARC, San Juan, P.R., 1989-90. Recipient Merit award Internat. Soc. Poets, 1992. Mem. Soc. Tech. Communicators. Office: Ralvec Ministries PO Box 9466 Plaza Carolina Sta Carolina PR 00628

VELDE, JOHN ERNEST, JR., business executive; b. Pekin, Ill., June 15, 1917; s. John Ernest and Alga (Anderson) V.; m. Shirley Margaret Walker, July 29, 1940 (dec. 1969); 1 dau., Drew; m. Gail Patrick, Sept. 28, 1974 (dec. July 1980); m. Gretchen Swanson Pullen, Nov. 7, 1981. A.B., U. Ill., 1938. Pres. Velde, Roelfs & Co., Pekin, 1955-60; dir. Herget Nat. Bank, 1948-75, Kroehler Mfg. Co., 1974-81; pres. Paisano Prodns., Inc., 1980-94, mng. ptnr., 1994—; mng. ptnr. The Gardner Partnership, 1994—. Trustee Pekin Pub. Library, 1948-69, Pekin Meml. Hosp., 1950-69, Everett McKinley Dirksen Rsch. Ctr., 1965-74, Am. Libr. Assn. Endowment, 1976-82, Joint Coun. Econ. Edn., 1977-83, Ctr. Am. Archeology, 1978-83, Western Heritage Mus., Omaha, 1994—; chmn. Am. Libr. Trustee Assn. Found., 1976; chmn. trustees, bd. dirs. Ctr. Ulcer Rsch. and Edn. Found., 1977-82; mem. bd. councilors Brain Rsch. Inst. UCLA, 1977-82; mem. Nat. Commn. on Libr. and Info. Sci., 1970-79; mem. adv. bd. on White House Conf. on Librs., 1976-80; bd. dirs. U. Ill. Found., 1977-83, Omaha Pub. Libr. Found., 1985-92, James Madison Coun. Libr. Congress, 1990—; vice chmn. U. Ill. Pres.' Coun., 1977-79, chmn., 1979-81, mem. fin. resources coun. steering com., 1976-78; mem. adv. coun. UCLA Grad. Sch. Libr. and Info. Sci., 1981-82; pres. Ill. Valley Library System, 1965-69; dir. Lakeview Ctr. for Arts and

Scis., Peoria, Ill., 1962-73; mem. Nat. Book Com., 1969-74. Served as lt. (j.g.) USNR, World War II. Mem. Am. Libr. Trustee Assn. (regional v.p. 1970-72, chmn. internat. rels. com. 1973-76), Internat. Boy Scouts (Baden-Powell fellow 1987—), Kappa Sigma. Clubs: Chgo. Yacht, Internat. (Chgo.); California (Los Angeles); Outrigger Canoe (Honolulu); Thunderbird Country (Rancho Mirage, Calif.); Chaine des Rotisseurs, Chevaliers du Tastevin; Circumnavigators (N.Y.C.); Omaha, Omaha Country; Old Baldy (Saratoga, Wyo.), Eldorado Country (Indian Wells, Calif.). Home: 8405 Indian Hills Dr Omaha NE 68114-4048 also: 40-231 Club View Dr Rancho Mirage CA 92270-3527 also: 123 Arapahoe Dr Saratoga WY 82331

VELICER, JANET SCHAFBUCH, elementary school educator; b. Cedar Rapids, Iowa, Aug. 27, 1941; d. Allan J. and Geraldine Frances (Stuart) Schafbuch; m. Leland Frank Velicer, Aug. 17, 1963; children: Mark Allan, Gregory Jon, Daniel James. BS, Iowa State U., 1963, MS, 1966; cert. Elem. Edn., Mich. State U., 1976. Tchr. chemistry Prendergast High Sch., Upper Darby, Pa., 1964-65; tchr. home econs. Cardinal O'Hara High Sch., Springfield, Pa., 1965-66; substitute tchr. Pa., Mich., 1967-76; elem. tchr. Winans Elem. Sch., Waverly, Mich., 1976-78, Wardcliff Elem. Sch., Okemos, Mich., 1978-94; tchr. gifted and talented alternative program grades 4 and 5 Hiawatha Elem. Sch., Okemos, 1994-95; tchr. grade 4 Wardcliff Elem. Sch., 1995—; computer coord., Great Books coord.; dist. com. mem. math, computer, substance abuse, cable TV, evaluation revision Okemos Pub. Schs., Instructional Coun. Author: (video) Wardcliff School Documentary, 1982, The Integrated Arts Program of the Okemos Elementary Schools, 1983. Citizens adv. com. to develop a five-yr. plan, 1982-83, Bldg. utilization adv. com., 1983-84, Community use of schs. adv. com., 1984-85, Strategic planning steering com., 1989-90, Taking our schs. into tomorrow com., 1990-91, Bonding election steering com., 1991; chmn. wellness com. Okemos Pub. Schs., 1993-95; bd. dirs. Okemos Music Patrons, 1981-86, pres., 1984-86; faculty rep. PTO. Recipient Classrooms of Tomorrow Tchr. award Mich. Dept. Edn., 1990. Mem. NEA, NAFE, Mich. Edn. Assn., Inst. Noetic Scis., Okemos Edn. Assn. (exec. coun.), Phi Kappa Phi, Mich. Coun. Tchrs. Math., Omicron Nu, Iota Sigma Pi. Democrat. Avocations: swimming, reading, hiking, travelogs,cultural events. Home: 2678 Blue Haven Ct East Lansing MI 48823-3804 Office: Okemos Pub Schs 4406 Okemos Rd Okemos MI 48864-2553

VELICK, SIDNEY FREDERICK, research biochemist, educator; b. Detroit, May 3, 1913; s. Harry Alexander and Ella (Stocker) V.; m. Bernadette Stemler, Sept. 5, 1941; children: William Frederick, Martha Elizabeth. B.S., Wayne State U., 1935; Ph.D., U. Mich., 1938. Research fellow parasitology Johns Hopkins U., 1939-40; research asso. chemistry Yale U., 1941-45; mem. biol. chemistry dept. Washington U. Sch. Medicine, St. Louis, 1946-63; prof. biol. chemistry Washington U. Sch. Medicine, 1958-64; prof., head dept. biol. chemistry U. Utah Coll. Medicine, 1964-79, prof. emeritus, 1988—; mem. biochemistry study sect. NIH. Assoc. editor: Archives Biochemistry and Biophysics; editorial bd.: Jour. Biol. Chemistry; contbr. papers on enzyme chemistry to tech. lit. Co-founder, pres. Alliance for the Mentally Ill Utah, 1980-85. Mem. NAS, AAAS, Am. Soc. Biol. Chemists, Am. Chem. Soc., Sigma Xi. Home: 4183 Parkview Dr Salt Lake City UT 84124-3436

VELIE, LESTER, journalist; b. Kiev, Ukraine, 1907; came to U.S., 1912, naturalized, 1922; s. Samuel and Sarah (Spector) V.; m. Frances Rockmore, Oct. 29, 1932; children: Alan R., Franklin Bell. BA, U. Wis., 1929. Reporter AP, N.Y., 1931-32; suburban editor Bklyn. Eagle, 1932-35; assoc. editor Jour. Commerce, N.Y.C., 1937-46; radio analyst Sta. WQXR, N.Y.C., 1941-45; assoc. editor Collier's, 1945-52; roving editor Reader's Digest, 1953-85. Author: Labor U.S.A, 1959, Labor U.S.A. Today, 1964, Countdown in the Holy Land, 1969, Desperate Bargain: Why Jimmy Hoffa had to Die, 1977, Murder Story: A Tragedy of Our Time, 1983; contbr. to Op Ed, N.Y. Times; ABC TV series Target the Corrupters based on mag. articles. Recipient Disting. Svc. award for mag. journalism Sigma Delta Chi, 1949, Sch. Bell award for mag. journalism NEA, 1966, Silver Gavel award ABA, 1973; Ford Found. grantee, 1981-82. Home and Office: 1022 Kings Rd Norman OK 73069

VELIOTES, NICHOLAS ALEXANDER, professional association executive, former ambassador and assistant secretary of state; b. Oakland, Calif., Oct. 28, 1928; s. Alexander and Irene (Kiskakis) V.; m. Patricia Jane Nolan, July 17, 1953; children: Christopher, Michael. BA, U. Calif.-Berkeley, 1952; MA, Woodrow Wilson Sch., 1954; student, Princeton U., 1969-70. Teaching asst. U. Calif.-Berkeley, 1952-54; commd. officer U.S. Fgn. Service, 1955; held various Fgn. Service posts Italy, India, Laos, Israel, Jordan, Egypt; Asst. Sec. of State Near East/South Asia, 1981-83; ambassador to Jordan, 1978-81, ambassador to Egypt, 1983-86; pres. Assn. Am. Pubs., 1986-87, pres. emeritus, 1997—. Bd. dirs. Fund for Free Expression, Amer. Acad. Diplomacy, Com. on Pres., Access and Amideast. Served with U.S. Army, 1946-48. Recipient Sec. of State and Presdl. Disting. Svc. awards, Anti-Defamation League, B'nai B'rith; decorated Chevalier des Arts et des Lettres (France). Mem. Council on Fgn. Relations, VFW, U. Calif. Berkeley Fellows. Office: Assn Am Pub 1718 Connecticut Ave NW Washington DC 20009-1148

VELISARIS, CHRIS NICHOLAS, financial analyst; b. Berwyn, Ill., June 2, 1961; s. Nicholas Chris and Panagiota Nicholas (Georgiou) V.; m. Mary Elizabeth Vlahos, July 23, 1994. BS, U. Ill., 1983; MS, U. Wash., 1985; MBA, Dartmouth Coll., 1990; postgrad., U. Naples, Italy, 1991-94. Rsch. engr. Amoco Chem. Co., Naperville, Ill., 1983, 85-94; cons. Orco Ltd., Athens, 1989; rsch. mgr. U. Wash., Seattle, 1990-94; sr. staff analyst fin. United Airlines, Chgo., Ill., 1994—; founder, prin. officer Velisaris Investment Cons. Svcs., Inc., Brookfield, Ill., 1994—; cons. in field. Author: Proc. 31st Ann. Nat. Sampe Symp., 1986, Polymer Engring. and Sci., 1986, 88, Proc. of the 5th European Conf. on Comp. Materials, 1992. Counselor Valleyview Correctional Ctr., Ill. Benedictine Coll., St. Charles, 1988; advisor Jr. Achievement of Chgo., Naperville, 1987-88. Mem. Tri-Orgn. of Amoco Corp. (bd. dirs. 1987-88). Greek Orthodox. Avocations: skiing, golf, tennis, chess, investing. Home: 59 Drexel Ave La Grange IL 60525-5845 Office: United Airlines World Hdqs WHQCJ PO Box 66100 Chicago IL 60666

VELLA, SANDRA RACHAEL, principal; b. Springfield, Mass., Jan. 19, 1946; d. Joseph James and Josephine Anna (DiMonaco) V. BA, Coll. of Our Lady Of Elms, 1967; MA, Westfield State Coll., 1974, postgrad., 1975. Cert. elem. sch. tchr., prin. Tchr. elem. sch. Samuel Bowles Sch., Springfield, Mass., 1967-86, prin. elem. sch., 1986—. Historian Italian Cultural Ctr., 1988—; bd. dirs. Springfield Preservation Trust, 1988-94; coord. Com. Dimonaco for Mayor, Springfield, 1989-90; co-author drug program Healthy Me Gov. Alliance vs. Drug, 1992-94; bd. dirs. Forest Park Civic Assn., 1990-92; bd. dirs. New Eng. Puppetry Theatre, 1984-92; mem. adv. coun. Springfield Cmty. Police sector, E. Springfield; grad. Citizen's Police Acad.; numerous ednl. and educational civic sub. coms. Recipient Serviam award Italian Cultural Ctr. Western Mass., 1992, Mass. Gov.'s Alliance vs. Drugs award, 1988-90. Mem. Springfield Elem. Prins. Assn., Alpha Delta Kappa (Kappa pres. 1991-94, state chaplain 1994-96). Democrat. Roman Catholic. Avocations: art, local history, gardening. Home: 99 Appleton St Springfield MA 01108-2945 Office: Samuel Bowles Sch 24 Bowles Park Springfield MA 01104-1510

VELLENGA, KATHLEEN OSBORNE, former state legislator; b. Alliance, Nebr., Aug. 5, 1938; d. Howard Benson and Marjorie (Menke) Osborne; m. James Alan Vellenga, Aug. 9, 1959; children: Thomas, Charlotte Vellenga Landreau, Carolyn Vellenga Berman. BA, Macalester Coll., 1959. Tchr. St. Paul Pub. Schs., 1959-60, Children's Ctr. Montessori, St. Paul, 1973-74, Children's House Montessori, St. Paul, 1974-79; mem. Minn. Ho. of Reps., St. Paul, 1980-94, mem. tax. com. and rules com., 1991—, chmn. St. Paul del., 1985-89, chmn. criminal justice div., 1989-90, chmn. crime and family law div., 1987-88, mem. Dem. steering com., 1987-94; chmn. judiciary Minn. Ho. of Reps., 1991, 92, chmn. edn. fin., 1992-93, 93-94; mem. St. Paul Family Svcs. Bd., 1994-95; exec. dir. St. Paul/Ramsey County Children's Initiative, 1994—. Chmn. Healthstart, St. Paul, 1987-91; mem. Children, Youth and Families Consortium, 1995—, Macalester Coll. Bd. Alumni, 1995—, Minn. Higher Edn. Svcs. Coun., 1995—. Mem. LWV (v.p. St. Paul chpt. 1979), Minn. Women Elected Ofcls. (vice chair 1994). Democrat. Presbyterian. Office: ST Paul Ramey County Childrens Inst 450 Syndicate St N Saint Paul MN 55104-4127

VELMANS, LOET ABRAHAM, retired public relations executive; b. Amsterdam, Netherlands, Mar. 18, 1923; s. Joseph and Anna (Cohen) V.; m. Pauline Edith Van Hessen, Mar. 29, 1949; children: Marianne and Hester (twins), Jessica. Grad., U. Amsterdam, 1947. Info. officer Dutch Govt. in, Singapore, 1945-47; with Hill & Knowlton, Inc., 1953-86; v.p. Hill Knowlton Internat., Geneva, 1959-69; pres. Hill Knowlton Internat., 1960-74; vice chmn. Hill Knowlton Internat., London, 1969-76; pres. Hill Knowlton Internat., N.Y.C., 1976-86; chmn. bd., chief exec. officer Hill Knowlton Internat., 1980-86. Contbr. articles on multinat. corps. to profl. jours. Bd. dirs. Lincoln Ctr. Inst., Netherland Am. Found., Global Pub. Affairs Inst. NYU. Decorated Grande Ufficiale Order of Merit, Italy, 1989. Club: Mid-Atlantic of N.Y. Inc (pres.). Home: PO Box 178 Sheffield MA 01257-0178

VELZ, JOHN WILLIAM, literature educator; b. Englewood, N.J., Aug. 5, 1930; s. Clarence Joseph and Harriet Josephine (O'Brien) V.; m. Sarah Elizabeth Campbell, Oct. 18, 1967; children: Jody, Emily; 3 children from previous marriage. BA in English with high distinction and honors, U. Mich., 1953, MA in English and French, 1954; PhD in English and Classical Greek, U. Minn., 1963. Instr. Coll. St. Thomas, St. Paul, 1958-60; asst. prof. English Rice U., Houston, 1963-69; prof. U. Tex., Austin, 1969-96, prof. emeritus, 1996—; vis. prof. U. Paul Valery, Montpelier, France, 1977-78, Julius Maximillians U., Wuerzburg, West Germany, 1981-82, 85-86; asst. dir., lit. adv. Odessa Shakespeare Festival, 1977; faculty mem. Oreg. Shakespeare Festival, 1979; lectr. tour Cen. and Ea. Europe univs., 1993; dir. acad. prodns. of Shakespeare and medieval drama; mem. Acad. Adv. Coun. Globe Theatre Ctr., 1981—; mem. U.S. Com. for Shakespeare's Globe, 1990—. Author: Shakespeare and the Classical Tradition, 1968 (ALA citation, Assn. Coll. and Rsch. Librs. citation); editor: Julius Caesar in MLA's New Variorum Shakespeare, 1966-95, (N.Am.) Cahiers Elisabethains, 1979-81; Shakespeare's English Histories: A Quest for Form and Genre, 1996; co-editor: Collected Papers of James G. McManaway, 1969, One Touch of Shakespeare: Letters of Joseph Crosby to Joseph Parker Norris 1875-1878, 1986; contbr. numerous scholarly, interpretive articles, mainly on Shakespeare and medieval drama, to profl. jours.; presenter numerous papers to learned socs., mem. editl. bd. Shakespeare Quar., 1975—, Classical and Modern Lit., 1981-85, Tex. Studies in Lit. and Lang., 1969-92, Shakespeare and the Classroom, 1993—; mem. editl. adv. bd. Complete Works of Shakespeare, 3d edit., 1980, 4th edit., 1992; cons. editor South Ctrl. Rev., 1989-92; mem. cons. com. Internat. Studies in Shakespeare and His Contemporaries, 1990—. Recipient Fulbright award, 1977-78, 81-82; recipient Oreon E. Scott award U. Mich., 1953; NEH fellow, 1967-68; Folger Library fellow, 1968. Mem. MLA (life), Assn. Lit. Scholars and Critics, Internat. Shakespeare Assn. (charter), Shakespeare Assn. Am., Malone Soc., Renaissance English Text Soc., Medieval and Renaissance Drama Soc., Marlowe Soc. of Am., Soc. for Textual Scholarship, H.W. Fowler Soc. (charter), Phi Beta Kappa, Phi Kappa Phi, Phi Eta Sigma. Home: 809 W 32nd St Austin TX 78705-2115 Office: U Tex Dept English Austin TX 78712 *Academic life is predicated on the obligation to teach as generously as we have been taught, to serve others as we have been served. This sense of mutuality has been a rationale for my professional life, though it would be impossible to pay all I owe.*

VELZY, CHARLES O., mechanical engineer; b. Oak Park, Ill., Mar. 17, 1930; s. Charles R and Ethel B. V.; m. Marilyn A. Gilman, Aug. 17, 1957; children: Charles Mark, Barbara Helen, Patricia Ethel. B.S.M.E., U. Ill., 1953, B.S. in Civil Engring., 1960, M.S. in San. Engring., 1959. Registered profl. engr., N.Y., 13 other states. Design engr., project engr. Nussbaumer, Clarke & Velzy, N.Y.C., 1959-66; sec.-treas., dir. Charles R Velzy Assos., Inc., Armonk, N.Y., 1966-76; pres. Charles R. Velzy Assoc., Inc., 1976-92; v.p. Roy F. Weston Inc., 1987-92; pres. Charles O. Velzy, P.E., Lyndonville, Vt., 1992—. Contbr. articles to profl. jours. Mem. White Plains (N.Y.) Bldg. Code Appeals Bd., 1970-92. With U.S. Army, 1954-56. Fellow ASME (chmn. solid waste processing divsn 1973-74, mem. policy bd. rsch. 1974-78, bd. govs. 1983-84, pres. 1989-90, Centennial medal 1980, medal of achievement 1981), Am. Cons. Engrs. Coun.; mem. ASTM, ASCE (life), NSPE, Am. Acad. Environ. Engrs. (trustee 1984-87, treas. 1993—), Am. Water Works Assn. (life), Water Environ. Fedn., Air Waste Mgmt. Assn. Methodist. *After deciding on what is needed in a specific situation, based on the facts, establish your objectives and goals and persist to a successful conclusion.*

VENABLE, ROBERT ELLIS, crop scientist; b. Clovis, N.Mex., Sept. 30, 1952; s. Charles Edward and Evelylee (Harvill) V.; m. Linda Sue Campbell, Oct. 9, 1976 (div. 1982); m. Melva Ivette Roman, Sept. 24, 1988; children: Jonathan Shelby, Stephen Blake. BA in Biology, Hendrix Coll., 1974; MS in Natural Sci., U. Ark., 1976. Quality control mgr. Thompson-Hayward Chem./Platte, Greenville, Miss., 1975-82; scientist Velsicol Chem./Sandoz, Chgo., 1982-88; surp. formulations devel. Ecogen, Inc., Langhorne, Pa., 1988-94, prin. formulation scientist, 1994-96, prin. formulation coord., 1996—. Mem. ASTM (pesticide com.), Soc. for Invertebrate Pathology. Achievements include research and development of water dispersable extruded pellets (herbicides, biofungicides and bioinsecticides) for crop protection, including improved stability for biological agricultural products with development of new methods of concentration. Office: Ecogen Inc 2005 Cabot Blvd W PO Box 3023 Langhorne PA 19047-3023

VENDITTI, CLELIA ROSE See PALMER, CHRISTINE

VENDLER, HELEN HENNESSY, literature educator, poetry critic; b. Boston, Mass., Apr. 30, 1933; d. George and Helen (Conway) Hennessy; 1 son, David. A.B., Emmanuel Coll., 1954; Ph.D., Harvard U., 1960; Ph.D. (hon.), U. Oslo; D.Litt. (hon.), Smith Coll., Kenyon Coll., U. Hartford; DLitt (hon.), Union Coll.; Fitchburg State U.; DLitt (hon.), Columbia U., Washington U.; D.Litt. (hon.), Marlboro Coll.; DHL (hon.), Dartmouth Coll., U. Mass., Bates Coll., U. Toronto, Ont., Can., Trinity Coll., Dublin, Ireland, Fitchburg State U. Instr. Cornell U., Ithaca, N.Y., 1960-63; lectr. Swarthmore (Pa.) Coll. and Haverford (Pa.) Coll., 1963-64; asst. prof. Smith Coll., Northampton, Mass., 1964-66; assoc. prof. Boston U., 1966-68, prof., 1968-85; Fulbright lectr. U. Bordeaux, France, 1968-69; vis. prof. Harvard U., 1981-85, Kenan prof., 1985—, Porter U. prof., 1990—, assoc. acad. dean, 1987-92, sr. fellow Harvard Soc. Fellows, 1981-93; poetry critic New Yorker, 1978—; mem. ednl. adv. bd. Guggenheim Found., 1991—, Pulitzer Prize Bd., 1991—. Author: Yeats's Vision and the Later Plays, 1963, On Extended Wings: Wallace Stevens' Longer Poems, 1969, The Poetry of George Herbert, 1975, Part of Nature, Part of Us, 1980, The Odes of John Keats, 1983, Wallace Stevens: Words Chosen Out of Desire, 1984; editor: Harvard Book of Contemporary American Poetry, 1985, Voices and Visions: The Poet in America, 1987, The Music of What Happens, 1988, Soul Says, 1995, The Given and the Made, 1995, The Breaking of Style, 1995, Poems, Poets, Poetry, 1995, The Art of Shakespear. Bd. dirs. Nat. Humanities Ctr., 1989-93. Recipient Lowell prize, 1969, Explicator prize, 1969, award Nat. Inst. Arts and Letters, 1975, Radcliffe Grad. Soc. medal, 1978, Nat. Book Critics award, 1980, Keats-Shelley Assn. award, 1994, Truman Capote award, 1996; Fulbright fellow, 1954, AAUW fellow, 1959, Guggenheim fellow, 1971-72, Am. Coun. Learned Socs. fellow, 1971-72, NEH fellow, 1980, 85, 94, Overseas fellow Churchill Coll., Cambridge, 1980, Charles Stewart Parnell fellow Magdalene Coll., Cambridge, 1996, hon. fellow, 1996—. Mem. MLA (exec. coun. 1972-75, pres. 1980), AAAL, English Inst. (trustee 1977-85), Am. Acad. Arts and Scis. (v.p. 1992-95), Norwegian Acad. Letters and Sci., Am. Philos. Soc., Phi Beta Kappa. Home: 54 Trowbridge St # 2 Cambridge MA 02138-4113 Office: Harvard U Dept English Barker Center Cambridge MA 02138-3929

VENEMA, JON ROGER, educator, pastor; b. Modesto, Calif., Apr. 11, 1953; s. Roger Edwin and Marilyn Ailene (Johnson) V.; m. Shelley Elizabeth, Mar. 29, 1974; children: Jordan Christopher Wilder, Susanna Lee. AA, Modesto (Calif.) Jr. Coll., 1974; BA magna cum laude, Simpson Coll., 1976; MDiv, Mennonite Brethren Bibl. Sem., 1980; PhD, Golden Gate Bapt. Theol. Sem., 1995. Instr. bibl. and religious studies Fresno Pacific Coll., Modesto, 1980-84; sr. pastor 1st Bapt. Ch., So. San Francisco, 1984-94; adj. faculty Fresno Pacific Coll., 1984-87, Simpson Coll., San Francisco, 1987-88; instr. St. James Coll., Pacifica, Calif., 1987-90; adj. prof. Golden Gate Bapt. Theol. Sem., Marin, Calif., 1992, Highland Christian Coll., San Bruno, Calif., 1992-93, We. Conservative Bapt. Theol. Sem., 1994—; acad. dean, devel. coord. We. Seminary, Sacramento, 1996—, asst. prof. N.T. lang. and lit., 1996—. Mem. Soc. Bibl. Lit., Delta Epsilon Chi. Republican. Avocations: sports, art and illustration, backpacking. Home: 2228 Canadian Cir Modesto CA 95356 Office: We Conservative Baptist Sem 2924 Becerra Way Sacramento CA 95821-3939

VENERABLE, SHIRLEY MARIE, gifted education educator; b. Washington, Nov. 12, 1931; d. John Henry and Jessie Josephine (Young) Washington; m. Wendell Grant Venerable, Feb. 15, 1959; children: Angela Elizabeth Maria Venerable-Joyner, Wendell Mark. PhB, Northwestern U., 1963; MA, Roosevelt U., 1976, postgrad., 1985. Cert. in diagnostic and prescriptive reading, gifted edn., finger math., fine arts, Ill. Tchr. Lewis Champlin Sch., 1963-74, John Hay Acad., Chgo., 1975-87, Leslie Lewis Elem. Sch., Chgo., 1988—; sponsor Reading Marathon Club, Chgo., 1991—; co-creator Project SMART (Stimulating Math. and Reading Techniques) John Hay Acad., Chgo., 1987-90, curriculum coord., 1985-87; creative dance student, tchr. Kathryn Duham Sch., N.Y.C., 1955-56; creative dance tchr. Doris Patterson Dance Sch., Washington, 1953-55; recorder evening divsn. Northwestern U., Chgo., 1956-62; exch. student tchr. Conservatory Dance Movements, Chgo., 1958-59; art cons. Chgo. Pub. Sch., 1967. Author primary activities Let's Act and Chat, 1991-94, Teaching Black History Through Classroom Tours, 1989-90. Solicitor, vol. United Negro Coll. Fund, Chgo., 1994; sponsor 21st Ward Reading Assn., Chgo., 1991-94; mem. St. Giles Coun. Cath. Women, 1985-96. Recipient Meritorious award United Negro Coll. Fund, 1990, 94, Recognition award Alderman Percy Giles, Chgo., 1993. Mem. ASCD (assoc., Recognition of Svcs. award 1989), Internat. Reading Assn., Eta Xi Sigma, Sigma Gamma Rho (Delta Sigma grad. chpt. 1963-93, Sigma chpt. 1992, Xi grad. chpt.), Phi Delta Kappa. Roman Catholic. Home: 1108 N Euclid Ave Oak Park IL 60302-1219

VENET, CLAUDE HENRY, architect, acoustic engineer; b. Lyon, France, Aug. 10, 1946; came to U.S., 1981; s. René Joseph and Marcellé (Michel) V.; m. Blanca Eppenstein Portella, Feb. 12, 1981 (div. Feb. 1984); m. Mouna Bennani-Smires, Feb. 29, 1992. Dipl. electronic engr., ESTA, Rochefort, France, 1968; Lic. Physics, U. Paris, 1971; MArch, So. Calif. Inst. Architecture, 1986. Mgr. Ling Dynamics/Altec U.K., Royston, Eng., 1971-72; mng. dir. CVE Enterprises, London, 1972-75; sales dir. Macinnes/Amcron France, Paris, 1975-77; tech. dir. Audio Cons. Coordination, Rio de Janeiro, 1977-81; cons. Paramount (Sound) Films Corp., Glendale, Calif., 1981-82; pres. Architecture and Engring. in Acoustics, Belleville, France, 1986-91, Archicoustics Inc., Uda, Fla., Rio de Janeiro, 1996—; lectr. U. Miami Sch. Architecture, 1995—. Vol. Architects Without Frontiers, Paris, 1990—. Cpl. French Air Force, 1962-67. Named Most Outstanding Consulting Engr., Miami AIA. Mem. AIA, AAAS, Am. Inst. Physics, Acoustical Soc. Am., Nat. Coun. Acoustical Cons., Audio Engring. Soc., N.Y. Acad. of Sci., Order French Architects, Chamber French Cons. Engrs. Achievements include design of computer-driven, polymorphic, multi-use theatre with continous variable acoustics/geometry, variable-shape, multi-acoustics polymorphous concept in recording studio design. Office: Archicoustics Corp 19860 Franjo Rd Miami FL 33157-8880

VENETSANOPOULOS, ANASTASIOS NICOLAOS, electrical engineer, educator; b. Athens, Greece, June 19, 1941; emigrated to Can., 1968; s. Nicolaos Anastasios and Elli (Papacondilis) V. Diploma, Athens Coll., 1960; diploma in elec. and mech. engring., Nat. Tech. U., Athens, 1965, hon. doctorate, 1994; MS, Yale U., 1966, MPhil, 1968. Registered profl. engr., Greece, Ont. Asst. in instrn. engring. and applied sci. Yale U., 1966-68, research asst., 1968-69; lectr. U. Toronto, Ont., Can., 1968-69; asst. prof. elec. engring. U. Toronto, 1970-73, assoc. prof., 1973-81, prof., 1981—, chmn. communications group dept. elec. engring., 1974-78, 81-86, assoc. chmn. elec. engring., 1978-79, mem. elec. engring. exec. com., 1974-78, 81-86, mem. elec. engring. curriculum com., 1972-79; acad. visitor Imperial Coll. Arts and Tech., U. London, 1979-80; vis. prof. Nat. Tech. U. Athens, spring 1979-80, Fed. U. of Technology of Lausanne, Switzerland, 1986-87, 93-94, U. Florence, Italy, summer 1987; cons. elec. engring. Consociates Ltd. Editor Can. Elec. Engring. Jour., 1981-83; contbr. over 500 articles to profl. jours. and to 25 books. Mem. allocations and agy. relations com. United Community Fund, Toronto, 1971-74; pres. Hellenic-Can. Cultural Soc., 1972-75; sec. gen. Greek Community Met. Toronto, 1973-75. Fulbright travel grantee in U.S., 1965; Def. Research Bd. Can. grantee, 1972-75, UN grantee; NSF grantee; J.P. Bickell Found. grantee; Natural Scis. and Engring. Research Council of Can. Fellow IEEE (fin. chmn. internat. symposium on circuit theory 1973, tech. program chmn. internat. conf. communications 1978, 86, vice-chmn. Toronto sect. 1976-77, chmn. 1977-79, assoc. editor transactions on circuits and systems 1985-87, guest editor spl. issue Transactions on Circuits and Systems in Image Processing 1987), Engring. Inst. Can.; mem. Assn. Profl. Engrs. Ont., Assn. Profl. Elec. Engrs. Greece, Assn. Profl. Mech. Engrs. Greece, Can. Soc. Elec. Engring. (chmn. Toronto sect. 1975-77, nat. dir. 1976-88, pres. 1983-86), Yale Sci. and Engring. Assn., N.Y. Acad. Scis., Tech. Chamber Greece, Am.-Hellenic Ednl. Progress Assn. (v.p. Toronto sect. 1973-75, pres. 1975-77), Intercultural Council (chmn. ednl. com. 1971-80, sr. v.p. 1977-80), Sigma Xi. Office: U Toronto, Dept Elec and Computer Engring, Toronto, ON Canada M5S 1A4

VENEZKY, RICHARD LAWRENCE, English educator; b. Pitts., Apr. 16, 1938; s. Bernard Jacob and Isabel (Zeisel) V.; m. Karen F. Gauz, Aug. 2, 1964; children: Dina Yael, Elie Michael. BEE, Cornell U., 1961, MA, 1962; postgrad., U. Calif., Berkeley, 1962-63; PhD, Stanford U., 1965. Sys. programmer, tech. writer Control Data Corp., Palo Alto, Calif., 1962-65; asst. prof. English and computer scis. U. Wis., Madison, 1965-69, assoc. prof. computer scis., 1969-74, prof., 1974-77, chmn. dept., 1975-77; Unidel prof. ednl. studies, prof. computer and info. sci., prof. linguistics U. Del., Newark, 1977—; Benton fellow in literacy U. Chgo., 1994-95; vis. rsch. assoc. Tel Aviv U., 1969-70, rsch. fellow, 1973; cons. Oxford English Dictionary Supplement; dir. computing Dictionary of Old English, 1971— co-dir. for R & D Nat. Ctr. on Adult Literacy, 1990-95. Author: The Structure of English Orthography, 1970, Testing in Reading, 1974, Random House Spelling Across the Curriculum, 1988; co-author: A Microfiche Concordance to Old English, 1981, Letter and Word Perception, 1980, PRS-Pre-Reading Skills Program, 1985, The Subtle Danger, 1987, World of Reading, 1989, The Intelligent Design of Computer-Assisted Instruction, 1991; co-editor: Orthography, Reading and Dyslexia, 1980, Toward Defining Literacy, 1990; contbr. articles to profl. jours., chpts. to books. Chmn. edn. commn Madison Jewish Community Coun., 1973-77; v.p. Jewish Fedn. Del., 1986-89; regional chmn. Am. Profs. for Peace in Mid. East, 1968-73. Named to Reading Hall of Fame, 1991; grantee Office of Edn., 1964-66, NSF, 1966-74, Nat. Inst. Edn., 1973-77, NEH, 1978-89, Office of Ednl. Rsch. and Improvement, Dept. Edn., 1990-95, Pew Charitable Trusts, 1995-97, Joyce Found., 1996—. Mem. Am. Psychol. Soc., Am. Edn. Rsch. Assn., Internat. Reading Assn., Reading Hall of Fame (pres. 1996-97), Assn. Computing Machinery. Democrat. Jewish. Home: 206 Hullihen Dr Newark DE 19711-3651

VENGROW, MICHAEL IAN, neurologist; b. Brookline, Mass., Apr. 10, 1949; s. Max and Mary V.; m. Lucy Lee Smith, Aug. 4, 1979; children: Robert David, Mary Elizabeth. BS in Chemistry magna cum laude, U. Mass., 1971; MD, U. Mass., Worcester, 1977. Diplomate Am. Bd. Psychiatry and Neurology, Am. Bd. Clin. Neurophysiology, Am. Bd. Electrodiagnostic Medicine, Am. Acad. Pain Mgmt., Nat. Bd. Med. Examiners. Rsch. chemist, asst. KFA-Julich, West Germany, 1970; rsch. chemist, asst. biomed. svcs. divsn. Damon Corp., Needham, Mass., 1971-72; rsch. chemist, head Shrine Burn Inst., Boston, 1972-73; intern Naval Regional Med. Ctr., San Diego, 1977-78; battalion med. officer Third Combat Engr. Battalion, Third Marine Divsn., Okinawa, Japan, 1978-79; resident, chief resident in neurology Nat. Naval Med. Ctr., Bethesda, Md., 1979-82; fellow in clin. neurophysiology Walter Reed Army Med. Ctr., Washington, 1982-83; neurologist, head divsn. diagnostic neurophysiology Naval Hosp. San Diego, 1983-85; neurologist Neurology Ctr. No. Ariz., Flagstaff, 1985-96, Neurology Cons. of Dallas, 1996—; sr. reviewer Ariz. Long Term Care Sys., Phoenix, 1986-94; dir. Alzheimer's unit Kachina Point Health Ctr., Sedona, Ariz., 1986-93, dir. neurol. rehab. unit, 1989-93; dir. neurophysiology lab. Kingman Regional Med. Ctr., 1985-95, Flagstaff Med. Ctr., 1985-95, Cmty. Med. Edn. dir., 1988, chief medicine, 1989; mem. profl. adv. bd. Epilipsy Soc., Phoenix, 1987-96, Multiple Sclerosis Soc., Phoenix, 1989-96, Quantum Health Resources; cons. First Western Med. Group, Fresno, Calif., 1991-93, Long Term Care Program Ariz. Long Term Care System, 1987-95, Marcus J. Lawrence Hosp., Cottonwood, Ariz., Pub. Health Svcs. Hosp., Tuba City, Ariz.; ind. med. examiner, Ariz.; agreed med. examiner, qualified med. examiner, electromyographer BH Mgmt. Med. Group, Fresno, 1993—; instr. emergency medicine L.A. C.C. Overseas, Uniformed Svcs. U. Health Scis., Bethesda; clin. lectr. dept. neurology sch. health scis. U. Ariz., Tucson; clin. asst. prof. neurology U. Tex. Southwestern Med. Sch.; rschr. in field; presenter in field. Contbr. articles to profl. pubs. Bd. dirs. Flagstaff Symphony, 1991-94; sponsor Am. Youth Soccer Orgn., 1988-90. LCDR, USN, 1978-85, capt. M.C., USNR. Pub. Health scholar, 1975, State Bd. Higher Edn. Scholar, 1967-71, 75, Armed Forces Health Svcs. Profl. scholarship, 1975-77, Religious High Edn. scholar, 1965; recipient letter commendation Operation Desert Storm, 1991. Fellow Am. Acad. Neurology (govt. section), Am. EEG Soc. (practice com.), Am. Assn. Electrodiagnostic Medicine, Am. Electromyographic Soc.; mem. AMA, Ariz. Med. Assn., Am. Mil. Surgeons U.S., Am. Epilepsy Soc., Uniformed Svcs. Neurology U.S., U.S. Navy Neurol. Soc., Am. Soc. Clin. Evoked Potentials, Am. Soc. Neuroimaging, Am. Med. EEG Assn., Naval Res. Assn, Am. Biographical Inst. Rsch. Assn., (life, dep. gov., bd. govs.), Am. Biographical Inst. (Man of Yr., 1992), Phi Eta Sigma, Phi Kappa Phi, Phi Beta Kappa. Avocations: scuba diving, rugby, bicycling, sailing, billiards. Home: 5945 W Parker Rd # 3112 Plano TX 75093

VENIARD, JOSE M., bank officer; b. Buenos Aires, Argentina, Feb. 11, 1935; came to U.S., 1970; s. Eduardo A. and Amalia (Bassi) V.; children: Maria, Sofia, Natalia, Clara. MS in Civil Engring., Buenos Aires U., 1962; MBA, Stanford U., 1972. Spl. asst. Minister of Pub. Works, Argentina, 1968-70; sr. ops. officer Stanford Rsch. Inst., Menlo Pk., Calif., 1971-73; sr. economist The World Bank, Washington, 1974-76, project mgr., 1976-81, 91—, asst. to v.p., 1981-85; ops. mgr. The World Bank, Beijing, 1985-91; cons. econ.-transp., 1963-68. Contbr. numerous articles, papers, to confs. and profl. publs. Fellow Econ. Devel. Inst. Home: 10005 Carter Rd Bethesda MD 20817

VENIS, LINDA DIANE, academic administrator, educator; b. Pasadena, Calif., Nov. 15, 1948; d. Ashton Harwood Venis and Grace (Bullock) Miller; m. Gary Arther Berg, Mar. 9, 1991; 1 child, Laura Grace Berg. BA magna cum laude, UCLA, 1970, PhD, 1978. Lectr. English UCLA, 1982-85, adj. asst. prof. Dept. English, 1987-90; lectr. Sch. Fine Arts U. So. Calif., L.A., 1985—; assoc. dir. studies UCLA/London & Cambridge Programs UCLA Extension, 1986-91, head writers program, 1985—, dir. dept. arts, 1992—. Contbr. articles to profl. jours. Recipient Profl. Contbrns. to Continuing Edn. award Continuing Edn. Assn., UCLA Disting. Tchg. award, 1985. Mem. PEN USA/West (bd. dirs. 1993—, adv. bd. 1992-93), Women in Film, Assn. Acad. Women. Office: UCLA Extension The Arts 10995 Le Conte Ave Los Angeles CA 90024-2400

VENKATA, SUBRAHMANYAM SARASWATI, electrical engineering educator, electric energy and power researcher; b. Nellore, Andhra Pradesh, India, June 28, 1942; came to U.S., 1968; s. Ramiah Saraswati and Lakshmi (Alladi) V.; m. Padma Subrahmanyam Mahadevan, Sept. 3, 1971; children: Sridevi Ramakumar, Harish Saraswati. BSEE, Andhra U., Waltair, India, 1963; MSEE, Indian Inst. Tech., Madras, 1965; PhD, U. S.C., 1971. Registered profl. engr., W.Va., Wash. Lectr. in elec. engring. Coimbatore (India) Inst. Tech., 1965-66; planning engr. S.C. Elec. & Gas Co., Columbia, 1969-70; postdoctoral fellow U. S.C., Columbia, 1971; instr. elec. engring. U. Mass., Lowell, 1971-72; asst. prof. W.Va. U., Morgantown, 1972-75, assoc. prof., 1975-79; prof. U. Wash., Seattle, 1979-96; prof., chmn. dept. elec. and computer engring. Iowa State U., Ames, 1996—; cons. Puget Sound Energy Co., Bellevue, Wash., 1980—, GEC/Alsthom, N.Y.C., 1991—; series editor, bd. dirs. PWS Pub. Co., 1991—. Author: Introduction of Electrical Energy Devices, 1987; patentee adaptive var compensators, adaptive power quality conditioner, distribution reliability based design software. Advisor Explorers Club, Morgantown, 1976-78; sec. Hindu Temple and Cultural Ctr. Pacific N.W., Seattle, 1990, chmn., 1991, 95. Recipient W.Va. U. Assocs. award W.Va. U. Found., 1974, 78. Fellow IEEE (best paper award 1985, 88, 91, Outstanding Power Engring. Educator award 1996); mem. Conf. Internat. des Grands Reseaux Electriques, Sigma Xi, Tau Beta Pi, Eta Kappa Nu. Democrat. Avocations: photography, tennis, table tennis. Home: 3109 Sycamore Rd Ames WA 50010-4592 Office: Dept Elec Computer Engring Iowa State U Ames IA 50011-3060

VENNAT, MICHEL, lawyer; b. Sept. 17, 1941; m. Marie-Anne Tawil; children: Catherine, Charles-Alexandre, Frédéric, Michèle Anne, Philippe-Olivier. B.A. magna cum laude, Coll. Jean-de-Brébeuf, Montreal, Que., Can., 1960; LL.L., U. Montreal, 1963; M.A., Oxford U., Eng., 1965. Bar: Que. 1966, Paris 1995; apptd. Queen's Counsel 1983, Office of the Orderof Can., 1995. Fgn. affairs officer Dept. External Affairs, Ottawa, Ont., Can., 1965; spl. asst. to Min. Fin., 1966-68; spl. asst. to Hon. Pierre E. Trudeau, Prime Min. of Can., 1968-70, spl. counsel, 1977; chmn. Can. Film Devel. Corp., Montreal, 1976-81; sr. ptnr. Stikeman, Elliott, Montreal, 1970-90; pres. Dumez Investments Inc., 1986-87, Westburne Internat. Industries Ltd., 1987; vice chmn. United Westburne Inc., 1990, vice chmn., CEO, 1991-93, chmn., CEO, 1993-94, also bd. dirs.; pres. Bastos du Canada Limitée, 1987—, also bd. dirs.; ptnr. Stikeman Elliot, Montreal, 1994—; lectr. in constl. law U. Montreal, 1970; bd. dirs. Nat. Bank of Greece (Can.), Meloche-Monnex Inc.; Hewlett-Packard (Can.) Ltd., Acklands Ltd., NAV Can.; pres. bd. Maxi-Krisp Can., Inc. Rhodes scholar, 1963-65. Mem. Barreau du Que., Barreau du Paris, Can. C. of C., French C. of C. (Can. bd. dirs.), Montreal Badminton and Squash Club, Mt. Bruno Country Club, Hillside Tennis Club, Mt. Royal Club, Hermitage Club. Avocations: squash, golf, tennis, skiing. Home: 22 Claude Champagne, Outremont, PQ Canada H2V 2X1 Office: Stikeman Elliott, 1155 René-Lévesque Blvd W, Montreal, PQ Canada H3B 3V2

VENNING, ROBERT STANLEY, lawyer; b. Boise, Idaho, July 24, 1943; s. William Lucas and Corey Elizabeth (Brown) V.; m. Sandra Macdonald, May 9, 1966 (div. 1976); 1 child, Rachel Elizabeth; m. Laura Siegel, Mar. 24, 1979; 1 child, Daniel Rockhill Siegel. AB, Harvard U., 1965; MA, U. Chgo., 1966; LLB, Yale U., 1970. Bar: Calif., U.S. Dist. Ct. (no. dist.) Calif., 1971, U.S. Dist. Ct. (cen. dist.) Calif. 1973, U.S. Ct. Appeals (9th cir.) 1977, U.S. Supreme Ct. 1977, U.S. Ct. Appeals (fed. cir.) 1986, U.S. Ct. Appeals (D.C. cir.) 1987. Assoc. Heller, Ehrman, White & McAuliffe, San Francisco, 1970-73, 73-76, ptnr., 1977—, mem. exec. com., 1991-94; vis. lectr. U. Wash., Seattle, 1973, Boalt Hall Sch. Law, U. Calif., Berkeley, 1982-85, 89, Sch. Bus., Stanford U., 1986-87. Editor Yale Law Jour., 1969-70. Early neutral evaluator U.S. Dist. Ct. (no. dist.) Calif., 1987—; mem. Natural Resources Def. Coun. Fellow Am. Bar Found.; mem. ABA, San Francisco Bar Assn. (past chair judiciary com.). Office: Heller White & McAuliffe 333 Bush St San Francisco CA 94104-2806

VENTO, BRUCE FRANK, congressman; b. St. Paul, Oct. 7, 1940; s. Frank A. and Ann (Sauer) V.; children: Michael, Peter, John. AA, U. Minn., 1961; BS, Wis. State U., River Falls, 1965. Tchr. sci., social studies Mpls. Pub. Schs.; mem. Minn. Ho. of Reps., 1971—; asst. majority leader 95th-103rd Congresses from 4th Minn. Dist., 1974-76; chmn. Ramsey County del., gen. legis. and vet. affairs com.; vice-chmn. jud. com.; chmn. natural resources subcom. on nat. pks., forests and pub. lands, 1985-94; mem. resource com., mem. subcom. on natural pks. and pub. lands, mem. subcom. on forests and forest health); mem. banking and fin. svcs. com., ranking mem. subcom. on fin. instns. and consumer credit, mem. subcom. on capital markets, securities and govt. sponsored enterprises; mem. housing and devel. subcom.; chmn. spkr.'s task force on homelessness 103d Congress. Mem. legis. rev. com. Minn. Commn. on Future Del.; Democratic Farmer Labor party Central com., 1972; chmn. Ramsey County com., 1972. Recipient numerous awards including Ansel Adams award Wilderness Soc.; NSF scholar, 1966-70. Mem. Minn. Fedn. Tchrs., Beta Beta Beta, Kappa Delta Phi. Office: US House of Reps 2304 Rayburn Bldg Washington DC 20515-2304

VENTO, M. THÉRÈSE, lawyer; b. N.Y.C., June 30, 1951; d. Anthony Joseph and Margaret (Stechert) V.; m. Peter Michael MacNamara, Dec. 23, 1977; children: David Miles, Elyse Anne. BS, U. Fla., 1974, JD, 1976. Bar: Fla. 1977, U.S. Dist. Ct. (so. and mid. dists.) Fla. 1982, U.S. Ct. Appeals (5th and 11th cirs.) 1981, U.S. Supreme Ct. 1985. Clk. to presiding justice U.S. Dist. Ct. (so. dist.) Fla., Miami, 1976-78; assoc. Mahoney, Hadlow & Adams, Miami, 1978-79; assoc. Shutts & Bowen, Miami, 1979-84, ptnr., 1985-95; founding ptnr. Gallwey Gillman Curtis Vento & Horn, P.A., Miami, 1995—. Trustee Miami Art Mus., 1988—, The Beacon Coun., 1995—. Mem. Dade County Bar Assn. (dir. young lawyers sect. 1978-83, editor newsletter 1981-83), Fla. Assn. for Women Lawyers, Fla. Bar Assn. (bd. govs., young lawyers div. 1983-85, civil procedure rules com. 1983-90, exec. coun. trial lawyers sect. 1996—), The Miami Forum (v.p. 1987-88, bd. dirs. 1989-91). Home: 3908 Main Hwy Miami FL 33133-6513 Office: Gallwey Gillman Curtis Vento & Horn 200 SE 1st St Ste 1100 Miami FL 33131-1909

VENTRE, FRANCIS THOMAS, environmental design and policy educator; b. Old Forge, Pa., Sept. 16, 1937; s. Thomas Anthony and Theresa Mary (Grippi) V.; m. Mary Alice Tibbals, Apr. 4, 1964; children—Antonina Alma, Emily Lucrezia. B.Arch., Pa. State U., 1961; M.C.P., U. Calif., Berkeley, 1966; Ph.D., M.I.T., 1973. City planner Louisville and Jefferson County (Ky.) Planning Commn., 1962-64; asst. prof. arch. and urban planning UCLA, 1966-68; research assoc. MIT-Harvard Joint Center Urban Studies, Cambridge, 1970-73; chief environ. design research div. Nat. Bur. Standards, Washington, 1973-83; prof. environ. design and policy, dir. Ctr. for Building Econs. and Industry Studies Va. Poly. Inst., Blacksburg, 1983-90, dir. Environ Systems Lab., 1983-87; prin. BuildingMeasure, cons. firm; mem. faculty U.Md., UCLA.; faculty mem. Va. Polytech. State U., 1983-93; faculty emeritus; mem. com. tech. advanced bldg. NAS, Nat. Acad. Engring., NRC, 1985-87; elected Consultative Coun. Nat. Inst. Bldg. Scis.; mem. Info. Com. co-founder, past assoc. editor, editorial adv. bd. Environ. and Behavior; mem. editorial bd. Jour. Archtl. and Planning Rsch., 1989-90; contbr. articles to profl. jours., chpts. to books. Mem. indsl. and profl. adv. coun. Pa. State Coll. Engring., 1979-84; del. State, Montgomery County, Va. Dem. Conv., 1989; libr. reader Nat. Gallery Art, 1989. With AUS, 1961-62. Mellon fellow in city planning, 1964-66; recipient award Pa. Soc. Architects, 1961; Stern Family Fund grantee, 1969; Catherine Bauer Wurster fellow, 1971-72; Nat. Endowment Arts grantee, 1984; NSF grantee, 1985, 87, Urban Land Inst. grantee, 1987. Mem. AIA (assoc.), Am. Inst. Cert. Planners, Am. Planning Assn., Environ. Design Rsch. Assn., ASTM, Internat. Facilities Mgmt. Assn., Archtl. Rsch. Ctrs. Consortium (founding sec., mem. panel on bldg. econs. and industry studies, 1984-90), AAUP (pres. Va. Poly. Inst. chpt.), Intelligent Bldgs. Inst. Found. (apptd. trustee), Va. Poly. Inst. Faculty Senate and Senate Cabinet, Montgomery County Stroke Club. Home: 4007 Rickover Rd Silver Spring MD 20902-2330

VENTRY, PAUL GUERIN, hysician, government official; b. Ossining, N.Y., Sept. 1, 1934; s. Victor and Catherine (Dillon) V.; BS, Manhattan Coll., 1957; MD, Syracuse U., 1962; m. Betty Anne Baildon, Aug. 20, 1960. Diplomate Am. Bd. Profl. Disability Cons., Am. Bd. Forensic Medicine. Commd. 1st lt. M.C., U.S. Army, 1962, advanced through grades to lt. col., 1971; intern Walter Reed Gen. Hosp., 1962-63, resident in internal medicine, physician to Pres. Eisenhower and Gen. Douglas MacArthur, 1963-66, fellow in immunology, 1966, fellow in allergy, 1967, chief med. outpatient clinic, 1971, allergy cons. to Surgeon Gen., Europe, 1967-70, chief medicine, 47th Mobile Army Surgical Hosp., ret., 1971; chief adult services Montgomery County Health Dept. (Md.), 1972; med. dir. Goddard Space Flight Ctr., NASA, 1973; ptnr. Med. Assocs. D.C., Washington, 1974; med. dir. Civilian Employees Health Svc., Dept. Def., Washington, Walter Reed Army Med. Ctr., also med. dir. Pentagon Drug and Alcohol Program and dir. Dept. Def. Blood Donor Program, med. dir. Def. Intelligence Agy., 1975-83; prin. med. cons. to Office Hearings and Appeals, Social Security Adminstrn., Arlington, Va., 1983—; asst. clin. prof. medicine George Washington U., 1973-79; chief med. surg. cons., med. officer in charge Social Security Adminstrn., 1983—; med. dir. Nat. Coun. Social Security Adminstrn. OHA, 1991, Am. Fedn. Govt. Employees # 3615, 1991—, Nat. Coun. Social Security Employees, Am. Fed. Govt. Coun. 215; med. surg. cons. Wash. Hq. Svc. Dept. Def.; chief cons. med. surg. medicare fraud divsn. HHS Med. Dir. Fellow Am. Occupl. Med. Assn., Am. Coll. Occupational and Environ. Medicine, Am. Acad. Disability Evaluating Physicians; mem. AMA, ACP, VFW, Fed. Physicians Assn. (treas.), Am. Pub. Health Assn., Am. Acad. Allergy, Royal Soc. Medicine, Brit. Allergy Soc., Am. Acad. Civil Svc. Physicians (treas.), Am. Coll. Physician Execs., Am. Bd. Forensic Examiners, Am. Legion, Assn. Mil. Surgeons, Nat. Fire Rev. Assn., Potomac C. of C., Washington Performing Arts Soc., D.C. Med. Soc., Montgomery County Med. Soc., Va. Med. Soc., Alpha Kappa Kappa. Contbr. articles to med. jours. Home: 7813 Masters Dr Potomac MD 20854

VENTURA, HECTOR OSVALDO, cardiologist; b. Buenos Aires, Mar. 21, 1951; came to U.S., 1981; s. Osvaldo Domingo and Nelida (Scocozza) V.; m. Laurie Anne Zeringue, Apr. 21, 1990; children: Austin Alejandro, Leighton Leandro, Kendra Mariel. BS, Nat. No. 10 Coll., Buenos Aires, 1968; MD, U. Buenos Aires, 1974. Diplomate Am. Bd. Internal Medicine with subspecialty in cardiovascular diseases. Resident in internal medicine Mil. Hosp., Argentina, 1975-78; rsch. fellow hypertension Ochsner Found., New Orleans, 1981-84; internal medicine resident Ochsner Found. Hosp., New Orleans, 1984-86, cardiology fellow, 1986-88; heart failure/heart transplant fellow Loyola U., Chgo., 1989; co-dir. heart failure heart transplant Ochsner Med. Inst., New Orleans, 1989—, transplant adv. bd., 1992—, mem. ethics com., 1995—; assoc. prof. medicine La. State U. Sch. Medicine, New Orleans; jour. manuscript reviewer. Editl. bd. Jour. Heart & Lung Transplantation, 1994; contbr. articles to profl. jours. 1st lt. Argentine Army, 1974-80. Ochsner Found. fellow, 1985, 86. Fellow Am. Coll. Cardiology; mem. Am. Soc. Transplant (organ thoracic com. 1993—), Am. Heart Assn. Roman Catholic. Avocations: tennis, aerobic exercise. Home: 3900 Wheat Dr Metairie LA 70002 Office: Ochsner Med Instn 1514 Jefferson Hwy New Orleans LA 70121-2429

VENTURA, MANUEL MATEUS, biochemist, educator; b. Fortaleza, Brazil, June 17, 1921; s. Antonio Rodrigues and Maria Raymunda (Lima) V.; m. Aglaeda Facó; children: Rita-Maria, Sandro, Manuel, Maria Monica. BSc, Agrl. Sch. Ceara, Fortaleza, 1943. Asst. prof. Agrl. Sch. Ceara, Fortaleza, 1945-48, prof., 1949-68; prof. Inst. of Chemistry of Fed. U. Ceara, Fortaleza, 1969-75; prof. biochemistry Inst. Biology, U. Brasilia, Brazil, 1975-91, prof. emeritus, 1992—; dir. Inst. Chemistry of Fed. U. Ceara, 1958-68. Contbr. articles to profl. jours. Recipient Anisio Teizeira prize Ministry of Edn., Brazil, 1981, Sci. Merit medal Fed. U. Ceara, 1988, Nat. Scientific Merit Order Ministry of Sci. and Tech., 1995. Mem. Brazilian Acad. Sci., N.Y. Acad. Sci., Protein Soc. Avocations: classical music, photography. Home: SQN 107 BL H Apto 504, 70743 Brasilia Brazil Office: U Brasilia Lab Biofisica-CEL-IB, Campus Universitario, 70910 Brasilia Brazil

VENTURA, ROBIN MARK, professional baseball player; b. Santa Maria, Calif., July 14, 1967. Student, Oklahoma State U. Mem. U.S. Olympic Baseball Team, Seoul, South Korea, 1988; with Chgo. White Sox, 1988—. Recipient Golden Glove award, 1991-93, 96, Golden Spikes award USA Baseball, 1988; named Sporting News Coll. Player of Yr., 1987-88, Third Basemen Sporting News All-Am. team, 1987-88; named to Am. League All-Star team, 1992. Office: Chgo White Sox 333 W 35th St Chicago IL 60616-3621*

VENTURI, ROBERT, architect; b. Phila., June 25, 1925; s. Robert C. and Vanna (Lanzetta) V.; m. Denise (Lakofski) Scott Brown, July 23, 1967; 1 child, James Charles. Grad., Episcopal Acad., 1943; A.B. summa cum laude, Princeton U., 1947, M.F.A., 1950, D.F.A. (hon.), 1983; D.F.A. (hon.), Oberlin Coll., 1977, Yale U., 1979, U. Pa., 1980, Phila. Coll. Art, 1985; LHD (hon.), N.J. Inst. Tech., 1984; Laurea Honoris Causa in Architecture, U. Rome "La Sapienza", 1994. Designer firms of Oskar Stonorov, Eero Saarinen and Assos., Louis I. Kahn, 1950-58; partner firm Venturi, Cope & Lippincott, Phila., 1958-61, Venturi and Short, Phila., 1961-64, Venturi and Rauch, Phila., 1964-80; ptnr. firm Venturi, Rauch & Scott Brown, Phila., 1980-89, Venturi, Scott, Brown and Assocs., Inc., 1989—; from asst. to assoc. prof. architecture U. Pa., 1957-65; Charlotte Shepherd Davenport prof. architecture Yale, 1966-70. Author: Complexity and Contradiction in Architecture, 1966, 2d edit., 1977, (with Denise Scott Brown and Steven Izenour) Learning from Las Vegas, 1972, 2d edit., 1977, (with Denise Scott Brown) A View from the Campidoglio, Selected Essays, 1953-84, Iconography and Electronics upon a Generic Architecture, 1996, others, also articles; prin. works include Vanna Venturi House, Phila., 1961, Guild House, Phila., 1961, Humanities Bldg., SUNY, 1972, Franklin Ct., Phila., 1972, addition to Allen Meml. Art Mus., Oberlin Coll., 1973, Inst. for Sci. Info. Corp. Hdqrts., Phila., 1978, Gordon Wu Hall, Princeton U., 1980, Seattle Art Mus., 1984, The Nat. Gallery, Sainsbury Wing, London, 1986, Fisher and Bendheim Halls, Princeton U., 1986, Gordon and Virginia MacDonald Med. Rsch. Labs. (with Payette Assocs.), UCLA, 1986, Charles P. Stevenson Jr. Libr., Bard Coll., 1989, Regional Govt. Bldg., Toulouse, France, 1992, Kirifuri Resort Facilities, Nikko, Japan, 1992, Trabant U. Ctr., U. Del., Newark, 1992, Meml. Hall Restoration and Addition, Harvard U., 1992, The Barnes Found. Restoration and Renovation, Merion, Pa., 1993, Disney Celebration (FLa.) Bank, 1993. Trustee Am. Acad. Rome, 1966-71. Recipient Nat. Medal of Arts, 1992, Pritzker Architecture prize, 1991, Benjamin Franklin medal The Royal Soc. for Encouragement of Arts, Mfrs. and Commerce, 1993; Rome Prize fellow Am. Acad. in Rome, 1954-56. Fellow AIA (awards 1974, 77, 78), Am. Acad. in Rome, Am. Acad. of Arts and Letters, Am. Acad. Arts and Scis., Royal Inst. of Brit. Architects (hon.), Royal Incorp. Architects of Scotland (hon.), Accademia Nazionale di San Luca; mem. Phi Beta Kappa. Office: 4236 Main St Philadelphia PA 19127-1603

VENUTI, RUTH LOUISE, secondary school educator, counselor; b. Spokane, Wash., July 1, 1957; d. Louis Jesse and Ruth Virginia (Mussetter) V. BA, Fla. So. Coll., 1979; MA in Counseling, Liberty U., Lynchburg, Va., 1990; specialist degree, Stetson U., 1992. Cert. elem., mid. sch. math. and secondary Spanish tchr., Fla. Elem. tchr. Polk County Sch. Bd., Auburndale, Fla., 1979, Bartow, Fla., 1979-84; jr. high sch. tchr. Volusia County Sch. Bd., Deltona, Fla., 1984-88, mid. sch. tchr., 1988—, NEAT observer, 1982, peer tchr., 1988-92, hosp./home bound program tutor, 1997; tutor Fla. Sheriff's Girls' Villa, Bartow, 1979-80, Fla. United Meth. Children's Home, Enterprise, 1984; ednl. dir. Rohr House, abuse shelter, Bartow, 1980-81. Recipient Cert. of Commendation from Pres. Nixon, 1974, Apple pin Volusia County Sch. Bd., 1988. Mem. Nat. Coun. Tchrs. Math., Am. Assn. Tchrs. Spanish and Portuguese, Kappa Delta Pi. Mem. Assembly of God Ch. Avocations: creative writing, music, sign language, church activities. Home: 670 Montclair Ave Orange City FL 32763-4842 Office: Galaxy Mid Sch 2400 Eustace Ave Deltona FL 32725-1765

VÉR, ISTVÁN LÁSZLÓ, noise control consultant; b. Tápiószecsö, Hungary, Dec. 22, 1934; came to U.S., 1965; s. István and Erzsebet G. (Darázs) V.; m. Elisabeth H. Waltering, Dec. 6, 1961; 1 child, Kristina M. BSEE, Tech. U., Budapest, 1956; MSEE, Tech. U., Aachen, Germany, 1960; PhD in Acoustics, Tech. U., Munich, 1963. R&d engr. Rohde and Schwarz, Munich, 1960-65; prin. cons. Bolt Beranek & Newman Inc., Cambridge, Mass., 1965—. Author, editor: Noise & Vibration Engineering, 1992; holder patents. Recipient U.S. Sr. Scientist award Alexander von Humboldt Found., Germany, 1978, Best Paper award Am. Soc. Heating and Refrigeration Engring., 1979. Fellow Acoustical Soc. Am.; mem. Inst. Noise Control Engring. USA (dir. 1976-77), German Acoustical Soc. Avocations: literature, philosophy, travel, tennis. Office: BBN Corp 10 Moulton St Cambridge MA 02138-1119

VERANO, ANTHONY FRANK, retired banker; b. West Harrison, N.Y., Jan. 4, 1931; s. Frank and Rose (Viscome) V.; m. Clara Cosentino, July 8, 1951; children—Rosemarie, Diana Lynn. Student, Am. Inst. Banking, 1956-60, Bank Adminstrn. Inst., U. Wis., 1962-64, RCA Programmers Sch., 1965, Burroughs Programmers Sch., 1965, N.J. Bankers Data Processing Sch., 1966-68. With County Trust Co., White Plains, N.Y., 1949-61; sr. auditor County Trust Co., 1960-61; with State Nat. Bank Conn., Bridgeport, 1961—; auditor State Nat. Bank Conn., 1962-79, exec. auditor, 1979—; exec. auditor Conn. Bank & Trust Co., 1983—; from v.p., auditor to sr. v.p., auditor Gateway Bank, Newtown, Conn., 1987-94, ret., 1994; tchr. bank auditing Am. Inst. Banking, 1976-78. Mem. adv. bd. Norwalk Community Coll., 1968—. Served with USN, 1951-52. Mem. Bank Adminstrn. Inst. (dir. Stamford chpt. 1967-68, sec. Western Conn. chpt. 1968-69, treas. 1969-70, v.p. 1970-71, pres. 1971-72), Am. Acctg. Assn., Inst. Internal Auditors (cert. bank auditor, cert. bank compliance officer, cert. fin. svcs. auditor). Home: 59 Bugg Hill Rd Monroe CT 06468-1710 *It is difficult to define the elements of success. There are those who say success is achieved through drive and ambition only. However, those who have achieved their goals in life using only these two principles have probably destroyed more than they have created. Success, I feel, is achieved when drive and ambition are tempered with honesty, fairness, and respect for others. An individual must have a sense of dedication not only to his work and for those with whom he works but, most importantly, for those who work for him. This has been my philosophy in achieving my success.*

VERBA, SIDNEY, political scientist, educator; b. Bklyn., May 26, 1932; s. Morris Harold and Recci (Salman) V.; m. E. Cynthia Winston, June 17, 1955; children—Margaret Lynn, Ericka Kim, Martina Claire. B.A., Harvard U., 1953; M.A., Princeton U., 1955, Ph.D., 1959. Asst. prof. polit. sci. Princeton U., 1960-63, assoc. prof., 1963-64; prof. Stanford U., 1964-68, U. Chgo., 1968-72; prof. govt. Harvard U., 1972—, now Carl H. Pforzheimer prof., dir. univ. library, chmn. dept. govt., 1976-80, asso. dean Faculty Arts and Scis., 1981—; dir. Harvard U. Library; chmn. bd. dirs. Harvard U. Press, 1991—; chmn. policy com. Social Sci. Rsch. Coun., 1980-86; mem. Commn. on Behavioral and Social Scis., NRC, 1986-91; Commn. on Preservation and Access, chair com. on internat. conflict and cooperation, NRC, 1991-93; vis. com. MIT Polit. Sci. Dept., Stanford U. Libr. Author: Small Groups and Political Behavior, 1961, The Civic Culture, 1963, Caste, Race and Politics, 1969, Participation in America, 1972, Vietnam and the Silent Majority, 1972, The Changing American Voter, 1976, Participation and Political Equality, 1978, Injury to Insult, 1979, Introduction to American Government, 1983, Equality in America, 1985, Elites and the Idea of Equality, 1987, Designing Social Inquiry, 1994, Voice and Equality, 1995. Guggenheim fellow, 1980-81. Fellow Am. Acad. Arts and Scis.; mem. NAS, Am. Polit. Sci. Assn. (exec. coun. 1971-74, v.p. 1979-81, pres.-elect 1993-94, pres. 1994-95, Gladys Kammerer award 1972, Woodrow Wilson Found. award 1976, James Madison award 1993), Internat. Studies Assn. (v.p. 1971-72). Jewish. Home: 142 Summit Ave Brookline MA 02146-2358 Office: Harvard U Harvard Univ Library Director Cambridge MA 02138

VERBOCKEL ROGERS, JOLENE MARY, auditor; b. Kaukauna, Wis., Nov. 17, 1964; d. Ralph and Elizabeth Louise (Sippel) Verbockel; m. Steven James Rogers, June 12, 1985; children: Tanner David, Thatcher Andrew. BBA, U. Wis., Oshkosh, 1990. CPA, Ill.; cert. mgmt. acct. Auditor, coord. ADP, Office Insp. Gen., U.S. Dept. Transp., Chgo., 1990—. Mem. Inst. Mgmt. Acct. (cert.), Assn. Govt. Accts. (meetings dir. 1996-97). Office: US Dept Transp OIG 111 N Canal St Ste 677 Chicago IL 60606-7203

VERBOUT, JAMES PAUL, recreational therapist; b. Sterling, Ill., July 7, 1957; s. Louis Pius and Agnes (Rajnowski) V.; m. Loretta Margaret Jaquet, May 30, 1981; children: Kimberly Noel, Brandon James. BS in Therapeutic Recreation, U. Wis., LaCrosse, 1979. Cert. therapeutic recreation specialist. Recreational therapist Glenwood (Iowa) State Hosp., 1979-80; recreational therapist Mayo Med. Ctr., Rochester, Minn., 1980—, lead recreational therapist, 1988—; S.E. Minn. dir. Minn. Therapeutic Recreation steering com., Burnsville, 1988-90; v.p. Advanced Speech Interface Sys., 1993-94. Author: (wuth Robert Steuck) Activity Fun for You, 1983. Bd. dirs. Rochester Area Disabled Athletics and Recreation, Inc., 1986-95, vice sec., 1986-87, v.p., 1991, pres., 1992-93; asst. coach Rochester Youth Baseball, 1995, Rochester Youth Soccer, 1995; vol. Rochester Area Courage Daycamp, 1996; den rep. Cub Scouts Pack 210, 1993-94, pack sec., 1994-95; St. Mary's Hosp. chair United Way, 1994, rehab. rep., 1990-94. Recipient Spirit award Rochester Area Disabled Athletics and Recreation, 1989-90, Outstanding Bd. Mem. award Rochester Area Disabled Athletics and Recreation, 1995. Mem. Am. Therapeutic Recreation Assn., Minn. Park and Recreation Assn., Nat. Closed Head Injury Found., State Closed Head Injury Found., S.E. Minn. Head Injury Support Group, KC (3d degree). Democrat. Roman Catholic. Avocations: fishing, reading, bowling. Home: 4911 22nd Ave NW Rochester MN 55901-2033 Office: Mayo Med Ctr 200 1st St SW Rochester MN 55902-3008

VERBURG, EDWIN ARNOLD, federal agency administrator; b. Lakehurst, N.J., Oct. 6, 1945; s. Edwin Donald Verburg and Dorothy (Orrell) Hoodless; m. Joyce Elaine Majack, Sept. 14, 1968; children: Adelle Kristine, Wendi Elizabeth. BS, Calif. Polytech. U., 1968; M in City Planning, U. Calif., Berkeley, 1970; D in Pub. Adminstrn., George Washington U., 1975. Asst. planner City of Inglewood (Calif.), 1970-71; planner City of Glendale (Calif.), 1971-72; grad. assoc. U.S. Army Corps Engrs., Washington, 1974-75; mgr. fiscal analysis Met. Washington Council Govts., 1975-77; sr. program analyst U.S. Fish and Wildlife Service, Washington, 1977-79, asst. div. chief, 1979-80, div. chief, 1980-82, asst. dir. planning and budget,

1982-86, dep. asst. dir. policy budget and adminstrn., 1986-87; dir. office of fin. U.S. Dept. Treas., Washington, 1987-88, dir. fin. svcs. directorate, 1988-91, dir. fin. svcs. directorate, dep. CFO, 1991-95; assoc. adminstr. adminstrn. FAA, 1995—. Author: Local State and Federal Fiscal Flows, 5 Vols., 1976; contbr. articles to fed. jours. Recipient Disting. Pub. Svc. award George Washington U., Sch. Bus. and Pub. Mgmt., 1994, Sec. of Treasury Disting Svc. award, 1995, Fin. Mgmt. Svc. Commrs. award, 1996. Mem. Am. Inst. Cert. Planners, Am. Planning Assn. (cert. govt. fin. mgr., Merit award Calif. chpt. 1973, First award Nat. Capital area chpt. 1980, Peer award for pub. svc. Dept. of Treasury 1990, sec. of treas. cert. appreciation 1991, Pres.'s Meritorious Svc. award 1991, Commr.'s Citation Fin. Mgmt. Svc. 1996). Home: 538 N Oakland St Arlington VA 22203-2219

VERCELLOTTI, JOHN RAYMOND, research chemist; b. Joliet, Ill., May 2, 1933; s. Joseph Francis and Mary Teresa (Walowski) V.; m. Sharon Cecile Vergez, Sept. 3, 1966; children: Ellen Theresa, Paul Auguste. BA, St. Bonaventure U., 1955; MS, Marquette U., 1960; PhD, Ohio State U., 1963. Lectr., rsch. assoc. Ohio State U., Columbus, 1963-64; asst. prof. Marquette U., Milw., 1964-67; assoc. prof. U. Tenn., Knoxville, 1967-70; prof. Va. Poly. Inst. & State U., Blacksburg, 1970-79; vis. prof. Inst. G. Ronzoni, Milan, Italy, 1977-78; sr. scientist Gulf South Res. Inst., New Orleans, 1980-85; rsch. chemist, rsch. leader So. Regional Rsch. Ctr. USDA, New Orleans, 1985-96; v.p. and sr. chemist V-Labs Inc., Covington, La., 1980-85, 96—; sr. rsch. advisor Sugar Processing Rsch. Inst., Inc., New Orleans, 1996—; adj. prof. chemistry and physics S.E. La. U., Hammond, 1986—. Contbr. over 185 articles to Elsevier & Am. Chem. Soc. Symposium Series; author, coauthor numerous book chpts., 1960—; contbr. numerous articles to profl. jours. U. Tenn. minority colls. grantee, 1968-70, NSF grantee, 1964—. Mem. Am. Chem. Soc. (sec. 1968-90, Melville L. Wolfrom award 1994), Inst. Food Technologists; fellow Sigma Xi. Democrat. Roman Catholic. Achievements include research on food flavor quality and agricultural commodity utilization, origin of flavor from carbohydrates, lipid oxidation products, and peptides. Avocations: golfing, fishing, gardening, playing accordion. Home: 113 E 25th Ave Covington LA 70433 Office: V-Labs Inc 423 N Theard St Covington LA 70433-2837

VERDERBER, JOSEPH ANTHONY, capital equipment company executive; b. Cleve., Nov. 30, 1938; s. Joseph Arthur and Dorothy Louise (Buchta) V.; m. Anita Barto, Sept. 10, 1960; children: Joseph Anthony, Lisa C., Paul A. BS in Mech. Engring., MIT, 1960, MS in Mech. Engring., 1961. Registered profl. engr., Ohio. Mgr. rsch. AM Internat., Cleve., 1964-70; dir. engring. Varityper div., East Hanover, N.J., 1971-73, product mgr., 1973-77; v.p. advanced bus. devel. multigraphics div., Mt. Prospect, Ill., 1977-81, gen. mgr. imaging systems group, Bedford, Mass., Chgo., 1981, pres. Varityper div., East Hanover, N.J., 1982-88; corp. v.p. bus. devel. AM Internat., Inc., Chgo., 1988-89; pres. Am. Splty. Products, Dayton, Ohio, 1989-90; pres. Barco Graphics, Inc., Dayton, 1990; pres. Gen. Scanning, Laser Sys. Divsn., Somerville, Mass., 1991—; lectr. Cleve. State U., 1962-67. Recipient Karl Taylor Compton prize MIT, 1960; NSF fellow, 1961; named Inventor of Yr., AM Internat., Chgo., 1980. Mem. ASME, Nat. Printing Equipment and Supply Assn. (bd. dirs. 1986-88, chmn. SEMI New Eng. Forum 1994—). Office: TLSI 32 Cobble Hill Rd Somerville MA 02143-4412

VERDERY, DAVID NORWOOD, broadcast programming executive; b. Waco, Tex., Dec. 12, 1943; s. David Paul and Ruthe (McCawley) V.; m. Randy Lee Mahan, June 6, 1968 (div. 1970); 1 child, David Roderick. Student, Baylor U., 1961-64. Announcer KEFC, Waco, 1962-64; announcer, producer KHFI, Austin, Tex., 1964-65; announcer, prodn. dir. KIXL, Dallas, 1965-66; program dir. KVIL, Dallas, 1967, KABL, San Francisco, 1968-69; nat. program coord. The McLendon Co., Dallas, 1969-73; v.p. programming TM Programming, Dallas, 1973-80, Bonneville Broadcasting Sys., Northbrook, Ill., 1980-86; music dir. KBIG, L.A., 1985-95, asst. program dir., music dir., 1996—. Mem. Project Angel Food, L.A., 1992-94; mem. Permanent Charities Com., L.A., 1995—, mem. Reading for the Blind, L.A., 1996—. Named Adult Contemporary Music Dir. of Yr., The Gavin Report, 1992, 93. Avocations: gourmet cooking, theater, travel, musical composing and arranging. Office: KBIG Radio 7755 W Sunset Blvd Los Angeles CA 90046-3911

VERDI, DAVID JOSEPH, broadcast news executive; b. Newark, Apr. 4, 1956; s. Joseph Peter and Georgina Alice (Meing) V.; m. Bernadette Rubino, June 26, 1982; children: Andriana Rubino, David Rubino, Stephen Rubino. BA in Journalism, U. No. Colo., 1979. Desk asst. ABC News, N.Y.C., 1980-82, prodn. assoc. Nightline, 1982-84, assoc. prodr. World News Tonight, 1984-86; field prodr. ABC News, St. Louis, 1986-88; prodr. This Week with David Brinkley ABC News, Washington, 1988-90; exec. news dir. NBC News, N.Y.C., 1990—. Office: NBC News 30 Rockefeller Plz New York NY 10112

VERDI, ROBERT WILLIAM, sports columnist; b. Bklyn., Aug. 31, 1946. BA in English, Lake Forest Coll., Ill., 1967. Reporter L.I. Press, Queens, N.Y., summers 1964, 65; sports columnist Chgo. Tribune, 1967—. Named Sportswriter of Yr. for Ill., Nat. Sportscasters and Sportswriters Assn., 1975-78, 80-82, 84-87, 89-90. Mem. Baseball Writers Assn. Am., Football Writers Assn. Am., Golf Writers Assn. Office: Chgo Tribune Sports Dept PO Box 25340 Chicago IL 60625-0340*

VERDINE, GREGORY LAWRENCE, chemist, educator; b. Somers Point, N.J., June 10, 1959; s. Richard Daniel and Therese Mary (Delaney) V.; m. Kasumi Koseki, Dec. 1, 1987; children: Vanessa Kaori, Lauren Arika, Erika Rose. BS, St. Joseph's U., Phila., 1982; MA, Columbia U., 1983, PhD, 1986; AB (hon.), Harvard U., 1995. Postdoctoral fellow MIT, Cambridge, Mass., 1986, 87, Harvard Med. Sch., Boston, 1987, 8; asst. prof. chemistry Faculty Arts and Scis. Harvard U., Cambridge, 1988-92, Thomas D. Cabot assoc. prof. chemistry, 1992-94, prof., 1994—; mem. sci. adv. bd. Ariad Pharms., Cambridge, 1992—, La Jolla (Calif.) Pharms., 1990—; cons. Hoffmann-LaRoche, Nutley, N.J., 1991—. Assoc. editor Chemistry and Biology, 1994—; contbr. numerous articles to profl. jours. Recipient Excellence in Chemistry award Zeneca Pharms., 1994; DuPont Young Faculty fellow, 1988, Searle scholar, 1990, Eli Lilly grantee, 1990, Alfred P. Sloan fellow, 1991, NSF Presdl. Young Investigator award, 1991, others. Mem. AAAS, Am. Chem. Soc. (Arthur C. Cope Scholar award 1994, Eli Lilly award 1995). Achievements include research in chemical genetics: the propagation, preservation and expression of genetic information. Office: Harvard U Dept Chemistry 12 Oxford St Cambridge MA 02138-2902

VERDON, GWEN (GWYNETH EVELYN), actress, dancer, choreographer; b. L.A., Jan. 13, 1925; d. Joseph William and Gertrude (Standring) V.; m. James Henaghan, 1942 (div. June 1947); children: James O'Farrell; m. Robert Louis Fosse, Apr. 3, 1960; 1 child, Nicole. Ed. pub. schs., studied dance with E. Belcher, Carmelita Marrachi, Jack Cole. Bd. dirs. Postgrad. Center for Mental Health. Broadway debut in Alive and Kicking, 1950; appeared in musical plays including: Can Can (Tony award 1954), 1953-54, Damn Yankees (Tony award 1956), 1955-56, New Girl in Town (Tony award 1958), 1957, Red Head (Tony award 1959), 1959, Sweet Charity, 1966, (starring role) Chicago, 1975; staged 2d co.: musical Dancin; also acted as dance mistress; appeared in play Love Letters, L.A., 1990; motion pictures: On The Riviera, 1951, Meet Me After the Show, 1951, David and Bathsheba, 1952, Mississippi Gambler, 1953, Damn Yankees, 1958, Cotton Club, 1984, Cocoon, 1986, Nadine, 1987, Cocoon II, 1988, Alice, 1990; TV series appearances include: MASH, Fame, All is Forgiven, Trapper John M.D., The Equalizer, Magnum P.I. (Emmy award nominee), Webster, Dear John, HBO's Dream On (Emmy award nominee), Homicide (Emmy award nominee). Recipient Donaldson award for acting and dancing, Lambs Gambol award for acting, Grammy award, 1959, Silver Bowl award Dance Mag., 1961. Office: care Shapiro & Lobel 111 W 40th St New York NY 10018-2506

VERDOORN, SID, food service executive; b. Albert Lea, Minn., Feb. 11, 1939; s. Cornelius Emery and Gwen (Pickell) V.; m. Carol Joyce Hoekstra, July 3, 1959; children: Jay Richard, Jeffrey Lee, James Dale. Student, Cen. Coll., Pella, Iowa. With sales C.H. Robinson Co., Mpls., 1963-66; mgr. C.H. Robinson Co., San Francisco, 1966-71; pers. dir. C.H. Robinson Co., Mpls., 1971-75, v.p., 1975-77, pres., chief exec. officer, 1977—; bd. dirs. Produce Mktg. Assocs., Newark, United Fruit and Produce, Washington. With U.S. Army, 1959-61. Republican. Avocations: hiking, water sports. Home: 28210 Woodside Rd Excelsior MN 55331-7950 Office: C H Robinson Co Inc 8100 Mitchell Rd Ste 200 Eden Prairie MN 55344-2178*

VERDORN, JERRY, actor; b. Sioux Falls, S.D.; married; children: Jacob, Peter. Student, Moorehead State U. Actor: (theatre) Black Elk Speaks, Are you Now or Have You Ever Been?, Man and Superman, The Star-Spangled Girl; (TV) Guiding Light, 1979—; (TV movie) The Cradle Will Fall, 1983. Recipient Best Supporting Actor Drama Series Daytime Emmy. Office: CBS Studio 222 E 44th St New York NY 10017-4334*

VERED, RUTH, art gallery director; b. Tel Aviv, Sept. 26, 1940; d. Abraham and Helen Rosenblum; children: Sharon, Oren. BA in Art History with honors, Bezalel U., Jerusalem, 1964. Freelance art cons., Israel and N.Y.C., 1965-75; dir. Vered Gallery, East Hampton, N.Y., 1977—. Sgt. paratroops Israeli Army, 1958-60. Home: 891 Park Ave New York NY 10021-0326 Office: Vered Gallery 68 Park Place Passage East Hampton NY 11937

VER EECKE, WILFRIED CAMIEL, philosopher, educator; b. Tielt, Belgium, Aug. 22, 1938; came to U.S., 1966; s. Jerome and Maria (Declercq) Ver E.; license philosophy, Cath. U. Leuven (Belgium), 1962, PhD, 1966; postgrad. U. Freiburg, 1966, Harvard U., 1966-67; MA in Econs., Georgetown U., 1972; m. Josiane Berten, Sept. 4, 1967; children: Mieke, Stefaan, Renaat, Jan. H.S. tchr., Heule, Belgium, 1962-63, Kortrijk, 1963-65; NSF research fellow, Belgium, 1965-69; asst. prof. Georgetown U., Washington, 1967-72, assoc. prof., 1972-80, prof., 1980—, chmn. dept. philosophy, 1980-83. Alexander von Humboldt fellow, Ger., 1975-76, 78. Mem. Am. Philos. Assn., Am. Cath. Philos. Assn., Hegel Soc. Am., Soc. Phenomenology and Existential Philosophy, Public Choice, Washington Forum Psychiatry-Humanities. Roman Catholic. Author: Negativity and Subjectivity, 1977; translator: Schizophrenia (La psychose) (A. De Waelhens), 1978; Saying No, 1984; contbr. articles to profl. jours. Home: 4100 Nebraska Ave NW Washington DC 20016-2736 Office: Dept Philosophy Georgetown U Washington DC 20057

VEREEN, BEN, actor, singer, dancer; b. Miami, Fla., Oct. 10, 1946; m. Nancy Vereen; children: Benjamin, Malakia, Naja, Kabara, Karon. Student, High Sch. of Performing Arts; LHD (hon.), Emerson Coll., 1977. Debut off-Broadway in The Prodigal Son, 1965; played Brother Ben in Sweet Charity, N.Y.C., Las Vegas, San Francisco, 1966, Daddy Brubeck in Can. tour, 1968, in Los Angeles co. of Hair, 1968, joined Broadway cast, 1969; played role of Judas in Jesus Christ Superstar, 1971 (Theatre World award); leading role in Pippin', 1972 (Tony award, Drama Desk award); appeared in Grind, 1985, Jelly's Last Jam, 1993; numerous theatrical appearances, including I'm Not Rappaport, San Francisco, 1989, A Christmas Carol, 1995, 96; appeared in TV movie Louis Armstrong-Chicago Style, 1976; created role of Chicken George in TV miniseries Roots, 1977 (TV Critics award); other TV miniseries include Ellis Island, 1984, A.D., 1985; appeared in TV spl. Ben Vereen-His Roots, 1978, Uptown-A Tribute to the Apollo Theatre; film appearances: Funny Lady, 1975, All That Jazz, 1979, Buy and Cell, 1989, Once Upon a Forrest, 1993 (voice only); TV appearances: Touched by an Angel, 1997; TV series include: Tenspeed and Brown Shoe, 1980, Webster, J.J. Starbuck, 1988; also nightclub appearances. Chmn. Dance for Heart campaign Am. Heart Assn.; internat. chmn. Sudden Infant Death Syndrome; established Naja Vereen Meml. Scholarship Fund, 1988; founder, pres. Celebrities for a Drug-Free Am. Recipient George M. Cohan award Am. Guild Variety Artists, 1976, Image award NAACP, 1978, 79, Israel's Cultural award, 1978, Israel's Humanitarian award, 1979, Eleanor Roosevelt Humanitarian award, 1983. Mem. Actor's Equity Assn., Am. Guild Variety Artists, AFTRA, SAG. Office: care Pamela Cooper 2968 Corral Canyon Malibu CA 90265 *I am like the turtle--determined and will stick my neck out; turtles also teach me patience.**

VEREEN, ROBERT CHARLES, retired trade association executive; b. Stillwater, Minn., Sept. 8, 1924; s. George and Leona Lucille (Made) Wihren; m. Rose Catherine Blair, Nov. 5, 1945; children: Robin, Stacy, Kim. Grad. high sch. Mng. editor Comml. West Mag., Mpls., 1946-50, Bruce Pub. Co., St. Paul, 1950-53, Nat. Retail Hardware Assn., Indpls., 1953-59; mng. dir. Liberty Distbrs., Phila., 1959-63; editor Hardware Retailing, Indpls., 1963-80; assoc. pub., dir. communications Nat. Retail Hardware Assn., 1980-84, sr. v.p., 1984-87; Vereen & Assocs., Mgmt., Mktg. Cons., 1987—; lectr. mgmt. insts.; guest lectr. on distbn. pub.; co-founder U.S.A. Direct; co-founder, ptnr. Eurotrade Mktg., 1988—. Author: (with Paul M. Doane) Hunting for Profit, 1965, The Computer Age in Merchandising, 1968, Perpetuating the Family-Owned Business, 1970, The How-To of Merchandising, 1975, The How-To of Store Operations, 1976, A Guide to Financial Management, 1976, Productivity: A Crisis for Management, 1978, Hardlines Rep Report Newsletter, 1984-94, Guidelines to Improve the Rep/Factory Relationships, 1992. Served with AUS, 1943-46. Mem. Am. Soc. Bus Press Editors (dir., v.p. 1966-70), Soc. Nat. Assn. Publs. (dir., pres. 1970-75, chmn. journalism edn. liaison com. 1976-79), Toastmasters (v.p., treas., sec. 1955-59), Am. Hardware Mfrs. Assn. (co-founder, sec.-treas. Young Execs. Club 1958-59, 63-65), Hardware-Housewares Packaging Expn. (founder 1960, chmn. com. packaging 1960-62, chmn. judging com. Hardware-Packaging Expn. 1975-78), Packaging Inst., Household Consumer Products Export Council (chmn. 1981-83), World-Wide DIY Council (exec. sec. 1981—). Home and Office: 4560 Lincoln Rd Indianapolis IN 46228-6706

VEREEN, WILLIAM JEROME, uniform manufacturing company executive; b. Moultrie, Ga., Sept. 7, 1940; s. William Coachman and Mary Elizabeth (Bunn) V.; m. Lula Evelyn King, June 9, 1963; children: Elizabeth King, William Coachman. BS in Indsl. Mgmt, Ga. Inst. Tech., 1963. With Riverside Mfg. Co., Moultrie, 1967—; v.p., then exec. v.p. Riverside Mfg. Co., 1970-77, pres., 1977-84, pres., treas., CEO, 1984—; also dir.; v.p., dir. Moultrie Cotton Mills, 1969—; exec. v.p. Riverside Industries, Inc., Moultrie, 1973-77; pres. Riverside Industries, Inc., 1977-84, CEO, 1984—, also dir.; v.p., bd. dirs. Riverside Uniform Rentals, Inc., Moultrie, 1971-80, pres., 1980-84, CEO, bd. dirs., 1984—; pres. Riverside Mfg. Co. (Ireland) Ltd., 1977—, Right Image Corp., Riverside Mfg. Co. GmbH, Germany, 1979—, also CEO, dir., 1984; pres., treas., CEO G.A. Rivers Corp., Riverside Mfg. Co. (U.K.) Ltd.; pres., treas. CEO, bd. dirs. Textile Clothing Tech. Corp.; chairholder Tyner eminent scholars, prof. coll. human scis. Fla. State U., 1993-94, mem. coll. human scis. devel. bd.; bd. dirs. Ga. Power Co., Gerber Sci., Inc., Blue Cross/Blue Shield Ga., Cerulean Cos., Inc., Ga. Bd. Industry, Trade and Tourism, Ga. Rsch. Alliance, Ga. Corp. Indsl. Devel.; mem. trilateral commn. apparel labeling NAFTA; so. regional dir. Nations Bank of Ga., N.A.; advisor textile and apparel tariffs and quotas U.S. Dept. State bd.; active Gov. Devel. Coun.; mem. trade and tourism bd. Ga. Dept. Industry, 1997—. Bd. dirs. Moultrie-Colquitt County (Ga.) Devel. Authority, 1973-77, Moultrie-Colquitt County United Givers, 1968-75, Moultrie YMCA, 1968-75, Colquitt County Cancer Soc., 1969-73; trustee Cmty. Welfare Assn. Moultrie, 1970—, Pineland Sch., Moultrie, 1971-75, Leadership Ga., 1972—, Ga. Coun. Econ. Edn.; trustee Am. Apparel Edn. Found.; adv. bd. Ga. Tech. sch. of textile and fiber engring.; elder 1st Presbyterian Ch. Capt. USMCR, 1963-67. Decorated Bronze Star, Purple Heart. Mem. Internat. Apparel Fedn. (2d v.p., 1st v.p., bd. dirs., exec. com., chmn. 1991-92), Am. Apparel Mfrs. Assn. (bd. dirs., exec. com., edn. found. com., 2d vice chmn., chmn. 1990-91), Nat. Assn. Uniform Mfrs. and Distbrs. (bd. dirs. 1988-91), Am. Apparel Edn. Found. (v.p., trustee), Capital City Club (Atlanta), Commerce Club (Atlanta), Sunset Country Club, Ga. C. of C. (vice chmn., bd. dirs., mem. exec. com., chmn. existing industry com.), Elks, Kiwanis, Sigma Alpha Epsilon. Home: 21 Dogwood Dr Moultrie GA 31768-6537 Office: PO Box 460 Moultrie GA 31776-0460

VERGANO, LYNN (MARILYNN BETTE VERGANO), artist; b. N.Y.C., Nov. 14; d. George and Sis Anagnostis (Helaine Haas); children: Scott, Stephen, Sandy, Sefton. Student, Pratt Inst., 1959-60; BA, NYU, Heights, 1963; MA, NYU, 1964. Lectr. art Morris County Coll., 1982; lectr. UN Pan Pacific and S.E. Asia Women's Assn., N.Y. chpt., 1996; lectr. in field; judge, art juror. Author/illustrator: (book) Paintings, 1980, Paintings by Lynn Vergano, 1997; one-woman shows include Paper Mill Playhouse, N.J., 1976, 79, 83, Fairleigh Dickinson U., N.J., 1977, Drew U., N.J., 1977, Rutgers U., N.J., 1978, 79, Hong Kong Arts Ctr., 1980, Am. Univ. Alumni, Bangkok, Thailand, 1980, Caldwell Coll., N.J., 1980, União Cultural Brasil-Estados Unidos, São Paulo, Brazil, 1982, Galleria Fenice, Venice, Italy, 1985, St. Sophia Mus., Istanbul, Turkey, 1988, Nat. Arts Club, N.Y.C., 1989, Centreplace, Hamilton, New Zealand, 1990, Women's Nat. Rep. Club, N.Y.C., 1997 and others; exhibited in group shows Monmouth Mus., Lincroft, N.J., 1976, 77, 82, Morris Mus., Morristown, N.J., 1977, 78, N.J. State Capital Mus., Trenton, 1979, Macculloch Hall Hist. Mus., N.J., Morristown, 1984, 87, 89, 92, 96, Nat. Audubon Artists, N.Y.C., 1981, Salmagundi Club, N.Y.C., 1981, World Trade Ctr., N.Y., 1981, Nat. Arts Club, N.Y.C., 1981-97, Bergen Mus., Paramus, N.J., 1983, Lincoln Ctr., N.Y.C., 1987, Bklyn. Botanic Gardens, N.Y., 1987, many others. Pres., chpt. charter mem., 1969-70, hon. mem. Welcome Wagon Club, Randolph, N.J., 1969—. Recipient UN 25th Anniversary Creative Writing award, 1970, John H. Miller award Morris County Coll., 1979, Grumbacher gold medallion, 1984, Torch award NYU, 1993. Mem. AAUW (hon.), UN Pan Pacific and S.E. Asia Women's Assn. Internat. (hon.), Am. Watercolor Soc. (assoc.), Nat. Arts Club (exhibiting), Nat. Soc. Arts and Letters (exec. bd. N.J. chpt. 1979—), Federated Art Assns. N.J. (trustee 1982—, pres., chmn. bd. dirs. 1982-88, Heritage plaque 1989), N.Y. Acad. Arts and Scis., Morris County Art Assn., Dover Art Assn., Kenilworth Art Assn. (hon.), Millburn-Short Hills Arts Ctr. Address: 229 Van Cortlandt Pk Ave Yonkers NY 10705-1520

VERGE, PIERRE, legal educator; b. Quebec City, Can., Jan. 9, 1936; s. Francis and Regina (Roy) V.; m. Colette Habel, June 29, 1963; children—Marc, Caroline, Louis. B.A., Laval U., 1956, LL.L., 1959, LL.D., 1971; M.A., McGill U., 1962, Cambridge U., 1977; LL.M., U. Toronto, 1968; 1971. Bar: Que. 1961, Queen's Counsel 1976. Pvt. practice law Quebec City, Can., 1961-66; mem. faculty Laval U. Faculty of Law, 1966—; dean Laval U. Faculty of Law (Faculty of Law), 1973-77. Commonwealth fellow St. John's Coll., Cambridge U., 1977-78. Mem. Assn. Can. Law Tchrs. (pres. 1972-73, chmn. conf. law deans 1975-76), Que. Bar, Canadian Bar, Royal Soc. Can. Home: 2542 de la Falaise, Sillery, PQ Canada G1T 1W3 Office: Cite Universitaire, Universite Laval, Quebec, PQ Canada

VERGER, MORRIS DAVID, architect, planner; b. Ft. Worth, Mar. 25, 1915; s. Joseph and Dora (Bunyan) V.; m. Florence Brown, June 21, 1939; children: Paul, Alice. B.Arch., U. Calif., Berkeley, 1943. Naval architect U.S. Navy Bur. Ships, San Pedro, Calif., 1943-45; draftsman various archtl. firms So. Calif., 1946-50; pvt. practice as architect and planner Los Angeles, 1951—; lectr. architecture UCLA Extension; vis. critic Calif. State U., San Luis Obispo; leader Seminar on Interactive Planning, San Francisco; cons. to legal profession, tech. witness. Works include program for City of Hope, Duarte, Calif., 1972, Terman Engring. Ctr., Stanford U., 1974, and design of Huntington Dr. Sch., L.A., 1975, Flax Artist Materials Bldg., L.A., 1976, Frank D. Lanterman H.S., L.A., 1978, exec. offices S.E. Rykoff & Co., L.A., 1982, condominiums, Stoneman Corp., L.A., 1988, 91; developed Discover-yBased Planning, 1994. Recipient design awards Westwood C. of C., 1974, 75. Fellow AIA (pres. So. Calif. chpt. 1975, v.p. environ. affairs Calif. council 1976, v.p. Calif. council 1979-80, pres. Calif. council 1980). Inventor (with E.H. Porter) Interactive Planning, evolved to Connective Planning; developed method for computer-design of Interstitial Space and computer-generated drawings for affordable housing using related dimensions and datum points to coordinate all trades. Home: 1362 Comstock Ave Los Angeles CA 90024-5315

VERGHESE, ABRAHAM CHEERAN, internist, writer, educator; b. Addis Ababa, Ethiopia, May 30, 1955; came to U.S., 1980; s. George and Mary Verghese; children: Steven, Jacob. MD, Madras (India) U., 1979; intern Govt. Gen. Hosp., Madras Med. Coll., India, 1979-80; from. res. to chief res., E. Tenn. State U., Johnson City, 1980-83; MFA, U. Iowa, 1991. Diplomate Am. Bd. Internal Medicine, Am. Bd. Infectious Diseases, Geriat., and Pulmonary Medicine. Instr. in medicine E. Tenn. State U., Johnson City, 1982-83, asst. prof. medicine, 1985-88, assoc. prof. medicine, 1988-90; teaching asst. medicine Boston U., 1983-85; chief infectious diseases VA Med. Ctr., Johnson City, 1986-90, asst. chief medicine, 1988-90; vis. assoc. U. Iowa, Iowa City, 1990-91; prof. medicine Tex. Tech. U., El Paso, Tex., 1991—; chief infectious diseases Tex. Tech. Regional Acad. Health Ctr., El Paso, 1991—. Author: My Own Country: A Doctor's Story of a Town and Its People in the Age of AIDS, 1994, (with others) Infection in the Nursing Home, 1990. Named Tchr. of Yr. Internat. Medicine residents and Alpha Omega Alpha E. Tenn. State U., 1989; recipient James Michener fellowship to Writer's Workshop U. Iowa. Fellow ACP (publs. coms.), Royal Coll. Physicians Can., Infectious Diseases Soc. Am., Coll. Chest Physicians; mem. Am. Geriat. Soc., Am. Fedn. for Clin. Rsch., Am. Soc. Microbiology, Soc. for Exptl. Biology and Medicine. Office: Tex Tech U 4800 Alberta Ave El Paso TX 79905-2709

VERGILIS, JOSEPH SEMYON, mechanical engineering educator; b. Odessa, Ukraine, Aug. 14, 1934; came to U.S., 1988; s. Semyon E. and Zinaida I. (Gleizerman) V.; m. Zhanna S. Berenfeld, Apr. 30, 1963; children: Helen, Irene. BS in Mfg. Engring., Poly. Inst., Odessa, 1958; PhD in Mech. Engring., Exptl. R&D Inst. Machine Tools, Moscow, 1973. Mfg. engr. Factory of Machine Tools, Odessa, 1958-66; sr. scientist R&D Inst. ENIMS, Moscow, 1966-87; cons. Beltran Assn., Inc., Bklyn., 1988-90; prof. mech. engring. Murray (Ky.) State U., 1990-92; cons. Russtrad, Inc., Richmond, Mass., 1992-93; prof. mech. engring. U. Turabo, Gurabo, P.R., 1993-94, CCNY, 1994—. Author: Fine-Boring Heads, 1972, Spindle Heads for Precision Tools, 1975; contbr. articles to profl. jours. Mem. ASME, Soc. Mfg. Engrs. (sr. mem.), Am. Soc. Engring. Edn. Republican. Jewish. Achievements include patents for tool holders for machine tools. Home: 868 E 24 St Brooklyn NY 11210 Office: CCNY Convent Ave at 135 St New York NY 10031

VERHALEN, ROBERT DONALD, consultant; b. Chgo., July 6, 1935; s. William Joseph and Pearl Evelyn (Anderson) V.; m. Phyllis Scandridge, Jan. 11, 1958; children: Elizabeth L., David S. BA, U. Iowa, 1963; MPH, U. N.C., 1965, DrPH, 1972. Expediter Fansteel Metall. Corp., North Chicago, Ill., 1957-58; tech. writer Collins Radio Co., Cedar Rapids, Iowa, 1958-59; rsch. aide Dept. Physics and Astronomy, Iowa City, 1960-63; sanitarian Lake County Health Dept., Waukegan, Ill., 1963-64; cons. safety mgmt. Ga. Dept. Pub. Health, Atlanta, 1965-68; instr. U. N.C., Chapel Hill, 1968-70; chief task force Pres.'s Commn. on Product Safety, Washington, 1969-70; asst. dir. Bur. Product Safety FDA, Washington, 1970-73; assoc. dir. U.S. Consumer Product Safety Commn., Washington, 1973-95; pres. Verhalen & Assocs., McLean, Va., 1995—; chmn., CEO Docutrol, McLean, 1997—; guest lectr. Sch. Pub. Health U. N.C., Chapel Hill, 1975—, Walter Reed Army Med. Ctr., Washington, 1982—. Mem. editorial bd. Jour. Safety Rsch.; developer Nat. Electronic Injury Surveillance System; contbr. articles to profl. jours. Mem. Conservative Network, Washington, 1985—. Sgt. USMC, 1953-57. Mem. Am. Coll. Epidemiology, Soc. Epidemiologic Rsch., Am. Pub. Health Assn., Am. Statis. Assn., Sr. Exec.'s Assn., Sr. Exec. Svc. Lutheran. Avocation: sailing. Home: 7209 Matthew Mills Rd Mc Lean VA 22101 Office: Verhalen & Assocs Ste 300 6867 Elm St McLean VA 22101

VERHESEN, ANNA MARIA HUBERTINA, counselor; b. Heerenveen, Friesland, Netherland, Dec. 6, 1932; came to U.S., 1968; d. Hendrikus H. and Henrika C. (Kluessjen) V. BS, Mercy Coll. of Detroit, 1981; MA, Sienna Height, Adrian, Mich., 1992. Childcare worker Schiedam, Netherland, 1952-54; social worker Rotterdam Halfweg, Netherland, 1954-59; childcare worker Mt. St. Ann's Home, Worcester and Lawrence, Mass., 1968-70; chem. dependency social worker St. Vincent Med. Ctr., Toledo, Ohio, 1970-75; social worker St. Joseph Hosp., Nashua, N.H., 1975-78; vocation dir. Grey Nuns, Lexington, Mass., 1978-79; coord. community svcs. St. Vincents Med. Ctr., Toledo, 1981-91; pvt. practice clin. therapist Sylvania, Ohio, 1992—; alcohol/drug addiction/mental health counselor for ex-prisoners; founder St. Vincent Med. Ctr. Alcoholism Detox and Rehab. Unit, Toledo, 1970-75. Co-founder Transitional Residences for the Homeless, Toledo, 1981-90, Ohio Coalition for the Homeless, Columbus, 1982-89; co-founder of a home for persons with AIDS; co-chair City of Toledo Housing Policy, 1985-90; coord. Housing Now, Toledo, 1988-90. Recipient Woman of Achievement award Women in Communication, Toledo, 1986, Spirit of '87 award N.W. Ordinance and U.S. Constn. Bicentennial Commn., Toledo, 1987, Gov.'s Spl. Recognition award, 1988, Man for Others award St. John's High Sch., 1991; named Woman of Toledo, St. Vincent Med. Ctr. Aux., 1988, Ohio Ho. of Reps., 1987; featured in various mags. Roman Catholic. Home: 219 Page St Toledo OH 43620-1430 Office: Elliott and Assocs Inc 5600 Monroe St Sylvania OH 43560-2731

VERHEY, JOSEPH WILLIAM, psychiatrist, educator; b. Oakland, Calif., Sept. 28, 1928; s. Joseph Bernard and Anne (Hanken) V.; BS summa cum laude, Seattle U., 1954; MD, U. Wash., 1958; m. Darlene Helen Seiler, July 21, 1956. Intern, King County Hosp., Seattle, 1958-59; resident Payne Whitney Psychiatric Clinic, N.Y. Hosp., Cornell Med. Center, N.Y.C., 1959-62, U. Wash. Hosp., Seattle, 1962-63; pvt. practice, Seattle, 1963-78; mem. staff U. Providence Hosp., 1963-78, Fairfax Hosp., 1963-78, VA Med. Center, Tacoma, 1978-83, chief inpatient psychiatry sect., 1983—; clin. instr. psychiatry U. Wash. Med. Sch., 1963-68, clin. asst. prof. psychiatry, 1968-82, clin. assoc. prof., 1982—; cons. psychiatry U.S. Dept. Def., Wash. State Bur. Juvenile Rehab.; examiner Am. Bd. Psychiatry and Neurology. Diplomate Am. Bd. Psychiatry and Neurology. Fellow N. Pacific Soc. Psychiatry and Neurology, Am. Psychiat. Assn.; mem. AMA, Am. Fedn. Clin. Rsch., World Fedn. Mental Health, Soc. Mil. Surgeons of U.S., Wash. Athletic Club, Swedish Club (life). Home: 1100 University St Seattle WA 98101 Office: VA Med Ctr Tacoma WA 98493

VERHEYEN, EGON, art historian, educator; b. Duisburg, Germany, Apr. 13, 1936; came to U.S., 1966; s. Franz and Klara (Läufer) V.; children: Peter David, Gero, Esther. Student, U. Mainz, Germany, 1956-58; Ph.D., U. Würzburg, Fed. Republic Germany, 1962. With German Nat. Museum, Nuremberg, 1961; Herodotos mem. Inst. for Advanced Study, Princeton, N.J., 1962-63, mem., 1983; research fellow Bayerische Staatsgemäldesammlungen, Munich, Fed. Republic Germany, 1965-66; asst. prof. history of art U. Mass., Amherst, 1966; asst. prof. U. Mich., Ann Arbor, 1967-70; assoc. prof. U. Mich., 1970-72; prof. dept history of art Johns Hopkins, 1972-87, chmn. dept., 1972-76; Clarence J. Robinson prof. humanities George Mason U., 1987—; research fellow Bibliotheca Hertziana, Rome, Italy, 1963-65; bd. dirs. Univ. Press Va. Author: Minoritenkirche Duisburg, 1959, Goldene Evangelienbuch von Echternach, 1963, Studiolo of Isabella d'Este, 1971, Palazzo del Te in Mantua, 1977; bd. editors: Emblemata, Architectura. Max Planck Gesellschaft grantee, 1963-65; Horace H. Rackham Found. grantee, 1968, 70; NEH grantee, 1972, 76, 77, 85, 90; Fritz Thyssen Gesellschaft grantee, 1965-66; U. Mich. travel grantee, 1971-72; Office Rsch. Adminstrn. grantee, 1971. Mem. Soc. Archtl. Historians (v.p. Latrobe chpt. 1990-91), Am. Goethe Soc. (pres. Md. chpt. 1984-86), Coll. Art Assn., Soc. for Emblem Studies, Internat. Soc. Classical Tradition. Office: MS1D6 George Mason U Fairfax VA 22030-4444

VERHOEK, SUSAN ELIZABETH, botany educator; b. Columbus, Ohio, 1942; m. S.E. Williams; 1 child. Student, Carleton Coll., 1960-62; BA, Ohio Wesleyan U., 1964; MA, Ind. U., 1966; PhD, Cornell U., 1975. Herbarium supr. Mo. Bot. Garden, St. Louis, 1966-70; asst. prof. Lebanon Valley Coll., Annville, Pa., 1974-82, assoc. prof., 1982-85, prof., 1985—; vis. researcher Cornell U., Ithaca, N.Y., 1982-83; content cons. Merrill Pub. Co., 1987-89; vis. profl. Chgo. Bot. Garden, 1991. Author: How to Know the Spring Flowers, 1982; contbr. articles to profl. jours., newspapers, and bulls. Trustee Lebanon Valley Coll., Annville, 1979-82, 84-90, 92—; dir. Lebanon Valley Coll. Arboretum, 1996—. Mem. Soc. for Econ. Botany (pres. 1985-86), Bot. Soc. Am., Am. Soc. Plant Taxonomists, Am. Assn. Bot. Gardens and Arboreta. Office: Lebanon Valley Coll Dept Botany Annville PA 17003-0501

VERHOEVEN, PAUL, film director; b. Amsterdam, Netherlands, July 18, 1938. PhD in Maths., Physics, U. Leiden. Dir. (films) Wat Zien Ik?, 1971, Turkish Delight, 1973, Keetje Tippel, 1975, Spetters, 1981, The Fourth Man, 1983, Robocop, 1987, Total Recall, 1990, Basic Instinct, 1992, Showgirls, 1995, Starship Troopers, 1996, Crusade, 1996, (episode of TV series) Hitchhiker (TV series) Floris, 1969, (documentary with the Royal Netherlands Navy) Het Korps Mariniers, 1965; dir., co-screenwriter Soldier of Orange, 1979, Flesh and Blood, 1985. Office: care Marion Rosenberg 8428 Melrose Pl Ste C West Hollywood CA 90069-5308 also: Robert Brenner Brenner & Glassberg 2049 Century Park E Ste 2450 Los Angeles CA 90067-3111*

VERING, JOHN ALBERT, lawyer; b. Marysville, Kans., Feb. 6, 1951; s. John Albert and Bernadine E. (Kieffer) V.; m. Ann E. Arman, June 28, 1980; children: Julia Ann, Catherine Ann, Mary Ann. BA summa cum laude, Harvard U., 1973; JD, U. Va., 1976. Bar: Mo. 1976, U.S. Dist. Ct. (we. dist.) Mo. 1976, U.S. Ct. Appeals (10th cir.), 1980, U.S. Ct. Appeals (4th cir.) 1987, Kans. 1990, U.S. Dist. Ct. Kans. 1990; arbitrator, mediator, Mo., Kans. Assoc. Dietrich, Davis, Dicus, Rowlands, Schmitt & Gorman, Kansas City, Mo., 1976-81, ptnr., 1982—. Editor: U. Va. Law Rev., 1974-76. Bd. dirs. Greater Kansas City YMCA Southwest Dist., 1987. Mem. Harvard Club (schs. com. Kansas City 1977-97, v.p. 1981-82, 92-93, pres. 1994-96). Democrat. Roman Catholic. Home: 1210 W 68th Ter Kansas City MO 64113-1904 Office: Armstrong Teasdale Schlafy & Davis 1700 City Ctr S 2345 Grand Blvd Ste 2000 Kansas City MO 64108-9999

VERINK, ELLIS DANIEL, JR., metallurgical engineering educator, consultant; b. Peking, China, Feb. 9, 1920; s. Ellis Daniel and Phoebe Elizabeth (Smith) V.; m. Martha Eulala Owens, July 4, 1942; children: Barbara Ann, Wendy Susan. B.S., Purdue U., 1941; M.S., Ohio State U., 1963, Ph.D., 1965. Registered profl. engr., Fla., Pa., Calif. Mgr. chem. sect., sales devel. div. Alcoa, New Kensington, Pa., 1946-59; mgr. chem. and petroleum indsl. sales Alcoa, Pitts., 1959-62; assoc. prof. metall. engring. U. Fla., Gainesville, 1965-68, prof. materials sci. and engring., 1968—; disting. service prof. U. Fla., 1984-91; prof. emeritus U. Fla., Gainesville, 1991—; pres. Materials Cons., Inc., 1970—; cons. Aluminum Assn., Washington, 1966-84; mem. U.S. nuclear waste tech. rev. bd., 1989-97. Author: Corrosion Testing Made Easy, The Basics, 1993; editor: Methods of Materials Selections, 1968, Material Stability and Environmental Degradation, 1988; contbr. articles to profl. jours. Pres. Gainesville YMCA, 1977. Recipient Sam Tour award ASTM, 1979, Donald E. Marlowe award Am. Soc. Engring. Edn., 1991; recipient Disting. Alumnus award Ohio State U., 1982, Disting. Faculty award Fla. Blue Key, 1983; named Tchr.-Scholar of Year U. Fla., 1979. Fellow Metall. Soc. of AIME (pres. 1984, Educator of Yr. award 1988), Am. Soc. Materials Internat., Nat. Assn. Corrosion Engrs. Internat. (bd. dirs. 1984-87, Willis Rodney Whitney award; mem. Masons, Shriners, Kiwanis, Sigma Xi, Tau Beta Pi. Republican. Presbyterian. Home: 4401 NW 18th Pl Gainesville FL 32605-3423 Office: U Fla Dept Materials Sci Eng Gainesville FL 32611

VERKADE, JOHN GEORGE, inorganic/organic chemistry educator, researcher; b. Chgo., Jan. 15, 1935; widowed; 3 children. BS, U. Ill., 1956, PhD in Inorganic Chemistry, 1960; AM, Harvard U., 1957. Sloan fellow, 1966-68; instr. to assoc. prof. Iowa State U., Ames, 1960-70, prof. inorganic chemistry, 1970—. Grantee NSF, 1961—, Petroleum Rsch. Found., 1963-66, 89—, NIH, 1972-78, DOE 1987-90, 92-97. Mem. Am. Chem. Soc., Sigma Xi. Office: Iowa State U Dept Chemistry 1275 Gilman Ames IA 50011-2010

VERKOUTEREN, ROBERT MICHAEL, chemist; b. Washington, Jan. 11, 1955; s. Theodore Robert and Marguerite (Norling) V.; m. Jennifer Renee Dennis, Feb. 6, 1988; children: Bryan Dennis, Lydia Ellen. BS, Tufts U., 1977; PhD, Purdue U., 1984. Rsch. chemist, sci. advisor Nat. Inst. Stds. and Tech., Gaithersburg, Md., 1984—; cons. Radon Testing Corp. Am., Elmsford, N.Y., 1986-88, Internat. Atomic Energy Agy., Vienna, Austria, 1993—. Contbr. article to profl. publs. Recipient Postdoctoral Rsch. award NRC, 1984-86. Mem. Am. Chem. Soc., Toastmasters Internat. (club pres. 1989-90, Advanced Toastmaster award 1997). Avocations: piano, sailing. Home: 14613 Dodie Ter Darnestown MD 20878-3978 Office: Nat Inst Stds and Tech Chem Sci & Tech Lab Analyt Chemistry Gaithersburg MD 20899

VERLICH, JEAN ELAINE, writer, public relations consultant; b. McKeesport, Pa., July 5, 1950; d. Matthew Louis and Irene (Tomko) V.; m. S(tanley) Wayne Wright, Sept. 29, 1979 (div. June 1988). Student, Bucknell U., 1968-69; BA, U. Pitts., 1971. Press sec. Com. to Re-elect President, S.W. Pa., 1972; adminstrv. asst. Pa. Rep. James B. Kelly III, 1972-73; reporter Beaver (Pa.) County Times, 1973-74; proofreader Ketchum, MacLeod & Grove, Pitts., 1975-76; community rels. specialist, PPG Industries, Pitts., 1976-77, editor PPG News, 1977-79, sr. staff writer, 1979-84, comm. coord., 1984-85; pub. rels. assoc. Glass Group, 1986-87; mgr. pub. rels. Glass Group PPG Industries, 1987-92; account mgr. Maddigan Comm., Pitts., 1992-93; owner JV Comm., Pitts., 1993—. Mem. Internat. Assn. Bus. Communicators (bd. dir. Pitts. chpt. 1981, v.p. pub. rels. Pitts. chpt. 1982, v.p. programs Pitts. chpt. 1985, pres. Pitts. chpt. 1986), Travelers Aid Soc. Pitts. (bd. dirs. 1992-95, v.p. 1994-95), Phi Beta Kappa, Delta Zeta. Office: JV Comm 3 Gateway Ctr Ste 1526 Pittsburgh PA 15222-1004

VERMA, RAM SAGAR, geneticist, educator, author, administrator; b. Barabanki, India, Mar. 3, 1946; came to the U.S., 1972; s. Gaya Prasad and Late Moonga (Devi) V.; m. Shakuntala Devi, May 4, 1962; children: Harendra K., Narendra K. BSc, Agra U., India, 1965, MSc in Quantitative Genetics, 1967; PhD in Cytogenetics, U. Western Ont., London, Ont., Can., 1972; diploma clinical cytogenetics, The Royal Coll. Pathologists, London, 1984. Diplomate The Royal Coll of Pathologists, London; lic. dir. clin. Cytogenetics, N.Y.C. and N.Y. state. Rsch. and teaching asst. dept. plant scis. U. Western London, Ont., Can., 1967-73; postdoctoral rsch. assoc. cytogenetics U. Colo. Dept. of Pediatrics, Denver, 1973-76; instr. to prof. human cytogenetics dept. of medicine Health Sci. Ctr. SUNY, Bklyn., 1976—, prof. dept. anatomy and cell biology, 1988—; chief cytogenetics div. hematology and cytogenetics Interfaith Med. Ctr. (formerly Jewish Hosp. and Med. Ctr. Bklyn.), 1980-86; chief div. genetics L.I. Coll. Hosp., Bklyn., 1986—; cons. WHO, Switzerland, 1982, Nat. Geog. Soc., Washington, 1982, Phototake, 1982-87; mem. cytogenetic adv. com. Prenatal Diagnosis Lab. N.Y.C. Dept. Health, 1978-90, Genetic Task Force N.Y. State, N.Y.C., 1976—; reviewer grants Nat. and Internat. Health Agys. and Socs.; lectr. colls., univs. and profl. assns. Author: Heterochromatin: Molecular and Structural Aspects, 1988, The Genome, 1990, (with A. Babu) Human Chromosomes: Manual of Basic Techniques, 1989, Human Chromosomes: Principles and Techniques; editor-in-chief: Advances in Genome Biology, 1989; contbr. over 350 abstracts and presentations and over 350 articles to profl. publs. including Am. Jour. Ob.-Gyn., Blood, Jour. Med. Genetics, Japanese Jour, Human Genetics, Oncology, Cytobios, Am. Jour. Human Genetics, Am. Jour. clin. Oncology, Internat. Jour. Cancer, Chromosoma, Cytogenetics. Apptd. to Adv. Coun. to Asst. Commr. City of N.Y. Dept. Health, Bur. Lab. Svcs., 1988. Nat. Merit scholar Gov. India, 1964-67, 1965-67; rsch. scholar Nat. Rsch. Coun. Can. and U. Western Ont., 1967-72, also teaching assistantship, 1972-73; rsch. grantee N.Y. State Dept. Health, Albany, 1985, 85-86, Cancer Treatment Fund, Cornell Med. Coll., 1985-86, United Leukemia Fund, Cornell Med. Coll., 1985-86, 86-87, Nat. Cancer Inst. of Health, Md., 1985-86, 86-87, 97-88, 88-90, Nat. Cancer Inst., 1976-77, 77-78, 78-80. Fellow AAAS, Royal Coll. Pathologists London, Assn. Clin. Scientists, The Inst. of Biology, N.Y. Acad. Scis., N.Y. Acad. Medicine (assoc.); mem. Am. Assn. Clin. Rsch., Am. Fedn. Clin. Rsch., Am. Genetic Assn. (life), Am. Soc. Cell Biology, Am. Soc. Human Genetics (life), European Soc. Human Genetics, Fedn. Am. Scientists, Genetic Soc. Am., Genetic Soc. Can., Genetic Toxicology Assn., Internat. Assn. Human Biologists, Indian Soc. Human Genetics (life), Soc. Exptl. Biology and Medicine. Achievements include research in differentiation of eukaryotic chromosomes with special interest on molecular aspects of structural organization of hetero-and euchromatin, cytological detection of cell damage using old and new classical methods of cytogenetics, application of animal models to understand the human genetic diseases, mechanisms of human cancer using DNA probes and blotting techniques, application of various banding techniques in basic and clinical cytogenetics, automation of human genome using computers. Home: 45-38 Springfield Blvd Bayside NY 11361-3556 Office: The L I Coll Hosp Div of Genetics Divsn Genetics Brooklyn NY 11201

VERMA, SURJIT K., school system administrator; b. India, May 17, 1940; arrived in Canada 1966; s. Sohara Lal and Gian Devi V.; m. Raj Verma; 1 child, Soania. MEd, St. Francis Xavier U., N.S., 1975; postgrad., Dalhousie U., N.S., U. Ottawa, Ont., Can, 1979. Cert. tchr. Nova Scotia. Sci. dept. head Halifax County Bedford Dist. Sch. Bd., N.S., Canada, 1968-88, curriculum supr., 1988—; served on C.T.F. Project Overseas Can. Teams, W.I., Nigeria, 1976, 77; mem. provincial sci. task force, biology rev. com., elem. sci.; mem. Internat. Sci. Symposium, 1979; worksop presenter numerous sci. workshops. Contbr. to profl. jours. Chmn. First Metro Halifax Dartmouth Reg Sci. Fair, 1975; co-chmn. Canada Wide Sci Fair, 1984. Recipient Sci. Tchg. Achievement Recognition award U.S. Nat. Sci. Tchrs. Assn. and Am. Gas Assn., 1993, Profl. Devel. award N.S. Tchrs. Union, Tchg. Excellence in Sci., Tech. and Math. award Prime Min. Can., 1993, 94, Sci. on Display award NASCO, 1993-94, Outstanding Achievement in Sci. Edn. award Halifax County Sch. Bd., 1993, Surjit Verma award for tchg. excellence created in his honor Halifax County Bedrod Dist. Sch. Bd., 1994, Michael Smith award Industry Can., 1996; U. Ottawa fellow, 1979, Dalhousie U. grad. fellow, 1980, Math. Sci. Tech. Edn. fellow Royal Bank Queen's U., 1994; Dalhousie U. Rsch. Devel. grantee, 1979; N.S. Tchrs. Union scholar, 1979; Can./N.S. Tech. Devel. grantee, 1995. Mem. Nat. Sci. Tchrs. Assn., Nova Scotia Assn. Sci. Tchrs., Nova Scotia Assn. Curriculum Suprs., Assn. for Suprs. and Curriculum Devel. (provincial sci. 10 task force and rev. com.). Avocations: jogging, yoga. Home: 49 Rosewood Ave, Timberlea, NS Canada B3T 1C6

VERMEER, MAUREEN DOROTHY, sales executive; b. Bronxville, N.Y., Mar. 21, 1945; d. Albert Casey and Helen (Valentine Casey) Vermeer; m. John R. Fassnacht, Feb. 11, 1966 (div. 1975); m. George M. Dallas Peltz IV, Oct. 26, 1985. Grad., NYU Real Estate Inst., 1976. Lic. real estate broker, notary pub., N.Y. With Douglas Elliman, N.Y.C., 1965-74, mgmt. supr., 1974-78, v.p., 1978-83; real estate broker Rachmani Corp., N.Y.C., 1983-84; v.p. sales and mktg. Carol Mgmt. Corp., N.Y.C., 1984-90; v.p. mktg. The Sunshine Group, N.Y.C., 1990; v.p., sec., bd. dirs. H.J. Kalikow & Co., N.Y.C., 1991—; mem. Real Estate Bd. N.Y.; speaker in field. Mem. Real Estate Bd. N.Y. (bd. dirs., residential mgmt. com.), Assn. Real Estate Women (sec., bd. dirs.). Republican. Presbyterian. Avocations: skiing, scuba diving. Home: 111 Broadway Norwood NJ 07648-1412 Office: H J Kalikow & Co 101 Park Ave New York NY 10178

VERMERSCH-DOUGLASS, SUSAN MARIE, nurse; b. San Antonio, Sept. 6, 1948; d. Robert Henry and Doris Inez (Thomas) Vermersch; married Edward; children: Lauren Marie, Christopher Michael; stepchildren: Jennifer, Michael. Diploma nursing, Brackenridge Hosp., Austin, Tex., 1969; BS in Nursing, U. Tex. Health Sci. Ctr., 1972, MS in Nursing, 1986. Staff nurse Med. Ctr. Hosp., San Antonio, 1969-72, clinician II, 1972-79, per diem coordinator, 1979-80, clinician III, 1980-81, dir. area I, 1981-82, adminstrv. dir. emergency ctr., 1982-95; adminstrv. dir. Regional Trauma System, San Antonio, 1995—. Active Conservation Soc., San Antonio, 1983—, March of Dimes, San Antonio, 1985-86; bd. dirs. Alamo Area Rape Crisis Ctr., 1986-88, pres., 1989; chair San Antonio Safe Kids Coalition, 1997; chair Trauma Coordinators Trauma Svc.; chair Pub. Info. Edn. Com. Recipient Dean Patty Hawken award for excellence in nursing adminstrn., 1994. Mem. Nat. League for Nursing, Emergency Nurses Assn. (San Antonio chpt., pres. 1987, sec. 1990—), Tex. Emergency Nurses Assn. (bd. dirs. 1989, sec. 1990—, pres. 1992), Nat. Emergency Nurses Assn. (nomination com. 1992, by-laws rev. com. 1992), U. Tex. San Antonio Nursing Sch. Alumni Assn. (bd. dirs. 1988-90), Sigma Theta Tau (Image Maker award 1994). Democrat. Roman Catholic. Home: 3539 Huntwick San Antonio TX 78230 Office: Univ Health Care Sys 4502 Medical Dr San Antonio TX 78229-4402

VERMETTE, RAYMOND EDWARD, clinical laboratories administrator; b. Lewiston, Maine, June 30, 1942; s. Edward Louis and Anna Lucy (Raymond) V.; m. Ernestine Pero, Dec. 28, 1963; children: Tamara, Gregory. BS in Bacteriology, U. Maine, 1964; MS in Biochemistry, U. Wis., 1966; cert. personnel mgmt. Va. Dept. Edn., Fairfax, 1969; MBA, Temple U., 1973; master tchrs.' cert., Cath. Diocese of Boston, 1981. Supr. animal toxicology Hazleton Labs., Vienna, Va., 1967-71; personnel mgr. Damon Clin. Lab., Phila., 1971-73, ops. mgr., 1973-75, gen. mgr., Needham, Heights, Mass., 1975-90; v.p. ops. Damon Corp., Needham Hts., 1983-87, corp. v.p., 1987-89, sr. v.p., 1990-93; sr. v.p., gen. mgr. Corning/MetPath, Westwood, Mass., 1994-95; ret. 1995; vis. lectr fin. mgmt. and bus. adminstrn. Framingham State Coll., 1978-84; instr. mgmt. Newbury Jr. Coll., Boston, 1976-79. Author: (with B. Kliman and E. Kolowrat) What You Should Know About Medical Lab Tests, 1979. V.p. fin. com. Framingham, Mass., 1982-84; mem. capital budget com., Town of Framingham, 1987; mem.-elect, Town Meeting, 1987—, mem. Govt. Study Com., 1995-97, mem. fin. com., 1997—; chmn. bd. religious edn. Cath. Ch., Framingham, 1981-84, co-chmn. Pre-Marriage Preparation Council, 1981—, organist, 1979—. Democrat. Home: 11 Willowbrook Dr Framingham MA 01702-5515

VERMEULE, CORNELIUS CLARKSON, III, museum curator; b. Orange, N.J., Aug. 10, 1925; s. Cornelius Clarkson, Jr. and Catherine Sayre (Comstock) V.; m. Emily Dickinson Townsend, Feb. 2, 1957; children—Emily D. Blake, Cornelius Adrian Comstock. Grad., Pomfret Sch., 1943; A.B., Harvard, 1949, M.A., 1951; Ph.D., U. London, Eng., 1953; DHL (hon.), Boston Coll., 1995. Instr. fine arts, then asst. prof. U. Mich., 1953-55; asst. prof. classical archaeology Bryn Mawr (Pa.) Coll., 1955-57; curator classical art Mus. Fine Arts, Boston, 1956-96, curator emeritus, 1996—; acting dir. Mus. Fine Arts, 1972-73; assoc. curator coins Mass. Hist. Soc., 1965-71, curator, 1971—; lectr. fine arts Smith Coll., 1960-64, Boston U., Harvard, Wellesley Coll.; vis. prof. Yale, 1969-70, 72-73; Thomas Spencer Jerome lectr. U. Mich., 1975-76; vis. prof. Boston Coll., 1978-97; vis. prof. U. Aberdeen, Scotland, 1993; pres. Internat. Com. to Save Jewish Catabombs of Italy, 1980-84, chmn., 1984—. Author: (with N. Jacobs) Japanese Coinage, 1948, 2d edit., 1972, Bibliography of Applied Numismatics, 1956, The Goddess Roma, 1959, 2d edit., 1974, Dal Pozzo-Albani Drawings, 1960, European Art and the Classical Past, 1964, Drawings at Windsor Castle, 1966, Roman Imperial Art in Greece and Asia Minor, 1968, Polykleitos, 1969, Numismatic Art in America, 1971, (with M. Comstock) Greek Etruscan and Roman Bronzes, 1972, (with N. Neuerburg) Catalogue of the Ancient Art in the J. Paul Getty Museum, 1973, Greek and Roman Sculpture in Gold and Silver, 1974, Greek and Roman Cyprus, 1976, (with M. Comstock) Sculpture in Stone, 1976, Greek Sculpture and Roman Taste, 1977, Roman Art: Early Republic to Late Empire, 1978, (with A Herrmann) The Ernest Brummer Collections, Vol. II, 1979, Greek Art: Socrates to Sulla, 1980, The Jewish Experience in Roman Art, 1981, Masterpieces of Greek and Roman Sculpture in America, 1982, Greek Art: Prehistoric to Perikles, 1982, Numismatic Studies, 1983, Alexander the Great Conquers Rome, 1985, The Cult Images of Imperial Rome, 1986, Numismatic Art of the Greek Imperial World, 1987, Philatelic Art in America, 1987, (with M. Comstock) Sculpture in Stone and Bronze, 1988, (with A. Brauer) Stone Sculptures, The Greek, Roman and Etruscan Collections of the Harvard University Art Museums, 1990, (with others) Le Sport dans la Grèce Antique, 1992, Du Jeu à la Compétition, 1992, (with others) El Deporte en la Grecia Antigua, La génesis del olimpismo, 1992-93, (with others) Vase-Painting in Italy, 1993. Trustee Cardinal Spellman Philatelic Mus., 1980-93. Served to 1st lt. AUS, 1943-47. Recipient Bicentennial medal Boston Coll., 1976; Fulbright fellow, 1951-53; Guggenheim fellow, 1968. Fellow AAAS, Am. Numis. Soc. (life), Royal Numis. Soc., Soc. Antiquaries; mem. Coll. Art Assn. (life), Archaeol. Inst. Am. (life) German Archaeol. Inst., Holland Soc. N.Y., Colonial Lords of Manors in Am., Mass. Hist. Soc. (hon.). Republican. Episcopalian. Club: Tavern (medalist 1986) (Boston). Home: 47 Coolidge Hill Rd Cambridge MA 02138-5509 Office: Mus Fine Arts 465 Huntington Ave Boston MA 02115-5523 *To teach, collect and record the past, as exemplar for the present, as prologue to the future, can there be any better use of a historian's and archaeologist's professional life?.*

VERMEULE, EMILY TOWNSEND (MRS. CORNELIUS C. VERMEULE, III), classicist, educator; b. N.Y.C., Aug. 11, 1928; d. Clinton Blake and Eleanor (Meneely) Townsend; m. Cornelius C. Vermeule III, Feb. 2, 1957; children: Emily Dickinson Blake, Cornelius Adrian Comstock. AB, Bryn Mawr Coll., 1950; student, Am. Sch. Classical Studies, Athens, 1950-51, St. Anne's Coll., Oxford U., 1953; MA, Harvard, 1954; PhD, Bryn Mawr Coll., 1956; DLitt, Douglass Coll.; D. Litt., Rutgers U., 1968, Tufts U., 1980, U. Pitts., 1983, Bates Coll., 1983, U. Miami, Oxford, Ohio, 1986; LL.D., Regis Coll., 1971; D. Fine Arts, U. Mass, Amherst, 1971; D.Litt., Smith Coll., 1972, Wheaton Coll., 1973, Trinity Coll., 1974; LHD, Emmanuel Coll., 1980, Princeton U., 1989, Bard Coll., 1994. Instr. Greek lang. Bryn Mawr Coll., 1956-57; instr. Wellesley (Mass.) Coll., 1957-58, prof. art and Greek, 1965-70, chmn. dept. art, 1966-67; asst. prof. classics Boston U., 1958-61, assoc. prof. classics, 1961-65; fellow for research Boston Mus. Fine Arts, 1965—; James C. Loeb vis. prof. classical philology Harvard, 1969; dir. univ. Cyprus expdn. Harvard U., 1971—, Samuel and Doris Zemurray Stone-Radcliffe prof., 1970-94; prof. emerita and Sather prof. U. Calif., Berkeley, 1975; Geddes-Harrower prof. Greek art and archaeology U. Aberdeen, 1980-81; Bernhard vis. prof. Williams Coll., 1986; excavations in Greece, Turkey, Libya, Cyprus. Author: Euripides v. Electra, 1959, Greece in the Bronze Age, 1964, The Trojan War in Greek Art, 1964, Götterkult, 1974, Toumba tou Skourou, The Mound of Darkness, 1975, Death in Early Greek Art and Poetry, 1978, (with U. Karageorghis) Mycenaean Pictorial Vase-Painting, 1982, (with F.Z. Wolsky) Toumba tou Skourou, A Bronze Age Potters' Quarter on Morphou Bay in Cyprus, 1990; contbr. articles to scholarly publs. Judge Nat. Book Award, 1977; bd. dirs. Humanities Rsch. Inst., U. Calif., 1988-91, bd. govs., 1988-90; trustee Isabella Stewart Gardner Mus., 1988-96. Recipient Gold medal for disting. achievement Radcliffe Coll. Grad. Soc., 1968; Guggenheim fellow, 1964-65. Fellow Soc. Antiquaries, Brit. Acad. (corr.), German Archaeol. Inst. (corr.); mem. AAAS, Am. Inst. Archaeology, Am. Philos. Soc. (v.p. 1978-81), Am. Philol. Assn. (Charles J. Goodwin award 1980, pres. 1995), Smithsonian Coun. (bd. scholars 1983-89), Hellenic Soc.

VERMILYE, PETER HOAGLAND, banker; b. N.Y.C., Jan. 17, 1920; s. Herbert Noble and Elise Tace (Hillyer) V.; m. Lucy Shaw Mitchell, Oct. 14, 1950; children: Peter H., Dana R., Andrew R., Mary S. AB, Princeton U., 1940. V.p. pension investments J.P. Morgan & Co. and Morgan Guaranty Trust, 1940-64; ptnr. State St. Research & Mgmt., Boston, 1965-69; pres. Alliance Capital Mgmt., N.Y.C., 1970-77; sr. v.p., chief investment officer Citibank, N.Y.C., 1977-84; chmn. Baring Am. Asset Mgmt., Boston, 1984-89; sr. advisor Baring Asset Mgmt., 1990-95, Harbor Capital Mgmt., Boston, 1989-96; chmn. bd. dirs. Huntington Theatre, 1989-96; bd. dirs. Baring Puma Fund, Fosterlane Mgmt. Trustee Boston U., 1970—. Clubs: Brook, Somerset, Myopia. Home: 157 School St Manchester MA 01944-1236 also: 107 Chestnut St Boston MA 02108-1038 Office: Harbor Capital Mgmt 125 High St Fl 26 Boston MA 02110-2704

VERMYLEN, PAUL ANTHONY, JR., oil company executive; b. N.Y.C., Dec. 5, 1946; s. Paul Anthony and Nancy Primrose (Barr) V.; m. Robin S. Collins, Jan. 24, 1970; children: Robert T.C., Nancy Barr, Sarah Morgan, Paul Anthony III. AB, Georgetown U., 1968; MBA, Columbia U., 1971. V.p. Citibank N.A., N.Y.C., 1971-78; treas. Commonwealth Oil Refining Co., San Antonio, 1978-81; v.p. fin., chief fin. officer Commonwealth Oil Refining Co., 1981-82; v.p., chief fin. officer, dir. Meenan Oil Co., Inc., Syosset, N.Y., 1982-91, pres., 1992—; pres. Meenan Oil Co., L.P., 1992—; bd. dirs. Petroleum Industry Rsch. Found., 1992—. Bd. dirs. Huntington Arts Coun., N.Y., 1983-89, v.p., 1986-87, pres., 1987-89; bd. dirs. Cold Spring Harbor Whaling Mus., 1995—; bd. advisors Cold Spring Harbor Lab. DNA Learning Ctr., 1991—. Mem. Empire State Petroleum Assn. (bd. dirs. 1994—), Cold Spring Harbor Beach Club, Seawanhaka Corinthian Yacht Club, N.Y. Yacht Club. Office: 6900 Jericho Tpke Syosset NY 11791-4407

VERNBERG, FRANK JOHN, marine and biological sciences educator; b. Fenton, Mich., Nov. 6, 1925; s. Sigurd A. and Edna (Anderson) V.; m. Winona M. Bortz, Sept. 7, 1945; children—Marcia Lynn, Eric Morrison, Amy Louise. A.B., DePauw U., 1949, M.A., 1950; Ph.D., Purdue U., 1951. Prof. zoology Duke Marine Lab., Beaufort, N.C., 1951-69; Belle W. Baruch prof. marine ecology, dir. Bell W. Baruch Marine Biology and Coastal Rsch. Inst., Columbia, 1969-96; interim dean Coll. Sci. and Math. Belle W. Baruch Coastal Research Inst., U. S.C., Columbia, 1993-94; dean Sch. of Environment U. S.C., Columbia, 1995-96, disting. prof. emeritus, 1996—; vis. prof. U. Coll. West Indies, Jamaica, 1957-58, U. Sao Paulo, Brazil, 1965; program dir. exptl. analytical biogeography of sea Internat. Biol. Program, 1967-69; mem. com. manned orbital research lab. Am. Inst. Biol. Scis.-NASA, 1966-68; pres. Estuarine Research Fedn., 1975-77. Contbr. articles to profl. jours.; spl. editor: Am. Zoologist, 1963; mem. editorial bd.: Biol. Bull., 1977-80; editor: Jour. Exptl. Marine Biology and Ecology, 1978—. Served with USNR, 1944-46. Recipient W.S. Proctor award Sigma Xi, 1983, award Drug Sci. Found., 1987; Guggenheim fellow, 1957-58; Fulbright-Hayes fellow, 1965. Fellow AAAS, Am. Soc. Zoologists (sec.-treas. divsn. comparative physiologists 1959-61, sec.-treas. edn. com. 1960-62, mem. coun. 1965-67, pres. 1982), Southeastern Estuarine Rsch. Soc. (pres. 1974-76), So. Assn. Marine Labs. (pres. 1993), Estuarine Rsch. Fedn. (pres. 1975-77), S.C. Wildlife Fedn. (Conservationist of Yr. 1983). Office: U SC Belle W Baruch Coastal Rsch Inst Columbia SC 29208

VERNER, JAMES MELTON, lawyer; b. Selma, Ala., Sept. 19, 1915; s. Singleton Foster and Jennie (Harris) V.; m. Gretchen Gores, Aug. 12, 1939; children: Ann Verner Picardo, James Singleton, William Melton. Student,

Biltmore Coll., 1932-34; A.B., U. N.C., 1936, LL.B., 1938. Bar: N.C. 1938, Tenn. 1947, D.C. 1950, Va., 1986. Assoc. firm Gover & Covington, Charlotte, N.C., 1938; law clk. atty. gen. N.C., 1938-40; atty. CAB, Washington, 1940-43; asst. gen. counsel Chgo. & So. Airlines, Memphis, 1946-47; atty. Air Transport Assn. Am., Washington, 1947-49; hearing examiner CAB, 1949-50, exec. asst. to chmn., 1950, exec. dir., 1950-53; atty. Turney & Turney, 1953-60, ptnr., 1954-60; ptnr. firm Verner, Liipfert, Bernhard, McPherson & Hand, Chartered (and predecessor firms), 1960-88, hon. mem. bd. dirs., 1988—; mem. policy adv. bd. Legal Counsel for the Elderly, Washington. Assoc. editor: N.C. Law Rev, 1937-38. Former mem., chmn. policy bd. Legal Counsel for Elderly, Washington. Served as lt. (j.g.) USNR, 1943-46; legal officer Naval Air Transport Svc., 1945-46. Mem. ABA, Order of Golden Fleece, Cosmos Club (Washington). Home: 3618 N Nelson St Arlington VA 22207-5319 Office: 901 15th St NW Washington DC 20005-2327 *My belief is that if you treat other people fairly and trust them, you will seldom be disappointed and will be the better for it.*

VERNEY, JUDITH LA BAIE, health program administrator; b. Buffalo, Mar. 23, 1937; d. Arthur W. and Mary B. (Grant) La Baie; m. George R. Verney, Dec. 27, 1958; children: Michael, Timothy, Christopher. BSN, Russell Sage Coll., 1958; MS, Rutgers State U., Newark, 1977. Cert. clin. specialist, cmty. health nurse; cert. pub. mgr. State coord. provider svcs. Healthstart N.J. State Dept. Health, Trenton; dir. HealthStart, Trenton; coord. preventive and primary care svcs. N.J. State Dept. Health, 1993—; clin. instr. grad. nursing program Rutgers U.; clin. preceptor Grad. Nurse Program, Kean Coll. Mem. ANA, N.J. Pub. Health Assn., N.J. State Nurses Assn. (Cmty. Health Nurse of Yr. award 1986), Nat. Soc. Cert. Pub. Mgrs., N.J. Assn. Pub. Health Nurse Adminstrs., N.J. Nat. Svc. Corp. Commn., Sigma Theta Tau.

VERNEY, RICHARD GREVILLE, paper company executive; b. Providence, Aug. 24, 1946; s. Gilbert and Virginia Ruth (Piggott) V.; m. Dorothy Howard, Aug. 26, 1967; children: Virginia F., Elizabeth I., Heather B., Eric G. AB, Brown U., 1968. Mgmt. trainee Monadnock Paper Mills, Bennington, N.H., 1969-70, asst. gen. mgr., 1970, exec. v.p., 1970-76, pres., 1977-85, chmn., chief exec. officer, 1978—. Mem. exec. com. Crotched Mt. Found., Greenfield, N.H., 1974-87, trustee, 1974—; trustee St. George's Sch., Newport, R.I., 1978-93, chmn., 1985-89, hon. trustee, 1993—, Monadnock Cmty. Hosp., 1993—, v.p., 1997; trustee Nantucket Cons. Found., Inc., 1994—. Mem. Am. Forest and Paper Assn. (bd. dirs. 1991—, chmn. splty. packaging and indsl. div. 1984-85, chmn. exec. bd. pulp consumers div. 1980-82, chmn. cover and text exec. com. 1989-91), Bus. Industry Assn. N.H. (bd. dirs. 1991—), Sales Assn. Paper Industry, Boston Paper Trade Assn. (pres. 1985-86), Algonquin Club (Boston), Nantucket Yacht Club (Mass.), N.Y. Yacht Club (N.Y.C.). Republican. Episcopalian. Home: The Verney Farm Bennington NH 03442 Office: Monadnock Paper Mills Inc Antrim Rd Bennington NH 03442

VERNIER, RICHARD, educator, author; b. Clermont-Ferrand, France, Feb. 1, 1929; came to U.S., 1951; s. Marcel Eugene Vernier and Marie Josè Font; m. Kathleen Manion, July 14, 1962; children: Matthew, John, Stephan. Student in pre-med., Université de Bordeaux, France, 1949; AB, U. Calif., Berkeley, 1958, PhD, 1965. Instr. Mills Coll., Oakland, Calif., 1961-62; lectr. CCNY, 1962-63; asst. prof. San Diego State Coll., 1963-66, U. Wash., Seattle, 1966-72; prof. French Wayne State U., Detroit, 1973-92, prof. emeritus, 1993—; cons. NEH, 1989. Author: Paul Eluard, 1971, Le Feu Parmi les Arbres, 1981, Yves Bonnefoy, 1985, La Patience, 1986, Parcours amèricain, 1991; Naufrage À Munising, 1995; mem. editorial bd. Swiss-French Studies, Wolfville, N.S., 1981-87. With U.S. Army, 1952-54, Korea. Decorated chevalier Palmes Académiques, Republic of France, 1981, officier, 1990. Avocations: long walks, ancient music. Home: 1326 Marion St Enumclaw WA 98022-2623

VERNIERO, PETER, state attorney general; married; 1 child. BA summa cum laude, Drew U., 1981; JD, Duke U., 1984. Law clk. to Justice Robert L. Clifford, 1984; with Pitney, Hardin, Kipp & Szuch, Morristown, N.J., 1985-87; dir. Herold & Haines P.A., Warren, N.J.; chief counsel, chief of staff Gov. Christine Whitman, Trenton, N.J.; atty. gen. State of N.J., Trenton, 1996—; adj. prof. bus. law County Coll. Morris, 1986. Exec. dir. Rep. State Com., 1989-90. Office: Office Atty Gen Justice Complex CN 080 Trenton NJ 08625*

VERNON, ARTHUR, educational administrator; b. N.Y.C., May 31, 1947; s. Chester M. and Lillian (Rosenfeld) V.; m. Michele Hope Levinthal, June 8, 1969; children: Ari, Devora, Shamar, Ronit. AB, Hunter Coll., 1968; BHL, Hebrew Union Coll./Jewish Inst. Religion, 1972; MA, HUC-JIR, 1973. Prin. Solomon Schecter Day Sch., Teaneck, N.J., 1974-76; cons. Bd. Jewish Edn., Washington, 1976-78; asst. dir. Bur. Jewish Edn., Cleve., 1978-85; exec. dir. Bur. Jewish Edn., Houston, 1985-89; dept. dir. Jewish Edn. Svc. N.Am., N.Y.C., 1989—; mem. adv. bd. Am. Jewish com. Petschek Ctr., N.Y.C., 1989—; mem. ednl. adv. com. Jewish Nat. Fund, N.Y.C., 1991—. Author curriculum pamphlet AIDS: A Jewish Response, 1990; editor mag. Pedagogic Reporter, 1991-92, Agenda: Jewish Education, 1992—. Bd. dirs. Open Congregation, Inc., N.Y.C., 1989—, treas., 1993-95, pres. 1996—; vice chmn. nat. Jewish Com. on Scouting, Irving, Tex., 1991—. Mem. Coun. for Jewish Edn. (v.p. 1991-95, treas. 1995-96, pres. 1996—), Religious Edn. Assn., Coalition for Advancement of Jewish Edn. Home: 22 Mountain Way West Orange NJ 07052-3717 Office: Jewish Edn Svc N Am 730 Broadway New York NY 10003-9511

VERNON, CARL ATLEE, JR., retired wholesale food distributor executive; b. Topeka, Aug. 15, 1926; s. Carl Atlee and Capitola May (Jarboe) V.; m. Marion Leila Colton, May 7, 1950; children—Mary Catherine, Matthew Fowler, Susan Elizabeth. B.S., Yale U., 1947. Merchandising mgr. Fleming Cos., Topeka, 1957-61, dir. merchandising, 1961-66, dir. info. services, 1966-72, v.p. info. services, 1972-74, v.p. regional systems, 1974-79; sr. v.p. mktg. services Fleming Cos., Oklahoma City, 1979-88. Chmn. Shawnee County chpt. ARC, Topeka, Kans., 1957-58. Served to ensign USNR, 1944-46. Republican. Episcopalian. Avocations: golf; gardening; travel.

VERNON, DAVID HARVEY, lawyer, educator; b. Boston, Aug. 9, 1925; s. Bernard Nathan and Ida E. (Cohen) V.; m. Rhoda Louise Sterman, June 1, 1947; children: Amy Lynne, Charles Adam. AB, Harvard U., 1949, LLB, 1952; LLM, NYU, 1953, JSD, 1960; DCL (hon.), U. Durham, Eng., 1988. Bar: Mass. 1952, Iowa 1966. Instr. NYU, 1953-54; asst. prof. law U. Houston, 1954-55; from asst. prof. to prof. law U. N.Mex., Albuquerque, 1955-64; assoc. dean, prof. law U. Wash., Seattle, 1964-66; prof. law U. Iowa, 1966—, dean Coll. Law, 1966-71, A.D. Vestal prof. law, 1986—, acad. v.p., 1988-90; vis. prof. Sch. Law, Washington U., St. Louis, 1974-75, U. Durham (Eng.), fall 1980, Victoria U. Wellington, New Zealand, 1986; vis. scholar Sch. Law, Washington and Lee U., Lexington, Va., spring 1991, So. Tex. Coll. Law, spring 1993, U. Ala. Law sch., spring 1997. Editor: (with Depew) General State Food and Drug Law, Annotated, 1955, Title XIV of the American Law of Mining, 1960, Conflict of Laws: Cases, Problems and Essays, 1973, supplement, 1979, Contracts: Theory and Practice, 1980, 2d edit., 1991, Conflict of Law: Theory and Practice, 1982, 2d edit., 1991, (with Weinberg, Reynolds and Richmond) Conflict of Law: Cases, Materials and Problems, 1991. Bd. dirs. Wash. State affiliate ACLU, 1964-66, Iowa Civil Liberties Union, 1966-72. With USNR, 1943-46. Fulbright travel awardee, New Zealand, 1986. Mem. ABA (ho. of dels. 1986-91, trustee law sch. admission coun. 1985-86), Iowa Bar Assn., Assn. Am. Law Schs. (mem. exec. com. 1978-80, pres. 1983, editor Jour. Legal Edn. 1987-92). Home: 327 Koser Ave Iowa City IA 52246-3036 Office: U Iowa Coll Law Iowa City IA 52242

VERNON, LILLIAN, mail order company executive; b. Leipzig, Germany; d. Herman and Erna Menasche; children: Fred, David. DCS (hon.), Mercy Coll., Dobbs Ferry, N.Y., 1984, Coll. New Rochelle, DSc in Bus. Adminstrn. (hon.), Bryant Coll., LLD (hon.), Baruch Coll., LHD (hon), Old Dominion U., DCS (hon.) Mercy Coll., DCS (hon.) Coll. New Rochelle; D in Bus. Adminstrn. (hon.) Bryant Coll., LLD (hon.) Baruch Coll. CEOLillian Vernon, New Rochelle, N.Y., 1951—; lectr. in field. Contbr. articles to profl. jours. Bd. dirs. Westchester County Assn., N.Y., Mental Health Assn. Westchester County, Ctr. Preventive Psychiatry, Va. Opera, Children's Mus. Arts, Retinitis Pigmentosa Found.; trustee Coll. Human Svcs., Bryant Coll.; mem. adv. bd. Giraffe Project, Girl Scout Coun. Tidewater, Women's News; mem. bd. overseers Columbia U. Bus. Sch., NYU; mem. adv. com. Citizen Amb. Program; mem. bus. com. Met. Mus. Art; bd. govs. The Forum; mem. nat. com. The Kennedy Ctr. for Performing Arts, Washington; active The Ellis Island Reopening Com., Women's News Bd. Advisors; bd. govs. The Forum. Recipient Dist. Achievement award Lab. Inst. Merchandising, Entrepreneural award Women's Bus. Owners of N.Y., 1983, Bravo award YWCA, Woman of Achievement award Woman's News, Nat. Hero award Big Bros./Big Sisters, Legend in Leadership award Emory U., A Woman Who Has Made A Difference award Inter. Womens Forum, medal of honor Ellis Island, Bus. Leadership award Gannett Newspapers, Outstanding Bus. Leader award Northwood Inst., Congl. Record Commendation award, Crystal award Coll. Human Svcs., City of Peace award Bonds of Israel, Svc. award Sr. Placement Bur., Excellence award Westchester Assn. Women Bus. Owners, Commendation in Congl. Record, Magnificent Seven award Bus. and Profl. Women, Woman of Distinction award Birmingham So. Coll.; named Va. Press Women Newsmaker of Yr., Woman of Yr., Women's Direct Response Group and Westchester County Fedn. Women's Clubs, Hampton Roads Woman of Yr., So. New England Entrepreneur Yr., Bravo award YWCA; named to Acad. Women Achievers, YWCA, Direct Mktg. Assn. Hall of Fame. Mem. Am. Bus. Conf. (dir.), Am. Stock Exch. (listed co. adv. com.), Com. of 200, Women's Forum, Nat. Retail Fedn. (bd. dirs.), Lotos Club. Office: Lillian Vernon Corp 543 Main St New Rochelle NY 10801-7214

VERNON, MIKE, professional hockey player; b. Calgary, Canada, Feb. 24, 1963. With Detroit Red Wings; played in NHL All-Star game, 1988-91, 93; mem. Stanley Cup championship team, 1989. Named WHL Most Valuable Player, 1981-82, 82-83, WHL Top Goaltender, 1981-82, 82-83, WHL Player of the Yr., 1981-82; named to WHL All-Star first team, 1981-82, 82-83, CHL All-Star second team, 1983-84, The Sporting News All-Star second team, 1988-89, NHL All-Star second team, 1988-89. Office: care Detroit Red Wings 600 Civic Center Dr Detroit MI 48226-4408

VERNON, RAYMOND, economist, educator; b. N.Y.C., Sept. 1, 1913; s. Hyman and Lillian (Sonnenberg) V.; m. Josephine Stone, Aug. 9, 1935; children: Heidi, Susan Patricia. A.B. cum laude, CCNY, 1933; Ph.D., Columbia U., 1941; M.A. (hon.), Harvard, 1959. Statistician SEC, 1935-42, asst. dir. trading and exchange div., 1942-46; asst. chief internat. resources div. Dept. State, 1946-48; became adviser on comml. policy, 1948; dep. dir. Office of Econ. Def. and Trade Policy, 1951, acting dir., 1954; staff mem. joint Presdl. Congl. Commn. on Fgn. Econ. policy, 1953- 54; planning and control dir. Hawley and Hoops, Inc., 1954-56; dir. N.Y. Met. Region Study, 1956-59; prof. Harvard U. Bus. Sch., 1959-78, dir. Harvard Devel. Adv. Service, 1962-65, dir. Ctr. for Internat. Affairs, 1973-78, prof. internat. relations, 1978-83, prof. emeritus, 1983—; bd. dirs. Cambridge Energy Rsch. Assocs.; lectr. Am. U., 1946-48, Princeton U., 1954-55, Swarthmore Coll., 1955-56; adj. prof. Fletcher Sch. Law and Diplomacy., 1979-81; mem. Mission on Japanese Combines, Tokyo, 1946; mem. U.S. del. GATT, Geneva, 1950, Torquay, Eng., 1951, vice chmn. U.S. del., Geneva, 1952; spl. cons. to undersec. Dept. State, 1962, Dept. Treasury, 1978-79; participant UN Conf. on Regional Devel., Tokyo, 1958; vis. prof. World Bank, 1987. Author: Regulation of Stock Exchange Members, 1941, America's Trade Policy and GATT, 1954, Organizing for World Trade, 1956, (with Edgar M. Hoover) Anatomy of a Metropolis, 1959, Metropolis 1985, 1960, The Dilemma of Mexico's Development, 1963, Myth and Reality of Our Urban Problems, 1965, Manager in The International Economy, 1968, Sovereignty at Bay, 1971, Storm over the Multinationals, 1976, Two Hungry Giants, 1983, Exploring the Global Economy, 1985, (with D.L. Spar) Beyond Globalism, 1988; editor: Public Policy and Private Enterprise in Mexico, 1964, How Latin America Views the U.S. Investor, 1966, The Technology Factor in International Trade, 1970, Big Business and the State, 1974, The Oil Crisis, 1976, State-owned Enterprises in the Western Economies, 1980, The Promise of Privatization, 1988, (with D.L. Spar and Glenn Tobin) Iron Triangles and Revolving Doors, 1991, (with Ethan Kapstein) Defense and Dependence in a Global Economy, 1992; founding editor Jour. Policy Analysis and Mgmt., 1981-85; contbr. articles to profl. jours. Recipient Meritorious Svc. award Dept. State, 1951, Disting. Svc. award Harvard Bus. Sch., 1986; decorated Order of Rising Sun (Japan), 1986; named Eminent scholar Internat. Studies Assn., 1994. Fellow Am. Acad. Arts and Scis., Acad. Internat. Bus.; mem. Council on Fgn. Relations, U.S./UN Assn., Phi Beta Kappa. Home: 1 Dunstable Rd Cambridge MA 02138-3341 Office: Harvard U Kennedy Sch Govt 79 Jfk St Cambridge MA 02138-5801

VERNON, SHIRLEY JANE, architect, educator; b. Mt. Kisco, N.Y., Dec. 9, 1930; d. J.H. and M.R. (Maher) V. B.Arch. cum laude, Pa. State U., 1953. Asso., coordinating architect for design, designer Vincent G. Kling and Assos., Phila., 1953-68; pvt. practice architecture Phila., 1968-74, 75—; mgr. archtl. design Ballinger Co., Phila., 1974-75; instr. architecture Drexel U., 1956-58, adj. asst. prof., 1959-64, adj. asso. prof., 1965-69, adj. prof., 1970-87; sr. advisor Phila. Coll. Art, 1980-81; prof. Moore Coll. Art and Design (formerly Moore Coll. Art), 1986-96, prof. emerita, 1996—. Recipient 25 Yr. Service award Drexel U., 1982. Fellow AIA (chpt. dir. 1973, 79, chpt. v.p. 1975); mem. Art Alliance Phila., Assn. Collegiate Schs. Architecture, EFAIA, Phila. Mus. Art, Tau Beta Pi. Office: 1704 Delancey St Philadelphia PA 19103-6715

VERNON, WESTON, III (WES VERNON), freelance journalist; b. N.Y.C., Aug. 23, 1931; s. Weston, Jr. and Adelaide (Neilson) V.; m. Alida Steinvoort, Oct. 5, 1951; children: Rosanne, Weston IV, Diane, John Randall. Student, Utah State U., 1949-50, Brigham Young U., 1953-54. Reporter, producer KBUH, Brigham City, Utah, 1950-51, KVRS, Rock Springs, Wyo., 1952, KOVO, Provo, Utah, 1952-54, Intermountain Network, Salt Lake City, 1954, KLO, Ogden, Utah, 1954, KBMY, Billings, Mont., 1954-63; news dir.-polit. specialist KSL Radio-TV, Salt Lake City, 1963-68; bur. chief Bonneville Internat. Corp., Washington, 1968-72; corr. CBS Radio Stas. News Service, CBS Radio, Washington, 1972-97; host CBS Crosstalk; bd. dirs. Am. Zephyr, Inc. Columnist The High Green, The Timetable; contbr. to Passenger Train jour., Railfan and Railroad. Bd. dirs. Winding-Orchard Citizens Assn., Wheaton-Glenmont, Md., 1974-77, 86—, pres., 1975-76. Served with AUS, 1951-52. Recipient Journalism awards Mont. A.P. Press Stas., 1960, Journalism awards Utah Bar Assn., 1965, Journalism awards Utah Broadcasters Assn., 1965-66. Mem. Radio-TV Corrs. Assn., Am. Legion (comdr. Yellowstone Post 4 1962-63), Railroad Enthusiasts (pres. Chesapeake divsn. 1992-94), Nat. Assn. Radio Talk Show Hosts. Office: 1605 Billman Ln Silver Spring MD 20902-1417

VERONIS, GEORGE, geophysics educator; b. New Brunswick, N.J., June 6, 1926; s. Nicholas Emmanuel and Angeliki (Efthimakis) V.; m. Anna Margareta Olsson, Nov. 8, 1963; m. Catherine Elizabeth, Jan. 29, 1949 (div. Nov. 1962); children—Melissa, Benjamin. A.B., Lafayette Coll., 1950; Ph.D., Brown U., 1954; M.A. (hon.), Yale U., 1966. Staff meteorologist Inst. Advanced Study, Princeton, 1953-56; staff mathematician Woods Hole Oceanographic Inst., Mass., 1956-64, mem. staff, dir. geophys. fluid dynamics summer program, 1959—, assoc. prof. MIT, Cambridge, 1961-64, research oceanographer, 1964-66; prof. geophysics and applied sci. Yale U., New Haven, 1966—, Henry Barnard Davis prof., 1985—, chmn. geology and geophysics, 1976-79, dir. applied math, 1979-93. Editor Jour. Marine Rsch., 1973—; contbr. articles to profl. jours. Served with USN, 1943-46. Fellow Am. Acad. Arts and Scis., Am. Geophys. Union; mem. NAS, Norwegian Acad. Scis. (Robert L. and Bettie P. Cody award 1989, Henry Stommel Rsch. award 1997). Greek Orthodox.

VERONIS, PETER, publisher; b. New Brunswick, N.J., June 15, 1923; s. Nicholas M. and Angeliki (Efthemakis) V.; m. Dorothy E. White, Sept. 8, 1947; 1 dau., Judith Anne Veronis Rodgers. Student, Columbia U., 1951-54. Nat. advt. mgr. Springfield (Mass.) Newspapers, 1954-57; v.p., gen. sales mgr. Ridder Johns Co., N.Y.C., 1957-62; corp. exec. Curtis Pub. Co., N.Y.C., 1963-64; assoc. sales mgr. Look mag., 1964-68; v.p., advt. dir. Psychology Today mag., 1968-71; v.p. advt. Saturday Rev., N.Y.C., 1971-73; pub. Book Digest, N.Y.C., 1973-80; pres. PV Pub. Inc., N.Y.C., 1980-81, Conn., 1988—; v.p., dir. CBS Mag. Network, N.Y.C., 1981-85, pres., 1985-87; pres. Diamandis Mag. Network, 1987-88. Served with USN, 1941-51. Home: 42 Thornwood Rd Stamford CT 06903-2613

VERPLANCK, WILLIAM SAMUEL, psychologist, educator; b. Plainfield, N.J., Jan. 6, 1916; s. William Samuel and Kathryn (Tracy) V. B.S., U. Va., 1937, M.A., 1938; Ph.D., Brown U., 1941. Asst. prof. Ind. U., 1946-50; asst. prof. Harvard, 1950-55, acting asso. prof., 1955-56; research asso. Stanford U., 1956-57; asso. prof. Hunter Coll., 1957-59; prof. U. Md., 1958-62; prof. psychology U. Tenn., 1963-81, head dept., 1963-73; founder, chmn. Resource Assocs., Inc., 1980-82; bd. dirs. Cambridge Ctr. for Behavioral Sci. Author: (with others) Modern Learning Theory, 1953. Bd. trustees Cambridge Ctr. Behavioral Studies. Served to lt. USNR, 1943-46. Recipient travel grant Am. Philos. Assn., 1953. Fellow APA, Am. Psychol. Soc., Assn. Study Animal Behavior, AAAS; mem. Ea. Psychol. Assn., Psychonomic Soc. (founder, past sec.-treas., bd. govs.), Sigma Xi, Sigma Alpha Epsilon. *The history of psychology is largely constituted of a succession of fads overlying the continuity given by a few plausible technological methods which have been progressively misapplied, with little critical concern for their social, political or scientific consequences.*

VERRILL, CHARLES OWEN, JR., lawyer; b. Biddeford, Maine, Sept. 30, 1937; s. Charles Owen and Elizabeth (Handy) V.; m. Mary Ann Blanchard, Aug. 13, 1960 (dec.); children: Martha Anne, Edward Blanchard, Ethan Christopher, Elizabeth Handy, Matthew Lawton, Peter Goldthwait; m. Diana Baber, Dec. 11, 1993. AB, Tufts U., 1959; LLB, Duke U., 1962. Bar: D.C. 1962. Assoc. Weaver & Glassie, 1962-64; assoc. Barco, Cook, Patton & Blow, 1964-66, ptnr., 1967; ptnr. Patton, Boggs & Blow, 1967-84, Wiley, Rein & Fielding, Washington, 1984—; adj. prof. internat. trade law Georgetown U. Law Ctr., Washington, 1978—, Charles Fahy Disting. adj. prof., 1993; conf. chmn. The Future of Internat. Steel Industry, Bellagio, Italy, 1984, U.S. Agenda for Uruguay Round, Airlie House, Warrenton, Va., 1986, Polish Joint Venture Law, Cracow, Poland, 1987, Internat. Steel Industry II, Bellagio, 1987, Bulgaria and the GATT, Washington, 1977; lectr. Duke U. Law Sch., 1970-73; chair, spkr. Protection of Intellectual Property from Theft and Piracy Abroad Southwestern Legal Found. Fgn. Investment Symposium, 1995, chair, panel on NAFTA 2 1/2 Years Later, 1996. Local dir. Tufts U. Am. Fund, 1965-69; mem. Duke Law Alumni Coun., 1972-75; trustee Internat. Law Inst., 1981—, chmn. bd. trustees, 1983-87; trustee Bulgarian Am. Friendship Soc., 1992—, Christ Ch., Dark Harbor, Maine; apptd. to roster of dispute settlement panelists World Trade Orgn., 1995. Mem. ABA, Internat. Bar Assn., D.C. Bar Assn., Order of Coif, Theta Delta Chi, Phi Delta Phi, Met. Club (Washington), Chevy Chase Club (Md.), Tarratine Club (Dark Harbor, Maine). Home: 3000 Q St NW Washington DC 20007-3080 Office: 1776 K St NW Washington DC 20006-2304

VERRILL, F. GLENN, advertising executive; b. N.Y.C., Dec. 17, 1923; s. Ralph Francis and Rose (Verner) V.; m. Jean Demar, Aug. 25, 1946; children: Gary, Joan. A.B., Adelphi Coll., 1949; A.M., Harvard U., 1950. With Batten, Barton, Durstine & Osborn, Inc., 1952—, v.p., 1964; creative dir. Batten, Barton, Durstine & Osborn, Inc. (Burke Dowling Adams div.), Atlanta, 1965-70, exec. v.p., gen. mgr., 1970-71, pres., 1971-88, chmn., 1988—, also dir. parent co. Author: Advertising Procedure, 1983, rev. edit., 1986, 88. Mem. adv. bd. U. Ga.; vice chmn. bd. overseers Coll. Bus. Adminstrn., Ga. State U.; bd. dirs. Atlanta Humane Soc., pres., 1980-81; chmn. Advanced Advt. Inst. Atlanta, 1981; mem. Peabody award com., 1984—; bd. dirs. Atlanta Coll. of Art, 1990. With USAAF, 1943-46. Mem. Am. Assn. Advt. Agys. (nat. dir. 1973—). Episcopalian. Clubs: Atlanta Athletic, Cherokee, Harvard (Atlanta). Home: 2600 W Wesley Rd NW Atlanta GA 30327-2036 Office: 3620 Cloudland Dr NW Atlanta GA 30327-2908

VERRILLO, RONALD THOMAS, neuroscience educator, researcher; b. Hartford, Conn., July 31, 1927; s. Francesco Paul and Angela (Forte) V.; m. Violet Silverstein, June 3, 1950; children—Erica, Dan, Thomas. B.A., Syracuse U., 1952; Ph.D., U. Rochester, 1958. Asst. prof. Syracuse U., 1957-62, research assoc., 1959-63, research fellow, 1963-67, assoc. prof., 1967-74, prof., 1974-94, prof. emeritus, 1995, assoc. dir. Inst. Sensory Research, 1980-84, dir., 1984-93, dir. grad. neurosci. program, 1984-93; advisor com. on hearing, bioacoustics and biomechanics NRC. Author: Adjustment to Visual Disability, 1961 (award 1962). Contbr. many chpts. to books, articles to profl. jours. Served with USN, 1945-46. Fellow Am. Found. for Blind, 1956, NATO, 1970; grantee NSF, 1969-72, 84-87, NIH, 1972—. Fellow Acoustical Soc. Am.; mem. Soc. for Neurosci. N.Y. Acad. Scis., Sigma Xi (research award 1982). Home: 312 Berkley Dr Syracuse NY 13210-3031 Office: Syracuse U Inst Sensory Rsch Merrill Ln Syracuse NY 13244

VERRONE, PATRIC MILLER, lawyer, writer; b. Glendale, N.Y.C., Sept. 29, 1959; s. Pat and Edna (Miller) V.; m. Margaret Maiya Williams, 1989; 1 child, Patric Carroll Williams. BA, Harvard U., 1981; JD, Boston Coll., 1984. Bar: Fla. 1984, Calif. 1988, U.S. Dist. Ct. (mid. dist.) Fla. 1984, U.S. Dist. Ct. (ctrl. dist.) Calif. 1995, U.S. Ct. Appeals (9th cir.) 1995. Assoc. Allen, Knudsen, Swartz, DeBoest, Rhoads & Edwards, Ft. Myers, Fla., 1984-86; writer The Tonight Show, Burbank, Calif., 1987-90; temp. judge L.A. Mcpl. Ct., 1995—. Dir., producer, writer The Civil War--The Lost Episode, 1991; writer The Larry Sanders Show, 1992-94, The Critic, 1993-95; producer, writer The Simpsons, 1994-95, Muppets Tonight!, 1995-97; editor Harvard Lampoon, 1978-84, Boston Coll. Law Rev., 1983-84, Fla. Bar Jour., 1987-88, L.A. Lawyer, 1994—; issue editor: Ann. Entertainment Law Issue, 1995-97; contbr. articles to profl. jours. including Elysian Fields Quar., Baseball and the American Legal Mind. Bd. dirs. Calif. Confedn. of Arts, Mus. Contemporary Art. Mem. ABA (vice chair arts, entertainment and sports law com.), Calif. Bar, Calif. Lawyers for Arts, L.A. County Bar Assn. (sec. barristers exec. com., chair artists and the law com., steering com. homeless shelter project, intellectual property and entertainment law sect., state appelate jud. evaluation com., legis. activity com.), Fla. Bar Assn., Writers Guild Am. West (exec. com. animation writers caucus), Harvard Club Lee County (v.p. 1985-86), Harvard Club So. Calif. Republican. Roman Catholic. Avocations: filmmaking, video, baseball. Home and Office: PO Box 1428 Pacific Palisades CA 90272-1428

VERSCHOOR, CURTIS CARL, business educator, consultant; b. Grand Rapids, Mich., June 7, 1931; s. Peter and Leonene (Dahlstrom) V.; m. Marie Emilie Kritschgau, June 18, 1952; children—Katherine Anne, Carolyn Marie, John Peter, Carla Michelle. BBA with distinction, U. Mich., 1951, MBA, 1952; EdD, No. Ill. U., 1977. CPA; cert. mgmt. acctg., cert. fin. planner, cert. fraud examiner, cert. internal auditor; chartered fin. cons. Pub. accountant Touche, Ross, Bailey & Smart (C.P.A.'s), 1955-63; with Singer Co., 1963-68, asst. controller, 1965-68; controller Colgate-Palmolive Co., 1968-69; asst. controller bus. products group Xerox Corp., 1969-72; controller Baxter Internat., 1972-73; v.p. finance Altair Corp., Chgo., 1973-74; prof. DePaul U., Chgo., 1974-94, ledger and quill alumni rsch. prof., 1994—; pres. C.C. Verschoor & Assocs., Inc., 1981—; part-time instr. Wayne State U., 1955-60. Contbg. editor: Jour. Accountancy, 1961-62, Jour. Internal Auditing, 1985—; editl. adv. bd. Acctg. Today, 1991—. Served with AUS, 1953-55. Recipient Elijah Watts Sells award Am. Inst. C.P.A.'s, 1953. Mem. AICPA, Ill. Soc. CPAs, Fin. Execs. Inst., Am. Acctg. Assn., Inst. Mgmt. Accts., Inst. Internal Auditors, Nat. Assn. Corp. Dirs., Beta Gamma Sigma, Beta Alpha Psi, Delta Pi Epsilon, Phi Kappa Phi, Phi Eta Sigma. Home: 231 Wyngate Dr Barrington IL 60010-4840 Office: DePaul Univ One E Jackson Blvd Chicago IL 60604-2287

VERSCHOOR, JOHN, IV, physician assistant; b. Phoenix, Mar. 19, 1949; s. John Verschoor III and Dorothy (Killman) Hibbard; m. Nancy Lorel Welsh, Jan. 24, 1970; children: Bianca Dawn, Jared Moroni, Renee Ann, Benjamin Thayer. AS, Ariz. Western Coll., Yuma, 1972; Assoc. Med. Sci., Emory U., 1975; MD, Spartan Health Sci. U., St. Lucia, West Cast, 1985. Lic. nurse, Ariz., Ga., Tex., physician asst., Ariz. Orderly Yuma Regional Med. Ctr., 1967-68, emergency rm. nurse, 1970-72; commd. U.S. Army, 1972, advanced through grades to maj., 1990; physician asst. S.W. Med., Yuma, 1975-80; comdr. 12th Spl. Force Group, Albuquerque, 1980-85; exec. officer 996th Med. Co., Glendale, Ariz., 1985-88; bn. comdr. indsl. facility Fitzsimmons Army Hosp., 1988-92; physician asst. Deseret Diagnostic Ctr., Mesa, Ariz., 1990—; med. svc. officer CIA, Langley, Va., 1988—; exec. officer Tripler Army Med. Ctr., HI, 1992—; Lectr. U. Utah, Salt Lake City, 1990-94; bd. dirs. Lazerus Group, Inc., Las Vegas, 1989—. V.p. Clnica de Mormona, Guadalajara, Mexico, 1981. Mem. Wilderness Med. Soc., Am. Acad. Physician Assts. Republican. LDS Ch. Avocations: orienteering, primitive camping. Office: Deseret Diagnostic Ctr 215 S Power Rd Ste 106 Mesa AZ 85206-5236

VERSFELT, DAVID SCOTT, lawyer; b. Mineola, N.Y., Feb. 17, 1951; s. William H. and Ruth (Gerland) V.; m. Mary Deborah Garber, Aug. 31, 1974; children: Christopher L., William S., Kathryn H. AB, Princeton U., 1973; JD, Columbia U., 1976. Bar: N.Y. 1977, U.S. Dist. Ct. (so. and ea. dists.) N.Y. 1977, U.S. Ct. Appeals (D.C. cir.) 1979, U.S. Ct. Appeals (2d and 7th cirs.) 1980, U.S. Supreme Ct. 1980, U.S. Ct. Appeals (9th cir.) 1981, U.S. Ct. Appeals (3d cir.) 1982, Ct. Internat. Trade 1990, U.S. Ct. Appeals (fed. cir.) 1994, U.S. Ct. Appeals (6th cir.) 1996. Mem. Coun. of Community Law Office; vol. div. Legal Aid Soc., N.Y.C., 1985-88; dir. Partnership for a Drug-Free Am., 1989—. Mem. ABA, Assn. Bar City N.Y. (com. on state legislation 1983-85), Phi Beta Kappa. Office: Donovan Leisure Newton & Irvine 30 Rockefeller Plz New York NY 10112

VERSIC, LINDA JOAN, nurse educator, research company executive; b. Grove City, Pa., Aug. 27, 1944; d. Robert and Kathryn I. (Fagird) Davies; m. Ronald James Versic, June 11, 1966; children: Kathryn Clara, Paul Joseph. RN, Johns Hopkins Sch. of Nursing, 1965; BS in Health Edn., Ctrl. State U., 1980. Asst. head nurse Johns Hopkins Hosp., Balt., 1965-67; staff Nurse Registry Miami Valley Hosp., Dayton, Ohio, 1973-90; instr. Miami Jacobs Jr. Coll. Bus., Dayton, 1977-79; pres. Ronald T. Dodge Co., Dayton, 1979-86, chmn. bd., 1987—; chmn. bd. dirs. A-1 Travel, Inc. instr. Warren County (Ohio) Career Ctr., 1980-84, coord. diversified health occupations, 1984—. Coord. youth activities, mem. steering com. Queen of Apostles Cmty. Recipient Excellence in Tchg. award, 1992, award for Project Excellence, 1992. Active Miami Valley Mil. Affairs Assn., Glen Helen, Friends of Dayton Ballet, Dayton Art Inst., Cin. Art Mus. Mem. Ohio Vocat. Assn., Am. Vocat. Assn., Vocat. Indsl. Clubs Am. (chpt. advisor 1982—). Roman Catholic. Club: Johns Hopkins, Yugoslav of Greater Dayton. Home: 1601 Shafor Blvd Dayton OH 45419-3103 Office: Ronald T Dodge Co PO Box 630 Dayton OH 45441-0630

VERSTANDIG, TONI GRANT, federal agency administrator; b. Pitts., Jan. 15, 1953; d. Louis A. and Ruth M. (O'Block) Grant; m. Lee L. Verstandig, Feb. 20, 1982; 1 stepchild, Scott B.; 1 child, Grant L. BA, Boston U., 1974; AD, Stephens Coll., 1972. Legis. asst. subcom. on agrl. labor House Com. on Edn. and Labor, 1976-77; staff dir. subcom. on accts. House Adminstrn. Com., 1977-78; mem. profl. staff subcom. on internat. security/sci. affairs House Com. on Fgn. Affairs, 1978-86; mem. profl. staff Com. on Fgn. Affairs, 1986-93; dep. asst. sec. of state Near Ea. affairs U.S. Dept. of State, Washington, 1993—; cons. to com. on fgn. affairs U.S. Ho. of Reps., 1978-93, staff dir. subcom. accts., com. on house adminstrn., prin. legis. asst. to Congressman John N. Dent. Vol. cons. on fgn. policy and nat. security Clinton-Gore Presdl. Campaign, 1992. Recipient Spl. Merit of Honor commendation Mayor Kevin White. Office: Dept of State Near Eastern Affairs 2201 C St NW Rm 6244 Washington DC 20520-0001

VER STEEG, CLARENCE LESTER, historian, educator; b. Orange City, Iowa, Dec. 28, 1922; s. John A. and Annie (Vischer) Ver S.; m. Dorothy Ann De Vries, Dec. 24, 1943; 1 child, John Charles. AB, Morningside Coll., Sioux City, Iowa, 1943; MA, Columbia U., 1946, PhD, 1950; LHD, Morningside Coll., 1988. Lectr., then instr. history Columbia U., N.Y.C., 1946-50; mem. faculty Northwestern U., Evanston, Ill., 1950—, prof. history, 1959—, dean grad. sch., 1975-86; vis. lectr. Harvard U., 1959-60; mem. council Inst. Early Am. History and Culture, Williamsburg, Va., 1961-64, 68-72, chmn. exec. com., 1970-72; vis. mem. Inst. Advanced Study, Princeton, N.J., 1967-68; chmn. faculty com. to recommend Master Plan Higher Edn. in Ill., 1962-64; mem. Grad. Record Exam. Bd., 1981-86, chmn., 1984-86; bd. dirs. Ctr. for Research Libraries, 1980-85, Council Grad. Schs. in U.S., 1983-87; pres. Assn. Grad. Schs., 1984-85; mem. steering com. Grad. Research Project, Consortium on Financing Higher Edn., 1981-85; mem. working group on talent Nat. Acad. Scis., 1984-87; mem. Higher Edn. Policy Adv. Com. to OCLC, Online Computer Library Ctr., 1984-87. Author: Robert Morris, Revolutionary Financier, 1954, A True and Historical Narraative of the Colony of Georgia, 1960, The American People: Their Historical, 1961, The Formative Years, 1607-1763, 1964 (Brit. edit.), 1965, The Story of Our Country, 1965, (with others) Investigating Man's World, 6 vols., 1970, A People and a Nation, 1971, The Origins of a Southern Mosaic: Studies of Early Carolina and Georgia, 1975, World Cultures, 1977, American Spirit, 1982, rev. edit., 1990; sr. author: Health Social Studies, 7 Vols., 1991, Planning at Northwestern University in the 1960s, 1993; editor: Great Issues in American History, From Settlement to Revolution 1584-1776, 1969; editl. cons.: Papers of Robert Morris, vols. I-VIII, 1973—; contbr. articles to profl. jours. Served with USAAF, 1942-45. Decorated Air medal with 3 oak leaf clusters; 5 Battle Stars; Social Sci. Research Council fellow, 1948-49, George A. and Eliza Gardner Howard Found. fellow, 1954-55, Huntington Library research fellow, 1955, Am. Council Learned Socs. sr. fellow, 1958-59, Guggenheim fellow, 1964-65, NEH sr. fellow, 1973. Mem. AAUP, Am. Hist. Assn. (nominating com. 1965-68, chmn. 1967-68, Albert J. Beveridge prize 1952, hon. mention 1991 Eugene Asher Disting. Teaching award), Orgn. Am. Historians (editorial bd. Jour. Am. History 1968-72), So. Hist. Assn. (nominating com. 1970-72). Presbyterian. Home: 2619 Ridge Ave Evanston IL 60201-1717 Office: Northwestern Univ Dean Grad Sch Evanston IL 60208

VER STEEG, DONNA LORRAINE FRANK, nurse, sociologist, educator; b. Minot, N.D., Sept. 23, 1929; d. John Jonas and Pearl H. (Denlinger) Frank; m. Richard W. Ver Steeg, Nov. 22, 1950; children: Juliana, Anne, Richard B. BSN, Stanford, 1951; MSN, U. Calif., San Francisco, 1967; MA in Sociology, UCLA, 1969, PhD in Sociology, 1973. Clin. instr. U. N.D. Sch. Nursing, 1962-63; USPHS nurse rsch. fellow UCLA, 1969-72; spl. cons., adv. com. on physicians' assts. and nurse practitioner programs Calif. State Bd. Med. Examiners, 1972-73; asst. prof. UCLA Sch. Nursing, 1973-79, assoc. prof., 1979-94, asst. dean, 1981-83, chmn. primary ambulatory care, 1976-87, assoc. dean, 1983-86, prof. emeritus (recalled 1994-96), chair primary care, 1994-96, emeritus, 1996—; co-prin. investigator PRIMEX Project, Family Nurse Practitioners, UCLA Extension, 1974-76; assoc. cons. Calif. Postsecondary Edn. Commn., 1975-76; spl. cons. Calif. Dept. Consumer Affairs, 1978; accredited visitor Western Assn. Schs. and Colls., 1985; mem. Calif. State Legis. Health Policy Forum, 1980-81; mem. nurse practitioner adv. com. Calif. Bd. RNs, 1995—. Contbr. chpts. to profl. books. Recipient Leadership award Calif. Area Health Edn. Ctr. System, 1989, Commendation award Calif. State Assembly, 1994; named Outstanding Faculty Mem. UCLA Sch. Nursing, 1982. Fellow Am. Acad. Nursing; mem. AAAS, ANA (pres. elect Calif. 1977-79, pres. Calif. 1979-81), ANA C interim chair Calif. 1995-96, Am. Soc. Law and Medicine, Nat. League Nursing, Calif. League Nursing, N.Am. Nursing Diagnosis Assn., Am. Assn. History Nursing, Assn. Health Svcs. Rsch., Stanford Nurses Club, Sigma Theta Tau (Gamma Tau chpt. Leadership award 1994), Sigma Xi. Home: 708 Swarthmore Ave Pacific Palisades CA 90272-4353 Office: UCLA Sch Nursing 700 Tiverton Ave Box 956919 Los Angeles CA 90095

VERTS, LITA JEANNE, university administrator; b. Jonesboro, Ark., Apr. 13, 1935; d. William Gus and Lolita Josephine (Peeler) Nash; m. B. J. Verts, Aug. 29, 1954 (div. 1975); 1 child, William Trigg. BA, Oreg. State U., 1973; MA in Lingustics, U. Oreg., 1974; postgrad., U. Hawaii, 1977. Librarian Forest Research Lab., Corvallis, Oreg., 1966-69; instr. English Lang. Inst., Corvallis, 1974-80; dir. spl. svcs. Oreg. State U., Corvallis, 1980—, faculty senator, 1988-96. Editor ann. book: Trio Achievers, 1986, 87, 88; contbr. articles to profl. jours. Precinct com. Rep. Party, Corvallis, 1977-80; adminstrv. bd. 1st United Meth. Ch., Corvallis, 1987-89, mem. fin. com., 1987-93, tchr. Bible, 1978—; bd. dirs. Westminster Ho., United Campus Ministries, 1994-95; adv. coun. Disabilities Svc., Linn, Benton, Lincoln Counties, 1990—, vice-chmn., 1992-93, chmn. 1993-94. Mem. N.W. Assn. Spl. Programs (pres. 1985-86), Nat. Coun. Ednl. Opportunities Assn. (bd. dirs. 1984-87), Nat. Gardening Assn., Alpha Phi (mem. corp. bd. Beta Upsilon chpt. 1990-96). Republican. Methodist. Avocations: gardening, photography, golf. Home: 530 SE Mayberry Ave Corvallis OR 97333-1866 Office: Spl Svcs Project Waldo 337 OSU Corvallis OR 97331

VERVILLE, ELIZABETH GIAVANI, federal official; b. N.Y.C., July 13, 1940; d. Joseph and Gertrude (Levy) Giavani. BA, Duke U., 1961; LLB, Columbia U., 1964. Bar: Mass. 1965, U.S. Supreme Ct. 1970, D.C. 1980. Assoc. Snow Motley & Holt, successor Gaston Snow & Ely Bartlett, Boston, 1965-67; asst. atty. gen. Commonwealth of Mass., Boston, 1967-69; atty. advisor for African affairs U.S. Dept. State, Washington, 1979-72, asst. legal adviser for East Asian and Pacific affairs, 1972-80, dep. legal adviser, 1980-89; dep. asst. sec. state Bur. Politico-Mil. Affairs Bur. Politico-Mil. Affairs, Washington, 1989-92; sr. coord. Bur. Politico-Mil. Affairs, 1992-95; dir. for global and multilateral affairs Nat. Security Coun., Washington, 1995—. Recipient presdl. rank of meritorious exec., 1985, 90, presdl. rank disting. exec., 1988. Mem. Am. Soc. Internat. Law, Coun. on Fgn. Rels. Home: 3012 Dumbarton Ave NW Washington DC 20007-3305 Office: Nat Security Coun The White House Washington DC 20504

VESCOVI, SELVI, pharmaceutical company executive; b. N.Y.C., June 14, 1930; s. Antonio and Desolina V.; BS, Coll. William and Mary, 1951; m. Elma Pasquinelli, Oct. 16, 1954; children: Mark, James, Anne. Salesman, Upjohn Co., N.Y.C., 1954-59, sales supr.,1959-62, product mgr. U.S. domestic pharm. dir., 1962-65, mgr. mktg. planning internat. div., 1965-71, v.p. Europe, 1971-74, group v.p. Europe, 1975-77, exec. v.p. Upjohn Internat., Inc., Kalamazoo, Mich., 1978-85, pres., gen. mgr., 1975-88, v.p. parent co., 1978-88; adj. prof. mgmt. Western Mich. U., Kalamazoo, 1988-92; chmn. bd. Carrington Labs; bd. dirs. Cytrx Pharms. Corp., Centaur Corp. 2d lt. M.C., U.S. Army, 1951-53. Mem. Internat. Pharm. Mfrs. Assn., NYAC (N.Y.). Republican. Roman Catholic. Office: Upjon Internat Co 7000 Portage Rd Kalamazoo MI 49001-0102

VESELL, ELLIOT SAUL, pharmacologist, educator; b. N.Y.C., Dec. 24, 1933; s. Harry and Evelyn (Jaffe) V.; m. Kristen Paige Peery, Mar. 24, 1968; children: Liane Clark, Hilary Peery. AB, Harvard U., 1955, MD, 1959; DSc (hon.), Phila. Coll. Pharmacy & Sci., 1988; PhD, Philipps U., Marburg, Germany, 1991. Intern, children's med. svc. Mass. Gen. Hosp., Boston, 1959-60; rsch. assoc. Rockefeller U., 1960-62; resident in medicine Peter Bent Brigham Hosp., Boston, 1962-63; clin. assoc. Nat. Inst. Arthritis and Metabolic Diseases, NIH, Bethesda, Md., 1963-65; head sect. pharmacogenetics Nat. Heart Inst., NIH, Bethesda, 1965-68; Evan Pugh prof. pharmacology, chmn. dept. Pa. State U., Hershey, 1968—, asst. dean grad. edn., 1973-96; Frohlich vis. prof. Royal Soc. Medicine, 1985, Pfizer vis. prof., Burroughs Wellcome vis. prof. Editor: The Life and Works of Thomas Cole, 1964, Progress in Basic and Clinical Pharmacology, 1990, numerous others; contbr. numerous articles to profl. jours. Recipient Von Humboldt award, 1988. Fellow AAAS, Royal Soc. of Medicine; mem. Assn. Am. Physicians, Am. Soc. for Clin. Investigation, Am. Soc. Pharmacology and Exptl. Therapeutics (sec.-treas. 1995-98, Exptl. Therapeutics award 1971, Harry Gold award in clin. pharmacology, 1985), Am. Coll. Clin. Pharmacology (pres. 1980-82), Am. Soc. Clin. Pharmacology and Therapeutics (Oscar B. Hunter Meml. award 1991). Office: Pa State U Coll Medicine Dept Pharmacology PO Box 850 Hershey PA 17033-0850

VESELY, ALEXANDER, civil engineer; b. Ladmovce, Czechoslovakia, Dec. 7, 1926; came to U.S., 1949; s. Joseph and Margaret (Lefkovitz) V.; m. Harriet Lee Roth, Aug. 11, 1957; 1 child, David Seth. BSCE, Carnegie Mellon U., 1952; postgrad. John Marshall Law Sch., 1955; MSCE, Ill. Inst. Tech., 1957. Registered profl. engr., Ind., Mass.; registered land surveyor, Ind. Staff engr., Amoco Oil Co., Whiting, Ind., 1952-62; mgr. engring. Borg Warner Chem. Co., Washington, W.Va., 1962-77; assoc. engr. Mobil Rsch. & Devel. Corp., Princeton, N.J., 1977-83; cons. engr. D.G. Peterson & Assocs. Inc., Greenfield, Mass., 1983-87; prin. Alexander Vesely & Assocs., 1987—; assoc. prof. Community Coll., Parkersburg, W.Va., 1965-67; chmn. Engrs. Week Com., Parkersburg, 1973. Pres. B'nai Israel Congregation, Parkersburg, 1976; bd. dirs. Bros. of Israel Congregation, Trenton, N.J., 1978-83. Served with U.S. Army, 1952-54. Carnegie Mellon U. scholar, 1950-52. Mem. Nat. Soc. Profl. Engrs. (pres. Parkersburg chpt. 1973-74), Am. Inst. Plant Engrs., ASCE, Scrabble Club, Chess Club, Bridge Club, Tau Beta Pi (life). Republican. Jewish. Avocations: ping-pong, tennis, swimming. Home and Office: 48 Hillcrest Dr Northampton MA 01060-1362

VESPA, NED ANGELO, photographer; b. Streator, Ill., May 31, 1942; s. Ned James and Evelyn Blanche (Flanigan) V.; m. Carol DeMasters, Sept. 11, 1976; 1 child, Nicole Marie; 1 son by previous marriage, James Paul. B.S., So. Ill. U., 1965. Photographer Milw. Jour. Co., 1965-95, Milw. Sentinel, 1965-95; ret., 1995, freelance, 1995—. Mem. Nat. Press Photographers Assn., Wis. News Photographers Assn. (past pres.), Milw. Press Photographers. Home: 38309 Genesee Lake Rd Oconomowoc WI 53066-8614

VESPER, CAROLYN F., newspaper publishing executive. Sr. v.p. and assoc. publisher USA TODAY, Arlington, Va. Office: USA Today 1000 Wilson Blvd Arlington VA 22209-3901*

VESPER, KARL HAMPTON, business and mechanical engineering educator; b. San Marino, Calif., Aug. 12, 1932; s. Karl Conrad and Roxie (Armstrong) V.; m. Joan Frantz, June, 1964; children—Karen, Linda, Holly, Nancy. B.S. in Mech. Engring, Stanford U., 1955; M.S. in Mech. Engring, 1965, Ph.D., 1969; M.B.A., Harvard U., 1960. Casewriter Harvard Bus. Sch., 1960-61; bus. mgr., mech. engr. Marine Advisers, 1961-62; cons. Dept. State, summer, 1963; dir. Hosmer Machine Co., Contoock, N.H., 1966-67; dir. summer insts. Stanford U., 1966, 67, dir. case devel., research asso., lectr. mech. engring., 1963-69, research asso., NASA faculty fellow in air pollution research design project, summer 1970; editor mech. engring. series McGraw Hill Book Co., N.Y.C., 1966-74; prof. bus. adminstrn., mech. engring. and marine studies U. Wash., Seattle, 1969—; Paul T. Babson prof. Babson Coll., 1980-81. Author: How To Write Engineering Cases, 1966, 73, Engineers at Work, 1975, The Entrepreneurial Function, 1977, Entrepreneurship Education, 1985, New Venture Strategies, 1980, rev. edit., 1990, Frontiers of Entrepreneurship Research, 1981-91, Entrepreneurship and National Policy, 1983, New Venture Mechanics, 1993, (with Paul Larson) Washington Entrepreneur's Guide, 1993, New Venture Experience, 1993, rev. edit., 1996; contbr. chpts. to books and articles to profl. jours. Served with USAF, 1955-57. Mem. Am. Inst. for Decision Scis., Acad. Mgmt., Sigma Xi. Home: 3721 47th Pl NE Seattle WA 98105-5224 Office: U Wash Sch Business Adminstrn Seattle WA 98195

VESSEL, ROBERT LESLIE, lawyer; b. Chgo., Mar. 21, 1942; s. Louis Frank and Margaret Ruth (Barber) V.; m. Diane White, Oct. 12, 1966; m. Lise Vessel, Dec. 19, 1992. BA, U. Ill., 1964; JD, Seton Hall U., 1973; LLM in Taxation, U. Miami, Coral Gables, Fla., 1980. Bar: N.J. 1973, Fla. 1981, U.S. Dist. Ct. (so. and mid. dists.) Fla. 1981, U.S. Ct. Appeals (11th cir.) 1981; bd. cert. civil trial, Fla. Assoc. Bennett & Bennett P.A., East Orange, N.J., 1973-76; ptnr. Kantor & Vessel, P.A., Wayne, N.J., 1976-81; assoc. Haddad Josephs & Jack, P.A., Coral Gables, Fla., 1981-85; ptnr. Mitchell Alley Rywant & Vessel, Tampa, 1985-89, Moffitt & Vessel, P.A., Tampa, 1989-94, Vessel & Morales, P.A., Tampa, 1994—. With USNR, 1964-66. Mem. Assn. Trial Lawyers Am., Nat. Inst. Trial Advocacy, Acad. Fla. Trial Lawyers, Hillsboro County Bar Assn. Avocation: sailing. Office: Vessel & Morales PA 5401 W Kennedy Blvd Tampa FL 33609-2428

VESSEY, JOHN WILLIAM, JR., army officer; b. Mpls., June 29, 1922; s. John William and Emily (Roche) V.; m. Avis Claire Funk, July 18, 1945; children: John William, David, Sarah. BS, U. Md., 1963; MS, George Washington U., 1967; LLD, Concordia Coll., St. Paul, 1978, U. Md., 1983, Concordia Sem., St. Louis, 1983; DMS (hon.), Norwich U., Northfield, Vt., 1985; grad., Command and Gen. Staff Coll., 1958, Indsl. Coll. Armed Forces, 1966. Commd. 2nd lt. U.S. Army, 1944, advanced through grades to gen., 1976; comdr. U.S. Army Support Command Thailand, 1970-71; chief Mil. Assistance Adv. Group Laos, 1972-73; dir. ops. Dept. Army Washington, 1973-74; comdr. 4th Inf. Div. Ft. Carson, Colo., 1974-75; dep. chief of staff-ops. Dept. Army Washington, 1975-76; comdr.-in-chief UN Command/U.S. Forces in Korea Seoul, 1976-79; comdr.-in-chief Republic of Korea/U.S. Combined Forces Command, 1978-79; vice chief of staff U.S. Army Washington, 1979-82, chmn. Joint Chiefs of Staff, 1982-85; ret. U.S. Army, 1985; presdl. emissary to Hanoi for POW/MIA matters, 1987-93. Bd. dirs. Nat. Flag Day Com.; with Mission Svcs. Luth. Ch., Mo.; chair bd. vistors UMUC; chmn. bd. Ctr. Preventive Action Def. Sci. Bd. Decorated D.S.C., Def. D.S.M., D.S.M., AF D.S.M., Navy D.S.M., Legion of Merit, Bronze Star, Air medal, Joint Svcs. Commendation medal, Army Commendation medal, Purple Heart (U.S.), Presdl. Medal of Freedom, decorated by govts. of Austria, Chile, Colombia, Fed. Republic Germany, France, Greece, Honduras, Korea, Luxembourg, Norway, Pakistan, Saudi Arabia, Spain, Thailand, Uruguay, Fed. Republic of Germany; recipient State of Minn. Disting. Svc. medal, Excellence in Diplomacy award Am. Acad. of Diplomacy, Sylvanus Thayer award USMA, Alumni Achievement award and Disting. Pub. Svc. award George Washington U., Disting. Alumnus award U. Md., Golden Plate award Am. Acad. Achievement, Adm. John M. Will award N.Y. Coun. Navy League, hon. award Nat. League Families, Excellence in Diplomacy award Am. Acad. Diplomacy. Mem. VFW (Eisenhower medal), Assn. U.S. Army (George Marshall medal), Army Aviation Assn., U.S. Armor Assn., Coun. Fgn. Rels. (chair bd. dirs. ctr. for prevention action), Phi Kappa Phi. Lutheran.

VESSOT, ROBERT FREDERICK CHARLES, physicist; b. Montreal, Que., Can., Apr. 16, 1930; s. Robert Charles Ulysses and Marguerite Yvonne (Giauque) V.; m. Norma Newman Wight, Apr. 18, 1959; children: Judith Norma, Margaret Anne, Nancy Elizabeth. B.A., McGill U., 1951, B.Sc., 1954, Ph.D., 1956. Mem. research staff MIT, 1956-60; mgr. Maser Research and Devel., Varian Assos., Hewlett Packard, Beverly, Mass., 1960-69; sr. physicist Harvard-Smithsonian Center for Astrophysics, Cambridge, Mass., 1969—. Contbr. articles to profl. jours. Served with RCAF, 1951-53. Recipient medal for outstanding sci. achievement NASA, 1978, I.I. Rabi award IEEE, 1993. Fellow Am. Phys. Soc.; mem. Eastern Yacht Club. Patentee in field. Office: 60 Garden St Cambridge MA 02138-1516

VEST, CHARLES MARSTILLER, academic administrator; b. Morgantown, W.Va., Sept. 9, 1941; s. Marvin Lewis and Winifred Louise (Buzzard) V.; m. Rebecca Ann McCue, June 8, 1963; children: Ann Kemper, John Andrew. BSME, W.Va. U., 1963; MSME, U. Mich., 1964, PhD, 1967; DEng (hon.), Mich. Tech. U., 1992, W.Va. U., 1994. Asst. prof., then assoc. prof. U. Mich., Ann Arbor, 1968-77, prof. mech. engring., 1977-90, assoc. dean acad. affairs Coll. Engring., 1981-86, dean Coll. Engring., 1986-89, provost, v.p. acad. affairs, 1989-90; pres. MIT, Cambridge, 1990—; bd. dirs. E.I. du Pont de Nemours and Co., IBM; vis. assoc. prof. Stanford (Calif.) U., 1974-75. Author: Holographic Interferometry, 1979; assoc. editor Jour. Optical Soc. Am., 1982-83; contbr. articles to profl. jours. Trustee Wellesley Coll., Woods Hole Oceanographic Inst., New Eng. Aquarium; adv. trustee Environ. Rsch. Inst. Mich. Recipient Excellence in Rsch. award U. Mich., 1980, Disting. Svc. award, 1972, Disting. Visitor award U. La Plata, Argentina, 1979, Centennial medal Am Soc. Engring. Edn., 1993. Fellow AAAS, Am. Acad. Arts and Scis., Optical Soc. Am.; mem. ASME, NAE, Sigma Xi, Tau Beta Pi, Pi Tau Sigma. Presbyterian. Office: MIT 77 Massachusetts Ave Cambridge MA 02139-4301

VEST, FRANK HARRIS, JR., bishop; b. Salem, Va., Jan. 5, 1936; s. Frank Harris and Viola Gray (Woodson) V.; m. Ann Jarvis, June 14, 1961; children: Nina Woodson, Frank Harris III, Robert Alexander. BA, Roanoke Coll., 1959; MDiv, Va. Theol. Sem., 1962, DD, 1985; DD (hon.), U. of South, 1987; LHD (hon.), St. Paul's Coll., 1991. Ordained to ministry Episcopal Ch. as deacon, 1962, as priest 1963. Curate St. John's Episcopal Ch., Roanoke, Va., 1962-64; rector Grace Episcopal Ch., Radford, Va., 1964-68; rector Christ Episcopal Ch., Roanoke, 1968-73, Charlotte, N.C., 1973-85; suffragan bishop Diocese of N.C., Raleigh, 1985-89; bishop coadjutor Diocese of So. Va., Norfolk, 1989-91, bishop, 1991—. Chmn. exec. com. Thompsons Children's Home, Charlotte, 1976-79; pres. Crisis Assistance Ministry, Charlotte, 1983-85; trustee Va. Theol. Sem., Alexandria, 1968-73, 91—, U. of South, Sewanee, Tenn., 1985-89, Episc. Radio TV Found., Atlanta, 19786-82; chair Dispatch of Bus., House of Bishops, 1988—. Democrat. Avocations: tennis, reading, walking, golf, fly-fishing. Office: Diocese of So Va 600 Talbot Hall Rd Norfolk VA 23505-4361*

VEST, G. WAVERLY, JR., lawyer; b. Temple, Tex., Nov. 13, 1947; s. George W. and Mary (knapp) V.; m. Judy Howard, May 15, 1971; children: Briggs, Deborah. BBA in Acctg. with honors, U. Tex., 1970, JD, 1973. Bar: Tex., D.C. Atty., ptnr. Bracewell & Patterson, Houston, 1973—; lectr. in field. Mem. St. Luke's United Meth. Ch. Lt. USAF, 1970-73. Recipient Acctg. Edn. Fund scholarship, 1969-70. Fellow Houston Bar Found.; mem. ABA (banking law com.), Tex. Bar Assn. (fin. institutions com.), Tex. Assn. Bank Counsel, D.C. Bar Assn., Houston Bar Assn., Phi Eta Sigma, Phi Kappa Phi, Beta Gamma Sigma, Beta Alpha Psi, Phi Delta Theta, Phi Delta Phi. Home and Office: 5619 Briar Dr Houston TX 77056-1003

VEST, GARY D., federal agency administrator; m. Camilla Bonzer; 1 child, Jason. BA in Polit. Sci., U. Idaho, 1968; M in Urban Planning, U. Washington, 1970. Assoc. city planner Redmond, Wash., 1969-71; chief programs, base master planner Laughlin AFB, 1971-72; asst. chief Air Tng. Command Master Planning, 1972-73; cmty. planner Hdqs. USAF, 1973-74; asst. to chief Air Force Environ. Divsn., 1974-83; dep. Air Force Environment, Safety and Occupl. Health, 1983-87, dep. asst. sec., 1987-93; prin. asst. dep. Sec. Def. Environ. Security. Recipient Presdl. Disting. and Meritorious Exec. Rank award, Exceptional Civilian Svc. award, Meritorious Svc. award, Straospheric Ozone Protection award EPA, SAME Tudor medal; inducted U. Idaho Alumni Hall of Fame, 1994. Mem. Am. Planning Assn., Am. Inst. Cert. Planners, Sr. Exec. Assn., Am. Def. Preparedness Assn., Soc. Am. Mil. Engrs., Air Force Assn., Air Force Hist. Found., Fed. Exec. Inst. Alumni Assn., Def. Fire Protection Assn. Office: Environ Security 3400 Defense Pentagon Washington DC 20301-3400*

VEST, GAYLE SOUTHWORTH, obstetrician and gynecologist; b. Duluth, Minn., Apr. 7, 1948; d. Russell Eugene and Brandon (Young) Southworth; m. Steven Lee Vest, Nov. 27, 1971; 1 child, Matthew Steven. BS, U. Mich., 1970. Diplomate Am. Bd. Ob-Gyn. Intern in ob-gyn. Milw. County Gen. Hosp., 1974-75, So. Ill. U. Sch. Medicine, 1975-78; pvt. practice Chapel Hill (N.C.) Ob-Gyn., 1978-80; asst. attending physician dept. ob-gyn. U. N.C. Sch. Medicine, Chapel Hill, 1978-80; clin. assoc. dept. ob-gyn. Duke U. Med. Ctr., Durham, N.C., 1978-80; pvt. practice Big Stone Gap (Va.) Clinic, 1980-88, Norwise Ob-Gyn. Assocs., Norton, Va., 1988—. Fellow Am. Coll. Obstetricians and Gynecologists; mem. Am. Soc. Reproductive Medicine, Va. Ob-Gyn. Soc., Va. Perinatal Assn., Med. Soc. Va., Wise County Med. Soc. Avocations: kayaking, travel. Office: Norwise Ob-Gyn Assocs Med Arts Bldg 3 102 15th St NW Norton VA 24273-1616

VEST, GEORGE SOUTHALL, diplomat; b. Columbia, Va., Dec. 25, 1918; s. George Southall and Nancy Margaret (Robertson) V.; m. Emily Barber Clemons, June 21, 1947; children—Jeannie, George, Henry. B.A., U. Va., 1941, M.A., 1947. Fgn. service duty SHAPE and NATO, Quito, Ottawa, Paris; dir. bur. polit. mil. affairs Dept. State; asst. sec. of state for European affairs Dept. State, Washington, 1977-81; ambassador to European Communities Brussels, 1981-85; dir. gen. Fgn. Svc. Dept. State, Washington, 1985-89; career amb. Dept. State, 1987-89, ret., 1989. Served to capt. U.S. Army, 1941-46, ETO. Mem. Phi Beta Kappa. Episcopalian. Avocations: bicycling, gardening. Home: 5307 Iroquois Rd Bethesda MD 20816-3104

VEST, HYRUM GRANT, JR., horticultural sciences educator; b. Salt Lake City, Sept. 23, 1935; s. Hyrum and Josephine Gwendolyn (Lund) V.; m. Gayle Pixton, Sept. 18, 1958; children: Kelly, Lani, Kari, Kamille, Kyle. B.S., Utah State U., 1960, M.S., 1964; Ph.D., U. Minn., 1967. Pathologist, agronomist U.S. Dept. Agr., Beltsville, Md., 1967-70; vegetable breeder Mich. State U., East Lansing, 1970-76; dept. head dept. hort. and landscape architecture Okla. State U., Stillwater, 1976-83; head dept. hort. scis. Tex A & M U., College Station, 1983-89; head dept. plants, soils and biometeorology Utah State U., Logan, 1989-95, assoc. dir. Utah Agrl. Experiment Sta., 1995—; mem. Nat. Plant Genetics Resource Bd., Washington, 1982-88. Served to 1st lt. U.S. Army, 1960-63. Univ. research fellow Utah State U., 1963-64. Fellow Am. Soc. Hort. Sci. Republican. Mem. LDS Ch. Home: 368 Spring Creek Rd Providence UT 84332-9432 Office: Utah State U Utah Agrl Experiment Sta Logan UT 84322-4810

VEST, JAMES MURRAY, foreign language and literature educator; b. Roanoke, Va., Mar. 27, 1947; s. Eddie Lewis and Irene (Cannaday) V.; m. Nancy Foltz, June 6, 1970; 1 child, Cecelia. BA, Davidson (N.C.) Coll., 1969; MA, Duke U., 1971, PhD, 1973. From asst. to assoc. prof. Rhodes Coll., Memphis, 1973-91, prof., 1991—; adminstr. Rhodes in Paris Program, France, 1978-87; organizer faculty teaching seminars, 1988—. Author: The French Face of Ophelia, 1989, The Poetic Works of Maurice de Guérin, 1991; contbr. articles to profl. jours. Chmn. Urban Outreach Commn., Memphis, 1978-81; leader youth groups, 1983—. Capt. U.S. Army Res., 1973—. Recipient campus svc. award Sears-Roebuck, 1990, Outstanding Teaching award Clarence Day Found., Memphis, 1984, Am. Assn. Higher Edn., 1988; Woodrow Wilson fellow, 1971, NDEA Title IV fellow, 1969. Mem. MLA, So. Atlantic Modern Lang. Assn., Am. Assn. of Tchrs. of

French. Avocations: cinema, hiking. Office: 2000 N Pkwy Rhodes C Memphis TN 38112

VEST, MARVIN LEWIS, mathematical educator; b. Elkins, W.Va., May 17, 1906; s. Marvin Johnson and Margaret (Kley) V.; m. Winifred Louise Buzzerd, Aug. 3, 1930; children: Marvin Lewis, Charles Marstiller. BS, Davis and Elkins Coll., 1927, ScD (hon.), 1970; MS, W.Va. U., 1932; AM, U. Mich., 1942, PhD in Math., 1948. Prin. Franklin (W.Va.) High Sch., 1927-28; instr. Elkins High Sch., 1928-31, 33-35; assoc. prof. math. Davis and Elkins Coll., 1935-38; mem. faculty W.Va. U., Morgantown, 1931-33, 38—, prof. math., 1955-73, emeritus, 1973—; cons. U.S. Bur. Mines, 1952-57. Mem. Am. Math. Soc., Math. Assn. Am., W.Va. Acad. Scis. (sec. 1934-37, pres. 1950-51), Sigma Xi, Pi Mu Epsilon. Republican. Presbyterian (elder). Lodge: Mason. Home: 417 Elm St Morgantown WV 26505-6507

VEST, R. LAMAR, church administrator. Dir. Ch. of God Media Ministries. Office: Ch of God PO Box 2430 Cleveland TN 37320-2430

VEST, ROSEMARIE LYNN TORRES, secondary school educator; b. Pueblo, Colo., Jan. 16, 1958; d. Onesimo Bernabe and Maria Bersabe (Lucero) Torres; m. Donald R. Vest, May 1, 1982. BA, U. So. Colo., 1979, BS, 1991; cert. travel agt., Travel Trade Sch., Pueblo, 1986. Cert. secondary tchr., Colo. Tutor U. So. Colo., Pueblo, 1977-79; sales rep. Intermountain Prodns., Colorado Springs, Colo., 1979-80; tutor, Pueblo, 1980-82, 84-85; travel agt. So. Colo. Travel, Pueblo, 1986-88; children's program facilitator El Mesias Family Support Program, Pueblo, 1987-88; substitute tchr. social studies Sch. Dist. 60, Pueblo, 1990—, Freed Mid. Sch., Pueblo, 1991, 92; Chpt. 1 Summer Reading Program, 1992, 93, 94, 95; instr. Travel and Tourism Dept. Pueblo C.C., 1994-95, Dept Social Studies, 1996-97. Tchr. Sunday sch., chairperson adminstrv. bd. cert. lay spkr., lay rep. to ann. conf. Ch. Evangelism, co-chmn. Trinity United Meth. Ch., Pueblo, 1989-94, parish coun. rep. to Trinity/Bethel Coop. Parish; sponsor United Meth. Youth United Meth. Ch.; tchr. Sunday Sch., co-coord. vacation Bible sch., edn. chairperson, 1994—, cert. lay spkr., ministerial program asst., lay leader Bethel United Meth. Ch., 1994—; craft facilitator Integrated Health Svcs., Pueblo, 1991—; spiritual devotions/worship leader Pueblo Manor Nursing Home, 1993—; vol. resident svcs. Pueblo County Bd. for Developmental Disabilities, 1989—; mem. conf. leadership team, parliamentarian Rocky Mountain Conf. United Meth. Ch., 1995, dist. rep., 1997—; ministerial candidate United Meth. Ch.; conf. rep. Rocky Mountain Conf. Coun. on Fin. and Adminstrn., 1996—. Recipient Excellence in Tchg. award Freed Mid. Sch., 1992, Vol. of Yr. award IHS of Pueblo, 1995. Mem. Assn. Am. Geographers, Nat. Oceanog. Soc., Nat. Geog. Soc. Democrat. Avocations: crafts, photography, reading, cross-stitch, listening to music. Home: 125 W Grant Apt C Pueblo CO 81004-2000

VEST, STEVEN LEE, gastroenterologist, hepatologist, internist; b. Mpls., July 30, 1948; s. Lee Herbert and Marian Mize (Rains) V.; m. Gayle Maureen Southworth, Nov. 27, 1971; 1 child, Matthew Steven. BA, U. Minn., 1970, MD, 1974. Diplomate Am. Bd. Internal Medicine, Am. Bd Gastroenterology. Intern internal medicine Milw. County Hosp., 1974-75; resident internal medicine So. Ill. U., Springfield, 1975-77; fellow in gastroenterology and hepatology Duke U. Med. Ctr., Durham, N.C., 1978-80; gastroenterology-hepatology and internal medicine cons. Lonesome Pine Hosp., Big Stone Gap, Va., 1980—; gastroenterology and internal medicine cons. St. Mary's Hosp., Norton, 1983—, Norton Community Hosp., Norton, Va., 1985—; chmn. med. care evaluation, Lonesome Pine Hosp., Big Stone Gap, 1984-88; chief of medicine Norton Community Hosp., 1991-93, bd. dirs., 1993—. Fellow ACP, Am. Coll. Gastroenterology; mem. Am. Gastroent. Assn., Am. Soc. Internal Medicine, Va. Med. Soc. (state del. 1992), Wise County Med. Soc. (treas. 1984-86, v.p. 1991-92, pres. 1992-93), Am. Assn. Christian Counselors. Methodist. Avocations: kayaking, jogging, skiing, photography, karate. Home: Powell Valley 1800 Egan Rd Big Stone Gap VA 24219 Office: NCH Med Arts Bldg #2 98 15th St NW Ste 202 Norton VA 24273-1600

VESTA, RICHARD V., meat packing company executive. Pres. Packerland Packing, Green Bay, Wis. Office: Packerland Packing PO Box 23000 Green Bay WI 54305*

VESTAL, JOSEPHINE BURNET, lawyer; b. Iowa City, June 13, 1949; d. Allan Delker and Dorothy (Walker) V. Student Williams Coll., 1970; B.A., Mount Holyoke Coll., 1971; J.D., U. Wash., 1974. Bar: Wash. 1974, U.S. Dist. Ct. (we. dist.) Wash. 1974, U.S. Ct. Appeals (9th cir.) 1984, U.S. Ct. Appeals (D.C. cir.) 1984, U.S. Dist. Ct. (ea. dist.) Wash. 1993. Ptnr. Selinker, Vestal, Klockars & Andersen, Seattle, 1974-80; assoc. Williams, Lanza, Kastner & Gibbs, Seattle, 1981-87, ptnr., 1988—. Mem. ABA (mem. labor and employment sect., mem. labor and employment sect. Def. Rsch. Inst.), Wash. State Bar Assn. (trustee young lawyers sect. 1974—), Seattle-King County Bar Assn. (trustee young lawyers sect. 1974—), Wash. Women Lawyers. Office: Williams Kastner & Gibbs 4100 Two Union Square 601 Union St Seattle WA 98101-2327

VESTAL, JUDITH CARSON, occupational therapist; b. Memphis, Dec. 22, 1939; d. Carl Thomas and Emma Winifred (Stewart) Carson; m. Tommy Vestal, June 22, 1974. BS in Elem. Edn., U. Tenn., 1961; BS in Occupl. Therapy, Washington U., St. Louis, 1964; MA in Guidance and Counseling, La. Tech. U., 1978; postgrad., Tex. Woman's U., 1993. Cert. occupl. therapist, La. Occupl. therapist Sewall Rehab. Ctr., Denver, 1964-67, Whittingham Hosp., London, 1967-70, The London Hosp., 1970-74, N.W. La. Rehab., Shreveport, 1975-77, Caddo Bossier Assn. for Retarded Children, Shreveport, 1977-81; occupl. therapist La. State U. Med. Ctr., Shreveport, 1981-87, asst. prof. occupl. therapy, 1986-92, assoc. prof. clin. occupl. therapy, 1992—. Editl. bd. Am. Jour. Occupl. Therapy, 1984-87; contbr. articles to profl. jours. Bd. dirs. Children's Learning Ctr., Shreveport, 1980-89; mem. Spl. Edn. Adv. Coun., Shreveport, 1985-91; mem., sec. vestry Ch. of Epiphany, Shreveport, 1992—. Mem. Am. Occupl. Therapy Assn. (sec. com. on state assn. pres. 1989-92, Svc. award 1992), La. Occupl. Therapy Assn. (v.p. 1983-86, pres. 1986-90, Pres.'s award 1991, Award of Merit 1994), Soc. for Rsch. in Child Devel., Neurodevelopmental Treatment Assn., Internat. Soc. for Alternative and Augmentative Comm., Phi Kappa Phi. Anglican Ch. Avocations: reading, travel, music. Home: 176 Preston Shreveport LA 71105-3306 Office: Louisiana State University Medical Center Sch Allied Health Prof 1501 Kings Hwy Shreveport LA 71103-4228

VESTAL, LUCIAN LAROE, financier; b. Whitewright, Tex., Aug. 10, 1925; s. Rolla C. and Lora A. (Robinson) V.; m. Gretalee Kranz Banzhaf, Nov. 8, 1994; 1 child, Denise Vestal Simon. Student, Baylor U., 1942-43; B.S., U. Pitts., 1947; postgrad., N.Y.U., 1948-50, Ill. Inst. Tech., 1960. Security analyst Lionel D. Edie & Co., N.Y.C., 1947-54; asst. dir. finance Champion Papers, Inc., Hamilton, Ohio, 1954-55; dir. research Rotan, Mosle & Co., Houston, 1955-58; dir. planning Pure Oil Co., Palatine, Ill., 1958-63; dir. planning and fin. services Weyerhaeuser Co., Tacoma, 1963-65; treas. Sunray DX Oil Co., Tulsa, 1965-68; asst. treas. Sun Oil Co., Phila., 1968-69; group v.p. Tesoro Petroleum Corp., San Antonio, 1969-72; sr. v.p. affiliate banking Palmer Bank Corp., Sarasota, Fla., 1973-75; trustee Citizens Growth Properties, 1969-78; chmn., dir. Palmer banks of Siesta Key, Village Plaza, N.A., Gulf Gate, Sarasota, Palmer Bank of Bradenton (N.A.), Fla., Palmer Bank & Trust Co. Naples (N.A.), Fla., Palmer Bank & Trust Co. Ft. Myers (N.A.), Fla.; pres., dir. Point Palma Sola, Inc., 1975-78, Cortez Yachts, Inc., 1975-78, So. Yachts, Inc., 1978-90; ceo, chmn., dir. Advantage Nat. Charge System, Sarasota, 1990; pres. Gen. Securities Transfer, 1995—; dir. Seaman Corp., Ohio; chmn. Trident Environ. Sys., Inc., Citizens Growth Properties, Omni Films Internat., Inc.; dir. Palmer Investment Adv. Co.; dir., pres. Partridge Inc. Served to 1st lt., inf. USMCR, 1943-45, 50-51. Decorated Navy Cross, Purple Heart. Mem. N.Y. Soc. Security Analysts, Retired Officers Club, U.S. Power Squadron, Sarasota Yacht Club (mem., dir.), Delta Tau Delta. Republican. Baptist. Home: 1648 Pine Harrier Cir Sarasota FL 34231-3353

VESTAL, THELMA SHAW, history educator; b. Spring Hill, Tenn., Apr. 19, 1946; d. Ester Lena McKissack; m. Danny Vestal, June 28, 1976; children: Danny La'Brian, Felecia De'Lece. BS, Tenn. State U., 1969, MS, 1972. Sec. Tenn. State U., Nashville, 1969-72, counselor, 1972-76; substitute tchr. Metro Pub. Schs., Nashville, 1977-85; U.S. history tchr. Dupont-Tyler Mid. Sch., Hermitage, Tenn., 1985—; Mem. Operation C.A.N., Nashville, 1985—. Active ARC, Nashville, 1988—. Named Educator of Yr., Nashville Mid. Sch. Assn., 1992-93; recipient Outstanding Christian award Schrader Lane Ch. of Christ, Nashville, 1989-90, Golden Apple award, 1996. Mem. Nat. Geographic Soc., Metro Nashville Coun. for Social Studies, Tenn. Edn. Assn., NEA, Nat. Coun. for Social Studies. Democrat. Ch. of Christ. Avocations: reading, bowling, music, dancing.

VESTAL, TOMMY RAY, lawyer; b. Shreveport, La., Sept. 19, 1939; s. Louie Wallace and Margaret (Golden) V.; m. Patricia Marie Blackwell, Jan. 24, 1981; children: Virginia Ann Hollingsworth, John Wallace Vestal, Douglas William Yancy. BSME, U. Houston, 1967, JD, 1970. Bar: Tex. 1970, U.S. Patent Office 1972, U.S. Ct. Appeals (D.C. cir.) 1975. Patent atty. Am. Enka Corp., Asheville, N.C., 1970-71, Akzona Inc., Asheville, 1971-84, Akzo Am., Inc., Asheville, 1985-86; sr. patent atty. Fibers div. BASF Corp., Enka, N.C., 1986-87, div. patent counsel, 1987-89, sr. patent counsel, 1989-90; pvt. practice law, 1990-91; dir. Geary Glast & Middleton, Dallas, 1992; ptnr. Falk, Vestal & Fish, Dallas, 1992-97; mgr. Law Offices Tom R. Vestal, Carrollton, 1997—. Mem. ABA, State Bar Tex., Am. Intellectual Property Law Assn. (mem. patent law com., alternate dispute resolution com.), Carolina Patent, Trademark and Copyright Law Assn. (bd. dirs. 1983-85, 2d v.p. 1985-86, 1st v.p. 1986-87, pres. 1987-88), Dallas Bar Assn. (mem. com. law in schs. and comm., schs. and the community bd.), DFW Patent Law Assn., Asheville C. of C. (chmn. legal affairs com.), Phi Alpha Delta. Republican. Lutheran. Lodge: Kiwanis (pres. 1982). Avocations: golf, fishing, hiking. Home: 3109 Squireswood Dr Carrollton TX 75006-5218 Office: 700 N Pearl St Dallas TX 75201-7424

VESTNER, ELIOT N., JR., bank executive; b. Bronxville, N.Y., Aug. 4, 1935; s. Eliot N. and Priscilla Alden (Fuller) V.; m. Elizabeth Gwin, Jan. 1, 1966 (div. 1992); children: Alice-Lee, Charles Fuller; m. Louise R. Cutler, Aug. 11, 1995. B.A., Amherst Coll., 1957; M.A., U. Mich., 1958; LL.B., Columbia U., 1962. Bar: N.Y. 1963. Assoc. Debevoise, Plimpton, Lyons & Gates, N.Y.C., 1962-68; spl. counsel N.Y. State Bank Dept., 1968-70; spl. asst. to Gov. Nelson A. Rockefeller, 1970-72; 1st dep. supt. N.Y. State, 1972-75, supt. banking, 1974-75; sr. v.p., gen. counsel Irving Trust Co., 1975-82, exec. v.p., 1982-87; exec. counsel Bank of Boston, 1987-96, exec. dir. pensions, 1996—; dir. Boston-AIG Co., 1994—; bd. dirs. Previnter, Mexico. Republican. Home: Devonshire Pl # 2605 Boston MA 02109 Office: Bank of Boston PO Box 2016 Boston MA 02106-2016

VETTER, HERBERT, physician, educator; b. Vienna, Austria, Aug. 24, 1920; m. Eleonore von Hacklaender, July 6, 1946 (div. 1969); 1 child, Barbara Weber; m. Brigitte Frei, Dec. 20, 1973 (div. 1993). M.D., U. Vienna, 1948. Physician, Allgemeines Krankenhaus, Vienna, Austria, 1948-60; Brit. Council research fellow, 1951; research fellow Sloan-Kettering Inst. Cancer Research, N.Y.C., 1954; head radioisotopes lab. 2d Med. Univ. Clinic, Vienna, 1951-60; asso. prof. medicine U. Vienna, 1959-67, prof., 1967—; sr. officer IAEA, 1958-81; chmn. sci. adv. council Austrian Soc. Energy Affairs, 1979—; v.p. Austrian Nuclear Tech. Soc., 1980—; bd. dirs. Austrian sect. Internat. Physicians for Prevention of Nuclear War, 1983-86; chmn. planning bd. IB, Internat. Commn. Radiation Units and Measurements, 1962-69, cons., 1969-89. Author: (with N. Veall) Radioisotope Techniques in Clinical Research and Diagnosis, 1958, Zwickmühle Zwentendorf, 1983; editor: Radioaktive Isotope in Klinik und Forschung, Vols. I-III, 1955-58, (with E.H. Belcher) Radioisotopes in Medical Diagnosis, 1971, Jour. Nuclear Medicine, 1959-95, Internat. Jour. Biomed. Engring., 1971-89. Recipient prize for art and sci. Republic of Austria, 1956, award of distinction Philippine Soc. Nuclear Medicine; Paul Harris fellow, 1983. Affiliate Royal Soc. Medicine; mem. Gesellschaft der Aerzte, Gesellschaft für Innere Medizin, Österreichische Roentgengesellschaft, Österreichische Gesellschaft für Nuklearmedizin (hon.). Club: Rotarian (pres. Vienna 1975-76). Home: Am Hausberg 1, 2344 Maria Enzersdorf Austria

VETTER, JAMES GEORGE, JR., lawyer; b. Omaha, Apr. 8, 1934; s. James George and Helen Louise (Adams) V.; m. Mary Ellen Froelich, June 25, 1960; 1 child, James G. III. BS, Georgetown U., 1954; JD, Creighton U., 1960. Bar: Nebr. 1960, Tex. 1967. Counsel IRS, Washington, 1960-64, Dallas, 1964-67; practiced in Dallas, 1967—; sr. ptnr. Vetter, Bates, Tibbals, Lee & DeBusk P.C., 1979-89; mem. Godwin & Carlton P.C., 1989—, mng. dir., 1994—; lectr. taxation seminars; bd. dirs. Pilgrim's Pride Corp., AFV Energy, Inc., VLSI Packaging Corp. Contbr. articles to profl. jours. Asst. sgt.-at-arms Tex. Dem. Conv., 1968; advisor selection com. Georgetown U., 1970-85; scoutmaster Boy Scouts Am., 1974-75. With USAF, 1954-57; capt. USAFR, ret. Mem. Nebr. Bar Assn., State Bar Tex. (cert. tax law 1983—), Coll. State Bar Tex., Dallas Bar Assn. (chmn. fee disputes com. 1985, chmn. publs. com. 1988, chmn. pictoral directory com. 1993), Real Estate Fin. Execs. Assn. (pres. 1982-83), Cash Alliance (pres. 1987-88), Creighton U. Alumni Assn. (pres. Dallas-Ft. Worth 1969-70), Ctrl. Dallas Assn. (bd. dirs. 1994—), Park Cities Club, City Club, Delta Theta Phi. Roman Catholic. Home: 11023 Rosser Rd Dallas TX 75229-3915 Office: Godwin & Carlton 2500 Nations Bank Plz Dallas TX 75202

VETTER, JAMES LOUIS, food research association administrator; b. St. Louis, Jan. 26, 1933; s. Charles W. and Dorothy (Smith) V.; m. Rose Marie Gentille, Aug. 21, 1954; children: Douglas John, Debra Dianne. AB, Washington U., St. Louis, 1954; MS, U. Ill., 1955, PhD, 1958. Food technologist Monsanto Co., St. Louis, 1958-63; dir. rsch. Keebler Co., Elmhurst, Ill., 1963-72; v.p. tech. dir. div. Standard Brands, Fraklin Park, Ill., 1972-75; pres. West Tex. Milling, Amarillo, 1975-77; v.p. Am. Inst. Baking, Manhattan, Kans., 1977—; adj. prof. Kans. State U., Manhattan, 1977—; tech. cons. Author: Food Labeling-Requirements for FDA Regulated Products, 1992, Food Laws and Regulations, 1996; editor: Adding Nutrients to Foods, 1982; Dairy Products for Cereal Processing, 1984. Contbr. articles to profl. jours. Patentee in field. Bd. dirs., pres. Wharton Manor Nursing Home, Inc., Manhattan, 1980-81. Fellow Inst. Food Technologists; mem. Am. Assn. Cereal Chemists (sec. 1983-85, pres. 1986-87), Kiwanis (bd. dirs.). Avocations: photography; golf. Home: 1947 Bluestem Ter Manhattan KS 66502-4530 Office: Am Inst Baking 1213 Bakers Way Manhattan KS 66502-4555

VEYSEY, ARTHUR ERNEST, reporter, administrator, biographer; b. Boulder, Colo., Sept. 28, 1914; s. Ernest Charles and Lillian (Larson) V.; m. Florence Jones, 1937 (dec. 1940); 1 dau., Priscilla Joan; m. Gwendolyn Morgan, 1946. B.A., U. Colo., 1935; L.H.D., Ill. Benedictine Coll., 1986. Reporter Denver Post, 1935-37, Scottsbluff (Neb.) Star-Herald, 1937-41, Omaha World-Herald, 1941-43; war corr. Southwest Pacific, Chgo. Tribune, 1943- 45, fgn. corr., 1946-50, chief London bur., 1950-75; gen. mgr. Cantigny Trust, 1975-86. Author: Death in the Jungle, 1966, (with Gwen Morgan) Halas by Halas, 1979, (with Gwen Morgan) Poor Little Rich Boy, Biography of Col. R.R. McCormick. Bd. dirs. The Forest Found. Recipient Norlin award U. Colo., 1986, Margaret Landon award, 1986. Address: 3 Cobham Ct, PO Box 232, Kerikeri Bay of Islands New Zealand

VEZERIDIS, MICHAEL PANAGIOTIS, surgeon, educator; b. Thessaloniki, Greece, Dec. 16, 1943; came to U.S., 1974; s. Panagiotis and Sofia (Avramidis) V.; m. Therese Mary Statz; children: Peter Statz, Alexander Michael. MD, U. Athens, 1967; MA (hon) ad eundem, Brown U., 1989. Diplomate Am. Bd. Surgery. Fellow surg. rsch. Harvard Med. Sch./Mass. Gen. Hosp., Boston, 1974-77; resident U. Mass., Worcester, 1977-80; fellow in surg. oncology Roswell Park Meml. Inst., Buffalo, 1980-81, attending surgeon, 1981-82; staff surgeon VA Med. Ctr., Providence, 1982-84; asst. prof. surgery Brown U., Providence, 1982-88; chief surg. oncology VA Med. Ctr., Providence, 1984—, assoc. chief surgery, 1986—; cons. in surgery R.I. Hosp., Providence, 1987—; surg. oncologist Roger Williams Med. Ctr., Providence, 1989—; assoc. dir. div. surg. oncology Brown U., Providence, 1989—, assoc. prof. surgery, 1988-94, prof., 1994—; chmn. profl. edn. com. R.I. div. Am. Cancer Soc., Providence, 1987-89, bd. dirs., 1987—, pres.-elect 1989-91, pres. 1991-93, 96, del. dir. to nat. bd. dirs., 1993-96, mem. nat. assembly, 1996—, mem. Nat. Assembly of the Am. Cancer Soc., 1997—; vis. prof. U. Patras (Greece) Med. Sch., 1988; mem. sci. adv. com. Clin. Rsch. Ctr., Brown U., Providence, 1989-91. Contbr. articles to profl. jours. and chpts. in med. books. Mem. parish coun. Ch. of Annunciation, Cranston, R.I., 1985-91; v.p. Hellenic Cultural Soc. Southeastern New Eng., Providence, 1987-89. Decorated Navy Commendation medal; named Profl. Fed. Employee of Yr., R.I. Fed. Exec. Coun., 1987; recipient St. George medal Am. Cancer Soc.; Merit Rev. Cancer Rsch. grantee VA, 1983-89. Fellow ACS; mem. Soc. Surg. Oncology, Assn. for Acad. Surgery, Am. Soc. Clin. Oncology, N.Y. Acad. Scis. (life), Soc. for Surgery Alimentary Tract, Am. Assn. for Cancer Rsch., Collegium Internat. Chirurgiae Digestivae, Assn. Mil. Surgeons U.S., Soc. for Metastasis Rsch., New Eng. Cancer Soc., New Eng. Surg. Soc., Quidnessett Country Club. Greek Orthodox. Avocations: classical music, reading, fencing, tennis, squash, cross-country skiing. Home: 50 Limerock Dr East Greenwich RI 02818-1643 Office: Roger Williams Med Ctr 825 Chalkstone Ave Providence RI 02908-4728

VEZIROGLU, TURHAN NEJAT, mechanical engineering educator, energy researcher; b. Istanbul, Turkey, Jan. 24, 1924; came to U.S., 1962; s. Abdul Kadir and Ferruh (Bürün) V.; m. Bengi Isikli, Mar. 17, 1961; children: Emre Alp, Oya Sureyya. A.C.G.I., City and Guilds Coll., London, 1946; B.Sc. with honors, U. London, 1947; D.I.C., Imperial Coll., London, 1948; Ph.D., U. London, 1951. Engring. apprentice Alfred Herbert Ltd., Coventry, U.K., 1945; project engr. Office of Soil Products, Ankara, Turkey, 1953-56; tech. dir. M.K.V. Constrn. Co, Istanbul, 1957-61; assoc. prof. mech. engring. U. Miami, Coral Gables, Fla., 1962-65; prof. U. Miami, Coral Fables, Fla., 1966—; dir. grad. studies mech. engring. U. Miami, Coral Gables, Fla., 1965-71, chmn. dept. mech. engring., 1971-75, assoc. dean research Coll. Engring., 1975-79, dir. Clean Energy Research Inst., 1974—; UNESCO cons., Paris; vis. prof. Middle East Tech. U., Ankara, 1969. Editor-in-chief: Internat. Jour. Hydrogen Energy, 1976—. Pres. Learning Disabilities Found., Miami, 1972-73, advisor, 1974-80. Recipient Turkish Presdl. sci. award Turkish Sci. and Tech. Research Found., 1975; named hon. prof. Xian Jiaotong U., China, 1982. Fellow AAAS, ASME, Instn. Mech. Engrs.; mem. Internat. Assn. Hydrogen Energy (pres. 1975), AIAA, Assn. Energy Engrs., Am. Nuclear Soc., Am. Soc. Engring. Edn., AAUP, Internat. Soc. Solar Energy, Systems Engring. Soc., Sigma Xi. Home: 4910 Biltmore Dr Miami FL 33146-1724 Office: U Miami Clean Energy Rsch Inst PO Box 248294 Miami FL 33124-8294 *Hydrogen energy system will provide the world with clean and abundant energy, while doing away with pollution, acid rains and the greenhouse effect. It is a noble and worthwhile goal to strive for.*

VIADERO, ROGER C., government official; b. N.Y.C.. BBA in Pub. Acctg., Pace U., MBA in Mgmt. Acctg. Former police officer and homicide investigator N.Y.C. Police Dept.; various positions FBI, 1979-94, chief internal auditor N.Y. div.; chief audit unit FBI, Washington; prof. FBI Nat. Acad., Quantico, Va.; insp. gen. USDA, Washington, 1994—. Contbr. numerous articles on law enforcement and mgmt. to profl. publs. Office: USDA Office Insp Gen Adminstrn Bldg 14th & Independence Ave SW Washington DC 20250*

VIALL, J(OHN) THOMAS, non-profit organization executive, fundraiser; b. Ft. Hood, Tex., Aug. 15, 1948; s. Otis DePry and Margaret Helen (Cowie) V.; m. Susan Jane Bright, Aug. 25, 1973 (div. Dec. 1980); m. Barbra Jill Baken, Oct. 17, 1982; children: Larissa Rachel, Alessandra Lauren. BA, Fairleigh Dickinson U., 1970, MA magna cum laude, 1972; postgrad., Columbia U., 1972-74; Tchg. Cert., Montclair State Coll., 1975. Tutor ED/LD Bd. of Edn., Bogota and Ridgefield Par, N.J., 1975-77; dir. devel. The Vail-Deane Sch., Elizabeth, N.J., 1977-83; dir. corp. devel. Save the Children, Westport, Conn., 1983-86, Thirteen/WNET, N.Y.C., 1986-87; exec. dir. Sister City Program of City of N.Y., Office of Mayor, 1987-91; dir. devel. Sister Cities Internat., Alexandria, Va., 1991-93; exec. dir. Internat. Coll. Surgeons, Chgo., 1993-96; exec. dir., CEO Orton Dyslexia Soc., 1996—; editor: N.Y.-Beijing Directory, 1987; project coord.: Hard Choices-Portraits of Poverty and Hunger in America, 1983. Recipient Key to City, Mayorof Owensboro, Ky., 1992. Achievements include negotiation of loan of 2 giant pandas from Beijing Zoo to N.Y. Zool. Soc. Avocations: golf, tennis, computer technology. Home: 3816 Palmetto Ct Ellicott City MD 21042 Office: Chester Bldg # 382 8600 Lasalle Rd Baltimore MD 21286-2001

VIANCO, PAUL THOMAS, metallurgist; b. Rochester, N.Y., Dec. 28, 1957; s. George William and Josephine Rose (Sardisco) V.; m. Karen Elaine Claghorn. BS in Physics, SUNY, 1980; MS in Mechanical and Aeronautical Engring., U. Rochester, 1981, PhD in Materials Sci., 1986. Sr. mem. tech. staff Sandia Nat. Labs., Alburquerque, 1987—. Mem. ASME, Am. Welding Soc. (chmn. subcom. 1992—), ASM Internat., The Metalurgical Soc., Sandia Skeet Club (treas.). Home: 4012 Shenandoah Pl NE Albuquerque NM 87111-4158 Office: Sandia Nat Labs PO Box 5800 MS 1411 Albuquerque NM 87185

VIANDS, DONALD REX, plant breeder and educator; b. Riverdale, Md., Apr. 1, 1952; s. Walter Leroy and Lydia (Zeh) V.; m. Janice Ann Ruppelt, Aug. 7, 1976; children: Jamie Christopher, April Suzanne. BS in Agronomy, U. Md., 1974; MS in Plant Breeding, U. Minn., 1977, PhD in Plant Breeding, 1979. Undergrad. rsch. asst. U. Md., College Park, 1969-74; grad. rsch. asst. U. Minn., St. Paul, 1974-79; asst. prof. Cornell U., Ithaca, N.Y., 1979-85, assoc. prof., 1985-92, prof., 1992—, assoc. dir. acad. programs, 1995—; mem. adv. com. biotech. sci. adv. com. EPA, Washington, 1987-95; mem. steering com. N.Y. State North Country Devel. Program, 1990—; adv. N.Y. State Forage and Grassland Coun., 1984-90, Alfalfa Crop Adv. Com., 1984-92. Contbr. articles to profl. jours., chpts. to books. Sunday sch. tchr. People's Bapt. Ch., Newfield, N.Y., 1988—, deacon, 1988-90, 93—, Awana comdr., 1993—. Named Most Influential Faculty Mem. for Merrill Presdl. Scholar, Cornell U., 1991. Mem. Am. Soc. Agronomy, Crop Sci. Soc. Am., Am. Seed Trade Assn. (mem. minimum distance com. 1988-94), N.Am. Alfalfa Improvement Conf. (sec. 1984-86, v.p. 1986-88, pres. 1988-90), Ea. Forage Improvement Conf., Am. Forage and Grassland Coun., N.Y. State Forage and Grasslands Coun. Republican. Achievements include development of 11 alfalfa varieties. Office: Cornell Univ Office Acad Programs 155 Roberts Hall Ithaca NY 14853-5905

VIANI, JAMES L., lawyer; b. Kincaid, Ill., Dec. 24, 1932; s. Frank Jerome and Alfonsina V.; m. Virginia Lee Wilson, Dec. 27, 1958; children: Theresa, Diana, Deborah. BS, Millikin U., 1954; LLB, Wash. U., St. Louis, 1957. Bar: Ill. 1957, Mo. 1957. Assoc. Blackmar, Swanson, Midgley, Jones & Eager, Kansas City, Mo., 1958-59, Stinson, Mag & Fizzell, Kansas City, 1960-62; ptnr. Stinson, Mag & Fizzel, Kansas City, 1962-87, chmn. corp. dept., 1979-87, cons. ptnr., 1988-92. Br. bd. chmn. YMCA, Kansas City, 1979-81. With U.S. Army, 1957-63. Mem. ABA, Phi Kappa Phi, Order of the Coif. Republican. Avocations: hiking, reading, farming. Home: 11106 Belleview Ave Kansas City MO 64114-5115 Office: Stinson Mag & Fizzell PO box 419251 1201 Walnut St Kansas City MO 64141-6251

VIANO, DAVID CHARLES, automotive safety research scientist; b. San Mateo, Calif., May 7, 1946; s. James Louis and Dorothy Marie (Clark) V.; m. Sharon Lynne Henderson, Dec. 7, 1975. BSEE, U. Santa Clara, 1968; MS in Applied Mechanics, Calif. Inst. Tech., 1969, PhD in Applied Mechanics, 1972; postdoctoral degree in biomed. sci., Swiss Inst. Tech., Zurich, 1974; MD, Karolinska Inst., 1997. Sr. rsch. engr. biomed. scis. dept., GM Rsch. Labs., Warren, Mich., 1974-76, staff rsch. engr., 1976-78, asst. dept. head, 1978-87, prin. rsch. scientist, leader safety rsch. program, 1987-92; mgr. global R&D programs, 1992—; tech. sec. med. com. for automotive safety biomed. scis. dept., GM Rsch. Labs., Warren, Mich., 1984—, mem. accident avoidance tech. com., 1989-93; adj. asst. prof. dept. mech. engring. Wayne State U., Detroit, 1981-86, adj. assoc. prof., 1986-89, adj. prof., 1989—; vis. prof. Chalmers U., Sweden, 1992—; chmn. indsl. adv. com. Bioengring. Ctr., Wayne State U., 1984—; mem. injury rsch. grant rev. com. CDC, HHS, Atlanta, 1986-88, mem. adv. com. for injury prevention and control, 1989-92; mem. indsl. adv. com. bioengring. divsn. U. Pa., Phila., 1988-95; mem. com. on fed. trauma rsch., NRC, NAS, 1984-85; mem. com. sch. bus. safety, 1987-89, com. on occupant restraint rsch. needs, 1988-92; mem. Transp. Rsch. Bd., NRC; com. to rev. CDC injury control program progress, NRC, 1988; mem. engring. directorate rev. panel bioengring. NSF, 1987. Assoc. editor Jour. Biomech. Engring., 1982-88, Accident Analysis and Prevention, 1988—; editl. cons. Jour. Trauma, 1988-92, emeritus, 1992—; tech. reviewer Handbook of Bioengineering, 1985, Protecting Your Bank From Injury, 1985; editor Jour. Traffic Medicine, 1996—. Mem. property tax assessment bd. rev. City of Bloomfield Hills, Mich., 1986—; bd. dirs., mem.-at-large Mich. Head Injury Alliance chpt. Nat. Head Injury Found., 1987-89, exec. com., bd. dirs. nat. orgn., Southborough, Mass., 1987-91, treas., chmn. fin. com., 1988-91; trustee Del. Harder Rehab. Fund Bd., 1987-89, pres., 1989, Rehab. Inst. Found., Detroit; bd. trustees Detroit Med. Ctr., clin. svcs. adv. bd. rehab. and post-acute svcs., 1989—. Recipient

Safety Engring. Excellence award Nat. Hwy. Traffic Safety Adminstrn., Dept. Transp., 1989, Best Paper award 30th Stapp Car Crash Conf., 1988, Bertil Aldman award IRCOBI, 1992. Fellow ASME (mem. transp. safety com. 1982-92, bioengring. honors com. 1982—, govt. rels. contact bioengring. div. 1980-92, program chmn. editor symposium, 1981), Soc. Automotive Engrs. (chmn. Stapp car crash adv. com., 1976-90, passenger protection com. 1980—, safety adv. com. 1985—, Ralph Isbrandt automotive safety engring. awards bd. 1987-89, organizer, editor 18 symposia 1982-86, mem. other coms., Isbrandt medals 1981, 85, 86, Forest R. McFarland Outstanding Svc. award 1982, Arch T. Colwell awards 1982, (3) 1988, (2) 1989), Assn. Advancement Automotive Medicine (chmn. ad hoc com. for impairment scaling, 1985—, mem. exec. bd. 1986-91, pres.-elect 1988, pres. 1989); mem. Am. Trauma Soc. (bd. dirs. 1989—), Motor Vehicle Mfrs. Assn. (mem. biomechanics task group 1976-84), U.S. Nat. Com. on Biomechanics (Soc. Automotive Engrs. del. 1982-89), Internat. Standards Orgn. (impact safety group 1976—), Am. Soc. Biomechanics, ACS (com. on truama and burns conjoint coun. surg. rsch. 1986—), Biomed. Engring. Soc. (sr.), AAAS. Republican. Home: 265 Warrington Rd Bloomfield Hills MI 48304-2952 Office: Gen Motors Rsch and Devel Ctr Warren MI 48090-9055

VIAULT, BIRDSALL SCRYMSER, history educator; b. Mineola, N.Y., Sept. 20, 1932; s. Joseph Choate and Helen Lee (Scrymser) V.; m. Sarah Reed Underhill, May 9, 1970. BS, Adelphi U., 1955, MA, 1956; MA, Duke U., 1957, PhD, 1963. Instr. history Adelphi U., Garden City, N.Y., 1959-63, asst. prof. history, 1963-68; assoc. prof. history Winthrop U., Rock Hill, S.C., 1968-72, prof. history, 1972—, chmn. dept. history, 1979-89; vis. assoc. prof. Duke U., Durham, N.C., 1970. Author: World History in the 20th Century, 1969, American History Since 1865, 1989, rev. edit., 1993, Western Civilization Since 1600, 1990, Modern European History, 1990, English History, 1992; author weekly column, 1979-87; contbr. articles and revs. to profl. jours. Mem. Nassau County (N.Y.) Dem. Com., 1961-68, S.C. Commn. for Archives and History, 1979-89, S.C. Bd. Rev. for Nat. Register of Hist. Places, 1988-96; del. S.C. State Dem. Conv., 1972, 74, 94, 96; leader ann. tours to Europe, 1977—. Ford Found. Coop. Program for Humanities Postdoctoral fellow U. N.C., Duke U., 1969-70. Mem. So. Hist. Assn., Am. Cath. Hist. Assn., Soc. Historians of Am. Fgn. Rels., S.C. Hist. Assn., Kiwanis Club Rock Hill, Phi Kappa Phi, Phi Alpha Theta, Zeta Beta Tau. Roman Catholic. Avocations: travel, photography, cooking. Home: 2186 Wentworth Dr Rock Hill SC 29732-1242 Office: Winthrop U Dept History Rock Hill SC 29733

VICE, JON EARL, hospital executive; b. Fairfield, Ala., July 1, 1947; s. Jon Walker Vice and Martha Ann (Lee) Cain; m. Sara Rose Romano Marino, July 26, 1967 (div. Feb. 1975); children: Jon E. Jr., Lisa Ann; m. Joanne Katherine Richter, June 28, 1975 (div. Mar. 1992); children: Jeffrey Walker, Jessica Lynn. BS, U. Ala., Tuscaloosa, 1970; MS, U. Ala., Birmingham, 1974. Asst. to adminstr. Children's Hosp. Ala., Birmingham, 1971-72, adminstr., chief operating officer, 1977-79; assoc. adminstr. Children's Hosp. Med. Ctr., Cin., 1972-76; exec. v.p., chief operating officer Children's Hosp. Wis., Milw., 1979-84, pres., chief exec. officer, 1984—; chmn., bd. dirs. Milw. Regional Med. Ctr., 1985—, Child Health Corp. Am., Kansas City, Mo.; pres., bd. dirs. Total Care Health Plan (HMO), Milw., 1985-87; mem. Greater Milw. Com.; bd. dirs. Milw. Ednl. Trust. Named Outstandng Alumnus Grad. Program in Health Adminstrn., U. Ala.-Birmingham Alumni Assn., 1987. Mem. Am. Coll. Healthcare Execs., Nat. Assn. Childrens Hosps. (exec. coun., bd. dirs. 1986—, chmn. 1989—), Westmoore Country Club (pres., bd. dirs.), Univ. Club. Presbyterian. Avocations: golf, skiing. Office: Children's Hosp Wis PO Box 1997 Milwaukee WI 53201-1997

VICE, LAVONNA LEE, lawyer; b. Lexington, Ky., May 27, 1952; d. Keith Romould and Helen (Singer) V. BA summa cum laude, U. Balt., 1980, JD, 1983. Bar: Md. 1983, U.S. Ct. Appeals (4th cir.) 1987, U.S. Dist. Ct. Md. 1988, D.C. 1989, U.S. Supreme Ct. 1989. Trial atty. Ellin & Baker, Balt., 1983—; lectr., writer, rschr., med. surg. and hosp. standards of care. Mem. ABA, ATLA, Md. State Bar Assn., D.C. Bar Assn., Balt. City. Bar Assn. Office: Ellin & Baker 1101 Saint Paul St Baltimore MD 21202-2662

VICENTE, ESTEBAN, artist; b. Turegano, Segovia, Spain, Jan. 20, 1903; came to U.S. 1941; s. Toribio Y Ruiz and Sofia Perez Y (Albarez); m. Harriet Godfrey, Dec. 1963. Art cert., Artes De San Fernando, Madrid, 1921-24; hon. PhD, Parsons Sch. Design, N.Y.C., 1984, Long Island U., South Hampton, N.Y., 1993. Faculty mem. art dept. various univs., 1949-74; tchr., artist-in-residence Vermont Studio Ctr., Johnson, Vt., 1985, Parsons Sch. Design, N.Y.C., 1991-93; founding mem., artist-in-residence N.Y. Studio Sch. Drawing, Painting & Sculpture, N.Y.C., 1964—. Recipient Lifetime Achievement in the Arts award Guild Hall Mus., East Hampton, N.Y., 1993, Gold Medal for fine arts Spanish Coun. of Ministers, Govt. of Spain, 1991. Mem. Am. Acad. Arts & Letters, Nat. Acad. of Design. Home: 1 W 67th St New York NY 10023

VICENZI, ANGELA ELIZABETH, nursing educator; b. N.Y.C., Aug. 19, 1938; d. Peter Christiaan and Angeline Elizabeth (Rudtke) Richard; m. Richard Emil Vicenzi, Nov. 11, 1961; children: Richard Martin, Paul Andrew, Stephen Mark, Douglas Emil. Diploma, St. Vincent's Hosp. Sch. Nursing, N.Y.C., 1959; BSN, Western Conn. State U., 1977; MEd in Cmty. Health Nursing, Columbia U., 1980, EdD in Health Edn., 1984. Pub. health nurse City of N.Y., 1960-61; pediat. staff nurse Norwalk (Conn.) Hosp., 1970-73; profl. nurse traineeship Columbia U. Tchrs. Coll., N.Y.C., 1978-80; clin. instr. Norwalk C.C., 1977-78; asst. prof. Sacred Heart U., Fairfield, Conn., 1980-83; from asst. prof. to assoc. prof. So. Conn. State U., New Haven, 1985-95, prof., 1995—; cons. Corp. Health Cons., Norwalk, 1980-90; pres. faculty senate So. Conn. State U., 1991-94. Editor, pub. Complexity & Chaos in Nursing Jour., 1994-97; contbr. articles to profl. jours. Mem. St. Jerome Parish Coun., Norwalk, 1995-97. Recipient Virginia A. Henderson award Conn. Nurses Assn., 1996; grantee Conn. State U., 1994-95, Profl. Nurse Traineeship grantee Health and Human Svcs., 1991-94. Mem. AAUP (treas. SCSU chpt. 1995—), Assn. Comty. Health Nursing Educators (program chair 1995), Mu Beta, Sigma Theta Tau (pres. 1992-94). Office: So Conn State U Dept Nursing 501 Crescent St New Haven CT 06515-1330

VICK, COLUMBUS EDWIN, JR., civil engineering design firm executive; b. Jacksonville, Fla., Nov. 8, 1934; s. Columbus Edwin Sr. and Lucretia (Dean) V.; m. Laura Anne McGowan, Mar. 20, 1964; children: Jennifer, Carolyn, Elizabeth. BSCE, N.C. State U., 1956, MSCE, 1960. Registered profl. engr., 15 states. Research asst. N.C. State Civil Engring. Dept., Raleigh, 1958-60; transp. planning engr. Harland Bartholomew & Assocs., Memphis, 1960-64; office and project mgr. Harland Bartholomew & Assocs., Raleigh, 1964-67; prin., co-founder Kimley-Horn and Assocs. Inc., Raleigh, 1967-72, pres., 1972-92; chmn., 1992—. Co-author: North Carolina Atlas; contbr. numerous research and tech. publs. in fields of transp. engring. planning and traffic engring. Past pres., bd. dirs. N.C. State U. Engring. Found.; past pres. bd. assocs. Meredith Coll.; past dir. N.C. State U. Alumni Assn.; past 2d v.p. Bapt. State Conv. of N.C.; bd. dirs. Assoc. Bapt. Press, Bibl. Recorder; bd. trustees Kenan Inst. for Engring. Tech. and Sci. Named Disting. Engring. alumnus N.C. State U., 1991. Fellow ASCE (Outstanding Young Engr. award ea. br. N.C. sect. 1966), Inst. Transp. Engrs. (Oustanding Individual Activity award so. sect. 1978, Disting. Svc. award so. sect. 1981, Lifetime Svc. award N.C. sect. 1995); mem. NSPE, Am. Con. Engrs. Coun., Am. Inst. Cert. Planners, Profl. Svcs. Mgmt. Assn. (Coll. of Fellow), N.C. Soc. Engrs. (Outstanding Engring Achievement award 1992). Baptist. Home: 2205 Nancy Ann Dr Raleigh NC 27607-3318 Office: Kimley-Horn and Assocs Inc 3001 Weston Pky Cary NC 27513-2301

VICK, FRANCES BRANNEN, publishing executive; b. Trinity, Tex., Aug. 14, 1935; d. Carl Andrew and Bess (courtney) B.; m. Ross William Vick Jr., June 23, 1956; children: Karen Lynn, Ross William III, Patrick Brannen. BA, U. Tex., 1958; MA, Stephen F. Austin State U., 1968. Teaching fellow Stephen F. Austin State U., Nacogdoches, Tex., 1966-68, lectr., 1968-69; lectr. Angelina Coll., Lufkin, Tex., 1969-71, Baylor U., Waco, Tex., 1974-75, 77-78; vice prin. Vanguard Sch., Waco, 1975-77; pres. E-Heart Press, Inc., Dallas, 1979—; co-dir. UNT Press U. North Tex., Denton, 1987-89, dir., 1989—. Publisher 150 books; editor 40 books. Leadership coun. Ann Richards Com., Austin, 1990-94; amb. Inst. Texan Cultures; mem. Tex. Commn. on Arts, Lit., 1991. Named to Tex. Inst. of Letters. Mem. AAUW, Book Pubs. Tex. (v.p. 1990-96, pres. 1996), Tex. Folklore Soc. (councillor 1991-93), Tex. Humanities Resource Ctr. (bd. dirs. 1990-91), Western Lit. Assn., Philos. Soc. Tex., Tex. Inst. of Letters, Pen Ctr. U.S.A. West, Tex. State Hist. Assn. (life), East Tex. Hist. Assn. (life), Soc. Scholarly Pub., Women in Scholarly Pub., Rocky Mountain Book Pubs. Assn., Leadership Tex., Leadership Am., Tex. Humanities Alliance, UNT League Profl. Women. Democrat. Episcopalian. Home: 3700 Mockingbird Ln Dallas TX 75205-2125 Office: U North Tex PO Box 13856 Denton TX 76203-6856

VICK, JAMES ALBERT, publishing executive, consultant; b. Norwalk, Conn., Feb. 5, 1945; s. James Albert and Madeline (Mayhew) V.; m. Deborah M. Ashley, Dec. 23, 1964 (div. Oct. 1974); children: James Ashley, Guy Robert; m. Susan Jane Collins, May 14, 1977; 1 child, Jonathan Scott. BS, Boston U., 1967. Dist. mgr. McGraw Hill Pub. Co., N.Y.C., 1969-75, Cahners Pub. Co., N.Y.C., 1975-79; mgr. advt. ASCE, N.Y.C., 1979-82; v.p. mktg. Bill Communications, N.Y.C., 1982-87; pub. Thomas Pub. Co., N.Y.C., 1987-95; v.p. Web Property Devel. Poppe Tyson, 1995-96; exec. v.p. sales/mktg. Lawyers Weekly Publs., Boston, 1996—; cons. Carvajal, Calle, Columbia, 1984, McLarens, London, 1987. Capt. USAR, 1967-70, Vietnam. Mem. Bus. Mktg. Assn. (cert. bus. communicator), Am. Bus. Press (pubs. com.), Soc. Plastics Engrs., Pharm Ad Club, Instrument Soc. Am., Indsl. Computing Soc., Princeton Club, Beacon Hill Country Club, Port Royal Golf Club, Elks. Episcopalian. Avocations: golf, sailing, antique restoration. Home: 75 Rodgers Rd Carlisle MA 01741-1866 Office: Lawyers Weekly Publs 41 West St Boston MA 02111-1203

VICK, NICHOLAS A., neurologist; b. Chgo., Oct. 3, 1939. MD, U. Chgo., 1965. Diplomate Am. Bd. Neurology. Intern U. Chgo. Hosps., 1965, resident in neurology, 1966-68; fellow in neurology NIH, Bethesda, Md., 1968-70; staff Evanston (Ill.) Hosp., 1975—; prof. neurology Northwestern U. Med. Sch., Evanston, Ill., 1978—. Office: Evanston Hosp Divsn Neurology 2650 Ridge Ave Evanston IL 60201-1718

VICK, SUSAN, playwright, educator; b. Raleigh, N.C., Nov. 4, 1945; d. Thomas B. Jr. and Merle (Hayes) V. MFA, Southern Meth. U., 1969; PhD, U. Ill., 1979. Prof. drama/theatre Worcester (Mass.) Poly. Inst., 1981—, dir. theatre programs; dir. theatre tech., playwright Excuse Me For Living Prodns., Cambridge, Mass., 1989—, Festival Fringe, Edinburgh, 1989—; playwright Ensemble Studio Theatre, Glasgow, N.Y.C., 1981-83; founder WPI Ann. New Voices Festival of Original Plays, 1982. Editor: (2 vols.) Playwrights Press, Amherst, 1988—; playwright plays including When I Was Your Age, 1982, Ord-Way Ames-Gay, 1982, Investments, 1985, Half Naked, 1989, Quandary, 1983, Meat Selection, 1984, Give My Love to Everyone But, 1989; appeared in plays including Rip Van Winkle, 1979, Why I Live at The P.O., 1982, The Play Group, 1984-85, Present Stage, 1985, Sister Mary Ignatius Explain It All, 1986, Wipeout, 1988, Bogus Joan, 1992, 93; dir. play Give My Love to Everyone But, 1990 (Edinburgh Festival); theatre editor: Sojourner The Women's Forum, 1995—; dramaturg, script cons. Clyde Unity Theatre, Glasgow, Scotland, 1992—. Dir., Women's Community Theatre, Amherst, 1981-84, Upstart, Wis., 1994. Faculty fellow U. Ill., 1976-77. Mem. Drama League, Dramatists Guild (assoc.), Soc. Stage Dirs. and Choreographers (assoc.), Alpha Psi Omega (Svc. to Students award 1996). Avocations: puppets, frogs. Office: Worcester Poly Tech Inst 100 Institute Rd Worcester MA 01609-2247

VICKER, RAY, writer; b. Wis., Aug. 27, 1917; s. Joseph John and Mary (Young) V.; m. Margaret Ella Leach, Feb. 23, 1944. Student, Wis. State U., Stevens Point, 1934, Los Angeles City Coll., 1940-41, U.S. Mcht. Marine Officers' Sch., 1944, Northwestern U., 1947-49. With Chgo. Jour. Commerce, 1946-50, automobile editor, 1947-50; mem. staff Wall St. Jour., 1950-83; European editor Wall St. Jour., London, Eng., 1960-75. Author: How an Election Was Won, 1962, Those Swiss Money Men, 1973, Kingdom of Oil, 1974, Realms of Gold, 1975, This Hungry World, 1976, Dow Jones Guide to Retirement Planning, 1985, The Informed Investor, 1990; also numerous articles. Served with U.S. Merchant Marine, 1942-46. Recipient Outstanding Reporting Abroad award Chgo. Newspaper Guild, 1959; Best Bus. Reporting Abroad award E. W. Fairchild, 1963, 67; hon. mention, 1965; Bob Considine award, 1979; ICMA Journalism award, 1983. Mem. Soc. Profl. Journalists, Authors Guild. Roman Catholic. Clubs: Overseas Press (Reporting award 1963, 67) (N.Y.C.); Press (Chgo.). Home and Office: 4131 E Pontatoc Canyon Dr Tucson AZ 85718-5227

VICKERS, JAMES HUDSON, veterinarian, research pathologist; b. Columbus, Ohio, Apr. 21, 1930; s. Carl James and Olga Elizabeth (Schaer) V.; m. Valerie Janet May, Apr. 5, 1964; 1 child, Dana Carlton. BS, Ohio State U., 1952, DVM, 1958; MS, U. Conn., 1966. Diplomate Am. Coll. Vet. Pathologists. Veterinarian Columbus Mcpl. Zoo, 1958-60; dir. pathology dept. Lederle Labs., Pearl River, N.Y., 1960-70; v.p., dir. rsch. Primelabs. Inc., Farmingdale, N.J., 1970-72; dir. spl. studies Johnson & Johnson, Washington Crossing, N.J., 1972-73; dir. pathology and primatology br. FDA, Bethesda, Md., 1973-92, dir. div. vet. svcs., 1992-95; pres. PathPro Assocs., Ijamsville, Md., 1995—; rep. interagy. rsch. animal commn. FDA, Bethesda, 1974-89; cons. Gov. Arab Republic Egypt, Cairo, 1976-84, Paul Erlich Inst., Frankfurt, Fed. Republic Germany, 1977-78; chmn. com. on animalcare Ctr. for Biologics, Bethesda. Contbr. chpts. to books. Spokesman Urbana (Md.) Civic Assn., 1987. Capt. U.S. Army, 1952-54. Recipient Presdl. citation Pres. James Carter, 1980, Alumni Svc. award Ohio State Coll. Vet. Medicine, 1987, FDA Commr.'s spl. citation, 1988; FDA Commr.'s Disting. Career Svc. award, 1995. Mem. Am. Vet. Med. Assn., Soc. Toxicology, Interant. Acad. Pathology, Ohio State Vet. Med. Assn., Zane Grey's West Soc. (rpes. 1987-95), Westerners Internat. Avocations: fine arts, books. Office: PathPro Assocs 2324 Oak Dr Ijamsville MD 21754-8650

VICKERS, ROGER SPENCER, physicist, program director; b. Hitchin, Hertfordshire, Eng., Nov. 13, 1937; came to U.S., 1963, naturalized, 1974; s. John Hector and Corona (McCarthy) V.; m. Solvi Loken, May 18, 1968; children: Michelle, Jacqueline, Kevin. BSc with honors, Southampton U., Eng., 1959, PhD, 1963. Physicist Ill. Inst. Tech. Research Inst., Chgo., 1963-66; rsch. assoc. Stanford U., 1966-68; v.p. sci. and applications E.R.A., Inc., Houston, 1969-70; assoc. prof. elec. engring. Colo. State U., 1970-73; dir. advanced radar program SRI Internat., Menlo Park, Calif., 1973—; cons. NSF. Mem. IEEE. Home: 1143 Los Altos Ave Los Altos CA 94022-1021 Office: SRI Internat Bldg G Menlo Park CA 94025

VICKERS, STANLEY, biochemical pharmacologist; b. Blackpool, Eng., Sept. 27, 1939; came to U.S., 1962, naturalized, 1979; s. Norman Stanley and Hannah (Snape) V.; m. Florence Margaret Foster, Jan. 6, 1975. BSc external, London U., 1962; PhD, SUNY, Buffalo, 1967. Fellow U. Kans., Lawrence, 1966-69; sr. rsch. pharmacologist Merck & Co., West Point, Pa., 1969-71, rsch. fellow, 1971-81, sr. rsch. fellow, 1981—. Contbr. articles to profl. jours.; patentee in field. Mem. AAAS, Am. Soc. Pharmacology and Exptl. Therapeutics, Am. Chem. Soc., N.Y. Acad. Scis. Avocations: golf, skiing, health club activities. Office: Merck Rsch Labs Bldg 26A-2044 West Point PA 19486

VICKERY, ANN MORGAN, lawyer; b. Anderson, S.C., June 25, 1944; d. Joseph Harold and Doris (Rogers) Morgan; m. Raymond Ezekiel Vickery, Jr., June 23, 1979; children: Raymond Morgan, Philip Dickens. AB History, Mary Baldwin Coll., 1965; JD, Georgetown U., 1978. Bar: D.C. 1978. Elem. sch. tchr. Chesterfield County, Va., 1965-66; legal publs. specialist Nat. Archives and Record Svc., Washington, 1966-69; speech writing staff to Pres., rsch. asst., chief rschr., staff asst. The White House, Washington, 1969-74; summer clerk Graham & James, Washington, 1975; various positions Dept. Treasury, Washington, 1975-78; atty. Hogan & Hartson, Washington, 1978—; health group dir. Hogan and Hartson, Washington, 1991—, exec. com., 1992-95, 96—; gen. counsel Nat. Hospice Orgn., 1982— (named Woman of the Yr. 1986); spkr. in field. Contbr. articles to profl. jours. Dir. Hospice No. Va., Arlington, 1987-93; trustee Nat. Hospice Found., 1996—. Mem. ABA, Nat. Health Lawyers Assn., D.C. Bar, Health on Wednesday, Phi Alpha Theta. Office: Hogan & Hartson Columbia Square 555 13th St NW Washington DC 20004-1109

VICKERY, RAYMOND EZCKIEL, JR., government official; b. Brookhaven, Miss., Apr. 30, 1942; s. Raymond Ezckiel and Clarene Helen (Dickens) V.; m. Raymond Claur Brown, Dec. 23, 1967 (div. June 1976); m. Ann Morgan, June 25, 1979; children: Raymond Morgan, Philip Dickens. AB, Duke U., 1964; postgrad., U. Sri Lanka, 1964-65; LLB, Harvard U., 1968. Assoc. Hogan & Hartman, Washington, 1968-77; ptnr. Johnson & Vickery, Vienna, Va., 1977-81, Reed Smith Shaw & McClay, McLean, Va., 1981-85, Hogan & HArtman, McLean, Va., 1985-93; asst. sec. for trade devel. U.S. Dept. Commerce, Washington, 1993—. Contbr. articles to profl. jours. Del. Va. Gen. Assembly, Richmond, 1974-80; mem. Dem. Com., Farifax County, Va., 1971-93; Dem. nominee for Congress, Va., 1992; mem. State Contra Com., Va., 1993; mem. Libt. Bd., Fairfax County, 1972-74. Fulbright scholar, 1964. Mem. ABA, Va. Bar Assn., D.C. Bar Assn., City Club, Phi Beta Kappa, Omicron Delta Kappa. Baptist. Avocations: fishing, horseback riding. Home: 2733 Willow Dr Vienna VA 22181 Office: US Dept Commerce 14th & Constitution Ave NW Washington DC 20230*

VICKERY, ROBERT BRUCE, oil industry executive, consultant; b. Shreveport, La., Aug. 25, 1938; s. Wilbur Claude and Clara Louise (Powell) V.; m. Margaret Lynn Gray, April 6, 1961; children: Joy Lynn, Andrew Gray, William Charles. Degree in Petroleum Engring., Colo. Sch. Mines, 1962; degree in Arctic Engring., U. Alaska, 1974. Petroleum engr. Pan Am. Petroleum Corp., Worland, Wyo., 1962-64; v.p. ops. Vickery Drilling Co., Inc., Evansville, Ind., 1964-73; mgr. drilling BP Alaska, Inc., Sohio-BP, Sohio Petroleum Corp., Anchorage, 1973-80; chmn. Artic Alaska Drilling Co., Inc., Anchorage, 1980-85; pres. Walker Energy Ptnrs., Houston, 1986-87; pres. Refuge Exploration, Inc., Houston, Tex., 1988—, Owensboro, Ky., 1988—. Author: World Oil, 1982. Pres. Boys Club of Alaska, 1978-80; trustee Boys Clubs Am., 1980-87; Alaska fin. chmn. Re-election of Pres. Reagan Com., 1984. Recipient Alaska Engr. of the Year award SPE of AIME, 1982. Mem. Soc. Petroleum Engrs., Ky. Oil and Gas Assn. (dir.), Ill. Oil and Gas Assn. (dir.). Office: Refuge Exploration Co Inc 700 Carlton Dr Owensboro KY 42303-7719

VICKREY, HERTA MILLER, microbiologist; b. San Gregorio, Calif.; d. John George and Hertha Lucy (Mehrstedt) Miller; m. William David Vickrey; children: Ellean H., Carlene L. Smith, Corrine A. Pochop, Arlene A.; m. Robert James Fitzgibbon, Dec. 28, 1979. BA, San Jose State U., 1957; MA, U. Calif., Berkeley, 1963, PhD in Bacteriology and Immunology, 1970. Cert. immunologist, pub. health microbiologist, med. technologist. Pub. health microbiologist Viral & Rickettsial Diseases Lab., Calif. Dept. Pub. Health, Berkeley, 1958-60, 61-62, 1964; postgrad. rsch. bacteriologist dept. bacteriology U. Calif., Berkeley, 1963-64; bacteriologist Children's Hosp. Med. Ctr. No. Calif., Oakland, 1958-70; asst. prof. U. Victoria, B.C., Can., 1970-72; rsch. assoc. rsch. dept. Wayne County Gen. Hosp., Wayne, Mich., 1972-83; lab. supr. med. rsch. and edn. U. Mich., Ann Arbor, 1977-83; pub. health lab. dir. Shasta County Pub. Health Svcs., Redding, Calif., 1983-84; sr. pub. health microbiologist, med. technologist Tulare County Pub. Health Lab., Tulare, Calif., 1984—; tech. supr. Tulare County Pub. Health Lab., Visalia, Calif., 1992-93; med. technologist Tulare County Pub. Health Lab., Tulare, Calif., 1994—; vis. scientist MIT, Cambridge, 1982; organizer, lectr. mycology workshop Tulare County Health Dept. Lab., Visalia, 1988; USPHS trainee U. Calif., Berkeley, 1965, 66. Author: Isolation and Identification of Mycotic Agents, 1987-88; contbr. articles to profl. jours. Fundraiser Battered Women's Shelter, Redding, 1983, Real Opportunities for Youth, Visalia, 1985, 86, Open Gate Ministries, Dinuba, Visalia, 1987-94. Fellow NIH, 1966-69, Dr. E.E. Dowdle rsch. fellow, U. Calif., 1969-70; grantee U. Victoria, 1970-72, Med. Rsch. and Edn. and Med. Adminstrn., U. Mich., 1973-83. Mem. No. Calif. Assn. Pub. Health Microbiologists, Calif. Scholarship Soc., Am. Soc. Clin. Pathologists (assoc.), Phi Beta Kappa, Delta Omega, Phi Kappa Phi, Beta Beta Beta. Avocations: biking, hiking, swimming. Home: 3505 W Campus Ave Apt 5 Visalia CA 93277-1869 Office: Tulare County Pub Health Lab 1062 S K St Tulare CA 93274-6421

VICKREY, WILLIAM SPENCER, economist, educator; b. Victoria, B.C., Can., June 21, 1914; came to U.S., 1914; s. Charles Vernon and Ada Eliza (Spencer) V.; m. Cecile Montez Thompson, July 21, 1951. B.A. in Math. with high honors (scholar), Yale, 1935; M.A., Columbia, 1937, Ph.D., 1947; D.H.L., U. Chgo., 1979; Social Sci. Research Council predoctoral field fellow, 1938-39. Jr. economist Nat. Resources Com., Washington, 1937-38; research asst. 20th Century Fund, 1939-40; economist OPA, 1940-41; sr. economist, div. tax research Treasury Dept., 1941-43; civilian pub. service assignee, 1943- 46, tax cons. to gov. P.R., 1946; mem. faculty Columbia U., N.Y.C., 1946-81; prof. econs. Columbia U., 1958-81; chmn. dept. Columbia, 1964-67, McVickar prof. polit. economy, 1971-81, prof. emeritus, from 1981; Cons. to govt. and industry, 1949-96; participant numerous confs., seminars; Ford research prof. Columbia, 1958-59; instr. IBM Systems Research Inst., 1964; vis. lectr. Monash U., Melbourne, Australia, 1971; inter-regional adviser UN, 1974-75. Author: Agenda for Progressive Taxation, 1947, Microstatics: Metastatics and Macroeconomics, 1964, Public Economics, 1994. Clk. Scarsdale (N.Y.) Friends Meeting, 1959-62. Fellow Inst. Advanced Study Behavioral Scis., Stanford, 1967-68. Fellow Am. Econ. Assn. (pres. 1992), Econometric Soc.; mem. Met. Econ. Assn., Am. Statis. Assn., Royal Econ. Soc., Ea. Econ. Assn., Atlantic Econ. Soc. (pres. 1992-93). Office: Econ Dept Columbia Univ New York NY 10027 *Having been born with considerable talent in an environment that encouraged its development and provided a modicum of recognition for its exercise, I can claim no special virtue for what this has enabled me to achieve. Indeed I have left undone many things that I ought to have done and can only hope that there is enough health left in me to make good some of the deficiency.Died Oct. 11, 1996.*

VICTOR, JAY, dermatologist; b. Detroit, Dec. 4, 1935; s. Ben and Pauline (Meisel) V.; m. Elana S. Lepler, Mar., 1965 (div. Aug., 1977); children: Pamela C., Daryl B.; m. Marianne Cook, sept. 4, 1978; children: Jonah A., Lauren. BA, U. Mich., 1958, MD, 1962. Diplomate Am. Bd. Dermatology. Intern Henry Ford Hosp., Detroit, 1962-63, resident, 1963-66; asst. prof. dermatology Wayne State U. Sch. of Medicine, Detroit, 1958-68; pvt. practice in dermatology Allen Park, Mich., 1966—; mem. active staff Oakwood Hosp., Dearborn, Mich., 1967—, courtesy staff Detroit Med. Ctr., 1967—; cons. Heritage Hosp. Taylor, Mich., 1980—. Fellow Am. Acad. Dermatology; mem. AMA, Mich. State Med. Soc. (del. 1980—), Wayne County Med. Soc. (del. 1980—), Mich. Dermatology Soc.. Jewish. Avocations: skiing, running, biking, sports. Office: Jay Victor MD 15201 Southfield Rd Allen Park MI 48101-2646

VICTOR, LORRAINE CAROL, critical care nurse; b. Duluth, Minn., June 14, 1953; d. George E. and Phyllis M. (Pierce) Drimel; m. Robert G. Victor. BA in Nursing, Coll. St. Scholastica, 1975; MS in Nursing, U. Minn., 1984. Cert. regional trainer for neonatal resuscitation program. Staff nurse St. Mary's Hosp., Rochester, Minn., 1975-79, 80-81, U. Wis. Hosp., Madison, 1979-80, U. Minn. Hosps., Mpls., 1981-84, 85-86; clin. instr. neonatal ICU, Children's Hosp. Inc., St. Paul, 1984-86; clin. nurse specialist neonatal ICU, Orlando (Fla.) Regional Med. Ctr., 1986-88, Children's Hosp. St. Paul, 1988—. Mem. AACN (Critical Care Nurse of Yr. award Greater Twin Cities chpt. 1992, cert. neonatal intensive care nursing), Nat. Cert. Corp. (cert. in neonatal intensive care nursing), Nat. Assn. Neonatal Nurses, Sigma Theta Tau. Office: Children's Health Care St Paul Birth Ctr 345 Smith Ave N Saint Paul MN 55102-2369

VICTOR, MICHAEL GARY, lawyer, physician; b. Detroit, Sept. 20, 1945; s. Simon H. and Helen (Litsky) V.; m. Karen Sue Hutson, July 20, 1975; children: Elise Nicole, Sara Lisabeth. Bars: Ill. 1980, U.S. Dist. Ct. (no. dist.) Ill. 1980, U.S. Ct. Appeals (7th cir.) 1981; diplomate Am. Bd. Legal Medicine. Pres., Advocate Adv. Assocs., Chgo., 1982—; asst. prof. medicine Northwestern U. Med. Sch., Chgo., 1982—; pvt. practice law, Barrington, Ill., 1982—; dir. emergency medicine Loretto Hosp., Chgo., 1980-85, chief. sect. of emergency medicine St. Josephs Hosp., Chgo., 1985-87; v.p. Med. Emergency Svcs. Assocs., Buffalo Grove, Ill., 1989; v.p. MESA Mgmt. Corp.; of counsel Bollinger, Ruberry & Garvey, Chgo. Author: Informed Consent, 1980; Brain Death, 1980; (with others) Due Process for Physicians, 1984, A Physicians Guide to the Illinois Living Will Act, The Choice is Ours!, 1989. Recipient Service awards Am. Coll. Emergency Medicine, 1973-83. Fellow Am. Coll. Legal Medicine (bd. govs. 1996-97, alt. del. to AMA House of Dels. 1996-97), Chgo. Acad. Legal Medicine; mem. Am. Coll. Emergency Physicians (pres. Ill. chpt. 1980, med.-legal-ins. council 1980-81, 83-84), ABA, Ill. State Bar Assn., Am. Soc. Law and Medicine, Chgo. Bar Assn. (med.-legal council 1981-83), AMA, Ill. State Med. Soc.

(med.-legal council 1980-86, 88), Chgo. Med. Soc. Jewish. Home and Office: 1609 Guthrie Cir Barrington IL 60010-5721

VICTOR, ROBERT EUGENE, real estate corporation executive, lawyer; b. N.Y.C., Dec. 17, 1929; s. Louis and Rebecca (Teitelbaum) V.; m. Dorothy Saffir, Oct. 14, 1951; children—Priscilla Saffir Victor Faubel, Pandora Saffir. LL.B., St. John's U., 1953, J.D., 1968. Bar: N.Y. bar 1953, Calif. bar 1965. With firm Szold and Brandwen, N.Y.C., 1953-54; atty. Dept. Army, Phila., 1955-56; with Hughes Aircraft Co., Culver City, Calif., 1956-62; v.p., gen. counsel Packard Bell Electronics Corp., Los Angeles, 1962-70; sr. v.p., gen. counsel Cordon Internat. Corp., Los Angeles, 1970-78; also dir.; gen. counsel Am. Harp Soc., 1969-85; pres. Vanowen Realty Corp., 1978-93, also dir. Mem. Los Angeles County Bar Assn. Club: Masons. Office: 722 Walden Dr Beverly Hills CA 90210-3125

VICTOR, WILLIAM WEIR, retired telephone company executive, consultant; b. Marshall, Ill., Apr. 16, 1924; s. Sturges L. and Esther (Weir) V.; m. Patricia Kelly, Sept. 7, 1946; children: William K., Jill Victor Buelsing, D. Gregory. Student, U. Okla., 1943-44; E.E., U. Cin., 1948, U. Ill., 1949. Various positions Cin. Bell Telephone, Ohio, 1947-69, v.p., 1972-85, sr. v.p., 1986-87; v.p. 195 Corp., N.Y., 1969-72; bd. dirs. Skidmore Sales and Distbn. Co. Trustee Goodwill Industries, Cin., 1973-91, WCET Ednl. TV Found., Cin., 1972-86, Bethesda Hosp., Cin., 1978, Herman Schneider Found., Cin., 1983, Armstrong Chapel Found., 1992; trustee, v.p. Millcreek Valley Conservancy Dist., 1990—. Sgt. USAR, 1943-45, ETO, lt. col. USAR, ret. Mem. IEEE, Engring. Soc. Cin., Cin. Country Club. Home: 5440 Windridge Ct Cincinnati OH 45243-2967

VICTORIN, HIS EMINENCE THE MOST REVEREND ARCHBISHOP See URSACHE, VICTORIN

VICTORSON, MICHAEL BRUCE, lawyer; b. Fairmont, W.Va., July 13, 1954; s. Morton Jerome and Deborah (Jacobson) V.; m. Janet Harris, Mar. 8, 1981; children: David Solomon, Sara Lorraine. BA, W.Va. U., 1976, JD, 1979. Bar: W.Va. 1979, U.S. Dist. Ct. (so. and no. dists.) W.Va. 1979, U.S. Dist. Ct. (ea. dist.) Ky. 1986, U.S. Ct. Appeals (4th cir.) 1980, U.S. Supreme Ct., 1992. Assoc. Love, Wise, Robinson and Woodroe, Charleston, W.Va., 1979-83; assoc. Robinson & McElwee, Charleston, 1983-84, ptnr., 1985—; speaker at profl. seminars. Contbr. articles to profl. publs. Chmn. appeal bd. U.S. Selective Svc. System, So. Dist. W.Va., Charleston, 1983—; lawyers' chmn. United Way Kanawha Valley, Charleston, 1988-90, 91-92, chmn. profl. div., 1992-93, mem. admissions com., 1990-92; bd. dirs. Med. Eye Bank W.Va., Charleston, 1989—; trustee B'nai Jacob Synagogue, 1992-94; mem. visiting com. W. Va. U. Coll. of Law, 1996—. Mem. ABA, Am. Law Firm Assn. (products liability steering com.), W.Va. Bar Assn., W.Va. State Bar Assn., Kanawha County Bar Assn., Def. Rsch. Inst., Def. Trial Counsel W.Va. (charter, bd. govs. 1992—), Nat. Assn. R.R. Trial Counsel, Order of Coif, Phi Beta Kappa, Phi Delta Phi, Phi Kappa Phi, Pi Sigma Alpha. Office: Robinson and McElwee PO Box 1791 Charleston WV 25326-1791

VIDAL, ALEJANDRO LEGASPI, architect; b. Kawit, Cavite, The Philippines, May 3, 1934; came to U.S. 1954; s. Antonio and Patrocinia Santonil (Legaspi) V.; m. Fe Del Rosario, Aug. 16, 1962; 1 child, Alex Anthony. BS in Architecture, Mapua Inst. Tech., 1962. Registered arch., The Philippines. Prin. A.L. Vidal Arch., Manila, The Philippines, 1962-63; staff arch. Vinnell Wall & Green, Agana, Guam, 1963-64; project engr. Dillingham Corp. of Nevada, Hawaii and Guam, 1964-74; sr. project mgr., preconstrn. svc. mgr. Fletcher-Pacific Constrn. Co. Ltd., Honolulu, 1974-96; prin. A.L. Vidal Constrn. Cons., Honolulu, 1996—, A.L. Vidal Arch., Cavite, The Philippines, 1996—. Designer, builder first application of integrated aluminum forming sys. for high rise concrete construction. Active Rep. Presdl. Task Force, Washington, 1980-88, Rep. Senatorial Com., Washington, 1980-88. With USN, 1954-58, Korea. Mem. Am. Concrete Inst., Am. Mgmt. Assn., Soc. Am. Mil. Engrs., Am. Legion, U. Hawaii Found., Chancellor's Club, Disabled Am. Vets., Comdrs. Club, Oxford Club. Roman Catholic. Avocations: golf, swimming, volunteer work. Home: 1051 Kaluanui Rd Honolulu HI 96825-1321

VIDAL, DAVID JONATHAN, insurance company executive, journalist; b. Bayamón, P.R., Oct. 11, 1946; s. Jesus Maria and Ercira Audacia (Mejia) V.; m. Watuza Leal, Jan. 25, 1975; 1 child, Katalyn. AB cum laude, Princeton U., 1968; student, Sch. Advanced Internat. Studies, Washington, 1982-83; MBA, Columbia U., 1991. Reporter The Caracas (Venezuela) Daily Jour., 1969-70; reporter, news editor AP, Caracas, N.Y., Sao Paulo, 1970-73; corr. AP, Brasilia, Brazil, 1973-75; reporter, bur. chief N.Y. Times, N.Y.C. and Rio de Janeiro, 1975-80; spl. asst., White House fellow Dept. State, Washington, 1980-81; cons. U.S. AID, Washington, 1981-82; dept. mgr. task force Pres.'s Pvt. Sector Survey on Cost Control, Washington, 1982-83; exec. dir. Nat. Commn. Secondary Schooling for Hispanics, Washington, 1983-84; dir. pub. affairs N.Y.C. Partnership, 1984-85; asst. v.p. Continental Ins., N.Y.C., 1985-95; v.p. Coun. on Fgn. Rels., N.Y.C., 1995—; adj. prof. journalism Columbia U. Grad. Sch. Journalism, N.Y.C., 1985-86; bd. dirs. Pub. Affairs Coun., Washington, 1988-95; trustee Found. for Pub. Affairs, Washington, 1989-95; mem. Contbns. Adv. Group, 1988-95, chmn., 1994-95; mem. corp. adv. group Schomburg Ctr. for Rsch. in Black Culture, 1988-95, Ad Hoc Com. on Charter Revision, 1988, Nat. Hispanic Agenda, 1988; mem. adv. group Latino Leadership Fund, 1991-95. Author newspaper series N.Y. Times, 1980; contbr. articles and reports in field. Trustee N.Y. Theol. Sem., N.Y.C., 1990—; elder, trustee West End Presbyn. Ch., N.Y.C., 1986—; mem. Coun. of Fgn. Rels.; prin. Coun. for Excellence in Govt., Washington, 1992—. Recipient Hispanic Achievement award Wall Street chpt. IMAGE, N.Y.C., 1989; Fulbright scholar, Washington and Venezuela, 1968. Mem. N.Y. Regional Assn. Grantmakers (dir., sec. 1988-95), Nat. Inst. Industry Assn. (corp. adv. group 1990-95), Nat. Civic League, Internat. Platform Assn., Coun. on Fgn. Rels. Democrat. Office: Coun on Fgn Rels 58 E 68th St New York NY 10021-5939

VIDAL, GORE, writer; b. West Point, N.Y., Oct. 3, 1925; s. Eugene L. and Nina (Gore) V. Grad., Phillips Exeter Acad., 1943. Author, 1946—. Author: (novels) Williwaw, 1946, In a Yellow Wood, 1947, The City and the Pillar, 1948, The Season of Comfort, 1949, A Search for the King, 1950, Dark Green, Bright Red, 1950, The Judgment of Paris, 1952, Messiah, 1954, Julian, 1964, Washington, D.C, 1967, Myra Breckinridge, 1968, Two Sisters, 1970, Burr, 1973, Myron, 1974, Kalki, 1978, Creation, 1981 (Prix Deauville 1983), Duluth, 1983, Lincoln, 1984, Empire, 1987, Hollywood/Live From Golgotha, 1990, (under name Edgar Box) Death in the Fifth Position, 1952, Death Before Bedtime, 1953, Death Likes It Hot, 1954, (short stories) A Thirsty Evil, 1956; (plays) Visit to a Small Planet, 1957, The Best Man, 1960, Romulus, 1962, Weekend, 1968, An Evening with Richard Nixon, 1972, (essays) Rocking the Boat, 1962, Sex, Death, and Money, 1968, Reflections upon a Sinking Ship, 1969, Homage to Daniel Shays, 1973, Matters of Fact and of Fiction, 1977, The Second American Revolution, 1982 (Nat. Book Critics Circle award for criticism 1982), Armageddon?, 1987 (London), United States: Essays 1952-1992, 1993 (Nat. Book award for nonfiction 1993), Live from Golgotha: The Gospel According to Gore Vidal, 1993; (films) The Catered Affair, 1956, I Accuse, 1958, The Left-Handed Gun, 1958, The Scapegoat, 1959, Suddenly Last Summer, 1959, The Best Man, 1964 (Cannes Critics prize 1964), Is Paris Burning?, 1966, The Last of the Mobile Hotshots, 1970; (teleplays) Barn Burning, 1954, Dark Possession, 1954, Smoke, 1954, Visit to a Small Planet, 1955, Dr. Jekyll and Mr. Hyde, 1955, A Sense of Justice, 1955, Summer Pavilion, 1955, The Turn of the Screw, 1955, Stage Door, 1955, A Farewell to Arms, 1955, The Death of Billy the Kid, 1955, Honor, 1956, The Indestructible Mr. Gore, 1959, Dress Gray, 1986, Billy the Kid, 1989; actor: Fellini Roma, 1978, Bob Roberts, 1992, With Honors, 1994, others, (memoirs) Screening History, 1992, Palimpsest, 1995. Mem. Pres.'s Adv. Com. on Arts, 1961-63; Dem.-Liberal candidate for U.S. Congress, 1960, candidate for Dem. nomination from Calif., 1982; co-chmn. The New Party, 1970-71. Served with AUS, 1943-46. Recipient Edgar Allan Poe award TV drama Mystery Writers of Am., 1955; named hon. citizen Ravello, Italy, 1983. •

VIDAL, MAUREEN ERIS, English educator, actress; b. Bklyn., Mar. 18, 1956; d. Louis and Lillian (Kaplan) Hendelman; m. Juan Vidal, June 25, 1974 (div. Sept. 1981); m. Guillermo Eduardo Uriarte, Dec. 22, 1986. BA, Bklyn. Coll., 1976, MS, 1981. English tchr. N.Y.C. Bd. Edn., 1976—. Mem. PETA Humane Soc. Mem. N.Y.C. Assn. Tchrs. English (exec. bd., v.p. 1990—, writing contest chair 1991—), Heights Players Theater Co. (actress, arranger theatrical performance for residents of homeless shelters 1986—, exec. bd., sec. 1993—), Delta Psi Omega. Avocations: world traveling, white water rafting, scuba diving, theater. Home: 3380 Nostrand Ave Brooklyn NY 11229 Office: I S 318 101 Walton St Brooklyn NY 11206-4311 also: Heights Players 26 Willow Pl Brooklyn NY 11201

VIDAS, VINCENT GEORGE, engineering executive; b. Phila., May 25, 1931; s. Joseph and Blanche (Misch) V.; m. Judith Weber, Oct. 15 1955; children: Lisa Louise, Jeffrey Vincent, Kristen Judith. BSEE, Drexel U., 1959, MSEE, 1964. Systems engr. RCA, Moorestown, N.J., 1959-65, Sci. Mgmt. Assn., Haddonfield, N.J., 1965-67; chief exec. officer, owner SEMCOR, Inc., Mt. Laurel, N.J., 1967—; also bd. dirs.; chmn., owner, bd. dirs. Edn. Mgmt. Corp., Cherry Hill, N.J., 1991-93. Staff Sgt. USAF, 1949-53. Mem. IEEE. Avocations: chess, tennis, photography, music. Office: SEMCOR Inc 815 E Gate Dr Mount Laurel NJ 08054-1208

VIDELL, JARED STEVEN, cardiologist; b. Phila., Apr. 9, 1947; s. Harry and Rose (Malken) V.; m. Cyla Trocki, Dec. 27, 1969; children: Haviv Elana, Mikhael Alon, Samara Pilar. AA, Miami-Dade Jr. Coll., Opalocka, Fla., 1966; BEd, U. Miami, 1969; DO, Phila. Coll. Osteo. Medicine, 1976. Resident and chief resident in internal medicine Atlantic City (N.J.) Med. Ctr., 1976-79; fellow in cardiovascular diseases Albert Einstein Med. Ctr., Phila., 1979-81; rsch. fellow in nuclear cardiology Deborah Heart and Lung Ctr., Browns Mills, N.J., 1981-82; dir. employee health svcs. Deborah Heart and Lung Ctr., Browns Mills, 1982-84; asst. dir. cardiology Pritikin Longevity Ctr., Downington, Pa., 1984-87; cardiologist, dir. clin. lab. Physician Care, P.C., Towanda, Pa., 1987-90; from co-chmn. intensive care to dir. cardiac stress lab. Meml. Hosp., Towanda, 1987-90; dir. house staff, intensive/cardiac care Lower Bucks Hosp., Bristol, Pa., 1992-94; dir. house staff ICU-Critical Care Unit North Phila. Health Systems, 1994—; med. dir. Am. Cancer Soc. chpt., 1989-90; mem. state peer rev. KEPRO, 1989-90. Contbr. rsch. articles to profl. jours. Fellow Am. Coll. Angiology; mem. AMA, Am. Coll. Chest Physicians, Am. Soc. Internal Medicine, Internat. Soc. Internal Medicine, Internat. Soc. Endovascular Surgery, Internat. Platform Assn., Pa. Med. Soc., Phila. County Med. Soc., Alumni Assn. Phila. Coll. Osteo. Medicine. Jewish. Avocations: squash, cycling, cross country skiing, traveling, fishing. Home: 408 N Exeter Ave Margate City NJ 08402-1868

VIDOVICH, DANKO VICTOR, neurosurgeon, researcher; b. Zagreb, Croatia, Dec. 29, 1958; came to U.S., 1991; s. Mladen and Zdenka (Radonichich) V. MD, Zagreb U., Croatia, 1982, MSc in Biology, 1990. Neurosurgeon Clin. Hosp. Sisters of Mercy, Zagreb, Croatia, 1986-91; sr. rschr. Allegheny Singer Rsch. Inst., Pitts., 1991—. Contbr. articles to profl. jours. Achievements include performing first laser assisted nerve anastomosis in humans; laser assisted embryonic tissue transplantation in spinal cord injury. Office: Allegheny Gen Hosp 320 E North Ave Pittsburgh PA 15212-4756

VIDRICKSEN, BEN EUGENE, food service executive, state legislator; b. Salina, Kans., June 11, 1927; s. Henry and Ruby Mae Vidricksen; m. Lola Mae Nienke, Jan. 20, 1950 (div.); children: Nancy, Janice, Ben, Penelope, Jeffery. AB, Kans. Wesleyan U., 1951. Field supt. Harding Creamery div. Nat. Dairy Products, Kearney, Kans., 1951-52; plant mgr. Kraft divsn. Nat. Dairy Products, O'Neill, Nebr., 1952-59; owner Vidricksen's Food Service, Salina, 1959—; cons. in field; mem. Kansas Senate, 1979—, asst. majority leader; chmn. joint bldg. constrn. com., legis. and congressional apportionment com., legis. post audit,econ. devel., transp. and utilities, pub. health and welfare, fed. and state affairs, govtl. orgn., spl. interim com. on efficiency in state govt., 1983; del. White House Conf. Small Bus., 1995, White House Conf. on Tourism and Travel, 1995; mem. Hennessy/USAF Worldwide Food Service Evaluation Team, 1978, 79. Mem. Salina Airport Authority, 1972-84, chmn., 1976-77; chmn. Republican Central Com., County of Saline, Kans., 1974-79; adv. council SBA, 1982—, chmn. adv. coun. small bus. devel. ctr.; mem. adv. bd. Salvation Army; past chmn. Salina Convention and Tourism Bur.; vice chmn. Kans. Turnpike Authority, 1995—. Served with USN, 1945-46. Recipient Salut au Restaurateur award Fla. State U., 1974, Gov.'s Spl. award Kans. Assn. Broadcasters, Guardian award Nat. Fedn. Indep. Bus., 1989, Promotion of Tourism and Travel award Travel Ind. Assn. Kans., 1989, Support of Kans. Nat. Guard award Kans. Adjutant Gen., 1990, Good Citizenship award Kans. Engring. Soc., 1991, 92, Freedom award NRA, 1994; named Nat. Rep. Legislator of Yr., Nat. Rep. Legislators Assn., 1991, Assoc. of Yr., Am. Womens Bus. Assn., 1992. Mem. USAF Assn., Assn. U.S. Army, Nat. Rep. Legislators Assn., Am. Legis Exch. Coun., Pan Am. Hwy. Assn. (Internat. Achievement award 1992, Road Builders award 1995), North Salina Bus. Assn. (past pres.), Internat. Bridge, Tunnel and Tpke. Assn., Kans. Restaurant Assn. (past pres., Restaurateur of Yr. 1973), Kans. Tourism and Travel Commn., Kans. Film Commn., Nat. Restaurant Assn. (dir. 1977—), Travel Industry Assn. Kans. (dir.) VFW (life), Salina C. of C. (past bd. dirs.), Am. Legion, Optimists, North Salina Lions Club, Elks, Moose, Eagles, Masons (knight commdr. Scottish rite, 1994), Shriners. Office: State Senate State Capitol Topeka KS 66612

VIE, RICHARD CARL, insurance company executive; b. St. Louis, Sept. 26, 1937; s. George William and Geraldine (Bell) V.; m. Joan Kay Wilschetz, June 4, 1960; children: Laura, Mark, Todd, Amy, Paul, Sarah. Student, St. Louis U., U. Mo. With Reliable Life Ins. Co., St. Louis, 1962-79; pres. Commonwealth Life Ins. Co., St. Louis, 1979-82; pres., chmn. bd. dirs. United Ins. Co. Am., Chgo., 1983—; sr. v.p., bd. dirs. Unitrin, Inc., 1990-92, pres., CEO, 1992—; chmn. Life Insurers Conf., 1994; trustee Life Underwriters Tng. Coun. Bd. dirs. Concordia U. Found., 1985-94, Valparaiso U., 1995—. Lt. USN, 1958-62. Mem. The Racquet Club St. Louis. Office: Unitrin Inc 1 E Wacker Dr Chicago IL 60601-1802

VIEHE, KARL WILLIAM, mathematics educator, lawyer, investment banker; b. Allentown, Pa., Aug. 12, 1943; s. John Sage and Margaret (Higgs) V. BA in Govt. and Econs., Am. U., 1965, MA in Econs., 1968; JD, Howard U., 1981; MLT in Taxation, Georgetown U., 1982. Bar: D.C. 1983, U.S. Ct. of Internat. Trade 1988, U.S. Tax Ct. 1984, U.S. Ct. Appeals (4th cir.) 1988, U.S. Ct. Appeals (D.C. cir.) 1985, U.S. Supreme Ct. 1988. Instr. math. and Russian lang. St. Alban's Sch., Washington, 1968-69; pres., CEO Investment-Futures Group, Washington, 1968-84; prof. math. and stats., U. D.C., Washington, 1971—; gen. counsel Promstroy Bank Russia, 1997—; adj. prof. internat. law and fin. Am. U., 1972—; adj. prof. internat. law and bus. George Washington U., 1986—; internat. advt. dir. Washingtonian Mag., 1972-75; mgmt. program chmn. Fla. Inst. Tech., 1983-85; adj. faculty Internat. Law Inst., Washington, 1986—, Internat. Devel. Law Inst., Rome, 1987—; various law positions at various firms, 1987—; v.p., gen. counsel James A. Tilley Co., Investment Bankers, Washington, Moscow, 1994-95; chmn., CEO, Horizons-Northstar Capital Mgmt. Co., Washington, 1995—; co-chmn. U.S. IRS Ann. Conf. on Current Issues in Internat. Taxation, 1986-88, Dept. Commerce Ann. Conf. on Current Issues in Internat. Trade, 1994—. Contbr. articles to profl. jours.; contbr. to textbooks; presenter in field. Mem. ABA, Am. Econ. Assn., Am. Fin. Assn., Am. Arbitration Assn. (comml. panel, internat. panel), Washington Fgn. Law Soc. (bd. dirs.), D.C. Bar Assn. Avocations: piano, photography, triathlons, marathons, tennis. Home: 2401 H St NW Apt 707 Washington DC 20037-2539 Office: Horizons & Northstar Capital Mgmt Co 1700 Pennsylvania Ave NW Washington DC 20006-4723

VIEIRA, NANCY ELIZABETH, biologist, researcher; b. New Bedford, Mass., Nov. 1, 1951; d. Francisco and Silvina Costa (Frias) V. BS, U. Md., 1973, MS, 1975. Physiologist Nat. Inst. Child Health & Human Devel., Bethesda, Md., 1976-77, biologist, 1977—. Co-author: Kinetic Models of Trace Elements and Mineral Metabolism, 1995; contbr. articles to profl. jours. Elem. sch. team leader, participating vol. tchr. NIH, Bethesda, 1994—; mem. equal employment opportunity adv. com. Nat. Inst. Child Health & Human Devel., 1993—; mem. Rebounders, College Park, Md., 1987—. Mem. AAAS, Am. Inst. Nutrition, Am. Chem. Soc., Am. Soc. Mass Spectrometry. Avocations: fishing, sailing, woodworking, music, automotive repair. Office: NIH NICHD LTPB 10 Center Dr Bldg 10 Rm 6 C208 Bethesda MD 20892

VIEMEISTER, TUCKER L., industrial designer; b. Dayton, Ohio, Aug. 14, 1948; s. Read and Beverly (Lipsett) V. B Indsl. Design, Pratt Inst., 1974. Jr. designer Vie Design Studios, Yellow Springs, Ohio, 1969; owner, mgr. Ohio Silver, Yellow Springs, 1971-73; designer Wyman & Cannon, N.Y.C., 1974-77; ptnr. Ted Muehling, N.Y.C., 1977-79; v.p. Smart Design Inc., N.Y.C., 1979-97; creative designer frogdesign, N.Y.C., 1997—; juror Ann. ID Design Rev., Archtl. Record, Pew Found., 1991 IDEA awards, design e7e 89, Nagoya, Japan; lectr. Form One Conf., 1986, Pratt Inst., 1985, 86, RISD, 1986, Cranbrook Acad. Art, 1986, Axis in Tokyo, 1989; faculty Parsons Sch. Design, 1986; sr. critic Yale U., 1996; del. Internat. coun. Socs. Indsl. Design Congress, Amsterdam, 1987; workshop condr. Contbr. articles to profl. publs. and confs.; represented in permanent collections Cooper-Hewitt Mus., Smithsonian Instn., N.Y.C., Staatliches Mus. fur Angewandte Kunst, Munich-Mus. Modern Art, N.Y.C.; work reviewed in numerous publs. Trustee Rowena Reed Kostellow Fund, Pratt Inst., 1989—. Recipient Presdl. Design Achievement award, 1984, best symbol award Archtl. League, 1986, award Neste, Finland, 1988, also others. Mem. Indsl. Designer Soc. Am. (co-chmn. N.Y. chpt. 1986-87, dir.-at-large 1991-92, nat. conf. chair 1995), Am. Inst. Graphic Designers, Am. Ctr. for Design (bd. dirs. 1996—), Archl. League N.Y. (bd. dirs. 1997—). Office: Smart Design Inc 137 Vermilyea Ave New York NY 10034-3202

VIENER, JOHN D., lawyer; b. Richmond, Va., Oct. 18, 1939; s. Reuben and Thelma (Kurtz) V.; m. Karin Erika Bauer, Apr. 7, 1969; children: John D. Jr., Katherine Bauer. BA, Yale U., 1961; JD, Harvard U., 1964. Bar: N.Y. State 1965, U.S. Supreme Ct. 1970, U.S. Dist. Ct. (so. dist.) N.Y. 1974, U.S. Tax Ct. 1975. Assoc. Satterlee, Warfield & Stephens, N.Y.C., 1964-69; sole practice N.Y.C., 1969-76; founder, bd. dirs., gen. counsel Foxfire Fund Inc., 1966-88; sr. ptnr. Christy & Viener, N.Y.C., 1976—; gen. counsel, bd. dirs. Landmark Communities, Inc., 1970—, NF&M Internat., Inc., 1976—, Singer Fund, Inc., 1979—; gen. counsel Nat. Cancer Found. Cancer Care, 1982-85, Am. Continental Properties Group, 1978—, Troster, Singer & Co., 1970-77; bd. dirs. Gen. Financiere Immob. et Commer. S.A., 1985-89; spl. counsel fin. instns., investment banking and securities concerns; real estate and tax advisor. Mem. Meeker Brook Sporting Assn., Fairfield County Hounds, Manursing Island Club, Washington Club, Palm Beach Polo. Home: 45 E 62nd St New York NY 10021-8025 also: 2474 Players Ct West Palm Beach FL 33414 Office: Christy & Viener 620 5th Ave New York NY 10020-2402

VIENNE, DOROTHY TITUS, school principal; b. Buffalo, May 8, 1939; d. Robert Paul and Bertha (Wissman) Titus; m. Richard Paul Vienne, Aug. 27, 1960; children: Richard Paul Jr., Kerstina Elaine. BS in Elem. Edn., SUNY, Brockport, 1960; MS in Elem. Edn., SUNY, Buffalo, 1964; postgrad., U. Buffalo, 1968-76, Canisius Coll., 1978. Cert. elem. tchr., N.Y. Elem. tchr. Lancaster (N.Y.) Cen. Schs., 1960-62, reading tchr., 1962-68, reading specialist, 1968-76; program supr. Kenmore-Town of Tonawanda, Kenmore, N.Y., 1976-79, 81-86; coordinator pupil personnel services Assn. for Retarded Children, Buffalo, 1980-81; prin. Thomas Edison Sch., Kenmore-Tonawanda Union Free Sch. Dist., Kenmore, 1986—; adj. prof. ednl. adminstrn. SUNY, Buffalo; apkr. Summer Inst. for Prins., 1987—, 1st Internat. Forum on Total Quality, Brazil, 1993; trainer 4MAT learning styles; author, presenter on total quality mgmt. in schs.; ednl. cons. U.S. Info. Svcs., Brazil, 1994. Named N.Y. State Disting. Elem. Prin., 1991. Mem. ASCD, Sch. Adminstrs. N.Y. State, Western N.Y. Women in Adminstrn. (bd. dirs., Woman Adminstr. of Yr. award 1990), Phi Delta Kappa (officer). Republican. Methodist. Avocations: skiing, travel, bridge. Home: 50 Gaylord Ct Elma NY 14059-9450 Office: Thomas Edison Elem Sch 236 Grayton Rd Tonawanda NY 14150-8620

VIERA, JAMES JOSEPH, financial executive; b. Erie, Pa., June 14, 1940; s. Joseph C. and Margaret (Kelly) V.; m. Cheryl Batchelder, Dec. 9, 1967; children: Robert, James Jay. BS, Rensselaer Poly. Inst., 1962; MBA, Columbia U., 1970. Fin. analyst Ford Motor Co., Dearborn, Mich., 1970-75; asst. compt. Pullman, Inc., Chgo., 1975-76; div. compt. The Pillsbury Co., Mpls., 1976-80; pres., chief fin. officer Jefferson Co., Mpls., 1980-87; chief fin. officer Cowles Media Co., Mpls., 1987—. Bd. dirs. Edina (Minn.) Hockey Assn., 1985-87, Edina Baseball Assn., 1985-87, Glenwood-Lyndale Cmty. Ctr., Sci. Mus. of Minn., 1990—. Mem. Mpls. C. of C. (bd. dirs. 1992—). Avocations: jogging, skiing. Home: 7131 Gleason Rd Minneapolis MN 55439-1610 Office: Cowles Media Co 329 Portland Ave Minneapolis MN 55415-1112

VIERECK, PETER, poet, historian, educator; b. N.Y.C., Aug. 5, 1916; s. George S. and Margaret (Hein) V.; m. Anya de Markov, June 1945 (div. May 1970); children: John-Alexis, Valerie Edwina (Mrs. John Gibbs); m. Betty Martin Falkenberg, Aug. 30, 1972. B.S. summa cum laude, Harvard, 1937, M.A., 1939, Ph.D., 1942; Henry fellow, Christ Ch., Oxford U., Eng., 1937-38; L.H.D. (hon.), Olivet Coll., 1959. Teaching asst. Harvard, 1941-42, instr. German lit., tutor history and lit. dept., 1946-47; instr. history U.S. Army U., Florence, Italy, 1945; asst. prof. history Smith Coll., 1947-48, vis. lectr. Russian history, 1948-49; assoc. prof. Modern European, Russian history Mt. Holyoke Coll., 1948-55, prof., 1955—; vis. lectr. Am. Culture Oxford U., 1953; Whittal lectr. in poetry Library of Congress, 1954, 63, 79; Fulbright prof. Am. poetry and civilization U. Florence, Italy, 1954-56; Elliston chair poetry lectr. U. Cin., 1956; vis. lectr. U. Calif. at, Berkeley, 1957; Disting. William R. Kenan prof. Mt. Holyoke Coll., 1979—; Charter mem. Council Basic Edn.; vis. poet Russian-Am. cultural exchange program Dept. State, USSR, 1961; vis. research scholar 20th Century Fund, USSR, 1962-63; vis. scholar Rockefeller Study Center at Bellagio, Italy, 1977; vis. artist and scholar Am. Acad. in, Rome, 1949-50, 78; dir. poetry workshop N.Y. Writers Conf., 1965-67; research fellow Huntington Library, San Marino, Calif., 1978. Author: Metapolitics—From the Romantics to Hitler, 1941 (Swedish edit., 1942, Italian, 1948), Terror and Decorum, poems, 1948, reprinted, 1972, Who Killed the Universe, novelette included in anthology New Directions Ten, 1948, Conservatism Revisited-The Revolt Against Revolt 1815-1949, 1949 (English edit, 1950), Strike Through the Mask, New Lyrical Poems, 1950, reprinted, 1972, The First Morning: New Poems, 1952, reprinted, 1972, Shame and Glory of the Intellectuals, 1953, rev. edit., 1965, reprinted 1978, Dream and Responsibility, The Tension Between Poetry and Society, 1953, The Unadjusted Man; a New Hero for Americans, 1956, reprinted, 1973, Conservatism: From John Adams to Churchill, 1956, reprinted, 1978, The Persimmon Tree, poems, 1956, Inner Liberty, The Stubborn Grit in the Machine, 1957, The Tree Witch: A Verse Drama, 1961, reprinted, 1973, Meta-politics, The Roots of the Nazi Mind, 1961, rev. expanded edit. 1965, Conservatism Revisited and The New Conservatives: What Went Wrong; rev. paperback edits., 1962, 65, reprinted hardcover, 1978, New and Selected Poems, 1932-67, 1967, Archer in the Marrow: The Applewood Poetry Cycles of 1967-87, 1987, Tide & Continuities: Last & First Poems, 1995; also author of selections in symposium books Towards a World Community, 1950, Midcentury American Poets, 1950, Arts in Renewal, 1951, The New American Right, 1955, Education in a Free Society, 1958, The Radical Right, 1962, Soviet Policy Making, 1967, Outside Looking In, 1972, A Question of Quality, 1976, The Southern California Anthology, 1987, rev. edits., 1987, 89, Decade: New Letters Anthology of the 80s, 1990; contbr. essays, poems to popular mags., and profl. jours., monograph on Conservatism in Ency. Brit., 1974. Sgt. U.S. Army, 1943-45, Africa and Italy. Decorated 2 battle stars; awarded Tietjens prize for poetry, 1948, Pulitzer prize for poetry, 1949; recipient Most Disting. Alumnus award Horace Mann School for Boys, 1958, Poetry Translation award Translation Center, Columbia U., 1978, Sadin poetry prize N.Y. Quar., 1977, Golden Rose award New Eng. Poetry Club, 1981, Varoujan prize, 1983; Guggenheim fellow Rome, 1949-50; Rockefeller Found. researcher in history Germany, summer 1958; NEH sr. rsch. fellow USSR, 1969; Mass. Artists Found. fellow, 1978. Mem. Am. Hist. Assn., Oxford Soc., Poetry Soc. Am., P.E.N., Phi Beta Kappa. Clubs: Harvard (N.Y.C. and London); Bryce (Oxford, Eng.). Home: 12 Silver St South Hadley MA 01075-1616 *After 81 years of books, scars, and sugar plums, my rock-bottom thought on life is a line of Vachel Lindsay: "Courage and sleep are the principal things."*

VIEREGG, ROBERT TODD, lawyer; b. Woodstock, Ill., Oct. 3, 1934; s. Robert and Mae (Todd) V.; m. Darla Jean Ax, Dec. 12, 1959 (div. Oct. 1983); children: Dorian Jean Griffin, Robert Todd II; m. Carilane Newman Awalt, May 25, 1985. Student, U. Ill., 1952-53; BA, Mich. State U., 1955; postgrad., U. Chgo., 1968-69; JD cum laude, Northwestern u., 1970. Bar: Ill. 1970, U.S. Dist. Ct. (no. dist.) Ill. 1970. From assoc. to ptnr. Sidley & Austin, Chgo., 1970—. Carrier jet fighter pilot USN, 1956-59. Mem. ABA, Ill. Bar Assn., Chgo. Bar Assn., Law Club Chgo., Union League (bd. dirs.

1987-88), Glen View Country Club (bd. dirs. 1995—). Republican. Office: Sidley & Austin 1 First Natl Plz Chicago IL 60603-2003

VIERHELLER, TODD, software engineering consultant; b. Winter Park, Fla., June 22, 1958; s. Irvin Theodore and Jeanne Marie (Zeller) V.; m. Susan Lindhe Watts, Dec. 22, 1984; children: Renate Jeanne, Clark, Lindhe Marie, Kent. BS in Computer Sci., U. Mo., Rolla, 1980; MA in Bibl. Studies, Multnomah Sch. Bible, Portland, Oreg., 1986. Tech. writer, software engr. Tektronix, Beaverton, Oreg., 1981-86, software engring. mgr., 1988-89; software engr., supr. Intel Corp., Hillsboro, Oreg., 1986-88; software engring. mgr. Summation, 1989-90; software cons. Quality First, Lynnwood, Wash., 1990—; software engring. cons. Digital Equipment Corp., Bellevue, Wash., 1990-91, GTE, Bothell, Wash., 1990-91, Frank Russell Co., Tacoma, Wash., 1992-93, InterConnections, Inc., Bellevue, 1993, Novell, San Jose, Calif., 1993, Heartstream, Inc., 1996, N.Am. Morpho Sys., Inc., 1996, Air Touch Cellular, 1996-97; software engring. mgmt. cons. Weyerhauser, Federal Way, Wash., 1991-92, Frank Russell, Tacoma, Wash., 1994, ConnectSoft, Inc., Bellevue, 1994, Microsoft, Redmond, Wash., 1995-96, Nordstrom, Seattle, 1997—; tech. writer, cons. Air Touch Cellular, Bellevue, Wash., 1996-97. Mem. IEEE, NRA, Upsilon Pi Epsilon, Kappa Mu Epsilon. Republican. Mem. Evang. Christian Ch. Avocations: camping, bicycling, shooting sports, kung fu. Home: 23617 36th Pl W Brier WA 98036-8411 Office: Quality First PO Box 6212 Lynnwood WA 98036-0212

VIERTEL, JACK, theatrical producer, writer; b. Stamford, Conn., Feb. 7, 1949; s. Joseph Maurice and Janet (Man) V.; m. Linda Gilmore, July 31, 1973; children: Joshua Louis, Anna Daisy. AB, Harvard Coll., 1971. Theater critic L.A. Reader, 1977-80; theater critic L.A. Herald Examiner, 1980-85, arts editor, 1984-85; dramaturg Mark Taper Forum Theater, L.A., 1986-87; creative dir. Jujamcyn Theaters, N.Y.C., 1987—. Co-author: (non-fiction) Becoming Parents, 1978; adaptor (play) Ghetto, 1986; prodr.: Smokey Joe's Cafe, 1995. Cert. judge Memphis-in-May Barbecue Contest Circuit, 1992—; mem. City Ctr. Encores Adv. Bd.; mem. Ethical-Fieldston Fund Bd. Mem. League Am. Theaters and Prodrs., Writers Guild Am. East, Theater Comm. Group (bd. dirs. 1997—). Democrat. Jewish. Avocations: guitar, cooking, scuba diving, travel. Office: Jujamcyn Theatres 246 W 44th St New York NY 10036-3910

VIESSMAN, WARREN, JR., academic dean, civil engineering educator, researcher; b. Balt., Nov. 9, 1930; s. Warren and Helen Adair (Berlinckee) V.; m. Gloria Marie Scheiner, May 11, 1953 (div. Apr. 1975); children: Wendy, Stephen, Suzanne, Michael, Thomas, Sandra; m. Elizabeth Gertrude Rothe, Aug. 8, 1980; children: Heather, Joshua. B in Engring., Johns Hopkins U., 1952, MS in Engring., 1958, DEng, 1961. Registered profl. engr., Md. Engr. W. H. Primrose & Assocs., Towson, Md., 1955-57; project engr. Johns Hopkins U., Balt., 1957-61; from asst. to assoc. prof. N.Mex. State U., Las Cruces, 1961-66; prof. U. Maine, Orono, 1966-68, U. Nebr., Lincoln, 1968-75; sr. specialist Libr. Congress, Washington, 1975-83; prof., chmn. U. Fla., Gainesville, 1983-90, assoc. dean for rsch. and grad. study, 1990-91, assoc. dean for acad. programs, 1991—; vis. scientist Am. Geophys. Union, 1970-71; Maurice Kremer lectr. U. Nebr., 1985; lectr. Harvard U. Water Policy Seminar, 1988; Wayne S. Nichols Meml. Fund lectr. Ohio State U., 1990; mem. steering com. on groundwater and energy U.S. Dept. Energy, 1979-80; mem. task group on fed. water rsch. U.S. Geol. Survey, 1985-87; mem. com. of water sci. and tech. bd. NAS, 1986-90; mem. water resources working group Nat. Coun. on Pub. Works Improvement, 1987; chmn., chief of engrs. Environ. Adv. Bd., Washington, 1991-93; chmn. solid and hazardous waste mgmt. adv. bd. State U. Sys. Fla. Co-author: Water Supply and Pollution Control, 1993, Water Management: Technology and Institutions, 1984, Introduction to Hydrology, 1996; contbr. over 145 articles to profl. jours. Mem. Water Mgmt. Com., Gainesville, 1983-88, Fla. Environ. Efficiency Study Commn., 1986-88. 1st lt. U.S. Army C.E., 1952-54, Korea. Fellow ASCE (Julian Hinds award 1989), Am. Water Resources Assn. (nat. pres. 1990, Icko Iben award 1983, Henry P. Caulfield Jr. medal 1996), Univs. Coun. on Water Resources (pres. 1987, Warren A. Hall medal 1994), Sigma Xi, Tau Beta Pi. Avocations: scuba diving, woodworking. Office: U Fla Coll Engring PO Box 116550 Gainesville FL 32611-6550

VIEST, IVAN M(IROSLAV), consulting structural engineer; b. Bratislava, Slovakia, Czechoslovakia, Oct. 10, 1922; came to U.S., 1947, naturalized, 1955; s. Ivan and Maria (Zacharova) V.; m. Barbara K. Stevenson, May 23, 1953. Ing., Slovak Tech. U., Bratislava, 1946; M.S., Ga. Inst. Tech., 1948; Ph.D., U. Ill., 1951. Registered profl. engr., Pa. Research asst. U. Ill., Urbana, 1948-50; research assoc. U. Ill., 1950-51, research asst. prof., 1951-55, research assoc. prof., 1955-57; bridge research engr. Am. Assn. State Hwy. Ofcls.; rd. test Nat. Acad. Scis., Ottawa, Ill., 1957-61; structural engr. Bethlehem Steel Corp., Pa., 1961-67; sr. structural cons. Bethlehem Steel Corp., 1967-70, asst. mgr. sales engring. div., 1970-82; pvt. cons. structural engr. IMV Cons., 1983—; lectr. in field. Author: Composite Construction, 1958, History of Engineering Foundation, 1991, Composite Construction--Design for Buildings, 1997. Recipient Constrn. award Engring. News Record, 1972. Fellow AAAS, Am. Concrete Inst. (Wason Rsch. medal 1956); mem. NAE, ASCE (hon., v.p. 1973-75, Rsch. prize, Ernest E. Howard award 1991), Internat. Assn. Bridge and Structural Engring., Transp. Rsch. Bd., Czechoslovak Soc. Arts and Scis. (exec. v.p. 1992-93), Earthquake Engring. Rsch. Inst., Saucon Valley Country Club (Bethlehem). Research, numerous publs. on various steel and concrete structures, especially bridges and bldgs., to profl. jours. Office: PO Box 132 Hellertown PA 18055-0132

VIETH, G. DUANE, lawyer; b. Omaha, Sept. 20, 1923; s. Walter E. and Irene E. (Horn) V.; m. Jane G. Richardson, Feb. 16, 1952; children: Peter D., Robert R., Jane G. BA, U. Iowa, 1947, JD, 1949. Bar: Iowa 1949, D.C. 1949, U.S. Dist. Ct. Iowa 1953, U.S. Dist. Ct. Md. 1955, U.S. Ct. Claims 1958, U.S. Ct. Appeals (3d cir.) 1960, U.S. Dist. Ct. (ea. dist.) Wis. 1965, U.S. Supreme Ct. 1966, U.S. Ct. Appeals (2d cir.) 1970, U.S. Ct. Appeals (7th cir.) 1971. Ptnr. Arnold & Porter, Washington, 1949—; mem. D.C. Commn. on Budget and Financial Priorities, 1989-90. Trustee Iowa Law Sch. Found., Iowa City, 1971-88, Fed. City Council, Washington, 1972—. With USAAF, 1942-45, ETO. Mem. ABA, D.C. Bar Assn., Iowa State Bar Assn., Columbia Country Club, Burning Tree Club, Met. Club. Lutheran. Avocation: golf. Home: 4407 Chalfont Pl Bethesda MD 20816 Office: Arnold & Porter 555 12th St NW Ste 955 Washington DC 20004-1200

VIETH, WOLF RANDOLPH, chemical engineering educator; b. St. Louis, May 5, 1934; s. Hans W. and Hedy (Fahrig) V.; m. Peggy Schira, July 6, 1957; children—Jane, Linda, Christopher, Mark. S.B. in Chem. Engring, Mass. Inst. Tech., 1956, Sc.D., 1961; M. Sc., Ohio State U., 1958. Registered profl. engr., N.J. From asst. prof. to assoc. prof. chem. engring. MIT, Cambridge, 1961-68, dir. Sch. Chem. Engring. Practice, 1965-68; prof. chem. and biochem. engring. Rutgers U., New Brunswick, N.J., 1968—, chmn. dept., 1968-78; cons. to govt. and industry; chmn. Gordon Research Conf. on Separation and Purification, 1975, Engring. Conf. on Biochem. Engring., 1978. Mem. econ. study subcom., planning bd. Montgomery (N.J.) Twp., 1970—. Served to 1st lt. AUS, 1961. Recipient DuPont Co. Invention award, 1960, St. Albert the Great medal for sci. Aquinas Coll., 1952; Vis. Fgn. Scientist award Japan Soc. for Promotion Sci., 1975; Ford postdoctoral fellow, 1961. Fellow Am. Inst. Chemists, N.Y. Acad. Scis.; mem. Am. Inst. Chem. Engrs., Am. Chem. Soc., Am. Soc. Engring. Edn., Sigma Xi, Phi Lambda Upsilon. Research on applied molecular biology, semipermeable membranes, polymers. Office: Chem Dept Heights Campus Rutgers Univ New Brunswick NJ 08903

VIETOR, HAROLD DUANE, federal judge; b. Parkersburg, Iowa, Dec. 29, 1931; s. Harold Howard and Alma Johanna (Kreimeyer) V.; m. Dalia Artemisa Zamarripa Cadena, Mar. 24, 1973; children: Christine Elizabeth, John Richard, Greta Maria. BA, U. Iowa, 1955, JD, 1958. Bar: Iowa 1958. Law clk. U.S. Ct. Appeals 8th Circuit, 1958-59; ptnr. Bleakley Law Offices, Cedar Rapids, Iowa, 1959-65; judge Iowa Dist. Ct., Cedar Rapids, 1965-79, chief judge, 1970-79; U.S. dist. judge U.S. Dist. Ct. for So. Dist. Iowa, Des Moines, 1979-96, chief judge, 1985-92, sr. U.S. dist. judge, 1997—; lectr. at law schs., legal seminars U.S. and Japan. Contbr. articles to profl. jours. in U.S. and Japan. Served with USN, 1952-54. Mem. ABA, Iowa Bar Assn. (pres. jr. sect. 1966-67), Iowa Judges Assn. (pres. 1975-76), 8th Cir. Dist. Judges Assn. (pres. 1986-88). Office: US Dist Ct 221 US Courthouse 123 E Walnut St Des Moines IA 50309-2035

VIETS, HERMANN, college president, consultant; b. Quedlinburg, Fed. Republic Germany, Jan. 28, 1943; came to U.S., 1949, naturalized, 1961; s. Hans and Herta (Heik) V.; m. Pamela Deane, June 30, 1968; children: Danielle, Deane, Hans, Hillary. BS, Polytech. U., 1965, MS, 1966, PhD, 1970. Postdoctoral fellow von Karman Inst., Brussels, 1969-70; group leader Wright-Patterson AFB, Dayton, Ohio, 1970-76; prof. Wright State U., Dayton, Ohio, 1976-81; assoc. dean W.Va. U., Morgantown, 1981-83; dean U. R.I., Kingston, 1983-91; pres. Milw. Sch. Engring., 1991—; chmn. bd. dirs. Precision Stampings, Inc., Beaumont, Calif., 1977—; bd. dirs. Astro Med, Inc., West Warwick, R.I., Wenthe-Davidson Engring. Co., New Berlin, Wis.; cons. USAF Aero Propulsion Lab., Dayton, 1976-80, Covington & Burling, Washington, 1976-77; cons. several cos. and govt. agys. Patentee in aero. field; contbr. numerous articles to tech. publs. Mem. Greater Milw. Com.; dir. Greater Milw. Edn. Trust, Competitive Wis., Gov. Regional H.S. Excellence Co., 1994, Gov.'s Export Strategy Commn., 1994; trustee Pub. Policy Forum. Recipient Tech. Achievement award USAF, 1974, Sci. Achievement award, 1975, Gov.'s Sci. and Tech. award State of R.I., 1987, Goodrich Pub. Svc. award, 1990, Citation R.I. Legislature, 1987, 90, 91, Outstanding Alumnus award aerospace engring. dept. Poly. U., 1994; Disting. Alumnus Poly. U., 1995; postdoctoral fellow NATO, 1969-70, NASA, 1965-69. Fellow AIAA (assoc., Best Tech. Paper award Allegheny-Pitts. sect. 1982); mem. Deutsche Gesellschaft fur Luft und Raumfahrt, Am. Soc. Engring. Edn., Japsn-Am. Soc. (bd. dirs. 1994), Soc. Mfg. Engrs., Rotary, Sigma Xi, Phi Kappa Phi, Tau Beta Pi, Sigma Gamma Tau. Avocations: antique automobiles; beer steins. Home: 4216 N Lake Dr Shorewood WI 53211-1722 Office: Milw Sch Engring 1025 N Broadway Milwaukee WI 53202-3109

VIETS, ROBERT O., utilities executive; b. Girard, Kans., Dec. 8, 1943; s. Willard O. and Caroline L. (Bollwinkel) V.; m. Karen M. Kreiter, June 13, 1980. BA in Econs., Washburn U., 1965; JD, Washington U., 1969. Bar: Kans. 1966, Mo. 1969, Ill. 1975; CPA, Kans. Auditor Arthur Andersen & Co., St. Louis, 1969-73; mgr. spl. studies Cen. Ill. Light Co., Peoria, 1973-76, mgr. rates and regulatory affairs, 1976-80, asst. v.p., regulatory affairs, 1980-81, v.p. fin. services, 1981-83, v.p. fin. group, 1983-86, sr. v.p., 1988—; sr. v.p. Cilcorp, Inc., Peoria, 1986-88; pres., chief exec. officer, chmn. bd. Cilcorp, Inc and Cen. Ill. Light Co., Peoria, 1988—; bd. dirs. First of Am. Bank, N.A., Ill., Lincoln Office Supply, Inc., RLI Corp.; pres., CEO, chmn. bd. QST Enterprises, Inc., 1996—. Bd. dirs. Meth. Health Svcs., Inc.; trustee Bradley U. Mem. ABA, Ill. Bar Assn., Peoria County Bar Assn., AICPA, Ill. Soc. CPAs. Republican. Lutheran. Lodge: Rotary (bd. dirs. 1985—, pres. 1986-87). Avocation: golf. Home: 11305 N Pawnee Rd Peoria IL 61615-9796 Office: Cilcorp Inc Hamilton Blvd Peoria IL 61602

VIG, VERNON EDWARD, lawyer; b. St. Cloud, Minn., June 19, 1937; s. Edward Enoch and Salley Johanna (Johnson) V.; m. Susan Jane Rosenow, June 10, 1961; 1 child, Elizabeth Karen. BA, Carleton Coll., 1959; LLB, NYU, 1962, LLM, 1963; postdoctoral Université de Paris, Faculté de Droit, 1964. Bar: N.Y. 1962, Avocat (France) 1992. Assoc. Cleary, Gottlieb, Steen & Hamilton, Paris, 1964-65; assoc. Donovan, Leisure, Newton & Irvine, N.Y.C. and Paris, 1965-72, ptnr., 1972-86; ptnr. LeBoeuf, Lamb, Greene & MacRae, N.Y.C., 1986—. Sr. warden Grace Ch., Bklyn., 1986—. George F. Baker scholar, Fullbright scholar, 1963-64, Ford Found. scholar, 1963-64. Mem. ABA (internat. trade com.), N.Y. State Bar Assn. (chmn. antitrust 1987-88), Assn. of Bar of City of N.Y., Internat. Bar Assn., Union Internationale des Avocats. Episcopalian. Clubs: Heights Casino (Bklyn.); Merriewold (Forestburgh, N.Y., bd. dirs. 1985-91). Office: LeBoeuf Lamb Greene & MacRae 125 W 55th St New York NY 10019-5369

VIGDOR, JAMES SCOTT, distribution executive; b. Bklyn., Oct. 12, 1953; s. Irving and Betty Jean (Wolkenbrod) V.; m. Mindy Sue Neirs, May 30, 1982; 1 child, Rachel Dyan. BA, Ohio State U., 1975. Regional distbn. mgr. Gestetner Corp., L.A., 1979-83; asst. ops. mgr. Wall-Pride, Inc., Van Nuys, Calif., 1983-88; ops. mgr. Opportunities for Learning, Inc., Chatsworth, Calif., 1988-89; dir. ops. Image Entertainment, Chatsworth, 1989-91; ops mgr. Cal-Abco and Legend Computer Products, Woodland Hills, Calif., 1991-95; dir. ops. HW Electronics, Van Nuys, Calif., 1995-97; v.p. ops. Micro Age Computer Ctr./Advanced Optical Distbn., Encino, Calif., 1997—. Office: Micro Age Computer Ctr Advanced Optical Distbn 16530 Ventura Blvd Ste 105 Encino CA 91436-4554

VIGEN, KATHRYN L. VOSS, nursing administrator, educator; b. Lakefield, Minn., Sept. 24, 1934; d. Edward Stanley and Bertha C. (Richter) Voss; m. David C. Vigen, June 23, 1956 (div. 1977); children: Eric. E., Amy Vigen Hemstad, Aana Marie. BS in Nursing magna cum laude, St. Olaf Coll., 1956; MEd, S.D. State U., 1975; MS, Rush U., 1980; PhD, U. Minn., 1987. RN. Staff nurse various hosps., Mpls, Boston, Chgo., 1956-68; nursing instr. S.E.A. Sch. Practical Nursing, Sioux Falls, S.D., 1969-74; statewide coord. upward mobility in nursing Augustana Coll., Sioux Falls, S.D., 1974-78; cons./researcher S.D. Commn. Higher Edn., 1974-79; gov. appointed bd. mem. S.D. Bd. Nursing, 1975-79; RN upward mobility project dir., chair/dir. div. of nursing Huron Coll. S.D. State U., 1978-79, mobility project dir., 1980-84; head dept. nursing, assoc. prof. Luther Coll., Decorah, Iowa, 1984-94; prof. nursing Graceland Coll., Independence, Mo., 1994—; cons. in field; developer outreach MSN programs Graceland Coll.; governing bd. mem. Midwest Alliance in Nursing, 1984-92; founder Soc. for Advancement of Nursing, Malta, 1992; developer Health Care in the Mediterranean Study Abroad Program, Greece and Malta, 1994, 96;developer summer internship for Maltese nursing students Mayo Med. Ctr. and Luther Coll.; presenter on internat. collaboration with Malta for nursing leadership 2d Internat. Acad. Congress on Nursing, Kansas City, 1996. Author: Role of a Dean in a Private Liberal Arts College, 1992; devel. and initiated 3 nursing programs in S.D., 1974-84 (named Women of Yr., 1982). Lobbyist Nursing Schs. in S.D., 1974-79; task force mem. Sen. Tom Harkin's Nurse's Adv. Com., 1986-94. Fellow to rep. U.S.A. ANA cand. in internat. coun. nursing 3M, St. Paul, 1978; recipient Leadership award Bush Found., St. Paul, 1979; tenure Luther Coll., 1986; Faculty fellow Minn. Area Geriatric Edn. Ctr. U. Minn., 1990-91; recipient Fulbright award Malta Coun. Internat. Exch. of Scholars, Washington, 1992—. Mem. AAUW, ANA, Am. Assn. Colls. Nursing (exec. devel. subcom. 1990—), Internat. Assn. Human Caring, Iowa Nurse's Assn. (bd. dirs. 1989-92, mem. nursing edn. com. 1989—, co-pres. 1989—), Midwest Alliance in Nursing (gov. bd. rep. Iowa 1989-92, chair membership com. 1989-92, S.D. gov. bd. rep. 1984-86, Rozella Schlotfeldt Leadership award 1993), Iowa Acad. Sci., Iowa Assn. Colls. Nursing Soc., Gerontol. Soc. Am., Rotary, Sigma Theta Tau. Democrat. Lutheran. Avocations: singing, travel and other cultures, meeting people, sailing, reading. Home: 4316 Northern Ave Apt 2633 Kansas City MO 64133-7249 Office: Graceland Coll Divsn Nursing 221 W Lexington Ave Independence MO 64050-3707

VIGIER, FRANÇOIS CLAUDE DENIS, city planning educator; b. Geneva, Oct. 14, 1931; s. Eugene Henri Rene and Françoise (Dupuy) V. BArch, MIT, 1955; M in City Planning, Harvard U., 1959, PhD, 1967. Architect UN Relief and Works Agy., Jordan, 1955-57; designer Town Planning Cons., Cambridge, Mass., 1957-58; mem. faculty Harvard Grad. Sch. Design, Cambridge, 1960—, prof. city planning and urban design, 1968-85, Charles Dyer Norton prof. regional planning, 1985—, dir. unit for housing and urbanization, 1987—, chmn. spl. programs, 1982-86; chmn. dept. urban planning and design, 1992—; vis. lectr. art Dartmouth Coll., 1962, 64; vis. critic urban design U. N.C., 1963; cons. Ford Found. Latin Am. program, 1964-65, Ednl. Svcs., Inc., 1966; dir. Harvard Ctr. Environ. Design Studies, 1967-69; pres. Nash-Vigier Inc., Cambridge, 1965-91. Author: Change and Apathy: Liverpool and Manchester During the Industrial Revolution, 1970, Housing in Tunis, 1987; contbr. articles to various periodicals. Decorated Knight, Order of Merit, France, 1995. Mem. Am. Inst. Cert. Planners, Am. Planning Assn. Home: 27 Fayerweather St Cambridge MA 02138-3329

VIGIL, CHARLES S., lawyer; b. Trinidad, Colo., June 9, 1912; s. J.U. and Andreita (Maes) V.; m. Kathleen A. Liebert, Jan. 2, 1943; children: David Charles Edward, Marcia Kathleen. LL.B., U. Colo., 1936. Bar: Colo. 1936. Dep. dist. atty. 3d Jud. Dist. Colo., 1937-42, asst. dist. atty., 1946-51; U.S. atty. Dist. Colo., 1951-53; pvt. practice law Denver.; Dir., sec. Las Animas Co. (Colo); ARC. Author: Saga of Casimiro Barela. Bd. dirs. Family and Children's Svc. Denver, Colo. Humane Soc., Animal Rescue Soc., Auraria Community Ctr.; mem. Bishop's com. on housing; Dem. candidate for U.S. Congress, 1988. Lt. USCG, 1942-46. Recipient award of civil merit Spain, 1960, award of civil merit Colo. Centennial Expn. Bd., 1976; award Colo. Chicano Bar Assn., 1979. Mem. Internat. Law Assn., ABA, Fed. Bar Assn., Colo. Bar Assn. (bd. govs.), So. Colo. Bar Assn., Hispanic Bar Colo. (bd. dirs.), Am. Judicature Soc., Internat. Bar Assn., Inter-Am. Bar, V.F.W. (comdr.), Am. Legion (comdr.), Nat. Assn. Def. Lawyers, Assn. Trial Lawyers Am., Lambda Chi Alpha, Elks, Eagles, Cootie. Home: 1085 Sherman St Denver CO 80203-2880 Office: 1715 Colo State Bank 1600 Broadway Denver CO 80202-4927 *Desire to serve and achieve in all matters related to public good as promoted and espoused by thoughts of father and mother-and family-brothers and sisters.*

VIGNELLI, MASSIMO, architecture and design executive; b. Milan, Italy, Jan. 10, 1931; came to U.S., 1965; s. Ettore and Noemi (Guazzoni) V.; m. Lella Elena Valle, Sept. 15, 1957; children: Luca, Valentina. Student, Brera Sch. Art, Milan, 1948-50, Politecnico di Milano, 1950-53, U. Venice, 1953-57; DFA (hon.), Parsons Sch. Design, 1983, Pratt Inst., 1987, R.I. Sch. Design, 1988, Istituto Universitario di Architettura, Venice, 1994, Corcoran Sch. Art, 1994. Prin. Lella & Massimo Vignelli Office Design and Architecture, Milan, 1960-64; dir., sr. v.p. design Unimark Internat., Milan and N.Y.C., 1965-71; pres. Vignelli Assocs., N.Y.C., 1971—; chmn. Vignelli Designs, Inc., N.Y.C., 1978—. Retrospective shows include: Parsons Sch. Design, N.Y.C., 1980, Padiglione d'Arte Moderna, Milan, 1980, Acad. of Art USSR, Moscow and Leningrad, 1989, Helsinki, 1989, London, 1990, Budapest, Barcelona, 1991, Copenhagen, Munich, 1992, Prague, Paris, 1992-93; represented in permanent collections Mus. Modern Art, N.Y.C., Cooper-Hewitt Mus., N.Y., Met. Mus. Art, N.Y., Bklyn. Mus., Die Neue Sammlung, Munich, Musée des Arts Décoratifs, Montreal, Tel Aviv Mus. Modern Art; designer: (dinnerware) Heller, 1964, (glass bakeware) 1975, (furniture), Sunar, 1979, Rosenthal, 1980, Knoll, 1985, Poltrona Frau, 1988, (tableware) Sasaki Crystal, 1985, (glassware) Steuben, 1993; interiors St. Peters Ch., Citicorp Ctr., N.Y.C., 1975, Inst. Fine Arts., Mpls., 1974; corp. image Knoll Internat., 1966, Lancia, 1978, Ciga Hotels, 1979, Solomon R. Guggenheim Mus., 1992—, Am. Ctr. in Paris, 1994, COSMIT, Milan, 1994, Bayerische Ruck, Munich, 1994—, Benetton Worldwide, 1995—, graphics Am. Airlines, 1967, Bloomingdales, 1972, books for Rizzoli Internat., 1980—; author: Knoll Design, 1981 (Am. Inst. Graphic Arts award). Recipient Indsl. Arts medal AIA, 1973, Presdl. Design award, 1985, Gold medal for design Nat. Arts Club, 1991, Fellowship of Excellence Interior Product Designers, 1992, Lifetime Achievement award Bklyn. Mus., 1995, Hon. Royal Designer for Industry award Royal Soc. of Arts, 1996; named to Hall of Fame N.Y. Art Dirs. Club, 1982, Compasso d'Oro, 1964, Interior Design Hall of Fame, 1988. Mem. Am. Inst. Graphic Arts (pres. 1976-77 Gold medal 1983), Indsl. Designers Soc. Am., Alliance Graphique Internationale (past pres.), Archtl. League N.Y. (v.p.). Office: Vignelli Assocs 475 10th Ave New York NY 10018-1120

VIGNERON, ALLEN HENRY, theology educator, rector, auxiliary bishop; b. Mt. Clemens, Mich., Oct. 21, 1948; s. Elwin E. and Bernadine K. (Kott) V. AB in Philosophy, Sacred Heart Sem., Detroit, 1970; STL in Fundamental Theology, Pontifical Gregorian U., 1977; PhD in Philosophy, Cath. U. Am., 1987. Ordained deacon Roman Cath. Ch., 1973, ordained priest, 1975, titular bishop, 1996. Assoc. pastor Our Lady Queen of Peace Ch., Harper Woods, Mich., 1975-79; asst. prof. philosophy and theology Sacred Heart Major Sem., Detroit, 1985—; addetto of the secretariat of his Holiness the Pope The Holy See, Vatican City, 1991-94; rector, pres. Sacred Heart Major Sem., Detroit, 1994—; auxiliary bishop Archdiocese of Detroit, 1996—; adj. prof. theology Pontifical Gregorian U., Rome, 1992-94. Office: Sacred Heart Major Sem 2701 W Chicago Detroit MI 48206-1704

VIGNOLO, BIAGIO NICKOLAS, JR., chemical company executive; b. New Brunswick, N.J., June 15, 1947; s. Biagio and Helen (Carleo) V.; m. Olga Tkachuk, Mar. 23, 1974; children: Adam, John. BS in Acctg., Rider Coll., 1970. Mgr. acctg. staff Peat, Marwick & Mitchell Co., Trenton, N.J., 1969-77; controller Revlon Inc., N.Y.C., 1977-83; v.p., controller Am. Bakeries Co., N.Y.C., 1983-88; sr. v.p. fin. Sun Chem. Corp., Ft. Lee, N.J., 1989—. Fellow Am. Inst. CPA's, N.J. Soc. CPA's. Republican. Roman Catholic. Office: Sun Chem Corp 222 Brg Plz S Fort Lee NJ 07024

VIGTEL, GUDMUND, museum director emeritus; b. Jerusalem, July 9, 1925; came to U.S., 1948, naturalized, 1966; s. Arne Jonsen and Elisabeth (Petri) V.; m. Solveig Lund, 1951 (div. 1964); 1 child, Elisabeth; m. Carolyn Gates Smith, July 18, 1964; 1 child, Catherine Higdon. BFA, U. Ga., 1952, MFA, 1953; DFA (hon.), Atlanta Coll. Art, 1991. Adminstrv. asst. Corcoran Gallery Art, Washington, 1954-61, asst. dir., 1961-63; dir. High Mus. Art, Atlanta, 1963-91, dir. emeritus, 1991—. Contbr. articles and essays to profl. publs. Served with Royal Norwegian Air Force, 1944-45. Decorated Chevalier des Arts et Lettres, Minister of Culture (France); recipient Order of Merit First Class Fed. Republic Germany, 1989. Home: 2082 Golf View Dr NW Atlanta GA 30309-1210

VIKEN, LINDA LEA MARGARET, lawyer; b. Sioux Falls, S.D., Oct. 27, 1945; d. Carl Thomas and Eleanor Bertha (Zehnpfennig) Crampton; m. Jerry Lee Miller, June 10, 1967 (div. 1975); m. Jeffrey Lynn Viken, Feb. 2, 1980. BS in Bus. Edn., U. S.D., 1967, JD in Law, 1977. Bar: S.D. 1978, U.S. Dist. Ct. S.D. 1978, U.S. Ct. Appeals (8th cir.) 1981. Tchr. Yankton (S.D.) High Sch., 1967-69, Edison Jr. High Sch., Sioux Falls, 1969-75; pvt. practice law Sioux Falls, 1978; ptnr. Finch, Viken, Viken, & Pechota, Rapid City, S.D., 1978-92, Viken, Viken, Pechota, Leach & Dewell, Rapid City, 1992—; part-time instr. Nat. Coll., Rapid City, 1978-80; magistrate judge Seventh Jud. Cir., Rapid City, 1983-84; chair S.D. Commn. on Child Support, 1985, 88, 96; mem. S.D. Bd. of Bar Examiners, 1987-88. Contbr. articles to profl. jours. State rep. S.D. Legislature Minnehaha County, 1973-76, Pennington County, 1988-92; state party vice chair S.D. Dem. party, 1978-80, 92-94; chair Pennington County Dem. Party, Rapid City, 1985-87. Named Woman Atty. of Yr. Law Sch. Women, 1987. Fellow Am. Acad. Matrimonial Lawyers; mem. ABA, S.D. Bar, S.D. Trial Lawyers Assn. Democrat. Roman Catholic. Avocations: poetry, skiing. Home: 4760 Trout Ct Rapid City SD 57702-4751 Office: Viken Viken Pechota Leach and Dewell 1617 Sheridan Lake Rd Rapid City SD 57702-3423

VIKIS-FREIBERGS, VAIRA, psychologist, educator; b. Riga, Latvia, Dec. 1, 1937; d. Karlis and Annemarie (Rankis) V.; m. Imants F. Freibergs, July 16, 1960; children: Karlis Roberts, Indra Karoline. B.A., U. Toronto, 1958, M.A., 1960; Ph.D., McGill U., 1965; LLD, Queen's U., 1991. Clin. psychologist Toronto (Ont.) Psychiat. Hosp., 1960-61; asst. prof. dept. psychology U. Montreal, Que., Can., 1965-72; asso. prof. U. Montreal, 1972-77, prof., 1977—; pres. Social Sci. Fedn. Can., 1980; chmn. NATO (spl. program panel on human factors), 1980; dir. Latvian Youth Ethnic Heritage Seminars Divreizdivi, 1979; mem. Sci. Council Can., 1980-89, vice chmn., 1984-89. Author: La Fréquence Lexicale au Quebec, 1974, The Amber Mountain, 1989, Against the Current, 1993; co-author: Latvian Sun Songs, 1988; editor: Linguistics and Poetics of Latvian Folk Songs, 1989; contbr. articles to profl. jours. Recipient Prof. A. Abele Meml. prize, 1979, Disting. Contbn. prize World Assn. Free Latvians, 1989, Order of the Three Stars, Republic of Latvia, 1995; Can. Coun. leave fellow, 1974-75; Killam Rsch. fellow Can. Coun., 1993-95. Fellow Can. Psychol. Assn. (pres. 1980), Royal Soc. Can. (Pierre Chauveau medal for disting. wk. in the humanities 1995); mem. Acad. Sci. Latvia (fgn; Grand medal 1997.), Assn. Advancement Baltic Studies (pres. 1984-86), Assn. Canadienne Francaise pour l'Avancement des Scis. (Marcel-Vincent prize and medal 1992), Sigma Xi. Lutheran. Home: 444 Grenfell Ave, Town of Mount Royal, PQ Canada H3R 1G5 Office: U Montreal Dept Psych CP 6128, Succursale Centre-ville, Montreal, PQ Canada H3C 3J7

VILA, ADIS MARIA, corporate executive, former government official, lawyer; b. Cuba, Aug. 1, 1953; came to U.S., 1962; d. Calixto Vila and Adis C. Fernandez. BA with distinction, Rollins Coll., 1974; JD with honors, U. Fla., 1978; LLM with high honors, Institut Universitaire de Hautes Estudes Internationales, Geneva, 1981; MBA, U Chgo., 1997—. Bar: Fla. 1979, D.C. 1984. Assoc. Paul & Thomson, 1979-82; White House fellow Office Pub. Liaison, Washington, 1982-83; spl. asst. to sec. state for inter-Am. affairs Dept. State, Washington, 1983-86; dir. Office of Mex. and Caribbean Basin, Dept. Commerce, Washington, 1986-87; sec. Dept. Adminstrn., State of Fla., 1987-89; asst. sec. for adminstrn. USDA, Washington, 1989-91; vis. asst., prof. Fla. Internat. U., 1993-94; vis. fellow Nat. Def. U., Washington,

1992-93; v.p. internat. devel. The Vigoro Corp., Chgo., 1994—; dir.,govt. rels. Nortel, 1997—; trustee So. Ctr. for Internat. Studies, 1987—. Bd. dirs. Rollings Coll. Alumni Coun., Winter Park, Fla., 1979—. Named one of 100 Most Influential Hispanics, 1988, Paul Harris fellow Rotary Internat., 1983, U.S.-Japan Leadership fellow, 1991-92, Eisenhower Exch. fellow, Beca Fiore, Argentina, 1992. Mem. Dade County Bar Assn. (bd. dirs. young and lawyers sect. 1979-87), Coun. Fgn. Rels (term mem. 1987-92), Am. Coun. Young Polit. Leaders (bd. dirs. 1984—), Women Execs. in State Govt. (bd. dirs. 1987—). Republican. Roman Catholic. Avocations: tennis, skiing, golf, theater, arts.

VILA, ROBERT JOSEPH, television host, designer, real estate developer; b. Miami, Fla., June 20, 1946; s. Roberto and Esperanza (Robles) V.; m. Diana Barrett, Oct. 3, 1975; children: Christopher, Monica, Susannah. AA in Architecture, Miami Dade Jr. Coll., 1966; BS in Journalism, U. Fla., 1969. Editor English Lang. Cons., Stuttgart, Fed. Republic of Germany, 1971; stagehand Wurttemburg State Theatre, Stuttgart, 1972; project mgr. Barrett Assocs., Boston, 1973-74; pres. R.J. Vila, Inc., Boston, 1975-85; host This Old House Sta. WGBH-TV, Boston, 1978-89; host Bob Vila's Home Again, Cape Cod and Chgo., 1990; host Plymouth, Mass., Naples, Fla., 1991—; host Martha's Vineyard and Malibu, Calif., 1991-92. Author: This Old House, 1980, Bob Vila's This Old House, 1982, Guide to Building Materials, 1986, Guide to Buying Your Dream House, 1990, Bob Vila's Tool Box, 1993, Bob Vila's Guide to Historic Homes of New England, 1993, Bob Vila's Guide to Historic Homes of the South, 1993, Bob Vila's Guide to Historic Homes of the Mid-Atlantic, 1993, Bob Vila's Workshop, 1994, Bob Vila's Guide to Historic Homes of the Midwest and Great Plains, 1994, Bob Vila's Guide to Historic Homes of the West, 1994, (A&E Special) Bob Vila's Guide to Historic Homes, 1996, Bob Vila's American Home mag., 1996. Bd. dirs. Plimouth Plantation, Plymouth, Mass., Nat. Alliance to End Homelessness, Washington. Emmy award New England Region, 1979, Nat., 1985. Mem. Am. Fedn. TV Radio Artists, Screen Actors Guild, Oyster Harbors Club (Osterville, Mass.), Friars Club (N.Y.C.). Roman Catholic. Avocations: sailing, fishing, cycling, gardening, woodworking. Home: PO Box 749 Marstons Mills MA 02648-0749 Office: BVTV PO Box 749 Marstons Mills MA 02648-0749

VILARDEBO, ANGIE MARIE, management consultant, parochial school educator; b. Tampa, Fla., July 15, 1938; d. Vincent and Antonina (Fazio) Noto; m. Charles Kenneth Vilardebo, June 26, 1960; children: Charles, Kenneth, Michele, Melanie. BA, Notre Dame Md., 1960; postgrad., Rollins Coll., 1980. Cert. tchr., Fla. Tchr. Sea Park Elem. Sch., Satellite Beach, Fla., 1960-61; office mgr. Computer Systems Enterprises, Satellite Beach, 1973-76; artist Satellite Beach, 1976-79; employment counselor Career Cons., Melbourne, Fla., 1979-80; tchr. Our Lady of Lourdes Parochial Sch., Melbourne, 1980-89; pres. Consol. Ventures, Inc., Satellite Beach, 1989—, Versatile Suppliers, Inc., Satellite Beach, 1989—; prin. search com. Diocese of Orlando, Fla., 1989-90. Patentee personal grading machine. V.p. Jaycees, Satellite Beach, 1976-77, pres., 1977-78. Recipient 1st Place Art award Fla. Fedn. Woman's Clubs, 1978, 2nd Place Art award, 1979, Honorable Mention, 1980. Mem. Satellite Beach Woman's Club, Paper Chaser's Investment Club, Brevard Arts Ctr. & Mus., Space Coast Art League (social chmn. 1987—). Roman Catholic. Avocations: bridge, writing, reading, oil painting, entrepreneurship. Home: 606 Barcelona Ct Melbourne FL 32937

VILCEK, JAN TOMAS, medical educator; b. Bratislava, Czechoslovakia, June 17, 1933; came to U.S., 1965, naturalized, 1970.; s. Julius and Friderika (Fischer) V.; m. Marica F. Gerhath, July 28, 1962. MD, Comenius U., Bratislava, 1957; CSc (PhD), Czechoslovak Acad. Sci., Bratislava, 1962. Fellow Inst. Virology, Bratislava, 1957-62, head of lab., 1962-64; asst. prof. microbiology NYU Med. Ctr., N.Y.C., 1965-68, assoc. prof., 1968-73, prof., 1973—, head biol. response modifiers, 1983—; lectr. Chinese Acad. Med. Sci., Beijing, 1981, 83, Osaka U., 1987-88; chmn. nomenclature com. WHO, 1981-86, cons. biol. standardization com., 1982-88; mem. adv. com. Cancer Soc., 1981-87, chmn., 1983; expert French Ministry Health, 1983-88; mem. sci. adv. bd. Max Planck Inst., Munich, 1987-95. Author: Interferon, 1969; editor in chief Jour. Archives of Virology, 1975-86, Cytokine and Growth Factor Revs., 1995—; editor: Interferons and the Immune Systems, 1984, Tumor Necrosis Factor: Structure, Function and Mechanism of Action, 1991; mem. editl. bd. Virology, 1979-81, Archives of Virology, 1986-92, Infection and Immunity, 1983-85, Antiviral Rsch., 1984-88, Jour. Interferon Rsch., 1988—, Jour. Immunological Methods, 1986—, Natural Immunity and Cell Growth Regulation, 1986-92, Jour. Immunology, 1987-89, Lymphokine Rsch., 1987-94, Jour. Biol. Chemistry, 1988-90, ISI Atlas Sci., Immunology, 1988-89, Jour. Cellular Physiology, 1988—, Cytokine, 1989—, Biologicals, 1989-95, Acta Virologica, 1991—, Internat. Archives of Allergy and Immunology, 1992—, Folia Biologica, 1993-96, Cellular Immunology, 1993, Jour. of Inflammation, 1994—; contbr. articles to profl. jours. Mem. rev. panel Israel Cancer Rsch. Fund, 1993-96; mem. fellowship rev. com. Am. Heart Assn., 1992-94. Recipient Rsch. Career Devel. award USPHS, 1968-73, Recognition award Japanese Inflammation Soc., 1989, Outstanding Investigator award Nat. Cancer Inst., NIH, 1991—, Elliott Osserman award for disting. svc. in support of cancer rsch., 1996; grantee USPHS, numerous other orgns. Mem. AAAS, Soc. Gen. Microbiology, Am. Soc. Microbiology, Am. Assn. Immunologists, Internat. Soc. Interferon Rsch., Czech Immunology Soc., Internat. Cytokine Soc. (v.p. 1997), Czechoslovak Soc. for Microbiology. Office: NYU Med Ctr 550 1st Ave New York NY 10016-6481

VILIM, NANCY CATHERINE, advertising agency executive; b. Quincy, Mass., Jan. 15, 1952; d. John Robert and Rosemary (Malpede) V.; m. Geoffrey S. Horner, Feb. 16, 1992; children: Matthew Edward Cajda, Megan Catherine Cajda, Margaret Horner. Student, Miami U., Oxford, Ohio, 1970-72. Media asst. Draper Daniels, Inc., Chgo., 1972-74; asst. buyer Campbell Mithun, Chgo., 1974-75; buyer Tatham, Laird & Kudner, Chgo., 1975-77; media buyer Adcom, Inc. div. Quaker Oats Corp., Chgo., 1977-79; media supr. G.M. Feldman, Chgo., 1979-81; v.p. media dir. Media Mgmt., 1981-83; v.p. broadcast dir. Bozell, Jacobs, Kenyon & Eckhardt, Chgo., 1983-88; v.p., media mgr. McCann-Erickson, Inc., 1989—; judge 27th Internat. Broadcast Awards, Chgo., 1987. Co-pres. Immaculate Conception Religious Edn. Parents Club, 1995-96. Recipient Media All Star awards Sound Mgmt. Mag., N.Y.C., 1987. Mem. Broadcast Advt. Club Chgo., Mus. Broadcast Communications, NAFE. Office: McCann-Erickson Inc 515 N State St Chicago IL 60610-4325

VILLA, JOHN KAZAR, lawyer; b. Ypsilanti, Mich., June 9, 1948; s. John Joseph and Susie (Hoogasian) V.; m. Ellen A. Edwards, June 3, 1990. AB, Duke U., 1970; JD, U. Mich., 1973. Bar: D.C. 1973. Trial atty. U.S. Dept. Justice, Washington, 1973-77; assoc. Williams & Connolly, Washington, 1977-81; ptnr. Williams & Connolly, 1981—. Author: legal treatises. Office: Williams & Connolly 725 12th St NW Washington DC 20005-3901

VILLABLANCA, JAIME ROLANDO, medical scientist, educator; b. Chillán, Chile, Feb. 29, 1929; came to U.S., 1971; naturalized, 1985; s. Ernesto and Teresa (Hernández) V.; m. Guillermina Nieto, Dec. 3, 1955; children: Amparo C., Jaime G., Pablo J., Francis X., Claudio I. Bachelor in Biology, Nat. Inst. Chile, 1946; licentiate médicine, U. Chile, 1953, MD, 1954. Cert. neurophysiology. Rockefeller Found. postdoctoral fellow in physiology John Hopkins and Harvard Med. Schs., 1959-61; Fogarty internat. rsch. fellow in anatomy UCLA, 1966-68, assoc. research anatomist and psychiatrist, 1971-72; assoc. prof. psychiatry and biobehavioral scis. UCLA Sch. Medicine, 1972-76; prof. psychiatry and biobehavioral scis. UCLA, 1976—, prof. neurobiology, 1977—; mem. faculty U. Chile Sch. Medicine, 1954-71, prof. exptl. medicine, 1970-71; vis. prof. neurobiology Cath. U. Chile Sch. Medicine, 1974; cons. in field. Author numerous rsch. papers, book chpts., abstracts; chief regional editor Developmental Brain Dysfunction, 1988—. Decorated Order Francisco de Miranda (Venezuela); recipient Premio Reina Sofia, Madrid, 1990, Fgn. Scientist Traveling grant Tokyo (Japan) Met. Govt., 1995; fellow Rockefeller Found., 1959-61, Fogarty Internat. Rsch. fellow NIH, 1966-68; grantee USAF Office Sci. Rsch., 1962-65, Found. Fund Rsch. Psychiatry, 1969-72, USPHS-Nat. Inst. Child Human Devel., 1972-96, USPHS-Nat. Inst. Drug Abuse, 1981-85, USPHS-Nat. Inst. Neurol. Disorders and Stroke, 1988-92. Mem. AAAS, AAUP, Am. Assn. Anatomists, Mental Retardation Rsch. Ctr., Brain Rsch. Inst., Internat. Brain Rsch. Orgn., Am. Physiol. Soc., Soc. for Neurosci., Assn. Venezolana Padres de Niños Excepcionales, Sci. Coun. Internat. Inst. Rsch. and Advice in Mental Deficiency (Madrid), Soc. Child and Adolescent Psychiatry and Neurology (Chile) (hon.), Sigma Xi. Home: 200 Surfview Dr Pacific Palisades CA 90272-2911 Office: UCLA Dept Psychiatry & Biobehavioral Scis Los Angeles CA 90024-1759

VILLAFRANCA, JOSEPH J., pharmaceutical executive, chemistry educator; b. Silver Creek, N.Y., Mar. 23, 1944; s. Joseph Nicholas and Mildred (Dolce) C.; children: Jennifer, June, Evan. BS, SUNY, Fredonia, 1965; PhD, Purdue U., 1969. From asst. prof. to prof. Pa. State U., University Park, 1971-76, Evan Pugh prof. chemistry, 1986—; cons. Monsanto Corp., St. Louis, 1985-89, Eastman Kodak Co., Rochester, N.Y., 1985-87. Author over 170 sci. publs. Mem. Am. Chem. Soc. (councilor 1986-89), Am. Soc. for Biochemistry and Molecular Biology, Biophys. Soc., Protein Soc. Avocation: skiing. Office: Bristol-Myers Squibb Pharm Res Inst PO Box 4000 Princeton NJ 08543

VILLA-KOMAROFF, LYDIA, molecular biologist, educator, university official; b. Las Vegas, N.Mex., Aug. 7, 1947; d. John Dias and Drucilla (Jaramillo) V.; m. Anthony Leader Komaroff, June 18, 1970. BA, Goucher Coll., 1970; PhD, MIT, 1975; DSc (hon.), St. Thomas U., 1996, Pine Manor Coll., 1997; PhD (hon.), Goucher Coll., 1997. Rsch. fellow Harvard U., Cambridge, 1975-78; asst. prof. dept. microbiology U. Mass. Med. Ctr., Worcester, 1978-81, assoc. prof. dept. molecular genetics micro, 1982-85; assoc. prof. dept. neurology Harvard Med. Sch., Boston, 1986-95; sr. rsch. assoc. neurology Children's Hosp., Boston, 1985-95, assoc. dir. mental retardation rsch. ctr., 1987-94; assoc. v.p. rsch., prof. dept. neurology Northwestern U., Evanston, Ill., 1996—; mem. mammalian genetics study sect. NIH, 1982-84, mem. reviewers rsch., 1989, mem. neurol. disorders program project rev. com., 1989-94; mem. adv. bd. Biol. Scis. Directorate, 1994—; mem. bd. dirs. Nat. Ctr. Genome Rsch., 1995—. Contbr. articles and abstracts to profl. jours.; patentee in field. Recipient Hispanic Engr. Nat. Achievement award, 1992, Nat. Achievement award Hispanic Mag., 1996; Helen Hay Whitney Found. fellow, 1975-78; NIH grantee, 1978-85, 89-96. Mem. Am. Soc. Microbiology, Assn. for Women in Sci., Soc. for Neurosci., Am. Coll. Cell Biology, Soc. for Advancement Chicanos and Native Ams. in Sci. (founding, bd. dirs. 1987-93, v.p. 1990-93). Office: Northwestern U 633 Clark St Evanston IL 60208-0001

VILLALOBOS PADILLA, FRANCISCO, bishop; b. Guadalajara, Mexico, Feb. 1, 1921. Ordained priest Roman Cath. Ch., 1949; named titular bishop of Colonnata, 1971; now bishop of Saltillo Mexico, 1975—. Office: Bishop's Residence, Obispado Apartado 25, Saltillo Coahuila, Mexico also: Hidalgo Sur 166, Apartado 25 CP25000, Saltillo Mexico Coahuila*

VILLAREAL, PATRICIA, lawyer; b. Sonora, Calif., Aug. 27, 1951. BA, Mount Vernon Coll., 1977; JD, Harvard U., 1980. Bar: Tex. 1980. Law clk. to Judge Sanders U.S. Dist. Ct. (no. dist.) Tex., 1980-82; mem. Jones, Day, Reavis & Pogue, Dallas; spl. asst. Ho. Reps. Jud. Com., 1975-77. Office: Jones Day Reavis & Pogue PO Box 660623 2300 Trammell Crow Ctr 2001 Ross Ave Dallas TX 75201-8001

VILLAR-PALASI, CARLOS, pharmacology educator; b. Valencia, Spain, Mar. 3, 1928; came to U.S., 1963; s. Vicente Villar Bolinaga and Teresa (Palasi-Pinazo); m. Amparo Gosalvez-Sobrino, Aug. 17, 1957 (dec. July 1978); children: Victor, Carlos, Juan Jose, Maria Amparo. MS in Chemistry, U. Valencia, Spain, 1951; PhD in Biochemistry, U. Madrid, Spain, 1955; MS in Pharmacy, U. Barcelona, Spain, 1962. Rsch. fellow med. sch. U. Hamburg, Fed. Republic of Germany, 1953-54, Spanish Rsch. Coun., Madrid, 1954-57, Case Western Res. U., Cleve., 1960-63; rsch. assoc. Spanish Rsch. Coun., Madrid, 1960-63, Case Western Res. U., Cleve., 1963-64; rsch. assoc. U. Minn., Mpls., 1964-65, asst. prof., 1965-69; assoc. prof. U. Va., Charlottesville, 1969-72, prof., 1972—; invited speaker Fedn. European Biochem. Soc., 1969, 96. March Found. fellow, 1957; recipient Rsch. award Cleve. Diabetes Found., 1960, NIH, 1967-69. Mem. AAAS (Rsch. award 1960-62), Am. Soc. Pharmacology, Am. Soc. Biol. Chemistry. Roman Catholic. Avocations: horse riding, camping. Home: PO Box 101 Ivy VA 22945-0101 Office: U Va Med Sch Dept Pharmacology 1300 Jefferson Park Ave Charlottesville VA 22903-3363

VILLARREAL, CARLOS CASTANEDA, engineering executive; b. Brownsville, Tex., Nov. 9, 1924; s. Jesus Jose and Elisa L. (Castaneda) V.; m. Doris Ann Akers, Sept. 10, 1948; children: Timothy Hill, David Akers. BA, U.S. Naval Acad., 1948; MS, U.S. Navy Postgrad. Sch., 1950; LLD (hon.), St. Mary's U., 1972. Registered profl. engr. Commd. ensign U.S. Navy, 1948, advanced through grades to lt., 1956; comdg. officer U.S.S. Rhea, 1951, U.S.S. Osprey, 1952; comdr. Mine Div. 31, 1953; resigned, 1956; mgr. marine and indsl. operation Gen. Electric Co., 1956-66; v.p. mktg. and adminstrn. Marquardt Corp., 1966-69; head Urban Mass Transit Adminstrn., Dept. Transp., Washington, 1969-73; commr. Postal Rate Commn., 1973-79, vice chmn., 1975-79; v.p. Washington ops. Wilbur Smith and Assocs., 1979-84, sr. v.p., 1984-86, exec. v.p., 1987—, also bd. dirs.; lectr. in field; mem. industry sector adv. com. Dept. Commerce; mem. sect. 13 adv. com. Dept. Transp., 1983-86. Contbr. to profl. jours. Mem. devel. com. Wolftrap Farm Park for the Performing Arts, 1973-78; mem. council St. Elizabeth Ch., 1982-86, chmn. fin. com.; mem. bd. edn. St. Elizabeth Sch.; bd. dirs. Assoc. Catholic Charities, 1983-86; mem. fin. com. Cath. Charities, U.S.A.; mem. John Carroll Soc. Decorated knight Sovereign Mil. Hospitaller Order St. John of Jerusalem of Rhodes and Malta, 1981, Knight Equestrian Order of the Holy Sepulchre of Jerusalem, 1995; recipient award outstanding achievement Dept. Transp. Fellow ASCE, Am. Cons. Engrs. Coun. (vice chmn. internat. com.); mem. IEEE, NSPE (pres. D.C. soc. 1986-87, bd. dirs. 1988-91), Am. Pub. Transit Assn., Soc. Naval Architects and Marine Engrs., Soc. Am. Mil. Engrs., Am. Rds. and Transp. Builders Assn. (chmn. pub. transp. adv. coun.), Transp. Rsch. Bd., Washington Soc. Engrs., Internat. Bridge, Tunnel and Turnpike Assn., Inst. Traffic Engrs., Intelligent Transp. Soc. Am. (chmn. fin. com., bd. dirs.), Univ. Club, Army-Navy Club. Republican. Roman Catholic. Office: Wilbur Smith Assocs 2921 Telestar Ct Falls Church VA 22042-1205

VILLARS, FELIX MARC HERMANN, physicist, educator; b. Biel, Switzerland, Jan. 6, 1921; came to U.S., 1949, naturalized, 1955; s. Jean Felix and Alma (Engel) V.; m. Jacqueline Dubois, June 25, 1949; children: J. Frederic, Cecile, Monique, Philippe. Diplome, Swiss Fed. Inst. Tech., Zurich, 1945, D.Sc.Nat., 1946. Research asst. Swiss Fed. Inst. Tech., 1946-49; vis. mem. Inst. Advanced Study at Princeton, 1949-50; research asso. MIT, 1950-52, asst. prof. physics, 1952-55, assoc. prof., 1955-60, prof., 1960-91, prof. emeritus, sr. lectr., 1991—; lectr. biophysics Harvard Med. Sch., 1974—. Served with Swiss Army, 1940-45. Fellow AAAS, Am. Acad. Arts and Scis., N.Y. Acad. Sci.; mem. Am. Phys. Soc. Home: 55 Orchard St Belmont MA 02178-3008 Office: Ctr for Theoretical Physics MIT 77 Massachusetts Ave Cambridge MA 02139-4301

VILLAVASO, STEPHEN DONALD, urban planner, lawyer; b. New Orleans, July 12, 1949; s. Donald Philip and Jacklyn (Tully) V.; m. Regina Smith, Apr. 17, 1971; children: Christine Regina, Stephen Warner. BS in Econs., U. New Orleans, 1971, M in Urban and Regional Planning, 1976; JD, Loyola U., New Orleans, 1981. Bar: La. 1982; recognized ct. expert in land use, planning and zoning. Urban and regional planner Barnard & Thomas, New Orleans, 1976-78; dir. analysis and planning Office of Mayor, City of New Orleans, 1978-81; counsel for planning and devel. Office of City Atty., City of New Orleans, 1983-84; dir. planning and environ. affairs Tecon Realty, New Orleans, 1981-83; v.p. for planning and project mgmt. Morphy, Makofsky, Mumphrey & Masson, New Orleans, 1984-89; bus. devel. mgr. Waste Mgmt., Inc., New Orleans, 1989-96; pres. Villavaso & Assocs., LLC, New Orleans, 1996—; bd. dirs. Regional Loan Corp.; guest lectr., adj. prof. Coll. of Urban and Pub. Affairs, U. New Orleans, 1976—; spl. instr. grad. studies in urban planning So. U. New Orleans, 1987—. Bd. dirs. New Orleans Traffic and Transp. Bur., 1981-86, Riverfront Awareness, New Orleans, 1984-86; bd. dirs. Vols. Am. Greater New Orleans, 1987-96, vice chmn., 1990, chmn. bd., 1992-95. With USN, 1971-74. Named one of Outstanding Young Men of Am., 1980, 82. Mem. ABA, Am. Inst. of Cert. Planners, Am. Planning Assn. (pres. La. div. 1980-84, disting. svc. award 1985), Urban Land Inst., La. Bar Assn., U. New Orleans Alumni Assn. (bd. dirs. 1990—), Phi Kappa Phi, Delta Sigma Pi (pres. 1971), Omicron Delta Kappa. Democrat. Roman Catholic. Avocations: philately, camping, travel. Home: 6304 Beauregard Ave New Orleans LA 70124-4502

VILLAVECES, JAMES WALTER, allergist, immunologist; b. San Luis Obispo, Calif., Nov. 4, 1933; s. Robert and Solita (Combariza) V. BA, UCLA, 1955; MD, U. Calif. Med. Sch., 1960. Cert. Am. Bd. Allergy and Immunology, recert. Rotating intern Santelle VA Hosp., L.A., 1960-61; preceptorship adult allergy L.A. County Hosp., Los Angeles, 1964-66; fellow allergy White Meml. CCM, L.A., 1966-67; chief allergy div. Ventura (Calif.) Med. Ctr., 1969-87; practice medicine specializing in allergy-immunology Ventura, 1984-96; cons. Bio-Dynamics Co., Ventura, 1975-80, Norwich-Eaton and Pharmacia and Fisons, Ventura, 1980-85; lectr. in field. Writer, prodr., editor films. Bd. dirs. Am. Lung Assn., Ventura, 1969-85, pres., 1974, advisor air pollution control com., 1971-74; judge Ventura Sci. Fair, 1970-85. Recipient Commendation, County Bd. Suprs., Ventura, 1974. Fellow Am. Acad. Allergy, Am. Coll. Allergists; mem. Calif. Soc. Allergy-Immunology, Calif. Med. Assn., Gold Coast Tri-County Allergy Soc. (pres. 1987), CAL Club (hon.), Ventura County Sports Hall of Fame (founder), Mensa. Republican. Avocations: writing, photography, lecturing, pistol target shooting. Home: 88 Eugenia Dr Ventura CA 93003-1502 Office: Dudley Profl Ctr 4080 Loma Vista Rd Ste M Ventura CA 93003-1811

VILLECCO, JUDY DIANA, substance abuse, mental health counselor, director; b. Knoxville, Tenn., Jan. 19, 1948; d. William Arthur and Louise (Reagan) Chamberlain; m. Tucker, June 10, 1965 (div. 1974); children: Linda Louise (Tucker) Smith, Constance Christine; m. Roger Anthony Villecco, May 3, 1979. BA in Psychology, U. West Fla., 1988, MA in Psychology, 1992. Lic. mental health counselor, Fla.; cert. addiction profl., Fla.; internat. cert. alcohol and drug counselor. Counselor Gulf Coast Hosp., Ft. Walton Beach, Fla., 1986-87; peer counselor U. West Fla., Ft. Walton Beach, 1987-89; family and prevention counselor Okaloosa Guidance Clinic, Ft. Walton Beach, 1988-89; family svc. dir. Anon Anew of Tampa (Fla.), Inc., 1989-91; dir. Renew Counseling Ctr., Ft. Walton Beach, 1990-92; substance abuse dept. dir. Avalon Ctr., Milton, Fla., 1992-93; adult coord. Partial & Rivendell, Ft. Walton Beach, 1994-95; pvt. practice Emerald Coast Psychiat. Care, P.A., Fort Walton Beach, 1994-95, Associated Psychotherapists, Ft. Walton Beach, 1995-97; with Aegis Behavioral Care, Ft. Walton Beach, 1997—; internat. substance abuse counselor, dir. and presenter in field. Author: Co-dependency Treatment Manual, 1992; creator Effective Treatment for Codependants, 1992. Named Outstanding Mental Health Profl. of Yr. Mental Health Assn., 1994. Mem. Internat. Assn. for Offender Counselors, Fla. Alcohol, Drug, Substance Abuse Assn. (bd. dirs., regional rep., Regional Profl. of Yr. 1992-93, 95-96), Am. Counseling Assn., Internat. Assn. for Marriage and Family Counseling, Phi Theta Kappa, Alpha Phi Sigma. Avocations: crafts, grandchildren, travel. Office: Aegis Behavioral Care Ste 37 348 Miracle Strip Pkwy SW Fort Walton Beach FL 32548-5264

VILLEE, CLAUDE ALVIN, JR., biochemistry educator; b. Lancaster, Pa., Feb. 9, 1917; s. Claude Alvin and Mary Elizabeth (Nestel) V.; m. Dorothy Theresa Balzer, Jan. 21, 1952; children: Claude Alvin III, Stephen Eric Fortney, Suzanne Villee, Charles Andrew. BS, Franklin and Marshall Coll., 1937; PhD, U. Calif.-Berkeley, 1941; AM (hon.), Harvard U., 1957; ScD (hon.), Franklin and Marshall Coll., 1991. Research fellow U. Calif. at Berkeley, 1941-42; asst. prof. U. N.C., 1942-45; mem. faculty Harvard, 1946—, prof. biol. chemistry, 1962-63, Andelot prof. biol. chemistry, 1964—; fellow Winthrop House, 1957—; tech. aide Nat. Acad. Scis., 1946-47; research assoc. Boston Lying in Hosp., 1950-66; dir. lab. reproductive biology Boston Hosp., 1966—; disting. vis. prof. U. Belgrade, Yugoslavia, 1974, 77; vis. prof. Mahidol U., Bangkok, Thailand, 1974; cons. NSF, Ford Found., Nat. Found./March of Dimes; mem. nat. adv. child health and human devel. council NIH; pres. Internat. Symposium Foeto-Placental unit, Milan, 1968. Author: Biology, 10th edit, 1993, General Zoology, 6th edit, 1984, Fallout from the Population Explosion, 1986, Metabolism, 1985, Introduction to Animal Biology, 1979, Control of Ovulation, 1961, Mechanism of Action of Steroid Hormones, 1960, The Placenta and Fetal Membranes, 1960, Gestation, Vols. 2-5, 1955-58, Respiratory Distress Syndrome, 1973, Biological Principles and Processes, 1976, The Placenta: A Neglected Experimental Animal, 1979, Human Reproduction, 1981, PDQ Biochemistry, 1986; mem. editorial bd. Paragon House Pus., 1984—; contbr. articles to profl. jours. Trustee Forsythe Dental Center, Boston, Winsor Sch.; trustee, v.p. Internat. Found. for Biochem. Endocrinology, 1980—; bd. dirs. Moors Assn., Falmouth, Mass. Lalor fellow, 1946-47; Guggenheim fellow, 1949-50; recipient Ciba award, 1956, Rubin award, 1957. Fellow Am. Acad. Arts and Scis., Am. Gynecol. Soc. (hon.), Am. Coll. Obstetrics and Gynecology (hon.), Soc. for Gynecol. Investigation (hon.), Serbian Acad. Arts and Scis. (hon.); mem. Moors Assn. Falmouth (pres.), Am. Soc. Biol. Chemists, Endocrine Soc. Am., Biochem. Soc. (Eng.), Am. Chem. Soc., Soc. Devel. Biology, Marine Biol. Lab. (Woods Hole, Mass). Home: 485 Elm Rd Falmouth MA 02540-2414 Office: 25 Shattuck St Boston MA 02115-6027

VILLELLA, EDWARD JOSEPH, ballet dancer, educator, choreographer, artistic director; b. L.I., N.Y., Oct. 1, 1936; s. Joseph and Mildred (DeGiovanni) V.; m. Janet Greschler (div. Nov. 1980); 1 child, Roddy; m. Linda Carbonetta, Apr. 1981; children: Christa Francesca, Lauren. BS in Marine Transp., N.Y. State Maritime Coll., 1957; LHD (hon.), Boston Conservatory, 1985; hon. degree, Skidmore Coll., Fordham U., Nazareth Coll., Siena Coll., Union Coll., Schenectady, N.Y., 1991; DHL (hon.), St. Thomas U., Miami, Fla., 1994. Mem. N.Y.C. Ballet, 1957, soloist, 1958-60, prin. soloist, 1960-83; artistic dir. Ballet Okla., Oklahoma City, 1983-86; founding artistic dir. Miami (Fla.) City Ballet, 1985—; vis. artist U.S. Mil. Acad., West Point, 1981-82; vis. prof. dance U. Iowa, 1981; resident Heritage chair arts and cultural criticism George Mason U.; lectr. in field. Performed dances in Symphony C, Scotch Symphony, Western Symphony, Donizetti Variations, Swan Lake, La Source, The Nutcracker, Agon, Stars and Stripes, The Prodigal Son; premiered in Balanchine works including The Figure in the Carpet, 1960, Electronics, 1961, A Midsummer Night's Dream, 1962, Bugaku, 1963, Tarantella, 1964, Harlequinade, 1965, The Brahms-Schoenberg Quartet, 1966, Jewels, 1967, Symphony in Three Movements, 1972, Schéhérazade, 1975; choreography includes Narkissas, 1966, Shostakovitch Ballet Suite, 1972, Shenandoah, 1972, Gayane Pas de Deux, 1972, Salute to Cole, 1973, Sea Chanties, 1974, Prelude, Riffs and Fugues, 1980; TV appearances include The Ed Sullivan Show, Bell Telephone Hour, Mike Douglas Show, (TV spl.) Harlequin, 1975 (Emmy award), summer theaters, festivals, U.S. and abroad, 1957—; co-author: (autobiography) Prodigal Son, 1991. Mem. Nat. Coun. of Arts, 1968-74; chmn. Commn. for Cultural Affairs City N.Y., 1978; bd. visitors N.C. Sch. for the Arts; mem. dance adv. panel Nat. Endowment for Arts; trustee Wolf Trap Found. for the Arts. Recipient Dance Mag. award, 1964, Lions of the Performing Arts award N.Y. Pub. Libr., 1987, Capezio Dance award, 1989, Gold medal Nat. Soc. Arts and Letters, 1990, William G. Anderson merit award AAHPERD, 1991; named Miamian of Yr., UNICO Nat., 1993; inductee Fla. Artists Hall of Fame, 1997.

VILLENEUVE, DONALD AVILA, biology educator; b. Ventura, Calif., Oct. 25, 1930; s. Victor Fredrick V.; and Florence Ann (Pelletier) Goodin; m. Marylyn Yvonne Peoples, Jan. 7, 1950; children: Debra Lynn, Theresa Dianne, Karen Elaine, Kathryn Anne. BS, U. Idaho, 1958; MS, Univ. of Pacific, 1960; MA, U. Colo., 1967; PhD, UCLA, 1976. Cert. tchr., Calif., cert. community coll. tchr., adminstr. Biology tchr. Glendora (Calif.) High Sch., 1960-61; prof. biology and environ. sci. Ventura Coll., 1961-76; dir. div. math. and sci. Moorpark (Calif.) Coll., 1976-78; asst. prof. biol. sci. Calif. Poly. U., San Luis Obispo, Calif., 1978; prof. biology and environ. sci. Ventura Coll., 1978-92 (ret.); pres. acad. senate Ventura Coll., 1985-87; bd. dirs. Calif. Acad. Partnership Program, Long Beach, 1985-88; curriculum cons. Calif. State Dept. Edn., Sacramento, 1986-87; mem. sci. tchr. preparatory panel Calif. Commn. on Tchr. Credentialing, Sacramento, 1988-93. Mem. City Coun. City of San Buenaventura, Ventura, 1987-91; mem. Calif. Coastal Commn., Santa Barbara, 1977-81; mem. planning commn. City of San Buenaventura, 1975-77, parks and recreation commn., 1974-75; v.p. Ventura County Symphony Assn., 1969-71; bd. dirs. Beach Erosion Authority, 1987-91, League for Coastal Protection, 1985—, League Calif. Cities, 1987-91; mem. Ventura County Ctr. Planned Parenthood Adv. Coun., 1991-94; pres. Cambria Dem. Club, 1996-97; mem. San Luis Obispo County Dem. Ctrl. Com.; pres. Cambria Friends of the Ranchland, 1994-96; pres., bd. dirs. Cambria Cmty. Svc. Dist., 1996; del. Assn. Calif. Water Agys.; mem. North Coast Adv. com., land use subcom. Sgt. U.S. Army, 1950-53. NIMH grantee, 1971-72. Mem. Faculty Assn. Calif. Community Colls., Calif. Fedn. Tchrs. (bd. dirs. 1985-87). Avocations: fishing, camping, hiking, boating. Home: 394 Orlando Dr Cambria CA 93428-4406

VILLENEUVE, JEAN-PIERRE, science association director, educator; b. Roberval, Que., Can., May 19, 1938; s. Pascal and Simone (Duval) V.; m. Céline Laroche, Feb. 9, 1962 (div.); children: Isabelle, Elise; m. Christiane Marcoux, Oct. 9, 1979. BScA in Civil Engring., U. Laval, Que., 1963; DES in Hydrodynamics, U. Toulouse, France, 1964, PhD in Hydraulics, 1966. Project engr. Natural Resources Can., Que., 1967; jr. lectr. U. Sherbrooke, Can., 1968-69, U. Que. è Chicoutimi, 1969-70; prof. U. Laval, 1966-70; prof. INRS-Eau, Ste. Foy, Que., 1970—, dir., 1990; pres. bd. dirs. Revue des Scis. de l'Eau, Que. and France, 1995, sci. dir., 1988-94. Contbr. numerous articles to profl. publs. Recipient prize for sci. excellence SNC Lavallin-AQTE, 1994. Mem. Am. Geophys. Union (mem. network design com. 1976-87), Club Tennis Montcalm (pres. 1984—). Achievements include development of software in field. Office: INRS-Eau, 2800 rue Einstein Ste 020, Quebec, PQ Canada G1X 4N8

VILLERS, PHILIPPE, mechanical engineer; b. Paris, June 20, 1935; came to U.S., 1940, naturalized, 1946; s. Raymond and Garda (Schmidt) V.; m. Annie Louise Young, July 13, 1957 (div. 1973); children: Jocelyn Anne (dec.), Renata Jane; m. Katherine Stephan, 1973; children: Noel Stephan, Carolyn Grace. AB in Applied Scis. cum laude, Harvard U., 1955; SM in Mech. Engring, Mass. Inst. Tech., 1960. Mem. mfg. tng. program Gen. Electric Co., 1955-58; project engr. Perkin-Elmer Corp., Wilton, Conn., 1959-62; project engr. Apollo Antenna pointings sensor Barnes Engring. Co., Stamford, Conn., 1962-65; project mgr. Advanced Products Center, Link Group, Gen. Precision, Inc., Binghamton, N.Y., 1965-67; mgr. advanced products Concord Control, Inc., Boston, 1967-69; co-founder, sr. v.p., dir. Computervision Corp., Bedford, Mass., 1969-80; founder, pres., dir. Automatix, Inc., Billerica, Mass., 1980-84; chmn. bd. Automatix Inc., Billerica, Mass., 1984-86; founder, pres., dir. Cognition Inc., 1985-88; bd. dirs. Xyvision, Inc., Wakefield, Mass., chair 1992-94; bd. dirs. Conflict Mgmt. Group, Cambridge, Mass., Energia Global, Wakefield, Grainpro Inc., Concord, Mass., pres., 1996—. Patentee process welding aluminum liners to steel surfaces, horizon sensor for visible wavelength, infrared roughness testing instrument, improved thermopile constrn. thermal die marker; pioneer design and feasibility solar sail applications for interplanetary probe propulsion and stblzn. Mem. Dem. Town Com., Wilton, Conn., 1963, Concord, Mass., 1978—, chmn., 1984-96; mem. Harvard Com. on Univ. Resources, 1981-92; mem. various vis. coms. MIT, 1981-91; mem. vis. com. Nat. Bur. Standards, 1981-84; trustee U. Lowell, 1985-91; founder, pres. Families U.S.A. Founds. (formerly Villers Found.), Washington, 1981—, Bay State Retiree Vol. Coun., Concord, 1989-92; del. Dem. Nat. Conv., 1988, 92. NSF grad. fellow, 1959-60. Mem. IEEE, ASME, Amnesty Internat. (bd. dirs. 1990-96, ombudsman 1992-96, exec. com. 1994-96, leadership coun. 1995—), Soc. Mfg. Engrs., ACLU (pres. com. 1981—, bd. dirs. Physicians for Human Rights 1991-94), Unitarian-Universalist Assn. (pres. coun. 1982-86), Sigma Xi. Home: 20 Whits End Rd Concord MA 01742-5411 Office: 97 Lowell Rd Ste 11-4 Concord MA 01742-1700

VILLFORTH, JOHN CARL, health physicist; b. Reading, Pa., Dec. 28, 1930; s. Carl and Grace L. (Fichthorn) V.; m. Joanne E. Heine, Sept. 12, 1953; children: Mary Jane Smith, Elaine, Jennifer Veazy. B.S. in San. Engring., Pa. State U., 1952, M.S., 1954; M.S. in Physics, Vanderbilt U., 1958. Cert. Am. Bd. Health Physics. With USPHS, 1961-90; dir. Ctr. for Devices and Radiol. Health, 1969-90, asst. surgeon gen., 1972-90, chief engr., 1985-89; pres. Food and Drug Law Inst., Washington, 1990—; bd. dirs. MiniMed Corp, NOMOS Corp. Served to capt. USAF, 1954-61. Recipient Meritorious Svc. medal USPHS, 1974, D.S.M., 1980, 84, Outstanding Svc. medal, 1986. Mem. Health Physics Soc. (pres. 1976-77, Elda Anderson award 1970), Drug Info. Assn., Assn. Food and Drug Ofcls., Internat. Radiation Protection Assn., Regulatory Affairs Profl. Soc., Commd. Officers Assn. Office: 1000 Vermont Ave NW Washington DC 20005-4903 *Understand the problem! Too much energy is wasted and too many relationships arestrained because we fail to understand the underlying problem before we embark on a solution.*

VILLINSKI, PAUL STEPHEN, artist; b. York, Maine, May 28, 1960; s. Paul Bernard and Jacqueline L. (Whalen) V. Student, Mass. Coll. Art, 1980-82; BFA, Cooper Union, 1984. adj. lectr. art history LaGuardia C.C., CUNY, L.I. City, 1990-93. Solo exhbns. include St. Peter's Ch. at Citicorp Ctr., N.Y.C., 1987, Midtown Payson Galleries, N.Y.C., 1989, Queens Mus. Art at Bulova Corp. Ctr., Jackson Heights, N.Y., 1990; group shows include Ridge St. Gallery, N.Y.C., 1986-87, Queens Mus. Art, Flushing, N.Y., 1987, Studio K Gallery, L.I., N.Y., 1987, 88, Midtown Payson Galleries, 1988, 89, The Barn Gallery, Ogunquit, Maine, 1990, PS Gallery Ogunquit, 1991, 92, DMB&B, N.Y.C., 1991, Cooper Union, N.Y.C., 1992, Nat. Acad. Design, N.Y.C., 1992, Paine Webber Art Gallery, N.Y.C., 1992, Fuel Gallery, Seattle, 1992, Herron Test-Site, Bklyn., 1992, Jamaica (N.Y.) Arts Ctr., 1992, 80 Washington Square Galleries, N.Y.C., NYU, 1993, Bklyn. Union Gas Co. Cmty. Galleries, 1993, PDG Gallery, 1993, Flushing Coun. on Culture and Arts Town Hall, 1994, Ronald Feldman Gallery, N.Y.C., 1995, The Cooper Union, N.Y.C., 1996, Sauce Gallery, Bklyn., 1996, Brookworld/Soho Arts Festival, N.Y.C., 1996, Crest Hardware, Bklyn., 1996, Clocktower Gallery, N.Y.C., 1996, 405 Broadway Gallery, N.Y.C., 1996, Art from Detrius/Nat. Convention for Recycling Convention, Pitts., 1996, Rotunda Gallery, Bklyn., 1997, St. Peter's Ch., N.Y.C., 1997, Ogunquit (Maine) Mus. Art, 1997, The Alternative Mus., N.Y.C., 1997; represented in permanent collections. Resident Millay Colony for Arts, Austerlitz, N.Y., 1987; grantee Nat. Endowment Arts, 1987; Agnes Bourne fellow in painting Djerassi Found., Woodside, Calif., 1988, fellow Montalvo Ctr. for the Arts, Saratoga, Calif., 1991, fellow Ucross Found., 1992. Home: 9-01 44th Dr Long Island City NY 11101-7012

VILLOCH, KELLY CARNEY, art director; b. Kyoto, Japan, July 22, 1950; d. William Riley and stepdaughter Hazel Fowler Carney; m. Joe D. Villoch, Aug. 9, 1969; children: Jonathan Christopher, Jennifer. A in Fine Arts, Dade C.C., Miami, Fla., 1971; student, Metro Fine Arts, 1973-74, Fla. Internat. U., 1985-88. Design asst. Lanvin, Miami, 1971—, Fieldcrest, Miami, 1974-77; art dir. Advercolor, Miami, 1977-78; art dir. copywriter ABC, Miami, 1978-89; writer Armed Forces Radio & TV Network; multimedia dir. ADVITEC, 1989-91; art dir. writer Miami Write, 1979—; owner Beach Point Prodns., 1992—; lectr. Miami Dade C.C., cons. Studio Masters, North Miami, 1979-89; writer Lucent techs., telephonetics, algorhythm, inter-tel, 1997—; conceptual artist. Prin. works include mixed media, 1974 (Best of Show 1974), pen and ink drawing, 1988 (Best Poster 1988); writer, dir., editor, prodr. (video film): Bif, 1988, Drink + Drive = Die, 1994; writer, dir., prodr. (pub. svc. announcement) Reading is the Real Adventure, 1990; film editor Talent Times Mag.; author: Winds of Freedom, 1994; art dir., exec. com. Miami Hispanic Media Conf., 1992, 93, 94; editor-in-chief, film editor: In Grove Miami Mag., 1994-96; webmaster, web content provider, website design cons., writer, graphic artist Guru Comms., 1996; editor-in-chief In Grove Miami Mag., 1994-96; web content provider WEBCOM; webmaster Guru Comm., 1996; web site designer, multimedia dir. State of Fla. grantee LimeLite Studios, Inc., 1990, William Douglas Pawley Found. grantee, Frances Wolfson scholar, Cultural Consortium grantee, 1993. Mem. Am. Film Inst., Phi Beta Kappa. Avocations: pen and ink drawing, printmaking, skin diving, boating, painting.

VILTER, RICHARD WILLIAM, physician, educator; b. Cin., Mar. 21, 1911; s. William Frederick and Clara (Bieler) V.; m. Sue Potter, Aug. 17, 1935; 1 son, Richard William. A.B., Harvard U., 1933, M.D., 1937. Diplomate: Am. Bd. Internal Medicine. Intern, resident internal medicine Cin. Gen. Hosp., 1937-42, founding dir. divsn. hematology/oncology, 1945-56, asst. dir. dept. internal medicine, 1953-56, dir., 1956-78; assoc. prof. medicine U. Cin. Coll. Medicine, 1948-56, Gordon and Helen Hughes Taylor prof., 1956-78, prof. medicine on spl. assignment, 1978-81, prof. medicine emeritus, 1981—, asst. dean, 1945-51; cons. VA, 1947—; cons. hematology Good Samaritan Hosp., Cin.; cons. physician Christ, Drake hosps., Cin.; mem. sci adv. bd. Nat. Vitamin Found., 1953-56; spl. cons. nutrition and anemias in Egypt WHO, 1954; cons. Pan Am. Sanitary Bur. Anemias of Kashiorkor in Guatemala and Panama, 1955; mem. Am. Cancer Soc. Com. on Investigation and Therapy of Cancer, 1960-64, chmn. 1964; chmn. hematology sect. NIH, 1965-69, nat. adv. com. anemia malnutrition Rsch. Ctr. Chiengmai, Thailand, 1967-75. Assoc. editor Jour. Clin. Investigation, 1951-52; contbr. to profl. publs. Recipient Joseph Goldberger award AMA, 1960, Daniel Drake medal U. Cin., 1985, Golden Apple award U. Cin., 1985, award for excellence U. Cin., 1990, Daniel Drake Humanitarian award Acad. Medicine, Cin., 1991, 1st recipient U. Cin. Coll. Medicine Lifetime Tchg. award, 1995. Master ACP (past gov. Ohio bd. regents, sec. gen. 1973-78, pres.-elect 1978-79, pres. 1979-80, pres. emeritus 1984); mem. Federated Coun. for Internal Medicine (chmn. 1979-80), Clin. and Climatol. Assn. (v.p. 1982-83), Assn. Am. Physicians, Am. Soc. Clin. Nutrition (pres. 1960-61), Am. Soc. Clin. Investigation, Ctrl. Soc. Clin. Rsch. (coun. mem. 1957-60), Am. Soc. Hematology, Am. Bd. Nutrition, Internat. Soc. Hematology, Cin. Lit. Club (pres. 1990-91), Phi Beta Kappa, Alpha Omega Alpha, Nu Sigma Nu. Home: 5 Annwood Ln Cincinnati OH 45206-1419 Office: U Cin Med Center Cincinnati OH 45267-0562

VINAY, PATRICK, university dean. Dean U. Montreal (Que., Can.) Faculty Medicine, Can. Office: U Montreal, PO Box 6128 Sta Centreville, Montreal, PQ Canada H3C 3J7

VINCE, CLINTON ANDREW, lawyer; b. Bklyn., May 31, 1949; s. Tibor Andrew and Priscilla (Ward) V.; m. Pamela Anne McHale, May 17, 1980; children: Matthew McHale, Jennifer Anne. AB, Trinity Coll., 1971; JD, Georgetown U., 1974. Bar: N.Y. 1975, U.S. Dist. Ct. (so. and ea. dists.) N.Y. 1975, U.S. Ct. Appeals (2nd cir.) 1975, D.C. 1976, U.S. Dist. Ct. D.C. 1976, U.S. Ct. Appeals (D.C. and 8th cirs.) 1976, U.S. Supreme Ct. 1979, U.S. Ct. Appeals (4th and 11th cirs.) 1984, U.S. Ct. Appeals (5th cir.) 1985, U.S. Ct. Appeals (10th cir.) 1988. Ptnr., co-chair exec. com. Verner, Liipfert, Bernhard, McPherson & Hand, Washington, 1984—; chief energy cons. City of New Orleans, 1983—; gen. counsel Southeastern Power Resources Com., Tucker, Ga., 1986—. Contbr. articles to profl. jours. Bd. dirs. Fed. City Coun., bd. trustees Keystone Energy; treas. bd. dirs. The Writers Ctr., One Voice. Mem. ABA, ATLA, Fed. Energy Bar Assn. (chmn. bd. dirs., chair Fed. Energy Law Jour. Found.), D.C. Bar Assn., Econ. Club Washington, City Tavern Club, Cosmos Club. Avocations: sailing, skiing, tennis, literature, writing. Office: Verner Liipfert Bernhard McPherson & Hand 901 15th St NW Washington DC 20005-2327

VINCENT, CHARLES EAGAR, JR., sports columnist; b. Beaumont, Tex., Mar. 24, 1940; s. Charles Eagar and Hazel Ruth (Balston) V.; m. Mary Jacquelyn Bertman, Aug. 8, 1959 (div. Jan. 1969); children: Lisa Marie, Dixie Ann, Charles Joseph, John Patrick; m. Patricia Helene Skinner, Mar. 28, 1970 (div. Apr. 1985); 1 child, Susanna Lee; m. Karen Judith Peterson, Aug. 17, 1985. Student, Victoria Coll., 1958-59. Reporter Victoria (Tex.) Mirror, 1958-59, Taylor (Tex.) Daily Press, 1959-60; sports writer Beaumont (Tex.) Jour., 1960-62; sports editor Galveston (Tex.) Tribune, 1962-63; sports writer San Antonio Express-News, 1963-69, Sandusky (Ohio) Register, 1969-70; sports writer Detroit Free Press, 1970-85, sports columnist, 1985—. Author: Welcome to My World, 1994. Recipient 4th Pl. award Nat. AP Sports Editors, 1981, 5th Pl., 1989, 92, Sister Mary Leila Meml. award, 1991, Mich. Columnist of Yr. award, 1991; Afro-Am. Night honoree, 1991. Mem. Baseball Writers Assn. Am. Avocations: traveling, cooking, genealogy. Office: Detroit Free Press 321 W Lafayette Blvd Detroit MI 48226

VINCENT, DAVID RIDGELY, management consulting executive; b. Detroit, Aug. 9, 1941; s. Charles Ridgely and Charlotte Jane (McCarroll) V.; m. Margaret Helen Anderson, Aug. 25, 1962 (div. 1973); children: Sandra Lee, Cheryl Ann; m. Judith Ann Gomez, July 2, 1978; 1 child, Amber; stepchildren: Michael Jr., Jesse Joseph Flores. BS, BA, Calif. State U.-Sacramento, 1964; MBA, Calif. State U.-Hayward, 1971; PhD Somerset U, 1991. Cert. profl. cons. to mgmt., 1994. Sr. ops. analyst Aerojet Gen. Corp., Sacramento, 1960-66; contr. Hexcel Corp., Dublin, Calif., 1966-70; mng. dir. Memorex, Austria, 1970-74; sales mgr. Ampex World Ops., Switzerland, 1974-76; dir. product mgmt. NCR, Sunnyvale, Calif., 1976-79; v.p. Boole & Babbage Inc., gen. mgr. Inst. Info. Mgmt., Sunnyvale, Calif., 1979-85; pres., CEO The Info. Group, Inc., Santa Clara, Calif., 1985—. Deacon Union Ch., Cupertino, Calif.; USSF soccer referee emeritus. Author: Perspectives in Information Management, Information Economics, 1983, Handbook of Information Resource Management, 1987, The Information-Based Corporation: stakeholder economics and the technology investment, 1990, Reengineering Fundamentals: Business Processes and the Global Economy, 1994-96; contbr. monographs and papers to profl. jours. Mem. Nat. Alliance Bus. Economists, Am. Electronics Assn., Soc. Competitive Intelligence Profls. Home: 2803 Kalliam Dr Santa Clara CA 95051-6838 Office: PO Box Q Santa Clara CA 95055-3756

VINCENT, EDWARD See BRACKEN, EDDIE

VINCENT, FREDERICK MICHAEL, SR., neurologist, educational administrator; b. Detroit, Nov. 19, 1948; s. George S. and Alyce M. (Borkowski) V.; m. Patricia Lucille Cordes, Oct. 7, 1972; children: Frederick Michael Jr., Joshua Peter, Melissa Anne. BS in Biology, Aquinas Coll., 1970; MD, Mich. State U., 1973. Diplomate Am. Bd. Psychiatry and Neurology (neurology and clin. neurophysiology), Am. Bd. Electrodiagnostic Medicine, Nat. Bd. Med. Examiners, Am. Bd. Forensic Examiners (fellow), Am. Bd. Forensic Medicine. Intern St. Luke's Hosp., Duluth, Minn., 1974-75; resident in neurology Dartmouth Med. Sch., Hanover, N.H., 1975-77, instr. dept. medicine, chief resident neurology, 1977-78; chief, neurology sect. Munson Med. Ctr., Traverse City, Mich., 1978-84; asst. clin. prof. medicine and pathology Mich. State U., East Lansing, 1978-84, chief sect. neurology Coll. Human Medicine, 1984-87; clin. prof. psychiatry and internal medicine Mich. State U., 1989—; clin. prof. medicine, 1990—; pvt. practice Neurology, Neuro-oncology and Electrodiagnostic Medicine, Lansing, Mich., 1987—; clin. and research fellow neuro-oncology Mass. Gen. Hosp., Boston, 1985; clin. Fellow in neurology Harvard Med. Sch., Boston, 1985; cons. med. asst. program Northwestern Mich. Coll., Traverse City, 1983-84; neurology cons. radio call-in show Sta. WKAR, East Lansing, 1984—, Sta. WCMU TV, 1987, 1993—. Author: Neurology: Problems in Primary Care, 1987, 2d edit., 1993; contbr. 80 articles to profl. jours. Fellow NSF, 1969, Nat. Multiple Sclerosis Soc., 1971. Fellow ACP, Am. Acad. Neurology (mem. program accreditation and devel. subcom. 1993—), Am. Assn. Electrodianostic Medicine (mem. computer and electronics com. 1995—); mem. Am. Coll. Legal Medicine, Am. Acad. Clin. Neurophysiology, Am. Heart Assn., Am. Soc. Clin. Oncology, Am. EEG Soc., Am. Fedn. Clin. Rsch., Am. Soc. Neurol. Investigation, Am. Epilepsy Soc., Soc. for NeuroSci., N.Y. Acad. Scis., Am. Bd. of Forensic Examiners, Am. Soc. for Neuro-Rehab., Movement Disorders Soc., Univ. Club, Alpha Omega Alpha. Roman Catholic. Office: 1515 Lake Lansing Rd Ste F1 Lansing MI 48912-3752

VINCENT, HAL WELLMAN, marine corps officer, investor; b. Pontiac, Mich., Sept. 27, 1927; s. Harold and Glenda (Wellman) V.; m. Virginia Bayler, June 9, 1951; children: David B., Dale W., Deborah K. Vincent Minder. Student, Navy V-5 program Western Mich. Coll./Colgate U., 1945; BS, U.S. Naval Acad., 1950; postgrad., Marine Officers Basic Sch., 1950, Flight Sch., 1952, Test Pilot Sch., 1955, Navy Fleet Air Gunnery Sch., 1958, Air Force Fighter Weapons Sch., 1959, Marine Corps Command and Staff Coll., 1964, Indsl. Coll., 1969, Marine Air Weapons Tng. Unit, 1972. Cert. flight and instrument instr. Commd. 2d lt. U.S. Marine Corps, 1950, advanced through grades to maj. gen., 1974; rifle and machinegun platoon comdr. Camp Lejeune, N.C., 1951; fighter pilot El Toro, Calif. and, Korea, 1953-54; test pilot Flight Test Div., Patuxent River, Md., 1955-57; ops. officer, squadron asst. and fighter pilot El Toro, 1958-59; conventional weapons project test pilot Naval Air Weapons Test Ctr., China Lake, Calif., 1960-62; squadron ops. and exec. officer El Toro and Japan, 1962-64; aviation specialist Marine Corps amphibious warfare presentation team and staff officer Quantico, Va., 1965-66; comdg. officer 2d Marine Aircraft Wing fighter-attack squadron, Beaufort, S.C., 1967-68; exec. officer Marine Aircraft Group, Vietnam, 1969; logistics staff officer Fleet Marine Force Pacific, Hawaii, 1970-72; comdg. officer Marine Aircraft Group, Yuma, Ariz., 1972-73; chief of staff 3d Marine Aircraft Wing, El Toro, 1973-76; dep. chief. of staff plans and policy to Comdr. in Chief Atlantic, Norfolk, Va., 1976-78; comdg. gen. 2d Marine Aircraft Wing, Cherry Point, N.C., 1978-80; dep. comdg. gen. Fleet Marine Force Atlantic, Norfolk, 1980-81; ret., 1981, pvt. investor, 1981—; flight test pilot; preliminary pilot, evaluator new mil. aircraft. Contbr. numerous articles on tactics and conventional weapons delivery, flight test stability and control to various mil. publs. Decorated Legion of Merit with 2 gold stars, D.F.C., Bronze Star with combat V, Air medal with star and numeral 14, Joint Svcs. Commendation medal U.S.; Honor medal 1st class; Cross of Gallantry with gold star (Republic of Vietnam). Mem. SAR, Soc. Exptl. Test Pilots, Marine Corps Assn., Early Pioneer Naval Aviators, Marine Corps Aviation Assn., Mach 2 Club, Marbella Country Club. Invented Triple Ejector Rack for delivery of conventional bombs, 1961; devel. fighter tactics in F8 and F4 aircraft, 1958-69; flew 165 models of fgn. and U.S. mil. aircraft; flew 8 models of fixed wing and helicopters on 242 combat missions; first Marine to fly MACH-2. *In all 36 years in the service I am convinced that war is bad, and little is accomplished in the long term by warfare. However when National policy dictates a war, then we must not limit what can be done. We must win! My thought then remains: "Winning isn't everything, it's the only thing!" When I must go to battle I want to be allowed to "fight to win."*

VINCENT, JAMES LOUIS, biotechnology company executive; b. Johnstown, Pa., Dec. 15, 1939; s. Robert Clyde and Marietta Lucille (Kennedy) V.; m. Elizabth M. Matthews, Aug. 19, 1961; children: Aimee Archelle, Christopher James. BSME, Duke U., 1961; MBA in Indsl. Mgmt., U. Pa., 1963. Mgr. Far East div. Tex. Instruments, Inc., Tokyo, 1970-72; pres. Tex. Instrument Asia, Ltd., Tokyo, 1970-72; v.p. diagnostic ops., pres. diagnostics div. Abbott Labs., North Chgo., Ill., 1972-74, group v.p., bd. dirs., 1974-81, exec. v.p., COO, bd. dirs., 1979-81; corp. group v.p., pres. Allied Health and Sci. Products Co. Allied Corp., Morristown, N.J., 1982-85; CEO Biogen, Inc., 1985-97, chmn. bd., 1997—. Bd. trustees Duke U.; bd. dirs. Found. for the Nat. Tech.; bd. overseers Wharton Grad. Bus. Sch. U. Pa. Recipient Young Exec. Achievement Young Execs. Club, Chgo., 1976, Disting. Alumni award Duke U., 1988. Mem. Biotech. Industry Orgn. (bd. dirs.), Econ. Club Chgo., Shoreacres Country Club, Algonquin Club, Boston Club, Chgo. Club, The Links (N.Y.C.). Republican. Presbyterian. Office: care Biogen Inc 14 Cambridge Ctr Cambridge MA 02142-1401

VINCENT, JEFFREY ROBERT, labor studies educator; b. Regensberg, Germany, Mar. 18, 1956; came to U.S., 1956; s. John J. and Norma J. (Trindle) V.; m. Patti Ann E. Knoff, Aug. 18, 1978; children: Natalie and Nicole (twins). BS in Ednl. Studies, U. Wis., Milw., 1978, MS in Indsl. Rels., 1984. Rsch. dir. Ind. U., Bloomington, 1985—; tchr., unions and labor mgmt. coms., Colo., Fla., Ill., Ind., Mich., Ohio and Tenn. Contbr. articles to profl. jours. Bd. dirs. Unitarian Universalist Ch. of Bloomington, Ind. Mem. AFL-CIO, Workers Edn. Local 189, Univ. and Coll. Labor Edn. Assn., Indsl. Rels. Rsch. Assn. Home: 3261 E Carowind Ct Bloomington IN 47401-9589 Office: Ind Univ Divsn Labor Studies Poplars 628 Bloomington IN 47405

VINCENT, JON STEPHEN, foreign language educator; b. Denver, Feb. 28, 1938; s. Joseph William and Lillian (Diamond) V.; m. Maria Louise Girard, June 13, 1962; children—Sean David, Tanya Maria. B.A., U. N.Mex., 1961, Ph.D., 1970. Instr., U. N.Mex., Albuquerque, 1963-64; asst. prof. U. Kans., Lawrence, 1967-74, assoc. prof., 1974-79, prof., 1979—, assoc. chmn. dept. Spanish, 1974-78, chmn., 1978-82; vis. prof. U. Costa Rica, San Jose, 1972; co-dir. Latin Am. Studies, 1987-89, dir., 1989-92. Author: Joao Guimaraes Rosa, 1978; assoc. editor Hispania, 1984-90, Brasil/Brazil, 1989—; asst. editor Latin Am. Theatre Rev., 1969—; mem. rev. staff World Lit. Today, 1983—. Served with U.S. Army, 1953-56. Mem. MLA (chmn. Luso-Brazilian div. 1982), Am. Assn. Tchrs. Spanish and Portuguese, Latin Am. Studies Assn., Fulbright Am. Republics, Kans. Fgn. Lang. Assn., Am. Republics Adv. Com. Democrat. Avocations: Fishing; hunting. Home: 1104 Centennial Dr Lawrence KS 66049-2700 Office: U Kans Dept Spanish And Portuguese Lawrence KS 66045

VINCENT, NORMAN FULLER, broadcasting executive; b. Boston, Oct. 5, 1930; s. Norman Harrison and Marian Bernice (Fuller) V.; m. Karen Ann Walter, June 21, 1969. B.A., Denison U., 1953. Sales mgr. Sta. WMBR, Jacksonville, Fla., 1956-62; gen. mgr. Sta. WZOK, Jacksonville, 1962-66; owner, pres. Norm Vincent Sound Recording Studios, Inc., Jacksonville, 1966-75; dir. radio ops. Sta. WJCT, Jacksonville, 1975-91; announcer, narrator radio, TV film and video, talking books, 1991—. Producer, host (radio): Swing Time with Norm Vincent, 1992—. Served with USN, 1953-56; to comdr. USNR, 1958-80. Mem. Navy League, Advt. Fedn. Am., Jacksonville C. of C. (armed services com.), Exchange Club. Republican. Episcopalian. Home: 2110 The Woods Dr Jacksonville FL 32246-1016

VINCENT, NORMAN L., retired insurance company executive; b. Milw., July 21, 1933; s. Victor V. Vincent and Hilda I. (Boedecker) Vincent Patlow; m. Arlene Page, Jan. 31, 1953 (div. 1978); children: J. Todd, Meg; m. Donna Jean Doll, Aug. 8, 1980. B.S., U. Wis., 1957; M.S., Purdue U., 1958, Ph.D., 1960. Diplomate Am. Bd. Profl. Psychology; registered psychologist., Ill., C.P.C.U., C.L.U. Supr. ag. research State Farm Ins. Cos., Bloomington, Ill., 1960-63, dir. agy. research., 1963-66, asst. v.p. agy., 1966-69, asst. v.p. exec., 1969-70, v.p. data processing, 1970-94; systems v.p., 1994-95. Pres. Bloomington Bd. Edn., 1974-77; bd. dirs. YMCA, Bloomington, 1971-85. Served with M.I. U.S. Army, 1953-55. Mem. AAAS. Home: W332n5861 Meadowlark Ct Nashotah WI 53058-9528

VINCENTI, SHELDON ARNOLD, law educator, lawyer; b. Ogden, Utah, Sept. 4, 1938; s. Arnold Joseph and Mae (Burch) V.; children: Matthew Lewis, Amanda Jo. AB, Harvard U., 1960, JD, 1963. Bar: Utah 1963. Sole practice law, Ogden, 1966-67; ptnr. Lowe and Vincenti, Ogden, 1968-70; legis. asst. to U.S. Rep. Gunn McKay, Washington, 1971-72, adminstrv. asst., 1973; prof., assoc. dean U. of Idaho Coll. of Law, Moscow, Idaho, 1973-83, dean, prof. law, 1983-95, prof. law, 1995—. Home: 2480 W Twin Rd Moscow ID 83843-9114 Office: U Idaho Coll Law 6th & Rayburn St Moscow ID 83843

VINCENTI, WALTER GUIDO, aeronautical engineer, emeritus educator; b. Balt., Apr. 20, 1917; s. Guido A. and Agnes (Nicolini) V.; m. Joyce H. Weaver, Sept. 6, 1947; children—Margaret Anna, Marc Guido. A.B., Stanford U., 1938, Aero. Engr., 1940. Aero. research scientist NACA, 1940-57; prof. aero. and astronautics and history of tech. Stanford U., 1957-83, prof. emeritus, 1983—; cons to industry, 1957—; mem. adv. panel engring. sec. NSF, 1960-63. Author: (with Charles H. Kruger, Jr.) Introduction to Physical Gas Dynamics, 1965, (with Nathan Rosenberg) The Britannia Bridge, 1978, What Engineers Know and How They Know It, 1990; also papers.; co-editor (with Milton Van Dyke) Annual Review of Fluid Mechanics, 1970-76. Served with USN, 1945-46. Recipient Gold medal Pi Tau Sigma, 1948; Rockefeller Pub. Service award, 1956; Guggenheim fellow, 1963. Fellow AIAA; mem. Internat. Acad. Astronautics (corr.), History of Sci. Soc., Soc. History Tech. (Usher prize 1984), Nat. Acad. Engring., Newcomen Soc., Phi Beta Kappa, Sigma Xi, Tau Beta Pi. Home: 13200 E Sunset Dr Los Altos CA 94022-3427 Office: Stanford U Stanford CA 94305

VINCENTI-BROWN, CRISPIN RUFUS WILLIAM, engineering executive; b. Epsom, Surrey, England, Sept. 20, 1951; came to U.S., 1989; s. Douglas Hector and Joan Margaret Patricia (Lowe) Brown; m. Terry Doreen Bennett, May 20, 1978 (dec. Oct. 1992); children: Genevieve Louise, Juliette Alexandra; m. Margaret Anna Vincenti, Feb. 13, 1993. BSc in Engring. Prodn., U. Birmingham, 1974. Mgr. Soc. M.O.M, Grans, France, 1975; prin. cons. Ingersoll Engrs. Inc., Rugby, England, 1975-79; pres., dir. Ingersoll Engrs. SA, Annecy, France, 1979-89; sr. ptnr. Ingersoll Engrs. Inc., Los Altos, Calif., 1989—; v.p. Groupe de Talloires, Geneva, 1987-89; bd. dirs. Ops. Mgmt. Assn., Waco, Tex. Fellow Inst. Elec. Engrs. (chartered engr.). Avocation: fixed wing and helicopter pilot. Home: 1098 Eastwood Ct Los Altos CA 94024-5015 Office: Ingersoll Engrs 5100 E State St Ste 4 Rockford IL 61108-2398

VINCI, JOHN NICHOLAS, architect, educator; b. Chgo., Feb. 6, 1937; s. Nicholas and Nicolina (Camiola) V. B.Arch., Ill. Inst. Tech., 1960. Registered architect, Ill., Mo. Draftsman Skidmore, Owings, Merrill, Chgo., 1960-61; with City of Chgo., 1961; stencil restorer Crombie Taylor, Chgo., 1961-62; designer Brenner, Danforth, Rockwell, Chgo., 1962-68; architect Vinci, Inc., Chgo., 1977-95; ptnr. Vinci/Hamp, Architects, Inc., Chgo., 1995—; lectr. Roosevelt U., Chgo., 1969-72, Ill. Inst. Tech., Chgo., 1972-90. Author: (booklet) Trading Room-Art Inst. Chgo., 1977; contbr. articles to profl. jours. Bd. dirs. Music of Baroque, Chgo., 1976-87, Campbell Ctr. Found.; mem. adv. com. Commn. on Chgo. Archtl. and Hist. Landmarks, 1971-83; exec. sec. Richard Nickel Com, Chgo., 1972—; chmn. Howard Van Doren Shaw Soc., 1994—; internat. arts adv. coun. Wexner Ctr. for the Arts, 1994—. Fellow AIA; mem. Soc. Archtl. Historians, Frank Lloyd Wright Home and Studio Found., Art Inst. Chgo., The Corp. of YADDO, Chgo. Hist. Soc., Arts Club of Chgo. Roman Catholic. Home: 3152 N Cambridge Ave Chicago IL 60657-4613 Office: Vinci/Hamp Architects Inc 1147 W Ohio St Chicago IL 60622-6472

VINEBURGH, JAMES HOLLANDER, banking executive; b. Hartford, Conn., July 17, 1943; s. Lawrence Harold and Dorothy Helen (Brandvein) V.; m. Nancy Cynthia Taylor; children: James Hollander Jr., Philip Lawrence Taylor. AB, Tufts U., 1966. CLU. From mgmt. trainee to sr. v.p. Conn. Gen. Life Ins. Co./CIGNA Corp., 1967-88; exec. v.p. Conn. Bank and Trust Co., N.A., Hartford, 1989-91; chmn., dir. Bank of New Eng. Trust Co., 1989-91; exec. v.p. Fleet Bank, N.A., Hartford, Conn., 1991-93; sr. v.p. The Pvt. Bank, Bank of Boston, 1994—. Class sec. The Hill Sch., Pottstown, Pa., 1986—; bd. dirs. Big Bros. Assn. Greater Boston, Boston Olympics Organizing Com.; trustee, pres. parent's com. Middlesex Sch., Concord, Mass., 19956; past chmn. bd. dirs. Child and Family Svcs., Hartford, 1983-93; past pres., bd. dirs. West Hartford Youth Baseball League, 1981-90; bd. dirs., exec. com. Riverfront Recapture, Hartford, 1986-94; adv. bd. WALKS Found., Simsbury, Conn., 1983-94; trustee Bushnell Meml. Hall, Hartford, 1992-94. Mem. Leadership Greater Hartford. Avocations: golf, politics, squash. Office: Bank of Boston 100 Federal St Boston MA 02110-1802

VINES, CHARLES JERRY, minister; b. Carroll County, Ga., Sept. 22, 1937; s. Charles Clarence and Ruby Johnson V.; m. Janet Denney, Dec. 17, 1960; children: Joy Vines Williams, Jim, Jodi, Jon. BA, Mercer U., 1959; BD, New Orleans Bapt. Sem., 1966; ThD, Luther Rice Sem., Jacksonville, Fla., 1974; DD (hon.), Criswell Coll., 1991, Liberty U., 1991. Pastor West Rome Bapt. Ch., Rome, Ga., 1968-74, 79-81, Dauphin Way Bapt. Ch., Moblie, Ala., 1974-79, 1st Bapt. ch., Jacksonville, Fla., 1981—. Author: Practical Guide to Sermon Preparation, An Effective Guide to Sermon Delivery, Great Events in the Life of Christ, I Shall Return - Jesus, Family Fellowship, Great Interviews of Jesus, God Speaks Today, Exploring the Epistles of John, Exploring Daniel, Exploring Mark, Wanted: Soul Winners, Wanted: Church Growers, Basic Sermons on the Ten Commandments. Pres. So. Bapt. Conv., 1988-89. Office: First Bapt Ch 124 W Ashley St Jacksonville FL 32202-3104*

VINES, GEORGIANA FRY, editor; b. Ft. Collins, Colo., Oct. 23, 1939; d. Geroge W. and Mary Helen (Flanagan) F.; m. Carl A. Vines, Jr., July 2, 1968 (dec. Nov. 1990); 1 child, Carla Jeanine; m. John David Fox, Oct. 23, 1993. BA, Fla. State U., 1961. Reporter Miami (Fla.) Herald, 1961, St. Petersburg (Fla.) Evening Ind., 1963, Milw. Sentinel, 1964-66; reporter, asst. city editor, metro editor, asst. mng. editor Knoxville (Tenn.) News-Sentinel, 1968-96, dep. mng. editor, 1996; editor El Paso (Tex.) Hearld-Post, 1996—. Mem. Leadershp Knoxville, 1992. Mem. Soc. Profl. Journalists (nat. pres. 1992-93), Sigma Delta Chi Found. (nat. sec. 1994—), Kappa Tau Alpha (hon.). Avocation: music. Office: Herald Post 300 N Campbell St El Paso TX 79901-1402

VINH, BINH, architect; b. Hue, Vietnam, Oct. 23, 1945; came to U.S., 1975; s. Tri and Chinh H. (Nguyen) Buu; m. Hang T. Nguyen, Jan. 22, 1975; 1 child, Michael. MArch and Urban Planning, U. Saigon, 1973; MArch, U. Pa., 1977; postgrad., Harvard U., 1991. Registered arch., Pa., N.J., N.C., S.C., Ala., Tenn., N.Y., Ark., Md., Tex., Ariz., Fla. Prin. BV Architects, Saigon, 1974-75; designer Berger Assocs., Harrisburg, Pa., 1975-77; project architect, designer Kling Partnership, Phila., 1977-89; ptnr., design prin. Kling Lindquist Partnership, Phila., 1989—; assoc. prof. Thu Duc (Vietnam) Poly. Inst., 1974-75; vis. critic U. Pa.; speaker and presenter in field. Prin. works include Ethyl Corp. Hdqs., Richmond, Va., Chester County Libr., Exton, Pa., C.C. Phila. (First Place Silver medal AIA Phila. chpt. 1982), Radnor/Plymouth Meeting (Pa.) Exec. Campus, SOHIO Corp. Rsch. Ctr., Cleve., Prudential Ins. Co., Roseland, N.J., Greyhound Terminal, Phila., E.I. du Pont de Nemours & Co., Inc. Life Scis. Complex, Wilmington, Del., Boehringer Ingelheim, Ltd. Corp. Hdqs. and R&D Ctr., Danbury and Ridgefield, Conn., NIH Bldg 29B, Bethesda, Md., Kennametal, Inc. Corp. Tech. Ctr., Latrobe, Pa. (Best Bld. in Westmorland County, Latrobe C. of C.), Ethyl Corp. Hdqs., Richmond, Va., Am. Cyanamid Co. Greenhouse Support Facility, Princeton, N.J., Ciba-Geigy Corp. Prodn. Facility, Suffern, N.Y., FAA Continuous Airworthiness Rsch. Facility, Jet Propulsion Testing and Fuels Rsch. Lab., Atlantic City (N.J.) Internat. Airport, Nat. Cancer Inst. Monoclonal Antibodies and Recombinant Protein Facility, Frederick, Md., Allied-Signal Corp. Charles W. Nichols, Jr. Tech. Ctr., Morristown, N.J. (Lab of Yr.'s High Honors award Rsch. and Devel. Mag.), Glaxo Inc. Rsch. and Devel. Facilities, Rsch. Triangle Park, N.C. (Triangle Devel. award 1992, Design Excellence award Archtl. Precast Assn. 1993, Best Mixed Use Project award Precast/Prestressed Concrete Inst. 1993, Exec. award for Bldg. Achievement 1994, Prog. Architecture award 1995), Miles, Inc. Pharm. Rsch. and Devel. Hdqs., West Haven, Conn., Glaxo Wellcome Medicines Rsch. Ctr. (Bldg. of the Yr. 1995, Brit. Constrn. Industry Supreme award 1995), Stevenage, Hertfordshire, Eng., Glaxo Wellcome Medicine Rsch. Ctr., FDA office Regulatory Affairs, Jefferson, Ark., Rohm & Haas Polymer & Resin Rsch. Facility, Spring House, Pa., Pfizer Hdqs. Health Group, West Chester, Pa., Wyeth Ayerst Pham. Sci. Bldg., Pearl River, N.Y., Saudi Arabia R&D Ctr., Dhahran, Hoechst Marion Roussel Rsch. Facility, Bridgewater, N.J., DuPont Agrl. Products R & D Hdqs., Newark, Del., semiconductor device lab. U. Va., Charlottesville; contbr. articles to, works featured in numerous profl. and popular jours. Bd. dirs. Harrisburg chpt. ARC; active Phila. Fellowship Commn. Mem. AIA (regional liaison Pa., coms. on design, environ. and internat. practice), Precast/Prestressed Concrete Inst., Union Internat. Archs., Fedn. Pan Am. Assn. Archs., L'Ordre Archs. D'lle de France, Pa. Soc. Archs., Phila. Solar Energy Assn., Phila. Philos. Consortium, Uran Ecology. Avocations: tennis, golf, music, travel, painting. Office: Kling-Lindquist Partnership 2301 Chestnut St Philadelphia PA 19103-3035

VINH, NGUYEN XUAN, aerospace engineering educator; b. Yen Bay, Vietnam, Jan. 3, 1930; came to U.S., 1962; s. Nguyen X. and Thao (Do) Nhien; m. Joan Cung, Aug. 15, 1955; children: Alphonse, Phuong, Phoenix, John. PhD in Aerospace Engring., U. Colo., 1965. Asst. prof. aerospace engring. U. Colo., Boulder, 1965-68; assoc. prof. aerospace engring. U. Mich., Ann Arbor, 1968-72, prof. aerospace engring., 1972—; vis. lectr. U. Calif., Berkeley, 1967; vis. prof. ecol. nat. sup. aero., France, 1974; chair prof. Nat Tsing Hua U., Taiwan, 1982. Co-author: Hypersonic and Planetary Entry Flight Mechanics, 1980; author: Optimal Trajectories in Atmospheric Flight, 1981, Flight Mechanics of High Performance Aircraft, 1993. Chief of staff Vietnam Air Force, 1957-62. Recipient Mechanics and Control of Flight award AIAA, 1994. Mem. Internat. Acad. Astronautics, Nat. Acad. Air and Space (France). Research in ordinary differential equations; astrodynamics and optimization of space flight trajectories; theory of nonlinear oscillations. Office: U Mich Dept Aerospace Engring 3001 FXB Bldg Ann Arbor MI 48109-2118

VINING, F(RANCIS) STUART, architect, consultant; b. Sanford, Fla., Oct. 11, 1934; s. J. Martyn Rufus and Hazel Leota Elizabeth (Greer) V. Cert. sr. divsn., Norton Sch. Fine Art, West Palm Beach, Fla., 1949; cert. archtl. drafting, Orange County Vocat. Tech., Orlando, Fla., 1957; BSCE, L.A. U., North Hollywood, Calif., 1970; BSArch (degree equivalency), Fla. State Bd. Architecture, Tallahassee, 1978. Registered architect, Fla. Draftsman, designer Broleman & Rapp, Orlando, Fla., 1957-60; indsl. labs. cons. Lockwood Greene, A-E, Spartanburg, S.C., 1967, archtl. design cons., 1977; archtl. design cons. Hayes, Saey, Mattern & Mattern, A-E, Roanoke, Va., 1969; structural precast cons. Xerox Corp., Webster, N.Y., 1969; structural, indsl. ventilation designer GE Capacitor Divsn., Irmo, Columbia, S.C., 1973; archtl. engring. designer Rogers, Lovelock & Fritz, A-E, Winter Park, Fla., 1974; cons. Proctor & Gamble, Cin., 1978; clean rm. labs. and indsl. interiors cons. IBM Gen. Techs. Divsn., Essex Junction, Vt., 1979; H.V.A.C. and indsl. interiors cons. Gen. Dynamics, Electric Boat Divsn., Groton, Conn., 1980; architect, indsl. cons. Am. Tech. Svcs. Group, Inc., Tucker, Ga., 1988-89; pres., CEO F. S. Vining and Co., Inc., Orlando, Fla., 1965—; student, computer-aided design Mid-Fla. Tech. Inst., Orlando, 1991—. Staff employment and transp. specialist Orange County Sheriff, Work Release Program, Orlando, 1991; adminstrv. staff, program asst. Mid-Fla. Tech. Inst., Orlando, 1992-94; adminstrv. staff fin. aid Orlando (Fla.) Tech., 1994—. Seaman USNR, 1951-55. Mem. AIA, Am. Concrete Inst., Am. Inst. Steel Constrn., Am. Mgmt. Assn., Constrn. Specifications Inst., Nat. Fire Protection Assn. Democrat. Roman Catholic. Avocations: study of history, native American culture, promotion of fine artists and musicians. Office: F S Vining and Co Inc PO Box 530006 Orlando FL 32853-0006

VINING, (GEORGE) JOSEPH, law educator; b. Fulton, Mo., Mar. 3, 1938; s. D. Rutledge and Margaret (McClanahan) V.; m. Alice Marshall Williams, Sept. 18, 1965; children: George Joseph IV, Spencer Carter. BA, Yale U., 1959, Cambridge U., 1961; MA, Cambridge U., 1970; JD, Harvard U., 1964. Bar: D.C. 1965. Atty. Office Dep. Atty. Gen., Dept. Justice, Washington, 1965; asst. to exec. dir. Nat. Crime Commn., 1966; assoc. Covington and Burling, Washington, 1966-69; asst. prof. law U. Mich., 1969-72, assoc. prof., 1972-74, prof., 1974-85, Hutchins prof., 1985—. Author: Legal Identity, 1978, The Authoritative and the Authoritarian, 1986, From Newton's Sleep, 1995. Bd. dirs. Am. Friends of Cambridge U. NEH sr. fellow, 1982-83, Bellagio fellow Rockfeller Found., 1997. Fellow Am. Acad. Arts and Scis.; mem. ABA, D.C. Bar Assn. Am. Law Inst., Century Assn. Office: U Mich 432 Hutchins Hall Ann Arbor MI 48109-1215

VINING, ROBERT LUKE, JR., federal judge; b. Chatsworth, Ga., Mar. 30, 1931; m. Martha Sue Cates; 1 child, Laura Orr. BA, JD, U. Ga., 1959. With Mitchell & Mitchell, 1958-60; ptnr. McCamy, Miner & Vining, Dalton, 1960-69; solicitor gen. Conasauga Judicial Cir., 1963-68; judge Whitfield County Superior Ct., Dalton, 1969-79; judge U.S. Dist. Ct. (no. dist.) Ga., 1979-95, chief judge, 1995—; now sr. judge. Served to staff sgt. USAF, 1951-59. Office: Richard B. Russell Fed Bldg Rm 2388 75 Spring St SW Atlanta GA 30335*

VINKEN, PIERRE JACQUES, publishing executive, neurosurgeon; b. Heerlen, The Netherlands, Nov. 25, 1927; MD, U. Utrecht, The Netherlands, 1955, postgrad. in psychiatry, neurology and neurosurgery, U. Amsterdam, 1957-63; hon. Dr., U. Paris, 1981. Staff neurosurgeon Univ. Clinic, Amsterdam, 1964-69; pres., chief editor Excerpta Medica Found., Amsterdam and Princeton, N.J., 1962-88 ; mng. dir. Elsevier Pub. Co., Amsterdam, 1972-78, chmn. bd. dirs., 1979-95; chmn. bd. dirs. Reed Elsevier, London, 1993-95; chmn. supervising bd. Elsevier, Amsterdam; chmn. Hiscom, Leyden, Commodore, Nieuw Vennep, Halder Holdings, The Hague, Port O' Call, Amsterdam, Blue Horse Prodns., Hilversum; bd. dirs. Wereldhave Investment Co., The Hague, Logica, London, Rotterdam, Aalberts Industries, Driebergen; dep. chmn. European Pubs. Coun.; prof. med. database informatics U. Leyden, 1975-93; mem. Nat. Sci. Policy Coun., The Hague, 1983-90; chmn. Netherlands del. Intergovtl. Unisist Conf., Paris, 1970; mem. Netherlands Unisist Commn., 1971-79. Chmn. Netherlands Commn. Bibliography and Documentation, 1972-81; pres. Internat. Congress Patient Counselling, 1976-79; chmn. bd. dirs. Reed Internat., London, 1993-95; chmn. The Lancet, London, 1991-95; bd. dirs. Pearson, London, 1988-91, The Economist, London, 1989-92; chmn. Mees Pierson Bank, Amsterdam, 1994-97. Mem. Royal Netherland Acad. Sci. (Academy award 1997), European Info. Providers Assn. (pres. 1980-83), Revord Neurol. Soc. India (hon.), French Neurol. Soc. (hon.), Amsterdam Neurol. Soc. (hon.), Peruvian Soc. Psychiat. Neurology and Neurosurgey (hon.). Founder, editor-in-chief: Handbook of Clinical Neurology, 66 vols.; editor sci. books; contbr. articles to profl. jours. Home: 142 Bentveldsweg, 2111 EE Aerdenhout The Netherlands

VINOCUR, M. RICHARD, publisher; b. Columbus, Ohio, Nov. 16, 1934; s. Louis O. and Edith (Solomon) V.; m. Carol S. Lennard, Oct. 26, 1957; chidren: Michael Drew, Lesle Jane. B.A. in Journalism, Ohio State U., 1956. Asso. editor R.H. Donnelley, 1956-59; v.p., pub. Vance Pub., N.Y.C., 1959-79; pub. Graphic Arts Monthly, N.Y.C., 1979-87, group pub. Fire Engring.; pres. Footprint Communications, Inc., N.Y.C., 1987—; pub. Footprints (twice monthly newsletter for printing industry execs.), Vue/Point:The Hard Copy Mag., Web Offset: The Hard Copy; columnist Am. Printer Mag., 1988—; organizing mgr., founder Vue/Point 90, 1990—; lectr. N.Y. U.; cons. CSV Found. Author: How to Win Occasionally, 1980. Pres. Greentree Assn.; sec. S. Harris Fund. Named Pub. of Yr., Hopkins Found., 1980, Internat. Assn. Printers and Craftsmen; recipient citizenship award Newcomb Club, 1979, Gutenberg media award Printing Industries, 1995, 96. Mem. Graphic Arts Tech. Found., Sigma Delta Chi. Republican. Jewish. Club: Bonat BG. Home: Apt 6F 1500 Palisade Ave Fort Lee NJ 07024 Office: Footprint Communications Inc PO Box 255 Tenafly NJ 07670-0255 also: Footprint Communications Inc 2400 Lemoine Ave Fort Lee NJ 07024-6204

VINROOT, RICHARD ALLEN, lawyer, mayor; b. Charlotte, N.C., Apr. 14, 1941; s. Gustav Edgar and Vera Frances (Pickett) V.; m. Judith Lee Allen, Dec. 29, 1964; children: Richard A., Laura Tabor, Kathryn Pickett. BS in BA, U. N.C., 1963, JD, 1966. Bar: N.C. 1966, U.S. Dist. Ct. (ea., mid. and we. dists.) N.C. 1969, U.S. Ct. Appeals (4th cir.) 1969. Ptnr. Robinson, Bradshaw & Hinson, P.A., Charlotte, 1969—; mayor City of Charlotte, N.C., 1991-95. Mem. Charlotte City Coun., 1983-91. Mem. ABA, N.C. Bar Assn., Mecklenburg County Bar Assn. (sec. 1976). Republican. Presbyterian.

VINSON, C. ROGER, federal judge; b. Cadiz, Ky., Feb. 19, 1940; m. Ellen Watson; children: Matt, Todd, Cate, Patrick, Joey. BS, U.S. Naval Acad., 1962; JD, Vanderbilt U., 1971. Commd. ensign USN, 1962, advanced through grades to lt., 1963, naval aviator, until 1968, resigned, 1968; assoc. to ptnr. Beggs & Lane, Pensacola, Fla., 1971-83; judge U.S. Dist. Ct. (no. dist.) Fla., Pensacola, 1983—; mem. Jud. Conf. Adv. Com. on Civil Rules, 1993—; mem. 11th Cir. Pattern Instrn. Com. Office: US Courthouse 100 N Palafox St Pensacola FL 32501-4839*

VINSON, JAMES SPANGLER, academic administrator; b. Chambersburg, Pa., May 17, 1941; s. Wilbur S. and Anna M. (Spangler) V.; m. Susan Alexander, Apr. 8, 1967; children: Suzannah, Elizabeth. B.A., Gettysburg Coll., 1963; M.S., U. Va., 1965, Ph.D., 1967. Asst. prof. physics MacMurray Coll., Jacksonville, Ill., 1967-71; asso. prof. physics U. N.C., Asheville, 1971-78; prof. physics U. N.C., 1974-78, chmn. dept. physics, dir. acad. computing, 1974-78; prof. physics, dean Coll. Arts and Scis. U. Hartford (Conn.), 1978-83; v.p. acad. affairs Trinity U., San Antonio, 1983-87; pres. U. Evansville, Ind., 1987—; computer cons. Contbr. articles to profl. jours. Mem. Am. Phys. Soc., World Future Soc., AAAS, Am. Assn. for Advancement of Humanities, Am. Assn. for Higher Edn., Am. Assn. Physics Tchrs., Phi Beta Kappa, Sigma Xi, Phi Sigma Kappa. Methodist. Office: U Evansville 1800 Lincoln Ave Evansville IN 47722-0001

VINSON, LAURENCE DUNCAN, JR., lawyer; b. Gadsden, Ala., Mar. 17, 1947. BS with hons., U. Ala., Tuscaloosa, 1969; JD, U. Ala., 1973. Bar: Ala., U.S. Dist. Ct. (no., mid. and so. dists.) Ala., U.S. Ct. Appeals (11th cir.), U.S. Supreme Ct. Assoc. Bradley Arant Rose & White, LLP, Birmingham, Ala., 1973-79; ptnr. Bradley Arant Rose & White, LLP, 1979—; Bar: Ala. 1973, U.S. Dist. Ct. (no. dist.) Ala. 1973, U.S. Supreme Ct. 1977, U.S. Ct. Appeals (11th cir.) 1981, U.S. Dist. Ct. (so. dist.) Ala. 1989, U.S. Dist. Ct. (mid. dist.) Ala. 1991. Chmn. Ala. Uniform Comml. Code Revisions Coms., Arts 3, 4, and 4A. Mem. ABA, Birmingham Bar Assn., Ala. State Bar, Ala. Law Inst., Order of Coif, Phi Beta Kappa, Omicron Delta Kappa. Office: Bradley Arant Rose & White LLP PO Box 830709 2001 Park Pl Ste 1400 Birmingham AL 35203-2736

VINSON, WILLIAM THEODORE, lawyer, diversified corporation executive. BS, USAF Acad., 1965; JD, UCLA, 1969. Bar: Calif. 1970. Judge advocate USAF, 1970-74; trial counsel Phillips Petroleum, San Mateo, Calif., 1974-75; corp. v.p., chief counsel Lockheed Martin Corp., Westlake Village, Calif. Office: Lockheed Martin Corp 310 N Westlake Blvd Ste 200 Westlake Village CA 91362-0001

VINYARD, ROY GEORGE, II, hospital administrator; b. St. Louis, June 19, 1955; s. Roy G. Sr. and Thelma E. (Adams) V.; m. Dina L. Strubinger, June 8, 1985; children; Kyle, Ryan. BS, St. Louis Coll. Pharmacy, 1979; MHA, Washington U., St. Louis, 1985. Exec. asst. Iowa Meth. Med. Ctr., Des Moines, 1985-88; asst. adminstr. Lester E. Cox Med. Ctrs., Springfield, Mo., 1988-91; assoc. adminstr. U. Kans. Hosp., Kansas City, 1991-94; chief adminstrn. officer Oreg. Health Scis. Univ. Hosp. & Clinics, Portland, 1994—. Bd. dirs. Big. Bros. Big Sisters, Springfield, 1991; mem. adv. bd. VNA, Springfield, 1991; participant Leadership Springfield, 1990. Mem. Am. Coll. Healthcare Execs. (diplomate), Rotary (bd. mem. West Linn site coun. 1996—), Lifeflight Consotrium (bd. mem. 1995—). Avocations: computers, softball, raquetball. Office: Oreg Health Scis U 3490 Belknap Dr West Linn OR 97068

VIOLA, BILL, artist, writer; b. N.Y.C., Jan. 25, 1951; s. William John and Wynne Viola; m. Kira Perov; children: Blake, Andrei. BFA, Syracuse U., 1973, DFA, 1995. Tech. dir. Art/Tapes/22 Video Studio, Florence, Italy, 1974-76; artist-in-residence Sta. WNET, N.Y.C., 1976-83, Sony Corp., Atsugi Labs., Japan, 1980-81, San Diego Zoo, 1984; instr. Calif. Inst. of Arts, Valencia, 1983; represented by Anthony d'Offay Gallery, London. Solo exhbns. include The Kitchen Ctr., N.Y., 1974, Everson Mus. Art, Syracuse, N.Y., 1975, Mus. Modern Art, N.Y.C., 1979, 87, Whitney Mus. Art, N.Y.C., 1982, Musée d'Art Moderne, Paris, 1983, Mus. Contemporary Art, L.A., 1985, Fukui Prefectural Mus. Art, Fukui City, Japan, 1989, Staditsche Kunsthalle Düsseldorf, 1992, Moderna Museet, Stockholm, 1993, Museo Nacional Centro de Arte Reina Sofia, Madrid, Spain, 1993, Musée Cantonal des Beaux-Arts, Lausanne, Switzerland, 1993, Whitechapel Art Gallery, London, 1993, Tel Aviv Mus. Art, 1994, Musée d'Art Contemporain, Montreal, Que., Can., 1993, Centro Cultural/Banco de Brazil, Rio de Janeiro, 1994, 46th Venice Biennale, 1995, Festival d'Automne à Paris, 1996; group exhbns. include De Saisset Art Gallery and Mus., Santa Clara, Calif., 1972, Whitney Mus. Am. Art, 1975-87, 89, 93, Stedelijk Mus., Amsterdam, The Netherlands, 1984, Carnegie Mus. Art, Pitts., 1988, Kölnischer Kunstverein, Cologne, Germany, 1989, Israel Mus., Jerusalem, 1990, Musée Nat. d'Art Moderne, Ctr. Georges Pompidou, Paris, 1990, Martin Gropius Bau, Berlin, 1991, Mus. Moderne Kunst, Frankfurt, Germany, 1991, Royal Acad., London, 1993, Denver Art Mus., Columbus (Ohio) Art Mus., 1994, Anthony d'Offay Gallery, London, 1995, Mus. Modern Art, N.Y.C., 1995, Tate Gallery, London, 1995; spl. screening film: Déserts, Vienna, Austria, 1994; commns. include The Stopping Mind, Mus. Moderne Kunst, Frankfurt, 1991, Nantes Triptych, Délégation aux Arts Plastiques, Nantes, France, 1992, Slowly Turning Narrative, Inst. Contemporary Art, Phila., Va. Mus. Fine Art, Richmond, 1992, Tiny Deaths, Biennale d'Art Contemporain de Lyon, France, 1993, Déserts, Konzerthause, Vienna, 1994, 3e Biennale d'Art contemporaire de Lyon, Musée d'art contemporain, Lyon, France, 1995, others; composer: (album) David Tudor-Rainforest IV, 1981; (video) Bill Viola: Selected Works, 1986, I Do Not Know What It Is I Am Like, 1986, The Passing, 1991. Japan/U.S. Creative Arts fellow NEA, 1980, Rockefeller Found. Video Artist fellow, 1982, Visual Artist fellow NEA, 1983-89, Guggenheim Meml. Found. fellow, 1985, Intercultural Film/Video fellow Rockefeller Found., 1991; recipient Jury prize U.S. Film and Video Festival, 1982, Grand prize, 1983, Jury prize Video Culture/Can., 1983, Grand prize for video art, 1984, First prize for video art Athens (Ohio) Film/Video Festival, 1984, Maya Deren award Am. Film Inst., 1987, First prize Festival Internat. d'Art Vidéo et des Nouvelles Images Electroniques de Locarno, 1987, John D. and Catherine T. MacArthur Found. award, 1989, Skowhegan medal, 1993, First prize Festival Internat. de Video, Cidade de Vigo, Spain, 1993, Medienkunstpreis, Siemens Kulturprogramm and Zentrum fur Kunst und Medientechnologie, Germany, 1993. Subject numerous books. Home: 282 Granada Ave Long Beach CA 90803-5520

VIOLA, HERMAN JOSEPH, museum director; b. Chgo., Feb. 24, 1938; s. Joseph and Mary (Incollingo) V.; m. Susan Patricia Bennett, June 13, 1964; children—Joseph, Paul, Peter. B.A., Marquette U., 1960, M.A., 1964; Ph.D., Ind. U., 1970. Founding editor Prologue: Jour. of Nat. Archives, 1969-72; dir. Nat. Anthrop. Archives, 1972-86; dir. quincentenary programs Mus. Natural History Smithsonian Inst., Washington, 1986-94; curator emeritus Smithsonian Instn., Washington, 1994—. Author: Thomas L. McKenney, Architect of America's Early Indian Policy, 1816-1830, 1974, The Indian Legacy of Charles Bird King, 1976, Diplomats in Buckskins: A History of Indian Delegations in Washington City, 1981, The National Archives of the United States, 1984, Magnificent Voyagers: The U.S. Exploring Expedition, 1938-42, 1985, Exploring the West: A Smithsonian Book, 1987, After Columbus: America's Indians Since 1492, 1990, Seeds of Change: Five Hundred Years Since Columbus, 1991, Ben Nighthorse Campbell: An American Warrior, 1993, Memoirs of Charles Henry Veil, 1994, North American Indians, 1996. Served with USNR, 1960-62. Mem. Western History Assn., Soc. Am. Archivists (program chmn. 1972). Home: 7307 Pinewood St Falls Church VA 22046-2725 Office: Mus Natural History Smithsonian Instn Washington DC 20560

VIOLAND-SANCHEZ, EMMA NATIVIDAD, school administrator, educator; b. Cochabamba, Bolivia, Nov. 5, 1944; came to U.S., 1961; d. Adalberto Violand and Emma Sanchez; children: James, Julia. BS, Radford U., 1966, MS, 1968; EdD, George Washington U., 1987. Postgrad. profl. lic. Tchr., counselor Am. Coop. Sch., La Paz, Bolivia, 1963, 71-76; instr. Ariz. Western Coll., Yuma, 1967-68; tchr., counselor St. Andrews Sch., La Paz, 1968-71; rschr. Instituto Boliviano Estudio Accion Social, La Paz, 1968-71; bilingual resource specialist Arlington (Va.) Pub. Schs., 1976-78, secondary project coord. Title VII, 1978-80, supr. ESOL, 1980—; adj. prof. U. Catolica, La Paz, 1974-75, George Mason U., Fairfax, Va., 1986-94, George Washington U., Washington, 1988—; cons. sch. dists., univs., Ministry of Edn. in Bolivia, 1976—, in El Salvador, 1996, in Escuela, Americana, San Salvador, Ministry of Devel. in Bolivia, 1996. Author: Vocational and Professional Handbook for Bolivia, 1971, Learning Styles in the ESL/EFL Classroom, 1995, (monographs) Ministry of Education, 1988, National Clearinghouse for Bilingual Education, 1990, 91. Founder, pres. coun. 4606 LULAC, Arlington, 1987-96; founder chair Immigration Rights Task Force, Arlington, 1989-92; bd. trustees United Way Nat. Capital Area, Washington, 1989-94; exec. bd. Com. of 100, Arlington, 1994-95. Named one of Notable Women of Arlington, Arlington County, 1993; recipient Outstanding Dissertation award Nat. Assn. Bilingual Edn., 1988, Award Arlington County Dept. of Human Svcs., 1996; Am. fellow AAUW, 1986-87; Fulbright Sr. scholar, 1995-96. Mem. ASCD, TESOL (rsch. bd. 1979—). Avocations: travel, research, Hispanic/Latin American issues, consulting, sports. Office: Arlington Pub Schs 1426 N Quincy St Arlington VA 22207-3646

VIOLENUS, AGNES A., retired school system administrator; b. N.Y.C., May 17, 1931; d. Antonio and Constance Violenus. BA, Hunter Coll., 1952; MA, Columbia U., 1958; EdD, Nova U., 1990. Tchr. N.Y. State Day Care, N.Y.C., 1952-53, N.Y.C. Bd. Edn., 1953-66; asst. prin. N.Y.C. Elem. and Jr. High Sch., 1966-91; student tchr. supr. dept. edn., adj. lectr. CCNY, 1997—; adj. instr. computer dept. continuing edn. divsn. York Coll., N.Y.C., 1985-88; adj. instr. tchr. mentor program grad. edn. divsn. CCNY, 1990-91; reviewer ednl. and instrnl. films; judge news and documentary Emmy awards NATAS, 1995, 97. Co-author: LOGO: K-12, 1980; contbr. articles to profl. jours. Mem. mid-Manhattan br. NAACP, mem. com. on Afro-Am. acad., cultural, and tech. olympics; life mem. Girl Scouts U.S., N.Y.C.; bd. visitors Manhattan Psychiat. Ctr., 1995; vol. advisor math., sci., computers Workshop Ctr., CCNY, 1995. Recipient Dedicated Svc. award Coun. Suprs. and Adminstrs., Appreciation award Aerospace Edn. Assn., 1985, Significant Contbn. award Am. Soc. for Aerospace Edn., 1985, Leaders' Day Cert. of Appreciation, Girl Scouts U.S., 1997. Mem. ASCE, Am. Ednl. Rsch. Assn., Assn. Advancement of Computing in Edn., Assn. Computers in Math. and Sci. Tchg., Soc. for Info. Tech. and Tchr. Edn., assn. for Women in Sci., N.Y. Acad. Scis. (scientists in schs. program 1995), Nat. Assn. Negro Bus. and Profl. Women's Clubs (scholarship com. 1989—, family math. com. 1995, rec. sec. 1994-95, profl. award 1997), Nat. Black Child Devel. Inst. (bd. dirs. 1991—, sci. exhibit com. 1995, pub.policy com. 1991—, Bridge Bldr.'s award 1995), Pub. Edn. Assn. (mem. good schs. exch. com. 1990), Schomburg Ctr. Rsch. in Black Culture (bd. trustee, co-chair corp. task force on African-Am. in math., sci. and tech. 1992—, pres. 1995), Doctorate Assn. N.Y. Educators, N.Y. Alliance Black Sch. Educators, Hunter Coll. Alumni Assn. (bd. dirs. 1993—, rec. sec. 1996—), Band St. Slumni Coun. Greater N.Y. (asst. sect. 1991—), Wistarians Alumni Hunter Coll. (exec. com. 1990—, pres. 1990-94). Democrat. Roman Catholic. Avocations: aeronautics and space science, music, collecting black education memorabilia, instructing survival strategies and techniques for women and children. Office: Farley Bldg PO Box 699 New York NY 10116

VIOLETTE, GLENN PHILLIP, construction engineer; b. Hartford, Conn., Nov. 15, 1950; s. Reginald Joseph and Marielle Theresa (Bernier) B.; m. Susan Linda Begam, May 15, 1988. BSCE, Colo. State U., 1982. Registered profl. engr., Colo. Engring. aide Colo. State Hwy. Dept., Glenwood Springs, Colo., 1974-79, hwy. engr., 1980-82; hwy. engr. Colo. State Hwy. Dept., Loveland, Colo., 1979-80; project engr. Colo. State Hwy. Dept., Glenwood Canyon, Colo., 1983—; guest speaker in field. Contbg. editor, author, photographer publs. in field. Recipient scholarship Fed. Hwy Adminstrn., 1978. Mem. ASCE, Amnesty Internat., Nat. Rifle Assn., Internat. Platform Assn., Siera Club, Audubon Soc., Nature Conservancy, World Wildlife

Fund, Cousteau Soc., Chi Epsilon. Office: Colo Dept Transp 202 Centennial Dr Glenwood Springs CO 81601-2845

VIORST, JUDITH STAHL, author; b. Newark, Feb. 2, 1931; d. Martin Leonard and Ruth June (Ehrenkranz) Stahl; m. Milton Viorst, Jan. 30, 1960; children: Anthony Jacob, Nicholas Nathan, Alexander Noah. BA, Rutgers U., 1952; grad., Washington Psychoanalytic Inst., 1981. Author: (children's books) Sunday Morning, 1968, I'll Fix Anthony, 1969, Try It Again Sam, 1970, The Tenth Good Thing About Barney, 1971 (Silver Pencil award 1973), Alexander and the Terrible Horrible No Good Very Bad Day, 1972, My Mama Says There Aren't Any Zombies, Ghosts, Vampires, Creatures, Demons, Monsters, Fiends, Goblins or Things, 1973, Rosie and Michael, 1974, Alexander, Who Used to Be Rich Last Sunday, 1978, The Good-Bye Book, 1988, Earrings!, 1990, The Alphabet from Z to A (with Much Confusion on the Way, 1994, Alexander, Who's Not (Do You Hear Me? I Mean It!) Going to Move, 1995; (poetry) The Village Square, 1965-66, It's Hard to Be Hip Over Thirty and Other Tragedies of Married Life, 1968, People and Other Aggravations, 1971, How Did I Get to Be Forty and Other Atrocities, 1976, If I Were in Charge of the World and Other Worries, 1981, When Did I Stop Being Twenty and Other Injustices, 1987, Forever Fifty and Other Negotiations, 1989, Sad Underwear and Other Complications, 1995; (with Milton Viorst) The Washington Underground Gourmet, 1970, Yes Married, 1972, A Visit From St. Nicholas (To a Liberated Household), 1977, Love and Guilt and the Meaning of Life, Etc., 1979, Necessary Losses, 1986, Murdering Mr. Monti, 1994; (musical) Love and Shrimp (book and lyrics), 1990; (HBO children's movie) Alexander and the Terrible, Horrible, No Good, Very Bad Day (book and lyrics), 1990). Recipient Emmy award for poems used in Anne Bancroft Spl., 1970. Jewish. Home: 3432 Ashley Ter NW Washington DC 20008-3238

VIORST, MILTON, writer; b. Paterson, N.J., Feb. 18, 1930; s. Louis and Betty (LeVine) V.; m. Judith Stahl, Jan. 30, 1960; children—Anthony, Nicholas, Alexander. B.A. summa cum laude, Rutgers U., 1951; student (Fulbright scholar), U. Lyon, France, 1952; M.A., Harvard U., 1955; M.S., Columbia U., 1956. Reporter Bergen (N.J.) Record, 1955-56, Newark StarLedger, 1956-57, Washington Post, 1957-61; Washington corr. N.Y. Post, 1961-64; syndicated columnist Washington Evening Star, 1971-75; staff writer The New Yorker, N.Y.C., 1987-93; Ferris prof. journalism Princeton (N.J.) U., 1995-96; lectr. in field. Author: Hostile Allies: FDR and de-Gaulle, 1965, Great Documents of Western Civilization, 1965, Fall from Grace: The Republican Party and the Puritan Ethic, 1968, Hustlers and Heroes, 1971, Fire in the Streets: America in the 1960's, 1980, Making a Difference: The Peace Corps at Twenty-five, 1986, Sands of Sorrow: Israel's Journey from Independence, 1987, Reaching for the Olive Branch: UNRWA and Peace in the Middle East, 1990, Sandcastles: The Arabs in Search of the Modern World, 1994; also articles.; contbg. corr. Washington Quar. Chmn. Fund for Investigative Journalism, 1969-78; bd. dirs. Georgetown Day Sch., 1977-80; mem. nat. adv. com. Middle East Policy Coun. Served as officer USAF, 1952-54. Recipient Columbia Journalism Alumni award, 1992; Woodrow Wilson sr. fellow, 1973-79, Alicia Patterson fellow, 1979; Middle East Inst. sr. scholar. Mem. PEN, Soc. Profl. Journalists, Author's Guild, Coun. on Fgn. Rels., Am. Peace Now, Phi Beta Kappa.

VIRGO, JOHN MICHAEL, economist, researcher, educator; b. Pressburry, Eng., Mar. 11, 1943; s. John Joseph and Muriel Agnes (Franks) V.; m. Katherine Sue Ulmrich, Sept. 6, 1980 (div. 1979); 1 child, Debra Marie. BA, Calif. State U., Fullerton, 1967, MA, 1969; MA, Claremont Grad. Sch., 1971, PhD, 1972. Instr. econs. Whittier (Calif.) Coll., 1970-71, Calif. State U., Fullerton and Long Beach, 1971-72, Claremont (Calif.) Grad. Sch., 1971-72; asst. prof. econs. Va. Commonwealth U., Richmond, 1972-74; assoc. prof. mgmt. So. Ill. U., Edwardsville, 1975-83, prof., 1984—; bd. dirs., founder Internat. Health Econ. & Mgmt. Inst., Edwardsville, 1983-87. Author: Legal & Illegal California Farmworkers, 1974; author, editor: Health Care: An International Perspective, 1984, Exploring New Vistas in Health Care, 1985, Restructuring Health Policy, 1986; founder, editor-in-chief Internat. Advances in Econ. Rsch. Served with USN, 1965-68. Mem. Internat. Hosp. Fedn., Am. Econ. Assn., Am. Hosp. Assn., Am. Soc. Assn. Execs., Royal Econ. Soc., Atlantic Econ. Soc. (founder, exec. v.p., mng. editor jour. 1973—), Allied Social Scis. Assn. (chmn. exec. confs. 1982-84), AMA, So. Econs. Assn., Sunset Hills Club (Edwardsville). Democrat. Roman Catholic. Avocations: tennis, skiing. Home: 5277 Lindell Blvd Saint Louis MO 63108-1223 Office: So Ill U Atlantic Econ Soc PO Box 1101 Edwardsville IL 62026

VIRGO, MURIEL AGNES, swimming school owner; b. Liverpool, Cheshire, Eng., Apr. 3, 1924; d. Harold Thornhill and Susan Ann (Duff) Franks; m. John Virgo, Aug. 13, 1942; children: John Michael, Angela Victoria, Barbara Ann, Collin Anthony, Donna Marie. Grad. parochial schs. Co-owner Virgo Swim Sch., Garden Grove, Calif., 1967—. Mem. Ancient Mystical Order Rosae Crucis, Traditional Martinist Order. Republican. Roman Catholic. Avocation: ballroom dancing. Home: 12751 Crestwood Cir Garden Grove CA 92841-5250 Office: Virgo Swim Sch 12851 Brookhurst Way Garden Grove CA 92841-5205

VIRKHAUS, TAAVO, symphony orchestra conductor; b. Tartu, Estonia, June 29, 1934; came to U.S., 1949; s. Adalbert August and Helene Marie (Sild) V.; m. Nancy Ellen Herman, Mar. 29, 1969. MusB U. Miami, 1955; MusM Eastman Sch. of Music, Rochester, 1957, DMA, 1967. Dir. music U. Rochester (N.Y.), also assoc. prof. Eastman Sch., Rochester, 1967-77; music dir., condr. Duluth (Minn.) Superior Symphony Orch., 1977-94; guest condr. Rochester Philharm., Minn. Orch., Balt. Symphony, Vancouver Symphony and others, 1972—; music dir., condr. Hunstville (Ala.) Symphony Orch., 1989—; guest condr. at Tallinn, Estonia, 1978, 88, 90, 92, 93, 94; lectr. U. Minn.-Duluth, U. of Wis.-Superior. With U.S. Army, 1957-58, USAR, 1957-61. Recipient Howard Hanson Composition award, 1966, Am. Heritage award JFK Libr. for Minorities, 1974; Fulbright scholar, Musickhochschule, Cologne, 1963. Mem. Am. Symphony Orch. League, Condrs. Guild, Am. Fedn. of Musicians. Composer: Violin Concerto, 1966, Symphony No. 1, 1976, Symphony No. 2, 1979, Symphony No. 3, 1984, Symphony No. 4, 1989, Symphony No. 5, 1994. Republican. Lutheran.

VIRKLER, DENNIS M., film editor. Editor: (films) Burnt Offerings, 1976, Xanadu, 1980, Continental Divide, 1981, Airplane II: The Sequel, 1982, Gorky Park, 1983, Independence Day, 1983, The River Rat, 1984, Secret Admirer, 1985, Nobody's Fool, 1986, (with William M. Anderson and Sheldon Kahn) Big Shots, 1987, Distant Thunder, 1988, (with John Wright) The Hunt for Red October, 1990 (Academy award nomination best film editing 1990), (with Don Brochu, Robert A. Ferretti, and Dov Hoenig) Under Siege, 1992, (with David Finfer) The Fugitive, 1993 (Academy award nomination best film editing 1993), Batman Forever, 1995. Office: Broder Kurland Webb Uffner Agy 9242 Beverly Blvd Ste 200 Beverly Hills CA 90210-3710*

VIRTEL, JAMES JOHN, lawyer; b. Joliet, Ill., May 15, 1944. BA cum laude, Loras Coll., 1966; JD cum laude, St. Louis U., 1969. Bar: Mo. 1969, Ill. 1969. Atty. Armstrong, Teasdale, Schlafly & Davis, St. Louis; adj. prof. law St. Louis U., 1995—; regent Loras Coll., Dubuque, Iowa, 1996—. Editor: St. Louis U. Law Jour., 1968-69. Fellow Am. Coll. Trial Lawyers; mem. Ill. State Bar Assn., Mo. State Bar Assn. Office: Armstrong Teasdale Schlafly & Davis 1 Metropolitan Sq Saint Louis MO 63102-2733

VISCHER, HAROLD HARRY, manufacturing company executive; b. Toledo, Oct. 17, 1914; s. Harry Philip and Hazel May (Patterson) V.; m. DeNell Meyers, Feb. 18, 1938; children: Harold Harry, Robert P., Michael L. B.B.A., U. Toledo, 1937. With Ohio Bell Telephone Co., 1937-38; with Firestone Tire & Rubber Co., Toledo, 1948-61; nat. passenger tire sales mgr. Firestone Tire & Rubber Co., 1953-57, dist. mgr., 1957-61; with Bandag Inc., Muscatine, Iowa, 1961-80; exec. v.p., pres. Bandag Inc. (Rubber and Equipment Sales group), 1975-80; also dir.; pres., gen. mgr. Hardline Internat., Inc., Jackson, Mich., 1980-82; chmn. Tred-X Corp., 1982—. Mem. City Council, Muscatine, 1964-76; chmn., mem. Dist. Export Council Iowa, 1964-81; chmn. Muscatine United Way, 1969-70; mem. adv. bd. Engring. Coll. Iowa State U., 1970-81; mem. Muscatine Light & Water Bd., 1979-80. Elected to Nat. Tire Dealers and Retreaders Assn. Hall of Fame, 1988, to Internat. Tire Retreading and Repairing Hall of Fame, 1990. Mem. Nat. Tire and Retreaders Suppliers Group Assn. (chmn. 1979-80, exec. com. 1977-80), Tire Retread Info. Bur. (exec. com. 1974-81), Am. Retreading Assn. (adv. bd. 1970-72), Retreading Industry Assn., Industry Man of Yr. 1979), Christian Business men's Com., Gideons, Rotary. Republican. Baptist. Home: 13500 Vischer Rd Brooklyn MI 49230-9022 Office: 116 Frost St Jackson MI 49202-2371

VISCI, JOSEPH MICHAEL, newspaper editor; b. Delaware, Ohio, Oct. 8, 1953; s. Leonard Albert and Alice Mary (Buzzelli) V. B.A., Ohio Wesleyan U., 1975; M.A., Ohio State U., 1977. Reporter Naples Daily News, Fla., 1975-76; editor Columbus Citizen-Jour., Ohio, 1977-78, Detroit Free Press, 1978—. Office: Detroit Free Press 321 W Lafayette Blvd Detroit MI 48226

VISCLOSKY, PETER JOHN, congressman, lawyer; b. Gary, Ind., Aug. 13, 1949; s. John and Helen (Kauzlaric) V. B.S. in Acctg., Ind. U.-Indpls., 1970; J.D., U. Notre Dame, 1973; LL.M. in Internat. and Comparative Law, Georgetown U., 1983. Bar: Ind., D.C., U.S. Supreme Court. Legal asst. Dist. Atty.'s Office, N.Y.C., 1972; assoc. Benjamin, Greco & Gouveia, Merrillville, Ind., 1973-76, Greco, Gouveia, Miller, Pera & Bishop, Merrillville, Ind., 1982-84; assoc. staff appropriations com. U.S. Ho. of Reps., Washington, 1976-80, assoc. staff budget com., 1980-82; mem. 99th-105th Congresses from 1st dist. Ind., 1985—; mem. Appropriations com., subcoms. treasury, postal svc., gen. govt. and military constrn. Democrat. Roman Catholic. Office: US House of Reps 2313 Rayburn Bldg Washington DC 20515-1401*

VISCOVICH, ANDREW JOHN, educational management consultant; b. Oakland, Calif., Sept. 25, 1925; s. Peter Andrew and Lucy Pauline (Razovich) V.; m. Roen Shirley Mulvana, Apr. 19, 1952 (div. Feb. 1985); children: Randal Peter, Andra Clair; m. Elena Beth Wong, Apr. 28, 1993; 1 child, Alison Wong. BA, U. Calif., Berkeley, 1949; MA, San Francisco State U., 1960; EdD, U. Calif., Berkeley, 1973; cert. labor dispute resolution, Golden Gate U., 1976. Assoc. supt. Oakland Unified Sch. Dist., Calif., 1970-77; supt. Palm Springs (Calif.) Unified Sch. Dist., 1976-79, Garvey Sch. Dist., Rosemead, Calif., 1979-88, Berkeley (Calif.) Unified Sch. Dist., Stockton, Calif., 1988-90; pres. Ctr. for Ednl. Rsch. in Adminstrn., Stockton, Calif., 1990—; state adminstr. Coachella Unified Sch. Dist., Sacramento, Calif., 1992; adj. prof. U. Calif., Berkeley, 1965-67, Calif. State U., Hayward, 1970-76, L.A., 1971-88; exec. dir. Marcus Foster Edn. Found., Oakland, 1975-76; cons. Spanish Ministry Edn., 1987—, Republic of China Ministry Edn., Taipei, Taiwan, 1986-89, Croatian Ministry Edn., Zagreb, 1993—, Marriott Sch. Svcs, 1992—, CSHQH, Idaho; pre-sch. dir. Oakland Unified Sch. Dist., 1974-76; asst. dir. Bay Area Bilingual Edn. League, 1971-75; dir. Bay Area Tchr. Ctr., 1974, asst. dir. Far West Ednl. Lab., 1974; adj. assoc. prof. Calif. State U. at L.A.and Hayward, U. South Fla., U. Oreg., Coll. of Holy Names; exec. dir. ANRO Cons., Inc., 1973-82. Author: Language Programs for the Disadvantaged, 1965, R.E.S. Plus, 1978; contbr. The School Principal, 1978. Chair United Way, Pasadena, Calif., 1985; pres. Croatian Scholarship Found., San Ramon, Calif., 1993-94. Served to ens. USNR, 1959-64. Recipient award for innovations in alternative schools Behavioral Rsch. Lab., San Francisco, 1973; named Knight of Civil Order of Merit King Juan Carlos of Spain, 1990. Mem. Am. Mgmt. Assn., Am. Assn. Sch. Adminstrs., Assn. Calif. Sch. Adminstrs., Calif. City Sch. Supts., Calif. Tchrs. Assn. (John Swett award 1978), Tau Kappa Epsilon. Avocations: golf, reading, travel. ultralite flying. Home: 3754 Fort Donelson Dr Stockton CA 95219-3211

VISEK, WILLARD JAMES, nutritionist, animal scientist, physician, educator; b. Sargent, Nebr., Sept. 19, 1922; s. James and Anna S. (Dworak) V.; m. Priscilla Flagg, Dec. 28, 1949; children: Dianna, Madeleine, Clayton Paul. B.Sc. with honors (Carl R. Gray scholar), U. Nebr., 1947; MSc (Smith fellow in agr.), Cornell U., 1949, Ph.D., 1951; M.D. (Peter Yost Fund scholar), U. Chgo., 1957; DSc (hon.), U. Nebr., 1980. Diplomate Nat. Bd. Med. Examiners, 1960. Grad. asst., lab. animal nutrition Cornell U., 1947-51; AEC postdoctoral fellow Oak Ridge, 1951-52; research assoc., 1952-53; research asst. pharmacology U. Chgo., 1953-57, asst. prof., 1957-61, assoc. prof., 1961-64; rotating med. intern U. Chgo. Clinics, 1957-58, 58-59, 59; prof. nutrition and comparative metabolism, dept. animal sci. Cornell U., Ithaca, N.Y., 1964-75; prof. clin. sci. (nutrition and metabolism) Coll. Medicine and dept. food sci. U. Ill. Coll. Agr., Urbana-Champaign, 1975—; prof. dept. internal medicine U. Ill. Coll. Medicine, Urbana-Champaign, 1986-93, prof. emeritus, 1993—; bd. dirs. Coun. Agriculture, Sci. and Tech., 1994-97; bd. sci. advisors Coun. Sci. and Health, 1994—; Brittingham vis. prof. U. Wis. Madison, 1982-83; Hogan meml. lectr. U. Mo., 1987; mem. subcom. dog nutrition com. animal nutrition NRC-Nat. Acad. Sci., 1965-71; adv. coun. Inst. Lab. Animal Resources, NRC-Nat. Acad. Sci., 1966-69; subcom. animal care faciltities Survey Inst. Lab. Animal Resources, 1967-70; cons., lectr. in field; mem. sci. adv. com. diet and nutrition cancer program Nat. Cancer Inst., 1976-81; mem. nutrition study sect. NIH, 1980-84; chmn. membership com. Am. Inst. Nutrition-Am. Soc. Clin. Nutrition, 1978-79, 80-83, 85; cons. VA, NSF, indsl. orgns.; Wellcome vis. prof. in basic med. scis. Oreg. State U., 1991-92; bd. sci. counselors USDA, 1989-91. Mem. editorial bd. Jour. Nutrition, 1980-84, editor, 1990—; contbr. articles to profl. jours. Bd. dirs. Coun. for Agrl. Sci. and Tech., 1994—; active local Boy Scouts Am. Served with AUS, 1943-46. Recipient alumni award Nebr. 4-H, 1967, 97, alumni award U. Chgo., 1997, Osborne and Mendel award, 1985, faculty merit award U. Ill. Coll. Medicine, 1988, Conrad Elvehjem award, 1996, Alumni Achievement award U. Nebr., 1997, U. Chgo., 1997; Nat. Cancer Inst. spl. fellow MIT, rsch. fellow Mass. Gen. Hosp., 1970-71; sr. scholar U. Ill., 1988. Fellow AAAS, Am. Inst. Nutrition, Am. Soc. Animal Sci. (chmn. subcom. antimicrobials, mem. regulatory agency com. 1973-78); mem. Soc. Pharmacology and Exptl. Therapeutics, Am. Inst. Nutrition (council 1980-83, 85-86), Soc. Exptl. Biology and Medicine, Am. Soc. Clin. Nutrition, Am. Therapeutic Soc., Am. Gastroenterol. Assn., Am. Bd. Clin. Nutrition, Innocents Soc., Fedn. Am. Socs. Exptl. Biology (sci. steering group life scis. rsch. office, adv. com. 1986-92), Am. Bd. Nutrition (bd. dirs.), Am. Soc. Nutritional Scis. (Conrad Elvehjem award 1996), Nat. Dairy Coun. (rsch. adv. com. 1987-91, vis. prof. nutrition program 1981-92), Gamma Alpha (pres. 1948-49), Phi Kappa Phi (pres. 1981-82), Alpha Gamma Rho (pres. 1946-47), Gamma Sigma Delta. Presbyterian (elder). Home: 1405 W William St Champaign IL 61821-4406 Office: U Ill 190 Med Sci Bldg 506 S Mathews Ave Urbana IL 61801-3618

VISHNIAC, ETHAN TECUMSEH, astronomy educator; b. New Haven, Sept. 29, 1955; s. Wolf Vladimir and Helen Frances (Simpson) V.; m. Ilene Joy Busch, June 13, 1976; children: Cady Anne, Miriam Rachel. BS and BA summa cum laude, U. Rochester, 1976; MA, Harvard U., 1980, PhD, 1980. Rsch. assoc. Princeton (N.J.) U., 1980-82; lectr. U. Tex., Austin, 1982-84, asst. prof., 1984-88, assoc. prof., 1988-93, prof., 1993—. Assoc. editor Phys. Rev. Letters; contbr. numerous articles to profl. jours. Recipient Presdl. Young Investigator, 1985; Alfred Sloan fellow, 1986. Mem. Am. Astron. Soc. (Helen B. Warner prize 1990), Internat. Astron. Union, Am. Phys. Soc. Office: U of Tex Dept Astronomy Austin TX 78712

VISKANTA, RAYMOND, mechanical engineering educator; b. Lithuania, July 16, 1931; came to U.S., 1949, naturalized, 1955; s. Vincas and Genovaite (Vinickas) V.; m. Birute Barbara Barpsys, Oct. 13, 1956; children: Renata, Vitas, Tadas. BSME, U. Ill., 1955; MSME, Purdue U., 1956, PhD, 1960; DEng (hon.), Tech. U. Munich, 1994. Registered profl. engr., Ill. Asst. mech. engr. Argonne (Ill.) Nat. Lab., 1956-59, student rsch. assoc., 1959-60, assoc. mech. engr., 1960-62; assoc. prof. mech. engring. Purdue U., West Lafayette, Ind., 1962-66, prof. mech. engring., 1966-86, Gross disting. prof. engring., 1986—; guest prof. Tech. U. Munich, Germany, 1976-77, U. Karlsruhe, Germany, 1987; vis. prof. Tokyo Inst. Tech., 1983. Contbr. over 500 tech. articles to profl. jours. Recipient Sr. U.S. Scientist award Alexander von Humboldt Found., 1975, Sr. Rsch. award Am. Soc. Engring. Edn., 1984, Nusselt-Reynolds prize, 1991, Thermal Engring. award for Internat. Activity, Japan Soc. Mech. Engrs., 1994; Japan Soc. for Promotion of Sci. fellow, 1983. Fellow ASME (Heat Transfer Meml. award 1976, Max Jakob Meml. award 1986, Melville medal 1988), AIAA (Thermophysics award 1979); mem. AAAS, NAE, Acad. Engring. Scis. Russian Fedn. (fgn.), Sigma Xi, Pi Tau Sigma, Tau Beta Pi. Home: 3631 Chancellor Way West Lafayette IN 47906-8809 Office: Purdue Univ 1288 Mechanical Engring Bui West Lafayette IN 47907

VISOCKI, NANCY GAYLE, data processing consultant; b. Dumont, N.J., May 13, 1952; d. Thomas and Gloria (Valle) V. BA in Maths., Manhattanville Coll., 1974; MS in Ops. Rsch. and Stats., Rensselaer Poly. Inst., 1977. Rsch. asst. Coll. Physicians and Surgeons Columbia U., N.Y.C., 1974-75; programmer analyst R. Shriver Assocs., Parsippany, N.J., 1977-79; sr. tech. rep. GE Info. Svcs. Co., East Orange, N.J., 1979-81; mgr. project office GE Info. Svcs. Co., Morristown, N.J., 1981-83, tech. dir., 1983-87, tech. mgr., 1988-89; area mgr. system devel. and consulting GE Info. Svcs. Co., Parsippany, 1989-92; area tech. mgr. system devel. and cons., Fin. Info. Systems GE Info. Svcs. Co., Parsippany, N.J., 1992-93, sr. cons. electronic commerce info. svcs., 1993—. Active Western Hills Christian Ch., Tranquility, N.J., 1986—; vol. Women's Ctr., Hackettstown, N.J., 1989-93; class fundraising and gift chmn. Rensselaer Poly. Inst., 1991-95; vol. Elfun Soc. Manhattanville Coll. grantee, Purchase, N.Y., 1970-71; tuition fellow Rensselaer Poly. Inst., Troy, N.Y., 1975-77. Mem. NAFE, Women of Accomplishment. Avocations: skiing, needlepoint, hiking, bicycling, reading. Home: 140 E Linden Ave Dumont NJ 07628-1916 Office: GE Info Svcs Co 20 Waterview Blvd Ste 302 Parsippany NJ 07054-1229 *Many people in business think that it takes time and costs money to be thoughtful and kind to others. It doesn't take time or money, but only a little effort to nurture a sincere concern and caring for others.*

VISOTSKY, HAROLD MERYLE, psychiatrist, educator; b. Chgo., May 25, 1924; s. Joseph and Rose (Steinberg) V.; m. Gladys Mavrich, Dec. 18, 1955; children: Jeffrey, Robin. Student, Herzl Coll., Chgo., 1943-44, Baylor U., 1944-45, Sorbonne, 1945-46; B.S., U. Ill., 1947, M.D. magna cum laude, 1951. Intern Cin. Gen. Hosp., 1951-52; resident U. Ill., Ill. Research and Ednl. Hosp., also Neuropsychiat. Inst., Chgo., 1952-55; asst. prof. U. Ill. Coll. Medicine, 1957-61, assoc. prof. psychiatry, 1965-69, dir. psychiat. residency tng. and edn., 1955-59; prof., chmn. dept. psychiatry and behavioral scis. Northwestern U. Med. Sch., Chgo., 1969-91; dir. Psychiat. Inst., chmn. dept. psychiatry Northwestern Meml. Hosp., 1969-91, dir. rsch. and edn. dept. psychiatry and behavioral sci., 1994—; polio respiratory ctr. psychiat. cons. Nat. Found. Infantile Paralysis, U. Ill., 1955-59; dir. mental health Chgo. Bd. Health divsn. mental health svcs., 1959-63; dir. Ill. Dept. Mental Health, 1962-70; examiner Am. Bd. Psychiatry and Neurology, 1964—; cons. Ctr. Mental Health and Psychiat. Svcs., Am. Hosp. Assn., 1979—; mem. 1st U.S. mission on mental health to USSR State Dept. Mission, 1967; chmn. task force V Joint Comm. on Mental Health of Children, 1967-69; mem. adv. com. on cmty. mental health svc. NIMH Ctr.; mem. profl. adv. group Am. Health Svcs., Inc.; mem. adv. com. Joint Commn. Accreditation Hosps., Coun. Psychiat. Facilities; mem. spl. panel mental illness for bd. dirs. ACLU; rector Lincoln Acad. of Ill. Faculty Social Svc.; mem. select com. psychiat. care and evaluation HEW; mem. faculty Practising Law Inst.; bd. overseers Spertus Coll. Judaica, Chgo., 1978-83; sr. cons. WHO-Mental Health Divsn., 1995—; mem. adv. coun. chair Ill. Dept Mental Health and Devel. Disabilities, 1995—; pres. Ctr. for Transcultural Studies, 1993—; bd. dirs. Alberto Culver Corp. Contbr. articles to psychiat. jours., chpts. psychiat. textbooks. Trustee Erikson Inst. Early Edn., Ill. Hosp. Assn., Mental Health Law Project, Washington; mem. Menninger Corp. Bd. Drirs., 1997—. Served with AUS, 1942-46. Decorated D.S.C., Purple Heart, Bronze Star; recipient Edward A. Strecker award Inst. Pa. Hosp., 1969; Med. Alumnus of Year award U. Ill., 1976; Disting. Service award Chgo. chpt. Anti-Defamation League B'nai B'rith, 1978. Fellow Am. Orthopsychiat. Assn. (dir. v.p. 1970-71, pres. 1976-77, Leadership in Cmty. Health Programs award 1986), Am. Psychiat. Assn. (chmn. coun. on mental health svcs. 1967-68, v.p. 1973-74, bd. trustees 1973-83, sec. 1981-83, chmn. coun. nat. affairs 1975-78, com. on abuse of psychiatry and psychiatrists 1980-84, chmn. coun. internat. affairs 1984-89, Adminstrv. Psychiatry award 1985, Simon Bolivar award 1982, Spl. Presdl. Commendation award 1988), AAAS, Am. Coll. Psychiatrists (charter, bd. regents 1976-79, v.p. 1980, pres. 1983-84, E.B. Bowis award 1981, gold medal for contbns. to psychiatry 1988), Chgo. Inst. Medicine, Am. Coll. Mental Health Adminstrs. (founding fellow); mem. Am. Assn. Chmn. Dept. Psychiatry, Am. Assn. Social Psychiatry (v.p. 1976, pres.-elect 1987, pres. 1988-90), Coun. Med. Splty. Socs., AMA, Ill. Psychiat. Soc. (pres. 1965-66), Am. Coll. Psychoanalysis, Mental Health Law Project (bd. trustees 1973-79), World Assn. Social Psychiatry (councilor, exec. coun. 1984—), World Psychiat. Assn. (exec. com. 1985—, sec. of meetings 1990-96, mem. WPA coun.), NAS, Inst. of Med. (commn. to develop methods useful for VA in estimating physician needs 1988—, expert rev. panel to set priorities for mental health 1989), Chgo. Consortium for Psychiat. Rsch. (chmn., bd. dirs. 1989—), Benj Rush Soc. (pres. 1997—), Alpha Omega Alpha. Office: Time-Life Bldg 303 E Ohio St Ste 550 Chicago IL 60611

VISSER, JOHN EVERT, university president emeritus, historian; b. Orange City, Iowa, Apr. 24, 1920; s. Arthur J. and Frances (TePaske) V.; m. Virginia Jean Schuyler, May 29, 1946; children: Betty Jean, Mary Frances, Nancy Ann, Martha Ellen. BA, Hope Coll., 1942, LittD (hon.), 1995; MA, U. Iowa, 1947, PhD, 1957; D honoris causa, Indsl. U. Santander, Bucaramanga, Colombia, 1968. Asst. prof. history Hope Coll., Holland, Mich., 1949-56; asst. registrar Western Mich. U., 1956-57; asst. dean Ball State U., 1957-58, exec. asst. to pres., prof. history, 1962-67; dean Grand Rapids (Mich.) Jr. Coll., 1958- 62; pres. Emporia (Kans.) State U., 1967-84; cons. U. Alaska, 1985-86; interim chancellor U. Alaska, Juneau, 1986-87; interim vice chancellor, U. Wis., Green Bay, 1987-88. Served to capt. inf. AUS, 1942-46. Inducted into Infantry OCS Hall of Fame, 1982. Mem. Nat. Assn. Intercollegiate Athletics (pres., mem. exec. com.), Am. Assn. State Colls. and Univs. (treas. 1971-75), Kans. Assn. Colls. and Univs. (pres. 1972-73), Blue Key, Phi Delta Kappa, Phi Alpha Theta. Presbyn. Club: Rotarian. Home: RR 1 Box 52 Vassar KS 66543-9716

VISSER, LESLEY, sports correspondent; b. Sept. 11, 1953. BA cum laude in English, Boston Coll., 1975; PhD (hon.), Coll. Our Lady of Elms, Mass., 1995. Sports staff Boston Globe, 1974-88; feature reporter, sports staff CBS Sports, 1988-94; corr. GameDay, SportsCenter ESPN, 1994—; sideline reporter coll. football, NFL and Super Bowl ABC, 1994—. Trustee Women's Sports Found., 1993—. Named outstanding woman sportswriter in Am., 1983, New England newswoman of yr.; recipient journalism award Women's Sports Found., 1992. Office: ESPN ESPN Plaza Bristol CT 06010

VISSER, VALYA ELIZABETH, physician; b. Chgo., Oct. 2, 1947; d. Roy Warren and Tania Eugenia (Morozoff) Nelson; children: Kira Elizabeth Visser, Michael Philip Visser. BS, Iowa State U., 1968; MD, U. Iowa, 1973. Diplomate Am. Bd. Pediatrics, Sub-Bd. Neonatal-Perinatal Medicine. Resident pediatrics U. Iowa Hosps. and Clinics, Iowa City, 1976; fellow neonatology Children's Mercy Hosp., Kansas City, 1978; asst. prof. pediatrics U. Kans. Sch. Medicine, Kansas City, 1978-81; staff pediatrician U.S. Army Med. Corps., Ft. Bragg, N.C., 1981-83; attending neonatologist Carolinas Med. Ctr., Charlotte, 1983—; acting chair dept. pediatrics Carolinas Med. Ctr., Charlotte, 1991-94; conf. chair Extracorporeal Life Support Orgn., Ann Arbor, Mich., 1993-95. Major Med. Corps., 1981-83. Fellow Am. Acad. Pediatrics; mem. Soc. for Critical Care Medicine. Mem. Unitarian-Universalist Ch. Avocations: parenting, music. Office: Carolinas Med Ctr Dept Pediatrics PO Box 32861 Charlotte NC 28232-2861

VISWANATH, DABIR SRIKANTIAH, chemical engineer; b. Bangalore, India, Aug. 5, 1934; s. Srikantiah and Kamalamma Viswanath; m. Pramila Viswanath, Jan. 5, 1967; 1 child, Arvind. BS, Mysore U., Bangalore, 1953; DIIS, Indian Inst. of Sci., Bangalore, 1956; MS, U. Rochester, 1960, PhD, 1962. Chemist Essen & Co., Bangalore, 1953-54; chem. engr. Sarabhai Chems., Bangalore, 1956-57; asst. prof. to prof., chmn. Indian Inst. of Sci., Barda, 1965-78; vis. prof. Tex. A&M, College Station, 1978-79; prof. U. Mo., Columbia, 1979-90, prof., chmn., 1990—. Co-author: Data Book on Viscosity of Liquids, 1989; contbr. articles to profl. jours. Pari Hargovandas fellowship Indian Inst. of Sci., Lever Bros. fellowship U. Rochester; recipient Halliburton Travel awards, Mo; grantee NSF, 1985, 1990-91, U. Wis., 1982-83, IBM Corp., 1988-91, USEPA-Kans. State, 1988-91, Waste Mgmt. of N.Am., 1992-93. Fellow AIChE, Am. Inst. Chemists; mem. AAAS, Am. Chem. Soc., Indian Inst. Chem. Engrs., Catalyst Soc. India, Rotary. Achievements include rsch. in the chemistry of ordorant compounds, generalized thermodynamic properties of real gases-generalized compressibility charts, thermodynamic properties of CC14, supercritical extraction, hydrocarbon oxidation, thermophysical properties of gases, liquids and polymer composites. Home: 507 Onofrio Ct Columbia MO 65203-0318 Office: U Mo Dept Chem Engring Columbia MO 65211

VITAGLIANO, KATHLEEN ALYCE FULLER, secondary education educator; b. Oneida, N.Y., May 3, 1949; d. Allen Herbert and Phyllis Ann

(Fearon) Fuller; m. Gene Angelo Vitagliano, Feb. 10, 1973; children: Marissa Ariana, Marc Anthony, Michael Allen. BA in English, SUNY, Buffalo, 1971, EdM in English Education, 1973; cert. Creative Studies, SUC, Buffalo, 1990. Cert. secondary English tchr. N.Y.; cert. sch. dist. adminstr., N.Y. Tchr. English grades 7-12 Buffalo Pub. Schs., N.Y., 1972-93, 95—, tchr. of gifted grades 5-8, 1992—; magnet sch. tchr. specialist Campus West Sch., Buffalo, 1993-95; facilitator Creative Problem Solving, 1990—; workshop presenter Buffalo Tchr. Ctr., N.Y., 1992—. Singer Buffalo Philharm. Chorus, N.Y., 1973—; mem. Just Buffalo Literary Ctr., 1991—; del. Buffalo Tchrs. Fedn., 1992—; bd. dirs. Parent, Tchr. and Student Cmty. Orgn. of City Honors Sch., 1993-97, v.p., 1994-97. Grantee NEH, 1985; recipient Pathfinders award for sch./bus. partnership, 1995; Western N.Y. Writing Project fellow Canisius Coll., 1995. Fellow Western N.Y. Writing Project (steering com., publs. com., workshop presenter 1990—, instr. 1992—, poetry anthology editor/contbr.); mem. NEA, ASCD, N.Y. State English Coun. (tchr. of Excellence award 1991), Nat. Coun. Tchrs. English, Grad. Sch. Edn. Alumni Assn. SUNY Buffalo, Creative Edn. Found., Creative Studies Alumni Assn. State U. Coll. Buffalo (newsletter editor 1991-95, v.p. 1992-96), Advocacy for Gifted and Talented Edn. N.Y., Internat. Creativity Network, Phi Delta Kappa. Avocations: singing, writing poetry, drama, reading. Home: 207 Saranac Ave Buffalo NY 14216-1931 Office: Campus West Sch 1300 Elmwood Ave Buffalo NY 14222-1004

VITALE, ALBERTO ALDO, publishing company executive; b. Vercelli, Italy, Dec. 22, 1933; came to U.S., 1960; s. Sergio and Elena (Segre) V.; m. Gemma G. Calori, Oct. 11, 1961; children—Raffaele Robert, Alessandro David. Dr. Econs. and Bus. Adminstrn., U. Turin, Italy, 1956, postgrad., 1956-57; postgrad. (Fulbright scholar), Wharton Sch. Finance, U. Pa., 1957-58. With Olivetti Corp. Am., 1959-72; dir. corp. planning Olivetti Corp. Am., N.Y.C., 1965-69; v.p. adminstrn. Olivetti Corp. Am., 1969-70; v.p. adminstrn., treas. Olivetti Corp. Am., N.Y.C., 1970-72; prin. officer IFI, Torino, 1972-75; exec. v.p., chief operating officer, dir. Bantam Books, Inc., N.Y.C., 1975-85, pres., 1985-87, co-chief exec. officer, 1985-86, chief exec. officer, 1986-87; pres., chief exec. officer Bantam, Doubleday, Dell Publishing Group, from 1987; now chmn. bd., pres., CEO Random House, N.Y.C.; bd. dirs. Transworld Pubs. Ltd. Mem. Assn. Am. Pubs. (dir. 1979, 86). Home: 505 Alda Rd Mamaroneck NY 10543-4002 Office: Random House Inc 201 E 50th St New York NY 10022-7703*

VITALE, DICK, commentator, sports writer; b. Garfield, N.J.; m. Lorraine Vitale; children: Terri, Sherri. Basketball coach East Rutherford (N.J.) High Sch., 1965-71; asst. basketball coach Rutgers U., New Brunswick, N.J., 1972; coll. basketball coach U. Detroit, 1973-77, athletic dir., 1978; pro basketball coach Detroit Pistons, Auburn Hills, Mich., 1978-79; TV commentator ESPN Sports, 1979—, ABC Sports, 1987—; sports radio commentator ABC Radio Network, 1987—; sports columnist Basketball Times, 1979—, Ea. Basketball, 1979—; radio commentator The J. P. McCarthy Show, Detroit; guest spkr., lectr. Co-author: (with Curay Kirk Patrick) Vitale: Just Your Average, Bald, One-Eyed Basketball Wacko Who Beat the Ziggy and Became a PTP'er, 1989, (with Dick Weiss) Time Out, Baby!, 1992, (with Mike Douchant) Tourney Time, It's Awesome Baby, 1994; co-author various computer games; appeared in TV commls. for Adidas, Taco Bell. Named Sports Personality of Yr., Am. Sportscasters Assn., 1989. Roman Catholic. Earned 5 sectional and 2 consecutive state championships as high sch. basketball coach. Office: IMG Peter Goldberg 22 E 71st St New York NY 10021-4911*

VITALE, PAUL, accountant; b. Bklyn., Oct. 7, 1958; s. Joseph A. and Joan J. (Pecoraro) V.; m. Marie N. Barbieri, Mar. 28, 1982; children: Michelle, Stephen, Jaclyn. BS in Acctg. magna cum laude, St. John's U., 1979. CPA, N.Y. Sr. mgr. Arthur Andersen & Co., Melville, N.Y., 1979-90; v.p. fin., treas., sec. Barron's Ednl. Series, Inc., Hauppauge, N.Y., 1990-93; sole practice in pub. acctg. Garden City, 1993—; bd. dirs. Comml. Capital Corp. Bd. dirs., treas. North Shore Child and Family Guidance Assn., 1995. Named Outstanding Young Man Am., 1985; recipient Regents scholarship N.Y. State Dept. Edn., 1976, St. John's U. Scholastic Excellence award, 1976. Mem. AICPA, N.Y. State Soc. CPAs (instr. Suffolk County chpt. 1991, 92), Mineola-Garden City Rotary Club (bd. dirs. 1996). Avocations: golf, collectibles. Office: 106 7th St Ste 201 Garden City NY 11530

VITALIANO, CHARLES J(OSEPH), geologist, educator; b. N.Y.C., Apr. 2, 1910; s. Joseph and Catherine (deBarberi) V.; m. Dorothy A. Brauneck, Oct. 19, 1940; children: Judith E., Peter W. B.S., CCNY, 1936; A.M., Columbia U., 1938, Ph.D. (James Furman Kemp fellow), 1944. Instr. extension div. Columbia U., 1938-40; instr. ceramics dept. Rutgers U., 1940-42; geologist U.S. Geol. Survey, 1942-47; asso. prof. geology Ind. U., Bloomington, 1947-57; prof. Ind. U., 1957-80, prof. emeritus, 1980—; prof. field geology Ind. U. Field Sta. in Mont., summers, 1948-50, 58-74; mem. sci. adv. com. Ind. U., 1979-81; chmn. Ind. U. Credit Union, 1967-68, bd. dirs., 1966-84; prof. field geology U.S. Geol. Survey, Nev. and N.Mex., summers 1950-58; cons. Earth Resources Tech. Satellite project, U. Mont., summer 1973; geol. cons. archaeol. projects, Greece, summers, 1971, 74, 78, 79. Contbr. articles to profl. jours. Fulbright sr. research fellow N.Z., 1954-55; Fulbright lectr. Australia, 1955; NSF grantee, 1957-61, 66-72; recipient Outstanding Teaching award Ind. U., 1982. Fellow Geol. Soc. Am. (chmn. archaeol. geology div. 1985—), AAAS, Mineral. Soc. Am.; mem. Geochem. Soc., Soc. Econ. Geologists. Unitarian.

VITALIANO, ERIC NICHOLAS, state legislator, lawyer; b. S.I., N.Y., Feb. 27, 1948; m. Helen M. Fleming, Sept. 9, 1983; children: Michael, Emma, Abigail. AB, Fordham Coll., 1968; JD cum laude, NYU, 1971; postgrad., U. Colo., 1977. Bar: N.Y. 1971. Law clk. to Mark A Costantino, U.S. Dist. Ct. for Ea. Dist. N.Y., N.Y.C., 1971-72; assoc. Simpson Thacher & Bartlett, N.Y.C., 1972-79; chief staff to Congressman John M. Murphy U.S. Ho. of Reps., N.Y.C., 1979-80; mem. Russo, Silverman & Vitaliano, N.Y.C., 1982-86, N.Y. Assembly, Albany, 1982—; counsel Behrins & Behrins, N.Y.C., 1995—; counsel to Behrins & Behrins, P.C., Staten Island, 1995—. Rsch. editor NYU Law Rev., 1970-71. Co-founder Citizens Against Bus Exhaust; co-founder Bodine Creek Civic Assn.; former parish chmn. Cardinal's Archdiocesan Appeal; mem. Dem. Com. Richmond County, N.Y.; past pres. N.Y. Conf. Italian-Am. State Legislators; past adv. Assumption Coun., K.C. Recipient Stella Falletta Meml. award Clifton Homeowners and Tenants Assn., S.I., 1986, Aldo R. Benedetto Outstanding Citizen award Am. Legion, 1994; named Dem. of Yr., Young Dems. Richmond County, 1980, Friend of Edn., Susan E. Wagner H.S., S.I., 1983, Legislator of Yr., N.Y. State Clks. Assn., 1987, Friend of Italian-Am. Inst. Inst., CUNY, 1990, Man of Yr., Italian Club S.I., 1991, Man of the Yr., Met. Police Conf. of N.Y. State, 1995. Mem. ABA, KC (past advisor Assumption coun. S.I.), Order of Coif. Home: 130 Chapin Ave Staten Island NY 10304-2927 Office: NY State Assembly 839 Legislative Office Bldg Albany NY 12248

VITEK, VACLAV, materials scientist; b. Olomouc, Czechoslovakia, Sept. 10, 1940; came to U.S., 1978; s. Josef and Ruzena V.; m. Ludovita Stankovicova, Aug. 5, 1972; children: Adrian Joseph, Clementine Mary. BSc in Physics, Charles U., Prague, 1962; PhD in Physics, Czechoslovakian Acad. Scis., Prague, 1966. Research assoc. dept. metall. materials sci. and research fellow Wolfson Coll., Oxford (Eng.) U., 1967-75; research officer Central Elec. Research Labs., Central Elec. Generating Bd., Leatherhead, Eng., 1975-78; prof. materials sci. and engring. U. Pa., 1978—; vis. prf. U. Groningen, The Netherlands, 1985-86. Recipient Humboldt award for sr. scientists, Germany, 1992-93, Acta metallurgica Gold medal, 1996. Fellow Inst. Physics (London), Am. Soc. Metals Internat.; mem. Am. Phys. Soc., Materials Rsch. Soc. Research on atomistic models of lattice defects, interfaces and amorphous structures, fracture processes and mechanisms, plastic deformation, intermetallic compounds. Office: U Pa Dept Materials Sci and Engring 3231 Walnut St Philadelphia PA 19104-6202

VITERBI, ANDREW JAMES, electrical engineering and computer science educator, business executive; b. Bergamo, Italy, Mar. 9, 1935; came to U.S., 1939, naturalized, 1945; s. Achille and Maria (Luria) V.; m. Erna Finci, June 15, 1958; children: Audrey, Alan, Alexander. SB, MIT, 1957, SM, 1957; PhD, U. So. Calif., 1962; DEng (honoris causa), U. Waterloo, 1990. Research group supr. C.I.T. Jet Propulsion Lab., 1957-63; mem. faculty Sch. Engring. and Applied Sci., UCLA, 1963-73, assoc. prof., 1965-69, prof., 1969-73; exec. v.p. Linkabit Corp., 1973-82; pres. M/A-Com Linkabit, Inc., 1982-84; chief scientist, sr. v.p. M/A-Com. Inc., 1985; prof. elec. engring. and computer sci. U. Calif., San Diego, 1985-94; vice chmn. Qualcomm Inc., 1985—; chmn. U.S. Commn. C, URSI, 1982-85; vis. com. dept. elec. engring. and computer sci. MIT, 1984—. Author: Principles of Coherent Communication, 1966, CDMA: Principles of Spread Spectrum Communications, 1995, (with J. K. Omura) Principles of Digital Communication and Coding, 1979; bd. editors: Information and Control, 1967, Transactions on Info. Theory, 1972-75. Recipient award for valuable contbns. to telemetry, space electonics and telemetry group IRE, 1962, best original paper award Nat. Electronics Conf., 1963, outstanding papers award, info. theory group IEEE, 1968, Christopher Columbus Internat. Comms. award, 1975, Aerospace Comm. award AIAA, 1980, Outstanding Engring. Grad. award U. So. Calif., 1986; co-recipient NEC Corp. C and C Found. award, 1992, S.O. Rice award, 1994, Edward Rhein Found. award, 1994; Marconi Internat. fellow, 1990. Fellow IEEE (Alexander Graham Bell medal 1984, Shannon lectr. internat. symposium on info. theory 1991); mem. NAE, NAS. Office: Qualcomm Inc 6455 Lusk Blvd San Diego CA 92121-2779

VITEZ, MICHAEL, reporter; b. Washington, 1957; m. Maureen Fitzgerald; children: Timmy, Sally, Jonathan. Degree, U. Va., 1979. Past reporter Hartford Courant, Washington Star, Virginian-Pilot, Norfolk; reporter Phila. Inquirer, 1985—. Office: Phila Inquirer PO Box 8263 Philadelphia PA 19101*

VITIELLO, JUSTIN, language educator; b. N.Y., Feb. 14, 1941; s. Michael and Ruth (Weishaupt) V.; 1 child, Domenic. BA in English and Spanish, Brown U., 1963; MA in Spanish, U. Mich., 1966, PhD in Comparative Lit., 1970. Asst. prof. comparative lit. U. Mich., Ann Arbor, 1970-73; from asst. prof. to assoc. prof. Italian Temple U., Phila., 1974-91, prof. Italian, 1991—. Author: Confessions of a Joe Rock, 1992, Poetics and Literature of the Sicilian Diaspora, 1993, (essays) Sicily Within, 1991, (poems) Vanzetti's Fish Cart, 1991, Subway Home, 1994. Grantee Fulbright, 1963-64. Mem. MLA, Arba Sicula (editl. bd.), Indsl. Workers World. Avocation: woodworking. Office: Temple U Dept French/Italian Philadelphia PA 19122

VITKOWSKY, VINCENT JOSEPH, lawyer; b. Newark, Oct. 3, 1955; s. Boniface and Rosemary (Ofack) V.; m. Mary Gunzburg, May 16, 1981 (div. 1997); children: Vincent Jr., Victoria. BA, Northwestern U., 1977; JD, Cornell U., 1980. Bar: N.Y. 1981. Assoc. Hart and Hume, N.Y.C., 1980-84, Kroll & Tract, N.Y.C., 1984-87; of counsel Nixon, Hargrave, Devans & Doyle, N.Y.C., 1988-89; ptnr. Buchalter, Nemer, Fields & Younger, N.Y.C., 1990-95, Edwards & Angell, N.Y.C., 1996—; lectr. industry and bar groups. Contbr. articles to profl. jours. Mem. ABA (com. chmn.), Am. Arbitration Assn., Internat. Bar Assn. (com. officer), Assn. Bar City of N.Y., Bus. Execs. for Nat. Security, Cornell Club, Amnesty Internat. Human Rights Watch. Home: 16 Weed St New Canaan CT 06840-6111 Office: Edwards & Angell 750 Lexington Ave New York NY 10022-1200

VITT, DAVID AARON, medical manufacturing company executive; b. Phila., Aug. 3, 1938; s. Nathan and Flora B.; m. Renee Lee Salkever, Oct. 20, 1963; children: Nadine Lori Einiger, Jeffrey Richard. BS, Temple U., 1961. Sales engr. Picker X-Ray Corp., Phila., 1961-65; sales engr. Midwest Am., Chgo., 1965-67, product mgr., 1967-68, product mgr. regional sales, 1968-70; dir. mktg. Valtronic & Living Wills, Bronx, N.Y., 1970-74; v.p. Siemens Med. Systems Inc., gen. mgr. dental div., Iselin, N.J., 1974-86, past corp. v.p.; CEO, pres. Pelton & Crane, Charlotte, N.C., 1986-89; v.p. govt. sales Siemens Med. Systems Corp. Officers, ret., 1994; founder, pres., CEO D.A.V., Inc., 1995—; founder, co-owner The Med. Inter Network, Ltd., 1997; industry rep. to Am. Nat. Standards Inst.; co. rep. U.S.-USSR Trade and Econ. Coun.; mem. exec. com. Jr. Achievement, Charlotte. Bd. dirs. Am. Fund for Dental Health; apptd. mem. Charlotte Mecklenburg Community Relations Com.; mem. bd. visitors, bd. vis. U. N.C., Charlotte; Jr. Achievement exec com. mem., officer. Served in USAR, 1961-68. Mem. Am. Mgmt. Assn. (bd. dirs. N.J. chpt.), Am. Mktg. Assn., Am. Dental Trade Assn. (bd. dirs.), Dental Mfrs. Am. (past pres.), Am. Acad. Dental Radiology, Charlotte C. of C. (bd. advisors), Acad. Gen. Dentists (bd. mem. found.), Masons (32 deg.), Shriners. Republican.

VITT, SAMUEL BRADSHAW, communications media services executive; b. Greensboro, N.C., Oct. 23, 1926; s. Bruno Caesar and Gray (Bradshaw) V.; m. Marie Foster, Oct. 30, 1955; children: Joanne Louise, Michael Bradshaw, Mark Thomas. A.B., Dartmouth Coll., 1950. Exec. asst. TV film CBS, N.Y.C., 1950-52; broadcast media buyer Benton & Bowles, Inc., N.Y.C., 1952-54; broadcast media buyer Biow Co., N.Y.C., 1954-55, assoc. account exec., 1955-56; advt. dir. Banking Law Jour., 1955-69; broadcast media buyer Doherty, Clifford, Steers & Shenfield, Inc., N.Y.C., 1956-57, media supr., 1958-59, v.p., media supr., 1960, v.p., assoc. media dir., 1960, v.p., media dir., 1960-63, v.p. in charge media and broadcast programming, 1963-64; v.p., exec. dir. media-program dept. Ted Bates & Co., Inc., N.Y.C., 1964-66, sr. v.p., exec. dir. media-program dept., 1966-69; dir. Advt. Info. Services, Inc., 1964-65; founder, pres. Vitt Media Internat., Inc., N.Y.C., 1969-81, chmn., CEO, 1982-91, chmn. emeritus, 1991—; lectr. in field, 1967—; lectr. advt. media NYU, 1973, 74, Am. Mgmt. Assn., 1974, 75, Assn. Nat. Advertisers, 1967, 69, 70, Advt. Age Media Workshop, 1975. Media columnist Madison Ave, 1963-68; editorial cons. Media/Scope, 1968-69; contbr. Advertising Procedure, 1969, rev. edit., 1973, 5th, 6th, 7th edits., 1977, Exploring Advertising, 1970; contbg. editor Handbook of Advertising Management, 1970; contbg. editor Nation's Bus., Broadcasting, Variety, Anny, TV/Radio Age, Sponsor, Printer's Ink; producer rec. album The Body in the Seine; cover story guest editor Media Decisions, 1967. Chmn. radio-TV reps. divsn. Greater N.Y. Fund, 1962, chmn. consumer pub. divsn., 1963; mem. Nat. UN Day Com., 1973, vice chmn., 1974, assoc. chmn. 1975, co-chmn., 1976-77; bd. dirs. UN Assn. Am., 1977; bd. dirs., chmn. Rsch. Inst. Hearing and Balance Disorders Ltd., 1979—; mem. advt. adv. com. The Acting Com., 1984; mem. Pres. Reagan's Joint Presdl. Congl. Steering Com., 1982, Bush Presdl. Roundtable, 1990—. Served to Lt. (j.g.) USN, 1944-46. Recipient Media awards Sta. WRAP, Norfolk, Va., 1962, award of Merit Greater N.Y. Fund, 1963, Gold Key Advt. Leadership award Sta. Reps. Assn., 1967, ann. honors Ad Daily, 1967, Cert. Merit Media/Scope, 1967, 69, Creative Pub. Statement Concerning Advt. award, Cert. of Appreciation, U.S. Congress, 1993, Rep. Congl. Order Liberty, Nat. Rep. Congl. Com., 1993, Order of Merit, Nat. Rep. Senatorial Com., 1994, Rep. Presdl. award Pres. Ronald Reagan and Rep. Senate Leadership, 1994, (with wife) Rep. Senatorial Medal of Freedom, 1994; named one of 10 Best Dressed Men in Advt. Cmty., Gentlemen's Quar., 1979; honoree (with wife) New Rochelle Hosp. Med. Ctr. Centennial Waldorf-Astoria Gala, 1992. Mem. Am. Assn. Advt. Agys. (broadcast media com. dir. corr. 1958-63, media operating com. on consumer mags. 1964-65), Internat. Radio and TV Soc. (time-buying and selling seminar com. dir. 1961-62), Internat. Radio and TV Found. (faculty seminar 1974), Nat. Acad. Arts Sci. (mem. com. dir.), Media Dirs. Coun., Sigma Alpha Epsilon, Manor Park Beach Club, N.Y. Athletic Club, Roxbury Run Club (N.Y., Denver). Presbyterian. Avocations: tennis, skiing, golf, swimming, chess. Home: 3 Roosevelt Ave Larchmont NY 10538-2912

VITTER, JEFFREY SCOTT, computer science educator, consultant; b. New Orleans, Nov. 13, 1955; s. Albert Leopold Jr. and Audrey Malvina (St. Raymond) V.; m. Sharon Louise Weaver, Aug. 14, 1982; children: Jillian St. Raymond, J. Scott Jr., Audrey Louise. BS in Math. with honors, U. Notre Dame, 1977; PhD in Computer Sci., Stanford U., 1980; AM (hon.), Brown U., 1986. Teaching fellow Stanford (Calif.) U., 1979; from asst. prof. to prof. Brown U., Providence, 1980-93; Gilbert, Louis and Edward Lehrman prof. computer sci. Duke U., Durham, N.C., 1993—, chmn. dept., 1993—; cons. IBM, 1981-86, Inst. for Def. Analyses, 1986, Ctr. for Computing Scis., 1992—, Lucent Technologies, Bell Labs., 1997; mem. rsch. staff Math. Scis. Rsch. Inst., Berkeley, 1986, Inst. Recherche en Informatique et en Automatique, Roquencourt, France, 1986-87; vis. prof. Ecole Normale Superieure, Paris, 1986-89; vis. and adj. prof. Tulane U., 1990—; lectr. Asian Sch. on Computer Sci., Bangkok, 1987; assoc. mem. Ctr. Excellence in Space Data and Info. Scis. Author: The Design and Analysis of Coalesced Hashing, 1987; editor Algorithmica, 1988, 94—, guest editor, 1994; guest editor Math. Sys. Theory: Internat. Jour. on Math. Computing Theory, 1991—, Soc. for Indsl. and Applied Math. Jour. on Computing, 1989—; contbr. articles to profl. jours.; patentee in field. Recipient Faculty Devel. award IBM, 1984, NSF Presdl. Young Investigator award, 1985; NSF grad. fellow, 1977-80; Guggenheim fellow, N.Y.C., 1986-87. Fellow IEEE (editor Trans. on Computers 1985, 87-91), Assn. for Computing Machinery (editor Comms. 1988-95, mem.-at-large spl. interest group on automata and computability theory 1987-91, vice chair spl. interest group on algorithms and computation theory 1991—); mem. Phi Beta Kappa, Sigma Xi. Avocations: reading, golf, basketball, baseball, football. Office: Duke U Dept Computer Sci Durham NC 27708-0129

VITTETOE, MARIE CLARE, retired clinical laboratory science educator; b. Keota, Iowa, May 19, 1927; d. Edward Daniel and Marcella Matilda Vittetoe. BS, Marycrest Coll., 1950; MS, W.Va. U., 1971, EdD, 1973. Staff technologist St. Joseph Hosp., Ottumwa, Iowa, 1950-70; instr. Ottumwa Hosp. Sch. Med. Tech., 1957-70, St. Joseph Hosp. Sch. Nursing, Ottumwa, 1950-70; asst. prof. U. Ill., Champaign-Urbana, 1973-78; prof. clin. lab. scis. U. Ky., Lexington, 1978-94. Contbr. articles to profl. jours. Recipient Kingston award for Creative Teaching; Recognition award for svc. to edn. Commonwealth of Ky. Coun. on Higher Edn., disting. grad. award Nat. Cath. Ednl. Assn., 1995, devel. of youth award Iowa 4-H Found., 1996; named Ky. Col. Mem. Am. Soc. for Med. Tech. (chmn. 1986-89, Profl. Achievement award 1991, Ky. Mem. of Yr. award 1994), Am. Soc. Clin. Lab. Scis., Am. Soc. Clin. Pathologists (assoc.), Alpha Mu Tau, Phi Delta Kappa, Alpha Eta. Avocation: bicycling.

VITTORINI, CARLO, publishing company executive; b. Phila., Feb. 28, 1929; s. Domenico and Helen (Whitney) V.; m. Alice Hellerman, Oct. 10, 1953 (div. Dec. 1993); children: Carolyn, Stephen Whitney; m. Nancy Braddock, Dec. 19, 1993. B.A., U. Pa., 1950. Promotion assoc. Chilton Co., Phila., 1950-51; merchandising mgr. Farm-Jour., Inc., Phila., 1951-53; advt. sales rep. Saturday Evening Post, Phila., 1953-61; assoc. advt. mgr. Look Mag., N.Y.C., 1961-65; publisher Redbook Mag., N.Y.C., 1965-75; pres. Charter Publishing, N.Y.C., 1975-78, Harlequin Publishing, N.Y.C., 1978—; chmn. pub., chief exec. officer Parade Publications subs. Advance Pubs. Inc., N.Y.C., 1979—. Trustee The Jackson Lab., Bar Harbor, Maine, 1973—; former mem. vestry St. Matthew's Ch., Bedford, N.Y. Served with USAR, 1950-57. Judge Advt. Hall of Fame, Am. Advt. Fedn. Mem. Advt. Coun. N.Y.C. (dir.-at-large 1974—), Mag. Pubs. Assn. (bd. dirs. 1970-79), Am. Advt. Fedn. (chmn. 1992-93), The Sky Club. Avocations: outdoor activities; tennis. Home: 40 Dusenberry Rd Bronxville NY 10708-2421 Office: Parade Publications 711 3rd Ave New York NY 10017-4014

VITZ, PAUL CLAYTON, psychologist, educator; b. Toledo, Aug. 27, 1935; m. Evelyn Birge; 6 children. BA high honors in Psychology, U. Mich., 1953; PhD, Stanford U., 1962. Instr. psychology Pomona (Calif.) Coll., 1962-64; asst. prof. NYU, 1965-70, assoc. prof., 1970-85, dir. psychology dept. undergrad. program, 1973-79, prof., 1985—, acting dir. master's program, 1988-89, 90-91, acting dir. grad. program, 1989-90; adj. prof. John Paul II Inst. on Marriage and Family, Washington, 1990—, Internat. Acad. Philosophy, 1994—; lectr. in field. Author: Psychology as Religion: The Cult of Self-Worship, 1977, 2d edit., 1994, (with A.B. Glimcher) Modern Art and Modern Science: The Parallel Analysis of Vision, 1984, Censorship: Evidence of Bias in Our Children's Textbooks, 1986, Sigmund Freud's Christian Unconscious, 1988; contbr. articles to profl. jours., chpts. to books. Rsch. grantee Nat. Inst. Mental Health, 1963-64, 64-66, 66-67, Nat. Inst. Neurol. Diseases and Blindness grantee, 1970-73, 73-74, Shalom Found. grantee, 1974-78, Nat. Inst. Edn. grantee, 1983, 84-85, Dept. Edn. grantee, 1986-87. Office: NYU Dept Psychology New York NY 10003

VIVERITO, LOUIS S., state legislator; m. Carolyn Strobl; children: Dean, Diane, Marianne. Mem. Ill. State Senate, 1995—. Mem. Stickney Twp. Dem. Com., 1969—; del. Dem. Nat. Conv., 1972; commr. Met. Sanitary Dist. Greater Chgo., 1980-86; mem. Cook County Zoning Bd. Appeals, 1987-95; local chmn. Chgo. Lung Assn., 1973—. Named Man of Yr., Joint Civic Com. Italian-Am., 1980; inductee Hall of Fame, Valentine Boys & Girls Club, 198. Mem. VFW (life), Am. Legion (life), Burbank C. of C., Burbank Sertoma Club (founder).

VIVIAN, GLADYS LILY, administrator social services; b. Rencuntre East, Can., Apr. 22, 1945; d. Waldron Keeping and Frances Mullins; m. John R. Courage, Dec. 27, 1963 (div. Jan. 1987); children: Angela, John; m. Herbert Alan Vivian, July 4, 1987. BSW, Meml. U., St. John's, Newfoundland, Can., 1980. Social worker Dept. of Social Svcs., St. John's, 1980-82; human rights officer Dept. of Justice, St. John's, 1982-86; exec. dir. Human Rights Commn., St. John's, 1986—, acting dir. labour stds., 1995—. Mem. Can. Assn. Statutory Human Rights Agys., Can. Assn. Adminstrs. Labour Legislation, Pub. Svc. Mgrs. Assn. Avocations: painting, walking, gardening, traveling. Office: Human Rights Commn, Box 8700, Saint Johns, NF Canada A1B 4J6

VIVIANO, SAM JOSEPH, illustrator; b. Detroit, Mar. 13, 1953; s. Thomas John Viviano and Prudy Katherine (DiGiuseppe) LaMendola; m. Diane E. Bloomfield, Sept. 3, 1988; 1 child, Alicia Catherine Viviano. BFA, U. Mich., 1975. Textile designer Manes Fabric Co., N.Y.C., 1976-77; freelance illustrator N.Y.C., 1976—; art instr. Sch. Visual Arts, N.Y.C., 1981-93, Pratt Manhattan Sch. Art, 1992—. Mem. Graphic Artists Guild (chmn. N.Y.C. chpt. 1981-87, treas. 1987-89). Office: 25 W 13th St New York NY 10011-7955

VIZARD, FRANK JOSEPH, journalist; b. N.Y.C., July 7, 1955; s. Matthew Joseph and Anne (Tierney) V. BA, NYU, 1977. News editor Paper Trade Jour., N.Y.C., 1977-78; mng. editor Paperboard Packaging, N.Y.C., 1978-80; editor Autosound & Communications, N.Y.C., 1980-84; freelance writer N.Y.C., 1984-90; electronics and photography editor Popular Mechanics mag., N.Y.C., 1990-96; tech. editor Popular Sci. mag., N.Y.C., 1996—. Avocations: basketball, Irish affairs, sports science. Office: Popular Mechanics Mag 224 W 57th St New York NY 10019-3212

VIZCAINO, JOSE LUIS PIMENTAL, professional baseball player; b. San Cristobal, Dominican Rep., Mar. 26, 1965. Grad. high sch., Dominican Rep. With L.A. Dodgers, 1989-90, Chgo. Cubs, 1991-93; infielder N.Y. Mets, 1994-96; with Cleve. Indians, 1996, San Francisco Giants, 1997—. Office: San Francisco Giants Candlestick Park San Francisco CA 94124*

VIZQUEL, OMAR ENRIQUE, professional baseball player; b. Caracus, Venezuela, Apr. 24, 1967. Grad. high sch., Caracus. With Seattle Mariners, 1989-93; shortstop Cleve. Indians, 1993—. Recipient Winner Am. League Golden Glove, 1993-96. Office: Cleve Indians 2401 Ontario St Cleveland OH 44115-4003*

VIZZA, ROBERT FRANCIS, hospital executive, former university administrator, marketing educator; b. N.Y.C., Apr. 2, 1933; s. Saverio and Agatha (Costanzo) V.; m. Joan Kilday, Dec. 11, 1954; children: Lorraine, Mary, Cathy, Robert. BBA, Pace Coll., 1954; MBA, CUNY, 1959; PhD, NYU, 1967; LLD (hon.), LaSalle Coll., 1978. Account exec. Diebold Inc., N.Y.C., 1954-61; asst. prof. mktg. St. John's U., 1962-66; assoc. prof. mktg., chmn. dept. bus. adminstrn. C.W. Post Coll., 1966-67; dean Sch. Bus., prof. mktg. Manhattan Coll., 1967-85; pres., CEO St. Francis Hosp., Roslyn, N.Y., 1985-95, vice chmn., 1995—; pres., CEO, St. Francis Corp., 1985-96, St. Francis Hosp. Found., Ind., 1985—, St. Francis Rsch. and Ednl. Corp., 1985—, St. Francis Mercy Corp., 1996—; cons. to industry; bd. dirs. Emery Air Freight Corp., Am. Assembly Collegiate Schs. Bus., The Green Point Savs. Bank, Phoenix Home Life, Ins., Green Point Fins., Holding Co., Greater N.Y. Hosp. Assn. Author: Improving Salesmen's Use of Time, 1962, Measuring the Value of the Field Sales Force, Training and Developing the Field Sales Manager, 1965, Basic Facts in Marketing, 1966, Adoption of the Marketing Concept, 1967, New Handbook of Sales Training, 1967, Time and Territory Management, 1972, Time and Territorial Management-A Programmed Learning Course, 1975, 2d edit., 1979; contbr. articles to profl. jours. Pres. bd. St. Mary's Sch.; bd. dirs. Pace U., Sch. of the Holy Child. Ford Found. fellow; recipient Jerome Levy Found. award. Fellow Internat. Acad. Mgmt.; mem. Middle Atlantic Assn. Colls. of Bus., Adminstrn. (v.p. 1970-71, pres. 1972-73, exec. com. 1969—), Sales Execs. Club N.Y. (bd. dirs.), Am. Mktg. Assn., Delta Sigma Pi, Delta Mu Delta, Pi Sigma Epsilon. Home: 3 Maria Ln Old Brookville NY 11545-2507 Office: St Francis Mercy Corp Northern Blvd Glen Head NY 11545

VLACH, JIRI, electrical engineering educator, researcher; b. Prague, Czechoslovakia, Oct. 5, 1922; emigrated to Can., 1969; s. Frantisek and Bozena (Papouskova) V.; m. Dagmar Gutova, Oct. 22, 1949; 1 son, Martin. Dipl.eng., Tech. U. Prague, 1947, C.Sc., 1957. With Research Inst. for Radio Communications, Prague, 1948-67; head math. dept. Research Inst. for Radio Communications, until 1967; vis. prof. U. Ill., Urbana, 1967-69; prof. elec. engring. U. Waterloo (Ont., Can.), 1969—. Author: Computerized Approximation and Synthesis of Linear Networks, 1969, (with others) Computer Methods for Circuit Analysis and Design, 1983, 2nd edit., 1994, Basic Network Theory with Computer Applications, 1992; assoc. editor IEEE Trans. on Circuits and Systems, 1979-80. Fellow IEEE; mem. Eta Kappa Nu. Home: 355 Craigleith Dr, Waterloo, ON Canada N2L 5B5 Office: University Waterloo, 200 University Ave West, Waterloo, ON Canada N2L 3G1

VLADECK, BRUCE CHARNEY, charitable organization executive; b. N.Y.C., Sept. 13, 1949; s. Stephen Charney and Judith (Pomarlen) V.; m. Fredda Wellin, Aug. 5, 1973; children—Elizabeth Charney, Stephen Isaiah, Abigail Sarah. B.A., Harvard U., 1970; M.A., U. Mich, 1972, Ph.D. in Polit. Sci., 1973. Assoc. social scientist N.Y.C.-Rand Inst., 1973-74; asst. prof. Columbia U., N.Y.C., 1974-78; assoc. prof. Columbia U., 1978-79; asst. commr. health planning and resources devel. N.J. Dept. Health, Trenton, 1979-82; asst. v.p. Robert Wood Johnson Found., Princeton, N.J., 1982-83; pres. United Hosp. Fund, N.Y.C., 1983—; now admstr. Dept. Health & Human Services, Washington; adj. prof. pub. adminstrn. NYU, 1984—; cons. U.S. Gen. Acctg. Office, other agys., Washington, 1984—; mem. N.Y. State Coun. on Health Care Financing, Albany, 1978—; mem. com. on nursing home regulation Inst. Medicine, Washington, 1983-85, chmn. com. on health care for homeless people, 1986-88, mem. prospective payment assessment com., 1986—. Author: Unloving Care: The Nursing Home Tragedy, 1981. Contbr. numerous articles to profl. publs. Fellow N.Y. Acad. Medicine; mem. Inst. Medicine, Nat. Acad. Scis., Phi Beta Kappa. Home: 161 W 15th St New York NY 10011 Office: Dept of Health & Human Services Healthcare Financing Admin 200 Independence Ave SW # 314G Washington DC 20201-0004*

VLADEM, PAUL JAY, investment advisor, broker; b. Chgo., Apr. 5, 1952; s. Arthur I. and Elaine A. (Ascher) V.; m. Sondra Joyce Berman, Dec. 27, 1981; children: Ashley Sherree, Evan David. BSBA with honors and high distinction, U. Ill., Chgo., 1974. Lic. brokerage securities, Fla., Ill., Ariz., Conn., Ga., Ind., N.C., Colo., Md., Nev., N.Y., Ohio, Calif., Utah; registered investment advisor; lic. ins. agt., Fla., Ill., Ind., Utah, Conn.; CPA, Fla., Ill.; lic. real estate agt., Fla. In charge acct. Peat Marwick, Fort Lauderdale, Fla., 1974-76; mgr. McGladrey & Pullen, CPA, Fort Lauderdale, 1976-85; sr. v.p. fin. Integrated Resources formerly Easter Kramer, Boca Raton, Fla., 1985-89; pres. Associated Investor Svcs., Fort Lauderdale, 1989—. Bd. dirs. Israel Bonds, Ft. Lauderdale, 1994, Jewish Family Svc., Ft. Lauderdale, 1993; chmn. CPA Com. on Israel Bonds, Ft. Lauderdale, 1994; chmn. investment com. Jewish Fedn. Found., Hollywood, Fla., 1994—, mem. prof. adv. com., 1992—. Named One of Top Ten Brokers of Yr. Registered Rep. Mag., 1994. Mem. AICPA (personal planning divsn.), Fla. Inst. CPAs (mem. personal fin. planning com., 1985), Internat. Platform Assn. Democrat. Jewish. Avocations: tennis, basketball, attending sporting events. Home: 11157 NW 18th Ct Coral Springs FL 33071 Office: Associated Investor Svcs 2699 Stirling Rd Ste A-200 Fort Lauderdale FL 33312-6517

VLCEK, DONALD JOSEPH, JR., food distribution company executive, consultant; b. Chgo., Oct. 30, 1949; s. Donald Joseph and Rosemarie (Krizek) V.; m. Claudia Germain Meyer, July 22, 1978 (div. 1983); 1 child, Suzanne Mae; m. Valeria Olive Russell, Nov. 11, 1989; children: James Donald, Victoria Rose. BBA, U. Mich., 1971. Gen. mgr. Popps, Inc., Hamtramck, Mich., 1969-76; pres. Domino's Pizza Distbn. Corp., Ann Arbor, Mich., 1978-93, chmn., 1993-94, also bd. dirs.; pres. Don Vlcek & Assocs., Ltd., Plymouth, Mich., 1994—; profl. speaker; trustee Domino's Pizza Ptnrs. Found.; bd. dirs. RPM Pizza Inc., Gulfport, Miss., Dimango Corp., South Lyon, Mich.; sr. v.p. distbn. and tech. Domino's Ohio Commissary, Zanesville; pres. Morel Mountain Corp.; judge 1994 Duck Stamp contest U.S. Dept. Interior, Jr. Fed. Duck Stamp Contest, 1995. Author: The Domino Effect, 1991 (Best of Bus. award ALA 1992, Soundview's Top 30 Business books of 1993), Supervisor, 1997, Job Planning and Review System Update Manual, 1997; (audio cassette tape series Super Vision; contbr. articles to profl. jours. Bd. dirs. Men's Hockey League of Oak Park, Mich., 1973-78. Named Person of Yr. Bd. Franchises, Boston, 1981; recipient Teal award Ducks Unltd., 1992, State Major Gifts Chmn. award, 1992, 93, State Chmn.'s award, 1992, State Major Gifts award, 1994. Mem. Mich. Steelheaders Assn. (life), Ducks Unltd. (life, Domino's Pizza chpt. treas., sponsor, chmn. 1988—, Mich. state bd. dirs., life sponsor, chmn. 1989, 91-92, state trustee 1992—, chmn. exec. com. 1992-94, major gifts chmn. 1993—, chmn. strategic devel. com. 1994, sponsor in perpetuity Grand Slam Life), Mich. United Conservation Club (life), Whitetails Unltd. (life), Pheasants Forever (life), Midstates Masters Bowling Assn. (bd. dirs. 1976-85), Barton Hills Country Club (golf com., capt. dist. team), U. Mich. Alumni Assn. (life), Domino's Lodge/Drummond Island Wildlife Habitat Found. (pres., chmn. bd.), Vlcek Family Wildlife Found. (pres., chmn. bd.), Elks (life), Die Hard Cubs Fan Club, Profl. Spkrs. Assn. of Mich. (bd. dirs. 1997—), Greater Detroit C. of C., Nat. Spkrs. Assn., Profl. Spkrs. Ill. Republican. Roman Catholic. Avocations: hunting, fishing, hockey, collecting wildlife art, coins, and sports cards and memorabilia. Home: 9251 Beck Rd N Plymouth MI 48170-3336 Office: Don Vlcek & Assoc Ltd PO Box 701353 Plymouth MI 48170-0963

VLIET, GARY CLARK, mechanical engineering educator; b. Bassano, Alta., Can., June 3, 1933. B.Sc. in Chem. Engring, U. Alta., 1955; M.S. in Mech. Engring, Stanford U., 1957, Ph.D., 1962. With Lockheed Research Labs., Palo Alto, Calif., 1961-71; mem. faculty U. Tex., Austin, 1971—; prof. mech. engring. U. Tex., 1979—, W. R. Woolrich prof. engring., 1985—. Contbr. articles to profl. jours. 02637624SME (Best Heat Transfer Paper award 1970, assoc. editor Jour. Solar Energy Engring.); mem. Am. Solar Energy Soc., Tex. Solar Energy Soc. (founder, bd. dirs. 1976—, pres. 1980, 94). Research areas include heat and mass transfer, solar energy. Office: U Tex Dept Mech Engr ETC 5.160 Austin TX 78712

VODRA, WILLIAM W., lawyer; b. L.A., Sept. 13, 1943. BA, Coll. of Wooster, 1965; JD, Columbia U., 1968. Bar: Ohio 1968, D.C. 1981. Atty. Bur. Narcotics and Dangerous Drugs/Drug Enforcement Adminstrn. Dept. Justice, 1971-74; atty. Office Gen. Counsel FDA Dept. Health Edn. and Welfare, 1974-79; vice chmn. Commn. Fed. Drug Approval Process, 1981-82; mem. Arnold & Porter, Washington. Office: Arnold & Porter Thurman Arnold Bldg 555 12th St NW Washington DC 20004-1202

VOEDISCH, LYNN ANDREA, reporter; b. Evanston, Ill., June 20, 1954; d. Robert William and Elaine Theresa (Strand) V.; m. Kent Van Meter, June 21, 1981 (div. 1987); 1 child, Erik Kyle. BA, Grinnell Coll., 1976. Reporter Pioneer Press, Wilmette, Ill., 1977-79, Los Angeles Times, 1979, Chgo. Sun-Times, 1980—. Recipient Stick O'Type award Chgo. Newspaper Guild, 1984. Democrat. Episcopalian. Avocations: singing, theater, baroque music, sewing. Office: Chgo Sun-Times 401 N Wabash Ave Chicago IL 60611-5642*

VOEGELI, VICTOR JACQUE, history educator, dean; b. Jackson, Tenn., Dec. 21, 1934; s. Victor Jacque and Winnie Lou (Lassiter) V.; m. Anna Jean King, Oct. 14, 1956; children: Victor Jacque, Charles Lassiter. B.S., Murray State Coll., 1956; M.A., Tulane U., 1961, Ph.D., 1965. Instr. history Tulane U., 1963-65, asst. prof., 1965-67; asst. prof. history Vanderbilt U., 1967-69, assoc. prof., 1969-73, prof. history, 1973—, chmn. history dept., 1973-76, dean Coll. Arts and Sci., 1976-92. Author: Free But Not Equal: The Midwest and the Negro During the Civil War, 1967. Served with U.S. Army, 1956-58. Nat. Endowment Humanities grantee, 1969-70, 72. Mem. So. Hist. Assn. Presbyterian. Home: 3704D Estes Rd Nashville TN 37215-1729 Office: Vanderbilt Hospital Nashville TN 37232

VOELKER, CHARLES ROBERT, archbishop, academic dean; b. Cleve., June 12, 1944; s. Charles Christ and Bertha Elizabeth (Zak) V. BA, Nat. Coll. Edn., 1968; MS, TCU, 1974; STL, Holy Trinity Sem., 1989; PhD, Internat. Sem., 1989. Ordained to ministry Orthodox Ch. as priest, 1974, as bishop, 1984. Parish priest Am. Orthodox Ch., Cleve., 1974-84; bishop Am. Orthodox Ch., Deltona, Fla., 1984—; tchr., adminstr. Ashtubula County Schs., 1971-76; acad. dean Internat. Sem., Plymouth, Fla., 1990-96; pres., rector Holy Trinity Sem., Deltona, 1985—; dir. human svcs. New London (Ohio) Hosp., 1981-84; pres. Eagles Fitness Ctr., Middleburg Heights, Ohio, 1977-84; tchr. Polaris Vocat. Ctr., Middleburg Heights, 1981-83. Mem. Order of St. Gregory the Illuminator (comdr. 1989—), Order of St. George (comdr. 1989—), Order St. John of Jerusalem. Home: 1088 Eastbrook Ave Deltona FL 32738-6925 Office: Internat Sem PO Box 1208 Plymouth FL 32768-1208 *The only limits are those of vision.*

VOELKER, MARGARET IRENE (MEG VOELKER), gerontology, medical, surgical nurse; b. Bitburg, Germany, Dec. 31, 1955; d. Lewis R. and Patricia Irene (Schaffner) Miller; 1 child, Christopher Douglas. Diploma, Clover Park Vocat.-Tech., Tacoma, 1975, diploma in practical nursing, 1984; ASN, Tacoma (Wash.) C.C., 1988; postgrad., U. Washington Tacoma, Tacoma, 1992-95; student nurse practitioner program, U. of Wash., 1995—. Cert. ACLS. Nursing asst. Jackson County Hosp., Altus, Okla., 1976-77; receptionist Western Clinic, Tacoma, 1983; LPN, Tacoma Gen. Hosp., 1984-88, clin. geriatric nurse, 1988-90, clin. nurse post anesthesia care unit perioperative svcs., 1990—; pre-admit clinic nurse, 1995—; mem. staff nurse coun. Tacoma Gen. Hosp., 1990-91, procedural sedation nurse, 1996—. Recipient G. Corydon Wagner endowment fund scholarship. Mem. PostAnesthesia Nurses Assn., Phi Theta Kappa, Sigma Theta Tau.

VOELZ, DAVID GEORGE, electrical engineer; b. Idaho Falls, Idaho, Feb. 24, 1959; s. George Leo and Emily Jane (Neunast) V.; m. Judi Rae Gore, Aug. 12, 1983. MSEE, U. Ill., 1983, PhD in Elec. Engring., 1987. Rsch. asst. U. Ill., Urbana, 1981-86; electronics engr. Phillips Lab. (formally USAF Weapons Lab.), Kirtland AFB, N.Mex., 1986—. Contbr. articles to Jour. of Geophysical Rsch., Applied Optics, and Optics Letters. Boy scout master Boy Scouts Am., Albuquerque, 1988-90. Recipient, Engineering Excellence award Optical Society of Am., 1995. Mem. IEEE, Soc. of Photo-Optical Instrumentation Engrs. (contbr. proceedings 1988-97), Optical Soc. Am. (Engring. Excellence award 1995). Republican. Lutheran. Home: 5232 Camino Sandia NE Albuquerque NM 87111-5769 Office: PL/LMI Kirtland AFB NM 87117

VOET, PAUL C., specialty chemical company executive; b. Cin., July 7, 1946; s. Leo C. and Claire G. (Burdick) V.; m. Judy A. Gates, Aug. 24, 1968; children—Jeffrey, Jeannette, Jamie, Jodie. B.A., U. Cin., 1968; M.B.A., U. Pa., 1970. Asst. to pres. KDI Corp., Cin., 1970; asst. to pres. Chemed Corp., 1970-72; v.p. Vestal Labs. div. Chemed, St. Louis, 1972-74, exec. v.p., 1974-76, pres., 1976-80; exec. v.p., chief operating officer Chemed Corp., Cin., 1986-88, exec. v.p., 1988—; pres., CEO Nat. Sanitary Supply Co. Mem. Pres.'s adv. council St. Louis U., 1979. Mem. Am. Mgmt. Assn. (president's coun.), Young Pres. Assn., Phi Beta Kappa, Beta Gamma Sigma (dir.'s table), Omicron Delta Epsilon, Phi Alpha Theta, Phi Eta Sigma. Avocations: scuba diving, photography, personal computers. Home: 8180 Graves Rd Cincinnati OH 45243-3631 Office: Chemed Corp 2900 Chemed Ctr 255 E 5th St Cincinnati OH 45202-4700 Also: Nat San Supply Co 255 E 5th St Cincinnati OH 45202-4700

VOGEL, ARTHUR ANTON, clergyman; b. Milw., Feb. 24, 1924; s. Arthur Louis and Gladys Eirene (Larson) V.; m. Katharine Louise Nunn, Dec. 29, 1947; children: John Nunn, Arthur Anton, Katharine Ann. Student, U. of South, 1942-43, Carroll Coll., 1943-44; B.D., Nashotah House Theol. Sem., 1946; M.A., U. Chgo., 1948; Ph.D., Harvard, 1952; S.T.D., Gen. Theol. Sem., 1969; D.C.L., Nashotah House, 1969; D.D., U. of South, 1971. Ordained deacon Episcopal Ch., 1946, priest, 1948; teaching asst. philosophy Harvard, Cambridge, Mass., 1949-50; instr. Trinity Coll., Hartford, Conn., 1950-52; mem. faculty Nashotah House Theol. Sem., Nashotah, Wis., 1952-71; asso. prof. Nashotah House Theol. Sem., 1954-56, William Adams prof. philosophical and systematic theology, 1956-71, sub-dean Sem., 1964-71; bishop coadjutor Diocese of West Mo., Kansas City, 1971-72; bishop Diocese of West Mo., 1972-89; rector Ch. St. John Chrysostom, Delafield, Wis., 1952-56; dir. Anglican Theol. Rev., Evanston, Ill., 1964-69; mem. Internat. Anglican-Roman Cath. Consultation, 1970-90; mem. Nat. Anglican-Roman Catholic Consultation, 1965-84, Anglican chmn., 1973-84; mem. Standing Commn. on Ecumenical Relations of Episcopal Ch., 1957-79; mem. gen. bd. examining chaplains Episcopal Ch., 1971-72; del. Episcopal Ch., 4th Assembly World Council Chruches, Uppsala, Sweden, 1968, and others. Author: Reality, Reason and Religion, 1957, The Gift of Grace, 1958, The Christian Person, 1963, The Next Christian Epoch, 1966, Is the Last Supper Finished?, 1968, Body Theology, 1973, The Power of His Resurrection, 1976, Proclamation 2: Easter, 1980, The Jesus Prayer for Today, 1982, I Know God Better Than I Know Myself, 1989, Christ in His Time and Ours, 1982, God, Prayer and Healing, 1995, Radical Christianity and the Flesh of Jesus, 1995; editor: Theology in Anglicanism, 1985; contbr. articles to profl. jours. Vice chmn. bd. dirs. St. Luke's Hosp., Kansas City, Mo., 1971, chmn., 1973-89. Research fellow Harvard, 1950. Mem. Am. Philos. Assn., Metaphys. Soc. Am., Soc. Existential and Phenomenological Philosophy, Catholic Theol. Soc. Am. Home: 524 W 119th Ter Kansas City MO 64145-1043

VOGEL, CARL-WILHELM ERNST, immunologist, biochemistry educator; b. Hamburg, Fed. Republic Germany, Mar. 9, 1951; came to U.S., 1979; s. Erich Hermann Walter and Lisbeth Klara (Barbulla) V; m. Candice G. McMullan-Vogel, 1989. MD, U. Hamburg, 1976, diploma in biology, 1980, PhD in Biochemistry, 1986. cert. lab. medicine (Germany). Predoctoral rsch. fellow Tropical Inst., Hamburg, 1973-75; intern Univ. Hosps., Hamburg and Kiel, Fed. Republic Germany, 1976-78; postdoctoral rsch. fellow Rsch. Inst. Scripps Clin., La Jolla, Calif., 1979-82, asst. prof. biochemistry and medicine Georgetown U., Washington, 1982-87, resident medicine, pathology, allergy/immunology, 1984-86, 88-89, assoc. prof. 1987-91, adj. prof., 1991—; mem. Vincent T. Lombardi Cancer Rsch. Ctr., Washington, 1982-92; mem. Internat. Ctr. for Interdisciplinary Studies of Immunology, Washington, 1982-94, sci. dir., 1987-91; prof., chmn. dept. biochemistry and molecular biology U. Hamburg, Germany, 1990—; vis. prof. pathology and lab. medicine Ind. U.-Purdue U. Med. Ctr., Indpls., 1996-97. Mem. editorial bd. Jour. Devel. and Comparative Immunology, 1984—; mem. and examiner Bd. Lab. Medicine (Germany); cons. to biomed. corps. Overseas research fellow Studienstiftung des Deutschen Volkes (Fed. Republic Germany), 1978-79; U.S.A. research fellow Deutsche Forschungsgemeinschaft (Fed. Republic Germany), 1980-92; NIH rsch. grantee, 1983-94; NCI/NIH Rsch. Career Devel. award. Mem. AMA, AAAS, Gesellschaft für Biologische Chemie, Am. Soc. Microbiology, Am. Assn. Immunologists, Am. Soc. Biochemistry and Molecular Biology, Am. Assn. Cancer Rsch., Am. Soc. Tropical Medicine and Hygiene, AAUP, Internat. Soc. Devel. and Comparative Immunology, Am. Fedn. of Med. Rsch., Gesellschaft für Immunologie, Gesellschaft Deutscher Chemiker, Am. Soc. Clin. Investigation, German Soc. Cell Biology, German Soc. Lab. Medicine, Japanese Biochem. Soc., Australasian Soc. Immunology, Am. Soc. Clin. Pathology, Sigma Xi. Office: U Hamburg-Dept Biochem & Mol Biology, Martin Luther King Pl 6, 20146 Hamburg Germany

VOGEL, CEDRIC WAKELEE, lawyer; b. Cin., June 4, 1946; s. Cedric and Patricia (Woodruff) V. BA, Yale U., 1968; JD, Harvard U., 1971. Bar: Ohio 1972, Fla. 1973, U.S. Tax Ct. 1972, U.S. Supreme Ct. 1975. Ptnr. Vogel, Heis, Wenstrup & Cameron, Cin., 1972-96; sole practice, 1997—; bd. dirs. Pro Srs., 1994—. Chmn. mem.'s com. Cin. Art Mus., 1987-88; chmn. auction Cin. Hist. Soc., 1985; local pres. English Speaking Union, 1979-81, nat. bd. dirs., 1981; chmn. Keep Cin. Beautiful, Inc., 1994-96; active Bravo! Cin. Ballet, 1989; chmn. Act II Nutcracker Ball, 1987-88; bd. dirs. Merc Libr., 1991—; bd. dirs. Cin. Preservation Assn., 1990-93; vice chmn. Children's Heart Assn. Reds Rally, 1989; bd. dirs. Cin. Country Day Sch., 1983; pres. Alumni Coun. and Ann. Fund, 1983. Mem. Cin. Bar Assn., Fla. Bar Assn., Harvard Law Sch. Assn. Cin., Heimlich Inst. (trustee 1987—), Yale Alumni Assn. (del. 1984-87), Cin. Yale Club (pres. 1980-81, 96-97), Cincinnatus, The Lawyers Club Cin. (pres. 1995), Harvard Club of Cin. (bd. dirs. 1996-98). Republican. Home: 2270 Madison Rd Cincinnati OH 45208-2659 Office: 817 Main St Ste 800 Cincinnati OH 45202-2183

VOGEL, DONALD STANLEY, gallery executive, artist; b. Milw., Oct. 20, 1917; s. Walter Frederick and Francis Osborne (Talmadge) V.; m. Margaret Katherine Mayer, Oct. 14, 1947 (dec. June 1974); children—Eric Stefan, Kevin Eliot, Katherine Barley; m. Erika Kjar Farkac, Oct. 4, 1980. Student Chgo. Art Inst., 1936. With WPA Easel Project, Chgo., 1940; tech. dir. Dallas Little Theatre, 1942-43; dir. Betty McLean Gallery, Dallas, 1951-54; dir., owner Valley House Gallery, Dallas, 1954—; dir., ptnr. Main Place Gallery, Dallas, 1968-70. Author: (with Margaret Mayer) Aunt Clara: The Paintings of Clara McDonald Williamson, 1966, Charcoal and Cadmium Red, 1989, Not for Revenge, 1991, King of the Hill, 1991, Transcendent Collector, 1992, Drawing for Paintings, 1992, The Untold Studio Secret, A Fantasy, 1992, The Boardinghouse, 1995, Prime Targets, 1996, Seeking the Intangible, 1996; also essays and catalogues. Mem. Art Dealers Assn. Am. Inc. Avocations: travel; swimming. Office: Valley House Gallery 6616 Spring Valley Rd Dallas TX 75240-8635

VOGEL, EUGENE L., lawyer; b. Balt., May 2, 1931; s. Phillip and Dorothy (Shor) V.; m. Sara Altman, Aug. 22, 1958; children—Jennifer L., Amanda J. B.S., U. Md., 1953; J.D. magna cum laude, Harvard U., 1958. C.P.A., Md. Bar: N.Y. Assoc. atty. Rosenman and Colin, N.Y.C., 1958-67, tax ptnr., 1967-77, sr. tax ptnr., 1977—; adj. prof. law NYU, 1977-88. Co-author: (with Ness): Taxation of the Closely-Held Corp., 5th edit. 1991; contbr. articles to profl. jours. Bd. dirs. The Appleseed Found., Washington; bd. dirs., treas. N.Y. Lawyers For Pub. Interest, N.Y.C., 1984-87; lectr. Practicing Law Inst. Served to 1st Lt. USAF, 1953-55. Mem. ABA, N.Y. State Bar Assn. (exec. com. tax sect.), Assn. of Bar of City of N.Y. (chmn. com. on personal income taxation 1991-94, coun. on taxation 1990—). Home: 245 E 50th St New York NY 10022-7752 Office: Rosenman & Colin 575 Madison Ave New York NY 10022-2511

VOGEL, EZRA F., sociology educator; b. Delaware, Ohio, July 11, 1930; s. Joseph H. and Edith (Nachman) V.; m. Suzanne Hall, July 5, 1953 (div.); children: David, Steven, Eva; m. Charlotte Ikels, Nov. 3, 1979. BA, Ohio Wesleyan U., 1950; MA, Bowling Green State U., 1951; PhD, Harvard U., 1958; LittD (hon.), Kwansai Gakuin, 1980, Wittenberg Coll., 1981, Bowling Green State U., 1982, U. Md., 1983, Albion Coll., 1988, Chinese U., Hong Kong, 1992; Ohio Wesleyan, 1996, U. Mass., Lowell, 1996. Research fellow Harvard (for work in Japan), 1958-60; asst. prof. Yale U., 1960-61; research assoc., lectr. Harvard U., 1961-67, prof., 1967—, Henry Ford II prof. social scis., 1990—, assoc. dir. East Asian Research Ctr., 1967-73, dir., 1973-77, chmn. council East Asian studies, 1977-80, dir. program on U.S.-Japan relations, 1980-87, hon. chmn. program on U.S.-Japan rels., 1988—, mem. faculty council, 1981-84; nat. intelligence officer for East Asia Nat. Intelligence Coun., 1993-95, dir. Fairbank Ctr. East Asian Studies, 1995—; Mem. Joint Com. on Contemporary China, 1968-75, Com. on Scholarly Communication with Peoples Republic China, 1975-78, Joint Com. Japanese Studies, 1977-79. Author: Japan's New Middle Class, 1963, Canton Under Communism, 1969, Japan As Number One, 1979, Comeback, 1985, The Impact of Japan on a Changing World, 1987, One Step Ahead in China, 1989, The Four Little Dragons, 1991; editor: (with Norman W. Bell) A Modern Introduction to the Family, 1960, Modern Japanese Organization and Decision-Making, 1975, (with George Lodge) Ideology and National Competitiveness, Living With China, 1997. Trustee Ohio Wesleyan U., 1970-75, 80-94. Served with AUS, 1951-53. Recipient Harvard faculty prize for book of year, 1970, Japan Found. prize, 1996; Guggenheim fellow, 1972. Mem. Assn. Asian Studies (bd. dirs. 1970-72), Am. Acad. Arts and Scis. Home: 14 Sumner Rd Cambridge MA 02138-3018

VOGEL, FREDERICK JOHN, diplomat; b. Annapolis, Md., July 11, 1943; s. Raymond William Vogel and Clair Patricia (O'Neill) Foley; m. Donsiri Kamak, Dec. 26, 1983; children: Chantharaphon M., Jenchira Erin, Thinarom Clair. BS in Engring., US Naval Acad., 1965; postgrad, Purdue U., 1961; cert. in Lao lang., Def. Lang. Inst., 1970; postgrad., U.S. Army War Coll., 1995-96; cert. in Thai lang., Union Lang. Sch., Bangkok, 1975; cert. Korean lang., Fgn. Svc. Inst., 1979. Lic. pvt. pilot, lic. tae kwon do instr., 2d Dan, lic. D parachutist, lic. 2d class diver. Commd. 2nd lt. USMC, 1965, advanced through grades to col., 1986; fgn. svc. officer on assignment to Pentagon Bangkok, London,, Washington, 1972-88; dept. of state rep. to conf. on disarmament Geneva, 1988-90; dep. chief of mission Am. Embassy, Vientiane, Laos, 1991-93, charge d' affaires, 1993; asst. dir. of fgn. mil. rights affairs, office of the Sec. of Def. The Pentagon, 1993-95; embassy rep. Thai-Am. Edn. Found., Bangkok, 1976-78; sec. martial arts com. Royal Bangkok Sports Club, 1984-86; chmn. Vientiane Internat. Sch. Bd., 1991-93. Active Am. Community Supprt Assn., Bangkok, 1984-85. Mem. Am. Fgn. Svc. Assn., Marine Corps Assn., U.S. Naval Acad. Alumni Assn., Force Recon Assn. Roman Catholic. Avocations: martial arts, parachuting, private flying, traveling, languages. Home: 1332 Cassia St Herndon VA 20170-2500

VOGEL, H. VICTORIA, psychotherapist, educator. BA, U. Md., 1968; MA, NYU, 1970, 1975; MEd, Columbia U., 1982, postgrad., 1982—; cert., Am. Projective Drawing Inst., 1983; bd. cert. expert in traumatic stress. Art Therapist Childville, Bklyn., 1962-64; tchr., Montgomery County (Md.) Jr. H.S., 1968-69; with H.S. div. N.Y.C. Bd. Edn., 1970—, guidance counselor, instructor, psychotherapist in pvt. practice; clinical counseling cons. psychodiagnosis and devel. studies, art/play therapy, The Modern School, 1984—; art/play therapist Hosp. Ctr. for Neuromuscular Disease and Devel. Disorders, 1987—; employment counselor-adminstr. N.Y. State Dept. Labor Concentrated Employment Program, 1971-72; intern psychotherapy and psychoanalysis psychiat. divsn. Cen. Islip Hosp., 1973-75; Calif. Grad. Inst., L.A.; Columbia U. Tchrs. Coll., N.Y. intern psychol. counseling and rehab. N.J. Coll. Medicine, Newark, 1979. Mem. com. for spl. events NYU, 1989; participant clin. and artistic perspectives Am. Acad. Psychoanalysis Conf., 1990, participant clin. postmodernism and psychoanalysis, 1996; auxilary police officer N.Y. Police Dept. Precinct 19, N.Y.C., 1994—; chair bylaws com. Columbia U., 1995—. Mem. APA, AAAS, Am. Psychol. Soc., Am. Orthopsychiat. Assn., Am. Soc. Group Psychotherapy & Psychodrama (publs. com. 1984—), Am. Counseling Assn., Am. Acad. Experts Traumatic Stress, N.Y.C. Art Tchrs. Assn., Art/Play Therapy, Assn. Humanistic Psychology (exec. sec. 1981), Tchrs. Coll. Adminstrv. Women in Edn., Phi Delta Kappa (editor chpt. newsletter 1981-84, exec. sec. Columbia U. chpt. 1984—, chmn. nominating com. for chpt. officers 1986—, nominating com. 1991, pub. rels. exec. bd. dirs. 1991, rsch. rep. 1986—), Phi Delta Kappa (v.p. programs NYU chpt. 1994—). Author: The Never Ending Story of Alcohol, Drugs and Other Substance Abuse, 1992, Variant Sexual Behavior and the Aesthetic Modern Nudes, 1992, Psychological Science of School Behavior Intervention, 1993, Joycean Conceptual Modernism: Relationships and Deviant Sexuality, 1995, Electronic Evil Eyes, 1995.

VOGEL, HENRY ELLIOTT, retired university dean and physics educator; b. Greenville, S.C., Sept. 16, 1925; s. Henry Lamprecht and Alice (Cousins) V.; m. Barbara Argyle Gladden, Aug. 16, 1953; children: Alisabeth, Henry L. II, Barbara Alice, Susan Marie. BS, Furman U., 1948; MS, U. N.C., 1950, PhD, 1962. Instr. dept. physics Clemson (S.C.) U., 1950-52, asst. prof. physics, 1952-59, assoc. prof., 1959-65, prof., 1965-67, prof., head physics dept., 1967-71; prof., dean Clemson (S.C.) U. Coll. Scis., 1971-87, prof. physics, 1987-90, dean emeritus, prof. emeritus dept. physics and astronomy, 1990—; mem. S.C. ad hoc com. for NSF exptl. program to stimulate competitive research, 1978-87; mem. tech. adv. bd. S.C. Research Authority, 1984-87. Served with AUS, 1943-45. Decorated Purple Heart. Mem. Am. Phys. Soc., Am. Assn. Physics Tchrs., Sigma Xi, Sigma Pi, Alpha Epsilon Delta. Address: 222 Wyatt Ave Clemson SC 29631-3003

VOGEL, HOWARD STANLEY, lawyer; b. N.Y.C., Jan. 21, 1934; s. Moe and Sylvia (Miller) V.; m. Judith Anne Gelb, June 30, 1962; 1 son, Michael S. B.A., Bklyn. Coll., 1954; J.D., Columbia U., 1957; LL.M. in Corp. Law, NYU, 1969. Bar: N.Y. 1957, U.S. Supreme Ct. 1964. Assoc. Whitman & Ransom, N.Y.C., 1961-66; with Texaco Inc., 1966—, gen. atty., 1970-73, assoc. gen. counsel, 1973-81, gen. counsel Texaco Philanthropic Found. Inc., 1979-82, gen. counsel Jefferson Chem. Co., Texaco Chems. Can. Inc., 1973-82, assoc. gen. tax counsel, gen. mgr. adminstrn., White Plains, N.Y., 1981—; gen. tax counsel Texaco Found. Inc., 1995—. Pres., dir. 169 E. 69th Corp., 1981—. Served to 1st lt. JAGC, U.S. Army, 1958-60. Mem. ABA, Assn. Bar City N.Y., Fed. Bar Council, Assn. Ex-Mems. of Squadron A (N.Y.C.). Club: Princeton (N.Y.C.). Home: 169 E 69th St Apt 9D New York NY 10021-5163 Office: 2000 Westchester Ave White Plains NY 10650-0001

VOGEL, JULIUS, consulting actuary, former insurance company executive; b. N.Y.C., Jan. 22, 1924; s. Max and Bertha V.; m. Corinne Iskowitz, Mar. 11, 1947; children: Robert, Charles. B.A., Bklyn. Coll., 1943. With

Prudential Ins. Co. Am., Newark, 1946-82; sr. v.p., chief actuary Prudential Ins. Co. Am., 1977-82; chmn. Pruco Services Inc., 1979-82, Prudential's Gibraltar Fund, 1980-82. Served with U.S. Army, 1944-46. Recipient Disting. Public Service award Dept. Navy, 1976. Fellow Soc. Actuaries (pres. 1979-80); mem. Am. Acad. Actuaries. Office: 72 Colt Rd Summit NJ 07901-3041

VOGEL, LINDA ANN, federal agency administrator; married; 1 child. Degree magna cum laude, U. Tex. Human health svc. mgmt. intern Dept. Health; coord. spl. fgn. currency program Orgn. Internat. Health, 1970-73, coord. bilateral program, 1973-75, past dep. dir.; dir. Office Internat. Affairs, 1994; past acting dir. Internat. and Refugee Health, Rockville, Md., dir., 1997—; active preparation report World Summit Children, U.S. Nat. Coun. Internat. Health, co-chmn. governing bd., 1991, 92, Pan Am. Health Orgn., U.S. del. meeting Pan Am. Sanitary Bur., 1994, alt. head coun. meetings, 1995, 96; formerly active Gore-Chernomyrdin Commn.; past U.S. rep. Second Hemispheric Conf. Children and Soc. Policy, N.Am., S.Am., Santiago, Chile; human health svc. mem. U.S. del. to exec. bd. UNICEF, 1984-95, past advisor to exec. dir.; U.S. mem. joint com. health policy UNICEF-WHO, 1986-95; U.S. del. World Health Assembly, 1995, 96; mem. other com. assignments, subcoms. Office: Internat and Refugee Health 5600 Fishers Ln Rockville MD 20857*

VOGEL, MARY ELLEN VIRGINIA, psychologist, learning consultant; b. Rochester, N.Y., May 19, 1938; d. Richard D. and Grace Margaret (Taylert) Krasucki; m. Emil Thomas Vogel Sr., Nov. 19, 1960; children: Pamela Ann, Emil Thomas Jr., Tobias Alan. BS, SUNY, Plattsburgh, 1959; MA, Fairleigh Dickinson U., N.J., 1983; PhD, Fordham U., N.Y., 1991. Cert. learning disabilities tchr. cons., sch. psychologist, psychologist, N.J. Tchr. Irondequoit N.Y. Bd. of Edn., Rochester, 1959-61, Rochester Bd. Edn., 1962-63; tchr., counselor, psychologist Ramsey (N.J.) Bd. Edn., 1972—. Mem., chair Jr. Women's Club, Ramsey, Parish Coun. St. Paul's Ch.; den leader Boy Scouts of Am.; leader Girl Scouts of Am. Named Tchr. of the Yr. Gov. Thomas Kean (N.J.), 1987. Mem. APA, AAUW, Nat. Assn. Sch. Psychologists, Kappa Delta Pi, Phi Delta Kappa, Psi Chi Nat. Honor Soc. Avocations: reading, gardening, cooking, writing, ice skating. Home: 105 Deer Trl Ramsey NJ 07446-2111

VOGEL, MICHAEL N., journalist, writer, historian; b. Buffalo, May 26, 1947; s. Ralph John and Florence Helen (Pohlmann) V.; m. Stasia Zoladz, Aug. 28, 1971; children: Charity Ann, Rebecca Marie, Alex Christian. BA in English, Canisius Coll., 1969; MA in English, So. Ill. U., 1970. Journalist Buffalo News, 1970—; assoc. prof. journalism Buffalo State U. Coll., 1979-80. Author: Maritime Buffalo, 1990, Echoes in the Mist, 1991, America's Crossroads, 1993. Pres. Buffalo Lighthouse Assn., Inc., 1985—; co-founder St. Michael's Sch. at Greycliff, Derby, N.Y., 1987; pres. Buffalo Newspaper Guild, 1994-96; bd. dirs. Landmark Soc. Niagara Frontier, 1990-91, Western N.Y. Heritage Inst., 1994—, Friends of N.Y. State Newspaper Project, 1996—; mem. Erie County Local Emergency Planning Com. 1st lt. U.S. Army, 1971-73. Recipient numerous awards including One to One Media award, 1978, 79, Newspaper Editorial Workshop award, 1979-80, N.Y. State AP award, 1982-90, Am. Planning Assn. award, 1987. Mem. AAAS, U.S. Lighthouse Soc., Nat. Assn. Sci. Writers, Gt. Lakes Hist. Soc., Buffalo & Erie County Hist. Soc. (Augspurger award 1989, Niederlander award 1990), Buffalo Mus. Sci. Roman Catholic. Avocations: sailing, photography, reading. Home: 6540 Lake Shore Rd Derby NY 14047-9755 Office: Buffalo News PO Box 100 1 News Plz Buffalo NY 14240*

VOGEL, NELSON J., JR., lawyer; b. South Bend, Ind., Oct. 13, 1946; s. Nelson J. and Carolyn B. (Drzewiecki) V.; m. Sandra L. Cudney, May 17, 1969; children: Ryan C., Justin M., Nathan J., Lindsey M. BS cum laude, Miami U., Oxford, Ohio, 1968; JD cum laude, U. Notre Dame, 1971. Bar: Ind. 1971, Mich. 1971, U.S. Dist. Ct. (no. dist.) Ind. 1971, Fla. 1972, U.S. Tax Ct. 1972, U.S. Ct. Appeals (5th cir.) 1975, U.S. Ct. Claims 1980. Acct. Coopers & Lybrand, South Bend, 1969-71; assoc. Barnes & Thornburg, South Bend, 1971-76, ptnr., 1977—; lectr. U. Notre Dame, South Bend, 1971, 74-80; instr. Ind. U., South Bend, 1971-74; mem. bd. advisors Goshen Coll. Family Bus. Program. Pres. Big Bros., Big Sisters, South Bend, 1978-79; bd. pres. South Bend Regional Mus. Art, 1984-86; mem. ethics com. Meml. Hosp., South Bend, 1986-94. Mem. Nat. Employee Stock Ownership Plan Assn. (sec.-treas. Ind. chpt. 1993-95), Am. Assn. Atty.-CPAs, Nat. Assn. State Bar Tax Sec. (exec. com. 1982-84), Ind. State Bar Assn. (chmn. taxation sect. 1981-82, Citation of Merit 1979), Mich. Bar Assn. (tax sect.), Fla. Bar Assn., Michiana World Affairs Coun. (bd. dirs. 1992-96), Michiana World Trade club (bd. dirs. 1992-96). Home: 1146 Dunrobbin Ln South Bend IN 46614-2150 Office: Barnes & Thornburg 600 1st Source Bank 100 N Michigan St South Bend IN 46601-1610

VOGEL, RICHARD WIEDEMANN, business owner, ichthyodynamicist, educator; b. N.Y.C., Apr. 12, 1950; s. Jack and Edna Jeanne (Wiedemann) V.; m. Pamela Jane Gordon, Aug. 7, 1974; children: Amy Jane, Katy Lynn, Gina Marie, Krista Jeanne. Grad. high sch., Calif. Owner, operator ichthyol. rsch. and comml. fishing vessel Santa Barbara, Calif., 1973-88; designer advanced hydrodynamic curvature Clark Foam Factory, Laguna Beach, Calif., 1994—; lectr. Surfrider Found. Conf., U. Calif., San Diego, 1994. Inventor in field. Episcopalian. Avocations: music, athletic tng. and fitness. Office: Ichthyodynamics PO Box 1167 Hanalei HI 96714-1167

VOGEL, ROBERT, retired lawyer, educator; b. Coleharbor, N.D., Dec. 6, 1918; s. Frank A. and Louella (Larsen) V.; m. Elsa Mork, May 29, 1942; children: Mary Lou, Sarah May, Frank, Robert. B.S., U. N.D., 1939; LL.B., Mpls. Coll. Law, 1942. Bar: N.D. 1943. Practiced in Garrison, 1943-54; state's atty. McLean County, 1948-54; U.S. atty. Fargo, 1954-61; mem. Vogel, Bair & Brown, Mandan, N.D., 1961-73; judge N.D. Supreme Ct., 1973-78; prof. U. N.D. Law Sch., Grand Forks, 1978-95; ret. Democratic candidate for U.S. Ho. of Reps., 2d Dist. N.D., 1962; mem., sec. Nonpartisan League State Exec. Com., 1952; mem. N.D. Parole Bd., 1966-73. Fellow Am. Bar Found.; mem. Am. Coll. Trial Lawyers, Am. Law Inst. Home: 524 Harvard St Grand Forks ND 58203-2845

VOGEL, ROBERT LEE, college administrator, clergyman; b. Phillipsburg, Kans., Sept. 27, 1934; s. Howard and Marie V.; m. Sally M. Johnson, June 3, 1956; children—Susan, Kirk. B.A., Wartburg Coll., 1956; B.D., M.Div., Wartburg Theol. Sem., 1960, D.D. (hon.), 1976. Ordained to ministry Am. Lutheran Ch., 1960. Organizing pastor Faith Luth. Ch., Golden, Colo., 1960-65; regional dir. div. youth activity Am. Luth. Ch., Chgo., 1965-67; dir. parish resources, div. youth activity Am. Luth. Ch., Mpls., 1967-69; sr. pastor Our Savior's Luth. Ch., Denver, 1969-73; exec. asst. to pres. Am. Luth. Ch., Mpls., 1973-80; pres. Wartburg Coll., Waverly, Iowa, 1980—; v.p. Internat. Luther League, Am. Luth. Ch., 1953-58, pres., 1958-60; ofcl. observer Luth. World Fedn. Assembly, 1957; mem. com. on laity Am. Luth. Ch., 1964-67. Recipient Alumni citation Wartburg Coll., 1978. Mem. Coun. Ind. Colls., Iowa Assn. Ind. Colls. and Univs. (chmn. bd. 1987-88), Luth. Ednl. Conf. N. Am. (pres. 1988-89), Nat. Assn. Ind. Colls. and Univs. (commn. mem.). Lodge: Rotary. Office: Wartburg Coll 222 9th St NW Waverly IA 50677-2215

VOGEL, ROBERT PHILIP, lawyer; b. N.Y.C., July 25, 1944; s. Stanley and Rita (Dembitz) V.; m. Joanne Fleisher; children: Lisa, Beth; m. Jean Jackes, Sept. 28, 1985; children: Eric, Kobey, Jaime. AB, Princeton U., 1966; LLB, Yale Law Sch., New Haven, 1969. Atty. Legal Aid Soc., Denver, 1969-71; asst. atty. gen. cmty. advocate unit Dept. Justice, Phila., 1971-77; from sr. atty. to v.p. gen. counsel Rohm & Haas Co., Phila., 1977—; bd. dirs. Edn. Law Ctr., Phila., 1994—, Pub. Interest Law Ctr., Phila., 1994—. Mem. Chem. Mfrs. Assn. (gen. counsel's group 1994—). Jewish. Home: 1463 Huntingdon Rd Philadelphia PA 19001 Office: Rohm & Haas Co 100 Independence Mall W Philadelphia PA 19106-2399

VOGEL, RONALD BRUCE, food products executive; b. Vancouver, Wash., Feb. 16, 1934; s. Joseph John and Thelma Mae (Karker) V.; m. Carol Vandecar, Mar. 16, 1958; children: Joseph S., Rhonda L., Theresa J., Denise R.; m. Donita Dawn Schneider, Aug. 8, 1970 (dec. June 1974); 1 child, Cynthia Dawn; m. Karen Cracknel, Feb. 14, 1992. BS in Chemistry, U. Wash., 1959. Glass maker Penberthy Instrument Co., Seattle, 1959-60; lab. technician Gt. Western Malting Co., Vancouver, 1960-62, chief chemist, 1962-67, mgr. corp. quality control, 1967-72, mgr. customer svcs., 1972-77, v.p. customer svcs., 1977-79, v.p. sales, 1979-84, gen. mgr., 1984-89, pres., CEO, 1989-95; ret. Chmn. bd. dirs. Columbia Empire Jr. Achievement, Portland, Oreg., 1991-92. With U.S. Army, 1954-56. Recipient numerous awards. Mem. Master Brewers Assn. Am. (pres. 1996), Am. Malting Barley Assn. (chmn. 1984-86, 89-91), Vancouver C. of C. (chmn. 1991-93), Applied Phytologics, Inc. (bd. dirs.). Home: 6521 Kansas St Vancouver WA 98661

VOGEL, SUSAN CAROL, nursing administrator; b. Hartford, Conn., Oct. 9, 1948; d. Morton B. and Esther (Riback) Worshoufsky. Diploma in nursing, Grace Hosp., New Haven, 1969; B in Healthcare Mgmt., U. La Verne, 1991, M in Health Adminstrn., 1994. RN, Calif.; cert. nephrology nurse, Nephrology Nurse Cert. Bd. Oper. rm. nurse New Britain (Conn.) Gen. Hosp., 1970-72; staff nurse oper. rm. Parkview Cmty. Hosp., Riverside, Calif., 1972-74; staff nurse dialysis, IV team Cedars-Sinai Med. Ctr., L.A., 1974-82; clin. nurse III dialysis UCLA, 1982-88; nurse mgr. inpatient dialysis UCLA Med. Ctr., 1988-93; adminstr. South Valley Regional Dialysis Ctr., Encino, Calif., 1993—; pres. Renal Replacement Therapies, Inc. Author: (with others) Review of Hemodialysis for Nurses and Dialysis Personnel, 1993, Vascular Access, Principles & Practices, 3rd edit., 1996. Mem. NAFE, Am. Orgn. Nurse Execs., Am. Nephrology Nurses Assn. (pres. L.A. chpt. 1990-92, 96-98, nat. chairperson hemodialysis spl. interest group 1993-95), Nat. Kidney Found. Avocations: traveling, skiing. Office: South Valley Regional Dialysis Ctr 17815 Ventura Blvd Ste 100 Encino CA 91316-3613

VOGEL, SUSAN MICHELLE, physician; b. London, June 17, 1961; d. John P. and Mary A. (Murphy) V.; m. Marco R. Siqueiros, Oct. 27, 1990; children: Nicholas, Alexander Maxwell. BS, Syracuse U., 1983; MD, SUNY, Syracuse, 1987. Resident U. Tex. Med. Sch., Houston, 1990-91, asst. prof., 1991—; pres., mng. physician Houston Internal Medicine Assocs., Houston, 1992-96; pres. Susan M. Vogel & Assocs. P.A., 1996—; pres. South East Tex. IPA, Houston, 1995-96; bd. dirs. St. Joseph Hosp., Houston. Mem. Tex. Med. Assn., Preaclarus. Office: 1315 Calhoun St Ste 1605 Houston TX 77002-8232

VOGEL, THOMAS TIMOTHY, surgeon, health care consultant, lay church worker; b. Columbus, Ohio, Feb. 1, 1934; s. Thomas A. and Charlotte A. (Hogan) V.; m. M.M. Darina Kelleher, May 29, 1965; children: Thomas T., Catherine D., Mark P., Nicola M. AB, Coll. of Holy Cross, 1955; MS, Ohio State U., 1960, PhD, 1962; MD, Georgetown U., 1965. Pvt. practice surgery Columbus, 1971—; chmn. liturgy com., pres. parish coun. St. Catharine Parish, Columbus, 1971-73; chmn. diocesan adminstrn. com. Diocesan Pastoral Coun., Columbus, 1972-73, chmn., 1973-75; vice prefect Sodality of Holy Cross, 1953-55; mem. Ohio Bishop's Adv. Coun., Columbus, 1976-79; clin. asst. prof. surgery Ohio State U., Columbus, 1974—; mem. med. adv. com. Ethix Corp., Dublin, Ohio; past trustee Peer Rev. Systems, Inc. Contbr. articles to profl. jours. Bd. dirs. St. Vincent's Children's Ctr., 1975-83, chmn., 1981-82; past chmn. bd. trustees St. Joseph Montessori Sch. Recipient Layman's award Columbus Ea. Kiwanis, 1972. Mem. Am. Coll. Surgeons, Am. Physiol. Soc., Assn. for Acad. Surgery, Ohio Med. Assn., Columbus Acad. Medicine, Sigma Xi, Delta Epsilon Sigma. Roman Catholic. Home: 247 S Ardmore Rd Columbus OH 43209-1701 Office: 621 S Cassingham Rd Columbus OH 43209-2403

VOGEL, VICTOR GERALD, medical educator, researcher; b. Bethlehem, Pa., Mar. 14, 1952; s. Victor Gerald Jr. and Margaret Moser (Smith) V.; m. Saralyn Sue Schaffner, June 25, 1977; children: Heather Marie, Christiaan Keith. Diplomate Am. Bd. Internal Medicine, Am. Bd. Preventive Medicine, Nat. Bd. Med. Examiners. Resident in internal medicine Balt. City Hosps., 1978-81; fellow in med. oncology Johns Hopkins Oncology Ctr., Balt., 1983-86; Andrew W. Mellon fellow Johns Hopkins Sch. Hygiene Pub. Health, Balt., 1984-86; asst. prof. medicine and epidemiology U. Tex./M.D. Anderson Cancer Ctr., Houston, 1986-93, assoc. prof. clin. cancer prevention, 1993-95; asst. prof. epidemiology U. Tex. Sch. Pub. Health, Houston, 1987-95; prof. medicine and epidemiology U. Pitts. Cancer Inst./Magee-Women's Hosp., 1996—, dir. comprehensive breast cancer program, 1996—; epidemiologist Tex. breast screening project Am. Cancer Soc., 1986—; Susan G. Komen Found. rsch. fellow, 1989; bd. dirs. Nat. Surg. Adjuvant Breast and Bowel Project, 1997—; lectr. in field. Contbr. articles to profl. jours. Served with USPHS, 1981-83. Named Med. Vol. of Yr., Am. Cancer Soc., 1983, award 1987, career devel. award, 1990-93. Fellow Am. Coll. Preventive Medicine, ACP; mem. Am. Soc. Clin. Oncology, Am. Soc. Preventive Oncology, Christian Med. and Dental Soc. Republican. Presbyn. Avocation: flying. Office: University of Pittsburgh Cancer Inst 802 Kaufmann Bldg 3471 5th Ave Pittsburgh PA 15213-3221

VOGELEY, CLYDE EICHER, JR., engineering educator, artist, consultant; b. Pitts., Oct. 19, 1917; s. Clyde Eicher and Eva May (Reynolds) V.; m. Blanche Wormington Peters, Dec. 15, 1947; children: Eva Anne, Susan Elizabeth Steele. BFA in Art Edn., Carnegie Mellon U., 1940; BS in Engring. Physics, U. Pitts., 1944, PhD in Math., 1949. Art supr. Pub. Sch. System, Spingdale, Pa., 1940-41; rsch. engr. Westinghouse Rsch. Labs., East Pitts., Pa., 1944-54; adj. prof. math. U. Pitts., 1954-64; sr. scientist Bettis Atomic Power Lab., West Mifflin, Pa., 1956-59; supr. tech. tng. Bettis Atomic Power Lab., West Mifflin, 1959-71; mgr. Bettis Reactor Engring. Sch., West Mifflin, 1971-77, dir., 1977-92; cons. U.S. Dept. Energy, Washington, 1992-95; cons. Bettis Atomic Power Lab., W. Mifflin, 1954-56; U.S. Navy Nuclear Power Schs., Mare Island, Calif., Bainbridge, Md., 1959-69. Author: (grad. sch. course) Non-linear Differential Equations, 1954; (rev. text) Ordinary Differential Equations, Rev. edit. 5, Shock and Vibration Problems, Rev. Edit. 6, 1991; rsch. report distributed to Brit., Can. and U.S. Govts. for use in design of airborne radar systems, 1944; oil painting represented in permanent Latrobe collection; acrylics, water colors and Christmas card designs in several pvt. collections; oil painting included in A Unique Vision of Art, 1997. Pres., trustee Whitehall (Pa.) Pub. Libr., 1985. Recipient letter of commendation naval reactors br. USN, 1992. Mem. IEEE (life), Am. Phys. Soc., Assoc. Artists Pitts. (hon.), Pitts. Watercolor Soc., Sigma Xi, Sigma Pi Sigma, Sigma Tau. Presbyterian. Achievements include patents for Automatic Continuous Wave Radar Tracking System, Modulating Signals Passing Along Ridged Waveguides, Ridged Waveguide Matching Device, Method for Joining Several Ridged Waveguides, Antenna Feed Modulation Unit, others. Home: 185 Peach Dr Pittsburgh PA 15236-2145 *My life as an artist, scientist, and teacher has been a wonderful journey - made richer by my family, teachers, friends, colleagues, and students. It has never seemed like work.*

VOGELGESANG, SANDRA LOUISE, federal government official; b. Canton, Ohio, July 27, 1942; d. Glenn Wesley and Louise (Forry) Vogelgesang; m. Geoffrey Ernest Wolfe, July 4, 1982. BA, Cornell U., 1964; MA, Tufts U., 1965, MA in Law and Diplomacy, 1966, PhD, 1971. With Dept. State, Washington, 1975—, policy planner for sec. state and European Bur., 1975-80, dir. Econ Analysis Office, Orgn. Econ. Coop. and Devel., 1981-82, econ. minister U.S. Embassy, Ottawa, Can., 1982-86, dep. asst. sec. Internat. Orgn. Affairs Bur., 1986-89; dep. asst. adminstr. Office Internat. Activities Environ. Protection Agy., Washington, 1989-92; with Dept. State, Washington, 1992; sr. policy advisor Agy. for Internat. Devel., 1993; U.S. amb. to Nepal Dept. State, Washington, 1994—; bd. dirs. Edward R. Murrow Ctr. for Pub. Diplomacy, Fletcher Sch., Medford, Mass., 1978-81; bd. advisors Am.'s Soc., N.Y.C., 1986-89. Author: Long Dark Night of the Soul, The American Intellectual Left and the Vietnam War, 1974, American Dream-Global Nightmare: The Dilemma of U.S. Human Rights Policy, 1980. Recipient Meritorious Service awards, 1973, 74, 82, 83, 86, Disting. Honor award, 1976 Dept. State, Pres.' Disting. Service award, 1985. Mem. Council on Fgn. Relations. Office: US Embassy Kathmandu Dept of State Washington DC 20521-6190 Address: Pani, Pokhari, Kathmandu Nepal

VOGELMAN, JOSEPH HERBERT, scientific engineering company executive; b. N.Y.C., Aug. 18, 1920; s. Jacob and Sabina (Weingarten) V.; m. Norma Schneider, Dec. 8, 1946; children: Jeffrey Allan, Leslie Sue, Linda Leigh. B.S., CCNY, 1940; M.E.E., Poly. Inst. Bklyn., 1948, D.Elec. Engring., 1957. Registered profl. engr., N.Y., N.J. Project engr. Signal Corps Engr. Labs., Belmar, N.J., 1943-45; chief devel. br. Watson Labs., Eatontown, N.J., 1945-50; chief scientist Rome Air Devel. Center, Griffiss AFB, N.Y., 1951-52; chief electronic warfare lab. Rome Air Devel. Center, 1953-56, dir. communications, 1956-59; v.p., dir. Capehart Corp., N.Y.C., 1959-64; dir. electronics Chromalloy Am. Corp., N.Y.C., 1964-67; gen. mgr. pocket fone div. Chromalloy Am. Corp., 1966-67, v.p., 1967-73; v.p., dir. Cro-Med Bionics Corp., 1968-73; vice chmn. bd., dir. Laser Link Corp., 1968-73; chief scientist, dir. Orentreich Found. for Advancement Sci., 1973—; pres. Vogelman Devel. Corp., 1973—; chmn. tech. adv. com. Compupix, Inc., 1984-86. Contbr. articles to profl. jours. and encys.; patentee in field. Served with AUS, 1942-43. Recipient Outstanding Performance award USAF, 1957. Fellow AAAS, IEEE; mem. Titulaire, Societe Francaise de Electroniciens et des Radio Electriciens, N.Y. Acad. Scis., Sigma Xi, Eta Kappa Nu. Home: 48 Green Dr Roslyn NY 11576-3221 Office: 910 5th Ave New York NY 10021-4155

VOGELSTEIN, BERT, oncology educator. BS, U. Pa., 1970; MD, Johns Hopkins U. Rsch. assoc. Nat. Cancer Inst., 1976-78; prof. dept. oncology Johns Hopkins U. Sch. Medicine, Balt., 1978—; advisor Nat. Insts. Health Scientific Review Groups, Nat. Cancer Inst. Assoc. editor Genes, Chromosomes and Cancer; mem bd. reviewing editors Science Magazine; contbr. article to profl. jours. Recipient Anne & Jason Farber Lecture award Am. Acad. Neurology, 1991, Gairdner Found. Internat. award Gairdner Found., 1992, Medal of Honor Am. Cancer Soc., 1992, Richard Lounsbery award Nat. Acad. Scis., 1993, Baxter Rsch. award Assn. Am. Med. Coll., 1994. G.H.A. Clowes Meml. award Am. Assn. Cancer Rsch. 1995; laureates Passano Found., 1994. Mem. NAS, Am. Acad. Arts Scis. Achievements include revolutionizing our understanding of complex genetic mutations that occur when an normal bowel epithelial cell is transformed into a malignant cell. Office: Johns Hopkins U Sch Med Dept Oncology 424 N Bond St Baltimore MD 21231-1001*

VOGELZANG, JEANNE MARIE, professional association executive, attorney; b. Hammond, Ind., Apr. 15, 1950; d. Richard and Laura Ann (Vanderaa) Jabaay; m. Nicholas John Vogelzang, May 17, 1971; children: Nick, Adam, Tim. BA, Trinity Christian Coll., Palos Heights, Ill., 1972; MBA, U. Minn., 1981; JD, U. Chgo., 1987. Bar: Ill. 1987; CPA, Ill. Tchr. Timothy Christian H.S., Elmhurst, Ill., 1972-74; tchg. assoc. in fin. U. Minn., Mpls., 1980-81; fin. analyst Quaker Oats Co., Chgo., 1982-84; atty. Baker & McKenzie, Chgo., 1987-89, Jenner & Block, Chgo., 1989-91; pres., owner J.M. Vogelzang & Assocs., Western Springs, Ill., 1991—; exec. dir. Structural Engrs. Assn. Ill., Chgo., 1992—, Nat. Coun. of Structural Engrs. Assn., Chgo., 1996—. Mem. jud. code com. Christian Reformed Ch. N.Am., Grand Rapids, Mich., 1991—; bd. dirs. Austin Christian Law Ctr., Chgo., 1989-92, Barnabas Found., Palos Heights, 1989-95; com. mem. Western Springs Planning Commn., 1991-95, village trustee, 1995—, chmn. fin. com.; mem. adv. bd. Coll. DuPage Internat. Trade Ctr., Glen Ellyn, Ill., 1992-94; bd. dirs., mem. acad. affairs com., planning com., exec. com. sec. Trinity Christian Coll., 1992—. Mem. ABA, Am. Soc. Assn. Execs., Ill. State Bar Assn., Chgo. Bar Assn. Mem. Christian Reformed Ch. Home: 5108 Fair Elms Ave Western Springs IL 60558-1808 Office: 203 N Wabash Ave Ste 1000 Chicago IL 60601-2412

VOGET, JANE J., city official, lawyer; b. Montréal, Que., Can., Jan. 2, 1949; d. Frederick Wilhelm and Mary Kay (Mee) V.; m. Frederick Walton Hyde, Oct. 9, 1988. BA in German and Anthropology, So. Ill. U., 1971, MS in Planning and Cmty. Devel., 1977; JD, Lewis and Clark Coll., 1990. Bar: Wash. 1991. Program mgr. Ill. Dept. Local Govt. Affairs, Springfield, 1975-78, U.S. Dept. Housing and Urban Devel., Washington, 1978; mem. staff The White House, Office Asst. to Pres. for Intergovtl. Affairs, Washington, 1979-80; exec. dir. Ctr. for Collaborative Problem Solving, San Francisco, 1981-83; hotel asst. mgr. Hyatt Regency Waikiki, Honolulu, 1983-85; housing project mgr. Multnomah County, Portland, Oreg., 1985-88; sr. project mgr. City of Seattle, 1989—; pvt. practice, Seattle, 1991—. Co-author govtl. publs. Vol. lawyer West Seattle Legal Clinic, 1994—; active 11th Dist. Dems., Seattle, 1993-95, Na Hanu 'O Kapuaku'ulei Aloha, 1996—. Mem. ABA (mem. affordable housing fin. com. 1991-96, forum housing & cmty. devel. law, probate and real property sect., state and local govt. sect.), Wash. State Bar Assn. (legal aid com.), King County Bar Assn. (mem. legis. com., govt. ops. subcom. 1995). Avocations: swimming, Hawaiian music and dance, animal rights advocate. Home: 5946 39th Ave SW Seattle WA 98136 Office: City of Seattle 618 2nd Ave Seattle WA 98104-2222

VOGL, OTTO, polymer science and engineering educator; b. Traiskirchen, Austria, Nov. 6, 1927; came to U.S., 1953, naturalized, 1959; s. Franz and Leopoldine (Scholz) V.; m. Jane Cunningham, June 10, 1955; children: Eric, Yvonne. Ph.D., U. Vienna, 1950; Doctorate (hon.), U. Jena, Germany, 1983, Poly. Inst. Iasi, Romania, 1992, Osaka U., Japan. Instr. U. Vienna, 1948-55; research asso. U. Mich., 1953-55, Princeton U., 1955-56; scientist E.I. Du Pont de Nemours & Co., Wilmington, Del., 1956-70; prof. polymer sci. and engring. U. Mass., 1970-83, prof. emeritus, 1983—; Herman F. Mark prof. polymer sci. Poly. U., Bklyn., 1983-95, prof. emeritus, 1996—; guest prof. Kyoto U., 1968, 80, Osaka U., 1968, 96, Royal Inst. Stockholm, 1971, 87, U. Freiburg, Germany, 1973, U. Berlin, 1977, Strasbourg U., 1976, Tech. U. Dresden, 1982, Kyoto Inst. Technology, Japan, 1996; guest Soviet Acad. Sci., 1973, Polish Acad. Sci., 1973, 75, Acad. Sci. Romania, 1974, 76; cons. in field. Chmn. com. on macromolecular chemistry Nat. Acad. Sci. Author: Polyaldehydes, 1967, (with Furukawa) Polymerization of Heterocyclics, 1973, Ionic Polymerization, 1976, (with Simionescu) Radical Co and Graftpolymerization, 1978, (with Donaruma) Polymeric Drugs, 1978, (with Donaruma and Ottenbrite) Polymers in Biology and Medicine, 1980, (with Goldberg and Donaruma) Targeted Drugs, 1983, (with Immergut) Polymer Science in the Next Decade, 1987, (with Kitoyama and Hatada) Macromolecular Design of Polymeric Materials; contbr. articles to profl. jours. Recipient Fulbright award, 1976, Humboldt prize, 1977, Chemistry Pioneer award, 1985, Gold medal City of Vienna, Austria, 1986, Exner medal, 1987, Mark medal, 1989, Honor Ring, City of Traiskirchen, 1989; Japan Soc. Promotion of Sci. sr. fellow, 1980. Fellow AAAS; mem. Am. Chem. Soc. (chmn. div. polymer chemistry 1974, chmn. Conn. Valley sect. 1974, award applied polymer chemistry 1990), Am. Inst. Chemistry, Austrian Chem. Soc., Japanese Soc. Polymer Sci. (award 1991), N.Y. Acad. Sci., Austrian Acad. Sci., Royal Swedish Acad. Sci., Pacific Polymer Fedn. (pres.), Slovak Chem. Soc. (hon. mem.), Croatian Chem. Soc. (hon. mem.), Soc. Polymer Sci. Japan (life), Sigma Xi. Home: 12 Canterbury Ln Amherst MA 01002-3536 Office: U Mass Dept Polymer Sci/Engring Amherst MA 01003

VOGLER, DIANE CLARK, elementary school principal; b. McGehee, Ark., Jan. 11, 1945; d. Stuart Emerson and Mamye Tompye (Campbell) Clark; m. Richard Joseph Vogler, June 16, 1968 (dec. Nov. 1979); children: Amy Diane, Jodi Leigh. BSE, Ark. A&M Coll., 1966; MSE, U. Ark., 1975, EdS, 1983. Cert. elem. adminstr., Ark. Tchr. 6th grade McGehee Pub. Schs., 1966-67; tchr. 5th grade North Little Rock (Ark.) Schs., 1967-68, tchr. 6th grade, 1970-73, tchr. math. grades 1-6, 1975-80; tchr. 6th grade Manhattan (Kans.) Pub. Schs., 1968-70; tchr. 1st grade Pulaski County Spl. Schs., North Little Rock, 1980-85, prin., 1985—; prin. Sylvan Hills Elem., Pulaski County Special Sch. Dist., Sherwood, Ark., 1990—. Mem., dean West Gulf Regional Sch. of Christian Mission United Meth. Women, North Little Rock, 1980—; del. Ark. Dems., Little Rock, 1988; active Sylvan Hills Elem. PTA; dir women's divsn. of the gen. bd. Global Ministries United Meth. Ch., 1996—. Recipient Tchr. of Yr. award Ark. PTA Coun., 1985, Ednl. Excellence award Greater Little Rock C. of C., 1985; named Elem. Prin. of Yr. Pulaski County Spl. Sch. Dist., 1994. Mem. ASCD, Internat. Reading Assn., Nat. Assn. Elem. Sch. Prins., Ctrl. Ark. Reading Coun., Ark. Assn. Elem. Prins. (zone dir. 1990-93), Pulaski County Adminstrs. Assn. (pres. 1989-90), Pulaski County Elem. Prins.' Forum (pres. 1993-94), Sherwood Rotary Club, Delta Kappa Gamma (pres. 1981-82), Phi Delta Kappa. Democrat. Avocations: music, needlework, travel. Office: Pulaski County Spl Sch Dist 402 Dee Jay Hudson Dr Sherwood AR 72120-2302

VOGLER, FREDERICK WRIGHT, French language educator; b. Burlington, Vt., May 27, 1931; s. Curtis Linville and Marion (Wright) V.; m. Mary Frances Angle, Aug. 27, 1965; 1 child, Robert. BA, U. N.C., 1953, MA, 1955, PhD, 1961; postgrad, U. Strasbourg, France, 1953-54. Instr. U. N.C., Chapel Hill, 1961-62, asst. prof., 1963-66, assoc. prof., 1966-78, prof. French, 1978—, assoc. dean arts and scis., 1976-87, dir. undergrad. studies French and Italian, 1989-95; asst. prof. U. Iowa, Iowa City, 1962-63; cons. Ednl. Testing Service, Princeton, N.J., 1967-70. Author: Vital d'Audiguier and the Early 17th Century French Novel, 1964; editor: Moliere Mocked: Three Contemporary Hostile Comedies, 1973; contbr. articles on French lit. and cultural history to profl. jours. Served to 1st lt. U.S. Army, 1955-65. Fulbright Commn. scholar, Washington, Paris, 1953; So. Fellowship Bd.

fellow, Chapel Hill, 1955. Mem. Am. Assn. Tchrs. French, Swiss Am. Hist. Soc. Episcopalian. Home: 1010 Dawes St Chapel Hill NC 27516-3010

VOGT, ALBERT R., forester, educator, program director. BS in Forest Mgmt., U. Mo., 1961, MS in Tree Physiology, 1962, PhD in Tree Physiology, 1966. Instr. in dendrology U. Mo., Columbia, 1965-66; asst. prof. rsch. tree physiology Ohio State U., 1966-69, assoc. prof., assoc. chmn. rsch. and adminstrn. forestry, 1969-76, prof., chmn. dept. adminstrn. and tchg. forestry, 1976-85; prof., dir. sch. natural resources U. Mo., 1985—; mem. Mo. Forest Heritage Initiative, Mo. Gov.'s Task Force on Environ. Edn., Mo. Gov.'s Energy Coalition, Mo. Citizen's Com. for Soil, Water, and State Parks; co-chair steering com. 3d Forestry Edn. Symposium, 1991; co-chair external rev. dept. forestry So. Ill. U., Carbondale, 1993, sch. forest resources Pa. State, 1995; chair external rev. forestry U. Wis., Madison, 1997. Office: Sch of Natural Resources 1-30 Agrl Bldg U Mo Columbia MO 65211

VOGT, CARL WILLIAM, lawyer; b. Houston, Apr. 20, 1936; s. Carl Wilhelm and Myrtle Jesse (Jones) V.; m. Margrit Wulff, July 27, 1968; children—Erika, Bianca. B.A., Williams Coll., 1958; LL.B., U. Tex., 1965. Bar: Tex. 1965, U.S. Dist. Dist. (so. dist.) Tex. 1966, U.S. Dist. Ct. D.C., U.S. Ct. Appeals (5th cir. 1968, U.S. Ct. Appeals (D.C. cir.), U.S. Ct. Appeals (4th cir.), U.S. Ct. Appeals (3d cir.), U.S. Supreme Ct. 1980. Assoc., Fulbright, Crooker, Freeman, Bates & Jaworski, Houston, 1966-68; assoc., ptnr. Thompson, Ogletree, Deakins & Vogt, Atlanta and Washington, 1968-72; assoc., ptnr. Fulbright & Jaworski, Washington, 1972—; presdl. appointee, bd. dirs. Nat. Passenger Ry. Corp. (Amtrak), 1991-92, Nat. Transportation Safety Bd., 1992-94, chmn. 1992-94; mem. White House Commn. on Aviation Safety and Security, 1996-97; dir. Flag Investors Funds, 1996—, Yellow Corp., 1996—, Naval Aviation Mus. Found., 1994—. Chmn., bd. dirs. Chinquapin Sch., Highlands, Tex., 1968-73; mem., hon. mem. bd. trustees Boy and Girls Club of Washington, 1978—; Served to capt. USMC, 1958-62. Fellow Am. Bar Found., Royal Aeronautical Soc.; mem. ABA (mem. adminstn. law sect., chmn. equal employment opportunity com. 1976-80, chmn. mgmt. com. 1984, mem. labor and employment law sect., mem. litigation sect.), Nat. Assn. Coll. and Univ. Attys. (chmn. nat. office com. 1978-81, mem. exec. bd. 1981—), State Bar Tex., Bar D.C., Flight Safety Found. (bd. gov., 1994), Republican. Club: Metropolitan (Washington). Office: Fulbright & Jaworski 801 Pennsylvania Ave NW Ste 500 Washington DC 20004-2615

VOGT, ERICH WOLFGANG, physicist, academic administrator; b. Steinbach, Man., Can., Nov. 12, 1929; s. Peter Andrew and Susanna (Reimer) V.; m. Barbara Mary Greenfield, Aug. 27, 1952; children: Edith Susan, Elizabeth Mary, David Eric, Jonathan Michael, Robert Jeremy. BS, U. Man., 1951, MS, 1952; PhD, Princeton U., 1955; DSc (hon.), U. Man., 1982, Queen's U., 1984, Carleton U., 1988; LLD (hon.), U. Regina, 1986, Simon Fraser U., 1996. Rsch. officer Chalk River (Ont.) Nuclear Labs., 1956-65; prof. physics U. B.C., Vancouver, 1965-95, prof. emeritus, 1995—, assoc. dir. TRIUMF Project, 1968-73, dir. TRIUMF Project, 1981-94, v.p. univ., 1975-81; chmn. Sci. Council B.C., 1978-80. Co-editor: Advances in Nuclear Physics, 1968—; Contbr. articles to profl. jours. Decorated officer Order of Can.; recipient Centennial medal of Can., 1967. Fellow Royal Soc. Can., Am. Phys. Soc.; mem. Can. Assn. Physicists (past pres., gold medal for achievement in physics 1988). Office: Triumf, 4004 Wesbrook Mall, Vancouver, BC Canada V6T 2A3

VOGT, EVON ZARTMAN, JR., anthropologist; b. Gallup, N.Mex., Aug. 20, 1918; s. Evon and Shirley (Bergman) V.; m. Catherine Christine Hiller, Sept. 4, 1941; children—Shirley Naneen (Mrs. Geza Teleki), Evon Zartman III, Eric Edwards, Charles Anthony. A.B., U. Chgo., 1941, M.A., 1946, Ph.D., 1948. Instr. Harvard U., 1948-50, asst. prof., 1950-55, assoc. prof., 1955-59, prof. anthropology, 1959-89, prof. emeritus, 1989—, dir. Harvard Chiapas project, 1957—, chmn. dept. anthropology, 1969-73, master Kirkland House, 1974-82; asst. curator Am. ethnology Harvard (Peabody Mus.), 1950-59, curator Middle Am. ethnology, 1960-89, hon. curator Middle Am. ethnology, 1990—; vis. prof. U. Hawaii, 1972; Mem. div. anthropology and psychology NRC, 1955-57. Author: Navaho Veterans, 1951, Modern Homesteaders, 1955, (with W.A. Lessa) Reader in Comparative Religion, 1958, (with Ray Hyman) Water Witching U.S.A., 1959, 2nd edit., 1970, Zinacantan: A Maya Community in The Highlands of Chiapas, 1969 (Harvard Press Faculty prize Sahagun prize 1969), The Zinacantecos of Mexico: A Modern Maya Way of Life, 1970, 2d edit. 1990, Tortillas for the Gods: A Symbolic Analysis of Zinacanteco Rituals, 1976, 2d edit., 1993, Fieldwork Among the Maya: Reflections on The Harvard Chiapas Project, 1994; editor: Desarrollo Cultural de Los Mayas, 1964, Los Zinacantecos, 1966, People of Rimrock, 1966, Handbook of Middle American Indians, vols. 7 and 8, 1969, Aerial Photography in Anthropological Field Research, 1974, (with Richard M. Leventhal) Prehistoric Settlement Patterns, 1983. Served from ensign to lt. USNR, 1942-46. Decorated Order Aztec Eagle Mexico; fellow Center for Advanced Study in Behavioral Sci., 1956-57. Fellow Am. Acad. Arts and Scis. (councilor 1974-78), Am. Anthrop. Assn. (exec. bd. 1958-60); mem. NAS (chmn. anthropology sect. 1981-84, class V behavioral and social scis. 1986-89), Soc. Am. Archaeology, Royal Anthrop. Inst. Gt. Britain and Ireland, Am. Ethnological Soc., Tavern Club. Home: 14 Chauncy St Cambridge MA 02138-2528 Office: Peabody Museum 35C Harvard Univ Cambridge MA 02138-6437

VOGT, EVON ZARTMAN, III (TERRY VOGT), merchant banker; b. Chgo., Aug. 29, 1946; s. Evon Zartman Jr. and Catherine C. (Hiller) V.; m. Mary Hewit Anschuetz, Sept. 26, 1970; 1 child, Elizabeth Christine. AB, Harvard U., 1968; MBA, U. Colo., 1976. Vol., then staff mem. U.S. Peace Corps., Brazil, 1968-72; v.p. Wells Fargo Bank, Sao Paulo, Brazil, 1977-81; mng. dir. Wells Fargo Internat. Ltd., Grand Cayman, 1982-84; mgr. global funding Wells Fargo Bank, San Francisco, 1984-86; pres. ARBI Transnational, Inc., San Francisco, 1986—; also bd. dirs. Arbi Transnational, Inc., San Francisco; bd. dirs. Magtech Recreational Products, Inc., Las Vegas, 1990—. Bd. dirs. Internat. Diplomacy Coun., San Francisco, 1990—, pres. 1995-97; active No. Calif. C.A.R.E. Found., 1993-95, The Mex. Mus., 1994-96; bd. dirs. World Affairs Coun. of No. Calif., 1996—. Recipient Order of Rio Branco, Brazilian Govt., 1996. Mem. Brazil Soc. No. Calif. (pres. 1989-94), Pan Am. Soc. Calif. (bd. dirs., pres. 1991-94), World Affairs Coun. No. Calif. (bd. dirs.). Office: ARBI Transnational Inc 601 California St San Francisco CA 94108

VOGT, JOHN HENRY, corporate executive; b. Ft. Madison, Iowa, Dec. 31, 1918; s. John Andrew and Edith Elizabeth (Cramer) V.; m. Jean Hilleary, Aug. 4, 1942; children: John Hilleary, Linda Jean, Lisa Louise. B.S.C., Iowa U., 1940. Retail exec. trainee Sears Roebuck & Co., 1940-41; mgmt. trainee, then chief standards engr. Nat. Pressure Cooker Co., Eau Claire, Wis., 1946; sr. indsl. engr. Continental Can Co., 1950-51; with aircraft engine div. Ford Motor Co., Chgo., 1951-57; asst. to gen. mgr. Ford Motor Co., 1956-57; exec. adminstr. Lions Internat., Chgo., 1957-71; exec. v.p. Dairy and Food Industries Supply Assn., Washington, 1971-73; pres. Nat. Eye Research Found., Chgo., 1973-79; exec. dir. North Bus. and Indsl. Council Chgo., 1979-80; exec. dir. Nat. Assn. Corp. Real Estate Execs., West Palm Beach, Fla., 1980-85, sr. mgmt. advisor, 1985-90. Mem. at large nat. coun. Boy Scouts Am.; bd. dirs. Nat. Eye Rsch. Found., 1973-79. Capt. USAAF, 1941-46. Mem. Am. Soc. Assn. Execs. (life), Internat. Assn. Attys. and Execs. in Corp. Real Estate (founder, exec. v.p. 1990—), Toastmasters (past pres. Chgo. chpt.), Lions, Execs. Club Chgo. Home and Office: 18421 Lakeview Cir E Tinley Park IL 60477-4810

VOGT, ROCHUS EUGEN, physicist, educator; b. Neckarelz, Germany, Dec. 21, 1929; came to U.S., 1953; s. Heinrich and Paula (Schaefer) V.; m. Micheline Alice Yvonne Bauduin, Sept. 6, 1958; children: Michele, Nicole. Student, U. Karlsruhe, Germany, 1950-52, U. Heidelberg, Germany, 1952-53; SM, U. Chgo., 1957, PhD, 1961. Asst. prof. physics Calif. Inst. Tech., Pasadena, 1962-65, assoc. prof., 1965-70, prof., 1970—, R. Stanton Avery Disting. Service prof., 1982—, chmn. faculty, 1975-77, chief scientist Jet Propulsion Lab., 1977-78, chmn. div. physics, math. and astronomy, 1978-83; acting dir. Owens Valley Radio Obs., 1980-81; v.p. and provost Calif. Inst. Tech., Pasadena, 1983-87; vis. prof. physics MIT, 1988-94; dir. Caltech/MIT Laser Interferometer Gravitational Wave Observatory Project, 1987-94. Author: Cosmic Rays (in World Book Ency.), 1978, (with R.B. Leighton) Exercises in Introductory Physics, 1969; contbr. articles to profl. jours. Fulbright fellow, 1953-54; recipient Exceptional Sci. Achievement medal NASA, 1981, Profl. Achievement award U. Chgo. Alumni Assn., 1981. Fellow AAAS, A. Phys. Soc. Achievements include research in astrophysics and gravitation. Office: Calif Inst Tech # 51-33 Pasadena CA 91125

VOGT, SHARON MADONNA, author, educator; b. St. Ann, Mo., June 12, 1963; d. Ralph Paul and Jane Louise (Sandberg) V. BS in Edn., Northeast Mo. State U., 1985; MAT, Webster U., 1989. Cert. tchr., Mo. Tchr., coord. math. St. Cletus Sch., St. Charles, Mo., 1986-88; writer, math. editor Ligature, Inc., St. Louis, 1989-90; tchr., math. adviser Pattonville Adult Edn., St. Ann, Mo., 1991-93; dir., cons. math. ednl. svcs. Vogt Cons., Merrimack, N.H., 1991—. Author: Math Review, 1991, Math Journal Writing and Problem Solving, 1991, vol. 2, 1995, Linking Math and Literature, 1992, Graphing, 1992, Money Fun, 1993, Multicultural Math., 1995, Middle School Multicultural Math. Activities, 1995, Geometry Activities, 1995, Middle School Journal Writing, 1995, Pre-Algebra, 1996, Geometry, 1996, Algebra, 1996, Problem Solving Test Bank, 1996, Multicultural Algebra Activities, 1996, Olympic Math., 1996. Mem. Nat. Coun. Tchrs. Math., Alpha Phi Sigma. Avocations: music, nature walks, racquetball, crafts. Home and Office: 93 Middlesex Rd Merrimack NH 03054

VOHRA, RANBIR, political scientist, educator; b. Lyallpur, Punjab, Pakistan, Mar. 5, 1928; came to U.S., 1964; s. Dualatram and Gurandevi V.; m. Meena Vincent, Jan. 14, 1954. BA with honours, Govt. Coll., Lahore, 1946; diploma in Chinese, Peking (China) U., 1959; MA, Harvard U., 1965, PhD, 1969. Program exec. All India Radio, 1947-64, head Chinese unit external svcs., 1959-64; tchg. fellow Harvard U., 1965-67, 68-69, instr., then lectr. history, 1969-71; assoc. prof. U. Calgary, Alta., Can., 1971-73; mem. faculty, Charles A. Dana prof. polit. sci. Trinity Coll., Hartford, Conn., 1973—, chmn. dept., 1973-85, 93-96; tutor Dudley House, Harvard U., 1966-71, vis. prof., summer 1972; vis. prof. Amherst Coll., spring 1974; vis. scholar Harvard Ctr. for East Asian Rsch., 1989-90. Author: Lao She and the Chinese Revolution, 1974, China's Path to Modernization, 1987, 2d edit., 1992, China: The Search for Social Justice and Democracy, 1990, The Making of India, 1997; editor: The Chinese Revolution 1900-1950, 1974. Ford Found. fellow Harvard U., 1964-68. Mem. Assn. Asian Studies, Internat. Polit. Sci. Assn., India Internat. Ctr. Home: 4 Shepard Rd Hartford CT 06110-2021 Office: Trinity Coll Hartford CT 06106

VOHS, JAMES ARTHUR, health care program executive; b. Idaho Falls, Idaho, Sept. 26, 1928; s. John Dale and Cliff Lucille (Packer) V.; m. Janice Hughes, Sept. 19, 1953; children: Lorraine, Carol, Nancy, Sharla. B.A., U. Calif., Berkeley, 1952; postgrad., Harvard Sch. Bus., 1966. Employed by various Kaiser affiliated orgns., 1952-92; chmn., pres., CEO Kaiser Found. Hosps. and Kaiser Found. Health Plan, INc., Oakland, Calif., 1975-92, chmn. emeritus; chmn. bd. dirs. Holy Names Coll., 1981-92; chmn. Marcus Foster Inst., 1981—; chmn. Fed. Res. Bank San Francisco, 1991-94. Bd. dirs. Oakland-Alameda County Coliseum Complex, 1986-96, Bay Area Coun., 1985-94, chmn., 1991-92; mem. Oakland Bd. Port Commrs., 1993-96. With AUS, 1946-48. Mem. NAS, Inst. Medicine.

VOIGHT, ELIZABETH ANNE, lawyer; b. Sapulpa, Okla., Aug. 6, 1944; d. Robert Guy and Garnetta Ruth (Bell) Voight; m. Bodo Barske, Feb. 22, 1985; children: Anne Katharine, Ruth Caroline. BA, U. Ark.-Fayetteville, 1967, MA, 1969; postgrad. U. Hamburg (W.Ger.), 1966-67; J.D., Georgetown U., 1978. Bar: N.Y. 1979. Lectr. German, Oral Roberts U., Tulsa, 1968-69; tchr. German, D.C. pub. schs., 1971-73; instr. German, Georgetown U., Washington, 1973-74, adminstrv. asst. to dean Sch. Fgn. Svc., 1974-77; law clk. Cole Corette & Abrutyn, Washington, 1977-78; atty. Walter, Conston, Alexander & Green, P.C., N.Y.C., 1978-88, Munich, 1990—, Hasche Eschenlohr Peltzer Riesenkampff Fischötter, Munich, 1990— . Translator articles for profl. jours. Chmn. regional screening Am. Field Svc., N.Y.C., 1981-86; founding mem. Am. Berlin Opera Found. German Acad. Exchange Program fellow, 1966-67. Mem. Assn. Bar City N.Y., N.Y. State Bar Assn., Internat. Fiscal Assn., Internat. Bar Assn., Am. C. of C. in Germany, Phi Beta Kappa, Kappa Kappa Gamma.

VOIGHT, JACK C., state official; b. New London, Wis., Dec. 17, 1945; s. Oscar C. and Thelma J. (Hamm) V.; m. Martha J. Wolfe, July 14, 1973; children: Carly, Emily. BS, U. Wis., Oshkosh, 1971. Claims adjuster U.S. F&G Ins. Co., Appleton, Wis., 1971-74; ins. agy. owner Voight Ins. Agy., Appleton, 1974—; state treas. State of Wis., Madison, 1995—; bank organizer Am. Nat. Bank, Appleton, 1992-94; real estate broker Voight Realty & Ins., Appleton, 1977-92. Pres. Appleton Northside Bus. Assn., 1982; alderman City Coun., City of Appleton, 1983-83, pres., 1992-93. Sgt. U.S. Army, 1968-70. Decorated Bronze Star; named Citizen of Yr., Appleton Northside Bus. Assn., 1990. Mem. Nat. Assn. State Treas., Midwest State Treass. Assn. (pres. 1996-97), Appleton Noon Optimist Club (pres. 1980). Republican. Presbyterian. Avocations: gardening, politics. Office: State Treas Wis PO Box 7871 Madison WI 53707-7871

VOIGT, CYNTHIA, author; b. Boston, Feb. 25, 1942; d. Frederick C. and Elise (Keeney) Irving; married, 1964 (div. 1972); m. Walter Voigt, Aug. 30, 1974; children: Jessica, Peter. BA, Smith Coll., 1963. High sch. tchr. English Glen Burnie, Md., 1965-67; tchr. English Key Sch., Annapolis, Md., 1968-69, dept. chmn., 1971-79, tchr., dept. chmn., 1981-88. Author: Homecoming, 1981, Tell Me If the Lovers Are Losers, 1982, Dicey's Song, 1982 (John Newbery medal 1983), The Callender Papers, 1983 (Edgar award 1984), A Solitary Blue, 1983, Building Blocks, 1984, Jackeroo, 1985, The Runner, 1985 (Silver Pencil award 1988, Deutscher Jugend Literator Preis 1989, ALAN award 1989), Come a Stranger, 1986, Izzy, Willy Nilly, 1986 (Calif. Young Reader's award 1990), Stories About Rosie, 1986, Sons From Afar, 1987, Tree by Leaf, 1988, Seventeen Against the Dealer, 1989, On Fortune's Wheel, 1990, The Vandemark Mummy, 1991, Orfe, 1992, Glass Mountain, 1991, David and Jonathan, 1992, The Wings of a Falcon, 1993, When She Hollers, 1994. *

VOIGT, PAUL WARREN, research geneticist; b. Ann Arbor, Mich., Mar. 20, 1940; s. Melvin John and Susie (Warkentin) V.; m. Josephine Bergeret, Aug. 24, 1963; children: Valorie Christine, Suzanna Jo, Peter Charles. BS, Iowa State U., 1962; MS, U. Wis., 1964, PhD, 1967. Rsch. geneticist Agrl. Rsch. Svc., USDA, Woodward, Okla., 1967-74, Temple, Tex., 1974-78; rsch. geneticist, rsch. leader Grassland Soil & Water Rsch. Lab., Temple, Tex., 1978-93; rsch. geneticist Appalachian Soil and Water Conservation Rsch. Lab., 1993—; v.p. Grass Breeder's Work Planning Conf., 1971-73, pres., 1973-75; mem. Nat. Cert. Grass Variety Rev. Bd., 1976-78, 84-87, Grass Crop Adv. Com., 1982-93. Author: (with others) The Science of Grassland Agriculture, 1985, Forages Vol. 1: An Introduction to Grassland Agriculture, 1995; contbr. numerous articles to profl. jours. Mem. Temple Civic Chorus, 1979-90. Fellow Am. Soc. Agronomy, Crop Sci. Soc. Am. (assoc. editor jour. 1980-82, tech. editor 1985-87); mem. Am. Forage and Grassland Coun., Soc. for Range Mgmt., Sigma Xi. Avocations: music, gardening, swimming, camping, photography. Office: Appalachian Soil & Water Conservation Rsch Lab PO Box 400 Beaver WV 25813-0400

VOIGT, RICHARD, lawyer; b. Oskaloosa, Iowa, Jan. 20, 1946; s. Franz Otto Wilhelm and Minni (Heilbrunn) V.; m. Annemarie H. Riemer, Oct. 2, 1976; children: Samuel, Nicholas. BA, Conn. Wesleyan U., 1968; JD, U. Va., 1974. Bar: Va. 1974, U.S. Dist. Ct. (ea. dist.) Va. 1979, Conn. 1981, U.S. Dist. Ct. Conn. 1982, U.S. Ct. Claims 1982, U.S. Ct. Appeals (4th cir.) 1982. Assoc. counsel regional litigation Solicitor's Office Osha Div., 1978-80; staff atty. U.S. Dept. Labor, Washington, 1974-78; prin. Siegel, O'Connor, Schiff, Zangari & Kainen, P.C., 1981-88, 87-88; ptnr. Cummings & Lockwood, Hartford, 1988—. Contbg. author: ABA Treatise on Occupational Safety and Health Law, 1988; contbr. articles to profl. jours. Bd. dirs. Urban League Greater Hartford, 1984-88, Isnt. for Non-Profit Tng. and Devel., 1991—, Hartford Proud and Beautiful, 1995—. Mem. ABA (labor and employment law sect., OSHA com., litigation sect.), Conn. Bar Assn. (labor employment law sect., employment discrimination com., com. on alternative dispute resolution). Avocations: acrylic design, history, sports. Office: 36th Floor Cityplace I Hartford CT 06103

VOIGT, ROBERT GARY, numerical analyst; b. Olney, Ill., Dec. 21, 1939; s. Donald E. and Jean C. (Fishel) V.; m. Susan J. Strand, Aug. 25, 1962; children: Christine, Jennifer. BA, Wabash Coll., 1961; MS, Purdue U., 1963; PhD, U. Md., 1969. Mathematician Naval Ship R & D Ctr., Washington, 1962-69, 71-72; vis. prof. U. Md., College Park, 1969-71; asst. dir. Inst. for Computer Application in Sci. and Engring., Hampton, Va., 1973-83, assoc. dir., 1983-86, dir., 1986-91; program dir. NSF, Arlington, Va., 1992-94; high performance computing and comm. coord. NSF, Arlington, 1994—; mem. tech. adv. bd. NSF, NASA, Dept. of Energy, and others. Co-author: Solution of Partial Differential Equations on Parallel and Vector Computers, 1985; co-editor 7 books; editor numerous jours.; contbr. 21 articles to profl. jours. Recipient Pub. Svc. award NASA, 1989. Mem. IEEE, Am. Math. Soc., Assn. for Computing Machinery, Soc. for Indsl. and Applied Math. (sec. 1987-91). Office: NSF 4201 Wilson Blvd Rm 1105 Arlington VA 22230-0001

VOINOVICH, GEORGE V., governor; b. Cleve., July 15, 1936; m. Janet Voinovich; 3 children. B.A., Ohio U., 1958; J.D., Ohio State U., 1961; LL.D. (hon.), Ohio U., 1981. Bar: Ohio 1961, U.S. Supreme Ct. 1968. Asst. atty. gen. State of Ohio, 1963-64; mem. Ohio Ho. of Reps., 1967-71; auditor Cuyahoga County, Ohio, 1971-76; commr., 1976-78; lt. gov. State of Ohio, 1979; mayor City of Cleve., 1979-90; gov. State of Ohio, 1991—; 1st v.p. Nat. League Cities, 1984-85, pres., 1985; trustee U.S. Conf. Mayors; chmn. Midwestern Govs. Conf., 1991-92, Coun. Gt. Lakes Govs., 1992-94. Recipient cert. of Merit award Ohio U., Humanitarian award NCCJ, 1986; named one of Outstanding Young Men in Ohio Ohio Jaycees, 1970; one of Outstanding Young Men in Greater Cleve. Cleve. Jaycees; Disting. Urban Mayor award Nat. Urban Coalition, 1987; named to All-Pro City Mgmt. team City & State Mag., 1987. Mem. Rep. Govs. Assn. (vice chmn. 1991-92, chmn. 1992-93), Nat. Govs. Assn. (chmn. edn. action team on sch. readiness 1991, chmn. child support enforcement work group 1991-92, mem. strategic planning task force 1991-92, mem. human resources com. 1991—, co-chmn. task force on edn. 1992-93, mem. exec. com. 1993—, co-lead gov. on fed. mandates 1993—), Omicron Delta Kappa, Phi Alpha Theta, Phi Delta Phi. Republican. Office: Office of Gov 77 S High St Fl 30 Columbus OH 43215-6108*

VOITLE, ROBERT ALLEN, college dean, physiologist; b. Parkersburg, W.Va., May 12, 1938; s. Ray Christian and Ruby Virginia (Hannaman) V.; m. Linda Ellen Loveday, Dec. 5, 1975; children: Robert Allen, Elizabeth Anne, Christian Blair, Vanessa Virginia. BS, W.Va. U., 1962; M.S., W.Va., 1965; Ph.D., U. Tenn., 1969. Asst. in poultry U. Tenn., Knoxville, 1965-69; asst. prof. physiology U. Fla., Gainesville, 1969-75, assoc. prof., 1975-79; prof., head dept. poultry Calif. Poly. State U., San Luis Obispo, 1979-81; assoc. dean Coll. Agr., Auburn U., Ala., 1981—; cons. Columbia Bank for Coops., S.C., 1972. Contbr. articles to sci. jours. Pres., other offices Alachua County Fair Assn., Gainesville, 1969-79. Recipient Pub. Service award Alachua County Commn., 1975; recipient Tchr. of Yr. award U. Fla., 1977, Golden Feather award Calif. Poly. Inst., 1982. Mem. Poultry Sci. Assn., So. Poultry Sci. Assn., Gainesville Jaycees (JCI senatorship), Sigma Xi, Gamma Sigma Delta. Episcopalian. Club: Elks. Home: 2247 Longwood Dr Auburn AL 36830-7105 Office: Auburn U Coll Agr Auburn AL 36849

VOJTA, PAUL ALAN, mathematics educator; b. Mpls., Sept. 30, 1957; s. Francis J. and Margaret L. V. B in Math., U. Minn., 1978; MA, Harvard U., 1980, PhD, 1983. Instr. Yale U., New Haven, 1983-86; postdoctoral fellow Math. Scis. Rsch. Inst., Berkeley, Calif., 1986-87; fellow Miller Inst. for Basic Rsch., Berkeley, 1987-89; assoc. prof. U. Calif., Berkeley, 1989-92, prof., 1992—; mem. Inst. for Advanced Study, Princeton, 1989-90, 96-97. Author: Diophantine Approximations and Value Distribution Theory, 1987. Recipient perfect score Internat. Math. Olympiad, 1975. Mem. Am. Math. Soc. (Frank Nelson Cole Number Theory prize 1992), Math. Assn. Am., Phi Beta Kappa, Tau Beta Pi. Avocations: computer, skiing. Office: Univ Calif Dept of Math Berkeley CA 94720

VOKETAITIS, ARNOLD MATHEW, bass-baritone, educator; b. East Haven, Conn., May 11, 1930; s. Mathew Joseph and Agnes Mary (Pilvelis) V.; m. Marion Lee Dever, June 1959 (div. 1967); children: Arnold Mathew Jr., Paul Stanley; m. Nijole Lipciute, Sept. 6, 1968. B.S. in Bus. Adminstrn, Quinnipiac Coll., 1954; postgrad., Yale U. Dir. opera program De Paul U., Chgo., 1987-89; lectr. on singing, acting Northwestern U., Evanston, Ill., 1986; mem. adv. panels in music and ethnic affairs Ill. Arts Coun.; mem. panel for opera and mus. theatre NEA; faculty mem. Brevard (N.C.) Summer Music Ctr., 1987, 88; artist-in-residence for opera Auburn U., Ala., 1990-93. Condr. master classes in singing; Operatic Debut with N.Y.C. Opera, 1958, European debut at, Liceo, Barcelona, Spain, 1968; mem., Met. Opera Nat. Co., appeared with maj. operatic and symphonic orgns. in U.S., Can., Mex., Cen. Am., S.Am., Lyric Opera of Chgo., 1966-84, 89, rec. artist for, Desto, Vox, Columbia, RCA, Turnabout; recitalist appearances on Pay-TV; classical soloist, U.S. Army Band, Washington. Served as sgt. U.S. Army, 1954-56. Recipient 1st place award Conn. Opera Assn. auditions, 1957, Rockefeller Found. award, 1964, Lithuanian Man of Yr. award, 1990, Disting. Alumni award Quinnipiac Coll., 1991. Mem. AFTRA, Am. Guild Mus. Artists (life), Actors Equity. Avocations: golfing, fishing, theater. *I have felt very strongly over the years that opera was written to be enjoyed, not revered, and that it cried out to be acted as well as sung. With television's influence on the viewer, necessity became reality and my hopes are being realized.*

VOLBERDING, PAUL ARTHUR, academic physician; b. Rochester, Minn., Sept. 26, 1949; s. Walter A. and Eldora M. (Prescher) V.; m. Juline Christofferson, June 15, 1971 (div. June 1976); m. Mary M. Cooke, June 6, 1980; children: Alexander, Benjamin, Emily. AB, U. Chgo., 1971; MD, U. Minn., 1975. Resident in internal medicine U. Utah, Salt Lake City, 1975-78; fellow in oncology U. Calif., San Francisco, 1978-81; dir. med. oncology San Francisco Gen. Hosp., 1981—, dir. AIDS program, 1983—; dir. Ctr. for AIDS Rsch. U. Calif., San Francisco, 1988—, prof. medicine, 1990—; bd. dirs. Dignity Ptnrs. Inc., 1996—. Editor: Medical Management in AIDS, 1986; editor Jour. of AIDS, 1990—. Fellow ACP, AAAS; mem. Internat. AIDS Soc. (founder, chmn. bd.). Office: San Francisco AIDS Program U Calif San Francisco 995 Potrero Ave San Francisco CA 94110-2859

VOLBERG, HERMAN WILLIAM, electronics engineer, consultant; b. Hilo, Hawaii, Apr. 6, 1925; s. Fred Joseph and Kathryn Thelma (Ludloff) V.; m. Louise Ethel Potter, Apr. 26, 1968; children: Michael, Lori. BSEE, U. Calif., Berkeley, 1949. Project engr. Naval Electronics Lab., San Diego, 1950-56; head solid state rsch. S.C. div. Gen. Dynamics, San Diego, 1956-60; founder Solidyne Solid State Instruments, La Jolla, Calif., 1958-60; founder, v.p. electronics divsn. Ametek/Straza, El Cajon, Calif., 1960-66; founder, cons. H.V. Cons., San Diego, 1966-69; sr. scientist Naval Ocean Systems Ctr., Oahu, Hawaii, 1970-77; chief scientist Integrated Scis. Corp., Santa Monica, Calif., 1978-80; founder, pres. Acoustic Sys. Inc., Goleta, Calif., 1980-84; founder, pres. Invotron, Inc., Lafayette, Calif., Murray, Utah, 1984—; tech. dir. Reson, Inc., Santa Barbara, Calif., 1992—; cons. U. Utah Ctr. for Engring. Design, 1991; cons. on autonomous underwater vehicle sonar systems Mitsui/U. Tokyo, 1992; lectr. solid state course UCLA and IBM, 1956-62; instr. Applied Tech. Inst., Columbia, Md., 1988—; contbr. to undersea acoustical rsch. and devel. programs European Union, 1990—. Contbr. articles to IRE Bull., IEEE Ocean Electronics Symposium. Mem. adv. panels for advanced sonar systems and for high resolution sonars, USN, 1970-77. 1st lt. U.S. Army, 1944-47, ETO. Recipient award of merit Dept. Navy, 1973, 94. Mem. IEEE, AAAS, NRA, Acoustical Soc. Am., Mine Warfare Assn., N.Y. Acad. Scis., Marine Tech. Soc., U.S. Naval Inst., Planetary Assn., Old Crows, Masons, Elks. Achievements include patents for device for detecting and displaying the response of tissue to stimuli, high rate neutralizer (HIRAN), crane high-voltage sensing system. Home and Office: 41 W 6830 S Murray UT 84107-7124

VOLBORTH, ALEXIS VON, geochemistry and geological engineering educator; b. Viipuri, Finland, July 11, 1924; came to U.S. 1955, naturalized; m. Nadia Hasso, 1947; children: Tatyana, Swetlana, Maria, Gregory, Anna, Nicholaus H.W., Elisabeth. PhC, U. Helsinki, 1950, PhLic and PhD in Geology-Mineralogy, 1954. Mineralogist, rsch. assoc., assoc. prof., prof. U. Nev., Reno, 1956-68; Killam vis. prof. geology, Killam rsch. prof. Dalhousie U., Can., 1968-72; vis. prof. NASA Lunar Sci. Inst., U. Houston, 1972-73; vis. rsch. chemist U. Calif., Irvine, 1973-76; prof. geology and chemistry N.D. State U., 1975-78; prof. geology, scientist Nucleaar Radiation Ctr., Wash. State U., Pullman, 1978-79; prof. geochemistry and chemistry Mont. Coll. Mineral Sci. and Tech., Butte, 1979-94, prof. geol. engring., 1987-92, dir. accelerator lab., 1983-86, sr. radiation safety officer,

1983-86; prof. emeritus Mont. Tech./U. Mont., Butte, 1995—; prin. investigator Stoichiometry Study Lunar Rocks, NASA, 1972-73; cons. AEC, 1961-63, NASA, 1965-73, Anaconda Co., 1968, Atomic Energy Orgn. Iran, 1975, Johns Manville Corp., Chevron, 1980-83, Pegasus Gold Inc., 1987, Placer Dome Inc., Echo Bay, Inc., 1990; U.S. rep., del. 2d Conf. on Natural Reactors, IAEC, Paris, 1977; U.S. rep. Internat. Geol. Correlation Program, 1990-96; interpreter, Russian translator in Soviet Siberia for U.S. and Can. mining cos., 1990-96. Contbr. articles to profl. jours. Traveling rsch. fellow Outokumpu Found., U. Vienna, U. Heidelberg, 1954-55, Hoover fellow Calif. Inst. Tech., 1955-56, sr. fellow Australian Acad. Sci., 1965, fellow Guggenheim Found., 1965-66. Fellow Mineral. Soc. Am., Am. Inst. Chemists; mem. Am. Chem. Soc., Am. Nuclear Soc., Soc. Econ. Geologists, Internat. Precious Metals Inst. Home and Office: PO Box 80 Dayton MT 59914-0080

VOLCKER, PAUL A., economist; b. Cape May, N.J., Sept. 5, 1927; s. Paul A. and Alma Louise (Klippel) V.; m. Barbara Marie Bahnson, Sept. 11, 1954; children: Janice, James. AB summa cum laude, Princeton U., 1949, LLD (hon.), 1982; MA, Harvard U., 1951, LLD (hon.), 1985. Economist Fed. Res. Bank N.Y., 1952-57; pres. Fed. Res. Bank of N.Y., 1975-79; economist Chase Manhattan Bank, N.Y.C., 1957-61, v.p., dir. planning, 1965-68; with Dept. Treasury, Washington, 1961-65, 69-74, dep. under sec. monetary affairs, 1963-65, under sec., 1969-74; chmn. bd. govs. Fed. Res. Bd., Washington, 1979-87; chmn. Fed. Res. Bd., N.Y.C., 1988-96; prof. internat. econ. policy Princeton U., 1988; chmn. Nat. Commn. on Pub. Svc., 1987-90, Trilateral Commn., Group of Thirty. Sr. fellow Woodrow Wilson Sch. Pub. and Internat. Affairs, 1974-75.

VOLCKHAUSEN, WILLIAM ALEXANDER, lawyer, banker; b. N.Y.C., Mar. 13, 1937; s. William Louis and Jessie (Rankin) V.; m. Grace Lyu, Aug. 2, 1968; children: Sharon, Alexander. AB, Princeton U., 1959; AM, U. Calif., Berkeley, 1963; JD, Harvard U., 1966. Bar: N.Y. 1967. Program officer Asia Found., N.Y.C. and San Francisco, 1966-69; mng. atty. Moblzn. for Youth Legal Services, N.Y., 1969-73; dep. supt., gen. counsel N.Y. State Banking Dept., N.Y.C., 1973-79; spl. counsel Hughes Hubbard & Reed, N.Y.C., 1979-80; exec. v.p., counsel, sec. The Dime Savs. Bank of N.Y. Fed. Savs. Bank, N.Y.C., 1980-89, sr. counsel, pub. affairs exec., 1989—; adj. prof. Cardozo Sch. Law Yeshiva U., N.Y.C., 1980-93. Bd. dirs. N.Y.C. Tech. Coll., Asian-Am. Fedn. of N.Y., 100 Yr. Assn., Circle in the Square Theatre, Bklyn. Legal Svcs.-Corp. A, Princeton-in-Asia. Bd. dirs. N.Y. Tech. Coll., Asian-Am. Fedn. of N.Y., 100 Yr. Assn., Circle in the Square Theatre, Bklyn. Legal Svcs.-Corp. A., Princeton-in-Asia, 1994—. Mem. ABA, Assn. of Bar of City of N.Y., Princeton Club (N.Y.C.). Democrat. Avocations: swimming, skiing, gardening, reading, travel. Home: 262 President St Brooklyn NY 11231-4346 Office: Dime Savs Bank 589 5th Ave Fl 2 New York NY 10017-1923

VOLGY, THOMAS JOHN, political science educator, organization official; b. Budapest, Hungary, Mar. 19, 1946. BA magna cum laude, Oakland U., 1967; MA, U. Minn., 1969, PhD, 1972. Prof. polit. sci. U. Ariz., Tucson; dir. Univ. Teaching Ctr.; mayor City of Tucson, 1987-91; exec. dir. Internat. Studies Assn., 1995—; chmn. telecom. com. U. Conf. Mayors, 1988—; cons. H.S. curriculum project Ind. U.; bd. dirs. Nat. League of Cities, 1989-91. Co-author: The Forgotten Americans, 1992; editor: Exploring Relationships Between Mass Media and Political Culture: The Impact of Television and Music on American Society, 1976; contbr. numerous articles to profl. jours.; producer two TV documentaries for PBS affiliate. Mem. Nat. Women's Polit. Caucus Conv., 1983, U.S. Senate Fin. Com., 1985, U.S. Ho. of Reps. Telecommunications Com., 1988—, Polit. Sci. Adminstrn. Com., 1986, Gov.'s Task Force on Women and Poverty, 1986, United Way, 1985-87; bd. dirs. Honors Program, 1981—, U. Teaching Ctr., 1988—, Tucson Urban League, 1981, Ododo Theatre, 1984, So. Ariz. Mental Health Care Ctr., 1987, Nat. Fedn. Local Cable TV Programmers; chmn. Internat. Rels. Caucus, 1981, 86—, Transp. and Telecommunications Com. Nat. League Cities, 1986, 88, 89-91. Recipient NDEA scholarship, 1964-76, NDEA fellowship, 1967-70, Oasis award for outstanding prodn. of local affairs TV programming; named Outstanding Young Am., 1981, Outstanding Naturalized Citizen of Yr., 1980; faculty research grantee U. Ariz., 1972-73, 73-74, 74-75, 77-78. Mem. Pima Assn. Govts., Nat. Fedn. Local Cable Programmers. Democrat. Jewish. Office: U Ariz Polit Dept Sci Tucson AZ 85721

VOLICER, LADISLAV, physician, educator; b. Prague, Czechoslovakia, May 21, 1935; came to U.S., 1969, naturalized, 1977; s. Ladislav and Vilma (Molnarova) V.; m. Olga Holeckova, July 14, 1959 (div. 1970); children: Irena, Katerina; m. Beverly J. Beers, May 20, 1972; children: Zuzka, Marika, Nadine. MD, Charles U., Prague, 1959; PhD in Pharmacology, Czechoslovak Acad. Scis., Prague, 1964. Research assoc. Czechoslovak Acad. Sci., Prague, 1966-68; research asst. prof. U. Munich, Fed. Republic Germany, 1968-69; from asst. to assoc. prof. pharmacology Boston U. Sch. Medicine, 1969-77, asst. prof. medicine, 1975—, prof. pharmacology, 1977—, prof. psychiatry, 1985—, mem. inst. rev. bd., 1975-78; clin. pharmacologist E.N. Rogers Meml. Vets. Hosp., Bedford, Mass., 1980-87, dep. dir. Geriatric Research Edn. Clin. Ctr., 1987-92, clin. dir., 1992—; mem. drug formulary com. State Mass., Boston, 1977-83; mem. inst. rev. bd. McLean Hosp., Belmont, Mass., 1980—. Editor: Clinical Aspects of Cyclic Nucleotides, 1977, Clinical Management of Alzheimer's Disease, 1988; contbr. papers to profl. publs. Grantee Nat. Inst. Aging, 1986—, Nat. Inst. Alcoholism and Alcohol Abuse, 1972-79, Nat. Inst. Drug Abuse, 1973-78, Merck, Sharp & Dohme, 1971; recipient Alcoholism Research award VA, 1979-85. Mem. Soc. for Neurosci., Am. Soc. Pharmacology Exptl. Therapeutics, Gerontol. Soc. Democrat. Unitarian. Home: 147A Andover Rd Billerica MA 01821 Office: EN Rogers Meml Vets Hosp 200 Springs Rd Bedford MA 01730-1114

VOLK, CECILIA ANN, elementary education educator; b. Greensburg, Ind., Mar. 8, 1956; d. Paul George and Ruth (Martin) Volk. BS, Purdue U., 1978; MA in Edn., Ball State U., 1984. Cert. K-Primary tchr., Ind. Tchr. spl. edn. Greensburg Community Schs., 1978-79; tchr. Decatur County Day Care, Greensburg, 1979-81; tchr. 1st grade St. Louis Sch., Batesville, Ind., 1983-91, kindergarten tchr., 1991—, tchr. kindergarten, 1991—. Mem. ASCD, Nat. Assn. Edn. Young Children, Ind. Assn. Edn. Young Chidren, Nat. Coun. Tchrs. Math., Ind. Home Econs. assn., Nat. Cath. Ednl. Assn. Home: 1035 N Broadway St Greensburg IN 47240-1309 Office: St Louis Sch 17 E Saint Louis Pl Batesville IN 47006-1353

VOLK, JAN, professional sports team executive; b. Davenport, Iowa; m. Lissa Volk; children: Shari, Matthew. Grad., Colby Coll., Maine, 1968; J.D., Columbia U., 1971. With Boston Celtics, 1971—, dir. ticket sales, mgr. equipment purchases, travel arrangements, bus. mgr., legal counsel, 1974-76, v.p., 1976-83, gen. mgr., 1983—, now also v.p. Office: Boston Celtics 151 Merrimac St Boston MA 02114-4714*

VOLK, KENNETH HOHNE, lawyer; b. Hackensack, N.J., Nov. 8, 1922; s. Henry L. and Constance (Brady) V.; m. Joyce Geary, May 11, 1954; children: Christopher H., Cynthia. BS, U.S. Naval Acad., 1946; LLB, Yale U., 1953. Ptnr. Burlingham, Underwood, N.Y.C., 1955-92; of counsel McLane, Graf, Raulerson & Middleton, Portsmouth, N.H., 1992—; speaker various symposia and confs. on maritime law. Contbr. articles to profl. jours. Pres. Maritime Assocs., N.Y.C., 1967-68; chmn. bd. dirs. Seamen's House YMCA, N.Y.C., 1971-76; sec., bd. dirs. Seamen's Ch. Inst., N.Y.C., 1977-92; bd. dirs. Strawbery Banke Mus., Portsmouth, N.H.; mem. adv. bd. Tulane Admiralty Law Inst.. Fellow Am. Bar Found., Am. Coll. Trial Lawyers; mem. ABA, Assn. Bar of City of N.Y., Maritime Law Assn. U.S. (exec. com. 1977-80, pres. 1990-92), Comite Maritime Internat. (titulary mem.), Quaker Hill Country Club (pres. 1976-78). Republican. Espicopalian. Avocations: reading, hiking, swimming. Office: McLane Graf Raulerson 30 Penhallow St Portsmouth NH 03801-3816

VOLK, KRISTIN, advertising agency executive; b. Phila., Feb. 26, 1953; d. Richard H. and Doris (Colasanti) V. BS in Biology, Tufts U., 1976; MPH, Boston U. Sch. Med., 1981. Rsch. technician Beth Israel Hosp., Boston, 1976; rsch. asst. Dana-Farber Cancer Inst., Boston, 1976-78; sr. rsch. asst. Beth Israel Hosp., Boston, 1978-81; rsch. supr. Schneider Parker Jakuc Advt., Boston, 1981-86; v.p., assoc. rsch. dir. HBM/Creamer, Boston, 1986-88, Della Femina McNamee, Boston, 1988-90; v.p., dir. rsch. Lawner Reingold Britton & Ptnrs., Boston, 1990-93; sr. v.p., dir. consumer insight group Arnold Fortuna Lawner & Cabot, Boston, 1993-95; exec. v.p., dir. consumer insight group Arnold Comm., Inc., Boston, 1995—; guest lectr. colls. and univs., Boston. Contbr. articles to profl. jours. Mem. Ad Club Boston. Office: Arnold Comm Inc 101 Arch St Boston MA 02110-1130

VOLK, ROBERT HARKINS, aviations company executive; b. East Orange, N.J., Nov. 27, 1932; s. Harry Joseph and Marion (Waters) V.; m. Barbara June Klint, Sept. 10, 1954; children: Christopher G., William W., Laura L., Elisabeth M. BA, Stanford U., 1954, LLB, 1958. Bar: Calif. 1959. Assoc. Adams Duque & Hazeltine, L.A., 1959-62; ptnr. Adams Duque & Hazelyine, L.A., 1962-67; commr. of corps. State of Calif., Sacramento, 1967-69; pres. Union Bancorp, L.A., 1969-73; pres., chmn. Union Am., L.A., 1973-79; owner, chief exec. officer Martin Aviation Inc., Santa Ana, Calif., 1980-90, Media Aviation L.P. Burbank, 1984—. Sgt. USAF, 1955-57. Mem. Calif. Bar Assn. Republican. Episcopalian. Avocations: skiing, golf, tennis. Home: 332 Conway Ave Los Angeles CA 90024-2604 Office: Media Aviation LP 3000 N Clybourn Ave Burbank CA 91505-1012

VOLK, STEPHEN RICHARD, lawyer; b. Boston, Apr. 22, 1936; s. Ralph and Miriam (Rose) V.; m. Veronica J. Brown, June 19, 1959 (dec. Feb. 1989); children: Jeffrey A., Andrew M., Michael J.; m. Diane Kemelman, Apr. 22, 1990; 1 child, Anne. Student, Dartmouth Coll., 1957; JD, Harvard U., 1960. Bar: N.Y. 1961. Assoc. Sherman & Sterling, N.Y.C., 1960-68, ptnr., 1968—, dep. sr. ptnr., 1988-91, sr. ptnr., 1991—; bd. trustees Consolidated Edison Co., N.Y.C., 1996—. Trustee St. Luke's/Roosevelt Hosp., N.Y.C., 1990; ptnr. N.Y.C. Partnership, 1991. Mem. ABA (com. on securities regulation 1974), Am. Law Inst., Assn. Bar City N.Y., Coun. on Fgn. Rels., Univ. Club, Phi Beta Kappa. Office: 599 Lexington Ave New York NY 10022-6030

VOLK, THOMAS, accountant; b. Stuttgart, Germany, July 30, 1970; came to U.S., 1971; s. Earl Walter and Erika (Theilmann) V. BS in Acctg. and Criminal Justice, U. Scranton, 1993, MBA in Acctg. and Finance, 1995. Asst. mgr. Catholic Youth Ctr., Scranton, Pa., 1990-93; acct. Internat. Soc. Animal Rights, Clarks Summit, Pa., 1993-94; head acct. Diocesan Guild Studios, Scranton, 1994—. Vol. Catholic Youth Ctr., Scranton, 1993—, Jr. Achievement Northeast Pa. Mem. Inst. Mgmt. Accts. Home: 101 Ben-Gar Dr Scranton PA 18505 Office: Diocesan Guild Studios 400 Wyoming Ave Scranton PA 18503-1226

VOLKER, DALE MARTIN, state senator, lawyer; b. Lancaster, N.Y., Aug. 2, 1940; s. Julius J. and Loretta (O'Neill) V.; m. Carol A. Suchyna, Nov. 28, 1970; children: Martin Andrew, Mark Dale, Meredith Ann. BA, Canisius Coll., 1963; JD, SUNY-Buffalo, 1966. Bar: N.Y. 1967. Police officer Village of Depew, N.Y., 1966-72; assemblyman State Assembly, Albany, N.Y., 1972-74; mem. N.Y. State Senate, Albany, 1975—; sole practice law, Lancaster. Mem. Erie County Bar Assn., Elks, Moose, Eagles. Republican. Roman Catholic. Home: 92 Center Dr Depew NY 14043-1706 Office: 708 Legislative Office Bldg Albany NY 12247 Address: 5441 Broadway St Lancaster NY 14086

VOLKHARDT, JOHN MALCOLM, food company executive; b. Chester, Pa., Apr. 13, 1917; s. George Thomas and Evelyn (Mitchell) V.; m. Linda J. Volkhardt; children—Jacqueline, Janet, Dana. A.B. cum laude, Brown U., 1939. Product mgr. Vick Chem. Co., N.Y.C., 1939-48; gen. mgr. Northam Warren Co., Stamford, Conn., 1948-56, Rit div. Best Foods Co., N.Y.C., 1956-58; with Best Foods div. CPC Internat. Inc., Englewood Cliffs, N.J., 1958-78, exec. v.p., 1968-71, pres., 1971-78; pres. North Am. div. CPC Internat. and exec. v.p. CPC Internat., 1978-82, group v.p., 1979; v.p. CPC, 1971-78, dir., 1977-82; pres., chmn. Full Circle Corp., Moss Creek, 1985-91; pres. Water Oak Utility, 1985-91. Chmn. bd. Keep Am. Beautiful, Inc., 1979-82, chmn. bd. trustees, 1982. Recipient Herbert Hoover award Nat. Assn. Wholesale Grocers Am.; honoree Nat. Jewish Hosp., 1976. Mem. Phi Beta Kappa.

VOLKMANN, FRANCES COOPER, psychologist, educator; b. Harlingen, Tex., May 4, 1935; d. Edward O. and Elizabeth (Bass) C.; m. John Volkmann, Nov. 1, 1958 (dec.); children: Stephen Edward, Thomas Frederick. A.B. magna cum laude, Mt. Holyoke Coll., 1957; M.A., Brown U., 1959, Ph.D., 1961; DSci., Mt. Holyoke Coll., 1987. Research assoc. Mt. Holyoke Coll., South Hadley, Mass., 1964-65; lectr. U. Mass., Amherst, 1964-65, Smith Coll., Northampton, Mass., 1966-67; asst. prof. Smith Coll., 1967-72, assoc. prof., 1972-78, prof. psychology, 1978—, dean faculty, 1983-88, Harold E. Israel and Elsa M. Siipola prof. psychology, 1988—, acting pres., 1991; vis. assoc. prof. Brown U., Providence, 1974, vis. prof., 1978-82; vis. scholar U. Wash., Seattle, summer 1977. Contbr. articles to profl. jours. Trustee Chatham Coll., 1987—. USPHS fellow, 1961-62; NSF grantee, 1974-78; Nat. Eye Inst. grantee, 1978-82. Fellow APA, AAAS, Optical Soc. Am.; mem. Ea. Psychol. Assn., Soc. Neurosci. Psychonomic Soc., Assn. Rsch. in Vision and Ophthalmology, New Eng. Assn. Schs. and Colls. (vice chair commn. instns. higher edn. 1991-93, chair 1993-95). Home: 40 Arlington St Northampton MA 01060-2003 Office: Smith Coll Northampton MA 01063

VOLKMER, HAROLD L., former congressman; b. Jefferson City, Mo., Apr. 4, 1931; m. Shirley Ruth Braskett; children: Jerry Wayne, John Paul, Elizabeth Ann. Student, Jefferson City Jr. Coll., 1949-51, St. Louis U. Sch. Commerce and Finance, 1951-52; LL.B., U. Mo., 1955. Bar: Mo. 1955. Individual practice law Hannibal, 1958—; asst. atty. gen. Mo., 1955; pros. atty. Marion County, 1960-66; mem. Mo. Ho. of Reps., 1966-76; chmn. judiciary com., mem. revenue and econs. com.; mem. 95th-104th Congresses from 9th Mo. Dist., 1977-96 (ret.); ranking minority mem. agr. subcom. livestock, dairy, & poultry. Served with U.S. Army, 1955-57. Recipient award for meritorious pub. service in Gen. Assembly St. Louis Globe-Democrat, 1972-74. Mem. Mo., 10th Jud. Circuit bar assns. Roman Catholic. Clubs: KC, Hannibal Lions. Home: 5542 N 11th St Arlington VA 22205 also: 719 Country Club Dr Hannibal MO 63401

VOLL, JOHN OBERT, history educator; b. Hudson, Wis., Apr. 20, 1936; s. Obert Frank and Ruth Olivia (Seaberg) V.; m. Sarah Lynne Potts, June 12, 1965; children: Sarah Layla, Michael Obert. AB summa cum laude, Dartmouth Coll., 1958, PhD (Ford Found. fellow), 1969; AM (Danforth fellow), Harvard U., 1960. Instr. history U. N.H., Durham, 1965-69, asst. prof., 1969-74, assoc. prof., 1974-82, prof., 1982-95, chair dept., 1988-91; prof. Georgetown U., Washington, 1995—, dep. dir. Ctr. for Muslim-Christian Understanding, 1996—; mem. history and social scis. adv. com. Coll. Bd. 1983-86, chmn. European history and world cultures achievement test com., 1985-88; tchg. fellow Harvard U., 1969. Author: Historical Dictionary of the Sudan, 1978, 2nd edit., 1992, Islam Continuity and Change in the Modern World, 2nd edit., 1994; (with others) The Sudan: Unity and Diversity, 1985, Eighteenth Century Renewal and Reform in Islam, 1987, Sudan: State and Society in Crisis, 1991, Islam and Democracy, 1996; contbr. articles to profl. jours. Mem. bd. Ecumenical Ministry U. N.H., 1974-78, pres., 1975-77; chmn. social action Durham Cmty. Ch., 1974-75, mem. ch. coun., 1977-78, deacon, 1986—. Sheldon traveling fellow, 1960-61, U. N.H. summer fellow, 1969, 89, NEH fellow, 1971-72, Fulbright faculty rsch. abroad fellow, 1978-79, Inst. Advanced Studies fellow Hebrew U., 1984-85; recipient Egyptian Presdl. medal, 1991. Mem. Am. Coun. Learned Socs. (del. 1989-96, del. exec. com. 1989-92, bd. dirs. 1990-92), New England Hist. Assn. (sec. 1975-78, v.p. 1981, pres. 1982), Sudan Studies Assn. (bd. dirs. 1981-82, co-exec. dir. 1990-94), N.H. Coun. on World Affairs (bd. dirs. 1978-95), Am. Hist. Assn., Mid. East Studies Assn. (bd. dirs. 1987-89, pres. 1992-93), Am. Coun. for Study of Islamic Socs. (bd. dirs. 1989—, v.p. 1989-91), N.H. Humanities Coun. (bd. dirs. 1991-95). Mem. United Ch. of Christ. Home: Apt 652B 4000 Cathedral Ave NW Washington DC 20016-5286 Office: Ctr Muslim Christian Understanding Georgetown U Washington DC 20057

VOLLBRECHT, EDWARD ALAN, school superintendent; b. Freeport, N.Y., July 22, 1941; s. Edward Chester and Lillian Elizabeth (Heinecke) V.; m. Catherine Ann Salgado, Dec. 2, 1977; 1 child, Matthew Grayson. BS, SUNY, New Paltz, 1963; MS, Hofstra U., 1968; PhD, Walden U., Naples, Fla., 1973. Adminstrv. asst. Pearl River (N.Y.) Sch. Dist., 1968-70, asst. prin., 1970-71; prin. Mark Twain Mid. Sch., Yonkers, N.Y., 1971-73; asst. dir. mid. schs. Yonkers Pub. Schs., 1973-74, dir. secondary edn., 1974-75; asst. supt. Bethlehem (Pa.) Area Sch. Dist., 1975-78; supt. schs. South Williamsport (Pa.) Area Sch. Dist., 1978-84, N.W. Area Sch. Dist., Shickshinny, Pa., 1984-88, Everett (Pa.) Area Sch. Dist., 1988—; cons. New Eng. Sch. Devel. Coun., Boston, 1973-75; adj. prof. Manhattan Coll., N.Y.C., 1975-76, Lehigh U., Bethlehem, 1978-79. Mem. Everett Area Indsl. Devel. Corp., 1988—, Wet Providence Indsl. Devel. Authority, Bedford County Devel. Authority, Bedford County Devel. Assn., Bedford County Planning Commn. Recipient Jenkins Meml. award Yonkers PTA, 1974, Svc. for Youth award YMCA, Yonkers, 1975. Mem. ASCD, Am. Assn. Sch. Adminstrs., Pa. Assn. Sch. Adminstrs., Pa. Sch. Bds. Assn., Bedford County Ednl. Found., Allegany C.C. Found., Lions, Rotary, Naurashank, Phi Delta Kappa. Republican. Roman Catholic. Home: 415 Locust Ct Dr Everett PA 15537 Office: Everett Area Sch Dist 15 South St Extension Everett PA 15537

VOLLEN, ROBERT JAY, lawyer; b. Chgo., Jan. 23, 1940; s. Ben N. and Rose (Belonsky) V.; m. Judith Paula Spector, Aug. 12, 1961; children: Steven, Neil, Jennifer. A.B., U. Mich., 1961; J.D., U. Chgo., 1964. Bar: Ill. 1964, D.C. 1965, U.S. Supreme Ct. 1975. Atty. appellate sect. Civil Div., U.S. Dept. Justice, Washington, 1964-65; asso. firm Schiff Hardin & Waite, Chgo., 1965-70; partner firm Schiff Hardin & Waite, 1971-72; gen. counsel BPI (Bus. and Profl. People for Pub. Interest), Chgo., 1972-83; ptnr. Schwartz & Freeman, Chgo., 1983-87. Mem. vis. com. U. Chgo. Law Sch., 1978-81. Mem. Chgo. Council Lawyers (gov. 1972-76, 79-81), ABA (ho. of dels. 1974-76). Home: 2 Kingswood Ln Deerfield IL 60015-1912

VOLLHARDT, KURT PETER CHRISTIAN, chemistry educator; b. Madrid, Mar. 7, 1946; came to U.S., 1972; Vordiplom, U. Munich, 1967; PhD, U. Coll., London, 1972. Postdoctoral fellow Calif. Inst. Tech., Pasadena, 1972-74; asst. prof. chemistry U. Calif., Berkeley, 1974-78, assoc. prof., 1978-82, prof., 1982—; prin. investigator Lawrence Berkeley Lab., 1975—; cons. Monsanto Corp., St. Louis, Exxon Corp., Annandale, N.J., Maruzen Corp., Tokyo; vis. prof. U. Paris-Orsay, 1979, U. Bordeaux, 1985, U. Lyon, 1987, U. Rennes, 1991, U. Paris VI, 1992, Tech. U. Munich, 1992. Author: Organic Chemistry, 1987, 2d edit., 1994; co-author: Aromatizität, 1972; assoc. editor: Synthesis, 1984-89; editor Synlett, 1989; contbr. articles to profl. jours.; patentee in field. Sloan fellow, 1976-90; Camille and Henry Dreyfus scholar, 1978-83; recipient Adolf Windaus medal, 1983, Humboldt Sr. Scientist award, 1985, 92, Otto Bayer prize, 1990, A.C. Cope scholar award, 1991, Japan Soc. for Promotion of Sci. award, 1995, German Sci. Book award, 1996; named one of Am.'s 100 Brightest Scientists Under 40, Sci. Digest, 1984. Mem. Am. Chem. Soc. (Organometallic Chemistry award 1987), German Chem. Soc., Chem. Soc. of London, Internat. Union Pure & Applied Chemistry (organic chemistry div. com.). Office: U Calif Berkeley Dept of Chemistry Berkeley CA 94720

VOLLMANN, JOHN JACOB, JR., cosmetic packaging executive; b. Elizabeth, N.J., Apr. 10, 1938; s. John Jacob and Marie Louise (Sirois) V.; m. Marian Ethel Snetsinger, May 29, 1976; children: Andrea Leah, John Jacob III. BA, Queen's U., Kingston, Ont., 1973, BA with honors, 1976; postgrad., Rutgers U., 1977; PhD, Walden U., Naples, Fla., 1991. Cert. hypnotherapist; criminal justice instr., Fla. V.p. No. Trading Co., Inc., Madawaska, Maine, 1976—, also chmn., bd. dirs., 1996—; instr. Sch. of Justice and Safety Adminstrn., Miami-Dade Community Coll., 1978—; bd. dirs. Edward Sagarin Inst. for Study of Deviance and Social Issues. Contbr. articles to profl. jours. Vice chmn. Police & Fire Pension Bd., Dania, Fla., 1984; chmn. Unsafe Structures Bd., Dania, 1984; code Enforcement Bd., Dania, 1984; adv. dep. Broward County Sheriff, Ft. Lauderdale, Fla., 1986-92; maj. Fla. Sheriff's Adv. Coun., 1992—. Recipient Richard A. McGhee award Am. Justice Inst., 1992. Mem. NRA, Am. Correctional Assn., Am. Soc. Criminology (life), Acad. Criminal Justice Scis. (life), Am. Jail Assn., Am. Probation and Parole Assn., Northeastern Criminal Justice Assn. (life), Fla. Criminal Justice Educators (pres. 1984-88), So. Assn. Criminal Justice (bd. dirs. 1981-90), Internat. Assn. for Study Organized Crime, N.Am. Assn. Wardens and Supts., Optimists (lt. gov. South Fla. dist. 1993-96, disting. lt. gov. 1996, lt. gov. New Eng. 1995-97), Internat. Assn. Chiefs of Police. Avocations: hunting, fishing. Home: 411 SE 3rd Pl Dania FL 33004-4703 Office: No Trading Co Inc 190-202 E Main St Madawaska ME 04756-1510

VOLLMAR, JOHN RAYMOND, electrical engineer; b. Phila., Nov. 8, 1929; s. William Gustav and Pauline Marie (Jesanker) V.; m. Sara Lois Jacob, Feb. 1, 1964; children—Paul Gary, Virginia Ann, Pamela Jean, Barbara Gayle, Thomas Edward, Timothy Morris. B.E.E., Drexel U., Phila., 1952. Registered profl. engr., Pa. Sales and application engr. Gen. Electric Co., Erie, Pa., 1955-59; rail transit and equipment engr. Louis T. Klauder & Assocs., Phila., 1959-65; ptnr. in charge r.r. and transit equipment engring. Louis T. Klauder & Assocs., 1965-84; v.p. LTK Engring. Svcs., Phila., 1985-92, sr. v.p., 1993-94; cons. emeritus, 1995—. Served with C.E. AUS, 1952-54. Decorated Army Commendation ribbon. Mem. Nat., Pa. socs. profl. engrs., IEEE, Am. Pub. Transit Assn. Methodist. Clubs: Union League (Phila.). Home: 727 Gregory Dr Horsham PA 19044-1123 Office: 2 Valley Sq Ste 300 Blue Bell PA 19422-2717

VOLLMER, JAMES E., consulting company executive; b. Phila., Apr. 19, 1924; s. Edward L. and Elizabeth (MacMichael) V.; m. Mary Campolieto, Nov. 16, 1946 (dec. July 1992); children: Jamie, Kurt, Kimarie; m. Avalon E. Kolar, Jan. 27, 1994. B.S., Union Coll., Schenectady, 1945; M.A., Temple U., Phila., 1951, Ph.D., 1956; grad., Advanced Mgmt. Program, Harvard U. Bus. Sch., 1971. Instr. physics Temple U., 1946-51; research supr. Honeywell Corp., Phila., 1952-59; with RCA, 1959—, dir. Advanced Tech. Labs., Camden, N.J., 1959-72; div. v.p., gen. mgr. Govt. Systems Group, RCA, Moorestown, N.J., 1972-79; corp. group v.p. Govt. Systems Div., Comml. Communications Div. and Picture Tube Div. RCA, Cherry Hill, N.J., 1979-83; corp. sr. v.p. RCA, Princeton, N.J., 1983-84; pres. James Vollmer Assocs. Inc., Jupiter Inlet Colony, Fla., 1984-89; disting. lectr. Am. Soc. Engring. Edn., 1972. Author; patentee in field. Vice pres. Palm Beach County (Fla.) United Way, 1974-75; exec. adv. council Fla. Atlantic U., Boca Raton, Fla., 1974-75; vice chmn. campaign Camden County (N.J.) United Way, 1980; bd. dirs. W. Jersey Hosp., Camden, 1980; bd. govs. Franklin Inst., Phila., 1980; chmn. bd. Bartol Rsch. Found., 1980-87. With USNR, 1943-45. Fellow IEEE, AAAS; mem. Am. Phys. Soc., Nat. Security Indsl. Assn. (nat. trustee, past pres. Phila. chpt.), World Affairs Coun. Phila. (bd. dirs. 1982-85), Navy League (life), S. Jersey C. of C. (dir. 1975-77), Northland C. of C., Tequesta Country Club, Phi Beta Kappa, Sigma Xi, Sigma Pi Sigma, Eta Kappa Nu. Home: 212 Turtle Creek Dr Tequesta FL 33469-1545 *Management is the process of making decisions in the presence of uncertainty. Success comes to those who recognize this and correctly evaluate their uncertainty, tolerance, and work to maximize it.*

VOLLMER, RICHARD WADE, federal judge; b. St. Louis, Mar. 7, 1926; s. Richard W. and Beatrice (Burke) V.; m. Marilyn S. Stikes, Sept. 17, 1949. Student, Springhill Coll., 1946-49; LLB, U. Ala., 1953. Bar: Ala. 1953, U.S. Dist. Ct. (so. dist.) Ala. 1956, U.S. Ct. Appeals (5th cir.) 1963, U.S. Ct. Appeals (11th cir.) 1983. Judge U.S. Dist. Ct. (so. dist.) Ala., 1990—. Mem. Mobile Bar Assn. (pres. 1990), Rotary (Paul Harris fellow 1988). Roman Catholic.

VOLLUM, ROBERT BOONE, management consultant; b. Abington, Pa., Sept. 13, 1933; s. Charles Milton and Marion (Yocum) V.; m. Gayle Lorraine Timmerman, July 8, 1956; children: Robert Boone III, Jeffrey Charles. BS in Engring. and Sci., U.S. Naval Acad., 1955. Sr. cons., group leader Stevenson, Jordan & Harrison, Inc., N.Y.C., 1959-65; asst. to pres., plant supt., sales engr. W.L. Gore & Assocs., Inc., Newark, Del., 1965-69; gen. mgr. Philmont Pressed Steel subs. Gulf & Western Industries, Inc., Bethayres, Pa., 1969-72, Air Shields div. Narco Sci. Industries, Inc., Hatboro, Pa., 1972-75; pres. Advanced Airflow Tech., Inc., Warminster, Pa., 1975-76, R.B. Vollum & Assocs., Huntingdon Valley, Pa., 1986—, RBV Mktg. Inc., Willow Grove, Pa., 1992—; chmn. bd. dirs., CEO SFM Technologies, Willow Grove, 1994—; prin. mfg. cons. Sperry Corp., Blue Bell, Pa., 1976-84; dir. cons. Creative Output, Inc., Milford, Conn., 1984-86; spkr. in field. Contbr. articles to profl. jours. Bd. dirs. Upper Moreland Little League, 1965-76. Served to lt. USN, 1955-59. Fellow Am. Prodn. and Inventory Control Soc. (chpt. pres. 1984-85); mem. soc. Mfg. Engrs (sr. mem.), Computer and Automated Systems Assn. (sr. mem.). Republican. Episcopalian. Home: 525 Overlook Ave Willow Grove PA 19090-2818 Office: PO Box 206 Huntingdon Valley PA 19006-0206

VOLMAN, DAVID HERSCHEL, chemistry educator; b. Los Angeles, July 10, 1916; s. Carl Herman and Blanche (Taylor) V.; m. Ruth Clare Jackson, Sept. 15, 1944; children: Thomas Peter, Susan Frances, Daniel Henry. B.A., UCLA, 1937; M.S., 1938; Ph.D. (Standard Oil Co. fellow), Stanford U., 1940. Mem. faculty U. Calif.-Davis, 1940-41, 46—, prof. chemistry, 1956-87, emeritus prof. chemistry, 1987—, chmn. dept., 1974-81, chmn. Acad. Senate, 1971-72; research chemist OSRD, 1941-46; research fellow Harvard U., 1949-50; Vis. prof. U. Wash. 1958. Editor: Advances in Photochemistry, 1983; mem. editorial bd. Jour. Photochemistry and Photobiology, 1972; contbr. articles to profl. jours. Grantee Research Corp. Am.; Grantee NIH; Grantee U.S. Army Research Office; Grantee NSF; Guggenheim fellow, 1949-50. Mem. Am. Chem. Soc., AAUP, Inter-Am. Photochem. Soc., Assn. Harvard Chemists, Sigma Xi. Office: U Calif-Davis Dept Chemistry Davis CA 95616

VOLPE, ANGELO ANTHONY, university administrator, chemistry educator; b. N.Y.C., Nov. 8, 1938; s. Bernard Charles and Serafina (Martorana) V.; m. Jennette Murray, May 15, 1965. B.S., Bklyn. Coll., 1959; M.S., U. Md., 1962, Ph.D., 1966; M.Engring. (hons.), Stevens Inst. Tech., 1975. Rsch. chemist USN Ordnance Lab., Silver Spring, Md., 1961-66; asst. prof. to prof. chemistry Stevens Inst. Tech., Hoboken, N.J., 1966-77; chmn. dept. chemistry East Carolina U., Greenville, N.C., 1977-80, dean. coll. arts and scis., 1980-83, vice chancellor for acad. affairs, 1983-87; pres. Tenn. Tech. U., 1987—; adj. prof. textile chem. N.C. State U., Raleigh, 1978-82; guest lect. Plastics Inst. Am., Hoboken, 1967-82. Contbr. articles to profl. jours. Recipient Ednl. Svc. award Plastics Inst. Am., 1973; named Freygang Outstanding Tchr., Stevens Inst. Tech., 1975. Mem. Am. Chem. Soc., Tenn. Acad. of Scis., Sigma Xi, Phi Kappa Phi. Democrat. Roman Catholic. Avocations: golf; reading. Home: Tenn Tech U Walton House Box 5007 Cookeville TN 38505 Office: Tenn Tech U Office of Pres Cookeville TN 38505

VOLPE, EDMOND L(ORIS), college president; b. New Haven, Nov. 16, 1922; s. Joseph D. and Rose (Maisano) V.; m. Rose Conte, May 20, 1950; children: Rosalind, Lisa. A.B., U. Mich., 1943; M.A., Columbia U., 1947, Ph.D., 1954. Instr. N.Y. U., 1949-54; mem. faculty City Coll. N.Y., 1954-74, prof. English, 1968-74, chmn. dept., 1964-70; pres. Richmond Coll., 1974-76, Coll. S.I., 1976-94; Fulbright prof. Am. lit., France, 1960-61. Author: A Reader's Guide to William Faulkner, 1964; also anthologies and coll. text books.; Co-editor: Eleven Modern Short Novels. Bd. dirs. Staten Island United Way, 1975—, S.I. council Boy Scouts Am., 1977-84, S.I. Doctors Hosp., 1977-78, Snug Harbor Cultural Ctr., 1978-83, St. Vincent's Hosp., 1979—; mem. N.Y.C. Mayor's Commn. on Bias, 1986-88. With AUS, 1943-46. Recipient Commendatore Order of Merit, Republic of Italy, Cmty. Svc. award Italian Club S.I., Humanitarian award S.I. Jewish Found. Sch., Mills G. Skinner award S.I. br. N.Y. Urban League, Christopher Columbus award Columbian Assn. Bd. Edn., Disting. Cmty. Svc. award YMCA, Cmty. Svc. award S.I. Women's divsn. Am. Com. on Italian Migration, Outstanding Achievement award Guiseppe Mazzini Lodge of Sons of Italy; named Educator of Yr. Am. Legion Richmond County. Mem. MLA, Am. Studies Assn., Assn. Dept. English (exec. com. 1969-71), Am. Assn. State Colls. and Univs. (task force ednl. opportunites for the aging, research and liason com., com. internat. programs, health affairs com.), Am. Assn. Higher Edn., Am. Assn. Colls. for Tchr. Edn., Am. Assn. Univ. Profs., Am. Council Edn., Am. Studies Assn., Assn. Colls. and Univs. N.Y., Assn. Depts. of English (nat. exec. com.), Coll. English Assn. (nat. bd. dirs.), Consortium Internat. Programs, Inst. Internat. Edn., Inc., Middle States Assn. Colls. and Schs. Club: Andiron N.Y. (pres. 1972-75).

VOLPE, EILEEN RAE, special education educator; b. Fort Morgan, Colo., Aug. 23, 1942; d. Earl Lester and Ellen Ada (Hearting) Moore; m. David P. Volpe, July 28, 1965 (div. 1980); children: David P. Jr., Christina Marie. BA, U. No. Colo., 1964, MA, 1978. Cert. fine art tchr., learning handicapped specialist, resource specialist. 5th grade tchr. Meml. Elem. Sch., Milford, Mass., 1967-68; fine arts jr./sr. high tchr. Nipmuc Regional Jr. Sr. H.S., Mendon, Mass., 1968-69; spl. edn. tchr. Saugus (Calif.) High Sch., 1979—; publicity dir. Sacred Heart Ch. Sch., Milford, Mass., 1974-75, float coord. bicentennial parade, 1975. Author: (poetry) Seasons to Come, 1994, Best Poems of 1997, The Other Side of Midnight, 1997. Mem. Calif. Tchr. Assn., Coun. for Exceptional Children, DAR, Phi Delta Kappa, Kappa Delta Pi. Republican. Avocations: arts and crafts, photography, travel, doll collecting and creation. Office: Saugus High Sch 219000 W Centurion Way Santa Clarita CA 91350

VOLPE, ELLEN MARIE, middle school educator; b. Bronx, N.Y., Aug. 2, 1949; d. George Thomas and Mary (Popadinecz) Soloweyko; m. Ronald Edward Volpe, May 22, 1971; children: Keith, Daniel, Christopher, Stephanie. BBA, Pace U., 1971; MA in Teaching, Sacred Heart U., 1986. Tchr. Conn. Bus. Inst., Stratford, 1979-80, Katherine Gibbs Sch., Norwalk, Conn., 1980-89; adj. instr. So. Cen. Community Coll., New Haven, 1986-87, Salt Lake C. C., Phillips Jr. Coll., Salt Lake City, 1992-93; instr. Bryman Sch., Salt Lake City, 1990-92; tchr. Indian Hills Mid. Sch., Sandy, Utah, 1993—; bus. team leader reaccreditation and tech. coms. Indian Hills Mid. Sch., 1996; mem. curriculum rev. com. Katharine Gibbs Sch., 1989-90. Mem., NEA, Am. Vocat. Assn., Nat. Bus. Edn. Assn., Western Bus. Edn. Assn. Avocations: ceramics, gardening. Home: 8390 Sublette Cir Sandy UT 84093-1164

VOLPE, ERMINIO PETER, biologist, educator; b. N.Y.C., Apr. 7, 1927; s. Rocco and Rose (Ciano) V.; m. 1991; children: Laura Elizabeth, Lisa Lawton, John Peter. B.S., City Coll. N.Y., 1948; M.A., Columbia, 1949, Ph.D. (Newberry award 1952), 1952. Asst. zoologist Columbia U., N.Y.C., 1948-51; instr. biology CCNY, N.Y.C., 1951-52; asst. prof. zoology Newcomb Coll., Tulane Uu., 1952-81, chmn. dept. zoology, 1954-64, 64-66, 69-79; W.R. Irby disting. prof. biology Tulane U., 1979-81, asso dean grad. sch., 1967-69; prof. basic med. scis. (genetics) Mercer U. Sch. Medicine, Macon, Ga., 1981—; cons. Nat. Commn. Undergrad. Edn. in Biol. Scis., 1964-71; mem. steering com. Biol. Scis. Curriculum Study, 1966-70; panelist NRC, 1967-70; mem. U.S. Nat. Commn. for UNESCO, 1968-72; regional lectr. Sigma Xi, 1970-72; lectr. Elderhostel, 1988—; chmn. Advanced Placement Test in Biology, Ednl. Testing Service, 1975-80. Author: (textbook) Understanding Evolution, 1985, Human Heredity and Birth Defects, 1971, Patterns and Experiments in Developmental Biology, 1973, Man, Nature, and Society, 1975, The Amphibian Embryo in Transplantation Immunity, 1980, Biology and Human Concerns, 1993, Patient in the Womb, 1984, Test-Tube Conception: A Blend of Love and Science, 1987; mem. editorial bd. jour. Copeia, 1962-63; asso. editor Jour. Exptl. Zoology, 1968-76, 84-85; editor (jour.) Am. Zoologist, 1975-80; contbr. articles to profl. jours. Served with USNR, 1945-46. Fellow AAAS; mem. Genetics Soc. Am., Am. Soc. Zoologists (pres. 1981), Am. Soc. Naturalists, Soc. Devel. Biology, Soc. Study Evolution, Am. Soc. for Cell Biology, Am. Soc. Human Genetics, Phi Beta Kappa (v.p. Tulane U. chpt. 1962), Sigma Xi (pres. Tulane U. chpt. 1964, faculty award 1972.). Office: Mercer Univ Sch Medicine PO Box 134 Macon GA 31207-0002

VOLPE, JOSEPH, opera company administrator. Gen. mgr. Met. Opera Assn., N.Y.C. Office: Met Opera Lincoln Ctr W 64th & Broadway New York NY 10023

VOLPE, PETER ANTHONY, surgeon; b. Columbus, Ohio, Dec. 17, 1936; s. Peter Anthony and Jeanette Katherine (Volz) V.; m. Suzanne Stephens, Sept. 5, 1959 (div. 1977); children: John David, Michael Charles; m. Kathleen Ann Townsend, Mar. 28, 1978; 1 child, Mark Christopher. BA cum laude, Ohio State U., 1958, MD summa cum laude, 1961. Diplomate Am. Bd. Surgery, Am. Bd. Colon and Rectal Surgery (pres. 1988). Pvt. practice San Francisco, 1969-86; sr. ptnr. Volpe, Russell, Chiu, Abel, MD's, San Francisco, 1987—; clin. prof. surgery U. Calif., San Francisco, 1995—; asst. clin. prof. surgery U. Calif., San Francisco, 1972-95, clin. prof., 1995—; chmn. dept. surgery St. Mary's Hosp. and Med. Ctr., San Francisco, 1978-90. Contbr. articles to profl. jours. Lt. USN, 1962-64. Fellow ACS (bd. govs. 1988-94), Am. Soc. Colon and Rectal Surgeons (treas. 1985-89, pres. 1990); mem. San Francisco Surg. Soc., San Francisco Med. Soc. Republican. Roman Catholic. Office: Volpe Russell Chiu Abel 3838 California St San Francisco CA 94118-1522

VOLPE, RALPH PASQUALE, insurance company executive; b. Souderton, Pa., Sept. 20, 1936; s. Pasquale S. and Katie M. (Hartzell) V.; m. Marie F. Romano, Feb. 6, 1965; children: William, Anthony, Lynda. BA in Polit. Sci., Pa. State U., University Park, 1963. Claim cons. Aetna Life & Casualty Co., King of Prussia, 1964—. Mem. Upper Merion Twp. Bd. Suprs., 1974-79, 82-87, 94—, chmn., 1984, 86, 87, 96, 97, vice chmn., 1985, 95, 2d. v.p. Montgomery County Assn. Twp. Ofcls., 1995-97, pres., 1997—; mem. exec. bd. Greater Valley Forge Transp. Mgmt. Assn., 1994—; mem. Upper Merion Govt. Study Commn., 1974, Rte 202 Exec. Com., 1994—; chmn. Upper Merion Dems., 1980-81; chmn. Montgomery County Dem. Campaign, 1975. With U.S. Army, 1959-61. Recipient Good Govt. award Upper Merion Jaycees, 1977, Excellence in Govt. award King of Prussia C. of C., 1997. Mem. Chapel Four Chaplains, Legion Hon. Mem., Optimists, Valley Forge Order Sons of Italy in Am. #1776, Valley Forge Hist. Soc. Republican. Roman Catholic. Home: 240 Strawberry Ln King Of Prussia PA 19406

VOLPÉ, ROBERT, endocrinologist, researcher, educator; b. Toronto, Mar. 6, 1926; s. Aaron G. and Esther (Shulman) V.; m. Ruth Vera Pullan, Sept. 5, 1949 (dec. Jan. 1997); children: Catherine, Elizabeth, Peter, Edward, Rose Ellen. MD, U. Toronto, 1950. Intern U. Toronto, 1950-51, resident in medicine, 1951-52, 53-55, fellow in endocrinology, 1952-53, NRC fellow, 1955-57, sr. rsch. fellow dept. medicine, 1957-62, McPhedran fellow, 1957-65, from asst. prof. to prof., 1962-92, prof. emeritus, 1992—, dir. divsn. endocrinology and metabolism, 1987-92, chmn. centennial com., 1987-88; attending staff St. Joseph's Hosp., Toronto, 1957-66; active staff Wellesley Hosp., Toronto, 1966—; dir. endocrinology rsch. lab. Wellesley Hosp., 1968—, physician-in-chief, 1974-87; trans-Atlantic vis. prof. Caledonia Endocrine Soc., 1985; Hashimoto Meml. lectr. Kyushu U., Fukuoka, Japan, 1992; K.J.R. Wightman vis. prof. Royal Coll. Physicians, Can., 1994; celebratory lectr. commemorating 200th anniversary of birth of Robert Graves, Dublin, Ireland, 1996. Author: Systematic Endocrinology, 1973, 2d edit., 1979, Thyrotoxicosis, 1978, Auto-immunity in the Endocrine System, 1981, Auto-immunity and Endocrine Disease, 1985, Thyroid Function and Disease, 1987, Autoimmunity in Endocrine Disease, 1990; also over 300 rsch. articles mostly on immunology of thyroid disease; past editl. bd. Jour. Clin. Endocrinology and Metabolism, Clin. Medicine, Clin. Endocrinology, Annals Internal Medicine, Endocrine Pathology; editl. bd.: Am. Jour. Physiology, Opinions in Endocrinolgy Metabolism, Thyroid, Jour. Royal Soc. Medicine. Served with Royal Can. Naval Vol. Res., 1943-45. Recipient Goldie medal for med. rsch. U. Toronto, 1971, Novo-Nordisk prize Irish Endocrine Soc., 1990; Med. Rsch. Coun. Can. grantee, 1960-97. Fellow Royal Coll. Physicians Can. (coun. 1988-96, chmn. ann. meetings com. 1988-94, sci. program com. 1988-94, chmn. rsch. com. 1994-96, v.p. medicine 1994-96), Royal Coll. Physicians Edinburgh and London, Royal Soc. Medicine (editl. bd.), ACP (gov. for Ont. 1978-83); mem. AAAS, Can. Soc. Endocrinology and Metabolism (past pres., Sandoz prize lectr. 1985, Disting. Svc. award 1990), Toronto Soc. Clin. Rsch. (Baxter prize lectr. 1984), Can. Soc. Clin. Investigation, Am. Thyroid Assn. (pres. 1980-81, Disting. Scientist award 1991), Assn. Am. Physicians, Endocrine Soc., Am. Fedn. Clin. Rsch., Can. Soc. Nuclear Medicine (Jamieson prize lectr. 1980), Can. Inst. Acad. Medicine, N.Y. Acad. Sci., European Thyroid Assn. (corr.), L.Am. Thyroid Assn. (corr.), Soc. Endocrinology and Metabolism of Chile (hon.), Caledonia Soc. Endocrinology (hon.), Japan Endocrine Soc. (hon., gold medal 1986), F+Donalda Club, Alpine Ski Club (bd. dirs. 1987-89), U. Toronto Faculty Club. Home: 3 Daleberry Pl, Don Mills, ON Canada M3B 2A5 Office: Wellesley Hosp, Toronto, ON Canada M4Y 1J3 *Rigid adherence to high standards and integrity is essential. Do what is worth doing now, not tomorrow.*

VOLPE, THOMAS J., advertising executive; b. Bklyn., Dec. 22, 1935; s. John G. and Josephine (Fontana) V.; m. Anita Mazzei, Nov. 24, 1957; children: Lisa, Lori, John. BS in Econs., Bklyn. Coll., 1957; MBA, CCNY, 1965. Mgr. Deloitte Haskins & Sells, N.Y.C., 1957-70; v.p., treas. Colgate Palmolive Co., N.Y.C., 1970-85; sr. v.p., fin. ops. Interpublic Group of Cos., N.Y.C., 1986—. Trustee St. Francis Coll., Bklyn., 1971—; bd. dirs., treas. Multiple Sclerosis Soc., N.Y.C. chpt., 1979—; bd. dirs. N.Y. Pub. Libr., 1995-97, Child Care Action Campaign. Mem. Fin. Execs. Inst. (com. chmn.), N.Y. State Soc. of CPA's (com. chmn.), Fin. Execs. Inst. (pres. N.Y. chpt. 1995). Office: The Interpub Group Cos Inc 1271 Avenue Of The Americas New York NY 10020-1300

VOLPERT, RICHARD SIDNEY, lawyer; b. Cambridge, Mass., Feb. 16, 1935; s. Samuel Abbot and Julia (Fogel) V.; m. Marcia Flaster, June 11, 1958; children: Barry, Sandy, Linda, Nancy. B.A., Amherst Coll., 1956; LL.B. (Stone scholar), Columbia U., 1959. Bar: Calif. bar 1960. Atty. firm O'Melveny & Myers, Los Angeles, 1959-86; ptnr. O'Melveny & Myers, L.A., 1967-86, Skadden, Arps, Slate, Meagher & Flom, L.A., 1986-95, Munger, Tolles & Olson, L.A., 1995—; pub. Jewish Jour. of Los Angeles, 1985-87. Editor, chmn.: Los Angeles Bar Jour, 1965, 66, 67, Calif. State Bar Jour, 1972-73. Chmn. community relations com. Jewish Fedn.-Council Los Angeles, 1977-80; bd. dirs. Jewish Fedn.-Council Greater Los Angeles, 1976—, v.p., 1978-81; pres. Los Angeles County Natural History Mus. Found., 1978-84, trustee, 1974—, chair bd. dirs., 1992—; chmn. bd. councilors U. So. Calif. Law Center, 1979-85; vice chmn. Nat. Jewish Community Relations Adv. Council, 1981-84, mem. exec. com., 1978-85; bd. dirs. U. Judaism, 1973-89, bd. govs., 1973-89; bd. dirs. Valley Beth Shalom, Encino, Calif., 1964-88; mem. capital program major gifts com. Amherst Coll., 1978-86; bd. dirs., mem. exec. com. Los Angeles Wholesale Produce Market Devel. Corp., 1978-95, v.p., 1981-93, pres. 1993-96; mem. exec. bd. Los Angeles chpt. Am. Jewish Com., 1967—; vice-chmn. Los Angeles County Econ. Devel. Council, 1978-81; bd. dirs. Jewish Community Found., 1981—, Brandeis-Bardin Inst., 1995—; mem. Pacific S.W. regional bd. Anti Defamation League B'nai B'rith, 1964—. Named Man of Year, 1978. Fellow Am. Bar Found.; mem. ABA, Urban Land Inst., Los Angeles County Bar Assn. (trustee 1968-70, chmn. real property sect. 1974-75), Los Angeles County Bar Found. (trustee 1977-80, 96—), Calif. Bar Assn. (com. on adminstrn. justice 1973-76), Am. Coll. Real Estate Lawyers (bd. govs. 1996—), Anglo-Am. Real Property Inst. (treas. 1995—), Amherst Club of So. Calif. (dir. 1968-85, pres. 1972-73), City Club (L.A.). Jewish. Home: 4001 Stansbury Ave Sherman Oaks CA 91423-4619 Office: Munger Tolles & Olson 355 S Grand Ave Los Angeles CA 90071-1560

VOLTZ, JEANNE APPLETON, author b. Collinsville, Ala.; d. James Lamar and Marie (Sewell) Appleton; m. Luther Manship Voltz, July 31, 1943 (dec. Aug. 1977); children: Luther Manship, Jeanne Marie; m. Frank B. MacKnight, Aug. 6, 1988 (div. Sept. 1994). AB, U. Montevallo, Ala., 1942. Corr., The Birmingham (Ala.) News, 1939-42; reporter The Press-Register, Mobile, Ala., 1942-45; reporter, feature writer The Miami Herald, 1947-53, food editor, 1953-60; food editor Los Angeles Times, 1960-73, Woman's Day, N.Y.C., 1973-84; free-lance writer, N.Y.C., 1984-88, Chapel Hill, N.C., 1988—; instr. wine and food in civilization UCLA, 1972-73; expert witness Senate Com. on Nutrition and Health, Ft. Lauderdale, Fla., 1980; adj. prof. Dept. Nutrition Hotel Mgmt. NYU, 1986—, Home Econs. Hotel Mgmt., 1987—; judge Hardee's Willow Creek Rib Cook-Off, Raleigh, N.C., 1993-96; Blue Ridge Barbecue and Rib Festival, Tryon, N.C., 1994-96. Author: The California Cookbook, 1970 (Tastemaker award 1970), The Los Angeles Times Natural Foods Cookbook, 1974, The Flavor of the South, 1976 (Tastemaker award 1976), An Apple A Day, 1983, Barbecued Ribs and Other Great Feeds, 1985 (Tastemaker award 1985), Community Suppers, 1987, Barbecued Ribs, Smoked Butts and Other Great Feeds, 1991; author: (with Burks Hamner) The L.A. Gourmet, 1971, (with Elayne Kleeman) How to Turn a Passion for Food into Profit, 1979, (with Caroline Stuart) The Florida Cookbook, 1993. Mem. N.C. Mus. Art, Raleigh. Recipient Vesta award Am. Meat Inst., 1962-72; Alumna of Yr. award U. Montevallo, 1981. Mem. Les Dames d'Escoffier (dir. 1976, pres. 1985-86, internat. pres. 1986-87), Inst. Food Technologists, Women in Communications, Soc. Women Geographers, Internat. Assn. Culinary Profls., The Authors' Guild N.Y., Am. Inst. Wine and Food (chairperson Piedmont chpt.), Culinary Historians N.Y., Phi Tau Sigma. Democrat. Methodist.

VOLZ, CHARLES HARVIE, JR., lawyer; b. Richmond, Va., Sept. 15, 1925; s. Charles Harvie and Mary V. (Mallory) V.; m. Constance A. Lewis, July 30, 1976; children: Charles Harvie III, Judith C. BS, U. Ala., 1950, JD, 1951. Bar: Ala. 1951. Spl. agt. FBI, 1951; claim mgr. Allstate Ins. Co., 1952-54; claims atty. State Farm Ins. Co., 1954-57; ptnr. Roberts, Orme & Volz, 1957-59; sole practice Montgomery, 1961-63; asst. dir. Dept. Indsl. Relations, State of Ala., 1959-62; ptnr. Volz, Capouano, Wampold & Prestwood, 1963-84, Volz & Volz, 1984-95, Volz, Prestwood & Hanan, 1995—. Note editor Ala. Law Rev, 1950-51. Campaign dir. March of Dimes, 1958, Am. Cancer Soc., 1967; exec. sec. Gov.'s Com. on Employment Physically Handicapped, 1959-62; mem. Pres.'s Com. on Employment Physically Handicapped, 1959-62; pres., bd. dirs. Montgomery chpt. Am. Cancer Soc. Served to 2d lt. USAAF, 1943-45. Recipient Outstanding Service award Am. Cancer Soc., 1967. Mem. Am. Arbitration Assn. (mem. nat. panel), ABA, Ala. Bar Assn., Assn. Trial Lawyers Am. (state committeeman 1973-75), Ala. Trial Lawyers Assn. (bd. govs.), Phi Alpha Delta. Methodist. Lodges: Masons, Kiwanis. Home: 1638 Cobblestone Ct Montgomery AL 36117-1713 Office: 350 Adams Ave Montgomery AL 36104-4204

VOLZ, WILLIAM HARRY, law educator, administrator; b. Sandusky, Mich., Dec. 28, 1946; s. Harry Bender and Belva Geneva (Riehl) V. B.A., Mich. State U., 1968; A.M., U. Mich., 1972; J.D., Wayne State U., 1975; M.B.A., Harvard U., 1978. Bar: Mich. 1975. Sole practice, Detroit, 1975-77; mgmt. analyst Office of Gen. Counsel, HEW, Woodlawn, Md., 1977; asst., then assoc. prof. bus. law Wayne State U., Detroit, 1978-85, interim dean sch. Bus. Adminstrn., 1985, prof. bus law, dean, 1985-95, interim dir. ctr. legal studies, 1996—; cons. Merrill, Lynch, Pierce, Fenner & Smith, N.Y.C., 1980-93 , City of Detroit law dept., 1982, Mich. Supreme Ct., Detroit, 1981; ptnr. Mich. C.P.A. Rev., Southfield, 1983-85. Author: Managing a Trial, 1982; contbr. articles to legal jours.; editorial bds. of bus. and law jours, AACSB visitation com.; internat. adv. bd., Inst. of Mgmt., Univ. of L'viv, Ukraine, Legal counsel Free Legal Aid Clinic, Inc., Detroit, 1976—, Shared Ministries, Detroit, 1981, Sino-Am. Tech. Exchange Council, People's Republic of China, 1982; chair advt. rev. panel Better Bus. Bur. Detroit, 1988-90; pres. Mich. Acad. Sci., Arts and Letters, Common Gound, PLAYERS; bd. dirs. Greater Detroit Alliance Bus., Olde Custodian Fund. Recipient Disting. Faculty award Wayne State Sch. Bus. Adminstrn., 1982. Mem. ABA, Amateur Mendicant Soc. (commissionaire 1981-85), Players, Golden Key, Alpha Kappa Psi, Beta Alpha Psi. Mem. Reorganized Ch. Latter Day Saints. Clubs: Detroit Athletic Club, Econ. of Detroit, Harvard Bus. Sch. of Detroit. Home: 3846 Wedgewood Dr Bloomfield Hills MI 48301-3949 Office: Wayne State U Sch Bus Adminstrn Cass Ave Detroit MI 48202

VOM BAUR, FRANCIS TROWBRIDGE, retired lawyer; b. Riverton, N.J., Sept. 17, 1908; s. Carl H. and Edith V. (Trowbridge) vom B.; m. Carolyn Bartlett Laskey, June 6, 1934 (dec. Aug. 1988); children: Nerissa Trowbridge, Daphne de Blois. BA, Amherst Coll., 1929; LLB, Harvard U., 1932. Bar: N.Y. 1934, D.C. 1948, Ill. 1952. Assoc. firm Milbank, Tweed & Hope, N.Y.C., 1933-42; spl. agt. War Dept., 1942; regional counsel Office Coordinator Inter-Am. Affairs (C.A.), Haiti, Panama, 1942-46; practiced law Washington, also Chgo., 1947-53; gen. counsel Dept. of Navy, Washington, 1953-60; mem. firm Hensel and vom Baur, 1960-62; sr. ptnr. vom Baur, Coburn, Simmons & Turtle (and successor firm Gage, Tucker & vom Baur), 1963-83; gen. counsel Naval Undersea Mus. Found., Washington, 1980-90; lectr. on govt. contracts, 1961-80. Author: Federal Administrative Law, 2 vols, 1942, Standards of Admission for Practice before Federal Administrative Agencies, a Report for the Survey of the Legal Profession, 1953, The Practical Lawyer's Manual on Memoranda of Law, 35th Anniversary, 1991; editor: Navy Contract Law, 2d edit, 1959; contbr. articles to profl. jours. Chmn. Republican finance com. D.C., 1975-77; mem. nat. fin. com. Mem. ABA (mem. ho. of dels. 1957, chmn. post conv. com. to visit Germany 1957, chmn. standing com. on unauthorized practice law 1958-62, chmn. sect. pub. contract law 1970-71, chmn. coordinating com. model procurement code 1972-83, chmn. emeritus 1983—, Extraordinary Service award 1979), Fed. Bar Assn. (pres. D.C. chpt. 1954-55, award for exceptionally disting. service 1972), Assn. of Bar of City of N.Y., Bar Assn. of D.C., Amherst Alumni Assn. (pres. Washington chpt. 1969-70, nat. v.p. 1971-80), Beta Theta Pi, Delta Sigma Rho. Clubs: Cosmos (Washington), City Tavern Assn. (Washington), Kennebunk River (Kennebunkport), Arundel Beach (Kennebunkport). Home: 8376 Meadows Rd Warrenton VA 20186-9603

VON ARX, DOLPH WILLIAM, food products executive; b. St. Louis, Aug. 30, 1934; s. Adolph William and Margaret Louise (Linderer) von A.; m. Sharon Joy Landolt, Dec. 21, 1957; children: Vanessa von Arx Gilvarg, Eric S., Valerie L. BSBA, Washington U., St. Louis, 1961; LHD, St. Augustine Coll., 1988. Account exec. Compton Advt., N.Y.C., 1961-64; v.p. mktg. Ralston Purina Co., St. Louis, 1964-69; exec. v.p. mktg. Gillette Personal Care Div., Chgo., 1969-72; exec. v.p. gen. mgmt. group T.J. Lipton Inc., Englewood Cliffs, N.J., 1973-87; pres., chief exec. officer R.J. Reynold Tobacco Co., Winston-Salem, N.C., 1987-88; chmn., chief exec. officer Planters LifeSavers Co., Winston-Salem, 1988-91; bd. dirs. Interat. Multi Food, Mpls., Ive Mackenzie, Toronto, Boca Raton, Fla., Village Bank, Naples, Fla., Cree Rsch. Inc., Durham, N.C., Ruby Tuesday Inc., BMC Fund Inc.; chmn. Morrison's F.C. Atlanta, 1992-96, Morrison Fresh Cooking, 1996—. Bd. visitors U. N.C., 1988-92; chmn. bd. trustees Wake Forest U. Grad. Sch. Mgmt., 1988—; pres. bd. trustees N.C. Dance Theater, Winston-Salem, 1989-90; bd. dirs. Forsyth Meml. Hosp., 1988-92, Naples Conservancy, Naples Philharmonic Ctr. for Arts, Wheeling Thunderbirds Hockey, Inc., Reynolds Mus. Am. Art, Naples Cmty. Hosp., chmn., 1994—, bd. dirs. health care sys., chmn., 1995—. Mem. Belle Haven Club (Greenwich) (bd. dirs. 1983-87), Naples Yacht Club, Univ. Club (N.Y.C.), Linville Ridge Country Club (Linville, N.C.), Collier Res. Club (Naples, Fla.). Avocation: tennis. Home: Pent House 1 4351 Gulf Shore Blvd N Naples FL 34103-3448

VON BERGEN WESSELS, PENNIE LEA, state legislator; b. Sterling, Ill., Mar. 19, 1949; d. Donald LeRoy and Mary Lou (Hammerle) von Bergen; m. Michael J. Wessels, Aug. 23, 1969. AA, Sauk Valley Coll., 1969; BSEd in English and Theater, No. Ill. U., 1971; postgrad., So. Ill. U., 1972-73; JD magna cum laude, U. Ill., 1983. Bar: Ill., 1983; cert. tchr., Ill. English and theater tchr. various schs., Ill., 1971-80; pvt. practice law Morrison, Ill., 1984-85; mem. Whiteside County Bd., Morrison, 1984-88, Ill. Gen. Assembly, Springfield, 1993-95. Bd. dirs. Ill. Citizens Utility Bd., 1989-92, Equip for Equality, 1994—, Ill. Alliance for Arts Edn., 1994—; del. candidate Dem. Nat. Convention, 1980, 92. Named Outstanding Working Woman of Ill. Ill. Bus. and Profl. Women, 1988; recipient Mounders Pride award Mt. Morris Sch. Dist., 1993, Friend of Agr. award Farm Bus. Activator Com., 1994, Outstanding Freshman Legislator award Ill. Edn. Assn., 1994. Unitarian. Avocation: theater. Home: 1300 Sinnissippi Park Rd Sterling IL 61081-4127

VON BERNUTH, CARL W., diversified corporation executive, lawyer. BA, Yale U., 1966, LLB, 1969. Bar: N.Y. 1970, Pa. 1990. Corp. atty. White & Case, 1969-80; assoc. gen. counsel Union Pacific Corp., N.Y.C., 1980-83, dep. gen. counsel fin. and adminstrn., 1984-88; v.p., gen. counsel Union Pacific Corp., Bethlehem, Pa., 1988-91, sr. v.p., gen. counsel, 1991—. Office: Union Pacific Corp 8th & Eaton Aves Bethlehem PA 18018

VON BERNUTH, ROBERT DEAN, agricultural engineering educator, consultant; b. Del Norte, Colo., Apr. 14, 1946; s. John Daniel and Bernice H. (Dunlap) von B.; m. Judy M. Wehrman, Dec. 27, 1969; children: Jeanie, Suzie. BSE, Colo. State U., 1968; MS, U. Idaho, 1970; MBA, Claremont (Calif.) Grad. Sch., 1980; PhD in Engring, U. Nebr., 1982. Registered profl. engr., Calif., Nebr. Agrl. product mgr. Rain Bird Sprinkler Mfg., Glendora, Calif., 1974-80; instr. agrl. engring. U. Nebr., Lincoln, 1980-82; from assoc. prof. to prof. U. Tenn., Knoxville, 1982-90; prof., chmn. Mich. State U., East Lansing, 1990—; v.p. Von-Sol Cons., Lincoln, 1980-82; prin. Von Bernuth Agrl. cons., Knoxville, East Lansing, 1982—. Patentee in field. With USNR, 1970-95, Vietnam. Decorated DFC (2); recipient Disting. Naval Grad. award USN Flight Program, Pensacola, Fla., 1970. Mem. ASCE, Am. Soc. Agrl. Engrs., Irrigation Assn. (Person of Yr. 1994), Naval Res. Assn. Avocations: flying, skiing, antique tractors. Office: Mich State U Dept Agrl Engring 215 Farrall Hall East Lansing MI 48824

VON BRANDENSTEIN, PATRIZIA, production designer. Prodn. designer films including Girlfriends, 1978, Heartland, 1979, Breaking Away, 1979, Ragtime, 1981 (Academy Award nomination best art direction 1981), Silkwood, 1983, Amadeus, 1984 (Academy Award best art direction 1984), Beat Street, 1984, A Chorus Line, 1985, The Money Pit, 1986, No Mercy, 1987, The Untouchables, 1987 (Academy Award nomination best art direction 1987), Betrayed, 1988, Working Girl, 1988, The Lemon Sisters, 1990,

Postcards From the Edge, 1990, State of Grace, 1990, Billy Bathgate, 1992, Sneakers, 1992, Leap of Faith, 1993, Six Degrees of Separation, 1993, The Quick and the Dead, 1995, Just Cause, 1995, The People vs. Larry Flynt, 1996; costume designer films including Between the Lines, 1977, Saturday Night Fever, 1977, A Little Sex, 1982. Address: 161 W 15th St Apt 7B New York NY 10011-6768 Address: 161 W 15th St #7B New York NY 10011

VON BRIESEN, EDWARD FULLER, builder, real estate developer; b. Glen Cove, N.Y., Sept. 21, 1948; s. Hans and Elizabeth Schermerhorn (Suydam) von B.; m. Alice Ruth Marvin. BSEE, Tufts U., 1970. Engr. L.I. Lighting Co., Hicksville, N.Y., 1970-72; pres. Briesmar Inc., Oyster Bay, N.Y., 1973-82, Breza Enterprises Inc., Oyster Bay, 1982—. Road commr. Inc. Village of Oyster Bay Cove, 1981—; sec. Grenville Baker Boys and Girls Club, Locust Valley, N.Y., 1996—; pres. L.I. Lead Assessment and Control, Inc., 1996—. Republican. Episcopalian. Club: Piping Rock (Locust Valley, N.Y.). Avocations: flying, restoring antique autos. Home and Office: 133 Horseshoe Rd Mill Neck NY 11765-1006

VON BUEDINGEN, RICHARD PAUL, urologist; b. Rochester, N.Y., Sept. 14, 1938; s. Wilmer Edward and Clara Elma von B.; BS, U. Wis., 1960, MA in Philosophy, 1961, MD, 1965; m. Bari Luwe Solesky, Nov. 26, 1966 (dec. 1992); children: Kirsten Karla, Christian Karl. Commd. ensign U.S. Navy, 1964, advanced through grades to capt., 1975, intern, U.S. Naval Hosp., St. Albans, N.Y., 1965-66, resident in internal medicine, in plastic and thoracic surgery, in urology affiliate programs Naval Regional Med. Ctr., Oakland, Calif., and U.S. Hosp., Oakland, U. Calif. San Francisco, Stanford U., 1969-73, fellow in pediatric urology, 1973, scientist astronaut trainee Naval Aerospace Med. Inst., Pensacola, Fla., 1966-67, group flight surgeon Marine Corp Air Sta., Beaufort, S.C., 1967-69, chief urology Naval Regional Med. Ctr., Long Beach, Calif., 1973-75, asst. clin. prof. urology, U. Calif., Irvine, 1973-75, resigned, 1975; pvt. practice urology, Aiken, S.C., 1975-80; bd. trustees, chief of surgery HCA Aiken Regional Med. Ctrs., 1985-91. Fellow Internat. Coll. Surgeons, ACS; mem. AMA, Am. Urol. Assn., S.C. Med. Assn. (com. on continuing edn. 1981-83), S.C. Urol. Assn., So. Med. Assn., Soc. Govt. Urologists, Aiken County Med. Soc., Am. Cancer Soc. (chmn. com. profl. edn. in S.C. 1980-82, nat. award for contbns. to profl. edn. 1982), Am. Diabetes Assn. (state bd. dirs., med. edn. com.), Am. Fertility Soc., Am. Lithotripsy Soc. Club: Edisto River Hounds (Master of Foxhounds). Contbr. articles to profl. publs. Home: 1500 Huntsman Dr Aiken SC 29803-5236 Office: 210 University Pky Ste 2300 Aiken SC 29801-6808

VON DER HEYDEN, KARL INGOLF MUELLER, manufacturing company executive; b. Berlin, July 18, 1936; came to U.S., 1957, naturalized, 1967; s. Werner and Erika (Mueller) von der H.; m. Mary Ellen Terrell, Aug. 17, 1963; children: Ellen, Eric. Student, Free U., Berlin, 1959-61; B.A., Duke, 1962; M.B.A., Wharton Sch. U. Pa., 1964. C.P.A., Pa. Mgmt. trainee Berliner Bank, Berlin, 1955-57; sr. staff accountant Coopers & Lybrand, Phila., 1963-66; asst. comptroller, corporate comptroller Pitney-Bowes, Inc., Stamford, Conn., 1966-74; v.p., controller PepsiCo., Inc., Purchase, N.Y., 1974-77; v.p. finance Pepsi-Cola Co., 1977-79, v.p. mfg., 1979-80; v.p. fin., treas. H.J. Heinz Co., Pitts., 1980-83, sr. v.p. fin., chief fin. officer; also bd. dirs., 1983-89; exec. v.p., chief fin. officer RJR Nabisco Inc., N.Y.C., 1989-93, co-chmn., CEO, 1993; pres., CEO Metallgesellschaft Corp., N.Y.C., 1993-94; sr. advisor The Clipper Group, 1994—; vice chmn. CFO PepsiCo, Inc., 1996—; bd. dirs. Federated Dept. Stores, Inc.; chmn. Fin. Acctg. Stds. Adv. Coun., 1995-96. Bd. trustees Duke U.; vice chmn. YMCA Greater N.Y. Mem. Univ. Club (N.Y.C.), Field Club (Greenwich, Conn.). Home: 15 Khakum Wood Rd Greenwich CT 06831-3728 Office: PepsiCo Inc 700 Anderson Hill Rd Purchase NY 10577-1403

VON DER HEYDT, JAMES ARNOLD, federal judge, lawyer; b. Miles City, Mont., July 15, 1919; s. Harry Karl and Alice S. (Arnold) von der H.; m. Verna E. Johnson, May 21, 1952. A.B., Albion (Mich.) Coll., 1942; J.D., Northwestern, 1951. Bar: Alaska 1951. Pvt. law practice Nome, 1953-59; judge superior ct. Juneau, Alaska, 1959-66; U.S. dist. judge Alaska, 1966—; U.S. commr. Nome, Alaska, 1951—; U.S. atty. div. 2 Dist. Alaska, 1951-53; mem. Alaska Ho. of Reps., 1957-59. Author: Mother Sawtooth's Nome, 1990. Pres. Anchorage Fine Arts Mus. Assn. Recipient Disting. Alumni award Albion Coll., 1995. Mem. Alaska Bar Assn. (mem. bd. govs. 1955-59, pres. 1959-60), Am. Judicature Soc., Sigma Nu, Phi Delta Phi., Sigma Nu. Club: Mason (32 deg.), Shriner. Avocation: researching Arctic bird life. Office: US Dist Ct 222 W 7th Ave Unit 40 Anchorage AK 99513-7504

VON DREHLE, DAVID JAMES, journalist; b. Denver, Feb. 6, 1961; s. Richard Reynolds and Dorothy Ann (Love) Von D.; m. Karen Janene Ball, Oct. 7, 1995. BA, U. Denver, 1983; M Letters, Oxford (Eng.) U., 1985. Sports aide Denver Post, 1978-83; staff writer Miami (Fla.) Herald, 1985-89; nat. corr. Miami (Fla.) Herald, N.Y.C., 1989-91; N.Y. bur. chief Washington Post, N.Y.C., 1991-93; nat. politics writer Washington Post, 1993-94, arts editor, 1994-95, asst. mng. editor, 1995—. Author: Among the Lowest of the Dead, 1995; co-author: Best Newspaper Writing, 1990, Best American Sportswriting, 1992, Best Newspaper Writing, 1995. Recipient Silver Gavel award ABA, 1989, Livingston award Mollie Parris Livingston Found., 1989, Deadline Writing award Am. Soc. Newspaper Editors, 1990; Marshall Aid Commemoration Commn. scholar, 1983. Episcopalian. Office: Washington Post 1150 15th St NW Washington DC 20071-0001

VON DREHLE, RAMON ARNOLD, lawyer; b. St. Louis, Mar. 12, 1930; s. Arnold Henry and Sylvia E. (Ahrens) Von D.; m. Gillian Margaret Turner, Sept. 13, 1980; children by previous marriage: Carin L., Lisa A., Courtney A. BS, Washington U., St. Louis, 1952; JD, U. Tex., Austin, 1957; postgrad, Parker Sch. Internat. Law, Columbia U., 1965. Bar: Tex. 1956, Mich. 1957, U.S. Supreme Ct. 1981. Sr. atty. Ford Motor Co., Dearborn, Mich., 1957-67; assoc., asst. gen. counsel Ford of Europe, Inc., Brentwood, Essex, Eng., 1967-75; v.p., gen. counsel Ford of Europe, Inc., 1975-79; v.p. legal Ford Motor Credit Co., Dearborn, 1979-87; v.p., gen. counsel Am. Road Ins. Co., Dearborn, 1979-87; exec. dir. legal affairs Ford Fin. Services Group, Dearborn, 1987-91; leader in residence Walsh Coll., Mich., 1992; panelist large complex case program Am. Arbitration Assn., 1993—; advisor to Czech Republic Ministry of Privatization, Prague, 1993-94; leader Russian Def. Conversion Project, 1995-96; lectr. in Ea. Europe, 1995; pres. Focus Internat. LLC, 1995—; mng. dir. McPherson Group, Washington, 1996—. Article editor: Tex. Law Rev, 1956-57. Trustee Birmingham Unitarian Ch., 1966-67. Served to 1st lt. AUS, 1952-54, Korea. Mem. ABA, Mich. Bar Assn., Tex. Bar Assn., Internat. Bar Assn., Am. Fin. Svcs. Assn. (chmn. 1990-91, bd. dirs. 1981-91), Fin. Svcs. Coun. (bd. dirs. 1987-91), Washington U. Alumni Club Detroit (past pres.), Order of Coif, Renaissance Club (Detroit), Tower Club (Tysons, Va.), Les Ambassadeur (London), Confrérie des Chevilier du Tastevin (France), Capitol Hill Club (Washington), Royal Automobile Club (London), Tau Beta Pi, Omicron Delta Kappa. Mem. Christ Ch. Home and Office: 519 Princess St Alexandria VA 22314

VON FETTWEIS, YVONNE CACHÉ, archivist, historian; b. L.A., Nov. 28, 1935; d. Boyd Eugene and Georgette Louisa (Tilmann) Adams; m. Maurice Lee Caché, Jan. 8, 1955 (div. 1962); children: Maurice C.B. II, Michele-Yvonne (Mrs. Vernon Young Sr.); m. Rolland Phillip von Fettweis, July 22, 1967. BA, Wagner Coll., 1954; postgrad, Am. U., 1973, Bentley Coll., 1981. Legal sec., asst. Judge, Davis, Stern, Orfinger & Tindall, Daytona Beach, Fla., 1961-66; head rec. sect., bd. dirs. 1st Ch. Christ Scientist, Boston, 1969-71, rsch. assoc., 1971-72, adminstrv. archivist, 1972-78, sr. assoc. archivist, 1979-84, records adminstr., 1984-91, div. mgr. records mgmt./orgnl. archives, 1991-92, divsn. mgr. ch. history, 1992—, divsn. mgr. ch. history and healing ministry, 1995; divsn. mgr. ch. history, 1995-96; ch. historian 1st Ch. Christ Scientist, Boston, 1996—; mem. Religious Pub. Rels. Coun. Co-author: Mary Baker Eddy: A Lifetime of Healing, 1997. Trustee Ch. Hist. Trust, 1995—; exec. sec. Volusia County Goldwater campaign, Daytona Beach, 1964. Mem. Soc. Am. Archivists (editor The Archival Spirit), Automated Records and Techniques Task Force, Am. Mgmt. Assn., Orgn. Am. Historians, Ctr. for Study Presidency, Religious Pub. Rels. Coun., New Eng. Archivists, Assn. Records Mgrs. and Adminstrs. (bd. dirs. 1983—), Assn. Coll. and Rsch. Librs., Bay State Hist. League, Order Ea. Star, Order Rainbow (bd. dirs. 1972-77). Republican. Christian Scientist. Home: 42 Edgell Dr Framingham MA 01701-3181 Office: 1st Ch Christian Sci 175 Huntington Ave # A221 Boston MA 02115-3117

VON FRAUNHOFER-KOSINSKI, KATHERINA, bank executive; b. N.Y.C.; m. Jerzy Kosinski, Feb. 15, 1987 (dec. May 3, 1991). Student, St. Joseph's Convent, London, Clark's Coll., London. Various positions Robert W. Orr & Assocs., N.Y.C., 1954-55; with traffic dept. Compton Advt., Inc., N.Y.C., 1956-63; acct. exec. J. Walter Thompson Co., N.Y.C., 1963-69; product mgr. Natural Wonder line Revlon Co., N.Y., 1969-71; pres. Scientia Factum, Inc., N.Y.C., 1971—; co-founder Polish Am. Resources Corp., N.Y.C., 1988—, pres., CEO, 1992—; founder, CEO, pres. Polish Am. Techs., L.P., N.Y.C., 1992—; chmn. bd. dirs. Am. Bank in Poland/AmerBank, Warsaw, 1991—. Co-founder Westchester Sports Club. Assoc. fellow Timothy Dwight Coll./Yale U., 1997—. Avocations: skiing, horse/polo, swimming, photography. Home: 60 W 57th St New York NY 10019-3911

VON FRIEDERICHS-FITZWATER, MARLENE MARIE, health communication educator; b. Beatrice, Nebr., July 14, 1939; d. Paul M. and Velma B. (von Friederichs) Fitzwater; children: Richard Nielson, Kevin T. Young, James L. Nielson, Paul M. Nielson. BS, Westminster Coll., 1981; MA, U. Nebr., Omaha, 1981; PhD, U. Utah, 1987; cert. in death edn., Temple U., 1982. Various pub. rels., writing and editing positions, 1957-78; teaching fellow in comm. U. Nebr., Omaha, 1978-83, U. Utah, Salt Lake City, 1978-83; asst. prof. mass comm. U. So. Colo., Pueblo, 1983-85; prof. comm. studies Calif. State U., Sacramento, 1985—, chair comm. studies, 1996—; asst. clin. prof. family practice Sch. Medicine U. Calif., Davis, 1987—; condr. workshops on communication skills for health care profls. Bergan Mercy Hosp., Omaha, 1980-81, Mercy Care Ctr., Omaha, 1980-81, Am. Cancer Soc., 1981-82, Hospice of Salt Lake, Utah, 1981-82; condr. seminars, workshops and courses on health communication, death and dying, patient edn. and compliance, other related topics, 1983—; presenter in health communication various profl. orgn. meetings and confs., 1981—; dir., co-founder The Health Communication Rsch. Inst., Sacramento, 1988—. Contbr. articles to profl. jours. Trainer United Way, Sacramento, project mgr., 1986—; pres. bd. dirs. Hospice Care Sacramento, Inc., 1986-87; instr. vol. tng. program Hospice Consortium Sacramento; hospice vol. 1980—. Recipient numerous state, regional and nat. awards for writing, editing, publ. design and photography. Fellow Am. Acad. on Physician & Patient; mem. Internat. Communication Assn. (health communication div., newsletter editor 1987-89, sec. 1989-91), AAUP, Assn. Behavioral Scis. and Med. Edn., Assn. Women in Sci., Pub. Rels. Soc. Am. (bd. dirs. Calif. Capital chpt. 1987-91), Soc. Tchrs. Family Medicine, Soc. Health Care Pub. Rels. and Mktg. No. Calif. Home: 5020 Hackberry Ln Sacramento CA 95841-4765 Office: Calif State U Communication Studies Dept 6000 J St Sacramento CA 95819-2605

VON FURSTENBERG, BETSY, actress, writer; b. Neiheim Heusen, Germany, Aug. 16, 1931; d. Count Franz-Egon and Elizabeth (Johnson) von F.; m. Guy Vincent de la Maisoneuve (div.); 2 children.; m. John J. Reynolds, Mar. 26, 1984. Attended Miss Hewitt's Classes, N.Y. Tutoring Sch.; prepared for stage with Sanford Meisner at Neighborhood Playhouse. Made Broadway stage debut in Second Threshold, N.Y., 1951; appeared in Dear Barbarians, 1952, Oh Men Oh Women, 1954, The Chalk Garden, 1955, Child of Fortune, 1956, Nature's Way, 1957, Much Ado About Nothing, 1959, Mary Mary, 1965, Paisley Convertible, 1967, Avanti, 1968, The Gingerbread Lady, 1970 (toured 1971), Absurd Person Singular, 1976; off Broadway appearances include For Love or Money, 1951; toured in Petrified Forest, Jason and Second Man, 1952; appeared in Josephine, 1953; subsequently toured, 1955; What Every Woman Knows, 1955, The Making of Moo, 1958 (toured 1958), Say Darling, 1959, Wonderful Town, 1959, Season of Choice, 1959, Beyond Desire, 1967, Private Lives, 1968, Does Anyone Here Do the Peabody, 1976; appeared in Along Came a Spider, Theatre in the Park, N.Y.C., 1985; appeared in film Women Without Names, 1950; TV appearances include Robert Montgomery Show, Ed Sullivan Show, Alfred Hitchcock Presents, One Step Beyond, The Mike Wallace Show, Johnny Carson Show, Omnibus, Theatre of the Week, The Secret Storm, As the World Turns, Movie of the Week, Your Money or Your Wife, Another World; writer syndicated column More Than Beauty; contbr. articles to newspapers and mags. including N.Y. Times Sunday Arts and Leisure, Saturday Rev. of Literature, People, Good Housekeeping, Art News, Pan Am Travel; co-author: (novel) Mirror, Mirror, 1988. Avocations: tennis, painting, photography. Office: care Don Buchwald 10 E 44th St New York NY 10017-3601

VON FURSTENBERG, DIANE SIMONE MICHELLE, fashion designer, writer, entrepreneur; b. Brussels, Belgium, Dec. 31, 1946; came to U.S., 1969; d. Leon L. and Liliane L. (Nahmias) Halfin; m. Eduard Egon von Furstenberg, July 16, 1969 (div.); children: Alexandre, Tatiana. Student, U. Madrid, 1965-66, U. Geneva, 1966-68. Founder, pres. Diane von Furstenberg Studio, N.Y.C., 1970—; pres. Diane Von Furstenberg Ltd., N.Y.C.; founder Salvy, Paris, 1985. Author: Diane Von Furstenberg's Book of Beauty; Beds, 1991, The Bath, 1993, The Table, 1996; contbg. editor Vanity Fair mag., 1993. Recipient Ellis Island Medal of Honor, 1986. Office: Diane Von Furstenberg Studio 745 5th Ave Ste 2400 New York NY 10151-2499 *Honesty in all ways—honest products, honest and straight approach to needs.*

VON FURSTENBERG, GEORGE MICHAEL, economics educator, researcher; b. Germany, Dec. 3, 1941; came to U.S., 1961; s. Kaspar Freiherr and Elisabeth Freifrau (von Boeselager) von F.; m. Gabrielle M. Freiin Koblitz von Willmburg, June 9, 1967; 1 child, Philip G. Ph.D., Princeton U., 1967. Asst. prof. econs. Cornell U., Ithaca, N.Y., 1966-70; assoc. prof. econs. Ind. U., Bloomington, 1970-73, prof., 1976-78, Rudy prof. econs., 1983—; sr. staff economist Council Econ. Advisors, Washington, 1973-76; div. chief research dept. IMF, Washington, 1978-83; project dir. Am. Coun. Life Ins., Washington, 1976-78; sr. advisor Brookings Instn., Washington, 1978-90; vis. sr. economist planning and analysis staff Dept. State, Washington 1989-90; Bissell-Fulbright vis. prof. Can.-Am. rels. U. Toronto, 1994-95. Contbg. author, editor: The Government and Capital Formation, 1980, Capital, Efficiency and Growth, 1980, Acting Under Uncertainty: Multidisciplinary Conceptions, 1990, Regulation and Supervision of Financial Institutions in the NAFTA Countries and Beyond, 1997; editor: International Money and Credit: The Policy Roles, 1983; assoc. editor Rev. of Econs. and Stats., 1987-92; contbr. articles to profl. jours. Fulbright grantee to Poland, 1991-92. Mem. Am. Econ. Assn., Am. Fin. Assn. Roman Catholic. Avocations: tennis; sailing. Office: Ind U Dept Econs Bloomington IN 47405

VON GIERKE, HENNING EDGAR, biomedical science educator, former government official, researcher; b. Karlsruhe, Germany, May 22, 1917; came to U.S., 1947, naturalized, 1977; s. Edgar and Julie (Braun) Von G.; married; 2 children. Dipl. Ing., Karlsruhe Tech., 1943, Dr. Engr., 1944. Asst. in acoustics Karlsruhe Tech., 1944-47, lectr., 1946; cons. Aerospace Med. Research Labs, Wright-Patterson AFB, Ohio, 1947-54; chief bioacoustics br. Aerospace Med. Research Labs, 1954-63, dir. biodynamics and bionics div., 1963-88; assoc. prof. Ohio State U., 1963-88; clin. prof. Wright State U., 1980—; mem. com. hearing bioacoustics and biomechanics NRC, 1953-93, chmn. 1990-93, bio-astronaut com., 1959-61; mem. adv. com., flight medicine and biology NASA, 1960-61. Author over 160 tech. publs., book chpts.; patentee in field. Recipient Dept. Def. Disting. Civilian Svc. award, 1963, Hubertus Strughold medal, 1980, Meritorious and Disting. Exec. Presdl. rank Pres. of U.S., 1980, 81, H.R. Lissner award ASME, 1983, Lord Rayleigh medal, 1988. Fellow Acoustical Soc. Am. (pres. 1979-80, Silver medal 1981), Aerospace Med. Assn. (v.p. 1966-67, E. Liljenkrantz award 1966, A.D. Tuttle award 1974), Inst. Environ. Scis. (hon.), Internat. Acad. Aviation and Space Medicine; mem. NAE, Inst. Noise Control Engring., Biomed. Engring. Soc., Internat. Acad. Astronautics. Researcher in bioacoustics, acoustics, biomechanics and bioengring. Home: 1325 Meadow Ln Yellow Springs OH 45387-1219 Office: Armstrong Aerospace Med Rsch Lab Dayton OH 45433

VON HAKE, MARGARET JOAN, librarian; b. Santa Monica, Calif., Oct. 27, 1933; d. Carl August and Inez Garnet (Johnson) von Hake;. BA, La Sierra U., 1955; MS in Library Sci., U. So. Calif., 1963. Tchr. Newbury Park (Calif.) Acad., 1955-60, librarian, 1957-60; librarian Columbia Union Coll., Takoma Park, Md., 1962-67, library dir., 1967—. Mem. ALA, Md. Libr. Assn., Congress of Acad. Libr. Dirs. of Md., Md. Ind. Coll.and Univ. Assn. Libr. Dirs. Round Table (chair 1996-98), Assn. Seventh Day Adventist Librs. (newsletter editor 1982, 83, pres. 1989-90), Paul Hill Chorale, Sligo Federated Music Club (pres. 1988-89). Republican. Office: Columbia Union Coll 7600 Flower Ave Silver Spring MD 20912-7796

VON HERZEN, RICHARD PIERRE, research scientist, consultant; b. L.A., May 21, 1930; s. Constantine Pierre Von Herzen and Elizabeth Martha (Hevener) Hough; m. Janice Elaine Rutter, Mar. 8, 1958; children—Brian P., Carol E. B.S., Calif. Inst. Tech., 1952; M.A., Harvard U., 1956; Ph.D., UCLA, 1960. Asst. researcher Scripps Inst. Oceanography, LaJolla, Calif., 1960-64, vis. investigator, lectr., 1974-75; dep. dir. office oceanography UNESCO, Paris, 1964-66; assoc. to sr. scientist Woods Hole Oceanog. Inst., Mass., 1966-96, emeritus, 1996—, chmn. dept. geology and geophysics, 1982-85. Author/co-author numerous peer-reviewed articles. Served with U.S. Army, 1953-55. Fellow Am. Geophys. Union (pres. Tectonics sect. 1986-88, assoc. editor Jour. Geophys. Research 1969-71). Avocations: sports; sailing; biking. Home: PO Box 271 Woods Hole MA 02543-0271 Office: Woods Hole Oceanog Inst Woods Hole MA 02543

VON HILSHEIMER, GEORGE EDWIN, III, neuropsychologist; b. West Palm Beach, Fla., Aug. 15, 1934; s. George E. Jr. and Dorothy Sue (Bridges) Von H.; m. Catherine Jean Munson, Dec. 27, 1968 (div. Oct. 1987); children: Dana Germaine, George E. IV, Alexandra; m. Jonnie Mae Warner, June 29, 1991. BA, U. Miami, 1955; PhD, Saybrook Inst., 1977. Diplomate Acad. Psychosomatic Medicine, Am. Bd. Behavioral Medicine, Am. Acad. Pain Mgmt., Am. Bd. Cert. Managed Care Providers, Am. Acad. Psychol. Treating Addiction, Nat. Register Neurofeedback. Sr. minister Humanitas, N.Y.C., 1959-64; cons. Pres. Kennedy's Commn. Nat. Vol. Svc., Juv. Del., Migration Labor, 1963-64; headmaster Summerlane Sch., North Branch, N.Y., 1964-69; supt. Green Valley Sch., Orange City, Fla., 1969-74; neuropsychologist Growth Insts., Twyman's Mill, Va., 1974-79, Growth Inst., DeLand, Fla., 1980-82; assoc. health profl. Maitland, 1982—; cons. Sci. Adv. Bd. EPA, Washington, 1974-84; chmn. Certification Bd., Internat. Coll. Environ. Medicine, 1991-94; mem. Bd. Assn. Diagnostic Efficiency and Brief Therapy, dir. curriculum, 1993-94. Author: How to Live With Your Special Child, 1970, Understanding Problems of Children, 1975, Allergy, Toxins and the LD Child, 1977, Psychobiology of Delinquents, 1978, Depression Is Not a Disease, 1989, Brief Therapy, 1993, Brief Therapy: Antecedent Scientific Principles, 1994; editor Human Learning, Washington, 1974-94. Mem. spl. bd. Fla. Symphony Orch., 1992-93. With mil. intelligence U.S. Army, 1957-59. Fellow Internat. Coll. Applied Nutrition, Acad. Psychosomatic Medicine; mem. Toastmasters, Phi Kappa Phi, Omicron Delta Kappa, Alpha Sigma Phi. Mem. Ch. of Brethren. Achievements include establishment of minor physical anomalies as significant predictor of physical and mental disease; demonstrated that treatment by neurofeedback significantly reduced criminal recidivism and that delinquency is a function of physical disease; demonstrated that ADHD and pain respond to neurofeedback; introduced treatment of schizophrenia by neurofeedback through Electro Dermal Response. Home: 160 W Trotters Dr Maitland FL 32751-5736 Office: AAT 175 Lookout Pl # 1 Maitland FL 32751-4494

VON HIPPEL, FRANK NIELS, public and international affairs educator; b. Cambridge, Mass., Dec. 26, 1937; s. Arthur Robert and Dagmar (Franck) von H.; m. Patricia Bardi, June, 1987; 1 child from previous marriage, Paul Thomas. S.B., MIT, 1959; Ph.D., Oxford U., 1962. Rsch. assoc. U. Chgo., 1962-64, Cornell U., Ithaca, N.Y., 1964-66; asst. prof. Stanford U., Calif., 1966-69; assoc. physicist Argonne Nat. Lab., Ill., 1970-73; research physicist Princeton U., N.J., 1974-83, prof. pub. and internat. affairs, 1983-93, 95—; asst. dir. for nat. security Pres.'s Office of Sci. and Tech. Policy, Washington, N.J., 1993-94; bd. dirs. Bull. of Atomic Scientists, Chgo., 1983-86, mem. editl. bd., 1996—, chmn. editl. bd., 1991-93. Author: Advice and Dissent, 1974, Citizen Scientist, 1991; chmn. editl. bd. Sci. and Global Security, 1989—; contbr. articles to profl. jours. Rhodes scholar, 1959-62; McArthur Found. Prize fellow, 1993-98. Fellow AAAS (bd. dirs. 1987-88, Hilliard Roderick prize in Sci., Arms Control and Internat. Security 1994); mem. Fedn. Am. Scientists (chmn. 1979-84, Pub. Svc. award 1989), Fedn. Am. Scientists Fund (chmn. 1986-93, 96—). Home: 3 University Way Princeton Junction NJ 08550-1617 Office: Princeton Univ Ctr for Energy & Environ Studies Princeton NJ 08544

VON HIPPEL, PETER HANS, chemistry educator; b. Goettingen, Germany, Mar. 13, 1931; came to U.S., 1937, naturalized, 1942; s. Arthur Robert and Dagmar (franck) von H.; m. Josephine Baron Raskind, June 20, 1954; children: David F., James A., Benjamin J. B.S., MIT, 1952, M.S., 1953, Ph.D., 1955. Phys. biochemist Naval Med. Research Inst., Bethesda, Md., 1956-59; from asst. prof. to assoc. prof. biochemistry Dartmouth Coll., 1959-67; prof. chemistry, mem. Inst. Molecular Biology U. Oreg., 1967-79, dir. Inst. Molecular Biology, 1969-80, chmn. dept. chemistry, 1980-87; rsch. prof. chemistry Am. Cancer Soc., 1989—; chmn. biopolymers Gordon Conf., 1968; mem. trustees vis. com. biology dept. MIT, 1973-76; mem. bd. sci. counsellors Nat. Inst. Arthritis, Metabolic and Digestive Diseases, NIH, 1974-78, mem. coun. Nat. Inst. Gen. Med. Scis., 1982-86, mem. dir.'s adv. com., 1987-92; mem. sci. and tech. ctrs. adv. com. NSF, 1987-89; bd. dirs. Fedn. Am. Socs. for Exptl. Biology, 1994—. Mem. editl. bd. Jour. Biol. Chemistry, 1967-73, 76-82, Biochem. Biophys. Acta, 1965-70, Physiol. Revs., 1972-77, Biochemistry, 1977-80, Trends in Biochem. Soc., 1987—, Protein Sci., 1990-95; editor Jour. Molecular Biology, 1986-94; contbr. articles to profl. jours., chpts. to books. Lt. M.S.C. USNR, 1956-59. NSF predoctoral fellow, 1953-55; NIH postdoctoral fellow, 1955-56; NIH sr. fellow, 1959-67; Guggenheim fellow, 1973-74. Fellow Am. Acad. Arts and Scis.; mem. AAAS, Am. Chem. Soc., Am. Soc. Biol. Chemists, Biophys. Soc. (mem. council 1970-73, pres. 1973-74), Nat. Acad. Scis., Fedn. Am. Scientists, Sigma Xi. Home: 1900 Crest Dr Eugene OR 97405-1753

VON HOFFMAN, NICHOLAS, writer, former journalist; b. N.Y.C., Oct. 16, 1929; s. Carl and Anna (Bruenn) von H.; m. Ann Byrne, 1950 (div.); children: Alexander, Aristodemos, Constantine; m. Patricia Bennett, 1979 (div.). Grad., Fordham Prep. Sch., 1948. Assoc. dir. Indsl. Area Found., Chgo., 1954-63; mem. staff Chgo. Daily News, 1963-66, Washington Post, 1966-76. Author: Mississippi Notebook, 1964, Multiversity, 1966, We Are The People Our Parents Warned Us Against, 1968, Two, Three, Many More, 1969, Left at The Post, 1970, (with Garry Trudeau) Fireside Watergate, 1973, Tales From the Margaret Mead Taproom, 1976, Make-Believe Presidents: Illusions of Power from McKinley to Carter, 1978, Organized Crimes, 1984, Citizen Cohn, 1988, Capitalist Fools, 1992; also articles.

VON HOLDEN, MARTIN HARVEY, psychologist; b. Bronx, N.Y., May 29, 1942; s. Leon and Gertrude (Fishbein) Von H.; m. Virginia T. Brown, Dec. 17, 1971; 1 child, Mark Walter; children by previous marriage: Sandi Gwen Bitton, David Lawrence; 1 stepchild, Theresa Ann Brilli-Rogers. B.A., NYU, 1964; M.A., U. Toledo, 1965; D.P.A., NYU, 1981. Sr. psychologist N.Y. State Dept. Mental Hygiene, Rockland State Hosp., Orangeberg, 1966-67, team leader, 1970-71, dir. interdisciplinary tng. team, 1971-73; chief of service Metro Unit Harlem Valley Psychiat. Ctr., Wingdale, N.Y., 1973-74, dep. dir. programs, 1974-75; dep. dir. treatment services Pilgrim Psychiat. Ctr., West Brentwood, N.Y., 1975-76; dir. Matteawan State Hosp., Beacon, N.Y., 1977, Central N.Y. Psychiat. Ctr., Marcy, N.Y., 1977-82; exec. dir. Rochester Psychiat. Ctr., Rochester, N.Y., 1982—; assoc. dir. Inst. for Motivation Rsch., Croton-on-Hudson, N.Y., 1965-73; dir. Martin H. Von Holden Assocs., motivation rsch., Fairlawn, N.J., 1970-74; cons. psychologist, group therapist Green Haven Correctional Facility, Stormville, N.Y., 1970-77; cons. psychologist, group therapist Auburn Correctional Facility, N.Y., 1977-94, Butler Correctional Facility, 1994-96, Willard Drug Treatment Ctr., 1997—; clin. assoc. prof. dept. psychiatry Sch. Medicine, U. Rochester, 1983—; spkr. nat. and internat. profl. confs. including 2d World Congress on Prison Health Care, 1983. Contbr. articles to profl. jours. Mem. adv. coun. N.Y. State Commn. Quality Care to Mentally Disabled, 1989—. Capt. MSC, U.S. Army, 1967-70. Recipient James Gordon Bennett prize NYU, 1964, Outstanding Achievement award United Way of N.Y. State, 1994. Fellow Am. Assn. Mental Health Adminstrs. (cert. mental health adminstr.); mem. Am. Psychol. Assn., Am. Correctional Assn., Am. Assn. Correctional Psychologists, Assn. Facility Dirs. N.Y. State Office Mental Health (pres. 1984-85), Order of Arrow, Psi Chi. Jewish. Home: 15 Waterbury Ln Rochester NY 14625-1361

VONK, HANS, conductor; b. Amsterdam, The Netherlands, June 18, 1942; s. Frans Vonk; m. Jessie Folkerts. Degree in Music, Ignatius Coll., Amsterdam; Degree in Law, City U., Amsterdam, 1964; trained with Franco

Ferrara, 1964-66. Condr. Nat. Ballet, Amsterdam, 1966-69; asst. condr. Concertgebouw Orch., Amsterdam, 1969-73; condr. Radio Philharm. Orch., Hilversom, The Netherlands, 1973-79; chief condr. Netherlands Opera, Amsterdam, 1976-85, Residentie Orkestra, Ben Haag, 1980-91, Staatskapelle, Dresden, Germany, 1985-90; assoc. condr. Royal Philharmonie, London, 1976-79; chief condr. Radio Symphonie Orch., Cologne, Germany, 1991-97; music dir., condr. St. Louis Symphony, 1996—; prin. guest condr. Netherlands Radio Philharm.; guest condr. l'Orchestre Nat. de France, Oslo Philharmonic, London Symphony, Norddeutsche Rendfunk, London Philharmonic, English Chamber Orch., Phila. Orch., Minn. Orch., Nat. Symphony Orch., Detroit Orch., Montreal Orch., Dallas Orch., Seattle Orch., Cleve. Orch., Boston Symphony Orch., Pitts. Orch., San Francisco Orch., Houston Orch., Balt. Orch., Mostly Mozart Festival Orch.; opera condr. La Scala, Rome, 1980, 88, Netherlands Opera, Dresden State Opera. Recs.: (with Christian Zacharias) 5 Beethoven piano concertos, Mozart overtures, The Nutcracker (Tchaikovsky), Der Rosenkavalier, Schumann symphonies and concertos, Bruckner Symphonies 4 and 6. Office: St Louis Symphony Orch Powell Symphony Hall 718 N Grand Blvd Saint Louis MO 63103-1011 also: c/o IMG Artists North AM 22 E 71st St New York NY 10021

VON KALINOWSKI, JULIAN ONESIME, lawyer; b. St. Louis, May 19, 1916; s. Walter E. and Maybelle (Michaud) von K.; m. Penelope Jayne Dyer, June 29, 1980; children by previous marriage: Julian Onesime, Wendy Jean von Kalinowski. BA, Miss. Coll., 1937; JD with honors, U. Va., 1940. Bar: Va. 1940, Calif. 1946. Assoc. Gibson, Dunn and Crutcher, L.A., 1946-52, ptnr., 1953-62, mem. exec. com., 1962-82, adv. ptnr., 1985—; CEO, chmn. Litigation Scis., Inc., Culver City, Calif., 1991-94, chmn. emeritus, 1994-96; chmn. emeritus Dispute Dyamics, Inc., Culver City, 1996—; bd. dirs., mem. exec. com. W.M. Keck Found.; mem. faculty Practising Law Inst., 1971, 76, 78, 79, 80; instr. in spl. course on antitrust litigation Columbia U. Law Sch., N.Y.C., 1981; mem. lawyers dels. com. to 9th Cir. Jud. Conf., 1953-73; UN expert Mission to People's Republic China, 1982. Contbr. articles to legal jours.; author: Antitrust Laws and Trade Regulation, 1969, desk edit., 1981; gen. editor: World Law of Competition, 1978, Antitrust Counseling and Litigation Techniques, 1984. With USN, 1941-46, capt. Res. ret. Fellow Am. Bar Found., Am. Coll. Trial Lawyers (chmn. complex litigation com. 1984-87); mem. ABA (ho. of dels. 1970, chmn. antitrust law sect. 1972-73), State Bar Calif., L.A. Bar Assn., U. Va. Law Sch. Alumni Assn., Calif. Club, L.A. Country Club, La Jolla Beach and Tennis Club, N.Y. Athletic Club, The Sky Club (N.Y.C.), Phi Kappa Psi, Phi Alpha Delta. Republican. Episcopalian. Home: 12320 Ridge Cir Los Angeles CA 90049-1151 Office: Dispute Dynamics Inc 6167 Bristol Pkwy Culver City CA 90230-6610

VON KANN, CLIFTON FERDINAND, aviation and space executive, software executive; b. Boston, Oct. 14, 1915; s. Alfred and Lyllian (Kaufman) von K.; m. Sallie Emery Flint, Oct. 6, 1938 (div. May 1965); children: Curtis Emery, Lisa Christine; m. Kathryn Heyne, July 18, 1965. AB cum laude, Harvard U., 1937, MBA, 1948, D in Aero. Sc. (hon.), 1984; grad., Arty. Sch., 1942, Command and Gen. Staff Sch., 1945, Armed Forces Staff Coll., 1954, Nat. War Coll., 1957. Commd. 2d lt., F.A. U.S. Army, 1938, advanced through grades to maj. gen., 1962; various combat assignments, North Africa, Sicily and Italy, 1942-45; mem. War Dept. gen. staff, 1945-46, with Office Comptr., Dept. of Army, 1948-51, with CIA, 1951-53, comdg. officer 7th Inf. Div. Arty., 8th Army, 1954; with Korean Mil. Adv. Group Korea, 1954-55; with Hdqrs. Army Forces Far East and 8th Army, Japan, 1955-56; asst. div. comdr. 82d Airborne Div. Ft. Bragg, N.C., 1957-59; dir. army aviation Dept. Army, 1959-61; J-3 U.S. Strike Command, Tampa, Fla., 1961-62; comdg. gen. 1st cavalry div. Korea, 1962-63; comdg. gen. U.S. Army Aviation Ctr. Ft. Rucker, Ala., 1963-65; ret., 1965; v.p. ops. and engring. Air Transport Assn. Am., 1965-70, sr. v.p. ops. and airports, 1970-80; pres. Nat. Aeron. Assn., 1980-89; chmn. bd. Nat. Aeronautic Assn., 1989-90, chmn. emeritus, 1992—; bd. dirs. the AVEMCO Corp., Frederick, Md.; chmn. bd. dirs. Traverse Techs., Inc., 1994-95. Decorated Silver Star, Legion of Merit; Cross of Mil. Valor (Italy); recipient Charles Edwin Webb Meml. medal Pa. Mil. Coll., 1964, mil. rev. award Command and Gen. Staff Coll., 1964, Clifford W. Henderson award for achievement, 1990, Dept. Transp./FAA award for disting. svc., 1990. Mem. Am. Helicopter Soc. (chmn. bd. 1962-63, pres. 1961-62), World Aerospace Edn. Assn. (bd. dirs. 1987-93, pres. 1990-91, Fedn. Aeronautique Internat. (v.p. 1980-88, pres. 1988-90), Black Tie Club (Washington; pres. 1978-79), Aero Club (Washington; pres. 1969), Harvard Varsity Club (Cambridge), Met. Club (Washington). Clubs: Harvard Varsity (Cambridge); Metropolitan, Nat. Aviation (pres. 1974-75). Home and Office: Apt 502 4200 Massachusetts Ave NW Washington DC 20016-4752

VON KAPPELHOFF, DORIS See DAY, DORIS

VON KLEMPERER, KLEMENS, historian, educator; b. Berlin, Nov. 2, 1916; came to U.S., 1938; s. Herbert O. and Frieda (Kuffner) Von K.; m. Elizabeth Lee Gallaher, Dec. 19, 1953; children—Catharine Lee, James Alfred. Abitur, Französisches Gymnasium, Berlin, 1934; M.A., Harvard U., 1940, Ph.D., 1949; MA, Cambridge U., 1974. Vis. prof. Stanford U., Palo Alto, Calif., 1960; prof. history Bonn U., Fed. Republic Germany, 1963-64; L. Clark Seelye prof. history Smith Coll., Northampton, Mass., 1960-87, prof. emeritus, 1987—; vis. prof. Amherst (Mass.) Coll., 1989, 91, 96; vis. fellow Trinity Coll., Oxford, Eng., 1982. Author: Germany's New Conservatism, 1957, Mandate for Resistance, 1969, Ignaz Seipel: Christian Statesman, 1972, German Resistance Against Hitler: The Search for Allies Abroad 1938-1945, 1992; editor: A Noble Combat. The Letters of Shiela Grant Duff and Adam von Trott, 1988, "Für Deutschland" Die Männer des 20 Juli, 1994; contbr. articles to profl. jours. Served with AUS, 1943-46, ETO. Guggenheim Found. fellow, 1957-58; Fulbright fellow, 1957-58, 63-64; Overseas fellow Churchill Coll., Cambridge, Eng., 1973-74; Inst. for Advanced Study fellow, Berlin, 1986; Am. Philos. Soc. grantee, 1977-78, Am. Council of Learned Socs. grantee, 1978-79. Mem. Am. Hist. Soc. (chmn. conf. group for central European history 1982-83). Club: Century (N.Y.C.). Avocations: playing recorder; mountaineering; hiking. Home: 23 Washington Ave Northampton MA 01060-2822 Office: Smith Coll Northampton MA 01063

VON KUTZLEBEN, BERND EBERHARD, nuclear engineer; b. N.Y.C., May 23, 1950; s. Siegfried Edwin and Ursula Herta (Klotz) von K.; m. Susan Eileen Thrane, Feb. 12, 1983 (div. 1991); children: John Hays Morgan, Alexander Joachim, Eric Raymond; m. Carolyn Alice Hays, Dec. 5, 1991. BS in Physics, U. Hamburg, 1974; BS in Physics Engring., Fachhochschule Wedel, 1976, MS, 1979. Nuclear test engr. Combustion Engring., Windsor, Conn., 1979-82, sr. nuclear test engr., 1982-85, nuclear test cons., 1985-90, nuclear test mgr., 1991-92; resident nuclear engring. mgr. Combustion Engring., Republic of Korea, 1992-95; nuclear engring. mgr. Combustion Engring., Windsor, Conn., U.S., 1996—; v.p. Treetop Water Corp., Fort Worth, 1990—. Mem. U.S. Nuclear Soc. Republican. Avocations: cooking, travel, foreign cultures and customs. Home: 35 Anvil Dr Avon CT 06001-3218

VON LAUE, THEODORE HERMAN, historian, educator; b. Frankfurt Main, Germany, June 22, 1916; came to U.S., 1937, naturalized, 1945; s. Max Felix and Magda (Milkau) Von L.; m. Hildegarde Hunt, Oct. 23, 1943 (dir. 1976); children: Christopher (dec.), Madeleine, Esther; m. Angela Turner, Nov. 13, 1976. A.B., Princeton U., 1939, Ph.D., 1944; cert. Russian Inst., Columbia U., 1948. Asst. prof. history U. Pa., Phila., 1948-49, Swarthmore Coll., (Pa.), 1949-51; lectr. Bryn Mawr Coll. and Swarthmore Coll., 1952-54; asst. prof. history U. Calif.-Riverside, 1955-59, assoc. prof., 1959-60, prof., 1960-64; prof. Washington U., St. Louis, 1964-70; Frances and Jacob Hiatt prof. history Clark U., 1970-82, Frances and Jacob Hiatt prof. history emeritus, 1983—; fgn. expert Shaanxi Tchrs. U., Xian, People's Republic of China, 1989-90. Author: Leopold Ranke, The Formative Years, 1950, Sergei Witte and the Industrialization of Russia, 1963, Why Lenin? Why Stalin?, 1964, The GLobal City, 1969, The World Revolution of Westernization: The Twentieth Century in Global Perspective, 1987, Why Lenin? Why Stalin? Why Gorbechev?, 1993, Faces of a Nation, 1996. Columbia U. Russian Inst. sr. fellow, 1951-52; Fulbright research fellow Finland, 1954-55; Guggenheim fellow, 1961-62, 74-75; Social Sci. Research Council grantee, 1951-52,58. Mem. Am. Hist. Assn., Am. Assn. Advancement Slavic Studies (dir. 1968-71), World History Assn. (coun. 1991-94, pres. New Eng. affiliate 1993-95). Quaker. Office: Clark U Dept History Worcester MA 01610

VON MANDEL, MICHAEL JACQUES, lawyer; b. Yokohama, Japan, Oct. 20, 1941; came to the U.S., 1946; s. Michael Maximillan and Suzanne (Jacques) V.M.; m. Mary Denise Bienvenue, Dec. 22, 1984; 1 child, Michelle Denise. AB in Econs., Georgetown U., 1964; JD, Cath. U., 1968; LLM in Taxation, NYU, 1970. Bar: Washington 1969, Conn. 1969, Ill. 1976, U.S. Dist. Ct. (no. dist.) Ill. 1976, Fla. 1977, U.S. Ct. Appeals (7th cir.) 1976. Trial atty. FTC, Washington, 1968-69; trial atty. tax divsn. U.S. Dept. Justice, Washington, 1970-76; pvt. practice Chgo., 1976-93; ptnr. Von Mandel & Von Mandel, Chgo., 1994—; adj. prof. grad. tax program DePaul U., Chgo., 1980-83. Contbr. chpts. to books. Mem. ABA (tax and litigation sects. 1976—), Chgo. Bar Assn. (fed. tax com. 1976—), Fed. Bar Assn. (bd. dirs. 1981-93), Bar Assn. 7th Fed. Cir., Union League Club. Roman Catholic. Office: von Mandel & von Mandel 135 S La Salle St Ste 2216 Chicago IL 60603-4108

VON MEHREN, ARTHUR TAYLOR, lawyer, educator; b. Albert Lea, Minn., Aug. 10, 1922; s. Sigurd Anders and Eulalia Marion (Anderson) von M.; m. Joan Elizabeth Moore, Oct. 11, 1947; children—George Moore, Peter Anders, Philip Taylor. S.B., Harvard U., 1942, LL.B., 1945, Ph.D., 1946; Faculty of Law, U. Zurich, 1946-47; Faculte de Droit, U. Paris, 1948-49; Doctor iuris (h.c.), Katholeke U., Leuven, 1985. Bar: Mass. 1950, U.S. Dist. Ct. Mass. 1980. Law clk. U.S. Ct. Appeals (1st cir.), 1945-46; asst. prof. law Harvard U., 1946-53, prof., 1953-76, Story prof., 1976-93, prof. emeritus, 1993—, dir. East Asian legal studies program, 1981-83; acting chief legislation br., legal div. Occupation Mil. Govt. U.S.,Germany, 1947-48, cons. legal div., 1949; tchr. Salzburg Seminar in Am. Studies, summers 1953, 54; Fulbright research prof. U. Tokyo, Japan, 1956-57, Rome, Italy, 1968-69; cons. legal studies Ford Found., New Delhi, 1962-63; vis. prof. U. Frankfurt, summer 1967, City Univ. Hong Kong, 1995; Ford vis. prof. Inst. Advanced Legal Studies, U. London, 1976; assoc. prof. U. Paris, 1977; Goodhart prof. legal sci. U. Cambridge, 1983-84, fellow Downing Coll., 1983-84, hon. fellow, 1984—; fellow Wissenschaftskolleg zu Berlin, 1990-91. Author: The Civil Law System, 1957, 2d edit. (with J. Gordley), 1977, Law in the United States: A General and Comparative View, 1988; co-author: The Law of Multistate Problems, 1965; bd. editors Am. Jour. Comparative Law, 1952-86; contbr. articles to profl. jours.; editor: Law in Japan-The Legal Order in a Changing Soc., 1963; mem. editorial com. Internat. Ency. Comparative Law, 1969—; mem. adv. bd. Internat. Ctr. for Settlement of Investment Disputes Rev.-Fgn. Investment Law Jour., 1985—. Mem. U.S. Del. Hague Conf. pvt. internat. law, 1966, 68, 76, 80, 85, 93, 96. Named to Order of the Rising Sun, golden rays Japanese Govt., 1989; Guggenheim fellow, 1968-69; inst. fellow Sackler Inst. Advanced Studies, 1986-87. Mem. ABA, Am. Acad. Arts and Scis., Internat. Acad. Comparative Law, Institut de Droit Internat., Japanese Am. Soc. Legal Studies, Am. Arbitration Assn. (comml. panel), Am. Soc. Comparative Law (bd. dirs., pres.), Am. Soc. Polit. and Legal Philosophy, Internat. C. of C., Inst. Internat. Bus. Law and Practice (acad. coun.), Institut Grand-Duchal (corr.), Phi Beta Kappa. Office: Harvard Law Sch Cambridge MA 02138

VON MEHREN, GEORGE M., lawyer; b. Boston, Nov. 2, 1950; s. Arthur Taylor and Joan Elizabeth (Moore) von M.; m. Laurie Beth Markworth, July 25, 1987; children: Paige Elizabeth, Reed Carl. AB, Harvard U., 1972, JD, 1977; BA, Cambridge U., Eng., 1974, MA, 1985. Bar: Ohio 1977. Assoc. Squire, Sanders & Dempsey, Cleve., 1977-86, ptnr., 1986—, mem. mgmt. com., 1990-93, chmn. creditors rights litig. practice group, 1992—; mem. adv. com. U.S. Dist. Ct. (no. dist.) Ohio, 1991-95. Editor: Harvard Law Rev., 1975-77. Mem. ABA, Fed. Bar Assn., Ohio State Bar Assn., Cleve. Bar Assn. Office: Squire Sanders & Dempsey 127 Public Sq Cleveland OH 44114-1216

VON MEHREN, JANE, editor, publisher; b. N.Y.C., Feb. 12, 1963; d. Robert Brandt and Mary Katharine (Kelly) von M.; m. Kenneth S. Diamond, Sept. 20, 1997. BA, Vassar Coll., 1985. Editorial asst. Crown Publs., Inc., N.Y.C., 1984-85, asst. editor, 1985-87, assoc. editor, 1987-89, editor, 1989-90; sr. editor Ticknor & Fields, N.Y.C., 1990-93; exec. editor Viking Penguin Books, N.Y.C., 1994-96, assoc. publ., 1997—; adj. lectr. NYU Sch. Continuing Edn., N.Y.C., 1990-94. Author: Editors on Editing, 1993, My First Year in Publishing, 1994. Mem. alumnae bd. Nightingale Bamford Sch., N.Y.C., 1984-86. Editl. fellow Jerusalem Internat. Bookfair, N.Y., 1993; Tony Godwin Meml. award, 1989. Mem. Women's Media Group (programming com. 1995-96), Women in Publ. (treas. 1988-90), PEN, Assn. Am. Pubs. (freedom to read com. 1997—). Office: Viking Penguin 375 Hudson St New York NY 10014-3658

VON MEHREN, ROBERT BRANDT, lawyer, retired; b. Albert Lea, Minn., Aug. 10, 1922; s. Sigurd Anders and Eulalia Marion (Anderson) von M.; m. Mary Katharine Kelly, June 26, 1948 (dec. Mar. 1985); children: Carl S., John M., Katharine, Jane, Margaret; m. Susan Heller Anderson, Apr. 2, 1988. BA summa cum laude with philosophical oration, Yale U., 1943; LLB magna cum laude, Harvard U., 1946. Bar: N.Y. 1946, U.S. Supreme Ct. 1954. Law clk. to Judge Learned Hand U.S. Ct. Appeals (2d cir.), 1946-47; law clk. to Assoc. Justice Stanley Reed U.S. Supreme Ct., 1947-48; assoc. Debevoise & Plimpton, N.Y.C., 1946, 48-57; ptnr. Debevoise & Plimpton, 1957-93, of counsel, 1994-95, ret., 1995; arbitrator in internat. and other matters; sr. lectr. in law Wharton Sch. U. Pa., Phila., 1985-86; legal counsel Prep. Commn. for Internat. Atomic Energy Agy., N.Y.C., 1956-57; trustee Practising Law Inst., N.Y.C., 1972-96, emeritus, 1996, pres., 1979-86, chmn. bd., 1986-96. Bd. editors Harvard Law Rev., 1944-46, Am. Jour. Internat. Law, 1981-89, hon. editor, 1990—; contbr. articles to profl. jours. Trustee Axe Houghton Found., N.Y.C., 1965—; bd. dirs. Legal Aid Soc., N.Y.C., 1966-70; pres. Harvard Law Sch. Assn. N.Y., 1982-83. Mem. Assn. Bar City N.Y., Internat. Law Assn. (vice chmn. 1989—, pres. Am. br. 1978-86, chmn. exec. com. 1986-92), Coun. on Fgn. Rels., Univ. Club, Century Assn. N.Y.C. Home: 925 Park Ave New York NY 10028-0210 Office: c/o Debevoise & Plimpton 875 3rd Ave New York NY 10022-6225

VON MERING, OTTO OSWALD, anthropology educator; b. Berlin, Germany, Oct. 21, 1922; came to Switzerland, 1933, to U.S., 1939, naturalized, 1954; s. Otto O. and Henriette (Troeger) von M.; m. Shirley Ruth Brook, Sept. 11, 1954; children: Gretchen, Karin, Gregory. Grad., Belmont Hill Sch., 1940; BA in History, Williams Coll., 1944; PhD in Social Anthropology, Harvard U., 1956. Instr. Belmont Hill Sch., Belmont, Mass., 1945-47, Boston U., 1947-48, Cambridge Jr. Coll., 1948-49; rsch. asst. lab. social rels. Harvard U., 1950-51, Boston Psychopathic Hosp., 1951-53; Russell Sage Found. fellow N.Y.C., 1953-55; asst. prof. social anthropology U. Pitts. Coll. Medicine, 1955-60, assoc. prof., 1960-65, prof. social anthropology, 1965-71; prof. child devel. and child care U. Pitts. Coll. Allied Health Professions, 1969-71; prof. anthropology and family medicine U. Fla., 1971-76, prof. anthropology in ob-gyn, 1979-84, prof. anthropology and gerontology, 1986—, joint prof. dept. medicine, coll. medicine, 1994-96; lectr. Sigmund Freud Inst., Frankfurt, Germany, 1962-64, Pitts. Psychoanalytical Inst., 1960–71, Interuniv. Forum, 1967-71; tech. adviser Maurice Falk Med. Fund; Fulbright vis. lectr., 1962-63; Richard-Merton guest prof. Heidelberg U., Germany, 1962-63; vis. prof. Dartmouth, 1970-71; vis. lectr. continuing edn. Med. Coll. of Pa., 1990-92, vis. lectr. U. Sheffield, Eng., Fall, 1995, U. Liverpool, 1995, U. Coll. London Med. Sch., fall 1997; bd. dirs. Tech. Assistance Resource Assocs., U. Fla., 1979-84; supr. grad. study program Ctr. Gerontologic Studies, U. Fla., 1983-85, assoc. dir. 1985-86, dir. 1986-95; mem. coordinating com. Geriatric Edn. Ctr., Coll. of Medicine, U. Fla.; mem. nat. tech. expert panel on long-term care Health Care Financing Adminstrn., Washington; chair, mem. adv. bd. Internat. Exchange Ctr. on Gerontology State U. System of Fla., 1987-92; adv. bd. Second Season Broadcasting Network, Palm Beach, Fla., 1989-92, Fla. Policy Exch. Ctr. on Aging, State U. System Fla., 1991-95, Assoc. Health Industries of Fla., Inc., Nat. Shared Housing Resource Ctr., Balt.; cons. mental hosps. Author: Remotivating the Mental Patient, 1957, A Grammar of Human Values, 1961, (with Mitscherlich and Brocher) Der Kranke in der Modernen Gesellschaft, 1967, (with Kasdan) Anthropology in the Behavioral and Health Sciences, 1970, (with R. Binstock and L. Cluff) The Future of Long Term Care, 1996; also articles; commentary editor: Human Organization, 1974-76; corr. editor Jour. Geriatric Psychiatry; mem. editl. bd. Med. Anthropology, 1976-84, Ednl. Gerontology, 1990—, Australasian Leisure for Pleasure Jour., 1995—. Mem. nat. adv. bd. Nat. Shared Housing Resource Ctr., 1994-95; pres. Dedicated Alt. Resources for the Elderly, 1996—; mem., bd. dirs. No. Ctrl. Fla. chpt. Alzheimer's Assn., 1996—. Recipient Fulbright-Hayes Travel award, 1962-63; grantee Wenner-Gren Found., N.Y., 1962-63, Am. Philos. Soc., 1962-63, Maurice Falk Med. Fund, 1970-71, US-DHHS, 1979-83, Walter Reed Army Inst. Rsch., 1987-91. US-ADA/Fla. Dept. of Elder Affairs, 1993-94; spl. fellow NIMH, 1971-72. Fellow AAAS, Am. Anthrop. Assn. (mem. James Mooney award com. 1978-81, vis. lectr. 1961,-62, 71-74, 91-92), Am. Gerontol. Soc., Royal Soc. Health, Acad. Psychosomatic Medicine, Am. Ethnological Soc., Soc. Applied Anthropology, Royal Anthrop. Inst.; mem. Assn. Am. Med. Colls., Assn. Anthrop. Gerontol. (pres.-elect 1991-92, pres. 1992-93), Am. Fedn. Clin. Research, Am. Public Health Assn., Canadian Assn. Gerontology, British Soc. Gerontology, Med. Group Mgmt. Assn., World Fedn. Mental Health, Internat. Assn. Social Psychiatry (regional counselor), Internat. Hosp. Fedn., Help Age Internat. (London). Home: 818 NW 21st St Gainesville FL 32603-1027 Office: U Fla Dept Anthropology 1350 Turlington Hall Gainesville FL 32611 *Three guides to conduct I value most: always search for the best fit of fact, argument, and experience. Every first remedy must be amended quickly. When the past disturbs the present, more work on the future is needed.*

VON MINCKWITZ, BERNHARD, publishing company executive; b. Göttingen, Germany, Aug. 11, 1944; s. Erasmus and Mary (von Lilienfeld) von M.; m. Cornelia Böhning; children: Alexis, Vanessa, Nicolas. Diploma, U. Berlin, 1971. Bd. dirs. Bertelsmann AG, Gütersloh, Fed. Republic Germany, Verband Bayerische Zeitschriftenverlage. Office: Bertelsmann Fachinformation, Neumarkter Strasse 18 PF 802020, 81673 Munich Germany

VONNEGUT, KURT, JR., writer; b. Indpls., Nov. 11, 1922; s. Kurt and Edith Sophia (Lieber) V.; m. Jane Marie Cox, Sept. 1, 1945 (div. 1979); children: Mark, Edith, Nanette; adopted nephews: James, Steven and Kurt Adams; m. Jill Krementz, 1979, 1 child, Lily. Student, Cornell U. 1940-42, U. Chgo., 1945-47; MA in Anthropology, U. Chgo., 1971. Reporter Chgo. City News Bur., 1946; pub. relations with Gen. Electric Co., 1947-50; freelance writer N.Y.C., 1950-65, 74—; lectr. writers workshop U. Iowa, Iowa City, 1965-67; lectr. in English Harvard U., Cambridge, Mass., 1970; disting. prof. CCNY, 1973-74. Author: (novels) Player Piano, 1951, Sirens of Titan, 1959, Mother Night, 1961, Cat's Cradle, 1963, God Bless You, Mr. Rosewater, 1964, Slaughterhouse-Five, 1969, Breakfast of Champions, 1973, Slapstick, or Lonesome No More, 1976, Jailbird, 1979, Deadeye Dick, 1982, Galápagos, 1985, Bluebeard, 1987, Hocus Pocus, 1990, Timequake, 1997, (collected stories) Welcome to the Monkey House, 1968; (play) Happy Birthday, Wanda June, 1970; (TV Script) Between Time and Timbuktu or Prometheus-5, 1972; (essays) Wampeters, Foma and Granfalloons, 1974; (Christmas Story with illustrations by Ivan Chermayeff) Sun Moon Star, 1980; (autobiographical collage) Palm Sunday, 1981, (collection of speeches and essays) Fates Worse Than Death, 1991, Timequake, 1997; also short stories, articles, revs. Served with inf. AUS, 1942-45. Guggenheim fellow, 1967-68. Mem. Nat. Inst. Arts and Letters (recipient Lit. award 1970). Office: care Donald C Farber 32d Fl 1370 Ave of the Americas New York NY 10019-4602

VON PRINCE, KILULU MAGDALENA, occupational therapist, sculptor, retired; b. Bumbuli, Lushoto, Tanzania, Jan. 9, 1929; came to U.S., 1949; d. Tom Adalbert and Juliane (Martini) Von P. BA in Occupational Therapy, San Jose State U., 1958, MS in Occupational Therapy, 1972; EdD, U. So. Calif., 1980. Registered occupational therapist; cert. work evaluator, work adjustment specialist. Commd. 2d lt. U.S. Army, 1959, advanced through grades to lt. col.; staff asst. U.S. Army, Denver, 1959-62; hand rehab. asst., hand therapy Walter Reed Army Med. Ctr., 1962-65; hand rehab. asst. occupational therapist 97th Gen. Hosp., U.S. Army, Frankfurt, Fed. Republic Germany, 1965-68; occupational therapist Inst. Surg. Rsch. U.S. Army, Ft. Sam Houston, Tex., 1967-70; occupational therapy dir., cons. U.S. Army, Honolulu, 1972-75; adminstr. occupational therapy clinic, cons. LAMC U.S. Army, Presido, Calif., 1975; asst. evening coll. program San Jose (Calif.) C.C., 1976-77; postdoctoral fellow allied health adminstrn. SUNY, Buffalo, 1978, Commonwealth U., Richmond, Va., 1978-79; project dir. Ctr. of Design, Palo Alto, 1980; part-time staff project developing pre-retirement program older adults De Anza Coll., Cupertino, Calif., 1980-81; part-time instr. Stroke Activity Ctr. Cabrillo Coll., Santa Cruz, Calif., 1981; dir. occupl. therapy Presbyn. Med. Ctr., 1981-86; ptnr., mgr. retail store, 1986-89; dir. rehab. therapy Merrithew Meml. Hosp. Contra Costa Med. Ctr., Martinez, Calif., 1990-93; sculptor, 1993—; part-time activity program coord. Calif. Women's Detention Facility, Chowchilla, Calif., 1994—; researcher, presenter workshops and seminars in field. Co-author: Splinting of Burned Patients, 1974; producer videos: Elbow Splinting of the Burned Patient, 1970, Self-Instruction Unit: Principles of Elbow Splinting, 1971; contbr. articles to profl. jours. Decorated Legion of Merit; recipient Disting. Alumni Honors award San Jose State U., 1982; grad. scholar U.S. Surgeon Gen.; Kellogg Found. postdoctoral fellow, 1979. Mem. Am. Occupational Therapy Assn., Occupational Therapy Assn. Calif. (award of excellence 1986, v.p. 1981-84, state chair pers. 1981-84, state chair continuing edn. 1984-86, Lifetime Achievement award 1994), Am. Soc. Hand Therapists (hon., life). Avocations: stone sculpture, gardening, kayaking, RV travel, fossil hunting. Home: 36141 Manon Ave Madera CA 93638-8613 Office: Calif Women's Detention Facility Chowchilla CA 93610-1501

VON RAFFLER-ENGEL, WALBURGA (WALBURGA ENGEL), linguist, lecturer, writer; b. Munich, Germany, Sept. 25, 1920; came to U.S., 1949, naturalized, 1955; d. Friedrich J. and Gertrud E. (Kiefer) von R.; m. A. Ferdinand Engel, June 2, 1957; children: Lea Maxine, Eric Robert von Raffler. DLitt, U. Turin, Italy, 1947; MS, Columbia U., 1951; PhD, Ind. U., 1953. Free-lance journalist, 1949-58; mem. faculty Bennett Coll., Greensboro, N.C., 1953-55, U. Charleston (formerly Morris Harvey Coll.), W.Va., 1955-57, Adelphi U., CUNY, 1957-58, NYU, 1958-59, U. Florence, Italy, 1959-60, Istituto Postuniversitario Organizzazione Aziendale, Turin, 1960-61, Bologna Center of Johns Hopkins U., 1964; assoc. prof. linguistics Vanderbilt U., Nashville, 1965-77, prof. linguistics, 1977-85, prof. emerita, sr. rsch. assoc. Inst. Pub. Policy Studies, 1985—; dir. linguistics program Vanderbilt U., 1978-86; chmn. com. on linguistics Nashville U. Ctr., 1974-79; Italian NSF prof. Psychol. Inst. U. Florence, Italy, 1986-87; prof. NATO Advanced Study Inst., Cortona, Italy, 1988; pres. Kinesics Internat., 1988—; vis. prof. linguistics Shanxi U., Peoples Republic China, 1985; vis. prof. U. Ottawa, Ont., Can., 1971-72, Lang. Scis. Inst., Internat. Christian U., Tokyo, 1976; grant evaluator NEH, NSF, Can. Coun.; manuscript reader Ind. U. Press, U. Ill. Press, Prentice-Hall; advisor Trinity U., Simon Frazer U.; lectr. in field; dir. internat. seminar Cross-Cultural Comm., 1986-87. Author: Il prelinguaggio infantile, 1964, The Perception of Nonverbal Behavior in the Career Interview, 1983, The Perception of the Unborn Across the Cultures of the World, Japanese edit., 1993, English edit., 1994 (transl. into Chinese); co-author: Language Intervention Programs, 1960-74, 75; editor, co-editor 12 books; author films and videotape; contbr. over 300 articles to scholarly jours., over 200 to profl. and popular publs. in various countries. Grantee Am. Coun. Learned Socs., NSF, Can. Coun., Ford Found., Kenan Venture Fund, Japanese Ministry Edn., NATO, UNESCO, Finnish Acad., Meharry Med. Coll., Internat. Sociol. Assn., Internat. Coun. Linguists, Tex. A&M U., Vanderbilt U., others. Mem. AAUP, Internat. Linguistic Assn., Linguistic Soc. Am. (chmn. Golden Anniversary film com. 1974, emerita 1985—), Linguistic Assn. Can. and the U.S., Internat. Assn. for Applied Linguistics (com. on discourse analyses, sessions chmn. 1978), Lang. Origins Soc. (exec. com. 1985-97, chmn. internat. congress, 1987), Internat. Sociol. Assn. (rsch. com. for sociolinguistics, session co-chmn. internat. conf. 1983, session chmn. profl. conf. 1983), Internat. Coun. Psychologists, Internat. Assn. for Intercultural Comms. Studies, Internat. Assn. for Study of Child Lang. (v.p. 1975-78, chmn. internat. conf. Tuscon Acad. Scis., Florence, Italy 1972), Inst. for Nonverbal Communication Research (workshop leader 1981), Southeastern Conf. on Linguistics, 1980— (hon. mem. 1985—), Semiotic Soc. Am. (organizing com. Internat. Semiotics Inst. 1981), Nat. Assn. Scholars, Tenn. Assn. Scholars (bd. dirs.), Internat. Assn. for Intercultural Comms. Studies, Internat. Coun. Psychologists. Home and Office: 116 Brighton Close Nashville TN 37205-2501 *In the social sciences theories come and theories go. Carefully collected and objectively analyzed data are useful for generations and the cleanest research design in the lab does not equal a moderately neat design in the naturalistic setting.*

VON RECUM, ANDREAS F., bioengineer; b. Dillingen, Bavaria, Germany, July 5, 1939; came to U.S., 1971; s. Bogdan Freiherr and Ilse Freifrau (von Rosenberg) von R.; m. Grudrun F. Bredenbröker-Hardt, Oct. 2, 1965; children: Derik F., Vera F., Uta F., Horst F., Thomas F., Elsa F. BS, U. Giessen, 1965; DVM, Free U. Berlin, 1968, PhD, 1969; PhD in Vet. Surgery, Colo. State U., 1974. Practitioner farm animal medicine and surgery Meitingen, Germany, 1968-69; clin. staff small animal clinic Free U. Berlin (Germany), Coll. Vet. Medicine, 1969-72; rsch. asst. surg. lab. Colo. State U., Coll. Vet. Medicine, Ft. Collins, 1972-74; dir. surg. rsch. lab. Sinai Hosp. Detroit, 1975-77; prof. dept. bioengring. Clemson (S.C.) U., 1978-93, head dept. bioengring., 1982-93; chmn. bioengring. alliance S.C. Coll. Engring., Clemson U., 1984-88; scientific staff Shriners Hosp., Greenville, S.C., 1989-95; prof. Hunter endowed chair bioengring. Clemson U. Coll. Engring., 1993-97; assoc. resident, prof. Coll. Vet. Medicine Ohio State U., Columbus, 1997—; adj. assoc. prof. comparative surgery Wayne State U. Sch. Medicine, Dept. Comparative Medicine, 1975-77; adj. prof. surgery U. S.C. Sch. Medicine, 1984—, Med. U. S.C., 1987-97; adj. prof. biomaterials Coll. Dentistry, U. Nijmegen, 1993—; prof. exptl. surgery, assoc. dean Coll. Vet. Medicine, Ohio State U.; chair internat. liaison com. World's Biomaterials Soc., 1996-2000; cons. in field. Editor Jour. Investigative Surg.; patentee in field. Recipient Fulbright Scientist award, 1990-91, Alexander von Humboldt Sr. Scientist award, 1990-91; nat. and internat. fellow Biomaterials Sci. and Engring., 1996. Mem. AVMA, Am. Soc. Lab. Animal Practitioners (governing body), Coll. Vet. Medicine (elected), Blue Ridge Vet. Med. Assn. (pres. 1984), Soc. Biomaterials (asst. editor 1986—, editl. bd. 1983, program chmn. 1990, sec.-treas. 1990-92, pres. 1993-94), Internat. Soc. Artificial Internal Organs, Am. Soc. Artificial Organs, Am. Heart Assn., Acad. Surg. Rsch. (founder 1982, pres. 1982-83, newsletter editor 1982-85), Biomed. Engring. Soc., Am. Soc. Engring. Edn., Assn. Advancement Med. Instrumentation. Presbyterian. Office: Ohio State U Coll Vet Medicine 1900 Coffey Rd Columbus OH 43210-1006

VON REYN, C. FORDHAM, infectious disease physician; b. Montour Falls, N.Y., Sept. 24, 1945; m. Janet Elizabeth Goldberger, June 18, 1967; children: Leah Edana, Adam Daniel, Charles Alexander. AB, Dartmouth Coll., 1967, BMS, 1969; MD cum laude, Harvard U., 1971. Diplomate Am. Bd. Internal Medicine, Am. Bd. Infectious Diseases. Intern in medicine Beth Israel Hosp., Boston, 1971-72, jr. resident in medicine, 1972-73, sr. asst. resident in medicine, 1975-76; clin. fellow in infectious disease Beth Israel Hosp., Children's Hosp. Med. Ctr., Dana-Farber Cancer Ctr., Boston, 1976-77; clin. assoc. in medicine U. N.Mex. Sch. Medicine, Albuquerque, 1973-75, clin. assoc. in family & cmty. medicine, 1974-75, outpatient attending dept. medicine, 1976-77, inpatient attending dept. medicine, 1978-79; instr. epidemiology sch. medicine Tufts U., Boston, 1974, 76; adj. asst. prof. clin. medicine Dartmouth Med. Sch., Hanover, N.H., 1978-85, lectr. microbiology, 1978—, adj. assoc. prof. clin. medicine, 1986-87, assoc. prof. clin. medicine, 1988-91; attending physician infectious disease svc. dept. medicine, co-dir. infectious disease block scientific basis of medicine Dartmouth Med. Sch., 1988—; assoc. prof. medicine Dartmouth Med. Sch., Hanover, N.H., 1991-94, prof. medicine, 1994—; dir. microbiology, hosp. epidemiologist infectious disease dept. Concord (N.H.) Hosp., 1977-88; cons. staff Mary Hitchcock Meml. Hosp., Hanover, 1977-88, clin. staff, 1988—; hosp. epidemiologist, chief infectious disease section Dartmouth-Hitchcock Med. Ctr., Hanover, 1988—; cons. physician infectious diseases Vets. Adminstrn. Hosp., White River Junction, Vt., 1990—; asst. physician Harvard U. Health Svcs., Cambridge, 1975-77; pres. Concord Clinic Inc., 1984-85; section chief internal medicine Concord divsn. Hitchcock Clinic, 1985-88; cons. global program on AIDS World Health Orgn., 1987. Mem. editl. bd. Current Issues in Public Health, 1993—; mem. internat. editl. adv. bd. AIDS and Society, 1989—; contbr. articles to profl. jours. and chpts. in books. Pres. Frontiers of Knowledge Found., Concord, N.H., 1982-83; v.p. Concord Cmty. Music Sch., 1984-85, pres., 1986-88; trustee Am. Red Cross, Concord, 1986-88, N.H. AIDS Found., Manchester, 1989—; chmn. N.Mex. Task Force on Rabies, 1974, U.S. del. Congress of the Internat. Physicians for the Prevention of Nuclear War, Helsinki, 1984; mem. N.H. AIDS Adv. Com., 1985-87; mem. Commr.'s Task Force on HIV/AIDS Divsn. of Pub. Health Svcs., N.H., 1990— and numerous others. Med. officer USPHS, 1973-75. Recipient Gov.'s Spl. award for Pub. Svc., Santa Fe, N.Mex., 1975. Fellow Infectious Disease Soc. Am.; mem. Am. Soc. Microbiology, Internat. Immunocomprised Host Soc., Internat. AIDS Soc., Northern New England Infectious Disease Soc. (v.p. 1990-92, pres. 1992-94), Physicians for Social Responsibility, Soc. for Hosp. Epidemiology Am., Alpha Omega Alpha. Home: 44 Waterman Hill Rd Norwich VT 05055-9686 Office: Dartmouth-Hitchcock Med Ctr Infectious Disease Sect One Medical Ctr Dr Lebanon NH 03756*

VON RHEIN, JOHN RICHARD, music critic, editor; b. Pasadena, Calif., Sept. 10, 1945; s. Hans Walter and Elsa Maryon (Brossmann) von R. AA, Pasadena City Coll., 1965; BA in Eng., UCLA, 1967; BA in Music, Calif. State U., Los Angeles, 1970. Music reviewer Hollywood (Calif.) Citizen-News, 1968-70; music editor and critic, dance critic Akron (Ohio) Beacon Jour., 1971-77; music critic Chgo. Tribune, 1977—; prof. music appreciation Rio Hondo Jr. Coll., Calif., 1970-71; lectr., TV host, rec. annotator. Author: (with Andrew Porter) Bravi; contbr. revs. and articles to World Book Ency., 1994 Yr. Book, 1995 Yr. Book, 1996 Yr. Book, 1997 Yr. Book., Stagebill, Opera News, High Fidelity/Mus. Am., Ovation, L.A. Times, Boston Globe, Vanity Fair, Fanfare, Am. Record Guide, others. Music Critics Assn.-Kennedy Center for Performing Arts fellow, 1972, 75. Mem. Music Critics Assn. (edn. com., dir. 1988), Ravinia Critics Inst. (dir. 1988). Office: Chgo Tribune Co 435 N Michigan Ave Chicago IL 60611

VON RINGELHEIM, PAUL HELMUT, sculptor; b. Vienna; s. Henry and Rosita (Altschuler) Von R. BS, Bklyn. Coll., 1956; MA, Fairleigh Dickinson U., 1958; postgrad., Art Students League, N.Y.C., 1958-59, Acad. Fine Arts, Munich, 1960-61. Tchr. printmaking Bklyn. Mus. Sch., 1957-58; prof. sculpture Sch. Visual Arts, N.Y.C., 1967-71. One-man shows include Niveau Art Gallery, N.Y.C., 1958, Am. House, Berlin, Munich and Hamburg, 1960-61, Rose Fried Gallery, N.Y.C., 1964, 67, Fairleigh Dickinson U., 1964, New Vision Galleries, London, 1964, N.Y. Cultural Center, 1975, O.K. Harris Gallery, N.Y.C., 1971-73, 76, 78, 80, 82, Mitzi Landau Gallery, Los Angeles, 1974, Amarillo Mus. of Art, 1987, Amarillo Art Ctr., Tex., 1987, Robert Berman Gallery, Los Angeles, 1988, Obelisk Gallery, 1992, 94; exhibited in group shows at Bklyn. Mus., 1958, Whitney Mus., 1963, 65, 68, 78, 82, 87, Mus. Modern Art, N.Y.C., 1964, 67, 69, 85, O.K. Harris Gallery, Providence, 1964, Ben Uri Gallery, London, 1965, Jewish Mus., N.Y.C., 1966, 68, 70, 74, Cleve. Mus., 1966, Obelisk Gallery, Boston, 1967, 69, Albright-Knox Gallery, Buffalo, 1967, Rose Art Mus., Brandeis U., 1967, Am. Embassy, Brussels, 1967, Meml. Hall, Boston, 1968, Finch Coll., N.Y.C., 1968, Frick Mus., Pitts., 1968, also in Rotterdam and Daensstadt, Cooper Hewitt, 1983, Internat. Airport Gallery, 1995, and numerous other galleries and museums; represented in permanent collections at Welton Becket Assos., Broadway Maintenance Corp., CBS, N.Y.C., Fairleigh Dickinson U., Martin Found., Mus. Modern Art, N.Y.C., Mus. Modern Art, Tel Aviv, Mus. Modern Art, Tokyo, Whitney Mus. Am. Art, Time and Life collections, N.Y.C., Smithsonian Instn., Internat. Sculpture Show, Hollycroft, Conn., others; archtl. commns. include World Peace Monument, U.S. Pavilion, World's Fair, 1964; Tangential 32 at Park Ave. and 55th St., N.Y.C., 1969; Variance inflatable at Internat. Sculpture Festival, Govt. Center, Boston, 1971; Fulcrum at Westinghouse Nuc. Ctr., Pitts., 1972; Vortex in Red for Main St. Ann. Art Festival, Houston, 1975, Nebr. Interstate 80 Bicentennial Sculpture Project, Houston Center, Tex. Eastern Corp.; also sculptures Columbia (N.C.) Mall, Taubman Corp., Century City, L.A., Diamond Shamrock, Dallas, Exec. Hdqrs. Becket Group, L.A.; also Endless Force for former Pres. Gerald R. Ford, Equinox for Diamond Shamrock Corp., fountain Exec. Hdqrs. Becket Group, L.A., Freeflight Lincoln Properties Co., San Jose, Calif., Perth, Australia, 1995, Edmonton, Can., 1995, Jakarta, Java, 1996. Recipient Outstanding Young Man of Yr. award N.Y. World's Fair, 1964; Fulbright scholar, 1974-75. Mem. Archtl. League City N.Y., Lambs Club (hon.), Explorers Club. Home: 9 Great Jones St New York NY 10012-1128

VON ROSENBERG, GARY MARCUS, JR., parochial school educator; b. Baumholder, Federal Republic of Germany, Feb. 22, 1956; s. Gary Marcus and Maria Gwendolyn (Pickett) Von R. BA, Cleve. State U., 1979; BS, U. Tex., 1991. Jr. high sch. sci. tchr. St. Andrew's Sch., Ft. Worth, 1982-86; math. tchr., coach, moderator Monsignor Nolan High Sch., Ft. Worth, 1986—. Creator jr. high Sci. Fair program. Capt. U.S. Army field artillery, 1979-82. Recipient Sci. Fair Tchr. award Ft. Worth Regional Sci. Fair, 1985, runner-up, 1984. Mem. ASCD, Nat. Coun. Tchrs. Math., The Math. Assn. Am., The Nat. Sci. Tchrs. Assn. Home: 1525 Lincolnshire Way Fort Worth TX 76134-5583

VON RYDINGSVARD, URSULA KAROLISZYN, sculptor; b. Deensen, Germany, July 26, 1942; cmae to U.S., 1950; d. Ignacy and Konegunda (Sternal) Karoliszyn; m. Pual Greengard. BA, MA, U. Miami, Coral Gables, Fla., 1965; postgrad., U. Calif., Berkeley, 1969-70; MFA, Columbia U., 1975; PhD (hon.), Md. Inst. Art, 1991. Instr. Sch. Visual Arts, N.Y.C., 1981-82; asst. prof. Pratt Inst., Bklyn., 1978-82, Fordham U., Bronx, N.Y., 1980-82; assoc. prof. Yale U., New Haven, 1982-86; prof. grad. divsn. Sch. Visual Arts, N.Y.C., 1986—. One-woman shows include Laumeier Sculpture Gallery, St. Louis, 1988, Capp St. Project San Francisco, 1990, Lorence-Monk Gallery, N.Y.C., 1990-91, Zamek Ujazdowski Contemporary Art Ctr., Warsaw, Poland, 1992, Storm King Art Ctr., Mountainville, N.Y., 1992-94, Galerie Lelong, N.Y.C., 1994, Weatherspoon Art Gallery, Grensboro, N.C., 1994, Univ. Gallery, Amherst, 1995, Mus. Art, Providence, 1996, Mus. Art R.I. Sch. Design, Providence, 1996, Yorkshire Sculpture Pk., Wakefield, England, 1997; exhibited in group shows at Contemporary Arts Ctr., Cin., 1987, Damon Brandt Gallery, N.Y.C., 1989, Met. Mus. Art, N.Y.C., 1989-93, Whitney Mus. Contemporary Art, 1990, Cultural Ctr., Chgo., 1991, Ctrl. Bur. Art Exhbns., Warsaw and Krakow, Poland, 1991, The Cultural Space/Exit Art, N.Y.C., 1992, Galerie Lelong, N.Y.C., 1993, Denver Art Mus. and Columbus Art Mus., 1994—, others; outdoor exhbns include Pelham Bay Park, Bronx, N.Y., 1978, Neuberger Mus., Purchase, N.Y., 1979, Artpark, Lewiston, N.Y., 1979, Laumeier Sculpture Park, St. Louis, 1989-94, Walker Art Ctr., Mpls., 1990-93, Oliver Ranch, Geyserville, Calif., Storm King Art Ctr., Mountainville, N.Y., 1992-93; contbr. articles to profl. jours. Fulbright Hays travel grantee, 1975; grantee N.Y. State Coun. Arts, Am. the Beautiful Fund, Nat. Endowment for Arts, Creative Artists Program Svc.; Griswald traveling grantee Yale U., 1985; Guggenheim fellow, 1983-84; Nat. Endowment for Arts individual artists grantee, 1986-87; recipient Alfred Jurzykowski Found. Fine Arts award, 1996. Studio: 429 S 5th St Brooklyn NY 11211-7425

VON SCHACK, WESLEY W., energy services company executive; b. N.Y., 1944; married. AB, Fordham U., 1965; MBA, St. John's U., Jamaica, N.Y., 1971; doctorate, Pace U., 1990. Chmn., CEO, pres. DQE, Pitts., 1989-96, ret., 1996; chmn., pres., CEO N.Y. State Electric and Gas Corp., Binghamton, 1996—; bd. dirs. Mellon Bank Corp., Mellon Bank, N.A., RMI Titanium Co. Vice chmn. bd. trustees Carnegie Mellon U. Office: NY State Elec and Gas Corp 4500 Vestal Pkwy East Binghamton NY 13902-3607

VON SCHWARZ, CAROLYN M. GEIGER, psychotherapist, educator; b. Greenville, Mich., May 16, 1949; d. Raymond Lavern and Bernice Clara (Schoenborn) Geiger; m. Jeffrey George von Schwarz, Apr. 25, 1970 (div. Sept. 1979); children: Sean Raymond, Laura Elizabeth. BA, Wayne State U., 1988, MEd, 1992. Lic. profl. counselor. Counselor Edn. Tng. Rsch. Found., 1986-89; dir., therapist von Schwarz Assocs., Grosse Pointe Farms, Mich., 1989—; pvt. practice Boysville, Mich., 1996—; spkr. in field. Vol. therapist, COO Grateful Home, Homeless Shelter, Treatment Shelter, Detroit, 1991-93; vol. Sacred Heart Ctr., Detroit, 1978—, SAC2, Grosse Pointe Farms, 1985—; cons. Treehouse Players, Grosse Pointe Woods. Mem. Psi Chi. Republican. Roman Catholic. Avocations: fitness, home restoration/renovation, traveling.

VON STADE, FREDERICA, mezzo-soprano; b. Somerville, N.J., June 1, 1945; m. Peter Elkus, 1973 (div.); children: Jennie, Lisa; m. Michael G. Gorman, Jan. 1991. Student, Mannes Coll. Music, N.Y.C., Ecole Mozart, Paris; DMus (hon.), Yale U., 1985. Former nanny, salesgirl; sec. Am. Shakespeare Festival. Debut in Die Zauberfloete with Met. Opera, 1970, later resident mem., Covent Garden debut, 1975; appeared with opera cos. including Paris Opera, San Francisco Opera, Salzburg Festival, London Royal Opera, Spoleto Festival, Boston Opera Co., Santa Fe Opera, Houston Grand Opera, La Scala; recital artist, soloist with symphony orchs.; appeared in operas The Marriage of Figaro, Faust, The Magic Flute, Don Giovanni, Tales of Hoffman, Rigoletto, Der Rosenkavalier, The Seagull, Werther, The Barber of Seville, The Dangerous Liasons, Le Nozze di Figaro; albums Frederica Von Stade Sings Mozart-Rossini Opera Arias, French Opera Arias, Pelleas and Melisande, Idomeneo, La Sonnambula, Simple Gifts with Mormon Tabernacle Choir, Songs of the Cat with Garrison Keillor; created roles of Nina in the Seagull (Pastieri), 1974, Tina in the Aspern Papers (Arganto), 1988; starred in Dominick Argento's Casa Guidi, 1985, Carnegie Hall, N.Y.C.; rec. artist EMI. Mem. Am. Guild Mus. Artists. Roman Catholic. Avocations: tennis, skiing, dancing. Office: Columbia Artists Mgt Inc Arbib/Treuhaft Div 165 W 57th St New York NY 10019-2201*

VON STUDNITZ, GILBERT ALFRED, state official; b. Hamburg, Germany, Nov. 24, 1950; came to U.S., 1954.; s. Helfrid and Rosemarie Sofie (Kreiten) von S.; m. Erica Lynn Hoot, May 26, 1990. BA, Calif. State U., L.A., 1972. Adminstrv. hearing officer State of Calif., Montebello, 1987-91; mgr. III driver control policy unit Dept. Motor Vehicles State of Calif., Sacramento, 1991-93; ops. mgr. Driver Safety Review, 1993-95; contract mgr. State Dept. Health Svcs., 1995-97; staff mgr. licensing ops. policy Dept. Motor Vehicles, Sacramento, 1997—. Author: Aristocracy in America, 1989; editor publs. on German nobility in U.S., 1986—. Active L.A. Conservancy, West Adams Heritage Assn., dir., 1989-91. Mem. Calif. State Mgrs. Assn., Assn. German Nobility in N.Am. (pres. 1985—), Driver Improvement Assn. Calif. (v.p. 1992-96, dir. media rels. 1996—), Benicia Hist. Soc., Sierra Club, Intertel, Mensa, Orders and Medals Soc. Am., Nat. Assn. Managed Care Regulators, Phi Sigma Kappa (v.p. chpt. 1978). Roman Catholic. Avocations: genealogical research, collecting. Home: 1101 W 2nd St Benicia CA 94510-3125

VON TAAFFE-ROSSMANN, COSIMA T., physician, writer, inventor; b. Kuklov, Slovakia, Czechoslovakia, Nov. 21, 1944; came to U.S., 1988; d. Theophil and Marianna Hajossy; m. Charles Boris Rossmann, Oct. 19, 1979; children: Nathalie Nissa Cora, Nadine Nicole. MD, Purkyne U., Brno, Czechoslovakia, 1967. Intern Valtice (Czechoslovakia) Gen. Hosp., 1967-68, resident ob-gyn, 1968-69; med. researcher Kidney Disease Inst., Albany, N.Y., 1970-71; resident internal medicine Valtice Gen. Hosp., 1972-73; gen. practice Nat. Health System, Czechoslovakia, 1973-74; pvt. practice West Germany, 1974-80; med. officer Baragwanath Hosp., Johannesburg, South Africa, 1984-85, Edendale Hosp., Pietermaritzburg, South Africa, 1985-86; pvt. practice Huntingburg, Ind., 1988-90, Valdosta, Ga., 1990—; med. researcher, 1966—. Contbr. articles on medicine to profl. jours.; inventor, patentee in field. Office: 2301 N Ashley St Valdosta GA 31602-2620

VON TERSCH, LAWRENCE WAYNE, electrical engineering educator, university dean; b. Waverly, Iowa, Mar. 17, 1923; s. Alfred and Martha (Emerson) Von T.; m. LaValle Sills, Dec. 17, 1948; 1 son, Richard George. B.S., Iowa State U., 1943, M.S., 1948, Ph.D., 1953. From instr. to prof. elec. engring. Iowa State U., 1946-56; dir. computer lab. Mich. State U., 1956-83, prof. elec. engring., chmn. dept., 1958-65, assoc. dean engring., 1965-68, dean, 1968-89, dean emeritus, 1989—. Author: (with A. W. Swago) Recurrent Electrical Transients, 1953. Mem. IEEE; mem. Sigma Xi, Tau Beta Pi, Eta Kappa Nu, Phi Kappa Phi, Pi Mu Epsilon. Home: 4282 Tacoma Blvd Okemos MI 48864-2734 Office: Michigan State U Coll Engring East Lansing MI 48823

VON TUNGELN, GEORGE ROBERT, retired university administrator, economics consultant; b. Golconda, Ill., July 18, 1931; s. Cecil Ernest and Rachel Elizabeth (Wright) von T.; m. Marilyn Ruth Burris, Nov. 6, 1955; children—Stuart, Cheryl, Brenda, Sonya, Eric. B.S., So. Ill. U., 1951, M.S., 1956; Ph.D., U. Ga., 1974. Asst. mgr. exptl. farms So. Ill. U., Carbondale, 1951-52; instr., research asst. Pa. State U., 1955-58; asst. prof. to prof. agrl. sci. Clemson (S.C.) U., 1958-85, asst. to dean internat. programs, 1977-85; cons. econs. and internat. econ. devel. El Paso, 1985—; Pres. P.T.O., 1973. Contbr. articles to profl. jours. Served with AUS, 1952-54. Mem. Assn. U.S. Univ. Dirs. Internat. Agrl. Programs, Partners of Americas, West Tex. Football Officials Assn., Phi Kappa Phi, Gamma Sigma Delta. Republican. Baptist. Clubs: S.C. Football Ofcls. Assn, Sertoma (chmn. bd. 1972). Home and Office: 547 Cocula Ave El Paso TX 79932-2731

VONTUR, RUTH POTH, elementary school educator; b. Beeville, Tex., Sept. 10, 1944; d. Robert Bennal and Ruth (Matejek) Poth; m. Robert F. Vontur, Aug. 8, 1964; children: Catherine Anne, Craig Robert, Cynthia Anne. BS in Edn., Southwest Tex. State U., 1966. Cert. health and phys. edn. tchr., biology tchr. Tex. Teachng asst. Blessed Sacrament Confraternity Christian Doctrine, Poth, Tex., 1958-64; phys. edn. tchr. Judson Ind. Sch. Dist., Converse, Tex., 1966-68; substitute tchr. St. Monica's Confraternity Christian Doctrine, Converse, 1974-96; substitute tchr. Judson Ind. Sch. Dist., Converse, 1972-75, 80, phys. edn. tchr., 1966-68, 81—, contact person elem. phys. edn., 1982-96; county adv. bd. Am. Heart Assn., San Antonio, Tex., 1985-88, jump rope for heart coord., 1984—, heart ptnr., 1992—. Pres. St. Monica's Coun. Cath. Women, Converse, 1975; sponsor Young Astronauts, 1993—, Hall Patrol, 1990-93, 96—, Flag Patrol, 1996—; contact person elem. phys. edn. Judson ISD, 1982-96. Mem. NEA, AAHPERD, Alamo Area Tex. Assn. Health, Phys. Edn., Recreation and Dance, Tex. Assn. Health, Phys. Edn., Recreation and Dance, Judson Tchrs. Assn. (exec. dir. 1993-95), Tex. State Tchrs. Assn., Judson Athletic Booster Club. Roman Catholic. Avocations: oil painting, tee shirt painting, sewing. Home: 105 Norris Dr W Converse TX 78109-1905 Office: Judson Ind Sch Dist Converse Elem Sch 102 School St Converse TX 78109-1320

VON WALDOW, ARND N., lawyer; b. Moenchen-Gladbach, Germany, Mar. 15, 1957; came to U.S., 1966; s. Hans Eberhard and Brigitte H. (Schulze-Kadelbach) von W.; m. Esther R. Haguel, May 25, 1987; children: Rachel J., Danielle M. BA, Syracuse U., 1980; JD, U. Pitts., 1983. Bar: La. 1983, Pa. 1989. Assoc. Sessions & Fishman, New Orleans, 1983-90, Eckert, Seamans, Cherin & Mellott, Pitts., 1990-91; ptnr. Meyer, Darragh, Buckler, Bebenek & Eck, Pitts., 1991—; mem. Product Liability Adv. Coun., Chgo., 1991—. Mem. ABA, Def. Rsch. Inst., Phi Beta Kappa. Home: 1738 Hempstead Ln Pittsburgh PA 15241-1376 Office: Meyer Darragh Buckler Bebeneck & Eck 2000 The Frick Bldg Pittsburgh PA 15219

VON WRIGHT, VICTOR, SR., actor, film producer; b. L.A., July 7, 1953; s. William and Helen (Twyman) Wright; m. Shari Von Wright; children: Denardo, Denote; children from previous marriage: Justus, Victor II. AS, Price Coll., 1990. Film producer 20th Century Fox, L.A., 1981-88, MGM Studios, L.A., 1988-90; producer Zulieka Entertainment, L.A., 1991—; chmn. Zulieka Entertainment, L.A., Zulieka Records, L.A., 1991—, Zulieka TV Films, L.A., 1991—, Zulieka Pub., L.A., 1991—, Zulieka Mgmt., L.A., 1991—, Zulieka Sound Tracks, L.A., 1991—; chmn., CEO Zulieka Comm. N.Y. and L.A., Studio City, L.A., 1991—; radio talk show host Am. Get It Off Your Chest; pres. Am. Voice News, Am. Get It Off Your Chest Pub., Am. Get It Off Your Chest Merchandising; chmn., nat. dir. The Found. for a Unified Am. Author: (screenplay) D.E.A. Connection, 1986, Time & Time, 1987. Fundraiser NAACP, L.A., 1986, Legal Rights Orgn., Washington, 1987; supporter Rep. Nat. Com., Washington, 1990. Recipient Best Film Producer award, 1990, Music Achievement award Fozzerlla Music Co., 1987, Outstanding Achievement in Film Prodn. award, 1980. Mem. Paralegal Assn. Am., Fedn. of Police, Royal Order of Police, Calif. Yacht Club. Office: Zulieka Motion Pictures 270 N Canon Dr Beverly Hills CA 90210-5323

VON ZERNECK, FRANK ERNEST, television producer; b. N.Y.C, Nov. 3, 1940; s. Peter and Beatrice (Francis) von Z.; m. Julie Hawthorne Mannix, Jan. 15, 1965; children: Danielle, Frank. BA in Speech and Drama, Hofstra Coll., 1962. Gen. mgr. JuJamcyn Theatres, N.Y.C., 1965-70, Ctr. Theatre Group, Los Angeles, 1970-74; ptnr. Moonlight Prodns., Hollywood, Calif., 1974-84; prin. Frank von Zerneck Films, Studio City, Calif., 1984—; cons. Found. for the Extension and Devel. of Am. Profl. Theatre, N.Y.C., 1970-77; v.p. League of Resident Theatres, N.Y.C., 1970-75; sec. Portrait of A Bookstore, North Hollywood, 1985—. Prodr. over 100 movies including: The Desperate Miles, 1975, 21 Hour at Munich, 1976, Sharon: Portrait of a Mistress, 1977, Portrait of a Stripper, 1979, Texas Rangers, 1980, Love Canal, 1982, Policewoman Centerfold, 1983, Summer Fantasy, 1984, Hostage Flight, 1985: (TV miniseries) Dress Gray, 1985, Queenie, 1987, To Heal a Nation, 1988, Billy the Kid, 1989, The Great Los Angeles Earthquake, 1990, Survive the Savage Sea, 1991, Too Young To Die, 1992, Jackie Collins' Lady Boss, 1992, The Broken Chain, 1994, Robin Cook's Mortal Fear, 1994, Take Me Home Again, 1994, The West Side Waltz, 1995, God's Lonely Man, 1996. Bd. dirs. Oakhill Sch., Los Angeles, 1984—. Recipient award of merit Nat. Cath. Broadcasters, N.Y.C., 1982, silver gavel award ABA, Washington, 1983, TV Prodr. of Yr. AFI, 1994. Mem. Caucus of Writers, Producers and Dirs., Producers Guild Am., League N.Y. Theatres and Prodns., Calif. Theatre Coun. (chmn. 1973-74), League Resident Theatres (v.p. 1972-73), ACI (bd. dirs. 1990-95). Home: 4355 Forman Ave Toluca Lake CA 91602-2909 Office: Frank von Zerneck Films 12001 Ventura Pl Ste 400 Studio City CA 91604-2629

VOOGT, JAMES LEONARD, medical educator; b. Grand Rapids, Mich., Feb. 8, 1944; married; 3 children. Student, Calvin Coll., 1962-64; BS in Biological Sci., Mich. Tech. Univ., 1966; MS in Physiology, Mich. State Univ., 1968, PhD in Physiology, 1970. Postdoc. fellow, lectr. dept. physiology U. Calif., San Francisco, 1970-71; asst. prof. dept. physiology and biophysics U. Louisville Sch. Medicine, 1971-77, assoc. prof. dept. physiology and biophysics, 1977; assoc. prof. dept. physiology U. Kans. Sch. Medicine, 1977-82, prof. dept. physiology, 1982—; assoc. in psychology, assoc. in oncology U. Louisville, 1973-77; assoc. dean rsch. U. Kans. Sch. Medicine, 1982-84, acting chmn. dept. physiology, 1987, chmn. dept. molecular and integrative physiology, 1993—; vis. prof. Erasmus U., 1985. Mem. editl. bd. Endocrinology, 1984-86, 89-92, Am. Jour. Physiology, 1984-88, Doody's Jour., 1995—; ad hoc reviewer Neuroendocrinology, Sci., Biology of Reproduction, Life Scis., Jour. Endocrinology, Molecular Cellular Neuroscis., Procs. Soc. Exptl. Biology and Medicine, biochm. endocrinology study sect. NIH, 1992—, reproductive endocrinology study sect., 1994—; reviewer grants NSF; editor scientific proceedings Research Week, 1982, 83; contbr. over 120 articles to prof. publs., 4 chpts. to books. Grantee NIH, 1972-80, 80-81, 82-85, 88—, 90-93, 94—, NSF, 1985-86, 91-94, Ctr. on Aging, 1988, Nat. Inst. Drug Abuse, 1991-93; fellow Japan Soc. Promotion of Sci., 1993; recipient Outstanding Young Alumni award Mich. Tech. Univ., 1974, Honors in Edn., Med. Student Voice, 1990. Mem. AAAS, Endocrine Soc., Internat. Soc. Neuroendocrinology (charter mem.), Am. Physiol. Soc. (pub. affairs adv. com. 1983-87) Soc. Neuroscis., Phi Kappa Phi, Sigma Xi. Office: Dept Physiology U Kans Med Ctr 3901 Rainbow Blvd Kansas City KS 66160-0001

VOOK, FREDERICK LUDWIG, physicist, consutlant; b. Milw., Jan. 17, 1931; s. Fred Ludwig and Hedwig Anna (Werner) V.; m. Frederica Jean Sandin, Aug. 16, 1958; children: Eric Robert, Dietrich Werner. BA with honors, U. Chgo., 1951, BS, 1952; MS, U. Ill., 1954, PhD in Physics, 1958. With Sandia Labs., Kirtland AFB East, N.Mex., 1958-94; div. supr., 1962-71, mgr. dept. research, 1971-78, dir. research, 1978-94; pvt. cons. Albuquerque, 1994—. Editor: Radiation Effects in Semiconductors, 1968; co-editor: Applications of Ion Beams to Metals, 1974. Mem. coll. engring. adv. bd. U. Ill.; mem. policy bd. Nat. Nanofabrication Facility Cornell U.; mem. basic engring. sci. adv. com. Panel on Value of Basic Rsch; mem. Okla. State Univ. Ctr. for Laser and Photonics Rsch. adv. bd. U. Chgo. and U. Ill. scholar and fellow. Fellow Am. Phys. Soc.; mem. IEEE (sr. mem.), Böhmische Physikalische Gesellschaft, Phi Beta Kappa, Sigma Xi.

VOOK, RICHARD WERNER, physics educator; b. Milw., Aug. 2, 1929; s. Fred Ludwig and Hedwig Anna (Werner) V.; m. Julia Deskins, Sept. 7, 1957; children: Katherine, Elizabeth, Richard S., Frederick W. BA, Carleton Coll., 1951; MS, U. Ill., 1952, PhD, 1957. Staff physicist IBM Rsch. Lab., Yorktown Heights, N.Y., 1957-61; sr. rsch. physicist Franklin Inst. Rsch. Labs., Phila., 1961-65; assoc. prof. of metallurgy Syracuse (N.Y.) U., 1965-70, prof. of materials sci., 1970-84, prof. of physics, 1984-93, prof. emeritus, 1993—, dir. solid state sci. and tech., 1984-87, 90-91; physicist/chemist U. Calif., Lawrence Livermore Nat. Lab., summers 1977-81; summer faculty mem. Sandia Nat. Lab., Albuquerque, 1983, 84; bd. editors Thin Solid Films, 1985—. Contbr. articles to profl. publs., chpts. to books. Recipient L. B. Pfeil medal and prize Metals Soc. of Great Britain, 1983. Mem. Am. Vacuum Soc., Electron Microscope Soc. Am., Materials Rsch. Soc., Phi Beta Kappa, Sigma Xi, Pi Mu Epsilon. Lutheran. Achievements include discovery of Auger R-factor characterization of thin film growth; development of theory of substrate-induced differential thermal expansion strains in thin films; first observation of Stranski-Krastanov growth mode in vapor deposited thin films, first use of flash evaporation to form high Tc superconducting thin films; discoverer of perpendicular electric field effect in copper surface electromigration. Office: Syracuse Univ 201 Physics Bldg Syracuse NY 13244-1130

VOORHEES, DAVID WILLIAM, editor, historian; b. Jersey City, Sept. 20, 1947; s. William Franklin Jr. and Irma Rose (Grissom) V. BA, NYU, 1974, MA, 1977, PhD, 1988. Reference history mng. editor Charles Scribner's Sons, N.Y.C., 1976-83; co-editor Papers of William Livingston, N.Y.C., 1983-88; editor-in-chief The Papers of Jacob Leisler Nat. Hist. Publs. and Records Commn., N.Y.C., 1988—; editor-in-chief de Halve Maen, N.Y.C., 1990—; rsch. asst. Bur. Applied Social Rsch. Columbia U., Metropolitan Mus. Art; instr. history NYU. Author: Centennial History of the Holland Society of New York, 1985; editor: Concise Dictionary of American History, 1983; compiler: Concise Dictionary of Huguenot Ancestors, 1985; mng. editor: Ency. Am. Fgn. Policy, 1978 (Am. Libr. Assn. award, Choice Mag. award 1980), Ency. Am. Econ. History, 1980 (Am. Libr. Assn. award 1980, Choice Mag. award 1980), Album of Am. History, 1981, Dictionary of Am. Biography: Supplement VII, 1981, Dictionary of Am. Biography: Biog. Index Guide, 1981, Ency. Am. Govt. and Politics, 1984; assoc. editor: Dictionary Am. History, 1976, Am. Writers, 1979, 81, Brit. Writers, 1979, 80, 81, Concise Dictionary Am. Biography, 1980, Dictionary Sci. Biography, 1970-81, Dictionary of Middle Ages, 1984, Ency. Am. Jud. Sys., 1987; contbr. numerous articles to history publs., conf. presentations. Recipient N.Y. State Hist. Assn. Manuscript award, 1990, Hendricks Manuscript award Friends of New Netherland, 1990, Huguenot Soc. Am. medal, 1993, N.Y. State Libr. Rsch. Residency award, 1995; named N.Y. State Coun. Humanities spkr., 1996—; grantee Am. Philos. Soc., 1989, Am. Coun. Learned Socs., 1990. Mem. Am. Hist. Assn., Assn. Documentary Editors, N.Y. Hist. Soc., N.Y. Geneal. and Biog. Soc., Holland Soc. N.Y. (trustee 1980—, Gold medal 1995), St. Nicholas Soc. (trustee 1985—). Liberal. Presbyterian. Avocations: swimming, hiking, drawing, painting. Home: 400 E 56th St New York NY 10022 Office: The Holland Soc NY 122 E 58th St New York NY 10022-1904

VOORHEES, JAMES DAYTON, JR., lawyer; b. Haverford, Pa., Nov. 14, 1917; s. James Dayton Voorhees and Elsa Denison Jameson; m. Mary Margaret Fuller, Sept. 5, 1942 (dec. Apr. 1991); children: J. Dayton III, Susan F. Voorhees-Maxfield, Jane Voorhees Kiss. BA, Yale U., 1940; JD, Harvard U., 1943. Bar: N.H. 1947, Colo. 1948, U.S. Dist. Ct. Colo. 1948, U.S. Ct. Appeals (10th cir.) 1949, U.S. Ct. Appeals (5th cir.) 1956, U.S. Supreme Ct. 1960. Assoc. Johnson & Robertson, Denver, 1947-50; atty. Conoco Inc., Denver, 1950-56; ptnr. Moran, Reidy & Voorhees, Denver, 1956-78, Kutak, Rock & Huie, Denver, 1978-80; ptnr., counsel Davis, Graham & Stubbs, Denver, 1980—; bd. dirs. Japex (U.S.) Corp., Houston, Mercury Internat. Techs., Tulsa. Mem. Denver Bd. Edn., 1965-71, pres. 1967-69. Lt. comdr. USNR, 1941-46, ATO, PTO. Mem. ABA, Colo. Bar Assn., Denver Bar Assn., Fed. Energy Bar Assn., Denver Country Club, University Club. Republican. Avocations: golf, skiing.

VOORHEES, JOHN LLOYD, columnist; b. DeWitt, Iowa, Aug. 30, 1925; s. Lloyd William and Elsie Irene (Bousselot) V. BA in History, U. Iowa, 1951; BA in Journalism, U. Wash., 1953. Tchr. Oelwein (Iowa) High Sch., 1951-52; columnist Seattle Post-Intelligencer, 1953-71; columnist, critic Seattle Times, 1971—. With U.S. Army, 1946-48. Democrat. Office: The Seattle Times Fairview Ave N & John St Seattle WA 98111

VOORHEES, LEE R., JR., lawyer; b. St. Joseph, Mo., Oct. 28, 1937; s. Lee R. and Nora Wilkinson (Bell) V.; m. Sandra Louise Day, Nov. 1965 (div.); children: Philip David, Alexandra Elizabeth; m. Joan Lind Heublein, Sept., 1992. AB, Yale U., 1959, JD, 1962. Bar: Wash. 1962, U.S. Supreme Ct. 1984. Assoc. Roberts & Shefelman, Seattle, 1966-71, ptnr., 1972-88; ptnr. Foster Pepper & Shefelman, Seattle, 1988—. Author: Taxable and Tax-Exempt Financing of Health Care Facilities, 1981. Lt. USNR, 1962-66. Mem. ABA, Wash. State Bar Assn., King County Bar Assn., Am. Acad. Hosp. Attys. (pres. 1987-88), Wash. State Soc. Hosp. Attys. (pres. 1979-80), Nat. Assn. Bond Lawyers, Wash. Coun. Sch. Attys., Wash. State Assn. Mcpl. Attys., Yale Alumni Assn. Western Wash. (pres. 1971-72), Yale Law Sch. Assn. (exec. com. 1981—), Rainier Club, Yale Club (N.Y.C.). Republican. Episcopalian. Avocations: skiing, boating. Home: 5211 W Mercer Pl Mercer Island WA 98040-4650 Office: Foster Pepper & Shefelman 34th Fl 1111 3rd Ave Seattle WA 98101

VOORHEES, RICHARD LESLEY, chief federal judge; b. Syracuse, N.Y., June 5, 1941; s. Henry Austin and Catherine Adeline (Fait) V.; m. Barbara Holway Humphries, 1968; children: Martha Northrop, Steven Coerte. BA, Davidson Coll., 1963; JD, U. N.C., Chapel Hill, 1968. Bar: N.C. 1968, U.S. Dist. Ct. (we. dist.) N.C. 1969, U.S. Tax Ct. 1969, U.S. Ct. Appeals (4th cir.) 1978, U.S. Dist. Ct. (mid. dist.) N.C. 1981. Mem., ptnr. Garland, Alala, Bradley & Gray, Gastonia, N.C., 1968-80; pvt. practice Gastonia, N.C., 1980-88; judge U.S. Dist. Ct., Charlotte, N.C., 1988—, chief judge, 1991—. Mem. N.C. State Rep. Exec. Com., Gaston County Rep. Com., chmn., 1979-83, U.S. Jud. Conf. Com., 1993—, case mgmt. and ct. adminstrn. com., 4th Cir. Ct. Appeals Jud. Coun., 1992-93; chmn. Gaston County Bd. Elections, Gastonia, 1985-86; alt. del. Rep. Nat. Conv., Kansas City, Kans., 1976. 1st lt. U.S. Army, 1963-65, U.S. Army Res., 1963-69. Mem. N.C. Bar Assn., Fed. Judges Assn., Dist. Judges Assn. Avocation: boating. Office: US Dist Ct WDNC 195 CR Jonas Fed Bldg 401 W Trade St Charlotte NC 28202-1619

VOORHESS, MARY LOUISE, pediatric endocrinologist; b. Livingston Manor, N.Y., June 2, 1926; d. Harry William and Helen Grace (Schwartz) V. BA in Zoology, U. Tex., 1952; MD, Baylor Coll., Houston, 1956. Diplomate Am. Bd. Pediatrics and Pediatric Endocrinology. Rotating intern Albany (N.Y.) Med. Ctr., 1956-57, asst. resident pediatrics, 1957-58, chief resident pediatrics, 1958-59; rsch. fellow pediatric endocrinology and genetics SUNY Health Sci. Ctr., Syracuse, 1959-61, asst. prof. pediatrics, 1961-65, assoc. prof. pediatrics, 1965-70, prof. pediatrics, 1970-76; prof. pediatrics SUNY Sch. Medicine and Biomed. Scis., Buffalo, 1976-91, prof. pediatrics emeritus, 1991-97; co-chief div. endocrinology Children's Hosp. Buffalo, 1976-91; retired, 1997; ad hoc reviewer Jour. Pediatrics, Pediatrics, Am. Jour. Diseases Children, other. Contbr. sci. articles to profl. jours., chpts. to books. Mem. adv. bd. Interim Healthcare inc., 1991-97; mem. devel. coun. Children's Hosp. Buffalo Found., 1991-97; med. dir. Children's Growth Found., Buffalo, 1976-97; cmty. advisor Assn. for Rsch. Childhood Cancer, Buffalo, 1990-97. Recipient rsch. career devel. award Nat. Caneer Inst., 1961-71, Dean's award SUNY Sch. Medicine and Biomed. Scis., 1991. Fellow Am. Acad. Pediatrics, AAAS; mem. Soc. Pediatric Rsch., Am. Pediatric Soc., Endocrine Soc., Lawson Wilkins Pediatric Endocrine Soc., Buffalo Pediatric Soc., Zonta Internat., Phi Beta Kappa, Alpha Omega Alpha. Presbyterian. Home: 6311 Chiswick Pk Williamsburg VA 23188-6369 Office: Children Hosp 219 Bryant St Buffalo NY 14222-2006

VOORSANGER, BARTHOLOMEW, architect; b. Detroit, Mar. 23, 1937; s. Jacob H. and Ethel A. (Arnstein) V.; m. Lisa Livingston, 1964; m. Catherine Hoover, Sept. 10, 1983; children—Roxanna Virginia (dec.), Matthew Ansley. A.B. cum laude, Princeton U., 1960; diplome, Fontainebleau, 1960; M.Arch., Harvard U., 1964. Assoc. Vincent Ponte, Montreal, Que., Can., 1964-67, I.M. Pei & Ptnrs., 1968-78; dir. I.M. Pei & Ptnrs., Iran, 1975-78; co-chmn. Voorsanger & Mills (Architects), N.Y.C., 1978-90; founder, prin. Voorsanger & Assocs., Architects, N.Y.C., 1990—; founder Taylor/Voorsanger Urban Designers, 1991; lectr. Bennington (Vt.) Coll., U. Pa., Columbia U., Harvard U.; guest critic, lectr. Yale U., Pratt Inst., CUNY, R.I. Sch. Design, U. Cin., Syracuse U., U. Tex., Arlington; mem. adv. bd. Parson Sch. Architecture; mem. archtl. rev. panel Port Authority of N.Y. & N.J.; advisor to Samsung Corp., Korea. Exhbns. include: NYU, Archtl. Assn., London, Harvard Grad. Sch. Design, Vacant Lots Housing Study, N.Y., Deutsches Architeckur Mus., Frankfurt, Mus. Finnish Architecture, Avery Lib.Centennial Exhbn. Columbia Univ., Helsinki, Bklyn. Mus.; major projects include: Le Cygne Restaurant, Neiman houseboat, NYU Midtown Ctr., NYU Bus. Sch. Library, La Grandeur housing, NYU dormitories, Hostos Community Coll., N.Y.; finalist Bklyn. Mus. masterplan internat. competition, expansion and master plan Pierpont Morgan Libr., Wethersfield Carriage Mus., Amenia, N.Y.; Montana and Wyoming Residences; Advanced Tng. Ctr., NYU, New York Apt., N.Y.C., Riverdale (N.Y.) Jewish Ctr.; fellow J. Pierpont Morgan Libr., N.Y. Mem. vis. com. R.I. Sch. Design, U. Tex., Arlington; mem. N.Y. Hist. Soc., also mem. archtl. cir. steering com.; chmn. bd. advisors Temple Hoyne Buell Ctr., Study Am. Architecture, Columbia U., N.Y.C., 1989—; mem. adv. bd. Parsons Sch. Architecture; chair archtl. rev. panel Port Authority N.Y. and N.J.; bd. dirs. Worldesign Found.; mem. Regent's Panel N.Y. State U., N.Y. State Regents' Com. on Schs. 1st lt. U.S. Army, 1960-61. Recipient awards N.Y.C. chpt. AIA, AIA/Better Homes, Bard City Club, Interiors mag., Stone Inst., AIA/Libr., Lumen, Pratt Inst., NYU, N.Y.C. Art Commn. Fellow AIA (bd. dirs. N.Y.C. chpt. 1979-81, v.p. 1987, chmn. Brunner award com. 1978-80, Bard award pres.-elect N.Y.C. chpt. 1984, Nat. Honor award, N.Y. State award); mem. Archtl. League N.Y.C. (bd. dirs.), Sir John Soane Mus. Found., N.Y. Found. for Arch. (bd. dirs.), Worldesign Found., N.Y., Century Assn., River Club, Wadawanuck Club, Alumni Coun. Grad. Sch. Design Harvard. Office: 246 W 38th St Fl 14 New York NY 10018-5805

VOOS, PAULA BETH, economics educator; b. Everett, Wash., Apr. 15, 1949; d. Paul Allen and Loualta (Peterson) Vogel; m. Keith Frederick Voos, May 30, 1970; children: Johanna, Michaela. AB in English, Whitman Coll., 1971; MA in Econs., Portland (Oreg.) State U., 1976; PhD in Econs., Harvard U., 1982. Instr. U. Mass., Boston, 1978-81; asst. prof. U. Wis., Madison, 1981-87, assoc. prof. econs., 1987-92, prof., 1992—; Mem. Commn. on the Future of Worker-Mgmt. Rels., 1993-94; pres. Inst. Wis.'s Future, 1995—. Contbr. articles to profl. jours. Mem. Am. Econs. Assn., Indsl. Rels. Rsch. Assn. (exec. bd. 1988-90, editor 1993—). Democrat. Home: 2710 Willard Ave Madison WI 53704-5755 Office: U Wis Industrial Relations Rsch Inst 4226 Social Science Bldg Madison WI 53706-1320

VORA, ASHOK, financial economist; b. Bombay, India, July 19, 1947; came to U.S., 1970; s. Kevalchand and Laxmi (Mehta) V.; m. Rama Kata, Dec. 12, 1982; children: Anjali Serena, Amit Raunak. B.Sc., U. Bombay, 1967; M.B.A., Indian Inst. Mgmt., 1970; Ph.D., Northwestern U., 1973. Asst. to chmn. Vora Automotives Ltd., Bombay, 1963-67, dir., 1967-70; asst. prof. fin. CUNY, 1973-80; vis. asst. prof. fin. U. Wis., Madison, 1977; vis. assoc. prof. fin. Northwestern U., Evanston, Ill., 1979-80; assoc. prof. fin. CUNY, 1980-84, prof. fin., 1984—; dir. fin. rsch. Fed. Home Loan Mortgage Corp., Reston, Va., 1987-88; vis. prof. fin. Hofstra U., Hempstead, N.Y., 1990-91; cons. in field. Contbr. articles to profl. jours. Mem. Am. Econ. Assn., Am. Fin. Assn., Fin. Mgmt. Assn., So. Fin. Assn., S.W. Fin. Assn., Western Fin. Assn., Mensa, Nat. Wildlife Fedn., Beta Gamma Sigma. Office: CUNY Box E0621 17 Lexington Ave New York NY 10010-5585

VORA, MANU KISHANDAS, chemical engineer, quality consultant; b. Bombay, India, Oct. 31, 1945; s. Kishandas Narandas and Shantaben K. (Valia) V., m. Nila Narotamdas Kothari, June 16, 1974; children: Ashish, Anand. BSChemE, Banaras (India) Hindu U., 1968; MSChemE, Ill. Inst. Tech., Chgo., 1970, PhD in ChemE, 1975; MBA, Keller Grad. Sch. Mgmt., Chgo., 1985. Grad. asst. Ill. Inst. Tech., 1969-74; rsch. assoc. Inst. Gas Tech., Chgo., 1976-77, chem. engr., 1977-79, engring. supr., 1979-82; mem. tech. staff AT&T Bell Labs. (now Lucent Techs.), Holmdel, N.J., 1983-84, Naperville, Ill., 1984—; mgr. customer safisfaction AT&T Bell Labs. (now Lucent Techs.), Naperville and Milw., 1990—; mem. faculty Ill. Inst. Tech., Chgo., part-time, 1993—; spkr. in field. Invited editor Internat. Petroleum Encyclopedia, 1980. Chmn. Save the Children Holiday Fund Drive, 1986—; trustee Avery Coonley Sch., Downers Grove, Ill., 1987-91; pres., dir. Blind Found. for India, Naperville, 1989—; dir. Nat. Ednl. Quality Initiatives, Inc., Milw., 1991—, fellow, 1992. Recipient Non-Supervisory AA award Affirmative Actions Adv. Com., 1987, 92, Outstanding Contbn. award Asian Am. for Affirmative Actions, 1989, Disting. Svc. award Save the Children, 1990, Ann. Merit award Chgo. Assn. Tech. Socs., 1992. Fellow Am. Soc. Quality Control (standing rev. bd. 1988—, editl. re. bd. 1989, tech. media com. 1989, mixed media rev. bd. 1994, nat. quality month regional planning com. 1989-94, nat. cert. com. 1989-94, chmn. cert. process improvements subcom. 1990-94, testimonial awards 1996, exec. bd. Chgo. sect., vice chmn. sect. affairs 1993-94, sect. chmn. 1994-95, nat. dir. at large, 1996-98, spl. award 1991, Century Club award 1992, Founders' award 1993, Joe Lisy Quality award 1994); mem. Ill. Team Excellence (chief judge 1993—, steering com. 1993—, award). Hindu. Avocations: reading, photography, travel, philanthropic activities. Home: 1256 Hamilton Ln Naperville IL 60540-8373 Office: Lucent Techs 2600 Warrenville Rd Lisle IL 60532-3640

VORAN, JAMES F., principal. Prin. Sealey Elem. Sch. Recipient Elem. Sch. Recognition award U.S. Dept. Edn., 1989-90. Office: Sealey Elem Sch 2815 Allen Rd Tallahassee FL 32312-2614*

VORBRICH, LYNN KARL, lawyer, utility executive; b. Iowa City, Feb. 12, 1939; s. William August and Anna Margaretha (Seibert) V.; m. Jody Nolan; children: Sally, Andrew, Peter, David, Peter, Jill, Jason. BS Indsl. Adminstrn., Iowa State U., 1960; JD, U. Iowa, 1962. Bar: Iowa 1962, Ill. 1962. Assoc. Seyfarth, Shaw, Fairweather & Geraldson, Chgo., 1962-64; assoc., ptnr. Dickinson, Throckmorton, Parker, et al, Des Moines, 1964-69; asst. counsel The Bankers Life Co., Des Moines, 1969-73; assoc. counsel Iowa Power, Des Moines, 1973-76, assoc. gen. counsel, 1976-78, sec., assoc. gen. counsel, 1978-79, sr. v.p., 1985, exec. v.p., 1986-89, pres., 1989-92; exec. v.p. Midwest Power Systems, Inc., Des Moines, 1992-95; pres. electric divsn. Mid-American Energy Co., Davenport, Iowa, 1995-96, exec. v.p., 1996—; bd. dirs. Bankers Trust Co., Des Moines, 1986-95, Preferred Risk Ins. Group, 1993—, Norwest Bank of Davenport. Trustee Davenport Mus. of Art, 1995-97; dir. Putnam Mus. of Natural History, Quad-City Econ. Devel. Group, Downtown Davenport Devel. Assn., Quad Cities United Way; mem. adv. com. Iowa State Boys Tng. Sch., Eldora, 1987-95, legis. study com. on juvenile justice, 1989-90; dean's adv. coun. Iowa State U. Coll. Bus. Adminstrn., Ames, 1987-90; pres. bd. Polk County Legal Aid Soc., 1970, Iowa Children's and Family Svcs., 1970, 78, Planned Parenthood of Mid-Iowa, 1983, Des Moines Area C.C. Found., 1986-87; chmn. Des Moines Human Rights Commn., 1970; bd. dirs. Golden Circle Incubator bd., Golden Circle Labor-Mgmt. Commn., Ankeny, Iowa, 1988-95, Civic Music Assn., Des Moines, 1986-87; mem. Bur. Econ. Devel. Coun. of the Greater Des Moines C. of C., 1989-95. Named Outstanding Young Alumnus Iowa State U., 1973. Mem. ABA, Iowa Bar Assn., Des Moines Club (trustee 1982-88), rock Island Arsenal Golf Club, Davenport Country Club. United Church of Christ. Office: Mid-American Energy Co PO Box 4350 Davenport IA 52801

VORE, MARY EDITH, pharmacology educator, researcher; b. Guatemala City, Guatemala, June 27, 1947; came to U.S., 1962; d. Charles Schrater and Sammye (Smith) V.; m. Edgar Tadasu Iwamoto, Dec. 27, 1976; children: Kenneth Edgar, Daniel Vore. BA, Asbury Coll., Wilmore, Ky., 1968; PhD, Vanderbilt U., Nashville, Tenn., 1972. Postdoctoral fellow Hoffman-LaRoche, Nutley, N.J., 1972-74; asst. prof. U. Calif., San Francisco, 1974-78; asst. prof. pharmacology U. Ky., Lexington, 1978-81, assoc. prof., 1981-86, prof., 1986—, vice chmn. dept., 1983-94, dir. grad. ctr. for toxicology, 1994—; cons. NIH, Bethesda, Md., 1983-87. Contbr. numerous articles to profl. jours., chpts. to books. Mem. Nat. Adv. Environ. Health Scis. Coun., 1991-94. USPHS grantee, 1979—. Mem. Soc. Toxicology, Am. Assn. Study of Liver Disease, Am. Soc. Pharmacology and Exptl. Therapeutics (sec., treas. 1986-89). Office: U Ky Coll Medicine 800 Rose St Lexington KY 40536-0001

VORENBERG, JAMES, lawyer, educator, university dean; b. Boston, Jan. 10, 1928; s. F. Frank and Ida (Muhlfelder) V.; m. Dorothy Greeley, Oct. 25, 1952; children: Jill, Amy, Eliza; m. Elizabeth Weiner Troubh, June 20, 1970. A.B., Harvard U., 1948, LL.B., 1951. Law clk. to Justice Frankfurter, 1953-54; with firm Ropes & Gray, 1954-62, partner, 1960-62; prof. law Harvard U., Cambridge, Mass., 1962—, Roscoe Pound prof. law, 1981—; dean Law Sch. Harvard U., 1981-89; dir. Office of Criminal Justice, 1964-65; exec. dir. Pres.'s Commn. on Law Enforcement and Adminstrn Justice, 1965-67; asso. spl. prosecutor Watergate Spl. Prosecution Force, 1973-75. Trustee Legal Def. Fund, NAACP; chmn. Mass. Ethics Commn., 1978-83. With USAF, 1951-53. Home: 9 Willard St Cambridge MA 02138-4836 Office: Harvard U Law Sch Cambridge MA 02138

VORHIES, MAHLON WESLEY, veterinary pathologist, educator; b. Fairfield, Iowa, June 26, 1937; s. Harold Wesley and Edith Mae (Bender) V.; m. Ilene Lanore Hoffman, Aug. 29, 1959; children—Susan Rae, Robert Wesley. D.V.M., Iowa State U., 1962; M.S., Mich. State U., 1967. Veterinarian in pvt. practice Riverside, Iowa, 1962-64; clin. instr. Mich. State U., East Lansing, 1964-67; vet. pathologist Iowa State U., Ames, 1962-72; vet. pathologist, dir., dept. head S.D. State U., Brookings, 1972-86; dir., dept. head Kans. State U. Coll. Vet. Medicine, Manhattan, 1986-95, dept. head, diagonostic medicine patho biology, 1995—; cons. NIH, Commonwealth Pa., Winrock Internat. Hdqrs., U.S. Dept. Agr., FAO-Fundagro/MIAC, LIFE, Quito, Ecuador, 1991. Contbr. articles to profl. jours. Trustee Brookings United Presbyn. Ch., 1975-78, elder, 1981-84; mem. adv. com. Pipestone Area Vocat. Tech. Inst., 1984. Mem. AVMA, Assn. Am. Vet. Med. Colls., S.D. Vet. Med. Assn. (Vet. of Yr. award 1979), Kans. Vet. Med. Assn., Am. Assn. Avian Pathologists, U.S. Animal Health Assn., Am. Assn. Vet. Lab. Diagnosticians (E.P. Pope award 1984, pres. 1977), North Central Conf. Vet. Lab. Diagnosticians (chmn. 1984, 94), Commn. Vet Medicine, Phi Zeta, Gamma Sigma Delta. Clubs: Brookings Country (dir. 1983-86). Lodge: Shrine (chmn. 1984-85). Home: 2035 Rockhill Cir Manhattan KS 66502-3952 Office: Coll Vet Medicine Kans State U Manhattan KS 66506

VORHOLT, JEFFREY JOSEPH, lawyer, software company executive; b. Cin., Feb. 20, 1953; s. Edward C. and Rita L. (Kinross) V.; m. Marcia Anne Meyer, Apr. 30, 1976; children: Kimberly Anne, Gregory Michael, Karen Michelle. BBA cum laude, U. Cin., 1976; MBA, Xavier U., Cin., 1978; JD, Chase Law Sch., 1983. Bar: Ohio, 1983; CPA, Ohio. Sec., treas. Cin. Bell Info. Systems, Inc., 1983-84, v.p., chief fin. officer, 1984-88, also bd. dirs.; v.p., controller Cin. Bell, Inc., 1988-89; sr. v.p. Cin. Bell Info. Systems, Inc., 1989-91, Cin. Bell Telephone Co., 1991-93; CFO Structural Dynamics Rsch. Corp., Milford, Ohio, 1994—. Voting mem. Cin. Playhouse, 1986—; mem. fin. planning com. ARC, Cin., 1986-89; trustee U. Health Maintenance Orgn., Inc., 1990-93, St. Joseph Infant and Maternity Home, Inc. Mem. ABA, AICPAs, Ohio Bar Assn., Aircraft Owners and Pilots Assn., Cin. Hist. Soc., Bankers Club of Cin. (bd. govs. 1990-97). Avocations: golf, tennis, hiking, photography. Office: Structural Dynamics Rsch Corp 2000 Eastman Dr Milford OH 45150-2712

VORIS, WILLIAM, academic administrator emeritus; b. Neoga, Ill., Mar. 20, 1924; s. Louis K. and Faye (Hancock) V.; m. Mavis Marie Myre, Mar. 20, 1949; children: Charles William II, Michael K. BS, U. So. Calif., 1947, MBA, 1948; PhD, Ohio State U., 1951; LLD, Sung Kyun Kwan U. (Korea), 1972, Eastern Ill. U., 1976. Teaching asst. Ohio State U., Columbus, 1948-50; prof. mgmt. Wash. State U., Pullman, 1950-52; prof., head dept. mgmt. Los Angeles State Coll., 1952-58, 60-63; dean Coll. Bus. and Pub. Adminstrn., U. Ariz., Tucson, 1963-71; pres. Am. Grad. Sch. Internat. Mgmt., Glendale, Ariz., 1971-89, pres. emeritus, 1989—, adj. prof., 1994—. Ford Found. research grantee Los Angeles State Coll., 1956; prof. U. Tehran (Iran), 1958-59; Ford Found. fellow Carnegie Inst. Tech., Pitts., 1961; prof. Am. U., Beirut, Lebanon, 1961, 62; cons. Hughes Aircraft Co., Los Angeles, Rheem Mfg. Co., Los Angeles, Northrop Aircraft Co., Palmdale, Calif., Harwood Co., Alhambra, Calif., ICA, Govt. Iran. Served with USNR, 1942-45. Fellow Acad. Mgmt.; mem. Ariz. Acad., Beta Gamma Sigma, Alpha Kappa Psi, Phi Delta Theta. Author: Production Control, Text and Cases, 1956, 3d edit., 1966; Management of Production, 1960. Research in indsl. future of Iran, mgmt. devel. in Middle East. Home: Thunderbird Campus Glendale AZ 85306

VOROUS, MARGARET ESTELLE, primary and secondary school educator; b. Charles Town, W.Va., Feb. 14, 1947; d. Benjamin Welton and Helen Virginia (Owens) Vorous. AA in Pre-Edn. (Laureate Scholar), Potomac State Coll., W.Va. U., 1967; BS in Elem. Edn., James Madison U., 1970, MS in Edn., 1975, postgrad., spring 1978, fall 1979, summer 1979, 81; postgrad. U. Va., summers 1977, 78, fall 1978, 89, 91, James Madison U., fall 1981-82, summer 1979, 81-82; MEd in Media Svcs., East Tenn. State U., 1988, 89. Cert. library sci., cert. adminstrn./supervisory. Tchr. 3d-4th grade Highview Sch., Frederick County, Va., 1968-69, 3d grade Kernstown Elem. Sch., Frederick County, 1970-71, E. Wilson Morrison Elem. Sch., Front Royal, Va., 1971-72, Stonewall Elem. Sch., Frederick County, 1972-78; tchr. 4th grade South Jefferson Elem. Sch., Jefferson County (W.Va.) Schs., 1978-79, Emergency Sch. Aid Act reading tchr./reading specialist, 1980-82, reading tchr./specialist Page Jackson Solar Elem. Sch., 1983-87; adult basic edn. tchr. Dowell J. Howard Vocat. Ctr., Winchester, Va., 1984-87, G.E.D. tchr., coordinator, 1985-87; libr., media specialist Powell Valley Middle Sch., 1988-91; ABE/GED/ESL tchr. for JOBS program Berkeley County Schs., 1992-94; libr., media specialist Northwestern Elem., 1994-95, first grade tchr., 1995—; tchr. 4th grade Ranson (W.Va.) Elem. Sch., 1979; reading tutor; reading tutor, trainer Laubach Literacy Internat., 1989—; art rep. Creative Arts Festival at Kernstown, 1971, Stonewall elem. schs., 1973-77; mem. cultural task force Frederick County Sch., 1974-75, music task force, 1973-74, textbook adoption com. for reading, writing, 1976-77. Founder, editor: The Reading Gazette, The Reading Tribune, Emergency Sch. Aid Act Reading Program, South Jefferson Elem. Sch., 1980-81, Shepherdstown Elem. Sch., 1981-82; creator numerous reading games, activities. Vol. fundraiser Am. Cancer Soc., Frederick County, Va., 1981; vol. blood donor Am. Red Cross, 1978—; mem. Frederick County Polit. Action Com., Jefferson County Polit. Action Com.; del. 103-109th Ann. Diocesan Convs., Episc. Ch., registrar of vestry Grace Episc. Ch., Middleway, W.Va., 1980-87, lic. lay reader, 1980-90, lic. chalice bearer, 1983-90; lic. lay reader, lay eucharistic min. St. Pauls's Episc. Ch.-on-the-Hill, Winchester, Va., 1996—; committeeperson Lebanon Dems., 1988-89; commd. mem. Order of Jerusalem, 1985—; VEMA leadership participant, 1989-91, 95; facilitator VEMA Conf., 1994; participant Seven Habits program Covey Leadership Ctr., 1993; Recipient various awards, including being named Miss Alpine Princess, award for Excellence in Adult Basic Edn. Dept. Edn., Charleston, W.Va., 1994, RIF Site Coord. for Honorable mention, 1995, Asst Coord. Pritt for Gov. Campaign (DEM), 1995-96, RIF Nat. Poster contest Storyteller for Chpt. I workshop and Ctrl. Elementary, 1994-96, Sigma Phi Omega, 1967. Mem. Internat. Reading Assn., NEA, Va. Reading Assn., Shenandoah Valley Reading Council, Assn. Supervision and Curriculum Devel., W.Va. Edn. Assn., NEA. Jefferson County Edn. Assn. (faculty rep.), Fauquier County Edn. Assn., Va. Edn. Assn., W.Va. Adult Edn. Assn., Va. Ednl. Media Assn., South Jefferson PTA, Potomac State Coll. Alumni Assn., James Madison U. Alumni Assn., Frederick County Dem. Women, Kappa Delta Pi, Phi Delta Kappa, Phi Kappa Phi.

VORSANGER, FRED S., university administrator; b. Calumet City, Ill., Apr. 20, 1928; s. Fred and Hannah (Steifel) V.; m. Doreen D. Carter, Apr. 24, 1965; children: Diana, Bruce, Bob;. B.S. in Bus. Adminstrn., Ind. U., 1951; M.B.A., George Washington U., 1970; postgrad., U. Ark., 1971. Acct. Ernst & Ernst, Chgo., 1951-53; internal auditor Purdue U., Lafayette, Ind., 1953-59; treas., bus. mgr. Am. Council on Edn., Washington, 1959-68; v.p. U. Ark., Fayetteville, 1968—; mgr. Walton Arena U. Ark.; exec. dir. U. Ark. Found., Inc., 1985-88, v.p. emeritus, 1988—; lectr. U. Ky. Mgmt. Inst., 1976—, U. Calif. Mgmt. Inst., 1976-85; adj. prof. Coll. Bus. Adminstrn., 1985—; trustee Common Fund, N.Y.C., chmn., 1982-85; bd. dirs. Tyson Foods, Inc., United Educators Ins. Risk Retention Co., McIlroy Bank and Trust, Ozark Guidance Ctr., Ozark Aging Found.; spl. cons. Meridian House Found., Washington, 1960-68; examiner North Central Commn. on Accrediting, 1971—. Author: (with Julian H. Levi) Patterns of Giving to Higher Education, 1968; contbr. articles to profl. jours.; mem. editorial adv. bd. Commerce Clearing House, Inc, 1963-68; mem. editorial adv. com. Coll. and Univ. Bus. Mag. Pres. Washington County unit Am. Cancer Soc., 1971-72; bd. dirs. Nationwide Edn. Conf. Centers, N.W. Ark. Regional Planning Commn., Ark. Regional Med. Program, U. Ark. Found., Fayetteville Community Concert Assn., Northwest Ark. Film Commn., 1983—; city dir. N.W. Ark. Econ. Devel. Dist., alderman, 1993—, mayor, 1991, Fayetteville, Ark. Served with U.S. Army, 1945-47. Mem. Nat. Assn. Land Grant Colls. and State Univs. (dir.), Nat. Assn. Ednl. Buyers (treas., dir.), Nat. Assn. Coll. and Univ. Bus. Officers (dir., pres. 1984-85, Disting. Bus. Officer award 1991), So. Assn. Coll. and Univ. Bus. Officers (pres.), Am. Coun. Edn., Fayetteville C. of C. (dir., pres.), Blue Key, Fayetteville Country Club, Capitol Club, Rotary Internat. (dist. gov.), Delta Sigma Pi, Sigma Phi Epsilon. Home: 1315 E Ridgeway Dr Fayetteville AR 72701-2616 *From standing in a public welfare relief line to being listed in Who's Who; Thank God for America.*

VORWERK, E. CHARLSIE, artist; b. Tennga, Ga., Jan. 28, 1934; d. James A. and Hester L. (Davis) Pritchett; m. Norman T. Vorwerk, Feb. 9, 1956; children: Karl, Lauren, Michael. AB, Ga. Coll. for Women, Milledgeville, 1955. Billboard design artist Vanesco Poster, Chattanooga, 1955; cartographic draftsman TVA, Chattanooga, 1955; fashion illustrator Loveman's, Chattanooga, 1956; freelance comml. artist Chattannoga, Charleston, S.C., 1957—; pvt. art instr. for children and adults, Chattanooga, Charleston, 1066—; art instr. continuing edn. Charleston So. U., 1979-82; exhbn. chmn. Charleston Artist Guild, Summerville Artist Guild; chair Flowertown Festival, Summerville, S.C., 1972—; co-coord. Picolo-Spoleto

Outdoor Art Exhibit, City of Charleston, 1983—, others. Illustrator: (jokes) Tales and Taradiddles, (elem. book) St. Paul's Epitahs, others. Mem. Bd. Archtl. Rev., Summerville, 1976—; mem. women's bd. St. Paul's Ch., Summerville, 1968-84; active Boy Scouts Am., Girl Scouts U.S.; vol. Mental Health Clinic. Recipient art show ribbons. Mem. Charleston Artist Guild, Summerville Artist Guild. Episcopalian. Avocations: gardening, cooking, sewing, photography, nature. Home and Office: 315 W Carolina Ave Summerville SC 29483

VORYS, ARTHUR ISAIAH, lawyer; b. Columbus, Ohio, June 16, 1923; s. Webb Isaiah and Adeline (Werner) V.; m. Lucia Rogers, July 16, 1949 (div. 1980); children: Caroline S., Adeline Vorys Cranson, Lucy Vorys Noll, Webb I.; m. Ann Harris, Dec. 13, 1980. BA, Williams Coll., 1945; LLB, JD, Ohio State U., 1949. Bar: Ohio 1949. From assoc. to ptnr. Vorys, Sater, Seymour & Pease, Columbus, 1949-82, sr. ptnr., 1982-93, of counsel, 1993—; supt. ins. State of Ohio, 1957-59; bd. dirs Vorys Bros., Inc., others. Trustee, past Children's Hosp., Greenlawn Cemetery Found.; trustee, former chmn. Ohio State U. Hosps.; regent Capital U.; del. Rep. Nat. Conv., 1968, 72. Lt. USMCR, World War II. Decorated Purple Heart. Fellow Ohio State Bar, Columbus Bar Assn.; mem. ABA, Am. Judicature Soc., Rocky Fork Headley Hunt Club, Rocky Fork Hunt and Country Club, Capital Club, Phi Delta Phi, Chi Psi. Home: 5826 Havens Corners Rd Columbus OH 43230-3142 Office: Vorys Sater Seymour & Pease PO Box 1008 52 E Gay St Columbus OH 43215-3161

VOS, FRANK, advertising and marketing executive; b. N.Y.C., Dec. 1, 1919; s. George W. and Anna (Lewis) V.; m. Mary C. Dempsey, June 24, 1951; children: George Andrew, Julia Elizabeth. Student, MIT, 1936-37; BA magna cum laude, Columbia U., 1982, MA, 1984, M of Philosophy, 1989. Copywriter firm Schwab & Beatty, N.Y.C., 1941-42, 46-48; sales promotion mgr. Doubleday & Co., N.Y.C., 1948-52; group head Kleppner Co., N.Y.C., 1952-57; founder, chmn. Vos & Co., N.Y.C., 1957, Vos & Co. (became Vos & Reichberg, 1965), Altman, Vos & Reichberg, Inc., 1970-76, Vos & White, Inc., 1976-79, Frank Vos Co. Inc., 1979-85; vis. lectr. NYU, 1961, 73, 75; chmn. Direct Mktg. Day, N.Y., 1972; spl. cons. dean Columbia U., 1983; instr. U. Conn., Stamford, 1986. Mem. adv. bd. The Ency. of N.Y.C. Bd. dirs. Stamford (Conn.) Symphony Soc., 1981-89. 1st lt. inf. AUS, World War II, ETO. Decorated Bronze Star U.S.; Knight's Cross Crown of Italy; recipient Silver Apple award N.Y.C. Direct Mktg. Club, 1985. Mem. Am. Hist. Assn., Orgn. Am. Historians, Urban History Soc., Lotos Club of N.Y.C. (chmn. lit. com. 1965-73, dir. 1971-79, admissions com. 1985—, Medal of Merit 1993), Stamford (Conn.) Yacht Club, Silvermine Golf Club (Conn.), Phi Beta Kappa. Home: 30 Windermere Lane Stamford CT 06902-1010

VOS, HUBERT DANIEL, private investor; b. Paris, Aug. 2, 1933; s. Marius and Aline (Porge) V.; m. Susan Hill, Apr. 18, 1958; children: Wendy, James. BA, Institut d'Etudes Politiques, U. Paris, 1954; M in Pub. Adminstrn., Princeton U., 1956. Internal auditor Internat. Packers Ltd., 1957-61, dir. fin., 1962-64; asst. to contr. Monsanto Co., 1964-66, contr. internat. div., 1966-69; v.p. planning and fin. Smith Kline Corp., 1969-72; sr. v.p. fin. Comml. Credit Co., Balt., 1972-74; sr. v.p. fin. and adminstrn., dir. Norton Simon Inc., N.Y.C., 1974-79; sr. v.p. fin., dir. Becton Dickinson and Co., Paramus, N.J., 1979-83; pres. Stonington Capital Corp., Santa Barbara, Calif., 1984—; bd. dirs. Rowe Price New Era Fund Inc., New Horizons Fund Inc., Equity Income Fund Inc., Capital Appreciation Fund, Inc., Sci. and Tech. Fund, Inc., Small Capital Appreciation Fund, Inc., Balanced Fund, Inc., Monarch Health Systems Inc. Bd. dirs. Surg. Eye Expdns. Internat. Mem. Am. Mgmt. Assn. (gen. mgmt. coun.), La Cumbre Golf and Country Club. Home: 800 Via Hierba Santa Barbara CA 93110-2222 Office: 1114 State St Ste 247 Santa Barbara CA 93101-2716

VOS, MORRIS, foreign languages educator, language services consultant; b. Mahaska County, Iowa, Dec. 10, 1944; s. Peter G. and Edith (De Vries) V.; m. Mary Elizabeth Posthuma, Aug. 16, 1966; children: Jeremy, Allison. AB in English and German, Calvin Coll., Grand Rapids, Mich., 1962-66; MA in German, Ind. U., 1968, PhD in German, 1975. Cert. oral proficiency tester in German. Assoc. instr. Ind. U., Bloomington, 1970-71; asst. prof. Western Ill. U., Macomb, 1971-79, assoc. prof., 1979-91, prof. German, 1991—; mem. internat. travel-study program faculty; cons. Ill. State Bd. Edn., Springfield, 1984-87; mem. adv. coun. Cen. States Conf. on Teaching Fgn. Langs., 1980—. Editor: Essays in Literature, 1986-93; contbr. articles to profl. jours. Adult leader Boy Scouts Am., Macomb, 1985-87. Grantee NEH, DAAD, Goethe Inst.; recipient Lt. Gov.'s award State of Ill. for enhancement of profession, 1993, AATG Goethe Inst. cert. merit, 1996. Mem. Am. Assn. Tchrs. German (cert. merit 1996), Am. Coun. on the Tchg. of Fgn. Langs. (charter), Ill. Coun. on the Tchg. of Fgn. Langs., Presbyn. No. Ill. (treas. 1985—). Presbyterian. Avocation: aerobic fitness activities. Home: 456 S Edwards St Macomb IL 61455-3015 Office: Western Ill U Fgn Langs and Lits 1 University Cir Macomb IL 61455-1367

VOSBECK, ROBERT RANDALL, architect; b. Mankato, Minn., May 18, 1930; s. William Frederick and Gladys (Anderson) V.; m. Phoebe Macklin, June 21, 1953; children: Gretchen, Randy, Heidi, Macklin. BArch, U. Minn., 1954. Various archtl. positions, 1956-62; ptnr. Vosbeck-Vosbeck & Assocs., Alexandria, Va., 1962-66, VVKR Partnership, Alexandria, 1966-79; exec. v.p. VVKR Inc., 1979-82, pres., 1982-88; prin. Vosbeck/DMJM, Washington and Alexandria, Va., 1989-94; archtl. cons., 1994—; mem. Nat. Capital Planning Commn., 1976-81, U.S./USSR Joint Group on Bldg. Design and Constrn., 1974-79; mem. Nat. Park System Adv. Bd., 1984-88. Archtl. works include Pub. Safety Ctr., Alexandria, Va., 1987, Yorktown (Va.) Visitors Ctr, 1976, Frank Reeves Mcpl. Office Bldg., Washington, 1986, Fed. Bldg., NOrfolk, Va., 1979, Jeff Davis Assocs. Office Complex, Arlington, Va., 1991, Westminster Continued Care Retirment Community, Lake Ridge, Va., 1993. Served as engr. officer USMC, 1954-56. Recipient Plaque of Honor Fedn. Colegios Architects (Republic of Mexico); named Acadamecian, Internt. Acad. Architecture, hon. fellow Royal Archtl. Inst. Can., Soc. Architects of Mexico; recipient hons. Colegios Architects Spain, Union Bulgarian Architects. Fellow AIA (bd. dirs. 1976-78, v.p. 1979-80, pres. 1981), Internat. Union Architects (coun. 1981-87), Nat. Trust Hist. Preservation, Alexandria C. of C. (pres. 1974-75). Presbyterian. Home and Office: Unit A 770 Potato Patch Dr Vail CO 81657-4441

VOSBURG, BRUCE DAVID, lawyer; b. Omaha, June 17, 1943; s. Noble Perrin and Dena V. (Ferrari) V.; m. Susan Simpson, May 27, 1972; children—Margaret Amy, Wendy Christine, Bruce David. B.A., U. Notre Dame, 1965, B.S.M.E., 1966; J.D., Harvard U., 1969. Bar: Nebr. 1969, Ill. 1970, U.S. Supreme Ct. 1974. Law clk. U.S. Dist. Ct. Nebr., 1969-70; assoc. Kirkland & Ellis, Chgo., 1970-72; ptnr. Fitzgerald & Schorr, Omaha, 1972—. Pres. Children's Crisis Ctr., 1984-85, bd. dirs., 1981-85; pres. Child Sav. Inst., 1986-88; pres. Omaha Tennis Assn., 1975-76, bd. dirs., 1973-84 ; pres. Nebr. Tennis Assn., 1976-77; chmn. grievance com. Missouri Valley Tennis Assn., 1978—, mem. exec. com., 1976—; mem. Leadership Omaha, 1979; chmn. bd. dirs. City of Omaha Parks and Recreation, 1985-92; founding dir. Friends of the Parks, 1988—; bd. dirs. Omaha Pub. Libr. Found., 1997—. Fellow Nebr. Bar Found.; mem. ABA, Nebr. Bar Assn. (chmn. securities com.), Omaha Bar Assn. (exec. council 1983-86), Nat. Assn. Bond Attys., Rotary (dir. 1993—), Tau Beta Pi. Republican. Roman Catholic. Author: Financing Small Businesses, 1981, Securities Law Practice, 1987, Securities Law-Going Public, 1989, Trade Secret Protection, 1994. Office: 1000 Woodmen Towers Omaha NE 68102

VOSBURGH, FREDERICK GEORGE, writer, editor; b. Johnstown, N.Y., Sept. 16, 1904; s. John Ross and Alice (Baker) V.; m. Doris Kennedy, Jan. 2, 1929 (div. 1948); children: Richard Kennedy, Alan Frederick; m. Valerie Paterson, May 28, 1949. A.B., Syracuse U., 1925; postgrad., George Washington U., 1938-39. Reporter, Syracuse (N.Y.) Jour., 1922-24; Reporter Syracuse Post-Standard, 1925-26, AP, N.Y.C. and Washington, 1927-33; joined editorial staff Nat. Geog. Mag., 1933, asst. editor, 1951-56, sr. asst. editor, 1956, asso. editor, 1957-67, editor, 1967-70. Author numerous articles in various fields. Served to lt. col. USAAF, 1942-45, overseas. Recipient Bronze Star, Air Medal. Mem. Nat. Geog. Soc. (v.p. 1958-70, trustee 1962-79, trustee emeritus 1979—), Phi Beta Kappa. Club: Nat. Press. Home: 8500 W Howell Rd Bethesda MD 20817-6827

VOSBURGH, MARGARET MURPHY, hospital administrator; b. Aug. 29, 1948; d. John Joseph and Rita (Ryan) Murphy. Diploma, St. Clare's Hosp., 1971; BSN, Mount Saint Mary Coll., 1976; MS in Nursing, Russell Sage Coll., 1979; MBA, U. So. Calif., 1989. Dir. nursing Albany (N.Y.) Med. Ctr. Hosp., 1976-86; dir. nursing svcs. Cedars-Sinai Med. Ctr., L.A., 1986-89; v.p. nursing svcs. Hoag Meml. Hosp., Newport Beach, Calif., 1989-92; v.p. patient care svcs. Hosp. of Good Samaritan, L.A., 1992-93; assoc. exec. dir. Swedish Health Sys., Seattle, 1993-96; v.p. Ctr. Health Policy Study, Albany, N.Y., 1996—. Wharton Fellow, 1983; recipient Fed. Traineeship award for Grad. Studies in Nursing. Mem. ANA, Am. Orgn. Nurse Execs., Orgn. Nurse Execs. Calif., Sigma Theta Tau.

VOSE, ROBERT CHURCHILL, JR., former art gallery executive; b. Boston, Mar. 30, 1911; s. Robert Churchill and Sarah Helen (Williams) V.; m. Ann Peterson, Mar. 8, 1941; children: Robert Churchill III, Abbot Williams. Student, Harvard, 1930-32. With Vose Galleries of Boston, Inc., 1932-85, treas., 1953-85, pres., 1976-80, chmn., 1980-85; ret., 1985; mem. Friends of Art, Boston U., 1957-59, Friends of Art, Colby Coll., 1959-89. Contbr. articles to profl. jours. Chmn. Community Fund drive, Dedham, Mass., 1952. Fellow Pilgrim Soc. (life); mem. Copley Soc. (dir. 1950-53, Copley medal 1987), Back Bay Assn. (v.p. 1958, dir. 1964-66), New Eng. Hist. Geneal. Soc. (coun. 1958-77, pres. 1971-74, trustee emeritus 1985—), Dedham Hist. Soc. (corr. sec. 1958), Boston Mus. Fine Arts, Bostonian Soc. (life), Albany Inst. History and Art, Conn. Hist. Soc., Duxbury Rural and Hist. Soc. (exec. com.), N.Y. State Hist. Assn., Mass. Hist. Soc. (chmn. house com., chmn. art com.), Colonial Soc. Mass., Back Bay Coun., Pilgrim Soc. (trustee 1992—), Neighbourhood Assn. Back Bay (dir. 1964-66), Plimouth Plantation, Harvard Club (Boston), Algonquin Club (Boston), Somerset Club (Boston). Republican. Unitarian (chmn. parish com. 1941). Address: 394 King Caesar Rd Duxbury MA 02332-3919

VOSKA, KATHRYN CAPLES, consultant, facilitator; b. Berkeley, Cal., Dec. 26, 1942; d. Donald Buxton and Ellen Marion (Smith) Caples; m. David Karl Nehrling, Aug. 15, 1964 (div. Nov. 1980); children: Sandra E. Nehrling-Swift, Barbara M. Nehrling, Melissa A. Nehrling-Holmgren; m. James Edward Voska, Aug. 31, 1985. BS, Northwestern U., 1964; MS, Nat.-Louis U., 1989. Cert. teacher, Ill. Tchr. Pub. Schs., Northbrook and Evanston, Ill., 1964-65; acting phys. dir. YWCA, Evanston, Ill., 1975; quality control technician Baxter Travenol, Morton Grove, Ill., 1978-80; sr. quality assurance analyst Hollister Inc., Libertyville, Ill., 1980-85; info. ctr. trainer, tech. training mgr. Rand McNally, Skokie, Ill., 1985-92; cons., facilitator Capka & Assocs., Skokie and Kansas City, 1992—; dir. edn. Nat. Office Machine Dealers, 1992-94; career mgmt. cons. Right Assocs., 1994—; pvt. practice estate conservator; bd. dirs. Coro/Kansas City, 1996—. Telephone worker Contact Chgo. Crisis Hotline, 1989-90; CPR instr. trainer Amer. Heart Assn., Chgo., 1977-89; aquatic dir. YMCA, Evanston, Ill., 1969-80; rep. Alumnae Panhellenic Coun., Evanston, 1969-75; grad. Leadership Overland Park, 1996, mem. 15th anniv. special task force. Mem. ASTD (bd. dirs. Kansas City chpt. 1997—), Soc. Human Resource Mgmt., Midwest Soc. Profl. Cons., Assn. for Mgmt. Orgn. Design, Assn. Suprs. Curriculum and Devel., Chicago Orgn. of Data Processing Educators, Chicago Computer Soc., Info. Ctr. Exch. of Chgo., Assn. Quality and Participation, Am. Soc. for Quality Control (teller N.E. Ill. section 1982-84), Internat. Soc. for Performance Improvement, The Learning Resource Network. Presbyterian. Avocations: scuba diving, swimming, hiking, camping, traveling. Home: 1001 E 118th Ter Kansas City MO 64131-3828 Office: Right Assocs 7300 W 110th St Overland Park KS 66210-2330

VOSS, ALI ANNELIES, history of art educator, antique dealer; b. Hamburg, Germany, July 24, 1917; Came to the U.S., 1948; d. Hans Joachim Meisterknecht-Von Brussel and Paula Dorothea Lisette (Rothenburg) Meisterkuecht; m. Thomas A. Beasley, Jan. 17, 1948 (div. Jan. 1968); m. Edgar O. Voss (dec.). Attended, Art Inst., Hamburg, U. Hamburg, Stockholm U.; PhD, Heidelberg (Germany) U., 1946, Cert. tchr., 1948. Tchr. Monterey (Calif.) Peninsula Coll.; part-owner Antiques Internat., La Jolla, Calif.; owner Antiques Internat., Moss Landing, Calif.; asst. prof. Heidelberg U., 1961-63. Mem. AAUW (life). Democrat. Avocations: all creatures great and small, the arts, music, wildlife preservation. Home: 111 17th St Pacific Grove CA 93950 Office: 2859 Ransford Ave Pacific Grove CA 93950-5110

VOSS, ANNE COBLE, nutritional biochemist; b. Richmond, Ind., Aug. 22, 1946; d. James Richard and Helen Lucille (Hoyt) Coble; m. Harold Lloyd Voss, July 20, 1969; children: Daniel, Jordan Matthew, Sarah Georgette. BS, Ohio State U., 1968, PhD, 1984. Registered dietitian. Therapeutic dietitian Johns Hopkins Hosp., Balt., 1968-69; clin. instr. Ohio State U. Hosps., Columbus, 1969-70; clin. dietitian U.S. Army Med. Clinic, Rothwesten, Fed. Republic Germany, 1970-72; clin. rsch. monitor Ross Labs., Columbus, 1978-79; rsch. asst. Ohio State U., Columbus, 1979-84, rsch. assoc., lectr., 1985-91; mgr. outcomes rsch. Ross Products divsn. Abbott Labs., Columbus, Ohio, 1992—; adj. asst. prof. Otterbein Coll., Westerville, Ohio, 1990-93; nutrition advisor Ohio Dental Assn., Columbus, 1977-93, ADA, Chgo., 1987-93; cons. Ohio Bd. Dietetics, Columbus, 1989-93; vis. scientist Rikshospitalet, Oslo, Norway, 1992. Author: Polyunsaturated Fatty Acids and Eicosanoids, 1987; author, editor: Nutrition Perspectives, 1990, 91, 2d edit., 1993; contbr. articles to profl. jours. Mem. exec. bd. Aux. to Ohio Dental Assn., Columbus, 1979-95; bd. dirs. Ohio Dental Polit. Action Com., Columbus, 1989-92, YWCA, Columbus, 1990-93; Gov.'s appointee, chmn. Ohio Bd. Dietetics. Recipient award Clement Found., Westerville, 1991, Disting. Alumni award Ohio State U., 1996; Nutrition Edn. in Tng. grant Ohio Dept. Edn., Columbus, 1978. Mem. Am. Dietetic Assn., Ohio Dietetic Assn., Med. Dietetics Assn. (founding mem., pres., v.p., sec. 1978—), Ohio Coun. Against Health Fraud (founding mem., bd. govs. 1987—), Ohio Nutrition Coun. (exec. bd. 1987-94), Columbus Dietetic Assn., Sigma Xi, Sigma Delta Epsilon (sec. 1985—). Methodist. Avocations: gardening, cooking, sewing, skiing. Home: 1526 Bridgeton Dr Columbus OH 43220-3908 Office: Abbott Labs Ross Products Divsn 625 Cleveland Ave Columbus OH 43215-1754

VOSS, EDWARD WILLIAM, JR., immunologist, educator; b. Chgo., Dec. 2, 1933; s. Edward William and Lois Wilma (Graham) V.; m. Virginia Hellman, June 15, 1974; children: Cathleen, Valerie. A.B., Cornell Coll., Iowa, 1955; M.S., Ind. U., 1964, Ph.D., 1966. Asst. prof. microbiology U. Ill., Urbana, 1967-71; assoc. prof. U. Ill., 1971-74, prof., 1974—, dir. cell sci. ctr., 1988-94, LAS Jubilee prof., 1990; mem. rev. panel USDA on molecular biology-gene structure, Washington, 1985, 86, U.S. Dept. of Energy Rsch., 1994; panel mem. in biol. scis. NSF Minority Grad. Fellowships, Washington, 1986, 87, 88; mem. sci. adv. bd. Biotech. Rsch. and Devel. Corp., 1989—; mem. Peer Review Com. AHA, 1993-96. Author, editor: Fluorescein Hapten: An Immunological Probe, 1984, Anti-DNA Antibodies in SLE, 1988; adv. editor: Immunochemistry, 1975-78, Molecular Immunology, 1980—; mem. editorial bd.: Applied and Environ. Microbiology, 1979—; contbr. articles to profl. jours. Apptd. to pres.'s coun. U. Ill. Found., 1995. Served with U.S. Army, 1956-58. NIH fellow, 1966-67, NSF fellow, 1975-77; NIH grantee, 1967—, NSF grantee, 1967—; recipient Disting. Lectr. award U. Ill., 1983; named 1st James R. Martin Univ. scholar, 1994; recipient Exemplary Contbn. award Lupus Found. Am., 1994. Ednl. Aid award E.I. DuPont, 1994, 95. Fellow Am. Inst. Chemists; mem. AAAS, Fedn. Am. Scientists, Am. Assn. Immunologists, Am. Assn. Biol. Chemists, Reticuloendothelial Soc., Am. Lupus Soc. (hon. bd. dirs. Cen. Ill. chpt. 1986—, named to Nat. Lupus Hall of Fame 1988, Cmty. Svc. award 1996), N.Y. Acad. Scis., U.S. Pharmacopeial Conv., Inc., Nat. Geog. Soc., Am. Chem. Soc. (tour speaker 1984-87), Protein Soc., Sigma Xi. Home: 2207 Boudreau Cir Urbana IL 61801-6601 Office: U Ill Dept Microbiology 131 Burrill Hall Urbana IL 61801 *Perserverance, determination and sacrifice only when coupled to appropriate goals in basic research and teaching yield results that justify the effort and commitment.*

VOSS, JACK DONALD, international business consultant, lawyer; b. Stoughton, Wis., Sept. 24, 1921; s. George C. and Grace (Tusler) V.; m. Mary Josephine Edgarton, May 7, 1955; children: Julia, Jennifer, Andrew, Charles. Ph.B., U. Wis., 1943; J.D., Harvard U., 1948. Bar: Ill. 1949, Ohio 1963. From assoc. to ptnr. Sidney & Austin predecessor firm, Chgo., 1948-62; gen. counsel Anchor Hocking Corp., Lancaster, Ohio, 1962-67, v.p., gen. counsel, 1967-72, gen. mgr. internat., 1970-86; pres. Anchor Hocking Internat. Corp., Lancaster, 1972-86; mng. ptnr. Voss Internat., Lancaster, 1986—; chmn. Internat. Coun. Conf. bd., 1985-87. Mem. Fairfield County Rep. Ctrl. and Exec. Com.; pres. Fairfield Heritage Assn., 1966-69; v.p. Lancaster Community Concert Assn., 1965-73; trustee, chmn. Ohio Info. Com. With USNR, 1943-46, ATO, MTO, PTO. Mem. ABA (internat. law & practice and bus. law sects.), Ohio Bar Assn. (chmn. corp. counsel sect. 1966), Columbus Bar Assn., Chgo. Bar Assn., Fairfield County Bar Assn., Licensing Execs. Soc., Am. Arbitration Assn. (panel mem.), Ctr. for Internat. Comml. Arbitration (panel mem.), Harvard Law Sch. Assn., Ohio Mfrs. Assn. (trustee, v.p. 1970-72), Symposiarch, Alpha Chi Rho. Lutheran. Clubs: Rotary (pres. Lancaster 1968), Racquet (Chgo.); Landsdowne (London). Home: 3375 Cincinnati-Zane Rd Lancaster OH 43130 Office: Voss Internat 212 S Broad St Lancaster OH 43130-4381

VOSS, JAMES FREDERICK, psychologist, educator; b. Chgo., Dec. 5, 1930; s. Leo Carl and Lydia (Isreal) V.; m. Marilyn Lydia Timm, June 20, 1953 (dec. Oct. 1982); children: Barbara Lynn, Katherine Ann, Mark Frederick, Carol Jean, David James; m. Deborah Jane Steinbach, Oct. 8, 1988; 1 child, Regina Lynn. B.A., Valparaiso (Ind.) U., 1952; M.S., U. Wis., 1954, Ph.D., 1956. Instr., asst. prof. Wis. State Coll., Eau Claire, 1956-58; asst. prof., asso. prof. Coll. of Wooster, Ohio, 1958-63; asso. prof. U. Pitts., 1963-66, prof., 1966—, chmn. dept. psychology, 1968-70, assoc. dir. Learning Rsch. and Devel. Ctr., 1985-92; prin. investigator Nat. Inst. Child Health and Human Devel., 1956-58, 59-70; Fulbright Disting. prof., lectr., USSR, 1979; NSF fellow Ind. U., 1960; vis. prof. U. Wis., 1964; vis. prof., NIMH spl. fellow U. Calif., Irvine, 1970—; vis. prof. Mershon Ctr., Ohio State U., 1989. Author: Psychology as a Behavioral Science, 1974; editor: Approaches to Thought, 1969, Topics in Human Performance, 1972, Informal Reasoning and Education, 1990; cons. editor: Jour. Exptl. Psychology, 1975-80, Jour. Verbal Learning and Verbal Behavior, 1981-87. Recipient Disting. Alumni award Valparaiso U., 1979. Fellow Am. Psychol. Assn., AAAS; mem. Midwestern, Eastern psychol. assns., AAAS, N.Y. Acad. Sci., Psychonomic Soc. (sec.-treas. 1978-80), Am. Diabetes Assn. (chmn. bd. Western Pa. affiliate 1974-77, 173-75), Internat. Soc. Political Psychology, Sigma Xi. Home: 115 Glen David Dr Pittsburgh PA 15238-1513

VOSS, JERROLD RICHARD, city planner, educator, university official; b. Chgo., Nov. 4, 1932; s. Peter Walter and Annis Lorraine (Hayes) V.; m. Jean Evelyn Peterson, Aug. 21, 1954; children—Cynthia Jean, Tania Hayes. B.Arch., Cornell U., 1955; M. City Planning, Harvard U., 1959; Ph.D. (Bus. History fellow, Univ. fellow, IBM fellow), 1971. Asst. prof. U. Calif., 1960-61; asst. prof., asso. prof. U. Ill., 1961-69; asso. prof. Harvard U., 1969-71; prof. city and regional planning Ohio State U., Columbus, 1971—; chmn. dept. city and regional planning Ohio State U., 1971-79; dir. Ohio State U. (Knowlton Sch. Architecture), 1981—; UN advisor to Govt. Indonesia, 1964-65; social affairs officer UN Secretariat, 1970-71; project mgr. UN Task Force on Human Environment, Thailand, 1975-76; dir. rsch. and devel. UN Ctr. for Human Settlements (Habitat), 1979-81; cons. Ill. Dept. Devel., J.S. Bolles & Assocs., UN Office Tech. Cooperation, UN Devel. Program, AID, Bechtel Nat. Inc., other pvt. and pub. orgns.; mem. external examiners team United Arab U., 1992—. Author: Human Settlements: Problems and Priorities; Contbr. articles to profl. jours. Mem. pub. policy com. Smithsonian Instn., 1970-73; bd. dirs. Champaign County United Community Council, 1965-69, Columbus Theatre Ballet Assn., 1972-75. Served to 1st lt. U.S. Army, 1955-57. Mem. Acad. for Contemporary Problems (asso.), Am. Am. Inst. Planners, Am. Soc. Engring. Edn., Internat. Center for Urban Land Policy (London). Office: 190 W 17th Ave Columbus OH 43210-1320

VOSS, KATHERINE EVELYN, international management consultant; b. Cleve., Sept. 2, 1957; d. Wendell Grant and Ann Terry (Miller) Voss; m. James Everett Mathias, Oct. 6, 1984 (div. Dec. 1988). BS, Bowling Green State U., 1979, MBA, 1981. Sci. systems analyst Eli Lilly & Co., Indpls., 1981-83, systems tng. cons., 1983-84; customer liaison mgr. Ind. U., Bloomington, 1985; prodn. ops. mgr. Ind. U., Indpls., 1985-86; prin. systems cons. Wang Labs., Inc., Carmel, Ind., 1986-93; mgmt. cons. AMT-Sybex (I) Ltd., Dublin, 1994—; cons. Ind. Univ., Bloomington, 1984-85, Allied Irish Bank, Dublin, Ireland, 1990-91. Contbr. (book) Introduction to Business, 1980, Introduction to Accounting, 1981, Computers and Data Processing, 1981. Presidental advisor Jr. Achievement, Indpls., 1982-83; pres. PEO Chpt. AM, Indpls., 1987-89, Irish rep., 1995—. Mem. Assn. for Image and Info. Mgmt. (Master of Info. Tech. award 1997), Irish Computer Soc., Beta Beta Beta. Republican. Presbyterian. Avocations: scuba diving, photography, biking, crafts. Home: Hill Cottage, Brennanstown Rd Cabinteely, Dublin 18, Ireland Office: AMT-Sybex (I) Ltd, Elm House, Leopardstown Office Park, Foxrock Dublin 18, Ireland

VOSS, OMER GERALD, truck company executive; b. Downs, Kans., Sept. 14, 1916; s. John and Grace (Bohlen) V.; m. Annabelle Katherine Lutz, June 20, 1940; children—Jerrol Ann, Omer Gerald. A.B., Ft. Hays (Kans.) State Coll., 1937; J.D., U. Kans., 1939. Bar: Kans. bar 1939. With Internat. Harvester Co., 1936-79, v.p. farm equipment div., 1962-66, exec. v.p., dir., 1966—, vice chmn., 1977-79. Served with USAAF, 1943-46. Clubs: Chicago, Commercial, Westmoreland Country.

VOSS, REGIS DALE, agronomist, educator; b. Cedar Rapids, Iowa, Jan. 4, 1931; s. Francis Joseph and Mary Valeria (Womichil) V.; m. Margaret Anne Mitchell, Nov. 24, 1956; children: Lori Anne, John Patrick, David James. BS, Iowa State U., 1952, PhD, 1962. cert. profl. agronomist. Agriculturist Tenn. Valley Authority, Muscle Shoals, Ala., 1962-64; prof. Iowa State U., Ames, 1964-; bd. dirs. fertilizer adv. Farmland Industries, Kansas City, Mo. Co-author: (chpt.) Sulfur in Agriculture, 1986, Organic Farming, 1984; assoc. editor Jour. Prodn. Agr., 1988-92. Pres. FarmHouse Frat. Alumni Assn. Bd., Ames, 1990. 1st lt. USAF, 1952-56, Korea. Recipient Agronomic Extension Edn. award Am. Soc. Agronomy, 1984, Agronomic Achievement award Am. Soc. Agronomy, 1989, Werner L. Nelson award Am. Soc. Agronomy, 1992, Burlington No. Found. award Iowa State U., 1990, Faculty Citation Iowa State U., 1992. Fellow AAAS, Am. Soc. Agronomy (bd. dirs. 1976-78), Soil Sci. Soc. Am. (bd. dirs. 1980-83). Republican. Roman Catholic. Achievements include development of field laboratory for training of crop advisors on diagnosis of crop problems; research on effects of soil amendments on chemical indices and crop yields and economic analysis of crop yield response to soil amendments. Office: Iowa State Univ Agronomy Hall Ames IA 50011

VOSS, WILLIAM CHARLES, retired oil company executive; b. Buffalo, Sept. 22, 1937; s. William T. and Dorathea S. (Grotke) V.; m. Marilyn Erickson, Sept. 6, 1958; children: William, John, Douglas. AB with honors, Harvard U., 1959, MBA with honors, 1961. With Northwestern Refining Co., St. Paul Park, 1961-70; v.p. adminstrn. Northwestern Refining Co., 1969-71; with Ashland Oil Inc., Ky., 1971-89, v.p., 1973-79, adminstrv. v.p., 1979-80, sr. v.p., group operating officer, 1980-89; pres. Ashland-Warren Inc., 1979-83, APAC, Inc., 1980-82, 83-86. Mem. Am. Chem. Soc. Republican. Home: 2660 Peachtree Rd NW Atlanta GA 30305-3673

VOTAW, JOHN FREDERICK, educational foundation executive, educator; b. Richmond, Va., May 9, 1939; s. Frederick Lee and Katherine (B.) V.; m. Joyce Marie Miller, June 8, 1961; children: Laura, Cynthia, Mary, John Jr. BS, U.S. Mil. Acad., 1961; MA in History, U. Calif., Davis, 1969; grad., U.S. Army Colls., 1970, 85; PhD in History, Temple U., 1991. Commd. 2d lt. U.S. Army, 1961, advanced through grades to lt. col., 1976; comdr. Company C 1st bn. 69th Armor U.S. Army, Hawaii, 1964-65; comdr. Troop A 1st Squadron 11th ACR U.S. Army, South Vietnam, 1966-67; comdr. C&C Squadron 11th ACR U.S. Army, Fulda, Germany, 1975-77; asst. prof. history U.S. Mil. Acad., West Point, N.Y., 1970-73, asst. dean for plans and programs, 1980-81, asst. prof., 1981-82; dep. dir. U.S. Army Mil. History Inst., Carlisle Barracks, Pa., 1983-86; ret. U.S. Army, 1986; dir. First Divsn. Mus., Wheaton, 1986—; exec. dir. Cantigny First Divsn. Found., Wheaton, 1991—; adj. asst. prof. history Dominican U. (formerly Rosary Coll.), River Forest, Ill., 1991—; dir. Col. Robt. R. McCormick Rsch. Ctr., Wheaton, 1991—; series editor Cantigny Mil. History Series. Contbg. author: The D-Day Ency., 1993, The Ency. of Am. Wars - The First World War, 1994, The European Powers in the First World War: An Ency., 1996, A Guide to the Study and Use of Military History, 1979; contbr. articles to profl. jours. Mem. adv. com. Ctr. for the Study of Force and Diplomacy, Temple U., 1996—. Decorated Legion of Merit, Bronze Star with "V" device, Purple

Heart (3 awards) and others. Mem. Am. Hist. Assn., Orgn. Am. Historians, Soc. for Mil. History, Am. Assn. Mus., U.S. Naval Inst. (life), U.S. Army War Coll. Alumni Assn. (life), Ret. Officers Assn. (life), Assn. Grads. U.S. Mil. Acad., U. Calif. Davis Alumni Assn. (life), Kiwanis (Wheaton club 1986—, pres. 1991-92), Phi Alpha Theta, Phi Kappa Phi (life). Avocations: reading, writing, classical music, golf. Office: First Divsn Mus at Cantigny 1 S 151 Winfield Rd Wheaton IL 60187-6097

VOTH, DOUGLAS W., academic dean. Intern U. Kans. Sch. Medicine, 1959-60, resident in internal medicine, 1960-61, 64-65; fellow in infectious diseases Upstate Med. Ctr., Syracuse, N.Y., 1961-64; mem. sect. infectious diseases Kans. U. Med. Ctr., 1965-73; prof. medicine U. Okla. Sch. Medicine, 1973-74; assoc. prof. medicine U. Kans. Sch. Medicine, 1971-73; prof. medicine, chair dept. and dir. residency program U. Kans. Sch. Medicine, Wichita, 1974-84, pres. corp., 1978-84; med. dir., chief med. svc. King Fahad Hosp, Al Baha, Saudi Arabia, 1985-86; overseas advisor Royal Coll. Physicians, U.K., 1987—; prof. medicine U. Okla. Coll. Medicine, Oklahoma City, 1987—, acting chair dept. neurology, 1990-92, exec. dean, 1992-96; trustee U.-Presbyn. Neurol. Inst., Oklahoma City, 1994-96; bd. dirs. Heartland Health Plan, Oklahoma City. Office: UAE U Fac Med and Health Scis, PO Box 17666, Al Ain United Arab Emirates

VOWELL, JACK C., former state legislator, investor; b. May 9, 1927; s. Jack C. and Daurice (McDaniel) V.; m. Mary Johnson, Apr. 19, 1957; 1 child, Janice Vowell Alexander. BS in Fgn. Svc., Georgetown U., 1948, MS in Fgn. Svc., 1952; MA in History, Tex. Western Coll., 1952; postgrad., Harvard U., 1953-55. Mem. faculty Sch. Fgn. Svcs. Georgetown U., Washington, 1948-49, U. Tex., El Paso, 1955-60; exec. v.p. Vowell Constrn. Co., El Paso, 1962-69, pres., chmn. bd. dirs., 1969-73; rep. Tex. Ho. of Reps., Austin, 1980-95, mem. numerous coms. 68th to 73rd legis., 1980-95; personal investor, 1973—; chmn. Tex. sunset commn., 1987-89. Pres. Yucca Coun., Boy Scouts Am., 1972-74, mem. adv. bd., 1987-92, adv. bd. we. region, 1993—; bd. dirs. South Ctrl. region, 1973-86, mem. adv. bd., 1987—, nat. coun., 1971-87; mem. adv. bd. Hotel Dieu Hosp., 1974-87; adv. dir. Tex. Art Alliance, 1981-83; bd. dirs. Goodwill Industries of El Paso, 1973-77, El Paso Indsl. Devel. Corp., 1962-82; pres. El Paso Hist. Soc., 1957-59, assoc. editor Password, 1962-64; chmn. pers. com. El Paso Pub. Libr. Sys., 1969-74, bd. dirs., 1969-74; adminstrv. adv. bd. City of El Paso, 1973-74; coun. state policy and planning agencies, 1989-92; adv. comm., 1985-89; Tex. coun. on disabilities, 1984-85; state coun. on child abuse, 1984-85. With U.S. Army, 1946-47. Recipient City of El Paso Conquistador award, 1967, 73, Goodwill Industries of El Paso Outstanding Svc. award to Handicapped Workers, 1972, Disting. Eagle award Boy Scouts Am., 1972, Silver Beaver award, 1973, Silver Antelope award, 1983, Tex. Assn. for Marriage and Family Therapy Recognition cert., 1982, U. Tex. El Paso Coll of Edn. Clin. Programs Assistance award, 1985, award for Commitment to Reshaping and Improvement of Svcs. MHMR, 1985, Texans for Children Support for Needy Children, 1985, U. Tex. El Paso Spl. Edn. commendation for Spl. Achievement Autism Program, 1985, Coalition of Texas with Disabilities Pub. Servant of Yr. award, 1985, Anti-Defamation League of El Paso Torch of Liberty award, 1985, Tex. Network of Youth Svcs. Outstanding Youth award, 1987, Nat. Coun. of State Human Svcs. Adminstrs. Nat. commendation, 1987, Disting. Svc. Award Tex. Assn. Deaf, 1987, Am. Public Welfare Assn. Nat. Recognition of Statesmanship in Tex. Ho. Reps., 1987, Better Life award Tex. Health Care Assn., 1987, Legis. Excellence award Tex. Health Care Assn., 1987, United Way of El Paso vol. of the year award, 1988, Am. Coll. of Health Care Adminstrs. Tex. chpt. award, 1988, award for contbn. developmentally delayed and at risk infants, 1988, 94, Tex. Head Injury Legislative award, 1991, Legis. award Tex. Rehab. Assn., 1991, Rio Grande Coun. Govt. Legislative Leadership in Human Svcs. award, 1992, Helen Farabee Leadership award Tex. Perinatal Assn., 1992, Friend of Child award Tex. Coalition Juvenile Justice, 1993, Alviane NO-AD, Public Svc. award, 1993, Unite El Paso Appreciation award, 1993, Gran Paseño award U. Tex. El Paso, 1994, Good Hands award Tex. Dept. Transp., 1994. Mem. El Paso C. of C. (bd. dirs. 1962-69), Rotary (bd. dirs. 1967-68, pres. 1968, Disting. Svc. award 1988). Republican. Episcopalian. Home: 201 W Sunset Rd El Paso TX 79922-1709 Office: 4849 N Mesa St Ste 310 El Paso TX 79912-5936

VOWLES, RICHARD BECKMAN, literature educator; b. Fargo, N.D., Oct. 5, 1917; s. Guy Richard and Ella (Beckman) V.; m. Ellen Noah Hudson, Aug. 1, 1942 (div. 1969); children: Elizabeth Ellen, Richard Hudson. B.S., Davidson Coll., 1938; postgrad., U. N.C., 1938-39, U. Stockholm, 1939-40; M.A., Yale U., 1942, Ph.D., 1950. Engr. Hercules Powder Co., Wilmington, Chattanooga, 1941-43; chemist Rohm & Haas, Knoxville, Tenn., 1943-44; econ. cons. War Dept., 1944; Am. vice consul Gothenburg, Sweden, 1945-46; asst. prof. English Southwestern U., Memphis, 1948-50, Queens U., N.Y.C., 1950-51; asso. prof. English U. Fla., 1951-60; prof. Scandinavian and comparative lit. U. Wis., Madison, 1960-85; prof. emeritus U. Wis., 1985—, chmn. comparative lit., 1962-63, 64-67, 71-72, chmn. Scandinavian studies, 1977-80; Am. specialist in Scandinavia Dept. State, summer 1963; vis. prof. N.Y.U., summer 1964, U. Helsinki, Finland, spring 1968, Stockholm, 1969; lectr., Sydney, Australia, 1975, Paris, 1975; master ceremonies Santa Fe Scandinavian Film Festival, 1984. Editor: Eternal Smile, 1954, Dramatic Theory, 1956, Comparatists at Work, 1968; Adv. editor: Nordic Council Series, 1965-70, Herder Ency. of World Lit; contbr. articles to profl. jours. Am.-Scandinavian Found. fellow Stockholm, 1939-40, Lassen fellow Am. Scandinavian Found., 1986; Fulbright fellow Copenhagen, 1955-56; Strindberg fellow Stockholm, 1973; Swedish govt. research award, 1978; Norwegian Govt. fellow, summer 1978. Mem. Modern Lang. Assn., Soc. Advancement Scandinavian Study (mem. exec. com.), Internat. Comparative Lit. Assn., Am. Comparative Lit. Assn. (adv. bd.), Strindberg Soc., Phi Beta Kappa. Home: 1115 Oak Way Madison WI 53705-1420

VRABLIK, EDWARD A., computer company executive, management consultant; b. Chgo., May 20, 1937; s. Edward Matthew and Helen Bertha (Felzan) V.; m. Carol Ann Kinzie, Apr. 29, 1961; children: Kevin Allen, Scott Edward. BSc, MIT, 1959; MSc, Northeastern U., 1963. Pres. Dimensional Sys., Inc., Lexington, Mass., 1969-73; mgr. CAD/CAM sys. Digital Equipment Corp., Maynard, Mass., 1973-78; v.p. R & D Computer Graphics Co., Denver, 1979-82; dir. workstation products Prime Computer, Natick, Mass., 1983-88; dir. tech. svcs. Maximum Claims Svc., Methuen, Mass., 1990-92; mgr. software engring. Baird Corp., Bedford, Mass., 1992-94; dir. product engring. Xionics, Burlington, Mass., 1995-96; with Azimuth Ptnrs., Inc., Stow, Mass., 1996—; cons./dir. Integrated Mgmt. Resources, Stow, Mass., 1990-93; dir. Massteck, Ltd., Littleton, Mass., 1992-95, Automated Billing Svcs., Methuen, 1993-94. Com. mem. MIT Class of 1959, Cambridge, 1984-94, chmn. reunion, 1994—. 2d lt. U.S. Army, 1959-60. Mem. Computer Graphics Pioneers (charter). Home: 2215 Swallow Hill Rd Pittsburgh PA 15220-1629 Office: Azimuth Ptnrs Inc 119 Adams Dr Stow MA 01775-1085

VRABLIK, EDWARD ROBERT, import/export company executive; b. Chgo., June 8, 1932; s. Steven Martin and Meri (Korbel) V.; m. Bernice G. Germer, Jan. 25, 1958; children: Edward Robert, II, Scott S. B.S. in Chem. Engring, Northwestern U., 1956; M.B.A., U. Chgo., 1961; postgrad., MIT, 1970. Registered profl. engr., Ill. Dir. indsl. mktg. Eimco Corp., 1956-61; dir. indsl. mktg. and planning Swift & Co., Chgo., 1961-68; v.p., gen. mgr. Swift Chem. Co., Chgo., 1968-73; pres., chief exec. officer Estech Gen. Chems. Corp., Chgo., 1973-86; pres. Kare Internat. Inc., Chgo., 1986—; pres. Julius and Assocs., Inc., Kare Internat., Inc.; bd dirs. Potash Phosphate Inst., Consol. Fertilizers, Ltd.; mem. mgmt. com. Esmark Inc., Korbel, Inc., Mister Lawn Care, Inc. Author. Bd. dirs., v.p. Northwestern U. Tech. Inst.; trustee Future Farmers Am. Mem. Internat. Superphosphate Mfrs. Assn. (dir.), Am. Inst. Chem. Engrs., Fertilizer Inst. (dir.). Lutheran. Clubs: Butler Nat. (Oak Brook, Ill.). Patentee in field. Home: 631 Thompsons Way Palatine IL 60067-4653 Office: 141 W Jackson Blvd Chicago IL 60604-2992

VRADENBURG, GEORGE, III, lawyer. AB cum laude, Oberlin Coll., 1964; LLB cum laude, Harvard U., 1967. Bar: N.Y., 1968, Calif. 1995. Sr. v.p., gen. counsel, sec. CBS Inc., N.Y.C., 1980-91; exec. v.p. Fox, Inc., L.A., 1991-95; ptnr., co-chair entertainment, sports & media industry practice group Latham & Watkins, L.A., 1995-97; sr. v.p., gen. counsel, sec. Am. Online, 1997—. Mem. Phi Beta Kappa.

VRANA, VERLON KENNETH, retired professional society administrator, conservationist; b. Seward, Nebr., June 25, 1925; s. Anton and Florence (Walker) V.; m. Elaine Janet Flowerday, June 5, 1949; children: Verlon Rodney, Timothy James, Carolyn Elaine, Jon David. Student, U. Nebr., 1959-62; BBA, George Washington U., 1967, MBA, 1970; mgmt. course, Harvard U., 1979. Field technician Soil Conservation Svc., USDA, Seward, 1948-58; watershed planner, cons. Soil Conservation Svc., USDA, Lincoln, Nebr., 1958-62; mem. pers. staff Soil Conservation Svc., USDA, Washington, 1962-72, dir. pers. div., 1972-76, asst. adminstr. for mgmt., 1976-79, assoc. dep. chief for adminstrn., 1979-80; chief planning div. Nebr. Natural Resources Com., Lincoln, 1980-88; owner-farmer Blue Ridge Farm, Seward, 1980-89; exec. v.p. Soil and Water Conservation Soc., Ankeny, Iowa, 1989-91; pres. Vrana Assocs., Seward, Nebr., 1992—; bd. dirs., sec. N.E. Natural Resources Dist., York, Nebr., 1988-89; bd. dirs. Cattle Nat. Bank, Seward; alt. dir. Renewable Natural Resources Foun., Washington, 1989-91. Contbr. articles to jours. in field. Mem. Com. on Ministry Presbyn. Ch. U.S.A., 1986-89, elder, 1970—; vice moderator Homestead Presbytery, 1989; treas. Nebr. Soil and Water Conservation Found., 1992—. Recipient N.E. Centennial Grass Seeding award N.E. Centennial Commn., Lincoln, 1967, N.E. Soil Steward award N.E. Natural Resources Commn., Lincoln, 1986. Fellow Soil and Water Conservation Soc. (pres. N.E. Coun. 1986, Presdl. citation 1989), Isaac Walton League (dir. Seward chpt. 1984-89), Nat. Wildlife Fedn. (soil conservationist of yr. award 1987), Seward Grange (officer 1984-89, 92—), Shriner. Home and Office: Vrana Assocs 131 N 1st St Seward NE 68434-2130

VRANCKEN, ROBERT DANLOY, facilities planner, designer and educator; b. Charleston, W.Va., June 28, 1936; s. Roger Joseph and Kathryn Elizabeth (Toben) V.; children: Robert, Brett, Paige, Mark. BFA, U. Notre Dame, 1958, MBA, 1984; PhD in Facilities Mgmt., Union Inst., 1992. Cert. facilities mgr. Designer Stone & Thomas, Wheeling, W.Va., 1962-63; pvt. practice in designing Wheeling, W.Va., 1962-63; asst. to pres. Lederman Elevator Co., Detroit, 1963-66; mgr. facilities planning and design Sperry Univac, Blue Bell, Pa., 1966-82; assoc. prof. mgmt. Grand Valley State U., Grand Rapids, Mich., 1982—; cons. space planning facilities design and mgmt., W.Va., Mich., Pa., 1963—; active Ops. Mgmt. Edn. Rsch. Found. Mem. Internat. Facilities Mgmt. Assn. (Educator of Yr. 1986), Nat. Assn. Corp. Real Estate Execs., Work Place Environment Group, Internat. Devel. Rsch. Coun., Notre Dame Club. Roman Catholic. Avocations: sailing, carpentry, tennis, singing. Office: Grand Valley State U 301 W Fulton St Grand Rapids MI 49504-6430

VRANICAR, MICHAEL GREGORY, lawyer; b. Hammond, Ind., Mar. 11, 1961; s. Melvin G. and Maryann R. (Szarek) V.; m. Marianna C. Livas, May 28, 1994. BSEE, U. Ill., 1983; JD, U. San Diego, 1987. Bar: Calif. 1987, Ill. 1988. Engr. Gen. Dynamics, San Diego, 1983-88; judge advocate USMC, Okinawa, Japan, 1988-91; assoc. Stellato & Schwartz, Chgo., 1992-94; ptnr. Plesha & Vranicar, Chgo., 1995—; arbitrator Cook County Arbitration Bd., Chgo., 1994—; judge regional competition Nat. Moot Ct., Chgo., 1992. Mem. Ill. State Bar Assn., Chgo. Bar Assn., Okinawa Bench & Bar Assn., Am. Legion. Republican. Roman Catholic. Office: 10540 S Western Ave Ste 103 Chicago IL 60643-2529

VRANISH, JOHN MICHAEL, electrical engineer, researcher; b. Brainerd, Minn., May 20, 1939; s. John Paul and Louise Ann (Jenkins) V.; m. Dorothy Jean Ward, June 27, 1980; children: John Christopher, Anthony Brian. BS, U.S. Mil. Acad., 1962; MSEE, George Washington U., 1973. Staff engr. robotics rsch. Naval Surface Weapons Ctr., White Oak, Silver Spring, Md., 1971-82, Nat. Bur. Standards, Gaithersburg, Md., 1982-86; staff engr. space mechanisms and space robotics Goddard Space Flight Ctr., Greenbelt, Md., 1986—; mem. tech. task force Office of Sec. Def., 1981-82, fact finding com., 1981; cons. U.S. Congress, 1983, 87, 96; spkr. in field. Inventor capaciflector, 3-D sprags, carrier-less anti-backlash transmission, robotic deriveter, magnetostrictive direct drive rotary motor, spin bearings, continuously variable planetary transmission; patentee in field; contbr. articles to books, jours. and various publs. Capt. U.S. Army, 1962-70. Mem. Robotics Internat. of Soc. Mfg. Engrs. (charter, award 1981). Avocations: sports, physical fitness, military history. Home: 900 Truro Ln Crofton MD 21114 Office: NASA/Goddard Space Flight Ctr. Code 723.4 Greenbelt MD 20771

VRATIL, KATHRYN HOEFER, federal judge; b. Manhattan, Kans., Apr. 21, 1949; d. John J. and Kathryn Ruth (Fryer) Hoefer; children: Alison K., John A., Ashley A. BA, U. Kans., 1971, JD, 1975; postgrad., Exeter U., 1971-72. Bar: Kans. 1975, Mo. 1978, U.S. Dist. Ct. Kans. 1975, U.S. Dist. Ct. (we. dist.) Mo. 1978, U.S. Dist. Ct. (ea. dist.) Mo. 1985, U.S. Ct. Appeals (8th cir.) 1978, U.S. Ct. Appeals (10th cir.) 1980, U.S. Ct. Appeals (11th dist.) 1983, U.S. Supreme Ct., 1995. Law clk. U.S. Dist. Ct., Kansas City, Kans., 1975-78; assoc. Lathrop Koontz & Norquist, Kansas City, Mo., 1978-83; ptnr. Lathrop & Norquist, Kansas City, 1984-92; judge City of Prairie Village, Kans., 1991-92; bd. dirs. Kans. Legal Svcs. Bd. editors Kans. Law Rev., 1974-75, Jour. Kans. Bar Assn., 1992—. Mem. Kansas City Tomorrow (XIV); bd. trustees, shepherd-deacon Village Presbyn. Ch.; nat. adv. bd. U. Kans. Ctr. for Environ. Edn. and Tng., 1993-95. Fellow Kans. Bar Foun., Am. Bar Found.; mem. ABA (edtl. bd. Judges Jour. 1995—), Am. Judicature Soc., Nat. Assn. Judges, Fed. Judges Assn., Kans. Bar Assn., Mo. Bar Assn., Kansas City Met. Area Bar Assn., Wyandotte County Bar Assn., Johnson County Bar Assn., Assn. Women Lawyers, Lawyers Assn. Kansas City, Supreme Ct. Hist. Soc., Kans. State Hist. Soc., U. Kans. Law Soc. (bd. govs. 1978-81), Kans. U. Alumni Assn. (mem. Kansas City chpt. alumni bd. 1990-92, nat. bd. dirs. 1991-96, bd. govs. Adams Alumni Ctr. 1992-95, mem. chancellor's club 1993—, mem. Williams ednl. fund 1993—, mem. Jayhawks for higher edn. 1993-95), Homestead Country Club Prairie Village (pres. 1985-86), Sons and Daus of Kans. (life), Rotary, Jr. League Wyandotte and Johnson Counties, Kans. State Hist. Soc., Order of Coif, Kans. Inn of Ct. (master 1993—), Overland Park Rotary, Univ. Club, Phi Kappa Phi. Republican. Presbyterian. Avocations: cycling, sailing. Office: 511 US Courthouse 500 State Ave Kansas City KS 66101-2403

VREDENBURG, DWIGHT CHARLES, retired supermarket chain executive; b. Lamoni, Iowa, Jan. 17, 1914; s. David Milton and Kate Emelyn (Putnam) V.; m. Ruth Irene Taylor, Apr. 25, 1937; children: John, Martha Vredenburg Kraklow, Charles. Student, Graceland Coll., 1931-34, LLD, 1988; BS in Commerce, U. Iowa, 1935. Store mgr. Hy-Vee Food Stores Inc., Chariton, Iowa, 1935-38, pres., from 1938, chief exec. officer, 1978-89; chmn. Hy- Vee Food Stores Inc., Chariton, Iowa, 1978-89; pres. Chariton Storage Co.; pres., dir. Iamo Realty Co. Served with USCGR, 1942-44. Named Citizen of Yr., 1965-66. Mem. Masons, Shriners, Des Moines Club. Home: 1105 Mallory Dr Chariton IA 50049-1161

VREDEVOE, DONNA LOU, research immunologist, microbiologist, educator; b. Ann Arbor, Mich., Jan. 11, 1938; d. Lawrence E. and Verna (Brower) V.; m. John Porter, Aug. 22, 1962; 1 child, Verna. B.A. in Bacteriology, UCLA, 1959, Ph.D. in Microbiology (Univ. fellow, USPHS fellow), 1963. USPHS postdoctoral fellow Stanford U., 1963-64; instr. bacteriology UCLA, 1963, postgrad. research immunologist dept. surgery Center Health Scis., 1964-65, asst. research immunologist dept. surgery Center Health Scis., 1964-67; asst. prof. Sch. Nursing, Center Health Scis., 1967-70, asso. prof., 1970-76, prof., 1976—, asso. dean Sch. Nursing, 1976-78, acting assoc. dean Sch. Nursing., 1985-86, asst. dir. space planning Cancer Center, 1976-78, dir. space planning, 1978-90, cons. to lab. nuclear medicine and radiation biology, 1967-80; acting dean Sch. Nursing Center Health Scis., 1995-96. Contbr. articles to profl. publs. Postdoctoral fellow USPHS, 1963-64; Mabel Wilson Richards scholar UCLA, 1960-61; research grantee Am. Cancer Soc., Calif. Inst. Cancer Research, Calif. div. Am. Cancer Soc., USPHS, Am. Nurses Found., Cancer Research Coordinating Com. U. Calif., Dept. Energy, UCLA. Mem Am. Soc. Microbiology, Am. Assn. Immunologists, Am. Assn. Cancer Research, Nat. League Nursing (2d v.p. 1979-81), Sigma Xi, Alpha Gamma Sigma., Sigma Theta Tau (nat. hon. mem.). Home: 355 21st Pl Santa Monica CA 90402-2503 Office: UCLA Sch Nursing Los Angeles CA 90095-1702

VREE, ROGER ALLEN, lawyer; b. Chgo., Oct. 2, 1943; s. Louis Gerard and Ruby June (Boersma) V.; m. Lauren Trumbull Gartside, Mar. 29, 1969; children: Jonathan Todd, Matthew David. BA, Wheaton Coll., 1965; MA, Stanford U., 1966, JD, 1969. Bar: Ill. 1969, U.S. Dist. Ct. (no. dist.) Ill. 1969. Assoc. Sidley & Austin, Chgo., 1969-75, ptnr., 1975—. Mem. ABA, Chgo. Bar Assn., Law Club, Legal Club. Club: Caxton Club (Chgo.), University (Chgo.). Office: Sidley & Austin 1 First Natl Plz Chicago IL 60603-2003

VREELAND, RUSSELL GLENN, accountant, consultant; b. Princeton, N.J., Apr. 27, 1960; s. Glenn Earl and Barbara Ann (Jungels) V.; m. Traci Ann Harbold, Dec. 17, 1988; children: Hans Russell, Anna Patricia. BSBA, Bloomsburg (Pa.) U., 1982. CPA, Pa., Md. Sr. acct. Louis H. Linowitz & Co., Trenton, N.J., 1982-85; tax supr. Horty & Horty, P.A., Wilmington, Del., 1985-87; tax mgr. Stewart Waddell & Co. P.A., Columbia, Md., 1988-92; assoc. in charge of tax Hillman & Glorioso, P.L.L.C., Vienna, Va., 1993—; pvt. practice acct., 1994—; speaker in field. Author: Foreign Sales Corporations - A Primer, 1992, Exporting-Are You Ready?, 1993; contbr. articles to profl. jours. Chmn. fin. com. Woodland Village Condominium Assn., 1989-90. Mem. AICPAs (tax. divsn., mgmt. consulting svcs. divsn.), Nat. Assn. Cert. Valuation Analysts, Md. Assn. CPAs (fed. taxation com. 1990-91), Greater Washington Soc. CPAs. Republican. Lutheran. Office: Hillman & Glorioso PLLC 1950 Old Gallows Rd Ste 700 Vienna VA 22182-3933

VROOM, VICTOR HAROLD, management consultant, educator; b. Montreal, Que., Can., Aug. 9, 1932; s. Harold Heard and Avice May (Brown) V.; m. Ann Louise Workman, June 12, 1956 (div. Jan. 1989); children: Derek Alan, Jeffrey James; m. Julia Ann Francis, Dec. 27, 1989; children: Tristan Alexander, Trevor Houston. B.Sc., McGill U., Montreal, 1953, M.Sc., 1955; Ph.D., U. Mich., 1958; M.A. (hon.), Yale, 1972. Lectr., study dir. U. Mich., Ann Arbor, 1958-60; asst. prof. psychology U. Pa., Phila., 1960-63; asso. prof. psychology and indsl. adminstrn. Carnegie-Mellon U., Pitts., 1963-66; prof. Carnegie-Mellon U., 1966-72; John G. Searle prof. orgn. and mgmt. Yale U., 1972—. Author: Work and Motivation, 1964, rev. edit. 1995, Leadership and Decision-Making, 1973, The New Leadership, 1988. Recipient Ford Found. Doctoral Dissertation award, 1958-59; McKinsey Found. research design award, 1967; Fulbright lectr. U.K., 1967-68. Fellow APA (James McKeen Cattell award 1970), APS Acad. Mgmt. Office: Yale U PO Box 1A New Haven CT 06520-0001

VU, HA MANH, city official; b. Dalat, Vietnam, Jan. 26, 1954; s. Thi Van Vu and Vy Thi Pham; m. Kim-Hoa Tran, July 21, 1984; children: Henry, Andrew. BA in Polit. Sci., NYU, 1979, MPA, 1981. Cert. assessment evaluator. City assessor N.Y.C. Dept. Fin., S.I., N.Y., 1983—. Mem. Internat. Assn. Assessing Officers, Am. Mgmt. Assn., N.Y. State Assessors' Assn. Democrat. Roman Catholic. Office: NYC Dept Fin 350 Saint Marks Pl Ste 203 Staten Island NY 10301-2416

VUCANOVICH, BARBARA FARRELL, former congresswoman; b. Fort Dix, N.J., June 22, 1921; d. Thomas F. and Ynez (White) Farrell; m. Ken Dillon, Mar. 8, 1950 (div. 1964); children: Patty Dillon Cafferata, Mike, Ken, Tom, Susan Dillon Stoddard; m. George Vucanovich, June 19, 1965. Student, Manhattanville Coll. of Sacred Heart, 1938-39. Owner, operator Welcome Aboard Travel, Reno, 1968-74; Nev. rep. for Senator Paul Laxalt, 1974-82; mem. 98th-104th Congresses from 2d Nev. dist., 1983-96; chmn. appropriations subcom. on military construction; Rep. natl. woman Nev. Rep. Party, 1996—. Pres. Nev. Fedn. Republican Women, Reno, 1955-56; former pres. St. Mary's Hosp. Guild, Lawyer's Wives. Roman Catholic. Club: Hidden Valley Country (Reno). Office: US Ho of Reps 2202 Rayburn Bldg Washington DC 20515-4501*

VUCKOVIC, GOJKO MILOS, public administration scholar; b. Belgrade, Yugoslavia, Feb. 27, 1952; came to U.S., 1989; s. Milos Boza and Zorka Milan (Cubra) V.; m. Ivana Vojin Ognjanovic, July 5, 1986; children: Ivan, Milosh. BA, U. Belgrade, 1976; MSM, Arthur D. Little Mgmt. Inst., 1990; MPA, Harvard U., 1991; PhD, U. So. Calif., 1995. Mgr. export-import Rudnap Inc., Belgrade, 1977; counselor Fed. Secretariat for Fgn. Econ. Rels., Belgrade, 1977-89; fellow UN Indsl. Devel. Orgn., Cambridge, Mass., 1989-90; cons. Compex Internat. Inc., Cambridge, 1991-92; project coord. Coro So. Calif., L.A., 1992-93; fellow Inst. for Study of World Politics, L.A. and Washington, 1994-95; affiliated scholar Ctr. for Multiethnic and Transnat. Studies, U. So. Calif., L.A., 1994—. Mem. Am. Soc. for Pub. Adminstrn., Am. Polit. Sci. Assn., Acad. Polit. Sci., Minza de Gunzberg Ctr. for European Studies, Pi Sigma Alpha, Pi Alpha Alpha. Avocations: rowing, soccer, theatre. Home: 3144 S Canfield Ave Apt 107 Los Angeles CA 90034-4377 Office: U So Calif Ctr Multiethnic & Transnational Studies Los Angeles CA 90089

VUILLEUMIER, FRANÇOIS, curator; b. Berne, Switzerland, Nov. 26, 1938; came to U.S., 1961; s. Willy Georges and Denise Geneviève (Privat) V.; m. Patricia Beryl Simpson, 1964 (div. 1971); m. Bonita Rae Johnson, 1972 (div. 1981); children: Alexis Brendan, Claire Anne; m. Rebecca Branch Finnell, Feb. 26, 1983; 1 child, Isabelle Finnell. Licence és sciences, U. Geneva, Switzerland, 1961; PhD, Harvard U., 1967. Instr. U. Mass., Boston, 1966-67, asst. prof., 1967-70, assoc. prof., 1971; prof. U. Lausanne, Switzerland, 1971-72; sr. researcher Marine Biol. Sta., Roscoff, France, 1972-73; assoc. curator Am. Mus. Natural History, N.Y.C., 1974-79, curator, 1979—; dir. Inst. Animal Ecology, U. Lausanne, 1971-72; vis. prof. U. Paris, 1973-74, U. of the Andes, Mérida, Venezuela, 1981; chmn. Dept. Ornithology, Chapman Fund, Am. Mus. Natural History, 1987-92. Author: High Altitude Tropical Biogeography, 1986; mem. editl. bd. Ornitologia Neotropical, Rivista Italiana di Orniblogia, Zoosystema, Revue d'Ecologie; contbr. 210 articles to jours. in field. Chapman fellow Am. Mus., 1967-68. Fellow AAAS, Am. Ornithologists Union; mem. French Ornithol. Soc. (hon.), Soc. for Study of Evolution, Neotropical Ornithol. Soc., Union Chilean Ornithologists. Achievements include research in evolutionary biology, zoogeography, speciation and biodiversity in South American birds. Avocations: painting, reading, foreign languages, birdwatching, cooking. Office: Am Mus Natural History Central Pk West At 79T St W New York NY 10024

VUJOVIC, MARY JANE, education and employment training planner; b. Huntington, N.Y., Dec. 3, 1951; d. Carl David Sr. and Alice Lucille (Hanson) B. BS in Psychology cum laude, U. Wash., 1973, postgrad., 1980-84. Spl. edn. tchr. Town of Huntington, 1972; adminstrv. asst. Daishowa Am. Corp., Seattle, 1973-74; with King County Work Tng. Program, Seattle, 1973-85, records sect. mgr., 1977-84, contracts mgr., 1984-85; tech. cons., program mgr. Refugee Ctr. of Clark County, Vancouver, Wash., 1985-87; instr., counselor S.W. Wash. Pvt. Industry Coun., Vancouver, 1986-87; planner Wash. Human Devel., Seattle, 1987, dir. planning and MIS, 1987-94; tech. cons. SJL and Assocs., Seattle, 1990—; dir. prog. devel. and evaluation Yakima Valley Opportunities Industrialization Ctr., 1994—; mem. planning and adv. com. Seattle-King County Pvt. Industry Coun., 1987-94; mem. Partnership for Tng. and Employment Careers, Washington, 1991-94. Bd. dirs. Slavia, Seattle, 1990—, St. James Refugee Program, Seattle, 1993-95. Mem. Phi Beta Kappa. Avocation: South Slavic dance and cultural preservation. Office: Yakima Valley Opportunities Indsl Ctr 815 Fruitvale Blvd Yakima WA 98902-1467

VUKSTA, MICHAEL JOSEPH, surgeon; b. Pitts., Apr. 25, 1926; s. Michael and Mary Sarah (Hanulya) V.; m. Dorothy Ann Bosak, Sept. 12, 1953; children: Patricia, Michael, Carol, Janet. BA, Youngstown State U., 1949; MD, Ohio State U., 1957. Diplomate Am. Bd. Surgery. Enlisted USN, advanced through grades to capt., 1974; intern St. Elizabeth Hosp., Youngstown, Ohio, resident in gen. surgery, 1958-62; pvt. practice gen. surgery Youngstown, 1962-89; head blue team surgery Oak Knoll U.S. Naval Hosp., Oakland, Calif., 1989-93. Capt. USN retired. Fellow ACS, Am. Coll. Sports Medicine, Southwestern Surg. Congress; mem. Nat. Athletic Trainers Assn. (advisor). Byzantine Catholic. Home: 131 Lovett Pl Pensacola FL 32506-5265

VULEVICH, EDWARD, JR., prosecutor; b. Nov. 5, 1933; s. Edward J. and Minnie R. V.; m. Diane Misko; children: Erin, Jan, John. AB, U. Ala., 1955, JD, 1957. Bar: Ala., U.S. Supreme Ct., U.S. Ct. Appeals (11th cir.) Ala., U.S. Ct. Appeals (5th cir.) Ala. Atty. U.S. Dept. Justice, Mobile, Ala., 1969—, 1st asst. atty. Office: US Attys Office 169 Dauphin St Ste 200 Mobile AL 36602-3271

VULGAMORE, MELVIN L., college president; b. Springfield, Ohio, July 19, 1935; s. Leo Beeman and Della Marie (McCoy) V.; m. Ethelanne Oyer,

Feb. 17, 1957; children: Allison Beth, Sarah Faith Vulgamore Evans. B.A. with honors, Ohio Wesleyan U., 1957; B.D., Harvard U., 1960; Ph.D., Boston U., 1963. Chmn., prof. religion Ohio Wesleyan U., Delaware, 1962-78, assoc. dean faculty, 1972-73, dean acad. affairs, 1973-78; v.p., provost U. Richmond, Va., 1978-83; pres. Albion Coll., Mich., 1983—; vis. prof. Am. U. Beirut, 1971-72; dir. Chem. Bank; vis. scholar Harvard U., 1995. Contbr. articles to profl. jours. Trustee Howe Mil. Sch., Ind., 1984—; mem. Mich. Coun. for Humanities, 1985-89, 96-97. Mem. Am. Acad. Religion, Tillich Soc. N.Am., Univ. Club N.Y., Detroit Athletics Club, Rotary, Univ. Club. N.Y., Phi Beta Kappa, Omicron Delta Kappa, Delta Sigma Rho, Pi Sigma Alpha. Avocations: bicycling, tennis, classical music, antique collecting and refinishing. Home: 1620 Van Wert Rd Albion MI 49224-9743 Office: Albion Coll Office of Pres Albion MI 49224

VYAS, GIRISH NARMADASHANKAR, virologist, immunohematologist; b. Aglod, India, June 11, 1933; came to U.S., 1965, naturalized, 1973; s. Narmadashankar P. and Rukshmani A. (Joshi) V.; m. Devi Ratilal Trivedi, Apr. 3, 1962; children: Jay, Shrikrishna. B.Sc., U. Bombay, 1954, M.Sc., 1956, Ph.D., 1964. Postdoctoral fellow Western Res. U., 1965-66; mem. faculty U. Calif., San Francisco, 1967—, chief blood bank, 1969-88; prof. lab. medicine U. Calif., 1977—; dir. transfusion rsch. program, 1985—; WHO cons., S.E. Asia, 1980; cons. in field; mem. com. viral hepatitis NRC, 1974-76; mem. task force blood processing Nat. Heart and Lung Inst., 1972-73; sci. program com. Am. Assn. Blood Banks, 1971-76; com. immunoglobulin allotypes WHO, 1974—; mem. U.S. del. immunologists to Romania and Hungary, 1980; mem. FDA com. on blood and blood products, 1987-92; cons. to VA on med. rsch., 1985, UN Devel. Program in India, 1986; and others; chmn. Transmed Biotech Inc., South San Francisco, 1989-95. Author: Hepatitis and Blood Transfusion, 1972, Laboratory Diagnosis of Immunological Disorders, 1975, Membrane Structure and Function of Human Blood Cells, 1976, Viral Hepatitis, 1978, Viral Hepatitis and Liver Disease, 1984, Use and Standardization of Chemically Defined Antigens, 1986, Transfusion-associated Infections and Immune Response, 1988, Molecular Approaches to Laboratory Diagnosis, 1996; also research papers. Recipient Julliard prize Internat. Soc. Blood Transfusion, 1969; named Outstanding Immigrant in Bay Area Communities Mayor of Oakland, Calif., 1969; Fulbright scholar France, 1980. Mem. AAAS, Am. Soc. Hematology (chmn. com. on transfusion medicine 1989-90), Am. Assn. Immunologists, Am. Soc. Clin. Pathologists, Internat. Assn. for Biol. Standarization (coun. 1992-96). Democrat. Hindu. Office: U Calif Lab Med S-555 San Francisco CA 94143-0134 *Truth alone wins. Truth in our actions manifests beauty in character. Beauty in character brings harmony into the home. Harmony in the home produces order in our society. Order in our society leads to peace in the nation. And peace in the nation can win for us universal prosperity and happiness for mankind, only if individuals practice truth in their actions.*

VYKUKAL, EUGENE LAWRENCE, wholesale drug company executive; b. Caldwell, Tex., June 26, 1929; s. Henry J. and Anna P. (Polansky) V.; m. Judith Anderson, Jan. 1, 1977; children—Anna K., Mark Roman, Laura Roman, Geni. B.S. in Pharmacy, U. Tex., Austin, 1952. Pharmacist Scarborough's Pharmacy, Baytown, Tex., 1952-53; pharmacist Gene Vykukal's Pharmacy, Clifton, Tex., 1953-57; with Southwestern Drug Corp. (name now Bergen Brunswig Drug Co.), 1957-86; gen. sales mgr. Southwestern Drug Corp., Dallas, 1966-67; v.p., dir. sales Southwestern Drug Corp., 1967-75, exec. v.p., dir. sales, 1975-81, exec. v.p., 1980-81, pres., chief exec. officer, 1981-86, vice chmn., 1985-86, dir., 1966-86; asst. dean for devel., lectr. Coll. Pharmacy U. Tex., Austin, 1991—, mem. adv. coun. Pharm. Found., chmn., 1978—; sr. v.p. profl. affairs Bergen Brunswig Corp., Bergen Brunswig Drug Co., 1986—. Mem. centennial endowment com. U. Tex., 1980—; bd. dirs. Baylor U. Med. Center Found., Dallas; mem. indsl. adv. coun. Coll. Pharmacy, U. Ky., 1990—. Recipient Disting. Alumni award U. Tex. Coll. Pharmacy, 1979, William J. Sheffield Disting. Alumni award U. Tex. at Austin Coll. Pharmacy, 1987. Mem. Nat. Wholesale Druggists Assn. (chmn. sales mgmt. com. 1972-73, dir. 1980—, chmn. bd. 1985-86, 1st vice chmn. 1983—, chmn. exec. com. 1987—, Timothy Barry award 1990), Am. Pharm. Assn., Tex. Pharm. Assn. (long range planning com. 1983—), Wholesale Druggist Assn. Tex. (pres. 1978-79), Drug Travelers Assn. Tex. (pres. 1977-78), Sales and Mktg. Execs. Dallas (dir. 1971-72). Roman Catholic. Office: U Tex Coll Pharmacy Pharmacy Bldg Austin TX 78712-1074 *The quality of life in our great country has been enhanced by the tremendous strides made in our health care delivery system over the past three decades. To have served in the pharmaceutical segment has been very rewarding.*

WAAGE, MERVIN BERNARD, lawyer; b. Spirit Lake, Iowa, May 12, 1944; s. Bernard and Pearl Peterson W.; m. Eileen Barbara Waage, Feb. 17, 1947; children: Love Lee, Mark Warren. BA, Northwestern Coll., Roseville, Minn., 1966; MDiv, Southwestern Sem., 1969; JD, So. Methodist U., 1974. Bar: Tex. 1974, U.S. Dist Ct. (no. dist.) Tex. 1974, U.S. Dist. Ct. (ea. dist.) Tex. 1976, U.S. Supreme Ct. 1977, U.S. Tax Ct. 1978, U.S. Ct. Claims, 1978, U.S. Dist. Ct. (we. dist) Tex. 1988, U.S. Ct. Appeals (5th cir.) 1989. Asst. dist. atty. Denton County (Tex.) Atty.'s Office, 1974-76; pvt. practice law Denton, Tex., 1977—; bankrupcy trustee, 1980-87. Mem. Tex. Bar Assn., Tex. State Bar (bankruptcy com.), Tex. Bd. Legal Specialization (cert. in consumer bankruptcy 1986, cert. in bus. bankruptcy 1988). Republican. Baptist. Avocations: singing, jogging, camping. Home: 107 Lexington Ln Denton TX 76205-5473 Office: Waage & Waage LLP 8350 S Stemmons St Denton TX 76205-2424

WAALAND, IRVING THEODORE, retired aerospace design executive; b. Bklyn., July 2, 1927; s. Trygve and Marie Waaland; m. Helen Rita Katz, Apr. 7, 1961; children: Theodore, Neil, Elizabeth, Scott, Diane. B of Aero. Engring. magna cum laude, NYU, 1953. Project engr. Grumman Corp., Bethpage, N.Y., 1953-74; v.p., B-2 Chief Designer Northrop Corp., Pico Rivera, Calif., 1974-93. Patentee in field. With USAF, 1946-48. Fellow AIAA (Aircraft Design award 1989, Aircraft Design cert. merit 1989, Wright Bros. lectr. in Aeronautics 1991); mem. NAE, Am. Def. Preparedness Assn. (Leslie E Simon award 1990), SAE (Aerospace Engring. Leadership award 1993). Home: 65 Rollingwood Dr Palos Verdes Peninsula CA 90274-2425

WAALKES, T. PHILLIP, physician, educator; b. Belmond, Iowa, Oct. 30, 1919; s. Albert Herman and Grace (Prins) W.; m. Frances Elizabeth Brewster, Aug. 18, 1945 (dec. Nov. 1988); children: Richard Hugh, Steven Albert, Michael Phillip, Robert Louis Brewster, Kelly, Marian; m. Helen Hayes Smith, Apr. 11, 1992. A.B. magna cum laude, Hope Coll., 1941; Ph.D. in Chemistry, Ohio State U., 1945; M.D. with honors, George Washington U., 1951. From grad. asst. to instr. dept. chemistry Ohio State U., 1941-48; asst. scientist Res. USPHS, Nat. Cancer Inst., Bethesda, Md., 1948-51; intern USPHS Hosp., Balt., 1951-52; resident in medicine USPHS Hosp., 1952-55; clin. staff Nat. Heart Inst., Bethesda, 1955-58; spl. asst. to chief cancer chemotherapy Nat. Service Center, Bethesda, 1958-59; chief clin. br. Nat. Service Center, 1959-63; assoc. dir. charge collaborative research Nat. Cancer Inst., 1963-65, charge extramural ops., 1965—; prof. oncology Med. Sch., John Hopkins U., 1976—; now prof. emeritus; Pres., Md. chpt. Am. Cancer Soc. Served to med. dir. USPHS, 1959—. Mem. AMA, AAAS, APHA, Am. Soc. Clin. Oncology, Am. Assn. for Cancer Rsch., Internat. Histamine Club, Sigma Xi, Phi Lambda Upsilon, Phi Chi. Home: 9801 Kendale Rd Potomac MD 20854-4246 Office: Johns Hopkins Oncology Center Johns Hopkins Oncology Ctr Baltimore MD 21205

WABLER, ROBERT CHARLES, II, retail and distribution executive; b. Dayton, Ohio, Dec. 14, 1948; s. Robert Charles Sr. and Eileen Marie (Langen) W.; m. Linda Adele Rayburn; 1 child, Robert Charles III. BS in Acctg. cum laude, U. Dayton, 1971; MS in Acctg. magna cum laude, U. Ga., 1976. Sr. auditor Touche Ross and Co., Dayton, 1971-73; internal auditor So. Company Services, Atlanta, 1974-75; acctg. mgr. Rich's div. Federated Dept. Stores, Atlanta, 1976-77; dir. auditing Munford, Inc., Atlanta, 1977-81, v.p., controller, 1982-83, v.p. fin. analyses, 1983-86; v.p. adminstrn. World Bazaar div. Munford, Inc., Atlanta, 1981-82, sr. v.p. fin., 1986-89; sr. v.p. fin. and administrn., sec. The Athlete's Foot Group, Inc., Atlanta, 1989-93; exec. v.p., CFO, treas. Just for Feet Inc., Birmingham, Ala., 1993—. Author: The Minimum Expenses Needed Technique, 1985. Mem. AICPA, Ga. Soc. CPAs, Inst. Internal Auditors, Assn. Systems Mgmt., EDP Auditor Assn. (bd. dirs. 1978-79). Home: 1541 Fairway View Dr Hoover AL 35244-1316 Office: Just For Feet Inc 153 Cahaba Valley Pkwy N Pelham AL 35124

WACHAL, ROBERT STANLEY, linguistics educator, consultant; b. Omaha, Mar. 13, 1929; s. Stanley William and Marie Frances (Rokusek) W.; m. Jane McCune, Sept. 15, 1968. B.A., U. Minn., 1952; M.S., U. Wis., 1959, Ph.D., 1966. Tchr. Mound Sch. Dist., Minn., 1955-59; faculty mem. U. Iowa, Iowa City, 1964—, prof. linguistics, 1975-97, chmn. dept., 1975-81; cons. Am. Coll. Testing Program, Iowa City, 1981-95, Ednl. Testing Svc., Princeton, N.J., 1996—, NSF, Washington, 1975-90, Can. Council, Ottawa, Ont., 1975-80, Nat. Endowment for Humanities, N.Y.C., 1978, 93; mem. editl. adv. com. Am. Speech, 1988-93. Fulbright prof. Athens, Greece, 1966-67; research grantee U.S. Office Naval Research, 1969-72, Can. Med. Research Council Victoria, B.C., 1967-74. Fellow Acad. Aphasia; mem. Am. Dialect Soc., Dictionary Soc. N.Am. Home: 8 Woodland Hts NE Iowa City IA 52240-9136 Office: 8 Woodland Hts NE Iowa City IA 52240-9136

WACHENDORF, MILES BENTON, naval officer; b. Munich, Sept. 21, 1952; (parents Am. citizens); s. Miles Lowell and Sara Elizabeth (Goff) W.; m. Kathryn Breen, June 12, 1976; children: Patrick Lowell, Elizabeth Teague, Maria Theresa. BS, U.S. Naval Acad., 1974; postgrad., U. Zurich, Switzerland, 1979-81, Harvard U., 1994; grad., Naval War Coll., Newport, R.I., 1984; MS in Engring., Cath. U. Am., 1995. Commd. ensign USN, 1974, advanced through grades to capt., 1994; comdg. officer USS Parche (SSN683), Mare Island, Calif., 1988-93; head undersea surveillance Office Chief Naval Ops., Washington, 1993-95; commdr. Submarine Devel. Group One, 1996—. Decorated D.S.M., Legion of Merit; Olmsted scholar U. Zurich, 1979-81. Home: 7909 Scott Ct Springfield VA 22153 Office: Office Chief Naval Ops 137 Sylvester Rd San Diego CA 92106-3520

WACHENFELD, WILLIAM THOMAS, lawyer, foundation executive; b. Orange, N.J., Feb. 9, 1926; s. William A. and Ann (Weir) W.; children: William S., Robin A., John C. A.B., Tufts U., 1947; LL.B., Duke U., 1950. Bar: N.J. 1949. Since practiced in Newark; mem. firm Lum, Biunno & Tompkins, 1957-58; pres. Charles Hayden Found., N.Y.C., 1968—; prof. law Jersey City divsn. Jersey City div. Rutgers U., 1954-56; v.p., assoc. gen. counsel Prudential Ins. Co. Am., 1965-84; of counsel Tompkins, McGuire & Wachenfeld, Newark, 1984—. Pres. Essex County Park Commn., 1960-65, Newark Acad., 1972-80; commr. pub. affairs, Orange, 1956-58; mem. N.J. Econ. Devel. Coun., 1980-88, 91-94; bd. govs. N.J. Hist. Soc., 1981-83; mem. adv. bd. Wildlife Conservation Soc., 1983-93; trustee Liberty Sci. Ctr., 1988-93. Fellow Am. Bar Found.; mem. ABA, N.J. Bar Assn., Essex County Bar Assn., N.Y. Regional Assn. Grantmakers (bd. dirs. 1992-97), Eastward Ho Country Club, HC Yacht Club (commodore 1992-97). Home: 40 Windsor Pl Essex Fells NJ 07021-1711 Office: Tompkins McGuire & Wachenfeld 4 Gateway Ctr 100 Mulberry St Newark NJ 07102-4004

WACHMAN, MARVIN, university chancellor; b. Milw., Mar. 24, 1917; s. Alex and Ida (Epstein) W.; m. Adeline Lillian Schpok, Apr. 12, 1942; children: Kathleen M., Lynn A. B.S., Northwestern U., 1939, M.A., 1940; Ph.D., U. Ill., 1942; LLD (hon.), U. Pa., 1964, Lincoln (Pa.) U., 1970, Del. Valley Coll. Sci. and Agr., 1973, Med. Coll. Pa., 1982, Bloomfield Coll., 1987, Albright Coll., 1991; DHL (hon.), Gratz Coll., 1973; LittD (hon.), Jewish Theol. Sem. Am., 1973, Drexel U., 1980; LHD (hon.), Colgate U., 1975, Widener U., 1976; DSc (hon.), Thomas Jefferson U., 1980. Asst. in history U. Ill., 1940-42; instr. Biarritz Am. U., Biarritz, France, 1945-46; vis. asst. prof. San Diego State Coll., summer 1948, U. Minn., 1950; assoc. prof. history U. Md. in Europe, 1952-53; from instr. to prof. Colgate U., 1946-61, dir. upper class core program, 1956-61; pres. Lincoln (Pa.) U., 1961-70; v.p. acad. affairs Temple U., 1970-73, pres., 1973-82, chancellor, 1982—, Dir. Salzburg Seminar in Am. Studies, 1958-60, pres. Fgn. Policy Rsch. Inst., 1983-89; acting exec. dir. Pa. Higher Edn. Assistance Agy., 1989; acting pres. Phila. Coll. Textiles and Sci., 1991; pres. Albright Coll., 1991-92; past chmn. Nat. Ctr. for Higher Edn. Mgmt. Sys.; specialist in Africa for State Dept., 1965, 68; mem. adv. coun. World Learning, Inc.; mem. Colgate Nat. Coun., Phila. Com. Fgn. Rels.; dir., chair COLLEGIS, Inc.; dir. emeritus Germantown Ins. Co. Author: History of Social-Democratic Party of Milwaukee, 1897-1910, 1945; contbr. articles to profl. jours. and newspapers, also chpts. in books. Mem. bd. overseers Coll. V.I.; hon. trustee Albright Coll.; hon. life trustee Temple U.; trustee, chmn. Phila. Coll. Textiles and Sci.; vice chair Fgn. Policy Rsch. Inst.; trustee emeritus Balch Inst. Ethnic Studies; mem. adv. coun. Greater Phila. Urban Affairs Coalition, World Affairs Coun.; mem. bd. mgrs. Phila. Found.; bd. dirs. Operation Understanding; hon. dir. Phila. Contributionship; alumni regent Phila. area Northwestern U. With AUS, 1942-46. Mem. NAACP, Am. Studies Assn. (past mem. exec. com.), AAUP (past pres. Colgate U. chpt.), Am. Hist. Assn., ACLU, Pa. Assn. Colls. and Univs. (past chmn., pres. 1993), Phi Beta Kappa. Office: Temple U Philadelphia PA 19122

WACHNER, LINDA JOY, apparel marketing and manufacturing executive; b. N.Y.C., Feb. 3, 1946; d. Herman and Shirley W.; m. Seymour Applebaum, Dec. 21, 1973 (dec. 1983). BS in Econs. and Bus., U. Buffalo, 1966. Buyer Foley's Federated Dept. Store, Houston, 1968-69; sr. buyer R.H. Macy's, N.Y.C., 1969-74; v.p. Warner divsn. Warnaco, Bridgeport, Conn., 1974-77; v.p. corp. mktg. Caron Internat., N.Y.C., 1977-79; chief exec. officer U.S. divsn. Max Factor & Co., Hollywood, Calif., 1979-82, pres., chief exec. officer, 1982-83; pres., chief exec. officer Max Factor & Co. Worldwide, 1983-84; mng. dir. Adler & Shaykin, N.Y.C., 1985-86; pres., CEO, chmn. Warnaco Inc., N.Y.C., 1986—; chmn., CEO Authentic Fitness Corp., 1991—; bd. dirs. The Travellers, Inc. Presdl. appointee Adv. Com. for Trade, Policy, Negotiations; trustee U. Buffalo Found., Carnegie Hall, Aspen Inst., Thirteen/WNET; bd. overseers Meml. Sloan-Kettering Cancer Ctr. Recipient Silver Achievement award L.A. YWCA; named Outstanding Woman in Bus. Women's Equity Action League, 1980, Woman of Yr., MS. Mag., 1986, one of the Yr.'s Most Fascinating Bus. People, Fortune Mag., 1986, one of 10 Most Powerful Women in Corp. Am., Savvy Woman Mag., 1989, 90, Am.'s Most Successful Bus. Woman, Fortune Mag., 1992, Queen of Cash Flow, Chief Exec. Mag., 1994. Mem. Am. Mgmt. Assn., Am. Apparel Mktg. Assn. (bd. dirs.), Bus. Roundtable, Coun. on Fgn. Rels. Republican. Jewish. Office: Warnaco Inc/Authentic Fitness Corp 90 Park Ave New York NY 10016

WACHS, DAVID V., retired apparel executive; b. Phila.. Attended, U Penn Wharton, 1948. With Charming Shoppes Inc., Bensalem, 1950-95, CEO, 1988-95; ret., 1995. Office: Charming Shoppes Inc 215 W Church Rd Ste 108 King Of Prussia PA 19406

WACHS, MARTIN, urban planning educator, author, consultant; b. N.Y.C., June 8, 1941; s. Robert and Doris (Margolis) W.; m. Helen Pollner, Aug. 18, 1963; children: Faye Linda, Steven Brett. B.C.E., CUNY, 1963; M.S., Northwestern U., 1965, Ph.D., 1967. Asst. prof. U. Ill.-Chgo., 1967-69, Northwestern U., Evanston, Ill., 1969-71; assoc. prof. urban planning UCLA, 1971-76, prof., 1976-96; dir. UCLA Inst. Transp. Studies, 1993-96; prof. civil and environ. engring and city and regional planning U. Calif., Berkeley, 1996—; dir. U. Calif. Transp. Ctr., 1996—; vis. disting. prof. Rutgers U., New Brunswick, N.J., 1983-84; mem. exec. com. Transp. Rsch. Bd., 1995—. Author: Transportation for the Elderly: Changing Lifestyles, Changing Needs, 1979, Transportation Planning on Trial, 1996; also numerous articles; editor: Ethics in Planning, 1984, The Car and the City, 1992. Mem. steering com. Los Angeles Parking Mgmt. Study, 1976-78; bd. dirs. Los Angeles Commuter Computer, 1978-94, mem. Calif. Commn. on Transp. Investment, 1995. Served to capt. Ordnance Corps, U.S. Army, 1967-69. Recipient Pike Johnson award Transp. Research Bd., 1976, Disting. Teaching award UCLA Alumni Assn., 1986, Disting. Planning Educator award Calif. Planners Found., 1986, vis. fellow Oxford U. (Eng.), 1976-77; Guggenheim fellow, 1977; Rockefeller Found. humanities fellow, 1980. Fellow Am. Coun. Edn.; mem. Am. Planning Assn., Am. Inst. Cert. Planners, Architects, Designers, Planners for Social Responsibility. Jewish. Home: 1106 Grizzly Peak Blvd Berkeley CA 94708-1704 Office: U Calif Transp Ctr 108 Naval Arch Bldg Berkeley CA 94720-1720

WACHSMAN, HARVEY FREDERICK, lawyer, neurosurgeon; b. Bklyn., June 13, 1936; s. Ben and Mollie (Kugel) W.; m. Kathryn M. D'Agostino, Jan. 31, 1976; children: Dara Nicole, David Winston, Jacqueline Victoria, Lauren Elizabeth, Derek Charles, Ashley Max, Marea Lane, Melissa Roseanne. B.A., Tulane U., 1958; M.D., Chgo. Med. Sch., 1962; J.D., Bklyn. Law Sch., 1976. Bar: Conn. 1976, N.Y. 1977, Fla. 1977, D.C. 1978, U.S. Supreme Ct. 1980, Pa. 1984, Md. 1986, Tex. 1987. Diplomate Nat. Bd. Med. Examiners; cert. Am. Bd. Legal Medicine, Am. Bd. Profl. Liability Attys. (pres.); cert. civil trial advocate Nat. Bd. Trial Advocacy (trustee). Intern surgery Kings County Hosp. Ctr., Bklyn., 1962-63; resident in surgery Kingsbrook Med. Ctr., Bklyn., 1964-65; resident in neurol. surgery Emory U. Hosp., Atlanta, 1965-69; practice medicine specializing in neurosurgery Bridgeport, Conn., 1972-74; ptnr. firm Wachsman & Wachsman, Great Neck, 1976—, Pegalis & Wachsman, Great Neck, N.Y., 1977—; adj. prof. neurosurgery SUNY, Stony Brook; adj. prof. law St. John's U. Sch. Law; bd. trustees SUNY, chmn. health sci. and hosp. com. Author: American Law of Medical Malpractice, Vol. I, 1980, 2d edit., 1992, American Law of Medical Malpractice, Vol. II, 1981, 2d edit., 1993, American Law of Medical Malpractice, Vol. III, 1982, 2d edit., 1994, Cumulative Supplement to American Law of Medical Malpractice, 1981, 82, 83, 84, 85, American Law of Medical Malpractice, 2d edit., Vols. I, II and II, Lethal Medicine, 1993; mem. editl. bd. Legal Aspects of Med. Practice, 1978-82. Trustee SUNY, chmn. health sci. and hosp. com. Fellow Am. Coll. Legal Medicine (mem. bd. govs. 1986, chmn. edn. com. 1983—, chmn. 1985 nat. meeting, New Orleans, chmn. 1988 nat. meeting, Va., bd. dirs. ACLM Found.), Am. Acad. Forensic Scis., Royal Soc. Medicine, Royal Soc. Arts (London), Royal Soc. Medicine (London), Roscoe Pound Found. of Assn. Trial Lawyers Am.; mem. ABA, Am. Soc. Law and Medicine, Congress Neurol. Surgeons, Assn. Trial Lawyers Am., Soc. Med. Jurisprudence (trustee), N.Y. Bar Assn., Conn. Bar Assn., Fla. Bar Assn., D.C. Bar Assn., N.Y. Acad. Scis., Assn. Trial Lawyers Am. (bd. govs.), N.Y. Trial Lawyers Assn., Conn. Trial Lawyers Assn., Fla. Acad. Trial Lawyers, Md. Trial Lawyers Assn., Tex. Trial Lawyers Assn., Pa. Trial Lawyers Assn., Nat. Bar Assn. (mem. com. on South Africa), Nassau County Bar Assn., Fairfield County Med. Soc., Nassau-Suffolk Trial Lawyers Assn. Club: Cosmos (Washington). Home: 55 Mill River Rd Oyster Bay NY 11771-2711 Office: 175 E Shore Rd Great Neck NY 11023-2430 *In my pursuit of knowledge and excellence in the fields of neurosurgery and the law, I Have found that arming oneself with the power of knowledge is truly the key to helping others. Let one's goal in life be to help others, and he shall always find fulfillment, challenge and hope.*

WACHSMANN, ELIZABETH RIDEOUT, reading specialist; b. Richmond, Va., Apr. 28, 1945; d. John Nelson and Lily Smith (Garter) Rideout; m. Marvin Rudolph Wachsmann, Aug. 14, 1966; children: Rebecca W. Campbell, Richard Nelson. BS, James Madison Univ., 1966; MEd in Adminstrn. and Supervision, Va. State U., 1989, MEd in Diagnosit and Remedial Reading, 1994. 1st grade tchr. Sussex (Va.) Pub. Schs., 1966-70; 6th grade tchr. Tidewater Acad., Wakefield, Va., 1978-89; 1st grade tchr. Surry (Va.) County Pub. Schs., 1989-92, reading specialist, 1992—. Named Tchr. of Yr. Daily Press/Newport News Shipbuilders, 1992. Mem. ASCD, Internat. Reading Assn., Richmond Area Reading Assn., Va. Br. ORton Dyslexic Soc., Assn. for Childhood Edn. Internat., Nat. Coun. Tchrs. of English, Va. Br. Orton Dyslexic Soc., Phi Delta Kappa, Kappa Delta Pi. United Methodist. Avocations: reading, handwork, cooking, gardening. Home: 13019 Robinson Rd Stony Creek VA 23882-3737 Office: Surry County Pub Schs PO Box 317 Surry VA 23883-0317

WACHSTETER, GEORGE, illustrator; b. Hartford, Conn., Mar. 12, 1911; s. Josef and Therese (Weiss) W.; m. Thelma Altshuler, July 29, 1939 (dec. 1991). Ed. pub. schs., Hartford. Illustrator Major Advt. Agys, Theatre and Motion Picture Prodns., 1936—, CBS, NBC, ABC Radio and TV Networks, 1937—; weekly illustrator and caricature to drama pages N.Y. Herald Tribune, 1941-50; contbr. illustration and caricature to drama and polit. pages N.Y. Times, 1938-50; caricaturist Theatre Guild On The Air, U.S. Steel, 1945-63; artist TV section N.Y. Times, 1950-51; featured drama artist N.Y. Jour. Am., 1956-63, artist TV mag. covers, 1958-63; artist TV mag. covers Hearst Syndicate, 1963-65; drama artist N.Y. World Telegram, 1964-66; syndicated feature illustrator Hallmark TV Drama Series, 1964-69. Illustrator, caricaturist (book) NBC Book of Stars, 1957; portrait Taft Meml. Fund Campaign, 1956; numerous work in pub. and pvt. collections. Jewish. Home: 85-05 Elmhurst Ave Elmhurst NY 11373-3357

WACHTEL, NORMAN JAY, lawyer; b. N.Y.C., June 1, 1941; s. A. Allen and Lillian (Rolnik) W.; m. C. Robin Fixler, June 12, 1969; children: Jonathan, Charles. AB, U. Pa., 1963, LLB, 1966; LLM, Boston U., 1967. Bar: N.Y. 1967. Assoc. Demov, Morris & Hammerling, N.Y.C., 1968-78, ptnr., 1978-87; ptnr. Rogers & Wells, N.Y.C., 1987-96, of counsel, 1996—; bd. advisors 1st Am. Title Ins. Co. N.Y., 1982—. Author: (chpt.) Real Estate Titles, 1984. Office: Rogers & Wells 200 Park Ave Ste 5200 New York NY 10166-0005

WACHTEL, THOMAS LEE, surgeon; b. Mansfield, Ohio, July 25, 1938; s. Earl J. and Lorena Fredona (Lehman) W.; m. Carolyn Coleman, May 15, 1965; children: John Matthew, David Earl-Martin, Julianne Maria. AB, Western Res. U., Cleve., 1960; MD, St. Louis U., 1964; cert. naval flight surgeon, Naval Flight Sch., Pensacola, Fla., 1970. Diplomate Am. Bd. Surgery; cert. added qualification in surg. critical care. Intern in surgery U. Ky., Lexington, 1964-65, resident in surgery, 1965-66; resident in surgery St. John's Mercy Hosp., St. Louis, 1966-69; pvt. practice Hamilton & Wachtel, Corbin, Ky., 1973-74; mem. surg. faculty U. N.Mex., Albuquerque, 1974-77; mem. surg. faculty U. Calif., San Diego, 1978-84, 91-96, burn dir., 1980-84, head trauma divsn., 1982-84; med. dir. trauma Samaritan Regional Med. Ctr., Phoenix, 1984-90; program dir. Phoenix Integrated Surg. Residency, 1986-90; med. dir. trauma Sharp Meml. Hosp., San Diego, 1990-96; chmn. bioengring. faculty Ariz. State U., 1984-90; dir. trauma Centura Health St. Anthony Hosp. Ctrl., Denver, 1996—; mem. surg. faculty F. Edward Hebert Sch. Medicine USPHS, Bethesda, 1988—; mem. surg. faculty U. Ariz., Tucson, 1993—; mem. nat. faculty Advanced Burn Life Support, Omaha, 1988—; mem. surg. faculty U. Colo., Denver, 1996—. Author: Medical Exploring, 2 edits., 1973, 76, Current Topics in Burn Care, 1983, Burns of the Head and Neck, 1984; editor: A Symposium on Burns, 1985. Mem. Nat. Commn. on Exploring Boy Scouts Am., Arlington, Tex., 1972-85; mem. Flynn Found. on Commn. on Med. Manpower, Phoenix, 1987-88. With USNR, 1969-97, capt. Res. Recipient Family Practice Teaching award Am. Acad. Family Practice, Phoenix, 1985; rsch. grantee U.S. Army, NIH, HSA-HEW. Fellow ACS (gov. 1995—), Am. Assn. Surgery of Trauma, Am. Coll. Critical Care Medicine; mem. Am. Burn Assn. (pres. 1989-90), Phi Gamma Delta, Phi Chi (pres. Phi Rho chpt. 1963-64), Omicron Delta Kappa, Sigma Delta Psi. Roman Catholic. Avocations: travel, hiking, woodworking, fishing, skiing. Office: Centura Health St Anthony Hosp Ctrl Trauma Dept 4231 W 16th Ave Denver CO 80204-1335

WACHTLER, SOL, retired judge, arbitration corporation executive, writer; b. N.Y.C., Apr. 29, 1930; s. Philip Henry and Fay (Sobel) W.; m. Joan Wolosoff, Feb. 23, 1952; children: Lauren Jane, Marjorie Dru, Alison Toni, Philip Henry. BA, Washington and Lee U., 1951, LLB, 1952, postgrad., 1980, LLD (hon.), 1981; LLD (hon.), New Eng. Sch. Law, 1978, Bklyn. Law Sch., 1978, Hofstra U., 1980, SUNY, 1981, Syracuse U., Dowling Coll., 1990, Thomas M. Cooley Law Sch., 1990, New. Eng. Law Sch.; LHD (hon.), LIU, Coll. of St. Rose. Bar: N.Y. 1956. Justice N.Y. State Supreme Ct., 1968-72; judge N.Y. State Ct. Appeals, Albany, 1972-84; chief judge State of N.Y., Albany, 1985-93; guest lectr. Bklyn. Law Sch., Hofstra Law Sch., Yale U. Sch. Law, Albany Law Sch., St. John's Law Sch., 1968-77, USIA, Munich, Germany, 1973, Stuttgart, Germany, 1977, U. Leyden, Amsterdam, Stockholm, 1988, Madrid, 1989; chmn. N.Y. State Fair Trial/Free Press Conf., N.Y. State Commn. on Bicentennial of U.S. Constitution.; bd. dirs. Confs. Cief Justices; mem. Nat Jud. Coun. Author: After the Madness, 1997; critic-at-large New Yorker mag., 1996; contbr. articles to legal jours. Councilman Town of North Hempstead, N.Y., 1963-65, chief exec., 1965-67; mem. Nassau County Bd. Suprs., 1965-67, chmn. com. pub. safety, 1965-67; trustee L.I. Jewish-Hillside Med. Ctr., 1970—, L.I. U.; bd. overseers Nelson A. Rockefeller Inst. Govt.; dist. chmn. Boy Scouts Am., 1968-69; trustee Cerebral Palsy Assn., Assn. for Help of Retarded Children, 1966-67. Mem. Am. Law Inst., Assn. N.Y. State Supreme Ct. Justices, ABA, N.Y. State Bar Assn., Nassau County Bar Assn., Order of Coif, Phi Delta Phi. Jewish. Home: 58 Fairway Dr Manhasset NY 11030-3906 *As a people, we are fond of the observation that ours is a nation of laws and not of men. It too, like the words of our great laws, seems to lend security, a sense of certainty, and a predictability to the paths we travel. In the law particularly, the thought that past generations have separated right from wrong and good from evil can be comforting. Yet, here again, if we will just scratch the surface, we will find that the greatest responsibility for our national welfare does not rest with statutes carved in stone but with the principles, conscience, and morality of the individuals who constitute this generation.*

WACHTMEISTER, COUNT WILHELM H. F., diplomat; b. Vanas, Sweden, Apr. 29, 1923; s. Gustaf and Margaretha (Trolle) W.; m. Ulla Leuhusen, 1947; children: Anna, Erik. LLD, U. Stockholm, Sweden, 1946. Attache Swedish Ministry for Fgn. Affairs, 1946-47; attache Swedish Embassy, Vienna, Madrid and Lisbon, 1947-50; 2d sec. Swedish Ministry Fgn. Affairs, Stockholm, Sweden, 1950-55; 1st sec. Swedish Embassy, Moscow, 1955-58; personal asst. to UN Sec. Gen., 1958-61; head UN sect. Fgn. Ministry, Stockholm, 1962-65, dep. under-sec. polit. affairs, 1965-66; ambassador to Algeria Swedish Embassy, 1966-67; under-sec. for polit. affairs Swedish Ministry Fgn. Affairs, Stockholm, 1968-74; Swedish ambassador to U.S. Swedish Embassy, Washington, 1974-89; dean diplomatic corps in Washington, 1986-89; sr. advisor to chmn. AB Volvo, 1989-94. Mem. Soc. Cin. (France), New World Found. (chmn.), Swedish-Am. C. of C. (chmn. 1993-95), Met. Club of Washington, Fed. City Club (Washington). Avocation: tennis. Home: 4202 48th Pl NW Washington DC 20016-2338

WACKENHUT, RICHARD RUSSELL, security company executive; b. Balt., Nov. 11, 1947; s. George Russell and Ruth Johann (Bell) W.; m. Mariane Hutson Ball, Mar. 13, 1971; children: Jennifer Anne, Lisa Renee, Ashley Elizabeth, Lauren Hutson. BA in Polit. Sci., The Citadel Mil. Coll., 1969; grad. bus. sch. advanced mgmt. program, Harvard U., 1987. With Wackenhut Corp., Coral Gables and Palm Beach Gardens, Fla. and Columbia, S.C., 1973—; v.p. ops. Wackenhut Corp., Coral Gables, 1981-82, sr. v.p. domestic ops., 1982-83, sr. v.p. ops., 1983-86, pres., chief operating officer, 1986—, also bd. dirs. various subs.; bd. dirs. Assoc. Industries of Fla. Mem. Internat. Assn. Chiefs Police, Internat. Security Mgmt. Assn., Am. Soc. Indsl. Security. Republican. Christian Scientist. Avocations: racquetball, jogging, boating. Office: Wackenhut Corp 4200 Wackenhut Dr Ste 100 Palm Bch Gdns FL 33410-4243

WACKER, FREDERICK GLADE, JR., manufacturing company executive; b. Chgo., July 10, 1918; s. Frederick Glade Wacker and Grace Cook Jennings; m. Ursula Comandatore, Apr. 26, 1958; children: Frederick Glade III, Wendy, Joseph Comandatore. BA, Yale U., 1940; student, Gen. Motors Inst. Tech., 1940-42; LLD (hon.), Northwood U., 1989, GMI Engring. and Mgmt. Inst., 1996. Efficiency engr. AC Spark Plug divsn. Gen. Motors Corp., 1940-43; with Ammco Tools, Inc., North Chicago, Ill., 1947-87, pres., 1948-87, chmn. bd., 1948-87; founder, pres. Liquid Controls Corp., North Chicago, 1954-87, chmn. bd., 1954—; chmn. bd. Liquid Controls Europe, Zurich, Switzerland, 1985-87; ltd. ptnr. Francis I. DuPont & Co., N.Y.C., 1954-70; mem. exec. coun. Conf. Bd., 1971-92, chmn., 1977. Condr. Freddie Wacker and His Orch., 1955-69, orch. has appeared on TV and radio, recs. for Dolphin and Cadet records. Bd. govs. United Rep. Fund Ill., Art Inst. Chgo., 1984—; trustee Lake Forest Acad., 1956-71, life trustee, 1992—; trustee Warren Wilson Coll., 1973-81, Chgo. chpt. Multiple Sclerosis Soc.; bd. govs. Lyric Opera Chgo., 1963-66; bd. advisers Nat. Schs. Com., 1966-88; adv. coun. Trinity Evang. Div. Sch., 1977-87; adv. bd. Internat. Coun. Biblical Inerrancy, 1981-88; bd. dirs., vice chmn. Rockford Inst., 1983-91; bd. govs. GMI Engring. and Mgmt. Inst., 1983-91; bd. regents Milw. Sch. Engring., 1981-91; mem. pres.'s coun. Ligonier Ministries, 1989—. Lt. (j.g.) USNR, 1943-45, PTO. Recipient Outstanding Bus. Leader award, Northwood, 1994; named to Hall of Fame Lake Forest Acad., 1987. Mem. Chief Execs. Forum, Young Pres. Orgn. (chmn. Chgo. chpt. 1965-66), Sports Car Club Am. (founder Chgo. region 1949, nat. pres. 1972-73), Ill. Mfrs. Assn. (bd. dirs. 1966-91, chmn. bd. 1975), Chgo. Pres. Orgn. (pres. 1972-73), Automotive Hall of Fame (life, bd. dirs. 1976-88, v.p. 1980-81, sec. 1981-88, Disting. Svc. Citation 1989, Chief Exec. Forum 1967-89), Soc. Automotive Engrs., World Bus. Coun., Waukegan C. of C. (bd. dirs. 1965-68), Art Inst. Chgo. (gov.), Chgo. Fedn. Musicians (life), Am. Motorcycle Assn. (life), Am. Legion (life mem. post 510), Big Band Acad. Am., Living Desert (life), Racquet Club (pres. 1960-61), Shoreacres Club, Onwentsia Club, Vintage Club, The Quarry. Presbyterian. Home: 1600 Green Bay Rd Lake Bluff IL 60044-2306 Office: Liquid Controls Corp 105 Albrecht Dr Lake Bluff IL 60044-2252

WACKER, SUSAN REGINA, cosmetic design director; b. Red Bank, N.J., Apr. 29, 1954; d. Durward Richard and Margaret Rose (Williams) W. BFA, Pratt Inst., 1978. Asst. art dir. Lesley-Hille Inc., N.Y.C., 1975-79; art dir. Kasica, Lefton, Brown, Inc., N.Y.C., 1980-82; sr. design dir. Elizabeth Arden Co., N.Y.C., 1982—. Patentee in field. Fellow Mus. Modern Art; supporting mem. Cooper Hewitt Mus.; friend mem. Whitney Mus.; active Met. Mus. Art. Recipient (4) DESI awards, 1980, ANDY award, 1980, Fragrance Found. award, 1988, 91, 92, Silver award N.J. Packaging Execs. Club, 1990, ADDY Excellence citation, 1991, Edison Best New Products Gold Medal award, 1991, (2) Gold awards Nat. Paperbox & Packaging Assn., 1992, (2) Gold awards, 1994, Silver award Paperboard Packaging Coun., 1993, Excellence award, 1993, Silver Excellence award Nat. Paperbox & Packaging Assn., 1993, (10) Silver Excellence awards, 1994, Mobius 1st Place Statuette award, 1995, Gold award Nat. Paperboard Coun., 1995, Prix Francois 1st de L'Emballage de Luxe, 1995, OMA Gold award, 1995, Oscar de L'Emballage Prestige à Lyon, 1995, Mobius award First Place Statuette for Elizabeth Taylor's Black Pearls perfume product line/package design, 1996, OMA Gold award for Elizabeth Arden's 5th Avenue tester display, 1996, OMA Bronze award for Elizabeth Taylor's Black Pearls tester display, 1996, CPC "Package of the Month" (October), Elizabeth Arden's 5th Avenue fragrance line, 1996, Natl. Paperboard Packaging Conc. award, 1996. Mem. Cosmetic Exec. Women Found., Fashion Group Internat. Avocations: skiing, tennis, horseback riding, photography. Office: Elizabeth Arden Co 1345 Avenue Of The Americas New York NY 10105-0302

WACKER, WARREN ERNEST CLYDE, physician, educator; b. Bklyn., Feb. 29, 1924; s. John Frederick and Kitty Dora (Morrissey) W.; m. Ann Romeyn MacMillan, May 22, 1948; children: Margaret Morrissey, John Frederick. Student, Georgetown U., 1946-47; M.D., George Washington U., 1951; M.A. (hon.), Harvard, 1968. Intern George Washington U. Hosp., 1951-52, resident, 1952-53; resident Peter Bent Brigham Hosp., Boston, 1953-55; Nat. Found. Infantile Paralysis fellow, 1955-57; investigator Howard Hughes Med. Inst., Boston, 1957-68; mem. faculty Harvard Med. Sch., Boston, 1955—; assoc. prof. medicine Harvard Med. Sch., 1968-71, Henry K. Oliver prof. hygiene, 1971-89, prof. hygiene, 1989-95, dir. univ. health services, 1971-89; Henry K. Oliver prof. hygiene emeritus, 1995; acting master Mather House Harvard Med. Sch., 1974-75, acting master Kirkland House, 1975-76, master Cabot House, 1978-84; sr. med. cons. Risk Mgmt. Found. of the Harvard Med. Instns., Cambridge, 1992—; vis. scholar St. Mary's Hosp. Med. Sch., 1964; vis. prof. U. Tel Aviv, 1987; chmn. bd. Applied mgmt. Sys., Burlington, Mass., Millipore Corp., Bedford, Mass., 1971-94; mem. editorial adv. bd. Toxilogical and Environ. Chemistry. Author: Magnesium and Man, 1981; sec., editorial adv. bd.: Biochemistry, 1962-76; assoc. editor: Magnesium; contbr. articles to med. and sci. jours. Vestryman St. Paul's Episc. Ch., Brookline, Mass., 1965-68, 76-79, 91-94; bd. dirs. Harvard Cmty. Health Plan, Boston, 1973-84, mem. fin. com., 1984-86, mem. corp., 1986—; bd. dirs. Bishop Rhinelander Found., Cambridge, 1973-76, 78-84, Controlled Risk Ins. Co., 1976-78; pres. bd. overseers Peter Bent Brigham Hosp., Boston, 1979-84; trustee Brigham and Women's Hosp., Boston, 1984-89,Risk Mgmt. Found., 1979-92; mem. mgmt. bd., med. bd. MIT, 1985-95; mem. corp. Mt. Auburn Hosp., Cambridge, 1986—; mem. adv. bd. hospitality program Episc. Diocese Mass., 1989-95. 1st lt. USAAF, 1942-45. Decorated Air medal, D.F.C., Liberation medal (Greece); named Disting. Alumnus, George Washington U., 1963; recipient Cert. of Merit, Soc. Magnesium Research, 1985. Mem. AMA, Am. Chem. Soc., Am. Soc. Biol. Chemistry, Am. Soc. Clin. Investigation, Mass. Med. Soc., A.C.P., Am. Coll. Health Assn. (pres. 1981, Boynton award 1986), Biochemistry Soc. (London), Am. Coll. Nutrition, Sigma Xi, Alpha Omega Alpha, Harvard Club (Boston). Home: 91 Glen Rd Brookline MA 02146-7764 Office: Risk Mgmt Found 840 Memorial Dr Cambridge MA 02139-3771

WACKERLE, FREDERICK WILLIAM, management consultant; b. Chgo., June 25, 1939; s. Fred and Babette (Buck) W.; m. Elaine Gately, Apr. 28, 1962 (div.); children: Jennifer, Ruth; m. Barbara L. Provus, Mar. 29, 1985. BA, Monmouth (Ill.) Coll., 1961. Prin. A.T. Kearney & Co., Chgo., 1964-66; v.p. Berry Henderson & Aberlin, Chgo., 1966-68, R.M. Schmitz & Co., Chgo., 1968-70; ptnr. McFeely-Wackerle-Shulman, Chgo., 1970—; dir. Rehab. Inst. Chgo. Trustee Monmouth Coll. Served with USAF, 1957-62. Mem. Assn. Exec. Search Cons. (bd. dirs., exec. v.p.), Tau Kappa Epsilon. Home: 3750 N Lake Shore Dr Apt 17F Chicago IL 60613-4234 Office: McFeely-Wackerle-Shulman 20 N Wacker Dr Ste 3110 Chicago IL 60606-3101

WADA, HARRY NOBUYOSHI, training company executive; b. North Platte, Nebr., Nov. 29, 1919; s. Gosaku and Hina (Arakawa) W.; m. Carol Tanaka, July 30, 1950; children: Sharon, Leslie, Gregg. B.S., Ill. Inst. Tech., 1954, M.S., 1956. Owner Palace Cafe, North Platte, 1946-50; mgr. purchases IIT Research Inst., Chgo., 1954-65; materials mgr. IIT Research Inst., 1965-76; dir. continuing edn. Nat. Assn. Purchasing Mgmt., 1976-83; pres. H. N. Wada & Assocs., 1983—; instr. Ill. Inst. Tech., Roosevelt U. Editor chpt. from George Aljians Handbook, 1973; contbr. articles to profl. jours. Mem. Bd. Standardization Cook County, Health and Hosps. Governing Commn. Served with AUS, 1942-46. Recipient J. Shipman Gold medal, 1976. Mem. Purchasing Mgmt. Assn. Chgo. (pres. 1969), Nat. Assn. Purchasing Mgmt. (chmn. dist. III profl. devel. 1970-71, program chmn. Internat. Conf. 1971, pres. 1974—, Brueggemann award 1974), Ill. C. of C., Ill. Inst. Tech. Alumni (bd. dirs.), Phi Eta Sigma, Sigma Iota Epsilon. Home and Office: 3128 Tarpon Dr #104 Las Vegas NV 89120

WADA, YUTAKA, electronics executive; b. Sapporo, Hokkaido, Japan, Feb. 2, 1932; s. Hiroshi and Toki (Hirano) W.; m. Makiko Hirate, Apr. 15, 1940; children: Takeshi, Kaori. BA, Tokyo U., 1953; Grad., London Sch. Economics, 1963. Cert. Nat. Civil Svc. With Ministry of Internat. Trade and Industry, Tokyo, 1953-64; dir. policy review and assessment sec. Small and Medium Enterprise Agy. MITI, Tokyo, 1968-70; counselor Japanese permanent delegation Internat. Orgn., Geneva, 1973-78; dir. gen. multilateral trade dept. MITI, Tokyo, 1975-76; dir. gen. first examination dept. Patent Office, Tokyo, 1978-79, dir. gen., gen. adminstrn. dept., 1979-80; dir. gen. Bur. of Equipment, Defense Agency, Tokyo, 1980-82; exec. dir., bd. dir. The Overseas Economic Cooperation Fund, Tokyo, 1982-84; with Sharp Corp., Osaka, 1984—, exec. dir., bd. dir., 1985—, group gen. mgr. internat. bus. group, 1986-89, sr. exec., dir., mem. of exec. com., 1989-91, sr. exec., v.p. for internat. bus., mem. exec. com., 1991-95, sr. exec. v.p., then corp. sr. exec. v.p. external rels., mem. exec. com., 1995—; interviewed by CNN Worldwide, 1994. Bimonthly articles contbr. (under Yasuhiko Hiromi) Keizai-kai Bus. Jour., 1978-80; contbr. articles Nippon Keizai Shinbun, 1994, The Nikkei Weekly, 1994, The Asian Wall Street Journal, 1994. Mem. Kansai Economic Fedn. (spl. com. on internat. bus. mgmt., 1993-94), The Osaka Indsl. Assn. (internat. community rels. com. 1993—), Osaka Fgn. Trade Assn. (dir. 1994—), Japan-China Investment Promotion Orgn. (dir. 1993—). Avocations: golf, swimming, skiing, go, reading. Office: Sharp Corp, 1-9-2 Nakase Mihama-ku, Chiba 261, Japan

WADDELL, HARRY LEE, editor, publisher; b. Monarch, Wyo., June 19, 1912; s. Edward Lee and Naomi (Epstein) W.; m. Eleanor Hazeltine, 1937 (dec.); children: Nancy, Caroline, Jessica; m. Helene Jamieson, Apr., 6, 1968 (dec.). A.B., Ohio U., 1933. Reporter, fin. editor, asst. city editor, news editor Buffalo Evening News, 1933-46; asst. mng. editor Bus. Week, McGraw-Hill, N.Y.C., 1946-49; editor Factory, 1949-53, pub. oil industry group, 1953-57, sr. v.p. mag. div., 1957-59, corp. exec. v.p., dir., 1959-65; gen. exec. Doubleday & Co., N.Y.C., 1966-69; with Simmons-Boardman Pub. Corp., N.Y.C., 1969—; chief editor Am. Bankers Assn. Banking Jour., 1971-82, editor emeritus, 1982-96, chmn. bd., 1972-82, vice chmn., 1982—; lectr. Am. Press Inst., Columbia U., 1946-59; Mem. Ednl. Adv. Bd., Garden City, N.Y., 1955-58, chmn., 1957-58. Trustee Orange County Citizens Found., 1983-96, v.p. 1987-93. Mem. Am. Bus. Press (dir. 1977-83), Phi Beta Kappa, Sigma Delta Chi, Beta Theta Pi. Republican. Presbyterian.

WADDELL, R. EUGENE, minister; b. Wayne County, N.C., Feb. 7, 1932; s. Robert Lee and Rena (Holland) W.; m. Elva Leah Nichols, July 22, 1954 (dec. Apr. 1962); children: Rhonda Waddell Sagraves, Robert, Paul, Marcia Waddell Thompson; m. Genevieve Johnson, July 4, 1963; children: Michael, John. BA, Free Will Bapt. Bible Coll., Nashville, 1954; MA, Columbia (S.C.) Bibl. Sem., 1966. Ordained to ministry Free Will Bapt. Ch., 1952. Pastor Bay Branch Free Will Bapt. Ch., Timmonsville, S.C., 1954-56, 1st Free Will Bapt. Ch., Portsmouth, Va., 1956-60, Garner (N.C.) Free Will Bapt. Ch., 1960-64, Cofer's Chapel Free Will Bapt. Ch., Nashville, 1964-81; assoc. dir. Free Will Bapt. Fgn. Missions Dept., Nashville, 1981-86, gen. dir., 1986—; bd. dirs. Free Will Bapt. Fgn. Missions, Nashville, 1959-78, bd. sec., 1971-78; founder, editor Free Will Bapt. Witness, Garner, 1962-63. Office: Free Will Bapt Fgn Missions 5233 Mount View Rd Antioch TN 37013-2306

WADDELL, THEODORE, painter; b. Billings, Mont., Jan. 6, 1941. Student, Bklyn. Mus. Art Sch., 1962; BS, Ea. Mont. Coll., 1966; MFA, Wayne State U., 1968. One-man shows include U. Calif., San Diego, 1984, Cheney Cowles Meml. Mus., Spokane, Wash., 1985, The New West, Colorado Springs, 1986, Bernice Stein Baum Gallery, N.Y., 1992; exhibited in group shows 38th Corcoran Biennial, Corcoran Gallery, Washington, 1983; represented in permanent collections Ea. Mont. Coll., Yellowstone Art Ctr., Billings, Sheldon Meml. Art Gallery, U. Nebr., Lincoln, City of Great Falls, Mont., Dallas Mus. Art, San Jose (Calif.) Mus. Office: care Stremmel Gallery 1400 S Virginia St Reno NV 89502-2806*

WADDELL, WILLIAM JOSEPH, pharmacologist, toxicologist; b. Commerce, Ga., Mar. 16, 1929; s. John Daniel and Lillian Marie (Vollrath) W.; m. Grace Carolyn Marlowe, Oct. 19, 1974; children: William Joseph, James Glenn, Martin Christie, Amy Alison. A.B. in Chemistry, U. N.C., 1951, M.D., 1955. Postdoctoral research fellow U. N.C. Sch. Medicine, 1955-58, asst. prof. pharmacology, 1958-62, asso. prof., 1962-72; asso. prof. oral biology U. N.C. Sch. Medicine (Dental Research Center), 1967-69, prof., 1969-72, asso. dir., 1968-72; prof. pharmacology U. Ky. Coll. Medicine, Lexington, 1972-77; prof., chmn. dept. pharmacology and toxicology U. Louisville, 1977—; Centennial Alumni Disting. vis. prof. U. N.C. Sch. Medicine, 1979. Contbr. articles to profl. jours. Fellow Acad. Toxicological Scis.; mem. Am. Soc. for Pharmacology and Exptl. Therapeutics, Am. Physiol. Soc., Am. Teratology Soc., Internat. Soc. for Study Xenobiotics, Soc. for Exptl. Biology and Medicine, Soc. Toxicology, Sigma Xi. Home: 14300 Rose Wycombe Rd Prospect KY 40059-9024 Office: U Louisville Dept Pharmacology Louisville KY 40292

WADDEN, RICHARD ALBERT, environmental engineer, educator, consultant, research director; b. Sioux City, Iowa, Oct. 3, 1936; s. Sylvester Francis and Hermina Lillian (Costello) W.; m. Angela Louise Trabert, Aug. 9, 1975; children—Angela Terese, Noah Albert, Nuiko Clare. Student, St. John's U., Collegeville, Minn., 1954-56; B.S. in Chem. Engring., Iowa State U., 1959; M.S. in Chem. Engring, N.C. State U., 1962; Ph.D. in Chem. and Environ. Engring., Northwestern U., 1972. Registered profl. engr., Ill.; cert. indsl. hygienist. Engr. Linde Co., Tonnawanda, N.Y., 1959-60, Humble Oil Co., Houston, 1962-65; instr. engring. Pahlavi U. Peace Corps, Shiraz, Iran, 1965-67; tech. adviser Ill. Pollution Control Bd., Chgo., 1971-72; asst. dir. Environ. Health Resource Ctr. Ill., Chgo., 1972-74; asst. prof. environ. and occupational health scis. Sch. Pub. Health U. Ill.-Chgo., 1972-75, assoc. prof., 1975-79, prof., 1979—, dir., 1984-86, 88-92; dir. Office Tech. Transfer U. Ill. Ctr. for Solid Waste Mgmt. and Resch., 1987-92; dir. indsl. hygiene and hazardous waste tng. programs Occupl. Safety and Health Ctr., U. Ill.-Chgo., Chgo.; vis. scientist Nat. Inst. Environ. Studies, Japan, 1978-79, invited scientist, 1983, 84, 88; cons. air pollution control, health implications of energy devel., indoor air pollution; vis. scholar dept. civil engring. Northwestern U., Evanston, Ill., 1997. Author: Energy Utilization and Environmental Health, 1978, (with P.A. Scheff) Indoor Air Pollution, 1983, Engineering Design for Control of Workplace Hazards, 1987; contbr. numerous articles to profl. publs. Sr. Internat. fellow Fogarty Internat. Ctr.-NIH, 1978-79, 83; WHO fellow, 1984. Mem. AIChE, Am. Chem. Soc., Am. Acad. Environ. Engrs. (diplomate), Am. Acad. Indsl. Hygiene (diplomate), Air and Waste Mgmt. Assn., Am. Indsl. Hygiene Assn., Am. Conf. Govtl. Indsl. Hygienists. Office: U Ill m/c 922 2121 W Taylor St Chicago IL 60612-7260

WADDEN, THOMAS ANTONY, psychologist, educator; b. Richmond, Va., Sept. 3, 1952; s. Thomas Antony Jr. and Mary Lloyd (Cradock) W.; m. Jan Robin Linowitz, Nov. 11, 1984; children: David Joseph, Michael James, Steven Zachary. AB magna cum laude, Brown U., 1975; PhD, U. N.C., 1981. Psychology intern Boston VA Med. Ctr., 1980-81; instr. in psychology U. Pa. Sch. Medicine, Phila., 1981-82, asst. prof. psychology, 1982-87, assoc. prof. psychology, 1987-91, prof. psychology, 1994—; prof. psychology, dir. clin. tng. Syracuse (N.Y.) U., 1992-93; clin. dir. Obesity Rsch. Group, U. Pa., Phila., 1983-91, dir. Weight and Eating Disorders Program, 1994—; dir. Ctr. for Health and Behavior, Syracuse U., 1992-93. Assoc. editor Annals of Behavioral Medicine, 1990-93; mem. editl. bd. Behavior Theraphy, Internat. Jour. Eating Disorders, Jour. Cons. and Clin. Psychology Obesity Rsch.; editor: (with T.B. VanItallie) Treatment of the Seriously Obese Patient, 1992, (with A.J. Stunkard) Obesity: Theory and Therapy, 1993; contbr. chpts. in books; writer numerous sci. papers. Recipient Nat. Rsch. Svc. award NIMH, 1983-85, Rsch. Scientist Devel. award, 1987-91, 94—. Mem. APA, Soc. Behavioral Medicine (bd. dirs. 1987-90), Assn. for Advancement of Behavior Therapy (New Rschr. award 1986), Acad. Behavioral Medicine, Phi Beta Kappa, Sigma Xi. Democrat. Avocations: tennis, squash, symphonic music, guitar. Home: 433 Bolsover Rd Wynnewood PA 19096-1301 Office: U Pa 3600 Market St Fl 738 Philadelphia PA 19104-2641

WADDILL, VAN HULEN, entomology educator; b. Brady, Tex., Aug. 24, 1947. BS, Tex. A&M U., 1970, MS, 1971; PhD, Clemson U., 1974. From asst. prof. to prof. entomology Inst. Food & Agrl. Sci. U. Fla., West Palm Beach, 1975—, ctr. dir.; mem. Coun. Agrl. Sci. & Tech. Mem. Entomol. Soc. Am. Office: U Fla Everglades Rsch Edn Ctr PO Box 8003 Belle Glade FL 33430-8003*

WADDINGHAM, JOHN ALFRED, artist, journalist; b. London, Eng., July 9, 1915; came to U.S., 1927, naturalized, 1943; s. Charles Alfred and Mary Elizabeth (Coles) W.; m. Joan Lee Larson, May 3, 1952; children: Mary Kathryn, Thomas Richard. Student, Coronado (Calif.) Sch. Fine Arts, 1953-54, Portland Art Mus., 1940-65, U. Portland, 1946-47; pupil, Rex Brandt, Eliot Ohara, George Post. Promotion art dir. Oreg. Jour., Portland, 1946-59; with The Oregonian, Portland, 1959-81; editorial art dir. The Oregonian, 1959-81; tchr. watercolor Ore. Soc. Artists, 1954-56; tchr. art Oreg. Sch. Arts and Crafts, 1981—, Portland Community Coll.; represented by several galleries, Oreg. and Wash. One man show includes Art in the Gov.'s Office Ore State Capitol, 1991; rep. mus. rental collections, Portland Art Mus., Bush House, Salem, Ore., U. Oreg. Mus., Vincent Price collection, Ford Times collection, also, Am. Watercolor Soc. Travelling Show; judge art events, 1946—, over 50 one-man shows; ofcl. artist, Kiwanis Internat. Conv., 1966; designed, dir. constrn. cast: concrete mural Genesis, St. Barnabas Episcopal Ch., Portland, 1960; spl. work drawings old Portland landmarks and houses; propr. John Waddingham Hand Prints, fine arts serigraphs and silk screen drawings, 1965—; featured artist: Am. Artist mag., May 1967, June 1990, published in numerous mags. Served with USAAF, 1942-46. Recipient gold medal Salone Internazionale dell' Umorismo, Italy, 1974, 76, 80; honored with a 45 yr. retrospective Assignment: The Artist as Journalist Oreg. Hist. Soc., 1991. Artist mem. Portland Art Mus.; mem. Portland Art Dirs. Club (past pres.), N.W. Watercolor Soc., Am. Watercolor Soc. (hon. assoc.), Watercolor Soc. Oreg., Oreg. Soc. Artists (watercolor tchr.), Multnomah Athletic Club, Jewish Community Ctr., Univ. Oreg. Med. Sch., Art in the Mounts., Oreg. Old Time Fiddlers, Clan Macleay Bagpipe Band. Home and Studio: 955 SW Westwood Dr Portland OR 97201-2744

WADDINGTON, BETTE HOPE (ELIZABETH CROWDER), violinist, educator; b. San Francisco; d. John and Marguerite (Crowder) Waddington; BA in Music, U. Calif. at Berkeley, 1945, postgrad.; postgrad. (scholarship) Juilliard Sch. Music, 1950, San Jose State Coll., 1955; MA in Music and Art, San Francisco U., 1953; violin student of Joseph Fuchs, Melvin Ritter, Frank Gittelson, Felix Khuner, Daniel Bonsack, D.C. Dounis, Naoum Blinder, Eddy Brown. Cert. tchr. music and art K-12 and jr. coll., Calif., libr. elem., secondary and jr. coll., Calif. Violinist Erie (Pa.) Symphony, 1950-51, Dallas Symphony, 1957-58, St. Louis Symphony, 1958-95. Cert. gen. elem. and secondary tchr., Calif.; life cert. music and art for jr. coll.; cert. in librarianship from elem. sch. to jr. coll., Calif. Toured alone and with St. Louis Symphony U.S., Can., Middle East, Japan, China, England, Korea, Europe, Africa; concert master Peninsula Symphony, Redwood City and San Mateo, Calif., Grove Music Soc., N.Y.C.; violinist St. Louis Symphony, 1958-95, violinist emeritus; numerous recordings St. Louis Symphony, 1958—. Mem. Am. String Tchrs. Assn., Am. Musicians Union (St. Louis and San Francisco chpts. life), U. Calif. Alumnae Assn. (Berkeley, life), San Francisco State U. Alumni Assn. (life), Am. String Tchrs. Assn., San Jose State U. Alumni Assn. (life), Sierra Club (life), Alpha Beta Alpha. Avocations: travel, art and archeology history, drawing, painting. Office: St Louis Symphony Orch care Powell Symphony Hall 718 N Grand Blvd Saint Louis MO 63103-1011

WADDINGTON, RAYMOND BRUCE, JR., English language educator; b. Santa Barbara, Calif., Sept. 27, 1935; s. Raymond Bruce and Marjorie Gladys (Waddell) W.; m. Linda Gayle Jones, Sept. 7, 1957 (div.); children: Raymond Bruce, Edward Jackson; m. Kathleen Martha Ward, Oct. 11, 1985. B.A., Stanford U., 1957; Ph.D., Rice U., 1963; postdoctoral (Univ. fellow in Humanities), Johns Hopkins U., 1965-66. Instr. English U. Houston, 1961-62; instr. U. Kans., 1962-63; asst. prof., 1963-65; asst. prof. English lit. U. Wis., Madison, 1966-68; asso. prof. U. Wis., 1968-74, prof., 1974-82; prof. English lit. U. Calif., Davis, 1982—. Author: The Mind's Empire, 1974; co-editor: The Rhetoric of Renaissance Poetry, 1974, The Age of Milton, 1980, The Expulsion of the Jews, 1994; mem. editl. bd. The Medal, 1991; sr. editor: Sixteenth Century Jour.; editor: Garland Studies in the Renaissance. Huntington Library fellow, 1967, 75; Inst. Research in Humanities fellow, 1971-72; Guggenheim fellow, 1972-73; NEH fellow, 1977, 83; Newberry Library fellow, 1978; Am. Philos. Soc. grantee, 1965. Mem. Renaissance Soc. Am., Milton Soc. Am., Am. Numismatic Soc., 16th Century Studies Conf. (pres. 1985), Logos Club. Home: 39 Pershing Ave Woodland CA 95695-2845 Office: U Calif Dept English Davis CA 95616

WADDLE, JOHN FREDERICK, former retail chain executive; b. Somerset, Ky., July 1, 1927; s. Lewis Everett and Anna Hail (Prather) W.; m. Catherine Joan Osborn, June 3, 1977; children: Lewis Victor, Joan Catherine, John Frederick. B.S., U. Ky., 1949; M.S., NYU, 1952. With Sears, Roebuck and Co., Chgo., 1949-85; nat. mgr. toys Sears, Roebuck and Co., 1969-72, asst. to sr. exec. v.p. merchandising, 1972-76, group nat. merchandising mgr., 1977-78, v.p. children's apparel, 1978-82; mng. dir., exec. v.p. Sears World Trade, Inc., Chgo., 1982-85. Served with USN, 1945-46. Republican. Presbyterian.

WADE, BEN FRANK, college administrator; b. Roanoke, Va., July 20, 1935; s. Frank Hart and Clyde Temple (Weaver) W.; m. Janice Marie Wine, June 14, 1958; children—Andrea Marie, Laurel Faye. B.A., Bridgewater Coll., 1957; M.Div. cum laude, United Theol. Sem., 1960; S.T.M., Boston U., 1961; M.S., Columbia U., 1966; Ph.D., Hartford Sem. Found., 1966. Prof. Shenandoah Coll., Winchester, Va., 1963-65, United Theol. Sem., Dayton, Ohio, 1965-69, James Madison U., Harrisonburg, Va., 1969-71; acad. dean Brevard Coll., N.C., 1971-73, Fla. So. Coll., Lakeland, Fla., 1973-77; pres. Westmar Coll., LeMars, Iowa, 1977-79; provost Bridgewater Coll., Va., 1979-85; v.p., acad. dean Fla. So. Coll., Lakeland, Fla., 1985-96, v.p., dean emeritus, 1996—; mem., chmn. accreditation visit teams So. Assn. Colls. and Schs., State Council Higher Edn. Va.; vis. lectr., cons. Div. chmn. YMCA Capital Funds Campaign, Lakeland, Fla., 1975. Named Disting. Alumnus, Bridgewater Coll., 1994, Hon. Alumnus, Fla. So. Coll., 1996; Hartzler fellow Hartford Sem. Found., 1961-62, 62-63. Mem. Theta Chi Beta, Phi Eta Sigma, Omicron Delta Kappa. Mem. Ch. of Brethren. Avocations: breadmaking; saddle horses; music. Home: 3733 Highland Fairways Blvd Lakeland FL 33810-5765

WADE, BENNY BERNAR, educational administrator; b. Crisp County, Ga., Oct. 3, 1939; s. Julius D. and Eleanor Eugenia (Boulware) W.; m. Merle Bailey Wade, Nov. 11, 1957; children: Noel, Tara. BS in Edn., Ga. So. Coll., 1964; MEd, U. Ga., 1968, Specialist Edn., 1973, EdD, 1977. Lic. reading specialist gifted, adminstrn. and supervision. Tchr., coach Turner County Bd. Edn., Ashburn, Ga., 1964-67; acad. skills coord. Ga. Southwestern Coll., Americus, 1968-71, asst. prof., 1978; curriculum dir. Dooly County Bd. Edn., Vienna, Ga., 1971-78; dir. edn. svcs. agy. Heart of Ga. Coop. Ednl. Svcs. Agy./Regional Ednl. Svcs. Agy., Eastman, 1979-94; exec. dir. RANREB Learning Enhancement Svcs., Inc., Eastman, Ga., 1994—; cons. parent edn., Eastman, 1977—; mem. Regional Ednl. Svcs. Agy. stds. task force Ga. Dept. Edn., Atlanta, 1988-91; mentor, coach So. Regional Ednl. Bd., 1993-94; owner Sylvan Learning Ctr., Albany, Ga., 1995—. Author: Benny's Book of Peruvian Proverbs, 1983; editor newsletter Ga. RESA Dirs., 1992. Organizer Four Dimensional Wellness Club, Eastman, 1991; activist Environ. Concers Agy., Eastman, 1989—. Exp. tchr. fellow U.

Ga., Athens, 1967; recipient Alumni award for ednl. leadership Ga. Southwestern Coll., Americus, 1980. Mem. Internat. Reading Assn. (local leadership chairperson 1992-93), Ga. Regional Ednl. Svcs. Agy. Dirs. (pres. 1984-85), Ga. Assn. Ednl. Leaders, Amarathine Runners Alliance of the Cosmos (founder), Eastman Rotary (pres. 1985-86), Phi Delta Kappa. Democrat. Methodist. Avocations: reading, writing, running, ruminating, renewing. Home: PO Box 334 Cordele GA 31010 Office: RANREB Learning Enhancement Svcs Inc PO Box 334 Cordele GA 31015-0334

WADE, EDWIN LEE, writer, lawyer; b. Yonkers, N.Y., Jan. 26, 1932; s. James and Helen Pierce (Kinne) W.; m. Nancy Lou Sells, Mar. 23, 1957; children: James Lee, Jeffrey K. BS, Columbia U., 1954; MA, U. Chgo., 1956; JD, Georgetown U., 1965. Bar: Ill. 1965; fgn. svc. officer U.S. Dept. State, 1956-57; mktg. analyst Chrysler Internat., S.A., Switzerland, 1957-61; intelligence officer CIA, 1961-63; industry analyst U.S. Internat. Trade Commn., 1963-65; gen. atty. Universal Oil Products Co., Des Plaines, Ill., 1965-72; atty. Amsted Industries, Inc., Chgo., 1972-73; chief counsel dept. gen. svcs. State of Ill., Springfield, 1973-75; sr. atty. U.S. Gypsum Co., Chgo., 1975-84; gen. atty., USG Corp., 1985, corp. counsel, 1986, asst. gen. counsel, 1987, corp. sec., 1987-90, corp. sec., asst. gen. counsel, 1990-93; prin. Edwin L. Wade, 1993-95; instr. Roosevelt U., Chgo., 1995-96. Author: (book) Constitution 2000: A Federalist Proposal for the Next Century, 1995; editor, pub. Let's Talk Sense, A Public Affairs Newsletter, 1994—. Fellow Chgo. Bar Assn. (life); mem. ABA, Ill. Bar Assn., Union League Club Chgo., Am. Philatelic Soc., Royal Philatelic Soc. Can., Toastmasters Internat. Home: 434 Mary Ln Crystal Lake IL 60014-7257 Office: Let's Talk Sense PO Box 6716 Chicago IL 60680-6716

WADE, GLEN, electrical engineer, educator; b. Ogden, Utah, Mar. 19, 1921; s. Lester Andrew and Nellie (Vanderwerff) W.; m. LaRee Bailey, Mar. 20, 1945; children: Kathleen Ann, RaLee, Lisa Jean, Mary Sue. B.S. in Elec. Engring, U. Utah, 1948, M.S., 1949; Ph.D., Stanford U., 1954. Research group leader, asso. prof. elec. engring. Stanford U., 1955-60; asso. dir. engring., microwave and power tube div. Raytheon Co., 1960-61, asst gen. mgr. research div., 1961-63; dir. Sch. Elec. Engring., Cornell U., 1963-66, J.P. Levis prof. engring., 1963-66; prof. elec. engring. U. Calif. at Santa Barbara, 1966—; indsl. advisor U. R.I., 1961-63; vis. lectr. Harvard, 1963; cons. to industry, 1956—; vis. prof. Tokyo U., 1971; Fulbright-Hays lectr., Spain, 1972-73; cons. mem. Dept. Def. Adv. Group Electron Devices, 1966-73; Spl. Chair prof. Nat. Taiwan U., 1980-81, internationally renowned fgn. scholar lectureship, 1988; UN vis. prof. Nanjing Inst. Tech., 1986; UN vis. prof. S.E. U. People's Republic of China, 1989, Nat. Com. Sci. and Tech. vis. prof. U. Guanajuato, Mex., 1994-97; elected mem. The Electromagnetics Acad., 1990. Editor: Transactions on Electron Devices, 1961-71, IEEE Jour. Quantum Electronics, 1965-68; series editor: Harcourt Brace Jovanovich, 1964—; contbr. articles to profl. jours. U.S. del. Tech. Cooperation Program internat. meeting, 1970. Served with USNR, 1944-46. Recipient ann. award Nat. Electronics Conf., 1959, Outstanding Teaching award Acad. Senate, U. Calif., Santa Barbara, 1977, Prof. of Yr. award U. Calif. at Santa Barbara Mortar Bd. Sr. Honor Soc., 1988, Hon. Chairmanship award Twentieth Acoustical Imaging, 1992. Fellow IEEE (life) (mem. adminstrv. com. profl. group election devices 1960-71, mem. publs. bd., chmn. info. processing com., mem. exec. com. 1971-72, dir. 1971-72, chmn. ednl. activities bd. 1971-72, editor proc. 1977-80, Centennial award 1984); mem. Am. Phys. Soc., Phi Kappa Phi, Tau Beta Pi, Sigma Xi, Eta Kappa Nu (Outstanding Young Elec. Engr. award 1955). Home: 1098 Golf Rd Santa Barbara CA 93108-2411

WADE, JAMES O'SHEA, publisher; b. Atlanta, June 17, 1940; s. Richard J. and Mary Clare (O'Shea) W.; m. Linda Norman, June 19, 1971; 1 child, Christopher Scott. AB magna cum laude, Harvard U., 1962. Editor Blaisdell Pub. Co., N.Y.C., 1963-65; asst. to pres., sr. editor Macmillan Co., 1966-69; editor-in-chief World Pub. Co., 1969-71; v.p., editorial dir. David McKay Co., 1971-74; founder, pres. Wade Pub. Co., Inc., N.Y.C., 1975-78; exec. v.p. Rawson, Wade Pubs., Inc., N.Y.C., 1978-82; sr. editor Crown Pubs., Inc., N.Y.C., 1982-85, exec. editor, 1985-95, v.p., 1988-95; with Ind. Editors Group, 1996—. Mem. Century Club (N.Y.C.), Iroquois/D.U. Club (Harvard), Hasty-Pudding Inst. 1770 (Harvard U.). Democrat. Home and Office: 1565 Baptist Church Rd Yorktown Heights NY 10598-5812

WADE, KAREN, national parks administrator; b. Cortez, Colo.; m. John W. Wade (div.); m. Lyman Jennings, 1990; children: Mylea, Michael. Student, U. Colo.; B.Bus., Ft. Lewis Coll.; postgrad., U. No. Ariz., U. Tenn., Knoxville. So. region trail coord. Appalachian trail Project Nat. Park Svc., 1978-83; mgmt. asst. Shenandoah Nat. Park, Va., 1983-85; supt. Ft. McHenry Nat. Monument and Historic Shrine Hampton Nat. Hist. Park, Balt., 1985-87; supt. Guadalupe Mountains Nat. Park, Tex., 1987-90, Wrangell-St. Elias Nat. Park and Preserve, Alaska, 1990-94, Great Smoky Mountains Nat. Park, Gatlinburg, Tenn., 1994—. Office: Great Smoky Mountains National Park 107 Park Hdqrs Rd Gatlinburg TN 37738

WADE, PAMELA SUE, women's health nurse; b. Gallup, N.Mex., June 19, 1950; d. Nolan Fisher and Claudia Jean (Coleman) Carter; m. Bill Wade, Apr. 3, 1987; children: Claudia Rebecca Sosa, Oscar Arturo Sosa Jr. Lic. vis. nurse, El Paso Community Coll., 1973, ADN, 1982; BSN, U. Tex. at El Paso, 1990. Cert. in in-patient obstetrics. Staff nurse Vista Hills Med. Ctr., El Paso, Providence Meml. Hosp., El Paso; home health nurse Sun City Home Care Inc., El Paso, patient care coord., 1996—; maternal-child nursing instr. N.Mex. State U., Alamagordo. Mem. Golden Key Honor Soc. Home: 115 Virginia Canyon Rd Ruidoso NM 88345-6645

WADE, ROBERT GLENN, engineering executive; b. Sturgeon, Mo., Nov. 21, 1933; s. Robert Clifford and Mildred Guinn (Bartee) W.; m. Geraldine Harris, Dec. 27, 1959; 1 child, Carolyn Ruth. BSCE, U. Mo., 1955. Registered profl. engr., Mo., Kans. Structural engr. Carter-Waters Corp., Kansas City, Mo., 1958-62; project mgr. Pfuhl & Stevson, Kansas City, 1962-76; prin. Stevson-Hall & Wade, Inc., Kansas City, 1976-82; pres. Structural Engring. Assocs., Inc., Kansas City, 1982-85, chmn., chief exec. officer, 1985—; mem. Mo. Bd. Architects, Engrs. and Land Surveyors, 1992—; mem. Midwest Concrete Industry Bd., pres., 1975-76. Contbg. author: Quality Assurance for Consulting Engineers, 1986. Com. mem. Downtown Coun., Kansas City, 1990. 1st lt. USAF, 1956-58. Recipient 1st merit award Midwest Concrete Industry Bd., 1976, award of excellence Am. Inst. Steel Constrn., 1982, Excellence in Design award Prestressed Concrete Inst., 1988. Fellow ASCE (pres. Kansas City sect. 1986-87, Leadership award 1987); mem. Am. Cons. Engrs. Coun. (firm rep., bd. dirs. 1987-88), Cons. Engrs. Coun. Mo. (firm rep., pres. 1986-87, Svc. award 1987). Avocation: golf. Office: Structural Engring Assocs 101 W 11th St Kansas City MO 64105-1803

WADE, ROBERT HIRSCH BEARD, international consultant, former government and educational association official; b. Tamaqua, Pa., Oct. 5, 1916; s. Edgar Gerber and Florence Annabelle (Hirsch) W.; m. Eleanor Marguerite Borden, Sept. 14, 1946; 1 son, Gregory Borden. A.B. magna cum laude, Lafayette Coll., 1937; diplome d'etudes universitaires, Bordeaux U., 1938; Ph.D., Yale U., 1942. Instr. French Yale U., 1939-42; chief Far Eastern analyst Office Naval Intelligence, 1946-54; asst. Office Nat. Security Coun. Affairs, Dept. Def., Washington, 1954-56, dir., 1956-61; spl. asst. to asst. sec. state for ednl. and cultural affairs, 1962; dir. multilateral and spl. activities Bur. Ednl. and Cultural Affairs, Dept. State, 1962-64; U.S. permanent rep. to UNESCO, with rank of minister, 1964-69; asst. dir. U.S. Arms Control & Disarmament Agy., Washington, 1969-73; exec. dir. Fgn. Student Service Council, Washington, 1974-77; dir. Washington office Am. Assembly Collegiate Schs. Bus., 1977-85; internat. cons., 1986—; Mem. U.S. del. to UNESCO Gen. Confs., 1962, 1964, 1966, 68; dep. U.S. mem. exec. bd. UNESCO, 1964-69; mem. U.S. Nat. Commn. for UNESCO, 1977-83, vice chmn., 1978-79. Author, editor: Management for XXI Century, 1982. Trustee Am. Coll. in Paris, 1967-78, chmn. bd., 1967-69. Served to lt. USNR, 1942-46, PTO. Recipient Merit Citation award Nat. Civil Service League. Fellow Acad. Internat. Bus.; mem. Am. Fgn. Svc. Assn., Friends of Vieilles Maisons Francaises, Phi Beta Kappa, Kappa Delta Rho (Ordo Honorium 1991). Republican. Christian Scientist. Clubs: Union Interalliee (Paris), Racing (Paris); Chevy Chase (Washington). Avocations: tennis, swimming, piano. Home and Office: 3049 W Lane Ky NW Washington DC 20007-3057

WADE, ROBERT PAUL, lawyer; b. Atlantic City, Aug. 22, 1936; s. John Joseph and Irene Madeline (Saxon) W.; m. Jeanne Krohn, Aug. 5, 1979; children: Elliott Saxon, Kellyn Deirdre. AB, George Washington U., 1963, JD, 1968. Bar: D.C. 1968, Md. 1990. Assoc. Denning and Wohlstetter, Washington, 1968-69; atty. Office Compt. Gen. U.S., Washington, 1969-72; gen. counsel Nat. Endowment for the Arts, Washington, 1972-83; ptnr. Lowe, Bressler & Wade, Washington, 1983-86, Silverberg and Wade, Washington, 1986-94, Robert Wade, Esq., Law Offices, 1994—; vis. lectr. in intellectual property, nonprofit and employment law Stanford U., NYU, George Washington U. With U.S. Army, 1955-58. Mem. Phi Sigma Tau, Nat. Honor Soc. (philosophy). Home: RR 1 Box 467 Bluemont VA 22012-9510 Office: Ste 450 1625 Massachusetts Ave NW Washington DC 20036-2246

WADE, ROYCE ALLEN, financial services representative; b. Medford, Wis., Apr. 30, 1932; s. Charles L. and Mildred H. (Clarin) W.; m. Corinne Mae Weber, June 30, 1956; children: Suzanne Mae, Debra Ann. BS (acad. scholar), U. Wis., Stevens Point, 1954; MDiv, Garrett Theol. Sem., Evanston, Ill., 1960; MS in Adult Edn., U. Wis., Milw., 1968; postgrad. U. Wis., Madison, 1970-75; grad. Realtors Inst. Ordained to ministry Meth. Ch., 1960; cert. pastoral counseling and interpersonal relations. Pastor Richmond (Wis.) Meth. Ch., 1956-58, Asbury United Meth. Ch., Janesville, Wis., 1958-61; tchr., guidance counselor Edgerton (Wis.) High Sch., 1961-62; assoc. pastor Community United Meth. Ch., Whitefish Bay, Wis., 1962-66; pastor Simpson and Gardner United Meth. Chs., Milw., 1966-68; assoc. pastor St. Luke United Meth. Ch., Sheboygan, Wis., 1968-69; pastor Poynette and Inch United Meth. Chs., 1969-74; dir. Adult Study Ctr., Portage, Wis., 1974-75; dir. growth and devel. Profl. Products & Services, Inc., Sauk City, Wis., 1976-83; realtor Dick Marquardt Agy., Poynette, 1983-86, Don Lee Realty, Inc., Portage, Wis., 1986-87, Noble Properties, Poynette, 1987, Anchor Real Estate Services, Madison, 1988-93; personal fin. analyst Primerica Fin. Svcs., Madison, 1992—; HRD cons., 1983-96; curriculum cons. U. Wis. Sch. Nursing, 1974-76, instr. small group seminar, 1974-76, supr. behavioral disabilities student tchrs., 1974-76; adult edn. instr. Wis. Conf. United Meth. Ch., 1964-69. Village trustee, Poynette, 1977-81; mem. Police Aux., Whitefish Bay; bd. dirs. North Shore Council Human Relations, Milw., Inter Faith Council, Milw., Poynette Area Community Devel. Orgn., 1983-87. Served with C.I.C., AUS., 1954-56. Mem. Adult Edn. Assn., Am. Soc. Tng. and Devel., Nat. Assn. Realtors, Wis. Realtors Assn., Phi Delta Kappa. Lodge: Optimists. Research on participation in adult intructional groups using Eriksonian ego-stage theory. Home: 131 N Cleveland St Poynette WI 53955-0115 Office: 6414 Copps Ave Ste 109 Madison WI 53716-3742

WADE, SAMUEL DAVID, medical products company executive; b. Hempstead, N.Y., Dec. 6, 1949; s. Samuel Davis and Pauline L. (Watkins) W.; m. Dorothy Elizabeth Dodge; 1 child, Alexander Andrew. BS, Colo. State U., 1971. Dir. internat. quality assurance and regulatory affairs Boston Scientific Internat., Watertown, Mass., 1982-89; dir. quality assurance and regulatory affairs Bard Vascular Systems divsn. C.R. Bard, Billerica, Mass., 1989-91, St. Jude Med., Chelmsford, Mass., 1991-94; v.p. quality and regulatory affairs Infusaid divsn. Pfizer Inc., Norwood, Mass., 1994-95; prin. The Acton (Mass.) Group, 1995-97; v.p. operations Telemed Systems, Inc., Marlborough, Mass., 1997—; bd. dirs. On Site Acad. Selectman Town of Maynard, Mass., 1982-84, mem. bd. of health, 1974-81; mem. adv. bd. County of Middlesex, Maynard, 1983; active Stow (Mass.) Conservation Commn., 1986. Recipient Community Svc. awards Mass. Ho. of Reps., 1984, Mass. Senate, 1984. Mem. Regulatory Affairs Profl. Soc., Am. Soc. for Quality Control, Soc. for Clin. Trials, Critical Incident Stress Debriefing Team, Am. Meteorol. Soc., N.Y. Acad. Scis. Avocations: birding, gardening, nature, photography, literature. Home: 12 Grasshopper Ln Acton MA 01720-4607

WADE, THOMAS EDWARD, electrical engineering educator, university research administrator; b. Jacksonville, Fla., Sept. 14, 1943; s. Wilton Fred and Alice Lucyle (Hedge) W.; m. Ann Elizabeth Chitty, Aug. 6, 1966; children: Amy Renee, Nathan Thomas, Laura Ann. BSEE, U. Fla.-Gainesville, 1966, MSEE, 1968, PhD, 1974. Cert. Rsch. Adminstr., 1992—. Interim asst. prof. U. Fla.-Gainesville, 1974-76; prof. elec. engring. Miss. State U., Starkville, 1976-85, state-wide dir. microelectronics rsch. lab., Miss., 1978-85, assoc. dean., prof. electrical engring. U. South Fla., Tampa, 1985—, dir. Engring. Indsl. Experiment Sta., 1986-93, exec. dir. Ctrs. for Engring. Devel. and Rsch., 1985-90, mem. presdl. faculty adv. com. for rsch. and tech. devel., 1986-88, mem. fed. demonstration project com. for contracts and grants, 1986-88; mem. adv. bd. USF Exec. Fellows Program, 1987-91; chmn. evaluation task force applied rsch. grants program High Tech. and Industry Coun. State of Fla., 1988-90, vice chmn. microelectronics and materials subcom. 1987-93, mem. telecom. subcom., 1988-89, chmn. legis. report com. FHTIC, 1989-90, chmn. U. sabbatical com., 1997-98; vice chmn. subcom. on microelectronics and materials Enterprise Fla. Innovation Partnership, 1993-94, chmn. univ. sabbatical com., 1997—; mem. Tampa Bay Internat. Super Task Force, 1986-92, vice chmn. edn. com. 1988; dir. Fla. Ctr. for Microelectronics Design and Test, 1986-88; bd. dirs. NASA Ctr. Comml. Devel. of Space Comm. Ctr., Fla., 1990-93; rev. panel govt.-univ.-industry rsch. round table for fed. demonstration project, NAS, 1988; solid state circuit specialist Applied Micro-Circuits Corp., San Diego, 1981-82; sr. scientist NASA Marshall Space Flight Ctr., Huntsville, Ala., 1983; scientist Trilogy Semiconductor Corp., Santa Clara, Calif., 1984; organizer, chmn. Very Large Scale Integrated/Ultra Large Scale Integrated Multilevel Interconnection Conf., Seminar and Exhbn., editor proceedings, 1991—; organizer, gen. chmn. Dielectrics for Ultra Large Scale Integrated Multilevel Interconnection Conf., 1995—, Chem.-Mech.-Polish Planarization for Ultra Large Scale Integrated Multilevel Interconnection Conf., 1996—, ; instr. short courses Dielectric and Chem.-Mech. Polish Planarization Ultra Large Scale Integration, 1996—; cons. in field. Author: Polyimides for Very Large Scale Integrated Applications, 1984, (U.S. Army handbook) Modern Very Large Scale Integrated Circuit Fabrication Processess, 1984, Photosensitive Polyimides for Very Large Scale Integrated Applications, 1986, Very Large Scale Multilevel Interconnection Tutorial, 1987—, Very Large Scale Multilevel Interconnection Tutorial, 1987—; contbr. to encys.; contbr. 120 articles to profl. jours. Treas. Tampa Palms Civic Assn., 1994-95; vol., United Fund, Miss. State U., 1983-85. Recipient Outstanding Engring. Teaching award Coll. Engring. U. Fla., 1976, Cert. of Recognition NASA (5 times), 1981-88, Outstanding Rsch. award Sigma Xi, 1984, Outstanding Contbn. to Sci. and Tech. award Fla. Gov., 1989, 90. Mem. AAAS, NSPE, IEEE (sr. mem., guest editor periodical 1982, gen. chmn. Internat. Very Large Scale Integrated Multilevel Interconnection Conf. annually 1984-90, editor conf. proceedings 1984-90, chmn. acad. affairs com. CHMT Soc. 1984-86, gen. chmn. univ./govt./industry microelectronics symposium, 1981, tech. program commn., 1991, bd. dirs. workshop on tungsten and other refractory metals 1987-90), Am. Soc. Engring. Edn. (gen. chmn. engring. research counc. ann. meeting 1987, chmn. engring. rsch. coun. adminstrv. com. 1987-90, chmn. coun., 1990-92, session chmn. ann. meeting 1990, 92, bd. dirs. 1990-92, mem. Nominations Com. 1992-94, mem. Long Range Planning Com. 1992-95, recipient ASEE Centennial Cert. 1992, 2d Century Cert. 1993), World Future Soc., Internat. Soc. Hybrid Microelectronics, Assn. U.S. Army (bd. dirs. Suncoast chpt. 1991-93), Soc. Photo Optical Instrumentation Engring., Univ. Faculty Senate Assn. of Miss. (organizer 1985), Am. Vacuum Soc., Am. Phys. Soc., Am. Electronics Assn., Am. Inst. Physics, Nat. Coun. Univ. Rsch. Adminstrs., Soc. Rsch. Adminstrs. (external rels. com. for SRA 1988-91), Fla. Engring. Soc. (v.p. edn. com. 1987-92, pres. 1989-90, bd. dirs. 1989-90, Fla. engring. found. trustee 1989-90, ann. meeting steering com. 1989-90, Outstanding Svc. to the Profession award 1992), Soc. Am. Mil. Engring., Order of Engrs., 1991, Sigma Xi (v.p. 1985), Tau Beta Pi (Fla. Alpha chpt. pres. 1969, 71, nat. outstanding chpt. award 1969, 71, faculty advisor Miss. Alpha chpt. 1977-85, faculty advisor Fla. Gamma chpt. 1986—, recipient outstanding hon. soc. advisor award, 1994), Eta Kappa Nu (pres. 1968), Sigma Tau, Omicron Delta Kappa, Soc. Am. Inventors, Fla. Blue Key (v.p. 1972, sec, 1971), Epsilon Lambda Chi (founder 1970, pres. 1971). Club: Downtown Tampa Rotary (Paul Harris Fellow 1987, perfect attendance award 1986—, chmn. com. on environ. issues 1990), Rotary Club New Tampa (organizer, charter mem., pres. 1995-96, v.p. 1996-97, dir. internat. svc. 1997—). Active First Bapt. Ch., Temple Terrace, Fla., vice-chmn. bd. deacons 1989-90, chmn. bd. deacons, 1990-91, 93-94, chmn. pastor search com. 1990-91, vice chmn. long range plannning com., 1989-91, vice chmn. pastor search com., 1994-95, dir. adult coed III Sunday sch. dept. 1993-94; ch. coun. 1994-95. Avocations: collecting antique furniture, carpentry, restoring antique sports cars, basketball. Home: 5316 Witham Ct E Tampa FL 33647-1026

WADEMAN, PATSY ANN, psychiatric, geriatrics nurse; b. Atlantic, Iowa, Nov. 20, 1943; d. Willie Hollesen and Annie Mae (Lewis) Hollesen Bennet; m. Fredrick N. Wademan, Sept. 11, 1966; children: Stephen, Linnea, Bethany. Diploma, Mercy Hosp., Council Bluffs, Iowa, 1966; BGS in Gerontology, U. Nebr., Omaha. Cert. psychiat. mental health nurse, gerontol. nurse. Nurse Nebraska City (Nebr.) Pub. Schs., 1966-68, St. Mary's Hosp., Nebraska City, 1973-74, 76-78; staff nurse Duffs Friendship Villa Nursing Home, Nebraska City, 1986-88; dir. nursing Nebraska City Manor, 1988-89; staff nurse Med. Ctr. U. Nebr. Med. Ctr., Omaha, 1989-97; health coord. Head Start, Tecumseh, Nebr., 1984-86; rsch. nurse intern I U. Nebr. Med. Ctr., Omaha, 1995—, rsch. nurse intern II, 1996-97; instr. Southeast C.C., Lincoln, Nebr., 1976-84; mem. Nat. Coun. on Aging. Mem. Am. Psychiat. Nurses Assn., Am. Gerontol. Nurses Assn., Nebr. Gerontol. Nurses Assn., Golden Key Nat. Honor Soc.

WADENBERG, MARIE-LOUISE GERTRUD, psychopharmacologist, researcher; b. Stockholm, Nov. 11, 1944; d. Sten Helge and Maj Gertrud (Vilgon) Borgendahl; m. Anders Einar Wadenberg, Aug. 4, 1973 (div. Dec. 1988); children: Andreas, Sofia, Mattias. Pianist diploma, Borgarskolan, Stockholm, 1971; BA, U. Stockholm, 1984, PhD, 1994. Piano playing instr. Stockholm, 1968-86; asst. rschr. Astra Pharms., Södertälje, Sweden, 1989-90; postdoctoral fellow, prin. investigator Scott & White Clinic, Temple, Tex., 1994—. Contbr. articles to profl. jours. and sci. meeting abstracts. Grantee Swedish Med. Rsch. Coun., Stockholm, 1994, Swedish Rsch. Coun. in Humanities and Social Scis., Stockholm, 1995, 96, Swedish Inst., Stockholm, 1994, 95. Mem. AAAS, Soc. Neurosci., Internat. Brain Rsch. Orgn., European Neurosci. Assn., Serotoni Club, J.B. Johnston Club. Avocations: music, skiing, arts. Office: Scott and White Clinic Dept Psychiatry 2401 S 31st St Temple TX 76508-0001

WADKINS, LANNY, professional golfer; b. Richmond, Va., Dec. 5, 1949; s. Jerry Lanston and Francis Ann (Burnett) W.; m. Rachel Irene Strong, Jan. 2, 1971; 1 child, Jessica. Student, Wake Forest U. Winner Sahara Invitational, 1972, PGA, 1977, World Series of Golf, 1977, Can. PGA, 1978, Tournament Players' Championship, 1979, 82, 83, Los Angeles Open, 1979, Phoenix Open, 1982, Greater Greensboro, 1983, Bob Hope Desert Classic, 1985, Doral Ryder, 1987, Hawaiian Open, 1988, Colonial Open, 1988, Anheuser Busch Classic, 1990, Hawaiian Open, 1991, Greater Hartford Open, 1992; mem. Ryder Cup Team, 1993. Office: care PGA Tour 112 Tpc Blvd Ponte Vedra Beach FL 32082-3046*

WADLER, ARNOLD L., lawyer; b. Bklyn., Aug. 15, 1943; s. Samuel and Anne (Lowenthal) W.; m. Elissa I. Devor, Sept. 17, 1967; children: Craig A., Todd J. BA, Bklyn. Coll., 1964; JD, NYU, 1967. Bar: N.Y. 1968, N.J. 1974. Asst. gen. counsel Metromedia, Inc., N.Y.C., 1968-82, assoc. gen. counsel, Los Angeles, 1982-85, v.p., gen. counsel, Secaucus, N.J., 1985-86; exec. v.p., gen. counsel, sec. Metromedia Internat. Group, Inc., East Rutherford, 1986—; pres., S&A Restaurant Corp., East Rutherford, 1992; sr. v.p., gen. counsel Metromedia Co., Inc., 1995, also bd. dirs. Mem. Zoning Bd. Adjustment, Marlboro Twp., N.J., 1980-82; exec. v.p. Marlboro Jewish Ctr., 1980-82. Mem. ABA, N.Y. Bar Assn. Lodge: KP (asst. sec. 1961-63). Office: Metromedia Co Met Exec Towers 1 Meadowlands Plz Fl 6 East Rutherford NJ 07073-2100

WADLEY, FREDIA STOVALL, state commissioner; b. Winchester, Tenn.. BS, Tenn Tech U., 1967; MD, U. Tenn., 1969; MSHPA, U. Cin., 1978. Diplomate Am. Bd. Pediats. Pediat. intern City of Memphis Hosp., 1970, pediat. resident, 1971-72; clin. instr. pediats. dept. pediats. U. Tenn. Ctr. for Health Scis., Memphis, 1973-74; pvt. practice Winchester, Tenn., 1974-75; instr. phys. assessment course dept. nursing U. Tenn., Chattanooga, 1975-76; dir. med. svcs. Dept. Health and Environ. Southeast Region, Chattanooga, 1975-80, regional dir., 1981-83; chief med. officer Dept. Health and Environ. Commr.'s Office, Nashville, 1984-87; dir. Met. Health Dept., Nashville, 1987-95; commr. Dept. Health, Nashville, 1995—; clin. asst. prof. dept. pediats. Meharry Med. Coll., 1985—; mem. faculty staff preventive medicine divsn. Quillen Dischner Med. Coll., 1985-87; vol. faculty mem. dept. nursing U. Tenn. Ctr. for Health Scis., Memphis, 1977-83, U. Tenn., Knoxville, 1977-83; mem. preventive medicine resident adv. com. Meharry Family Medicine Dept., 1988—; adj. assoc. prof. nursing dept. family and cmty. health Vanderbilt U., 1988—; presenter in field. Contbr. articles to profl. jours. Mem. HSA III Task Force on Ambulatory Health Care Problems, 1977, HSA III Bd., 1981-82; mem. southeast Tenn. regional placement com. Tenn. Med. Loan Scholarship Program, 1978-79; bd. dirs. Southeast Tenn. Chpt. Kidney Found., 1981, Vol. Healthcare Sys., Inc., 1988-90, Vanderbilt AIDS Project, 1990, United Way Mid. Tenn., 1992-95, ARC, 1992; mem. Tenn. Sch. health Coalition, 1985—, Cmty. Coalition for Minority Health, 1988, Mayor's Substance Abuse Action Team, 1990; active Brentwood United Meth., Sunday Sch. tchr. 6th grade, 1984-87; chmn. Tenn. AIDS Adv. Com., 1987-88, Davidson County Child Fatality Rev. Team, 1994-95, others. Mem. AMA, APHA (Charles G. Jordan award for outstanding accomplishments in field of pub. health so. br. 1981), Southern Health Assn. (chmn. awards com. and governing coun. 1981-83, pres. 1989-90, spl. meritorious award for outstanding contbns. to orgn. and pub. health 1992), Tenn. Pub. Health Assn. (pres. 1990-91, spl. meritorious award 1993), Tenn. Health Officers, Tenn. Pediat. Soc., Tenn. Med. Assn., Nashville/Davidson County Acad. Medicine, Davidson County Pediat. Soc. Address: 909 Lakemont Dr Nashville TN 37220-2112

WADLEY, M. RICHARD, consumer products executive; b. Lehi, Utah; s. Merlyn R. and Verla Ann (Ball) W.; m. Nancy Zwiers; children: Lisa Kathleen, Staci Lin, Eric Richard, Nicole Marie. BS, Brigham Young U., 1967; MBA, Northwestern U., 1968. Brand asst. packaged soap and detergent divsn. Procter & Gamble Co., Cin., 1968-69, asst. brand mgr. packaged soap and detergent divsn., 1970-71, brand mgr. Dawn detergent, 1972-73, copy supr. packaged soap and detergent divsn., 1974-75, brand mgr. Tide detergent, 1975-77, assoc. advt. mgr. packaged soap and detergent divsn., 1977-81; corp. product dir. Hallmark Cards, Inc., Kansas City, Mo., 1982-83, corp. product dir. Ambassador Cards divsn., 1983-85; v.p., gen. mgr. feminine protection divsn. Tambrands Inc., Lake Success, N.Y., 1986-88; sr. v.p. Bongrain, Inc., N.Y.C., 1988-89; pres., CEO Alta-Dena Inc., Divsn. of Bongrain, Inc., 1989-91; pres. The Summit Group, 1991—; chmn., CEO T-Chem Products Inc., 1993—; bd. dirs. T-Chem Products. Bd. dirs. Long Beach Opera, 1991-95, L.I. Friends of the Arts, 1986-88; mem. adv. bd. Bus. Sch. Calif. State U., Long Beach, 1991-93. Avocations: Civil War history, tennis, travel.

WADLEY, SUSAN SNOW, anthropologist; b. Balt., Nov. 18, 1943; d. Chester Page and Ellen Snow (Foster) W.; m. Bruce Woods Derr, Dec. 28, 1971 (div. July 1989); children: Shona Snow, Laura Woods; m. Richard Olanoff, July 4, 1992. BA, Carleton Coll., Northfield, 1965; MA, U. Chgo., 1967, PhD, 1973. Instr. Syracuse U., 1970-73, asst. prof., 1973-76, dir. fgn. and comparative studies program, 1978-83, prof., 1982, dir. So. Asia Ctr., 1985—. Ford-Maxwell prof. South Asian Studies, 1996—, chair anthropology dept., 1990-95; trustee Am. Inst. Indian Studies, Chgo., 1984—, exec. com., 1991-94; mem. joint com. South Asia Social Sci. Rsch. Coun., 1982-89. Author: Shakti: Power in the Conceptual Struture of Krimpur Women, 1975, Women in India: Two Perspectives, 1978, revised, 1989, 95, Struggling with Destiny in Karimpur, 1925-84, 1994; editor: Power of Tamil Women, 1980, Oral Epics in India, 1989, Media and the Transformation of Religion in South Asia, 1995. Pres. Edward Smith Parent Tchr. Orgn., Syracuse, 1988-89. Grantee NSF, 1967-69, U.S. Dept. Edn., 1983-84, Smithsonian Instn., 1983-84, Am. Inst. Indian Studies, 1989, Social Scis. Rsch. Coun., 1989, NEH, 1995. Mem. Am. Anthropological Soc., Am. Folklore Soc., Soc. for Ethnomusicology, Assn. for Asian Studies. Home: 302 Carlton Dr Syracuse NY 13214-1906 Office: Syracuse U Maxwell Sch Syracuse NY 13244

WADLINGTON, WALTER JAMES, law educator; b. Biloxi, Miss., Jan. 17, 1931; s. Walter and Bernice (Taylor) W.; m. Ruth Miller Hardie, Aug. 20, 1955; children: Claire Hardie, Charlotte Taylor Griffith, Susan Miller, Derek Alan. AB, Duke U., 1951; LLB, Tulane U., 1954. Bar: La. 1954, Va. 1965. Pvt. practice New Orleans, 1954-55, 58-59; asst. prof. Tulane U., 1960-62; mem. faculty U. Va., 1962—, prof law, 1964—, James Madison prof., 1970—; prof. legal medicine U. Va. Med. Sch., 1979—; Harrison Found. rsch. prof. U. Va., 1990-92; tutor civil law U. Edinburgh, Scotland, 1959-60; vis. Tazewell Taylor prof. law Coll. William and mary, spring 1986; program dir. Robert Wood Johnson Med. Malpractice Program, 1985-91; mem. adv. bd. Robert Wood Johnson clin. scholars program, 1989—; chmn. nat. adv. bd. Improving Malpractice Precention and Compensation Sys., 1994—; Disting. Health Law Tchr. Am. Soc. Law, Medicine and Ethics; trustee-at-large Ednl. Commn. Fgn. Med. Credentials, 1996—. Author: Cases and Materials on Domestic Relations, 1970, 3d edit., 1995; (with Waltz and Dworkin) Cases and Materials on Law and Medicine, 1980; (with Whitebread, Scott and Davis) Children in the Legal System, 1983, 2d edit., 1997; editor-in-chief Tulane U. Law Rev., 1953-54. Fulbright scholar U. Edinburg. Mem. Va. Bar Assn., Am. Law Inst., Inst. Medicine of NAS, Order of Coif. Home: 1620 Keith Valley Rd Charlottesville VA 22901-3018 Office: U Va Sch Law 580 Massie Rd Charlottesville VA 22903-1738

WADLINGTON, WARWICK PAUL, English language educator; b. New Orleans, May 2, 1938; s. Robert Lee and Della Frances (Guerin) W.; m. Elizabeth Bernard, Dec. 26, 1963 (div. 1988); children: Laura, Mark, Paul; m. Elizabeth H. Harris, Feb. 18, 1995. BS, U.S. Mil. Acad., 1961; MA, Tulane U., 1966, PhD, 1967. Asst. prof. English U. Tex., Austin, 1967-72, assoc. prof., 1972-78, prof., 1978—, Joan Negley Kelleher Centennial prof., 1987—. Author: The Confidence Game in American Literature, 1975, Reading Faulknerian Tragedy, 1987, As I Lay Dying: Stories Out of Stories, 1992; contbr. articles to profl. jours. With U.S. Army, 1961-64. Decorated Air medal. Mem. MLA, Faulkner Soc., Am. Studies Assn. Office: U Tex Dept English Austin TX 78712

WADLOW, JOAN KRUEGER, academic administrator; b. LeMars, Iowa, Aug. 21, 1932; d. R. John and Norma I. (IhLe) Krueger; m. Richard R. Wadlow, July 27, 1958; children: Dawn, Kit. B.A., U. Nebr., Lincoln, 1953; M.A. (Seacrest Journalism fellow 1953-54), Fletcher Sch. Law and Diplomacy, 1956; Ph.D. (Rotary fellow 1956-57), U. Nebr., Lincoln, 1963; cert., Grad. Inst. Internat. Studies, Geneva, 1957. Mem. faculty U. Nebr., Lincoln, 1966-79; prof. polit. scis. U. Nebr., 1964-79, assoc. dean Coll. Arts and Scis., 1972-79; prof. polit. scis., dean Coll. Arts and Scis., U. Wyo., Laramie, 1979-84, v.p. acad. affairs, 1984-86; prof. polit. sci., provost U. Okla., Norman, 1986-91; chancellor U. Alaska, Fairbanks, 1991—; cons. on fed. grants; bd. dirs. Key Bank Alaska; mem. Commn. Colls. N.W. Assn. Author articles in field. Bd. dirs. Nat. Merit Scholarship Corp., Lincoln United Way, 1976-77, Bryan Hosp., Lincoln, 1978-79, Washington Ctr., 1986—, Key Bank of Alaska; v.p., exec. commr. North Cen. Assn., pres., 1991; pres. adv. bd. Lincoln YWCA, 1970-71; mem. def. adv. com. Women in the Svcs., 1987-89; mem. community adv. bd. Alaska Airlines. Recipient Mortar Board Teaching award, 1976, Disting. Teaching award U. Nebr., Lincoln, 1979; fellow Conf. Coop. Man, Lund, Sweden, 1956. Mem. NCAA (divsn. II subcom. of pres. commn. 1997—), Internat. Studies Assn. (co-editor Internat. Studies Notes 1978-91), Nat. Assn. State Univs. and Land-Grant Colls. (exec. com. coun. acad. affairs 1989-91, chair internat. affairs counsel 1996-97), Western Assn. Africanists (pres. 1980-82), Assn. Western Univs. (pres. 1993), Coun. Colls. Arts and Scis. (pres. 1983-84), Greater Fairbanks C. of C., Gamma Phi Beta. Republican. Congregationalist. Office: U Alaska Fairbanks Singers Hall Ste 320 Fairbanks AK 99775

WADMAN, WILLIAM WOOD, III, educational director, technical research executive, consulting company executive; b. Oakland, Calif., Nov. 13, 1936; s. William Wood, Jr., and Lula Fay (Raisner) W.; children: Roxanne Alyce Wadman Hubbling, Raymond Alan (dec.), Theresa Hope Wadman Boudreaux; m. Barbara Jean Wadman; stepchildren: Denise Ellen Varine Skrypkar, Brian Ronald Varine. M.A., U. Calif., Irvine, 1978. Cert. program mgr. tng. Radiation safety specialist, accelerator health physicist U. Calif. Lawrence Berkeley Lab., 1957-68; campus radiation safety officer U. Calif., Irvine, 1968-79; dir. ops., radiation safety officer Radiation Sterilizers, Inc., Tustin, Calif., 1979-80; prin., pres. Wm. Wadman & Assocs. Inc., 1980—; mem. operational review team Princeton U. Rsch. Campus TOKOMAK Fusion Test Facility, 1993-94; technical project mgr. for upgrades projects Los Alamos Nat. Lab. 1994-96, tech. project mgr. for 3 projects, 1995—; mem. team No. 1, health physics appraisal program NRC, 1980—, operational readiness review team to Princeton U. Rsch. Campus TOKOMAK Fusion Test Facility, 1993-94; cons. health physicist to industry; lectr. sch. social ecology, 1974-79, dept. community and environ. medicine U. Calif., Irvine, 1979-80, instr. in environ. health and safety, 1968-79, Orange Coast Coll., in radiation exposure reduction design engring. Iowa Electric Light & Power; trainer Mason & Hanger-Silas Mason Co., Los Alamos Nat. Lab.; instr. in medium energy cyclotron radiation safety UCLBL, lectr. in accelerator health physics, 1966, 67; curriculum developer in field; subject matter expert Los Alamos Nat. Lab., Earth and Environ. Scis., Tech. Support Office. Active Cub Scouts; chief umpire Mission Viejo Little League, 1973. Served with USNR, 1955-63. Recipient award for profl. achievement U. Calif. Alumni Assn., 1972, Outstanding Performance award U. Calif., Irvine, 1973. Mem. Health Physics Soc. (treas. 1979-81, editor proc. 11th symposium, pres. So Calif. chpt. 1977, Professionalism award 1975), Internat. Radiation Protection Assn. (U.S. del. 4th Congress 1977, 8th Congress 1992), Am. Nuclear Soc., Am. Public Health Assn. (chmn. program 1978, chmn. radiol. health sect. 1979-80), Campus Radiation Safety Officers (chmn. 1975, editor proc. 5th conf. 1975), ASTM, Project Mgmt. Inst. Club: UCI Univ. (dir. 1976, sec. 1977, treas. 1978). Contbr. articles to tech. jours. Achievements include research in radiation protection and environmental sciences; Avocations: sailing, Tae Kwon Do, wood working, numesmantics. Home: 3687 Red Cedar Way Lake Oswego OR 97035-3525 Office: 675 Fairview Dr Ste 246 Carson City NV 89701-5468 *Personal philosophy: The continuous practice of patience, openmindedness, and open communication provide the essential ingredients for a full, satisfying personal and professional life. The timing of major decisions is not a matter of heart, but the culmination of the effective use of the practices above.*

WADSWORTH, CHARLES WILLIAM, pianist; b. Barnesville, Ga., May 21, 1929; s. Charles and Ethel (Capps) W.; m. Susan Popkin, June 5, 1966; 1 dau., Rebecca; children from previous marriage—David, Beryl. Student, U. Ga., 1946-48; BS, Juilliard Sch. Music, 1951, MS, 1952. Founder, artistic dir. Chamber Music Concerts of Spoleto (Italy) Festival, 1960-77; founder Chamber Music Concerts of the Spoleto Festival, Charlesston, S.C., 1977; founder, artistic dir., pianist Chamber Music Soc. of Lincoln Ctr., N.Y.C., 1969-89; artistic dir. chamber music Spoleto/USA, Charleston, 1994—, chamber music concerts, 1997, 1996 Olympic Arts Festival, Atlanta; pianist in recitals with Beverly Sills, Hermann Prey, Jennie Tourel, Shirley Verrett, Pinchas Zukerman, Dietrich Fischer-Dieskau. Decorated Cavaliere Ufficiale nel Ordine di Merito dalla Reppublica Italiana, 1975, Chevalier in the Order of Arts and Letters, France, 1986; recipient Mayors award for excellence in the arts N.Y.C., 1979, Handel medallion of City of N.Y. Mayor Edward Koch, 1989. Office: Chamber Music Soc of Lincoln Ctr 70 Lincoln Center Plz New York NY 10023-6548 Office: c/o Judith Kurz Enterprises PO Box 157 Charleston SC 29402-0157*

WADSWORTH, DYER SEYMOUR, lawyer; b. N.Y.C., June 16, 1936; s. Seymour and Phoebe Armistead (Helmer) W.; m. Beverley Allen Dunn Barringer, Feb. 2, 1963; children: Sophia, Jennifer. B.A., Yale U., 1959; J.D., Harvard U., 1962. Bar: N.Y. 1963, Pa. 1979. Assoc. Humes, Andrews & Botzow, N.Y.C., 1962-64; with Inco Ltd. and subs., N.Y.C., 1964-96; asst. gen. counsel Inco Ltd., N.Y.C., 1982-96; pres. Inco U.S., Inc., N.Y.C., 1993-96; chmn., bd. dirs. Barringer Crater Co., Flagstaff, Ariz.; chmn., CEO, treas., dir. Cass County Iron Co., Linden, Tex. Gen. counsel Baseline Fin. Svcs., Inc., N.Y.C., 1997—, The Sailors Snug Harbor, Sea Level, N.C., 1987—; chmn., bd. dirs. Amsterdam Nursing Home Corp., N.Y.C., 1986—; trustee Isaac Tuttle Fund for the Aged, N.Y.C., 1968-96; bd. dirs. N.Y. Health Care Network, Inc., N.Y.C. Named Trustee of Yr. N.Y. Assn. Homes and Svcs. for the Aging, 1995. Mem. Assn. of Bar of City of N.Y., Meteoritical Soc. Clubs: Down Town Assn., Union, Pilgrims (N.Y.C.). Home: 215 E 48th St New York NY 10017-1538

WADSWORTH, FRANK WHITTEMORE, foundation executive, literature educator; b. N.Y.C., June 14, 1919; s. Prescott Kingsley and Elizabeth (Whittemore) W.; m. Roxalene Harriet Nevin, Oct. 22, 1943 (dec. 1979); Susan, Roxalene; m. Deborah Yohalem, Dec. 22, 1980. A.B., Princeton U., 1946, Ph.D., 1951. Instr. English Princeton (N.J.) U., 1949-50; instr. to assoc. prof. English UCLA, 1950-61; prof. English, dean div. humanities U. Pitts., 1962-67; acad. v.p. SUNY-Purchase, 1967-78, prof. lit., 1967-89, emeritus, 1989—; nat. rep. Woodrow Wilson Nat. Fellowship Found., 1958-61, trustee, 1973—; vice-chmn. bd. trustees, 1992—; trustee Wenner-Gren Found., N.Y.C., 1970—, chmn. bd. trustees, 1977-87. Author: The Poacher from Stratford, 1958; contbr. articles to publs. Trustee Rye Country Day Sch., N.Y. Served to lt. (j.g.) USNR, 1942-45. Woodrow Wilson fellow, 1946-47; Scribner fellow, 1948-49; Folger Shakespeare Library fellow, 1961; Guggenheim fellow, 1961-62. Mem. MLA, Am. Soc. Theatre Research, Malone Soc., Phi Beta Kappa. Clubs: Princeton; Conanicut Yacht (R.I.). Home: 430 Sterling Rd Harrison NY 10528-1404

WADSWORTH, HAROLD WAYNE, lawyer; b. Logan, Utah, Oct. 12, 1930; s. Harold Maughan and Nellie Grace (Grosjean) W.; m. Laila Anita Ingebrigtsen, Dec. 27, 1957; children: Warren, Kenneth, Jeffrey, Theresa, Erik. BS, Utah State U., 1952; JD with honor, George Washington U., 1959. Bar: D.C. 1959, Utah 1961, U.S. Dist. Ct. Utah 1961, U.S. Ct. Appeals (10th cir.) 1962, U.S. Ct. Appeals (9th cir.) 1978, U.S. Supreme Ct. 1972. Spl. agt. FBI, Atlanta and Macon, 1959-60; assoc. atty., ptnr. Hanson, Wadsworth & Russon, Salt Lake City, 1961-77; ptnr. Watkiss & Campbell, Salt Lake City, 1978-89, Watkiss & Saperstein, Salt Lake City, 1990-91, Ballard, Spahr, Andrews & Ingersoll, Salt Lake City, 1992-95, Jones Waldo Hollbrook & McDonough, Salt Lake City, Utah, 1996—. 1st lt. U.S. Army, 1952-54. Republican. Mem. LDS Ch. Avocations: horsemanship, hunting, fishing, opera, Shakespeare. Office: Jones Waldo Holbrook & McDonough 1500 1st Intersate Plz 170 S Main St Salt Lake City UT 84101-1605

WADSWORTH, JACQUELINE DORÈT, private investor; b. San Diego, June 15, 1928; d. Benjamin H. Dilley and Georgia E. (Elliott) Dilley Waters; m. Charles Desmond Wadsworth Jr., June 16, 1954 (dec. 1963); 1 child, Georgia Duncan Wadsworth Barber. BS, U. Oreg., 1946-50; MA, San Diego State U., 1950-52. Cert. tchr. Calif., Oreg. Dir. Jr. Red Cross, San Diego County chpt. ARC, 1952-59; asst. dir. leadership ctrs. for 8 western states ARC, Calif., 1954-59; pvt. investor, comml. real estate and property devel., 1974—; interior designer J. Wadsworth Interiors, La Jolla, Calif., 1990—. Vol. chairperson nat. conv. ARC, San Diego, 1966; vol., fundraiser San Diego Symphony Orch. Orgn., 1974-83; mem. Gold Ribbon Patron com. San Diego Symphony, 1995—; friends mem., vol. San Diego Mus. Art, 1958—, Asian Arts Com., 1996—; mem. Scripps Found. for Medicine and Sci., 1990—; life mem., bd. dirs. programs chairmanships, Mercy Hosp. Aux., 1965—; life mem., chairperson, bd. dirs. Social Svc. Aux., 1968—. Recipient Svc. awards Mercy Hosp. Aux., 1967-70. Mem. Caridad Internat., Globe Gilders Theatre Aux. (activity chairperson 1966-85), San Diego Zool. Soc. (curator 1976—), Country Friends Charities La Jolla Group, Mus. Contemporary Art San Diego. Republican.

WADSWORTH, MICHAEL A., athletic director, former ambassador; b. Toronto, ON, Canada, 1943. Professional football player Toronto Argonauts, CFL, 1966-70; lawyer, 1971-81; ambassador to Ireland Canadian Foreign Min., 1989-94; athletic dir. U. Notre Dame, 1995—. Office: U Notre Dame Dept of Athletics Notre Dame IN 46556

WADSWORTH, ROBERT DAVID, advertising agency executive; b. Prestbury, Cheshire, Eng., May 20, 1942; came to U.S., 1978; s. Eric and Irene (Thorpe) W.; m. Kathleen O'Meara, Dec. 13, 1968; children: Tracey, Charles Robert. B.A., U. Natal, S. Africa, 1963. With Lever Bros. S. Africa, 1960-66, sr. brand mgr., 1964-66; sr. brand mgr. Gen. Foods S. Africa, 1967; account exec. London Press Exch., S. Africa, 1968, Grant Advt., S. Africa, 1969; dir., then mng. dir. Cen. Advt., Johannesburg, S. Africa, 1970-73; dir. new bus. coord. McCann-Erickson, South Africa, 1973-78; sr. v.p., mng. rep., new bus. coord. McCann-Erickson, Inc., N.Y.C., 1978-82; client dir., exec. v.p. Lintas, N.Y.C., 1983-90; dir. corp. strategy, regional dir. So. Africa Lintas Worldwide, N.Y.C., 1991-97. Home: 20 Hobson St Stamford CT 06902-8114 Office: Lintas Worldwide 1 Dag Hammarskjold Plz New York NY 10017-2201

WAECHTER, ARTHUR JOSEPH, JR., lawyer; b. New Orleans, Nov. 20, 1913; s. Arthur Joseph and Elinor (Reckner) W.; m. Peggy Weaver, Feb. 20, 1939; children: Susan Porter Waechter McClellan, Sally Ann Waechter McGehee, Robert. AB, Tulane U., 1934, LLB, 1936. Bar: La. 1936. Since practiced in New Orleans; ptnr. Jones, Walker, Waechter, Poitevent, Carrere & Denegre, 1942—; prof. law Sch. Law Tulane U., 1947-68, prof. emeritus, 1968—; bd. dirs. Canal Barge Co., Inc. Bd. visitors Tulane U., 1959-64; bd. advisers to editors Tulane Law Rev. Assn., 1960—; bd. adminstrs. Tulane Ednl. Fund, 1968-83, emeritus bd. adminstrs., 1983—. Served to lt. (j.g.) USNR, 1943-46. Mem. ABA, La. Bar Assn. (gov. 1968-70), New Orleans Bar Assn. (pres. 1961-62), Internat. Assn. Def. Counsel, Tulane U. Alumni Assn. (pres. 1962-63), Maritime Law Assn. U.S., Am. Law Inst., Am. Judicature Soc., Am. Coll. Real Estate Lawyers (gov. 1983-86), Order of Coif, Pickwick Club, Boston Club, Stratford Club, La. Club, So. Yacht Club, The Plimsol (New Orleans), Phi Kappa Sigma, Phi Delta Phi. Home: 100 Christwood Blvd Covington LA 70433 Office: Jones Walker Waechter Poitevent Carrere & Denegre 201 Saint Charles Ave New Orleans LA 70170-1000

WAELDE, LAWRENCE RICHARD, chemist; b. Teaneck, N.J., Dec. 27, 1951; s. Clinton Brewster and Eileen Florence (Kennedy) W.; m. Soledad Nelita Acedillo, May 24, 1975; children: Christine Ann, Richard Adams. BS, Fairleigh Dickinson U., 1976; postgrad., Syracuse U., 1969-72. Project leader Muralo Paints, Bayonne, N.J., 1974-79; lab. mgr. Lazon Paints, Fair Lawn, N.J., 1979-84; plant mgr. Stevens Paint Co., Yonkers, N.Y., 1984-86; mgr. powder coatings Troy Chem. Corp., Newark, 1986—. Mem. N.Y. Soc. Coating Tech. (tech. chmn. 1990-93, symposium chmn. 1993, 95, treas. 1995-96, sec. 1996-97, pres. elect 1997-98, Roy H. Kienle award 1994), Powder Coating Inst. (tech. mem.). Office: Troy Chem Corp 1 Avenue L Newark NJ 07105-3805

WAELSCH, SALOME GLUECKSOHN, geneticist, educator; b. Danzig, Germany, Oct. 6, 1907; came to U.S., 1933, naturalized, 1938; d. Ilya and Nadia Gluecksohn; m. Heinrich B. Waelsch, Jan. 8, 1943; children: Naomi Barbara, Peter Benedict. Student, U. Konigsberg, Germany, U. Berlin, 1927-28; PhD, U. Freiburg, Germany, 1932; DSc (hon.), Columbia U., 1995. Rsch. assoc. in genetics Columbia U., 1936-55; assoc. prof. anatomy Albert Einstein Coll. Medicine, 1955-58, prof., 1958-63, prof. molecular genetics, 1963—, chmn. dept. genetics, 1963-76; mem. study sects. NIH. Contbr. numerous articles on devel. genetics. Recipient Nat. Medal of Sci., Pres. Clinton, 1993. Fellow AAAS, Am. Acad. Arts and Scis.; mem. NAS, N.Y. Acad. Scis. (hon. life), Am. Soc. Zoologists, Am. Assn. Anatomists, Genetics Soc., Soc. Devel. Biology, Am. Soc. Naturalists, Am. Soc. Human Genetics, The Royal Soc. (fgn. mem.), Sigma Xi. Office: Albert Einstein Coll Med Dept Molecular Genetics 1300 Morris Park Ave Bronx NY 10461-1926

WAETJEN, WALTER BERNHARD, academic administrator emeritus; b. Phila., Oct. 16, 1920; s. Walter E. and Marguerite D. (Dettmann) W.; m. Betty Walls, Sept. 28, 1945; children: Walter Bernhard, Kristi Waetjen Jenkins, Daniel G. BS, U. Pa., Millersville, 1942; MS, U. Pa., 1947; EdD, U. Md., 1951; LittD (hon.), Hanyang U., Seoul, Korea, 1980; LLD (hon.), Gama Filho U., Brazil, 1980; LHD (hon.), Cleveland State U., 1992, Ashland U., 1993. Profl. football player Detroit Lions and Phila. Eagles, 1942-45; tchr. Sch. Dist. Phila., 1945-48; rsch. fellow U. Md., 1948-50, mem. faculty, 1950-73, prof. ednl. psychology, 1957-65; dir. Bur. Ednl. Rsch. and Field Svcs., 1962-65; gen. dir. Interprofl. Rsch. Commn. Pupil Pers. Svcs., 1963-65, v.p. adminstrv. affairs, 1965-70, v.p. gen. adminstrn., 1970-73; pres. Cleve. State U., 1973-88; vis. prof. Cambridge U., 1988-89; sr. fellow Internat. Tech. Edn. Assn., 1989; interim pres. Ashland (Ohio) U., 1992-93; vis. rsch. fellow U. Edinburgh, Scotland, 1991; Patty Hill Smith Meml. lectr. U. Louisville, 1964; psychol. cons. to sch. systems, 1951—; bd. dirs. Overseas Capital Corp.; mem. governing bd. St. Vincent Quadrangle, Inc.; bd. dirs. Talbot Philanthropies, Inc., 1994; mem. pres.'s commn. NCAA, 1984-88; chmn. Internat. Tech. Edn. Adc. Coun.; Nat. Coun. on Sci. and Tech., 1991—. Co-author in field.; contbr. articles to ednl. jours. Trustee Woodruff Found.; mem. governing bd. St. Vincent Charity Hosp. and Health Ctr. Corp. Recipient Disting. Alumni award Pa. State Coll., 1972, Commdr's. Cross of Order of Merit award, Fed. Republic Germany, 1986, Order Yugoslav Flag Govt. of Yugoslavia, 1988. Mem. ASCD, AAAS (mem. nat. coun. on sci. and tech. edn. 1990—), Assn. Mid-Continent Univs. (pres. 1983), Soc. Rsch. Child Devel., Assn. Urban Univs. (chmn. 1984—), Am. Edn. Rsch. Assn., Aesculapian Soc., Blue Key, Iota Lambda Sigma, Phi Delta Kappa, Phi Kappa Phi, 50 Club, Union Club, Masons. Home and Office: 4790 Sailors Retreat Rd Oxford MD 21654-1739

WAFFENSCHMIDT, LORI ANN, television executive producer; b. Sauk City, Wis., Nov. 8, 1957; d. Lyman Arno and Irene Agnes (Grass) W.; m. Daniel Leo Ronan, Oct. 5, 1985; children: Daniel Henry, Matthew George. Grad., U. Wis., 1980. Announcer WVLR Radio, Sauk City, 1974-76; from prodr. to asst. news dir. Wis. Pub. Radio, Madison, 1977-82; newscaster Nat. Pub. Radio, Washington, 1982-84; from writer/prodr. to sr. prodr. CNN World Report, Atlanta, 1988-95; exec. prodr. The CNN Computer Connection, Atlanta, 1995—. Office: CNN One CNN Ctr Atlanta GA 30303

WAGAMAN, JAMES BRIAN, environmentalist; b. Waynesboro, Pa., Oct. 23, 1963; s. Elvin C. and Margaret Madeline (Peiffer) W.; m. Cheri Louise Ross, Jan. 28, 1994. AA, Pa. State U., Mont Alto, 1994; BHumanities, Pa. State U., Harrisburg. Lic. water purification, Pa. Operator, asst. supt., acting supt. Waynesboro (Pa.) Water Treatment Plant, 1980-91; pub. housing restoration coord. Franklin County Housing Authority, Chambersburg, 1992; coord. new constrn. Borough of Mont Alto (Pa.) Water Dept., 1994—. Mem. MLA, Am. Water Resources Assn., Am. Water Works Assn., Popular Culture Assn (Dan Walden award 1994), N.E. MLA, Mid-Atlantic Popular Culture Assn. (area chair culture and the environment). Republican. Home: 555 Mountainview Rd Middletown PA 17057 Office: Borough of Mont Alto Water Dept Mont Alto PA 17057

WAGEMAKER, DAVID ISAAC, human resources development executive; b. Grand Rapids, Mich., Feb. 10, 1949; s. Raymond Ogden and Inez Loraine W. BA in Philosophy, Grand Valley State U., 1971; MA in Orgn. Mgmt., U. Phoenix, 1997. Owner Edn. Ctr., Grand Rapids, 1970-72; cons. Am. Leadership Coll., Washington, 1972-78, Wagemaker Co., Honolulu, 1978-80; edn. cons. Batten, Batten, Hudson & Swab, Inc., San Diego, 1980-81, mgr., 1981; securities broker, ins. agt. The Equitable Assurance Co., San Diego, 1982; assoc. cons. Pacific S.W. Airlines, San Diego, 1982-83; project mgr. GM Hughes Electroncis, Westchester, Calif., 1983—; mgmt. cons. Mgmt. Devel. Ctr., San Diego State U., 1980—. Co-author: Build A Better You Starting Now, 1982; author: (cassette program) Effective Time Management, 1979, (with others) How To Organize Yourself To Win, 1988; featured in tng. film Managing Diversity, 1991. Mem. Acad. Mgmt., Hughes Mgmt. Club, Hughes Golf Club, Sigma Chi, Zeta Nu. Republican. Congregationalist. Avocations: golf, public speaking, snow skiing. Home: 2227 Robinson St # A Redondo Beach CA 90278-2019

WAGEMAN, LYNETTE MENA, librarian; b. Trinidad, West Indies, Aug. 18, 1934; came to U.S., 1955.; d. Hubert and Alma (Sampath) Jagbandhansingh. BA in Modern Fgn. Langs., Park Coll., Parkville, Mo., 1959; MLS, U. Hawaii, 1966, MA in Asian Studies, 1976. Serials asst. East-West Ctr. Libr., Honolulu, 1962-66; catalog libr. U. Hawaii, Honolulu, 1966-71, South Asia specialist, 1971-93, acting head Asia collection, 1991-93, head, 1993—, collection devel. mgr. Asia collection, pub. svc. head rep., 1991—; exec. com. Ctr. South Asian Studies, 1973-75, 77-79, 81-83, 85-86, 87-90, acting dir., 1988, 90, 92. Mem. Hawaii Libr. Assn. (mem. bd. 1990-92, co-editor newsletter 1990-92), Assn. Asian Studies (exec. bd. com. on South Asian Librs. and Documentation 1983-85, 90—, chairperson 1992—, exec. com. Asian Libr. Liaison com. 1991—, adv. com. Bibliography Asian Studies 1992—), Internat. Assn. Orientalist Librs., South Asian Lit. Assn., Com. on Women in Asian Studies. Avocations: cultivating Bromeliads and other exotic plants. Office: U Hawaii Asia Collection Hamilton Libr 2550 The Mall Honolulu HI 96822-2233

WAGEMAN, VIRGINIA FARLEY, editor, writer; b. Jersey City, N.J., Feb. 18, 1941; d. James Christopher and Charlotte Carter (Stebbins) Farley; m. Steven Lipson, Dec. 26, 1962 (div. 1964); 1 child, Melissa; m. James Carter Wageman, Apr. 22, 1968; children: Robinson Michael, Sarah Carter. BA, Bard Coll., 1964. Book editor, prodn. asst. AICPA, N.Y.C., 1964-67; prodn. mgr. U. Hawaii Press, 1967-68; asst. dir. office univ. rels. U. Md., Balt., 1968-70; dir. publs. art mus. Princeton U., 1971-81; writer, editor Hirshhorn Mus. and Sculpture Garden, Washington, 1982-86; freelance editor, 1986—; sr. editor Hudson Hills (N.Y.) Press, 1988-89; mgr. publs. Coll. Art Assn., N.Y.C., 1989-96; editor, writer various publications, 1996—. Recipient Smithsonian Commendation for Exceptional Svc. Mem. Art Table, Assn. Freelance Art Editors (pres. 1984-86), Princeton Rsch. Forum. Home: 78 6795 Walua Rd Kailua Kona HI 96740

WAGENER, HOBART D., retired architect; b. Sioux Falls, S.D., May 10, 1921; s. Frank Samuel and Beatrice (Hobart) W.; m. Violet LaVaughn, Dec. 16, 1944; children: Diane Kay Wagener Welch, Jeffrey Scott, Shaw Bradley. BArch, U. Mich., 1944. Registered architect, Colo. Draftsman Eggers & Higgins, Architects, N.Y.C., 1946-47, Pietro Belluschi, Architect, Portland, Oreg., 1947-50; designer James Hunter, Architect, Boulder, Colo., 1950-53; prin. Hobart D. Wagener Assocs., Boulder, 1953-77; prin. ptnr. Wagener VanderVorste, Architects, Boulder, 1977-86; ret., 1986; mem. selection com. Colo. Supreme Ct., Denver, 1968-72. Co-author: The School Library, 1962; work pub. in Archtl. Record, Sunset mag., N.Y. Times, House Beautiful, 25 Years of Record Houses. Chmn. Boulder Planning Commn., 1966; pres. Boulder C. of C., 1971. Lt. (j.g.) USN, 1944-46, PTO. Named Outstanding Designer for past 50 yrs. Hist. Boulder, 1983; also numerous nat. and regional design awards. Fellow AIA (pres. Colo. 1973, Colo. Architect of Yr. award 1985), Lions (pres. Boulder 1965). Avocations: travel, golf. Address: 1730 Avenida Del Mundo Apt 1607 Coronado CA 92118-3028

WAGENKNECHT, EDWARD, author; b. Chgo., Mar. 28, 1900; s. Henry E. and Mary (Erichsen) W.; m. Dorothy Arnold, Aug. 3, 1932; children: Robert Edward, David Arnold, Walter Chappell. PhB, U. Chgo., 1923, MA, 1924; PhD, U. Wash., 1932. Prof. of English Boston U., 1947-65, prof. emeritus, 1965—; editor Boston U. Studies in English, 1954-57; Lowell lectr., 1958. Author: many critical and biog. works, including The Man Charles Dickens, 1929, rev. edit., 1966, Mark Twain, The Man and His Work, 1935, rev., 1961, 67, Cavalcade of the English Novel, 1943, rev. edit., 1954, Cavalcade of the American Novel, 1952, A Preface to Literature, 1954, Longfellow, A Full Length Portrait, 1955, The Seven Worlds of Theodore Roosevelt, 1958, Nathaniel Hawthorne, Man and Writer, 1961, Washington Irving: Moderation Displayed, 1962, The Movies in the Age of Innocence, 1962, Edgar Allan Poe: The Man Behind the Legend, 1963, Chicago, 1964, Seven Daughters of the Theater, 1964, Harriet Beecher Stowe, The Known and The Unknown, 1965, Dickens and the Scandalmongers, 1965, Merely Players, 1966, Henry Wadsworth Longfellow: Portrait of an American Humanist, 1966, John Greenleaf Whittier: A Portrait in Paradox, 1967, The Personality of Chaucer, 1968, As Far As Yesterday: Memories and Reflections, 1968, William Dean Howells: The Friendly Eye, 1969, The Personality of Milton, 1970, James Russell Lowell: Portrait of a Many-Sided Man, 1971, Ambassadors for Christ: Seven American Preachers, 1972, The Personality of Shakespeare, 1972, Ralph Waldo Emerson: Portrait of a Balanced Soul, 1974; Nine Before Fotheringhay: A Novel about Mary Queen of Scots (under pseud. Julian Forrest), 1966, The Glory of The Lilies, A Novel about Joan of Arc (under pseud. Julian Forrest), 1969; (with Anthony Slide) The Films of D.W. Griffith, 1975, A Pictorial History of New England, 1976, Eve and Henry James: Portraits of Women and Girls in His Fiction, 1978; (with Anthony Slide) Fifty Great American Silent Films, 1912-20, 1980, Henry David Thoreau: What Manner of Man?, 1981, American Profile, 1900-1909, 1982, Gamaliel Bradford, 1982, The Novels of Henry James, 1983, Daughters of the Covenant, 1983, The Tales of Henry James, 1984, Henry Wadsworth Longfellow: His Poetry and Prose, 1986, Stars of the Silents, 1987, Nathaniel Hawthorne, The Man, His Tales and Romances, 1989, Sir Walter Scott, 1991, Seven Masters of Supernatural Fiction, 1991, Willa Cather, 1994; editor: Mrs. Longfellow: Selected Letters and Journals, 1956, The Supernaturalism of New England (John Greenleaf Whittier), 1969, The Letters of James Branch Cabell, 1974; also numerous anthologies including The Fireside Book of Christmas Stories, 1945, The Collected Tales of Walter de la Mare, 1950, An Introduction to Dickens, 1952, Chaucer: Modern Essays in Criticism, 1959, Stories of Christ and Christmas, 1963, The Stories and Fables of Ambrose Bierce, 1977, Washington Irving's Tales of the Supernatural, 1982. Home: 177 Leo Dr Gardner MA 01440-1213

WAGER, DEBORAH MILLER, researcher, consultant; b. Phila., Sept. 5, 1938; d. Albert S. and Pauline (Goldberg) Miller; m. Robert J. Wager, July 3, 1966; 1 child, James M. BA, Skidmore Coll., 1960; MAT, Columbia U., 1963. Editor Toy Quality and Safety Report, Washington, 1972-88; cons. Wager Rsch., Washington, 1989—; devel. rschr. Sidwell Friends Sch., Washington, 1988-89, 92— ; trustee Sheridan Sch., Washington, 1978-84. Author: Good Toys, 1986. Mem. Assn. Profl. Rschrs. Advancement. Office: Wager Rsch Consulting 4545 29th St NW Washington DC 20008-2144

WAGER, DOUGLAS CHARLES, artistic director; b. Gloversville, N.Y., June 11, 1949; s. George Robert and Jane Margaret (Upright) W.; m. Cary Anne Spear, June 20, 1981 (div. Nov. 23, 1993). BA in English Lit. and Theater, SUNY, Albany, 1971; MFA in Directing, Boston U., 1974. Intern Arena Stage, Washington, 1974, asst. stage mgr., 1974-75, stage mgr., 1975-76, asst. prodn. coord., 1976-77, lit. mgr., 1977-80, assoc. dir., 1980-83, assoc. producing dir., 1983-91, artistic dir., 1991—; assoc. prof. drama Colo. Coll., Colorado Springs, 1981, 84, guest artist summer theatre inst., 1985, 86. Dir. (stage prodns.) Madmen, 1975, Singers, Scooping, 1976, Gemini Trappers, 1977, The Curse of the Starving Class, 1978, The Past, 1978, Conjuring an Event, 1978, You Can't Take It With You, 1979, The Man Who Came to Dinner, 1980, 89, The Child, 1980, A Lesson from Aloes, 1981, Tomfoolery, 1981, 83, Animal Crackers, 1981, On the Razzle, 1982, Candide, 1982, As You Like It, 1983, Accidental Death of an Anarchist, 1983, 84, Man and Superman, 1984, Execution of Justice, 1984 (Helen Hayes awards for Outstanding Direction and Outstanding Resident Prodn.), Women and Water, 1985, The Philadelphia Story, 1985, The Taming of the Shrew, 1985, Measure for Measure, 1986, Glengary Glen Ross, 1986, Don Pasquale, 1986, All the King's Men, 1987, The Rivers and Ravines, 1987, The Cocoanuts, 1987 (Helen Hayes award for Outstanding Resident Musical), L'Amico Fritz, 1987, A Lie of the Mind, 1988, On the Town, 1988, Merrily We Roll Along, 1989, Our Town, 1990, Pygmalion, 1990, The Seagull, 1990, A Wonderful Life, 1991, The Father, 1991, The Visit, 1991, Of Thee I Sing, 1992, The Skin of Our Teeth, 1992, Twelfth Night, 1993, The Revengers' Comedies, 1994, The Odyssey, 1994, Long Day's Journey Into Night, 1995, The Matchmaker, 1995, Candide, 1996. Recipient Creative Achievement in Theatre award Boston U. Sch. Arts Alumni Assn., 1989. Avocations: wine collection, tennis, hiking, biking. Office: Arena Stage 6th And Maine Ave SW Washington DC 20024*

WAGER, MICHAEL, company executive. Pres. Robert H. Wager Co. Address: Forum 52 Industrial Park 570 Montroyal Rd Rural Hall NC 27045

WAGER, PAULA JEAN, artist; b. Lansing, Mich., Dec. 19, 1929; d. Mervin Elihu and Cora Della (Raymer) Fowler; m. William Douglas Wager, May 4, 1952; children: Pamela Ann, Scott Alan. Student, Mich. State U., 1949-52. Music tchr. Toledo, Ohio, 1968-72, Union Lake, Mich., 1972-76; tchr. art, artist Paula Wager's Art Studio, Commerce Twp., Mich., 1984—; hostess Artistic Touch with Paula, Cable Comcast channel 44, Waterford, Mich., 1991-94, 96—, TCI West Oakland, Walled Lake, Mich., Channel 10, 1991-94, Channel 14, 1996—. Exhibited in group shows including Village Art Supplies, 1982-88, Pontiac Oakland Soc. Artists, 1983—, Pontiac Galleria, 1983, Oakland C.C., Commerce Twp., 1985, Red Piano Gallery, Hilton Head, S.C., 1985-89, Mich. State U., East Lansing, 1986, Silver Pencil Gallery, Pontiac, 1987-89, Wooden Sleight, Vestaburg, Mich., 1988-93, Art Pad, Keego Harbor, Mich., 1990-93, Local Color Gallery, Union Pier, Mich., 1992-94, Mich. Assn. Artists, Southfield Civ. Ctr. Mich. 1995, Swann Gallery, Detroit, 1995—; solo exhbns. include Waterford Pub. Lib., 1996, Waterland Pub. Libr., 1996—, Millers Artist Supplies, Ferndale, Mich., 1996, Waterford Twp. Hall, 1996; represented in pvt. collections; juror Village of Fine Arts Assn., 1996. Recipient Outstanding Achievement award in instructional programming Comcast Cable TV, Waterford, 1992, 1st place, Waterford Friends of the Arts Art Show, 1988, Pontiac Oakland Soc. Artists Cmty. Rm., 1990, Am. Biog. Inst. Woman of Yr. Commemorative medal, 1995; Waterford Cable Commn. grantee, 1991, 93, Charter Twp. of Waterford grantee, 1991-94. Mem. Nat. Assn. Female Exec. Pontiac Oakland Soc. Artists, Waterford Friends of the Arts, Mich. Watercolor Soc., Birmingham Bloomfield Art Assn., Colored Pencil Soc. Am., Colored Pencil Soc. Detroit, Village Fine Arts Assn., Paint Creek Ctr. for the Arts. Avocations: music, art. Home and Studio: 3316 Greenlawn Ave Commerce Township MI 48382-4629

WAGER, WALTER HERMAN, author, communications director; b. N.Y.C., Sept. 4, 1924; s. Max Louis and Jessie (Smith) W.; m. Sylvia Liebowitz Leonard, May 6, 1951 (div. May 1975); 1 child, Lisa Wendy; m. Winifred McIvor, June 4, 1975. BA, Columbia U., 1943; LLB, Harvard U., 1946; LLM, Northwestern U., 1949. Bar: N.Y. 1946. Spl. asst. to Israel dir. Civil Aviation, 1951-52; freelance writer N.Y.C., 1952-54; sr. editor UN, N.Y.C., 1954-56; freelance TV and mag. writer N.Y.C., 1956-63; editor-in-chief Playbill mag., N.Y.C., 1963-66; editor Show mag., N.Y.C., 1965; cons. pub. rels. and editorial dept. ASCAP, N.Y.C., 1966-72, dir. pub. relations, 1972-78; cons. pub. relations Nat. Music Pub. Assn., N.Y.C., 1978-84; dir. communications Juilliard Sch., N.Y.C., 1985-86; counsel pub. relations Mann Music Ctr., Phila., 1986-87, Eugene O'Neill Theater Ctr., N.Y.C., 1987-89; dir. pub. info. U. Bridgeport, 1991-93; tchr. Northwestern U., 1949, Columbia U., 1955-56; spl. asst. to atty. gen. N.Y. State investigation hate lit. in elections, 1962; bd. dirs. Jazz Hall of Fame, 1975-77. Author: Death Hits the Jackpot, 1954, Operation Intrigue, 1956, I Spy, 1965, Masterstroke, 1966, Superkill, 1966, Wipeout, 1967, Countertrap, 1967, Death Twist, 1968, The Girl Who Split, 1969, Sledgehammer, 1970, Viper Three, 1971 (filmed as Twilights's Last Gleaming 1977), Swap, 1972, Telefon, 1975 (filmed in 1977), My Side-By King Kong, 1976, Time of Reckoning, 1977, Blue Leader, 1979, Blue Moon, 1980, Blue Murder, 1981, Designated Hitter, 1982, Otto's Boy, 1984, 58 Minutes, 1987 (filmed as Die Hard 2, 1990), The Spirit Team, 1996; (non-fiction) Camp Century, 1962, Playwrights Speak, 1967, (with Mel Tillis) Stutterin' Boy, 1984. Pres. Columbia Coll., class 1944. Fulbright fellow Sorbonne, Paris, 1949-50, Northwestern U. Law Sch. fellow, 1948-49. Mem. Writers Guild Am., Mystery Writers Am. (bd. dirs. 1988-94, 1997—, exec. v.p.). Democrat. Jewish. Avocation: traveling. Home and Office: 200 W 79th St New York NY 10024-6212

WAGES, ROBERT COLEMAN, equity investor; b. Casablanca, Morocco, Aug. 28, 1963; came to U.S., 1963; s. Dan Sims and Sara Mae (Miller) W.; m. Tara Shamattee Sarwan, July 18, 1992; children: John Coleman, Thomas Sims; 1 stepchild, Jason Anthony Squillace. AB in Chemistry with honors, Princeton U., 1985. Cons. Oliver, Wyman & Co., N.Y.C., 1985-87; assoc. Castle Harlan, Inc., N.Y.C., 1987-90, v.p., 1990—; bd. dirs. Dearborn Risk Mgmt., Inc., Chgo., Tradesco Mold Ltd., Toronto, Ont., Can. Sponsor Student/Sponsor Partnership, N.Y.C., 1987-91. Republican. Episcopalian. Avocations: sailing, travel, photography, scuba diving. Office: Castle Harlan Inc 150 E 58th St New York NY 10155-0099

WAGGENER, RONALD EDGAR, radiologist; b. Green River, Wyo., Oct. 6, 1926; s. Edgar Fleetwood and Mary Harlene (Hutton) W.; m. Everina Ann Stalker, Aug. 1, 1948; children: Marta, Nancy, Paul, Daphne. Student, Colo. A&M U., 1944; student, Oreg. State U., 1945; BS, U. Nebr., 1949, MS, 1952, PhD, 1957, MD cum laude, 1954, postgrad., 1955-58; postgrad., St. Bartholomew's, London, 1956-57. Diplomate Am. Bd. Radiology. Intern U. Nebr. Hosp., 1954-55, resident, 1955-56, 57-58; radiation therapist Nebr. Meth. Hosp., Omaha, 1965-70, chmn. cancer com., 1964-89, dir. cancer and radiation therapy, 1964-89, dir. dept. radiology, 1970-89, dir. cancer fellowship program, 1977-89; instr. radiology U. Nebr., Omaha, 1958, asst. prof., 1959-61, radiation therapist, 1959-65, assoc. prof., 1962-80, clin. assoc. prof., 1981—; pres. Highland Assocs. Ltd., Omaha, 1977-89; mem. cancer com. Children's Meml. Hosp., Omaha, 1970-89. Contbr. articles to profl. jours. With C.E., U.S. Army, 1944-46. Fellow AEC, 1952-53, Am. Cancer Soc., 1956-57. Fellow Am. Coll. Radiologists; mem. Nebr. Radiology Soc. (pres. 1963-64), Sigma Xi, Alpha Omega Alpha, Phi Nu. Home: 1227 S 109th St Omaha NE 68144-1813 Office: 13304 W Center Rd Omaha NE 68144-3453

WAGGONER, JAMES VIRGIL, chemicals company executive; b. Judsonia, Ark., Oct. 29, 1927; s. Loren Dye and Vera (Meacham) W.; m. M.E. June Howell; children: Liz Waggoner Quisenberry, Jay. BS in Chemistry and Math., Ouachita Bapt. U., 1948, DSc (hon.), 1990; MS in Organic Chemistry and Math., U. Tex., 1950. Successively rsch. chemist, sales asst., asst. sales mgr., sales mgr. Monsanto, Texas City, Tex., 1950-57; dir. sales Monsanto, Springfield, Mass., 1957-59; product adminstr. Monsanto, St. Louis, 1959-61, dir. sales, 1961-63, dir. mktg., 1963-67, bus. dir., 1967-68, gen. mgr. petrochems. div., 1972-76, gen. mgr. cycle-safe div., 1976, corp. v.p., mng. dir. Plastics & Resins Co., 1977, group v.p., 1978-80; pres. petrochem. and plastics unit El Paso Co., Odessa, Tex., 1980-83; cons. to petrochem. industry Houston, 1984-85; pres., chief exec. officer Sterling Chems., Inc., Houston, 1986—; mem. adv. bd. 1st Comml. Bank, N.A., Little Rock; bd. dirs. Kirby Corp., Houston, Mail-Well Holdings, Inc., Englewood, Colo. Chmn. adv. coun. Coll. Natural Scis., U. Tex., Austin; mem. devel. coun. Ouachita Bapt. U.; bd. dirs. Tex. Rsch. League; bd. dirs., chmn. Good Samaritan Found., 1993-94; supporter, patron Star of Hope Mission; corp. leader, contbr. United Way, Texas City, LaMarque Area, Houston; mem. chmn.'s adv. bd. Rep. Nat. Conv. Mem. Nat. Petroleum Refiners Assn. (v.p., bd. dirs., exec. com.), Tex. Assn. Taxpayers (bd. dirs.). Avocations: golf, art collecting. Home: 11 Shadder Way Houston TX 77019-1415 Office: 1200 Smith St Ste 1900 Houston TX 77002-4312 *In my opinion, the greatest single character trait that separates those who excel and achieve from those who don't is their constant committment to excellence and to strive for continuing improvement.*

WAGGONER, LAWRENCE WILLIAM, legal educator; b. Sidney, Ohio, July 2, 1937; s. William J. and Gladys L. Waggoner; m. Lynne S. Applebaum, Aug. 27, 1963; children: Ellen, Diane. BBA, U. Cin., 1960; JD, U. Mich., 1963; PhD, Oxford U. (England), 1966. Assoc. Cravath, Swaine & Moore, N.Y.C., 1963; prof. law U. Ill., Champaign, 1968-72; prof. law U. Va., Charlottesville, 1972-74; prof. law U. Mich., Ann Arbor, 1974-84, James V. Campbell prof. law, 1984-87; Lewis M. Simes prof. law, 1987—; dir. rsch., chief reporter joint editorial bd. for Uniform Probate Code, 1986-94, dir. rsch., 1994—; adviser restatement (2d) of property, 1987-90; reporter restatement (3d) of property, 1990—. Served to capt. U.S. Army, 1966-68. Fulbright scholar Oxford U., 1963-65. Mem. Am. Law Inst., Am. Coll. Trust and Estates Counsel, Internat. Acad. Estate and Trust Law. Author: Estates in Land and Future Interests in a Nutshell, 1981, 2nd edit., 1993, Federal Taxation of Gifts, Trusts, and Estates (2d edit.), 1982, Family Property Law: Wills, Trusts, and Future Interests, 1991. Office: U Mich Law Sch 625 S State St Ann Arbor MI 48109-1215

WAGGONER, LELAND TATE, insurance company executive; b. Greensboro, Ga., Feb. 5, 1916; s. Andrew B. and Blanche (Proffitt) W.; m. Florence Adelaide Gee, Feb. 15, 1942; children: Frederick Charles, Leonora Blanche. AB, Maryville Coll., 1938; MBA with honors, NYU, 1972; CLU, 1941; LLD (hon.), Maryville Coll., 1987. Mgr. Mut. of N.Y., Boston, 1946-54; v.p. Western sect. Mut. of N.Y., San Francisco, 1954-57; v.p. sales Life Ins. Co. N.Am., Phila., 1957-63, Home Life Ins. Co., N.Y.C., 1963-69; sr. v.p., dir. Home Life Ins. Co., 1969-81; pres. Home Life Equity Sales Corp., 1970-81, Creative Mktg., Inc., 1981—; chmn. Va. Life Ins. Co. of N.Y., 1983—, chmn. emeritus; sr. dir. Warring & Assocs. Internat. Cons., 1983—; instr. Stanford Grad. Sch. Bus. Adminstrn., 1957; exec. vis. prof. Ga. State U., 1981—; past mem. bd. CLU Inst.; mem. agy. officers round table Life Ins. Mktg. and Research Assn.; life ins. pub. relations council Inst. Life Ins.; adv. bd. N.Y. State Ins. Dept.; past mem. agy. officers roundtable. Author: You Can See the World in Forty Days!; contbg. author: other booklets. Life Ins. Sales Mgmt. Handbook; Sr. editor: CLU Jour, 1946—; co-editor: The Life Insurance Policy Contract; cons. editor, contbg. author: Life and Health Insurance Handbook; interviewed for: Am. Coll.'s Oral History of Life Ins. Bd. dirs. and exec. com. Am. Bible Soc.; past bd. dirs. Maryville Coll., U. Tampa, Foster Parents Plan. Served to lt. comdr. USNR, 1942-45. Recipient Leland T. Waggoner distinguished lecture series in life and health ins. established at Ga. State U.; L. T. Waggoner room of Am. Colls. Grad. Center named for him.; N.J. Room of Am. Coll. Grad. Center named in his honor. Mem. Internat. Ins. Soc. (bd. govs.), Tenn Soc., Baltusrol Golf Club. Episcopalian. Home: 3747 Peachtree Rd NE # 803-5 Atlanta GA 30319-1360

WAGGONER, PAUL EDWARD, agricultural scientist; b. Appanoose County, Iowa, Mar. 29, 1923; s. Walter Loyal and Kathryn (Maring) W.; m. Barbara Ann Lockerbie, Nov. 3, 1945; children—Von Lockerbie, Daniel Maring. S.B., U. Chgo., 1946; M.S., Iowa State Coll., 1949, Ph.D., 1951. From asst. to chief scientist Conn. Agrl. Expt. Sta., New Haven, 1951-71; vice dir. Conn. Agrl. Expt. Sta., 1969-71, dir., 1972-87, disting. scientist, 1987—; lectr. Yale Forestry Sch., New Haven, 1962—; mem. panels on policy implications of global warming NAS, 1989-91. Contbr. articles to profl. jours. Served to capt. USAAF, 1943-46. Guggenheim fellow, 1963. Fellow AAAS (chmn. climate changes and water resources com. 1986-89), Am. Phytopath. Soc.; mem. NAS, Am. Meteorol. Soc. (Outstanding Achievement in Biometeorology award 1967), Conn. Acad. Sci. and Engring., Recipient of the Anton-de- Bary Medal, 1996, Grads Club. Achievements include mathematical simulation of plant disease epidemics; hydrologic role of foliar pores; impact of climate change on agriculture and water resources; how much ten billion can spare for nature. Home: 314 Vineyard Point Rd Guilford CT 06437-3255 Office: Conn Agrl Expt Sta PO Box 1106 New Haven CT 06504-1106

WAGGONER, SUSAN MARIE, electronics engineer; b. East Chicago, Ind., Sept. 1, 1952; d. Joseph John and Elizabeth Vasilak; m. Steven Richard Waggoner, July 31, 1976; children: Kenneth David, Michael Christopher. AS, Ind. U., 1975, BA in Journalism, 1976, BS in Physics, 1982, M in Pub. Affairs, 1991. Engring. technician Naval Surface Warfare Ctr., Crane, Ind., 1978-82, electronics engr. test and measurement equipment, 1982-91, electronics engr. batteries, 1991—. Mem. AIAA, Am. Soc. Naval Engrs., Fed. Mgrs. Assn., Federally Employed Women, Am. Rose Soc., Am. Hort. Soc., Mensa, Theatre Circle Ind. U., Sigma Pi Sigma. Home: RR 5 Box 387 Loogootee IN 47553-9337 Office: Naval Surface Warfare Ctr 300 Hwy 361 Crane IN 47522-5001

WAGGONER, WILLIAM JOHNSON, lawyer; b. Salisbury, N.C., Oct. 13, 1928; s. James Martin and Julia (Johnson) W.; m. Martha Anne Garwood, Aug. 8, 1953; children—William Johnson, Ellen Christine, David Garwood. A.B., U. N.C., Chapel Hill, 1951, LL.B., 1954. Bar: N.C. 1954. Ptnr., Weinstein, Muilenburg, Waggoner & Bledsoe, 1954-57; asst. U.S. atty. Western Dist. N.C., 1957-59; ptnr. Weinstein, Waggoner & Sturgess, 1959-70, Waggoner, Hasty & Kratt, Charlotte, N.C., 1970-84, Waggoner, Hamrick, Hasty, Monteith, Kratt, Cobb & McDonnell, 1985-88, Waggoner, Hamrick, Hasty, Montieth & Kratt PLLC, 1989—. Gen. counsel Mecklenburg Rep. Exec. Com., 1963-73; bd. deacons Lutheran Ch.; chmn. Charlotte Bd. Adjustment, 1970-72; mem. N.C. Bd. Elections, 1973-77. Served with AUS, 1946-47. Mem. Charlotte C. of C., Am. Arbitration Assn. (panel arbitrators), ABA, N.C. Bar Assn., Fed. Bar Assn., N.C. Bar Assn., Assn. Trial Lawyers Am., Am. Judicature Soc., Kappa Alpha Order. Club: Hornet Toastmasters (past pres.). Office: Waggoner Hamrick Hasty Monteith & Kratt PLLC Two First Union Ctr Ste 2750 Charlotte NC 28282

WAGMAN, GERALD HOWARD, retired biochemist; b. Newark, Mar. 4, 1926; s. David and Sophie (Milinsky) W.; B.S., Lehigh U., 1946; M.S., Va. Poly. Inst. and State U., 1947; m. Rhoda Kirschner, Dec. 9, 1948; children: Jan Donald, Neil Mark. Tech. research asst. Squibb Inst. for Med. Research, New Brunswick, N.J., 1947-49, research asst., 1954-57; mgr. Yankee Radio Corp., N.Y.C., 1950-54; assoc. biochemist Schering Corp. (now Schering-Plough Rsch. Inst.), Kenilworth, N.J., 1957-58, biochemist, 1958-65, sr. biochemist, 1966-68, sect. leader, 1969-70, mgr. antibiotics dept., 1970-74, assoc. dir. microbiol. scis.-antibiotics, 1974-76, assoc. dir. microbiol. scis. and head screening lab., 1977-78, dir. microbiol. strain lab., 1979-84, antibiotics isolation, 1984-85, microbial products chem. screening, 1985-87, prin. scientist, 1987-89, mgr. libr. info. ctr., 1989-93; ret., 1993; freelance tech. writing, editor, cons. 1993—; mem. adv. bd. Nat. Cert. Commn. in Chemistry and Chem. Engring., 1985-88. Coun. mem. Troop 23 Boy Scouts Am., 1964-66; communications officer East Brunswick Civil Def. and Disaster Control, 1966-71; mem. sci. adv. com. East Brunswick Bd. Edn., 1960-68; bd. dirs. Tamarack N. Homeowners Assn., 1983-84, 89—, pres., 1989-93, treas. 1994—. Recipient Public Svc. award Am. Radio Relay League, 1965. Chartered chemist, Gt. Britain. Fellow Am. Inst. Chemists; mem. AAAS, ALA, Spl. Librs. Assn., Am. Chem. Soc., Am. Soc. Microbiology, Am. Inst. Biol. Scis., Soc. Indsl. Microbiology, Soc. Applied Bacteriology (Gt. Britain), Royal Soc. Chemistry, Sigma Xi, Tau Delta Phi. Author: Chromatography of Antibiotics, 1973, rev. edit., 1984; mem. editorial bd. Antimicrobial Agents and Chemotherapy, 1971-74; co-editor: Isolation, Separation and Purification of Antibiotics, 1978, Natural Products Isolation, 1989; The Handy HamBook, 1994; contbr. articles to profl. jours. and books. Patentee in field. Home and Office: 17 Crommelin Ct East Brunswick NJ 08816-2406 *Serendipity often plays a big part in research. One may discover something entirely different from the object of the research, but you must have an open mind and a wide angle of observation.*

WAGMAN, ROBERT JOHN, journalist, author; b. Chgo., Nov. 11, 1942; s. Albert Alan and Rosamond (Horner) W.; m. Carol Ann Mueller, Jan. 30, 1965; children: Jennifer, Robert, Patricia, Marilyn. A.B., St. Louis U., 1966, M.A., 1968, J.D., 1971. Analyst Dun & Bradstreet, 1965-67; with CBS News, 1967-71, 74-77; asst. to dean St. Louis U. Sch. Law, 1971-74; Washington bur. chief N.Am. Newspaper Alliance, 1977-80, Ind. News Alliance, 1980-82; columnist Newspaper Enterprise Assn., 1980-95; pub. Fed. Real Estate Letter, 1995—. Author, co-author: Hubert Humphrey, The Man and His Dream, 1978, Citizens Guide to the Tax Revolt, 1979, Asbestos: The Silent Killer, 1982, Lord's Justice, 1985, Instant Millionaires, 1986, The Nazi Hunters, 1988, The First Amendment Book, 1991, 2d edit., 1996, World Almanac Guide to the Supreme Court, 1993, Blood Oath, 1994, Hong Kong, 1997, And Beyond, 1997; editor: World Almanac of U.S. Politics, 1988—. Recipient Thomas Stokes award in journalism.

WAGNER, ALAN BURTON, entrepreneur; b. Balt., June 8, 1938; s. Robert Ellsworth and Anna Margaret (Schnitzlein) W.; B.Engring. Sci. (scholastic leadership award) Johns Hopkins, 1960; M.M.E., Case-Western Res. U., 1962, Ph.D. in Bus. Mgmt., 1965; m. Lynn Felton Wynant, June 26, 1964; children: Brian Alan, David Scott, Elizabeth Lynn. Mgr. orgn. planning and devel. Internat. Minerals & Chem. Corp., Libertyville, Ill., 1964-67, dir., 1967-70, dir., v.p., 1970-73, corp. v.p., 1973-78; pres., dir. Taylor Tot Products, Inc., Frankfort, Ky., 1979-80, Fed. Mining Co., 1980-82, Wagner Mgmt. Corp., 1982—; prin., pres. Hilliard-Lyons, Wagner Assoc., 1982-92, Ky. Metals, Inc., Carolina Metal, Inc., Fla. Metals, Inc., Tex. Almet, Inc., Control Machine, Inc., FM Properties, Wagner Industries, Inc.; lectr. in field. Trustee, Union Coll., Furman U. Fellow Alfred P. Sloan Nat. Found.; mem. Chgo. Assn. Commerce and Industry, Chem. Industries Council of Midwest, ASME, Am. Mgmt. Assn., ASHRAE, (Homer Addams award), AAAS, Ky. Coal Assn. (dir.), Sigma Xi, Omicron Delta Kappa. Clubs: Knollwood (Lake Forest, Ill); Greenbrier, Lafayette (Lexington). Home: 1523 Lakewood Ct Lexington KY 40502-2567 Office: 651 Perimeter Dr Ste 600 Lexington KY 40517-4139

WAGNER, ALAN CYRIL, television and film producer; b. N.Y.C., Oct. 1, 1931; s. Joseph and Isabelle (Chanson) W.; m. Martha Celia Dreyfus, Mar. 11, 1956; children: David Mark, Susan Jill, Elizabeth Celia. BA, Columbia U., 1951, MA in English, 1952. Mgr. network programs Benton & Bowles, Inc., N.Y.C., 1957-61; dir. program devel. CBS, N.Y.C., 1961-68; v.p. program devel. CBS, Hollywood, Calif., 1968-73; v.p. program planning and devel. CBS, N.Y.C., 1973-75, v.p. nighttime programs, 1975-78, v.p. programs, 1978-82; pres., chief exec. officer The Disney Channel, N.Y.C., 1982-83, Alan Wagner Prodns., Inc., N.Y.C., 1983—; exec. v.p. feature and TV devel. and prodn. Grosso-Jacobson Entertainment Corp., N.Y.C., 1985-90; pres. Boardwalk Entertainment, N.Y.C., 1990—; adj. assoc. prof. visual arts NYU, 1993—. Prodr., dir., host program Living Opera, Stas. WNYC-WNYC-FM, N.Y.C., 1958-68; host radio broadcasts N.Y.C. Opera Co., 1978-80; panelist Met. Opera broadcast Quiz, 1996—; exec. prodr. film Reunion at Fairborough, 1985; prodr. TV pilot We're Puttin' on the Ritz, 1986; author: Prima Donnas and other Wild Beasts, 1961; exec. com. The Gunfighters, Diamonds; supervising prodr. Cop Talk: Behind the Shield, 1988, 89, True Blue, TV movie and series, 1989, A Family for Joe, TV movie and series, 1989-90, TV series Counterstrike, 1990-93, Top Cops, 1989-94; exec. prodr. TV movies Spenser: Ceremony, Spenser: Pale Kings and Princes, 1993, Spenser: The Judas Goat, Spenser: A Savage Place, 1994, Wounded Heart, 1995, Hearts Adrift, Reasons of the Heart, 1996, TV series The Marriage Counselor, 1994. Lt. (j.g.) USNR, 1953-57. Recipient Evelyn Burkey Meml. award Writers Guild Am., 1983. Mem. NATAS, Internat. Radio and TV Soc., Acad. Cable Programming, Columbia U. Alumni Assn. Avocations: opera, other music, sound reproduction, baseball, other sports. Office: Boardwalk Entertainment 210 E 39th St New York NY 10016-0911 *A decent and abiding respect for the opinions and talents of the creative community on one hand, and the consuming community on the other, has always served as the necessary framework for any decision making in both my professional and personal life. The doers and the thinkers are crucially important, but no more so than those for whom they do and think. If I can serve as an effective middle man, a good part of my life's objective is realizable.*

WAGNER, ALLAN RAY, psychology educator, experimental psychologist; b. Springfield, Ill., Jan. 6, 1934; s. Raymond August and Grace (Johnson) W.; m. Barbara Rae Meland, Nov. 21, 1959, (dec. Nov. 1994); children: Krystn Rae, Kathryn Rae. B.A., U. Iowa, 1956, M.A., 1958, Ph.D., 1959; M.A. hon., Yale U., 1970. Asst. prof. psychology Yale U., New Haven, 1959-64, assoc. prof., 1964-69, prof., 1970-89, chmn. psychology dept., 1983-89, James Rowland Angell prof. psychology, 1990—, chmn. philosophy dept., 1991-93, dir., divsn. of the soc. sci., 1992—; cons. NIMH, 1968-71; mem. Pres. Biomed. Research Panel, 1975-76; adv. bd. Cambridge Ctr. Behavioral Studies, 1982—; mem. psychobiology panel NSF, 1984-85, com. on basic research in behavioral and social scis. NRC, 1984-87. Author: Reward and Punishment, 1965; assoc. editor: Learning and Motivation, 1969-74, Animal Learning and Behavior, 1972-74; editor: Jour. Exptl. Psychology, 1974-81, Quantitative Analyses of Behavior, Vol. 3, 1982, Vol. 4, 1983, Vol. 7, 1988. Fellow NSF, 1958 (grantee 1960—), NIMH, 1963. Fellow APA, AAAS (mem. coun. 1988-91), Soc. Exptl. Psychologists (Howard Crosby Warren medal 1991), Am. Psychol. Soc.; mem. NAS, Psychonomic Soc., So. Quantitative Analysis of Behavior (sec. 1983-92), Ea. Psychol. Assn. (bd. dirs. 1985-88), Sigma Xi, New Haven Law Club. Home: 1405 Ridge Rd North Haven CT 06473-3051 Office: Yale U Dept Psychology PO Box 208205 New Haven CT 06520-8205

WAGNER, ARTHUR WARD, JR., lawyer; b. Birmingham, Ala., Aug. 13, 1930; s. Arthur Ward and Lucille (Lockheart) W.; m. Ruth Shingler, May 11, 1957; children: Celia Wagner Minter, Julia Wagner Dolce, Helen Wagner McAfee. BSBA, U. Fla., 1954, JD, 1957. Bar: Fla. 1957, U.S. Dist. Ct. (so. dist.) Fla. 1957, U.S. Dist. Ct. (mid. dist.) Fla. 1975. Ptnr. Wagner, Johnson, & McAfee, P.A., West Palm Beach, Fla., 1959—; lectr. in field. Author: Art of Advocacy: Jury Selection, 1981; co-author: Anatomy of Personal Injury Lawsuit I & II, 1968 and 1981. Mem. 15th Jud. Nominating Com., Palm Beach City, 1979-82, 4th Dist. Nominating Commn., Palm Beach City, 1982-86; mem. pres.'s coun. U. Fla.; vestry, chancellor Holy Trinity Parish; bd. dirs. U. Fla. Found., 1996-2000. Fellow Internat. Acad. Trial Lawyers, Am. Coll. Trial Lawyers, Internat. Soc. Barristers, Am. Bd. Trial Advs.; mem. Assn. Trial Lawyers Am. (pres. 1975-76, hon. life trustee Roscoe Pound Found.), So. Trial Lawyers Assn. (pres. 1991), U. Fla. Law Coll. Alumni (mem. bd. govs.). Democrat. Episcopalian. Office: Wagner Nugent Johnson & McAfee PA 1818 S Australian Ave West Palm Beach FL 33409-6487

WAGNER, BRUCE STANLEY, marketing communications executive; b. San Diego, Aug. 1, 1943; s. Robert Sheldon and Janet (Lowther) W.; m. Elizabeth Pearsall Winslow, Oct. 4, 1975; children: Sage Elizabeth, Alexander Winslow. BA, Dartmouth Coll., 1965; MBA, U. Pa., 1984. Sr. v.p. Grey Advt., Inc., N.Y.C., 1967-81; exec. v.p., chief operating officer Campaign '76 Media Communications, Inc., Washington, 1975-76; exec. v.p., bd. dirs. Ross Roy, Inc., Bloomfield Hills, Mich., 1981-91, Ross Roy Group, Inc., Bloomfield Hills, Mich., 1991-94; v.p. comm. ITT Automotive Inc., Auburn Hills, Mich., 1995—. Mem. Am. Assn. Advt. Agys. (bd. govs. ctrl. region 1988-94, chmn., bd. govs. Mich. coun. 1985-86), Wharton Alumni Assn. (chmn. 1983-85), Wharton Club of Mich. (bd. dirs. 1985—), Detroit Athletic Club, Orchard Lake Country Club, Birmingham Athletic Club. Home: 975 Arlington Rd Birmingham MI 48009-1684 Office: ITT Automotive Inc 3000 University Dr Auburn Hills MI 48326-2356

WAGNER, BURTON ALLAN, lawyer; b. Milw., June 13, 1941; s. Irwin and Jennie (Oxman) W.; m. Georgia Olchoff, Aug. 29, 1964; children: Andrew, Laura. B.B.A. in Acctg, U. Wis., 1963, J.D., 1966, M.A. in Health Services Adminstrn, 1976. Bar: Wis. 1966. Assoc. legal counsel U. Wis., 1968-74; asst. to vice chancellor, legal counselor U. Wis. Hosps., 1974-77; asst. sec. Wis. Dept. Health and Social Services, 1977-83, adminstr. div. community services, 1979-83; clin. assoc. prof. health adminstrn. U. Wis.;

ptnr. Thomas Harnisch & Wagner, Madison, 1983-85, Whyte & Hirschboeck, Madison, 1985-90; ptnr. (of counsel) Katten Muchin and Zavis, Madison, 1990-93; ptnr. Reinhart Boerner Van Deuren Norris & Rieselbach, Madison, 1993—. Chmn. personnel com. Dane County chpt. ARC, 1977-90. Served with USAR, 1966-68, Vietnam. Decorated Bronze Star. Mem. Soc. Law and Medicine, Wis. Bar Assn., Dane County Bar Assn. Jewish. Office: PO Box 2020 Madison WI 53701-2020

WAGNER, CARRUTH JOHN, physician; b. Omaha, Sept. 4, 1916; s. Emil Conrad and Mabel May (Knapp) W. A.B., Omaha U., 1938; B.Sc., U. Nebr., 1938, M.D., 1941, D.Sc., 1966. Diplomate: Am. Bd. Sugery, Am. Bd. Orthopaedic Surgery. Intern U.S. Marine Hosp., Seattle, 1941-42; resident gen. surgery and orthopaedic surgery USPHS hosps., Shriners Hosp., Phila., 1943-46; med. dir. USPHS, 1952-62; chief orthopaedic service USPHS Hosp., San Francisco, 1946-51, S.I., N.Y., 1951-55; health mblzn. USPHS Hosp., 1959-62; asst. surgeon gen. dep. chief div. hosps. UPHS, 1957-59; chief div. USPHS, 1962-65, USPHS (Indian Health), 1962-65; dir. Bur. Health Services, 1965-68; Washington rep. AMA, 1968-72; health services cons., 1972-79; dept. health services State of Calif., 1979—. Contbr. articles to med. jours. Served with USCGR, World War II. Recipient Pfizer award, 1962; Meritorious award Am. Acad. Gen. Practice, 1965; Disting. Svc. medal, 1968, Calif. Dept. Health Svcs. Pub. Health Recognition award, 1995. Fellow A.C.S. (bd. govs.), Am. Soc. Surgery Hand, Am. Assn. Surgery Trauma, Am. Geriatrics Soc., Am. Acad. Orthopaedic Surgeons; mem. Nat. Assn. Sanitarians, Am. Pub. Health Assn. Sanitarians, Am. Pub. Health Assn., Washington Orthopaedic Club, Am. Legion, Alpha Omega Alpha. Lutheran. Club: Mason (Shriner). Home: 6234 Silverton Way Carmichael CA 95608-0757 Office: PO Box 638 Carmichael CA 95609-0638 *My success can best be summarized as the result of efforts of other people. First my family, particularly my mother, then my teachers and preceptors, and finally my associates. Throughout my life there has been a key individual who created an environment where I could exercise my maximum capabilities. Later in life when it became possible for me to provide similar opportunities for associates I found the benefits I derived far exceeded anything I could have achieved on my own. In summary, success means getting things done, getting planned things done, and getting planned things done largely through other people.*

WAGNER, CHARLES LEONARD, electrical engineer, consultant; b. Pitts., Nov. 23, 1925; s. Charles Fredrick and Ada Sophia (Hanna) W.; m. Rachel Mae Arbogast, Nov. 15, 1952 (dec. Mar. 1978); children: Charles John, Virginia Ann, Robert Alan. BSEE, Bucknell U., 1945; MSEE, U. Pitts., 1949. Registered profl. engr., Pa. Engr. Westinghouse Elec. Corp., Pitts., 1946-50, sponsor engr., 1950-67, mgr. transmission engring., 1967-76, cons. engr., 1976-85; pvt. cons. Export, Pa., 1985—; adj. instr. U. Pitts., Carnegie-Mellon U., 1952-85. Contbr. articles to profl. jours. Lt. (j.g.) USN, 1943-46. Fellow IEEE (C.P. Steinmetz award, Standards medallion, Centennial medal, Switchgear Com. Dist. Svc. award 1982, Relay Com. Dist. Svc. award 1985, Tech. Coun. Meritorious Svc. award 1990); mem. Internat. Conf. Large High Voltage Electric Systems (Attwood Assoc. award), Power Engring. Soc. of IEEE (chmn. tech. coun. 19771-81, v.p. 1981-83, pres. 1984-85, Meritorious Svc. award 1989, Paper prizes 1970, 90), Tau Beta Pi, Pi Mu Sigma. Presbyterian. Avocations: golf, woodworking, computing. Home and Office: 4933 Simmons Dr Export PA 15632-9330

WAGNER, CHRISTIAN NIKOLAUS JOHANN, materials engineering educator; b. Saarbrucken-Dudweiler, Germany, Mar. 6, 1927; came to U.S., 1959, naturalized, 1969; s. Christian Jakob and Regina (Bungert) W.; m. Rosemarie Anna Mayer, Apr. 5, 1952; children—Thomas Martin, Karla Regine, Petra Susanne. Student, U. Poitiers, France, 1948-49; Licence es Sci., U. Saar, Ger., 1951, Diplom-Ingenieur, 1954, Dr.rer.nat., 1957. Research asst. Inst. fur Metallforschung, Saarbrucken, 1953-54; vis. fellow M.I.T., 1955-56; research asso. Inst. fur Metallforschung, 1957-58; teaching, research asst. U. Saarbrucken, 1959; asst. prof. Yale U., New Haven, Conn., 1959-62; assoc. prof. Yale U., 1962-70; prof. dept. materials engring. UCLA, 1970-91, prof. emeritus, 1991—, chmn. dept., 1974-79, asst. dean undergrad. studies Sch. Engring. and Applied Sci., 1982-85, acting chmn., 1990-91; vis. prof. Tech. U., Berlin, 1969, U. Saarbrücken, 1979-80. Contbr. articles to profl. jours. Recipient U.S. Sci. Humboldt award U. Saarbrucken, 1989-90, 92. Fellow Am. Soc. Metals Internat.; mem. Am. Crystallographic Assn., Minerals, Metals and Materials Soc. Home: 37621 Golden Pebble Ave Palm Desert CA 92211-1430 Office: UCLA 6532 Boelter Hall Los Angeles CA 90095-1595

WAGNER, CURTIS LEE, JR., judge; b. Kingsport, Tenn., Nov. 8, 1928; m. Jeanne E. Allen (dec.); children: Curtis L. III, Rex A. Student Tenn. Poly. Inst., 1947-49; LLB, U. Tenn., 1951. Bar: Tenn. 1952. Assoc. Kramer, Dye, McNabb and Greenwood, Knoxville, Tenn., 1951-54; atty.-adv. gen. crimes and fraud sect. Criminal Div., Dept. Justice, Washington, 1954-56, trial atty. Dept. Justice, 1954-60, assigned to Ct. of Claims sect. Civil Div., 1956-60; spl. asst. to JAG for communications, transp. and utilities, Office JAG, Dept. Army, Washington, 1960-64, chief Regulatory Law Div., 1964-74, mem. civilian lawyer career com., 1960-74, chmn. JAG incentive awards com. 1960-74, mem. Army Staff Awards Bd., 1964-74, mem. Army Environ. Policy Council, 1972-74. Adminstrv. law judge FERC, Washington, 1974-79, chief adminstrv. law judge, 1979—. Dist. commr. Nat. Capital Area council Boy Scouts Am., 1967-69; mem. Bd. Govts. Watergate of Alexandria Condo, 1996—; commr. Alexandria Redevel. and Pub. Housing Commn., 1996—. Decorated Meritorious Civilian Service award, Exceptional Civilian Service award; recipient citation for outstanding performance Dept. Army, 1961-74; Scouter's Tng. award Boy Scouts Am., 1965, Scoutmaster's Key, 1966, Commr.'s Key, 1968, Commr.'s Arrowhead Honor, 1966, Silver Beaver award, 1969. Mem. Order of Arrow. Methodist. Clubs: Annapolis Yacht (parliamentarian). Office: Fed Energy Regulatory Commn 888 1st St NE Washington DC 20426-0001

WAGNER, CYNTHIA GAIL, editor, writer; b. Bethesda, Md., Oct. 3, 1956; d. Robert Cheney and Marjory Jane (Kletzing) W. BA in English, Grinnell Coll., 1978; MA in Comms., Syracuse U., 1981. Editorial asst. The Futurist/World Future Soc., Bethesda, Md., 1981-82, staff editor, 1982-85, asst. editor, 1985-91, sr. editor, 1991-92, mng. editor, 1992—. Author: (plays) Discriminating Dining, 1993, Limited Engagement, 1993; columnist 3-2-1 Contact, 1994; contbr. Encyclopedia of the Future, 1995. Mem. Theatre Comm. Group, Soc. Profl. Journalists. Avocation: theater. Office: The Futurist World Future Soc 7910 Woodmont Ave Ste 450 Bethesda MD 20814-3015

WAGNER, D. WILLIAM, lawyer; b. Dixon, Ill., Jan. 14, 1943; s. Earl L. and Lois Mae Wagner; m. Susan A. Aldrich; children: Peter Alan, Nicholas William. BA, Northwestern U., 1965, JD, 1968. Bar: Ill. 1968, U.S. Dist. Ct. (no. dist.) Ill. 1969, U.S. Ct. Appeals (7th cir.) 1971, Calif. 1982. Ptnr. firm Sidley & Austin, Chgo. and L.A., 1969—. Dir. Housing Options for People to Excell, Inc., 1992-94, 96—. Co-author: Illinois Municipal Law: Subdivisions and Subdivisions in Controls, 1978, 81. Mem. ABA, Internat. Assn. Attys. and Execs. in Corp. Real Estate, Ill. State Bar Assn., Chgo. Bar Assn. (chmn. real property land use com. 1980-81), L.A. County Bar Assn., Beverly Hills Bar Assn. (chmn. real estate sect. 1986-87). Presbyterian. Clubs: Legal (Chgo.); Beach (Santa Monica). Home: 20 Ocean Park Blvd Unit 25 Santa Monica CA 90405-3557 Office: Sidley & Austin 555 W 5th St Ste 4000 Los Angeles CA 90013-3000

WAGNER, DANIEL A., human developement educator, academic administrator; b. Chgo., July 18, 1946; married; 2 children. BS in Ops. Rsch. Engring., Cornell U., 1968; MA in Exptl. Psychology, U. Mich., 1971, PhD in Developmental Psychology, 1976. Vis. postdoctoral fellow lab. of human devel. Harvard U., Cambridge, Mass., 1979-81; prof. human devel. Grad. Sch. Edn. U. Pa., Phila., dir. Internat. Literacy Inst., dir. Literacy Rsch. Ctr.; dir. Nat. Ctr. on Adult Literacy, U.S. Dept. Edn., 1990-95. Contbr. articles to profl. publs. Spencer Fedn. fellow, 1983-85; recipient Nat. Rsch. Svc. award NIMH, 1980-81; grantee Nat. Inst. Child Health and Human Devel., 1981-84, NSF, 1990-93, UNESCO, USAID, 1991-96. Fellow AAA, APA. Office: U Pennsylvania Nat Ctr on Adult Literacy 3910 Chestnut St Philadelphia PA 19104-3111

WAGNER, DAVID JAMES, lawyer; b. Cleve., Feb. 7, 1946; m. Martha Wilson, June 22, 1979; 1 child, Diana Jane. BS, USAF Acad., 1969; JD, Georgetown U., 1973. Bar: Colo. 1973, U.S. Supreme Ct. 1975, U.S. Dist. Ct. of Colo. 1973, U.S. Tax Ct. 1974. Asst. assoc. gen. counsel Presdl. Clemency Bd., Washington, 1974-75; sec., gen. counsel Cablecomm-Gen. Inc., Denver, 1975-77; adj. prof. law Metro. State Coll., Denver, 1975-80; atty., mng. prin. Wagner & Waller, P.C., Denver, 1977-84; chmn. bd. GILA Comm., Inc., Denver, 1987; pvt. practice David Wagner & Assocs., P.C., Englewood, Colo., 1984—. Editor Am. Criminal Law Rev., Georgetown U. Law Sch., 1972-73. Trustee Kent Denver Sch., Cherry Hills Village, Colo., 1990-96, treas., 1992, pres., 1992-96; treas., dir. Denver Chamber Orch., 1979-81; dir. Leadership Denver Assn., 1978-80. Capt. USAF, 1973-75. Republican. Episcopalian. Office: David Wagner & Assocs PC Penthouse 8400 E Prentice Ave Englewood CO 80111-2912

WAGNER, DIANE M(ARGARET), theology educator; b. Hancock, Mich., Apr. 22, 1943; d. Benjamin Philip and Eunice Rose (La Mothe) W. BA, Alverno Coll., Milw., 1965; MA, Mundelein Coll., Chgo., 1972; student, Clin. Pastoral Edn., Milw., 1979-80. Cert. advanced standing chaplain, 1982. Tchr. grade 1 St. Peter Sch., Skokie, Ill., 1964-65; tchr. grades 1 and 2 St. Cecelia Sch., Hubbell, Mich., 1965-67; tchr. grades 1, 2, 4-6 St. Joseph Sch., Wilmette, Ill., 1967-71; tchr. grade 5. middle grade coord. St. Mary Sch., Buffalo Grove, Ill., 1971-73; tchr. grade 5 St. Alphonsus Sch., Greendale, Wis., 1973-74; recruiter Sch. Sisters of St. Francis, Milw., 1974-79; chaplain, dir. pastoral care Tau Home Health Care Agy., Milw., 1980-88, dir. vols., 1981-88; chaplain, dir. pastoral care St. Mary's Hill Hosp., Milw., 1988-92; tchr. theology, assoc. chaplain Divine Savior Holy Angels High Sch., Milw., 1993—; mem. Chaplain Adv. Bd., Milw., 1982-88, pres., 1985-88. Author: (tape) College of Chaplains, 1986. Vice pres bd. dirs. Clare Towers, Inc., Milw., 1981-87. Recipient Cert. Appreciation, Clare Towers, Inc., 1987. Mem. Nat. Assn. Cath. Chaplains (sec. regional bd. dirs. 1986-88), Milw. Area Dirs. Pastroal Care Assn. (pres. 1987-88). Democrat. Roman Catholic. Avocations: reading, camping, golfing. Home: 2619 N 39th St Milwaukee WI 53210-2503 Office: Divine Savior Holy Angels High Sch 4257 N 100th St Milwaukee WI 53222-1313

WAGNER, DONALD ARTHUR, securities group executive; b. Bklyn., July 9, 1963; s. Nathan and Jeanette (Rabinowitz) W. BA in Physics summa cum laude, Harvard U., 1985. Cons. analytical systems group Morgan Stanley & Co., N.Y.C., 1981-83; assoc. corp. fin. dept. Lazard Frères & Co., N.Y.C., 1985-87; ptnr. capital markets group Lazard Bros. & Co. Ltd., London, 1987-89; sr. v.p. high yield securities and capital markets group Lazard Frères & Co., N.Y.C., 1989-95, mng. dir., 1996—. Mem. Phi Beta Kappa. Office: Lazard Frères & Co 30 Rockefeller Plz New York NY 10112

WAGNER, DONALD BERT, health care consultant; b. York, Pa., July 27, 1930; s. Bert Daniel and Mary Elizabeth (Roelke) W.; m. Janet Louise Bankert, July 12, 1952; children: Kimberly, Susan, David, John. Student, Franklin & Marshall, 1948-50; BS in Phys. Therapy, Columbia U., 1952; MHA, Baylor U., 1960. Commd. 2d lt. USAF, 1952, advanced through grades to brig. gen., 1981; physical therapist Randolph AFB, San Antonio, 1952-55; asst. adminstr. USAF/RAF S. Ruislip, London; adminstr. USAF/RAF Bentwaters, Ipswich, Eng., 1955-58; various adminstrv. roles USAF Hosps. and Commands, Europe and U.S., 1958-73; dep. comdr. USAF Sch. Health Care Sci., Wichita Falls, Tex., 1973-75; adminstr. Wilford Hall Med. Ctr., San Antonio, 1975-79; chief med. svc. corps Office Surgeon Gen. USAF, San Antonio, 1979-82; dep. surgeon gen. USAF Med. Svc. Ctr., San Antonio, 1981-82, ret., 1982; adminstr., assoc. v.p. M. D. Anderson/U. Tex. Cancer Ctr., Houston, 1982-85; chief exec. officer Meml. Southwest Hosp., Houston, 1985-91; v.p. Meml. Hosp. System, Houston, 1985-91, cons., 1992—; dir. residency edn., grad. program in healthcare adminstrn. U. Houston, Clear Lake; adj. prof. Baylor and Trinity U., San Antonio, 1975-82; assoc. prof. U. Houston, St. Louis U., 1982-88. Bd. dirs. Hospice at the Med. Ctr., Child Advocates, Houston, 1985-89, Kidney Found., Houston, 1985-88, Westland YMCA, Houston, 1985-88, 90-94, Greater Houston Hosp. Coun., 1983-87, Sam Houston area Alzheimer's Assn. 1990-94; chmn. external adv. bd. Sch. Allied Health, U. Tex. Med. Br. Named Disting. Alumnus Baylor U. Program in Healthcare Adminstrn., 1993. Fellow Am. Coll. Healthcare Execs. (edn. com.), Royal Soc. Health; mem. Am. Hosp. Assn. (bd. dirs. hosp. rsch. and edn. found. 1990—), Tex. Hosp. Assn., Assn. Mil. Surgeons U.S. (Ray E. Brown award 1982, Outstanding Sr. Level Healthcare Exec. Ache Regents award 1991), Am. Mgmt. Soc. Republican. Methodist. Avocation: music. Home: 1746 Carriage Way Sugar Land TX 77478-4201 Office: Meml Healthcare System 7737 Southwest Fwy Houston TX 77074-1807

WAGNER, DOROTHY MARIE, retired senior creative designer, artist; b. Chgo., Jan. 12, 1926; d. William Christopher and Margaret Frances (Rowell) W. Student, Kalamazoo Coll., 1943-45; BS, Western Mich. U., 1947; BFA, Art Ctr. Coll. Design, L.A., 1962. Dir. electroencephalography lab. Bronson Hosp., Kalamazoo, 1945-51; dir. EEG lab. Terr. Hosp., Kaneohe, Hawaii, 1951-55, UCLA Med. Ctr., 1955-60; sr. creative designer GM Tech. Ctr. Styling, Warren, Mich., 1962-82; cons. in EEG, Army Hosp., Honolulu, 1950-55; dir. sales and rental gallery Pt. Huron (Mich.) Mus., 1989-93, art and painting instr., 1992-96. Recipient Best of Show award Ea. Mich. Internat. Art Show, 1992, 1st pl. award, 1988, 89, 94. Mem. Blue Water Art Assn. (pres. 1990-96), Orion Art Ctr. Episcopalian. Avocations: horseback riding, showing in dressage, breeding and raising racing greyhounds, water color and acrylic painting, stained glass design and fabrication. Home: 14841 Pine Knoll Rd Capac MI 48014-1913

WAGNER, DOUGLAS WALKER ELLYSON, journal editor; b. Orange, N.J., Nov. 5, 1938; s. Norman Raphael and Virginia (Taylor) W. B.A., Yale U., 1960. Editorial coordinator Med. World News, N.Y.C., 1965-69, assoc. editor, 1969-70; writer, assoc. editor Emergency Medicine, N.Y.C., 1970-76, sr. editor, 1976-81, editor-in-chief, 1981-87; editor, pub. Pediatric Primary Care (formerly Pediatric Therapeutics and Toxicology, Jersey City, 1987—; editor, publ. Pediatric Emergency and Critical Care (formerly Pediatric Trauma and Acute Care), 1988—; editor-in-chief Transition: Medicine and the Aging Process, N.Y.C., 1983. Mem. Nat. Assn. Sci. Writers, Am. Med. Writers Assn., Soc. for Acad. Emergency Medicine (assoc.), Soc. Pediatric Emergency Medicine, Am. Acad. Clin. Toxicology. Home: PO Box 23 72 Sussex St PO Box 23 Jersey City NJ 07303-0023 Office: Riverpress Inc PO Box 23 Jersey City NJ 07303-0023

WAGNER, DURRETT, former publisher, picture service executive; b. El Paso, Tex., Feb. 27, 1929; s. Francis and Florence (Durrett) W.; m. Betty Jane Brown, June 7, 1951; children—Gordon, Velma, Kendra. B.A., Baylor U., 1950; M.Div., Yale, 1954; postgrad., U. Chgo., 1954-59. Chmn. social sci. div. Kendall Coll., Evanston, Ill., 1959-63; dean Kendall Coll., 1963-67; partner v.p.; Swallow Press Inc., Chgo., 1967-92; owner, partner, pres. Hist. Pictures Service, Inc., Chgo., 1975-92; now pres. Bookworks, Inc., Chgo. Home and Office: 614 Ingleside Pl Evanston IL 60201-1742

WAGNER, EDWARD FREDERICK, JR., investment management company executive; b. Columbus, Ohio, Nov. 26, 1938; s. Edward Frederick and Margaret Ann (List) W.; m. Diana Beth Pietraszweski, Jan. 14, 1989; children: Edward Frederick III, John Patrick, James Francis, Caroline Elizabeth. BS, Xavier U., Cin., 1960; MBA, Miami U., Oxford, Ohio, 1965. Registered prin. and ops. rep. N.Y. Stock Exch., Am. Stock Exch.; registered rep. Nat. Assn. Securities Dealers. Investment analyst The Equitable Life Assurance Soc. U.S., N.Y.C., 1965-68; security analyst H.C. Wainwright & Co., N.Y.C., 1968-71; v.p. William D. Witter, Inc., N.Y.C., 1971-76, Wainwright Securities, Inc., N.Y.C., 1976-78, Blyth Eastman Dillon & Co., Inc., N.Y.C., 1978-79, Salomon Bros., Inc., N.Y.C., 1979-81, Lehman Bros., Kuhn Loeb & Co., Inc., N.Y.C., 1981-84; sr. v.p. Gabelli & Co., Inc., Rye, N.Y., 1984—, Gabelli Asset Mgmt. Co. (GAMCO Investors, Inc.), Rye, 1984—. 1st lt. U.S. Army, 1961-63. Mem. N.Y. Soc. Security Analysts Inc., Assn. for Investment Mgrs. and Rsch., Racquet and Tennis Club (N.Y.C.), The Rockaway Hunting Club (Cedarhurst, N.Y.), Southampton (N.Y.) Club, The Brook Club (N.Y.C.). Office: Gamco Investors Inc Corp Ctr at Rye Rye NY 10580-1430

WAGNER, EDWARD KURT, publishing company executive; b. N.Y.C., Sept. 29, 1936; s. Kurt Henry and Julia Marie (Selesky) W.; m. Ann Marie Philbin, Jan. 31, 1959; children: Denise, Steven, Kenneth, Jeanne. B.B.A., St. Francis Coll., 1961. With Pitman Pub. Corp., N.Y.C., 1952-75, v.p., treas., 1968-71, exec. v.p., 1971-75; financial mgr. Dun-Donnelley Pub. Corp., N.Y.C., 1975-76, contr. gen. book div., 1976-77; sr. mgr. contr.'s dept. Dun & Bradstreet, Inc., N.Y.C., 1977-78, asst. contr., 1978-83, contr., 1983-88, v.p., contr., 1989-96; ret., 1996—. Home: 1660 Goldspire Rd Toms River NJ 08755-0891

WAGNER, ELLYN E. See SANTI, ELLYN E.

WAGNER, ERIC ARMIN, sociology educator; b. Cleve., May 31, 1941; s. Armin Erich and Florence (Edwards) W. AB, Ohio State U., 1964; MA, U. Fla., 1968, PhD, 1973. Instr. sociology Ohio U., Athens, 1968-73, asst. prof., 1973-75, assoc. prof., 1975-83, prof., 1983—, chmn. sociology and anthropology, 1974-78, 86-91, 94-97, vice chmn. faculty senate, 1982-84. Dir. Planned Parenthood of Southeast Ohio, 1990-96, pres. 1992-94. Mem. Internat. Sociol. Assn., North Cen. Sociol. Assn., Midwest Assn. for Latin Am. Studies (pres. 1979-80), U.S. Orienteering Fedn. (dir. 1976-82, sec.-treas. 1976-78, v.p. 1979-80, sec. 1980-82), Delta Sigma Phi. Presbyterian. Contbr. books and articles on internat. sport and society to various pubs. Home: 10030 Oxley Rd Athens OH 45701-9647 Office: Ohio U Dept Sociology Athens OH 45701

WAGNER, FLORENCE ZELEZNIK, telecommunications executive; b. McKeesport, Pa., Sept. 23, 1926; d. George and Sophia (Petros) Zeleznik; BA magna cum laude, U. Pitts., 1977, MPA, 1981; m. Francis Xavier Wagner, June 18, 1946; children: Deborah Elaine Wagner Franke, Rebecca Susan Wagner Schroettinger, Melissa Catherine Wagner Good, Francis Xavier, Robert Francis. Sec. to pres. Tube City Iron & Metal Co., Glassport, Pa., 1944-50; cons. Raw Materials, Inc., Pitts., 1955; gen. mgr. Carson Compressed Steel Products, Pitts., 1967-69; ptnr. Universal Steel Products, Pitts., 1970-71; gen. mgr. Josh Steel Co., Braddock, Pa., 1971-78; owner Wagner's Candy Box, Mt. Lebanon, Pa., 1979-80; borough sec./treas. Borough of Pennsbury Village, Allegheny County, Pa., 1980-88; ptnr. Tele-Communications of Am., Burgettstown, Pa., 1984-86; trustee Profit-Sharing trust, Pension trust Josh Steel Co., 1986—, Consol, Inc., Upper St. Clair, Pa., 1989—; mem. Foster Parents, Jefferson Twp. Planning Commn., Washington County, Pa.; mem. sch. bd. St. Bernard Cath. Elem. Sch., Mt. Lebanon, Pa., sec., 1995—. Mem. AAUW, Pitts. Symphony Soc., Pitts. Ballet Theater Guild; GED literacy vol. Pitts.-Carlow, 1997—. Mem. Soc. Pub. Adminstrn. (founder U. Pitts. br.), Acad. Polit. Sci., U.S. Strategic Inst., Southwestern Pa. Sec. Assn., Alpha Sigma Lambda (past treas., sec., pres.). Republican. Home: 1611 Upper Saint Clair Dr Pittsburgh PA 15241

WAGNER, FREDERICK BALTHAS, JR., historian, retired surgery educator; b. Phila., Jan. 18, 1916; s. Frederick Balthas and Gertrude Louise (Mattes) W.; m. Jean Lockwood, June 30, 1945; children: Frederick B. III, Theodore Walter. AB, U. Pa., 1937; MD, Thomas Jefferson U., 1941, LHD (hon.), 1996. Diplomate: Am. Bd. Surgery. Clin. prof. surgery Jefferson Med. Coll. Thomas Jefferson U., Phila., 1954-78, Grace Revere Osler prof. surgery, 1978-84, historian, 1984—. Author: Twilight Years of Lady Osler, 1985; editor: Thomas Jefferson University: Tradition and Heritage, 1989. Recipient Alumni Achievement award Jefferson Med. Coll., 1987. Fellow Phila. Acad. Surgery (pres. 1985-86), Coll. Physicians Phila.; mem. Meigs Med. Assn. (pres. 1989-91), Jefferson Alumni Assn. (pres. 1975), Union League Phila. Republican. Methodist. Home: 800 Chauncey Rd Narberth PA 19072-1304

WAGNER, FREDERICK REESE, language professional; b. Phila., Apr. 15, 1928; s. Fred Reese and Mildred Wagner; m. Barbara Alexander Brady, May 9, 1959 (div. 1968); 1 child, Christopher A. BA summa cum laude, Duke U., 1948, MA, 1949, PhD, 1971. Advt mgr. Prentice-Hall, Inc., N.Y.C., 1955-57; promotion mgr. Harper & Row, N.Y.C., 1957-65; instr. English Duke U., Durham, N.C., 1967-69; asst. prof. Hamilton Coll, Clinton, N.Y., 1969-73, assoc. prof., 1973-78, prof. English, chmn. dept., 1978-90; prof. English Hamilton Coll, Clinton, 1990-95. Author: Famous Underwater Adventurers, 1962; Submarine Fighter of the American Revolution, 1963; Patriot's Choice: The Story of John Hancock, 1964; Robert Morris, Audacious Patriot, 1976. Mem. Thoreau Soc. (pres. 1984-86), Hawthorne Soc., Phi Beta Kappa. Home: 28 Dwight Ave Clinton NY 13323-1630

WAGNER, FREDERICK WILLIAM (BILL WAGNER), lawyer; b. Daytona Beach, Fla., Apr. 13, 1933; s. Adam A. and Nella (Schroeder) W.; m. Ruth Whetstone; children: Alan Frederick, Darryl William, Thomas Adam. BA, U. Fla., 1955, LLB with honors, 1960. Bar: Fla. 1960, U.S. Supreme Ct. 1967, D.C. 1989. Pvt. practice law Miami, Fla., 1960-63, Orlando, Fla., 1963-65, Tampa, Fla., 1965—; ptnr. law firm Nichols, Gaither, Beckham, Colson, Spence & Hicks, Tampa, Fla., 1965-67; partner law firm Wagner, Vaughan & McLaughlin (P.A. and predecessor names), 1967-87; mem. Gov.'s Judicial Nominations Commn., 1971-72, Constnl. Judicial Nominations Commn., 1972-75; mem. Fla. Bd. Bar Examiners, 1974-77; chmn. Civil Procedure Rules Com. Fla. Bar, 1977-78; bd. govs. Fla. Bar, 1978-83; trustree Roscoe Pound Found, 1984—. Contbr. articles to profl. jours. Capt. USAF, 1955-57. Fellow Am. Bar Found., Am. Coll. Trial Lawyers, Internat. Acad. Trial Lawyers; mem. Assn. Trial Lawyers Am. (bd. govs. 1973-80, 84-89, chmn. pub. affairs dept. 1984-89, treas. 1982-84, v.p. 1986-87, pres.-elect 1987-88, pres. 1988-89), Acad. Fla. Trial Lawyers (bd. dirs. 1965—, pres. 1972-73), Bay Area Trial Lawyers Assn. (v.p. 1966-68), Am. Law Inst. (coun. 1993—), Lawyer-Pilots Bar Assn., Fla. Bar Found., U. Fla. Alumni Assn., Nat. Bd. Trial Advocacy (cert. civil). Democrat. Methodist. Home: 78 Martinique Ave Tampa FL 33606-4053 Office: Wagner Vaughan & McLaughlin 601 Bayshore Blvd Ste 910 Tampa FL 33606-2761

WAGNER, GEORGE FRANCIS ADOLF, naval officer; b. S.I., N.Y., Mar. 24, 1941; s. George and Cornelia F. (Cosmen) W.; m. Sarah Elizabeth Lilly, June 6, 1962; children: Kristine, Gregory, Karin. BS, U.S. Naval Acad., 1962; MS, MIT, 1968, Naval Engr., 1968. Commd. ensign USN, 1962, advanced through grades to rear adm., 1991; staff fleet introduction officer Naval Sea Systems Command, Washington, 1977-79; instr. Sr. Officer Materiel Readiness Course, Idaho Falls, Idaho, 1979-81; comdg. officer USS John Rodgers (DD-983), Charleston, S.c., 1981-83; program mgr. Cruise Missiles Project, Washington, 1983-87; dep. and asst. Chief of Naval Rsch., Washington, 1987-89; mem. pers. policy staff Bur. Naval Pers., Washington, 1989-90; warfare system engr. Space and Naval Warfare System Command, Washington, 1990-91; program exec. officer cruise missiles projects and unmanned aerial vehicle joint project Washington, 1991-95; comdr. Space and Naval Warfare Sys. Command, Washington, 1995—. Decorated Def. Superior Svc. medal, Legion of Merit with oak leaf cluster. Episcopalian. Office: San Diego:COMPSAWARSYSCOM COMPSAWARSYCOM 53560 Hull St San Diego CA 92152-5801

WAGNER, GÜNTER PAUL, biologist educator; b. Vienna, Austria, May 28, 1954; came to U.S., 1991; s. Otto Karl and Käthe Auguste (Birke) W.; m. Herta Ruttner Brinkmann, Dec. 31, 1978 (div. 1985); 1 child, Susanne Karoline; m. Michaela Sabine Hauser, July 19, 1985; children: Veronika Eszter, Nikolas Frederik. PhD, U. Vienna, Austria, 1979; MA (hon.), Yale U., 1992. Asst. prof. U. Vienna, 1985-90, assoc. prof., 1990-91; prof. biology, chmn. dept. ecology and evolutionary biology Yale U., New Haven, 1996—; bd. dirs. Orgn. for Tropical Studies; vis. prof. Northwestern U., Evanston, Ill., 1987-88, U. Basel. Switzerland, 1991, U. Leiden, The Netherlands, 1995; Gompertz lectr. U. Calif., Berkeley, 1993; disting. lectr. Internat. Inst. for Applied Sys. Analysis, 1995; Sewell Wright lectr. U. Chgo., 1996. Publ. com. mem. Yale U. Press, New Haven, 1992-95; contbr. articles to profl. jours. Bd. dirs. Ctr. Computational Ecology, New Haven. Recipient MacArthur prize MacArthur Found., 1992. Mem. AAAS, European Soc. Evolutionary Biology (editl. bd. 1988-92), Austrian Acad. Scis. (corr.), Soc. for Study of Evolution (assoc. editor Jour. Exptl. Zoology 1994-97, editor 1997—), Soc. Systematic Biology, German Zool. Soc. Lutheran. Avocations: sailing, canoeing, horseback riding, literature, music. Office: Yale Univ 165 Prospect St New Haven CT 06511-2106

WAGNER, HAROLD A., industrial gas and chemical company executive; b. Oakland, Calif., Nov. 12, 1935; s. Harold A. and Lurline Frances (Madsen) W.; m. Marcia Kenaston, July 14, 1956; children: Sandra Wagner Boyce, Kristi Wagner, Schwiering, Tracey, Erik. BS in Mech. Engring., Stanford U., 1958, SEP, 1982; MBA, Harvard U., 1963. Regional sales mgr. ind. gases U.S. Air Products & Chems., Allentown, Pa., 1963-70; mgr. GM ind. gases U.K.Air Products & Chems., 1970-76; regional sales mgr. GM Ind.

Gases Continental Europe, 1976-80, GM Ind. Gases U.S., 1980-81; v.p. sales ind. gases div. FM, 1981-82; v.p. corp. planning Air Products & Chems., 1982-87, v.p. bus. div. chems., 1987-88; pres. AP Europe, 1988-90, exec. v.p., 1990-91, pres., COO, 1991-92, past chmn. pres., CEO; now chmn., pres., CEO, dir. Air Products and Chems. 1st Lt. USAF, 1958-61. Avocations: squash, photography. Home: 1306 Prospect Ave Bethlehem PA 18018-4917 Office: Air Prods & Chems Inc 7201 Hamilton Blvd Allentown PA 18195-1526*

WAGNER, HARVEY ALAN, finance executive; b. Detroit, Feb. 11, 1941; s. Max and Anne (Levine) W.; m. Arlene F. Tasman, Jan. 26, 1963 (dec. June 1988); children: Brooke D., Jennifer D; m. Arlene L. Rittenberg-Gelb, June, 1992. BBA in Acctg., U. Miami, 1963. Sr. acct. Hoch, Frey and Zugman, Ft. Lauderdale, Fla., 1963-67; contr. Canaveral Internat. Corp., Miami, Fla., 1967-68, Systems Engring. Lab., Ft. Lauderdale, 1968-70; dir. fin. and adminstrn., western area Arcata Comms., Inc., Menlo Park, Calif., 1971-73; sec., treas., contr. Commodore Bus. Machines Inc., Palo Alto, Calif., 1973-75; group contr. Fairchild Camera and Instrument Corp., Mountainview, Calif., 1975-83; v.p. contr. internat. GTE Corp., Phoenix, 1983-86; v.p. fin., sec., CFO Am. Microsystems, Inc., Santa Clara, Calif., 1986-89; v.p. fin., CFO Datapoint Corp., San Antonio, 1989, Computervision Corp., Bedford, Mass., 1989-94; v.p. fin., CFO, treas. Scientific-Atlanta, Inc., 1994—. Chmn. bd. Tech. Fed. Credit Union, San Jose, Calif., 1980-82, chmn. supervisory com., 1986-88, 78-80; v.p., founding dir. The Wellness Comty., Atlanta; mem. pres.'s adv. bd. U. Miami, 1995—; mem. Wharton Exec. Edn. Adv. Bd., 1995—. With USAR, 1959-67. Mem. Inst. Mgmt. Accts., Fin. Exec. Inst. (bd. dirs.), Assn. for Corp. Growth, Buckhead Club (bd. govs. 1995). Republican. Jewish. Avocations: golf, travel, art collecting. Office: Scientific-Atlanta Inc 1 Technology Pkwy S Norcross GA 30092-2928

WAGNER, HARVEY ARTHUR, nuclear engineer; b. Ann Arbor, Mich., Jan. 2, 1905; s. Emanuel M. and Emma (Kiebler) W.; m. Eleanor Mary Bond, July 6, 1929. B.S. in Mech. Engring., U. Mich., 1927; D.Eng., Lawrence Inst. Tech., 1969. With Procter & Gamble Co., 1927-28; with Detroit Edison Co., 1928-70, exec. v.p., 1969-70; cons. engr., 1970-96; chmn., dir. Overseas Adv. Assocs., Inc., 1974-96; Mem. Detroit Bd. Water Commrs., 1952-60; Trustee Nat. Sanitation Found., 1965-82. Author papers in field. Recipient Disting. Alumnus award U. Mich. Coll. Engring., 1953, Outstanding Alumni Achievement award, 1989; Sesquincentennial award as outstanding exec. and nuclear power cons. U. Mich., 1967; cert. pub. service Fed. Power Commn., 1964. Fellow ASME, Am. Nuclear Soc. (Cisler Award, 1994), Engring. Soc. Detroit (pres. 1968-69); mem. Nat. Acad. Engring., Tau Beta Pi, Phi Kappa Phi. Home: 932 Trombley Rd Grosse Pointe Park MI 48230-1860

WAGNER, HENRY NICHOLAS, JR., physician; b. Balt., May 12, 1927; s. Henry N. and Gertrude Loane W.; m. Anne Barrett Wagner, Feb., 1951; children—Henry N., Mary Randall, John Mark, Anne Elizabeth. A.B., Johns Hopkins U., 1948, M.D., 1952; D.Sc. (hon.), Washington Coll., Chestertown, Md., 1972, Free U., Brussels, 1985; M.D. (hon.), U. Gottingen, 1988. Chief med. resident Osler Med. Service, Johns Hopkins Hosp., Balt., 1958-59; asst. prof. medicine, radiology Johns Hopkins Med. Instns., 1959-64, asso. prof., 1964-65, prof. environ health scis., dir. divs. nuclear medicine and radiation health sci., 1965—. Author numerous books in field.; contbr. articles to med. jours. Served with USPHS, 1955-57. Recipient Georg von Hevesey medal, 1976. Fellow ACP; mem. Inst. Medicine of NAS, AMA (coun. sci. affairs, Sci. Achievement award 1991), Balt. City Med. Soc. (past pres.), World Fedn. Nuclear Medicine and Biology (past pres.), Am. Bd. Nuclear Medicine (founding mem.), Soc. Nuclear Medicine (past pres.), Am. Fedn. Clin. Research (past pres.), Research Socs. Council (past pres.), Assn. Am. Physicians, Am. Soc. Clin. Investigation, Phi Beta Kappa. Home: 5607 Wildwood Ln Baltimore MD 21209-4520 Office: John's Hopkins Med Instns 600 N Wolfe St Baltimore MD 21205-2128*

WAGNER, JAMES WARREN, engineering educator; b. Washington, July 12, 1953; s. Robert Earl and Bernice (Bittner) W.; m. Debbie Kelley, July 31, 1976; children: Kimberly Renee, Christine Kelley. BSEE, U. Del., 1975; MS, Johns Hopkins U., 1978, PhD, 1984. Electronics engr. U.S. FDA, Washington, 1975-84; asst. prof. Johns Hopkins U., Balt., 1984-88, assoc. prof., 1988-93, prof., 1993—, chmn. dept. materials scis. and engring., 1993—. Contbr. articles to profl. jours. Regional v.p. Chesapeake Bay Yacht Racing Assn., Annapolis, Md., 1982; elder Presbyterian Ch. U.S.A. Mem. IEEE, Optical Soc. Am., Materials Rsch. Soc., Laser & Electro-Optics Soc., Biomed. Engring., Am. Soc. for Nondestructive Evaluation, Soc. Exptl. Mechanics (Peterson award 1988), Nat. Materials Adv. Bd. Presbyterian. Achievements include contributions to the field of optical metrology applied to materials characterization, especially advanced holographic and laser-based ultrasonic methods. Office: Johns Hopkins Univ Materials Sci & Engring 3400 N Charles St # 102 Md Baltimore MD 21218-2608

WAGNER, JOHN GARNET, pharmacologist, educator; b. Weston, Ont., Can., Mar. 28, 1921; came to U.S., 1949; naturalized, 1993; s. Herbert William and Coral (Cates) W.; m. Eunice Winona Kelsey, July 4, 1946; children: Wendie Lynn, Linda Beth. Pharm.B., U. Toronto, Ont., 1947; B.S. in Pharmacy, U. Sask., Can., 1948, B.A., 1949; Ph.D., Ohio State U., 1952, D.Sc. (hon.), 1980. Asst. prof. pharm. chemistry Ohio State U., 1952-53; with Upjohn Co., Kalamazoo, 1953-56, head pharmacy rsch. sect., 1956-63, sr. rsch. scientist med. rsch. divsn., 1963-68; prof. pharmacy Coll. Pharmacy U. Mich., Ann Arbor, 1968-81, Albert B. Prescott prof. pharmaceutics, 1982-86, John G. Searle prof. pharmaceutics, 1986-91, John G. Searle prof. emeritus, 1991—, prof. pharmacology Sch. Medicine, 1986-91, prof. pharmacology emeritus, 1991—; asst. dir. R. and D. Pharmacy Service, Univ. Hosp., 1968-72; mem. staff Upjohn Center for Clin. Pharmacology, 1973-91; cons. Bur. of Drugs, FDA, Washington, 1971-73, Upjohn Co., 1968-90, Key Pharms., Miami, Fla., 1980-91, Warner-Lambert, Ann Arbor, Mich., 1983-84. Author: Biopharmaceutics and Relevant Pharmacokinetics, 1971, Fundamentals of Clinical Pharmacokinetics, 1975, Pharmacokinetics for the Pharmaceutical Scientist, 1993; also numerous articles.; mem. editorial bd.: Internat. Jour. Clin. Pharmacology, 1967-91, Clin. Pharmacol. Therapeutics, 1973-91, Biopharmceutics and Drug Disposition; cons. editor: Jour. Pharmacokinetics and Biopharmaceutics. Served with RCAF, 1941-45. Recipient L. George R. Parke Meml. scholarship and silver medal, 1946, John Roberts Gold medal for pharmacy and chemistry U. Toronto, 1947, Dr. William E. Upjohn award, 1960, Centennial Achievement award Ohio State U., 1970, Høst Madsen medal Fédération Internationale Pharmaceutique, 1972, Volwiler award Am. Assn. Colls. of Pharmacy, 1983, Rsch. Achievement award in pharmacokinetics, pharmacodynamics, drug metabolism, 1992; fellow Am. Found. Pharm. Edn., 1949-51; FDA grantee, 1969-76, Am. Assn. Pharm. Sci. fellow, 1986. Fellow AAAS, Am. Coll. Clin. Pharmacology and Chemotherapy, Acad. Pharm. Sci. (Stimulation of Rsch. award 1983, Pharmaceutics award 1984, Rsch. Achievement award 1984); mem. Am. Soc. Clin. Pharmacology and Therapeutics (bd. regents 1968-72, v.p. 1972, vice chmn. sect. on pharmacokinetics 1970-74), Am. Pharm. Assn. (Ebet prize 1961, rsch. award 1983, 84, Takeru Higuchi prize 1992), N.Y. Acad. Scis., Sigma Xi, Phi Lambda Upsilon, Rho Chi. Home: 908 Ivanhoe Dr Florence SC 29505-3614

WAGNER, JOHN LEO, federal judge, lawyer; b. Ithaca, N.Y., Mar. 12, 1954; s. Paul Francis and Doris Elizabeth (Hoffschneider) W.; m. Marilyn Modin, June 18, 1987. Student, U. Nebr., 1973-74; BA, U. Okla., 1976, JD, 1979. Bar: Okla. 1980, U.S. Dist. Ct. (we. dist.) Okla. 1980, U.S. Dist. Ct. (no. and ea. dists.) Okla. 1981, U.S. Ct. Appeals (10th cir.) 1982. Assoc. Franklin, Harmon & Satterfield Inc., Oklahoma City, 1980-82; ptnr. Franklin, Harmon & Satterfield, Inc., Oklahoma City, 1982; assoc. Kornfeld, Franklin & Phillips, Oklahoma City, 1982-85, ptnr., 1985; magistrate judge U.S. Dist. Ct. for No. Dist. Okla., Tulsa, 1985—. Pres. U. Okla. Coll. Law Assn., 1991-92. Mem. ABA, Fed. Magistrate Judge's Assn. (dir. 10th cir. 1987-89), 10th Cir. Edn. Com., Okla. Bar Assn., Council Oak Am. Inn of Cts. (pres. 1992-93), Jud. Conf. U.S. (com. ct. adminstrn. and case mgmt. 1992—). Republican. Office: US Magistrate Judge 333 W 4th St Rm 3355 Tulsa OK 74103-3819

WAGNER, JOSEPH CRIDER, retired university administrator; b. North Manchester, Ind., Feb. 19, 1907; s. Arthur Augustus and Grace (Crider) W.; A.B., Manchester Coll., 1929, LL.D., 1961; M.A. in Econs., U. Mich., 1936; postgrad. U. Wis., 1930, U. Chgo., 1931-32, Columbia, 1935; m. Geraldine B. Garber, June 30, 1933; 1 dau., Joene Henning. Tchr. Hartford City (Ind.) High Schs., 1929-35, prin., 1936-37, supt. schs., 1937-45; supt. schs., Crawfordsville, Ind., 1946; bus. mgr., treas. Ball State U., Muncie, Ind., 1946-61, v.p. for bus. affairs, 1961-73, v.p. emeritus, 1973—, treas., prof., gen. bus. adminstrn.; nat. chmn., 1976 Annual Fund. Drive; lectr. Mem. Ind. Common Sch. Bldg. Commn., 1960—. Active United Fund of Delaware County. Trustee Ind. Heart Found., Manchester Coll.; mem. ins. trust of Am. Assn. Ret. Persons and Nat. Ret. Tchrs. Assn.; bd. dirs. Muncie YMCA, Ind. State Tchrs. Retirement Fund. Mem. gen. bd. edn., nat. cons. in fin. Methodist Ch. in U.S. Paul Harris fellow Rotary; named Sagamore of the Wabash State of Ind. Gov's. Bowen and Orr, 1976, 88; recipient Friend of Journalism award, Friend of Music Citation, Retiree Recognition award Ball State U., 1992. Mem. Ind. Schoolmen's Club (pres. 1949), Ind. State Tchrs. Retirement Fund (bd. trustees 1975, pres. 1987-88), Retired Sch. Supt. Assn. Ind., Internat. Platform Assn., Am. Assn. Ret. Persons (ins. trust, Retiree Recognition award), Tau Kappa Alpha, Delta Pi Epsilon, Phi Delta Kappa (Cert. of Recognition), Sigma Alpha Epsilon. Mason, Rotarian (past pres.). Contbr. articles to profl. and religious jours. Home: 629 N Forest Ave Muncie IN 47304-3818

WAGNER, JOSEPH EDWARD, veterinarian, educator; b. Dubuque, Iowa, July 29, 1938; s. Jacob Edward and Leona (Callahan) W.; m. Kay Rose (div. Apr. 1983); children: Lucinda, Pamela, Jennifer, Douglas. DVM, Iowa State U., 1963; MPH, Tulane U., 1964; PhD, U. Ill., 1967. Asst. prof. U. Kans. Med. Ctr., Kansas City, 1967-69; assoc. prof. U. Mo. Coll. Vet. Medicine, Columbia, 1969-72, prof. vet. medicine, 1972—, Curator's prof., 1989—; cons. Harlan Sprague Dawley, Indpls., 1984—. Author: The Biology and Medicine of Rabbits and Rodents, 1989, 4th edit., 1995. Recipient award of excellence in lab. animal medicine Charles River Found., Wilmington, Mass., 1986. Mem. AMVA, Am. Coll. Lab. Animal Medicine (pres. 1985-86), Am. Assn. Lab. Animal Scis. (pres. 1980-81). Office: U Mo-Coll of Veterinary Medicine Dept of Vet Pathobiology 1600 W Rollins Rd Columbia MO 65203-1756

WAGNER, JOSEPH M., church administrator. Exec dir. Division for Ministry of the Evangelical Lutheran Church in America, Chgo. Office: Evangelical Lutheran Church Am 8765 W Higgins Rd Chicago IL 60631-4101*

WAGNER, JUDITH BUCK, investment firm executive; b. Altoona, Pa. Sept. 25, 1943; d. Harry Bud and Mary Elizabeth (Rhodes) B.; m. Joseph E. Wagner, Mar. 15, 1980; 1 child, Elizabeth. BA in History, U. Wash., 1965; grad. N.Y. Inst. Fin., 1968. Registered Am. Stock Exch., N.Y. Stock Exch., investment advisor. Security analyst Morgan, Olmstead, Kennedy & Gardner, L.A., 1968-71; security analyst Boettcher & Co., Denver, 1972-75; pres. Wagner Investment Mgmt., Denver, 1975—; chmn., bd. dirs. The Women's Bank, N.A., Denver, 1977-94, organizational group pres., 1975-77; chmn. Equitable Bankshares Colo., Inc., Denver, 1980-94; bd. dirs. Equitable Bank of Littleton, 1983-88, pres., 1985; bd. dirs. Colo. Growth Capital, 1979-82; lectr. Denver U., Metro State, 1975-80. Author: Woman and Money series Colo. Woman Mag., 1976; moderator 'Catch 2' Sta. KWGN-TV, 1978-79. Pres. Big Sisters Colo., Denver, 1977-82, bd. dirs., 1973-83; bd. fellows U. Denver, 1985-90; bd. dirs. Red Cross, 1980, Assn. Children's Hosp., 1985, Colo. Health Facilities Authority, 1978-84, Jr. League Community Adv. Com., 1979-92, Brother's Redevel., Inc., 1979-80; mem. agy. rels. com. Mile High United Way, 1978-81, chmn. United Way Venture Grant com., 1980-81; bd. dirs. Downtown Denver Inc., 1988-95; bd. dirs., v.p., treas. The Women's Found. Colo., 1987-91; treas., trustee, v.p., Graland Country Day Sch., 1990—, pres. 1994—; trustee Denver Rotary Found., 1990-95; trustee Hunt Alternatives Fund, 1992—. Recipient Making It award Cosmopolitan Mag., 1977, Women on the Go award, Savvy mag., 1983, Minouri Yasoui award, 1986, Salute Spl. Honoree award, Big Sisters, 1987; named one of the Outstanding Young Women in Am., 1979; recipient Woman Who Makes A Difference award Internat. Women's Forum, 1987. Fellow Assn. Investment Mgmt. and Rsch.; mem. Women's Forum of Colo. (pres. 1979), Women's Found. Colo., Inc. (bd. dirs. 1986-91), Denver Soc. Security Analysts (bd. dirs. 1976-83, v.p. 1980-81, pres. 1981-82), Colo. Investment Advisors Assn., Rotary (treas. Denver chpt. found., pres. 1993-94), Leadership Denver (Outstanding Alumna award 1987), Pi Beta Phi (pres. U. Wash. chpt. 1964-65). Office: Wagner Investment Mgmt Inc Ste 240 3200 Cherry Creek South Dr Denver CO 80209-3245

WAGNER, JULIA A(NNE), retired editor; b. Alexandria, Va., Feb. 15, 1924; d. Luigi and Domenica (Di Giammarino) Coppa; Widowed. B.A., George Washington U., 1948, M.A., 1950. With U.S. Govt., Washington, 1941-55, publs. editor, 1951-55; editorial asst. Dell Pub. Co., N.Y.C., 1956-59, mng. editor, 1959-72, editor-in-chief, 1973-87. Mem. Am. Fedn. Astrologers. Democrat. Roman Catholic.

WAGNER, LINDSAY J., actress; b. L.A., June 22, 1949; d. Bill Nowels and Marilyn Louise (Thrasher) W.; m. Alan Rider (div.); m. Michael Brandon, Dec. 1976 (div.); m. Henry Kingi, 1981 (div.); m. Lawrence Mortorff, 1990 (div.); children: Dorian Henry, Alex Nathan. Student, U. Oreg., 1967. Tchr. acting children Founders Sch. Los Angeles, 1975. Actress numerous TV shows Universal Studios, Universal City, Calif., 1971-74; motion picture picture appearances include: Two People, 1972, The Paper Chase, 1973, Second Wind, 1976, Nighthawks, 1981, Martin's Day, 1984, Ricochet, 1991; TV series include The Bionic Woman, 1976-78, Jessie, 1984, Peaceable Kingdom, 1989; appeared in TV miniseries Scruples, 1980, Princess Daisy, 1983, The Dead of the Night, 1989, Voices of the Heart, 1990, To Be the Best, 1991; TV films include: The Two Worlds of Jennie Logan, 1979, The Incredible Journey of Dr. Meg Laurel, 1979, I Want to Live, 1983, Two Kinds of Love, 1983, Callie and Son, 1983, Passion, 1984, This Child is Mine, 1985, The Other Lover, 1985, Nightmare at Bitter Creek, 1988, The Taking of Flight 847, 1988, Shattered Dreams, 1990, Babies, 1990, A Message from Holly, 1992, Once in a Lifetime, 1994, Bionic Ever After, 1994, Fighting for My Daughter, 1995, A Mother's Instinct, 1996, Sins of Silence, 1996, Contagious, 1997, Second Channel, 1997; author book, video, film: (with others) Lindsay Wagner's New Beauty: The Acupressure Facelift; co-author: The High Road to Health, 1990. Office: care Jim Wyatt Internat Creative Mgmt 8942 Wilshire Blvd Beverly Hills CA 90211-1934

WAGNER, LOUIS CARSON, JR., retired army officer; b. Jackson, Mo., Jan. 24, 1932; s. Louis Carson and Margaret Marie (Macke) W.; m. Judith Gifford, Sept. 24, 1955; children: Susan, Amy. B.S., U.S. Mil. Acad., 1954; M.S. in Applied Mechanics, U. Ill., 1961; grad., U.S. Naval War Coll., 1971. Commd. 2d lt. U.S. Army, 1954, advanced through grades to gen., 1987; served in Vietnam, Germany, Alaska; dep. dir. material plans and programs Office Dept. Chief Staff Research, Devel. and Acquisition, Washington, 1976-78, dir. combat support systems, 1978-80; comdg. gen. Armor Ctr., Ft. Knox, 1980-83; asst. dep. chief of staff for ops. and plans ODCSOPS, USA, Washington, 1983-84, dep. chief of staff for research, devel. and acquisition, 1984-87; comdg. gen. U.S. Army Materiel Command, Alexandria, Va., 1987-89; ret., 1989; sr. fellow Inst. of Land Warfare Assn. of U.S. Army, Arlington, Va., 1990—. Decorated D.S.C., D.S.M. with oak leaf cluster, Silver Star, Legion of Merit with oak leaf cluster, Bronze Star, Air medal with oak leaf cluster, Purple Heart, Meritorious Service medal, Army Commendation medal with 2 clusters, Combat Inf. badge. Mem. Assn. Grads. U.S. Mil. Acad., Armor Assn., Assn. U.S. Army, Ret. Officers Assn. (chmn. bd. dirs.), Am. Def. Preparedness Assn., Army Aviation Assn. Am., Nat. Eagle Scout Assn. (bd. regents), S.C. Rsch. Authority (bd. advisors). Office: 6309 Chaucer Ln Alexandria VA 22304-3537

WAGNER, MARILYN FAITH, elementary school educator; b. Salinas, Calif.; d. Clay Chester and Gladys Edna (Wiley) W. AA, Hartnell Coll., Salinas, 1956; BA, San Jose (Calif.) State U., 1958; MA in Computer Edn., U.S. Internat. U., San Diego, 1987; diploma, Inst. Children's Lit., Redding Ridge, Conn., 1981. Cert. elem. tchr., Calif.;cert. in cross-cultural lang. acad. devel., Calif. Tchr. Hollister (Calif.) Elem. Sch., Greenfield (Calif.) Schs., Alum Roc, Union Sch. Dist., San Jose. Mem. NEA, Calif. Tchrs. Assn., Spartan Found.

WAGNER, MARY KATHRYN, sociology educator, former state legislator; b. Madison, S.D., June 19, 1932; d. Irving Macaulay and Mary Browning (Wines) Mumford; m. Robert Todd Wagner, June 23, 1954; children: Christopher John, Andrea Browning. BA, U. S.D., 1954; MEd, S.D. State U., 1974, PhD, 1978. Sec. R.A. Burleigh & Assocs., Evanston, Ill., 1954-57; dir. resource ctr. Watertown (S.D.) Sr. High Sch., 1969-71, Brookings (S.D.) High Sch., 1971-74; asst. dir. S.D. Com. on the Humanities, Brookings, 1976-90; asst. prof. rural sociology S.D. State U., 1990-96; mem. S.D. Ho. of Reps., 1981-88, S.D. Senate, 1988-92. Mem., pres. Brookings Sch. Bd., 1975-81; chair fund dr. Brookings United Way, 1985; bd. dirs. Brookings Chamber music Soc., 1981—, Advance and Career Learning Ctr. Named Woman of Yr., Bus. and Profl. Women, 1981, Legislator Conservationist of Yr., Nat. and S.D. Wildlife Fedn., 1988. Mem. Population Assn. Am., Midwest Sociol. Soc., Rural Sociol. Soc., Brookings C. of C. (mem. indsl. devel. com. 1988—), PEO, Rotary. Republican. Episcopalian. Avocations: reading, gardening, music, golf, bridge. Home: 929 Harvey Dunn St Brookings SD 57006-1347

WAGNER, MARY MARGARET, library and information science educator; b. Mpls., Feb. 4, 1946; d. Harvey F.J. and Yvonne M. (Brettner) W.; m. William Moore, June 16, 1988; children: Lebohang Y.C., Nora M. BA, Coll. St. Catherine, St. Paul, 1969; MLS, U. Wash., 1973. Asst. libr. St. Margarets Acad., Mpls., 1969-70; libr. Derham Hall High Sch., St. Paul, 1970-71; youth worker The Bridge for Runaways, Mpls., 1971-72; libr. Guthrie Theater Reference and Rsch. Libr., Mpls., 1973-75; asst. br. libr. St. Paul Pub. Libr., 1975; assoc. prof. dept. info. mgmt. Coll. St. Catherine, St. Paul, 1975—; del. Minn. Gov.'s Pre-White House Conf. on Librs. and Info. Svcs., 1990; mem. Minn. Pre-White House Program Com., 1989-90, Continuing Libr. Info. and Media Edn. Com. Minn. Dept. Edn., Libr. Devel. and Svcs., 1980-83, 87—; mem. cmty. faculty Met. State U., St. Paul, 1980—; mem. core revision com. Coll. St. Catherine, 1992-93, faculty budget adv. com., 1992-95, faculty pers. com., 1989-92, acad. computing com. 1991-96; chair curriculum subcom. Minn. Vol. Cert. Com., 1993—. Contbr. articles to profl. jours. Bd. dirs. Christian Sharing Fund, 1976-80, chair, 1977-78. Grantee: U.S. Embassy, Maseru, Lesotho, Africa, Brit. Consulate, Maseru, various founds.; Upper Midwest Assn. for Intercultural Edn. travel grantee Assoc. Colls. Twin Cities. Mem ALA (libr. book fellows program 1990-91), Am. Soc. Info. Sci., Am. Soc. Indexers, Spl. Libr. Assn., Minn. Libr. Assn. (pres. 1981-82, chair continuing edn. com. 1987-90, steering com. Readers Adv. Roundtable, 1989-91), Minn. Ednl. Media Orgn., Twin Cities Women in Computing. Office: Coll St Catherine Dept Info Mgmt 2004 Randolph Ave Saint Paul MN 55105-1750

WAGNER, MURIEL GINSBERG, nutrition therapist; b. N.Y.C., Apr. 6, 1926; d. Irving A. and Anna Ginsberg; divorced; 1 child, Emily Lucinda Faith. BA, Wayne State U., 1948, MS, 1951; PhD, U. Mich., 1982. Registered dietitian. Nutritionist Merrill-Palmer Inst., Detroit, 1951-74; pvt. practice, nutritional therapist Southfield, Mich., 1976—; cons. select com. on nutrition U.S. Senate, 1973-74, Ford Motor Co., Dearborn, Mich., 1975-78, Detroit Dept. Consumer Affairs, 1979—; adj. faculty mem. Wayne State U., Detroit, 1970-80, U. Mich., Dearborn, 1974-79. Author: (cookbook) Tun...ahhh, 1993; contbr. articles to profl. publs. Vol. Am. Heart Assn. of Mich.; also various local and nat. govtl. groups. Recipient Outstanding Cmty. Svc. award Am. Heart Assn., 1990; named Outstanding Profl., Mich. Dietetic Assn., 1974. Fellow Am. Dietetic Assn. (organizer Dial-A-Dietitian); mem. Am. Diabetes Assn. Avocations: cooking, recipe development, gardening. Office: 4000 Town Ctr Ste 8 Southfield MI 48075-1401

WAGNER, NORMAN ERNEST, corporate education executive; b. Edenwold, Sask., Can., Mar. 29, 1935; s. Robert Eric and Gertrude Margaret (Brandt) W.; m. Catherine Hack, May 16, 1957; children: Marjorie Dianne, Richard Roger, Janet Marie. BA, U. Sask., 1958, MDiv, 1958; MA, U. Toronto, 1960, PhD in Near Eastern Studies, 1965; LLD, Wilfrid Laurier U., 1984. Asst. prof. Near Eastern studies Wilfrid Laurier U., Waterloo, Ont., 1962-65, assoc. prof., 1965-69, prof., 1970-78, dean grad. studies and rsch., 1974-78; pres. U. Calgary, Alta., Can., 1978-88; chmn. bd. Alta. Natural Gas Co., Ltd., 1988—; pres. emeritus U. Calgary, Can., 1988-95; chmn. Knowledge at Work Found., 1995—; bd. dirs., chmn. Terry fox Humanitarian Award Program; pres. The Corp. Higher Edn. Forum, 1996—. Author: (with others) The Moyer Site: A Prehistoric Village in Waterloo County, 1974. Mem. Adv. Coun. on Adjustment, OCO '88, Alta. Heritage Found. for Med. Rsch., Nat. Adv. Bd. Sci. and Tech., Internat. Trade Adv. Com. Decorated officer Order of Can. Mem. Can. Soc. Bibl. Studies. Lutheran. Home: Box 5 Site 33 RR # 12, Calgary, AB Canada T3E 6W3 Office: The Corp Higher Edn Forum, 440 1010 8th Ave SW, Calgary, AB Canada T2P 1J2

WAGNER, PATRICIA HAMM, lawyer; b. Gastonia, N.C., Feb. 1, 1936; d. Luther Boyd and Mildred Ruth (Wheeler) Hamm; married; children: David Marion, Michael Marion, Laura Marion. AB summa cum laude, Wittenberg U., 1958; JD with distinction, Duke U., 1974. Bar: N.C. 1974, Wash. 1984. Asst. univ. counsel Duke U., Durham, N.C., 1974-75, assoc. univ. counsel health affairs, 1977-80; atty. N.C. Meml. Hosp., 1975-77; assoc. N.C. Atty. Gen. Office, 1975-77; assoc. Powe, Porter & Alphin, Durham, 1980-81, prin., 1981-83; assoc. Williams, Kastner & Gibbs, 1984-86, Wickwire, Goldmark & Schorr, 1986-88; spl. counsel Heller, Ehrman, White & McAuliffe, 1988-90, ptnr., 1990—; arbitrator Am. Arbitration Assn., 1978—; arbitrator, pro tem judge King County Superior Ct., 1986—; tchr. in field. Mem. bd. vis. Law Sch. Duke U., 1992—; bd. dirs. Seattle Edn. Ctr., 1990-91, Metroctr. YMCA, 1991-94, Cmty. Psychiat. Clinic, Seattle, 1984-86; bd. dirs., sec.-treas. N.C. Found. Alternative Health Programs, Inc., 1982-84; bd. dirs., sec.-treas. N.C. Ctr. Pub. Policy Rsch., 1976-83, vice-chmn., 1977-80; mem. task force on commitment law N.C. Dept. Human Resources, 1978; active Def. Rsch. Inst. 1982-84; bd. dirs. Law Fund, 1992—, v.p., 1993—. Fellow Am. Bar Found.; mem. ABA (mem. ho. dels. Seattle-King County Bar Assn. 1991-94, mem. litigation sect.), Am. Soc. Hosp. Attys., Wash. State Bar Assn. (mem. domestic rels. task force 1991-93), Seattle-King Bar Assn. (mem. bd. trustees 1990-93, sec. bd. 1989-90, chair judiciary and cts. com. 1987-89, mem. King County Superior Ct. delay reduction task force 1987-89, mem. gender bias com. 1990-94, chair 1990-91), Wash. Def. Trial Lawyers (chmn. ct. rules and procedures com. 1987, co-editor newsletter 1985-86), Wash. State Soc. Hosp. Attys., Wash. Women Lawyers (treas. 1986, 87). Office: Heller Ehrman White & McAuliffe 6100 Columbia Ctr 701 5th Ave Seattle WA 98104-7016

WAGNER, PAUL ANTHONY, JR., education educator; b. Pitts., Aug. 28, 1947; s. Paul A. and Mary K. Wagner; children: Nicole S., Eric P., Jason G. BS, N.E. Mo. State U., 1969; MEd, U. Mo., 1972; MA in Philosophy, 1976, PhD in Philosophy of Edn., 1978. Internal expeditor electromotive div. GM, La Grange, Ill., 1970-71; instr. Moberly (Mo.) Jr. Coll., 1972-73; instr. U. Mo., Columbia, 1973-78, dir. univ. self-study, acting dir. instl. rsch. and planning, 1990-92; instr. Mo. Mil. Acad., 1978-79; prof. edn. and philosophy U. Houston-Clear Lake, 1979—, Atrium Ctr. Disting. Rsch. Prof., 1980, Chancellor's Disting. Svc. Prof., 1985; dir. Inst. Logical and Cognitive Studies, 1980—; dir. Project in Profl. Ethics, 1992—; chmn. dept. edn. U. Houston-Clear Lake, 1989-92; adj. prof. bus. mgmt. U. Houston-Victoria, 1995—; pres. Wagner & Assocs. Ednl. Consulting, 1988-93; dir. Tex. Ctr. for Study Profl. Ethics in Tchg., 1988-95; rsch. assoc. Ctr. for Moral Devel., Harvard U., 1985-86; vis. scholar Stanford U., Palo Alto, Calif., 1981; cons. to various sch. dists., 1979—; cons. in total quality mgmt. Golden Gate U., 1992-93, M.D. Anderson Cancer Ctr. & Hosp., 1992-93, U. Houston-Victoria, 1993, Houston Chronicle Newspaper, 1997; chair So. Accreditation of Colls. and Schs. steering com., U. Houston-Clear Lake, 1990-93; chair univ. planning com., 1993-94; mem. faculty Senate exec. com., 1993-95; mem. bd. dirs., chair planning and budgeting com. Houston Tenneco Marathon, 1992—; mem. steering com. Trilateral Conf. and Supershow Greater Human Partnership, 1994-95; cons. and ethics trainer Am. Leadership Forum, 1995-96; chair faculty devel. and post tenure review taskforce U. Houston-Clear Lake, 1996—. Author: (with F. Kierstead) The Ethical Legal and Multicultural Founds. of Teaching, 1992, Understanding Professional Ethics, 1996; contbr. articles on sci. edn., mgmt. theory and philosophy of edn. to profl. jours. Mem. editorial bd. Jour. of Thought, 1981—, Focus on Learning, 1982-85; editorial cons. Instrnl. Scis., 1981-83; editorial assoc. Brain and Behavioral Scis., 1986—. Mem. Human Rights Commn., Columbia, Mo., 1976-79, vice chmn., 1978-79; Sunday sch. tchr. Mary Queen Cath. Ch., Friendswood, Tex., 1979-85; founding bd. mem. Bay Area Symphony Soc., 1983-85; capital campaign com. Soc. Prevention Cruelty to Animals, 1989-91; publicity com. Am. Cancer Soc., Houston chpt., 1989-92; mem. Houston-Tenneco Marathon bd., 1989—, chair steering com. for strategic planning, 1993, chair planning and budgeting com., 1993—; cons. in strategic planning to M.D. Anderson Cancer Ctr. vol. divsn.; mem.

steering com. City of Houston Emerging Bus. Conf., 1994-95, Trilateral Conf., Greater Houston Partnership, 1994-95; acctive Houston Bus. Promise; chair strategic planning com. Leadership Houston, 1996-97. Sgt. Mo. N.G., 1970-76. Recipient Cert. of Appreciation, City of Columbia, 1978; K.E. Graessle scholar, 1968, Mo. Peace Studies Inst. grantee, 1971. Mem. Assn. Applied and Profl. Ethics, Am. Assn. Pub. Adminstrs. (ethics com.), Am. Philos. Assn., Assn. Philosophers in Edn. (exec. bd., v.p.), Philosophy of Edn. Soc. (exec. sec.-treas., hospitality chair 1995-96), Am. Ednl. Studies Assn., Philosophy Sci. Assn., S.W. Philosophy Edn. Soc., Tex. Network for Tchr. Tng. in Philosophy for Children (bd. dirs. 1983-90), Tex. Ctr. for Ethics in Edn. (bd. dirs. 1988—), Tex. Ednl. Found. Soc. (pres. 1986—), Tex. Assn. Coll. Tchrs., So. Assn. Colls. Coord., Houston Bar Assn. (mem. steering com. NAFTA Conf. 1993-94), Informal Logic Assn., Leadership Houston, Friends Hermann Pk., Clearlake Cir. (chair 1979-85), Phi Delta Kappa, Kappa Delta Pi. Roman Catholic. Avocations: running, racquetball, reading, opera, ballet. Address: RR 4 Box 217 Navasota TX 77868 Office: U Houston 2700 Bay Area Blvd # 338 Houston TX 77058-1002

WAGNER, PETER EWING, physics and electrical engineering educator; b. Ann Arbor, Mich., July 4, 1929; s. Paul Clark and Charlotta Josephine (Ewing) W.; m. Caryl Jean Veon, June 23, 1951; children: Ann Frances, Stephen Charles. Student, Occidental Coll., 1946-48; AB with honors, U. Calif., Berkeley, 1950, PhD, 1956. Teaching rsch. asst. U. Calif., 1950-56; rsch. physicist Westinghouse Rsch. Labs., Pitts., 1956-59; assoc. prof. elec. engring. Johns Hopkins, 1960-65, prof., 1965-73; dir. Ctr. for Environ. and Estuarine Studies U. Md., 1973-80, prof., 1973-81; vis. prof. physics U. Ala., Huntsville, 1980-81, prof., 1981; vice chancellor for acad. affairs, prof. physics U. Miss., 1981-84; provost, prof. physics and elec. engring. Utah State U., 1984-89; v.p. acad. affars and provost SUNY, Binghamton, 1989-92, prof. physics and elec. engring., 1989—; spl. projects engr. State of Md., 1971-72; mem. Gov.'s Sci. Adv. Coun., 1973-77, Md. Power Plant Siting Adv. Com., 1972-80; cons. in field. Contbr. articles to profl. jours.; patentee in field. Trustee Chesapeake Rsch. Consortium, 1974-80, chmn. bd. trustees, 1979-80. Guggenheim fellow Oxford U., 1966-67. Mem. Nat. Assn. State Univs. and Land Grant Colls. (mem. coun. acad. affairs, mem. affirmative action com. 1986-89, chmn. nominating com. 1988-89, chmn. libr. commn. 1989-92), Ctr. Rsch. Librs. (bd. dirs. 1991-97, mem. budget and fin. com. 1991-93, vice chairperson 1992-93, chairperson 1993-94, chair nominating com. 1994-95), Blue Key, Gold Key, Phi Beta Kappa, Phi Beta Kappa Assocs. (life, bd. dirs. 1995—, chairperson membership com. 1996—), Sigma Xi (life), Phi Kappa Phi, Eta Kappa Nu. Home: 261 Loretta Ln Vestal NY 13850

WAGNER, RAYMOND THOMAS, JR., lawyer; b. St. Louis, June 8, 1959; s. Raymond T. and Loretto (Muenster) W.; m. Ann L. Trousdale, Feb. 20, 1987. BA, St. Louis U., 1981, MBA, 1984; JD, U. Mo., Kansas City, 1985; LLM in Taxation, Washington U., St. Louis, 1993. Bar: Mo. 1985, Ill. 1986, U.S. Supreme Ct. 1989, U.S. Tax Ct. 1989. Legal rsch. and writing instr. U. Mo., Kansas City, 1983-84; law clk. to chief justice Mo. Supreme Ct., Jefferson City, 1985-86; assoc. Gilmore & Bell, St. Louis, 1986-87, Suelthaus & Kaplan P.C., St. Louis, 1987-89; gen. counsel Mo. Dept Revenue, 1989-90; counsel to gov. State of Mo., Jefferson City, 1990-91; dir. revenue Mo. Dept. Revenue, 1991-93; of counsel Armstrong Teasdale Schlafly & Davis, St. Louis, 1993; dir. revenue Ill. Dept Revenue, Springfield, 1993-95; legal and legis. dir., asst. v.p. Enterprise Rent-A-Car, St. Louis, Mo., 1995—; adj. prof. law LLM taxation program sch. law Washington U., St. Louis, 1993—; chmn. Gov.'s Ethics Com., 1991-92, Mo. Hwy. Reciprocity Commn., 1991-93; commr. Multistate Tax. Commn., 1991-93, Mo. Mil. Adv. Commn., 1991-93. Twp. coord. Jefferson Twp., Webster Groves, Mo., 1988; precinct capt. Gravois Twp., Webster Groves, 1988; bd. dirs. Shelter the Children, St. Louis, 1988-95, INd. Charities Am., 1993-95, Foster Care Coalition St. Louis; chmn. platform com. Mo. Rep. Conv., 1992; counsel Ashcroft for Senate Campaign., 1993-94; exec. bd. dirs. St. Louis U. Sch. Bus. Mem. ABA, Ill. Bar Assn., Mo. Bar Assn., Bar Assn. Met. St. Louis (chmn. law student svcs. com. 1986-87, chmn. social com. 1987-88, mem. exec. com. young lawyers assn. 1988-89, co-chmn. administrv. law com., govt. liaison com. young lawyers sect. 1989-90, chmn. legis. com. 1991—), Regional Commerce and Growth Assn. (vice chair pub. policy coun. 1996, chair pub. policy coun. 1997—), Associated Industries Mo. (bd. dirs. 1996—). Republican. Roman Catholic. Home: 313 Saint Andrews Ct Ballwin MO 63011-2504 Office: Enterprise Rent-A-Car 600 Corporate Park Dr Saint Louis MO 63105-4204

WAGNER, RICHARD, business executive, former baseball team executive; b. Central City, Nebr., Oct. 19, 1927; s. John Howard and Esther Marie (Wolken) W.; m. Gloria Jean Larsen, May 10, 1950; children—Randolph G., Cynthia Kaye. Student, pub. schs., Central City. Gen. mgr. Lincoln (Nebr.) Baseball Club, 1955-58; mgr. Pershing Mcpl. Auditorium, Lincoln, 1958-61; exec. staff Ice Capades, Inc., Hollywood, Calif., 1961-63; gen. mgr. Sta. KSAL, Salina, Kans., 1963-65; dir. promotion and sales St. Louis Nat. Baseball Club, 1965-66; gen. mgr. Forum, Inglewood, Calif., 1966-67; asst. to exec. v.p. Cin. Reds, 1967-70, asst. to pres., 1970-74, v.p. adminstrn., 1975, exec. v.p., 1975-78, gen. mgr., 1977-83, pres., 1978-83; pres. Houston Astros Baseball Club, 1985-87; spl. asst. Office of Baseball Commr., 1988-93; asst. to chmn. Major League Exec. Coun., 1993-94; pres. RGW Enterprises, Inc., Phoenix, 1978—. Served with USNR, 1945-47, 50-52. Named Exec. of Yr., Minor League Baseball, Sporting News, 1958. Mem. Internat. Assn. Auditorium Mgrs. Republican. Methodist.

WAGNER, ROBERT EARL, agronomist; b. Garden City, Kans., Mar. 6, 1921; s. Fay Arthur and Margaret (Longbottom) W.; m. Bernice Bittner, Aug. 7, 1948; children—Robert Earl, James Warren, Douglas Alan. B.S., Kans. State Coll., 1942; M.S., U. Wis., 1943, Ph.D., 1950. Forage crops specialist Ft. Hays Expt. Sta., Hays, Kans., 1943-45; asso. agronomist Plant Industry Sta., U.S. Dept. Agr., Beltsville, Md., 1945-48; research agronomist, asst. project leader pasture and range project Plant Industry Sta., U.S. Dept. Agr., 1951-54, research agronomist, project leader western pasture and range project, 1954-56; prof., head dept. agronomy U. Md., 1956-59; regional dir. American Potash Inst., 1959-66, also Found. for Internat. Potash Research, v.p. both orgns., 1966-67; dir. Coop. Extension Service, U. Md., 1967-75; pres., bd. dirs. Potash Inst., 1975-77; pres., bd. dirs. Potash and Phosphate Inst., 1977-88, pres. emeritus, 1988—; chmn., bd. dirs. Potash & Phosphate Inst. Can., 1975-88; pres., bd. dirs. Found. for Agronomic Rsch., 1980-87; owner Wagner Performance Cattle, Stone Mountain, Ga., 1985—; bd. dirs., mem. exec. com. Internat. Fertilizer Devel. Ctr., 1975—; bd. dirs. African Ctr. for Fertilizer Devel., 1988—; chmn. Nat. Ext. Com. on Orgn. and Policy; mem. U.S. del. 7th Internat. Grassland Congress, New Zealand. Author tech., popular publs.; Editor: Proc. Sixth Internat. Grassland Congress. Recipient Medallion award Am. Forage and Grassland Coun., Disting. Grasslander award, 1994; award Md. Farm Bur.; Disting. Svc. award in agr. Kansas State U., 1985, Disting. Alumnus award, 1990; Cert. of Disting. Citizenship, State of Md.; Robert E. Wagner Efficient Agr. award established in his honor; Disting. Grasslander award Am. Forages Md. Grassland Coun., 1994. Fellow AAAS, Am. Soc. Agronomy (chmn. grassland com., mem. exec. com., bd. dirs., pres. N.E. br.), Crops Sci. Soc. Am., Soil Sci. Soc. Am.; mem. Grassland Coun. (pres.), Am. Soc. Range Mgmt., Cosmos Club (Washington), Atlanta Athletic Club, Sigma Xi, Alpha Zeta, Gamma Sigma Delta, Phi Kappa Phi. Presbyterian. Home: 1934 Mountain Creek Dr Stone Mountain GA 30087-1016 Office: 655 Engineering Dr Norcross GA 30092-2822

WAGNER, ROBERT RODERICK, microbiologist, oncology educator; b. N.Y.C., Jan. 5, 1923; s. Nathan and Mary (Mendelsohn) W.; m. Mary Elizabeth Burke, Mar. 23, 1967. A.B., Columbia U., 1943; M.D., Yale U., 1946. Intern, asst. resident physician Yale-New Haven Med. Center, 1946-47, 49-50; research fellow Nat. Inst. Med. Research, London, Eng., 1950-51; instr., then asst. prof. medicine Yale U., 1951-55; asst., then assoc. prof. medicine Johns Hopkins U., Balt., 1956-59, assoc. prof. microbiology, 1959-64, asst., then assoc. dean med. faculty, 1957-63, prof. microbiology, 1964-67; vis. fellow, mem. Common Room All Souls Coll. Oxford U., 1967, 76; prof. microbiology U. Va., 1967-97; chmn. dept. microbiology, 1967-94; Marion McNulty Weaver and Malvin C. Weaver prof. oncology U. Va., 1984-97, prof. emeritus, 1997—; dir. Cancer Ctr., 1984-94; vis. scientist Chinese Acad. Med. Scis., 1982; vis. prof. Univs. Giessen and Wuerzburg (W. Ger.), 1983; Cons. Am. Cancer Soc. Mem. coms.; USPHS, NSF, Assn. Am. Med. Colls., AMA, Nat. Bd. Med. Examiners.; bd. dirs. W. Alton Jones Cell Sci. Center, Lake Placid, N.Y., 1982—. Editor-in-chief: Jour. Virology, 1966-82. Served to lt. USNR, 1947-49. Rockefeller Found. resident scholar Villa Serbelloni, Bellagio, Italy, 1976; Macy Found. Faculty scholar Oxford U., 1976; recipient Disting. U.S. Scientist award Alexander von Humboldt Found., 1983. Fellow AAAS (councillor); mem. Assn. Am. Physicians, Am. Soc. Clin. Investigation, Am. Soc. Biol. Chemists, Am. Assn. Immunologists, Am. Soc. for Microbiology (councillor), Assn. Med. Sch. Microbiology Chmn. (pres. 1974), Am. Soc. Virology (pres. 1984). Office: Univ of Va Dept Microbiology Box 441 Charlottesville VA 22908

WAGNER, ROBERT TODD, university president, sociology educator; b. Sioux Falls, S.D., Oct. 30, 1932; s. Hans Herman and Helen Emilie (Castle) W.; m. Mary Kathryn Mumford, June 23, 1954; children: Christopher, Andrea. BA, Augustana Coll., Sioux Falls, 1954; MDiv, Seabury Western Theol. Sem., 1957, STM, 1970; PhD, S.D. State U., 1972; DHL, Augustana Coll., 1994. Ordained to ministry Episc. Ch., 1957. Staff analyst AMA, Chgo., 1954-57; vicar Ch. of Holy Apostles, Sioux Falls, 1957-64; chaplain All Saints Sch., Sioux Falls, 1962-64; rector Trinity Episcopal Ch., Watertown, S.D., 1964-69; prof. sociology S.D. State U., Brookings, 1971—, acting head dept. sociology, 1978, asst. to v.p. for acad. affairs, 1980-84, pres., 1985—; v.p. Dakota State U., Madison, S.D., 1984-85; cons. sociologist Devel. Planning and Research, Manhattan, Kans., 1976-85; bd. dirs. Deuel County Nat. Bank, Clear Lake, S.D., Found. Seed Stock. Bd. dirs. Karl Mundt Found., Prairie Repertory Theatre, REACH, S.D. 4-H Found., S.D. State U. Found., SA Found., Griffith Charitable Trust, F.O. Butler Found., Christian Edn. Camp and Conf. of Episcopal Dioceses of S.D. Arthur Vinning Davis Found. fellow, 1969-70, Episcopal Ch. Found. fellow, 1969-71, Augustana Coll. fellow, 1977. Mem. Nat. Assn. State Univs. and Land Grant Colls., Brookings C. of C., Phi Kappa Phi, Phi Kappa Delta, Pi Gamma Mu, Alpha Kappa Delta, Alpha Lambda Delta, Sigma Gamma Delta. Republican. Lodges: Elks, Rotary. Avocations: railroading, gardening, cooking. Home: 929 Harvey Dunn St Brookings SD 57006-1347 Office: SD State U Adminstrn Bldg 222 Office of Pres Brookings SD 57007-2298

WAGNER, ROBERT WALTER, photography, cinema and communications educator, media producer, consultant; b. Newport News, Va., Nov. 16, 1918; s. Walter George and Barbara Anna W.; m. Betty Jane Wiles, Nov. 21, 1948; children—Jonathan R., Jeffrey A., Jennifer J. B.Sc., Ohio State U., 1940, M.A., 1941, Ph.D., 1953. Motion picture writer-dir. Office War Info., N.Y.C. and Washington, 1942-43; writer-dir. Office Coordinator Interam. Affairs for South and Central Am., 1943-44; chief info. Div. Mental Hygiene, Ohio Dept. Pub. Welfare, 1944-46; dir. div. motion pictures Ohio State U., 1946-58, prof. communications, photography and cinema, 1960—, chmn. dept. photo-cinema, 1966-74; pres. Univ. Film Found., 1979-85; writer, dir. James Thurber's Columbus Town, 1990, Images of the Depression, 1990; internat. cons. communications; bd. dirs. Am. Film Inst., 1974-81; mem. faculty U. So. Calif., 1958-59, U. P.R., 1961, 66, 68, San Jose State U., 1967, Ariz. State U., 1971, Concordia U., Montreal, Que., Can., 1980, 81, Danish Nat. Film Sch., 1983, 84, Emerson Coll., Boston, 1987. Ency. Brit. fellow, 1953; Sr. Fulbright fellow, Peru, 1976; recipient Disting. Svc. award Columbus Cmty. Film Council, 1986, Disting. Svc. award Ohio State U., 1988. Fellow Soc. Motion Picture and TV Engrs. (Eastman Gold Medal award 1981); mem. Acad. TV Arts and Scis. (Disting. Svc. award 1966, Ohioana Pegasus award 1985), Univ. Film/Video Assn. (bd. editors jour. 1975-85, editor jour. 1956-75), Internat. Congress Schs. Cinema and TV (v.p. 1964-82), Assn. Ednl. Communication and Tech. (bd. editors jour. 1976—). Club: Torch (Columbus, Ohio). Author film series: Series of Motion Picture Documents on Communication Theory and New Educational Media, 1966; co-author: The American Tintype, 1996; editor: Education of Film Maker, 1975; coprodr. Cognizant Films StudioCity, 1997. Home: 1353 Zollinger Rd Columbus OH 43221-2939

WAGNER, ROBIN SAMUEL ANTON, stage and set designer; b. San Francisco, Aug. 31, 1933; s. Jens Otto and Phyllis Edna (Smith-Spurgeon) W.; children: Kurt, Leslie, Christie. Student, Calif. Sch. Fine Arts, 1953-54. Pres. Scarab Prodns., Inc., 1975—; prof. theatre arts Columbia U., 1988—; sr. v.p. The Design Edge, 1989—; adv. com. Broadway Theatre Inst. Designer on Broadway including The Life, Big, Death Defying Acts, Victor/Victoria, Angels in America, Millenium Approaches Perestroika, Crazy for You, Jelly's Last Jam, City of Angels, Jerome Robbins's Broadway, Teddy and Alice, Chess, Song and Dance, Merlin, Dreamgirls, 42nd Street, A Chorus Line, One the Twentieth Century, Ballroom, Mack and Mabel, Seesaw, Sugar, Jesus Christ Superstar, The Great White Hope, Promises, Promises, Lenny, Inner City, Hair; designer off Broadway, including: Putting It Together, Hamlet 90, In White America, View from the Bridge, Mahogony, The Prodigal, Between Two Thieves, Cages; designer regional theatres including Joseph Papp Pub. Theatre, Arena State, Washington, Actor's Workshop, San Francisco, Met Opera, San Francisco Balet, Am. Ballet Theatre, Am. Shakespeare Festival, Eliot Feld Ballet, N.Y. Shakespeare Festival, Ensemble Studio Theatre, N.Y.C. Ballet, Vienna State Opera, Hamburg State Opera, Malmo Music Theatre, Sweden, Royal Opera at Covent Garden, Rolling Stones Tour of Ams., 1975, (London prodns.), Gothenberg Opera, 1996, Crazy For You, City of Angels, Chess, 42d Street, A Chorus Line, Promises, Promises, Hair, (Tokyo prodns.), A Chorus Line, Dream Girls, 42nd St., City of Angels, Crazy For You. Mem. adv. bd. Nat. Corp. Theatre Fund, Theatre Adv. Coun. for City of N.Y.; mem. art adv. com. N.Y. Internat. Festival of the Arts; bd. trustees N.Y. Shakespeare Festival. Recipient Tony award for On the Twentieth Century, 1978, City of Angels, 1990, also numerous nominations; Drama Desk award, 1971, 78, 82, 90, Theatre World award, 1975, Outer Circle Critics award, 1978, 90, 92, Maharam award, 1973, 75, 82, Lumen award, 1975, Dramalogue award, 1980, Boston Critics award, 1974, 92, award for excellence in theatre Ensemble Studio Theatre, 1990, Dora award, 1995, New Eng. Theatre Conf. 1996 Lifetime Achievement award, En Garde Arts honoree, N.Y.C., 1996. Mem. United Scenic Artists. Office: Robin Wagner Studio 890 Broadway New York NY 10003-1211

WAGNER, ROD, library director; b. Oakland, Nebr., Sept. 14, 1948; s. Francis Lynn and Doris Jean (Egbers) W.; m. M. Diane Kennedy, June 14, 1969; children: Jennifer, Brian, James. BA Social Sci. Edn., Wayne (Nebr.) State Coll., 1970; MA Polit. Sci., U. Nebr. Lincoln, 1971; MA Libr. Sci., U. Mo., 1981. Rsch. coord. Nebr. Libr. Commn., Lincoln, 1972, planning, evaluation, rsch. coord., 1972-73, adminstrv. asst., 1973-74, dep. dir., 1974-87, dir., 1988—; bd. dirs. Nebr. Ctr. for the Book, Nebr. Devel. Network. With U.S. Army Nat. Guard, 1970-77. Mem. ALA (contbr. yearbook 1981-84), Nat. Mgmt. Assn., Mountain Plains Libr. Assn., Nebr. Libr. Assn. (pres.-elect 1993-94, pres. 1994-95), Chief Officers State Libr. Agencies, Western Coun. State Librs. (pres. 1992-93). Presbyterian. Home: 3205 W Pershing Rd Lincoln NE 68502-4844 Office: NE Libr Commn 1200 N St Ste 120 Lincoln NE 68508-2020

WAGNER, ROY, anthropology educator, researcher; b. Cleve., Oct. 2, 1938; s. Richard Robert and Florence Helen (Mueller) W.; m. Brenda Sue Geilhausen, June 14, 1968 (div. Dec. 1994); children: Erika Susan, Jonathan Richard. AB, Harvard U., 1961; AM, U. Chgo., 1962, PhD, 1966. Asst. prof. anthropology So. Ill. U., Carbondale, 1966-68; assoc. prof. Northwestern U., Evanston, Ill., 1969-74; prof. U. Va., Charlottesville, 1974—, chmn. dept., 1974-79; mem. cultural anthropology panel NSF, Washington, 1981-82. Author: Habu, 1972, The Invention of Culture, 1975, Lethal Speech, 1978, Symbols That Stand for Themselves, 1986. Social Sci. Research Council faculty research grantee, 1968; NSF postdoctoral research grantee, 1979. Fellow Am. Anthropol. Assn. Avocation: student hot-air balloon pilot. Home: 726 Cargil Ln Charlottesville VA 22902-4302 Office: U Va Dept Anthropology University Station Charlottesville VA 22906

WAGNER, SAMUEL, V, secondary school English language educator; b. West Chester, Pa., Dec. 28, 1965; s. Samuel and Mary Ann (Baker) W.; m. Allison Lee Lewis, May 25, 1991; 1 child, Samuel Jackson. BS in English Lit., Haverford Coll., 1988; MEd, U. New Orleans, 1995. Intern in English, asst. coach Westtown (Pa.) Sch., spring 1989; tchr. upper sch. English Metairie (La.) Pk. Country Day Sch., 1989-97; head upper sch. Hutchison Sch., Memphis, 1997—; asst. varsity soccer coach Metairie Pk. Country Day Sch., 1989-94; advisor to student senate Metairie Country Day Sch., 1990-95, chairperson/headmaster adv. com., 1994—, coll. counselor, 1995—; presenter ann. conf. Ind. Sch. Assn. of the South, New Orleans, 1992, 96. Mem. NASAA, NASSP, So. Assn. for Coll. Admissions Counseling, Nat. Assn. of Coll. Admissions Officers, Nat. Coun. Tchrs. of English, La. Coun. Tchrs. of English, Alpha Theta Epsilon, Phi Delta Kappa, Kappa Delta Pi. Republican. Mem. Soc. of Friends. Home: 416 Severn Ave Metairie LA 70001-5145 Office: Hutchison Sch 1740 Ridgeway Rd Memphis TN 38119-5314

WAGNER, SAMUEL ALBIN MAR, records management executive, educator; b. Brighton, Colo., Feb. 23, 1942; s. Jacob Doer and Leota Garnet (Wilson) W.; m. Donna Dee Person, Mar. 20, 1987; children: Andrea, Kurt, Autumn, Jan, Arthur. BA in History, U. Colo., 1964, MA in History, 1965; STB (MTS) in History of World Religions, Harvard U., 1968; cert. in archival adminstrn., U. Denver, 1978. cert. records mgr., 1993, cert. archivist, 1994. Archival asst. Harvard U. & Harvard Bus. Sch., 1965-68; asst. curator we. hist. collections U. Colo., 1968-70; sr. asst. archivist Cornell U., Ithaca, N.Y., 1971-73; editor Brighton Blade, Ft. Lupton Press, Colo., 1973-77; city archivist City of Providence, 1978-80; state records analyst Wyo. State Archives, Cheyenne, 1979-83; records mgr. Ft. Collins (Colo.) Police Dept., 1984-87; pres. Records Mgmt. Cons. Internat., 1984—; pub. records adminstr. State R.I., Providence, 1987-90; asst. prof. Master Archival Studies program U. B.C., Vancouver, Can., 1990-93; editor Mo. State Archives, Jefferson City, 1994-96; prodr. community access Sta. JCTV, Jefferson City, 1994-96; chief N.J. Bur. Records Mgmt., Trenton, 1996—; pres. Historic Rsch. Svcs., Trenton, 1996—; instr. Chapman, U., 1981-87, Colo. State U., 1985-87, Lincoln U., 1995-96; speaker at nat. and internat. confs. Author: Brighton Reflections, 1976, Adams County: Crossroads of the West, 1977, Directory of Automated Records Management Systems, 1987, 88, 89, 90, 91, Crossroads of the West: A History of Brighton and the Platte Valley, 1987; editor The Fort Lupton Story, 1987; contbr. numerous articles to profl. jours. Officer, bd. dirs. Adams County Hist. Soc., 1973-77; county historian Adams County, Brighton, 1976-77; mem. Brighton Human Rels. Commn., 1977-78; bd. dirs. Brighton Bicentennial Com., 1975-76, Ft. Lupton Bicentennial Com., 1975-76, R.I. RSVP, 1978-80, R.I. Pub. Records Adv. Coun., 1987-90, R.I. Hist. Records Adv. Bd., 1987-90; chair info. profls. legis. task force Freedom of Info. and Privacy Assn., 1991-93; chair oral history project Cole County Hist. Soc., 1996. Recipient Hist. Preservation award Adams County Hist. Soc., 1978, award Freedom of Info. and Privacy Assn., 1993; Ethnic Heritage Project grantee Colo. Humanities Council, 1977, Humanities and Social Scis. grantee U. B.C., 1993, Nat. Historic Pub. & Records grantee, 1988-92; Ford Found. fellow, 1964. Mem. Assn. Records Mgrs. and Adminstrs. (pres. No. Colo. chpt. 1984-85, v.p. Ocean State chpt. 1987-90, bd. dirs., editor Vancouver chpt. 1991, chmn. various coms., mem. records mgmt. standards and glossary task forces, Mem. Yr. 1985, microcomputer/PC industry action com., chmn. 1984-86, editor Software Dir. 1985-91, dir. Automated Records Sys. 1986-91, co-chmn. tech. applications com. 1989-90, chmn. Archives ISG 1997—), Inst. Cert. Records Mgrs. (regional coord., exam proctor, grader 1982—, cert. records mgr. 1993), Soc. Am. Archivists (com. automated records and techniques 1990-94, select com. task force on automated records and techniques 1994—, chair MicroMARC users group 1994-96, rep. joint SAA-ARMA Com. 1996—), Nat. Assn. Govt. Archivists an Records Adminstrs., Archives Assn. B.C. (freedom of info. and privacy legis. com. 1990-93), Assn. Can. Archivists (electronic records select com. 1991-93, Acad. Cert. Archivists (cert. 1994, mem. outreach com.). Democrat. Unitarian. Avocations: local historian, art, photography, film and TV production, hiking. Home: 231 Hobbs Ave Cheyenne WY 82009-4720

WAGNER, SIGURD, electrical engineering educator, researcher; came to U.S., 1968; naturalized in 1990; s. Richard A. and Pauli (Steiner) W.; m. Erika Freiberger, 1968; children: Matthias, Wolfgang. PhD, U. Vienna, Austria, 1968. Univ. postdoctoral fellow Ohio State U., 1969-70; mem. tech. staff Bell Labs., Murray Hill, N.J., 1970-73, Holmdel, N.J., 1973-78; chief photovoltaic research br. Solar Energy Research Inst., Golden, Colo., 1978-80; prof. elec. engring. Princeton U., N.J., 1980—. Contbr. articles on macroelectronics and solar cells to profl. jours.; assoc. editl. bd. Materials Letters, 1982—; patentee electronic materials and devices. Fellow Am. Phys. Soc.; mem. IEEE, Electrochem. Soc., Am. Chem. Soc., Materials Rsch. Soc.

WAGNER, SUSAN ELIZABETH, secondary school educator; b. Shelby, Ohio, Jan. 22, 1951; d. Joseph H. and Patricia A. (Shoup) W. BS, U. Dayton, 1973. Cert. tchr., Tex., Ohio. Tchr. health and phys. edn. Copperas Cove (Tex.) High Sch., 1973—, dept. chairperson, 1979—, head coach cross country and track, 1986—, girls athletic coord., 1994, asst. athletic dir., 1995; mem. bd. govs. Copperas Cove High Sch., 1993. Mem. AAHPERD, Am. Assn. Health Educators, Tex. Alliance Health, Phys. Edn., Recreation and Dance, Tex. Classroom Tchrs. Assn., Tex. Girls Coaches Assn., Athletic Congress USA (cert. official), Nat. Sports and Phys. Edn. Home: 701 N 19th St Copperas Cove TX 76522-1202 Office: Copperas Cove High Sch 400 S 25th St Copperas Cove TX 76522-2054

WAGNER, TERESA ANN, business owner; b. Spokane, Wash., Jan. 5, 1954; d. Alexander Lazarus and Pauline Joyce (Hodgson) Birch; m. Robert Earl Hurt, Aug. 11, 1973 (div. Jan. 1986); 1 child, Melinda Eslie Ann; m. Gary William Wagner, Aug. 25, 1996. AAS in Paralegal Studies, Spokane C.C., 1995. Cert. in behavioral profiling and forensic document exams., Am. Bd. Forensic Examiners, 1993; cert. in document exam., Nat. Assn. Document Examiners, 1995. Owner Profl. Handwriting Analysis, Spokane, 1986—; instr. Spokane Falls C.C., 1989-92, 92-94. Mem. Am. Handwriting Analysis Found. (cert., com. mem.), Coun. Graphological Soc., Nat. Assn. Document Examiners (treas., cert. document examiner), Northwest Fraud Investigators Assn. Avocations: writing, sewing, humor, legal studies. Office: Profl Handwriting Analysis 10 N Post St Ste 550 Spokane WA 99201-0705

WAGNER, THOMAS JOSEPH, lawyer, insurance company executive; b. Jackson, Mich., June 29, 1939; s. O. Walter and Dorothy Ann (Hollinger) W.; m. Judith Louise Bogardus, Jan. 15, 1961; children—Ann Louise, Mark Robert, Rachel Miriam. B.A., Earlham Coll., 1957; J.D., U. Chgo., 1965. Bar: Ill. 1968, U.S. Supreme Ct. 1975. Asst. to gov. State of Ill., Springfield, 1966-67, legal counsel, adminstrv. asst. to treas., 1967-70; adminstrv. asst. to U.S. senator Adlai E. Stevenson, Washington, 1970-77; sr. v.p. govt. affairs div. Am. Ins. Assn., Washington, 1977-80; staff v.p. Ina Corp., 1980-82; v.p., chief counsel Property Casualty Group, CIGNA Corp., Phila., 1982-86, v.p., assoc. gen. counsel, 1986-88, sr. v.p., corp. sec., 1988-91, exec. v.p., gen. counsel, 1992—; trustee Eisenhower Exchange Fellowships, Inc.; bd. dirs. Inst. Law and Econs., U. Penn. Past chmn. Phila. Crime Commn. Africa-Asia Pub. Svc. fellow Syracuse U., 1965-66. Mem. ABA (bus. law com.), Am. Corp. Counsel Assn., U.S.-Pacific Econ. Cooperation Coun., Forum for U.S.-European Union Legal Affairs. Office: Cigna Corp PO Box 7716 1 Liberty Place 55th Fl Philadelphia PA 19192-1550

WAGNER, WARREN HERBERT, JR., botanist, educator; b. Washington, Aug. 29, 1920; s. Warren Herbert and Harriet Lavinia (Claflin) W.; m. Florence Signaigo, July 16, 1948; children: Warren Charles, Margaret Frances. A.B., U. Pa., 1942; Ph.D., U. Calif. at Berkeley, 1950; spl. student, Harvard, 1950-51. Instr. Harvard, summer 1951; vis. prof., 1991; faculty U. Mich. at Ann Arbor, 1951—, prof. botany, 1962-91, prof. emeritus, 1991—, curator pteridophytes, 1961—, dir. Bot. Gardens, 1966-71, chmn. dept. botany, 1975-77; spl. rsch. higher plants, origin and evolution ferns, groundplan/divergence methods accurate deduction phylogenetic relationships fossil and living plants, pteridophytes of Hawaii, 1962-65; prin. investigator project evolutionary characters ferns NSF, 1960—, monograph grapeferns, 1980—, pteridophytes of Hawaii, 1991—; chmn. Mich. Natural Areas Coun., 1958-59; mem. Smithsonian Coun., 1967-72, hon. mem., 1972—; cons. mem. Survival Svc. Commn., Internat. Union for Conservation of Nature and Natural Resources, 1971—; mem. nat. hist. bd. Nat. Mus., 1989—. Trustee Cranbrook Inst. Scis. Recipient Distinguished Faculty Achievement award U. Mich., 1975, Amoco Outstanding Tchr. award, 1980, Disting. Sr. Lectr. award U. Mich., 1986. Fellow AAAS (sec. sect. bot. scis., v.p. sect. 1968), Am. Acad. Arts and Scis.; mem. NAS, Am. Fern Soc. (sec. 1952-54, curator, libr. 1957-77, pres. 1970, 71, hon.), Am. Soc. Plant Taxonomists (coun. 1958-65, pres. 1966, Asa Gray award 1990), Soc. for Study Evolution (v.p. 1965-66, coun. 1967-69, pres. 1972), Am. Soc. Naturalists, Internat. Assn. Pteridologists (v.p. 1981-87, pres. 1987-93), Bot. Soc. Am. (pres. 1977, Merit award 1978), Mich. Bot. Club (pres. 1967-71), Torrey Bot. Club, New Eng. Bot. Club, Internat. Soc. Plant Morphologists, Internat.

Assn. Plant Taxonomy, Sigma Xi, Phi Beta Kappa, Phi Kappa Tau. Home: 2111 Melrose Ave Ann Arbor MI 48104-4067

WAGNER, WILLIAM BURDETTE, business educator; b. Oswego, N.Y., Apr. 27, 1941; s. Guy Wesley and Gladys M. (Redlinger) W.; divorced; 1 child, Geoffrey D. BA with highest honors, Mich. State U., 1963; MBA, Ohio State U., 1965, PhD, 1967. Research and teaching asst. Ohio State U., Columbus, 1966-68; prof. mktg. and logistics U. Mo., Columbia, 1969—; guest prof. mktg. U. Nanjing, Peoples Republic of China, 1985-87, Prince of Songla U., Hat Yai, Thailand, 1990, 92; expert witness petroleum industry, 1989—; adv. dir. Mo. State Bank, St. Louis, 1981-93. Contbr. articles to profl. jours. Univ. coordinator book procurement program for minorities McDonnell Douglas, St. Louis, 1972—; mem. St. Louis-Nanjing Sister City Com., 1985—; faculty ambassador U. Mo. Alumni Assn., 1987—; mem. speakers bur., high sch. liaison team U. Mo., 1987—; Mizzou Outreach prof., 1987—; bd. dirs. Cen. Mo. Sheltered Enterprises for Handicapped, Columbia, 1985-92. Recipient Civic Svc. award McDonnell Douglas, 1977, Educator of Yr. award Jr. C. of C., 1983, Prof. of Yr. award Coll. of Bus. and Pub. Adminstrn., 1987, Golden Key Honor Soc. Faculty Mem. of Yr. award, 1987, Faculty Mem. of Yr. award Beta Theta Pi, 1990, Prof. of Yr. award Kans. City Alumni Assn., 1990; named Mktg. Prof. of Yr., U. Mo., 1987-88, 89-91; rsch. grantee SBC, Econ. Devel. Adminstrn., U. Mo.; NDEA fellow Ohi State U., 1963-66, William T. Kemper Teaching fellow, 1991, Wakonse Teaching fellow, 1995; Fulbright scholar, Korea, 1992. Mem. Nat. Assn. Purchasing Mgmt., St. Louis Purchasing Mgmt. Assn., Coun. Logistics Mgmt., Nat. Fulbright Assn., Nat. Eagle Scout Assn., Am. Soc. Transp. and Logistics (pres. Mo. chpt. 1974-75, bd. govs. 1970-74, 75-82), Delta Sigma Pi, Beta Gamma Simga, Omicron Delta Epsilon, Rotary Internat. (Paul Harris fellow), Mo. Athletic Club (St. Louis), Country Club of Mo. (Columbia), Univ. Club (Columbia), Jefferson Club. Methodist. Avocations: stamp and coin collecting, bridge, golf, swimming, jogging. Home: 2401 Bluff Blvd Columbia MO 65201-8613 Office: Univ Mo 324 Middlebush Hall Columbia MO 65211

WAGNER, WILLIAM CHARLES, veterinarian; b. Elma, N.Y., Nov. 12, 1932; s. Frederick George and Doris Edna (Newton) W.; m. Donna Ann McNeill, Aug. 14, 1954 (div. May 1993); children: William Charles, Elizabeth Ann, Victoria Mary, Kathryn Farrington; m. Victoria Sandberg Eggleton, Oct. 21, 1995. D.V.M., Cornell U., 1956, Ph.D., 1968. Gen. practice vet. medicine Interlaken, N.Y., 1956-57; research veterinarian Cornell U., 1957-65, NIH postdoctoral fellow dept. animal sci., 1965-68; asst. prof. vet. medicine Vet. Med. Research Inst., Iowa State U., Ames, 1968-69; assoc. prof. Vet. Med. Research Inst., Iowa State U., 1969-74, prof., 1974-77; prof. physiology, head dept. vet. biosci. U. Ill., Urbana, 1977-90, assoc. dean for rsch. and grad. studies Coll. Vet. Medicine, 1990-93; prin. vet. scientist USDA Coop. State Rsch. Edn. & Extension Svc., 1993—; gen. sec. Internat. Congress on Animal Reprodn., urbana, 1984, pres. standing com., 1988—; v.p. Conf. Rsch. Workers in Animal Disease, 1987-88, pres., 1988-89; prin. vet. scientist USDA-Coop. State Rsch. Svcs., Washington, 1990-91. Pres. Ames Community Theater, 1972-73, 76-77. Recipient Alexander von Humboldt U.S. Scientist award Humboldt Stiftung, Freising-Weihenstephan, W. Ger., 1973-74; Fulbright prof., W. Ger., 1984-85. Mem. Am. Coll. Theriogenologists (diplomate; Bartlett award and lectr. 1995), AVMA (mem. coun. on edn. 1987-93), Nat. Acad. of Practice Vet. Medicine, Physiol. Soc., Am. Soc. Animal Sci., Soc. Study Reprodn., Soc. Study Fertility, N.Y. Acad. Scis., Sigma Xi, Phi Kappa Phi, Phi Zeta, Gamma Sigma Delta, Alpha Zeta. Lutheran. Home: 20676 Cutwater Pl Sterling VA 20165-7340 Office: USDA CSREES Ag Box 2220 901 D St SW Washington DC 20250-2220 *I believe that it is important to be friendly to others, to try to understand the other person's position or feelings and deal with colleagues and subordinates in an impartial and fair manner. One should always remember that talents are a gift to be used wisely and to the fullest extent possible.*

WAGNER, WILLIAM GERARD, university dean, physicist, consultant, information scientist, investment manager; b. St. Cloud, Minn., Aug. 22, 1936; s. Gerard C. and Mary V. (Cloone) W.; m. Janet Agatha Rowe, Jan. 30, 1968 (div. 1978); children: Mary, Robert, David, Anne; m. Christiane LeGuen, Feb. 21, 1985 (div. 1989); m. Yvonne Naomi Moussette, Dec. 4, 1995; children: Mark, David, Paul, Jonathan. B.S., Calif. Inst. Tech., 1958, Ph.D. (NSF fellow, Howard Hughes fellow), 1962. Cons. Rand Corp., Santa Monica, Calif., 1960-65; sr. staff physicist Hughes Research Lab., Malibu, Calif., 1960-69; lectr. physics Calif. Inst. Tech., Pasadena, 1963-65; asst. prof. physics U. Calif. at Irvine, 1965-66; assoc. prof. physics and elec. engring. U. So. Calif., L.A., 1966-69, prof. depts. physics and elec. engring., 1969—, dean div. natural scis. and math. Coll. Letters, Arts and Scis., 1973-87, dean interdisciplinary studies and developmental activities, 1987-89, spl. asst. automated record services, 1975-81; founder program in neural, informational & behavioral scis., 1982—; chmn. bd. Malibu Securities Corp., L.A., 1971—; cons. Janus Mgmt. Corp., L.A., 1970-71, Croesus Capital Corp., L.A., 1971-74, Fin. Horizons Inc., Beverly Hills, Calif., 1974—; allied mem. Pacific Stock Exch., 1974-82; fin. and computer cons. Hollywood Reporter, 1979-81; mem. adv. coun. for emerging engring. techs. NSF, 1987—. Contbr. articles on physics to sci. publs. Richard Chase Tolman postdoctoral fellow, 1962-65. Mem. Am. Phys. Soc., Nat. Assn. Security Dealers, Sigma Xi. Home: 2828 Patricia Ave Los Angeles CA 90064-4425 Office: U So Calif Hedco Neurosci Bldg Los Angeles CA 90089

WAGNON, JOAN, former state legislator, association executive; b. Texarkana, Ark., Oct. 17, 1940; d. Jack and Louise (lucas) D.; m. William O. Wagnon Jr., June 4, 1964; children: Jack, William O. III. BA in Biology, Hendrix Coll., Conway, Ark., 1962; MEd in Guidance and Counseling, U. Mo., 1968. Sr. research technician U. Ark. Med. Sch., Little Rock, 1962-64; sr. research asst. U. Ark. Med. Sch., Columbia, Mo., 1964-68; tchr. No. Hills Jr. High Sch., Topeka, 1968-69, J.S. Kendall Sch., Boston, 1970-71; counselor Neighborhood Youth Corps, Topeka, 1973-74; exec. dir. Topeka YWCA, 1977-93; mem. Kans. Legislature, 1983-94; with Kans. Families for Kids, 1994-97; mayor City of Topeka, 1997—. Mem. Health Planning Rev. Commn., Topeka, 1984-85. Recipient Service to Edn. award, Topeka NEA, 1979, Outstanding Achievement award, Kans. Home Econs. Assn., 1985; named Woman of Yr. Mayors Council Status of Women, 1983; named one of Top Ten Legislators Kans. Mag., Wichita, 1986. Mem. Topeka Assn. Human Svc. Execs. (pres. 1981-83), Topekans for Ednl. Involvement (pres. 1979-82), Women's Polit. Caucus (state chair). Democrat. Methodist. Lodge: Rotary. Avocations: music, swimming, boating. Home: 1606 SW Boswell Ave Topeka KS 66604-2729 Office: Kans Families for Kids 2209 SW 29th St Topeka KS 66611-1908

WAGONER, DAVID RUSSELL, author, educator; b. Massillon, Ohio, June 5, 1926; s. Walter Siffert and Ruth (Banyard) W.; m. Patricia Lee Parrott, July 8, 1961 (div. June 1982); m. Robin Heather Seyfried, July 24, 1982; children: Alexandra Dawn, Adrienne Campbell. B.A. in English, Pa. State U., 1947; M.A. in English, Ind. U., 1949. Instr. English DePauw U., 1949-50; instr. Pa. State U., 1950-53; asst. prof. U. Wash., 1954-57, assoc. prof., 1958-66, prof., 1966—; Elliston lectr. U. Cin., 1968; editor Poetry NW, 1966—; poetry editor Princeton U. Press, 1977-81, Mo. Press, 1983—. Author: (poetry books) Dry Sun, Dry Wind, 1953, A Place to Stand, 1958, The Nesting Ground, 1963, Staying Alive, 1966, New and Selected Poems, 1969, Working Against Time, 1970, Riverbed, 1972, Sleeping in the Woods, 1974, Collected Poems, 1976, Who Shall Be the Sun?, 1978, In Broken Country, 1979, Landfall, 1981, First Light, 1983, Through the Forest, 1987, Walt Whitman Bathing, 1996, (novels) The Man in the Middle, 1954, Money, Money, Money, 1955, Rock, 1958, The Escape Artist (also film 1982), 1965, Baby, Come on Inside, 1968, Where is My Wandering Boy Tonight?, 1970, The Road to Many a Wonder, 1974, Tracker, 1975, Whole Hog, 1976, The Hanging Garden, 1980; editor: Straw for the Fire: From the Notebooks of Theodore Roethke, 1943-63, 1972. Recipient Morton Dauwen Zabel prize Poetry mag., 1967, Blumenthal-Leviton-Blonder prize, 1974, 2 Fels prizes Coordinating Coun. Lit. Mags., 1975, Tietjens prize, 1977, English-Speaking Union prize, 1980, Sherwood Anderson award, 1980, Ruth Lilly Poetry prize, 1991, Levinson prize, 1994; Guggenheim fellow, 1956, Ford fellow, 1964, Nat. Inst. Arts and Letters grantee, 1967, Nat. Endowment for Arts grantee, 1969. Mem. Acad. Am. Poets (chancellor 1978—), Soc. Am. Magicians, Nat. Assn. Blackfeet Indians (asso.). Home: 5416 154th Pl SW Edmonds WA 98026-4348 Office: U Wash 4045 Brooklyn Ave NE Seattle WA 98105-6210

WAGONER, GERALDINE VANDER POL, music educator; b. Kankakee, Ill., Sept. 16, 1931; d. Ralph and Josie (Mieras) VanderPol; BA, Central U. of Iowa, 1954; MA, Montclair State Coll., 1968; postgrad. Juilliard Sch. Music, 1955, 56, 66, 67, NYU, Royal Conservatory, Toronto, 1971, Mozarteum, Salzburg, Austria, 1972; children: Joel Timothy, Stephanie Anne. Music coach, piano pedagog, cons. Bd. Edn., Edison, N.J., Englewood and Ridgewood, N.J., 1954-74; music specialist, Ridgewood, 1975-95; owner, mgr., CEO Musical Spheres Co., 1995—; cons. NYU spl. project; cons. Project Impact. Trustee, Hudson Symphony Orch., 1965-71; mem. Met. Mus. of Art. Teaching fellow NYU, 1990-91; adj. prof. music William Paterson Coll., Wayne, N.J. Mem. Profl. Music Tchrs. Guild (cert. for highest goals and achievements 1966), Nat. Music Tchrs. Assn., N.J. Music Tchrs. Assn., Am. Orff Schulwerk Assn., NEA, Music Educators Assn., Bergen County Music Educators Assn., Theater Devel. Found., Met. Opera Guild, Netherland-American Found., Collegiate Chorale, Silver Bay Assn. (trustee 1975—). Clubs: Knickerbocher Rep., Netherland, Overseas Yacht Club. Composer creative tonal and rhythm curriculum for children and assessing beginning instrumental music instructional strategies.

WAGONER, JENNINGS LEE, JR., history educator; b. Winston-Salem, N.C., July 26, 1938; s. Jennings Lee and Carolyn Nelme (Phifer) W.; m. Shirley Canady, Aug. 12, 1962; children: David Carroll, Brian Jennings. BA, Wake Forest U., 1960; MATeaching, Duke U., 1961; PhD, Ohio State U., 1968. Tchr. High Point Pub. Schs., N.C., 1960-62; instr. Wake Forest U., 1962-65; teaching assoc. Ohio State U., 1965-68; from asst. prof. to prof. history of edn. U. Va., Charlottesville, 1968—, dir. Ctr. for Study Higher Edn., 1975-85, chmn. leadership and policy studies, 1985-87, disting. prof. Curry Sch. Edn. U. Va., 1987, William C. Parrish Jr. Endowed prof., 1994—; vis. research scholar Harvard U., 1972, U. Calif., Berkeley, 1984; vis. prof. Monash U., Melbourne, Australia, 1992. Author: Thomas Jefferson and the Education of a New Nation, 1976; co-author: American Education: A History, 1996; contbr. articles to profl. jours.; co-editor: Changing Politics of Education, 1978; editorial bd. History of Edn. Quar., Ednl. Studies jour. Recipient Disting. Prof. award U. Va. Alumni Assn., 1996. Sesquicentennial fellow U. Va., 1972, 84, 90. Mem. History of Edn. Soc. (pres. 1983-85, bd. dirs. 1979-81), Am. Ednl. Research Assn. (v.p. div. F 1981-83), Orgn. Am. Historians, Am. Ednl. Studies Assn. (bd. dirs.), Assn. Study Higher Edn., Raven Soc., Sierra Club, Outward Bound, Kappa Delta Pi, Phi Delta Kappa, Omicron Delta Kappa (faculty advisor), Golden Key Nat. Honor Soc. Avocations: hiking, fishing, canoeing. Home: 468 Dry Bridge Rd Charlottesville VA 22903-7456 Office: U Va 405 Emmet St Charlottesville VA 22903-2495

WAGONER, PORTER, country music singer, composer; b. nr. West Plains, Mo., Aug. 12, 1927; s. Charles and Bertha W.; children: Richard, Denise, Debra. Former clerk, butcher. Singer, composer, radio and TV personality, 1950—, rec. artist, RCA Record Co., MCA/DOT Records, 1986—, radio and TV appearances include radio, KWPM, West Plains, Mo., 1950, KWTO, Springfield, Mo., 1951, Jubilee, U.S.A, ABC-TV, 1955, radio, WSM Grand Ole Opry, Nashville, Tenn., 1957—, Porter Wagoner TV Show; Records include A Satisfied Mind, Heartwarming Songs, Porter Wagoner Today, Best of Porter Wagoner, Porter & Dolly, Two of a Kind; composer songs including (with Gary Walker) Trade Mark, 1953, (with Michael Pearson) Bottom of the Fifth, 1982; albums include Greatest Songs, 1995, Greatest Hits, 1996. Recipient (with Dolly Parton) Vocal Group of Yr. award, Vocal Duo of Yr. award Country Music Assn., 1970, 71. Address: Pair Records Inc Essex Entertainment Inc 560 Sylvan Ave Englewood NJ 07632 Address: PO Box 290785 Nashville TN 37229-0785*

WAGONER, RALPH HOWARD, academic administrator, educator; b. Pitts., May 30, 1938; s. Richard Henry and Charlotte (Stevenson) W.; m. Wilma Jo Staup, Dec. 21, 1961; children: Amanda Jane, Joseph Ryan. AB in Biology, Gettysburg Coll., 1960; MS in Ednl. Adminstrn., Westminster Coll., 1963; PhD, Kent State U., 1967; postgrad., MIT, 1973, Dartmouth Coll., 1979. Prin., tchr., coach Williamsfield (Ohio) Elem. and Jr. High Sch., 1960-62; dir. elem. edn. Pymatuning Valley (Ohio) Local Schs., 1962-64, asst. supt. instrn., 1964-65; acad. counselor, asst. to dean coll. edn. Kent (Ohio) State U., 1965-66, instr. edn., 1966-67; asst. prof. Drake U., Des Moines, Iowa, 1967-70, assoc. prof., 1970-71, chmn. dept. elem. edn., 1968-70, chmn. dept. tchr. edn., 1970-71, acad. adminstrn. intern Am. Council Edn., Office of Pres., 1971-72, asst. to pres., 1972-77, dir. devel., 1975-77; v.p. pub. affairs and devel., prof. Western Ill. U., Macomb, 1977-87, pres., 1987-93; pres. Augustana Coll., Sioux Falls, S.D., 1993—; adj. prof. San Francisco Theol. Sem., 1971; mem. senate Drake U., 1968-77; sponsor interhall council Western Ill. U., 197893, mem. BOG/UPI task force on incentives for faculty excellence, co-chmn., faculty mentor, 1985-93; cons. in field. Co-author: (with L. Wayne Bryan) Societal Crises and Educational Response: A Book of Readings, 1969, (with Robert L. Evans) The Emerging Teacher, 1970, (with William R. Abell) The Instructional Module Package System, 1971, Writing Behavioral Objectives or How Do I Know When He Knows, 1971; contbr. articles to profl. jours. Chmn. Mid-Ill. Computer Consortium, 1980, 85, Western Ill. Corridor of Opportunity, 1987-93; mem. Pres.' Regional Adv. Coun., 1977-87; mem. investments com. McDonough County YMCA; mem. exec. com. Macomb Area Indsl. Corp.; trustee Robert Morris Coll., 1983-88, Chgo. and Carthage, Ill., 1983-88; bd. dirs. Ill. Coun. Econ. Edn., 1987-93, McDonough County United Way Dr., 1980-82; bd. trustees The Cornerstone Found. LSS of Ill., 1990-96; mem. Sioux Falls Tomorrow Task Force, 1993-94; bd. dirs. S.D. Symphony, 1993—, Edn. Telecomms. State of S.D., 1993—, Sioux Falls Devel. Found., 1993—, Children's Inn, 1993—, Sioux Valley Physicians Alliance, 1995—, LECNA, 1996—; life trustee Lutheran Social Svcs., 1996—. Recipient Man of Yr. award Andover Rotary Club, 1964, Quax Honor award, 1969-70, Disting. Alumni award Gettysburg (Pa.) Coll., 1991; named McDonough County Citizen of Yr., Elks, 1982. Fellow Am. Coun. Edn. (cons. fund raising 1984-87); mem. Am. Assn. State Colls. and Univs. (com. econ. devel. 1988, com. on athletics 1987), Ednl. Computing Network (chmn. policy bd. 1985-87), Assn. Midcontinent Univs. (coun. dels. 1987-93), Gateway Conf. (coun. dels. 1987-93), Coun. for Advancement and Support of Edn. (discussion leader, speaker, 1975, 77, 80, 84, 86, 91, 92, 93, 94, Citation award 1981, 83, Grand award 1982, Bronze award 1985, Silver award 1986), Macomb C. of C. (exec. com., bd. dirs.), Ill. Chamber Econ. Devel. Policy Task Force, Blue Key (hon.), Omicron Delta Kappa, Phi Eta Sigma (hon.), Phi Mu Alpha. Lutheran. Lodge: Rotary. Home: 2817 S Grange Ave Sioux Falls SD 57105-4616 Office: Augustana Coll 29th and Summit Sioux Falls SD 57197*

WAGONER, ROBERT HALL, engineering educator, researcher; b. Columbus, Ohio, Jan. 8, 1952; s. Robert H. and Leorra (Schmucker) W.; m. Robyn K. O'Donnell, Aug. 30, 1980; children: Erin A. Wagoner Hansgen, Amy J. BS, Ohio State U., 1974, MS, 1975, PhD, 1976. NSF postdoctoral rschr. U. Oxford, Eng., 1976-77; staff rsch. scientist GM Rsch. Labs., Warren, Mich., 1977-83; assoc. prof. material sci. engring. Ohio State U., Columbus, 1983-86, prof., 1986—, chmn. dept., 1992-96; maitre de recherche Ecole des Mines de Paris, Sophia Antipolis, France, 1990-91; dir. Ohio State U. Rsch. Found., 1991-94, Ctr. Advt. Materials Mfg. Auto Components, 1994—; trustee Orton Found., 1992-96. Co-author: Fundamentals of Metal Forming, 1997; editor: Novel Techniques in Metal Deformation, 1983, Forming Limit Diagrams, 1989. Recipient Raymond Meml. award AIME, 1981, 83; Disting. Scholar award Ohio State U., 1990, Harrison award for tchg. excellence, 1988; Presdl. Young Investigator award NSF, 1984; NSF postdoctoral fellow Oxford (Eng.) U., 1976. Fellow ASM Internat.; mem. Nat. Acad. Engring., Minerals, Metals and Materials Soc. (founding mem., dir. 1991-95, Mathewson Gold medal 1988, Hardy Gold medal 1981, v.p. 1996-97, pres. 1997—), Am. Inst. Mining, Metall., and Petroleum Engring. (trustee 1997—). Developed SHEET-3 and SHEET-S, sheet forming simulation programs for indsl. use; introduced first quantitative test for planetensile work hardening; invented formability test and friction test. Office: Ohio State U Dept Material Sci Engring 2041 N College Rd Columbus OH 43210-1124

WAGONER, ROBERT VERNON, astrophysicist, educator; b. Teaneck, N.J., Aug. 6, 1938; s. Robert Vernon and Marie Theresa (Clifford) W.; m. Lynne Ray Moses, Sept. 2, 1963 (div. Feb. 1986); children: Alexa Frances, Shannon Stephanie; m. Stephanie Nightingale, June 27, 1987. B.M.E., Cornell U., 1961; M.S., Stanford U., 1962, Ph.D., 1965. Research fellow in physics Calif. Inst. Tech., 1965-68, Sherman Fairchild Disting. scholar, 1976; asst. prof. astronomy Cornell U., 1968-71, asso. prof., 1971-73; asso. prof. physics Stanford U., 1973-77, prof., 1977—; George Ellery Hale disting. vis. prof. U. Chgo., 1978; mem. Com. on Space Astronomy and Astrophysics, 1979-82, theory study panel Space Sci. Bd., 1980-82, physics survey com. NRC, 1983-84; grant selection com. NSERC (Can.), 1990-93. Contbr. articles on theoretical astrophysics and gravitation to profl. publs., mags.; co-author Cosmic Horizons. Sloan Found. rsch. fellow, 1969-71; Guggenheim Meml. fellow, 1979; grantee NSF, 1973-90, NASA, 1982—. Fellow Am. Phys. Soc.; mem. Am. Astron. Soc., Internat. Astron. Union, Tau Beta Pi, Phi Kappa Phi. Patentee. Office: Stanford U Dept Physics Stanford CA 94305-4060

WAGONSELLER, JAMES MYRL, real estate executive; b. Zanesville, Ohio, July 29, 1920; s. Myrl H. and Florence L. (Pfeiffer) W.; m. Mary J. McCauley, Nov. 16, 1943; children—Thomas James, John Myrl, Anne Elizabeth Wagonseller Bauswein. Grad. high sch. Draftsman apprentice machinist Hermann Mfg. Co., Lancaster, Ohio, 1945-47; advt. sales Lancaster (Ohio) Eagle-Gazette, 1947-50, classified mgr., 1950-52, dir. advt. sales, 1952-54; real estate salesman Larkin Durdin (Realtor), Lancaster, 1954-60; ptnr. Lancaster Realty Co., 1960-65, Simons & Wagonseller (Realtors), Lancaster, 1965-77; prin. James M. Wagonseller, Appraiser; Pres. Lancaster Bd. Realtors, 1965; mem. Bd. Zoning Appeals Lancaster, 1972-74. Pres. Community Service Council, 1944, United Appeal, 1968; Mem. central, exec. coms. Fairfield County Democratic Com., 1960-70, mem. exec. com., 1976—. Served with USAF, 1941-45. Decorated D.F.C., Air medal with 3 clusters; named to Ohio Vets. Hall of Fame, 1996. Mem. Lancaster C. of C. (pres. 1970), Nat. Assn. Real Estate Brokers, Ohio Assn. Real Estate Brokers, Am. Assn. Cert. Appraisers, Am. Legion (nat. comdr. 1974-75). Democrat. Roman Catholic. Lodges: Kiwanis (pres.), Elk (Ann. Citizen award 1975). Home and Office: 1973 Coldspring Dr Lancaster OH 43130-1458

WAHAAB, JAY, entrepreneur; b. Arima, Trinidad, West Indies, Jan. 31, 1961; arrived in Can., 1976; came to U.S., 1981; s. A. Wahaab and Maria Sankar. AA, Westchester Bus. Inst., 1990. Prin. MJ Mktg., White Plains, N.Y., 1986—. Sgt. USMC, 1984-94. Mem. Beneath the Sea (ad dir. 1987—, Disting. Svc. award 1989), Marine Corps League (chmn. Toys for Tots 1990—, Disting. Svc. award 1992). Avocations: scuba diving, outdoor activities, sports, camping, hiking. Office: MJ Mktg PO Box 1734 White Plains NY 10602

WAHBA, GRACE, statistician, educator; b. Washington; d. Harry and Anne Goldsmith; 1 child, Jeffrey A. BA, Cornell U.; MA, U. Md.; PhD, Stanford U. Prof. statistics U. Wis., Madison, 1967-87, Bascom prof., 1987—; fellow Weizmann Inst., Israel, St. Cross Coll., Oxford (Eng.) U.; Lady Davis fellow Technion, Israel, Australian Nat. U., Canberra; Clare Booth Luce vis. prof. Yale U.; cons. to industry and govt. Author: Spline Models for Observational Data, 1990; assoc. editor; SIAM Jour. Sci. Computing, 1985—; adv. bd. Jour. Computational Graphical Stats., 1990—. Recipient Emanuel and Carol Parzen prize for Statis. Innovation, 1994, NSF Creativity award, 1994. Fellow AAAS, Inst. Math. Statis. (Neyman lectr. nat. meeting 1994), Am. Statis. Assn., Internat. Statis. Inst.; mem. Soc. Indsl. and Applied Math. (plenary speaker nat. meeting 1994), Bernoulli Soc., Am. Math. Soc., Am. Meteorol. Soc. Achievements include development of new methods of curve and surface smoothing, of new statistical methods in biology and meteorology, of new methods for multivariate response function estimation, of analysis of variance in function spaces, of approximate solution of ill posed explicit and implicit inverse problems with noisy data, and of the assimilation of data from heterogenous sources. Office: U Wis Dept Stats 1210 W Dayton St Madison WI 53706-1613

WAHL, ARTHUR CHARLES, retired chemistry educator; b. Des Moines, Sept. 8, 1917; s. Arthur C. and Mabel (Mussetter) W.; m. Mary Elizabeth McCauley, Dec. 1, 1943; 1 child, Nancy Wahl Miegel. BS, Iowa State Coll., 1939; PhD, U. Calif., Berkeley, 1942. Group leader Los Alamos (N.Mex.) Nat. Lab., 1943-46; assoc. prof. chemistry Washington U., St. Louis, 1946-53, Farr prof. of radiochemistry, 1953-83, prof. emeritus, 1983—; cons. Los Alamos Nat. Lab., 1950—. Author, editor: Radioactivity Applied to Chemistry, 1951; contbr. articles to profl. jours. NSF fellow, 1967; recipient Sr. Vis. Scientist Humboldt award Humboldt Found., 1977. Mem. Am. Chem. Soc. Office: Los Alamos Nat Lab MS # 514 Los Alamos NM 87545

WAHL, FLOYD MICHAEL, geologist; b. Hebron, Ind., July 7, 1931; s. Floyd Milford and Ann Pearl (DeCook) W.; m. Dorothy W. Daniel, July 4, 1953; children: Timothy, David, Jeffrey, Kathryn. A.B., DePauw U., 1953; M.S., U. Ill., 1957, Ph.D., 1958. Cert. profl. geologist. Prof. geology U. Fla., Gainesville, 1969-82, assoc. dean Grad. Sch., 1974-80, acting dean, 1980-81; exec. dir. Geol Soc Am., Boulder, Colo., 1982-94; ret., 1994. Contbr. articles to profl. jours. Served to cpl. U.S. Army, 1953-55. Recipient Outstanding Tchr. award U. Ill., 1967. Fellow Geol. Soc. Am. (Outstanding Svc. award 1994); mem. Mineral Soc. Am., Am. Inst. Profl. Geologists (chpt. pres.), Sigma Xi.

WAHL, HOWARD WAYNE, retired construction company executive, engineer; b. Hitterdal, Minn., Jan. 17, 1935; s. Milo Ormenzo and Esther Marie (Sorenson) W.; m. Carroll May Pollock, Aug. 16, 1958; children: Jeffrey David, Michael Edward, Nancy Elizabeth. BCE, U. Washington, 1957. Registered engr., Calif., N.Y., Mich., Ohio, Md. Structural engr. Bechtel Corp., San Francisco, 1956-69; project engr. Bechtel Corp., Gaithersburg, Md., 1969-72; chief civil engr. Bechter Power Corp., San Francisco, 1972-74; mgr. engring. and constrn. Bechter Power Corp., 1975-78; v.p., mgr. Ann Arbor Power Div.-Bechtel, Mich., 1978-84; dir. Bechtel Group, Inc., 1982-92; pres. Bechtel Ea. Power Corp., Gaithersburg, 1984-88; mng. dir. Bechtel Power Corp., San Francisco, 1988-89; pres. European region Bechtel Corp., Paris, 1989-91; ret., 1991; pres. Pacific Voice Track, Las Vegas, 1996—; dir. Ann Arbor Bank-1st Am., 1978-84. Contbr. articles to profl. jours. Campaign chmn. Washtenaw County United Way, Ann Arbor, 1982; chmn. Turkish-U.S. Bus. Coun., Washington, 1988-90; mem. exec. coun. Boy Scouts Am., Ann Arbor, 1978-84; mem. devel. coun. U Wash. Coll. Engring.; trustee Desert Rsch. Inst. U. Nev., Reno. Mem. ASCE, Am. Concrete Inst., U. Mich. Pres. Club and Victors Club, U. Washington Pres. Club, Olympic Club (San Francisco). Republican. Presbyterian. Avocations: woodworking, gardening, cooking, boating, hiking. Home: PO Box 7601 Incline Village NV 89452-7601

WAHL, JONATHAN MICHAEL, mathematics educator; b. Washington, Jan. 29, 1945; s. Marvin C. and Blanche (Genauer) W.; m. Deborah R. Sody, Dec. 27, 1970; 1 child, Elizabeth Rachel. BS, MA, Yale U., 1965; PhD, Harvard U., 1971. Instr. U. Calif., Berkeley, 1970-72; asst. prof. U. N.C., Chapel Hill, 1973-75, assoc. prof., 1975-80, prof., 1980—. Office: U NC Dept Math Chapel Hill NC 27599-3250

WAHL, WILLIAM JOSEPH, JR., information systems specialist; b. Pottsville, Pa., Jan. 19, 1947; s. William Joseph and Edith (Adams) W.; m. Mary Ellen Trautman, Oct. 17, 1964; children: Patricia Marie, William Joseph III, Monica Marie, Michael Anthony. MS in Bus. Policy, Columbia U., 1983. Dir. info. sys. IBM Gen. Bus. Group Internat., White Plains, N.Y., 1979-81; dir. info. systems programs IBM Corp. Hdqrs., White Plains, N.Y., 1982; dir. info. systems IBM Info. Systems and Communications Group, White Plains, N.Y., 1983-84; group dir. mgmt. control systems IBM Info. Systems and Tech. Group, Harrison, N.Y., 1985-87; group dir. info. systems and telecommunications IBM Enterprise Systems, Somers, N.Y., 1988-92; chief info. officer IBM Personal Systems, Somers, N.Y., 1992-94; dir. worldwide fulfillment sys. tech. IBM Corp Hdqs, Somers, N.Y., 1995—; rsch. affiliate NYU Stern Sch. Bus., N.Y.C., 1991—; ops. mgmt. advisor Columbia Grad. Sch. Bus., N.Y.C., 1988—. Mem. Beta Gamma Sigma. Avocations: fishing, philately, music. Home: 36 Pleasant Hill Rd Hopewell Junction NY 12533-7411 Office: IBM RR 1 Somers NY 10589-9801

WAHLBERG, MARK, actor. Appeared in films The Substitute, 1993, Renaissance Man, 1994, The Basketball Diaries, 1995, No Fear, 1995, Boogie Nights, 1997. Office: c/o Provideng Fin Mgmt 268 Newberry St 4th Fl Boston MA 02116*

WAHLBERG, PHILIP LAWRENCE, former bishop; b. Houston, Jan. 18, 1924; s. Philip Lawrence and Ella Alieda (Swenson) W.; m. Rachel Conrad, June 1, 1946; children: David, Christopher, Pauli, Sharon. AA, Tex. Luth.

Coll., 1942, DD (hon.), 1963; BA, Lenoir Rhyne Coll., Hickory, N.C., 1944; MDiv, Luth. Theol. Sem., Columbia, S.C., 1946. Ordained to ministry United Luth. Ch. in Am., 1946. Pastor St. Luke Luth. Ch., Thunderbolt, Ga., 1946-50, Redeemer Luth. Ch., Wilmington Island, Ga., 1946-50, St. Mark Luth. Ch., Corpus Christi, Tex., 1950-59; pres. Tex.-La. Synod, United Luth. Ch. Am., Austin, Tex., 1959-62; bishop Tex.-La. Synod, Luth. Ch. Am., Austin, 1963-87; acting dir. devel. Lutheran Outdoor and Retreat Ministries Southwest, 1987-88; legis. liaison Tex. Impact, Austin, 1989-91; interim coord. Regional Ctr. for Mission Evang. Luth. Ch. in Am., Dallas, 1991-92; mem. devel. staff Luth. Sem. Program of Southwest, 1992—; mem. com. on appeals, also chmn. Evang. Luth. Ch. in Am., 1988-95, hearing officer, 1995—; also mem. exec. coun. Luth. Ch. in Am., N.Y.C., 1980-87, chmn. com. on legal matters, 1984-87; mem. mgmt. com. Div. for Mission in N.Am., N.Y.C., 1972-80, chmn., 1972-76; bd. dirs. Bd. Am. Missions, N.Y.C., 1963-72, chmn., 1968-72; bd. dirs. Luth. Sch. Theology, Chgo., 1967-87. Author articles in religious jours., sermons; author theol. cassette, 1973. Named Disting. churchman Tex. Luth. Coll., 1978; Disting. Alumnus, Lenoir Rhyne Coll., 1962; named Man of Year, Thunderbolt, Ga. C. of C., 1950. Mem. Interfaith Impact. Democrat. Avocations: winemaking, golf, choral singing. Office: 5804 Cary Dr Austin TX 78757-3108

WAHLEN, EDWIN ALFRED, lawyer; b. Gary, Ind., Mar. 12, 1919; s. Alfred and Ethel (Pearson) W.; m. Alice Elizabeth Condit, Apr. 24, 1943 (div. 1983); children: Edwin Alfred, Virginia Elizabeth, Martha Anne; m. Elizabeth L. Corey, Nov. 23, 1984. Student, U. Ala., 1936-38; A.B., U. Chgo., 1942, J.D., 1948. Bar: Ill. 1948. Practiced in Chgo., 1948—; mem. firm Haight, Goldstein & Haight, 1948-55; ptnr. Goldstein & Wahlen, 1956-59, Arvey, Hodes, Costello & Burman (and predecessor), 1959-91, Wildman, Harrold, Allen & Dixon, 1992—. Author: Soldiers and Sailors Wills: A Proposal For Federal Legislation, 1948. Served to 2d lt. AUS, 1942-46. Decorated Silver Star medal, Bronze Star medal. Mem. ABA, Ill. Bar Assn., Chgo. Bar Assn., Order of Coif, Phi Beta Kappa, Phi Alpha Delta. Home: 1250 Breckenridge Ct Lake Forest IL 60045 Office: 225 W Wacker Dr Chicago IL 60606-1224

WAHLKE, JOHN CHARLES, political science educator; b. Cin., Oct. 29, 1917; s. Albert B.C. and Clara J. (Ernst) W.; m. Virginia Joan Higgins, Dec. 1, 1943; children: Janet Parmely, Dale. A.B., Harvard U., 1939, M.A., 1947, Ph.D., 1952. Instr., asst. prof. polit. sci. Amherst (Mass.) Coll., 1949-53; assoc. prof. polit. sci. Vanderbilt U., Nashville, Tenn., 1953-63; prof. polit. sci. SUNY, Buffalo, 1963-66, U. Iowa, 1966-71, SUNY, Stony Brook, 1971-72, U. Iowa, Iowa City, 1972-79; prof. polit. sci. U. Ariz., Tucson, 1979-87, prof. emeritus, 1987—. Author: (with others) The Legislative System, 1962, Government and Politics, 1966, The Politics of Representation, 1978; co-author: Introduction to Political Science—Reason, Reflection, and Analysis, 1997;. Served to capt., F.A. AUS, 1942-46. Decorated Air medal with 2 oak leaf clusters. Mem. AAAS, Am. Polit. Sci. Assn. (past pres.), Internat. Polit. Sci. Assn., So. Polit. Sci. Assn., Midwest Polit. Sci. Assn. (past pres.), Western Polit. Sci. Assn., Southwestern Polit. Sci. Assn., Assn. Politics and the Life Scis. Home: 5462 N Entrada Catorce Tucson AZ 85718-4851 Office: U Ariz Dept Polit Sci Tucson AZ 85721

WAHOSKE, MICHAEL JAMES, lawyer; b. Ripon, Wis., June 4, 1953; m. Marcia Wilson; children: Jennifer, John. BA with highest honors, U. Notre Dame, 1975, JD summa cum laude, 1978. Bar: Minn. 1978, U.S. Dist. Ct. Minn. 1979, U.S. Ct. Appeals (7th cir.) 1979, U.S. Ct. Appeals (8th and 9th cirs.) 1980, U.S. Ct. Appeals (10th cir.) 1982, U.S. Supreme Ct. 1982, U.S. Ct. Appeals (6th cir.) 1988, U.S. Ct. Appeals (fed. cir.) 1989, U.S. Ct. Appeals (D.C. cir.) 1992, U.S. Ct. Appeals (4th cir.) 1994, U.S. Ct. Appeals (11th cir.) 1996, Supreme Ct. of Winnebago Tribe of Nebr., 1996. Law clk. to judge Luther M. Swygert U.S. Ct. Appeals (7th cir.), Chgo., 1978-79; law clk. to chief justice Warren E. Burger U.S. Supreme Ct., Washington, 1979-80; assoc. Dorsey & Whitney, Mpls., 1980-85, ptnr., 1986—; adj. prof. law U. Minn., Mpls., 1981-83. Exec. editor U. Notre Dame Law Rev., 1977-78; co-editor: Freedom & Education: Pierce v. Society of Sisters Reconsidered, 1978. Recipient Vol. Recognition award Nat. Assn. Attys. Gen., 1993, Supreme Ct. Reception hons. State and Local Legal Ctr., 1991, 92, 93, 95. Mem. ABA, Fed. Bar Assn., Minn. Bar Assn., Hennepin County Bar Assn., Phi Beta Kappa. Office: Dorsey & Whitney LLP 220 S 6th St Minneapolis MN 55402-4502

WAILAND, GEORGE, lawyer; b. Munich, Fed. Republic Germany, Mar. 14, 1947; came to U.S., 1951; s. Max and Bella (Grylak) W.; m. Adele M. Rosen, Aug. 20, 1972; children: J. Zachary, William J. BS, NYU, 1969, JD, 1972. Bar: N.Y. 1973, U.S. Supreme Ct. 1976, U.S. Dist. Ct. (so., ea. dists.) N.Y. 1973, U.S. Dist. Ct. (no. dist.) N.Y. 1981, U.S. Claims Ct. 1979, U.S. Tax Ct., 1979, U.S. Ct. Appeals (2d cir.) 1973, U.S. Ct. Appeals (fed. cir.) 1982, U.S. Ct. Appeals (4th cir. and 9th cir.) 1986, U.S. Ct. Appeals (7th cir.) 1987. Assoc. Cahill Gordon & Reindel, N.Y.C., 1972-80, ptnr., 1980—. John Norton Pomeroy scholar NYU, 1970. Mem. ABA, Fed. Bar Council. Home: 1050 Park Ave New York NY 10028-1031 Office: Cahill Gordon & Reindel 80 Pine St New York NY 10005-1702

WAIN, CHRISTOPHER HENRY FAIRFAX MORESBY, actuary, insurance and investment consultant; b. Toronto, Ont., Can., Nov. 21, 1918; came to U.S., 1923; s. Andrew Martin and Eve Margaret (Fairbain) W.; m. Jeane Crawford Thomas, June 26, 1948; children: Christopher H. Jr., Margot Crawford. BA, UCLA, 1940. CLU. Actuarial student Occidental Life of Calif., L.A., 1946-48; various positions including v.p., actuary Prudential Ins. Co. Am., Newark and L.A., 1948-83; ins. and investment cons. L.A., 1984—; mem. various coms. Am. Coun. Life Ins., Washington, 1965-83. Capt. U.S. Army, 1941-45. Regents scholar UCLA, 1938-39. Fellow Soc. Actuaries; mem. Am. Acad. Actuaries.

WAINBERG, ALAN, footwear company executive; b. Zelechow, Poland, June 25, 1937; came to U.S., 1949; s. Jaime M. and Pearl (Boruchowicz) W.; m. Karen Sue Schneider, July 31, 1966; children: David, Laura, Daniel. BS in Indsl. Engring., U. Miami, 1964; MS in Ops. Rsch., NYU, 1965. Indsl. engr. U.S. Naval Propellant Plant, Indian Head, Md., 1964; sr. cons., mgr. Arthur Andersen & Co., N.Y.C., 1965-70; sr. cons. Alexander Grant & Co., Miami, 1970-71; sr. v.p., sec., treas., dir. Suave Shoe Corp., Miami, 1971-75, 78-84; group v.p. G.H. Bass & Co., Falmouth, Maine, 1984-86, pres., 1986-88; pres. Alan Wainberg & Assocs., Cumberland Center, Maine, 1988; v.p. Internat. New Balance Athletic Shoes Inc., Boston, 1991-95; v.p. sourcing strategic devel. Stride Rite Corp., Lexington, Mass., 1995—; owner, cons., pres. Mgmt. Cons. Services, Miami, 1975-77; dir., pres. Damaron Investment Services, Miami, 1975-78; vis. com. Coll. Engring. U. Miami. Mem. Footwear Industries Am. (mem. tech. steering com., chmn. new tech. com., 1981, bd. dirs. 1986—), U. Miami Coll. Engring. Alumni Assn. (bd. dirs., officer). Office: Stride Rite Corp 191 Spring St Lexington MA 02173-8030

WAINERDI, RICHARD ELLIOTT, medical center executive; b. N.Y.C., Nov. 27, 1931; s. Harold Roule and Margaret (Greenhut) W.; m. Angela Lampone, June 2, 1956; children: Thomas Joseph, James Cooper. B.S. in Petroleum Engring, Okla. U., 1952; M.S., Pa. State U., 1955, Ph.D., 1958. Registered profl. engr., Tex. Research asst., fellow petroleum engring. Pa. State U., 1953-55; mem. faculty Tex. A. and M. U., College Station, 1957-77; prof. chem. engring. Tex. A. and M. U., 1961-77, assoc. v.p. acad. affairs, 1974-77, also founder, head activation analysis lab., 1957-77; sr. v.p. 3D/Internat., Houston, 1977-82; coord. nuclear activities Dresser Industries Inc., Dallas, 1956-57; head Nuclear Sci. Ctr. Tex. Engring. Expt. Sta., 1957-59; pres. Gulf Research & Devel. Co. div. Gulf Oil Corp., Houston, 1982-84; pres., chief exec. officer Tex. Med. Ctr., Houston, 1984—. Author: Modern Methods of Geochemical Analysis, 1971; regional editor: Internat. Jour. Radioanalytical Chemistry; contbg. editor: Producers Monthly, 1957-69; assoc. editor: Radiochemical and Radioanalytical Letters; mem. editorial adv. bd. Talanta jour., 1969; contbr. to profl. jours. Served with USAF, 1952-53. Recipient 1st pl. presentation award Am. Inst. Chem. Engrs. and Chem. Inst. Can., 1961, faculty disting. rsch. award Tex. A. and M. U., 1962, George Hevesy medal, 1977, others. Mem. Am. Nuclear Soc. (chmn. isotopes and radiation divsn. 1964), Internat. Union Pure and Aplied Chemistry (chmn. com. on analytical radiochemistry), Am. Chem. Soc., River Oaks Country Club, Ramada Club, Sigma Xi, Tau Beta Pi, Phi Kappa Phi, Sigma Tau, Pi Epsilon Tau, Phi Eta Sigma. Office: Tex Med Ctr 406 Jesse H Jones Libr Bldg Houston TX 77030

WAINESS, MARCIA WATSON, legal management consultant; b. Bklyn., Dec. 17, 1949; d. Stanley and Seena (Klein) Watson; m. Steven Richard Wainess, Aug. 7, 1975. Student, UCLA, 1967-71, 80-81, Grad. Sch. Mgmt. Exec. Program, 1987-88, grad. Grad. Sch. Mgmt. Exec. Program, 1988. Office mgr., paralegal Lewis, Marenstein & Kadar, L.A., 1977-81; office mgr. Rosenfeld, Meyer & Susman, Beverly Hills, Calif., 1981-83; adminstr. Rudin, Richman & Appel, Beverly Hills, 1983; dir. adminstrn. Kadison, Pfaelzer, L.A., 1983-87; exec. dir. Richards, Watson and Gershon, L.A., 1987-93; legal mgmt. cons. Wainess & Co., Beverly Hills, 1993—; faculty mem. UCLA Legal Mgmt. & Adminstrn. Program, 1983, U. So. Calif. Paralegal Program, L.A., 1985; mem. adv. bd. atty. asst. tng. program, UCLA, 1984-88; adj. faculty Univ. of West L.A. Sch. Paralegal Studies, 1997—. Mem. ABA (chair Displaywrite Users Group 1986, legal tech. adv. coun. litig. support working group 1986-87), Inst. Mgmt. Consultants, L.A. County Bar Assn. (exec. com. law office mgmt. sect.), San Fernando Valley Bar Assn., Assn. Legal Adminstrs. (bd. dirs. 1990-92, asst. regional v.p. Calif. 1987-88, regional v.p. 1988-89, pres. Beverly Hills chpt. 1985-86, membership chair 1984-85, chair new adminstrn. sect. 1982-84, mktg. mgmt. sect. com. 1989-90, internat. conf. com.), Beverly Hills Bar Assn. (exec. com. law practice mgmt. sect.), Internat. Platform Assn., Cons. Roundtable of So. Calif. Avocations: historic preservation, antiques, interior design. Office: 415 N Camden Dr Beverly Hills CA 90210-4403

WAINTROOB, ANDREA RUTH, lawyer; b. Chgo., Dec. 23, 1952; d. David Samuel and Lees (Carson) W. AB, Brown U., 1975; JD, U. Chgo., 1978. Bar: Ill. 1978, U.S. Dist. Ct. (no. dist.) Ill. 1978, U.S. Dist. Ct. (cen. dist.) Ill. 1996, U.S. Ct. Appeals (7th cir.) 1982, U.S. Supreme Ct. 1989. Assoc. Vedder, Price, Kaufman and Kammholz, Chgo., 1978-84; ptnr. Vedder, Price, Kaufman, Chgo., 1984-94, Franczek Sullivan, P.C., Chgo., 1994—; lectr. indsl. relations Grad. Sch. Bus. U. Chgo. Mem. Chgo. Bar Assn., Nat. Coun. Sch. Attys. Home: 1345 E 54th St Chicago IL 60615-5318 Office: Franczek Sullivan 300 S Wacker Dr Ste 3400 Chicago IL 60606-6703

WAINWRIGHT, CARROLL LIVINGSTON, JR., lawyer; b. N.Y.C., Dec. 28, 1925; s. Carroll Livingston and Edith Katherine (Gould) W.; m. Nina Walker, July 2, 1948; children: Delos Walker, Mark Livingston. A.B., Yale U., 1949; LL.B., Harvard U., 1952. Bar: N.Y. 1953. With Milbank, Tweed, Hadley & McCloy (and predecessor), N.Y.C., 1952-58, 60-62, ptnr., 1963—; asst. counsel Gov. N.Y., 1959-60; mem. State Commn. Jud. Conduct, 1974-83; dir. U.S. Trust Corp.; trustee U.S. Trust Co. N.Y.; adj. prof. law Washington and Lee U. Sch. Law, 1991—; mem. governing bd. N.Y. Community Trust, 1991—. Hon. trustee Am. Mus. Natural History; trustee Edward John Noble Found., Boys' Club N.Y., 1966—, pres., 1986-94; vice-chmn. Cooper Union Advancement Sci. and Art, 1988-95, trustee; trustee Ch. Pension Fund and Affiliates, 1974-91, treas. 1974-78; mem. univ. coun. Yale U., 1978-81; mem. vestry Trinity Ch., N.Y.C., 1983-90. Served with USMCR, 1943-46. Mem. ABA, N.Y. State Bar Assn., Assn. Bar City N.Y. (treas. 1970-73, v.p. 1975-76), Union Club, Down Town Assn. (pres. 1985-92), Maidstone Club (pres. 1970-73). Home: 825 5th Ave New York NY 10021-7268 Office: Milbank Tweed Hadley & McCloy 1 Chase Manhattan Plz New York NY 10005-1401

WAINWRIGHT, CYNTHIA CRAWFORD, banker; b. N.Y.C., July 5, 1945; d. Townsend Wainwright and Rosalie deForest (Crosby) Gevers; m. Stephen Berger, Sept. 24, 1977; children: Robin Wainwright Berger, Diana Wainwright Berger. MBA, Columbia Bus. Sch., 1984. Sec., adminstrv. asst. Time-Life Broadcast, N.Y.C., 1965-68; adminstrv. asst. Downe Comms., N.Y.C., 1968-69, Office of the Mayor, N.Y.C., 1969-71; program mgr. Dept. of Correction, N.Y.C., 1972-73, dir. adminstrn., 1973-75, dep. commr., 1978-79; dir. of spl. projects N.Y. State Dept. Correctional Svcs., Albany, 1975-76; asst. dir. Offender-Based Transaction Svcs./Divsn. Criminal Justice, Albany, 1976-77; various positions Chem. Bank, N.Y.C., 1979-96; dir. corp. soc. resp. Chase Bank, N.Y.C., 1996—. Chmn. adv. comms. N.Y. State Office of Parks, N.Y.C., 1986-95; bd. dirs., chmn. Hist. House Trust of N.Y.C., 1989—; bd. dirs., past pres. The Bridge, Inc., N.Y.C., 1984—; trustee, past pres. Preservation League of N.Y. State, Albany, 1984—; trustee The Chapin Sch., Ltd., N.Y.C., 1989—. Named Woman of the Yr. East Manhattan C. of C., 1984; recipient Mental Health award The Bridge, Inc., N.Y.C., 1992, award for acad. excellence Columbia Bus. Sch., N.Y.C., 1983. Avocations: horseback riding, tennis, cooking. Office: Chase Bank 600 5th Ave Fl 3 New York NY 10020-2302

WAINWRIGHT, DAVID STANLEY, intellectual property professional; b. New Haven, May 23, 1955; s. Stanley Dunstan and Lillian (Karelitz) W.;m. Catherine Demetra Kefalas, Aug. 11, 1984; children: Maxwell Stanley Hector, Eric George Alexander. BSc with 1st class honors in Physics, Dalhousie U., Halifax, N.S., 1976; MSc in Physics, U. B.C., Vancouver, 1979. Registered patent agt., U.S., Can. Model plant supr., scientist, technician Moli Energy Ltd., Maple Ridge, B.C., Can., 1978-84, project leader cell devel., 1984-88, cell devel. mgr., 1988-90; cell devel. mgr. Moli Energy (1990) Ltd., Maple Ridge, 1990-92, mgr. intellectual property, 1992—. Contbr. articles to profl. jours. Mem. Patent and Trademark Inst. Can. Home: 2585 W 1st Ave, Vancouver, BC Canada V6K 1G8 Office: Moli Energy Ltd Maple Ridge, 20000 Stewart Crescent, Maple Ridge, BC Canada V2X 9E7

WAINWRIGHT, PAUL EDWARD BLECH, construction company executive; b. Annapolis, Md., Jan. 28, 1917; s. Richard and Alice Sorrel (Blech) W.; m. Helen Mae Rogers, July 10, 1941; children—Richard, Paul Edward Blech, John. B.S. in Civil Engring, Va. Mil. Inst., 1938. Cost engr. Turner Constrn. Co., N.Y.C., 1938-40; cost engr., asst. supt. Turner Constrn. Co., 1945-46; cost. engr. for contractors Pacific Naval Air Bases, Honolulu, 1940-42; with Dillingham Corp., Honolulu, 1946-82; asst. v.p., then v.p. Dillingham Corp., 1961-69, group v.p. constrn., 1969-82; cons. constrn. Honolulu, 1982—. Bd. dirs. Hawaii Visitors Bur., 1967, Goodwill Industries Hawaii, 1965-70; pres. Citizens Adminstrn. of Justice Found., 1968, Hawaii Epilepsy Soc., 1975. Served with AUS, 1942-45. Decorated Legion of Merit, Bronze Star, Air medal. Mem. Am. Soc. Mil. Engrs., Beavers, Gen. Contractors Assn. Hawaii (pres. 1966), Hawaii C. of C. (dir. 1964-65). Republican. Episcopalian. Clubs: Waikiki Yacht, Outrigger Canoe. Home: 4301 Providence Point Pl SE Issaquah WA 98029-6270

WAISANEN, CHRISTINE M., lawyer, writer; b. Hancock, Mich., May 27, 1949; d. Frederick B. and Helen M. (Hill) W.; m. Robert John Katzenstein, Apr. 21, 1979; children: Jeffrey Hunt, Erick Hill. BA with honors, U. Mich., 1971; JD, U. Denver, 1975. Bar: Colo. 1975, D.C. 1978. Labor rels. atty. U.S. C. of C., Washington, 1976-79; govt. rels. specialist ICI Americas, Inc., Wilmington, Del., 1979-87; dir. cultural affairs City of Wilmington, 1987; founder, chief writer Hill, Katzenstein & Waisanen, 1988—. Chmn. Delaware State Coastal Zone Indsl. Control Bd., 1993—. Mem. Fed. Bar Assn., Jr. League of Wilmington (v.p. 1985-86), Women's Rep. Club of Wilmington (bd. dirs. 1988-93). Republican. Presbyterian. Home: 1609 Mt Salem Ln Wilmington DE 19806-1134

WAIT, CAROL GRACE COX, organization administrator; b. L.A., Dec. 20, 1942; d. Earl George Atkinson Sr. and Virginia Rose (Clanton) Boggs; m. David L. Edwards (div. 1974); children: Nicole Rose Smith, Alexandra Edwards; m. Gary G. Cox, Jan. 25, 1975 (div. 1982); m. Robert Atwood Wait, July 4, 1991. AA in Pre Law, Cerritos Coll., 1966; AB in History, Whittier Coll., 1969. Probation counselor Los Angeles County Probation Dept., Downey, Calif., 1967-69; corp. sec., mgr. Dennis and Dennis Personnel, Santa Ana, Calif., 1969-71; owner, pres. Cox Edwards & Assocs., Santa Ana, 1971-73; adminstrv. services officer County of Santa Cruz (Calif.), 1973-74; cons. State of Calif., Sacramento, 1974-75; project dir. Nat. Assn. Counties, Washington, 1975-77; legis. dir. U.S. Senate Com. on the Budget, Washington, 1977-81; pres. Com. for a Responsible Budget, Washington, 1981—, Carol Cox & Assocs., Washington, 1984—; bd. dirs. Cigna Corp.; cons. to bus. and other orgns. on the fed. budget, the budget process and other econ. issues; writer and speaker on the budget and budget process. Am. participant USIS/Brazilian Senate Symposium on Budget Process, Brazilia, Brazil, 1985—, Ampart speaker on 1990 budget agreement France, Ger., 1990. Named one of 150 Who Make a Difference Nat. Jour., 1986; recipient Nat. Disting. Svc. award Am. Assn. Budget and Program Analysis. Mem. Washington Women's Forum, Internat. Women's Forum (pres.). Republican. Episcopalian. Avocations: party bridge, wing shooting, tennis. Office: Com Responsible Fed Budget 10648 Old Valley Pike Mount Jackson VA 22842-2900*

WAIT, CHARLES VALENTINE, banker; b. Albany, N.Y., May 28, 1951; s. Newman Edward Jr. and Jane Caroline (Adams) W.; m. Candace Ellin Hollar, May 27, 1978; children: Charles Valentine Jr., Christopher David, Alexandra Dallas Wait. BA, Cornell U., 1973; cert. in banking, Rutgers U., 1981. Asst. v.p. The Adirondack Trust Co., Saratoga Springs, N.Y., 1974, treas., 1978-81, sec., treas., 1981-84, pres., 1984—, also bd. dirs.; bd. trustees N.Y. Bus. Devel., 1997; nom. com. Fed. Reserve Bank N.Y.; nat. adv. bd. Deluxe Corp.; mem. Yaddo Corp., Saratoga Springs, 1996—; bd. dirs. N.Y. Bus. Devel. Corp. Trustee Skidmore Coll., Saratoga Springs, 1984—, Nat. Mus. Dance, Saratoga Springs, 1987—, N.Y. Racing Assn., Nat. Mus. Racing, 1988-91, v.p., 1989-91; trustee Chrles R. Wood Found., 1991—; chmn. Saratoga Springs City Ctr. Authority, 1983-89; treas. Saratoga Performing Arts Ctr., 1987, chmn., 1989-97. Named Outstanding New Yorker, N.Y. State Jaycees, 1984; recipient Pvt. Sector Initiative award Pres. Ronald Reagan, Commitment to Community award, N.Y. State Bus. Coun., 1983, Liberty Bell award Saratoga County Bar Assn. for community svc., Good Scout award Twin Rivers Coun., 1997; Paul Harris fellow Dist. 7190, 1997. Mem. Ind. Bankers Assn. of N.Y. State (bd. dirs., sec. 1986-87), N.Y. Bankers Assn. (bd. dirs. 1987, treas. 1995—, chmn. 1997—), N.Y. State Bankers Retirement System (trustee 1987—, vice chmn., chmn. 1992-94), Am. Inst. Banking (Counsel of Yr. 1976), Greater Saratoga C. of C., Pillar Soc., Rotary (hon.), Elks. Republican. Home: 658 N Broadway Saratoga Springs NY 12866-1624 Office: The Adirondack Trust Co 473 Broadway Saratoga Springs NY 12866-2203

WAIT, JAMES RICHARD, electrical engineering educator, scientist; b. Ottawa, Ont., Can., Jan. 23, 1924; came to U.S., 1955, naturalized, 1960; s. George Enoch and Doris Lillian (Browne) W.; m. Gertrude Laura Harriet, June 16, 1951; children: Laura, George. BASc, U. Toronto, Ont., 1948, MASc, 1949, PhD, 1951. Research engr. Newmont Exploration, Ltd., Jerome, Ariz., 1949-52; sect. leader Def. Research Telecommunications Establishment, Ottawa, 1952-55; scientist U.S. Dept. Commerce Labs., Boulder, Colo., 1955-80; adj. prof. elec. engring. U. Colo., Boulder, 1961-80; prof. elec. engring., geosci. U. Ariz., Tucson, 1980-88, Regents prof., 1988-90, emeritus Regents prof., 1990—; prin. Geo-Em Cons., Tucson, 1990—; fellow Coop. Inst. Rsch. Environ. Scis., 1968-80; sr. scientist Office of Dir. Environ. Rsch. Labs., Boulder, 1967-70, 72-80; vis. rsch. fellow lab. electromagnetic theory U. Denmark, Copenhagen, 1961; vis. prof. Harvard, 1966-67, Catholic U., Rio de Janeiro, 1971; vis. prof. elec. engring. U. B.C., Vancouver, Can., 1987; mem.-at-large U.S. nat. com. Internat. Sci. Radio Union, 1963-65, 69-72, del. gen. assemblies, Boulder, 1957, London, 1690, Tokyo, 1963, Ottawa, 1969, Warsaw, Poland, 1972, Lima, Peru, 1975, Helsinki, Finland, 1978; sec. U.S. nat. com., 1976-78; Lansdowne lectr. U. Victoria, B.C., Can., 1992.; adj. prof. in mining and geol. engring. U. Ariz., Tucson, 1995—. Founder Jour. Rsch. Radio Sci, 1959, editor, 1959-68; assoc. editor: Pure and Applied Geophysics, 1964-75, Geoexploration, Ludea, Sweden, 1983-91; co-editor internat. series monographs on electromagnetic waves Pergamon Press, 1961-73, Instn. Elec. Engrs, London, 1974-97. Served with Canadian Army, 1942-45. Recipient Gold medal Dept. Commerce, 1958; Samuel Wesley Stratton award Nat. Bur. Standards, 1962; Arthur S. Flemming award Washington C. of C., 1964; Outstanding Publ. award Office Telecommunications, Washington, 1972; Rsch. and Achievement award Nat. Oceanic and Atmospheric Adminstrn., 1973; Van der Pol gold medal, 1978; Evans fellow Otago U., New Zealand, 1990. Fellow IEEE (adminstrv. com. on antennas and propagation 1966-73, Harry Diamond award 1964, Centennial medal 1984, Disting. Achievement award geosci. and remote sensing 1985, Disting. Achievement award antennas and propagation soc. 1990, Heinrich Hertz medal 1992), AAAS, Sci. Rsch. Soc. Am. (Boulder Scientist award 1960); mem. Soc. Exploration Geophysicists (hon.), Internat. Union Radio Sci. (mem. editl. adv. bd. Radio Sci. Bull. 1995—). Home and Office: 2210 E Waverly St Tucson AZ 85719-3848

WAIT, SAMUEL CHARLES, JR., academic administrator, educator; b. Albany, N.Y., Jan. 26, 1932; s. Samuel C. and Isabel M. (Cassedy) W.; m. Carol D. Petrie, June 6, 1957; children: Robert J., Alison R. BS in Chemistry, Rensselaer Polytechnic Inst., 1953, MS in Physical Chemistry, 1955, PhD in Physical Chemistry, 1956. Postdoc. teaching fellow U. Minn., 1958-59; visiting asst. prof. Carnegie Inst. Tech., 1959-60; rsch. sci. Nat. Bur. Standards, 1960-61; from asst. prof. to prof. of chemistry Rensselaer Poly. Inst., Troy, N.Y., 1961—, from asst. dean of sci. to assoc. dean of sci., 1974—, acting dean of sci., 1978-80, 88-89; dir. Cooperative Coll. Sci. Improvement Program, Troy, 1972-73, Rsch. Participation for High Sch. Tchrs., Troy, 1962-67; asst. dir., prof. M of Sci. in Natural Scis. Program, Troy, 1962-74. Author: Scattering of Laser Radiation, 1971; contbr. articles to profl. jours. Pres. dist. 2 Niskayuna (N.Y.) Fire Co., 1970-72; mem. Niskayuna Bd. Fire Commrs., 1978-83; v.p., trustee Dudley Obs., 1990-91, pres., 1991—; mem. math., sci. and tech. adv. com. Schenectady County C.C., 1976—, chmn., 1977-78; vice chmn. Schenectady County Fire Adv. Bd., 1978-79; mem. Schenectady County Hazardous Materials Team, 1991—. Recipient Disting Faculty award Rensselaer Alumni Assn., 1988, Alumni Key award, 1994, Rensselaer Alumni Admission award of excellence, 1993, Rensselaer Alumni Assn. Albert Fox Demers medal, 1997; named fellow Rsch. Corp., 1954-55, Eastman Kodak Co., 1955-56; Fulbright scholar, 1956-58. Mem. Am. Chem. Soc., Optical Soc. Am., Coblentz Soc., Rensselaer Premed. Soc., Sigma Xi, Alpha Epsilon Delta, Phi Theta Kappa. Office: Rensselaer Poly Inst 1C 05 Sci Ctr 110 8th St Troy NY 12180-3522

WAITE, CHARLES MORRISON, food company executive; b. Chgo., Oct. 1, 1932; s. Norman and Lavinia M. (Fyke) W.; m. Barbara Chowning Wham, Aug. 21, 1954; children: Susan R., Charles M., John B., David T. B.A., Yale, 1954; M.B.A., Harvard, 1958. Mgr. planning and analysis Standard Fruit & Steamship Co., New Orleans, 1958-62; v.p., exec. v.p. Standard Fruit & Steamship Co., 1969-72, dir., 1972-76; div. mgr. Standard Fruit Co., La Ceiba, Honduras, 1962-69; dir. Standard Fruit Tropical Charities, Inc., 1970-76; sr. v.p. Castle & Cooke, Inc., Honolulu, 1972-76; exec. v.p. Castle & Cooke Foods, San Francisco, 1974-76; pres. United Fruit Co., Boston, 1976-77; sr. v.p. United Brands Co., Boston, 1976-77; pres. Genoa Packing Co., Boston, 1977-78, Catelli Foods Inc., 1979-90; pres. Howard Foods Inc., Danvers, Mass., 1990—, also bd. dirs.; bd. dirs. Rock of Ages Corp., Barre, Vt., Swenson Granite Co., Concord, N.H. Served to 1st lt. USAF, 1955-57. Mem. Zeta Psi. Republican. Episcopalian. Club: Harvard (Boston). Home: 520 Cherry Valley Rd Gilford NH 03246-7841 Office: Howard Foods Inc 5 Ray St Danvers MA 01923-3531

WAITE, DANIEL ELMER, retired oral surgeon; b. Grand Rapids, Mich., Feb. 19, 1926; s. Charles Austin and Phoebe Isabel (Smith) W.; m. Alice Darlene Carlile, June 20, 1948; children—Christine Ann, Thomas Charles, Peter Daniel, Julie Marilyn, Stuart David. AA, Graceland Coll., 1948; DDS, State U. Ia., 1953, MS Grad. Coll., 1955. Diplomate: Am. Bd. Oral Surgery. Resident oral surgery State U. Ia. Hosps., 1953-55; instr. oral surgery State U. Ia. Coll. Dentistry, 1955-56, asst. prof., 1956-57, asso. prof., acting head dept. oral surgery, 1957-59, prof. head dept., 1959-63; mem. staff Mayo Clinic, Mayo Grad. Sch. Medicine, Rochester, Minn., 1963-68; prof., also chmn. div. oral surgery U. Minn., 1968-84; chmn. dept. oral and maxillofacial surgery, asst. dean for hosp. affairs Baylor Coll. Dentistry, Dallas, 1984-90, prof. emeritus, 1990—, asst. dean emeritus, 1990—; clin. prof. U. Mo. Dental Sch., Kans. City, 1993—; vis. prof. U. Adelaide, Australia, 1980, U. Jinan, Guangzhou, China, 1987, U. Costa Rica, 1988; mem. Health Mission Team, Bolivia, 1991, Honduras, 1992. Author: Textbook of Practical Oral Surgery, 1972, 3d edit., 1986; contbr. over 100 articles to sci. jours., author of 7 book chpts. Active People to People Found.; with Project HOPE, Peru, 1962, Sri Lanka, 1969, Egypt, 1975; trustee Graceland Coll., Lamoni, Iowa, 1960-78, Park Coll., Parkville, Mo., 1972-78, 90—, Outreach Internat., 1990—; bd. dirs. Hennepin County unit Am. Cancer Soc., 1970-73; evangelist Reorganized LDS Ch.; pres. med. and dental assn. health missions, Bolivia, 1990, Honduras, 1991, 92, 93. With USAAF, 1944-46; sr. dental surgeon USPHS Res. Recipient Novice award Internat. Assn. Dental Rsch., 1955, Disting. Alumni award Graceland Coll., 1989; named Man of Yr. U. Minn. Sch. Dentistry Century Club, 1980, Hon. Fellow Sch. Dentistry, U. Minn., 1990; Daniel E. Waite Lectureship established in his honor U. Minn., 1991—. Fellow Am. Coll. Dentists, Am. Soc. Oral Surgeons; mem. Christian Med. Soc., Midwestern Soc. Oral Surgeons, Ia. Soc. Oral Surgeons (sec. 1958-61, pres. 1962), Minn. Soc. Oral Surgeons (pres. 1974), Am. Dental Assn., Internat. Assn. Dental Research (sec. Ia. sect. 1957-62),

Tex. Soc. of Oral & Maxillofacial Surgeons, Southwestern Soc. of Oral and Maxillofacial Surgeons, Kans. City Soc. of Oral and Maxillofacial Surgeons, Sigma Xi, Omicron Kappa Upsilon. Home: 319 NW Blue Beech Pt Lees Summit MO 64064-1813

WAITE, DENNIS VERNON, investor relations consultant; b. Chgo., Aug. 26, 1938; s. Vernon George and Marie G. Waite; m. Christine Rene Hibbs; 1 child, Kip Anthony. BA, U. Ill., 1968; MS in Journalism, Northwestern U., 1969. Fin. reporter, columnist Chgo. Sun-Times, Chgo., 1969-76; asst. prof. Northwestern U., Evanston, Ill., 1978-79; assoc. prof. Mich. State U., East Lansing, 1979-82; ptnr. Fin. Rels. Bd., Inc., Chgo., 1982-90, sr. ptnr., 1991—; reporter, producer econ. affairs Sta. WTTW-TV, Sta. WBBM-TV, Chgo., 1973-76. Mem. editorial adv. bd. alumni relations U. Ill., Chgo., 1980-84, 90-94. With USAF, 1956-60, PTO. Rutgers U. fellow, 1972. Mem. Medill Alumni Assn. (bd. dirs. 1989-92). Avocations: reading, tennis, fishing. Office: Financial Relations Bd John Hancock Ctr 875 N Michigan Ave Chicago IL 60611-1803

WAITE, DONALD EUGENE, medical educator, consultant; b. Columbus, Ohio, Aug. 25, 1925; s. Sidney B. and Louise Alice (Lipsey) W.; children: David L., Larry R., James A., Steve C., Debra J., Julie A., Craig D., Tracy E., Christopher R. DO in Osteopathic Medicine, U. Osteo. Medicine and Health Scis., 1955; MPH, U. Calif., Berkeley, 1989. Intern Doctors Hosp., Columbus, Ohio, 1955-56; pvt. practice Columbus, 1956-72; prof. family medicine Mich. State U., East Lansing, 1972-90, prof. emeritus, 1990—; cons. Environ. Health Conss., Columbus, East Lansing, 1990—. Author: Your Environment, Your Health and You, 1991, Environmental Health Hazards, 1994. Med. examiner FAA, East Lansing, 1964-90; asst. scoutmaster Boy Scouts Am., East Lansing, 1980-83. With USN, 1943-45. Mem. Am. Osteo. Assn., Am. Coll. Occupl. Medicine, Aerospace Med. Assn., Ohio Osteo. Assn., Mich. Assn. Osteo. Physicians. Avocations: skiing, fishing, hunting. Home: 117 Agate Way Williamston MI 48895-9434 Office: Mich State U Dept Family Medicine East Lansing MI 48824

WAITE, ELLEN JANE, vice president of academic services; b. Oshkosh, Wis., Feb. 17, 1951; d. Earl Vincent and Margaret (Luft) W.; m. Thomas H. Dollar, Aug. 19, 19 1977 (div. July 1984); m. Kent Hendrickson, Mar. 26, 1994 (div. Dec. 1995). BA, U. Wis., Oshkosh, 1973; MLS, U. Wis., Milw., 1977. Head of cataloging Marquette U., Milw., 1977-82; head catalog librarian U. Ariz., Tucson, 1983-85; assoc. dir. libraries Loyola U., Chgo., 1985-86, acting dir. libraries, 1986-87, dir. libraries, 1987-94, v.p. acad. svcs., 1994-97; assoc. provost for info. svcs. U. Richmond, 1997—; cons. Loyola U., Chgo., 1984, Boston Coll., 1986, U. San Francisco, 1989; bd. trustees Online Computer Lib. Ctr., Dublin, Ohio, 1994—. Contbg. author: Research Libraries and Their Implementation of AACR2, 1985; author: (with others) Women in LC's Terms: A Thesaurus of Subject Headings Related to Women, 1988. Mem. ALA. Avocation: photography. Office: Loyola U 25 E Pearson St Chicago IL 60611-2001

WAITE, HELEN ELEANOR, funeral director; b. Richmond, Va., Aug. 7, 1947; d. Julia F. (Braxton) Candia; m. Malcolm L. Waite, July 24, 1982. AB, Va. State U., 1968, MA, 1977; degree in funeral svc., Northampton C.C., Bethlehem, Pa., 1994. Cert. tchr., Pa., N.J. Tchr. Westmoreland County Schs., Montross, Va.; tchr. English Rittenhouse Acad., Phila.; funeral dir. T.W. Waite Funeral Home, Phila. Mem. Nat. Coun. Tchrs. English, Pa. Coun. Tchrs. English, Nat. Funeral Dirrs. Assn., Pa. Funeral Dirs. Assn. Home: 820 N 65th St Philadelphia PA 19151-3303

WAITE, LAWRENCE WESLEY, osteopathic physician; b. Chgo., June 27, 1951; s. Paul J. and Margaret E. (Cresson) W.; m. Courtnay M. Snyder, Nov. 1, 1974; children: Colleen Alexis, Rebecca Maureen, Alexander Quin. BA, Drake U., 1972; DO, Coll. Osteo. Medicine and Surgery, Des Moines, 1975; MPH, U. Mich., 1981. Diplomate Nat. Bd. Osteo. Examiners. Intern Garden City Osteo. Hosp., Mich., 1975-76; practice gen. osteo. medicine, Garden City, 1979-82, Battle Creek, 1982-96, La Crosse, Wis., 1996—; assoc. clin. prof. Mich. State U. Coll. Osteo. Medicine, East Lansing, 1979—; dir. med. edn. Lakeview Gen. Osteo. Hosp., Battle Creek, Mich., 1983-87; cons. Nat. Bd. Examiners Osteo. Physicians and Surgeons, 1981-88; chief med. examiner Calhoun County, 1991-93. Writer TV program Cross Currents Ecology, 1971; editor radio series Friendship Hour, 1971-72. Bd. dirs., instr. Hospice Support Services, Inc., Westland, Mich., 1981-86; mem. profl. adv. council Good Samaritan Hosp., Battle Creek, 1982-83; bd. dirs. Neighborhood Planning Council 11, Battle Creek, 1982-92; mem. population action council Population Inst., 1984—; exec. bd. officer Battle Creek Area Urban League, 1987-91; vestryman St. Thomas Episcopal Ch., 1990-93; exec. bd. Primary Care Network, 1994-96; leader Boy Scouts Am. Served to lt. comdr. USN, 1976-79. State of Iowa scholar, 1969. Mem. AMA, APHA, Aerospace Med. Assn., Nat. Eagle Scouts Assn. (life), Am. Osteo. Assn., S. Cen. Osteo. Assn. (officer, state del. 1983-96), Am. Acad. Osteopathy, Bermuda Hist. Soc. (life). Avocations: geography, medieval history, genealogy. Home: 2110 Evenson Dr Onalaska WI 54650-8772 Office: Gundersen Luthern 3100 S Kinney Coulee Rd Onalaska WI 54650-8152

WAITE, NORMAN, JR., lawyer; b. Chgo., Mar. 16, 1936; s. Norman and Lavinia (Fyke) W.; m. Jaqueline A. Hurlbutt; children: Leslie Catherine, Lindsay H., Norman III. BA, Yale U., 1958; LLB, Harvard U., 1963. Bar: Ill. 1963. Assoc. Winston & Strawn, Chgo., 1963-69, ptnr., 1969-78, capital ptnr., 1978—, exec. com., 1978-95, vice chmn., 1989—. Bd. dirs. Met. Family Svcs., Jr. Achievement, Chgo., Steadman/Hawkins Sports Medicine Found. Lt. (j.g.) USN, 1958-60. Mem. ABA, Chgo. Bar Assn., Univ. Club Chgo., The Tavern Club Chgo., Indian Hill Club (Winnetka, Ill.), Econ. Club, Eagle Springs Club (Vail, Colo.). Republican. Home: 1710 N Burling St Chicago IL 60614-5102 Office: Winston & Strawn 35 W Wacker Dr Chicago IL 60601-1614

WAITE, PETER ARTHUR, literacy educator, educational consultant; b. San Mateo, Calif., Jan. 8, 1951; s. James Bishop and Beverly Jane (Petrich) W.; m. Lauren Chapman Singer, Sept. 10, 1977; children: Hillary, Christopher, Hannah. BA, U. Vt., 1973, MEd, 1976; EdD, Seattle U., 1986. Cert. tchr. Tchr. Winooski (Vt.) High Sch., 1972-73; program developer NEA, Washington, 1973-74; coord. Ctr. for Svc. Learning, Burlington, Vt., 1974-76; instr. Champlain Coll., Burlington, 1975-76; exec. dir. Winooski Youth Commn., 1976-79, Wash. Literacy, Inc., Seattle, 1979-82, Laubach Literacy Action, Syracuse, N.Y., 1982—; sr. policy advisor Bus. Coun. for Effective Literacy, N.Y.C., 1982—; bd. dirs. Literacy Network, Mpls., 1987—; mem. exec. com. Nat. Coalition for Literacy, Chgo., 1989—. Author: Handbook for Industry-Literacy, 1986. Del. Seattle Dem. Com., 1981; bd. dirs. Friends of VISTA, Washington, 1986—; founder Concerned Citizens Skaneateles (N.Y.), 1987—. Named Ky. col. State of Ky., 1985, hon. citizen City of Memphis, 1986, San Diego County, 1988; recipient state achievement award State of Okla., 1988. Mem. Assn. for Adult and Continuing Edn., Am. Literacy Assn., Community Edn. Assn., Ind. Sector. Democrat. Episcopalian. Avocations: running, skiing, sailing, mountain climbing, book collecting. Office: Laubach Literacy Internat 1320 Jamesville Ave Syracuse NY 13210

WAITE, RIC, cinematographer; b. Sheboygan, Wis., July 10, 1933; s. Howard Pierce and Bertha Ann (Pippert) W.; m. Judy Lescher, Apr. 24, 1965; children: Richard R., Burgandy B. Student, U. Colo. Cinematographer: (films) Adventures in Babysitting, 1988, Cobra, 1988, Great Outdoors, 1989, Marked for Death, 1990, Price of Our Blood, 1990, 48 Hours, Uncommon Valor, Rep Dawn, Long Riders, The Border, Tex, Class, Volunteers, On Deadly Ground, Truth or Consequences, N.Mex., 1996. 1st lt. USAF, 1951-56. Recipient Emmy award, 1976. Mem. Am. Soc. Cinematographers. Avocations: sailing, flying. Home: PO Box 1322 Friday Harbor WA 98250-1322 Office: 1216 Roulac Ln Friday Harbor WA 98250-9572 also: Irv Shechter Agy 9300 Wilshire Blvd Beverly Hills CA 90210

WAITE, ROBERT GEORGE LEESON, history educator; b. Cartwright, Manitoba, Can., Feb. 18, 1919; came to U.S., 1929, naturalized, 1943; s. George Lloyd and Alice (Carter) W.; m. Anne Barnett, Sept. 8, 1943; children: Geoffrey, Peter. AB, Macalester Coll., 1941; MA, U. Minn., 1946, Harvard U., 1947; PhD, Harvard U., 1949; postgrad., U. Munich, 1953-54. Teaching asst. Macalester Coll., 1941; Emerton fellow history Harvard U., Cambridge, Mass., 1947, teaching fellow, 1947-49; asst. prof. history Williams Coll., 1949-53, assoc. prof., 1953-58, prof., 1958-88, Brown prof., 1960-88, chmn. dept., 1967-72; dir. History Insts., 1968, 69; vis. prof. U. Minn., summer 1957, U. Tex., Austin, 1974; sr. assoc. mem. St. Antony's Coll. Oxford U., 1978, 82; sr. fellow Inst. Humanities, Williams Coll., 1989-91. Author: Vanguard of Nazism: The Free Corps Movement in Postwar Germany, 1918-23, 1952, 69, The Psychopathic God: Adolf Hitler, 1977, rev. 1993, Kaiser and Führer: A Comparative Study of Personality and Politics, 1997; editor, contbr. Hitler and Nazi Germany, 1965, 69; mem. editorial bd. Jour. Modern History, 1957-60; contbr. World Book, 1958, Collier's Ency, 1961, Afterword to the Mind of Adolf Hitler, 1972, Human Responses to the Holocaust, 1981, Genocide and the Modern Age, 1987, War: The Psychological Dimension, 1990; co-translator: (Erich Eyck) A History of the Weimar Republic, 2 vols., 1962, 70; cons. History of Third Reich Time-Life Mag., 1989-91. Guggenheim fellow, 1953-54; sr. Fulbright research fellow Germany, 1953-54; Am. Council Learned Socs. grantee, 1967, 82; grantee Social Sci. Research Council, 1967. Mem. Am. Hist. Assn., Central European Study Group (sec.-treas. 1970-72). Conglist. (bd. deacons). Home: PO Box 451 Williamstown MA 01267-0451

WAITE, STEPHEN HOLDEN, lawyer; b. Rochester, N.Y., Dec. 5, 1936; s. Richard Holden and Judith H. (Lapp) W.; m. Sarah T. Caswell, Aug. 20, 1960 (dec. Mar. 1960); m. Martha Gay Stewart, Jan. 4, 1997; children: Sarah T., Richard H. B.A., Amherst Coll., 1958; J.D., Yale U., 1961. Bar: N.Y. 1961. Mem. firm Nixon, Hargrave, Devans & Doyle, Rochester, N.Y., 1961-69; v.p., counsel Lincoln First Banks Inc., Rochester, 1969-73, sr. v.p., 1973-77, exec. v.p., 1978-81; chief fin. officer Lincoln First Banks Inc., 1973-81; sr. v.p. Schlegel Corp., 1981-82; mem. firm Harris, Beach, Wilcox, Rubin & Levey, Rochester, 1982-88, Underberg & Kessler, Rochester, 1988—; bd. dirs. Mercy Flight Ctrl., Inc. Past chmn. Rochester Area Hosp. Assn.; past bd. dirs. Highland Hosp., Monroe County Long Term Care, Inc., Rochester Regional Rsch. Libr. Coun., Hosp. Assn. N.Y. State, Health Futures for Rochester, Harley Sch., Hearing and Speech Ctr. Rochester; mem. strategic planning comm. Monroe Cmty. Hosp.; bd. dirs., treas. Hosp. Trustees N.Y. State; bd. dirs., past chmn. Ctr. for Govtl. Rsch. With U.S. Army, 1962. Mem. ABA, N.Y. State Bar Assn., Monroe County Bar Assn., Country Club Rochester. Home: 7 Woodcliff Terrace Fairport NY 14450 Office: 1800 Chase Sq Rochester NY 14604-1910

WAITER, SERGE-ALBERT, retired civil engineer; b. Paris, Feb. 8, 1930; came to the U.S., 1959; s. Bernard and Anny (Suskind) W.; 1 child, Thomas-Bernard. DSc, Sorbonne-Paris U., 1954. Registered civil engr., France. Engr. Onera, Chatillon, France, 1949-51; flight test engr. Fouga, Aire S/ Adour, France, 1951-53; mgr. prototype Sud Aviation, Courbevoie, France, 1953-59; rsch. scientist USC/EC, L.A., 1959-62; sr. specialist Rockwell Internat., Downey, Calif., 1962-88, ret., 1988; sr. cons. Dassault Aviation, St. Cloud, France, 1988-92, ret., 1992; attaché scientifique, cons. Contbr. articles to profl. jours. Fellow (assoc.) AIAA; mem. Ingenieurs Scientifiques de France. Achievements include work on Apollo, Shuttle, and Hermes programs. Home: 801 Crest Vista Dr Monterey Park CA 91754-3749

WAITES, CANDY YAGHJIAN, former state official; b. N.Y.C., Feb. 21, 1943; d. Edmund Kirken and Dorothy Joanne (Candy) Yaghjian; children: Jennifer Lisa, Robin Shelley. B.A., Wheaton Coll., Mass., 1965. Elected county councilwoman Richland County, S.C., 1976-88, mem. S.C. Ho., 1988-94; dir. external programs The Leadership Inst., Columbia Coll., 1993—; vice chmn. Adv. Commn. on Intergovtl. Relations, S.C., 1977-87; bd. dirs. Interagy. Council on Pub. Transp., S.C., 1977-85, Central Midlands Regional Planning Council, Columbia, S.C., 1977-84; dir. Wachovia Bank. Vice pres. bd. dirs. United Way of Midlands, 1977-89; trustee Columbia Mus. Art, 1982-88; bd. dirs. Rape Crisis Network, 1984-87; chmn. County Coun. Coalition; mem. C. of C. Leadership Forum, S.C. Fedn. of the Blind; mem. adv. bd. U. S.C. Hunanities and Social Scis. Coll., Family Shelter, Nurturing Ctr.; pres Trinity Housing Corp.; found. bd. Richland Meml. Hosp., 1995. Named Outstanding Young Career Woman, Columbia YWCA, 1980, YWCA Hall of Fame, 1993, Columbia Housing Authority Bd., Outstanding Young Woman of Yr., Columbia Jaycees, 1975, Pub. Citizen of Yr. Nat. Assn. Social Workers, hon. mem. Mortar Bd. Soc., 1994; recipient Ann. Legis. award Common Cause S.C., 1990, 91, Legis. Yr. award by S.C. Assn. Counties, 1992. Mem. S.C. Women in Govt. (vice chmn. 1984-86), S.C. Assn. Counties (bd. dirs. 1982-88 , Pres's award 1983), Network Female Execs., LWV (pres. 1973-76), Omicron Delta Kappa. Democrat. Episcopalian. Club: Univ. Assocs. (Columbia). Avocations: exercising, drawing, gardening, walking. Home: 3419 Duncan St Columbia SC 29205-2705 Office: Columbia Coll Leadership Inst 1301 Cola Coll Dr Columbia SC 29203

WAITS, JOHN A., lawyer; b. Greenville, Miss., June 6, 1947. BA summa cum laude, U. Miss., 1969; MA with honors, U. Va., 1973; JD, NYU, 1977. Bar: N.Y. 1978, U.S. Dist. Ct. (ea. and so. dists.) N.Y. 1978, D.C. 1988. Counsel to Ho. Agrl. Subcom. U.S. Ho. of Reps., Washington, 1979-80, asst. to Congressman David R. Bowen, 1980-82; ptnr. Winston & Strawn, Washington. Fulbright scholar. Mem. Assn. Bar City N.Y. Office: Winston & Strawn 1400 L St NW Washington DC 20005-3509

WAITS, THOMAS ALAN, composer, actor, singer; b. Pomona, Calif., Dec. 7, 1949; s. Frank W. and Alma (Johnson) McMurray; m. Kathleen Patricia Brennan, Aug. 10, 1980; children: Kellesimone Wylder, Casey Xavier, Sullivan Blake. Composer 14 albums including Closing Time, 1973, The Heart of Saturday Nite, 1974, Nighthawks at the Diner, 1975, Small Change, 1976, Foreign Affairs, 1978, Heartattack and Vine, 1980, Swordfishtrombones, 1983, Rain Dogs, 1985, Anthology, 1985, Frank's Wild Years, 1987, Big Time, 1988, Bone Machine, 1992, The Black Rider, 1993; composer (film scores) One from the Heart, 1983, Streetwise, 1985, Night on Earth, 1991; co-author music and songs (with Kathleen Brennan) for Night on Earth, 1991, film American Heart; composer songs and music for The Black Rider opera, Hamburg, Germany, 1990, Alice in Wonderland opera, Hamburg, 1992; actor (musical) Frank's Wild Years, 1986, (stage play) Demon Wine, 1989; appeared in films Paradise Alley, 1978, The Outsiders, 1983, Rumble Fish, 1983, The Cotton Club, 1984, Down by Law, 1986, Ironweed, 1987, Candy Mountain, 1987, Big Time, 1988, Cold Feet, 1989, The Bearskin, 1991, Queen's Logic, 1991, At Play in the Fields of the Lord, 1991, Bram Stoker's Dracula, 1992, Short Cuts, 1993. Recipient Acad. Award nomination Best Song Score for One from the Heart, 1983; Grammy award for best alternative album Bone Machine, 1992. Mem. ASCAP, Musicians Union Local 47, SAG, AFTRA, Motion Picture Acad. Office: care Howard Grossman 10960 Wilshire Blvd Ste 2150 Los Angeles CA 90024-3807*

WAITT, TED W., computer company executive. CEO Gateway 2000, 1992—, chmn., pres. Office: Gateway 2000 610 Gateway Blvd North Sioux City SD 57049-3199*

WAITZKIN, HOWARD BRUCE, physician, sociologist, educator; b. Akron, Ohio, Sept. 6, 1945; s. Edward and Dorothy (Lederman) W.; m. Stephany Borges, Mar. 13, 1983; 1 stepchild, Daren; 1 child, Sofia. BA summa cum laude, Harvard U., 1966, MA, 1969, MD, PhD, 1972. Diplomate Am. Bd. Internal Medicine, Am. Bd. Geriatric Medicine. Resident in medicine Stanford (Calif.) U. Med. Ctr., 1972-75, Robert Wood Johnson clin. scholar depts. sociology-medicine, 1973-75; sr. resident in medicine Mass. Gen. Hosp., Boston, 1977-78; assoc. prof. sociology, clin. asst. prof. medicine U. Vt., Burlington, 1975-77; vis. assoc. prof. health and med. scis. U. Calif., Berkeley, 1978-82; clin. asst. prof. medicine U. Calif., San Francisco, 1978-82; internist La Clínica de la Raza, Oakland, Calif., 1978-82; prof. medicine and social scis. U. Calif., Irvine, 1982-96, chief div. gen. internal medicine and primary care, 1982-90; med. dir. U. Calif.-Irvine-North Orange County Community Clinic, Anaheim, 1982-90; prof., dir. divsn. cmty. medicine U. N.Mex., Albuquerque, 1997—; regional rep., nat. sec. bd. dirs. Physicians for Nat. Health Program, Cambridge, Mass., 1989-91; cons. documentary Health Care Across the Border, Nat. Pub. TV, N.Y.C., 1989-90, documentary on U.S. health care system Nat. TV Austria, 1991; cons. BBC, 1992, Pew Health Professions Commn., 1992-94, Assn. Am. Med. Colls., 1992-93, Robert Wood Johnson Found., 1992, Rsch. and Tng. Group in Social Medicine, Santiago, Chile, 1990—, Eisenhower Rural Health Ctrs., Idyllwild, Calif., 1995—; lectr. med. sociology U. Amsterdam, The Netherlands, 1977; vis. prof. Northwestern U., 1994, U. Ill., Chgo., 1994, U. Wash., 1996, U. N.Mex., 1996, U. Ky., 1996; mem. expert panel on comms. with elderly patients Nat. Inst. Aging, 1997. Co-author: The Exploitation of Illness in Capitalist Society, 1974; author: The Second Sickness: Contradictions of Capitalist Health Care, 1983, paperback edit., 1986, The Politics of Medical Encounters: How Patients and Doctors Deal with Social Problems, 1991, paperback edit., 1993. Cons. on health policy Jesse Jackson Presdl. Campaign, 1988; bd. dirs., mem. com. on litigation Orange County Pub. Law Ctr., 1990-96. Fellow in ind. study & rsch. NEH, 1984-85, Fulbright fellow, 1983, 88-90, 93-94, sr. fellow NIA, 1989-91, Fogarty Internat. Ctr., NIH, 1994—. Fellow ACP, Am. Acad. Physician and Patient; mem. APHA, Am. Sociol. Assn. (nat. coun.-at-large med. sociology sect. 1989-92, coord. resolution process concerning nat. health program 1990-91, Leo G. Reeder award for disting. career in medicine and social scis. 1997), Soc. Gen. Internal Medicine, Phi Beta Kappa. Avocations: music, athletics, gardening, mountain hiking. Office: U NMex Sch Medicine Divsn Cmty Med 2400 Tucker NE Albuquerque NM 87131-5261

WAIXEL, VIVIAN, journalist; b. Norfolk, Va., July 22, 1946; d. Julius and Julia (Heimann) W.; m. Steven E. Scharbach, Aug. 24, 1969. BS in Communication, Simmons Coll., 1967; MA in Communication, U. Wis., 1971. Teaching asst. U. Wis., Madison, 1967-69; reporter Wis. State Jour., Madison, 1969-72, The Record, Hackensack, N.J., 1972-74; bus. editor The Record, Hackensack, 1974-76, assignment editor, 1976-86, sports editor, 1986-88, chief news editor, 1988-92, mng. editor, 1992-97, editor, 1997—. Recipient Tribute to Women and Industry award, YWCA, 1976. Avocations: snorkeling, fitness walking, music, reading. Office: The Record 150 River St Hackensack NJ 07601-7110

WAJENBERG, ARNOLD SHERMAN, retired librarian, educator; b. Indpls., Apr. 11, 1929; s. Henry and Hazel L. (Johnson) W.; m. Joyce E. Dunham, Sept. 6, 1952; 1 child, Earl S. B.A., Butler U., Indpls., 1951, M.A., 1953; M.A., U. Chgo., 1955. Cataloger U. Chgo. Library, 1953-69; catalog librarian U. Ill., Chgo., 1969-74; asst. catalog librarian U. Ill., Champaign-Urbana, 1974-78, prin. cataloguer, 1979-94; retired, 1994; prof. library adminstrn. U. Ill., Champaign-Urbana; prin. educator, Ill. Tng. Program for Implementation of Anglo-Am. Cataloguing Rules, 2d edit., 1979-80; mem. editorial policy com. Dewey Decimal, 1981-92; Ill. rep. cataloging adv. com., Online Computer Libr. Ctr. 1979-82, cataloging and database svcs. adv. com., 1989-92. Author: FLC FEDLINK AACR 2 Cataloging Manual for Federal Libraries, 1981; contbr. articles to profl. jours. Mem. ALA (com. on cataloging: description and access 1981-86, mem.-at-large exec. com. cataloging and classification sect. 1982-86). Avocations: walking, science fiction. Home: Apt 505 99 Clinton St Concord NH 03301

WAJER, RONALD EDWARD, management consultant; b. Chgo., Aug. 31, 1943; s. Edward Joseph and Gertrude Catherine (Rytelny) W.; m. Mary Earlene Hagan, July 5, 1969; children: Catherine, Michael. BSIE, Northwestern U., 1966; MBA, Loyola U., Chgo., 1970. Cert. mgmt. cons. Project engrng. mgr. Procter & Gamble, Chgo., 1966-67; indsl. engrng. mgr. Johnson & Johnson, Bedford Park, Ill., 1967-71; project mgr. Jewel Cos., Franklin Park, Ill., 1971-73; divsn. engrng. mgr. Abbott Labs., North Chicago, Ill., 1973-79; pres. bus. engrng. divsn. R.E. Wajer & Assocs., Northbrook, Ill., 1979—. Contbr. articles to profl. jours. Sec. Downtown Redevel. Commn., Mt. Prospect, Ill., 1977-78; fundraising vol. Maryville Acad., Des Plaines, 1985—; bd. dirs. Lattof YMCA, Des Plaines, 1994-96; profl. advisor Sch. for New Learning, DePaul U., 1994—; mem. indsl. sector com. Lincoln Found. for Bus. Excellence, 1997—. Recipient Cmty. Svc. award Chgo. Lighthouse for the Blind, 1989, Cert. of Merit, Village of Mt. Prospect, 1978. Mem. Inst. Indsl. Engrs. (cmty. svc. chmn. 1984), Inst. Mgmt. Cons. (exec. v.p., bd. dirs. 1987-94), Assn. Mgmt. Cons. (ctrl. regional v.p. 1985-87), Midwest Soc. Profl. Cons., Northwestern Club Chgo. Roman Catholic. Office: Bus Engring 5 Revere Dr Ste 200 Northbrook IL 60062-8000

WAKE, DAVID BURTON, biology educator; b. Webster, S.D., June 8, 1936; s. Thomas B. and Ina H. (Solem) W.; m. Marvalee Hendricks, June 23, 1962; 1 child, Thomas Andrew. BA, Pacific Luth. U., 1958; MS, U. So. Calif., 1960, PhD, 1964. Instr. anatomy and biology U. Chgo., 1964-66, asst. prof. anatomy and biology, 1966-69; assoc. prof. zoology U. Calif., Berkeley, 1969-72, prof., 1972-89, prof. integrative biology, 1989-91, John and Margaret Gompertz prof., 1991—; dir. Mus. Vertebrate Zoology U. Calif., Berkeley, 1971—. Author: Biology, 1979; co-editor: Functional Vertebrate Morphology, 1985, Complex Organismal Functions: Integration and Evolution in the Vertebrates, 1989. Mem. nat. bd. Nat. Mus. Natural History. Recipient Quantrell Teaching award U. Chgo., 1967, Outstanding Alumnus award Pacific Luth. U., 1979; grantee NSF, 1965—; Guggenheim fellow, 1982. Fellow AAAS, NRC (bd. biology 1986-92); mem. Internat. Union for Conservation of Nature and Natural Resources (chair task force on declining amphibian populations 1990-92), Am. Soc. Zoologists (pres. 1992), Am. Soc. Naturalists (pres. 1989), Am. Soc. Ichthyologists and Herpetologists (bd. govs.), Soc. Study Evolution (pres. 1983, editor 1979-81), Soc. Systematic Biology (coun. 1980-84), Herpetologist's League (Disting. Herpetologist 1984), Am. Philos. Soc., Am. Acad. Arts & Scis., (1997). Home: 999 Middlefield Rd Berkeley CA 94708-1509

WAKE, MADELINE MUSANTE, nursing educator. Diploma, St. Francis Hosp. Sch. Nursing, 1963; BS in Nursing, Marquette U., 1968, MS in Nursing, 1971; PhD, U. Wis., Milw., 1986. Clin. nurse specialist St. Mary's Hosp., Milw., 1971-74, asst. dir. nursing, 1974-77; dir. continuing nursing edn. Marquette U., Milw., 1977-92, asst. prof., 1977-90, assoc. prof., 1991—, dean Coll. Nursing, 1993—. Chmn. bd. dirs. Trinity Meml. Hosp., Cudahy, Wis., 1991-96. Recipient Profl. Svc. award Am. Diabetes Assn.-Wis. affiliate, 1978, Excellence in Nursing Edn. award Wis. Nurses Assn., 1989; named Disting. Lectr. Sigma Theta Tau Internat., 1991. Fellow Am. Acad. Nursing; mem. ANA, AACN, Am. Orgn. Nurse Execs. Office: Marquette Univ Sch Nursing Milwaukee WI 53201-1881

WAKE, MARVALEE HENDRICKS, biology educator; b. Orange, Calif., July 31, 1939; d. Marvin Carlton and Velvalee (Borter) H.; m. David B. Wake, June 23, 1962; 1 child, Thomas A. BA, U. So. Calif., 1961, MS, 1964, PhD, 1968. Teaching asst./instr. U. Ill., Chgo., 1964-68, asst. prof., 1968-69; lectr. U. Calif., Berkeley, 1969-73, asst. prof., 1973-76, assoc. prof., 1976-80, prof. zoology, 1980-89, chmn. dept. zoology, 1985-89, chmn. dept. integrative biology, 1989-91, assoc. dean Coll. Letters and Sci., 1975-78, prof. integrative biology, 1989—; mem. NAS/NRC Bd. on Sustainable Devel., 1995—. Editor, co-author: Hyman's Comparative Vertebrate Anatomy, 1979; co-author: Biology, 1978; contbr. articles to profl. jours. NSF grantee, 1978—; Guggenheim fellow, 1988-89. Fellow AAAS, Calif. Acad. Sci. (trustee 1992—); mem. Am. Soc. Ichthyologists and Herpetologists (pres. 1984, bd. govs. 1978—), Internat. Union Biol. Scis. (U.S. nat. com. 1986-95, chair 1992-95; sec.-gen. 1994—), World Congress of Herpetology (sec.-gen. 1994—). Home: 999 Middlefield Rd Berkeley CA 94708-1509 Office: U Calif Dept Integrative Biology Berkeley CA 94720

WAKE, RICHARD W., food products executive; b. 1953. With Aurora (Ill.) Eby-Brown Co., Inc., 1975—; co-pres. Aurora (Ill.) Eby-Brown Co., Inc., Naperville, Ill. Office: Eby-Brown Co L P 280 Shuman Blvd Ste 280 Naperville IL 60563-8456*

WAKE, THOMAS G., food products executive. Co-pres. Eby-Brown Co., Naperville, Ill., now co-chief exec. Office: Eby Brown Co 280 Shuman Blvd Ste 280 Naperville IL 60563-8456*

WAKE, WILLIAM S., wholesale distribution executive; b. 1926. MBA, U. Mich., 1948. With Aurora (Ill.) EBy-Brown Co., Inc., 1948-56, chmn. bd., CEO, 1956. With USN, 1944-46. Office: Eby-Brown Co 280 Shuman Blvd Ste 280 Naperville IL 60563-8456*

WAKEFIELD, BENTON MCMILLIN, JR., banker; b. Monroe, La., Apr. 8, 1920; s. Benton McMillin and Adele (Rhodes) W.; m. Cindy Walton, May 19, 1951; children: Benton McMillin, III, Will Walton. BS in Commerce summa cum laude, Washington and Lee U., 1941; postgrad., Grad. Sch. Banking, U. Wis., 1949-51. Asst. v.p. First Nat. Bank Memphis, 1946-52; v.p. Ouachita Nat. Bank, Monroe, La., 1952-63; pres., CEO, bd. dirs. Merc. Nat. Bank Ind., Hammond, 1963-72; pres., CEO 1st Bank and Trust Co., South Bend, Ind., 1972-79, FBT Bancorp., 1972-79; chmn., CEO First Nat. Bank of Jefferson Parish, 1979-84; chmn., pres., CEO First Fin. Bank, New

Orleans, 1984-88; prin. Bank and Thrift Cons. Group, New Orleans, 1988—; dir. Eureka Homestead Soc., New Orleans, 1995—; cons., including trial expert testimony Fin. Litigation Support, 1988—; bd. dirs. 10 banks, Mich. and Ind., 1972-79, Carpetland U.S.A., Chgo.; mem. fin. adv. coun. Fed. Res. Bank Atlanta; mem. visitors com. Loyola U. Bus. Sch.; Chpt. 11 bankruptcy trustee Kirk Mfg. Inc. Bd. dirs. Econ. Devel. Com. New Orleans, Bur. Govt. Research, United Way. Served to lt. comdr. USNR, 1941-46. Mem. Am. Bankers Assn. (econ. policy com.), U.S. C. of C. (fin. com.), New Orleans Country Club, Bienville Club, Phi Beta Kappa, Sigma Alpha Epsilon, Omicron Delta Kappa, Beta Gamma Sigma, Rotary, Royal Soc. St. George, Huguenot Soc. Methodist. Home: 5301 Marcia Ave New Orleans LA 70124-1050 Office: 5301 Marcia Ave New Orleans LA 70124-1050

WAKEFIELD, DAN, author, screenwriter; b. Indpls., May 21, 1932; s. Benjamin H. and Brucie (Ridge) W. B.A., Columbia U., 1955; Nieman fellow, Harvard U., 1963-64. News editor Princeton (N.J.) Packet, 1955; staff writer Nation mag., 1956-59; free lance writer, 1959—; contbg. editor The Atlantic Monthly, 1968-80; staff Bread Loaf Writers Conf., 1964, 66, 68, 70, 86; contbn. writer GQ mag., 1992—; vis. lectr. U. Mass., Boston, 1965-66; vis. lectr. journalism U. Ill., 1968; writer-in-residence Emerson Coll., 1989-92; Disting. vis. writer Fla. Internat. U., 1995—. Creator, story cons. TV show James at 15, 1977-78, Heartbeat, 1988; author: Island in the City: The World of Spanish Harlem, 1959, Revolt in the South, 1961, Ananthology, 1963, Between the Lines, 1966, Supernation at Peace and War, 1968, Going All the Way, 1970 (Nat. Book Award nomination), Starting Over, 1973, All Her Children, 1976, Home Free, 1977, Under the Apple Tree, 1982, Selling Out, 1985, Returning: A Spiritual Journey, 1988, The Story of Your Life: Writing a Spiritual Autobiography, 1990, New York in the Fifties, 1992, Expect a Miracle, 1995, Creating from the Spirit, 1996; editor: The Addict: An Anthology, 1963; (teleplay) The Innocents Abroad (Mark Twain) for PBS, 1983; writer, co-prodr. TV movie The Seduction of Miss Leona, 1980; contbg. editor: Atlantic Monthly, 1969-80. Bernard DeVoto fellow Bread Loaf Writers Conf., 1957, Rockefeller Grant in Creative Writing, 1968; short story prize, Nat. Council of Arts, 1968. Mem. Authors Guild Am., Writers Guild Am., Nat. Writers Union, Vestry of King's Chapel. Address: c/o Janklow & Nesbit 598 Madison Ave New York NY 10022*

WAKEFIELD, RICHARD ALAN, energy consulting firm executive; b. Exeter, N.H., June 22, 1947; s. Frederick Irving and Helen (Smith) W.; m. Priscilla Jean Warnock, Aug. 16, 1969; 1 child, Laura Katherine. BSEE magna cum laude, U. N.H., 1969; MSEE, U. Ill., 1970; PhD in Elec. Engring., U. Wash., 1975. Project engr. Air Force Avionics Lab., Wright-Patterson AFB, Ohio, 1973-77; sr. engr., project mgr. Mathtec, Inc., Arlington, Va., 1977-81; v.p. CSA Energy Cons., Arlington, 1981-88, sr. v.p., 1988-90, pres., 1991—, also chmn. bd. dirs. Bd. dris. Arlington Cmty. Residences, Inc., 1983-88, chmn., 1988-89; bd. dirs. Arlington Cmty. Svcs., 1989-95. Capt. USAF, 1973-77. Recipient Nat. Capital award D.C. Coun. Engring. and Archtl. Socs., Washington, 1982, Perske award Assn. for Mentally Retarded, Arlington, 1983. Mem. IEEE (sr., mem. Power Engring. Soc. 1983-90, mem. sys. planning subcom. Power Engring. Soc. 1985—, mem. energy policy com. 1992—, vice chair energy policy com. 1997—), AAAS, Conf. Internat. Grands Réseaux Electriques a Haute Tension (Cigré). Democrat. Roman Catholic. Avocations: tennis, fly fishing. Office: CSA Energy Cons Inc 1901 Fort Myer Dr Ste 503 Arlington VA 22209-1604

WAKEFIELD, STEPHEN ALAN, lawyer; b. Olney, Ill., Oct. 18, 1940; s. George William and Blanche Lucille (Sheesley) W.; children from previous marriage: Melissa Cox, Tracy Lenz, Stephen Alan Jr.; m. Patricia Ann McGuire, Nov. 29, 1980; 1 child, Mark. LLB, U. Tex., Austin, 1965. Bar: Tex. 1965. Assoc. Baker & Botts, Houston, 1965-70, ptnr., 1974-84, sr. ptnr., chmn. energy dept., 1986-89; atty. Federal Power Commn., Washington, 1970-72; dep. asst. sec. energy programs Dept. Interior, Washington, 1972-73, asst. sec. energy and minerals, 1973-74; asst. adminstr. Fed. Energy Office, Washington, 1973-74; vice chmn., gen. counsel United Energy Resources, Inc., Houston, 1985-86; pres. United Gas Pipe Line Co., Houston, 1985-86; exec. v.p. MidCon Corp., 1985-86; gen. coun. Dept. Energy, Washington, 1989-91; ptnr. Akin, Gump, Strauss, Hauer & Feld, L.L.P., 1991—. Bd. dirs. Houston Advanced Rsch. Ctr.; bd. visitors M.D. Anderson Cancer Ctr. Mem. ABA, Tex. Bar Assn., Houston Bar Assn. Clubs: River Oaks Country, Coronado (Houston). Home: 16 West Ln Houston TX 77019-1008 Office: Akin Gump Strauss Et Al 711 Louisiana St Ste 1900 Houston TX 77002-2720

WAKEFIELD, WESLEY HALPENNY, church official; b. Vancouver, B.C., Can., Aug. 22, 1929; s. William James Elijah and Jane Mitchell (Halpenny) W.; m. Mildred June Shouldice, Oct. 24,1959. Ed. pub. schs., 1936-45, student tech. inst., 1945-47, student theology, 1947-51. Ordained to ministry The Bible Holiness Movement, 1951. Pastor Penticton, B.C., 1949-56; itinerant evangelist, 1956-59; internat. leader, bishop-gen. The Bible Holiness Movement, Vancouver, 1949—; mission to native Indians in Alta., Can., 1960-65, to Nigeria and Liberia, 1966, to drug culture youth in Pacific N.W., 1969—, among alcoholics, 1956-59, 64-66, 73; guest speaker, dir. Bible Broadcast, 1952-56, Freedom Broadcast, 1984-85; sec.-treas. Penticton Ministerial Assn., 1956; mgr. Evang. Book Svc., 1964—, Liberty Press, 1964—; presented opening prayer Fall legis. session, B.C., 1972; lectr. in field. Author: Bible Doctrine, 1951, Bible Basis of Christian Security, 1956, Jesus Is Lord, 1976, How to Incorporate a Nonprofit Society, 1976, Foundations of Freedom, 1978, Fire from Heaven, 1987, Bringing Back the Ark, 1987, John Wesley: The Burning Heart, 1988, Like Lightning, 1990, Antinomianism: The Curse of the Ages, 1990; legis. rsch. submissions: Effects of Marijuana and Youth, 1969, Labour Legislation Clauses, 1973, Religious Liberty in the Constitution, 1978, Alternatives to Electro-shock Therapy, 1988, 90, Present Day Slavery, 1973, 90; editor Hallelujah mag. (formerly Truth on Fire!), 1949—, Christian Social Vanguard, 196-61, Canadian Church and State, 1977-90, Hallelujah Songbook, 1981-83, Wesleyan Annotated Edition of the Bible, 1980—, Miniature Railways (quar.), 1988—. Chmn. Christians Concerned for Racial Equality, 1975—; v.p. Can. United for Separation of Ch. and State, 1977-90; chmn. Religious Freedom Coun. of Christian Minorities, 1978—; rsch. dir. United Citizens for Integrity, 1979—; v.p. Can. Coun. Japan Evang. Band, 1988—; chmn. Religious Info. Ctr., 1978—; Western Can. rep. Can. for the Protection of Religious Liberty, 1979—. Recipient Internat. Community Svc. award Gt. Britain, 1976, 79, Religious Liberty Advocacy award Religious Freedom Crusade, 1986, 87. Mem. NAACP, Anti-Slavery Soc., Can. Bible Soc., Bible Sci. Assn., Christian Holiness Assn. (com. mem.), Nat. Black Evang. Assn. (denomination rep. 1980-86), Wesley Study Bible (reference com. 1988-90), Evangs. for Social Action, Internat. Platform Assn., Salvation Army Hist. Soc. Avocation: miniature railways. Office: Bible Holiness Movement, PO Box 223 Postal Sta A, Vancouver, BC Canada V6C 2M3 *The real Christian is one who has exchanged the love of life for a life of love and desires the whole will of God—nothing else, nothing less, and nothing more. This consistency of service is the jewel of life and holiness its crowning glory.*

WAKEHAM, HELMUT RICHARD RAE, chemist, consulting company executive; b. Hamburg, Germany, Apr. 15, 1916; s. Rae G. and Augusta (Beiss) W.; m. Kathleen Ferguson, June 22, 1939; children: Stuart, Susan, Rosemary. B.A., U. Nebr., 1936, MA, 1937; PhD, U. Calif.-Berkeley, 1939. Research chemist Standard Oil Co. Calif., 1939-41, So. Regional Research Lab., U.S. Dept. Agr., 1941-47; research assoc. Inst. Textile Tech., Charlottesville, Va., 1947-49; project head chem.-physics sect. Textile Research Inst., also research dir., 1949-56; dir. Ahmedabad (India) Textile Industries Research Assn., 1956-58; staff asst. for research to v.p. Philip Morris, Inc., 1958-59, dir. research and devel., 1959-61, v.p., dir. research and devel., 1961-65, v.p. corporate research and devel., 1965-75, v.p. sci. and tech., 1975-80, v.p. world tobacco tech. group, 1980-82; pres. HRW Tech. Assocs. Inc., 1982-93; chmn. MEGG Assocs., Inc., 1984—; pres. Vigor Corp., 1985-87; mem. Sci. Commn. of CORESTA (internat. tobacco research orgn.), 1966-72; gen. chmn. CORESTA/TCRC Conf., Williamsburg, Va., 1972; chmn. Nat. Conf. Adminstrn. Research, 1970; mem. gen. adv. com. Textile Research Inst., 1961-65; mem. tobacco working group Nat. Cancer Inst., 1967-76; session chmn. Nat. Cancer Plan Workshop, 1971. Pres. Robert E. Lee council Boy Scouts Am., 1972-75; pres. Sci. Mus. of Va. Found., 1974-77, Va. Ctr. for Performing Arts, 1980-85; chmn. Carpenter Ct. for Performing Arts; exec. v.p. Richmond Symphony, 1976-79, pres., 1979-81, chmn., 1981-83. Cultural Laureate in sci. and tech. State of Va., 1977; Angel award Internat. Soc. Performing Arts Adminstrs., 1985. Fellow Am. Inst. Chemists, Textile Inst. (Great Britain), Va. Acad. Sci., AAAS; mem. Am. Chem. Soc. (chmn. local program sect. 1943-45, Disting. Chemist award Va. sect. 1982), Fiber Soc. (program chmn., councilor 1950-55), Am. Inst. Physics. Home: 8905 Norwick Rd Richmond VA 23229-7715 Office: 2716 Enterprise Pky Richmond VA 23294-6334

WAKEHAM, MATTHEW S., electronics marketing manager; b. Yonkers, N.Y., Aug. 15, 1961; s. Edwin Wakeham and Margaret Scanlon. BSEE, Pratt Inst., 1984. Elec. engr. Underwriters Labs., Melville, N.Y., 1984-92; mktg. mgr. Leviton Mfg. Co., Little Neck, N.Y., 1992—. Mem. IEEE (chmn. surge protection com. 1994—), Nat. Elec. Mfrs. Assn. (chmn. TVSS wiring devices 1996—), Nat. Fire Protection Assn. Avocations: theater, playwriting, music, art, baseball. Home: 55 W 74th St New York NY 10023

WAKEMAN, FREDERIC EVANS, JR., historian educator; b. Kansas City, Kans., Dec. 12, 1937; s. Frederic Evans and Margaret Ruth (Keyes) W.; divorced; children: Frederic Evans III, Matthew Clark, Sarah Elizabeth. B.A., Harvard Coll., 1959; postgrad., Institut d'Etudes Politiques, U. Paris, 1959-60; M.A., U. Calif.-, Berkeley, 1962, Ph.D., 1965. Asst. prof. history U. Calif., Berkeley, 1965-67, assoc. prof., 1968-70, prof., 1970-89, Haas prof. Asian Studies, 1989—, dir. Ctr. Chinese Studies, 1972-79; humanities research prof., vis. scholar Corpus Christi Coll., U. Cambridge, Eng., 1976-77, Beijing U., 1980-81, 85; acad. adviser U.S. Ednl. Del. for Study in China; chmn. Joint Com. Chinese Studies Am. Coun. Learned Socs./Social Sci. Rsch. Coun.; sr. adviser Beijing office NAS; pres. Social Sci. Rsch. Coun., 1986-89, chmn. com. on scholarly comm. with China, 1995—; dir. Inst. East Asian Studies, Berkeley, 1990—. Author: Strangers at the Gate, 1966, History and Will, 1973, The Fall of Imperial China, 1975, Conflict and Control in Late Imperial China, 1976, Ming and Qing Historical Studies in the People's Republic of China, 1981, The Great Enterprise, 1986, Shanghai Sojourners, 1992, Policing Shanghai, 1995, Shanghai Badlands, 1996. Harvard Nat. scholar, 1955-59; Tower fellow, 1959-60; Fgn. Area fellow, 1963-65; Am. Coun. Learned Socs. fellow, 1967-68; Guggenheim fellow, 1973-74; NRC fellow, 1985. Mem. Am. Acad. Arts and Scis., Coun. on Fgn. Rels., Am. Hist. Assn. (pres.). Home: 702 Gonzalez Dr San Francisco CA 94132-2234 Office: University of California Inst East Asian Studies Berkeley CA 94720

WAKEMAN, OLIVIA VAN HORN, marketing professional; b. Starkville, Miss.; d. Thomas Oliver and Mary Jeanne (Walker) W. BA in Mgmt., Eckerd Coll., St. Petersburg, Fla., 1980; MIM in Mktg./Advt., Am. Grad. Sch. Internat. Mgmt., 1982. Bus. analyst Dun & Bradstreet, Tampa, Fla., 1980; mgmt. cons. Cardinal Mgmt. Assocs., L.A., 1982-83; asst. account exec. McCann-Erickson, N.Y.C., 1984-86; account exec. Hearst Mag., N.Y.C., 1986-87, Ribaudo & Schaefer, N.Y.C., 1987-88; dir. pub. affairs/bus. soc. and ethics program Carnegie Coun. on Ethics and Internat. Affairs, N.Y.C., 1989-93; sr. mgr. client svcs. Burson-Marsteller, Inc., 1994—; adult edn. mktg. prof. Touro Coll., N.Y.C., 1989; mktg. comm. cons. Hoffmann-La Roche, Inc., McGraw-Hill Inc., Daniel J. Edelman, Inc., Dilenschneider Group, Stingray Ptnrs., N.Y.C., 1993-94. Reading vol. Vol. Svcs. for Children, N.Y.C., 1991-93. Episcopalian. Avocation: scuba diving.

WAKEMAN, RICHARD JOHN, psychologist, neuropsychologist; b. Chgo., Ill., Apr. 3, 1948; s. Richard Frank and Leilani Margaret (Wongwai) W.; m. Pamela Anne Bonura, May 26, 1973; children: Jared John, Devin John. BA with honors, Loyola U., New Orleans, 1970; MA with honors, U. of Southern Miss., 1973, PhD with honors, 1975. Diplomate Am. Bd. Psychology; cert. in neuropsychology, La. and Tex. Internship Walter Reed Army Med. Ctr., Washington, 1974-75; asst. chief, psychology Brooke Army Med. Ctr., San Antonio, 1975-80; head of dept. psychology Ochsner Clinic, New Orleans, 1980—; clin. assoc. prof. psychology, dept. psychiatry/neurology Tulane Sch. Medicine, New Orleans, 1988—; Mem. State Bd. of Examiners, State of La., Baton Route, 1984-85; cons. Dupont Corp., Delisle, Miss., 1986—, Entergy Corp., New Orleans, 1988—, Mobil Oil Co., New Orleans, 1993—. Contbr. articles and editor for prof. jours. Capt. U.S. Army Med. Svc. Corp., 1974-80. Fellow Am. Acad. Clinical Psychology, 1994; recipient Milton H. Erickson award Am. Soc. of Clinical Hypnosis, 1979, 1988. Mem. APA, Internat. Neuropsychol. Soc., Southeastern Psychol. Assn., La. Psychol. Assn., Nat. Acad. Neuropsychologists. Republican. Roman Catholic. Avocations: jazz drumming, running, alpine skiing, reading, baseball. Home: 1907 Octavia St New Orleans LA 70115-5651

WAKEMAN, RICK, musician, composer; b. Middlesex, Eng., May 18, 1949; s. Cyril and Mildred W.; m. Nina Carter, 1983; children: Jemma, Oscar; children from previous marriages: Oliver, Adam, Benjamin. Educated, Royal Coll. Music, London. Keyboard and composition tng. Royal Coll. Music, 1968. Performed with group Strawbs, 1970-71; with Yes, 1971-72, 77-79, 91; with Anderson Bruford Wakeman Howe, 1989; formed own group, 1973—; rec. artist A & M Records, 1971-80, Charisma Records, from 1980, others; composed film score based on works of Liszt for film Lisztomania, 1975; original film scores White Rock, 1976, The Burning, 1982, G'Olé, 1983, Crimes of Passion, 1984; albums include Journey to the Centre of the Earth, 1974, Six Wives of Henry VIII, 1974, Myths and Legends of King Arthur, 1975, No Earthly Connection, 1976, Criminal Record, 1977, Best Known Works, 1978, 81, 84, Rhapsodies, 1979, Silent Nights, 1985, Live at Hammersmith, 1985, The Family Album, 1987, (with Tony Fernandez) Zodiaque, 1988, A Suite of Gods, 1988, Time Machine, 1988, Black Knights in the Court of Ferdinand IV, 1990, Phantom Power, 1990, Aspirant Sunset, 1990, Aspirant Sunrise, 1990, Softsword, King John & the Magna Carta, 1991, Greater Hits, 1994, numerous others; toured U.S. with Nat. Philharm. Orch. and Chorus, 1974, with own group, 1975, with Yes, 1977, 78, 79, 91, with Anderson Bruford Wakeman Howe, 1989. Address: Bajonor Ltd, Bajonor House, 2 Bridge St, Peel Isle of Man Office: Atlantic Records 75 Rockefeller Plz New York NY 10019-6908*

WAKIL, SALIH JAWAD, biochemistry educator; b. Kerballa, Iraq, Aug. 16, 1927; s. Jawad and Milook (Attraqchi) W.; m. Fawzia Bahrani, Nov. 30, 1952; children: Sonya, Aida, Adil, Youssef. B.Sc., Am. U., Beirut, 1948; Ph.D., U. Wash., 1952. Research fellow U. Wash., 1949-52; research fellow U. Wis., Madison, 1952-56, asst. prof., 1956-59; asst. prof. Duke U., 1959-60, assoc. prof., 1960-65, prof., 1965-71; prof. biochemistry, chmn. dept. Baylor Coll. Medicine, Houston, 1971—, Lodwick T. Bolin prof., chmn. dept. biochemistry, 1984—, prof. biotechnology, 1986-95, Disting. Svc. prof., 1990—. Recipient Paul Lewis award in enzyme chemistry Am. Chem. Soc., 1967, Disting. Duke Med. Alumnus award, 1973, Chilton award U. Tex. Southwestern Med. Ctr., Dallas, 1985, Kuwait prize Kuwait Found. Advancement Sci., 1988, Disting. Svc. award Arab Am. Med. Assn., 1990, Supelco Rsch. award Am. Oil Chemists Soc., 1993; John Simon Guggenheim fellow, 1968-69. Fellow Am. Acad. Microbiology; mem. NAS, Assn. Med. and Grad. Depts. Biochemistry (pres. 1988-89). Office: Baylor Coll Medicine Biochemistry Dept 1 Baylor Plz Houston TX 77030-3411

WAKIM, FAHD GEORGE, physicist, educator; b. Mieh-Mieh, Lebanon, Aug. 6, 1933; s. George Hanna and Marriam (Semaan) W.; m. Bertha Villarreal. BSc in Physics, Am. U. Beirut, 1956; MA in Solid State Physics, U. Tex., 1960, PhD in Solid State Physics, 1964. Rsch. physicist Itek Corp., Lexington, Mass., 1965-70; investigator Tex. Christian U., Ft. Worth, 1970-71; assoc. prof. Am. U. Cairo, 1971-73; prof. physics Kuwait U., Kuwait, 1973-84; assoc. prof. dept. elec. engring U. Mass., Lowell, 1984—, coord. for EET program, 1996—; Presenter numerous seminars. Patentee process for producing images with photosensitive materials and their products; contbr. articles to profl. jours. Grantee Kuwait Inst. for Sci. Rsch., 1978, 79, 91, Kuwait U., 1979. Mem. IEEE, Am. Phys. Soc., Materials Rsch. Soc. Office: U Mass-Lowell 1 University Ave Lowell MA 01854-2827

WAKLEY, JAMES TURNER, manufacturing company executive; b. Springfield, Ohio, Feb. 17, 1921; s. James Henry and Edith Lynn (Welsh) W.; m. Mary Pennell, May 18, 1945; children: Ruth Nadine, Gary James, Martin Pennell. Student, pub. schs., Springfield. Regional sales mgr. Nat. Supply Co., 1947-54; exec. v.p. Kanawha Sand Co., 1956-60; pres. Ohio River Sand & Gravel Co., Parkersburg, W.Va., 1960-77; v.p., bd. dirs. McDonough Co., Parkersburg, 1960-81; pres. McDonough Found., 1981—; chmn. bd. dirs. Marmac Corp., Parkersburg, 1981-95. Chmn. Parkersburg Urban Renewal Authority, 1968-75; trustee Ohio Valley Improvement Assn., Marietta Coll., W.Va. Found. Ind. Colls. Decorated DFC, Air medal. Mem. Nat. Sand and Gravel Assn. (bd. dirs. 1976-79). Lutheran. Home: 1906 Washington Ave Parkersburg WV 26101-3608 Office: PO Box 1825 Parkersburg WV 26102-1825

WAKOSKI, DIANE, poet, educator; b. Whittier, Calif., Aug. 3, 1937; d. John Joseph and Marie Elvira (Mengel) W. BA in English, U. Calif., Berkeley, 1960. Writer-in-residence Mich. State U., East Lansing, 1976—, Univ. disting. prof., 1990—; vis. writer Calif. Inst. Tech., 1972, U. Va., 1972-73, Wilamette U., 1973, Lake Forest Coll., 1974, Colo. Coll., 1974, U. Calif., Irvine, 1974, Macalester Coll., 1975, U. Wis., 1975, Hollins Coll., 1974, U. Wash., 1978, Whitman Coll., 1976, Emory U., 1980-81, U. Hawaii, 1978. Author: books Coins and Coffins, 1962, Discrepancies and Apparitions, 1966, Inside The Blood Factory, 1968, The George Washington Poems, 1967, The Magellanic Clouds, 1969, The Motorcycle Betrayal Poems, 1971, Smudging, 1972, Dancing On The Grave of A Son Of A Bitch, 1973, Trilogy, 1974, Virtuoso Literature For Two and Four Hands, 1976, Waiting For the King of Spain, 1977, The Man Who Shook Hands, 1978, Cap of Darkness, 1980, The Magician's Feastletters, 1982, The Collected Greed: Parts I-XIII, 1984, The Rings of Saturn, 1986, Emerald Ice: Selected Poems 1962-87, 1988 (William Carlos Williams prize 1989), Medea The Sorceress, 1991, Jason the Sailor, 1993, The Emerald City of Las Vegas, 1995, Argonaut Rose, 1997. Cassandra Found. grantee, 1970; N.Y. State Cultural Council grantee, 1971-72; Nat. Endowment for Arts grantee, 1973-74; Guggenheim grantee, 1972-73; Fulbright grantee, 1984; Mich. Arts Coun. grantee, 1988; recipient Mich. Arts Found. award, 1989, Disting. Faculty award Mich. State U., 1989, Univ. Disting. Prof., 1990. Office: Mich State U 207 Morrill Hall East Lansing MI 48824-1036

WAKS, JAY WARREN, lawyer; b. Newark, Dec. 6, 1946; s. Isadore and Miriam Waks; m. Harriet S. Siedman, July 27, 1969; children: Jonathan Warren, Allison Lindsay. BS, Cornell U., 1968, JD, 1971. Bar: N.Y. 1972, U.S. Ct. Appeals (2d cir.) 1972, U.S. Dist. Ct. (no. dist.) N.Y. 1972, U.S. Dist. Ct. (so. & ea. dists.) N.Y. 1973, U.S. Ct. Appeals (3d cir.) 1983, U.S. Dist. Ct. D.C. 1985, U.S. Supreme Ct. 1991. Law clk. to Hon. Inzer B. Wyatt U.S. Dist. Ct. So. Dist. N.Y., 1971-72; assoc. Kaye, Scholer, Fierman, Hays & Handler, N.Y.C., 1972-80, ptnr., 1981—, co-chmn. labor and employment law dept., chmn. health care law practice group and ADR practice group; gen. counsel, sec. to bd. dirs. Work in Am. Inst., Inc., Scarsdale, N.Y., 1989—, exec. com., 1995—; mem., chair faculty numerous employment and labor law confs., 1982—; chair Ann. Employment Law and Litigation Conf., 1992—; participant NYU 40th Nat. Conf. on Labor, 1987, 43d Nat. Conf. on Labor, 1990; spkr. Nat. Law Jours. Gen. Coun. Conf., 1988—, Am. Employment Law Coun. Bus. watch columnist Nat. Law Jour., 1990—; contbg. author numerous articles to profl. jours. Mem. employment disputes com. CPR Inst. for Dispute Resolution, 1988—, chair, 1991—; chmn. 20th and 25th reunion campaigns Cornell Law Sch., Ithaca, N.Y., 1991-96, mem. nat. chair dean's spl. leadership commn., 1996—. Named among nation's best litigators in employment law, The Nat. Law Jour., 1992; named among best lawyers in N.Y. and among 7 best corporate side labor/employment lawyers, N.Y. Mag., 1995. Mem. ABA, State Bar Calif., N.Y. State Bar Assn. (co-chair employment alternative dispute resolution com., labor and employment law sect.), Assn. Bar of City of N.Y. (chmn. labor and employment law com. 1990-93), N.Y. C. of C. and Industry (chmn. adv. panel on employment litigation 1986—). Avocations: swimming, tennis, skiing, bicycling, rollerblading. Home: 44 Eton Rd Larchmont NY 10538-1424 Office: Kaye Scholer Fierman Hays & Handler LLP 425 Park Ave New York NY 10022-3506

WAKSBERG, JOSEPH, statistical company executive, researcher; b. Kielce, Poland, Sept. 20, 1915; s. Harry and Anna (Kalichstein) W.; m. Roslyn Karr, Dec. 25, 1941; children: Arlene, Mark. BS, CCNY, 1936; postgrad., NYU, 1936-37, Am. U., 1941-43. Project dir. WPA, Phila., 1938-40; assoc. dir. stats. U.S. Bur. Census, Washington, 1940-73; chmn. bd. dirs. Westat, Inc., Rockville, Md., 1973—; tchr. U. Mich., Ann Arbor, 1968-75; statis. cons. CBS, N.Y.C., 1967-90, UN, 1975-81, Voter News Svc., N.Y.C., 1992—. Editor: Telephone Survey Methodology, 1988; assoc. editor Survey Methodology, 1992—; contbr. articles to profl. jours. Mem. tech. adv. com. Coun. Jewish Fedns., N.Y.C., 1978—. Recipient Gold medal U.S. Dept. Commerce, 1965. Fellow Am. Statis. Assn. (bd. dirs., chair several sects.); mem. Internat. Statis. Inst., Internat. Assn. Survey Statisticians (mem. coun. 1975-77). Office: Westat Inc 1650 Research Blvd Rockville MD 20850-3195

WAKSMAN, BYRON HALSTED, neuroimmunologist, experimental pathologist, educator, medical association administrator; b. N.Y.C., Sept. 15, 1919; s. Selman A. and Bertha (Mitnik) W.; m. Joyce Ann Robertroy, Aug. 11, 1944; children: Nan, Peter. BS, Swarthmore Coll., 1940; MD, U. Pa., 1943. Intern Michael Reese Hosp., Chgo., 1944; fellow Mayo Found., 1946-48; NIH fellow Columbia U. Med. Sch., 1948-49; assoc., then asst. prof. bacteriology and immunology Harvard Med. Sch., 1949-63; research fellow, then assoc. bacteriologist (neurology) Mass. Gen. Hosp., 1949-63; prof. microbiology Yale U., 1963-74, prof. pathology, 1974-78, chmn. dept., 1964-70, 72-74, prof. pathology and biology, 1979-89; v.p. rsch. programs Nat. Multiple Sclerosis Soc., N.Y.C., 1979-87; v.p. research and med. programs Nat. Multiple Sclerosis Soc., N.Y.C., 1987-89; adj. prof. pathology NYU, 1979—; vis. scientist in neurology Harvard U., 1990—; mem. expert panel immunology WHO, 1963-83; microbiology fellowships panel and study sect. mem. NIH, 1961-69; bd. trustees Found. for Microbiology, 1968—, pres., 1970—; bd. trustees Biosis, 1988-91; dir. sci. writing fellowships program Marine Biol. Lab., Woods Hole, Mass., 1990-95; Humboldt prof. Max Planck Inst., Munich, 1991-92; dir. European Initiative for Communicators Sci., 1992-95. Author numerous articles on thymus, cell-mediated immunity, tolerance, lymphokines, lymphocyte stimulation mechanisms, autoimmunity; editor: Progress in Allergy/Chemical Immunology, 1962—; mem. editl. adv. bd. Cellular Immunology, 1970-95, Immunol. Comms., 1970-95, Annales d'Immunologie, 1970-78, Pathologie et Biologie, 1975-89, Inflammation, 1975-90; assoc. editor: Bacteriol. Revs., 1963-67, Jour. Immunology, 1962-66, Internat. Archives Allergy and Applied Immunology, 1962-95. Served as psychiatrist AUS, 1944-46. Mem. Am. Assn. Immunologists (councillor 1965-70, pres. 1970-71), British Soc. Immunology, Am. Soc. Microbiology (councillor 1967-69). Home: 300 E 54th St New York NY 10022-5018 Office: NYU Med Ctr Dept Pathology 550 1st Ave New York NY 10016-6481

WAKSMAN, TED STEWART, lawyer; b. N.Y.C., July 4, 1949; s. Alfred and Helen (Greenberger) W.; m. Lois J. Lichter, Dec. 26, 1970; children: Scott, Michael. BS, Cornell U., 1970; JD, NYU, 1973. Bar: N.Y. 1974. Ptnr. Weil, Gotshal & Manges, N.Y.C., 1973—. Mem., assoc. editor NYU Law Rev., 1971-73. Mem. ABA (comml. fin. services com.), N.Y. State Bar Assn. Office: Weil Gotshal & Manges 767 5th Ave New York NY 10153-0001

WAKUMOTO, YOSHIHIKO, electronics company executive, grants executive; b. Bunkyo-Ku, Tokyo, June 4, 1931; s. Yoshitaro and Fumie (Oka) W.; m. Reiko Tanaka, Mar. 28, 1959; children: Yoshiaki, Yoshiyuki. BA, Tokyo U., 1955; postgrad., Columbia U., 1960-61. Dep. mgr. license negotiation Toshiba Corp., Tokyo, 1964-67, mgr. overseas mfg. ops., 1967-72, mgr. fin. divsn., 1972-74, gen. mgr. internat. fin. divsn., 1974-81, gen. mgr. internat. affairs divsn., 1981-88, v.p., dep. group exec.-internat. staff group, 1988-91, exec. v.p. for corp. planning, info. sys. and group cos., 1991-95, exec. v.p. for internat. rels., 1995-96, bd. dirs., advisor, 1996—; exec. dir. Japan Found. Ctr. for Global Partnership, Tokyo, 1996—; bd. dirs. Schlumberger Ltd., Tokyo, 1997—; bd. dirs. Schlumberger Ltd. Co-author: Foreign Exchange Risk and International Financial Strategy, 1973, The Run-up of 21st Century, 1991; translator: Management By Exception, 1968. Mem. Internat. House of Japan, Am.-Japan Soc., Fgn. Corr. Club Japan (assoc.), Bus. Rsch. Inst., Inc. (trustee). Home: 3-43-18 Hongo Bunkyo-ku, Tokyo 113, Japan Office: Toshiba Corp, 1-1-1 Shibaura Minato-Ku, Tokyo 105, Japan

WALASH, EILEEN ROBIN (LEE WALASH), promotions and public relations specialist; b. Bklyn., Jan. 30, 1964; d. Myron and Marilyn Estelle (Rosner) W. BA, Miami U., Oxford, Ohio, 1986. Asst. editor Gralla Publs., N.Y.C., 1986-88; market editor Women's Wear Daily, N.Y.C., 1988-89; account supr. The Rowland Co., N.Y.C., 1989-92; pub. rels. and promotions cons., freelance writer N.Y.C., 1992-95; ind. promotions contractor Radio City Music Hall, N.Y.C., 1994-95, promotions mgr., 1995—. Vol. N.Y.

Cares, N.Y.C., 1993—, Gay Men's Health Crisis, 1995—. Mem. Pub. Rels. Soc. Am., N.Y. Alumni Assn. Miami U. (steering com.). Democrat.

WALASZEK, EDWARD JOSEPH, pharmacology educator; b. Chgo., July 4, 1927; married; two children. BS, U. Ill., 1949; PhD in Pharmacology, U. Chgo., 1953; MD honoris causa, U. Helsinki, 1990. Rsch. fellow U. Edinburgh, 1953-55; asst. prof. neurophysiology and biochemistry U. Ill., 1955-56; asst. prof. pharmacology U. Kans. Sch. Medicine, Kansas City, 1957-59; assoc. prof. U. Kans. Sch. Medicine, 1959-62, prof., 1962—, chmn. dept., 1964-92; USPHS spl. rsch. fellow, 1956-61; mem. health study sect. med. chemistry NIH, 1962-66, mem. health study sect. on rsch. career devel. award, 1966-70, mem. health study sect. on pharmacology-toxicology, 1974-78, rsch. career award, 1963; mem. com. tchg. of sci. Internat. Coun. Sci. Unions; mem. adv. coun. Internat. Union Pharmacology, 1972-81, chmn. sect. teaching, 1975-85; chmn. bd. Computer Assisted Teaching Systems Consortium. Editorial bd.: Med. Biology, 1974-84, Arch. int. Pharmacodyn, 1977. Recipient vice-chancellor's award U. Kans., 1974, Rector's medal U. Helsinki, 1975, Recognition medal Vanderbilt U., 1991, Arstiteaduskond medal Tartu U., Estonia, 1993. Fellow Am. Coll. Clin. Pharmacologists, AAAS, Am. Chem. Soc., Soc. Pharmacology, Soc. Neurosci.; mem. Finnish Acad. Sci. and Letters (fgn.), Finnish Pharm. Soc. (hon.), Hungarian Pharm. Soc. (hon.), Sigma Xi, Alpha Omega Alpha, Rho Chi. Office: U Kans Sch Medicine Dept Pharmacology Kansas City KS 66160

WALBERG, HERBERT JOHN, psychologist, educator, consultant; b. Chgo., Dec. 27, 1937; s. Herbert J. and Helen (Bauer) W.; m. Madoka Bessho, Aug. 20, 1965; 1 child, Herbert J. III. BE in Edn. and Psychology, Chgo. State U., 1959; ME in Counseling, U. Ill., 1960; PhD in Ednl. Psychology, U. Chgo., 1964. Instr. psychology Chgo. State U., 1962-63, asst. prof., 1964-65; lectr. edn. Rutgers U., New Brunswick, N.J., 1965-66; asst. prof. edn. Harvard U., Cambridge, Mass., 1966-69; assoc. prof. edn. U. Ill., Chgo., 1970-71, prof., 1971-84, rsch. prof., 1984—, external examiner, 1981; external examiner, 1981; ednl. cons. numerous orgns.; external examiner Monash U., 1974, 76, Australian Nat. U., 1977; speaker in field; former coord. worldwide radio broadcasts on Am. Edn. Voice of Am., USIA, Office Pres. U.S., cons. Ctr. for Disease Control U.S. Pub. Health Svcs., 1985-90. Author, editor 49 books; chmn. editl. bd. Internat. Jour. Ednl. Rsch., 1985—; contbr. over 350 articles to profl. jours., chpts. to books. Mem. Chgo. United Edn. Com., also other civic groups, 1971-86; bd. dirs. Family Study Inst., 1987; chmn. bd. dirs. Heartland Inst., 1995. Nat. Inst. Edn. rsch. grantee, 1973, NSF rsch. grantee, 1974, March of Dimes rsch. grantee, 1976, numerous others. Fellow AAAS, Am. Psychol. Assn., Royal Statis. Soc.; mem. Internat. Acad. Edn. (founding), Am. Ednl. Rsch. Assn., Assn. for Supervision and Curriculum Devel., Brit. Ednl. Rsch. Assn., Nat. Soc. for Study Edn., Evaluation Rsch. Soc., Internat. Acad. Scis., Phi Delta Kappa (Disting. Rsch. award U. Chgo. chpt. 1971, cert. of recognition 1985), Phi Kappa Phi (hon.). Lutheran. Avocation: travel. Home: 180 E Pearson St Apt 3607 Chicago IL 60611-2135 Office: U Ill PO Box 4348 Chicago IL 60680-4348

WALBORSKY, HARRY M., chemistry educator, consultant; b. Lodz, Poland, Dec. 15, 1923; came to U.S., 1929; s. Israel and Sarah (Miedowicz) Wolborski; m. Paula Levitt, Nov. 28, 1970; children: Edwin, Eric, Lisa, Irene. BS, CCNY, 1945; PhD, Ohio State U., 1949. Rsch. assoc. Calif. Inst. Tech., Pasadena, 1948; rsch. assoc. UCLA Med. Sch., 1949-50, rsch. assoc. chemistry dept. UCLA, 1950; instr. Fla. State U., Tallahassee, 1950-51, asst. prof. chemistry, 1951-54, assoc. prof., 1954-59, prof., 1959—, Disting. prof., 1980—; cons. Dow Chem. Co., Midland, Mich., 1956-72. Contbr. over 150 articles to profl. jours., 1949—. Recipient Sr. Scientist award von Humboldt Soc., Federal Republic of Germany, 1987; USPH fellow, 1951, Japanese Soc. for Promotion Sci. fellow, 1977. Mem. Am. Chem. Soc. (award Fla. chpt. 1978), N.Y. Acad. Sci., Chem. Soc. London, Sigma Xi, Phi Lambda Upsilon. Avocations: tennis, bridge. Office: Fla State U Dept Chemistry Tallahassee FL 32306

WALBRIDGE, WILLARD EUGENE, broadcasting executive; b. Republic, Pa., Mar. 11, 1913; s. Peter D. and Anna (Higbee) W.; m. Marietta H. Arner, Nov. 15, 1941; 1 child, Peter F. A.B., U. Mich., 1936. Salesman, Sta. WWJ, Detroit, 1939-43; mgr. Sta. WWJ-TV, Detroit, 1946-53; exec. v.p., gen. mgr. Sta. WJIM AM-TV, Lansing, Mich., 1953-54, Sta. KTRK-TV, Houston, 1954-70; sr. v.p. corp. affairs Capital Cities Communications, Inc., 1970-78, cons., 1978-81; dir. Houston Lighting & Power Co., Houston Industries, Inc., 1975-83, Internat. Systems & Controls, Inc., Tex. Commerce Med. Bank. Pres., Greater Houston Community Found.; bd. dirs. Salvation Army, Houston Area council Boy Scouts Am., Houston Grand Opera Assn.; mem. nat. bd. govs. ARC, 1974-80, also bd. dirs. Houston chpt., 1965-83, chmn. Houston chpt., 1972-75; chmn. bd. TV Info. Office, N.Y.C., 1965-70; trustee Mus. Broadcasting, 1978-82. Served from ensign to lt. USNR, 1943-46. Decorated Silver Star. Mem. Maximum Service Telecasters (dir. 1971-81), Houston Assn. Community TV (dir. 1972-82), Internat. Radio and TV Fedn. (dir. 1969-76), Nat. Assn. Broadcasters (dir. 1965-70, chmn. bd. 1970-71), U.S. C. of C. (dir. 1975-81), Houston C. of C. (dir. 1971-83, chmn. bd. 1975-76), Houston Council Fgn. Relations (chmn. 1977-78). Home: 2828 Bammel Ln Apt 1203 Houston TX 77098-1132 Office: 1 E Greenway Plz Ste 716 Houston TX 77046-0103 also: Hill & Knowlton Innc 1415 Louisiana Ste 2601 Houston TX 77002-2546

WALBURN, JOHN CLIFFORD, mental health services professional; b. Marion, Ind., Apr. 6, 1945; s. Rex Raymond and Norma Jane (Clifford) W.; m. Linda Sue Spall, Sept. 21, 1968 (div. Dec. 1987); 1 child, Geoffrey Jacob; m. Mitzi Lynn Johnson, June 20, 1992; 1 child, Abigail Rae. BS, Ball State U., 1969, MA, 1975; JD, I.U., Indpls., 1991. Bar: Ind. 1992. Planner Metro. Planning Commn., Muncie, Ind., 1970-72; dir. adult svcs. Del. County Assn. for Retarded, Muncie, Ind., 1972-76; exec. dir. Fayette-Union Assn. for Retarded, Connersville, Ind., 1976-83; cons. Ind. Protection and Advocacy, Indpls., 1984-86; case mgr. Ind. Dept. Mental Health, Indpls., 1986-87; v.p. Cardinal Svc. Mgmt., New Castle, Ind., 1987—; ofcl. Ind. Spl. Olympics, 1973—; chmn. Ind. Residential Mgmt. Com., 1991—; cons. DLG Cons. and Mktg. Svc., Ind., 1992. Co-author: Feldman/Walburn Habilitation System, 1988; photo, drawing artist, 1978—. With USN, 1965-67. Named Ky. Col., Commonwealth of Ky., 1978. Mem. Am. Assn. Mental Retardation (bd. dirs. 1991—), Ind. Assn. Rehab. Facilities (bd. dirs. 1996—). Avocations: sports, playing/listening to music, movies, art, reading fiction. Home: 1121 Indiana Ave New Castle IN 47362-4620 Office: Cardinal Svc Mgmt Inc PO Box 505 New Castle IN 47362-0505

WALCH, TIMOTHY GEORGE, library administrator; b. Detroit, Dec. 6, 1947; s. George Louis Walch and Margaret Mary (Shields) DeSchryver; m. Victoria Irons, June 24, 1978; children: Thomas Emmet, Brian Edward. BA, U. Notre Dame, 1970; PhD, Northwestern U., 1975. Assoc. dir. Soc. Am. Archivists, Chgo., 1975-79; grants analyst Nat. Hist. Publ. Commn., Washington, 1979-81; budget analyst Nat. Archives, Washington, 1981-82, editor Prologue, 1982-88; asst. dir. Hoover Presdl. Libr., West Branch, Iowa, 1988-93, dir., 1993—. Author: Catholicism in America, 1989, Pope John Paul II, 1989, Parish School, 1996, others; editor: Herbert Hoover & Harry S Truman, 1992, Immigrant America, 1994, At the President's Side, 1997, and others; assoc. editor: U.S. Cath. Historian, 1983—; mem. editl. bd. Soc. Am. Archivists, 1982-86; guest columnist Cedar Rapids Gazette, 1996—. Recipient Achievement and Svc. awards Nat. Archives, 1980, 83, 87, 89, 93, Journalism award U.S. Cath. Press Assn., 1986, 1st place publ. award Nat. Assn. Govt. Communicators, 1988, Iowa Gov.'s Vol. award, 1995, 97. Mem. Soc. Am. Archivists, Orgn. Am. Historians, U.S. Cath. Hist. Soc., Rotary Internat. Home: 65 N Westminster St Iowa City IA 52245-3833 Office: Hoover Presdl Libr PO Box 488 West Branch IA 52358-0488

WALCHER, ALAN ERNEST, lawyer; b. Chgo., Oct. 2, 1949; s. Chester R. and Dorothy E. (Kullgren) W.; m. Penny Marie Walcher; children: Dustin Alan, Michael Alan, Christopher Ray; 1 stepchild, Ronald Edwin Culver. BS, U. Utah, 1971, cert. in internat. rels., 1971, JD, 1974. Bar: Utah 1974, U.S. Dist. Ct. Utah 1974, U.S. Ct. Appeals (10th cir.) 1977, Calif. 1979, U.S. Dist. Ct. (cen. dist.) Calif. 1979, U.S. Ct. Appeals (9th cir.) 1983, U.S. Dist. Ct. (ea., no., and so. dists.) Calif. 1994. Sole practice, Salt Lake City, 1974-79; ptnr. Costello & Walcher, L.A., 1979-85, Walcher & Scheuer, 1985-88, Ford & Harrison, 1988-91, Epstein Becker & Green, 1991—; judge pro tem Los Angeles Mcpl. Ct., 1986-91; dir. Citronia, Inc., Los Angeles, 1979-81. Trial counsel Utah chpt. Common Cause, Salt Lake City, 1978-79. Robert Mukai scholar U. Utah, 1971. Mem. Soc. Bar and Gavel (v.p. 1975-77), ABA, Fed. Bar Assn., Los Angeles County Bar Assn., Century City Bar Assn., Assn. Bus. Trial Lawyers, Phi Delta Phi, Owl and Key. Club: Woodland Hills Country (Los Angeles). Home: 17933 Sunburst St Northridge CA 91325-2848 Office: Epstein Becker & Green 1875 Century Park E Ste 500 Los Angeles CA 90067-2506

WALCOTT, CHARLES, neurobiology and behavior educator; b. Boston, July 19, 1934; s. Charles Folsom and Susan (Cabot) W.; m. Jane Clayton Taylor, Aug. 14, 1976; children: Thomas Stewart, Samuel Cabot. AB, Harvard U., 1956; PhD, Cornell U., 1959. Asst. prof. div. engring. and applied physics Harvard U., Cambridge, Mass., 1961-65; asst. prof. biology Tufts U., Medford, Mass., 1965-67; assoc. prof. dept. biology SUNY, Stony Brook, 1967-74, prof. dept. biology, 1974-81; prof., exec. dir. Cornell Lab. of Ornithology, Ithaca, N.Y., 1981-93, Louis Agassiz Fuertes dir., 1992-95; prof. neurobiology and behavior Cornell U., 1995—; cons., dir. Elem. Sci. Study, Watertown, Mass., 1961-67; dir. 3-2-1- Contact, Children's TV Workshop, N.Y.C., 1978—; dir. L.A. Fuertes. Contbr. many rsch. papers to sci. jours. Dir. sci. TV, Mass. Audubon, Lincoln, 1959-61. Avocations: gardening, sailing, photography. Home: 84 Besemer Hill Rd Ithaca NY 14850-9636 Office: Cornell U Sect Neurobiology Behavior W255 Seeley Mudd Hall Ithaca NY 14853

WALCOTT, DELORES DEBORAH, psychologist, educator. BA in Psychology, Chgo. State U., 1976, MS in Corrections, 1978; cert. group treatment with adolescents, Youth Guidance Tng. Inst., 1981; cert. law program for cmty. developers and social workers, John Marshall Law Sch., 1982; cert. MMPI-2 and MMPI-A clin. workshops, Western Mich. Psychol. Assn., 1992; PhD in Clin. Psychology, Ill. Sch. Profl. Psychology, Chgo., 1993. Cert. in sex edn.; cert. family life edn. tng.; licensed clin. psychologist, Ill., Mich. Psychologist, correction specialist, alcohol youth prevention specialist Bobby E. Wright Comprehension Inc., Chgo., 1978-84; child welfare worker Habilitative Sys., Inc., Chgo., 1984-85; program coord. Brass Found., Essence House, Chgo., 1985-86; social worker Kaleidoscope, Inc., Chgo., 1986-87; psychology extern, adult unit Ill. State Psychiat. Inst., Chgo., 1990-91; coord. family life edn. program Nia Comprehensive Ctr. for Developmental Disabilities, Inc., Chgo., 1987-92; clin. psychology intern Western Mich. U., Kalamazoo, 1992-93; clin. psychologist Onarga (Ill.) Acad.-Nexus Inc., 1993-95; asst. prof. Counseling Ctr. Western Mich. U., Kalamazoo, Mich., 1995—. Mem. APA, Am. Profl. Soc. Abuse of Children, Nat. Black Alcoholism Coun., Nat. Black Psychol. Assn., Western Mich. Psychol. Assn., Chem. People Task Force, Human Resource Devel. Inst. (Vol. award), Westside Youth Booster (bd. dirs. 1983-84), Alumni Assn. The Family Inst. Home: 8122 S Green St Chicago IL 60620-3143 Office: Western Mich U Counseling Ctr Kalamazoo MI 49008

WALCOTT, DEREK ALTON, poet, playwright; b. Castries, St. Lucia, Jan. 23, 1930; s. Warwick and Alix W.; m. Fay Moston, 1954 (div. 1959); 1 son; m. Margaret Ruth Maillard, 1962 (div.); 2 daus.; m. Norline Metivier (div.). BA, U. West Indies, Kingston, Jamaica, 1953, DLitt, 1972. Former tchr. St. Lucia, Grenada, Jamaica; poet-in-residence Hollins Coll., Roanoke, VA, 1980; prof. English Boston U.; founding dir. Trinidad Theatre Workshop, 1959—; lectr. Rutgers U., Yale U.; vis. prof. Columbia U., 1981, Harvard U., 1982, Boston U., 1985. Author: (poetry) Twenty-Five Poems, 1948, Epitath for the Young: A Poem in XII Cantos, 1949, Poems, 1953, In A Green Night: Poems, 1948-1960, 1962, Selected Poems, 1964, The Castaway and Other Poems, 1965 (Heinemann award Royal Soc. Lit. 1966), The Gulf and Other Poems, 1969 (Cholmondeley award 1969), Another Life, 1973 (Jock Campbell/New Statesman prize 1974), Sea Grapes, 1976, Selected Verse, 1976, The Star-Apple Kingdom, 1979, The Fortunate Traveller, 1981 (Heinemann award Royal Soc. Lit. 1983), Selected Poetry, 1981, Midsummer, 1984, Collected Poems, 1948-1984, 1986 (L.A. Times Book Rev. prize 1986), The Arkansas Testament, 1987, Omeros, 1990 (W.H. Smith Literary award 1991), Selected Poetry, 1993, Antiles: Fragments of Epic Memory, 1993; (plays) Henry Christophe: A Chronicle in Seven Scenes, 1950, Henry Dernier, 1951, Wine of the Country, 1953, The Sea at Dauphin: A Play in One Act, 1953, Ione: A Play with Music, 1957, Drums and Colours: An Epic Drama, 1958 (Jamaica Drama Festival prize 1958), Ti-Jean and His Brothers, 1958, Malcochon; or, Six in the Rain, 1959, Dream on Monkey Mountain, 1967 (Obie award 1971), In a Fine Castle, 1970, The Joker of Seville, 1974, The Charlatan, 1974, O Babylon!, 1976, Remembrance, 1977, Pantomime, 1978, The Isle Is Full of Noises, 1982, The Last Carnival, 1986, Beef, No Chicken, 1986, A Branch of the Blue Nile, 1986, The Odyssey, 1992. Recipient Guinness award, 1961, Nat. Writer's Coun. prize Welsh Arts Coun., 1979, Queen Elizabeth II Gold Medal for poetry, 1988, Nobel Prize for Lit., 1992; Rockefeller Found. fellow, 1957, 58; Eugene O'Neill Found.-Wesleyan U. fellow, 1969; MacArthur Found. grantee, 1981; decorated Order of the Hummingbird, Trinidad and Tobago, 1969. Founded Trinidad Theater workshop. Home: 71 Saint Marys St Boston MA 02215-2957 Office: 165 Duke of Edinburgh Ave, Diego Martin Trinidad and Tobago also: care Farrar Straus & Giroux 19 Union Sq W New York NY 10003-3304*

WALCOTT, DEXTER WINN, allergist; b. Greenville, Miss., Dec. 20, 1954; s. Charles DeWitt and Ruth LaFon (Stillions) W.; m. Virginia Shackelford, Sept. 20, 1980; children: Arrington, Winn. Grad. cum laude, U. Miss., 1977; postgrad., U. Miss. Sch. Medicine, 1978-82. Diplomate Am. Bd. Pediatrics, Am. Bd. Allergy and Immunology; lic. physician, Miss. Intern U. Miss. Med. Ctr., Jackson, 1982-83, resident in pediatrics, 1983-85; pvt. practice Oxford, Pa., 1985-91; with Miss. Asthma and Allergy Clinic, Jackson, 1993—; pres. house staff U. Med. Ctr., 1984-85, U. Med. Ctr. del. to Miss. State Med. Soc., 1985; ethics com. mem. North Miss. Retardation Ctr.; rev. physician Miss. Found. for Med. Care; participant vs. clinician program LeBonheur Children's Hosp.; mem. staff Miss. Bapt. Med. Ctr., Meth. Med. Ctr., River Oaks Hosp., St. Dominic's Med. Ctr., U. Med. Ctr. dept. pediatrics divsn. allergy/immunology; spkr. in field. Allergy/Immunology fellow La. State U. Med. Ctr., 1991-93. Fellow Am. Bd. Allergy and Immunology; mem. AMA, Am. Coll. Allergy/Immunology, Am. Acad. Allergy and Immunology, Am. Acad. Pediatrics, Miss. State Med. Assn., Miss. State Acad. Pediatrics, Ctrl. Miss. Med. Soc. (exec. com. mem. 1994—), Ctrl. Miss. Pediatric Soc. (pres. 1996), Alpha Epsilon Delta, Order of Omega, Eta Sigma Phi, Beta Beta Beta, Sigma Alpha Epsilon (pres. 1976-77). Office: Miss Asthma & Allergy Clin 940 N State St Jackson MS 39202-2646

WALCOTT, ROBERT, healthcare executive, priest; b. Boston, July 31, 1942; s. Robert and Rosamond (Pratt) W.; m. Diane Palmer, Sept. 1, 1966; 1 child, Sara. BA, Coll. of Wooster, 1964; MDiv, Ch. Div. Sch., Berkeley, Calif., 1967; M Healthcare Adminstrn., Ohio State U., 1972. Ordained Episc. priest, 1968. Planning specialist Health Planning and Devel. Coun., Wooster, Ohio, 1972-73, asst. dir., 1974-75; asst. dir. St. Joseph Hosp., Lorain, Ohio, 1975-78, assoc. dir., 1978-81; CEO, Lakeside Meml. Hosp., Brockport, N.Y., 1981-85; adminstr. Dent Neurologic Inst., Buffalo, 1986-87, Oak Hills Nursing Ctr., Lorain, 1994; pastor Ch. of Transfiguration, Buffalo, 1988-91, St. Michael and All Angels Ch., Uniontown, Ohio, 1991-93; adminstr.-in-tng. Chapel Hill Cmty., Canal Fulton, Ohio, 1993; interim adminstr. Regina Health Ctr., Richfield, Ohio, 1994-95; adminstr. Ohio Pythian Sisters Home, Sophia Huntington Parker Home, Medina, 1995—. Mem. long range planning com. Tremont Devel. Corp., Cleve., 1994—, bd. dirs.; mem. steering com. Habitat for Humanity, Cleve., 1994—. Fellow Am. Coll. Healthcare Execs.; mem. Am. Coll. Health Care Adminstrs. Democrat. Avocations: travel, reading. Home: 2672 W 14th St Cleveland OH 44113-5216 Office: Ohio Pythian Sisters Homes 550 Miner Dr Medina OH 44256-1472

WALD, BERNARD JOSEPH, lawyer; b. Bklyn., Sept. 14, 1932; s. Max and Ruth (Mencher) W.; m. Francine Joy Weintraub, Feb. 2, 1964; children—David Evan, Kevin Mitchell. B.B.A. magna cum laude, CCNY; J.D. cum laude, NYU, 1955. Bar: N.Y. 1955, U.S. Dist. Ct. (so. dist.) N.Y. 1960, U.S. Dist. Ct. (ea. dist.) N.Y. 1960, U.S. Ct. Appeals (2d cir.) 1960, U.S. Supreme Ct. 1971. Mem. Herzfeld & Rubin, P.C. and predecessor firms, N.Y.C., 1955—. Mem. ABA, N.Y. State Bar Assn., Assn. Bar City N.Y., N.Y. County Lawyers Assn. Office: Herzfeld & Rubin PC 40 Wall St Ste 5400 New York NY 10005-2301

WALD, DONNA GENE, advertising executive, media specialist; b. Peekskill, N.Y., July 24, 1947; d. David and Blossom (Karlin) W. BA, Rider Coll., 1969; MA, Hunter Coll., 1974. Broadcast traffic rep. SSC&B Inc., N.Y.C., 1969-74; broadcast buyer J. Walter Thompson, N.Y.C., 1974-78, regional broadcast supr., v.p., Dallas, 1978-81; v.p., regional broadcast supr., Los Angeles, 1981-85; prof. UCLA, 1984; sr. v.p., account dir. Western Internat. Media, Calif., 1985-95, exec. v.p., regional dir. account svcs., 1995—. Mem. Advt. Industry Emergency Fund, Hollywood Radio and TV Soc., Assn. Broadcast Execs. of Tex. (bd. dirs. 1979-80, sec. 1980-81). Home: 14844 Dickens St Apt 106 Sherman Oaks CA 91403 Office: Western Internat Media Corp 8544 W Sunset Blvd West Hollywood CA 90069-2310

WALD, FRANCINE JOY WEINTRAUB (MRS. BERNARD J. WALD), physicist, academic administrator; b. Bklyn., Jan. 13, 1938; d. Irving and Minnie (Reisig) Weintraub; student Bklyn. Coll., 1955-57; BEE, CCNY, 1960; MS, Poly. Inst. Bklyn., 1962, PhD, 1969; m. Bernard J. Wald, Feb. 2, 1964; children: David Evan, Kevin Mitchell. Engr., Remington Rand Univac div. Sperry Rand Corp., Phila., 1960; instr. Poly. Inst. Bklyn., 1962-64, adj. rsch. assoc., 1969-70; lectr. N.Y.C. C.C., Bklyn., 1969, 70; instr. sci. Friends Sem., N.Y.C., 1975-76, chmn. dept. sci., 1976-94; instr. sci., chmn. dept. sci. Nightingale-Bamford Sch., N.Y.C., 1994—; adj. asst. prof. NYU. NDEA fellow, 1962-64. Mem. Am. Phys. Soc., Am. Assn. Physics Tchrs., Assn. Tchrs. in Ind. Schs., N.Y. Acad. Scis., Nat. Sci. Tchrs. Assn., AAAS, Sigma Xi, Tau Beta Pi, Eta Kappa Nu.

WALD, MICHAEL LEONARD, economist; b. Balt., Jan. 5, 1951; s. Leonard Marvin and Frances (Kosinski) W.; m. Marlena Malmstedt, June 10, 1972. BA, Am. U., 1972. Mgr. Woodward and Lothrop Dept. Store, Washington, 1972-75, Hecht Co., Washington, 1975-76; store mgr. W.J. Sloane & Co., Washington, 1976-77; economist U.S. Bur. of Labor Stats., Balt., 1977-85, Washington, 1985-86; economist U.S. Bur. of Labor Stats., Atlanta, 1986-96, S.E. regional economist, 1996—; lectr. on fed. compensation issues; peer reviewer ACA Jour. Editl. bd. HR Atlanta, 1993-95; contbr. articles on compensation issues to profl. publs.; reviewer Monthly Labor Rev., 1992—; peer reviewer ACA Jour., 1995—. Bd. dirs. Athens (Ga.) Habitat for Humanity, 1990-93; venue mktg. liaison mgr. 1996 Centennial Olympic Games. Mem. Am. Compensation Assn. (cert. compensation profl.), Atlanta Compensation Assn. (v.p. 1992, 93, 94, pres. 1996), Am. Sociol. Assn. (co-chair software vendor fair 1996), Alpha Tau Omega. Avocations: reading, home improvement, travel, computers. Home: 5015 Fawn Valley Dr Loganville GA 30249 Office: US Bur Labor Stats 61 Forsyth St SW Ste 7t50 Atlanta GA 30303-8916

WALD, NIEL, medical educator; b. N.Y.C., Oct. 1, 1925; s. Albert and Rose (Fischel) W.; m. Lucienne Hill, May 24, 1953; children: David, Philip. A.B., Columbia U., 1945; M.D., NYU, 1948. Sr. hematologist Atomic Bomb Casualty Commn., Hiroshima, Japan, 1954-57; head biologist health physics div. Oak Ridge Nat. Lab., 1957-58; med. rsch. and teaching specializing in radiation medicine and cytogenetics Pitts., 1958—; mem. faculty U. Pitts. Grad. Sch. Pub. Health and Med. Sch., 1958—, prof. radiation health, 1962-91, prof. environ. and occupational health, 1991—, prof. radiology, 1965—; prof. human genetics U. Pitts., 1991—; chmn. dept. radiation health U. Pitts. Grad. Sch. Pub. Health and Med. Sch., 1969-76, 77-89, chmn. dept. occupational health, 1975-76, chmn. dept. indsl. environ. health scis., 1976-77; dir. radiation medicine dept. Presbyn.-Univ. Hosp., 1966—; med. dir. Clin. Cytogenetics Lab., U. Pitts., 1982—; cons. U.S. Nuclear Regulatory Commn. Office of Nuclear Materials Safety and Safeguards, mem. adv. panel for decontamination of Three Mile Island Nuclear Power Sta. Unit 2, 1981-93, cons. adv. com. on reactor safeguards, 1989-94; mem. U.S. working group on health effects, U.S.-USSR Joint Coordinating Com. for Civilian Nuclear Reactor Safety, 1989-92; cons. USN, nuclear industries and utilities; chmn. radiol. health study sect. USPHS, 1967-71; mem. Nat. Coun. Radiation Protection and Measurements, 1969-81, consociate mem., 1981—; mem. Gov. Pa. Adv. Com. Atomic Energy Devel. and Radiation Control, 1966-84, chmn., 1974-76; mem. Pa. Dept. Environ. Protection adv. com. on low level radioactive waste disposal, 1985—. Contbr. numerous articles to sci. and med. publs. Served to capt. M.C. USAF, 1952-54. Recipient Health Physics Faculty Rsch. award U.S. Dept. Energy, 1992-95. Mem. Health Physics Soc. (pres. 1973-74), Am. Pub. Health Assn. (governing council 1971-73, program devel. bd. 1973-74), Radiation Rsch. Soc. (assoc. editor jour. 1965-68), Soc. Nuclear Medicine (assoc. editor jour. 1959-69), Am. Soc. Human Genetics, Am. Coll. Occupational & Environ Medicine, AAAS, AMA, Internat. Soc. Hematology. Achievements include research in the diagnosis and treatment of accidental human radiation injury, in human radiation dosimetry by automatic image analysis of radiation-induced chromosome aberrations, and in the cytogenetics of murine radiation induced leukemia. Office: U Pitts Grad Sch Pub Health A-744 Crabtree Hall Pittsburgh PA 15261

WALD, PATRICIA MCGOWAN, federal judge; b. Torrington, Conn., Sept. 16, 1928; d. Joseph F. and Margaret (O'Keefe) McGowan; m. Robert L. Wald, June 22, 1952; children—Sarah, Douglas, Johanna, Frederica, Thomas. BA, Conn. Coll., 1948; LLB, Yale U., 1951; HHD (hon.), Mt. Vernon Jr. Coll., 1980; LLD (hon.), George Washington Law Sch., 1983, CUNY, 1984, Notre Dame U., John Jay Sch. Criminal Justice, Mt. Holyoke Coll., 1985, Georgetown U., 1987, Villanova U. Law Sch., Amherst Coll., N.Y. Law Sch., 1988, Colgate U., 1989, Hofstra Law Sch., 1991, New Eng. Coll., 1991, Hoffstra U., 1991, Vermont Law Sch., 1995. Bar: D.C. 1952. Clk. to judge Jerome Frank U.S. Ct. Appeals, 1951-52; asso. firm Arnold, Fortas & Porter, Washington, 1952-53; mem. D.C. Crime Commn., 1964-65; atty. Office of Criminal Justice, 1967-68, Neighborhood Legal Svc., Washington, 1968-70; co-dir. Ford Found. Project on Drug Abuse, 1970, Ctr. for Law and Social Policy, 1971-72, Mental Health Law Project, 1972-77; asst. atty. gen. for legis. affairs U.S. Dept. Justice, Washington, 1977-79; judge U.S. Ct. Appeals (D.C. cir.), 1979—, chief judge, 1986-91. Author: Law and Poverty, 1965; co-author: Bail in the United States, 1964, Dealing with Drug Abuse, 1973; contbr. articles on legal topics. Trustee Ford Found., 1972-77, Phillips Exeter Acad., 1975-77, Agnes Meyer Found., 1976-77, Conn. Coll., 1976-77; mem. Carnegie Council on Children, 1972-77. Mem. ABA (exec. bd. 1994—, bd. editors ABA Jour. 1978-86), Am. Law Inst. (coun. 1979—, exec. com. 1985—, 2d v.p. 1988-93, 1st v.p. 1993—), Inst. Medicine, Am. Acad. Arts and Scis., Phi Beta Kappa. Office: US Ct Appeals US Courthouse 3rd & Constitution Ave NW Washington DC 20001

WALD, RICHARD CHARLES, broadcasting executive; b. N.Y.C.; s. Joseph S. and Lily (Forstate) W.; m. Edith May Leslie; children: Matthew Leslie, Elizabeth Tole, Jonathan Simon. BA, Columbia U., MA; AB, Clare Coll., Cambridge. From reporter to mng. editor N.Y. Herald Tribune, 1955-66; asst. mng. editor Washington Post, 1967; exec. v.p. Whitney Communications Corp., N.Y.C., 1968; pres. NBC News, 1968-77; sr. v.p. ABC News, 1978; dir. Worldwide TV News; chmn. bd. Columbia Daily Spectator. Annotator: (with James Bellows) The World of Jimmy Breslin, 1967. Office: ABC News 47 W 66th St New York NY 10023-6201

WALD, SYLVIA, artist; b. Phila., Oct. 30, 1915. Ed., Moore Inst. Art, Sci. and Industry. One-woman shows include U. Louisville, 1945, 49, Kent State Coll., 1945, Nat. Serigraph Soc., 1946, Grand Central Moderns, N.Y.C., 1957, Devorah Sherman Gallery, Chgo., 1960, New Sch., 1967, Book Gallery, White Plains, N.Y., 1968, Benson Gallery, Bridgehampton, L.I., 1977, Knoll Internat., Munich, Germany, 1979, Amerika Havs, Munich, 1979, Aaron Berman Gallery, N.Y.C., 1981, Hirschtadler Gallery, 1994, New Britain (Conn.) Mus., 1994, Dongah Art Gallery, Seoul, Korea, 1995, Hanlim Art Gallery, Daejun, 1995-96, Kwanju City Art Mus, Pusanm Korea, Dong Shin U., Kwangju, 1996; group shows include Nat. Sculpture Soc., 1940, Sculpture Internat., Phila., 1940, Chgo. Art Inst., 1941, Bklyn. Mus., 1975, Library of Congress, 1943, 52, 58, Smithsonian Instn., 1954, Internat. Print Exhbn., Salzburg and Vienna, 1952, 2d Sao Paulo Biennial, 1953, N.Y. Cultural Center, 1973, Mus. Modern Art, N.Y.C., 1975, Benson Gallery, Bridgehampton, L.I., 1982, Dumon-Landis Gallery, New Brunswick, N.J., 1982-83, Suzuki Gallery, N.Y.C., 1982, Sid Deutch Gallery, N.Y.C., 1983, Aaron Berman Gallery, N.Y.C., 1983, Full House Gallery, Kingston, N.J., 1984, Worcester Mus., 1991, Boston Mus. Fine Arts, 1991, Hirschl & Adler Gallery, N.Y.C., 1993, others; represented in permanent collections Aetna Oil Co., Am. Assn. U. Women, Ball State Tchrs. Coll., Bibliotheque Nationale, Paris, Bklyn. Mus., Howard U., State U. Iowa, Library of Congress, U. Louisville, Nat. Gallery, Mus. Modern Art, Phila. Mus., N.C. Mus., Rose Mus. Art at Brandeis U., Whitney Mus., N.Y.C., Finch Coll. Mus., N.Y.C., U. Nebr., Ohio U., U. Okla., Princeton, Victoria and Albert Mus., Walker Gallery, Worcester (Mass.) Art Mus., Guggenheim

Mus., N.Y.C., Grunewald Mus., U.Calif. Los Angeles, Rutgers Mus., N.J., Aschenbach Collection Mus., San Francisco, Grunewald Coll. Mus. UCLA; Contbr. to profl. publs. Address: 417 Lafayette St New York NY 10003-7005

WALDBAUER, GILBERT PETER, entomologist, educator; b. Bridgeport, Conn., Apr. 18, 1928; s. George Henry and Hedwig Martha (Gribisch) W.; m. Stephanie Margot Stiefel, Jan. 2, 1955; children: Gwen Ruth, Susan Martha. Student, U. Conn., 1949-50; BS, U. Mass., 1953; MS, U. Ill., Urbana, 1956, PhD, 1960. Instr. entomology U. Ill., Urbana, 1958-60, asst. prof., 1960-65, assoc. prof., 1965-71, prof., 1971—, prof. agrl. entomology Coll. Agr., 1971—, prof. emeritus, 1995—; sr. scientist Ill. Natural History Survey; vis. scientist ICA, Palmira, Colombia, 1971; vis. sr. scientist Internat. Rice Rsch. Inst., 1978-79; cons. AID, 1985; vis. prof. U. Philippines, 1978-79. Author: Insects Through the Seasons, 1996; contbg. author: Insect and Mite Nutrition, 1972, Introduction to Insect Pest Management, 1975, Evolution of Insect Migration and Diapause, 1978, Sampling Methods in Soybean Entomology, 1980, Mimicry and the Evolutionary Process, 1988, Ann. Rev. Entomology, 1991; contbr. numerous articles to profl. jours. Served with AUS, 1946-47, PTO. Grantee Agrl. Rsch. Svc. USDA, 1966-71, 83-90, Nat. Geog. Soc., 1972-74, NSF, 1976-79, 82-90. Mem. AAAS, Entomol. Soc. Am., Entomol. Soc. Washington, Soc. for Study of Evolution, Mich. Entomol. Soc., Sigma Xi, Phi Kappa Phi. Home: 807A Ramblewood Ct Savoy IL 61874-9568 Office: U Ill Dept Entomology 320 Morrill Hall Urbana IL 61801

WALDBAUM, JANE COHN, art history educator; b. N.Y.C., Jan. 28, 1940; d. Max Arthur and Sarah (Waldstein) Cohn. BA, Brandeis U., 1962; MA, Harvard U., 1964, PhD, 1968. Rsch. fellow in classical archaeology Harvard U., Cambridge, Mass., 1968-70, 72-73; asst. prof. U. Wis.-Milw., 1973-78, assoc. prof., 1978-84, prof. art history, 1984—, chmn. dept., 1982-85, 86-89, 91-92; Dorot rsch. prof. W.F. Albright Inst. Archaeol. Rsch., Jerusalem, 1990-91. Author: From Bronze to Iron, 1978; Metalwork from Sardis, 1983; author (with others), co-editor Sardis Report I, 1975; mem. editorial bd. Bull. Am. Schs. Oriental Rsch., 1994—; contbr. numerous articles to profl. jours. Woodrow Wilson Found. fellow, dissertation fellow, 1962-63, 65-66, NEH post-doctoral rsch., Jerusalem, 1989-90; grantee Am. Philos. Soc., 1972, NEH, summer 1975, U. Wis.-Milw. Found., 1983. Mem. Am. Schs. Oriental Research, Soc. for Archaeol. Sci., Archaeol. Inst. Am. (exec. com. 1975-77, chmn. com. on membership programs 1977-81, nominating com. 1984, chmn. com. on lecture program 1985-87, acad. trustee 1993—, com. profl. responsibilities 1993—, fellowships com. 1993—, gold medal com. 1993—, mem. Ancient Near East com. 1993—, chair 1996-97), W.F. Albright Inst. Archaeol. Rsch. (trustee 1996—, mem. governance com. 1996—), Wis. Soc. Jewish Learning (trustee 1993—), Milw. Soc. Archaeol. Inst. (bd. dirs. 1973—, pres. 1983-85, 91-95), Phi Beta Kappa. Office: U Wis Dept Art History PO Box 413 Milwaukee WI 53201-0413

WALDECK, JOHN WALTER, JR., lawyer; b. Cleve., Sept. 10, 1949; s. John Walter Sr. and Marjorie Ruth (Palenschat) W.; m. Cheryl Gene Cutter, Sept. 10, 1977; children: John III, Matthew, Rebecca. BS, John Carroll U., 1973; JD, Cleve. State U., 1977. Bar: Ohio 1977. Product applications chemist Synthetic Products Co., Cleve., 1969-76; assoc. Arter & Hadden, Cleve., 1977-85, ptnr., 1986-88; ptnr. Porter, Wright, Morris and Arthur, Cleve., 1988-90, ptnr. in charge, 1990-96; ptnr. Walter & Haverfield, Cleve., 1996—. Chmn. Bainbridge Twp. Bd. Zoning Appeals, Chagrin Falls, Ohio, 1984-94; trustee Greater Cleve. chpt. Lupus Found. Am., 1978-91, sec., 1979-86; trustee LeBlond Housing Corp., Cleve., 1990-96, sec., 1996—, Univ. Circle, Inc., 1993-97, Fairmount Ctr. for Performing and Fine Arts, Novelty, Ohio, 1993—, sect., 1994-95; bd. dirs. Geauga County Mental Health Alcohol and Drug Addiction Svc. Bd., Chardon, Ohio, 1988—, treas., 1991-93, vice-chmn., 1993-95, chmn., 1995—; mem. bd. advisors Palliative Care Svcs., Cleve. Clinic Cancer Ctr., 1989-91. Mem. ABA (real property sect. bd. govs. 1992), Greater Cleve. Bar Assn. (real property, corp. banking sect, co-chair real estate law inst. 1990, 95, 96), The Union Club, Chagrin Valley Athletic Club. Democrat. Roman Catholic. Avocations: beekeeping, gardening, jogging. Home: 18814 Rivers Edge Dr W Chagrin Falls OH 44023-4968 Office: Walter & Haverfield 50 Public Square 1300 Terminal Tower Cleveland OH 44113

WALDEN, DANIEL, humanities and social sciences educator; b. Phila., Aug. 1, 1922; s. Benjamin and Reba (Freedman) Weinroth; m. Beatrice Schulman, Oct. 12, 1957; children: Moss Carl, Ruth E. Walden Turek. BA, CCNY, 1959; MA, Columbia U., 1961; PhD, NYU, 1964. Lectr. Queens Coll., N.Y.C., 1960-63; asst. prof. Mich. State U., East Lansing, 1963-66; prof. Pa. State U., University Park, 1966—. Co-editor: On Being Black, 1970, W.E.B. DuBois, The Crisis Writings, 1972, On Being Jewish, 1974, Twentieth Century American Jewish Fiction Writers, 1984, The World of Chaim Potok, 1985, The World of Cynthia Ozick, 1987, Bernard Malamud: in Memoriam, 1988, American Jewish Poets: The Roots and the Stems, 1990, Herbert Gold and Beyond, 1991, Jewish Identity: From Midrash to Modernity, 1991, American Jewish Women Writers, 1992, The Changing Mosaic: Cahan to Malamud and Ozick, 1993, New Voices in an Old Tradition, 1994, Bernard Malamud's Literary Imagination: A New Look, 1995, The Tragedy of Joy, 1996. Mem. ALA, MLA (MELUS pres. 1977-78, Disting. MELUS award 1993), N.E. MLA (pres. 1991-92), Soc. Am. Jewish Lit. (pres. 1991-92, Disting. Svc. award 1992), Am. Studies Assn., Am. Culture Assn., Soc. for Utopian Studies. Democrat. Jewish. Avocations: reading, music, photography. Office: Dept English/Am Studies Pa State U University Park PA 16802

WALDEN, JAMES WILLIAM, accountant, educator; b. Jellico, Tenn., Mar. 5, 1936; s. William Evert and Bertha L. (Faulkner) W.; m. Eva June Selvia, Jan. 16, 1957 (dec. Aug. 1988); 1 child, James William; m. Hattie Nan Lamb, Jan. 6, 1990 (div. June 1992); m. Janet Faulkner, Aug. 12, 1993. BS, Miami U., Oxford, Ohio, 1963; MBA, Xavier U., Cin., 1966. CPA, Ohio. Tchr. math. Middletown (Ohio) City Sch. Dist., 1963-67, Fairfield (Ohio) High Sch., 1967-69; instr. accounting Sinclair Community Coll., Dayton, Ohio, 1969-72, asst. prof., 1972-75, assoc. prof., 1975-78, prof., 1978-89, prof. emeritus, 1991—; cons., public acct. Group comdr., fin. officer Ohio Wing, CAP. Served with USAF, 1954-59. Mem. Butler County Torch Club, Pub. Accts. Soc. Ohio (pres. S.W. chpt. 1985-86), Inst. Mgmt. Accts., Nat. Soc. Pub. Accts., Greater Hamilton Estate Planning Coun., Ohio Soc. CPAs, Beta Alpha Psi. Home: PO Box 469 Springboro OH 45066-0469 Office: Sinclair C C 444 W 3rd St Dayton OH 45402-1421

WALDEN, LINDA LEE, lawyer; b. Dallas, Aug. 16, 1951; d. Leslie LaFayette Jr. and Neva Irene (McBee) W.; m. David Lee Finney, June 9, 1984. BA, Tex. Women's U., 1972; JD, St. Mary's U., 1975. Bar: Tex., 1975, U.S. Supreme Ct., 1979, U.S. Tax Ct., 1988. Asst. city atty. City of Amarillo, Tex., 1976-77; asst. dist. atty. 84th Jud. Dist., Borger, Tex., 1977-79; asst. atty. gen. Office Atty. Gen. Tex., Austin, 1979-84; litigation atty. Friedman & Ginsberg, Dallas, 1984-86, Bradford & Snyder, Dallas, 1986-88; corp. counsel Occidental Chem. Co., Dallas, 1988-96. Home: 2209 Greenview Dr Carrollton TX 75010-4110 Office: Occidental Chem Corp 5005 Lyndon B Johnson Fwy Dallas TX 75244-6100

WALDEN, PHILIP MICHAEL, recording company executive, publishing company executive; b. Greenville, S.C., Jan. 11, 1940; s. Clemiel Barton and Carolyn Hayes (McClendon) W.; m. Peggy Hackett, Sept. 13, 1969; children: Philip Michael, Amantha Starr. A.B. in Econs., Mercer U., 1962. Pres. Phil Walden & Assocs., 1961, Capricorn Records, Inc., 1969—. Campaign chmn. Macon Muscular Dystrophy Assn., 1975; chmn. Macon Heritage Found.; mem. In-Town Macon Neighborhood Assn.; Mem. nat. finance com. Jimmy Carter for Pres.; mem. Com. for Preservation of the White House; mem. nat. adv. bd. NORML; bd. dirs. Brandywine Conservancy; mem. Presdl. Inaugural Com., 1977; trustee Ga. Trust for Historic Preservation.; founder Otis Redding Scholarship Fund, Mercer U., Phil Walden scholarship. Served to 1st lt. Adj. Gen. Corps AUS, 1963-65. Recipient Gold and Platinum Record awards, pub. awards; Big Bear award Mercer U., 1975; Martin Luther King, Jr. Humanitarian award, 1977; Human Relations award Am. Jewish Com., 1978. Mem. Common Cause, Middle Ga. Hist. Soc., Nat. Assn. Rec. Arts and Scis., Rec. Industry Assn. Am. (dir.), Nat. Assn. Rec. Merchandisers, Phi Delta Theta Alumni Assn. Home: 2740 Habersham Rd Atlanta GA 30303

WALDEN, ROBERT THOMAS, physicist educator, consultant; b. Paducah, Ky., Mar. 25, 1939; s. Charles Robert and Anna Catherine (Robertson) W.; m. Nellie Sue Clayton, June 9, 1962; children: Clayton Thomas, Alan Keith. BS, Murray State U., 1961, MS, 1968; PhD, Miss. State U., 1973. Tchr. math. Dongola (Ill.) High Sch., 1962-63; instr. physics Paducah C.C., 1963-68; asst. prof. Ky. Wesleyan Coll., Owensboro, 1968-70; chair sci. Miss. Gulf Coast C.C., Perkinston, 1973-87; staff scientist Nat. Ctr. Phys. Acoustics, U. Miss., University, 1987-91; prof. physics Mid-Continent Coll., Mayfield, Ky., 1991-96, dean gen. edn., 1995-96; cons. Walden Assocs., Paducah, 1990—; vis. prof. U. Miss., University, 1986-87; cons. Paducah Gaseous Diffusion Plant, 1992—; organizer, chair 1st nat. symposium on agroacoustics; organizer, chair Miss. Alliance Sci. Advancement. Contbr. articles to Jour. Molecular Spectroscopy, Jour. Miss. Acad. Sci. Dir., founder Stone County Jr. Basketball League, Wiggins, Miss., 1979-82; vice-chmn. Stone Coutny Hosp. Bd., Wiggins, 1983-85. Mem. Acoustical Soc. Am., Rotary (Rotarian of Yr. Wiggins unit 1981), Sigma Pi Sigma, Phi Kappa Phi. Baptist. Achievements include initiation of acoustic remote sensing of bark beetles. Home: 420 Hutchinson Ave Paducah KY 42003-5726 Office: Walden Assocs 453 Hutchinson Ave Paducah KY 42003-5725

WALDEN, STANLEY EUGENE, composer, clarinetist; b. Bklyn., 1932. BA in Music with honors, Queens Coll.; studied composition with Ben Weber, clarinet with David Weber. Faculty C.W. Post Coll.; guest lectr. U. Wis., Yale Drama Sch.; mem. dance faculty (music) Juilliard Sch., N.Y.C., 1965-71; faculty Sarah Lawrence Coll., 1973-75, SUNY, Purchase, 1973-78; prof., chmn. musical/show dept. H.D.K. Berlin, 1990. Guest composer: So. Meth. U., 1984, Eastman Sch., 1985; pianist for Martha Graham, Anna Sokolow; music dir. Tamaris-Nagrin Dance Co., Horseman, Pass By, 1967, Am. Dance Festival, 1984; solo clarinetist Contemporary Chamber Ensemble, Bennington Composers Conf., Penn Contemporary Players; guest artist N.Y. Woodwind Quintet.; commns. include Dance Sonata for Daniel Nagrin, Stretti for Group for Contemporary Music Columbia, Image for Harkness Ballet, (with Anna Sokolow) Manhattan Festival Ballet, Invisible Cities for Phila. Orch., 1985, 3 Ladies for Jan De Gaetani and Gilbert Kalish, Songs and Dances for Joel Krosnick and Gilbert Kalish, 1986; composer incidental music Off-Broadway prodn. Scuba Duba, 1967; mem. Open Theater (The Serpent, Mutation Show) 1968-72; music for Pinkville, Am. Place Theater, 1970, The Kid, 1972, Sigmunds Freude, Bremen Stadt Theater, 1975, Weewis for Joffrey Ballet, 1971; film The Crazy American Girl, Paris, 1975, Desperado City, 1980 (winner Camera d'Or at Cannes 1981), Frohes Fest (winner 1st Prize Mannheim Festival), The Open Window Trio; solo recitals, albums for Vanguard, Three Views; commd. and recorded (as mem.) Louisville Orch., 1969; music and lyrics Oh! Calcutta!, 1969; new score The Caucasian Chalk Circle, Arena Theater, Washington, 1978, musical Back Country, 1978, Shylock, 1978, My Mother's Courage, 1979, Untergang der Titanic, 1980, Hamlet, 1980; dir. We Each Got a Reason for Being Here Tonight, Vienna Festival, 1981, Der Voyeur; actor Berlin Festival, 1982, Jubiläum for Bochum Schauspielhaus, 1983, opera Doctor Faustus Lights the Lights (G. Stein), Cologne Schauspielhaus, 1983, Peepshow (G. Tabori), Bochum, 1984, The Beggars Opera, Renaissance Theater, Berlin, 1984, Claire, Bochum, 1985, U Ber Die Städte, Burg Theater, Vienna, 1986, Mein Kampf (G. Tabori) Burg Theater, 1987; co-dir. Der Tod Dankt Ab, 1987, Sigmunds Freude, 1987; Pour La Seconde Fois (J.C. Carrière) actor/composer-Der Kreis, Vienna, 1988; musical Bahn Frei! for Hochschule der Künste, Berlin, 1989, Lear's Schatten, Bregenz Festival, 1989, Othello-Burg Theater, 1990, Miami Lights-Coconut Grove Playhouse, 1990, Faust-Bad Hersfeld Festspiele, 1990, Endangered Species, 1990, BAM Nextwave Fest, Babylon Blues, 1991, Goldberg Variationen at Burg Theater, Vienna, 1991, Miami Lights at Theater Works, Palo Alto, Calif., 1991, Kasimir and Karoline, Schloss Park Theater, Berlin, 1991, Abendwind and Mrozek, Schlosspark Theater, Berlin, 1992, Der Grossinquisitor (Tabori), Seville, 1992, Munich Residenz Theater, Potsdam; condr. Cividale Mittelfest, 1992, Pottsdam, 1993, Requiem Fur Einen Spion (Tabori) Burg Theatre, 1993, Memini Mortuarum, Eastman and Potsdam, 1993, Brandenburg Philharmonic, 1993, Die 25te Stunde (Tabori), Burg Theater, 1994; recitals with Hanna Schygulla, Hebbel Theater, Berlin, 1994., Delirium (Enzensberger) Thalia Theatre, Hamburg, 1994, Die Massenmörderin (Tabori) Akademie Theater, Vienna, 1995, Ballade von Wiener Schnitzel (Tabori), 1996, Liebster Vater, Chamber Opera after Kafka, Stadttheatre, Bremen, Berliner Kammeroper, 1997, Nat. Theater, Weimar, 1997; author: (with Barbara Walden) Life Upon the Wicked Stage, 1997. Address: 60 Miller Hill Rd Hopewell Junction NY 12533-6829

WALDERA, WAYNE EUGENE, crisis management specialist; b. Cayuga, N.D., Mar. 23, 1930; s. Bernard Cyril and Eleanor Nee (Kugler) W.; m. Eva Jenzene Personius, Jan. 13, 1958; children: Anthony, Lori, Mia, Shauna. BSBA, N.D. State U., 1952. With Gamble-Skogmo, 1954-88; pres. Gamble div. Gamble-Skogmo, Mpls., 1972-88; pres., CEO Retail Resource Co., Mpls., 1988-89; pres., CEO Amdura Corp., Denver, 1989-92, also bd. dirs.; chmn. Sullivan Waldera, Inc., Mpls., 1992-93; prin., CEO Waldera & Co. Inc., Mpls., 1993—. 1st lt. USAF, 1952-54. Home: 12125 62nd St Waconia MN 55387-9411 Office: Waldera & Co Inc 15500 Wayzata Blvd Ste 604-208 Wayzata MN 55391-1438

WALDFOGEL, MORTON SUMNER, prefabricated housing/plywood company executive; b. Somerville, Mass., Nov. 5, 1922; s. Benjamin and Gertrude (Levins) W.; m. Lillian Thelma Gouse, June 16, 1949; children: Peter Douglas, Jane Leslie. AB, Harvard U., 1944; MBA, Boston U., 1948. Assoc. prof. math. econs. Boston U., 1947-48; mgr. Roddis Plywood Co., Cambridge, Mass., 1948-51; partner East Coast Mill Sales, 1951—; chmn. bd., chief exec. officer Allied Industries Inc., Charlestown, Mass., 1954-89; chmn., chief exec. officer Gilwal Industries, Charlestown, Mass., 1982—; pres. United Internat. Inc., Boston, 1990—. Served with USNR, 1942-47. Decorated Letter of Commendation. Jewish. Home: 16 Brown Rd Swampscott MA 01907-1608 Office: Gilwal Industries PO Box 580 Charlestown MA 02129-0001

WALDHAUSEN, JOHN ANTON, surgeon, editor; b. N.Y.C., May 22, 1929; s. Max. H. and Agnes H. (Stettner) W.; m. Marian Trescher, June 4, 1957; children: John H., Robert Rodney, Anthony Gordon Scarlett. B.S. magna cum laude, Coll. Great Falls, 1950; M.D., St. Louis U., 1954. Diplomate Am. Bd. Surgery (bd. dirs. 1985-88), Am. Bd. Thoracic Surgery (bd. dirs. 1989-95). Intern Johns Hopkins Hosp., 1954-55, resident, 1955-57; clin. asst. Nat. Heart and Lung Inst., NIH, 1957-59; resident Hosp. U. Pa., 1959, Ind. U. Med. Center, 1960-62; practice medicine specializing in cardiothoracic surgery Indpls., 1962-66, Phila., 1966-70; mem. staff Milton S. Hershey (Pa.) Med. Ctr., 1969-96; from instr. to asst. prof. Ind. U. Med. Ctr., 1962-66; assoc. prof. surgery U. Pa., Phila., 1966-70; prof. surgery Pa. State U. Coll. Medicine/Milton S. Hershey Med. Ctr., Hershey, 1966-83, 94—, J.W. Oswald prof., 1983-94, assoc. dean and dir. Univ. Physicians, 1993-96, sr. mem. grad. faculty, 1970-94, chmn. dept. surgery, 1969-94, vice chmn. med. policy bd., 1971-72, interim provost, dean, 1972-73, assoc. dean health care, 1973-75. Mem. editl. bd. Jour. Cardiovascular Surgery, 1985-93, Jour. Pediatric Surgery, 1972-78, Jour. Thoracic and Cardiovascular Surgery, 1982, editor, 1994—; cons. editor Archives of Surgery, 1972-74; contbr. chpts. to books and articles to med. jours. Served with USPHS, 1957-59. Recipient Career Devel. award USPHS, 1964. Mem. AMA, AAAS, ACS (chpt. pres. 1974-75, gov. 1979-85, chmn. adv. coun. Conn. surgery 1992—), Am. Acad. Pediatrics, Am. Assn. Surgery of Trauma, Am. Coll. Cardiology (sec. 1981-82, trustee 1984-89, mem. editorial bd. jour. 1983, assoc. editor 1986-89), Am. Fedn. Clin. Rsch., Am. Heart Assn., Am. Physiol. Soc., Am. Soc. Artificial Internal Organs, Am. Assn. Thoracic Surgery (1st v.p. 1990-91, pres., 1991-92), Am. Surg. Assn. (1st v.p. 1984-85), Central Surg. Assn., Internat. Cardiovascular Soc. (chpt. recorder 1969-74), Pa. Assn. Thoracic Surgery (pres. 1977-78), Thoracic Surgery Dirs. Assn. (pres. 1977-79), Societe Internationale de Chirurgie (membership chmn. 1987-92, treas. 1992-94), Soc. Clin. Surgery (treas. 1971-80, v.p. 1981-82, Pres. 1982-83), Soc. Surg. Chairmen, Soc. Thoracic Surgeons, Soc. Univ. Surgeons, Soc. Vascular Surgery, So. Surg. Assn., Sigma Xi, Alpha Omega Alpha. Home: RR 1 Box 158G Annville PA 17003-9704 Office: Pa State U Coll Med MS Hershey Med Ctr PO Box 850 Hershey PA 17033-0850

WALDINGER SEFF, MARGARET, special elementary education educator; b. N.Y.C., June 12, 1949; d. Herbert Francis Waldinger and Michelle (Rubin) Cohen; children: Dylan Paul Seff, Cortney Sara Seff, Blake Adam Seff. BA, Hofstra U., 1971; postgrad., NYU, 1971-73; MA, Fairleigh Dickinson U., 1986. Cert. elem. sch. tchr., tchr. of handicapped, learning disability tchr. cons., N.J. Tchr. pub. schs., N.J., N.Y., 1984-88; learning specialist Manchester (Vt.) Elem. Sch., 1988—; adv., ednl. therapist, N.J., 1983-88.. Reading grantee Tuxedo Park Sch., 1986, Bennington Rutland Supervisory Union, 1992. Avocations: sports, reading, home restorations. Home: RR 1 Box 2291 Manchester Center VT 05255-9738 Office: Manchester Elem Sch Memorial Dr Manchester Center VT 05255

WALDMAN, ALAN I. (ALAWANA), songwriter, composer, lyricist, computer programmer; b. Elkins Park, Pa., Jan. 20, 1955; s. Harry and Anna Waldman. Student, U. Okla., 1973-76, U. Oreg., 1978, 79; BS in Econs., U. Wis., 1979; MS in Stats., U. Iowa, 1985. Performing songwriter, composer, lyricist Deerfield Beach, Fla., 1986—; ind. computer programmer; cons. Internet and World Wide Web. Author: Poetic Universe Collection, How to Form Your Own Publishing Entity and Operating it Thereafter; lyricist, composer (song collections) Hit The Market, Down to Home, Sphere of Influence, Next Galaxy, Quality Rainbow, Predicaments of Life, Great Guidelines for Living, Collection of Alawana, Vol. I, 1993, The Artist Dimension Song Collection, Vols. II, III, Artsist Dimension Collection. Charter mem. Rep. Presdl. Task Force, Washington, 1984-92. Mem. U. Iowa Alumni Assn. Republican. Avocations: listening to music, computer trade mags., internat, walking, travel. Home: PO Box 4581 Deerfield Beach FL 33442-4581

WALDMAN, ANNE LESLEY, poet, performer, editor, publisher, educational administrator; b. Millville, N.J., Apr. 2, 1945; d. John Marvin and Frances (Le Fevre) W.; m. Reed Eyre Bye; 1 son, Ambrose. B.A., Bennington Coll., 1966. Dir. The Poetry Project, St. Marks Ch. In-the-Bowery, N.Y.C., 1968-78; dir. Jack Kerouac Sch. of Disembodied Poetics at Naropa Inst., Boulder, Colo., 1974—; adj. faculty Inst. Am. Indian Arts, Santa Fe; bd. dirs. Com. for Internat. Poetry, Eye and Ear Theatre, N.Y.C.; poet-in-residence with Bob Dylan's Rolling Thunder Rev. Author: (poetry) On the Wing, 1968, O My Life, 1969, Baby Breakdown, 1970, Giant Night, 1970, No Hassles, 1971, Life Notes, 1973, Fast Speaking Woman, 1975, Journals and Dreams, 1976, Shaman, 1977, Countries, 1980, Cabin, 1981, First Baby Poems, 1982, Makeup on Empty Space, 1983, Invention, 1986, Skin Meat Bones, 1986, The Romance Thing, 1987, Blue Mosque, 1988, Helping the Dreamer: New and Selected Poems, 1989, Not a Male Pseudonym, 1990, Lokapala, 1991, Troubairitz, 1993, Iovis: All is Full of Jove, 1993, Kill or Cure, 1994, Iovis II, 1997; editor: Nice To See You: Homage to Ted Berrigan, 1991, The Beat Book, 1996, (anthologies) The World Anthology, 1969, Another World, 1972, Talking Poetics From Naropa Institute vol. 1, 1978, vol. 2, 1979, Out of This World, 1991, (with Andrew Schelling) Disembodied Poetics: Annals of the Jack Kerovac School, 1994; translator (with Andrew Schelling) Sons & Daughters of the Buddha, 1996; publisher: anthologies Angel Hair Books, N.Y.C., Full Ct. Press, N.Y.C.; recordings: The Dial-a-Poem Poets Disconnected, Anne Waldman/John Giorno, Fast Speaking Woman, The Nova Convention, Big Ego, Uh-oh Plutonium!, 1982, Crack in My World, 1986, Assorted Singles, 1990; performance videos include Eyes in All Heads, 1990, Live at Naropa, 1991, Battle of the Bards, 1991; featured on nat. pub. radio show All Things Considered, also featured in the poetry documentary Poetry In Motion. Dir. summer writing program Naropa; organizer Surrealist, Objectivist, Feminist, Pan Am. Ecology, Performance Confs., and The Robert Creeley Symposium. Recipient Dylan Thomas Meml. award New Sch., N.Y.C., 1967, Blue Ribbon Am. Film Festival, Nat. Literary Anthology award, 1970; named Heavyweight Champion Poet, 1989, 90; Cultural Artists Program grantee, 1976-77; NEA grantee, 1979-80; recipient Shelley Meml. award, 1996. Mem. PEN Club, Amnesty Internat. Office: care Naropa Inst 2130 Arapahoe Ave Boulder CO 80302-6602

WALDMAN, BART, lawyer; b. Stamford, Conn., Oct. 24, 1948; s. Murry Robert and Beatrice Carol (Goldstein) W.; m. Nancy Vivian Smith, Jan. 1, 1981; children: Marcy Nicole, Tracy Michelle. AB, Harvard U., 1970; JD, Georgetown U., 1978. Bar: Wash. 1978. Spl. asst. to pres. Assn. of Am. Med. Colls., Washington, 1971-78; ptnr. Perkins Coie, Seattle, 1978—. Trustee Mcpl. League of King County, 1995—; sec. Puget Sound Sr. Baseball League, 1996—. Mem. ABA, Wash. Bar Assn., Seattle-King County Bar Assn., Sports Lawyers Assn. Office: Perkins Coie 1201 3rd Ave Fl 40 Seattle WA 98101-3099

WALDMAN, JAY CARL, judge; b. Pitts., Nov. 16, 1944; s. Milton and Dorothy (Florence) W.; m. Roberta Tex Landy, Aug. 28, 1969. B.S., U. Wis., 1966; J.D., U. Pa., 1969. Bar: Pa. 1970, D.C. 1976, U.S. Supreme Ct. 1976. Assoc., Rose, Schmidt, Dixon & Hasley, Pitts., 1970-71; asst. U.S. atty. western dist. Pa., Pitts., 1971-75; dep. asst. U.S. Atty. Gen., Washington, 1975-77; counsel Gov. of Pa., Harrisburg, 1978-86; sr. ptnr., Dilworth, Paxson, Kalish & Kauffman, Phila., 1986-88; judge U.S. Dist. Ct. (ea. dist.) Pa., 1988—. Dir. Thornburgh for Gov. campaign., Pa., 1977-78; commr. Pa. Convention Ctr. Authority, 1986-88. Fellow Am. Bar Found.; mem. ABA, Fed. Bar Assn., Union League Phila. Republican. Office: US Dist Ct Pa 9613 US Courthouse 601 Market St Philadelphia PA 19106-1713

WALDMAN, PAUL, artist; b. Erie, Pa., 1936. Student, Bklyn. Mus. Art Sch., 1955, Pratt Inst., 1956. vis. artist Ohio State U., 1966; artists-in-residence, The Clamworks Studio Workshop, N.Y., 1982. One man shows include Allan Stone Gallery, N.Y., 1963, 65, Albright Gallery of Art, Hax Art Ctr., St. Joseph, Mo., 1966, Leo Castelli Gallery, N.Y.C., 1973, 75, 78, 81, 84, 88, 91, 95, Blum-Helman Gallery, N.Y.C., 1978, Kunsthalle Tranegarden, Copenhagen, 1981, Norblyllands Kunstmuseum, Aalborg, Denmark, 1981, Castelli Graphics, N.Y.C., 1984, Fariden Cadot Gallery, Paris, 1987, 88, 91, Phyllis Kind Gallery, Chgo., 1988, Leo Castelli Gallery, N.Y.C., 1991; exhibited in group shows include Allan Stone Gallery, 1961, Louis Alexander Gallery, N.Y.C., 1962, Gallery of Modern Art, Washingotn, 1963, 64, Wadworth Atheneum, Hartford, Conn., 1964, Rutgers U., New Brunswick, N.J., 1964, Knoedler Gallery, 1965, Art Mus., U. of Ind., Bloomington, 1965, Richard Feigen Gallery, Chgo., 1965, Ark. Arts Ctr., Little Rock, 1966, Ithaca Coll. Mus. Art, N.Y., 1967, Smithsonian Inst., 1967-68, Kansas City Art Inst., Mo., 1967, Newark Mus., 1968, Leo Castelli Gallery, 1973, 75, 78, 81, 84, 88, Castelli Graphics, 1976, 82, 84, Phila. Coll. Art., 1976, Guggenheim Mus., 1977, 79, 84, La Jolla Mus. Art, 1982, Jan van Eyck Acad., Maastricht, Germany, 1985, Cooper-Hewitt Mus., N.Y.C., 1987, Williams Coll. Mus. Art, 1990, Thread Waxing Space, 1993, Lennon Weinberg, N.Y.C., 1993; represented in permanent collections Mus. Modern Art, Newark Mus., Bklyn. Mus., L.A. County Mus. Art, NYU, Hirshhorn Mus. and Sculpture Garden, Smithsonian Inst., Des Moines Mus., Guggenheim Mus., Mus. Fine Arts, Houston, Balt. Mus. Art, Carnegie Mus., Dallas Mus. Fine Arts, DeCordova Mus., Norbyllands Kunstmuseum, Aalborg, Denmark, Denver Art Mus., Allen Meml. Art Mus., Oberlin Coll., Dartmouth Coll., Solomon R. Guggenheim Mus., Russell Sage Collection, Storm King Art Ctr., Rose Art Mus., Brandeis U., Smithsonian Inst., Palace Legion Honor Achenbach Found., MIT, L.A. County Mus. Art, U. Mass., Fairleigh Dickinson U., others. Grantee Ford Found., 1965.

WALDMANN, ROBERT, hematologist; b. Budapest, Hungary, Aug. 17, 1935; s. Gyula and Elizabeth (Vajda) W.; m. Denise Bartz, Dec. 24, 1960; 1 child, Rodena. BS, St. Louis Coll. Pharmacy, 1958; DO, Kansas City Coll. Osteo., 1967. Diplomate Am. Bd. Internal Medicine, Am. Bd. Hematology. From resident internal medicine to staff hematologist Henry Ford Hosp., Detroit, 1971-82; staff Sinai Hosp., Detroit, 1982—; staff Harper Hosp., Detroit, 1986—; staff St. Joseph Mercy Hosp., Detroit, 1982—, chmn. dept. medicine, 1990-92. Bd. dirs. Children's Leukemia Found., Detroit, 1983-86. Mem. AMA, Am. Soc. Hematology, Am. Soc. Clin. Oncology, Am. Osteopathic Assn., Mich. Med. Assn., Mich. Assn. Osteopathic Physicians. Democrat. Jewish. Avocations: travel, sports. Home: 1288 W Long Lake Rd Bloomfield Hills MI 48302-1332 Office: 43555 Dalcoma Dr Clinton Township MI 48038-6310

WALDMANN, THOMAS ALEXANDER, medical research scientist, physician; b. N.Y.C., Sept. 21, 1930; s. Charles Elizabeth (Sipos) W.; m. Katharine Emory Spreng, Mar. 29, 1958; children—Richard Allen, Robert James, Carol Ann. A.B., U. Chgo., 1951; M.D., Harvard U., 1955; PhD (hon.), U. Med. Sch., Debrecin, Hungary, 1991. Diplomate Am. Bd. Allergy and Immunology. Intern Mass. Gen. Hosp., Boston, 1955-56; clin. assoc. Nat. Cancer Inst. NIH, Bethesda, Md., 1956-58, sr. investigator, 1958-68, head immunophysiology sect., 1968-73, chief metabolism br., 1971—; cons. WHO, 1975, 78; bd. dirs., v.p. Found. for Advanced Edn. in Scis., Bethesda, 1980—, treas., 1988-90, v.p., 1990-92; William Dameshek vis. prof. U. Calif.,

Irvine, 1984; mem. med. adv. bd. Howard Hughes Med. Inst., 1987-93; vis. com. mem. Harvard Med. Sch., Boston, 1988-94; mem. sci. adv. com., chmn. Mass. Gen. Hosp., 1992-96; cons. HealthCare Investment Corp., Edison, N.J., 1986—. Author: Plasma Protein Metabolism, 1970; contbr. over 570 articles to profl. jours. With USPHS, 1956-58, 59-63, 75-94. Recipient Henry M. Stratton medal Am. Hemotology Soc., 1977; named Man of Yr. Am. Leukemia Soc., 1980; recipient G. Burroughs Mider award NIH, 1980; Disting. Service medal Dept. Health and Human Services, 1983. Fellow Am. Acad. Allergy (Bela Schick award 1974, John M. Shelton award 1984, Lila Gruber prize 1986, Simon Shubitz prize 1987, CIBA-GEIGY Drew award 1987, Milken Family Med. Found. Disting. Basic Scientist prize, Artois Latour Internat. Rsch. prize 1991, Bristol-Myers Cancer prize 1992); mem. NAS (chmn. 1985—), Am. Acad. Arts and Scis., Inst. Medicine, Nat. Acad. Scis., Assn. Am. Physicians, Am. Soc. Clin. Investigation (mem. editorial bd. 1978-80, 83-88), Clin. Immunology Soc. (pres. 1988). Achievements include the defining of structure of multisubunit IL-2 receptor; identifying novel cytokine IL-15; introduction of different forms of IL-2R-directed therapy using alpha- and beta-emitting radionuclide chelate versions of humanized monoclonal antibodies for treatment of cancer; introduction of analysis of immunoglobulin gene rearrangements to define clonality and classifying human lymphoid neoplasia; discovered intestinal lymphagectasia and allergic gastroenteropathy. Office: Nat Inst Health 9000 Rockville Pike Bethesda MD 20814-1436

WALDMEIR, PETER NIELSEN, journalist; b. Detroit, Jan. 16, 1931; s. Joseph John and Helen Sarah (Nielsen) W.; m. Marilyn C. Choma; children—Peter William, Patti Ann, Lindsey Marilyn, Christopher Norman. Student, Wayne State U., 1949-58. With Detroit News, 1949—, sports columnist, 1962-72, gen. columnist, 1972—. Trustee, Cleary Coll., Ypsilanti, Mich., 1985—; pres. Old Newsboys Goodfellow Fund, Detroit, 1988; chmn. bd. dirs. Doorstep Homeless Shelters, Detroit, 1996—. Served with USMC, 1951-53. Recipient Headliners award Nat. Headliners Club, 1971; named Mich. Sports Writer of Yr., Nat. Sportscasters and Sportswriters, 1967, 69, 71; Heart award Variety Club Internat., 1985. Mem. Sigma Delta Chi. Roman Catholic. Office: Detroit News 615 W Lafayette Blvd Detroit MI 48226-3124

WALDO, BURTON CORLETT, lawyer; b. Seattle, Aug. 11, 1920; s. William Earl and Ruth Ernestine (Corlett) W.; m. Margaret Jane Hoar, Aug. 24, 1946; children: James Chandler, Bruce Corlett. BA, U. Wash., 1941, JD, 1948. Bar: Wash. 1949. Assoc. Vedova, Horswill & Yeomans, Seattle, 1949-50, Kahin, Carmody & Horswill, Seattle, 1950-54; ptnr. Keller Rohrback & predecessor firms, Seattle, 1954-86; mng. ptnr. Keller Rohrback & predecessor firms, 1978-83, sr. ptnr., 1983-86, of counsel, 1986—. Mem. Seattle Bd. Theater Suprs., 1958-61, Mcpl. League of Seattle/King County, 1965—. Capt. U.S. Army, 1942-46, ETO. Mem. ABA, Am. Judicature Soc., Internat. Assn. Def. Counsel, Fedn. Ins. and Corp. Counsel, Wash. Bar Assn., Wash. Def. Trial Lawyers Assn., Seattle-King County Bar Assn. (trustee 1965-68), Fedn. Fly Fishers (life), S.R., Puget Sound Civil War Roundtable, Rainier Club, Wash. Athletic Club, The Steamboaters, Flyfishers Club Oreg., Hope Island King-50 Club, Delta Tau Delta, Phi Delta Phi, Alpha Kappa Psi. Avocation: fly fishing.

WALDO, (CLIFFORD) DWIGHT, political science educator; b. DeWitt, Nebr., Sept. 28, 1913; s. Cliff Ford and Grace Gertrude (Lindley) W.; m. Gwendolyn Payne, Sept. 17, 1937; children: Mary Grace, Martha Gwen, Margret Ann. B.A., Nebr. State Tchrs. Coll., Peru, 1935; M.A., U. Nebr., 1937; Ph.D., Yale U., 1942. Instr. polit. sci. Yale U., 1941-42; price analyst OPA, 1942-44; adminstrv. analyst Exec. Office Pres., 1944-46; mem. faculty U. Calif. at Berkeley, 1946-67, prof. polit. sci., 1953-67, dir. Inst. Govt. Studies, 1958-67; Albert Schweitzer prof. humanities Syracuse U., 1967-79, emeritus prof., 1979—; Carl Hatch prof. law and pub. adminstrn. U. N.Mex., 1984-85; vis. disting. prof. Fla. Internat. U., 1989; resident fellow Woodrow Wilson Internat. Center for Scholars, Smithsonian Instn., Washington, 1979-81. Author: The Administrative State, 1948, The Study of Public Administration, 1955, Perspectives on Administration, 1956, Political Science in the U.S.A, 1956; Editor: Public Administration in a Time of Turbulence, 1972, others; editor-in-chief: Pub. Adminstrn. Rev, 1966-77. Mem. Am. Polit. Sci. Assn. (v.p. 1961-62), Am. Soc. Pub. Adminstrn. (v.p. 1985-86), Internat. City Mgmt. Assn. (hon. life), Nat. Assn. Schs. Pub. Affairs and Adminstrn. (v.p. 1976-77, pres. 1977-78), Nat. Acad. Pub. Adminstrn. Home: Apt 1411W 3713 S George Mason Dr Falls Church VA 22041-3738

WALDO, JAMES CHANDLER, lawyer; b. Seattle, Oct. 23, 1948; s. Burton Chandler and Margaret (Hoar) W.; m. Sharon B. Barber; children: Sara K., William K., John J. Grad., Whitman Coll., 1970; JD, Willamette U., 1974. Bar: Wash. 1974, U.S. Ct. Appeals (9th cir.) 1976. Exec. asst. Dept. of Labor, Washington, 1974-76; asst. U.S. atty. Justice Dept., Seattle, 1976-79; of counsel ESTEP & LI, Seattle, 1979-80; ptnr. Gordon, Thomas, Honeywell, Malanca, Peterson & Daheim, P.L.L.C., Seattle, 1981—; chmn. N.W. Renewable Resources Ctr., Seattle, 1984—, Wash. State Energy Strategy Com., Olympia, 1991-93; mem. Wash. Dept. Natural Resources Aquatic Lands Program Adv. Com., 1994, U. Wash. Tacoma Br Environ. Mgr. Program Adv. Bd., 1994. Trustee Western Wash. U., Bellingham, 1981-93. Recipient Outstanding Alumnus of Yr. Whitman Coll., 1994, Dir.'s award Wash. Dept. Fisheries, 1986, Pres.'s award Assn. Wash. Bus., 1988, Outstanding Citizen award Western Assn. Fish & Wildlife Agys., 1987. Republican. Office: Gordon Thomas Honeywell Malanca Peterson & Daheim 1201 Pacific Ave Tacoma WA 98402-4301 Address: PO Box 1157 Tacoma WA 98401-1157

WALDO, ROBERT LELAND, retired insurance company executive; b. Pittsville, Wis., Sept. 1, 1923; s. Elmer Harley and Edith Viola (Senter) W.; m. Elaine Anne Jossie, June 4, 1947; children: Daniel Robert, Thomas Parker, Susan Jeanne. BA, U. Wis., 1949, JD, 1951. Assoc. atty. Foley & Lardner, Milw., 1951-59; asst. sec., asst. gen. counsel Wis. Gas Co., Milw., 1959-69; v.p., gen. counsel Verex Corp. and Subss., Madison, Wis., 1969-72; exec. v.p., sec. Verex Corp. and subs., Madison, Wis., 1972-78, pres., chief operating officer, 1978-82, pres., chief exec. officer, 1982-85, chmn., chief exec. officer, 1985-86. Served as sgt. U.S. Army, 1943-46, ETO. Mem. Wis. Bar Assn., Dane County Bar Assn., Mortgage Ins. Co.'s Am. (pres. 1980-82), Maple Bluff Country Club. Republican. Methodist. Avocations: travel, golf. Home: 818 Charing Cross Rd Madison WI 53704-6010

WALDON, ALTON RONALD, JR., state senator; b. Lakeland, Fla., Dec. 21, 1936; s. Alton Ronald and Rupert Juanita (Wallace) W.; m. Barbara De Costa, June 6, 1961; children: Alton III, Dana Olive, Ian Patrick. BS, John Jay Coll., 1968; JD, N.Y. Law Sch., 1973. Capt. N.Y.C. Housing Authority Police Dept., 1962-75; dep. commr. N.Y. State Divsn. Human Rights, 1975-82; assemblyman N.Y. State Assembly, 1983-86; congressman U.S. Ho. Reps., Washington, 1986-87; commr. N.Y.C. Investigation Commn., 1987-90; senator N.Y. State, 1991—; bd. dirs. USO Met. N.Y. Recipient Thurgood Marshall fellow, N.Y. State Trial Lawyers Assn., 1970-73. Mem. Met. Block Bar Assn., Macon B. Allen Bar Assn. Democrat. Roman Catholic. Avocation: sports.

WALDRON, ELLIS LEIGH, retired political science educator; b. Denver, Feb. 21, 1915; s. Grover C. and Maud M. (Dolbeer) W.; m. Phyllis Schwoegler, May 16, 1941; 1 child, Jean Madelene. BA, Ohio State U., 1936; MA, U. Wis., 1939, PhD, 1952; student, Duke, 1939-40. Staff polit. corr. U.P., Columbus, Ohio, 1941-44; instr. polit. sci. extension div. U. Wis., 1946-49, fellow polit. sci., 1949-50; faculty dept. polit. sci. U. Mont., 1950—, prof. polit. sci., 1957—; dean U. Mont. (Grad. Sch.), 1957-61, emeritus, 1980—; fellow law and polit. sci. Harvard Law Sch., 1963-64. Author: Montana Legislators 1864-1979: Profiles and Biographical Directory, Mont. Politics Since 1864, An Atlas of Elections, 1958; (with Paul B. Wilson) Atlas of Montana Elections 1889-1976, 1978, Social and Economic Dimensions of Popular Vote on 110 State Ballot Issues in Montana, 1926-86, 1990-91. Mem. Mont. Constl. Conv. Commn., 1971-72. Served with AUS, 1944-46. Mem. Am. Polit. Sci. Assn. (coun. 1969-71), Phi Beta Kappa, Kappa Sigma, Phi Kappa Phi. Home: 53 Oak Creek Trl Madison WI 53717-1509

WALDRON, KENNETH JOHN, mechanical engineering educator, researcher; b. Sydney, NSW, Australia, Feb. 11, 1943; came to U.S., 1965; s. Edward Walter and Maurine Florence (Barrett) W.; m. Manjula Bhushan, July 3, 1968; children: Andrew, Lalitha, Paul. BEngring., U. Sydney, 1964, M Engring. Sci., 1965; PhD, Stanford U., 1969. Registered profl. engr., Tex. Acting asst. prof. Stanford (Calif.) U., 1968-69; lectr., sr. lectr. U. NSW, Sydney, 1969-74; asst. prof. U. Houston, 1974-79; assoc. prof. mech. engring. Ohio State U., Columbus, 1979-81, prof., 1981—, Nordholt prof., 1984—, chmn. dept. mech. engring., 1993—. Co-author: Machines That Walk, 1988; editor: Advanced Robotics, 1989; contbr. over 215 articles to profl. jours. and conf. procs. Recipient Robotics Industries Assn. Engelberger award, 1997. Fellow ASME (tech. editor Trans. Jour. Mech. Design 1988-92, Leonardo da Vinci award 1988, Mechanisms award 1990, Machine Design award 1994); mem. Soc. Automotive Engrs. (Ralph R. Teetor award 1977), Am. Soc. for Engring. Edn. Achievements include work on adaptive suspension vehicle project. Office: Ohio State U 206 W 18th Ave Columbus OH 43210-1189

WALDRON, ROBERT LEROY, II, physician; b. Carbondale, Ill., Feb. 6, 1936; s. Robert Leroy and Violet Mae (Thompson) W.; m. Sandra Sellers; children: Richard, Robert Leroy III, Ryan, Burton Johnson. AB, Princeton U., 1958; MD, Harvard U., 1962. Diplomate Am. Bd. Radiology; cert. added qualifications in neuroradiology. Intern, Mass. Gen. Hosp., Boston, 1962-63; resident in radiology Columbia-Presbyn. Med. Center, N.Y.C., 1965-68; instr. radiology Coll. Physicians and Surgeons, Columbia U. and spl. fellow in neuroradiology Neurol. Inst., N.Y.C., 1968-69; clin. asst. in radiology Harvard Med. Sch., asst. radiologist Mt. Auburn Hosp. and MIT, Cambridge, 1969-71; assoc. prof. clin. radiology Coll. Physicians and Surgeons, 1971-73; dir. radiology French Hosp. and French Med. Clinic, San Luis Obispo, 1973-80, v.p., dir., 1976-77; assoc. clin. prof. radiology Loma Linda U. Sch. Medicine, 1977-80; dir. radiology Richland Meml. Hosp., Columbia, S.C., 1980-90; chief radiology svcs. Richland Meml. Hosp., 1982-90, trustee, 1990—; prof. radiology U. S.C. Sch. Medicine, Columbia, 1985—; mng. ptnr. Richland Radiol. Assn., Columbia, 1988-90; founder Chilean N.Am. Hosp. Corp., 1989; pres. MedBill, 1984-95; Bd. dirs. Am. Cancer Soc., San Luis Obispo. With USPHS, 1963-65. Recipient grants James Picker Found., Am. Cancer Soc., NRC, Nat. Acad. Scis., Nat. Cancer Inst. Fellow Am. Coll. Radiology, Soc. Internat. Med. Sci. Cooperation; mem. AMA, Am. Roentgen Ray Soc., Radiol. Soc. N.Am., Am. Soc. Neuroradiology, Western Neuroradiol. Soc., Southeastern Neuroradiol. Soc., S.C. Med. Assn., San Luis Obispo County Med. Soc. (pres. 1979), Columbia Med. Soc., Sierra-Cascade Trauma Soc. (pres. 1983-84), S.C. Radiol. Soc. (pres. 1992-93). Republican. Methodist. Clubs: Ivy of Princeton; Wildewood, Capital City (Columbia). Contbr. articles to profl. jours. Home: 1420 Adger Rd Columbia SC 29205-1406 Office: 1814 Bull St Columbia SC 29201-2506

WALDROP, BERNARD KEITH, English educator; b. Emporia, Kans., Dec. 11, 1932; s. Arthur and Opal Irene (Mohler) W.; m. Rosmarie Sebald, Jan. 22, 1959. B.A., Kans. State Tchrs. Coll., Emporia, 1955; M.A., U. Mich., Ann Arbor, 1958, Ph.D., 1964. Mem. faculty Brown U., Providence, 1968, prof. English, 1980—; editor Burning Deck Press, Providence, 1961—. Author: (poems) A Windmill Near Calvary, 1968, The Garden of Effort, 1977, The Ruins of Providence, 1984, A Ceremony Somewhere Else, 1984, Selected Poems, 1990, Shipwreck in Haven, 1992, The Locality Principle, 1995; (prose) Hegel's Family, 1989, Light While There is Light, 1993. Served with U.S. Army, 1953-55. Mem. PEN Am. Ctr. Home: 71 Elmgrove Ave Providence RI 02906-4132 Office: Brown U English Dept 79 Waterman St Providence RI 02912-9079

WALDROP, FRANCIS NEIL, physician; b. Asheville, N.C., Oct. 5, 1926; s. Troy Lester and Emma Louise (Ballard) W.; m. Eleanor Dorothy Wickes, June 10, 1950; children—Mark Lester, Barbara Louise. A.B., U. Minn., 1946; M.D., George Washington U., 1950. Intern George Washington U. Hosp., Washington, 1950-51; resident St. Elizabeth's Hosp., Washington, 1951-54; med. officer St. Elizabeth's Hosp., 1951-71; dir. manpower and tng. programs NIMH, Rockville, Md., 1972-75; dep. adminstr. Alcohol, Drug Abuse and Mental Health Adminstrn., HEW, Rockville, 1975-79; ret., 1979; clin. prof. psychiatry George Washington U. Recipient Superior Service award HEW, 1962, Disting. Service award, 1964. Fellow Am. Psychiat. Assn. (Vestermark award 1980). Research, publs. in field. Home: 1775 Elton Rd Silver Spring MD 20903-1726

WALDROP, GIDEON WILLIAM, composer, conductor, former president music school; b. Haskell County, Tex., Sept. 2, 1919; s. Gideon William and Margaret (Pierson) W. MusB, Baylor U., 1940; Mus M, U. Rochester, 1941, PhD, 1952. Asso. prof. music Baylor U., Waco, Tex., 1946-51; condr. Waco-Baylor Symphony Orch., 1946-51; editor Rev. Recorded Music, N.Y.C., 1952-54, Musical Courier, N.Y.C., 1953-58; cons. div. arts and humanities Ford Found., N.Y.C., 1958-61; asst. to pres. Juilliard Sch. Music, N.Y.C., 1961-63, dean, 1963-86, acting pres., 1983-84; pres. Manhattan Sch. Music, N.Y.C., 1986-89; mem. adv. com. Toscanini Archives; cons. to Minister Edn., Israel, summers 1972-74, Portugal, summer 1979, Fundacion Isaac Albeniz, Madrid, Spain, 1989—. Condr. Shreveport Symphony, 1941-42; composer (symphony overture) Prelude and Fugue for Orchestra, chamber music, choral works and songs.; commd. by, San Antonio Symphony Soc., 1958, 63. Served to maj. USAAF, 1942-46, ETO. Decorated Bronze Star. Mem. ASCAP, Phi Beta Kappa, Phi Mu Alpha. Democrat. Clubs: Players, Bohemians, N.Y. Athletic, Century (N.Y.C.).

WALDROP, LINDA MCGILL, medical administrator; b. Jefferson County, Ala., Oct. 24, 1942; d. Luther Grady Jr. and Anna Katherine (Gray) McGill; m. Bennie Lee Waldrop Jr., Mar. 14, 1961; children: Tracy L., Terry L. AS, Jefferson State Jr. Coll., 1971; BSN, Samford U., 1985; MA, U. Ala., Birmingham, 1989. Head nurse open heart ICU Bapt. Med. Ctr.-Montclair, Birmingham, 1976-82, head nurse telemetry unit, 1985-87, head nurse med. unit, 1983-85, head nurse oncology unit, 1987-90, edn. coord.; internal auditor Bapt. Med. Ctr.-Montclair, 1991; dir. med.-surg. telemetry nursing Shelby Med. Ctr. (now Shelby Bapt. Med. Ctr.), Alabaster, Ala., 1991-96, dir. gastroenterol. svcs., 1993-95, nursing internal auditor, 1993—, dir. women's svcs., 1994-95, dir. edn., 1996—. Mem. ANA (cert. nursing adminstrn.), AACN, Oncology Nursing Soc., Nat. Mgmt. Assn., Ala. Orgn. Nurse Execs., Birmingham Regional Orgn. Nurse Execs.

WALDROP, MARY LOUISE, nursing educator; b. Spartanburg, S.C., Feb. 7, 1947; d. Clarence Daniel and Esther Lorena Waldrop. BSN, U. S.C., 1975; MSN, Med. Coll. Ga., 1978; ABD, U. Ga., 1984. Lic. perinatal nurse, women's health nurse practitioner; cert. ACLS, advance practice, Ga. Bd. Nursing, pediat. advanced life support. Staff nurse labor and delivery Greenville (S.C.) Hosp. Sys., 1968-70; head nurse CCU/ICU St. Francis Comty. Hosp., Greenville, 1970-73; team coord. adolescent psychology Marshall I. Pickens Psych./Mental Health, Greenville, 1973-74; DON, patient care coord. Piedmont Health Care Corp., Greenville, 1975-76; teaching assoc. ADN program U. S.C., Spartanburg, 1976-77; instr. maternal child nursing Clemson (S.C.) U., 1978-84; asst. prof. Med. Coll. Ga., Augusta, 1985-86; nurse practitioner prem. prev. project Med. Coll. Ga./Ga. Human Resource, Augusta, 1986-87; joint appt. asst. prof., clinician Incarnate World Coll./Santa Rosa Med. Ctr., San Antonio, 1987-88; mem. faculty obstets. Bapt. Hosp. Sch. Nursing, San Antonio, 1988-90; mem. faculty pediatrics St. Phillips Coll., San Antonio, 1990-91; asst. dir. nursing, program dir. Howard Coll., Del Rio, Tex., 1992-93; asst. prof. Valdosta (Ga.) State U., 1992—; coord. 3d Ann. Women's Health Seminar, 1985; prodr. workshop continuing edn. dept. Clemson U., Greenville; adv. bd. Head Start, Valdosta, 1994; adv. com. Nursing Ctr., Valdosta State U., 1994. Co-author: (videotape) Complemental Nursing Care, 1975; group author: (newspaper column) Pregnancy & Nutritive During Holidays, 1984. Vol. Greenville chpt. ARC, 1981—. Recipient Nat. Disting. Svc. award Libr. of Congress, 1988; univ. rsch. grantee, 1984. Mem. ANA (item writer cert. exam 1987), AAUP, S.C. Nurses Assn. (mem. coun. on edn. 1982-84), S.C. Perinatal Assn. (program com. 1928-84), Ga. Nurses Assn. (1st v.p. 1993—, exec. bd. 1995—), Tex. Nurses Assn. (program com. 1991-92). Avocations: gardening, music, small animals. Home: 113 Runnymeade Ln Spartanburg SC 29301-2621 Office: Valdosta State U Coll of Nursing Brookwood Hall Valdosta GA 31601

WALDSTEIN, SHELDON SAUL, physician, educator; b. Chgo., June 23, 1924; s. Herman S. and Sophia (Klapper) W.; m. Jacqueline Sheila Denbo, Apr. 2, 1952; children: Sara Jean, Peter Denbo, David John. Student, Harvard U., 1941-43; M.D., Northwestern U., 1947. Diplomate: Am. Bd. Internal Medicine. Intern Cook County Hosp., 1947-48, resident in internal medicine, 1948-51; chief Northwestern Med. Service, 1954-62, exec. dir. dept. medicine, 1962-64, chmn. dept. medicine, 1964-69; exec. dir. North Suburban Assn. Health Resources, 1969-72; mem. faculty Northwestern U. Med. Sch., 1954-61, assoc. prof. medicine, 1961-66, prof. medicine, 1966—, assoc. dean health services, dir. Northwestern U. Med. Assos., 1974-77; exec. v.p. Nat. Ctr. for Advanced Med. Edn., Chgo., 1977-91; pres. Nat. Ctr. Advanced Med. Edn., Chgo., 1961-96. Contbr. articles to med. jours. Trustee Nat. Ctr. Advanced Med. Edn., Chgo., 1961-96. Served to capt. M.C., AUS, 1952-54. Fellow Am. Coll. Physicians, Am. Coll. Endocrinology; mem. AMA, Chgo. Med. Soc., Cen. Soc. Clin. Rsch., Endocrine Soc., Am. Assn. Clin. Endocrinology, Am. Fedn. Med. Rsch., Chgo. Soc. Internal Medicine, Alpha Omega Alpha. Home: 601 Mulberry Pl Highland Park IL 60035-3670 Office: 541 N Fairbanks Ct Chicago IL 60611-3319

WALEN, HARRY LEONARD, historian, lecturer, author; b. Winchester, Mass., June 26, 1915; s. Harry Leonard and Alice (Garland) W.; m. Elizabeth Rowe Benson, June 26, 1939; children: Harry Benson, Kimball Frederick, Robert Leonard. AB cum laude, Harvard U., 1937, AM, 1942. Tchr. Los Alamos (N.M.) Ranch Sch., 1937-42, head English dept., 1939-42; tchr. English Groton (Mass.) Sch., 1942-46; instr. English, faculty marshal Newton Jr. Coll., 1946-51; tchr. English and journalism Newton High Sch., Newtonville, Mass., 1946-51, adminstr., 1951-55; directing editor secondary sch. English textbooks Ginn and Co., Boston, 1955-61; prin. Needham (Mass.) High Sch., 1961-72, career and post secondary guidance counselor, 1972-79; Mem. Regional Interviewing Com. for Overseas Grants and Fellowships, 1961-84; mem. planning com. Task Force on High Sch. Graduation Requirements, Mass Dept. Edn., 1976-80. Author: (books) The Family Travel-Camper, 1955, (with E. Gordon and others) Types of Literature, American Literature, English Literature, 1964, The Memory Book of the New England Association of Teachers of English, 1981, The Sons of the American Revolution 1962-82: An Historical Anthology, 1984; (monographs) English Learning Environments, 1972, History of the Order of Founders and Patriots of America, 1982, Centennial History, 1996; co-author Alluring Rockport, rev. edit. 1986, (poetry) The Little Old Meeting House and How It Grew, Images and Perceptions, 1996; editor The English Leaflet, 1947-54; cons. editor on career edn. New Voices Series, 1978; contbr. chpts., articles, poems to books, profl. jours. and periodicals. Alderman City of Newton, Mass., 1961-72; corp. mem. USS Mass. Meml. Com., Inc., 1972—, bd. dirs., 1984-91, honorary dir., 1995—; chmn. edn. com. N.E. Conf. NCCJ, 1972-82, mem. study mission to Israel, 1974; vice chmn. New Eng. Conf. on Quality of Life, Boston, 1973; mem. Newton Regional Adv. Manpower Planning Bd., 1973-77; pres. counseling svcs. YMCA, Greater Boston, 1976-7; chmn. Newton Highlands Bd. Christian Edn., 1974-75; pres. bd. trustees weekday ch. sch. 1st Congl. Ch., Rockport, Mass., ch. historian, 1982—; del. Mass. Conf. United Ch. Christ, 1989-96. John Hay fellow, 1965, Mass. Dept. Edn. Commonwealth fellow, 1971; recipient citation U.S. Commr. Edn., 1971, citation New Eng. Assn. Schs. and Colls., 1984, cert. of Appreciation, City of Newton, 1971, Service award, YMCA, 1978. Mem. Nat. Council Tchrs. English (assoc. chmn. nat. conv. 1965, chmn., co-founder Emeritus Assembly 1979-83, various other coms. and offices, Citation 1969), Nat. Assn. Secondary Sch. Prins., Headmasters Assn. (life), New Eng. Assn. Tchrs. English (life, past pres., chmn. ann. C. S. Thomas award com. 1975-96, historian 1978—, Thomas award 1978), Mass. Secondary Sch. Prins. Assn. (diploma standards com. 1973-78, Bronze plaque 1974), Mass. Council Tchrs. English (co-founder), Mass. Schoolmasters Club (past pres., hon. life), Mensa, Friends of Jackson Homestead, Newton Hist. Soc. (life, past pres.), Los Alamos (N.Mex.) Hist. Soc. (life), Sandy Bay Hist. Soc. (pres. 1983-86), Essex County Geneal. Soc., Greater Boston Guidance Club (hon.), Nat. Gavel Soc., New Eng. Hist. and Geneal. Soc., SAR (pres. state 1979-81, nat. trustee 1981-83, historian gen. 1983-86, sec. Mus. Bd. 1982-88, Minuteman award 1985), Gen. Soc. Mayflower Descs. (mem. nat. exec. com. 1990-93), Mass. Soc. Mayflower Descs. (gov. 1985-88, dep. gov. gen. 1988-93), Pilgrim John Howland Soc. (pres. 1987—, led pilgrimage to Eng., 1989), Mass. Huguenot Soc. (pres. 1990-92, nat. del. 1983-92), Descs. Colonial Clergy, Soc. Colonial Wars, Navy League U.S. (life), Sons and Daus. of 1st Settlers of Newbury (pres. 1982-84), Piscataqua Pioneers (pres. 1990-91), Order of Crown of Charlemagne, Order Founders and Patriots (nat. treas. 1978-81, dep. gov. gen. 1981-84, exec. com. 1992—, councillor gen. Mass. 1984—, N.H., 1987-90, 93—, gov. 1992-95, councillor gen. 1993—, Nat. Disting. Svc. award 1996), Boston Athenaeum, Harvard Club, Boston Authors Club (pres. 1995-96), English Lunch Club (pres. 1975-82), Friday Evening Club (most venerable 1979-86), Sandy Bay Yacht Club, Masons (32d degree, 50-Yr. award). Home: Penzance Rd Rockport MA 01966

WALEN, JAMES ROBERT, engineering specialist; b. N.Y.C., Nov. 23, 1947; s. John Nicholas and Carol Susan (Rannbury) W.; m. Lisa L. Burdick, Sept. 27, 1993; children from previous marriage: Heather Renee, Aaron James. Grad., Citrus Coll., 1966, Orange Coast Coll., 1970. Assoc. engr. Hughes Aircraft Co., Irvine, Calif., 1966-78; ptnr., chief engr. D&L Engring., Irvine, 1978-80; design supr. Interconics, Irvine, 1980-85; engring. specialist Packard-Hughes Interconnect, Irvine, 1985—; instr. Inst. for Interconnecting & Pkg. Electronic Circuits, 1979, 82. Inventor, patentee in field. Mem. Rep. Nat. Com., 1981—, Nat. Rep. Congl. Com., 1988—, Ronald Reagan Presdl. Found., 1989—; vol. Friendship Home of Laguna Beach, Calif., 1992—. With U.S. Army, 1968. Mem. San Onofre Surfing Club (bd. dirs. 1985-88). Avocation: surfing, watercolor painting, crafts, hiking, sailing. Office: Packard-Hughes Interconnect 17150 Von Karman Ave Irvine CA 92614-0901

WALENGA, JEANINE MARIE, medical educator, researcher; b. Evergreen Park, Ill., Nov. 21, 1955; d. Eugene Adam and Therese Marie (Podsiadlik) W. BS, U. Ill., Chgo., 1978; Diplome d'Etudes Approfondies, U. Paris VI, 1984, PhD, 1987; postgrad., Loyola U., Maywood, Ill., 1981-84. Cert. med. technologist. Med. technologist MacNeal Hosp., Berwyn, Ill., 1978-79; rsch. asst. Loyola U. Med. Ctr., Maywood, 1979-80, hemostasis rsch. lab. supr., 1980-87, co-dir. hemostasis rsch. lab., 1987—, asst. prof. thoracic/cardiovascular surgery/pathology, 1988-94, assoc. prof., 1994—; mem. Cardiovascular Inst., Loyola U., 1995—; cons. in field; lectr. in field; observer Nat. Com. for Clin. Lab. Stds., 1988—; del. US Pharmacopeia, 1990—. Contbr. articles to profl. jours. Named Alumnus of Yr., U. Ill., 1990; NHLBI rsch. grantee, 1989—; recipient Investigator Recognition award, 1993. Fellow Am. Coll. Angiology; mem. Internat. Inst. for Thrombotic Diseases (sec. 1989—), Am. Assn. Pathologists, Am. Soc. Hematology, Internat. Soc. Thrombosis and Hemostasis (sci. and standardization subcom. on heparin 1990-93), Am. Soc. Clin. Pathologists, Am. Heart Assn., Am. Soc. Med. Tech. Avocations: photography, archeology, gardening, birding, travel.

WALENTIK, CORINNE ANNE, pediatrician; b. Rockville Centre, N.Y., Nov. 24, 1949; d. Edward Robert and Evelyn Mary (Brinskele) Finno; m. David Stephen Walentik, June 24, 1972; children: Anne, Stephen, Kristine. AB with honors, St. Louis U., 1970, MD, 1974, MPH, 1992. Diplomate Am. Bd. Pediatrics, Am. Bd. Neonatal and Perinatal Medicine. Resident in pediatrics St. Louis U. Group Hosps., 1974-76, fellow in neonatalogy, 1976-78; neonatalogist St. Mary's Health Ctr., St. Louis, 1978-79; co-dir. neonatal unit St. Louis City Hosps., 1979-83, dir. neonatal unit, 1983-85; dir. neonatalogy St. Louis Regional Med. Ctr., 1985-96; asst. prof. pediatrics St. Louis U., 1980-94, assoc. clin. prof., 1994—; supr. nursery follow up program Cardinal Glennon Children's Hosp., St. Louis, 1979—, neonatologist, physician exec. for managed care and pub. policy, 1997—. Contbr. articles to profl. jours. Mem. adv. com. Mo. Perinatal Program., 1983-86. Fellow Am. Acad. Pediats.; mem. APHA, Mo. Pub. Health Assn. (pres. St. Louis chpt. 1995-96), Mo. Perinatal Assn. (pres. 1983), Nat. Perinatal Assn. (coun. 1984-87), Mo. State Med. Assn., St. Louis Met. Med. Soc. Roman Catholic. Avocations: bridge, baseball, sports. Home: 7234 Princeton Ave Saint Louis MO 63130-3027 Office: Cardinal Glennan Children's Hosp 1465 S Grand Ave Saint Louis MO 63104

WALES, GWYNNE HUNTINGTON, lawyer; b. Evanston, Ill., Apr. 18, 1933; s. Robert Willett and Solace (Huntington) W.; m. Janet McCobb, Feb. 8, 1957; children—Thomas Gwynne, Catherine Anne, Louise Carrie. A.B., Princeton U., 1954; J.D., Harvard U., 1961. Bar: N.Y. 1962. Asso. White & Case, N.Y.C., 1961-69; partner White & Case, 1969—; resident partner White & Case, Brussels, 1969-75. Served with USN, 1954-58. Mem. ABA, N.Y. State Bar Assn., Am. Law Inst., Union Internat. des Avocats. Club: Round Hill (Greenwich, Conn.). Home: 185 W Old Mill Rd Greenwich CT 06831 Office: White & Case 1155 Ave Of The Americas New York NY 10036-2711

WALES, PATRICE, school system administrator; b. Washington, Sept. 9, 1935; d. Robert Corning and Bernadette Mary (Dyer) W. BA, Dunbarton Coll. of Holy Cross, 1957; MTS, Cath. U. Am., 1978; PhD, U. Md., 1993. Cert. tchr., supt., Md. Tchr. mid. sch. St. Marys, Laurel, Md., 1960-61; tchr. high sch. St. Vincent Pallotti High Sch., Laurel, Md., 1962-65; instr. nursing sch. St. Mary's Sch. Nursing, Huntington, W.Va., 1965-66; tchr. St. Vincent Pallotti High Sch., Laurel, 1967-76, adminstr., 1976—, chair sci. dept., 1962-80, dean students, 1976-87, sponsorship dir., 1988—; bd. dirs. St. Vincent Pallotti H.S., Laurel, 1988—; trustee St. Joseph's Hosp., Buckhannon, W.Va., 1990—; dir. German Exch. Program, Laurel, Ahlen, Germany, 1976—, Maesawa H.S. Exch., Japan, 1997. Senator Sisters Senate Archdiocese of Washington, 1993—. NSF grantee, 1967, 69, 71. Mem. ASCD, Nat. Cath. Edn. Assn., Nat. Soc. Daughters of Am. Revolution. Roman Catholic. Avocations: walking, hiking, biking. Home: 404 8th St Laurel MD 20707-4032 Office: St Vincent Pallotti High Sch 113 8th St Laurel MD 20707-4099

WALES, ROSS ELLIOT, lawyer; b. Youngstown, Ohio, Oct. 17, 1947; s. Craig C. and Beverly (Bromley) W.; m. Juliana Fraser, Sept. 16, 1972; children: Dod Elliot, James Craig. AB, Princeton U., 1969; JD, U. Va., 1974. Bar: Ohio 1974, U.S. Dist. Ct. (so. dist.) Ohio 1974, U.S. Ct. Appeals (5th cir.) 1979. Assoc. Taft, Stettinius & Hollister, Cin., 1974-81, ptnr., 1981—; pres. U.S. Swimming, Inc., Colorado Springs, 1979-84, U.S. Aquatic Sports, Inc., Colorado Springs, 1984-88, 94—. Pres. Cin. Active to Support Edn., 1987-88; chmn. sch. tax levy campaign, Cin., 1987; trustee The Childrens Home Cin., 1987—, v.p., 1995—; bd. sec. Cin. State Tech. and C.C., 1995—; sec. Greater Cin. Arts and Edn. Ctr., 1996—. Mem. ABA, Ohio Bar Assn., Cin. Bar Assn., Internat. Swimming Fedn. of Lausanne, Switzerland (sec. 1988-92, v.p. 1992—). Presbyterian. Office: 1800 Star Bank Ctr 425 Walnut St Cincinnati OH 45202

WALES, WALTER D., physicist, educator; b. Oneonta, N.Y., Aug. 2, 1933; s. Walter D. and Anna Laura (Brockway) W.; m. Margaret Irene Keiter, June 19, 1955; children: Stephen Dirk, Carolyn Sue. B.A., Carleton Coll., 1954; M.S., Calif. Inst. Tech., 1955, Ph.D., 1960. Instr. physics U. Pa., Phila., 1959-62, asst. prof., 1962-64, assoc. prof., 1964-72, prof., 1972—, chmn. dept. physics, 1973-82, assoc. dean, 1982-87, acting dean, 1987-88; assoc. dean U. Pa., 1988-92, dep. provost, 1992-95, interim dean, 1996-97; assoc. dir. Princeton-Pa. Accelerator, Princeton, N.J., 1968-71; staff physicist AEC, 1972-73. Fellow Am. Phys. Soc.; mem. Am. Assn. Physics Tchrs. Research in exptl. particle physics. Home: 404 Drew Ave Swarthmore PA 19081-2406 Office: 209 S 33rd St Philadelphia PA 19104

WALETSKY, LUCY ROCKEFELLER, psychiatrist; b. N.Y.C., Mar. 9, 1941; d. Laurance Spelman and Mary Billings (French) Rockefeller; m. Jeremy Peter Waletsky (div. 1984); children: Jacob Peter, Naomi French. BA, Wellesley Coll., 1963; MD, Columbia U., 1968. Cert. Am. Bd. Psychiatry and Neurology. Pvt. practice Chevy Chase, Md., 1975-81; co-dir., co-founder Med. Illness Counseling Ctr., Chevy Chase, Md., 1982-95; asst. dir. Stress Medicine Group, Pleasantville, N.Y., 1995—; founder, pres. DateABLE, Chevy Chase, 1987—. Fellow Am. Psychiatric Assn. (Significant Achievement award 1993), Am. Holistic Med. Assn., Am. Soc. Psycho-oncology/AIDS. Episcopalian. Avocations: golf, hiking, birdwatching. Office: Stress Medicine Group 444 Bedford Rd Pleasantville NY 10570-3031

WALGREEN, CHARLES RUDOLPH, III, retail store executive; b. Chgo., Nov. 11, 1935; s. Charles Rudolph and Mary Ann (Leslie) W.; m. Kathleen Bonsignore Allen, Jan. 23, 1977; children: Charles Richard, Tad Alexander, Kevin Patrick, Leslie Ray, Chris Patrick; stepchildren—Carleton A. Allen Jr., Jorie L. Allen Grassie. B.S. in Pharmacy, U. Mich., 1958. With Walgreen Co., Chgo., 1952—, adminstrv. asst. to v.p. store ops., 1963-65, 65-66, dist. mgr., 1966-69, regional dir., 1968-69, v.p., pres., 1969-71, pres., chief exec. officer, 1971-76, chmn., chief exec. officer, 1976—, also bd. dirs. Mem. bus. adv. coun. Chgo. Urban League.; bd. dirs. Jr. Achievement Chgo. Mem. Nat. Assn. Chain Drug Stores (bd. dirs.), Ill. Retail Mchts. Assn. (bd. dirs. 1966—), Am. Pharm. Assn., Ill. Pharm. Assn., Comml. Club of Chgo., Great Lakes Cruising Club, Exmoor Country Club (Highland Park, Ill.), Key Largo (Fla.) Anglers Club, Sailfish Point Club (Stuart, Fla.), Conway Farms Golf Club (Lake Forest, Ill.), Delta Sigma Phi. Office: Walgreen Co 200 Wilmot Rd Deerfield IL 60015-4620

WALHOUT, JUSTINE SIMON, chemistry educator; b. Aberdeen, S.D., Dec. 11, 1930; d. Otto August and Mabel Ida (Tews) S.; m. Donald Walhout, Feb. 1, 1958; children: Mark, Timothy, Lynne, Peter. BS, Wheaton Coll., 1952; PhD, Northwestern U., 1956. Instr. Wright City Community Coll., Chgo., 1955-56; asst. prof. Rockford (Ill.) Coll., 1956-59, assoc. prof., 1959-66, 81-89, prof., 1989-96, prof. emeritus, 1996—, dept. chmn., 1987-95; cons. Pierce Chem. Co., Rockford, 1968-69; trustee Rockford (Ill.) Coll., 1987-91. Contbr. articles to profl. jours. Mem. Ill. Bd. Edn., 1974-81. Mem. AAUW (Ill. bd. mem. 1985-87), Am. Chem. Soc. (councilor 1993—), Rockford LWV (bd. dirs. 1983-85), Sigma Xi. Presbyterian. Home: 320 N Rockford Ave Rockford IL 61107-4547 Office: Rockford Coll 5050 E State St Rockford IL 61108-2311

WALI, MOHAN KISHEN, environmental science and natural resources educator; b. Kashmir, India, Mar. 1, 1937; came to U.S., 1969, naturalized, 1975; s. Jagan Nath and Somavati (Wattal) W.; m. Sarla Safaya, Sept. 25, 1960; children: Pamela, Promod. BS, U. Jammu and Kashmir, 1957; MS, U. Allahabad, India, 1960; PhD, U. B.C., Can., 1970. Lectr. S.P. Coll., Srinagar, Kashmir, 1963-65; rsch. fellow U. Copenhagen, 1965-66; grad. fellow U. B.C., 1967-69; asst. prof. biology U. N.D., Grand Forks, 1969-73, assoc. prof., 1973-79, prof., 1979-83, Hill rsch. prof., 1973, dir. Forest River Biology Area Field Sta., 1970-79, Project Reclamation, 1975-83, spl. asst. to univ. pres., 1977-82; staff ecologist Grand Forks Energy Rsch. Lab., U.S. Dept. Interior, 1974-75; prof. Coll. Environ. Sci. and Forestry, SUNY, Syracuse, 1983-89, dir. grad. program environ. sci., 1983-85; prof. Sch. Natural Resources, 1990—; dir., Sch. Nat. Resources, assoc. dean, Coll. Agr., 1990-93; vice chmn. N.D. Air Pollution Adv. Council, 1981-83; co-chair IV Internat. Congress on Ecology, 1986. Editor: Some Environmental Aspects of Strip-Mining in North Dakota, 1973, Prairie: A Multiple View, 1975, Practices and Problems of Land Reclamation in Western North America, 1975, Ecology and Coal Resource Development, 1979, Ecosystem Rehabilitation-Preamble to Sustainable Development, 1992; co-editor Agriculture and the Environment, 1993; sr. editor Reclamation Rev., 1976-80, chief editor, 1980-81; chief editor Reclamation and Revegetation Rsch., 1982-87; contbr. articles to profl. jours. Recipient B.C. Gamble Disting. Teaching and Svc. award, 1977. Fellow AAAS, Nat. Acad. of Scis. India; mem. Ecol. Soc. Am. (chmn. sect. internat. activities 1980-84), Brit. Ecol. Soc., Can. Bot. Assn. (dir. ecology sect. 1976-79, v.p. 1982-83), Ohio Acad. Sci., Torrey Bot. Club, Am. Soc. Agronomy, Am. Inst. Biol. Sci. (gen. chmn. 34th ann. meeting), Internat. Assn. Ecology (co-chmn. IV Internat. Congress Ecology), Internat. Soc. Soil Sci., N.D. Acad. Sci. (chmn. editorial com. 1979-81), Sigma Xi (nat. lectr. 1983-85, pres. Ohio State chpt. 1993-94, pres. Syracuse chpt. 1984-85, Outstanding Rsch. award U. N.D. chpt. 1975). Office: Ohio State U Sch Natural Resources 2021 Coffey Rd Columbus OH 43210-1044

WALICKI, ANDRZEJ STANISLAW, history of ideas educator; b. Warsaw, Poland, May 15, 1930; came to U.S., 1986, naturalized 1993.; s. Michal Walicki and Anna (Szlachcinska) Chmielewska; m. Janina Derks, Mar. 10, 1953 (div. June 1970); m. Maria Wodzynska, June 17, 1972 (div. May 1985); children: Malgorzata, Adam; m. Marzena Balicka, July 27, 1985. MA, Warsaw U., 1953; PhD, Polish Acad. Scis., 1957. Asst. prof. Warsaw U., 1958-60; asst. prof. Polish Acad. Scis., Warsaw, 1960-64, assoc. prof., 1964-72, prof., head dept. Inst. Philosophy, 1972-81; sr. rsch. fellow Australian Nat. U., Canberra, 1981-86; O'Neill prof. history U. Notre Dame, Ind., 1986—; vis. Kratter prof. history Stanford U. Author: The Slavophile Controversy, 1975, A History of Russian Thought, 1979, Philosophy and Romantic Nationalism, 1982, Legal Philosophies of Russian Liberalism, 1987, Marxism and the Leap to the Kingdom of Freedom: The Rise and Fall of the Communist Utopia, 1995; also 13 others. Recipient award A. Jurzykowski Found., N.Y.C., 1983; Rsch. grantee Ford Found., N.Y.C., 1960, vis. fellow All Souls Coll., U. Oxford, 1966-67, 73, Guggenheim fellow J.S. Guggenheim Meml. Found., 1991. Mem. Am. Assn. for Advancement Slavic Studies, Polish Acad. Scis. (corr. mem. 1994—). Roman Catholic. Office: U Notre Dame Dept History Notre Dame IN 46556

WALINSKY, LOUIS JOSEPH, economic consultant, writer; b. London, Apr. 19, 1908; came to U.S., 1912; s. Ossip Joseph and Rose (Newman) W.; m. Michele Benson, 1936 (div. 1947); 1 child, Adam; m. Dorothy Monie; children—Marian, Louisa. B.A. in Econs. with honors, Cornell U., 1929; postgrad., U. Berlin, CCNY, New Sch. Social Research. Tchr. econs. N.Y.C. Bd. Edn., 1930-43; econ. cons. War Prodn. Bd., Washington, 1943-47; fin. dir., dir. Germany-Austria ops., sec.-gen. World ORT Union, N.Y.C., 1947-49; v.p. Robert Nathan Assocs., Washington, 1950-63; econ. cons. Washington and Cohasset, Mass., 1963—; exec. sec. combined pulp and paper com. Combined Raw Materials Bd., 1944-45; dir. office of econ. rev. and analysis Civilian Prodn. Adminstrn., 1946-47; mem. and/or leader econ. missions to Korea, Afghanistan, El Salvador, Brazil, East Africa, Israel, Iran, India, Bolivia, Venezuela, Newfoundland, Papua-New Guinea and P.R.; chief resident econ. adviser Govt. Burma, Rangoon, 1953-58; spl. advisor Asia Dept. World Bank, 1971-72; cons. OECD, 1978. Author: Heil Hitler!, 1936, (dramatization) Brave New World, 1939, Economic Development in Burma, 1962, Planning and Execution of Economic Development, 1963, (wth others) Planning Economic Development, 1963, Work, Youth and Unemployment, 1968, Man, State and Society in Contemporary Southeast Asia, 1969, Issues Facing World Jewry, 1981, Coherent Defense Strategy, 1982; editor: Unfinished Business of Land Reform, 1977; contbr. articles to profl. jours. Mem. nat. bd. Ams. for Dem. Action, Washington, 1950-51; dir. internat. commn. World Jewish Congress, N.Y.C., 1979-80; vice chmn. Am. Friends Democracy in Burma, 1991—. Avocations: golf; music; reading. Home and Office: 4000 Massachusetts Ave NW Washington DC 20016-5105

WALINSKY, PAUL, cardiology educator; b. Phila., June 21, 1940; s. Aaron and Bess (Kleiman) W.; m. Stephanie Sosenko, Nov. 27, 1971; children: Shira, Daniel. BA, Temple U., 1961; MD, U. Pa., 1965. Cert. Nat. Bd. Med. Examiners, Am. Bd. Internal Medicine Cardiovascular. Instr. medicine Thomas Jefferson U., Phila., 1973-75, asst. prof. medicine, 1975-79, assoc. prof. medicine, 1979-82, prof. medicine, 1982—; cons. EP Technologies, Mountain View, Calif., 1991-93, Baxter Edwards, Irvine, Calif.,1 988-91, C.R. Bard, Billerica, Mass., 1994. Contbr. articles to profl. jours.; inventor method for high frequency ablation, percutaneous microwave catheter angioplasty. Capt. USAF, 1967-69. Fellow Am. Coll. Cardiology, ACP; mem. AMA, Pa. Med. Soc., Phila. County Med. Assn. Achievements include 13 U.S. patents in field of perfusion balloon catheter, microwave aided balloon angioplasty with lumen measurement, intravascular ultrasonic imaging catheter and method for making same, and acoustic catheter with rotary drive. Office: Thomas Jefferson U 111 S 11th St Philadelphia PA 19107-4824

WALIZE, REUBEN THOMPSON, III, health research administrator; b. Williamsport, Pa., May 28, 1950; s. Reuben Thompson Jr. and Marion Marie (Smith) W.; m. Kathleen Anne Smith, Aug. 13, 1979; children: Heather, Amanda, Reuben IV. BS, Pa. State U., 1972; MPH magna cum laude, U. Tenn., 1975; cert. exec. mgmt., Boston U., 1978. Manpower planner North ctrl. Pa. Area Health Edn. Sys. The Inst. for Med. Edn. and Rsch. Geisinger Med. Ctr., Danville, Pa., 1975-76; asst. dir. Northcentral Pa. Area Health Edn. System, Danville, 1976, exec. dir., 1976-78; health mgr. Seda-Cog, Timberhaven, Pa., 1978; exec. asst. VA Med. Ctr., Erie, Pa., 1978-81; trainee VA Med. Ctr., Little Rock, 1981; adminstrv. officer rsch. svc. VA Med. Ctr., White River Junction, Vt., 1981-88; mgmt. analyst Dept. Vets. Affairs Med. Ctr., Roseburg, Oreg., 1988-90, health systems specialist, 1990-92; adminstrv. officer rsch. Vets. Affairs Med. Ctr. Am. Lake, 1992-95; EEO investigator Dept. Vet. Affairs, Washington, 1995—; adminstrv. officer rsch. dept. vets. affairs Am. Lake divsn. VA Puget Sound Health Care System, Tacoma, 1995—; exec. dir. American Lake Biomed Rsch. Inst., 1996—; exec. dir. Am. Lake Biomed. Rsch. Inst., 1996—; mem. Pa. Coun. Health Profls., 1975-77, Ctrl. Pa. Health Sys. Agy. Manpower Com., 1975-77; mem. Interagy. Coun. Geisinger Med. Ctr., Danville, 1976-78; liaison for rsch. Dartmouth Med. Sch., Hanover, N.H., 1981-88; mem. instnl. rev. bd. Madigan Army Med. Ctr., 1994—; EEO investigator; cons. in field. Recipient Man of Achievement award Queens Coll., Eng., 1978, Student Am. Med. Assn. Found. award, 1975; 1st pl. Douglas County Lamb Cooking Contest, 1992. Mem. APHA, AAAS, N.Y. Acad. Scis., Soc. Rsch. Adminstrs., Assn. Hosps., Pa. State Alumni Assn., Nat. Audubon Soc., Steamboaters, Nat. Wildlife Fedn., Record Catch Club, VIP Club. Avocations: fly fishing, fly tying, gardening, photography, gourmet cooking. Home: 1103 25th Ave SE Puyallup WA 98374-1362

WALK, RICHARD DAVID, retired psychology educator; b. Camp Dix, N.J., Sept. 25, 1920; s. Arthur Richard and Elsie (Roberts) W.; m. Lois MacDonald, Apr. 1, 1950; children: Joan MacDonald Scharf, Elizabeth Walk Robbins, Richard David Jr. AB, Princeton U., 1942; MA, U. Iowa, 1947; PhD, Harvard U., 1951. Research assoc. Human Resource Research Office, George Washington U., Washington, 1952-53, from assoc. prof. to prof., 1959-91; asst. prof. Cornell U., Ithaca, N.Y., 1953-59, prof. emeritus, 1991—; vis. prof. MIT, Cambridge, 1965-66, London Sch. Econs., U. London, 1981. Author: Perceptual Development, 1981; editor: (with H.L. Pick Jr.) Perception and Experience, 1978, Chinese edit., 1987, Intersensory Perception and Sensory Integration, 1981; contbr. articles to profl. jours., chpts. to books. Served to 1st lt. U.S. Army, 1942-45, ETO, 1951-52. Fellow AAAS, Am. Psychol. Soc.; mem. Am. Psychol. Assn., Soc. for Rsch. in Child Devel., Psychonomic Soc., Brit. Psychol. Assn. (fgn. assoc.), Sigma Xi, Vet. OSS. Democrat. Episcopalian. Club: Princeton Terrace (N.J.); Princeton, Harvard (Washington). Home: 7100 Oakridge Ave Chevy Chase MD 20815-5170

WALKE, DAVID MICHAEL, public relations executive; b. Mt. Vernon, N.Y., Dec. 30, 1954; s. Charles Philip and Elinor Mae (Denner) W.; m. Linda Susan Berkover, Nov. 26, 1978; children: Evan Matthew, Hilary Rose. BS in Acctg., Syracuse U., 1976. Account exec. Ecom Cons., Inc., N.Y.C., 1976-79, Anametrics, Inc., N.Y.C., 1979-81, Ruder, Finn & Rotman, Inc., N.Y.C., 1981-82; prin. Morgen-Walke Assocs., Inc., N.Y.C., 1982—, ptnr. Mem. Nat. Investor Rels. Inst. Office: Morgen-Walke Assocs Inc 380 Lexington Ave Ste 5100 New York NY 10168-0002*

WALKER, A. HARRIS, lawyer, manufacturing executive, retired; b. Lincoln, Ill., Feb. 7, 1935; s. Arthur M. and Margaret (Harris) W.; m. Ann Pontious, Aug. 27, 1960; children: Christine, Stuart, Melinda. BA, Northwestern U., 1956; JD, U. Mich., 1963; MBA, U. Chgo., 1969. Bar: Ill. 1963, U.S. Dist. Ct. (no. dist.) Ill. 1964, U.S. Ct. Appeals (7th cir.) 1963. Assoc. Peterson, Lowry, Rall, Barber & Ross, Chgo., 1963-66; atty. Am. Hosp. Supply Co., Evanston, Ill., 1966-71; sr. atty. A.B. Dick Co., Chgo., 1971-74, asst. gen. counsel, 1974-86, v.p., gen. counsel, sec., 1986-97, also bd. dirs., officer of various subs.; retired, 1997. Presbyterian. Office: AB Dick Co 5700 W Touhy Ave Niles IL 60714-4628

WALKER, ALICE MALSENIOR, author; b. Eatonton, Ga., Feb. 9, 1944; d. Willie Lee and Minnie (Grant) W.; m. Melvyn R. Leventhal, Mar. 17, 1967 (div. 1976); 1 dau., Rebecca Walker Leventhal. BA, Sarah Lawrence Coll., 1966; PhD (hon.), Russell Sage U., 1972; DHL (hon.), U. Mass., 1983. Co-founder, pub. Wild Trees Pr., Navarro, Calif., 1984-88; writer in residence, tchr. black studies Jackson State Coll., 1968-69, Tougaloo Coll., 1970-71; lectr. literature Wellesley Coll., 1972-73, U. Mass., Boston, 1972-73; disting. writer Afro-American studies dept. U. Calif., Berkeley, 1982; Fannie Hurst Prof. of Literature Brandeis U., Waltham, Mass., 1982; cons. Friends of the Children of Miss., 1967. Author: Once, 1968, The Third Life of Grange Copeland, 1970, Five Poems, 1972, Revolutionary Petunias and Other Poems, 1973 (Nat. Book award nomination 1973, Lillian Smith award So. Regional Coun. 1973), In Love and Trouble, 1973 (Richard and Hinda Rosenthal Found. award Am. Acad. and Inst. of Arts and Letters 1974) Langston Hughes: American Poet, 1973, Meridian, 1976, Goodnight, Willie Lee, I'll See You in the Morning, 1979, You Can't Keep a Good Woman Down, 1981, The Color Purple, 1982 (Nat. Book Critics Circle award nomination 1982, Pulitzer Prize for fiction 1983, Am. Book award 1983), In Search of Our Mothers' Gardens, 1983, Horses Make a Landscape Look More Beautiful, 1984, To Hell With Dying, 1988, Living By the Word: Selected Writings, 1973-1987, 1988, The Temple of My Familiar, 1989, Her Blue Body Everything We Know: Earthling Poems, 1965-1990, 1991, Finding the Green Stone, 1991, Possessing the Secret of Joy, 1992, (with Pratibha Parmar) Warrior Marks, 1993, (with others) Double Stitch: Black Women Write About Mothers & Daughters, 1993, Everyday Use, 1994, Alice Walker Banned: The Banned Works, 1996, Everything We Love Can Be Saved: A Writer's Activism: Essays, Speeches, Statements and Letters, 1997; editor: I Love Myself When I'm Laughing... And Then Again When I'm Looking Mean and Impressive, 1979. Recipient first prize Am. Scholar essay contest, 1967, O. Henry award for "Kindred Spirits", 1986, Nora Astorga Leadership award, 1989, Fred Cody award for lifetime achievement Bay Area Book Reviewers Assn., 1990, Freedom to Write award PEN Ctr. USA West, 1990; Bread Loaf Writer's Conf. scholar, 1966; Merrill writing fellowship, 1967, McDowell Colony fellowship, 1967, 77-78; National Endowment for the Arts grantee, 1969, 77; Radcliffe Inst. fellowship, 1971-73; Guggenheim fellow, 1977-78. Address: Random House Inc 201 E 50th St New York NY 10022*

WALKER, ANN YVONNE, lawyer; b. San Francisco, Sept. 26, 1954; d. C. Richard and Athene (Henderson) Walker. B.S. with distinction in Math., Stanford U., 1976, J.D., 1979. Bar: Calif. 1979. Assoc. Wilson, Sonsini, Goodrich & Rosati, Palo Alto, Calif., 1979-86, ptnr., 1986—. Violinist Redwood Symphony Orch., 1985—, mem. cast Stanford Gilbert & Sullivan group, 1979—. Mem. ABA, Calif. State Bar Assn. (corps. com. 1992—), Santa Clara County Bar Assn., Phi Beta Kappa. Office: Wilson Sonsini Goodrich & Rosati 2 Palo Alto Sq Palo Alto CA 94306-2122

WALKER, ANNETTE, counseling administrator; b. Birmingham, Ala., Sept. 20, 1953; d. Jesse and Luegene (Wright) W. BS in Edn., Huntingdon Coll., 1976; MS in Adminstrn. and Supervision, Troy State U., 1977, 78, MS in Sch. Counseling, 1990, AA in Sch. Adminstrn., 1992; diploma, World Travel Sch., 1990; diploma in Cosmetology, John Patterson Coll., 1992; MEd in higher Edn. Adminstrn., Auburn (Ala.) U., 1995. Cert. tchr., adminstr., Ala.; lic. cosmetologist, Ala. Tchr. Montgomery (Ala.) Pub. Sch. System, 1976-89, sch. counselor, 1989—; gymnastics tchr. Cleveland Ave. YMCA, 1971-76; girls coach Montgomery Parks and Recreation, 1973-76; summer sch. sci. tchr. grades 7-9, 1977-88; chmn. dept. sci. Bellingrath Sch., 1987-90, courtesy com., 1987-88, sch. discipline com., 1977-84; recreation asst. Gunter AFB, Ala., 1981-83; calligraphy tchr. Gunter Youth Ctr., 1982; program dir. Maxwell AFB, Ala., 1983-89, vol. tchr. Internat. Officer Sch., 1985—, Ala. Goodwill Amb., 1985—, day camp dir., 1987, calligraphy tchr., 1988; trainer internat. law for sec. students, Ala., 1995—; leader of workshops in field; evening computer tchr. high sch. diploma program, 1995—; sales rep. Ala. World Travel, 1990—; behavior aid Brantwood Children's Home, 1996—; computer tchr. h.s. diploma program Montgomery County Sch., 1995—; behavior aide Brantwood Children's Home, 1995—; hotel auditor, 1995—. Mem. CAP; tchr. Sunday sch. Beulah Bapt. Ch., Montgomery; vol. zoo activities Tech. Scholarship Program for Ala. Tchrs. Computer Courses, Montgomery, Ala.; bd. dirs. Cleveland Ave. YMCA, 1976-80; sponsor Bell-Howe chpt. Young Astronauts, 1986-90, Pate Howe chpt. Young Astronauts, 1991-92; judge Montgomery County Children Festival Elem. Sci. Fair, 1988-90; bd. dirs. Troy State U. Drug Free Schs., 1992—; chmn. Maxwell AFB Red Cross-Youth, 1986-88; goodwill amb. sponsor to various families (award 1989, 95); State of Ala. rep. P.A.T.C.H.-Internat. Law Inst., 1995. Recipient Outstanding high Sch. Sci./Math. Tchr. award Sigma Xi, 1989, Most Outstanding Youth Coun. Leader award Maxwell AFB Youth Ctr., 1987, Outstanding Ala. Goodwill Amb. award, 1989, 95; named Tchr. of the Week, WCOV-TV, 1992, Ala. Tchr. in Space Program , summer 1989, Local Coodr. Young Astronaut Program, 1988, Tchr. of Yr. award Paterson Sch., 1990, Career Infusion Award (Most Appreciated Tchr. award 1987), Montgomery Pub. Sch., 1982, 84. Mem. NEA, Internat. Platform Assn., Nat. Sci. Tchrs. Assn., Ala. Sch. Counselors, Montgomery Sch. Counselors Assn., Montgomery County Ednl. Assn., Space Camp Amb., Huntingdon Alumni Assn. (sec.-treas.), Ala. Goodwill Amb., Montgomery Capital City Club, Young Astronauts, Ea. Star, Zeta Phi Beta, Chi Delta Phi, Kappa Pi. Avocations: international travel, calligraphy, international food, cruising. Home: 2501 Westwood Dr Montgomery AL 36108-4448 Office: Bellingrath Sch 3488 S Court St Montgomery AL 36105-1608

WALKER, BETSY ELLEN, computer products and services company executive; b. Atlanta, Sept. 14, 1953; d. John Franklin and Betty Louise (Brown) W.; 1 child, William Franklin. BA summa cum laude, Duke U., 1974; MBA, Harvard U., 1978. Mgmt. trainee, First Atlanta, 1974, officer, 1975-76; analyst Coca Cola, Atlanta, 1977; bus. analyst Am. Mgmt. Systems Inc., N.Y.C., 1978-80, prin., 1981, v.p., 1982—, dir. fin. svcs. group, 1982-90, IBM Svcs. sector group, 1990-92, fin. strategic initiatives group, 1993, dir. fin. industry Strategic Alliance Group, 1994-96, area dep. dir. fin. industry groups, 1996—; mem. mgmt. policy com. Am. Mgmt. Systems, 1988—, mem. corporate operating group, 1994—. J. Spenser Love fellow Harvard U., 1976-78. Mem. Alexandria North Ridge Citizens Assn. (exec. bd.), Phi Beta Kappa, Pi Mu Epsilon (bd. mgrs. Madison Green 1990-91, treas.), Harvard Bus. Sch. Club, Downtown Athletic Club (N.Y.C.). Office: Am Mgmt Systems Inc 4050 Legato Rd Fairfax VA 22033-4087

WALKER, BRADFORD C., architect; b. Oshkosh, Wis., Feb. 27, 1960. BS in Architecture, U. Va., 1982; MArch, Harvard U., 1985. Registered arch., Mass.; cert. Nat. Coun. Archtl. Registration Bd. Sr. assoc. Peter Forbes & Assocs., Inc., Boston, 1985-95; prin. Bradford C. Walker, Architect, 1995-96, Walker Architects, Inc., 1996—; mem. design studio faculty Boston Archtl. Ctr., 1984, 85, 86, mem. design theory faculty, 1987; mem. faculty architecture Roger Williams Coll., Bristol, R.I., 1988; mem. design studio faculty RISD, Providence, 1989; critic core curriculum Harvard U., Cambridge, Mass., 1992. Editor: Harvard Architecture Rev., Vol. 6.

WALKER, BRIGITTE MARIA, translator, linguistic consultant; b. Stolp, Germany, Sept. 20, 1934; came to U.S., 1957; d. Joseph Karl and Ursula Maria Margot Ehrler; m. John V. Kelley (div.); 1 child, John V. Jr.; m. Edward D. Walker, July 3, 1977. Grad., Erlangen Translator's Sch., Germany, 1956; grad. fgn. corres., Berlitz Sch., Germany, 1956. Bilingual sec., translator Spencer Patent Law Office, Washington, 1959-62; office mgr., translator I. William Millen, Millen and White, Patent Law, Washington, 1962-67; prin. Tech. Translating Bur., Washington, 1967-68, St. Petersburg Beach, Fla., 1968—; cons. for patent law offices, Washington, 1962—; ofcl. expert for ct. Paul M. Craig, Patent Atty., Rockford, Ill., 1981; cons. to sci. editor Merriam-Webster, Inc., Springfield, Mass., 1987—. Author: German-English/English-German Last-Resort Dictionary for Technical Translators, 1991, (poetry) The Other Side of the Mirror, 1992 (Poetry award Nat. League Am. Pen Women 1994); co-translator: The Many Faces of Research, 1980; holder of trademark in field. Evaluator fgn. textbooks Pinellas County Sch. Bd., St. Petersburg, 1987, German judge, 1988. Recipient Recoginition award Pinellas County Sch. Bd., 1988, Meritorious Pub. Svc. award City of St. Petersburg Beach, 1987, poetry award Nat. League Am. Pen Women, 1994, essay award, 1996, short story award, 1997. Mem. Mensa (Winner Nat. award Best Fiction 1996). Democrat. Lutheran. Avocations: swimming, aerobics, piano, painting. Home and Office: 7150 Sunset Way Apt 1007 Saint Petersburg FL 33706-3650

WALKER, BRUCE EDWARD, anatomy educator; b. Montreal, Que., Can., June 17, 1926; s. Robinson Clarence and Dorothea Winston (Brown) W.; m. Lois Catherine McCuaig, June 26, 1948; children—Brian Ross, Dianne Heather, Donald Robert, Susan Lois. B.S., McGill U., 1947, M.S., 1952, Ph.D., 1954; M.D., U. Tex. at Galveston, 1966. Instr. anatomy McGill U., 1955-57; asst. prof. anatomy U. Tex. Med. Br., 1957-61, assoc. prof. anatomy, 1961-67; prof. Mich. State U., East Lansing, 1967—, chmn. dept., 1967-75. Contbr. articles to profl. jours. Mem. Am. Assn. Anatomists, Teratology Soc., Am. Assn. for Cancer Research. Office: Mich State U Anatomy Dept East Lansing MI 48824

WALKER, CAROLYN PEYTON, English language educator; b. Charlottesville, Va., Sept. 15, 1942; d. Clay M. and Ruth Peyton. BA in Am. History and Lit., Sweet Briar Coll., 1965; cert. in French, Alliance Francaise, Paris, 1966; EdM, Tufts U., 1970; MA in English and Am. Lit., Stanford U., 1974, PhD in English Edn., Stanford U., 1977. Tchr. Elem. and jr. high schs. in Switzerland, 1967-69; tchr. elem. grades Boston Sch. System, 1966-67, 69-70; Newark (Calif.) Unified Sch. System, 1970-72; instr. div. humanities Canada Coll., Redwood City, Calif., 1973, 76-78; instr. Sch. Bus., U. San Francisco, 1973-74; evaluation cons. Inst. Profl. Devel., San Jose, Calif., 1975-76; asst. dir. Learning Assistance Ctr., Stanford U., Calif., 1972-77, dir., 1977-84, lectr. Sch. Edn., 1975-84, dept. English, 1977-84, supr. counselors, tutors and tchrs., 1972-84; assoc. prof. dept. English, San Jose State U., Calif., 1984-93; dir. English dept. Writing Ctr., 1986-93, Steinbeck Rsch. Ctr., 1986-87; mem. faculty U. Calif., Berkeley and Santa Cruz, 1995—;

corp. trainer, 1993—; pres. Waverley Edn., Inc., Ednl. Cons., 1983-91, tchr. writing and Am. culture for fgn. profls., U. Calif. at Berkeley, 1995—, pvt. prac. corp. trng., 1983—; head cons. to pres. to evaluate coll.'s writing program, San Jose City Coll., 1985-87; cons. U. Tex., Dallas, 1984, Stanford U., 1984, 1977-78, CCNY, 1979, U. Wis., 1980, numerous testing programs; cons. to pres. San Diego State U., 1982, Ednl. Testing Svc., 1985-88, also to numerous univs. and colls.; condr. reading and writing workshops, 1972—; reviewer Random House Books, 1978—, Rsch. in the Teaching of English, 1983—, Course Tech., Inc., 1990—; cons. Basic Skills Task Force, U.S. Office Edn., 1977-79, Right to Read, Calif. State Dept. Edn., 1977-82, Program for Gifted and Talented, Fremont (Calif.) Unified Sch. Dist., 1981-82; bd. dirs. high tech. sci. ctr., San Jose, 1983-84; speaker numerous profl. confs. Author: (with Patricia Killen) Handbook for Teaching Assistants at Stanford University, 1977, Learning Center Courses for Faculty and Staff: Reading, Writing, and Time Management, 1981, How to Succeed as a New Teacher: A Handbook for Teaching Assistants, 1978, ESL Courses for Faculty & Staff: An Additional Opportunity to Serve the Campus Community, 1983, (with Karen Wilson) Tutor Handbook for the Writing Center at San Jose State University, 1989, (with others) Academic Tutoring at the Learning Assistance Center, 1980, Writing Conference Talk: Factors Associated with High and Low Rated Writing Conferences, 1987, Lifeline Mac: A Handbook for Instructors in the Macintosh Computer Classrooms, 1989, Communications with the Faculty: Vital Links for the Success of Writing Centers, 1991, Coming to America, 1993, Teacher Dominance in the Writing Conference, 1992, Instant Curriculum: Just Add Tutors and Students, 1993; contbr. chpts. to Black American Literature Forum, 1991; contbr. articles to profl. jours. Vol. fundraiser Peninsula Ctr. for the Blind, Palo Alto, Calif., 1982—, The Resource Ctr. for Women, Palo Alto, 1975-76. Recipient Award for Outstanding Contbns., U.S. HEW, 1979, award ASPIRE (federally funded program), 1985, two awards Student Affirmative Action, 1986, award Western Coll. Reading & Learning Assn., 1984; numerous other awards and grants. Mem. MLA, Coll. Reading & Learning Assn. (treas. 1982-84, bd. dirs. 1982-84), Nat. Coun. Tchrs. English, No. Calif. Coll. Reading Assn. (sec.-treas. 1976-78), Am. Assn. U. Profs., Jr. League Palo Alto (bd. dirs. 1977-78, 83-84). Home: 2350 Waverley St Palo Alto CA 94301-4143

WALKER, CAROLYN SMITH, college services administrator, counselor; b. Atlanta, May 9, 1946; d. George Taft and Lonnie Bell (Bates) Smith; 1 child from previous marriage, Gary Sherard Walker II. BA in Psychology, Clark Coll., Atlanta, 1970; MS in Counseling & Guidance, U. Nebr., Omaha, 1975. Lic. profl. counselor, Ga. Adult basic edn. instr. Atlanta Pub. Schs., 1970-71, adult basic edn. site coord., 1971; adult basic edn. instr. Omaha-Nebr. Tech. C.C., Omaha, 1971-74, dir. adult basic edn., 1974; guidance counselor Omaha Pub. Schs., 1974-76; recruitment counselor Minority Women Employment Program, Atlanta, 1976-77; career planning and employment preparation instr. Discovery Learning Inc., Job Tng. and Pntrship Act, Atlanta, 1985-86; dir. counseling and testing svcs. Atlanta Met. Coll., 1977—; test supr. Ednl. Testing Svc., Princeton, N.J., 1980—, Psychology Corp., San Antonio, 1991—, Law Sch. Admissions Test, Newtown, Pa., 1991—; cons. Commn. on Colls., So. Assn. Colls. and Schs., Atlanta, 1978—; jr. c.c. rep. Placement & Coop. Edn., Atlanta, 1987-90. Editor newsletters Romar On-Line, 1997, The Brief, 1984, 85, Guided Studies News, 1974; contbg. author: (manual) AJC Self-Study, 1981; author: (manual) Policies and Procedures for Coordinated Counseling, 1981, 2d edit., 1991, Policies and Procedures for Learning Disability Services Women's Coalition for Habitat for Humanity in Atlanta, 1993-95, 97. Pres. Atlanta Barristers Wives Inc., 1984, 85; mem. steering com. Atlanta Mayor's Masked Ball, 1987; mem. memberships sales com. Atlanta Arts Festival, 1986, Neighborhood Arts Ctr., 1986; state host Dem. Nat. Conv., Atlanta, 1988; mem. Heritage Valley Cmty. Neighborhood Assn., 1982—. Recipient Outstanding Svc. award Nat. Orientation Dirs. Assn., 1985, 86, Literacy Action, Inc., 1978, Atlanta Met. Coll., 1987, others. Mem. Ga. Coll. Personnel Assn., Ga. Mental Health Counselors Assn., Nat. Coun. Student Devel., Univ. System Counseling Dirs., 100 Women Internat. Inc. (charter mem.), Am. Assn. Community and Jr. Colls., The Links Inc., Ga. Assn. Women Deans, Counselors and Adminstrs., Ga. Coll. Consclors Assn. Democrat. Methodist. Avocations: tennis, travel, horticulture. Home: 3511 Toll House Ln SW Atlanta GA 30331-2330 Office: Atlanta Metro Coll 1630 Stewart Ave SW Atlanta GA 30310-4448

WALKER, CHARLES ALLEN, chemical engineer, educator; b. Wise County, Tex., June 18, 1914; s. Jackson Lamar and Eula (Hamilton) W.; m. Bernice Rolf, Dec. 24, 1942; children: Allen Rolf, John Lamar, Laurence Gordon. BS, U. Tex., 1938, MS, 1940; DEng, Yale U., 1948. Mem. faculty Yale U., New Haven, 1942-84, prof. chem. engring., 1956-84, master Berkeley Coll., 1959-69, chmn. dept. engring. and applied sci., 1974-76, Raymond John Wean prof., 1979-84, prof. emeritus, 1984—, chmn. dept. chem. engring., 1981-84; mem. staff Yale Instn. for Social and Policy Studies, 1970-84; cons. chem. engr., 1942—. Bd. dirs. Conn. Fund for the Environ., 1978-86. Fellow AAAS; mem. AICE, Sci. Rsch. Soc. Am. (past nat. dir., treas. 1968-73), Am. Chem. Soc. (petroleum rsch. fund adv. bd. 1970-81, chmn. 1972-81), Am. Soc. Engring. Edn., Conn. Acad. Sci. and Engring., Conn. Acad. Arts and Scis., Yale Club, Phi Beta Kappa (hon.), Sigma Xi (bd. dirs. 1976-78), Tau Beta Pi, Phi Lambda Upsilon. Home: 1155 Whitney Ave Hamden CT 06517-3434

WALKER, CHARLES DODSLEY, conductor, organist; b. N.Y.C., Mar. 16, 1920; s. Marshall Starr and Maude Graham (Marriott) W.; m. Janet Elizabeth Hayes, May 30, 1949; children: Peter Hayes, Susan Starr. BS, Trinity Coll., 1940; AM, Harvard U., 1947. Organist, choirmaster Am. Cathedral, Paris, 1948-50, Ch. of the Heavenly Rest, N.Y.C., 1951-88; music dir. Blue Hill Troupe, Ltd., N.Y.C., 1955-90, The Chapin Sch., N.Y.C., 1961-85; mem. organ faculty Union Theol. Sem., N.Y.C., 1962-73, NYU, 1968-80; dean, music dir. Berkshire Choral Inst., Sheffield, Mass., 1982-91; organist, choirmaster Trinity Episcopal Ch., Southport, Conn., 1988—. Contbr. articles to profl. jours. Lt. comdr. USNR, 1942-46. Recipient Disting. Alumnus award Cathedral Choir Sch., 1988. Fellow Am. Guild of Organists (nat. pres. 1971-75); mem. Am. Fedn. of Musicians, Canterbury Choral Soc. (founder, conductor 1952—), Saint Wilfrid Club, The Bohemians. Avocations: travel, photography. Home: 160 W 96th St Apt 15N New York NY 10025-9212 Office: Trinity Episcopal Ch 651 Pequot Ave Southport CT 06490-1416

WALKER, CHARLES MONTGOMERY, lawyer; b. St. Louis, Sept. 30, 1915; s. Charles J. and Gertrude (Zoll) W.; m. Gertrude E. Acton, Apr. 30, 1943. A.B., U. Mo., 1937, LL.B., 1939. Bar: Mo. 1939, Calif. 1941, D.C. 1977. Practiced law Los Angeles, 1941—; mem. Brady, Nossaman & Walker, 1941-62; partner Paul, Hastings, Janofsky & Walker, 1962-75, 77-81, counsel, 1981—; asst. sec. treasury for tax policy Washington, 1975-77. Served with AUS, 1942-46. Decorated Bronze Star. Fellow Am. Bar Found., Am. Coll. Tax Counsel (bd. regents 1987-93), Am. Bar Retirement Assn. (bd. dirs., pres. 1986), Am. Tax Policy Inst. (pres. 1990-93); mem. ABA (chmn. taxation sect. 1979-80, coms.), L.A. Bar Assn., Am. Law Inst., State Bar Calif., Order of Coif, L.A. Country Club, Met. Club, Sigma Chi. Home: 9255 Doheny Rd West Hollywood CA 90069-3201 Office: 1299 Ocean Ave Santa Monica CA 90401-1038

WALKER, CHARLES NORMAN, retired insurance company executive; b. Buchanan, Mich., Mar. 8, 1923; s. Leland Seymour and Beatrice (Fairchild) W.; m. Rosemary McElwee, Aug. 21, 1919 (dec.); children: James Charles, Christopher Hugh. Student, Western Mich. U., 1939-41; B.S., U. Mich., 1945, M.A., 1947. With Lincoln Nat. Life Ins. Co., Ft. Wayne, Ind., 1947-75; asst. v.p., mgr. accident and sickness Lincoln Nat. Life Ins. Co., 1957-60, 2d v.p., 1960-64, v.p., 1964-75; v.p. selection and issue New Eng. Mut. Life Ins. Co., Boston, 1975-83. Served to 1st lt. USAF, 1943-46. Fellow Soc. Actuaries; mem. Am. Acad. Actuaries. Episcopalian. Home: 506 Mill Rd Woodstock VA 22664-2308

WALKER, CHARLES THOMAS, physicist, educator; b. Chgo., Sept. 5, 1932; s. Charles William and Velma Rose (Reich) W.; m. Alice Ann Pawlak, Dec. 26, 1953 (div. 1973); children: David John, Valerie Anne, Carolyn Marie; m. Carrie Anna Ramsey, Sept. 14, 1973. A.B. in Math., U. Louisville, 1956, M.S. in Physics, 1958; PH.D. in Physics, Brown U., 1961. Research assoc Cornell U., Ithaca, N.Y., 1961-63; asst. prof. Northwestern U., Evanston, Ill., 1963-67, assoc. prof., 1967-71; prof. physics Ariz. State U., Tempe, 1971-85, chmn. dept., 1981-85; corp. scientist 3M Co./Photonics Rsch. Lab., St. Paul, 1985—; cons. U.S. Dept. Def., Washington, 1966-71, Coronet Films, Chgo., 1969-71, Motorola, Inc., Phoenix, 1974-78. Contbr. articles to profl. jours. Served to sgt. U.S. Army, 1953-55. Guggenheim Found. fellow, 1967-68; Alexander von Humboldt Found. sr. U.S. scientist, 1978-79. Fellow Am. Phys. Soc.; mem. AAAS, Optical Soc. Am. Home: 163 Riverview Acres Rd Hudson WI 54016-6753 Office: 3M Co/Photonics Rsch Lab Corp Rsch Lab 3M Center # 05 Saint Paul MN 55144-0001

WALKER, CHARLES URMSTON, retired university president; b. Bolivar, Pa., June 20, 1931; s. Charles William and Frances May (Urmston) W.; m. Cherie Hall Duckworth, Aug. 7, 1959; children: Douglas Leland, Christy Lynn. BA, U. Pitts., 1953; MA, Columbia U., 1958; PhD, Stanford U., 1964; LLD (hon.), Kanto Gakuin U., 1979; LHD (hon.), Linfield Coll., 1992. Asst. prof. English Rockford (Ill.) Coll., 1958-61; dept. head, residence dir. Menlo Coll., Menlo Park, Calif., 1961-64; v.p., dean Hamline U., St. Paul, 1964-70; pres. Russell Sage Coll., Troy, N.Y., 1970-75; pres. Linfield Coll., McMinnville, Oreg., 1975-92, pres. emeritus, 1992—; ednl. cons., 1992—; dir. Ford scholar program Ford Family Found., Roseburg, Oreg., 1994—; chmn. bd. dirs. 1st Fed. Savs. & Loan, McMinnville; bd. dirs. Wespro Ins. Co., Oreg. Mut. Ins. Co.; mem. Univ. Pres. Initiative, IIE/USIA/NATO, Brussels, 1991. Mem. bd. dirs., pres. Hillside Manor, McMinnville, 1990; bd. dirs. South Tillamook County Libr., 1994, Coll. and Univ. Partnership Program, Memphis; pres. Newkowin (Oreg.) Chamber Music; chmn. long range planning First Bapt. Ch., McMinnville; bd. dirs., mem. exec. com. Oreg. Coun. Humanities; trustee Ford Family Found. Warg scholar U. Pitts., 1949-51; Univ. fellow Stanford U., 1963-64; Hill Found. grantee, St. Paul, 1970; Paul Harris fellow Rotary Internat., 1987; recipient Community Svc. award Troy, N.Y. Troy C. of C., 1975, First Citizen award McMinnville, Oreg., 1989; named Man of Yr., Troy C. of C., 1975.. Mem. Univ. Club (Portland), Rotary (past pres. McMinnville). Home: 1324 SW Gilorr St Mcminnville OR 97128-6617

WALKER, CHARLS EDWARD, economist, consultant; b. Graham, Tex., Dec. 24, 1923; s. Pinkney Clay and Sammye D. (McCombs) W.; m. Harmolyn Hart, June 24, 1949; children: Carolyn, Charls Edward. BBA, U. Tex., 1947, MBA, 1948; PhD in Econs., U. Pa., 1955. Instr. fin. U. Tex., 1947-48, asst. prof., then assoc. prof., 1950-54; instr. fin. U. Pa. Wharton Sch., 1948-50; fin. economist Fed. Res. Bank Phila., 1953; with Fed. Res. Bank Dallas, 1954-61, v.p., econ. adviser, 1958-61; economist Republic Nat. Bank Dallas, 1955-56; asst. to sec. treasury, 1959-61; exec. v.p. Am. Bankers Assn., N.Y.C., 1961-69; under sec. treasury, 1969-72, dep. sec., 1972-73; adj. prof. U. Tex., Austin, 1986—, Georgetown U., Washington, 1996—; bd. dirs. Enron Corp., Washington Campus. Co-editor: The Bankers Handbook, New Directions in Federal Tax Policy, The Consumption Tax: A Better Alternative, 1987, Intellectual Property Rights and Capital Formation, 1988, The U.S. Savings Challenge, 1990; contbr. articles to profl. jours. and newspapers, chpts. to books. Founder, chmn. Am. Coun. for Capital Formation; co-founder Com. on the Present Danger, chmn. Pres.'s adv. coun. on minority enterprise, 1973-75; co-chmn. Presdl. Debates, 1976; founder, chmn. Bretton Woods Com.; chmn. Ronald Reagan's Task Force on Tax Policy, 1980; sr. advisor Nat. Issues Conv., U. Tex., 1996. Recipient Alexander Hamilton award U.S. Dept. Treasury, Urban League award, Baker award for Exemplary Svc. to Econ. Edn.; named Disting. Alumnus, U. Tex., 1994. Mem. Coun. Fgn. Rels., Burning Tree Club, Congressional Club (Bethesda, Md.), The Hills of Lakeway Club (Austin, Tex.). Home: 10120 Chapel Rd Potomac MD 20854-4143 *What's good for the public interest ultimately is good for every person, business, or other group in the nation. This, combined with modern application of the Golden Rule, about sums it up.*

WALKER, CLARENCE EUGENE, psychology educator; b. Monongahela, Pa., Jan. 8, 1939; s. Lewis G. Walker and Olga T. Brioli; divorced; children: Chad Eugene, Kyle Lewis, Cass Emanuel. BS in Psychology summa cum laude, Geneva Coll., 1960; MS in Clin. Psychology, Purdue U., 1963, PhD in Clin. Psychology, 1965. Lic. psychologist, Okla. Asst. prof. Westmont Coll., 1964-68; pvt. practice clin. psychology Santa Barbara, Calif., 1965-68; from asst. prof. to assoc. prof. Baylor U., 1968-74; pvt. practice clin. psychology Waco, Tex., 1970-74; assoc. prof. med. sch. U. Okla., Oklahoma City, 1974-80; chief pediatric psychology svc. Okla. Children's Meml. Hosp., 1974-80, dir. out-patient pediatric psychology clinic, 1974-80; prof. med. sch., dir. pediatric psychology tng. program U. Okla., Oklahoma City, 1980-95, prof. emeritus, 1995; assoc. chief mental health svcs. Children's Hosp. Okla., 1980-95; intern in clin. psychology Riley Children's Hosp., West 10th St. VA Hosp., Indpls., 1963-64; psychology trainee West 10th St. VA Hosp., Indpls., 1963; cons. Head Start Program, Waco, 1968-70, VA Hosp, Waco, 1969-74, VA Ctr., Temple, Tex., 1969-74, Region XII Ednl. Svc. Ctr., Waco, 1971-74, Rusk (Tex.) State Hosp., 1972-74, Bapt. Children's Home, Oklahoma City, 1975-79; rsch. cons. Los Alamos (N.Mex.) Pub. Schs., 1975-79; chmn. div. edn. and psychology Westmont Coll., 1966-68; consulting psychologist, 1995—. Author: Learn to Relax, 1975, 2nd edit., 1991, (with P. Clement, A. Hedberg and L. Wright) Clinical Procedures for Behavior Therapy, 1981, (with B.L. Bonner and K. Kaufman) The Physically and Sexually Abused Child, 1988, others; editor: The History of Clinical Psychology in Autobiography, Vol. I, 1992, Vol. II, 1993, (with M.C. Roberts) Handbook of Clinical Child Psychology, 1992; contbr. articles to profl. jours. Fellow APA; mem. AAAS, Southwestern Psychol. Assn. (pres. 1977), Okla. Psychol. Assn. (pres. 1983), Soc. Pediat. Psychology (pres. 1986), Ctrl. Tex. Psychol. Assn. (pres. 1973), Sigma Xi. Avocations: reading, wine tasting, travel. Office: U Okla Med Sch PO Box 26901 920 S L Young Blvd Oklahoma City OK 73190

WALKER, CLARENCE WESLEY, lawyer; b. Durham, N.C., July 19, 1931; s. Ernie Franklin and Mollie Elizabeth (Cole) W.; m. Ann-Heath Harris, June 5, 1954; children: Clare Ann, Wesley Gregg. A.B., Duke U., 1953, LL.B., 1955. Bar: N.C. 1955. Assoc. Mudge Stern Baldwin & Todd, 1955-59; ptnr. Kennedy, Covington, Loddell & Hickman, Charlotte, N.C., 1959—; bd. dirs. Lawyers Mut. Liability Ins. Co., Legal Services Corp. N.C., Oakwood Home Corp. Glendale Hosiery Co.; lectr. N.C. Bar Found. Continuing Legal Edn. Insts., N.C. Jud. Planning Com., 1978-79; pres. Pvt. Adjudication Found. Chmn. bd. mgrs. Charlotte Meml. Hosp. and Med. Ctr., 1981-87; trustee N.C. Ctrl. U., 1979-83; vice-chmn. Charlotte-Mecklenburg Hosp. Authority; adv. bd. Ctrl. Piedmont Paralegal Sch.; pres. Charlotte-Mecklenburg Hosp. Found.; trustee Charlotte Country Day Sch., 1977-81; state chmn. Nat. Found. March of Dimes, 1968-70; chmn. Charlotte Park and Recreation Commn., 1970-73; bd. dirs. Charlotte Symphony, 1965-71, Bethlehem Ctr., 1975-77, N.C. Recreators Found., 1973-75; adv. bd. Charlotte Children's Theatre, 1972; bd. dirs. Charlotte C. of C., 1970-72; bd. visitors Duke U. Law Sch.; dir., gen. campaign chmn. United Way Ctrl. Carolinas, 1985. Fellow Am. Bar Found.; mem. N.C. Bar Assn. (pres. 1978-79, gov. 1971-75), ABA (state del. 1980-89, assembly del.) 26th Jud. Dist. Bar Assn., Mecklenburg Bar Found. (trustee), Am. Law Inst., Order of Coif, Phi Eta Sigma, Phi Beta Kappa. Democrat. Methodist. Home: 1047 Ardsley Rd Charlotte NC 28207-1815 Office: Kennedy Covington Lobdell & Hickman NationsBank Ctr 100 N Tryon St Ste 4200 Charlotte NC 28202-4000

WALKER, CRAIG MICHAEL, lawyer; b. Vt., 1947; m. Patricia A. Magruder; two children. BA, Williams Coll., 1969; JD, Cornell U., 1972. Bar: N.Y. 1973, U.S. Dist. Ct. (so. dist.) N.Y. 1975, U.S. Ct. Appeals (2d cir) 1975, U.S. Supreme Ct 1976. Assoc. Alexander & Green, N.Y.C., 1972-80, ptnr., 1980-86, chmn. litigation dept., 1985-86; ptnr. Walter, Conston, Alexander & Green P.C., N.Y.C., 1987-89, Rogers & Wells, N.Y.C., 1990—. Contbr. author: New York Forms of Jury Instruction, 1992; contbr. articles to profl. jours. Fellow Am. Bar Found.; mem. ABA, N.Y. State Bar Assn., Def. Rsch. Inst., Fed. Bar Coun. Democrat.

WALKER, DALE RUSH, financial company executive; b. High Point, N.C., Jan. 14, 1943; s. Raymond Lowe and Virginia (Rush) W.; m. Linda Gates, 1990; children by previous marriage: Virginia Ashley, Whitney Beaumont. BS in Math., Wake Forest U., 1965; MBA, U. N.C., 1967. Asst. cashier Citibank, N.Y.C., 1967-70; sr. v.p. Union Bank, San Francisco, 1970-75, regional v.p., 1975-78; regional v.p. Union Bank, Oakland, Calif., 1978-80; chief mktg. officer Wells Fargo Leasing, San Francisco, 1980-81, chmn. bd., CEO, 1986-89; exec. v.p. and group head real estate group Wells Fargo Bank, San Francisco, 1981-92; exec. v.p. chief credit officer ITT Fin. Corp., St. Louis, 1993-95; chmn., pres., CEO ITT Lyndon Ins. Cos., St. Louis, 1993-95; pres. AIG Consumer Fin. Group, N.Y.C., 1995—; vice chmn. bd. SPC Credit, Ltd., Hong Kong. Chmn. Pacific Vision Found., 1989-93. Democrat. Presbyterian. Avocations: skiing, piano, golf. Office: AIG Consumer Fin Group 125 Maiden Ln New York NY 10038-4912

WALKER, DAVID A(LAN), finance educator; b. York, Pa., Jan. 5, 1941; s. Arthur Benjamin and Alva (Strasbougher) W.; m. Audrey Thayer, Aug. 21, 1982; children Matthew, Billett, Elizabeth, Penniman, Billartz. BA, Pa. State U., 1962; MS, Iowa State U., 1964, PhD, 1968. Asst. prof. Pa. State U., 1968-70; economist FDIC, 1970-76, 78-80; vis. assoc. prof. Northwestern U., 1976-77; dir. rsch. Office Compt. Currency, 1977-78; assoc. prof. fin. Georgetown U., 1980-82, prof., 1982-92, assoc. dean, 1985-87, John A. Largay Scholar, 1992—; dir. Ctr. for Bus. and Govt. Rels., 1989—; advisor U.S. Dept. Treas., U.S. SBA; cons. in field. Co-author textbooks; editor Jour. Fin. Rsch., 1981-87; co-editor Jour. Small Bus. Fin., 1992-95; mem. editl. bd. Jour. Fin. Rsch., Fin. Mgmt., J.F.Q.A., Fin. Rev., Quarterly Rev. Econs. and Fin., Jour. Small Bus. Fin.; contbr. articles to profl. jours. NDEA fellow, 1962-64. Mem. Am. Econ. Assn., So. Fin. Assn. (bd. dirs.), Ea. Fin. Assn. (bd. dirs.), Fin. Mgmt. Assn. (v.p. 1990-91, pres.-elect 1993-94, pres. 1994-95, bd. trustees 1995—). Republican. Home: 4845 Loughboro Rd NW Washington DC 20016-3454 Office: Georgetown U Sch Bus Washington DC 20057

WALKER, DAVID BRADSTREET, political science educator; b. Salem, Mass., May 7, 1927; s. George Lincoln and Mildred (Bradstreet) W.; m. Jeanne Hallahan, Sept. 1955; children: Melissa J., Stephen B., Justin D. BA, Boston U., 1949, MA, 1950; PhD, Brown U., 1956. Instr. in govt. Bowdoin Coll., Brunswick, Maine, 1956-57; ass.t prof. in govt. Bowdoin Coll., 1957-63; staff dir. subcom. on intergovt. relations U.S. Senate, Washington, 1963-66; asst. dir. for govt. structure & function Adv. Commn. on Intergovt. Relations, Washington, 1966-84; prof. polit. sci. U. Conn., Storrs, 1984—; dir. Inst. Pub. & Urban Affairs, U. Conn., Storrs, 1986-90; publ. and urban affairs keynote speaker ann. meetings of nat. orgns.; speaker at polit. sci. and govtl. orgns.; Fulbright prof. U. Göttingen, Germany, 1990-91. Author: Toward a Functioning Federalism, 1981, (with others) Managing Public Programs, 1989, (with others) The Great Society and its Legacy, 1986, The Rebirth of Federalism, 1995; contbr. articles to profl. jours. Citizen mem. Conn. Adv. Commn. on Intergovt. Rels., Hartford, 1985-96, chmn., 1986-90. With U.S. Army, 1945-47. Recipient Disting. Citizen award Nat. Mcpl. League, 1986, Donald C. Stone award for Significant Contbn. to Intergovt. Mgmt. in Acad./Rsch. Areas Membership, Nat. Acad. Pub. Adminstrn., Bosworth Meml. award Conn. chpt. Mem. Am. Soc. Pub. Adminstrn., Am. Polit. Sci. Assn. (spl. achievement award 1995), Nat. Acad. Pub. Adminstrn. (bd. dirs.), Phi Alpha Alpha, Phi Beta Kappa. Democrat. Episcopalian. Avocations: swimming, gardening, white water rafting, fishing. Home: 31 Edgewood Lane Ext Mansfield Center CT 06250-1210 Office: Inst Pub and Urban Affairs U 106 / U Conn 421 Whitney Road Ext Storrs Mansfield CT 06269-1106

WALKER, DAVID ELLIS, JR., educator, minister, consultant; b. Richmond, Va., Oct. 5, 1938; s. David Ellis and Laura Eloise (Vaughan) W.; m. Sandra Suzanne Barnes, Feb. 3, 1964; children: David Ellis III, Virginia Suzanne Walker Frizzell, Cindy Poole Key, Michelle Poole. BA, David Lipscomb U., 1960; MA, U. Fla., 1961, PhD, 1969. Ordained to ministry Ch. Christ, 1954. Instr. Jacksonville (Fla.) U., 1963-65; min. Ch. of Christ, 1954—; prof. Middle Tenn. State U., Murfreesboro, 1965—; cons. 1981—; acting chmn. dept. speech Middle Tenn. State U., summer 1984, fall 1990, dir. debate, 1965-70, pres. faculty senate, 1983-84. Author: Aletheia, 1991; editor Jour. of NonTraditional Education, 1992-96; contbr. articles to profl. jours. and Ency. U.S.A. Grad. fellow U. Fla., 1961-63; grantee Mid. Tenn. State U., 1967, 72, 77, 78, 88, 89, 90, 92, 93, 94, David Walker scholarship Mid. Tenn. State U., 1993—. Mem. Tenn. State Comm. Assn. (v.p. 1973-74, pres. 1974-75, editor Jour. Tenn. Speech Comm. Assn. 1977-85), Tenn. Intercollegiate Forensic Assn. (pres. 1966-67, exec. sec. 1967-68), Pi Kappa Delta (gov. province of S.E. 1966-68), Phi Kappa Phi (chpt. treas. 1989-90). Avocations: reading, walking. Home: 2644 E Compton Rd Murfreesboro TN 37130-6848 Office: Dept of Speech and Theatre Mid Tenn State U Murfreesboro TN 37132

WALKER, DAVID MICHAEL, human capital consultant, accountant; b. Birmingham, Ala., Oct. 2, 1951; s. David Sellers and Dorothy Ann (West) W.; m. Mary Carmel Etheredge, June 12, 1971; children: Carol Marie, James Andrew. BS in Acctg., Jacksonville U., 1973; Sr. Exec. Govt. Cert., Harvard U., 1986. CPA, Fla., Tex., Ga. Sr. auditor Price Waterhouse & Co. and Coopers & Lybrand, Jacksonville, Fla., 1973-76; dir. personnel Coopers & Lybrand, Atlanta and Houston, 1976-79; Ea. regional mgr. Source Services Corp., Washington, 1979-83; acting exec. dir. and dep. exec. dir. Pension Benefit Guaranty Corp., Washington, 1983-85; dep. asst. sec. U.S. Dept. of Labor, Washington, 1985-87, asst. sec., 1987-89; worldwide mng. ptnr. human capital svcs. practice Arthur Andersen LLP, Atlanta, 1989—; speaker in field. Author: Retirement Security-Understanding and Planning Your Financial Future, 1996; contbr. articles, editorial adv. bd. several profl. jours. Asst. Pvt. Pension and Welfare Plans; dir., former chmn. Investment and Acctg. Issues Com.; former vice-chmn. chair legis. affairs com. So. Employee Benefits Inst.; sec. of labor Erisa Adv. Coun.; former trustee Social Security and Medicare Trust Funds. Recipient numerous industry and achievement awards for outstanding svc. and contbns. Mem. AICPA (past chmn. employee benefit plans com.), Fla. Inst. CPAs, Ga. Soc. CPAs, Nat. Acad. Social Ins., ESOP Assn., Internat. Found. of Employee Benefit Plans, Coun. for Excellence in Govt. Republican. Methodist. Home: 997 Peachtree Battle Ave NW Atlanta GA 30327-1315 Office: Arthur Andersen 133 Peachtree St Atlanta GA 30303

WALKER, DEWARD EDGAR, JR., anthropologist, educator; b. Johnson City, Tenn., Aug. 3, 1935; s. Deward Edgar and Matilda Jane (Clark) W.; m. Candace J. Arroyo; children: Alice, Deward Edgar III, Mary Jane, Sarah, Daniel, Joseph Benjamin. Student, Ea. Oreg. Coll., 1953-54, 56-58, Mexico City Coll., 1958; BA in Anthropology with honors, U. Oreg., 1960-61, PhD in Anthropology, 1964; postgrad., Wash. State U., 1962. Asst. prof. anthropology George Washington U., Washington, 1964-65; asst. prof. anthropology Wash. State U., Pullman, 1965-67, research collaborator, 1967-69; assoc. prof., chmn. dept. Sociology/Anthropology, lab. dir. U. Idaho, Moscow, 1967-69; prof. U. Colo., Boulder, 1969—, research assoc. in population processes program of inst. behavioral sci., 1969-73, assoc. dean Grad. Sch., 1973-76; v.p. Walker Rsch. Group, Ltd., Boulder, Colo. Founder, co-editor Northwest Anthropol. Rsch. Notes, 1966—; editor, Plateau Vol.: Handbook of North American Indians, 1971; author, co-author 135 books, reports, articles and papers. Mem. tech. steering panel Hanford Environ. Dose Reconstrn. Project, 1988-95, Basalt Waste Isolation Project, Hanford, 1986-88; advisor on Native Am. affairs. With U.S. Army, 1954-62. Fellow NSF, 1961, NDEA, 1961-64. Fellow Am. Anthropol. Assn. (assoc. editor Am. Anthropologist 1973-74), Soc. Applied Anthropology (hon. life, exec. com. 1970-79, treas. 1976-79, chmn. 1980-95, cons., expert witness tribes of N.W., editor Human Orgn. 1970-76, rsch. over 65 projects with 135 monographs, articles, reports, and papers); mem. AAAS, Am. Acad. Polit. and Social Scis., N.W. Anthropol. Conf. Avocations: geology, mining. Home: PO Box 4147 Boulder CO 80306-4147 Office: U Colo PO Box 233 Boulder CO 80309-0233 *I have been both lucky and happy to have had the opportunities to do so many wonderful things in my life as an anthropologist.*

WALKER, DONALD ANTHONY, economist, educator; b. Mar. 6, 1934; s. Timothy Anthony and Helen (Walker) W.; m. Patricia Ann McKeage, Feb. 14, 1961; 1 dau., Valerie Alana. A.B., S.W. Tex. State U., 1952; M.A., U. Tex., 1956; Ph.D., Harvard U., 1961. Asst. prof. econs. Miami U., Oxford, Ohio, 1961-67; assoc. prof. econs. Miami U., 1967-69; prof. econs. Indiana U. Pa., 1969-88, chmn. dept., 1969—, Univ. prof., 1988—. Author: Walras's Market Models, 1996, Advances in General Equilibrium Theory, 1997; editor: William Jaffé's Essays on Walras, 1983, Money and Markets: Essays by Robert W. Clower, 1984, Perspectives on the History of Economic Thought, 1989, Welfare Economics and the Theory of Economic Policy, 1995, Jour. of the History of Econ. Thought; contbr. articles to profl. jours. Recipient Commonwealth of Pa. Disting. Acad. Service award, 1974, Ind. U.-Pa. Disting. Research Award, 1984; Harvard fellow, 1956-57, 57-58; Henry Lee Meml. fellow, 1957-58. Mem. History of Econs. Soc. (pres. 1987-

88). Home: 48 Shady Dr Indiana PA 15701-3245 Office: Indiana U of Pennsylvania Dept Econs McElhaney Hall Indiana PA 15705-1087

WALKER, DONALD EDWIN, history educator; b. Hammond, Ind., Feb. 6, 1941; s. Carl Thurston and Verla Irene (Cutler) W.; m. Julie Ann Woerpel, Dec. 20, 1960; children: Theodore R., Susan J. Walker. BA, Ind. U., 1963; MA, U. S.D., 1964; postgrad., U. Wyo., 1964-65; PhD, Mich. State U., 1982. Asst. prof. Olivet (Mich.) Coll., 1965-74, assoc. prof., 1974-82, prof., 1982—; cons. Score Cards, Westport, Conn., 1991. Co-author: Baseball and American Culture, 1995; contbr. articles to profl. jours. City coun. mem. Olivet City Coun., 1977—; police commr. Olivet Police Dept., 1984—; mayor pro tempore City of Olivet, 1983—. Mem. Orgn. of Am. Historians, Western History Assn., Phi Alpha Theta, Phi Kappa Phi, Omicron Delta Kappa, Phi Mu Alpha. Methodist. Avocations: gardening, music, reading, traveling, walking. Home: PO 516 407 Washington Olivet MI 49076 Office: Olivet Coll Dept History Mott Bldg Olivet MI 49076

WALKER, DONALD EZZELL, retired academic administrator; b. Springfield, Mo., July 13, 1921; s. Edward Everett and Cecilia (Ezzell) W.; m. Ann Lathrop, Dec. 17, 1943; 1 son, Craig Lathrop. A.B., U. So. Calif., 1943, M.Th., 1947; Ph.D., Stanford U., 1954; L.H.D. (hon.), Southeastern Mass. U., 1973. Recreational dir. club work All Nations Found., Los Angeles, 1941-42, Wilshire Meth. Ch., Los Angeles, 1942-43; asst. minister Vincent Meth. Ch., Los Angeles, 1943-44; minister Encinitas Meth. Ch., 1945-47; teaching asst. Stanford U., 1947-49; instr. sociology San Diego State Coll., 1949-51, asst. prof. sociology, 1951-54, assoc. dean students, counseling, 1954-56, dean counseling, 1956-58, v.p. acad. affairs, 1968-71, acting pres., 1971-72; dean of students San Fernando Valley State Coll., Northridge, Calif., 1958-60; pres. Idaho State U., 1960-64; dean of students Sonoma State Coll., Rohnert Park, Calif., 1964-66; vice chancellor student affairs U. Calif., Irvine, 1966-68, sr. lectr. Grad. Sch. Administrn., 1967-68, fellow Univ. Coll., 1967-68; pres. Southeastern Mass. State U., N. Dartmouth, 1972-83; chancellor Grossmont-Cuyamaca Community Coll. Dist., El Cajon, Calif., 1983-92; ret., 1992. Author: (with others) Readings in American Public Opinion; The Effective Administrator: A Practical Approach to Problem-Solving, Decision-Making, and Campus Leadership, 1979; contbr. (with others) articles to profl. jours. Home: 8661 Lake Murray Blvd Apt 19 San Diego CA 92119-2837

WALKER, DORIS ANN, education educator; b. Oxford, Miss., Aug. 6, 1950; d. Earnest Jr. and Mildred (Blackmon) McEwen; m. Grady Walker Jr., June 19, 1971 (div. Aug. 1990); children: Maleika Rene, Cheo Da'Mu. BS, No. Mich. U., 1971; MS, Mich. State U., 1975, PhD, 1981. Cert. tchr. 7-12, secondary adminstr. 5-12, supt. endorsement, Mich.; tchr., adminstr., Nev.; secondary adminstr., supt., Ind., Wash. Tchr. Flint (Mich.) Sch. Dist., 1972; tchr., sch. adminstr. Lansing (Mich.) Sch. Dist., 1973-86; prof. U. Nev., Reno, 1986-88, 96—; asst. prin. Waverly H.S., Lansing, 1988-91; prin. East Lansing (Mich.) H.S., 1991-94; assoc. prof. Ind. U., South Bend, 1994-96; asst. supt. Edmonds Sch. Dist. 15, Lynnwood, Wash., 1996—; edn. cons. Nev. State Dept. Edn., Carson City, 1986-88. Contbr. articles to profl. jours. Bd. dirs. Lansing Art Gallery; past advisor Boy Scouts Am.; cadette leader Mich. Capitol Girl Scouts; mem. nominating bd. YWCA; trustee meml. Hosp.; mem. urban youth adv. bd. YMCA. Mem. ASCD, NAACP, Nat. Assn. Secondary Sch. Prins., Nat. Alliance Black Sch. Educators, Am. Assn. Sch. Adminstrs., Mich. Assn. Secondary Sch. Prins., Ind. Assn. Secondary Sch. Prins., Optimist Club, Phi Delta Kappa, Delta Sigma Theta. Avocations: reading, computers, multimedia. Home: 710 Elm Pl W Edmonds WA 98020 Address: 900 Fifth Ave S #300 Edmonds WA 98020

WALKER, DOUGLASS WILLEY, retired pediatrician, medical center administrator; b. Thomaston, Maine, Aug. 3, 1913; s. Lee Wilson and Eliza Ann (Willey) W.; m. Janet Franklin Stockbridge, Mar. 21, 1942; children: Barbara, Elizabeth, Ann. BS, Bowdoin Coll., 1935, ScD (hon.), 1977; MD, Yale U., 1939. Diplomate Am. Bd. Pediatrics. Resident in pediatrics Yale Med. Sch.-New Haven Hosp., 1939-41, 46; pvt. practice, Laconia, N.H., 1946-63; pres. Laconia Clinic, 1963; asst. prof., asst. dean Johns Hopkins U. Med. Sch., Balt., 1963-67, assoc. prof., assoc. dean, 1967-70; med. dir. Maine Med. Ctr., Portland, 1970-75, v.p. med. affairs, 1975-78, corporator, 1970—; ret., 1978; assoc. clin. prof. Tufts U. Med. Sch., Boston, 1970-78; trustee Penobscot Bay Med. Ctr., Rockport, Maine, 1985-91; incorporator N.E. Health, Camden, Maine, 1985—. Mem. editl. bd. History of Preventive Medicine, World War II, 8 vols., 1955-76. Chmn. child health com. N.H. White House Conf., 1960; mem. adv. bd. So. Maine Vocat. Tech. Inst., South Portland, 1978-84; bd. mgrs. Park Danforth Home, Portland, 1980-82; sec., past pres. Martin Point Improvement Assn. Lt col. M.C., AUS, 1941-46. Decorated Legion of Merit. Mem. New Eng. Pediatric Soc. (past pres.). Republican. Methodist. Avocations: sailing, gardening, bridge. Home: PO Box 40 Friendship ME 04547-0040

WALKER, DUARD LEE, medical educator; b. Bishop, Calif., June 2, 1921; s. Fred H. and Anna Lee (Shumate) W.; m. Dorothea Virginia McHenry, Aug. 11, 1945; children: Douglas Keith, Donna Judith, David Cameron, Diane Susan. A.B., U. Calif. - Berkeley, 1943, M.A., 1947; M.D., U. Calif. - San Francisco, 1945. Diplomate Am. Bd. Microbiology. Intern, U.S. Naval Hosp., Shoemaker, Cal., 1945-46; asst. resident internal medicine Stanford U. Service San Francisco Hosp., 1950-52; asso. prof. med. microbiology and preventive medicine U. Wis., Madison, 1952-59; prof. med. microbiology U. Wis., 1959-88, prof., chmn. med. microbiology, 1970-76, 81-88, Paul F. Clark prof. med. microbiology, 1977-88, prof. emeritus, 1988—; cons. Naval Med. Rsch. Unit., Gt. Lakes, Ill., 1958-74; mem. microbiology tng. com. Nat. Inst. Gen. Med. Scis., 1966-70; mem. nat. adv. Allergy and Infectious Diseases Coun., 1970-74; mem. adv. com. on blood program rsch. ARC, 1978-79; mem. study group on papovaviridae Internat. Com. on Taxonomy of Viruses, 1976-90; mem. vaccines and related biol. products adv. com. FDA, 1985-89; mem. rev. panel postdoct. rsch. fellowships for physicians Howard Hughes Med. Inst., 1990-93. Mem. editorial bd. Infection and Immunity, 1975-83, Archives of Virology, 1981-83, Microbial Pathogenesis, 1985-90. Served to lt. comdr. USNR, 1943-46, 53-55. NRC postdoctoral fellow virology Rockefeller Inst. Med. Research, N.Y.C., 1947-49; USPHS fellow immunology George Williams Hooper Found., U. Calif. - San Francisco, 1949-50. Fellow Am. Pub. Health Assn., Am. Acad. Microbiology, Infectious Diseases Soc. Am.; mem. NAS, Am. Assn. Immunologists, Am. Soc. Microbiology, AAAS, Soc. Exptl. Biology and Medicine (editorial bd. Procs.), Reticulendothelial Soc. AAUP, Am. Soc. Virology, Wis. Acad. Scis., Arts and Letters. Home: 618 Odell St Madison WI 53711-1435 Office: U Wis Med Sch 1300 University Ave Madison WI 53706-1510

WALKER, E. JERRY, retired clergyman; b. Seattle, May 31, 1918; s. Septimus and Mae Ruth (Roys) W.; m. Holly Rae Harding, Nov. 10, 1941; children: Jerrianne, Dale Harding, Barbara Rae. AB, Seattle Pacific U., 1940; MDiv, Garrett Theol. Sch., 1945; DD, Wiley Coll., 1958, Northland Coll., 1971. Ordained to ministry United Meth. Ch. Teaching fellow State Coll. Wash., 1940-41; dir. edn. Prairie Farmer Sta. WLS, Chgo., 1942-45; dir. radio Internat. Coun. Religious Edn., 1945-48; freelance writer, dir. radio and TV Sta. WBKB-TV, Chgo., 1948-53; pastor St. James Meth. Ch., Chgo., 1953-62, First United Meth. Ch., Duluth, 1962-74; freelance daily commentary Sta. KDAL-TV, Duluth, Minn., 1964-76; exec. dir. Ctr. for Family Studies, Duluth, 1972-82; ptnr. SoundVideo Prodns., Tahuya, Wash., 1987—; cons. environ. grants, 1987—; project dir. Hood Canal Wetlands Interp Ctr., 1988—; bd. dirs. Pacific N.W. WRiters Conf., Wash., 1983-88; mem. gen. bd. Nat. Coun. Chs., 1954-66. Author: Five Minute Stories from the Bible, 1948, Stories from the Bible, 1955, Seeking a Faith of Your Own, 1961, Sinner's Parish, 1963, (plays) Checkerboard, Kyrie, The Unpainted Wall; also numerous articles. Bd. dirs. Chgo. chpt. NCCJ, 1955-62, nat. bd. trustees, 1974-76; mem. Kenwood-Ellis Cmty. Renewal Commn., 1957-62, Gov. Ill.'s Adv. Commn. on Aged, 1958-62, S.E. Chgo. Commn., 1958-62, United Fund Survey Com., 1968-70; co-chmn. Duluth Citizens Com. Secondary Edn., 1963-64; bd. dirs. Mary E. Theler Cmty. Ctr., Belfair, Wash., 1988-91; cons. Mason County United Way, 1990-94, co-chmn. needs assessment com., 1992-94; cons. Bremerton Hist. Ships Assn., 1994—. Recipient Human Rels. award Chgo. Commn. Human Rels., 1954, Friend of Youth award Southside Community Com., 1955, Disting. Citizen award Com. of One Hundred, 1962, Achievement award Freedom Found., 1963-65, Broadcast Journalism award Minn. Coun. Chs., 1971, Appreciation award North Mason Sch. Dist., 1990, Environ. Pride award Pacific Northwest Mag., 1992; named Chicagoan of Yr. Chgo. Jaycees, 1962. Mem. Internat. Platform Assn., Seattle Free Lances, Kiwanis. Democrat. Avocation: boating. Home: 18341 E State Highway 106 Belfair WA 98528-9588 Office: North Mason Sch Dist PO Box 167 Belfair WA 98528-0167

WALKER, EDWARD KEITH, JR., business executive, retired naval officer; b. Annapolis, Md., Jan. 23, 1933; s. Edward Keith and Miriam (Whitmore) W.; m. Carol Ann Turner, June 12, 1954; children: Lynn Walker Streett, Wendy Louise. BS, U.S. Naval Acad., 1954; postgrad., Armed Forces Staff Coll., 1966; MBA in Fin. Mgmt., George Washington U., 1970. Commd. ensign U.S. Navy, 1954, advanced through grades to rear admiral, 1981; force supply officer COMSUBLANT Norfolk, Va., 1975-78; exec. officer SPCC Mechanicsburg, Pa., 1978-80; comdr. Naval Supply Ctr., Puget Sound, Bremerton, Wash., 1980-81; Atlantic Fleet supply officer CINCLANTFLT Norfolk, 1981-83; asst. comptroller Navy Dept., Washington, 1983-84; comdr. Naval Supply Systems Command and 35th chief supply corps Washington, 1984-88; v.p. adminstrn. and corp. strategy Resource Cons. Inc., Vienna, Va., 1989—. Decorated D.S.M., Legion of Merit (3 awards); recipient Def. Superior Service medal, 1983. Mem. Vinson Hall Corp. (bd. dirs.), Naval Acad. Found. (trustee), U.S. Navy Meml. Found. (bd. dirs., treas.), Supply Corps Found. (past pres.), Supply Corps Assn. (past pres.), Am. Soc. Mil. Comptrs., U.S. Naval Inst., Am. Soc. Naval Engrs., Soc. Logistics Engrs., Nat. Security Indsl. Assn., Naval Submarine League, Naval Order U.S., Navy League U.S., Am. Def. Preparedness Assn., N.Y. Yacht Club, Chesapeake Yacht Club. Republican. Episcopalian. Home: 3520 Saylor Pl Alexandria VA 22304-1831 Office: Resource Cons Inc 1960 Gallows Rd Vienna VA 22182-3824 *There is no greater satisfaction than to see your people succeed, and then to insure they get the credit.*

WALKER, EDWARD S., JR., diplomat; b. Abington, Pa., June 13, 1940; s. Edward Stanley and Rosabel Dunlop (Gould) W.; m. Wendy Jane Griffiths, Apr. 7, 1973; Kathryn Erica, Christopher James. BA, Hamilton Coll., 1963; MA, Boston U., 1965. Joined Fgn. Svc., Dept. State, Washington, 1967; polit. officer Am. Embassy, Tel Aviv, 1969-73; staff asst. Nr. Ea. affairs Fgn. Svc., Dept. State, Washington, 1974-75; Arabic lang. trainee Fgn. Svc. Inst., Lebanon, Tunis, Egypt, 1975-77; polit. officer Am. Embassy, Damascus, Syria, 1977-79; spl. asst. Pres.'s personal rep., Washington, 1980-82; exec. dir. Office of Dep. Sec. State, Washington, 1982-84; mem. Royal Coll. Def. Studies, London, 1984-85; dep. chief of mission Am. Embassy, Riyadh, Saudi Arabia, 1985-88; dep. asst. sec. Dept. State, 1988-89; U.S. amb. to United Arab Emirates Abu Dhabi, 1989-92; dept. permanent rep. to UN, N.Y.C., 1993-94; U.S. amb. to Egypt Cairo, 1994—. With U.S. Army, 1962-65. Recipient Superior Honor award Dept. State, 1975, Meritorious Honor award, 1976, Abu Dhabi, Order of Independence, 1992. Mem. Internat. Inst. Strategic Studies. Episcopalian. Office: US Embassy Unit 64900 Box 1 APO AE 09839-4900

WALKER, ELJANA M. DU VALL, civic worker; b. France, Jan. 18, 1924; came to U.S., 1948; naturalized, 1954; student Med. Inst., U. Paris, 1942-47; m. John S. Walker, Jr., Dec. 31, 1947; children: John, Peter, Barbara. Pres., Loyola Sch. PTA, 1958-59; bd. dirs. Santa Claus shop, 1959-73; treas. Archdiocese Denver Catholic Women, 1962-64; rep. Cath. Parent-Tchr League, 1962-65; pres. Aux. Denver Gen. Hosp., 1966-69; precinct committeewoman Arapahoe County Republican Women's Com., 1973-74; mem. re-election com. Arapahoe County Rep. Party, 1973-78, Reagan election com., 1980; block worker Arapahoe County March of Dimes, Heart Assn., Hemophilia Drive, Muscular Dystrophy and Multiple Sclerosis Drive, 1978-81; cen. city asst. Guild Debutante Charities, Inc. Recipient Distinguished Service award Am.-by-choice, 1966; named to Honor Roll, ARC, 1971. Mem. Cherry Hills Symphony, Lyric Opera Guild, Alliance Franciase (life mem.), ARC, Civic Ballet Guild (life mem.), Needlework Guild Am. (v.p. 1980-82), Kidney Found. (life), Denver Art Mus., U. Denver Art and Conservation Assns. (chmn. 1980-82), U. Denver Women's Library Assn., Chancellors Soc, Passage Inc., Friends of the Fine Arts Found. (life), CHildren's Diabetes Found. (life). Roman Catholic. Clubs: Union (Chgo.); Denver Athletic, 26 (Denver); Welcome to Colo. Internat. Address: 2301 Green Oaks Dr Greenwood Village CO 80121

WALKER, ESPER LAFAYETTE, JR., retired civil engineer; b. Decatur, Tex., Sept. 22, 1930; s. Esper Lafayette and Ruth (Mauldin) W.; B.S., Tex. A&M U., 1953; B.H.T., Yale U., 1958; m. Sara Lynn Dunlap, Oct. 2, 1955; children: William David, Annette Ruth. Design engr. Tex. Hwy. Dept., Austin, 1956-57; dir. Dept. Traffic Engring., High Point, N.C., 1958-63, 63-68, Columbia, S.C.; v.p. Wilbur Smith & Assos., Houston, 1968-89, sr. v.p., 1989-94, bd. dirs., 1994-95; ret., 1994. Pres. Meadow Wood PTA, 1976-77; chmn. Pack 902 com. Sam Houston council Boy Scouts Am., 1973-74, treas. Troop 904 com., 1976-80; treas. Stratford High Band, 1981-82, bd. dirs., 1980-82; baseball team mgr. Spring Br. Sports Assn., 1975-77; mem. adminstrv. bd. Meml. Drive Meth. Ch., 1971-77, 83-89, 90-94, 95-98, bldg. com., 1974-82, 94-97, fin. com., 1975-77, 83-85, trustee, 1983-94, chmn. bd. trustees, 1990-94. Served to 1st lt. C.E., AUS, 1953-56. Recipient Key Man award High Point Jaycees, 1962. Registered profl. engr., Tex., S.C., Colo., Ark., Wis., La., Okla., N.Mex., Wyo. Mem. Nat., Tex. socs. profl. engrs., High Point Jaycees (dir.), Tex. A&M U. Alumni Assn. (ctr. urban affairs council 1985-90, vice chmn. 1988), Houston C. of C. (chmn. transit com. 1975-79), Inst. Transp. Engrs. (pres. So. sect. 1963). Clubs: Galveston Country Club, Plaza, Westlake and Gov. Club. Home: 14216 Kellywood Ln Houston TX 77079-7410

WALKER, EVELYN, retired television executive; b. Birmingham, Ala.; d. Preston Lucas and Mattie (Williams) W.; AB, Huntingdon Coll., 1927; student Cornell U., 1927-28; MA, U. Ala., 1963; LHD, Huntingdon Coll., 1974. Speech instr. Phillips High Sch., Birmingham, 1930-34; head speech dept. Ramsay High Sch., Birmingham, 1934-52; chmn. radio and TV, Birmingham Pub. Schs., 1944-75, head instructional TV programming svcs., 1969-75; mem. summer faculty extension div. U. Va., 1965, 66, 67; former regional cons. ednl. TV broadcasting; Miss Ann, broadcaster children's daily radio program, Birmingham, 1946-57; prodr. Our Am. Heritage radio series, 1944-54; TV staff prodr. programs shown daily Ala. Pub. TV Network, 1954-75; past cons. Gov.'s Ednl. TV Legis. Study Com., 1953; nat. del. Asian-Am. Women Broadcasters Conf., 1966; former regional cons. Ednl. TV Broadcasting. Mem. emerita Nat. Def. Adv. Com. on Women in Svcs.; past TV-radio co-chmn. Gov.'s Adv. Bd. Safety Com.; past chmn. creative TV-radio writing competition Festival of Arts; past audio-visual chmn. Ala. Congress, also past mem. Birmingham coun. PTA; media chmn. Gov.'s Commn. on Yr. of the Child; bd. dirs. Women's Army Corps Mus., Fort MiClellen, 1960-93. Recipient Alumnae Achievement award Huntingdon Coll., 1958; Tops in Our Town award Birmingham News, 1957; Air Force Recruiting plaque, 1961; Spl. Bowl award for promoting arts through Ednl. TV. Birmingham Festival of Arts, 1962; citation 4th Army Corps., 1962; cert. of appreciation Ala. Multiple Sclerosis Soc., 1962; Freedoms Found. at Valley Forge Educator's medal award, 1963; Top TV award ARC, 1964; Ala. Woman of Achievement award, 1964; Bronze plaque Ala. Dist. Exch. Clubs, 1969; cert. of appreciation Birmingham Bd. Edn., 1975; Obelisk award Children's Theatre, 1976; 20-Yr. Svc. award Ala. Ednl. TV Commn.; key to city of Birmingham, 1966; named Woman of Yr., Birmingham, 1965; named Ala. Woman of Yr., Progressive Farmer mag., 1966; hon. col. Ala. Militia. Mem. Am. Assn. Ret. Persons, Ala. Assn. Ret. Tchrs., Huntingdon Coll. Alumnae Assn. (former internat. pres.), Former Am. Women in Radio and TV, Arlington Hist. Assn. (dir., pres. 1981-83), Magna Charta Dames (past state sec.-treas.), DAR (former pub. rels. com. Ala., TV chmn., state program chmn. 1979-85, state chmn. Seimes Microfilm com. 1985-88, state chmn. Motion Picture, Radio TV com. 1988-94, tricom. chmn. 1988-94), Colonial Dames 17th Century, U.S. Daus. 1812 (past state TV chmn.), Daus. Am. Colonists (past 2d v.p. local chpt., past state TV and radio chmn.), Ams. Royal Descent, Royal Order Garter, Plantagenets Soc. Am., Salvation Army Women's Aux., Symphony Aux., Humane Soc. Aux., Eagle Forum, Nat. League Am. Pen Women, Womens's Com. 100 for Birmingham (bd. dirs.), Royal Order Crown, Women in Communications (past local pres., nat. headliner 1965), Internat. Platform Assn., Birmingham-Jefferson Hist. Soc., Delta Delta Delta (mem. Golden Circle), Ladies Golf Assn., Birmingham Country Club, The Club. Methodist. Home: Kirkwood By The River 3605 Ratliff Rd Birmingham AL 35210-4512

WALKER, FLOYD LEE, lawyer; b. Kiefer, Okla., Mar. 27, 1919; s. Willis and Sarah Josephine (McFarl) W.; children by previous marriage: Mary Lea Walker Byrd, Cheryl Sue Walker Newman, James M.; m. Virginia Gifford Raines, Oct. 8, 1971. LLB, Tulsa U., 1949. Bar: Okla. 1949. Claims atty. Standard Ins. Co., Tulsa, 1949-53; pvt. practice Tulsa, 1953—. 1st lt. USAAF, 1942-45. Decorated DFC, Air medal with 3 oak leaf clusters. Fellow Am. Coll. Trial Lawyers; mem. ABA, ATLA, Okla. Bar Assn. (bd. govs. 1979-82), Tulsa County Bar Assn. (pres. 1973), Okla. Trial Lawyers Assn. Home: 1502 S Boulder Ave Apt 7B Tulsa OK 74119-4022 Office: 900 Oneok Plz Tulsa OK 74103

WALKER, FRANCIS JOSEPH, lawyer; b. Tacoma, Aug. 5, 1922; s. John McSweeney and Sarah Veronica (Meechan) W.; m. Julia Corinne O'Brien, Jan. 27, 1951; children: Vincent Paul, Monica Irene Hylton, Jill Marie Nudell, John Michael, Michael Joseph, Thomas More. B.A., St. Martin's Coll., 1947; J.D., U. Wash., 1950. Bar: Wash. Asst. atty. gen. State of Wash., 1950-51; pvt. practice law, Olympia, Wash., 1951—; gen. counsel Wash. Cath. Conf., 1967-76. Lt. (j.g.) USNR, 1943-46; PTO. Home and Office: 2723 Hillside Dr SE Olympia WA 98501-3460

WALKER, FRANK BANGHART, pathologist; b. Detroit, June 14, 1931; s. Roger Venning and Helen Frances (Reade) W.; m. Phyllis Childs; children: Nancy Anne, David Carl, Roger Osborne, Mark Andrew. BS, Union Coll., N.Y., 1951; MD, Wayne State U., 1955, MS, 1962. Diplomate Am. Bd. Pathology (trustee 1982-94, treas. 1984-91, v.p. 1991-92, pres. 1993-94). Intern Detroit Meml. Hosp., 1955-56; resident Wayne State U. and affiliated hosps., Detroit, 1958-62; pathologist, 1962-93; dir. labs. Detroit Meml. Hosp., 1984-87, Cottage Hosp., Grosse Pointe, Mich., 1984-93; pathologist, dir. labs. Macomb Hosp Ctr. (formerly South Macomb Hosp.), Warren, Mich., 1966-93, Jennings Meml. Hosp., Detroit, 1971-79, Alexander Blain Hosp., Detroit, 1971-85; ptnr. Langston, Walker & Assocs., P.C., Grosse Pointe, 1968-93; instr. pathology Wayne State U. Med. Sch., Detroit, 1962-72, asst. clin. prof., 1972-94, assoc. clin. prof., 1994—. Pres. Mich. Assn. Blood Banks, 1969-70; mem. med. adv. com. ARC, 1972-83; mem. Mich. Higher Edn. Assistance Authority, 1975-77; trustee Alexander Blain Meml. Hosp., Detroit, 1974-83, Detroit-Macomb Hosp. Corp., 1974-93, 95—; bd. dirs. Wayne State Fund, 1971-83. Capt. M.C., U.S. Army, 1956-58. Recipient Disting. Svc. award Wayne State U. Med. Sch., 1990. Fellow Detroit Acad. Medicine (pres.-elect 1995-96, pres. 1996-97); mem. AMA (coun. on long-range planning and devel. 1982-88. vice chmn. 1985-87, chmn. 1987-88, trustee 1988-96), Coll. Am. Pathologists (Disting. Svc. award 1989), Am. Soc. Clin. Pathologists (sec. 1971-77, pres. 1979-80, Disting. Svc. award 1989), Mich. Soc. Pathologists (pres. 1980-81), Wayne County Med. Soc. (pres. 1984-85, trustee 1986-91, chmn. 1990-91), Mich. Med. Soc. (bd. dirs. 1981-90, vice chmn. 1985-88, chmn. 1988-90), Am. Assn. Blood Banks, Mich. Assn. Blood Banks, Wayne State U. Alumni Assn. (bd. govs. 1968-71), Wayne State U. Med. Alumni Assn. (pres. 1969, trustee 1970-85, Disting. Alumni award 1974), Econ. Club Detroit, Detroit Athletic Club, Lochmoor Club, Mid-Am. Club, Alpha Omega Alpha, Phi Gamma Delta, Nu Sigma Nu. Republican. Episcopalian. Home and Office: 14004 Harbor Place Dr Saint Clair Shores MI 48080-1528

WALKER, FRANK DILLING, market research executive; b. Indpls., Dec. 31, 1934; s. Frank D. and Dorothy Mae (Cole) W.; m. Jane Tatman, Aug. 25, 1979; children—Steven F., Leah R. B.A., DePauw U., 1957. Chmn., CEO Walker Group, Indpls., 1960-95, Walker Clin. Evaluations, Inc., Indpls., 1986-95; chmn. Walker Info., 1995—; bd. dirs. Am. United Life Ins. Co., NBD Ind. Nat. Bank, State Life Ins. Co.; frequent speaker on market rsch. to various groups. Contbr. articles trade publs. Past mem. Indpls. Hist. Preservation Commn.; bd. dirs. Ind. Repertory Theatre, Meth. Hosp., United Way of Greater Indpls.; adv. council Indpls. Mus. Art, Buchanan Counseling Center; former chmn. Central Ind. Better Bus. Bur.; former chmn. Indpls. Econ. Devel. Corp.; trustee Children's Mus. Indpls., Univ. Indpls.; former bd. dirs. Jr. Achievement Central Ind., mem. adv. council; trustee The Children's Mus., YMCA Found.; bd. dirs. Citizens Gas and Coke Utility. With USAF, 1958-60. Mem. Council Am. Survey Research Orgns. (past chmn. bd.), Am. Mktg. Assn. (past pres. Ind. chpt.), Indpls. Sales and Mktg. Execs. Assn. (past pres.), Indpls. C. of C. (past chmn.), Mktg. Rsch. Assn. (hon. life), Sigma Chi. Republican. Methodist. Office: Walker Info 3939 Priority Way South Dr Indianapolis IN 46240-1496

WALKER, FRED ELMER, broadcasting executive; b. Trenton, N.J., May 31, 1931; s. Elmer and Adele F. (Decker) W.; m. Catharine Middleton Sullivan, Nov. 26, 1952; children: Catharine Walker Bergstrom, Elizabeth Walker Phillips, Frederick Christopher. Student, Trenton State Coll., 1952, NYU, 1953. Dir. pub. relations Sta. WPTZ-TV, Phila., 1953; v.p., gen. mgr. Sta. WTTM-AM, Trenton, 1956-59; gen. sales mgr. Sta. KYW-AM, Cleve., 1959-62; v.p., gen. mgr. Sta. KDKA-AM, Pitts., 1962-65, Sta. KYW-TV, Phila., 1965-67, Sta. KPIX-TV, San Francisco, 1967-69, Sta. WLWT-TV, Cin., 1969-71; pres. Broad St. Communications Corp., New Haven, 1971-85; v.p. radio group Westinghouse Broadcasting, N.Y.C., 1985-88; exec. v.p. Broad St. Ventures, N.Y.C., 1988—; pres. Broad St. TV Corp., 1988—, Broad. St. Mgmt. Corp., 1988—; bd. dirs. Broadcast Music, Inc., 1984-87, Call for Action, Washington, 1993—. Bd. dirs. Long Wharf Theatre, New Haven; chmn. Long Wharf Theatre Future Fund campaign, 1983-85, chmn. devel., 1986-90, chmn. and pres., 1990-97; mem. Pres.'s Coun. Albertus Magnus Coll.; trustee Hamden Hall Country Day Sch., chmn. devel. com.; chmn. 250th fund dr. United Ch. Christ, 1987—; chmn. Call For Action, Washington, 1994—. Recipient Alfred P. Sloan award, 1954, Ohio State Ednl. award, 1953; fellow Berkeley Coll. Yale U., 1976. Mem. Radio Advt. Bur. (dir.), TV Bur. Advt., Nat. Assn. Broadcasters, New Haven C. of C. (vice chmn.), New Haven Lawn Club, Quinnipiac Club. Republican. Office: Sturbridge Commons North Haven CT 06473 also: Long Wharf Theatre 222 Sargent Dr New Haven CT 06511-5919

WALKER, GARY LINN, materials and logistics executive, consultant; b. Cin., Apr. 26, 1947; s. Ward Walkie and Cora Lee (Reynolds) W.; m. Mary Lee Robertson, Aug. 30, 1969; 1 child, Charlotte Anne. BA, Samford U., 1969. Cert. fellow in prodn. and inventory mgmt. Prodn. planner, prodn. foreman, indsl. engr., Cin., 1969-74; mfg. mgr. Xomox Inc., 1974-77; materials mgr. Textron Inc.-Sprague Meter Divsn., 1977-80; dir. materials and mgmt. info. Fairchild Inc., Beckley, W.Va., 1980-83; materials mgr., corp. mgr. distbn. and logistics Pelikan Inc./Dennison Mfg. Co., Franklin, Tenn., 1983-94; internat. mgr. mfg. and logistics Pelikan Inc./Dennison Mfg. Co., Franklin, 1983-94; application cons. The Everest Group, Nashville, 1994-97; cons. Nukote/Pelikan, Derry, Pa., 1995-97, Pelikan Europa, Egg, Switzerland, 1989-94, Magnetic Marelli, USA, 1997—. V.p. Young Dems., Samford U., 1967-69. With U.S. Army, 1970-71. Avocation: golf. Home: 2049 Long Point Trail Sanford NC 27331 Office: Magnoti Marelli PO Box 548 Sanford NC 27331

WALKER, GEORGE KONTZ, law educator; b. Tuscaloosa, Ala., July 8, 1938; s. Joseph Henry and Catherine Louise (Indorf) W.; m. Phyllis Ann Sherman, July 30, 1966; children: Charles Edward, Mary Neel. BA, U. Ala., 1959; LLB, Vanderbilt U., 1966; AM, Duke U., 1968; LLM, U. Va., 1972; postgrad. (Sterling fellow), Law Sch. Yale U., 1975-76. Bar: Va. 1967, N.C. 1976. Law clk. U.S. Dist. Ct., Richmond, Va., 1966-67; assoc. Hunton, Williams, Gay, Powell & Gibson, Richmond, 1967-70; pvt. practice Charlottesville, Va., 1970-71; asst. prof. Law Sch. Wake Forest U., Winston-Salem, N.C., 1972-73, assoc. prof. Law Sch., 1974-77, prof. Law Sch., 1977—; mem. bd. advisors Divinity Sch. Wake Forest U., 1991-94; Charles H. Stockton prof. internat. law U.S. Naval War Coll., 1992-93; vis. prof. Marshall-Wythe Sch. Law, Coll. William and Mary, Williamsburg, Va., 1979-80, U. Ala. Law Sch., 1985; cons. Naval War Coll., 1976—, Nat. Def. Exec. Res., 1991—, Naval War Coll., Operational Law Adv. Bd., 1993—. Co-author: Moore's Federal Practice, 3rd edit., 1997; contbr. articles to profl. jours. With USN, 1959-62, capt. USNR, ret. Woodrow Wilson fellow, 1962-63; recipient Joseph Branch Alumni Svc. award, Wake Forest, 1988; named Hon. Atty. Gen. N.C., 1986. Mem. ABA, Va. Bar Assn., N.C. Bar Assn. (chair internat. law & practice sect. 1995-96), Am. Soc. Internat. Law (exec. coun. 1988-91), Internat. Law Assn., Am. Judicature Soc., Am. Law Inst., Maritime Law Assn., Order of Barristers, Piedmont Club, Phi Beta Kappa, Sigma Alpha Epsilon, Phi Delta Phi. Democrat. Episcopalian. Home: 3321 Pennington Ln Winston Salem NC 27106-5439 Office: Wake Forest U Sch Law PO Box 7206 # U Winston Salem NC 27109

WALKER, GEORGE THEOPHILUS, JR., composer, pianist, music educator; b. Washington, June 27, 1922; s. George Theophilus Sr. and Rosa (King) W.; children: Gregory, Ian. MusB, Oberlin Coll., 1941; student of,

Rudolf Serkin, Rosario Scalero; Artist Diploma, Curtis Inst. music, 1945; D of Mus. Arts, U. Rochester, 1957; DFA (hon.), Lafayette Coll., 1982; MusD (hon.), Oberlin Coll., 1983; student of, Nadia Boulanger; MusD (hon.), Curtis Inst. Music, 1997; DHL (hon.), Montclair State U., 1997, Bloomfield Coll., 1997. Instr. Dillard U., New Orleans, 1953-54; instr. Dalcroze Sch. Music, N.Y.C., 1960-61, New Sch. Social Research, N.Y.C., 1961; instr. to assoc. prof. Smith Coll., Northampton, Mass., 1961-68; assoc. prof. U. Colo., Boulder, 1968-69; disting. prof. Rutgers U., Newark, 1976-92, prof. emeritus, 1992; concert pianist Nat. Concert Artists, N.Y.C., 1950-53, Columbia Artists, N.Y.C., 1959-60; adj. prof. Peabody Inst. Johns Hopkins U., Balt., 1973-76; disting. prof. U. Del., Newark, 1975-76. Composer: Sonata for 2 Pianos (Harvey Gaul prize 1963), numerous sonatas, cantatas and concertos, Concerto for Cello and Orch., 1982, Sinfonias for Orch. Bd. dirs. Am. Bach Found., 1988. Recipient award Am. Acad. and Inst. Arts and Letter, 1982, Koussevitsky award, 1988, Pulitzer prize, 1996, L.J. Govs. award 1997; grantee Smith Coll., U. Colo., Rutger U. Rsch. Coun., NEA, N.J. State Coun. for Arts; Fulbright fellow, 1957, John Hay Whitney fellow, 1958, Guggenheim fellow, 1969, 88, Rockefeller fellow, 1971, 74; Disting. scholar U. Rochester, 1996; commd. N.Y. Philharm., Kennedy Ctr., Cleve. Orch., Boston Symphony. Mem. ASCAP, Am. Bach Found. (bd. dirs. 1988), Am. Symphony League. Democrat. Avocations: tennis, photography, audio. Home: 323 Grove St Montclair NJ 07042-4223

WALKER, GEORGE W., bishop. Bishop, treas. Bd. Bishops AME Zion Ch., flossmoor, Il. Office: AME Zion Church 3654 Poplar Rd Flossmoor IL 60422-2239*

WALKER, GORDON T., lawyer; b. June 12, 1942; M. Nancy Geary; children: Angus, Gwendolyn. AB, Tufts U., 1964; LLB, Harvard U., 1967. Bar: Mass. 1968, U.S. Dist. Ct. Mass., U.S. Ct. Appeals (1st cir.), U.S. Supreme Ct. Assoc., then ptnr. Hale and Dorr, Boston, 1968-82; ptnr. Finnegan, Stanzler, Nadeau & Walker, Boston, 1982-84; ptnr., head litigation dept. McDermott, Will & Emery, Boston, 1984—; mem. Mass. Joint Bar Com. on Jud. Nominations, 1994-97, chmn., 1996-97. Mem. ABA (co-chmn. litigation sect. alternative dispute resolution com. 1986-91, vice chmn. 1993-94), Am. Arbitration Assn., Boston Bar Assn. (chair com. internat. dispute resolution 1992-94). Office: McDermott Will & Emery 75 State St Ste 1700 Boston MA 02109-1807

WALKER, H. LAWSON, lawyer; b. Cin., Feb. 10, 1949; s. H. Lawson and Lucille (Kerr) W.; m. Peggy L. Walker, June 1, 1974; children: Erin, Jonathan. BBA, U. Coll. of Bus., Cin., 1972; JD, U. Cin. Coll. of Law, Cin., 1975. Bar: 6th cir. 1975, U.S. Dist. Ct. (Ohio dist.) 1975, ED Ky. 1975, Ohio 1975, Ky. 1976. Assoc. Riggs & Riggs, Erlanger, Ky., 1975-80; ptnr. Riggs, Riggs & Walker, Erlanger, Ky., 1980-87, Dinsmore & Shohl, Florence, Ky., 1987-92, Brown, Todd & Heyburn, Covington, Ky., 1992—; dir. Liberty Nat. Bank of No. Ky. State rep. Ky. Legislature, Frankfort, 1987; chmn. Rep. Party, Fenton County, Ky., 1980, 85; chmn. No. Ky. Legis. Caucus, 1991-93; dist. chmn. Powderhorn dist. Boy Scouts Am., 1995—; bd. dirs. No. Ky. Easter Seals, Covington, 1982—, Sanitation Dist. of Kenton, Campbell and Boone Counties; deacon Lakeside Christian Ch., Ft. Mitchell, Ky., 1983—. Recipient Leadership award, Ky. C. of C., Frankfort, 1988. Mem. Ohio Bar Assn., Ky. Bar Assn., No. Ky. Bar Assn., Ky. Sch. Bd. Atty. Assn., Ky. Acad. Trial Attys., U. Cin. Alumni Assn. (bd. dirs. 1988-95). Republican. Christian. Home: 28A Linden Hill Dr Crescent Springs KY 41017-1308 Office: Brown Todd & Heyburn 50 E Rivercenter Blvd Covington KY 41011

WALKER, HAROLD BLAKE, minister; b. Denver, May 7, 1904; s. Herbert R. and Ethel G. (Blake) W.; m. Mary Alice Corder, Feb. 1, 1930; children—Herbert Elwood, Howard Deane, Timothy Blake. AB, U. Denver, 1925, DD, 1952; AM, Boston U., 1927; BD, McCormick Theol. Sem., 1932; postgrad., U. Chgo., 1933-34; DD, Emporia Coll., 1944, Hamilton Coll., 1949, U. Denver, 1952, Rocky Mountain Coll., 1971; LHD, Lake Forest U., 1959, Nat. Coll. Edn., 1970; STD, Northwestern U., 1970. Editor, writer A.P., Kansas City, 1927-30; ordained to ministry Presbyn. Ch., 1932; minister Fullerton-Covenant Ch., Chgo., 1932-36; minister First Ch., Utica, N.Y., 1936-42, Oklahoma City, 1942-47; minister 1st Presbyn. Ch., Evanston, Ill., 1947-69; columnist Splty. Salesman mag., 1954-67, Chgo. Tribune-N.Y. News syndicated columnist, 1954-81; lectr. homiletics McCormick Theol. Sem.; lectr., bd. dirs. Harold Blake Walker chair pastoral theology; cons. W. Clement Stone Enterprises, 1970-74; sem. v.p. Bd. Fgn. Missions Presbyn. Ch. U.S.A.; Nat. Commn. Evangelism, 1946-47; dir. Presbyn. Tribune, 1943-55; mem. Presbyn. Commn. on Consolidation, 1957-58, Commn. on Ecumenical Mission Relations, 1958-61. Author: Going God's Way, 1946, Ladder of Light, 1951, Upper Room on Main Street, 1954, Power to Manage Yourself, 1955, (with wife) Venture of Faith, 1959, Heart of the Christian Year, 1962, Faith for Times of Tension, 1963, Thoughts to Live By, 1965, To Conquer Loneliness, 1966, Prayers to Live By, 1966, Memories to Live By, 1968, Inspirational Thoughts for Everyday, 1970, Days Demanding Courage, 1978, History of St. John's of Red Cross of Constantine, 1985, Caring Community, 1986; contbr. to religious publs. Bd. dirs. Nat. Presbyn. Ch. and Ctr., Washington; bd. dirs. McCormick Theol. Sem., pres., 1953-55, 57-71; bd. dirs. Ill. Masonic Med. Center, Chgo., Lake Forest Coll.; trustee Maryville Coll. Recipient DeMolay Legion of Honor; Freedoms Found. sermon prize, 1950, 55, 77; citations Protestant Fund. Greater Chgo., 1970; Chgo. Inst. Medicine Citizens fellow, 1987; citations Chgo. Friends of Lit., 1971, 79; Disting. Alumnus award McCormick Theol. Sem., 1979. Mem. Utica Council Chs. (pres. 1940), Am. Theol. Soc. Chgo. Cleric, Pi Kappa Alpha. Clubs: Univ. (Chgo.). Lodge: Masons (Chgo., Evanston) (Shriner, 33 deg., grand chaplain N.Y. 1940-41). Home: 422 Davis St Evanston IL 60201-4610

WALKER, HERSCHEL, professional football player; b. Wrightsville, Ga., Mar. 3, 1962; m. Cindi Di Angelis. BS in Criminal Justice, U. Ga., 1984. Football player N.J. Generals, 1983-85, Dallas Cowboys, 1986-89, 96—, Minn. Vikings, 1989-91, Phila. Eagles, 1992-95, N.Y. Giants, 1995. Named to Sporting News coll. All-Am. team, 1980-82, United States Football League All-Star team, 1983, 85, Pro Bowl, 1987, 88; recipient Heisman trophy, 1982; named Sporting News Coll. Football Player of Yr., 1982, Sporting News United States Football League Player of Yr., 1985. Office: Dallas Cowboys 1 Cowboys Pky Irving TX 75063*

WALKER, HOWARD ERNEST, lawyer; b. Mobile, Ala., Mar. 3, 1944; s. Ernest W. and Denise (Kearney) W.; m. Michelle Ann Pinsonneault, June 20, 1992. BA, U. Ill., 1966; JD, Boston U., 1974. Bar: R.I. 1974. Assoc. Hinckley, Allen & Snyder, Providence, R.I., 1974-80, ptnr., 1980—. Trustee Providence Pub. Libr., 1978—, pres., 1988-92; trustee R.I. Wild Plant Soc., 1995—; trustee R.I. Civic Chorale & Orchestra, 1988-95. Lt. USNR, 1967-71. Mem. ABA, R.I. Bar Assn. (chmn. superior ct. bench/bar com. 1990-93, 94-95), Maritime Law Assn. of U.S., Nat. Assn. R.R. Trial Counsel, Def. Rsch. Inst., Phi Kappa Phi, Phi Beta Kappa. Avocations: Western Americana, nat. hist. Home: 39A Berrie Ln PO Box 118 Rockville RI 02873-0118 Office: Hinckley Allen & Snyder 1500 Fleet Ctr Providence RI 02903

WALKER, IRVING EDWARD, lawyer; b. Balt., Jan. 31, 1952; s. Bertram and Mildred (Shapiro) W.; m. Laura Sachs, May 21, 1978; children: Brandon Harris, Aaron Seth, Emily Celeste. BA, Duke U., 1973; JD, U. Md., 1978. Bar: Md. 1978, U.S. Dist. Ct. Md. 1978, U.S. Ct. Appeals (4th cir.) 1980, U.S. Supreme Ct. 1995. Assoc. Frank, Bernstein, Conaway & Goldman, Balt., 1978-85, ptnr., 1986-91; ptnr. Miles & Stockbridge, Balt., 1991—; chair Bankruptcy & Creditors Rights Group, 1991—, bd. dirs., 1995—. Contbg. author: Bankruptcy Deskbook, 1986. Bd. dirs. Jewish Community Ctr. Greater Balt., 1986-88, Temple Emanuel of Balt., Inc. Mem. ABA (mem. chpt. 11 subcom. 1993, co-chairperson task force 3rd, 4th and D.C. cirs.), Md. Bar Assn., Bar Assn. Balt. City (chmn. bankruptcy and bus. law com. 1989-90), Am. Bankruptcy Inst., Bankruptcy Assn. Dist. Md. (pres. 1992-93, chmn. Balt. chpt. 1989-91), Order of Coif. Avocation: sports. Office: Miles & Stockbridge 10 Light St Baltimore MD 21202-1435

WALKER, JAMES BRADLEY, academic institution administrator; b. N.Y.C., Apr. 10, 1948; s. James Bradley and Mary Jane (Thayer) W.; m. Virginia Lynn, Apr. 11, 1969; children: Carol Renee, Laura Jane. BS, Calif. Poly. State U., 1975. Comptroller Albuquerque Western Industries, 1975-78; CFO U. N.Mex. Hosp., Albuquerque, 1978-84, Univ. Hosp., Portland, Oreg., 1984-92; v.p. fin. and adminstrn. Oreg. Health Scis. U., Portland, 1992—. Sgt. USAF, 1969-72. Avocations: golfing, travel. Office: Oreg Health Scis U Hosp 3181 SW Sam Jackson Park Rd Portland OR 97201-3011

WALKER, JAMES ELLIOT CABOT, physician; b. Bryn Mawr, Pa., Sept. 28, 1926; s. Arthur Meeker and Sylvia (Cabot) W.; m. Audrey Crowder Wakeman, July 11, 1965; children—Holly Barnwell, James Elliot Cabot. B.A., Williams Coll., 1949; M.D., U. Pa., 1953; M.S. in Hygiene, Harvard U., 1966. Intern and resident in medicine U. Wis., 1953, U. Mich., 1954-55, Peter Bent Brigham Hosp., 1958-60; assoc. dir., sr. assoc. dept. medicine Peter Bent Brigham Hosp., Boston; also research asst., lectr. Harvard U. Med. Sch., 1959-65; chmn. dept. community medicine U. Conn. Med. Sch., Farmington, 1966-86, prof. medicine, 1966—; vis. prof. St. Thomas' Hosp., London, 1975-76, Harvard Med. Sch., Cambridge, Mass., 1986-87; pres. Northeast Can./Am. Health Coun., 1978-87; dir. Ctr. for Internat. Cmty. Health Studies, 1981-86; assoc. dir. Traveler's Ctr. on Aging, 1987—; chmn. Alzheimers Coalition of Conn., 1992-94; med. dir. Avery Heights Retirement Cmty., 1992—. Author articles, monograph in field. Served with Am. Field Service, 1945; to capt. M.C. U.S. Army, 1955-58. Fellow ACP, AGS. Home: 111 Westmont St West Hartford CT 06117-2929 Office: U Conn Health Center Farmington CT 06032

WALKER, JAMES KENNETH, judge; b. Decatur, Tex., Jan. 10, 1936; s. James Bluford and Elmer Vernice (Clark) W.; m. Mary Frank Garrett, July 9, 1960 (dec. Nov. 1976); children—James Garrett, Steven Wade; m. Jo Beth Robertson, July 28, 1978; 1 child, Ann Elizabeth. LLB, Baylor U., 1960. Bar: Tex. 1960. Practice law Lubbock, Tex., 1960-63, Morton, Tex., 1963-84; judge 286th Dist. Ct., 1984-91; Cochran County atty., 1965-73, 79-84. Bd. dirs. Morton Indsl. Found. Mem. ABA, Tex. Bar Assn. Methodist. Club: Lion. Home: 218 Sandalwood Ln Levelland TX 79336-6816

WALKER, JAMES ROY, microbiologist; b. Chestnut, La., Nov. 8, 1937; s. Clint Cortez and Annie Mae (Holland) W.; m. Barbara Ann Fess, Aug. 8, 1959; children: James Bryan, Melinda Lee. BS, Northwestern State U., 1960; PhD, U. Tex., 1963. Asst. prof. U. Tex., Austin, 1967-71, assoc. prof., 1971-78, prof., 1978—, chmn. dept. microbiology, 1981-93; mem. sci. adv. com. U. Tex. Health Science Ctr., Science Park Cancer Ctr., 1984-88. Contbr. articles to profl. jours. Served to capt. U.S. Army, 1963-65. Fellow NIH, 1965-67, Rosalie B. Hite U. Tex., 1960-63; grantee NIH, 1967-91, NSF, 1978-84, 91-95, Am. Cancer Soc., 1976-91, The Welch Found., 1982-91, Tex. Adv. Rsch. Program, 1992-93, Am. Heart Assn., 1995, Coun. for Tobacco Rsch., 1996—. Mem. Am. Soc. Microbiology (vis. professorship at Fed. U. Rio de Janeiro 1977). Home: 8504 Greenflint Ln Austin TX 78759-8131 Office: U Tex Dept Microbiology Austin TX 78712-1095

WALKER, JAMES SILAS, college president; b. LaFollette, Tenn., Aug. 21, 1933; s. John Charles and Ruth Constance (Yeagle) W.; m. Nadine Leas Mortenson, May 28, 1954; children: Steven J., David K., Bradley P., Scott C. BA, U. Ariz., 1954; BDiv, McCormick Theol. Sem., 1956; postgrad. U. Basel, Switzerland, 1956-57; PhD, Claremont Coll., 1963. Ordained to ministry Presbyn. Ch., 1956. Asst. pastor Central Presbyn. Ch., Denver, 1957-60; prof. Huron Coll., S.D., 1963-66; prof. Hastings (Nebr.) Coll., 1966-75, dir. devel., 1975-79, dean, 1979-83; pres. Jamestown Coll., N.D., 1983—; adj. faculty mem. Luther Northwestern Theol. Sem., St. Paul, 1984—. Author: Theology of Karl Barth, 1963. Rotary Internat. Found. fellow, 1956-57; Nat. Def. Title IV grantee, 1960-63. Mem. Assn. Presbyn. Colls. and Univs., Presbytery of No. Plains (coun.), Rotary (dist. 563 gov. 1978-79). Republican. Avocations: travel, hunting, photography. Office: Jamestown Coll Office of Pres # 6080 Jamestown ND 58405

WALKER, JEFFREY CLEMENS, venture capitalist; b. Knoxville, Tenn., Sept. 22, 1955; s. William Clemens and Joyce Hazel (Harkins) W.; m. Suzanne Marie Connelly, Apr. 27, 1984; children: Courtney, Ryan, Morgan. BS, U. Va., 1977; MBA, Harvard U., 1981. CPA, Tex.; cert. mgmt. acct., Tex. Sr. auditor, cons. Arthur Young & Co., Houston, 1977-79; assoc. Chem. Bank, N.Y.C., 1981-82, v.p., 1982-83; ptnr. Chase Capital Ptnrs., N.Y.C., 1984-87, mng. ptnr., 1988—; bd. dirs. Timothys, Inc., Toronto, Monet Corp., N.Y.C., Guitar Ctr., L.A., Seymour (Ind.) Housewares, Metroplex Corp., N.J., PTN Holding Corp., N.Y.C., Six Flags Theme Parks, N.J., Doane Products, Mo., Harris Chem. Corp., N.Y. Mem. Young Pres. Orgn.; chmn. Bd. Edn., Wilton, Conn.; bd. dirs. WPA Theatre, N.Y.C.; found. bd. McIntire Sch., U. Va. Mem. AICPA, Nat. Venture Capital Assn., Nat. Assn. Small Bus. Investment Cos. (bd. govs., vice chmn.), Silver Spring Country Club, Pawling Mountain Hunt Club, wilton Riding Club, Beta Gamma Sigma. Republican. Unitarian. Home: 360 New Canaan Rd Wilton CT 06897-3331 Office: Chase Capital Ptnrs 12th Fl 380 Madison Ave Fl 12 New York NY 10017-2513

WALKER, JERALD CARTER, university administrator, minister; b. Bixby, Okla., May 22, 1938; s. Joseph Carter and Trula Tosh (Jackson) W.; m. Virginia Canfield, Apr. 14, 1963; children: Elisabeth Katherine, Anne Carter. BA in Sociology, Oklahoma City U., 1960; BD, U. Chgo., 1964; D of Religion, Sch. Theology at Claremont, 1966; LHD (hon.), Shiller U., 1994. Ordained to ministry Meth. Ch., 1964. Dir., campus minister Campus Christian Assn., Chgo., 1961-64; minister of outreach Temple Meth. Ch., San Francisco, 1965-66; chaplain, asst. prof. religion Nebr. Wesleyan U., Lincoln, 1966-69; pres. John J. Pershing Coll., Beatrice, Nebr., 1969-70; v.p. univ. rels., assoc. prof. Southwestern U., Georgetown, Tex., 1970-74; pres. Baker U., Baldwin, Kans., 1974-79, Oklahoma City U., 1979—; ednl. adv. to bd. dirs. Tianjin U. Commerce, People's Republic of China; participant Okla. Ann. Conf. of United Meth. Ch. Co-author: The State of Sequoyah: An Impressionistic View of Eastern Oklahoma, 1985; contbr. chpt. book, articles to profl. jours. Bd. dirs., past chmn. Okla. Ind. Coll. Found. Recipient Alumni Recognition award Nebr. 4H Club, 1970, Okla. 4H Club, Disting. Alumni award Oklahoma City U., 1974, Outstanding Citizen award Dist. 575 Rotary Internat., 1990, Award for Excellence Asia Soc. Okla., 1990, Humanitarian award for Okla/Ark. region NCCJ, 1992, Nat. Police Adminstrn. award for promotion or peace and order Rep. of China, 1992, Francis Asbury award for fostering United Meth. Ministries in Higher Edn., 1994, Excellent Leader award Mgmt. Devel. Inst. Singapore, 1996, Benjamin Franklin award Downtown Olka. City Sertoma Club, 1992, Excellent Leader award Mgmt. Devel. Inst. of Singapore, 1996. Mem. Nat. Assn. Schs. and Colls. of United Meth. Ch. (past pres.), Nat. Assn. Colls. and Univs. (bd. dirs.). Office: Oklahoma City U 2501 N Blackwelder Ave Oklahoma City OK 73106-1402

WALKER, JIMMIE KENT, mechanical engineer; b. Lawton, Okla., May 1, 1940; s. James K. and Ruth L. (Fleming) W.; m. Carol T. Walker, Mar. 22, 1962; (div. Aug. 1979); children: Mollie Walker Freeman, Keith M.; m. Joan F. Korth, Feb. 11, 1983; 1 stepson, Raymond Van Buskirk. BSME, Okla. U., 1963; MBA, U. S.D., 1991. Registered profl. engr. Iowa. Design engr. Cessna Aircraft, Hutchinson, Kans., 1965-68, 72-75; chief engr. Lyons (Kans.) Mfg. Corp., 1968-72; sales engr. Prince Mfg. Co., Sioux City, Iowa, 1975-79, mfg. mgr., 1979-83, dir. engring., 1983—. Treas. Hutchinson Jaycees, 1968; pres. Lyons Jaycees, 1970; mem. adv. bd. adult edn. Western Iowa Tech., Sioux City, 1980-90, Cosmo, 1992-93; judge Physics Olympics, 1992-94; bd. dirs. Jr. Achievement Sioux City, 1993-94. Maj. U.S. Army, 1972. Mem. Welding Soc., Am. Soc. Metals, Soc. Profl. Engrs., Tau Beta Pi, Sigma Tau, Beta Gamma Sigma. Roman Catholic. Achievements include patents for square wire, internal piston lock for hydraulic cylinders, design of high efficiency, square wire lock for telescopic hydraulic cylinder stop rings, low speed tractor pto pump, design of durable series/rephase implement carrier wheel cylinders, unique zero leakage telescopic, constant speed telescopic cylinder. Home: 4816 Royal Ct Sioux City IA 51104-1128 Office: Prince Mfg Co PO Box 537 Sioux City IA 51102-0537

WALKER, JOHN DENLEY, foundation director, former government official; b. Petersburg, Va., July 15, 1921; s. John Otey and Evelyn Mildred (Denley) W.; m. Diana Taylor, Apr. 30, 1949 (div. 1980); children—Walker Diana, John Denley, Joseph Warren; m. Helen Hoogerwerff, Mar. 15, 1984; step children—Saskia Roskam, Hugo, Frederick. B.A., U. N.C.-Chapel Hill, 1944; postgrad., U. Pa., 1950-51. Superintendant N.J. Bell, 1946-48; asst. dir. labor div. ECA, Paris, France, 1948-50; mgmt. cons., 1951-53; fgn. service res. officer U.S. Govt., Paris, Malta, Israel, Australia, 1953-77; exec. dir. English Speaking Union of U.S., N.Y.C., 1978-87. Contbr. articles to profl. jours. Bd. dirs. Am. Student Ctr., Paris, 1953-57; v.p. Ctr. for Security Studies, 1988—. Lt. USN, 1942-45. Episcopalian. Clubs: Pilgrims, Standrews (N.Y.C.); Univ. (Washington); Chevy Chase (Md.). Lodges: Legion of Valor, Soc. Cin., Order of St. Johns of Jerusalem. Home: River Place 1021 Arlington Blvd # 819 Arlington VA 22209

WALKER, JOHN MERCER, JR., federal judge; b. N.Y.C., Dec. 26, 1940; s. John Mercer and Louise (Mead) W.; m. Cristy West, June 20, 1980 (div. Apr. 1983); m. Katharine Kirkland, Feb. 14, 1987. BA, Yale U., 1962; JD, U. Mich., 1966. Bar: N.Y. 1969, U.S. Dist. Ct. (so. dist.) N.Y. 1971, U.S. Ct. Appeals (2d cir.) 1972, U.S. Supreme Ct. 1977, U.S. Ct. Appeals (D.C. cir.) 1982. Maxwell Sch. Pub. Adminstrn. fellow, state counsel Republic of Botswana, Africa, 1966-68; assoc. Davis, Polk and Warwell, N.Y.C., 1969-70; asst. U.S. atty. U.S. Dist. Ct. (so. dist.) N.Y., N.Y.C., 1971-75; assoc. to ptnr. Carter, Ledyard and Milburn, N.Y.C., 1975-81; asst. sec. enforcement ops. Dept. Treasury, Washington, 1981-85; judge U.S. Dist. Ct. (so. dist.) N.Y., 1985-89, U.S. Ct. Appeals (2nd cir.), 1989—; adj. prof. NYU Law Sch., 1995—; gen. counsel Nat. Coun. on Crime and Deliquency, N.Y.C., 1977-81; chmn. Fed. Law Enforcement Tng. Ctr., Washington, 1981-85; spl. counsel Adminstrv. Conf. U.S., Washington, 1986-92; mem. budget com. jud. conf. Inst. Jud. Adminstrn., 1992—, dir., 1992—. Del. Rep. Nat. Conv., Detroit, 1980. With USMCR, 1963-67. Recipient Alexander Hamilton award Sec. of Treas., Washington, 1985, Secret Service Honor award, 1985. Mem. ABA, D.C. Bar Assn., Assn. Bar City of N.Y., Fed. Judges Assn. (pres. 1993-95). Republican. Episcopalian. Office: US Cir Ct US Courthouse FOLEY SQUARE New York NY 10007*

WALKER, JOHN NEAL, agricultural engineering educator; b. Erie, Pa., Feb. 19, 1930; s. Gordon Durwood and Marie Katherine (Beck) W.; m. Betty Jane Bloeser, Aug. 14, 1954; children: David Thomas, Janet Ann. B.S. in Agrl. Engring, Pa. State U., M.S., 1958; Ph.D., Purdue U., 1961. Registered profl. engr., cons., Ky. Extension agrl. engr. Pa. State U., 1954-58; mem. faculty U. Ky., 1960-96, prof. agrl. engring., 1966-74, chmn. dept., 1974-81, acting dir. Inst. Mining and Minerals Research, 1981-82, assoc. dean Coll. Agr., 1982-88, assoc. dean Coll. Engring., 1989-96, dir. Ctr. for Robotics and Mfg. Systems, 1991-96; retired, 1996; Duggar lectr. Auburn (Ala.) U., 1976. Author articles in field, chpts. in books. Officer USNR, 1951-77. Named Gt. Tchr. U. Ky. Alumni Assn., 1974. Fellow Am. Soc. Agrl. Engrs. (exec. coun. 1984-87, 88-91, v.p. adminstrv. coun. 1984-87, pres. 1989-90, MBMA award 1974); mem. Order Ky. Cols.

WALKER, JOHN PATRICK, theater producer, actor; b. Elgin, Ill., Apr. 21, 1956; s. John Patrick and Ruth Ellen (Borror) W.; m. Pamela Jean Gay, Dec. 5, 1981; children: Miranda, Caitlin. BA, Notre Dame U., 1978; cert., Am. Conservatory Theatre, San Francisco, 1980. Actor Peninsula Players, Door County, Wis., 1978-84, gen. mgr., 1984-86; house mgr. Civic Ctr. Performing Arts, Chgo., 1984-86; gen. mgr. Royal George Theater, Chgo., 1986-89, Cullen, Henaghan, Platt, Chgo., 1989-91; mng. dir. Victory Gardens Theater, Chgo., 1991—; past pres. League of Chgo. Theaters. Avocations: fly fishing, skiing. Office: Victory Gardens Theater 2257 N Lincoln Ave Chicago IL 60614-3717

WALKER, JOHN SUMPTER, JR., lawyer; b. Richmond, Ark., Oct. 13, 1921; s. John Sumpter, Martha (Wilson) W.; m. Eljana M. duVall, Dec. 31, 1947; children: John Stephen, Barbara Monika Ann, Peter Mark Gregory. BA, Tulane U., 1942; MS, U. Denver, 1952, JD, 1960; diploma Nat. Def. U., 1981. Bar: Colo. 1960, U.S. Dist. Ct. Colo. 1960, U.S. Supreme Ct., 1968, U.S. Ct. Appeals (10th cir.) 1960, U.S. Tax Ct., 1981. With Denver & Rio Grande Western R.R. Co., 1951-61, gen. solicitor, 1961-89 ; pres. Denver Union Terminal Ry. Co. Apptd. gen. counsel Moffat Tunnel Commn., 1991; life mem. Children's Diabetes Fund. With U.S. Army, 1942-46. Decorated Bronze Star. Mem. Colo. Bar Assn., Arapahoe County Bar Assn., Alliance Francaise (life), Order of St. Ives, U. Denver Chancellors' Soc., Cath. Lawyers Guild. Republican. Roman Catholic. Club: Denver Athletic.

WALKER, JOSEPH, retired research executive; b. Rockford, Ill., Dec. 28, 1922; s. Joseph H. and Elizabeth (McEachran) W.; m. June Farley Enerson, Jan. 22, 1944; children—Joseph A., Amy E., Richard H., Jeanne A. B.S. with high honors, Beloit Coll., 1943; M.S., U. Wis., 1948, Ph.D., 1950. Sr. research chemist Pure Oil Co. Research Center, Crystal Lake, Ill., 1950-51; project technologist Pure Oil Co. Research Center, 1952-54, sect. supr., 1954-58, div. dir. analytical research and service div., 1958-64, research coordinator, 1964, dir. research, 1965; assoc. dir. research Union Oil Co. of Calif., Research Center, Brea, Calif., 1966-78; v.p. chem. research Union Oil Co. of Calif., Research Center, 1979-85. Pres. Sch. Bd., Crystal Lake, 1963-65. Served to lt. (j.g.) USNR, 1943-46. Mem. Am. Chem. Soc., Am. Petroleum Inst., Phi Beta Kappa, Sigma Xi, Phi Lambda Upsilon, Sigma Alpha Epsilon. Home: 2821 Caminito Merion La Jolla CA 92672-5479

WALKER, KATHRINE L., museum educational administrator, educator; b. San Jose, Calif., Mar. 12, 1962; d. Paul D. and Barbara (White) W. BA with honors, Stanford U., 1984; MA, Coll. William and Mary, 1985; cert. mus. mgmt., U. Colo., 1996. Archaeologist Va. Rsch. Ctr. for Archaeology, Newport, 1984-85; curatorial asst. Colonial Williamsburg Found., Va., 1985-86; asst. curator, coord. edn. Nantucket (Mass.) Historical Assn., 1986-88; dir. edn. Webb-Deane-Stevens Mus., Wethersfield, Conn., 1988-91, Lyman Allyn Art Mus., New London, Conn., 1991-94, Beach Mus. Art, Kans. State U., Manhattan, 1994—; mem. Mass. Arts Lottery Coun., Nantucket, 1988-89; chair diversity subcom. Regional Adv. Com. on Edn. Reform, 1994; adv. bd. Manhattan Arts Coun., 1995-96; panelist Kans. Arts Commn., 1995; steering com. Take a Stand Ednl. Collaborative. Author: (curriculum) The Outsiders, 1990, The Face in Art, 1994, (gallery guide) From Distaff Side, 1992; author: (with others) Cultural Diversity in Literature, Art and Music, 1992, The American Collection 1620-1920: Guide to the Palmer Gallery, 1994. Vol. tchr. Nantucket Learning & Resource Ctr., 1988; mem. New London Culture and Tourism Alliance, 1991—; Manhattan C. of C. Edn. com., 1996; Big Brothers, Big Sisters, 1996. Grantee Inst. Mus. Svcs., Nantucket, 1987, 88, Rockefeller Found./Conn. Humanities Coun., New London, 1991-92; scholar Conn. Humanities Coun., 1989—. Mem. Am. Assn. Mus. (rep. bd. 1990-93, 95—, edn. com. 1988—, Excellence and Equity award) Nat. Art Edn. Assn., New Eng. Mus. Assn. (edn. com. 1988-94, chair 1991-94), Mountain Plains Mus. Assn. (chair edn. com. 1995—), Conn. Art Docents Network (bd. dirs. 1991—), Alliance of Cultural Educators of Hartford, Nat. Art Edn. Assn., Kans. Art Edn. Assn., Manhattan C. of C. (edn. com. 1996). Avocations: the arts, multicultural education, skiing, writing. Office: Beach Mus Art 701 Beach Ln Manhattan KS 66506-0600

WALKER, KENNETH DALE, automotive service company executive; b. Ft. Worth, Feb. 25, 1948; s. Billy Glenn and Jo Ann (Prestridge) W.; m. Cheri Lee Propp, Feb. 28, 1969 (div. Aug. 1980); children: Joel Glenn, Corbett Dale; m. Vickie Lynn Franklin, Sept. 27, 1980; children: Kristi Lynn, Carolyn Christine. BBA, U. Tex., 1970. CPA, Tex. Mgr. Arthur Young & Co., Ft. Worth, 1970-76; controller, v.p. fin. Big 4 Automotive, Ft. Worth, 1976-80, v.p. ops West Tex., 1980-82, v.p. retail, 1982-84; chief fin. officer southwest region AI Automotive Corp., Ft. Worth, 1984-86, v.p. ops., chief operating officer southwest region, 1986-88; owner Kenneth D. Walker Consulting Turn Around Mgmt. Projects, 1988; pres. CEO Cardis Corp., Buena Park, Calif., 1989-92, Parts Industry Corp., Memphis, 1992-96, Meineke Discount Muffler Shops, Inc., 1996—. Instr. project bus. Jr. Achievement, Ft. Worth, 1981; bd. dirs. All Pro Program, Inc., Andolusia, Ala., 1978-84. Bumper to Bumper Program, Ft. Worth, 1987-88. Recipient Automotive Replacement Edn. award Northwood Inst., 1987. Mem. Inst. Internal Auditors (v.p. 1975-76, pres. 1976), Automotive Warehouse Distbr. Assn. (chmn. fin. stats. com. 1984-87, chmn. univ. faculty 1986-87, bd. govs. 1986—, chmn. bd. dirs. 1995, Pursuit of Excellence award 1986), TPC-Southwind Club. Methodist. Avocations: golf, skiing. Office: Meineke Discount Muffler 128 S Tryon St Ste 900 Charlotte NC 28202-5001

WALKER, KENNETH HENRY, architect; b. N.Y.C., June 11, 1940; s. Matthew and Lillian (Goldfarb) W. B.A., Brown U., 1962; M.Arch., Harvard U., 1966. Founder, pres. Walker Grad, 1973-76; founder, pres. Walker Group, N.Y.C., 1976-85, WalkerGroup/CNI, N.Y.C., 1985-93; pres. Retail Options, Inc., N.Y.C., 1993—; lectr. on design. Prin. works include Isetan Dept. Store, Tokyo, Saks 5th Ave., N.Y.C., John Wanamaker, Phila., Bloomingdales, Boca Raton, Fla., FAO Schwarz, N.Y.C., Citibank (nationally), Galeries Lafayette, France; contbr. articles to Time mag., Fortune, Interior Design, Archtl. Record, others; exhibited indsl. designs at Whitney Mus. Past pres. Art Adv. Com., Brown U., Providence, 1979-83; mem. architecture and design commn. Mus. Modern Art, N.Y.C., 1976-93; trustee Village of Dering Harbor, Shelter Island, N.Y., 1982-87; pres. alumni coun. Harvard U. Grad. Sch. Design, 1985-88. Named to Interior Design Hall of Fame, Interior Design mag., 1985. Fellow AIA (over 20 design awards); mem. Young Pres.'s Orgn., Inst. Store Planners, Harvard U. Alumni Assn. Office: Retail Options Inc 15 E 26th St New York NY 10010-1505

WALKER, KENT, lawyer; b. Geneva, Ill., Oct. 4, 1944; s. Robert and Jean (McCullough) W.; m. Helene Feinberg, Sept. 14, 1984; children: Forrest, Lowell, Molly. BA, Wheaton Coll., 1966; JD, Northwestern U., Evanston, Ill., 1969. Bar: Ill. 1969, Del. 1970, Pa. 1984; U.S. Dist. Ct. Del. 1971, U.S. Dist. Ct. D.C. 1973, U.S. Dist. Ct. (ea. dist.) Pa. 1984; U.S. Ct. Appeals (3rd cir.) 1972, U.S. Ct. Appeals D.C. 1972; U.S. Tax Ct. 1975. Dep. atty. gen. Del. Dept. Justice, Wilmington, 1971-72, state solicitor and chief civil divsn., 1972-74; acting U.S. atty. U.S. Dept. Justice, Wilmington, 1977, 1st asst. U.S. atty., 1975-78; assoc. Garfinkel & Volpicelli, Phila., 1984-86; assoc., ptnr. Mesirov, Gelman, Jaffe, Cramer & Jamieson, Phila., 1986-89; ptnr. Ballard, Spahr, Andrews & Ingersoll, Phila., 1989-95; shareholder Buchanan Ingersoll, Phila., 1995—. Mem. ABA, Pa. Bar Assn., Phila. Bar Assn., Del. State Bar Assn. Republican. Episcopalian. Office: Buchanan Ingersoll 11 Penn Ctr 14th Fl 1835 Market St Philadelphia PA 19103-2968

WALKER, L. T., bishop. Bishop of Ark. ch. of God in Christ, Little Rock. Office: Ch of God in Christ 2315 S Chester St Little Rock AR 72206-2021*

WALKER, LANNON, foreign service officer; b. Los Angeles, Jan. 17, 1936; s. James Orville and Esther W.; m. Arlette Daguet, July 14, 1954; children: Rachelle, Anne. B.S., Georgetown U., 1961. Fgn. service officer Dept. State, 71961; polit. officer Dept. State, Rabat, Morocco, 1962-64; prin. officer Dept. State, Constantine, Algeria, 1964-66; assigned Exec. Secretariat Dept. State, 1966-69; econ. counselor Dept. State, Tripoli, Libya, 1969-70; dep. chief mission Dept. State, Yaounde, Cameroon, 1971-73; adminstrv. counselor Dept. State, Saigon, Viet Nam, 1973-74; dep. chief mission Dept. State, Kinshasa, Zaire, 1974-77; dep. asst. sec. African Affairs Dept. State, Washington, 1977-82; spl. adviser African affairs Dept. State, 1983-84, dep. insp. gen., 1984-85, ambassador to Senegal, 1985-88, amb. to Nigeria, 1989-92; mem. Policy Planning Coun. Dept. of State, Washington, 1993-95; ambassador to Cote d'Ivoire Abidjan, 1995—; employed in pvt. sector, 1982-83; sr. assoc. Carnegie Endowment, 1988-89. Served with USAF, 1953-58. Mem. Am. Fgn. Service Assn. (chmn. 1966-69). Roman Catholic.

WALKER, LARRY KENNETH ROBERT, professional baseball player; b. Maple Ridge, B.C., Dec. 1, 1966. Grad. high sch., B.C., Can. With Montreal Expos, 1989-94; outfielder Colo. Rockies, 1995—. Named "The Sporting News" Nat. League All-Star Team, 1992, "The Sporting News" NAt. League Silver Slugger Team, 1992; recipient Gold Glove as outfielder, 1992-93. Office: Colo Rockies 2001 Blake St Denver CO 80205-2008*

WALKER, LAWRENCE D., lawyer; b. Syracuse, N.Y., July 10, 1948. BA, Fordham U., 1970; JD, Northwestern U., 1973. Bar: Ohio 1973. Ptnr. Taft, Stettinius & Hollister, Columbus, Ohio. Office: 21 E State St Columbus OH 43215-4228

WALKER, LELAND JASPER, civil engineer; b. Fallon, Nev., Apr. 18, 1923; s. Albert Willard and Grayce (Wilkinson) W.; m. Margaret Frances Noble, Jan. 21, 1946; children: Thomas, Margaret, Timothy. B.S. in Civil Engring, Iowa State U., 1944; D. Eng. (hon.), Mont. State U., 1983. Engr. with various govtl. depts., 1946-51, 53-55; v.p. Wenzel & Co. (cons. engrs.), Great Falls, Mont., 1955-58; pres., chmn. bd. No. Engring. and Testing, Inc., Great Falls, 1958-88; pres. Ind. Labs. Assurance Co., 1977-79; bd. dirs. Mont. Power Co., Entech Inc., 1982-92, Lewis and Clark Biologicals, Inc., 1989-92, Applied Tech., Inc. Pres., trustee Endowment and Rsch. Found. Mont. State U., 1969-82, Mont. Deaconess Hosp., Great Falls, 1959-67. McLaughlin Rsch. Inst. Biol. Scis., 1989-92, Mont. Sch. Deaf and Blind Found., 1984—; trustee Rocky Mountain Coll., 1977-80, Dufresne Found., 1979-87; chmn., bd. dirs. Mont. Tech. Svcs. Adv. Coun. adv. coun. Engring. Coll. Mont. State U.; bd. dirs. Mont. State Fair, Engring. Socs. Commn. on Energy, 1977-79, Mont. Bd. Sci. and Tech., 1983-88, Great Falls Chamber Found., 1989-91, trustee Great Falls Public Libr. Found., 1995—. Fellow ASCE (pres. 1976-77), AAAS, Cons. Engrs. Coun. (pres. Mont. 1971), Accrediting Bd. Engring. and Tech. (v.p. 1978-79, pres. 1980-83); mem. Nat. Acad. Engring., Am. Coun. Ind. Labs. (hon. sec. 1973-76), Meadowlark Country Club, Pachyderm Club (bd. dirs., v.p. 1992-94), Chi Epsilon (nat. hon.), Tau Beta Pi (hon.). Republican. Methodist. Home: 1200 32nd St S Apt 9 Great Falls MT 59405-5333 Office: PO Box 7425 Great Falls MT 59406-7425

WALKER, LEROY TASHREAU, university chancellor, coach; b. Atlanta, June 14, 1918; s. Willie and Mary Elizabeth (Thomas) W.; m. Katherine McDowell, Dec. 31, 1938 (dec.); children—LeRoy, Carolyn. BS, Benedict Coll., 1940, PhD (hon.); MA, Columbia U., 1941; PhD, NYU, 1957; PhD (hon.), Defiance Coll.; D of Sports Sci., U.S. Sports Acad.; LLD (hon.), Ea. Ky. U. and N.C. Cen. U., Wake Forest U., 1993, Morehouse U., 1993; DHL (hon.), Tuskegee U., 1993, Duke U., 1995; LHD (hon.), U. N.C., 1995, Queens Coll., 1995; Dr.Humanities, Princeton U., 1996. Chmn. dept. phys. edn., coach basketball, football, track and field Benedict Coll., Columbia, S.C., 1941-42; chmn. dept. phys. edn., coach basketball, football, track and field Bishop Coll., Marshall, Tex., 1942-43, Prairie View State U., 1943-45; chmn. dept. phys. edn. and recreation, coach basketball, football, track and field N.C. Cen. U., Durham, 1945-73; vice-chancellor for univ. relations N.C. Cen. U., 1974-83, chancellor, 1983-86, chancellor emeritus, 1986—; ednl. specialist Cultural Exchange Program, Dept. State, 1959, 60, 62,; dir. program, planning and tng. Peace Corps, Africa, 1966-68; coach Ethiopian and Israeli teams Olympic Games, Rome, 1960; adviser track and field teams throughout world; mem. U.S. Collegiate Sports Coun., 1971; chmn. Coll. Commrs. Assn., 1971-74; chmn. track and field com. Athletic Union U.S.A., 1973-75; head coach U.S. track and field team Olympic Games, Montreal, 1976; chmn. bd. U.S. Olympic Festival, 1987—; mem. exec. bd., treas. U.S. Olympic Com., pres., 1992—; chef de mission for 1992 Barcelona Olympic Games, 1991—; sr. v.p. sports Atlanta Com. for the Olympic Games 1996, 1991—. Author: Manual of Adapted Physical Education, 1960; Physical Education for the Exceptional Student, 1965; Championship Techniques in Track and Field, 1969, Track and Field for Boys and Girls, 1983; also articles. Bd. dirs. U.S.A.-China Rels. Com.; bd. trustees U.S. Olympic Com.; pres. Athletic Congress, U.S. Olympic Com., 1992—. Recipient James E. Shepard Outstanding Tchr. award Hamilton Watch Co., 1964, U. N.C. Systems Bd. Govs. award, 1989; Achievement award Cen. Intercollegiate Athletic Assn., 1967; Disting. Alumnus award Benedict Coll., 1968, Disting. Service award Kiwanis Internat., 1971, City of Durham, 1971, Durham C. of C., 1973, Gov.'s Ambassador of Goodwill award, 1974; O. Max Gardner award, 1976; N.C. Disting. Citizen award, 1977; Achievement in Life award Ency. Brit., 1977, Achievement award Sertoma; Heritage award YMCA, 1988, Robert Giegengack award The Athletics Congress, 1990, Amb. award Pres.' Coun. on Phys. Fitness and Sports, 1991, Disting. Alumni award NYU, 1993, Jim Corbett award Nat. Assn. Coll. Athletic Dirs., 1993; named to N.C. Hall of Fame, 1975, S.C. Hall of Fame, 1977, Nat. Assn. Sport and Phys. Edn. Hall of Fame, 1977, N.C. Cen. U. Hall of Fame, 1984, U.S. Olympic Hall of Fame, 1987, Ga. Hall of Fame, 1988, Benedict Coll. Hall of Fame, N.C. Soc. award The Olympic Order by Internat. Olympic Com., 1995, Toastmasters Golden Camel award, 1996, 100 Blackmen Disting. Leadeship award, 1996. Mem. Am. Alliance Health, Phys. Edn., Recreation, and Dance (nat. pres.; Honor award 1972, Gulick award), NEA, U.S. Track Coaches Assn. (Nat. Track Coach of Yr. 1972), N.C. Assn. Health, Phys. Edn., Recreation and Dance (Honor award 1971; v.p. div., dir.), Internat. Assn. Athletic Fedns. (U.S. rep. 1976—), Sigma Delta Psi, Alpha Phi Omega, Omega Psi Phi. Episcopalian.

WALKER, LESLEY, film editor. Editor: (films) Portrait of an Artist as a Young Man, 1979, The Tempest, 1980, Eagle's Wing, 1980, Richard's Things, 1981, Ill Fares the Land, 1982, Meantime, 1983, Winter's Flight, 1984, Letter to Brezhnev, 1985, Mona Lisa, 1986, Cry Freedom, 1987, Buster, 1988, Shirley Valentine, 1989, The Fisher King, 1991, Waterland, 1992, Born Yesterday, 1993, Shadowlands, 1993, (TV movies) Winston Churchill: The Wilderness Years, 1983, The Secret Life of Ian Fleming, 1990. Office: Sandra Marsh Mgt 9150 Wilshire Blvd Ste 220 Beverly Hills CA 90212-3429*

WALKER, LINDA ANN, financial planner; b. Denver, May 10, 1956; d. John Bruce Elmer and Ruth Evelyn (Rogers) Metsker; m. Sidney Carr Walker III, Feb. 9, 1992; 1 child. BA, U. Colo., 1978. CFP. Account exec. E.F. Hutton, Boulder, 1980-84; with Fin. Planning and Mgmt., Boulder, 1984-91, pres., 1989-91; pres. Premier Planning Assocs., Boulder, 1991-95; pvt. practice, 1995—; cons. Lighting Co., Boulder, 1987-88. Actress (play) Shadow of a Gunman, 1991, La Ronde, 1992 (dancer) Who's There, 1991. Bd. dirs. Nancy Spanier Dance Theatre, Boulder, 1986-91; mem. Win/Win, Boulder, 1989-91. Mem. Internat. Assn. Fin. Planners, Inst. CFP. Democrat. Avocations: reading, writing, meditating, horseback riding. Office: CFP Linsco/Pvt Ledger 5150 E PCH Ste 520 Long Beach CA 90804

WALKER, LINDA LEE, lawyer; b. Phila., Jan. 24, 1954; d. M. Lorenzo and Romaine Yvonne (Smith) W.; m. Bruce McIntyre, Sept. 16, 1981; children: Jessica Marie, Nicole Yvonne. BA with honors, U. Pa., 1975; JD, Yale U., 1978. Bar: N.Y. 1979, U.S. Dist. Ct. (so. and ea. dists.) N.Y. 1982, U.S. Ct. Appeals (1st cir.) 1982. Asst. regional atty. U.S. Dept. Health & Human Svcs., N.Y.C., 1978-82; assoc. Shea & Gould, N.Y.C., 1982-85; v.p., sr. assoc. counsel Chase Manhattan Bank, N.A., N.Y.C., 1985-89; v.p., assoc. gen. counsel Citicorp Credit Svcs., N.Y.C., 1989—. Mem. ABA, Phi Beta Kappa. Office: Citicorp Credit Svcs Inc 1 Court Sq Long Island City NY 11120-0001

WALKER, LOREN HAINES, electrical engineer; b. Bartow, Fla., Sept. 25, 1936; s. Robert Ellsworth and Vera May (Williams) W.; m. Barbara Gray Doss, Aug. 26, 1961; children: Linda Gray, Katherine Leigh, Virginia Kent. BEE, U. Fla., 1958; SM, MIT, 1961. Registered profl. engr., Va. Program engr. GE Corp., 1958-59; sr. design engr. specialty control dept. GE Corp., Waynesboro, Va., 1959-70; elec. engr. R & D GE Corp., Schenectady, N.Y., 1972-76; cons. engr. drive systems GE Corp., Salem, Va., 1976-96; sr. devel. engr. Exide Power Systems div. ESB, Raleigh, N.C., 1970-72. Inventor 53 patents in field. Active Presbyn. Ch. Recipient IR-100 award Indsl. Rsch., 1974. Fellow IEEE (1st prize conf. papers 1979, 2d prize 1989).

WALKER, LORENZO GILES, surgeon, educator; b. Phila., June 29, 1957; s. Manuel Lorenzo and Romaine Yvonne (Smith) W.; m. Anne Marie Gazzo, Aug. 13, 1990; children: Zachary Giles, Benjamin Lee. BA cum laude, U. Pa., 1978; MD, Harvard U., 1982. Diplomate Am. Bd. Orthopaedic Surgery, Nat. Bd. Med. Examiners; lic. surgeon, Mass., Calif.; cert. added qualification hand surgery, 1993. Intern in surgery New England Deaconess-Harvard Surg. Svc., Boston, 1982-83, asst. resident in surgery, 1983-84; resident in orthopaedic surgery Harvard U., Boston, 1985-88; fellow in hand surgery UCLA, 1988-89, asst. clin. prof. orthopaedic surgery, 1988—, attending physician dept. orthopedics Hand Clinic; ptnr. Ventura (Calif.) Orthopaedic Hand and Sports Med. Group, 1994—; staff physician St. John's Plasant Valley Hosp., Camarillo, Calif., St. John's Regional Med. Ctr., Oxnard, Calif., Cmty. Meml. Hosp., Ventura, Calif.; attending physician, cons. Sepulveda (Calif.) VA Hosp.; presenter in field. Cons. reviewer Clin. Orthopaedics and related Rsch., 1990-92; contbr. numerous articles to profl. jours. Vol. Spl. Olympics, Ventura, 1994—, Direct Relief Internat., Santa Barbara, Calif., 1994—, Ventura County Rescue Mission, 1994—. Recipient Cert. of Appreciation, Am. Heart Assn., 1994; UCLA faculty fellow, 1988-89. Mem. Am. Soc. for Surgery of the Hand, Am. Assn. for Hand Surgery, AMA, Calif. Med. Assn., Calif. Orthopaedic Assn., Ventura County Med. Soc., Internat. Soc. Aquatic Medicine, Western Orthopaedic Assn., Orthopaedic Overseas, UCLA Hand Club, Arthroscopy Assn. N.Am., Alpha Epsilon Delta, Onyx Honor Soc., Philomathean Soc. Avocations: photography, scuba diving, sports, fishing, travel. Home: Ventura Orthopaedic Hand & Sports Med Group 11090 E Las Posas Rd Camarillo CA 93012 Office: 2100 Solar Dr Oxnard CA 93030-2661

WALKER, MACK, historian, educator; b. Springfield, Mass., June 6, 1929; s. Gilbert Creighton and Lavinia Pillsbury (Mack) W.; m. Irma Julianne Wiesinger, 1954; children: Barbara B., Gilbert C., Benjamin F. AB, Bowdoin Coll., 1950; PhD, Harvard U., 1959. Instr. RISD, Providence, 1957-59; instr., asst. prof. Harvard U., Cambridge, Mass., 1959-66; assoc. prof., prof. Cornell U., Ithaca, N.Y., 1966-74; prof. Johns Hopkins U., Balt., 1974—, dept. chmn., 1979-82. Author: Germany and the Emigration, 1964, German Home Towns, 1971, Johann Jakob Moser, 1981, The Salzburg Transaction, 1993, Der Salzburger Handel, 1997; editor: Metternich's Europe, 1968, Plombières, 1968. Sgt. U.S. Army, 1951-53. Fellow Inst. for Advanced Study, Princeton, 1977, Wissenschaftskolleg zu Berlin, 1982-83, Max-Planck-Inst. für Geschichte, Göttingen, 1987-88; recipient Forschungspreis Alexander von Humboldt Found., 1989. Fellow Am. Acad. Arts and Scis. Office: Johns Hopkins U Dept of History Baltimore MD 21218

WALKER, MALLORY, real estate executive; b. Washington, Apr. 13, 1939; s. Oliver Mallory and Elizabeth Powell (Dunlop) W.; m. Diana Hardin Walker; children—Taylor Scott Walker, William Mallory. Ed., U. Va., 1958-63. Joined Walker & Dunlop, 1963, v.p., 1968-71, dir., 1969—, exec. v.p., 1971-76, pres., 1976—; cons. and lectr. in field; bd. dirs. Atlantic Trust Co., 1993-94, Charles E. Smith Residential Realty Inc., 1994—, Fed. Nat. Mortgage Assn., 1981-94, Fannie Mae Found.; trustee Group Hospitalization and Med. Svcs., Inc., 1989-93. Trustee Fed. City Coun., 1977—, Greater Washington Rsch. Ctr., 1977—, Eugene and Agnes E. Meyer Found., 1977-89, vice chmn. 1981-83, chmn. 1983-89. Mem. Am. Soc. Real Estate Counselors, Urban Land Inst., Mortgage Bankers Assn. Am. (bd. govs. 1986-90, exec. com. 1986-87). Office: Walker & Dunlop 7500 Old Georgetown Rd Ste 800 Bethesda MD 20814-6133

WALKER, MALLORY ELTON, tenor; b. New Orleans, May 22, 1935; s. James Hugh and Edith Mamie (Gilmore) W.; m. Carolyn Pryor, Dec. 21, 1956; children: Maria Vanessa, Anthony Hugh, Jamie Eugene. BA, Occidental Coll., 1957. Vocal instr. Boston Conservatory of Music, 1974-77. Prin. artist Met. Opera, N.Y.C., 1978-89; appeared with Dallas Opera, Cologne Opera, Stuttgart Opera, Miami Opera, L.A. Music Ctr. Opera; soloist Robert Shaw Chorale, 1960, also with L.A. Philharm., Cleve. Symphony, Boston Symphony, Phila. Orch., Chgo. Symphony. With U.S. Army Chorus, 1957-60. Rockefeller Found. grantee, 1962-63; Ford Found. grantee, 1963. Mem. Am. Guild Mus. Artists, AFTRA, SAG. Home: 11250 Morrison St Apt 108 N Hollywood CA 91601-5343

WALKER, MARGARET SMITH, real estate company executive; b. Lancashire, Eng., Oct. 14, 1943; came to U.S., 1964; d. Arthur Edward and Doris Audrey (Dawson) Smith; m. James E. Walker, Feb. 6, 1992. Lic. real estate agt., Hawaii. Broker Lawson-Worrall Inc. (now Worrall-McCarter), Honolulu, 1974-81; pres. Maggie Parkes & Assocs., Inc., Honolulu, 1981—. Bd. dirs. Hawaii Combined Tng. Assn., Honolulu, 1985—; com. chmn. Hist. Hawaii Found., Honolulu, 1990; com. chmn. Hawaii Opera Theatre, 1997, chmn. Opera Ball, 1997. Mem. Am. Horse Shows Assn., Hawaii Horse Shows Assn., Outrigger Canoe Club. Episcopalian. Avocations: dressage riding, horse show management. Office: PO Box 25083 Honolulu HI 96825-0083

WALKER, MARIE FULLER, elementary education educator; d. Gladys Fuller; m. Frederick T. Walker; children: Frederick T. Jr., Nicole Marie. BA in History, U. Philippines, 1969; MEd, West Chester U., 1992. Cert. elem. tchr., Calif., Pa., N.C., Okla., Ala.; cert. elem. adminstr., prin., Pa. Tchr. ESL Royal Thai Army Sch. Nursing, Bangkok, Thailand, 1975; tchr. 2d grade Ruam Rudee Internat. Sch., Bangkok, Thailand, 1975-76; tchr. 3d grade St. Adelaide Sch., Highland, Calif., 1976-77; tchr. Midwest City (Okla.) Sch., 1980-82; tchr. 4th grade Rainbow Elem. Sch., Coatesville, Pa., 1989—. Administered vol. programs ARC, Ft. Bragg and Pope AFB, recruited and trained vols., official community spokesperson, nat. cons., Washington, vol. cons., 1984 (Vol. of Yr. award N.C., 1983, Achievements awards 1983, 84, 85, Clara Barton award 1984). Recipient N.C. Outstanding Vol. Adminstr./Coord., Gov., 1984, Gift of Time award Family Inst., 1992, Dir. Edn. Excellence award IST PDE, 1994; grantee Math, 1994, Ecology, 1995, Butterfly Garden, 1995, Arts Spl. Edn., 1995, 96, Arts in Edn., 1995, 96, Math. Lab., 1996, Hist. Rsch. Tech., 1996. Mem. NEA, NAESP, PTA, Pa. Assn. Elem. Sch. Prins., Phi Delta Kappa. Avocations: reading, walking, gardening, travel. Home: 17 Willow Pond Rd Malvern PA 19355-2888 Office: Rainbow Elem Sch 50 Country Club Rd Coatesville PA 19320-1813

WALKER, MARK A., lawyer; b. N.Y.C., June 24, 1941; s. Joseph and Eleanor (Junger) W.; m. Tania Khodjamirian; children: Marie, Andrew. BA, Stanford U., 1963; LLB, Yale U., 1966. Bar: N.Y. 1967, U.S. Dist. Ct. (so. dist.) N.Y. 1977. Assoc. Cleary, Gottlieb, Steen & Hamilton, Paris, Brussels and N.Y., 1966-75; ptnr. Cleary, Gottlieb, Steen & Hamilton, N.Y.C., 1975—. Mem. Assn. Bar City N.Y.

WALKER, MARY DIANE, secondary school educator; b. Royal Oak, Mich., Sept. 11, 1955; d. Thomas Walker and Mary Jo Brown Stevenson. BS in Med. Records Adminstrn., U. Ctrl. Fla., 1979; MEd, U. South Fla., 1995. Registered records adminstr.; cert. secondary sci. and biology tchr., Fla. Tchr. Key Tng. Ctr., Lecanto, Fla., 1982-87; tchr. biology, ecology, environ. sci. and gen. sci. Lecanto H.S., 1987—; tchr. Withlacoochee Environ. Tng. Ctr., 1992, teaching fellow, 1993-96; facilitator Project WILD. Mem. NEA, Nat. Audubon Soc., League Environ. Educators Fla., Fla. Assn. Sci. Tchrs., Phi Kappa Phi. Methodist. Avocations: music, playing piano, sewing, camping, aerobics. Home: PO Box 1121 Floral City FL 34436-1121 Office: Lecanto High Sch 3810 W Educational Path Lecanto FL 34461-9488

WALKER, MARY L., lawyer; b. Dayton, Ohio, Dec. 1, 1948; d. William Willard and Lady D. Walker; 1 child, Winston Samuel. Student, U. Calif., Irvine, 1966-68; BA in Biology/Ecology, U. Calif., Berkeley, 1970; postgrad., UCLA, 1972-73; JD, Boston U., 1973. Bar: Calif. 1973, U.S. Supreme Ct. 1979. Atty. So. Pacific Co., San Francisco, 1973-76; from assoc. to ptnr. Richards, Watson, & Gershon, L.A., 1976-82; dep. asst. atty. gen. lands div. U.S. Dept. Justice, Washington, 1982-84; dep. solicitor U.S. Dept. Interior, Washington, 1984-85; asst. sec. for environment, safety and health U.S. Dept. Energy, Washington, 1985-88; spl. cons. to chmn. bd. Law Engring., Atlanta, 1988-89; v.p., West Coast and the Pacific Law Environ., Inc., San Francisco, 1989; ptnr., head environ. law dept. Richards, Watson & Gershon, San Francisco, 1989-91; ptnr. Luce, Forward, Hamilton & Scripps, San Diego, 1991-94; ptnr. and head San Diego Environ. Practice Group Brobeck, Phleger & Harrison, San Diego, 1994—; U.S. commr. InterAm. Tropical Tuna Commn., 1989-95. Bd. dirs. Endowment for Comty. Leadership, 1987—. Mem. Calif. Bar Assn., San Diego Bar Assn., San Diego BioCommerce Assn. (bd. dirs. 1991-96, pres. 1994), Profl. Women's Fellowship-San Diego (co-founder, pres. 1996—), World Affairs Coun., Renaissance Women. Republican.

WALKER, MICHAEL CHARLES, SR., retirement services executive; b. Rochester, N.Y., Mar. 4, 1940; s. Charles Boyle and Evelyn Esther (Young) W.; m. Patricia Ann Camelio, Feb. 2, 1963; children: Michael Charles Jr., Lyn, Lea, Matthew. BA, U. Colo., 1962; MBA, Columbia Pacific U., 1982, DBA, 1984. Adminstrv. trainee Lincoln Rochester (N.Y.) Trust Co., 1962-64, mktg. officer, 1964-68; asst. v.p. Lincoln First Bank of Rochester, 1968-72, v.p., 1972-77; pres. M.C. Walker Co., Inc., Spencerport, N.Y., 1977-80; exec. dir. The Valley Manor, Rochester, 1980-85; pres., CEO Presbyn. Residence Ctr. Corp., Rochester, 1985—; lectr. SUNY, Brockport, 1982-89; v.p., dir. Kilian and Caroline Schmitt Found., Rochester, 1985—; mem. adv. bd. Chase Lincoln 1st Bank, Rochester, 1989-92; trustee Rochester Hearing and Speech Ctr., 1989-95, chmn., 1993-94; bd. dirs. Genesee Region Home Care Assn., Rochester, 1990—, chmn., 1995—; trustee Greater Rochester Metro C. of C., 1981-89. Author: Introduction to Bank Marketing Research, 1969, rev. edit., 1972, Practical Handbook of Marketing Definitions, 1970; contbr. articles to profl. jours. Leader task force Spencerport Ctrl. Schs. Bd. Edn., 1977, 80-81, 85; chmn. Monroe County Svs. Bond Com., Rochester, 1972—; mem. United Way Evaluation Team, 1990-94; bus. adv. bd. SUNY, Brockport, 1993—; mem. N.Y. State Bd. Profl. Med. Conduct, 1993—; profl. adv. com. Self Help for Hard of Hearing, 1994-96. Recipient Pres.'s Geneseekers award Rochester Area C. of C., 1979, Innovation of Yr. award NYAHSA, 1989. Mem. Am. Assn. Homes for Aging (various coms.), Am. Mktg. Assn. (pres. Rochester chpt. 1969-70), N.Y. State Bankers Assn. (pres. residential mortgage com. 1975-76), N.Y. Assn. Homes and Svcs. for Aging (various coms.), Ridgemont Country Club, Rochester Rotary. Episcopalian. Avocations: golf, reading, travel, physical fitness. Office: Presbyn Residence Ctr Corp 1570 East Ave Rochester NY 14610-1610

WALKER, MICHAEL CLAUDE, finance educator; b. Sherman, Tex., June 8, 1940; s. Andrew Jackson and Alice Lorene (Curry) W.; m. Martha Ellen Hindman, Sept. 10, 1966; children: Stephanie Elizabeth, Rebecca Elaine, Priscilla Eileen. BA, Austin Coll., 1965; MA, Ohio State U., 1966; PhD, U. Houston, 1971. Instr. U. Houston, 1969-70; asst. prof. Ga. State U., Atlanta, 1971-75; assoc. prof. U. Okla., Norman, 1975-78; prof., head dept. fin., ins. and real estate North Tex. State U., Denton, 1978-85; prof. U. Cin., 1985-88, dept. head, 1985—, Virgil M. Schwarm prof. fin. and investments, 1988—. Co-editor: Cases in Financial Institutions, 1979; contbr. articles to profl. jours. Served with AUS, 1958-61. Recipient Leonard P. Ayers fellowship award, 1973. Mem. Am. Fin. Assn., Fin. Execs. Inst., Fin. Mgmt. Assn., So. Fin. Assn. (bd. dirs. 1983-85, sec.-treas. 1986-88, v.p. 1988-89, pres. 1989-90), Southwestern Fin. Assn. (bd. dirs. 1986-88), Ea. Fin. Assn., Midwest Fin. Assn., Beta Gamma Sigma, Omicron Delta Epsilon. Methodist. Office: U Cin Fin Dept Mail Location 195 Cincinnati OH 45221-0195

WALKER, MICHAEL LEON, education educator; b. Cin., May 17, 1942; s. Degree and Annie (Wynn) W. BA, Wayne State U., 1970, EdD, 1991; MA, U. Detroit, 1978. Asst. prof. La. State U., Shreveport, 1991-92, U. Nebr., Lincoln, 1992-94, SUNY, Plattsburgh, 1994-95, Ea. Mich. U., 1995—. Mem. Martin Luther King Club, Plattsburgh, 1994. Recipient award for Svc. to Children, Salvation Army, Lincoln, 1993, 1994. Mem. Nat. Coun. Tchrs. of English, Internat. Reading Assn., Nat. Reading Conf., Phi Delta Kappa. Democrat. Baptist. Avocations: reading, organ, piano. Office: EMU 714 Pray Harrold Hall Ypsilanti MI 48197-2210 also: Mich Acad Reading Improvement 22150 Greenfield Ste 203 Oak Park MI 48237

WALKER, MOIRA KAYE, sales executive; b. Riverside, Calif., Aug. 2, 1940; d. Frank Leroy and Arline Rufina (Roach) Porter; m. Timothy P. Walker, Aug. 30, 1958 (div. 1964); children: Brian A., Benjamin D., Blair K., Beth E. Student, Riverside City Coll., 1973. With Bank of Am., Riverside, 1965-68, Abitibi Corp., Cucamonga, Calif., 1968-70; with Lily div. Owens-Illinois, Riverside, 1970-73; salesperson Lily div. Owens-Illinois, Houston, 1973-77; salesperson Kent H. Landsberg div. Sunclipse, Montebello, Calif., 1977-83, sales mgr., 1983-85; v.p., sales mgr. Kent H. Landsberg div. Sunclipse, Riverside, 1985—. Mem. NAFE, Women in Paper (treas. 1978-84), Kent H. Landsberg President's Club (1st female to make club, 1994, 95, 96). Lutheran. Office: Kent H Landsberg Div Sunclipse 1180 W Spring St Riverside CA 92507-1327

WALKER, MORT, cartoonist; b. El Dorado, Kans., Sept. 3, 1923; s. Robin A. and Carolyn (Richards) W.; m. Catherine Prentice, Aug. 24, 1985; children: Greg, Brian, Polly, Morgan, Marjorie, Neal, Roger, Whitney, Cathy, Jr., Priscilla. Student, Kansas City Jr. Coll., 1941-42, Washington U., St. Louis, 1943-44; B.A., U. Mo., 1948; LL.D., William Penn Coll., 1981. Designer Hallmark Greeting Cards, 1941; editor Dell Pub. Co., 1948-49; free lance cartoonist Saturday Evening Post, other popular mags., 1948-50; scholar in residence Mo. U., 1992. Comic strip artist King Features, 1950—; creator Beetle Bailey, 1950, Hi and Lois, 1954, Sam's Strip, 1961, Boner's Ark, 1968, Sam and Silo, 1977, The Evermores, 1982, Betty Boop and Felix, 1984, (for United Features) Gamin and Patches, 1987; author: Most, 1971, Land of Lost Things, 1973, Backstage at the Strips, 1975, The Lexicon of Comicana, 1981, The Best of Beetle Bailey, 1984; contbr. to numerous anthologies and textbooks. Mem. Pres.'s Com. to Hire Handicapped, People to People Com. Exhbn. touring group show Met. Mus. Art, N.Y.C., 1951; chmn. Internat. Mus. Cartoon Art. Served to 1st lt. AUS, 1943-46, ETO. Recipient Outstanding Cartoonist award The Banshees, 1955, Il Secolo XIX award (Italy), 1972, Adamson award (Sweden), 1975, 88, Segar award, 1977, 4th Estate award Am. Legion, The Jester, 1979, Power of Printing, 1977; named Man of Yr. NCCJ, 1988. Mem. Nat. Cartoonists Soc. (pres. 1959-60, Reuben award 1953, award for best humor strip of 1966, 69, Mus. Cartoon Art Hall of Fame 1989), Artists and Writers, Newspaper Features Coun. Authors Guild, Soc. Illustrators, Nat. Press Club, Silvermine Club (Norwalk,

Conn.), Greenwich Country Club, Quechee Club (Vt.), Boca Raton Resort and Club (Fla.), Kappa Sigma (Man of Yr. 1988). Office: care King Features Syndicate 235 E 45th St New York NY 10017-3305 *If I enjoy my own life that's one life enjoyed. But if I can help others enjoy their lives more, many lives are made more enjoyable.*

WALKER, OLENE S., lieutenant governor; b. Ogden, Utah, Nov. 15, 1930; d. Thomas Ole and Nina Hadley (Smith) W.; m. J. Myron Walker, 1957; children: Stephen Brett, David Walden, Bryan Jesse, Lori, Mylene, Nina, Thomas Myron. BA, Brigham Young U., 1954; MA, Stanford U., 1954; PhD, U. Utah, 1986. V.p. Country Crisp Foods; mem. Utah Ho. of Reps. Dist. 24; lt. gov. State of Utah, 1993—. Mem. Salt Lake Edn. Found. bd. dirs. 1983-90; dir. community econ. devel.; mem. Ballet West, Sch. Vol., United Way, Commn. on Youth, Girls Village, Salt Lake Conv. and Tourism Bd. Mormon. Office: Lieutenant Governor 203 State Capitol Building Salt Lake City UT 84114-1202*

WALKER, PHILIP CHAMBERLAIN, II, health care executive; b. Big Spring, Tex., July 7, 1944; s. Philip Chamberlain and Mary Catherine (St. John) W.; m. Linda Jane Holsclaw, Jan. 21, 1978; children: Shannon M., Meghan M. BA, Cen. Wash. State Coll., 1970; MS, U. Idaho, 1971. Exec. dir. Multnomah Found. for Med. Care, Portland, Oreg., 1972-81; chief exec. officer Peer Rev. Orgn. for Wash. State, Seattle, 1981-84; dir. Preferred Provider Orgn. devel. Provident Life and Accident, Chattanooga, 1984-88; v.p. Maxicare Health Plans, L.A., 1988-91; v.p., gen. mgr. Maxicare Health Plans Midwest, Chgo., 1991-92; pres. Health Plus, Peoria, Ill., 1992—; CEO, chmn. bd. Kepple & Co., Peoria, 1992—; sr. v.p. Health Care Horizons, Albuquerque, 1992—; bd. dirs. RMR Group; cons. to numerous orgns. Contbr. articles to profl. jours. Bd. dirs. Hult Health Edn. Ctr. With USAF, 1961-66, Vietnam. Office: 209 W 5th St Peoria IL 61605-2502

WALKER, PHILLIP R., agricultural products supplier. Pres. Tenn. Farmers Coop., La Vergne, Tenn., Dyer Lauderdale Farmers, Inc., Dyersburg, Tenn. Office: Tenn Farmers Coop PO Box 3003 200 Waldron Rd La Vergne TN 37086 also: Dyer Lauderdale Farmers Inc Dyersburg TN 38024*

WALKER, RALPH CLIFFORD, lawyer; b. Bradenton, Fla., Apr. 30, 1938; s. Julius Clifford and Dorothy (Hefner) W.; m. Sarah Mildred Walker, Sept. 9, 1959 (div. Sept. 1971), 1 child, Laura Elizabeth; m. Katherine Marie Christensen, Oct. 10, 1971; children: Mark Clifford, Tyler Lanier. BA cum laude, Vanderbilt U., 1959; LLB, U. Calif., Berkeley, 1965. Bar: Calif. Ptnr. Orrick Herrington & Sutcliffe, San Francisco, 1965—. Town councilman Town of Ross, Calif., 1970-72.Lt. (j.g.) USN, 1959-62. Mem. ABA, State Bar Calif., San Francisco Bar Assn., University Club (San Francisco, dir. 1986-88, counsel 1983—), Meadow Club (Fairfax, Calif.), Order of Coif. Republican. Presbyterian. Avocations: golf, wine, youth sports. Office: Orrick Herrington & Sutcliffe 400 Sansome St San Francisco CA 94111-3304

WALKER, RANDALL WAYNE, lawyer; b. Pampa, Tex., Mar. 13, 1956; s. Jimmy Wayne and Dorothy Evelyn (Mercer) W.; m. Patricia Gale Vernon Walker, Dec. 12, 1992; children: Alissa Gail Walker Warner, Angie Marie Walker, Cory Wayne Walker, Nicholas Russell Rattan Walker. AA, Clarendon (Tex.) Coll., 1980; BS, West Tex. State U., Canyon, 1984; JD, Tex. Tech. U., Lubbock, 1986. Bar: Tex., 1987. Pvt. practice Clarendon, Tex., 1987-91; asst. atty. gen. Tex. Atty. Gen. Office, Wichita Falls, Tex., 1991—. Cubmaster Boy Scouts Am., Clarendon, 1988-89. Mem. State Bar Tex., Wichita County Bar Assn., Lions (v.p. Clarendon 1989). Avocations: fishing, camping, woodworking. Office: Attorney General Office 813 8th St Wichita Falls TX 76301-3305

WALKER, RICHARD BRIAN, chemistry educator; b. Quincy, Mass., May 14, 1948; s. George Edgar and Eva Mary (Taylor) W. BS in Biochemistry, U. So. Calif., 1970; PhD in Pharm. Chemistry, U. Calif., San Francisco, 1975. Rsch. assoc. Oreg. State U., Corvallis, 1975-76, U. Wash., Seattle, 1976-78; lectr. U.S. Internat. U., San Diego, 1978-81, Hamdard Sch. Pharmacy, New Delhi, India, 1981-82; rsch. scientist Biophysica Found., San Diego, 1982-83; assoc. prof. chemistry U. Ozarks, Clarksville, Ark., 1983-84; asst. to assoc. prof. chemistry U. Ark., Pine Bluff, 1984-96, prof. chemistry, 1996—; prin. investigator minority biomed. rsch. support program NIH, Bethesda, Md., 1986—; project dir. Ark. Systemic Sci. Initiative. Contbr. articles to profl. jours. Coord. home Bible fellowship The Way Internat., Pine Bluff, 1984—; judge Ctrl. Ark. Sci. Fair, Little Rock, 1986—. NIH rsch. grantee, 1986, 89, 93. Mem. Am. Chem. Soc., Ark. Acad. Scis., Coun. on Undergrad. Rsch., Sigma Xi. Avocations: fishing, golf, skiing. Office: U Ark Dept Chemistry 1200 University Dr Pine Bluff AR 71601-2799

WALKER, RICHARD HAROLD, pathologist, educator; b. Cleve., Dec. 2, 1928; s. Harold Deford and Bernice Margaret (Wright) W.; m. Carolyn Franklin, Sept. 28, 1954; children: Bruce, Lynn, Cara, Leah. BS, Emory U., 1950, MD, 1953. Intern City Memphis Hosps., 1953-54; resident in pathology U. Tenn. Coll. Medicine, Memphis, 1954-55, 57-59; Am. Cancer Soc. clin. fellow U. Tenn. Coll. Medicine, 1957-59; med. dir. blood bank and transfusion service City of Memphis Hosps., 1961-70; prof. pathology Coll. Medicine, U. Tenn., Memphis, 1966-70; chief of blood bank and transfusion service William Beaumont Hosp., Royal Oak, Mich., 1970-95; med. dir. Sch. Med. Tech. William Beaumont Hosp., 1970-91; clin. prof. pathology Wayne State U. Sch. Medicine, Detroit, 1982-95. Contbr. articles on blood transfusion, blood group genetics and transfusion medicine to med. jours. With USNR, 1955-76. Recipient Murray Thelin Humanitarian award Memphis chpt. Nat. Hemophilia Found., 1968. Mem. AMA, Coll. Am. Pathologists, Am. Soc. Clin. Pathologists (Disting. Svc. award 1977, Ward Burdick award 1992), Am. Assn. Blood Banks (pres. 1976-77, John Elliott Meml. award 1986), Tenn. Assn. Blood Banks (L.W. Diggs award 1986), Internat. Soc. Blood Transfusion, Am. Soc. for Histocompatibility and Immunogenetics. Republican. Presbyterian. Home: 4204 Fleet Landing Blvd Atlantic Beach FL 32233

WALKER, RICHARD K., lawyer; b. Knoxville, Tenn., Oct. 21, 1948. BA with honors, U. Kans., 1970, JD, 1975; student, U. Bonn, Germany. Bar: Ariz. 1975, D.C. 1977, U.S. Supreme Ct. 1977. Asst. prof. law U. S.C., 1977-81, assoc. prof. law, 1981-82; ptnr. Bishop, Cook, Purcell & Reynolds, Washington, 1981-90, Winston & Strawn, Washington, 1990-93; dir. Streich Lang, Phoenix, 1993—. Bd. trustees Ariz. Theatre Co., 1995—. Fulbright scholar. Mem. ABA, Labor and Employment Law Sec. (mem. equal employment opportunity law com. 1979—), Ariz. Assn. Def. Counsel (bd. dirs. 1997—). Office: Streich Lang Renaissance One 2 N Central Ave Phoenix AZ 85004-2391

WALKER, RICHARD LOUIS, former ambassador, educator, author; b. Bellefonte, Pa., Apr. 13, 1922; s. Robert Shortlidge and Genevieve (Bible) W.; m. Celeno Claypole Kenly, Mar. 29, 1945; children: Geoffrey Kenly, Dorothy Anne, Stephen Bradley. BA, Drew U., 1944; cert. Chinese lang. and area, U. Pa., 1944; MA, Yale U., 1947, PhD, 1950; LLD (hon.), Coll. of Charleston, 1985, Drew U., 1986, The Citadel, 1990; D of Polit. Sci. (hon.), Seoul Nat. U., 1982; D. Pub. Svc., U. S.C., 1991. Asst. prof. history Yale U., 1950-57; prof. internat. studies U. S.C., 1957—, James F. Byrnes prof. internat. relations, 1959—, prof. emeritus, 1992—; U.S. amb. to Republic of Korea, 1981-86; amb.-in-residence U. S.C., 1986—; vis. assoc. prof. Nat. Taiwan U., Taipei, China, 1954-55; vis. prof. U. Wash., 1959, 65; prof. polit. affairs Nat. War Coll., 1960-61; spl. rsch. internat. rels., Far East; lectr., cons. U.S. Govt., 1953—, Dept. Def., 1969—; rep. U.S. Dept. State, USIS, 1973-74; lectr. numerous confs., major U.S. govt. svc. schs. and univs. in Asia, Australia and Europe. Author: Western Language Periodicals on China, 1949, Multi-State System of Ancient China, 1953, China Under Communism, 1955, China and the West, 1956, The Continuing Struggle, 1958, Democracy Confronts Communism in World Affairs, 1965, Edward R. Stettmius, Jr., 1965, The China Danger, 1966, Ancient China, 1969, Prospects in the Pacific, 1972, Asia in Perspective, 1974, Ancient Japan, 1975; contbr. articles to various symposium vols., learned jours. Bd. dirs. Nat. Com. U.S.-China Rels., 1968-94, U.S. Strategic Inst., 1977—, U. S.C. Ednl. Found., 1958—, Conf. on European Problems, 1967—. With AUS, 1942-46, PTO. Recipient Alumni Achievement award in arts Drew U., 1958; Disting. Service award Air U., 1970; Fgn. Service Inst. award, 1971; Armed Forces Staff Coll. award, 1978; Fulbright-Social Sci. Research Council research scholar Academia Sinica Republic China, 1965-66. Mem. Assn. Asian Studies, Am. Assn. for China Studies (pres. 1994-95, nat. pres. 1995-97), Aurelian Honor Soc., Forest Lake Club, Torch Club, Pi Gamma Mu, Omicron Delta Kappa. Episcopalian. Home: 700 Spring Lake Rd Columbia SC 29206-2111

WALKER, ROBERT DIXON, III, surgeon, urologist, educator; b. Rochester, N.Y., July 22, 1936; s. Robert Dixon, Jr. and Virginia (Weir) W.; m. Joyce Ann Copeland, June 23, 1961; children—Sherri Lynn, Lisa Marie, Jeffrey Alan. B.A., B.S., Carson-Newman Coll., 1959; M.D., U. Miami, Fla., 1963. Intern Wake Forest U., 1964; resident in surgery U. Fla., 1968, asst. prof., 1970-74, assoc. prof., 1974-76, prof. surgery, 1976—, dir. admissions Coll. Medicine, 1976-79; instr. U. Tenn., 1969-70; chief of staff Shands Teaching Hosp., 1976. Assoc. editor: Jour. Urology. Served to comdr. USNR, 1968-70. Fellow ACS (gov.); mem. Assn. Univ. Urologists, Am. Urol. Assn. (editorial bd. Update Series), Am. Assn. Genitourinary Surgeons, Soc. Pediatric Rsch., Soc. Pediatric Urology (exec. com., sec., pres.), Am. Acad. Pediatrics (sec., chmn. urology sect.), Fla. Urologic Soc. (sec., pres.). Home: 6322 SW 37th Way Gainesville FL 32608-5105 Office: Div of Urology Box J 247 JHM Health Center Gainesville FL 32610

WALKER, ROBERT HARRIS, historian, author, editor; b. Cin., Mar. 15, 1924; m. Grace Burtt; children: Amy, Rachel, Matthew. BS, Northwestern U., 1945; MA, Columbia U., 1950; PhD, U. Pa., 1955. Edn. specialist U.S. Mil. Govt., Japan, 1946-47; instr. Carnegie Inst. Tech., 1950-51, U. Pa., 1953-54; asst. prof., dir. Am. studies U. Wyo., 1955-59; assoc. prof. George Washington U., 1959-63, prof. Am. civilization, 1963-94, dir. Am. studies program, 1959-66, 68-70; first dir. edn. and pub. programs NEH, 1966-68; fellow Woodrow Wilson Internat. Ctr., 1972-73, Rockefeller Rsch. Ctr., 1979, Hoover Instn., Huntington Libr., 1980; specialist grants to Japan, Germany, Thailand, Iran, Greece, Israel, Brazil, China, People's Republic of Korea, Hong Kong, 1964-91; Fulbright lectr., Australia, New Zealand, Philippines, 1971, Sweden, France, West Germany, Norway, all 1987; Am. Coun. Learned Socs. alt. del. UNESCO Gen. Info. Program, 1978—; cofounder Algonquin Books, 1982. Author: Poet and Gilded Age, 1963, Life in the Age of Enterprise, 1967, American Society, 1981, 2d edit., 1995, Reform in America (nominated for Pulitzer prize in history), 1985, (with R.H. Gabriel) Course of American Democratic Thought, 3d edit., 1986, Cincinnati and the Big Red Machine, 1988, Everyday Life in Victorian America, 1994; editor, compiler: American Studies in the U.S., 1958, American Studies Abroad, 1975, Reform Spirit in America, 1976, 85, American Studies: Topics and Sources, 1976; editor: Am. Quar., 1953-54; sr. editor: Am. Studies Internat., 1970-80, Am. studies series for Greenwood Press, 1972-96. Founding mem. Japan-U.S. Friendship Commn., 1977-80; pres. Friends of Raoul Wallenberg Found., 1989—. With USNR, 1943-46, 50. Mem. Am. Studies Assn. (nat. pres. 1970-71), Cosmos Club, Phi Beta Kappa. Office: 4006 County Road 115 Glenwood Springs CO 81601-9020

WALKER, ROBERT MOWBRAY, physicist, educator; b. Phila., Feb. 6, 1929; s. Robert and Margaret (Seivwright) W.; m. Alice J. Agedal, Sept. 2, 1951 (div. 1973); children: Eric, Mark; m. Ghislaine Crozaz, Aug. 24, 1973. B.S. in Physics, Union Coll., 1950, D.Sc., 1967; M.S., Yale U., 1951, Ph.D., 1954; Dr honoris causa, Université de Clermont-Ferrand, 1975. Physicist Gen. Electric Research Lab., Schenectady, 1954-62, 63-66; McDonnell prof. physics Washington U., St. Louis, 1966—; dir. McDonnell Center for Space Scis., 1975—; vis. prof. U. Paris, 1962-63; adj. prof. metallurgy Rensselaer Poly. Inst., 1958, adj. prof. physics, 1965-66; vis. prof. physics and geology Calif. Inst. Tech., 1972, Phys. Research Lab., Ahmedabad, India, 1981, Institut d'Astrophysique, Paris, 1981; nat. lectr. Sigma Xi, 1984-85; pres. Vols. for Internat. Tech. Assistance, 1960-62, 65-66, founder, 1960; mem. Lunar Sample Analysis Planning Team, 1968-70, Lunar Sample Rev. Bd., 1970-72; adv. com. Lunar Sci. Inst., 1972-75; mem. temporary nominating group in planetary scis. Nat. Acad. Scis., 1973-75, bd. on sci. and tech. for internat. devel., 1974-76, com. planetary and lunar exploration, 1977-80, mem. space sci. bd., 1979-82; bd. dirs. Univs. Space Research Assn., 1969-71; mem. organizing com. Com. on Space Research-Internat. Astron. Union, Marseille, France, 1984; mem. task force on sci. uses of space sta. Solar System Exploration Com., 1985-86; mem. Antarctic Meteorite Working Group, 1985-92; mem. NASA Planetary Geosci. Strategy Com., 1986-88; mem. European Sci. Found. Sci. Orgn. Com., Workshop on Analysis of Samples from Solar System Bodies, 1990; chmn. Antarctic Meteorite Working Group, 1990-92. Decorated officer de l'Ordre des Palmes Academiques (France); recipient Disting. Svc. award Am. Nuclear Soc., 1964, Yale Engring. Assn. award for contbn. to basic and applied sci., 1966, Indsl. Rsch. awards, 1964, 65; Exceptional Sci. Achievement award NASA, 1970; E.O. Lawrence award AEC, 1971; Antarctic Svc. medal NSF, 1985; NSF fellow, 1962-63. Fellow AAAS, Am. Phys. Soc., Meteoritical Soc. (Leonard medal 1993), Am. Geophys. Union, Indian Inst. of Astrophycis (hon.); mem. NAS (mem. polar rsch. bd. com. 1995, J. Lawrence Smith medal 1991), Am. Astron. Soc., St. Louis Acad. Scis. (Peter Raven Lifetime Scientific Achievement award 1997). Achievements include research and publs. on cosmic rays, nuclear physics, geophysics, radiation effects in solids, particularly devel. solid state track detectors and their application to geophysics and nuclear physics problems; discovery of fossil particle tracks in terrestrial and extra-terrestrial materials and fission track method of dating; application of phys. scis. to art and archaeology; lab. studies of interplanetary dust and interstellar grains in primitive meteorites. Home: 3 Romany Park Ln Saint Louis MO 63132-4211

WALKER, ROBERT SMITH, former congressman; b. Bradford, Pa., Dec. 23, 1942; s. Joseph Eddman and Rachael Viola (Smith) W.; m. Sue Ellen Albertson, Apr. 13, 1968. BS, Millersville (Pa.) U., 1964; MA in Polit. Sci, U. Del., 1968. Tchr. Penn Manor High Sch., Lancaster, Pa., 1964-67; legis. asst. to Congressman Edwin D. Eshleman, 1967-74, adminstrv. asst., 1974-76; mem. 95th-104th Congresses from 16th Pa. dist., Washington, D.C., 1977-96; chmn. House Com. Sci. Co-author: Congress-The Pennsylvania Dutch Representatives, 1774-1974. Can You Afford This House, 1978, House of Ill Repute, 1987; contbr. articles to profl. jours. Served with Pa. NG, 1967-73. Republican. Office: US House of Reps 2369 Rayburn Bldg Ofc Bldg Washington DC 20515-0909 *When you decide to seek public office, you accept a trust. The responsibilities of that trust involve not only your talents, your wisdom and your energies, but also your integrity, your character and your commitment to a better tomorrow.**

WALKER, ROGER GEOFFREY, geology educator, consultant; b. London, Mar. 26, 1939; s. Reginald Noel and Edith Annie (Wells) W.; m. Gay Parsons, Sept. 18, 1965; children—David John, Susan Elizabeth. B.A., Oxford U., Eng., 1961; D.Phil., Oxford U., 1964. NATO postdoctoral fellow Johns Hopkins U., Balt., 1964-66; geology faculty McMaster U., Hamilton, Ont., Can., 1966—; prof. McMaster U., 1973—; vis. scientist Marathon Oil Research Ctr., Littleton, Colo., 1973-74, Amoco Can., Calgary, Alta., 1982; vis. prof. Australian Nat. U., Canberra, 1981; tchr. 80 profl. short courses on various aspects of oil exploration in clastic reservoirs, Can., U.S., Brazil, Australia, Japan, Italy; mem. grant selection com. earth scis. sect. Nat. Scis. and Engring. Rsch. Coun. Can., 1981-84. Editor: Facies Models, 1979, 3d edit., 1992; contbr. over 1400articles to profl. jours. Recipient operating and strategic grants Nat. Scis. and Engring. Rsch. Coun. Can., 1966—. Fellow Royal Soc. Can.; mem. Geol. Assn. Can. (assoc. editor 1977-80, Past President's medal 1975, Disting. Svc. award 1994), Can. Soc. Petroleum Geologists (Link award 1983, R.J.W. Douglas Meml. medal 1990), Am. Assn. Petroleum Geologists (Disting. lectr. 1979-80), Soc. Econ. Paleontologists and Mineralogists (pres. eastern sect. 1975-76, coun. for mineralogy 1979-80, hon. mem. 1991, assoc. editor 1970-78, Francis J. Pettijohn medal 1997), Can. Assn. Univ. Tchrs., Internat. Assn. Sedimentologists. Avocations: skiing, classical music, photography, model railroading. Home: 71 Robin Hood Dr, Dundas, ON Canada L9H 4G2 Office: McMaster U Dept Geology, 1280 Main St W, Hamilton, ON Canada L8S 4M1

WALKER, RONALD C., magazine publisher; m. Lou Ann Walker; two children. BA, U. Nebr. Market rsch. mgr. Lane Pub., Menlo Park, Calif., 1967-69, marketing dir., 1969-74, v.p., circulation dir., 1974-84, v.p., gen. mgr. Sunset mag., 1984-90; pub. Smithsonian mag., D.C., 1991—, Air & Space/Smithsonian mag., D.C., 1991—. Office: Smithsonian Mag 900 Jefferson St NW Washington DC 20011-2906*

WALKER, RONALD EDWARD, psychologist, educator; b. East St. Louis, Ill., Jan. 23, 1935; s. George Edward and Marnella (Altmeyer) W.; m. Aldona M. Mogenis, Oct. 4, 1958; children: Regina, Mark, Paula, Alexis. B.S., St. Louis U., 1957; M.A., Northwestern U., 1959, Ph.D., 1961. Lectr. psychology Northwestern U., 1959-61; faculty dept. psychology Loyola U., Chgo., 1961—; asst., then asso. prof. Loyola U., 1961-68, prof., chmn. dept., 1965—; acting dean Loyola U. (Coll. Arts and Scis.), 1973-74, dean, 1974-80, academic v.p., 1980-81, sr. v.p., dean faculties, 1981-89, exec. v.p., 1989—; Cons. VA, Chgo., 1965-74; Am. Psychol. Assn.-NIMH; vis. cons., 1969; vis. scientist Am. Psychol. Assn. NSF, 1968; Cook County (Ill.) rep. from Ill. Psychol. Assn., 1969-72; cons.-evaluator North Cen. Assn., 1986—. Contbr. articles to profl. jours. Trustee St. Francis Hosp., Evanston, Ill., 1986-92, Chgo. Archdiocesan Sems., 1985—, Loyola Acad., Wilmette, Ill., 1987-93, St. Louis U., 1988—. Mem. AAAS, APA (coun. rep. 1970-72), Ill. Psychol. Assn. (chmn. student devel. com. 1965-67, chmn. acad. sec. 1966-67, disting. psychologist of yr. award 1986), Sigma Xi, Psi Chi, Phi Beta Kappa. Home: 2712 Park Pl Evanston IL 60201-1337 Office: 820 N Michigan Ave Chicago IL 60611-2103

WALKER, RONALD F., corporate executive; b. Cin., Apr. 9, 1938; married. BBA, U. Cin., 1961. V.p. Kroger Co., Cin., 1962-72; with Am. Fin. Corp., Cin., 1972—, exec. v.p., 1978-84, pres., COO, bd. dirs., 1984-95; exec. v.p. Gt. Am. Ins., Cin., 1972-80, pres., 1980-87, vice chmn., 1987—; pres., COO Penn Cen. Corp., 1987-92, COO, 1987-92; pres., CEO Gen. Cable Corp., 1992-94; also bd. dirs.; bd. dirs. Chiquita Brands Internat., Cin., Am. Fin. Enterprises, Cin., Am. Annuity Gruop, Inc., Tejas Gas Corp. Office: Gt Am Ins Co 580 Walnut St Cincinnati OH 45202-3110 also: Am Fin Corp 1 E 4th St Cincinnati OH 45202-3717

WALKER, RONALD HUGH, executive search company executive; b. Bryan, Tex., July 25, 1937; s. Walter Hugh and Maxine (Tarver) W.; m. Anne Lucille Collins, Aug. 8, 1959; children: Lisa, Marjorie, Lynne. BA, U. Ariz., 1960. With Allstate Ins. Co., Pasadena, Calif., 1964-67, Hudson Co., 1967-69; asst. to sec. interior, 1969-70; founder, 1st dir., staff asst. to Pres. U.S. White House Advance Office, 1970-72; spl. asst. to Pres., 1972-73; dir. Nat. Park Service, Washington, 1973-75; cons. Saudi Arabia, 1975; assoc. dir. World Championship Tennis, 1975-77; pres. Ron Walker & Assocs., Inc., Dallas, 1977-79; sr. officer, mng. dir. Korn/Ferry Internat., Washington, 1979—; bd. dirs. Guest Svcs. Inc., NOVAFAX. vol. Nixon/Agnew Campaign, 1968, transition and inauguration, 1969; founder, chmn. emeritus Order of Raft, 1972; mem. spl. presdl. del. to Prime Min. Indira Gandhi's funeral, New Delhi, 1984, Games of XXIV Olympiad, Seoul, 1988; trustee Nat. Outdoor Leadership Sch., Nat. Fitness Found., Pres.'s Coun. on Phys. Fitness and Sports, 1981-85; vice chmn., mem. Pres.'s Commn. on Bicentennial U.S. Constn., 1985—; mem. U.S. Olympic Com., 1989-93; bd. dirs., mem. exec. com. NCAA Found.; bd. dirs. Meridian Internat.; mem. Ctr. for Study of Presidency, 1988—, Coun. for Excellence in Govt., 1988—; chmn. Freedom Found. at Valley Forge, 1989—; trustee Ford's Theater, Washington; men's chair Project Hope Ann. Ball, 1989, 90, 91; chmn. ann. dinner Boys and Girls Clubs Am., 1993; chmn. 50th Presdl. Inauguration, Dedication Richard Nixon Libr., Birthplace, 1990, bd. dirs., 1990—; mgr. 1984 Rep. Nat. Conv.; sr. advisor Rep. Nat. Conv., 1988, 92, 96, Bush/Quayle Presdl. Campaign, 1988; nat. chair Celebrities & Sports for Bush/Quayle; mem. oversite com. U.S. Rowing, 1993; active Commn. for Preservation of White House, 1973-75, Nat. Park adv. bd., 1973-75, Nat. Park Found., 1973-75, John F. Kennedy Ctr. for Performing Arts, 1973-75, Friends of Nancy Hanks Ctr., Meridian House Internat. Bd. Trustees, 1992—, USA Gymnasium Found., 1993—. Capt. U.S. Army, 1961-64. Recipient Disting. Citizen award U. Ariz., 1973, Outstanding Svc. award Dept. Interior, 1975, Centennial Medallion award U. Ariz., 1989, Ellis Island Congl. medal of honor, 1992. Mem. NCAA (bd. dirs. 1992—, exec. com. 1992—), Econs. Club of Washington, Met. Club of Washington, Congl. Country Club, Georgetown Club, City Club of Washington, Univ. Club. of N.Y., Burning Tree Club, Phi Delta Theta (named to Hall of Fame, 1991). Republican. Methodist. Office: Presidential Pla 900 19th St NW Washington DC 20006-2105

WALKER, RONALD R., writer, newspaper editor, educator; b. Newport News, Va., Sept. 2, 1934; s. William R. and Jean Marie (King) W.; m. O. Diane Mawson, Apr. 16, 1961; children: Mark Jonathan, Steven Christopher. BS, Pa. State U., 1956; postgrad. (Nieman fellow) Harvard U., 1970-71. Reporter, news editor, sr. editor, editorial page editor, mng. editor San Juan Star (P.R.), 1962-73, Washington columnist, 1982-84, city editor, 1984-87; instr. journalism Pa. State U., State College, 1973-74; asst. prof. Columbia U. Grad. Sch. Journalism, N.Y.C., 1974-76; editor The Daily News, V.I., 1976-77; press sec. Gov. V.I., 1978-79; special asst., chief of staff Rep. James H. Scheuer, U.S. Congress, 1980-82, special asst., chief of staff, Resident Commr. Jaime B. Fuster, U.S. Congress, 1987-92, spl. asst., press sec. Resident Commr. Antonio J. Colorado, 1992-93; independent profl. writer, weekly columnist editl. page San Juan Star, 1993—. Contbr. articles to nat. mags. and jours. Served with U.S. Army, 1957-59. Mem. Soc. Nieman Fellows., Leica Hist. Soc. Am. Address: PO Box 1358 Saint John VI 00831-1358 also: 5500 Friendship Blvd Apt 1522N Chevy Chase MD 20815-7208

WALKER, RUTH ANN, journalist; b. Elmhurst, Ill., June 22, 1954; d. Robert F. and Jeanne (Carsman) W. AB, Oberlin (Ohio) Coll., 1976. Staff reporter Aiken (S.C.) Standard, 1977-78; various editing and writing positions Christian Sci. Monitor, Boston, 1978-83, bus. corr., 1983-85, editorial writer, 1985-88, asst. editor editorial page, 1988, asst. mng. editor, 1988-90, dep. editor, 1990-94, assoc. editor, 1994-95, sr. correspondent Europe, 1995—. Recipient Exceptional Merit Media award Nat. Women's Polit. Caucus, 1987. Christian Scientist. Home and Office: Muensterstr 20, D53111 Bonn Germany

WALKER, SALLY BARBARA, retired glass company executive; b. Bellerose, N.Y., Nov. 21, 1921; d. Lambert Roger and Edith Demerest (Parkhouse) W. Diploma Cathedral Sch. St. Mary, 1939; AA, Finch Jr. Coll., 1941. Tchr. interior design Finch Coll., 1941-42; draftsman AT&T, 1942-43; with Steuben Glass Co., N.Y.C., 1943—, exec. v.p., 1959-62, exec. v.p. ops., 1962-78, exec. v.p. ops. and sales, 1978-83, exec. v.p., 1983-88, ret. 1988. Pres. 116 E. 66th St. Corp. Mem. Fifth Ave. Assn. Republican. Episcopalian. Clubs: Rockaway Hunting, Lawrence Beach, U.S. Lawn Tennis, Colony, English-Speaking Union. Home: 116 E 66th St New York NY 10021-6547

WALKER, SAMMIE LEE, retired elementary education educator; b. Elkhart, Tex., July 10, 1927; d. Samuel and Mary (Pigford) Nathaniel; m. R.L. Walker, Oct. 12, 1952 (dec. 1994); children: Winfred, Frederick, Mary, Pearlene, Gladys, Robert, Ethel. BS, Tex. Coll., 1951; MEd, Tex. So. U., 1979. Cert. tchr., home econs. educator, elem. educator. Seamstress Madonna Guild Factory, Houston, 1958-60; presch. tchr. Project Head Start, Houston, 1961-64; tchr. Houston Ind. Schs., 1964-86; tchr. Harris County Youth Authority, Clear Lake, Tex., 1985; costume maker CETA program Houston Ind. Sch. Dist., 1984. Tchr. Trinity Garden Ch. of Christ, 1956—; phys. fitness coord. Kashmere Garden Sr. Citizen Club, Houston, 1986-92; home care provider Tex. Home Health Care, Houston, 1988-93. Recipient Friendship award Houston Christian Inst., 1993. Mem. NEA. Avocations: sewing, cooking, travel, volunteer work for local charities and school districts. Home: 7911 Shotwell St Houston TX 77016-6548

WALKER, SANDRA, mezzo-soprano; b. Richmond, Va., Oct. 1, 1946; d. Phillip Loth and Mary Jane W.; m. Melvin Brown, May 17, 1975; 1 child, Noel Christian Brown. MusB, U. N.C., 1969; postgrad., Manhattan Sch. Music, 1971-72. Artist-in-residence Ky. Opera Assn., 1980. Recorded Ned Rorem's song cycle King Midas on Desto Records, 1974; debut San Francisco Opera, 1972, re-engaged 1986, Chgo. Lyric Opera, 1973, 88, re-engaged 1988, Washington Opera Soc., 1973, Phila. Lyric Opera, 1973, Teatro Communale, Florence, Italy, 1985, Met. Opera, N.Y.C., 1986, re-engaged 1989, Opernhaus Zurich, 1987, Stadt Theater Wiesbaden, 1987, Rigoletto, Eugene-Onegin, Met. Opera. 1989, Netherlands Opera, 1989, Orlands Furioso, San Francisco Opera, 1989, Ring Cycle, 1990; leading mezzo soprano N.Y.C. Opera, 1974—, Stadt Theater, Würzburg, Germany, 1980-82, Stadt Theater Gelsenkirchen, Fed. Republic Germany, 1983-85, Stadt Theater Essen, Fed. Republic Germany, 1984, Frankfurt Opera, Fed. Republic Germany, 1985; soloist Orchestra Santa Cecilia Academia, Rome, 1987, New Orch. Paris, 1988; singer in major U.S. and European music festivals Tanglewood, Caramoor, Spoleto-U.S.A. and Spoleto Festival of Two Worlds in, Italy; soloist, Am. Symphony, San Francisco Symphony, 1980; appeared in: PBS nat. telecasts Manon, The Ballad of Baby Doe, Saint of Bleeker Street, 1981, on Great Performances: in The Consul and Eugene

Onegin, 1986; Met. Opera nat. broadcast Samson, 1986, Eugene Onegin, 1989; orchestral appearances with Nat. Symphony, Washington, St. Louis Symphony, Chgo. Symphony, Richmond (Va.) Symphony, Houston Symphony, San Francisco Symphony, Charlotte Symphony, Cleve. Orch.; comml. video prodns. Eugene Onegin, Manon, Orlando Furioso; opera appearances include Falstaff, Calgary Opera, 1991, Mephistofiles, Chgo. Lyric Opera, 1991, Barber of Seville, Phila. Lyric Opera, 1991, Theatre De Capitole Toulouse France, 1992, Paris Opera, 1993, Blossom Festival Clev. Opera, 1993, Met. Opera, 1994, Met. Opera, 1995, Recording Die Walkuere with Cleve. Orch. Recipient Nat. Endowment for Arts Affiliate Artist grant sponsored by Va. Opera Assn. and Sears Roebuck Co., 1978. Office: care Columbia Artists Mgmt Inc 165 W 57th St New York NY 10019-2201*

WALKER, SAVANNAH T., executive assistant, legislative assistant; b. Lubbock, Tex., Nov. 23, 1930; d. John Hansford and Lenore Belle (Muecke) Tunnell; m. Julius Waring Walker, Jr., July 29, 1956; children: Savannah Waring, Lucile Lenore, George Julius Stewart. BA, Tex. Tech. U., 1951; student, Radcliffe Coll., 1951. Cert. secondary sch. tchr., Tex. Tchr., English and journalism Phillips (Tex.) Ind. Sch. Dist., 1951-52; asst. to congressman Mahon U.S. Congress, Washington, 1952-54, admisntrv., exec. asst., 1954-58, 63-66; legis. asst. to chmn. House Appropriations U.S. Ho. of Reps., Washington, 1973-78; exec. asst. to v.p. Nat. Assn. Mfrs., Washington, 1985-89; exec. asst. to pres. Ogilvy Adams & Rinehart, Washington, 1990—. Vol., fundraiser for charitable orgns., Chad and Eng., 1966-73; pres. Am. Women in London, 1971-72, Am. Women in Liberia, Monrovia, 1979-80. Mem. AAUW, PEO, Am. Women in the Arts Mus., DAR, Internat. Women's Club (founder pres.) (Ouagadougou, Burkina, Faso), Delta Delta Delta. Avocations: church work, bridge, reading, needlework, writing. Home: 3801 Jenifer St NW Washington DC 20015 Office: Ogilvy Adams & Rinehart 1901 L St NW Ste 300 Washington DC 20036-3515

WALKER, SHARON LOUISE, gifted education educator; b. St. Paul, Mar. 26, 1944; d. John Franklin and Catherine G. (Keiffer) Corkill; m. David Glenn Smith, June 11, 1964 (div. Feb. 1980); 1 child, Carina Ann Smith; m. William Laurens Walker III, Nov. 10, 1981. BS in Edn., U. Md., 1971; M in Adminstrn. and Supervision, U. Va., 1990. Cert. elem. sch. prin., K-12 tchr. of gifted, 1-7 classroom tchr., K-12 tchr. art, Va. Tchr. 3rd and 4th grades Seat Pleasant (Md.) Elem. Sch., 1971-75; tchr. 4th grade Venable Elem. Sch., Charlottesville, Va., 1975-79; tchr. 3rd and 4th grade gifted edn. Quest program Charlottesville City Schs., 1979—; coord. acad. summer sch. Summer Discovery grades kindergarten through 4 Charlottesville City Schs., 1988-94, mem. various curriculum, staff devel., award coms., 1990—; seminar leader summer enrichment program U. Va., Charlottesville, 1986-89. Mem., chairperson placement com. Jr. League, Charlottesville, 1977—; mem. edn. com. Bayly Art Mus., Charlottesville, 1984-89; bd. dirs., devel. chairperson Charlottesville Albemarle Youth Orch., 1991-93; bd. dirs., mem. program com. Madison Ho., U. Va., 1994—, bd. dirs., co-chair, 1996—. Mem. Charlottesville Edn. Assn., Phi Delta Kappa (U. Va. chpt.), Delta Kappa Gamma (v.p. 1993-95, chair rsch. com. 1996—). Home: 1180 Old Garth Rd Charlottesville VA 22901-1916 Office: Quest Ctr 406 14th St NW Charlottesville VA 22903-2305

WALKER, SONIA EVADNE, osteopath; b. Apr. 22, 1957; d. Albert and Beryl Adassa (Goffe) Adamson; m. Denzel Hugh Walker; 1 child, Norville Hugh. BS in Environ. Health, York Coll. CUNY, 1979; MS in Med. Biology/Nutritional Sci., L.I. U., 1983; DO, N.Y. Coll. Osteo. Medicine, 1992. Bd. cert. family practice physician. Cancer immunology rsch. tech. Meml. Sloan Kettering Hosp., 1983-90; resident Luth. Med. Ctr., Bklyn., 1992-95. Active Cmty. Civic Assn., 1994-95; vol. Healthcare Internat. Recipient Resident Tchr. award Soc. Tchrs. Family Medicine, Service by a Resident to Her Cmty. award N.Y. State Acad. Family Physicians, others. Mem. AMA, Physicians for Social Responsibility, Am. Coll. Gen. Practice in Osteo. Medicine and Surgery, Am. Acad. Family Physicians. Avocations: reading, community activities, church activities, theater. Home: 9 Oakdale Dr Westbury NY 11590 Office: Family Med Svcs PC 11481 177th Pl Jamaica NY 11434-1405

WALKER, STANLEY P., publishing executive; b. Arkham, Mass., May 23, 1955; s. Gerald Jeffrey and Rebecca (Chamberlain) W.; m. Faith Darwin, Aug. 17, 1977; children: Erin, Emily, Amy. BA in English, Oberlin Coll., 1977; MFA in Creative Writing, Western Mich. U., 1979; MA in English Lit., Columbia U., 1982, PhD in English Lit., 1983. Sr. editor Farrar Straus Giroux, N.Y.C., 1980-83; assoc. prof. creative writing, early English lit. Columbia U., N.Y.C., 1983-87; pres., editor-in-chief Walker Press, N.Y.C., 1987-90; pres. Walker/Sturgeon Publs., Inc., New Providence, N.J., 1990—; vis. assoc. prof. Grinnell (Iowa) Coll., 1985-86; adj. prof. CUNY, 1987-90; cons. Farrar Straus Giroux, N.Y.C., 1990—. Author: (short story collections) The Rudeness of Youth, 1989, Life in the Sour Patch, 1991; co-author: (with L.Q. Sturgeon) Succeeding in Small-Scale Publishing, 1991; book reviewer numerous publs., N.Y.C., 1987—; contbr. articles to profl. jours. Trustee Grinnell Coll., 1990—; soccer coach, referee Am. Youth Soccer League, New Providence, 1990—. Mem. Writers Guild, Mensa, Ragnarok Lumberjacks, Phi Beta Kappa. Avocations: Old and Middle English writings, linguistics, music criticism, soccer, poker. Office: Reed Elsevier New Providence 121 Chanlon Rd New Providence NJ 07974-1541

WALKER, STEVEN FRANK, management consultant; b. Indpls., Dec. 31, 1957; s. Frank Dilling and Beverly (Trudgen) W.; m. Brenda Anne Brost, July 11, 1986; children: Jack. BS, Boston U., 1980. Acct. R.A. Boston & Co., Boston, 1980-81; staff acct. NEECO, Needham, Mass., 1981-82; sr. project dir. Walker Research Inc., Phoenix, 1982-84; account exec. Walker Research Inc., Walnut Creek, Calif., 1984-85; group mgr. Walker Research Inc., Indpls., 1985-87; v.p. new bus. Walker Research Inc., 1987-88, v.p. new ventures and corp. devel., 1988—; bd. dirs. Walker Clin. Evaluations, Indpls., 1989—; lectr. in field. Contbr. articles to profl. ours. Bd. dirs. Boys Clubs of Indpls., 1987—; mem. mktg. com. Indpls. Zoo, 1988; capt. fund raising Indpls. C. of C., 1987-88, Children's Mus., 1986-88; charter mem. Young Leadxers for Mutz, 1988. Mem. Am. Mktg. Assn., Mktg. Research Assn., Advt. Research Found. Republican. Roman Catholic. Avocations: golf, wine, auto racing. Office: Walker Research Inc 3939 Priority Way South Dr Indianapolis IN 46240-1496

WALKER, THOMAS H., federal agency administrator; b. Hattiesburg, Miss., Nov. 11, 1950; s. Thomas Ray and Mary Ella (Bennett) W.; m. Cynthia Kay Sherer, June 5, 1993; children: Ty, Kelly, Rachel, Stacey. BS in Engring., Miss. State U., 1972; MBA, U. West Fla., 1982; postgrad., Nat. Def. U., 1987-88, Harvard U., 1990, Fed. Exec. Inst., 1992. Registered profl. engr., Va. Indsl. engr. Navy Pub. Works Ctr., Norfolk, Va., 1973-75, Atlantic Divsn. Naval Facility Engring. Commn., Norfolk, Va., 1975-76; supervisory gen. engr. Naval Comm. Sta., Exmouth, Australia, 1976-78; indsl. engr. Western Divsn. Naval Facility Engring. Commn., San Bruno, Calif., 1978-79; head facilities mgmt. Navy Pub. Works Ctr., Pensacola, Fla., 1979-82, Subic Bay, The Philippines, 1982-85; dep. dir. facilities mgmt. USMC, Washington, 1985-89; asst. commr. GSA, Washington, 1989-92, dep. asst. regional adminstr., 1992-93; asst. regional adminstr. pub. bldgs. GSA, Kansas City, Mo., 1993—; bd. dirs. Kansas City BOMA. Coach Little League Baseball, Fairfax, Va., 1986-92, Girls Softball Team, Lees Summit, Va., 1995. cub scout den father Boy Scouts Am., Fairfax, 1987-88. Miss. State U. Disting. Engring. fellow, 1992; recipient Arthur S. Fleming award Washington Jaycees, 1989, Presdl. rank award, 1996, v.p. Hammer award, 1996. Mem. NSPE, Va. Soc. Profl. Engrs., Bldg. Owners and Mgrs. Assn. (mem. govt. bldgs. com. 1991—, chmn. 1993—, mem. corp. facilities com. 1991—, nat. adv. coun. 1995—), Internat. Facilities Mgmt. Assn. (mem. pub. sector com. 1991—, Golden Cir. award 1994), Sr. Execs. Assn., Phi Kappa Phi, Alpha Pi Mu, Gamma Beta Phi. Methodist. Avocation: golf. Home: 328 NE Sunderland Ct Lees Summit MO 64064-1610 Office: GSA 1500 E Bannister Rd Kansas City MO 64131-3009

WALKER, TIMOTHY BLAKE, lawyer, educator; b. Utica, N.Y., May 21, 1940; s. Harold Blake and Mary Alice (Corder) W.; m. Sandra Blake; children: Kimberlee Corder, Tyler Blake, Kelley Loren. AB magna cum laude, Princeton U., 1962; JD magna cum laude, U. Denver, 1967, MA in Sociology, 1969. Bar: Colo. 1968, Calif. 1969, Ind. 1971. Asst. prof. law U. Pacific, 1968-69; vis. assoc. prof. U. Toledo, 1969-70; assoc. prof. Indpls. Law Sch., Ind. U., 1970-71; assoc. prof. U. Denver, 1971-75, prof., 1975—, dir. adminstrn. of justice program, 1971-78; sole practice law Denver, 1972-79; of counsel Robert T. Hinds, Jr. & Assocs. (P.C.), Littleton, Colo., 1980-85; ptnr., of counsel Cox, Mustain-Wood, Walker & Schumacher, Littleton, 1985—; cons. in field; rsch. on lay representation in adminstrv. agys., Colo., 1975-76. Contbr. articles to profl. publs.; lectr., symposium editor: Denver Law Jour., 1966-67; editor-in-chief: Family Law Quar., 1983-92. Mem. Ind. Child Support Commn., 1970-71; pres. Shawnee (Colo.) Water Consumers Assn., 1975-84, 93-95; del. Colo. Rep. Conv., 1978. Colo. Bar Assn. grantee, 1975-76. Fellow Am. Sociol. Assn., Am. Acad. Matrimonial Lawyers, Internat. Acad. Matrimonial Lawyers; mem. ABA (vice chmn. child custody subcom., sec. sect. family law 1992-93, vice-chairperson, sec. family 1993-94, chairperson-elect sect. family law 1994-95, chairperson sect. family law 1995-96, mem. child custody task force, chmn. alimony maintenance and support com.), Calif. Bar Assn., Colo. Bar Assn., Ind. Bar Assn., Colo. Trial Lawyers Assn. (cons.). Presbyterian. Home: 7329 Rochester Ct Castle Rock CO 80104-9281 Office: 1900 Olive St Denver CO 80220-1857 also: 6601 S University Blvd Littleton CO 80121-2913 *Law and justice require the combination of intellectual self-discipline and an awareness of human dignity. The path of the law is often twisted and circuitous, and my goal has been to leave the trail better than I found it.*

WALKER, VAUGHN R., federal judge; b. Watseka, Ill., Feb. 27, 1944; s. Vaughn Rosenworth and Catharine (Miles) W. AB, U. Mich., 1966; JD, Stanford U., 1970. Intern economist SEC, Washington, 1966, 68; law clk. to the Hon. Robert J. Kelleher U.S. Dist. Ct. Calif., L.A., 1971-72; assoc. atty. Pillsbury Madison & Sutro, San Francisco, 1972-77, ptnr., 1978-90; judge U.S. Dist. Ct. (no. dist.) Calif., San Francisco, 1990—; mem. Calif. Law Revision Commn., Palo Alto, 1986-89. Dir. Jr. Achievement of Bay Area, San Francisco, 1979-83, St. Francis Found., San Francisco, 1991—. Woodrow Wilson Found. fellow U. Calif., Berkeley, 1966-67. Fellow Am. Bar Found.; mem. ABA (jud. rep., antitrust sect. 1991-95), Lawyers' Club of San Francisco (pres. 1985-86), Assn. Bus. Trial Lawyers (dir. 1996—), Am. Law Inst., Am. Saddlebred Horse Assn., San Francisco Mus. Modern Art, Bohemian Club, Olympic Club. Office: US Dist Ct 450 Golden Gate Ave San Francisco CA 94102

WALKER, W. LAWRENCE, JR., newspaper publishing executive. Pres., CEO San Antonio Express-News. Office: San Antonio Express-News PO Box 2171 Ave E & 3d St San Antonio TX 78205

WALKER, WALDO SYLVESTER, academic administrator; b. Fayette, Iowa, June 12, 1931; s. Waldo S. and Mildred (Littelle) W.; m. Marie J. Olsen, July 27, 1952 (div.); children: Martha Lynn, Gayle Ann; m. Rita K. White, June 16, 1984. BS cum laude, Upper Iowa U., Fayette, 1953; MS, U. Iowa, 1957, PhD, 1959. Mem. faculty Grinnell (Iowa) Coll., 1958, assoc. dean coll., 1963-65, chmn. div. Natural Scis., 1968-69, dean of adminstrn., 1969-73, exec. v.p., 1973-77, dean coll., 1973-80, provost, 1977-80, exec. v.p., 1980-90, exec. v.p. and treas., 1988-90, v.p. for coll. svcs., 1990-95, prof. biology, 1968—; research assoc. U. B.C. Dept. of Botany, 1966-67. Author articles on plant physiology, ultrastructural cytology. Served with U.S. Army, 1953-55. Fellow NSF Sci. Faculty, 1966-67; recipient NSF research grants, 1960-63, 68. Mem. Am. Assn. Colls., Am. Conf. Acad. Deans (nat. chmn. 1977-78), Am. Assn. Higher Edn., Sigma Xi. Home: 1920 Country Club Dr Grinnell IA 50112-1130 Office: Grinnell Coll PO Box 805 Grinnell IA 50112-0805

WALKER, WALTER FREDERICK, professional basketball team executive; b. Bradford, Pa., July 18, 1954; m. Linda Walker. Diploma, U. Va.; MBA, Stanford U., 1987; BA, U. Va., 1976. Chartered Fin. Analyst. Player Portland (Oreg.) Trail Blazers, 1976-77; player Seattle SuperSonics, 1977-82, pres., gen. mgr., 1994—; player Houston Rockets, 1982-84; with Goldman Sachs and Co., San Francisco, 1987-94; prin. Walker Capital, Inc., San Francisco, 1994; mem. USA gold medal World Univ. Games basketball team, 1973; broadcaster basketball Raycom Network, 1989-94; cons. Seattle SuperSonics, 1994. Vice chmn. Capital Campaign; bd. dirs. Red Hook Ale Brewery; bd. dirs. Interpoint Corp., Gargoyles Performance Eyeware. Named 1st team Acad. All-Am. U. Va.; named to Pa. State Sports Hall of Fame. Office: Seattle SuperSonics 190 Queen Anne Ave N Ste 200 Seattle WA 98109-4926*

WALKER, WALTER GRAY, JR., small business owner, program statistician; b. Newport News, Va., June 6, 1931; s. Walter Gray and Verna Elizabeth (Haughton) W.; divorced; children: James Gray, Thomas Shelton, Martha Anne Crute. AB, William and Mary Coll., 1956; AAS magna cum laude, No. Va. Community, 1983; D of Noetic Scis. (hon.), Fergle U., 1987. Broadcast engr. Sta. WGH, Hampton, Va., 1957-58; instr. Chesterfield Sch. Bd., Va., 1958-63; asst. coord. Va. Mental Health Study Commn., Richmond, Va., 1964; asst. dir. Community Action Agency, Hampton, Va., 1965; statistician U.S. Govt., Washington, 1966-78; pres. Diversified Svcs. Co., Arlington, Va., 1980—; automotive tech. instr. No. Va. Community Coll., Alexandria, Va., 1983; radio electronics officer OMI Corp., N.Y.C., 1991; real estate broker Va. Real Estate Commn., Richmond, Va., 1962; bd. dir. Chesterfield Hosp. Corp., Va., 1963-64. Author: Public Housing Review, 1973, Automotive Technical Document Study of Northern Virginia Community College, 1983. Treas. 1st Congregational Ch., Washington, 1972; del. Arlington (Va.) Dem. Party, 1992. With USNR, 1949-53; petty officer 2d class USN, 1950-52, Korea. Mem. Am. Radio Assn., World Federalist Assn., Vets. for Peace, UN Assn. of the Nat. Capitol Area, Chesterfield Jaycees (external affairs rep. 1962-63, Common Cause, Ams. for Dem. Action, Arlington Amateur Radio Club (treas. 1988-89). Democrat. Unitarian. Home: 900 N Livingston St Arlington VA 22205-1423 Office: Diversified Svcs Co PO Box 5315 Arlington VA 22205-0415

WALKER, WALTER HERBERT, III, lawyer, writer; b. Quincy, Mass., Sept. 12, 1949; s. Walter H. Jr. and Irene M. (Horn) W.; m. Anne M. DiScuillo, June 17, 1982; children: Brett Daniel, Jeffrey St. John. BA, U. Pa., 1971; JD, U. Calif., San Francisco, 1974. Bar: Calif. 1974, Mass. 1981. Appellate atty. ICC, Washington, 1975-77; trial atty. Handler, Baker, Greene & Taylor, San Francisco, 1977-80; ptnr. Sterns and Walker and predecessor firm Sterns, Smith, Walker & Grell, San Francisco, 1981-88; ptnr. firm Walker & Durham, San Francisco, 1988—. Author: A Dime to Dance By, 1983 (Best 1st Novel by Calif. Author), The Two Dude Defense, 1985, Rules of The Knife Fight, 1986, The Immediate Prospect of Being Hanged, 1989, The Appearance of Impropriety, 1992. Mem. ATLA, Consumer Attys. of Calif., San Francisco Trial Lawyers Assn., Mystery Writers Am., Consumer Attys. of Calif. Democrat. Club: Hastings Rugby. Home: 604 Seminary Dr Mill Valley CA 94941-4907 Office: 50 Francisco St Ste 160 San Francisco CA 94133-2108

WALKER, WANDA GAIL, special education educator; b. Montgomery, Ala., June 7, 1946; d. Carter Warren Gamaliel and Ruth Jones (Carter) Walker. BS in Elem. Edn., Campbell U., 1968; MA in Christian Edn., Scarritt Coll., 1970; cert. in tchg. of learning disabled, Pembroke U., 1994. Cert. tchr. class A, N.C. Dir. Christian edn. United Meth. Ch., Roxboro, N.C., 1970-76; diaconal min. United Meth. Ch., Hamlet, N.C., 1976-77, Rockingham, N.C., 1977-85; head teller Montgomery Savs. and Loan, Rockingham, 1985-87; loan officer-credit R.W. Goodman Co., Rockingham, 1987-89; tchr. spl. edn. Richmond County Schs., Hamlet, 1987—; active Richmond County Reading Coun., Hamlet, 1989—. Bd. dirs. Sandhill Manor Group Home, Hamlet, 1977—. Eisenhower grantee U. N.C., 1994; recipient Mission award United Meth. Women, N.C. Conf., 1990; named Best Working Mem., Women's Club Hamlet, 1991. Mem. Woman's Club Hamlet (treas. 1989-91, 1st v.p. 1992-94). Democrat. Avocations: church activities, reading, volunteer work. Home: 344 Raleigh St Hamlet NC 28345-2750 Office: Richmond County Schs Hamlet Ave Hamlet NC 28345

WALKER, WARREN STANLEY, English educator; b. Bklyn., Mar. 19, 1921; s. Harold Stanley and Althea (Luscher) W.; m. Barbara Jeanne Kerlin, Dec. 9, 1943; children—Brian, Theresa. BA, SUNY-Albany, 1947, MA, 1948; PhD, Cornell U., 1951; LittD (hon.), Selcuk U., 1989. Prof., chmn. dept. English Blackburn Coll., Carlinville, Ill., 1951-59; prof., dean arts and scis. Parsons Coll., Fairfield, Iowa, 1959-64; Fulbright lectr. Am. lit. Ankara (Turkey) U., 1961-62; prof. English Tex. Tech U., Lubbock, 1964-86; Horn prof. Tex. Tech U., 1972-86; dir. Archive Turkish Oral Narrative, 1971; adv. council Tex. Cultural Alliance, 1975. Author: Nigerian Folktales, 1961, Twentieth-Century Short Story Explication, 14 vols., 1961-93, James Fenimore Cooper, 1962, Leatherstocking and the Critics, 1965, Tales Alive in Turkey, 1966, Archive of Turkish Oral Narrative: Catalogue 1, 1975, Plots and Characters in the Fiction of J.F. Cooper, 1978, A Bibliography of American Scholarship on Turkish Folklore and Ethnography, 1982, Turkish Games for Health and Recreation, 1983, Archive of Turkish Oral Narrative: Catalogue 2, 1988, Catalogue 3, 1994, The Book of Dede Korkut-A Turkish Epic, 1991, More Tales Alive in Turkey, 1992, A Turkish Folktale: The Art of Behçet Mahir, 1996; mem. editorial bd. Definitive Edit. Works of James Fenimore Cooper, 1968; bibliographer Studies in Short Fiction, 1973. Served with USAAF, 1943-45. Recipient Tex. Writers award, 1967; citation Turkish Ministry Edn., 1967, Turkish Ministry State, 1973; research grantee Am. Council Learned Socs., 1973, 79; Am. Philos. Soc., 1974, Tex. Tech U., 1971-74, 76, 83, Republic of Turkey, 1983, Inst. Turkish Studies, 1984. Mem. MLA, Am. Folklore Soc., Nat. Coun. Tchrs. English, Internat. Soc. Folk Narrative Rsch., Middle East Studies Assn., Tex. Assn. Middle East Scholars (exec. coun.), Turkish Studies Assn., Atatürk Supreme Coun. on Turkish Culture (hon.). Home: 3703 66th St Lubbock TX 79413-5325 Office: Tex Tech U Archive Turkish Oral N Lubbock TX 79409

WALKER, WELMON, JR. (RUSTY WALKER), publisher, consultant; b. Chgo., Dec. 28, 1947; s. Welmon Sr. and Mary Ann (Befford) W.; m. Nedra Kay Carlson, Dec. 30, 1972; children: Welmon III, Whitney O. Student, U. Alaska, 1970-74; AA, Tanana Valley Community Coll., 1984; BS, U. of the State of N.Y., 1985; MBA, U. Phoenix, 1996. Gen. mgr. Sta. KMPS (name now Sta. KSUA-FM), Fairbanks, Alaska, 1971-74; duty dir. Sta. KUAC-TV, Fairbanks, 1973-74; staff photographer Sta. KFAR-TV, Fairbanks, 1974-75; bus. mgr. Nat. Painting Corp., Fairbanks, 1975-76; instr. Fairbanks Native Assn., 1975-76; asst. mgr. Wometco-Lathrop Co., Fairbanks, 1978-79; pres. That New Pub. Co., Fairbanks, 1977-93, Honolulu, 1993—; instr. U. Alaska, Fairbanks, 1979-80. Author: Hawaii Corp. Manual, 1970, Alaska Corp Manual, 1977, Publishing Manual, 1987, Finding The Lowest Quality Print Bid For Your Short Run Book Project, 1997; contbr. articles to profl. jours. Dir. Lost Lake Camp, Midnight Sun Coun. Boys Scouts Am., 1986-87, bd. dirs., 1978—; pres., bd. dirs. Fairbanks Youth Svcs., Inc., 1979—; dir. Bapt. Tng. Union, St. John Bapt. Ch., Fairbanks, 1969; pres., 1994-95, bd. dirs., 1993— Luth. Ch. of Honolulu; student affairs chmn. univ. assembly U. Alaska, 1971-74. With U.S. Army, 1968-70. Mem. Small Pubs. Assn. N.Am. (charter), Pubs. Mktg. Assn., Star Fleet Club (lt. comdr. 1983—), Rotary. Avocations: computer programming, chess. Office: That New Pub Co PO Box 621 Aiea HI 96701-0621

WALKER, WESLEY M., lawyer; b. Union, S.C., Jan. 28, 1915; s. John Frost and Cornelia (Greer) W.; m. Martha Bratton, Nov. 8, 1941; children—Martha Bratton, Wesley M., Nancy F. A.B., U. S.C., 1936, LL.B., 1938. Bar: S.C. 1938. Now partner firm Leatherwood, Walker, Todd & Mann, Greenville, S.C.; city atty. Greenville, 1949-51; spl. circuit judge York County, 6th Jud. Circuit, 1962. Served to lt. USNR, 1941-45. Fellow Am. Bar Found. (50 Yr. award 1994); mem. ABA (ho. of dels. 1952-54, 72-86, mem. com. law lists 1955-68, chmn. 1965-68, bd. govs. 1976-79), S.C. Bar Assn. (state del. 1973-77), Greenville Bar Assn. (pres. 1973), Am. Law Inst., Am. Coll. Trust and Estate Counsel, Phi Delta Phi. Home: 233 Camille Ave Greenville SC 29605-1703 Office: 100 E Coffee St Greenville SC 29601-2707

WALKER, WILLARD BREWER, anthropology educator, linguist; b. Boston, July 29, 1926; s. William Henry Clowes and Helen (Brewer) W.; m. C. Pearline Large, Oct. 18, 1952; children: Christopher William, Andrew Francis. AB, Harvard U., 1950; MA, U. Ariz., 1953; PhD, Cornell U., 1964. Teaching fellow dept. modern langs. Cornell U., Ithaca, N.Y., 1960-61; rsch. asst. comparative study codes and models Cornell U., Nat. Inst. Mental Health, Ithaca, N.Y., 1963; rsch. assoc. dept. anthropology U. Chicago, Tahlequah, Okla., 1964-66; asst. prof. anthropology Wesleyan U., Middletown, Conn., 1966-70, assoc. prof., 1970-77, prof., 1977-89, prof. emeritus, 1989—, chmn. anthropology dept., 1971, 74-77, chmn. linguistics program, 1986-89. Author: Cherokee Primer, 1965, Workin' for Galatti's Lira: An AFS Driver's Recollections of Cross-Cultural Encounters in World War II, 1996; co-author: Cherokee Stories, 1966, A History of World's End, 1973, 1984; co-editor: Hopis, Tewas, & the American Road, 1983, 1986; contbr. numerous articles to profl. jours. Fellow Am. Anthrop. Assn.; mem. Am. Ethnological Soc., Linguistic Soc. Am., Am. Soc. Ethnohistory, Soc. for the Study of Indigenous Langs. of the Americas. Democrat. Avocation: forestry. Address: RR 2 Box 3310 Canaan ME 04924-9714

WALKER, WILLIAM BOND, painter, retired librarian; b. Brownsville, Tenn., Apr. 15, 1930; s. Marshall Francis and Mary Louise (Taylor) W. B.A., State U. Iowa, 1953; M.L.S., Rutgers U., 1958. Librarian-trainee Donnell br. N.Y. Public Library, N.Y.C., 1955-57; reference librarian/cataloger Met. Mus. Art, N.Y.C., 1957-59; chief librarian Bklyn. Mus., 1959-64; supervisory librarian Library of Nat. Collection Fine Arts and Nat. Portrait Gallery, Smithsonian Instn., Washington, 1964-80; Arthur K. Watson chief librarian Thomas J. Watson Library, Met. Mus. Art, N.Y.C., 1980-94; ret., 1994; adj. lectr. Columbia U. Sch. Library Service, 1987-88. Author: annotated bibliography American Sculpture, 18th-20th Century, 1979; retrospective exhbn. paintings, 1954-96, Pittsfield, Mass., 1996-97. Mem. ALA, Art Librs. Soc. N.Am (pres. 1975, Disting. Svc. award), Geneal. and Biog. Soc. (corr.), Phi Beta Kappa. Home: 54 Queechy Lake Dr PO Box 237 Canaan NY 12029

WALKER, WILLIAM EASTON, surgeon, educator, lawyer; b. Glasgow, Scotland, Aug. 7, 1945; came to U.S., 1969; s. William Telfer and Josephine Blair (Easton) W.; m. Mary Fraley Cooley, June 23, 1973; children—Sarah Cooley, Blair Easton, Denton Arthur Cooley, William Easton, II. M.D., Glasgow U., Scotland, 1968; Ph.D., Johns Hopkins U., 1975; JD, South Tex. Coll Law, 1993. Diplomate Am. Bd. Surgery, Am. Bd. Thoracic Surgery, Am. Bd. Vascular Surgery. Intern, resident Johns Hopkins U., Balt., 1969-75; resident Vanderbilt U., Nashville, 1976-79; assoc. prof., dir. div. thoracic and cardiovascular surgery U. Tex. Med. Sch., Houston, 1979—; cons. M.D. Anderson Hosp., Houston, 1979—. Recipient Harwell Wilson award Vanderbilt U., Nashville, 1979. Fellow ACS, So. Surg. Assn., Royal Coll. Surgeons, Am. Coll. Cardiology; mem. Am. Assn. Thoracic Surgery, Coun. Fgn. Rels., Confrérie de la Chaine de Rôtisseurs, Houston Country Club, Belle Meade Country Club, Cosmos Club (Washington), Krewe of Endymion (New Orleans), Phi Beta Kappa, Sigma Xi. Republican. Presbyterian. Avocations: law, golf, flying, backgammon, bridge. Home and Office: 2831 Sackett St Houston TX 77098-1125

WALKER, WILLIAM OLIVER, JR., educator, university dean; b. Sweetwater, Tex., Dec. 6, 1930; s. William Oliver and Frances Baker (White) W.; m. Mary Scott Daugherty, Dec. 22, 1955 (div. Dec. 1978); children: William Scott, Mary Evan, Michael Neal. BA, Austin Coll., 1953; MDiv, Austin Presbyn. Sem., 1957; MA, U. Tex., 1958; PhD, Duke U., 1962. Instr. religion Austin Coll., Sherman, Tex., 1954-55, Duke U., 1960-62; from asst. to prof. religion Trinity U., San Antonio, 1962—, chair dept., 1980-88, acting dean divsn. Humanities and Arts, 1988-89, dean, 1989—. Contbr. articles and book revs. to profl. jours. Editor: The Relationships, 1978, The HarperCollins Bible Pronunciation Guide, 1994; assoc. editor HarperCollins Bible Dictionary, 1996. Mem. Studiorum Novi Testamenti Soc., Soc. Bibl. Lit. (regional sec.-treas. 1980-86), Am. Acad. Religion (regional pres. 1966-67), Soc. Sci. Study Religion, Cath. Bibl. Assn. Am., Coll. Theology Soc. Democrat. Presbyterian. Avocations: tennis, traveling, photography. Home: 315 Cloverleaf Ave San Antonio TX 78209-3822 Office: Trinity U Office Dean Humanities & Arts 715 Stadium Dr San Antonio TX 78212-3104

WALKER, WILLIAM TIDD, JR., investment banker; b. Detroit, Sept. 5, 1931; s. William Tidd and Irene (Rhode) W.; m. Patricia Louise Frazier, Sept. 10, 1953; children—Louise, Carol Ann, Sally Lynn, Alyssa Jane. Student, Stanford, 1950. Rep. William R. Staats & Co., Los Angeles, 1952-57; sales mgr. William R. Staats & Co., 1957-58, syndicate partner, 1958-65; sr. v.p. Glore Forgan, William R. Staats Inc., N.Y.C., 1965-68; partner, exec. com. Lester, Ryons & Co., Los Angeles, 1968; exec. v.p. Bateman Eichler, Hill Richards Inc., Los Angeles, 1969-85; past pres., bd. dirs. Delhi Co., L.A.; pres., CEO, WTW Inc.; chmn., CEO Walker Assocs., bd. dirs. Go-Video, Inc., Elevision, Inc., Fortune Petroleum Corp., Aviation Distbrs., Inc., Aquajet, Inc., Jugular, Inc.; adv. mem. Am. Stock Exch., 1981—. With USAF, 1949-52. Mem. Securities Industry Assn. (dir. nat. syndicate com., chmn. Calif. Dist. 10), Pacific Coast Stock Exch. (bd. govs. 1971-72), Investment Bankers Assn. (nat. pub. rels. com. 1966—), Bond

Club L.A. (pres. 1973—), Calif. Yacht Club, Newport Harbor Yacht Club. Office: Walker Assocs PO Box 10684 Beverly Hills CA 90213-3684

WALKER-LAROSE, LINDA WALESKA, elementary education educator; b. New Haven, Conn., June 19, 1952; d. Edward Lawrence and Waleska Katherine (Bussmann) W.; m. Mr. LaRose, Aug. 17, 1996. BS, So. Conn. State Coll., 1974, postgrad., 1979. Tchr. 4th grade Union Sch., West Haven, Conn., 1974-75, tchr. 2d grade, 1975-76; tchr. 3d grade Washington Sch., West Haven, 1976-81; tchr. 1st grade Washington Magnet Sch., West Haven, 1981—; unit leader Washington Magnet Sch., 1991—; coop. tchr., mentor Conn. Dept. Edn., West Haven, 1987—. Mem. PTA (2d v.p. 1987—), Schooner Inc., New Haven, New Haven Preservation Trust. Mem. Conn. Fedn. Tchrs., Vintage Truck Assn. Avocations: knitting, restoration of Victorian home, making Victorian lampshades, collecting and restoring old cars and trucks. Office: Washington Magnet Sch 369 Washington Ave New Haven CT 06516-5328

WALKLET, JOHN JAMES, JR., publishing executive; b. Trenton, N.J., June 14, 1922; s. John James and Katherine Helen (Slamin) W.; m. Gretchen Crowell, Aug. 21, 1948; children: John III, Philip, Deborah, Preston, Richard, Colin, Keith, Christopher, Megan. BL in Journalism, Rutgers U., 1943. Reporter Montclair (N.J.) Times, 1943; prodn. editor Macmillan Pub. Co., N.Y.C., 1946-52, dir. mfg. sch. div., 1969-88, asst. v.p., 1982, v.p., 1983-88, cons., 1989, ret.; tech. writer Shell Chem. Corp., N.Y.C., 1952-54; dir. publs. Colonial Williamsburg, Williamsburg, Va., 1954-69; cons. book prodn. U. Press of Va., Charlottesville, 1963-69. Author, designer: Adventure in Williamsburg, 1960 (So. Books Competition award), A Window on Williamsburg, 1966 (So. Books Competition award); designer: The Journal of John Harrower, 1963 (One of 50 Books of Yr. award Am. Inst. Graphic Arts). Pres. Kiwanis Club of Williamsburg, 1969; bd. dirs. Edenton-Chowan Kiwanis Club, 1996—; cons. Va. Travel Coun., Richmond, 1960-69. Sgt. U.S. Army, 1943-46. Mem. Assn. Am. Pubs. (mfg. com. rep. Adv. Commn. Textbook Specifications 1980-84, vice chmn. mfg. com. 1984-86, chmn. mfg. com. 1986-88), Williamsburg Stirrup Club (bd. dirs. 1965-69), James Iredell Assn. (bd. dirs. Edenton soc. 1989-97). Republican. Roman Catholic. Avocations: reading, piano and organ, golf, fishing, spectator sports. Home: 1222 Sound Shore Dr Edenton NC 27932-8916 *In one's career, success is augmented by the willingness of dedicated professionals to share their knowledge and experience and teach those individuals whose desire to learn and contribute is beyond measure.*

WALKLET, JUDITH KULA, printing company executive; b. Boston, May 18, 1958; d. Eric Bertil and Gulli Ingegerd (Ahs) K. BA, Middlebury Coll., 1980; postgrad., Radcliffe U., 1980, Harvard U., 1991. Sales rep. R.R. Donnelley & Sons Co., N.Y.C., 1980-87; sales rep. Maxwell Communication Corp., N.Y.C., 1987-88, v.p. sales, 1988, sr. v.p. sales, 1988-90; sr. v.p. sales Quebecor Printing (USA) Corp., N.Y.C., 1990-93, sr. v.p. strategic planning, 1994—. Recipient Luminaire award Women In Prodn., N.Y.C., 1990, Good Scout award Graphic Arts divsns. Boy Scouts Am., 1996. Mem. Mag. Publishers Assn., Graphic Communications Assn., Gravure Assn. Am. Avocations: running, skiing, photography, travel, languages. Office: Quebecor Printing USA Corp 301 Howard St Ste 1330 San Francisco CA 94105

WALKOWIAK, VINCENT STEVEN, lawyer, educator; b. Chgo., Apr. 22, 1946; s. Vincent Albert and Elizabeth (Modla) W.; m. Linda Kae Schweigert, Aug., 1968; children—Jenifer, Steven. B.A., U. Ill., 1968, J.D., 1971. Bar: Ill. 1971, Tex. 1981, U.S. Ct. Appeals (8th cir.) 1971, U.S. Ct. Appeals (5th cir.) 1982, U.S. Dist. Ct. (ea., we., so. and no. dists. Tex.) 1982. Assoc., Dorsey, Marquart, Windhorst, West & Halladay, Mpls., 1971-74; ptnr. Fulbright & Jaworski, Houston, 1982—; prof. Fla. State U., Tallahassee, 1974-76, So. Meth. U., Dallas, 1976-84. Editor: Uniform Product Liability Act, 1980; Trial of a Product Liability Case, vol. 1, 1981, vol. 2, 1982; Preparation and Presentation of Product Liability, 1983, Attorney Client Privilege in Civil Litigation, 1997. Office: Fulbright & Jaworski 2200 Ross Ave Ste 2800 Dallas TX 75201-2750

WALKOWITZ, DANIEL J., historian, filmmaker, educator; b. Paterson, N.J., Nov. 25, 1942; s. Sol and Selda (Margel) W.; m. Judith Rosenberg, Dec. 26, 1965; 1 child, Rebecca Lara. AB, U. Rochester, 1964, PhD, 1972; postgrad., U. Grenoble, France, 1965. Lectr. in history U. Rochester, N.Y., 1967-69; instr. history Rensselaer Poly. Inst., Troy, N.Y., 1969-71; asst. prof. history Rutgers U., New Brunswick, N.J., 1971-78, NYU, N.Y.C., 1978-81; assoc. prof. NYU, 1981-88, co-dir. pub. history program, 1981-89, prof., 1988—, dir. met. studies, 1989—; ptnr., film producer PastTimes Prodns., N.Y.C., 1982—; vis. prof. Johns Hopkins U., 1991-92, U. Calif. Irvine, 1982; editorial sec. Radical History Rev., N.Y.C., 1985-89; bd. dirs. N.Y. Marxist Sch., 1987-90. Author: Worker City, Company Town, 1978; co-author: Workers of the Donbass Speak, 1995; film project dir. The Molders of Troy, 1980; co-editor: Workers in the Industrial Revolution, 1974, Working-Class America, 1984; video dir., co-prodr., dir., writer: Perestroika From Below, 1990; co-prodr., writer Public History Today. Grantee, Nat. Endowment Humanities, 1976, 78, 82. Mem. Nat. Coun. Pub. History (bd. dirs. 1986-89), Am. Hist. Assn., Orgn. Am. Historians, Oral History Assn. Avocation: international folk dance. Office: NYU Dept Met Study Porgram New York NY 10003

WALKUP, JOHN KNOX, state official; m. Betsy Walkup; children: Alice, Margaret. BA magna cum laude, Centre Coll. Ky.; JD, Harvard U. Law clk. to Chief Justice Tenn. Supreme Ct., 1972-73; formerly in pvt. practice Burson & Walkup, Memphis; chief counsel, staff dir. subcom. govtl. affairs U.S. Senate, 1977-84, former legis. dir.; chief dep. atty. gen. State of Tenn., 1985-89, solicitor gen., 1989-93, atty. gen., 1997—; former ptnr. Gullett, Sanford, Robinson & Martin, Nashville; former part-time asst. county atty. Shelby County, Tenn.; lectr. Law Sch. Vanderbilt U., 1993-95. Mem. ABA, Tenn. Bar Assn., Nashville Bar Assn. Office: Office Atty Gen 450 James Robertson Pky Nashville TN 37243-0485*

WALL, BARBARA WARTELLE, lawyer; b. New Orleans, Sept. 30, 1954; d. Richard Cole and Ruth Druhan (Power) W.; m. Christopher Read Wall, June 21, 1980; children: Christopher, Louisa. BA, U. Va., 1976, JD, 1979. Bar: N.Y. 1980, U.S. Dist. Ct. (so. and ea. dists.) N.Y. 1980. Assoc. Satterlee & Stephens, N.Y.C., 1979-85; asst. gen. counsel Gannett Co., Inc., Arlington, Va., 1985-90, sr. legal counsel, 1990-93, v.p., sr. legal counsel, 1993—. Mem. ABA (chair forum on comm. law), N.Y. State Bar Assn., Assn. of Bar of City of N.Y. Republican. Roman Catholic. Home: 5026 Tilden St NW Washington DC 20016-2334 Office: Gannett Co Inc 1100 Wilson Blvd Arlington VA 22209-2297

WALL, BENNETT HARRISON, history educator; b. Raleigh, N.C., Dec. 7, 1914; s. Bennett Louis and Evie David (Harrison) W.; m. Neva White Armstrong, Sept. 7, 1968; children by previous marriage: Maie (Mrs. John E. Clark) (dec.), Diana Wall Freckman, Ann Bennett. AB, Wake Forest Coll., 1933; MA, U. N.C., 1941, PhD, 1947. Instr. N.C. State U., 1942-43; instr. U. N.C., 1943-44; instr. U. Ky., 1944-46, asst. prof., 1946-52, assoc. prof., 1952-64; prof. history dept. Tulane U., New Orleans, 1965-80; head dept. Tulane U., 1968-73; dir. Tulane Center Bus. History Studies, 1974-79; lectr. U. Ga., 1980-85. Author: Growth in a Changing Environment: History of Standard Oil Company New Jersey, 1950-1972, Exxon Corporation 1972-75, 1988; co-author Teagle of Jersey Standard, 1974; contbr. numerous articles to profl. jours. Fellow La. History Assn. (pres. 1974-75, McGinty award 1991); mem. Orgn. Am. Historians, Agrl. History Soc., Bus. History Soc., Econ. History Soc., So. History Assn. (sec., treas. 1952-85, v.p. 1986-87, pres. 1987-88), N.C. History Assn., S.C. Hist. Soc., Ga. History Soc., Omicron Delta Kappa, Phi Alpha Theta. Home: 150 Ashton Dr Athens GA 30606-1618

WALL, BRIAN ARTHUR, sculptor; b. London, Sept. 5, 1931; s. Arthur Francis and Dorothy (Seymour) W.; m. Sylvia Brown, Oct. 27, 1973; children—Nathaniel, Gideon. Student, Luton (Eng.) Coll. Art, 1951. First asst. to Dame Barbara Hepworth, St. Ives, Cornwall, Eng., 1954-59; instr. Ealing Coll. Art, Middlesex, Eng., 1961-62; prin. lectr. Central Sch. Art and Design, London, 1962-72; head dept. sculpture Central Sch. Art and Design, 1962-72; vis. lectr. U. Calif., Berkeley, 1969-73; lectr. U. Calif., 1973-75, asst. prof., 1975-77, assoc. prof., 1977-81, prof., 1981-93; prof. emeritus, 1993—. One-man shows U. Nev., Las Vegas, 1976, Braunstein Gallery, San Francisco, 1974, 76, 78, Sculpture Now, N.Y.C., 1977, 78, Max Hutchinson Gallery, Houston, 1979, May Hutchinson Gallery, N.Y.C., 1981, Seattle Art Mus., 1982, San Francisco Mus. Modern Art, 1983, John Berggruen Gallery, San Francisco, 1983, Lowinsky Gallery, N.Y.C., 1987, Francis Graham-Dixon Gallery, London, 1992, Jernigan Wicker Fine Arts, 1995, Sheldon Meml. Art Gallery, U. Nebr., 1995; exhibited in group shows, including Mus. Modern Art, Paris, 1961, U. Tex., Dallas, 1976, Crocker Art Mus., Sacramento, 1979, Tate Gallery, London, 1985; works represented in permanent collections Tate Gallery, Mus. Art, Dublin, Art Gallery NSW, Australia, Univ. Art Mus., Berkeley, U. Houston, Sheldon Meml. Art Gallery, Seattle Art Mus., Towson State U., Balt., Oakland Mus.; works include Thornaby, 1968, Alai, 1978. Mem. Arts Council Gt. Brit., 1969-72; trustee San Francisco Art Inst., 1974-77; mem. San Francisco Twin Bicentennial Arts Com., 1975-76. Served with RAF, 1950-52. U. Calif. at Berkeley Humanities Rsch. Fellowship Program grantee, 1978-79; recipient prize BART Sculpture Competition, 1975. Subject of numerous profl. articles. Home: 306 Lombard St San Francisco CA 94133-2415

WALL, CLARENCE VINSON, state legislator; b. Athens, Ga., Oct. 17, 1947; s. Clarence Jacob and Fannie Lucile (Clark) W.; m. Linda Gail Mason, Dec. 6, 1969 (div. 1980); 1 child, Jeffrey Vinson. Grad. high sch., Lawrenceville, Ga., 1965. Rep. Ga. Ho. of Reps., Lawrenceville, 1973-82, 85-96. Staff sgt. Ga. ANG, 1967-73. Republican. Baptist. Home: 164 E Oak St Lawrenceville GA 30245-4900

WALL, DIANE EVE, political science educator; b. Detroit, Nov. 17, 1944; d. Albert George and Jean Carol (Young) Bradley. BA in History and Edn., Mich. State U., 1966, MA in History, 1969, MA in Polit. Sci., 1979, PhD in Polit. Sci., 1983. Cert. permanent secondary tchr., Mich. Secondary tchr. Corunna (Mich.) Pub. Schs., 1966-67, N.W. Pub. Schs., Rives Junction, Mich., 1967-73; lectr. Tidewater Community Coll., Chesapeake, Va., 1974-77; instr. Lansing (Mich.) Community Coll., 1981-83; prof. dept. polit. sci. Miss. State U., 1983—, undergrad. coord., 1993—; instr. Wayne State U., Detroit, fall 1980, Ctrl. Mich. U., Mt. Pleasant, spring 1982; pre-law advisor Miss. State U., 1990-93, chair, 1993—. Contbr. articles, revs. to profl. jours., chpt. to book. Evaluator Citizen's Task Force, Chesapeake, Va., 1977; panelist flag burning program Ednl. TV, Mississippi State, 1990, prayer in pub. sch., Starkville Cmty. TV, 1995. Recipient Paideia award Miss. State U. Coll. Arts and Scis., 1988, Miss. State U. Outstanding Woman Teaching Faculty award Pres.'s Commn. on Status of Women, 1994, Acad. Advising award Miss. State U., 1994, Outstanding Advisor award Nat. Acad. Advising Assn., 1995; Grad. Office fellow Mich. State U., 1980; Miss. State U. rsch. grantee, 1984. Mem. ASPA (exec. bd. Sect. for Women 1987-90, Miss. chpt. pres. 1992-93), LWV (Chesapeake charter pres. 1976-77), Miss. Polit. Sci. Assn. (exec. dir. 1991-93), Miss. State U. Soc. Scholars (pres. 1992-93), Miss. State U. Faculty Women's Assn. (v.p. 1985-86, pres. 1986-88, scholar 1987-89), Phi Kappa Phi (v.p. 1985-86, pres. 1986-88), Pi Sigma Alpha (Ann. Chpt. Activities award 1991). Democrat. Methodist. Avocations: dog obedience training, Corvette activities, gardening. Office: Miss State U PO Drawer PC Mississippi State MS 39762

WALL, DONALD ARTHUR, lawyer; b. Lafayette, Ind., Mar. 17, 1946; s. Dwight Arthur and Myra Virgina (Peavey) W.; m. Cheryn Lynn Heinen, Aug. 29, 1970; children: Sarah Lynn, Michael Donald. BA, Butler U., 1968; JD, Northwestern U., 1971. Bar: Ohio 1971, U.S. Dist. Ct. (no. dist.) Ohio 1973, U.S. Ct. Appeals (6th cir.) 1982, U.S. Supreme Ct. 1980, Ariz. 1982, U.S. Dist. Ct. (no. dist.) W.Va. 1982, U.S. Dist. Ct. Ariz. 1983, U.S. Ct. Appeals (9th and 10th cir.) 1984, U.S. Ct. Appeals (5th cir.) 1988. Assoc. Squire, Sanders & Dempsey, Cleve., 1971-80, ptnr., 1980-82, Phoenix, 1983—; speaker at profl. meetings; program moderator. Contbr. articles to profl. jours. Mem. adminstrv. bd. Ch. of Saviour, Cleve. Heights, Ohio, 1980-83; trustee Ch. of the Saviour Day Center, Cleve. Heights, 1979-82; fin. com. Paradise Valley (Ariz.) United Meth. Ch., 1986-87; bd. dirs., div. commr. North Scottsdale (Ariz.) Little League, 1983-92; bd. dirs. Epilepsy Found. N.E. Ohio, 1976-82, pres., 1981-82; bd. dirs. N.E. Cmty. Basketball Assn., 1993-96. Mem. ABA (torts and ins. practice and litigation sect., past chmn. r.r. law com., litigation sect.), Def. Research Inst., Ariz. Bar Assn. (labor and trial practice sects.), Maricopa County Bar Assn., Am. Judicature Soc., Ariz. Assn Def. Counsel. Methodist. Office: Squire Sanders & Dempsey 40 N Central Ave Phoenix AZ 85004-4424

WALL, FREDERICK THEODORE, retired chemistry educator; b. Chisholm, Minn., Dec. 14, 1912; s. Peter and Fanny Maria (Rauhala) W.; m. Clara Elizabeth Vivian, June 5, 1940; children: Elizabeth Wall Ralston, Jane Vivian Wall-Meinike. B.Chemistry, U. Minn., 1933, Ph.D., 1937. Mem. faculty chemistry dept. U. Ill., 1937-64, dean grad. coll., 1955-63; prof., chmn. dept. chemistry U. Calif., Santa Barbara, 1964-66, vice chancellor rsch., 1965-66; vice chancellor grad. studies and research, prof. chemistry U. Calif. at San Diego, 1966-69; exec. dir. Am. Chem. Soc., Washington, 1969-72; prof. chemistry Rice U., Houston, 1972-78; Pres. Assn. Grad. Schs., 1961; trustee Inst. Def. Analyses, 1962-64; mem. governing bd. Nat. Acad. Scis.-NRC, 1963- 67. Author: Chemical Thermodynamics, 1958; editor Jour. Phys. Chemistry, 1965-69. Mem. Am. Chem. Soc. (Pure Chemistry award 1945, dir. 1962-64), Finnish Chem. Soc. (corr.), Am. Acad. Arts and Scis., Nat. Acad. Scis. Achievements include early work on Monte Carlo computer simulation of macromolecular configurations and of basic reaction probabilities. Home: 2468 Via Viesta La Jolla CA 92037-3935

WALL, JAMES EDWARD, telecommunications, petroleum and pharmaceutical executive; b. Santa Barbara, Calif., Nov. 24, 1947; s. Charles Caswell II and Lydia (Sinn) W.; m. Judith Ann Hochman, Aug. 1, 1976. AA, Bakersfield Coll., 1967; BS, Calif. State U., Los Angeles, 1969; MBA, UCLA, 1970; D of Profl. Studies, Pace U., 1985; PMD, Harvard U. Sch. Bus., 1987. CPA, Calif. Agt. IRS, Los Angeles, 1971-74; agt. service office internat. ops. IRS, Washington, 1974-76; mgr. fin. forecasts Am. Ultramar, Ltd., Mt. Kisco, N.Y., 1976-80, treas., 1980-85, v.p., treas., 1985-91; exec. dir. fin. and adminstrn. Ultramar Exploration, London, 1991; v.p., treas. Ultramar Corp., Greenwich, Conn., 1992-94; v.p., corp. treas. ICN Pharms., Costa Mesa, Calif., 1994-95; treas. AirTouch Comms., Inc., San Francisco, 1995—; chief fin. officer Enstar Corp., Indonesia; mem. bd. mgmt. Unimar Co., 1985-91. Recipient award in acctg. UCLA, 1972, award in gen. bus. mgmt., 1973. Mem. AICPA, Fin. Execs. Inst., Nat. Assn. Corp. Treas., UCLA Grad. Sch. Alumni Assn., Harvard U. Bus. Sch. Alumni Assn. Office: AirTouch Comms Inc 9th Fl One California St San Francisco CA 94111

WALL, JAMES MCKENDREE, minister, editor; b. Monroe, Ga., Oct. 27, 1928; s. Louie David and Lida (Day) W.; m. Mary Eleanor Kidder, Sept. 11, 1953; children: David McKendree, Robert Kidder, Richard James. Student, Ga. Inst. Tech., 1945-47; BA, Emory U., 1949, BD, 1955, LHD (hon.), 1985; MA, U. Chgo., 1960; LittD (hon.), Ohio No. U., 1969; DHL (hon.), Willamette Coll., 1978; DD (hon.), MacMurray, 1981; DHL (hon.), Coe Coll., 1987. Ordained to ministry United Meth. Ch., 1954. Staff writer, sports dept. Atlanta Jour., 1948-50; asst. minister East Lake Meth. Ch., Atlanta, 1953; asst. to dean students Emory U., Atlanta, 1954-55; pastor North Ga. Conf. Moreland, Luthersville Meth. Chs., Ga., 1955-57, Bethel United Meth. Ch., Chgo., 1957-59; mng. editor Christian Adv. mag., Park Ridge, Ill., 1959-63, editor, 1963-72; editor Christian Century mag., Chgo., 1972—. Author: Church and Cinema, 1971, Three European Directors, 1973, Winning the War, Losing Our Soul, 1991, Hidden Treasures: Searching for God in Modern Culture, 1997; author, editor: Theologians in Transition, 1981, A Century of the Century, 1987, How My Mind Has Changed, 1991. Del. Dem. Nat. Conv., 1972, 76, 80, 92; mem. Dem. Nat. Com., 1976-80, Dem. State Cen. Com., 1974-86, Pres. Commn. White House Fellowships, 1976-80. Served to 1st lt. USAF, 1950-52. Mem. Alpha Tau Omega, Omicron Delta Kappa, Sigma Delta Chi. Home: 451 S Kenilworth Ave Elmhurst IL 60126-3928 Office: Christian Century 407 S Dearborn St Ste 1405 Chicago IL 60605-1119

WALL, LEONARD J., bishop; b. Windsor, Ont., Can., Sept. 27, 1924; Ordained Roman Catholic priest, June 11, 1949; ordained titular bishop of Leptiminus and aux. bishop of Toronto, 1979-92; archbishop of Winnipeg Archdiocese of Winnipeg, 1992—. Office: Archdiocese of Winnipeg, 1495 Pembina Hwy, Winnipeg, MB Canada R3T 2C6*

WALL, M. DANNY, finance company executive. BArch, N.D. State U., 1963. Exec. dir. Urban Renewal Agy., Fargo, N.D., 1964-71, Salt Lake City Redevel. Agy., 1971-75; dir. legis. Office U.S. Senator Jake Garn, Washington, 1975-78; minority staff dir. Senate Com. for Banking, Housing and Urban Affairs, Washington, 1979-80, staff dir., 1980-86, Rep. staff dir., 1987; chmn. Fed. Home Loan Bank Bd./Fed. Home Loan Mortgage Corp., Washington, 1987-89; dir. Office Thrift Supervision (formerly Fed. Home Loan Bank Bd.), 1989-90; fin. svcs. cons., 1990—; sr. v.p. Dougherty Funding L.L.C., 1997—.

WALL, MATTHEW J., JR., surgeon, scientist; b. June 22, 1958; s. Matthew J. and Anne V. (Connolly) W.; m. Barbara M. Ford; children: Christopher Matthew, Patrick Joseph. BS, Rice U., Houston, 1980; MD, Baylor Coll. Medicine, Houston, 1984. Diplomate Am. Bd. Surgery, Am. Bd. Thoracic Surgeons. Resident gen. surgery Baylor Affiliated Hosp., Houston, 1984-89, resident cardiothoracic surgery, 1989-91; asst. prof. surgery Baylor Coll. Medicine, Houston, 1991-95, assoc. prof. surgery, 1995—; dir. trauma and critical care svcs. Ben Taub Gen. Hosp., Houston, 1993—, dep. chief surgery, 1993—. Contbr. chpts. to books, articles to jours. Fellow Am. Coll. Surgeons, Am. Assn. Surgery Trauma, Soc. Thoracic Surgeons; mem. Assn. Academic Surgeons, Tex. Surg. Soc. Office: Baylor Coll Medicine One Baylor Plz Houston TX 77030

WALL, ROBERT ANTHONY, JR., lawyer; b. Hartford, Conn., Mar. 3, 1945; s. Robert Anthony and Eileen (Fitzgerald) W.; divorced; children: Andrea, Melanie, Victoria, Robert, Natalie. BA, Georgetown U., Washington, 1968; JD, Am. U., Washington, 1973. Bar: Conn. 1974, U.S. Ct. Appeals (D.C. cir.) 1974, U.S. Dist. Ct. Conn. 1974, U.S. Supreme Ct. 1977. Ptnr. Wall, Wall & Frauenhofer, Torrington, Conn., 1974-87; pvt. practice Torrington, 1987—. Mem. State of Conn. Rep. Ctrl. Com., 1976-79. Mem. Conn. Trial Lawyers Assn. (bd. govs. 1984-86), Ct. Washington #67 Foresters of Am. (trustee 1988—). Roman Catholic. Home: 55 Quail Run Torrington CT 06790-2550 Office: 8 Church St Torrington CT 06790-5247

WALL, ROBERT EMMET, educational administrator, novelist; b. N.Y.C., Apr. 29, 1937; s. Robert Emmet and Sabina (Daly) W.; m. Regina Palasek, Aug. 1, 1959; children—Elizabeth, Nina, Amy, Christopher, Craig. BA, Holy Cross Coll., 1960; MA, Yale U., 1961, PhD, 1965. Asst. in instrn. Yale U., New Haven, 1963; instr. history Duke U., Durham, N.C., 1963-65; asst. prof. Mich. State U., East Lansing, 1965-69, asso. prof. history, 1970; asso. prof. Concordia U. (Sir George Williams U.), Montreal, Que., Can., 1971-72, prof., 1972-80, chmn. dept., 1972-77, dean, 1977-80; provost, acting v.p. Fairleigh Dickinson U., Rutherford, N.J., 1980-85; v.p. academic affairs Gannon U., Erie, Pa., 1986-92; acad. v.p. Fairfield (Conn.) U., 1992—. Author: Massachusetts Bay, The Crucial Decade, 1640-1650, 1972, The Canadians, Vol. I (Blackrobe), 1981, Vol. II (Bloodbrothers), 1981, Vol. III (Birthright), 1982, Vol. IV (The Patriots), 1982, Vol. V (The Inherators), 1983, Vol. VI (Dominion), 1984, Vol. VII (Brotherhood), 1985, The Acadians, 1984, Sierre Gold, 1987, Membership of The Massachusetts Bay General Court, 1630-1686, 1990, The Cat and The Rat, 1991. Home: 1232 Windward Rd Milford CT 06460-1765

WALL, ROBERT F., lawyer; b. Chgo., Jan. 7, 1952. BA with distinction, Northwestern U., 1973; JD summa cum laude, U. Santa Clara, 1977. Bar: Ill. 1977, U.S. Dist. Ct. (no. dist.) Ill. 1977. Ptnr. Winston & Strawn, Chgo. Mem. editorial bd. M&A and Corp. Control Law Reporter, 1988—. Mem. ABA. Office: Winston & Strawn 35 W Wacker Dr Chicago IL 60601-1614

WALL, ROBERT THOMPSON, secondary school educator; b. Luray, Va., May 31, 1943; s. Robert Alexander and Mary Ann (Coffman) W.; m. Sarah S. Wall, Aug. 19, 1967; children: Melissa Coffman, Jennifer Grey. BA, Va. Poly. Inst. and State U., 1966; MA, Radford (Va.) U., 1971; postgrad., U. Fla., 1978. Tchr. instrumental and choral music Halifax County Schs., Halifax, Va.; tchr. instrumental music Montgomery County Schs., Christiansburg, Va.; chmn. fine arts dept. Christiansburg Middle Sch., 1991—; judge, clinician and adjudicator for marching and concert bands; curriculum and instrn. clin. affiliate Va. Poly. Inst. and State U., Blacksburg, Radford (Va.) U.; clinician, guest condr. for mid-Atlantic band camps Ferrum Coll., Va.; guest condr. all-dist. bands in Va., N.C., S.C. Composer: Published Windsor Portrait, 1990, Adagio for horn and piano, 1982, Nocturne for flute and piano, 1987, Royal Brigade, 1988, Prelude and tarantelle, 1991, An American Tattoo, 1994; compositions commd. by Va. State Symphony Orch., Charlotte (N.C.) Mecklenburg County Schs., Rural Retreat (Va.) H.S., Va. Dist. VI and Dist. V Band Dirs. Assn.; music performed at Va. Music Educators Conf., 1990, 95, Midwest Band Conv., Chgo., 1990, Finland Radio, 1993, Great Britain, 1993, 94, France, 1995. Recipient Young composers award Va. Music Clubs, 1960, Va. Govs. Sch. Presdl. citation, 1990, 92, Teaching award Halifax County Schs., 1972. Mem. ASCAP, Music Educators Nat. Conf., Nat. Band Assn., Va. Music Educators Assn. (exec. bd.), Va. Band and Orch. Dirs. Assn. (instrumental chmn. dist. VI), Modern Music Masters (life, past adv. coun., exec. bd.), Phi Beta Mu, Phi Delta Kappa. Home: 2810 Mt Vernon Ln Blacksburg VA 24060-8121

WALL, ROBERT WILSON, JR., former utility executive; b. Monticello, Ark., June 11, 1916; s. Robert Wilson and Thursa (Cotham) W.; m. Joyce Esther Hoffman, Sept. 27, 1943; children: Mary Lynn Wall Sykes, Kathy Ann Wall Theros. B.A., U. Miss., 1938, J.D., 1940; grad. exec. program bus. adminstrn., Columbia U., 1974. Bar: Miss. bar 1940. With FBI, 1940-41, 47-53, spl. agt. in charge Miami (Fla.) office, 1951-53; with U.S. Fgn. Service, 1941-46; legal attache embassy U.S. Fgn. Service, Mexico City, 1944-46; personnel dir. Phillips Petroleum Co., Caracas, Venezuela, 1946-47; with Fla. Power & Light Co., Miami, 1953-81; v.p. Fla. Power & Light Co., 1963-73, sr. v.p., 1973-81; asst. chmn. Nat. Alliance Businessmen, 1966-70; bd. dirs. Southeastern Legal Found.; adv. bd. U. Miami Sch. Bus. Adminstrn. Div. chmn. United Fund Dade County, 1964-67; bd. dirs. Miami Better Bus. Bur., 1955-62, Goodwill Industries Miami, 1964-66, Miami council Girl Scouts Am., 1971-72. Mem. Am. Bar Assn., Am. Soc. Corp. Secs., Am. Arbitration Assn. (panel 1987), Soc. Former Spl. Agts. FBI, Miss. Bar Assn., Greater Miami C. of C. (dir. 1963, exec. com. 1964), Blue Key, Phi Delta Theta, Phi Delta Phi, Omicron Delta Kappa. Republican. Home: 16 Kituhwa Trl Brevard NC 28712-9438

WALLACE, ALICEANNE, civic worker; b. Chgo., Sept. 28, 1925; d. Alexander and Mary (Zurek) Zalac; m. Henry Clay Wallace, Jr., Apr. 10, 1948; children: Laura Lillian Wallace Bergin, Christine Claire Wallace Stockwell. Student, St. Teresa Coll., Winona, Minn., 1944-45, DePaul U., 1946-48, North Tex. State U., 1971, 72. City sec. City of Southlake, Tex., 1969-77; pres. AZW, Inc., real estate sales, Roanoke, Tex., 1977-84. Mem. Trinity Valley Mental Health-Mental Retardation, Ft. Worth, 1971-72; chmn. ways and means Tex. Silver-Haired Legis., Austin, 1986-90, parliamentarian, 1991-94; treas. TSHL Found., 1990-92, pres., 1992-96; sec., bd. dirs. Sr. Citizens Activities, Inc., Temple, Tex., 1989-90; sec. CTCOG Area Agy. on Aging, Citizens Adv. Comm. Bd., Belton, Tex., 1991; bd. dirs. Tex. Dept. on Aging, Austin, 1991-97; congl. sr. intern U.S. Ho. of Reps., Washington, 1991; pres. Tri-County Tex. Dem. Women, 1990-94; congl. del. White House Conf. on Aging, 1995; del. Nat. Silver Haired Congress, Inaugural Convention, 1997; elected State Dem. Exec. Com. Senatorial Dist. #24, 1994—. Mem. Am. Assn. Ret. Persons (legis. chmn. Temple chpt. 1990-94, regional coord. VOTE 1991-96, assoc. state coord. 1996—), Tex. Fedn. Women's Clubs (state legis. chmn. 1990-92, resolutions chmn. 1992-94, parliamentarian Capitol dist. 1990-92), North Ctrl. Tex. Secy. Assn. (pres. 1976), City Fedn. Women's Clubs (corr. sec. 1991-92, records custodian 1991—), Triangle Forum (pres. 1992-94), Daus. Republic Tex. (assoc.), Internat. Inst. Mcpl. Clks. (state cert.), Epsilon Eta Phi. Home: RR 2 Box 2585 Belton TX 76513-9611

WALLACE, ANDREW GROVER, physician, educator, medical school dean; b. Columbus, Ohio, Mar. 22, 1935; s. Richard Homes and Eleanor Bradley (Grover) W.; m. Kathleen Barrick Altvater, June 22, 1957; children: Stephen Andrew, Michael Bradley, Kathleen Claude. BS, Duke U., 1958, MD, 1959. Diplomate Am. Bd. Internal Medicine. Intern medicine Duke U. Hosp., Durham, N.C., 1959-60, asst. resident, 1960-61; fellow NIH, Bethesda, Md., 1961-63; chief resident medicine Duke U., Durham, 1963-64, asst. prof., 1965-67, assoc. prof., 1967-71, chief, divsn. cardiology, 1970-81, prof. medicine, 1971—, Walter Kempner prof. medicine, 1973; vice chancellor health affairs, chief exec. officer Duke U. Hosp., Durham, 1981-87; v.p. health affairs Duke U., 1987-90; dean Dartmouth Med. Sch., Hanover, N.H., 1990—; v.p. for health affairs Dartmouth Coll., 1990—; cons.

program project com., cardiology adv. com. and pharmacology study sect. Nat. Heart and Lung Inst., cardiovascular merit rev. bd. VA. Co-author: (with R.S. Williams) Biological Effects of Physical Activity, 1989; mem. editl. bd. Am. Jour. of Physiology, 1965-70, Jour. of Pharmacology and Exptl. Therapeutics, 1966-71, Jour. of Molecular and Cellular Cardiology, 1970-75, Jour. of Clin. Investigation, 1973-78. Pres. Durham YMCA Swim Assn., 1975-77; bd. dirs. Durham C. of C.; co-chmn. Nat. Jr. Olympics, 1976; mem. adv. bd. Ledyard Bank. Markle scholar, 1965-70. Mem. AAAS, AAMC, NAS, Inst. of Medicine, Am. Fedn. for Clin. Rsch. (coun.), Am. Soc. Internal Medicine, Am. Soc. Clin. Investigation, Am. Heart Assn. (coun. on clin. cardiology), Am. Physiol. Soc., Biomed. Engring. Soc., Soc. Med. Adminstrs., Assn. Am. Med. Colls. (adv. com. electronic residency 1992-94, generalist initiative 1993-95, mission and orgn. 1994—, exec. coun. 1996—), N.H. Med. Soc., So. Soc. Clin. Investigation. Home: 62 Oak Ridge Rd West Lebanon NH 03784-3113 Office: Dartmouth Coll Med Sch Office of Dean Hanover NH 03755-3833

WALLACE, ANTHONY FRANCIS CLARKE, anthropologist, educator; b. Toronto, Ont., Can., Apr. 15, 1923; s. Paul A.W. and Dorothy Eleanor (Clarke) W.; m. Betty Louise Shillott, Dec. 1, 1942; children: Anthony, Daniel, Sun Ai, Samuel, Cheryl, Joseph. B.A., U. Pa., 1948, M.A., 1949, Ph.D., 1950; L.H.D. (hon.), U. Chgo., 1983. Instr. anthropology Bryn Mawr Coll., 1948-50; asst. instr. anthropology U. Pa., research sec. Behavioral Research Council, 1951-55; research asst. prof. U. Pa., 1952-55, vis. assoc. prof., 1955-61, prof., 1961—, chmn. dept., 1961-71, Geraldine R. Segal prof. Am. social thought, 1980-83, Univ. prof. anthropology, 1983-88, prof. emeritus, 1988—; sr. research assoc. anthropology Eastern Pa. Psychiat. Inst., 1955-60, dir. clin. research, 1960-61, med. research scientist, III, 1961-80; mem. tech. adv. com. N.J. Psychiat. Inst., 1958; cons. disaster studies NRC, 1956-57; cons. Phila. Housing Authority, 1952; mem. research adv. com. Commonwealth Mental Health Research Found., 1960-61, U.S. Office Edn., 1965-68; mem. behavioral scis. study sect. NIMH, 1964-68; mem. NRC, 1963-66; mem. various adv. coms. NIMH, 1962—; mem. social sci. adv. council NSF, 1969-72. Author: King of the Delawares: Teedyuscung, 1700-1763, 1949, Culture and Personality, 1961, rev. edit., 1970, Religion: An Anthropological View, 1966, Death and Rebirth of the Seneca, 1970, Rockdale: The Growth of an American Village in the Early Industrial Revolution, 1978, Social Context of Innovation, 1983, St. Clair, 1987, The Long, Bitter Trail, 1993. Bd. mgrs. Founds. Fund for Research in Psychiatry, 1969-71. Served AUS, 1942-45. Recipient Bancroft prize in Am. History, 1979, Dexter prize in History of Technology, 1989; Guggenheim fellow, 1978-79. Fellow Am. Anthrop. Assn. (pres. 1971-72),; mem. Nat. Acad. Scis., Am. Philos. Soc., Am. Acad. Arts and Scis. Office: Univ PA Dept Anthropology 33rd and Spruce Sts Philadelphia PA 19104

WALLACE, ARTHUR, JR., college dean; b. Muskogee, Okla., June 12, 1939; s. Arthur and Edna (Collins) W.; m. Claudina Young, Oct. 4, 1969; children: Dwayne, Jon, Charles. BS, Langston U., 1960; MS, Okla. State U., Stillwater, 1962, PhD, 1964. Dir. commodity rsch. Gen. Foods Corp., White Plains, N.Y., 1964-67; v.p., sr. economist Merrill Lynch & Lionel D. Edie & Co., N.Y.C., 1968-71; econ. cons. Wall St. fin. instns. Group IV Econs., N.Y.C., 1972-76; mgr. U.S. and Can. econs. Internat. Paper Co., N.Y.C., 1976-78, chief economist, 1978-82, dir. corp. affairs and policy analysis, 1982-83; corp. sec. Internat. Paper Co., Purchase, N.Y., 1983-87; v.p., corp. sec. Internat. Paper Co., 1987-93; pres. Internat. Paper Co. Found., 1983-93; dean coll. bus. San Francisco State U., 1993—. Home: 1085 Greenwich St Apt 1 San Francisco CA 94133-2545 Office: San Francisco State U School of Business 1600 Holloway Ave San Francisco CA 94132-1722

WALLACE, BARBARA BROOKS, writer; b. Soochow, China, Dec. 3, 1922; came to U.S., 1938; d. Otis Frank and Nicia Brooks; m. James Wallace Jr., Feb. 27, 1954; 1 child, James V. BA, UCLA, 1945. Script sec. Foote, Cone & Belding, Hollywood, Calif., 1946-49; tchr. Wright MacMahon Secretarial Sch., Beverly Hills, Calif., 1949-50; head fund drive Commerce and Industry Divsn. ARC, San Francisco, 1950-52. Author: Claudia, 1969 (Nat. League of Am. Pen Women Juvenile Book award 1970), Andrew the Big Deal, 1970, The Trouble with Miss Switch, 1971, Victoria, 1973, Can Do, Missy Charlie, 1974, The Secret Summer of L.E.B. (Nat. League of Am. Pen Women Juvenile Book award 1974), Julia and the Third Bad Thing, 1975, Palmer Patch, 1976, Hawkins, 1977, Peppermints in the Parlor, 1980 (William Allen White award 1983), The Contest Kid Strikes Again, 1980, Hawkins and the Soccer Solution, 1981, Miss Switch to the Rescue, 1981, Hello, Claudia, 1982, Claudia and Duffy, 1982, The Barrel in the Basement, 1985, Argyle, 1987, 92, Perfect Acres, Inc., 1988, The Twin in the Tavern, 1993 (Edgar award Mystery Writers Am. 1994), Cousins in the Castle, 1996, Sparrows in the Scullery, 1997. Mem. Children's Book Guild of Washington, Alpha Phi. Episcopalian. Home and Office: 2708 George Mason Pl Alexandria VA 22305-1620

WALLACE, CHRISTOPHER, broadcast television correspondent; b. Chgo., Oct. 12, 1947; s. Mike and Norma (Kaphan) W.; m. Elizabeth Farrell, May 12, 1973; children: Peter Farrell, Margaret Coleman, Andrew Farrell, Catherine Farrell. BA, Harvard U., 1969. Nat. reporter Boston Globe, 1969-73; polit. reporter Sta. WBBM-TV, Chgo., 1973-75; investigative reporter Sta. WNBC-TV, N.Y.C., 1975-78; polit. reporter NBC News, Washington, 1978-81; anchor Today Show, 1981-82; corr. White House, 1982-89, Prime Time Live, ABC-TV, 1989—; anchor Meet The Press, 1987-88. Reporter, writer: documentaries NBC The Migrants, 1980, Protection For Sale: The Insurance Industry, 1981, Nancy Reagan, The First Lady, 1985. Recipient Peabody award U. Ga., 1978, Emmy award NATAS, 1981, 90, award Overseas Press Club, 1981, Humanitas Found. award, 1981, Investigative Reporters and Editors award U. Mo. Sch. Journalism, 1990, 95, George Polk award, 1992. Office: PrimeTime Live 1717 Desales St NW Washington DC 20036-4401

WALLACE, DAVID DUNSMORE, architect, planner, urban designer; b. Haverhill, Mass., Oct. 26, 1928; s. Henry Arthur and Doris Stanley (Conley) W.; m. June A. Feuer, June 7, 1953; children—Susan, Andrew, Gordon. B.A., Middlebury Coll., 1950; B.Arch., M.I.T., 1952, M. Arch., 1956. Registered architect, Mass., Vt., Nat. Council Archtl. Registration Bds. Prin. architect Geometrics, Inc., Cambridge, Mass., 1961-70, Wallace, Floyd, Ellenzweig, Moore, Inc., Cambridge, 1970-81, Wallace, Floyd, Assocs. Inc., Boston, 1981-95, pvt. practice, 1995—. Prin. archtl. works include univ. bldgs., pub. housing renovation, mass transit and train stations, also Boston's Ctrl. Artery/Tunnel Project; exec. arch. Middlebury Coll. Trustee Schwamb Mill Preservation Trust, Arlington, 1970—; mem. town Meeting, Arlington, 1965-72, Conservation Commn., Arlington, 1967-72; incorporator Cambridge Sch. of Weston, Mass., 1979-85. Voorhis, Walker, Smith & Smith research fellow MIT, 1955-56; Fulbright research grantee, 1960. Fellow AIA; mem. Am. Planning Assn. Avocations: watercolor painting; photography; tennis. Office: Wallace Floyd Assocs Inc 286 Congress St Boston MA 02210-1038

WALLACE, DON, JR., law educator; b. Vienna, Austria, Apr. 23, 1932; s. Don and Julie (Baer) W. (parents Am. citizens); m. Daphne Mary Wickham, 1963; children: Alexandra Jane, Sarah Anne, Benjamin James. B.A. with high honors, Yale U., 1953; LL.B. cum laude, Harvard U., 1957. Bar: N.Y. 1957, D.C. 1978. Assoc. Fleischmann, Jaeckle, Stokes and Hitchcock, N.Y.C., 1959-60, Paul, Weiss, Rifkind, Wharton and Garrison, N.Y.C., 1957-58, 60-62; rsch. asst. to faculty mem. Harvard Law Sch., Cambridge, Mass., 1958-59; regional legal adv. Middle East AID, Dept. State, 1963-65, dep. asst. gen. counsel, 1965-66; assoc. prof. law Georgetown U. Law Ctr., Washington, 1966-71, prof., 1971—; chmn. Internat. Law Inst., Washington, 1969—; cons. AID, 1966-70, UN Centre on Transnat. Corps., 1977-78; counsel Wald, Harkrader & Ross, Washington, 1978-86, Arnold & Porter, 1986-89, Shearman & Sterling, 1989—; legal advisor State of Qatar, 1979-82; chmn. adv. com. on tech. and world trade Office of Tech. Assessment, U.S. Congress, 1976-79; mem. Sec. of State's Adv. Com. on Pvt. Internat. Law, 1979—; mem. U.S. del. UN Conf. on State Succession in Respect of Treaties, Vienna, 1978; mem. U.S. del. new internat. econ. order working group UN Commn. Internat. Trade Law, Vienna, 1981—; vis. com. Harvar dLaw Sch., 1996—. Co-author: Internat. Business and Economics: Law and Policy; author: International Regulation of Multinational Corporations, 1976, Dear Mr. President: The Needed Turnaround in America's International Economic Affairs, 1984; editor: A Lawyer's Guide to International Business Transactions, 1977-87; contbr. numerous articles on internat. trade and law to profl. jours., books revs. on law and bus. to profl. jours. Coord. Anne Arundel County (Md.) Dem. Nat. Com., 1972-79; sec. Chesapeake Found., 1972-73; nat. chmn. Law Profs. for Bush and Quayle, 1988, 92, for Dole and Kemp, 1996; v.p., bd. govs. UNIDROIT Found., Rome, 1997—.$Dat. co-chmn. Law Profs. for. Fulbright fellow, 1967, Eisenhower Exch. fellow, 1976. Mem. ABA (chmn. sect. internat. law 1978-79), Ho. of Dels. 1982-84), Am. Law Inst., Internat. Law Assn., Shaybani Soc. of Internat. Law (v.p.), Ctrl. and Ea. European Law Initiative (mem. adv. bd.), World Trade Orgn. (mem. panel of judges), Cosmos Club, Met. Club. Home: 2800 35th St NW Washington DC 20007-1411 Office: Georgetown U Law Ctr 600 New Jersey Ave NW Washington DC 20001-2075

WALLACE, DOROTHY ALENE, special education administrator; b. Wright County, Mo., Sept. 11, 1942; d. Stephen Foster and Lois Alene (Breman) Dudley; widowed; children: Michael Dean Huckaby, David Lee. BS in Edn., Drury Coll., 1975, MS in Edn., 1978; Specialist in Ednl. Adminstrn., Southwest Mo. State U., 1988. Cert. tchr. and adminstr., Mo. Tchr. 3rd grade Mansfield (Mo.) R-IV Schs., 1975-78, tchr. 1st grade, 1978-85, tchr. learning disabled, 1985-89, adminstr. spl. edn., 1989-92, adminstr. spl. svcs., 1992—; active sch. coms. on curriculum and nutrition Mansfield R-IV Schs., mem. sch./cmty. adv. coun., 1992—. Mem. Am. Salers Assn., Mo. State Tchrs. Assn., Mo. Coun. Adminstrs. of Spl. Edn., Coun. for Exceptional Children, Coun. Adminstrs. of Spl. Edn., Local Adminstrs. of Spl. Edn., Cmty. Tchrs. Assn. Avocations: raising beef cattle, writing, collecting antiques. Home: 3489 Jerico Rd Seymour MO 65746-9784

WALLACE, EDITH, biology educator; b. Jersey City, N.J.; d. Clarence William Winchel and Edith (Johnson) W.; m. Gordon Johnson, Dec. 22, 1956; children: Eric, Jennifer, Karen. BA, Montclair State Coll., 1956, MA, 1961; PhD, Rutgers U., 1969. Prof. biology William Paterson Coll., Wayne, N.J., 1968—. Achievements include research in effects of selenium deficiency on mouse sperm mitochonoria. Office: William Paterson Coll 300 Pompton Rd Wayne NJ 07470-2103

WALLACE, F. BLAKE, aerospace executive, mechanical engineer; b. Phoenix, Az., Jan. 10, 1933. BMechE, Calif. Inst. Tech., 1955; MS in Engring., Ariz. State U., 1963, PhD in Engring., 1967. Preliminary design engr. Pratt & Whitney, East Hartford, Conn., 1955-59; chief engr. advanced tech. Garrett Corp., Phoenix, 1959-80; mgr. advanced plans and programs Aircraft Engine Group GE, Evendale, Ohio, 1981-83; gen. mgr. Allison div. GM, Indpls., 1983-93; v.p. GM, 1987-93; chmn. & CEO Allison Engine Co., Indpls., 1993-95; retired, 1995. Author numerous tech. papers. Fellow AIAA (chmn. air breathing propulsion tech. com. 1977-78, Air Breathing Propulsion award 1991), U.S. Advanced Ceramic Assn. (chmn. 1987-89).

WALLACE, FRANKLIN SHERWOOD, lawyer; b. Bklyn., Nov. 24, 1927; s. Abraham Charles and Jennie (Etkin) Wolowitz; student U. Wis., 1943-45; BS cum laude, U.S. Mcht. Marine Acad., 1950; LLB, JD, U. Mich., 1953; m. Eleanor Ruth Pope, Aug. 23, 1953; children: Julia Diane, Charles Andrew. Bar: 1954. Practiced in Rock Island; ptnr. firm Winstein, Kavensky & Wallace; asst. state's atty. Rock Island County, 1967-68; local counsel UAW at John Deere-J.I. Case Plants. Former bd. dirs. Tri City Jewish Ctr.; former trustee United Jewish Charities of Quad Cities; bd. dirs. Blackhawk Coll. Found. Mem. ABA, Ill. Bar Assn. (chmn. jud. adv. polls com. 1979-84), Rock Island County Bar Assn., Am. Trial Lawyers Assn., Ill. Trial Lawyers Assn., Nat. Assn. Criminal Def. Lawyers, Ill. Appellate Lawyers Assn., Am. Orthopsychiat. Assn., Am. Judicature Soc., Blackhawk Coll. Found. Democrat. Jewish. Home: 3405 20th Street Ct Rock Island IL 61201-6201 Office: Rock Island Bank Bldg Rock Island IL 61201

WALLACE, G. DAVID, magazine editor; b. New Castle, Pa., Jan. 4, 1941; s. Glenn Wright and Luise (McAfee) W.; m. Ann Byrne Bransfield, June 23, 1972; children: Kevin, Colin, Shannon. BA, Coll. Wooster, Ohio, 1962. Gen. assignment reporter Titusville (Pa.) Herald, 1962-63; reporter Associated Press, Washington, 1966-77; correspondent Reuters, Washington, 1977-80, Bus. Week, Washington, 1980-83; editor Bus. Week, N.Y., 1983-91, asst. mng. editor, 1992—. Author: (book) Money Basics, 1984. Recipient John Hancock Financial Journalism award Fordham U. Journalism Sch., 1992. Mem. Am. Soc. Mag. Editors, Nat. Assn. Science Writers. Office: Business Week 1221 6th Ave 39th Flr New York NY 10020

WALLACE, GEORGE CORLEY, former governor; b. Clio, Ala., Aug. 25, 1919; s. George C. and Mozell (Smith) W.; m. Lurleen Burns, May 23, 1943 (dec.); children: Bobbie Jo, Peggy Sue, George Corley, Janie Lee; m. Cornelia Ellis Snively, Jan. 1971 (div. Jan. 1978); m. Lisa Taylor, Sept. 1981 (div. Jan. 1987). LLB, U. Ala., 1942. Bar: Ala. 1942. Asst. atty. gen. State of Ala., 1946-47, mem. Barbour County Legis., 1947-53, judge 3d jud. dist., 1953-58, gov., 1963-66, 71-79, 83-87; sole practice Clayton, Ala., 1958-62; dir. rehab. resources U. Ala., Birmingham, 1979-83; chair pub. adminstrn. Troy State U., Montgomery, Ala., 1987-95; pres. Ala. Bd. Edn. Sponsor, Wallace Act for state trade schs., 1947. Candidate for pres. Am. Ind. Party, 1968, Dem. primary, 1972, 76; bd. dirs. Ala. Tb Assn.; past Sunday sch. tchr. and supt. Meth. Ch. Served with USAAF, 1942-45, PTO. Mem. Am. Legion, VFW, DAV. Lodges: Masons, Shriners, Moose, Elks, Modern Woodman of World, Order Eastern Star, Civitan Internat. Home: 3140 Fitzgerald Rd Montgomery AL 36106-2633 Office: The Wallace Found PO Box 667 Montgomery AL 36101

WALLACE, GLADYS BALDWIN, librarian; b. Macon, Ga., June 5, 1923; d. Carter Shepherd and Dorothy (Richard) Baldwin; m. Hugh Loring Wallace, Jr., Oct. 14, 1941 (div. Sept. 1968); children: Dorothy, Hugh Loring III. BS in Edn., Oglethorpe U., 1961; MLS, Emory U., 1966; EdS, Ga. State U., 1980. Libr. pub. elem. schs., Atlanta, 1956-66; libr. Northside High Sch., Atlanta, 1966-87, Episc. Cathedral St. Philip. Author: The Time of My Life, 1994. Mem. High Mus. Art, Madison-Morgan Cultural Ctr. Ga. Dept. Edn. grantee, 1950, NDEA grantee, 1963, 65. Mem. AAUW, Nat. Audubon Soc., The Cousteau Soc., Atlanta Bot. Garden, Am. Assn. Ret. Persons, Ga. Conservancy, Ga. Geneal. Soc., Oglethorpe U. Nat. Alumni Assn., Emory U. Alumni Assn., Ga. State U. Alumni Assn., Atlanta Hist. Soc., Ga. Trust for Historic Preservation. Home: NC 6 136 Peachtree Memorial Dr NW Atlanta GA 30309-1030

WALLACE, HAROLD JAMES, JR., physician; b. South Hadley Falls, Mass., Aug. 15, 1930; s. Harold James and Evelyn (Mason) W.; m. Dorothy Ann Green, July 4, 1959; children—Harold James III, Elizabeth Marie, John Hill. BA, U. Vt., 1954, MD cum laude, 1958. Intern Mary Fletcher Hosp., Burlington, Vt., 1958-59; resident Mary Fletcher Hosp., 1959-62; practice medicine specializing in oncology Buffalo, 1970-79, Rutland, Vt., 1979—; assoc. chief dept. medicine Roswell Pk. Meml. Inst., Buffalo, 1970-75; dir. Cancer Control Rehab. and Adolescent Program, 1976-79; oncologist Rutland Hosp., 1979-96, Southwestern Vt. Regional Cancer Ctr., 1996—; dir. Cmty. Cancer Ctr., Rutland Regional Med. Ctr., 1989-93; rsch. prof. medicine Darmouth Med. Sch.; exec. officer Cancer and Leukemia Group B, 1992-95. Mem. Am. Cancer Soc. (pres. Vt. div. 1983-84, Nat. div. award 1969), Am. Assn. for Cancer Research, Am. Soc. Clin. Oncology, Green Mountain Oncology Group (chmn. 1983-96), Alpha Omega Alpha. Congregationalist. Office: Southwestern Vt Regional Cancer Ctr Medical Center Dr Bennington VT 05201

WALLACE, HARRY LELAND, lawyer; b. San Francisco, June 26, 1927; s. Leon Harry and Anna Ruth (Haworth) W.; 1 child, Mary Ann Wallace Frantz. A.B. in Govt.; B.S. in Bus, Ind. U., 1949; J.D., Harvard U., 1952. Bar: Wis. 1953. Law clk. U.S. Supreme Ct. Justice Sherman Minton, Washington, 1952-53; assoc. firm Foley & Lardner, Milw., 1953-61; partner Foley & Lardner, 1961-96, retired, 1996; officer and/or dir. various corps. treas. Mequon-Thiensville Sch. Bds., 1966-67, 71-73, pres., 1965-66, 67-71, 73-75; bd. dirs. Milw. County Assn. for Mental Health, 1970-76, Milw. Mental Health Found., 1983-94; chmn. public policies com. Gov.'s Commn. on Edn., 1969-70; mem. Gov.'s Task Force on Sch. Financing and Property Tax Reform, 1972-73; chmn. Gov.'s Commn. on State-Local Rels. and Fin. Policies, 1975-76; trustee Pub. Policy Forum, 1976-92, sec., 1984-86, pres., 1986-88. With USN, 1945-46. Mem. ABA, Wis. Bar Assn., Am. Law Inst., Phi Beta Kappa, Beta Gamma Sigma, Delta Tau Delta. Methodist. Club: Milwaukee. Home: 1913 Somerset Ln Northbrook IL 60062-6067

WALLACE, HELEN MARGARET, physician, educator; b. Hoosick Falls, N.Y., Feb. 18, 1913; d. Jonas and Ray (Schweizer) W. AB, Wellesley Coll., 1933; MD, Columbia U., 1937; MPH cum laude, Harvard U., 1943. Diplomate Am. Bd. Pediatrics, Am. Bd. Preventive Medicine. Intern Bellevue Hosp., N.Y.C., 1938-40; child hygiene physician Conn. Health Dept., 1941-42; successively jr. health officer, health officer, chief maternity and new born div., dir. bur. for handicapped children N.Y.C. Health Dept., 1943-55; prof., dir. dept. pub. health N.Y. Med. Coll., 1955-56; prof. maternal and child health U. Minn. Sch. Pub. Health, 1956-59; chief profl. tng. U.S. Children's Bur., 1959-60, chief child health studies, 1961-62; prof. maternal and child health U. Calif. Sch. Pub. Health, Berkeley, 1962-80; prof., head divsn. maternal and child health Sch. Pub. Health San Diego State U., 1980—; Univ. Research lectr. San Diego State U., 1985—; cons. WHO numerous locations, including Uganda, The Philippines, Turkey, India, Geneva, Iran, Burma, Sri Lanka, East Africa, Australia, Indonesia, China, Taiwan, 1961—, traveling fellow, 1989—; cons. Hahnemann U., Phila., 1993, Ford Found., Colombia, 1971; UN cons. to Health Bur., Beijing, China, 1987; fellow Aiiku Inst. on Maternal and Child Health, Tokyo, and NIH Inst. Child Health and Human Devel., 1994; dir. Family Planning Project, Zimbabwe, 1984-87. Author, editor 14 textbooks; contbr. 325 articles to profl. jours. Mem. coun. on Disabled Children to Media, 1991; dir. San Diego County Infant Mortality Study, 1989—, San Diego Study of Prenatal Care, 1991. Recipient Alumnae Achievement award Wellesley Coll., 1982, U. Minn. award, 1985; Ford Found. study grantee, 1986, 87, 88; fellow World Rehab. Fund, India, 1991-92, Fulbright Found., 1992—, NIH Inst. Child Health and Human Devel., 1994, Aiiku Inst. of Maternal-Child Health, Tokyo, 1994. Fellow APHA (officer sect., Martha May Eliot award 1978, chair com. on internat. MCH), Am. Acad. Pediatrics (Job Smith award 1980, award 1989); mem. AMA, Assn. Tchrs. Maternal and Child Health, Am. Acad. Cerebral Palsy, Ambulatory Pediatric Assn., Am. Sch. Preventive Medicine. Home: 850 State St San Diego CA 92101-6046

WALLACE, HELEN MARIE, secondary school educator, coach; b. Chgo., Mar. 4, 1939; d. James and Birdie (Burdett) W. BS in Health and Phys. Edn., George Williams Coll., 1963, MS in Counseling Psychology, 1973, MS in Adminstrn., 1973. Cert. tchr. and adminstr., Ill. Girls and boys track, volleyball, and swimming coach Chgo. Pub. H.S.; adminstrv. asst. Chgo. Commn. on Urban Opportunity, summers 1965-68; phys. instr. Chgo. Park Dist., 1958-64; phys. edn. tchr. Chgo. Pub. Sch. Sys., 1963—, athletic dir. Harrison H.S., 1967-87, phys. edn. tchr. Lincoln Park H.S., 1987—, mem. citywide objectives for phys. edn. com., 1993-94, mem. health edn. curriculum com., 1992-94, 96-97, mem. co-chair girls track com., 1983—; phys. edn. tchr., dept. chair Lincoln Park H.S.; mem. state track com. Ill. H.S.; co-author health edn. curriculum Chgo. Pub. H.S.'s; cons. for devel. of health and phys. edn. programs, adminstrv. guidelines, inter-intra-mural sport programs. Jr. ch. organist, celestial choir dir., organist First Bapt. Congl. Ch.; dir. and orgnaist for women's chorus Original Providence Bapt. Ch.; soprano soloist numerous functions. Mem. AAHPERD, Am. Choral Dirs. Assn., Gospel Music Workshop Am. Office: Lincoln Park HS 2001 N Orchard St Chicago IL 60614-4415

WALLACE, J. CLIFFORD, federal judge; b. San Diego, Dec. 11, 1928; s. John Franklin and Lillie Isabel (Overing) W.; m. Elaine J. Barnes, Apr. 8, 1996; 9 children. B.A., San Diego State U., 1952; LL.B., U. Calif., Berkeley, 1955. Bar: Calif. 1955. With firm Gray, Cary, Ames & Frye, San Diego, 1955-70; judge U.S. Dist. Ct. (so. dist.) Calif., 1970-72; judge U.S. Ct. Appeals (9th cir.), 1972-91, sr. circuit judge, 1996. Contbr. articles to profl. jours. Served with USN, 1946-49. Mem. Am. Bd. Trial Advocates, Inst. Jud. Adminstrn. Mem. LDS Ch. (stake pres. San Diego East 1962-67, regional rep. 1967-74, 77-79). Office: US Ct Appeals 9th Cir 940 Front St Ste 4192 San Diego CA 92101-8941 *My principles, ideals and goals and my standard of conduct are embodied in the Gospel of Jesus Christ. They come to fruition in family life, service, industry and integrity and in an attempt, in some small way, to make my community a better place within which to live.*

WALLACE, JACK HAROLD, employee development specialist, educator; b. Pleasant Ridge, Mich., Dec. 3, 1950; s. Jack Alfred and Mary Hilda (Hemming) W.; m. Laura Jeannine Placer, May 20, 1978. AA, Oakland Community Coll., 1972; BA, Oakland U., 1974; postgrad., Cen. Mich. U., 1984; MeD, Wayne State U., 1986, postgrad., 1988—. Cert. secondary tchr., Mich. Supply systems analyst TACOM, Warren, Mich., 1979-84; employee devel. specialist Army Tank Automotive Command, Tng. and Dev. Div., Warren, 1985—; site coord. TA COM long distance learning program Nat. Tech. U., Warren, 1993—; v.p. acad. affairs Virtual U., Bloomfield Hills, Mich., 1994—; instr. Ferndale (Mich.) Bd. of Edn., 1976-86; instr., cons. Jordan Coll., Detroit, 1986—, Detroit Coll. Bus., Dearborn, Mich., 1986—; trainer, instr. govt. agys. Co-author: (book) Balancing the Scales of Justice, 1986, (cable TV prodn.) A Course in Law and Application in Everyday Living, 1989. Mem. Am. Soc. for Tng. and Devel., Assn. for Ednl. Comm. and Tech., Fed. Mgrs. Assn., Mich. Soc. Instructional Tech., Phi Delta Kappa. Lutheran. Avocations: reading, camping, fishing, public speaking, travel. Home: 3005 Kenmore Rd Berkley MI 48072-1684 Office: TACOM AMSTA-RM-PRT Warren MI 48397-5000

WALLACE, JAMES HAROLD, JR., lawyer; b. Atlanta, Feb. 8, 1941; s. James Harold Sr. and Ruth (Cocking) W. BSEE, U. S.C., 1963; JD, Georgetown U., 1966. Bar: D.C. 1967. Patent examiner U.S. Patent & Trademark Office, Washington, 1966-67; trial atty. antitrust div. U.S. Dept. Justice, Washington, 1967-70; from assoc. to ptnr. Kirkland & Ellis, Washington, 1970-83; ptnr. Wiley, Rein & Fielding, Washington, 1983—; mem. adv. bd. BNA Patent, Trademark & Copyright Jour., Washington, 1971—. Contbr. articles to profl. jours. Mem. ABA. Home: 3029 Cambridge Pl NW Washington DC 20007-2914 Office: Wiley Rein & Fielding 1776 K St NW Washington DC 20006-2304

WALLACE, JAMES WENDELL, lawyer; b. Clinton, Tenn., July 13, 1930; s. John Nelson and Rose Ella (Carden) W.; m. Jeanne Mary Ellen Newlin; children: Karen Wallace Young, Michael James. Student, Syracuse U., 1952-53; BS, U. Tenn., Knoxville, 1959, JD, 1958. Bar: Calif. 1959, U.S. Dist. Ct. (cen. dist.) Calif. 1959, U.S. Ct. Appeals (9th cir.) 1977, U.S. Supreme Ct. 1964. Sec., legal counsel Guidance Tech., Inc., Santa Monica, Calif., 1958-65; sr. atty., asst. sec. Varian Assocs., Palo Alto, Calif., 1965-67; gen. counsel, asst. sec. Electronic Splty. Co., Pasadena, Calif., 1967-69; asst. gen. counsel, asst. sec. The Times Mirror Co., L.A., 1969-75, assoc. gen. counsel, asst. sec., 1976-85, assoc. gen. counsel, sec., 1985-89; dir., v.p. and sec. Flintridge Asset Mgmt. Co., San Marino, Calif., 1990—. Mem. editorial bd. Tenn. Law Rev., 1956-58. Served with USAF, 1951-55. Mem. Jonathan Club, Phi Delta Phi, Phi Kappa Phi. Home: 5822 Briartree Dr La Canada Flintridge CA 91011-1825

WALLACE, JANE HOUSE, geologist; b. Ft. Worth, Aug. 12, 1926; d. Fred Leroy and Helen Gould (Kixmiller) Wallace; A.B., Smith Coll., 1947, M.A., 1949; postgrad. Bryn Mawr Coll., 1949-52. Geologist, U.S. Geol. Survey, 1952—, chief Pub. Inquiries Offices, Washington, 1964-72, spl. asst. to dir., 1974—, dep. bur. ethics counselor, 1975—, Washington liaison Office of Dir., 1978—. Recipient Meritorious Service award Dept. Interior, 1971, Disting. Svc. award, 1976, Sec.'s Commendation, 1988, Smith Coll. medal, 1992. Fellow Geol. Socs. Am., Washington (treas. 1963-67); mem. Sigma Xi (asso.). Home: 3003 Van Ness St NW Washington DC 20008-4701 Office: Interior Bldg 19th and C Sts NW Washington DC 20240 also: US Geol Survey 103 National Ctr Reston VA 22092

WALLACE, JEANNETTE OWENS, state legislator; b. Scottsdale, Ariz., Jan. 16, 1934; d. Albert and Velma (Whinery) Owens; m. Terry Charles Wallace Sr., May 21, 1955; children: Terry C. Jr., Randall J., Timothy A., Sheryl L., Janice M. BS, Ariz. State U., 1955. Mem. Los Alamos (N.Mex.) County Coun., 1981-82; cons. County of Los Alamos, 1983-84; chmn., vice chmn. Los Alamos County Coun., 1985-88; cons. County of Los Alamos, Los Alamos Schs., 1989-90; rep. N.Mex. State Legislature, 1991—; mem. appropriations and fin. govt. and urban affairs, N.Mex., 1991—, legis. fin. com., Indian affairs, radioactive and hazardous materials, co-chmn. Los Alamos County's dept. energy negotiating com., 1987-88; mem. legis. policy com. Mcpl. League, N.Mex., 1986-88. Bd. dirs. Tri-Area Econ. Devel., 1988-94, 96—, Crime Stoppers, Los Alamos, 1988-92, Los Alamos Citizens Against Substance Abuse, 1989-94; mem. N.Mex. First, Albuquerque, 1989-96; legis. chmn. LWV, 1990; mem. Los Alamos Rep. Women, pres., 1989-90.

Mem. Los Alamos Bus. & Profl. Women (legis. chmn. 1990), Los Alamos C. of C., Mana del Norte, Kiwanis. Methodist. Avocations: tennis, needlework, reading. Home: 146 Monte Rey Dr S Los Alamos NM 87544-3826

WALLACE, JESSE WYATT, pharmaceutical company executive; b. Canton, Ga., Jan. 24, 1925; s. Jesse Washington and Lula (Wyatt) W.; m. Myra Brown, Jan. 2, 1949; children: Karin, Kimberly, Stephen, David. BBA magna cum laude, U. Ga., 1954; MS, Ga. Inst. Tech., 1960. Chmn. svc. groups Ga. Tech, Atlanta, 1953-57; adminstrv. mgr. Am. Viscose Corp., Marcus Hook, Pa., 1957-61; various exec. positions FMC Corp., Phila., 1961-85; pres. Wallco Internat. Corp., Wilmington, Del., 1985-89, 96—, pres., dir., 1996—; v.p., sec. Pharm. Svc. and Tech., Inc., Woodbury, N.J., 1989-95; bd. dirs. Artist Alive, Inc.; adv. bd. Pharm. Tech. Conf., 1986—. Editor: Controlled Release Systems, 1988; contbr. Encyclopedia, 1989; contbr. articles to profl. jours; author (manual) Problem Solver, 1980. Vice chmn. Ch. Deacons, Wilmington; v.p., pres. Wilmington Gideons, 1969-71; v.p. ACA Acad., 1971-73; vice chmn. Del. Family Found., 1990—. Lt. USN, 1943-46, 50-53. Recipient Publ. award Pharm. Technology, 1989. Fellow Acad. Pharm. Scis., Am. Asnsn. of Pharm. Scientists; mem. Internat. Platform Assn., La. Fedn. Internat. Pharm., Am. Assn. Pharm. Scientists, Mensa, Delta Sigma Pi (life), Delta Mu Delta. Republican. Avocations: reading, golf, racquet ball, travel, family. Home: 1106 Grinnell Rd Wilmington DE 19803-5126 Office: Wallco Internat Corp 1106 Grinnell Rd Wilmington DE 19803-5126

WALLACE, JOAN SCOTT, psychologist, social worker, international consultant; b. Chgo., Nov. 8, 1930; d. William Edouard and Esther (Fulks) Scott; m. John Wallace, June 12, 1954 (div. Mar. 1976); children: Mark, Eric, Victor; m. Maurice A. Dawkins, Oct. 14, 1979. A.B., Bradley U., 1952; M.S.W., Columbia U., 1954; postgrad., U. Chgo., 1965; Ph.D., Northwestern U., 1973; H.H.D. (hon.), U. Md., 1979; L.H.D. (hon.), Bowie State Coll., 1981; LLD (hon.), Ala. A&M U., 1990. Asst. prof., then assoc. prof. U. Ill.-Chgo., 1967-73; assoc. dean, prof. Howard U., Washington, 1973-76; v.p.-programs Nat. Urban League, N.Y.C., 1975-76; v.p. adminstrn. Morgan State U., Balt., 1976-77; asst. sec. adminstrn. USDA, Washington, 1977-81, adminstr. Office Internat. Cooperation and Devel., 1981-89; rep. to Trinidad and Tobago Inter Am. Inst. for Cooperation in Agr., USDA, 1989; internat. cons. U.S. Partnerships Internat., Ft. Lauderdale, 1993—; speaker in field. Pub. Toward Democracy newsletter. Chair Binat. Agrl. Research and Devel. Fund, 1987. Recipient Disting. Alumni award Centurian Soc., Bradley U., 1978, Meritorious award Delta Sigma Theta, 1978, award for leadership Lambda Kappa Mu, 1978, award for outstanding achievement and svc. to nation Capital Hill Kiwanis Club, 1978, Links Achievement award, 1979, Presdl. Rank for Meritorious Exec., 1980, NAFEO award, 1989, Community Svc. award Alpha Phi Alpha, 1987, Pres.' award for outstanding pub. svc. Fla. A&M U., 1990. Mem. APA, NASW, AAAS, Am. Consortium for Internat. Pub. Adminstrn. (exec. com., governing bd. 1987), Soc. Internat. Devel. (Washington chpt.), Sr. Exec. Assn., Soc. for Internat. Devel., White House Com. on Internat. Sci., Engring. and Tech., Internat. Sci. and Edn. Coun. (chmn. 1981-89), Am. Evaluation Assn., Consortium Internat. Higher Edn. (adv. com.), Caribbean Studies Soc., Caribbean Assn. of Agriculture Economists, Assn. Polit. Psychologists, Assn. of Mng. Psychologists, Pi Gamma Mu. Presbyterian. Avocations: painting, collecting international arts. Office: Ams for Democracy in Africa 1825 I St NW Washington DC 20006

WALLACE, JOHN LOYS, aviation services executive; b. Decatur, Tex., July 31, 1941; s. John K. and Flora Viola (Lumsden) Montgomery W.; m. Linda M. Jackson, May 18, 1962; children—John, Amy Lynn, Katherine Lea, Elizabeth D'Ann. Student, U. Tex.-Arlington, 1961-65, North Tex. State U., Denton, 1960-61. V.p. acctg. svcs. Cooper Airmotive, Dallas, 1975-77, v.p. fin., 1977-80, exec. v.p., gen. mgr. Gen. Aviation div., 1980-82; exec. v.p. fin., adminstrn. Aviall, Dallas, 1982-85; exec. v.p., chief oper. officer Aviall, Inc., Dallas, 1985-89, pres. Gen. Aviation Svcs. div., 1989-93; pres. Ryder Aviall Inc., ret. 1993. Mem. Fin. Execs. Inst., N. Dallas C. of C., U.S./Mex. C. of C. (bd. dirs.), Chief Exec.'s Round Table, Delta Sigma Phi. Republican. Presbyterian. Clubs: Univ., Cotton Creek Club. Avocation: gardening, fishing, golf. Home: 3651 Pinehurst Cir Gulf Shores AL 36542-9052

WALLACE, JOHN ROBERT, county administrator; b. Princeton, Ind., Mar. 24, 1939; s. Robert Floyd and Marjorie Eloise (Steele) W.; m. Karen Sue Katilius, June 18, 1967 (div. Mar. 1985). BS in Engring. with honors, USCG Acad., 1961; BS in Civil Engring. with honors, U. Ill., 1967. Commd. ensign USCG, 1961, advanced through grades to capt., 1982; facilities engr. Coast Guard Res. Tng. Ctr., Yorktown, Va., 1975-77; chief engr. Coast Guard Activities Europe, Am. Embassy, London, 1977-80; mem. planning/plans evaluation staff USCG Chief of Staff, Washington, 1980-82; dep. chief civil engring. USCG Office Engring., Washington, 1982-83; chief, dep. chief office USCG Office Rsch. and Devel., Washington, 1983-86; commanding officer, sr. engr. USCG Facilities Design and Constrn. Ctr., Norfolk, Va., 1986-89; asst. county adminstr. planning and community devel. Pittsylvania County, Chatham, Va.; county adminstr. County of Amelia, Va., 1992—. Recipient Man of Yr. award Optimists, 1982, Spl. award Kennedy Found., 1984, Haskel Small USO Vol. awards, Washington, 1985, 86. Fellow Soc. Am. Mil. Engrs.; mem. VFW, NRA (life), Am. Def. Preparedness Assn., U.S. Lighthouse Soc., Naval Airship Assn., Royal Nat. Lifeboat Instn. Eng., Scottish Soc. Tidewater, St. Andrews Soc. Tidewater, Clan Wallace Soc., Scottish-Am. Mil. Soc., Am. Legion, Retired Officers Assn., Am. Planning Assn., Va. Citizen's Planning Assn., Va. Econ. Developers Assn., Va. Assn. County Ofcls., Coast Guard Combat Vets. Assn., Va.-Carolina Scottish Soc., Lions. Office: County of Amelia PO Box A Amelia Court House VA 23002-0066

WALLACE, JOYCE IRENE MALAKOFF, internist; b. Phila., Nov. 25, 1940; d. Samuel Leonard and Henrietta (Hameroff) Malakoff; A.B., Queens Coll., City U. N.Y., 1961; postgrad. Columbia U., 1962-64; M.D. State U. N.Y., 1968; m. Lance Arthur Wallace, Aug. 30, 1964 (div. 1974); 1 dau., Julia Ruth; m. Arthur H. Kahn, Oct. 7, 1979 (div. 1986); 1 son, Aryeh N. Kahn. Intern, St. Vincent's Hosp. Med. Center, N.Y.C., 1968-70; resident Manhattan VA Hosp., N.Y.C. and Nassau County Med. Center, East Meadow, N.Y., 1972-73; practice medicine, N.Y.C., 1970-71, North Conway, N.H., 1974-75; practice medicine specializing in internal medicine, N.Y.C., 1976—; mem. attending staff Nassau County Med. Center, 1974, St. Vincent's Hosp. and Med. Center, N.Y.C., 1977—; asst. prof. medicine Mt. Sinai Med. Sch., N.Y.C.; pres. Found. for Research on Sexually Transmitted Diseases, Inc., 1986-89, exec. and med. dir., 1989—. Diplomate Am. Bd. Internal Medicine. Fellow ACP, N.Y. Acad. Medicine; mem. Am. Med. Women's Assn., N.Y. County, N.Y. State med. socs. Office: 369 8th Ave New York NY 10001-4852

WALLACE, JULIA DIANE, newspaper editor; b. Davenport, Iowa, Dec. 3, 1956; d. Franklin Sherwood and Eleanor Ruth (Pope) W.; m. Doniver Dean Campbell, Aug. 23, 1986; children: Emmaline Livingston Campbell, Eden Jennifer Campbell. BS in Journalism, Northwestern U., 1978. Reporter Norfolk (Va.) Ledger-Star, 1978-80, Dallas Times Herald, 1980-82; reporter, editor News sect. USA Today, Arlington, Va., 1982-89, mng. editor spl. projects, 1989-92; mng. editor Chgo. Sun-Times, 1992-1996; exec. editor Statesman Jour., 1996—. Mem. Am. Soc. Newspaper Editors. Office: Statesman Journal 280 Church St NE Salem OR 97301-3734

WALLACE, KEN, magazine publisher. BBA, St. John's U. With Reader's Digest mag., 1967-1983; v.p. advt. Sylvia Porter's Personal Finance mag., 1983-87; v.p., advt. dir. Parade mag., 1987-93; v.p., pub. Prevention mag., Emmaus, Pa., 1993—. Office: Prevention 733 3rd Ave Fl 15 New York NY 10017-3204 also: Prevention 33 East Minor St Emmaus PA 18098

WALLACE, KENNETH ALAN, investor; b. Gallup, N.Mex., Feb. 23, 1938; s. Charles Garrett and Elizabeth Eleanor (Jones) W. A.B. in Philosophy, Cornell U., 1960; postgrad. U. N.Mex., 1960-61; m. Rebecca Marie Odell, July 11, 1980; children: Andrew McMillan, Aaron Blue, Susanna Garrett, Megan Elizabeth, Glen Eric. Comml. loan officer Bank of N.Mex., Albuquerque, 1961-64; asst. cashier Ariz. Bank, Phoenix, 1964-67; comml. loan officer Valley Nat. Bank, Phoenix, 1967-70; pres. WWW, Inc., Houston, 1970-72; v.p. fin. Hometels of Am., Phoenix, 1972-77, Precision Mech. Co., Inc., 1972-77; ptnr. Schroeder-Wallace, 1977-93; chmn. Shalako Corp., Phoenix; mng. ptnr., pres. Blackhawk, Inc., Phoenix, 1977—, also, bd. dirs.; pres., chmn. bd. AlphaSat Corp., Phoenix, 1990—; pres. chmn. bd. dirs. Black Diamond Cable Co., LLC, Park City, Utah; gen. ptnr. Wallco Enterprises, Ltd., Mobile, Ala., Am. Entertainment Network, LLC, Phoenix; mng. gen. ptnr. The Village at University Heights, Flagstaff; mem. AEN Cable Ventures, LLC. Loaned exec. Phoenix United Way, 1966, Tucson United Way, 1967; mem. Valley Big Bros., 1970—; bd. dirs. Phoenix Big Sisters, 1985-87; mem. Alhambra Village Planning Com.; fin. dir. Ret. Sr. Vol. Program, 1973-76; mem. Phoenix Men's Arts Coun., 1968—, dir., 1974-75; mem. Phoenix Symphony Coun., Packards Internat. Campaign committeeman Rep. gubernatorial race, N.Mex., 1964; mem. AEN CableVentures, LLC; treas. Phoenix Young Reps., 1966; mem. Cornell U. adv. coun., 1996—, Coll. Arts and Scis. Coun. Cornell U., 1996—; bd. dirs. Devel. Authority for Tucson, 1967. Mem. Soaring Soc. Am. (Silver badge), Am. Rifle Assn. (life), Nat. Mktg. Assn. (Mktg. Performance of Year award 1966), Nat. Assn. Skin Diving Schs., Pima County Jr. C. of C. (bd. dir. 1967), Phoenix Little Theatre, Phoenix Musical Theatre, S.W. Ensemble Theatre (bd. dir.), Wheelmen of Am., Cornell Univ. Coun., Cornell Univ. Arts & Scis., Packards Internat., Masons, Shriners, Kona Kai Club (San Diego), Paradise Valley Country Club, Alpha Tau Omega. Office: The Wallace Group of Cos PO Box 7703 Phoenix AZ 85011-7703

WALLACE, KENNETH DONALD, lawyer; b. Spokane, Wash., Oct. 2, 1918; s. Donald and Adillah (Mason) W.; m. Ida H. Harvey, June 6, 1946 (div. 1965); children: Ann H., Jane B.; m. Betty Casey Major, July 31, 1965. AB summa cum laude, Wash. State U., 1940; LLB, Columbia U., 1946. Bar: N.Y. 1947, Conn. 1971. Pvt. practice law N.Y.C. and Conn., 1947—; with Cahill, Gordon, Reindel & Ohl, 1946-60; gen. counsel, sec. Bigelow-Sanford, Inc., 1960-70; v.p., dir. Oconee Realty Corp.; dir. JAI Press, Inc., 1984—; of counsel Philip E. Silberberg, N.Y.C.; gen. counsel Johnson Assocs., Inc., JAI Press, Inc., Alpen Pantry, Inc. Editor: Columbia Law Review, 1946. Trustee Bigelow-Charitable Trust. Served to 1st lt. USAAF, 1942-46. Decorated D.F.C. with oak leaf cluster, Air medal with oak leaf cluster; recipient Presdl. citation, medal, pilot's wings, Republic of China. Mem. ABA, Am. Acad. Polit. Sci. (life), Fed. Bar Coun., N.Y. State Bar Assn., Conn. Bar Assn., Assn. Bar City N.Y., Stamford/Darien Bar Assn., Am. Soc. Corp. Secs., Hump Pilor's Assn. (life), Phi Beta Kappa, Phi Sigma Kappa. Home and Office: PO Box 843 947 Ridge Rd New Canaan CT 06840-0843

WALLACE, KENNY, professional race car driver; b. St. Louis, Aug. 23, 1963; m. Kim Wallace; children: Brooke, Brandy, Brittany. Profl. race car driver NASCAR Winston Cup, 1990—. Named ASA Rookie of Yr., 1986, NASCAR Busch Rookie of Yr., 1993. Office: Kenny Wallace Fan Club PO Box 3050 Concord NC 28025

WALLACE, MARY ELAINE, opera director, author; m. Robert House. BFA cum laude, U. Nebr., Kearney, 1940; MusM, U. Ill., 1954; postgrad., Music Acad. West, Santa Barbara, Calif., 1955, Eastman Sch. Music, 1960, Fla. State U., 1962. Prof. voice, dir. opera La. Tech. U., Ruston, 1954-62, SUNY-Fredonia, 1962-69, So. Ill. U.-Carbondale, 1969-79; dir. Marjorie Lawrence Opera Theatre, Opera on Wheels; adminstrv. adviser Summer Playhouse, Carbondale; stage mgr. Chautauqua Opera Co., N.Y., 1963; asst. mus. dir., condr. Asolo Festival, Sarasota, Fla., 1961; music editor, critic The Chautauquan Daily; adjudicator Met. Opera auditions; exec. sec. Nat. Opera Assn., 1981-91. Co-author: Opera Scenes for Class and Stage, 1979, (with Robert Wallace) More Operas Scenes for Class and Stage, 1990, Upstage Downstage, 1992. Mem. Nat. Opera Assn. (pres. 1974, 75), Music Tchrs. Nat. Assn., Nat. Assn. Tchrs. Singing, AAUP, AAUW, Met. Opera Guild, Mortar Bd., Sigma Tau Delta, Pi Kappa Lambda, Phi Beta, Alpha Psi Omega, Delta Kappa Gamma. Address: 3106 Lakeside Dr Rockwall TX 75087-5319

WALLACE, MARY MONAHAN, elementary and secondary schools educator; b. Teaneck, N.J., Nov. 22, 1943; d. Thomas Gabriel and Louise Grace (Monaco) Monahan; m. James Anthony Wallace, Nov. 22, 1978; (dec. May, 1992); 1 child, Meg. BS, Fordham U., 1967; MA, 1971; postgrad. in Supervision, Montclair U., 1978; postgrad. in Edn., various colls. Cert. tchr. language arts, supr., N.Y. 1st and 4th grades tchr. Holy Rosary Sch., Harlem, N.Y., 1963-65; 7th grade tchr. Immaculate Conception Sch., Bronx, N.Y., 1965-66; 8th grade tchr. St. Finbar Sch., Bklyn., 1966-68, St. Patrick Mil. Acad., Harriman, N.Y., 1968-69; English tchr. St. Stephen H.S., Bklyn., N.Y., 1969-70, Holy Rosary Acad., Union City, N.J., 1970-71, Harriman (N.Y.) Coll., 1971-72, Montclair (N.J.) Coll., 1981-82; English tchr. elem. and secondary schs. Fairlawn (N.J.) Schs., 1972—; advisor Fair Lawn H.S. Yearbook, 1977-80, Nat. Lang. Arts Olympiad, Fair Lawn, 1987-89; mem. Mid. Sch. Task Force Fair Lawn Schs., 1991-93, dist. wide steering com. Edn. Recognition Day, Fair Lawn, 1992, 93, mem. steering com. Fair Lawn Mid. Schs., 1994—. Editor (newsletter) Concern, 1970-72; mem. editorial staff (newsletter) Flea Bytes, 1988, 89, 90. Participant Summer in the City U.S. Antipoverty Program, Staten Island, N.Y., 1965; pres. Bear Pond Improvement Assn., 1996—. Named Meml. Sch. Tchr. of Yr. N.J. Gov.'s Recognition Program, 1993. Mem. NEA, N.J. Edn. Assn., N.J. Middle Sch. Assn., Nat. Coun. Tchrs. of English, Fair Lawn Edn. Assn. (treas. 1990-93, pres. 1993—). Roman Catholic. Avocations: reading, swimming, boating, travel. Home: 20-18 Saddle River Rd Fair Lawn NJ 07410-5933 Office: Fair Lawn Edn Assn 3-13 4th St Fair Lawn NJ 07410

WALLACE, MIKE, television interviewer and reporter; b. Brookline, Mass., May 9, 1918; s. Frank and Zina (Sharfman) W.; m. Lorraine Perigord (dec.); children: Peter (dec.), Christopher, Pauline; m. Mary Yates, June 28, 1986. AB, U. Mich., 1935-39, hon. degree, 1987; hon. degree, U. Mass., 1978, U. Pa., 1989. Associated with radio, 1939—, TV, 1946—; commentator, CBS-TV, 1951-54, TV interviewer, reporter, 1951—, CBS news corr., 1963—; co-editor: 60 Minutes, CBS; Author: Mike Wallace Asks, 1958, Close Encounters, 1984. Recipient Robert Sherwood award, 18 ATVAS Emmy awards, George Foster Peabody awards, 1963-71, DuPont Columbia Journalism award, 1972, 83, Carr Van Anda award, 1977, Thomas Hart Benton award, 1978. Mem. Century Assocs., Sigma Delta Chi. Office: CBS News 60 Minutes 524 W 57th St New York NY 10019-2902

WALLACE, NORA ANN, lawyer; b. Phila., May 24, 1951. AB, Vassar Coll., 1973; JD cum laude, Harvard U., 1976. Bar: N.Y. 1977. Mem. Willkie Farr & Gallagher, N.Y.C. Bd. trustees Bklyn. Acad. Music. Office: Willkie Farr & Gallagher 1 Citicorp Ctr 153 E 53rd St New York NY 10022-4611

WALLACE, PAUL EDWARD, JR., health services management; b. Balt.; s. Paul E. and Frances (Tindal) W.; children from previous marriage: Gregory, Demetria, Denise, Eli. BS, Morgan State U., 1974; MA, U. Pitts., 1976, PhD, 1979, MPH, 1981. Adminstrv. fellow Mercy Hosp., Pitts., 1980-81; asst. adminstr. Norfolk (Va.) Gen. Hosp., 1981-85; v.p. profl. svc. Forsyth Meml. Hosp., Winston, N.C., 1985-88; chmn., assoc. prof. Howard U., Washington, 1988—; cons. OAS, Washington, 1989-91. Bd. dirs. Am. Heart Assn., Washington, 1991-95, Franciscan Health Sys., Aston, Pa., 1994. Recipient Recognition award Area Health Edn. Ctr., 1985, J.B. Johnson award Am. Heart Assn., 1992. Fellow Am. Coll. Healthcare Execs. (regent 1994). Presbyterian. Avocations: golf, reading, racquetball. Office: Urban Med Inst 2600 Liberty Heights Ave Baltimore MD 21215-7804

WALLACE, RALPH, superintendent; b. Halifax, Nova Scotia; s. Ralph and Alberta (Warren) W.; m. Haunani Wallace, Aug. 1, 1980; children: Lianne, Travis. BEd, U. British Columbia, 1968, MEd, 1976; postgrad., U. Conn., 1986; CAGS, Boston U., 1987, EdD, 1992. Cert. supt., int. adminstr., Conn. Asst. supt. West Vancouver (B.C.) Bd. Edn., 1967-83; prin. Farmington (Conn.) Bd. Edn., 1983-85; prin. Granby (Conn.) Bd. Edn., 1985-88, supt., 1988-92; supt. Cheshire (Conn.) Bd. Edn., 1992—; apptd. Pres. Nat. Excellence Panel. Contbr. articles to profl. jours. Dir. Gov.'s Sch., Conn. State U.; mem. Conn. Tech. Commn. Recipient Nat. Excellence award U.S. Dept. Edn.; named Conn. Supt. of Yr., 1992. Mem. ASCD, SDE (Conn. tech. com.), PDK, Am. Assn. Sch. Adminstrs., Conn. Assn. Pub. Sch. Supts. (legis), Am. Edn. Rsch. Assn., Edn. Rsch. Svc., Conn. Transp. Commn. (hon.), Conn. Tech. Commn. Home: 40 Dorset Ln Farmington CT 06032-2330 Office: Cheshire Pub Schs 29 Main St Cheshire CT 06410-2405

WALLACE, RICHARD, editor, writer; b. Bronxville, N.Y., May 25, 1947; m. Elisabeth Wallace; 1 child, Eric B. BA, Columbia U., 1974. Reporter, editor, contbr. varius industry and bus. pubs., Electronic News, EE Times, 1976-92; editor-in-chief Electronic Engring Times, Manhasset, N.Y., 1992—. Mem. Internat. Platform Assn. Democrat. Avocations: running, writing, reading, orchardist. Office: CMP Pubs Inc Electronic Engring Times 600 Community Dr Manhasset NY 11030-3847*

WALLACE, RICHARD CHRISTOPHER, JR., school system administrator, educator; b. Haverhill, Mass., Jan. 3, 1931; s. Richard C. and Anna Catharine (Rogan) W.; m. Rita Wallace, June 18, 1957; children: Monica, Margaret, Mona. BS in Edn., Gorham State Coll., Maine, 1953; MEd, Boston Coll., 1960, EdD, 1966; postgrad., Stanford U., 1968-69. Dir. Eastern Regional Inst. Edn., Syracuse, N.Y., 1969-70, 1970-71; deputy dir. program planning and evaluation U. Tex., Austin, 1971-73; supt. Fitchburg (Mass.) Pub. Schs., 1973-80, Pitts. Pub. Schs., 1980-92; prof. U. Pitts., 1993—; chmn. nat. adv. panel ctr. sch. restructuring U. Wis., 1990-95; sch. assoc. Learning Rsch. and Devel. Ctr. U. Pitts., 1983—; chmn. nat. adv. panel Ctr. Effective Secondary Schs., U. Wis., Madison, 1986-90, mem. Coun. of Great City Schs. Exec. Com., 1980-92, Coun. of Great City Schs. Bylaws and Personnel Policies Com., 1986-87. Contbr. articles to profl. jours. Trustee Chatham Coll., 1984-95; bd. dirs. Urban League Pitts, 1985-92, Sta. WQED-TV, Pitts., 1987, Carnegie Found. for Advancement of Teaching, 1990. Named Man of Yr. Edn. Vectors, Pitts., 1981; recipient Shaw medal Boston Coll., Chestnut Hill, Mass., 1985, Leadership for Learning award Am. Assn. Sch. Adminstrs., Washington, 1987, Harold W. McGraw Jr. prize, 1990. Mem. ASCD, Am. Assn. Sch. Adminstrs., Am. Ednl. Research Assn. Democrat. Roman Catholic. Lodge: Rotary (chmn. youth com. 1980) (Pitts.). Office: U Pitts Rm 5P20 Forbes Quad 230 S Bouquet St Pittsburgh PA 15213-4015*

WALLACE, ROBERT BRUCE, surgeon, retired; b. Washington, Apr. 12, 1931; s. William B. and Anne E. W.; m. Betty Jean Newel, Aug. 28, 1955; children: Robert B., Anne E., Barbara N. B.A., Columbia U., 1953, M.D., 1957. Diplomate: Am. Bd. Surgery, Am. Bd. Thoracic Surgery. Chmn., prof. dept. surgery Mayo Clinic and Mayo Med. Sch., Rochester, Minn.; bd. govs. Mayo Clinic, 1968-79; prof. dept. surgery Georgetown U. Sch. Medicine, 1980—, chmn. dept. surgery, 1980-95, surgeon and chief univ. hosp., 1980-95; retired, 1995. Trustee Mayo Found., 1970-78. Mem. ACS (bd. govs. 1975-79), Am. Surg. Assn., Soc. Clin. Surgery, Am. Assn. Thoracic Surgery (pres. 1994-95), Internat. Cardiovascular Soc., Soc. Vascular Surgery. Home: 1322 Darnall Dr Mc Lean VA 22101-3009

WALLACE, ROBERT EARL, geologist; b. N.Y.C., July 16, 1916; s. Clarence Earl and Harriet (Wheeler) W.; m. Gertrude Kivela, Mar. 19, 1945; 1 child: Alan R. BS, Northwestern U., 1938; MS, Calif. Inst. Tech., 1940, PhD, 1946. Geologist U.S. Geol. Survey, various locations, 1942—; regional geologist U.S. Geol. Survey, Menlo Park, Calif., 1970-74; chief scientist Office of Earthquakes, Volcanoes and Engring. U.S. Geol. Survey, Menlo Park, 1974-87, emeritus, 1987—; asst. and assoc. prof. Wash. State Coll., Pullman, 1946-51; mem. adv. panel Nat. Earthquake Prediction Evaluation Coun., 1980-90, Stanford U. Sch. Earth Sci., 1972-82; mem. engring. criteria rev. bd. San Francisco Bay Conservation and Devel. Commn., chmn. 1981-92. Contbr. articles to profl. jours. Recipient Alfred E. Alquist award Calif. Earthquake Safety Found., 1995. Fellow AAAS, Geol. Soc. Am. (chair cordillidan sect. 1967-68), Earthquake Engring. Rsch. Inst., Calif. Acad. Scis. (hon. 1991); mem. Seismol. Soc. Am. (medalist 1989). Avocations: birding, ham radio, water color painting. Office: US Geol Survey MS-977 345 Middlefield Rd Menlo Park CA 94025-3561

WALLACE, ROBERT GEORGE, retired construction company executive, civil engineer; b. Flagstaff, Ariz., Apr. 30, 1928; s. William Robert Francis and Maeclaire (Wright) W.; m. Gloria Mae Reid, Oct. 29, 1960. B.S.C.E., U. Ariz., Tucson, 1953. Registered profl. civil engr. Pres. Wallace & Royden Equipment Co., Phoenix, 1956-67; v.p. Royden Constrn. Co., Phoenix, 1953-67; v.p. The Tanner Cos., Phoenix, 1967-81, exec. v.p., 1971-82, pres., 1982-88, also dir.; nat. bd. dirs. Scripps Rsch. Inst., Kasler Holding Co., The Fenton Cos. Bd. dirs. Assn. Gen. Contractors, 1973-80, The Road Information Rrogram 1978-82, The Beavers, 1982-88, Western Force, 1972-78. Served with USN, 1946-48; PTO. Recipient award of Disting. Service Ariz. Assoc. Gen. Contractors, 1967; Disting. Citizen award U. Ariz. Engring. Coll., 1983. Mem. La Jolla Country Club, La Jolla Beach and Tennis Club, Masons (32d degree). Republican. Episcopalian. Home: 1001 Genter St Ph 8F La Jolla CA 92037-5527

WALLACE, RUSTY, race car driver; b. St. Louis, Aug. 14, 1956; m. Patti Wallace; children: Greg, Katie, Stephen. Stock race car driver, 1980—; mem. Miller Genuine Draft team. Winner NASCAR Winston Cup, 1989; has finished 1st 39 times; 1st place finishes include Goodwrench 500, Budweiser 500, Hanes 500, UAW-GM Teamwork 500, Miller Genuine Draft 400, Goody's 500 (twice), SplitFire Spark Plug 500 (all 1994); 2d place finishes Pontiac Excitement 400, First Union 400, Coca-Cola 600, Charlotte, N.C. (all 1994), winner Hanes 500, 1995, Miller Genuine Draft 400, 1995. Office: NASCAR PO Box 2875 Daytona Beach FL 32120-2875*

WALLACE, SPENCER MILLER, JR., hotel executive; b. Portland, Maine, Aug. 17, 1923; s. Spencer M. and Caroline (Clark) W.; m. Margaret Keeler, May 12, 1956; 1 son, Daniel Walker. With Hotels Statler, 1944-54, Hilton Hotels Corp., 1954-57, Hilton Hotels, Internat., 1957-61; exec. v.p., dir. Hotel Syracuse Corp., N.Y., 1961-80; chmn. Onondaga County Tourism and Conv. Com.; mem. N.Y. State Tourism Adv. Council. Trustee Milton J. Rubenstein Mus. Sci. and Tech. Mem. N.Y. State Hotel Assn., Am. Hotel and Motel Assn. (past dir.), N.Y. State Hotel and Motel Assn. (past pres.), Am. Diabetes Assn. (bd. dirs. N.Y. state affiliate), N.Y. Srs. Golf Assn. (past pres.), Ea. Srs. Golf Assn., Rotary (Syracuse Club), Masons (Shriner, Jester). Episcopalian. Clubs: Mason (Shriner, Jester), Onondaga Golf and Country (bd. dirs.). Home: 11 Wheeler Ave Fayetteville NY 13066-2530 Office: 6875 E Genesee St Fayetteville NY 13066-1009

WALLACE, TERRY CHARLES, SR., technical administrator, researcher, consultant; b. Phoenix, May 18, 1933; s. Terry Milton Wallace and Fair June (Hartman) Wallace Timberlake; m. Yvonne Jeannette Owens, May 21, 1955; children: Terry Charles, Randall James, Timothy Alan, Sheryl Lynn, Janice Marie. BS, Ariz. State U., 1955; PhD, Iowa State U., 1958. Mem. staff Los Alamos Nat. Lab., 1958-71, dep. group leader, 1971-80, group leader, 1980-83, assoc. div. leader, 1983-89, tech. program coord., 1989-91, retired, 1991; sr. tech. adv. SAIC, Inc., 1994-95; ptnr. Stonewall Enterprises, Los Alamos, 1966-71. Contbr. chpts., numerous articles to profl. publs. Patentee in field. Fundraiser Los Alamos County Republican Party, N.Mex., 1983-84. Served to 1st lt. Chem. Corps, U.S. Army, 1959-61. Mem. Am. Chem. Soc., AAAS, Lab. Retiree Group, Inc. (Los Alamos, treas. 1995, bd. dirs. 1995—). Methodist. Home: 146 Monte Rey Dr S Los Alamos NM 87544-3826 Office: 146 Monte Rey Dr S Los Alamos NM 87544-3826

WALLACE, THOMAS C(HRISTOPHER), editor, literary agent; b. Vienna, Austria, Dec. 13, 1933; came to U.S., 1938; s. Don and Julia (Baer) W.; m. Lois Kahn, July 19, 1962; 1 son, George Baer. Grad., Peddie Sch., 1951; BA, Yale U., 1955, MA in History, 1957. Editor G.P. Putnam Sons, N.Y.C., 1959-63; with Holt, Rinehart & Winston, N.Y.C., 1963-81, editor-in-chief gen. books div., 1968-81; v.p., sr. editor Simon and Schuster, N.Y.C., 1981; editor W.W. Norton, N.Y.C., 1982-87; v.p. Wallace Lit. Agy., N.Y.C., 1987—; bd. dirs. Roger Klein Found. Mem. PEN, Yale Club, Century Assn. (N.Y.C.), Pound Ridge (N.Y.) Tennis Club. Home: 45 E 82nd St New York NY 10028-0326 Office: Wallace Lit Agy 177 E 70th St New York NY 10021-5109

WALLACE, WALTER C., lawyer, government official; b. N.Y.C., Mar. 25, 1924; m. Frances Helm, Apr. 5, 1963; 1 dau., Laura. BA magna cum laude, St. John's U., Hillsdale, N.Y., 1948; LLB with distinction, Cornell U., 1951. Bar: N.Y. 1952, Calif. 1954, D.C. 1975, U.S. Dist. Ct. (no. dist.) Calif. 1954, U.S. Ct. Appeals (9th cir.) 1954, D.C. 1975, U.S. Dist. Ct. D.C. 1975, U.S. Ct. Appeals (D.C. cir.) 1975. Assoc. Cahill, Gordan & Reindel, N.Y.C., 1951-54; exec. asst. sec. of labor Dept. of Labor, Washington, 1955-60, asst. sec. of labor, 1960-61; gen. counsel Presdl. R.R. Commn., Washington, 1961; v.p. labor rels. Hudson Pulp & Paper Corp., N.Y.C., 1963-73; pres. Bituminous Coal Operators Assoc., Washington, 1974-75; ptnr. Ables & Wallace,

Washington, 1977-80; prin. Law Offices Walter C. Wallace, N.Y.C., 1981-82; mem. Nat. Mediation Bd., Washington, 1982—, chmn., 1983, 85, 88; U.S. del. Internat. Labor Orgn. Conf. on Labor Rels. in Timber Industry, Geneva, 1958. Mem. bd. editors Cornell Law Quar., 1950-51. Bd. dirs. Nat. Safety Coun., Washington, 1974-75; asst. to chmn. United Givers Fund, Washington, 1956, mem. admission and allocations com., 1957-58. Staff sgt. U.S. Army, 1943-45, ETO. Decorated Bronze Star; recipient Presdl. commendation Pres. Eisenhower, Washington, 1961, Disting. Svc. award United Givers Fund, 1956, Disting. Svc. award Nat. Mediation Bd., 1990. Mem. Calif. Bar Assn., N.Y. State Bar Assn., D.C. Bar Assn., Order of Coif. Republican. Roman Catholic. Home: 55 Central Park W New York NY 10023-6003

WALLACE, WALTER L., sociologist, educator; b. Washington, Aug. 21, 1927; s. Walter L. and Rosa Belle (Boisseau) W.; children: Jeffrey Richard, Robin Claire, Jennifer Rose. B.A., Columbia U., 1954; M.A., Atlanta U., 1955; Ph.D., U. Chgo., 1963. Instr. Spelman Coll., Atlanta U., 1955-57; from lectr. to prof. sociology Northwestern U., Evanston, Ill., 1963-71; prof. sociology Princeton, 1971—; staff sociologist Russell Sage Found., N.Y.C., 1969-77, vis. scholar, 1968; fellow Ctr. for Advanced Study in Behavioral Scis., Stanford, Calif., 1974-75. Author: Student Culture, 1966, Logic of Science in Sociology, 1971, (with James E. Conyers) Black Elected Officials, 1975, Principles of Scientific Sociology, 1983, A Weberian Theory of Human Society, 1994; editor, author: Sociological Theory, 1969; mem. social scis. adv. com. World Book, 1977-94, editorial bd. Social Forces, 1984-87, The Am. Sociologist, 1988-91, Sociol. Quar., 1989-92, Am. Sociol. Rev., 1997—. Mem. exec. com. Assembly of Behavioral and Social Scis. Nat. Rsch. Coun., 1974-77. With AUS, 1950-52. Mem. Am. Sociol. Assn. (council 1971-74, theory sect. 1988—), Sociol. Rsch. Assn. Office: Princeton U Dept Sociology Princeton NJ 08544

WALLACE, WILLIAM, III, engineering executive; b. Bklyn., June 7, 1926; s. William and Ruth (Fitch) W.; m. Dorothy Ann Reimann, Aug. 2, 1969 (dec.); 1 child, Andrew William. B.E.E., Union Coll., 1947. Registered prof. engr., 22 states. Test engr. Gen. Electric Co., Schenectady, 1947; engr. Ebasco Services Inc., N.Y.C., 1948-67, chief elec. engr., 1967-70, mgr. projects, 1970-73; v.p. Atlanta office Ebasco Services Inc., Norcross, Ga., 1973-76; exec. v.p. Ebasco Services Inc., N.Y.C., 1976-80, dir., pres., chief exec. officer, 1980-82, chmn., chief exec. officer, 1982-86, also bd. dirs.; cons., 1986—; bd. dirs. McNab Corp. Chmn. bd. advisors Sch. engring., N.C. State U., 1986-89; mem. adv. bd. trustees Union Coll.; trustee Poly. Prep. Country Day Sch.; v.p. Saddle River Day Sch.; deacon West Side Presbyn. Ch., Ridgewood, N.J., 1988-90, 96—, elder, 1990-93. Mem. IEEE (sr.), NSPE, N.J. State Soc. Profl. Engrs., World Rehab. Fund (bd. dirs.), N.Y.C. C. of C. and Industry (bd. dirs. 1980-88), Delta Upsilon (vice chmn. Ednl. Found.). Republican. Home and Office: 84 Buckhaven Hl Upper Saddle River NJ 07458

WALLACE, WILLIAM AUGUSTINE, philosophy and history educator; b. N.Y.C., May 11, 1918; s. William Augustine and Louise Cecilia (Teufel) W. BEE, Manhattan Coll., 1940, LHD (hon.), 1975; MS in Physics, Cath. U. Am., 1952; PhD in Philosophy, U. Freiburg, Switzerland, 1959, STD, 1962; Lector of Sacred Theology, Dominican House of Studies, Washington, 1954, M of Sacred Theology, 1967; DSc (hon.), Providence Coll., 1973; DLitt (hon.), Molloy Coll., 1974; LHD (hon.), Fairfield U., 1986. Entered Dominican Order, 1946; ordained priest Roman Cath. Ch., 1953. Elec. engr. Consol. Edison, N.Y.C., 1940-41; rsch. engr. Naval Ordnance Lab., Washington, 1941-43; lector philosophy Dominican House of Philosophy, Dover, Mass., 1954-62; philosophy editor New Cath. Ency., Washington, 1962-65; rsch. assoc. Harvard U., Cambridge, Mass., 1965-67; regent of studies Dominican House of Studies, Washington, 1967-70; prof. philosophy and history Cath. U. Am., Washington, 1970-88, prof. emeritus, 1988—; prof. philosophy U. Md., College Park, 1988—; mem. Inst. for Advanced Study, Princeton, 1976-77; fellow Woodrow Wilson Ctr. for Scholars, Washington, 1983-84; dir. gen. Leonine Commn., Washington, 1976-87. Author: The Scientific Methodology of Theodoric of Freiberg, 1959, The Role of Demonstration in Moral Theology, 1963, Causality and Scientific Explanation, vol. 1, 1972, vol. 2, 1974, The Elements of Philosophy, 1977, From a Realist Point of View, 1979 2d edit. 1983, Prelude to Galileo, 1981, Galileo and His Sources, 1984, Galileo, the Jesuits, and the Medieval Aristotle, 1991, Galileo's Logic of Discovery and Proof, 1992, The Modeling of Nature, 1996; editor, translator: Thomas Aquinas: Cosmogony, 1967, Galileo's Early Notebooks: the Physical Questions, 1977, Galileo's Logical Treatises, 1992; editor: Reinterpreting Galileo, 1986, Albertus Magnus, 1996; co-editor: Galileo Galilei: De praecognitionibus and De demonstratione, 1988; mem. editorial bd. Rev. of Metaphysics, The Thomist; contbr. over 325 articles to jours., encys. and books. Lt. Comdr. USN, 1941-46, PTO. Decorated Legion of Merit; recipient Alumni Achievement award Manhattan Coll., 1967, Alumni Achievement award Cath. U. Am., 1986; grantee NSF, 1965-84, NEH, 1981-89. Mem. Am. Cath. Philos. Assn. (pres. 1969-70, Aquinas medal 1983), History of Sci. Soc. (mem. coun. 1974-77, 88-91), Philosophy of Sci. Assn., Phi Beta Kappa, Sigma Xi. Democrat.

WALLACE, WILLIAM C., airline executive; b. Pittsburg, Tex., July 12, 1941; m. Joyce Johnson, Apr. 22, 1978; children: Kristin, Kari, Michael. BBA, U. Tex., Arlington, 1965. Various positions Am. Airlines, Dallas, Ft. Worth, 1967-79, mgr. passenger svcs., 1979-82; div. mgr. reservations Am. Airlines, L.A., 1982-84; mgr. airport terminal svcs. Am. Airlines, Dallas, Ft. Worth, 1984-85, dir. idea systems, 1985-87; regional mgr. Am. Airlines, Nashville, 1987-88, v.p. field svc., 1990—; exec. v.p. Nashville Eagle (Am. Eagle), 1988-89, pres., 1989-90. Exec. bd. Nashville Symphony, 1990-93; adv. bd. Girl Scouts Am., Nashville, 1990-93; bd. dirs. Mid. Tenn. coun. Boy Scouts Am., 1991-93. Capt. U.S. Army, 1965-70. Mem. Nashville C. of C. (bd. govs. 1991-93). Republican. Episcopalian. Avocations: photography, gardening. Office: Am Airlines Inc PO Box MD 1110 619616 Dallas TX 75261

WALLACE, WILLIAM EDWARD, engineering educator,scientist; b. Fayette, Miss., Mar. 11, 1917; s. James D. and Mattie (Rogers) W.; m. Helen Meyer, June 21, 1947; children: Richard Glen, Donald Alan, Marcia Louise. BS, Miss. Coll., 1936; PhD, U. Pitts., 1940. Teaching asst. U. Pitts., 1936-40, rsch. assoc. chemistry, 1941-45, mem. faculty, 1945-83, prof. chemistry, chmn. dept., 1963-77, prof. materials and metall. engring., 1973-83, prof. chem. engring., 1977-83; prof. applied sci. and engring. Carnegie-Mellon U., Pitts., 1983—; rsch. assoc. manhattan project Ohio State U., 1945; cons. Wright-Patterson AFB, 1962—, Du Pont, 1977—, Gen. Motors, 1974—, Amoco, 1977—; Union Oil Co., 1979—; mem. Pa. Gov.'s Sci. Com., Pa. Sci. and Engring. Found.; fellow Carnegie Instn., Washington, 1940-42; pres. Advanced Materials Corp., 1986-93. Recipient Frank Spedding award 1978, Morley award, 1983; Buhl fellow, 1942-44; Guggenheim fellow, 1954-55. Fellow AAAS; mem. Am. Chem. Soc., Phi Beta Kappa (hon.), Sigma Xi, Phi Lambda Upsilon. Research on metals and intermetallics, hydrogen as a fuel, magnetic materials. Home: 201 Pinecrest Dr Pittsburgh PA 15237-3652

WALLACE, WILLIAM HALL, economic and financial consultant; b. Senatobia, Miss., Aug. 8, 1933; s. Woodard Harvey and Cellie (Carter) W.; m. Margaret Jaeger, Mar. 7, 1964 (dec. 1978); children—Amy Margaret, William Douglas, John Richard Bruce; m. Virginia Wilson, Aug. 25, 1979. B.B.A., U. Miss., 1955, M.B.A., 1956; Ph.D., U. Ill., 1962. Asst. prof. econs. Duke U., Durham, N.C., 1962-67; v.p. Fed. Res. Bank Richmond, Va., 1967-73; prof. econs. N.C. State U., Raleigh, 1973-74; staff dir. Fed. Res. Bd., Washington, 1974-80; 1st v.p., chief oper. officer Fed. Res. Bank Dallas, 1981-91; prof. fin., dean Coll. Bus. and Pub. Adminstrn. Old Dominion U., Norfolk, Va., 1991-94; ret., 1994; pres. Wallace Cons., Inc., 1994—; co-dir. Eurasia Found. Program in Banking & Fin. Markets for Russia and CIS, 1994-95. Trustee Dallas Hist. Soc.; mem. Dallas Com. Fgn. Rels. Served to 1st lt. U.S. Army, 1956-58. Mem. Am. Econs. Assn., Am. Statis. Assn., Cen. Dallas Assn. (exec. com.), Greater Dallas C. of C. (edn. com. 1984-88, chmn. edn. com. 1989-90), Rotary. Methodist. Home: 6 Mansilla Way Hot Springs National Park AR 71909-4312 Office: Wallace Consultants Inc Hot Springs National Park AR 71909

WALLACH, ALAN, art historian, educator; b. Bklyn., June 8, 1942; s. Israel and Vivian (Esner) W.; m. Phyllis Rosenzweig, Jan. 3, 1988. BA, Columbia U., 1963, MA, 1965, PhD, 1973. Assoc. prof. Kean Coll., Union, N.J., 1974-89; Ralph H. Wark prof. art and art history Coll. William and Mary, Williamsburg, Va., 1989—; vis. prof. UCLA, 1982-83, Stanford (Calif.) U., 1987, CUNY, 1988, U. Mich., 1989; co-curator Nat. Mus. Am. Art, Washington, 1991-94. Author: (with William Truettner) Thomas Cole: Landscape into History, 1994; Exhibiting Contradiction: Essays on the Art Museum in the United States, 1997; contbr. articles to profl. jours. Sr. Postdoctorate Rsch. award Smithsonian Inst., 1985-86. Mem. Am. Studies Assn., Coll. Art Assn. (bd. dirs. 1996-2000), Assn. Art Historians. Home: 2009 Belmont Rd NW Washington DC 20009-5449 Office: Coll William and Mary Dept Art and Art History Williamsburg VA 23187-8795

WALLACH, AMEI MARIONE, journalist, art critic; b. N.Y.C., Sept. 21, 1941; d. Gert M.K. and Gerda (Lewenz) W.; m. William Edwards, 1989; student U. Chgo., 1959-61; B.S. in Comparative Lit., Columbia U., 1965. Editorial trainee McGraw Hill, Inc., N.Y.C., 1965, asso. editor cover stories and features Merchandising Week, 1966-68; reporter, reviewer UPI, 1968-69; editor Modern Living sect. Newsday, Garden City, N.Y., 1969-72, cultural affairs writer, 1972-83, chief art critic N.Y. Newsday, N.Y.C., 1984-95; arts essayist The MacNeil/Lehrer Newshour, 1987-95; lectr., seminar leader in field. Recipient Front Page award in columnist category Newswomen's Club of N.Y., 1970, 85, 94, Clarion award for article Andrew Wyeth, a Painter's World; Nat. Endowment Humanities profl. journalism fellow Stanford U., 1983-84; Newsday Publisher's award, 1986. Am. Women in Communication, 1977. Among initiators Newsday Part II, expanded modern living sect.; initiated international art coverage; contbr. to N.Y. Times, Vanity Fair, Vogue, Elle, Elle Decor, Archtl. Digest, MS Mag., German Esquire, Art in Am., Lears, Coll. Art Jour., L.A. Times, Art News, Antiques World, Portfolio, N.Y. Mag., Village Voice, MSNBC. Author intro. to Tetrascroll (Buckminster Fuller), 1982, intro. to Universal Limited Art Editions, 1989, Ilya Kabakov: The Man Who Never Threw Anything Away, 1996. Mem. Art Table (v.p. 1985), Internat. Assn. Art Critics (bd. dirs. USA sect.).

WALLACH, ANNE JACKSON See JACKSON, ANNE

WALLACH, EDWARD ELIOT, physician, educator; b. N.Y.C., Oct. 8, 1933; s. David Abraham and Madeleine (Spiro) W.; m. Joanne Levey, June 24, 1956; children: Paul, Julie. BA, Swarthmore Coll., 1954; MD, Cornell U., 1958; MA (hon.), U. Pa., 1970. Diplomate Am. Bd. Ob-gyn. (bd. dirs. 1989—, dir. divsn. reproductive endocrinology 1989—), subcert. in reproductive endocrinology. Intern 2d med. div. Bellevue Hosp., N.Y.C., 1958-59; resident obstetrics and gynecology Kings County Hosp., Bklyn., 1959-63; asst. instr. State U. N.Y. Downstate Med. Center, Bklyn., 1962-63; mem. faculty U. Pa. Sch. Medicine, 1965-84, prof. obstetrics and gynecology, 1971-84, chief endocrinology sect., div. human reprodn., dept. obstetrics and gynecology, 1968-71, mem. admissions com., 1970-73, mem. community health com., 1966-71, mem. student adv. com., 1966-84, mem. com. for appointments and promotions, 1972-77, chmn., 1974-77; dir. dept. obstetrics and gynecology Pa. Hosp., 1971-84, sec., treas. profl. staff, 1972-75; prof., chmn. dept. ob-gyn. Johns Hopkins U. Sch. Medicine, 1984-94, chmn. med. staff, 1991-94, prof., 1984-94; vis. prof. ob-gyn. U. Kyoto Sch. Medicine, 1981; vis. prof. Keio U. Sch. Medicine, 1987; mem. fertility and maternal health drugs adv. com. FDA, 1992-96. Assoc. editor: Fertility and Sterility, 1974—; co-editor: Modern Trends in Infertility and Conception Control; editor-in-chief Postgrad. Obstetrics and Gynecology, 1980—; mem. editorial bd. Fertility and Sterility, 1970—, Obstetrics and Gynecology, 1976-79, Contemporary Obstetrics and Gynecology, 1976—, Biology of Reproduction, 1978-84; editor-in-chief Current Opinion in Obstetrics and Gynecology, 1989-93; contbr. to med. jours. Trustee Marriage Council Phila., 1970-78; chmn. finance com. Phila. Coordinating Council for Family Planning, 1972-73, chmn. med. adv. com., 1973-76; trustee Balt. Chamber Orch., 1989—. Served as surgeon USPHS, 1963-65. Trainee NIH, 1961-62; recipient Lindback Found. Disting. Teaching award U. Pa., 1971. Fellow Am. Coll. Ob-Gyn., Am. Fertility Soc. (dir. 1977-81, pres. 1985-86); mem. AAAS, Am. Gynecol. and Obstet. Soc. (v.p. 1983-84), Endocrine Soc., Soc.Gynecol. Investigation (pres. 1986-87), Am. Bd. Ob-Gyn. (bd. dirs. 1989—, dir. divsn. reproductive endocrinology 1989—), Phila. Endocrine Soc., Obstet. Soc. Phila. (program chmn. 1969-70, 70-71, 71-72, mem. coun. 1972-83, v.p. 1976-77, pres. 1979-80), Soc. Study Reprodn., Inst. Medicine/NAS, Am. Fertility Soc. (pres. 1985-86), Soc. Gynecol. Investigation (pres. 1986-87), Am. Gynecol. and Obstet. Soc. (v.p. 1984), Phila. Obstet. Soc. (pres. 1980), Alpha Omega Alpha. Office: Johns Hopkins Med Instn 600 N Wolfe St Baltimore MD 21205-2110

WALLACH, ELI, actor; b. Bklyn., Dec. 7, 1915; s. Abraham and Bertha (Schorr) W.; m. Anne Jackson, Mar. 5, 1948; children: Peter Douglas, Roberta Lee, Katherine Beatrice. AB, U. Tex., 1936; MS in Edn, CCNY, 1938; student, Neighborhood Playhouse Sch. of Theatre, 1940; hon. doctorate, Emerson Coll., Boston, Sch. for Visual Arts, 1991. Corp. mem., dir. Neighborhood Playhouse Sch. Theatre. Actor, 1945—; Broadway plays include Antony and Cleopatra, 1948, Mr. Roberts, 1949-50, Rose Tatoo, 1950-52, Camino Real, 1953, Mademoiselle Colombe, 1953, Teahouse of the August Moon, 1954-55, London prodn., 1954, Twice Around the Park, 1983, Major Barbara, 1956, Rhinoceros, 1961, Luv, 1964, Promenade All, 1972, Opera Comique, Kennedy Ctr. Performing Arts, 1987, The Flowering Peach, Fla., 1987, Broadway, 1994, Cafe Crown, 1989; appeared off-Broadway prodn. Typists and the Tiger, 1962-63, London prodn., 1964, Saturday, Sunday, Monday, 1974, (with wife and 2 daus.) Diary of Anne Frank, 1977-78; appeared in: nat. tour co. Waltz of the Toreadors, 1973-74; appeared in TV film Murder By Reason of Insanity, 1985, TV series Our Family Honor, 1985, TV miniseries Christopher Columbus, 1985, Executioner's Song, 1986; motion pictures include Baby Doll, 1955, The Misfits, 1960, The Victors, 1962, Lord Jim, 1964, How To Steal a Million, The Good, the Bad and the Ugly, The Tiger Makes Out, Band of Gold, Zig-Zag, Cinderella Liberty, 1973, Crazy Joe, 1973, Movie, Movie, 1976, Sam's Son, 1985, Tough Guys, 1986, Rocket to the Moon,1986, Nuts, 1987, The Impossible Spy, 1987, Godfather III, 1990, The Two Jakes, 1990, Article 99, Mistress, 1991, Night and the City, 1991, Honey, Sweet Love, 1993, Two Much, 1995, The Associate, 1996. Served to capt. Med. Adminstrn. Corps AUS, World War II. Recipient Donaldson, Theatre World, Variety, Antoinette Perry, Drama League awards, Brit. Film Acad. award, 1956, Disting. Alumnus award U. Tex., 1989. Original mem. Actors Studio.

WALLACH, ERIC JEAN, lawyer; b. N.Y.C., June 11, 1947; s. Milton Harold and Jacqueline (Goldschmidt) W.; m. Miriam Grunberger, Mar. 21, 1976; children: Katherine, Emily, Peter. BA, Harvard Coll., 1968, JD, 1972. Bar: N.Y. 1973, U.S. Dist. Ct. (so. and ea. dists.) N.Y. 1973, U.S. Dist. Ct. (no. dist.) N.Y. 1989, U.S. Ct. Appeals (2nd cir.) 1973, (3d cir.) 1996, U.S. Tax Ct. 1976. Assoc. Webster & Sheffield, N.Y.C., 1972-77; assoc. Rosenman & Colin, N.Y.C., 1977-80, ptnr., 1981-96, mem. mgmt. com., 1993-96, chmn. employment practice group, 1985-96; ptnr., chmn. employment practice group Kasowitz, Benson, Torres & Friedman LLP, N.Y.C., 1996—. Mem. editl. bd. You and the Law, 1992-96; contbr. articles to profl. jours. Sec., treas. Art Dealers Assn. Am., Inc., N.Y.C., 1985-96; trustee C.G. Jung Found. for Analytical Psychology; trustee Am. Jewish World Svc., Inc., N.Y.C., 1989—, chmn., 1995—. Mem. Harvard Club N.Y.C. (admissions com. 1992-94), Sunningdale Country Club, Poughkeepsie Tennis Club. Democrat. Avocations: sports, travel, reading. Home: 20 W 64th St New York NY 10023-7129 Office: Kasowitz Benson Torres Friedman LLP 1301 Ave of Ams New York NY 10019 Home: 16 Buttonwood Ln Rhinebeck NY 12572-2402

WALLACH, IRA DAVID, lawyer, business executive; b. N.Y.C., June 3, 1909; s. Joseph and Della (Kahn) W.; m. Miriam Gottesman, Dec. 25, 1938. AB, Columbia U., 1929, JD, 1931, LLD (hon.), 1983; LLD (hon.), U. Maine, 1983. Bar: N.Y. 1932. Practiced in N.Y.C., 1932-45; exec. v.p. Gottesman & Co., Inc. (name changed to Central Nat.-Gottesman Inc. 1984), N.Y.C., 1952-56; pres., CEO Gottesman & Co., Inc. (name changed to Central Nat.-Gottesman Inc. 1984), 1956-74, chmn., CEO, 1974-79, chmn., 1979—, dir., 1947—; exec. v.p. Ctrl. Nat. Corp., N.Y.C., 1952-56, pres., CEO, 1956-74, chmn., CEO, 1974-79, chmn., 1979—, dir., 1948—; exec. v.p. Eastern Corp., Bangor, Maine, 1951-52, dir., 1947-58; dir., pres. Sejak Corp., N.Y.C., dir., exec. v.p. Cenro Corp., N.Y.C. Pres. D. S. and R. H. Gottesman Found., 1956—, bd. dirs., 1941—; chmn., dir. Miriam and Ira D. Wallach Found., 1956—; bd. dirs. Internat. Peace Acad., People for the Am. Way. Lt. USNR, 1943-46. Mem. Am. Bar Assn., Assn. of Bar of City of N.Y., N.Y. Co. Lawyers Assn. Home: 5 Sherbrooke Rd Scarsdale NY 10583-4429 Office: 3 Manhattanville Rd Purchase NY 10577-2116

WALLACH, LESLIE ROTHAUS, architect; b. Pitts., Feb. 4, 1944; s. Albert and Sara F. (Rothaus) W.; m. Susan Rose Berger, June 15, 1969; 1 child, Aaron. BS in Mining Engring., U. Ariz., 1967, BArch, 1974. Registered architect, Ariz.; registered contractor, Ariz. Prin. Line and Space, Tucson, 1978—. Representative projects include Ariz. Sonora Desert Mus. Restaurant Complex, Tucson, Elgin Elem. Sch., Ariz., Hillel Student Ctr. U. Ariz., Tucson, Boyce Thompson Southwestern Arboteum Vis. Ctr., Superior, Ariz., San Pedro Riparian Ctr., Sierra Vista, Ariz., Nat. Hist. Trails Ctr., Casper, Wyo., 1996; contbr. Sunset Mag., Architecture Mag. and Fine Homebuilding; exhibited at U. Ariz., AIA Nat. Conv., Washington. Bd. dirs Tucson Regional Plan, Inc. Recipient Roy P. Drachman Design award, 1982, 85, 93, Electric League Ariz. Design award, 1987, 88, Gov. Solar Energy award, 1989, Desert Living awards citation, 1991, Ariz. Architect's medal, 1989, also 25 additional design awards, including 4 received in 1995. Fellow AIA (Ariz. Honor award 1989, 92, 96, AIA/ACSA Nat. Design award 1991, Western Mountain region Design award 1992, 96, CA AIA/Phoenix Homes and Gardens Home of the Yr. Honor award 1992, 96, Western Region Silver medal 1996); mem. SAC AIA (past pres., Design award 1985, 88, 90). Office: Line and Space 627 E Speedway Blvd Tucson AZ 85705-7433

WALLACH, MARK IRWIN, lawyer; b. Cleve., May 19, 1949; s. Ivan A. and Janice (Grossman) W.; m. Karla L. Wallach, 1996; children: Kerry Melissa, Philip Alexander. BA magna cum laude, Wesleyan U., 1971; JD cum laude, Harvard U., 1974. Bar: Ohio 1974, U.S. dist. ct. (no. dist.) Ohio 1974, U.S. Ct. Appeals (6th cir.) 1985, U.S. Supreme Ct. 1985. Law clk. U.S. Dist. Ct., Cleve., 1974-75; assoc. Baker & Hostetler, Cleve., 1975-79; chief trial counsel City of Cleve., 1979-81; assoc. Calfee, Halter & Griswold, Cleve., 1981-82, ptnr., 1982—, exec. com., 1997—; mem. fed. ct. adv. com. U.S. Dist. Ct. (no. dist.) Ohio, 1991-95. Author: Christopher Morley, 1976. Chmn. bd. trustees Ohio Group Against Smoking Pollution, 1986-90; trustee Cleve. chpt. Am. Jewish Com., 1986—, sec. 1989-91, v.p., 1991-95, pres., 1995—; bd. trustees Citizens League of Greater Cleve., 1978-79, 87-92; pres. Wesleyan Alumni Club Cleve., 1983-87, 1992—; trustee Lyric Opera, Cleve., 1995—, pres., 1996—, Ratner Schs., 1994-96. Mem. ABA, Ohio Bar Assn., Fed. Bar Assn., Cuyahoga County Law Dirs. Assn., The Cleve. Racquet Club, Greater Cleve. Bar Assn., The Club at Soc. Ctr. Avocations: reading, bicycling, space exploration, politics. Home: 23950 Lyman Blvd Shaker Hts OH 44122 Office: Calfee Halter & Griswold 1400 McDonald Investment Ctr 800 Superior Ave E Cleveland OH 44114-2601

WALLACH, PATRICIA, mayor; b. Chgo.; m. Ed Wallach; 3 children. Grad., Pasadena City Coll. Mem. city coun. City of El Monte, Calif., 1990-92, mayor, 1992—; tchr.'s aide Mountain View Sch. Dist. Past trustee El Monte Union High Sch. Dist., L.A. County High Sch. for the Arts; chief amb. of goodwill Zamora, Michoacan, Mex., Marcq-en-Baroeul, France, Yung Kang, Hsiang, Republic of China, Minhang, Peoples Republic of China; mem. L.A. County Libr. Commn.; mem. air quality com. West San Gabriel Valley; chairperson of bd. Cmty. Redevel. Agy.; mem. bd. El Monte Cmty. Access TV Corp.; mem. PTA, Little League Assns.; v.p. exec. bd. Foothill Transit. Mem. League of Calif. Cities, San Gabriel Valley Assn. of Cities, Independent Cities Assn., Bus. and Profl. Women, U.S./Mex. Sister Cities Assn., Sister Cities Internat. Office: 11333 Valley Blvd El Monte CA 91731-3210

WALLACH, PHILIP C(HARLES), financial, public relations consultant; b. N.Y.C., Nov. 17, 1912; s. Edgar Smith and Rix Wallach; m. Magdalena Charlotta Falkenberg, Mar. 5, 1950. Student, NYU, 1930-33. Editor, writer Hearst Publs., N.Y.C., 1933-42; editor Shell Oil Co., N.Y.C., 1943-46; editor, dir. pub. relations W.R. Grace & Co., N.Y.C., 1946-54; dir. pub. relations and advt. H.K. Porter & Co., N.Y.C., 1954-58; pres. Wallach Assocs., Inc., N.Y.C., 1958-85; officer and v.p. investor rels. Occidental Petroleum Co., L.A., 1985-91; v.p. Occidental Internat. Corp., N.Y.C., 1987-91, cons., 1991-92. Pres. St. Paul Guild, N.Y.C., 1959-68, bd. dirs., 1964-72; pres. Cath. Inst. Press, N.Y.C., 1959-75; co-founder Air Force Assn., Washington, 1946; nat. committeeman Rep. Party, N.Y., 1945-60; mem. Rep. Nat. Com., Greenwich, Conn., 1982-91; bd. dirs., mem. exec. com. U.S. Pakistan Econ. Coun. With USAF, 1942-43. Mem. Overseas Press Club. Home: 126 W Lyon Farm Dr Greenwich CT 06831-4352

WALLACH, STANLEY, medical educator, consultant, administrator; b. Bklyn., Dec. 10, 1928; s. Abraham and Ida Helen (Pevin) W.; m. Pearl Small, 1973; children: Sara Lynn, Rhonda, Peter, Francine, Shellie, Allen, Corinne, Mara. AB, Cornell U., 1948; MA in Phys. Chemistry, Columbia U., 1949; MD, SUNY Downstate Med. Ctr., 1953. Diplomate Am. Bd. Internal Medicine, Am. Bd. Endocrinology and Metabolism. Intern Kings County Hosp., Bklyn., 1953-54; resident in internal medicine VA Hosp./Salt Lake Gen. Hosp., Salt Lake City, 1954-56; fellow in endocrinology and metabolism Mass. Gen. Hosp., Boston, 1956-57; attending physician Kings County Hosp., Bklyn., 1957-73, SUNY Hosp., Bklyn., 1966-73, Albany (N.Y.) Med. Ctr., 1973-83; chief of med. svc. VA Med. Ctr., Albany, 1973-83, Bay Pines, Fla., 1983-90; cons. VA Med. Ctr., Tampa, Fla., 1991-92; attending physician Tampa Gen. Hosp., 1991—, Moffitt Cancer Ctr., 1991-92; dir. med. edn. Cath. Med. Ctr., Jamaica, N.Y., 1992-93; dir. endocrinology and osteoporosis ctr. Hosp. for Joint Diseases, N.Y.C., 1993—; instr. in medicine SUNY Downstate Med. Ctr., 1957-58, from asst. prof. to assoc. prof., 1960-71, prof., 1971-73; prof., asst. chmn. dept. medicine Albany Med. Coll., 1973-77, prof., assoc. chmn. dept. medicine, 1977-83; prof. internal medicine Coll. Medicine U. South Fla., 1983-92, assoc. chmn. dept. internal medicine, 1988-92; exec. dir. Am. Coll. Nutrition, 1993—; clin. prof. medicine NYU Sch. Medicine, N.Y.C., 1995—; pres. Certification Bd. for Nutrition Specialists, 1992-96; career scientist Health Rsch. Coun., City of N.Y., 1967-71; program dir. USPHS Clin. Rsch. Ctr., SUNY Downstate Med. Ctr., 1966-73; rsch. collaborator Brookhaven Nat. Lab., Upton, N.Y., 1970-82; vice-chmn. Gordon Rsch. Conf. on Magnesium in Biochem. Processes and Medicine, 1987, chmn., 1990; cons. NIH, NSF, USDA, Nat. Osteoporosis Found., Nat. Arthritis Found., U.S. Pharmacopeial Conf. Mem. editl. bd. Jour. Am. Coll. of Nutrition, 1981—, Magnesium and Trace Elements, 1982—, Jour. Trace Elements in Exptl. Medicine, 1987—; reviewer Am. Jour. Medicine, Annals of Internal Medicine, Archives of Internal Medicine, Jour. Clin. Endocrinology and Metabolism, Endocrinology, Metabolism, Calcified Tissue Internat., Jour. Bone and Mineral Rsch., Osteoporosis Internat., Procs. of Soc. Exptl. Biology and Medicine, Jour. Nutritional Biochemistry; contbr. numerous articles to profl. jours. Capt. USNR, 1957-88. Co-recipient Hektoen Silver award AMA Conv., 1959, John B. Johnson award Paget's Disease Found., 1989. Fellow ACP (emeritus), Am. Coll. Clin. Pharmacology, Am. Coll. Endocrinology, Am. Coll. Nutrition (bd. dirs. 1982-93, v.p. 1983-85, pres.-elect 1985-87, pres. 1987-89, sec., treas. 1991-93, exec. dir. 1993—); mem. Assn. Am. Physicians, Am. Soc. for Clin. Investigation (emeritus), Am. Fedn. Clin. Rsch. (emeritus), Am. Soc. Bone and Mineral Rsch., Am. Soc. for Clin. Nutrition, Am. Inst. of Nutrition, Am. Assn. Clin. Endocrinology, Endocrine Soc., Confedn. of Nutrition Socs., European Calcified Tissue Soc., Paget's Disease Found. (bd. dirs. med. adv. panel), Internat. Bone and Mineral Soc., Internat. Soc. Trace Element Rsch. in Humans. Office: Hosp for Joint Diseases 301 E 17th St New York NY 10003-3804

WALLACH, STEPHEN JOSEPH, cardiologist; b. Bklyn., Dec. 16, 1942; s. Frank and Sylivia B. (Meisel) W.; m. Vicki Wallach, June 30, 1968; children: Jonathan, Rachel. BS, L.I. U. Pharmach, 1965; MD, U. Okla., 1969. Intern Emory Affiliated, Atlanta, 1960-70, med. resident, 1970-71; gen. med. officer USN, 1971-74; med. resident USN Naval Res. Med. Ctr., Phila., 1974-75, fellow cardiology, 1975-76, mem. staff interstat medicine, 1976-77; asst. prof. John Adams Sch. Medicine, Honolulu, 1977-78; pvt. practice cardiology Queens Med. Ctr., Honolulu, 1978—, chief dept. medicine, 1993—. Bd. dirs. Am. Heart Assn., Honolulu, 1980-86, pres. Honolulu chpg., 1994-95. Ltd. comdr. USNR, 1971. Fellow Am. Coll. Cardiology; mem. Honolulu County Med. Assn. (pres. 1990-91), Hawaii Med. Assn. (pres. 1991-92), Hawaii Soc. Internal Medicine (pres. 1996—). Jewish. Avocations: movies, hiking, music. Home: 268 Iliaina St Kailea HI 96734 Office: 1329 Lisistra # 804 Honolulu HI 96813

WALLACH-LEVY, WENDEE ESTHER, retired secondary school educator; b. N.Y.C., Dec. 29, 1948; d. Leonard Morris and Annette (Cohen) W.; m. David H. Levy, Mar. 23, 1997; 1 child, Nanette Renè. BS in Edn., SUNY, Cortland, 1970; MA in Teaching, N.Mex. State U., 1975. Cert.

tchr., N.Mex. Tchr. phys. edn. Las Cruces (N.Mex.) Pub. Schs., 1970-96; mem. Shoemaker-Levy Observing Team, 1996—; coord. Jarnac Obs., Vail, Ariz., 1997—; intramural and athletic coord. White Sands Sch., 1970-93; instr. swimming N.Mex. State U. Weekend Coll., Las Cruces, 1986-96; dir., coord. learn to swim program ARC, Las Cruces, 1973-96; instr. phys. edn., coach volleyball and track, athletic coord. Sierra Mid. Sch., 1993-96. Instr. trainer water safety ARC, 1973—, CPR, 1974—; instr. life guard, trainer, health and safety specialist, 1988-96, instr., trainer standard first aid, 1991—; chair com. health and safety svcs. Don Ana County Red Cross. Named Water Safety Instr. of Yr. ARC, Las Cruces, 1986, 89, 25 Yr. Svc. award, 1992. Mem. AAHPERD, N.Mex. Alliance Health, Phys. Edn. Recreation and Dance (spkr. 1988, 92, 93, aquatic chmn. 1990-92), Nat. Intramural-Recreational Sports Assn., N.Mex. H.S. Athletic Dirs. Assn. Democrat. Jewish. Avocations: skywatching, swimming, needlework, square dancing, photography. Home and Office: 2500 E Wetstones Rd Vail AZ 85641

WALLACK, RINA EVELYN, lawyer; b. Pitts.; d. Erwin Norman and Gloria A. (Schacher). AD in Nursing, Delta Coll., 1973; BS cum laude in Psychology, Eastern Mich. U., 1980; JD cum laude, Wayne State U., 1983. Registered nurse Mich.; bar: Calif. 1983. Psychiat. head nurse Ypsilanti (Mich.) State Hosp., 1973-77, instr., nursing educator, 1977-80; teaching asst. contracts Wayne State U., Detroit, 1981-83; legal asst. Wayne County Prosecutor's Office, 1982-83; atty. NLRB, L.A., 1983-86, dir. employee rels. legal svcs. Paramount Pictures Corp., L.A., 1986-89, v.p., 1989—. Contbr. articles to profl. jours. Instr. ARC, Mich., 1978-80. Recipient Am. Jurisprudence Book award, 1983. Mem. ABA, L.A. County Bar Assn., Am. Trial Lawyers Assn., Mich. Bar Assn., Calif. Bar Assn., Order of Coif. Avocations: shooting, movies, dancing, reading, photography.

WALLANCE, GREGORY J., lawyer; b. Washington, Oct. 24, 1948; s. Donald Aaron Wallance and Shula Cohen; m. Elizabeth Van Veen, Jan. 4, 1981; children: Daniel, Carina, Lisanne. BA, Grinnell Coll., 1970; JD, Bklyn. Law Sch., 1976. Bar: N.Y. 1977, U.S. Dist. Ct. (ea. dist.) N.Y. 1977, U.S. Dist. Ct. (so. dist.) N.Y. 1978, U.S. Ct. Appeals (2d cir.) 1980, U.S. Dist. Ct. (no. dist.) 1989. Clk. to Hon. Jacob Mishler N.Y.C., 1976-77; assoc. Paul, Weiss, Rifkind, Wharton & Garrison, N.Y.C., 1977-79; asst. U.S. atty., U.S. Atty's. Office, N.Y.C., 1979-85; assoc. Kaye Scholer Fierman Hays & Handler, N.Y.C., 1985-88; ptnr. Kaye, Scholer, Fierman, Hays & Handler, 1988—; chief litigation counsel Kidder Peabody & Co., Inc., 1995—. Author: Papa's Game, 1981; assoc. prodr. (HBO) Sakharov, 1981; columnist Nat. Law Jour., 1993—; contbr. articles to profl. jours. Vol. VISTA, N.Y.C., 1970-72. Mem. ABA, Assn. for Bar of City of N.Y. Office: Kaye Scholer Fierman Hays & Handler 425 Park Ave New York NY 10022-3506

WALLCRAFT, MARY JANE LOUISE, religious organization executive, songwriter, author; b. Deloraine, Man., Can., Nov. 2, 1933; d. Norman Zephaniah and Mary Jane (McKinney) Sexton; m. James Orval Wallcraft, Oct. 13, 1956; children: Angela Mae, Ronald Clarke. Assoc. in piano, Royal Conservatory Toronto, Brandon, Man., 1952; AA, Victor Valley Coll., 1973. Tchr. piano Souris, Man., 1963-67; church organist St. George's Anglican, Brandon, 1960-63, St. Lukes Anglican, Souris, Man., 1963-67, Victorville (Calif.) United Meth. Ch., 1970-74; tchr. piano Hines House of Music, Victorville, 1969-72; ch. sec. Fredericksburg (Va.) United Meth. Ch., 1977-79; med. transcriptionist Mary Washington Hosp., Fredericksburg, 1985-87, Shady Grove Adventist, Rockville, Md., 1987-89; founder, pres. Make Me a Blessing Ministries, Inc., Zellwood, Fla., 1992—. Author: Make Me a Blessing, 1991, Sing Your Way to Victory, Reflections, 1994, A Modern Day Psalter, Shadows, Symbols and Strategies, 1994, Sing to the Lord a New Song Every Day of the Year, 1996; songwriter (albums) Make Me a Blessing, 1992, Grandkid's Praise, 1993, Grandma Jane's Unity Rap, 1993, A Word of Encouragement from Make Me a Blessing, Music from the Psalms, Vol. 1, 1995, vols. 2 and 3, 1996; completion of 5-yr investigation of Benny Hinn; choir accompanist New Hope Presbyn. Ch., 1995, 96; recommenced ministry to Care Homes, 1996. Republican. Avocations: writing and compiling daily devotional book and putting the scriptures to music, playing piano and organ, cooking, walking. Home and Office: 4162 Greenbluff Ct Zellwood FL 32798-9005

WALLEIGH, ROBERT SHULER, consultant; b. Washington, Mar. 31, 1915; s. Charles Henry and Martha (McDaniel) W.; m. Catherine Richarde Coulon, Feb. 22, 1938; children—Margaret Coulon (Mrs. Shaffer), Catherine Richarde (Mrs. Carnevale). B.S. in Elec. Engring, George Washington U., 1936. Test engr. Gen. Electric Co., 1936-38; rating examiner Civil Service Commn., 1938-39; adminstrv. asst. Pub. Roads Adminstrn., Washington, 1939-42; elec. engr. to dep. asst. dir. for adminstrn. Nat. Bur. Standards, 1943-53, asso. dir for adminstrn., 1955-75, acting dep. dir., 1975-79, sr. adv. internat. affairs, 1978-79; asst. for adminstrn. Diamond Ordnance Fuze labs. Dept. Army, 1953-55; cons. IEEE, Washington, 1979—. Recipient Naval Ordnance Devel. award, 1945; Exceptional Service award with gold medal Dept. Commerce, 1967; Engr. Alumni Achievement award George Washington U., 1975; others. Methodist. Home: 5701 Springfield Dr Bethesda MD 20816-1237

WALLEN, LINA HAMBALI, educator, consultant; b. Garut, West Java, Indonesia, Mar. 24, 1952; came to U.S., 1986; d. Mulyadi and Indra (Hudiyana) Hambali; m. Norman E. Wallen, Apr. 16, 1986. BA, IKIP, Bandung, Indonesia, 1975, DRA, 1984; PhD in Psychology, Columbia Pacific U., San Rafael, Calif., 1990; MA in Economics, San Francisco State U., 1993. Cert. tchr. Clk. PT Radio Frequency Communication, Bandung, 1972-74; adminstrv. mgr. CV Electronics Engring., Jakarta, Indonesia, 1974-76; exec. sec. PT Tanabe Abadi, Bandung, 1977-81; br. mgr. PT Ama Forta, Bandung, 1982-84; tchr. SMA Pembangunan, Bandung, 1976-83, Patuha Coll., Bandung, 1980-84.

WALLENSTEIN, JAMES HARRY, lawyer; b. N.Y.C., Oct. 28, 1942; s. Ira Jerome and Jane Irene (Hoffman) W.; m. Marcia Faye Michaelson, July 9, 1967; children: Julie, Debbie. BA cum laude, Washington and Lee U., 1964; LLB cum laude, So. Meth. U., 1967. Bar: Tex. 1967, U.S. Ct. Appeals (5th cir.) 1967. Law clk. to justice U.S. Ct. Appeals (5th cir.), Dallas, 1967-68; assoc. Johnson, Bromberg & Leeds, Dallas, 1970-73; pvt. practice law Dallas, 1973-78; ptnr. Wallenstein & St. Claire, Dallas, 1978-81, Jenkens & Gilchrist, Dallas, 1981-88, Jenkens & Gilchrist, P.C., Dallas, 1988—; adj. prof. So. Meth. U. Law Sch., 1978-91; lectr. numerous orgns. including U. Tex., So. Meth. U. Law Sch., State Bar Tex., N.W. Ctr. for Profl. Edn., 1974—. Editor in chief S.W. Law Jour., 1966-67; contbr. articles to profl. jours. Capt. U.S. Army, 1969-70, Vietnam. Mem. ABA (lectr., chair opinion letter com. real property, probate and trust law sect. 1985-89), Tex. Bar Assn. (lectr., coun. sect. on real estate, probate and trust law 1976-84, 86-89, chair sect. 1988-89, chair opinion letter com. 1983—, chair subcom. legal fees paid by title cos. 1985-89, editor newsletter 1981-84), Dallas Bar Assn. (lectr., chair real property sect. 1980-81), Am. Coll. Real Estate Lawyers (lectr.), Dallas Area Real Estate Lawyers' Discussion Group (founder, chair 1976—), Order of Coif, Barristers. Democrat. Jewish. Avocations: reading, swimming. Office: Jenkens & Gilchrist PC 1445 Ross Ave Ste 3200 Dallas TX 75202-2770

WALLENTINE, MARY KATHRYN, secondary educator; b. Moscow, Idaho, Dec. 27, 1943; d. Elwood Vernon and Mary Berenice (Hillard) White; m. William Edward Wallentine, Dec. 29, 1977; 1 child, Vicki. BA, Whitman Coll., 1966. Tchr. math. and art Mt. Rainier H.S., Des Moines, Wash., 1966-85; pres. Highline Edn. Assn., Seattle, 1985-88; tchr. math., dept. head Tyee H.S., SeaTac, Wash., 1988-96, ret.; tchr. leadership cadre Highline Sch. Dist., 1988-92, co-chair dist. site-based decision making com., 1989-92; tchr. leadership cadre Tyee H.S., 1995—, sr. class advisor, graduation advisor, 1994-96. Dir., editor, photographer, prodr. sr. class video Fly Me to the Moon, Tyee H.S., 1995-96. Precinct committeeperson Dem. Ctrl. Com., King County, Wash., 1980-92, state committeewoman, 1982-88, del. nat. conv., 1980; campaign office mgr. Supt. of Pub. Instrn., 1996. Recipient award Women's Polit. Caucus, 1997. Mem. NEA (PULSE dir. 1992—, resolutions com. 1987-92, nat. del. 1980-96), Nat. Coun. Tchrs. Math. (spkr.), Wash. Edn. Assn. (ret., bd. dirs.), Highline Edn. Assn. (pres. 1986-89). Episcopalian. Avocations: gardening, politics, visual arts, community service. Home: 860 100th Ave NE Apt 34 Bellevue WA 98004-4132

WALLER, EDWARD MARTIN, JR., lawyer; b. Memphis, July 2, 1942; s. Edward Martin and Freda (Lazarov) W.; m. Laura Jayne Rhodes, June 18, 1982; children: Lauren Elizabeth, Jonathan. B.A., Columbia U., 1964; J.D., U. Chgo., 1967. Bar: Fla. 1967. Assoc. Fowler, White, Gillen, Boggs, Villareal & Banker, P.A., Tampa, Fla., 1967-72, ptnr., 1972—. Mem. ABA (standing com. professionalism chmn. 1995—, banking and fin. transactions com., litigation sect. 1978-82, co-chmn. 1983-87, coun. 1990-92, budget officer 1996—, litigation sect.), Fla. Bar Assn., Hillsborough County Bar Assn., Bay Area Legal Svcs. (bd. dirs. 1996—). Democrat. Jewish. Office: Fowler White Gillen Boggs Vilareal & Banker PO Box 1438 Tampa FL 33601-1438

WALLER, EPHRAIM EVERETT, retired professional association executive; b. Sioux City, Iowa, Aug. 10, 1928; s. Everett and Ruth Emma (Little) W.; m. Virginia Louise Harper, Oct. 3, 1959. BA, U. Iowa, 1951, MA, 1959; grad., Strategic Intelligence Sch., 1955, Army Security Agy. Sch., 1962, Nat. Cryptologic Sch., 1966; grad. with honors, Comd. and Gen. Staff Coll., 1966, State Dept. Fgn. Svc. Inst., 1967, Turkish Lang. Sch., 1968; grad., Indsl. Coll. Armed Forces, 1972; EdD, U. S.D., 1981. Cert. fgn. area specialist, cryptologist. Commd. 2d lt. U.S. Army, 1951, advanced through grades to lt. col., 1967, retired, 1979; exec. dir. Midwest Agrl. Chems. Assn., Sioux City, Iowa, 1981-95; cons., 1996—; mem. sci. and regulatory oversight coun. Am. Crop Protection Assn., Washington, 1990-95; mem. interregional coord. coun. Joint Body U.S. Regional Agrl. Assns., Dawson, Ga., 1991-95. Contbr. numerous articles to profl. jours. Mem. coms. 1st Congrl. Ch., Sioux City, 1937—. Decorated Bronze Star, Cross of Gallantry with Silver Star, Legion of Merit with oak leaf cluster, Chinese and Vietnamese Honor medals, Meritorious Svc. medal with oak leaf cluster, Joint Svc. Commendation medal with oak leaf cluster, Army Commendation medal with oak leaf cluster, Army Gen. Staff badge, Vietnamese Combad Merit medal. Mem. Retired Officers Assn., Siouxland C. of C. (com. mem. 1981-95), Interprofessional Inst., Scottish Rite, Masons, Eastern Star, Phi Delta Kappa, Delta Sigma Rho. Avocations: swimming, hiking, travel, stamp collecting, writing.

WALLER, GARY FREDRIC, English language educator, administrator, poet; b. Auckland, N.Z., Jan. 3, 1944; came to U.S., 1983; s. Fred and Joan Elsie (Smythe) W.; m. Jennifer Robyn Denham, July 2, 1966 (div. 1980); children: Michael, Andrew; m. Kathleen Ann McCormick, Nov. 12, 1988; one child, Philip. BA, U. Auckland, 1965, MA, 1966; PhD, Cambridge U., Eng., 1970. Donaldson Bye fellow Magdalene Coll., Cambridge, New Zealand, 1967-69; assoc. prof. English U. Auckland, Nova Scotia, New Zealand, 1969-72, Delhousie U., Nova Scotia, Can., 1972-78; head, prof. English Wilfrid Lawrie U., Waterloo, Can., 1978-83; head, prof. lit. and cultural studies Carnegie Mellon U., Pitts., Conn., 1983-92; dean arts and scis., prof. lit. and cultural studies U. Hartford, West Hartford, Conn., 1992-95; v.p. acad. affairs, prof. lit. and cultural studies Purchase (N.Y.) Coll., SUNY, 1995—. Author: The Strong Necessity of Time, 1976, The Triumph of Death, 1977, Pamphilia to Amphilanthus, 1977, Dreaming America, 1979, Mary Sidney Countess of Pembroke, 1979, Sir Philip Sidney and the Interpretation of Renaissance Culture, 1984, Sixteenth Century Poetry, 1986, 2d edit., 1993, Reading Texts, 1986, Lexington Introduction to Literature, 1987, Shakespeare's Comedies, 1991, Reading Mary Wroth, 1991, The Sidney Family Romance, 1993, Edmund Spenser: A Literary Life, 1994, Lady Mary Sidney's Antonie and a Discourse of Life and Death, 1996; (poems) Other Flights, Always, 1991, Impossible Futures Indelible Pasts, 1983.

WALLER, GEORGE MACGREGOR, historian, educator; b. Detroit, June 7, 1919; s. George and Marguerite (Rowl) W.; m. Martha Huntington Stifler, Oct. 16, 1943; children: Susan, Marguerite, Elizabeth, Donald, Richard. Grad., Deerfield Acad., 1937; AB, Amherst Coll., 1941; MA, Columbia U., 1947, PhD, 1953. Comml. rep. Detroit Edison Co., 1941-42; lectr. Hunter Coll., 1946-47; instr. Amherst Coll., 1948-52; chief Am. history research center Wis. Hist. Soc., 1952-54; prof., head dept. history and polit. sci. Butler U., Indpls., 1954-84, McGregor prof. history, 1987-89, McGregor prof. history emeritus, 1989—; Fulbright sr. scholar U. Southampton, Eng., 1961-62; vis. prof. Ind. U., 1967-69. Author: Samuel Vetch. Colonial Enterpriser, 1960, The American Revolution in the West, 1976; editor: Puritanism in Early America, 1950, rev., 1973, Pearl Harbor, Roosevelt and the Coming War, 1953, 65, 3d edit., 1976; contbr. to: Ency. So. History, World Book Ency., Dictionary of Can. Biography, Vol. I., Ency. of Indpls. Mem. Ind. Am. Revolution Bicentennial Commn., 1971-82. Served to lt. comdr. USNR, 1943-46. Recipient Holcomb award, 1960, Daus. of Founders and Patriots of Am. award, 1977, Disting. Hoosier award, 1989, Sagamore of the Wabash award, 1990. Mem. Ind. Acad. Social Scis. (pres. 1983), Ind. Mus. Soc. (past pres.), Internat. Platform Assn., Phi Beta Kappa (past pres. Ind. chpt.), Phi Kappa Phi, Phi Alpha Theta. Home: 740 Broad Ave S Naples FL 34102-7330

WALLER, HAROLD MYRON, political science educator; b. Detroit, Oct. 12, 1940; s. Allan L. and Lillian R. (LeVine) W.; m. Diane Carol Goodman, June 28, 1966; children: Sharon, Dahvi, Jeffrey. SB, MIT, 1962; MS, Northwestern U., 1966; PhD, Georgetown U., 1968. Asst. prof. McGill U., Montreal, 1967-71, assoc. prof., 1971-93, prof., 1993—, chmn. polit. sci. dept., 1969-74, 89-90, acting chmn., 1980-81, 86-87, assoc. dean (acad.) faculty arts, 1991-94, acting dean faculty arts, 1994-95; pres. McGill Assn. Univ. Tchrs., Montreal, 1978-79; fellow Jerusalem Ctr. Pub. Affairs, 1980—; dir. Can. Ctr. Jewish Community Studies, Montreal, 1980—. Co-author: Maintaining Consensus: The Canadian Jewish Polity in the Postwar World, 1990; co-editor: Canadian Federalism: From Crisis to Constitution; contbg. editor: Middle East Focus; mem. editorial bd. Jewish Political Studies, Patterns of Prejudice; chmn. editorial bd. Viewpoints; contbr. numerous articles to profl. jours. and books in field. Com. chmn. Can. Jewish Congress, Montreal, 1971-74; chair, nat. exec. Can. Profs. for Peace in Middle East, Toronto, 1975-85; pres. Akiva Sch., Montreal, 1984-85; com. chmn. Jewish Edn. Council, Montreal, 1986-88. Recipient Nat. Jewish Book award Jewish Book Coun., N.Y.C., 1991; Grad. fellowship NSF, Washington, 1965-66; leave fellowship Social Sci. Humanities Rsch. Council, Ottawa, 1981-82. Mem. Am. Polit. Sci. Assn., Can. Polit. Sci. Assn., Assn. Jewish Studies, Assn. Sociol. Study of Jewry, Assn. Israel Studies, Sigma Xi, Pi Sigma Alpha. Jewish. Club: MIT Hillel (Cambridge, Mass.) (pres. 1961-62). Avocations: travel, athletics, reading, politics. Office: McGill U Dept Polit Sci, 855 Sherbrooke St W, Montreal, PQ Canada H3A 2T7

WALLER, JIM D., holding company executive. CEO Ithaca Holdings, Wilkesboro, N.C. Office: Ithaca Industries Inc Hwy 268 Wilkesboro NC 28697*

WALLER, JOHN HENRY, JR., judge; b. Mullins, S.C., Oct. 31, 1937; s. John Henry and Elnita (Rabon) W.; m. Jane McLaurin Cooper, Nov. 16, 1963 (div.); children: John Henry III, Melissa McLaurin; m. Debra Ann Meares, May 9, 1981; children: Ryan Meares, Rand Ellis. AB in Psychology, Wofford Coll., 1959; LLB, JD, U. S.C., 1963. Mem. S.C. Ho. of Reps., 1967-77, S.C. Senate, 1977-80; judge S.C. Cir. Ct., 1980-94, S.C. Supreme Ct., 1994—; mem. S.C. Cir. Ct. Adv. Com., 1981-94, chmn., 1991-94; mem. S.C. Jud. Std. Com., 1991-94, chmn., 1992-94. Capt. U.S. Army, 1959-60. Mem. Millins Rotary Club (1st pres.), Masons, Shriners. Avocations: woodworking, golf, water sports, snow skiing. Office: SC Supreme Ct Courthouse Main St Marion SC 29571

WALLER, JOHN LOUIS, anesthesiology educator; b. Loma Linda, Calif., Dec. 1, 1944; s. Louis Clinton and Sue (Bruce) W.; m. Jo Lynn Marie Haas, Aug. 4, 1968; children: Kristina, Karla, David. BA, So. Coll., Collegedale, Tenn., 1967; MD, Loma Linda U., 1971. Diplomate Am. Bd. Anesthesiology. Intern Hartford (Conn.) Hosp., 1971-72; resident in anesthesiology Harvard U. Med. Sch.-Mass. Gen. Hosp., Boston, 1972-74, fellow, 1974-75; asst. prof. anesthesiology Emory U. Sch. Medicine, Atlanta, 1977-80, assoc. prof., 1980-86, prof., chmn. dept., 1986—; chief anesthesiology Emory U. Hosp., Atlanta, 1986-94, 97—, med. dir., 1993-95; assoc. v.p. info. svcs. Woodruff Health Scis. Ctr., 1995—; chief info. officer Emory U. System Healthcare, Atlanta, 1995—; cons. Arrow Internat., Inc., Reading, Pa., 1988—; bd. dirs. Clifton Casualty Co., Colo.; mem. adv. com. on anesthetic and life support drugs FDA, Washington, 1986-92; numerous vis. professorships and lectures. Contbr. articles to med. jours. Maj. M.C., USAF, 1975-77. Recipient cert. of appreciation Office Sec. Def., 1983. Fellow Am. Coll. Anesthesiologists, Am. Coll. Chest Physicians; mem. AMA, Am. Soc. Anesthesiologists, Soc. Cardiovascular Anesthesiologists (pres. 1991-93), Internat. Anesthesia Rsch. Soc. (trustee 1984—, sec. 1993—), Assn. Univ. Anesthetists, Soc. Acad. Anesthesia Chairmen (councillor 1989—), Assn. Cardiac Anesthesiologists. Avocations: tennis, sailing, swimming. Office: Emory U Hosp Dept Anes 1364 Clifton Rd NE Atlanta GA 30322-1059

WALLER, JOHN OSCAR, English language educator; b. L.A., Oct. 29, 1916; s. David Oscar and Susan Veva (Williams) W.; m. Elaine Louise Johnson, Jan. 6, 1946. B.A., San Diego State Coll., 1941; M.A., U. So. Calif., 1949; Ph.D., 1954. Instr. San Diego State Coll., 1946-48; dir. publs. Oxnard (Calif.) Union High Sch., 1951-52; mem. faculty Walla Walla Coll., College Place, Wash., 1952-60; prof. English Andrews U., Berrien Springs, Mich., 1960-88, chmn. dept., 1963-79. Author: A Circle of Friends: The Tennysons and the Lushingtons of Park House; author articles on lit. history; mem. editl. bd. Abstracts of English Studies, 1967-80; contbr. articles to profl. jours., 1988-95. Served with USNR, 1941-45. Mem. Seventh Day Adventist Ch. Home: 8886 George Ave Berrien Springs MI 49103-1406

WALLER, PATRICIA FOSSUM, transportation executive, researcher, psychologist; b. Winnipeg, Man., Can., Oct. 12, 1932; d. Magnus Samuel and Diana Isabel (Briggs) Fossum; m. Marcus Bishop Waller, Feb. 27, 1957; children: Anna Estelle, Justin Magnus, Martha Wilkinson, Benjamin Earl. AB in Psychology cum laude, U. Miami, Coral Gables, 1953, MS in Psychology, 1955; PhD in Psychology, U. N.C., 1959. Lic. psychologist, N.C. Psychology intern VA Hosp., Salem, Va., 1956; psychology instr. Med. Sch. U. N.C., Chapel Hill, 1957; USPHS postdoctoral fellow R.B. Jackson Lab., Bar Harbor, Maine, 1958-60; psychologist VA Hosp., Brockton, Mass., 1961-62; psychology lectr. U. N.C., Chapel Hill, Greensboro, 1962-67; assoc. dir. driver studies Hwy. Safety Rsch. Ctr. U. N.C., Chapel Hill, 1967-89, dir. Injury Prevention Rsch. Ctr., 1987-89; dir. Transp. Rsch. Inst. U. Mich., Ann Arbor, 1989—; bd. dirs. Intelligent Transp. Soc. Am., Washington, 1991—, Traffic Safety Assn. Mich., Lansing, 1991—; bd. advisors Eno Transp. Found., Inc., Landsdowne, Va., 1994—; chair group 5 coun. Transp. Rsch. Bd. of NRC, Washington, 1992-95, chmn. Task Force Operator Regulations, 1974-76, mem. study com. devel. ranking rail safety R&D projects, 1980-82, chmn. group 3 coun. operation, safety and maintenance transp. facilities, 1980-83, mem. IVHS-IDEA tech. rev. panel, 1993—, chair workshop human factors rsch. in hwy. safety, 1992, chair ad hoc com. environ. activies, 1992, mem. task force on elderly drivers, 1990-93, mem. com. vehicle user characteristics, 1983-86, mem. com. planning and adminstrn. of transp. safety, 1986-92, mem. com. alcohol, other drugs and transp., 1986—, numerous other coms., mem. spl. coms. including Inst. Medicine Dana Award com., 1986-90, com. of 55MPH nat. maximum speed limit, 1983-84; mem. motor vehicle safety rsch. adv. com. Dept. Transp., Washington, 1991-95; reviewer JAMA, Jour. Studies on Alcohol, Jour. of Gerontology, Am. Jour. Pub. Health; apptd. Pres. Coun. Spinal Cord Injury, 1981; apptd. advisor Nat. Hwy. Safety Adv. Com. to Sec. U.S. Dept. Transp., 1979-80, 80-83; author numerous reports on transp. to govtl. coms. and univs. Author: (with Paul G. Shinkman) Instructor's Manual for Mogan and King: Introduction to Psychology, 1971; author: (with others) Psychological Concepts in the Classroom, 1974, Drinking: Alcohol in American Society—Issues and Current Research, 1978, The American Handbook of Alcoholism, 1982, The Role of the Civil Engineer in Highway Safety, 1983, Aging and Public Health, 1985, Young Driver Accidents: In Search of Solutions, 1985, Alcohol, Accidents and Injuries, 1986, Transportation in an Aging Society: Improving the Mobility and Safety for Older Persons, 1988, Young Drivers Impaired by Alcohol and Drugs, 1988; mem. editorial bd. Jour. Safety Rsch., 1979—; assoc. guest editor Health Edn. Quar., 1989; assoc. editor Accident, Analysis, and Prevention, 1978-84, mem. editorial bd., 1976-87; contbr. articles to profl. jours. Grantee HHS, 1982, 92-97, NIH; named Widmark laureate Internat. Coun. Alcohol, Drugs and Traffic Safety, 1995. Mem. AAAS, APA (Harold M. Hildreth award 1993), APHA (injury control and emergency health svcs. sect., Disting. Career award 1994, transp. rsch. bd., Roy W. Crum award for rsch. contbns. 1995), Assn. for the Advancement of Automotive Medicine (chmn. human factors sect. 1978-80, bd. dirs. 1979-82, pres. 1981-82), Coun. Univ. Transp. Ctrs. (exec. com. 1991-93), Transp. Rsch. Bd., Ea. Psychol. Assn., Sigma Xi. Democrat. Avocations: gardening, reading. Office: U Mich Transp Rsch Inst 2901 Baxter Rd Ann Arbor MI 48109-2150

WALLER, ROBERT JAMES, writer; b. Aug. 1, 1939; s. Robert Sr. and Ruth W.; m. Georgia Ann Wiedemeier; 1 child, Rachael. Student, U. Iowa, 1957-58, U. No. Iowa, 1958; PhD, Ind. U., 1968. Prof. mgmt. U. No. Iowa, Cedar Falls, 1968-91, dean bus. sch., 1979-85. Author: Just Beyond the Firelight: Stories & Essays, 1988, One Good Road is Enough: Essays, 1990, The Bridges of Madison County, 1992, Slow Waltz in Cedar Bend, 1993, Old Songs in a New Cafe: Selected Essays, 1994, Border Music, 1995; recorded album The Ballads of Madison County, 1993. Recipient Literary Lion award New York Public Library, 1993. Office: care Aaron Priest Literary Agy 708 3rd Ave Fl 23 New York NY 10017-4201*

WALLER, ROBERT REX, ophthalmologist, educator, foundation executive; b. N.Y.C., Feb. 19, 1937; s. Madison Rex and Sally Elizabeth (Pearce) W.; m. Sarah Elizabeth Pickens, Dec. 27, 1963; children: Elizabeth, Katherine, Robert Jr. BA, Duke U., 1958; MD, U. Tenn., 1963. Diplomate Am. Bd. Ophthalmology (dir. 1982—, vice chmn. 1988-89, chmn. 1989—). Intern City of Memphis Hosps., 1963-64; resident internal medicine Mayo Grad. Sch. Medicine, Rochester, Minn., 1966-67, resident in ophthalmology, 1967-70, mem. faculty, 1970—; assoc. prof. ophthalmology Mayo Clinic, Rochester, Minn., 1974-78, prof., 1978—; chmn. dept. ophthalmology Mayo Med. Sch., Rochester, Minn., 1974-84, cons., 1970—, mem. bd. govs., 1978-93, chmn., 1988-93; trustee Mayo Found., Rochester, 1978—, pres., chief exec. officer, 1988—. Contbr. chpts. to books, articles to profl. jours. Elder 1st Presbyn. Ch., Rochester, 1975-78; mem. Rochester Task Force on Pub. Assembly Facilities, 1983-84. Sr. asst. surgeon USPHS, 1964-66. Ocuplastic surgery fellow U. Calif. San Francisco, 1973. Mem. AMA, Minn. State Med. Assn., Zumbro Valley Med. Assn., Am. Acad. Ophthalmology, Am. Ophthalmol. Soc., Am. Soc. Plastic and Reconstructive Surgery, Orbital Soc., Am. Soc. Ophthalmic Plastic and Reconstructive Surgery, Minn. Acad. Ophthalmology and Otolaryngology, Rochester Golf and Country Club, Augusta Nat. Golf Club, Alpha Omega Alpha, Delta Tau Delta. Presbyterian. Avocations: golf, travel, photography, dogs. Home: 800 12th Ave SW Rochester MN 55902-2071

WALLER, STEPHEN, air transportation executive; b. 1949. Student, New Zealand U., 1970-74. Courier, country mgr., european mktg. mgr. DHL Airways, Inc., London, 1975-80, Tehran, Iran, 1975-80; sr. v.p. DHL Airways, Inc., Redwood City, Calif., 1981—. Office: DHL Airways Inc 333 Twin Dolphin Dr Redwood City CA 94065-1401

WALLER, WILHELMINE KIRBY (MRS. THOMAS MERCER WALLER), civic worker, organization official; b. N.Y.C., Jan. 19, 1914; d. Gustavus Town and Wilhelmine (Claflin) Kirby; m. Thomas Mercer Waller, Apr. 7, 1942. Ed., Chapin Sch., N.Y.C. Conservation chmn. Garden Club Am., 1959-61, pres., 1965-68, chmn. nat. affairs, 1968-74, dir., 1969-71; mem. adv. com. N.Y. State Conservation Commn., 1959-70; mem. Nat. Adv. Com. Hwy. Beautification, 1965-68; trustee Mianus River Gorge Conservation Com. of Nature Conservancy, 1955—, Arthur W. Butler Meml. Sanctuary, 1955-79; dir. Westchester County Soil and Water Conservation Dist., 1967-74; adviser N.Y. Gov.'s Study Commn. Future of Adirondacks, 1968-70; adv. com. N.Y. State Parks and Recreation Commn., 1971-72; adv. com. to sec. state UN Conf. Human Environment, 1971-72; mem. Pres.'s Citizens Adv. Com. on Environ. Quality, 1974-78. Mem. planning bd., Bedford, 1953-57; mem. Conservation adv. coun., Bedford, N.Y., 1968-70, Westchester County Planning Bd., 1970-88; bd. govs. Nature Conservancy, 1970-78; Mem. Lyndhurst council Nat. Trust for Historic Preservation, 1965-74; bd. dirs. Scenic Hudson, Inc., 1985-88. Recipient Frances K. Hutchinson medal Garden Club Am., 1971, Holiday mag. award for beautiful Am., 1971, Conservation award Am. Motors Corp., 1975, Oak Leaf award Nature Conservancy, 1988. Mem. Nat. Soc. Colonial Dames, Huguenot Soc. Am., Daus. of Cincinnati. Address: Tanrackin Farm Bedford Hills NY 10507

WALLERSTEIN, GEORGE, astronomy educator; b. N.Y.C., Jan. 13, 1930; s. Leo and Dorothy (Calman) W. B.A., Brown U., 1951; M.S., Calif. Inst. Tech., 1954, Ph.D., 1958. Research asso. Calif. Inst. Tech., Pasadena, 1957-58; instr. U. Calif., Berkeley, 1958-60; asst. prof. U. Calif., 1960-64, asso.

prof., 1964-65; prof., chmn. astronomy U. Wash., Seattle, 1965-80; prof. astronomy U. Wash., 1980—. Trustee Brown U., Providence, 1975-80. Served with U.S. Navy, 1951-53. Mem. Am. Astron. Soc., Astron. Soc. Pacific, AAAS, Arctic Inst. N. Am. Home: 7040 17th Ave NE Seattle WA 98115 Office: U Wash Astronomy Seattle WA 98195 *It is not sufficient "to follow knowledge like a sinking star, beyond the utmost bounds of human thought." One must endeavor to create knowledge, and beyond that to create understanding.*

WALLERSTEIN, MITCHEL BRUCE, government official; b. N.Y.C., Mar. 8, 1949; s. Melvin Julian and Rita Helen (Nomburg) W.; m. Susan Elyse Perlik, June 29, 1974; children: Matthew, Leah. AB, Dartmouth Coll., 1971; MPA, Syracuse U., 1972; MS, MIT, 1977, PhD, 1978. Assoc. dir. Internat. Food Policy Program MIT, Cambridge, Mass., 1978-83, lectr. dept. polit. sci., 1978-83; asst. prof. dept. polit. sci. Holy Cross Coll., Worcester, Mass., 1979-81; exec. dir. Office Internat. Affairs NAS, Washington, 1983-89; dep. exec. officer NAS, Washington, 1989-93; dep. asst. sec. for counterproliferation policy U.S. Dept. Def., Washington, 1993—; adj. prof. Sch. Advanced Internat. Studies, Johns Hopkins U., Washington, 1992—; adj. prof. Sch. Fgn. Svc., Georgetown U., Washington, 1989-93. Author: Food for War - Food for Peace: The Politics of U.S. Food Aid, 1979; author, dir. reports in field including multiple NAS reports on tech. transfer and nat. security. Recipient Sec. Def. medal for Outstanding Pub. Svc., 1997. Mem. AAAS, Internat. Inst. Strategic Studies, Coun. Fgn. Rels. Democrat. Office: US Dept Def Office Asst Sec Def/Counterproliferation Rm 4B 856 The Pentagon Washington DC 20301-2600

WALLERSTEIN, RALPH OLIVER, physician; b. Dusseldorf, Germany, Mar. 7, 1922; came to U.S., 1938, naturalized, 1944; s. Otto R. and Ilse (Hollander) W.; m. Betty Ane Christensen, June 21, 1952; children: Ralph Jr., Richard, Ann. A.B., U. Calif., Berkeley, 1943; M.D., U. Calif., San Francisco, 1945. Diplomate Am. Bd. Internal Medicine (bd. govs. 1975-83, chmn. 1982-83). Intern San Francisco Hosp., 1945-46, resident, 1948-49; resident U. Calif. Hosp., San Francisco, 1949-50; research fellow Thorndike Meml. Lab., Boston City Hosp., 1950-52; chief clin. hematology San Francisco Gen. Hosp., 1953-87; mem. faculty U. Calif., San Francisco, 1952—, clin. prof. medicine, 1969—. Served to capt. M.C. AUS, 1946-48. Mem. AMA, ACP (gov. 1977-87, chmn. bd. govs. 1980-81, regent 1981-87, pres. 1988-89), Am. Soc. Hematology (pres. 1978), San Francisco Med. Soc., Am. Clin. and Climatol. Assn., Am. Fedn. Clin. Rsch., Am. Soc. Internal Medicine, Am. Assn. Blood Banks, Inst. Medicine, Calif. Acad. Medicine, Internat. Soc. Hematology, Western Soc. Clin. Rsch., Western Assn. Physicians, Gold Headed Cane Soc. Republican. Home: 3447 Clay St San Francisco CA 94118-2008

WALLERSTEIN, ROBERT SOLOMON, psychiatrist; b. Berlin, Jan. 28, 1921; s. Lazar and Sarah (Guensberg) W.; m. Judith Hannah Saretsky, Jan. 26, 1947; children—Michael Jonathan, Nina Beth, Amy Lisa. B.A., Columbia, 1941, M.D., 1944; postgrad., Topeka Inst. Psychoanalysis, 1951-58. Assoc. dir., then dir. rsch. Menninger Found., Topeka, 1954-66; chief psychiatry Mt. Zion Hosp., San Francisco, 1966-78; tng. and supervising analyst San Francisco Psychoanalytic Inst., 1966—; clin. prof. U. Calif. Sch. Medicine, Langley-Porter Neuropsychiat. Inst., 1967-75, prof., chmn. dept. psychiatry, also dir. inst., 1975-85, prof. dept. psychiatry, 1985-91, prof. emeritus, 1991—; vis. prof. psychiatry La. State U. Sch. Medicine, also New Orleans Psychoanalytic Inst., 1972-73, Pahlavi U., Shiraz, Iran, 1977, Fed. U. Rio Grande do Sul, Porto Alegre, Brasil, 1980; mem., chmn. rsch. scientist career devel. com. NIMH, 1966-70; fellow Ctr. Advanced Study Behavioral Scis., Stanford, Calif., 1964-65, 81-82, Rockefeller Found. Study Ctr., Bellagio, Italy, 1992. Author 18 books and monographs; mem. editl. bd. 19 profl. jours; contbr. over 225 articles to profl. jours. Served with AUS, 1946-48. Recipient Heinz Hartmann award N.Y. Psychoanalytic Inst., 1968, Disting. Alumnus award Menninger Sch. Psychiatry, 1972, J. Elliott Royer award U. Calif., San Francisco, 1973, Outstanding Achievement award No. Calif. Psychiat. Soc., 1987, Mt. Airy gold medal, 1990, Mary Singleton Sigourney award, 1991. Fellow ACP, Am. Coll. Psychoanalysts, Am. Psychiat. Assn., Am. Orthopsychiat. Assn.; mem. Am. Psychoanlytic Assn. (pres. 1971-72), Internat. Psychoanalytic Assn. (v.p. 1977-85, pres. 1985-89), Group for Advancement Psychiatry, Brit. Psycho-Analytical Soc. (hon.), Phi Beta Kappa, Alpha Omega Alpha. Home: 290 Beach Rd Belvedere CA 94920-2472 Office: 655 Redwood Hwy Ste 261 Mill Valley CA 94941-3011

WALLESTAD, PHILIP WESTON, retired business owner; b. Madison, Wis., May 14, 1922; s. John Oscar and Dorothy Francis (White) W.; BA, U. Wis., 1947, MD, 1954; m. Edith Stolle, Jan. 15, 1949 (div. Mar. 1967); children: Kristin Eve, Ingrid Birgitta, Erika Ann; m. 2d, Muriel Annette Moen, June 22, 1968; children: Thomas John, Scott Philip. Intern, Calif. Luth. Hosp., L.A., 1954, resident in surgery, 1955-56; pvt. practice medicine, Fredonia and Port Washington Wis., 1957-72, Libby, Mont., 1972-74; staff physician VA Hosp., Fort Harrison, Mont., 1974-77, Tomah, Wis., 1977-78, VA Hosp., Iron Mountain, Mich., 1978-88, ret., 1989; owner Wallestad's Arms, mil. antique collectables store, Sturgeon Bay, Wis., 1989-95, ret., 1995. Mem. Conservative Caucus. Served with AUS, 1943-46; ETO; lt. col. USAF Res., 1979-82. Mem. NRA Golden Eagles, DAV, VFW, Am. Legion, Air Force Assn., Conservative Caucus, Res. Officers Assn., Sons of Norway, Coun. for Inter-Am. Security, U. Wis. Alumni Assn., Nat. W Club, Rotary. Republican. Presbyterian Ch. (elder). Home: 443 N 12th Ave Sturgeon Bay WI 54235-1313

WALLEY, BYRON See CARD, ORSON SCOTT

WALLFESH, HENRY MAURICE, business communications company executive, editor, writer; b. N.Y.C., June 15, 1937; s. David Shibe and Rose (Silk) W.; m. Suzanne Krakowitch, Dec. 26, 1960; children: Saundra Kay, Gerald Bruce. Grad. indsl. and labor rels., Cornell U., 1958. Editor, copub. Indsl. Rels. News, N.Y.C and Stamford, Conn., 1960-67; pres., chief exec. officer RAI div. Hearst Bus. Communications, N.Y.C., 1968-91, sr. v.p., editor at large, 1991; pres. Whale Communications, Inc., Stamford, Conn., 1992—; pres. Indsl. Rels. Inst., Stamford, 1964-67; founder, bd. dirs. Internat. Soc. Pre-Retirement Planners, 1975-88; bd. dirs. VSOP Mktg., Boston. Author: Implications of the Age Discrimination in Employment, 1977, When a CEO Retires, 1978. Bd. dirs. Aging in Am., N.Y.C., 1985-90, N.Y.C. Anti-Defamation League, 1987-89; mem. alumni bd. dirs. Cornell Inst. Labor Rels., 1995—. Capt. inf. USAR, 19658-67. Recipient Corp. Achievement award Nat. Assn. for Sr. Living Industries, 1990; inducted into Internat. Soc. Pre-Retirement Planners Hall of Fame, 1988. Mem. Roxbury Swim and Tennis Club (bd. dirs. 1975-78), Cornell Club. Jewish. Avocations: tennis, theatre, writing. Home and Office: 1616 Long Ridge Rd Stamford CT 06903-3902

WALLIN, JACK ROBB, research plant pathology educator; b. Omaha, Nov. 21, 1915; s. Carl O.A. (Wallin) and Elizabeth Josephine (Smith) W.; m. Janet Mary Melhus, Sept. 25, 1937; children: Jack I.M., Robb M. B.S., Iowa State U., 1939, Ph.D., 1944. Rsch. asst. prof. Iowa State U., Ames, 1944-47; rsch. prof., rsch. plant pathologist Agr. Rsch. Svc. USDA/Iowa State U., 1947-75; prof. plant pathology, researcher Agrl. Rsch. Svc. USDA/U. Mo., Columbia, 1975-87; ret., 1986; disaster assistance employee region 7 Fed. Emergency Mgmt. Agy., Kansas City, 1989—; U.S. rep. World Meteorol. Orgn., Geneva, 1959-61; mem. aeriobiology com. Nat. Acad. Sci., NRC, Washington, 1976-80. Patentee (in field). Recipient 1st Peterson award Internat. Soc. Biometeorology, 1966. Mem. Internat. Assn. Aerobiology, Am. Phytopathol. Soc. (sec. treas. N. Central div. 1964-65), Internat. Soc. Plant Pathology, Mo. Acad. Sci. (chmn. agrl. div. 1976-81). Republican. Presbyterian. Lodge: Rotary. Home: 4036 Fletcher Blvd Ames IA 50010-4183 *My genetic constitution must be basically responsible for those talents and abilities that have been expressed in any success that I have attained. Along with reasonable intelligence, I have been endowed with determination, tenacity and loyalty in the desire to achieve set goals. A sense of humor has enabled me to survive mistakes and failures. An agricultural scientist father-in-law inspired me to make a useful contribution to mankind. A supportive wife provided encouragement along the way. Always remember to dedicate your life to helping others less fortunate, we pass this way but once!.*

WALLIN, JAMES PETER, lawyer; b. Huntington, N.Y., May 9, 1958; s. Jerome Peter and Margaret Mary (Gilvarry) W.; m. Julia Katherine Springen, Aug. 11, 1984; children: James Peter Jr., Thomas George, Katherine Grace, Sarah Elizabeth. BA in Econs., SUNY, Stony Brook, 1980; JD, N.Y. Law Sch., 1983. Bar: N.Y. 1984. Counsel Alliance Capital Mgmt., N.Y.C., 1982-86; assoc. Cole & Dietz (now Winston & Strawn), N.Y.C., 1986-87; counsel The Dreyfus Corp., N.Y.C., 1987-88; gen. counsel Yamaichi Capital Mgmt. Inc., N.Y.C., 1988-92, Yamaichi Internat. (Am.) Inc., N.Y.C., 1992-94, Evergreen Asset Mgmt. Corp., 1994—; mem. faculty Practicing Law Inst., N.Y.C., 1992—. Author: (seminar materials) Broker Dealer Regulation, 1992. Avocations: aviation, skiing. Home: PO Box 151 Cold Spring Harbor NY 11724 Office: Evergreen Asset Mgmt Corp 2500 Westchester Ave Purchase NY 10577-2515

WALLIN, LELAND DEAN, artist, educator; b. Sioux Falls, S.D., Oct. 14, 1942; s. Clarence Forrest and Leona Mae (McInnis) W.; m. Meredith Maria Hawkins, Mar. 26, 1977; 1 child, Jessica Hawkins. Student, Columbus Coll. Art and Design, 1961-62; BFA in Painting, Kansas City (Mo.) Art Inst., 1965; MFA in Painting, U. Cin. and Cin. Art Acad., 1967. Prof., coord. drawing St. Cloud (Minn.) State U., 1967-86; prof. Queens Coll., CUNY, Flushing, 1983-84; prof., coord. MFA painting Marywood Coll., Scranton, Pa., 1985-90; prof. painting and drawing East Carolina U., Greenville, N.C., 1993—; lectr. Carnegie-Mellon U., Pitts., 1988; juror Belin Arts Grant Com., Waverly, Pa., 1989; curator Philip Pearlstein Retrospective Exhibit, Scranton, 1988; vis. prof. painting East Carolina U., Greenville, N.C., 1992-93; judge/juror No. Nat. Art Competition, 1993. One man shows include Mpls. Coll. Art and Design, 1978, Harold Reed Gallery, 1983, Gallery Henoch, N.Y.C., 1991, others; group shows at The Bklyn. Mus., 1979, Greenville County Mus. of Art, 1983, The Mus. of Modern Art, 1993, Huntsville Mus. Art, 1994, Sacramento Fine Arts Ctr. Internat., 1995, San Bernardino County Mus. Internat., Calif., 1995, Contemporary Realism, '96 Internat., Phila.; represented in permanent collections N.Y.C. Gallery, Gallery Henoch, 1986—; contbr. articles to profl. jours. Named Outstanding Tchr., East Carolina U., 1994, 95; recipient numerous rsch. awards East Carolina U., 1992—. Mem. Coll. Art Assn. Am., Pa. Soc. Watercolor Painters. Home and Studio: 218 York Rd Greenville NC 27858

WALLING, CHEVES THOMSON, chemistry educator; b. Evanston, Ill., Feb. 28, 1916; s. Willoughby George and Frederika Christina (Haskell) W.; m. Jane Ann Wilson, Sept. 17, 1940; children—Hazel, Rosalind, Cheves, Janie, Barbara. A.B., Harvard, 1937; Ph.D., U. Chgo., 1939. Rsch. chemist E.I. duPont de Nemours, 1939-43, U.S. Rubber Co., 1943-49; tech. aide Office Sci. Research, Washington, 1945; sr. rsch. assoc. Lever Bros. Co., 1949-52; prof. chemistry Columbia U., N.Y.C., 1952-69; Disting. prof. chemistry U. Utah, Salt Lake City, 1970-91, prof. chemistry emeritus, 1991—. Author: Free Radicals in Solution, 1957, Fifty Years of Free Radicals, 1995; also numerous articles. Fellow AAAS; mem. Nat. Acad. Scis., Am. Acad. Arts and Scis., Am. Chem. Soc. (editor jour. 1975-81, James Flack Norris award 1970, Lubrizol award 1984). Home: PO Box 537 Jaffrey NH 03452-0537

WALLINGTON, PATRICIA MCDEVITT, computer company executive; b. Phila., July 29, 1940; d. James J. and Mary (Eschbach) McDevitt; m. William R. Wallington; 1 child, Colleen Xydis. BBA, U. Pa., 1975; MBA, Drexel U., 1978; postgrad. mgmt. devel., Harvard U., 1981. Project mgr. Fidelity Mut., Phila., 1965-72, Penn Mut. Ins. Co., Phila., 1972-77; mgr. info. systems Sun Info. Svcs., Phila., 1977-81; dir. info. systems Sun Exploration & Prodn. Co., Dallas, 1981-87; sr. v.p., chief info. officer Mass. Mut. Life Ins. Co., Springfield, 1987-89; corp. v.p., chief info. officer Xerox Corp., Rochester, N.Y., 1989—; mem. MBA adv. bd. Baylor U., Waco, Tex., 1986-88; bd. dirs. FINA, Inc., Middlesex Mut. P&C Co. Mem. adv. bd. Handicap Ctr.-HUP, Phila., 1978-80; v.p. fin. Girls Club Dallas, 1986-87. Named one of Top 100 Women in Tech., 1994. Mem. Soc. for Info. Mgmt. Office: Xerox Corp 800 Long Ridge Rd Stamford CT 06902-1227

WALLIS, CARLTON LAMAR, librarian; b. Blue Springs, Miss., Oct. 15, 1915; s. William Ralph and Tellie (Jones) W.; m. Mary Elizabeth Cooper, Feb. 22, 1944; 1 child, Carlton Lamar. B.A. with spl. distinction, Miss. Coll., 1936; M.A., Tulane U., 1946; B.L.S., U. Chgo., 1947; L.H.D., Rhodes Coll., Memphis, 1980. English tchr., coach Miss. Pub. Schs., 1936-41; teaching fellow Miss. Coll. and Tulane U., 1941-42; chief librarian Rosenberg Library, Galveston, Tex., 1947-55; city librarian Richmond, Va., 1955-58; dir. Memphis Pub. Library, 1958-80, ret., 1980. Author: Libraries in the Golden Triangle, 1966; contbr. articles to library jours. Trustee Belhaven Coll., 1978-82, Nat. Ornamental Metal Mus., 1989—. Served as chief warrant officer AUS, 1942-46. Decorated Bronze Star. Mem. ALA (chmn. library mgmt. sect. 1969-71), Pub. Library Assn. (dir. 1973-77), Tex. Library Assn. (pres. 1952-53), Va. Library Assn., Southwestern Library Assn. (exec. bd. 1950-55), Southeastern Library Assn. (chmn. pub. library sect. 1960-62), Tenn. Library Assn. (pres. 1969-70, Distinguished Service award 1979). Presbyterian (elder). Club: Egyptian (pres. 1973-74). Home: 365 Kenilworth Pl Memphis TN 38112-5405

WALLIS, DIANA LYNN, artistic director; b. Windsor, Eng., Dec. 11, 1946; d. Dennis Blackwell and Joan Williamson (Gatcombe) W. Grad., Royal Ballet Sch., Eng., 1962-65. Dancer Royal Ballet Touring Co., London, 1965-68; ballet mistress Royal Ballet Sch., London, 1969-81, dep. ballet prin., 1981-84; artistic coord. Nat. Ballet of Can., Toronto, 1984-86, assoc. artistic dir., 1986-87, co-artistic dir., 1987-89; free-lance prod., tchr. London; dep. artistic dir. English Nat. Ballet, London, 1990-94; artistic dir. Royal Acad. Dancing, 1994—. Fellow Imperial Soc. Tchrs. Dancing. Home: 41 Musard Rd, London W68NR, England

WALLIS, DONALD WILLS, lawyer; b. Wilkes-Barre, Pa., Aug. 22, 1950; s. Donald and Hazel (Jansen) W.; m. Kathryn Macon Waggoner, Aug. 28, 1971; children: Neill Jansen, Kathryn Spencer. AB, Duke U., 1971, JD, 1974. Bar: Fla. 1974, U.S. Tax Ct. 1975, U.S. Dist. Ct. (mid. dist.) Fla. 1977, U.S. Ct. Appeals (5th cir.) 1978, U.S. Claims Ct. 1978, U.S. Supreme Ct. 1979. Assoc. Mahoney, Hadlow, Chambers & Adams, Jacksonville, Fla., 1974-78; mem. firm Fisher, Tousey & Wallis, P.A., Jacksonville, Fla., 1978-89; ptnr. Holland & Knight, Jacksonville, Fla., 1989—. Co-author: Bank Holding Companies: A Practical Guide to Bank Acquisitions and mergers, 1978; tax notes editor: The Florida Probate System, 1977; contbg. editor Jour. Partnership Taxation, 1989-95. Chmn. Duke U. Alumni Admissions Adv. Com., Jacksonville, 1986—; chmn. Beaches Fine Arts Series, Inc., Jacksonville Beach, Fla., 1990—. Mem. ABA (taxation sect.), Fla. Bar (tax sect., bd. cert. tax atty.), Jacksonville Bar Assn. (tax sect.), Duke U. Alumni assn. (admissions com. 1986—), Selva Marina Country Club, Inc. (bd. govs. 1987-89). Episcopalian. Avocations: Jacksonville symphony chorus, sailing, scuba diving, backpacking, cycling. Office: Holland & Knight 50 N Laura St Ste 3900 Jacksonville FL 32202-3622

WALLIS, ERIC G., lawyer; b. Astoria, N.Y., Jan. 8, 1950. AB magna cum laude, U. Pacific, 1972; JD, U. Calif., Hasting Coll. of Law, 1975. Bar: Calif. 1975. Mem. Crosby, Heafey, Roach & May P.C., Oakland, Calif. Editorial assoc. Hastings Law Jour., 1974-75. Mem. ABA (sect. litigation), State Bar Calif., Alameda County Bar Assn. Office: Crosby Heafey Roach & May PC PO Box 2084 Oakland CA 94604-2084

WALLIS, GRAHAM BLAIR, engineer, educator; b. Rugby, Warwickshire, Eng., Apr. 1, 1936; came to U.S., 1957; s. Alfred Stanley and Dora (Fleming) W.; m. Suzanne Harriet White, Sept. 12, 1959; children: Iain, Tasha, Peter, Jeremy. B.A., Cambridge U., Eng., 1957; Ph.D., Cambrige U., Eng., 1961; M.S., MIT, 1959. Registered profl. engr., N.H. Asst. prof. Dartmouth Coll., Hanover, N.H., 1962-65, assoc. prof., 1966-72, prof., 1972—, assoc. dean, 1989-93; prof. engring. Sherman Fairchild, 1991—; interim dean engring., 1994-95; cons. Creare Inc., Hanover, 1964—. Author: One-Dimensional Two-Phase Flow, 1959. Recipient Inst. Mech. Engring. Ludwig Mond prize, 1962, Fluids Engineering awardAm. Soc. of Mechanical Engineers, 1994. Mem. ASME (Moody award 1971, Centennial award and medal 1980, Fluids Engring. award 1994). Home: Blood Rd Norwich VT 05055 Office: Dartmouth Coll Thayer Dept of Engring Sch Hanover NH 03755

WALLIS, JOHN JAMES (JIMMY WALLIS), comedian, impressionist, ventriloquist, comedy writer, video production executive; b. Searcy, Ark., Mar. 21, 1939; s. Prentiss Bascom and Maxine (James) W.; children: Lori Diana Wallis Waterman, Shauna Kathleen. Grad., Okla. U., 1960. advisor Am. Acad. for Entertainment at U.S. Vets. Hosps., N.Y.C., 1988—. Nat. TV debut Art Linkletter's Hollywood Talent Scouts, 1966; entertained troops in S.E. Asia, 1967-70; performed with Ann Murray, Lou Rawls, Lola Falana, Ben Vereen, Al Hirt, Debbie Reynolds, Rip Taylor, Suzanne Somers, others; performed in numerous clubs including Tropicana, Las Vegas, The Sahara, Las Vegas, The Flamingo, Las Vegas, Chauteau Champlain, Montreal, The Cave, Vancouver, The Paradise Island Casino, The Bahamas, The Superstar Theater, Atlantic City, Riviera, Las Vegas, Harrah's, Reno, The Reno Hilton, Las Vegas Hilton, Flamingo Hilton; featured in Royal Caribbean Cruise Lines, Premier's Disney Theme Cruises, Norwegian Cruise Lines, Holland Am. and Celebrity Cruise Lines, Night of the Stars, Las Vegas. Named Okla.'s Top Comedian, Okla. Ho. of Reps.; recipient Am. Legion medal. Mem. Nat. Park and Conservation Assn., Planetary Soc., Nat. Space Soc., Smithsonian Assocs., NRA. Presbyterian. Avocations: photography, scuba diving, computers, tennis, target shooting. Office: PO Box 276100 Boca Raton FL 33427-6100

WALLIS, MICHAEL VAN, financial consultant, insurance agent; b. Galesburg, Ill., Sept. 4, 1961; s. Raymond Albert Wallis and Marelyn Mae (Vander Wert) Verner; 1 child, Alexander Joel. BS in Adminstrv. Scis., So. Ill. U., Carbondale, 1983. Ops. supr., acct. rep., terminal mgr. Roadway Express, Inc., St. Louis, Ill., 1983-94; branch mgr. The Fruehauf Trailer Corp., St. Louis, 1994-96; registered rep. EQ Fin. Cons., Inc., St. Louis; agt. Equitable Life Assurance Soc. U.S., Clayton, Mo. Mem. U.S. Parachute Assn., Aircraft Owners and Pilots Assn., World Trade Club St. Louis. Republican. Methodist. Avocations: private pilot, exhibition parachutist, advanced open water scuba diver. Home: 1001 Oak Glen Cir Ballwin MO 63021-7481 Office: 8182 Maryland Ave Ste 1000 Saint Louis MO 63105-3786

WALLIS, RICHARD FISHER, physicist, educator; b. Washington, May 14, 1924; s. William F. and Alberta (Sigelen) W.; m. Mary Camilla Williams, Aug. 20, 1955; children: Maria Fisher, Sylvia Camilla. BS, George Washington U., 1945, MS, 1948; PhD, Cath. U. Am., 1952. Postdoctoral fellow (U. Md.), College Park, 1951-53; chemist Applied Physics Lab. Johns Hopkins U., Silver Spring, Md., 1953-56; physicist Naval Rsch. Lab., Washington, 1956-66, 67-69, head semiconductors br., 1958-66, 67-69; prof. physics U. Calif., Irvine, 1966-67, 69—; prof. emeritus, 1993—; chmn. dept. physics U. Calif., Irvine, 1972-75, 80-83; cons. Gen. Motors, Naval Rsch. Lab.; vis. prof. U. Paris, 1975-76, 79, 85. Author: (with Maradudin and Dobrzynski) Handbook of Surfaces and Interfaces, 1980, (with Balkanski) Many-Body Aspects of Solid State Spectroscopy, 1986; editor: Lattice Dynamics, 1965, Localized Excitations in Solids, 1968 (with Stegeman) Electromagnetic Surface Excitations, 1986, (with Birman and Sebenne) Elementary Excitations in Solids, 1992; contbr. articles to profl. jours. Served with U.S. Army, 1945-46. Recipient Pure Sci. award Naval Rsch. Lab., 1964, Disting. Alumni Achievement award George Washington U., 1991. Fellow Am. Phys. Soc., AAAS; mem. Philos. Soc. Washington, Phi Beta Kappa, Sigma Xi. Home: 2635 Alta Vista Dr Newport Beach CA 92660-4102 Office: U Calif Dept Physics Irvine CA 92717

WALLIS, RICHARD JAMES, lawyer; b. Hagerstown, Md., June 24, 1954; s. O. Lee and Teresa Marie (Rigley) W.; m. Leslie Wallis; children: Rory Evan, Rebecca Erin, Ryan Christopher. BA magna cum laude, Duquesne U., 1976; JD magna cum laude, U. Pitts., 1979. Bar: Wash. 1979, U.S. Dist. Ct. (we. dist.) Wash. 1979, U.S. Ct. Appeals (9th cir.) 1982, U.S. Supreme Ct. 1985. Assoc. Bogle & Gates, P.L.L.C., Seattle, 1979-86, mem., 1987—; CEO Bogle & Gates, P.L.L.C., 1993—. Author: (with others) Antitrust Counselling and Litigation Techniques, 1984; editor Washington Antitrust Law Developments, 1985 and Washington Antitrust Law Developments, 2d edit. 1988. Mem. ABA (antitrust sect. coun. 1995—, chair pvt. lit. com. 1992-95), Fed. Bar Assn. of Western Dist. Wash. (pres. 1990-91), Wash. State Bar Assn. (chmn. antitrust sect. 1989-90, chmn. disciplinary bd. mem. 1996-97), Rotary. Democrat. Roman Catholic. Clubs: Sahalee Golf and Country, Columbia Tower (Seattle), Washington Athletic. Avocations: hiking, climbing, fly fishing, golf. Office: Bogle & Gates Two Union Sq 601 Union St Seattle WA 98101-2327

WALLIS, ROBERT RAY, psychologist, entrepreneur; b. Hardwood, Okla., Sept. 1, 1927; s. Walter William and Osie Oma (Luckett) W.; m. Joan Elaine Martino, Sept. 10, 1955; children: Rosalie, Glenn, Damon, Gina, Darren. Student, Southwestern Inst. Tech., 1945; B.A., U. Okla., 1951, Ed.M., 1960, Ph.D., 1963. Lic. psychologist, Pa., N.J. From psychology intern to dir. div. psychology Greater Kansas City Mental Health Found., 1962-71; from fellow to chief psychologist Western Mo. Mental Health Center, Kansas City, 1965-71; from program dir. to exec. dir. Horizon House Inc., Phila., 1971-79; chief exec. officer Ancora Psychiat. Hosp., Hammonton, N.J., 1979-81; individual practice clin. and cons. psychology, Medford, N.J., 1981—; propr. Wallis Printing Ctr., Phila., 1984-91; clin. supr. Alcoholism and Psychotherapy Assocs., Medford, N.J., 1985—, Middlesex Counseling Assocs., Cranbury, N.J., 1985-89; from asst. prof. to chmn. div. psychology dept. psychiatry, U. Mo., Kansas City Sch. Medicine, 1965-71. Contbr. articles to profl. jours. Served with USNR, 1945-46. Mem. Am. Psychol. Assn. Home and Office: 32 Schoolhouse Dr Medford NJ 08055-9209 *Treat each person with respect and dignity, without regard to rank or power.*

WALLIS, W(ILSON) ALLEN, economist, educator, statistician; b. Phila., Nov. 5, 1912; s. Wilson Dallam and Grace Steele (Allen) W.; m. Anne Armstrong, Oct. 5, 1935 (dec. Oct. 1994); children: Nancy Wallis Ingling, Virginia Wallis Cates. AB, U. Minn., 1932, postgrad., 1932-33; postgrad. fellow, U. Chgo., 1933-35, Columbia U., 1935-36; DSc, Hobart and William Smith Colls., 1973; LLD, Roberts Wesleyan Coll., 1973, U. Rochester, 1984; LHD, Grove City Coll., 1975; D of Social Scis., Francisco Marroquin U., Guatemala, 1992. Economist Nat. Resources Com., 1935-37; instr. econs. Yale U., 1937-38; asst. to assoc. prof. econs. Stanford U., 1938-46; Carnegie rsch. assoc. Nat. Bur. Econ. Rsch., 1939-40, 41; dir. war rsch. Statis. Rsch. Group Columbia U., 1942-46; prof. stats. and econs. U. Chgo., 1946-62, chmn. dept. stats., 1949-57, dean Grad. Sch. Bus., 1956-62; pres. (title later chancellor) U. Rochester, N.Y., 1962-82; under sec. for econ. affairs U.S. Dept. State, Washington, 1982-89; resident scholar Am. Enterprise Inst., Washington, 1989—; staff Ford Found., 1953-54; fellow Ctr. for Advanced Study in Behavioral Scis., 1956-57. mem. math. div. NRC, 1958-60; bd. dir. Nat. Bur. Econ. Rsch., 1953-74; spl. asst. Pres. Eisenhower, 1959-61; pres. Nat. Commn. Study of Nursing and Nursing Edn., 1967-70; chmn. Commn. Presdl. Scholars, 1969-78; mem. Pres.'s Commn. on All-Vol. Armed Force, 1969-70; chmn. Pres.'s Commn. Fed. Stats., 1970-71; mem. Nat. Coun. Ednl. Rsch., 1973-75; chmn. Adv. Coun. Social Security, 1974-75; bd. dirs. Corp. Pub. Broadcasting, 1975-78, chmn., 1977-78. Author: (with others) Consumer Expenditures in the United States, 1939, A Significance Test for Time Series and Other Ordered Observations, 1941, Sequential Analysis of Statistical Data: Applications, 1945, Techniques of Statistical Analysis, 1947, Sampling Inspection, 1948, Acceptance Sampling, 1950, Statistics: A New Approach, 1956, The Nature of Statistics, 1962, Welfare Programs: An Economic Appraisal, 1968; An Overgoverned Society, 1976; co-compiler: The Ethics of Competition and Other Essays by Frank H. Knight, 1935; chmn. editorial adv. bd.: Internat. Ency. Social Scis., 1960-68; contbr. articles to profl. jours. Trustee Tax Found., 1961-82, chmn. bd., 1972-75, chmn. exec. com., 1975-78; bd. overseers Hoover Instn. War, Revolution and Peace, 1972-78; trustee Eisenhower Coll., 1969-79, Nat. Opinion Rsch. Ctr., 1957-62, 64-68, Com. Econ. Devel., 1965-71, Colgate Rochester Div. Sch., 1963-82, Ctr. Govtl. Rsch., Inc., 1962-82, Internat. Mus. Photography at George Eastman House, 1963-82, Robert A. Taft Inst. Govt., 1973-77, Ethics and Pub. Policy Ctr., 1980-82, 89—; mem. Com. on the Present Danger, 1980-82, 1989-92; chmn. bd. overseers Ctr. Naval Analyses, 1967-82. Recipient Sec.'s Disting. Svc. award Dept. of State, Washington, 1988. Fellow Am. Soc. Quality Control, Inst. Math. Stats., Am. Statis. Assn. (editor Jour. 1950-59, pres. 1965, Wilks medal 1980), Am. Acad. Arts and Scis.; mem. Am. Econ. Assn. (exec. com. 1962-64), Rochester C. of C. (trustee 1963-68, 70-75), Mont Pelerin Soc. (treas. 1949-54), Washington Inst. Fgn. Affairs, Cosmos Club (Washington), Bohemian Club (San Francisco), Phi Beta Kappa, Chi Phi, Beta Gamma Sigma. Office: Am Enterprise Inst 1150 17th St NW Washington DC 20036-4603

WALLISON, FRIEDA K., lawyer; b. N.Y.C., Jan. 15, 1943; d. Ruvin H. and Edith (Landes) Koslow; m. Peter J. Wallison, Nov. 24, 1966; children: Ethan S., Jeremy L., Rebecca K. AB, Smith Coll., 1963; LLB, Harvard U., 1966. Bar: N.Y. 1967, DC 1982. Assoc. Carter, Ledyard & Milburn, N.Y.C.,

1966-75; spl. counsel, div. market regulation Securities & Exchange Commn., Washington, 1975; exec. dir., gen. counsel Mcpl. Securities Rulemaking Bd., Washington, 1975-78; ptnr. Rogers & Wells, N.Y.C. and Washington, 1978-83; ptnr. Jones, Day, Reavis & Pogue, N.Y.C., and Washington, 1983—; mem. Govtl. Acctg. Standards Adv. Council, Washington, 1984-90, Nat. Council on Pub. Works Improvement, Washington, 1985-88; vice chair environ. fin. adv. bd. EPA, 1988-92. Fellow Am. Bar Found.; mem. Nat. Assn. Bond Lawyers, N.Y.C. Bar Assn. Contbr. articles to profl. jours. Office: Jones Day Reavis & Pogue 1450 G St NW Ste 600 Washington DC 20005-2001

WALLMAN, CHARLES JAMES, historian; b. Kiel, Wis., Feb. 19, 1924; s. Charles A. and Mary Ann (Loftus) W.; m. Charline Marie Moore, June 14, 1952; children: Stephen, Jeffrey, Susan, Patricia, Andrew. Student Marquette U., 1942-43, Tex. Coll. Mines, 1943-44; BBA, U. Wis., 1949. Sales promotion mgr. Brandt, Inc., Watertown, Wis., 1949-65, v.p., 1960-70, exec. v.p., 1970-80, v.p. corp. devel., 1980-83, past dir.; written formal paper to the inst. "The 48ers of Watertown", presented orally at Symposium U. Wis.-Madison (Inst. for German-Am. Studies), 1986, written formal paper "Business, Industry and the German Press in Early Watertown, Wis., 1853-65", presented orally at symposium U. Wis.-Madison Inst. for German-Am. Studies, 1987; guest spkr. dept. German, U. Wis.-Madison, 1987; former dir., former sec. The Friends of the Max Kade Inst. for German Am. Studies U. Wis.-Madison. Author: Edward J. Brandt, Inventor, 1984, Pioneer Memoirs of Early Watertown, 1986, The Joe Davies Scholars, 1988, The German-Speaking Forty-Eighters: Builders of Watertown, Wisconsin, 1990, Built on Irish Faith, 150 Years at St. Bernard's, 1994, (with others) The Prisoners of War of the 12th Armored Division, 1988. Former mem. exec. bd. Potawatomi coun. Boy Scouts Am., also former v.p. coun.; former bd. dirs., former pres. Earl and Eugenia Quirk Found., Inc. Trustee, mem. Joe Davies Scholarship Found.; former bd. dirs., former exec. com. mem. Watertown Meml. Hosp., dir. emeritus. Served with armored inf. AUS, 1943-45; ETO. Decorated Bronze Star; recipient Local History Award of Merit, State Hist. Soc. Wis., 1994. Mem. Am. Legion (life), E. Central Golf Assn. (past pres.), Mid-States Golf Assn. (past pres.), Wis. Alumni Assn. (local pres. 1950-52, 89-91, bd. dirs. nat. orgn. 1989-91), 12th Armored Div. Assn. (life), Watertown Hist. Soc. (life, past bd. dirs.), Am. Ex-Prisoners of War, Inc. (life), Phi Delta Theta (mem. Golden Legion). Republican. Roman Catholic. Club: Watertown County (past dir.). Lodges: Rotary (past pres., former bd. dirs., Paul Harris fellow), Elks (life, past officer). Home: 604 Votech Dr Watertown WI 53098-1124

WALLMAN, GEORGE, hospital and food services administrator; b. N.Y.C., Apr. 10, 1917; s. Joseph and Celia (Kascawal) W.; m. Benita B. Kaufman, June 11, 1941. Student public schs., N.Y.C. Dir. food and banquet services Normandy Hotel, Hollywood, Calif., 1945-47; dir. food services Med. Center, N.Y.C., 1947-64; menucologist and cons. to hosps., 1964-67; dir. food services Montefiore Hosp., Pitts., 1967—; cons. public schs., homes and hosps. for aged, 1947—, cons. new food products various cos., 1967—; mem. Cancer Rehab. Project, U. Pitts., 1973—; lectr. on food to various profl. orgns., 1947—. Lectr.: program Exercise is Not Enough, Sta. NBC-TV, 1976; narrator, CBS Evening News; show Hosp. Gourmet, 1974; Contbg. editor, feature writer: Today's Chef, 1978—. Mem. Nat. Restaurant Assn., Am. Hosp. Assn., Am. Fedn. Musicians. Home: 1420 Centre Ave Pittsburgh PA 15219-3517 Office: Montefiore Hosp Fifth Ave Pittsburgh PA 15213 *My goals are to continue to maintain the ultimate in high level quality food service enhanced with the very best of culinary skill. Ten years ago I wrote an article in a national food trade magazine titled 'The Great Captive Audience in White'. I stated that hospitals should serve a beautiful orchestrated food tray to romanticize the pleasure of fine food, rather than the usual adequate meal that is merely nutritionally sufficient. It would mean so much to the patients. Let each dinner be serendipity, each dinner a dining event not just eating.*

WALLMAN, STEVEN MARK HARTE, lawyer; b. N.Y.C., Nov. 14, 1953; s. Eugene and Doris (Lee) W.; m. Kathleen M. Harte, May 5, 1985. BS, MIT, 1975, MS, 1976; postgrad., Harvard U., 1976-77; JD, Columbia U., 1978. Bar: D.C. 1978, Va. 1986. Assoc. Covington & Burling, Washington, 1978-86, ptnr., 1986-94; commr. SEC, Washington, 1994—. Home: 9332 Ramey Ln Great Falls VA 22066-2025 Office: SEC 450 5th St NW Washington DC 20001-2739

WALLMANN, JEFFREY MINER, author; b. Seattle, Dec. 5, 1941; s. George Rudolph and Elizabeth (Biggs) W.; BS, Portland State U., 1962; PhD, U. Nev., 1997. Pvt. investigator Dale Systems, N.Y.C., 1962-63; asst. buyer, mgr. pub. money bidder Dohrmann Co., San Francisco, 1964-66; mfrs. rep. electronics industry, San Francisco, 1966-69; dir. pub. rels. London Films, Cinelux-Universal and Trans-European Publs., 1970-75; editor-in-chief Riviera Life mag., 1975-77; cons. Mktg. Svcs. Internat., 1978—; instr. U. Nev., Reno, 1990—; books include: The Spiral Web, 1969, Judas Cross, 1974, Clean Sweep, 1976, Jamaica, 1977, Deathtrek, 1980, Blood and Passion, 1980; Brand of the Damned, 1981; The Manipulator, 1982; Return to Conta Lupe, 1983; The Celluloid Kid, 1984; Business Basic for Bunglers, 1984, Guide to Applications Basic, 1984; (under pseudonym Leon DaSilva) Green Hell, 1976, Breakout in Angola, 1977; (pseudonym Nick Carter) Hour of the Wolf, 1973, Ice Trap Terror, 1974; (pseudonym Margaret Maitland) The Trial, 1974, Come Slowly, Eden, 1974, How Deep My Cup, 1975; (pseudonym Amanda Hart Douglass) First Rapture, 1972, Jamacia!, 1978; (pseudonym Grant Roberts) The Reluctant Couple, 1969, Wayward Wives, 1970; (pseudonym Gregory St. Germain) Resistance #1: Night and Fog, 1982, Resistance #2: Maygar Massacre, 1983; (pseudonym Wesley Ellis) Lonestar on the Treachery Trail, 1982, numerous others in the Lonestar series; (pseudonym Tabor Evans) Longarm and the Lonestar Showdown, 1986; (psyeudonym Jon Sharpe) Trailsman 58: Slaughter Express, 1986, numerous others in Trailsman series; also many other pseudonyms and titles; contbr. articles and short stories to Argosy, Ellery Queen's Mystery Mag., Alfred Hitchcock's Mystery Mag., Mike Shayne's Mystery Mag., Zane Grey Western, Venture, Oui, TV Guide; also (under pseudonym William Jeffrey in collaboration with Bill Pronzini) Dual at Gold Buttes, 1980, Border Fever, 1982, Day of the Moon, 1983. Mem. Mystery Writers of Am., Sci. Fiction Writers Am., Western Writers Am., Nat. Coun. Tchrs. English, Crime Writers Assn., Nev. State Coun. Tchrs. English, Esperanto League N.Am., Western Literature Assn., Internacia Societo De Amikeco Kaj Bonvolo, Science Fiction Rsch. Assn., Internat. Assn. of the Fantastic in the Arts, Nat. Assn. Sci. Tech. & Sci., Soc. Internat. d'Amitié et Bonne Volonté, Nat. Coun. Tchrs. English, Western Lit. Assn. Office: Jabberwocky Lit Agy 41-16 47th Ave Ste 2D Sunnyside NY 11104-3040

WALLOT, JEAN-PIERRE, archivist, historian; b. Valleyfield, Que., Can., May 22, 1935; s. Albert and Adrienne (Thibodeau) W.; m. Denyse Caron; children: Normand, Robert, Sylvie. B.A., Coll. Valleyfield, 1954; lic. es lettres, U. Montreal, 1957, M.A. in History, 1957, Ph.D. in History, 1965; D (hon.), U. Rennes, France, 1987, U. Ottawa, Can., 1996. Reporter Le Progres de Valleyfield, 1954-61; lectr. U. Montreal, 1961-65, asst. prof., 1965-66, prof. dept. history, 1973-85, chmn. dept., 1973-75, vice dean studies faculty arts and scis., 1975-78, vice dean research Faculty Arts and Scis, 1979-82, academic v.p., 1982-85; nat. archivist, Can., 1985—; historian Nat. Mus. Man, Ottawa, Ont., 1966-69, assoc. prof. U. Toronto, 1969-71; prof. Concordia U., Montreal, Que., 1971-73; dir. Etude Associé Ecole Pratique des Hautes Etudes en Sciences Sociales, Paris, 1975, 79, 81, 83, 85, 87, 89, 94. Author: Intrigues françaises et americaines au Canada, 1965, (with John Hare) Les Imprimés dans le Bas-Canada, 1967, Confrontations, 1971, (with G. Paquet) Patronage et Pouvoir dans le Bas-Canada, 1973, Un Quebec qui bougeait, 1973; Editor: (with R. Girard) Memoires de J.E. McComber, bourgeois de Montreal, 1981; (with J. Goy) Evolution et eclatement du monde rural, 1986. Pres. internat. adv. com. on memory of the world, UNESCO, 1993-97. Decorated officer Order Arts et Lettres (France), 1987; officer Order of Can., 1991; recipient Marie Tremaine medal, 1973, Tyrrell medal, 1982, Royal Soc. Centenary medal, 1994. Fellow Royal Soc. Can. (sect. pres. 1985-87, pres. elect 1997); mem. Am. Antiquarian Soc., Acad. des Lettres du Quebec, Inst. d'Histoire l'Amerique Francaise (pres. 1973-77), Can. Hist. Assn. (pres. 1982), Assn. Can.-Francaise l'Avancement Scis. (pres. 1981-83, emeritus mem.), Assn. Archivists Que., Assn. Can. Archivists, Internat. Coun. on Archives (v.p. 1988-92, pres. 1992-96, pres. emeritus). Roman Catholic. Office: Nat Archives, 395 Wellington St, Ottawa, ON Canada K1A 0N3

WALLRAFF, BARBARA JEAN, magazine editor, writer; b. Tucson, Mar. 1, 1953; d. Charles Frederick and Evelyn Pauline (Bartels) W.; m. Julian Hart Fisher, Apr. 25, 1992. BA in Polit. Sci. and Philosophy, Antioch Coll., 1972. Sect. editor Boston Phoenix, 1979-83; assoc. editor The Atlantic Monthly, Boston, 1983-89, sr. editor, 1989—; freelance writer, 1978—. Columnist Word Court, 1995—. Office: Atlantic Monthly 77 N Washington St Boston MA 02114-1908

WALLS, CARL EDWARD, JR., communications company official; b. Magnolia, Ark., Sept. 9, 1948; s. Carl E. and Melba Rene (Garrard) W.; m. Doris Duhart, Aug. 1, 1970; children: Carl Edward, Forrest Allen. Student San Antonio Coll., 1966-68. Div. mgr. Sears Roebuck & Co., San Antonio, 1967-73, area sales mgr., 1973-78; service cons. Southwestern Bell, 1978-79, account exec., 1979-82; account exec., industry cons. AT&T Info. Systems, 1983-88, account mgr., 1988-89; gen. mgr. Tex. State Govt., 1989—. Mem. citizens advisory com. Tex. Senate, 1975-81; legis. aide Tex. Ho. of Reps., 1981-85; commr. Alamo Area council Boy Scouts Am., 1970-79, Capitol Area council, 1980—, nat. jamboree staff, 1973, 77, 81, 85, 89, 93; mem. Republican Nat. Com., 1980—, Rep. Presdl. Task Force, 1980—, Rep. Senatorial Club, 1981—. Recipient Patriotic Service award U.S. Treasury Dept., 1975-76; Scouters Key and Commrs. award Boy Scout Am., Dist. Merit award Boy Scouts Am., 1978. Mem. Scouting Collectors Assn. (pres. South Central region 1979-80, v.p. region 1980-81, sec. 1983-86), U. Ark. Alumni Assn. (life), Am. Legion. Baptist. Home: 11712 D K Ranch Rd Austin TX 78759-3770 Office: 1624 Headway Cir Austin TX 78754-5109

WALLS, CARMAGE, newspaper publishing executive; b. Crisp County, Ga., Oct. 28, 1908; s. Benjamin Gaff and Anna (Byrd) W.; m. Odessa Dobbs (div.); children: Carmage Lee, Ronald Eugene (dec.), Mark Thomas (dec.), Dinah Jean Garcich; m. Martha Ann Williams, Jan. 2, 1954; children: Byrd Cooper, Lissa Walls Vahldiek. Ed. pub. schs., Fla. Bus. mgr. Orlando (Fla.) Newspaper, Inc., 1934-40; pub. Macon (Ga.) Telegraph News, 1940-47; pres. Gen. Newspapers, Inc., Gadsden, Ala., 1945-59, So. Newspapers, Inc., Montgomery, Ala., 1951-69; also dir.; pub. Montgomery (Ala.) Advt.-Jour., 1963-69; chmn. bd., dir. Galveston Newspapers, Inc., Tex.; owner Walls Investment Co., Houston.; bd. dirs. Tex. City Newspapers, Inc. Pres. Macon Area Devel. Commn., 1943-44, Macon C. of C., 1945; trustee Birmingham-So. Coll., 1971-7. Mem. So. Newspaper Pubs. Assn., Soc. Profl. Journalists, The Houstonian. Episcopalian. Home: 623 Shartle Cir Houston TX 77024-5521 Office: 1050 Wilcrest Dr Houston TX 77042-1608

WALLS, CARMAGE LEE, JR., newspaper executive, consultant; b. Cleveland, Tenn., May 4, 1962; s. Carmage Lee Walls Sr. and Sarah (Smith) Bailey; m. Jeanne Marie Waller, June 4, 1989; children: Courtney Marie, Kathryn Jessica. BA in Journalism and English, U. Ala., Birmingham, 1988. Writer Birmingham News, 1987; exec. v.p. Cleveland Newspapers Inc., Birmingham, 1987—; pres. Walls New Media, Inc., 1997—. Republican. Methodist. Avocations: bicycle racing.

WALLS, CHARLES WESLEY, football player; b. Batesville, Miss., Feb. 26, 1966. Student, U. Miss. Tight end San Francisco 49ers, 1989-93, New Orleans Saints, 1994-96, Carolina Panthers, 1996—. Named to Pro Bowl, 1996. Office: care Carolina Panthers 800 S Mint St Charlotte NC 28202-1502*

WALLS, MARTHA ANN WILLIAMS (MRS. B. CARMAGE WALLS), newspaper executive; b. Gadsden, Ala., Apr. 21, 1927; d. Aubrey Joseph and Inez (Cooper) Williams; m. B. Carmage Walls, Jan. 2, 1954; children: Byrd Cooper, Lissa Walls Vahldiek. Student pub. schs., Gadsden. Pres., dir. Walls Newspapers, Inc., 1969-70; sec., treas., dir. Summer Camps, Inc., Guntersville, Ala., 1954-69; CEO, pres., dir. So. Newspapers, Inc., Houston, 1970—; v.p., dir. Scottsboro (Ala.) Newspapers, Angleton (Tex.) Times, Ft. Payne (Ala.) Newspapers, Inc.; v.p., dir. Bay City (Tex.) Newspapers, Inc.; sec., dir. Mil. Pubs., Inc., Portales, N.Mex.; bd. dirs. Liberal (Kans.) Newspapers, Inc., Monroe (Ga.) Newspapers, Inc., Moore Newspapers, Inc., Dumas, Tex., Jefferson Pilot Corp., Greensboro, N.C., Jefferson-Pilot Life Ins. Co., Jefferson Pilot Communications. Bd. dirs. Montgomery Acad., 1970-74. Mem. Soc. Profl. Journalists, The Houstonian. Episcopalian. Office: So Newspapers Inc 1050 Wilcrest Dr Houston TX 77042-1608

WALLS, RON M., emergency medicine physician, educator, health facility administrator; b. Prince George, B.C., Can., Sept. 20, 1954; m. Barbara A. Walls; children: Andrew, Blake, Alexa. BSc, U. B.C., Vancouver, Can., 1975, MD, 1979. Diplomate Am. Bd. Emergency Medicine. Resident Denver Gen. Hosp., 1982-84; asst. prof. emergency medicine George Washington U., 1984-87; assoc. prof. surgery, chmn. emergency medicine Vancouver Gen. Hosp., 1987-93; assoc. prof. medicine Harvard U., Boston, 1993—; chmn. emergency medicine Brigham and Women's Hosp., Boston, 1993—. Assoc. editor: Emergency Medicine: Concepts and Clinical Practice, 1993-97; assoc. editor Jour. Emergency Medicine, 1988-93. Fellow Royal Coll. Physicians Can., Am. Coll. Emergency Physicians, Am. Acad. Emergency Medicine; mem. AMA, Soc. Acad. Emergency Medicine. Office: Brigham and Womens Hosp Emergency Medicine 75 Francis St Boston MA 02115-6110

WALLS, THOMAS FRANCIS, management consultant; b. Phila., June 4, 1947; s. Thomas Francis and Margaret Mary (Whalen) W.; m. Kathleen Cecilia Lyons, Dec. 7, 1968; children: Thomas, James, Eleanor. ABA in Econs., U. Pa., 1974, BBA in Mgmt., 1977. Programmer Gen. Elec. Reentry Sys., King of Prussia, Pa., 1965-69; mgr. Keane Assocs., Paoli, Pa., 1969-73, Alco Std. Corp., Valley Forge, Pa., 1973-80, Comserv Corp., Mendota Heights, Minn., 1980-88; mgr. Andersen Cons., Chgo., 1988-89, Phila., 1989-95; dir. SAP tng. Andersen Cons., St. Charles, Ill., 1995-97; corp. resource JGI, Inc., Exton, Pa., 1997—. Contbg. author: APICS Dictionary. With USNR, 1967-68, Vietnam. Mem. Am. Prodn. and Inventory Control Soc. (cert. practitioner inventory mgmt.). Roman Catholic. Avocations: family, rowing, soccer, reading. Office: JGI Inc 825 Springdale Dr Exton PA 19341-2843

WALLS, WILLIAM HAMILTON, judge; b. Atlantic City, Nov. 28, 1932; s. Clifford Hamilton and Nannette Verneice (Anderson) W.; married, Aug. 6, 1960 (div. 1985); children: Claire Alexia, Peter Graves. AB, Dartmouth Coll., 1954; LLB, Yale U., 1957. Bar: N.J. 1959, U.S. Ct. Appeals (3d cir.) 1966. Asst. corp. counsel City of Newark, 1966-68; judge Mcpl. Ct., City of Newark, 1968-70; corp. counsel City of Newark, 1970-73, bus. adminstr., 1974-77; judge County of Essex, Newark, 1977-79, N.J. Superior Ct., Newark, 1979—. Mem. Yale Law Alumni N.J. (Achievement award 1978), Phi Beta Kappa. Avocations: photography, hiking, travel. Office: NJ Superior Ct PO Box 999 50 Walnut St Rm 4046 Newark NJ 07101-0999*

WALLS, WILLIAM WALTON, JR., management consultant; b. Phila., Oct. 3, 1932; s. William Walton and Mary Crown (Elliott) W.; m. Nina Catherine deAngeli, July 1, 1961; 1 child, Deborah. BSME, Swarthmore Coll., 1959. With Boeing Helicopters, Phila., 1959-96, v.p. light helicopter joint venture, 1988-91, v.p. devel. programs, 1991-92, v.p. rsch. and engring., 1992-96; small high-tech. bus. cons. Ridley Park, Pa., 1996—; cons. in field. Chmn. aerospace adv. coun. Pa. State Coll., 1974-79; mem. NATO Indsl. Advisors Group, 1988-93; mem. bd. advisors Rotocraft Ctr. Excellence, Rensselaer Polytech. Inst., 1982-84. Mem. Am. Helicopter Soc. (pres. 1988-89, chmn. 1989-90). Republican. Avocations: skiing, jogging, personal computer applications. Home: 502 Harrison St Ridley Park PA 19078-3208

WALLWORK, WILLIAM WILSON, III, automobile executive; b. Fargo, N.D., Mar. 8, 1961; s. William Wilson Jr.; m. Shannon Wallwork, July 12, 1991. AA in Automotive Mktg., Northwood Inst., 1981; student, San Diego State U., Moorhead State U. Lease rep. Wallwork Lease and Rental, 1984-86; sales mgr. W.W. Wallwork, Inc., Fargo, N.D., 1986-87, v.p., 1987-91, pres., 1991—; v.p. Valley Imports Inc, Fargo, N.D., 1986-91; pres. Valley Imports Inc., Fargo, N.D., 1991—; vice chmn. Kenworth 20 Group, 1992-93, chmn., 1994-96; mem. PACCAR Chmn.'s Meeting, 1993; mem. Rockwell Internat. Dealer Adv. Bd., 1995—. Mem. Fargo-Moorhead Automobile Dealers Assn. (v.p. 1986-88, pres. 1988-90). Avocation: skiing. Office: W W Wallwork Inc 4001 Main Ave Fargo ND 58103-1145

WALMAN, JEROME, psychotherapist, publisher, consultant, critic; b. Charleston, W.Va., June 19, 1937; s. Joe and Madeline Minnie (Levy) W.; m. Mary Joan Granara, Sept. 5, 1960. Student, U. W.Va.; student, Boston U., Berkley Sch. Music, Boston. Producer, composer, writer mus. compositions Carnegie Hall, Broadway Theatre, 1962, 63; pvt. practice psychotherapy in spl. hypnosis and music therapy, 1964—; designer Jerome Walman Systems Applied Hypnosis, 1969; travel-restaurant-wine-entertainment critic Sta. WNCN-FM Radio; critic travel, food, wine Sta. WNCN-FM Radio, Fodor's N.Y. restaurant sect.; marriage and family counselor; lectr. dir. tng. programs in memory improvement and speed reading; cons. personal image, wine and food Dept. Def., NYU; cons., dir. Cooking for Relaxation and Wieght Control; restaurant publicist; condr. courses in wine appreciation and food; restaurant, wine and food critic Sta. WCNC-GAF Radio; host travel, restaurant and wine show Sta. WEVD Radio. Dir., producer syndicated TV show Enterprises Unltd., 1978—; producer, composer I Murdered Mary, N.Y.C., 1976, Last Call, N.Y.C., 1977, TV Mag., 1978; lectr. East-West Ctr., N.Y.C., 1978, Actors Tng. and Acting Therapy Ctr. Am., Westwinds Learning Ctr., The Learning Exchange, 1986; editor Punch In Internat. Electronic Travel, Wine and Restaurant mag.; pub. Wine On Line mag., The Computer User's Survival Newsletter and Syndicated Column; originator facimile news svc. Fax It To Me; author papers on hypnosis, psychic phenomena and memory, music therapy, biofeedback and meditation application; featured in various publs. including Fortune, Gentleman's Quar., Cosmopolitan, Leaders mag., Mademoiselle; editor Punch in Internat. Wine, Restaurant and Travel Electronic mag.; syndicated columnist travel and wine Cab Mag.; reviewer Wine-on-Line Internat. Wire Svc., The Computer User's Survival Newsletter; contbg. writer Chocolatier Mag., Troika Mag.; contbr. The Official Airline Guides Electronic Edition, Fodor's N.Y. Sunday in N.Y. and Pocket N.Y. Travel Guide. Mem. Music Therapy Internat., Meditation and Mental Devel. Ctr. N.Y., Memory Improvement and Concentration Ctr. Am., Delphi-Gen. Videotex Svc.-Nynex Info-Logic, Internat. Foods, Wine & Travel Writers Assn. Office: Punch In Syndicate 400 E 59th St Apt 9F New York NY 10022-2344

WALMER, EDWIN FITCH, lawyer; b. Chgo., Mar. 24, 1930; s. Hillard Wentz and Anna C. (Fitch) W.; m. Florence Poling, June 17, 1952; children: Linda Diane Walmer Dennis, Fred Fitch. BS with distinction, Ind. U., 1952, JD with high distinction, 1957. Bar: Wis. 1957, U.S. Dist. Ct. (ea. dist.) Wis. 1957. Assoc. Foley & Lardner, Milw., 1957-65, ptnr., 1965-90, ret., 1990. Served to 1st lt. U.S. Army, 1952-54. Recipient Cal. C. Chambers award Culver (Ind.) Mil. Acad., 1948. Fellow Am. Coll. Trust and Estate Counsel; mem. Order of Coif, Dairymen's Country Club (Boulder Junction, Wis.), Vineyards Country Club (Naples, Fla.), Phi Eta Sigma, Beta Gamma Sigma. Republican. Congregationalist. Avocations: golf, fishing. Office: Foley & Lardner 777 E Wisconsin Ave Milwaukee WI 53202-5302

WALNER, ROBERT JOEL, lawyer; b. Chgo., Dec. 22, 1946; s. Wallace and Elsie W.; m. Charlene Walner; children: Marci, Lisa. BA, U. Ill., 1968; JD, De Paul U., 1972; M in Mgmt. with distinction, Northwestern U., 1991. Bar: Ill. 1972, U.S. Dist. Ct. (no. dist.) Ill. 1972, U.S. Ct. Appeals (7th cir.) 1972, Fla. 1973. Atty. SEC, Chgo., 1972-73; pvt. practice Chgo., 1973—; adminstrv. law judge Ill. Commerce Commn., Chgo., 1973-76; atty. Allied Van Lines, Inc., Broadview, Ill., 1976-79; sr. v.p., gen. counsel, sec. The Balcor Co., Skokie, Ill., 1979-92; prin. fin. ops. Balcor Securities divsn. The Balcor Co., Skokie, 1984-92, pres., 1989-92; of counsel Lawrence, Walner & Assocs., Ltd., Chgo., 1992-93; sr. v.p., gen. counsel, sec. Grubb & Ellis Co., San Francisco, 1994—; mem. securities adv. com. to Ill. Sec. of State, 1984-94; mem. editl. bd. Real Estate Securities Jour., Real Estate Securities and Capital Markets; program chmn. Regulators and You seminar. Contbr. chpts. to books, articles on real estate and securities law to profl. jours.; assoc. editor De Paul U. Law Rev. Mem. Kellogg Career Devel. Com., 1992-94, Kellogg Bus. Adv. Com., 1992—; mem. enterprise forum MIT, 1992—, mem. exec. com., 1993-94. With USAR, 1968-73. Mem. ABA, Ill. Bar Assn., Chgo. Bar Assn., Am. Real Estate Com. (pres. com. 1985-90), Real Estate Syndication Com. (chmn. 1982-85), Ill. Inst. Continuing Legal Edn., N.Am. Securities Adminstrs. Assn. Inc. (industry adv. com. to real estate com., 1987-89), Real Estate Securities and Syndication Inst. of Nat. Assn. Realtors (chmn. regulatory and legis. com., 1984, 87, specialist, real estate investment, group v.p., 1987, exec. com. 1987-90), Nat. Real Estate Investment Forum (chmn. 1985, 88), Real Estate Investment Assn. (founder, exec. com. 1990-92), Kellogg Alumni Club (bd. dirs., event chmn. 1996—), Beta Gamma Sigma.

WALPIN, GERALD, lawyer; b. N.Y.C., Sept. 1, 1931; s. Michael and Mary (Gordon) W.; m. Sheila Kainer, Apr. 13, 1957; children: Amanda Eve, Edward Andrew, Jennifer Hope. BA, CCNY, 1952; LLB cum laude, Yale Law Sch., 1955. Bar: N.Y. 1955, U.S. Supreme Ct. 1965, U.S. Ct. Appeals (2d cir.) 1960, (6th cir.) 1969, (3d cir.) 1976, (8th cir.) 1982, (9th cir.) 1983, (llth cir.) 1983, (7th cir.) 1984, U.S. Ct. Claims 1984. Law clk. to Hon. Justice E.J. Dimock U.S. Dist. Ct. (so. dist.) N.Y., N.Y.C.; law clk. to hon. F.P. Bryan U.S. Dist. Judge (so. dist.) N.Y., N.Y.C., 1955-57; asst. U.S. atty., chief spl. prosecutions U.S. Atty. Office, N.Y.C., 1960-65; sr. ptnr. Rosenman & Colin and predecessor firm, N.Y.C., 1965—, chmn. litigation dept., 1985—; mem. adv. com. Fed. Ct. So. Dist. N.Y., 1991—; co-chmn. Lawyers div. Anti-Defamation League, N.Y., 1994—. Editor Yale Law Jour., 1953-54, mng. editor, 1954-55; contbr. articles to profl. jours. Pres., trustee Parker Jewish Geriatric Inst., New Hyde Park, N.Y., 1979-87, chmn., trustee, 1987—; bd. dirs. Fund for Modern Cts., N.Y.C., 1985-91; mem. law com. Am. Jewish Com., 1980—; mem. Com. for Free World, N.Y.C., 1983-91; trustee, mem. exec. com. United Jewish Appeal-Fedn. Jewish Philanthropies, N.Y.C., 1984—; mem. Nassau County Crime Commn., 1970; pres. Kensington Civic Orgn., Gt. Neck, N.Y., 1972-73. Recipient Quality of Life award United Jewish Appeal Fedn., 1978, Human Rels. award Am. Jewish Com., 1982, Gift of Life award Jewish Inst. Geriatric Care, 1987, Learned Hand award Am. Jewish Com., 1990. Mem. ABA, Assn. Bar City N.Y., Fed. Bar Coun. (chmn. modern cts. com. 1989, v.p. 1991-95, chmn. bench and bar liaison com. 1994-95, vice chmn. 1995—), Federalist Soc. (chmn. litigation sect. 1996—), Univ. Club, Yale Club. Republican. Jewish. Home: 875 Park Ave New York NY 10021-0341 Office: Rosenman & Colin 575 Madison Ave New York NY 10022-2511 *My life should be an appropriate response to God and this country for providing me with the opportunities I have had: Contribution to our society and strengthening of our country's steadfast opposition to discrimination for or against anyone based on race, religion or sex.*

WALPOLE, ROBERT, heavy manufacturing executive. BA, Principia Coll., 1962; MBA, Washington U., 1964. Distbn. sales office, planning and distbn. mgr. Ford Motor Co., Atlanta, 1964-70; officer Walbro Corp., Cass City, Mich., 1970—; now v.p. Walbro Corp., Cass City; pres. Walbro Asia Pacific, 1991—. Office: Walbro Corp 6242 Garfield Ave Cass City MI 48726-1342

WALRATH, HARRY RIENZI, minister; b. Alameda, Calif., Mar. 7, 1926; s. Frank Rienzi and Cathren (Michlar) W.; AA, City Coll. San Francisco, 1950; BA, U. Calif. at Berkeley, 1952; MDiv, Ch. Div. Sch. of Pacific, 1959; m. Dorothy M. Baxter, June 24, 1961; 1 son, Gregory Rienzi. Dist. exec. San Mateo area council Boy Scouts Am., 1952-55; ordained deacon Episcopal Ch., 1959, priest, 1960; curate All Souls Parish, Berkeley, Calif., 1959-61; vicar St. Luke's, Atascadero, Calif., 1961-63, St. Andrew's, Garberville, Calif., 1963-64; asso. rector St. Luke's Ch., Los Gatos, 1964-65, Holy Spirit Parish, Missoula, Mont., 1965-67; vicar St. Peter's Ch., also headmaster St. Peter's Schs., Litchfield Park, Ariz., 1967-69; chaplain U. Mont., 1965-67; asst. rector Trinity Parish, Reno, 1969-72; coordinator counciling svcs. Washoe County Council Alcoholism, Reno, 1972-74; adminstr. Cons. Assistance Svcs., Inc., Reno, 1974-76; pastoral counselor, contract chaplain Nev. Mental Health Inst., 1976-78; contract mental health chaplain VA Hosp., Reno, 1976-78; mental health chaplain VA Med. Ctr., 1978-83, staff chaplain, 1983-85, chief, chaplain service, 1985-91, also triage coord. for mental health, ret., 1991; per diem chaplain Washoe Med. Ctr., Reno, 1993; assoc. priest Trinity Episcopal Ch., Reno, 1995; assoc. Mountain Ministries, Susanville, Calif., 1995—; dir. youth Paso Robles Presbytery; chmn. Diocesan Commn. on Alcoholism; cons. teen-age problems Berkeley Presbytery; mem. clergy team Episcopal Marriage Encounter, 1979-85, also Episc. Engaged Encounter. Author: God Rides the Rails-Chapel Cars on American Railroads at the Turn of the Century, 1994. Mem. at large Washoe dist. Nev. area council Boy Scouts Am., scoutmaster troop 73, 1976, troop 585, 1979-82, asst. scoutmaster troop 35, 1982-92, assoc. adviser area 3

Western region, 1987-89, regional com. Western Region, 1989-90; lodge adviser Tannu Lodge 346, Order of Arrow, 1982-87; docent coun. Nev. Hist. Soc., 1992; South Humboldt County chmn. Am. Cancer Soc. Trustee Community Youth Ctr., Reno. Served with USNR, 1944-46. Decorated Pacific Theater medal with star, Am. Theater medal, Victory medal, Fleet Unit Commendation medal; recipient dist. award of merit Boy Scouts Am., St. George award Episc. Ch.-Boy Scouts Am., Silver Beaver award Boy Scouts Am., 1986, Founders' award Order of the Arrow, Boy Scouts Am., 1985; performance awards VA-VA Med. Ctr., 1983, 84; named Arrowman of Yr., Order of Arrow, Boy Scouts Am. Cert. substance abuse counselor, Nev. Mem. Ch. Hist. Soc., U. Calif. Alumni Assn., Nat. Model R.R. Assn. (life), Sierra Club Calif., Missoula Council Chs. (pres.), Alpha Phi Omega. Democrat. Club: Rotary. Home: 4822 Ramcreek Trail Reno NV 89509-8029 *The study of history has taught me one thing: that human nature has not changed, only the means of its execution. This same study has also taught me that human nature reveals the glory of God in our quest for our future.*

WALRATH, PATRICIA A., state legislator; b. Brainerd, Minn., Aug. 11, 1941; d. Joseph James and Pansy Patricia (Drake) McCarvill; m. Robert Eugene Walrath, Sept. 1, 1961; children: Karen, Susan, David, Julie. BS, Bemidji State U., 1962; MS, SUNY, Oswego, 1975. Cert. secondary math. tchr., N.Y., Mass. Programmer analyst Control Data Corp., Mpls., 1962-65; crewleader dept. commerce U.S. Census, Middlesex County, Mass., 1979-80; selectman Town of Stow, Mass., 1980-85; tchr. math. Hale Jr. High Sch., Stow, 1981-82; instr. math. Johnson & Wale Coll. Hanscom AFB, Bedford, Mass., 1983-84; test examiner Hanscom AFB, Bedford, 1983-84; state rep. 3d Middlesex dist. State of Mass., Boston, 1985—; mem. House Ways and Means com., 1987-92, 96, joint coms. on local affairs, 1993-95, pub. svc., 1993-96, election law, 1985-86, 95-96, sci. and tech. com., 1995-96, commerce and labor, 1996, govt. rels., 1996; chair house com. long term debt and capital spending, 1997—. Chmn. Mass. Indoor Air Pollution Commn., Boston, 1987-88; mem. Stow Dem. Com., 1988—; merit badge counselor Boy Scouts Am., Stow and Hudson, Mass., 1990—; bd. dirs. Hudson Arts Alliance, 1991—. Recipient Disting. Svc. award Auburn N.Y. Jaycees, 1976. Mem. LWV (pres. 1973-76, dir. fin. 1977-78), Am. Legis. Exch. Coun., Mass. Legislators' Assn., Mass. Dem. Leadership Coun. (v.p. 1991-92, co-chmn. 1993-94, treas. 1995—), Mass. Women's Legis. Caucus (chair 1986). Roman Catholic. Avocations: gardening, stamp collecting, travel. Home: 20 Middlemost Way Stow MA 01775-1363 Office: State Capital RM4665 Boston MA 02133

WALRAVEN, JOSEPH WILLIAM (BILL WALRAVEN), writer, publisher; b. Dallas, July 1, 1925; s. Orange Daniel Sr. and Valerie (Garrison) W.; m. Marjorie Kathryn Yeager, May 28, 1950; children: Valerie Ruth, Wilson Frederick, Joseph William Jr. BA, Tex. A&I U., 1950; postgrad. sch. profl. writing, U. Okla., 1950-51. Copy editor San Antonio Light, 1951-52; reporter Corpus Christi (Tex.) Caller-Times, 1952-68, daily columnist, 1968-89; pub. Sandcrab Press, Corpus Christi, 1983—, Javelina Press, Corpus Christi, 1989—; freelance writer Corpus Christi, 1989—. Author, pub.; Real Texans Don't Drink Scotch in Their Dr Pepper, 1983; author: Corpus Christi, History of a Texas Seaport, 1983, Walraven's World or Star Boarder (and other) Wars, 1985, El Rincon, A History of Corpus Christi Beach, 1990, (with Marjorie Kathryn Walraven) The Magnificent Barbarians, Little-Told Tales of The Texas Revolution, 1993, All I Know Is What's On TV, 1995, Gift of the Wind: The Corpus Christi Bayfront, 1997. V.p. South Tex. Hist. Soc., 1978; active Tex. State Hist. Assn. With USN, 1943-45, PTO. Recipient 1st pl. gen. interest column Harte-Hanks Newspapers, 1979, 2nd prize, 1987; recipient 2nd pl. news story Tex. AP, 1954, 1st pl. features, 1958; recipient 2nd prize series Animal Def. League Tex., 1987; award recipient Corpus Christi Police Officers Assn., 1967, ARC, 1970, Tex. Hist. Commn. and Tex. Hist. Found., 1980, 81, Corpus Christi Landmark Commn., 1987, Nueces County Hist. Commn., 1989; named Civic Salesman of Yr., Sales and Mktg. Execs. Corpus Christi, 1984. Mem. Nat. Soc. Newspaper Columnists, Corpus Christi Press Club (v.p. 1964, pres. 1965, many awards). Democrat. Methodist. Avocations: reading, travel, flounder fishing. Home: 4609 Wilma Dr Corpus Christi TX 78412-2357 Office: Sandcrab Press PO Box 1479 Corpus Christi TX 78403-1479

WALROD, DAVID JAMES, retail grocery chain executive; b. Toledo, Dec. 9, 1946; s. Maynard Elmer and Isabella (Soldwish) W.; m. Judith Kay Stevens, Aug. 17, 1968; children—David, Bryant, Marc. Student, Michael Owens Coll.; student in food distbn. mgmt. mktg., Toledo U., 1968. With Seaway Food Town, Inc., Maumee, Ohio, 1963—, grocery merchandiser, 1971-74, v.p. supermarket ops., 1974-77, corp. v.p. ops., 1977-80, sr. v.p. ops., 1980-88, exec. v.p., chief oper. officer, 1988—; bd. dirs. Ohio Grocers Assn. Bd. dirs. Toledo Mud Hens, Riverside Hosp., St. Francis Desales H.S., Toledo, Corp. for Effective Govt., Junior Achievement, Toledo City Parks Commn., Labor Mgmt. Coun., Bishop's Edn. Coun. Cath. Diocese of Toledo; trustee Maumee C. of C. Mem. Brandywine Country Club. Office: Seaway Food Town Inc 1020 Ford St Maumee OH 43537-1820

WALSER, MACKENZIE, physician, educator; b. N.Y.C., Sept. 19, 1924; s. Kenneth Eastwood and Jean (Mackenzie) W.; m. Elizabeth C. Gearon, Sept. 17, 1988; children from previous marriage: Karen D., Jennifer McK., Cameron M., Eric H. Grad., Phillips Exeter Acad., 1941; A.B., Yale, 1944; M.D., Columbia, 1948. Diplomate: Am. Bd. Internal Medicine. Intern Mass. Gen. Hosp., Boston, 1948-49; asst. resident in medicine Mass. Gen. Hosp., 1949-50; resident Parkland Hosp., Dallas, 1950-52; staff mem. Johns Hopkins Hosp., Balt., 1957—; instr. U. Tex. at Dallas, 1950-51, asst. prof., 1951-52; investigator Nat. Heart Inst., Bethesda, Md., 1954-57; asst. prof. pharmacology Johns Hopkins Med. Sch., 1957-61, assoc. prof., 1961-70, prof., 1970—, asst. prof. medicine, 1957-64, assoc. prof., 1964-74, prof., 1974—; Med. dir. USPHS, 1970—, pharmacology study sect., 1968-72. Co-author: Mineral Metabolism, 1969, Handbook of Physiology, 1973, The Kidney, 1976, 5th edit., 1996, also articles; co-editor: Branched-Chain Amino and Ketoacids, 1981, Nutritional Management, 1984. Served with USNR, 1942-45; to lt. M.C. USNR, 1952-54. Recipient Research Career Devel. award USPHS, 1959-69. Mem. AAAS, AAUP (pres. Johns Hopkins 1970), Am. Soc. Clin. Investigation, Assn. Am. Physicians, Am. Fedn. Clin. Rsch., Am. Physiol. Soc., Biophys. Soc., Am. Soc. Pharmacology and Exptl. Therapeutics (Exptl. Therapeutics award 1975), Am. Soc. Nephrology, Am. Inst. Nutrition, Am. Soc. Clin. Nutrition (Hermann award 1988), Internat. Soc. Nutrition and Metabolism in Renal Disease (Addis award 1994), Century Assn. Club. Home: 7513 Club Rd Baltimore MD 21204-6418 Office: Johns Hopkins U Sch Medicine Baltimore MD 21205

WALSH, ANNMARIE HAUCK, research firm executive; b. N.Y.C., May 5, 1938; d. James Smith and Ann-Marie (Kennedy) Hauck; m. John F. Walsh, Jr., Aug. 20, 1960; children: Peter Hauck, John David. BA, Barnard Coll., 1961; MA, Columbia U., 1969, PhD, 1971. Sr. staff mem. Inst. Pub. Adminstrn., N.Y.C., 1961-72, pres., 1982-89, trustee, Gulick scholar, 1989—, dir. programs in Ctrl. Europe and NIS, 1991—; dir. Ctr. for Urban and Policy Studies, CUNY Grad. Ctr., N.Y.C., 1972-79, Govs.' Task Force on Regional Planning, N.Y., Conn., N.J., 1979-81; disting. vis. prof. Bklyn. Coll., 1991-93; cons. pub. enterprise, civil svc., urban and regional mgmt., tng., pub. fin. adminstrn. reform UN, China, Indonesia, Bangladesh, Czech Republic and Slovakia, Poland, Macedonia, Uzbekistan, Kazakstan, state and local govts., U.S. Postal Svc., U.S. Dept. Transp., senate com. govt. ops. Author: Urban Government for Zagreb, Yugoslavia, 1968, Urban Government for Lagos, Nigeria, 1968, Urban Government for the Paris Region, 1968, The Urban Challenge to Government: An International Comparisons of Thirteen Cities, 1969, The Public's Business: Politics and Practices of Government Corporations, 1978, 2d edit., 1980, Designing and Managing the Procurement Process, 1989, Privatization-Implications for Public Management, 1996; editor: Agenda for a City, 1970. Project dir. 20th Century Fund, Pub. Enterprise, 1972-76, pub.-pvt. partnerships, 1989-93; bd. dirs. Ralph Bunche Inst., UN, 1978-82, Regional Plan Assn., 1987-91. Herbert Lehmann fellow, 1966-69. Fellow, Nat. Acad. Pub. Adminstrn. (bd. dirs. 1996—); mem. Phi Beta Kappa. Office: Inst Pub Admistrn 55 W 44th St New York NY 10036-6609

WALSH, ARTHUR CAMPBELL, psychiatrist; b. Vancouver, B.C., Can., Dec. 21, 1919; came to U.S., 1964; s. William Charles and Kathleen (Patterson) W.; m. Bernice Martha Hessom, Dec. 26, 1944; children: Kathleen, David, Thomas. MD, U. Alta., Edmonton, 1943. Intern Vancouver Gen. Hosp., B.C., 1943; pvt. practice Vancouver, B.C., 1945-64; resident psychiatry U. Pitts., 1964-67, clin. asst. prof. psychiatry, 1967-89; pvt. practice Pitts., 1968—; pres. Ctr. Senility Studies Alzheimer Treatment Rsch. Ctr., Pitts., 1969—; psychiat. cons. VA, Pitts., 1969-89, Woodville State Hosp., Pitts., 1969-86. Author: Conquering Senility; co-author: Mental Capacity: Medical Legal Aspects of Assessment and Treatment, 1975, 2d edit., 1994; contbr. med. articles to profl. jours. With Royal Can. Army Med. Corps, 1943-45. Mem. AMA, Am. Psychiat. Assn., Pa. Med. Soc. Home: 307 S Dithridge St Apt 202 Pittsburgh PA 15213-3514 Office: Alzheimer Treatment Rsch Ctr Ctr Senility Studies 161 N Dithridge St Pittsburgh PA 15213-2646

WALSH, CHARLES RICHARD, banker; b. Bklyn., Jan. 30, 1939; s. Charles John and Anna Ellen Walsh; m. Marie Anne Goulden, June 24, 1961; children: Kevin C., Brian R., Gregory M. BS, Fordham U., 1960; MBA, St. John's U., 1966, D of Comml. Scis. (hon.), 1985. V.p. Mfrs. Hanover Trust Co., Hicksville, N.Y., 1974-80, sr. v.p., 1980-86, exec. v.p., 1986-90, group exec., mem. mgmt. com., 1990-92; exec. v.p., group exec. Chem. Banking Corp., Hicksville, N.Y., 1992-95, The Chase Manhattan Corp., 1995—; bd. dirs. Mastercard Internat.; bd. dirs., former chmn. Eastern States Monetary Svcs., Lake Success, N.Y., 1978-88; former pres., CEO, bd. dirs. The Bankcard Assn., Hicksville, 1988-91. Sustaining mem. Rep. Nat. Com., 1978—; vice chmn. adv. bd. St. John's U., 1982—. With USAR, 1960, 61-62. Mem. N.Y. State Bankers Assn. (former bd. dirs., mem. gov. coun., chmn. consumer banking divsn.), Am. Bankers Assn. (mem. govt. rels. coun., chmn. bank card divsn., mem. exec. com., former mem. comms. coun. and chmn. edn. com.), Am. Mgmt. Assn., N.Y. Credit and Fin. Mgmt. Assn., Soc. Cert. Consumer Credit Execs. (cert.), Beta Gamma Sigma, Omicron Delta Epsilon, North Hempstead Country Club, Gov.'s Club Kiawah Island (S.C.). Republican. Home: 9 Blueberry Ln Oyster Bay NY 11771-3901 also: 121 Turnberry Dr Johns Island SC 29455-5726 Office: 100 Duffy Ave Hicksville NY 11801-3639

WALSH, DANIEL FRANCIS, bishop; b. San Francisco, Oct. 2, 1937. Grad., St. Joseph Sem., St. Patrick Sem., Catholic U. Am. Ordained priest, Roman Catholic Ch., 1963. Ordained titular bishop of Tigia, 1981; aux. bishop of San Francisco, 1981-87, bishop of Reno-Las Vegas, 1987—. Home: 2809 Cameo Cir Las Vegas NV 89107-3213 Office: Diocese of Reno-Las Vegas Office of Bishop PO Box 18316 Las Vegas NV 89114-8316*

WALSH, DAVID GRAVES, lawyer; b. Madison, Wis., Jan. 7, 1943; s. John J. and Audrey B. Walsh; married; children: Michael, Katherine, Molly, John. BBA, U. Wis., 1965; JD, Harvard U., 1970. Bar: Wis. Law clk. Wis. Supreme Ct., Madison, 1970-71; ptnr. Walsh, Walsh, Sweeney & Whitney, Madison, 1971-86; ptnr.-in-charge Foley & Lardner, Madison, 1986—; bd. dirs. Nat. Guardian Life, Madison, 1981—; lectr. U. Wis., Madison, 1974-75, 77-78. Chmn. State of Wis. Elections Bd., Madison, 1978. Lt. USN, 1965-67, Vietnam. Maple Bluff Country Club (Madison) (pres. 1987). Roman Catholic. Avocations: tennis, golf, fishing. Home: 41 Fuller Dr Madison WI 53704-5962 Office: Foley & Lardner 150 E Gilman PO Box 1497 Madison WI 53701-1497

WALSH, DENNY JAY, reporter; b. Omaha, Nov. 23, 1935; s. Gerald Jerome and Muriel (Morton) W.; m. Peggy Marie Moore, Feb. 12, 1966; children by previous marriage—Catherine Camille, Colleen Cecile; 1 son, Sean Joseph. B.J., U. Mo., 1962. Staff writer St. Louis Globe-Democrat, 1961-68; asst. editor Life mag., N.Y.C., 1968-70; assoc. editor Life mag., 1970-73; reporter N.Y. Times, 1973-74, Sacramento Bee, 1974—. Served with USMC, 1954-58. Recipient Con Lee Kelliher award St. Louis chpt. Sigma Delta Chi, 1962; award Am. Polit. Sci. Assn., 1963; award Sigma Delta Chi, 1968; Pulitzer prize spl. local reporting, 1969; 1st prize San Francisco Press Club, 1977. Office: Sacramento Bee 21st and Q Sts Sacramento CA 95813

WALSH, DIANA CHAPMAN, academic administrator, social and behavioral sciences educator; b. Phila., July 30, 1944; d. Robert Francis and Gwen (Jenkins) Chapman; m. Christopher Thomas Walsh, June 18, 1966; 1 child, Allison Chapman Walsh. BA, Wellesley Coll., 1966; MS, Boston U. Sch. of Pub. Comm., 1971; PhD, Boston U., 1983; LHD (hon.), Boston U, 1994, Amer. Coll. of Greece, Athens, 1995. Mgr. spl. events Barnard Coll., N.Y.C., 1967-70; dir. info., edn. Planned Parenthood League, Newton, Mass., 1971-74; sr. program assoc. Dept Pub. Health, Boston, 1974-76; assoc. dir. Boston U. Health Policy Inst., 1985-90; prof. Sch. Pub. Health, Sch. Medicine, Boston U., 1987-90, prof., 1988-90, adj. prof. pub. health, 1990—; adj. prof. Harvard Sch. Pub. Health, 1993—; pres. Wellesley Coll., 1993—. Author: (book) Corporate Physicians, 1987; editor: Women, Work, and Health: Challenges to Corporate Policy, 1980, (book series) Industry and Health Care, 1977-80; contbr. articles to profl. jours. Bd. dirs. Planned Parenthood League of Mass., 1974-79, 1981-85, bd. of overseers 1993-94; trustee Occupational Physicians Scholarship Fund, 1987-94; trustee WGBH Educational Found., 1993—. Kellogg Nat. fellow, 1987-90. Mem. AAAS. Intersts include: gender and health, leadership studies, social policy, the craft of writing, skiing. Office: Wellesley Coll Office of the Pres 106 Central St Wellesley MA 02181-8203*

WALSH, DIANE, pianist; b. Washington, Aug. 16, 1950; d. William Donald and Estelle Louise (Stokes) W.; m. Henry Forbes, 1969 (div. 1979); m. Richard Pollak, 1982. MusB, Juilliard Sch. Music, 1971, MusM, Mannes Coll., 1982. N.Y.C. debut Young Concert Artists Series, 1974; founding mem. Mannes Trio, 1983-94; solo appearances include: Kennedy Ctr. for Performing Arts, Washington, 1976, Met. Mus., N.Y.C., 1976, Wigmore Hall, London, 1980, Merkin Concert Hall, 1989, Miller Theatre, 1994, 96; with Mannes Trio: Lincoln Ctr.'s Alice Tully Hall, Library of Congress, 1987; appeared with maj. orchs. worldwide, including St. Louis Symphony, Indpls. Symphony, San Francisco Symphony, Bavarian Radio Symphony of Munich, Berlin Radio Symphony, Radio Symphony Frankfurt, Radio Symphony Stuttgart; has toured Europe, N.Am., S.Am., C.Am., former Soviet Union, Marlboro Festival, 1982, Bard Festival, 1990-97, Chopin Festival, Marianske Lazne, Czech Republic ; recs. for Nonesuch Records, 1980, 82, Book-of-Month Records, 1985, Music and Arts, 1990, CRI, 1991, Koch, 1995, Biddulph Records, 1997; mem. piano and chamber music faculty Mannes Coll. Music, 1982-96; vis. assoc. prof. Hunter Coll., CCNY, 1991-92, Vassar Coll., 1992-93. Recipient 3d prize Busoni Internat. Piano Competition, Italy, 1974, 2nd prize Mozart Internat. Piano Competition, Salzburg, Austria, 1975, 1st prize Munich Internat. Piano Competition, 1975, Naumburg Chamber Music award, 1986; NEA grantee, 1981.

WALSH, DON, marine consultant, executive; b. Berkeley, Calif., Nov. 2, 1931; s. J. Don and Marguerite Grace (Van Auker) W.; m. Joan A. Betzmer, Aug. 18, 1962; children—Kelly Drennan, Elizabeth McDonough. BS, U.S. Naval Acad., 1954; MS, Tex. A&M U., 1967, PhD, 1968; MA, San Diego State U., 1968. Commd. ensign USN, 1954, advanced through grades to capt., 1974; officer-in-charge Bathyscaph Trieste USN, Trieste, 1959-62; comdr. in USS Bashaw USN, 1968-69; dir. Inst. Marine and Coastal Studies, prof. ocean engring. U. So. Calif., Los Angeles, 1975-83; pres., chief exec. officer Internat. Maritime, Inc., Los Angeles, 1976—; mng. dir. Deep Ocean Engring., Inc., 1990—, also bd. dirs.; dir. Ctr. for Marine Transp. Studies, U. So. Calif., 1980-83, Coastal Resources Ctr., 1990-94; trustee USN Mus. Found., 1989—; mem. Nat. Adv. Com. on Oceans and Atmosphere, 1979-85; bd. govs. Calif. Maritime Acad., 1985-95; pres. Parker Diving, 1989-94. Editor, contbr.: Law of the Sea: Issues in Ocean Resource Management, 1977, Energy and Resources Development of Continental Margins, 1980, Energy and Sea Power: Challenge for the Decade, 1981, Waste Disposal in the Oceans: Minimizing Impact, Maximizing Benefits, 1983; editor Jour. Marine Tech. Soc., 1975-80; mem. editorial bd. U.S. Naval Inst., 1974-75. Decorated Legion of Merit (2), Meritorious Service medal (2); Woodrow Wilson Internat. Ctr. for Scholars fellow, 1973-74. Fellow Marine Tech. Soc., Acad. Underwater Arts and Scis., Explorers Club (hon. life, bd. dirs. 1994—), Royal Geog. Soc. (Eng.); mem. AAAS, Soc. Naval Archs. and Marine Engrs., Am. Soc. Naval Engrs., Navy League, Navy Inst., Adventurers Club (hon. life). Office: Internat Maritime Inc HC-86 Box 101 Myrtle Point OR 97458-9726

WALSH, DONNIE, sports club executive; married; 5 children. Grad., U. N.C.; attended, N.C. Law Sch. Bar: 1977. Assoc. head coach U. N.C.; staff coach Denver Nuggets, head coach, 1979-81; asst. coach Ind. Pacers, 1984-86, exec. v.p., gen. mgr., 1986-92, pres., 1992—. Office: Ind Pacers Market Sq Arena 300 E Market St Indianapolis IN 46204-2603*

WALSH, EDWARD JOSEPH, toiletries and food company executive; b. Mt. Vernon, N.Y., Mar. 18, 1932; s. Edward Aloysius and Charlotte Cecilia (Borup) W.; m. Patricia Ann Farrell, Sept. 16, 1961; children: Edward Joseph, Megan Simpson, John, Robert. BBA, Iona Coll., 1953; MBA, NYU, 1958. Sales rep. M & R Dietetic Labs., Columbus, Ohio, 1955-60; with Armour & Co., 1961-71, Greyhound Corp., 1971-87; v.p. toiletries div. Armour Dial Co., Phoenix, 1973-74; exec. v.p. Armour Dial Co., 1975-77; pres. Armour Internat. Co., Phoenix, 1978-84; pres. The Dial Corp. (formerly Armour-Dial Co.), Phoenix, 1984-87, chief exec. officer, 1984-87; pres., chief exec. officer Purex Corp., 1985; chmn., chief exec. officer The Sparta Group Ltd., Scottsdale, Ariz., 1988—; bd. dirs. Guest Supply Inc., New Brunswick, N.J., WD-40 Co., San Diego, Nortrust Ariz. Holding Corp., Phoenix, No. Trust Bank of Ariz., N.A., Exec. Svcs. Corps. of Ariz., Inc. Bd. trustees Scottsdale Meml. Health Found.; pres. Mt. Vernon Fire Dept. Mems. Assn., 1960-61. Served with U.S. Army, 1953-55, Germany. Mem. Am. Mgmt. Assn., Nat. Meat Canner Assn. (pres. 1971-72), Cosmetic, Toiletries and Fragrance Assn. (bd. dirs. 1985—), Nat. Food Processors Assn. (bd. dirs.). Republican. Roman Catholic. Office: The Sparta Group Ltd 6623 N Scottsdale Rd Scottsdale AZ 85250-4421

WALSH, EDWARD PATRICK, federal agency administrator; b. N.Y.C., Nov. 21, 1937; s. Edward P. and Marion B. (Burnich) W.; m. Kathleen F. Ringrose, Nov. 25, 1967; children: Megan, Brendan. BS in Econs., Villanova U., 1959. Patrol inspector U.S. Border Patrol Immigration and Naturalization Svc., Harlingen, Tex., 1962-65; spl. agt. U.S. Secret Svc., 1965-86; dep. asst. dir. U.S. Secret Svc., Washington, 1986; dir. Bur. Investigations FMC, Washington, 1986, mng. dir., 1986—. Trustee, assoc. Villanova U., 1990—. With U.S. Army, 1959-61, Korea. Recipient Presdl. Rank award, 1989. Mem. Internat. Assn. Chiefs of Police, Assn. Former Secret Svc. Agts., Fed. Exec. Inst. Alumni Assn., Sr. Exec. Assn.

WALSH, FRANCIS RICHARD, law educator; b. Newark, Jan. 1, 1924; s. Loretta Anne (Norton) W.; m. Ethel Anne Walsh, Mar. 12, 1944; 1 child, Jeffrey R. BSBA, Seton Hall U., 1943; JD, Georgetown U., 1948. Prof. Law Sch. Georgetown U., Washington, 1949-51; law clk. to presiding justice U.S. Ct. Appeals (9th cir.), San Francisco, 1948-49; chief broadcast bur. FCC, Washington, 1970-71; pvt. practice San Francisco, 1954-70; prof. law U. San Francisco, 1951-54, 71-74, dean, prof. law, 1957-70; prof. law Hastings Coll. of Law, U. Calif., San Francisco, 1974—. Lt. USNR, 1934-46, PTO. Avocations: golf, travel. Home: 28 Spring Rd San Rafael CA 94904-2625 Office: Hastings Coll Law 200 Mcallister St San Francisco CA 94102-4707

WALSH, GARY L., consumer products company executive; b. 1942. Sr. mgmt. Sara Lee Corp. and Sysco Foods, 1966-77; CEO Miller Cascade Foodsvc. of Am., 1977-1990; chmn., pres., CEO Core-Mark Internat., Inc., South San Francisco, 1990—. Office: Core-Mark International Inc 395 Oyster Point Blvd Ste 415 South San Francisco CA 94080-1932 also: Core Mark Interrlated Cos 311 Reed Cir Corona CA 91719-1349*

WALSH, GEORGE WILLIAM, publishing company executive, editor; b. N.Y.C., Jan. 16, 1931; s. William Francis and Madeline (Maass) W.; m. Joan Mary Dunn, May 20, 1961; children—Grail, Simon. B.S., Fordham U., 1952; M.S., Columbia U. Sch. Journalism, 1953. Copy editor, reporter Cape Cod Standard-Times, Hyannis, Mass., 1955; communications specialist IBM, N.Y.C., 1955-58; editorial trainee Time, Inc., 1958-59; writer-reporter Sports Illus., N.Y.C., 1959-62; book editor Cosmopolitan, N.Y.C., 1962-65; mng. editor Cosmopolitan, 1965-74; editor-in-chief, v.p. Ballantine Books div. Random House, N.Y.C., 1974-79, Macmillan Pub. Co., N.Y.C., 1979-85; pub. cons., 1985—. Author: Gentleman Jimmy Walker, 1974, Public Enemies, 1980. Served with AUS, 1953-55. Mem. Assn. Am. Pubs. Roman Catholic. Clubs: Univ. (N.Y.C.); Pamet Harbor Yacht and Tennis (Truro, Mass.). Home: 35 Prospect Park W Brooklyn NY 11215-2370

WALSH, GEORGE WILLIAM, engineering executive; b. Teton County, Idaho, Mar. 22, 1923; s. Raymond Eugene and Maude Ethel (Brack) W.; m. Catherine Mary Yunker, July 1, 1950; children: Dwight, Maureen, John. BSEE, U. Idaho, 1947; MEE, Rensselaer Poly. Inst., 1960. Registered profl. engr., N.Y. With GE, 1947-94; test engr. GE, Cleve. and Schenectady, N.Y., 1947-49; design engr. GE, Pittsfield, Mass., 1949-50; power system engr. GE, Schenectady, 1950-66, mgr. power system engring., 1966-85, mgr. power system cons. engring., 1985-93, cons., 1993-94; profl. cons. engr., 1994—. Contbr. numerous papers and articles relating to electric power system engring. to profl. publs. Recipient GE Power Systems Engring. awards for Outstanding Tech. Contbn., 1986, and Outstanding Profl. and Social Svcs., 1991. Fellow IEEE (life, Centennial medal 1984, Richard Harold Kaufmann field award for outstanding contbn. to indsl. engring. 1993); mem. IEEE Industry Applications Soc. (pres., mem. exec. bd., adminstrv. and tech. coms., Power Systems Achievement award 1980, Outstanding Achievement award 1990), IEEE Power Engring. Soc., Sigma Xi, Sigma Tau. Home and Office: 26 St Stephens Ln E Schenectady NY 12302-4221

WALSH, GERALDINE FRANCES, nursing administrator; b. Phila., July 3, 1946; d. Raymond S. and Marie Ruth (Lipsett) Lore; m. Harry G. Walsh, Jan. 29, 1966; children: Michael, Gregory. AA, No. Va. Community Coll., 1979; BS, St. Joseph's Coll., Windham, Maine, 1987, postgrad. Cert. in nursing adminstrn.; cert. instr. basic life support; cert. dir. nursing adminstrn. long term care. Charge nurse, asst. head nurse Parkview Hosp., Phila., 1968-73; staff nurse JFK Med. Ctr., Edison, 1973-76; clin. nursing supr., charge nurse med.-surg. Loudoun Hosp. Ctr., Leesburg, Va., 1976-88; asst. dir. nursing Loudoun Long Term Care Ctr., Leesburg, 1988-95; dir. nursing Cameron Glen Care Ctr., Reston, Va., 1995—. Recipient Nursing Achievement award. Fellow Nat. Assn. Dirs. Nursing; mem. ANA, NAFE, Nat. League Nursing, Va. League Nursing, Va. Nurses Assn., Am. Coll. Healthcare Execs. (student assoc. mem.), Nat. Assn. for Healthcare Quality, Assn. Healthcare Adminstrs. of Nat. Capitol Area. Address: 20380 Harmony Ct Ashburn VA 22011-3300

WALSH, GREGORY SHEEHAN, optical systems professional; b. Buffalo, Dec. 24, 1955; s. John Kevin and Ruth (Murphy) W.; m. Patricia DelGiudice, Apr. 8, 1976; children: James, Kevin, Patrick. BBA, U. North Fla., 1989; cert. in submarine periscope design, Dept. of Navy, 1992. Optical systems specialist Naval Aviation Depot, Jacksonville, Fla., 1984-91, Trident Refit Facility, Kings Bay, Ga., 1991—; tech. adv. Naval Tech. Tng., Pensacola, Fla., 1992; bd. dirs. Strategic Bus. Plan Naval Aviation Depot, Jacksonville, 1989; cons. Small Bus. Adminstrn., Jacksonville, 1989. Coach Orange Park (Fla.) Soccer Assn., 1989—; com. mem. Olympic devel. Fla. Youth Soccer Assn. With USN, 1974-78. Achievements include performed the first retrofit to the trident submarine periscope system at an IMA; design of submarine periscope stadimeter sling, submarine optical periscope bushing, submarine optical periscope torque sleeve, submarine optical quick evacuation plug puller, aircraft optical hot mock-up; performed the first article acceptance test on the FA-18 aircraft optical systems. Home: 450 Sigsbee Ct Orange Park FL 32073-3409

WALSH, JAMES ANTHONY (TONY WALSH), theater and film educator; b. Bklyn., Aug. 21, 1947; s. Henry Michael and Clara (Nappi) W. BA in Theater, Hofstra U., 1968; MA in Theater, Adelphi U., 1976. Tchr., dir. theater N.C. Sch. of Arts, Winston-Salem, 1976-81; artistic dir. Cross and Sword/State Play of Fla., St. Augustine, 1982-91; dean Fla. Sch. of Arts, Palatka, 1982-91; dir. Inst. of Entertainment Technologies Valencia C.C., Orlando, Fla., 1992-93, dir. Ctr. Profl. Devel., 1993—; producing dir. TV and video prodn. Valencia Coll., Orlando, 1996—; freelance theater dir., acting coach, N.Y.C., 1973-76; cons. Network of Performing and Visual Arts Schs., Washington, 1980—, Inst. Outdoor Drama, Chapel Hill, N.C., 1989—, Univ. Film and Video Assn., Sarasota, Fla., 1992, Internat. Film Workshops, Rockport, Maine, 1992, Dir. Guild Am. Educators Workshop, L.A., 1993, Dir.'s Workshop, 1996, Acad. TV Arts and Scis. Educators Seminar, L.A., 1995. Writer PBS documentary World of Family, NCCJ, 1995; exptl. theater playwright; lyricist (off-Broadway mus.) Sugar Hill, 1990. bd. dirs. Enzian Film Theatre. NEH grantee, 1978; recipient playwriting fellowships Atlantic Ctr. for Arts, 1983, Fla. Divsn. Cultural

Affairs, 1983; named Winner Fla. Playwrite Competition, 1994, Winner Best Video, Fla. Assn. C.C., 1996. Mem. Assn. Theater in Higher Edn., Fla. Motion Picture and TV Assn. (bd. dirs., v.p.), Ctrl. Fla. Film Commn. (bd. dirs.), Fla. Inst. for Film Edn. (bd. dirs.) Actors Equity Assn., Dramatists Guild N.Y.C., Players Club (N.Y.C.). Home: 100 Detmar Dr Winter Park FL 32789-3901 Office: Valencia CC PO Box 3028 Orlando FL 32802-3028

WALSH, JAMES JEROME, philosophy educator; b. Seattle, May 23, 1924; s. John Jerome and Agnes (Counihan) W.; m. Carol Jean Paton, Sept. 16, 1946; children—John Jerome II, James Paton. B.A., Reed Coll., 1949, Oxford (Eng.) U., 1951; M.A., Oxford (Eng.) U., 1956; Ph.D., Columbia U., 1960. Mem. faculty Columbia U., 1954-90, prof. philosophy, 1966-90, prof. emeritus, 1990—, dir. grad. studies philosophy dept., 1963-66, 73-88, chmn. dept., 1967-73, acting chmn. dept., 1982-83; vis. instr. U. Calif.-Berkeley, 1958; cons. TV series G.E. Coll. Bowl, 1965-70. Author: Aristotle's Conception of Moral Weakness, 1963, Philosophy in the Middle Ages, 1967, 2d edit., 1983; Editor Jour. Philosophy, 1965-90. Mem. Rockland County Democratic Com., 1960-63. Served with AUS, 1943-45. Decorated Purple Heart.; Rhodes scholar, 1949; Ford Found. fellow, 1958; Am. Coun. Learned Socs. fellow, 1962; Guggenheim fellow, 1966. Mem. Soc. Medieval and Renaissance Philosophy. Home: 300 Haverstraw Rd Suffern NY 10901-3137

WALSH, JAMES THOMAS, congressman; b. Syracuse, N.Y., June 19, 1947. BA, St. Bonaventure U., 1970. Agrl. extension agt. Peace Corps, 1970-72; mktg. exec. telecommunications co., 1974-88; exec.-in-residence telecommunications inst. Coll. Tech. SUNY, Utica, Rome, N.Y., 1986-87; common councilor City of Syracuse, 1977-85, pres. common coun., 1986-88; mem. 101st-present Congresses from 27th (now 25th) N.Y. dist., Washington, D.C., 1989—. Republican. Office: US House of Reps 2351 Rayburn Bldg Washington DC 20515-3225 also: 1340 Federal Bldg Syracuse NY 13261-7306 also: One Lincoln St Auburn NY 13021

WALSH, JAMES WILLIAM, mental health professional; b. Pottsville, Pa., Aug. 15, 1948; s. William John and Anna Mae (Carl) W.; m. Celia Marie Ruggiero, Sept. 14, 1974; children: Tara Marie, Christine Ann, James William, Jr. Student, Wilmington Coll., 1971-72, Pa. State U., 1972-74; BA, Bapt. Christian Coll., 1985; MA, La. Bapt. U., 1991, postgrad., 1995—. With Residential Pilot Program for Developmentally Disabled United Cerebral Palsy, Pottsville, Pa., 1974; with Direct Care with Developmentally Disabled Regional Devel. Corp., Pottsville, 1982-83; vocat. program specialist Habilitation Inc., Pottsville, 1992-96; mental health profl. Kids Peace, Temple, 1996—; mem. steering com. Habilitation, Inc., Pottsville, 1993-94; mem. behavior intervention com., policy & procedure subcom. Schuylkill County, Pottsville, 1995; mem. behavior intervention com. United Cerebral Palsy, Pottsville, 1995; mem. middle Atlantic states accreditation presentation com. Kids Peace, 1996; mem. Mental Health Profl. Family Svc. Agy., Pottsville, 1997. Author: Don't Take Any Wooden Nickels, 1994. With USCG, 1966-70. Democrat. Methodist. Avocations: bicycling, reading, writing. Home: 238 W Bacon St Pottsville PA 17901

WALSH, JOANNE ELIZABETH, art educator, librarian; b. Chgo., Nov. 25, 1942; d. Joseph Frank and Elizabeth Margaret (Gretz) Fiali; m. John Kerwin Walsh, July 17, 1976; 1 child, Kevin Joseph. BA in English, Mundelein Coll., Chgo., 1965; MEd Ednl. Adminstrn. and Supervision, Loyola U., Chgo., 1969. Tchr. Chgo. Pub. Schs., 1965-83, prin., 1983-89; tchr. libr. Burbank (Ill.) Dist III, 1990-93; tchr. art Tate Sch. of Discovery, Knoxville, Tenn., 1994-95. Vol. Palos Community Hosp., Palos Park, Ill., 1990, Palos Heights Libr., 1993; Rainbow facilitator, 1992, 93; mem. St. John Neumann Cath. Ch. Recipient Tchr. of Yr. award McCord Sch., 1992-93. Mem. Chgo. Prins. Club, Aquin Guild, Knoxville Welcome Wagon Club, Knoxville Newcomers Club. Avocations: reading, boating, gardening, crafts, golf. Home: 12301 Butternut Cir Knoxville TN 37922-4682

WALSH, JOHN, museum director; b. Mason City, Wash., Dec. 9, 1937; s. John J. and Eleanor (Wilson) W.; m. Virginia Alys Galston, Feb. 17, 1962; children: Peter Wilson, Anne Galston, Frederick Matthiessen. B.A., Yale U., 1961; postgrad., U. Leyden, Netherlands, 1965-66; MA, Columbia U., 1965, PhD, 1971. Lectr., rsch. asst. Frick Collection, N.Y.C., 1966-68; assoc. higher edn. Met. Mus. Art, N.Y.C., 1968-71; assoc. curator European paintings Met. Mus. Art, 1970-72, curator dept. European paintings, 1972-74, vice-chmn., 1974-75; adj. asso. prof. art history Columbia U., N.Y.C., 1969-72; adj. prof. Columbia U., 1972-75; prof. art history Barnard Coll., Columbia U., N.Y.C., 1975-77; Mrs. Russell W. Baker curator paintings Mus. Fine Arts, Boston, 1977-83; dir. J. Paul Getty Mus., Malibu, Calif., 1983—; vis. prof. fine arts Harvard U., 1979; mem. governing bd. Yale U. Art Gallery, 1975—, Smithsonian Coun., 1990—. Contbr. articles to profl. jours. Mem. Dem. County Com., N.Y.C., 1968-71; mem. vis. com. Fogg Mus., Harvard U., 1982-87; bd. fellows Claremont U. Ctr. and Grad. Sch., 1988—. With USNR, 1957-63. Fulbright grad. fellow The Netherlands, 1965-66. Mem. Coll. Art Assn., Am. Assn. Mus., Archaeol. Inst. Am., Am. Antiquarian Soc., Assn. Art Mus. Dirs. (trustee 1986—, pres. 1989-90), Century Assn. N.Y.C. Office: J Paul Getty Museum PO Box 2112 Santa Monica CA 90407*

WALSH, JOHN BREFFNI, aerospace consultant; b. Bklyn., Aug. 20, 1927; s. George and Margaret Mary (Rigney) W.; m. Marie Louise Leclerc, June 18, 1955; children: George Breffni, John Leclerc, Darina Louise. B.E.E., Manhattan Coll., 1948; M.S., Columbia U., 1950; postgrad., NYU, 1954-62. Asst., instr. Columbia U., N.Y.C., 1948-51, asst. prof., asst. dir. Electronics Research Labs., 1953-66; various positions through tech. dir. Intelligence and Reconnaissance Div., Rome Air Devel. Center, N.Y., 1951-53; dep. for research to asst. sec. Air Force, 1966-71; sr. staff mem. Nat. Security Council, 1971-72, asst. to Pres.'s sci. advisor, 1971-72; dep. dir. Def. Research and Engring., 1972-77; asst. sec. gen. for def. support NATO, 1977-80; holder chair in systems acquisition mgmt., dean exec. inst. Def. Systems Mgmt. Coll., Ft. Belvoir, Va., 1981-82; prof. emeritus Def. Systems Mgmt. Coll., Ft. Belvoir, 1982—; v.p., chief scientist Boeing Mil. Airplane Co., Wichita, Kans., 1982-89; v.p. rsch. and engring. programs Boeing Aerospace and Electronics div., Seattle, 1990-92; v.p. strategic analysis Boeing Defense and Space Group, Seattle, 1992-93; prin. John B. Walsh Assocs., 1993—; mem. aeros. adv. com. NASA; mem. Congl. Adv. Com. on Aeros., 1984-85; assoc. Def. Sci. Bd.; mem. indsl. adv. bd. Wichita State U. Coll. Engring., adj. prof. elec. engring., 1989-90; chmn. tech. working group Def. Trade Adv. Group Dept. State, 1992-95. Author: Electromagnetic Theory and Engineering Applications, 1960, (with K.S. Miller) Introductory Electric Circuits, 1960, Elementary and Advanced Trigonometry, 1977; contbr. tech. papers to publs.; patentee in field. Mem. planning bd., Cresskill, N.J., 1964-66; commr. Kans. Advanced Tech. Commn., 1985-86; bd. dirs. Kans. Inc., 1986-90; mem. math. scis. edn. bd. NRC, 1989-92. Served with U.S. Army, 1946-47. Recipient Air Force Exceptional Civilian Service award, 1969; recipient Dept. Def. Meritorious Civilian Service award, 1971, Disting. Civilian Service award, 1977, Air Force Assn. citation of honor as outstanding Air Force civilian employee of year, 1971, Theodore von Karman award Air Force Assn., 1977. Fellow IEEE (life), AIAA (v.p. tech. 1987-89); mem. N.Y. Acad. Scis., GPS Internat. Assn., Electromagnetics Acad., Sigma Xi, Eta Kappa Nu. Roman Catholic. Office: 8800 Prestwould Pl Mc Lean VA 22102-2231

WALSH, J(OHN) B(RONSON), lawyer; b. Buffalo, Feb. 20, 1927; s. John A. and Alice (Condon) W.; m. Barbara Ashford, May 20, 1966; 1 child, Martha. AB, Canisius Coll., 1950; JD, Georgetown U., 1952. Bar: N.Y. 1953, U.S. Supreme Ct. 1958, U.S. Ct. Internat. Trade 1969, U.S. Ct. Customs and Patent Appeals 1973. Trial atty. Garvey & Conway, N.Y.C., 1953-54; vol. atty. Nativity Mission, N.Y.C., 1953-54; ptnr. Jaeckle, Fleischmann, Kelly, Swart & Augspurger, Buffalo, 1955-60; pvt. practice Buffalo, 1961-75; ptnr. Jaeckle, Fleischmann & Mugel, Buffalo, 1976-80; with Walsh & Cleary, P.C., Buffalo, 1980-84; pvt. practice, 1984—; spl. counsel Ecology and Environment, Inc., Lancaster, N.Y., 1989—; trial counsel antitrust div. Dept. Justice, Washington, 1960-61; spl. counsel on disciplinary procedures N.Y. Supreme Ct., 1960-76; appointee legal disciplinary coordinating com. State of N.Y., 1971; legis. counsel, spl. counsel to mayor Buffalo, 1995—; counsel to sheriff Erie County, 1969-72; legis counsel Niagara Frontier Transp. Authority; cons. Norfolk So. R.R., Ecology and Environment on Govtl. Affairs; guest lectr. univs. and profl. groups. Author: (TV series) The Law and You (Freedom Found. award, ABA award, Internat. Police Assn. award). Past pres. Ashford Hollow Found. Visual and Performing Arts; past trustee Dollar Bills, Inc.; past co-producer Grand Island Playhouse and Players. With U.S. Army, 1945-46. Recipient Gold Key Buffalo Jr. C. of C., 1962, award Freedom Found., 1966. Fellow Am. Bar Found.; mem. ABA (del. internat. conf. Brussels 1963, Mexico City 1964, Lausanne, Switzerland 1964, Award of Merit com. 1961-70, sec., vice chair, chmn. sect. bar activities 1965-69, mem. ho. of dels. 1969-70, mem. crime prevention and control com. 1968-70, vice chair sr. lawyers divsn., com. legislation and adminstrn. regulations 1992—, vice chair sr. lawyers divsn. membership com. 1993-94), N.Y. Trial Lawyers Assn., Am. Immigration Lawyers Assn., Am. Judicature Soc., N.Y. State Bar Assn. (past exec. sec.), Erie County Bar Assn., Buffalo Bar Assn., Nat. Pub. Employer Labor Relations Assn., Capital Hill Club of Buffalo, Am. Assn. Airport Execs., N.Y. State Bus. Coun. (environ. law subcom., chmn. subcom.), Buffalo Irish Club (bd. dirs.), Buffalo Athletic Club (past bd. dirs., past v.p.), Buffalo Canoe Club, Buffalo Club, Ft. Orange of Albany Club, KC, Knights of Equity, Leoknights, Phi Delta Phi. Roman Catholic. Home: 95 North Dr Eggertsville NY 14226-4158 Office: 368 Pleasant View Dr Lancaster NY 14086-1316 also: 210 Ellicott Sq Bldg Buffalo NY 14203

WALSH, JOHN CHARLES, metallurgical company executive; b. Indpls., Sept. 8, 1924; s. John Charles and Nell (O'Neil) W.; m. Mary Louise Dreiss, Feb. 5, 1949; children: Michael S., Carolyn Ann, Anne D. B.S., Notre Dame U., 1949. Auditor Herdrich Boggs & Co., Indpls., 1949-50; with P.R. Mallory & Co., Inc., 1949-80; pres. Walgang Co. Inc., Indpls., 1980—; v.p., treas. P.R. Mallory & Co., 1971. Served with USMCR, 1943-45. Mem. Fin. Execs. Inst., Indpls. C. of C., Ind. Hist. Soc., Econ. Club, Notre Dame Club, Rotary. Home and Office: 4974 Shadow Rock Cir Carmel IN 46033-9500

WALSH, JOHN E., JR., business educator, consultant; b. St. Louis, Apr. 28, 1927; s. John E. and Ann M. (Narkewicz) W. B.S., U.S. Naval Acad., 1950; M.B.A., Washington U., St. Louis, 1957; D.B.A., Harvard U., 1960. Asst. prof. Washington U., St. Louis, 1959-60; assoc. prof. Washington U., 1960-68, prof., 1968—; vis. assoc. prof. Stanford U., 1964-65; vis. prof. INSEAD, Fontainebleau, France, 1970. Author: Preparing Feasibility Studies in Asia, 1971, Guidelines for Management Consultants in Asia, 1973, Planning New Ventures in International Business, 1976, (with others) Strategies in Business, 1978, Management Tactics, 1980, International Business Case Studies: For the Multicultural Market Place, 1994. Served to 1st lt. USAF, 1950-54. Zurn Found. fellow, 1958. Mem. Harvard Club N.Y.C. Home: 5471 Charglow Dr Saint Louis MO 63129-3564 Office: Washington U Grad Sch Bus PO Box 1133 1 Brookings Dr Saint Louis MO 63130-4889

WALSH, JOHN HARLEY, medical educator; b. Jackson, Miss., Aug. 22, 1938; s. John Howard and Aimee Nugent (Shands) W.; m. Courtney Kathleen McFadden, June 12, 1963 (div. 1979); children: Courtney Shands (Mrs. Peter Phleger), John Harley Jr.; m. Mary Carol Territo, Feb. 4, 1989. BA, Vanderbilt U., 1959, MD, 1963. Diplomate Am. Bd. Internal Medicine, Am. Bd. Gastroenterology. Intern N.Y. Hosp., N.Y.C., 1963-64; resident N.Y. Hosp. Cornell Med. Ctr., N.Y.C., 1964-67; rsch. assoc. Bronx VA Hosp., N.Y., 1969-70; fellow gastroenterology Wadsworth, Va., LA, 1970-71; clin. investigator Wadsworth VA Hosp., L.A., 1971-73; asst. to assoc. prof. UCLA, 1970-78, prof. medicine, 1978—, dir. Integrated Gastroenterology Tng. Program, 1983-89, dir. Div. Gastroenterology, 1988-93, Dorothy and Leonard Straus prof., 1989—; rsch. dir. CURE Digestive Diseases Rsch. Ctr., L.A., 1993—; dep. dir. Ctr. Ulcer Rsch. and Edn., L.A., 1974-80, assoc. dir., 1980-87, dir. 1987—, CURE Digestive Diseases Rsch. Ctr., 1995—; adv. coun. mem. NIH, Bethesda, Md., 1982-85; mem. Nat. Digestive Disease Adv. Bd., 1987-91. Assoc. editor: Gastroenterology Jour., 1976-86; mem. editorial bd. Am. Jour. Physiology, Jour. Clin. Endocrinology and Metabolism, Peptides Jour.; contbr. articles to profl. jours. Served with USPHS, 1967-69. Recipient AGA Fiterman/Kirsner Clinical Rsch. award, 1993, Rorer award So. Calif. Soc. Gastroenterology, 1972, Western Gastroent. Rsch. prize Western Gut Club, 1983, Merit award NIH, 1987. Mem. Am. Gastroent. Assn. (v.p., 1992-93, pres.-elect 1993-94, pres. 1994-95), Am. Soc. Clin. Investigation, Assn. Am. Physicians, Endocrine Soc., Western Soc. Clin. Investigation (counselor 1978-81). Episcopalian. Avocations: tennis, golf, ballet, modern fiction. Home: 247 S Carmelina Ave Los Angeles CA 90049-3903 Office: CURE Digestive Diseases Rsch Ctr 11301 Wilshire Blvd Los Angeles CA 90073-1003

WALSH, JOHN JOSEPH, medical school administrator, physician; b. N.Y.C., July 31, 1924; s. Patrick Joseph and Elizabeth (Lawless) W.; m. Gloria Paolini (dec. 1971); children: Maureen Walsh Garland, John Joseph Jr., Kathleen Walsh Saer; m. Dorothy B. Ray, 1989. Student, Fordham U., 1941-43, Cornell U., 1943-44; MD, L.I. Coll. Medicine, 1948; postdoctoral, Tulane U., 1957-58; ScD (hon.), SUNY, 1989. Diplomate Am. Bd. Internal Medicine. Commd. USPHS, 1948, advanced through grades to rear admiral, 1966; intern USPHS Hosp., Staten Island, N.Y., 1948-49; resident USPHS Hosp., Seattle, 1951-54; asst. chief medicine USPHS Hosp., New Orleans, 1954-56, dep. chief, 1956-57, chief research activities, 1958-64, chief med. service, 1963-64, med. dir., med. officer in charge, 1964-66; asst. surgeon gen., dir. div. direct health services USPHS, 1966-68, ret., 1968; instr. Tulane U. Sch. Medicine, New Orleans, 1957-58, asst. prof., 1958-60, assoc. prof., 1960-67, prof., 1967-89, prof. medicine emeritus, 1989—, dean, 1968-69; dean, coordinator health sci. and programs Tulane U. Med. Ctr., New Orleans, 1968-69, v.p. health affairs, 1969-78, chancellor, 1973-89; chancellor emeritus Tulane U. Med. Ctr., 1989—; acting dean sch. pub. health and tropical medicine Tulane U. Med. Ctr., New Orleans, 1974, Jack R. Aron prof. in adminstrv. medicine, 1978-89; adj. prof. Tulane U. Sch. Pub. Health and Tropical Medicine, 1978-89; pres., CEO Mahorner Clinic, Kenner, La., 1989-92; cons. VA Hosp., New Orleans, 1969-89, VA Hosp., Alexandria, La., 1969-89, USPHS Hosp., New Orleans, 1968-89; vis. physician Charity Hosp., New Orleans, 1957-66, sr. vis. physician, 1966-89, chief service Tulane div., 1968-69, acting chief service Tulane div., 1972; instr. La. State U. Sch. Medicine, New Orleans, 1956-57; mem. bd. cons. to comdr. Naval Med. Command Dept. Navy, Washington, 1983-86; mem. adv. com. to dir. NIH, 1983-85. Contbr. articles to profl. jours. Mem. planning com. Touro Infirmary, New Orleans; bd. dirs., mem. exec. com. Am. Cancer Soc., Internat. House, 1978-82, 83-84; mem. New Orleans Area Health Planning Council, 1968-70, task force in health manpower; trustee La. Sci. Ctr., 1983-85, La. Regional Med. Programs, 1969; bd. dirs. Friends of Charity Inc., 1986-89, Blue Cross, Washington, 1966-68, New Orleans Area/Bayou-River Health Systems Agy., 1978-82, Tuberculosis Assn. Greater New Orleans, 1968—, Flint-Goodridge Hosp., New Orleans, 1978-82. Fellow Tulane U. Sch. Medicine, 1957-58; recipient Outstanding Alumni award Downstate Med. Ctr., 1973. Fellow ACP, Am. Coll. Cardiology, Am. Coll. Chest Physicians, Am. Coll. Clin. Pharmacology and Chemotherapy; mem. AMA (com. on emergency health service), Am. Thoracic Soc. (councilor), La. Thoracic Soc. (pres. 1964), Nat. Adv. Rsch. Resources Coun. (mem. health care tech. study sect. 1970-74, chmn. 1972-74), Am. Lung Assn. La. (hon. life.), Delta Omega, Kappa Delta Phi, Alpha Epsilon Delta, Omicron Delta Kappa, Alpha Omega Alpha. Roman Catholic. Office: Tulane Univ Medical Ctr Office Chancellor New Orleans LA 70112*

WALSH, JOSEPH BRENNAN, ophthalmologist; b. Troy, N.Y., Mar. 6, 1941; s. Joseph Edward and Edna Margaret (Molloy) W. BS in Biology, Georgetown U., 1962, MD, 1966. Diplomate Am. Bd. Ophthalmology. Intern SUNY Upstate Med. Ctr., Syracuse, 1966-67; resident in medicine Univ. Hosp., Boston, 1967-68; resident in ophthalmology The N.Y. Eye and Ear Infirmary, N.Y.C., 1970-73; retina fellow Montefiore Hosp. and Med. Ctr./Albert Einstein Coll. Medicine, Bronx, 1973-74; from instr. to assoc. prof. dept. ophthalmology Montefiore Med. Ctr./Albert Einstein Coll. of Medicine, Bronx, N.Y., 1973-88; chmn., prof. dept. ophthalmology N.Y. Eye and Ear Infirmary/N.Y. Med. Coll., N.Y.C., 1988—; lectr. in field. Capt. USAF, 1968-70, Vietnam. Decorated Knight Hospitaller U.S. Priory of the Most Venerable Order of Hosp. St. John Jerusalem. Fellow N.Y. Acad. Medicine, N.Y. Acad. Sci., Royal Coll. Ophthalmologists; mem. Am. Acad. Ophthalmology, Assn. for Rsch. in Vision and Ophthalmology, Ophthalmic Laser Surg. Soc. (pres. 1991-94), Macula Soc., Retina Soc., N.Y. Soc. for Clin. Ophthalmology (pres. 1993-94). Office: NY Eye and Ear Infirmary 310 E 14th St New York NY 10003-4201

WALSH, JOSEPH LEO, III, lawyer; b. St. Louis, Dec. 7, 1954; s. Joseph Leo and Joan Marie (Bocklage) W.; m. Eileen Rose Boland, June 11, 1982; children: Katie Rose, Joseph L. IV, Brian James, John Patrick, Mary Elizabeth. BS cum laude, Loras Coll., 1977; JD, St. Mary's U., 1984. Bar: Tex. 1984, U.S. Dist. Ct. (so. dist.) Tex. 1985, Mo. 1986, U.S. Dist. Ct. (ea. dist.) Mo. 1989, U.S. Ct. Appeals (8th cir.) 1989, U.S. Supreme Ct. 1991. Assoc. Chamberlain, Hrdlicka, White, Johnson & Williams, Houston, 1984-86; atty. Haley, Fredrickson & Walsh, St. Louis, 1986-88; assoc. Gray & Ritter, St. Louis, 1988-95; sole practitioner St. Louis, 1995—; pro bono legal clinic St. Patrick Ctr., 1991—, Holy Guardian Angel Settlement, 1995—; jud. clk. U.S. Dist. Ct. (we. dist.) Tex., 1984. Co-author: Missouri Bar CLE Treatise on Torts, 2d edit., 1990; sr. assoc. editor St. Mary's U. Sch. Law Jour., 1983-84. Mem. Holly Hills Neighborhood Assn., 1991-93. Recipient Torts and Evidence award Lawyers' Co-op Pub. Co., 1982; named to Nat. Order Barristers, 1984. Mem. Assn. Trial Lawyers Am., Mo. Assn. Trial Attys., Bar Assn. Met. St. Louis, Lawyers Assn. St. Louis, Phi Delta Phi (pres. 1984). Roman Catholic. Home: 10469 White Bridge Ln Saint Louis MO 63141-8415 Office: Joseph L Walsh PC 10469 White Bridge Ln Saint Louis MO 63141-8415

WALSH, JOSEPH MICHAEL, magazine distribution executive; b. N.Y.C., Jan. 19, 1943; s. John Redmond and Bridget Judith (Donovan) W.; m. Theresa Rose Vericker, Oct. 3, 1964; children—Joseph, Matthew, Teresa Ann, John, James. B.B.A. in Acctg., Iona Coll., 1964. With Peat, Marwick, Mitchell & Co., C.P.A.s, N.Y.C., 1964-70, audit supr., until 1970; asst. to chmn. bd. and pres. Cadence Industries Corp., West Caldwell, N.J., 1970-71, v.p., 1971-74, exec. v.p., 1974-87; pres. subs. Curtis Circulation Co., 1972-74, chmn., chief exec. officer, 1982—; pres. Data Services for Health, 1976-77, U.S. Pencil and Stationery Co., 1977-79, Perfect Subscription Co. (merger Perfect Sch. Plans, Perfect Telephone Plan, Moore Cottrell and Keystone Readers Service), 1980-83. Mem. AICPA, N.Y. State Soc. CPAs, K.C. Home: 730 River Rd Woodcliff Lake NJ 07646-3048 Office: Curtis Circulation Co 730 River Rd New Milford NJ 07646-3048

WALSH, JOSEPH THOMAS, state supreme court justice; b. Wilmington, Del., May 18, 1930; s. Joseph Patrick and Mary Agnes (Bolton) W.; m. Madeline Maria Lamb, Oct. 6, 1955; children: Kevin, Lois, Patrick, Daniel, Thomas, Nancy. BA, LaSalle Coll., 1952; LLB, Georgetown U., 1955. Bar: D.C. 1955, Del. 1955. Atty. Ho. of Reps., Dover, Del., 1961-62; chief counsel Pub. Svc. Commn., Dover, 1964-72; judge Del. Superior Ct., Wilmington, 1972-84; vice chancellor Ct. of Chancery, Wilmington, 1984-85; justice Del. Supreme Ct., Wilmington, 1985—. Capt. U.S. Army, 1955-58. Democrat. Roman Catholic. Office: Del Supreme Ct 820 N French St Fl 11 Wilmington DE 19801-3509*

WALSH, KENNETH ALBERT, chemist; b. Yankton, S.D., May 23, 1922; s. Albert Lawrence and Edna (Slear) W.; m. Dorothy Jeanne Thompson, Dec. 22, 1944; children: Jeanne K., Kenneth Albert, David Bruce, Rhonda Jean, Leslie Gay. BA, Yankton Coll., 1942; PhD, Iowa State U., 1950. Asst. prof. chemistry Iowa State U., Ames, 1950-51; staff mem. Los Alamos Sci. Lab., 1951-57; supr. Internat. Minerals & Chem. Corp., Mulberry, Fla., 1957-60; mgr. Brush Beryllium Co., Elmore, Ohio, 1960-72; assoc. dir. tech. Brush Wellman Inc., Elmore, 1972-86; cons., patentee in field. Democratic precinct chmn., Los Alamos, 1956, Fremont, Ohio, 1980. Mem. AIME, Am. Chem. Soc. (sect. treas. 1956), ASM Internat., Toastmasters Internat., Theta Xi, Phi Lambda Upsilon. Methodist. Home: 2106 Kensington Dr Tyler TX 75703-2232

WALSH, KENNETH ANDREW, biochemist; b. Sherbrooke, Que., Can., Aug. 7, 1931; s. George Stanley and Dorothy Maud (Sangster) W.; m. Deirdre Anne Clarke, Aug. 22, 1953; children: Andrew, Michael, Erin. BSc in Agr., McGill U., 1951; MS, Purdue U., 1953; PhD, U. Toronto, 1959. Postdoctoral fellow U. Wash., Seattle, 1959-62, from asst. prof. to assoc. prof. Biochemistry, 1962-69, prof. Biochemistry, 1969—; chair, 1990—. Author (book) Methods in Protein Sequence Analysis, 1986. Mem. The Protein Soc. (sec.-treas. 1987-90), Am. So. Biochemistry/Molecular Biology. Office: U Wash Dept Biochem Box 357350 Seattle WA 98195

WALSH, KENNETH T., journalist. BA in Journalism, Rutgers U.; MA in Comm., Am. U. Sr. writer, chief White House corr. U.S. News & World Report; former polit. reporter, columnist, Washington corr. Denver Post; former newsman AP, Denver; adj. prof. comm. Am. U. Author: Feeding the Beast: The White House Versus the Press, 1996. Recipient Aldo Beckman award, 1991, Gerald R. Ford prize, 1993. Office: US News & World Report 2400 N St NW Washington DC 20037-1196

WALSH, LAWRENCE EDWARD, lawyer; b. Port Maitland, N.S., Can., Jan. 8, 1912; came to U.S., 1914, naturalized, 1922; s. Cornelius Edward and Lila May (Sanders) W.; m. Mary Alma Porter; children: Barbara Marie, Janet Maxine (Mrs. Alan Larson), Sara Porter, Dale Edward, Elizabeth Porter (Mrs. Joseph Wells). A.B., Columbia, 1932, LL.B., 1935; LL.D., Union U., 1959, St. John's U., 1975, Suffolk U., 1975, Waynesburg Coll., 1976, Vt. Law Sch., 1976. Bar: N.Y. 1936, D.C. 1981, Okla. 1981, U.S. Supreme Ct. 1951. Spl. asst. atty. gen. Drukman Investigation, 1936-38; dep. asst. dist. atty. N.Y. County, 1938-41; assoc. Davis Polk Wardwell Sunderland & Kiendl, 1941-43; asst. counsel to gov. N.Y., 1943-49, counsel to gov., 1950-51; counsel Pub. Service Commn., 1951-53; gen. counsel, exec. dir. Waterfront Commn. of N.Y. Harbor, 1953-54; U.S. judge So. Dist. N.Y., 1954-57; U.S. dep. atty. gen., 1957-60; partner firm Davis, Polk & Wardwell, 1961-81; counsel firm Crowe & Dunlevy, Oklahoma City, 1981—; ind. counsel Iran/Contra investigation, 1986-93; chmn. N.Y. State Moreland Commn. Alcoholic Beverage Control Law, 1963-64; pres. Columbia Alumni Fedn., 1968-69; dep. head with rank of amb. U.S. del. meetings on Vietnam, Paris, 1969; counsel to N.Y. State Ct. on Judiciary, 1971-72; 2d crct. mem. U.S. Crct. Judge Nominating Commn., 1978-80. Trustee emeritus Columbia U., Mut. Life Ins. Co., N.Y.; trustee William Nelson Cromwell Found. Recipient medal for excellence Columbia U., 1959, Law Sch., Columbia U., 1980, John Jay award Columbia Coll., 1989. Fellow Am. Bar Found., Am. Coll. Trial Lawyers; mem. Am. Law Inst. (coun.), ABA (pres. 1975-76), N.Y. State Bar Assn. (pres. 1966-67), Oklahoma County Bar Assn., Okla. State Bar Assn., Internat. Bar Assn., Assn. of Bar of City of New York, N.Y. County Lawyers Assn., Fed. Bar Coun.; hon. mem. Law Soc. Eng. and Wales, Can. Bar Assn., Mexican Bar Assn., Beta Theta Pi. Presbyterian. Clubs: N.Y. India House, The Century, Oklahoma City Golf and Country; Petroleum (Oklahoma City), Beacon (Oklahoma City). Home: 1902 Bedford Dr Oklahoma City OK 73116-5306 Office: 1800 Mid Am Towers Oklahoma City OK 73102

WALSH, MARIE LECLERC, nurse; b. Providence, Sept. 11, 1928; d. Walter Normand and Anna Mary (Ryan) Leclerc; m. John Breffni Walsh, June 18, 1955; children: George Breffni, John Leclerc, Darina Louise. Grad., Waterbury Hosp. Sch. Nursing, Conn., 1951; BS, Columbia U., 1954, MA, 1955. Team leader Hartford (Conn.) Hosp., 1951-53; pvt. duty nurse St. Luke's Hosp., N.Y.C., 1953-57; sch. nurse tchr. Agnes Russel Ctr., Tchrs. Coll. Columbia U., N.Y.C., 1955-56; clin. nursing instr. St. Luke's Hosp., N.Y.C., 1957-58; chmn. disaster nursing ARC Fairfax County, Va., 1975; course coord. occupational health nursing U. Va. Sch. Continuing Edn., Falls Church, 1975-77; mem. disaster steering com. No. Va. C.C., Annandale, 1976; adj. faculty U. Va. Sch. Continuing Edn., Falls Church, 1981; disaster svcs. nurse ARC, Wichita, Kans., 1985-90; disaster svcs. nurse Seattle-King County chpt. ARC, Seattle, 1990-96; rsch. and statis. analyst U. Va. Sch. Continuing Edn. Nursing, Falls Church, 1975; rsch. libr. Olive Garvey Ctr. for Improvement Human Functioning, Inc., Wichita, 1985. Sec. Dem. party, Cresskill, N.J., 1964-66; county committeewoman, Bergen County, N.J., 1965-66; pres., v.p., Internat. Staff Wives, NATO, Brussels, Belgium, 1978-80; election officer, supr. Election Bd., Wichita, 1987, 88. Mem. AAAS, AAUW, N.Y. Acad. Sci., Pi Lambda Theta, Sigma Theta Tau. Avocation: travel, gardening. Home: 8800 Prestwould Pl Mc Lean VA 22102

WALSH, MASON, retired newspaperman; b. Dallas, Nov. 27, 1912; s. Herbert C. and Margaret (Hayes) W.; m. Margaret Anne Calhoun, Mar. 7, 1947; children: Margaret Anne (Mrs. James G. Dunn), Timothy Mason, Kevin Calhoun. B.A. in Polit. Sci., So. Meth. U., 1934. Staff Dallas Evening Jour., 1929-37; staff Dallas Dispatch-Jour. (later Dallas Jour.), 1938-42; editor Austin (Tex.) Tribune, 1942; dir. employee relations N.Am. Aviation, Dallas, 1942-45; with Dallas Times-Herald, 1945-60, mng. editor, 1952-60; mng. editor Phoenix Gazette, 1960-66; gen. mgr. Phoenix Newspapers, Inc., 1966-75, asst. pub., 1975-78; pub. Ariz. Republic and Phoenix Gazette, 1978-80, pub. emeritus, 1980—. Profl. musician, 1929-35. Chmn.

Ariz. Dept. Econ. Planning and Devel. Bd., 1968-71; bd. dirs., v.p. Goodwill Industries Central Ariz., 1978-84, v.p., 1982-83; bd. dirs. Western Newspaper Found., 1974-81; trustee Desert Found., Scottsdale, 1982-85; mem. Nat. Def. Exec. Res., 1964-80. Mem. A.P. Mng. Editors Assn. (dir. 1956-63, pres. 1963), A.P. Assn. Calif., Ariz., Hawaii and Nev. (pres. 1976-77), Ariz. Acad. (dir. 1973-81, v.p. 1980-81), Valley Forward Assn. (dir. 1970-87), Newcomen Soc., Phoenix 40, Sigma Delta Chi. Episcopalian. Club: Arizona. Home: 4102 N 64th Pl Scottsdale AZ 85251-3110

WALSH, MICHAEL FRANCIS, advertising executive; b. Pitts., June 22, 1956; s. Peter Paul and Joan Brooks (Murdoch) W.; m. Lisa Ann Ruscillo, May 14, 1983; children: Megan, Allison, Ann. BA, Duquesne U., 1978; MBA, U. Pitts., 1990. Asst. media planner Ketchum Advt./Pitts., 1978-79, media planner, 1979-82, media supr., 1982-84, v.p., assoc. media dir., 1984-86, dir. media ops., 1986-87, media dir., 1987-88, sr. v.p., media dir., 1988-92, dir. ops. and fin., 1993—; part-time mem. faculty U. Pitts., 1990—; adj. faculty Point Park Coll., 1992—. Contbr. articles to advt. jours. Mem. Pitts. Radio and TV Club (bd. dirs. 1988-91), Info. Tech. Media Adv. Coun. (pres. 1995—), Bus. and Profl. Advt. Internat., Inc. (bd. dirs., exec. com. 1991—), U. Pitts. Alumni Assn. (pres.). Office: Ketchum Communications Inc 6 Ppg Pl Pittsburgh PA 15222-5406

WALSH, MICHAEL J., lawyer; b. Portland, Oreg., Sept. 4, 1932; s. Frank M.J. and Elisemary (Derbes) W.; m. June Griffin, Nov. 28, 1959; children: Molly, Erin, Kathryn (dec.), Anne. BA, U. Portland, 1954; JD, Georgetown U., 1959. Bar: D.C. 1959, Oreg. 1959, U.S. Ct. Appeals (fed. and 9th cirs.) 1959, U.S. Tax Ct. 1959, U.S. Supreme Ct. 1968. Law ck. to presiding justice Oreg. Supreme Ct., Salem, 1959-60; mng. ptnr. Rankin, Walsh, Ragen and Roberts, Portland, 1960-75; sole practice Portland, 1976-81; ptnr. Walsh and Conolly, Portland, 1982-83; of counsel McEwen, Hanna, Gisvold and Rankin, Portland, 1983-85, Bullivant, Houser, Bailey, Pendergrass, & Hoffman, Washington, 1985—; chmn. Employees Compensation Appeals Bd. U.S. Dept. Labor, Washington, 1985—; legal counsel to Reagan-Bush '84, Nat. Hdqtrs., Washington, 1983-84. Chmn. legal dev. March of Dimes, 1967; chmn. admissions Georgetown U., Oreg., 1972-83; trustee Christie Sch., 1974-78; trustee Cath. Charities Oreg., 1966-72, pres. 1971; trustee Parry Ctr. for Children, 1967-73, v.p. 1970-71; trustee Portland Tennis Ctr. Assn., 1972-83, pres. 1976-82; bd. dirs. Portland Traffic Safety Commn., 1981-83. Served with JAGC, USAF, capt. res. Mem. Am. Judicature Soc., Am. Trial Lawyers Assn., Nat. Assn. Coll. and Uiv. Attys., Am. Arbitration Assn., D.C. Bar Assn., Oreg. Bar Assn. (mem. various coms.), Multnomah County Bar Assn., Portland C. of C. (bd. dirs. 1975-78, chmn. legis. coun. 1975). Club: Georgetown Univ. (Oreg.) (pres. 1966). Home: 3273 Sutton Pl NW # B Washington DC 20016-3537

WALSH, MICHAEL S., lawyer; b. Chgo., Sept. 29, 1951. AB, Colgate U., 1973; MBA, Cornell U., 1975; JD, So. Meth. U., 1978. Bar: Ill. 1978, U.S. Dist. Ct. (no. dist.) Ill. 1978, U.S. Ct. Appeals (fed. cir.) 1983, U.S. Ct. Appeals (9th cir.) 1985. Mem. Jenner & Block, Chgo. Mem. ABA, Fed. Bar Assn., Chgo. Bar Assn. Office: Jenner & Block 1 IBM Plz Chicago IL 60611-3586

WALSH, PATRICK CRAIG, urologist; b. Akron, Ohio, Feb. 13, 1938; s. Raymond Michael and Catherine N. (Rodden) W.; m. Margaret Campbell, May 23, 1964; children—Christopher, Jonathan, Alexander. A.B., Case Western Res. U., 1960, M.D., 1964. Intern in surgery Peter Bent Brigham Hosp., Boston, 1964-65; asst. resident in surgery Peter Bent Brigham Hosp., 1965-66; asst. resident in pediatric surgery Children's Hosp. Med. Center, Boston, 1966-67; resident in urology U. Calif.-Los Angeles Med. Center, 1967-71; dir. Brady Urol. Inst., urologist-in-chief Johns Hopkins Hosp., Balt., 1974—; prof., dir. dept. urology Johns Hopkins U. Sch. Medicine, 1974—. Contbr. articles to med. jours. Served to comdr. M.C. USN, 1971-73. Recipient Charles F. Kettering medal GM Cancer Rsch. Found., 1996. Mem. Soc. Univ. Surgeons, Am. Assn. Genitourinary Surgeons, Clin. Soc. Genitourinary Surgeons, Am. Urol. Assn., Endocrine Soc., Am. Surg. Assn. Inst. Medicine of NAS, Alpha Omega Alpha. Roman Catholic. Office: Johns Hopkins Med Inst 600 N Wolfe St Baltimore MD 21205-2110

WALSH, PAUL S., food products executive. Chmn., pres., CEO Pillsbury Co., Mpls. Office: Pillsbury Co 200 S 6th St Minneapolis MN 55402-1403

WALSH, PETER JOSEPH, physics educator; b. N.Y.C., Aug. 21, 1929; s. Peter and Mary Ellen (Kelly) W.; m. Rosemarie Imundo, May 13, 1952; children: Kathleen, Mary Ellen, Susan, Carole, Karen. B.S., Fordham U., 1951; M.S., N.Y.U., 1953, Ph.D., 1960. Research physicist Westinghouse Elec. Co., Bloomfield, N.J., 1951-60; supervisory physicist Am. Standard, Piscattaway, N.J., 1960-62; prof. Fairleigh Dickinson U., 1962-93; prof. emeritus, 1993—; vis. rsch. scientist MIT, 1977; vis. prof. electronics and elec. engring. U. Sheffield, 1978-79; NASA fellow U. Santa Clara, 1980; Am. Soc. Engring. Edn. Navy fellow Naval Rsch. Labs., 1981, 82, 86, NASA Langley, 1987, Air Force fellow Hanscom AFB, 1988, Kirtland AFB, 1990; vis. prof. U. Genoa, 1984; vis. scholar Stanford U., 1984-85, cons. physics to 20 labs., 1963—; chmn. bd. trustees EMS Ednl. Corp., 1982—. Author: Dark Side of Knowledge, articles in field. Mem. Am. Phys. Soc., AAAS, N.J. Acad. Sci., Sigma Xi (sec. 1969). Patentee in field. Home: 40 St Joseph Dr Stirling NJ 07980-1224

WALSH, PHILIP CORNELIUS, retired mining executive; b. Harrison, N.J., May 23, 1921; s. Philip Cornelius and Frances Walsh (Prendergast) W.; m. Alexandra Somerville Tuck, May 19, 1945 (dec. Sept. 1993); children: Eugenie Philbin Flaherty, Philip C.C., Frances Cornelia Cummings, Alexander Tuck, Nicholas Holladay, Elizabeth Lovering; m. Peggy Flanigan McDonnell, Oct. 13, 1996. BA, Yale U., 1943; member of the Class of 1944. With W.R. Grace & Co., Lima, Peru and N.Y.C., 1946-71; v.p. parent co., chief operating officer Latin Am. group, 1961-71, group exec. corp. adminstrv. group, 1970-71; v.p. Cerro Corp., 1972-74, Newmont Mining Corp., 1974-80; chmn. bd. Foote Mineral Co., Exton, Pa., 1979-80; vice chmn. St. Joe Minerals Corp., 1980-85; chmn. bd. Chilean Lithium Co. Ltd., 1980-94; dir. So. Pera Copper Co., 1973-80, Cyprus Minerals Co., 1985-93, Piedmont Mining Co., 1985-94; bd. dirs. T. Rowe Price Assocs., Inc.; mem. Nat. Strategic Minerals and Metals Program Adv. Commn. Mem. Harding Twp. Bd. Edn., N.J., 1960-66; mem. Harding Twp. Com., 1966-72, police commr., 1966-72; trustee Morristown Meml. Hosp., 1969-79; vis. com. Colo. Sch. Mines, Global Systems and Cultures. 1st lt. F.A., U.S. Army, 1943-46. Decorated Silver Star, Purple Heart. Mem. AIME (Saunders gold medal 1992, Disting. Mem. award 1993), Pan Am. Soc. U.S. (past vice chmn.), Am. Soc. (hon. dir.), Am. Assn. Order of Malta (chancellor, bd. councillors 1983-96), Racquet and Tennis Club, Edgartown Yacht Club (commodore 1993-95), Edgartown Golf Club, Edgartown Reading Rm., Phi Beta Kappa, Sigma Xi. Republican. Roman Catholic. Home: Pleasant Valley Peapack NJ 07977

WALSH, RICHARD GEORGE, agricultural economist; b. Seward, Nebr., Aug. 16, 1930; s. Thomas George and Francis Kathryn (Pape) W.; m. Patricia Burke Bard, 1976; children by previous marriage: Cathryn M., Susan E., Thomas R., Robert J. B.S., U. Nebr., 1952, M.A., 1955; Ph.D., U. Wis., 1961. From asst. prof. to prof. agrl. econs. U. Nebr., 1958-68; prof. dept. agrl. and resource econs. Colo. State U., Ft. Collins, 1968-97, prof. emeritus, 1997—; intergovt. exchange EPA, 1973-74; cons. FTC, 1965-66, 72, 78-79, U. P.R., 1967, Justice Dept., 1971, U.S. Forest Service, 1972, 82, 86, Bur. Land Mgmt., 1973, 85, Nat. Park Service, 1975-79; vis. prof. U. Md., 1965, Stanford Research Inst., 1971, U. Newcastle upon Tyne, 1991. Author: Economics of the Baking Industry, 1963, Market Structure of the Agricultural Industries, 1966, The Structure of Food Manufacturing, 1966, Organization and Competition in Food Retailing, 1966, Economic Benefits of Improved Water Quality, 1982, Wilderness Resource Economics, 1982, Wild and Scenic River Economics, 1985, Recreation Economic Decisions: Comparing Benefits and Costs, 1986, Long-Run Forecasts of Participation in Fishing, Hunting and Nonconsumptive Wildlife Recreation, 1987, Economic Demand Studies with Nonmarket Benefit Estimates, 1988, Recreation Value of Ranch Open Space, 1994, Benefits of Ranch Open Space to Local Residents, 1996; contbr. articles to profl. jours. Bd. dirs. North Ft. Collins Sanitation Dist., 1971-73. Served to lt. (j.g.) USNR, 1952-54. Mem. Am. Agrl. Econs. Assn. (Outstanding Published Research award 1964), Assn. Environ. & Resource Econs., Western Agrl. Econs. Assn., European Assn. Environ. & Resource Econs., Internat. Soc. Ecological Economics. Office: Colo State U Dept Agrl and Resource Eco Fort Collins CO 80523

WALSH, RICHARD MICHAEL, lawyer; b. Portland, Oreg., Nov. 8, 1958; s. Robert Thomas and Elizabeth Ann (Stott) W.; m. Teresa Ann Emfinger; children: Samantha Ann, Michael Richard, Kevin Collier. BS in Polit. Sci., Portland State U., 1983; JD, U. Oreg., 1986. Bar: Oreg. 1986. Assoc. Schouboe Marvin & Furniss, Portland, 1986-88; ptnr. Olson Rowell & Walsh, Salem, Oreg., 1988-93; pvt. practice Salem, 1993—. Atty. Oreg. Workers Compensation. Oreg. Law Sch. Alumni scholar, 1983-84, Oreg. Law Found. scholar, 1985. Mem. ABA, Oreg. State Bar, Oreg. Trial Lawyers Assn., Oreg. Fed. Dist. Bar., Am. Trial Lawyers Assn., Lions Club, Phi Delta Phi. Democrat. Roman Catholic. Avocations: bicycling, backpacking, racquetball. Office: 876 Welcome Way SE Ste 200 Salem OR 97302-3936

WALSH, RODGER JOHN, lawyer; b. Kansas City, Mo., Apr. 20, 1924; s. John Joseph and Margaret Mary (Halloran) W.; m. Patricia Ann O'Brien, Nov. 18, 1950; children—Regina, Martin, Eileen, Daniel, Veronica, Bernard, Kathleen. B.S., Rockhurst Coll., 1947; J.D., Georgetown U., 1950. Bar: Mo. 1950, D.C. 1950, U.S. Ct. Appeals (8th cir.) 1955, U.S. Supreme Ct. 1960. Spl. agt. FBI, Washington, 1950-53; ptnr. Linde-Thomson Van Dyke Fairchild, Kansas City, Mo., 1953-63, Biersmith & Walsh, 1963-69; v.p., asst. gen. counsel Riss Internat., 1969-83, exec. v.p., gen. counsel, 1983-87; pvt. practice law Independence, Mo., 1987—; chmn., mem. Mo. State Pers. Adv. Bd., Jefferson City, 1979-84; mem. Mo. State Environ. Improvement Authority, 1977-83. Bd. dirs. Mo. Bus and Truck Assn., Jefferson City, 1983-87, Democracy Inc., Kansas City, Mo., 1960—; hon. dir. Rockhurst Coll., 1960—. With U.S. Army, 1942-45; ETO. Decorated Air Medal with 5 oak leaf clusters. Mem. Mo. Bar Assn., Fed. Bar Assn., Kansas City Bar Assn., Am. Legion, Soc. Former FBI Agts. Democrat. Roman Catholic. Home: 10512 Mersington Ave Kansas City MO 64137-1626 Office: 115 W Lexington Ave Independence MO 64050-3705

WALSH, SEMMES GUEST, retired insurance company executive; b. Annapolis, Md., June 15, 1926; m. Annette Hunt Cromwell, Aug. 23, 1952; children: Semmes. G. Jr., Annette T., Marion H., Jacquelyn C. BE, Yale U., 1946; MBA, Harvard U., 1950. Gen. ptnr. Baker, Watts & Co., Balt., 1962-74, mng. ptnr., 1974-80; exec. v.p., chief fin. officer Monumental Corp., Balt., 1980-89, ret., 1989. Bd. dirs. Wm. G. Baker Meml. Fund, Jas. L. Kernan Hosp. Found. Lt. (j.g.) USNR, 1943-46. Republican. Episcopalian. Avocations: tennis, golf. Home: 230 Hopkins Ln Owings Mills MD 21117-4327

WALSH, THOMAS A., production designer. Prodn. designer: (IMAX films) Flyers, 1980, Speed, 1984, The Discoverers, 1993, (TV movies) Miss Lonely Hearts, 1981, A Gathering of Old Men, 1986 (Emmy award nomination outstanding art direction 1987), Eugene O'Neill, 1986, War Story: Vietnam, 1988, Without Warning: The James Brady Story, 1990 (Emmy award nomination outstanding art direction 1991), Blindspot, 1992, In Search of Dr. Seuss, 1994, (documentaries) John Huston, 1988, MGM: When the Lion Roars, 1992 (Emmy award outstanding art direction 1993), (feature films) The Handmaid's Tale, 1990, Prayer of the Rollerboys, 1990. *

WALSH, THOMAS CHARLES, lawyer; b. Mpls., July 6, 1940; s. William G. and Kathryne M. Walsh; m. Joyce Williams, Sept. 7, 1968; children: Brian Christopher, Timothy Daniel, Laura Elizabeth. BS in Commerce magna cum laude, St. Louis U., 1962, LLB cum laude, 1964. Bar: Mo. 1964, U.S. Supreme Ct. 1971, U.S. Dist. Ct. (ea. dist.) Mo. 1964, U.S. Ct. Appeals (8th cir.) 1968, U.S. Ct. Appeals (6th cir.) 1972, U.S. Ct. Appeals (5th cir.) 1974, U.S. Ct. Appeals (D.C. cir.) 1980, U.S. Ct. Appeals (7th cir.) 1982, U.S. Ct. Appeals (9th cir.) 1987, U.S. Ct. Appeals (4th cir.) 1989, U.S. Ct. Appeals (11th and Fed. cirs.) 1992, U.S. Ct. Appeals (2d and 10th cirs.) 1993. Jr. ptnr. Bryan, Cave, McPheeters & McRoberts, St. Louis, 1964-73, ptnr. Bryan Cave, LLP, 1974—, mem. exec. com., 1980-96; mem. 8th Cir. Adv. Com., 1983-86. Bd. dirs. St. Louis Symphony Soc., 1983-95. Served with U.S. Army, 1965-66, to lt. USNR, 1966-71. Fellow Am. Coll. Trial Lawyers, Am. Acad. Appellate Lawyers; mem. ABA, Mo. Bar, St. Louis Bar Assn., Am. Law Inst., Mo. Athletic Club, Noonday Club, Bellerive Country Club. Roman Catholic. Office: Bryan Cave LLP 1 Metropolitan Sq 211 N Broadway Saint Louis MO 63102-2733

WALSH, THOMAS GERARD, actuary; b. N.Y.C., Jan. 14, 1942; s. Martin Joseph and Margaret Ellen (Moyles) W.; children: Brian, Kristen, Meghan, Jacqueline. B.S., Manhattan Coll. Exec. v.p. Tchr. Ins. & Annuity Am./ CREF, N.Y.C. Fellow Soc. Actuaries. Office: Tchrs Ins & Annuity Assn Am 730 3rd Ave New York NY 10017-3206

WALSH, THOMAS JAMES, JR., lawyer; b. Memphis, Oct. 22, 1947; s. Thomas James and Lois Rhine (Gibson) w.; m. Jean Clay McKee, May 31, 1969; children: Courtney Michelle, Meredith McKee. BA, Yale Coll., 1969; JD, U. Va., 1975. Bar: Tenn. 1975, U.S. Dist. Ct. (we. dist.) Tenn. 1976, U.S. Ct. Appeals (5th cir.) 1982, U.S. Ct. Appeals (6th cir.) 1985, U.S. Ct. Appeals (11th cir.) 1986, U.S. Supreme Ct. 1986, U.S. Ct. Appeals (10th cir.) 1991, U.S. Ct. Appeals (8th cir.) 1992. Assoc. Canada, Russell & Turner, Memphis, 1975-78; assoc. Wildman, Harrold, Allen, Dixon & McDonnell, Memphis, 1978-80, ptnr., 1981-89; ptnr. McDonnell, Boyd, Smith & Solmson, Memphis, 1989-90, McDonnell Boyd, Memphis, 1990-94; atty. Wolff Ardis, P.C., Memphis, 1995—; hearing officer Bd. of Profl. Responsibility Supreme Ct. Tenn., 1988-95. Chmn. bd. dirs. Multiple Sclerosis Soc. mid-south chpt., Memphis, 1978, World Affairs Coun. Memphis, 1985—; vol. atty. pro bono panel for sr. citizens, Memphis, 1982—; v.p. Bapt. Peace Fellowship of N.Am., Memphis, 1984-89; coun. chmn. Prescott Meml. Bapt. Ch., Memphis, 1993-95. Mem. Class award Leadership Memphis, 1985, Community Class award Unitarian Universalist Fellowship, Memphis, 1989. Mem. ABA, Tenn. Bar Assn., Memphis Bar Assn. Democrat. Avocations: photography, baseball. Office: 6055 Primacy Pky Ste 360 Memphis TN 38119-5724

WALSH, THOMAS JOSEPH, neuro-ophthalmologist; b. N.Y.C., Sept. 18, 1931; s. Thomas Joseph and Virginia (Hughes) W.; m. Sally Ann Maust, June 21, 1958; children—Thomas Raymond, Sara Ann, Mary Kelly, Kathleen Meghan. BA, Coll. Fordham, 1954; MD, Bowman Gray Med. Sch., 1958. Intern St. Vincent's Hosp., N.Y.C., 1958-59; resident ophthalmology Bowman Gray Med. Sch., Winston-Salem, N.C., 1961-64; fellow neuro-ophthalmology Bascom Palmer Eye Inst., Miami, Fla., 1964-65; practice medicine specializing in neuro-ophthalmology Stamford, Conn., 1965—; dir. neuro-ophthalmology service, asst. prof. ophthalmology and neurology Yale Sch. Medicine, New Haven, 1965-74; assoc. prof. Yale Sch. Medicine, 1974-79, prof., 1979—, also bd. permanent officers; dir. ophthalmology Stamford Hosp., 1978-83; mem. staff St. Joseph Hosp., Yale New Haven Hosp.; cons. to surgeon gen. army in neuro-ophthalmology Walter Reed Hosp., Washington, 1966—, VA Hosp., West Haven, 1965—, Silver Hill Found., New Canaan, Conn., 1974—; frequent lectr. various univs. Contbr. articles to various publs. Mem. adv. bd. Stamford Salvation Army, 1972-92; mem. med. bd. Darien Nurses Assn., Conn., 1972—; surgeon Darien Fire Dept., 1969—. With AUS, 1959-61. Decorated Knight of Malta, 1983; Centennial fellow Johns Hopkins, 1976. Mem. AMA, Conn., Fairfield County med. socs., Acad. Ophthalmology, Oxford Ophthal. Congress, Acad. Neurology, Am. Assn. Neurol. Surgeons, Internat. Neuro-Ophthalmology Soc., Soc. Med. Cons. to Armed Forces, Cosmos Club (Washington), Darien County Club, Yale Club (N.Y.C), Lions, Army-Navy Club. Office: 1100 Bedford St Stamford CT 06905-5305

WALSH, W. TERENCE, lawyer; b. Toledo, Ohio, Nov. 18, 1943; s. Walter James and Ann (Gifford) W.; m. Patricia Jane Walker, Dec. 17, 1966; children: Christopher O'Brien, Ryan Kerrick, Ann Elisabeth. AB, Brown U., 1965; JD, Emory U., 1970. Bar: Ga., 1971, U.S. Dist. Ct. (no. dist.) Ga., 1971, U.S. Ct. Appeals (11th cir.), 1971. Assoc. Alston, Miller & Gaines, Atlanta, 1970-76, ptnr., 1976-83; ptnr. Alston & Bird, Atlanta, 1983—; lectr. various seminars on appellate procedure, juvenile law, ethics, and professionalism. Contbr. articles to profl. jours. Bd. dirs. Georgians for Children, 1993—, The Bridge, 1992—, Ga. Justice Project, 1987—; bd. dirs. Atlanta Legal Aid Soc., Inc., 1976—, pres., 1987; bd. dirs. Capital Area Mosaic, chmn., 1994-95; chmn. sch. bd. Christ the King Sch., 1982-84; alumni trustee Brown U., 1994—; chmn. KIND, Inc., 1993—; chmn. State Bar Com. on Children and the Cts. Fellow Ga. Bar Found.; mem. ABA, State Bar Ga. (bd. govs. 1979—, pres. young lawyers sect. 1980-81, H. Sol Clark award 1987), Atlanta Bar Assn. (bd. dirs. 1987-93, pres. 1991-92, Charles E. Watkins award 1994), Gate City Bar Assn., Emory Law Alumni Assn. (exec. com. 1990—). Avocations: sports, gardening, reading. Office: Alston & Bird 1201 W Peachtree St NW Atlanta GA 30309-3400

WALSH, WILLIAM, former football coach; b. Los Angeles, Nov. 30, 1931. Student, San Mateo Jr. Coll.; BA, San Jose State U., 1954, MA in Edn., 1959. Asst. coach Monterey Peninsula Coll., 1955, San Jose State U., 1956; head coach Washington Union High Sch., Fremont, Calif., 1957-59; asst. coach U. Calif., Berkeley, 1960-62, Stanford U., 1963-65, Oakland Raiders, Am. Football League, 1966-67, Cin. Bengals, 1968-75, San Diego Chargers, Nat. Football League, 1976; head coach Stanford U., 1977-78; head coach, gen. mgr. San Francisco 49ers, NFL, 1979-89, exec. v.p., 1989; broadcaster NBC Sports, 1989-91; head coach Stanford U., 1992-95; cons. San Francisco Forty Niners, 1996—. Named NFL Coach of Yr., Sporting News, 1981; coached Stanford U. winning team Sun Bowl, 1977, Bluebonnet Bowl, 1978, Blockbuster Bowl, 1993, San Francisco 49ers to Super Bowl championships, 1981, 84, 88; elected to Pro Football Hall of Fame, 1993. Office: Bill Walsh Enterprises 3000 Sand Hill Rd Ste 200 Menlo Park CA 94025-7116

WALSH, WILLIAM ALBERT, management consultant, former naval officer; b. Gilman, Ill., Aug. 15, 1933; s. Lawrence Eugene and Myrtle R. (Mulder) W.; m. Joan Elizabeth Kennedy, Dec. 28, 1957; children: Kathryn, Michael, Julie. B.S. in Commerce, U. Notre Dame, 1955; M.S. in Mgmt. with distinction, U.S. Naval Postgrad. Sch., Monterey, Calif., 1962; M.S. in Internat. Affairs with honors, George Washington U., 1972. Commd. ensign U.S. Navy, 1955, advanced through grades to rear adm., 1981; exec. asst. to dep. chief naval ops. (Surface Warfare), Washington, 1974-76; comdg. officer USS Juneau, San Diego, 1976-78; comdr. Amphibious Squadron Three, San Diego, 1978-79; head plans and policy div., comdr. rapid deployment naval forces Comdr. in Chief U.S. Pacific Fleet, Honolulu, 1979-81; comdr. Amphibious Group Eastern Pacific, San Diego, 1981-82; dir. surface warfare div. Office Chief Naval Ops., Pentagon, Washington, 1983-85; ret., 1985; pres. Air/Space Am., San Diego, 1986-89, W.A. Walsh Enterprises, 1990—. Decorated Legion of Merit with 2 gold stars, Bronze Star, Navy Commendation medal U.S.; Disting. Service Order 2d Class Vietnam.

WALSH, WILLIAM ARTHUR, JR., lawyer; b. Washington, Mar. 17, 1949; children: Jesse Creighton, Patrick McKay. BS in Econs. and Fin., U. Md., 1972; JD, U. Richmond, 1977. Bar: Va. Ptnr. Hunton & Williams, Richmond, Va.; mem. adv. bd. for law rev. U. Richmond. Bd. trustees Va. Commonwealth U. Real Estate Found.; mem, bd. dirs. Local Initiatives Support Corp.; mem., adv. bd. U. Richmond Law Rev.; mem. Va. Commonwealth U. Real Estate Circle of Excellence. Mem. ABA, Va. Bar Assn., Richmond Bar Assn. Home: 4705 Leonard Pky Richmond VA 23226-1337 Office: Hunton & Williams Riverfront Pla East Tower 951 E Byrd St Richmond VA 23219-4040

WALSH, WILLIAM DESMOND, investor; b. N.Y.C., Aug. 4, 1930; s. William J. and Catherine Grace (Desmond) W.; m. Mary Jane Gordon, Apr. 5, 1951; children: Deborah, Caroline, Michael, Suzanne, Tara Jane, Peter. BA, Fordham U., 1951; JD, Harvard U., 1955. Bar: N.Y. State bar 1955. Asst. U.S. atty. So. dist. N.Y., N.Y.C., 1955-58; counsel N.Y. Commn. Investigation, N.Y.C., 1958-61; mgmt. cons. McKinsey & Co., N.Y.C., 1961-67; sr. v.p. Arcata Corp., Menlo Park, Calif., 1967-82; gen. ptnr. Sequoia Assocs., 1982—; pres., chief exec. officer Atacra Liquidating Trust, 1982-88; bd. dirs. Consol. Freightways Corp., Menlo Park, Calif., Clayton Group, Inc., Tampa, Fla., Newell Mfg. Corp., Lowell, Mich., Newell Indsl. Corp., Roanoke, Va., URS Corp., San Francisco, Basic Vegetable Products, San Francisco, Golden Valley Produce, Bakersfield, Calif., Nat. Edn. Corp. of Irvine, Calif. Mem. bd. visitors Harvard Law Sch., co-chair dean's adv. bd.; trustee Fordham U., Neurosci. Inst., Scripps Inst.; chmn. bd. trustees, bd. overseers Hoover Instn. Mem. N.Y. State Bar Assn., Harvard Club (N.Y.C. and San Francisco), Fordham Club No. Calif., Knights of Malta. Home: 279 Park Ln Atherton CA 94027-5448 Office: 3000 Sand Hill Rd Ste 140 Menlo Park CA 94025-7116

WALSH, WILLIAM EGAN, JR., electronics executive; b. Springfield, Mass., Dec. 2, 1948; s. William Egan and Veronica (Maroney) W.; m. Terese Anne Sullivan, Oct. 25, 1952; children: Brian, Kathleen, John, Kevin. BA in Physics, Holy Cross, 1970; MS in Physical Oceanography, U.S. Naval Sch., Monterey, Calif., 1971; MBA, U. North Fla., 1975. Oceanographer Sippican, Inc., Marion, Mass., 1975-77, mktg. mgr., 1977-80, from v.p. to sr. v.p., 1980-90, pres., 1990—, also bd. dirs.; bd. dirs. Phys. Scis., Inc., Andover, Mass. Lt. USN, 1970-75, lt. comdr. USNR, 1976-80. Mem. Marine Tech. Soc. Roman Catholic. Avocations: boating, jogging, racquetball, photography. Office: Sippican Inc 7 Barnabas Rd Marion MA 02738-1421

WALSHE, AUBREY PETER, political science educator; b. Johannesburg, South Africa, Jan. 12, 1934; s. Aubrey John and Joan Kathleen (Evans) W.; m. Catherine Ann Pettifer, Jan. 28, 1957; children: Sally, Jane, Dominic, Emma. BA, Wadham Coll., Oxford, Eng., 1956, MA, 1959; PhD, St. Antony's Coll., Oxford, 1968. Vis. asst. prof. U. Notre Dame, Ind., 1962-63, asst. prof. dept. govt. and internat. studies, 1967-71, dir. African studies, 1971-77, assoc. prof., 1971-77, prof., 1977—; sr. assoc. fellow St. Antony's Coll., Oxford, 1972-73; dir. ann. Missionary Inst. on Sub-Saharan Africa, U.Notre Dame, 1969—; lectr. and cons. in field; found. mem. So. African Rsch. Archival Project;l mem. N.Am. Support Com., Ecumenical Dialogue of Third World Theologians. Contbr. articles to profl. jours.; author: The Rise of African Nationalism in South Africa, 1971, 2d edit. 1988, Black Nationalism in South Africa: A Short History, 1975, Church Versus State in South Africa, 1983, Prophetic Christianity and the Liberation Management in South Africa, 1997; contbr. revs. to numerous jours.; occasional reader: U. Calif. Press, U. Notre Dame Press, Rev. of Politics, Social Scis. and Humanities Rsch. Coun. of Can., Ottawa, Ind. U. African Studies Pubs. Com., Cath. Inst. for Internat. Rels., London, U. Queensland, Australia. Mem. edn. com. cath. Inst. for Internat. Rels., London; adv. bd. Storypoint Ctr., Presbyn. Ch. U.S.A., N.Y.C.; cons. Nat. Coun. of Chs. of Christ, Convocation of the Kairos Document: Challenge to the Ch. in South Africa. Walsh-Price fellow Ctr. for Mission Studies, Maryknoll, N.Y., 1980-81, Helen Kellogg Inst. for Internat. Studies fellow, 1983, Inst. for Internat. Peace Studies fellow, 1987; MacArthur Found. grantee, 1989-90. Ecumenical Christian. Home: 1302 Hillcrest Rd South Bend IN 46617-1107 Office: Univ Notre Dame Dept Govt Notre Dame IN 46556

WALSHE, BRIAN FRANCIS, management consultant; b. White Plains, N.Y., June 8, 1958; s. Kevin D. and Anna G. (Touhy) W. BSCE, Northeastern U., 1981; MBA, U. Mich., 1986. Assoc. engr. Stone & Webster Engring. Corp., Boston, 1981-82, engr., 1982-84; assoc. Metzler and Assocs., Deerfield, Ill., 1986-87, sr. assoc., 1987-90, mgr., 1990-94; energy specialist McKinsey & Co., Atlanta, 1994-96; ind. cons., 1996—; guest lectr. in field; expert witness testimony in constrn. mgmt. Mem. Am. Soc. Cost Engrs., Am. Nuclear Soc., Inst. Mgmt. Cons., Fin. Mgmt. Assn., MENSA. Republican. Home and Office: Ste 1209 3329 E Bayaud Ave Denver CO 80209

WALSKE, M(AX) CARL, JR., physicist; b. Seattle, June 2, 1922; s. Max Carl and Margaret Ella (Fowler) W.; m. Elsa Marjorie Nelson, Dec. 28, 1946; children: C. Susan, Steven C., Carol A. BS in Math. cum laude, U. Wash., 1944; PhD in Theoretical Physics, Cornell U., 1951. Staff, asst. theoretical divsn. leader Los Alamos Sci. Lab., 1951-56; dep. rsch. dir. Atomics Internat., Canoga Park, Calif., 1956-59; sci. rep. AEC in U.K., London, 1961-62; theoretical physicist RAND Corp., 1962-63; sci. attache U.S. missions to NATO and OECD, Paris, 1963-65; staff mem. Los Alamos Sci. Lab., 1965-66; asst. to sec. def. atomic energy, 1966-73; pres., COO Atomic Indsl. Forum, Inc., Washington, 1973-87; chmn. Dept. Def. Mil. Liaison Com. to U.S. AEC, 1966-73; mem. U.S. del. Conf. Suspension Nuclear Tests, Geneva, 1959-61; chair reunion com. U. Wash., 1994-95; mem. fin. com. Ctrl. Kitsap Sch. Dist., 1994-96. Chmn. Upper Hood Canal Watershed Mgmt. Com., 1994—; budget steering com. Kitsap County, 1996, participant strategic planning, 1997. Lt. (J.G.) USNR, 1973-46. Recipient Disting. Civilian Service medal Dept. Def. Fellow Explorers Club, Am. Phys. Soc.; mem. Am. Nuclear Soc., U.S. Power Squadrons (comdr. Agate

Pass squadron 1995-96), Poulsbo Yacht Club (trustee 1996—), Phi Beta Kappa, Sigma Xi. Home: PO Box 370 Silverdale WA 98383-0370 *To seek out positions which appeared the most challenging and personally satisfying; to gain my reward through self-respect rather than public recognition; to expend extra effort as an offset to my limitations.*

WALSTON, RAY, actor; b. Laurel, Miss., Nov. 2, 1924; s. Harry Norman and Mittie (Kimbrell) W.; m. Ruth Calvert, Nov. 3, 1943; 1 dau., Katharine Ann. Grad. high sch., New Orleans. Appeared at Margo Jones Theatre, Houston, 1938-43, Cleve. Playhouse, 1943-45; Broadway appearances include GI Hamlet, 1945, Front Page, 1946, The Survivors, 1947, The Insect Comedy, 1948, Richard III, 1949, Summer and Smoke, 1949 (Clarence Derwent award 1949), The Rat Race, 1949, South Pacific, 1950, Me and Juliet, 1953, House of Flowers, 1954, Damn Yankees, 1955 (Tony award 1955); films include Kiss Them for Me, 1957, South Pacific, 1957, Damn Yankees, 1958, Tall Story, 1958, The Apartment, 1959, Portrait in Black, 1960, Wives & Lovers, 1963, Kiss Me Stupid, 1964, Paint Your Wagon, 1968, Who's Minding the Store, Caprice, The Sting, 1973, The Silver Streak, 1976, Popeye, 1980, Fast Times at Ridgemont High, 1982, Johnny Dangerously, 1984, From the Hip, 1986, Fine Gold, 1987, A Man of Passion, 1988, Popcorn, 1989, Ski Patrol, 1989, Of Mice and Men, 1991; dir.: Broadway musical Damn Yankees, 1974; TV series My Favorite Martian, 1963-66, Picket Fences, 1993— (Emmy awards, Supporting Actor - Drama Series, 1995, 96); TV movies include: The Stand, 1994. Recipient Emmy award, 1945, 46. Mem. Actors Studio, Players Club. *Regarding success in any field, two of the most important words in the English language, or any language for that matter, are persistence and determination. They are all-powerful; nothing can match them.*

WALSTON, RODERICK EUGENE, state government official; b. Gooding, Idaho, Dec. 15, 1935; s. Loren R. and Iva M. (Boyer) W.; m. Margaret D. Grandey; children: Gregory Scott W., Valerie Lynne W. A.A., Boise Jr. Coll., 1956; B.A. cum laude, Columbia Coll., 1958; LL.B. scholar, Stanford U., 1961. Bar: Calif. 1961, U.S. Supreme Ct. 1973. Law clk to judge U.S. Ct. Appeals 9th Cir., 1961-62; dep. atty. gen State of Calif., San Francisco, 1963-91, head natural resources sect, 1969-91, chief asst. atty. gen. pub. rights div., 1991—; spl. dep counsel Kings County, Calif., 1975-76; mem. environ. and natural resources adv. coun. Stanford (Calif.) Law Sch. Contbr. articles to profl. jours.; bd. editors: Stanford Law Rev., 1959-61, Western Natural Resources Litigation Digest, Calif. Water Law and Policy Reporter; spl. editor Jour. of the West. Co-chmn. Idaho campaign against Right-to-Work initiative, 1958; Calif. rep. Western States Water Coun., 1986—; environ. and natural resources adv. coun., Stanford Law Sch. Nat. Essay Contest winner Nat. Assn. Internat. Rels. Clubs, 1956, Stanford Law Rev. prize, 1961; Astor Found. scholar, 1956-58. Mem. ABA (chmn. water resources com. 1988-90, vice chmn. and conf. chmn. 1985-88, 90—), Contra Costa County Bar Assn., U.S. Supreme Ct., Hist. Soc., Federalist Soc., World Affairs Coun. No. Calif. Office: Calif Atty Gen's Office 1300 I St Ste 1720 Sacramento CA 95814-2913

WALT, HAROLD RICHARD, rancher; b. Berkeley, Calif., Jan. 30, 1923; s. Ralph Sidney and Frances Kathryn (Leahy) W.; m. Kathleen Dorothy O'Connell, Dec. 20, 1947; children: Michael Lowney, Timothy Gordon, Kimberly Ann, Patrick Randolph, Jennifer Joan, Carolyn Marie. B.S. in Forestry, U. Calif.-Berkeley, 1948, B.S. in Bus. Adminstrn., 1950, M.B.A. in Corp. Fin., 1953. Vice chancellor fin., lectr. bus. adminstrn. U. Calif., Berkeley, 1948-60; asst. budget dir. Kaiser Industries Corp., Oakland, Calif., 1961-64; dep. dir. fin. State of Calif., 1965-66; dir. civil systems Aerojet-Gen. Corp., El Monte, Calif., 1967-68; exec. v.p. SysteMed Corp., Newport Beach, Calif., 1969-71; pres. William L. Pereira Assos., Los Angeles, 1972-74; dean Coll. Bus. Adminstrn., U. San Francisco, 1978-89, prof. mgmt., 1989; rancher, co-owner, mgt. Box D Ranch, Ashland, Oreg., 1989—; vis. prof. fin. San Francisco State U., 1978; chmn. bd. Fidelity Savs. & Loan Assn., 1982; bd. dirs. Homestead Savs.vis. scholar, 1981; bd. dirs. Eureka Savs. & Loan; adv. com. Fed. Home Loan Mortgage Corp., Washington, 1980-83; vis. scholar Coll. Natural Resources, U. Calif., 1984; S.J. Hall lectr. in indsl. forestry U. Calif., Berkeley, 1986; vis. prof. forest policy U. Calif., 1987, 88. Contbr. over 50 articles related to bus. and forestry. Mem. Calif. Gov.'s Commn. Ocean Resources, 1965-66, Gov.'s Com. Econ. Devel., 1965-66; chmn. Calif. State Bd. Forestry, 1983-90; chmn. bd. Children's Hosp., Stanford, Calif., 1974-80; bd. dirs. Calif. Dept. Forestry, 1990-91, Nat. Forest Found., 1992-94. Served with USMCR, 1942-47. Fellow Fund Adult Edn., 1958; named Calif. Forester of Yr., Calif. Assn. Resource Conservation Dists., 1986. Mem. Soc. Am. Foresters, Am. Forestry Assn. (bd. dirs.), Fin. Execs. Inst., Bay Area Pub. Affairs Council, Acad. Mgmt., Security Analysts Soc., Town Hall of Calif. (bd. dirs. 1972-74), Beta Gamma Sigma, Pi Sigma Alpha, Alpha Zeta, Xi Sigma Pi, Theta Delta Chi, Delta Sigma Pi, Beta Alpha Psi. Republican. Roman Catholic. Clubs: Bohemian (San Francisco); Sutter (Sacramento). Home: PO Box 1267 Ashland OR 97520-0043

WALT, MARTIN, physicist, consulting educator; b. West Plains, Mo., June 1, 1926; s. Martin and Dorothy (Mantz) W.; m. Mary Estelle Thompson, Aug. 16, 1950; children: Susan Mary, Stephen Martin, Anne Elizabeth, Patricia Ruth. B.S., Calif. Inst. Tech., 1950; M.S., U. Wis., 1951, Ph.D., 1953. Staff mem. Los Alamos Sci. Lab., 1953-56; research scientist, mgr. physics Lockheed Missiles and Space Co., Palo Alto (Calif.) Rsch. Lab., 1956-71, dir. phys. scis., 1971-86, dir. research, 1986-93; cons. prof. Stanford U., 1986—; mem. adv. com. NRC, NASA, Dept. Def., U. Calif. Lawrence Berkeley Lab. Author 2 books; contbr. articles to sci. jours. Served with USNR, 1944-46. Wis. Research Found. fellow, 1950-51; AEC fellow, 1951-53. Fellow Am. Geophys. Union, Am. Phys. Soc.; mem. Am. Inst. Physics (bd. govs.), Bd. Overseers for Superconducting Supercollider, Fremont Hills Country Club. Home: 12650 Viscaino Ct Los Altos CA 94022-2517 Office: Stanford U Starlab Durand 317 Stanford CA 94305

WALTER, DONALD ELLSWORTH, federal judge; b. Jennings, La., Mar. 15, 1936; s. Robert R. and Ada (Lafleur) D'Aquin; m. Charlotte Sevier Donald, Jan. 5, 1942; children: Laura Ney, Robert Ellsworth, Susannah Brooks. BA, La. State U., 1961, JD, 1964. Bar: La. 1964, U.S. Supreme Ct. 1969. Assoc. Cavanaugh, Brame, Holt & Woodley, 1964-66, Holt & Woodley, Lake Charles, La., 1966-69; U.S. atty. U.S. Dept. Justice, Shreveport, La., 1969-77; lawyer Hargrove, Guyton, Ramey & Barlow, Shreveport, La., 1977-85; judge U.S. Dist. Ct. (west. dist.) La., Monroe, 1985-92, Shreveport, La., 1993—. Served with AUS, 1957-58. Office: US Dist Ct 300 Fannin St Rm 2b12 Shreveport LA 71101-3141*

WALTER, HELEN JOY, executive director, teacher; b. Bronx, May 22, 1938; d. David and Frieda (Halpern) Presby; m. Wolfgang Walter, Feb. 4, 1962; children: Cheryl, Rochelle, Laurie. BA, Yeshiva U., 1961; MEd, Northeastern U., Boston, 1979. Tchr. Maimonides Day Sch., Brookline, Mass., N.Y.C. Pub. Schs.; counselor Northeastern U.; exec. dir. Brookline C. of C., 1979—. Office: Brookline C of C 1330 Beacon St Brookline MA 02146-3202

WALTER, INGO, economics educator; b. Kiel, Fed. Republic of Germany, Apr. 11, 1940; s. Hellmuth and Ingeborg (Moeller) W.; m. Jutta Ragnhild Dobernecker, June 24, 1963; children: Carsten Erik, Inga Maria. AB summa cum laude, Lehigh U., 1962, MS, 1963; PhD, NYU, 1966. Asst. prof. econs. U. Mo., St. Louis, 1965-67, assoc. prof., chmn. dept., 1967-70; prof. econs. and fin. Stern Sch. Bus. Adminstrn. NYU, N.Y.C., 1970—, assoc. dean academic affairs, 1970-79, chmn. internat. bus. and fin. depts., 1980-85, Dean Abraham L. Gitlow chair, 1987-90; Charles Simon chair, dir. NYU Salomon Ctr., 1990—; Swiss Bank Corp. prof. internat. mgmt. (joint appointment) INSEAD, Fontainebleau, France, 1985—; cons. in field. Author. editor 24 books including Secret Money, 1985, 2d edit., 1990, Global Financial Services, 1990, 2d edit., 1996, Universal Banking in the United States, 1994, Street Smarts, 1997; contbr. articles to profl. jours. Recipient Bernhard Harms medal, 1992; Ford Found. fellow, 1974-76, Rockefeller Found. fellow, 1977-78. Mem. Am. Econ. Assn., Am. Fin. Assn., Acad. Internat. Bus., Royal Econ. Soc., So. Econ. Assn., Phi Beta Kappa, Beta Gamma Sigma, Omicron Delta Epsilon. Home: 77 Club Rd Montclair NJ 07043-2528 Office: NYU Stern Sch Bus 44 W 4th St New York NY 10012-1106

WALTER, J. JACKSON, foundation executive, consultant; b. Abington, Pa., Nov. 6, 1940; s. Joseph Horace and Edith Wilson (Jackson) W.; m. Susan Draude, Feb. 3, 1978; 1 child, Allison K. Mabe. A.B., Amherst Coll., Mass., 1962; LL.B., Yale U., New Haven, 1966. Sec. Fla. Dept. Bus. Regulation, Tallahassee, 1976-79; dir. U.S. Office Govt. Ethics, Washington, 1979-82; pres. Nat. Acad. Pub. Adminstrn., Washington, 1982-84, Nat. Trust Historic Preservation, Washington, 1984-92; exec. dir. Waterford (Va.) Found.; cons. in field. Co-author: America's Unelected Government, 1983. Contbr. articles to profl. jours. Bd. dirs. George Washington U. North Va. Campus, Sabre Found., Boston, 1983—, Am. Alliance for Rights and Responsibilities, Washington. Mem. Nat. Acad. Pub. Adminstrn., ABA, Met. (Washington) Club.

WALTER, JAMES FREDERIC, biochemical engineer; b. Arlington, Va., Dec. 3, 1956; s. John Emory and Barbara (Ward) W.; m. Paula Ann Hanchak, Apr. 19, 1983; children: Jonathan Anthony, James Alexander. BS, U. Va., 1979; PhD, U. Calif., Berkeley, 1983. Rsch. engr. W.R. Grace, Columbia, Md., 1983-85, sr. rsch. engr., 1985-88, mgr. biochem. engring., 1988-93; dir. R&D Grace Biopesticide, 1994-96; dir. rsch. Thermo Trilogy Corp., Columbia, Md., 1996-97; mgr. turf and ornamentals product R&D, Rohm & Haas, Phila., 1997—; lectr. U. Md., College Park, 1985-87. Contbr. chpts to books; contbr. articles to Chem. Engring. Jour., Phytopathology. Named Outstanding Young Leader Optimists, 1974. Mem. AAAS, AIChE, Am. Entomol. Soc., Am. Phytopathol. Soc., Trigon (sec. 1974-75), Alpha Chi Sigma. Achievements include 36 patents including storage of stable azadirachtin formulations, selective production of L-serine derivative isomers, a novel vermiculite formulation with fermentor biomass of biocontrol fungi to control soilborne pathogens, use of neem oil as a fungicide, others. Office: Rohm & Haas 100 Independence Mall W Philadelphia PA 19106

WALTER, JOHN, newspaper editor. Mng. editor Atlanta Jour. and Constn. Office: Journal-Constitution PO Box 4689 72 Marietta St NW Atlanta GA 30303-2804*

WALTER, JOHN ROBERT, printing company executive; b. Pitts., Jan. 20, 1947; s. Jack and Helen (Sech) W.; m. Carol Ann Kost, Sept. 6, 1969; children: Lindsay, Ashley. BBA, Miami U., Oxford, Ohio, 1969. With R.R. Donnelley & Sons Co., Chgo., 1969—, various sales positions, 1969-77, v.p. sales, 1977-81, sr. v.p. sales, 1981-83, dir. mfg. div., 1983-85, group pres., 1985-86, exec. v.p., 1986-87, pres., 1987-89, pres., chmn., CEO, 1989, chmn., CEO, 1990—; bd. dirs. Abbott Labs., Deere & Co., Dayton Hudson Corp., NAM; mem. bus. adv. com. Miami U., 1987—. Trustee Chgo. Symphony Orch.; mem. univ. assocs. bd. Northwestern U.; CEO bd. advisors U. So. Calif.; bd. dirs. Evanston (Ill.) Hosp., Steppenwolf Theatre Co. Mem. Am. Soc. Corp. Execs., Internat. Adv. Coun. of Singapore Econ. Devel. Bd., Bus. Coun., Bus. Round Table (policy com.), Comml. Club Chgo., Chgo. Commonwealth Club, Exec. Club (bd. dirs.), Links Club (N.Y.), River Club (N.Y.), Chgo. Club, Econ. Club Chgo., Historic Georgetown Club. Republican. Lutheran. Avocations: golfing, tennis, sailing.

WALTER, JUDITH ANNE, government executive; b. Ames, Iowa, Feb. 13, 1941; d. Gordon Escher and Eileen Anna (Womeldorff) Walter; m. Irvin B. Nathan; stepchildren: Daniel Nathan, Jonathan Nathan. BA, U. Wis., 1964; MA, U. Calif., Berkeley, 1968, MBA, 1976. Intelligence analyst Nat. Security Agy., Ft. Meade, Md., 1964-66; asst. v.p. internat. Wells Fargo Bank, San Francisco, 1969-75; spl. asst. to under sec. State Dept., Washington, 1975-76; exec. asst. to pres. Am. U., Washington, 1976-77; v.p. corp. banking Wells Fargo Bank, San Francisco, 1977-79; dep. dir. strategic analysis Office of the Comptroller of the Currency, Washington, 1979-82, dir. strategic planning, 1982-85, dep. comptroller ops., 1985-86, sr. dep. comptroller adminstrn., 1986—. Bd. dirs., chmn. governance com. Girl Scout Coun. of Nation's Capital, Washington; bd. govs. The Shakespeare Theatre Guild, Washington. Mem. White House Fellows Assn. (pres.), Women in Housing and Fin. Office: Office of the Comptroller of the Currency 250 E St SW Washington DC 20024-3202

WALTER, MELINDA KAY, health department evaluator; b. Taylorville, Ill., Aug. 6, 1957; d. Ray and Betty (Jones) W.; m. Laurence M. Nakrin, Dec. 21, 1983. BA, Millikin U., 1979; MPA, Sangamon State U., 1981. Acctg. intern Archer Daniels Midland, Decatur, Ill., 1978; econ. devel. intern City of Decatur, 1979; resident dir. Millikin U., Decatur, 1978-79; classification analyst Ill. Dept. Personnel, Springfield, 1979-81; rules analyst Ill. Gen. Assembly, Springfield, 1981-84; regulatory cons. Ill. Dept. Pub. Health, Chgo., 1984-85; asst. to div. chief Ill. Dept. Pub. Health, 1985-88; health planner Lake County Health Dept., Waukegan, Ill., 1988-89; program evaluator Lake County Health Dept., 1989—; cons., Waukegan St. People Task Force, 1990-91; mem. pub. health com., Lake County Coalition for Homeless, Grayslake, Ill., 1990-91; legis. com. mem., Ill Pub. Health Assn., Springfield, 1989-90. Named Student Marshall, Sangamon State U., 1981, Outstanding Young Women Am., 1983. Mem. AAUW, Am. Soc. Pub. Adminstrn. (exec. bd. Springfield, Chgo. 1983-84), Am. Evaluation Assn., Ill. Pub. Health Assn., Ill. Farmers Union, Chgo. Area Health Planning Mktg. Assn. Avocations: bicycling, travel, museums, art galleries, cooking. Home: 801 Browning Ct Vernon Hills IL 60061-1401 Office: Lake County Health Dept 3010 Grand Ave Waukegan IL 60085-2321

WALTER, PAUL HERMANN LAWRENCE, chemistry educator; b. Jersey City, N.Y., Sept. 22, 1934; s. Helmuth Justus and Adelaide C. J. (Twardy) W.; m. Grace Louise Carpenter, Aug. 25, 1956; children: Katherine Elizabeth Walter Bousquet, Marjorie Allison Walter Moran. BS, MIT, 1956; PhD, U. Kans., 1960. Rsch. scientist DuPont Cen. Rsch. Dept., Wilmington, Del., 1960-67; prof. chemistry Skidmore Coll., Saratoga Springs, N.Y., 1967-96, chair chemistry and physics, 1975-85, prof. emeritus, 1996—. Translator: (book) Foundations of Crystal Chemistry, 1968; contbr. articles to sci. publs. Fellow Chem. Inst. Can.; mem. AAAS, AAUP (pres. 1984-86), Am. Chem. Soc. (bd. dirs. 1991—, chmn. 1993-95, pres.-elect 1997), Sociedad Quimica de Mexico (hon.). Democrat. Presbyterian. Achievements include patents in field. Home: 3 Benedictine Retreat Savannah GA 31311-1621

WALTER, PRISCILLA ANNE, lawyer; b. Chgo., Feb. 9, 1943; d. William M. and Anne (Rogers) McConnell; m. Douglas H. Walter, Sept. 6, 1964; children: Kristin Lynn, Nicholas D. BA, Wellesley Coll., 1965; MSc, London Sch. Econ., 1967; JD magna cum laude, Northwestern U., 1978. Bar: Chgo. 1978. Law clk. to presiding justice 7th Cir. Ct. Appeals, Chgo., 1978-79; ptnr. Gardner, Carton & Douglas, Chgo., 1979—. Pres. bd. trustees The Latin Sch., Chgo., 1988-90; mem. bd. govs., mem. exec. com. Met. Planning Coun.; co-chair Field Mus. of Natural History Founder's Coun., 1993-96; bd. dirs. Shakespeare Repertory. Elected one of 100 Top Women in Computing, Open Computing mag., 1995. Mem. Info. Industry Assn. (mem. proprietary rights com.), Computer Law Assn., Am. Bar Found. Office: Gardner Carton & Douglas 321 N Clark St Ste 3400 Chicago IL 60610-4717

WALTER, RICHARD LAWRENCE, physicist, educator; b. Chgo., Nov. 1, 1933; s. Lawrence Barnabas and Marie Ann (Boehmer) W.; m. Carol Elizabeth Goethals, Dec. 27, 1958; children—Timothy, Susan, Matthew. B.S., St. Procopius Coll., 1955; Ph.D., Notre Dame U., 1960. Teaching asst., research asst. Notre Dame U., 1955-59; research asso. dept. physics U. Wis., 1960-61, instr., 1961-62; asst. prof. physics Duke U., Durham, N.C., 1962-67; asso. prof. Duke U., 1967-74, prof., 1974—; vis. staff mem. Los Alamos Sci. Lab., 1964, 70, 75; vis. prof. Max Planck Inst. fur Kernphysik, Heidelberg, Germany, 1970-71, Fudan U., Shanghai and Tsinghua U., Beijing, People's Republic of China, 1985, 88, 91, 94, 95, 96; staff mem. Triangle Univs. Nuclear Lab., 1970—. Contbr. articles to profl. jours. Fulbright scholar, 1970-71. Mem. Am. Phys. Soc., Environ. Metals Group (council 1973-76), Sigma Xi, Sigma Pi Sigma (nat. council 1964-68). Home: 2818 McDowell Rd Durham NC 27705-5621 Office: Duke Univ Dept Physics PO Box 90305 Durham NC 27708-0305

WALTER, ROBERT D., wholesale pharmaceutical distribution executive; b. 1945. BMechE, Ohio U., 1967; MBA, Harvard U., 1970. With Cardinal Foods Inc. (acquired by Roundy's Inc. 1988), Dublin, Ohio, 1971-88; CEO, chmn. bd. Cardinal Health, Inc., Dublin, 1979—. Office: Cardinal Health Inc 5555 Glendon Ct Dublin OH 43016-3249

WALTER, ROBERT IRVING, chemistry educator, chemist; b. Johnstown, Pa., Mar. 12, 1920; s. Charles Weller and Frances (Riethmiller) W.; m. Farideh Asghari, Oct. 17, 1973. AB, Swarthmore Coll., 1941; MA, Johns Hopkins U., 1942; PhD, U. Chgo., 1949. Instr. U. Colo., 1949-51, U. Conn., 1953-55; rsch. assoc. Rutgers U., 1951-53; assoc. physicist Brookhaven Nat. Lab., 1955-56; mem. faculty Haverford Coll., 1956-68, prof. chemistry, 1963-68; prof. U. Ill., Chgo., 1968—, prof. emeritus, 1990—; vis. lectr. Stanford (Calif.) U., winter 1967; acad. guest U. Zurich, 1976; U.S. NAS exch. visitor to Romania, 1982, 88. Mem. Adv. Council Coll. Chemistry, 1966-70. Served with USNR, 1944-46. Grantee U.S. Army Signal Research and Devel. Lab., NIH, NSF, Dept. Energy; NSF fellow, 1960-61. Fellow AAAS; mem. Am. Chem. Soc. (vis. scientist div. chem. edn. 1964-73), Sigma Xi. Achievments include special research preparation, proof of structure, chemical and physical properties of stable aromatic free radicals, C1 reactions and mechanisms in heterogeneous catalysis, reactions of porphyrin bases. Home: 987 Inverleith Rd Lake Forest IL 60045-1607

WALTER, SHERYL LYNN, lawyer; b. Morris, Ill., July 18, 1956; d. C. Frank and Margaret (Juhl) W. BA in History cum laude, Grinnell (Iowa) Coll., 1978; JD cum laude, U. Minn., 1984. Bar: Minn. 1984, U.S. Dist. Ct. Minn. 1987, U.S. Ct. Appeals (8th cir.) 1987, D.C. 1989, U.S. Dist. Ct. D.C. 1989, U.S. Ct. Appeals (D.C. cir.) 1989. Law clk. to presiding judge 3d Jud. Dist. of Minn., Rochester, 1984-85; law clk. to Chief Judge Donald P. Lay U.S. Ct. Appeals (8th cir.), St. Paul, 1985-87; assoc. Mayer, Brown & Platt, Washington, 1987-89; gen. counsel Nat. Security Archive, Washington, 1989-94, Assn. Records Review Bd., 1994-95, Commn. Protecting and Reducing Govt. Secrecy, 1995-97; dep. spl. counsel Senate Vets. Affairs Spl. Investigation on Persian Gulf War Illnesses, 1997—; cons. Amnesty Internat., Washington, 1988-89. Mem. ABA (vice chmn. adminstrv. law sect. govt. info. subcom. 1990-96), D.C. Bar Assn. (steering com., adminstrv. law sect. 1990-97), Am. Soc. Access Profls. (bd. dirs. 1990—, pres. 1996-97), Brit.-Am. Security Info. Coun. (bd. dirs. 1994—), Lawyers Alliance for World Security (bd. dirs. 1994—). Office: 2201 C St NW Rm 225 Washington DC 20522-0001

WALTER, VIRGINIA LEE, psychologist, educator; b. Temple, Tex., Oct. 30, 1937; d. Luther Patterson and Virginia Lafayette (Wilkins) W.; m. Glen Ellis, 1958 (div.); children: Glen Edward, David Walter; m. Robert Reinehr, 1963 (div.); 1 son, Charles Allen; m. Robert Bruininks, 1975 (div.). B.S., U. Tex.-Austin, 1959, M.Edn., 1967; postgrad. internship program in spl. Edn. Adminstrn., 1970; Ed.D., U. Houston, 1973. Tchr. elem. sch. Austin Ind. Sch. Dist., 1959-60, Houston Ind. Sch. Dist, 1965; teaching asst. and research asst. dept. ednl. psychology U. Tex.-Austin, 1965-66; intern Austin State Hosp., 1967; curriculum specialist Spl. Ednl. Instructional Materials Ctr. U. Tex., 1967-68; dir. field activities Edn. Personnel Devel., Austin, 1969-70; parent trainer-communication coordinator Edn. Service Ctr., Austin, 1970-71; grad. asst. U. Houston, 1971-72, teaching fellow, summer 1972, evaluator lab. experiences Tchrs. Inst. Program, 1972-73, grad. asst., advisor in curriculum and instrn. student services ctr., 1972-73, teaching fellow dept. curriculum and instrn., 1973; prof. ednl. psychology dept. ednl. psychology U. Minn., Mpls., 1973-85; pres. Sch. Resource Ctr., Austin, Tex., 1985-90; tchr. Llano Pub. Schs., 1988—; chmn. State Adv. Council for Inservice Tng. Regular Classroom Tchrs., 1977-79; cons. spl. ednl. various sch. dists., state depts. and agys.;. Editorial cons.: Jour. Ednl. Psychology, 1979, Reading Research Quar., 1982; assoc. editor: Exceptional Children, 1979-84; assoc. editor Teaching Exceptional Children, 1985-89; contbr. articles to profl. jours., papers to profl. confs. Named Minn. Spl. Educator of Yr., 1978; recipient Service award Internat. Council Exceptional Children, 1978; HEW Office of Human Devel. Services grantee, 1976-80; Dept. Edn. contractee, 1980-83. Mem. Council for Exceptional Children, Nat. Assn. Children with Learning Disabilities (dir. Minn. chpt. 1978-80), Nat. Assn. Retarded Citizens, AAUP, Assn. Supervision and Curriculum Devel. Home and Office: PO Box 493 Llano TX 78643-0493

WALTERS, ARTHUR SCOTT, neurologist, educator, clinical research scientist; b. Balt., Feb. 20, 1943; s. Charles Henry and Jean Vivian (Scott) W.; m. Bokyun Kim, May 18, 1985 (div. Oct. 1992); m. Lesley J. Gill, Dec. 19, 1992. BA, Kalamazoo Coll., 1965; MS, Northwestern U., 1967; MD, Wayne State U., 1972. Diplomate Am. Bd. Psychiatry and Neurology; diplomate Am. Bd. Sleep Medicine. Intern Oakwood Hosp., Dearborn, Mich., 1972-73; resident in neurology SUNY Downstate Med. Ctr., Bklyn., 1976-79; movement disorder fellow Neurol. Inst., N.Y.C., 1982-84; asst. prof. neurology Robert Wood Johnson Med. Sch., U. Medicine & Dentistry N.J., New Brunswick, 1984-91, assoc. prof. neurology, 1991—; asst. chief divsn. neurology Lyons (N.J.) VA Med. ctr., 1985-89; neurology cons. Lyons (N.J.) VA Med. Ctr., 1984—; nat. chmn. med. adv. bd. Restless Legs Syndrome Found., 1992—; organizer Internat. Restless Legs Study Group, 1992—; head Restless Legs Syndrome and Periodic Limb Movement Coun. for the Nat. Sleep Found., 1994-96; neurology cons. Coney Island Hosp., Bklyn., Bklyn. Jewish Hosp., 1980-81; presenter in field. Contbr. articles, abstracts, to profl. publs., chpts. to books, organizer symposia. Grantee UMDNJ, 1984-86, VA RAG, 1985-86, Sandoz Corp., 1985-88, VA Merit Rev., 1989—, Clemente Found., 1994-95. Fellow Am. Acad. Neurology, Am. Sleep Disorders Assn.; mem. AAAS, Sleep Rsch. Soc., Movement Disorder Soc., N.Y. Acad. Scis., N.J. Sleep Soc. (sec. 1995-96, treas. 1996—). Home: 207 S Adelaide Ave Highland Park NJ 08904-1605 Office: UMDNJ-Robert Wood Johnson Med Sch Dept Neurology CN19 1 Robert Wood Johnson Pl New Brunswick NJ 08901-1928

WALTERS, BARBARA, television journalist; b. Sept. 25, 1931; d. Lou and Dena (Selett) W.; 1 child, Jacqueline. Grad., Sarah Lawrence Coll., 1953; LHD (hon.), Ohio State U., Marymount Coll., Tarrytown, N.Y., 1975, Wheaton Coll., 1983. Former writer-producer WNBC-TV; then with Stas. WPIX and CBS-TV; joined Today Show, 1961, regular panel mem., 1964-74, co-host, 1974-76; moderator syndicated program Not For Women Only, 1974-76; newscaster ABC Evening News (now ABC World News Tonight), 1976-78; host The Barbara Walters Spls., 1976—; co-host ABC TV news show 20/20, 1979—. Contbr. to ABC programs Issues and Answers. Author: How To Talk With Practically Anybody About Practically Anything, 1970; contbr. to Reader's Digest, Good Housekeeping, Family Weekly. Recipient award of yr. Nat. Assn. TV Program Execs., 1975, Emmy award Nat. Acad. TV Arts and Scis., 1975, Mass Media award Am. Jewish Com. Inst. Human Relations, 1975, Hubert H. Humphrey Freedom prize Anti-Defamation League-B'nai B'rith, 1978, Matrix award N.Y. Women in Communications, 1977, Barbara Walters' Coll. Scholarship in Broadcast Journalism established in her honor Ill. Broadcasters Assn., 1975, Pres.'s award Overseas Press Club, 1988, Lowell Thomas award Marist Coll., 1990, Lifetime Achievement award Internat. Women's Media Found., 1992; named to 100 Women Accomplishment Harper's Bazaar, 1967, 71, One of Am.'s 75 Most Important Women Ladies' Home Jour., 1970, One of 10 Women of Decade Ladies' Home Jour., 1979, One of Am.'s 100 Most Important Women Ladies' Home Jour., 1983, Woman of Year in Communications, 1974, Woman of Year Theta Sigma Phi, Broadcaster of Yr. Internat. Radio and TV Soc., 1975, One of 200 Leaders of Future Time Mag., 1974, One of Most Important Women of 1979 Roper Report, One of Women Most Admired by Am. People Gallup Poll, 1982, 84, to Hall of Fame Acad. TV Arts and Scis., 1990. Office: 20/20 147 Columbus Ave Fl 10 New York NY 10023-5900 also: Barwall Productions The Barbara Walters Specials 825 7th Ave Fl 3 New York NY 10019-6014*

WALTERS, BETTE JEAN, lawyer; b. Norristown, Pa., Sept. 5, 1946. BA, U. Pitts., 1967; JD, Temple U., 1970, LLM in Taxation, 1974. Bar: Pa. 1970, U.S. Dist. Ct. (ea. dist.) Pa. 1971. Law clk., assoc. William R. Cooper, Lansdale, Pa., 1969-72; spl. asst. to pub. defender Montgomery County (Pa.), 1973; pvt. practice North Wales, Pa., 1972-73; assoc. counsel Alco Standard Corp., Valley Forge, Pa., 1973-79, group counsel mfg., 1979-83; v.p., gen. counsel, sec. Alco Industries, Inc., Valley Forge, 1983—, also bd. dirs., 1983—. Mem. corp. sponsors com. Zool. Soc. of Phila. Mem. ABA, DAR, Pa. Bar Assn., Montgomery County Bar Assn., Am. Corp. Counsel Assn., Licensing Execs. Soc.. Republican. Office: Alco Industries Inc PO Box 937 Valley Forge PA 19482-0937

WALTERS, BILL, state senator, lawyer; b. Paris, Ark., Apr. 17, 1943; s. Peter Louis and Elizabeth Cecelia (Wilhelm) W.; m. Joyce Leslie Garrett Moore, Jan. 9, 1964 (div. 1970); children: Jamie, Sherry Ann; m. Shirley Ann Dixon, Aug. 20, 1971; 1 child, Sandra. BS, U. Ark., 1966, JD, 1971. Bar: Ark. 1971, U.S. Dist. Ct. Ark. 1971. Asst. prosecuting atty. 12th Jud. Dist. Ark., Ft. Smith, 1971-74; pvt. practice Greenwood, Ark., 1975—; mem. Ark. Senate, Little Rock, 1982—; bd. dirs. 1st Ark. Title Co., Pine Bluff; bd. dirs., sec.-treas. Mineral Owners Collective Assn. Inc., Greenwood; v.p., bd. dirs. Sebastian County Abstract & Title Ins. Co., Greenwood and Ft. Smith, Ark.; mem. Ark. Real Estate Commn., Ark. Abstract and Title Commn. Committeeman Rep. Ctrl. Com. Ark., Ft. Smith, 1980; search pilot CAP, Ft. Smith. Decorated Silver Medal of Valor; recipient Cert. of Honor Justice for Crime's Victims, 1983. Mem. Ark. Bar Assn., South Sebastian County Bar Assn. (pres. 1991-94), Profl. Landmen's Assn. Roman Catholic. Home: PO Box 280 Greenwood AR 72936-0280 Office: 44 Town Square St Greenwood AR 72936-4019

WALTERS, DANIEL RAYMOND, political columnist; b. Hutchinson, Kans., Oct. 10, 1943; s. Howard Duke and Glenna Lucille (Hesse) W.; m. Doris K. Winter, June 16, 1995; children: Danielle, Staci. Mng. editor Hanford (Calif.) Sentinel, 1966-69, Herald News, Klamath Falls, Oreg., 1969-71, Times-Standard, Eureka, Calif., 1971-73; polit. writer and columnist Sacramento (Calif.) Union, 1973-84; polit. columnist Sacramento Bee, 1984—. Author: The New California: Facing the 21st Century, 1986; founding editor Calif. Polit. Almanac, 1989. Office: The Sacramento Bee 925 L St Ste 1404 Sacramento CA 95814-3704*

WALTERS, DAVID MCLEAN, lawyer; b. Cleve., Apr. 4, 1917; s. William L. and Marguerite (McLean) W.; m. Betty J. Latimer, Mar. 25, 1939 (dec. 1983); 1 child, Susan Patricia (Mrs. James Edward Smith); m. Rebecca Brewer, Feb. 14, 1991. BA, Baldwin-Wallace Coll., 1938, LHD (hon.); LLB, Cleve. Sch. Law, 1943; JD, U. Miami, 1950; LHD (hon.), St. Thomas of Villanova U. Bar: D.C. 1950, Fla. 1950, Fed. 1950. Judge adminstrv. practices U.S. Dept. Justice, Washington, 1940-50; sr. law ptnr. firm Walters & Costanzo, Miami, Fla., 1950-80; of counsel firm Walters, Costanzo, Russell, Zyne, 1980-85; amb. to Vatican, 1976-78; fellow internat. medicine, bd. advisors Med. Sch., Boston U., 1985. Chmn. Fla. Harbor Pilot Commn., 1952-54, City of Miami Seaport Commn., 1953-54, Nat. Leukemia Soc., 1965-66, Archbishops Charities Dr., 1975-76; spl. bond counsel Dade County, 1957-58; gen. counsel Dade County Port Authority, 1957-58; vice-chmn. Nat. Dem. Fin. Coun., 1960-77; mem. Gov.'s Adv. Bd. on Health and Rehabilitative Svc., 1976-77; sec.-treas. Inter-Am. Ctr. Authority, 1960-74; bd. advisor St. Thomas Law Sch., 1985-88; personal rep. Pres. Reagan F.D.R. Meml. Commn., 1985; bd. dirs. Barry U.; chmn. bd. trustees Variety Children's Hosp.; pres. Miami Children's Hosp. Found., 1980—; trustee Gregorian Inst. Found., Rome. Served with Counter Intelligence Corps, U.S. Army, 1943-46. Decorated Bronze Star medal., Knight of the Grand-cross, Order St. Gregory the Great; recipient Silver medallion NCCJ, Resolution of Commendation award for civic contbn. Fla. Legislature, 1988. Mem. Am., Fla., Fed., D.C., Interam. bar assns., Am. Assn. Knights of Malta (v.p.), Serra Club, Sovereign Mil. Order Malta (master knight 1975—, exec. com. papal visit to U.S. 1987), Omicron Delta Kappa, Lambda Chi Alpha. Democrat. Roman Catholic. Home: 9202 SW 78th Pl Miami FL 33156-7590 Home (summer): 5 St Helens, Marine Parade Sandycove, Dublin Ireland Office: 3000 SW 62nd Ave Miami FL 33155-3065

WALTERS, DENNIS H., lawyer; b. Rochelle, Ill., Mar. 2, 1950; s. Harold R. and Helen M. (Eshbaugh) W.; m. Marilyn E. Hoban, Jan. 1, 1984. BA, Ill. Wesleyan U., 1972; MS in Bus. Adminstrn., Boston U., 1975; JD, Harvard U., 1979. Bar: Wash. 1979, Alaska, 1985, U.S. Ct. Appeals (9th cir.) 1991, U.S. Supreme Ct. 1991; lic. comml. pilot, flight instr. Assoc. Karr Tuttle Campbell, Seattle, 1979, shareholder, 1987—, head of appellate practice, 1991—. Trustee, pres. Vision Svcs., Seattle, 1980-86; trustee Literacy Coun. of Kitsap, 1993-96. With U.S. Army, 1972-76. Named Citizen of Day, Sta. KIXI, Seattle, 1985. Mem. ABA, Seattle-King County Bar Assn. (chmn. aviation sect. 1984-85), Lawyer-Pilots Bar Assn., Wing Point Golf and Country Club. Avocations: flying, golf, boating. Home: 25853 W Canyon Rd NW Poulsbo WA 98370-9503 Office: Karr Tuttle Campbell 1201 3rd Ave Ste 2900 Seattle WA 98101-3028

WALTERS, DORIS LAVONNE, pastoral counselor, counseling services facility administrator; b. Peachland, N.C., Feb. 24, 1931; d. H. Lloyd and Mary Lou (Helms) W. AA, Gardner Webb U., 1959; BA cum laude, Carson-Newman Coll., 1961; MRE, Southwestern Bapt. Theol. Sem., 1963; MA in Pastoral Counseling, Wake Forest U., 1982; DMIn in Pastoral Counseling, Southeastern Bapt. Theol. Sem., 1988. Min. of edn. and youth First Bapt. Ch., Orange, Tex., 1963-66; assoc. prof. Seinan Jo Gakuin Jr. Coll., Japan, 1968-72; dir. Fukuoka (Japan) Friendship House, 1972-88, pastoral counselor, chaplain, 1983-86; Tokyo lifeline referral counselor (in English) Hiroshima-South, Fukuoka, 1983-86; supr. Japanese and Am. staff Fukuoka Friendship House, 1972-86; with chaplaincy Med. Coll. Va., Richmond, 1976; resident chaplain N.C. Bapt. Hosp., Winston-Salem, 1981-82, counselor-in-tng. pastoral care dept., 1986-88; dir. missionary counseling and support svcs. Pastoral Care Found. N.C. Bapt. Hosp., Winston-Salem, 1989-93; dir. Missionary Family Counseling Svcs., Inc., Winston-Salem, 1993—; mem. Japan Bapt. Mission Exec. Com., Tokyo, 1973-76. Author: An Assessment of the Reentry Issues of the Children of Missionaries, 1991, 2d printing with title Missionary Children: Caught between Cultures, 1996; translator: The Story of the Craft Dogs, 1983. Named Alumnus of Yr., Gardner Webb U., 1993; J.M. Price scholar Southwestern Bapt. Theol. Sem., 1962; First Bapt. Ch. Blackwell grantee Southeastern Sem., 1986-88. Mem. Assn. for Clin. Pastoral Counselors (assoc.), Am. Assn. Pastoral Counselors (pastoral affiliate). Democrat. Avocations: photography, travel, reading, classical music, concerts. Home: 208 Oakwood Sq Winston Salem NC 27103-1914 Office: Missionary Family Counseling Svcs Inc 514 S Stratford Rd Winston Salem NC 27103-1823

WALTERS, GLEN ROBERT, banker; b. Mpls., Sept. 11, 1943; s. Sterling Thomas and Mildred Eunice (Parkinson) W.; m. Gail Elvira Engelsen, June 11, 1966; children—Nicole Marie, Brent Aaron, Hillary Renee. B.A., U. Minn., Mpls., 1965, postgrad., 1965-67; banking degree, Stonier Grad. Sch. Banking, Rutgers U., New Brunswick, N.J., 1982. Comml. banker 1st Nat. Bank, Mpls., 1967-83, sr. v.p. human resources, 1983-90; sr. v.p. Firstar Bank Minn., Mpls., 1990—. Served to sgt. USNG, 1967-73. Republican. Presbyterian. Office: Firstar Bank 1550 E 79th St Minneapolis MN 55425-1139

WALTERS, GOMER WINSTON, lawyer; b. Johnstown, Pa., Sept. 24, 1937; s. Philip Thomas and Margaret Elizabeth (Peat) W.; m. Jean Mary Jester, June 13, 1964 (divorced 1988); children: Bruce Joseph, Matthew Howel, Melinda Jean. BE, Yale U., 1960; JD, George Washington U., 1965. Bar: Ill. 1965, Pa. 1972, U.S. Dist. Ct. (no. dist.) Ill. 1965, U.S. Dist. Ct. (we. dist.) Pa. 1972, U.S. Dist. Ct. (no. dist.) Ohio 1973, U.S. Ct. Appeals (3 and 7th cirs.) 1981, U.S. Supreme Ct. 1982, U.S. Ct. Appeals (fed. cir.) 1982. Assoc. Kirkland & Ellis, Chgo., 1965-70, ptnr., 1970-72; patent atty. Westinghouse Electric Corp., Pitts., 1972-73; assoc. Walsh, Case & Coale, Chgo., 1973-74, Lee & Smith, Chgo., 1975; ptnr. Haight & Hofeldt, Chgo., 1975-90, Wood, Phillips, Van Santen, Clark & Mortimer, Chgo., 1990-95; pvt. practice, Chgo., Ligonier, Pa., 1995—; dir. R2 Corp., 1981-84, Vast Research Co., 1981-87; chmn.'s council Crow Canyon Archaeol. Ctr., 1987—, trustee, 1996—; dir., treas. Primitive Arts Soc. of Chgo., 1991-96. Mem. ABA, Chgo. Bar Assn., Am. Intellectual Property Law Assn., Intellectual Property Law Assn., Univ. Club Chgo., The Tower Club. Republican. Office: Cliffwood 1300 Route 271 S Ligonier PA 15658-9248

WALTERS, JANE, state agency administrator. MusB, Rhodes Coll., BA in Music History; MA in Counseling, U. Memphis; PhD in Sch. Adminstrn., Duke U. Tchr., counselor Messick H.S., Memphis, asst. prin.; asst. dir. computer svcs. Memphis City Schs.; prin. Craigmont Jr. H.S., 1974-79, Craigmont Jr. and Sr. H.S., 1979-95; 21st commr. edn. State Dept. Edn., Nashville, 1995—; adv. com. edn. depts. Rhodes Coll, Christian Brothers Com., Tenn. Arts Acad.; cons. College Bd. advanced placement program. Grant reader NEA; mem. Goals for Memphis Edn. Com.; bd. dirs. World Affairs Coun, Nat. Coun. Christians and Jews, Memphis Coun. Internat. Visitors, Memphis Youth Symphony, Am. Cancer Soc., Memphis chpt. Office: Tenn State Dept Edn 6th Fl Andrew Johnson Tower 710 James Robertson Pkwy Nashville TN 37219-1219*

WALTERS, JEFFERSON BROOKS, musician, retired real estate broker; b. Dayton, Ohio, Jan. 20, 1922; s. Jefferson Brooks and Mildred Frances (Smith) W.; m. Mary Elizabeth Espey, Apr. 6, 1963 (dec. July 22, 1983); children: Dinah Christine Basson, Jefferson Brooks; m. Carol Elaine Clayton Gillette, Feb. 19, 1984. Student, U. Dayton, 1947. Composer, cornetist Dayton, 1934—, real estate broker, 1948-88; ret., 1988. Condr., composer choral, solo voice settings of psalms and poetry Alfred Lord Tennyson; composer Crossing the Bar (meml. performances U.S. Navy band), 1961; composer The Yorktown Grand March (Good Citizenship medal SAR, 1988). Founder Am. Psalm Choir, 1965; apptd. deferred giving officer Kettering (Ohio) Med. Ctr., 1982-85. Served with USCGR, 1942-45, PTO, ETO. Mem. SAR, Greater Dayton Antique Study Club (past pres.), Dayton Art Inst., Montgomery County Hist. Soc., Masons (32d deg.). Brethren Ch. Home: 4113 Roman Dr Dayton OH 45415-2423

WALTERS, JOHN LINTON, electronics engineer, consultant; b. Washington, Mar. 8, 1924; s. Francis Marion Jr. and Roma (Crow) W.; m. Grace Elizabeth Piper, June 19, 1948; children: Richard Miller, Gretchen Elizabeth, Christopher Linton, John Michael, Kim Anne. BS, U.S. Naval Acad., 1944; SM, Harvard U., 1949; DrEng, Johns Hopkins U., 1959. Staff mem. Los Alamos (N.Mex.) Sci. Lab., 1949-52; rsch. assoc. Johns Hopkins U., Balt., 1952-59; assoc. elec. engr. Brookhaven Nat. Lab., Upton, N.Y., 1959-62; rsch. scientist Johns Hopkins U., Balt., 1962-70; electronics engr. Naval Rsch. Lab., Washington, 1970—; asst. sci. advisor Comdr. 6th Fleet, Gaeta, Italy, 1979-80; lectr. dept. elec. engring. Johns Hopkins U., 1964-65. Lt. (j.g.) USN, 1944-47, PTO. Recipient commendation Dir. of Navy Labs., 1979. Mem. IEEE, Sigma Xi. Achievements include research on electronic countermeasures, refinements to measurement techniques used in particle accelerators, analysis of radar and jamming phenomena, measurement and analysis of anomalous propagation in atmosphere. Home: 212 Beach Dr Annapolis MD 21401-5856 Office: Radar Divsn Naval Rsch Lab Washington DC 20375

WALTERS, JOHN SHERWOOD, retired newspaperman; b. Junction City, Ark., May 15, 1917; s. John Thomas and Cora (McBride) W.; m. Claire Dailey, June 1, 1941; children: Elizabeth Claire, Mary Dailey (dec.). B.A., La. Tech. Inst., 1939; M.A., La. State U., 1941. Editor Ruston (La.) Daily Leader, 1940; reporter Baton Rouge Morning Adv., 1941; rating examiner Jacksonville Naval Air Sta., 1941-42; reporter Fla. Times-Union, Jacksonville, 1943, 44-53; city editor Fla. Times-Union, 1953-60; exec. editor Times-Union and Jacksonville Jour., 1960-78, asso. pub., 1978-82, ret., 1982; asst. prof. journalism La. Tech. Inst., 1943-44; mem. jud. Nominating Commn., 1st Dist. Ct. Appeals of Fla. Bd. dirs. Duval County chpt. A.R.C., chmn., 1966-67; charter trustee U. North Fla. Found., Inc., pres., 1973-75; chmn. council advisers U. North Fla., 1975; bd. dirs. Health Planning Council, N.E. Fla. Cancer Program, Jacksonville Blood Bank. Mem. Am. Soc. Newspaper Editors, Fla. Soc. Newspaper Editors (pres. 1971-72), Alpha Lambda Tau, Sigma Delta Chi. Democrat. Methodist. Clubs: Rotarian (Jacksonville) (sec. 1970-71, pres. 1971-72); Timuquana Country, River. Home: 1750 Dogwood Pl Jacksonville FL 32210-2202

WALTERS, JOHNNIE MCKEIVER, lawyer; b. nr. Hartsville, S.C., Dec. 20, 1919; s. Tommie Ellis and Lizzie Lee (Grantham) W.; m. Donna Lucile Hall, Sept. 1, 1947; children: Donna Dianne Walters Gent, Lizbeth Kathern Walters Kukorowski, Hilton Horace, John Roy. AB, Furman U., 1942, LLD, 1973; LLB, U. Mich., 1948. Bar: Mich. 1948, N.Y. 1955, S.C. 1961, D.C. 1973. Atty. office chief counsel IRS, Washington, 1949-53; asst. mgr. tax div. law dept. Texaco, Inc., N.Y.C., 1953-61; ptnr. firm Geer, Walters, & Demo, Greenville, S.C., 1961-69; asst. atty. gen. tax div. Dept. Justice, Washington, 1969-71; commr. IRS, 1971-73; ptnr. firm Hunton & Williams, Washington, 1973-79, Leatherwood Walker Todd & Mann, P.C., Greenville, 1979-95; exec. v.p., gen. counsel Colonial Trust Co., 1996—; bd. dirs. Textile Hall Corp., Greenville, Santee Cooper, Moncks Corner, S.C. Mem. S.C. Coun. on Competitiveness, 1987-91; bd. dirs. Greenville Hosp. System Found., S.C. State Mus. Found. With USAAF, 1942-45. Fellow Am. Coll. Tax Counsel (founding regent), Am. Coll. Trust and Estate Counsel, Am. Bar Found., S.C. Bar Found. (bd. dirs. 1988-92); mem. ABA (taxation sect.), S.C. Bar (chmn. taxation sect. 1983-84), Rotary (pres. local club 1968-69). Republican. Baptist. Office: 12 N Spring St Greenville SC 29601-2807 Home: 1804 N Main St Greenville SC 29609-4729

WALTERS, LAWRENCE CHARLES, advertising executive; b. Cin., Apr. 1, 1948; s. Lawrence Simpson and Mary Josephine (Koerner) W.; m. Ann Morley Reifenrath, Jan. 15, 1983. Assoc. in Advt., U. Cin., 1969. Art dir. J. Walter Thompson, Chgo., 1972-78; sr. art dir. Needham Harper and Steers, Chgo., 1978-81; advt. creative dir. ACOM, Quaker, Chgo., 1981-83; co. group creative dir. Tatham, Laird, Kudner, Chgo. With the USMC, 1966-69. Democrat. Roman Catholic. Avocations: music writing, white water canoe racing, tennis, water color painting. Office: Tatham Laird Kudner 980 N Michigan Ave Chicago IL 60611-4501

WALTERS, MILTON JAMES, investment banker; b. Hornell, N.Y., May 21, 1942; s. James Henry and Frances Eleanor (Simmons) W.; m. Caroline Houck, May 24, 1963; children: Melissa Ann, Gregory Thomas, Timothy Allen. BA, Hamilton Coll., 1964. Trainee Mfrs. Hanover, 1964-65; with A.G. Becker Paribas Inc., N.Y.C., 1965-84, v.p., 1969-78, mng. dir., 1978-84; sr. v.p. corp. fin., mng. dir. Smith Barney, N.Y.C., 1984-88; pres. Tri-River Capital Group, 1988—; trustee Hamilton Coll., Clinton, N.Y., 1983-88, Friends Acad., Locust Valley, N.Y., 1981-91. Mem. Econ. Club N.Y., Mill River Club. Republican. Presbyterian. Office: Tri River Capital Group Inc 689 5th Ave New York NY 10022-3133

WALTERS, PHILIP RAYMOND, foundation executive; b. Frankfort, Ind., Jan. 26, 1938; s. Raymond and Ruth Edna (Grimes) W.; m. Sharon Pearl Wilfong, May 31, 1958 (div. Nov. 1992); children: Raymond (dec.), Robert, Sharon Ruth; m. Candace Gina Oden, Jan. 29, 1994. BSBA, Olivet Nazarene Coll., 1959; JD, Ind. U., Indpls., 1969; postgrad., NYU, 1969-70. Bar: Ind. 1969, U.S. Dist. Ct. (so. dist.) Ind. 1969. Co-corp. counsel Ind. Farm Bur. Ins., Indpls., 1975-79; dir. gift and estate planning Orlando (Fla.) Regional Healthcare Found., 1991-96; regional dir. planned giving Arthritis Found., Longwood, Fla., 1996—; dep. atty. gen. State of Ind., Indpls.; planned giving officer Wheaton (Ill.) Coll.; campaign dir. Ketchum, Inc., Pitts.,; dir. planned giving Presbyn. Sch. Christian Edn., Richmond, Va.; presenter in field. Contbr. articles to profl. jours. Mem. Wekiva Presbyn. Ch., Longwood. Mem. Nat. Soc. Fundraising Execs, Ctrl. Fla. Planned Giving Coun. Republican. Avocation: running. Home: 897 Cutler Rd Longwood FL 32779-3525

WALTERS, RAYMOND, JR., newspaper editor, author; b. Bethlehem, Pa., Aug. 23, 1912; s. Raymond and Elsie (Rosenberg) W. A.B., Swarthmore Coll., 1933; postgrad., Princeton U., 1933-35; M.A., Columbia U., 1937, Ph.D., 1942. Editorial staff Current History mag., 1937-39; editorial staff Saturday Rev., 1946-58, book rev. editor, 1948-58; editor Encore mag., 1946-48; editor, columnist N.Y. Times Book Rev., 1958—; Mem. fiction jury Pulitzer Prize adv. bd., 1968. Author: Alexander James Dallas: Lawyer, Politician, Financier, 1943, Albert Gallatin: Jeffersonian Financier and Diplomat, 1957 (named One of Notable Books of Year, ALA), The Virginia Dynasty, 1965, Paperback Talk, 1985; Contbr. articles to profl. jours. Served with USAAF, 1942-46; hist. office hdqrs. USAAF, 1943-46. Mem. Am. Hist. Assn., Soc. Am. Historians (v.p.), P.E.N., Authors Guild. Episcopalian. Home: 315 E 68th St New York NY 10021-5692

WALTERS, ROBERT ANCIL, II, protective services coordinator; b. Washington, Sept. 21, 1945; s. Robert Ancil and Etha Jane (McKinley) W.; m. Sandra Faye Roy, June 30, 1969; children: Anthony Wayne, Byron Edward. Student, Western Ky. U., 1964-65, Internat. Acad., 1965-66, U. Md., 1969-70. Cert. fire tng instr., Ky., emergency med. technician, Ky., profl. emergency mgr., Md. Computer operator U.S. Naval Weapons Lab., Dahlgren, Va., 1969-70; instr. computer programming Brentwood Acad., Lexington, Ky., 1970-71; data control supr. Dept. Child Welfare, State of Ky., Frankfort, 1971-74; military personnel supr. Ky. Army Nat. Guard, Frankfort, 1974-77; area coord. Ky. Disaster and Emergency Svcs., Somerset, Ky., 1977—. Chmn. bd. dirs. Somerset-Pulaski County Rescue Squad, Ky., 1982-86, active mem., 1978-89; bd. dirs. Nancy Fire Dept., 1986-87, active mem., 1979-95; bd. dirs., disaster chmn. Lake Cumberland (Ky.) chpt. ARC, 1982-86, instr. CPR and first aid, 1979-88; mem. prospect listing and evaluation com. Ptnrs. in Progress, Somerset C.C., 1994. Sgt. U.S. Army, 1968-69, Vietnam. Recipient Ky. Commendation medal, 1975, 77, 79, Ky. Merit citation, 1976, 80, 892, Ky. Humanitarian citation, 1974, 77, Ky. Achievement medal, 1978, 82, 93. Mem. Ky. Disaster and Emergency Svcs Assn., Ky. Emergency Mgmt. Assn., Nat. Emergency Mgrs. Assn., Order of Kentucky Colonels, Somerset Colonel, Adair County General. Democrat. Baptist. Home: 1063 Prather Dr Nancy KY 42544-8722

WALTERS, RONALD OGDEN, finance company executive; b. Holcombe, Wis., July 13, 1939; s. Ogden Eugene and Josephine Ann (Hennekens) W.; m. Margaret Ellen Weisheipl, July 14, 1962; children—Laurie, Cheryl, Michael, Patrick. Student, U. Wis. Mgr. Thorp Fin., LaCrosse, Wis., 1962-65; regional mgr. Thorp Fin., Milw., 1965-69, ITT Consumer Fin. Corp., Milw., 1969-74; sr. v.p. ITT Consumer Fin. Corp., Brookfield, Wis., 1974—, exec. v.p. adminstrn., CEO, 1991-93; CEO Ideal Fin. Corp., 1994-97, USA Funding Corp., Brookfield, Wis., 1997—. Mem. Wis. Fin. Services Assn. (pres. 1980). Republican. Roman Catholic. Avocations: boating; fishing; hunting. Home: N62w15763 Skyline Dr Menomonee Falls WI 53051-5748 also: 17035 Wisconsin Ave Brookfield WI 53005

WALTERS, WILLIAM LEE, accountant; b. New Orleans, Feb. 26, 1946; s. Elton E. and Helen (England) W.; m. Wanda Lovorn, Aug. 24, 1968; 1 child, Jack. BS in Acctg., Miss. State U., 1969. CPA, Miss. Acct. Ellis & Hirsberg, CPA's, Clarksdale, Miss., 1969-75; prin. W.L. Walters, CPA's, Clarksdale, 1975—. Founding dir. Found. for N.Am. Wild Sheep, Cody, Wyo., 1978-82; com. man U.S. Golf Assn., Far Hills, N.J., 1986—; panel mem. Golf Digest 100 Greatest Courses, 1985—; bd. dirs. Lula-Rich Ednl. Found., Clarksdale, 1995—. Mem. AICPA, Miss. Soc. CPAs, Miss. State U. Alumni Assn. (pres. Coahoma County chpt. 1996), Clarksdale Country Club (pres. 1980, 85), Bulldog Club (bd. dirs. 1986—), Old Waverly Golf Club. Methodist. Avocations: golf, hunting, bodybuilding, competitive water skiing. Home and Office: PO Box 896 Clarksdale MS 38614-0896

WALTERS, WILLIAM LEROY, physics educator; b. Racine, Wis., Mar. 30, 1932; s. Robert N. and Elsie (Ahrens) W.; m. Darlene A. Kessenich, Feb. 5, 1955; children: Judy, Sandra, Robert, James. BS, U. Wis., 1954, MS, 1958, PhD, 1961. Assoc. dean scis. Coll. Letters and Sci. U. Wis., Milw., 1965-67, spl. asst. to chancellor, 1967-68, exec. asst. chancellor, 1968-69, asst. chancellor, acting dean Coll. Applied Sci. and Engring., 1969-70, vice chancellor univ., 1971-81, prof. physics, 1981-95, emeritus prof. physics, 1996—; sci. edn. grant adminstr., cons. Contbr. articles to physics jours. With U.S. Army, 1954-56. Mem. AAAS, Am. Assn. Physics Tchrs., Am. Phys. Soc., Nat. Assn. State Univs. and Land Grant Colls. (mem., chmn. exec. com. coun. acad. affairs 1978), Physics Club Milw. (dir. 1964-67, 82-92). Home: 2100 E Jarvis St Milwaukee WI 53211-2003

WALTERS-PARKER, KIMBERLY KAY, secondary school educator; b. Mt. Sterling, Ky., Apr. 9, 1961; d. Robert Wendell and Lagene Kay (Stull) Walters; m. Steve Robert Parker, July 3, 1992; 1 child, Blake. BA, Georgetown Coll., 1983; MA, Morehead State U., 1985; Rank I Cert., U. Ky., 1990. Cert. secondary English educator, reading specialist, Ky. Instr. Eastern Ky. U., Richmond, 1985-87; reading specialist Bryan Sta. High Sch. Fayette County Pub. Schs., Lexington, Ky., 1987—, dir. writing ctr., 1990—; co-owner Walters/Parker Learning Ctr., Inc., 1993-96; cons. tech. writing and rsch. skills Ky. Sci. and Tech. Coun., 1993. Recipient Merit of Excellence award County of Fayette; grantee Ky. Dept. Edn., 1991-92, 93, Lexington Edn. Assistance Found., 1992, 96. Mem. ASCD, Nat. Coun. Tchrs. English, Internat. Reading Assn., Ky. Coun. Tchrs. English. Avocations: PhD coursework in ednl. psychology. Home: 4201 Ridgewater Dr Lexington KY 40515-6009

WALTHALL, LEE WADE, artistic director, dancer; b. Houston, Nov. 12, 1953; s. L.W. and Martha Virginia (Tacker) W. Student, Sch. of Am. Ballet, N.Y.C., 1973-75; BA cum laude, U. Wash., 1994. Prin. dancer Dutch Nat. Ballet, Amsterdam, 1975-82, Pacific N.W. Ballet, Seattle, 1982-90; dancer, ballet master Ballet Austin, Tex., 1990-91; artistic dir. Eastside Dance Theatre, Seattle, 1993-94, The Evergreen City Ballet, 1994—; dir. Evergreen City Ballet Acad., 1995—; artist in residence Hong Kong Ballet, 1991; guest artist Nureyev Internat. Ballet Festival, Kazan, Russia, 1994. Guest appearances throughout Europe and U.S.; starring role in Nutcracker-The Movie, 1986. Study grantee U. Wash. Dept. Dance, 1991-94.

WALTHER, JOSEPH EDWARD, health facility administrator, retired physician; b. Indpls., Nov. 24, 1912; s. Joseph Edward and Winona (McCampbell) W.; m. Mary Margaret Ruddell, July 11, 1945 (dec. July 1983); children: Mary Ann Margolis, Karl, Joanne Landman, Suzanne Conran, Diane Paczesny, Kurt. BS, Ind. U., 1936, MD, 1936; postgrad., U. Chgo., Harvard U., U. Minn., 1945-47. Diplomate Nat. Bd. Med. Examiners, Am. Bd. Internal Medicine, Am. Bd. Gastroenterology. Intern Meth. Hosp. and St. Vincent Hosp. of Indpls., 1936-37; physician, surgeon U.S. Engrs./Pan Am. Airways, Midway Island, 1937-38; chief resident, med. dir. Wilcox Meml. Hosp., Lihue, Kauai, 1938-39; internist, gastroenterologist Meml. Clinic Indpls., 1947-83, med. dir., pres., chief exec. officer, 1947—; founder, pres. Doctors' Offices Inc., Indpls., 1947—; founder, pres., chief exec. officer Winona Meml. Found. and Hosp. (now Walther Cancer Inst.), Indpls., 1956—; clinical asst. prof. medicine Ind. U. Sch. Medicine, Indpls., 1948-93, clin. asst. prof. emeritus, 1993—. Author: (with others) Current Therapy, 1965; mem. edit. rsch. bd. Postgrad. Medicine, 1982-83; contbr. articles to profl. jours. Bd. dirs. March of Dimes, Marion County div., 1962-66, Am. Cancer Soc., Ind. div., 1983-92. Col. USAAF, 1941-47, PTO. Decorated Bronze Star, Silver Star, Air medal; recipient Clevenger award Ind. U. 1989;, Disting. Alumnus award Ind. U. Sch. Med., 1989, Sagamore of Wabash award State of Ind., 1995; Dr. Joseph E. Walther Disting. Physician's award named in honor Winona Meml. Hosp., 1995. Master Am. Coll. Gastroenterology (pres. 1970-71, Weiss award 1988); mem. AMA (del. 1970-76), Soc. Cons. to Armed Forces, Ind. Med. Assn., Marion County Med. Assn., Ind. U. Alumni Assn. (life), Hoosier Hundred (charter), Highland Golf and Country Club (hon.), Waikoloa Golf and Country Club (Hawaii), Indpls. Athletic Club, 702 Club. Republican. Home: Ste 104 3266 N Meridian St #104 Indianapolis IN 46208 Office: Walther Cancer Inst 3202 N Meridian St Indianapolis IN 46208-4646

WALTNER, JOHN RANDOLPH, banker; b. San Diego, Dec. 11, 1938; s. Glenn H. and Pauline B. (Hoffman) W.; m. Janice L. McNamara, Nov. 23, 1963; children: Mary E., Ann L. BSBA, U. S.D., 1961, MBA, 1989. Trainee 1st Nat. Bank, Freeman, S.D., 1961-62, v.p., cashier and bd. dirs., 1968-87, pres., CEO and bd. dirs., 1988—; ops. officer Wells Fargo Bank, Monterey, Calif., 1964-67; bd. dirs. S.D. Blue Shield; mem. faculty U. S.D., Vermillion, 1990—, bus. adv. coun. Sch. of Bus., 1985—, chmn., 1992; mem. S.D. Investment Coun., 1994—, S.D. Lottery Commn., 1996—. Mem. S.D. Lottery Commn., 1996—; mem. Freeman Cmty. Devel. Corp., 1967—, past pres.; pres. Freeman Sch. Bd., 1981-84; treas. City of Freeman, 1961-62. With U.S. Army, 1962-64. Mem. Am. Bankers Assn. (govt. rels. coun. 1995—), S.D. Bankers Assn. (bd. dirs., v.p. 1991, pres.-elect 1992, pres. 1993-94), Freeman C. of C. (past sec.-treas.), Beta Gamma Sigma. Republican. Mennonite. Avocations: pub. speaking, community theater, amateur radio, astronomy, chess. Home: 541 S Poplar St PO Box 566 Freeman SD 57029 Office: 1st National Bank PO Box H Freeman SD 57029

WALTON, ALAN GEORGE, venture capitalist; b. Birmingham, Eng., Apr. 3, 1936; s. Thomas George and Hilda (Glover) W.; m. Jasmin Yvonne Christensen, Sept. 1, 1958 (dec. Nov. 1970); children: Kimm A., Keir D.A.; m. Elenor Jean McElliott, Aug. 6, 1977; children: Kristin M., Sherri L. Ph.D., U. Nottingham, Eng., 1960, D.Sc., 1973. Research assoc. Ind. U., Bloomington, 1960-62; asst. prof. chemistry Case Western Res. U., Cleve., 1962-66, assoc. prof., 1966-69, assoc. prof. macromolecular sci., 1969-71, prof., 1971-81, dir. Lab. for Biol. Macromolecules, 1972-81; pres., chief exec. officer Univ. Genetics Co., 1981-86, chmn., 1986-87; ptnr. Oxford Ptnrs., Westport, Conn., 1987—; chmn. Oxford Biosci. Corp., 1992—; vis. lectr. biol. chemistry Harvard Med. Sch., 1971; mem. Pres. Carter's Task Force on Sci. and Tech.; U.S. project officer Rudjer Boskovic Inst., Zagreb, Yugoslavia, 1967-75; bd. dirs. Collaborative Clin. Rsch. Inc., Cardio Pulmonary Corp.; chmn. AVID Corp., Gene Logic Inc.; chmn. Exelixis Pharms. Corp.; bd. govs. Nat. Ctr. Genome Resources. Author: Formation and Properties of Precipitates, 1967, Biopolymers, 1973, Structure and Properties of Amorphous Polymers, 1980, Polypeptide and Protein Structure, 1981, Recombinant DNA, 1981, Yearbook of Genetic Engineering and Biotechnology, 1983, 85, 88. Recipient Israel State medal, 1972, Case Inst. Centennial Scholar medal, 1981. Mem. Nat. Venture Capital Assn., Conn. Venture Group, Sigma Xi (Research award 1973), Pi Kappa Alpha. Home:

17 Walnut Ln Weston CT 06883-1417 Office: Oxford Biosci Corp 315 Post Rd W Westport CT 06880-4739

WALTON, ANTHONY JOHN (TONY WALTON), theater and film designer, book illustrator; b. Walton on Thames, Eng., Oct. 24, 1934; s. Lancelot Henry Frederick and Hilda Betty (Drew) W.; m. Julie Andrews, May 10, 1959 (div. 1968); 1 child, Emma Kate; m. Genevieve LeRoy, Sept. 12, 1991; 1 stepchild, Bridget. Student, Oxford Sch. Tech. Art and Commerce, 1949-52, Slade Sch. Fine Art, London, 1954-55. Designer settings, costumes for theater prodns., London, off-Broadway, 1957-60, Broadway, 1961—; Broadway prodns. include Pippin, 1972 (Tony award 1972-73, Drama Desk award 1972-73), Shelter, 1973 (Drama Desk award 1972-73), Sophisticated Ladies, 1981, The Real Thing, 1984, Hurlyburly, 1984, I'm Not Rappaport, 1985, House of Blue Leaves, 1986 (Tony award 1985-86), Drama Desk award 1985-86), Front Page, 1986, Social Security, 1986 (Drama Desk award 1985-86), Anything Goes, 1987, Grand Hotel, 1989, Six Degrees of Separation, 1990, The Will Rogers Follies, 1991, Death and the Maiden, 1992, Conversations with My Father, 1992, Four Baboons Adoring the Sun, 1992, Guys and Dolls, 1992 (Tony award 1991-92, Drama Desk award 1991-92), Tommy Tune Tonight, 1992, She Loves Me, 1993, A Grand Night for Singing, 1993, Laughter on the 23rd Floor, 1993, Picnic, 1994, A Christmas Carol, N.Y.C., 1994, Company, 1995, Moonlight, 1995, A Fair Country, 1996, A Funny Thing Happened on the Way to the Forum, 1996, The Shawl, 1996; designer settings, costumes for theather prodns., dir. The Importance of Being Earnest, 1996; dir. Noel Coward in Two Keys Bay St. Theatre Festival, 1996; ballets, principally San Francisco Ballet Co., Am. Ballet Theatre; films include Mary Poppins, A Funny Thing Happened on the Way to the Forum, Murder on the Orient Express, The Wiz, All That Jazz (Acad. award with Philip Rosenberg 1980), Prince of the City, Star 80, The Glass Menagerie, 1987, Regarding Henry, 1991; operas in London, 1963-68, Spoleto, Italy, 1965, Santa Fe, 1975, San Francisco, 1992, Chgo., 1993; author: Adelie Penguin in Wonders, 1981; illustrator Wonders, 1981, The Importance of Being Earnest, 1973, Lady Windemere's Fan, 1973, Popcorn, 1972, God Is a Good friend, 1969, Witches Holiday, 1971, others. Served with RAF, 1952-54. Recipient Emmy award Death of a Salesman, 1986; named to Theatre Hall of Fame, 1991; elected to Interior Design Hall of Fame, 1993. Mem. United Scenic Artists, Costume Designers Guild Calif., Acad. Motion Picture Arts and Scis. Office: care Martino ICM 40 W 57th St New York NY 10019-4001

WALTON, BILL (WILLIAM THEODORE WALTON, III), sportscaster, former professional basketball player; b. La Mesa, Calif., Nov. 5, 1952; s. Theodore and Gloria W.; m. Susan Walton; children: Adam, Nathan, Luke. Grad., UCLA, 1974. Team center Portland Trail Blazers, 1974-79, capt., 1976-77; with Los Angeles Clippers (formerly San Diego Clippers), 1979-85, Boston Celtics, 1985-87; sportscaster NBC Sports, 1993—; mem. NCAA Divisional Championship Team, 1972-73, NBA Championship Teams, 1977, 86. Recipient James E. Sullivan Meml. award, 1974, James Naismith award, 1972, 73, 74, Adolph Rupp trophy, 1972, 73, 74, NBA Sixth Man award, 1986; named NBA Most Valuable Player, 1978. Office: NBC Sports General Electric Corp 30 Rockefeller Plz New York NY 10112*

WALTON, BRIAN, labor union executive; b. London, Dec. 24, 1947; came to U.S., 1966; s. Frank William and Irene Mary (Thornton) W.; (div.); children: Robert, Sarah; m. Deborah R. Baron. BA with honors, Brigham Young U., 1969, MA in Polit. Sci., 1971; JD, U. Utah, 1974. Bar: Calif. 1974, U.S. Dist. Ct. (ctrl., so. and no. dists.) Calif. 1974. Law clk. to Hon. J. Allan Crockett Utah Supreme Ct., 1974; assoc. Reavis & McGrath and predecessor firms, L.A., 1974-82; ptnr. Selvin and Weiner, L.A., 1982-85; exec. dir. Writers Guild Am., West, Inc., L.A., 1985—; teaching asst. Coll. Law, Utah U., 1973, asst. to v.p. of spl. projects, 1971-73, rsch. asst. Coll. Law, 1972-74, tchr., dir. legal skills seminar Coll. Law, 1974. Contbr. articles to law jours. Edwin S. Hinckley scholar. Mem. ABA (antitrust sect.), L.A. County Bar Assn. (antitrust sect., intellectual property and unfair competition sect.), Assn. Bus. Trial Lawyers, Internation Assn. des Avocats du Droit d'Auteur. Office: Writers Guild of Am 7000 W 3rd St Los Angeles CA 90048-4329

WALTON, CAROLE LORRAINE, clinical social worker; b. Harrison, Ark., Oct. 20, 1949; d. Leo Woodrow Walton and Arlette Alegra (Cohen) Armstrong. BA, Lambuth Coll., Jackson, Tenn., 1971; MA, U. Chgo., 1974. Diplomate Clin. Social Work, Acad. Cert. Social Workers; bd. cert. diplomate; lic. clin. social worker. Social worker Community Mental Health, Flint, Mich., 1971-72; clin. social worker Community Mental Health, Westchester, Ill., 1974-76; dir. self-travel program Chgo. Assn. Retarded Citizens, 1976-78; coord. family svcs. Inner Harbors Psych. Hosp., Douglasville, Ga., 1976-83; sr. mental health clinician Northside Mental Health Ctr., Atlanta, 1983—. Mem. NASW, Ga. Soc. for Clin. Work (pres. 1981-82, pres. 1993-95). Avocation: tennis. Office: Northside Mental Health Ctr 5825 Glenridge Dr NE Bldg 4 Atlanta GA 30328-5387

WALTON, CHARLES MICHAEL, civil engineering educator; b. Hickory, N.C., July 28, 1941; s. Charles O. and Virginia Ruth (Hart) W.; m. Betty Grey Hughes; children: Susan, Camila, Michael, Gantt. BS, Va. Mil. Inst., 1963; MCE, N.C. State U., 1969, PhD, 1971. Research asst. N.C. State U., Raleigh, 1967-71; transp. planning engr. N.C. Hwy. Commn., Raleigh, 1970-71; asst. prof. civil engring. U. Tex., Austin, 1971-76, assoc. prof., 1976-83, prof., 1983—, Bess Harris Jones Centennial prof. natural resource policy studies, 1987-91, Paul D. and Betty Robertson Meek Centennial prof. engring., 1991-93, Ernest H. Cockrell Centennial chair engring., 1993—, chmn. dept. civil engring., 1988-96; transp. cons., 1970—; assoc. dir. Ctr. for Transp. Rsch. U. Tex., 1980-88; chmn., exec. com. Transp. Rsch. Bd., NRC, 1991, Disting. Lectr., 1994. Contbr. articles to profl. jours. Past chmn. Urban Transp. Commn., Austin. Recipient Disting. Engring. award N.C. State U., 1995, Joe J. King Profl. Engring. Achievement award U. Tex. at Austin, 1995-96. Fellow ASCE (Harland Bartholomew urban planning award 1987, Frank M. Masters transp. engring. award 1987, James Laurie prize 1992), Inst. Transp. Engrs.; mem. NSPE, NAE, Intelligent Transp. Soc. Am. (vice chair tech. coord. coun., immediate past chair tech. com. on comml. vehicle ops.), Soc. Automotive Engrs., Urban Land Inst., Inst. for Ops. Rsch. and Mgmt. Scis., Soc. Am. Mil. Engrs., Internat. Rd. Fedn. (bd. dirs.), Internat. Rd. Ednl. Found. (bd. dirs.), Austin C. of C. (Leadership Austin program). Democrat. Methodist. Home: 3404 River Rd Austin TX 78703-1031 Office: U Tex Dept Civil Engring Dept Civil Engring ECJ Hall Ste 6.3 Austin TX 78712

WALTON, CLIFFORD WAYNE, chemical engineer, researcher; b. Phila., May 14, 1954; s. John Robert and Elizabeth Baird (Hamilton) W. BSChemE, Drexel U., 1976; MSChemE, Tex. A&M U., 1977, PhD, 1987. Registered profl. engr., Nebr.; cert. electroplater-finisher. Instr. U. Coll. div. U. Md., Stuttgart, Germany, 1978-79, Tex. A&M U., College Station, 1982-84; rsch. engr. Dow Chem. Co., Freeport, Tex., 1985; asst. prof. U. Nebr., Lincoln, Nebr., 1987-91; assoc. prof. U. Nebr., Lincoln, 1991-92; cons. Walton & Assocs., Lincoln, 1987-94; rsch. assoc. FMC Corp., Princeton, N.J., 1994—; cons. Lincoln Plating Co., 1987-94, Mitsui Engring. and Shipbuilding Co., Ltd., Tokyo, 1989-93, Nat. Ctr. for Mfrs. Scis., Ann Arbor, 1990-94, J.P. Industries, Ann Arbor, 1990-94. Editl. bd. Plating and Surface Finishing, 1989-95; internat. editl. bd. Jour. of Clearner Prodn., 1990—; contbr. articles to profl. jours. Treas. Nebr. Wrestling Booster Club, Lincoln, 1990-92. 1st lt. U.S. Army, 1977-80. Named Outstanding Young Man in Am., U.S. Jaycees, 1982; recipient Ralph R. Teetor award Soc. Automotive Engrs., 1990. Mem. AIChE (sec.-treas. Nebr. br. 1989-91), ASTM (tech. com. 1989-96), Am. Electroplaters and Surface Finishers Soc. (br. pres. 1988-91, publs. bd. 1989-95, scholarship com. 1989-92, chair scholarship com. 1992-94, 95-96), Electrochem. Soc. Inc. (sec. IEEE divsn. 1996—, symposium organizer 1989-90, 92, 96, 97). Avocation: physical fitness, amateur wrestling, boxing, church choir. Office: FMC Corp Chem Rsch & Devel Ctr PO Box 8 Princeton NJ 08543-0008

WALTON, G. CLIFFORD, family practice physician; b. Richmond, Va., Jan. 5, 1968; s. Eugene Marion and Mary Ann (McNabb) W. BS summa cum laude, Hampden-Sydney Coll., 1990; MD, Med. Coll. Va., 1994. Intern Med. Coll. Va., Richmond, 1994-95; resident Blackstone (Va.) Family Practice, 1995—; physician Patient First, Richmond, 1996—; med. examiner Va. Dept. Health, Richmond, 1996—; housestaff coun. Med. Coll. Va., 1995-97. Sci. fair judge Southside Va. H.S., Farmville, 1988—. Mem. AMA, Am. Acad. Family Physicians, Med. Soc. Va., Phi Beta Kappa, Omicron Delta Kappa, Sigma Xi. Baptist. Avocations: baseball card collecting, gardening, photography. Home: 1618 Cedar Ln Powhatan VA 23139 Office: Blackstone Family Practice 820 S Main St Blackstone VA 23824-2600

WALTON, GERALD WAYNE, English educator, university officiala; b. Union, Miss., Sept. 11, 1934; s. Willie Jay and Ruby Elizabeth (Williamson) W.; m. Juliet Katherine Hart, Aug. 26, 1960; children: Katherine Hart, Dorothy Elizabeth, Margaret Stevens. A.A., East Central Jr. Coll., 1954; B.S., U. So. Miss., 1956; M.A., U. Miss., 1959, Ph.D., 1967. Tchr. asst. U. Miss., 1956-59, instr. English, 1959-62, asst. prof., 1962-67, assoc. prof., 1967-70, prof., 1970—, assoc. dean Coll. Liberal Arts, 1970-76, dean, 1976-82, assoc. vice chancellor for acad. affairs, 1982-94, interim vice chancellor for acad. affairs, 1994-96, provost, 1996—. Contbr. articles to profl. jours. Vice-pres. Oxford Human Rels. Coun., 1968; mem. adminstrv. bd. Oxford U. Meth. Ch., chmn. bd. trustees, 1971-72; bd. dirs. Yoknapatawpha Arts Coun., 1980-81; sec.-treas. So. Lit. Festival, 1965. Tri-Univ. fellow in linguistics U. Nebr., 1969-70. Mem. MLA, Am. Dialect Soc., Miss. Folklore Soc., Friends of Arts in Miss., Miss. Assn. English Tchrs. (sec. 1968), Miss. Inst. Arts and Letters (sec. 1979-80), Nat. Coun. Tchrs. English, William Faulkner Soc., Miss. Hist. Soc., Rotary, Golden Key, Phi Kappa Phi, Sigma Tau Delta, Omicron Delta Kappa. Home: 106 Ole Miss Dr Oxford MS 38655-2615 Office: U Miss Vice Chancellor Acad Affairs University MS 38677

WALTON, GLORIA JEAN, secretary; b. Mpls., July 7, 1942; d. Harvey William and Edna May (Akins) Nash; m. Louis Edward Walton, Aug. 23, 1964; children: Lisa, Louis Jr., Timothy, Teresa. AA, U. Minn., 1985, BS, 1991. Lic. minister Assemblies of God, 1997. Clerk typist St. Paul (Minn.) Urban League, 1959-62; with Norwest Bank, Mpls., 1962-65; clerk typist Munsingwear, Mpls., 1967-68; transcriber typist Hennepin County Dept. Ct. Svcs., Mpls., 1968-70; sec. Trinity Tabernacle Assembly of God, Mpls., 1970—; clerk typist Stivers Temporary Pers., Mpls., 1985-90. Recipient Bus. scholarship Pragmateia Sorority, 1960, recognition for faithful ministry of music Trinity Tabernacle, 1986. Mem. U. Minn. Alumni Assn. (life), Women's Ministries (pres. 1980-95). Avocations: photography, sewing, home improvement, bike riding, poetry reading. Home: 2206 Queen Ave N Minneapolis MN 55411-2437

WALTON, HAROLD VINCENT, former agricultural engineering educator, academic administrator; b. Christiana, Pa., June 17, 1921; s. Howard King and Alice Lauretta (Kirk) W.; m. Velma Purvis Braun, June 24, 1946; children: H. Richard, Marilyn J. Walton Friedersdorf, Carol A. B.S. in Agrl. Engring., Pa. State U., 1942, M.S. in Agrl. Engring., 1950; Ph.D. in Agrl. Engring., Purdue U., 1961. Test engr. Gen. Electric Co., Schenectady, 1943-45; instr. Pa. State U., 1947-50, asst. prof. agrl. engring., 1950-52, assoc. prof., 1952-61, prof., 1961, 76-85, head dept. agrl. engring., 1976-85, ret., 1985; prof.-in-charge, chmn. dept. agrl. engring. U. Mo.-Columbia, 1962-69; chief of party U. Mo.-Columbia, Bhubaneswar, India, 1969-71; prof. U. Mo.-Columbia, 1971-76; cons. OAS, Trinidad and Tobago, 1980, Ptnrs. of Ams., Brazil, 1984. Served with U.S. Army, 1945-46. Fulbright scholar, Cyprus, 1989-90. Fellow Am. Soc. Agrl. Engrs. (bd. dirs. 1967-69, 85-87). Republican.

WALTON, JAMES M., investment company executive; b. Pitts., Dec. 18, 1930; m. Ellen Carroll; 4 children. B.A., Yale U.; M.B.A., Harvard U. With Gulf Oil Corp., Phila., Houston, Pitts., Tokyo, Rome, 1958-67; pres. Carnegie Inst., Pitts., 1968-84, Carnegie Mus. Natural History and Mus. of Art, Pitts., 1968-84, Carnegie Library, Pitts., 1968-84; life trustee, pres. emeritus Carnegie Inst. and Carnegie Library, Pitts., 1984—; vice chmn. bd. dirs. MMC Group Inc.; bd. dirs. Irish Investment Fund, Inc. Mem. sponsoring com. Penn's Southwest Assn.; life trustee Carnegie-Mellon U.; treas. Carnegie Hero Fund Commn.; dir. World Affairs Coun. of Pitts., One Hundred Friends of Pitts. Art; trustee Sarah Scaife Found. Inc., Scaife Family Found.; chmn. Vira I. Heinz Endowment; mem. Cultural Dist. Devel. Com. Lt. U.S. Army, 1954-56. Office: 525 William Penn Pl Rm 3902 Pittsburgh PA 15219-1707

WALTON, JON DAVID, lawyer; b. Clairton, Pa., Sept. 18, 1942; s. Thomas Edward and Matilda Lucy (Sunday) W.; m. Carol Jeanne Rowland, Sept. 15, 1964; children: David Edward, Diane Elizabeth. BS, Purdue U., 1964; JD, Valparaiso U., 1969. Bar: Pa. 1969. Atty. U.S. Steel Corp. (now USX Corp.), Pitts., 1969-73; asst. gen. counsel Harbison-Walker Refractories, Pitts., 1973-75; gen. counsel Harbison-Walker Refractories, 1975-81, v.p., gen. counsel, 1981-83; regional gen. counsel Dresser Industries, Inc. (now Indresco Corp.), Pitts., 1983-86; gen. counsel, sec. Allegheny Ludlum Corp., Pitts., 1986-90, v.p., gen. counsel, sec., 1990-96; v.p., gen. counsel, sec. Allegheny Teledyne Inc., Pitts., 1996—. Pres., bd. dirs. Music for Mt. Lebanon, 1996—; chmn. bd. dirs. Pitts. Youth Golf Found., 1991—. Mem. ABA, Pa. Bar Assn., Allegheny County Bar Assn., Am. Soc. Corp. Secs. (former pres. regional group), Pa. Chamber Bus. and Industry (bd. dirs., exec. com.), Am. Corp. Counsel Assn., Am. Arbitration Assn. (panel arbitrators), Duquesne Club, Valley Brook Country Club, Rolling Rock Club. Home: 137 Hoodridge Dr Pittsburgh PA 15228-1803 Office: Allegheny Teledyne Inc 1000 Six PPG Pl Pittsburgh PA 15222-5479

WALTON, MATT SAVAGE, retired geologist, educator; b. Lexington, Ky., Sept. 16, 1915; m. Kathryn Ralston, Dec. 6, 1940 (div.); m. Nalda Robison, May 22, 1969 (dec.); m. Kay Ann Thorson, June 21, 1970; children: Matt Savage III, Kate Johns, Lisa Baar, Anne Elizabeth, Owen Hardwick. B.A., U. Chgo., 1936; M.A. (James Furman Kemp fellow), Columbia U., 1947, Ph.D., 1951. Geologist U.S. Geol. Survey, 1942-46; asso. prof. Yale U., New Haven, 1948-65; geologist N.Y. State Geol. Survey, summers, 1947-57; cons. geologist, 1947-73; regents lectr. environ. sci. and engring. UCLA, 1970-71; dir. Minn. Geol. Survey, U. Minn., 1973-86, prof. geology and geophysics, 1973-86, prof. emeritus, 1986—; cons. on geologic conditions affecting excavation and undergroung constrn., 1995—; dir. Deep Observation and Sampling of the Earth's Continental Crust, Inc., 1984-86; mem. exec. com. Great Lakes Internat. Project. Contbr. articles on engring. geology to sci. jours. Pres. Old Town Restorations, Inc., St. Paul, 1974-79; bd. dirs. Summit Hill Assn., 1974-79. Fellow Geol. Soc. Am.; mem. Assn. Am. State Geologists. Avocations: writing, consulting. Home: 30 Crocus Pl Saint Paul MN 55102-2810

WALTON, MORGAN LAUCK, III, lawyer; b. Woodstock, Va., July 30, 1932; s. Morgan Lauck Jr. and Frances (Allen) W.; m. Jeannette Freeman Minor, Mar. 4, 1961; children: Morgan Lauck IV, Charles Lancelot Minor, Christopher Allen, Laura Cathlyn. BA, Randolph-Macon Coll., 1953; LLB, U. Va., 1959. Bar: Va. 1959, N.Y. 1959, U.S. Ct. Appeals (2d cir.) 1959, U.S. Dist. Ct. (ea. and so. dists.) N.Y. 1960, U.S. Dist. Ct. (we. dist.) Va. 1988. Assoc. Donovan Leisure Newton & Irvine, N.Y.C., 1959-68; ptnr. Donovan, Leisure, Newton & Irvine, N.Y.C., 1968-84; counsel FDIC, Washington, 1989-90, asst. gen. counsel, 1990—. Contbr. articles to legal jours. Trustee Randolph-Macon Acad., Front Royal, Va., 1987-92, Unitarian Ch. Shenandoah Valley, Stephens City, Va., 1987—; mem. coun. Law Sch. U. Va., 1989-92; treas. Shenandoah Valley Music Festival, Woodstock, 1986-87; chmn. bd. All Souls Ch., N.Y.C., 1974-76. With U.S. Army, 1953-56. Mem. ABA (co-chmn. long term planning com. govt. lawyers divsn. 1993-94, chmn. Clayton Act com. antitrust sect. 1976-78), Assn. of Bar of City of N.Y., Univ. Club, Collectors Club, Order of Coif, Phi Beta Kappa. Democrat. Home: 908 Kern Springs Rd Woodstock VA 22664-3216 Office: FDIC 550 17th St NW H6018 Washington DC 20429-0001

WALTON, RALPH GERALD, psychiatrist, educator; b. Darlington, Eng., Aug. 18, 1942; came to U.S., 1950; s. Kenneth and Paula (Weissman) W.; m. Ellen Paula Liebling, Feb. 15, 1970 (div. 1980); children: Deborah, Rachel; m. Mary Elaine Hultburg, Sept. 27, 1981; children: Lisa, Jonathan. AB, U. Rochester, 1963; MD, SUNY, Syracuse, 1967. Diplomate Am. Bd. Psychiatry and Neurology. Intern Strong Meml. Hosp., Rochester, N.Y., 1967-68, resident in psychiatry, 1968-71; asst. prof. psychiatry Sch. Medicine U. Rochester, N.Y., 1973-76; chief psychiatry Jamestown (N.Y.) Gen. Hosp., 1976-88; commr. mental health Chautauqua County, Jamestown, 1985-88; chmn. dept. psychiatry Western Res. Care System, Youngstown, Ohio, 1988—; prof. psychiatry N.E. Ohio Univs. Coll. of Medicine, Rootstown, Ohio, 1988—; med. dir. Profl. Recovery Plus Alcoholic Clinic, Youngstown, 1992—. Contbr. chpt. to: Dietary Phenylalanine and Brain Function, 1988; contbr. foreword to: Katherine It's Time, 1989; contbr. articles to profl. jours., 1972—. Maj. U.S. Army, 1971-73, Panama. Fellow Am. Psychiat. Assn. Jewish. Office: 725 Boardman Canfield Rd Youngstown OH 44512-4380

WALTON, RICHARD EUGENE, business educator; b. Pulaski, Iowa, Apr. 15, 1931; s. Lee Richard and Florence (King) W.; m. Sharon Claire Doty, Apr. 13, 1952; children—John, Elizabeth, Margaret, Andrew. B.S., Purdue U., 1953, M.S., 1954; postgrad., Victoria U., New Zealand, 1953; D.B.A., Harvard, 1959. Faculty Harvard Bus. Sch., 1968—, Edsel Bryant Ford prof. bus., 1970-76, dir. rsch. div., 1970-76, now Wallace Brett Donham prof. bus.; cons. various indsl. firms, govt. agys. including Dept. State; bd. dirs. Champion Internat. Corp. Author: A Behavioral Theory of Labor Negotiations: An Analysis of a Social Interaction System, 1965, (with R.B. McKersie) The Impact of the Professional Engineering Union, 1961, (with M. Beer and others) Human Assets, 1984, (with P. Lawrence) Human Resource Management Trends and Challenges, 1985, Managing Conflict, 1987, Innovating to Compete, 1987, Up and Running, 1989, (with Joel Cutcher-Gershenfeld and Robert B. McKersie) Strategic Negotiations: A Theory of Change in Labor-Management Relations, 1994, (with Joel Cutcher-Gershenfeld and Robert B. McKersie) Pathways to Change: Case Studies of Strategic Negotiations, 1995. Served with AUS, 1954-56. Ford Found. faculty grantee U. Mich., 1962-63. Home: 109 Beaver Rd Weston MA 02193-1035 Office: Harvard Bus Sch Dept of Bus Boston MA 02163

WALTON, ROBERT LEE, JR., plastic surgeon; b. Lawrence, Kans., May 30, 1946; s. Robert L. and Thelma B. (Morgan) W.; m. Laura Lake, May 1, 1971; children: Marc, Morgan, Lindsey. BA, U. Kans., 1968; MD, U. Kans., Kansas City, 1972. Diplomate Am. Bd. Surgery, Am. Bd. Plastic Surgery. Resident in surgery Johns Hopkins Hosp., Balt., 1972-74, Yale-New Haven (Conn.) Hosp., 1974-78; chief of plastic surgery San Francisco Gen. Hosp., 1979-83; prof. and chmn. dept. plastic surgery U. Mass. Med. Ctr., Worcester, 1983-94; prof., chmn dept. plastic surgery U. of Chicago, 1994—. Contbr. articles to profl. jours. Founder Projecto Mira Found. for Handicapped Children, Santurce, P.R., 1990. Mem. Am. Assn. Plastic Surgeons, Am. Coll. Surgeons, Am. Soc. Plastic and Reconstructive Surgery, Am. Soc. Surgery of the Hand, Alpha Omega Alpha. Office: U of Chicago Divsn Plastic Surgery MC6035 5841 S Maryland Ave Chicago IL 60637-1463

WALTON, RODNEY EARL, lawyer; b. Corvallis, Oreg., Apr. 28, 1947; s. Ray Daniel Jr. and Carolyn Jane (Smith) W. BA, Coll. of Wooster, 1969; JD, Cornell U., 1976. Bar: Fla. 1976, U.S. Dist. Ct. (so. dist.) Fla. 1976, U.S. Dist. Ct. (mid. dist.) Fla. 1977, U.S. Supreme Ct. 1980, U.S. Ct. Appeals (11th cir.) 1981. Assoc. to jr. ptnr. Smathers & Thompson, Miami, Fla., 1976-87; ptnr. Kelley, Drye and Warren, Miami, 1987-93; atty. Heinrich Gordon Hargrove Weihe & James, P.A., Ft. Lauderdale, 1994—. Sec. bd. dirs. Kings Creek Condominium Assn., Miami, 1984-89, treas., 1984, pres., 1990-91. 1st lt. U.S. Army, 1969-73, Vietnam. Decorated Bronze Star. Mem. ABA, Fla. Bar, Broward County Bar Assn., Maritime Law Assn. Republican. Methodist. Avocations: travel, reading, sports. Home: 2331 NW 33rd St Apt 301 Fort Lauderdale FL 33309-6444 Office: Heinrich Gordon PA 500 E Broward Blvd Ste 1000 Fort Lauderdale FL 33394-3002

WALTON, ROGER ALAN, public relations executive, mediator, writer; b. Denver, June 25, 1941; s. Lyle R. and Velda V. (Nicholson) W.; m. Helen Anderson. Attended, U. Colo., 1960-63. Govt. rep. Continental Airlines, Denver, 1964-72; dir. pub. affairs Regional Transp. Dist., Denver, 1972-77; pub. affairs cons. Denver, 1977—; res. pub. info. officer Fed. Emergency Mgmt. Agy., 1995-96; pres. Colo. Times Pub. Co. Author: Colorado-A Practical Guide to its Government and Politics, 1973, 6th rev. edit., 1990, Colorado Gambling - A Guide, 1991; columnist The Denver Post newspaper, 1983—, The Rocky Mountain Jour., 1977-81. Mem. U.S. Presdl. Electoral Coll., Washington, 1968; commr. U.S. Bicentennial Revolution Commn., Colo., 1972-76, U.S. Commn. on the Bicentennial of U.S. Constn., Denver, 1985-90, pres.; trustee Arapahoe County (Colo.) Libr. Bd., 1982-86; chmn. lobbyist ethics com. Colo. Gen. Assembly, 1990-91. Republican. Avocations: reading, fishing, photography. Home and Office: 12550 W 2nd Dr Lakewood CO 80228-5012

WALTON, RUSSELL SPAREY, foundation administrator; b. Trenton, N.J., Nov. 28, 1921; s. Lewis Kirk and Edna Russell (Sparey) W.; m. Ila E. Lappe, Aug. 23, 1969. Student, King's Coll., 1938-39, DHL (hon.), 1991; student, Temple U., 1940-41. Mgr. publs. and pub. rels. Rexall Drug Co., L.A., 1946-49; mgr. advt. and pub. rels. Gladding McBean & Co., Glendale, Calif., 1949-51; editor, pub. San Bruno (Calif.) Herald, 1951-52; dir. pub. affairs West Divsn. Nat. Assn. Mfgrs., Palo Alto, Calif., 1952-62; exec. dir. United Rep. Calif., Los Altos, 1962-66; sec. program devel. Gov. Calif., Sacramento, 1967-71; columnist, radio commentator newspapers in Calif. and Midwest, 1971-74; mng. editor Third Century Pub., Washington, 1974-76; exec. dir. Plymouth Rock Found., Marlborough, N.H., 1976—. Author: One Nation Under God, 1978, Fundamentals for American Christians, 1979, Biblical Solutions to Contemporary Problems, 1984. Capt. U.S. Army Air Corps, 1941-46. Baptist. Office: Plymouth Rock Found Fisk Mill on Water St Marlborough NH 03455

WALTON, STANLEY ANTHONY, III, lawyer; b. Chgo., Dec. 10, 1939; s. Stanley Anthony and Emily Ann (Pouzar) W.; m. Karen Kayser, Aug. 10, 1963; children: Katherine, Anne, Alex. BA, Washington and Lee U., 1962, LLB, 1965. Bar: Ill. 1965, U.S. Dist. Ct. (no. dist.) Ill. 1966, U.S. Ct. Appeals (7th cir.) 1966. Ptnr. Winston & Strawn, Chgo., 1965-89, Sayfarth Shaw Fairweather, Chgo., 1989-96. Trustee Village of Hinsdale (Ill.), 1985-89; bd. dirs. Washington and Lee Law Sch., Lexington, Va., 1975-78, bd. dirs. univ. alumni, 1983-87, pres. 1986-87; bd. dirs. UNICEF, Chgo., 1983; pres. Hinsdale Hist. Soc., 1979-81, St. Isaac Jogues PTA, 1980 . Mem. ABA, Phi Alpha Delta. Republican. Roman Catholic. Club: Hinsdale Golf. Home and Office: 6679 Snug Harbor Dr Clarendon Hills IL 60514-1826

WALTON, THOMAS EDWARD, research scientist, educator; b. McKeesport, Pa., Dec. 2, 1940; s. Thomas E. and Matilda S. Walton; m. Mary Louise Monahan, Apr. 10, 1987; children: Anne L., Leigh E., Thomas A. DVM, Purdue U., 1964; PhD, Cornell U., 1968. Diplomate Am. Coll. Vet. Microbiologists. Vet. med. officer Mid. Am. Rsch. Unit, Ancon, Panama Canal Zone, 1968-72, Animal Diseases Rsch. Lab., Denver, 1972-74; rsch. leader USDA, Denver, 1974-85, Laramie, Wyo., 1985-92; nat. program leader USDA, Beltsville, Md., 1992-95; dir., supervisory vet. med. officer Nat. Animal Disease Ctr., Ames, Iowa, 1995—; prof. Iowa State U., Ames, 1996—; affiliate faculty mem. Colo. State U., Fort Collins, 1974—; adj. prof. vet. sci. U. Wyo., Laramie, 1986—; adj. prof. vet. microbiology and internat. vet. medicine Purdue U., West Lafayette, 1996—; tech. adv. assignments, sci. field studies, or cons. in Australia, Austria, Belice, Colombia, Costa Rica, Egypt, El Salvador, England, France, Greece, Guadeloupe, Guatemala, Honduras, Israel, Mexico, Netherlands, Nicaragua, Panama, Poland, Puerto Rico, Spain, Switzerland, Venezuela. Presenter in field; contbr. numerous articles to profl. jours. Mem. Soc. for Tropical Vet. Medicine (treas. 1991—). Address: 2906 Ridgetop Rd Ames IA 50014-4513

WALTRIP, DARRELL LEE, professional stock car driver; b. Owensboro, Ky., Feb. 5, 1947; s. Leroy and Margaret Jean (Evans) W.; m. Stephanie Hamilton Rader, Aug. 15, 1969; children: Jessica Leigh, Sarah. Student, Ky. Wesleyan Coll. Driver for Junior Johnson & Assocs., Rick Hendrick Motor Sports; owner Darrell Waltrip Honda Volvo, 1994—. Named Driver of Yr., Nat. Motorsports Press Assn., 1977, Olsonite Driver of Yr., 1979; winner Winston Cup, 1982, Nat. Assn. Stock Car Auto Racing Championship, 1985, Winston Cup Championship, 1981, 82, 85, numerous auto races including Coca Cola 600, 1985, 88, 89, Wrangler 500, 1985, Busch 500, 1986, Budweiser 400, 1986, Holly Farms 400, 1986, Goody's 500, 1987, 88, 89, Motorcraft 500, 1989, Daytona 500, 1989, Champion Spark Plug 500, 1991. Mem. Nat. Assn. Stock Car Auto Racing. Republican. Presbyterian. Top Motor Sport money winner worldwide with more than 7.5 million dollars. Office: 1450 Murfreesboro Rd Franklin TN 37064*

WALTZ, JON RICHARD, lawyer, educator, author; b. Napoleon, Ohio, Oct. 11, 1929; s. Richard R. and Lenore (Tharp) W. B.A. with honors in Polit. Sci, Coll. Wooster, 1951; J.D., Yale U., 1954. Bar: Ohio 1954, Ill.

1965. Assoc. Squire, Sanders & Dempsey, Cleve., 1954-64; chief prosecutor City of Willowick (Ohio), 1958-64; assoc. prof. law Northwestern U. Sch. Law, Chgo., 1964-65; prof. law Northwestern U. Sch. Law, 1965-78, Edna B. and Ednyfed H. Williams prof. law emeritus; instr. med. jurisprudence Northwestern Med. Sch., 1969—; book critic Washington Post, Chgo. Tribune, others; Disting. vis. prof. law Ill. Inst. Tech.-Chgo.-Kent Coll. Law, 1974; lectr. Author: The Federal Rules of Evidence—An Analysis, 1973, Criminal Evidence, 1975, Chinese lang. ed., 1994, Evidence: A Summary Analysis, 1976, Introduction to Criminal Evidence, 1991, Chinese lang. edit., 1993; co-author: The Trial of Jack Ruby, 1965, Cases and Materials on Evidence, 1968, Principles of Evidence and Proof, 1968, Medical Jurisprudence, 1971, Cases and Materials on Law and Medicine, 1980, Evidence: Making the Record, 1981, Criminal Prosecution in the People's Republic of China and the United States of America: A Comparative Study, 1995; note and comment editor Yale Law Jour., 1953-54; mem. editorial adv. bd. Harcourt Brace Law Group,. 1978—; contbr. numerous articles to profl. jours. Mem. Ill. adv. com. U.S. Commn. on Civil Rights, 1971-74; mem. Ill. Criminal Justice System Policy and Planning Com., 1973-74, Ill. Jud. Inquiry Bd., 1980-88; mem. com. med. edn. AMA, 1982-83; mem. Gov.'s Task Force on Med. Malpractice, 1985; Rep. candidate Ill. Appellate Ct., 1978. Capt. AUS, 1955-58. Decorated Commendation medal; recipient Disting. Svc. award Soc. Midland Authors, 1972, Disting. Alumni award Coll. Wooster, 1987. Mem. Assn. Am. Law Schs., Judge Advs. Assn., Soc. Am. Law Tchrs., Order of Coif, Phi Alpha Delta, Pi Sigma Alpha. Presbyterian. also: 4005 Lakeridge Dr Holland MI 49424-2263 Office: Northwestern U Sch Law 357 E Chicago Ave Chicago IL 60611-3008

WALTZ, JOSEPH MCKENDREE, neurosurgeon, educator; b. Detroit, July 23, 1931; s. Ralph McKinley and Bertha (Seeley) W.; m. Janet Maureen Journey, June 26, 1954; children: Jeffrey McKinley, Mary Elaine, David Seelye, Stephen McKendree; m. Marilyn Liska, June 5, 1967; 1 child, Tristana McKendree. Student, U. Mich., 1950; B.S., U. Oreg., 1954, M.D., 1956. Diplomate Am. Bd. Neurol. Surgery. Surg. intern U. Mich. Hosp., 1956-57, gen. surg. resident, 1957-58, clin. instr. neurosurgery, 1960-63; neurosurg. assoc. St. Barnabas Hosp., N.Y.C., 1963—; assoc. dir. Inst. Neurosci., 1974—, dir. dept. neurol. surgery, 1977—; assoc. cons. in neurosurgery Englewood (N.J.) Hosp., 1964—; assoc. prof. neurosurgery NYU Med. Str., 1974—; asst. prof. dept. surgery (neurosurgery) N.Y. Coll. Osteo. Medicine, 1989—; bd. dirs. Neurol. Surgery Rsch. Found., 1978; mem. alumni bd. U. Mich. Med. Ctr., 1995. Author papers on functional neurosurg. treatment of abnormal movement disorders cerebral palsy, others; cryothalamectomy-cryopulvinectomy and implantation brain pacemakers; chpt. in book on cryogenic surgery; contbr. chpts. to Cryogenic Surgery, Neurology, 1982, Advances in Neurology, 1983. Patentee 4-electrode quadrapolar computerized spinal cord stimulator. Mem. sci. adv. bd. Dystonia Med. Research Found., 1980—; trustee St. Barnabas Hosp., 1980—. Served to capt. M.C. AUS, 1958-60. Recipient Bronze award Am. Congress Rehab. Medicine, 1967, World Cmty. Svc. award Rotary, Disting. Trustee award United Hosp. Fund, 1995. Mem. AMA, Am. Paralysis Assn., World Soc. Stereotactic and Functional Neurosurgery, Congress Neurol. Surgeons, Math. Assn. Am., Internat. Neural Network Soc., Soc. for Cryobiology, N.Y. State Med. Soc., Bronx County Med. Soc., N.Y. State Neurosurg Soc., Nat. Ski Patrol, Phi Beta Pi. Achievements include spl. rsch. on neurophysiology and treatment of epilepsy, basal ganglia disorders, abnormal movement disorders, cerebral palsy, also neurosurg. application stereotactic thalamic surgery and spinal cord stimulation. Home: Four B Island South 720 Milton Rd Rye NY 10580-3258 Office: St Barnabas Hosp Dept Neurosurgery New York NY 10457

WALTZ, KENNETH NEAL, political science educator; b. Ann Arbor, Mich., June 8, 1924; s. Christian Benjamin and Luella (Braun) W.; m. Helen Elizabeth Lindsley, June 4, 1949; children: Kenneth L., Thomas E. (dec.), Daniel E. AB, Oberlin Coll., 1948; MA, Columbia U., 1950, PhD, 1954; D honoris causa, Copenhagen U., 1995. Instr., then asst. prof. Columbia U., 1953-57; from assoc. prof. to prof. politics Swarthmore Coll., 1957-66; research assoc. Center Internat. Affairs, Harvard, 1963-64, 68-69, 72; prof. politics Brandeis U., Waltham, Mass., 1966-71, Adlai E. Stevenson prof. internat. politics, 1967-71; Ford prof. polit. sci. U. Calif., Berkeley, 1971-94, Ford prof. emeritus, 1994—; vis. sr. research assoc. King's Coll., U. London, 1986-87; cons. govt. agys.; vis. scholar philosophy London Sch. Econs., 1976-77; vis. scholar Rsch. Sch. Pacific Studies, Australian Nat. U., 1978; vis. scholar dept. internat. politics Beijing U., 1982, 91, 96, Fudan U., Shanghai, 1991, USAF Acad., 1991-92. Author: Man, The State and War, 1959, Foreign Policy and Democratic Politics, 1967, Theory of International Politics, 1979, The Spread of Nuclear Weapons, 1981; co-author: The Spread of Nuclear Weapons: A Debate, 1995; co-author, co-editor: Conflict in World Politics, 1971, The Use of Force, 1971, 4th edit., 1993; mem. edtl. bd. Jour. Strategic Studies, ABC Polit. Sci. Served to 1st lt. AUS, 1944-46, 51-52. NSF grantee, 1968-71; Guggenheim fellow, 1976-77; fellow Woodrow Wilson Center, Internat. Center for Scholars, 1979-80; Heinz Eulau award for best article in the Am. Polit. Sci. Rev., 1990. Fellow Am. Acad. Arts and Scis.; mem. Am. Polit. Sci. Assn. (sec. 1966-67, pres. 1987-88), Internat. Studies Assn. (pres. New Eng. sect. 1966-67), Coun. Fgn. Rels., Am. Acad. Arts and Scis., Phi Beta Kappa. Office: U Calif at Berkeley Polit Sci Dept 210 Barrows Hall Berkeley CA 94720-1951

WALUBO, ANDREW, clinical pharmacologist, researcher; b. Mulago, Kampala, Uganda, Feb. 15, 1960; s. Febiano and Ferectasi (Nabirye) K.; m. Elizabeth Mukisa, Sept. 25, 1985; children: Kabere Christine, Kirunda Kelvin. MB ChB, Makerere U., Uganda, 1986; MPhil in Pharmacology, Chinese U. Hong Kong, 1991; MD, U. Cape Town, South Africa, 1995. Registered physician Uganda Med. and Dental Coun., South African Med. and Dental Coun. Med. officer Ministry of Health, Uganda, 1986-88, Venda Hosp., Louis Trichard, South Africa, 1991-92; lectr. U. Cape Town, 1992-95; clin. fellow in pharmacology Vanderbilt U., Nashville, 1995-97; sr. clin. pharmacologist, sr. lectr. Med. U. of S. Africa, Pretoria, 1997—. Contbg. author: South African Medical Formulary, 3d edit., 1995. Commonwealth fellow, 1989, Merck internat. fellow, 1995; grantee Med. Rsch. Coun. South Africa, 1993-96. Mem. AAAS, Internat. Soc. for Study Xenobiotics. Avocations: soccer, golf, cricket. Office: Med U South Africa, Dept Pharmacology, PO Box 225, Medunsa 0204, South Africa

WALVOORD, JOHN FLIPSE, academic administrator, theologian; b. Sheboygan, Wis., May 1, 1910; s. John Garrett and Mary (Flipse) W.; m. Geraldine Lundgren, June 28, 1939; children: John Edward, James Randall, Timothy, Paul. A.B., Wheaton Coll., 1931, D.D., 1960; B.Th., Dallas Theol. Sem., 1934, M.Th., 1934, D.Th., 1936; A.M., Tex. Christian U., 1945; D.Litt. (hon.), Liberty Bapt. Sem. Registrar Dallas Theol. Sem., 1935-45, prof. systematic theology, 1936-52, prof., 1952-85, regent, 1940-86, asst. to pres., 1945-52, pres., 1952-86, chancellor, 1986—; editor Sem. Bull., 1940-53; pastor Ft. Worth, 1935-50; editor Bibliotheca Sacra, 1952-85. Author: The Doctrine of the Holy Spirit, 1943, The Holy Spirit, 1954, The Return of the Lord, 1955, The Thessalonian Epistles, 1956, The Rapture Question, 1957, The Millennial Kingdom, 1959, To Live Is Christ, 1961, Israel in Prophecy, 1962, The Church in Prophecy, 1964, The Revelation of Jesus Christ, 1966, The Nations in Prophecy, 1967, Jesus Christ Our Lord, 1969, Philippians, 1971, Daniel, 1971, The Holy Spirit at Work Today, 1973, Major Bible Themes, 1974, Armageddon, Oil and the Middle East Crisis, 1974, 2d edit., 1990, Matthew: Thy Kingdom Come, 1975, The Blessed Hope and the Tribulation, 1976, Prophecy Knowledge Handbook, 1990, What We Believe: Discovering the Truths of Scripture, 1990, Major Bible Prophecies, 1991; contbr. to: Four Views of Hell, 1992, Prophecy: 14 Essential Keys to Understanding the Final Drama, 1993; editor: Inspiration and Interpretation, 1957, Truth for Today, 1963; co-editor: The Bib Sac Reader, 1983, The Bible Knowledge Commentary, N.T. edit., 1983, Old Testament edit., 1985; editor: Lewis Sperry Chafer Systematic Theology, abridged edit., 1988. Named Alumnus of Yr. Wheaton Coll., 1981. Mem. Evang. Theol. Soc., Wheaton Coll. Scholastic Honor Soc. Home: 1302 El Patio Dr Dallas TX 75218-3209

WALWER, FRANK KURT, dean, legal educator; b. 1930; s. Kurt and Beatrice (Ahlert) W.; m. Maryann Pancake, Apr. 15, 1961; 1 child, Gregory F. AB, Columbia U., 1952, LLB, 1956. Bar: N.Y. 1959. Assoc. dean Columbia U., 1972-80; dean, prof. U. Tulsa, 1980-91, trustee's prof. law, 1991-94, dean, prof. Tex. Wesleyan U. Law Sch., 1994—, chmn. Grad. and Profl. Sch. Fin. Aid Svc., 1976-78, pres. Law Sch. Admission Coun. , 1983-84; bd. dirs. The Coun. on Postsecondary Accreditation, 1989-92. Mem. Assn. Am. Law Schs. (chmn. sect. econs. of legal edn. 1974-76), ABA (accreditation com. 1988-94, chair legal edn. and bar admissions sect. 1986-87, lawyer competency com. 1986-92, standards rev. com. 1986-94, AALS/ABA comm. on financing), Am. Bar Fellows, Am. Inns of Court. Office: 6335 W NW Hwy Apt 1811 Dallas TX 75225

WALWORTH, ARTHUR, author; b. Newton, Mass., July 9, 1903; s. Arthur Clarence and Ruth Richardson (Lippincott) W. Grad., Phillips Andover Acad., 1921; B.A., Yale U., 1925. Ednl. dept. Houghton Mifflin Co., 1927-43; staff OWI, 1943; Staff Medomak Camp, Washington, Maine, summers 1943-63. Author: School Histories at War, 1938, Black Ships Off Japan, 1946, Cape Breton, 1948, The Medomak Way, 1953, Woodrow Wilson, 2 vols, 1958, 1 vol., 1967, 78, America's Moment: 1918, 1977, Wilson and his Peacemakers, 1986. Recipient Pulitzer prize in biography, 1958. Clubs: Cosmos; Graduates (New Haven). Home: North Hill 865 Central Ave Apt C201 Needham MA 02192-1338

WALZER, JUDITH BORODOVKO, academic administrator, educator; b. N.Y.C., May 27, 1935; d. Isidore and Ida (Gins) Borodovko; m. Michael L. Walzer, June 17, 1956; children—Sarah, Rebecca. B.A., Brandeis U., 1958, M.A., 1960, Ph.D., 1967. Dir. office women's edn. Radcliffe Coll., Cambridge, Mass., 1974-77, assoc. dean., 1976-77; Allston Burr sr. tutor, asst. dean for co-edn. Harvard Coll., Cambridge, Mass., 1977-80; asst. to the pres. Princeton U., N.J., 1980-85; provost New Sch. for Social Research, N.Y.C., 1985—. Mem. alumni fund com. Brandeis U., Waltham, Mass., 1983—; mem. adv. com. Overseas Sch., Hebrew U. in Jerusalem, 1989—; bd. dirs., v.p. Woodrow Wilson Found., Princeton U., 1991—. Democrat. Jewish. Office: New Sch for Social Rsch 66 W 12th St New York NY 10011-8603

WALZER, MICHAEL LABAN, political science educator; b. N.Y.C., Mar. 3, 1935; s. Joseph P. and Sally (Hochman) W.; m. Judith Borodovko, June 17, 1956; children: Sarah, Rebecca. B.A., Brandeis U., 1956; Ph.D., Harvard U., 1961. Fulbright fellow Cambridge (Eng.) U., 1956-57; asst. prof. Princeton U., 1962-66; faculty Harvard U., 1966-80, prof. govt., 1968-80; prof. Sch. Social Scis., Inst. Advanced Study, Princeton, N.J., 1980—. Author: The Revolution of the Saints, 1965, Obligations: Essays on Disobedience, War and Citizenship, 1970, Political Action, 1971, Regicide and Revolution, 1974, Just and Unjust Wars, 1977, Radical Principles: Reflections of an Unreconstructed Democrat, 1980, Spheres of Justice: A Defense of Pluralism and Equality, 1983, Exodus and Revolution, 1985, Interpretation and Social Criticism, 1987, The Company of Critics: Social Criticism and Political Commitment in the Twentieth Century, 1988, What It Means To Be an American, 1993, Thick and Thin: Moral Argument at Home and Abroad, 1994, (with David Miller) Pluralism, Justice, and Equality, 1995, On Toleration, 1997; mem. editl. bd. Dissent mag., 1960—; contbg. editor New Republic, 1976—. Bd. govs. Hebrew U., Jerusalem, 1975—; trustee Brandeis U., 1983-88 ; chmn. faculty adv. cabinet United Jewish Appeal, 1977-81. Home: 103 Linwood Cir Princeton NJ 08540-3625

WALZER, NORMAN CHARLES, economics educator; b. Mendota, Ill., Mar. 17, 1943; s. Elmer J. and Anna L. (Johnston) W.; m. Dona Lee Maurer, Aug. 22, 1970; children: Steven, Mark. BS, Ill. State U., Normal, 1966; MA, U. Ill., 1969, PhD, 1970. Rsch. dir. Cities and Villages Mcpl. Problems Com., Springfield, Ill., 1974-84; vis. prof. U. Ill., Urbana, 1977-78; prof. econs. Western Ill. U., Macomb, 1978—, chmn. dept. econs., 1980-89, dir. Ill. Inst. Rural Affairs, 1988—, interim dean coll. bus. and tech., 1993-95. Author: Cities, Suburbs and Property Tax, 1981; Government Structure and Public Finance, 1984; editor: Financing State and Local Governments, 1981, Rural Community Economic Development, 1991; co-editor: Financing Local Infrastructure in Non Metro Areas, 1986, Financing Economic Development in The 1980s, 1986, Financing Rural Health Care, 1988, Rural Health Care, 1992, Rural Community Economic Development, 1992, Local Economic Development: International Trends and Issues, 1995, Community Visioning Programs: Practice and Principles, 1996. Mem. Am. Econs. Assn., Ill. Econs. Assn. (pres. 1979-80), Mid-Continent Regional Sci. Assn. (pres. 1985-86). Home: 727 Auburn Dr Macomb IL 61455-3002 Office: Western Ill U Ill Inst Rural Affairs 518 Stipes Hall Macomb IL 61455

WALZOG, NANCY LEE, film and television executive; b. Balt., Feb. 12, 1963; d. William Richard and Barbara Jane (Lombardi) W. BFA, NYU, 1983; MBA, Pace U., 1991. Dir. TV sales and mktg. Internat. Film Exch., N.Y.C., 1984-86; producer ABC Entertainment, N.Y.C., 1984; comml. producer Nancy Walzog Film and TV, Ltd., N.Y.C., 1982-84; v.p. Tapestry Internat., Ltd., N.Y.C., 1986-94, pres., 1994—. Recipient Emmy award, Acad. TV Arts and Scis., N.Y.C., 1987, Emmy nominiation, 1990, ACE award, Nat. Acad. Cable TV Programming, Washington, 1987, Gold award San Francisco Internat. Film Festival, 1987, Hugo award Chgo. Internat. Film Festival, 1988. Office: Tapestry Internat 920 Broadway 16th Fl New York NY 10010-6004

WAMBAUGH, JOSEPH, author; b. Pitts., Jan. 22, 1937; s. Joseph Aloysius and Anne (Malloy) W.; m. Dee Allsup, Nov. 26, 1955; children: Mark (dec.), David, Jeannette. BA, Calif. State Coll., L.A., 1960; MA, Calif. State Coll., Los Angeles, 1968. Police officer, L.A., 1960-74. Author: The New Centurions, 1971, The Blue Knight, 1972, The Onion Field, 1973 (Edgar Allan Poe award Mystery Writers Am. 1974), The Choirboys, 1975, The Black Marble, 1978, The Glitter Dome, 1981, The Delta Star, 1983, Lines and Shadows, 1984 (Rodolfo Walsh prize Internat. Assn. Crime Writers 1989), The Secrets of Harry Bright, 1985, Echoes in the Darkness, 1987, The Blooding, 1989, The Golden Orange, 1990, Fugitive Nights, 1992, Finnegan's Week, 1993, Floaters, 1996;. Served with USMC, 1954-57. •

WAMP, ZACH P., congressman; b. Ft. Benning, Ga., Oct. 28, 1957; m. Kim Wamp; 2 children. Student, U. N.C., U. Tenn. Chmn. Hamilton County Rep. Party, 1987; regional dir. Tenn. Rep. Party, 1989; v.p. Charter Real Estate Corp., 1989-92; real estate broker Fletcher Bright Co., 1992-94; mem. 104th and 105th Congress from 3d Tenn. dist., 1995—, mem. house appropriations coms. Office: US House Reps 423 Cannon Bldg Ofc Bldg Washington DC 20515-4203

WAMPLER, BARBARA BEDFORD, entrepreneur; b. New Bedford, Mass., July 23, 1932; d. William and Mary (Fitzpatrick) Bedford; m. John H. Wampler, Oct. 21, 1950; children: John H. Jr., William C., James B., Robert T. AS, Tunxis C.C., 1975; MEd, Cambridge Coll., 1996. Lic. real estate agt., Mass., 1986-95. Counselor Wampler Rehab. Counseling Svcs., Farmington, Conn., 1975-85; owner, mgr. Wampler Mktg., Farmington, 1980-84, Earth Campgrounds I and II, Otis, Mass., 1984-97; pres., mgr. Earth Works (name now Earth Enterprises), Otis, Mass., 1984-97; founder, pres. Advt. Matters, Otis, 1989-96; v.p. Mastery Books, Otis, 1989—; mem., clk. Zoning Bd. Appeals, Otis, Mass., 1988-92; notary pub., 1986—; aft. Primerica Fin. Svcs., 1992-94. Author: Do It Yourself Empowerment; creator Calendar Journal; contbr. articles to profl. jours. Dir. music First Congl. Ch., Otis, 1985—, trustee, 1994-96; family counselor Berkshire Coun. Alcoholism and Addiction, 1994-96, Mediation OPTIONS/PLUS, 1994—. Faculty scholar U. Hartford, 1976. Mem. Acad. Family Mediators, Am. Assn. Christian Counselors, Bus. Mgrs. Assn., Kiwanis. Avocations: vocal soloist, organist, choir director. Home and Office: Mediation Option Plus 1824 S Main Rd # 690 Otis MA 01253-9707

WAMPLER, LLOYD CHARLES, retired lawyer; b. Spencer, Ind., Nov. 4, 1920; s. Charles and Vivian (Hawkins) W.; m. Joyce Ann Hoppenrath, Sept. 28, 1950 (dec. 1954); 1 child, Natalie Gay (dec.); m. Mary E. Shumaker, Sept. 16, 1952. AB, Ind. U., 1942, JD, 1947. Bar: Ind. 1947, U.S. Supreme Ct. 1971. Instr. bus. law U. Kans., 1947-49; dep. atty. gen. Ind., 1949-50; mem. legal com. Interstate Oil Compact Commn., 1950; asst. pub. counselor Ind., 1950-53; mem. Stevens, Wampler, Travis & Fortin, Plymouth, 1953-83; claim counsel Am. Family Ins. Group, Indpls., 1983-88; ret., 1988. Mem. Ind. Rehab. Services Bd., 1978-86; Dem. nominee for judge Ind. Supreme Ct., 1956. With USNR, 1942-46. Mem. ABA, Am. Judicature Soc., Ind. Bar Assn. (bd. mgrs. 1975-77), Indpls. Bar Assn., Ind. Acad. Sci., Ind. Def. Lawyers Assn. (bd. dirs. 1967-72, v.p. 1970, pres. 1971-72), Ind. Hist. Soc., Marshall County Hist. Soc. (bd. dirs. 1969-75), Sagamore of the Wabash, Am. Legion, Phi Delta Phi. Home: 4000 N Meridian St Indianapolis IN 46208-4034

WAMSLEY, BARBARA SIMBORSKI, public administration educator; b. Holden, W.Va., July 6, 1945; d. Joseph and Katie (Stepson) Simborski; m. Dennis Edward Wamsley, Dec. 27, 1969. MPA, Harvard U., 1985. Analyst U.S. Govt. Dept. HEW, Washington, 1963-82; deputy asst. sec. U.S. Govt. Dept. Health & Human Svcs., Washington, 1982-86, sr. policy/mgmt. position, 1986-88; dep. dir. fed. programs Nat. Acad. Pub. Adminstrn., Washington, 1988-93, sr. advisor to dep. sec., 1993-95; fellow Syracuse Maxwell Ctr. for Advanced Pub. Adminstrn., 1995—; prin. LMA Internat.; fellow Ctr. for Am. Govt., Johns Hopkins U., 1996—; fellow Nat. Acad. Pub. Adminstrn., 1996—; spkr. in field. Author, editor: Modernizing Federal Classification, 1991, Leading People in Change, 1993; contbr. articles to profl. jours. Labauch tutor Literacy Coun., Charles County, 1992. Littauer fellow Harvard U., Cambridge, 1985. Fellow Am. Soc. Polit. Sci., Nat. Acad. Pub. Adminstrn.; mem. Am. Soc. Pub. Adminstrn. Avocations: flying, water coloring, col. work, history. Home: Pomonkey Landing 2900 Creedon Dr Indian Head MD 20640

WAMUTOMBO, DIKEMBE MUTOMBO MPOLONDO MUKAMBA JEAN JACQUE See MUTOMBO, DIKEMBE

WAN, FREDERIC YUI-MING, mathematician, educator; b. Shanghai, Jan. 7, 1936; arrived in U.S., 1947; s. Wai-Nam and Olga Pearl (Jung) W.; m. Julia Y.S. Chang, Sept. 10, 1960. SB, MIT, 1959, SM, 1963, PhD, 1965. Mem. staff MIT Lincoln Lab., Lexington, 1959-65; instr. math. MIT, Cambridge, 1965-67, asst. prof., 1967-69, assoc. prof., 1969-74; prof. math., dir. Inst. Applied Math. and Stats. U. B.C., Vancouver, 1974-83; prof. applied math. and math. U. Wash., Seattle, 1983-95, chmn. Dept. Applied Math., 1984-88, assoc. dean scis. coll. arts and scis., 1988-92; prof. math., prof. mech. and aero. engring. U. Calif., Irvine, 1995—, vice chancellor rsch., dean grad. studies, 1995—; program dir. Divsn. Math. Sci. NSF, 1986-87, divsn. dir., 1993-94; cons. indsl. firms and govt. agys.; mem. MIT Ednl. Coun. for B.C. Area of Can., 1974-83. Assoc. editor Jour. Applied Mechanics, 1991-95, Can. Applied Math. Quar., Studies in Applied Math., Jour. Dyn. Discrete, Continuous and Impulsive Sys., Internat. Jour. Solids & Structures; contbr. articles to profl. jours. Sloan Found. award, 1973, Killam sr. fellow, 1979. Fellow AAAS, ASME, Am. Acad. Mechanics (sec. fellows 1984-90, pres.-elect 1992-93, pres. 1993-94), Soc. Indsl. and Applied Math., Can. Applied Math. Soc. (coun. 1980-83, pres. 1983-85, Arthur Beaumont Disting. Svc. award 1991), Am. Math. Soc., Math. Assn. Am., Sigma Xi. Home: 22 Urey Ct Irvine CA 92612-4045 Office: U Calif Irvine Office Rsch & Grad Studies 155 Administration Irvine CA 92697-3175

WANAMAKER, ELLEN PONCE, tax specialist; b. Newark, June 27, 1956; d. Arthur Zachary and Charlotte Rhoda (Frisch) Ponce; m. William A. Wanamaker, Aug. 8, 1979; 1 child, Marlee Ann. AS in Dental Hygiene, Fairleigh Dickinson U., 1978, BS in Dental Hygiene, 1979; student, H&R Block tax tng. seminars, Wayne, N.J., 1984-90, William Paterson Coll., 1975-76 90—. Registered dental hygienist, N.J., dental hygiene specialist, N.J.; cert. dental asst. patient accounts mgr., inst. dental assisting; accredited tax perparer; accredited tax advisor; IRS licensure-enrolled agt. status. Dental hygienist, dental asst. Arthur Ponce, DDS, Bloomingdale, N.J., 1972-80; dental asst., dental hygienist various dentists, N.J., 1977-80; instr., dept. chmn. Berdan Inst., Totowa, N.J., 1980-83; prodn. coord., cons. performer These Days Prodns., Ltd., Pompton Lakes, N.J., 1981—; tax preparer H&R Block, Wayne, N.J., 1985-90; mgr. William Paterson Coll., Wayne, N.J., 1975-76, 90-91; pvt. practice tax advisor, tax preparer Bloomingdale, 1985—; pvt. instrn. dental assts. and dental hygienists, Ellen Wanamaker, Bloomingdale, 1981-83; instr. County Coll. of Morris, Randolph, N.J., 1979-80. Vol. dental asst. N.E. Regional Bd. Dental Licensing Exams., 1978-86, Head Start Program, 1979, Bloomingdale Saturday Sch. Bloomingdale Bd. of Health, 1981, Ann. Bloomingdale Health Fair, 1983-93, 94-97. Recipient Gold cert. Music Educators Assn., 1967-69. Mem. NOW, Am. Speech and Hearing Assn., Am. Dental Hygiene Assn., Nat. Assn. Tax Practitioners, Nat. Soc. Pub. Accts., Nat. Assn. Dental Assts., N.J. Dental Assn., FDU Dental Hygiene Assn., FDU Alumni Assn., Phi Omega Epsilon. Avocations: gourmet cooking, rug hooking, music, sign language. Office: William A Wanamaker DMD MS 14 Leary Ave Bloomingdale NJ 07403-1612

WANAMAKER, ROBERT JOSEPH, advertising company executive; b. Oak Park, Ill., Nov. 24, 1924; s. Daniel John and Mabel (Maloney) W.; m. Carol Anne George, Apr. 20, 1968; children: Stacey Lynne, Bethanne. Ed., Northwestern U., 1949. Vice pres., copy dir. Edward H. Weiss & Co., Chgo., 1957-62; sr. v.p., U.S. creative dir. Clinton E. Frank, Inc., Chgo., 1962-72; sr. v.p., creative dir. Grey-North, Inc., Chgo., 1972-76; sr. v.p., dir. creative services Y & R/Buchen, Reincke, Chgo., 1976-79; v.p., dir. creative services Pollenex, Chgo., 1979-86; pres. Robert Wanamaker "Getting Thru" Mktg. Comms., River Forest, Ill., 1987—. Served with AUS, 1943. Named one of 100 top advt. creative people in U.S.A. Ad Daily U.S.A., 1975. Home and Office: 7225 Division St River Forest IL 60305-1267 *One of the biggest problems with success in worldly things is keeping your sense of values in proper perspective. Affluence can dull your sensitivity to the needs and aspirations of those less fortunate. You can become obsessed with building your own financial assets. The misguided fear of losing your status, your luxuries, your comforts can be abnormally painful. Every once in awhile you have to chasten your thinking and remind yourself that the only three riches in life are love, health, and being at peace with yourself and your God.*

WAND, PATRICIA ANN, librarian; b. Portland, Oreg., Mar. 28, 1942; d. Ignatius Bernard and Alice Ruth (Suhr) W.; m. Francis Dean Silvernail, Dec. 20, 1966 (div. Jan. 19, 1986); children: Marjorie Lynn Silvernail, Kirk Dean Silvernail. BA, Seattle U., 1963; MAT, Antioch Grad. Sch., 1967; AMLS, U. Mich., 1972. Vol. Peace Corps, Colombia, S.Am., 1963-65; secondary tchr. Langley Jr. High Sch., Washington, 1965-66; asst. libr. Wittenberg U. Libr., Springfield, Ohio, 1967-69; secondary tchr. Caro (Mich.) High Sch., 1969-70; assoc. libr. Coll. of S.I. (N.Y.) Libr., 1972-77; head, access svcs. Columbia U. Librs., N.Y.C., 1977-82; asst. univ. libr. U. Oreg., Eugene, 1982-89; univ. libr. The Am. U., Washington, 1989—; cons. Bloomsburg (Pa.) U. Libr., 1990. Contbr. articles to profl. jours. Pres. West Cascade Returned Peace Corps Vols., Eugene, 1985-88; v.p. Friends of Colombia, Washington, 1990—; speaker on Peace Corps, 1965—, libr. and info. svcs., 1979—. Honors Program scholarship Seattle U., 1960-62, Peace Corps scholarship Antioch U., 1965-66; recipient Beyond War award, 1987, Fulbright Sr. Lectr. award Fulbright, 1989, Disting. Alumnus award Sch. of Info. and Libr. Studies, U. Mich., 1992. Mem. ALA, Assn. Coll. and Rsch. Librs. (chair budge and fin. bd. dirs. 1987-89, chair WHCLIS task force 1989-92), On-line Computer Librs. Ctr. (adv. com. on coll. and univ. librs. 1991-96), D.C. Libr. Assn. (bd. dirs. 1993—, pres. 1996—). Home: 4854 Bayard Blvd Bethesda MD 20816-1785 Office: Am Univ Libr 4400 Massachusetts Ave NW Washington DC 20016-8001

WANDER, HERBERT STANTON, lawyer; b. Cin., Mar. 17, 1935; s. Louis Marvin and Pauline (Schuster) W.; m. Ruth Cele Fell, Aug. 7, 1960; children: Daniel Jerome, Susan Gail, Lois Marlene. AB, U. Mich., 1957; LLB, Yale U., 1960. Bar: Ohio 1960, Ill. 1960. Law clk. to judge U.S. Dist. Ct. (no. dist.) Ill., 1960-61; ptnr. Pope Ballard Shepard & Fowle, Chgo., 1961-78, Katten Muchin & Zavis, Chgo., 1978—; trustee Michael Reese Found., 1991—; bd. dirs. Tel. & Data Systems, Chgo.; mem. legal adv. com. to the bd. govs. N.Y. Stock Exch., 1989-92; mem. legal adv. bd. Nat. Assn. Securities Dealers, Inc., 1996—. Contbr. numerous articles to profl. jours. Bd. dirs. Jewish Fedn. Met. Chgo., 1972—, pres., 1981-83; bd. dirs. Jewish United Fund, 1972—, pres., 1981-83, chmn. pub. affairs com., 1984-87, gen. campaign chmn., 1993; former regional chmn. nat. young leadership cabinet United Jewish Appeal; vice chmn. large city budgeting conf. Council Jewish Fedns., 1979-82, bd. dirs., 1980—, exec. com., 1983-84. Editor (jour.) Bus. Law Today, 1992-93; editor-in-chief (jour.) The Bus. Lawyer, 1993-94. Mem. ABA (sec. bus. law sect. 1992-93, vice-chair 1993-94, chair-elect 1994-95, chair 1995-96), Chgo. Bar Assn., Ill. State Bar Assn., Yale Law Sch. Assn. (exec. com. 1982-86), Phi Beta Kappa. Clubs: Standard, Econ. (Chgo.); Northmoor Country (Highland Park, Ill.). Home: 70 Prospect Ave Highland Park IL 60035-3329 Office: Katten Muchin & Zavis 525 W Monroe St Ste 1600 Chicago IL 60661-3629

WANDERS, HANS WALTER, banker; b. Aachen, Germany, Apr. 3, 1925; came to U.S., 1929, naturalized, 1943; s. Herbert and Anna Maria (Kusters) W.; m. Elizabeth Knox Kimball, Apr. 2, 1949; children: Crayton Kimball, David Gillette. BS, Yale U., 1947; postgrad. Grad. Sch. Banking, Rutgers

U., 1961-64. With GE, 1947-48, Libbey-Owens-Ford Glass Co., 1948-53, Allied Chem. Co., 1953-55, McKinsey & Co., Inc., 1955-57; from asst. cashier to v.p. No. Trust Co., Chgo., 1957-65; v.p. Nat. Blvd. Bank, Chgo., 1965-66, pres., 1966-70; exec. v.p. Wachovia Bank & Trust Co., N.A., Winston-Salem, N.C., 1970-74, chmn., 1977-85, vice chmn., 1985-88, also bd. dirs.; pres. Wachovia Corp., Winston-Salem, 1974-76, 85-87, chmn., 1977-85, vice chmn., 1987-88, also bd. dirs.; pres., chief exec. officer 1st Wachovia Corp. Services, Inc., Winston-Salem, 1986-88, ret., 1988; dir. Exxon Supply Co., 1989-94, Goody's Pharmaceuticals, 1989-94; dir. Gulf USA, Inc., 1989-92. Chmn. Winston-Salem Found. Com., 1981-82; bd. dirs. N.C. Textile Found., N.C. Engring. Found., Inc., 1971-88; trustee, mem. exec. com. Salem Coll. and Acad., 1986-91, Tax Found., 1982—, vice chmn., 1984-86, chmn., 1986-88, chmn. exec. com., 1989; mem. bd. visitors Fuqua Sch. Bus., Duke U., 1978-89; mem. nat. corps. com. United Negro Coll. Fund; mem., chmn. N.C. Bd. Econ. Devel., 1989-93; corporator Belmont Hill Sch., 1996—. Lt. USNR, 1943-46, 51-53. Mem. Am. Bankers Assn. (chmn. mktg. divsn. 1979-80, dir. 1971-73), Assn. Res. City Bankers, Conf. Bd. (So. regional adv. coun.), Assn. Bank Holding Cos. (bd. dirs., exec. com. 1981-83), Chgo. Club, Commonwealth Club Chgo., Twin-City Club Winston Salem, Old Town Club Winston-Salem, Roaring Gap Club N.C. Home: 10 Graylyn Pl Winston Salem NC 27106 Office: Wachovia Corp 420A W 4th St Winston Salem NC 27101

WANDYCZ, PIOTR STEFAN, history educator; b. Krakow, Poland, Sept. 20, 1923; s. Damian Stanislaw and Stefania (Dunikowska) W.; m. Maria Teresa Chrzaszcz, Aug. 13, 1963; children: Anna, Joanna, Antoni. B.A., Cambridge U., 1948, M.A., 1952; Ph.D., London U., 1951; M.A. (hon.), Yale U., 1968; PhD (hon.), Wroclaw U., Poland, 1993; DHC, Sorbonne U., Paris, 1997. Instr. to assoc. prof. history Ind. U., 1954-66; fellow Harvard's Russian Research Center, 1963-65; assoc. prof. history Yale U., 1966-68, prof., 1968-89, chmn. Russian and East European council, 1974-76, 81-83, Bradford Durfee prof., 1989—; vis. prof. history Columbia U., 1967, 69, 74. Author: Czechoslovak-Polish Confederation and Great Powers, 1956, France and Her Eastern Allies, 1962, Soviet-Polish Relations, 1969, The Lands of Partitioned Poland, 1974, United States and Poland, 1980, August Zaleski, 1980, Polska i Zagranica, 1986, The Twilight of French Eastern Alliances, 1988, Z Dziejow dyplomacji, 1988, Polish Diplomacy 1914-1945, 1988, The Price of Freedom, 1992, Die Freiheit und ihr Preis, 1993, Pod zaborami, 1994, Cena wolnosci, 1995; contbr. articles to profl. jours.; mem. editl. bd. Slavic Rev., Internat. History Rev., Polish Rev., Polin., East European Politics and Soc. Served as 2d lt. Polish Army, 1942-45. Decorated Comdr.'s Cross of Polonia Restituta; recipient Alfred Jurzykowski Found. award in history, 1977; fellow Guggenheim Found., Ford Found., Rockefeller Found., Am. Philos. Soc., Am. Coun. Learned Socs., Social Sci. Rsch. Coun., Internat. Rsch. and Exchs. Bd. Mem. AAAS (Wayne Vucinich prize 1989), Am. Hist. Assn. (George Louis Beer prize 1962, 89), Polish Hist. Assn. (hon.), Polish Acad. Arts and Scis., Polish Acad. Scis., Polish Inst. Arts and Scis. Abroad (A. Lenkszewicz prize 1991), Czechoslovak Acad. of Scis. (Hlavka medal 1992), Czechoslovak Soc. Arts and Scis. Home: 27 Spring Gardens St Hamden CT 06517-1913 Office: Yale U Dept History New Haven CT 06520

WANEK, WILLIAM CHARLES, public relations executive; b. Ridgewood, N.Y., Oct. 21, 1932; s. William John and Anna (Benes) W.; m. Robbie Gene Fairbanks, Feb. 14, 1974; children: William Robert, Jennifer Leigh. BA in English, CCNY, 1954; MA in Psychology, The New Sch. Social Rsch., N.Y.C., 1982. Asst. editor Soap Chem. Spltys. Mag., N.Y.C., 1956-58; editor in chief Maintenance Supplies Mag., N.Y.C., 1958-60; acct. exec. O.S. Tyson & Co. Inc., N.Y.C., 1960-62; dir. advt. and pub. rels. Pa. Glass Sand Corp., N.Y.C., 1962-64; sr. acct. exec. McCann-Erickson Inc., N.Y.C., 1964-66; acct. supr. Burson-Marsteller Assocs., N.Y.C., 1966-71; exec. v.p. Gibbs & Soell Inc., N.Y.C., 1971—. With U.S. Army, 1954-56. Mem. Am. Agrl. Editors Assn., Nat. Agri-Mktg. Assn. (bd. dirs. ea. chpt. 1974-76), Nat. Assn. Farm Broadcasters. Presbyterian. Avocations: horticulture, classical music, theater, reading, swimming. Office: Gibbs & Soell Inc 600 3rd Ave New York NY 10016-1901

WANG, ALBERT JAMES, violinist, educator; b. Ann Arbor, Mich., Nov. 19, 1958; s. James and Lydia (Ebenhoch) W.; m. Bridget Renee Becker, June 30, 1987; children: Ona Lenore, Kevin Lewis. BM, Ind. U., 1979; MM, U. Mich., 1981; DMA, Am. Conservatory, 1993. Prin. second violin Baton Rouge Symphony Orch., 1981-82; first violin Valcour String Quartet, Baton Rouge, 1981-82, Loyola String Quartet, 1982-83; mem. Lyric Opera Chgo. Orch., 1982—; mem. Orch. Ill., Chgo., 1982-88; prin. 2d violin Internat. Symphony Orch., Port Huron, Mich., 1984; 1st violin Internat. String Quartet, Port Huron, 1984; concertmaster, soloist Chgo. Chamber Orch., 1985-88, Chgo. Philharm., 1985—; mem. Grant Park Symphony Orch., Chgo., 1986-87; concertmaster, soloist Birch Creek Music Festival, Wis., Woodstock (Ill.) Mozart Festival Orch., 1988-90; concertmaster Rockford (Ill.) Symphony Orch., 1990-91, Northwestern Music Festival Orch., 1990—; soloist, concertmaster Pro Musica Orch. of Mauritius, 1992-93; soloist, concertmaster China tour Classical Symphony Orch., 1994, 95; soloist, concertmaster Midwest Symphony Orch., 1995-96; music dir. Baroque Masterplayers, 1994—; soloist, concertmaster Met. Arts Orch., 1995—; artist-in-residence St. Clair Coll., Port Huron, 1984, Elgin C.C., 1994—; lectr. Am. Conservatory Music, Chgo., 1989-92; Fulbright lectr. Francois Mitterand Conservatory of Music, Quatre Bornes, Mauritius, 1992-93; asst. prof. violin Roosevelt U., 1993—. Numerous solo, recital and chamber music appearances and master classes throughout U.S., Can., Mauritius and China; recs. and broadcasts by Mauritian Nat. Radio and WFMT Chgo. Fine Arts Sta., PBS, Nat. Pub. Radio, and Chinese Nat. Radio & TV; numerous world premiers; adjudicator for state and nat. music competitions; contbr. articles and revs. to profl. jours. Vol. ARC, Literacy Vols. Am., Chgo. Pub. Librs., United Way; bd. advisors Prism Music Festival, 1984—, Am. Chamber Symphony, 1985, Symphony II, 1993-94. Fulbright grantee, 1992-93; recipient 1st prize Ann Arbor (Mich.) Symphony Competition, 1976, Soc. Am. Musicians Competition, Chgo., 1984, Internat. Concerts Atlantique Competition, N.Y.C., 1989, Chgo. Park Dist. Competition, 1991, 2nd prize Biennial Adult Artist Competition, 1992; selected to Arts Am. Touring Artist Roster, 1993; finalist Lilly Fellows Program in Humanities and the Arts, Valparaiso U., 1994, Harry and Sarah Zelzer Fellowship and prize; recipient Leo Sowerby medal, 1994. Mem. Am. Fedn. Musicians, Am. String Tchrs. Assn., Coll. Music Soc., Chamber Music Am., Am. Music Ctr., Music Tchrs. Nat. Assn. Avocations: powerlifting, fishing, travel, woodworking. Office: Roosevelt U 430 S Michigan Ave Chicago IL 60605-1301 also: Lyric Opera Chgo 20 N Wacker Dr Chicago IL 60606-2806 also: Elgin CC 1700 Spartan Dr Elgin IL 60123-7189 also: Baroque Masterplayers 5528 S Hyde Park Blvd Ste 1002 Chicago IL 60637-1938

WANG, ARTHUR CHING-LI, law educator, lawyer; b. Boston, Feb. 4, 1949; s. Kung Shou and Lucy (Chow) W.; m. Wendy F. Hamai, May 22, 1976 (div. 1981); m. Nancy J. Norton, Sept. 1, 1985; children: Alexander Xinglin, Sierra Xinan. BA, Franconia Coll., 1970; JD, U. Puget Sound, 1984. Bar: Wash. 1984. Printer Carmel Valley (Calif.) Outlook, 1970-73; project coord. Tacoma (Wash.) Cmty. House, 1973-76; rsch. analyst Wash. Ho. of Reps., Olympia, Wash., 1977-80, mem., 1981-94; of counsel Davies Pearson, P.C., Tacoma, 1984-94; adj. prof. U. Puget Sound Law Sch., Tacoma, 1987-93, Seattle U. Law Sch., Tacoma, 1995—; chmn House Capital Budget Com., 1993-94, Revenue Com., 1989-92, Commerce and Labor Com., 1985-88; mem. Wash. Pers. Appeals Bd., Olympia, 1994-96; chief adminstrv. law judge Washington Office Adminstrn. Hearings, 1997—. Assoc. editor U. Puget Sound Law Review, 1983-84. Vista vol. Tacoma Urban League, 1973-74; del. Dem. Nat. Conv., 1976. Named Chinese Am. Man of Yr., Seattle Chinese Post, 1991, Legislator of Yr., Wash. Health Care Assn., 1992, Alumni of Yr., U. Puget Sound Law Sch. Alumni Assn., 1993. Democrat. Avocation: birding. Home: 3319 N Union Ave Tacoma WA 98407-6043

WANG, ARTHUR WOODS, publisher; b. Port Chester, N.Y., Oct. 7, 1918; s. Israel and Madolin (Woods) W.; m. Mary Ellen Mackay, Aug. 13, 1955; 1 son, Michael Anthony. B.S., Bowdoin Coll., 1940; postgrad., Columbia U., 1949-51. Advt. research McCann-Erickson, Inc., 1940-41; editor Doubleday & Co., 1942-43, Alfred A. Knopf, Inc., 1943, T.Y. Crowell (Pub.), 1943-47; with E.M. Hale & Co., Eau Claire, Wis., 1947-52; editor A.A. Wyn, Inc., 1952-56; co-founder, pres., editor-in-chief Hill & Wang, Inc., 1956-71; pub., editor-in-chief Hill & Wang div. Farrar, Straus & Giroux, Inc., N.Y.C., 1971-87; sr. editor Hill and Wang div. Farrar, Straus & Giroux, Inc., 1988—. Home: 150 E 69th St New York NY 10021-5704 Office: Hill & Wang 19 Union Sq W New York NY 10003-3304

WANG, CHAO-CHENG, mathematician, engineer; b. Peoples Republic of China, July 20, 1938; came to U.S., 1961; s. N.S. and V.T. Wang; m. Sophia C.L. Wang; children: Ferdinand, Edward. BS, Nat. Taiwan U., 1959; PhD, Johns Hopkins U., 1965. Registered profl. engr., Tex. Asst. prof. Johns Hopkins U., Balt., 1966-68, assoc. prof., 1968-69; prof. Rice U., Houston, 1968-79, Noah Harding prof., 1979—, chmn. math. sci. dept.,, 1983-89, chmn. mech. engring. and materials sci., 1991-94. Author numerous books in field; contbr. articles to profl. jours. Named Disting. Young Scientist Md. Acad. Sci., 1968. Mem. ASME, Soc. Natural Philosophy (treas. 1985-86), Am. Acad. Mechs. Office: Rice Univ Dept Mech Engring Materials Sci Houston TX 77251

WANG, CHARLES B., computer software company executive; b. Shanghai, Rep. China, Aug. 19, 1944. BS, Queens Coll., 1967. Chmn., CEO Computer Assocs., Islandia, N.Y., 1976—. Office: Computer Assocs Internat Inc 1 Computer Assocs Plz Islandia NY 11788-7000

WANG, CHEN CHI, electronics company executive, real estate executive, finance company executive, investments services executive, international trade executive; b. Taipei, Taiwan, Aug. 10, 1932; came to U.S., 1959, naturalized, 1970; s. Chin-Ting and Chen-Kim Wang; m. Victoria Rebisoff, Mar. 5, 1965; children: Katherine Kim, Gregory Chen, John Christopher, Michael Edward. B.A. in Econs., Nat. Taiwan U., 1955; B.S.E.E., San Jose State U., 1965; M.B.A., U. Calif., Berkeley, 1961. With IBM Corp., San Jose, Calif., 1965-72; founder, chief exec. officer Electronics Internat. Co., Santa Clara, Calif., 1968-72, owner, gen. mgr., 1972-81, reorganized as EIC Group, 1982, now chmn. bd., chief exec. officer; dir. Systek Electronics Corp., Santa Clara, 1970-73; founder, sr. ptnr. Wang Enterprises (name changed to Chen Kim Entrprises 1982), Santa Clara, 1974—; founder, sr. ptnr. Hanson & Wang Devel. Co., Woodside, Calif., 1977-85; chmn. bd. Golden Alpha Enterprises, San Mateo, Calif., 1979—; mng. ptnr. Woodside Acres-Las Pulgas Estate, Woodside, 1980-85; founder, sr. ptnr. DeVine & Wang, Oakland, Calif., 1977-83; Van Heal & Wang, West Village, Calif., 1981-82; founder, chmn. bd. EIC Fin. Corp., Redwood City, Calif., 1985—; chmn. bd. Maritek Corp., Corpus Christi, Tex., 1988-89; chmn. EIC Internat. Trade Corp., Lancaster, Calif., 1989—, EIC Capital Corp., Redwood City, 1990—. Served to 2d lt., Nationalist Chinese Army, 1955-56. Mem. Internat. Platform Assn., Tau Beta Pi. Mem. Christian Ch. Author: Monetary and Banking System of Taiwan, 1955, The Small Car Market in the U.S., 1961. Home: 195 Brookwood Rd Woodside CA 94062-2302 Office: EIC Group Head Office Bldg 2055 Woodside Rd Redwood City CA 94061-3355

WANG, CHIA PING, physicist, educator; came to U.S., 1963, naturalized; (parents Chinese citizens).; s. Guan Can and Tah (Lin) W. BS, U. London, 1950; MS, U. Malaya (now U. Singapore), 1951; PhD in Physics, U. Malaya (now U. Singapore) and U. Cambridge, 1953; DSc in Physics, U. Singapore, 1972. Asst. lectr. U. Malaya, 1951-53; mem. faculty Nankai U., Tientsin, 1954-58, prof. physics, 1956-58, head electron physics div., 1955-58, mem. steering com. nuc. physics divsn., 1956-58; head electron physics Lanchow Atomic Project, 1958; mem. faculty Hong Kong U.; mem. faculty Chinese U., Hong Kong, 1958-63, prof. physics, 1959-63, acting head physics, math. depts., 1959; rsch. assoc. lab. nuclear studies Cornell U., Ithaca, N.Y., 1963-64; assoc. prof. space sci. and applied physics Cath. U. Am., Washington, 1964-68; assoc. prof. physics Case Inst. Tech. Case Western Res. U., Cleve., 1966-70; vis. scientist, vis. prof. U. Cambridge (Eng.), U. Leuven (Belgium), U.S. Naval Rsch. Labs., U. Md., MIT, 1970-75; rsch. physicist radiation lab. U.S. Army Natick (Mass.) R & D Command, 1975—, mem. steering com. sci. and tech. directorate, 1993—; pioneer in fields of nuclear sub-structure (now often referred to as parton), nucleon sub-unit structure, multiparticle prodn., cosmic radiation, picosecond time to pulse-height conversion, thermal physics, lasers, microwaves. Contbg. author: Atomic Structure and Interactions of Ionizing Radiations with Matter in Preservation of Food by Ionizing Radiation, 1982; contbr. numerous articles to profl. jours. Recipient Outstanding Performance award Dept. Army, 1980, Quality Increase award, 1980. Mem. AAAS, Am. Nuclear Soc., Am. Phys. Soc., Inst. Physics London, N.Y. Acad. Scis., Sigma Xi. Home: 28 Hallett Hill Rd Weston MA 02193-1753 Office: US Army Natick R&D Ctr Natick MA 01760

WANG, DANIEL I-CHYAU, biochemical engineering educator; b. Nanking, China, Mar. 12, 1936; s. Shou Chin and Ling Nyi (Vee) W.; m. Victoria Dawn, Aug. 27, 1966; 1 child, Keith Fredric. B.S., MIT, 1959, M.S., 1961; Ph.D., U. Pa., 1963. Process engr. Esso. Research and Devel. Co., Linden, N.Y., 1963; asst. prof. MIT, Cambridge, 1965-70; assoc. prof. MIT, 1970-74, prof. biochem. engring., 1974—, Chevron prof. chem. engring., 1985—, dir. Biotech. Process Engring. Ctr., 1985—. Co-author 3 books; contbr. articles to profl. jours. Served with U.S. Army, 1963-65. Recipient Outstanding Tchr. award MIT, 1972, 78, 89, Sci. Appreciation award Republic of China, 1978; AMF fellow, 1962-63. Mem. NAE, Am. Inst. Chem. Engrs. (food, pharm. and bioengring. award 1981, Inst. lectr. 1986), Am. Chem. Soc. (M.J. Johnson award 1983, David Perlman Meml. lectr. 1991), Am. Soc. Microbiology, Inst. Food Technologists (sci. lectr. 1984-87), Am. Acad. Arts and Scis., Sigma Xi, Tau Beta Pi. Patentee in field. Office: MIT 77 Massachusetts Ave Cambridge MA 02139-4301

WANG, DEHUA, chemist; b. Shaoxing, China, Sept. 27, 1937; m. Xiaolong Xu, Nov. 7, 1967; children: Kathy Yu, Wendy Lu. PhD, Syracuse U., 1985. Spectroscopist Atlanta U., 1985-86; prof. Wuhan Inst. Physics, China, 1986-89; vis. prof. Coll. Staten Island, N.Y., 1989-90; NMR rsch. scientist Kimberly-Clark Corp., Roswell, Ga., 1990—. Office: Kimberly-Clark Corp 1400 Holcomb Br Rd Roswell GA 30076

WANG, FREDERICK MARK, pediatric ophthalmologist, medical educator; b. N.Y.C., Feb. 17, 1948. Student, Northwestern U., 1968; MD, Yeshiva U., 1972. Diplomate Am. Bd. Ophthalmology, Am. Bd. Pediats., Nat. Bd. Med. Examiners. Intern in pediats. H.C. Moffitt-U. Calif. San Francisco Hosps., 1972-73; resident in pediats. Bronx Mcpl. Hosp. Ctr.-Albert Einstein Coll. Medicine, 1973-74, resident in ophthalmology, 1976-79; Heed fellow in ophthalmology and strabismus Children's Hosp. Nat. Med. Ctr., Washington, 1979-80; asst. prof. ophthalmology Albert Einstein Coll. Medicine, Bronx, 1980-82, asst. clin. prof., 1982-85, assoc. clin. prof., 1985-95, clin. prof., 1995—, asst. prof. pediats., 1980-82, asst. clin. prof. pediats., 1982-92; dir. pediat. ophthalmology and strabismus svc. Montefiore Med. Ctr., Bronx, 1980-90; cons. ophthalmologist Children's Evaluation & Rehab. Ctr., Rose Kennedy Ctr. for Rsch. in Mental Retardation and Human Devel., Bronx, 1980—, Craniofacial Ctr., Montefiore Med. Ctr., Bronx, 1980—; attending physician in ophthalmology Bronx Mcpl. Hosp./Montefiore Med. Ctr., 1980—; asst. attending physician in ophthalmology North Ctrl. Bronx Hosp., 1980—; assoc. attending physician in ophthalmology N.Y. Eye & Ear Infirmary, N.Y.C., 1982—; attending physician Strabismus Svc., N.Y. Eye & Ear Infirmary, N.Y.C., 1982—; mem. dept. ophthalmology Lenox Hill Hosp., N.Y.C., 1988—; sci. reviewer Jour. Am. Acad. Ophthalmology, 1980-86; mem. profl. adv. bd. Found. for Children with Learning Disabilities, N.Y.C., 1983-89; mem. sci. adv. bd. The Glaucoma Found., N.Y.C., 1986—; mem. profl. adv. bd. Nat. Assn. for Visually Handicapped, N.Y.C., 1988—; coord. pediat. sect. Greater N.Y. Ophthalmology Clin. Lectr. Series, 1990-93; mem. Velo-Cardio-Facial Syndrome Ednl. Found., 1994—, nominating com., 1995—. Contbr. chpts. to books and articles to profl. jours. Maj. med. officer USAF, 1974-76. Mem. Am. Acad. Pediats., Am. Acad. Ophthalmology, Am. Assn. for Pediat. Ophthalmology and Strabismus, N.Y. Soc. for Pediat. Ophthalmology and Strabismus (program chmn. 1987-89, pres. 1990-92), N.Y. Soc. for Clin. Ophthalmology (corr. sec. 1988-90, membership chmn. 1990-91, program chmn. 1991-92, pres. 1992-93), N.Y. Acad. Medicine (sec. sect. on ophthalmology 1993-94, sect. chmn. 1995-96), Alpha Omega Alpha. Avocations: chess, swimming. Office: Pediat Ophthalmology of NY 30 E 40th St New York NY 10016-1201

WANG, GUNG H., management consultant; b. Ningpo, Zhejiang, China, Feb. 3, 1909; s. Cheng V. and Zhao S. (Zhu) W.; m. Gladys Chen Wang, Sept. 10, 1938; children: Edward, Jo-Ann, Nancy, James. BA, U. Shanghai, China, 1928; MA, Tulane U., New Orleans, 1952; LLD (hon.), Loyola U., Chgo., 1989. Staff officer Mil. Fgn. Affairs, Nanking, China, 1928-30; vice cons. Consulate Gen. China, Chgo., 1930-38; cons. Consulate of China, New Orleans, 1938-50; exec. dir. Chinese Am. Civic Council, Chgo.; mng. dir. Chinatown Devel. Inc., Chgo., 1960-64; asst. dir. Chgo. Dwellings Assn., 1964-69; housing specialist Model Cities Program, Chgo., 1969-73; dir. Neighborhood Housing Services, Dept. Human Services, 1973-76; owner G.H. Wang Assocs., Chgo., 1976—; sec. Chinese Del. UN Gen. Assembly, Lake Success, N.Y., 1946-47; alt. del. UN Temporary Commn. on Korea, Seoul and Paris, 1948; pres. Neighborhood Redevel. Assn. Inc., Chgo., 1972—; exec. dir. South Side Planning Bd., 1977; adminstr. fund for intercultural edn. NRAI, 1989—. Author: The Chinese Mind 1946, Kinsiskt Tankande, 1948; contbr. articles to profl. jours. 1948-51. Mem. Nat. Assn. Housing and Redevel. Ofcls., Am. Planning Assn., Rotary Club Chgo., Phi Sigma Alpha. Presbyterian. Avocation: writing. Home: 8200 S Indiana Ave Chicago IL 60619-4725

WANG, GWO JAW, university educator. Recipient U. Va. Pres.'s Report award, 1992. Office: U Va Sch Medicine Charlottesville VA 22906

WANG, HENGTAO (HANK T. WANG), lawyer; b. Tianjin, China, Apr. 8, 1953; came to U.S., 1989; s. Shiying and Yungqiu W.; m. Shenzhong L. Wang, June 5, 1978; 1 child, Lenny. BA in English Lit. with honor, Normal U., Dalian, China, 1974, MA in English Lit., 1977; JD, St. Louis U., 1992. Bar: Mo. 1992, Ill. 1993, U.S. Dist. Ct. (ea. dist.) Mo. Prof., vice chair dept. langs. and internat. studies Dalian Naval Acad., China, 1985-88; mem. Chinese Nat. Linguistic Profs. Soc., China, 1985-88; atty. Mcpl. Fgn. Bus. Legal Office, Dalian, China, 1988-89; assoc. Armstrong, Teasdale, Schlafly & Davis, St. Louis, 1992-96; sr. counsel, group leader Asia/China Practice Group, St. Louis, 1996—. Co-author: Maritime English Textbook Series, 1985-87; author: U.S. Naval Training & Educational System, 1987; contbr. essays to profl. jours. Advisor, bd. dirs. Asian Am. Coalition, Mo., Ill., 1991, Orgn. Chinese Ams. St. Louis Chpt., 1990—; mem. World Affairs Coun., St. Louis, 1993—, St. Louis-Nanjing Sister City Com., 1993—. Comdr. Navy, 1969-88, China. Recipient Acad. Achievements award St. Louis U., 1991, Best Author of Yr. award Navy Mag., 1986. Mem. ABA (bus. law com., internat. law assn.), Am. Immigration Lawyers Assn., Asian-Am. Lawyers Assn., Mo. Bar Assn., Bar Assn. of Met. St. Louis, Ill. Bar Assn., Alpha Sigma Nu. Avocations: ping pong, boating, music, drawing. Home: 15641 Clayton Rd Ballwin MO 63011-2363 Office: Bryan Cave LLP One Metropolitan Sq Saint Louis MO 63102-2740

WANG, HERBERT FAN, geophysics educator; b. Shanghai, China, Sept. 14, 1946; came to U.S., 1948; s. Chu-Kia and Wei-Woh (Sun) W.; m. Rosemary Jane Dugan, June 3, 1968; children: Michelle Q., Melissa Y., Michael Benjamin, Matthew Alexander. BA, U. Wis., 1966; AM, Harvard U., 1968; PhD, MIT, 1971. Asst. prof. geophysics U. Wis., Madison, 1972-77, assoc. prof., 1977-82, prof., 1982—; program scientist Dept. Energy, Germantown, Md., 1980-81; vis. scientist Lawrence Livermore (Calif.) Nat. Lab., 1986-87; vis. prof. SUNY, Albany, 1989-90. Author: Introduction to Groundwater Modeling, 1982; also numerous articles. Mem. Am. Geophys. Union. Home: 5118 Juneau Rd Madison WI 53705-4744 Office: U Wis 1215 W Dayton St Madison WI 53706-1600

WANG, HUAI-LIANG WILLIAM, mechanical engineer; b. Hsinchu, Taiwan, Republic of China, Apr. 4, 1959; came to U.S., 1984; s. Feng-Chi and Hu-Mei (Chou) W.; m. Wen-Pei Chen, June 28, 1986; children: James, Edward. BSME, Tatung Inst. of Tech., Taipei, Taiwan, 1981; MSME, Okla. State U., 1985. Asst. engr. Teco Electric and Machinery Corp., Taipei, Taiwan, 1984; electro-mech. engr. Microsci. Internat. Corp., Sunnyvale, Calif., 1987-89; engr. Lockheed Engring. and Scis. Co., Houston, 1989-91, sr. engr., 1991-92; mgr. mech. engring. Orbiter Tech. Co., Fremont, Calif., 1992; sr. engr. Avatar Sys. Corp., Milpitas, Calif., 1993, Quantum Corp., Milpitas, 1994—. Mem. IEEE, ASME. Office: Quantum Corp 500 Mccarthy Blvd Milpitas CA 95035-7908

WANG, I-TUNG, atmospheric scientist; b. Peking, People's Republic of China, Feb. 16, 1933; came to U.S., 1958; s. Shen and Wei-Yun (Wen) W.; m. Amy Hung Kong; children: Cynthia P., Clifford T. BS in Physics, Nat. Taiwan U., 1955; MA in Physics, U. Toronto, 1957; PhD in Physics, Columbia U., 1965. Rsch. physicist Carnegie-Mellon U., Pitts., 1965-67, asst. prof., 1967-70; environ. systems engr. Argonne (Ill.) Nat. Lab., 1970-76; mem. tech. staff Environ. Monitoring and Svcs. Ctr. Rockwell Internat., Creve Coeur, Mo., 1976-80, Newbury Park, Calif., 1980-84; sr. scientist, combustion engr. Environ. Monitoring and Svcs. Inc., Newbury Park, Camarillo, 1984-88; sr. scientist ENSR Corp (formerly ERT), 1988; pres. EMA Co., Thosand Oaks, Calif., 1989—; tech. advisor Bur. of Environ. Protection, Republic of China, 1985; environ. cons. ABB Environ, 1989-92, ARCO, 1990-91, Du Pont (SAFER Sys. Divsn.), 1992-93, So. Calif. Edison, 1993-95, So. Coast Air Quality Mgmt. Dist., 1995—. Contbr. papers to profl jours. Grantee Bureau of Environ. Protection, Taiwan, 1985. Mem. N.Y. Acad. of Scis., Air and Waste Mgmt. Assn., Sigma Xi. Avocations: violin and chamber music. Office: EMA Co Ste 435 2219 E Thousand Oaks Blvd Thousand Oaks CA 91362-2930 *Personal philosophy: The pursuit of science is much like the pursuit of art. It requires one's complete involvement and devotion.*

WANG, JAMES CHIA-FANG, political science educator; b. Nanling, China, Apr. 4, 1926; came to U.S., 1946, naturalized, 1962; s. Chien-Yu and Lilian W.; m. Sarah Cutter, May 7, 1960; children—Sarah, Eric. BA in Polit. Sci., Oberlin Coll., 1950; postgrad., N.Y. U., 1951; PhD in Polit. Sci, U. Hawaii, 1971. Rsch. asst., internat. study group Brookings Instn., 1951-53; adminstrv. and tng. officer UN Secretariat, N.Y.C., 1953-57; editor-in-charge UN Documents Edit., Readex Corp., N.Y.C., 1957-60; lectr. far eastern politics NYU, N.Y.C., 1957-60; instr. Asian history and econs. Punahou Sch., Honolulu, 1960-64; program officer Inst. Student Interchange, East-West Ctr., Honolulu, 1964-69, acting dir. participant svcs., 1970, adminstrv. officer admissions, 1969-71; dir. freshmen integrated program Hilo (Hawaii) Coll., 1971-72; asst. prof. polit. sci. and internat. studies U. Hawaii, Hilo, 1971-72, assoc. prof., 1973-76, prof., 1976—; mem. U. Hawaii Contemporary China Study Group), Hilo, 1971—; chmn. dept. polit. sci. U. Hawaii, Hilo, 1973-75, 84—; profl. assoc. East-West Communications Inst., Honolulu, 1978, East-West Communications Inst. (Resource System Inst.), 1980-81; adviser to AAUW, Hawaii, 1978-79; cons. World Polit. Risk Forecast, Frost & Sullivan, Inc., N.Y.C., 1980-81. Author: The Cultural Revolution in China: An Annotated Bibliography, 1976, Contemporary Chinese Politics: An Introduction, 1980, rev. edit., 1985, 89, 92, 95, Hawaii State and Local Politics, 1982, Study Guide for Power in Hawaii, 1982, Ocean Law and Politics, 1992 (selected One of 1993 Outstanding Acad. Books ALA), Comparative Asian Politics, 1994; contbr. articles to profl. jours. Mem. Hawaii County Bicentennial Com., 1988-89; vice chmn. Dem. Party, County of Hawaii, 1972-76, chmn., 1982-84; mem. Dem. State Ctrl. Com., 1982-84; chmn. univ. adv. com. to Hawaii County Coun.; mem. coordinating com. Hawaii Polit. Studies Assn., 1986—; mem. Hawaii State Campaign Spending Commn., 1990-94, chmn., 1994—. U. Hawaii Rsch. Found. grantee, 1972-78. Mem. Assn. Asian Studies, Internat. Studies Assn., Coun. Ocean Law and the Law of the Sea Inst., Big Island Press Club. Home: PO Box 13 Hilo HI 96721-0013 Office: U Hawaii Dept Polit Sci Hilo HI 96720

WANG, JAW-KAI, agricultural engineering educator; b. Nanjing, Jiangsu, People's Republic of China, Mar. 4, 1932; came to U.S., 1955; s. Shuling and Hsi-Ying (Lo) W.; m. Kwang Mei Chow, Sept. 7, 1957 (div. Oct. 1989); children: Angela C.C., Dora C.C., Lawrence C.Y. BS, Nat. Taiwan U., 1953; MS in Agrl. Engring., Mich. State U., 1956, PhD, 1958. Registered profl. engr., Hawaii. Faculty agrl. engring. dept. U. Hawaii, Honolulu, 1959-93; assoc. prof., chmn. dept. U. Hawaii, 1964-68, prof., 1968—, chmn. dept. agrl. engring., 1968-75, dir. Aquaculture Program, 1990-96; prof. biosystems engring. dept. U. Hawaii-Manoa, Honolulu, 1994—; spl. asst., Internat. Rsch. Dept., Office of Internat. Cooperation and Devel. U.S. Dept. Agr., 1988; pres. Aquaculture Tech., Inc., 1990—; co-dir. internat. sci. and ednl. coun. USDA; vis. assoc. dir. internat. programs and studies office Nat. Assn. State Univs. and Land-Grant Colls., 1979; vis. prof. Nat. Taiwan U., 1965, U. Calif., Davis, 1980; cons. U.S. Army Civilian Adminstrn., Ryukus, Okinawa, 1966, Internat. Rice Rsch. Inst., The Philippines, 1971, Pacific Concrete and Rock Co. Ltd., 1974, AID, 1974, Universe Tankships, Del., 1980-81, World Bank, 1981, ABA Internat., 1981-85, Internat. Found. for Agrl. Devel./World Bank, 1981, Rockefeller Found., 1980, Orizaba, Inc., 1983, Agrisys./FAO, 1983, Info. Processing Assocs., 1984, County of Maui,

1984, 85, Dept. of State, 1985, Alexander and Baldwin, 1986; mem. expert panel on agrl. mechanization FAO/UN, 1984-90; sr. fellow East-West Ctr. Food Inst., 1973-74; dir. Info. Sys. and Svcs. Internat., Inc., 1986-90; mem. Am. Soc. Agrl. Author: Irrigated Rice Production Systems, 1980; editor: Taro-A Review of Colocasia Esculenta and its Potentials, 1983; mem. editl. bd. Aquacultural Engring., 1982—. Recipient Exemplary State Employee award State of Hawaii, 1986, State of Hawaii Employee of Yr. award Office of Gov., 1990. Fellow Am. Soc. Agrl. Engrs. (chmn. Hawaii sect. 1962-63, chmn. grad. instrn. com. 1962-63, various coms., Engr. of Yr. 1976, Tech. Paper award 1978, Kishida Internat. award 1991), Am. Inst. Med. and Biol. Engring.; mem. Nat. Acad. Engring., Aquaculture Engring. Soc. (pres. 1993-95), Sigma Xi, Gamma Sigma Delta (pres. Hawaii chpt. 1974-75), Pi Mu Epsilon. Office: U Hawaii Biosystems Engring Dept 3050 Maile Way Honolulu HI 96822-2231 *To be allowed a continuing search for truth even when you are doubting its existence, is to be blessed.*

WANG, JOHN CHENG HWAI, communications engineer; b. Beijing, Feb. 12, 1934; s. Hwa Lung and Shu Shiang (Shia) W.; m. Rosa Jenny Chu, Sept. 9, 1967; children: Sophia, Maria, Nina, Amy. BS, U. Md., 1959; MS, U. Pitts., 1968. Engr. Chesapeake Instrument Corp., Shadyside, Md., 1959-64; rsch. scientist Rsch. Ctr. U.S. Steel Corp., Monroeville, Pa., 1964-67; asst. prof. Pa. State U., New Kensington, 1967-69; rsch. engr. FCC, Washington, 1969—; chmn. working party medium wave propagation Internat. Radio Consultative Com., Geneva, 1983—. Contbr. articles to profl. jours. Fellow IEEE. Avocations: astronomy, bridge, Chinese history. Office: FCC 1919 M St NW Washington DC 20036-3521

WANG, JONAS CHIA-TSUNG, pharmaceutical executive; b. Canton, People's Republic of China, July 21, 1944; came to U.S., 1977; s. Gin-Han and Gin (Lai) W.; m. Huey-Wen An, Nov. 15, 1969; children: Jeremy, Joseph, JoAnn. BS in Pharmacy, Nat. Def. Med. Ctr., Taipei, Republic of China, 1967; PhD in Phys. Pharmacy, U. Iowa, 1982. Registered pharmacist, Republic of China. Instr. in pharm. chemistry Nat. Def. Med. Ctr., 1968-77; chief quality control dept. Ret. Serviceman's Pharm. Plant, Taipei, 1968-77; teaching asst. U. Iowa, Iowa City, 1977-81; assoc. dir. R & D Bristol-Myers Squibb, Buffalo, 1981-88; dir. R & D Johnson & Johnson Consumer Products, Inc., Skillman, N.J., 1988-94, v.p. Rsch. and Tech. & Tech. Rsch. Ctr., 1994—; adj. prof. cosmetic sci. program Coll. Pharmacy, U. Cin., 1985—; mem. coun. biology dept. Canisius Coll., Buffalo, 1984-88; reviewer Pharm. Rsch., 1986-94; mem. faculty spl. seminar IV Internat. Symposium on Psoriasis, Stanford U., 1986; tech. cons. Western N.Y. Tech. Transfer Com., 1984-88; lectr., presenter in field; vis. prof. Sch. Pharmacy Nat. Def. Med. Ctr., 1986. Contbr. articles to profl. publs.patentee in field. Maj. Rep. of China armed forces, 1965-67. Mem. Acad. Pharm. Sci., Soc. Cosmetic Chemists (mem. Merit award com. 1991), Am. Assn. Pharm. Scientists, Am. Acad. Dermatology, Nat. Def. Med. Ctr. Alumni Assn. (pres. N.Y. chpt. 1991-93), Chinese Pharm. Soc., Asian Pharm. Assn. Avocations: tennis, skiing, ballroom dancing, swimming. Home: 23 Ellsworth Dr Robbinsville NJ 08691-3513 Office: Johnson & Johnson Consumer Products Inc Grandview Rd Skillman NJ 08558

WANG, JOSEPHINE L. FEN, physician; b. Taiwan, China, Jan 2, 1948; came to U.S., 1974; d. Pao-San and Ann-Nam (Chen) Chao; m. Chang-Yang Wang, Dec. 20, 1973; children: Edward, Eileen. MD, Nat. Taiwan U., Taipei, 1974. Diplomate Am. Bd. Pediatrics, Am. Bd. Allergy and Immunology. Intern Nat. Taiwan U. Hosp., 1973-74; resident U. Ill. Hosp., Chgo., 1974-76; fellow Northwestern U. Med. Ctr., Chgo., 1976-78, instr. pediatrics, 1978—; cons. Holy Cross Hosp., Chgo., 1978—, Meth. Hosp. Ind., 1979—, St. Anthony Hosp., 1985—, Christ Hosp., 1995—. Fellow Am. Coll. Allergy; mem. AMA, Am. Acad. Allergy. Office: 9012 Connecticut Dr Merrillville IN 46410-7170 also: 4901 W 79th St Burbank IL 60459-1554

WANG, JUI HSIN, biochemistry educator; b. Beijing, Republic of China, Mar. 16, 1921; s. Lieh and Sun Li (Sun) W.; m. Yen Chan Yang, Apr. 2, 1949 (dec.); children: Jane, Nancy. BS, Nat. SW Assoc. U., Kunming, Republic of China, 1945; PhD, Washington U., St. Louis, 1949; MA (hon.), Yale U., 1960. Postdoctoral fellow radiochemistry Washington U., 1949-51; faculty Yale U., New Haven, Conn., 1951—, prof. chemistry, 1960-62, Eugene Higgins prof. chemistry, 1962-65, Eugene Higgins prof. chemistry and molecular biophysics, 1965-72; Einstein prof. sci. SUNY, Buffalo, 1972—; rschr. molecular structure and biochem. activity, superconductivity. Contbr. articles to profl. jours., chapters in books. Guggenheim fellow Cambridge U., 1960-61. Fellow AAAS, Am. Acad. Arts and Scis.; mem. Am. Chem. Soc., Am. Soc. Microbiology, Yale Chemists Assn., Am. Soc. for Biochemistry and Molecular Biology, Am. Phys. Soc., Biophys. Soc., Academia Sinica, Materials Rsch. Soc., Sigma Xi. Home: 477 Lebrun Rd Buffalo NY 14226-4218 Office: SUNY Dept Chemistry Buffalo NY 14260-3000

WANG, JUN, engineering educator; b. Dalian, China, July 11, 1954; came to U.S., 1986; s. Jingxian Wang and Shuofang Qi; m. Li Jin, Apr. 12, 1984; 1 child, Shuo. BSEE, Dalian U. Tech., 1982, MS, 1985; PhD, Case Western Res. U., 1991. Mem. faculty Dalian U. Tech., 1985-86; teaching asst., rsch. asst. Case Western Res. U., Cleve., 1986-89; tech. staff mem. Zagar, Inc., Cleve., 1989-90; asst. prof. dept. indsl. tech. U. N.D., Grand Forks, 1990-93, assoc. prof., 1993-95; assoc. prof. mech. and automation engring. Chinese U. of Hong Kong, 1995—; presenter at profl. confs. Editor: Neural Networks in Design and Manufacturing, 1993; co-editor: Neural Networks for Optimization, 1996; guest editor Neural Networks and Ops. Rsch.Mgmt. Sci. European Jour. Operational Rsch.; contbr. articles to profl.jours. Experimental Program to Stimulate Competitive Rsch. grantee NSF, 1992. Mem. IEEE (sr.) Inst. Indsl. Engrs. (sr.), Internat. Neural Network Soc., Inst. Ops. Rsch. and Mgmt. Sci. Office: Chinese U of Hong Kong, Dept Mech & Automation Engring, Shatin New Territories Hong Kong

WANG, KUO-KING, manufacturing engineer, educator. BSME, Nat. Ctrl. U., China, 1947; MSME, U. Wis., 1962, PhD in Mech. Engring., 1968. Sibley prof. mech. engring. Cornell U., Ithaca, N.Y.; founder, dir. Cornell Injection Molding Program, 1974—; cofounder Cornell Mfg. Engring. and Productivity Program, Advanced CAE Tech., Inc. Recipient Disting. Svc. citation U. Wis., 1990. Fellow ASME (Blackall Machine Tool and Gage award 1968, William T. Ennor Mfg. Tech. award 1991), Soc. Mfg. Engrs. (Frederick W. Taylor Rsch. medal 1987); mem. CIRP, ASM Internat., Nat. Acad. Engring., Am. Welding Soc. (Adams Meml. Membership award 1976), Soc. Plastic Engrs., Polymer Processing Soc. Achievements include pioneering research in injection molding, friction welding and applications of solid modeling to CAD/CAM. Office: Cornell Univ Dept Mech/Aero Engring Upson Hall Ithaca NY 14853

WANG, L. EDWIN, church official; b. Medford, Oreg., Nov. 2, 1919; s. Lorang Edwin and Laura (Thomas) W.; m. Astrid H. Wikander, Sept. 4, 1942; children: David M., Linnea M., Judith L. Extension student, U. Calif., 1947-48, U. Minn., 1956-65; LHD, Midland Luth. Coll., 1970. CLU. Field underwriter, then asst. mgr. Mut. of N.Y., 1943-51; mgr. Standard Ins. Co., Oakland, Calif., 1951-56; exec. sec. Augustana Pension & Aid Fund, Mpls., 1956-62; pres. bd. pensions Luth Ch. Am., 1962-87; acting ins. commr., Minn., 1967; part-time ins. instr. Oakland Jr. Coll., Contra Costa Jr. Coll., 1954-56; pres. Oakland-East Bay Life Underwriters Assn., 1951, Oakland Mgrs. and Gen. Agts. Assn., 1955; pres. Ch. Pensions Conf., 1967; mem. pension research council U. Pa. Wharton Sch. Fin., 1971-92. Bd. dirs. Nat. Found. for Philanthropy, 1981—; pres. Lewis and Clark Trail Heritage Found. Inc., 1985-86; pres. Luth. Ch. Libr. Assn. 1988-90, bd. dirs., 1988—. Recipient Outstanding Service award Gov. Minn. Mem. Am. Risk and Ins. Assn., Am. Soc. CLU's (bd. dirs. 1980-84), Mpls. Chpt. CLU's (pres. 1973-74). Home: 6013 St Johns Ave Minneapolis MN 55424-1834

WANG, PAUL WEILY, materials science and physics educator; b. Kao-Hsiung, Taiwan, Republic of China, Nov. 4, 1951; came to U.S., 1979; s. Yao Wen Wang and Yue Hua Lo; m. Diana Chung-Chung Chow, June 9, 1979; children: Agnes J., Carol H., Alfred Z. PhD, SUNY, Albany, 1986. Rsch. asst. prof. Vanderbilt U., Nashville, 1986-90; asst. prof. U. Tex., El Paso, 1990-96, assoc. prof., 1996—; hon. prof. Dalian Inst. Light Industry, 1995—; cons. EOTec Inc., 1987-88, Midtex Comm. Instruments Inc., 1996—. Contbr. articles to Jour. Applied Physics, Nuclear Instru. and Math., Springer Series in Surface Scis., Applied Surface Sci., Applied Optics, Jour. of Am. Ceramic Soc., Jour. Materials Sci., Jour. Luminescence, Jour. Non-cyrs. Solids, Lasers, Thin Solid Films, Jour. Materials Chemistry and Physics. Fellow Inst. for Study of Defects in Solids; mem. Am. Ceramic Soc., Am. Phys. Soc., Materials Rsch. Soc., Am. Vacuum Soc. Achievements include iron in silicon gettered by thermally grown silicon dioxide thin film, dopants effects on the structure of fluoride glasses, surface modification of heavy metal doped glasses under x-ray and electron irradiations, luminescence centers in silica stimulated by particle bombardments, defects introducted by gamma-ray radiation enhance the luminescence in silica, development of defects creation mechanism in silica by 5 and 50 eV photons, investigation of silver diffuses and precipitates thermally on the surface in ion exchange sodium calcium silicate glass, investigate the radiation effects on lead silicate glasses, electron beam processing on trimethylsilane covered Si(100) surface, aluminum nitride/aluminum oxide composite films grown by plasma, conduct and manage numerous research projects in materials research. Home: 6890 Orizaba Ave El Paso TX 79912-2324 Office: U Tex Dept Physics and Materials Rsch El Paso TX 79968

WANG, SHIH-HO, electrical engineer, educator; b. Kiangsu, China, June 29, 1944; came to U.S., 1968; s. C.C. Wang and Man Shih. BEE, Nat. Taiwan U., Taipei, 1967; MEE, U. Calif., Berkeley, 1970, PhD in Elec. Engring., 1971. Asst. prof. elec. engring. U. Colo., Colo. Springs, 1973-76, Boulder, 1976-77; asst. prof. electrical engring. U. Md., College Park, 1977-78, assoc. prof., 1978-84; prof. U. Calif., Davis, 1984—; cons. Lawrence Livermore (Calif.) Nat. Lab., 1986—; scientific officer Office Naval Research, Arlington, Va., 1983-84. Assoc. editor Internat. Jour. Robotics and Automation, 1986—. Served to 2d lt. China Air Force, Taiwan, 1967-68. Mem. IEEE (hon. mention award control systems soc. 1975). Office: Univ Calif Dept Elec/Computer Engring Davis CA 95616

WANG, SU SUN, chemical company executive, chemist; b. Taipei, Taiwan, China, Jan. 11, 1934; s. Tuan King and Shane (Lai) W.; m. Beth Song-hwa, Aug. 6, 1964; children: Albert W., Fritz W. BS, Nat. Taiwan U., 1957, MS, 1959; PhD, U. Calif., Berkeley, 1966. Sr. chemist Hoffmann-La Roche Inc., Nutley, N.J., 1970-79; ptnr. Peninsula Labs. Inc., Belmont, Calif., 1979-81; founder, pres. Am. Biochems., San Carlos, Calif., 1981-82; v.p. Alpha 1 Biomeds. Inc., Bethesda, 1982—. invited vis. scholar Ministry Edn., Academia Sinica, Taipei Inst. Biochemistry, 1986. Patentee in field. U.S. Dept. Health and Edn. fellow Rockefeller U., 1968-70. Mem. AAAS, Am. Chem. Soc., Fedn. Am. Socs. for Exptl. Biology, Chinese Biochem. Soc. Republican. Home: 1512 Chula Vista Dr Belmont CA 94002-3614

WANG, TAYLOR GUNJIN, science administrator, astronaut, educator; b. Shanghai, China, June 16, 1940; came to U.S., 1963; m. Beverly Fung, 1966; children: Kenneth, Eric. BS, UCLA, 1967, MS, 1968, PhD, 1971. Mgr. microgravity sci. and applications program Jet Propulsion Lab., Pasadena, Calif., 1972-88, cons., 1987-89; Space Shuttle astronaut-scientist NASA, 1983-85; Centennial prof., dir. Ctr. for Microgravity Rsch. and Applications Vanderbilt U., Nashville, 1988—. Contbr. over 170 articles to profl. jours.; inventor living cells encapsulation tech. as cure of hormone deficiency states in humans; over 20 patents in field. Bd. dirs. Com. of 100. Fellow Acoustical Soc. Am.; mem. AIAA, Am. Phys. Soc., Assn. Space Explorers-USA (pres. 1988), Sigma Xi. Office: Vanderbilt U Sta B Box 6079 Nashville TN 37235

WANG, WILLIAM KAI-SHENG, law educator; b. N.Y.C., Feb. 28, 1946; s. Yuan-Chao and Julia Ying-Ru (Li) W.; m. Kwan Kwan Tan, July 29, 1972; 1 child, Karen You-Chuan. B.A., Amherst Coll., 1967; J.D., Yale U., 1971. Bar: Calif. 1972. Asst. to mng. partner Gruss & Co., N.Y.C., 1971-72; asst. prof. law U. San Diego, 1972-74, asso. prof., 1974-77, prof., 1977-81; prof. Hastings Coll. Law, U. Calif., San Francisco, 1981—; vis. prof. law U. Calif., Davis, 1975-76, U. Calif., L.A., 1990; cons. to White House Domestic Policy Staff, Washington, 1979; vis. prof. Hastings Coll. Law, U. Calif., 1980; chair investment policy oversight group Law Sch. Admissions Coun.; mem. com. on audit and assn. investment policy Assn. of Am. Law Schs. Co-author: Insider Trading, 1996; contbr. articles to newspapers, mags., scholarly jours. Mem. State Bar Calif., Am. Law Inst. Home: 455 39th Ave San Francisco CA 94121-1507 Office: U Calif Hastings Coll Law 200 Mcallister St San Francisco CA 94102-4707

WANG, WILLIAM SHI-YUAN, linguistics educator; b. Shanghai, China, Aug. 14, 1933; came to U.S., 1948, naturalized, 1960; s. Harper and Lily W.; children: Eugene, Yulun, Yumei, Yusi. A.B., Columbia U., 1955; M.A., U. Mich., 1956, Ph.D., 1960. Assoc. prof., chmn. dept. linguistics Ohio State U., Columbus, 1963-65; prof. linguistics U. Calif., Berkeley, 1966—, dir. Project on Linguistic Analysis, 1966—; prof. grad. sch., 1994—; fellow Center Advanced Studies in Behavioral Scis., 1969-70, 83-84; sr. Fulbright lectr. in, Sweden, 1972, India, 1979. Author: Explorations in Language, 1991; editor: The Lexicon in Phonological Change, 1977, Human Communication, 1982, Language Writing and the Computer, 1986; co-editor: Individual Differences in Language Ability and Language Behavior, 1979; assoc. editor Language, 1967-73; founding editor Jour. Chinese Linguistics, 1973—; contbr. numerous articles to profl. jours. Guggenheim Found. fellow, 1978-79. Mem. Linguistic Soc. Am., Acoustical Soc. Am., Academia Sinica, Internat. Assn. Chinese Linguistics (pres. 1992-93). Office: U Calif 2222 Piedmont Ave Berkeley CA 94720-2171 *Because language penetrates so many aspects of life, my attempt to understand its nature has frequently led me into anthropology, biology, etc. These forays into neighboring fields have enhanced my awareness of the unity of knowledge, and of the importance of a broad perspective in any serious intellectual venture.*

WANG, XIAODONG, corporate executive, consultant; b. Yunhe, Zhejiang, China, Sept. 10, 1957; s. Wendou and Huizhong (Yang) W.; m. Hong Xue, Oct. 1, 1982; 1 child, Cindy. Med. practitioner cert., Yunhe Med. Sch., China, 1977; BS, Zhejiang U., Hangzhou, China, 1983; MBA, Boise State U., 1993. Practitioner Shaxi Hosp., Yunhe, China, 1977-78; sect. chief Lishui Hosp., China, 1983-84; project engr. Fujian Investment & Enterprise Co., Fuzhou, China, 1984-86; dep. dir. SHP Corp., Fuzhou, 1986-90; project coord. Simplot Co., Boise, Idaho, 1992-93, gen. mgr. China ops., 1994—; cons. Chendou Hydro Design Inst., Chendou, China, 1988-90, Hunan (China) Electric Power Bur., 1989-90. Author: Poems, Essays and Short Stories, 1972-82 (Best Works 1982). Mem. Mgmt. Assn. China, Collegiate Entrepreneur Assn., MBA Assn. (advisor 1991-92). Home: 5656 S Snapdragon Pl Boise ID 83705-6917 Office: Simplot Co 6360 Federal Way Boise ID 83716-9617

WANG, XINWEI, aeronautics educator; b. Wu County, Jiangsu, China, Feb. 25, 1948; s. Shiheng and Meizhen (Jiang) W.; m. Guoying Zhang, Dec. 2, 1975; children: Xia Ping, Xiongfei. BS, Nanjing Aero. Inst., China, 1975, MS, 1981; PhD, U. Okla., 1989. Farmer Constrn. People's Commune, Jiangsu, 1968-72; asst. prof. Nanjing Aero. Inst., 1976-78, lectr., 1981-84; vis. scholar UCLA, 1984-85; vis. rsch. prof. U. Okla., 1985-86, vis. asst. prof., 1989-92; prof. Nanjing U. Aeronautics and Astronautics, 1992—, dir. structural mechanics and strenght divsn., 1994—; vis. prof. UMBC, 1995-96. Mem. ASME (assoc.), Am. Acad. Mechanics, Chinese Soc. Theoretical and Applied Mechanics (Jiangsu br. dir.), Chinese Soc. Aeronautics, Chinese Soc. Vibration Engring., Chinese Soc. Composite Materials. Avocations: traveling, American football, basketball, football, reading. Office: NUAA Dept, Dept Aircraft Engring, Nanjing 210016, China

WANG, ZENG-YU, neurologist, immunologist; b. Dongan,, Hunan, China, July 27, 1962; came to U.S., 1993; s. Xian-Zhun and Yue (Lu) W.; m. Jianhua, Oct. 1, 1989; 1 child, Rachel. MB, Hunan (China) Med. U., 1984, M of Medicine in Neurology, 1987; PhD, Karolinska Inst., Stockholm, Sweden, 1993. Resident Hunan Med. U., 1987-90; rsch. asst. Karolinski Inst., Stockholm, 1990-93; postdoctoral assoc. U. Minn., St. Paul, 1993-96; rsch. assoc. U Minn., 1996—. Contbr. articles to profl. jours. Recipient Rsch. fellowship Karolinska Inst., 1991, Rsch. fellowship Swedish NHR-fonden, 1992, Rsch. fellowship Muscular Dystrophy Assn., 1994. Mem. AAAS, N.Y. Acad Scis. Achievements include induction of oral tolerance to experimental myasthenia gravis. Avocations: fishing, badminton, classical music. Home: 1619 Carl St Apt 15 Saint Paul MN 55108-1242 Office: U Minn Dept Biochemistry 1479 Gortner Ave Saint Paul MN 55108-1041

WANGER, OLIVER WINSTON, federal judge; b. L.A., Nov. 27, 1940; m. Lorrie A. Reinhart; children: Guy A., Christopher L., Andrew G., W. Derek, Oliver Winston II. Student, Colo. Sch. Mines, 1958-60; BS, U. So. Calif., 1963; LLB, U. Calif., Berkeley, 1966. Bar: Calif. 1967, U.S. Dist. Ct. (ea. dist.) Calif. 1969, U.S. Tax Ct. 1969, U.S. Dist. Ct. (cen. dist.) Calif. 1975, U.S. Dist. Ct. (so. dist.) Calif. 1977, U.S. Dist. Ct. (no. dist.) Calif. 1989, U.S. Ct. Appeals (9th cir.) 1989. Dep. dist. atty. Fresno (Calif.) County Dist. Atty., 1967-69; ptnr. Gallagher, Baker & Manock, Fresno, 1969-74; sr. ptnr. McCormick, Barstow, Sheppard, Wayte & Carruth, Fresno, 1974-91; judge U.S. Dist. Ct. (ea. dist.) Calif., Fresno, 1991—; adj. prof. law Humphreys Coll. Law, Fresno, 1968-70. Fellow Am. Coll. Trial Lawyers, Internat. Acad. Trial Lawyers; mem. Am. Bd. Trial Advs. (pres. San Joaquin Valley chpt. 1987-89, nat. bd. dirs. 1989-91), Am. Bd. Profl. Liability Attys. (founder, diplomate), Calif. State Bar (mem. exec. com. litigation sect. 1989-92, mem. com. on fed. cts. 1989-90), San Joaquin Valley Am. Inn of Ct. (pres. 1992-93), Beta Gamma Sigma. Office: US Dist Ct 5104 US Courthouse 1130 O St Fresno CA 93721-2201

WANGLER, MARK ADRIAN, anesthesiologist; b. Coldwater, Ohio, Sept. 29, 1955; s. William Henry and Rita Francis (Vielkind) W.; m. Kathleen Sara Schlarman, May 6, 1977; children: Nathan, Aaron. BS in Biology, Wright State U., 1977; MD, Ohio State U., 1981. Diplomate Am. Bd. Anesthesiology. Intern Ohio State U., Columbus, 1981-82, resident, 1982-84, chief resident, 1983-84; asst. prof. anesthesiology Northeastern Ohio Coll. Medicine, Canton, 1984-86; dir. anesthesiology Mercer County Joint Twp. Community Hosp., Coldwater, 1987-90; ptnr. Anesthesia Assocs. of Lima, Inc., 1990—; dir. rsch. Northeastern Ohio Coll. Medicine, Canton, 1985-86, dir. pain clinic, 1985-86; dir. pain clinic Mercer County Cmty. Hosp., Coldwater, 1986-90, St. Rita's Med. Ctr., 1994—. Contbr. articles to numerous profl. jours. Mem. Mercer County Hist. Soc., Celina, Ohio, 1988; patron Lighthouse Ministries, Celina, 1988. Grantee, NIH, Bethesda, Md., 1978. Mem. AMA, Internat. Anesthesia Rsch. Soc., Am. Soc. Anesthesiologists, Ohio Med. Assn., Ohio Soc. Anesthesiologists, Allen County Acad. of Medicine. Republican. Avocations: biking, camping, reading. Home: 860 Yorkshire Dr Lima OH 45804-3300 Office: 1103 Bank One Twr Lima OH 45801

WANGLER, WILLIAM CLARENCE, retired insurance company executive; b. Buffalo, Dec. 7, 1929; s. Emil A. and Viola M. (Roesser) W.; m. Carol B. Sullivan, Aug. 17, 1957; children: Jeffrey W., Eric J. BS, SUNY, Cortland, 1951. Claims adjuster Liberty Mut. Ins. Co., Buffalo, 1954-60; claims supr. Liberty Mut. Ins. Co., Miami, Fla., 1960-65; home office examiner Liberty Mut. Ins. Co., Boston, 1965-68; asst. claims mgr. Liberty Mut. Ins. Co., Cleve., 1968-69; claims mgr. Liberty Mut. Ins. Co., Cleve, 1969-73; div. claims service mgr. Liberty Mut. Ins. Co., Pitts., 1973-79, div. claims mgr., 1979-86; v.p. asst. gen. claims mgr. adminstrn. Liberty Mut. Ins. Co., Boston, 1986-94; ret., 1994; pres. Claims Mgrs. Counsel, Cleve., 1970; chmn. Nationwide Intercompany Arbitration, Cleve., 1969-70. Loaned exec. Mass. Bay United Way, Boston, 1964; account exec. Pitts. United Way, 1985-86. Served to capt. USMC, 1951-54. Republican. Roman Catholic. Home: 64 Trout Farm Ln Duxbury MA 02332-4609

WANK, GERALD SIDNEY, periodontist; b. Bklyn., Jan. 20, 1925; s. Joseph and Sadie (Ikowitz) W.; m. Gloria Baum, June 4, 1949; children: David, Stephen, Daniel. B.A., NYU, 1945, D.D.S., 1949; cert. in orthodontia, Columbia U., 1951, cert. in periodontia, 1956. Intern in oral surgery Bellevue Hosp., 1949-50; practice dentistry specializing in oral rehab. and periodontal prosthetics N.Y.C., Great Neck, N.Y., 1949—; instr. dept. periodontia, oral medicine NYU Dental Sch., 1956-63, asst. clin. prof. dept. periodontia, 1963-67, asst. prof. periodontia, oral medicine, former postgrad. dir. periodontal-prosthesis dept. fixed partial prosthesis, 1970—, clin. assoc. prof. periodontia and oral medicine, 1970-77, clin. prof., 1977—, postgrad. dir. periodontia, 1986-71; staff lectr. periodontology Harvard U. Sch. Dental Medicine, 1973-74; vis. lectr. N.Y.C. Community Coll. Sch. Dental Hygiene, 1960-65, Albert Einstein Coll. Medicine, 1967-96; sr. asst. attending staff North Shore Univ. Hosp., 1974-77, sr. asst. attending div. surgery, 1977—; cons. orthodontic panel N.Y. State, N.Y.C. depts. health, 1953-80; cons. periodontal prosthesis, Goldwater Meml. Hosp., N.Y.C.; former postgrad. instr. 1st Dist. Dental Soc. Postgrad. Sch.; lectr. various socs. N.Y. U.; mem. com. admissions N.Y. U. Coll. Dentistry, 1975—, chmn. fund raising, 1976—; cons. N.Y. VA Hosp. Contbr. to: Practice of Periodontia, 1960, Dental Clinics of North America, 1972, 81, Manual of Clinical Periodontics, 1973; contbr. articles to profl. jours. Served to capt. USAF, 1953-55. Recipient Alumni Meritorious Service award N.Y. U., 1981, Coll. Dentistry Alumni Achievement award N.Y. U., 1983. Fellow Acad. Gen. Dentistry, N.Y. Acad. Dentistry, Internat. Coll. Dentists, Am. Coll. Dentists, Am. Acad. Oral Medicine (pres. N.Y. sect. 1971-72), Am. Pub. Health Assn.; mem. N.Y. Coll. Dentists (dir.), ADA, Dental Soc. N.Y.C. (dir. 1st dist., chmn. ethics com. 1985-86), Fedn. Dentaire Internat., Am. Assn. Dental Schs., N.Y. State Pub. Health Assn., AAUP, Pan Am. Med. Assn. (life), AAAS, ADA, Am. Acad. Periodontology, Sci. Rsch. Soc. Am., Northeastern Soc. Periodontia, Am. Acad. Dental Medicine, Acad. Gen. Dentistry, Internat. Acad. Orthodontia, Am. Acad. Endodontia (life), Am. Acad. Periodontia (life), Am. Acad. Oral Medicine (life), NYU Coll. Dentistry Alumni Assn. (dir., sec. 1973-74, v.p. 1974-75, pres. 1976-77), Am. Soc. Anesthesiology, Am. Assn. Endodontists, NYU Coll. Dentistry Dental Assocs. (charter), Acad. Oral Rehab. (hon.), First Dist. Dental Soc. (program chmn. 1984, chmn. continuing edn. 1983, sec., 1985, v.p. Eastern Dental Soc. br. 1986, pres.-elect 1987, pres. br. 1988, bd. dirs. 1989—, Meritorious Svc. award 1997), Am. Acad. Osseointegration, NYU Gallatin Assos., Alumni Fedn. N.Y. U. (dir. 1976-81), Omicron Kappa Upsilon, Alpha Omega. Jewish. Clubs: Fresh Meadow Country (Great Neck, N.Y.); N.Y. U. (charter N.Y. U. Coll. Dentistry), Century (charter N.Y. U. Coll. Dentistry); Masons. Home and Office: 40 Bayview Ave Great Neck NY 11021-2819 Office: 310 Madison Ave New York NY 10017-6009

WANKAT, PHILLIP CHARLES, chemical engineering educator; b. Oak Park, Ill., July 11, 1944; s. Charles and Grace Leona (Pryor) W.; m. Dorothy Nel Richardson, Dec. 13, 1980; children: Charles, Jennifer. BS in Chem. Engring., Purdue U., 1966, MS in Edn., 1982; PhD, Princeton U., 1970. From asst. prof. to prof. chem. engring. Purdue U., West Lafayette, Ind., 1970—, head freshman engring., 1987-95, interim dir. continuing engring. edn., 1996; cons. pharm. firm, 1985-94. Author: Large Scale Ads and Chromatog, 1986, Equil Staged Separations, 1988, Rate Controlled Separations, 1990, Teaching Engineering, 1993; patentee in field. With AUS, 1962-64. Recipient award in Separations Sci. and Tech., Am. Chem. Soc., 1994. Mem. AIChE, Am. Soc. Engring. Edn., Am. Chem. Soc. Avocations: fishing, canoeing, camping. Office: Purdue U Dept Chem Engring Dept Chemical Engring West Lafayette IN 47907-1283

WANKE, RONALD LEE, lawyer; b. Chgo., June 22, 1941; s. William F. and Lucille (Kleinwachter) W.; m. Rose Klonowski, Oct. 23, 1987. BSEE, Northwestern U., 1964; JD, DePaul U., 1968. Bar: Ill. 1968. Assoc. Wood, Dalton, Phillips, Mason & Rowe, Chgo., 1968-71, ptnr., 1971-84; ptnr. Jenner & Block, Chgo., 1984--; lectr. John Marshall Law Sch., Chgo., 1985-94. Contbr. articles to Software Law Jour., 1987, Internat. Legal Strategy, 1995. Mem. ABA, Chgo. Bar Assn. (lectr. 1985-87, chmn. computer law com. 1987-88), Computer Law Assn., Intellectual Property Law Assn. Chgo. (chmn. inventor svcs. com. 1976, chmn. fed. rules com. 1981). Home: 1806 N Sedgwick St Chicago IL 60614-5306 Office: Jenner & Block 1 E Ibm Plz Chicago IL 60611-3586

WANNER, ERIC, foundation executive; b. Wilmington, Del., Mar. 14, 1942; s. Edwin and Isabel Smith (Speakman) W.; m. Patricia Attix, June 13, 1964 (div. 1976); children: Noel Edwin, Erin Cole; m. Carla Francesca Seal, June 18, 1983; children: Lindzay Elizabeth. BA, Amherst Coll., 1963; PhD, Harvard U., 1969. Asst. to assoc. prof. Harvard U., Cambridge, Mass., 1968-76; behavioral sci. editor Harvard U. Press, Cambridge, Mass., 1976-82; program officer Alfred P. Sloan Found., N.Y.C., 1982-84, v.p., 1984-86; pres. Russell Sage Found,, N.Y.C., 1986—; mem. adv. bd. Malcolm Weiner Ctr. for Social Policy, Harvard U., 1988—; trustee Ctr. for Advanced Study in Behavioral Scis., 1993—; bd. dirs. Life Trends Inc. Author: Remembering, Forgetting and Understanding Sentences, 1974; editor: Language Acquisition: the State of the Art, 1982; contbr. articles to profl. jours. Fulbright fellow Sussex U., Brighton, Eng., 1979, fellow N.Y. Inst. for Humanities, NYU, 1985-93, Am. Acad. Arts and Scis., 1994—. Mem. APA, Cognitive Sci. Soc., N.Y. Acad. Scis., Century Club, Sigma Xi. Office: Russell Sage Found 112 E 64th St New York NY 10021-7307

WANNSTEDT, DAVID RAYMOND, professional football team coach; b. Pitts., May 21, 1952; m. Jan Wannstedt; children: Keri, Jami. Student, U. Pitts. Player Green Bay Packers, 1974; asst. coach U. Pitts., 1975-79, Okla. State U., 1979-82, U. So. Calif., 1983-85; def. coord. U. Miami, 1986-89, Dallas Cowboys, 1989-93; head coach Chgo. Bears, 1993—. Named to NCAA 2nd team All-East; inducted into Western Pa. Hall of Fame, 1990. Office: Chgo Bears Halas Hall 250 Washington Rd Lake Forest IL 60045-2459

WANTLAND, WILLIAM CHARLES, bishop, lawyer; b. Edmond, Okla., Apr. 14, 1934; s. William Lindsay and Edna Louise (Yost) W. BA, U. Hawaii, 1957; JD, Okla. City U., 1967; D in Religion, Geneva Theol. Coll., Knoxville, Tenn., 1976; DD (hon.), Nashotah House, Wis., 1983, Seabury-Western Sem., Evanston, Ill., 1983. With FBI, various locations, 1954-59, Ins. Co. of N.Am., Oklahoma City, 1960-62; law clk.-atty. Bishop & Wantland, Seminole, Okla., 1962-77; vicar St. Mark's Ch., Seminole, 1963-77, St. Paul's Ch., Holdenville, Okla., 1974-77; presiding judge Seminole Mcpl. Ct., 1970-77; atty. gen. Seminole Nation of Okla., 1969-72, 75-77; exec. dir. Okla. Indian Rights Assn., Norman, 1972-73; rector St. John's Ch., Oklahoma City, 1977-80; bishop Episcopal Diocese of Eau Claire, Wis., 1980—; interim bishop of Navajoland, 1993-94; adj. prof. Law Sch. U. Okla., Norman, 1970-78; instr. canon law Nashotah House, 1983—; mem. nat. coun. Evang. & Cath. Mission, Chgo., 1977-90; mem. Episcopal Commn. on Racism, 1990-92, Episcopal Coun. Indian Ministries, 1990-95, Standing Commn. on Constn. and Canons, 1992-95. Author: Foundations of the Faith, 1982, Canon Law of the Episcopal Church, 1984, The Prayer Book and the Catholic Faith, 1994; co-author: Oklahoma Probate Forms, 1971; contbr. articles to profl. jours. Pres. Okla. Conf. Mcpl. Judges, 1973; v.p. South African Ch. Union, 1985-95; trustee Nashotah House, Wis., 1981—, chmn., 1992—; bd. dirs. SPEAK, Eureka Springs, Ark., 1983-89; mem. Wis. adv. com. U.S. Civil Rights Commn., 1990-91; mem. support com. Native Am. Rights Fund, 1990—; co-chmn. Luth.-Anglican-Roman Cath. Commn. of Wis., 1989-95; pres. Wis. Episc. Conf., 1995-97. Recipient Most Outstanding Contbn. to Law and Order award Okla. Supreme Ct., 1975, Outstanding Alumnus award Okla. City U., 1980, Wis. Equal Rights Coun. award, 1986, Manitou Ikwe award Indian Alcoholism Coun., 1988, Episcopal Synod Pres.'s award, 1995. Mem. Okla. Bar Assn., Okla. Indian Bar Assn., Living Ch. Found., Oklahoma City Law Sch. Alumni Assn. (pres. 1968), Wis. Conf. Chs. (pres. 1985-86). Democrat. Avocations: canoeing, skin-diving, cross-country skiing. Home: 145 Marston Ave Eau Claire WI 54701-3911 Office: Diocese of Eau Claire 510 S Farwell St Eau Claire WI 54701-3723 *If we truly believe that God reigns, we will so order our lives that such a belief is clearly reflected in all that we do and say; further, such a belief will shape our relations, not only with all other people, but all of God's created order.*

WANZER, ROBERT, retired basketball player; b. N.Y.C., June 4, 1921. Student, Seton Hall. With Rochester Royals, 1947-57; coach Rochester Royals, Cin., 1957-58; player, coach Rochester Royals, 1955-57. With U.S. Marines. Named to Basketball Halll of Fame, 1987. Achievements include All-City selection on two Ben Franklin (N.Y.) H.S. state championship teams, 1940, 41; All-Am., Seton Hall, 1947, All-Time team, number retired Seton Hall; mem. Championship Team, NBA, 1951; two-time All-NBA Second Team selection; five-time All-Star Team selection. Office: c/o Basketball Hall of Fame PO Box 179 Springfield MA 01101-0179

WAPIENNIK, CARL FRANCIS, manufacturing firm executive, planetarium and science institute executive; b. Donora, Pa., Oct. 10, 1926; s. Karl and Rose (Kidzinski) W.; m. Elva Louise Bartron, Nov. 27, 1953; children: Carl Eric, Ellen Louise. B.S., U. Pitts., 1953. Prodn. supr. RCA, Canonsburg, Pa., 1953-54; staff physicist Buhl Planetarium and Inst. Popular Sci., Pitts., 1954-64; exec. dir. Buhl Planetarium and Inst. Popular Sci., 1964-82; owner, operator Work-o-Art Miniatures (small mfg. firm), 1983—. Mem. Rostraver Twp. Planning Commn., 1965-67; mem. adv. bd. Allegheny C. of C. (formerly North Side Pitts. C. of C.), 1966-67, dir., 1968-73, pres., 1970; mem. adv. coun. Salvation Army, 1978-82; bd. dirs. Bapt. Homes, Pitts., 1982-94; chmn. Rostraver Twp. Mcpl. Water Authority, 1990-94. With USNR, 1945-46. Recipient Man of Yr. award in sci. Pitts. Jaycees, 1969. Mem. Service Core Ret. Execs., Pitts. Bapt. Assn. (bd. dirs. 1976-82), Phi Beta Kappa, Sigma Pi Sigma. Patentee means for controlling liquid flow. Home: 602 Salem Church Rd Belle Vernon PA 15012-9457 Office: Work-o-Art Miniatures 602 Salem Church Rd Belle Vernon PA 15012-2906

WAPNER, SEYMOUR, psychologist, educator, administrator; b. Bklyn., Nov. 20, 1917; s. Hyman and Rose S. (Liese) W.; m. Lorraine E. Gallant, June 4, 1946; children: Jeffrey Gallant, Amy Beth. A.B., NYU, 1939; A.M., U. Mich., 1940, Ph.D., 1943. Instr., dir. U. Rochester Office Com. Selection and Tng. Aircraft Pilots, NRC, N.Y., 1943-46, 45-46; asst. prof. Bklyn. Coll., 1946-48, acting chmn. psychology dept., 1947-48; assoc. prof. dept. psychology Clark U., Worcester, Mass., 1948-56, prof., 1956-63, chmn. dept., 1960-86, G. Stanley Hall prof. genetic psychology, 1963-88; prof. emeritus Clark U., 1988—; chmn. exec. com. H. Werner Inst. Devel. Analysis, 1957—; mem. exec. bd. Council Grad. Depts. of Psychology, 1981-84; mem. U.S. Nat. Com. for Man and the Biosphere Directorate, 1975-86. Author: (with H.A. Watkin, et al), Personality Throuth Perception, 1954, (with H. Werner) Perceptual Development, 1957; editor: The Body Percept, 1965, (with W.A. Koelsch) Freud In Our Time, 1988, (with S.B. Cohen, B. Kaplan) Experiencing the Environment, 1976, (with B. Kaplan) Toward a Holistic Developmental Psychology, 1983, Perspectives in Psychological Theory, 1960, (with M. Bertini and L. Pizzamiglio) Field Dependence in Psychological Theory, Research and Application, 1986, (with L. Cirillo) Value Presuppositions in Theories of Human Development, 1986, (with L. Cirillo and B. Kaplan) Emotions in Ideal Human Development, 1989, (with J. Demick) Field Dependence-Independence, 1991, (with T. Yamamoto) Developmental Psychology of Life Transitions, 1992, Relations Between Psychology and Allied Fields, 1995, (with J. Demick, T. Yamamoto, T. Takahashi) Handbook of Japan-US Environment-behavior research: Towards a transactional approach, 1997. Fellow APA, AAAS; mem. AAUP, Soc. Rsch. in Child Devel., Eastern Psychol. Assn. (dir. 1968-70, 71-74, 85-88, 93—, pres. 1979-80), New Eng. Psychol. Assn. (pres. 1979-80), Mass. Psychol. Assn., Phi Beta Kappa, Sigma Xi. Office: Clark U Werner Inst for Devel Analysis 950 Main St Worcester MA 01610-1400

WAPPNER, REBECCA SUE, pediatrics educator; b. Mansfield, Ohio, Feb. 25, 1944; d. William Henry and Helen Elizabeth (Gilmore) W. BS in Zoology, Ohio U., 1966; MD, Ohio State U., 1970. Cert. Am. Bd. Pediatrics, clin. and clin. biochem. Am. Bd. Med. Genetics. Intern in pediatrics The Children's Hosp., Ohio State U., Columbus, 1970-71, resident in pediatrics, 1971-72, asst. chief resident, 1972-73; fellow in pediatric metabolism and genetics Ind. U. Sch. Medicine, Indpls., 1973-75, asst. prof. dept. pediatrics, 1975-78, assoc. prof. dept. pediatrics, 1978-92, prof. dept. med. & molecular genetics, 1993—, prof. pediats., 1992—. Mem. Am. Acad. Pediatrics, Am. Soc. for Human Genetics, Soc. for Inherited Metabolic Disease, Soc. for the Study of Inborn Errors of Metabolism, Soroptimist Internat., Mortar Bd., Iota Sigma Pi, Sigma Xi, Phi Beta Kappa. Office: Riley Hosp 702 Barnhill Dr Rm 0907 Indianapolis IN 46202-5128

WARBURTON, RALPH JOSEPH, architect, engineer, planner, educator; b. Kansas City, Mo., Sept. 5, 1935; s. Ralph Gray and Emma Frieda (Niemann) W.; m. Carol Ruth Hychka, June 14, 1958; children: John Geoffrey, Joy Frances W. Tracey. B.Arch., MIT, 1958; M.Arch., Yale U., 1959, M.C.P., 1960. Registered architect, Colo., Conn., Fla., Ill., La., Md., N.J., N.Y., Va., D.C.; registered profl. engr., Conn., Fla., N.J., N.Y.; registered cmty. planner, Mich., N.J.; lic. interior designer, Fla. With various archtl. planning and engring. firms Kansas City, Mo., 1952-55, Boston, 1956-58, N.Y.C., 1959-62, Chgo., 1962-64; chief planning Skidmore, Owings & Merrill, Chgo., 1964-66; spl. asst. for urban design HUD, Washington, 1966-72, cons., 1972-77; prof. architecture, archtl. engring. and planning U. Miami, Coral Gables, Fla., 1972—, chmn. dept. architecture, archtl. engring. and planning, 1972-75, assoc. dean engring. and environ. design, 1973-74; dir. grad. urban and regional planning program, 1973-75, 81,, 87-93; advisor govt. Iran, 1970; advisor govt. France, 1973, govt. Ecuador, 1974, govt. Saudi Arabia, 1985; cons. in field, 1972—, lectr., critic design juror in field, 1965—; mem./chmn. Coral Gables Bd. Archts., 1980-82. Assoc. author: Man-Made America: Chaos or Control, 1963; editor: New Concepts in Urban Transportation, 1968, Housing Systems Proposals for Operation Breakthrough, 1970, Focus on Furniture, 1971, National Community Art Competition, 1971, Defining Critical Environmental Areas, 1974; contbg. editor: Progressive Architecture, 1974-84; editl. adv. bd.: Jour. Am. Planning Assn., 1983-88, Planning for Higher Edn., 1986-94, Urban Design and Preservation Quar., 1987-94; contbr. over 100 articles to profl. jours.; mem. adv. panel Industrialization Forum Quar., 1969-79, archtl. portfolio jury Am. Sch. and Univ., 1993. Mem. Met. Housing and Planning Coun., Chgo., 1965-67; mem. exec. com. Yale U. Arts Assn., 1965-70; pres. Yale U. Planning Alumni Assn., 1983—; mem. ednl. adv. com. Fla. Bd. Architecture, 1975; mem. grievance com. The Fla. Bar, 1996—. Recipient W.E. Parsons medal Yale U., 1960; recipient Spl. Achievement award HUD, 1972, commendation Fla. Bd. Architecture, 1974, Fla. Trust Historic Preservation award, 1983, Group Achievement award NASA, 1976; Skidmore, Owings & Merrill traveling fellow MIT, 1958; vis. fellow Inst. Architecture and Urban Studies, N.Y.C., 1972-74; NSF grantee, 1980-82. Fellow AIA (nat. housing com. 1968-72, nat. regional devel. and natural resources com. 1974-75, nat. sys. devel. com. 1972-73, nat. urban design com. 1968-73, bd. dirs. Fla. S. chpt. 1974-75), ASCE, Fla. Engring. Soc., Nat. Acad. Forensic Engrs.; mem. NSPE, Am. Inst. Cert. Planners (exec. com. dept. environ. planning 1973-74), Am. Soc. Engring. Edn. (chmn. archtl. engring. divsn. 1975-76), Nat. Sculpture Soc. (allied profl.), Nat. Soc. Arch. Engrs. (founding), Nat. Trust Hist. Preservation (principles and guidelines com. 1967), Am. Soc. Landscape Architects (hon., chmn. design awards jury 1971, 72), Am. Planning Assn. (Fla. chpt. award excellence 1983), Am. Soc. Interior Designers (hon.), Urban Land Inst., Omicron Delta Kappa, Sigma Xi, Tau Beta Pi. Home: 6910 Veronese St Coral Gables FL 33146-3846 Office: 420 S Dixie Hwy Coral Gables FL 33146-2222 also: U Miami Sch Architecture Coral Gables FL 33124-5010 *My contribution to society is made through comprehensive determination, design and development activity leading to habitats most suited to the optimum continuing progress of mankind.*

WARCH, RICHARD, academic administrator; b. Hackensack, N.J., Aug. 4, 1939; s. George William and Helen Anna (Hansen) W.; m. Margot Lynn Moses, Sept. 8, 1962; children: Stephen Knud, David Preston, Karin Joy. B.A., Williams Coll., 1961; B.D., Yale Div. Sch., 1964; Ph.D., Yale U., 1969; postgrad., U. Edinburgh, 1962-63; H.H.D., Ripon Coll., 1980. Asst. prof. history and Am. studies Yale U., 1968-73, asso. prof., 1973-77; asso. dean Yale Coll.; dir. summer plans Yale U., 1976-77; asso. dir. Nat. Humanities Inst., New Haven, 1975-76; v.p. acad. affairs Lawrence U., Appleton, Wis., 1977-79; pres. Lawrence U., 1979—; cons. Nat. Humanities Faculty; ordained to ministry United Presbyn. Ch. in U.S.A., 1968; dir. Bank One of Appleton. Author: School of the Prophets, Yale College, 1701-1740, 1973; editor: John Brown, 1973. Rockefeller Bros. Theol. fellow, 1961-62. Mem. Am. Studies Assn., Soc. for Values in Higher Edn., Winnebago Presbytery. Club: Rotary. Home: 229 N Park Ave Appleton WI 54911-5414 Office: Lawrence U PO Box 599 Appleton WI 54912-0599

WARD, ALAN S., lawyer; b. Wilmington, Del., Jan. 1, 1931; s. Gilbert Hughes and Sarah Anna (Sparks) W.; m. Mariette S. Schneider, Apr. 4, 1959; children: Kathryn Ann Ward Koch, Guy Gilbert, Carolyn Alice. AB, Wesleyan U., 1952; JD, U. Chgo., 1955. Bar: Del. 1955, U.S. Supreme Ct. 1959, N.Y. 1962, D.C. 1964. Law clk. to judge U.S. Dist. Ct., Wilmington, 1955-56; trial atty. Antitrust div. Dept. Justice, Washington, 1956-61, asst. chief spl. litigation sect., 1960-61; assoc. Breed, Abbott & Morgan, N.Y.C., 1961-63; ptnr. Hollabaugh & Jacobs, Washington, 1963-70; dir. Bur. Competition, FTC, Washington, 1970-73; ptnr. Baker & Hostetler LLP, Washington, 1973—; mem. mng. com. Baker & Hostetler, Washington, 1977-87; lectr. law George Washington U., 1967-70; lectr. profl. assns. Mem. bd. trustees Wesleyan U., 1986-89. Mem. ABA (chmn. antitrust com. litigation sect. 1986-87), Assn. of Bar of City of N.Y., Bar Assn. D.C., Del. Bar Assn., Wesleyan U. Alumni Assn. (chmn. 1983-86), Univ. Club, Union Club (N.Y.C.), Union Club (Cleve.), Columbia County Club (Chevy Chase, Md.), Farmington Country Club (Charlottesville, Va.). Republican. Methodist. Avocations: squash, golf, tennis, sailing. Home: 3577 Hamlet Place Chevy Chase MD 20815-4822 Office: Baker & Hostetler LLP 1050 Connecticut Ave NW Washington DC 20036

WARD, CARL EDWARD, research chemist; b. Albuquerque, Oct. 16, 1948; s. Joe E. and Loris E. (Wenk) W.; m. Bertha R. Schloer, June 9, 1970. BS in Chemistry, N.Mex. Inst. Mining and Tech., 1970; MS in Chemistry, Oreg. Grad. Ctr., 1972; PhD in Chemistry, Stanford U., 1977. Research chemist Union Carbide Corp., Charleston, W.Va., 1977-79, Dynapol Corp., Palo Alto, Calif., 1979-80; research chemist Chevron Chem. Co., Richmond, Calif., 1980-85, sr. research chemist, 1986-88; apptd. supr. chemical synthesis Chevron Chem. Co., Richmond, 1988-90; sr. rsch. assoc. Chevron Rsch. & Tech. Co., Richmond, 1990-91, staff scientist, 1991—; staff scientist Chevron Products Co.-Global Lubricants, Richmond, 1997—. Referee Jour. Organic Chemistry, 1983—; patentee in field; contbr. articles to profl. jours. Recipient NSF traineeship, Stanford U., 1972-73; Upjohn fellow, Stanford U., 1976-77; recipient Clarence E. Earle Meml. award, 1995. Mem. Soc. Tribologists and Lubrication Engrs., Nat. Lubricating Grease Inst. (Clarence E. Earle Meml. award 1995), Am. Chem. Soc., Calif. Acad. Sci., N.Mex. Inst. Mining and Tech. Pres. Club, Stanford U. Alumni Assn. Democrat. Avocations: gardening, camping, fishing. Home: 1355 Nisich Dr San Jose CA 95122-3061 Office: Chevron Rsch & Tech Co PO Box 1627 Richmond CA 94802-1796

WARD, CHARLES RAYMOND, systems engineer; b. Lansing, Mich., Oct. 23, 1949; s. George Merrill and Dorothy Irene (Hupp) W.; m. Sarah Hopkins Eddy, June 23, 1979; children: Katherine Emily, Rachel Elizabeth. BS in Math., Purdue U., 1971; MSEE, Naval Postgrad. Sch., 1977. Commd. ensign USN, 1971, advanced through grades to lt. commdr., served on USS Barbel, 1972-75, served on USS James Madison, 1978-81, served on USS Alabama, 1983-85; strategic navigation project mgr. Strategic Systems Programs, Arlington, Va., 1985-91; surveillance towed array sensor sys., mgr. sys. engring. Govt. Info. Sys. divsn. TRW, McLean, Va., 1991-95; integrated undersea surveillance sys., mgr. internat. programs TRW Systems Svcs. Co., McLean, 1995—. Editor: Trident Navigation Standard Operating Prcedures, 1991, Acoustic Warfare Operating Doctrine, 1992, Surveillance Towed Array Sensor Passive User's Guide, 1994. Chmn. grounds com. Burke (Va.) United Meth. Ch., 1989—, chmn. worship com., 1993-94. Mem. IEEE, Eta Kappa Nu, Sigma Xi. Republican. Achievements include research in automatic depth and pitch control for a near surface submarine. Office: TRW Systems Svcs Co PO Box 10400 Fairfax VA 22031-0400

WARD, CHARLES RICHARD, extension and research entomologist, educator; b. Tahoka, Tex., Mar. 25, 1940; s. James Henry and Bertrice Opha (Moore) W.; m. Norma Faye Martin, Aug. 25, 1960; children: Beverly Jan, Charles Edward. AA, South Plains Coll., 1960; BS, Tex. Tech U., 1962, MS, 1964; PhD, Cornell U., 1968. Entomology specialist N.Mex. State U., Santa Cruz, Bolivia, 1976-78; rsch. assoc., assoc. prof. entomology N.Mex. State U., Las Cruces, 1978-80; pest mgmt. specialist N.Mex. State U., Artesia, 1980-82, 1984-85; chief party, entomologist N.Mex. State U., San Pedro Sula, Honduras, 1983-84; supt. agrl. sci. ctr., prof. entomology N.Mex. State U., Alcalde, N.Mex., 1985-86; extension and rsch. entomologist, prof. N.Mex. State U., Albuquerque, 1986-96; cons. entomologist Internat. Irrigation Ctr., Logan, Utah, 1985-86, Consortium for Internat. Crop Protection, College Park, Md., 1986-93, Cornell U., Ithaca, N.Y., 1993—, Tropical Rsch. and Devel., Gainesville, Fla., 1989—. Contbr. numerous articles to profl. jours. Mem. Bd. Cert. Entomologists (chair elect 1996-97, chair 1997-98, Outstanding Contbrn. award 1981), Entomol. Soc. Am. (sec. subsect. ea. 1992-93), Southwestern Entomol. Soc. (pres. 1993-94), Extension Specialists Assn., N.Mex. Acad. Sci. Avocations: insect collecting, hunting, fishing. Home: 12105 El Dorado Pl NE Albuquerque NM 87111-4059

WARD, CHESTER LAWRENCE, physician, retired county health official, retired military officer; b. Woodland, Yolo, Calif., June 8, 1932; s. Benjamin Briggs and Nora Elizabeth (Cash) W.; m. Sally Diane McCloud, Dec. 10, 1960; children: Katharine, Lynda. BA, U. Calif., Santa Barbara, 1955; MD, U. So. Calif., 1962; MPH, U. Calif., Berkeley, 1966; grad., Indsl. Coll. Armed Forces, 1978. Commd. 2d lt., inf. U.S. Army, 1954; advanced through grades to brig. gen., 1980; chief aviation medicine, preventive medicine and aeromed. consultation service Ft. Rucker, Ala., 1967-68; surgeon Aviation Brigade and USA Vietnam Aviation Medicine Cons., 1968-69; flight surgeon Office of U.S. Army Surgeon Gen., 1970-71; physician The White House, Washington, 1971-75, 76; dir. environ. quality research U.S. Army Med. Research and Devel. Commd., 1975-76; comdr. Womack Community Hosp.; surgeon XVIII Airborne Corps, Ft. Bragg, N.C., 1978-80; comdr. William Beaumont Army Med. Center, El Paso, Tex., 1980-82; med. dir. Union Oil Co., Schaumburg, Ill., 1982-83; dir. domestic medicine Union Oil Co., Los Angeles, 1983-84; exec. dir. continuing med. edn. and clin. prof. emergency medicine U. So. Calif. Sch. Medicine, Los Angeles, 1984-85; dir., health officer Dept. Health, Butte County, Caif., 1985-95; cons., contractor, pvt. med. practice, 1996—. Apptd. by Gov. Wilson Calif. Commn. Emergency Med. Svcs. Decorated D.S.M., Legion of Merit (2), Bronze Star, Air medal (5). Fellow Am. Coll. Preventive Medicine, Aerospace Med. Assn., Butte-Glenn County Med. Soc. (past pres.), Calif. Med. Assn. (del.), Calif. Commn. Emergency Med. Svcs., No. Calif. Emergency Med. Svcs. (dir.), Butte Coll. Found. (bd. dirs.), Emergency Svcs. Found. (bd. dirs.). Home: 4 Lemon Hill Ct Oroville CA 95966-3708 Office: Enloe Outpatient Ctr 888 Lakeside Vlg Commons Chico CA 95928-3979

WARD, DANIEL THOMAS, bishop; b. Umri, Yavatmal, India, Apr. 8, 1942; s. Thomas Tuckker and Sudina Thomas (Suhasini) W.; m. Suhasini Daniel, Nov. 27, 1968; children: Vandan, Prerana. BA, Amolakchand Coll., Yavatmal, 1964; BD, Union Bibl. Sem., Yavatmal, 1967; ThM, Fuller Sem., Pasadena, Calif., 1982. Bishop Free Meth. Ch. of N.Am., Indpls.; deacon, minister Free Meth. Ch., Yavatmal, 1969-71, elder, 1971-91, dist. supt., 1986-87, bishop, 1989—; mem. hosp. bd. Free Meth. Ch., Yavatmal, 1989, mem. sem. faculty, 1983, registrar, 1984, bishop on U.S. bd., 1989—. Editor, author (newsletter) Christ-Jyot, 1974, (monthly publ.) Ankur, 1985, (quar. publ.) The New Day, 1989. Speaker All Religions Platform Meeting Lions Club, Yavatmal, 1986, Nat. Integrity, 1987. Avocations: soccer, badminton, cricket, basketball, volleyball. Home: Bishop House Maharashtra, PO Box 27 Vanjari Fail Rd, 445001 Yavatmal India Office: Free Meth Ch N Am, PO Box 27, Bishop House, 445001 Yavatmal Maharashtra, India Office: PO Box 535002 Indianapolis IN 46253-5002*

WARD, DAVID, academic administrator, educator; b. Manchester, Eng., July 8, 1938; came to U.S., 1960; s. Horace and Alice (Harwood) W.; m. Judith B. Freifeld, June 11, 1964; children: Michael J.H., Peter F.B. BA, U. Leeds, Eng., 1959; MA, U. Leeds, 1961; MS, U. Wis., 1961, PhD, 1963; LittD, U. Leeds, 1992. Lectr. Carleton U., Ottawa, Ont., Can., 1963-64; asst. prof. Univ. B.C., Vancouver, Can., 1964-66; asst. prof. U. Wis., Madison, 1966-67, assoc. prof., 1967-70, prof., 1970—, chmn. geography dept., 1974-77, assoc. dean Grad. Sch., 1980-88, provost and vice chancellor acad. affairs, Andrew Clark prof. geography, 1989—; now chancellor U. Wis. Madison; mem. exec. com. Argonne (Ill.) Nat. Lab., 1990-93; dir.-at-large Social Sci. Rsch. Coun., 1991-93; mem. Kellogg Commn. on Future of Land Grant Univs. Author: Cities and Immigrants, 1970, Geographic Perspectives on Americas Past, 1978, Poverty Ethnicity and the American City, 1989, Landscape of Modernity, 1992; contbr. articles to profl. jours. Guggenheim fellow, 1970, Einstein fellow Hebrew U., 1980, Fulbright fellow, Australian Nat. U., 1979. Mem. Assn. Am. Geographers (pres. 1989). Office: U Wis-Madison 161 Bascom Hall 500 Lincoln Dr Madison WI 53706-1314

WARD, DAVID ALLEN, sociology educator; b. Dedham, Mass., June 21, 1933; s. Theodore Allen and Jessie Miller (Ketchum) W.; m. Carol Jane Barton, June 10, 1957 (div. 1964); children: Douglas Allen, Andrew Barton; m. Reneé Ellen Light, Mar. 10, 1967. BA, Colby Coll., 1955; PhD, U. Ill., 1960. Asst. prof. Wash. State U., Pullman, 1960-61; asst. research sociologist UCLA, 1961-64; assoc. prof. U. Minn., Mpls., 1965-68, prof., 1968—, chmn. dept. sociology, 1984-88, 92-95; chmn. Salzburg (Austria) Seminar in Am. Studies, 1977; cons. jud. com. U.S. Ho. Reps., Washington, 1984. Co-author: Women's Prison, 1965, Prison Treatment, 1971; co-editor: Delinquency, Crime and Social Process, 1969, Confinement in Maximum Custody, 1981; editorial cons. Jour. Criminal Law and Criminology, 1968—. Rev. bd. Mpls. Civilan Police Bd., 1991-94. Liberal Arts fellow Harvard U. Law Sch., 1968-69; Fulbright research fellow, 1971-72; research fellow Norwegian Fgn. Office, Oslo, 1976. Mem. Am. Sociol. Assn. (chmn. sect. criminology 1976-77), Law and Soc. Assn., Am. Soc. Criminology. Office: Univ of Minn Dept of Sociology 909 Social Sci Bldg Minneapolis MN 55455

WARD, DAVID HENRY (DAVE WARD), television news reporter, anchorman; b. Dallas, May 6, 1939; s. H. M. and Mary W.; m. Glenda Lois Odom, Nov. 10, 1959 (div.); children—Linda Ann, David H.; m. 2d, Debra Rene Holland, Apr. 25, 1976 (div.); children: Jonathan H., Christopher H. Student Tyler Jr. Coll., Tex., 1957-59. Announcer Sta. KGKB, Tyler, 1958-60; program director Sta. WACO (Tex.), 1960-62; news dir. Sta. KNUZ, Houston, 1962-66; news reporter, photographer, writer, producer Sta. KTRK-TV, 1966—; freelance writer, producer, cons.; chmn. pub. affairs adv. bd. Houston Bus. Council; pub. info. com. Am. Cancer Soc.; pres. bd. dirs. Easter Seal Soc., Harris, Fort Bend counties. Recipient Best TV Newscast award Tex. UPI, 1968, 72, 73-80; TV Service award Houston Jaycees, 1982; named Man of Yr., Houston Sertoma Club, 1973; TV Personality of Yr. Am. Women in Radio and TV, 1983, Best TV Anchor, Houston Press, 1995, 96. Mem. Sigma Delta Chi. Baptist. Club: Press (Houston). Office: Channel 13 PO Box 13 3310 Bissonnet Houston TX 77005

WARD, DAVID SCHAD, screenwriter, film director; b. Providence, Oct. 24, 1947; s. Robert McCollum and Miriam (Schad) W.; children: Joaquin Atwood, Sylvana Soto. B.A., Pomona Coll., 1967; M.F.A., UCLA, 1970. Scriptwriter: films include Steelyard Blues, 1971, The Sting, 1973 (Acad. award best original screenplay 1973), The Milagro Beanfield War, 1988, (with Nora Ephron and Jeff Arch) Sleepless in Seattle, 1993 (Academy award nominee Best Original Screenplay 1993); writer, dir. films include Cannery Row, 1981, Major League, 1989, King Ralph, 1991, The Program, 1993, Major League II, 1995, Down Periscope, 1996. Mem. Dirs. Guild Am., Acad. Motion Picture Arts and Scis. Office: care CAA/Ken Stovitz 9830 Wilshire Blvd Beverly Hills CA 90212-1804

WARD, DENITTA DAWN, lawyer; b. Gardner, Kans., Apr. 29, 1963; d. Gerald Dee Ascue and Patricia Diane (Henderson) Ray; m. Kent Alan Ward, July 6, 1991; 1 child, Alexander Patrick. BA, U. Kans., 1985; JD magna cum laude, Georgetown U., 1989. Bar: Md. 1989, U.S. Ct. Appeals (fed. cir.) 1990, D.C. 1991, U.S. Ct. Internat. Trade 1991. Rsch. asst. Georgetown U., Washington, 1988-89; jud. clk. U.S. Ct. Appeals for Fed. Cir., Washington, 1989-90; assoc. Donovan Leisure Rogovin Huge & Schiller, Washington, 1990-94; atty. Fed. Election Commn., Washington, 1994-96, Marriott Internat., Inc., 1996—. Mng. editor Law and Policy in Internat. Bus., 1988-89. Mem. ABA, Ct. of Appeals for Fed. Cir. Bar Assn., Ct. of Appeals of Fed. Cir. Former Jud. Clks. Assn., Order of Coif, Omicron Delta Kappa, Pi Sigma Alpha. Avocations: travel, gardening. Home: 5711 25th St N Arlington VA 22207-1401 Office: Marriott Internat Inc Marriott Dr Washington DC 20058

WARD, EDITH BURNETTE, business educator; b. Wakulla, Fla., Sept. 3, 1930; d. Andrew Joshua and Delia Leanna (Green) Hargrett. BS, Fla. Agrl. and Mech. U., 1951; MEd, Am. U., 1964; EdD, Va. Poly. Inst. and State U., 1992. Cert. of advanced grad. studies. Sec. Fla. Agrl. and Mech. U., Tallahassee, 1951-52; sec., adminstrv. asst. Fed. Govt., Washington, 1952-64; tchr. D.C. Pub. Schs., 1964-90; acad. advisor Va. Poly. Inst. and State U., Blacksburg, 1990-92; asst. prof. St. Augustine's Coll., Raleigh, N.C., 1992—, acting chair divsn. bus., 1995-96. Chairperson fin. com. Tabernacle Bapt. Ch., Washington, 1982-90; treas. PTA, Washington, 1975-87; tchr. Mayor's Summer Youth Program, Washington, 1980-89; advisor Future Bus. Leaders of Am., Washington, 1975-90; vol. Dem. Party, Prince George's County, Md., 1988, NAACP, Washington, 1958-64; vol. tutor Sargeant Meml. Presbyn. Ch., Washington, 1963; sec. Hyde Park Cmty. Families, 1993—; bd. trustees Annie Malone Scholarship Fund, 1997. Mem. Am. Vocat. Assn., Washington Tchrs. Union, Fla. Agrl. and Mech. U. Alumni Assn. (D.C. chpt. sec. 1970-85), Phi Eta Sigma, Delta Pi Epsilon, Phi Delta Kappa, Omicron Tau Theta, Sigma Gamma Rho (Nu chpt. advisor 1996-97). Democrat. Avocations: bowling, puzzles, reading. Home: 1316 Oakwood Ave Apt C Raleigh NC 27610 Office: Saint Augustine's College 1315 Oakwood Ave Raleigh NC 27610-2247

WARD, EDWARD WELLS, telecommunications executive; b. Jacksonville, Fla., Nov. 17, 1947; s. Joe Terrell and Dorothy Robyn (Wells) W. AA, Fla. Jr. Coll., 1976; MBA, Jacksonville U., 1986; MA, George Washington U., 1991. Cert. data processor, systems profl. Tech. dir. Trader Glick's Dinner Theatre, Jacksonville, 1969-70; prodn. asst. William Cook Advt., Jacksonville, 1970-74; various positions Computer Power, Inc., Jacksonville,

1974-84, communications svcs. mgr., 1984-87; CEO, founder PractiComm, Jacksonville, 1984-86; network svcs. mgr. Am. Mgmt. Systems, Inc., Arlington, Va., 1987-93; dir. data and voice communications Am. Mgmt. Systems, Inc., Fairfax, Va., 1993-94; European network mgr. Am. Mgmt. Systems, Inc., The Hague, The Netherlands, 1995—; instr. Jones Coll., Jacksonville, 1985; dir. credit union Am. Mgmt. Systems, 1988-89. Contbr. articles to profl. jours. With U.S. Army, 1968. Mem. North Am. ISDN User's Forum (svc. ind. chmn. 1990-91), Met. Washington Area Mensa (testing coord. 1994), No. Va. Royal Scottish Country Dance Soc. (chmn. 1994). Avocations: skiing, Scottish country dancing, tennis. Office: Am Mgmt Systems Inc 4050 Legato Rd Fairfax VA 22033-4087

WARD, ELAINE, artist; b. Boston, June 4, 1927; d. Robert and Gertrude (Toibb) Winston; m. William Ward (dec.); 1 child, Heather; m. Arthur Lee Dann. BA, Ecole des Beaux Arts, Paris, 1958; student, Art Students League, N.Y.C.; hon. degree, Ecole des Beaux Arts, Cannes, France. Mem. Phoenix Gallery, N.Y.C., 8 yrs. Solo show at Phoenix Gallery, 1989, East End Art Coun., Riverhead, N.Y., 1997; group shows include Lever House, N.Y.C., 1987-89, 93, 95, Guild Hall, Easthampton, N.Y., 1988, 95, Phoenix Gallery, N.Y.C., 1992-94, Elaine Benson Gallery, Bridgehampton, N.Y., 1992, Palmas Del Mar, P.R., 1993, C.W. Post Coll., 1993, Agora Gallery, N.Y.C., 1994, Meadowlands Ctr. for Arts, N.J., 1995, Marcella Geltman Gallery, N.J., 1995; East End Art Coun., N.Y.C., 1995 (winner), Focus on Art, Livingston, N.J., 1995 (prize); represented in collections at Coastal Steel Co., Carteret, N.H., Pandora and Co., Conway, N.H., Ardan Assocs., Ltd., N.Y.C.; subject of articles. Winner Juried Show, East End Arts Coun., 1995. Mem. Nat. Arts Club, Nat. Assn. Women Artists, Guild Hall Mus., Parrish Mus.

WARD, FRED, actor; b. 1943. Film appearances include Escape From Alcatraz, 1979, Tilt, 1979, Carny, 1980, Southern Comfort, 1981, Timerider: The Adventures of Lyle Swann, 1982, Silkwood, 1983, Uncommon Valor, 1983, The Right Stuff, 1984, Swing Shift, 1984, Secret Admirer, 1985, UFOria, 1985, Remo Willaims: The Adventure Begins..., 1985, Train of Dreams, 1987, The Prince of Pennsylvania, 1988, Big Business, 1988, Off Limits, 1988, Tremors, 1990, Henry and June, 1990, Backtrack, 1990, Miami Blues, 1990 (also co-exec. prodr.), Thunderheart, 1992, The Player, 1992, Bob Roberts, 1992, Equinox, 1993, Short Cuts, 1993, The Naked Gun 33 1/3: The Final Insult, 1994, The Blue Villa, 1995, Tremors II: Aftershocks, 1995, Chain Reaction, 1996; TV appearances (movies) Belle Star, 1980, Florida Straights, 1986, Cast A Deadly Spell, 1991, Four Eyes and Six Guns, 1992, (spls.) Noon Wine, 1985, ...First do no harm, 1997. *

WARD, GEOFFREY CHAMPION, author, editor; b. Newark, Ohio, Nov. 30, 1940; s. Frederick Champion and Duira Rachel (Baldinger) W.; m. Diane Raines; children—Nathan, Kelly; 1 stepchild, Garrett Keim. BA, Oberlin Coll., 1962; DHL (hon.), Wilkes U., 1995. Sr. picture editor Ency. Britannica, Chgo., 1964-68; co-founder, editor Audience mag., Boston, 1969-73; mng. editor Am. Heritage Mag., N.Y.C., 1976-78; editor Am. Heritage Mag., 1978-82. Author: Lincoln's Thought and the Present, 1978, Treasures of the Maharajas, 1983, Before the Trumpet: Young Franklin Roosevelt, 1882-1905, 1985, A First-Class Temperament: The Emergence of Franklin Roosevelt, 1989 (Nat. Book Critics Cir. award, Francis Parkman prize Soc. Am. Historians, L.A. Times biography prize, Ohioana award), The Civil War: An Illustrated History, 1990, American Originals: The Private Worlds of Some Singular Men and Women, 1991; (with Diane Raines Ward) Tiger Wallahs, Encounters with the Men Who Tried to Save the Greatest of the Great Cats, 1993, Baseball: An Illustrated History, 1994, Closest Companion: The Unknown Story of the Intimate Friendship between Franklin Roosevelt and Margaret Suckley, 1995, The West: An Illustrated History, 1996; editor: The Best American Essays of 1996; (TV documentaries) Huey Long, 1985, Thomas Hart Benton, 1989, Lindbergh, 1990, Nixon, 1990 (Writer's Guild Am. award), The Civil War, 1990 (Emmy award), Reminiscing in Tempo, 1991, Empire of the Air, 1992, The Kennedys, 1992 (Emmy award), George Marshall and the American Century, 1993, Baseball, 1994 (Emmy award), Daley: The Last Boss, 1995, The West, 1996, Theodore Roosevelt, 1996, Thomas Jefferson, 1997; contbr. articles to mags., jours. Recipient Christopher awards for The Statue of Liberty and Theodore Roosevelt, The Christophers, The Civil War, New Eng. Booksellers Assn. award, Am. Booksellers award, Lila Acheson Wallace Readers Digest writers award. Mem. Soc. Am. Historians, Writers Guild Am., East Inc., Century Assn. Home: 17 C 290 W End Ave New York NY 10023-8106 Office: Brandt & Brandt care Carl Brandt 1501 Broadway New York NY 10036-5601

WARD, GEORGE FRANK, JR., foreign service officer; b. Jamaica, N.Y., Apr. 9, 1945; s. George Frank and Hildegard Louisa (Evans) W.; m. Peggy Elizabeth Coote, June 12, 1965; 1 child, Pamela Ward Priester. BA, U. Rochester, 1965; MPA, Harvard U., 1980. U.S. vice consul Am. Consulate, Hamburg, Germany, 1970-72; ops. officer Office Sec. State, Washington, 1972-74; U.S. consul Am. Consulate Gen., Genoa, Italy, 1974-76; polit. officer Am. Embassy, Rome, 1976-77, exec. asst., 1977-79; polit. officer Am. Embassy, Bonn, Germany, 1984-85, dep. chief mission, 1989-92; polit.-military officer U.S. Dept. State, Washington, 1980-84, deputy dir. European Security and Polit. Affairs, 1985-88, prin. dep. asst. sec. Bur. Internat. Orgns., 1992-96; U.S. ambassador to Namibia U.S. Dept. State, 1996—. Capt. USMC, 1965-69. Decorated Vietnamese Cross Gallantry (Vietnam); Naval Commendaton medal; recipient Presdl. Meritorious Svc. awards, 1992, 94. Mem. Am. Fgn. Svc. Assn., Phi Beta Kappa. Episcopalian. Avocations: classical music, running, skiing, tennis. Home: 51 Chalsedoon St, Windhoek Namibia Office: Am Embassy Windhoek Dept of State Washington DC 20521-2540

WARD, GEORGE TRUMAN, architect; b. Washington, July 24, 1927; s. Truman and Gladys Anna (Nutt) W.; m. Margaret Ann Hall, Sept. 10, 1949; children: Carol Ann Ward Dickson, Donna Lynne Ward Solomon, George Truman, Robert Stephen. BS, Va. Poly. Inst., 1951, MS, 1952; postgrad., George Washington U., 1966. Registered profl. architect, Va., Md., D.C., W.Va., Ohio, N.J., Del., N.C. Archtl. draftsman Charles A. Pearson, Radford, Va., 1950; head archtl. sect. Hayes, Seay, Mattern & Mattern, Radford and Roanoke, 1951-52; with Joseph Saunders & Assos., Alexandria, Va., 1952-57, assoc. architect, 1955-57; ptnr. Vosbeck-Ward & Assos., Alexandria, 1957-64, Ward/Hall Assocs., Fairfax, Va., 1964—; dir. Crestar Bank/Greater Washington Region. Pres. PTA Burke (Va.) Sch., 1970-71; mem. bd. mgrs. Fairfax (Va.) County YMCA, 1964-76; chmn. adv. com. Coll. Architecture, Va. Poly. Inst., 1984-90; bd. dirs., mem. investment com. Va. Tech. Found., Inc., 1986-91, 93—; pres. Springfield Rotary Found., 1978-79; chmn. county adv. bd. Salvation Army, 1978-79, 86-95, co-chmn. Fairfax County Salvation Army Capital Campaign, 1991-95; mem. Gen. Bd. Va. Bapts., deacon, moderator; mem. bd. visitors Va. Poly. Inst. & State U., 1984-87; trustee Fairfax County Pub. Schs. Edn. Found., Inc. With AUS, 1946-47. Paul Harris fellow; recipient William H. Ruffner medal Va. Tech., 1996. Fellow Coll. AIA, mem. AIA (corp., charter Octagon Soc.), No. Va. Soc. AIA (chmn. polit. action com. 1991-93, Disting. Svc. award 1990, treas. Va. soc. 1994—, Outstanding Achievement award 1996), Rowe Fellowship (charter mem. 1988), Alumni Assn. Va. Poly. Inst. & State U. (bd. dirs., v.p. 1992, pres. 1994), Interfaith Forum on Religion, Art and Architecture, Va. Found. for Architecture (trustee), Va. Assn. Professions, Va. C. of C., No. Va. Angus Assn. (pres. 1987-88), Va. Tech. Alumni Assn. (hon., life, bd. dirs., Disting. Svc. award 1988), Masons, Shriners, KT, Rotary (charter mem., pres. Springfield 1973-74, Dist. Svc. award dist. 7610 1995), Tau Sigma Delta, Omicron Delta Kappa, Phi Kappa Phi, Pi Delta Epsilon, Ut Prosim. Baptist. Home: Glenara Farm 10239 Glenara Ln Marshall VA 20115-2728 Office: Ward Hall Assoc AIA 12011 Lee Jackson Memorial Hwy Fairfax VA 22033-3310

WARD, HAROLD WILLIAM COWPER, oncologist, educator; b. Southend-On-Sea, Essex, Eng., Nov. 24, 1925; came to U.S., 1976; s. William Samuel and Winifred (Marjorie) W.; m. Barbara Mary Sanderson, Oct. 6, 1982; children: Belinda Mary Jane Morris, Rosemary Sylvia, Timothy Harold. MB BS, U. London, 1953; diploma in med. radiation therapy, Royal Coll. Physicians London, 1957. Cert. therapeutic radiology Am. Bd. Radiology, cert. basic cardiopulmonary resuscitation Am. Heart Assn. Intern Charing Cross Hosp., London, 1953, resident in radiotherapy, 1955-56; intern Royal Postgrad. Med. Sch., London, 1954-55; intern in surgery The Bolinbroke Hosp., London, 1954; sr. resident in radiotherapy Edinburgh (Scotland) Royal Infirmary, London, Scotland, 1958-59; rsch. fellow in radiotherapy St. Bartholomew's Hosp., London, 1959-65; cons. radiotherapist Queen Elizabeth Hosp., Birmingham, Eng., 1965-75; clin. lectr. U. Birmingham, 1965-75; dir. radiation oncology Parkland Meml. Hosp., Dallas, 1976-78; prof. radiology U. Tex. Southwestern Med. Sch., Dallas, 1976-78; clin. prof. radiology divsn. radiation oncology U. Cin., 1978-82, assoc. prof. medicine divsn. hematology, 1980-82; dir. radiation oncology Meml. Med. Ctr., Corpus Christi, Tex., 1982-95; clin. assoc. prof. radiation oncology U. Tex. Med. Br., Galveston, 1984-90; mem. Oncology Assocs., Inc., Cin., 1978-82; travelling fellow in radiotherapy Meml. Hosp. for Cancer and Allied Diseases, N.Y.C., M.D. Anderson Hosp., Houston, U. Calif. Med. Sch., San Francisco, 1965; mem. U.K. Med. Rsch. Coun. Working Party for study of embryonal tumors of childhood, 1967-75; mem. steering com. U.K. Nat. Ovarian Cancer Clin. Survey, 1967-75; site vis. team NCI, 1984-87; physician advisor Tex. Med. Found. Peer Rev. Orgn., 1985—; mem. regional quality rev. com., 1989—. Mem. exec. com. Symphony Orch., Corpus Christi, 1992-95. Fellow Royal Coll. Radiology; mem. AMA, Internat. Soc. for Pediatric Oncology, Royal Coll. Surgeons Eng., Royal Coll. Physicians, Soc. Apthecaries, Am. Soc. Therapeutic Radiologists, Am. Soc. Clin. Oncology, Am. Coll. Radiology, Am. Cancer Soc. (Nueces County br. 1984-88), Brit. Inst. Radiology, Brit. Med. Assn., Brit. Assn. for Cancer Rsch., Tex. Med. Assn., Southwestern Oncology Group, Nueces County Med. Soc. (pub. rels., environ.. pollution control, Cancer adv. com. 1984—, consultative fee rev. com. 1988—). Episcopalian. Avocations: music, gardening. Home: 131 Naples St Corpus Christi TX 78404-1828 Office: 1201 S 19th St Corpus Christi TX 78405-1527

WARD, HARRY PFEFFER, physician, university chancellor; b. Pueblo, Colo., June 6, 1933; s. Lester L. and Alysmai (Pfeffer) W.; m. Betty Jo Stewart, Aug. 20, 1955; children—Stewart, Leslie, Elizabeth, Mary Alice, Amy. A.B., Princeton U., 1955; M.D., U. Colo., 1959; M.S., U. Minn., 1963. Intern Bellevue Hosp., N.Y.C., 1959; resident Mayo Clinic, Rochester, Minn., 1960-63; practice medicine specializing in hematology; chief medicine Denver VA hosp., 1968-72; dean, assoc. v.p. U. Colo. Sch. Medicine, 1972-78, prof. medicine, 1972; chancellor U. Ark. Med. Sci., Little Rock, 1979—; clin. investigator VA, 1964-67. Chmn. Assn. Acad. Health Ctr., 1993-94. Mem. ACP, AMA, Am. Fedn. Clin. Research, Central Soc. Clin. Investigation, Am. Soc. Hematology, Internat. Soc. Hematology, Western Soc. Clin. Research. Home: 369 Valley Club Cir Little Rock AR 72212-2900 Office: U Ark Med Scis 4301 W Markham St Little Rock AR 72205-7101

WARD, HILEY HENRY, journalist, educator; b. Lafayette, Ind., July 30, 1929; s. Hiley Lemen and Agnes (Fuller) W.; m. Charlotte Burns, May 28, 1951 (div. 1971); children: Dianne, Carolee, Marceline, Laurel; m. Joan Bastel, Aug. 20, 1977. BA, William Jewell Coll., 1951; MA, Berkeley (Calif.) Bapt. Div. Sch., 1953; MDiv, McCormick Theol. Sem., Chgo., 1955; summer, evening student, Northwestern U., 1948, 54, 56-57; PhD, U. Minn., 1977. News asst. Christian Advocate, 1953-55; editor jr. publs. David C. Cook Pub. Co., 1956-59; editor Record, Buchanan, Mich., 1960; religion editor Detroit Free Press, 1960-73; asst. prof. journalism Mankato (Minn.) State U., 1974-76; assoc. prof. journalism Wichita (Kans.) State U., 1976; prof. journalism Temple U., Phila., 1977-96, prof. emeritus, 1997—, dir. news-editorial sequence, journalism dept., 1977-80, chmn. dept., 1978-80; instr. journalism Oakland U., Rochester, Mich., evenings 1963-66. Author: Creative Giving, 1958, Space-age Sunday, 1960, Documents of Dialogue, 1966, God and Marx Today, 1968, Ecumania, 1968, Rock 2000, 1969, Prophet of the Black Nation, 1969, The Far-out Saints of the Jesus Communes, 1972, Religion 2101 A.D., 1975, Feeling Good About Myself, 1983, Professional Newswriting, 1985, My Friend's Beliefs: A Young Reader's Guide to World Religions, 1988, Reporting in Depth, 1991, Magazine and Feature Writing, 1993, Mainstreams of American Media History, 1997; editor: Media History Digest, 1979-94; exec. editor: Kidbits, 1981-82; book editor: Editor and Publisher, 1989—; contbr. articles to profl. jours., feature articles to newspapers and mags.; also short stories and poems. Religious Pub. Rels. Coun. fellow, 1970; recipient citation Religious Heritage Am., 1962, Leidt award Epsic. Ch., 1969, citation U.S. Am. Revolution Bicentennial Adminstrn., 1976. Mem. Religion Newswriters Assn. (pres. 1970-72), Am. Soc. Journalists and Authors, Am. Journalism Historians Assn. (bd. dirs. 1994-96), Overseas Press Club. Home: PO Box 399 1263 Folly Rd Warrington PA 18976-1422 Office: Temple U Dept Journalism Philadelphia PA 19122

WARD, HIRAM HAMILTON, federal judge; b. Thomasville, N.C., Apr. 29, 1923; s. O.L. and Margaret A. W.; m. Evelyn M. McDaniel, June 1, 1947; children: William McDaniel, James Randolph. Student, Wake Forest Coll., 1945-47; J.D., Wake Forest U., 1950, LLD (hon.), 1996. Bar: N.C. bar 1950. Practiced law Denton, N.C., 1950-51; staff atty. Nat. Prodn. Authority, Washington, 1951-52; partner firm DeLapp, Ward & Hedrick, Lexington, N.C., 1952-72; U.S. dist. judge Mid. Dist. N.C., 1972—, chief judge, 1982-88, sr. judge, 1988—; mem. com. on Codes of Conduct of Jud. Conf., U.S., 1990-95; mem. Fourth Cir. Jud. Coun., 1984-87. Contbr. legal opinions to Fed. Supplement, F.2d & F.R.D., 1972—. Bd. visitors Wake Forest U. Sch. Law, 1973—; Mem. N.C. Bd. Elections, 1964-72; trustee Wingate Coll., 1969-72. Served with USAAF, 1940-45. Decorated Air medal, Purple Heart; recipient Liberty Bell award N.C. Bar Assn., 1994. Mem. ABA, N.C. Bar Assn., Am. Judicature Soc., N.C. State Bar, Masons, Lions, Phi Alpha Delta (hon. life). Republican. Baptist. Home: 188 Forest Park Dr Denton NC 27239 Office: US Courthouse 246 Fed Bldg 251 N Main St Winston Salem NC 27101-3914

WARD, HORACE TALIAFERRO, federal judge; b. LaGrange, Ga., July 29, 1927; m. Ruth LeFlore (dec.); 1 son (dec.). AB, Morehouse Coll., 1949; MA, Atlanta U., 1950; JD, Northwestern U., 1959. Bar: Ga. 1960. Instr. polit. sci. Ark. A.M. and N. Coll., 1950-51, Ala. State Coll., 1951-53, 55-56; claims authorizer U.S. Social Security Adminstrn., 1959-60; assoc. firm Hollowell Ward Moore & Alexander (and successors), Atlanta, 1960-69; individual practice law Atlanta, 1971-74; judge Civil Ct. of Fulton County, 1974-77, Fulton Superior Ct., 1977-79; U.S. Dist. Ct. judge No. Dist. Ga., Atlanta, 1979—; lectr. bus. and sch. law Atlanta U., 1965-70; dep. city atty., Atlanta, 1969-70, asst. county atty., Fulton County, 1971-74. Former Trustee Friendship Baptist Ch., Atlanta; mem. Ga. adv. com. U.S. Civil Rights Commn., 1963-65; assisting lawyer NAACP Legal Def. and Edn. Fund, Inc., 1960-70; mem. Jud. Selection Commn., Atlanta, 1972-74, Charter Commn., 1971-72; mem. Ga. Senate, 1964-74, jud. com., rules com., county and urban affairs com.; mem. State Democratic Exec. com., 1966-74; former bd. dirs. Atlanta Legal Aid Soc.; bd. dirs. Atlanta Urban League, Fed. Defender Program, No. Dist. Ga.; trustee Met. Atlanta Commn. on Crime and Delinquency, Atlanta U., Fledgling Found. Mem. Am. Bar Assn., Nat. Bar Assn. (chmn. jud. council 1978-79), State Bar Ga., Atlanta Bar Assn., Gate City Bar Assn. (pres. 1972-74), Atlanta Lawyers Club, Phi Beta Kappa, Alpha Phi Alpha, Phi Alpha Delta, Sigma Pi Phi. Office: US Dist Court 2388 US Courthouse 75 Spring St SW Atlanta GA 30303-3309

WARD, JACQUELINE ANN BEAS, nurse, healthcare administrator; b. Somerset, Pa., Oct. 23, 1945; d. Donald C. and Thelma R. (Wable) Beas; divorced; children: Charles L. Jr., Shawn M. BS in Nursing, U. Pitts., 1966; MA in Counseling and Guidance, W.Va. Coll. Grad. Studies, 1976; MBA, Columbus Coll., 1983. Cert. in advanced nursing adminstrn. Staff nurse W.Va. U. Hosp., Morgantown, 1966-67; staff nurse, head nurse Meml. Hosp. Charleston, W.Va., 1967-69; staff nurse Santa Rosa Hosp., San Antonio, 1969; staff nurse, supr. Bexar County Hosp., San Antonio, 1970; charge, staff nurse Rocky Mountain Osteo. Hosp., Denver, 1971; staff nurse Charleston Area Med. Ctr., 1971-74, asst. dir. nursing, 1974-82; dir. nursing H.D. Cobb Meml. Hosp., Phenix City, Ala.; clin. instr. Chattahoochie Valley C.C., Phenix City, 1982-84; v.p. nursing Venice (Fla.) Hosp., 1984-90, v.p. ops., 1990-94, exec. dir., v.p. Life Counseling Ctr., Osprey, Fla., 1994-95, dir. skilled unit and spl. projects Bon Secours/Venice Hosp., 1995—; support svcs. cons. Bon Secours Healthcare, Fla., 1996—. Am. Orgn. of Nurse Execs. (pres. regon II south Fla. 1985-86, 90-94), Fla. Orgn. Nurse Execs., Fla. Commn. on Nursing. Office: Bon Secours-Venice Hosp 540 The Rialto Venice FL 34285-2900

WARD, JAMES FRANK, pension fund administrator; b. Chgo., May 29, 1938; s. Frank William and Josephine (Calderone) W.; m. Judith Evelyn Drake, Nov. 22, 1957 (dec. Sept. 1981); children: Jeffrey Thomas, Jason Banning. BEd in Acctg., Ill. State U.; MBA, DePaul U., 1967. Chartered fin. analyst. Asst. traffic mgr. Witco Chem. Co., Stickney, Ill., 1958-59; office mgr. R.E. Chatterton Indsl. Diamonds, Chgo., 1960-62; acctg. tchr. Chgo. Bd. Edn., 1963-66; asst. exec. dir. Chgo. Tchrs. Pension Fund, 1967-76, exec. dir., 1977—. Author, editor numerous newsletters, bulletins. Speaker on pension topics various civic & tchr. orgns. Mem. Nat. Coun. on Tchr. Retirement, Nat. Conf. Pub. Employee Retirement Systems, Govt. Fin. Officers Assn. U.S. & Canada (cert. of excellence in achievement for fin. acctg. & disclosures 1989, 90), Investment Analysts Soc. Chgo., Assn. for Investment Mgmt. & Rsch. Avocations: instrumental music, tennis, skiing. Home: 300 N State St Apt 5233 Chicago IL 60610-4808 Office: Chgo Tchrs Pension Fund 55 W Wacker Dr Chicago IL 60601

WARD, JAMES GORDON, education administration educator; b. Auburn, N.Y., June 28, 1944; s. Gordon J. and Alice A. Ward; m. Lynn Elizabeth Harmon, Jan. 19, 1981; children: Heather Anne, James Thomas, Audrey Lynn. BA, SUNY, Albany, 1966, MPA, 1975, MA, 1968; EdD, Va. Poltechnic Inst., 1984. Tchr. social studies Waterloo (N.Y.) Central Schs., 1967-72; policy analyst N.Y. State United Tchrs., Albany, 1972-77; dir. rsch. Am. Fedn. Tchrs., Washington, 1977-85; asst. prof. U. Ill., Champaign, 1985-89, assoc. prof. edn. adminstrn., 1989-93, prof. edn. adminstrn., 1993, assoc. dean edn., 1990-95; cons. in field; mem. Urbana Bd. Edn., 1991-96. Contbr. over 80 chpts. to books and articles to profl. jours. Mem. Am. Soc. Pub. Adminstrn., Am. Edn. Fin. Assn. (bd. dirs. 1980-86, pres. 1986-87), Am. Ednl. Rsch. Assn. Home: 703 W Iowa St Urbana IL 61801-4037 Office: Univ Ill 1310 S 6th St Champaign IL 61820-6925

WARD, JANET LYNN, magazine editor, sports wire reporter; b. Albany, Ga., Feb. 20, 1955; d. Andrew Johnson and Dorothy Iris (Pepera) W.; m. William Thomas Hankins III, Apr. 25, 1981 (div. Feb. 1990); m. Jack Wilkinson, May 22, 1993. AB in Journalism, U. Ga., 1977; JD, Woodrow Wilson Coll. Law, 1984. Sports editor Marietta (Ga.) Daily Jour., 1977-79, North Fulton extra-Atlanta Jour. Constitution, 1979-80; asst. editor In town extra-Atlanta Jour. Constitution, 1980-84; lawyer Atlanta, 1984-89; editor Am. City & County Mag., Atlanta, 1989—. Democrat. Roman Catholic. Avocations: sports, reading. Home: 372 Oakdale Rd NE Atlanta GA 30307-2070 Office: Am City & County 6151 Powers Ferry Rd NW Atlanta GA 30339-2959

WARD, JEANNETTE POOLE, psychologist, educator; b. Honolulu, June 19, 1932; d. Russell Masterton and Bessie Naomi (Hammett) Poole; children: John Russell Ward, Lisa Joy Ward. BA, Birmingham (Ala.) So. Coll., 1963; PhD in Psychology, Vanderbilt U., 1969. NSF summer rsch. asst. U. Iowa, Iowa City, 1962; NSF summer rsch. asst. Vanderbilt U., Nashville, 1963, NASA fellow, 1963-66, NIH postdoctoral fellow, 1966-67; spl. rsch. fellow Duke U., Durham, N.C., 1970-71; asst. prof. psychology Memphis State U., 1967-72, assoc. prof. psychology, 1972-77, prof. psychology, 1977—. Editor: Current Research in Primate Laterality, 1990, Primate Laterality, 1992; mem. editl. bd. Jour. Comparative Psychology, 1988-95, Internat. Jour. of Comparative Psychology, 1995—; contbr. chpts. to books and articles to profl. jours. Fellow Am. Psychol. Soc.; mem. Psychonomic Soc., Animal Behavior Soc., Am. Psychol. Assn., Am. Primatology Soc., Southeastern Psychol. Assn., Soc. for Neuroscis., Internat. Soc. for Comparative Psychology (treas. 1989-90, pres.-elect 1996—), Sigma Xi (pres. Memphis State U. chpt. 1989-90, rsch. award 1985). Democrat. Avocations: dogs, reading, art, music. Office: Univ of Memphis Dept Psychology Memphis TN 38152

WARD, JO ALICE, computer consultant, educator; b. Ft. Worth, Aug. 14, 1939; d. Boyd Wheeler and Frances Elizabeth (Wheeler) Patton; m. John Oliver Ward, Mar. 19, 1960 (div. Feb. 1976); children: Russell Scott, Pamela Joan Ward Watson. BA in Math., North Tex. State U., 1961, MA in Math., 1965, postgrad., 1969-72. Instr. math. North Tex. State U., Denton, 1965-67, grad. asst., 1968-72; instr. math. Tarrant County Jr. Coll., Ft. Worth, 1967-68; math. tchr. Aldine Ind. Schs., Houston, 1973-76; math. instr. U. Houston Downtown, 1974-80; sys. analyst Conoco Inc, Houston, 1981-93; computer cons. Quality First Computer Svcs., Houston, 1994—. Vol. facilitator for family violence program Houston Area Women's Ctr., 1993-94; adminstrv. vol. Citizens for Animal Protection, 1993—; vol. Bering Comty. Svc. Found., 1995—, bd. trustees, 1997—. Recipient Outstanding Adminstrv. Vol. award Citizens for Animal Protection, 1995. Home: 11943 Briar Forest Dr Houston TX 77077-4132

WARD, JOHN MILTON, music educator; b. Oakland, Calif., July 6, 1917; s. John Milton and Maud (Van Alstyne) W.; m. Ruth Marie Neils, Jan. 9, 1945. B.A., San Francisco State Coll., 1941; M.Mus., U. Wash., 1942; Ph.D., NYU, 1953; A.M. (hon.), Harvard U., 1955. Instr. lit. and fine arts Mich. State U., 1947-53; asst., later assoc. prof. music U. Ill., 1953-55; assoc. prof. music Harvard U., 1955-58, prof., chmn. dept., 1958-62, William Powell Mason prof., 1961-85, William Powell Mason prof. emeritus, 1985—. Author: The Dublin Virginal Manuscript, 1954, 3d edit., 1983, A Dowland Miscellany, 1977, Sprightly and Cheerful Musick, 1981, Music for Elizabethan Lutes, 1992, The Lute Music of John Johnson, 1994; editor series Pantomime, Dance, and Ballet; contbr. articles to profl. jours. Chmn. bd. dirs. Laura Boulton Found.; mem. adv. bd. London Entertainment, 1660-1800; hon. curator music and dance Harvard Theatre Collection. Mem. Am. Acad. Arts and Scis., Am. Musicol. Soc. (hon.), Internat. Musicological Soc., Internat. Coun. for Traditional Music, Soc. Ethnomusicology, Royal Mus. Assn. (hon. fgn. mem.), Lute Soc. (hon.). Home: 20 Follen St Cambridge MA 02138-3503

WARD, JOHN ROBERT, physician, educator; b. Salt Lake City, Nov. 23, 1923; s. John I. and Clara (Elzi) W.; m. Norma Harris, Nov. 5, 1948; children: John Harris, Pamela Lyn, Robert Scott, James Alan. BS, U. Utah, 1944, MD, 1946; MPH, U. Calif., Berkeley, 1967; Masters, Am. Coll. of Rheumatology, 1990. Diplomate Am. Bd. Internal Medicine. Intern Salt Lake County Gen. Hosp., 1947-48, asst. resident, 1949-50, resident physician internal medicine, 1950-51, asst. physician, 1957-58, assoc. physician, 1958-69; clin. fellow medicine Harvard U., Boston, 1955-57; instr. medicine U. Utah Med. Sch., Salt Lake City, 1954-58, asst. prof., 1958-63, assoc. prof., 1963, prof., 1966-93, chmn. dept. preventive medicine, 1966-70, emeritus prof. internal medicine, 1993—, chief div. rheumatology, 1957-88; prof. internal medicine emeritus U. Utah. Med. Sch., Salt Lake City, 1994—; attending physician internal medicine Salt Lake City VA Hosp., 1957-70; Nora Eccles Harrison prof. medicine, Am. Coll. Rheumatology. Served as capt. M.C. AUS, 1951-53. Master Am. Coll. Rheumatology; fellow ACP; mem. Am. Coll. Rheumatology (Disting. rheumatologist award 1994), Utah State Med. Assn. (hon. pres. 1994-95), U. Utah Sch. Medicine Alumni Assn. (Disting. Alumnus 1996). Home: 1249 E 3770 S Salt Lake City UT 84106-2446 Office: U Utah Health Scis Ctr 50 N Medical Dr Salt Lake City UT 84132-0001

WARD, JOHN WESLEY, retired pharmacologist; b. Martin, Tenn., Apr. 8, 1925; s. Charles Wesley and Sara Elizabeth (Little) W.; m. Martha Isabelle Hendley, Dec. 7, 1947; children: Judith Carol, Charles Wesley, Richard Little. A.A., George Washington U., 1948, B.S., 1950, M.S., 1955; Ph.D., Georgetown U., 1959. Research assoc. in pharmacology Hazleton Labs., Falls Church, Va., 1950-55; head dept. pharmacology Hazleton Labs., 1955-58, chief depts. biochemistry and pharmacology, 1958-59; with A. H. Robins Co., Richmond, Va., 1959-90, dir. biol. research, 1978-80, dir. research, 1980-82, v.p. research, 1982-89, v.p., gen. mgr. R & D div., 1989-90; ret., 1990; lectr. in pharmacology Med. Coll. Va., 1960-64, adj. assoc. prof. pharmacology, 1982-90; guest lectr. Seminar on Good Lab. Practices, FDA, Washington, 1979, Chgo., 1979, San Francisco, 1979; apptd. expert pharmacologue toxicologue, France, 1986. Contbr. articles on pharmacology, toxicology and medicinal chemistry to profl. publs. Served with USMC, 1943; Served with USN, 1944-46; Served with U.S. Army, 1944. Mem. AAAS, N.Y. Acad. Sci., Va. Acad. Sci., Am. Chem. Soc., Soc. Toxicology (charter), Am. Soc. Pharmacology and Exptl. Therapeutics, Internat. Soc. Regulatory Toxicology and Pharmacology (charter), Pharm. Mfrs. Assn. (chmn. animal care and use com. 1971-88), Am. Assn. for Accreditation Lab. Animal Care (chmn. bd. trustees 1976-80), Sigma Xi. Clubs: Willow Oaks (Richmond); Cosmos (Washington), Masons (Washington). Achievements include patents in field. Home: 10275 Cherokee Rd Richmond VA 23235-1107 *An appreciation of the responsibility we have to society has set the standards by which I live. These responsibilities are as* *important as the rights to be gained from society. Those who are unwilling to assume responsibility should have no rights.*

WARD, KATHERINE MARIE, school system administrator; b. Raton, N.Mex., Oct. 31, 1936; d. Robert Lee and Lucille (Gasperetti) Davis; m. Leonard Carlin Ward, Aug. 30, 1953; children: Kathy Ann, Ronnie, Tonia, Jess. BS, Ea. N.Mex. U., 1972, MEd, 1977; edn. specialist, U. N.Mex., 1981. Data reduction tech. phys. sci. lab. N.Mex. State U., Las Cruces, 1955-61; 3d and 4th grade tchr. Clayton Pub. Schs., Amistad, N.Mex., 1972-74; 4th grade tchr. Grants/Cibola County (N.Mex.) Schs., 1974-76, Title I reading tchr., 1976-77, Title I coord., 1977-82, Chpt. I coord., 1982-89, coord. Chpt. I and drug free schs. and cmtys., 1989-90, coord. Chpt. I, drug free, DARE and Title II, 1990-92, coord. Chpt. I, Title I, drug free and Title II, 1992-96, fed. program coord., 1996—. Leader Girl Scouts U.S., Las Cruces, 1966-67, 4-H, Grants, 1977-80; mem., sec. Fighting Back Robert Wood Johnson Found. Prevent Drug and Alcohol Use Grants, 1991-96. Recipient Adminstrn. award N.Mex. Study and Rsch. Coun., 1986, Chpt. I Exemplary award U.S. Dept. Edn., 1988, Merit award DARE program Grants Police Dept., 1991. Mem. Internat. Reading Assn., Malpais Internat. Reading Assn. (pres. 1977-79, Literacy award 1979), N.Mex. Internat. Reading Assn. (Land of Enchantment Book award com. 1983-86). Avocations: grandchildren, travel, writing children's literature, recreational reading. Home: PO Box 188 2100 Ann St Grants NM 87020 Office: Grants Cibola County Schs Grants NM 87020

WARD, LARRY THOMAS, social program administrator; b. Abingdon, Va., Sept. 10, 1951; s. Manuel Thomas and Virginia June (Meade) W.; m. Jacqueline June Moore, Aug. 7, 1982 (div. June 1995); 1 child, Nicholas Lawrence. BSW cum laude in Clin. Social Work, Philosophy, U. Md., 1983, MSW in Social Program Adminstrn. and Community Orgn., 1984; PhD in Counseling Psychology, Columbia U., 1997. Lic. social worker. Legis. lobbyist Citizen Action Coalition, Balt., 1982-83; mgmt. cons. United Way of Md., Balt., 1983-84; program adminstr. Adams County Office for Aging, Gettysburg, Pa., 1985-86; dir. social work Margaret E. Moul Home, York, Pa., 1986-87, Employee Assistance Program coordinator, family service supr., Family and Children's Service, Harrisburg, Pa., 1987-92; cons. Drug and Alcohol, Gettysburg, 1984-86; pres., CEO Impact Seminars, Guffey, Colo., 1988-97; pub. Guffey, Co., 1992—; pres., CEO Family Adv., Guffey, 1997—. Author: Meditations on Descartes, 1979, A Philosophical Perspective, 1979, Heracles Reborn, 1983, Protective Services for the Elderly, 1984, Why A Psychiatrist, 1985, The Blue Ridge Summit Project, 1986, The Effects of Office Design on the Delivery of Therapeutic Social Work Services, 1987, Emotional Disorders of the Chronically Disabled Adolescent, 1987, Resistance to School-based EAPs, 1989, 2nd edit., 1993, What Healthy Couples Seem to Know, 1990, Good Relationships Have Certain Traits, 1991; exec. prodr. film on courtroom survival techniques, 1996. Ex-officio bd. dirs. Grass Roots, Inc., Columbia, Md., 1984; del. Gov.'s Youth Adv. Council, Annapolis, Md., 1970-72; mem. consumer adv. council Met. Edison Co., Harrisburg, 1986-87. Recipient Original Art award Md. Pub. Broadcasting, 1969. Democrat. Avocations: tennis; baseball. Home: 365 Eagles Nest Trl Guffey CO 80820-9624 Office: PO Box 324 Guffey CO 80820-0324

WARD, LESLIE ALLYSON, journalist, editor; b. L.A., June 3, 1946; d. Harold Gordon and Marilyn Lucille (Dahlstead) W.; m. Robert L. Biggs, 1971 (div. 1977); m. Colman Robert Andrews, May 26, 1979 (div. 1988). AA, Coll. San Mateo, 1966; BA, UCLA, 1968, MJ, 1971. Reporter, researcher L.A. Bur. Life mag., 1971-72; reporter, news asst. L.A. bur. N.Y. Times, 1973-76; sr. editor New West mag., L.A., 1976-78, 79-80; L.A. bur. chief US mag., 1978-79; Sunday style editor L.A. Herald Examiner, 1981-82, editor-in-chief Sunday mags., 1982-83, Olympics editor, 1984, sports editor, 1985-86, sr. writer, 1986; sr. editor L.A. Times Mag., 1988-90; travel editor L.A. Times, 1990—. Democrat. Office: LA Times Times Mirror Sq Los Angeles CA 90053*

WARD, LESTER LOWE, JR., arts executive, lawyer; b. Pueblo, Colo., Dec. 21, 1930; s. Lester Lowe and Alysmai (Pfeffer) W.; m. Rosalind H. Felps, Apr. 18, 1964; children: Ann Marie, Alison, Lester Lowe. AB cum laude, Harvard U., 1952, LLB, 1955. Bar: Colo. 1955. Pvt. practice Pueblo, 1957-89; ptnr. Predovich, Ward & Banner, Pueblo, 1974-89; pres., COO Denver Ctr. for Performing Arts, 1989—. Trustee, Thatcher Found., Frank I. Lamb Found., Helen G. Bonfils Found.; pres. bd. trustees Pueblo Pub. Library, 1960-66; trustee St. Mary-Corwin Hosp., 1972-80, pres., 1979-80. With U.S. Army, 1955-57. Named Outstanding Young Man of Yr., Pueblo Jaycees, 1964. Fellow Am. Coll. Trust and Estate Counsel; mem. ABA (ho. of dels. 1986-88), Colo. Bar Assn. (bd. govs. 1977-79, 82-88, pres. 1983-84), Pueblo County Bar Assn. (Outstanding Young Lawyer award 1965, 67, pres. 1976-77), Denver Metro C. of C. (bd. dirs.), Denver Civic Ventures, Harvard Law Sch. Assn. Colo. (pres. 1972), Kiwanis (pres. 1969). Democrat. Roman Catholic. Home: 1551 Larimer St Apt 2601 Denver CO 80202-1638 Office: Denver Ctr Performing Arts 1050 13th St Denver CO 80204-2157

WARD, LLEWELLYN O(RCUTT), III, oil company executive; b. Oklahoma City, July 24, 1930; s. Llewellyn Orcutt II and Addie (Reisdorph) W.; m. Myra Beth Gungoll, Oct. 29, 1955: children: Casidy Ann, William Carlton. Student, Okla. Mil. Acad. Jr. Coll., 1948-50; BS, Okla. U., 1953; postgrad. Harvard U., 1986. Registered profl. engr., Okla. Dist. engr. Delhi-Taylor Oil Corp., Tulsa, 1955-56; ptnr. Ward-Gungoll Oil Investments, Enid, Okla., 1956—; owner L.O. Ward Oil Ops., Enid, 1963—; mem. Okla. Gov.'s Adv. Coun. on Energy; rep. to Interstate Oil Compact Commn.; bd. dirs. Community Bank and Trust Co. Enid. Chmn. Indsl. Devel. Commn., Enid, 1968—; active YMCA; mem. bd. visitors Coll. Engring., U. Okla.; mem. adv. coun. Sch. Bus., trustee Phillips U., Enid, Univ. Bd., Pepperdine, Calif.; Okla. chmn. U.S. Olympic Com., 1986—; chmn. bd. Okla. Polit. Action Com., 1974—, Bass Hosp.; Rep. chmn. Garfield County, 1967-69; Rep. nat. committeeman from Okla.; bd. dirs. Enid Indsl. Devel. Found. Served with C.E., U.S. Army, 1953-55. Mem. Ind. Petroleum Assn. Am. (chmn. 1996—), Okla. Ind. Petroleum Assn. (pres., bd. dirs.), Nat. Petroleum Council, Enid C. of C. (v.p., then pres.), Alpha Tau Omega. Methodist. Clubs: Toastmasters (pres. Enid chpt. 1966), Am. Bus. (pres. 1964). Lodges: Masons, Shriners, Rotary (pres. Enid 1990-91). Home: 900 Brookside Dr Enid OK 73703-6941 Office: 502 S Fillmore St Enid OK 73703-5703

WARD, LLOYD D., appliance company executive; m. Lita; 2 sons. BS Engring, Mich. State U., 1970; MBA, Xavier U. Design engr., group leader engring., product devel., operations, advertising Proctor & Gamble Co., 1970-88, gen. mgr. dish care products, 1988; v.p. ops. Pepsi Cola East, 1988-91; pres. Frito-Lay West PepsiCo, 1991-92, pres. Frito-Lay central divsn., 1992-96; exec. v.p., pres. Maytag Appliances, Newton, Iowa, 1996—; special assignment PepsiCo restaurant internat. bus. Recipient Exec. Yr. award Black Enterprise mag. 1995. Office: 403 W 4th St N Newton IA 50208-3026*

WARD, LOUIS EMMERSON, retired physician; b. Mt. Vernon, Ill., Jan. 19, 1918; s. Henry Ben Pope and Aline (Emmerson) W.; m. Nan Talbot, June 5, 1942; children—Nancy, Louis, Robert, Mark; m. Marian Mansfield, Jan. 27, 1979. A.B., U. Ill., 1939; M.D., Harvard, 1943; M.S. in Medicine, U. Minn., 1949. Intern Ill. Research and Ednl. Hosp., Chgo., 1943; fellow medicine Mayo Found., 1946-49; cons. medicine, rheumatology Mayo Clinic, 1950-83, chmn. bd. govs., 1964-75. Contbr. articles to profl. jours. Vice chmn. bd. trustees Mayo Found., 1964-76; past bd. dirs. Fund for Republic, Ctr. for Study Democratic Instns., Arthritis Found.; mem. Nat. Council Health Planning and Devel., 1976-83. Recipient U. Ill. Achievement award, 1968; co-valedictorian, U. Ill. Class of 1939; recipient disting. alumnus award Mayo Found., 1983. Master Am. Coll. Rheumatology (pres. 1969-70); mem. AMA, Nat. Soc. Clin. Rheumatologists (pres. 1967-69), Ctrl. Soc. Clin. Rsch., Minn. Med. Soc., Zumbro Valley Med. Soc., So. Minn. Med. Assn., Phi Beta Kappa, Sigma Xi, Alpha Omega Alpha, Phi Delta Theta. Home: 30 Raeburn Ct Port Ludlow WA 98365-9796

WARD, LYNDA SUE SCOVILLE, special education educator, writer; b. Pampa, Tex., Jan. 5, 1945; d. Kenneth E. and Opal Myrle (Turner) Scoville; m. Bruce C. Ward, Oct. 1, 1976; children: J. Wade Bainum, Jennifer L. Bainum. BS in Edn., Emporia (Kans.) State U., 1967; MS in Edn., U. Kans., 1973; postgrad., Wichita (Kans.) State U. Cert. learning disabled, educable mentally handicapped, psychology, composition and lit., Kans., Tex. Tchr. educable mentally handicapped and learning disabled Shawnee Mission (Kans.) Pub. Schs., 1967-69; tchr. headstart program Hutchinson Pub. Schs., 1968; tchr. educable mentally handicapped Chanute High Sch., Iola, Kans., 1974-76; tchr. learning and behavior disabled Sedgwick County Area Spl. Edn. Svcs. Coop., Goddard, Kans., 1979-80; tchr. learning disabled coun. spl. edn. program Butler County Sch. Bd., El Dorado, Kans., 1986-87; tchr. learning disabled Wichita Pub. Schs., 1987-89; writer and researcher, Andover, Kans., 1989-91; legal adminstrv. asst., 1992-94; tchr. learning and behavior disabled So. Tex. Ind. Sch. Dist., Mercedes, 1995-96. Author: A Scoville Branch in America: A Genealogy and Story (1660-1990). Grantee U. Kans. Mem. AAUW, ASCD, DAR (Eunice Sterling chpt. registrar), Nat. Fedn. Paralegal Assns., Coun. for Exceptional Children, Kans. Paralegal Assn., Psi Chi.

WARD, MARVIN MARTIN, retired state senator; b. Newport News, Va., Feb. 10, 1914; s. Charles Tilden and Nora Belle (Martin) W.; m. Mary June Darden, Aug. 23, 1941; children: Elizabeth Darden Ward Cone, Marvin Thomas. BS, Appalachian U., 1934; MA, U. N.C., 1940. Tchr. Bethel Sch., Midland, N.C., 1934-37, Reynolds High Sch., Winston-Salem, N.C., 1937-46; prin. Granville Elem. Sch., Winston-Salem, N.C., 1946-49; asst. supt. Winston-Salem City Schs., 1949-62, supt., 1962-63; supt. Winston-Salem/Forsyth County Schs., 1963-76; mem. N.C. State Senate, Raleigh, 1979-94; ret., 1994; mem. exec. com. N.C. Pub. Sch. Forum, Raleigh, 1986—; mem. edn. com. Nat. Cong. State Legis., Denver, 1985—. Sunday sch. tchr. Centenary Meth. Ch., Winston-Salem, 1941—; mem. Forsyth County Emergency Planning Com., Winston-Salem, 1987—. Recipient Valand award Mental Health Assocs. Inc., Raleigh, 1982, Leadership award N.C. Assn. Educators, 1985; named Disting. Alumni Appalachian State U., 1986, The Educator A. Phillip Randolph Inst., 1989, Legis. of Yr. N.C. Nurses Assn., 1989. Mem. Winston-Salem C. of C., Lions, Ardmore Community Club (pres. 1950). Democrat. Avocations: golf, fishing, travel, photography, wood carving. Home: 641 Yorkshire Rd Winston Salem NC 27106-5541

WARD, MICHAEL DELAVAN, social services administrator, former Congressman; b. Jan. 7, 1951; s. Jasper Dudley III and Lucretia (Baldwin) W.; m. Christina Heavrin, July 18, 1975; children: Jasper Dudley IV, Kevin Michael. BS, U. Louisville, 1975. Salesperson Matthew Bender & Co., Louisville, 1979-83; owner Campaign Svcs., Polit. Cons., Louisville, 1983—; campaign mgr. Ron Mazzoli for Congress, Louisville, 1984; salesman Sta. WAVG, Louisville, 1984-85; spl. asst. Jefferson County, Louisville, 1985-88; state rep. Ky. Gen. Assembly, Frankfort, 1988-93; mem. 3rd congl. dist. U.S. Ho Reps., 1995-97; assoc. dir. The Peace Corps, Washington, 1996—. State chair Common Cause/Ky. Louisville, 1975-77, 79-80; treas. Jefferson County Dem. Com., Louisville, 1984-91; bd. dirs. Ohio Valley March of Dimes, 1987-88. Mem. Kentuckiana Hemophilia Soc. (bd. dirs. 1987—), Action League for Physically Handicapped Adults (bd. dirs. 1987—). Home: 1905 Deer Park Ave Louisville KY 40205-1201 Office: 1990 K St NW Washington DC 20526

WARD, MILTON HAWKINS, mining company executive; b. Bessemer, Ala., Aug. 1, 1932; s. William Howard and Mae Ivy (Smith) W.; m. Sylvia Adele Randle, June 30, 1951; children: Jeffrey Randle, Lisa Adele. BS in Mining Engring., U. Ala., 1955, MS in Engring., 1981; MBA, U. N.Mex., 1974; DEng (hon.), Colo. Sch. of Mines, 1994. Registered profl. engr., Tex., Ala. Supr., engr. San Manuel (Ariz.) Copper Corp., 1955-60; mine supt., divsn. supt., gen. supt. of mines, divsn. engr. Kerr-McGee Corp., Oklahoma City and Grants, N.Mex., 1960-66; gen. mgr. Homestake Mining Co., Grants, 1966-70; v.p. ops. Ranchers Exploration & Devel. Corp., Albuquerque, 1970-74; v.p., bd. dirs. Freeport Minerals Co., N.Y.C., 1974-85; pres., COO Freeport-McMoRan, Inc., New Orleans, 1985-92, also bd. dirs.; chmn., pres. CEO Cyprus Amax Minerals Co., Englewood, Colo., 1992—; chmn., CEO Amax Gold Inc., 1993—; bd. dirs. Mineral Info. Inst., Inc., Internat. Copper Assn. Contbr. articles to profl. jours. Bd. trustees Western Regional Coun.; bd. dirs. Smithsonian Nat. Mus. Natural History, Nat. Mining Hall of Fame and Mus.; mem. adv. bd. bus. coun. Tulane U. Sch. Bus.; disting. engring. fellow U. Ala., also mem. mining engring. adv. coun., mem. Pres.'s cabinet. Recipient Daniel C. Jackling award and Saunders gold medal Soc. Mining, Metallurgy and Exploration, 1992; inductee Am. Mining Hall of Fame, State of Ala. Engring. Hall of Fame, 1996. Fellow Inst. Mining and Metallurgy (London); mem. NAE, AIME (former sect. chmn., Disting. Mem. award), Am. Mining Congress, Nat. Mining Assn. (dir.), Am. Australian Assn., Mining and Metall. Soc. Am. (pres. 1981-83, exec. com.), Can. Inst. Mining and Metall., NAM (natural resources com.), Internat. Copper Assn. (bd. dirs.), Copper Club, Cherry Hills Country Club (Englewood), Met. Club (Washington), Met. Club (Englewood). Republican. Presbyterian. Office: Cyprus Amax Minerals Co 9100 E Mineral Cir Englewood CO 80112-3401

WARD, PETER ALLAN, pathologist, educator; b. Winsted, Conn., Nov. 1, 1934; s. Parker J. and Mary Alice (McEvoy) W. B.S., U. Mich., Ann Arbor, 1958, M.D., 1960. Diplomate: Am. Bd. Anat. Pathology, Am. Bd. Immunopathology. Intern Bellevue Hosp., 1960-61; resident U. Mich. Hosp., Ann Arbor, 1961-63; postdoctoral fellow Scripps Clinic, La Jolla, Calif., 1963-65; chief immunobiology br. Armed Forces Inst. Pathology, Washington, 1967-71; prof. dept. pathology, chmn. dept. U. Conn. Health Center, Farmington, 1971-80; prof., chmn. dept. pathology U. Mich., Ann Arbor, 1980—; interim dean U. Mich. Med. Sch., 1982-85, 1st Godfrey D. Stobbe prof. pathology, 1987; Disting. faculty lectr. U. Mich. Biomed. Rsch. Coun., 1989; cons. VA Hosp., 1980—; mem. rsch. rev. com. NHLBI, NIH, Bethesda, Md., 1978-82, Inst. Medicine/NAS, 1990—; trustee Am. Bd. Pathology, 1988—, pres., 1996; bd. dirs. Univs. Assoc. for Rsch. and Edn. in Pathology, Inc., 1978—, pres. bd. dirs., 1988-90; chmn., mem. sch. adv. bd. Armed Forces Inst. Pathology, Washington, 1981-83; mem. pathology A study sect. NIH, 1972-76, chmn., 1976-768; pres.-elect U.S./Can. Acad. Pathology, 1991-92, pres., 1992-93, past pres., 1993-94. Capt., M.C. U.S. Army, 1965-67. Recipient Borden Rsch. award U. Mich. Med. Sch., Ann Arbor, 1960, R&D and Devel award U.S. Army, 1969, Meritorious Civilian Svc. award Dept. Army, 1970, Parke-Davis award Am. Soc. Exptl. Pathology, 1971, Rous-Whipple award Am. Soc. Investigative Pathology, 1996. Mem. Am. Assn. Pathologists (pres. 1978-79), Am. Soc. Clin. Investigation, Assn. Am. Physicists, Am. Assn. Immunologists, U.S. and Can. Acad. Pathologists (past pres. 1993-94), Assn. Pathology Chmn., Assn. Am. Physicians, Mich. Soc. Pathologists. Office: U Mich Med Sci I PO Box 0602 1301 Catherine Rd #M5240 Ann Arbor MI 48109-0602

WARD, R. J., bishop. Bishop of Ea. Md. Ch. of God in Christ, St. Louis. Office: Ch of God in Christ 4724 Palm St Saint Louis MO 63115-2017*

WARD, RICHARD JOSEPH, university official, educator, author; b. Beverly, Mass., Nov. 7, 1921; s. Ralph Woodbury and Margaret (Lyons) W.; m. Cecilia Butler, Sept. 1, 1951; children: Timothy, Mary, Richard, Christopher. BS, Harvard U., 1946; MA, U. Mich., 1948, PhD, 1958. Dir. planning U.S. Aid Mission to Jordan, 1961-63; chmn. econ. dept. C.W. Post Coll., L.I. U., 1960-61, 63-65; chief planning Bur. for Near East, S. Asia, U.S. Agy. for Internat. Devel., 1965-69; mgr. internat. cons. Peat, Marwick, Mitchell & Co., Washington, 1969-75; dean U. Mass. Coll. Bus., Dartmouth, 1975-87, dean, dir. rsch., prof., 1990—, Chancellor prof., 1996; dir. U.S. Internat. U. Sch. Bus., London, 1988-89; cons. in field. Author: Principles of Economics, 1967, Development Problems, 1973, The Palestine State, 1978, Development Horizon '80, 1980; editor: The Challenge of Development, 1967; editor Third Wave, 1995-96; contbr. articles to profl. jours. Bd. dirs. Indsl. Found., 1976-82, New Bedford Symphony, 1982-85; bd. dirs. Jr. Achievement, 1977—, also past pres.; mem. exec. com. World Congress on Violence and Human Co-existence. Lt. USN, 1943-46, PTO. Recipient Disting. Svc. award AID, Jordan Mission, 1963, Univ. Svc. award U. Mass. Alumni Assn., 1983; fellow Ford Found., 1957. Mem. Assn. Social Econs. (pres. 1970-71), Ea. Econ. Assn. (exec. com.), Am. Econ. Assn., Harvard Club (pres. 1984-87, regional bd. dirs. Mass. and R.I. 1989-92), U.S. Signatory/Found. for Human Co-Existence. Home: 20 Pleasant St South Dartmouth MA 02748-3813

WARD, RICHARD VANCE, JR., management executive; b. Montreal, Que., Can., Jan. 19, 1929; s. Richard Vance Ward and Isobel Eugene Moseley; m. Elizabeth Anne Gareau, Aug. 15, 1953; children: Carolyn, Jennifer, Philip, Karen, Katherine. BSc, McGill U., Montreal, 1951; diploma in bus. adminstrn., U. Western Ont., London, Can., 1952. Indsl. engr. CIL Inc., Montreal, 1952-63, prodn. mgr., 1963-65; prodn. dir. ICI Am. Inc., Stamford, 1965-73; prodn. dir. CIL Inc., Montreal, 1973-76, v.p., 1976-84; pres. CIL Corp. of Am., Stamford, Conn., 1984-89, Ward Assocs. Mgmt. Cons., 1989—; bd. dirs. Cornwall Chems. Inc., CIL Corp. Am., Cansco Chems. Inc., Can., Interstate Resources Inc.; bd. dirs. Chlorine Inst., Washington, exec. com., 1984-86, Friends of McGill, Inc., N.Y.C. Mem. Chem. Mfrs. Assn., Sr. Men's Club (dir., pres.). Avocations: sailing, hiking, curling, skiing. Home: 45 Brushy Ridge Rd New Canaan CT 06840-4207

WARD, ROBERT, composer, conductor, educator; b. Cleve., Sept. 13, 1917; s. Albert E. and Carrie (Mollenkopf) W.; m. Mary Raymond Benedict, June 19, 1944; children: Melinda, Johanna, Jonathon, Mark, Timothy. B.Mus., Eastman Sch. Music, 1939; cert., Juilliard Grad. Sch. Music, 1946; student composition with, Bernard Rogers, Howard Hanson, Frederick Jacobi, Aaron Copland; conducting with, Albert Stoessel, Edgar Schenkman; D.F.A., Duke, 1972; Mus.D., Peabody Inst., 1975; D.F.A., U. N.C., Greensboro, 1992. Tchr. Juillard Sch. Music, 1946-56; mng. editor, exec. v.p. Galaxy Music Corp., until 1967, dir., 1967—; exec. v.p. Highgate Press, 1967; pres. N.C. Sch. Arts, Winston-Salem, 1967-74; tchr. composition N.C. Sch. Arts, 1974-79; prof. composition Duke U., Durham, N.C., 1978-87, Mary Duke Biddle prof. music, 1978-87; chmn. bd. Triangle Music Theater Assocs. Composer: 1st Symphony, 1942, Hush'd Be the Camps Today, 1943, Second Symphony, 1947, Third Symphony, 1951, Fourth Symphony, 1958, Divertimento for Orchestra, 1961, Earth Shall Be Fair, 1960, He Who Gets Slapped (Pantaloon) (opera in 3 acts); opera in 4 acts The Crucible, 1962 (Pulitzer Prize in music); Hymn and Celebration (for orch.), 1962; for orch. Invocation and Toccata, 1963; opera in 2 acts The Lady From Colorado, 1964; Let the Word Go Forth, 1965; cantata Sweet Freedom's Song, 1965, Hymn To The Night, 1966; First String Quartet, 1966, Concerto for Piano and Orchestra, 1968; opera Claudia Legare, 1974; Fifth Symphony-Canticles for America, 1976, Sonic Structure (for orch.), 1980; opera Abelard and Heloise, 1981, Minutes Till Midnight, 1982, Dialogues for Violin, Cello and Orchestra, 1983, Concerto for Saxophone and Orchestra, 1984, Raleigh Divertimento for Wind Quintet, 1986, Festival Triptych, 1987, Sixth Symphony, 1988, First Symphonic Set for the New South, 1988, Fanfare, 1988, Second Symphonic Set, 1988, Appalachian Ditties and Dances, 1988, 5x5, 1989, Images of God, 1989, Ballet Music on The Scarlet Letter, 1990, Second Sonata for Violin and Piano, 1990, Bath County Rhapsody, 1991, Serenade for Mallarmé, 1991, By The Way of Memories for Orchestra, 1997, one act opera Roman Fever, 1993, Love's Seasons, 1994, song cycle Sacred Carticles, 1994, The Hill Song, 1996, Brass Ablaze for British Brass Band, 1996, Night Under the Big Sky for Wind Quintet and Piano, 1997, Trio for Clarinet, Cello and Piano, 1997. Bd. dirs. Martha Baird Rockefeller Fund for Music, 1971-82, Am. Symphony Orch. League, 1977-89, Nat. Inst. Music Theatre, 1977-85; mem. music com. Henry St. Settlement; bd. dirs. Durham Arts Coun. Served with AUS, 1942-46. Decorated Bronze Star; MacDowell Colony fellow, 1938; recipient Juilliard Pub. award, 1942, Fine Arts award State of N.C., 1975, Gold Baton award Am. Symphony Orch. League, 1991, Disting. Faculty Alumnus award U. N.C., 1992, A.I. DuPont award of Del. Symphony, 1995; Alice M. Ditson fellow Columbia U., 1944, Guggenheim fellow, 1950, 52, 66-67; Am. Acad. Arts and Letters grantee, 1946. Mem. Nat. Acad. Arts and Letters. Home: The Forest at Duke # 4029 2701 Pickett Rd Durham NC 27705-5654

WARD, ROBERT ALLEN, JR., advertising executive; b. Summit, N.J., Sept. 25, 1937; s. Robert Allen and Edith Allen (Edith) Seiberling; m. Nancy Prescott, Oct. 3, 1964; children: Victoria, Jennifer, Robert. BA, Yale U., 1959. Analysis and account exec. U.S. Trust Co., N.Y.C., 1959-62; v.p., dir. Progressive Mktg. Svcs., N.Y.C., 1962-63, Coin Depot Corp., Elizabeth, N.J., 1963-68; pres. J.S. Riley Co., Wayne, N.J., 1964-70; pres., dir., C.G.W. Enterprises, Butler, N.J., Carelli, Glynn & Ward Advt. Co., 1969-95, All Hours Answering Svc., Pompton Lakes, N.J., 1969-93; v.p., dir. N.J. Exchange, 1969-93, v.p. direct Anserve Inc., 1993—; pres., dir. B.E.K., Inc., real estate mgmt. co., Wayne, N.J., Litho Four Printers, 1970-88, Health-serve, 1996—; dir. Devon Pubs., Butler, N.J., 1977-78. Pres., Kinnelon PTA, N.J., 1972-73; councilman Kinnelon Borough Coun., 1978-83; police commr., Kinnelon, 1978-83; mem. Kinnelon Drug Adv. Coun., 1978-83; vestry St. David Episc. Ch., Kinnelon, 1969-72, 78-87, 90-93, sr. warden, 1978-87; bd. dirs. Morris Area Coun. Girl Scouts U.S.A., 1977-80; dir. Inner City Ensemble, 1983-90, Willing Hands, 1989—; mem. sports awards dinner com. North Jersey March of Dimes, 1986-90; chmn. Yale Alumni Schs. commn., 1984—. Served with USMC, 1959-60; served to capt. USAR, 1960-72. Mem. No. N.J. Advt. Club (bd. dirs. 1970-72), Commerce and Industry Assn. of N.J. (Penpac bd. dirs. 1982-90), N.J. Home Builder Assoc. (bd. dirs. 1967-70), Bank Mktg. Assn., Hugueuot Soc., S.A.R., Inner City Ensemble/N.J. Dance Troupe (bd. dirs. 1983-89). Republican. Clubs: Yale (trustee, v.p. 1981—, pres. 1993-96, Montclair); Nippon (N.Y.C.); Smoke Rise (Kinnelon), Smoke Rise Paddle Tennis (pres. 1988—). Home: 393 Ski Trl Kinnelon NJ 07405-2247 Office: Anserve 1250 State Route 23 Butler NJ 07405-2026

WARD, ROBERT CLEVELAND, research mathematician, science administrator; b. Sparta, Tenn., Dec. 7, 1944; s. James C. and Mary E. (Pharris) W.; m. C. Gayle Gillen, Sept. 3, 1965; children: Kimberly M. Ward Smith, Jonathan R. BS in Math., Tenn. Tech. U., 1966; MS in Math., Coll. of William and Mary, 1969; PhD in Applied Math., U. Va., 1974. Mathematician NASA Langley Rsch. Ctr., Hampton, Va., 1966-74; rschr. Oak Ridge (Tenn.) Nat. Lab., 1974-77, head math rsch. sect., 1977-82, head math. sci., 1982-90, dir. engring. physics and math., 1990—; prof., head computer sci. dept. U. Tenn., Knoxville, 1995—. Fellow AAAS; mem. IEEE Computer Soc., Soc. Indsl. and Applied Math. (various offices 1974—), Assn. for Computing Machinery, Sigma Xi. Achievements include devel., analysis and improvement numerical techniques in areas of numerical linear algebra and scientific computing. Office: U Tenn Dept Computer Sci 107 Ayres Hall Knoxville TN 37996-1301

WARD, ROBERT EDWARD, retired political science educator and university administrator; b. San Francisco, Jan. 29, 1916; s. Edward Butler and Claire Catherine (Unger) W.; m. Constance Regina Barnett, Oct. 31, 1942; children: Erica Anne, Katherine Elizabeth. B.A., Stanford U., 1936; M.A., U. Calif.-Berkeley, 1938, Ph.D., 1948. Instr. in polit. sci. U. Mich., 1948-50, asst. prof. polit. sci., 1950-54, assoc. prof., 1954-58, prof., 1958-73; prof. Stanford U., 1973-87, dir. Center for Research in Internat. Studies, 1973-87; cons. in field; advisor Center for Strategic and Internat. Studies, Washington, 1968-87. Author: Modern Political Systems: Asia, 1963, Political Modernization in Japan and Turkey, 1964. Mem. nat. council Nat. Endowment for Humanities, Washington, 1968-73; mem. Pres.'s Commn. on Fgn. Lang.-Internat. Studies, 1978-79; chmn. Japan-U.S. Friendship Commn., 1980-83; mem. Dept. Def. Univ. Forum, 1982-87. Served to lt. (j.g.) USN, 1942-45. Recipient Japan Found. award Tokyo, 1976; recipient Order of Sacred Treasure 2d class (Japan), 1983. Fellow Am. Acad. Arts and Scis.; mem. Am. Polit. Sci. Assn. (pres. 1972-73), Assn. Asian Studies (pres. 1972-73), Social Sci. Research Council (chmn. 1969-71), Am. Philos. Soc. Home: Box 8129 501 Portola Rd Portola Valley CA 94028

WARD, ROBERT JOSEPH, federal judge; b. N.Y.C., Jan. 31, 1926; s. Joseph G. and Honor V. (Hess) W.; m. Florence C. Maisel, Apr. 15, 1951 (dec. Mar. 1994); children: Laura Alice, Carolyn; m. Renée J. Sokolow, May 28, 1995. SB, Harvard Coll., 1945, LLB, 1949. Bar: N.Y. 1949. Practiced in N.Y.C., 1949-51, 61-72; asst. dist. atty. N.Y. County, 1951-55; asst. U.S. atty. So. Dist. N.Y., 1956-61; judge U.S. Dist. Ct. (so. dist.) N.Y., 1972—. With USNR, 1944-46. Mem. ABA, N.Y. State Bar Assn., Assn. of Bar of City of N.Y., Fed. Bar Coun. Office: US Dist Ct US Courthouse Foley Sq New York NY 10007-1501

WARD, ROBERTSON, JR., architect; b. Boston, Sept. 7, 1922; s. Robertson and Sylvia (Whiting) W.; m. Sara Weeks, June 2, 1948 (div. 1953); 1 child, Robin Regina. A.B. cum laude, Harvard Coll., 1944, M.Arch., 1951. Mem. faculty dept. advanced bldg. research Ill. Inst. Tech., Chgo., 1951-52; research designer Arnold Rosner, Chgo., 1952; architect Skidmore, Owings & Merrill, Tokyo, 1953, Breuer, Nervi and Zehrfuss, UNESCO, Paris, 1953-54; head dept. design research Skidmore, Owings & Merrill, Chgo., 1954-60; pvt. practice architecture, bldg. systems, research Chgo., from 1960; rep., cons. UNESCO archtl. environ. info. system, 1976-79, U.S. Nat. Com./Coun. Internat. Bldg. Rsch., 1973-78; rep. from U.S. Econ. Commn. for Europe, 1972; mem. Chgo. Urban Renewal Rev. Commn., 1965; mem. tech. adv. bd. U.S. Dept. Commerce, 1967; dir. ARCC/NSF Office

Environ. Rsch., 1984—, AIA/R.W. Johnson Found./Health Facilities Rsch. Program on Oper. Costs., 1992—, others. Archtl. works include Sci., Visual and Performing Arts Centers, Bennington Coll., Exptl. Theater, Vassar Coll., Sci. Center, Deerfield Acad. Served with USNR, 1944-46. Recipient Gov. of Calif.'s Design award, 1966; Graham Found. fellow, 1963, 75; NSF grantee 1984, 89. Fellow AIA, 1970; mem. Illuminating Engring. Soc., U.S. Inst. Theater Tech., Environ. Design Research Assn. Clubs: Harvard (N.Y.C.), Tavern. Home: 17 Brimmer St Boston MA 02108-1010 Office: MIT Rm 5-41B Architecture/Bldg Tech Grp Cambridge MA 02139

WARD, RODMAN, JR., lawyer; b. Wilmington, Del., Apr. 8, 1934; s. Rodman and Dorcas (Andrews) W.; m. Susan Speakman Hill, Oct. 10, 1959; children: Margery Ward Garnett, Emily Ward Neilson, Rodman III, Jennifer Ward Oppenheimer. BA, Williams Coll., 1956; LLB, Harvard U., 1959. Bar: Del. 1959, D.C. 1959. Partner Prickett, Ward, Burt & Sanders, Wilmington, 1967-79, Skadden, Arps, Slate, Meagher & Flom, Wilmington, 1979—; bd. dirs. WMB Holdings, Inc. Author: (with Folk and Welch) Folk on the Delaware General Corporation Law, 1987; contbr. articles to profl. jours. Trustee, mem. fin. com. Med. Ctr. of Del. Served to capt. USAF, 1960-63. Fellow Am. Coll. Trial Lawyers, Am. Bar Found.; mem. ABA, Am. Law Inst., Del. State Bar Assn. (pres. 1989-90), D.C. Bar Assn., Assn. of Bar of City of N.Y., Am. Judicature Soc., Wilmington Club, Wilmington Country Club, Vicmead Hunt Club. Home: 52 Selborne Dr Wilmington DE 19807-1216 Office: PO Box 636 Wilmington DE 19899-0636

WARD, ROGER COURSEN, lawyer; b. Newark, June 19, 1922; s. Waldron Merry and Aline Toppin (Coursen) W.; m. Katharine More Stevens, Oct. 22, 1949; children: James Olney, Alexander More. Grad., Phillips Exeter Acad., 1940; A.B., Princeton U., 1943; LL.B., Columbia U., 1949. Bar: N.J. 1949. Law clk. to justice N.J. Supreme Ct., 1951; since practiced in Newark, Morristown, Montclair, N.J.; ptnr. Pitney, Hardin, Kipp & Szuch, 1959-91, counsel, 1991-92; counsel Schwartz, Tobia & Stanziale, 1993—; bd. advisors Am. Inst. Law Tng. Within Office, Phila. 1986-88, Law Hiring and Tng. Report, Chgo., 1983-88. Bd. dirs. United Hosps. Newark, 1965-78, pres., 1973; trustee, v.p. Newark Mus. Assn., 1969-92; bd. dirs. Better Bus. Bur. Greater Newark, 1970-84; mem. Summit Zoning Bd. Adjustment, 1966-70; trustee Eye Inst. N.J., 1973, Pingry Sch., 1966-68, Summit YMCA, 1960-62, Newark Council Social Agys., 1956-60; vice chmn. Newark Mayor's Commn. on Youth, 1958-60. Served to lt. (j.g.) USNR, 1943-46, PTO, ETO. Harlan Fiske Stone scholar Columbia U., 1949. Mem. N.J. State Bar Assn., Essex County Bar Assn., Princeton Club N.Y., Short Hills (N.J.) Club, Phi Beta Kappa. Office: Schwartz Tobia Stanziale Becker Rosensweig & Sedita 22 Crestmont Rd Verona NJ 07044-2902

WARD, ROSCOE FREDRICK, engineering educator; b. Boise, Idaho, Dec. 5, 1930; s. Roscoe C. W. and Alice E. (Ward); m. Julia Duffy, June 8, 1963; children: Eric R., David C. Student, U. Oreg., 1949-50; B.A., Coll. of Idaho, 1953; postgrad., U. Wash., 1955-57; B.S., Oreg. State U., 1959; M.S., Wash. State U., 1961; Sc.D., Washington U., St. Louis, 1964. Registered profl. engr., Ohio. Asst. prof. civil engring. U. Mo., Columbia, 1963-65, Robert Coll., Istanbul, Turkey, 1965-67; assoc. prof. civil engring. Asian Inst. Tech., Bangkok, Thailand, 1967-68; assoc. prof. civil engring., assoc. dean Sch. Engring. U. Mass., Amherst, 1968-75; prof. Bogazici U., Istanbul, 1974-75; br. chief biomass energy Dept. Energy, Washington, 1975-79; interregional advisor UN/World Bank, N.Y.C., 1979-83; dean Sch. Applied Scis. Miami U., Oxford, Ohio, 1983-88; prof. paper sci. and engring. Sch. Applied Scis. Miami U., Oxford, 1983—; vis. scientist Csir, Republic of South Africa, 1990-91. Contbr. chpts. to books, articles to profl. jours. Fellow ASCE. Home: 4818 Bonham Rd Oxford OH 45056-1423

WARD, SHERMAN CARL, III (BUZZ WARD), theater manager; b. Camden, N.J., Apr. 21, 1958; s. Sherman Carl Jr. and Ann Laura (Bodie) W. BA, Princeton U., 1980; MBA, Harvard U., 1986. Contr.'s asst. McCarter Theatre Co., Princeton, N.J., 1977-80; spl. projects analyst Madison Fin. Corp., Nashville, 1980-81, dir. client svcs., 1981-83; tchr. English, vol. rschr. Nan, Thailand, 1983-84; studio ops. Walt Disney Pictures, Burbank, Calif., summer 1985; contr. Coconut Grove Playhouse, Miami, Fla., 1986-87, dir. ops., 1987-88; gen. mgr. Yale Sch. Drama, Yale Repertory Theatre, New Haven, Conn., 1988-92; exec. dir. Cin. Playhouse in the Park, 1992—. Recipient Letter of Appreciation, King of Thailand, 1984. Mem. Actor's Equity Assn. Avocations: travel, singing, dancing, golf, volleyball. Office: Cin Playhouse in the Park 962 Mount Adams Cir Cincinnati OH 45202-6023

WARD, SUSAN MARIE, cultural organization administrator; b. Detroit, Jan. 29, 1954; d. Richard Guerin and Helen Marie (Stone) W. BA in Art History, Wayne State U., 1983; MA in Decorative Arts, Parsons Sch. Design/Cooper-Hewitt Mus., 1985. Intern Met. Mus. Art, N.Y.C., 1985; asst. curator Biltmore Estate, Asheville, N.C., 1985-86, curator, 1987-92; exec. dir. Travellers Rest, Nashville, 1992-94; founder, dir. Heritage Comm., Brentwood, Tenn., 1994—; sec. Biltmore Village Hist. Mus., Asheville, 1989-91; adj. prof. O'More Coll. Design, Franklin, Tenn., 1995—; instr. Watkins Inst. of Design, Nashville. Author: The Gilded Age at Biltmore Estate, 1990. Vol. Big Bros. and Sisters, Asheville, 1988-92; com. mem. Bele Cher, Asheville, 1989; vol. cons. Jr. Achievement, 1994. Mem. Am. Assn. State and Local History (state membership chmn. 1989), N.C. Mus. Coun. (chmn. computers and museums com.), Southeast Museums Conf. (chmn. intern staff devel. com.), Asheville Mus. of Art (bd. dirs. 1991-92).

WARD, THOMAS JEROME, lawyer; b. New Kensington, Pa., May 6, 1936; s. Richard Thomas and Renatha Ann (Hruscienski) W.; m. Lindley Ann Bennett, Aug. 20, 1960; children: Christine Lester, Janice Nolte, Thomas, James, Jeffrey, Matthew. BS, Duquesne U., 1958; JD, Villanova U., 1961. Tax atty. Westinghouse Electric Corp., Pitts., 1961-65; successively atty., sr. atty., assist. gen. atty. Rockwell Mfg. Co., Pitts., 1965-71, mgr. corp. devel., 1971-73; v.p., gen. counsel, sec. Disston Inc., Pitts., 1973-78; ptnr. Meyer, Darragh, Buckler, Bebenek & Eck, Pitts., 1978-84; v.p. fin. and law, gen. counsel, sec. Dravo Corp., Pitts., 1984-87, sr. v.p. fin. and adminstrn., 1987-88, exec. v.p., 1988-90; sr. atty. Buchanan Ingersoll. PC, Pitts.; dir. Buchanan Ingersoll (Europa), Frankfurt, Fed. Republic Germany, 1990-91; sr. v.p., gen. counsel Federated Svcs. Co., Pitts., 1991—. Editor Villanova Law Rev., 1960-61. Bd. dirs., past pres. Cath. Charities of Pitts.; past bd. advisors Duquesne U. Sch. Bus. and Adminstrn., Pitts.; mem. bd. dirs., pres. Bethel Park Cmty. Found. Mem. ABA, Pa. Bar Assn., Allegheny County Bar Assn., Am. Soc. Corp. Secs., Century Club Dining. Alumni, Duquesne U. Democrat. Roman Catholic. Club: Duquesne. Office: Federated Investors Tower Pittsburgh PA 15222

WARD, THOMAS LEON, engineering educator; b. Norfolk, Va., May 12, 1930; s. Thomas Leon and Emma Anna (Meyer) W. B.S. in Physics, U. Tex., 1953; M.S. in Systems Engring., West Coast U., 1969; M.S. in Indsl. and Systems Engring., U. So. Calif., 1972, Ph.D. in Engring., 1975. Registered profl. engr., Ky., Calif. Engr. Glenn L. Martin Co., Balt., 1953-55, Convair, Edwards AFB, Calif., 1955-58; prin. engr. Rep. Aviation Corp., Edwards AFB, 1958-59; group engr. Giannini Controls Corp., Passadena, Calif., 1959-62; chief engr. Parsons Electronics, Pasadena, 1962-63; engr. Delta Semicondrs., Inc., Newport Beach, Calif., 1963-64; sr. engr. Electro-Optical Systems, Pasadena, 1964-65, 67-68; group engr. Hycon Mfg. Co., Morovia, Calif., 1965-66; mem. engring. staff Truesdail Labs., Los Angeles, 1966-67, 70-76; engring. specialist Aerojet-Gen. Corp., Azusa, Calif., 1968-69; chief engr. Giannini-Voltex, Whittier, Calif., 1969-70; lectr. indsl. and systems engring. U. So. Calif., 1972-75, asst. prof., 1975-78; prof., chmn. indsl. and mfg. engring. Calif. State Poly. U., Pomona, 1978-80; mem. tech. staff Jet Propulsion Lab., Calif. Inst. Tech., 1980-81; prof., chmn. dept. indsl. engring. Speed Sci. Sch., U. Louisville, 1981-86, prof., 1986—; dir. Instn. for Fuzzy Systems and Intelligent Control. Sr. mem. Am. Inst. Indsl. Engrs., IEEE, Soc. Mfg. Engrs.; mem. AAAS, ASME, Sigma Xi, Alpha Pi Mu, Omega Rho., Tau Beta Pi. Democrat. Office: Speed Sci Sch Louisville KY 40292

WARD, THOMAS MONROE, lawyer, law educator; b. Raleigh, N.C., Mar. 6, 1952; s. Melvin Francis and Margaret Alice (Fulcher) W.; m. Ann Frances Sharky, July 28, 1980. B.S.B.A., U. N.C., 1974, J.D., 1978. Bar: N.C. 1978, U.S. Dist. Ct. (ea. dist.) N.C. 1978. Ptnr. Ward, Ward, Willey & Ward, New Bern, N.C., 1978-96; Harris, Shields, Creech & Ward, PA, 1997—; instr. bus. law Craven Community Coll., New Bern, 1982-85. Bd. dirs. Footlight Theatre/Lollipop Playhouse Inc., New Bern, 1980-89, Craven Chpt. N.C. Cmty. Found., 1994—; vol. Craven County Recreation Dept., New Bern, 1982-86; chmn. Richard Dobbs Spaight Constl. Commemorative Com., 1985-89; dir. Craven county affiliate N.C. Commns. Found. Mem. Craven County Bar Assn., N.D. Bar Assn., N.C. Acad. Trial Lawyers, Assn. Trial Lawyers Am., Phi Beta Kappa, Beta Gamma Sigma. Democrat. Methodist. Lodge: Rotary. Office: Harris Shields Creech & Ward PA 325 Pollock St PO Drawer 1168 New Bern NC 28563-1168

WARD, VERNON GRAVES, internist; b. Palisade, Nebr., Mar. 5, 1928; s. Charles Bennett and Mildred Belle (Graves) W.; m. Eleanore Mae Farstveet, Aug. 28, 1952; children: Margo, Alison, Barry. BA, Nebr. Wesleyan U., 1948; MD cum laude, U. Nebr., Omaha, 1954. Diplomate Am. Bd. Internal Medicine. Instr. in anatomy Columbia U., N.Y.C., 1948-50; intern U. Wis., Madison, 1954-55, resident internal medicine, 1955-58, chief resident, physician, 1957-58; fellow in neurophysiology and psychosomatic medicine U. Okla., Oklahoma City, 1960-61; asst. clin. prof. medicine U. Wis., Madison, 1961-62; pvt. practice internal medicine Kearney, Nebr., 1962-67; asst. prof. U. Nebr. Coll. Medicine, Omaha, 1967-69; assoc. clin. prof. medicine U. Nebr., Omaha, 1969—; pvt. practice internal medicine Omaha, Nebr., 1969—; chmn. dept. internal medicine Clarkson Hosp., Omaha, 1976-78, 96—. Contbr. articles to profl. jours. including JAMA, Nebr. State Med. Jour., Wis. State Med. Jour., Am. Heart Jour., Postgrad. Medicine. Pres. Nebr. chpt. Arthritis Found., 1969-71. Lt. Commdr. USNR, 1958-60. Named Hutton Traveling Scholar Coll. of Physicians, 1965. Fellow ACP, Am. Coll. Rheumatology; mem. AMA, Nebr. State Med. Soc., Omaha Med. Soc., Am. Soc. Internal Medicine, Am. Psychosomatic Soc., Nebr. Soc. Internal Medicine (pres. 1980-82, Disting. Internist award 1990), Phi Kappa Phi, Alpha Omega Alpha (pres. Nebr. chpt. 1984-85), Phi Chi (grand sec.-treas. 1986—, co-chmn. nat. conv. Omaha 1953), Phi Kappa Tau. Republican. Lutheran. Home: 302 N 54th St Omaha NE 68132-2813 Office: 201 S Doctor's Bldg Omaha NE 68131

WARD, WILLIAM BINNINGTON, agricultural communicator; b. Idaho Falls, Ida., July 16, 1917; s. William A. and Daisy (Binnington) W.; m. Thora Bracken, Sept. 12, 1939; children—Ann Lyn, William Bracken, Cristen Lee, Alan Miller. B.S., Utah State Agrl. Coll., 1940; M.S., U. Wis., 1941. With editorial dept. Post Register (daily newspaper), Idaho Falls, 1935-36; asst. to extension editor Utah State Agrl. Coll., Logan, 1937-40; corr. A.P. and Rocky Mountain newspapers, 1938-40; asst. to extension editor, grad. instr. agrl. journalism U. Wis., 1940-41; information specialist dairy marketing, handling pub. relations on milk marketing agreements and orders U.S. Dept. Agr., 1941-42; chief information sect. Agrl. Marketing Adminstrn., then Food Distbn. Adminstrn., 1943-44; prof., head dept. communication arts, editor, chief of publs. N.Y. State Coll. Agr. Life Scis. and Human Ecology, Cornell U., Ithaca, N.Y., 1945-72; prof. N.Y. State Coll. Agr. Life Scis., Cornell U., 1973-88, prof. emeritus, 1988—; chmn. nat. adv. com. on information U.S. Dept. Agr., 1953-55; agr. com. adviser U. Philippines, 1956-57, 65; communications adviser Argentine Govt., 1961-62; agr. communications cons. Ford Found., India, 1968-69, 70; communication adviser, chief of party U. Tenn./U.S. AID India Agrl. Programs, 1972; cons. ICRISAT, India, 1973, World Bank, Bangladesh, 1974—; vis. scientist Internat. Inst. Tropical Agr., Africa, 1976-77, cons., 1978-89, 92—; cons. Boyce Thompson Inst. Plant Research, 1981-82; communications cons., Indonesia, 1978-81, 87, Internat. Center Argrl. Rsch. in Dry Areas, 1981-86; cons., mem. adv. bd. Acad. Ednl. Devel., 1985-88. Author: Agricultural News in the Daily Press, 1941, Reporting Agriculture, 2d edit, 1959, Science and Rice in Indonesia, 1985; contbr. articles to internat., nat., regional agrl. publs. Mem. Am. Assn. Agrl. Coll. Editors (pres.), Agrl. Communicators in Edn., Rotarian Club, Blue Key, Sigma Delta Chi. Home: 402 Savage Farm Dr Ithaca NY 14850

WARD, WILLIAM E., mayor. Mayor City of Chesapeake, Chesapeake, VA., 1990—. Office: Office of Mayor PO Box 15225 Chesapeake VA 23328

WARD, WILLIAM FRANCIS, JR., real estate investment banker; b. Everett, Mass., Aug. 23, 1928; s. William Francis and Helen (Schriber) W.; m. Elaine L. Wilson, June 11, 1950 (dec. Oct. 1993); children: Jeffrey W., Gary T., Michelle A., Gregory W., Suzanne M.; m. Marie-Louise Buchheit, Nov. 5, 1994. B.S., U.S. Mil. Acad., 1950; M.B.A., Harvard U., 1956; LLB, La Salle U., 1966; LLD (hon.), Southern Vermont U., 1996. Econ. analyst E.I. duPont de Nemours & Co., Inc., Wilmington, Del., 1956-58; sec. N.Y. State Bridge Authority, Poughkeepsie, 1958-60; div. controller, dir. marketing services GAF Corp., N.Y.C., 1960-63; asst. to pres. Grosset & Dunlap, Inc., 1963-65, v.p., 1965-67; controller Dun & Bradstreet, 1967-71, v.p., 1968-71; chmn. bd., pres. Dun-Donnelley Pub. Corp., 1971-77; v.p., treas. Gestam, Inc., 1981-83, pres., 1983-86; chief Army Res., 1986-91; chmn., pres. Realicam, 1985—; bd. dirs. Quotron Electronics, Inc., Empire Nat. Bank, Eastern Savs. Bank, Apple Bank for Savs., Greater N.Y. Bank for Savs.; trustee All-City Funds; faculty N.Y. U. Sch. Commerce, 1960-64. Pres. Ramapo Central Sch. Dist., 1966-72, 1982-87; mem. facilities and planning bd. Good Samaritan Hosp., 1980-85; County chmn. Citizen for Kennedy and Johnson, 1960; Dem. candidate for Ho. of Reps., 1962; chmn. Young Citizens for Johnson and Humphrey, 55 counties N.Y., 1964; exec. v.p. Am. Cancer Soc., 1976-81; bd. dirs. N.Y.C. div. Aerospace Edn. Found., U.S. Army War Coll. Found., West Point Fund, 1979, Franciscan Sisters of the Poor Found., 1980-92; trustee N.Y. Mil. Acad., 1982-86, 91—, Assn. Grads. U.S. Military Acad., 1993—, Hist. Soc. Rockland County, 1993—. Served to capt. AUS, 1950-54; maj. gen. U.S. Army Res. Decorated D.S.M. with 1 oak leaf cluster, Legion of Merit, Meritorious Service medal with oak leaf cluster, Air medal with 3 oak leaf clusters, Army Commendation medal with oak leaf cluster, Purple Heart. Mem. West Point Soc. (Washington chpt., Space Coast chpt., N.Y. chpt., pres. 1974-76), Antrim Players, Soc. Harvard Engrs. and Scientists, Fin. Execs. Inst., Newcomen Soc., Res. Officers Assn., Am. Friends of Viet Nam (nat. chmn.), VFW, Am. Legion, Disabled Am. Vets., Pilgrim Soc., Army and Navy Club, Squadron "A" Club, Univ. Club (N.Y.), Harvard Club (Washington), Nat. Press Club, KC. Roman Catholic. Home: Summit View Farm RJ17A PO Box 150 Goshen NY 10924 also: 1271 Continental Ave Melbourne FL 32970

WARD, WILLIAM REED, composer, educator; b. Norton, Kans., May 20, 1918; s. Joseph Aloysius and Maude (Jones) W.; m. Elizabeth Jane Adam, Aug. 8, 1943; children—Claudia Christine, Joseph Andrew, John David. Mus.B., Mus.Edn.B., U. Kans., 1941; Mus.M., Eastman Sch. Music, 1942, Ph.D., 1954; student, Charles S. Skilton, L.E. Anderson, Robert Palmer, Bernard Rogers, Howard Hanson. Instr. music Colo. State U., 1942-44; asst. prof. music, head composition and theory curriculum Lawrence U., 1944-47; faculty San Francisco State U., 1947-88, head music dept., 1954-69, prof. music, 1959—; asso. dean San Francisco State U. (Sch. Creative Arts), 1977-80; Lectr. panelist music Idyllwild Inst. Arts; Lectr. panelist music Cal. Music Tchrs. Assn., Choral Condrs. Guild Calif., Am. Guild Organists, Music Educators Nat. Conf., Music Tchrs. Nat. Assn. Choir dir., First Christian Ch., Ft. Collins, Colo., 1942-44, Meml. Presbyn. Ch., Appleton, Wis., 1944-47, First Bapt. Ch., Burlingame, Calif., 1949-63, United Meth. Ch., 1967—; dir., Asian Arts Acad. and Music of Whole Earth Festival, San Francisco, 1978, World Arts Acad., San Francisco, 1979; compositions performed by Eastman-Rochester, Indpls., Oklahoma City, San Francisco symphony orchs., numerous others; composer: Lullaby for a Pinto Colt, 1941, A Vision of the World, 1955, Psalm 136, 1959, Fray Junipero Serra, The Great Walker; dramatic oratorio, 1960, Symphony 1, 1938, 2, 1947, 3, 1954, Variations on a Western Tune, 1948, Suite for Woodwind Quintet, 1954, A Psalm of Praise, 1964, The Crucufixion, 1971, Fun, Love, Joy, Trains, 1971, In Town Again, 1973, Arcs, 1973, O For A Thousand Tongues, 1973, They Shall Mount Up With Wings, 1980, Four Old American Songs of Merriment, 1994, Fantasia on St. Dunstan's Tune, 1996, others.; Author: Examples for the Study of Musical Style, rev. edit, 1970, American Bicentennial Song Book, 2 vols, 1975. Mem. City of Burlingame Beautification Commn., 1988—; mem. artistic adv. com. Music at Kohl Mansion, 1987—. Recipient Nat. Arrangers contest award, 1947. Mem. Assn. Univ. Composers, ASCAP, Music Tchrs. Nat. Assn., Music Educators Nat. Conf., Choral Condrs. Guild, AAUP. Home: 120 Occidental Ave Burlingame CA 94010-5268

WARD, WILLIAM WEAVER, electrical engineer; b. Dallas, Feb. 19, 1924; s. Carroll Ross Ward and Dorothy Jane (Weaver) O'Rourke; m. Lydia Maeve McPeek, June 4, 1955; children: Geoffrey William, Christopher Andrew. BSEE, Tex. A & M Coll., 1948; MSEE, Calif. Inst. Tech., 1949, PhD in Elec. Engring., 1952. Registered profl. elec. engr., Mass. Engr. Texaco Geophys. Lab., Bellaire, Tex., summer 1948, Hughes Aircraft Co., Culver City, Calif., summer 1949, 50; teaching asst. Calif. Inst. Tech., Pasadena, 1949-52; staff mem. to group leader to mgr. satellite ops. Lincoln Lab., MIT, Lexington, 1952-94; cons. on various tech. matters U.S., Can., British, and Australian govts.; presenter, lectr. in field. Vestryman, treas. local ch., Newton Highlands, Mass. With U.S. Army, 1943-46, PTO. Mem. IEEE (reviewer, named regional outstanding lectr. 1974, disting. lectr. 1995—), AIAA (disting. lectr. 1986-87), Nat. Soc. Profl. Engrs., Mass. Soc. Profl. Engrs., Dalhousie Lodge, Masons, Sigma Xi, Tau Beta Pi. Democrat. Episcopalian. Achievements include research and development on UHF airborne-early-warning radar; development of worldwide tracking range for Project Mercury, ballistic-missile tracking, UHF and EHF satellites for military communication. Home: 22 Carver Rd Newton MA 02161-1008 Office: Lincoln Lab MIT 244 Wood St Lexington MA 02173-6426

WARD, YVETTE HENNIG, advertising executive; b. St. Paul, June 15, 1910; d. Leo J. and Adele (Hennig) Borer; m. Charles Saunders, Nov. 30, 1931 (div.); 1 child, Charlene; m. Charles Allen Ward, Feb. 29, 1940 (dec. May 1959); children—Allen, Vida, Herbert. Publisher Hudson (Wis.) Star-Observer, 1952-58; with Brown & Bigelow, 1942—, pres., 1959—. Profl. dancer, 1918-28, free-lance interior decorator, 25 yrs; Author: Russia Through Women's Eyes, 1956, Around the World in 32 Days, 1958. Chmn. fine arts and jewelry funding Compas 11, Phoenix.; Chmn. bd. Hudson Meml. Hosp.; bd. dirs. Heard Mus., Phoenix, Barrows Neurol. Inst., trustee; trustee Harrington Arthritis Research Ctr., St. Luke's Hosp., Phoenix Art Mus.; bd. dirs. Florence Crittenton Home.; bd. dirs. Western Arts. The Nat. Livestock show honors Yvette Ward as a Pioneer Stockman and mem. of the Ariz. Living-Stockman Hall of Fame, 1991. Mem. Phoenix Zoo Aux., Phoenix Symphony Aux., Costume Design Inst. Club: Phoenix Country. Office: Brown & Bigelow 106 E San Miguel Ave Phoenix AZ 85012-1339

WARD DIDIO, PATTY, special education educator, educational diagnostician; b. McCamey, Tex., Dec. 10, 1934; d. Frank and Bertha Ellen (Hancock) McIlhaney; m. Arthur Ward Sr., Oct. 31, 1958 (div. May 1985); children: Candice Kama, Arthur Jr., Karen Guile; m. Ugo J. DiDio, June 26, 1989. BS, U. Tex., El Paso, 1974, MEd, 1979; PhD, U. So. Miss., 1988. Cert. supt., elem. adminstr., elem. supr., spl. subject supr., psychometrist, Miss.; cert. mid mgmt. adminstr., profl. supr., profl. ednl. diagnostician, profl. counselor, profl. spl. edn. counselor, tchr., Tex. Tchr. El Paso (Tex.) Ind. Sch. Dist., 1974-79, ednl. diagnostician, 1979-86, asst. prin., 1990-91; coord. assessment Ysleta Ind. Sch. Dist., El Paso, 1991-94; ednl. diagnostician Clint (Tex.) Ind. Sch. Dist., 1991—; part time instr. U. Tex., El Paso, 1990-93. Contbr. chpts. to book. Mem. Tex. Ednl. Diagnosticians Assn. Republican. Baptist. Avocations: reading, music, writing poetry, traveling. Home: 2205 Sea Palm Dr El Paso TX 79936-3032

WARDELL, DAVID JOSEPH, travel industry specialist; b. Portland, Oreg., Feb. 4, 1956; s. Joseph Lindsay and Alice Freda (Salvisburg) W.; m. Lydia Wilhelm. Computer software developer, svc. bur. operator PDQ Data Systems, Portland, 1973-76; owner The Book House, Portland, 1974-76; agt., account exec. Gateway Travel, Portland, 1976-83; v.p. tech. services Sontag, Annis & Assocs., Inc., Rockville, Md., 1984-87; various positions including v.p. mgr. product devel., dir. bus. devel., mng. dir. vendor rels. Citicorp Info Mgmt. Services, Rockville, 1987-90; aviation, hospitality and travel industry cons., 1990-91; chief info. officer, v.p. info. svcs. US Travel, Rockville, Md., 1991-94; v.p. bus. devel. Global Travel Computer Svcs., Toronto and Vienna, Va., Ont., Can., 1994-95; sr. v.p. info. systems OAG Travel Svcs. (Reed Elsevier), Secaucus, N.J., 1995-96; exec. v.p., COO Travelogue, Inc., Washington, 1996—; pres. U.S. Matrix, Washington and Toronto, 1997—; cons. software and travel, sys. design, planning and integration; featured speaker and seminar dir. Travel Weekly, Am. So. Travel Agts., Assn. Retail Travel Agts., other groups; program dir. Travel Weekly Conf., 1996. Pub., editor: (newsletter) Automation Guidelines, 1982-84, Tech. Reality, 1993—; columnist: (trade jour.) Travel Weekly, 1985—; author of textbooks; contbr. over 300 articles to profl. jours. and gen. interest publs. Mem. IEEE, Am. Soc. Artificial Intelligence, Soc. Bibl. Lit. Republican. Mem. LDS Ch. Avocations: computer science, machine intelligence, patristics, writing, history. Home: PO Box 1746 Vienna VA 22183-1746 Office: US Matrix LLC, 7550 Birchmount Rd, Markham, ON Canada

WARDELL, JOE RUSSELL, JR., pharmacologist; b. Omaha, Nov. 11, 1929; s. Joe Russell and Marie Hamilton (Waugh) W.; m. Leta Harris, July 14, 1952 (div. Oct. 1981); children: Michael R., Susan E., John D.; m. Doris Erway, Aug. 27, 1983. BS in Pharmacy, Creighton U., 1951; MS in Pharmacology, U. Nebr., Omaha, 1959, PhD in Pharmacology, 1962. Lic. pharmacist Nebr. Pharmacist Osco Drug, Waterloo, Iowa, 1953-56; grad. asst. Coll. of Medicine U. Nebr., Omaha, 1956-62; sr. pharmacologist Smith Kline & French Labs., Phila., 1962-64, advanced to assoc. dir. biol. rsch., 1974-78; dir. R & D compound acquistions R&D, 1978-86; pres. Wardell Assocs., Park City, Utah, 1986—. Author: more than 40 articles in profl. pubs.; inventor/co-inventor 4 patents respiratory and cardiovascular drugs. Asst. scoutmaster, Boy Scouts of Am., N.J., 1969-75. Recipient Merck Award Creighton U., 1951. Mem. Soc. of Parmacology & Experiemental Therapeutics, Am. Acad. of Pharmaceutical Scis., Am. Chem. Soc., Licensing Exec. Soc., Am. Arbitration Assn. Panel Neutrals. Avocations: recreational flying, skiing, fly fishing. Home and Office: Wardell Assocs 55 Thaynes Canyon Dr Park City UT 84060-6713

WARDEN, GAIL LEE, health care executive; b. Clarinda, Iowa, May 11, 1938; s. Lee Roy and Juanita (Haley) W.; m. Lois Jean Johnson, Oct. 9, 1965; children: Jay Christopher, Janna Lynn, Jena Marie. BA, Dartmouth Coll., 1960; MHA, U. Mich., 1962. Adminstrv. asst. Blodgett Meml. Hosp., Grand Rapids, Mich., 1962; adj. Dewitt Hosp., Ft. Belvoir, Va., 1963-65; adminstrv. asst. Presbyn.-St. Luke's Hosp., Chgo., 1965-68, asst. to pres., 1968, v.p. adminstrn., 1968-69; exec. v.p. Rush-Presbyn.-St. Luke's Med. Center, Chgo., 1970-76, Am. Hosp. Assn., Chgo., 1976-81; pres., CEO Group Health Coop. Puget Sound, Seattle, 1981-88, Henry Ford Health System, Detroit, 1988—; past chmn. Am. Hosp. Assn.; bd. dirs. Medicus Systems Corp., Evanston, Ill., Comerica Bank; mem. governing coun. Inst. Medicine of NAS. Contbr. articles to profl. jours. Bd. dirs. Robert Wood Johnson Found. Served to capt. AUS, 1965. Named one of Ten Outstanding Young Men in Chgo., Jr. Assn. Commerce and Industry, 1968, Nat. Health Care award B'nai B'rith Internat., 1992, CEO award Am. Hosp. Assn.'s Soc. for Healthcare Planning and Mktg., 1993. Mem. NAS, Am. Coll. Hosp. Adminstrs. (named Young Adminstr. of Yr. 1972), Am. Pub. Health Assn., Am. Healthcare Systems, Alpha Chi Rho. Office: Henry Ford Health System 1 Ford Pl Detroit MI 48202-3450

WARDEN, HERBERT EDGAR, surgeon, educator; b. Cleve., Aug. 30, 1920; s. Fred Edgar and Eva Alethea (Powers) W.; m. Audrey Eleanor Flaten, June 14, 1958; children: Karen Eleanor, Bradford Edgar, Douglas Edward, Suzanne Elise. BS, Washington and Jefferson Coll., 1942, ScD (hon.), 1996; MD, U. Chgo., 1946. Diplomate Am. Bd. Surgery, Am. Bd. Thoracic Surgery. Intern U. Chgo. Clinics, 1946-47; med. officer U.S. Naval Hosp., Mare Island, Calif., 1947-49; surgeon USAF Hosp., Travis AFB, Calif., 1949-50; asst. resident in surgery U. Minn., Mpls., 1951-56, rsch. asst. cardio vascular surgery, 1953-56, chief resident, 1956-57, instr., 1957-60; assoc. prof. surgery W.Va. U., Morgantown, 1960-62, head cardiovascular surgery, 1960-82, prof., 1962-96, vice chmn. dept. surgery, 1968-76, prof. emeritus, 1996; cons. Louis A. Johnson VA Hosp., Clarksburg, W.Va., 1962—; bd. dirs. W.Va. U. Med. Corp., Morgantown, 1987-94; physician football team W.Va. U.; bd. dirs. First Nat. Bank, Morgantown. Contbr. articles to profl. jours. Trustee Drummond Chapel, Morgantown, 1974-78; bd. dirs. Am. Heart Assn., 1968-73, Washington and Jefferson Coll., Washington, Pa., 1974—. Lt. M.C., USNR, 1947-49. Recipient Albert Lasker award APHA, 1955, Disting. Svc. awards W. Va. Heart Assn., 1973, W. Va. U., 1976; named to the Order of Vandalia, W.Va. U., 1995; named Disting. Alumnus Washington and Jefferson Coll., 1968, U. Chgo., 1996. Fellow ACS (gov. 1988-95), Am. Coll. Cardiology (gov. 1982-85), Southeastern Surg. Congress; mem. AMA (Hektoen Gold medal 1957), Am. Surg. Assn., Am. Assn. Thoracic Surgery, Soc. Univ. Surgeons, Soc. Thoracic Sugeons (founder, chair program com. 1983-84, Chamberlin award 1985), So. Thoracic Surg. Assn., Halsted Soc., Lillehei Surg. Soc. (pres. 1988), Wangensteen Soc. (pres. 1972), Alpha Kappa Alpha, Alpha Omega Alpha,

Sigma Xi. Republican. Methodist. Avocations: golfing, fishing, gardening, reading. Home: 616 Schubert Pl Morgantown WV 26505-2330 Office: Health Scis Ctr N W Va U Morgantown WV 26505

WARDEN, JOHN L., lawyer; b. Evansville, Ind., Sept. 22, 1941; s. Walter Wilson and Juanita (Veatch) W.; m. Phillis Ann Rodgers, Oct. 27, 1960; children: Anne W. Clark, John L., W. Carson. AB, Harvard U., 1962; LLB, U. Va., 1965. Bar: N.Y. 1966, U.S. Ct. Appeals (2d cir.) 1966, U.S. Dist. Ct. (so. and ea. dists.) N.Y. 1967, U.S. Ct. Appeals (10th cir.) 1971, U.S. Supreme Ct. 1972, U.S. Ct. Appeals (D.C. cir.) 1980. Assoc. Sullivan & Cromwell, N.Y.C., 1965-73, ptnr., 1973—. Trustee U. Va. Law Sch. Found., Am. Ballet Theatre. Fellow Am. Coll. Trial Lawyers; mem. ABA, Am. Law Inst., N.Y. State Bar Assn., Assn. of Bar of City of N.Y., N.Y. County Lawyers Assn., Knickerbocker Club, Down Town Assn. Club, Bedford Golf and Tennis Club, Lyford Cay Club. Republican. Episcopalian. Editor-in-chief Va. Law Review, 1964-65. Office: Sullivan & Cromwell 125 Broad St New York NY 10004-2400

WARDEN, RICHARD DANA, government labor union official; b. Great Falls, Mont., Dec. 10, 1931; s. Robert Dickinson and Helen (Leach) W.; m. Barbara Freeman; children: Denise, Michael, Joseph, Jerome. B.A., Mont. State U., 1957, M.A., 1958. Reporter, then state editor Gt. Falls (Mont.) Tribune, 1959-61; legis. asst. to U.S. Senator Lee Metcalf of Mont., 1962-63; adminstrv. asst. to U.S. Congressman James G. O'Hara of Mich., 1963-67; dep. dir. Office Civil Rights, HEW, 1967-68; legis. rep. AFL-CIO, 1969-70; dir. Washington Research Project Action Council, 1970-72; legis. rep. UAW, 1972-75, legis. dir., 1975-77, 79-91, ret., 1991; asst. sec. legis. HEW, 1977-79. Served with USN, 1951-54. Congressional fellow, 1961-62; recipient Pub. Affairs Reporting award Am. Polit. Sci. Assn., 1960. Home: 515 School Ln Rehoboth Beach DE 19971

WARDER, MICHAEL YOUNG, think tank executive; b. Buffalo, June 29, 1946; s. Thomas Grayston and Norma A. (Young) W.; m. Cheryl Lynn Gilkerson, Feb. 8, 1975; children: Maureen, Amy, Michael Jr. BA, Stanford U., 1968. Tchr. Drew Sch., San Francisco, 1968-69; pres. Internat. Re-edn. Found., San Francisco, 1970-73; sec.-gen. Internat. Conf. on the Unity of Scis., N.Y.C., 1974-79; pres., pub. Newsworld Comm., N.Y.C., 1976-69; dir. adminstrn. Heritage Found., Washington, 1980-83; exec. v.p. Ethics and Pub. Policy Ctr., Washington, 1983-84, The Rockford (Ill.) Inst., 1985-95; v.p. devel. The Claremont (Calif.) Inst., 1995—; radio commentator (bi-weekly) Sta. WNIJ-FM NPR Affiliate, DeKalb, Ill., 1991-95, (weekly) KMNY-AM, Pomona, Calif., 1996—; del. leader People to People, USSR, 1991, Rockford Inst., Lithuania, Latvia, Estonia, 1994; del. to London Claremont Inst., 1996, del. to Hong Kong, 1997, Claremont Inst., 1997; spkr. in field. Op-ed columnist The Wall Street Jour., USA Today, The Chgo. Tribune, Chgo. Sun Times, San Francisco Chronicle, St. Louis Post Dispatch, Indpls. Star, 1985—; host/prodr. (TV weekly public affairs show) Stateline Newsmakers, 1990-92; columnist (weekly) Rockford Register Star, 1991-92, Herald Tribune, Pasadena, 1997—. Recipient Silver Dome award Ill. Broadcasters Assn., 1993, 95, 96; grantee Earhart Found., 1988. Mem. Nat. Strategy Forum (mem. rsch. comm.), Phila. Soc., L.A. World Affairs Coun., Sigma Delta Chi. Republican. Avocations: travel abroad, women's coll. basketball, history, geography. Office: The Claremont Inst 250 W 1st St Ste 330 Claremont CA 91711-4744

WARDER, RICHARD CURREY, JR., dean, mechanical aerospace engineering educator; b. Nitro, W.Va., Sept. 30, 1936; s. Richard Currey and Edith Irene (Moser) W.; m. Carolyn Strickler, Mar. 7, 1964 (div. Dec. 1978); children: Jennifer, Jeffrey W.; m. Marjorie Dianne Forney, Jan. 10, 1981. B.S., S.D. Sch. Mines, 1958; M.S., Northwestern U., 1959, Ph.D., 1963. Registered profl. engr., Mo., Tenn. Asst. prof. Northwestern U., Evanston, Ill., 1963-65; mgr. energy processes research Litton Industries, Beverly Hills, Calif., 1965-68; assoc. prof. mech. and aerospace engring. U. Mo., Columbia, 1968-72, prof., 1972-94, James C. Dowell prof., 1989-94, chmn. mech. aerospace engring., 1988-94; dean Herff Coll. of Engring. U. Memphis, Tenn., 1994—; program mgr., head resources sect. NSF, Washington, 1974-76; cons. to industry U.S. govt. Bd. dirs. Columbia Montessori Soc., 1971-73; bd. dirs. Columbia Soccer Club, 1976-80, pres., 1978-80; referee Maj. Indoor Soccer League, 1979-83. Fellow AIAA (assoc.); mem. AAAS, Am. Phys. Soc., ASME, Am. Soc. Engring. Edn., Am. Assn. for Aerosol Research, Am. Soc. Heating, Refrigerating and Air Conditioning Engrs. Methodist.

WARDLOW, BILL, record industry consultant, entertainer; b. Columbus, Ohio, Jan. 2, 1921; s. Clayton Jesse and Angeline Naomi (Peckham) W. B.B.A., Ohio State U., 1942; cert., Am. Mgmt. Assn., N.Y.C., 1964. Vice pres. Capitol Records, Los Angeles, 1947-56; gen. mgr. Columbia Record Club, N.Y.C., 1957-61; exec. v.p. Hammond Industries, N.Y.C., 1961-64; assoc. pub. Billboard Mag., N.Y.C., 1964-83; pres. Bill Wardlow & Assocs., Los Angeles, 1983—; ptnr. Dealmakers Connection, Inc., Los Angeles, 1983—; cons. to disco industry, worldwide, 1974-83. Author preface: This Business of Disco, 1976; TV appearances include 60 Minutes, Merv Griffin Show, Mike Douglas Show, Ted Turner Network. Named Father of Disco Rec. Industry Am., 1976; reipient numerous Gold and Platinum records, 1974-83. Episcopalian. Club: Regines (N.Y.C.). Home and Office: care Williams 11012 Ventura Blvd # 138 Studio City CA 91604-3546 *Always be interested in the careers of those around you; i.e., recording artists. Discover them, help in every way possible for them to achieve stardom. And by helping others reach their goals, you have automatically reached yours.*

WARD NEVILLE, JOHANNA (ANNE), government official; b. Amersfoort, Geldland, The Netherlands, Aug. 25, 1947; arrived in Canada, 1952; d. Teunis and Maria (Van De Wetering) Schimmel; m. John Neville, Apr. 27, 1967 (div. Dec. 1985); 1 child, tracy; m. Timothy Keith Ward, Dec. 27, 1986; children: Jeffrey, Darren. BSW, U. Calgary, Alta., 1981; MSc in Econs., London Sch. Econs., 1984. Registered psychiat. nurse. Staff nurse psychiat. ward Holy Cross Hosp., Calgary, 1968-74, team leader, 1973-74; child welfare worker Govt. of Alta., Calgary, 1974-76, dist. mgr. social svcs., 1976-83; dir. audit br. social svcs., cmty. health Govt. of Alta., Edmonton, 1985-86; regional dir. social svcs. Govt. of Alta., 1986-93; exec. dir. income and employment programs br. Govt. of Alta., Edmonton, 1993—, project mgr. welfare programs, 1993-96; critic Doubleday Books. Mem. Victoria Bus. Ladies Golf Club. Avocations: reading, travel, walking, golf. Office: Alberta Family & Social Svc, 7th St Plz 10030 107 St 14th Fl, Edmonton, AB Canada T5J 3E4

WARDROPPER, BRUCE WEAR, language educator; b. Edinburgh, Scotland, Feb. 2, 1919; came to U.S., 1945; s. Joseph Blair and Edna (Bruce) W.; m. Joyce Vaz, Dec. 15, 1942 (dec. Mar. 1959); 1 son, Ian Bruce; m. Nancy Hélène Palmer, July 19, 1960. Student, King Edward's Sch., Birmingham, Eng., 1932-36; B.A., U. Cambridge, 1939, M.A., 1942; Ph.D., U. Pa., 1949. Head modern lang. dept. Wolmer's Sch., Kingston, Jamaica, 1940-45; instr. U. Pa., 1945-49; asst. prof. Johns Hopkins U., 1949-53, asso. prof., 1953-55, chmn. dept. Romance langs., 1954-55, prof. Spanish, 1959-62; William H. Wannamaker prof. Romance langs. Duke U., 1962-89, William H. Wannamaker prof. Romance studies emeritus, 1989—; prof. Spanish, Ohio State U., 1955-59; vis. Andrew Mellon prof. Romance langs. U. Pitts., 1965; vis. prof. U. N.C., 1967-68; cons. bd. overseers U. Louisville, 1976-78; NEH Fellowships in Residence Program, 1977-78; seminar dir. NEHSummer Seminars for Coll. Tchrs., 1975, 76, 81; mem. ednl. adv. bd. John Simon Guggenheim Meml. Found., 1978-82. Author: Introducción al teatro religioso, 1953, Historia de la poesía lírica a lo divino, 1958, Critical Essays on the Theatre of Calderón, 1965, Poesía elegíaca española, 1967, Teatro español del Siglo de Oro, 1970, Spanish Poetry of the Golden Age, 1971; co-author: Teoría de la comedia: La comedia española del Siglo de Oro, 1978; mem. editorial bd., PMLA (MLA), 1962-69, 73-75; assoc. editor: Purdue U. Monographs in Romance Langs., 1978-90; editor, translator: (Calderon) El Magico Prodigioso, 1982; editor Historia y Critica de la Literatura Española, vol. 3: Barroco, 1983. Guggenheim fellow, 1952, 59; Recipient award Am. Philos. Soc., 1957, award Am. Council Learned Socs., 1959, fellow, 1969. Mem. MLA (editorial bd. PMLA 1973-75), Internat. Assn. Hispanists (exec. com. 1971-77), Renaissance Soc. Am., South Atlantic MLA, Acad. Lit. Studies (membership com. 1973-78), Assn. Hispanists Gt. Britain and Ireland, Modern Humanities Research Assn. (Am. com. 1976-80), Cervantes Soc. Am. (v.p. 1980-83, pres. 1983-85, Am. com. 1976-90). Home: 3443 Rugby Rd Hope Valley Durham NC 27707

WARDROPPER, IAN BRUCE, museum curator, educator; b. Balt., May 11, 1951; s. Bruce Wear and Joyce (Vaz) W.; stepmother: Nancy Hélène (Palmer) W.; m. Laurel Ellen Bradley, May 22, 1982; 1 child, Chloe Bradley. BA, Brown U., 1973; MA, NYU, 1976, PhD, 1985. Asst. curator European sculpture Art Inst. Chgo., 1982-85, assoc. curator European decorative arts and sculpture, 1985-89, Eloise W. Martin curator European decorative arts and sculpture, and classical art, 1989—; adj. instr. Drew U., N.J., 1982; vis. asst. prof. Northwestern U., Evanston, Ill., 1986, Sch. of Art Inst. Chgo., 1988; guest scholar J. Paul Getty Mus., Malibu, Calif., 1995; Rhoades lectr. U. Chgo., 1997. Co-author: European Decorative Arts in the Art Institute of Chicago, 1991, Austrian Architecture and Design beyond Tradition in the 1990s, 1991, News from a Radiant Future: Soviet Porcelain from the Collection of Craig H. and Kay A. Tuber, 1992, Chiseled with a Brush: Italian Sculpture, 1860-1925, from The Gilgore Collections, 1994; contbr. articles to profl. jours. Mem. sculpture and garden ornament com. Chgo. Bot. Garden, Glencoe, Ill., 1988—. NEA fellow, 1976-77, Chester Dale fellow Met. Mus. Art, 1978-79; Kress Found. rsch. grantee, Paris, 1979-81, Am. Philos. Soc. grantee, 1991; named Chicagoan of the Yr. in Arts Chicago Tribune, 1994. Mem. Phi Beta Kappa. Office: The Art Inst Chgo 111 S Michigan Ave Chicago IL 60603-6110

WARD-STEINMAN, DAVID, composer, music educator, pianist; b. Alexandria, La., Nov. 6, 1936; s. Irving Steinman and Daisy Leila (Ward) W.-S.; m. Susan Diana Lucas, Dec. 28, 1956; children: Jenna, Matthew. MusB cum laude, Fla. State U., 1957; MusM, U. Ill., 1958, DMA, 1961; studies with Nadia Boulanger, Paris, 1958-59; postdoctoral vis. fellow, Princeton U., 1970. Grad. instr. U. Ill., 1957-58; mem. faculty San Diego State U., 1961—, prof. music, 1968—, dir. comprehensive musicianship program, 1972—, composer in residence, 1961—, univ. research lectr., 1986-87; mem. summer faculty Eastman Sch. Music Workshop, 1969; Ford Found. composer in residence Tampa Bay (Fla.) Area, 1970-72, Brevard Music Ctr., N.C., summer 1986; acad. cons. U. North Sumatra (Indonesia), 1982; concert and lecture tour U.S. Info. Agy., Indonesia, 1982; mem. faculty Coll. Music Soc. Nat. Inst. for Music in Gen. Studies, U. Colo., 1983, 84, Calif. State Summer Sch. for the Arts, Loyola Marymount U., 1988; master tchr. in residence Atlantic Ctr. for the Arts, New Smyrna Beach, Fla., summer 1996; vis. artist in residence Victorian Ctr. for the Arts, Melbourne, Australia, summer 1997. Composer: Symphony, 1959, Prelude & Toccata for orch., 1962, Concerto No. 2 for chamber orch., 1962, ballet Western Orpheus, 1964, Cello Concerto, 1966, These Three ballet, 1966, The Tale of Issoumbochi chamber opera, 1968, Rituals for Dancers and Musicians, 1971, Antares, 1971, Arcturus, 1972, The Tracker, 1976, Brancusi's Brass Beds, 1977; oratorio Song of Moses, 1964; Jazz Tangents, 1967, Childs Play, 1968; 3-act opera Tamar, 1977; Golden Apples, 1981; choral suite Of Wind and Water, 1982; Christmas cantata And In These Times, 1982; Moiré for piano and chamber ensemble, 1983, And Waken Green, song cycle on poems by Douglas Worth, 1983, Olympics Overture for orchestra, 1984, Children's Corner Revisited, song cycle, 1984, Summer Suite for oboe and piano, 1984, Quintessence for double quintet and percussion, 1985, Chroma concerto for multiple keyboards, percussion and chamber orch., 1985, Winging It for chamber orchestra, 1986, Elegy for Astronauts, for orchestra, 1986, What's Left for piano, 1987, Gemini for 2 guitars, 1988, Intersections II: Borobudur, Under Capricorn, 1989, 1989 Voices from the Gallery, 1990, Cinnabar for viola and piano, 1991, Seasons Fantastic for chorus and harp, 1992, Cinnabar Concerto for Viola and Chamber Orchestra, 1993, Night Winds Quintet # 2 for woodwinds, 1993, Double Concerto for Two Violins and Orchestra, 1995, Prisms and Reflections (3rd Piano Sonata), 1996; recs. include Fragments from Sappho, 1969; Duo for cello and piano, 1974, Childs Play for bassoon and piano, 1974, The Tracker, 1989, Brancusi's Brass Beds, 1984, concert suite from Western Orpheus, 1987, Sonata for Piano Fortified, 1987, Moiré, 1987, 3 Songs for Clarinet and Piano, 1987, Concerto #2 for Chamber Orchestra, 1990; commd. by Chgo. Symphony, Joffrey Ballet, numerous others; author: (with Susan L. Ward-Steinman) Comparative Anthology of Musical Forms, 2 vols, 1976, Toward a Comparative Structural Theory of the Arts, 1989. Recipient Joseph H. Bearns prize in Music Columbia U., 1961, SAI Am. Music award, 1962, Dohnanyi award Fla. State U., 1965, ann. BMI awards, 1970—, Broadcast Music prize, 1954, 55, 60, 61; named Outstanding Prof., Calif. State Univs. and Colls., 1968, Outstanding Alumnus of Yr., Fla. State U., 1976; Fulbright sr. scholar La Trobe U. and Victorian Coll. Arts, Victorian Arts Ctr., Melbourne, Australia, 1989-90. Mem. Coll. Music Soc. (nat. bd. for composition 1991-93), Broadcast Music, Inc., Soc. of Composers, inc., Nat. Assn. of Composers U.S.A., Golden State Flying Club. Presbyterian. Office: San Diego State U Dept Music San Diego CA 92182

WARDWELL, ALLEN, art historian; b. N.Y.C., Jan. 18, 1935; s. Edward Rogers and Lelia (Morgan) W.; m. Sarah Williams Tilghman, June 29, 1957; children: William Thomas, Lelia Morgan, Alexander Tilghman. Grad., Groton Sch., 1953; BA, Yale, 1957; MA, NYU, 1960. Asst. curator primitive art dept. Art Inst. Chgo., 1960-62, curator, 1962-73, acting curator decorative arts dept., 1963-70, asst. dir. mus. svcs., 1969-72; dir. Gallery Asia Soc., N.Y.C., 1974-84, Isamu Noguchi Garden Mus., 1985-90; sr. cons. on tribal art Christie's, N.Y.C., 1992—; vis. prof. art history Princeton (N.J.) U., 1994-95. Trustee Yale Art Gallery; adv. coun. U. Notre Dame Art Gallery, 1970-84; mem. mus. panel Indo-U.S. Subcommn. Edn. and Culture, 1975-84; mem. vis. com. Asian Art Met. Mus. Art, 1977—. Mem. Coll. Art Assn., Am. Mus. Assn. Office: 88 Central Park W New York NY 10023-5209

WARE, BRENDAN JOHN, retired electrical engineer and utility executive; b. Dublin, Ireland, Aug. 27, 1932; came to U.S., 1959, naturalized, 1967; s. Michael and Rose Anna (Ryan) W.; m. Jane Mills Orth, Oct. 7, 1961; children—Michael, Henry, Frieda. B.E. with honors, Nat. U. Ireland, Dublin, 1954; M.S.E.E., Newark Coll. Engring., 1967. Various engring. positions Am. Elec. Power Service Corp., N.Y.C., 1960-76; mgr. elec. research and tech. svcs. Am. Elec. Power Service Corp., Columbus, Ohio, 1976-96. Contbr. articles to profl. jours. Fellow IEEE; mem. Conf. Internat. de Grand Reseau. Roman Catholic. Home: 2478 Bryden Rd Columbus OH 43209-2132

WARE, D. CLIFTON, singer, educator; b. Newton, Miss., Mar. 15, 1937; s. Durward Clifton and Emma Edna (Blount) W.; m. Elizabeth Jean Oldham, June 20, 1958; children: Jon Clifton, David Michael, Stephen Alan. B.A., Millsaps Coll., 1959; MusM, U. So. Miss., 1962; MusD, Northwestern U., 1970. Voice instr. U. So. Miss., Hattiesburg, Miss., 1964-69; coord. voice instrn., chmn. Roy A. Schuessler Vocal Arts Ctr. U. Minn., Mpls., 1970—; clinician, cons., adjudicator. Author: (book, song collection and video) Voice Adventures, 1988, (text, song collection, audio cassette, CD) Adventures in Singing, 1995; made recs. St. Nicolas, 1977, Paul Bunyan, 1988; tenor soloist opera, oratorio, recitals. Mem. Nat. Assn. Tchrs. Singing (pres. Minn. chpt. 1972-73, 81-82, bd. dirs. 1995—), Nat. Opera Assn. (pres. 1978-79), Pi Kappa Lambda, Phi Kappa Delta, Phi Mu Alpha Sinfonia, Pi Kappa Alpha. Avocations: travel, hiking, reading. Home: 1923 3rd St NW New Brighton MN 55112-7254 Office: U Minn Sch Music 100 Ferguson Minneapolis MN 55455

WARE, JAMES EDWIN, retired international company executive; b. Athens, Ga., Jan. 27, 1925; s. James Edwin and Marguerite (McCue) W.; m. Petronella J. Knoors, Dec. 13, 1952; children: Marguerite Linda, Jennifer Ellen. Student, St. Petersburg Jr. Coll., Fla., 1942-43, Rutgers U., 1943-44; M.E., Stevens Inst. Tech., 1948. Salesman Chgo. Pneumatic Tool Co., N.Y.C., N.Y., 1948-61; gen. sales mgr. Hoke, Inc., Cresskill, N.J., 1961-63; mgr. instrument systems sales McKiernan Terry div. Litton Industries, Clifton, N.J., 1963-66; dir. marketing, mining and constrn. div. Joy Mfg. Co., Claremont, N.H., 1966-67; v.p., gen. mgr. Picker X-Ray Co., White Plains, N.Y., 1967-70; pres., gen. mgr. Northrop Archtl. Systems, City of Industry, Calif., 1971-82; v.p. Northrop Corp., 1971-82, dir. comml. internat. offset trade program, 1982-84; dir. Shinko-Northrop, Japan, dir. Société d'Etudes et de Prefabrication, France., dir. Industry Mfrs. Council, City of Industry, Calif., 1971-74. Served with inf. AUS, World War II, ETO. Decorated Bronze Star. Home: 10952 Cherry Hill Dr Santa Ana CA 92705-2442

WARE, JAMES W., federal judge; b. 1946. BA, Calif. Luth. U., 1969; JD, Stanford U., 1972. Assoc. Blase, Valentine & Klein, Palo Alto, Calif., 1972-77, ptnr., 1977; judge Santa Clara County Superior Ct., U.S. Dist. Ct. (no. dist.) Calif., 1990—; pro bono East Palo Alto Law Project. Active Am. Leadership Forum; mem. bd. visitors Stanford Law Sch.; active Martin Luther King Papers Project. 2nd lt. USAR, 1969-86. Office: US Dist Cts US Courthouse Rm 4150 280 S 1st St San Jose CA 95113-3002*

WARE, LUCILE MAHIEU, child psychiatrist, educator, researcher; b. Kansas City, Mo., Feb. 23, 1929; d. Robert Georges and Lucile (Bailey) Mahieu; m. Jean Andre Demonchaux, Sept. 4, 1958; children: Elisabeth (dec.), Catherine, Theodore. AB cum laude, Bryn Mawr Coll., 1949; MD, Columbia U., 1953. Diplomate Am. Bd. Psychiatry and Neurology, Am. Bd. Child Psychiatry. Staff psychiatrist, Children's Div. Menninger Clinic, Topeka, 1968-93, dir. Presch. Day Treatment Ctr., 1972-93; dir. admissions and diagnosis Children's Div. Menninger Clinic, 1974-75,77,78; cons. No. Topeka Head Start, 1976-93, co-principle investigator, DHHS-NIMH (CPR) MH#39895, 1982-87; mem. faculty Karl Menninger Sch. of Psychiatry, Topeka, 1969-93, Topeka Inst. for Psychoanalysis, 1974—; cons. C.F. Menninger Hosp. and Children's Hosp., Topeka, 1975-93, rschr. The Menninger Clinic, 1982—. Contbr. articles to profl. jours. Assoc. leader Campfire Girls, Topeka, 1968-72; bd. dirs. Dance Arts of Topeka, 1974-77; bd. dirs., founder Ballet Midwest, 1977-88; bd. dirs. Shawnee County Med. Soc., 1992-94. Fellow Albert Einstein Coll. Med. N.Y.C., 1957-58, Seeley Fellow Menninger Found. Children's Div.; named Kenworthy Prof., Menninger Found., 1983-84. Fellow Am. Assn. Child and Adolescent Psychiatry, Am. Psychiatric Assn. (life); mem. Kans. Assn. for Infant Mental Health (founder, pres., bd. dirs.). Club: Alliance Francaise (Topeka). Home: 1925 SW Wayne Ave Topeka KS 66604-3138 Office: Menninger Clinic Rsch Dept PO Box 829 Topeka KS 66601-0829

WARE, PEGGY JENKINS, photographer, writer, artist, dancer; b. Santa Monica, Calif., Sept. 6, 1947; d. Stanley Lauder Mahony and Patricia Lou Chapman Covo; m. James Michael Jenkins, Feb. 5, 1966 (div. May 1982) 1 child, Cheryl Denise Jenkins; m. Wiley Neal Ware, Jan. 1, 1988. Dance student of Eugene Loring, U. Calif., Irvine, 1979; dance student Valentina Oumansky, Dramatic Dance Ensemble, North Hollywood, Calif., 1969-72; dance student, Jerry Bywaters Cochran, Dallas, 1972-75; photography student of James Baker, U. Tex., Dallas, Richardson, 1984-86; BA in English, U. Tex. at Dallas, Richardson, 1986, postgrad., 1987. Propr. Mahony/Jenkins & Assocs., Richardson, 1980-82; mng. editor, writer Happenings Mag., Dallas, 1983; prodn. supr. Publishing Concepts, Dallas, 1983-85; mem. book prodn. team David Marquis/Robin Sachs-Corp. for Edn., Dallas, 1990; freelance photographer and artist Dallas, 1984-95, Sedona, Ariz., 1995—; rsch. editor Prin. Fin. Securities, Dallas, 1994; dance rsch. interviewer Simon Semenoff, Ballet Russe, Sol Hurok, Impressario. Exhbns. include Allen St. Gallery, Dallas, 1985, Oak Cliff Art Festival, Dallas, 1991, 500 Inc. Artfest, Dallas, 1992, Sedona Art and Wine Festival, 1993, Good Dog/Bad Dog, Dallas, 1994, Internat. FotoFest, 1994, Lakewood Svc. League, Dallas, 1995, Bath House Cultural Ctr., 1995, Irvine (Calif.) Fine Arts Ctr., 1995-96, Select Art Gallery, Sedona, 1996, Sedona Arts Festival, 1996; transcribing editor: I Am a Teacher, A Tribute to America's Teachers, 1990; photographer: Photo Essay of the Berlin Wall, 1988; contbr. articles and photos to mags. Exec. bd. Friends of Photography, Dallas Mus. Art, 1993-94; bd. dirs., trustee Dancers Unltd. Repertory Co., Dallas, 1990-91; contbr. photographer Lakewood Svc. League, Dallas, 1992; writer, video producer Women's Conf., Women's Caucus for Art, Dallas, 1986. Home: 62 Morning Sun Dr Sedona AZ 86336 Office: PO Box 1891 Sedona AZ 86339-1891

WARE, RICHARD ANDERSON, foundation executive; b. N.Y.C., Nov. 7, 1919; s. John Sayers and Mabelle (Anderson) W.; m. Lucille Henney, Mar. 20, 1942 (div. 1972); children: Alexander W., Janet M., Bradley J., Patricia E.; m. Beverly G. Mytinger, Dec. 22, 1972. BA, Lehigh U., 1941; M in Pub. Adminstrn., Wayne State U., 1943; D in Social Sci. (honoris causa), Francisco Marroquin U., Guatemala, 1988. Research asst. Detroit Bur. Govt. Research, 1941-42; personnel technician Lend-Lease Adminstrn., Washington, 1942-43; research asso. to asst. dir. Citizens Research Council, Detroit, 1946-56; sec. Earhart and Relm Founds., Ann Arbor, Mich., 1951-70; trustee, pres. Earhart and Relm Founds., 1970-84, trustee, pres. emeritus, 1985—; prin. dep. asst. sec. def. for internat. security affairs, Washington, 1969-70; cons. Office Asst. Sec. Def., 1970-73; dir. Citizens Trust Co., 1970-87. Vice pres. Ann Arbor United Fund and Community Svcs., 1968, pres., 1969; asst. dir. Mich. Joint Legis. Com. on State Reorgn., 1950-52; sec. Gov.'s Com. to Study Prisons, 1952-53; com. to chmn. Ann Arbor City Planning Commn., 1958-67; mem. Detroit Com. on Fgn. Rels., 1971-87; mem. coun. Woodrow Wilson Internat. Center for Scholars, 1977-85; vis. com. div. social scis. U. Chgo., 1977-85; mem. adv. com. The Citadel, 1977-85; mem. adv. coun. internat. studies program Fletcher Sch., Tufts U., 1979-85; trustee Greenhills Sch., 1973-80, Ann Arbor Area Found., 1977-83, Inst. Fgn. Policy Analysis, 1985—, Inst. Polit. Economy, 1985—, Ctr. for Study Social and Polit. Change Smith Coll., 1988—, Pequawket Found., 1989—, Intercollegiate Studies Inst., 1996—; polit. analyst Republican Nat. Com., Washington, 1964; bd. dirs. The Liberty Fund, Inc., Indpls., 1980—, Bd. Fgn. Scholarships, 1984-90, chmn., 1987-89. With USAAF, 1943-46. Recipient Civilian Meritorious Service medal Dept. Def., 1970. Mem. Govtl. Research Assoc. (trustee, v.p. 1955-56), Am. Polit. Sci. Assn., Mont Pelerin Soc., Phi Beta Kappa, Phi Alpha Theta. Congregationalist. Clubs: Ann Arbor; North Conway Country, Cosmos (Washington). Home: PO Box 310 Intervale NH 03845-0310 Office: 2200 Green Rd Ste H Ann Arbor MI 48105-1569

WARE, THADDEUS VAN, government official; b. High Point, N.C., Mar. 31, 1935; s. Elsec and Irene (Myers) W.; m. Doretha Ardella Lee, June 18, 1960; children—Kimberly Melissa, Chrystal Lynn. B.A. cum laude, Va. Union U., 1957; J.D., Howard U., 1960. Bar: Va. bar 1961, D.C. bar 1970, U.S. Supreme Ct. bar 1970. Gen. atty. Office of Solicitor, Dept. Labor, 1961-66; trial counsel Chief Counsel's Office, Fed. Hwy. Adminstrn., 1966-69; staff asst. to Pres. Richard M. Nixon, 1969-70; chief adminstrv. judge, chmn. Bd. Contract Appeals, Dept. Transp., 1987—. Served with AUS, 1960-61. Mem. Va., D.C., U.S. Supreme Ct., Fed. Bar Assns., Urban League, NAACP, Bd. Contract Appeals Judges Assn. (pres. 1988-89), Alpha Phi Alpha, Sigma Delta Tau, Alpha Kappa Mu. Home: 2213 Parallel Ln Silver Spring MD 20904-5446 Office: 400 7th St SW Washington DC 20590-0001

WARE, THOMAS EARLE, building consultant; b. Cleve., Apr. 13, 1931; s. Orval Bertele and Dorothy Lillian (Brammar) W.; m. Ann Sanborn Gilkey, Dec. 21, 1955 (div. Dec. 1960); 1 child, Thomas Earle Jr.; m. Gillian May Arnold, June 8, 1968 (div. Dec. 1983); 1 child, Elizabeth; m. Mary Erin Chandler, Apr. 19, 1994. BArch, Cornell U., 1955. Assoc. ptnr. Kelly and Kress and Assocs., Architects and Planners, Cleve., 1955-59; project architect J. Gordon Lorimer, F.A.I.A., N.Y.C., 1959; gen. mgr., ptnr. Project Design, Inc., Cleve., 1960-64; project architect, mgr. Cleve. dist. and hdqrs. The Austin Co., 1961-68; project architect, mgr., asst. and acting chief bldg. systems sect., bldg. rsch. divsn. Inst. Applied Tech., Nat. Bur. Standards U.S. Dept. Commerce, Washington, 1968-71; sr. program specialist, Office of the Sec., Office of Asst. Sec. for Sci. and Tech., Office of Dep. Asst. Sec. for Environ. Affairs U.S. Dept. Commerce, 1971-72; with Bldg. Cons., Reston, Va., 1972-73; v.p., dir. Bldg. Tech., Inc., Silver Spring, Md., 1973—, TCSB, Inc., Silver Spring, Md., Tehran and Shiraz, Iran, 1974-82; instr. continuing engring. edn. program, Sch. Engring. and Applied Sci., George Washington U., 1969-71; lectr. dept. architecture The Cath. U. Am., 1969-71; lectr., discussion leader U. Wis.-Ext., 1980-83; presenter in field. Contbr. articles to profl. jours. Named Architect of Yr., D.C. Coun. Engring. and Archtl. Socs., 1971; recipient Sci. and Tech. fellowship U.S. Dept. Commerce, 1971. Mem. Nat. Inst. Bldg. Scis., Am. Soc. Am. Mil. Engrs., Constrn. Specifications Inst. Home: 11478 Links Dr Reston VA 22190-4814 Office: Bldg Tech Inc 1109 Spring St Silver Spring MD 20910-4002

WARE, WILLIAM BRETTEL, education educator; b. Glen Ridge, N.J., June 17, 1942; s. Howard Brettel and Helen Burd (Dickson) W.; m. Andrea Lou Gartley, June 24, 1967 (div. May 1989); children: Emily Dickson, Matthew Brettel, Erin Johanna Ware; m. Barbara Ann McClave Reynolds, Dec. 26, 1991; stepchildren: Dianne Catherine, Kristin Elise. AB, Dartmouth Coll., 1964; MA in Tchg., Northwestern U., 1965, PhD, 1968. Classroom tchr. Chgo. Pub. Schs., 1964-65; asst. prof. U. Fla., Gainesville,

1968-73, assoc. prof., 1973-76, prof., 1976-78; prof. U. N.C., Chapel Hill, 1978—. Contbr. chpts. to books and articles to profl. jours. Mgr. youth soccer team Ctrl. Carolina Youth Soccer Assn., Chapel Hill, 1980-86. Recipient J. Minor Gwynn professorship Sch. Edn., U. N.C., 1994-95, Chancellor's Award for Disting. Tchg., 1995. Mem. Am. Ednl. Rsch. Assn., Nat. Coun. on Measurement in Edn., N.C. Assn. for Rsch. in Edn. (bd. dirs. 1991—, pres. 1996-97), Psychometric Soc., Am. Evaluation Assn. Home: 110 Princeton Rd Chapel Hill NC 27516-3222 Office: Sch Edn U N C CB #3500 Chapel Hill NC 27599-3500

WARE, WILLIAM LEVI, physical education educator, researcher; b. Greenwood, Miss., May 15, 1934; s. Leslie and Catherine (Bowden) W.; m. Lottie Herger, Apr. 26, 1958; children: Felicia Rogene, Trevor Lesleo, Melvinia Simone. BS, Mississippi Valley State U., 1957; MA, Calif. State U., L.A., 1969; PhD, U. So. Calif., 1978. Tchr., coach Greenwood Pub. Schs., 1957-63, Bellflower (Calif.) Unified Sch. Dist., 1963-72; teaching asst. U. So. Calif., L.A., 1972-73; asst. prof. Calif. State U., Northridge, 1973-79; assoc. prof. Miss. State U., Starkville, 1979-90; prof. phys. edn., chmn. dept. Mississippi Valley State U., Itta Bena, 1990—, asst. to pres., 1996—; presenter in field; chmn. Delta Algebra Project Planning & Coordinating Group, 1991-93. Advisor Affirmative Action Adv. Coun., Whittier, Calif., 1977-78; bd. dirs. United Way, Starkville, 1983-86. Recipient Outstanding Svc. award Kiwanis Internat., 1985, Outstanding Educator award Greenwood Cultural Club, 1986, Presdl. citation Nat. Assn. for Equal Opportunity in Higher Edn., 1989; Inducted into Southwestern Athletic Conf. Hall of Fame, 1993; Faculty fellow Found. for Mid-South, 1994. Mem. Phi Delta Kappa (svc. award 1989), Greenwood/Leflore C. of C. (chmn. Leadership Tomorrow 1992-93). Avocations: racquetball, jogging. Office: Miss Valley State U PO Box 620 Itta Bena MS 38941-0620

WARE, WILLIS HOWARD, computer scientist; b. Atlantic City, Aug. 31, 1920; s. Willis and Ethel (Rosswork) W.; m. Floy Hoffer, Oct. 10, 1943; children—Deborah Susanne Ware Pinson, David Willis, Alison Floy Ware Manoli. B.S.E.E., U. Pa., 1941; M.S.E.E., MIT, 1942; Ph.D. in Elec. Engring, Princeton U., 1951. Research engr. Hazeltine Electronics Corp., Little Neck, N.Y., 1942-46; mem. research staff Inst. Advanced Study, Princeton, N.J., 1946-51, North Am. Aviation, Downey, Calif., 1951-52; mem. corp. research staff Rand Corp., Santa Monica, Calif., 1952—; adj. prof. UCLA Extension Service, 1955-68; first chmn. Am. Fedn. Info. Processing Socs., 1961, 62; chmn. HEW sec.'s Adv. Com. on Automated Personal Data Systems, 1971-73; mem. Privacy Protection Study Commn., 1975-77, vice chmn., 1975-77; mem. numerous other adv. groups, spl. coms. for fed. govt., 1959—. Author: Digital Computer Technology and Design, vols. I and II, 1963. Recipient Computers Scis. Man of Yr. award Data Processing Mgmt. Assn., 1975, Exceptional Civilian Svc. medal USAF, 1979, Disting. Svc. award Am. Fedn. Info. Processing Socs., 1986, Nat. Computer Sys. Security award Nat. Computer Sys. Lab./Nat. Computer Security Ctr., 1989, Computer Pioneer award IEEE Computer Soc., 1993, Pioneer award Electronic Frontier Found., 1995; named one of Fed. 100 of 1994, Fed. Computer Week. Fellow IEEE (Centennial medal 1984), AAAS, Assn. for Computing Machinery; mem. NAE, AIAA, Sigma Xi, Eta Kappa Nu, Pi Mu Epsilon, Tau Beta Pi. Office: The Rand Corp 1700 Main St Santa Monica CA 90401-3208

WAREHAM, RAYMOND NOBLE, investment banker; b. Rochester, N.Y., Nov. 20, 1948; s. Simon Harold and Barbara (Snell) W.; m. Cornelia Lee Clifford, June 28, 1975; children: Ellinor Park, Laura Stewart, Cornelia Ashley. BS in Indsl. Engring., Northwestern U., 1970; MBA, Harvard U., 1975. With J.P. Morgan & Co., N.Y., 1975-80; head-corp. fin. J.P. Morgan & Co., Tokyo, 1980-85; exec. dir. J.P. Morgan Securities Ltd., London, 1986-87; mngr. dir., head banking industry group J.P. Morgan & Co., N.Y., 1988-92; mng. dir. corp. fin. dept. J.P. Morgan Securities, N.Y.C., 1992—. Pres. bd. trustees Spence Sch., N.Y.C.; trustee Am. Sch., Tokyo, 1982-85; elder Brick Presbyn. Ch., N.Y.C., 1989-92; bd. dirs. Brick Ch. Day Sch., 1989-92. Lt. Supply Corps, USN, 1970-73. Mem. DERU (Northwestern hon.), Union Club (N.Y.), Duxbury Yacht Club, Century Club (Harvard Bus. hon.). Republican. Avocations: athletics, Japanese antique furniture, secondary school education. Home: 1148 Fifth Ave New York NY 10128-0807 Office: JP Morgan Securities Inc 60 Wall St New York NY 10005-2836

WAREN, ALLAN DAVID, computer information scientist, educator; b. Toronto, Ontario, Can., Nov. 23, 1935; s. David and Sirkka Siiri (Kahara) W.; m. Marion Veronica Halligan, Jan. 25, 1962; children: David, Melissa, Melanie, Jessica. BASc, U. Toronto, 1960; MSEE, Case Inst. Tech., Cleve., 1962, PhD, 1964. Profl. engr., Ontario. Staff engr. Clevite Electronics Research Div., Cleve., 1963-66; assoc. prof. Cleve. State U., 1966-69, prof., 1971-93, prof. emeritus, 1993—, interim dean Coll. Bus. Adminstrn., 1990-91; pres. Com-Share Ltd., Toronto, 1969-71; cons. Gould, Cleve., 1974-84, Texaco, Houston, 1987-88, PPG Industries, Cleve., 1988-92, LTV Steel, 1993-96, Transat Corp., Cleve., 1996—; v.p. Optimal Methods, Austin, Tex., 1993—; expert witness Rose Law Firm, 1993-95. Co-author: Modeling and Optimization with Gino, 1986, Optimization with the IBM Optimization Subroutine Library, 1994, Handbook for IBM OSL, 1994; co-developer computer software GRG2, 1973, What-If-Solver, 1988, Excel Solver, 1991, Borland Quatro Pro Solver, 1991; co-author case study, 1985 (runner-up best case 1985); contbr. articles to profl. jours. Recipient Disting. Faculty Rsch. award, Cleve. State U., 1979, First Annual Faculty Rsch. award, Nance Coll. of Bus. Adminstrn., 1993, grant in Ohio Rsch. Challenge Program, State of Ohio, 1988, various other rsch. grants, 1973-84. Mem. IEEE (sr.), Assn. Computing Machinery, Ops. Rsch. Soc. Am., Math. Programming Soc. Avocations: Oriental objects of art, philately. Home: 9155 Woodsway Dr Willoughby OH 44094-9370 Office: Cleve State U E 24th and Euclid Ave Cleveland OH 44115

WAREN, STANLEY A., university administrator, theatre and arts center administrator, director; b. N.Y.C., Mar. 22, 1919; s. Maurice and Minnie (Rosen) W.; m. Florence Rigal, Nov. 21, 1949; 1 child, Mark. B.S.S., CCNY, 1938; M.A., Columbia U., 1939, Ph.D., 1953. Exec. producer, dir. theatre U.S. and abroad, 1953-70; prof., chmn. dept. speech and theatre CCNY, 1967-72; prof., exec. officer Ph.D. program theatre CUNY, 1972-81, v.p., provost, dep. pres. Grad. Sch., 1981-84; dir. Ctr. for Advanced Study in Theatre Arts, N.Y.C., 1979-82, 84-86; reviewer NEH, 1978-91; advisor humanities com. Bklyn. Acad. Music, N.Y.C., 1980-81; spl. edn. cons. Double Image Theatre, N.Y.C., 1982-90; mem. adv. council Roundabout Theatre, N.Y.C., 1985—; Fulbright-Hayes vis. prof. Nat. Taiwan U., 1986-87; vis. prof. Shanghai Drama Inst., 1988. Dir. musical The Chess King (Taiwan) 1987, Old B Hanging on the Wall (Shanghai), 1988, Judas, Mexico (N.Y.), 1989. Bd. dirs. Women's Inter. Art Ctr., N.Y.C., 1978-82; mem. grants panel N.Y.C. Dept. Cultural Affairs, 1979; bd. dirs. Frank Silvera Workshops for Writers, N.Y.C., 1979-81. Served to capt. USAF, 1942-46. Grantee Herman Goldman Found., 1980-82, NEH, 1980-81, N.Y. Coun. Humanities, USIA/Arts Am., Singapore, 1990. Mem. AAUP, Soc. Stage Dirs. and Choreographers, Profl. Staff Congress CUNY. Democrat. Club: The Century Assn. (resident 1984—). Avocations: arts; tennis; swimming. Home: 465 W End Ave New York NY 10024-4926 Office: CUNY Grad Sch 33 W 42nd St New York NY 10036-8003

WARFEL, JOHN HIATT, medical educator, retired; b. Marion, Ind., Mar. 3, 1916; s. Robert A. and Mary (Hiatt) W.; m. Marjorie Jane Wolfe, Oct. 28, 1942; children: Barbara, Susan, David. BS, Capital U., 1938; MS, Ohio State U., 1941; PhD, Case Western Res. U., 1948. Assoc. prof. anatomy SUNY, Buffalo, 1949-86; ret., 1986. Author: The Extremities, 6th edit., 1993, The Head, Neck and Trunk, 6th edit., 1993. Lt. (s.g.) USNR, 1942-46. Mem. Am. Assn. Anatomists, Mason, Sigma Xi. Methodist.

WARFIELD, GERALD ALEXANDER, composer, writer; b. Ft. Worth, Feb. 23, 1940; s. George Alexander and Geraldine (Spencer) W. Student, Tex. Christian U., 1958-61; B.A., North Tex. State U., 1963, M.Mus., 1965; M.F.A., Princeton U., 1967; postgrad., Tanglewood, summers 1963-64. Instr. Princeton, 1968-71; asso. dir. Index of New Mus. Notation, N.Y.C., 1971-75; lectr. contemporary music notation. Mem. conf. com. Internat. Conf. on New Mus. Notation, Belgium, 1974; chmn. program com. 2d Nat. Conf. Music Theory, 1977. Author: A Beginner's Manual of Music 4B, 1967, Layer Analysis: a Primer of Elementary Tonal Structures, 1976, Writings on Contemporary Music Notations, 1977, How to Write Music Manuscript, 1977, (with others) Layer Dictation, 1978, The Investor's Guide to Stock Quotations, 1982, How To Buy Foreign Stocks and Bonds, 1984, How to Read the Financial News, 1986; (with others) Export-Import Financing, 1986; No Nonsense Guides to the Stock Market, Mutual Funds, Tax-Free Bonds, 1991, Managing Your Stock Portfolio, Money Market Funds, 1993, (with others) Feng Shui Revealed, 1997; composer: Variations and Metamorphoses, 1973 (1st prize Ariz. Cello Soc.); filmstrip Introduction to Musical Notation, 1976; Fantasy Quintet, 1978 (2d prize New Music for Young Ensembles); contbr.: Grove's Dictionary of Music and Musicians, 1976; editor: Longman Music Series, 1976-85; contbr. articles to profl. jours. Mem. Soc. Composers, Inc (chmn. exec. com. 1972-74, conf. chmn. 9th Ann. Conf., 1974, founding editor Jour. of Music Scores, gen. mgr. 1977—), Am. Composers Alliance (treas. 1979-96), Coll. Music Soc. (coun., conf. chmn. 1981), Broadcast Music Inc. Home: 205 W 22nd St New York NY 10011-2702

WARFIELD, JOHN NELSON, engineering educator, consultant; b. Sullivan, Mo., Nov. 21, 1925; s. John Daniel and Flora Alice (Land) W.; m. Rosamond Arline Howe, Feb. 2, 1948; children: Daniel, Nancy, Thomas. BA, U. Mo., 1948, BSEE, 1948, MSEE, 1949; PhD, Purdue U., 1952. Assoc. prof. Pa. State U., University Park, 1949-55, U. Ill.-Urbana, 1955-57, Purdue U., West Lafayette, Ind., 1957-58; prof. elec. engring U. Kans., Lawrence, 1958-66; sr. research leader Battelle Meml. Inst., Columbus, Ohio, 1966-74; prof. elec. engring U. Va., Charlottesville, 1974-83; sr. mgr. Burroughs Corp., 1983-84; dir. Inst. for Info. Tech. George Mason U., Fairfax, Va., 1984-87, dir. Inst. for Advanced Study in Integrative Scis., 1987—; cons. IBM, Armonk, N.Y., 1979-82, Saudi Arabian Nat. Ctr. Sci. and Tech., Riyadh, 1978-82, Ghana Coun. for Sci. and Indsl. Rsch., Accra, 1989—, Niagara-Mohawk Power Co., 89, Ford Motor Co., 1990—, Defense Systems Mgmt. Coll., 1990—. Author: Societal Systems, 1976, A Science of Generic Design, 1990, A Handbook of Interactive Management, 1994; inventor interpretive structural modeling, 1973; editor: IEEE Transactions on Systems, Man, and Cybernetics, 1968-73, Systems Research, 1981-90. Recipient Excellence in Instrn. award Western Electric Co., 1966, Peace Pipe award Ams. for Indian Opportunity, 1987, Best Paper award European Conf. Cyberneti s and Systems, 1988, Mayour's cert. City of Austin, 1993, Plaque of Recognition, Mex. Ministry of Social Devel., 1994, Spl. Recognition award Internat. Soc. Design and Process Sci., 1995. Fellow IEEE (life, outstanding contbn. award 1977, Centennial medal 1984), Soc. for Design and Process Sci. (fellow award, 1996); mem. Systems, Man and Cybernetics Soc. (pres. 1972), Soc. Gen. Systems Research (pres. 1982-83), Assn. for Integrative Studies, Internat. Soc. Panetics. Home: 4308 Wakefield Dr Annandale VA 22003-3611 Office: George Mason U Inst. Advanced Study in Integrative Sci Fairfax VA 22030

WARFIELD, WILLIAM CAESAR, singer, actor, educator; b. West Helena, Ark., Jan. 22, 1920; s. Robert Elza and Bertha (McCamery) W.; m. Leontyne Price, Aug. 31, 1952 (div. Dec. 1972). MusB, Eastman Sch. Music, 1942; LLD (hon.), U. Ark., 1972; MusD (hon.), Lafayette Coll., 1978. Prof. music dept. U. Ill., Champaign, 1974—; Bd. dirs. N.Y. Coll. Music; also trustee; trustee Berkshire Boys Choir, 1966-70, Nat. Assn. Negro Musicians. Actor nat. co. Call Me Mister, 1946-47; Broadway plays include Regina, 1948-49; Town Hall debut, 1950, tour of, Australia, 1950; motion picture Showboat, 1951; toured with: govt. sponsored European prodn. Porgy and Bess; singing role of Porgy govt. sponsored European prodn., 1952, concerts, radio and TV appearances; Symphony soloist recitals, 1950—, concert tour for, Dept. State; as soloist with Phila. Orch. for its continental debut, 1955, tour, Africa, Nr. East, Europe, 1956, Asia, Australia, 1958, Cuba, 1959, Europe, 1966, recital, Brussels Fair, 1958; starred as De Lawd in: Green Pastures, NBC-TV, 1957, 59; star: N.Y.C. Opera revival Porgy and Bess, 1961, 64; also Vienna prodn., 1965-72; featured soloist, Casals Festival, P.R. and N.Y.C., 1962-63, Athens Festival, Greece, 1966; starred in: Richard Rodgers' prodn. Show Boat for, Music Theater of Lincoln Center, 1966; German lang. Show Boat for Vienna Volksoper, 1971-72; soloist (with Pablo Casals) German lang., Geneva, Switzerland, Pacem in Terris II Convocation, 1967; title role in: German lang. Mendelssohn's Elijah, 1969; presented by Central City Opera (Colo.) as: star prodn. Puccini opera Gianni Schicchi, 1972; performed concert, Carnegie Hall, 1975. Recipient hon. citation Eastman Sch. Music, 1954, Grammy award Nat. Acad. Rec. Arts and Scis., 1984. Mem. Actors Equity, Am. Guild Mus. Artists, Screen Actors Guild, AFTRA, NAACP (life), Phi Mu Alpha Sinfonia (life). Home: 247 E Chestnut St Apt 701 Chicago IL 60611-2405

WARG, PAULINE, artist, educator; b. Detroit, Mich., Oct. 15, 1951; d. Clifford Rudolf and Marguerite Evelyn (Kaiser) W.; m. Gary Dean Snider, Apr. 14, 1990. Student, Bowling Green State U., 1969-72, diploma, 1972-75; postgrad., U. So. Maine, 1992—. Cert. Spl. Needs Vocat. Instr. Maine. Owner, pres. Warg Designs Inc., Scarborough, Maine, 1975—; instr. The Jewelry Inst., Providence, R.I., 1983-87; resident instr. Lexington Arts & Crafts Ctr., Lexington, Mass., 1987; asst. mgr. cons. J.S. Ritter Jewelers Tool & Supply Co., Portland, Maine, 1991-92; instr. Maine Coll. of Art, Portland, 1992—; owner, dir. metalsmithing program Future Builders, Inc., Scarborough, Maine, 1992—; lectr. Paul Revere House Mus., Boston, 1981, juror League of N.H. Craftsmen, Concord, N.H., 1985-87, stds. com. juror League of N.H. Craftsman, Concord, 1985-87, exhbn. juror Boston Mus. Sch., Boston, 1992. Contbr. articles to profl. jours. Founding mem. Portsmouth Artisans, Portsmouth, N.H., 1975-77, founding owners, treas. Sail Loft Cmty. Arts Program, Portsmouth, 1977-79. Mem. Soc. Am. Silversmiths (artisan mem. 1992—), Maine Crafts Assn. Democratic. Avocations: bicycling, canoeing, photography, gardening, travel. Office: Warg Designs Inc Pine Point Business Park 15 Holly St Ste 106 Scarborough ME 04074-8867

WARGA, JACK, mathematician, educator; b. Warsaw, Poland, Dec. 5, 1922; came to U.S., 1943, naturalized, 1944; s. Herman and Czarna (Lichtenstein) W.; m. Faye Kleinman, Feb. 27, 1949; children—Charna Ruth, Arthur David. Student, Brussels (Belgium) U., 1939-40; BA, Carleton Coll., 1944; PhD, NYU, 1950. Assoc. mathematician Reeves Instrument Corp., N.Y.C., 1951-52; Chief engring. computing sect. Republic Aviation Corp., Farmingdale, N.Y., 1952-53; head math dept. Burroughs Corp., Pasadena, Cal., 1954-56; mgr., math dept. Avco Research and Devel., Wilmington, Mass., 1957-66; prof. math. Northeastern U., Boston, 1966-93, prof. emeritus, 1993—. Author: Optimal Control of Differential and Functional Equations, 1972, expanded Russian transl., 1977; contbr. articles to profl. jours. Served with AUS, 1944-46. Weizmann Meml. fellow, 1956-57. Fellow AAAS; mem. Am. Math. Soc., Soc. Indsl. and Applied Math. (editor Jour. on Control and Optimization 1963-89). Home: 233 Clark Rd Brookline MA 02146-5847 Office: Northeastern U Dept Math Boston MA 02115

WARGO, ANDREA ANN, public health official, commissioned officer; b. Pottsville, Pa., Dec. 27, 1941; d. John Andrew and Anna Mary (Blischok) W.; m. Roger Fredrick Sies, Mar. 31, 1981. B.S. in Biology, Chestnut Hill Coll., 1972; Ph.D. in Biology, Georgetown U., 1978. Educator, adminstr. Catholic Archdiocese Phila., 1961-74; teaching asst. Georgetown U., Washington, 1974-78, postdoctoral fellow, 1978-80; acting br. chief FDA, Silver Spring, Md., 1980-86, acting chief gen. hosp. and personal use devices, 1986-88; assoc. adminstr. Agy. for Toxic Substances and Disease Registry, Washington, 1988—. Contbr. articles to sci. pubs. Grantee NSF, 1972, 73, Kidney Found., 1979-80. Mem. Assn. Women in Sci. (treas. Washington-Balt. chpt. 1979-80), Commd. Officers Assn., Georgetown U. Alumni Assn., Toastmistress Club (pres. Bethesda, Md. chpt. 1978-79), Pub. Health Service (scientist profl. adv. com., exec. sec. 1984-86, vice-chmn. 1986-87, chairperson 1987-88), Sigma Xi. Avocations: gardening; computers; financial planning; handwriting analysis. Home: 15521 Quail Run Dr North Potomac MD 20878 Office: 200 Independence Ave SW Washington DC 20201-0004

WARIN, ROGER E., lawyer; b. Des Moines, Iowa, June 14, 1945; s. Roger Francis and Mary (Gray) W.; m. Diane Whyte-Warin, May 31, 1974; children: Elizabeth, Patricia, Christopher, Michael. BA, Creighton U., 1967; JD, Georgetown U., 1970. Law clerk to Judge Oliver Gasch, Washington, 1970-71; assoc. Steptoe & Johnson, Washington, 1971-77, ptnr., 1978—; adj. law instr. Am. U., Washington, 1981-83. Mem. ABA, Washington Lawyer Com. Civil Rights. Avocation: skiing. Home: 3508 36th St N Arlington VA 22207-5310 Office: Steptoe & Johnson 1330 Connecticut Ave NW Washington DC 20036-1704

WARING, MARY LOUISE, social work administrator; b. Pitts., Feb. 15, 1928; d. Harold R. and Edith (McCallum) W. AB, Duke U., 1949; MSS, Smith Coll., 1951; PhD, Brandeis U., 1974. Lic. clin. social worker, Tenn. Sr. supervising social worker Judge Baker Guidance Ctr., Boston, 1955-65; dir. social svc. Cambridge (Mass.) Mental Health Ctr., 1965-70; assoc. prof. Sch. Social Work Fla. State U., Tallahassee, 1974-77; prof. Fordham U., N.Y.C., 1977-82; cons. Dept. Human Svc., N.J., 1983-84; cons., sr. staff mem. Family Counseling Svc. Bergen County, Hackensack, N.J., 1984-86; dir. Step One Employee Assistance Program Fortwood Ctr., Inc., Chattanooga, 1986-96; part-time psychotherapist Greenleaf Svcs., Chattanooga, 1996—, pvt. practice, 1996—; mem. ethics com. Chattanooga Rehab. Hosp., 1995. Contbr. articles to profl. jours. Mem. Citizen Amb. Program Human Resource Mgmt. Delegation to Russia, 1993; active Nat. Trust for Hist. Preservation, Nature Conservancy, Hunter Mus. Am. Art, Chattanooga Symphony and Opera Assn., Friends of Hamilton County Bicentennial Libr. Recipient Career Tchr. award Nat. Inst. Alchohol and Alchohol Abuse, 1972-74; traineeship NIMH, 1949-51. Mem. NASW (charter), Acad. Cert. Social Workers, Nat. Mus. Women in Arts (charter), Smithsonian Assocs., Cmty. Svcs. Club Greater Chattanooga (pres. 1995, 96, v.p. 1994, 97). Office: Greenleaf Svcs 602 Belvoir Ave Chattanooga TN 37412-2602

WARING, WALTER WEYLER, English language educator; b. Sterling, Kans., May 13, 1917; s. Walter Wray and Bonnie Laura (Weyler) W.; m. Mary Esther Griffith, Feb. 8, 1946; children: Mary Laura, Helen Ruth, Elizabeth Anne, Claire Joyce. B.A., Kans. Wesleyan U., 1939; M.A., U. Colo., 1946; Ph.D., Cornell U., 1949. Tchr., English and chemistry Belleville (Kan.) High Sch., 1939-41; instr. U. Colo., Boulder, 1941-42, 46-47; mem. faculty Kalamazoo Coll., 1949—, prof. English, 1955-85, prof. emeritus, 1985—, chmn. dept., 1953-78, dir. humanities, 1978-83; Ednl. TV lectr.; vis. prof. Kenyon Coll., 1984-86, 90-91. Painter watercolors.; author: Thomas Carlyle, 1978, also articles. Served to 1st lt. AUS, World War II, PTO. Decorated Legion of Merit. Mem. Phi Beta Kappa. Home: 156 Monroe St Kalamazoo MI 49006-4475

WARING, WILLIAM WINBURN, pediatric pulmonologist, educator; b. Savannah, Ga., July 20, 1923; s. Antonio Johnston and Sue Cole (Winburn) W.; m. Nell Pape Williams, July 19, 1952; children—William Winburn, Benjamin Joseph, Antonio Johnston, Peter Ayraud, Patrick Houstoun. Grad., Hotchkiss Sch., Lakeville, Conn., 1942; student, Yale U., 1942-43; M.D., Harvard U., 1947. Diplomate Am. Bd. Pediatrics (subbd. of pediatric pulmonology 1985-89). Intern Children's Hosp., Boston, 1947-48; intern, then resident Johns Hopkins Hosp., Balt., 1948-52; practice medicine specializing in pediatrics Jacksonville, Fla., 1955-57; instr. dept. pediatrics Sch. Medicine, Tulane U., New Orleans, 1957-58, asst. prof., 1958-61, assoc. prof., 1961-66, prof., 1966—, Jane B. Aron Prof. Pediatrics, 1987—; dir. Pediat. Pulmonary Ctr., New Orleans, 1969-88, Cystic Fibrosis Ctr., Tulane U., New Orleans, 1963-88; chmn. profl. tng. com. Cystic Fibrosis Found., 1978-86; cons. La. State Handicapped Children's Assn., 1963-88; mem. pulmonary diseases adv. com. NIH, 1978-80. Co-author, editor: Practical Manual of Pediatrics, 1975, 2d edit., 1982; editor: Harriet Lane Handbook: A Manual for Pediatric House Officers, 1952, Hospital Pediatric Manual, 1958; contbg. author books on pediatric pulmonary disease, also articles in field; assoc. editor Am. Jour. Diseases of Children, 1989-91; mem. editl. bd. Pediatric Pulmonology, 1985-94. Served to capt. M.C., U.S. Army, 1952-54. Recipient Research Career Devel. award NIH, 1970-72. Fellow Am. Acad. Pediatrics (exec. com. 1966-71), Am. Coll. Chest Physicians; mem. Am. Pediatric Soc., Am. Thoracic Soc. (v.p. 1977). Republican. Roman Catholic. Clubs: Boston, So. Yacht, Wyvern (New Orleans). Avocations: fly fishing; running; computing. Home: 123 Walnut St Ste 905 New Orleans LA 70118 Office: Tulane U Sch of Medicine Dept of Pediatrics 1430 Tulane Ave New Orleans LA 70112-2699

WARK, ROBERT RODGER, art curator; b. Edmonton, Can., Oct. 7, 1924; came to U.S., 1948, naturalized, 1970; s. Joseph Henry and Louise (Rodger) W. B.A., U. Alta., 1944, M.A., 1946, LLD (hon.), 1986; A.M., Harvard, 1949, Ph.D., 1952. Instr. art Harvard U., 1952-54; instr. history art Yale U., 1954-56; curator art Henry E. Huntington Library and Art Gallery, San Marino, Calif., 1956-90; lectr. art Calif. Inst. Tech., 1960-91, UCLA, 1966-80. Author: Sculpture in the Huntington Collection, 1959, French Decorative Art in the Huntington Collection, 1961, Rowlandson's Drawings for a Tour in a Post Chaise, 1963, Rowlandson's Drawings for the English Dance of Death, 1966, Isaac Cruikshank's Drawings for Drolls, 1968, Early British Drawings in the Huntington Collection 1600-1750, 1969, Drawings by John Flaxman, 1970, Ten British Pictures 1740-1840, 1971, Meet the Ladies: Personalities in Huntington Portraits, 1972, Drawings from the Turner Shakespeare, 1973, Drawings by Thomas Rowlandson in the Huntington Collection, 1975, British Silver in the Huntington Collection, 1978; editor: Sir Joshua Reynolds: Discourses on Art, 1959. Served with RCAF, 1944-45; Served with RCNVR, 1945. Mem. Coll. Art Assn. Home: 1330 Lombardy Rd Pasadena CA 91106-4120 Office: Huntington Library San Marino CA 91108

WARLICK, CHARLES HENRY, mathematician/computer science educator; b. Hickory, N.C., May 8, 1930; married; 3 children. BS, Duke U., 1952; MA, U. Md., 1955; PhD, U. Cin., 1964. Mathematician U.S. Dept. Army, 1952-53; programmer IBM Corp., 1954; from applied mathematician to supervisor applied math. GE Co., 1955-65; from lectr. to sr. lectr., dir. computer ctr. U. Tex., Austin, 1965-96, exec. dir. acad. info. sys., 1987-93; v.p. VIM Users Orgn. Control Data Corp., 1966-70, pres., 1970-71; mem., vice chair, bd. commrs. Tex. Dept. Info. Resources, 1981-87; mem., chair, trustee EDUCOM, 1989-95. Mem. Assn. Computing Machinery. Office: U Tex Austin Computation Ctr Austin TX 78712

WARLICK, ROGER KINNEY, history educator, assistant dean; b. San Diego, Oct. 1, 1930; s. John Portland and Bernice Catherine (Johnson) W.; m. Claudette Evans, Aug. 22, 1953 (div. 1972); m. Lorraine Vanden Bout, Dec. 13, 1973; children: David, Andrea, Kathryn, Dawn, Elizabeth, Sarah, Amy. BA, Ariz. State U., 1957; PhD, Boston U., 1965. Asst. to assoc. prof. history Bentley Coll., Boston and Waltham, Mass., 1963-70; prof., head history dept. Armstrong Atlantic State U. (formerly Armstrong State Coll.), Savannah, Ga., 1970-93, asst. dean Arts and Scis., 1993-94, prof. emeritus, 1994—; asst. program dir. Brit. studies U. Ga. system, London, 1982, 83, program dir., 1988, 89, 90, 92, 93, 94. Author: As Grain Once Scattered, 1988; contbr. articles to profl. jours. Bd. dirs. Hist. Savannah Found., 1980-86, Savannah Park and Tree Commn., 1976-87, vice chmn., 1983-87; gov. appointed mem. Ga. Hist. Records Adv. Bd., 1993—. Staff sgt. USAF, 1951-55. Cokesbury, resident fellow Boston U., 1961-63. Mem. Ga. Hist. Soc. (pres. 1990-94), Ga. Assn. Historians (various coms. 1978—), Savannah Symphony Soc. (bd. dirs. 1983-86).

WARM, JOEL SEYMOUR, psychology educator; b. Bklyn., Sept. 28, 1933; s. Abraham and Stella (Kaplan) W.; m. Frances Goldberg, July 31, 1966; children: Eric Jay, Ellen Sue. BS, CCNY, 1956, MS, 1958; PhD, U. Ala., 1966. Rsch. assoc. U.S. Army Med. Rsch. Lab., Ft. Knox, Ky., 1958-60; rsch. intern VA, Tuscaloosa, Ala., 1960-63; instr. U. Bridgeport (Conn.), 1963-64; adj. asst. prof. U. Louisville, 1964-67; asst. prof. U. Cin., 1967-72, assoc. prof., 1972-75, prof. psychology, 1975—; chair Fellows of the Grad. Sch., 1996—. Co-author: Psychology of Perception, 1979, Ergonomics and Human Factors, 1987; editor: Sustained Attention in Human Performance, 1984; editorial bd. Human Factors, 1989—, Jour. Gen. Psychology, 1992—, Internat. Rev. Rsch. in Mental Retardation, 1992—. Fellow Grad. Sch. U. Cin., 1986, chair, 1996-97; Knothole mgr. Finneytown (Ohio) Athletic Assn., 1980. Lt. (j.g.) USNR, 1963-70. Fellow Grad. Sch., U. Cin., 1984—, sr. postdoctoral fellow NRC, Cin., 1986, Disting. Summer Faculty fellow Naval Air Warfare Ctr., Warminster, Pa., 1992; grantee Fragrance Rsch. Fund, N.Y.C., 1987-89, NASA, 1992, Naval Air Warfare Ctr., 1995, Procter and Gamble Corp., 1995-97. Fellow AAAS, APA, Am. Psychol. Soc., Human Factors Soc. (pres. Tri-State chpt. 1988); mem. Psychonomic Soc., So. Soc. Philosophy and Psychology (pres. 1991-92), Sigma Xi (treas. U. Cin. chpt. 1988-91, pres.-elect 1991, pres. U. Cin. chpt. 1992). Jewish. Office: Dept Psychology U Cin ML #376 Cincinnati OH 45221

WARMAN, ARTURO GRYJ, Mexican government official; b. Mexico City, Sept. 9, 1937; m. Theresa Rojas. Diploma in ethnology, Nat. Sch. Anthropology; MA in Anthropology, UNAM. Acad. rschr. U. Iberoamericana, UNAM, U. Nat. Autonoma Metro., 1969-88; dir. Inst. Indigenous People and Agrarian Ombudsman, 1988-92; sec. Agrarian Reform Govt. Mex., 1995—. Author works on Mexican population and state. Recipient Nat.

Prize for Social Sci., 1976. Mem. Instl. Revolutionary Party. Office: Palacio Nacional, Patio de hono 20 Piso, Mexico City DF 06067, Mexico*

WARMBROD, JAMES ROBERT, agriculture educator, university administrator; b. Belvidere, Tenn., Dec. 13, 1929; s. George Victor and Anna Sophia (Zimmerman) W.; m. Catharine P. Phelps, Jan. 30, 1965. B.S., U. Tenn., 1952, M.S., 1954; Ed.D. (Univ. fellow), U. Ill., 1962. Instr. edn. U. Tenn., Knoxville, 1956-57; tchr. high sch. Winchester, Tenn., 1957-59; asst. prof. U. Ill., Urbana, 1961-66; assoc. prof. U. Ill., 1966-67; prof. agrl. edn. Ohio State U., Columbus, 1968-95; ret., Presdl. prof., 1989, Presdl. prof. emeritus, 1995, Disting. univ. prof. emeritus, 1995—, chmn. dept., 1978-86, acting assoc. dean Coll. Agr., 1989, acting v.p. agrl. adminstrn., dean Coll. Agr., 1989-91; vis. prof. Pa. State U., 1970, U. Minn., 1971, Iowa State U., 1974, La. State U., 1986; vis. scholar Va. Poly. Inst. and State U., 1976, Univ. Coun. Vocat. Edn., 1988-89; mem. com. on agr. in secondary schs. Nat. Acad. Scis., 1985-87. Author: Review and Synthesis of Research on the Economics of Vocational Education, 1968, The Liberalization of Vocat. Education, 1974, (with others) Methods of Teaching Agriculture, 1986, 2d edit. 1993; editor: Agrl. Edn. mag., 1968-71. Served with USAF, 1954-56. Recipient Tchg. award Gamma Sigma Delta, 1977. Fellow Am. Assn. Agrl. Edn.; mem. Am. Vocat. Assn. (v.p. 1976-79, Outstanding Svc. award 1987), Am. Ednl. Rsch. Assn., Am. Vocat. Edn. Rsch. Assn. (pres. 1976), Am. Assn. Tchr. Educators in Agr. (Disting. Svc. award 1974, Disting. lectr. 1974). Home: 3853 Surrey Hill Pl Columbus OH 43220-4778 Office: 2120 Fyffe Rd Columbus OH 43210-1010

WARMENHOVEN, DANIEL JOHN, communications equipment executive; b. Jersey City, Nov. 27, 1950; s. Peter F. and Roseann E. (Fedkenheuer) W.; m. Charmaine C. Andre, June 16, 1973; children: Eric A., Laura A. BS in Elec. Engring., Princeton U., 1972. Program mgr. communication products div. IBM Corp., Research Triangle Park, N.C., 1972-85; gen. mgr. Info. Networks Group Hewlett-Packard Co., Cupertino, Calif., 1985-89; chmn., pres., chief exec. officer Network Equipment Techs., Redwood City, Calif., 1989—; pres., chief exec. officer Network Appliance, Santa Clara, Calif. Avocations: golf, amatuer photography. Office: Network Appliance 2770 San Tomas Expy Santa Clara CA 95051-0952

WARMER, RICHARD CRAIG, lawyer; b. Los Angeles, Aug. 12, 1936; s. George A. and Marian L. (Paine) W.; children: Craig McEchron, Alexander Richard. AB, Occidental Coll., 1958; MA, Tufts U., 1959; LLB, NYU, 1962. Bar: Calif. 1963, D.C. 1976. Assoc. O'Melveny & Myers, Los Angeles, 1962-69, ptnr., 1970-75; mng. ptnr. O'Melveny & Myers, Washington, 1976-92, mem. mgmt. com., 1986-92; with O'Melveny & Myers, San Francisco, 1994—; speaker in field. Contbr. articles to profl. jours. Trustee Law Ctr. Found. NYU, 1981-94. Mem. ABA, D.C. Bar, State Bar Calif., Order of Coif, Phi Beta Kappa, Cosmos Club. Home: 550 Davis St Apt 26 San Francisco CA 94111-1953 Office: O'Melveny & Myers Embarcadero Ctr W 275 Battery St San Francisco CA 94111-3305

WARNATH, MAXINE AMMER, organizational psychologist, mediator; b. N.Y.C., Dec. 3, 1928; d. Philip and Jeanette Ammer; m. Charles Frederick Warnath, Aug. 20, 1952; children: Stephen Charles, Cindy Ruth. BA, Bklyn. Coll., 1949; MA, Columbia U., 1951, EdD, 1982. Lic. psychologist, Oreg. Various profl. positions Hunter Coll., U. Minn., U. Nebr., U. Oreg., 1951-62; asst. prof. psychology Oreg. Coll. Edn., Monmouth, 1962-77; assoc. prof. psychology, chmn. dept. psychology and spl. edn. Western Oreg. U., Monmouth, 1978-83, prof. 1983-96, prof. emeritus, 1996—, dir. organizational psychology program 1983-96; pres. Profl. Perspectives Internat., Salem, Oreg., 1987—; cons., dir. Orgn. R & D, Salem, Oreg., 1983-87, seminar leader Endeavors for Excellence program. Author: Power Dynamism, 1987. Mem. APA (com. pre-coll. psychology 1970-74), Am. Psychol. Soc., N.Y. Acad. Sci., Oreg. Acad. Sci., Oreg. Psychol. Assn. (pres. 1980-81, pres.-elect 1979-80, legis. liaison 1977-78), Western Psychol. Assn. Office: Profl Perspectives Internat PO Box 2265 Salem OR 97308-2265

WARNE, RONSON JOSEPH, mathematics educator; b. East Orange, N.J., June 14, 1930; s. Ronson Joseph and Mildred (Morton) W.; m. Gloria Jane La France, Oct. 24, 1950. BA, Columbia U., 1953; MS, NYU, 1955; PhD, U. Tenn., 1959. Teaching asst., instr. U. Tenn., Knoxville, 1955-59; asst. prof. Math. La. State U., New Orleans, 1959-63; assoc. prof. Math. Va. Polytech. Inst., Blacksburg, 1963-64; prof. Math. W.Va. U., Morgantown, 1964-70, U. Ala., Birmingham, 1970-89, King Fahd U. of Petroleum and Minerals, Dhahran, Saudi Arabia, 1989—. Contbr. articles to profl. jours. Oak Ridge Nat. Lab. fellow, 1960, Dryser fellow, U. Tenn., 1957; vis. rsch. scholar U. Calif., Berkeley, 1982. Mem. Am. Math. Soc. Avocations: body building, weightlifting, running. Office: KFUPM # 1564, Dhahran 31261, Saudi Arabia

WARNE, WILLIAM ROBERT, economist; b. Washington, Nov. 30, 1937. BA, Princeton U., 1960; MA, Johns Hopkins U., 1974. Provincial advisor U.S. Mission, Vinh Binh, Vinh Long, Vietnam, 1962-64; officer in charge trade, devel. and fin. policy U.S. Mission to European Communities, Brussels, 1974-77; dep. dir. East Asian Econ. Policy, 1977-79; dir. Caribbean affairs U.S. Dept. State, Kingston, Jamaica, 1979-81, charge d'affaires, dep. chief mission, 1981-84; dir. Latin Am. Econ. Policy U.S. Dept. State, Washington, 1984-86; counselor for trade, energy, social affairs and agr. U.S. Delegation OECD, Paris, 1986-88; v.p. Midwest Ctr. Exec. Coun. on Fgn. Diplomats, Indpls., 1988-89; pres. Korea Econ. Inst. Am., Washington, 1990—. With U.S. Army, 1960-62. Office: Korea Econ Inst Am 1101 Vermont Ave NW Ste 401 Washington DC 20005-3521

WARNECKE, MICHAEL O., lawyer; b. Chgo., June 28, 1941. BS, ME, Purdue U., 1963; JD, George Washington U., 1967. Bar: Ill. 1967. Ptnr. Mayer, Brown & Platt, Chgo.; lectr. in field. Fellow Am. Coll. of Trial Lawyers; mem. ABA, Am. Arbitration Assn. (mem. panel arbitrators), Am. Intellectual Property Law Assn., Chgo. Bar Assn., Bar Assn. 7th Cir., Intellectual Property Law Assn. Chgo., Internat. Patent and Trademark Assn. Office: Mayer Brown Platt 190 S La Salle St Chicago IL 60603-3410

WARNER, ALVINA (VINNIE WARNER), principal; b. Des Moines, Nov. 3, 1936; d. Harry and Pearl Walker; m. Robert M. Warner, June 8, 1958. BS, U. Mo., 1958; MEd, Saint Louis U., 1969. Adv. cert. specialist-prin. S.E. Mo., 1972. Tchr. Centralia (Mo.) Pub. Schs., 1958-59; tchr., curriculum coord., asst. prin. Webster Groves Sch. Dist., 1959-74; prin. Barretts Sch. Parkway Sch. Dist., Saint Louis County, 1974-96; ret., 1996; organizer Barretts Sch. Centennial Celebration, 1994-95. Recipient Elem. Sch. Recognition, Blue Ribbon Sch. of Excellence award, U.S. Dept. Edn., 1989-90. Home: 169 Horseshoe Dr Kirkwood MO 63122-3714

WARNER, BARRY GREGORY, geographer, educator; b. Cambridge, Ont., Can., July 20, 1955; s. Gregory O. and Alma (Jansen) W. B in Environ. Studies, U. Waterloo, 1978, MS, 1980; PhD, Simon Fraser U., Burnaby, Can., 1984. Rsch. asst. prof. U. Waterloo, Ont., Ont., 1985-89; rsch. assoc. prof. U. Waterloo, Ont., 1989-91; assoc. prof. geography U. Waterloo, Ont., Ont., 1991-96; prof. geography U. Waterloo, Ont., 1996—; interim dir. Wetlands Rsch. Inst., 1991—; U. Neuchatel; vis. prof. U. Neuchatel, 1993; chair Can. Nat. Wetlands Working Group, 1993—; bd. dirs. Internat. Mire Conservation Group. Editor: Methods in Quaternary Ecology, 1990; co-editor: Wetlands: Envigradients, Boundaries and Buffers, 1996; contbr. articles to profl. jours. Postdoctoral fellow Natural Scis. and Engring. Rsch. Coun. of Can., 1984-85, rsch. fellow, 1985-90; fellow Suisse Nat. Res. Fond, 1993. Fellow Geol. Assn. Can. Office: Univ of Waterloo, Dept Geography, Waterloo, ON Canada N2L 3G1

WARNER, CECIL RANDOLPH, JR., lawyer; b. Ft. Smith, Ark., Jan. 13, 1929; s. Cecil Randolph and Reba (Cheeves) W.; m. Susan Curry, Dec. 10, 1955 (div. 1982); children: Susan Rutledge, Rebecca Jane, Cecil Randolph III, Matthew Holmes Preston, Katherine Mary; m. Barbara Ragsdale, May 26, 1983. B.A. magna cum laude, U. Ark., 1950; LL.B. magna cum laude, Harvard U., 1953, Sheldon fellow, 1953-54. Bar: Ark. 1953. Ptnr. Warner & Smith and predecessor firm, 1954-89; pres., CEO, Fairfield Communities Inc., Little Rock, 1973-81; chmn., CEO Fairfield Communities Inc., 1981-85, chmn., pres., CEO, 1985-91; chmn., pres., CEO Environ. Systems Co., Little Rock, 1991-93; cons., 1993-95; chmn. bd. Wortz Co., Poteau, Okla., 1993-97; instr. U. Ark. Sch. Law, 1954, 56; vi ce chmn. Ark. Constl. Revision Study Commn., 1967; v.p. 7th Ark. Constl. Conv., 1969-70. Scoutmaster troop 23 Boy Scouts Am., Fort Smith, 1955-58; commr. Ark. State Police Commn., 1970. Fellow Am. Bar Found., Ark. Bar Found.; mem. ABA, Ark. Bar Assn. (past chmn. exec. com., past chmn. young lawyers sect.), Pulaski County Bar Assn., Am. Law Inst., Fifty for the Future, Phi Beta Kappa, Phi Eta Sigma, Omicron Delta Kappa, Sigma Alpha Epsilon. Methodist. Office: PO Box 7462 Little Rock AR 72217-7462 also: One Treetop Ln Little Rock AR 72201

WARNER, CHARLES COLLINS, lawyer; b. Cambridge, Mass., June 19, 1942; s. Hoyt Landon and Charlotte (Collins) W.; m. Elizabeth Denny, Aug. 24, 1964; children: Peter, Andrew, Elizabeth. BA, Yale U., 1964; JD cum laude, Ohio State U., 1970. Bar: Ohio 1970. Assoc. Porter, Wright, Morris & Arthur and predecessor, Columbus, 1970-76, ptnr., 1976—, also mgr. labor and employment law dept., 1988-92. Pres. Peace Corps Svc. Coun., Columbus, 1974-76, Old Worthington (Ohio) Assn., 1976-78, Alliance for Quality Edn., Worthington, 1987-89, Worthington Ednl. Found., 1994-96; chmn. lawyers sect. United Way, Columbus, 1983-84. Mem. ABA (subcom. chmn. EEO com. 1986-89, exec. com. Met. Bar Caucus 1992-94, chmn. state & local bar ADR com.), Ohio State Bar Assn. (coun. of dels. 1993—, chmn. fed. cts. com. 1992-94), Ohio Met. Bar Assn. (pres. 1991-92), Columbus Bar Assn. (pres. 1991-92, bd. govs. 1982-87, 88-93), FBA, Ohio Assn. Civil Trial Attys. (exec. bd. 1988—), Nat. Coun. Ohio State U. Law Alumni Assn., Capital Club, Univ. Club, Yale Club (pres. 1979-81). Avocations: clarinet, singing, tennis. Home: 145 E South St Worthington OH 43085-4129 Office: Porter Wright Morris & Arthur 41 S High St Columbus OH 43215-6101

WARNER, DENNIS ALLAN, psychology educator; b. Idaho Falls, Idaho, Apr. 27, 1940; s. Perry and Marcia E. (Finlayson) W.; m. Charyl Ann DeHart, Dec. 12, 1962; children: Lisa Rae, Sara Michelle, David Perry, Matthew Arie. BS, Brigham Young U., 1964; MS with honors, U. Oreg., 1966, PhD, 1968. Asst. prof. edn. Wash. State U., Pullman, 1968-72, assoc. prof. edn., 1972-78, prof. edn., 1978-85, dir. tchr. edn., 1983-85, prof., chmn. ednl. counseling psychology, 1985-93, interim dir. Partnership Ctr., 1993-94; prof. edn. leadership and counseling psychology Wash. State U., Pulman, 1994—; vis. asst. prof. psychology U. Idaho, Moscow, 1971. Author: Interpreting and Improving Student Test Performance, 1982; contbr. articles to profl. jours. Postdoctoral research assoc. U. Kans., 1976-77. Mem. Am. Psychol. Assn., Council for Exceptional Children, Phi Delta Kappa. Mem. LDS Ch. Home: 645 SW Mies St Pullman WA 99163-2057 Office: Wash State Univ Dept Ednl and Counsel Psych Rm 371 Cleveland Hall Pullman WA 99164-2131

WARNER, DON LEE, dean emeritus; b. Norfolk, N.B., Jan. 4, 1934; s. Donald A. and Cleo V. (Slagel) W.; m. Patricia Ann Walker, Feb. 24, 1957; children: Mark J., Scott Lee. BS in Geol. Engring., Colo. Sch. Mines, 1956, MSc in Geol. Engring., 1961; PhD in Engring. Sci., U. Calif., Berkeley, 1964. Registered profl. engr., Mo., geologist, Mo. Geol. engr. Gulf Oil Corp., Casper, Wyo., 1956, Calif. Exploration Co., Guatemala, 1957-58; civil engr. U.S. Forest Svc., Gunnison, Colo., 1958-59; teaching asst. Colo. Sch. Mines, Golden, 1959-61; rsch. asst. U. Calif., Berkeley, 1962-64; rsch. geologist and engr. U.S. Pub. Health Svc., Cin., 1964-67; chief, earth scis. Ohio Basin Region Fed. Water Pollution Control Adminstrn., 1967-69; prof. geol. engring. U. Mo., Rolla, 1969-92, prof. emeritus geol. engring., 1992—, dean emeritus Sch. Mines and Metallurgy, 1992—, chmn., geol. engring., 1980-81, dean Sch. Mines and Metallurgy, 1981-93; bd. dirs. Underground Injection Practices Coun., 1985-89; mem. adv. com. to Sec. of Interior for Mineral Resources Rsch., 1985-92. Author: Subsurface Wastewater Injection, 1977. Special award scholarship Colo. Sch. Mines, 1951-56, grad. fellowship Colo. Sch. Mines, 1959-51, rsch. fellowship U. Calif., 1962-64; recipient Best Paper award Am. Water Works Assn., 1971. Mem. Am. Assn. Petroleum Geologists (cert.), ASTM, Geol. Soc. Am. (ground water protection coun.), Nat. Ground Water Assn. (sci. award 1984, disting. lectr. 1986), Blue Key, Soc. Petroleum Engrs., Scabbard and Blade, Theta Tau, Tau Beta Pi. Avocations: fishing, boating, tennis, golf. Office: U Mo-Rolla Sch Mines and Metallurgy 1870 Miner Cir Rolla MO 65409-0001

WARNER, DOUGLAS ALEXANDER, III, banker; b. Cin., June 9, 1946; s. Douglas Alexander Jr. and Eleanor (Wright) W.; m. Patricia Grant, May 13, 1977; children: Alexander, Katherine, Michael. BA, Yale U., 1968. Officer's asst. J.P. Morgan & Co. Inc., N.Y.C., 1968-70; asst. treas. J.P. Morgan & Co., Inc., N.Y.C., 1970-72, asst. v.p., 1972-75; v.p. Morgan Guaranty Trust Co., N.Y.C., 1975-85; sr. v.p. J.P. Morgan & Co. Inc., N.Y.C., 1983-87, exec. v.p., 1987-89; mng. dir. Morgan Guaranty Trust Co., N.Y.C., 1989-90, pres., 1990-95, chmn., pres., CEO, 1995—, also bd. dirs.; bd. counselors Bechtel Group, Inc.; bd. dirs. GE Co., Anheuser-Busch Cos., Ind.; vice chmn. bd. mgrs. Meml. Sloan-Kettering Cancer Ctr.; vice chmn. The Bus. Coun. Trustee Pierpont Morgan Libr., Cold Spring Harbor Lab. Mem. Bankers Roundtable, Links Club, River Club, Meadowbrook Club (L.I.). Avocations: golf, skiing, shooting. Home: PO Box 914 New York NY 10268-0914 Office: J P Morgan & Co Inc 60 Wall St New York NY 10005-2836

WARNER, E. JOHN, manufacturing financial executive; b. Chgo., Sept. 28, 1942; s. Eugene John and Kathryn (Jones) W.; m. Nan Shipley, Aug. 21, 1965; children: John Warner, Thomas Shipley. BSBA, Ohio State U., 1965; MCS, Harvard U., 1978; PEE, Carnegie Mellon U., 1981. Mgmt. trainee GM, Flint, Mich., 1965-68; asst. prodn. mgr. Diebold Inc., Canton, Ohio, 1968-70, prodn. mgr., 1970-77, gen. mgr. Wooster (Ohio) divsn., 1977-85, dir. strategic planning, 1985-88; pres. W.L. Jenkins Co., Canton, 1988—; guest lectr. Harvard U. Bus. Sch., Boston, 1979. Bd. dirs. United Way, Canton, 1987—, gen. campaign chmn., 1987; bd. dirs. Jr. Achievement, Wooster, 1980-85, YMCA, Wooster, 1980-85. Mem. Canton City Club, Glemoor Country Club. Episcopalian. Avocations: tennis, swimming, sailing, fishing, golf. Home: 3304 Croydon Dr NW Canton OH 44718-3220 Office: WL Jenkins Co 1445 Whipple Ave SW Canton OH 44710-1321

WARNER, EDWARD L., III, federal agency administrator; b. Detroit, 1940; m. Pam Melton; children: Kelly, Erika. BS, U.S. Naval Acad., 1962; MS in Politics, Princeton U., 1967, PhD in Politics, 1975; grad., Armed Forces Staff Coll., 1975; grad. in Russian, Def. Lang. Inst., 1976. Commd. 2d lt. USAF, 1962; analyst Office Strategic Rsch., CIA; asst. prof. polit. sci. USAF Acad., Colorado Springs, Colo.; asst. air attache Am. Embassy, Moscow; dep. chief strategy div. Hdqs. USAF, Washington, head staff group Office Chief of Staff; ret., 1982; sr. def. analyst RAND Corp., Washington, 1982-93; asst. sec. def. for strategy and requirements Dept. Def., Washington, 1993—; condr. grad. seminars on Soviet def. and arms control policy George Washington U., Johns Hopkins U. Sch. Advanced Internat. Studies, Princeton U., Columbia U.; former mem. mil. adv. panel to Nat. Intelligence Coun.; former mem. polit. consultative group Office Slavic and Eurasian Analysis, CIA. Mem. Coun. Fgn. Rels. Office: Dept Def Pentagon Washington DC 20301-2900*

WARNER, EDWARD WAIDE, JR., lawyer; b. St. Louis, Oct. 17, 1951; s. Edward Waide Sr. and Barbara (Hardy) W.; m. Cecilia Tso, Oct. 1, 1983; children: Edward Waide Tso, Sarah Liang, Rebecca Li, Genevieve An Hardy. AB magna cum laude, Boston Coll., 1973; JD, Rutgers U., 1977; postgrad., U. Chgo., 1974. Bar: Mo. 1978, N.Y. 1980. Law clk. to sr. cir. judge U.S. Ct. Appeals (8th cir.), St. Louis, 1977-78; assoc. Davis, Polk & Wardwell, N.Y.C., 1978-85, ptnr., 1986—; bd. advisors Morin Ctr. Banking Law Studies, Boston U. Sch. Law, 1989-94. Trustee Episcopal Sch., N.Y.C., 1994—. Mem. ABA, Internat. Bar Assn., Assn. of Bar of City of N.Y., Mo. Bar Assn., Phi Beta Kappa. Home: 151 E 74th St New York NY 10021-3226 Office: Davis Polk & Wardwell 450 Lexington Ave New York NY 10017-3911

WARNER, ELIZABETH ROSE, librarian, educator; b. Phila., Pa., Dec. 10, 1952; d. Charles Hoffman and Elizabeth Mathilda Warner; m. Michael Joseph Dunn, Oct. 12, 1979; children: Brian Joseph Charles Warner Dunn, Colin Joseph Patrick Warner Dunn. BA, Holy Family Coll., 1974; MLS, Villanova U., 1977. Med. librarian JFK Meml. Hosp., Stratford, N.J., 1975-77; lib. coord. N.J. Sch. Osteopathic Medicine, Stratford, 1976-77; extension librarian Coll. Physicians Phila., 1977-79, reader's svcs. asst., 1975-77; med. librarian Crozer-Chester (Pa.) Med. Ctr., 1979-86; reference librarian Scott Meml. Lib. Thomas Jefferson U., Phila., 1986-90, edn. svcs. librarian, instr. info. skills workshops Scott Meml. Lib., 1991—; vol. librarian Mummers Mus., Phila., 1976; cons., presenter in field. Contbr. numerous articles to profl. jours. Mem. Am. Lib. Assn., Med. Lib. Assn. (chair legis. com. Phila. Regional chpt. 1980-81, pres. elect, program chair, 1981-82, pres. 1982-83, mem. com. 1981-83, rep. chpt. coun. 1985-87, nominating com. 1987-88, 94-95, Achievement award 1994, edn. com. nursing and allied health resources sect. 1988-89, sec., treas. 1991-93, nominating com. 1988-89, 93-94, editor newsletter, 1992—, course designer 1993—, instr. 1993—, com. chair pub. svcs. sect., 1985-87, jury chair Ida and George prize 1992-94, Disting. mem. Acad. Health Info. Profls. 1990—), Grtr. Phila. Health Care Congress, Phila. Area Reference Librarians Info. Exchange (Bibliotecaire Sans Sobriete cert. 1993), Kappa Gamma Pi, Phi Kappa Phi. Democrat. Roman Catholic. Home: 421 E Melrose Ave Westmont NJ 08108-2510 Office: Thomas Jefferson U Scott Meml Lib 1020 Walnut St Philadelphia PA 19107-5567

WARNER, FRANK WILSON, III, mathematics educator; b. Pittsfield, Mass., Mar. 2, 1938; s. Frank Wilson Jr. and Charlotte (Walton) W.; m. Ada Woodward, June 6, 1958; children: Bruce Woodward, Clifford Powell. BS, Pa. State U., 1959; PhD, MIT, 1963. Instr. MIT, Cambridge, 1963-64; acting asst. prof. U. Calif., Berkeley, 1964-65, asst. prof., 1965-68; assoc. prof. U. Pa., Phila., 1968-73, prof. math., 1973—, assoc. dean Sch. Arts and Scis., 1992-95, dep. dean Sch. Arts and Scis., 1995—. Author: Foundations of Differentiable Manifolds and Lie Groups, 1971; contbr. articles to scholarly jours. Fellow Guggenheim Found., 1976. Fellow AAAS; mem. Am. Math. Soc., Math. Assn. Am., Sigma Xi. Achievements include research on the conjugate locus of a Riemannian manifold, on existence and conformal deformation of metrics with prescribed gaussian and scalar curvatures, on great circle fibrations of spheres. Office: U Pa 116 College Hall Philadelphia PA 19104-6377

WARNER, HAROLD CLAY, JR., banker, investment management executive; b. Knoxville, Tenn., Feb. 24, 1939; s. Harold Clay and Mary Frances (Waters) W.; m. Patricia Alice Rethorst, Sept. 1, 1961; children—Martha Lee, Carol Frances. B.S. in Econs, U. Tenn., 1961, Ph.D., 1965. Asst. to pres. First Fed. Savs., Savannah, Ga., 1965-67; v.p. and economist No. Trust Co., Chgo., 1967-73; sr. v.p. and chief economist Crocker Nat. Bank, San Francisco, 1974-79; sr. v.p. liability mgmt. Crocker Nat. Bank, 1979-82; exec. v.p., dir. fixed income mgmt. BA Investment Mgmt. Corp., 1982-84, dir., pres., chief operating officer, 1984-86; dir., pres. Montgomery St. Income Securities, Inc., 1984-86; sr. v.p. Bank of Am., San Francisco, 1982-86; chmn. BA Investment Mgmt. Internat., Ltd., 1985-86; pres. Arthur D. Gimbel, Inc., San Mateo, Calif., 1986-87; exec. v.p., chief investment officer Riggs Nat. Bank Washington, 1987-88; chmn. Riggs Investment Mgmt. Corp., 1988-89; sr. v.p., chief economist Bank of Calif., San Francisco, 1989-93; pres., chief investment officer MERUS Capital Mgmt., San Francisco, 1989-93; pres. Govett Asset Mgmt. Co., 1993-95, Govett Fin. Svcs. Ltd., 1993-95; pres., COO Fisher Investments, Inc., Woodside, Calif., 1996; pres. Warner Fiduciary Counsel, LLC, San Francisco, 1997—; lectr. dept. econs. U. Tenn., 1962-63, Grad. Sch. Bus., Loyola U., Chgo., 1969-73; lectr. Pacific Coast Banking Sch., U. Wash., 1978-79. NDEA fellow, 1961-64. Mem. Burlingame Country Club, Phi Gamma Delta, Phi Eta Sigma, Beta Gamma Sigma, Omicron Delta Kappa, Phi Kappa Phi. Home: 1960 Broadway San Francisco CA 94109-2216 Office: 1960 Broadway San Francisco CA 94109-2216

WARNER, HARRY BACKER, JR., retired journalist, freelance writer; b. Chambersburg, Pa., Dec. 19, 1922; s. Harry Backer, Sr. and Margaret Caroline (Klipp) W. Student, Hagerstown, Md. Reporter, editor, columnist Herald-Mail Co., Hagerstown, 1942-82; ret., 1982. Author: All Our Yesterdays, 1969, A Wealth of Fable, 1976; editor, author (amateur jour.) Horizons, 1939—. Com. mem. Community Action Coun., Hagerstown, Civic Music Assn., Hagerstown, Washington County Adult Edn., Hagerstown; mem. publicity com. Washington County United Fund, Hagerstown. Recipient Hugo award World Sci. Fiction Convs., 1968, 72, 93, Hist. Preservation award Washington County Commrs., 1980, First Fandom Hall of Fame award, 1995. Mem. Spectator Amateur Press Soc. (v.p. 1982-97), So. Fandom Pubs. Alliance. Republican. Lutheran. Avocations: science fiction fandom, classical music. Home: 423 Summit Ave Hagerstown MD 21740-6229

WARNER, HARRY HATHAWAY, financial consultant; b. Staunton, Va., Nov. 30, 1935; s. Morris Thompson and Virginia Drury (Worthington) W.; m. Mary Elizabeth Patrick, Sept. 24, 1960; children—Harry Hathaway, Cabell Worthington, Ann Morris, Morris Patrick. B.A., Va. Mil. Inst., 1957; grad., U. Va. Sch. Bank Mgmt., 1963, Stonier Grad. Sch. Banking, 1969. With Met. Nat. Bank, Richmond, Va., 1965-71; exec. v.p. Met. Nat. Bank, 1969-71; pres., dir. Transohio Fin. Corp., Cleve., 1971-78; exec. v.p. VMI Found., Lexington, Va., 1978-90; cons. in field; bd. dirs. Chesapeake Corp., Pulaski Furniture Corp. Va., Am. Filtrona Corp., Allied Rsch. Corp. Served as 2d lt. AUS, 1957. Recipient Distinguished Service award Richmond Jaycees, 1969. Mem. Commonwealth Club, Lexington Country Club. Episcopalian. Address: PO Box 1577 Lexington VA 24450-1577

WARNER, HEIDI C., clinical research nurse; b. Thomasville, N.C., Nov. 7, 1962. BSN, N.C. U., Charlotte, 1985. RN, N.C.; cert. in audiometry. Clin. rsch. assoc. tng. The Blethen Group, Research Triangle Park, N.C.; contract in-house monitor Intercardia, Inc., Research Triangle Park, N.C. Walter C. Teagle Found. nursing scholar, Exxon Co. USA. Mem. N.C. Health Info. Mgmt. Sys. Soc., Phi Eta Sigma.

WARNER, JOHN ANDREW, foundry executive; b. Kansas City, Mo., Jan. 1, 1924; s. Richard G. and Margaret (Falconer) W.; m. Patricia Pooley, Feb. 25, 1950; children: Katherine, Amanda. Sec. Warner Oil Co., Oklahoma City, 1948-50; pres., chief exec. officer Tyler Pipe Industries, Tex., 1950-89; ret., 1989; bd. dirs. Tex. Power & Light Co., Dallas. Past chmn. East Tex. Hosp. Found.; trustee Tex. Chest Found.; former mem. Tex. Gov.'s Commn. on Phys. Fitness. Served with USCGR, 1942-46. Named Tyler's Most Outstanding Citizen, 1973. Mem. Tyler C. of C. (dir., past pres.), Cast Iron Soil Pipe Inst. (dir., past pres.), Am. Foundrymen's Soc., Tex. Assn. Bus. (dir., past state chmn.), Country Club of the Rockies, Willow Brook Country Club (dir., past pres. Tyler), Masons, Shriners, Sigma Alpha Epsilon. Presbyterian. Home: 608 Rosemont Pl Tyler TX 75701-8643

WARNER, JOHN EDWARD, advertising executive; b. Troy, N.Y., Mar. 26, 1936; s. George Edward and Ann Frances (Teson) W.; m. Anne Elizabeth Hibbard, Sept. 19, 1959; children—Matthew J., Barbara A., Peter J., Christopher J. B.S. in Chemistry and Philosophy, Coll. Holy Cross, 1957. Promotion mgr. Union Carbide Corp., N.Y.C., 1957-62; account exec. McCann-Erickson, Inc., N.Y.C., 1962-64; pres. Warner, Bicking & Fenwick, Inc., N.Y.C., 1964-84; chmn. Warner, Bicking, Morris & Ptnrs. Inc., 1984—; Pres. Transworld Advt. Agy. Network, 1987—; speaker confs. advt. mktg. assns. Columnist advt. and mktg. pubs. Home: 706 Hillcrest Rd Ridgewood NJ 07450-1110 Office: 866 UN Pla New York NY 10017

WARNER, JOHN HILLIARD, JR., technical services, military and commercial systems and software company executive; b. Santa Monica, Calif., Mar. 2, 1941; s. John Hilliard and Irene Anne (Oliva) W.; m. Helga Magdalena Farrington, Sept. 4, 1961; children: Tania Renee, James Michael. BS in Engring. with honors, UCLA, 1963, MS in Engring., 1965, PhD in Engring., 1967. Mem. staff Marquardt Corp., Van Nuys, Calif., 1963; mem. faculty West Coast U., Los Angeles, 1969-72; mem. staff TRW Systems Group, Redondo Beach, Calif., 1967-70, sect. mgr., 1970-73; mem. staff Sci. Applications Internat. Corp., San Diego, 1973-75, asst. v.p., 1975-77, v.p., 1977-80, corp. v.p., 1980-81, sr. v.p., 1981-87, sector v.p., 1987-89; exec. v.p. Sci. Applications Internat Corp., San Diego, 1989-96, bd. dirs., 1988—; corp. exec. v.p. Sci. Applications Internat. Corp., San Diego, 1996—; cons. Rand Corp., Santa Monica, 1964-66. Contbr. articles to profl. jours. AEC fellow, 1963, 66, NSF fellow, 1964, 65. Mem. AIAA, Healthcare Info. and Mgmt. Sys. Soc., Assn. U.S. Army, Air Force Assn. Am. Def. Preparedness Assn., Am. Security Coun., Armed Forces Communications and Electronics Assn., Navy League U.S., La Jolla Chamber Music Soc. (bd. dirs. 1990—), Sigma Nu, Tau Beta Pi. Methodist. Avocations: bicycling, fishing, water skiing, music. Office: SAIC 10260 Campus Point Dr San Diego CA 92121-1522

WARNER, JOHN WILLIAM, senator; b. Washington, DC, Feb. 18, 1927; s. John William and Martha Stuart (Budd) W.; children: Mary Conover,

Virginia Stuart, John William IV. BS Engring., Washington and Lee U., 1949; LL.B., U. Va., 1953. Law clk. to U.S. judge, 1953-54, spl. asst. to U.S. atty., 1956-57; asst. U.S. atty. Dept. Justice, 1957-60; ptnr. Hogan & Hartson, 1960-68; owner, operator Cattle Farm, 1961—; undersec. of navy, 1969-72, sec. of navy, 1972-74; adminstr. Am. Revolution Bicentennial Adminstrn., 1974-76; U.S. senator from Va., 1979—; mem. armed svcs. com., environment and pub. works com., labor and human resources com., rules and adminstrn. com., small bus. aging com., nat. Rep. senatorial com. Served with USNR, 1944-46; to capt. USMCR, 1949-52. Mem. Bar Assn. D.C. Republican. Episcopalian. Club: Metropolitan. Office: US Senate 225 Russell Senate Bldg Washington DC 20510-4601*

WARNER, JUDITH (ANNE) HUSS, educator; b. Plainfield, N.J., June 15, 1936; d. Charles and Martha McMullen (Miller) Huss; m. Howard R. Warner, June 14, 1958; children: Barbara, Robert. BS in Elem. Edn., Russell Sage Coll., 1959. Elem. tchr. Pitts. Bd. Edn., 1959-60; home tchr. Napa (Calif.) Sch. Bd., 1974-77; substitute tchr. Allegheny Intermediate Unit, Pitts., 1977—. Leader Girl Scouts U.S.A., Pitts., 1966-70; vol. Children's Hosp., PItts., 1967-74, Jefferson Hosp., Pitts., 1977-88; pres., trustee Whitehall Libr., Pitts., 1984-92; pres., bd. dirs. Friends of Whitehall Libr., Pitts., 1969-94. Mem. AAUW, DAR. Republican. Methodist. Avocations: sailing, skiing, swimming, hiking, travel. Home: 4985 Wheaton Dr Pittsburgh PA 15236-2064

WARNER, KENNETH E., public health educator, consultant; b. Washington, Jan. 25, 1947; s. Edgar W. Jr. and Betty (Strasburger) W.; m. Patricia A. Hilty, Oct. 1, 1977; children—Peter, Andrew. A.B., Dartmouth Coll., 1968; M.Phil., Yale U., 1970, Ph.D., 1974. Lectr. dept. health mgmt. and policy Sch. Pub. Health, U. Mich., Ann Arbor, 1972-74; asst. prof. Sch. Pub. Health, U. Mich., 1974-77, assoc. prof., 1977-83, prof., 1983—, chmn., 1982-88, 92-95; Richard D. Remington Collegiate prof. pub. health, 1995—; cons. Office of Tech. Assessment, U.S. Congress, Washington, 1976-95, Office on Smoking and Health, USPHS, Rockville, Md., 1978—, Inst. Medicine, Nat. Acad. Scis., Washington, 1984—, numerous additional pub. and pvt. orgns.; mem. bd. sci. counselors divsn. cancer prevention and control Nat. Cancer Inst., Bethesda, Md., 1985-89. Author: (with Bryan Luce) Cost-Benefit & Cost Effectiveness Analysis in Health Care, 1982; contbr. articles to profl. jours. Trustee Am. Lung Assn., Mich., Lansing, 1982; mem. subcom. on smoking Am. Heart Assn., Dallas, 1983-87; mem. com. on tobacco and cancer Am. Cancer Soc., N.Y.C., 1984-92. Hon. Woodrow Wilson fellow, 1968; W.K. Kellog Found. fellow, 1980-83; vis. scholar Nat. Bur. Econ. Research, Stanford, Calif., 1975-76; recipient Surgeon Gen.'s medallion Dr. C. Everett Koop, 1989. Fellow Assn. Health Svcs. Rsch.; mem. APHA (leadership award 1990), Am. Econ. Assn., Inst. Medicine, Nat. Assn. Pub. Health Policy (sec. council on smoking prevention 1983-84), Phi Beta Kappa. Office: U Michigan Dept Health Sch Pub Health Mgmt Policy 109 Observatory St Ann Arbor MI 48109-2029

WARNER, KENNETH WILSON, JR., editor, association publications executive; b. Chgo., Dec. 22, 1928; s. Kenneth Wilson and Ann S. (Knapp) W.; m. Deborah Ann Bollo, Dec. 28, 1982 (div. Apr. 1995); 1 child, Joseph; children by previous marriages: Sara, Seth, Katharin. B.S. Ed., No. Ill. U., 1950. Staff editor Bldg. Supply News, Chgo., 1953-56; staff editor Elec. Merchandising, 1956-60; free-lance writer Sarasota, Fla., 1960-66; editor Gunsport Mag., Alexandria and Falls Church, Va., 1966-67; editor Gunfacts Mag., Arlington, Va., 1968-70, pub., 1968-70; exec. editor Am. Rifleman, Nat. Rifle Assn., Washington, 1971-78, asst. dir. publs. div., 1972-78; editor Am. Hunter, 1973-78, Am. Rifleman, 1976-78; dir. publs. NRA, Washington, 1977-78; editor in chief Gun Digest, Knives Annual-DBI Books Inc., Greenville, W.Va., 1979—; design cons. Blackjack Knives, Effingham, Ill. Author: The Practical Book of Knives. 1976; The Practical Book of Guns, 1978. Editor: The Bolt Action, 1976. Contbr. articles to profl. jours. Cpl. U.S. Army. 1951-53. Recipient Cutlery Hall of Fame. Mem. NRA (life), Knifemaker's Guild. Am. (assoc.). Office: Gun Digest Editorial Office PO Box 52 Greenville WV 24945-0052

WARNER, LAVERNE, education educator; b. Huntsville, Tex., Aug. 14, 1941; d. Clifton Partney and Velma Oneta (Steely) W. BS, Sam Houston State U., 1962, MEd, 1969; PhD, East Tex. State U., 1977. Cert. elem. sch. tchr., Tex. First grade tchr. Port Arthur (Tex.) Ind. Sch. Dist., 1962-64; kindergarten tchr. Burlington (Vt.) Community Schs., 1964-66; first grade tchr. Aldine Sch. Dist., Houston, 1967-68; music tchr. Crawfordsville (Ind.) Community Schs., 1968-71; prof. early childhood edn. Sam Houston State U., Huntsville, 1975—, chmn. faculty senate, 1988-89; chair faculty senate Sam Houston State U., 1990-91, chair-elect, 1989-90; educator preparation Improvement Initiative, 1996-97. Author: (with P. Berry) Tunes for Tots, 1982, (with K. Craycraft) Fun with Familiar Tunes, 1987, Language in Centers: Kids Communicating, 1991, Theme Escapades, 1992, What If...Themes, 1993; contbg. editor Good Apple, Inc., Carthage, Ill., 1986-88, 91-93; contbr. over 60 articles to profl. jours. Mem. Huntsville Leadership Inst., 1986-88, chmn. adv. bd. 1987-88, chmn. 1987-88; Community Child Care Assn., Huntsville, 1988-90. Recipient Sam Houston State U. Excellence in Teaching award, 1992, Tchr. Educator of Yr. award Tex. Assn. for Edn. Young Children, 1992, Sammy award Divsn. of Student Life, 1996. Mem. Tex. Assn. Coll. Tchrs. (life, past pres.), Nat. Assn. for Edn. Young Children (life), Tex. Elementary-Kindergarten Nursery Educators (state pres. 1982-84), Tex. Assn. for Edn. Young Children (v.p. 1988-89, newsletter editor, 1991-93, Teacher Educator of Yr. 1992, pres.-elect 1993-95, pres. 1995-97), Huntsville Leadership Inst. Alumni Assn. (pres. 1988-89), Phi Delta Kappa (area 3H coord. 1986-92, Svc. Key 1987), Sam Houston Assn. for Edn. Young Children (charter, pres-elect, 1991-92, pres. 1992-93), Sam Houston Univ. Women (pres. 1985-86), Huntsville High Sch. Ex-Students Assn. (charter, pres. 1989-91), Sam Houston Alumni Assn. (bd. dirs. 1996—). Mem. Ch. of Christ. Avocations: music, reading, shopping. Office: Sam Houston State U Coll Edn and Applied Sci Huntsville TX 77341

WARNER, MARK ROY, film editor. Editor: (films) (with Freeman Davies and Billy Weber) 48 Hours, 1982, (with Don Zimmerman) Rocky III, 1982, (with Zimmerman) Staying Alive, 1983, (with Caroline Biggerstaff) A Soldier's Story, 1984, (with Christopher Lebenzon and Scott Wallace) Weird Science, 1985, (with Steve Mirkovich and Edward A. Warschilka) Big Trouble in Little China, 1986, (with Warschilka and John Wright) The Running Man, 1987, Cocoon: The Return, 1988, Driving Miss Daisy, 1989 (Academy award nomination best film editing 1989), Pacific Heights, 1990, Rush, 1992, (with John F. Burnett and Zimmerman) Leap of Faith, 1992, Rich in Love, 1992, Intersection, 1994, Dolores Claiborne, 1995. Home: 20567 Paradise Ln Topanga CA 90290-3735*

WARNER, MINER HILL, investment banker; b. N.Y.C., Aug. 13, 1942; s. Bradford Arnold and Nancy (Hill) W.; m. Ellen C. Murphy, Mar. 18, 1972; children—Alix Mallet-Prevost, Lily Wolcott. A.B., Harvard U., 1964; C.E.P., Institut d'Etudes Politiques, Paris, 1963; M.Sc. in Econs., London Sch. Econs., 1965; LL.B., U. Pa., 1968; postgrad., NYU. Grad. Sch. Bus. Adminstrn., 1971-73. Bar: N.Y. 1969. Assoc. Shearman & Sterling, N.Y.C., 1968-71; assoc. Salomon Bros. Inc., N.Y.C., 1971-73; v.p. Salomon Bros. Internat. Ltd., London, 1974-78; v.p., mgr. Salomon Bros. Inc., N.Y.C., 1979-87; dir. Merrill Lynch & Co., 1988-92; pres. Pub. Resources Internat., 1992—; former advisory dir. Council of the Americas, 1991-93, former dir. Woodwin Mgmt. Inc. Pres.'s Pvt. Sector Survey on Cost Control, Washington, 1982-83; sr. warden St. John's Ch., Fishers Island, N.Y.; regent Cathedral of St. John the Divine, N.Y.; Pilgrims, N.Y.C.; trustee N.Y. Hist. Soc. 1985, chmn. 1994—, Econ. Club, N.Y.; former dir. Hay Harbor Club, Fishers Island. Recipient Order of St. John of Jerusalem. Mem. Mayflower Soc. Republican. Episcopalian. Clubs: Brook (sec.), Links, River, Downtown Assn. (N.Y.C.); Metropolitan (Washington); Fishers Island. Home: 148 E End Ave New York NY 10028-7503 Office: Pub Resources Internat 780 3rd Ave Rm 2805 New York NY 10017-2024

WARNER, PETER DAVID, publishing executive; b. Phila., Aug. 15, 1942; s. Robert and Myra (Spector) W.; m. Ruth Bluestein (div. 1982); m. Jill Sansone, 1983; children: Emily, Cynthia, Nicholas. BA, NYU, 1964. Asst. dir. membership and devel. Mus. Modern Art, N.Y.C., 1973-76; editor, promotion dir. Book-of-the-Month Club, N.Y.C., 1976-79; pres. Thames and Hudson, N.Y.C., 1979—. Author: Loose Ends, 1972, Lifestyle, 1986. Mem. The Writers Room (bd. dirs.). Office: Thames & Hudson Inc 500 5th Ave New York NY 10110

WARNER, RAWLEIGH, JR., oil company executive; b. Chgo., Feb. 13, 1921; s. Rawleigh and Dorothy (Haskins) W.; m. Mary Ann deClairmont, Nov. 2, 1946; children: Alison W. Pyne, Suzanne W. Parsons. Grad., Lawrenceville (N.J.) Sch., 1940; A.B. cum laude, Princeton U., 1943. Sec., treas. Warner Bard Co., Chgo., 1946-48; with Continental Oil Co., 1948-53; asst. treas. Continental Oil Co., Houston, 1952-53; treas. Socony-Vacuum Overseas Supply Co., 1953-55; asst. treas. Mobil Overseas Oil Co., 1955-56; mgr. econs. dept., then mgr. Middle East dept. Socony Mobil Oil Co. Inc., 1956-59; regional v.p. Mobil Internat. Oil Co., 1959-60, exec. v.p., 1960-63, pres., 1963-64; exec. v.p., dir. Mobil Oil Corp. (formerly Socony Mobil Oil Co., Inc.), 1964, pres., 1965-69, chmn. bd., chief exec. officer, 1969-86; chmn. Mobil Corp., 1976-86. Served to capt. F.A., AUS, 1943-45. Decorated Purple Heart, Bronze Star, Silver Star. Mem. Am. Petroleum Inst. Republican. Presbyn. Clubs: Augusta (Ga.) Nat. Golf; Links (N.Y.C.) ; New Canaan Country; Blind Brook (Rye Brook, N.Y.); Jupiter Island (Hobe Sound, Fla.); Chicago; Seminole (North Palm Beach, Fla.). Office: Mobil Corp PO Box 2072 New York NY 10163-2072

WARNER, ROBERT MARK, university dean, archivist, historian,; b. Montrose, Colo., June 28, 1927; s. Mark Thomas and Bertha Margaret (Rich) W.; m. Eleanor Jane Bullock, Aug. 21, 1954; children: Mark Steven, Jennifer Jane. Student, U. Denver, 1945; B.A., Muskingum Coll., 1949, LL.D. (hon.), 1981; M.A., U. Mich., 1953, Ph.D., 1958; H.H.D. (hon.), Westminster (Pa.) Coll., 1981; L.H.D. (hon.), DePaul U., 1983. Tchr. high sch. Montrose, Colo., 1949-50; lectr. dept. history U. Mich., 1958-66, asso. prof., 1966-71, prof., 1971—, prof. Sch. Info. and Library Studies, 1974—, dean Sch. Info. and Library Studies, 1985-92, univ. historian, 1992—, interim dir. Univ. Libraries, 1988-90; asst. in rsch. Bentley Hist. Libr., 1953-57, asst. curator, 1957-61, asst. dir., 1961-66, dir., 1966-80; archivist of U.S., 1980-85; mem. exec. com. Bentley Hist. Libr., 1988—; bd. visitors Sch. Libr. Sci., Case Western Res. U., 1976-80, chmn., 1980-84, Maxwell Sch. Govt., Syracuse U., 1982-87; chmn. Gerald R. Ford Presdl. Libr. Bldg. Com., 1977-79; bd. dirs., sec. Gerald R. Ford Found., 1987—; trustee Woodrow Wilson Internat. Ctr. for Scholars, 1980-85, chmn. fellowship com., 1983-85; chmn. Nat. Hist. Publs. and Records Commn., 1980-85; mem. exec. com. Internat. Coun. on Archives, 1984-88; pres. 2d European Conf. on Archives, 1989; comptroller gen. U.S. Rsch. and Edn. Adv. Com., 1988—; rsch. adv. com. Online Computer Libr. Ctr., 1990-93; bd. govs. Clements Libr., 1988-90, 93—, Clark Hist. Libr. Ctrl. Mich. U., 1987—; vis. prof. UCLA, 1993. Author: Chase S. Osborn, 1860-1949, 1960, Profile of a Profession, 1964, (with R. Bordin) The Modern Manuscript Library, 1966, (with C.W. Vanderhill) A Michigan Reader: 1865 to the Present, 1974, (with F. Blouin) Sources for the Study of Migration and Ethnicity, 1979, Diary of a Dream: A History of the National Archives Independence Movement, 1980-1985, 1995. Served with U.S. Army, 1950-52. Recipient Disting. Svc. award Muskingum Coll., 1990, Disting. Svc. award Nat. Hist. Pub. and Records Commn., 1992. Fellow Soc. Am. Archivists; mem. Am. Hist. Assn. (council 1981-85), Orgn. Am. Historians, ALA (council 1986-91), Assn. for Library and Info. Sci. Edn., Presbyn. Hist. Soc. (bd. dirs. 1987-91), Am. Assn. State and Local History, Hist. Soc. Mich. (trustee 1960-66, v.p. 1972-73, pres. 1973-74), Soc. Am. Archivists (mem. council 1967-71, sec., exec. dir. 1971-73, v.p. 1974-75, pres. 1976-77), Am. Antiquarian Soc., Phi Alpha Theta, Beta Phi Mu. Presbyterian. Club: U. Mich. Research. Lodge: Rotary. Home: 1821 Coronada Dr Ann Arbor MI 48103-5066 Office: U Mich Sch Info & Libr Studies 550 E University Ave Ann Arbor MI 48109-1092

WARNER, ROBERT S., company director, former accountant; b. Erie, Pa., Apr. 9, 1907; s. Spencer Roycraft and Anna Edith (MacDonald) W.; m. Doris Jean Squarey, June 29, 1931 (dec. Sept. 1987); children: Elizabeth S. (Mrs. Richard W. Bakenhus), Robert S. (dec.); m. Mary Catherine Moore, Oct. 13, 1990. Litt.B., Rutgers U., 1928. With Lybrand, Ross Bros. & Montgomery, C.P.A.s, N.Y.C., 1928-72; charge St. Louis office Lybrand, Ross Bros. & Montgomery, C.P.A.s, 1936-49; charge Los Angeles office Lybrand, Ross Bros. & Montgomery, C.P.A.s, Los Angeles, 1949-72; mem. firm Lybrand, Ross Bros. & Montgomery, C.P.A.s, 1944-72; mem. exec. com.; exec. com. Coopers & Lybrand; dir. Bixby Ranch Co. Trustee J.B. and Emily Van Nuys Charities, L.A., South Coast Med. Ctr. Found., South Laguna. Mem. Calif., N.Y. socs. C.P.A.s, Am. Inst. C.P.A.s. Clubs: Bohemian (San Francisco); Big Canyon Country (Newport Beach, Calif.). Home: 32 N La Senda Dr Laguna Beach CA 92677-3365

WARNER, SCOTT DENNIS, investment banker; b. York, Pa., July 13, 1963; s. Earl Dennis and Sandra Glee (Barnhart) W. SB in Elec. Engring., MIT, 1986, SB in Computer Sci. and Engring., 1986, SM in Elec. Engring. and Computer Sci., 1986; MBA in Fin., U. Chgo., 1990. Rschr., teaching asst. MIT Lab. for Computer Sci., Cambridge, Mass., 1982-86; intern IBM Corp., Yorktown Heights, N.Y., 1983-86; fin. analyst Merrill Lynch & Co., N.Y.C., 1986-88, assoc., 1990-94, v.p., 1994-95; summer assoc. Goldman, Sachs & Co., N.Y.C., 1989; v.p. Lipper & Co., N.Y.C., 1995—. Nat. Merit scholar, 1981, ROTC scholar, 1981, teaching asst. scholar MIT, 1985, 86; Leon C. Marshall scholar U. Chgo., 1988. Mem. Nat. Eagle Scout Assn., Delta Upsilon Frat. Republican. Presbyterian. Home: 235 E 95th St Apt 23E New York NY 10128 Office: Lipper & Co 101 Park Ave New York NY 10178

WARNER, SETH L., mathematician, educator; b. Muskegon, Mich., July 11, 1927; s. Seth LeMoyne and Agnes (Brustad) W.; m. Susan Emily Rose, June 16, 1962; children: Susan Emily, Sarah Southall, Seth Lawrence. B.S., Yale U., 1950; M.A., Harvard U., 1951, Ph.D., 1955. Rsch. instr. Duke U., 1955-57, asst. prof., 1957-61, asso. prof., 1961-65, prof. math., 1965-95, dir. grad. studies math., 1966-68; prof. emeritus math., 1995—; chmn. Duke U., 1968-70, 73-82; mem. Inst. Advanced Studies, 1959-60; vis. disting. prof. math. Reed Coll., 1970-71; visitor U. Paris, 1964-65, U. Oslo, 1982-83. Author: Modern Algebra, vols. I and II, 1965, re-issued, 1990, Classical Modern Algebra, 1971, Topological Fields, 1989, Topological Rings, 1993. Served with Med. Service Corps AUS, 1946-48. Mem. Phi Beta Kappa, Sigma Xi. Episcopalian. Home: 2433 Wrightwood Ave Durham NC 27705-5823 Office: Duke U Math Dept Box 90320 Durham NC 27708-0320

WARNER, THEODORE KUGLER, JR., lawyer; b. Phila., Sept. 13, 1909; s. Theodore Kugler and Anna (Allen) W.; m. Dorothy Wark Hoehler, Nov. 23, 1935 (dec. 1985); children: Betsy Ann, Peter Joyce; m. Lynn Howell, May 20, 1995. A.B., U. Pa., 1931, LL.B. cum laude, 1934. Bar: Pa. 1934. With Pa. R.R., Phila., 1934-70; chief tax counsel Pa. R.R., 1952-58, dir. taxation, 1958-68, v.p. taxes, 1968, v.p. accounting and taxes, 1968-69, v.p. corp. adminstrn., 1969-70; pres. Can. So. Ry., 1968-70; v.p. Pitts. & Lake Eric R.R., 1968-70; officer, dir. other Penn Central cos., 1968-70; counsel Duane, Morris & Heckscher, Phila., 1970-71, Harper & Driver, 1975—; lectr. on consol. returns various tax forums. Bd. suprs. Easttown Twp., Pa., 1962-70, chmn., 1966-70; bd. dirs. Independence Found., 1991—, sec. 1993, pres., 1993-95, sec.-treas., 1996—. Mem. Nat. Tax Assn. (pres. 1965-66), Am. Law Inst. (life mem.), ABA, Pa. Bar Assn., Order of Coif, Aronimink Golf Club, Union League, Masons (33 deg., mem. com. on masonic homes 1970-84, chmn. 1975-77, 81-83, Franklin medal 1983, bd. dirs., treas. Masonic libr. and mus. 1991—), Tau Kappa Epsilon. Republican. Lutheran. Home: 39 Old Covered Bridge Rd Newtown Square PA 19073-1211 Office: 1000 N American St Philadelphia PA 19123-1512

WARNER, VINCENT W., bishop. Bishop Diocese of Olympia, Seattle, 1990—. Office: Diocese of Olympia PO Box 12126 1551 10th Ave E Seattle WA 98102-4298*

WARNER, WALTER DUKE, corporate executive; b. Davenport, Iowa, Feb. 26, 1952; s. Robert Martin and Opal Louise (Gibbons) W.; m. Susan Dee Hafferkamp, Nov. 15, 1975 (div. 1982); 1 child, Natalie. BS, Drake U., 1975. Ops. officer Iowa-Des Moines Nat. Bank, 1975-78; from v.p. ops. to v.p. mktg. and pub. rels. Cen. Savs. and Loan Assn., San Diego, Calif., 1978-84; pres. The Lomas Santa Fe Cos., Solana Beach, Calif., 1985-91; pres., co-founder Ebert Composites Corp., San Diego, 1991—, also bd. dirs.; bd. dirs. Torrey Pines Bank, Solana Beach, Lomas Group Inc., Del Mar, Calif., Madison Valley Properties, Inc., La Jolla, Calif., Nature Preserved of Am. Inc., San Clemente, Calif.; pres., bd. dirs. Regents Pk. Comml. Asns., La Jolla. Bd. dirs. Inst. of the Ams., La Jolla, 1986—, mem. internat. council, 1986—; chmn. bd. dirs., pres. San Diego chpt. Arthritis Found., 1985-87; dir., pres. Gildred Found., Solana Beach, 1986—; founding dir., treas. Golden Triangle Arts Found. Mem. The Exec. Com., Calif. League of Savs. and Loans (mem. mktg. and ops. com. 1982-84), Internat. Forum for Corp. Dirs., Iowa Club of San Diego (founding dir. 1984-85). Republican. Protestant. Avocations: tennis, piano.

WARNER, WILLIAM HAMER, applied mathematician; b. Pitts., Oct. 6, 1929; s. John Christian and Louise (Hamer) W.; m. Janet Louise West, June 29, 1957; 1 dau., Katherine Patricia. Student, Haverford Coll., 1946-48; B.S., Carnegie Inst. Tech., 1950, M.S., 1951, Ph.D., 1953. Research asso. grad. div. applied math. Brown U., Providence, 1953-55; asst. prof. dept. aerospace engring. and mechanics U. Minn., Mpls., 1955-58; asso. prof. U. Minn., 1958-68, prof., 1968-95, prof. emeritus, 1995—. Author: (with L.E. Goodman) Statics, 1963, Dynamics, 1964; contbr. articles to profl. jours. Mem. Am. Math. Soc., Soc. Indsl. and Applied Math., Math. Assn. Am., Soc. Natural Philosophy. Office: U Minn 107 Akerman Hall Minneapolis MN 55455

WARNICK, WALTER LEE, mechanical engineer; b. Balt., May 31, 1947; s. Marvin Paul and Freda (Wilt) W.; m. Metta Ann Nichter, May 2, 1970; children: Ashlie Colleen, Leah Brooke. BS in Engring., Johns Hopkins U., 1969; PhD, U. Md., 1977. Registered profl. engr., Md. Engr. Westinghouse Electric Co., Linthicum, Md., 1969-71, U.S. Naval Rsch. Lab., Washington, 1971-77; engr. U.S. Dept. Energy, Washington, 1977-85, sr. exec., 1985—; Dept. Energy rep. Nat. Acid Precipitation Assessment Program, Washington, 1981-96, dir. Office of Scientific and Tech. Info., Washington, 1997—. Author: Warnick Families of Western Maryland, 1988, 95, Wilt Families of Western Maryland, 1991. Pres. citizen's adv. com. to Howard County Bd. of Edn., Ellicott City, Md., 1980-82. Mem. ASME, Sigma Xi. Office: US Dept Energy Washington DC 20585

WARNKE, DETLEF ANDREAS, geologist, educator; b. Berlin, Fed. Republic of Germany, Jan. 29, 1928; came to U.S., 1955; s. Aloys and Martha (Konetzky) W.; m. Holly M. Menkel, Nov. 14, 1964 (div. 1993); children: Erik, D. Christian. Diploma in Geology, U. Freiburg, Fed. Republic of Germany, 1953; PhD in Geology, U. So. Calif., 1965. Jr. exploitation engr. Shell Oil, Houston and Los Angeles, 1956-58; research asst. U. So. Calif., Los Angeles, 1959-61; instr. various colls., Los Angeles and Long Beach, Calif., 1959-63; research assoc., asst. prof. Fla. State U., Tallahassee, 1963-71; from asst. prof. to prof. geology Calif. State U., Hayward, 1971—, chair dept. geology, 1994—; exchange prof. Free U. Berlin, 1980-81. Contbr. articles to profl. jours. Fulbright scholar, 1987-88; NSF grantee. Mem. Geol. Soc. Am., Soc. Sedimentary Geology, Am. Geophys. Union, Am. Quaternary Assn., Geologische Vereinigung, Sigma Xi. Avocations: skiing, hiking. Office: Calif State U Hayward Dept Geol Scis Hayward CA 94542

WARNKE, PAUL CULLITON, lawyer; b. Webster, Mass., Jan. 31, 1920; s. Paul Martin and Lillian (Culliton) W.; m. Jean Farjeon Rowe, Sept. 9, 1948; children: Margaret Farjeon, Georgia Culliton, Thomas Martin, Stephen August, Benjamin Hyatt. A.B., Yale U., 1941; LL.B., Columbia U., 1948; LL.D. (hon.), Northland Coll., 1979, Franklin and Marshall Coll., 1983, George Washington U., 1984, Grinnell Coll., 1985, Amherst Coll., 1985, Haverford Coll., 1989. Bar: D.C. 1948. Assoc. Covington & Burling, Washington, 1948-57; ptnr. Covington & Burling, 1957-66; gen. counsel Dept. Def., 1966-67, asst. sec. def. for internat. security affairs, 1967-69; ptnr. Clifford, Warnke, Glass, McIlwain & Finney, 1969-77; dir. U.S. Arms Control and Disarmament Agy., Washington, 1977-78; chief U.S. arms control negotiator, 1977-78; ptnr. Clifford & Warnke, Washington, 1978-91, Howrey & & Simon, Washington, 1991—; adj. prof. Georgetown U. Sch. Fgn. Svc., 1996-97; spl. cons. to sec. state, 1978-81; mem. Md. and D.C. adv. coms. to U.S. Commn. Civil Rights, 1962-66; trustee Lawyers Com. for Civil Rights Under Law; dir. Internat. Vol. Svcs., 1973-76; exec. com. Trilateral Commn., 1973-77; mem. China coun. Asia Soc., 1976-77; mem. Presdl. Adv. Bd. on Arms Proliferation Policy, 1995-96; mem. sci. and policy adv. commn. ACDA, 1995—; mem. disciplinary bd. D.C. Bar, 1973-75, bd. govs., 1976-77. Trustee Potomac Sch., 1958-66, chmn. bd., 1965-66; bd. dirs. Health and Welfare Coun. Nat. Capital Area, 1966-67, Franklin and Eleanor Roosevelt Inst., 1991—, Georgetown U., 1979-92, Wolftrap Found., 1978-83; trustee Northland Coll., 1970-76, Columbia U., 1984-90; mem. bd. visitors Columbia U. Sch. Law; chmn. selection com. Albert Einstein Peace Prize Found., 1991-93; mem. governing bd. Common Cause, 1983-86. Lt. USCGR, 1942-46. Fellow Am. Bar Found.; mem. ABA, Fed. Bar Assn., D.C. Bar Assn., Coun. Am. Ambs., Am. Soc. Internat. Law, Coun. Fgn. Rels., Atlantic Coun. of the U.S. (sr. councillor), Am. Acad. Diplomacy. Democrat. Clubs: Met. (Washington); Yale (N.Y.C.), West Chop (Martha's Vineyard, Mass.). Home: 5037 Garfield St NW Washington DC 20016-3465 Office: Howrey & Simon 3rd Fl 1299 Pennsylvania Ave NW Ste 3 Washington DC 20004-2400

WARNKE, ROGER ALLEN, pathology educator; b. Peoria, Ill., Feb. 22, 1945; s. Delmar Carl and Ruth Armanelle (Peard) W.; m. Joan Marie Gebhart, Nov. 18, 1972; children: Kirsten Marie, Lisa Marie. BS, U. Ill., 1967; MD, Washington U., St. Louis, 1971. Diplomate Am. Bd. Pathology. Intern in pathology Stanford (Calif.) U. Med. Sch., 1971-72, resident in pathology, 1972-73, postdoctoral fellow in pathology, 1973-75, postdoctoral fellow in immunology, 1975-76, asst. prof. pathology, 1976-82, assoc. prof., 1983-90; prof., 1991—; cons. Becton Dickinson Monoclonal Ctr., Mountain View, Calif., 1982-88, IDEC, Mountain View, 1985-90; sci. advisor Ventana Med. Systems, Inc., Tucson, 1986-94. Contbr. over 200 articles to med. jours., chpts. to books. Recipient Benjamin Castleman award Mass. Gen. Hosp., 1981; Agnes Axtel Moule faculty scholar Stanford U., 1979-82; Nat. Cancer Inst. and NIH rsch. grantee, 1978—. Mem. So. Bay Pathology Soc., Calif. Soc. Pathologists, U.S. Can. Acad. Path., Am. Assn. Pathologists, Soc. for Hematopathology, European Assn. for Haematopathology. Home: 845 Tolman Dr Stanford CA 94305-1025 Office: Stanford U Dept Pathology Stanford CA 94305

WARNOCK, DAVID GENE, nephrologist; b. Parker, Ariz., Mar. 5, 1945. MD, U. Calif., San Francisco, 1970. Diplomate Am. Bd. Internal Medicine, Am. Bd. Nephrology. Intern U. Calif., San Francisco, 1970-71, resident, 1971-73; fellow nephrology NIH, Bethesda, Md., 1973-75; prof. medicine and pharmacology U. Calif., San Francisco, 1983; prof. U. Ala., Birmingham, 1988—; chief nephrology sect. VA Med. Ctr., Birmingham, 1983-88; prof., dir. divsn. nephrology U. Ala., Birmingham, 1988—, prof. medicine & physiology, 1988—. Mem. AAAS, Am. Physiol. Soc., Am. Soc. Clin. Investigation, Am. Soc. Nephrology. Office: U Ala Nephrology Rsch & Tng Ctr UAB Sta Birmingham AL 35294

WARR, ROBERT, producer. Appeared in film Let Him Have It, 1991. Recipient Best Music Video-Long Form Grammy award, 1996. Office: Vivid Prodns Centro House 1st Fl, 23 Mandela St, London NW1 ODY, England*

WARREN, ALBERT, publishing executive; b. Warren, Ohio, May 18, 1920; s. David and Clara W.; m. Margaret Virginia Yeomans, Jan. 9, 1947; children: Ellen, Paul, Claire, Daniel, Thomas, Joan. BA in Journalism, Ohio State U., 1942. Assoc. editor TV Digest, Washington, 1945-50, sr. editor, 1950-58, chief Washington Bur., 1958-61; pres., editor, pub. Warren Pub., Inc., Washington, 1961—; lectr. Columbia Grad. Sch. Journalism, N.Y.C., 1962-75; mem. alumni adv. coun. Ohio State U., Columbus, 1982-88. Contbr. articles to profl. jours. Mem. adv. coun. sch. of journalism Ohio State U., 1982—. With USNR, 1942-45, PTO. Recipient Disting. Alumnus award Ohio State U. Sch. Journalism, 1995. Mem. Ind. Newsletter Assn. (co-founder 1963, pres. 1965-66), Newsletter Pubs. Assn. (Pub. of Yr. 1985), Broadcast Pioneers (Annual Recognition award 1982), Cable TV Pioneers, Internat. Radio and TV Soc. Pubs., Mus. of TV & Radio, White House Corr. Assn., U.S. Congress Periodical Gallery, Soc. Profl. Journalists (Hall of Fame 1991). Home: 26 W Kirke St Chevy Chase MD 20815-4261 Office: Warren Pub Inc 2115 Ward Ct NW Washington DC 20037-1209

WARREN, ALVIN CLIFFORD, JR., lawyer, educator; b. Daytona Beach, Fla., May 14, 1944; s. Alvin Clifford and Barbara (Barnes) W.; m. Judith Blatt, Aug. 20, 1966; children—Allison, Matthew. B.A., Yale U., 1966; J.D., U. Chgo., 1969. Bar: Conn. 1970, Pa. 1975. Prof. law U. Conn.-West Hartford, 1969-73, Duke U., Durham, N.C., 1973-74, U. Pa., Phila., 1974-79, Harvard U. Law Sch., Cambridge, Mass., 1979—. Mem. ABA (tax sect.). Contbr. articles to law jours. Office: Law Sch Harvard U Cambridge MA 02138

WARREN, CHARLES DAVID, library administrator; b. Martin, Tenn., June 12, 1944; s. Charles Alton and Evelyn (Bell) W.; m. Linda Ann Hild, July 10, 1971; children: Aaron David, Meredith Hild, Julia Myers. BS, U. Tenn., 1967; MS, U. Ill., Urbana, 1969. cert. pub. library adminstr. Dir. Shiloh Regional Library, Jackson, Tenn., 1969-72, Cumberland County Pub. Library, Fayetteville, N.C., 1973-79; exec. dir. Richland County Pub. Library, Columbia, S.C., 1979—; v.p. LHW Creations, Inc., 1979—. Bd. dirs. Civic Music Assn., Fayetteville, N.C., 1973-79, Fayetteville Symphony, 1973-78, Fayetteville Arts Commn., 1975, Friends of Librs. U.S.A., 1994—; mem. Columbia Coord. Coun., 1987-88; chmn. Richland County History Commn., 1987-93; mem. John Cotton Dana Awards Commn., 1994—. Recipient Lucy Hampton Bostick award, 1993, S.C. Pub. Adminstr. Yr. award, 1993; named Young Man of Yr., Fayetteville Jaycees, 1977, S.C. Libr. of Yr., 1991. Mem. ALA (pres. Jr. Member Roundtable 1977, chmn. awards com. 1984), Southeastern Libr. Assn. (pres. pub. libr. sect. 1978), S.C. Libr. Assn. (bd. dirs. 1980), Caprician Club, Spring Valley Country Club, Rotary, Kiwanis, Beta Phi Mu. Democrat. Episcopalian. Home: 217 Cricket Hill Rd Columbia SC 29223-3003 Office: Richland County Pub Libr 1431 Assembly St Columbia SC 29201-3101

WARREN, CHRISTOPHER COLLINS, professional football player; b. Silver Spring, Md., Jan. 24, 1967. Degree in psychology, Ferrum Coll. Running back Seattle Seahawks, 1990—. Selected to Pro Bowl, 1993-94. Office: c/o Seattle Seahawks 11220 NE 53rd St Kirkland WA 98033-7505*

WARREN, CLAY, communication educator; b. Lexington Park, Md., Aug. 11, 1946; s. Cassius Clay and Dorothy Dean Warren; m. Gitte Bonde Kolind, May 1, 1985; children: Laura Kolind, Daniel Clay Kolind. BS, U.S. Naval Acad., 1968; MA, U. Colo., 1973, PhD, 1976. Instr. U. Colo., Boulder, 1973-76; asst. prof. semester-at-sea program Inst. Shipbd. Edn., Laguna Hills, Calif., 1977; vis. asst. prof. U. Coll. Cape Breton, Sydney, N.S., Can., 1978, assoc. prof., 1984-90; asst. prof. Shepherd Coll., Shepherdstown, W.Va., 1978-79, U. Hawaii at Manoa, Honolulu, 1979-82; sr. lectr. Internat. People's Coll., Elsinore, Denmark, 1982-84; assoc. prof. George Washington U., Washington, 1990-91, Chauncey M. Depew prof., 1991—; assoc. cons. M J Solutions, Westport, Conn., 1986—; dir. comm. program George Washington U., Washington, 1990—, Warren Consulting, Washington, 1990—. Author: Coming Around, 1986; editor: Inner Visions, Outer Voices, 1988; contbr. articles to scholarly jours. Mem. site team Mil. Installation Vol. Edn. Rev. Project Office of Asst. Sec. of Def., 1992—. Lt. USN, 1968-71. Latin Am. Teaching fellow Tufts U., 1977, Tompkins Inst. Rsch. fellow, 1987-89; Rudolf Dreikurs Meml. scholar Internat. Com. for Adlerian Summer Schs. and Insts., 1988; named Princeton Seminarian Acad. Consciousness Studies, Princeton U., 1994. Mem. AAUP (v.p. George Washington U. chpt. 1994—), Internat. Comm. Assn., N.Am. Soc. Adlerian Psychology, Folk Edn. Assn. Am. (exec. coun. 1992—). Avocations: certified scuba diver, sport parachutist, pvt. pilot, pianist, creative writer. Office: George Washington U Ste 709 2130 H St NW Washington DC 20037-2515

WARREN, CRAIG BISHOP, flavor and fragrance company executive, researcher; b. Phila., Oct. 21, 1939. AB, Franklin and Marshall Coll., 1961; MS, Villanova U., 1963; PhD, Cornell U., 1968. Rsch. chemist Monsanto Co., St. Louis, 1968-70, sr. rsch. chemist, 1970-72, rsch. specialist, 1973-75; group leader Internat. Flavors & Fragrances, Union Beach, N.J., 1975-77, sr. group leader, 1977-79, rsch. dir., 1979-83, v.p., 1983—. Editor: Odor Quality and Chemical Structure, 1981, Use of Computers in Flavor and Fragrance Research, 1983; contbr. 40 articles to profl. jours.; patentee in field. Mem. exec. coun. Boy Scouts Am., Monmouth County, N.J., 1981-85. Rsch. fellow NIH, 1964-68. Mem. Assn. Rsch. Dirs. (pres. 1989-90), Am. Chem. Soc. (chmn. Monmouth Country chpt. 1980-81), N.Y. Acad. Sci., Indsl. Rsch. Inst., ASTM. Avocations: bicycling, sailing, skiing, tropical fish, personal computers. Office: Internat Flavors & Frangrance 1515 State Route 36 Keyport NJ 07735-3542

WARREN, DAVID GRANT, lawyer, educator; b. Chgo.; m. Marsha White, 1959. A.B., Miami U., Oxford, Ohio, 1958; J.D., Duke U., 1964. Bar: N.C. 1964. Prof. Med. Ctr., Duke U., Durham, N.C., 1975—; exec. dir. N.C. Med. Malpractice Study Commn., 1986, Gov.'s Inst. on Alcohol and Substance Abuse, 1991—; faculty mem. U.N.C., U. London, Georgetown U., McGill U. News editor Jour. Health Politics, Policy and Law, 1977—. Office: Duke U Med Ctr PO Box 3834 Durham NC 27710-3834

WARREN, DAVID HARDY, psychology educator; b. Chelsea, Mass., July 28, 1943; s. Roland Leslie and Margaret (Hodges) W.; m. Katherine V. Warren; children: Michael Jonathan Warren, Gabriel Kristopher Coy. A.B. in Psychology, Yale U., 1965; Ph.D. in Child Devel, U. Minn., 1969. Prof. psychology U. Calif., Riverside, 1969—, dean Coll. Humanities and Social Scis., 1977-85, dir. Univ. honors program, 1989-92, chair dept. psychology, 1992-94, exec vice chancellor, 1994—. Author: Blindness and Early Childhood Development, 1977, 84, Blindness and Children: An Individual Differences Approach, 1994; contbr. articles to profl. jours. Mem. Psychonomic Soc., AAAS. Office: U Calif Office of Exec Vice Chancellor Riverside CA 92521

WARREN, DAVID LILES, educational association executive; b. Goldsboro, N.C., Sept. 15, 1943; s. James Hubert and Katherine (Liles) W.; m. Ellen Elizabeth LeGendre, Mar. 1, 1969; children—Jamison, Mackenzie, Katrin. B.A. in English, Wash. State U., 1965; M. Urban Studies, Yale U., 1970, M.Div., 1970; Ph.D., U. Mich., 1976; LittD, Elmhurst Coll., 1994, Moravian Coll., 1994; LLD, Rider U., 1996. Gen. sec. Dwight Hall, Yale U., New Haven, 1969-76, bd. dirs., 1976—; assoc. dir. community relations Yale U., New Haven, 1976-78; sr. v.p., provost Antioch U., N.Y.C. and Yellow Springs, Ohio, 1978-82; chief adminstrv. officer City of New Haven, 1982-84; pres. Ohio Wesleyan U., Delaware, 1984-93, Nat. Assn. Indep. Colls. and Univs., Washington, 1993—; cons. to hosps., sch. systems, colls., univs.; bd. dirs. Delaware County Bank; chmn. NCAA Pres. Commn., Div. III, 1990-92. Contbr. chpts. to books, articles to Yale Alumni Mag. Mem. NEw Haven Bd. Alderman, 1973-75; vice chmn. New Haven Commn. on Poverty, 1981-82; pres. North Coast Athletic Conf., 1988-90; justice of peace New Haven Dem. Party, 1974-76; state chmn. People to People, 1987; chmn. Gov.'s Task Force on Dep. Registrar, 1987; chmn. Ohio Five Coll. Commn., 1985-95, Campus Compact Nat. Exec. Com., 1987-88; bd. dirs. U.S. Health Corp., Coun. Ethics and Econs.; exec. com. Great Lakes Colls. Assn., Ctrl. Ohio Symphony Orch.; chmn. Ohio Ethics commn. Fulbright scholar Wash. State U., 1965-66; Rockefeller fellow Yale U., 1966; disting. Centennial Alumnus Wash. State U. Mem. Am. Assn. Higher Edn., Assn. Ind. Colls. Univs. (sec. 1987-88), Phi Beta Kappa. Democrat. Methodist. Clubs: University (Columbus, Ohio); Graduate (New Haven). Avocations: jogging; writing; tennis. Office: Nat Assn Ind Colls & Univs 1025 Connecticut Ave NW Ste 700 Washington DC 20036-5420

WARREN, DEAN STUART, artist; b. Mpls., June 30, 1949; s. Jefferson Trowbridge and Dorothy Ann (Edin) W.; m. Betty Sharon Poe, Aug. 14, 1971; children: Jeremy, Adam. BFA, Fla. Atlantic U., 1973; MA, Northwestern State U., 1975; MFA, Stephen F. Austin State U., 1980. Instr. art Cisco (Tex.) Jr. Coll., 1976-78; staff craftsworker Walt E. Disney Show Prodn. Walt Disney World, Lake Buena Vista, Fla., 1981-83, staff craftsworker staff shop, 1983, property craftsworker, 1983-87, artist preparator animation dept., 1987—; lead prodn. artist Marvac, Inc., Seminole County, Fla., 1983; founder Dean S. Warren Studio, 1991—; cons. Mt. Dora (Fla.) Ctr. for Arts Children's Edn. Program; instr. Bok Tower Gardens Art Ctr. Workshop, Lake Wales, Fla., 1996. Author: Runemaster, 1991; project artist Youth Art Symposium, U. Ctrl. Fla., 1993, Children's Art program, Atlantic Ctr. for arts, 1993, 95, Children's Art Program Mount Dora Ctr. for Arts, 1995, Edn. Ctr., 1996; one-man shows include Ormond Beach (Fla.) Meml. Art Gallery and Gardens, 1987, U. Ctrl. Fla. Art Gallery, Orlando, 1991, Harris House Atlantic Ctr. for Arts, New Smyrna Beach, Fla., 1993; exhibited in group shows at U. Miami (Fla.) Sculpture Invitational, 1982, Valencia C.C. Fine Arts Gallery, Orlando, 1989, Polk C.C. Fine Arts Gallery, Winter Haven, Fla., 1990, U. Ga., Athens, 1990, U. Tampa (Fla.) Scarfone Gallery, 1991, World Cup Soccer, Valencia C.C., 1994, Mt. Dora Ctr. of Arts, 1996, others. Recipient Artist in the Schs. grant Tex. Commn. on the Arts, 1980, awards U. Ga. Bot. Gardens, Athens, 1980, Valencia C.C., East Campus, Orlando, 1983, Arts on The Park, Lakeland, Fla., 1995. Home: 8069 Wellsmere Cir Orlando FL 32835-5361

WARREN, DONALD WILLIAM, physiology educator, dentistry educator; b. Bklyn., Mar. 22, 1935; s. Sol B. and Frances (Plotkin) W.; m. Priscilla Girardi, June 10, 1956; children: Donald W. Jr., Michael C. BS, U. N.C., 1956, DDS, 1959; MS, U. Pa., 1961, PhD, 1963; d Odontology honoris causa, U. Kuopio, Finland, 1991. Asst. prof. dentistry U. N.C., Chapel Hill, 1963-65, dir. Craniofacial Ctr., 1963—, assoc. prof., 1965-69, prof., 1969-80, chmn. dept. dental ecology, 1970-85, Kenan prof., 1980—, rsch. prof. otolaryngology, 1985—; cons. NIH, Bethesda, Md., 1967—, R. J. Reynolds-Nabisco, Winston-Salem, N.C., 1986—. Contbr. articles to profl. jours. Recipient Honor award Am. Cleft Palate Assn./Craniofacial Assn., 1992, O. Max Garner award U. N.C. Bd. Govs., 1993. Fellow AAAS, Internat. Coll. Dentists, Am. Speech and Hearing Lang. Assn., Internat. Assn. Dental Rsch., Acoustical Soc. Am., Am. Cleft Palate Assn. (pres. 1981-82, Disting. Svc. award 1984), Am. Cleft Palate Edn. Found. (pres. 1976-77). Avocations: horse related activities, running, farming. Home: PO Box 1356 Southern Pines NC 28388-1356 Office: U NC Sch Dentistry CB # 7450 Chapel Hill NC 27599

WARREN, EDUS HOUSTON, JR., investment management executive; b. Danville, Va., Dec. 9, 1923; s. Edus Houston and Edith (Farley) W.; children: Ann Farley Warren, Ralph Lounsbury, Sarah W. Fenton, Edus Houston III; m. Harriet C. Higgins, May 5, 1990. A.B., Harvard U., 1946. With Spencer Trask & Co., Inc., N.Y.C., 1951-77; gen. partner Spencer Trask & Co., Inc., 1959-68, pres., chief exec. officer, dir., 1974-77; vice chmn. Hornblower, Weeks, Noyes & Trask, Inc., (merger Spencer Trask & Co., Inc./Hornblower, Weeks, Hemphill, Noyes), 1977-78; exec. v.p., mem. fin. com., mem. exec. com. Loeb Rhoades, Hornblower & Co.; vice chmn. Capital Guardian Research Co., N.Y.C., 1978-88; sr. v.p. Capital Internat. Ltd., London, 1989-95; sr. v.p., dir. Capital Guardian Trust Co., 1989-96; sr. ptnr. Capital Group Cos.; treas., trustee Fin. Acctg. Found., 1981-89. Served to 1st lt. USAAF, 1943-45. Decorated D.F.C., Air medal. Mem. N.Y. Soc. Security Analysts, Fin. Analysts Fedn. (chmn.), Securities Industry Assn., Inst. Chartered Financial Analysts. Republican. Episcopalian. Home: 1157 Lynch Mountain Rd Sautee Nacoochee GA 30571

WARREN, HARRY VERNEY, geological sciences educator, consulting geological engineer; b. Anacortes, Wash., Aug. 27, 1904; s. Victor Mackenzie and Rosamond Ellice Burrell (Campion) W.; m. Margaret Bessie Tisdall, July 14, 1934; children: Charlotte Louisa Verney, Victor Henry Verney. BA, U. B.C., Vancouver, Can., 1926, BASc, 1927, DSc (hon.), 1978; postgrad., Rhodes Sch. for B.C., 1926-29; MSc, Oxford U., Eng., 1928, DPhil, 1929; DSc (hon.), Waterloo U., Ont., Can., 1975. Registered profl. engr., B.C. Lectr. U. B.C., 1932-35, asst. prof. geol. scis., 1935-39, assoc. prof., 1939-45, prof., 1945-73, hon. prof., 1973—; Commonwealth Fund fellow Calif. Inst. Tech., 1929-32. Contbr. articles to profl. jours. Mem. coun. Vancouver Bd. Trade, 1939-81 (life); pres. B.C. and Yukon Chamber of Mines, Vancouver, 1952-54, UN Assn. Can. (Vancouver br.), 1956-58. Decorated officer Order of Can., 1971, Order of B.C., 1991; named Disting. lectr. Can. Inst. Mining and Metallurgy, 1971; Hon. fellow Royal Coll. Gen. Practitioners, Eng., 1973; recipient "Spud" Huestis disting. prospectors award B.C./Yukon Chamber of Mines, 1986, Disting. Citizen award City of Vancouver Centennial, 1986, Disting. Svc. award Prospector and Developer's Assn. Can., 1990, Can. 125th Commemorative medal, 1992; inductee B.C. Sports Hall of Fame, 1990, U. B.C. Sports Hall of Fame, 1993. Fellow Inst. Mining and Metallurgy (life), Royal Soc. Can. (life), Geol. Soc. Am. (life); mem. Can. Coun. (Killam award), Assn. Profl. Engrs. B.C. (life), Sigma Xi. Mem. Ch. of England. Avocations: field hockey, rugby, cricket. Home: 1816 Western Pkwy, Vancouver, BC Canada V6T 1V4

WARREN, IRWIN HOWARD, lawyer; b. N.Y.C., May 16, 1950; s. Milton and Shirley (Glatman) W.; m. Elizabeth Vogel, Aug. 11, 1974. BA, Columbia U., 1971, JD, 1974. Bar: N.Y., U.S. Ct. Appeals (1st, 2d, 3d, 4th, 5th, 6th, 8th cirs.), U.S. Dist. Ct. (so. and ea. dists.). Assoc. Weil, Gotshal & Manges, N.Y.C., 1974-82, ptnr., 1982—. Contbr. articles to profl. jours. Mem. ABA (litigation sect., co-chair task force on ind. lawyer). Office: Weil Gotshal & Manges 767 5th Ave New York NY 10153-0001

WARREN, J. BENEDICT, retired history educator; b. Waterflow, N.Mex., June 30, 1930; s. Benedict Alfred and Mary Ursula (Clark) W.; m. Patricia Susan Hyde, June 15, 1968. BA, Duns Scotus Coll., 1953; postgrad., Holy Family Sch. Theology, 1953-57, Cath. U. of Am., 1957-58; MA, U. N.Mex., 1960, PhD, 1963. Franciscan priest various chs., 1957-67; asst. prof. history U. Md., Coll. Park, 1968-70, assoc. prof. hist., 1970-77, prof. history, 1977-93; ret., 1993; cons. Library of Congress, Washington, 1967-77. Author: Vasco de Quiroga and His Pueblo-Hospitals of Santa Fe, 1963 (rev. Spanish edits. 1977, 90), Hans P. Kraus Collection of Hispanic American Manuscripts, a Guide, 1974, La conquista de Michoacán, 1521-1530, 1977 (rev. edit., 1989,rev. English version, 1985); editor: books including Diego Basalenque, Arte, 1994, Gonzalo Gómez primer poblador espanol de Guayangareo (Morelia), 1991, Diccionario grande de la lengua de Michoacan, 1991 (2 vol.), Maturino Gilberti, Arte, 1987, Vocabulario, 1989, Juan Baptista de Lagunas, 1983, Latin America: a Guide to the Historical Literature, 1971; editor: The Americas: A Quarterly Rev. of Inter-Am. Cultural History, 1963-66. John Carter Brown Library fellow, 1965, Fulbright fellow 1981-82. Mem. Conf. on Latin Am. History, Academia Mexicana de la Historia (corr.). Democrat. Avocation: gardening. Office: Lic J Ma Mendoza Pardo 99, Col Nueva Chapultepec, 58280 Morelia Michoacan, Mexico

WARREN, JACK HAMILTON, former diplomat and trade policy advisor; b. Apr. 10, 1921; m. Hilary J. Titterington; children: Hilary Warren Nicolson, Martin, Jennifer Warren Part, Ian. Student, Queens U., Kingston, Ont., Can., 1938-41. Joined Dept. External Affairs, 1945; assigned London, 1948-51; fin. counsellor Washington, 1954-57; asst. dep. minister trade and commerce, 1958-64, dep. minister industry, trade and commerce, 1964-71, high commr. to U.K., 1971-75, ambassador to U.S., 1975-77, Can. coordinator for multilateral trade negotiations, 1977-79; vice chmn. Bank of Montreal, Que., Can., 1979-86; prin. trade policy advisor Govt. Que., 1986-94. Served with Royal Canadian Navy, 1941-45; officer Order of Can., 1982. Home: PO Box 282 RR 1, 37 Chemin Larrimac, Chelsea, PQ Canada J0X 1N0

WARREN, JAMES RONALD, retired museum director, author, columnist; b. Goldendale, Wash., May 25, 1925; stepson H.S. W.; m. Gwen Davis, June 25, 1949; children: Gail, Jeffrey. B.A., Wash. State U., 1949; M.A., U. Wash., 1953, Ph.D., 1963. Adminstrv. v.p. Seattle Community Coll., 1965-69; pres. Edmonds Community Coll., Lynnwood, Wash., 1969-79; dir. Mus. of History and Industry, Seattle, 1979-89; lectr. in field. Author history books; columnist Seattle Post Intelligencer, 1979-92, Seattle Times, 1992-96. Served with U.S. Army, 1943-45, ETO, prisoner-of-war, Germany. Mem. VFW, Am. Ex-POW Assn., 42d (Rainbow) Div. Vets., Rotary, also others. Home and Office: 3235 99th Ave NE Bellevue WA 98004-1803

WARREN, JOHN COOLIDGE, private school dean, history educator; b. Boston, May 16, 1956; s. William Bradford and Mary-Elizabeth (Coolidge) W.; m. Laura Parker Appell, June 18, 1983; children: Ethan Reynolds Appell, Amanda Pfaltzgraff Appell. BA, Stanford U., 1978, MA, 1980; MEd, Harvard U., 1991, EdD, 1994. Tchr. history Robert Louis Stevenson Sch., Pebble Beach, Calif., 1979-81; tchr. history Milton (Mass.) Acad., 1981—, chmn. dept. history, 1992-95, acad. dean, 1995—; faculty cons. Ednl. Testing Svc., Princeton, 1990—, William Joiner Ctr., Boston, 1992—; editl. cons. Longman Inc., White Plains, N.Y., 1991—. Editor: America's Intervention in Vietnam, 1987. NEH fellow, 1985, advanced doctoral fellow, Harvard U., 1993. Mem. Am. Hist. Assn., Orgn. Am. Historians, Assn. Asian Studies, World History Assn., Boston Athenaeum, Colonial Soc. Mass., Mass. Hist. Soc., Phi Beta Kappa. Avocations: canoeing, fishing. Home and Office: Milton Acad 170 Centre St Milton MA 02186-3338

WARREN, JOHN WILLIAM, professional society administrator; b. Clarksville, Ark., June 27, 1927; s. Frederick H. and Fannie Emily (Casey) W.; m. Marguerette Christine Cohoon, Oct. 9, 1948 (dec. Dec. 1987); children: Catherine Gail, Carolyn Anne, Eve Colette; m. Anna Jane Taylor, Feb. 10, 1990. BA, Abilene Christian U., 1949; MA, U. Ark., 1951; PhD, U. Tenn., 1961. Instr. U. Tenn., Knoxville, 1954-61; assoc. prof. David Lipscomb Coll., Nashville, 1961-62; prof., chmn. English Tenn. Tech. U., Cookeville, 1962-88; assoc. exec. dir. Phi Kappa Phi, Baton Rouge, 1988-92, exec. dir., 1992—. Author Ofcl. Lit. Map of Tenn., 1976; author: Tennessee Belles-Lettres-Guide to Tennessee Literature, 1976. Mem. Rotary (Cookeville pres. 1972-73), Phi Kappa Phi (Tenn. Tech. U. chpt. pres. 1980, SE region v.p. 1982-88, nat. bd. dirs. 1982-88). Republican. Mem. Ch. of Christ. Avocations: gardening, travel. Office: Honor Soc Phi Kappa Phi PO Box 16000 LSU Baton Rouge LA 70893

WARREN, MARK EDWARD, shipping company executive, lawyer; b. Rochester, Minn., Nov. 26, 1951; s. Edward Joseph and Eunice (Golberg) W.; m. Jasmine Margaret Syracuse, Feb. 18, 1984; children: Natalie, Stephanie. Cert., Instituto de Estudios Europeos, Madrid, 1972; BA, Gustavus Adolphus Coll., St. Peter, Minn., 1974; JD, U. Minn., 1977. Bar: Calif. 1977, U.S. Dist. Ct. (no. and cen. dists.) Calif. 1978, U.S. Ct. Appeals (9th cir.) 1985, U.S. Dist. Ct. (ea. dist.) Calif. 1986, U.S. Dist. Ct. (so. dist.) Calif. 1987, D.C. 1989, U.S. Supreme Ct. 1989, U.S. Ct. Appeals (D.C. cir.) 1989, U.S. Dist. Ct. (D.C. dist.) 1989, U.S. Dist. Ct. Md. 1991, Va. 1992. Assoc. Gibson, Dunn & Crutcher, L.A., 1977-78; spl. asst. to V.P. Walter Mondale Washington, 1979-80; assoc. Gibson, Dunn & Crutcher, L.A., 1980-84; ptnr. Gibson, Dunn & Crutcher, L.A. and Washington, 1985-93; sr. v.p., gen. counsel Princess Cruises, L.A., 1993-96. Mem. U. Minn. Law Alumni Assn. (bd. dirs.). Home: 2227 Wingfield Rd Charlottesville VA 22901

WARREN, PATRICIA J., arts association executive; b. Seattle, Dec. 12, 1950; d. Vernon Sidney and Ernestine Abernathy (Bilan) W. BA, U. Wash., 1972, BS, 1975, JD, 1978, MA, 1990. Atty. City Kirkland, Wash., 1978-80, City Bellevue, Wash., 1980-86; mus. dir. Jefferson County Hist. Soc., Port Townsend, Wash., 1990-94. Precinct chair 46th Dist., Seattle, 1985-88; mem. Jefferson County AIDS Task Force, Port Townsend, 1991-94; mem. Greater Seattle Bus. Assn., 1994—. U. Wash. fellow, 1988-89. Mem. Wash. State Bar Assn., Wash. Mus. Assn. (trustee 1991-93, v.p. 1993-95, pres. 1995—). Democrat. Office: Pratt Fine Arts Ctr 1902 S Main St Seattle WA 98144-2206

WARREN, RICHARD JORDAN, newspaper publisher; b. Bangor, Maine, May 28, 1945; s. Richard Kearney Warren and Joanne (Jordan) Van Namee; m. Barbara Burrowes Hall, Mar. 9, 1968 (div.); m. Elizabeth Carter, June 21, 1978; children: Courtney, George, Anne. BA, Trinity Coll., Hartford, Conn., 1968; postgrad. smaller cos. mgmt. program Harvard Bus. Sch., 1977-80. Reporter, The Courant, Hartford, Conn., 1968-71; asst. pub. The Bangor Daily News 1971-84, v.p., 1974—, editor, 1980—, pub., 1984—; pres. Northeast Pub. Co., Presque Isle, Maine; dir. Bangor Pub. Co., Northeast Pub. Co., Rockland Courier-Gazette, Inc., Alta Group Newspapers, Inc., Eastern Maine Med. Ctr., Affiliated Health Care, New Eng. Newspaper Assn., Action Com. Fifty, Quebec-Labrador Found., Maine Coast Heritage Trust, Nature Conservancy Maine chpt., Am. Mus. Fly Fishing, Atlantic Salmon Found., Bangor Symphony Orch.; mem. Am. Soc. Newspaper Editors, Maine Daily Newspaper Assn., Bangor Mechanic Assn., Land for Maine's Future Bd., Kent Moot Ct., Columbia U. Law Sch., N.Y.C.; adv. bd., past trustee Unity Coll. Served to 1st lt., Air N.G.. Mem. Alexander Graham Bell Assn. Deaf Centennial Bd. (steering com.), Nat. Press Club, Univ. Club, Anglers Club, Penobscot Salmon Club. Office: Bangor Daily News 491 Main St Bangor ME 04401-6296*

WARREN, RICHARD KEARNEY, newspaper publisher; b. N.Y.C., Apr. 13, 1920; s. George Earle and Anna (Kearney) W.; m. Joanne Jordan, Sept. 18, 1943 (div. Oct. 1969); children: Richard J., Carolyn; m. Susan Atwood Thibodeau, Oct. 1, 1970. B.S., Yale U., 1942; Litt.D., Ricker Coll., 1971. Shift supt. W.Va ordnance works Gen. Chem. Co., Point Pleasant, 1942-43; dir. Bangor Pub. Co., Maine, chmn. exec. com.; pres. Rockland Courier-Gazette, Inc., also dir.; bd. dirs. N.E. Pub. Co. Past bd. dirs. William A. Farnsworth Libr. and Art Mus.; past trustee Ricker Coll.; past bd. dirs. Bangor YMCA. Lt. (j.g.) USNR, 1943-46. Mem. Maine Daily Newspaper Assn. (pres. 1953-54, 73-74), N.E. Daily Newspaper Assn. (pres. 1959-60), Newspaper Assn. Am., New Eng. Soc. N.Y., N.E. Harbor Fleet Club (Maine), Penobscot Valley Country Club, Yale Club (N.Y.C.), N.E. Harbor Tennis Club, Rotary. Home: 28 W Broadway Bangor ME 04401-4541 Office: 96 Harlow St Ste F Bangor ME 04401-4920 also: 3 Huntington Pl Northeast Harbor ME 04662-0663

WARREN, RICHARD M., experimental psychologist, educator; b. N.Y.C., Apr. 8, 1925; s. Morris and Rae (Greenberg) W.; m. Roslyn Pauker, Mar. 31, 1950. BS in Chemistry, CCNY, 1946; PhD in Organic Chemistry, N.Y. U., 1951. Flavor chemist Gen. Foods Co., Hoboken, N.J., 1951-53; rsch. assoc. psychology Brown U., Providence, 1954-56; Carnegie sr. rsch. fellow Coll. Medicine NYU, 1956-57; Carnegie sr. rsch. fellow Cambridge (Eng.) U., 1957-58, rsch. psychologist applied psychology Rsch. Unit, 1958-59; rsch. psychologist NIMH, Bethesda, Md., 1959-61; chmn. psychology Shimer Coll., Mt. Carroll, Ill., 1961-64; assoc. prof. psychology U. Wis., Milw., 1964-66, prof., 1966-73, rsch. prof., 1973-75, disting. prof., 1975-95, adj. disting. prof., 1995—; vis. scientist Inst. Exptl. Psychology, Oxford (Eng.) U., 1969-70, 77-78. Author: (with Roslyn Warren) Helmholtz on Perception: Its Physiology and Development, 1968, Auditory Perception: A New Synthesis, 1982; contbr. articles on sensation and perception to profl. jours. Fellow APA, Am. Psychol. Soc.; mem. AAAS, Acoustical Soc. Am., Am. Chem. Soc., Am. Speech and Hearing Assn., Sigma Xi. Office: U Wis Dept Psychology Milwaukee WI 53201

WARREN, RICHARD WAYNE, obstetrician and gynecologist; b. Puxico, Mo., Nov. 26, 1935; s. Martin R. and Sarah E. (Crump) W.; m. Rosalie J. Franzola, Aug. 16, 1959; children: Lani Marie, Richard W., Paul D. BA, U. Calif., Berkeley, 1957; MD, Stanford U., 1961. Intern, Oakland (Calif.) Naval Hosp., 1961-62; resident in ob-gyn Stanford (Calif.) Med. Ctr., 1964-67; practice medicine specializing in ob-gyn, Mountain View, Calif., 1967—; mem. staff Stanford and El Camino hosps.; pres. Warren Mexical Corp.; assoc. clin. prof. ob-gyn Stanford Sch. Medicine. Served with USN, 1961-64. Diplomate Am. Bd. Ob-Gyn. Fellow Am. Coll. Ob-Gyn; mem. AMA, Am. Fertility Soc., Am. Assn. Gynecologic Laparoscopists, Calif. Med. Assn., San Francisco Gynecol. Soc., Peninsula Gynecol. Soc., Assn. Profs. Gynecology and Obstetrics, Royal Soc. Medicine, Shufelt Gynecol. Soc. Santa Clara Valley. Contbr. articles to profl. jours. Home: 102 Atherton Ave Menlo Park CA 94027-4021 Office: 2500 Hospital Dr Mountain View CA 94040-4106

WARREN, ROBERT WILLIS, federal judge; b. Raton, N.M., Aug. 30, 1925; s. George R. and Clara (Jolliffe) W.; m. Laverne D. Voagen, Aug. 23, 1947; children: Cheryl Lynn, Iver Eric, Gregg Alan, Treiva Mae, Lyle David, Tara Rae. BA magna cum laude, Macalester Coll., 1950; MA, U. Minn., 1951; JD, U. Wis., 1956; postgrad., Fgn. Service Inst., 1951-52. Bar: Wis. 1956. Fgn. affairs officer U.S. Dept. State, 1951-53; mem. firm Godfrey, Godfrey & Warren, Elkhorn, 1956-57; ptnr. firm Warren & Boltz, Attys., Green Bay, 1957-59, Smith, Will & Warren, 1965-69; asst. dist. atty. Brown County, Wis., 1959-61; dist. atty., 1961-65; mem. Wis. Senate, 1965-69; atty. gen. Wis., 1969-74; U.S. dist. judge Milw., 1974—; now sr. judge; Mem. Gt. Lakes Commn., Wis. Council on Criminal Justice, Wis. Bd. Commrs. Pub. Lands, Four Lakes council Boy Scouts Am., Wis. Controlled Substances Bd., Wis. Council on Drug Abuse, Wis. State Urban Affairs. Served with AUS, 1943-46, ETO. Decorated Purple Heart. Mem. ABA, Wis. Bar Assn., Nat. Assn. Attys. Gen. (pres. 1973-74), Midwestern Conf. Attys. Gen., Wis. Dist. Attys. Assn., VFW, DAV. Republican. Methodist. Club: Optimist. Office: US Dist Ct 364 US Courthouse 517 E Wisconsin Ave Milwaukee WI 53202-4504*

WARREN, ROSANNA, poet; b. Fairfield, Conn., July 27, 1953; d. Robert Penn Warren and Eleanor Clark; m. Stephen Scully, 1981; children: Katherine, Chiara; stepson, Benjamin. BA summa cum laude, Yale U., 1976; MA, Johns Hopkins U., 1980. Private art tchr., 1977-78; clerical worker St. Martin's Pr., N.Y.C., 1977-78; asst. prof. English Vanderbilt U., Nashville, 1981-82; vis. asst. prof. Boston U., 1982-88, asst. prof. English and modern fgn. langs., 1989-95, assoc. prof. English, 1995—; poetry cons., contbg. editor Partisan Rev., 1985—; poet-in-residence Robert Frost Farm, 1990. Author: The Joey Story, 1963, Snow Day, 1981, Each Leaf Shines Separate, 1984, Stained Glass, 1993; editor, contbr.: The Art of Translation: Voices from the Field, 1989; editor: Eugenio Montale's Cuttlefish Bones, 1993; translator (with Stephen Scully) Euripides' Suppliant Women, 1995; contbr. to periodicals including Agni Rev., Am. Poetry Rev., Antioch Rev.,

Atlantic Monthly, Chelsea, Chgo. Rev., Georgia Rev., Nation, New Republic, New Yorker, N.Y. Times, Paris Rev., Threepenny Rev., Partisan Rev., Ploughshares, Southern Rev., Washington Post. Recipient McLaughlin English prize Yale U., 1973, Charles E. Clark award Yale U., 1976, Nat. Discovery award in poetry 92nd St. YMHA-YWCA, 1980, Newton Arts Coun. award, 1983, Lavan Younger Poets prize Acad. Am. Poets, 1992, Lamont Poetry prize Acad. Am. Poets, 1993, Lila Wallace Writers' Fund award, 1994, Witter Bynner prize in poetry Acad. Arts and Letters, 1994, May Sarton award New Eng. and Poetry Club, 1995; named Scholar of House Yale U., 1975-76; Yaddo fellow, 1980; Ingram Merrill grantee, 1983, 93; Guggenheim fellow, 1985-86; Am. Coun. Learned Societies grantee, 1989-90. Mem. MLA, ALTA, ALSC, PEN. Home: 11 Robinwood Ave Needham MA 02192 Office: Univ Professors Program Boston Univ 745 Commonwealth Ave Boston MA 02215-1401

WARREN, RUSSELL GLEN, academic administrator; b. Balt., Apr. 29, 1942; s. Clarence N. and Kathryn (Butler) W. BBA, U. Richmond, 1964; PhD, Tulane U., 1968. Asst. prof., then assoc. prof. U. Richmond (Va.), 1971-74, dean of Richmond Coll., 1974-76, asst. to univ. v.p., then. asst. to univ. pres., 1976-78; v.p. for acad. affairs U. Montevallo, Ala., Ala., 1978-84; v.p. for acad. affairs James Madison U., Harrisonburg, Va., 1984-90, acting pres., 1986-87; pres. N.E. Mo. State U., Kirksville, 1990-95; Disting. prof. econs. and mgmt. Hardin-Simmons U., Abilene, Tex., 1995—, dir. Ctr. for Rsch. on Teaching and Learning, 1995—. Author: Antitrust in Theory and Practice, 1976, Carpe Diem, 1995. Bd. Dirs. Va. Rural Devel. Corp., Richmond, 1988-90. Capt. U.S. Army, 1969-71. Named One of Outstanding Young Men of Va., Va. Jaycees, 1976. Mem. Am. Assn. Colls. and Univs. (bd. dirs. 1994-95). Methodist. Avocations: golf, collecting cars. Home: 71 Tamarisk Cir Abilene TX 79606 Office: Hardin-Simmons U Sch Bus Box 16220 Abilene TX 79698

WARREN, RUSSELL JAMES, investment banking executive, consultant; b. Cleve., July 28, 1938; s. Harold Fulton and Agnes Elmina (Hawkswell) W.; BS, Case Western Res. U., 1960; MBA, Harvard U., 1962. CPA, Ohio; m. Doris Helen Kenyeres, June 6, 1964. With Ernst & Whinney, Cleve., 1962-87, ptnr. in charge merger and acquisition svcs., 1976-87; pres. The TransAction Group, 1987—. Co-author: Implementing Mergers and Acquisitions in the Fin. Svcs. Industry, 1985; assoc. editor Jour. Corp. Growth, 1986-87, mem. editorial bd., 1988; contbg. editor Jour. Buyouts and Acquisitions, 1984-86; contbg. author venture capital financing study conducted in five selected countries for Asian Devel. Bank, Malaysia, Indonesia, Pakistan, Sri Lanka, Thailand, 1986. Trustee Case Western Res. U., 1980—, chmn. audit com., 1991—, Cleve. Bot. Garden, 1995—, Western Res. Hist. Soc., 1996—, Fairmount Presbyn. Ch., 1987-93, elder, 1991-93, Cmty. Improvement Corp. Summit, Medina and Portage Counties, 1992—, Cascade CDC, 1992—; dir. Univ. Tech., Inc., 1986-88; adv. bd. Shaker Investments, 1992—; v.p. M & A Internat., Inc., 1990-91, pres., 1992; bd. zoning appeals City of Lyndhurst, 1978—, chmn., 1980-82, 91-93; mem. vis. com. Weatherhead Sch. Mgmt. Mem. AICPA, Brit.-Am. C. of C., Ohio Soc. CPAs, Assn. for Corp. Growth (bd. dirs internat. orgn. 1988, 91-96, pres. 1994), Cleve. Com. on Fgn. Rels., Cleve. World Trade Assn. Clubs: Union, Mayfield Country, Catawba Island (Port Clinton, Ohio), Put-in-Bay (Ohio) Yacht. Lodge: Jesters. Office: The TransAction Group 500 Hanna Bldg Cleveland OH 44115

WARREN, THOMAS PAUL, consulting executive; b. Atlanta, Oct. 2, 1952; s. Thomas J. and Irma Louise (Denson) W.; m. Cheryl M. Barringer, Apr. 8, 1978; 1 child, Thomas Peyton. BS, BA, St. Andrews Coll., Laurinburg, N.C., 1974; BS, Ga. Tech., 1975; MBA, Ga. State U., 1977. V.p. investment banking Merrill Lynch White Weld, N.Y.C., 1977-82; mng. dir. Brooks Internat., Montvale, N.J., 1982-85; sr. v.p. C4 practice Gemini Consulting, Paris, 1985-94; mng. ptnr. comm. and media practice Perot Systems Corp., Dallas, 1994—; bd. dirs. Mancon Inc., Anderson, S.C., 1982-85. Bd. dirs. Juvenile Diabetes Found., Atlanta, 1989-92, Camp Twin Lakes, Atlanta. Rsch. fellow NSF, 1975. Mem. Golf Club Ga. (charter). Avocations: golf, tennis, photography. Office: Perot Systems Corp 12377 Merit Dr Dallas TX 75251

WARREN, W. K., JR., oil industry executive; b. 1911. Vice chmn. The William K. Warren Found., Tulsa; also with Warren Am. Oil Co., Tulsa, 1938—, now pres. and chmn. bd. Office: The William K Warren Found PO Box 470372 Tulsa OK 74147-0372

WARREN, WILLIAM BRADFORD, lawyer; b. Boston, July 25, 1934; s. Minton Machado and Sarah Ripley (Robbins) W.; children: John Coolidge, Sarah Robbins; m. Arete B. Swartz, Sept. 20, 1985. AB magna cum laude, Harvard U., 1956, LLB cum laude, 1959. Bar: N.Y. 1960. Assoc. Dewey Ballantine, N.Y.C., 1959-68; ptnr. Dewey Ballantine, 1968—; lectr. Inst. Fed. Taxation, N.Y. U., So. Fed. Tax Inst., Practicing Law Inst. Pres. Cintas Found., N.Y.C.; bd. dirs. John Carter Brown Libr., Providence, R.I. Mem. Am. Law Inst., Am. Coll. Trust and Estate Counsel (former regent), Acad. Am. Poets (bd. dirs.), Internat. Acad. Estate and Trust Law (former exec. coun.), N.Y. State Bar Assn. (chmn. com. taxation of trust and estates sect. 1980-83), Assn. Bar City N.Y., Soc. Mayflower Descs., Harvard Club, Knickerbocker Club, Century Club, Grolier Club (pres.). Home: 520 E 86th St New York NY 10028-7534 Office: Dewey Ballantine 1301 Avenue Of The Americas New York NY 10019-6022

WARREN, WILLIAM CLEMENTS, law educator; b. Paris, Tex., Feb. 3, 1909; s. Archibald Levy and Elma (Clements) W.; m. Diana June Peel Willock, Jan. 13, 1945; children: Robert Peel, Larissa Eve, William Liversidge. AB, U. Tex., 1930, AM, 1931; LLB, Harvard U., 1935; LLD (hon.), L.I. U., 1955, Columbia U., 1981; D in Polit. Sci., U. Basle, 1965. Bar: Ohio 1937, N.Y. 1952, D.C. 1959. Assoc. Davis, Polk & Wardwell, N.Y.C., 1935-37, Holiday, Grossman & McAfee, Cleve., 1937-42, Milbank, Tweed, Hadley & McCloy, N.Y.C., 1942-47; prof. law Western Res. U., Cleve., 1937-42; mem. faculty Columbia Law Sch., N.Y.C., 1946-82, Kent prof. law, 1959-77, Kent prof. emeritus, 1977—, dean, 1952-70, dean emeritus, 1970—; ptnr., of counsel Roberts & Holland, N.Y.C., 1952; bd. dirs. Guardian Life Ins. Co. Am., Sterling Nat. Bank & Trust Co. N.Y.C., Barnwell Industries, Inc., Sterling Bancorp, CSS Industries, Aston-Martin LaGonda Group, Aladan Corp.; hon. chmn. bd. dirs. Sandoz U.S.; mem. N.Am. adv. bd. Swissair. Served as lt. col. U.S. Army, 1943-46. Decorated Bronze Star (2), Legion of Merit; comdr. Order of the Crown (Italy); recipient Medal for execellence Columbia Law Sch. Alumni Assn., 1969. Mem. ABA, Am. Judicature Soc., Am. Law Inst., Assn. of Bar of City of N.Y., N.Y. County Lawyers Assn., N.Y. State Bar Assn., Inst. Internat. Edn. (trustee), Order Moral Scis. (fgn. corr.), Accademia delle Scienze dell' Instituto di Bologna (fgn. corr. mem.; Order Moral Scis. 1971). Presbyterian. Clubs: Broad Street, Century Assn., Cosmos, Links, Metropolitan, Univ. Co-author: U.S. Income Taxation of Foreign Corporations and Nonresident Aliens, 1966; Cases and Materials on Accounting and the Law, 1978; Cases and Materials on Federal Wealth Transfer Taxation, 1982; Cases and Materials on Federal Income Taxation, Vol. I, 1972, supplement, 1983, Vol. II, 1980; pres., dir. Columbia Law Rev. Office: Roberts & Holland 825 8th Ave New York NY 10019-7416

WARREN, WILLIAM HERBERT, business administration educator; b. Newport News, Va., July 21, 1924; s. William Herbert and Helen Virginia (Cofer) W.; m. Mary Virginia Shaw, Sept. 11, 1948; children: Katherine Warren Butt, Constance Warren Desaulniers, Suzanne Warren Huhn, David, John. BSBA, U. Richmond, 1948; MS, Purdue U., 1950, PhD, 1969. Dir. indsl. rels., plant mgr. Albemarle Paper Co. div. Ethyl Corp., 1954-66; dir. labor relations, cons. Newport News Shipbldg. div. Tenneco, 1970-73; asst. prof. U. Richmond, Va., 1950-53; assoc. prof. Purdue U., 1966-70; mem. faculty Coll. William and Mary, Williamsburg, Va., 1972—, D. Hillsdon Ryan prof. bus. adminstrn., 1979-92; prof. emeritus Williamsburg, Va., 1992—; cons. to industry and govt.; labor arbitrator. Served with USN, 1943-46. Mem. APA, Acad. Mgmt., Kiwanis, Omicron Delta Kappa. Republican. Baptist. Home: 110 Bowstring Dr Williamsburg VA 23185-4952 Office: Sch Business Coll William and Mary Williamsburg VA 23185

WARREN, WILLIAM KERMIT, electronic publishing consultant; b. Harlem, Ga., May 27, 1941; s. William Kermit and Willie Garnell (Thaxton) W.; m. Nancy Carolyn Andrews, Sept. 5, 1964; children—Wendy Karen, William Kermit. B.A. in Journalism, U. Ga., 1964. Reporter Augusta Ga. Chronicle, Ga., 1964-65; reporter Chattanooga Times, Tenn., 1965-66, reporter, city editor, 1971-80; mng. editor Roanoke (Va.) Times & World News, 1980-95; electronic pub. cons., 1995—. Served to capt. USAF, 1966-70. Recipient Best Feature Story award Ga, AP, 1964. Mem. AP Mng. Editors Assn., Sigma Delta Chi. Episcopalian. Avocation: reading. Home: 3355 Dawn Cir Roanoke VA 24018-3837 Office: Times World Corp PO Box 2491 201-209 W Campbell Ave Roanoke VA 24010

WARRICK, KENNETH RAY, dermatologist, cosmetic surgeon; b. Charleston, S.C., Dec. 15, 1946; s. Ray Lawrence and Evelyn Lila (Hughes) W.; m. Linda Diane Painter, Oct. 11, 1975; 1 child: Michael Todd. BS in Chemistry, Coll. of Charleston, S.C., 1967. Diplomate Am. Bd. Dermatology. Pvt. practice dermatology Charleston, 1975—; clin. instr. dermatology Med. U. S.C., Charleston, 1976-85, clin. assoc. prof. dermatology; med. adv. bd. Am. Electrolysis Assoc.; cons. S.C. Bd. Cosmetology; co-chmn. S. C. Gov.'s Adv. Com. Bd. on Medicaid Formulary. Recipient Pres.'s Award, Am. Electrolysis Assn., 1986. Fellow Am. Acad. Dermatology; mem. S.C. Med. Assn., S.C. Dermatol. Assn. (pres. 1986-87), Charleston County Med. Soc. Luth. Lodge: Rotary (North Charleston). Avocation: computing. Office: Ashley Cooper Dermatology and Cosmetic Surgery Clinic 9304 Medical Plaza Dr Ste A Charleston SC 29406-9143 also: Atlantic Dermatology 2021 N Myrtle Point Blvd Ste 103 North Myrtle Beach SC 29582

WARRINER, WILLIAM ERNEST, government official; b. Regina, Sask., Can., Nov. 10, 1950; s. William Robert and Carol (Geris) W.; m. Wannie Thompson, Dec. 31, 1981; children: William James Robert, Catherine Anne Marie. Postgrad., Carleton U., 1980-81; student, London Internat. Film Sch., 1976; BA in Econs., U. Regina, 1976, BA in Social Studies with honors, 1977, MA in Social Studies, 1979. Mem. staff dept. sociology and social studies U. Regina, 1975-81; rsch. asst. dept. sociology and demography Carleton U., 1980-81; rsch. cons. Sask. Industry, Trade and Commerce, 1980; from rsch. officer to policy cons. pensions br. Sask. Dept. Labor, 1981-84; sr. policy analyst policy, planning and evaluation br. Sask. Dept. Justice, 1984-85; economist econ. and policy analysis br. Sask. Employment Devel. Agy., 1985-86, mgr. policy analysis, 1986-87; mgr. policy and rsch. planning, policy and comms. divsn. Sask. Dept. Human Resources, Labor and Employment, 1987-93, sr. policy analysis br., 1993-94; intergovtl. affairs officer fed.-provincial rels. br. Sask. Intergovtl. Affairs, Regina, 1994—. Home: 3606 21st Ave, Regina, SK Canada S4S 0V2 Office: 1919 Saskatchewan Dr, Regina, SK Canada S4P 3V7

WARRINGTON, WILLARD GLADE, former university official; b. Macomb, Ill., Oct. 24, 1920; s. Henry K. and Farie V. (Prather) W.; m. A. Irene Windser, Aug. 9, 1945 (dec. 1969); m. Janette Moffatt Cooper, Apr. 26, 1972; children: David, Steven, Douglas, Jane Ann, Stephen Cooper. B.Ed., Western Ill. State Tchrs. Coll., 1941; M.S., U. Ill., 1949, U. Ill., 1950; Ed.D., U. Ill., 1952. Tchr. public high schs. Ill., 1941-42, 45-48; mem. faculty Mich. State U., 1952-58, dir. office evaluation services, 1958-74, asso. dean Univ. Coll., 1974-78, acting dean Univ. Coll., 1978-80, dir. undergrad. univ. div., 1980-85, dir., prof. emeritus, 1986—; cons. edn.; Ford Found. cons. U. Philippines. Contbr. articles on ednl. measurement to profl. publs.; editorial bd.: Ednl. and Psychol. Measurement, 1968-85. Active Boy Scouts Am., 1957-68. Served to lt. col. USAAF, 1942-45. Mem. Nat. Council on Measurement in Edn. (pres. 1973-74), Am. Ednl. Research Assn., Assn. for Gen. and Liberal Studies (sec.-treas. 1973-79). Methodist. Home: 9 Ashleigh Ct Lansing MI 48906-1540

WARSAWER, HAROLD NEWTON, real estate appraiser and consultant; b. N.Y.C.; s. Sidney L. and Alice W.; m. Sally Kingsbury; children: Alice Cooper, Nancy Arkuss, Carole Greenblatt. BA, U. Mo.; MBA, Harvard U. Property mgr. and real estate broker Sidney L. Warsawer & Son, N.Y.C., 1950—; pres., dir. Consol. Capital, N.Y.C., 1962-68; pres. Atlantic Appraisal Co., Inc., N.Y.C., 1960—; pres., dir. Contemporary Enterprises, N.Y.C., 1974-76; pres. Mem. editorial bd. The Appraisal Jour., 1970-85. Candidate Teaneck (N.J.) Sch. Bd.; chmn. bldg. com. Temple Emeth, Teaneck, 1954-64. Mem. Appraisal Inst. (pres. N.Y. chpt. 1977, bd. dirs. 1970-80, 90-92, gov. counselor 1978), Nat. Assn. Rev. Appraisers, Real Estate Bd. N.Y., Nat. Realty Conf. (pres. 1992, bd. dirs.), Am. Arbitration Assn., Haworth Golf Club. Avocations: golf, clocks. Home: 430 Rutland Ave Teaneck NJ 07666-2823 Office: Ste 1446 60 E 42nd St Rm 1446 New York NY 10165-1499

WARSHAUER, IRENE CONRAD, lawyer; b. N.Y.C., May 4, 1942; d. A. Alfred and Sylvia (Bober) Conrad; m. Alan M. Warshauer, Nov. 27, 1966; 1 dau., Susan L. B.A. with distinction, U. Mich., 1963; LL.B. cum laude, Columbia U., 1966. Bar: N.Y. 1966, U.S. Dist. Ct. (so. and ea. dists.) N.Y. 1969, U.S. Ct. Appeals (2d cir.) 1969, U.S. Supreme Ct. 1972, U.S. Dist. Ct. (no. dist.) N.Y. 1980. With First Jud. Dept., N.Y. State Mental Health Info. Service, 1966-68; assoc. Chadbourne Parke Whiteside & Wolff, 1968-75; mem. Anderson Kill Anderson Kill & Olick, P.C., N.Y.C., 1975—; lectr. Def. Research Inst., Aspen Inst. Humanistic Studies, ABA, Rocky Mountain Mineral Law Found., CPR Inst. Dispute Resolution, panelist Am. Arbitration Assn., 1973—; mediator U.S. Dist. Ct. So. Dist., N.Y. Contbr. articles, chpts. to profl. lit. Mem. Democratic County Com., 1968—. Named to Hon. Order Ky. Cols. Mem. Assn. of Bar of City of N.Y. (judiciary com. 1982-84), N.Y. State Bar Assn. (chairperson subcom. mentally disabled and community 1978-82), ABA. Avocations: gardening, cooking, birding. Office: Anderson Kill Olick & Oshinsky 1251 Avenue Of The Americas New York NY 10020-1104

WARSHAVSKY, ELI SAMUEL, media company chief executive; b. Tel Aviv, July 2, 1930; s. Yechiel and Zipora Warshavsky; m. Carmela Warshavsky; children: Ofer Bernard, Sharon-Rina. Student, Tel Aviv U., 1952. Foodstuff wholesaler Tel Aviv, 1952; v.p. Imex Ltd., Ghana, 1952-58; dir. operations Super-Sol Ltd. Supermarkets, Israel, 1958-64; gen. mgr. Chen-Paldag Ltd., Israel, 1958-64, Jantzen (Israel) Bathing Suits Mfg., 1964-69; pres. Maximedia Group Outdoor Advt., Media, Ramat-Gan, Israel, 1969—, Golden-Wheels Ltd., Telruf Ltd., Terminal (Airports & Railways Advt.), Barak Silk Screen Printing Ltd., 1969—; acad. lectr. Author: Outdoor Advertising - the Powerful Medium; contbr. articles to profl. jours. Recipient Quality Mgmt. award Israel, CBI Yakir award Jerusalem. Mem. Internat. Advt. Assn. (world bd. dirs. 1986—, internat. adv. assn. N.Y., Internat. Medal for Merit 1992 Barcelona, pres. Israel chpt.), Forum Israeli Outdoor Advt. Assn. (chmn.), Coun. Beautiful Israel (hon. world treas. 1980—), Fe-Pe European Outdoor Advt. Fedn. Paris (bd. dirs.). Mem. D'Honneur FEPE (Rome) World Outdoor Advt. Assn. Home: 42 King David St, 46661 Herzliyya Israel

WARSHAW, ALLEN CHARLES, lawyer; b. Harrisburg, Pa., Aug. 27, 1948; s. Julius and Miriam (Nepove) W.; m. Shirley Anne Nes, Aug. 23, 1970; children: Christopher James, Andrew Charles, William Robert. BA, U. Pa., 1970; JD, Villanova U., 1973. Bar: Pa. 1973, U.S. Dist. Ct. (ea. and mid. dists.) Pa. 1974, U.S. Ct. Appeals (3d cir.) 1975, U.S. Supreme Ct. 1977, Calif. 1978. Staff atty. Office Atty. Gen., State of Pa., Harrisburg, 1973-79, chief civil litigation, 1979-85, dir. civil law, 1985-86; ptnr. Duane, Morris & Heckscher, Harrisburg, 1986—. Coach, pres. Mechanicsburg Soccer Assn. Fellow Am. Bar Found.; mem. ABA, Am. Bankruptcy Inst., Pa. Bar Assn., Pa. Def. Inst. Home: 1035 Mccormick Rd Mechanicsburg PA 17055-5970 Office: Duane Morris & Heckscher 305 N Front St Harrisburg PA 17101-1236

WARSHAW, ANDREW LOUIS, surgeon, researcher; b. N.Y.C., Feb. 18, 1939; s. David and Florence (Rand) W.; m. Brenda Rose Flavin, Jan. 4, 1986; children: Jordan, Abigail, Daniel; stepchildren: Heather, Gretchen, Brenda. AB, Harvard U., 1959, MD, 1963. Diplomate Am. Bd. Surgery. Intern in surgery Mass. Gen. Hosp., Boston, 1963-64, resident in surgery, 1964-65, 67-70, rsch. fellow in medicine, 1970, chief resident in surgery, 1971; clin. assoc. in gastroenterology NIH, Bethesda, Md., 1965-67; from instr. surgery to prof. surgery Harvard Med. Sch., Boston, 1972-90, Harold & Ellen Danser prof. surgery, 1990—; assoc. chief surg. svcs. Mass. Gen. Hosp., Boston, 1990—, chief gen. surgery, 1992—. Editor: Pancreatitis, 1989, Current Practice of Surgery, 1993; contbr. over 400 articles to med. jours., revs., 8 med. ednl. films, videos; editor-in-chief Surgery, 1997. Lt. comdr. USPHS, 1965-67. Mem. Am. Bd. Surgery (chmn. 1992-93, dir. 1985-93), New Eng. Surgical Soc. (pres. 1993-94), Am. Coll. Surgeons (pres. Mass. chpt. 1991-92). Avocations: photography, fly fishing. Office: Mass Gen Hosp WACC-336 Boston MA 02114

WARSHAW, JOSEPH BENNETT, pediatrician, educator; b. Miami Beach, Fla., July 17, 1936; s. Phillip Robert and Mona (Monashefsky) W.; m. Cynthia Ann Stober, June 6, 1961; children: Deborah, Kathryn, Lawrence. B.S., U. Fla., 1957; M.D., Duke U., 1961; M.S. (hon.), Yale U., 1976; M.D. (hon.), Catholic U.; Josiah Macy Jr. faculty scholar, U. Oxford, 1979-80. Diplomate Am. Bd. Pediatrics., subsplty bd. in neonatal-perinatal medicine. Intern, resident in pediatrics Strong Meml. Hosp., Rochester, N.Y., 1961-63; resident in pediatrics Duke Hosp., Durham, N.C., 1963-64; research assoc. NIH, 1964-66, Retina Found., Boston, 1966-68; assoc. in pediatrics Harvard U., 1968-71, asst. prof. pediatrics, 1971-72, assoc. prof., 1972-73; assoc. prof. pediatrics and ob-gyn Yale U., 1973-76, prof. pediatrics and ob-gyn, 1976-82; prof., chmn. dept. pediatrics U. Tex. Health Sci. Ctr., Dallas, 1982-87; chief staff Children's Med. Ctr., Dallas, 1982-87; chief pediatrics Parkland Meml. Hosp., Dallas, 1982-87; prof., chmn. dept. pediatrics Yale U. Sch. Medicine, New Haven, 1987—; physician-in-chief Children's Hosp. at Yale New Haven Hosp., 1987—, dep. dean for clin. affairs, 1995—; dep. dean clin. affairs Sch. Medicine Yale U., New Haven; mem. human embryology and devel. study sect. NIH, 1974-78, nat. adv. council nat. inst. child health and human devel., 1987-91. Editor: Seminars in Perinatology, Principles and Practice of Pediatrics; contbr. articles on pediatrics, perinatology, devel. biology and biochemistry to profl. jours. Clin. research adv. com. Nat. Found. March of Dimes, 1978-92; mem. rsch. com. United Cerebral Palsy, 1987—. Served with USPHS, 1964-66. Fellow Am. Acad. Pediatrics; mem. Inst. Medicine of NAS, Am. Pediatric Soc. (coun. mem. 1988-94), Am. Soc. Clin. Investigation, Am. Soc. Biol. Chemistry, Am. Soc. Cell Biology, Soc. Devel. Biology, Soc. Pediatric Rsch. (pres. 1981-82), Assn. Am. Physicians, Internat. Pediatric Rsch. Found. (chmn. bd. 1989-93), Conn. Acad. Arts and Scis., Conn. Acad. Sci. & Engring. Home: 350 Vineyard Point Rd Guilford CT 06437-3255 Office: Yale Sch Medicine PO Box 208064 New Haven CT 06520

WARSHAW, LEON J(OSEPH), physician; b. N.Y.C., July 20, 1917; s. Samuel and Bessie (Olken) W.; m. Mona Glassman, Aug. 31, 1941; children: Peter M., David C. A.B., Columbia U., 1938, M.D., 1942. Diplomate Am. Bd. Internal Medicine, Am. Bd. Preventive Medicine (occupational medicine). Intern, house physician 1st med. div. Bellevue Hosp., N.Y.C., 1942-44; from clin. asst. vis. physician to asso. vis. physician Bellevue Hosp., 1942-59; clin. asst., then adj. Beth Israel Hosp., N.Y.C., 1944-49; asso. attending physician Beth Israel Hosp., 1949-87, chief adult cardiac clinic, 1950-62; practice internal medicine N.Y.C., 1944-55, med. dir. and/or med. cons. various corps., 1944-69; with Equitable Life Assurance Soc., N.Y.C., 1967-80; v.p., chief med. dir. Equitable Life Assurance Soc., 1970-75, v.p., corp. med. dir., 1975-80; on leave as dep. dir. N.Y.C. Mayor's Office of Ops., 1978-80; clin. prof. environ. medicine NYU, 1980—; cons. health care delivery, 1980—; exec. dir. N.Y. Bus. Group on Health, 1980-94; mem. N.Y. Gov.'s Health Adv. Coun., 1978-84, N.Y. State Adv. Coun. on Alcoholism Svcs., 1988—, chmn., 1990—; mem. faculty Columbia U. Coll. Physicians and Surgeons, 1944-60, NYU Med. Sch., 1945-47; chmn. bd. Equitable Environ. Health, Inc., Woodbury, N.Y., 1973-75, dir., 1975-78; trustee Ins. Med. Scientist Scholarship Fund, 1975-78; mem. adv. bd. Ctr. Productive Aging, N.Y. Ctr. for Policy on Aging; bd. dirs. Med. & Health Rsch. Assn.; mem. nat. adv. com. Pres.'s Com. Employment Handicapped, 1965-89; mem. Pres.'s Coun. Phys. Fitness and Sports, 1970-85; bd. sponsors Twin Cities Health Care Devel. Project, 1972-75; chmn. med. adv. com. Washington Bus. Group Health, 1977-79; mental health adv. bd. Cornell U., 1970-80; Sappington Meml. lectr. Indsl. Med. Assn.; dir. Health Sys. Agy. N.Y.C., 1987-93; Thackrah lect. Soc. Occupl. Medicine/Leeds U., 1988. Author: Malaria: Biography of a Killer, 1949, Managing Stress, 1979, The Heart in Industry, 1969, Enhancing the Health of the Public: The New York Academy of Medicine 1947-1997, 1997; assoc. editor: Encyclopedia on Occupational Health and Safety, 1994—; contbr. articles to profl. jours.; mem. editorial bd. jours. Fellow Am. Coll. Occupational & Environ. Medicine, Am. Coll. Cardiology, ACP, Am. Coll. Preventive Medicine, Am. Occupational Medicine Assn. (past dir.), N.Y. Acad. Scis.; mem. AMA, N.Y. State, N.Y. County med. socs., Am. Arbitration Assn. (adv. health council 1972-80), Am. Heart Assn. (chmn. heart industry com. 1966-68, dir. 1969-73), Conf. Board, Nat. Safety Council (dir. 1972-74, v.p. research 1972-74), Greater N.Y. Safety Council (1970), N.Y. C. of C., N.Y. Heart Assn. (dir. 1968-70, 76-82), Occupational Health Inst. (dir. 1970-87), N.Y. Acad. Medicine (chmn. sec. occupational medicine 1964-66), N.Y. State Soc. Occupational Medicine (pres. 1965-67, exec. com. 1967-77), Occupational Psychiatry Group, Soc. Occupational Medicine, Med. and Health Rsch. Assn. N.Y.C. (bd. dirs.), Alpha Omega Alpha, Beta Sigma Rho, Phi Delta Epsilon. Office: 180 W End Ave Apt 6C New York NY 10023-4933

WARSHAW, MARTIN RICHARD, marketing educator; b. N.Y.C., Sept. 17, 1924; s. Irving Gregg and Adelaide (Klein) W.; m. Alice M. Present, Mar. 28, 1948; children: Gregg, Mark, Lynn, Laurie. A.B., Columbia U., 1947; M.B.A., U. Mich., 1957, Ph.D., 1960. Salesman Daniels Jewelry Co., Battle Creek, Mich., 1947-50; store mgr. Daniels Jewelry Co., 1950-55; v.p., dir. Daniels Jewelry Co., Lansing, Mich., 1955-64; instr. mktg. U. Mich., 1957-60, asst. prof., 1960-64, assoc. prof., 1964-67, prof., 1967-89, prof. emeritus, 1989—, chmn. mktg. faculty, 1973-79, 81-84. Author: (with Taylor and Scott) Introduction To Marketing Management, 5th edit, 1985, (with Engel and Kinnear) Promotional Strategy, 8th edit., 1994. Served with C.E. U.S. Army, 1943-46. Mem. Am. Mktg. Assn. (past pres. Detroit chpt.). Home: 5424 Parkgrove Rd Ann Arbor MI 48103-9202 Office: U Mich Sch Bus Adminstrn Ann Arbor MI 48109

WARSHAW, MICHAEL THOMAS, lawyer; b. Jersey City, June 29, 1950; s. Thomas T. and June C. (Lancaster) W.; m. Mary Jane Egidio, July 12, 1986. BA in Sociology, Coll. of the Holy Cross, 1972; JD, Bklyn. Law Sch., 1975. Bar: N.J. 1976, U.S. Dist. Ct. N.J. 1976, U.S. Ct. Appeals (3d cir.) 1982, N.Y. Ct. of Appeals 1987, U.S. Supreme Ct. 1982. Law sec. to judge N.J. Superior Ct., 1975-76; assoc. Drazin & Warshaw PC, Red Bank, N.J., 1976-88, Magee & Graham, Wall, N.J., 1988-90; pres. Michael T. Warshaw, P.C., Red Bank, 1990-95; shareholder Warshaw & Barnes, P.C., Red Bank, 1995—; adj. prof. bus. law Brookdale Community Coll., Lincroft; speaker Mock Trial Sem., Young Lawyers div. N.J. Bar Assn., 1984, Discovery Sem., 1986; mem. com. on mcpl. cts. N.J. Supreme Ct., 1984-88. Atty., advisor mock trial team CBA, 1983-90; chair Red Bank Cath. H.S. Devel. Adv. Coun., 1994—, elder law seminar Trenton Diocese, 1996; trustee Brookdale C.C. Found., 1995—. Mem. ABA, N.J. Bar Assn. (young lawyers divsn., exec. com. 1983-86), N.J. Bar Found. (spkrs. bur.), Monmouth County Bar Assn. (civil practice com. 1985—, chair alternative dispute resolution com.), Christian Bros. Acad. Alumni Assn. (pres. 1993-95), Phi Delta Phi. Republican. Roman Catholic. Avocations: golf, youth athletics. Home: 18 Quaker Rd Middletown NJ 07748-3193 Office: 10 W Bergen Pl Ste 202 Red Bank NJ 07701-1500

WARSHAW, ROBERTA SUE, lawyer, financial specialist; b. Chgo., July 10, 1934; d. Charles and Frieda (Feldman) Weiner; m. Lawrence Warshaw, July 5, 1959 (div. June 1978); children: Nan R., Adam; m. Paul A. Heise, Apr. 2, 1994. Student, U. Ill., 1952-55; BFA, U. So. Calif., 1956; JD, Northwestern U., 1980. Bar: Ill. 1980. Atty., fin. specialist Housing Svcs. Ctr., Chgo., 1980-84, Chgo. Rehab. Network, 1985-91, 92-95; dir. housing State Treas., State of Ill., Chgo., 1991; sole practitioner, 1995—; legal worker Sch. of Law, Northwestern U. Legal Clinic, Chgo., 1977-80; real estate developer, mgr., marketer, Chgo., 1961-77; bd. dirs. Single Room Housing Assistance Corp. Co-author: (manual) The Cook County Scavenger Sale Program and The City of Chicago Reactivation Program, 1991, (booklet) Fix the Worst First, 1989; co-editor: The Caring Contract, Voices of American Leaders, 1996. Alderman 9th ward City of Evanston, Ill., 1985-93, mem. planning and devel., rules com., unified budget com., chair flood and pollution control com.; pres. Sister Cities Found.; mem. cmty. and econ. devel. policy Nat. League Cities, 1990-93; mem. Dem. Nat. Com.; bd. dirs. Dem. Ctrl. Com. Evanston, 1973—; elected committeeman Evanston Twp. Dem. Com., 1994—; del. Dem. Nat. Conv., 1996. Mem. ABA (affordable housing com.), Ill. State Bar Assn., Chgo. Bar Assn. (real estate coms.), Decalogue Soc. Lawyers, Chgo. Coun. Lawyers (housing com.). Avocations: politics, travel, hiking, camping, athletic activities. Home: 550 Sheridan Sq Apt 5G Evanston IL 60202-3171

WARSHAW, STANLEY IRVING, government official; b. Boston, Nov. 5, 1931; s. Alec and Sarah (Laserson) W.; m. Wanda Faye Capino, Feb., 12, 1992; 1 child from previous marriage, Karen Beth. B.S. in Ceramic Engring, Ga. Tech. Inst., 1957; Sc.D. in Ceramics, M.I.T., 1961; grad., Advanced

Mgmt. Program, Harvard Bus. Sch., 1978. Sr. scientist research div. Raytheon Co., Waltham, Mass., 1961-64; with Am. Standard, Inc., New Brunswick, N.J., 1964-75, gen. mgr. engring. and devel., 1972-75; dir. Ctr. for Consumer Product Tech., Nat. Inst. Stds. and Tech. (formerly Nat. Bur. Stds.), Washington, 1975-80, dir. Office Product Standards Policy, 1981-86, assoc. dir., 1987-89; dir. Office Standards Svcs. Nat. Inst. Stds. and Tech. (formerly Nat. Bur. Stds.), Gaithersburg, Md., 1989-93; sr. policy advisor for stds. and tech. U.S. Dept. Commerce, Gaithersburg, 1994—. Served to capt. U.S. Army, 1951-53. Fellow N.Y. Acad. Scis., Washington Acad. Scis. Home: 8051 Rising Ridge Rd Bethesda MD 20817-6951 Office: US Dept Commerce Rm 326 NIST North Gaithersburg MD 20899-0001

WARSHAWSKY, ISIDORE, physicist, consultant; b. N.Y.C., May 27, 1911; s. Morris and Esther (Sherman) W. BS, CCNY, 1930. Physicist Nat. Adv. Com. Aeronautics, Langley Field, Va., 1930-42; chief instrumentation sect. Nat. Adv. Com. Aeronautics, Cleve., 1942-50; chief instrument rsch. br. Nat. Adv. Com. Aeronautics/ NASA, Cleve., 1950-72; instrumentation cons. NASA, Cleve., 1972-90, ret., 1990, disting. rsch. cons. (unsalaried), 1990-95. Author: (textbook) Foundations of Measurement and Instrumentation, 1990; author 10 NACA/NASA tech. reports; contbr. 20 articles to sci. jours. and books. Fellow Instrument Soc. Am., Am. Phys. Soc., Combustion Inst., Am. Vacuum Soc.

WARSHELL, JAY, systems engineer. BSME, Drexel U., 1984, MSEE, 1990. Cert. engr. in tng., Pa. Software engr. Computer Task Group, Inc., Media, Pa., 1984-89; sys. engr. All-Control Sys., Inc., West Chester, Pa., 1989-93, Astra Merck, Inc., Wayne, Pa., 1993—. Mem. IEEE. Avocation: scuba diving. Home: 208 Canford Dr Broomall PA 19008 Office: Astra Merck Inc 725 Chesterbrook Blvd Wayne PA 19087-5637

WARSICK-RINZIVILLO, MARY KATRINA, counselor, educator; b. Tampa, Fla., Aug. 3, 1956; d. Frank McDonough and Mary Margaret (Laxton) W.; m. Ronald Carl Rinzivillo, Nov. 18, 1990. BA in English Edn., U. South Fla., 1979, MA in Counselor Edn., 1984. Lic., cert. mental health counselor, Fla.; nat. cert. counselor; cert. English and mass comm. tchr., Fla. Tchr. Mango (Fla.) Bapt. Sch., 1979-80; tchr. English Eisenhower Jr. High Sch., Gibsonton, Fla., 1980-84; counselor, chair guidance svcs. Dowdell Jr. High Sch., Tampa, 1984-85; counselor Lake Weir Mid. Sch., Summerfield, 1985-87; counselor West Hernando Mid. Sch., Spring Hill, 1987—, counselor, chair guidance svcs., 1989—; pvt. practice Cen. Fla. Counseling Ctr., 1992; contract therapist Cath. Charities, 1992—; therapist Family Svc. Ctr., 1996—. Co-facilitator Parent Support Group, Hernando County, Fla., 1988-89, Parents Anonymous, 1990-92, various Cath. charities, 1992-95. Named Counselor of Yr., Hernando County Mid. Sch., 1987, 88, 91-92. Mem. Hernando County Assn. Counseling and Devel. (pres. 1989-90), Phi Kappa Phi, Phi Delta Kappa. Presbyterian. Avocations: reading, biking, swimming. Office: Hernando County Schs 14325 Ken Austin Pky Brooksville FL 34613-4907

WARTELL, ROGER MARTIN, biophysics educator; b. N.Y.C., Feb. 24, 1945; s. Hugh H. and Jennie (Silbermann) W.; m. Aila Irmeli Salo, Sept. 18, 1945; children: Zachary, Arlena. BSc, Stevens Inst. Tech., Hoboken, N.J., 1966; PhD, U. Rochester, N.Y., 1971. Postdoctoral fellow U. Wis., Madison, 1971-73; prof. physics and biology Ga. Inst. Tech., Atlanta, 1974—, dir. Sch. Biology, 1991—, dir. Bioscis. Ctr., 1991-95; vis. fellow U. Wis., Madison, 1978-79; vis. scientist NIH, Bethesda, Md., 1986-87; cons. SCI-EXPO Inc., Tucson, 1984-86. Contbr. articles to profl. jours. Mem. Biophys. Soc., ACS. Office: Ga Inst Tech Sch of Biology Atlanta GA 30332

WARTELLA, ELLEN ANN, communications educator, consultant; b. Kingston, Pa., Oct. 16, 1949; d. Nicholas and Margaret (Lipko) W.; m. D. Charles Whitney, Aug. 1, 1976; children: David Charles, Stephen Wright. BA, U. Pitts., 1971; MA, U. Minn., 1974, PhD, 1977. Asst. prof. Ohio State U., Columbus, 1976-79; rsch. asst. prof. communications U. Ill., Champaign, 1979-83, rsch. assoc. prof., 1983-89, rsch. prof., 1989-93; dean Coll. Comm., Walter Cronkite Regents Chair in Comm. U. Tex., Austin, 1993—; vis. prof. U. Calif., Santa Barbara, 1992-93; cons. Children's TV Workshop, N.Y.C., 1988-89, FTC, Washington, 1978, 1991-92, FCC, Washington, 1979. Co-author: How Children Learn to Buy, 1977; editor: Mass Communications Review Yearbook, 1982-83, Rethinking Communication, vols. I and II, 1989. Mem. bd. advisors Am. Children's TV Festival, Chgo., 1988; bd. trustees Children's TV Workshop, 1996—; bd. dirs. Headliners Found., Austin, Sta. KLRU-TV (ex officio), Austin. Recipient Krieghbaum award Assn. for Edn. in Journalism and Mass Communication, 1984; Univ. scholar U. Ill., 1989-93; Gannett Ctr. for Media Studies fellow, 1985-86. Fellow Internat. Comm. Assn. (pres. 1992-93), Broadcast Edn. Assn. (bd. dirs. 1990-94), Speech Comm. Assn., Soc. for Rsch. in Child Devel.

WARTELLA, ROSANNE KAREN, occupational therapy assistant; b. Allentown, Pa., Apr. 1, 1948; d. Stephen William Sr. and Georgine Gloria (Kemmerer) Cicon; m. Richard Alan Biehl, Aug. 31, 1968 (div. Mar. 1987); children: Bradford Alan, Christine Denise; m. Stephen Wartella III, Oct. 9, 1993. AAS in Occupational Therapy, Lehigh County C.C., 1984. Lic. occupational therapy asst., Pa. Primary therapist Penn Found. for Mental Health, Sellersville, 1984-89; occupational therapy asst. Grand View Hosp., Sellersville, 1989-97, Manor Care, Devon, Pa., 1997—; mem. spkrs. bur. Arthritis Found. Ea. Pa., 1995-96, GVH, 1993-97, clin. educator, 1985-96, facilitator Arthritis Club, 1992-97. Chair person craft show Penn Found. for Mental Health, 1992-95. Avocations: reading, antiquing, gardening. Home: 2020 Clover Mill Rd Quakertown PA 18951

WARTH, ROBERT DOUGLAS, history educator; b. Houston, Dec. 16, 1921; s. Robert Douglas and Virginia (Adams) W.; m. Lillian Eleanor Terry, Sept. 18, 1945. B.S., U. Ky., 1943; M.A., U. Chgo., 1945, Ph.D., 1949. Instr. history U. Tenn., Knoxville, 1950-51; instr. Rutgers U., Newark, 1951-54; asst. prof. Rutgers U., 1954-58; vis. prof. Paine Coll., Augusta, Ga., 1960; asso. editor Grolier, Inc., N.Y.C., 1960-62, 63-64; lectr. Hunter Coll., N.Y.C., part time, 1962-63; asso. prof. S.I. Community Coll., 1964-68; prof. history U. Ky., Lexington, 1968-92; prof. emeritus history U. Ky., 1992—; Pres. So. Conf. Slavic Studies, 1982-83. Author: The Allies and the Russian Revolution, 1954, Soviet Russia in World Politics, 1963, Joseph Stalin, 1969, Lenin, 1973, Leon Trotsky, 1977. Served with AUS, 1943-44. Sr. scholar award So. Conf. Slavic Studies, 1992. Mem. Am. Hist. Assn., Am. Assn. Advancement Slavic Studies, AAUP. Home: 640 W Cooper Dr Lexington KY 40502-2277 Office: U Ky Dept History Lexington KY 40506

WARTHEN, HARRY JUSTICE, III, lawyer; b. Richmond, Va., July 8, 1939; s. Harry Justice Jr. and Martha Winston (Alsop) W.; m. Sally Berkeley Trapnell, Sept. 7, 1968; children: Martha Alsop, William Trapnell. BA, U. Va., 1961, LLB, 1967. Bar: Va. 1967, U.S. Ct. Appeals (4th cir.) 1967, U.S. Dist. Ct. (ea. dist.) Va. 1969. Law clk. to judge U.S. Ct. Appeals (4th cir.), Richmond, Va., 1967-68; assoc. Hunton & Williams, Richmond, 1968—; lectr. U. Va. Law Sch., Charlottesville, 1975-77, in field. Trustee exec. com. Hist. Richmond Found., 1986-95, 96—; dir. exec. com. Preservation Alliance of Va., 1991—, pres., 1994-96; elder, trustee endowment fund Grace Covenant Presbyn. Ch.; moderator Hanover Presbytery, Presbyn. Ch. (USA), 1988. Lt. U.S. Army, 1962-64. Fellow Am. Coll. Trust and Estate Counsel, Va. Law Found.; mem. ABA, Richmond Bar Assn., Va. Bar Assn. (chmn. sect. on wills, trusts and estates 1981-89), Antiquarian Soc. Richmond (pres. 1977-78), Country Club Va., Deep Run Hunt Club. Republican. Home: 1319 Shallow Well Rd Manakin-Sabot VA 23103-2305 Office: Hunton & Williams Riverfront Plaza East Tower 951 E Byrd St Richmond VA 23219-4040

WARTHEN, JOHN EDWARD, construction, leasing and finance executive; b. Cedar City, Utah, May 8, 1922; s. Mark Tew and Emma (Simkins) W.; student Branch Agrl. Coll. So. Utah, Cedar City, 1940-41; m. Norma Jane Hansen, June 22, 1943; children—Russel Edward, John Merrill, Judith Lally, Linda Fahringer, Carla Jean Thompson, Lauri Janette Sherratt. Pres., mgr. St. George Service, Inc. (Utah), 1945-61, Warthen Constrn. Co., Las Vegas, 1961—, Warthen Buick, 1961—; pres., gen. mgr. Diversified Investment & Leasing Corp., Las Vegas. Councilman, City of St. George, 1950-54. Past trustee, treas. Latter Day Saint Br. Geneal. Library, Las Vegas, 1964-76 ; co-founder Ctr. for Internat. Security Studies; past dist. dir. Freeman Inst.; past nat. dir. Liberty Amendment Com.; past chmn. Citizens for Pvt. Enterprise, Las Vegas; mem. Coun. Inter-Am. Security, Americanism Ednl. League; past fin. chmn. Boy Scouts Am.; past state chmn. Nev. Dealer Election Action Com.; mem. Nev. Devel. Authority. Mem. Ludwig Von Misses Inst. Econs. (charter), SAR (Good Citizenship award nat. soc.). Mormon (bishop 1957-61). Clubs: Rotary, Kiwanis. Home: 2475 E Viking Rd Las Vegas NV 89121-4109 Office: 3025 E Sahara Ave Las Vegas NV 89104-4315

WARTHIN, THOMAS ANGELL, physician, educator; b. Ann Arbor, Mich., Aug. 11, 1909; s. Aldred Scott and Katharine Louise (Angell) W.; m. Virginia Carver Whittier, Oct. 15, 1938 (dec. Nov. 1995); children: Jonathan Carver, Richard Scott, Thomas Whittier. AB, U. Mich., 1930; MD cum laude, Harvard U., 1934. Diplomate Am. Bd. Internal Medicine. Intern medicine Boston City Hosp., 1934-36; resident intern medicine New Haven Hosp., Conn., 1936-37; fellow intern medicine Johns Hopkins Med. Sch., Balt., 1937-39; practice medicine Mass. Gen. Hosp., Boston, 1939-42; chief med. svc. VA Hosp., W. Roxbury, Mass., 1946-75; prof. of medicine Harvard Med. Sch., Boston, 1955-76, prof. of medicine emeritus, 1976—; cons. Surgeon Gen. U.S. Army, Washington, 1960-69, Internal Medicine VA Hosp., W. Roxbury, Mass., 1976-84. Contbr. articles to profl. jours. Brigadier Gen. U.S. Army, 1942-69. Recipient Legion of Merit, U.S. Army, 1969. Mem. ACP (master), Soc. Med. Cons. Armed Forces (pres. 1964), Internat. Soc. Internal Medicine (hon.), Mass. Med. Soc., Am. Clin. and Climatol. Assn. (coun., v.p. 1982), Aesculapian Club (pres. 1962), Alpha Omega Alpha. Avocation: gardening. Home: 180 Main St Apt 120 Walpole MA 02081-4033

WARTOFSKY, LEONARD, medical educator; b. N.Y.C., July 14, 1937; s. Harry and Sadie (Gondelman) W.; m. Donna L. Brodsky, Dec. 18, 1959; 1 child, Michael. BS, George Washington U., 1959, MS, 1961, MD, 1964; MPH, 1995. Diplomate Am. Bd. Internal Medicine, Am. Bd. Endocrinology. Intern Washington U., St. Louis, 1964-65, resident, 1965-66; resident Albert Einstein Coll., Bronx, N.Y., 1966-67; fellow Harvard U., Boston, 1967-69; chief dept. medicine Walter Reed Med. Ctr., Washington, 1990-93; prof. medicine Uniformed Svcs. U., Washington; chmn. dept. medicine Washington Hosp. Ctr., 1993—; clinical prof. Georgetown Howard, George Washington Univ. Assoc. editor: Principles and Practice of Endocrinology, 1991; contbr. 200 articles to profl. jours. Mem. ACP (master), Am. Thyroid Assn. (bd. dirs. 1986-89, nat. sec. 1988-93, pres. 1995), Am. Fedn. Clin. Rsch., Endocrine Soc., Am. Soc. Clin. Invstigation, Assn. Am. Physicians. Democrat. Jewish. Office: Washington Hosp Ctr 110 Irving St NW Washington DC 20010-2931

WARWICK, DIONNE, singer; b. East Orange, N.J., Dec. 12, 1940; m. Bill Elliott (div. 1975); children: David, Damon. Ed., Hartt Coll. Music, Hartford, Conn. As teen-ager formed Gospelaires and Drinkard Singers, then sang background for rec. studio, 1966; debut, Philharmonic Hall, N.Y. Lincoln Center, 1966; appearances include London Palladium, Olympia, Paris, Lincoln Ctr. Performing Arts, N.Y.C.; records include Don't Make Me Over, 1962, Walk On By, Do You Know The Way to San José, What The World Needs Now, Message To Michael, I'll Never Fall In Love Again, I'll Never Love This Way Again, Deja Vu, Heartbreaker, That's What Friends are For; albums include Valley of the Dolls and Others, 1968, Promises, Promises, 1975, Dionne, 1979, Then Came You, Friends, 1986, Reservations for Two, 1987, Greatest Hits, 1990, Dionne Warwick Sings Cole Porter, 1990, Hidden Gems; The Best of Dionne Warwick, Vol. 2, 1992, (with Whitney Houston) Friends Can Be Lovers, 1993, Dionne Warwick and Placido Domingo, 1994, Aquarela Do Brasil, 1994, From the Vaults, 1995; TV appearance in Sisters in the Name of Love, HBO, 1986; screen debut Slaves, 1969, No Night, So Long, also, Hot! Live and Otherwise; co-host: TV show Solid Gold; host: TV show A Gift of Music, 1981; star: TV show Dionne Warwick Spl. Founder Dionne Warwick Scholarship Fund, 1968, charity group BRAVO (Blood Revolves Around Victorious Optimism), Warwick Found. to Help Fight AIDS; spokeswoman Am. Sudden Infant Death Syndrome; participant U.S.A for Africa; Am. Amb. of Health, 1987. Recipient Grammy awards, 1969, 70, 80; NAACP Key of Life award, 1990. Address: Arista Records Inc 6 W 57th St New York NY 10019-3913*

WARWICK, SHARON BRENDA, elementary art educator; b. El Paso, Tex., Dec. 18, 1946; d. George Clark and Charlene (Walker) W.; m. Alfonso Cortes, Sept. 14, 1978 (div. 1980); 1 child, Clark Lewis Cortes. BA, U. Tex., 1971; MEd, Tex. Woman's U., 1981, MFA, 1984. Cert. tchr. elem., art, secondary English., Tex. Art specialist Roger Williams Middle Sch., Providence, 1971-76; prof. English Instituto Allende, San Miguel de Allende, Mexico, 1977; tchr. English Krum (Tex.) High Sch., 1980-86; art specialist Borman Elem. Sch., Denton, Tex., 1986-92, Lakewood Elem. Sch., Euless, Tex., 1992-93, Shady Brook Elem. Sch., Bedford, Tex., 1993—; adj. instr. Cooke County Coll., Gainesville, Tex., 1984-85, Tex. Woman's U., Denton, 1985-86, U. North Tex., Denton, 1986-87; tchr. Cen. Jr. H.S., 1994-95; v.p. It Works Inc. Pub. Co., Denton, 1979-80; assoc. rep. Tex. State Tchrs. Assn., Denton, 1989-91; guest educator Meadows Mus. Art, So. Meth. U., Dallas, 1994-96; part-time faculty Tarrant County Jr. Coll., 1995—; presenter in field. Solo exhbns. include Tex. Woman's U., Denton, 1984, Bath House Cultural Ctr., Dallas, 1989, Studio W Gallery, El Paso, Tex., 1991, Chilton Hall U. N. Tex., Denton, 1991, African Meth. Episcopal Ch., Denton, 1992, Ctr. for Visual Arts, Denton, 1996; group shows include Saguarro Gallery, Denton, 1987, Lamar State U., 1989, Waterworks Gallery, 1989, Trammell Crow Ctr., Dallas, 1992, Trading Sisters Gallery, South Padre, 1993, Ctr. for Visual Arts, Denton, 1996, others; solo slide/lectr. Dallas Mus. Art; contbg. author: Art Works, 1987, Spectra, 1988, Milagros, 1994, Portfolios, 1996. Hospitality chair Delta Kappa Gamma, Denton, 1992; exhbn. com. chair Greater Denton Arts Coun., 1987-97; del. Tex. Dem. Conv., Dallas, Houston, 1985-86. Recipient Yellow Rose of Tex., Gov. Ann Richards, 1991, PTA Tchr. of Yr., Shady Brook PTA, 1993-94, Founders award Denton Area Art Edn. Assn., 1996, various art awards, 1988—. Mem. Nat. Art Edn. Assn., Am. Craft Assn., Tex. Art Edn. Assn. (elem. div. chair 1989-91, newsletter editor, bus. mgr., regional dir. visual arts scholastic event 1995—, Tex. Outstanding Art Educator - Mid. Divsn. 1996), Dallas Mus. Art, Modern Art Mus. Ft. Worth, Kimbell Mus. Art, North Tex. Inst. for Educators in the Visual Arts (leadership group, 1992), League United Latin Am. Citizens. Democrat. Unitarian. Avocations: potter, sculptor, painter. Home: 1003 Aileen St Denton TX 76201-2527 Office: Cen Jr H S 3191 W Pipeline Rd Euless TX 76040-6235

WASAN, DARSH TILAKCHAND, university official, chemical engineer educator; b. Sarai, Salah, West Pakistan, July 15, 1938; came to U.S., 1957, naturalized, 1974; s. Tilakchand Gokalchand and Ishari Devi (Obhan) W.; m. Usha Kapur, Aug. 21, 1966; children: Ajay, Kern. BSChemE, U. Ill., 1960; PhD, U. Calif., Berkeley, 1965. Asst. prof. chem. engring. Ill. Inst. Tech., Chgo., 1964-67, assoc. prof., 1967-70, prof., 1970—, chmn. dept., 1971-77, 78-87, acting dean, 1977-78, 87-88, v.p. rsch. and tech., 1988-91, provost, 1991—, provost and sr. v.p., 1995-96, v.p., internat. and Motorola chair, 1996—; cons. Inst. Gas Tech., 1965-70, Chgo. Bridge & Iron Co., 1967-71, Ill. EPA, 1971-72, NSF, 1971, 78-79, 87-89, Nelson Industries, 1976—, B.F. Goodrich Chem. Co., 1976-78, Exxon Rsch. & Engring. Co., 1977-89, Stauffer Chem. Co., 1980-88, ICI Ams., 1988-92. Editor-in-chief Jour. colloid and Interface sci.; mem. publs. bd. Chem. Engring. Edn. Jour.; mem. adv. bd. Interant. Jour. Powder Tech., Jour. Separations Tech., Surfaces and Colloids Jour., Current Opinion in Colloid and Interface Sci., Jour. of Dispersion Sci. and Tech.; contbr. articles to profl. jours. Recipient Donald Gage Stevens Disting. Lectureship award Syracuse U., 1991, Jakob J. Bikerman Lectureship award Case Western U., 1994, Robert Gilpin Lectr. award Clarkson U., 1995, MacMoran Disting. Lectrureship award Tulane U., 1996, Sidney Ross lectr. award, 1996. Fellow Am. Inst. Chem. Engrs. (Ernest Thiele award 1989); mem. AAAS, Am. Chem. Soc., Soc. Rheology, Am. Soc. Engring. Edn. (Western Electric award 1972, 3M Lectureship award chem. engring. divsn. 1991), Am. Physics Inst., Fine Particles Soc. (pres. 1976-77, Hausner award 1982), Sigma Xi. Home: 8705 Royal Swan Ln Darien IL 60561-8433 Office: Ill Inst Tech 3300 S Federal St Chicago IL 60616-3732

WASELL, GÖSTA, retired auditor; b. Hudiksvall, Sweden, Mar. 14, 1930; s. Per-Alef and Henny (Bengtsson) W.; m. Siv Ingegerd Berggård, Aug. 13, 1955; children: Åsa-Helen, Per-Anders. Student, Stockholm U., 1952-55. Cert. internal auditor. Part-time railway and bldg. worker Swedish State Railways, 1946-51; officer, internal auditor, office mgr. Folksam Ins. Group, Stockholm, 1954-76; internal auditor, v.p. Swedish Trade Coun., Stockholm, 1976-81; mgr. audit dept. Swedish Trade Union Confederation, Stockholm, 1981-92; elected external auditor Stockholm, 1981-95; ret., 1995. Fellow Nils Ferlin Soc.; mem. Inst. Internal Auditors. Social Democrat. Lutheran. Avocations: playing organ, reading biographies and memoirs, travel abroad. Home: Sparrisbacken 35, 16561 Hasselby Sweden

WASFI, SADIQ HASSAN, chemistry educator; b. Basrah, Iraq, July 1, 1936; established residency in the U.S., 1978; s. Hassan Mohammed and Seniye (Omar) W.; m. Ellen Olivia Schwarz, Nov. 15, 1968; children: Yasmine, Dahlia, Ammar. BS in Chemistry Edn., Baghdad (Iraq) U., 1961; MS in Analytical Chemistry, Georgetown U., 1966, PhD in Inorganic Chemistry, 1971. Lectr. chemistry Basrah U., 1971-77; rsch. assoc. U. Hawaii, Honolulu, 1975-76, Georgetown U., Washington, 1977-78; assoc. prof. Montgomery Coll., Takoma Park, Md., 1978-79; prof. chemistry Del. State U., Dover, 1979—; vis. assoc. prof. Georgetown U., 1980, 81. Contbr. articles to profl. jours; patent in antimony oxometalate complexes having anti-viral activity, 1991. Mem. Am.-Arab Anti-Discrimination Com. Mem. Am. Chem. Soc., Sigma Xi. Muslim. Home: 286 Pine Valley Rd Dover DE 19904-7111 Office: Del State Univ Dept Chemistry 1200 N Dupont Hwy Dover DE 19901-2202

WASFIE, TARIK JAWAD, surgeon, educator; b. Baghdad, Iraq, July 1, 1946; m. Barina Y. Wasfie, Mar. 11, 1975; children: Giselle, Nissan. BS, Central U., Iraq, 1964; MD, Baghdad Med. Sch., 1970. Cert. gen. surgeon. Surg. rsch. assoc. Sinai Hosp. of Detroit/Wayne State U., 1981-85; clin. fellow Coll. Phys. & Surg., Columbia U., N.Y.C., 1985-91, postdoctoral rsch. scientist, 1987-91; attending surgeon Mich. State U./McLaren Hosp., Flint, 1991—. Contbr. articles to profl. jours. NIH grantee, 1984. Fellow ACS (assoc.), Internat. Coll. Surgeons; mem. AMA, Mich. State Med. Soc., Flint Acad. Surgeons, Am. Soc. Artificial Internal Organs, Internat. Soc. Artificial Organs, Soc. Am. Gast. Endoscopic Surgeons. Achievements include production of antiidiotypic antibodies and their role in transplant immunology; development of percutenous access device. Home: 1125 Kings Carriage Rd Grand Blanc MI 48439-8715

WASHBURN, BARBARA POLK, cartographer, researcher, explorer; b. Boston, Nov. 10, 1914; m. Bradford Washburn, Apr. 27, 1940; children: Dorothy, Edward, Elizabeth. Grad., Smith Coll., 1935; DSc (hon.), U. Alaska, 1995, D (hon.), 1995; DSc (hon.), Boston U., 1996. Sec. Harvard Biol. Labs., 1936-38; exec. sec. Mus. of Sci., 1939-40; remedial reading tchr. Shady Hill Sch., Cambridge, Mass.; asst. to Henry Bradford Washburn Jr.; first ascent of Mt. Bertha, Alaska, 1940, Mt. Hayes, Alaska, 1941; first woman to climb Mt. McKinley, Alaska, 1947; worked with husband on numerous sci. expdns., including Mt. McKinley, the Grand Canyon, Bangkok, London, Nepal, China, Alaska, Zurich, Milan, 1945—; participated in remapping the Grand Canyon for Nat. Geographic/Mus. of Sci., 1971-76; cons. to Govt. of Alaska State Parks Recreational Area in Tokositna Valley, 1980. Editor new chart of Swan Lake, 1977, new map of Presdl. Range, N.H., 1989; contbr. articles to Anchorage Daily News, 1987. Bd. dirs. Boston Children's Svc. Assn.; overseer Brigham & Women's Hosp., Boston; mem. corp. Fernald Sch., 1976; mem. Cambridge LWV, 1945-50, Mt. Auburn Hosp. Aux., Cambridge, 1945-60; pres. Women's Travel Club of Boston, 1949-51; pres. Cambridge Smith Coll. Club, 1952-54; bd. svc. league Mus. of Sci., 1959-62, sec., 1961-62; chmn. personal interview program for Smith, Alumnae Fund in Boston, 1964-65. Recipient Achievement award 100th Ann. Dinner of the Girl's Latin Sch. Alumni Assn., 1978; honored by Mus. of Sci. with plaque for yrs. of work, 1974, gold medal Royal Scottish Geog. Soc. for Outstanding Contbns. to Cartographic Rsch., 1979, Smith medal for Lifetime Exploration and Mapmaking, 1980, 1st Alexander Graham Bell award of Nat. Geog. Soc., 1980, Centennial award, 1988, award of Yukon Ter. Commr., 1997. Home: 220 Somerset St Belmont MA 02178-2011

WASHBURN, BRADFORD (HENRY B. WASHBURN, JR.), museum administrator, cartographer, photographer; b. Cambridge, Mass., June 7, 1910; s. Henry Bradford and Edith (Hall) W.; m. Barbara Teel Polk, Apr. 27, 1940; children: Dorothy Polk, Edward Hall, Elizabeth Bradford. Grad., Groton Sch., 1929; A.B., Harvard U., 1933, A.M., 1960, D.H.L. (hon.), 1975; postgrad., Inst. Geog. Exploration, 1934-35; postgrad. hon. degrees; PhD, U. Alaska, 1951; DSc, Tufts U., 1957, Colby Coll., 1957, Northeastern U., 1958; D.Sc., U. Mass., 1972; DSc, Curry Coll., 1982; DFA, Suffolk U., 1965; DHL, Boston Coll., 1974; LLD, Babson Coll., 1980. Instr. Inst. Geog. Exploration, Harvard U., 1935-42; dir. Mus. Sci., Boston, 1939-80, chmn. of the corp., 1980-85, hon. dir., 1985—; dir. Mountaineer in Alps, 1926-31; explorer Alaska Coast Range, 1930-40; served as leader numerous mountain, subarctic area explorations; cons. various govtl. agys. on Alaska and cold climate equipment; leader in spl. expdns. investigating high altitude cosmic rays, Alaska, 1947; rep. Nat. Geog. Soc., 17th Internat. Geog. Congress, 1952; leader Nat. Geog. mapping expdns. to, Grand Canyon, 1971-75; chmn. Mass. Com. Rhodes Scholars, 1959-64; chmn. arts and scis. com. UNESCO conf., Boston, 1961; mem. adv. com. John F. Kennedy Library, 1977; mem. vis. com. Internat. Mus. Photography, 1978; mem. U.S. Nat. Commn. for UNESCO, 1978; lectr. work of Yukon Expdn., Royal Geog. Soc., London, 1936-37, on mapping Grand Canyon, 1976; lectr. Mus. Imaging Tech., Bangkok, 1989, Royal Geog. Soc., London, on mapping Mt. Everest, 1990; lectr. Antarctica, 1994. Contbr. articles, photographs on Alaska, Alps, glaciers, and mountains to mags., books.; editor, pub. 1st large-scale map Mt. McKinley, Am. Acad. Arts and Scis.-Swiss Found. Alpine Rsch., Bern, 1960; mapped Mt. Kennedy for Nat. Geog. Soc., 1965, Grand Canyon, 1971-74, Muldrow Glacier (Mt. McKinley), 1977; editor new chart, Squam Lake, N.H., 1968, new Grand Canyon map for Nat. Geog. Soc., 1978, Bright Angel Trail map, 1981; photo-mapped Mt. Everest for Nat. Geog. Soc., 1984; dir., pub. large-scale map of Mt. Everest for Nat. Geog. Soc., 1984-88; project chief new 1:50,000 map of Mt. Everest for Nat. Geog. Soc. and Boston Sci. Mus., 1988; pub. Tourist Guide to Mt. McKinley, 1971, new map of Presdl. Range, N.H, 1989; completed new large-scale relief model Mt. Everest, 1990; one-man photographic shows Whyte Art Mus., Banff, Can., Internat. Mus. Photography, N.Y.C., Rochester, N.Y. Bd. overseers Harvard, 1955-61; trustee Smith Coll., 1962-68, Richard E. Byrd Found., 1979-84, Mt. Washington Obs., 1979—; mem. Task Force on Future Financing of Arts in Mass., 1978; hon. bd. dirs. Swiss Found. Alpine Research, 1984—. Recipient Royal Geog. Soc. Cuthbert Peek award for Alaska Exploration and Glacier Studies, 1938, Burr prize Nat. Geog. Soc., 1940, 65, Stratton prize Friends of Switzerland, 1970, Lantern award Rotary Club, Boston, 1978, New Englander of Yr. award New Eng. Coun., 1974, Gold Research medal Royal Scottish Geog. Soc. (with wife), 1979, Alexander Graham Bell award Nat. Geog. Soc., 1980, Disting. Grotonian award Groton Sch., 1979, Explorers medal Explorers Club, 1984, award for lifelong contbns. to cartography and surveying Engring. Socs. New Eng., 1985, King Albert medal of merit, 1994; named Bus. Statesman of Yr. Harvard Bus. Sch. Assn., Boston, 1970; named to Acad. Disting. Bostonians Boston C. of C., 1983; one of nine Photographic Masters, Boston U., prize for outstanding contbn. to pub. understanding of geology Am. Geol. inst., 1996. Fellow Royal Geog. Soc. London, Harvard Travelers Club (Gold medal 1959), Nat. Geog. Soc. (with wife, Centennial award 1988), AAAS, Am. Acad. Arts and Scis., Am. Geog. Soc. (hon., major photographic exhibit for ann. conv. 1993—). Clubs: Commercial, Harvard Varsity, St. Botolph (hon. life), Aero Club of New Eng. (hon.), Harvard Mountaineering (Boston) (hon., past pres.); American Alpine (N.Y.C.) (hon.); Alpine (London) (hon.); Sierra of San Francisco (hon.); Mountaineers (Seattle) (hon.); Mountaineering Club of Alaska (hon.); hon. mem. several clubs. Leader 1st ascent Mt. Crillon, Alaska, 1934, Nat. Geog. Soc. Yukon Expdn., 1935; leader 1st aerial photog. exploration Mt. McKinley, 1936, ascended its summit, 1942, 47, 51; leader 1st aerial exploration St. Elias range, 1938; 1st ascents Mount Sanford and Mount Marcus Baker in Alaska, 1938, Mt. Lucania, Yukon, 1937, Mt. Bertha, Alaska, 1940, Mt. Hayes, Alaska, 1941; 1st ascent West side Mt. McKinley 1951; leader Nat. Geog. Soc. Mt. Everest mapping project, 1981-88; expdn. to S.E. Asia, guest Chinese Acad. Scis., met with King of Nepal, 1988; leader expdn. to Nepal, 1992; 1st laser-distance observation to summit of Mt. Everest, 1992; 50th trip to Alaska to open exhibit of own photos Anchorage Art Mus., 1993; 57th Alaska-Yukon trip on occasion of 60th anniversary of Lucania ascent, 1997. Home: 220 Somerset St Belmont MA 02178-2011 Office: Science Park Boston MA 02114

WASHBURN, DAVID THACHER, lawyer; b. Claremont, N.H., May 2, 1930; s. Walter Henry and Josephine Emmeline (Dana) W.; m. Joycemarie Springer, June 10, 1957 (div. Dec. 1975); children: Margaret Dana, David Thacher Jr., Robert Springer, John Putnam. BA, U. Vt., 1952; JD, NYU,

1955. Bar: N.Y. 1956, D.C. 1970, U.S. Supreme Ct 1970. From assoc. to ptnr. Paul, Weiss, Rifkind, Wharton & Garrison, N.Y.C., 1955-95, counsel, 1996—; adj. prof. CUNY Law Sch., 1997—. Trustee Rye Neck Bd. Edn., Mamaroneck, N.Y., 1971-73, Cambridge (Mass.) Coll., 1980-88, The Yard, N.Y.C., 1986-95, ARIA Found., Inc., Williston, Vt., 1991—; trustee, mem. exec. com. Rare Ctr. for Tropical Bird Conservation, Phila., 1979-80; dir. Sanctuary for Families, Inc., N.Y.C., 1994—, treas. 1995—. Mem. ABA, N.Y. State Bar Assn., Assn. of Bar of City of N.Y., The Coffee House, Doubles, Westchester Country Club. Home: 10 W 66th St New York NY 10023-6206 Office: Paul Weiss Rifkind Wharton & Garrison 1285 Avenue Of The Americas New York NY 10019-6028

WASHBURN, DONALD ARTHUR, transportation executive; b. Mankato, Minn., Sept. 24, 1944; s. Donald and Geraldine Helen (Pint) W.; m. Christine Carvell, Aug. 24, 1968; children: Timothy, Abigail. BBA with high honors, Loyola U., Chgo., 1971; MBA, Northwestern U., 1973, JD cum laude, 1978. Bar: Ill. 1978. With prodn. mgmt. dept. J.T. Ryerson/Inland Steel, Chgo., 1963-68; asst. to the pres. G.B. Frank, Inc., 1969-70; cons. Intec, Inc., 1970-72; mktg. mgmt., atty. Quaker Oats, Co., 1972-79; sr. cons. Booz, Allen & Hamilton, 1979-80; corp. v.p., then sr. v.p. Marriott Corp., Washington, 1980-90; sr. v.p. N.W. Airlines, Mpls., 1990-94, exec. v.p., 1994—; bd. dirs. Mesaba Holdings, Inc., Princess House, Inc., Children's Cancer Rsch. Fund. Contbr. articles to profl. jours. Mem. ABA, Ill. Bar Assn., Chgo. Bar Assn., Alpha Sigma Nu, Beta Gamma Sigma. Unitarian Universalist. Office: Northwest Airlines Inc Dept A5010 5101 Northwest Dr Dept A5010 Saint Paul MN 55111-3027

WASHBURN, HARRIET CAROLINE, secondary education educator; b. Hallock, Minn., Mar. 15, 1920; d. John W. and Anna Melinda (Younggren) Swanson; m. Edward James Washburn, Jan. 22, 1971 (dec. 1993); children: Jacqueline Ann Batt, stepchild, Margaret; m. Ohls Batt. BA cum laude, Macalester Coll., 1941; MA in Pupil Personnel Svcs., San Jose State U., 1969. Tchr. Latin, English, phys. edn. Renville (Minn.) Pub. Sch., 1941-43; tchr. phys. edn. St. Cloud (Minn.) Jr. H. S., 1943-44, Fremont (Calif.) Unified Sch. Dist., 1958-69; recreation specialist City Recreation Dept., Lincoln, Nebr., 1946-50; dir. youth activities Trinity Meth. Ch., Lincoln, 1950-53; counselor Milpitas (Calif.) Unified Sch. Dist., 1969-75, head counselor, 1975-80; cons., trainer, speaker Stockton, Calif., 1980—; coord. bank acct. Bank of Stockton, 1989—; mem., presenter Internat. Tng., Anaheim, 1978—; cons. personal, profl. devel. Personal Dynamics, Inc., Mpls., 1980-87. Guest speaker Kiwanis, Lions, Candy Stripers, Ctrl. Meth. Ch., MCClellan AFB, and numerous others, 1980—, presenter Asian Am. Found., Stockton, 1995—. With USN, 1944-46. Recipient Sch. Counselor Svc. award Calif. Sch. Counselor Assn., Milpitas, 1980. Mem. AAUW, Beginners Luck Investment Club, Alliance for the Mentally Ill of S.J. County, Rep. Women's Club. Presbyterian. Avocations: bridge, Bible study, reading, writing. Office: Bank of Stockton 301 E Miner Ave Stockton CA 95202-2501

WASHBURN, ROBERT BROOKS, university dean, composer; b. Bouckville, N.Y., July 11, 1928; s. Robert Phelps and Florence (Brooks) W.; m. Beverly Jean Darnell, July 10, 1952; children: Brooks, Roberta. BS, SUNY, Potsdam, 1949, MS, 1956; PhD, Eastman Sch. Music, 1960. Dean, prof. music SUNY, Potsdam, 1954-95, dean emritus, sr. fellow music, 1995—; cons. NEH, Ogdensburg, N.Y., 1984-87, N.Y. State Sch. Music Assn., 1976-80, U.S. Office Edn., Washington, 1978-80; del. Music Educators Nat. Conf. Composer over 150 mus. works, 1955—. Served as sgt. USAF, 1950-54. Nat. Endowment for the Arts grantee, 1979; fellow Danforth Found., 1958-59, Ford Found. grantee, 1959-60, Fulbright fellow, 1986. Mem. ASCAP, Soc. for Ethnomusicology. Avocation: traveling. Home: 87 State Hwy 72 Potsdam NY 13676-3478 Office: SUNY Crane Sch Music Potsdam NY 13676

WASHBURN, STAN, artist; b. N.Y.C., Jan. 2, 1943; s. Sherwood Larned and Henrietta (Pease) W.; m. Andrea Aall Stub, Mar. 5, 1966; children: Anne Elizabeth, John Larned. MFA, Calif. Coll. Arts and Crafts, 1968. Founding ptnr. The Griffin Co., Oakland, Calif., 1968-70. Author: George's Dragon, 1974, A Moral Alphabet of Vice and Folly, 1986, Intent to Harm, 1994, Into Thin Air, 1996; one-man shows include Achenbach Found., San Francisco, 1977, St. Botolph Club, Boston, 1977, Pucker/Safrai, Boston, 1975, 77, 80, 85, Ames, Berkeley, Calif., 1974, 78, 81, 84, Thackrey & Robertson, San Francisco, 1981, 86, Charles Campbell, San Francisco, 1983, 86, 88, 90, 91, Bannatyne, Santa Monica, 1990, North Point, San Francisco, 1993, 96; represented in permanent collections at Bklyn. Mus., Achenbach Found., Chgo. Art Inst., Libr. of Congress, Houghton Libr., Phila. Mus. Art, Boston Mus. Fine Arts. Mem. Berkeley Police Res., 1973-78; mem. Berkeley Police Rev. Commn., 1979-83; trustee The Coll. Prep. Sch., Oakland, 1986—. Address: 2010 Virginia St Berkeley CA 94709-2138

WASHBURN, WILCOMB EDWARD, historian, educator; b. Ottawa, Kans., Jan. 13, 1925; s. Harold Edward and Sidsell Marie (Nelson) W.; m. Lelia Elizabeth Kanavarioti, July 14, 1951 (div. June 1981); children: Harold Kitsos, Edward Alexandros; m. Kathryn Lafler Cousins, Jan 2, 1985. Grad., Phillips Exeter Acad., 1943; AB summa cum laude, Dartmouth Coll., 1948; MA, Harvard U., 1951, PhD, 1955; HHD (hon.), St. Mary's Coll. Md., 1970, Assumption Coll., 1983, St. Lawrence U., 1991, Salisbury State U., 1996. Teaching fellow history and lit. Harvard, 1954-55; fellow Inst. Early Am. History and Culture, Williamsburg, Va., 1955-58; instr. Coll. William and Mary, 1955-58; curator div. polit. history Smithsonian Instn., U.S. Nat. Mus., Washington, 1958-65; dir. Am. studies program Smithsonian Instn., 1965-97; Professorial lectr. Am. U., 1961-63, adj. prof., 1963-69; cons. in research Grad. Sch. Arts and Scis., professorial lectr. in Am. civilization George Washington U., 1966—; adj. prof. U. Md., 1975—; Civil info. and edn. officer Toyama Mil. Govt. Team, Toyama Prefecture, Japan, 1946-47. Author: The Governor and the Rebel: A History of Bacon's Rebellion in Virginia, 1957, Red Man's Land/White Man's Law: A Study of the Past and Present Status of the American Indian, 1971, revised edit., 1995, The Assault on Indian Tribalism: General Allotment Law (Dawes Act) of 1887, 1975, The Indian in America, 1975, (with others) The Federal City: Plans and Realities, The Exhibition, 1976; editor: (with others) The Indian and the White Man, 1964, Proc. of the Vinland Map Conf., 1971, The American Heritage History of the Indian Wars, 1977; contbr. articles to profl. jours. Past pres. Hist. Soc. of Washington; active Am. Hist Assn., Va. Hist. Assn., Md. Hist. Assn., Mass. Hist. Soc. With USMCR, 1943-45, 51-52. Fellow Am. Anthropol. Assn.; mem. AAAS, Am. Soc. Ethnohistory (past pres.), Am. Studies Assn. (past pres.), Colonial Soc. Mass., Am. Antiquarian Soc., Orgn. Am. Historians, Japan-Am. Soc. Washington (past trustee), Instituto Histórico e Geográfico Brasileiro, Anthropol. Soc. Washington, Phi Beta Kappa, Cosmos Club. Club: Cosmos (Washington). Home: 2122 California St NW Washington DC 20008

WASHINGTON, ADRIENNE MARIE, elementary school educator; b. Chgo., June 26, 1950; d. Henry and Emily Marguerite (Sims) Robertson; m. Gregory Blake, Mar. 26, 1967 (div.); children: Emily M., Gregory D.; m. Donald Booker Washington, Apr. 18, 1990. BA, U. Mich., 1976, MA, 1977; Specialist in Arts, Ea. Mich. U., 1991. Cert. tchr., Mich. Head tchr. Second Bapt. Day Care, Ann Arbor, Mich., 1977; tchr. Willow Run Pub. Schs., Ypsilanti, 1977—; workshop presenter Nat. Black Child Devel. Inst., detroit, 1984; pub. rels./crisis chair WREA; founder What Black History Means to Me essay contest. Youth leader NAACP, Ypsilanti, 1980's; campaign asst. Dem. orgn., Ypsilanti, 1988, 91; canvasser Mar. Dimes; corr. sec. Brown Chapel A.M.E. Ch., tchr. Bible sch., co-chair sesquicentinnel anniversary. Hon. Citizen City of Nashville, 1992, State of Tenn., 1992. Mem. Nat. Assn. Black Bus. and Profl. Women's Clubs (pres. 1984-86, Spl. Appreciation award 1997), Tenn. Black Caucus of State Legislators (hon. mem.), Elks (pres. PSP Club of Mich. 1988-95, fin. sec. Anna G. Parker Temple No. 1283). Avocations: travel, reading, sewing. Home: 1835 Manchester Dr Ypsilanti MI 48198-3646

WASHINGTON, CLARENCE EDWARD, JR., insurance company executive; b. New Orleans, Nov. 20, 1953; s. Clarence Edward and Alice Mildred (Jones) W.; m. Denise Sandra Agard, June 29, 1985. BS cum laude, Xavier U., 1983. Mgr. Time Saver, Inc., New Orleans, 1972-79; budget, fin. analyst Equitable Life Assurance, N.Y.C., 1983-84; actuarial asst. Prudential Life Assurance, Newark, 1984-87; pension mgr. Am. Internat. Life, N.Y.C., 1987—. Mem. Fiske Terrace Assns. (bd. dirs.), Am. Mus. Natural History (assoc.), Internat. Platform Assn. Democrat. Roman Catholic. Office: Am Internat Life 80 Pine St Fl 13 New York NY 10005-1702

WASHINGTON, DENNIS, production designer. Prodn. designer: White Men Can't Jump, 1992, Nowhere to Run, 1993, The Fugitive, 1993, Angels in the Outfield, 1994. Office: Smith/Gosnell/Nicholson & Assocs PO Box 1166 1515 Palisades Dr Pacific Palisades CA 90272*

WASHINGTON, DENNIS, construction executive. CEO Washington Cos., Missoula, Mont. Office: Washington Corp 101 International Way Missoula MT 59802-1549*

WASHINGTON, DENZEL, actor; b. Mt. Vernon, N.Y., Dec. 28, 1954; m. Pauletta Pearson; children: John David, Katia, Malcolm and Olivia (twins). BA in Journalism, Fordham U.; student, Am. Conservatory Theatre, San Francisco. With N.Y. Shakespeare Festival, Manhattan Theatre Club, New Fed. Theatre. Actor: (stage prodns.) Coriolanus, 1979, Spell No. 7, The Mighty Gents, Richard III, One Tiger to a Hill, Ceremonies in Old Dark Men, When the Chicken Comes Home to Roost (Audelco award), A Soldier's Play (Obie award 1981), Checkmates, 1988, Split Second, (feature films) Carbon Copy, 1981, A Soldier's Story, 1981, Power, 1986, Cry Freedom, 1987, For Queen and Country, 1988, The Mighty Quinn, 1989, Glory, 1989 (Golden Globe award 1989, Acad. award 1990, NAACP Image award 1990), Heart Condition, 1990, Mo' Better Blues, 1990, Ricochet, 1991, Mississippi Masala, 1992, Malcolm X, 1992, Much Ado About Nothing, 1993, Philadelphia, 1993, The Pelican Brief, 1993, Crimson Tide, 1995, Virtuosity, 1995, Devel in a Blue Dress, 1995, Courage Under Fire, 1996 (NAACP Image award 1997), The Preacher's Wife, 1996; (TV Movies) Wilma, 1977, License to Kill, 1984, The George McKenna Story, 1986, (TV miniseries) Flesh and Blood, 1979; regular (TV series) St. Elsewhere, 1982-88. Recipient Harvard Found. award, 1996; Am. Conservatory Theater scholar. Avocations: basketball, reading, cooking. Office: care ICM 8942 Wilshire Blvd Beverly Hills CA 90211-1934

WASHINGTON, GROVER, JR., musician, producer, composer, arranger; b. Buffalo, Dec. 12, 1943; m. Christine; children: Grover III, Shana. Student, Wurlitzer Sch. Music, Temple U.; also pvt. instrn.; DFA (hon.), U. Arts Phila., 1997. Worked for record distbr., 1969-70; pres. pub. co. G.W. Jr. Music, Inc.; pres. prodn. co. G-Man Prodns., Inc.; tchr. seminars and master classes throughout U.S. Played with musical group Four Clefs, to 1963, with Keith McAllister, 1963-65, 19th Army Band, 1965-67; played with various groups in Phila. and N.Y., with Billy Cobham, with Don Gardner's Sonotones, 1967-68, Charles Earland, 1971; rec. for Kudu Records, Elektra Records, now under contract with Columbia Records; plays soprano, tenor, alto, baritone saxophones; over 25 solo albums including Come Morning, Mr. Magic, Winelight, The Best Is Yet to Come, Then and Now, Time Out of Mind, Next Exit, All My Tomorrows, Soulful Strut; numerous recs. as sideman or featured artist with Randy Weston, Bob James, Ralph MacDonald, Kathleen Battle, John Williams and London Symphony, Don Sebesky, others; numerous TV and personal appearances throughout U.S., Can., Europe, Japan; performs Nat. Anthem regularly for Phila. Eagles and Phila. 76ers; prodr. 3 albums for group Pieces of a Dream, Jean Carne; first album of music from the Cosby Show. Performed at Inaugural events for Pres. Bill Clinton, 1993; participant Pres. Clinton's 50th Birthday celebration Radio City Music Hall, Presdl. Summit Vol., 1997. Recipient numerous record industry awards including Grammy awards, 6 gold albums, platinum albums, also many prestigious industry, charitable and cmty. awards.

WASHINGTON, JAMES WINSTON, JR., artist, sculptor; b. Gloster, Miss., Nov. 10, 1909; s. James and Lizie (Howard) W.; m. Janie R. Miller, Mar. 29, 1943. Student, Nat. Landscape Inst., 1944-47; D.F.A., Center Urban-Black Studies, 1975. tchr. summer class N.W. Theol. Union Seattle U., 1988. One man shows U.S.O. Gallery, Little Rock, 1943, Foster-White Gallery, Seattle, 1974, 78, 80, 83, 89 (also at Bellevue Art Mus., 89), Charles and Emma Frye Art Mus., Seattle, 1980, 95, Mus. History and Industry, Seattle, 1981; exhibited in group shows Willard Gallery, N.Y.C., 1960-64, Feingarten Galleries, San Francisco, 1958-59, Grosvenor Gallery, London, Eng., 1964, Lee Nordness Gallery, N.Y.C, 1962 Woodside Gallery, Seattle, 1962-65, Foster-White Gallery, Seattle, 1974, 76, 89, 92, Smithsonian Instn., 1974, San Diego, 1977, others; retrospective exhbn. Bellevue Art Mus., Washington, 1989; represented in permanent collections Seattle, San Francisco, Oakland art museums, Seattle First Nat. Bank, Seattle Pub. Libr. YWCA, Seattle, Meany Jr. H.S., Seattle World's Fair, Expo 70 Osaka, Japan, Whitney Mus. Am. Art, N.Y.C.; commd. sculpture: Bird With Covey, Wash. State Capitol Mus., Olympia, 1983, Obelisk with Phoenix and Esoteric Symbols of Nature in granite, Sheraton Hotel Seattle, 1982, Life Surrounding the Astral Alter, In Matrix, owner T.M. Rosenblume, Charles Z. Smith & Assocs., Seattle, 1986, The Oracle of Truth (6 1/2 ton sculpture) Mt. Zion Bapt. Ch., Seattle, 1987, commd. sculptures King County Arts Commn., 1989, Bailey Gatzent Elem. Sch., Seattle, 1991, Twin Eaglets of the Cosmic Cycle (Quincy Jones), 1993, Fountain of Triumph (Bangasser Assocs. Inc.), 1992-93, Seattle, 1993-94, 94-95, Child in Matrix, 1995, Blunt Tail Owl, 1996, Bunny Rabbit and Robbin, 1996. Passover leader Mt. Zion Baptist Ch., Seattle, 1974-87; founder James W. Washington, Jr. and Mrs. Janie Rogella Washington Found. Recipient Spl. Commendation award for many contbns. to artistic heritage of state Gov., 1973, plaque City of Seattle, 1973, plaque Benefit Guild, Inc., 1973, arts service award King County Arts Commn., 1984, cert. of recognition Gov. of Wash., 1984, Editor's Choice award Outstanding Achievement in Poetry Nat. Libr. Poetry, 1993; named to Wash. State Centennial Hall of Honor, Wash. State Hist. Soc., 1984; home and studio designated historic landmark (city and state), 1991. Mem. Internat. Platform Assn., Internat. Soc. Poets (life, awards 1993), Profl. Artists Phila., Masons (33d degree). Home: 1816 26th Ave Seattle WA 98122-3110

WASHINGTON, JOHN AUGUSTINE, physician, pathologist; b. Istanbul, Turkey, May 29, 1936; (parents Am. citizens); s. Samuel Walter and Simone (Fleisher) Washington; m. Maaja Harms, July 11, 1959; children: Stephen L., Richard R., Mikaela A. BA with honors, U. Va., 1957; MD, Johns Hopkins U., 1961. Diplomate Am. Bd. Pathology, (Clin. Pathology, Med. Microbiology). Intern Duke U. Med. Ctr., Durham, N.C., 1961-62, resident in surgery, 1962-63; resident in clin. pathology NIH, Bethesda, Md., 1965-67, asst. chief microbiology svc., 1966-67; assoc. cons. microbiology Mayo Clinic, Rochester, Minn., 1967-68, dir. bacteriology lab., 1968-71, head sect. clin. microbiology, 1971-86; chmn. dept. microbiology Cleve. Clinic Found., 1986-92, vice chmn. divsn. pathology and lab. medicine, 1992-96, chmn. dept. clin. pathology, 1992-96, head microbiology sect., 1992—; trustee Am. Bd. Pathology, Tampa, Fla., 1989-94. Mem. editl. bd. European Jour. Clin. Microbiology and Infectious Diseases; sect. editor Infectious Diseases in Clin. Practice; contbr. more than 300 articles to profl. jours.; author numerous chapters in books. Lt. comdr. USPHS, 1963-67. Fellow ACP, Coll. Am. Pathologists, Am. Soc. Clin. Pathologists, Am. Coll. Chest Physicians, Infectious Diseases Soc. Am., Am. Acad. Microbiology. Independent. Avocations: gardening, swimming. Office: Cleve Clin Found 9500 Euclid Ave Cleveland OH 44195-0001

WASHINGTON, MALIVAI, professional tennis player; b. Swartz Creek, MI, June 20, 1969. Student, U. Mich. Ranked 6th in U.S. Tennis Assn., 1993. Named All-American NCAA, 1988-89; mem. U.S. Davis Cup Team, 1993; winner of Australian Open, 1994, U.S. Clay Courts Championship, 1992. Office: c/o US Tennis Assn 70 W Red Oak Ln White Plains NY 10604-3602*

WASHINGTON, REGINALD LOUIS, pediatric cardiologist; b. Colorado Springs, Colo., Dec. 31, 1949; s. Lucius Louis and Brenette Y. (Wheeler) W.; m. Billye Faye Ned, Aug. 18, 1973; children: Danielle Larae, Reginald Quinn. BS in Zoology, Colo. State U., 1971; MD, U. Colo., 1975. Diplomate Nat. Bd. Med. Examiners, Am. Bd. Pediatrics, Pediatric Cardiology. Intern in pediatrics U. Colo. Med. Ctr., Denver, 1975-76, resident in pediatrics, 1976-78, chief resident, instr., 1978-79, fellow in pediatric cardiology, 1979-81, asst. prof. pediatrics, 1982-1988, assoc. prof. pediatrics, 1988-90, assoc. clin. prof. pediatrics, 1990—; staff cardiologist Children's Hosp., Denver, 1981-90; v.p. Rocky Mountain Pediatric Cardiology, Denver, 1990—; chmn. dept. pediatrics Presbyn./St. Luke's Med. Ctr.; mem. admissions com. U. Colo. Sch. Medicine, Denver, 1985-89; chmn., bd. dirs. Coop. Health Care Agreements, 1994—; chmn. dept. pediatrics Presbyn./St. Lukes MC, Denver. Cons. editor Your Patient and Fitness, 1989-92. Chmn. Coop. Health Care Agreements Bd., State of Colo., 1994—; adv. bd. dirs. Equitable Bank of Littleton, Colo., 1984-86; bd. dirs. Ctrl. City Opera, 1989-95, Cleo Parker Robinson Dance Co., 1992-94, Rocky Mountain Heart Fund for Children, 1984-89, Raindo Ironkids, 1989—; nat. bd. dirs. Am. Heart Assn., 1992-96; bd. dirs. Nat. Coun. Patient Info. and Edn., 1992—, Children's Heart Alliance, 1993-94, Regis U., Denver, 1994—, Colo. State U. Devel. Coun., 1994—; trustee Denver Ctr. Performing Arts, 1994—; mem. Gov.'s Coun. Phys. Fitness, 1990-91; bd. trustees Regis U.; mem. Colo. State Bd. Agr., 1996—. Named Salute Vol. of Yr. Big Sisters of Colo., 1990; honoree NCCJ, 1994, Physician of Yr., Nat. Am. Heart Assn., 1995. Fellow Am. Acad. Pediatrics (cardiology subsect.), Am. Coll. Cardiology, Am. Heart Assn. (coun. on cardiovascular disease in the young, exec. com. 1988-91, nat. devel. program com. 1990-94, vol. of yr. 1989, pres. Colo. chpt. 1989-90, Torch of Hope 1987, Gold Heart award Colo. chpt. 1990, bd. dirs. Colo. chpt., exec. com. Colo. chpt. 1987—, grantee Colo. chpt. 1983-84, mem. editorial bd. Pediatric Exercise Scis. 1988—, Nat. Physician of the Yr., 1995), Soc. Critical Care Medicine; mem. Am. Acad. Pediatrics/Perinatology, , Am. Acad. Pediatrics/Pediatric Cardiology (exec. com. 1996—), N.Am. Soc. Pediatric Exercise Medicine (pres. 1986-87), Colo. Med. Soc. (chmn. sports medicine coun. 1993-94), Leadership Denver 1990, Denver Athletic Club, Met. Club, Glenmoor Golf Club. Democrat. Roman Catholic. Avocations: skiing, golf, fishing. Home: 7423 Berkeley Cir Castle Rock CO 80104-9278 Office: Rocky Mountain Pediatric Cardiology 1601 E 19th Ave Ste 5600 Denver CO 80218-1255

WASHINGTON, ROBERT ORLANDA, educator, former university official; b. Newport News, Va., Feb. 8, 1935; s. Robert Lee and Fannie (Bates) W.; m. Mary Louise Lewis, Apr. 7, 1955; children: Robert, Glynis, Cheryl, Nathan, Allyson, Terrence, Candace. B.S., Hampton Inst., 1956; M.S., Marquette U., 1966; M.A., U. Mo., 1968; Ph.D., Brandeis U., 1973. Pub. Milw. Post, weekly newspaper, 1960-64; rsch. assoc. Greenleigh Assocs., N.Y.C., 1968-72; instr. social work Simmons Coll., Boston, 1970-72; prof. Case Western Res. U., Cleve., 1972-74; dean Ohio State U. Sch. Social Work, Columbus, 1976-82, U. Ill., Champaign, 1982-86; pres., CEO, Social Policy Rsch. Group, Inc., Boston, 1986-88; vice chancellor for rsch. and grad. studies U. New Orleans, 1988-93; cons. U.S. AID, Nigeria, 1970, 72, Cairo, 1975, 77; commr. accreditation Coun. on Social Work Edn., N.Y.C., 1978-81; cons. HHS, Washington, 1981. Author: Program Evaluation in the Human Services, 1980, (with others) Social Policy and Social Welfare, 1980, Marco Practice in Social Work, 1982, Social Work in the 1980's, 1982, Children in Need of Roots, 1985, Social Work in Schools, 1985, Toward a Theory of Social Planning, 1994; editor Jour. Planning Edn. and Rsch. NDEA fellow, 1967. Mem. NASW, Coun. on Social Work Edn., Assn. Collegiate Schs. of Planning, Am. Planning Assn., Urban Affairs Assn., Phi Kappa Phi. Democrat. Home: 7135 Benson Ct New Orleans LA 70127-2001 Office: U New Orleans Dept Social Work Lakefront New Orleans LA 70148

WASHINGTON, SHELLEY LYNNE, dancer; b. Washington, Nov. 3, 1954; d. Edward Freeman and Geraldine (Butler) W. Student, Interlochen Arts Acad., 1969-72, Juilliard Acad., N.Y.C., 1972-74. Dancer Martha Graham, N.Y.C., 1974-75, Twyla Tharp Dance Found., N.Y.C., 1975—, Am. Ballet Theatre, N.Y.C., 1988-91; ballet mistress and artistic assoc. dir. for Twyla Tharp, including repertory for Boston Ballet, Hubbard St. Dance Co., Martha Graham Dance Co., Am. Ballet Theatre, The Royal Ballet, London, The Australian Ballet, Tharp. Dancer in film Hair, 1978; in Broadway show Singin in the Rain, 1985-86. Recipient Bessie Schonberg award for Outstanding Performing, 1987. Office: Twyla Tharp Dance Found Tharp Prodns 336 Central Park W New York NY 10025-7111

WASHINGTON, VALORA, foundation administrator; b. Columbus, Ohio, Dec. 16, 1953; d. Timothy Washington and Elizabeth (Jackson) Barbour; children: Omari, Kamilah. BA in Social Sci. with honors, Mich. State U., 1974; PhD, Ind. U., 1978; PhD (hon.), Bennett Coll., 1992. Assoc. instr. sch. edn. Ind. U., Bloomington, 1975-77; dir., cons. Urban League Ind., Indpls., 1977-78; substitute tchr. Indpl. Pub. Schs., 1978; dir. U. N.C., Chapel Hill, 1980-82; congrl. sci. fellow Soc. for Rsch. in Child Devel., Washington, 1981-82; prof. edn. U. N.C., Chapel Hill, 1978-83; asst. dean, assoc. prof. Howard U., Washington, 1983-86, Am. U., Washington, 1986-87; prof., v.p. Antioch Coll., Yellow Springs, Ohio, 1987-90; v.p. Kellogg Found., Battle Creek, Mich., 1990—; cons. Ford Found., N.Y.C., 1990; project evaluator Carnegie Corp., N.Y.C., 1989-90, Ohio Bd. Regents, Columbus, 1990—. Author: (with others) Creating New Linkages for the Adoption of Black Children, 1984, Project Head Start: Past, Present and Future Trends in the Context of Family Needs, 1987, Black Children and American Institutions: An Ecological Review and Resource Guide, 1988, Affirmative Rhetoric, Negative Action: The Status of Black and Hispanic Faculty in Higher Education, 1989; contbr. articles to profl. jours; contbr. chapters to numerous books. Recipient Capital U. award, 1990, award Springfield Alliance Black Educators, 1989; named one of Ten Outstanding Young Women Am., 1980, Outstanding Young Woman N.C., 1980, one of 100 Young Women of Promise Good Housekeeping Mag., 1985, one of 25 Most Influential Working Mothers, Working Mothers Mag., 1997. Mem. Nat. Coun. Negro Women (chmn. 1982-83), Am. Assn. for Higher Edn. (sec. black caucus 1989), Soc. for Rsch. in Child Devel. (pres. black caucus 1987-89), Nat. Assn. for the Edn. of Young Children (sec. of bd. dir. 1990—), Phi Delta Kappa, Delta Kappa Gamma.

WASHINGTON, VIVIAN EDWARDS, social worker, former government official; b. Claremont, N.H., Oct. 26, 1914; d. Valdemar and Irene (Quashie) Edwards; m. George Luther Washington, Dec. 22, 1950; 1 child, Valdemar Luther. AB, Howard U., 1938, MA, 1946, MSW, 1956; LHD (hon.), U. Balt., 1993. Tchr., guidance counselor, sch. social worker, asst. prin., prin. Edgar Allan Poe Sch. Program for Pregnant Girls, Balt., 1966-73; cons. Office Adolescent Pregnancy Programs, HEW, Washington, 1978-80, program devel. specialist, 1980-81; exec. dir. Balt. Coun. on Adolescent Pregnancy, Parenting and Pregnancy Prevention Inc., 1982-86, cons., 1986—; Author: I Am Somebody, I Am Me, 1986; contbr. articles to profl. jours. Bd. dirs. Nat. Alliance Concerned with Sch.-Age Parents, 1970-76, pres., 1970-72; YWCA, Balt., 1944-69, United Way Central Md., 1972-85; mem. bd. visitors U. Balt., 1976-80, U. Balt. Ednl. Found., 1980, 92-94, chair, 1992-94; adv. commn. on social services City of Balt., 1978-85, Govs. Coun. on Adolescent Pregnancy, 1986; chmn. Md. Gov.'s Commn. on Children and Youth, 1972-77, active 1987. Recipient Alumni award Howard U. Sch. Social Work, 1966, Clementine Peters award United Way, 1979, Sojourner Truth award Nat. Bus. and Profl. Women, 1979, Vashti Turley Murphy award Balt. chpt. Delta Sigma Theta, 1981, Balt.'s Best Blue and Silver award, 1983, Pvt. Sector Vol. Svc. award Pres. Reagan, 1984, United Way Community Svc. award, 1985, H. Mebane Turner Svc. award U. Balt. Alumni Assn., 1991, 94, Disting. Black Marylander award Towson State U., 1992, Cmty. Svc. award For Sisters Only, 1994, Learn and Earn Program Pioneer award Balt. City 4-H, 1993, Citizen Citation City of Balt., 1995; named to Balt. Women's Hall of Fame, 1989, Md.'s Outstanding Ch. Woman Nat. Episc. Triennial, 1991; Paul Harris fellow Balt. Rotary, 1985. Mem.Great Cir. Md. Living Legend, Nat. Assn. Social Work, LWV, Nat. Coun. Negro Women (life), Balt. Urban League (Equal Opportunity award 1987, Whiting Moore Young Jr. award 1997), Balt. Mus. Art, Delta Sigma Theta (nat. treas. 1958-63, Las Amigas Svc. award Balt. chpt. 1973), Pietian Club. Democrat. Episcopalian. Home: 3507 Ellamont Rd Baltimore MD 21215-7422

WASHINGTON, WALTER, retired academic administrator; b. Hazlehurst, Miss., July 13, 1923; s. Kemp and Mable (Comous) W.; m. Carolyn Carter, July 31, 1949. BA, Tougaloo Coll., 1948, LLD (hon.), 1972; MS, Ind. U., 1952, LLD (hon.), 1983; Edn. Specialist, Peabody Coll., 1958; postgrad., Yale, 1953; EdD, U. So. Miss., 1969; postgrad., Harvard U., 1989; DSc (hon.), Purdue U., 1993. Tchr. Holtzclaw High Sch., Crystal Springs, Miss., 1948-49; asst. prin., tchr. Parrish High Sch., Hazlehurst, 1949-52; prin. Utica Jr. Coll. High Sch., Miss., 1951-54; dean Utica Jr. Coll., 1954-55, pres., 1957-69; prin. Sumner Hill High Sch., Clinton, Miss., 1955-57; pres. Alcorn (Miss.) State U., 1969-94, pres. emeritus, 1994—; past ptnr. Klinger Industries, Ltd.; bd. dirs. Blue Cross and Blue Shield Miss. Pres. Nat. Pan-Hellenic Council, 1964-67, Nat. Alumni Council of United Negro Coll. Fund, 1959-60; past. mem. adv. council Miss. Vocational Edn. Program, Miss. Regional Med. Programs; mem. Miss. Econ. Council; mem. S.E. regional exec. com. Boy Scouts Am.; mem. exec. com. Andrew Jackson council; past mem. adv. council Miss. 4-H Clubs; bd. dirs. Miss. Mental Health Assn., Miss. Easter Seal Soc.; past bd. dirs. Miss. Heart Assn. Recipient Presdl. citation for outstanding leadership to Univ./Industry Cluster, 1980-81, Disting. Alumni award Vanderbilt-Peabody, 1991, George Washington Carver Lifetime Achievement award Tuskegee Inst., 1993; named to U. So. Miss. Alumni Hall of Fame, 1987; Walter Washington Bldgs. named in his honor U. So. Miss., 1993, Alcorn State U., 1994. Mem. NEA, ASCD, Am. Assn. Sch. Adminstrs. (So. Regional Edn. bd.), Nat. Assn. State Univs. and Land Grant Colls., So. Assn. Colls. Secondary Schs. (past bd. dirs., past chmn. secondary commn., past chmn. commn. on colls., past trustee), Miss. Educators Assn. (pres. 1964-65), Miss. Tchrs. Assn., Nat. Soc. for Study of Higher Edn., Tougaloo Nat. Alumni Assn. (pres. 1960), George Peabody Coll. Alumni Assn. (past v.p. exec. com., Disting. Alumni of Yr. 1991), John Dewey Soc., Delta Kappa Pi, Phi Delta Kappa, Alpha Kappa Mu, Alpha Phi Alpha (gen. pres. 1974-76).

WASHINGTON, WARREN MORTON, meteorologist; b. Portland, Oreg., Aug. 28, 1936; s. Edwin and Dorothy Grace (Morton) W.; m. LaRae Herring, July 30, 1959 (div. Aug. 1975); children: Teri, Kim, Marc (dec.), Tracy; m. Jona Ann, July 3, 1978 (dec. Jan. 1987); m. Mary Elizabeth Washington, Apr., 1995. B.S. in Physics, Ore. State U., 1958, M.S. in Meteorology, 1960; Ph.D. in Meteorology, Pa. State U., 1964. Dir. of climate and global dynamics div. Nat. Center Atmospheric Research, Boulder, Colo., 1978-95; affiliate prof. meteorology oceanography U. Mich. at Ann Arbor, 1968-71; mem. Nat. Adv. Com. for Oceans and Atmospheres, 1978-84; mem. sec. of energy adv. bd. U.S. Dept. Energy, 1990-93. Contbr. articles to meteorol. jours. Mem. Boulder Human Relations Commn., 1969-71; mem. Gov.'s Sci. Adv. Com., 1975-78. Recipient Disting. Alumni award Oreg. State U., 1991, E.B. Lemon Disting. Alumni award Pa. State U., 1991; inductee NAS portrait collection African Am. in Sci., Engring., and Medicine, 1997. Fellow AAAS (bd. dirs.), Am. Meteorol. Soc. (pres. 1994); mem. Am. Geog. Union, Nat. Sci. Bd. Home: 725 Pinehurst Ct Louisville CO 80027-3285 Office: PO Box 3000 Boulder CO 80307-3000

WASIELE, HARRY W., JR., diversified electrical manufacturing company executive; b. Chgo., June 29, 1926; s. Harry W. and Antoinette (Tuleja) W.; m. Loretta K. Anderson, Jan. 3, 1948; children: Kathleen Ann Wasiele Bach, Brian David, Larry Scott, Mark Thomas. Grad. high sch. Asst. sales mgr. Drake Mfg. Co., Chgo., 1950-55; sales engr. AMP, Inc., Chgo., 1955, Detroit, 1956-57; product mgr. AMP, Inc., Harrisburg, Pa., 1958-61; industry mgr. AMP, Inc., 1961-67, dir. marketing, 1967-68; div. gen. mgr. Brand-Rex div. Am. Enka Corp., Willimantic, Conn., 1968-70; pres. Brand-Rex Co., subs. Akzona Inc., 1970-83; chmn. Brand-Rex Ltd., Glenrothes, Scotland, 1974-83; v.p. sales and corp. devel. Cablec Corp., New City, N.Y., 1985—; dir. Berkel Inc.; chmn., pres. Tarpon Springs (Fla.) Internat. Tannery, Inc., 1990—. Bd. dirs. Ea. Conn. State Coll. Found., 1972-83; trustee Windham Cmty. Hosp., Willimantic, 1969-83, trustee emeritus, 1983—, pres. bd. trustees, 1981-83; trustee YMCA of Martin County Found. Mem. Nat. Elec. Mfrs. Assn. (chmn. wire and cable div., bd. govs. 1982-84), Conn. Bus. and Industry Assn. (emeritus dir.), New Seabury Country Club, Mariner Sands Country Club. Republican. Roman Catholic. Home (summer): 53 Shore Dr W PO Box 826 New Seabury MA 02649 Home (winter): Mariner Sands 6755 SE Barrington Dr Stuart FL 34997-8639

WASIK, JOHN FRANCIS, editor, writer, publisher; b. Chgo., July 2, 1957; s. Arthur Stanley and Virginia Frances (Gray) W.; m. Kathleen Rose. BA in Psychology, U. Ill., Chgo., 1978, MA in Communication, 1988. Sr. editor Consumers Digest Inc., Chgo., 1986—; editor, pub. Conscious Consumer and Co. Newsletters. Author: Electronic Business Information Sourcebook, 1987, Green Company Resource Guide, 1992, The Green Supermarket Shopping Guide, 1993, The Investment Club Book, 1995. Mem. Soc. Profl. Journalists, Soc. Environ. Journalists. Office: Consumers Digest Inc 5705 N Lincoln Ave Chicago IL 60659-4707

WASILEWSKI, VINCENT THOMAS, retired lawyer; b. Athens, Ill., Dec. 17, 1922; s. Alex and Anna (Gillespie) W.; m. Patricia Callery, June 17, 1950 (dec. 1989); children: Jan, Susan, Catherine, Terese, Thomas, James; m. Marjorie Nohowel, June 19, 1992. A.B. in Polit. Sci, U. Ill., 1948, J.D., 1949. Bar: Ill. 1950, D.C. 1980. Mem. staff Nat. Assn. Broadcasters, Washington, 1949-82; v.p. govt. affairs Nat. Assn. Broadcasters, 1960-61, exec. v.p., 1961-65, pres., 1965-82; trustee Mus. Broadcasting. Served with USAAF, 1942-45. Decorated D.F.C. with oak leaf cluster; Air medal with oak leaf cluster.; Recipient David Sarnoff award, Am. Women in Radio and TV Silver Satellite award, Commonwealth award. Mem. ABA, Nat. Assn. Broadcasters (Disting. Svc. award 1982), Fed. Comms. Bar Assn., Internat. Radio and TV Soc., Internat. Club (Washington), Burning Tree Club (Washington), George Town Club (Washington), Congl. Club (Potomac, Md.), John's Island Club (Vero Beach, Fla.), Knights of Malta, Order of Coif, Sigma Phi Epsilon, Phi Kappa Phi, Phi Alpha Delta. Home: 6111 Davenport Ter Bethesda MD 20817-5827 Office: Dow Lohnes & Albertson 1255 23rd St NW Washington DC 20037-1125

WASIOLEK, EDWARD, literary critic, language and literature educator; b. Camden, N.J., Apr. 27, 1924; s. Ignac and Mary (Szczesniewska) W.; m. Emma Jones Thomson, 1948; children: Mark Allan, Karen Lee, Eric Wade. B.A., Rutgers U., 1949; M.A., Harvard, 1950, Ph.D., 1955; postgrad., U. Bordeaux, France, 1950-51. Teaching fellow Harvard U., Cambridge, Mass., 1953-54, research fellow Russian Research Ctr., 1952-54; instr. English Ohio Wesleyan U., 1954-55; asst. prof. U. Chgo., 1955-60, assoc. prof. English and Russian, 1960-64, prof. Russian and comparative lit., 1964-69, Avalon prof. comparative lit. and Russian, 1969-76, Disting. Services prof. of English, comparative lit., and Slavic studies, 1976—, chmn. comparative lit. program, 1965-83, chmn. dept. Slavic langs. and lit., 1971-77; vis. prof. Slavic and comparative lit. Harvard, 1966-67. Author: (with R. Bauer) Nine Soviet Portraits, 1955, Crime and Punishment and the Critics, 1961, Dostoevsky: The Major Fiction, 1964, The Notebooks for Crime and Punishment, 1967, The Brothers Karamazov and the Critics, 1967, The Notebooks for the Idiot, 1968, The Notebooks for the Possessed, 1968, The Notebooks for A Raw Youth, 1969, The Notebooks for the Brothers Karamazov, 1970, The Gambler, with Paulina Suslova's Diary, 1972, Tolstoy's Major Fiction, 1978, Critical Essays on Tolstoy, 1986, Fathers and Sons: Russia at the Crossroads, 1993. Addressed UN on Tolstoy, 1988. With USNR, 1943-46. Recipient Quantrell teaching prize U. Chgo., 1961; Laing Press prize, 1972; Research fellow USSR, 1963; Guggenheim fellow, 1983-84. Mem. Modern Lang. Assn., Phi Beta Kappa, Lambda Chi Alpha. Home: 1832 Butterfield Ln Flossmoor IL 60422-2107 Office: Univ Chicago Dept English Chicago IL 60637 *I believe in the life of the mind and I believe with Albert Camus that man's dignity lies in his lucidity: in seeing his fate clearly and in having the courage to accept it. Man is capable of sensitivity, courage, love, and compassion, and all of these are more human because he can think. He is also capable of cruelty, hatred, and destruction, and these are more tolerable because he can reason. Man is not man without reason.*

WASKO-FLOOD, SANDRA JEAN, artist, educator; b. N.Y.C., Mar. 12, 1943; d. Peter Edmund and Margaret Dalores (Kubek) Wasko; m. Michael Timothy Flood, June 28, 1969. BA, UCLA, 1965, postgrad., 1968-69; postgrad., Calif. State U., Northridge, summer 1968; student, Otis Art Inst., L.A., 1969, Marie Kaufman, Rio de Janeiro, 1970-72, Museo de Arte Moderno, Rio de Janeiro, 1970-73, Foothill Coll., Los Altos, Calif., 1973-74, Claremont (Calif.) Coll., 1975, U. Wis., Janesville, 1977, Beloit (Wis.) Coll., 1977-78, U. Wis., 1977-78; grad. etching student, Warrington Colescott. Instr. printmaking Washington Women's Arts Ctr., 1983; artist-in-residence U. Md., College Park, 1984; instr. printmaking Arlington (Va.) Arts Ctr., 1984-85; prof. St. Mary's (Md.) Coll., 1985; instr. printmaking Arlington County Lee Arts Ctr., 1989-95; workshop coord. cultural affairs div. Arlington County Parks, Recreation and Community Resources, 1989-96. One woman shows include Wisconsin Women in the Arts Gallery, Madison, 1977, Mbari Art, Washington, 1981, Miya Gallery, Washington, 1981, Slavin Gallery, Washington, 1982, Stuart Mott House, Washington, 1983, Washington Printmakers Gallery, 1986, 88, 91, St. Peter's Ch., N.Y.C., 1989, Montana Gallery, Alexandria, Va., 1991, Montpelier Cultural Arts Ctr., Laurel, Md., 1992, Gallery 10, Washington, 1994, 96, Sch. 33, Balt., 1996; mus. and internat. shows include Boston Printmakers: The 39th North Am. Print Exhbn., Framingham, Mass., Jan.-Mar., 1986, Internat. Graphic Arts Found. and Silvermine Guild Arts Ctr., New Canaan, Conn., Feb., 1988, prints: Washington, The Phillips Collection, Washington, Sept.-Oct., 1988, Contemporary Am. Graphics, Book Chamber Internat., Moscow, 1990, Gallery 10 Artists of Washington D.C. Vartai Gallery, Lithuania, 1994, Peninsula Fine Arts Ctr., Newport News, Va., 1995-96, Riva Sinistra Arte, Florence, Italy, 1997 and numerous others; juried shows include Washington Women's Arts Ctr.: Printmakers VII show, 1985, Washington Women's Arts Ctr., 1981, 82, Seventh Ann. Faber Birren Color Show Nat. Juried Open Exhibit, Stamford, Conn., 1987, Acad. of the Arts 25th Ann. Juried Exhbn., 1989, Fla. Printmakers Nat., 1994, S.W. Tex. State U., 1995, and numerous others; invitational shows include Office of the Mayor, Mini Art Gallery, Washington, "Glimpses: Women Printmakers", 1981, Pyramid Paperworks, Balt., 1984, Gallery 10 "Nightmare Show": Washington, D.C., 1987, The Intaglio Process, The Benedicta Art Ctr. Gallery, St. Joseph, Minn., 1988, Women's Caucus for Art, Washington Artists in Perspective, Westbeth Gallery, N.Y.C., 1990, 91, Wesley Theol. Sem., 1992, Balt. City Hall, N.Am. Print Alliance, 1993, The Five Elements Women's Caucus For Art, 1994, and numerous others; galleries: Slavin Gallery, Washington, D.C., 1981-83, Washington Printmakers Gallery, Washington, 1985-96, White Light Collaborative, Inc., N.Y.C., 1988-89, Montana Gallery, Alexandria, Va., 1989-91, Gallery 10, Washington, 1992-97, and numerous others; collections include Nat. Mus. of Women in the Arts, Washington, Corcoran Gallery of Art, Washington, Museo de Arte Moderno, Buenos Aires, Cultural Found., USSR, Coll. Notre Dame, Balt. Pres. Washington Area Printmakers, Washington, D.C., 1985-86; pub. rels. dir. Washington Women's Arts Ctr., 1980; bd. dirs. Washington Women's Arts Ctr., 1981-82. Grantee Friends of the Torpedo Factory Art Ctr., Alexandria, Va., 1989, Va. Commn. on the Arts, 1994; recipient Award of Honorable Mention Nat. Gallery of Art, 1989, Best of Show, Artists Equity Exhibit, Gallery 901, Washington, 1991. Mem. Nat. Print Orgn., Pyramic Atlantic, So. Graphics Coun., Women's Caucus for Art, Coalition Washington Artists, L.A. Printmaking Soc., Washington Ctr. for Photography, Md. Printmakers, Calif. Printmakers, Calif. Printmaking Soc., Am. Print Alliance, Corcoran Gallery/Washington Project for the Arts, Washington Sculpture Group, Artists Equity. Avocations: classical music, hiking, reading. Home: 8106 Norwood Dr Alexandria VA 22309-1331 Studio: 57 N St NW Washington DC 20001-1254

WASKOW, ARTHUR OCEAN, theologian, educator; b. Balt., Oct. 12, 1933; s. Henry B. and Hannah (Osnowitz) W.; m. Irene Elkin, 1956 (div. 1978); children: David, Shoshana; m. Phyllis Ocean Berman, 1986. B.A., Johns Hopkins, 1954; M.A., U. Wis., 1956, Ph.D., 1963. Legis. asst. Ho. of Reps., Washington, 1959-61; sr. staff mem. Peace Rsch. Inst., Washington, 1961-63; fellow Inst. Policy Studies, Washington, 1963-77; colleague Pub. Resource Ctr., Washington, 1977-82; faculty Reconstructionist Rabbinical Coll., Phila., 1982-89; dir. Shalom Ctr., 1983—; fellow ALEPH Alliance for Jewish Renewal, 1990—: mem. adv. bd. Temple of Understanding; vis. prof. religion Swarthmore Coll., 1982-83, Temple U., 1976-77, 87-88, Drew U., 1997—; sec.-treas. Conf. On Peace Rsch. in History, 1969-74. Author: The Limits of Defense, 1962, (with Stanley L. Newman) America in Hiding, 1962, Worried Man's Guide to World Peace, 1963, From Race Riot to Sit-In, 1966, The Freedom Seder, 1969, Running Riot, 1970, The Bush Is Burning, 1971, Godwrestling, 1978, Seasons of Our Joy, 1982, These Holy Sparks, 1983, (with David and Shoshana Waskow) Before There Was a Before, 1984, (with Howard Waskow) Becoming Brothers, 1993, Down-to-Earth Judaism: Food, Money, Sex, and the Rest of Life, 1995, Godwrestling—Round 2: Ancient Wisdom, Future Paths, 1996, (with Phyllis O. Berman) Tales of Tikkun: New Jewish Stories to Heal the Wounded World, 1996; editor: Debate Over Thermonuclear Strategy, 1965, Menorah Jour., 1979—; screenwriter: In Every Generation, 1988; editl. bd. Tikkun. Alt. del. Dem. Nat. Conv., 1968; fellow Chs. Ctr. for Theology and Pub. Policy, 1977-82; Gamaliel chair Luth. Student Ctr., Milw., 1996; wisdom-keeper UN Conf. on Habitat II, 1996; adv. bd. Found. for Ethics and Meaning, 1996—. Coolidge fellow Assn. Religion and Intellectual Life, 1983. Fellow Am. Acad. Arts and Scis. (colloquium on disarmament 1962); mem. Nat. Writers Union, Fabrangen, Nat. Havurah Com. (bd. dirs. 1979-80, 83-87), P'nai Or (bd. dirs. 1984-93), Aleph bd. dirs. 1993-95), Internat. Coord. Com. on Religion and Earth (steering com. 1990-93), Phi Beta Kappa. Address: 6711 Lincoln Dr Philadelphia PA 19119-3119 *For about 500 years the human race has made no "Sabbath" from ceaseless working, making, producing, doing and it therefore has raced to the brink of destroying itself and much of life on the planet. Just as individuals need rhythmic rest, so do societies—a spiritual truth that we should again learn from Torah. Time to be!.*

WASKOW, JOYCE ANN, school administrator; b. Meriden, Iowa, Aug. 15, 1941; d. Clarence Emory and Lucille Dorothy (Horstman) Smith; m. James R. Waskow, July 6, 1963; children: Susan, Brent. BS, Iowa State U., 1963; MA, U. Mo., St. Louis, 1992. Cert. edn. specialist, Mo. Home econs./sci. tchr. Collins (Iowa) H.S., 1963-64; home economist Met. Sewer Dist., Omaha, Nebr., 1964-65; home econs. tchr. Westbrook Jr. H.S., Omaha, 1965-67; home economist The Merchandising Group, N.Y.C., 1970-76; home econs. tchr. Pattonville H.S., St. Louis, 1976-79, Maplewood-Richmond Hts. H.S., St. Louis, 1979-80, Webster Groves H.S., St. Louis, 1980-93; dir. Tchr.'s Acad. Network for Ednl. Devel., St. Louis, 1989-92; asst. prin. Lafayette H.S., St. Louis, 1993—; spkr./workshop leader Network for Edn. Devel., 1987—. Mem. ASCD, Nat. Assn. Secondary Sch. Prins., Am. Home Econs. Assn. (nominating com.), Suburban Home Econs. Assn. (pres. 1986-87), Nat. Assn. Vocat. Home Econs. Tchrs. (Disting. Svc. award 1989), Mo. Home Econs. Tchrs. Assn. (Tchr. of the Yr. 1987, nominating com. 1987-88). Avocations: reading, whitewater rafting, hiking, antiquing, orienteering. Office: Lafayette High School 17050 Clayton Rd Ballwin MO 63011-1792

WASMUTH, CARL ERWIN, physician, lawyer; b. Pitts., Feb. 16, 1916; s. Edwin Hugo and Mary Blanche (Love) W.; m. Martha Conn., Aug. 25, 1939; children: Carl Erwin; m. Gertrude White Ruth, June 19, 1984; m. Wilhelmina Waterman Devine, May 12, 1990. BS, U. Pitts., 1935, MD, 1939; LLB, Cleve.-Marshall Law Sch., 1959. Diplomate Am. Bd. Anesthesiology. Bar: Ohio 1959. Intern Western Pa. Hosp., Pitts., 1939-40; fellow anesthesiology Cleve. Clinic Found., 1949-51, mem. emeritus staff, 1976—; pvt. practice medicine Dry Run, Pa., 1942-45, Scottdale, Pa., 1945-49; mem. dep. anesthesia Cleve. Clinic, 1951—, head dept., 1967-69; asso. prof. law Cleve.-Marshall Law Sch., 1959-66; adj. prof. Cleve. Marshall Law Sch., 1966-73. Author: Anesthesia and the Law, 1961, Law for the Physician, 1966, Law and the Surgical Team, 1968; Editor: Legal Problems in the Practice of Anesthesiology, 1973; contbg. editor: Hale's Anesthesiology; editorial bd.: Med. World News; Contbr. articles to profl. jours. Trustee Cleve.- Marshall Law Sch., chmn., 1969-71; bd. dirs. Scottdale Hosp. Found; chmn. bd. govs. Cleve. Clinic, 1969-77; trustee Cleve. Clinic Found., 1969-76, v.p., 1973-76; trustee Cleve. Clinic Ednl. Found., 1969-76, v.p., 1973-76; chmn. bd. trustees, pres. Cleve. Marshall Ednl. Found., 1972-81; bd. overseers Coll. Law, Cleve. State U., 1972-76; vis. com. Coll. Law, Case-Western Res. U., 1973-76; trustee United Torch Svcs., Tucson Symphony Soc., 1983-84, 88; trustee Santa Cruz Med. Found., 1977, pres., 1978; bd. govs. Ohio World Trade Center; trustee Cancer Center Cleve., Ohio Coll. Podiatric Medicine, 1976, Am. Coll. Legal Medicine Research Found., 1984—; mem. U. Ariz. Found., 1978, World Congress Med. Law, 1967—, Keynoter 3d World Congress, 1971; sec. Commn. Med. Malpractice, HEW, 1972-73; vestryman St. Francis-in-the-Valley Episcopal Ch., Green Valley. Named Distinguished Eagle Scout Nat. Council Boy Scouts Am., 1977; named Outstanding Citizen Eagle Cuyahoga council, 1976; Citizen of Year Cleve. Area Bd. Realtors, 1976. Fellow Am. Coll. Anesthesiologists, Am. Coll. Legal Medicine (pres. bd. govs. 1966-69), A.C.P., Am. Coll. Chest Physicians, Law Sci. Acad.; mem. Am. Soc. Anesthesiologists (dir., pres. 1968, speaker ho. of dels.), Ohio Soc. Anesthesiologists (dir. 1960-69), Cleve. Soc. Anesthesiologists (pres. 1963), Internat. Anesthesia Research Soc., World Fedn. Soc. Anesthesiologists (vice chmn. Am. delegation 1967), Acad. Anesthesiology (chmn. program com. 1967), Am., Ohio med. assns., N.Y. Acad. Scis., Nat. Acad. Sci., NRC, Com. Cadaver Utilization, Cleve. Acad. Medicine, AAAS, Transplantation Soc. (charter), Am., Ohio, Cuyahoga County, Cleve. bar assns., Phi Rho Sigma, Delta Theta Phi, Masons, Lions (past pres. local clubs), Old Pueblo Club, Tucson Club, Country of Green Valley Club, Pleasant Valley Country Club, Mt. Kenya Safari Club, Nanyuki, Kenya. Home: 727 W Quail Dr Green Valley AZ 85614-1740

WASS, HANNELORE LINA, educational psychology educator; b. Heidelberg, Germany, Sept. 12, 1926; came to U.S., 1957, naturalized, 1963; d. Hermann and Mina (Lasch) Kraft; m. Irvin R. Wass, Nov. 24, 1959 (dec.); 1 child, Brian C.; m. Harry H. Sisler, Apr. 13, 1978. B.A., Tchrs. Coll., Heidelberg, 1951; M.A., U. Mich., 1960, Ph.D., 1968. Tchr. W. Ger. Univ. Lab. Schs., 1958-60; mem. faculty U. Mich., Ann Arbor, 1958-60, U. Chgo. Lab. Sch., 1960-61, U. Mich., 1963-64, Eastern Mich. U., 1965-69; prof. ednl. psychology U. Fla., Gainesville, 1969-92; prof. emeritus, 1992—; faculty assoc. Ctr. for Gerontol. Studies U. Fla., Gainesville; cons., lectr. in thanatology. Author: The Professional Education of Teachers, 1974, Dying-Facing the Facts, 1979, 2d edit., 1988, 3d edit., 1995, Death Education: An Annotated Resource Guide, 1980, vol. 2, 1985, Helping Children Cope With Death, 1982, 2d edit., 1984, Childhood and Death, 1984; founding editor (jour.) Death Studies, 1977—; cons. editor: Ednl. Gerontology, 1977-92, (book series) Death Education, Aging and Health Care; contbr. approximately 200 articles to profl. jours. and chpts. in books. Mem. Am. Psychol. Assn., Gerontol. Soc., Internat. Work Group Dying, Death and Bereavement (bd. dirs.), Assn. Death Edn. and Counseling. Home: 6014 NW 54th Way Gainesville FL 32653-3265 Office: U Fla 346 Norman Hall Gainesville FL 32611-2053

WASS, WALLACE MILTON, veterinarian, clinical science educator; b. Lake Park, Iowa, Nov. 19, 1929; s. Authur Carl and Esther (Moberg) W.; m. Doreen McCollum, May 31, 1953; children: Karen, Kimberly, Christopher, Kirby. Student, Minn. Jr. Coll., 1947-48; B.S., U. Minn., 1951, D.V.M., 1953, Ph.D., 1961. Diplomate: Am. Coll. Vet. Internal Medicine. Veterinarian Medford Vet. Clinic, Wis., 1953-58; instr. U. Minn. Coll. Vet. Medicine, St. Paul, 1958-63; prof. vet. medicine Iowa State U., Ames, 1964—, head dept. vet. clin. scis., 1964-83, prof., 1983—; cons. U.S. AID, Bogota, Columbia, 1963, U. Yola, Nigeria, 1983; staff veterinarian for med. rsch. sect. Brookhaven Nat. Lab., Upton, N.Y., 1963-64; cons. investigator fur seal harvest U.S. Dept. Commerce, Pribilof Islands, 1971, South Africa, 1974; use of antibiotics in animal feed U.S. FDA, 1972; cons. Farmland Ins. Co., 1971—; spl. cons. Kasetsart U., Bangkok, Thailand, 1974, Min. of Edn., Thailand, 1994. Contbr. articles, papers in field to profl. lit. Chmn. collegiate-ch. paster parish rels. com. United Methodist Ch., 1979, chmn. stewardship and fin. com., 1982. Served to 1st lt. USAF, 1953-55. Mem. AVMA (del. 1973-88), Iowa Vet. Med. Assn., Central Iowa Vet. Med. Assn. (pres. 1977), Am. Assn. Vet. Clinicians (pres. 1971-73), Phi Kappa Phi (sec. 1984-88, Iowa State U. chpt. pres. 1989-90), Phi Zeta, Alpha Zeta, Gamma Sigma Delta. Club: Wiltco Flying (sec. 1966-74). Home: 2166 Ashmore Dr Ames IA 50014-7840 Office: Iowa State U Dept Vet Clin Scis Ames IA 50011

WASSEEN, MARJORIE, rehabilitation nurse, administrator; b. Kylertown, Pa., Jan. 3, 1944; d. Raymond George and Dorcas Carolyn (Hoover) Watts; m. James Wasseen, Sept. 17, 1966; children: Melissa, James II, Julie. Diploma, York (Pa.) Hosp. Sch. Nursing, 1966. Cert. rehab. nurse. Head nurse oper. rm. Broaddus Hosp., Philippi, W.Va.; dir. nursing Camelot Hall Nursing Home Med. Facilities of Am., Richmond, Va.; nurse mgr. med.-surg. unit Richmond Meml. Hosp.; nurse mgr., dir. clin. support svcs. Sheltering Arms Rehab. Hosp., Richmond. Mem. Am. Orgn. Nurse Execs., Assn. Rehab. Nurses, Va. Assn. Rehab. Nurses.

WASSENICH, LINDA PILCHER, health policy analyst, fund raiser; b. Washington, Aug. 27, 1943; d. Mason Johnson and Vera Bell (Stephenson) Pilcher; m. Mark Wassenich, May 14, 1965; children: Paul Mason, David Mark. BA magna cum laude, Tex. Christian U., 1965; MSW, U. N.C., 1970. Licensed advanced practitioner, cert. social worker, Tex. Counselor family ct. Dallas County Juvenile Dept., Dallas, 1970-73, 75-76; dir. govt. rels. Vis. Nurse Assn., Dallas, 1980-84, exec. officer of hospice, 1984-85; exec. dir. Incest Recovery Assn., Dallas, 1985-86; assoc. exec. dir. Lone Star Coun. Camp Fire, Dallas, 1986-89; exec. v.p. Vis. Nurse Assn. Found., Dallas, 1989-91; dir. policy & resource devel. Vis. Nurse Assn. Tex., Dallas, 1992—. Contbr. articles to profl. publs. Bd. dirs. Women's Coun. Dallas County, 1986-95, pres., 1992-93; chmn. Dallas County Welfare Adv. Bd., 1991-95; bd. dirs. United Way of Met. Dallas, 1992-94, Youth Impact Ctrs., Dallas, 1993-94; mem. adv. bd. Maternal Health and Family Planning Dallas, 1990-94; mem. Leadership Dallas, 1988-89. Recipient AAUW, Dallas, Laurel award, 1995. Mem. NASW (Tex. bd. dirs., nominating chmn. 1990-92, co-chmn. Dallas unit 1981-82, Social Worker of Yr. award 1988), LWV (bd. dirs. Dallas 1974-80, 95—, pres. 1995-99), Acad. Cert. Social Workers, Nat. Soc. Fundraising Execs. (cert., bd. dirs. Dallas chpt. 1994-99, v.p. governance 1995-96). Home: 6948 Kenwhite Dr Dallas TX 75231-5640 Office: 1440 W Mockingbird Ln Dallas TX 75247-6911

WASSER, HENRY, retired English educator; b. Pitts., Apr. 13, 1919; s. Nathan and Mollie (Mendelson) W.; m. Solidelle Felicité Fortier, Aug. 20, 1942; children: Michael Frederick (dec.), Eric Anthony (dec.), Frederick Anthony, Felicity Louise. B.A., M.A., Ohio State U., 1940; Ph.D., Columbia U., 1951. Teaching fellow George Washington U., 1940-42; analyst USAAF intelligence, 1941-43; chemist Goodyear Synthetic Rubber Co., 1943-45; from tutor to assoc. prof. City Coll., CUNY, 1946-66; prof. English, dean faculties Richmond Coll., CUNY, 1966-73; v.p. for acad. affairs Calif. State U., Sacramento, 1973-74; prof. English Coll. S.I., CUNY, 1974-89; dir. Center for European Studies, Grad. Sch. CUNY, 1979-93, prof. emeritus of sociology and English, 1989—; Fulbright prof. U. Salonika, Greece, 1955-56; Higher Edn. Seminar assoc. Columbia U., 1961—, co-chair, 1982-87, chair, 1987-89; mem. Colloquium on Higher Edn., Yale U., 1974-75; Fulbright prof. Am. Lit. U. Oslo, 1962-64, dir., prof. Am. Inst., 1963-64; vis. prof. U. Sussex, Eng., 1972; lectr. in field, Sweden, Norway, Eng., Germany, Poland, Yugoslavia, Italy, Turkey, Greece, Bulgaria; Fulbright prof. Am. Lit. and Civilization U. Bergen, Norway, 1989-90, U. Aveiro, Portugal, 1993; rsch. scholar comparative higher edn. CUNY, 1989—. Author: The Scientific Thought of Henry Adams, 1956, (with others) Higher Education in Western Europe and North America: A Selected and Annotated Bibliography, 1979, American Literature and Language: A Selected and Annotated Bibliography, 1980; editor: (with Sigmund Skard) Americana Norvegica; Norwegian Contributions to American Studies, 1968, (with others) The Compleat University, 1983, Problems of the Urban University: A Comparative Perspective, 1984, Impact of Changing Labor Force on Higher Education, 1987; editor (with Ulrich Teichler) German and American Universities: Mutual Influences, 1992; mem. bd. editors History of European Ideas, 1986—, guest editor, summer, 1987; guest editor Higher Edn. Policy, spring, 1994, contbr. articles to newspapers and profl. jours. Faculty trustee CUNY, 1981-86, trustee emeritus, 1986—; bd. dirs. Scandinavian Seminar, 1978-86, sec., 1980-83, vice chmn., 1983-86. Recipient Am. Scandinavian Found. award, 1969, 71, German Acad. Exchange Service award, 1973, 80, Swedish Info. Service award, 1979, Norwegian Ministry of Culture award, 1983, NEH award, 1984, Foscolo medal U. Pavia, Italy, 1986, German Marshall Fund award, 1985, 87, Atheneum medal U. Pavia, Italy, 1988; Finnish Ministry Culture grantee, 1989. Mem. Am. Studies Assn. (pres. Met. N.Y. chpt. 1961-62, mem. nat. exec. council 1968-74), Melville Soc. Am. (historian 1969-74), MLA, Am. Scandinavian Found. (fellow 1971), Internat. Assn. Univ. Profs. English, Assn. Upper Level Colls. and Univs. (2d v.p. 1971-72), Assn. for World Edn. (internat. council), Phi Beta Kappa (sec. City Coll. chpt. 1957-62, 64-67, pres. CUNY Acad. for Humanities and Scis. 1991—), Internat. Conf. Higher Edn. (steering com. 1989—), Henry Adams Soc. (exec. coun. 1994—, pres. 1996—). Home: 333 E 34th St Apt 16C New York NY 10016-4950 also: 5517 Fieldston Rd Bronx NY 10471 Office: CUNY Academy Grad Sch 33 W 42nd St New York NY 10036-8003

WASSERBURG, GERALD JOSEPH, geology and geophysics educator; b. New Brunswick, N.J., Mar. 25, 1927; s. Charles and Sarah (Levine) W.; m. Naomi Z. Orlick, Dec. 21, 1951; children: Charles David, Daniel Morris. Student, Rutgers U.; BS in Physics, U. Chgo., 1951, MSc in Geology, 1952, PhD, 1954, DSc (hon.), 1992; Dr. Hon. Causa, Brussels U., 1985, U. Paris, 1986; DSc (hon.), Ariz. State U., 1987. Research assoc. Inst. Nuclear Studies, U. Chgo., 1954-55; asst. prof. Calif. Inst. Tech., Pasadena, 1955-59, assoc. prof., 1959-62, prof. geology and geophysics, 1962-82, John D. MacArthur prof. geology and geophysics, 1982—; served on Juneau Ice Field Rsch. Project, 1950; cons. Argonne Nat. Lab., Lamont, Ill., 1952-55; former mem. U.S. Nat. Com. for Geochem., com. for Planetary Exploration Study, NRC, adv. coun. Petroleum Rsch. Fund, Am. Chem. Soc.; mem. lunar sample analysis planning team (LSAPT) manned Spacecraft Ctr., NASA, Houston, 1968-71, chmn., 1970; lunar sample rev. bd., 1970-72; mem. Facilities Working Group LSAPT, Johnson Space Ctr., 1972-82; mem. sci. working panel for Apollo missions, Johnson Space Ctr., 1971-73; advisor NASA, 1968-88, phys. scis. com., 1971-75, mem. lunar base steering com., 1984; chmn. com. for planetary and lunar exploration, mem. space sci. bd. NAS, 1975-78; chmn. divsn. Geol. and Planetary Scis., Calif. Inst. Tech., 1987-89; vis. prof. U. Kiel, Fed. Republic of Germany, 1960, Harvard U., 1962, U.

Bern, Switzerland, 1966, Swiss Fed. Tech. Inst., 1967, Max Planck Inst., Mainz and Heidelberg, Fed. Republic of Germany, 1985; invited lectr., Vinton Hayes Sr. fellow Harvard U., 1980, Jaeger-Hales lectr. Australian Nat. U., 1980, Harold Jeffreys lectr. Royal Astron. Soc., 1981, Ernst Cloos lectr. Johns Hopkins U., 1984, H.L. Welsh Disting. lectr. U. Toronto, Can., 1986, Danz lectr. U. Washington, 1989, Goldschmidt Centennial lectr. Norwegian Acad. Sci. and Letters, 1989, Lindsay lectr. Goddard Space Flight Ctr., 1996; plenary spkr. 125th Anniversary Geol. Soc. Sweden, 1996; 60th Anniversary Symposium spkr. Hebrew U., Jerusalem, 1985. Served with U.S. Army, 1944-46. Decorated Combat Inf. badge. Recipient Group Achievement award NASA, 1969, Exceptional Sci. Achievement award NASA, 1970, Disting. Pub. Svc. medal NASA, 1973, J.F. Kemp medal Columbia U., 1973, Profl. Achievement award U. Chgo. Alumni Assn., 1978, Goldschmidt medal Geochem. Soc., 1978, Disting. Pub. Svc. medal with cluster NASA, 1978, Wollaston medal Geol. Soc. London, 1985, Sr. Scientist award Alexander von Humboldt-Stiftung, 1985, Crafoord prize Royal Swedish Acad. Scis., 1986, Holmes medal, 1987, Regents fellow Smithsonian Inst., Gold medal Royal Astron. Soc., 1991; named Hon. Fgn. fellow European Union Geoscis., 1983. Fellow Am. Acad. Arts and Scis., Geol. Soc. London (hon.), Am. Geophys. Union (planetology sect., Harry H. Hess medal 1985), Geol. Soc. Am. (life, Arthur L. Day medal 1970), Meteoritical Soc. (pres. 1987-88, Leonard medal 1975), Geochemical Society and the European Assn. for Geochemistry, 1996; mem. Nat. Acad. Scis. (Arthur L. Day prize and lectureship 1981, J. Lawrence Smith medal 1985), Norwegian Acad. Sci. and Letters, Am. Phil. Soc. Research interests include geochemistry and geophysics and the application of the methods of chemical physics to problems in the earth scis. Major researches have been the determination of the time scales of nucleosynthesis, connections between the interstellar medium and solar material, the time of the formation of the solar system, the chronology and evolution of the earth, moon and meteorites, the establishment of dating methods using long-lived natural radio-activities, the study of geologic and cosmic processes using nuclear and isotopic effects as a tracer in nature, the origin of natural gases, and the application of thermodynamic methods to geologic systems. Office: Calif Inst of Tech Divsn Geol & Planetary Scis Pasadena CA 91125

WASSERMAN, ALBERT, writer, director; b. N.Y.C., Feb. 9, 1921; s. Martin S. and Beatrice (Schaffer) W.; m. Della Newmark, Aug. 5, 1943 (div. Mar. 1965); children—Paul, Vicki; m. Barbara Alson, June 19, 1968. B.S., Coll. City N.Y., 1941. Pres. Wasserman Prodns., Inc., N.Y.C., 1968-75. Writer documentary, ednl. and indsl. films, 1946-53; free lance writer, dir. TV documentary films, 1953-55; staff writer, dir., producer, CBS-TV, 1955-60; producer, dir., writer: NBC News, 1960-67; producer: 60 Minutes, 1976-86; writer, prod., dir.: Out of Darkness; writer film: First Steps; writer, dir. films for: CBS Pub. Affairs Series The Search; prod., writer dir.: NBC White Paper programs; prod., dir.: TV Spl. The Making of the President, 1972; (Sylvania TV award, Robert Flaherty film award, Acad. award 1947, Peabody award CBS Pub. Affairs series.). Recipient Lasker Med. Journalism awards (2); Edinburgh Film Festival silver medal, 1948, George Polk award, 1960, Journalism award Ohio State U., 1961. Mem. Writers Guild Am. East (treas. 1965-66), Dirs. Guild Am. (eastern regional council 1965-66, 69-70). Home: 259 W 11th St New York NY 10014-2412

WASSERMAN, ANTHONY IRA, software company executive, educator; b. Bronx, N.Y., Mar. 1, 1945; s. Joseph K. and Frances (Hirsch) W.; m. Susan Gail Cohen, June 11, 1966; children: Mark, Michelle. AB in Math. and Physics, U. Calif., Berkeley, 1966; MS in Computer Sci., U. Wis., 1967, PhD in Computer Sci., 1970. Prof. med. info. sci. U. Calif., San Francisco, 1973-88; pres., CEO Interactive Devel. Environments, Inc., San Francisco, 1983-93, also chmn. bd. dirs.; pres. Software Methods and Tools, San Francisco, 1997—; lectr. computer sci. U. Calif., Berkeley, 1971-86, vis. prof., 1996. Editor: Software Development Environments, 1981, Software Design Techniques, 4th edit., 1983, others; contbr. articles to prol. jours. Recipient Silver Core award Internat. Fedn. Info. Processing, 1986. Fellow IEEE, Assn. Computing Machinery (editor-in-chief ACM Computing Surveys 1983-86, Disting. Svc. award 1995). Democrat. Avocations: running, photography.

WASSERMAN, BARRY L(EE), architect; b. Cambridge, Mass., May 25, 1935; s. Theodore and Adelaide (Levin) W.; m. Wilma Louise Greenfield, June 21, 1957 (div. 1971); children: Tim Andrew, Andrew Glenn; m. Judith Ella Michalowski, Apr. 22, 1979. B.A., Harvard U., 1957, M. Arch., 1960. Registered architect, Calif. Assoc. John S. Bolles Assocs., San Francisco, 1960-69; prin. Wasserman-Herman Assocs., San Francisco, 1969-72; prin., dir. Office Lawrence Halprin U Assocs., San Francisco, 1972-76; dep. state architect State of Calif., Sacramento, 1976-78, state architect, 1978-83; prof. dept. architecture, dir. Inst. Environ. Design, Sch. Environ. Design Calif. State Poly. U., Pomona, 1983-87, chair dept. architecture, Coll. Environ. Design, 1988-96; cons. architecture, Sacramento, 1983—; program advisor Fla. A&M U., Tallahassee, 1981-83. Architect Wasserman House, San Rafael, Calif., 1963 ((AIA-Sunset Mag. award of Merit) 1965-66), Anna Waden Library, San Francisco, 1969 ((AIA award of Merit 1970)), Capitol Area Plan, Sacramento, 1977 (Central Valley chpt. AIA Honor award 1979). Recipient Awards citation Progressive Architecture 26th awards Program, 1979. Fellow AIA chmn. architecture in govt. com. (1979). Democrat. Jewish. Home: 6456 Fordham Way Sacramento CA 95831-2218

WASSERMAN, CHARLES, banker; b. Guayaquil, Ecuador, Aug. 31, 1929; came to U.S., 1948, naturalized, 1960; s. Mendel and Mary Wasserman; m. Jacqueline Royer, Oct. 4, 1960 (dec. June 1996); children: Roger, Mark. BA, Farleigh Dickinson U., 1949; MBA, U. Havana, 1956. Trainee internat. dept. Chase Manhattan Bank, N.Y., 1958-60, Swiss Bank Corp., N.Y., 1960-64; area sr. credit analyst Am. Express Bank, N.Y., 1965-66; exec. v.p. Republic Nat. Bank, N.Y., 1967—, cons. to World Bank, 1989; chmn., pres. Republic Internat. Bank N.Y., L.A., 1988-89; hon. chmn. Meridian Capital Corp. Named Hon. Chmn., Meridian Capital Corp., 1994. Mem. Internat. Exec. Svc. Corps, Internat. Platform Assn. Home: 224 Nassau Ave Manhasset NY 11030-2440 Office: 127 E 59th St Rm 222 New York NY 10022-1225

WASSERMAN, DALE, playwright; b. Rhinelander, Wis., Nov. 2, 1917; s. Samuel and Hilda (Paykel) W. founder, artistic dir. Midwest Profl. Playwrights Lab.; Trustee, founding mem. Eugene O'Neill Theatre Center. Writer, producer, dir. for TV, motion pictures, theatre; author: (with Bruce Geller) musical Livin' the Life, 1957; stage plays The Pencil of God, 1961, 998, 1962, One Flew Over the Cuckoo's Nest, 1963, Man of La Mancha, 1965 (Tony award for best musical 1966, N.Y. Drama Critics' Circle award for best musical 1966, Outer Circle award 1966, Variety award 1966, Spanish Pavilion award 1966, others), Play with Fire, 1978, Great Big River, 1981, Shakespeare and The Indians, 1983; screenplays World of Strangers, 1955, The Vikings, 1958, Two Faces to Go, 1959, Aboard the Flying Swan, 1962, Jangadeiro, 1962, Cleopatra, 1963, Quick, Before It Melts, 1964; writer, coprodr.: motion pictures Mister Buddwing, 1965, A Walk With Love and Death, 1969, Man of LaMancha, 1972; also numerous TV plays including Elisha and the Long Knives, 1954 (Publishers Guild award 1954), The Fog, 1957 (Writers Guild of Am. award 1957), Eichmann, 1958, Engineer of Death, 1959, The Citadel, 1959 (Writers Guild of Am. award 1959), I, Don Quixote, 1959, (Writers Guild of Am. award 1960), The Power and the Glory, 1960, The Lincoln Murder Case, 1961 (Writers Guild of Am. award 1961), Stranger, 1962, Burden of Proof, 1976, Scheherazade, 1977, The Seventh Dimension, 1984, My Name Is Esther, 1985, The Whole Truth, 1987, Green, 1987, A Fine American Family, 1988, Players in a Game, 1989, Murder Among the Saints, 1989, The Girl From Botany Bay, 1990, (mus.) Western Star, 1992, Beggar's Holiday, 1994, (plays) An Enchanted Land, 1997, How I Saved the Whole Damn World, 1997, (movie) The Game, 1997; short stories and articles to Variety, others. Recipient hon. degree U. Wis., 1980. Mem. ASCAP, ALA, Writers Guild Am. East (nat. coun. 1960-64), Writers Guild Am. West, Dramatists Guild, Am. Acad. Motion Picture Arts and Scis., French Soc. Authors and Composers, The Jaques Brel Found. (gov.), Players Club, Monte Cristo Soc. Office: care Harold Orenstein Atty 157 W 57th St New York NY 10019-2210

WASSERMAN, DAVID H., medical educator, researcher; b. New Orleans, Aug. 24, 1957; m. Doris S.; children: Micah Joseph, Mira Rose. BSc in Kinesiology, UCLA, 1979, MSc in Kinesiology, 1981; PhD in Physiology, U. Toronto, 1985. Rsch. asst. dept. respiratory physiology and medicine UCLA, 1979-81, tchg. asst. gen. physiology dept. kinesiology, 1980-81; tchg. asst. gen. physiology dept. physiology U. Toronto, 1982-84; rsch. assoc. dept. molecular physiology and biophysics Vanderbilt U. Sch. Medicine, Nashville, 1985-87, lab. instr. med. sch. physiology dept. molecular physiology and biophysics, 1986-88, course coord., lectr. exercise physiology dept. molecular physiology and biophysics, 1986—, rsch. instr. dept. molecular physiology and biophysics, 1987-88, asst. prof. dept. molecular physiology and biophysics, 1988-92, lectr. tutorials in physiology dept. molecular physiology and biophysics, 1989-90, lectr. metabolic regulation in vivo dept. molecular physiology and biophysics, 1989—, lectr. history physiology dept. molecular physiology and biophysics, 1991-92, assoc. prof. dept. molecular physiology and biophysics, lectr. med. sch. physiology dept. molecular physiology and biophysics, 1992—, lectr. interdisciplinary grad. program physiology dept. molecular physiology and biophysics, 1992-94, course coord. interaction cell sys. sect. interdisciplinary grad. program, 1994—, course coord., instr. tutorials in physiology dept. molecular physiology and biophysics, 1995—. Mem. editl. bd. Am. Jour. Physiology: Endocrinology and Metabolism, 1992—, Jour. Applied Physiology, 1996—; assoc. editor: Metabolism, 1996—. Mem. Am. Diabetes Assn. (mem. rsch. coun. on exercise 1988—, co-advisor tech. report on diabetes and exercise 1993-94, mem. grant review panel 1993-96), Am. Coll. Sports Medicine, Am. Physiol. Soc. (mem. program adv. com. 1988-92, head organizing com. interactions of endocrine and cardiovasc. sys. in health and disease 1989-91, sec./treas. endocrinology and metabolism sect. 1992-95, mem. organizing com. integrated biology of exercise 1993—), Juvenile Diabetes Found. Internat. (bd. dirs. Tenn. chpt. 1995—, chmn. govt. rels. com. Tenn. chpt. 1996—), European Assn. for Studies in Diabetes. Office: Vanderbilt U Med Sch Dept Molecular Physiology and Biophysics Med Rsch Bldg Rm 702 Nashville TN 37232

WASSERMAN, EDWARD ARNOLD, psychology educator; b. L.A., Apr. 2, 1946; s. Albert Leonard and May (Sabin) W. BA, UCLA, 1968; PhD, Ind. U., 1972. Postdoctoral fellow U. Sussex, Brighton, Eng., 1972; from asst. prof. to prof. psychology U. Iowa, Iowa City, 1972-83, prof., 1983—; pres. faculty senate U. Iowa, 1997-98. Contbr. articles to profl. jours., chpts. to books; assoc. editor several jours. Bd. dirs. Big Bros., Big Sisters, Johnson County, Iowa, 1982-85. Ind. U. fellow, 1968, U. Iowa fellow, 1975, 82, NAS fellow, former USSR, 1976, James Van Allen Natural Scis. fellow, 1994-95. Fellow APA, Am. Psychol. Soc.; mem. Psychonomic Soc., Midwestern Psychol. Assn., Phi Beta Kappa. Office: U Iowa Dept Psychology Iowa City IA 52242

WASSERMAN, FRED, III, internist; b. Phila., May 17, 1955; m. Susan Valesky; 1 child, Sara Elisabeth. MBA, U. South Fla., 1990; MD, U. Miami, 1981. Diplomate Am. Bd. Internal Medicine. Resident in gen. surgery U. Miami (Fla.) Affiliated Hosps., 1981-82; resident in internal medicine Baylor Coll. Medicine Affiliated Hosps., Houston, 1982-85; chief med. officer, clin. of jurisdiction Dept. Vets. Affairs Bay Pines (Fla.) VA Med. Ctr., 1991—. Mem. ACP, Am. Coll. Physician Execs. Office: Dept Vets Affairs Bay Pines VAMC Bay Pines FL 33744

WASSERMAN, HELENE WALTMAN, art dealer, artist; b. Phila., Jan. 29, 1929; d. William T. and Bertha (Brener) Waltman; m. Richard M. Wasserman, June 23, 1950 (div. 1972); children: Ann Zelver, Ellen Rubinfeld, Stephen; m. Mark C. Cooper, Jan. 22, 1988. BFA, U. Pa., 1951. Pvt. practice art dealer, 1972—; apptd. appraiser Supreme Ct., State of N.Y., 1978. One-woman shows at Philmont Gallery, Phila., 1964, Roko Gallery, N.Y., 1965; exhibited in group shows at Phila. Mus. Art, Pa. Acad. Fine Arts, Philbrook Mus., Tulsa, Woodmere Gallery, Roko Gallery, 1953-68. Active Nassau County Art Commn., 1968-72; trustee, Sculpture Ctr., N.Y.C., bd. dirs., 1991. Mem. Pvt. Art Dealers Assn., Cosmopolitan Club, Nature Conservancy. Avocations: painting, sculpting, garden design.

WASSERMAN, JACK F., exercise science educator; b. Dayton, Ohio, July 29, 1941; s. Lee Simond and Louise (Cockerill) W.; m. Susan Ainsworth, June 5, 1965 (div. May 1975); children: Ric, Andrea; m. Betty M. McClain, July 29, 1978; 1 child, Michel. BS, Purdue U., 1964; MS, U. Cin., 1971, PhD, 1975; cert. physician asst., Cin. Tech. Coll., 1977. Registered profl. engr., Ohio. Assoc. prof. U. Tenn., Knoxville, 1979—, cons. Meml. Rsch. Ctr. Hosp., 1979—, adj. assoc. prof. Inst. Agr., 1983—, prof., 1986, adj. prof. exercise sci., 1996—; pres. ops., acting v.p. Hydro Force Corp.; adj. assoc. prof. U. Cin., 1975-79, rsch. assoc., 1975-79; vis. prof. U.S. Army Aeromed. Rsch. Lab., Ft. Rucker, Ala., summer 1984. Inventor acoustic aneurysm detector and associated method. Mem. Am. Acad. Physician's Asst., Am. Soc. Biomechanics, ASME (membership chmn., biomed. divsn.), Acoustic Soc. Am., Orthopedic Rsch. Soc., Tenn. Acad. Scis. Avocations: mountain biking, aerobics, water aerobics. Home: 4512 Westover Ter Knoxville TN 37914-5055 Office: U Tenn MAES Dept 310 Perkins Hall Knoxville TN 37996-2030

WASSERMAN, LEW R., film, recording and publishing company executive; b. Cleve., Mar. 15, 1913; m. Edith T. Beckerman, July 5, 1936; 1 dau., Lynne Kay. D (hon.), Brandeis U., NYU. Nat. dir. advt. and publicity Music Corp. Am., 1936-38, v.p., 1938-39, became v.p. charge motion picture div., 1940; now chmn., chief exec. officer, dir., mem. exec. com. MCA, Inc., also chmn. bd., chief exec. officer, dir. subsidiary corps.; now chmn. emeritus; chmn. emeritus Assn. Motion Picture and TV Producers. Trustee John F. Kennedy Libr., John F. Kennedy Ctr. Performing Arts, Jules Stein Eye Inst., Carter Presdl. Ctr., Lyndon Baines Johnson Found.; pres. Hollywood Canteen Found.; chmn. Rsch. to Prevent Blindness Found.; hon. chmn. bd. Ctr. Theatre Group L.A. Music Ctr.; bd. dirs. Amateur Athletic Found. of L.A. (chmn. fin. com.), L.A. Music Ctr. Found.; bd. gov.'s Ronald Reagan Presdl. Found. Recipient Jean Hersholt Humanitarian award Acad. Motion Picture Arts and Scis., 1973. Democrat. Office: Universal City Studios Inc 100 Universal City Plz Universal Cty CA 91608-1002*

WASSERMAN, LOUIS ROBERT, physician, educator; b. N.Y.C., July 11, 1910; s. Jacob and Ethel (Ballin) W.; m. Julia B. Wheeler, Feb. 20, 1957. A.B., Harvard U., 1931; M.D., U. Chgo., 1935. Diplomate: Am. Bd. Internal Medicine. Intern Michael Reese Hosp., Chgo., 1935-37; research fellow hematology Mt. Sinai Hosp., N.Y.C., 1937-39; research asst. Mt. Sinai Hosp., 1940-42, dir. dept. hematology, 1953-72, hematologist to hosp., 1950-72; research fellow med. physics U. Cal. at Berkeley, 1946-48, cons. radiation labs., 1948-51; asst. prof. Columbia Coll. Phys. and Surg., 1950-60, asso. clin. prof., 1960-66; prof. medicine Mt. Sinai Sch. Medicine, 1966-72, chmn. dept. clin. sci., 1967-72, Distinguished Service prof., 1972-79, emeritus, 1979—, Albert A. and Vera G. List prof. medicine (hematology), 1977-79, emeritus, 1979—; Research collaborator Brookhaven Nat. Labs., 1960-71; cons. practice specializing in hematology, N.Y.C., 1950—; Mem. nat. cancer planning com., chmn. polycythemia vera study group Nat. Cancer Inst., NIH, 1967—, mem. diagnostic research adv. com., 1972-75, co-chmn., 1975-77, chmn. bd. sci. counselors div. cancer treatment, 1974-76. Served to maj. AUS, 1942-46. Fellow ACP, AMA, N.Y. Acad. Medicine, N.Y. Acad. Sci., Internat. Soc. Hematology (v.p. 1972, counselor at-large 1973—); mem. Assn. Am. Physicians, Am. Soc. Hematology (exec. com. 1964-66, pres. 1968-69, adv. council 1969-74), Soc. Nuclear Medicine, Societe de Hopitaux de Paris, Soc. Exptl. Biology and Medicine, Harvey Soc., Soc. Study Blood, Am. Fedn. Clin. Research, Am. Soc. Clin. Nutrition, Am. Assn. Cancer Research, Am. Soc. Clin. Oncology, Reticulo-Endothelial Soc., Alpha Omega Alpha. Office: Mt Sinai Hosp 19 E 98th St # 1410 New York NY 10029-6501

WASSERMAN, MARTIN P., human health administrator; m. Barbara; children: Brad, Torrey. Grad., John Hopkins Sch. Medicine, 1968. Dir. pediat. care on Navajo reservation Gallup, N.Mex.; med. dir. Mt. Washington Pediat. Hosp., Balt.; dir. pediat. outpatient clinic and emergency room U. Md. Hosp., 1974-76; health officer Montgomery County, Md., Prince George's County, Md.; dir. human svcs. Arlington County, Va.; sec. Md. Dept. Health and Mental Hygiene; chair U.S. Surgeon Gen.'s Lifestyles Task Force. Mem. AMA, ABA, APHA, Am. Acad. Pediats. Office: Dept Health and Mental Hygiene 201 W Preston St Baltimore MD 21201-2323

WASSERMAN, PAUL, library and information science educator; b. Newark, Jan. 8, 1924; s. Joseph and Sadie (Ringelescu) W.; m. Krystyna Ostrowska, 1973; children: Jacqueline R., Steven R. BBA, Coll. City N.Y., 1948; MS in L.S., Columbia, 1949, MS, 1950; PhD, U. Mich., 1960; postgrad., Western Res. U., 1963-64. Advt. mgr. Zuckerberg Co., N.Y.C., 1946-48; asst. to bus. libr. Bklyn. Pub. Library, 1949-51, chief sci. and industry div., 1951-53; librarian, asst. prof. Grad. Sch. Bus. and Pub. Adminstrn., Cornell U., 1953-56, libr., assoc. prof., 1956-62, librarian, prof., 1962-65; dean U. Md. Coll. Library and Info. Scis., 1965-70, prof., 1970-97, prof. emeritus, 1997—; vis. prof. U. Mich., summers 1960, 63, 64, Asian Inst. Tech., U. Hawaii, U. Hong Kong, summer 1988, Chulalongkorn U., Bangkok, 1990, U. Wash., summer 1991, U. Wis., summer 1991, U. Wis., summer 1992, C.W. Post Coll., L.I. U., 1993, Inst. Sci. and Tech. China, Beijing, 1996; Isabel Nichol lectr. Denver U. Libr. Sch., 1968; market rsch. cons. Laux Advt., Inc., 1955-59, Gale Rsch. Co., Detroit, 1959-60, 63-64; rsch. planning cons. Ind. U. Sch. Bus., 1961-62; cons. to USPHS as mem. manpower tng. rev. com. Nat. Libr. Medicine, 1966-69, Ohio Bd. Regents, 1969, Omngraphics Inc., 1988-91, VITA, summer 1987; dir. Documentation Abstracts, Inc., 1970-73, v.p., 1971-73; Fulbright prof. Warsaw U., 1993-94; rsch. project dir. Kellogg Study, 1996—. Author: Information for Administrators, 1956, (with Fred Silander) Decision Making, 1958, Measurement and Evaluation of Organization Performance, 1959, Sources of Commodity Prices, 1960, 2d edit., 1974, Sources for Hospital Administrators, 1961, Decision Making: An Annotated Bibliography, supplement, 1958-63, 1964, Librarian and the Machine, 1965; Book rev. editor: Adminstrv. Sci. Quar, 1956-61; editor: Service to Business, 1952-53, Directory of University Research Bureaus and Institutes, 1960, Health Organizations of the U.S. and Canada, 1961, and 2d to 4th edit., 1977, Statistics Sources, 1962 and 4th to 8th edits., 1984, (with Bundy) Reader in Library Adminstration, 1968, Reader in Research Methods in Librarianship, 1969; mng. editor: Mgmt. Information Guide Series, 1963-83, Consultants and Consulting Organizations, 1966, 4th edit., 1979, 5th edit., 1982, Who's Who in Consulting, 1968, 2d edit., 1974, Awards, Honors and Prizes: A Sourcebook and Directory, 1969, 2d edit., 1972, 4th edit. Vol. 1, 1978, International and Foreign Awards, 1975, New Consultants, 1973-74, 76-77, 78-79, Readers in Librarianship and Information Science, 1968-78, Ency. Bus. Information Sources, 1971, 3d edit., 1976, 4th edit., 1980, 5th edit., 1983, Library and Information Services Today, 1971-75, Consumer Sourcebook, 1974, 2d edit., 1978, 3d edit., 1980, 4th edit., 1983; series editor: Contributions in Librarianship and Information Science, 1969—; coordinating mgmt. editor: Information Guide Library, 1971-83, The New Librarianship-A Challenge for Change, 1972; mng. editor: Museum Media, 1973, Library Bibliographies and Indexes, 1975, Ethnic Groups in the United States, 1976, 2d edit., 1982, Training and Development Organizations, 1978, 2d edit., 1983, Speakers and Lecturers: How to Find Them, 1979, 2d edit., 1982, Learning Independently, 1979, 2d edit., 1983, Recreation and Outdoor Life Directory, 1979, Law and Legal Information Directory, 1980, 2d edit., 1982, Ency. Health Info. Sources, 1986, Ency. Sr. Citizen Info. Sources, 1987, Ency. Pub. Affairs Info. Sources, 1987, Ency. Legal Info. Sources, 1987; mem. editorial bd. Social Scis. Citation Index, Inst. Scientific Info., 1972—, Jour. Library Adminstrn., 1979-89, Social Sci. Info. Studies, 1979—, 1991 Education for Info.: The Internat. Rev. of Education and Tng. in Library and Info. Sci., 1983-88. Active U.S. Com. on Edn. and Tng. for Internat. Fedn. for Info. and Documentation, 1993-94. Served with U.S. Army, 1943-46. Decorated Purple Heart, Bronze Star; Fulbright scholar, Sri Lanka, 1986-87. Mem. AAUP, ALA, Am. Soc. Info. Sci., Spl. Librs. Assn. (editor, chmn. publ. project., Disting. Mem. award bus. divsn. 1996—). Home: 4940 Sentinel Dr Apt 203 Bethesda MD 20816-3552 Office: U Md Coll Libr and Info Svcs College Park MD 20742

WASSERMAN, RICHARD LAWRENCE, pediatrician, educator; b. Bklyn., Oct. 28, 1948; s. Isidore and Gladys (Glazer) W.; m. Tina D. Rice; children: Jonathan A., Leslie R. BS in Chemistry, Hobart Coll., 1970; PhD, CUNY, 1975; MD, U. Tex. Southwest, Dallas, 1977. Diplomate Am. Bd. Pediatrics, Am. Bd. Allergy and Immunology. Intern Children's Hosp. Phila., resident in pediatrics, 1977-79, fellow in immunology, 1979-80; rsch. assoc. in immunology Rockefeller U., N.Y.C., 1980-82; asst. prof. pediatrics and microbiology U. Tex. S.W. Med. Ctr., Dallas, 1982-88, asst. clin. prof. pediatrics, 1988—; asst. chief pediatrics Baylor U. Med. Ctr., Dallas, 1989; dir. Immunology Clinic Children's Med. Ctr., Dallas, 1983—; adj. attending physician Mt. Sinai Hosp., N.Y.C., 1981-82; cons. Am. Assn. Blood Banks, Arlington, Va., 1983-95; test devel. com. Nat. Bd. Med. Examiners, 1992—; med. dir. pediatric allergy and immunology Columbia Hosp. at Med. City, Dallas, 1994—. Mem. Am. Assn. Immunologists, Clin. Immunology Soc., Am. Assn. Allergy Asthma and Immunology, So. Soc. for Pediatric Rsch. (coun. 1986-87, Founder's award 1988), Phi Beta Kappa Zeta. Home: 7153 Lavendale Ave Dallas TX 75230-3650

WASSERMAN, RICHARD LEO, lawyer; b. Balt., Aug. 6, 1948; s. Jack B. and Claire (Gutman) W.; m. Manuele Delbourgo, May 13, 1973; children: Alexander E., Lauren E. AB, Princeton U., 1970; JD, Columbia U., 1973. Bar: N.Y. 1975, Md. 1978, U.S. Dist. Ct. (so. and ea. dists.) N.Y. 1975, U.S. Dist. Ct. Md. 1978, U.S. Ct. Appeals (2d cir.) 1975, U.S. Ct. Appeals (4th cir.) 1979, U.S. Supreme Ct. 1982. Law clk. to hon. Roszel C. Thomsen U.S. Dist. Ct. Md., Balt., 1973-74; assoc. Proskauer Rose Goetz & Mendelsohn, N.Y.C., 1974-78; assoc. Venable, Baetjer & Howard, Balt., 1978-81, ptnr., 1982—. Mem. ABA (bus. bankruptcy com.), Md. Bar Assn. (sec. coun. bus. law sect. 1989-92), Bar Assn. Balt. City (chmn. banking, bankruptcy and bus. law com. 1987-88), Bankruptcy Bar Assn. Dist. Md. (bd. dirs. 1988—, pres. 1990-91), Assn. Bar City N.Y., Am. Bankruptcy Inst., Princeton U. Alumni Assn. Md. (bd. dirs. 1980—, pres. 1985-87), Suburban Club Baltimore County (bd. govs. 1982-89, 94—, 2d v.p. 1986-87, sec. 1987-88, pres.-elect 1994-95, pres. 1995-97). Democrat. Jewish. Avocations: tennis, bridge. Office: Venable Baetjer & Howard LLP 1800 Mercantile Bank Bldg Baltimore MD 21201

WASSERMAN, ROBERT HAROLD, biology educator; b. Schenectady, Feb. 11, 1926; s. Joseph and Sylvia (Rosenberg) W.; m. Marilyn Mintz, June 11, 1950; children: Diane Jean, Arlene Lee, Judith Rose. B.S., Cornell U., 1949, Ph.D., 1953; M.S., Mich. State U., 1951. Research assoc. AEC project U. Tenn., Oak Ridge, 1953-55; sr. scientist med. div. Oak Ridge Inst. Nuclear Studies, 1955-57; asso. prof. dept. phys. biology N.Y. State Vet. Coll., Cornell U., 1957-63, prof., 1963—, James Law prof. physiology, 1989—, acting head phys. biology dept., 1963-64, 71, 75-76, chmn. dept. / sect. physiology, 1983-87, mem. exec. com. div. biol. sci., 1983-87; vis. fellow Inst. Biol. Chemistry, Copenhagen, 1964-65; chmn. Conf. on Calcium Transport, 1962; co-chmn. Conf. on Cell Mechanisms for Calcium Transfer and Homeostasis, 1970; mem. adv. bd. Vitamin D Symposia, 1976—; mem. adv. bd. Symposia Calcium-Binding Proteins, 1977-88, chmn., 1977; mem. food and nutrition bd. NRC; cons. NIH, Oak Ridge Inst. Nuclear Studies; mem. pub. affairs com. Fedn. Am. Socs. Exptl. Biology, 1974-77 ; chmn. com. MPI, NRC. Bd. editors: Calcified Tissue Research, 1977-80, Procs. Soc. Exptl. Biol. Medicine, 1970-76, Cornell Veterinarian, Jour. Nutrition; contbr.: articles to profl. jours. Served with U.S. Army, 1944-45. Recipient Mead Johnson award, 1969, Andre Lichtwitz prize INSERM, 1982, W.F. Neuman award Am. Soc. Bone and Mineral Rsch., 1990, merit award NIH, 1993-96; Guggenheim fellow, 1964-65, 72, fellow NSF-OECD, 1964-65. Fellow Am. Inst. Nutrition, mem. Am. Physiol. Soc., Soc. Exptl. Biology and Medicine, AAAS, Nat. Acad. Scis., Sigma Xi, Phi Kappa Phi, Phi Zeta. Home: 207 Texas Ln Ithaca NY 14850-1758

WASSERMAN, STEPHEN IRA, physician, educator; b. Los Angeles, Dec. 17, 1942; m. Linda Morgan; children: Matthew, Zachary. BA, Stanford U., 1964; MD, UCLA, 1968. Diplomate Am. Bd. Internal Medicine, Am. Bd. Allergy and Immunology. Intern, resident Peter B. Brigham Hosp., Boston, 1968-70; fellow in allergy, immunology Robert B. Brigham Hosp., Boston, 1972-75; asst. prof. medicine Harvard U., Boston, 1975-79, assoc. prof., 1979; assoc. prof. U. Calif.-San Diego, La Jolla, 1979-85, prof., 1985—, chief allergy tng. program Sch. Medicine, 1979-85, chief allergy div. Sch. Medicine, 1985-93, acting chmn. dept. medicine, 1986-88, chmn. dept. medicine, 1988—, Helen M. Ranney prof., 1992—; co-dir. allergy sect. Robert B. and Peter B. Brigham Hosps., 1977-79; dir. Am. Bd. Allergy and Immunology, Am. Bd. Internal Medicine. Contbr. articles to profl. jours. Served to lt. comdr. USPHS, 1970-72, San Francisco. Fellow Am. Acad. Allergy and Immunology (pres.-elect 1997—); mem. Am. Soc. Clin. Investigation, Assn. Am. Physicians, Am. Assn. Immunologists, Collegium INternationale Allergologicum, Phi Beta Kappa, Alpha Omega Alpha. Office: U Calif Med Ctr 402 Dickinson St Ste 380 San Diego CA 92103-6902

WASSERMAN, STEPHEN MILES, communications manager; b. Chgo., Apr. 26, 1945; s. Samuel Isreal and Rayna (Krassner) W.; m. Faye Rita Samuelson, Oct. 17, 1971; children: Rayna, Alyssa. BA in Journalism, Bradley U., 1967. Mgr. corp. comm. Underwriters Labs., Inc., Northbrook,

Ill., 1991—; mem. pub. rels. and fundraising com. Ill. Math. and Sci. Acad., Aurora, 1992-96; comms. chair Nat. Electric Safety Found., Washington, 1994-96. campaign chmn. United Way, Buffalo Grove, Ill., 1991-93, pres., 1994-95. Mem. Nat. Press Club. Office: Underwriters Labs Inc 333 Pfingsten Rd Northbrook IL 60062-2002

WASSERMAN, STEVE, editor; b. Vancouver, Wash., Aug. 3, 1952; s. Abraham and Ann (Dragoon) W.; m. Michelle Krisel, Mar. 7, 1982; children: Claire, Paul, Isaac. AB in Criminology, U. Calif., Berkeley, 1974. Asst. editor City Mag. of San Francisco, 1975-76; dep. editor opinion sect. Los Angeles Times, 1977-83; editor in chief New Republic Books The New Republic, N.Y.C., 1984-87; pub. Hill and Wang div. Farrar, Straus and Giroux Inc., N.Y.C., 1987-90, The Noonday Press div. Farrar, Straus and Giroux Inc., N.Y.C., 1987-90; editorial dir. Times Books divsn. Random House, N.Y.C., 1990-96; editor L.A. Times Book Rev., 1996—; cons. editor The Threepenny Rev., Berkeley, Calif., 1980-86, Tikkun, Oakland, Calif., 1986-90. Contbr. articles and revs. to mags. and newspapers. Mem. PEN. Office: LA Times Times Mirror Sq Los Angeles CA 90053

WASSERMAN, STEVE, broadcast executive. BA in Mass Comm., U. Miami. News mgmt. positions Post-Newsweek stas., Miami, Jacksonville, Fla., Detroit; news dir. WCBS-TV, N.Y.C.; v.p., gen. mgr. WJXT-TV, Jacksonville, KPRC-TV Channel 2, Houston, 1994—. Mem. bds. United way of Gulf Coast, ARC, Jr. Achievement, Nat. Conf. Christians and Jews, March of Dimes, John Cooper Sch. in the Woodlands. Office: KPRC-TV PO Box 2222 Houston TX 77252-2222

WASSERMAN, SUSAN VALESKY, accountant; b. St. Petersburg, Fla., June 5, 1956; d. Charles B. Valesky and Jeanne I. (Schulz) Morgan; m. Fred Wasserman III, May 19, 1990; 1 child, Sara Elisabeth. BS in Merchandising, Fla. State U., 1978; BA in Acctg., U. South Fla., 1983; ChFC, Am. Coll., 1991. CPA, Fla.; ChFC, Fla. Mgmt. trainee Burdines Dept. Stores, Miami, Fla., 1978-79; store mgr. Levi Straus Inc., San Francisco, 1979; pvt. practice St. Petersburg, Fla., 1980—; internet practice, 1996—. Paintings shown at Longboat Key (Fla.) Art Ctr. Watercolor 10 Art Show, 1993, Fla. Suncoast Watercolor Soc. Aqueous Show, Sarasota, 1994; quoted in The Tax Advisor (nat. syndicated column); developer 1st worldwide Internet discussion group on fin. planning. Mem. AICPA (personal fin. specialist), Am. Soc. CLUs and ChFCs (bd. dirs.), Fla. Inst. CPAs. Avocation: watercolor painting. Office: PO Box 48247 Saint Petersburg FL 33743-8247

WASSERSTEIN, WENDY, playwright; b. Bklyn., Oct. 18, 1950; d. Morris and Lola W. BA, Mt. Holyoke Coll., 1971; MA, CCNY, 1973; MFA, Yale Drama Sch., 1976. Author: (plays) Any Woman Can't, 1973, Happy Birthday, Montpelier Pizz-zazz, 1974, (with Christopher Durang) When Dinah Shore Ruled the Earth, 1975, Uncommon Women and Others, 1975, Isn't It Romantic, 1981, Tender Offer, 1983, The Man in a Case, 1986, Miami, 1986, The Heidi Chronicles, 1988 (Pulitzer prize for drama 1989, Outer Critics Cir. award for best play 1989, N.Y. Drama Critics Cir. award 1989, Susan Smith Blackburn prize 1989), The Sisters Rosensweig, 1991 (Outer Critics Cir. award 1993); (essays) Bachelor Girls, 1990; (screenplays) Uncommon Women and Others, 1978, The Sorrows of Gin, 1979, (with Durang) House of Husbands, Isn't It Romantic, The Heidi Chronicles; (children's book) Pamela's First Musical, 1995. Bd. dirs. Channel Thirteen MacDowell Colony, British Am. Arts. Assn. Am. Playwrights Project grantee, 1988, Brit.-Am. Arts Assn. grantee, Hale Matthews Found. award, Commissioning Program Phoenix Theater grantee, Guggenheim fellow, 1983. Mem. Coun. Dramatists Guild. *

WASSHAUSEN, DIETER CARL, systematic botanist; b. Jena, Germany, Apr. 15, 1938; came to U.S., 1950, naturalized, 1957; s. Heinz P. and Elizabeth A. (Mueller) W.; m. Merrilee M. Locklin, Dec. 23, 1961; children—Lisa A., David B. B.S., George Washington U., 1962, M.S., 1965, Ph.D., 1972. Assoc. curator dept. botany Smithsonian Instn., Washington, 1969-76; chmn., curator dept. botany Nat. Mus. Natural History, Washington, 1976—. Recipient Smithsonian Research Found. awards, 1974, 75, Willdenow medal, 1979. Mem. Am. Soc. Plant Taxonomists, Internat. Assn. Plant Taxonomy, Neotropical Field Botanists Assn., Am. Inst. Biol. Scis., AAAS, Assn. Tropical Biology, Sigma Xi. Presbyterian. Research on systematics of neotropical Acanthaceae, floristic studies in Graminea of Brazil, floristic studies in Begoniaceae, revision of Nat. List Sci. Plant Names. Home: 9406 Chatteroy Pl Gaithersburg MD 20879-1424 Office: Nat Mus Natural History 10th St and Constitution Ave NW Washington DC 20560

WASSNER, STEVEN JOEL, pediatric nephrologist, educator; b. N.Y.C., Dec. 16, 1946; s. Abraham and Clara (Weitzner) W.; m. Enid K. Kling, June 11, 1972; children: Adam Jacob, Nancy Shane. B.S., CCNY, 1968; M.D., NYU, 1972. Diplomate Am. Bd. Pediatrics, Am. Bd. Pediatrics Nephrology. Intern, resident Children's Hosp. L.A., 1972-74, fellow in pediatric nephrology, 1974-75; research fellow in pediatric nephrology UCLA, 1975-77; asst. prof. pediat. Pa. State U. M.S. Hershey Med. Ctr., Hershey, 1978-83, assoc. prof., 1983-91, prof., 1991—, vice chmn. dept., 1978—, chief div. pediat. nephrology, 1990—, chief div. pediatric nephrology and diabetes, 1991—; vis. prof. human biochemistry Hebrew U., Hadassah Hosp., 1985-86; dir. Pediatric Diabetes Svc., 1988-91; bd. dirs. dialysis program for Pa. State U. students. Contbr. articles to med. jours. Mem. adv. bd. Kidney Found. South Ctrl. Pa., Harrisburg, 1980-90, sci. adv. coun. for pediatric nephrology/urology Nat. Kidney Found., 1986-92, Harrisburg com. for Hebrew U.; bd. dirs. Jewish Family Svc., Harrisburg, 1979-85, United Jewish Fedn., 1983-85, 94—, Yeshiva Acad., 1987-90. Recipient Rsch. Career Devel. award NIH, 1983; Musclar Dystrophy Assn. grantee, 1979-81; Sr. Internat. fellow Fogarty Internat. Ctr. NIH, 1985. Fellow Am. Acad. Pediatrics, Am. Bd. Pediatrics; mem. Am. Pediatrics Soc., Soc. Pediatric Rsch., Am. Soc. Nephrology, Internat. Soc. Nephrology, Am. Soc. Pediatr, Nephrology, Am. Physiol. Soc., Am. Diabetes Assn., Internat. Soc. Pediatric Nephrology, Internat. Pediatric Nephrology Assn. (counsellor 1989-95). Office: MS Hershey Med Ctr PO Box 850 Hershey PA 17033-0850

WASSON, JAMES WALTER, aircraft manufacturing company executive; b. Pitts., Dec. 9, 1951; s. George Fredrick and Dolores Helen (Wuerl) W.; m. Evelyn Fay Gonzales, Dec. 28, 1974; children: Robert, Brian. AST, Pitts. Inst. Aeronautics, 1972; BSET, Northrop U., Inglewood, Calif., 1981; MBA, U. Phoenix, 1988, govt. contracts mgmt. cert., 1989. Avionics technician various cos., 1972-74; electronics prodn. mgr. Ostgaard Industries, Gardena, Calif., 1974-75; sr. avionics design engr. Allied Signal Garrett Airesearch Aviation Co., L.A., 1975-81; v.p. engring., co-founder Avionics Engring. Svcs., Inc., Tucson, 1980-81; sr. tech. specialist Northrop Aircraft Div., Hawthorne, Calif., 1981-84; prog. mgr. McDonnell Douglas Helicopter Co., Mesa, Ariz., 1984-86; tech. devel. mgr. McDonnell Douglas Helicopter Co., 1986-93; exec. v.p., co-founder Leading Edge Technologies, Inc., Mesa, 1991-95; mgr. bus. devel. McDonnell Douglas Helicopter Sys., Mesa, 1993-95; dir. tech. mktg. Smiths Aerospace, Grand Rapids, Mich., 1995—; adj. prof. govt. contract mgmt., program mgmt., proposal devel., strategic mgmt., mktg., tech. mgmt., rsch. projects U. Phoenix, 1990—; cons. in field. Author: Avionics Systems Operation and Maintenance, 1993, Business Opportunities in Artificial Intelligence, 1988; contbr. articles to profl. jours. Inventor in field. Com. chmn. industry adv. bd. Northrop U., 1981; chmn. bd. dirs., pres. Alta Mesa Community Assn., 1989; organizer Boy Scouts Am., Mesa, 1988. Named Engr. of Yr., Northrop U., 1980; recipient Disting. Alumnus award Pitts. Inst. Aeronautics, 1981, U. Phoenix, 1996; named to Hall of Fame, Career Colls. Assn., 1991. Mem. IEEE, NSPE, Assn. Avionics Educators, Soc. Automotive Engrs., Army Aviation Assn. (chpt. sr. v.p. 1988-91, treas. 1993—), Am. Def. Preparedness Assn., Am. Helicopter Soc. (chmn. avionics com. 1990), Assn. Avionics Educators. Republican. Roman Catholic. Avocations: flying, scuba diving, hiking, golf, camping.

WASSON, RICHARD HOWARD, English language educator; b. Chgo., Oct. 7, 1930; s. Robert Rock W. and Anna Hilbert Witt; m. Audrey Dohmeyer, 1956 (div. 1971); 1 child, Kristen Anna Wasson-Mirskin. BA, Cornell Coll., 1952; MA, U. Iowa, 1956; PhD, U. Wisc., 1962. Profl. Cert. English. Instr. U. W.Va., Morgantown, 1956-57; teaching asst. U. Wis., Madison, 1956-62; asst. prof. U. Ill., Champaign, Urbana, 1962-70; prof. Rutgers U., New Brunswick, N.J., 1970-96, now prof. emeritus; freshman com. dir. Rutgers U., 1977-81. Recipient Georgina Smith award for Creative and Disting. Leadership, Rutgers Coun. AAUP Chpt., 1992. Mem. AAUP (grievance chair 1987, 89, 92-95, pres. New Brunswick chpt. 1990-93, founder retiree assembly 1997), MLA. Home: 12 Talbot St Somerset NJ 08873-4639

WASTAK, JOHN RUDOLPH, health care executive, educator; b. Passiac, N.J., July 5, 1940; s. John S. and Rosemarie (Simek) W.; m. Isobel Adam Gray, Sept. 27, 1974; children: Scott Adam, Jonathan William. BS, St. Peter's Coll., Jersey City, 1962; MPA in Health Svcs. Adminstrn., NYU, 1972; MBA in Fin. and Mktg., Case Western Reserve U., 1985. Lic. Nursing Home Adminstr. Adminstrv. dir. Hackensack (N.J.) Hosp. Med. Ctr., 1972-76; exec. dir., CEO Cuyahoga Comty. Mental Health Bd., N.Y., 1976-86; project adminstr., regional v.p. Health Industries of Am., 1987-90; adminstr. Lehigh Valley Health Svcs. Network, Allentown, Pa., 1990—. Mem. Am. Coll. Healthcare Execs., Med. Group Mgmt. Assn., Am. Coll. Med. Practice Execs., Health Industries Am. Avocations: golf, swimming, white water rafting. Home: 7930 Woodsbluff Run Fogelsville PA 18051 Office: Lehigh Valley Hosp Cedar Crest I 78 PO Box 689 Allentown PA 18105-1556

WASTERLAIN, CLAUDE GUY, neurologist; b. Courcelles, Belgium, Apr. 15, 1935; s. Desire and Simone (De Taeve) W.; m. Anne Marguerite Thomsin, Feb. 28, 1967; 1 child, Jean Michel. Cand. Sci., U. Liege, 1957, MD, 1961; LS in Molecular Biology, U. Brussels, 1969. Resident Cornell U. Med. Coll., N.Y.C., 1964-67, instr. neurology, 1969-70, asst. prof., 1970-75, assoc. prof., 1975-76; assoc. prof. UCLA Sch. Medicine, 1976-79, prof., 1979—, vice chair dept. neurology, 1976—; chief neurology svc. VA Med. Ctr., Sepulveda, Calif., 1976—; cons. neurologist Olive View Med. Ctr., Sylmar, Calif., 1976—; attending neurologist UCLA Ctr. Health Scis., 1976—. Author, editor: Status Epilepticus, 1984, Neonatal Seizures, 1990, Molecular Neurobiology and Epilepsy, 1992; contbr. articles to med. jours. William Evans fellow, U. Auckland, New Zealand, 1984; recipient N.Y. Neurol. Soc. Young Investigator award, 1965, Rsch. Career Devel. award NIH, 1973-76, Worldwide AES award, 1992, Golden Hammer Teaching award, 1996. Fellow Am. Acad. Neurology; mem. Am. Neurol. Assn., Am. Soc. Neurochemsitry (coun. mem. 1991—), Internat. Neurochemistry, Am. Epilepsy Soc., Royal Soc. Medicine. Avocations: tennis, skiing, jazz, theatre. Office: VA Med Ctr 1611 Plummer St Sepulveda CA 91343

WATABE, NORIMITSU, biology and marine science educator; b. Kure, Hiroshima, Japan, Nov. 29, 1922; came to U.S., 1957; s. Isamu and Matsuko (Takamatsu) W.; m. Sakuko Kobayashi, Dec. 12, 1952; children: Shoichi, Sachiko. BS, 1st Nat. High Sch., Tokyo, 1945; MS, Tohoku U., Sendai, Japan, 1948, DSc, 1960. Rsch. investigator Fuji Pearl Co., Mie-ken, Japan, 1948-52; instr. Prefect U. Mie, Tsu, Mie-ken, Japan, 1952-55, asst. prof., 1955-59; rsch. assoc. Duke U., Durham, N.C., 1957-70; assoc. prof. U. S.C., Columbia, 1970-72, prof. biology, marine sci., 1972-93, disting. prof., 1993-94; disting. prof. emeritus, 1994—. dir. Electron Microscopy Ctr., 1970-95; cons. in field. Author: Studies on Pearls, 1959. Editor: Mechanisms of Mineralization, 1976; Mechanisms of Biomineralization, 1980, Hard Tissue Mineralization and Demineralization, 1991. Contbr. numerous sci. articles to profl. jours. Recipient Pearl Research award Elmer W. Ellsworth, 1952, Alexander Von Humboldt award Govt. of Germany, 1976, Russel award U. S.C., 1981; grantee NIH, 1971-76, NSF, 1973-95. Fellow AAAS, Royal Micros. Soc. Gt. Britain; mem. Am. Micros. Soc. (rev. bd.), Am. Malacological Union (rev. bd.), Am. Soc. Zoologists, Micros. Soc. Am. Avocations: music; piano playing. Home: 3510 Greenway Dr Columbia SC 29206-3416 Office: Dept Biol Sci Univ S Carolina Columbia SC 29208

WATANABE, AUGUST MASARU, physician, scientist, medical educator, corporate executive; b. Portland, Oreg., Aug. 17, 1941; s. Frank H. and Mary Y. W.; m. Margaret Whildin Reese, Mar. 14, 1964; children: Nan Reiko, Todd Franklin, Scott Masaru. BS, Wheaton (Ill.) Coll., 1963; MD, Ind. U., 1967. Diplomate Am. Bd. Internal Medicine. Intern Ind. U. Med. Center, Indpls., 1967-68; resident Ind. U. Med. Center, 1968-69, 71-72, fellow in cardiology, 1972-74; clin. asso. NIH, 1969-71; clin. instr. medicine Georgetown U. Med. Sch., Washington, 1970-71; mem. faculty Ind. U. Sch. Medicine, Indpls., 1972—, prof. medicine and pharmacology, 1978—, chmn. dept. medicine, 1983-90; dir. Regenstrief Inst. for Health Care Ind. U. Sch. of Medicine, Indpls., 1984-90; from v.p. to group v.p. rsch. labs. Eli Lilly & Co., Indpls., 1990-94, v.p., pres. labs, 1994-95; exec. v.p. sci. and tech. Eli Lilly and Co., Indpls., 1996—, also bd. dirs., 1994—; mem. pharmacology study sect. NIH, 1979-81, chmn., 1981-83; mem. cardiovasc.-renal adv. com. FDA, 1982-85; mem. com. A, Nat. Heart, Lung and Blood Inst., 1984-88, chmn., 1986-88; cons. to fed. govt. and industry. Contbr. articles to profl. jours.; editorial bds. sci. jours. Dir. Ind. U. Found., 1989—, Indpls. Symphony Orch., 1994—, Regenstrief Found., 1995—. NIH grantee, 1972-92. Fellow ACP, Am. Coll. Cardiology, Am. Heart Assn. (councils on clin. cardiology and circulation, research rev. com. Ind. affiliate 1978-82, research and adv. com. North Central region 1978-82, adv. com. cardiovascular drugs 1976-79, chmn. com. 1979-81, chmn. program com. council on basic sci. 1982-84, chmn. com. on sci. sessions programs 1985-88, bd. dirs. 1985-88), Am. Coll. Cardiology (govt. relations com. 1979-81, trustee 1982-87); mem. Am. Fedn. Clin. Research (councilor Midwest sect. 1976-77, chmn.-elect Midwest sect. 1977-78, chmn. sect. 1978-79, chmn. sect. nominating com. 1979-80), Am. Soc. Clin. Investigation, Am. Soc. Clin. Pharmacology and Therapeutics, Am. Soc. Pharmacology and Exptl. Therapeutics (exec. com. div. clin. pharmacology 1978-81), Cardiac Muscle Soc., Central Soc. Clin. Research (councillor 1983-86, pres.-elect 1989, pres. 1990), Internat. Soc. Heart Research, Assn. Am. Physicians, Assn. Profs. of Medicine, Sigma Xi. Office: Eli Lilly & Co Drop Code 1209 Lilly Corp Ctr Indianapolis IN 46285

WATANABE, KYOICHI A(LOYSIUS), chemist, researcher, pharmacology educator; b. Amagasaki, Hyogo, Japan, Feb. 28, 1935; s. Yujiro Paul and Yoshiko Francisca (Hashimoto) W.; m. Kikyoko Agatha Suzuki, Nov. 22, 1962; children: Kanna, Kay, Kenneth, Kim, Kelly, Katherine. BA, Hokkaido U., 1958, PhD, 1963. Lectr. Sophia U., Tokyo, 1963; rsch. assoc. Sloan-Kettering Inst., N.Y.C., 1963-66, assoc., 1968-72, assoc. mem., 1972-81, mem., prof., 1981-95; rsch. fellow U. Alta., Edmonton, Can., 1966-68; assoc. prof. Cornell U. Med. Coll., N.Y.C., 1972-81, prof. pharmacology, 1981—; dir. organic chemistry Codon Pharm., Inc., Gaithersburg, Md., 1996—; mem. study sect. NIH, Washington, 1981-84. Mem. Polish Chem. Soc. (hon.), Russian Acad. Sci. (bd. sci. cons. Engelhardt Inst. Molecular Biology 1994—). Achievements include total synthesis of nucleoside antibiotics, novel heterocycle ring transformation, C-nucleose chemistry; antiviral and anticancer nucleosides; intercalating agents; modified oligonucleotides. Office: Codon Pharm Inc 200 Perry Pkwy Gaithersburg MD 20877-2171

WATANABE, MAMORU, former university dean, physician, researcher; b. Vancouver, B.C., Can., Mar. 15, 1933; s. Takazo and Nao (Suginobu) W.; m. Marie Katie Bryndzak, June 1, 1974; 1 child, David. M.D., McGill U., 1957, Ph.D., 1963. Intern Royal Victoria Hosp., Montreal, 1957-58, resident in medicine, 1958-63; prof. medicine U. Alta., Edmonton, 1967-74; head internal medicine U. Calgary, Alta., 1974-76, assoc. dean edn., 1976-80, assoc. dean research, 1980-81, acting dean medicine, 1981-82, dean faculty medicine, 1982-92; med. staff Foothills Hosp., Calgary, 1974—. Fellow Royal Coll. Physicians and Surgeons (Can.); mem. Endocrine Soc., Can. soc. Clin. Investigation, Can. Soc. Endocrinology and Metabolism, Can. Hypertension Soc. Home: 162 Pumpridge Place SW, Calgary, AB Canada T2V 5E6 Office: U Calgary, 3330 Hospital Dr NW, Calgary, AB Canada T2N 1N4

WATANABE, MARK DAVID, pharmacist, educator; b. Santa Monica, Calif., Dec. 7, 1955; s. Jack Shigeru and Rose Nobuko (Iida) W. BA in Chemistry, U. Calif., Irvine, 1977, BS in Biol. Sci., 1978; PharmD, U. Calif., San Francisco, 1982, PhD in Pharm. Chemistry, 1990. Lic. pharmacist, Calif., Oreg., Tex., Ill. Pharmacy intern various locations, San Francisco, 1979-82; pharmacist Kaiser Permanente, San Francisco, 1981-87; clin. scis. rsch. fellow in psychiat. pharmacy U. Tex., Austin, 1987-89; clin. asst. prof. pharmacy practice U. Ill., Chgo., 1989—; rsch. asst. U. Calif., San Francisco, 1980-87; clin. pharmacy cons. Ill. Dept. Mental Health & Devel. Disabilities, 1994—. Regents scholar U. Calif., San Francisco, 1979-82; recipient Excellence in Teaching award Long Found., San Francisco, 1984. Mem. Am. Coll. Clin. Pharmacy, Am. Soc. Health-Sys. Pharmacists, Am. Assn. Colls. Pharmacy, Am. Pharm. Assn., Amnesty Internat., Mensa, Rho Chi. Unitarian Universalist. Avocations: individual and fitness sports, reading, travel, music. Home: 440 W Barry Ave Apt 605 Chicago IL 60657-5500 Office: U Ill 1601 W Taylor St Rm 534 W Chicago IL 60612-4310

WATANABE, TOSHIHARU, ecologist, educator; b. Kyoto, Japan, June 6, 1924; s. Seizo and Fusa Watanabe; m. Sumiko Isebo, Nov. 3, 1952; children: Ikuko, Naoki. DSc, Kyoto U., 1961. Prof. Nat. Kanazawa (Japan) U., 1972-75, Nat. Nara (Japan) Women's U., 1975-88; prof. fgn. studies Kansai U., Hirakata/Osaka, Japan, 1988—; owner Diamond Resort Hawaii Owner's Club, 1989—; pres. Inst. Sci. Rsch. to Hydrospherical Ecology, 1990-95, adviser, 1995—. Author: Encyclopedia of Environmental Control Technology, 1990; editor: Japanese Jour. Diatomology, 1985—, Japanese Jour. Water Treatment Biology, 1971—. Profl. mem. Ministry of Constrn., Kinki dist., 1980-96; vice-chmn. Com. on environ. pollution, Nara Prefecture and City, 1982-96, chmn., 1997—, com. mem. Wakayama, 1980—; pres. Environ. Coun., Nara Prefecture, 1996—, Nara City, 1997—. Recipient Blue Ribbon Order of the Navy, 1961. Avocations: Indian ink drawing, music. Home: Higashigawa-cho 518, Shinkyogoku St Nakagyo-ku, Kyoto 604, Japan Office: Kansai U Fgn Studies, Kitakatahoko-cho 16-1, Hirakata Osaka 573, Japan

WATANABE, WADE OSAMU, marine biologist; b. Honolulu, Sept. 19, 1951; s. Charles Shujiro and Clara Mieko (Hasegawa) W.; m. Colleen Aiko Sasaki, June 26, 1976; children: Skye, Laine, Landon. BS in Zoology, Oreg. State U., 1973; MS in Zoology, U. Hawaii, 1975, PhD in Zoology, 1982. Lab. technician Fish Physiology Lab., Oceanic Inst., Hawaii, 1976-77, rsch. asst., 1977-81; marine biologist Internat. Ctr. for Living Aquatic Resources Mgmt., Manila, Philippines, 1982-84; chief scientist Caribbean Marine Rsch. Ctr., Vero Beach, Fla., 1986-95, Sea Change Found., Vero Beach, Fla., 1996-97; assoc. rsch. scientist U. N.C., Wilmington, 1997—; adj. grad. faculty mem. Dept. Biol. Scis., Fla. Inst. Tech., 1991—; cons. in field; lectr. in field; grant reviewer NSF, Nat. Coastal Resources Rsch. and Devel. Inst., Univ. Hawaii Sea Grant Coll. Program, Nat. Marine Fisheries Svc. Co-editor: Aquaculture of the Milkfish, 1986; reviewer Aquaculture Jour., Jour. World Aquaculture Soc., Aquaculture Engring., Can. Jour. Zoology, Jour. Fish Biology, Aquatic Living Resources, Jour. Applied Aquaculture, Asian Fisheries Soc., Gulf and Caribbean Fisheries Inst., Jour. Aquaculture in the Tropics; contbr. articles to profl. jours. Grad. rsch. assistantship Hawaii Inst. Marine Biology, 1975; Jessie Smith Noyes Found. pre-doctoral fellow, 1977-81, Rockfeller Found. postdoctoral rsch. fellow, 1982-84; grantee Caribbean Marine Rsch. Ctr., 1987-91, 92, Oceanic Inst. Hawaii, 1993, 94, George F. Baker Trust, 1993, 94, 95, Marine Scis. and Tech. Ctr./U. Conn., 1995, 96. Mem. Am. Tilapia Assn. (bd. dirs. 1991-92), Fla. Foodfish, Gamefish and Aquatic Bait Farmers Assn. (bd. dirs. 1992), Internat. Ctr. for Living Aquatic Resources Mgmt. (affiliate scientist 1984-88), World Aquaculture Soc., Asian Fisheries Soc., Caribbean Aquaculture Assn. (bd. dirs. 1993-96), Fla. Aquaculture Assn., Network of Tropical Aquaculture Scientists. Avocation: youth baseball coach. Home: 5846 62nd Ln Vero Beach FL 32967-5263 Office: U NC Ctr Marine Sci Rsch 7205 Wrightsville Ave Wilmington NC 28403-7224

WATARU, WESTON YASUO, civil engineer; b. Honolulu, Mar. 30, 1957; s. Ralph Mitsuo and Anna Setsuko (Ogami) W.; m. Celine Jacqueline Teasdale, Nov. 1, 1986; children: Maile, Hope, Amber, Adam. BS, U. Hawaii, 1980. Registered profl. engr., Hawaii. Asst. engr. Dames and Moore, Honolulu, 1980-82; civil engr. I City and County of Honolulu Dept. Pub. Works, 1982-84, civil engr. IV, 1985-87, civil engr. V, 1987-89, svc. engr., civil engr. VI, 1989—; mem. utilities coord. com. City and County of Honolulu, 1989—, mem. permit streamlining task force, 1995—. Mem. ASCE, NSPE, Am. Pub. Works Assn., Hawaii Govt. Employees Assn. Avocations: family, sporting events, basketball, reading. Office: City and County of Honolulu Dept Pub Works 650 S King St Honolulu HI 96813-3017

WATCHORN, WILLIAM ERNEST, diversified manufacturing executive; b. Toronto, Ont., Can., Aug. 8, 1943; s. Roy Elgin and Josephine (Swyrida) W.; m. Maureen Emmett, Dec. 28, 1967; 1 child, Meghan. Chartered Acct., Toronto, 1967. Mgr. fin. planning Found. Group of Cos., Toronto, 1968-70; cons. Pahang Tengarra Regional Master Planning Study, Malaysia, 1970-72; controller Selkirk Holdings, Ltd., Toronto, 1972-75; corp. contr. Torstar Corp., Toronto, 1975-78; v.p. fin. Canwest Capital Corp., Winnipeg, Man., 1978-82; exec. v.p. Kaiser Resources Ltd., Vancouver, B.C., 1982; sr. v.p., chief fin. officer Fed. Industries Ltd., Winnipeg, 1982-88; pres., chief exec. officer Fed. Industries Indsl. Group, Winnipeg, 1989-91, Ensis Corp., Inc., Winnipeg, 1991—; bd. dirs. Ensis Corp. Inc., Heron Cable Industries Ltd., Milltronics Ltd., Neo Industries Inc., Neo Europe, S.A. Chmn. Balmoral Hall Sch. Found., Winnipeg, Manitoba Capital Fund; bd. dirs., vice-chmn. western region com. C.D. Howe Inst., Toronto; dir. Can. Stds. Assn.; vice chmn. Assocs.; co-chmn. Internat. Adv. Coun., faculty mgmt. U. Manitoba. Mem. Can. Inst. Chartered Accts., Fellowship Inst. of Chartered Accts., Man. Inst., Chartered Accts., Ont. Inst. Chartered Accts., Winter Club, St. Charles Country Club. Avocations: squash, golf, tennis. Home: 6453 Southboine Dr, Winnipeg, MB Canada R3R 0B7 Office: Ensis Corp Inc, Ste 1120/200 Graham Ave, Winnipeg, MB Canada R3C 4L5

WATERBURY, LARRY, physician, educator; b. Ft. Worth, May 30, 1937; m. Marcia Winkelman, 1968. Student, Princeton U., 1955-57, S.W. Tex. Coll., 1957-58; MD, U. Tex., Galveston, 1962. Diplomate Am. Bd. Internal Medicine, Am. Bd. Hematology, Am. Bd. Oncology. Intern U. Okla. Hosps., Oklahoma City, 1962-63; resident internal medicine parkland Meml. Hosp., Dallas, 1965-67; instr. dpet. Medicine U. Tex., Dallas, 1969-70; from instr. to assoc. prof. sch. medicine Johns Hopkins U., Balt., 1970-82, assoc. prof. medicine, 1982—, assoc. prof. oncology, 1986—; asst. chief physician Balt. City Hosps., 1970—, dir. blood bank, 1970-73; chief divsn. hematology, oncology Francis Scott Key Med. Ctr., Balt., 1978—; cons. Perry Point Vets. Hosp., Fort Howard Vets. Hosp.; mem. adv. com. Johns Hopkins Home Health Care Hospice, 1995—. Author: Hematology for the House Officer, 1981, 4th edit., 1996, (chpt.) Clinical Pathology, 1973, Complications of Neoplastic Disorders, 1979, Guide to Hematologic Disorders, 1980; co-author: (chpt.) Clinical Anesthesia, Vol. 3, 1968; author, co-author: (chpt.) Principles and Practice of Medicine, 19th edit., 1976, Principles of Ambulatory Medicine, 3d edit., 1991; contbr. articles to profl. jours. With U.S. Army Spl. Forces, 1963-65, Vietnam. Mem. Am. Soc. Hematology, Am. Soc. Clin. Oncology. Home: 5713 Visitation Way Baltimore MD 21210 Office: Johns Hopkins Bayview Med Ctr Divsn Hematology Oncology 4940 Eastern Ave Baltimore MD 21224-2735

WATERMAN, DANIEL, mathematician, educator; b. Bklyn., Oct. 24, 1927; s. Samuel and Anna (Robson) W.; m. Mudite Upesleja, Nov. 4, 1960; children—Erica, Susan, Scott. B.A., Bklyn. Coll., 1947; M.A., Johns Hopkins U., 1948; Ph.D., U. Chgo., 1954. Research assoc. Cowles Commn. Research in Econs., Chgo., 1951-52; instr. Purdue U., West Lafayette, Ind., 1953-55, asst. prof., 1955-59; asst. prof. U. Wis.-Milw., 1959-61; prof. Wayne State U., Detroit, 1961-69; prof. Syracuse (N.Y.) U., 1969-96, prof. emeritus, 1996—, chmn. math dept., 1988-94; cons. Martin-Marietta, Denver, 1960-61; researcher in real and Fourier analysis. Editor: Classical Real Analysis, 1985; contbr. articles to profl. jours. Fulbright fellow U. Vienna, 1952-53. Mem. Math. Assn. Am., Am. Math. Soc. (council mem.-at-large 1975-78), Sigma Xi. Home: 116 Donridge Dr Syracuse NY 13214-2344 Office: Syracuse U Dept Math Syracuse NY 13244-1150

WATERMAN, DIANE CORRINE, artist, educator, writer; b. Bklyn., Feb. 9, 1949; d. Beverly D. and Bernice Iona (Dowling) Waterman; children: Christopher, Tutankhamon, Joy, Derrick, Idiah, Kia. BA, Hunter Coll., 1984; postgrad., L.I. U., 1984-86. Cert. leisure profl., N.Y. Art instr./ adminstr. Afro-Am. Experience, Hempstead, N.Y., 1968-73; art specialist/ adminstr. MLK Youth Ctr., Westbury, N.Y., 1968-71; substance abuse counselor 5 Town Cmty. Ctr., Lawrence, N.Y., 1969-71; adminstr., counselor UJAMAA Acad., Hempstead, 1971-75; adminstr. asst. Inservice Learning Program Hunter Coll., 1981-84; unit mgr., youth divsn. counselor N.Y. State Divsn. for Youth, Bklyn., 1986-89; dean of women Claflin Coll., Orangeburg, S.C., 1989-90; dir. recreation and art therapy Dept. Homeless Svcs., N.Y.C., 1984-95; adj. prof. Touro Coll., Bklyn., 1995—; founder Renaissance Woman Cons., N.Y.C., 1984—; pres., founder Better Living Gen. Svc., N.Y.C., 1988—; designer Ethnic Wear, Empress Fashions, N.Y.C., 1993—; founder Artist in Focus, N.Y.C., 1991-94. Mem. PTA (pres. Bklyn. 1985), Citizens Com. N.Y.C., 1986, Dynamics of Leadership, Bklyn., 1995. Recipient Outstanding Cooperation award Dept. Homeless Svcs., 1994, Outstanding Svc. award N.Y.C. Tech. Coll., 1987, Cert. of Appreciation Edwin Gould Svcs. for Children, 1984. Mem. Lioness Club, Zeta Iota Phi (sec. 1968—). Democrat. Jewish. Avocations: art, writing, dancing, jogging. Home and Office: PO Box 466 Westbury NY 11590

WATERMAN, MICHAEL SPENCER, mathematics educator, biology educator; b. Coquille, Oreg., June 28, 1942; s. Ray S. and Bessie E. (Payne) W.; m. Vicki Lynn Buss, Aug. 14, 1962 (div. Mar. 1977); 1 child, Tracey Lynn. B.S., Oreg. State U., 1964, M.S., 1966; M.A., Mich. State U., 1968, Ph.D., 1969. Assoc. prof. Idaho State U., Pocatello, 1969-75; mem. staff Los Alamos Nat. Lab., 1975-82, cons., 1982—; USC Assocs. Endowed Chair U. So. Calif., L.A., prof. math. and biology, 1982—, U. So. Calif. Assocs. Endowed Chair, 1991—; vis. prof. math. U. Hawaii, Honolulu, 1979-80; vis. prof. structural biology U. Calif.-San Francisco, 1982; vis. prof. Mt. Sinai Med. Sch., N.Y.C., 1988. author: Introduction to Computational Biology, 1995; editor: Mathematical Methods for DNA Sequences; assoc. editor Bull. Math. Biology; mem. editl. bd. Jour. Advances in Applied math. jour., Molecular Phylongenetics and Evolution, Genomics, Soc. for Indsl. and Applied Math. Jour. Applied Math.; sr. editor: Jour. Computational Biology; contbr. numerous articles on math. stats., biology to profl. jours. Grantee NSF, 1971, 72, 75, Los Alamos Nat. Lab, 1976, 81, 88—, Sys. Devel. Found., 1982-87, NIH, 1986—, Sloan Found., 1990-91; Guggenheim Found. fellow, 1995. Fellow AAAS, Am. Acad. Arts and Scis., Inst. Math. Stats.; mem. Am. Statis. Assn., Soc. Math. Biology, Soc. Indsl. and Applied Math. Office: U So Calif Dept Math Los Angeles CA 90007

WATERS, BETTY LOU, newspaper reporter, writer; b. Texarkana, Tex., June 13, 1943; d. Chester Hinton and Una Erby (Walls) W. AA, Texarkana Jr. Coll., 1963; BA, East Tex. State U., 1965. Gen. assignment reporter Galveston County Pub. Co., Galveston and Texas City, 1965-68; news and feature writer Ind. and Daily Mail, Anderson, S.C., 1968-69; reporter Citizen-Times newspaper, Asheville, N.C., 1969-74; edn. and med. reporter News Star World Pub. Co., Monroe, La., 1974-79; reporter, writer Delta Democrat Times, Greenville, Miss., 1980-89; staff writer Tyler (Tex.) Morning Telegraph, 1990—. Recipient 1st place award for articles La. Press Women's Contest, 1978, 1st place for interview, 1979; news media award N.C. Easter Seal Soc., 1973; 3d place award for feature writing Miss. Press Assn., 1984, for gen. news, 1983, for investigative reporting, 1988, 1st place for best series of articles, 1990; hon. mentions Tex. AP, 1966. Mem. Sigma Delta Chi.

WATERS, CHERYL DIANE, accountant; b. Kalamazoo, Mich., May 24, 1966; d. Milton Oneal and Delores Roberta (Holloway) W. BA, U. Mich., Dearborn, 1989; postgrad., U. Phoenix, 1996—. Valuation specialist, Mich., 1993. Loan counselor Source One Mortgage, Farmington Hills, Mich., 1989-91; substitute tchr. Detroit Pub. Schs., 1991; Student Employee In Tng. program Mich. Dept. Transp., Lansing, 1993-94; lead worker, prin. clerk City of Lansing, 1994-96; accountant Holland Sys. Corp., Lansing, 1996—. Mem. Mich. Assn. CPAs, Inst. Mgmt. Accts., U. Mich. Alumni Assn., Delta Sigma Theta (asst. leader minerva circle 1990-91). Avocations: horseback riding, reading, swimming, bicycle riding.

WATERS, CYNTHIA WINFREY, media advertising specialist; b. Atlanta, Feb. 25, 1951; d. Tommie Lee Winfrey; m. Leroy Hollaway Jr., June 7, 1970 (div. 1981); children: Marechalnelle, Geoffrey; m. Leamond Howard Waters, Sept. 1, 1985. Cert. in acctg., Atlanta Area Tech. Inst., 1982; cert. in human relations, Chattahoochee Tech. Inst., 1988. Customer svc. rep. Atlanta Gaslight Co., 1975-83; asst. mktg. mgr. Vorwerk, U.S.A., Atlanta, 1983-86; fgn. sec. coord. Focal Point Inc., Atlanta, 1986-91, safety facilitator, 1988-91; pub. svc. dir. Sta. WYZE Radio, Atlanta, 1991—, media advt. specialist, 1996—; TV host A New Look in Gospel, Atlanta, 1991—; sec. Emory U., Atlanta, 1993-94; owner operator Water Print Media Creations, 1995—. Mem. Atlanta Prevention Connection, Edwin Hawkins Arts & Music Seminar Choir Metro Atlanta chpt.,Gateway Baptist Church youth job training pgm., cons. Avocations: reading, activities with youths, writing, comm. Home: 2968 Chipmunk Trl Marietta GA 30067 Office: PO Box 813056 Smyrna GA 30081-8056

WATERS, DONALD EUGENE, academic administrator; b. Muncie, Ind., Mar. 28, 1941; s. William James and Mary Harriet (Peare) W.; m. Kathryn Elaine Small, Aug. 17, 1963; children: Jill Maras, Janet Schulenburg. BS in Social Studies and English, Ball State U., 1963, MS in Guidance, 1964; EdD in Adminstrn. and Higher Edn., U. Mo., 1973. Dir. residence hall Ball State U., Muncie, 1964-66; asst. dean of students U. No. Iowa, Cedar Falls, 1966-70; with U. Mo., Columbia, 1970-73; dir. community edn. Muscatine (Iowa) Community Coll., 1973-75, dean arts and scis., 1975-77; asst. to pres. Elgin (Ill.) Community Coll., 1977-88, v.p. corp. devel., 1988-96. Councilman City of Elgin, 1980-87; mem. policy steering com. Nat. League of Cities, Washington, 1986-87; v.p., bd. dirs. United Way of Elgin, 1986-94, chair, bd. dirs. Golden Corridor Steering Com., Ill., 1986-90. Mem. Nat. Coun. Resource Devel. (pres. 1993, treas., bd. dirs. 1986-90, Lifetime Svc. award 1994), Ill. Resource Devel. Commn. (pres. 1986-87), Kiwanis (dist. pres. 1983-84). Methodist. Avocations: reading, model trains, exercise, boating.

WATERS, DONALD JOSEPH, information services administrator; b. Balt., Sept. 16, 1952; s. Richard Hunter and Annette Catharine (Hannan) W.; m. Beverly Ann Brent, Apr. 5, 1974; children: Laura Elizabeth, Sarah Elizabeth. BA, U. Md., 1973; M Phil, Yale U., 1976, PhD, 1982. Resource specialist Yale Computer Ctr., New Haven, 1982-84; dir. computer services Yale Sch. Mgmt., New Haven, 1984-87; head, systems office Yale U. Library, New Haven, 1987-92, dir., libr. and adminstrv. systems, 1992-93, assoc. univ. librarian, 1993—. Author: Strange Ways and Sweet Dreams: Afro-American Folklore From the Hampton Institute, 1983. Mem. AAAS, ALA, Am. Soc. Info. Sci. Roman Catholic. Avocations: jazz, rowing, cabinet making. Home: 40 Overbrook Rd Madison CT 06443-1834 Office: Yale U Libr 120 High St New Haven CT 06511-6644

WATERS, GEORGE BAUSCH, newspaper publisher; b. Syracuse, N.Y., July 4, 1920; s. Louis Addison and Mildred Elaine (Bausch) W.; m. Shirley Kessinger Barnard, Sept. 23, 1943; children: Peter, Stephen, Nancy, Kristin, Dean. BA, Syracuse U., 1943. With Rome (N.Y.) Sentinel Co. Pub., 1947—, asst. gen. mgr., 1954-60, gen. mgr., 1960-66, pub., 1966-93, pres., 1993—; bd. dirs. N.Y. State Photonics Devel. Corp. Chmn. Rome Art and Community Ctr., 1967-85; trustee Stevens Kingsley Found., N.Y.C., 1966—, Kirkland Coll., Clinton, N.Y., 1973-79, Utica Coll. Syracuse U., Utica, 1963-78; past mem. Rome Bd. Edn., Rome Hosp.; bd. dirs. Cen. Assn. Blind. Capt. inf. U.S. Army, 1943-47, ETO. Mem. Am. Newspaper Pubs. Assn., N.Y. State Newspaper Pubs. Assn., N.Y. State Associated Dailies (pres. 1974), Am. Soc. Newspaper Editors, Jervis Libr. Assn. (pres. 1959-65), Soc. Profl. Journalists, Ft. Schuyler Club, Yale Club, Washington Press Club, Delta Kappa Epsilon. Republican. Presbyterian. Office: Rome Sentinel Co 333 W Dominick St Rome NY 13440-5701

WATERS, GWENDOLYN, human services administrator; b. Columbus, Ohio, Jan. 10, 1954; d. Harry Amos and Bertha Beatrice (Meadows) W.; 1 child, Harry B. BA, Holy Cross Coll., 1976; postgrad., Capital Law Sch., 1977-79. Income maintenance worker Franklin County Dept. Human Svcs., Columbus, 1977-79; accounts payable clk. Assn. for Developmentally Disabled, Columbus, 1979-80, cmty. aide, 1980-84; mgmt. evaluation reviewer Ohio Dept. Human Svcs., Cleve., 1985-89, pub. assistance coord., 1989—. Violinist Heights Civic Orch., Cleveland Heights, Ohio, 1985-90, pres. bd. dirs., 1990; mem. Libr. of Congress, African Am. Mus., Nat. Mus. of the Am. Indian. Recipient Blue Ribbon, Ohio State Fair, 1978-84, Cuyahoga County Fair, 1985-95, Grand prize Ohio State Fair, 1989-90. Mem. Assn. for Study of African-Am. Life and History, Smithsonian Instn. Avocations: knitting, sewing, reading, playing violin, traveling. Office: Ohio Dept Human Svcs 615 W Superior Ave Ste 990 Cleveland OH 44113-1801

WATERS, H. FRANKLIN, federal judge; b. Hackett, Ark., July 20, 1932; s. William A. and Wilma W.; m. Janie C. Waters, May 31, 1958; children—Carolyn Denise, Melanie Jane, Melissa Ann. B.S., U. Ark., 1955; LL.B., St. Louis U., 1964. Engr., atty. Ralston-Purina Co., St. Louis, 1958-66; ptnr. Crouch, Blair, Cypert & Waters, 1967-81; judge U.S. Dist. Ct. (we. dist.) Ark., from 1981, now chief judge. Former bd. dirs. Springdale Schs.; former bd. govs. Washington Regional Med. Ctr. Mem. ABA, Ark. Bar Assn., Springdale C. of C. (past bd. dirs.). Office: US Dist Ct Rm 523 PO Box 1908 Fayetteville AR 72702-1908

WATERS, JAMES LOGAN, analytical instrument manufacturing executive; b. Lincoln, Nebr., Oct. 7, 1925; s. Leland L. and Marian L. (Yungblut) W.; m. Faith Cabot Pigors, Sept. 11, 1948; children: Richard Cabot, Barbara Faith. B.S., Columbia U., 1946; DSc (hon.), Northeastern U., 1993. Project mgr. Baird Assocs., Inc., Cambridge, Mass., 1947; founder, pres. James L. Waters, Inc., Framingham, Mass., 1947-58, Waters Assocs., Inc., Milford, Mass., 1958-72; chmn. bd. Waters Assocs., Inc., 1972-80; founder, pres. Waters Bus. Systems, Inc., Framingham, 1978—; bd. dirs. Applied Analytical Industries Wilmington, N.C., Transtek Corp., Ellington, Conn. Mem. Framingham Town Meeting, 1952-61; mem. Framingham Sch. Com., 1961-70, chmn., 1962, 64; trustee Babson Coll., Wellesley, Mass., 1979-85; founder, trustee Waters Found., 1955—; trustee Northeastern U., 1984—. Served as ensign USNR, 1943-46. Mem. Tau Beta Pi. Patentee in field. Home: 1153 Grove St Framingham MA 01701-3779 Office: New York Ave Framingham MA 01701

WATERS, JENNIFER NASH, lawyer; b. Bridgeport, Conn., Dec. 21, 1951; d. Lewis William and Patricia (Cousins) W.; m. Todd David Peterson, Sept. 19, 1981; children: Elizabeth, Andrew. BA, Radcliffe, 1972; JD, Harvard, 1976. Bar: D.C. 1977, U.S. Supreme Ct. 1980. Clk. U.S. Ct. Appeals (D.C. cir.), Washington, 1976-77; assoc. Jones, Day, Reavis & Poque, Washington, 1977-79; assoc. Crowell & Moring, Washington, 1979-83, ptnr., 1983—. Mem. Fed. Energy Bar Assn. (bd. dirs. 1988-94, v.p. 1994-95, pres. 1996-97). Office: Crowell & Moring 1001 Pennsylvania Ave NW Washington DC 20004-2505

WATERS, JOHN, film director, writer, actor; b. Balt., Apr. 22, 1946; s. John Samuel and Patricia Ann (Whitaker) W. Student, NYU, 1966. Speaker various colls., comedy clubs, U.S., Europe, Australia, 1968—. Writer, dir. films Roman Candles, 1966, Eat Your Makeup, 1968, Mondo Trasho, 1969, Multiple Maniacs, 1970, Pink Flamingos, 1972, Female Trouble, 1974, Desperate Living, 1977, Polyester, 1981, Cry-Baby, 1990, Serial Mom, 1994; writer, dir., actor film Hairspray, 1987; actor Something Wild, 1988, Homer and Eddie, 1990, (TV show) 21 Jump Street, 1990; author: Shock Value, 1981, Crackpot, 1986, Trash Trio, 1988; contbr. articles to N.Y. Times, Am. Film, other mags. Fund raiser AIDS Action Balt.; spokesperson Anti-Violence Campaign, N.Y.C., 1991. John Waters Day named in his honor State of Md., 1985; John Waters Week named in his honor City of Balt., 1988. Mem. AFTRA, SAG, Dirs. Guild Am., Writers Guild Am., Acad. Motion Picture Arts and Scis. Avocation: study of extreme Catholic behavior before the Reformation.

WATERS, JOHN B., lawyer; b. Sevierville, Tenn., July 15, 1929; s. J. B. and Myrtle (Paine) W.; m. Patsy Temple, Apr. 8, 1953; children: John B., Cynthia Beth. BS, U. Tenn., 1952, JD, 1961, D in Environ. Sci. (hon.), Milligan Coll., 1993. Bar: Tenn. 1961, U.S. Dist. Ct. (ea. dist.) Tenn. 1961, U.S. Dist. Ct. D.C. 1970, U.S. Supreme Ct. 1969. Ptnr. Long, Ragsdale & Waters, P.C., Knoxville, Tenn. Mem. hearing com. Bd. Profl. Responsibility, Supreme Ct., 1974-80, 95—, Fed. co-chmn. Appalachian Regional Commn., 1969-71; chmn. Sevier County Indsl. Bd., Sevierville Library Found.; mem. Gov.'s Com. Econ. Devel.; Tenn. rep. to So. Growth Policies Bd., 1970-74; appointed dir. by Pres. Reagan Tenn. Valley Authority, Knoxville, 1984, appointed chmn. bd. dirs. by Pres. Bush 1992; trustee East Tenn. Baptist Hosp., Knoxville; mem. Tenn.-Tombigbee Waterway Authority, 1978-84; mem. bd. Met. Knoxville Airport Authority; bd. dirs. Inst. Nuclear Power Ops., 1985; chmn. Leadership Sevier, 1996—. Lt. USN, 1952-55. Fellow Am. Bar Found.; mem. Tenn. Bar Assn. (pres. 1983-84), Sevier County Bar Assn. (past pres.). Republican. Baptist. Home: Waters Edge 405 Burridge Dr Sevierville TN 37862 also: 119 Commerce St Sevierville TN 37862-3524

WATERS, JOHN W., minister, educator; b. Atlanta, Feb. 5, 1936; s. Henry and Mary Annie (Randall) W. Cert., U. Geneva, Switzerland, 1962; BA, Fisk U., 1957; STB, Boston U., 1967, PhD, 1970. Ordained to ministry Bapt. Ch., 1967. Min. religious edn. Ebenezer Bapt. Ch., Boston, 1965-67, assoc. min., 1967-69; min. Myrtle Bapt. Ch., West Newton, Mass., 1969, Greater Solid Rock Bapt. Ch., Atlanta, 1980—; prof. Interdenominational Theol. Ctr. , Atlanta, 1976-86, trustee, 1980-83; bd. dirs. Habitat for Humanities, Atlanta, 1984-90; chmn. South Atlanta Joint Urban Ministries, 1983-93. Contbr. articles to profl. jours. Mem. Va. Highlands Neighborhood Assn., Atlanta, 1977-87, Butler St. YMCA, 1980-86, South Atlanta Civic League, 1983, others; treas. Prison Ministries with Women, Inc.; v.p. South Met. Ministries Fellowahip, Atlanta, 1990-94. Fund for Theol. Edn. fellow, 1965-67, Nat. Fellowship Fund fellow, 1968-70, Rockefeller doctoral fellow, 1969. Mem. AAUP (chpt. pres. 1971-72), Am. Acad. Religion, Soc. Bibl. Lit., Blacks in Bibl. Studies, New Era Missionary Bapt. Conf. Ga., So. Bapt. Conv. Democrat. Home: 1516 Niskey Lake Trl SW Atlanta GA 30331-6318 Office: The Greater Solid Rock Bapt Ch 6280 Camp Rd Riverdale GA 30296-2803 *In life, each of us faces a variety of choices. The choices made determine our destiny, fate. When more of us assume responsibility and accountability for the choices made, the world in which we live will be decisively better.*

WATERS, LAUGHLIN EDWARD, federal judge; b. L.A., Aug. 16, 1914; s. Frank J. and Ida (Bauman) W.; m. Voula Davanis, Aug. 22, 1953; children: Laughlin Edward, Maura Kathleen, Deirdre Mary, Megan Ann, Eileen Brigid. A.B., UCLA, 1939; J.D., U. So. Calif., 1946. Bar: Calif. 1946. Dep. atty. gen. Calif., Los Angeles, 1946-47; individual practice law Los Angeles, 1947-53; sr. ptnr. Nossaman, Waters, Krueger & Marsh, 1961-76; U.S. atty. So. Dist. Calif., 1953-61; judge U.S. Dist. Ct. (cen. dist.) Calif., 1976—; cons. U.S. Dept. State in London, 1970; mem. U.S. Del. to Conf. Environ. Problems in Prague, 1971, White House Conf. on Aging, 1970-71; sr. dist. judge rep. Jud. Coun.; judge Atty Gen.'s Adv. Inst. Mem. Calif. Legislature, 1946-53; vice chmn. Rep. State Ctrl. Com., 1950-51, chmn., 1952-53; bd. dirs. Legal Aid Found., 1954-60; past pres. Cath. Big Brothers. Served as capt. U.S. Army, 1942-46. Decorated Bronze Star with oak leaf cluster, Purple Heart with oak leaf cluster, Combat Inf. badge. Fellow Am. Bar Found., Am. Coll. Trial Lawyers; mem. ABA (chmn. com. on housing and urban devel. 1977-79), Fed. Bar Assn. (founder, past pres.), L.A. County Bar Assn., Am. Judicature Soc., Assn. Bus. Trial Lawyers, U. So. Calif., UCLA Law Assn., Am. Legion , U. So. Calif. Legion Lex, Order Blue Shield, Town Hall, Polish Order Merit Cross with Swords, Hon. Citizen of Chambois, Trun, France, 10th Polish Dragoons (hon.), Soc. Friendly Sons St. Patrick (past pres., Medallion of Merit award), Knights of Malta, Anchor Club, Calif. Club, L.A. Club (past pres.). Roman Catholic. Office: US Dist Ct 255 E Temple St Los Angeles CA 90012-3334

WATERS, LOU, anchorman, correspondent; b. Mpls., July 7, 1938; s. Louis Joseph and Anne Marie Riegert; m. Martha Lee Morin Waters, Feb. 15, 1975; children: Scott, Christopher, Alexander. Student, U. Minn. Reporter Sta. KDWB, Mpls., 1959, Sta. WWTC, Mpls., Sta. KFWB, L.A., Sta. WLBS-FM, N.Y.C., Sta. KNEW, San Francisco; reporter, anchor Sta. KVOA-TV, Tucson, news dir.; news dir. Sta. KCST-TV, San Diego; asst. sta. mgr., evening anchor Sta. KOLD-TV, CBS, Tucson; co-anchor CNN Today CNN, Atlanta, 1980—, co-anchor Earlyprime, 1991—. Avocations: golf, photography, music. Office: CNN One CNN Ctr Atlanta GA 30348

WATERS, M. BRUCE, engineering technician; b. Houston, Apr. 17, 1950; s. Wayland O. and Snellah G. (Holt) W.; m. Jean H. Sudduth, June 26, 1971; 1 child, Tegan Joy. Student, La. State U., 1968-69, 70-74, U. Houston, 1969, San Jacinto Jr. Coll., Deer Park, Tex., 1969. Engrng. aide I La. Dept. Highways, Baton Rouge, 1971-73, engrng. aide II, 1973-74; sta. mgr. Cliff Brice Gas Stas., Boulder, Colo., 1975; mill worker Red Dale Coach, Longmont, Colo., 1975; engrng. aide B Colo. Dept. Highways, Boulder, 1975-76, engrng. aide C, 1976-91, engrng tech. I, 1991—. Blood donor Belle Bonfils, Boulder, Colo., 1975—; mem. Vols. for Outdoor Colo.; sec. Libertarian Party of Boulder County, 1991-93, 95-96. Eagle Scout, 1967. Mem. Nat. Inst. Cert. Engrng. Techs., Chpt. C Freewheelers (sec. 1993-95), Am. Motorcyclist Assn., Soc. for Preservation and Encouragement of Barbershop Quartet Singing in Am. Avocations: collecting antique motorcycles, skiing, reading, music. Office: Colo Dept Transp 1050 Lee Hill Dr Boulder CO 80302-9404

WATERS, MAXINE, congresswoman; b. St. Louis, Aug. 15, 1938; d. Remus and Velma (Moore) Carr; m. Sidney Williams, July 23, 1977; children: Edward, Karen. Grad. in sociology Calif. State U., L.A.; hon. doctorates, Spelman Coll., N.C. Agrl. & Tech. State U., Morgan State U. Former tchr. Head Start; mem. Calif. Assembly from dist. 48, 1976-91, Dem. caucus chair, 1984; mem. 102nd-105th Congresses from Dist. 35, Calif., 1991—; mem. Banking, Fin., Urban Affairs com., Ho. subcom. on banking, capitol subcom. on banking, employment and tng. subcom. on vets., veterans affairs com. Mem. Dem. Nat. Com., Dem. Congrl. Campaign com.; del. Dem. Nat. Conv., 1972, 76, 80, 84, 88, 92, mem. rules com. 1984; mem. Nat. Adv. Com. for Women, 1978—; bd. dirs. TransAfrica Found., Nat. Women's Polit. Caucus, Ctr. Nat. Policy, Clara Elizabeth Jackson Carter Found. Spellman Coll., Nat. Minority AIDS Project, Women for a Meaningful Summit, Nat. Coun. Negro Women, Black Women's Agenda; founder Black Women's Forum. Office: US Ho of Reps 2344 Rayburn Washington DC 20515*

WATERS, RICHARD, retired publishing company executive; b. Sterling, Mass., May 13, 1926; s. Sherman Hoar and Viola (Arnold) W.; m. June Hollweg Dorer, Aug. 27, 1949; children: Karl (dec.), Kurt, Kris. B.A., Hobart Coll., 1950, LL.D. hon., 1970; M.B.A., Harvard U., 1951. Assoc. acct. Hunter & Weldon, N.Y.C., 1953-55; exec. v.p., chief fin. officer Reader's Digest Assn., Pleasantville, N.Y., 1955-77; assoc. dean Harvard U. Bus. Sch., Boston, 1977-81; pres., chief exec. officer Sporting News, St. Louis, 1981-90, ret., 1990; bd. dirs. Republic Bank for Savs. (formerly Manhattan Savs. Bank), N.Y.C., Republic Nat. Bank, N.Y.C. Trustee Hobart Coll., 1971-91, William Smith Coll., 1971-91; regional v.p. Associated Industries N.Y. State, Albany, 1965-79; chmn. bd. Westchester Heart Assn., Port Chester, N.Y., 1975-76; bd. dirs., vice-chmn. Gateway chpt. Nat. Multiple Sclerosis Soc., 1991-95, chmn., 1996—. With USN, 1944-46, PTO; 1st lt. USAF, 1951-53. Mem. Nat. Assn. Pub. Accts.; mem Baseball Writers Assn. Am. Republican. Clubs: Old Warson Country; University (St. Louis); Sky (N.Y.C.). Home: 20 Somerset Downs Saint Louis MO 63124-1007

WATERS, ROGER, rock musician; b. Cambridge, England, Sept. 6, 1947. Bassist Sigma-6, T-Set, Megga Death, Screaming Abdabs, Pink FLoyd Sound, Pink Floyd, 1964-86; solo musician, 1987—. Albums include Music from the Body, 1970, The Pros & Cons of Hitchhiking, 1986, Radio KAOS, 1987, The Wall: Berlin 1990, 1990, Amused to Death, 1992; (with Pink Floyd) Piper at the Gates of Dawn, 1967, More, 1969, Atom Heart Mother, 1970, Relics, 1971, Darkside of the Moon, 1973, Wish You Were Here, 1976, The FInal Cut, 1983, A Collection of Great Dance Songs, 1994, The Division Bell, 1994, (with Jeff Beck, Don Henley, others) Amused to Death. Office: Columbia Records 550 Madison Ave New York NY 10019*

WATERS, RONALD W., educator, church executive, pastor; b. Kokomo, Ind., July 23, 1951; s. Ronald Lee and Carolyn Elizabeth (Myers) W.; m. Norma Lee Grumbling Waters, June 16, 1973; 1 child, Melinda Ronee Waters. BA magna cum laude, Ashland (Ohio) Coll., 1973; MA in Comms. with high honors, Wheaton (Ill.) Coll., 1975; MDiv with high honors, Ashland (Ohio) Theol. Seminary, 1985; postgrad., Asbury Theol. Seminary, Wilmore, Ky., 1993—. Ordained elder Brethren Ch., 1986; lic. minister, 1985-86. Asst. to dir. Bd. of Christian Edn. The Brethren Ch., Ashland, Ohio, 1971-74; mng. editor of publs. Brethren Pub. Co., Ashland, Ohio, 1975-78, asst. to dir. and gen. mgr., 1978-80, exec. dir., 1980-82; dir. of Denom. Bus. The Brethren Ch. Nat. Office, Ashland, Ohio, 1982-84; cons. in mgmt. and computer applications, 1984-85; pastor Mt. Olive Brethren Ch., McGaheyville, Va., 1985-89; dir. Brethren Ch. Ministries The Brethren Ch. Nat. Office, Ashland, Ohio, 1989-95; asst. prof. evangelism Ashland (Ohio) Theol. Sem., 1996—; cons. for evangelism and ch. growth The Brethren Ch. Nat. Office, Ashland, 1996—; bd. dirs. corp. sec. Brethern Printing Co., Ashland, 1989-96; mem. mission bd. Brethren Ch. Southeastern Dist., 1987-89; mem. statement of faith task force Gen. Conf. Brethern Ch., 1981-84, polity com. 1986-91, bd. ref. congl. adv. The Andrew Ctr., Elgin, Ill., 1994—; founder, tchr. Young Adult Sunday Sch. class Park St Brethern Ch., Ashland, 1990-93; adv. com. Ashland Theol. Sem., 1990-95; mem. Evangelism Mgmt. Team, Elgin, 1992—; spkr. in field. Author: Promise for the Future, 1993, Leader's Manual for Inviting and Welcoming New People, 1995; editor: The Brethren Evangelist mag., 1975-78, New Beginnings mag., 1995—; contbr. numerous articles to religious jours. Adv. coun. World Relief Corp., Wheaton, Ill., 1990-92. Mem. Am. Soc. Ch. Growth, Nat. Assn. Brethern Ch. Elders, Acad. Evangelism Theol. Edn. Avocation: gardening. Office: Ashland Theological Sem 910 Center St Ashland OH 44805-4007

WATERS, RUDOLPH EARL, university administrator; b. Brookhaven, Miss., May 21, 1932; s. Leonard Douglas and Annie Mae (Thadison) W.; m. Kathleen Graham; children Rudolph E. Jr., Veronica. BSC, DePaul U., 1954; EdM, Boston U., 1958; PhD, Kans. State U., 1977. Registrar Utica (Miss.) Jr. Coll., 1954-55, dean of instrn., 1955-57; dean of students Alcorn State U., Lorman, Miss., 1957-58; dean of instrn. Alcorn State U., Lorman, 1958-70, coord. of title III programs, 1967-75, v.p., 1970-93, exec. v.p., 1993—, interim pres., 1994-95; mem. adv. com. So. Growth Policies Bd., 1995—. Alumni fellow Kans. State U., 1988. Mem.ASCD, Am. Assn. for Higher Edn., Nat. Soc. for the Study of Edn., Am. Assn. of Univ. Adminstrs., Phi Delta Kappa (chpt. pres. 1992), Delta Mu Delta, Sigma Pi Phi. Home: RR 2 Box 29C Lorman MS 39096-9705 Office: Alcorn State U 1000 Asu Dr # 329 Lorman MS 39096-9400

WATERS, SYLVIA, dance company artistic director. Prin. dance Alvin Ailey Am. Dance Theater, N.Y.C.; artistic dir. Alvin Ailey Repertory Ensemble, N.Y.C., 1974—. Office: Alvin Ailey Repertory Ensemble 211 W 61st St Fl 3 New York NY 10023-7832*

WATERS, WILLIE ANTHONY, opera and orchestra conductor; b. Goulds, Fla., Oct. 11, 1951. BMus, U. Miami, 1973; postgrad., Memphis State U. Music dir. Greater Miami (Fla.) Opera, 1983-84, artistic dir., 1984-92, prin. condr., 1992-95; music dir. San Antonio Festival, 1983-85; guest condr. Detroit Symphony, Indpls. Orch., Norwegian Radio Orch., Philharm. Orch. Fla., Essen Philharm., Bavarian Radio Orch., Baden-Baden Radio Orch., Cologne Opera. Condr. San Diego Opera, Mich. Opera Theatre, Conn. Opera, San Francisco Opera, Australian Opera, Sydney, Ópera De Montréal; conducted Otello, Salome, Die Walkure, Bianca e Falliero (U.S. premiere), other operas; appeared in concert with Detroit Symphony, Norwegian Radio Orch., Fla. Philharm., Dayton Philharm., Brucknerhaus Orch., Linz, Austria; rec. Philips Co. Recipient Prix de Martell, 1991. Office: care John J Miller 801 W 181st St Apt 20 New York NY 10033-4518*

WATERSTON, SAMUEL ATKINSON, actor; b. Cambridge, Mass., Nov. 15, 1940; s. George Chychele and Alice Tucker (Atkinson) W.; m. Lynn Louisa Woodruff, Jan. 26, 1976; children: Graham C., Elisabeth P., Katherine B.; child by previous marriage: James S. B.A., Yale U., 1962; student, Sorbonne, Paris, 1960-61. Theatrical appearances include: Indians, Oh Dad Poor Dad, Halfway Up the Tree, Lunch Hour, Hamlet, The Tempest, Measure for Measure, Much Ado About Nothing (Obie, Drama Desk awards), Benefactors, 1986, A Walk in the Woods, 1988, Abe Lincoln in Illinois, 1993-94 (Drama League award 1994), Shakespeare & Szekspir, 1994; film appearances include: The Great Gatsby, 1975, Rancho Deluxe, 1976, Capricorn One, 1978, Interiors, 1978, Sweet William, 1978, Heaven's Gate, 1979, Eagle's Wing, 1983, The Killing Fields, 1984 (Acad. nomination best leading actor), Warning Sign, 1985, Savages, Hopscotch, 1980, Hannah and Her Sisters, 1986, Just Between Friends, 1986, The Devil's Paradise, September, 1987, Welcome Home, 1989, Crimes and Misdemeanors, 1990, Captive in the Land, 1990, Crimes and Misdemeanors, The Man in the Moon, 1991, Mindwalk, 1991, Serial Mom, 1994, Nixon, 1995, Proprietor, 1996, Shadow Conspiracy, 1997; TV films include: Much Ado About Nothing, 1974, The Glass Menagerie, 1975, Diabolique, 1975, Friendly Fire, 1978, Oppenheimer, 1982; TV series Q.E.D., 1982, Terrorist on Trial: The United States vs. Salim Ajami; TV miniseries appearance: Oppenheimer, 1980, 82, Gore Vidal's Lincoln, 1988, Nightmare Years, 1989, Lost Civilizations, 1995 (Emmy award for best documentary 1996); regular TV series Q.E.D., 1979, I'll Fly Away, NBC-TV, 1991-93 (Emmy award nomination, Lead actor, Drama, 1993), I'll Fly Away: Then and Now, PBS, 1993 (Emmy nomination, Lead Actor - Special, 1994), Law and Order. 1994—. Mem.

Actors Equity Assn., Screen Actors Guild, AFTRA. Office: care Addis/Wechsler & Assocs 955 Carrillo Dr Fl 3 Los Angeles CA 90048-5400

WATERSTON, WILLIAM KING, minister, educator, academic administrator; b. Elizabeth, N.J., Feb. 12, 1937; s. John Robert and Sylvia (Eadie) W.; m. Judith Jane Schramm, Aug. 29, 1959; children: John Scott, Gregory Glenn, Robert Ormsby; m. Kathryn Larsen, Dec. 17, 1983; 1 child, Chad. AB, Bates Coll., 1959; BD, Eastern Bapt. Sem., 1962, M.Div., 1973. Ordained to ministry Am. Bapt. Chs. USA, 1962. Bus. mgr., editorial asst. Missions Mag., 1962-66, Crusader Mag., 1964-66; assoc. dir. radio and TV Am. Bapt. Chs. USA, 1966-69, dir. electronic media, 1969-72; host Dialogue TV Show, Phila., 1969-85; assoc. dir. communications div. Am. Bapt. Chs. USA, 1972-73; Parker Ford Bapt. Ch., 1973-81; dir. group homes ch. rels. devel. Bapt. Children's Svcs., Phila., 1981-92; sr. minister First Bapt. Warren, Warren, Pa., 1992-95; pres. Warren County Ministerium, 1971-85; instr. Eastern Bapt. Coll., 1973-85, Eastern Bapt. Sem., 1970-85. Editor Mediathink, 1973. Lodge: Rotary (pres. Cen. Perkiomen 1968). Home: 747 Ball Ave Watertown NY 13601 Office: First Baptist Watertown 207 State St Watertown NY 13601-2604

WATHEN, DANIEL EVERETT, state supreme court chief justice; b. Easton, Maine, Nov. 4, 1939; s. Joseph Jackson and Wilda Persis (Dow) W.; m. Judith Carol Foren, July 14, 1960; children: Julanne Carol, Daniel Arthur. AB, Ricker Coll., 1962; JD, U. Maine, 1965; LLM (hon.), U. Va. Law Sch., 1988. Bar: Maine 1965. Atty. Wathen & Wathen, Augusta, Maine, 1965-77; trial judge Superior Ct. Maine, Augusta, 1977-81; appellate judge Supreme Jud. Ct. Maine, Augusta, 1981-92; state chief justice Supreme Jud. Ct. Maine, 1992—.

WATHNE, CARL NORMAN, hospital administrator; b. Johnstown, Pa., Oct. 16, 1930; s. Odd and Alice (Anderson) W.; m. Alice Adele Tucker, Jan. 25, 1958; children: John M., Carl K. BS, U. Pitts., 1952; MS, Columbia U., 1958. Asst. adminstr. Bayonne (N.J.) Hosp., 1958-60; assoc. adminstr. Binghamton (N.Y.) Gen. Hosp., 1960-63; chief exec. officer Putnam Community Hosp., Carmel, N.Y., 1963-65; v.p. A.J.J. Rourke, Inc., New Rochelle, N.Y., 1965-72; exec. dir. Lahey Clinic, Boston, 1972-79; pres., chief exec. officer Leonard Morse Health System, Natick, Mass., 1980-85, Leominster (Mass.) Health System, 1985-92; pres. Wathne Health Strategists, 1992—; adj. asst. prof. Boston U., 1981—; pres. Cen. New Eng. PHO, Leominster, 1991-92; hosp. cons. Contbr. articles to profl. jours. Mem. Mass. Hosp. Assn. (pres. 1987-88, chmn. 1987), New Eng. Hosp. Supts. Club (pres. 1986-88), North Cen. Mass. C. of C. (dir. 1988-91). Avocations: painting, sailing, photography. Home: 6 Colony Rd Lexington MA 02173-2004 Office: Wathne Health Strategists 9 Warren St Salem MA 01970-3119

WATKIN, DAVID, film director, cinematographer; b. Margate, Eng., Mar. 23, 1925. Filmmaker, 1948—; asst. cameraman Brit. Transport Films, 1950-55, cameraman, 1955-61; ind. filmmaker, 1961—. Motion pictures include The Knack, 1964, Help!, 1965, Marat/Sade, 1966, How I Won the War, 1967, Charge of the Light Brigade, 1968, Catch 22, 1970, The Devils, 1971, The Boyfriend, 1971, The Homecoming, A Delicate Balance, 1973, The Three Musketeers, 1974, The Four Musketeers, 1976, Jesus of Nazareth, Mahogany, 1975, To The Devil a Daughter, 1976, Robin and Marian, 1976, Joseph Andrews, 1977, Cuba, 1979 Endless Love, 1981, Chariots of Fire, 1981, Yentil, 1983, The Hotel New Hampshire, 1984, White Nights, 1985, Out of Africa (Acad. award 1985), Return of Oz, 1985, Sky Bandits, 1986, Moonstruck, 1987, The Good Mother, 1988, Masquerade, 1988, Memphis Belle, 1990, Hamlet, 1990, An Object of Beauty, 1991, The Cabinet of Dr. Ramirez, 1991, Used People, 1992, The Boy's Life, 1993, Bopha, 1993, Milk Money, 1993, Jane Eyre, 1994, Bogus, 1995, Night Falls on Manhatten, 1995, Through Roses, 1996, Critical Care, 1996, Critical Care, 1996. Home: 6 Sussex Mews, Brighton BN2 1GZ, England

WATKINS, BIRGE SWIFT, real estate investment executive; b. Grand Rapids, Mich., May 2, 1949; s. Robert Goodell and Betty Jane (Swift) W.; m. Elizabeth Beverly Price, Nov. 28, 1985; children: Elizabeth Porter, Benjamin Thorne Swift, Robert William MacIntosh. BA, Alma Coll., 1971; MBA, London Bus. Sch., 1981; MPA, Harvard U., 1989. Staff asst. to Pres. of U.S. Washington, 1974-77; congl. press sec. U.S. Ho. of Reps., Washington, 1977; v.p. Arbor Internat. Inc., McLean, Va., 1980-81; asst. office dir. AID, Washington, 1982-88; asst. dir. Pres.'s Task Force on Internal Pvt. Enterprise, Washington, 1983-85; dep. asst. sec. USDA, Washington, 1989-90; dir. investor outreach Resolution Trust Corp., Washington, 1991-94; ptnr. Benton Resources, Washington, 1994-95; cons. Com Mac, Washington, 1995; mng. dir. Thornfalcon Internat., 1996—; bd. dirs. Corp. Healthcare Svcs. Inc., Springfield, Va., Asia Forum - Japan; cons. Washington Campus Inc., 1977, Va. Med. Assocs. Inc., Springfield, 1988. Mem. campaign staff Reagan-Bush campaign, Washington, 1980, Bush for President, 1988; mem. transition team office of Pres.-elect Bush, 1988. Mem. Urban Land Inst., Harvard Club (Washington). Avocations: skiing, running, contemporary art. Home: 832 Blackwell Rd Warrenton VA 20186-2216 Office: 832 Blackwell Rd Warrenton VA 20186-2216

WATKINS, CARLTON GUNTER, retired pediatrician; b. Wilmington, N.C., Aug. 25, 1919; s. Edison Lee and Maysie (Gunter) W.; m. Charlotte Jean Metcalf, Mar. 21, 1943; children—Lloyd Dixon Hollingsworth, Carlton Gunter, Mary Melissa, Charlotte Lou. A.B., U. N.C., 1939; M.D., Washington U., St. Louis, 1943. Rotating intern, asst. resident, resident pediatrics St. Louis City Hosp., 1943-45; resident pediatrics Duke Hosp., 1945-46; pvt. practice Charlotte, N.C., 1946-51, 53-73; chmn. dept. pediatrics Charlotte Meml. Hosp., 1958-61, 63-67; founder, sr. mem. Charlotte Pediatric Clinic, 1963-73; med. dir. Mecklenburg Center for Human Devel., Charlotte, 1973-89. Contbr. articles to med. jours. Pres. Charlotte-Mecklenburg Assn. for Children with Learning Disabilities, 1971-73, Mecklenburg Sr. Dems., 1993-94; mem. profl. adv. bd. Epilepsy Assn. N.C., 1976-86, v.p., 1986-88; mem. cons. bd. CPC Cedar Spring Hosp., 1992-98; mem. Charlotte-Mecklenburg Bd. Edn., 1966-74, Mecklenburg Human Svcs. Coun., 1994—; mem. Mecklenburg Surface Water Investigation Mgmt., 1997—. Capt. M.C., U.S. Army, 1951-53. Fellow Am. Acad. Pediatrics (life); mem. AMA (life), N.C. Med. Soc., Mecklenburg County Med. Soc., N.C. Pediatric Soc., Charlotte Pediatric Soc. (founder, 1st sec. 1950, pres. 1962), N.C. PTA (life), N.C. Zool. Soc. (life), Friends of U. N.C. Charlotte (life), Alpha Kappa Kappa, Old Catawba (Charlotte) Club. Home: 8713 Gainsford Ct Charlotte NC 28210-5850

WATKINS, CAROL CHARLES, hotel, timeshare, apartments and shopping center executive, fundraiser; b. Walsenberg, Colo., Sept. 7, 1933; d. Iestyn Martin and Marion Lucretia (Lammé) Charles; m. James McKenzie Watkins, Sept. 11, 1954; children: Kathleen Watkins Leeger, Kristina Watkins McCubbins, James M. Jr., Karen Charisse Watkins Vafiadis. Student, U. Oreg., U. Wyo. Worked in display advt. San Dieguito Citizen newspaper, Visalia Times-Delta, 1966-68; co-owner Winners Circle Resorts Internat., Calif., 1968—; freelance writer; establisher chain pie shops including Mr. Pie Man, The Sugar Plum, 4 art galleries including Vintage Press, Christmas Carol's, Destiny Gallery, Grunion's Run. Contbr. articles to newspapers. First chairwoman J. F. Duffy Sheriff Found. Benefit, Del Mar, Calif., 1984; chairperson, tournament dir. Bacharach-Shoemaker Horsemen's Benevolent and Protective Assn., Celebrity Tennis Charities,; founder Turn in a Pusher program, So. Calif.; chairwoman Bruce Jenner Benefit for Free Arts Clinic for Battered and Abused Children; hon. dep. San Diego Sheriff; fundraiser San Dieguito Boys and Girls Club, YMCA, Guide Dogs of the Desert, Caine Companions. Mem. Del Mar (Calif.) C. of C. (Woman of the Year 1981), A.A., Toastmasters, Laughmasters, Rotary Internat. (Paul Harris fellow), Kappa Kappa Gamma. Avocations: professional and amateur theatre, painting, writing, dress designing, tennis. Home: 16043 Via Del Alba PO Box 1262 Rancho Santa Fe CA 92067 Office: Winners Circle Resorts Internat P O Box 99 Statford 58 Del Mar CA 92014

WATKINS, CATHY COLLINS, corporate purchasing agent; b. Memphis, Sept. 20, 1952; d. Amos Verlyn and Ruby Etoile (Mayo) Collins; m. Lewis McGill Watkins Jr., May 21, 1988. AA, Clarke Coll., 1972; BMus, William Carey Coll., 1974. Sales assoc., mgr. inventory and receiving Waldoff's Inc., Hattiesburg, Miss., 1974-80; buyer Forrest Gen. Hosp., Hattiesburg, 1980-81; asst. mgr. Ward's Fast Food of Laurel (Miss.), Inc., 1981-82; buyer, sole purchasing agent Eagle Distbrs., Hattiesburg, 1982-85; inventory coord., purchasing agent Miss. Music, Inc., Hattiesburg, 1985—. Photographer campus yearbook Carey Crusader, 1974; editor: (newsletter) Mississippi Bandmaster, 1988—. Mem. Nat. Assn. Music Merchants. Baptist. Avocations: music, cooking, needlework. Home: 105 Elaine Cir Hattiesburg MS 39402-3305 Office: Miss Music Inc PO Box 1705 222 S Main Hattiesburg MS 39401

WATKINS, CHARLES BOOKER, JR., mechanical engineering educator; b. Petersburg, Va., Nov. 20, 1942; s. Charles Booker and Haseltine Lucy (Thurston) W.; m. Judith Griffin; children: Michael, Steven. B.S. in Mech. Engrng. cum laude, Howard U., 1964; M.S., U. N.Mex., 1966, Ph.D., 1970. Registered profl. engr., D.C. Mem. tech. staff Sandia Nat. Labs., Albuquerque, 1964-71; asst. prof. dept. mech. engrng. Howard U., Washington, 1971-73; prof., chmn. dept. mech. engrng. Howard U., 1973-86; Herbert G. Keyser prof. mech. engrng. dean Sch. Engrng. CCNY, 1986—; cons. U.S. Army, U.S. Navy, NSF, pvt. industries, 1984-85; bd. dirs. Parsons Brinkerhoff, Inc., 1994—. Research grantee NSF, U.S. Navy, Nuclear Regulatory Commn.; research grantee Dept. Energy, NASA; recipient Ralph R. Teetor award Soc. Automotive Engrs., 1980; Sandia Labs. doctoral fellow; NDEA fellow. Fellow ASME, AIAA (assoc.); mem. AAAS, Soc. Automotive Engrs., Am. Soc. Engrng. Edn., Sigma Xi, Omega Psi Phi, Tau Beta Pi. Home: 171 Sherman Ave Teaneck NJ 07666-4121 Office: CCNY Sch Engrng Convent Ave New York NY 10031

WATKINS, CHARLES REYNOLDS, medical equipment company executive; b. San Diego, Oct. 28, 1951; s. Charles R. and Edith A. (Muff) W.; children: Charles Devin, Gregory Michael. BS, Lewis and Clark Coll., 1974; postgrad., U. Portland, 1976. Internat. salesman Hyster Co., Portland, Oreg., 1975-80, Hinds Internat. Corp., Portland, 1980-83; mgr. internat. sales Wade Mfg. Co., Tualatin, Oreg., 1983-84; regional sales mgr. U.S. Surg., Inc., Norwalk, Conn., 1984-86; nat. sales mgr. NeuroCom Internat., Inc., Clackamas, Oreg., 1986-87; pres. Wave Form Systems, Inc., Portland, 1987—. Bd. dirs. Portland World Affairs Coun., 1980. Mem. Am. Soc. Laser Medicine and Surgery, Am. Fertility Soc., Am. Assn. Gynecol. Laparoscopists, Portland City Club. Republican. Avocations: flying, photography, travel. Office: Wave Form Systems Inc PO Box 3195 Portland OR 97208-3195

WATKINS, CHERYL DENISE, special education educator; b. Chgo., Dec. 15, 1963; d. Henry Eugene and Jean (Ingram) W. BS Edn. in Spl. Edn., Chgo. State U., 1987; MEd, U. Ill., 1992. Tchr. children with spl. needs Chgo. Bd. Edn., 1987—; cons. in field; adj. faculty Columbia Coll., Chgo., 1993, Nat. Louis U., Chgo. State U., Elmhurst Coll.; spkr. edn1. topics Chgo., St. Louis, Ill., Iowa, Fla., Md., Ala., Tex. Author: You Can Do Anything: A Story for Ryan, 1993, Living with Autism, 1995. Vol. workshops Cabrini Green Tutoring Program, Chgo. Recipient Golden Apple award Golden Apple Found., 1991, Disting. Alumni award Nat. Assn. for Equal Opportunity in Higher Edn./Chgo. State U., 1992, Kizzy award, 1992, Tchr. Achiever award Michael Jordan Found. Edn. Club, 1993, Swanegan Tchr. award Trinity United Ch. of Christ, 1996, Kathy Osterman award for superior pub. svc., Chgo., 1997; named Outstanding Young Woman in Am., 1986. Mem. Nat. Bd. Profl. Teaching Standards (spl. needs com.), Kappa Delta Pi, Phi Delta Kappa, Delta Sigma Theta. Avocations: roller skating, reading, cake decorating, writing, traveling.

WATKINS, CURTIS WINTHROP, artist; b. Pontiac, Mich., Apr. 9, 1946; s. Robert James and Arvella Marquitta (Chenoweth) W.; student Ann Arbor Art Center, 1964-66, Kendall Sch. Design, 1966-68, Kraus Hypnosis Center, 1966, 70, Arons Ethical Hypnosis Tng. Center, 1977; m. Gayle Lynn Blom, Dec. 19, 1975; 1 dau., Darcy Ann. Illustrator, instr. Ann Arbor Art Center, 1969-71; owner, dir. Hypno-Art Research Center and Studio, Howell, Mich., 1971—; research on visualization process of subconscious by doing art work under hypnosis; lectr. hypnosis convs. and schs.; one-man shows include: LeVern's Gallery, 1969, Rackham Gallery, 1973, Hartland Gallery, 1974, Platt Gallery, 1975, Detroit Artists Guild Gallery, 1975, Golden Gallery, 1977, Cromaine Gallery, 1982, Driggett Gallery, 1982, Mill Gallery, 1983, Walnut Street Gallery, 1983, Merrill Gallery, 1986, Corbino Gallery, 1986, VanAntwerp, 1991; group shows include Mich. All-State Show, 1980, Mich. State Fine Arts Exhibit, 1980, Washington Internat., 1981, Lansing Art Gallery (Mich.), 1981, Capitol City Arts Show, 1981, Mich. Ann., 1981, Mich. Ann., 1982-83; illustrator: Handbook of Hypnotic Techniques, 1988; bd. dirs. 9th Ann. Hartland Art Show, 1975, Livingston Arts and Crafts Assn., 1977-79, Hartland Art Council, 1974-78. Recipient Dr. Garland H. Fross award, 1989, numerous awards of excellence in art. Mem. Internat. Soc. Artists, Assn. Advance Ethical Hypnosis, Am. Assn. Profl. Hypnologists, Internat. Soc. Profl. Hypnosis, Internat. Platform Assn. Presbyterian. Home and Studio: 1749 Pinckney Rd Howell MI 48843-8825

WATKINS, DAYTON J., federal agency administrator. BA in Econs., Howard U.; BS in Acctg., U. Md.; MA in Mgmt. and Adminstrn., Ctrl. Mich. U.; MBA, Mount Vernon Coll. Economist U.S. Dept. of Transp., 1972-74; various fin. positions, 1974-76; acad. advisor U. Md., 1976-78; prin. acctg. firm, 1987; asst. treas./cash mgr. D.C. Dept. of Fin. and Revenue, 1978-80, dept. comptr., 1980-82, chief real estate taxation divsn., 1982-84; exec. asst. to the dir. D.C. Dept. of Housing and Community Devel., 1984-86, gen. mgr. bur. of real estate, 1986-90; acting dep. dir. of program ops., 1990-92; acting SBA adminstr. U.S. SBA, 1993, coun. to the adminstr., 1993-94; with Dept. Agrl. Rural Bus. and Coopr Svc., Washington, 1994—. Office: Dept of Agrl Rural Bus & Coop Svc 14th & Independence Ave SW Washington DC 20250

WATKINS, DEAN ALLEN, electronics executive, educator; b. Omaha, Oct. 23, 1922; s. Ernest E. and Pauline (Simpson) W.; m. Bessie Ena Hansen, June 28, 1944; children—Clark Lynn, Alan Scott, Eric Ross. B.S., Iowa State Coll., 1944; M.S., Calif. Inst. Tech., 1947; Ph.D., Stanford, 1951. Engr. Collins Radio Co., 1947-48; mem. staff Los Alamos Lab., 1948-49; tech. staff Hughes Research Labs., 1951-53; asso. prof. elec. engring. Stanford, 1953-56; prof., dir. Electron Devices Lab., 1956-64, lectr. elec. engring., 1964-70; co-founder, pres., chief exec. officer, dir. Watkins Johnson Co., Palo Alto, Calif., 1957-67; chmn., chief exec. officer, dir. Watkins Johnson Co., 1967-80, chmn., dir., 1980—; cons. Dept. Def., 1956-66; mem. White House Sci. Coun., 1988-89. Patentee in field; contbr. articles to profl. jours. Legis. chmn., dir. San Meteo County Sch. Bds. Assn., 1959-69; gov. San Francisco Bay Area Coun., 1966-75; Rep. precinct capt. Portola Valley, 1964; vice chmn. San Mateo County Fin. Com., 1967-69; mem. Calif. Rep. Ctrl. Com., 1964-68; trustee Stanford, 1966-69; regent U. Calif., 1969-96, chmn., 1972-74; mem. governing bd. Sequoia Union H.S. Dist., 1964-68, chmn., 1967-68; mem. governing bd. Portola Valley Sch. Dist., 1958-66; mem. bd. overseers Hoover Instn. on War, Revolution and Peace, Stanford, 1969—, chmn., 1971-73, 85-86; adv. policy commn. Santa Clara County Jr. Achievement; trustee Nat. Security Indsl. Assn., 1965-78. Served from pvt. to 1st lt. C.E., O.R.C. AUS, 1943-46. Fellow IEEE (7th region Achievement award 1957, Frederik Philips award 1981), AAAS; mem. Am. Phys. Soc., Am. Mgmt. Assn., Western Electronic Mfrs. Assn. (chmn. San Francisco coun. 1967, v.p., dir.), Calif. C. of C. (dir. 1965-92, treas. 1978, pres. 1981), Nat. Acad. Engring., Mounted Patrol San Mateo County (spl. dep. sheriff 1960-70), San Mateo County Horseman's Assn., San Benito County Farm Bur., Calif. Cattlemen's Assn., Delta Upsilon. Clubs: Palo Alto (Palo Alto), University (Palo Alto); Shack Riders (San Mateo County); Commonwealth (San Francisco); Rancheros Visitadores. Office: Watkins-Johnson Co 3333 Hillview Ave Palo Alto CA 94304-1204

WATKINS, GEORGE DANIELS, physics educator; b. Evanston, Ill., Apr. 28, 1924; s. Paul F. and Lois V. (Daniels) W.; m. Carolyn Lenore Nevin, June 19, 1949; children: Lois Roberta, Paul Brent, Ann Romaine. B.S., Randolph-Macon Coll., 1943; D.Sc. (hon.), 1976; M.A., Harvard U., 1947, Ph.D., 1952. Research physicist Gen. Electric Research Lab., Schenectady, 1952-75; adj. prof. Rensselaer Poly. Inst., 1962-65, SUNY-Albany, 1969-72; Sherman Fairchild prof. physics Lehigh U., Bethlehem, Pa., 1975-95, prof. emeritus, 1995—; chmn. Gordon Research Conf. on Defects in Semiconductors, 1981; mem. solid state adv. com. Oak Ridge Nat. Lab., 1980-85. Mem. editorial bd. Phys. Rev. B, 1978-82; contbr. articles to profl. jours. Served to lt. (j.g.) USNR, 1943-46. NSF fellow, 1966-67; named Virginian of Yr. Va. Press Assn., 1980; recipient Alexander von Humboldt sr. U.S. Scientist award, 1983, 91. Fellow Am. Phys. Soc. (Oliver E. Buckley award 1978), AAAS, Nat. Acad. Scis. Democrat. Unitarian. Office: Lehigh U Dept Physics Bethlehem PA 18015

WATKINS, HAROLD ROBERT, minister; b. Wauseon, Ohio, July 30, 1928; s. Orra Lynn and Florence Margaret (Bruner) W.; m. Evelyn Norma Earlywine, June 18, 1950; children: Mark Edwin, Nancy Jo Watkins. AB, Bethany Coll., 1950; BD, Lexington Theol. Sem., 1953; DD, Phillips U., 1985, Christian Theol. Sem., Indpls., 1995. Ordained minister Disciples of Christ, 1950. Min. Park Ave. Christian Ch., Tucson, 1953-56, First Christian Ch., Tuscaloosa, Ala., 1956-57; gen. ch. adminstr. Bd. Ch. Extension of Disciples of Christ, Indpls., 1958-95, pres., 1980-95; mem. faculty Lexington Theol. Sem., 1996-97; chmn. bd. dirs. Discipledata, Inc., Indpls. Trustee Bethany (W.Va.) Coll., 1976—, Nat. City Christian Ch. Corp., Washington, 1981—; bd. dirs. Ecumenical Ch. Loan Fund, Geneva; pres. World Conv. Chs. of Christ, Nashville, 1988-92. Recipient Outstanding Alumnus award Bethany Coll., 1975. Mem. Interfaith Forum on Religion, Art and Arch. (dir. officer 1979-95, pres. 1981-82, Elbert M. Conover award 1989). Home: 7402 Somerset Bay Apt 118 Indianapolis IN 46240-3495

WATKINS, HAYS THOMAS, retired railroad executive; b. Fern Creek, Ky., Jan. 26, 1926; s. Hays Thomas Sr. and Minnie Catherine (Whiteley) W.; m. Betty Jean Wright, Apr. 15, 1950; 1 son, Hays Thomas III. BS in Acctg., Western Ky. U., 1947; MBA, Northwestern U., 1948; LLD (hon.), Baldwin Wallace Coll., 1975, Alderson Broaddus Coll., 1980, Coll. of William and Mary, 1982, Va. Union U., 1987. CPA, Ill., Ohio. With C. & O. Ry. Cleve., 1949-80, v.p. fin., 1964-67, v.p. adminstrv. group, 1967-71, pres., chief exec. officer, 1971-73, chmn. bd., chief exec. officer, 1973-80; with B. & O. R.R., 1964-80, v.p. finance, 1964-71, pres., chief exec. officer, 1971-73, vice chmn. bd., chief exec. officer, 1973-80; chmn., chief exec. officer Chessie System, Inc., 1973-80; pres. and co-chief exec. officer CSX Corp. (merger of Chessie System, Inc. and Seaboard Coast Line Industries, Inc.), Richmond, Va., 1980-82, chmn. bd., chief exec. officer, 1982-89, chmn. bd., 1989-91; chmn. emeritus, 1991—. Vice rector bd. visitors Coll. William and mary, 1984-87, rector, 1987-93. With AUS, 1945-47. Named Man of Yr., Modern R.R. mag., 1984; recipient Excellence in Mgmt. award Industry Week mag., 1982. Mem. Nat. Assn. Accts., Am. Inst. C.P.A.'s. Clubs: Commonwealth (Richmond, Va.); Country of Va. (Richmond). Home: 22 Lower Tuckahoe Rd W Richmond VA 23233-6108 Office: CSX Corp PO Box 85629 Richmond VA 23285-5629

WATKINS, HORTENSE CATHERINE, middle school educator; b. St. Louis, Nov. 29, 1924; d. Isaiah S. and Katie M. (Phelps) W. BA, Harris-Stowe State Coll., St. Louis, 1946; MEd, U. Ill., 1953; postgrad. U. Chgo., InterAm. U., Saltillo, Coahuila, Mex.; postgrad., U. Seville, Spain, Webster U., St. Louis. Cert. life tchr., reading specialist, Mo. Coord. urban rural programs Carver-Dunbar Schs., St. Louis, 1975-76; adminstrv. asst. Shaw Visual Performing Arts Sch., St. Louis, 1978-82; team IV leader Woerner IGE, St. Louis, 1982-87; tchr., head lang. arts dept. Nottingham Mid. Sch., St. Louis, 1987-92; tutor fgn.-speaking religious, presenter, lectr. numerous workshops; curriculum advisor St. Louis Pub. Schs. Active numerous comty. orgns.; bd. dirs. St. Louis Cathedral Sch., St. Louis Metro Singers, Concert Series of St. Louis Cathedral. Mem. ASCD, Nat. Coun. Tchrs. English, Mo. State Tchrs. Assn., Greater St. Louis Coun. Social Studies, Delta Sigma Theta (Golden life), Delta Kappa Gamma. Home: 5070A Enright Ave Saint Louis MO 63108-1008

WATKINS, JAMES DAVID, food products executive; b. Rochester, Minn., Sept. 17, 1947; s. John Frederick and Lillian Kay (Johnson) W.; m. Elizabeth Smith Cieslowski; children: James David Jr., Joseph John. BA, U. Minn., 1969. Venture mgr. Pillsbury, Mpls., 1971-78; chief exec. officer Golden Valley Microwave Foods, Mpls., 1978—; bd. dirs. Country Lake Foods, Mpls. Bd. dirs. Big Brothers/Big Sisters, 1987.

WATKINS, JAMES DAVID, government official, naval officer; b. Alhambra, Calif., Mar. 7, 1927; s. Edward Francis and Louise Whipple (Ward) W.; m. Sheila Jo McKinney, Aug. 19, 1950 (dec. Sept. 1996); children: Katherine Marie, Laura Jo, Charles Lancaster, Susan Elizabeth, James David, Edward Francis. BS, U.S. Naval Acad., 1949; MS, Naval Postgrad. Sch., 1958; LHD (hon.), Marymount Coll., 1982, N.Y. Med. Coll., 1988; DSc (hon.), Dowling Coll., 1983, U. Ala., 1991; LLD (hon.), Cath. U., 1985, Mt. Sinai Sch. Medicine, 1993, Calif. U. Pa., 1994. Commd. ensign USN, 1949, advanced through grades to adm., 1979, comdg. officer U.S.S. Snook, 1964-66, exec. officer U.S.S. Long Beach, 1967-69; head submarine/nuclear power distbn. control br. Bur. Naval Pers., Dept. Navy, Washington, 1969-71, dir. enlisted pers. div., 1971-72; asst. chief of naval pers. for enlisted pers. control Bur. Naval Personnel, Dept. Navy, Washington, 1972-73; comdr. Cruiser-Destroyer Group 1 USN, 1973-75; dep. chief naval ops. manpower Navy Dept., Washington, 1975-78, chief of naval pers., 1975-78, chief Bur. Naval Pers., 1975-78; comdr. U.S. Sixth Fleet USN, 1978-79; vice chief naval ops. Navy Dept., 1979-81, comdr.-in-chief U.S. Pacific Fleet, 1981-82, chief naval ops., 1982-86; chmn. Presdl. Commn. on Human Immunodeficiency Virus Epidemic, 1987-88; sec. Dept. of Energy, Washington, 1989—. Decorated D.S.M. with 1 gold star, Legion of Merit with 2 gold stars, Bronze Star medal with Combat V; recipient Disting. Alumni award Naval Postgrad. Sch., 1958, Chairman's award Am. Assn. Engrng. Socs., 1991. Mem. U.S. Naval Acad. Alumni Assn. Roman Catholic. Lodge: Knights of Malta.

WATKINS, JERRY WEST, retired oil company executive, lawyer; b. Vernon, Tex., Dec. 10, 1931; s. Terrell Clark and Daisy (West) W.; m. Elizabeth Jill Cole, Sept. 3, 1955. Student, Hendrix Coll., 1949-50, La. Poly. Inst., 1950-51; JD, U. Ark., 1954. Bar: Ark. 1954. Law clk. Supreme Ct. Ark., Little Rock, 1954-55; with Murphy Oil Corp., El Dorado, Ark., 1955-89, sec., gen. atty., 1966-71, sec., gen. counsel, 1971-88, v.p., dir., 1975-88, exec. v.p., 1991-92, also dir., 1975-89; chief exec. officer, bd. dirs. Ocean Drilling and Exploration Co., New Orleans, 1989-91; mem. Ark. Bd. Law Examiners, 1969-74. Trustee Ark. State U., 1982-87; mem. Barton Libr. Bd., El Dorado, 1966-89; bd. dirs. South Ark. Arts Ctr., El Dorado, 1979-82, 85-88, Warner Brown Hosp., El Dorado, 1984-87, South Ark. Med. Systems, 1987-89. Mem. ABA, Ark. Bar Assn., Union County Bar Assn. Home: 111 Watkins Dr El Dorado AR 71730-2752

WATKINS, JOAN MARIE, osteopath, occupational medicine physician; b. Anderson, Ind., Mar. 9, 1943; d. Curtis David and Dorothy Ruth (Beckett) W.; m. Stanley G. Nodvik, Dec. 25, 1969 (div. Apr. 1974). BS, West Liberty State Coll., 1965; Cert. of Grad. Phy. Therapy, Ohio State U., 1966; DO, Phila. Coll. Osteo., 1972; M of Health Professions Edn., U. Ill., Chgo., 1986; MPH, U. Ill., 1989. Diplomate Osteo. Nat. Bds., Am. Bd. Preventive Medicine. Emergency osteo. physician Cooper Med. Ctr., Camden, N.J., 1974-79, Shore Meml. Hosp., Somers Point, N.J., 1979-81, St. Francis Hosp., Blue Island, Ill., 1981-82; emergency osteo. physician Mercy Hosp. and Med. Ctr., Chgo., 1982-90, dir. emergency ctr., 1984-88; resident in occupational and preventive medicine U. Ill., 1988-90; corp. med. dir. occupl. health svc. Univ. Cmty. Hosp., Tampa, 1992—. Fellow Am. Coll. Occupl. and Environ. Medicine, Am. Co.. Preventive Medicine. Avocations: sailing, needlework, swimming. Home: 4306 Harbor House Dr Tampa FL 33615-5408 Office: U Community Hosp Occupational Health Svcs 3100 E Fletcher Ave Tampa FL 33613-4613

WATKINS, JOHN CHESTER ANDERSON, newspaper publisher; b. Corpus Christi, Tex., Oct. 2, 1912; s. Dudley Warren and Ruth (Woodruff) W.; m. Helen Danforth, Nov. 20, 1943 (div. 1959); children: Fanchon Metcalf Burnham, Robert Danforth, Stephen Danforth, Jane Pierce; m. Izetta Jewel Smith, Feb. 1960 (dec. 1989). Litt.D., Bryant Coll.; D.J., Roger Williams Coll., 1983. Reporter, makeup editor, aviation editor Dayton (Ohio) Jour. and Herald, 1934-35; reporter, aviation editor, mil. corr. Balt. Sun, 1935-41; asst. to pub., assoc. pub. Providence Jour.-Bull., 1945-54, pub., 1954-79; chmn. Providence Jour. Co., 1961-85, chmn. emeritus, 1985—; pres. Interam. Press Assn., 1971-72; also mem. adv. council. Served as fighter pilot USAAF, 1941-45; ops. officer 325th Fighter Group MTO. Decorated D.F.C., Air medal with 9 oak leaf clusters; knight comdr. Order of Merit Italy), R.I. Heritage Hall of Fame. Fellow New Eng. Acad. Journalists (Yankee Quill award); mem. Air Force Assn., Am. Soc. Newspaper Editors, New Eng. Daily Newspaper Assn. (pres. 1966-68), Hope Club, Agawam Hunt Club, Cruising Am. Club, N.Y. Yacht Club, Spouting Rock Beach Assn. Home: PO Box 1085 Providence RI 02901-1085 Office: Providence Jour Co 75 Fountain St Providence RI 02902-0050

WATKINS, JOHN FRANCIS, management consultant; b. Alhambra, Calif., May 21, 1925; s. Edward F. and Louise (Ward) W.; divorced; children—Stephen, Katherine, John Francis, William. BSCE, U. Tex., Austin, 1947. With Earle M. Jorgensen Co., Lynwood, Calif., 1947-90, sr. v.p. adminstrn., 1978-90, ret.; owner John F. Watkins Assocs., Pasadena, Calif., 1990—. Bd. dirs. Boys Republic, Chino Hills, Calif., 1970—, pres., 1977-80; bd. dirs. St. Luke Hosp., Pasadena, 1979-86, chmn. bd., 1982-86; pres. bd. Poly. Sch., Pasadena, 1978-80, Holy Family Sch., 1994—; bd. dirs. Econ. Literacy Coun. Calif., 1980-87, Pasadena Hist. Mus., 1990—, Greater Pasadena Bus. Ptnrs., 1995—; tri-sch. consortium mem., commn. on cath. schs. mem. Archdiocese L.A., 1995—; pres. coun. Coll. Sci. and Engring./ Loyola Marymount U.; posse sheriff Huntington Westerners; adv. bd. Bishop Mora Salesian H.S., 1994—; mem. Edn. Found. Archdiocese L.A., 1995—; St. Gabriel pastoral region bd. dirs. Cath. Charities, 1994—. Mem. U.S. Navy League (nat. bd. dirs. 1989—, pres. Pasadena coun. 1992-93), Calif. Club, Annandale Golf Club, Serra Club (pres. 1995—), Valley Club (San Marino, Calif.). Republican. Roman Catholic. Home & Office: 410 California Ter Pasadena CA 91105-2419

WATKINS, JOHN GOODRICH, psychologist, educator; b. Salmon, Idaho, Mar. 17, 1913; s. John Thomas and Ethel (Goodrich) W.; m. Evelyn Elizabeth Browne, Aug. 21, 1932; m. Doris Wade Tomlinson, June 8, 1946; m. Helen Verner Huth, Dec. 28, 1971; children: John Dean, Jonette Alison, Richard Douglas, Gregory Keith, Rodney Philip, Karen Stroobants, Marvin R. Huth. Student, Coll. Idaho, 1929-30, 31-32; BS, U. Idaho, 1933, MS, 1936; PhD, Columbia U., 1941. Instr. high sch. Idaho, 1933-39; faculty Ithaca Coll., 1940-41, Auburn U., 1941-43; assoc. prof. Wash. State Coll., 1946-49; chief clin. psychologist U.S. Army Welch Hosp., 1945-46; clin. psychologist VA Hosp., American Lake, Wash., 1949-50; chief clin. psychologist VA Mental Hygiene Clinic, Chgo., 1950-53, VA Hosp., Portland, Oreg., 1953-64; prof. psychology U. Mont., Missoula, 1964-84; prof. emeritus U. Mont., 1984—, dir. clin. tng., 1964-80; lectr. numerous univs.; clin. asso. U. Oreg. Med. Sch., 1957; pres. Am. Bd. Examiners in Psychol. Hypnosis, 1960-62. Author: Objective Measurement of Instrumental Performance, 1942, Hypnotherapy of War Neuroses, 1949, General Psychotherapy, 1960, The Therapeutic Self, 1978, (with others) We, The Divided Self, 1982, Hypnotherapeutic Techniques, 1987, Hypnoanalytic Techniques, 1992, Ego States: Theory and Therapy, 1997; contbr. articles to profl. jours. Mem. Internat. Soc. Clin. and Exptl. Hypnosis (co-founder, pres. 1965-67, recipient awards 1960-65), Soc. Clin. and Exptl. Hypnosis (pres. 1969-71, Morton Prince award), Am. Psychol. Assn. (pres. divsn. 30 1975-76, recipient award 1993), Sigma Xi, Phi Delta Kappa. Home and Office: 413 Evans Ave Missoula MT 59801-5827 *For a complete life one needs a job, a home, a love, a friend, and an enemy. My "enemies" are injustice, war, poverty, illness, and suffering, not people. Make your existence as meaningful as possible. Enjoy life fully, and when it comes time to leave, have no fear or regrets. Seek to leave this world a little better off because you lived. These are my values. Would that I were mature enough always to live up to them.*

WATKINS, LLOYD IRION, university president; b. Cape Girardeau, Mo., Aug. 29, 1928; s. Herman Lloyd and Lydia Mina (Irion) W.; m. Mary Ellen Caudle, Aug. 14, 1949; children: John Lloyd, Joseph William, Robert Lawrence. BEd, Southeast Mo. State U., 1949; MS, U. Wis., 1951, PhD, 1954; DH (hon.), U. Dubuque, 1974; EdD (hon.), Srinakharinwirot U., Thailand, 1986. Tchr. Jackson (Mo.) High Sch., 1948-50; asst. prof. Moorhead State Coll., 1954-56; asst., assoc. prof. Ohio U., 1956-64, asst. to acad. v.p., assoc. prof., 1964-66; exec. v.p. Ida. State U., 1966-69; pres. Iowa Assn. Pvt. Colls. and Univs. Des Moines, 1969-73, West Tex. State U., 1973-77; pres. Ill. State U., Normal, 1977-88, prof., pres. emeritus, 1988-91, pres. emeritus, 1991—. Contbr. articles to profl. jours. Recipient Baker grant for Research Ohio U., 1963, Alumni Merit award S.E. Mo. State U., 1978. Mem. McLean County Humane Soc., McLean County Hist. Soc., Citizens' Com., The Alumni Club, Crestwicke Country Club, Kappa Delta Pi, Phi Alpha Theta, Rotary. Home: RR 13 Box 111 Bloomington IL 61704-8917

WATKINS, LOIS IRENE, English educator; b. Sterling, Nebr., Mar. 12, 1926; d. August Ralph and Magdalena Anna (Foss) Bargman; m. Morris Grant Watkins, Dec. 28, 1947 (dec. May 1996); children: Sharon Thomas, Stephen, Mark, Paul, Debra Walters, Joanna Hutchinson, David. Student, Concordia Tchrs. Coll., 1945-47; BA in Applied Linguistics, Calif. State U., Fullerton, 1976, MA in Applied Linguistics, 1978. 2d grade tchr. Canoga Park (Calif.) Luth. Sch., 1961-62; asst. prof. William Carey U., Pasadena, Calif., 1978-80; asst. to pres. All Nations Lit., Calif., Ind., Wash., 1972-92; dir. literature and literacy All Nations Lit., Colorado Springs, Colo., 1992-94, pres., bd. dirs., 1994-96; ESL program coord. Internat. Bible Soc., Colorado Springs, Colo., 1996—; missionary wife Luth. Ch.-Mo. Synod, Uyo, Nigeria, 1950-52, Ogojo, Nigeria, 1959-63. Author, sr. instr. manual and video series Bridge of Love, 1994; co-editor: All Nations English Dictionary, 1990. Mem. Rep. Nat. Com., Washington. Mem. Luth. Soc. for Missiology (bd. dirs. 1994—). Avocations: reading, writing, gardening, computer graphics. Home: 5475 Jennifer Ln Colorado Springs CO 80917

WATKINS, PAUL B., academic research center administrator, medical educator; b. Schenectady, N.Y., Feb. 17, 1953; s. George Daniels and Carolyn Lenore (Nevin) W.; m. Joanne Carol Spalty, July 4, 1981; children: Andrew James, Melanie Ann. BA, Cornell U., 1975, MD, 1979. Intern N.Y. Hosp., 1979-80, resident, 1980-82; fellow Medical Coll. Va., 1982-84; physician admission ward Khao-I-Dang Cambodian Refuge Camp, Thailand, 1982; from instr. to asst. prof. Med. Coll. Va., 1984-86; asst. prof. U. Mich., Ann Arbor, 1986-91, assoc. prof. medicine, 1991-97, prof. medicine, 1997—, assoc. dir. clin. rsch. ctr., 1991, dir. clin. rsch. ctr., 1991—; advisor toxic waste orgn. Inst. Medicine, Washington, 1993-96; mem. toxicology study sect. NIH, Bethesda, Md., 1992-96; sci. cons. Parke-Davis Pharm., Organon Internat., Wyeth-Ayerst, Proctor and Gamble, Abbott Labs., Bristol-Meyers Squibb; FDA cons., 1997—. Contbr. articles to profl. jours. Mem. St. Andrews Ch., Ann Arbor, 1990—. Recipient VA Career Devel. Associate Investigator award, 1984-86, Rsch. Assoc. award, 1987-91. Fellow ACP; mem. AAAS, Am. Soc. Clin. Investigation (elected), Am. Assn. Study Liver Disease, Am. Gastroent. Assn., Am. Fedn. Clin. Rsch., Midwest Gut Club, Ctrl. Soc. Clin. Rsch., Internat. Assn. Study Liver, Internat. Soc. Study Xenobiotics. Avocations: jogging, skiing, wind surfing, tennis, scuba diving. Home: 2112 Wallingford Rd Ann Arbor MI 48104-4563 Office: U Mich Hosp Gen Clin Rsch Ctr 1500 E Med Ctr Dr A7119 Ann Arbor MI 48109-0108

WATKINS, RUFUS NATHANIEL, newspaper professional; b. Laurel, Miss., Sept. 27, 1963; s. Rufus Sr. and Mary Helen (Washington) W. AA, City Coll. of San Francisco, 1983; BA in Speech Communications, Baylor U., 1987. Sr. news copy clk. San Francisco Chronicle, 1988—. Area coord. Terence Hallinan Supervisory Campaign, 1987-88, John Burton Asssembly Campaign, 1987-88, mem. Mayor Frank Jordan Transition Team, San Francisco, 1992, mem. Housing and Econ. Devel. Team, 1992, Citizens Com. on Cmty. Devel. Adv. Bd., 1992-96, cmty. budget forum panel, 1993, subcoms. cmty. facilities, pub. open space, emergency shelters, housing, 1993—; mem. election panel Robert F. Kennedy Bus. Dem. Club, 1992; mayor's cmty. rep. Re-elect Mayor Frank Jordan Com., 1995; precinct organizer Kathleen Brown for Gov. Campaign, 1994, Rufus Watkins for Bd. of Edn. Com., 1996, Party Smart Assn., 1990—; bd. dirs. San Francisco Cmty. Action Network, 1994-95; mem. com. Rufus Watkins Bd. Edn., 1996; mem. Jobs for Youth, 1997—, Com. to elect Rufus Watkins Bd. Edn., 1996; vol. San Francisco Zoo Campaign, San Francisco Sch. Bd. Campaign, San Francisco Human Rights Commn. youth & Edn. Com.; precinct proposition capt. David F. Campaign, 1997. Recipient Scholar of Yr., San Francisco Police Athletic League, 1977. Mem. World Affairs Coun. (internat. forum steering com. 1993—, pub. rels. subcom. 1993—, logistics subcom. 1993—, edn. subcom. 1993-94, tech. subcom. 1993-94, donations subcom. 1993-94, polit. subcom. 1994—, social events subcom. 1994-95, cmty. svcs. subcom. 1994-95, bus. and careers subcom. 1994—, membership com. 1995—, comembership vice chair 1994-95, vice chair 1995-96, chair polit. sub.-com. 1995-96, chair cmty. svc. subcom. 1995-96, 1st officer pub. rels. subcom. 1996-97, facilitator, organizer 1997—), San Francisco Jr. C. of C. (dir. pub. rels. 1989-90, chair ann. Halloween party youth 1990-93, v.p. membership devel. 1990-91, chmn. bd. 1991-94, pres. 1993-94, chairperson Project Open Hand food drive 1992-94, Mem. of Month Oct. 1989, Officer of Yr. 1989, Presdl. award 1990, 91, Calif. Presdl. award 1992-93), Internat. Platform Assn., Toastmasters Internat. (treas. Pacific Heights/Nob Hill chpt. 1993, v.p. membership devel. 1993-94, pres. 1993-94, Competent Spkr. award 1994), Commonwealth Club of Calif. (mem. Bay Area platform sect. 1994-95), No. Calif. Baylor U. Alumni, St. Ignatius Coll. Preparatory Alumni Assn., St. Dominic's Sch. Alumni Assn., San Francisco C. of C., Diplomat Club, Chinese Am. Dem. Club, Robert F. Kennedy Dem. Club (PAC com. 1997—, membership com. 1997—). Avocations: researching politics, running, weightlifting, music. Home: 2060 Ofarrell St Apt 102 San Francisco CA 94115-3410 Office: San Francisco Chronicle 901 Mission St San Francisco CA 94103-2905

WATKINS, SHERRY LYNNE, elementary school educator; b. Bloomington, Ind., Oct. 13, 1944; d. Quentin Odell and Velma Ruth W. BSEd, Ind. U., 1966, MSEd, 1968. Tchr. 4th grade North Grove Elem. Sch., Ctr. Grove Sch. Dist., Greenwood, Ind., 1966-68; tchr. 4th and 6th grades John Strange Sch., Met. Dist. of Wash. Twp., Indpls., 1968-91; tchr. 4th grade Allisonville Sch. Met. Sch. Dist. of Wash. Twp., Indpls., 1991—. Mem. People for Ethical Treatment of Animals. Mem. NEA (nat. del. 1978—), ACLU, AAUW, Ind. Tchrs. Assn. (state del. 1966—), Washington Twp. Edn. Assn. (pres. 1986-89), World Confedn. Orgn. of Tchg. Profls. (del. Costa Rica 1990), Delta Kappa Gamma (chpt. pres. 1992-94, chmn. coord. coun. Indpls. area 1994-96), Alpha Omicron Pi. Avocations: traveling, cultural activities. Office: Allisonville Sch 4920 E 79th St Indianapolis IN 46250-1615

WATKINS, STEPHEN EDWARD, accountant; b. Oklahoma City, Sept. 1, 1922; s. Ralph Bushnell and Jane (Howell) W.; m. Suzanne Fowler, Aug. 16, 1976; children—Elizabeth Ann Watkins Racicot, Stephen Edward. B.B.A., U. N.Mex., 1944. C.P.A., N.Mex. With Peat, Marwick, Mitchell & Co., 1944-67; pres. The New Mexican, Santa Fe, 1967-78, 90—; pvt. practice pub. acctg. Santa Fe, 1978—. Vestryman Ch. of Holy Faith; trustee St. Vincent Hosp., 1979-85, Orchestra Santa Fe, 1976-82, Hist. Santa Fe Found. (pres. 1990). Mem. AICPA, Sons of Am. Revolution, Rotary. Home: 1325 Don Gaspar Ave Santa Fe NM 87505-4627 Office: 223 E Palace Ave Santa Fe NM 87501-2044

WATKINS, SYDNEY LYNN, sports administrator; b. Hartford, Conn., Sept. 12, 1964; s. Robert Lee and Joan (Hardy) W. BS, Howard U., 1986, MS, 1989. Cert. U.S. Olympic Acad., Sport Adminstrn. Facility Mgmt. Inst. Water safety instr. Howard U. Satellite Youth Program, Washington, 1986; water safety instr. D.C. Dept. Recreation, Washington, 1986-87, phys. therapeutic recreation specialist, 1987-88; account rep. AT&T, Silver Spring, Md., 1988-90; program assoc. Amateur Athletic Found., L.A., 1991-95; program mgr. L.A. Team Mentoring, 1995-96; ind. cons., 1996—; pharm. sales cons. Wyeth-Ayerst Labs., 1997—; spl. asst. to pres. Dr. LeRoy T. Walker Found., Durham, N.C., 1993. African Am. Summit fellow NAACP, L.A., 1994; Patricia Roberts Harris grantee Howard U., 1989. Mem. AAHPERD, Alpha Kappa Alpha. Home: 1233 1/2 S Citrus Ave Los Angeles CA 90019-1603

WATKINS, TED ROSS, social work educator; b. Terrell, Tex., Dec. 2, 1938; s. Daniel Webster and Iva Lucy (Lowrie) W.; m. Betty Diane Dobbs, May 30, 1959; children: Evan Scott, Brett Dobbs, James David. BA in Psychology, U. North Tex., 1961; MSW, La. State U., 1963; D of Social Work, U. Pa., 1976. Staff social worker Mercer County Mental Health Ctr., Sharon, Pa., 1963-65; chief social worker, assoc. exec. Talbot Hall Treatment Ctr., Jonestown, Pa., 1965-70; chief social worker Harrisburg (Pa.) Mental Health Ctr., 1970-71; asst. prof. social work U. Tex., Arlington, 1971-76; dir. counseling svcs. Family Svcs., Inc., Ft. Worth, 1976-79; assoc. prof. social work U. Tex., 1979-85, dir. criminal justice, 1985-87, chair dept. sociology, 1987-91, assoc. prof., grad. advisor social work, 1991—; cons. in field. Author: (with James Callicutt) Mental Health Policy and Practice Today. Tex. del. to Pres.'s Commn. in Mental Health, Austin, 1978. Recipient Golladay Teaching award Coll. Liberal Arts, Arlington, 1990; named Outstanding Profl. Human Svcs., 1972. Mem. NASW (state bd. dirs. 1976-78, 80-82, unit chair, vol. lobbyist 1982), Acad. Cert. Social Workers (lic. master social worker, advanced clin. practitioner). Democrat. Methodist. Avocations: music, painting, camping. Office: U Tex Box 19129 UTA Arlington TX 76019

WATKINS, WESLEY WADE, congressman; b. DeQueen, Ark., Dec. 15, 1938; s. L. V. and Mary J. W.; m. Elizabeth Lou Rogers, June 9, 1963; children: Sally, Martha, Wade. B.S., Okla. State U., 1960, M.S., 1961. With USDA, Washington, 1961; asst. dir. admissions Okla. State U., 1963-66; exec. dir. Kiamichi Econ. Devel. Dist. of Okla., 1966-68; founder, owner constrn. and land devel. bus., 1968-76; mem. Okla. Senate, 1975-76, 95th-105st Congresses from Okla.; mem. house appropriations com. Pres. Higher Edn. Alumni Council of Okla.; Okla. chmn. Nat. Future Farmers Am. Found.; mem. Okla. Health Planning Council.; Pres. Ada (Okla). Growth and Devel. Assn. Served with Air N.G., 1961-67. Recipient Nat. Security Leadership award U.S. Air N.G., 1967, Okla. 4-H Alumni Recognition award, 1978, Disting. Alumnus award Okla. State U. Alumni Assn., 1978, others; named Policymaker of the Yr. Am. Vocational Assn., One of 3 Outstanding Young Men in Okla., Okla. Jaycees, 1968; named to Okla. State U. Hall of Fame, 1989. Mem. C. of C. Republican. Presbyterian. Clubs: Masons, Lions. Office: US Ho Reps 2312 Rayburn Bldg Washington DC 20515-0005

WATKINS, WILLIAM, JR., electric power industry executive; b. Jersey City, N.J., Aug. 12, 1932; s. William James and Willie Ree (Blount) W.; m. Sylvia I. Mulzac, Oct. 16, 1955; children: Cheryl, Rene, Linda. BBA, Pace U., 1954; MBA, NYU, 1962; postgrad. advanced mgmt. program, U. Mich., 1979; postgrad. exec. program, Edison Electric Inst., 1988. Staff asst. Consol. Edison Co. N.Y., N.Y.C., 1957-64; sys. mgr. Volkswagen Am., Englewood Cliffs, N.J., 1964-71; v.p., dir. adminstrn. New Eng. Power Svc. Co., Westboro, Mass., 1972-82, v.p., dir. human resources, 1986-92; v.p., dist. mgr. Narragansett Electric Co., Providence, 1982-86, exec. v.p., 1992—; bd. dirs. Peerless Precision Corp., Lincoln, R.I., 1982-91. Chmn. R.I. Urban Project, Providence, 1984, R.I. Coun. for Econ. Edn., Providence, 1984; mem. Gov.'s Commn. on Health Care Reform, 1993-94; trustee R.I. Hosp., 1995-96, Lifespan, 1996—, Roger Williams U., Bristol, R.I., 1991-94; bd. dirs. R.I. Hosp. Trust Nat. Bank, Providence, 1987—, R.I. Hosp. Fin. Corp., Providence, 1987-91, Inroads, 1993—, Leadership R.I., 1993-95, NCCJ, 1993—; mem. resource and devel. commn. Episcopal Diocese Mass., 1988-92; vice chmn. bd. trustees RISD, 1995—. Recipient Cmty. Svc. award Urban League R.I., 1986, Paris V. Sterett award John Hope Settlement House, 1987, Small Bus. Adminstrn. Adv. of the Yr. award, 1994; named Developer of Yr., Am. Econ. Devel. Coun., 1996. Mem. N.E. Indsl. Developers Assn. (bd. dirs. 1993—), R.I. Urban Bankers Assn., Kappa Alpha Psi. Avocations: swimming, biking, hiking, traveling, golf. Home: 509 Corey Ln Middletown RI 02842 Office: Narragansett Electric Co 280 Melrose St Providence RI 02907-2152

WATKINS, WILLIAM LAW, retired lawyer; b. Anderson, S.C., Dec. 26, 1910; s. Thomas Franklin and Agnes (Law) W.; m. Frances Sitton, Oct. 23, 1937; children: Sarah Watkins Marshall, Anna Watkins Hattaway, Elizabeth Watkins Kinghorn, Jane Watkins Mudd. A.B., Wofford Coll., 1932; LL.B., U. Va., 1933; LLD, Anderson (S.C.) Coll., 1996. Bar: S.C. 1933. Practice law Anderson, S.C., 1933; mem. Watkins & Prince, 1934-46, Watkins & Watkins, 1946-54, Watkins, Vandiver & Freeman, 1954-64, Watkins, Vandiver, Kriven & Long, 1964-67, Watkins, Vandiver, Kirven, Long & Gable, 1968-77; ptnr. Watkins, Vandiver, Kirven, Gable & Gray, 1977-85, of counsel, 1985-92; bd. dirs. Duke Power Co., 1975-84, Perpetual Bank, F.S.B., 1953-92. Mem. S.C. Ho. of Reps., 1935-36; mem. S.C. Probation, Parole and Pardon Bd., 1954-69; trustee Presbyterian Coll., Clinton, S.C., 1966-75, Anderson County Hosp. Assn., S.C., 1964-74. Served with AUS, 1942-46. Decorated Bronze Star with oak leaf cluster. Fellow Am. Coll. Trial Lawyers, Am. Bar Found.; mem. ABA, S.C. Bar, Anderson Bar Assn., Order of the Palmetto, Phi Beta Kappa, Sigma Alpha Epsilon. Presbyterian. Lodge: Rotary. Home: 317 North St Anderson SC 29621-5814

WATKINSON, PATRICIA GRIEVE, museum director; b. Merton, Surrey, Eng., Mar. 28, 1946; came to U.S., 1972; d. Thomas Wardle and Kathleen (Bredl) Grieve. BA in Art History and Langs. with honors, Bristol U., Eng., 1968. Sec. Mayfair Fine Arts and The Mayfair Gallery, London, 1969-71; adminstr. Bernard Jacobson, Print Pub., London, 1971-73; freelance exhbn. work, writer Kilkenny Design Ctr., Davis Gallery, Irish Arts Council in Dublin, Ireland, 1975-76; curator of art Mus. Art, Wash. State U., Pullman, 1978-83, dir., 1984—; asst. prof. art history Wash. State U., Pullman, 1978. Co-author, co-editor: Gaylen Hansen: The Paintings of a Decade, 1985. Mem. Assn. Am. Colls. and Univ. Mus. and Galleries (western regional rep. 1987-89), Art Mus. Assn. Am. (Wash. state rep. 1986-87), Internat. Coun. Mus. (modern art com. 1986-89), Wash. Mus. Assn. (bd. dirs. 1984-87), Am. Fedn. Arts (western region rep. 1987-89), Wash. Art Consortium (pres. 1993-95), Western Mus. Assn. (bd. dirs. 1996—). Office: Wash State U Mus Art Pullman WA 99164-7460

WATKISS, ERIC JOHN, naval flight officer; b. East Point, Ga., May 17, 1964; s. George Philip Watkiss and Barbara Anne Seaman; m. Lynne Lee Novak, Nov. 25, 1989. B of Aerospace Engring., Ga. Inst. Tech., 1986; MS in Aero. Engring., Naval Postgrad. Sch., 1994; grad., U.S. Naval Test Pilot Sch., 1995. Airport mgr. Aerocountry Airport, McKinney, Tex., 1981-86; advanced through grades to lt. comdr. USN, 1996, naval flight officer, 1986—, naval flight test officer, 1995-96, naval test pilot sch. instr., 1996—; test pilot instr., 1996—. Decorated two Navy Achievement medals. Mem. AIAA (winner 1st pl. aircraft design competition 1993. 94), MENSA. Republican. Episcopalian. Avocations: flying, mountain biking, skiing. Home: 20705 Hermanville Rd Lexington Park MD 20653 Office: US Naval Test Pilot Sch Aircraft Divsn Naval Air Warfare Ctr Patuxent River MD 20670-5304

WATLINGTON, JOHN FRANCIS, JR., banker; b. Reidsville, N.C., Mar. 23, 1911; s. John Francis and Frances (Byers) W.; m. Margaret Jones, Feb. 22, 1947; children: John Francis III, Anne Wilson Watlington Curtis. A.B., Washington and Lee U., 1933. With Wachovia Bank & Trust Co., Winston-Salem, N.C., 1933-82; transit clk., asst. cashier, asst. v.p., v.p., sr. v.p. Wachovia Bank & Trust Co., 1933-56, pres., 1956-74, chmn., 1974-76, chmn. exec. com., 1977-82, also chmn. Charlotte office, 1946-56; chmn. Wachovia Corp., 1968-76; chmn. exec. com., 1977-82; ret. dir. Piedmont Natural Gas Co., Inc.; dir. emeritus USAir Group Inc. Trustee Union Theol. Sem.; chmn. Union Theol-Sem., 1980-82; hon. life trustee Va. Found. for Ind. Colls.; hon. chmn. bd. visitors Bowman Gray Sch. Medicine; dir., past pres. Presbyn. Ch. U.S.A. Found. Mem. Winston-Salem C. of C. (pres. 1958-59), N.C. Citizens Assn. Presbyterian. Home: 17 Graylyn Place Ln Winston Salem NC 27106-5816 Office: 100 N Main St Winston Salem NC 27101-4047

WATNE, ALVIN L., surgeon, educator; b. Shabbona, Ill., Jan. 13, 1927; m. Diana Folio, Dec. 3, 1966; children: Carrie, Matthew, Andrew, Valerie. B.S., U. Ill.-Chgo. Coll. Medicine, 1950, M.D., 1952, M.S., 1956. Diplomate: Am. Bd. Surgery. Intern Indpls. Gen. Hosp., 1952-53; resident U. Ill. Research and Edn. Hosps., Chgo., 1954-58; assoc. cancer surgeon Cancer Research, Roswell Park, Buffalo, N.Y., 1958, assoc. chief cancer research, 1959; assoc. prof. surgery W.Va. U., 1962-67, prof., 1967-72, acting chmn. dept. surgery, 1973-75, prof., chmn. dept. surgery, 1975-86; prof., chmn. dept. surgery U. Ill., Peoria, 1986-91; dir. Cancer Ctr. of Ga., 1991-94; assoc. dir. dept. surgery Ga. Bapt. Med. Ctr., 1994-97; cons. surgery VA, Clarksburg, W.Va., 1963—. Author: Gardner's Syndrome, 1977, (2d edit.), 1979, Melanoma of Head and Neck, 1981, Polyposis Coli, 1982. Pres. W. Va. div. Am. Cancer Soc., 1967-68, 80—, v.p., 1981. Recipient Hektoen Gold medal AMA, 1958; recipient Hektoen Silver medal AMA, 1960. Mem. ACS (pres. W.Va. chpt. 1972-73, chmn. local com. 1978—, gov. 1985—), Southeastern Surg. Congress (councilor 1980—), Soc. Surg. Oncology (exec. council 1980), Soc. Head and Neck Surgeons (pres. 1982), Am. Cancer Soc. (dir.-at-large 1985—). Office: Ga Baptist Med Ctr 303 Parkway Dr NE Atlanta GA 30312-1212

WATNE, DARLENE CLAIRE, state legislator; b. Minot, N.D., Feb. 11, 1935; d. Charles and Anna (Fjeld) Widdel; m. Clair A. Watne, 1954; children: Carmen (Watne) Hadreas, Steven, Nancy (Watne) Mitchell, Matthew. Cert. ct. reporting, Minot Bus. Coll., 1975. Cert. residential specialist; grad. Real Estate Inst.; residential mktg. master. Senator N.D. State Senate, Bismarck, 1994—; assoc. broker Watne Inc. Realtors; bd. dirs. Minot Bd. Realtors, 1993, No. States Power, 1995—; vice chmn. judiciary com. polit. subdivsn. com. N.D. State Senate. Bd. dirs. Minot YWCA, 1989-92, Minot Symphony Assn., 1986-91, 95—; mem. Minot Area Coun. Arts, 1995—; dir. ARC, 1996—; mem. N.D. Ct. Svcs. Commn., 1995—, N.D. Joint Legal Svcs. Commn., 1995—, Mayors Office, 1995—, Minot Commn. on Aging, 1996—. Named Woman of Distinction in Bus. and Industry, Minot YWCA, 1993. Mem. Nat. Bd. Realtors, N.D. Realtors Assn., N.D. Shorthand Reporters Assn., Rotary. Home: 520 28th Ave SW Minot ND 58701-7065 Office: 408 N Broadway Minot ND 58703-2310

WATRING, WATSON GLENN, gynecologic oncologist, educator; b. St. Albans, W.Va., June 2, 1936; m. Roberta Tawell. BS, Washington & Lee U., 1958; MD, W.Va. U., 1962. Diplomate Am. Bd. Ob-Gyn, Am. Bd. Gynecol. Oncology. Intern The Toledo Hosp., 1963; resident in ob-gyn Ind. U., Indpls., 1964-66, Tripler Gen. Hosp., Honolulu, 1968-70; resident in gen. and oncologic surgery City of Hope Nat. Med. Ctr., Duarte, Calif., 1970-71, assoc. dir. gynecol. oncology, sr. surgeon, 1973-77; fellow in gynecol. oncology City of Hope Nat. Med. Ctr. and UCLA Med. Ctr., 1972-74; asst. prof. ob-gyn UCLA Med. Ctr., 1972-77; assoc. prof., sr. gynecologist, sr. surgeon Tufts New Eng. Med. Ctr. Hosp., Boston, 1977-80, asst. prof. radiation therapy, 1978-80; practice medicine specializing in ob-gyn Boston, 1980-82; assoc. prof. ob-gyn U. Mass., Worcester, 1982; regional dir. gynecol. oncology So. Calif. Permanente Med. Group, Los Angeles, 1982—, asst. dir. residency tng., 1985—; dir. gynecol. oncology St. Margarets Hosp. for Women, Dorchester, Mass., 1977-80; clin. prof. ob-gyn U. Calif., Irvine, 1982—. Contbr. articles to profl. jours. Mem. ch. council Luth. Ch. of the Foothills, 1973-75. Served to lt. col. M.C., U.S. Army, 1965-71. Fellow Am. Coll. Ob-Gyn, Los Angeles Obstet. and Gynecol. Soc.; mem. AAAS, ACS (Calif. and Mass. chpts.), Boston Surg. Soc., AMA, Mass. Med. Soc., Mass. Suffolk Dist. Med. Soc., Internat. Soc. Gynecol. Pathologists, Western Soc. Gynecologists and Obstetricians, Am. Soc. Clin. Oncology, Soc. Gynecol. Oncologists, Western Assn. Gynecol. Oncologists (sec.-treas. 1976-81, program chmn. 1984, pres. 1985—), New Eng. Assn. Gynecol. Oncologists (chmn. charter com.), New Eng. Obstet. and Gynecol. Soc., Obstet. Soc. Boston, Am. Radium Soc., Soc. Study Breast Disease, New Eng. Cancer Soc., Internat. Gynecol. Cancer Soc., Daniel Morton Soc., Sigma Xi. Republican. Avocations: golf, skiing, horticulture.

WATROUS, ROBERT THOMAS, academic director; b. Cleve., Apr. 20, 1952; s. Frank Thomas and Marie Anne (Kmeicik) W.; m. Robin Joyce Braun, Mar. 14, 1981 (div. 1993); 1 child, Michael Francis. BS, U. Dayton, 1974, MS, 1977. Dir. student ctr. for off campus community rels. Univ. Dayton, Ohio, 1974-76; resident dir. Univ. Dayton, 1976-78; dir. of housing St. Bonaventure Univ., Olean, N.Y., 1978-81; asst. dean of student life/ housing Kutztown (Pa.) Univ. of Pa., 1981-86, dir. commuter and jud. affairs, 1986-89, 92-95; faculty senate Kutztown (Pa.) U., 1986-89, 92-95; mem. Pa. Task Force on Intergroup Behavior in Higher Edn., 1991-94; trainer Pa. Interagy. Task Force on Civil Tension, Harrisburg, Pa., 1989—; exec. coun. Adult Learners Consortium, Bloomsburg, Pa., 1990-91; mem. Lehigh Valley Svc. Learning Consortium, 1994—. Bd. mgr. Tri Valley YMCA, Fleetwood, Pa., 1983-94; adv. bd. Crossroads, Kutztown, 1989-94; bd. dirs. Jr. Achievement of Berks County, Reading, Pa., 1990, Reading, Pa., 1990, Reading and Berks Coun. YMCA, 1992-96; mem. Leadership Berks, Reading, 1990; bd. dirs. Leadership Berks, 1995—; co-founder Leading Sch. Bds., 1994—; mem. YMCA cultural diversity and internat. awareness com., 1994—. Mem. Nat. Assn. Student Pers. Adminstrs. (profl. affiliate), Hawk Mt. Coun. Boy Scouts Am. (sustaining mem.), Berks County C. of C. (sch. bd. governance com. 1993—), Fleetwood Youth Soccer Club (treas.), Fleetwood Youth Basketball Assn. (coach 1995-96). Avocations: golf, sports, gardening. Office: Kutztown Univ PO Box 37 Kutztown PA 19530-0037

WATROUS, WILLIAM RUSSELL, trombonist, composer, conductor; b. Middletown, Conn., June 8, 1939; s. Ralph Jarvas and Edna (Little) W.; m. Mary Ann Ackerman, Oct. 1978; children: Melody, Cheryl, Jason. Student pub. schs., New London, Conn. lectr. jazz edn., participant music seminars, brass confs.; bd. dirs. Internat. Trombone Workshop. Trombonist with bands of Woody Herman, Quincy Jones, Count Basie, leader own band, Manhattan Wildlife Refuge (now Calif. Wildlife Refuge), from 1970, composer: Dirty Dan and others (Voted Number One Trombonist, Downbeat Reader's Poll, 1975, 76, 77, 78, 79, 80, Internat. Critics Poll 1976, 77). Albums include The Tiger of San Pedro, Bone Straight Ahead, Watrous in

Hollywood, I'll Play For You, Coronary Trombossa, La Zorra, Roarin' Back Into New York, New York, Someplace Else, 1986, Reflections, 1987, Bonefied, 1992, A Time for Love, 1993. Served with USNR, 1956-60. Mem. ASCAP, Am. Fedn. Musicians. Address: care Welk Records 1299 Ocean Ave Ste 800 Santa Monica CA 90401-1040*

WATSON, ALEXANDER FLETCHER, organization executive, former ambassador; b. Boston, Aug. 8, 1939; s. Fletcher G. and Alice Victoria (Hodson) W.; m. Judith Dawson Tuttle, June 23, 1962; children: David F., Caitlin H. BA, Harvard U., 1961; MA, U. Wis., 1969. Consular officer Am. Embassy, Santo Domingo, Dominican Republic, 1962-64, Madrid, 1964-66; internat. relations officer Dept. State, Washington, 1966-68, 73-75; polit. officer Am. Embassy, Brasilia, Brazil, 1969-70; prin. officer Am. Consulate, Salvador, Brazil, 1970-73; spl. asst. Dept. State, Washington, Brazil, 1975-77, dir. Office of Devel Fin., 1978-79; dep. chief of mission Am. Embassy, La Paz, Bolivia, 1979-81; dep. chief of mission Bogota, Colombia, 1981-84, Brasilia, Brazil, 1984-86; U.S. ambassador to Lima, Peru, 1986-89; dep. U.S. permanent rep. to UN, 1989-93; asst. sec. of state for inter-Am. affairs Dept. of State, Washington, 1993-96; v.p., exec. dir. L.Am. and Caribbean program The Nature Conservancy, Arlington, Va., 1996—. Bd. dirs. Inter-Am. Found., Pan Am. Devel. Found., Banco La Caja, Caribbean/Latin Am. Action. Decorated Order of San Carlos, Govt. of Colombia, 1984; Order of the Condor, Govt. of Bolivia, 1985; Labor Justice Order of Merit, Govt. of Brazil, 1987; Order of the Sun, Govt. of Peru, 1989. Mem. Am. Soc., Am. Fgn. Svc. Assn., Coun. on Fgn. Rels. Office: The Nature Conservancy Internat Hdqs 1815 N Lynn St Arlington VA 22209-2003

WATSON, ANDREW SAMUEL, psychiatry and law educator; b. Highland Park, Mich., May 2, 1920; s. Andrew Nicol and Eva Arvel (Barnes) W.; m. Catherine Mary Osborne, Sept. 1942; children: Andrew Nicol, John Lewis, David Winfield, Steven; m. Joyce Lynn Goldstein, July 21, 1967. BS in Zoology, U. Mich., 1942; MD, Temple U., 1950, M in Med. Sci., 1954. Intern, U. Pa. Grad. Hosp., 1950-51; resident in psychiatry Temple U., Phila., 1951-54; spl. lectr. Sch. Social Work, Bryn Mawr Coll., 1955-59; mem. med. faculty U. Pa., 1954-59, law faculty, 1955-59; prof. psychiatry U. Mich., Ann Arbor, 1959-80, mem. law faculty, 1959-90, prof. emeritus psychiatry and of law, 1990; pvt. practice medicine, specializing in psychiatry, Ann Arbor, 1959—. Mem. Mich. Law Enforcement and Criminal Justice Commn., 1968-72. Served to capt. Med. Service Corps, AUS, 1942-46. Recipient Issac Ray award Am. Psychiat. Assn., 1978. Mem. Am. Psychiat. Assn., Am. Coll. Psychiatry, ABA (assoc.). Democrat. Unitarian. Author: Psychiatry for Lawyers, rev. edit., 1978; The Lawyer in the Interviewing and Counseling Process, 1976; others. Home: 21 Ridgeway St Ann Arbor MI 48104-1739 Office: 555 E William St Apt 21D Ann Arbor MI 48104-2427

WATSON, ARTHUR DENNIS, government official; b. Brownsville, Pa., May 11, 1950; s. Arthur Francis Puglia and Margaret Teresa Mastile; stepson of John Leslie Watson; m. Kathleen Frances Zaccardo, July 16, 1983; 1 child, Fiona Kathleen. BSBA, U. Richmond, 1972; MS in Bus.-Govt. Rels. Am. U., 1977, MA in Lit., 1979; PhD in English Lang. and Lit. Cath. U., 1987. Statisical asst. U.S. Postal Svc. Hdqrs., Washington, 1972-73, economist assoc., 1973-74, staff economist, 1974-77, mktg. analyst, 1977; rate analyst U.S. Postal Rate Commn., Washington, 1977-79, dir. pub. affairs, 1979-82; pub. affairs officer ICC, Washington, 1982-89, dep. dir. pub. affairs, 1989-93, assoc. dir. congl. and pub. affairs, 1993-95, assoc. dir. congressional and external affairs surface transp. bd., U.S. DOT, 1996—; pres. Arthur D. Watson and Co., Clifton, Va., 1983—. Washington corr. Linn's Stamp News, Sidney, Ohio, 1983-84; pub. rels. columnist Arundel Communications, Reston, Va., 1991-92; contbr. articles to profl. jours.; reader Washington Ear, WETA-FM radio side channel, 1977. With USCG, 1972-78. Recipient Meritorious Svc. medal, Pub. Svc. award ICC, 1989. Mem. E. Claiborne Robins Sch. Bus. Alumni Assn., Assn. Transp. Law, Logistics and Policy, USS Natoma Bay Assn., Pub. Rels. Soc. Am. Roman Catholic. Avocations: classical music, reading, writing, model building, travel. Home: 6521 Rockland Dr Clifton VA 20124-2415 Office: Surface Transp Bd 1925 K St NW Rm 842 Washington DC 20006-1105

WATSON, BERNARD CHARLES, foundation administrator; m. Lois Lathan, July 1, 1961; children: Barbra, Bernard Jr. BS, Ind. U., 1951; MEd, U. Ill., 1955; PhD, U. Chgo., 1967; postdoctoral work, Harvard U., 1968; LHD (hon.), Allen U., 1981, LaSalle U., 1987, Spring Garden Coll., Elizabethtown Coll, Beaver Coll., 1988, Harris-Stowe State Coll., Morris Brown Coll., 1989, Millersville U., 1991; LLD (hon.), Morgan State U., 1992, Lincoln U., 1974, Fla. Meml. Coll., 1984, Temple U., 1986, Med. Coll. Pa., 1986, Tuskegee U., 1991, Lincoln U., 1992, Phila. Coll. Pharmacy and Sci., 1994, Bethune-Cookman Coll., 1995; HHD (hon.), Wilberforce U., 1979; DFA, Univ. of the Arts, 1992; D of Pedagogy, Drexel U., 1992. Tchr., prin. Roosevelt Jr. and Sr. H.S., Gary, Ind., 1955-65; staff assoc. Midwest Adminstrn. Ctr. U. Chgo., 1965-67; assoc. supt. innovative programs Sch. Dist. Phila., 1967-68, dep. supt. for planning, 1968-70; prof., chmn. dept. urban edn. Temple U., Phila., 1970-75, also prof. social foundations Coll. Edn. and prof. urban studies Coll. Liberal Arts, 1970-75, v.p. acad. adminstrn., 1976-81, presdl. scholar, 1994—; pres., CEO William Penn Found, Phila., 1982-93; chmn. HMA Found., Phila., 1994—; bd. dirs. Comcast Corp., First Union Bancorp North, First Union Bank, Keystone AAA Club, Keystone Ins. Co., Phila. Contributionship; assoc. edn. Grad. Sch. Edn. Harvard U., 1970-72, mem. vis. com., 1981-87; mem. vis. com. dept. Afro-Am. studies Harvard Coll., 1974-78. Author: In Spite of the System: The Individual and Educational Reform, 1974; editor in chief Cross Reference: A Jour. Pub. Policy and Multi-Cultural Edn., 1976-79, Testing Its Origin, Use and Misuse, 1997, Colored, Negro, Black: Chasing the American Dream, 1997; contbr. numerous articles to profl. jours., chpts. to books. Mem. steering com., mem. exec. com. Nat. Urban Coalition, 1973-89; vice chmn. Nat. Adv. Coun. Edn. Professions Devel., 1967-70, Pa. Coun. on Arts, 1986-93; mem. Nat. Coun. Ednl. Rsch., 1980-82, William T. Grant Found. Commn. Work, Family and Citizenship, 1987-88; sr. vice chmn. bd. trustees Nat. Urban League, 1983-96; vice chmn. bd. dirs. Pa. Conv. Ctr. Authority, 1986—; trustee Thomas Jefferson U., 1993-95; sec. bd. N.J. State Aquarium, 1988-93; chmn. Ave. the Arts Inc., 1992—; mem. fed. judiciary nominating com. Pa., 1981-89. Recipient numerous honors and awards for leadership in edn., the arts, and civil rights. Mem. Am. Philosophical Soc., Am. Acad. Polit. and Social Sci., Phi Delta Kappa, Kappa Delta Pi. Office: TUCC 1616 Walnut St Ste 1 Philadelphia PA 19103-5301

WATSON, BOB, professional baseball executive. Gen. mgr. Houston Astros. Office: Houston Astros PO Box 288 Houston TX 77001-0288

WATSON, CATHERINE ELAINE, journalist; b. Mpls., Feb. 9, 1944; d. Richard Edward and LaVonne (Slater) W.; m. Al Sicherman (div.); children: Joseph Sicherman, David Sicherman. B.A. in Journalism, U. Minn., 1967; M.A. in Teaching, Coll. of St. Thomas, 1971. Reporter Mpls. Star Tribune, 1966-72; editor Picture mag., 1972-78, Travel sect., 1978—; editor in chief Galena (Ill.) Gazette, 1990-91. Author: Travel Basics, 1984. Contbr. articles to newspapers and travel mags. and books. Recipient Newspaper Mag. Picture Editor's award Pictures of Yr. Competition, 1974, 75, awards for writing and photography Soc. Am. Travel Writers, 1983-96, Photographer of Yr. award, 1990, Alumna of Notable Achievement award U. Minn. Coll. Liberal Arts, 1994; named Lowell Thomas Travel Journalist of Yr., 1990. Mem. Am. Newspaper Guild, Soc. Am. Travel Writers, Phi Beta Kappa, Kappa Tau Alpha, Alpha Omicron Pi. Office: 425 Portland Ave Minneapolis MN 55415-1511

WATSON, DAVID SCOTT, financial services executive; b. Westfield, Mass., June 28, 1959; s. Donald King and Cynthia Ann (Johnson) W.; m. Carol Anne Brekus, Oct. 26, 1991; children: Brooke Catherine, Andrew Donald. BA in Econs. and Polit. Sci., Drew U., 1981; MBA in Fin., Syracuse U., 1995. Credit trainee Horizon Bancorp, Princeton, N.J., 1981-82; asst. v.p. Ctr. Fin. Corp., Waterbury, Conn., 1982-86; v.p., regional mgr. Citytrust Bancorp, Bridgeport, Conn., 1986-91; v.p., group lending mgr. Chase Manhattan Bank, Bridgeport, Conn., 1991—; mem. New Haven Home Loan Adv. Com., 1993-95, Conn. Mortgage Intermediary Task Force, Hartford, 1994—, Bankers Regional Reinvestment Compact, 1993-95; mem. Fairfield County adv. bd. Local Initiatives Support Corp., 1995—. Bd. chmn. Bridgeport (Conn.) Cmty. Health Ctr., 1992—; dir., treas. Hall Neighborhood House, Bridgeport, 1992—; bd. dirs. Bridgeport Neighborhood Fund, 1996—, Conn. Preservation Loan Fund, 1996—; vol. United Way, Waterbury, Conn., 1982-86; mem. Madison (Conn.) Police Retirement Bd., 1993—. Recipient Vol. Action award, Pres. of U.S., 1994. Mem. Internat. Econs. Honor Soc., Grad. Club. Republican. Episcopalian. Avocations: golf, oenology, volunteer work, computers, private pilot. Home: 85 Overbrook Rd Madison CT 06443-1934 Office: Chase Manhattan Bank 999 Broad St Bridgeport CT 06604-4328

WATSON, DENNIS WALLACE, microbiology educator, scientist; b. Morpeth, Ont., Can., Apr. 29, 1914; came to U.S., 1938, naturalized, 1946; s. William and Sarah (Verity) W.; m. Alicemay Whittier, June 15, 1941; children: Catherine W., William V. BSA, U. Toronto, 1934; MS, Dalhousie U., 1937; PhD, U. Wis., 1941, DSc (hon.), 1981. Rsch. assoc. U. Wis., 1942, asst. prof., 1946-49; vis. investigator Rockefeller Inst., 1942; investigator Connaught Lab. Med. Rsch. U. Toronto, 1942-44; assoc. prof. U. Minn., Mpls., 1949-52; prof. U. Minn., 1953-63, head dept. microbiology, 1964-84, Regents prof. microbiology, 1980-84, Regents prof. emeritus, 1984—; vis. prof. Med. Sch. U. Wash., 1950; mem. Commn. Immunization Armed Forces Epidemiology Bd., 1946-59; mem. bd. sci. counselors, div. biol. standards NIH, 1957-59, mem. allergy and immunology study sect., 1954-58; chmn. tgn. grant com. Inst. Allergy and Infectious Diseases, 1964, mem. adv. coun., 1967-71; mem. microbiology panel Office Naval Rsch., 1963-66; vice chmn. Am. Soc. Microbiology Found., 1973; bd. dirs. Nat. Found. Infectious Diseases, 1976-81. Editorial bd. Infection and Immunity, 1971-72; editorial cons. Medcom Faculty Medicine, 1973—. With AUS, 1944-46. Recipient USPHS Research Career award, 1962-64; Spl. research fellow USPHS, 1960-61. Mem. AAAS, Am. Assn. Immunologists, Am. Chem. Soc., Am. Acad. Microbiology (vice chmn. bd. govs. 1967), Am. Soc. Microbiology (pres. 1969, v.p. Found. 1972-73), Soc. Exptl. Biology and Medicine (coun. 1977-79, pres. 1976-77), Lancefield Soc., Sigma Xi, Phi Zeta. Home: 2106 Hendon Ave Saint Paul MN 55108-1419 Office: U Minn Med Sch Dept Microbiology PO Box 196 Minneapolis MN 55455

WATSON, DOC (ARTHEL LANE WATSON), vocalist, guitarist, banjoist, recording artist; b. Deep Gap, N.C., Mar. 2, 1923; s. General Dixon and Annie (Greer) W.; m. Rosa Lee Carlton; children—Eddy Merle (dec.), Nancy Ellen. Ind. rec. artist, touring performer. Made first appearance at Boone (N.C.) Fiddler's Conf., rec. artist for Folkways in 1960's, signed with Vanguard Records, 1964, also recorded for United Artists, Columbia, Poppy, Sugar Hill, Verve and Flying Fish labels; performed at Newport Folk Festival, 1963, Smithsonian Inst., White House, 1980, Carnegie Hall, 1985; toured in Africa for Dept. State, 1970, also toured in Europe and Japan; albums include (many with Merle Watson) Southbound, Red Rocking Chair, The Guitar Album, Riding the Midnight Train (Grammy award for Best Traditional Folk album, 1986), Portrait, Songs for Little Pickers, On Praying Ground (Grammay award for best traditional folk album 1990); performed music for film Places in the Heart. Recipient Grammy award Nat. Acad. Rec. Arts and Scis., 1973, 74, 79, 86, 90, N.C. award State of N.C., 1985, Carolina prize N.Y. Times Corp., 1985, Grammy award for Best Traditional Folk Rec., 1990. Office: care Folklore Inc 1671 Appian Way Santa Monica CA 90401-3258

WATSON, DONALD RALPH, architect, educator, author; b. Providence, Sept. 27, 1937; s. Ralph Giles W. and Ethel (Fletcher) Pastene; m. Marja Palmqvist, Sept. 8, 1966 (div. Jan. 1984); children: Petrik, Elise; m. Judith Criste, Jan. 3, 1986. A.B., Yale U., 1959, B.Arch., 1962, M.Ed., 1969. Lic. architect Nat. Council Archtl. Registration Bds. Architect Peace Corps, Tunisia, 1962-64; archtl. cons. Govt. of Tunisia, 1964-65; pvt. practice, Trumbull, Conn., 1969—; dean Sch. Architecture, Rensselaer Poly. Inst., Troy, N.Y., 1990-95, prof., 1990—; Frederick C. Baker vis. prof. U. Oreg., 1995; chmn. environ. design program, Yale U., 1979-90; cons. UN, Bhutan, 1976, World Bank, North Yemen, 1979, Dept. of Energy, 1979, NAS, 1982, U.S. Advanced Bldg. Tech. Coun., 1991. Author: Designing and Building a Solar House, 1977, Energy Conservation Through Building Design, 1979, Climatic Design, 1983, Energy Design Handbook, 1993; editor: Time Saver Standards: Architectural Fundamentals, 1997; editor in chief Design Data. Bd. dirs. Save the Children Fedn., 1979-82. Recipient Honor Design award Conn. Soc. Architects, 1974, Honor Design award region AIA, 1978, 84, 1st award Owens Corning Energy Conservation Bldg. Design Program, 1983, Excellence in housing award Energy Efficient Bldg. Assn., 1988, Lifetime Achievement award Passive and Low Energy Architecture, 1990; Assn. of Collegiate Schs. of Architecture/Am. Metals Climax rsch. fellow, 1967-69; rsch. fellow Rockefeller Found., 1978. Fellow AIA; mem. Am. Solar Energy Soc. (editor). Home and Office: 54 Larkspur Dr Trumbull CT 06611-4652 Office: Rensselaer Poly Inst 110 Eighth St Troy NY 12180

WATSON, ELIZABETH MARION, protective services official; b. Phila., Aug. 25, 1949; d John Julian and Elizabeth Gertrude (Judge) Herrmann; m. Robert LLoyd Watson, June 18, 1976; children: Susan, Mark, David. BA in Psychology with honors, Tex. Tech. U., 1971. With Houston Police Dept., 1972-92, detective homicide, burglary and theft, 1976-81, lt. records div. northeast patrol div., 1981-84, capt. inspections div., auto theft div., 1984-87, dep. chief west patrol bur., 1987-90, police chief, 1990-92; with Austin, Tex. Police Dept., 1992—, police chief, 1992—; mem. adv. bd. S.W. Law Enforcement Inst., Richardson,Tex., 1990—. Mem. editorial bd. Am. Jour. Police, 1991—. mem. Internat. Assn. Chiefs of Police (mem. major cities chiefs, mem. civil rights com.), Police Exec. Rsch. Form, Tex. Police Chiefs Assn. Roman Catholic. Office: Police Department 715 E 8th St Austin TX 78701-3300

WATSON, GEORGE HENRY, JR., broadcast executive, journalist; b. Birmingham, Ala., July 27, 1936; s. George Henry and Grace Elizabeth (Carr) W.; m. Ellen Havican Bradley, July 13, 1979; children—George H., III, Ellen Havican. B.A., Harvard U., 1959; M.S., Columbia U., 1960. Reporter Washington Post, 1960-61; corr. ABC News, 1962-75, Moscow bur. chief, 1966-69, London bur. chief, 1969-75, v.p., Washington bur. chief, 1976-80; v.p., mng. editor Cable News Network, 1980; v.p. news ABC News, N.Y.C., 1981-85; exec. in charge ABC News Viewpoint ABC News, 1981-85, v.p., Washington bur. chief, 1985-93, sr. contbg. editor, 1993—. Bd. advisors Grad. Sch. Journalism, Berkeley.Served with U.S. Army, 1958. Recipient Peabody award, 1982, DuPont Columbia award, 1983, nat. news Emmy award, 1984. Mem. Radio Television News Dirs. Assn., Soc. Profl. Journalists, Nat. Press Club, Overseas Press Club (award for best television documentary 1971, citation for excellence 1974), Washington Press Club, Com. to Protect Journalists. Club: Fed. City. Office: ABC News 1717 Desales St NW Washington DC 20036-4401

WATSON, GEORGIANNA, librarian; b. Lock Haven, Pa., Feb. 18, 1949; d. George and Anna (Eisenhower) Rhine; children: Sharga Nicolle, George Winfield-Martin. BS in Edn., Lock Haven State U., 1971; MLS, Brigham Young U., 1978; M in Pub. Adminstrn., John Jay Coll. Criminal Justice, N.Y.C., 1986. Tchr. Mifflin County Sch. Dist., Lewistown, Pa., 1971-72; librarian Shiprock Boarding Sch. Bur. Indian Affairs, Shiprock, N.Mex., 1972-79, Ft. Sill Indian Sch. Bur. Indian Affairs, Lawton, Okla., 1979-80; librarian U.S. Mil. Acad., West Point, N.Y., 1980-83, head pub. services, library, 1983—. Mem. Southeastern N.Y. Library Resource Council (mem. continuing edn. com., chairperson govt. documents interest group), Southeastern N.Y. Reference Library Interest Group, Am. Quarter Horse Assn., Internat. Arabian Horse Assn., Pi Alpha Alpha. Republican. Home: 8 St Michaels Ln Walden NY 12586-2443 Office: US Mil Acad Dept Army West Point NY 10996-1799

WATSON, HARLAN L(EROY), federal official, physicist, economist; b. Macomb, Ill., Dec. 17, 1944; s. Joseph Carroll and Helen Louise (Sanders) W.; m. Sharon Ann Rinkus Diguette, Apr. 22, 1977. BA in Physics, Western Ill. U., 1967; PhD in Physics, Iowa State U., 1973; MA in Econs., Georgetown U., 1981. Postdoctoral fellow Argonne (Ill.) Nat. Lab., 1973-75; project scientist, then sr. scientist B-K Dynamics, Inc., Rockville, Md., 1975-78; tech. staff TRW Energy Systems Planning Group, Mc Lean, Va., 1978-80; profl. staff mem. subcom. on energy nuclear proliferation and govt. processes Com. on Govtl. Affairs, U.S. Senate, Washington, 1980-81; tech. and sci. cons. Com. on Sci. and Tech., U.S. Ho. of Reps., 1981-86; rep. energy and environ., coord. Com. on Sci., Space and Tech., U.S. Ho. of Reps., 1986-89; sci. adviser to sec. Dept. Interior, Washington, 1989-93, dep. asst. sec for sci.-water and sci., 1989-90, prin. dep. asst. to sec. for water and sci., 1990-93; rep. spl. asst. subcom. energy, com. sci., space, tech. U.S. Ho. of Reps., Washington, 1993-95, staff dir. subcom. energy and environment, com. sci., 1995—. Contbr. articles to profl. jours. Home: 6719 Tomlinson Ter Cabin John MD 20818-1328 Office: B 374 Rayburn House Office Bldg Washington DC 20515

WATSON, HAROLD GEORGE, ordnance company executive, mechanical engineer; b. Phoenix, Oct. 19, 1931; s. Clarence Elmer and Eunice A. (Record) W.; m. Ruth May Thomas, Aug. 30, 1951 (dec.); children: Patricia Ruth, Linda Darlene, Harold George; m. Katherina Anna Kish, Sept. 22, 1990. B.S., U. Ariz., 1954. Engr. Shell Oil Co., L.A., 1954; project engr. Talco Engrng. Co., Hamden Conn., 1956, area mgr., Mesa, Ariz., 1956-57, chief engr. Rocket Power, 1958-61, dir. engrng., 1961-64; dir. engrng. Space Ordnance Systems, El Segundo, Calif., 1964-68; dir. engrng. Universal Propulsion Co., Riverside, Calif., 1968-70, gen. mgr., v.p. engrng., Tempe, Ariz., 1970-76, v.p., mgr., 1976-77, pres., gen. mgr., Phoenix, 1977—. Patentee in field. 1st lt. USAR, 1954-56. Mem. Am. Mgmt. Assn., SAFE Assn. (past pres.), AIAA, Air Force Assn., Internat. Pyronetics Soc., Am. Def. Preparedness Assn. Office: Universal Propulsion Co Inc 25401 N Central Ave Phoenix AZ 85027-7837

WATSON, HELEN RICHTER, educator, ceramic artist; b. Laredo, Tex., May 10, 1926; d. Horace Edward and Helen Mary (Richter) Watson. B.A., Scripps Coll., 1947; M.F.A., Claremont Grad. Sch. and U. Ctr., 1949; post-grad. Alfred U., 1966; Swedish Govt. fellow Konstfackskolan, Stockholm, 1952-53. Mem. faculty Chaffey Coll., Ontario, Calif., 1950-52; chmn. ceramics Mt. San Antonio Coll., Walnut, Calif., 1955-57; prof., chmn. ceramics dept. Otis Art Inst., Los Angeles, 1958-81; mem. faculty Otis-Parsons Sch. Design, 1983-88, ret. 1988; studio ceramic artist, Claremont, Calif. and Laredo, Tex., 1949—; design cons. Interpace, Glendale, Calif., 1963-64; artist-in-residence Clarement Men's Coll., 1977. Claremont Grad. Sch. fellow, 1948-49; Swedish Govt. grantee, 1952-53; recipient First Ann. Scripps Coll. Disting. Alumna award, Claremont, 1978. Mem. Artists Equity, Nat. Ceramic Soc., Am. Craftsmen's Council, Los Angeles County Mus. Art, Mus. Contemporary Art Los Angeles. Republican. Episcopalian. Address: 220 Brooks Ave Claremont CA 91711-4026 also: 1906 Houston St Laredo TX 78040-7709

WATSON, JACK CROZIER, retired state supreme court justice; b. Jonesville, La., Sept. 17, 1928; s. Jesse Crozier and Gladys Lucille (Talbot) W.; m. Henrietta Sue Carter, Dec. 26, 1958; children: Carter Crozier (dec.), Wells Talbot. BA, U. Southwestern La., 1949; JD, La. State U., 1956; completed with honor, Appellate Judges Seminar, N.Y. U., 1974, Sr. Appellate Judges Seminar, 1980. Bar: La. 1956. Atty. King, Anderson & Swift, Lake Charles, La., 1956-58; prosecutor City of Lake Charles, 1960; asst. dist. atty. Calcasieu Parish, La., 1961-64; ptnr. Watson & Watson, Lake Charles, 1961-64; judge 14th Jud. Dist., La., 1964-72; judge ad hoc Ct. Appeals, 1st Circuit, Baton Rouge, 1972-73; judge Ct. Appeals, 3rd Circuit, Lake Charles, 1973-79; assoc. justice La. Supreme Ct., New Orleans, 1979-96, ret., 1996; faculty advisor Nat. Coll. State Judiciary, Reno, 1970, 73; adj. prof. law summer sch. program in Greece, Tulane U., 1988-97; del. NEH Seminar, 1976; La. del to Internat. Conf. Appellate Magistrates, The Philippines, 1977; mem. La. Jud. Coun., 1986-92. 1st lt. USAF, 1950-54. Mem. ABA, La. Bar Assn., S.W. La. Bar Assn. (pres. 1973), Law Inst. State of La., La. Coun. Juvenile Ct. Judges (pres. 1969-70), Am. Judicature Soc., S.W. La. Camellia Soc. (pres. 1973-74), Am. Legion (post comdr. 1963), Lake Charles Yacht Club (commodore 1974), Blue Key, Sigma Alpha Epsilon, Phi Delta Phi, Pi Kappa Delta. Democrat. Baptist. Address: 868 Del Mar Downs Rd Solana Beach CA 92075

WATSON, JACK H., JR., lawyer; b. El Paso, Tex., Oct. 24, 1938; children: Melissa Woodward, Lincoln Hearn. BA, Vanderbilt U., 1960; LLB, Harvard U., 1966. Bar: Ga. 1965, D.C. 1978. Assoc. King & Spalding, Atlanta, 1966-71; partner King & Spalding, 1972-77; asst. to Pres. for intergovtl. affairs and sec. to cabinet Washington, 1977-80; chief of staff White House, 1980-81; ptnr. Long, Aldridge & Norman, Atlanta, 1981—; mem. vis. com. Harvard Law Sch., 1987-93; permanent chmn. Ga. Joint Commn. on Alt. Dispute Resolution, 1990-93, chmn. Ga. Commn. on Dispute Resolution, 1993—. Counsel Met. Atlanta Commn. Crime and Juvenile Delinquency, 1966-67; trustee, vice chair Milton S. Eisenhower Found., 1994—; pres. Met. Atlanta Mental Health Assn., 1971-72; chmn. Gov.'s Study Commn. Alcohol, 1971-72, Ga. Alcoholism Adv. Council, 1972; chmn. bd. Ga. Dept. Human Resources, 1972-77; candidate gov. of Ga., 1982; mem. nat. adv. com. Ctr. for Study of Presidency, 1983; mem. Franklin D. Roosevelt Library Bd., 1986—; chmn. 20th Century Fund Task Force on the U.S. Vice Presidency, 1987-88; active Franklin and Eleanor Roosevelt Instnl. Bd., 1990—. Served as officer USMC. Named One of Atlanta's Five Outstanding Young Men Jaycees, 1970. Mem. ABA (standing com. on dispute resolution 1991-93, coun. mem. sect. dispute resolution 1993—, chmn. ABA task force on N.Am. Free Trade Agreement 1993), State Bar Ga., Atlanta Bar Assn., Atlanta Lawyers Club, Phi Beta Kappa, Phi Eta Sigma, Omicron Delta Kappa. Office: Long Aldridge & Norman 701 Pennsylvania Ave NW Ste 600 Washington DC 20004-2624

WATSON, JAMES DEWEY, molecular biologist, educator; b. Chgo., Apr. 6, 1928; s. James Dewey and Jean (Mitchell) W.; m. Elizabeth Lewis, 1968; children: Rufus Robert, Duncan James. BS, U. Chgo., 1947, DSc (hon.), 1961; PhD in Zoology, Ind. U., 1950, DSc (hon.), 1963; LLD (hon.), U. Notre Dame, 1965; DSc (hon.), L.I. U., 1970, Adelphi U., 1972, Brandeis U., 1973, Albert Einstein Coll. Medicine, 1974, Hofstra U., 1976, Harvard U., 1978, Rockefeller U., 1980, Clarkson Coll., 1981, SUNY, 1983; MD (hon.), U. Buenos Aires, Argentina, 1986; DSc (hon.), Rutgers U., 1988, Bard Coll., 1991, U. Cambridge, 1993, Fairfield U., 1993, U. Stellenbosch, 1993, U. Oxford. Rsch. fellow NRC, U. Copenhagen, 1950-51; Nat. Found. Infantile Paralysis fellow Cavendish Lab., Cambridge U., 1951-52, 55-56; sr. rsch. fellow biology Calif. Inst. Tech., 1953-55; asst. prof. biology Harvard U., 1955-58, assoc. prof., 1958-61, prof., 1961-76; dir. Cold Spring Harbor Lab., N.Y., 1968—, pres., 1994—; assoc. dir. Nat. Ctr. for Human Genome Rsch. NIH, 1988-89, dir. Nat. Ctr. for Human Genome Rsch., 1989-92; pres. Cold Spring Harbor (N.Y.) Lab.; Newton-Abraham vis. prof. Oxford U., 1994. Author: Molceular Biology of the Gene, 1965, 4th edit., 1986, The Double Helix, 1968, (with John Tooze) The DNA Story, 1981, (with others) The Molecular Biology of the Cell, 1983, 2d edit., 1989, 3d edit. 1994, (with John Tooze and David Kurtz) Recombinant DNA, A Short Course, 1983, 2d edit., 1992. Named Hon. fellow Clare Coll., Cambridge U.; recipient (with F.H.C. Crick) John Collins Warren prize Mass. Gen. Hosp., 1959, Eli Lilly award in biochemistry Am. Chem. Soc., 1959, Albert Lasker prize Am. Pub. Health Assn., 1960, (with F.H.C. Crick) Rsch. Corp. prize, 1962, (with F.H.C. Crick and M.H.F. Wilkins) Nobel prize in medicine, 1962, Presdl. Medal of Freedom, 1977, Kaul Found. award for excellence, 1993, Nat. Biotech. Venture award, 1993, Copley Medal, 1993, Charles A. Dana award, 1994, Lomonosov medal Russian Acad. Sci., 1995, Nat. medal of Sci., 1997. Mem. NAS (Carty medal 1971), Am. Philos. Soc., Am. Assn. Cancer Rsch., Am. Acad. Arts and Scis., Am. Soc. Biol. Chemistry, Royal Soc. (London) (Copley medal 1993), Acad. Scis. Russia, Danish Acad. Arts and Scis. Home: Bungtown Rd Cold Spring Harbor NY 11724 Office: Cold Spring Harbor Lab PO Box 100 Cold Spring Harbor NY 11724-0100

WATSON, JAMES LOPEZ, federal judge; b. N.Y.C., May 21, 1922; s. James S. and Violet (Lopez) W.; m. D'Jaris Hinton Watson, July 14, 1956 (dec. Nov. 1989); children: Norman, Karen, Kris. B.A. in Govt, N.Y. U., 1947; LL.B., Bklyn. Law Sch., 1951. Bar: N.Y. bar 1951. Mem. N.Y. Senate from 21st Senatorial Dist., 1954-63; judge Civil Ct. N.Y., 1964-66; acting judge N.Y. State Supreme Ct., 1965; judge U.S. Customs Ct., 1966-80, U.S. Ct. Internat. Trade, 1980—. Bd. dirs. N.Y.C. Police Athletic League. Served with inf. AUS, World War II, ETO. Decorated Purple Heart, Combat Inf. badge. Mem. ABA, N.Y. State Bar Assn., Fed. Bar Council, World Peace Through Law. Home: 676 Riverside Dr New York NY 10031-5529 Office: US Ct Internat Trade 1 Federal Plz New York NY 10278-0001

WATSON, JAMES RAY, JR., education educator; b. Anniston, Ala., Dec. 6, 1935; s. James Ray and Mary Garrity (Profumo) W.; m. Shirley Jean Lesesne, 1960 (div. 1972); children: Laura Catherine, Gregory Andrew, Jennifer Ann; m. Louise Edmonds, 1973. BS in Animal Sci., Auburn U., 1957, MS in Agronomy, 1960; PhD in Botany, Iowa State U., 1963. Rsch. asst. dept. agronomy Auburn (Ala.) U., 1958-60; rsch. asst. dept. botany Iowa State U., Ames, 1960-61, teaching asst. dept. botany, 1961-63; asst. prof.

dept. botany Miss. State U., Mississipi State, 1963-68, assoc. prof. dept. botany, 1968-77, head dept. botany, 1975-78, prof. dept. botany, 1977-78, prof. dept. biol. sci., 1978—; participant Smithsonians Summer Inst. Systematics, Washington, 1968; vis. scholar U. Mich., Ann Arbor, 1964-65. Contbr. articles to profl. jours. Mem. The Nature Conservancy. With U.S. Army, 1957-58. NSF postdoctoral fellow U. Mich., 1963-64; Nat. Natural Landmarks Miss. grantee, 1973-74. Mem. Natural Areas Assn., Bot. Soc. Am. (paleobot. sect.), Miss. Native Plant Soc., Sigma Xi, Xi Sigma Pi. Republican. Roman Catholic. Avocation: pocket watch collector. Home: 217 Seville Pl Starkville MS 39759-2133 Office: Miss State U Dept Biol Sci PO Drawer GY Mississippi State MS 39762

WATSON, JAMES STANLEY, secondary education educator; b. Glen Ridge, N.J., Feb. 2, 1948; s. James G. and Bernice T. (Frail) W. BS in Natural Sci. Edn., U. Tenn., 1971; MA in Environ. Edn., Glassboro State Coll., 1978; postgrad., U. Tenn., 1984, 89, Coll. Atlantic, U. Maine, 1986. Cert. secondary sci. curriculum, Tenn. Tchr. geology, chemistry, biology and applied sci., asst. coach wrestling Red Bank High Sch., Chattanooga, 1972-76; tchr. earth sci. 8th grade Red Bank Jr. High Sch., Chattanooga, 1976-78; tchr. gen. sci. and ecology, coach wrestling Ooltewah High Sch., Chattanooga, 1978-81; tchr. biology, earth sci., chemistry, gen. sci., geology and physical sci., coach boys and girls soccer, asst. coach wrestling Red Bank High Sch., 1981-92; tchr. honors biology, asst. coach boys and girls soccer Soddy-Daisy High Sch., Chattanooga, 1992—; textbook reviewer for scis. Tenn. Dept. Edn., 1996—, Praxis reviewer for earth sci., 1996; writer, tchr. new geology course Red Bank High Sch., 1973, new ecology course Ooltewah High Sch., 1979; writer energy conservation plan Hamilton County Sch. Dist., 1978, gen. sci. curriculum guide, 1979; planner, contributing writer tchr. workshop field activity design and procedures Chattanooga Nature Ctr., Keystone (Colo.) Sci. Sch., 1985, tchr. workshop volcanoes Mt. St. Helens Nat. Monument, Washington, 1986, tchr. workshop marine mammals in Gulf of Maine, 1989; writer solar energy sect. Tenn. Valley Authority Energy Source Book for Tchrs., 1985; participant Tenn. Valley Authority Water Quality Monitoring Network, 1986; presenter environ. edn. conf. N.Am. Assn., Eugene, Oreg., 1986; mem. task force on earth sci. curriculum Tenn. Dept. Edn., 1988; mem. adoption com. sci. textbooks Hamilton County Sch. Dist., 1990; textbook reader, evaluator geology, gen. sci. and phys. sci. Tenn. Dept. Edn., 1990; asst. to instr. dept. geoscis. U. Tenn., 1990, 91; presenter workshops Ctr. Excellence for Sci. and Math. Edn. Tenn. Dept. Edn., 1991. sponsor winner Chattanooga Sci. Fair, 1973, runner-up, 1974; mem. dual team championships wrestling rules com. Tenn. Secondary Sch. Athletic Assn., 1987, speaker bureau Tenn. River Aquarium, 1990, 91, ednl. adv. com. Spangler Farm Environ. Edn. Ctr., 1991, adv. coun. Chattanooga YMCA Earth Sci. Corps, 1992; horticulture vol. Tenn. River Aquarium, 1992. Grantee Lyndhurst Found., 1982, 84, 86, Pub. Edn. Found., 1990, 94, Pub. Edn. Found., 1994, GeoTrek, 1996; recipient Soccer Coach of Yr. award News Free Press, 1985, 89, Mini-grant Chattanooga Jr. League, 1985, 87. Mem. NEA, Am. Littoral Soc., Nat. Assn. Geology Tchrs. (Outstanding Earth Sci. Tchr. award 1992, 96), Nat. Marine Edn. Assn., Ga. Assn. Marine Edn., Tenn. Edn. Assn., Hamilton County Edn. Assn. (Outstanding Svc. award 1980, trustee Hamilton County Sch. Dist. Sick Leave Bank 1982—), Tenn. Conservation League, Chattanooga Nature Ctr., Internat. Oceanographic Found., Nature Conservancy, Tenn. Earth Sci. Tchrs. Assn. (pres. 1995-97). Baptist. Avocations: hiking, mineral rock collecting, water sports, biking, yard work. Office: Soddy-Daisy High Sch 618 Sequoyah Access Rd Soddy Daisy TN 37379-4049

WATSON, JERRY CARROLL, advertising executive; b. Greenville, Ala., Aug. 22, 1943; s. William J. and Georgia Katherine (Mixon) W.; m. Judith Zeigler Brooks, Sept. 16, 1988; 2 child, Theodore William, Hunter Brooks. BS, U. Ala., Tuscaloosa, 1967; MS, U. Va., 1995. Staff writer Phillips, Eindhoven, The Netherlands, 1967-68; mgr. mktg. Fuller & Dees Mktg., Montgomery, Ala., 1968-70; v.p. Univ. Programs, Washington, 1970-73; pres. Coll. & Univ. Press, Washington, 1973-80; ptnr. Direct Response Consulting Svcs., McLean, Va., 1981-96; bd. dirs. Foxhall Corp., The Art Co. Founding mem. Am. Inst. Cancer Rsch. Mem. Direct Mktg. Assn., Non-Profit Mailer Fedn., Promotional Mktg. Assn., Nature Conservancy, Sierra Club, Falls Church (Va.) C. of C. (bd. dirs.). Avocation: gardening, astronomy. Home: 850 Dolley Madison Blvd Mc Lean VA 22101-1821 Office: Direct Response Cons Svcs 6849 Old Dominion Dr Ste 300 Mc Lean VA 22101-3705

WATSON, JOANN FORD, theology educator; b. Ashland, Ohio, Apr. 11, 1956; d. Laurence Wesley and Edna Lucille (Garber) F.; m Duane Frederick Watson, June 2, 1984; 1 child, Christina Lucille. BA, DePauw U., 1978; MDiv, Princeton Theol. Sem., 1981; PhD, Northwestern U., 1984. Ordained to ministry, Presbyn. Ch. Asst. prof. hist. theology Ashland Theol. Sem., 1984-86, assoc. prof. theology, chair dept. ch. history and theology, 1989-95, H.R. Gill Prof. of theology, 1996—; chaplain Grady Meml. Hosp., Atlanta, 1986-87; co-pastor Tri-Ch. Parish United Meth. Chs. Northwestern, N.Y., 1987-89; pastor Camroden Presbyn. Ch., Rome, N.Y., 1987-89; clergy commr. del. Gen. Assembly of Presbyn. Ch., 1995. Author: Manna for Sisters in Christ, 1989, Mutuality in Christ, 1991, Meditations on Suffering, 1993, Study of Karl Barth's Doctrine of Man and Woman, 1995. Missionary vol. Mother Teresa's Missionaries of Charity, Calcutta, 1988; mem. Hospice Ashland County chpt., 1989-93; assoc. mem. Women's Symphony League, Ashland Symphony Orch., 1989-94. Doctoral fellowship Northwestern U., 1982-84. Mem. Internat. Assn. of Women Mins. (exec. bd., trustee 1990-95), Presbyn. Women in Leadership, Nat. Assn. of Presbyn. Clergywomen, Soc. of Biblical Lit., Am. Acad. of Religion, Alpha Lambda Delta, Phi Beta Kappa. Republican. Avocations: travel, music, water sports. Office: Ashland Theolog Sem 910 Center St Ashland OH 44805-4007

WATSON, JOHN ALLEN, lawyer; b. Ft. Worth, Sept. 18, 1946; s. John and Mary (Barlow) W.; m. Patricia L. Clardy, Oct. 24, 1946; 1 child, Virginia E. B.A., Rice U., 1968; J.D., U. Tex., Austin, 1971. Bar: Tex. 1971. Assoc. Fulbright & Jaworski, Houston, 1971-78, ptnr., 1978—. Mem. ABA. Office: Fulbright & Jaworski LLP 1301 Mckinney St Ste 5100 Houston TX 77010-3095

WATSON, JOHN LAWRENCE, III, former trade association executive; b. Rome, Ga., Jan. 14, 1932; s. John Lawrence and Mary (Cowen) W.; m. Dorothy Palmer McLanahan, Aug. 9, 1958; children: Mary Palmer Watson Gard, Valerie Catherine Watson Bilbrough, John Lawrence IV. BS, Auburn U., 1954. Trader-over the counter J.C. Bradford & Co., Atlanta, 1957-58; with Robinson Humphrey & Co., Atlanta, 1958-64, dept. head-over the counter, 1964-74, dir. equity trading, 1974-83, dir. capital markets, 1983-85; pres. Security Traders Assn., N.Y.C., 1985-96. Mem. bd. visitors Babcock Sch. Mgmt. Wake Forest U.; past chmn. Parent's Coun. Wofford Coll.; life trustee Pace Acad.; trustee Securities Industry Found. for Econ. Edn. Named Man of Yr., Equities mag. Mem. Nat. Assn. Securities Dealers (dist. chmn. 1982, bd. govs. 1983-85), Am. Mus. Fin. History (trustee), Capital City Club, Piedmont Driving Club (Atlanta), Ponte Vedra Club, Sawgrass Country Club (Ponte Vedra), Univ. Club (N.Y.C.). Home: 505 Ponte Vedra Blvd Ponte Vedra Beach FL 32082-4153

WATSON, JOSEPH GARTRELL, medical facility administrator; b. Atlanta, Feb. 8, 1940; s. Joseph and Johnnie Mae (Lo Max) W.; m. Juanita Leona Brown, Oct. 27, 1962; children: Joseph Gartrell Jr., Andrea D. Watson Fiendenburg, Stephanie L. BA in Sociology, CUNY, 1984; BS in Psychology/Polit. Sci., U. State N.Y., Albany, 1987; MA in Bus. Mgmt., SUNY, Stony Brook, 1994; grad., Am. Inst. of Hypnotherapy, 1996. N.Y. State advanced cert. in labor/mgmt. studies; cert. hypnotherapist; registered hypnotherapist. Unit mgr. surgery SUNY-Univ. Hosp., Stony Brook, 1985-88, mgr. hosp. svc. adminstrn., 1989-90, sr. staff adminstrv. asst., patient rep., 1990-91, sr. staff adminstrv. asst. human resources, 1991-92; coord. emergency medicine L.I. Jewish Med. Ctr., New Hyde Park, N.Y., 1991-94, patient svc. mgr. hosp.-wide, 1995-96; occupational therapy cons., Fresh Meadow, N.Y., 1995—. Served with USAR, 1967-95. Recipient 25 yrs. svc. award N.Y. State Office Mental Health, Queens Village, N.Y., 1988, Achievement medal U.S. Army War Office Sec. of Army, Washington, 1989. Mem. Am. Coll. Health Care Execs. (assoc.), Am. Occupational Therapy Assn. (cert. occupational therapy asst.). Avocation: classical music. Home: 67-25C 186 Lane 2C Fresh Meadows NY 11365

WATSON, JOYCE LESLIE, elementary educator; b. Riverside, N.J., May 31, 1950; d. Robert Eugene and Doris Virginia (Robinson) Stockton; 1 child, Michelle Leslie. BS, Trenton State Coll., 1972, MEd, 1978. Cert. elem. tchr., N.J., Pa. Tchr. elem. Willingboro (N.J.) Sch. Dist., 1972-81, Pennsbury Sch. Dist., Fallsington, Pa., 1987—; tchr. gifted/talented Pennsbury Sch. Dist., Fallsington, 1987-88, 92—; elem. demonstration tchr. Pennsbury Sch. Dist., 1995—; coach Odyssey of Mind, Pennwood Mid Sch., Yardley, Pa., 1993-94; participant 8th Ann. Capital Area Space Orientation Program, Washington, 1996. Mem. NEA, ASCD, Coun. Exceptional Children, Talented and Gifted, Pa. Assn. for Gifted Edn., Pa. State Edn. Assn., Airplane Owners and Pilots Assn., Nat. Aero. Assn., Phi Delta Kappa. Home: 10 Shelley Ln Yardley PA 19067-7320 Office: Makefield Elem Sch Makefield Rd Yardley PA 19067

WATSON, JULIAN See BLAKE, BUD

WATSON, KATHARINE JOHNSON, art museum director, art historian; b. Providence, Nov. 11, 1942; d. William Randolph and Katharine Johnson (Badger) W.; m. Paul Luther Nyhus, Dec. 17, 1983; stepchildren: Kristina Victoria, Karen Ida, Katharine Ellen. BA, Duke U., 1964; MA, U. Pa., 1967, PhD, 1973. Teaching asst. U. Pa., 1966-67; instr., curator exhbns. U. Pitts., 1969-70; curator of art before 1800 Allen Meml. Art Mus., Oberlin, Ohio, 1973-77; lectr. Oberlin Coll., 1973-77; dir. Peary-MacMillan Artic Mus. Bowdoin Coll., Brunswick, Maine, 1977-83, dir. Mus. of Art, 1977—; trustee Mus. Art of Ogunquit, 1977-89, Regional Art Conservation Lab., Williamstown, 1977-90, Surf Point Found., York, Maine; mem. Smithsonian Coun. Author: Pietro Tacca, 1983; author text for exhbn. catalogues; co-editor: Allen Meml. Art Mus. Bull, 1974-77; contbr. articles to profl. jours. Mem. profl. adv. com. Victoria Soc. Maine, 1988-93; mem. adv. coun. Archives of Am. Art, 1982-90. Kress Found. fellow, 1967-68, Chester Dale Fellow, 1970-71, Am. Coun. Learned Socs. fellow, 1977-78, Villa I Tatti fellow, 1977-78. Mem. Am. Assn. Art Mus. Dirs., Am. Assn. Museums, Coll. Art Assn. Office: Bowdoin Coll Mus Art Walker Art Bldg Brunswick ME 04011

WATSON, KEITH STUART, lawyer; b. Phila., July 25, 1942; s. Alfred Nelson and Elizabeth (Dixon) W.; m. Susan Calano; children: Tara, Taylor. BA, Trinity Coll., Hartford, Conn., 1964; MA, Conn. Coll., 1970; JD, Harvard U., 1967. Instr. USCG Acad., New London, Conn., 1968-70; mng. ptnr. Wald, Harkrader & Ross, Washington, 1970-85; ptnr. Piper & Marbury, Washington, 1986-93, Wiley, Rein & Fielding, 1993—; bd. dirs. Northland Terr., Inc., Columbus, Ohio. Contbr. numerous articles to profl. jours. Pres. bd. trustees Woodley House, Washington, 1980-94. Lt. (j.g.) USCG, 1968-70. Recipient Edgerton Achievement award ACLU, 1987. Mem. ABA. Avocations: tennis, travel.

WATSON, KENNETH MARSHALL, physics educator; b. Des Moines, Sept. 7, 1921; s. Louis Erwin and Irene Nellie (Marshall) W.; m. Elaine Carol Miller, Mar. 30, 1946; children: Ronald M., Mark Louis. B.S., Iowa State U., 1943; Ph.D., U. Iowa, 1948; Sc.D. (hon.), U. Ind., 1976. Rsch. engr. Naval Rsch. Lab., Washington, 1943-46; mem. staff Inst. Advanced Study Princeton (N.J.) U., 1948-49; rsch. fellow Lawrence Berkeley (Calif.) Lab., 1949-52, mem. staff, 1957-81; asst. prof. physics U. Ind., Bloomington, 1952-54; asso. prof. physics U. Wis., Madison, 1954-57; prof. physics U. Calif., Berkeley, 1957-81; prof. oceanography, dir. marine physics lab. U. Calif., San Diego, 1981-93; cons. Mitre Corp., Sci. Application Corp.; mem. U.S. Pres.'s Sci. Adv. Com. Panels, 1962-71; adviser Nat. Security Coun., 1972-75; bd. dirs. Ctr. for Studies of Dynamics, 1979-88; mem. JASON Adv. Panel; mem. sci. adv. bd. George C. Marshall Inst., 1989—. Author: (with M.L. Goldberger) Collision Theory, 1964, (with J. Welch and J. Bond) Atomic Theory of Gas Dynamics, 1966, (with J. Nutall) Topics in Several Particle Dynamics, 1970, (with Flatté, Munk, Dashen) Sound Transmission Through a Fluctuating Ocean, 1979. Mem. Nat. Acad. Scis. Home: PO Box 9726 Rancho Santa Fe CA 92067-4726 Office: U Calif Marine Physics Lab La Jolla CA 92093

WATSON, LINDA ANNE, library director; b. New Milford, Conn., Nov. 26, 1951. Student, Georgetown U., 1969-71; BA summa cum laude, U. Conn., 1972; MLS, Simmmons Coll., 1973. Libr., project mgr. Tracor-Jitco, Inc., Rockville, Md., 1974-75, libr. assoc., then AVLINE coord., 1975-79; asst. head selection and acquisitions sect. Nat. Libr. Medicine, NIH, Bethesda, Md., 1979-80, chief materials utilization br., 1980-82, head audiovisual resources sect., 1982-85; dir. info. svcs. Houston Acad. Medicine-Tex. Med. Ctr. Libr., 1985-86, assoc. dir. for pub. svcs., 1986-89, assoc. exec. dir. for libr. ops., 1989-90; dir. Claude Moore Health Scis. Libr., U. Va. Health Scis. Ctr., Charlottesville, 1990—, mem. gen. med. faculty, 1990—; sr. assoc. Cooper and Assocs., Charlottesville, 1985—; mem. adv. com. arthritis info. clearinghouse NIH, 1980-82, diabetes info. clearinghouse, 1984-85; mem. adv. com. combined health info. database HHS, 1983-85; adj. asst. prof. Baylor Coll. Medicine, Houston, 1986-90; adj. asst. prof. U. Tex. Med. Sch., Houston, 1986-90; mem. pub. rels. adv. coun. Tex. Med. Ctr., 1987-89; mem. planning panel on edn. and tng. health sci. librs. Nat. Libr. Medicine, 1993-94; presenter in field. Contbr. articles to profl. jours. Mem. Leadership Charlottesville, 1990—. Grantee Nat. Libr. Medicine, 1990-93, 94-95, Va. State Libr. and Archives, 1993-94, NSF, 1993-94. Mem. ALA, Assn. Coll. and Rsch. Librs., Libr. Adminstrn. and Mgmt. Assn., Am. Med. Informatics, Va. Libr. Assn., Med. Libr. Assn. (chmn. ann. meeting nat. program com. 1992-95, bd. dirs. 1996—, treas. 1997—), Acad. Health Info. Profls. (disting.), Assn. Acad. Health Scis. Libr. Dirs. (vice chmn. joint legis. task force with Med. Libr. Assn. 1990-94, ann. stats. editl. bd. 1997-2001), Va. Coun. Health Scis. Librs. (chmn. 1991-94). Avocations: horses, sports. Home: 200 George Rogers Rd Charlottesville VA 22911-8402 Office: U Va Health Scis Ctr HSC # 234 Claude Moore Health Sci Lib Charlottesville VA 22908

WATSON, MARY ALICE, academic administrator; b. Dublin, Ga., Apr. 10, 1943; d. Jonnie Cecil and Annie Hudson (Temples) Raffield; m. Ray James Watson, Sept. 1, 1963; children: Ray Jeffry, John Adam (dec.), Sally Ann Watson-Hall. BS in Bus. Edn., Ga. Coll., 1973, MEd in Bus. Edn., 1976; Ednl. Specialist in Vocat. Edn., U. Ga., 1982; EdD, Nova Southeastern U., 1995. Cert. postsecondary edn. adminstr., secondary tchr. and adminstr. Tchr. bus. edn. Treutlen County High Sch., Soperton, Ga., 1973-74, East Laurens High Sch., Dublin, 1974-77; coord. program edn. and career exploration East Laurens Elem. Sch., Dublin, 1977-80; dep. prin. East Laurens Comprehensive High Sch., Dublin, 1980-83; v.p. instrnl. svcs. Heart of Ga. Tech. Inst., Dublin, 1983—; mem. on-site evaluation team SACS-COEI, Houston, 1989, Paducah, Ky., 1990, Ochsner Allied Health Programs, Oschner Found. Hosp., New Orleans, 1993; presenter practicum Nova U. Summer Inst., 1989; George T. Baker Aviation Sch., Miami, 1993; Ft. Sam Houston Med. Programs, San Antonio, 1993; East Ctrl. Consortium VPISC chair, 1994-96; pres. Instrnl. Svcs. Coun., 1996—; Pinellas Tech. Edn. Ctr., Clearwater, Fla., 1996; participant various seminars and workshops. Vol. Cancer Crusade, 1983—. Mem. Nat. Coun. Community Svcs. and Continuing Edn., Am. Tech. Edn. Assn., Internat. Tech. Edn. Assn., Nat. Coun. Instrnl. Adminstrs., Nat. Coun. Local Adminstrs. Vocat. Edn., Am. Vocat. Assn., Women Bus., Ga. Vocat. Assn., Ga. Assn. Local Adminstrs. Vocat. Edn., Dublin-Laurens County C. of C., Dodge County C. of C., Order Blarney Stones, Pi Omega Pi, Iota Lambda Sigma (v.p. 1994—). Baptist. Avocations: golf, walking, gardening, reading, sewing. Office: Heart of Ga Tech Inst 560 Pine Hill Rd Dublin GA 31021-1521

WATSON, MARY ELLEN, ophthalmic technologist; b. San Jose, Calif., Oct. 29, 1931; d. Fred Sidney and Emma Grace (Capps) Doney; m. Joseph Garrett Watson, May 11, 1950; children: Ted Joseph, Tom Fred, Pamela Kay Watson. Cert. ophthalmic med. technologist and surg. asst. Ophthalmic technician Kent W. Christoferson, M.D., Eugene, 1965-80; ophthalmic technologist, surg. asst., adminstr. I. Howard Fine, M.D., Eugene, 1980—; course dir. Joint Commn. Allied Health Pers. in Ophthalmolgy, 1976—, lectr., mem. faculty, 1983—, skill evaluator and site coord., Eugene, 1988—; intermat. instr. advanced surgical techniques. Contbr. articles to profl. jours. Recipient 5-Yr. Faculty award Joint Commn. for Allied Health Pers. in Ophthalmology, 1989. Mem. Allied Tech. Pers. in Ophthalmology, Internat. Women's Pilots Assn. Avocation: flying. Home: 2560 Chaucer Ct Eugene OR 97405-1217 Office: I Howard Fine MD 1550 Oak St Eugene OR 97401-7701

WATSON, MATHEW D., optical scientist; b. L.A., Feb. 9, 1958. BS in Physics, San Jose State U., 1984; MS in Optical Scis., U. Ariz., 1989, PhD in Optical Scis., 1991. Mem. tech. staff Uniphase, Inc., San Jose, Calif., 1984-86; rsch. assoc. Optical Scis. Ctr., Tucson, Ariz., 1986-91; electro optical engr. ILX Lightwave, Inc., Bozeman, Mont., 1991-93; sr. optical engr. Quest Integrated, Inc., Kent, Wash., 1994-96; pres. Eclipse Optical Rsch., Bellevue, Wash., 1997—. Contbr. articles to profl. jours.; patentee in field. Grad. rsch. scholar Optical Scis. Ctr., 1989; recipient ARCS scholarship ARCS Found., 1983. Mem. Optical Soc. Am., IEEE/Laser and Electro-optic Soc., Soc. Photometric and Instrumentation Engrs. Home: 10439 NE 28th Pl Bellevue WA 98004-2043 Office: Eclipse Optical Rsch 10439 NE 28th Pl Bellevue WA 98004-2043

WATSON, MAX P., JR., computer software company executive; b. 1946. Graduate, La. U. With IBM Corp., Houston, 1967-83, Wang Labs., Houston, 1985-90; with BMC Software, Inc., Houston, 1990—, now pres., ceo, chmn. Office: BMC Software Inc 2101 Citywest Blvd Houston TX 77042-2827

WATSON, PATRICIA L., library director; b. Jan. 15, 1939; m. Jack Samuel Watson, 1960; children: Bradley, Amanda. BA, Univ. Tenn., 1961, MS in Libr. and Info. Sci., 1975. Cataloging asst. tech. svcs. dept. Knoxville Pub. Libr., 1961-65; adminstrv. asst. Knoxville-Knox County Pub. Libr., 1975-78, head West Knoxville br. libr., 1978-85; dir. Knox County Pub. Libr. System, 1985—. Bd. dirs. Tanasi Girl Scout Coun., 1981-86; treas. Univ. Tenn. Grad. Sch. Libr. and Info. Sci. Alumni Orgn., 1983-84; elder Farragut Presbyn. Ch. Mem. ALA, Tenn. Libr. Assn. (pres. 1992-93), East Tenn. Libr. Assn. (pres. 1988-89), Rotary Internat. Office: Knox County Pub Libr System 500 W Church Ave Knoxville TN 37902-2505

WATSON, PATTY JO, anthropology educator; b. Superior, Nebr., Apr. 26, 1932; d. Ralph Clifton and Elaine Elizabeth (Lance) Andersen; m. Richard Allan Watson, July 30, 1955; 1 child, Anna Melissa. M.A., U. Chgo., 1956, Ph.D. in Anthropology, 1959. Archaeologist-ethnographer Oriental Inst.-U. Chgo., 1959-60, research assoc., archaeologist, 1964-70; instr. anthropology U. So. Calif., Los Angeles, 1961, UCLA, 1961, L.A. State U., 1961; asst. prof. anthropology Washington U., St. Louis, 1969-70, assoc. prof., 1970-73, prof., 1973—, Edward Mallinckrodt disting. univ. prof., 1993—; mem. rev. panel NSF, Washington, 1974-76; fellow Ctr. Advanced Study in Behavioral Scis., Stanford, Calif., 1981-82, 91-92. Author: The Prehistory of Salts Cave, Kentucky, 1969, Archaeological Ethnography in Western Iran, 1979, (with others) Man and Nature, 1969, Explanation in Archaeology, 1971, Archaeological Explanation, 1984, Girikihaciyan, A Halafian Site in Southeastern Turkey; author, editor: Archaeology of the Mammoth Cave Area, 1974, Prehistoric Archaeology Along the Zagros Flanks, 1983; co-editor: The Origins of Agriculture, 1992, Of Caves and Shell Mounds, 1996. Grantee NSF, 1959-60, 68, 70, 72-74, 78-79, NEH, 1977-78, Nat. Geog. Soc., 1969-75. Fellow Am. Anthropol. Assn. (editor for archaeology 1973-77, Disting. Lectr. award 1994, Disting. Svc. award 1996); mem. AAAS (chair sect. H 1991-92), NAS, Soc. Am. Archaeology (exec. com. 1974-76, 82-84, editor Am. Antiquity 1984-87, Fryxell medal 1990), Cave Rsch. Found., Assn. Paleorient (sci. bd.), Nat. Speleological Soc. (hon. life, editorial bd. bull. 1979—). Office: Dept Anthropol CD #1114 Washington U Saint Louis MO 63130-4899

WATSON, PAUL, photojournalist, correspondent. Photographer The Toronto Star, 1986—, Africa bur. chief, 1992-94, Asian bur. chief, 1994—. Recipient Robert Capa gold medal for photography, 1993, Nat. Newspaper award for spot news photography, 1994, Pulitzer Prize for spot news photography, 1994, Nat. Newspaper award for internat. reporting, 1996. Office: The Toronto Star, One Yonge St, Toronto, ON Canada M5E 1E6*

WATSON, PAULA D., library administrator; b. N.Y.C., Mar. 6, 1945; d. Joseph Francis and Anna Julia (Miksza) De Simone; m. William Douglas Watson, Aug. 23, 1969; children—Lucia, Elizabeth. A.B., Barnard Coll., 1965; M.A., Columbia U., 1966; M.S.L.S., Syracuse U., 1972. Reference librarian U. Ill., Urbana, 1972-77, city planning and landscape architecture librarian, 1977-79, head documents library, 1979-81; asst. dir. gen. services U. Ill. Library, Urbana, 1981—, acting dir. gen. svcs., 1988-93, dir. ctrl. pub. svcs., 1989-93, asst. univ. libr., 1993-95, dir. electronic info. svcs., 1995—. Contbr. articles to profl. jours. N.Y. State Regents fellow Columbia U., N.Y.C., 1965-66; Council on Library Resources profl. edn. and tng. for librarianship grantee, 1983. Mem. ALA (sec. univ. librs. sect. ALA-Assn. Coll. and Rsch. Librs. 1989-91, mem. libr. adminstrn. mgmt. sect. com. on comparative libr. orgn. 1988-89, mem. conf. planning com. optical disk interest group 1988), Ill. Library Assn. Avocation: gardening. Home: 715 W Delaware Ave Urbana IL 61801-4806 Office: U Ill 246 A Library 1408 W Gregory Dr Urbana IL 61801-3607

WATSON, RAYMOND COKE, JR., engineering executive, academic administrator; b. Anniston, Ala., Aug. 31, 1926. BS, Jacksonville State U.; MSE, U. Ala.; MS, U. Fla.; MBA and PhD in Engring. Sci., Calif. Coast U. Chief engr. Dixie Svc. Co., 1948-54; head dept. physics and engring. Jacksonville State U., 1954-60; v.p. engring. and rsch. Teledyne Brown Engring., 1960-70, chief engr., chief scientist, 1990—; dir. continuing edn., engring. and math. U. Ala., Huntsville, 1970-76; pres., prof. engring. and math. Southeastern Inst. Tech., Huntsville, 1976—; adj. assoc. prof. U. Ala., Huntsville, 1961-70; cons. various def. industries, 1970—. Contbr. articles to profl. jours. Recipient NASA Pub. Svc. award; NSF Sci. Faculty Fellow. Mem. IEEE, AIAA, Optical Soc. Am., Ops. Rsch. Soc. Am., Inst. Mgmt. Sci., Internat. Soc. Optical Engrs., Inst. Indsl. Engrs. Achievements include research in defense systems, space systems and electro-optics. Home: 1801 Inspiration Ln SE Huntsville AL 35801-1150 Office: Teledyne Brown Engineering PO Box 070007 300 Sparkman Dr NW Huntsville AL 35807-7007

WATSON, RICHARD ALLAN, philosophy educator, writer; b. New Market, Iowa, Feb. 23, 1931; s. Roscoe Richard and Daisy Belle (Penwell) W.; m. Patty Jo Andersen, July 30, 1955; 1 child, Anna Melissa. B.A., U. Iowa, 1953, M.A., 1957, Ph.D. in Philosophy,, 1961; M.S. in Geology, U. Minn., 1959. Instr. philosophy U. Mich., Ann Arbor, 1961-64; asst. prof. Washington U., St. Louis, 1964-67; assoc. prof. Washington U., 1967-74, prof., 1974—; pres. Cave Research Found., Mammoth Cave, Ky., 1965-67; trustee Nat. Parks and Conservation Assn., Washington, 1969-81. Author: The Downfall of Cartesianism, 1966, Under Plowman's Floor, 1978, The Runner, 1981, The Philosopher's Diet, 1985, The Breakdown of Cartesian Metaphysics, 1987, The Philosopher's Joke, 1990, Writing Philosophy, 1992, Niagara, 1993, Caving, 1994, The Philosopher's Demise, 1995, Representational Ideas, 1995, Good Teaching, 1997;(with others) Man and Nature, 1969, The Longest Cave, 1976; editor: Classics in Speleology, 1968-73, Speleologia, 1974-79, Cave Books, 1980—, Jour. History of Philosophy, 1983, Jour. History of Philosophy Monograph Series, 1985-95. Served to 1st lt. USAF, 1953-55. NEH grantee, 1975; fellow Ctr. Advanced Study in Behavioral Scis., Stanford, Calif., 1967-68, 81-82, 91-92, Am. Coun. Learned Socs., 1967-68, Princeton Ctr. Internat. Studies, 1975-76, Camargo Found., 1995. Mem. Nat. Speleological Soc. (hon. life), AAAS, Am. Philos. Assn., Cave Research Found. Office: Washington U Dept Philosophy Saint Louis MO 63130-4899

WATSON, RICHARD THOMAS, lawyer; b. Lakewood, Ohio, Aug. 21, 1933; s. Thomas Earl Watson and Sara Lucille (Whapham) Hadfield; m. Judith C. Briggs, Aug. 6, 1960; children: David, Andrew, Susan (dec.). AB, Harvard U., 1954, JD, 1960. Bar: Ohio 1960. Assoc. Spieth, Bell, McCurdy & Newell, Cleve., 1960, ptnr., 1965, mng. ptnr., 1987—; bd. dirs. numerous corps. Chancellor Episcopal Diocese of Ohio, Cleve., 1986—; mem. Harvard U. Univ. Resources, 1992—; v.p. bd. trustees Cleve. Mus. Art, 1991—; trustee Case Western Res. U., 1993—. Mem. Union Club Cleve. Office: Spieth Bell McCurdy & Newell 925 Euclid Ave Cleveland OH 44115

WATSON, ROBERT, professional sports team executive; b. L.A., Apr. 10, 1996; m. Carol; children: Keith, Kelley. Student, Harbor Jr. Coll., Wilmington, Calif. Baseball player Astros, Houston, 1965-79; gen. mgr., 1993-95; baseball player Red Sox, Boston, 1979, Yankees, N.Y.C., 1980-82; gen. mgr., 1996—; baseball player Braves, 1982-84; coach, instr. Oakland, 1984-88; asst. gen. mgr. Astros, Houston, 1988-93. All-star Nat. League, 1973. Office: NY Yankees Yankee Stadium 161st St and River Ave Bronx NY 10451

WATSON, ROBERT JOE, hospital administrator, retired career officer; b. Wellington, Kans., Nov. 12, 1934; s. Charles Bruce and Marguerite B. (Scholes) W.; m. Ursula Eschenroeder, Dec. 26, 1983; children: Stephanie, Stacy Watson Bruce, Susannah Watson Gold; stepchildren: Jurgen Wanke, Claudia Wanke. MS in Edn., Kans. State Tchrs. Coll., 1963; MBA, U. Hawaii, 1969; MHA, George Washington U., 1973, EdD, 1976; student, Command-Gen. Staff Coll., 1973, U.S. Army War Coll., 1986. Commd. 2nd lt. U.S. Army, 1963, advanced through grades to col., 1989; stationed at Tripler Army Med. Ctr., Honolulu, 1967-69, USARV Surgeons Office, Long Binh, Vietnam, 1969-70, Surgeon Gen.'s Office, Washington, 1970-74, Walter Reed Med. Ctr., Washington, 1974-76, Acad. Health Svcs., Ft. Sam Houston, Tex., 1976-80, 87-89, 68th Med. Group, Ziegenberg, Germany, 1980-82, U.S. Army Hosp., Ft. Riley, Kans., 1982-84, 34th Gen. Hosp., Augsburg, Germany, 1984-87; ret., 1989; assoc. dir. Student Health Ctr. U. Fla., Gainesville, 1989—. Fellow Am. Coll. Healthcare Execs. (adv., regent 1982-84). Episcopalian. Avocations: tennis, golf, gardening. Office: U Fla Student Health Ctr Gainesville FL 32611

WATSON, ROBERT R., lawyer; b. Buffalo, N.Y., Mar. 10, 1944. BA, Wheaton Coll., 1967; JD, U. Chgo., 1972. Bar: Ill. 1972. Law clerk to Hon. Richard W. McLaren U.S. Dist. Ct. (no. dist.), Ill., 1972-74; ptnr. Sidley & Austin, Chgo. Office: Sidley & Austin 1 First Natl Plz Chicago IL 60603-2003

WATSON, ROBERT TANNER, physical scientist; b. Columbus, Ohio, Sept. 25, 1922; s. Rolla Don and Gladys Margaret (Tanner) W.; m. Jean Mehlig, Oct. 7, 1944; children—Melinda Jean, Parke Tanner, John Mehlig, Todd Pennell, Kate Ann. B.A., DePauw U., 1943; Ph.D., MIT, 1951. With photo products dept. E. I. duPont de Nemours & Co., Inc., Parlin, N.J., 1951-55; with electron tube div. RCA, Marion, Ind., 1955-59; with Internat. Tel. & Tel. Corp., 1959-71, v.p., gen. mgr. indsl. labs. div., 1962-63, pres., 1963-68; dept. tech. dir., other positions Aerospace and Def. Group, 1968-71; gen. phys. scientist OT and NTIA U.S. Dept. Commerce, 1971-90. Mem. Gov.'s Air Pollution Control Bd., 1966-70; Allen County chmn. Ind. Sesquicentennial, 1965; trustee Ind. Ednl. Services Found., 1968-71; bd. dirs. YMCA of Greater Ft. Wayne and Allen County, 1966-69. Served to lt. (j.g.) USNR 1943-46, combat, PTO; USNR, 1946-55. Mem. Am. Inst. Mgmt. (fellow pres.'s council 1970), Ft. Wayne C. of C. (dir. 1966-68), Allen County-Ft. Wayne Hist. Soc. (Old Fort com.), Optical Soc. Am., IEEE, Sigma Xi, Phi Eta Sigma, Beta Theta Pi. Research and engring. in x-ray diffraction, radioactive scattering, solid state energy levels, electron emission, magnetic and photog. media, electro-optical, Laser and telecommunication systems. Mgr. several engring. firsts. Patentee in field. Home: 1770 Lang Dr Crofton MD 21114-2145

WATSON, ROBERT WINTHROP, poet, English language educator; b. Passaic, N.J., Dec. 26, 1925; s. Winthrop and Laura Berdan (Trimble) W.; m. Elizabeth Ann Rean, Jan. 12, 1952; children: Winthrop, Caroline. BA, Williams Coll., 1946; postgrad., U. Zurich, 1947; MA, Johns Hopkins, 1950, PhD in English, 1955. Instr. English Williams Coll., 1946, 47-48, 52-53, Johns Hopkins, 1950-52; mem. faculty U. N.C., Greensboro, 1953—; prof. English U. N.C., 1963-90; vis. poet, prof. English Calif. State U., Northridge, 1968-69. Author: (poetry) A Paper Horse, 1962, Advantages of Dark, 1966, Christmas in Las Vegas, 1971, Selected Poems, 1974, Island of Bones, 1977, Night Blooming Cactus, 1980, The Pendulum: New and Selected Poems, 1995; (novels) Three Sides of the Mirror, 1966, Lily Lang, 1977. Swiss-Am. exch. fellow, 1947; grantee Nat. Endowment for Arts, 1973; recipient Am. Scholar Poetry prize, 1959, Lit. award Am. Acad. Inst. Arts Letters, 1977. Home: 9D Fountain Manor Dr Greensboro NC 27405-8001

WATSON, SHARON GITIN, psychologist, executive; b. N.Y.C., Oct. 21, 1943; d. Louis Leonard and Miriam (Myers) Gitin; m. Eric Watson, Oct. 31, 1969; 1 child, Carrie Dunbar. B.A. cum laude, Cornell U., 1965; M.A., U. Ill., 1968, Ph.D., 1971. Psychologist City N.Y. Prison Mental Health, Riker's Island, 1973-74; psychologist Youth Services Ctr., Los Angeles County Dept. Pub. Social Services, Los Angeles, 1975-77, dir. clin. services, 1978, dir. Youth Services Ctr., 1978-80; exec. dir. Crittenton Ctr. for Young Women and Infants, Los Angeles, 1980-89, Assn. Children's Svcs. Agys. of So. Calif., L.A., 1989-92, L.A. County Children's Planning Coun., 1992—. Contbr. articles to profl. jours. Mem. Commn. for Children's Svcs. Family Preservation Policy Com., Mayor's Com. on Children, Youth and Families, L.A. Learning Ctrs. Design Team, Interagy. Coun. Child Abuse and Neglect Policy Com., L.A. Unified Sch. Dist. Bd. Edn.'s Com. on Student Health and Human Svcs.; bd. dirs. L.A. Roundtable for Children, 1988-94, Adolescent Pregnancy Childwatch, 1985-89; trustee L.A. Ednl. Alliance for Restructuring Now; co-chmn. Los Angeles County Drug and Alcohol Abuse Task Force, 1990; mem. Cmty. Adv. Coun. Dept. Children's Svcs., 1989-90; mem. steering com. western region Child Welfare League Am., 1985-87. Mem. APA, Calif. Assn. Svcs. for Children (sec.-treas. 1983-84, pres. elect 1985-86, pres. 1986-87), Assn. Children's Svcs. Agys. So. Calif. (sec. 1981-83, pres. elect 1983-84, pres. 1984-85), Town Hall Calif., U.S. Figure Skating Assn. (bd. dirs., chair, membership com., sanctions and eligibility 1993-96), Pasadena Figure Skating Club (bd. dirs., pres. 1985-87, 89-90). Home: 4056 Camino Real Los Angeles CA 90065-3928 Office: LA County Children's Planning Coun 500 W Temple St Rm B-26 Los Angeles CA 90012-2713

WATSON, SOLOMON BROWN, IV, lawyer, business executive; b. Salem, N.J., Apr. 14, 1944; s. Solomon Brown and Denise Amelia W.; m. Bernadette Aldrich, Mar. 18, 1967 (div.); children: Katitti Madrid, Kira Pallis (twins); m. Brenda J. Wilson, Apr. 28, 1984. B.A. in English, Howard U., 1966; J.D., Harvard U., 1971. Bar: Mass. 1972, N.Y. 1977. Assoc. Bingham, Dana & Gould, Boston, 1971-74; corp. sec., asst. gen. counsel N.Y. Times Co., N.Y.C., 1979-89, gen. counsel, 1989-90, v.p., gen. counsel, 1990-96, sr. v.p., gen. counsel, 1996—. Active Vols. Legal Svc., Jobs for Youth Inc., until 1989; v.p. N.Y. Vietnam Vets. Leadership Program, Inc., until 1992, Agent Orange Assistance Fund, Vets. Adv. Bd. Lt. U.S. Army, 1966-68. Decorated Bronze Star with oak leaf cluster, Army Commendation medal with oak leaf cluster and V. Mem. ABA (com. on corp. law depts.), Am. Arbitration Assn. (bd. dirs.), Am. Corp. Counsel Assn. (dir.), Assn. Bar City N.Y., Mass. Bar Assn., Newspaper Assn. Am. (mem. legal affairs com.), Legal Aid Soc. (bd. dirs.). Home: 341 W 87th St New York NY 10024-2635 Office: NY Times Co 229 W 43rd St New York NY 10036-3913

WATSON, STANLEY ELLIS, clergyman, financial company executive; b. New Orleans, July 25, 1957; s. Joseph and Dorothy (Jones) W.. EdB, Jarvis Christian Coll., Hawkins, Tex., 1977; MRE, Tex. Christian U., Ft. Worth, 1979; spl. edn., So. U. A&M, Baton Rouge, 1986; grad., U.S. Acad. Pvt. Investigation, 1991; DD (hon.), Charter Ecumenical Ministries, 1994. Cert. tchr.; registered notary Mich. Asst. min. Jarvis Christian Coll., Hawkins, Tex., 1974-77; tchr. pub. sch., Daingerfield, Tex., 1977-78; asst. min. Park Manor Christian Ch., Chgo., 1980-81; asst. mgr. K Mart, Shreveport, La., 1981-82; min. United Christian Ch., Jackson, Miss., 1982-83; tchr. pub. sch., Napoleonville, La., 1986-87, Zachary, La., 1987-88; min. Vermont Christian Ch., Flint, Mich., 1988-90; sr. pastor Mich., 1990—; owner Waton Diversified Fin. Co., 1989—. Mem. NAACP, NEA. Christian Women's fellow, 1975-77, St. Louis Bd. Edn. fellow, 1977-79, Tex. Christian U. Brite Div. Sch. scholar, 1977; Jarvis Christian Coll. cert. of Honor, Merit, 1974-77; named Rev. Stanley Watson Day City of Flint, Mich., 1989. Mem. Nat. Assn. Investigative Specialists, Am. Inst. Profl. Bookeepers, Am. Fin. Coord. Assn. (fin. coord.), Christian Counselors Assn., Nat. Assn Investigative Specialist, Nat. Assn Federated Tax Preparers, Am. Soc. Notaries, Aircraft Owners and Pilots Assn. Coun. for Exceptional Children, Forgotten Man Ministries, Jarvis Christian Coll. Alumni Assn. (v.p.), NAACP, Urban League of Flint, Urban Coalition of Greater Flint, Flint C. of C., Internat. Reading Assn., NEA, Phi Beta Sigma, Kappa Delta Pi. Dem. Avocations: bee keeping. Office: Watson's Detective Agy PO Box 1664 Donaldsonville LA 70346-1664

WATSON, STEPHEN ALLISON, III, lawyer; b. Spokane, Wash., Aug. 17, 1957; s. Stephen Allison Jr. and Joan (Sauter) W.; m. Jeanie Watson; 1 child, Angelie. BA in Polit. Sci., Northwestern U., 1979; JD, Case We. U., 1982. Bar: Ohio 1983, U.S. Dist. (no. dist.) Ohio 1983. Counsel, environ. claims mgr. Argonaut Ins. Co., Chgo., 1982-86; mgr. hazardous waste unit Zurich Ins. Co., Schaumburg, Ill., 1989-91; mgr. environ. line bus. Zurich Ins. Co., Schaumburg, 1991-94; program exec., dir. regulatory svcs. Foster Wheeler Environ. Corp., Livingston, N.J., 1995—; cons. Office Spl. Dep., Chgo., 1995-96; lectr. in field. Contbr. articles to profl. jours. Mem. ABA (natural resource, energy and environ. law sect.), Def. Rsch. Inst. (environ. law com.). Republican. Avocations: golf, photography, sailing. Office: Foster Wheeler Environ Corp 8 Peach Tree Hill Rd Livingston NJ 07039

WATSON, STEWART CHARLES, construction company executive; b. Brock, Sask., Can., Sept. 17, 1922; s. Samuel Henry and Elva Jane (St. John) W.; student U. Buffalo; m. Irene Lillian Ahrens, Aug. 4, 1943; children: Judith Gail (Mrs. David Stafford), Wendy Carolyn (Mrs. Rocco Amuso), Ronald James, Candyce Louise. With Acme Steel & Malleable Iron Works, Buffalo, 1940-42; with Acme Hwy. Products, Buffalo, 1946-69, internat. mktg. mgr., 1955-69; pres. Watson-Bowman Assocs., Inc., Buffalo, 1970—, pres., Kinematics, 1984—. chmn. bd. Air Stewart Inc.; Internat. lectr. on kinetics of civil engring. structures; mem. U.S. Transp. Rsch. Bd.; bd. dirs. Internat. Bridge of Peace for Bering Strait Crossing. Served with AUS, 1943-45; ETO. Fellow Am. Concrete Inst. (dir. 1984—, Delmar Bloehm award 1984, Charles S. Whitney Medal 1987, hon. mem.); mem. Internat. Joints & Bearings Rsch. Coun. (chmn. 1988—), Internat. Activities Commn., ASTM, NAS, Masons (32 degree), Shriners. Home: 272 Lake Shore Rd, Fort Erie, ON Canada L2A 1B3

WATSON, THOMAS C., lawyer; b. Poplar Bluff, Mo., Feb. 26, 1945; s. William C. and Dorothy E. (Whitson) W.; children: Thomas II, Nathan, Edward, Clay, Luke; m. Sharlene Wonders, Mar. 19, 1994. BS, U. Memphis, 1967, MEd, 1968; JD, Washington U., St. Louis, 1972. Bar: Mo. 1972, D.C. 1973. Assoc. Morgan, Lewis & Bockius, Washington, 1973-78, ptnr., 1978-79; ptnr. Crowell & Moring, Washington, 1979-95, Watson & Renner, 1996—. Avocations: hiking, biking. computers, hunting wild fowl. Office: Watson & Renner 1001 Pennsylvania Ave NW Washington DC 20004

WATSON, THOMAS CAMPBELL, economic development consulting company executive; b. Pensacola, Fla., Feb. 19, 1931; s. Thomas Campbell (dec.) and Lucie Davis (Yonge) (dec.) W.; m. Norma Lynn Lofberg, June 20, 1959; children: Thomas C., Valerie Lynn, Pamela Lucie. Student, The Citadel, 1949-50; B.S., U.S. Naval Acad., 1954; B.S.E.E., U.S. Naval Postgrad. Sch., 1962; postgrad., Armed Forces Staff Coll., 1978. Commd. ensign U.S. Navy, 1954, advanced through grades to rear adm., 1980; comdg. officer Attack Squadron 81, 1970-72, comdr. Carrier Air Wing 9, 1972-73, comdr. Light Attack Wing 1, 1973-75; exec. asst. DCNO Air Warfare, The Pentagon Washington, 1975-76; comdg. officer USS Truckee, 1976-78, comdg. officer USS Independence, 1978-80; dep. dir. for current ops. Joint Chiefs of Staff, The Pentagon Washington, 1980-82; ret. U.S. Navy, 1982; pres. Mars Electronics, U.S.A., West Chester, Pa., 1982-88, ret., Omega Ventures, 1988—; exec. dir. Mus. Sci. and History, Jacksonville, Fla., 1989; pres. CAVUAssoc., 1990—. Decorated Legion of Merit, D.F.C., Bronze Star, Air medal. Mem. Assn. Naval Aviation, Naval Acad. Alumni Assn. Roman Catholic. Club: Rotary. Home: 2371 Bridgette Way Green Cove Springs FL 32043-8763

WATSON, THOMAS STURGES, professional golfer; b. Kansas City, Mo., Sept. 4, 1949; s. Raymond Etheridge and Sarah Elizabeth (Ridge) W.; m. Linda Tova Rubin, July 8, 1973; children: Margaret Elizabeth, Michael Barrett. BS, Stanford U., 1971. Profl. golfer, 1971—. Winner Western Open, 1974, 1977, 1984; winner Byron Nelson Tournament, 1975, 78, 79, 80; winner Brit. Open, 1975, 77, 80, 82, 83; winner, U.S. Open, 1982; winner World Series, 1975, 80; winner Andy Williams San Diego Open, 1977, 80; winner El Prat, 1977; winner Masters, 1977, 81; winner Bing Crosby Nat. Pro-Am Golf Tournament, 1977, 78; winner Tucson Open, 1978, 84; winner Colgate Hall of Fame Classic, 1978, 79; winner Anheuser Busch Golf Classic, 1978; winner Meml. Tournament, 1979; winner Heritage Classic, 1979, 83; winner Tournament of Champions, 1979, 80, 84; Los Angeles Open, 1980, 82; Greater New Orleans Open, 1980, 81; Dunlop Phoenix, 1980, Atlantic Classic, 1981; Nabisco Championship, 1987, Hong Kong Open, 1992; Recipient Vardon Trophy, 1977, 78, 79, Byron Nelson award, 1977-78, 79-80; named to Ryder Cup Team, 1977, 81, 83, 89 (elected capt. 1992—); named Player of Year Profl. Golf Assn., 1977, 78, 79, 80, 82, 84; elected to PGA World Golf Hall of Fame, 1988, Kans. Golf Hall of Fame, 1991, William H. Richardson award 1990. Mem. U.S. Golf Assn., Profl. Golfers Assn., Golf Course Supts. Assn. of Am. (Old Tom Morris award 1992), Butler Nat. Golf Club, Shadow Glen Club, Preston Trails Golf Club, Oakwood Country Club, Par Club, Blue Hills Country Club, Kansas City Country Club. Leading money winner PGA, 1977-80, 84. Office: 1901 W 47th Pl Ste 200 Shawnee Mission KS 66205-1834

WATSON, W. H., bishop. Bishop of N.W. Tex. Ch. of God in Christ, Lubbock. *

WATSON, W(ALLACE) ROBERT, financial executive; b. Corvallis, Oreg., Sept. 3, 1943; s. John Ernest and Sara (Rice) W.; m. Janice Gayle Blair, Mar. 18, 1978; children: Shelly, Rhonda, Melody, Brian. BS in Fin., Fla. State U., 1965, MBA, 1968. Mktg. mgr. Coca-Cola U.S.A., Atlanta, 1969-79, mgr. strategic planning, 1979-82, dir. fin. svcs., 1982-88; sr. v.p. Tex. Commerce Bank, Houston, 1988-89; pres. Watson & Assocs., Inc., Marietta, Ga., 1989-94; pres., CEO Harrison Direct, Inc., Atlanta, 1994-96; chmn., CEO Fidelity Family Svcs., Inc.; pres., CEO Watson & Assocs., L.L.C., Marietta, 1996—. Elder Presbyn. Ch., Marietta, 1985-86; deacon Johnson Ferry Bapt. Ch.; mem. Fla. State U. Boosters Club, President's Club. Capt. U.S. Army, 1965-67.

WATSON, WELLS, lawyer; b. Lake Charles, La., Apr. 11, 1963; s. Jack Crozier and Sue (Carter) W. BA, U. Miss., 1987; JD cum laude, Tulane U., 1990. Bar: La. 1990. Law clk. for Chief Judge Fred Heebe U.S. Dist. Ct., New Orleans, 1990-91; lawyer Baggett, McCall & Burgess, Lake Charles, La., 1991—. Mem. La. Trial Lawyers Assn. (chmn. new lawyers, bd. govs. 1994), Am. Trial Lawyers (La. gov. of new lawyers). Home: 6916 Shadow Ln Lake Charles LA 70605 Office: Baggett McCall & Burgess 3006 Country Club Rd Lake Charles LA 70605-5920

WATSON, WILLIAM D., lawyer; b. Buffalo, Sept. 1, 1943; s. William E. and Dorothy J. (Bowman) W.; m. Andrea L. Ehudin, Dec. 18, 1971; children: William A., Graham H. BA, Princeton U., 1965; LLB, Harvard U., 1968. Atty. Holme Roberts & Owen, LLP, Denver, 1970—; dir. Colo. Oil & Gas Assn. Author: The Gas Sellers Companion, 1992; editor Public Land and Resource Law Digest, 1990—. Capt. U.S. Army, 1968-70, Vietnam. Decorated 8 Bronze stars. Mem. Colo. Bar Assn., Fed. Energy Bar Assn., Rocky Mountain Princeton Club (pres. 1991-94). Office: Holme Roberts & Owen LLP 1700 Lincoln St Ste 4100 Denver CO 80203-4541

WATSON-BOONE, REBECCA A., library & information studies educator, researcher; b. Springfield, Ohio, Mar. 7, 1946; d. Roger S. and Elizabeth Lupton (Walker) Boone; m. Dennis David Ash, 1967 (div. 1975); m. Frederick Kellogg, 1979 (div. 1988); m. Peter G. Watson-Boone, May 26, 1989. Student, Earlham Coll., 1964-67; BA, Case Western Res. U., 1968; MLS, U. N.C., 1971; PhD, U. Wis., 1995. Asst. reference libr. Princeton (N.J) U., 1970-76; head cen. reference dept. U. Ariz., Tucson, 1976-83, assoc. dean Coll. Arts and Scis., 1984-89; loaned exec. Ariz. Bd. Regents, 1988-89; pres. Ctr. for Study of Info. Profls., 1995—. Contbr. articles to profl. jours. Mem. ALA (div. pres. 1985-86, councilor 1988-92), Assn. for Libr. and Info. Sci. Edn., NAFE. Mem. Soc. of Friends. Office: 4721 W Parkview Dr Mequon WI 53092-2022

WATT, DEAN DAY, retired biochemistry educator; b. McCammon, Idaho, Sept. 21, 1917; s. George William and Mary Amelia (Day) W.; m. Frances Elaine Murdock, Aug. 23, 1945; children: Sharon (Mrs. William E. Shull, Jr.), Nola Jean (Mrs. Thomas E. Barzee, Jr.), Barbara (Mrs. Robert Lauritzen), David, Stuart. Student, Idaho State U., 1936-37, 38-40; BS, U. Idaho, 1942; PhD, Iowa State U., 1949; postgrad., Case-Western Res. U., 1946-47. Research chemist Westvaco Chlorine Products, Newark, Calif., 1942-44; instr. Iowa State U., 1947-49; asst. prof. Purdue U., 1949-53; head dept. physiol. scis. Southeast La. Hosp., Mandeville, 1953-60; asso. prof. Tulane U., 1955-60, Ariz. State U., 1960-63; prin. biochemist Midwest Research Inst., Kansas City, Mo., 1963-69; prof. biochemistry Creighton U., 1969-88, prof. emeritus, 1988—. Fellow AAAS; mem. Internat. Soc. Toxinology (founding mem.), Sigma Xi. Mem. Ch. of Jesus Christ of Latter-day Saints. Research on animal venoms, biochemistry mental diseases. Home: 618 S 130th St Omaha NE 68154-2910

WATT, DOUGLAS (BENJAMIN WATT), writer, critic; b. N.Y.C., Jan. 20, 1914; s. Benjamin Douglas and Agnes Rita (Neimann) W.; m. Ray Mantel, Nov. 5, 1937 (div.); children—Richard David, James Douglas; m. Ethel Madsen, Aug. 13, 1951; children—Patricia, Katherine. A.B., Cornell U., 1934. Copy boy N.Y. News, 1936-37, radio columnist, 1937-40, drama reporter, 1940-71, sr. drama critic, 1971-87, critic-at-large, 1987-93; staff writer New Yorker mag., 1946-95; profl. song writer; columnist Small World, 1955-70. Pres. Hampton Animal Shelter, 1965-79. Served with USAAF, World War II. Mem. ASCAP, N.Y. Drama Critics Circle (pres. 1975-77). Club: Dutch Treat (N.Y.C.) (bd. govs.). Home: 27 W 86th St New York NY 10024-3615 *To say one has achieved success, except perhaps in isolated instances, is an exercise in vanity and contrary to man's experience. At best, some satisfaction can be gained in one's career, and then almost always because of intense effort.*

WATT, (ARTHUR) DWIGHT, JR., computer programming and microcomputer specialist; b. Washington, Jan. 25, 1955; s. Arthur Dwight and Myrtle Lorraine (Putnam) W.; m. Shari Elizabeth Gambrell, July 30, 1988. BA, Winthrop U., 1977, MBA, 1979; EdD, U. Ga., 1989. Cert. computer profl. Inst. Cert. Computer Profls.; cert. instr. cmty. first aid and safety, ARC; cert. Home Fire Arms Safety, NRA. Data processing instr. York Tech. Coll., Rock Hill, S.C., 1977-78; computer ctr. asst. Winthrop U., Rock Hill, 1976-79; data processing instr. Brunswick (Ga.) Coll., 1979-80; system operator, asst. programmer Sea Island (Ga.) Co., The Cloister, 1981; pvt. practice data processing cons. Swainsboro, Ga., 1981—; computer programming/microcomputer specialist instr. Swainsboro Tech. Inst., 1981-96; sr. programmer/analyst Policy Mgmt. Sys. Corp., Columbia, S.C., 1996—; cons., speaker in field; chmn. exec. bd. computer curricula Ga. Dept. Tech. and Adult Edn., 1990-92, mem. exec. bd. computer curricula, 1994-96; chmn. East Ctrl. Ga. Consortium for Computer Occupations, 1990-93, 94-96. Author: District Revenue Potential and Teachers Salaries in Georgia, 1989; co-author: District Property Wealth and Teachers Salaries in Georgia, 1990, Factors Influencing Teachers Salaries: An Examination of Alternative Models, 1991, Local Wealth and Teachers Salaries in Pennsylvania, 1992, School District Wealth and Teachers' Salaries in South Carolina, 1993, Structured COBOL for Technical Students, 1997. Chmn. Emanuel County chpt. ARC, Swainsboro, 1989-90, 92-93, bd. dirs., 1989—; pres. United Meth. Men. Swainsboro, 1984-86; trustee Greater Swainsboro Tech. Inst. Found., Inc., 1995-96. Recipient Nat. Tech. Tchr. of Yr. finalist award Am. Tech. Edn. Assn., 1994; named Olympic Cmty. Hero Torchbearer, 1996. Mem. Ga. Bus. Edn. Assn. (dir. dist. 1 1986, 96, dist. sec.-treas. 1993-95, dist. 1 dir.-elect 1995-96, Dist. 1 Postsecondary Tchr. of Yr. 1985, state postsecondary tchr. of yr. 1995), Ga. Vocat. Assn., Data Processing Mgmt. Assn., Swainsboro Jaycees (Outstanding Young Citizen 1985, treas. 1984-89, pres. 1987-88, pres. S.E. Ga. Jaycee Fair 1995, treas. S.E. Ga. Jaycee Fair 1995), Ga. Jaycees (v.p. area C. mem. 1988-89, chaplain 1989-90, dir. region 6 1990-91, chmn. state shooting edn. 1991-92), U.S. Jr. C. of C. (nat. rep. shooting edn. program 1992-95, Shooting Edn. State Program Mgr. of Yr. 1992). Methodist. Home: 8100 Bayfield Rd Apt 24-E Columbia SC 29223 Office: Policy Mgmt Sys Corp PO Box 10 Columbia SC 29223

WATT, JOHN H., financial executive; b. Jersey City, Aug. 31, 1927; s. John and Mary (Tollan) W.; m. Margaret Johnstone, Feb. 15, 1958; children: John, Jennifer, Andrew, R. Cameron. BS, Rutgers U., 1953; MBA cum laude, Fairleigh Dickinson U., 1965. Mgr. bus. planning NL Industries, Inc., N.Y.C., 1960-65, fin. mgr., 1965-69, asst. treas., 1969-82, treas., 1982-87; treas. Omnicom Group Inc., N.Y.C., 1988-92; prin. John H. Watt Assocs., Weston, Conn., 1993—. Served with USN, 1945-46, U.S. Army, 1953-55. Mem. Nat. Assn. Corp. Treas., Soc. Internat. Treas., University Club (N.Y.C.).

WATT, JOHN REID, retired mechanical engineering educator; b. Seattle, Nov. 15, 1914; s. Paul Harris and Roberta Gertrude (Frye) W.; m. Sarah Elizabeth Craven, Oct. 25, 1939 (dec. Jan. 1961); children: John David, Louisa Catherine; m. Lillian A. Mann, May 4, 1962; 1 child, Madeleine Megan. BSME, U. Wash., 1937, MA in Econs., 1942, ME, 1950; MS in Mech. Engring., U. Tex., 1954, PhD in Mech. Engring., 1960; postgrad., Harvard U., 1937-39. Registered profl. engr., Tex. Instr. econs. U. Tex., Austin, 1941-43, instr. mech. engring., 1943-46, asst. prof., 1948-56, assoc. prof., 1956-71; rsch. engr. C.W. Murchison Enterprises, Dallas, 1946-48; vis. prof. indsl. engring. Ga. Inst. Tech., Atlanta, 1971-72, prof. health systems, 1973-75; ret., 1975; chmn. EFC Assocs., Greensboro, N.C., 1977-82; owner Energy Conservation Labs., Inc., Atlanta, 1989-93; pres. Watt Properties Co., Inc., Atlanta, 1982-93; dir. rsch. in evaporative air cooling U.S. Naval Civil Engring. Rsch. and Evaluation Lab., Port Hueneme, Calif., 1952-53; dir. rsch. Nat. Assn. Home Builders and Nat. Warm Air Assn., Austin, 1954-56. Author: Evaporative Air Conditioning, 1963, Introduction to Typical U.S. General Hospital, 1968, rev. edit., 1975, Evaporative Air Conditioning Handbook, 1986, rev. edit., 1997, Pioneering From Covered Wagons Onward, 1995, also articles, tech. films, TV tapes; patentee for Polar Chips automatic icemaker, others. Fellow ASHRAE (chpt. newsletter editor 1958-59, evaporative cooling com. 1953-60, 84-93, rsch. award 1958); mem. ASME (life), Indsl. Engring. Club (founding pres. Austin, now chpt. Am. Inst. Indsl. Engrs.), Sigma Xi, Pi Tau Sigma. Avocations: writing, research, gardening. Home and Office: 300 Camden Rd NE Atlanta GA 30309-1513

WATT, KENNETH EDMUND FERGUSON, zoology educator; b. Toronto, July 13, 1929; s. William Black Ferguson Watt and Irene Eleanor (Hubbard) Dodd; m. Genevieve Bernice Bendig, Oct. 28, 1955; children: Tanis Jocelyn, Tara Alexis. BA with honor, U. Toronto, 1951; PhD in Zoology, U. Chgo., 1954; LLD, Simon Fraser U., 1970. Biometrician Rsch. div. Dept. Lands and Forests, Ont., Canada, 1954-57; sr. biometrician Can. Dept. Agr., Ottawa, Ont., 1957-60; head, statis. rsch. and svcs. Canadian Dept. Forestry, Ottawa, 1960-63; from assoc. prof. to prof. dept. zoology Dept. Zoology, U. Calif., Davis, 1963—. Author: Ecology and Resource Management, 1968, Principles of Environmental Sciences, 1973, Understanding the Environment, 1982, Taming the Future, 1991; editor-in-chief The Macloscope. Recipient Gold medal Entomol. Soc., 1969. Achievements include development of new approach to forecasting future based on exhaustive statistics testing of nonlinear math. equations to long runs of historical data; discovery that change through time in real world systems violates Markov principles. Home: 2916 Quail St Davis CA 95616-5711 Office: U Calif Dept Evolution and Ecology Davis CA 95616 *The actual causes of present events are much further back in time than most people suspect. Failure to understand this is why forecasting is such a disaster area.*

WATT, MELVIN L., congressman, lawyer; b. Mecklenburg County, N.C., Oct. 26, 1945; m. Eulada Paysour; children: Brian, Jason. BS in Bus. Adminstrn., U. N.C., 1967; JD, Yale U., 1970. Atty. Ferguson, Stein, Watt, Wallis, Adkins, & Grensham, 1971—; U.S. senator from N.C. 95th Congress, 1985-86; co-owner East Towne Manor, 1989—; mem. 103rd-105th Congress from 12th N.C. dist., Washington, D.C., 1993—; mem. banking and fin. svcs.; pres. Mecklenburg County Bar. Active Ctrl. Piedmont C.C. Found., Legal Aid of Southern Piedmont, N.C. NB Community Devel. Corp., Auditorium-Coliseum-Civic Ctr. Authority, United Way, Mint Mus., Family Housing Svcs., Pub. Edn. Forum, Dilworth Community Devel. Assn., Cities in Schs., Housing Authority Scholarship Bd., Morehead Scholarship Selection Com.; bd. visitors Johnson C. Smith Univ. Mem. N.C. Assn. Black Lawyers, N.C. Acad. Trial Lawyers, Charlotte C. of C. (sports action coun.), West Charlotte Bus. Incubator, Inroads Inc., Phi Beta Kappa. Democrat. Presbyterian. Office: US Ho of Reps 1230 Longworth Ho Office Bldg Washington DC 20515-3312*

WATT, STUART GEORGE, engineering contracting company executive; b. Warsaw, N.Y., Apr. 26, 1934; s. George James and Elizabeth Fern (Fullington) W.; m. Dorothy Elayne McLeod, Aug. 13, 1957; children: Stuart George II, Eric Duncan. BS in Mineral Engring., Pa. State U., 1956, MS in Mineral Engring. (NSF fellow), 1958. Ops. research cons. Lukens Steel Co., Coatesville, Pa., 1959; sr. research engr. Internat. Minerals & Chems. Co., Mulberry, Fla., 1959-62; project mgr. Internat. Minerals & Chems. Co., Skokie, Ill., 1962-64; prodn. mgr. Internat. Minerals & Chems. Co., Carlsbad, N.Mex., 1964-66; exec. engr. Davy Powergas, Inc., Lakeland, Fla., 1966-69, v.p. bus. devel., 1970-71, sr. v.p., 1972-74; exec. v.p., chief exec. ops.

Davy Powergas, Inc., Houston, 1974-78; exec. v.p. Davy Internat. Inc., 1978—, also dir.; exec. v.p. Davy McKee, 1979—; pres. Stuart G. Watt & Co., Pensacola, Fla.; bd. dirs. McKee-Kearney, Bricmont Enterprises, Aker Oil and Gas Tech., Inc., Aker Omega Inc. Mem. Am. Inst. Mining and Metal. Engrs., Pa. State Alumni Assn., Toastmasters Club, Jr. Achievement, Sigma Gamma Epsilon. Republican. Lutheran. Clubs: Houston University, Lone Palm Golf; Lakeside Country (Houston); University (Salt Lake City); Walden Golf. Home and Office: 14456 River Rd Pensacola FL 32507-9684

WATT, THOMAS LORNE, dermatologist; b. Denver, July 14, 1935; s. Sherman Alvin and Lois May (Hitt) W.; m. Mette Arup, Aug. 22, 1959; children: Charles Thomas, Sherman Alexander, Kathryn Anne. AB, Dartmouth Coll., 1957; D, Harvard U., 1960. Diplomate Am. Bd. Dermatology. Intern, resident Dartmouth-Hitchcock Hosp., Hanover, N.H., 1960-65; dermatologist Monroe (Wis.) Clinic, 1965-71, U.S. Army Med. Corps, El Paso, Tex., 1968-70; pvt. practice, dermatology Bangor, Maine, 1971—; head, sect. dermatology, Ea. Maine Med. Ctr., Bangor, 1973-97; mem. Maine Bd. Registration in Medicine, Augusta, 1987-93. Bd. dirs., pres., Bangor Symphony Orch., 1988-94. Lt. col. U.S. Army Med. Corps, 1968-69, Viet Nam. Decorated Bronze Star. Fellow New England Dermatol. Soc. (pres. 1996-97), Am. Acad. Dermatology, Can. Dermatology Assn.; mem. Penobscot County Med. Soc. (pres. 1971-72). Republican. Episcopalian. Avocations: cross-country skiing, golf, sailing. Office: 263 State St Bangor ME 04401-5435

WATT, WILLIAM JOSEPH, academic administrator, chemistry educator; b. Carbondale, Ill., Dec. 15, 1925; s. Phillip Clinton and Ella (Dickey) W.; m. Helen Stevens Gravatt, Sept. 1, 1956; children: John Gravatt, Phyllis Cary, William Joseph. Student, U. Mich., 1943; B.S. in Chemistry, U. Ill., 1949; M.S., Cornell U., 1951, Ph.D., 1956. Asst. prof. chemistry Davidson (N.C.) Coll., 1951-53; asst. prof. to assoc. prof. Washington and Lee U., Lexington, Va., 1955-65, prof. chemistry, 1965-94; prof. and dean emeritus, 1994—; assoc. dean of coll. Washington and Lee U., Lexington, Va., 1968-71, dean, 1971-84, head dept. chemistry, 1986-91; vis. prof. NSF Inst. High Sch. Tchrs., Ala. Coll., summers 1959-61, U. Va., summers 1964-66; Summer research participant Cornell U., 1956; Oak Ridge Nat. Lab., 1957, 58, U. Va., 1962. Contbr. articles to profl. jours. Pres. Rockbridge chpt. Va. Mus. Fine Arts, 1963-65; bd. dirs. Rockbridge Concert Theater Series, 1960—, pres., 1971-77; trustee Episcopal High Sch., 1974-80; vestryman, sr. warden Episcopal Ch.; bd. dirs. Botetourt-Rockbridge Regional Library, 1971-80, chmn., 1975-77; sec.-treas. Conf. Acad. Deans of So. States, 1978-79, v.p., 1979-80, pres., 1980-81; chmn. Nat. Deans Conf., 1983, Commn. Ministry Higher Edn. Diocese of Southwestern Va., 1989—. Served with AUS, 1944-46. Mem. AAAS, Am. Chem. Soc., English-Speaking Union (nat. bd. dirs. 1993—), Va. Acad. Sci., Phi Eta Sigma, Alpha Chi Sigma, Omicron Delta Kappa (hon.). Democrat. Home: 7 Providence Pl # 753 Lexington VA 24450-1833 Office: Washington and Lee U Dept Chemistry Lexington VA 24450

WATT, WILLIAM STEWART, physical chemist; b. Perth, Scotland, Feb. 25, 1937. BSc, U. St. Andrews, Scotland, 1959; PhD in Phys. Chemistry, U. Leeds, 1962. Fellow Cornell U., 1962-64; rsch. chemist Cornell Aeronautics Lab., Buffalo, 1964-71; head chem. laser sect. Naval Rsch. Lab., 1971-73, dep. head laser physics br., 1973-76, head laser physics br. optical sci. divsn., 1976-79; gen. mgr. wash ops. W. J. Schafer Assoc., Arlington, Va., 1979-80, v.p. program devel., 1980-90, sr. v.p., dir. programs, 1991-94; CEO Lawrence Assocs., Inc., Arlington, 1994-95; pres. WSW Consulting Inc., McLean, Va., 1996—. Recipient J. B. Cohen Rsch. prize, 1962. Mem. IEEE (assoc. editor Jour. Quantum Electronics), Am. Phys. Soc., Combustion Inst., Sigma Xi. Achievements include research in laser physics and development, laser-induced chemistry, energy transfer and reaction rate measurements, optical diagnostics. Office: WSW Consulting Inc PO Box 121 Mc Lean VA 22101

WATT, WILLIAM VANCE, surgeon; b. Thomasville, Ga., Apr. 10, 1924; s. Charles Hansell and Elizabeth Gilkeson (Pancake) W.; m. Mary Mercer Pendleton, Apr. 7, 1951; children: Mercer Pendleton Watt Pember, Elizabeth Vance Watt Finch, Philip Cargill. Student, Davidson Coll., 1942-43, Duke U., 1943-44; MD, Johns Hopkins U., 1948. Diplomate Am. Bd. Surgery. Intern Union Meml. Hosp., Balt., 1948-49; resident surgery Jefferson Hosp., Roanoke, Va., 1949-51, 53-54; fellow surgery Lahey Clinic, Boston, 1954-55; mem. surg. staff Archbold Meml. Hosp., Thomasville, Ga., 1955-94. Founder Brookwood Sch., Thomasville, 1970, All Saints Episcopal Ch., Thomasville, 1980, mem. vestry, 1996—. Recipient Silver Beaver award Boy Scouts Am., 1974, Golden Eagle award, 1995. Mem. ACS, AMA, Am. Soc. Gastrointestinal Endoscopy, Southeastern Surg. Soc., Rotary. Republican. Episcopalian. Avocations: hunting, golfing, fishing. Home: 1104 Old Monticello Rd Thomasville GA 31792

WATT, WILLIS MARTIN (BILL WATT), academic administrator, communications educator; b. Ottawa, Kans., Dec. 20, 1950; s. Gerald Omry and Shirley Arlene (Tush) W.; m. Katherine Ann Young, Feb. 14, 1970; 1 child, Derek Lee. BS in Christian Edn., Manhattan Christian Coll., 1976; BS in Secondary Edn.-Speech/Drama, Kans. State U., 1976, MA in Speech/Drama, 1978, PhD in Curriculum/Instrn./Speech, 1980. Ordained to ministry Christian Ch., 1976. Grad. tchg. asst. dept. speech, theatre and dance Kans. State U., Manhattan, 1976-78, instr., 1978-80; teaching intern speech/drama Manhattan (Kans.) Christian Coll., 1979; asst. prof. dept. speech comm. Iowa State U., Ames, 1980-84; dir. forensics dept. comm. Ft. Hays (Kans.) State U., 1984-91, chair, 1991-97; v.p. acad. affairs Manhattan (Kans.) Christian Coll., 1997—; dir. Talking Tiger Rsch. Inst., Hays, 1985-91, Comm. Tng. Consulting Svcs., Hays, 1986-97; exec. dir. Chi Rho Players Religious Drama Troupe, Ames, Iowa, 1981-84; adjudicator Am. Coll. Theatre Festival, Region V, 1982—. Author: Fundamentals of Speech, 1988, Theory and Application for Effective Bus. and Profl. Presentations, 1994, Fundamentals of Oral Communication: Theory and Practice, 1995; editor Kans. Speech Jour., 1994—; assoc. editor Nat. Forensic Jour., 1987-97. Edn. divsn. leader United Way of Ellis County, Hays, 1989, Ft. Hays State U. chmn. leader, 1992; baseball coach Little League, Ames, Iowa and Hays, 1982-86; bd. dirs. Actors Cmty. Theatre, Ames, 1982-84. With U.S. Army, 1971-74. Recipient Bronze award Ellis County United Way, 1996. Mem. World Comm. Assn., Speech Comm. Assn., Speech Comm. Assn. P.R., Ctrl. State Comm. Assn., Kans. Speech Comm. Assn. (mem. exec. bd., Outstanding Coll. Tchr. award 1996), Theta Alpha Phi (hon. drama), Pi Kappa Delta (gov. plains province 1986-88, 90-91, Exemplary Svc. award 1987, 91, Svc. award 1993, Order of Highest Distinction 1995), Pi Delta Kappa, Alpha Psi Omega (hon. drama). Avocations: racketball, chess, reading, writing, travel. Home: Box 394 Welda KS 66091 Office: Manhattan Christian Coll 1415 Anderson Ave Manhattan KS 66502-4030

WATTEL, HAROLD LOUIS, economics educator; b. Bklyn., Sept. 30, 1921; s. David Max and Carolyn (Abrams) W.; m. Sara Gordon, Sept. 1, 1946; children: Karen, Jill. B.A., Queens Coll., 1942; M.A., Columbia U., 1947; Ph.D. magna cum laude, New Sch. Social Research, 1954. Jr. economist WPB, 1942; economist Dept. Agr., 1946; econ. cons. Boni, Watkins & Mounteer, 1952; economist Bur. Bus. and Community Research, Hofstra U., 1954, 57, dir., 1957-58; prof. econs. Bur. Bus. and Community Rsch., Hofstra U., 1957-86, prof. emeritus, 1986—, chmn. dept. econs., 1957-61, chmn. div. bus., 1961—, dean Sch. Bus., 1965-73; econ. cons. to consumer counsel, staff Gov. N.Y., 1956-58; cons. N.Y. State Moreland Commn. on Alcoholic Beverage Control Law, 1963-64, Legislative Reference Bur., U. Hawaii, 1966, Schenley Industries, 1967—, Ralston Purina Co., 1967—, Am. Can Co., 1965—; econ. cons. Nat. Millinery Planning Bd., 1959-70; ednl. cons. U.S. Mcht. Marine Acad., Kings Point, 1972, Bulova Watch Co., 1975-82. Author ann. publ.: The Millinery Industry; Editor: Planning in Higher Education, 1975, Chief Executive Officer Compensation, 1978, The Gross Personal Income Tax, 1981; Contbr. chpts. to books, encys., dictionaries, also reports.; Editor, contbr.: L.I. Bus, 1954-59. Mem. Comprehensive Health Planning Coun., 1970-75; bd. dirs., v. p., N.Y. State unit Am. Lung Assn.; pres. Nassau-Suffolk unit; bd. dirs. Comprehensive Health Planning Coun., Nassau-Suffolk, N.Y., N.Y. State Citizen Coun., Regional Med. Program Nassau-Suffolk, consumer rep., bd. dirs. Island Peer Rev. Orgn. , 1990; treas. Parodneck Found. Lt. USNR, 1942-46. Edn. fellow, 1949; Hazen Found. fellow, 1952; Ford Found. regional fellow, 1960. Mem. AAUP (chpt. pres. 1953), Middle Atlantic Assn. Colls. Bus. Adminstrn. (pres. 1970-71), Am., Met. econs. assns., N.Y. State Environ. Health Assn. (v.p.), Island Peer Rev. Orgn. (consumer/AARP rep. 1990—), Pi Gamma Mu, Omicron Chi Epsilon, Beta Gamma Sigma (hon. assoc.). Home: 181 Shepherd Ln Roslyn Heights NY 11577-2525 Office: Hofstra U Dept Econ Hempstead NY 11550

WATTENBERG, ALBERT, physicist, educator; b. N.Y.C., Apr. 13, 1917; s. Louis and Bella (Wolff) W.; m. Alice von Neumann, May 23, 1992; children from a previous marriage: Beth, Jill, Nina Diane. B.S., Coll. City N.Y., 1938; M.A., Columbia, 1939; Ph.D., U. Chgo., 1947. Spectroscopist Schenley Distilleries, N.Y.C., 1939-42; physicist Manhattan Project, Metall. Lab., Chgo., 1942-46; group leader Argonne Nat. Lab., Chgo., 1946-50; asst. prof. U. Ill., Urbana, 1950-51; prof. physics U. Ill., 1958—; research physicist Mass. Inst. Tech., 1951-58. Recipient award for 1st nuclear reactor Am. Nuclear Soc., 1962; Nuclear Pioneer award Soc. Nuclear Medicine, 1977; NSF fellow U. Rome, 1962-63. Pioneered controlled nuclear reactor.

WATTENMAKER, RICHARD JOEL, archive director, art scholar; b. Phila., Feb. 22, 1941; s. Nathan H. and Frances (Rynes) W.; m. Eva Augusta Oscarsson, June 25, 1968; children: Adrian Ezra, Barnaby Leo. B.A., U. Pa., 1963; M.A., NYU Inst Fine Arts, 1965; Ph.D., NYU Inst Arts, 1972; student, The Barnes Found., 1959-66. With The Barnes Found., 1959-66, Rutgers U. Art Gallery, New Brunswick, N.J., 1966-69; chief curator Art Gallery Ont., Toronto, Can., 1972-78; dir. Chrysler Mus., Norfolk, Va., 1979-80, Flint (Mich.) Inst. Arts, 1980-88, Archives of Am. Art, Smithsonian Instn., Washington, 1990—; lectr. Barnes Found., 1991-92. Author: The Art of Charles Prendergast, 1968, The Art of Jean Hugo, 1973, Puvis de Chavannes and the Modern Tradition, 1975, Maurice Prendergast, 1994. Trustee Intermus. Conservation Lab., Oberlin, Ohio, 1982-88. Recipient Founders Day award NYU, 1972. Office: Smithsonian Instn Archives of Am Art 8th and G Sts NW Washington DC 20560

WATTERS, EDWARD MCLAIN, III, lawyer; s. Edward McL. and Lucy F. (Disston) W.; m. Susan Secor, May 12, 1979; children—Jennifer Susan, Ann Elizabeth. B.A. cum laude, Yale U., 1965; J.D. cum laude, U. Pa., 1970. Bar: Pa. 1970. Ptnr., Pepper, Hamilton & Scheetz, Phila., 1977—; lectr. programs on estate planning and will drafting Pa. Bar Inst. Bd. dirs. Children's Cruise and Playground Soc. Pa., Sanitarium Playgrounds of N.J., others. Served to lt. USNR, 1965-75. Fellow Am. Coll. Trust and Estate Counsel (mem. com. state laws); mem. Phila. Bar Assn. , Pa. Bar Assn. (past chmn. legis. com. probate sect.), ABA (mem. com. on significant legislation probate sect.), Phila. Estate Planning Council (past pres.), Yale Club of Phila., Penn Club, Merion Golf Club. Office: Pepper Hamilton & Scheetz 1235 Westlakes Dr Ste 400 Berwyn PA 19312-2416

WATTERS, RICHARD DONALD, lawyer; b. Midland, Mich., May 3, 1951; s. Donald Wayne and Madalyn Bird (Tinetti) W.; m. Ann Elizabeth Hutchison, May 24, 1975; children: Kelly E., Nathan Paul. BS in Indsl. Engrng., Bradley U., 1973; JD cum laude, St. Louis U., 1976. BAr: Mo. 1976, U.S. Dist. Ct. (we. and ea. dists.) Mo. 1976, Ill. 1977, U.S. Ct. Appeals (8th cir.) 1981. Assoc. Lashly & Baer, P.C., St. Louis, 1976-81, ptnr., 1981—, dept. chmn., 1989—; instr. St. Louis U. Sch. Law, 1977-79. Chmn., pres. United Cerebral Palsy Assn. St. Louis, 1985-88; bd. dirs. Canterbury Enterprises, sheltered workshop, St. Louis, 1988-94, participant Leadership St. Louis, 1988-89. Mem. Am. Acad. Hosp. Attys., Mo. Soc. Hosp. Attys. (bd. dirs. 1988-94, pres. 1990-91), Mo. Bar Assn. (vice chmn. health and hosp. com. 1988-90), Bar Assn. Metro. St. Louis (co-chmn. med.-legal com.). Republican. Avocation: sailing. Office: Lashly & Baer PC 714 Locust St Saint Louis MO 63101-1603

WATTERS, RICHARD JAMES, professional football player; b. Harrisburg, Pa., Apr. 7, 1969. Degree in design, U. Notre Dame. With San Francisco 49'ers, 1991-94; running back Phila. Eagles, 1995—. Selected to Pro Bowl, 1992-94. Achievements include member San Francisco 49'ers Super Bowl XXIX Champions, 1994, holds NFL postseason single game for most points (30), most touchdowns (5), Jan. 15, 1994 vs N.Y. Giants. Office: Philadelphia Eagles 3501 S Broad St Philadelphia PA 19148-5249*

WATTERS, THOMAS ROBERT, geologist, museum administrator; b. West Chester, Pa., Feb. 1, 1955; s. Frank Edward Sr. and Beatrice Josephine (Speirs) W.; m. Nancy Rae Tracey, June 18, 1983; children: James T. Samantha E., Adam T. BS in Earth Scis., West Chester U., 1977; MA in Geology, Bryn Mawr Coll., 1979; PhD in Geology, George Washington U., 1985. Rsch. fellow Am. Mus. Natural History, 1978-80; rsch. asst. dept. terrestrial magnetism Carnegie Instn. Washington, 1980-81; rsch. geologist Ctr. for Earth and Planetary Studies Smithsonian Instn., Washington, 1981-89, supervisory geologist Ctr. for Earth and Planetary Studies, Nat. Air and Space Mus., 1989—, acting. chmn. Ctr. for Earth and Planetary Studies, 1989-92, chmn. Ctr. for Earth and Planetary Studies, 1992—; lectr. in field. Author: Plants: A Smithsonian Guide; contbr. over 100 abstracts and papers. Active Plum Point Elem. PTA, 1991—, mem. exec. bd. 1991-92; coach Calvert T-Ball, 1992-93; coach Babe Ruth League, 1994-96. William P. Phillips Meml. scholar; grantee NASA, 85-89, 86-88, 87-88, 87-90, 89-94, 89-95, 91-95, 95—; recipient cert. award Nat. Air Space Mus., 1983, 86, 89-94. Mem. AAAS, Geol. Soc. Am. (mem. editl. bd. GEOLOGY 1993—), Am. Geophys. Union (Editor's citation 1992), Nat. Youth Sports Coaches Assn., Kappa Delta Phi. Achievements include research in terrestrial and planetary tectonics and tectonophysics; morphological and structural comparisons of tectonic features on the terrestrial planets and analogous features on Earth; geologic mapping of Mars. Office: Smithsonian Instn Nat Air & Space Museum Rm 3789 Ctr Earth & Planetary Studies Washington DC 20560

WATTERSON, SCOTT, home fitness equipment manufacturer. Chmn., CEO ICON Health & Fitness, Inc., Logan, Utah. Office: ICON Hlth & Fitness Inc 1500 S 1000 W Logan UT 84321-8206*

WATTLEWORTH, ROBERTA ANN, family practice physician, nursing home director; b. Sioux City, Iowa, Dec. 26, 1955; d. Roland Joseph and Elizabeth Ann (Ahart) Eickholt; m. John Wade Wattleworth, Nov. 7, 1984; children: Adam, Ashley. BS, Morningside Coll., Sioux City, 1978; D of Osteopathy, Coll. Osteopathic Medicine and Surgery, Des Moines, 1981. Intern Richmond Heights (Ohio) Gen. Hosp., 1981-82, resident in anesthesiology, 1982-84; anesthesiologist Doctor's Gen. Hosp., Plantation, Fla., 1984-85; resident in family practice J.F. Kennedy Hosp., Stratford, N.J., 1985-87; educator family practice U. Osteopathic Medicine and Health Scis., Des Moines, 1987-89; family practitioner McFarland Clinic, P.C., Jewell, Iowa, 1989-94; med. dir. nursing home Bethany Manor, Story City, Iowa, 1990—, Jewell Vol. Fire and Rescue Squad, 1990—. Bd. dirs., v.p. Heartland Sr. Svcs., 1995—. Mem. Am. Osteopathic Assn., Am. Coll. Gen. Practitioners in Osteopathic Medicine and Surgery, Am. Med. Dirs. Assn. (sec.-treas. Iowa chpt. 1997—), Am. Geriatric Assn., Am. Coll. Osteopathic Family Physicians (pres. Iowa chpt. 1995-96), Iowa Osteopathic Med. Assn. (bd. trustees). Lutheran. Avocations: gardening, cooking, painting. Office: 212 Lafayette Ave Story City IA 50248-1454

WATTMAN, MALCOLM PETER, lawyer; b. N.Y.C., June 27, 1941; s. William and Irma (Turtletaub) W.; m. Donna Weber, Sept. 1, 1963. BS in Indsl. Engring., U. Buffalo, 1963; postgrad., Syracuse U., 1963-64; JD, Fordham U., 1968. Bar: N.Y. 1969. Engr. US Air Material Command, Rome, N.Y., 1963-64, Uniroyal, Passaic, N.J., 1964-66, M&M Candies, Hackettown, N.J., 1966-68; cons. Touche Ross Co., N.Y.C., 1968-69; assoc. Cadwalader Wickersham & Taft, N.Y.C., 1969-78, ptnr., 1978—. Mem. ABA, N.Y. State Bar Assn., Assn. of Bar of City of N.Y. Home: 1185 Park Ave Apt 8K New York NY 10128-1310 Office: Cadwalader Wickersham & Taft 100 Maiden Ln New York NY 10038-4818

WATTS, ANDRÉ, concert pianist; b. Nüremberg, Germany, June 20, 1946; s. Herman and Maria Alexandra (Gusmits) W. Student, Phila. Mus. Acad.; grad., Peabody Conservatory, Balt.; hon. doctorate, Yale U., 1973; HHD, Albright Coll., 1975; MusD (hon.), U. Pa., 1984. First pub. appearance at age 10, Phila. Orch. Children's Concerts, 1955, performed with Phila. Orch., 1956, with Leonard Bernstein and the N.Y. Philharm., 1963, European debut, London Symphony Orch., 1966, made world concert tour to 16 Asian and Western European cities for U.S. State Dept., 1967, including an appearance at the Berlin Festival, Soviet Union tour with San Francisco Symphony, 1972, appearances as soloist with all major U.S. and European orchs., solo tours, Europe, U.S., Japan, Israel; TV appearances include Live from Lincoln Ctr., Great Performers series Lincoln Ctr., NET TV Spl. with Zubin Mehta and L.A. Philharm., Eugene Ormandy and the Phila. Orch., Casals Festival in P.R. on Arts and Entertainment Network (Emmy award nomination for Outstanding Individual Achievement in Cultural Programming); rec. artist with Angel/EMI and Telarc labels. Decorated Order of Zaire Congo; recipient Grammy award Nat. Acad. Rec. Arts and Scis., 1963; Lincoln Center medallion, 1974, Avery Fisher prize, 1988. Address: c/o IMG Artist 420 W 45th St New York NY 10036

WATTS, BARBARA GAYLE, law academic administrator; b. Covington, Ky., Oct. 18, 1946; d. William Samuel and LaVerne Barbara (Ziegler) W. BA, Purdue U., 1968; MEd, U. Cin., 1969, JD, 1978. Bar: Ohio 1978, U.S. Dist. Ct. (so. dist.) Ohio 1978. Residence dir. Ohio State U., Columbus, 1969-71, asst. dean students, 1971-75; assoc. Frost & Jacobs, Cin., 1978-81; asst. dean U. Cin. Coll. Law, 1981-84, assoc. dean, 1984—. Trustee Summerfair Inc., Cin., 1982-85; bd. dirs. Pro-Srs., 1995—; mem. Summerfair Cmty. Adv. Com. Schleman fellow Purdue U., 1968, Castleberry fellow AAUW, 1977. Mem. ABA, Ohio State Bar Assn., Cin. Bar Assn. (trustee 1992—, sec.1993-94), Nat. Assn. Women in Edn., Order of Coif, Chi Omega. Democrat. Office: U Cin Coll Law Clifton & Calhoun Sts Cincinnati OH 45221-0040

WATTS, BEVERLY L., civil rights executive; b. Nashville, Feb. 4, 1948; d. William E. and Evelyn L. (Bender) Lindsley; 1 child, Lauren. BS, Tenn. State U., 1969; MS, So. Ill. U., 1973. Mgr., exec. sec. State of Ill. Minority and Female Bus. Enterprise Program, Chgo.; equal opportunity specialist U.S. Dept. of Health, Edn., and Welfare, Chgo.; regional dir., civil rights/equal employment opportunity USDA, Chgo. Grad. Leadership Louisville, 1994, Leadership Ky., 1995, Duke U. Strategic Leadership for State Execs.; mem. long term planning commn. Ky. Health Policy Bd.; mem. Ohio Valley March of Dimes; mem. equal opportunity com. Ky. Coun. on Higher Edn., Louisville Met. Housing Coalition; mem. Ky. housing adv. com. Leadership Louisville Found. Bd., Bus. & Profl. Women Rover City Bd. Recipient Chgo. Forum Gavel award, BEEP Gold Seal award. Mem. Nat. Urban Affairs Coun., Ky. Women's Leadership Network, Chgo. Forum, Affirmative Action Assn., Chgo. Urban Affairs Coun. (pres.), Coalition 100 Black Women. Office: Ky Commn on Human Rights 322 W Broadway Fl 7 Louisville KY 40202-2106

WATTS, CHARLES DEWITT, retired surgeon, corporate medical director; b. Atlanta, Sept. 21, 1917; s. Lewis G. and Ida H. (Hawes) W.; m. Constance Merrick, Jan. 5, 1945; children: Eileen Constance Watts Welch, Deborah Hill (dec.), Charles D., Winifred Anita Watts Hemphill. B.S., Morehouse Coll., 1938; M.D., Howard U., 1943; LHD (hon.), St. Pauls Coll., 1984; DSc (hon.), Duke U., 1991. Diplomate Am. Bd. Surgery. Practice medicine specializing in surgery Durham, N.C., 1950-97; med. dir. N.C. Mut. Life Ins. Co., Durham, 1960-97; ret., 1997; mem. faculty dept. surgery Howard U. Coll. Medicine, 1947-50; instr. surgery Howard U., Washington; asst. clin. prof. surgery Duke Med. Center; attending surgeon Durham County Gen. Hosp.; chmn. bd. Capital Health Systems Regional Agy., 1976; founder, dir. Lincoln Community Health Center, Durham, 1970. Trustee Howard U., Washington. Fellow ACS; mem. Inst. of Medicine of NSF. Home: 829 E Lawson St Durham NC 27701-4534 *As one looks back, he is impressed with the fact that whatever one accomplished was done with the help of others. It is an humbling experience to realize how interdependent we are as we go through life.*

WATTS, CHARLES HENRY, II, university administrator; b. N.Y.C., Oct. 17, 1926; s. Charles Henry and Mabel (Lamborn) W.; m. Patricia Dorothy McQuillen, June 9, 1951; children: Katharine L., Caroline W. Collins, Charles Henry III. AB, Brown U., 1947, PhD, 1953, LLD, 1975; MA, Columbia, 1948; LittD, Franklin Coll., 1965; LLD, Dickinson Sch. Law, 1968; HHD, Alderson-Broaddus Coll., 1969; LHD, Bucknell U., 1979. Mem. English dept. faculty Brown U., 1948-62, dean coll., 1958-62; exec. assoc. Am. Council on Edn., 1962-64; pres. Bucknell U., 1964-76; pres., chief exec. officer Wolf Trap Found. Performing Arts, 1976-77; cons., 1977-78; dir. campaign Brown U., 1978-80; dir. Beneficial Corp., Wilmington, Del., 1953—, gen. dir., 1980-87. Trustee emeritus Bucknell U., Lewisburg, Pa.; trustee St. John's Coll. Ensign USNR, WWII. Mem. Century Assn. (N.Y.C.), Knickerbocker Club (N.Y.C.), St. Botolph Club. Home: 191 Commonwealth Ave Apt 41 Boston MA 02116-2211

WATTS, CLAUDIUS ELMER, III, retired air force officer; b. Bennettsville, S.C., Sept. 22, 1936; s. Claudius Elmer and Blanche Robey (Wannamaker) W.; m. Patricia Jane Sims, July 23, 1960; children: Claudius Elmer IV, Patricia Watts Heck. A.B. in Polit. Sci., The Citadel, 1958; postgrad. (Fulbright scholar), London Sch. Econs. and Polit. Sci., 1958-59; M.B.A., Stanford U., 1967. Commd. officer USAF, 1958, advanced through grades to lt. gen., 1986; comdr. 438th Mil. Airlift Group USAF, McGuire AFB, N.J., 1978-80; comdr. 63d Mil. Airlift Wing USAF, Norton AFB, Calif., 1980-82; asst. dep. chief staff plans Mil. Airlift Command USAF, Scott AFB, Ill., 1982-83, dep. chief staff plans Mil. Airlift Command, 1983-84; dir. budget Hdqrs. U.S. Air Force, Washington, 1984-85; sr. mil. asst. to dep. sec. def. U.S. Dept. Def., Washington, 1985-86; compt. USAF, Washington, 1986-89; pres. The Citadel, Charleston, S.C., 1989-96; ret.; former mem. adv. coun. grad. sch. bus. Stanford U.; former mem. bd. visitors Air U.; former mem. NCAA Coun., rep. on acad. requirements, chmn. peer rev. teams for cert.; bd. dirs. First Cmty. Bank S.C. Past bd. trustees Palmetto Partnership; chmn. Marion Sq. Commn.; bd. dirs., mem. fin. com. Air Force Aid Soc. Decorated Def. Disting. Svc. medal, USAF Disting. Svc. medal, Legion of Merit with oak leaf cluster, DFC with two oak leaf clusters, Air Medal with 10 oak leaf clusters, Gallantry Cross with Palm (Vietnam), Vietnamese Svc. Cross with 2 svc. stars. Mem. Air Force Assn., Am. Soc. Mil. Comptrollers, Mil. Order World Wars, Air Force Sgts. Assn., Airlift Assn., VFW, Royal Order of St. Stanislas, Order of Daedalians, Assn. Mil. Colls. and Schs. of U.S. (exec. com.), Aerospace Edn. Found. (trustee), Air Force Aid Soc. (bd. dirs., mem. finance com.). Methodist. Avocations: golf; reading. Office: Mil Coll of SC MSC # 150 The Citadel Charleston SC 29409

WATTS, DAVE HENRY, retired corporate executive; b. Montgomery, Ala., Jan. 18, 1932; s. Lawson Tate and Annie (Sherman) W.; m. Eleanor Lewis, Nov. 5, 1950; children—Anne Watts Durham, Martha Watts Keens, Susan Watts Balla. Student, U. Ala., 1950, U. Va., 1962; B.B.A., George Washington U., 1968, M.B.A., 1970, D.B.A., 1974. Constrn. clk. So. Ry., Birmingham, Ala., 1950-51, safety supr., various other positions, 1951-77; v.p. personnel So. Ry., Washington, 1977-82; v.p. personnel and corp. devel. Norfolk So. Corp., Va., 1982-85, exec. v.p. planning and devel., 1985-86, exec. v.p. mktg., 1986-95, vice-chmn., 1995-97; lectr. George Washington U., 1974—. Contbr. articles to publs. in field. Mem. Va. Opera Bd.; bd. trustees Va. Wesleyan Coll. Mem. Nat. Freight Transp. Assn. (exec. com.), Nat. Indsl. Transp. League, Washington Golf and Country Club (Arlington, Va.), Princess Anne Country Club (Virginia Beach, Va.), Town Pt. Club (Norfolk, Va., bd. dirs.). Methodist. Avocations: tennis; golf.

WATTS, DAVID EIDE, lawyer; b. Fairfield, Iowa, June 13, 1921. B.A., U. Iowa, 1941, J.D., 1942; postgrad., Columbia Law Sch., 1946-47. Bar: Iowa 1942, Mass. 1950, N.Y. 1954. Instr. U. Iowa, Iowa City, 1947-48; asst. prof. U. Pa., 1948-49, Harvard Law Sch., 1949-52; ptnr. Dewey Ballantine, N.Y.C., 1958-90; of counsel Dewey Ballantine, N.Y.C., 1990—; adj. assoc. prof. NYU, 1952-55; vis. lectr. Columbia U., 1954. Contbr. articles to legal jours. Mem. ABA, N.Y. State Bar Assn., Assn. Bar City N.Y., Am. Law Inst., Am. Coll. Tax Counsel, Am. Inst. Tax Policy. Home: 33 W 74th St New York NY 10023-2402 Office: Dewey Ballantine 1301 Avenue Of The Americas New York NY 10019-6022

WATTS, EMILY STIPES, English language educator; b. Urbana, Ill., Mar. 16, 1936; d. Royal Arthur and Virginia Louise (Schenck) Stipes; m. Robert Allan Watts, Aug. 30, 1958; children: Benjamin, Edward, Thomas. Student, Smith Coll., 1954-56; A.B., U. Ill., 1958, M.A. (Woodrow Wilson Nat. fellow), 1959, Ph.D., 1963. Instr. English U. Ill., Urbana, 1963-67, asst. prof., 1967-73, assoc. prof., 1973-77, prof., dir. grad. studies dept. English, 1977—; bd. dirs. U. Ill. Athletic Assn., chmn., 1981-83; mem. faculty adv. com. Ill. Bd. Higher Edn., 1984—, vice chmn., 1986-87, chmn., 1987-88. Author: Ernest Hemingway and The Arts, 1971, The Poetry of American Women from 1632 to 1945, 1977, The Businessman in American Literature, 1982; contbg. editor: English Women Writers from the Middle Ages to the

Present, 1990; contbr. articles on Jonathan Edwards, Anne Bradstreet to lit. jours. John Simon Guggenheim Meml. Found. fellow, 1973-74. Mem. MLA, AAUP, Midwest MLA, Am. Inst. Archaeology, Authors Guild, Ill. Hist. Soc., Phi Beta Kappa, Phi Kappa Phi. Presbyterian. Home: 1009 W University Ave Champaign IL 61821-3317 Office: U Ill 208 English Urbana IL 61801

WATTS, ERNEST FRANCIS, manufacturing company executive; b. Chgo., Mar. 23, 1937; s. Ernest Francis and Frances A. (Roche) W.; student Spring Hill Coll., 1955-57; student No. Ill. U., 1958-59; m. Sept. 10, 1960; children: Ernest Francis, Peggy, Colin. Sales rep. Binks Mfg. Co., Dallas, 1960-62, Memphis, 1962-65, asst. regional mgr., Dallas, 1971, v.p., gen. mgr., Mexico City, 1971-75, v.p. gen. mgr., Toronto, 1975-81, v.p. mktg., Franklin Park, Ill., 1981-96, v.p. market devel., 1996—; dir. Binks Can., Australia. Trustee, mem. exec. bd. Fenwick High Sch., 1983-89, lifetime trustee, 1989; trustee Rosary Coll., 1990-96. Served with USAR, 1960. Republican. Roman Catholic. Club: K.C. Office: Binks Mfg Co 9201 Belmont Ave Franklin Park IL 60131-2807

WATTS, GLENN ELLIS, union official; b. Stony Point, N.C., June 4, 1920; s. George Dewey and Nellie Viola (Ellis) W.; m. Bernice Elizabeth Willett, Nov. 8, 1941; children: Glenn Ellis II, Sharon Elizabeth Ann, Marianne Elizabeth Watts Erickson. With Chesapeake & Potomac Telephone Co., Washington, 1941-48; with Communications Workers Am., Washington, 1942-85, pres. div. 36, 1948-51, dir. dist. 2, 1951-56, asst. to pres., 1956-65, v.p., 1965-69, sec.-treas. union, 1969-74, pres., 1974-85, pres. emeritus, 1985—; v.p. exec. council AFL-CIO, 1974-85, v.p. emeritus, 1985—; v.p. indsl. union dept., 1968-85, mem. exec. bd. maritime trades dept., 1974-85; mem. Nat. Labor Com. for U.S. Savs. Bonds, 1975; nat. adv. bd. Labor Council for Latin Am. Advancement, 1975-85; mem. labor policy adv. com. for trade negotiations Dept. Labor, 1975-79; mem. industry-labor council White House Conf. on Handicapped Individuals, 1976; chmn. labor subcom. Pres.'s Com. on Employment of Handicapped, 1977; mem. sec.'s adv. council Dept. Commerce, 1976-77; mem. Pres.'s Commn. on Mental Health, 1977-78. Mem. Pres.'s Commn. on the Holocaust, 1978-79; mem. U.S. Holocaust Meml. Coun., 1979-93; past mem. D.C. Appeals and Rev. Bd., D.C. Wage and Hour Rev. Panel, Home Rule for D.C. Com.; mem. nat. advisory com. Nat. Congress Community Econ. Devel., 1974; past chmn. community chest relations com. Nat. Capital Area council Boy Scouts Am., past chmn. James E. West Dist., 1969-71; pres. Health and Welfare Council of Nat. Capital Area, 1967-69; mem. Inter-Am. adv. com. Postal Tel. and Tel. Internat., 1968-74, mem. exec. com., 1977-85, v.p., 1978-81, pres., 1981-85; gen. chmn. United Giver's Fund, 1968, pres., 1971-75; sec. United Way of Am., 1971-76; bd. dirs., treas. United Way Internat., 1974-78; mem.-at-large Dem. Nat. Com., 1974-85, mem. incomes policy study group of domestic affairs task group, 1974-76; trustee, sec.-treas. Am. Inst. Free Labor Devel., 1974-85; mem. U.S. Assn. for Club of Rome, 1978-80; trustee AFL-CIO Human Resources Devel. Inst., 1974-85, George Meany Ctr. for Labor Studies, 1976-85; trustee Ford Found., 1976-88; trustee Aspen Inst. for Humanistic Studies, 1974-89, trustee emeritus, 1989—; trustee Nat. Planning Assn., 1974-80; governing bd. Common Cause, 1974-77; sec.-treas. Ctr. for Mgmt. Services, 1974; hon. vice chmn. Am. Trade Union Council for Histadrut, 1974; mem. nat. adv. council Ariz. Heart Inst., 1974-80; bd. dirs. Am. Arbitration Assn., 1975-79, Am. Productivity Ctr., 1978-82, New Directions, 1977-80, Alliance to Save Energy, 1977-80; mem. nat. com. on coping with interdependence Aspen Program of Humanistic Studies, 1975-77; bd. dirs. Council on Fgn. Rels., 1987-90, Initiative Com. for Nat. Econ. Planning, 1975-76, Overseas Devel. Council, 1987-91; trustee, mem. exec. com. Joint Council Econ. Edn., 1976-79, Collective Bargaining Forum, 1983—, co-chmn. 1983-87, adv. bd. Collective Bargaining Inst. George Washington U., 1987-92; mem. Commn. on a Nat. Inst. Justice, 1976-79, Trilateral Commn., 1977—, Helsinki Watch, 1978-90, commn. Future U.S.-Mex. Relations, 1987-89, exec. com. Am. Agenda, 1988. Recipient Urban Trade Unionist award Nat. Urban Coalition, 1978, Silver Beaver award, 1965. Unitarian.

WATTS, HAROLD WESLEY, economist, educator; b. Salem, Oreg., Sept. 30, 1932; s. Elton and Claire W.; m. Doris A. Roth, Sept. 28, 1951 (div. 1973); children—Michael Lee, Suzanne, Jane Marie, Kristin. B.A., U. Oreg., 1954; M.A., Yale U., 1956, Ph.D., 1957. From instr. to assoc. prof. Yale U., New Haven, 1957-63; from assoc. prof. to prof. econs. U. Wis., Madison, 1963-76, dir. Inst. Research on Poverty, 1966-71; prof. econs. and pub. policy Columbia U., N.Y.C., 1976—, dir. Pub. Policy Rsch. Ctr., 1988-93; sr. fellow Mathematica Policy Research Princeton, N.J., 1979-92; sr. rsch. assoc. Urban Inst., 1994-95. Recipient Paul Lazarsfeld award, 1980; Guggenheim fellow, 1975. Fellow Assn. Pub. Policy Analysis and Mgmt., Econometric Soc.; mem. Am. Econ. Assn., Am. Statis. Assn. Democrat. Home: 448 Riverside Dr # 82 New York NY 10027-6801 Office: Columbia U Dept Economics New York NY 10027

WATTS, HELEN CASWELL, civil engineer; b. Brunswick, Maine, July 28, 1958; d. Forrest and Frances Caswell; m. Austin Watts. BS in Civil Engrng., U. N.H., 1980; cert. 5th yr. pulp and paper, U. Maine, 1983. Registered profl. engr., Maine. Constrn. engr., 1980-82, Oklahoma Dept. Transp., Okla. City, 1983-84; design engr. Structural Design Cons., Inc., Portland, Maine, 1985; facility engr. Bath (Maine) Iron Works, 1986-96; cons. engr. Watts Engrng., Bowdoin, Maine, 1996—. Judge New Eng. Regional ASCE Concrete Canoe Race, 1994. Mem. ASCE (assoc.), Tech. Assn. Pulp and Paper Industry (assoc.). Achievements include permits and construction of 300 ton transporter roadway across wetlands and mitigation site; planning and construction of a four story medical building and permits for dredge material landspreading. Office: Watts Engring RR 2 Box 4161 Bowdoin ME 04008-0370

WATTS, HELENA ROSELLE, military analyst; b. East Lynne, Mo., May 29, 1921; d. Elmer Wayne and Nellie Irene (Barrington) Long; m. Henry Millard Watts, June 14, 1940; children: Helena Roselle Watts Scott, Patricia Marie Watts Foble. B.A., Johns Hopkins U., 1952, postgrad., 1952-53. Assoc. engr., Westinghouse Corp., Balt., 1965-67; sr. analyst Merck, Sharp & Dohme, Westpoint, Pa., 1967-69; sr. engr. Bendix Radio div. Bendix Corp., Balt., 1970-72; sr. scientist Sci. Applications Internat. Corp., McLean, Va., 1975-84; mem. tech. staff The MITRE Corp., McLean, 1985-94, ret., 1994; adj. prof. Def. Intelligence Coll., Washington, 1984-85. Contbr. articles to tech. jours. Mem. IEEE, AAAS, AIAA, Nat. Mil. Intelligence Assn., U.S. Naval Inst., Navy League of U.S., Air Force Assn., Assn. Former Intelligence Officers, Assn. Old Crows, Mensa, N.Y. Acad. Sci. Republican. Roman Catholic. Avocations: photography, gardening, reading. Home: 4302 Roberts Ave Annandale VA 22003-3508

WATTS, J. C., JR., congressman; b. Eufaula, Okla., Nov. 8, 1957; m. Frankie Watts; 5 children. BA in Journalism, U. Okla., 1981. Profl. football player Ottawa and Toronto Teams Can. Football League, 1981-86; youth min. Sunnylane So. Bapt. Ch., Del City, 1987-94; mem. Okla. Corp. Commn., 1990-94, chmn., 1993-94; mem. 104th Congress from 4th Okla. dist., 1995—; mem. Nat. Drinking Water Adv. Coun.; mem. electricity com. Nat. Assn. Regulatory Utility Commrs. Republican. Office: US House Reps 1210 Longworth Bldg Washington DC 20515-3604

WATTS, JOHN RANSFORD, university administrator; b. Boston, Feb. 9, 1930; s. Henry Fowler Ransford and Mary Marion (Macdonald) W.; m. Joyce Lannon, Dec. 20, 1975; 1 child, David Allister. AB, Boston Coll., 1950, MEd, 1965; MFA, Yale U., 1953; PhD, Union Grad. Sch., 1978.Prof., asst. dean Boston U., 1958-74; prof., dean of fine arts Calif. State U., Long Beach, 1974-79; dean and artistic dir. The Theatre Sch. (Goodman Sch. of Drama), DePaul U., Chgo., 1979—; mng. dir. DePaul U. Blackstone Theatre, 1988—; gen. mgr. Boston Arts Festival, 1955-64; adminstr. Arts Programs at Tanglewood, 1966-69; producing dir. Theatre Co. of Boston, 1973-75. Chmn., Mass. Council on Arts and Humanities, 1968-72; dir., v.p. Long Beach (Calif.) Pub. Corp. for the Arts, 1975-79; mem. theatre panel, Ill. Arts Council, 1981-90. Served with U.S. Army, 1953-55. Mem. Mass. Ednl. Communications Commn., Am. Theatre Assn., Nat. Council on Arts in Edn., Met. Cultural Alliance, U.S. Inst. Theatre Tech., League Chgo. Theatres, Chgo. Internat. Theatre Festival, Phi Beta Kappa, Phi Kappa Phi. Clubs: St. Botolph (Boston); University (Chgo.). Office: De Paul U The Theatre Sch 2135 N Kenmore Ave Chicago IL 60614-4111

WATTS, JUDITH-ANN WHITE, academic administrator; b. Moline, Ill., Nov. 11, 1955; d. Harry Cameron and Jennie Elizabeth (Brockevelt) White. BSEd, Ill. State U., 1976; MSEd, Western Ill. U., 1987; postgrad., George Mason U., 1992-96, U. So. Calif., 1996-97. English tchr. United Twp. High Sch., East Moline, Ill., 1976-77, English tchr., curriculum designer/asst. theatre dir., 1978-84; county coord. Simon for Senate Campaign, Rock Island, Ill., 1984; legis. asst. U.S. Sen. Paul Simon, Washington, 1985-89; program devel. specialist NEA, Washington, 1989-90; dir. constituent rels. Nat. Coun. Accreditation Tchr. Edn., Washington, 1990-92; exec. assoc. policy devel. Nat. Bd. Profl. Teaching Standards, Washington, 1992-93; spl. asst. to pres. Va. State U., Petersburg, 1993-96; exec. asst. ofc. of the dean U. So. Calif. Sch. of Edn., L.A., 1996-97; v.p. bd. dirs. Rappahannock Mediation Ctr., Fredericksburg, Va., mediator, 1989—, trainer, 1991—. Mem. Fredericksburg Singers, 1990—, Fredericksburg Community Chorus, 1990—; precinct capt. Spotsylvania County (Va.) Dem. Com., 1989—; campaign worker various polit. campaigns, Va., Ill., 1972—; exec. com. of vestry St. George's Ch., Fredericksburg, mem. ch. choir, 1990—. Mem. NEA, ASCD, Am. Ednl. Rsch. Assn., Am. Assn. Sch. Adminstrs., Nat. Assn. Sec. Sch. Prins., Ill. Edn. Assn. (regional vice chair 1982-84, regional pub. rels. chair 1982-84), Va. Edn. Assn., Va. Meditation Network. Episcopalian. Avocations: sewing, singing, crafts, community theater, exercise/fitness. Home: 120 21st St Huntington Beach CA 92648-3918

WATTS, MALCOLM S(TUART) M(CNEAL), physician, medical educator; b. N.Y.C., Apr. 30, 1915; s. Malcolm S.M. and Elizabeth (Forbes) W.; m. Genevieve Moffitt, July 12, 1947; children: Pauline, Elizabeth, Malcolm, James. A.B., Harvard U., 1937; M.D., 1941. Diplomate: Pan Am. Med. Assn. Group practice internal medicine San Francisco, 1948-76; clin. prof. medicine U. Calif. Sch. Medicine, 1972-89, assoc. dean, 1966-89, clin. prof. medicine emeritus, 1989—, dir. Extended Programs in Med. Edn., 1973-82; dir. Calif. Statewide Area Health Edn. System, 1979-89; chmn. bd. trustees San Francisco Consortium, 1968-74, trustee, 1974-80, exec. dir., 1981-94; dir. Soc. Med. Coll. Dirs. Continuing Med. Edn., 1975-82, pres., 1980-81; trustee Hospice of San Francisco, v.p., 1979-85; pres. Alliance Continuing Med. Edn., 1979-81. Editor Western Jour. Medicine, 1968-90, Jour. Continuing Edn. in the Health Professions, 1988-91. Served to capt. M.C. AUS, 1942-46. Recipient Outstanding Community Funds and Councils Am., 1964, U. Calif. San Francisco medal, 1983, Disting. Svc. award Alliance for Continuing Med. Edn., 1990, Disting. Svc. award soc. Med. Coll. Dirs. of Continuing Med. Edn., 1991. Master ACP; fellow Am. Coll. Hosp. Adminstrs. (hon.); mem. AMA, AAAS, Calif. Acad. Scis., Calif. Acad. Medicine, Am. Med. Writers Assn. (John T. McGovern award 1986), San Francisco Med. Soc. (pres. 1961), Am. Soc. Internal Medicine (pres. 1964-65), Calif. Med. Assn. (bd. dirs. 1962-90), Nat. Inst. Medicine, Soc. Med. Friends Wine, Acad. Mexicana Ciencias Mexicano de Cultura (corr.). Home: 270 Sea Cliff Ave San Francisco CA 94121-1028

WATTS, MARVIN LEE, minerals company executive, chemist, educator; b. Portales, N.Mex., Apr. 6, 1932; s. William Ellis and Jewel Reata (Holder) W.; m. Mary Myrtle Kiker, July 25, 1952; children: Marvin Lee, Mark Dwight, Wesley Lyle. BS in Chemistry and Math., Ea. N.Mex. U., 1959, MS in Chemistry, 1960; postgrad. U. Okla., 1966, U. Kans., 1967. Analytical chemist Dow Chem. Co., Midland, Mich., 1960-62; instr. chemistry N.Mex. Mil. Inst., Roswell, 1962-65, asst. prof., 1965-67; chief chemist AMAX Chem. Corp., Carlsbad, N.Mex., 1967-78, gen. surface supt., 1978-84; pres. N.Mex. Salt and Minerals Corp., 1984—; chem. cons. Western Soils Lab., Roswell, 1962-67; instr. chemistry N.Mex. State U., Carlsbad, 1967—; owner, operator cattle ranch, Carlsbad and Loving, N.Mex., 1969—; bd. dirs. Mountain States Mutual Casualty Co., 1991; gen. mgr. Eddy Potash, Inc., 1987—; pres. Carlsbad Dept. Devel., 1996, N.Mex. BLM Resource Adv. Coun., 1994; chmn. Eddy County Land USF Commn., Eddy County Labor Rels. Bd.; dir. Soil Conservation Svc.; mem. Roswell dist. adv. bd. Bur. Land Mgmt. bd. dirs. Southeastern N.Mex. Regional Sci. Fair, 1966; mem. adv. bd. Roswell dist. Bur. Land Mgmt.; mem. Eddy County Fair Bd., 1976—, chmn., 1978, 82; mem. pub. sch. reform com.; chmn. higher edn. reform com.; mem. sponsor of N.Mex. Pub. Sch. Reform Act; bd. dirs. Carlsbad Regional Med. Ctr., 1976-78; pres. bd. Carlsbad Found., 1979-82; adv. bd. N.Mex. State U. at Carlsbad, 1976-80; vice chmn. bd. Guadalupe Med. Ctr.; bd. dirs. N.Mex. State U. Found.; state senator N.Mex. Legis., 1984-89. Mem. Rep. State Exec. com., 1972—; Rep. chmn. Eddy County (N.Mex.), 1970-74, 78-82. dirs. Conquistador coun. Boy Scouts Am., Regional Environ. Ednl. Rsch. and Improvement Orgn. Served with Mil. Police Corps, AUS, 1953-55; Germany. Recipient Albert K. Mitchell award as outstanding Rep. in N.Mex., 1976; hon. state farmer N.Mex. Future Farmers Am.; hon. mem. 4-H. Fellow N.Mex. Acad. Sci.; mem. Am. Chem. Soc. (chmn. subsect.), Western States Pub. Lands Coalition, Carlsbad C. of C. (dir. 1979-83), N.Mex. Mining Assn. (dir.), AIME (chmn. Carlsbad potash sect. 1975), Carlsbad Mental Health Assn., N.Mex. Inst. Mining and Tech. (adv. bd. mining dept.), Am. Angus Assn., Am. Quarter Horse Assn., N.Mex. Cattle Growers Assn. (bd. dirs. 1989—), Carlsbad Farm and Ranch Assn., Nat. Cattleman's Assn. Baptist. Kiwanis (Disting. lt. gov.), Carlsbad Mental Health Assn. (pres. 1994—), Elks. Home: PO Box 56 Carlsbad NM 88221-0056 Office: PO Box 31 Carlsbad NM 88221-5601

WATTS, OLIVER EDWARD, engineering consultancy company executive; b. Hayden, Colo., Sept. 22, 1939; s. Oliver Easton and Vera Irene (Hockett) W.; m. Charla Ann French, Aug. 12, 1962; children—Erik Sean, Oliver Eron, Sherilyn. BS, Colo. State U., 1962. Registered profl. engr., Colo., Calif.; profl. hand surveyor, Colo. Crew chief Colo. State U. Rsch. Found., Ft. Collins, 1962; with Calif. Dept. Water Resources, Gustine and Castaic, 1964-70; land and water engr. CF&I Steel Corp., Pueblo, Colo., 1970-71; engrng. dir. United Western Engrs., Colorado Springs., Colo., 1971-76; ptnr. United Planning and Engring Co., Colorado Springs, 1976-79; owner Oliver E. Watts, Cons. Engr., Colorado Springs, 1979—. Dir. edn. local Ch. of Christ, 1969-71, deacon, 1977-87, elder, 1987-96. 1st lt. C.E., AUS, 1962-64. Recipient Individual Achievement award Colo. State U. Coll. Engring., 1981. Fellow ASCE (v.p. Colorado Springs br. 1975, pres. 1978); mem. NSPE (pres. Pike's Peak chpt. 1975, sec. Colo. sect. 1976, v.p. 1977, pres. 1978-79, Young Engr. award 1976, Pres.'s award 1979), Cons. Engrs. Coun. Colo. (bd. dirs. 1981-83), Am. Cons. Engrs. Coun., Profl. Land Surveyors Colo., Colo. Engrs. Coun. (del. 1980—), Colo. State U. Alumni Assn. (v.p., dir. Pike's Peak chpt. 1972-76), Lancers, Lambda Chi Alpha. Home: 7195 Dark Horse Pl Colorado Springs CO 80919-1442 Office: 614 Elkton Dr Colorado Springs CO 80907-3514

WATTS, QUINCY DUSHAWN, track and field athlete; b. Detroit, June 19, 1970. Student, U. So. Calif., 1993. Olympic track and field participant Barcelona, Spain, 1992; Gold medalist and world record holder (with Valmon, Reynolds, Johnson) 4 x400 relay World Track and Field Championships, Stuttgart, Germany, 1993. Recipient 400m Track and Field, 4x4 Relay Gold medals Olympics, Barcelona, 1992. Office: c/o First Team Mktg 10100 Santa Monica Blvd Ste 46 Los Angeles CA 90067-4003*

WATTS, ROBERT GLENN, retired pharmaceutical company executive; b. Norton, Va., Apr. 28, 1933; s. Clifford Amburgey and Stella Lee (Cornette) W.; m. Doris Juanita Slaughter, Aug. 29, 1953 (dec. 1980); children: Cynthia L. Watts Waller, Robert Glenn, Kelly L.; m. Sara Lowry Childrey, Aug. 20, 1982; stepchildren: J. Eric Alexander, Matthew R. Alexander. B.A., U. Richmond, 1959. Dir. ops. A.H. Robins Co., Inc., Richmond, Va., 1967-71, asst. v.p., 1971-73, v.p., 1973-75, sr. v.p., 1975-79, exec. v.p., 1979-92; ret., 1992; bd. dirs. Little Oil Co., Richmond, Fidelity Fed. Savs. Bank, Richmond. Bd. dirs. United Way, Richmond, 1982—; Pvt. Industry Council, Richmond, 1983—; sec. YMCA, Richmond, 1984—. Served with USN, 1952-56. Mem. Met. Richmond C. of C. (chmn. 1985-86), Bull and Bear Club, Hermitage Country. Episcopalian. Home: 2409 Islandview Dr Richmond VA 23233-2525

WATTS, RONALD LESTER, retired military officer; b. Seneca, Mo., June 27, 1934; s. Lester N. and Naomi (Montgomery) W.; m. Anita Abelquist, Sept. 26, 1981; 1 child, Christina; children by previous marriage—Elizabeth Ann, Ronald Allen. B.S. in Edn., Pitts. State U., 1956; M.S. in Polit. Sci., Auburn U., 1976. Commd. officer U.S. Army, 1956, advanced through grades to lt. gen., 1987; asst. div. comdr. 1st Inf. Div., Ft. Riley, Kans., 1981-83; comdg. gen. U.S. Army Readiness, Fort Meade, Md., 1983; dep. comdg. gen. 1st U.S. Army, Fort Meade, Md., 1983-84; comdg. gen. 1st Inf. Div., Ft. Riley, Kans., 1984-86; chief staff Hdqrs. Forces Command, Ft. McPherson, Ga., 1986-87; commdg. gen. VII Corps, 1987-89, ret., 1989; pres. Watts Leadership Devel. Svcs., Greensboro, Ga., 1990—. Decorated D.S.M. with oak leaf cluster, Legion of Merit with 2 oak leaf clusters, Bronze Star, Air medal with 10 oak leaf clusters, Combat Inf. badge, Def. Superior Svc. medal with cluster.

WATTS, ROSS LESLIE, accounting educator, consultant; b. Hamilton, Australia, Nov. 10, 1942; came to U.S., 1966; s. Leslie R. and Elsie B. (Horadam) W. m. Helen Clare Firkin, Jan. 15, 1966; children: Andrew David, James Michael. B. Commerce with honors (Commonwealth Govt. scholar 1960-65), U. Newcastle (Australia), 1966; MBA (Ford Found. fellow 1967-68), U. Chgo., 1968, PhD, 1971. Audit clk. Forsythe & Co., Newcastle, Australia, 1960-64, acct., 1964-66; instr. Grad. Sch. Bus., U. Chgo., 1969-70; asst. prof. Simon Sch. Mgmt., U. Rochester (N.Y.), 1971-78, assoc. prof., 1978-84, prof., 1984-86; endowed chair Rochester Telephone Corp., 1986—; prof. commerce U. Newcastle, 1974-76; hon. prof. City U. Hong Kong, 1996—; cons. to bus. firms, 1972—; disting. lectr. Hong Kong Univ. Sci. and Tech., 1994. Contbr. articles on acctg. rsch. to profl. jours.; assoc. editor Jour. Acctg. Rsch., 1972-78, Jour. Fin. Econs., 1974-89, Australian Jour. Mgmt., 1976-81; co-editor Jour. Acctg. and Econs., 1979—; editor Jour. Acctg. Abstracts, 1995—; mem. adv. bd. Midland Corp. Fin. Jour., 1983-88, Continental Bank Jour. of Applied Corp. Fin., 1988-94, Bank Am. Jour. Applied Corp. Fin., 1994—; mem. editorial bd. Contemporary Acctg. Rsch., 1983-85. Recipient Notable Contbn. award AICPA, 1979, 80, award Alpha Kappa Psi Found., 1985. Mem. Am. Acctg. Assn., Am. Fin. Assn., Inst. Chartered Accts. in Australia. Home: 17 Burncoat Way Pittsford NY 14534-2215 Office: U Rochester Simon Sch Mgmt Wilson Blvd Rochester NY 14627-2241

WATTS, STEPHEN HURT, II, lawyer; b. Lynchburg, Va., Feb. 21, 1947; s. James Owen Jr. and Sarah Webb (Key) W.; m. Beverley Allan Brockenbrough, July 16, 1969 (div. 1986): children: Day Lowry, Stephen Hurt Jr.; m. Sally Yates Wood, May 24, 1986 (div. 1995). BA, Washington & Lee U., 1968; JD, U. Va., 1972. Bar: Va. 1972, W.Va. 1973. Law clk. Taylor, Michie & Callahan, Charlottesville, Va., 1970-72; assoc. Spilman, Thomas, Battle & Klostermeyer, Charleston, W.Va., 1972-75; ptnr. Watts & Watts, Lynchburg, Va., 1975-77; v.p., counsel Commonwealth Gas Pipeline Corp., Richmond, 1977-81; gen. counsel Commonwealth Natural Resources, Inc., Richmond, 1980-81; assoc. McGuire, Woods & Battle, Richmond, 1981-83; ptnr. McGuire, Woods, Battle & Boothe, L.L.P., Richmond, 1983—. Bd. dirs. Lower Fan Civic Assn., Richmond, 1987-91, TheatreVirginia, Richmond, 1992-93, Va. Oil and Gas Assn., 1993; pres., bd. dirs. Studio Theatre Richmond, 1991-93; chmn. outreach com. Grace and Holy Trinity Episcopal Ch., Richmond, 1993. Mem. ABA, Va. State Bar (dir. adminstrv. law sect., chmn. 1995-96), Fed. Energy Bar Assn. Home: 3420 Grove Ave Richmond VA 23221-2734 Office: McGuire Woods Battle et al One James Center 901 E Cary St Richmond VA 23219-4057

WATZ, HALLET N., emergency physician; b. New Orleans, Dec. 31, 1951; s. Nels Peter and Lena Mae (Brazelton) W.; m. Susan G. Watz, June 22, 1974; children: Hans E., Danielle N., Erik P. BS in Chemistry, Bowling Green State U., 1974; MD, Med. Coll. of Ohio of Toledo, 1977; MBA in Fin., U. Colo., 1996. Diplomate Am. Bd. Emergency Medicine. Resident So. Colo. Family Med. Residency Program, 1977-80; physician emergency dept. St. Mary Corwin Hosp., Pueblo, Colo., 1980-81, Parkview Hosp., Pueblo, 1981; physician emergency dept. Penrose-St. Francis Health Svcs., Colorado Springs, Colo., 1981—, chief med. staff, 1985—, chief dept. emergency medicine, 1989-94; v.p. Bd. Preferred Physicians, Inc., 1991-93; CEO Pikes Peak Emergency Specialists, 1987-94; pres. Front Range Emergency Specialists, 1994—; dir. Penrose Paramedic Program, 1984-94; clin. faculty dept. family medicine Colo. Med. Sch., 1981-86; ACLS affiliate faculty, 1984—. Physician advisor Cunty One Vol. Fire Dept., 1982—; bd. dirs. Metro YMCA, 1993—; bd. dirs. Garden Ranch YMCA, 1990—, chmn. bd. dirs., 1993-95, chair ptnrs. campaign, 1996—. Mem. Am. Coll. Emergency Physicians, El Paso County Med. Soc. Office: Front Range Emergency Specialists PC 2131 N Tejon St # 6-3 Colorado Springs CO 80907-6957

WATZ, MARTIN CHARLES, brewery executive; b. St. Louis, Oct. 31, 1938; s. George Michael and Caroline Theresa (Doggendorf) W.; m. Deborah Perkowski; children: Pamela, Kathlene, Karen. BS in Chemistry and Microbiology, SE Mo. State U., 1961; MBA, Washington U., 1966-67. Safety engr. McDonnell-Douglas, 1962-64; sr. brewing chemist Anheuser-Busch, Inc., St. Louis, 1965-68, asst. brewmaster, Columbus, Ohio, 1968-79, sr. asst. brewmaster, St. Louis, 1979-82, resident brewmaster, Baldwinsville, N.Y., 1982-84, Williamsburg, Va., 1984-87; v.p. bakers yeast divsn. Anheuser-Busch Indsl. Products Corp., St. Louis, 1987-88, dir. brewing ops., 1988-89; sr. resident brewmaster Anheuser-Busch, Ft. Collins, Colo., 1989—. Patentee in field. With USAF, 1962-65. Mem. Master Brewers Assn. Am. (pres., nat. bd. govs.), Am. Soc. Brewing Chemists, Internat. Food Tech. Assocs., Aircraft Owners and Pilots Assn., U.S. Pilots Assn. Avocation: flying. Home: 1417 North County Rd # 3 Fort Collins CO 80524-9312 Office: Anheuser-Busch Ft Collins Brewery 2351 Busch Dr Fort Collins CO 80524-9400

WAUD, ROGER NEIL, economics educator; b. Detroit, Mar. 26, 1938; s. Othneil Stockwell and Mary Josephine (Gough) W.; children: Heather, Neil. B.A., Harvard U., 1960; M.A., U. Calif., Berkeley, 1962; Ph.D. (Ford Found. fellow), U. Calif., Berekley, 1965. Asst. prof. bus. econs. Grad. Sch. Bus. U. Chgo., 1964-69; assoc. prof. econs. U. N.C., Chapel Hill, 1969-72; prof. U. N.C., 1972—; sr. economist, bd. govs. Fed. Res. System, Washington, 1973-75; cons. Dept. Labor; mem. adv. bd. Taxpayers Ednl. Coalition, 1981; research assoc. Nat. Bur. Econ. Research, 1982-92; mem. N.C. Energy Policy Council, 1986-92. Author: Macroeconomics, 5th edit., 1992, Microeconomics, 5th edit., 1992; contbr. articles to profl. jours.; mem. editorial bd.: So. Econ. Jour, 1970-73, Studies in Econs. & Fin., 1995—. Mem. Am. Econ. Assn., Econometric Soc., So. Econ. Assn. (exec. com. 1977-79). Office: Univ NC Dept Econs Chapel Hill NC 27599-3305

WAUGAMAN, RICHARD MERLE, psychiatrist, psychoanalyst, educator; b. Easton, Pa., Apr. 27, 1949; s. Charles Hoffmeier and Ruth Alviene (Melee) W.; m. Elisabeth Leone Pearson, June 20, 1970; children: Adele Marie, Garrett Dennis. AB, Princeton U., 1970; MD, Duke U., 1973. Cert. psychiatry, 1978, psychoanalysis, 1984. Resident in psychiatry Sheppard-Pratt Hosp., Towson, Md., 1973-76; mem. faculty Washington Sch. Psychiatry, 1983-96; grad. Washington Psychoanalytic Inst., 1984, tng. and supervising analyst, 1989—; from clin. instr. to clin. assoc. prof. Georgetown U. Sch. Medicine, Washington, 1978-92, clin. prof. psychiatry, 1992—; staff psychiatrist Chestnut Lodge, Rockville, Md., 1986—; cons. psychiat. residency program Nat. Naval Med. Ctr., Bethesda, Md., 1994—. Contbr. articles to profl. jours. Mem. Washington Psychoanalytic Soc., Am. Psychoanalytic Assn. (exec. coun. 1995-97), Internat. Psychoanalytic Assn., Am. Psychiat. Assn. Methodist. Home: 8109 Horseshoe Ln Potomac MD 20854-3834 Office: Chestnut Lodge 500 W Montgomery Ave Rockville MD 20850-3892

WAUGH, DOUGLAS OLIVER WILLIAM, pathology educator; b. Hove, Sussex, Eng., Mar. 21, 1918; emigrated to Can., 1918; s. Oliver Sayles and Helen (Champion) W.; m. Sheila Louise Duff, Jan. 16, 1971. Student, U. Man., 1935-38; M.D.C.M., McGill U., 1942, M.S., 1948, Ph.D., 1950; LL.D. (hon.), Dalhousie U., 1992. Assoc. prof. pathology U. Alta., Edmonton, Can., 1950-51, McGill U., Montreal, Que., Can., 1951-57; assoc. prof. Queens U., Kingston, Ont., Can., 1958-60, prof., 1960-64, dean medicine, 1970-75, vice prin. health sci., 1971-72; prof., head pathology Dalhousie U., Halifax, N.S., Can., 1964-70; exec. dir. Assn. Can. Med. Colls., Ottawa, Ont., 1975-83; free-lance writer, essayist, biographer, 1983—; columnist Can. Med. Assn. Jour., 1983-97; adj. prof. pathology U. Ottawa, 1978-83; chmn. adv. com. Can. Tumour Reference Ctr., NCI, Toronto, Ont., 1958-70; chmn. med. rsch. coun. Survey Path. Rsch., Ottawa, 1967; cons. Lab. Tech. Govt., B.C., 1977; sec. com. on accreditation Can. Med. Schs., 1978-83; mem. bd. accreditation Can. Assn. Univ. Schs. Nursing, 1984-93, cons. Ont. region, 1983. Editor: ACMC Forum, 1975-83; contbr. articles to profl. jours. Served to capt. M.C., RCA, 1942-46. Named Prof. of Yr. Med. Undergrads., Dalhousie U., 1967; recipient Jubilee medal Queen Elizabeth II, 1977. Mem. Can. Med. Assn. (sr.), Can. Cytology Coun., Nat. Cancer Inst. Can. (pres. 1974-76), Social and Behavior Coun., Alcoholic Beverages Med. Rsch. Found., Royal Coll. Physicians and Surgeons Can. (coun. 1969-70), Can

Authors Assn. (nat. v.p. 1991-94, Alan Sangster award 1995). Home: 183 Marlborough Ave, Ottawa, ON Canada K1N 8G3

WAUGH, JOHN STEWART, chemist, educator; b. Willimantic, Conn., Apr. 25, 1929; s. Albert E. and Edith (Stewart) W.; married 1983; children: Alice Collier, Frederick Pierce. AB, Dartmouth Coll., 1949; PhD, Calif. Inst. Tech., 1953; ScD (hon.), Dartmouth Coll., 1989. Rsch. fellow in physics Calif. Inst. Tech., 1952-53; mem. faculty MIT, Cambridge, 1953—, prof. chemistry, 1962—, Albert Amos Noyes prof. chemistry, 1973-88, inst. prof., 1989—, emeritus, 1996—; vis. prof. U. Calif.-Berkeley, 1963-64; lectr. Robert Welch Found., 1968; Falk-Plaut lectr. Columbia U., 1973; DuPont lectr. U. S.C., 1974; Lucy Pickett lectr. Mt. Holyoke Coll., 1978; Reilly lectr. U. Notre Dame, 1978; Spedding lectr. Iowa State U., 1979; McElvain lectr. U. Wis., 1981; Vaughan lectr. Rocky Mountain Conf., 1981; G.N. Lewis meml. lectr. U. Calif., 1982; Dreyfus lectr. Dartmouth Coll., 1984; G.B. Kistiakowsky lectr. Harvard U., 1984; O.K. Rice lectr. U. N.C., Chapel Hill, 1986, Baker lectr. Cornell U., 1990; Smith lectr. Duke U., 1992; sr. fellow Alexander von Humboldt-Stiftung; also vis. prof. Max Planck Inst., Heidelberg, 1972; vis. scientist Harvard U., 1976; mem. chemistry adv. panel NSF, 1966-69, vice chmn., 1968-69; mem. rev. com. Argonne Nat. Lab., 1970-74; mem. sci. and edn. adv. com. Lawrence Berkeley Lab., 1980-86; exchange visitor USSR Acad. Scis., 1962, 75; mem. vis. com. Tufts U., 1966-69, Princeton, 1973-78; mem. fellowship com. Alfred P. Sloan Found., 1977-82; Joliot-Curie prof. École Supérieure de Physique et Chemie, Paris, 1985, 96. Author: New NMR Methods in Solid State Physics, 1978; editor: Advances in Magnetic Resonance, 1965-87; assoc. editor: Jour. Chem. Physics, 1965-67, Spectrochimica Acta, 1964-78; mem. editorial bd. Chem. Revs., 1978-82, Jour. Magnetic Resonance, 1989—, Applied Magnetic Resonance, 1989—. Recipient Irving Langmuir award, 1976, Gold Pick Axe award, 1976, Pitts. award Spectroscopic Soc. Pitts., 1979, Wolf prize, 1984, Pauling medal, 1985, Calif. Inst. Tech. disting. alumnus award, 1987, Killian award, 1988, ISMAR prize, 1989, Richards medal, 1992, Evans award, 1994, Ea. Acad. Symposium award 1996; Sloan fellow, 1958-62, Guggenheim fellow, 1963-64, 72; Sherman Fairchild scholar Calif. Inst. Tech., 1989. Fellow AAAS, Am. Acad. Arts and Scis., Am. Phys. Soc. (chmn. divsn. chemistry and physics 1983-84); mem. NAS, Internat. Soc. Magnetic Resonance (mem. coun. 1989-95, mem. exec. com. 1996—, v.p. 1997—), Slovenian Acad. Sci. and Arts (fgn. corr.), Phi Beta Kappa, Sigma Xi. Office: MIT 77 Massachusetts Ave Cambridge MA 02139-4301

WAUGH, THEODORE ROGERS, orthopedic surgeon; b. Montreal, Sept. 21, 1926; s. Theodore Rogers and Anne Maude (Lawlor) W.; children: Susanne Rogers, Margaret Stewart, Theodore Rogers. BA, Yale U., 1949; MD, CM, McGill U., 1953; D Med.Sci., U. Goteborg, Sweden, 1968. Diplomate Am. Bd. Orthopaedic Surgery. Intern Royal Victoria Hosp., Montreal, 1953-54; asst. resident in pathology McGill U., 1954-55; asst. resident in surgery N.Y. U. Bellevue Med. Center, 1955-56; asst. resident, resident, fellow N.Y. Orthopedic Hosp., Columbia U., 1958-62, instr., clin. asst. prof. orthopedic surgery, 1962-68; asst. attending Presbyn. Hosp., N.Y.C., 1962-68; prof., chief div. orthopedic surgery U. Calif., Irvine, 1968-78; prof., chmn. dept. orthopedic surgery N.Y.U. Med. Center, 1978-96, emeritus prof., 1997—. Contbr. numerous articles to profl. jours. Capt., M.C. USAF, 1956-58. Fellow ACS, Royal Coll. Surgeons (Can.), Am. Acad. Orthopaedic Surgeons, Scoliosis Research Soc., Assn. Bone and Joint Surgeons, Am. Orthopaedic Assn., Am. Orthopaedic Soc. for Sports Medicine.; mem. Soc. Colonial Wars, Alpha Omega Alpha. Presbyterian. Club: 20th Century Orthopedic. Designer surg. devices used in orthopedic surgery. Office: NYU Med Ctr 550 1st Ave New York NY 10016-6481

WAUGH, WILLIAM HOWARD, biomedical educator; b. N.Y.C., May 13, 1925; s. Richey Laughlin and Lyda Pearl (Leamer) W.; m. Eileen Loretta Garrigan, Oct. 4, 1952; children: Mark Howard, Kathleen Cary, William Peter. Student, Boston U., 1943, W.Va. U., 1944; MD, Tufts U., 1948, postgrad., 1949-50. Cardiovascular rsch. trainee Med. Coll. Ga., Augusta, 1954-55, asst. rsch. prof. physiology, 1955-60, assoc. medicine, 1957-60; assoc. prof. medicine U. Ky., Lexington, 1960-69; Ky. Heart Assn. Chair in cardiovascular rsch. Ky. Heart Assn., Lexington, 1963-71; prof. medicine U. Ky., Lexington, 1969-71; prof. medicine and physiology East Carolina U., Greenville, N.C., 1971—; head renal sect. U. Ky. Coll., Lexington, 1960-68; chmn. dept. clin. scis. E.Carolina U., Greenville, 1971-75; chmn. E. Carolina U. Policy and Rev. Com. on Human Rsch., Greenville, N.C., 1971-90. Contbr. articles to profl. jours. With AUS, 1943-46; capt. USAF, 1952-54. Fellow ACP; mem. AAAS, Am. Physiology Soc., Am. Heart Assn., Am. Soc. Nephrology, Microcirculatory Soc. Republican. Achievements include basic advances in excitation contraction coupling in vasc. smooth muscle; basic advances in autoregulation of renal blood flow and urine flow; adj. therapy in acute lung edema; noncovalent antisickling agents in sickle cell hemoglobinopathy. Home: 119 Oxford Rd Greenville NC 27858-4954 Office: E Carolina U Sch Medicine Dept Physiology Greenville NC 27858

WAVLE, ELIZABETH MARGARET, music educator, college official; b. Homer, N.Y., Jan. 18, 1957; d. John Andrew Jr. and Louise Hayford (Estey) W. BMus, SUNY, Potsdam, 1979; AM in Libr. Sci., U. Mich., 1980; MS in Edn., Elmira Coll., 1990. Sr. libr. asst. U. Mich., Ann Arbor, 1979-80; pub. svcs. libr. Elmira (N.Y.) Coll., 1980-84, instr. music, 1981—, head tech. svcs., 1984—, coord. women's studies, 1992, 96-97; mem. South Ctrl. Rsch. Libr. Coun. Interlibr. Loan Adv. Com., Ithaca, N.Y., 1991-93; mem. South Ctrl. Rsch. Libr. Coun. Regional Automation Com., Ithaca, 1994-95, resource sharing com., 1996—. Contbr. revs., essays to profl. publs. Mem. Ithaca Concert Band, 1st Unitarian Ch. of Ithaca. Mem. ALA. Democrat. Avocations: music, reading, antiques. Home: 700 Comfort Rd Spencer NY 14883-9622 Office: Elmira Coll 1 Park Pl Elmira NY 14901-2085

WAVLE, JAMES EDWARD, JR., pharmaceutical company executive, lawyer; b. N.Y.C., July 19, 1942; s. James Edward and Florence Marie (Kehoe) W.; children from previous marriage: James Edward, William Patrick, Robert Thomas, Stephanie Elizabeth; m. Elizabeth Edith Symons Tallett; 1 child, Christopher Andrew; stepchildren: James E. Tallett, Alexander M. Tallett. B.A., Adelphi U., 1964; J.D., Georgetown U., 1967; LL.M., N.Y. U., 1968. Bar: N.Y. bar 1967. With Warner-Lambert Co., Morris Plains, N.J., 1968-87; internat. counsel Warner-Lambert Co., 1971-74, assoc. gen. counsel, 1974-77, v.p., gen. counsel, 1977-80, sr. v.p., gen. counsel, 1980-81; corp. sr. v.p. and pres. Parke-Davis Group, 1982-87; pres., CEO Centocor Inc., Malvern, Pa., 1987-92; chmn. Dioscor Inc., Stockton, N.J., 1993-97; chmn., pres., CEO Therics Inc., Princeton, N.J., 1997—. Mem. Am. Bar Assn. Clubs: Lookaway Golf, Stamford Yacht. Office: Therics Inc 115 Campus Dr Princeton NJ 08540-6400

WAX, ARNOLD, physician; b. Bklyn., Mar. 11, 1949; s. Emanuel and Eleanor (Greenfield) W.; m. Francine Wax; children: Erin, Racheal, Adam, Benjamin. BS in Pharm. Scis., Columbia U., 1971; MD, SUNY, Buffalo, 1976. Diplomate Nat. Bd. Med. Examiners, Am. Bd. Internal Medicine, Am. Bd. Quality Assurance and Utilization Rev. Physicians, Am. Acad. Pain Mgmt.; lic. physician, Fla., Calif., N.D., Minn., N.Y., Nev., Ariz. Intern, resident Millard Fillmore Hosp., Buffalo, 1976-79; clin. asst. instr. SUNY, 1977-79; instr. medicine U. Rochester, N.Y., 1979-81; dir. internal medicine U. N.D., Grand Forks, 1982-83, clin. asst. prof., 1982-85; pvt. practice Las Vegas, Nev., 1987—; mem. staff Sunrise Hosp., Las Vegas, Desert Springs Hosp., Las Vegas, Nathan Adelson Hospice, Las Vegas, Valley Hosp., Las Vegas, U. Med. Ctr., Las Vegas, St. Rose Dominican Hosp., Henderson, Nev., Lake Mead Hosp., North Las Vegas. Contbr. articles to profl. jours. Grantee So. Nev. Cancer Rsch. Found., Ea. Coop. Oncology Group, Gynecol. Oncology Group, North Ctrl. Cancer Treatment Group, S.W. Oncology Group. Fellow Am. Coll. Physicians; mem. AMA, Am. Cancer Soc. (fellow 1979), Am. Soc. Clin. Oncology, Nev. Med. Soc., Clark County Med. Soc. (trustee, peer rev. com.), Nev. Peer Rev. Orgn., U. Nev. Las Vegas Found., Nev. Dance Theater, Nev. Opera Theater, Las Vegas Symphony, Nev. Inst. Contemporary Art, Lied Mus., Allied Arts Coun., James Platt White Soc., U. Buffalo Found., Rho Chi (Bronze medal 1971). Home: 2224 Chatsworth Ct Henderson NV 89014 Office: 3920 S Eastern Ave Ste 202 Las Vegas NV 89119-5171

WAX, BERNARD, research and development consultant, lecturer; b. Phila., Apr. 4, 1930; s. Samuel and Anna (Kaminker) W.; m. Dolores Helen Nemchek, Mar. 21, 1953; children—Ann Susan Wax Loeb, Steven Albert, Stuart Michael, Rebecca Mara. B.A., U. Chgo., 1950, M.A., 1955; postgrad., U. Wis., 1955-59. Field rep., field services supr. Ill. State Hist. Library, 1959-66; dir. Am. Jewish Hist. Soc., Waltham, Mass., 1966-91, dir. spl. projects, 1991-93, dir. emeritus, 1993—; mem. Ill. State Records Commn., 1961-66, Cook County State Records Commn., 1961-66. Editor: Assn. Jewish Libraries Bull, 1970-72, Bay State Hist. League Bull, 1971-73. Co-founder Joint Cultural Appeal, 1972; pres. Coun. on Archives and Rsch. Librs. in Jewish Studies, 1983-85. With Signal Corps, U.S. Army, 1953-55. Mem. Bay State Hist. League (editor, bd. dirs. 1971-76, pres. 1976-78). Home: 21 Blake Rd Brookline MA 02146-5803

WAX, GEORGE LOUIS, lawyer; b. New Orleans, Dec. 6, 1928; s. John Edward and Theresa (Schaff) W.; LL.B., Loyola U. of South, 1952, B.C.S., 1960; m. Patricia Ann Delaney, Feb. 20, 1965; children: Louis Jude, Joann Olga, Therese Marie. Admitted to La. bar, 1952, practiced in New Orleans, 1954—. Served with USNR, 1952-54. Mem. La., New Orleans bar assns., Am. Legion. Roman Catholic. Kiwanian. Clubs: New Orleans Athletic, Suburban Gun and Rod, Southern Yacht. Home: 6001 Charlotte Dr New Orleans LA 70122-2731 Office: Nat Bank Commerce New Orleans LA 70112

WAX, NADINE VIRGINIA, retired banker; b. Van Horne, Iowa, Dec. 7, 1927; d. Laurel Lloyd and Viola Henrietta (Schrader) Bobzien; divorced; 1 child, Sharlyn K. Wax Munns. Student, U. Iowa, 1970-71; grad. Nat. Sch. Real Estate and Fin., Ohio State U., 1980-81. Jr. acct. McGladrey, Hansen, Dunn (now McGladrey-Pullen Co., CPAs), Cedar Rapids, Iowa, 1944-47; office mgr. Iowa Securities Co. (now Norwest Mortgage Co.), Cedar Rapids, 1954-55; asst. cashier Mchts. Nat. Bank (now Firstar Bank), Cedar Rapids, 1956-75, asst. v.p., 1976-78, v.p., 1979-90; ret., 1990. Bd. dirs., v.p. Kirkwood C.C. Facilities Found., Cedar Rapids, 1970-97; bd. dirs., treas. Kirkwood C.C., 1984-91; trustee Indian Creek Nature Ctr., Cedar Rapids, 1974—, pres., 1980-81; vol. St. Luke's Hosp. Aux., Cedar Rapids, 1981-85; mem. Linn County Regional Planning Commn., 1982-92, Cedar Rapids-Marion Fine Arts Coun., 1994—; bd. suprs. Compensation Commn. for Condemnation, 1987-92; bd. dirs. Am. Heart Assn., Cedar Rapids, 1983-94; mem. Iowa Employment and Tng. Coun., Des Moines, 1982-83. Recipient Outstanding Woman award Cedar Rapids Tribute to Women and Industry, 1984. Mem. Fin. Women Internat. (state edn. chmn. 1982-83), Am. Inst. Banking (bd. dirs. 1968-70), Soc. Real Estate Appraisers (treas. 1978-80), Linn. County Bankers Assn. (pres. 1979-80), Cedar Rapids Bd. Realtors, Cedar Rapids C. of C. (bus.-edn. com. 1986-91), Cedar Rapids Country Club. Republican. Lutheran. Avocations: travel, reading, walking. Home: 147 Ashcombe SE Cedar Rapids IA 52403-1700

WAX, WILLIAM EDWARD, photojournalist; b. Miami, Fla., Dec. 7, 1956; s. Ira and Rita (Gunshor) W. A.S., Berry Coll., Rome, Ga., 1976; B.S. in Engring., U. Fla., 1983. With Ind. Fla. Alligator, Gainesville, Fla., 1977-79; staff photographer Gainesville (Fla.) Sun, 1979-87; photo cons. N.Y. Times regional newspapers, 1984—; freelance photographer Miami, 1987—; pres. Wax Photographics, Inc., Miami Beach, Fla., 1989—, Waxcom, Miami Beach, 1996—; owner Studio SoBe, Miami Beach, 1992—; guest lectr. various univs.; faculty So. Short Course in News Photography, 1985—. named Photographer of Yr., NPPA/U. Mo. and Nikon, 1980, So. Photographer of Yr., 1980, Regional Photographer of Yr., 1979, 82, 85; recipient Mark of Excellence, Sigma Delta Chi, 1978, Best of Show award Atlanta Seminar on Photojournalism, 1982, Best of Show and Silver medal Hearst awards, 1978, Design Gold award Fla. Tech. Writers Assn., 1992, Design award, Gold award, Excellence award Soc. Tech. Comm. Internat. Tech. Art Competition, 1993, 94, Best of Show, 1994, Disting. Design award, 1993, Excellence Design award, 1993, 2 Design Excellence awards and award of merit, 1995, Best of Show award Ann. Report Fla. Pub. Rels., 1995, Silver and Bronze awards Fla. Mag. Assn., 1994, 96, Gold, Silver and Bronze awards Fla. Mag. Assn., 1995, Merit award STC, 1995, Apex Design awards 1996, Global award/Ann. Report Photography, 1996; nominated for Pulitzer prize, 1979, 89, STC Internat. Design, 1996. Mem. Nat. Press Photographers Assn., Fla. Mag. Assn., Profl. Photographers Am., Nikon Profl. Svcs., Fla. Press Photographers Assn. Democrat. Jewish. Office: Wax & Co 350 Lincoln Rd Ste 516 Miami FL 33139-3148

WAXENBERG, ALAN M., publisher; b. Davenport, Iowa, Mar. 1, 1935; s. George and Rose Waxenberg; m. Suzanne C. Ecker, Oct. 26, 1958; children: Robin Lynn, Scott Stephen. BA, U. Iowa, 1956. Cen. advt. dir. Look mag., Detroit, 1958-71; mgr. Petersen Pub. Co., Detroit, 1971-72; v.p. nat. advt. dir. Petersen Pub. Co., N.Y.C., 1972-76; pub. Motor, N.Y.C., 1976-79; v.p., pub. Redbook, N.Y.C., 1982-88; sr. v.p., pub. Good Housekeeping, Hearst Pub. Co., N.Y.C., 1988-96; exec. v.p., pub. Vicotria, Hearst Pub. Co., N.Y.C., 1996—. Active United Jewish Appeal Fedn., Anti-Defamation League, Jr. Achievement, United /fund; bd. dirs. adv. coun. Am. Health Found. Served with U.S. Army, 1956-58. Mem. Am. Advt. Fedn. (bd. dirs.), Mag. Pubs. Assn., Adcraft Club Detroit, U. Iowa Alumni Assn. Clubs: Metropolis Country (White Plains, N.Y.); University (N.Y.). Office: Victoria Hearst Mags 224 W 57th St New York NY 10019-3212

WAXLER, BEVERLY JEAN, anesthesiologist, physician; b. Chgo., Apr. 11, 1949; d. Isadore and Ada Belle (Gross) Marcus; m. Richard Norman Waxler, Dec. 24, 1972; 1 child, Adam R. BS in Biology, No. Ill. U., 1971; MD, U. Ill., Chgo., 1975. Diplomate Am. Bd. Anesthesiology, Am. Bd. Pathology. Intern dept. pathology Northwestern U., Chgo., 1975-76, resident, 1976-79; instr. Rush Presbyn. St. Luke's Med. Ctr., Chgo., 1979-81; asst. prof. pathology Loyola U., Maywood, Ill., 1981-84; resident dept. anesthesiology Cook County Hosp., Chgo., 1984-87, attending anesthesiologist, 1987—; clin. asst. prof. U. Ill., Chgo., 1988-95, Rush Med. Coll., Chgo., 1996—. Contbr. papers to Tissue and Cell, British Jour. Exptl. Pathology, Biochem. Medicine, Calcified Tissue Internat., Jour. Lab. Clin. Med. Recipient B.B. Sankey Anesthesia Advancement award Internat. Anesthesia Rsch. Soc., 1989; Nat. Rsch. Svc. award fellow Nat. Cancer Inst., 1980; grantee Varlen Corp., 1982. Mem. AAAS, Internat. Anesthesia Rsch. Soc., Am. Soc. Anesthesiologists, Sigma Xi. Achievements include research with future implications for the delivery of anesthesia for cancer patients and the effects of anesthetics on proteinase inhibitors and tumor behavior. Home: 7615 Church St Morton Grove IL 60053-1618 Office: Cook County Hosp Chicago IL 60612

WAXMAN, DAVID, physician, university consultant; b. Albany, N.Y., Feb. 7, 1918; s. Meyer and Fannie (Strosberg) W.; m. Jane Zabel; children: Gail, Michael, Dan, Ann, Steve, Abby. B.S., Syracuse U., 1942, M.D., 1950. Intern Grace Hosp., Detroit, 1950-51; resident in medicine, fellow in cardiology Kans. U. Med. Ctr., Kansas City, 1958-61; instr. internal medicine Kans. U. Med. Ctr., 1961-64; asst. prof. internal medicine Kans. City Med. Ctr., 1964-69, assoc. prof., 1969-77, prof., 1977—, dir. dept. medicine outpatient service, 1970-74, asst. dean, 1970-71, assoc. dean for student affairs, 1971-72, dean of students, 1972-74, vice chancellor for students, 1974-76, vice chancellor, 1976-77, exec. vice chancellor, 1977-83, spl. cons. to chancellor for health affairs, 1983-94; ret.; nat. cons. to surgeon gen. USAF. Contbr. articles to med. jours. Mem. Kans. State Bd. Healing Arts, 1984-88. Maj. gen. USAFR ret. Decorated D.S.M., Legion of Merit with one oak leaf cluster. Fellow ACP, Alpha Omega Alpha; mem. Kans. Med. Soc., Soc. Med. Cons. to the Armed Forces. Office: Kans U Med Ctr 39th and Rainbow Blvd Kansas City KS 66103

WAXMAN, HENRY ARNOLD, congressman; b. Los Angeles, Sept. 12, 1939; s. Louis and Esther (Silverman) W.; m. Janet Kessler, Oct. 17, 1971; children: Carol Lynn, Michael David. B.A. in Polit. Sci, UCLA, 1961, J.D., 1964. Bar: Calif. 1965. Mem. Calif. State Assembly, 1969-74, chmn. com. on health, until 1994; mem. 94th-104th Congresses from 24th (now 29th) Calif. dist., 1975—, ranking minority mem. house subcom. on health and environment, 1979—; mem. govt. reform & oversight com. Pres. Calif. Fedn. Young Democrats, 1965-67. Mem. Calif. Bar Assn., Guardians Jewish Home for Aged, Am. Jewish Congress, Sierra Club, B'nai B'rith, Phi Sigma Alpha. Office: US Ho of Reps 2408 Rayburn HOB Washington DC 20515

WAXMAN, RONALD, computer engineer; b. Newark, Nov. 28, 1933; s. Benjamin and Rose (Lifson) W.; m. Pearl Latterman, June 19, 1955; children: David, Roberta, Benjamin. BSEE, N.J. Inst. Tech., 1955; MEE, Syracuse U., 1963. Engr. IBM, Poughkeepsie, N.Y., 1955-56, 58-64, East Fishkill, N.Y., 1964-70, Poughkeepsie and Kingston, N.Y., 1970-80; sr. engr. IBM, Manassas, Va., 1980-87; prin. scientist U. Va., Charlottesville, 1987—; IEEE rep. and tech. advisor to Internat. Elec. Commn. U.S. tech. activities group for internat. design automation stds.; mem. steering com. very high speed integrated circuits hardware description lang. VHDL Users Group, 1987-91. Contbr. numerous articles to profl. jours. and tech. presentations. 1st lt. USAF, 1956-58. Fellow IEEE, IEEE Computer Soc. (bd. govs. 1989-94, 96-98, chmn. fellows evaluation com. 1995-96, chmn. audit com., 1997, founder, chmn. design automation stds. subcom. 1983-88, steering com. 1989—, chmn. design automation tech. com. 1988-90, steering com. 1991—, vice-chmn. tech. activities bd. 1991-92, chmn. awards com. 1993, disting. visitor 1986-88, v.p. mem. activities bd. 1994, Meritorious Svc. cert. 1988, Disting. Svc. cert. 1994, TAB Pioneer award 1989), Internat. Fedn. Info. Processing Orgns. (working group hardware description langs. rep. to tech. com.), Assn. for Computing Machinery (spl. interest group DA). Achievements include patents in field. Office: U Va Ctr for Semicustom Integrated Systems Dept EE Thornton Hall Charlottesville VA 22903

WAXMAN, SETH PAUL, lawyer; b. Hartford, Conn., Nov. 28, 1951; s. Felix H. and Frieda (Goodman) W.; m. Debra F. Goldberg, Mar. 20, 1977; children: Noah, Sarah, Ethan. AB summa cum laude, Harvard U., 1973; JD, Yale U., 1977. Bar: D.C. 1978, U.S. Dist. Ct. D.C., U.S. Ct. Appeals (D.C., 3d, 4th, 5th, 9th and 11th cirs.) 1979, U.S. Supreme Ct. 1981. Law clk to Judge Gerhard A. Gesell Washington, 1977-78; mng. ptnr. Miller Cassidy Larroca & Lewin, Washington, 1978-94; assoc. dep. atty. gen. U.S. Dept. Justice, Washington, 1994-96, dep. solitor gen., 1996—, acting dep. atty. gen., 1997—; instr. Nat. Inst. for Trial Advocacy. Contbr. numerous articles on litigation to legal jours. Michael C. Rockefeller fellow Harvard U., 1973-74; recipient Cardozo award for civil rights Anti-Defamation League, 1987. Mem. ABA (steering com. postconviction death penalty representation project, com. chmn. litigation sect., Pro Bono Publico award 1988), Jud. Conf. U.S. Office: US Dept Justice Rm 4201 Washington DC 20530

WAXMAN, SHELDON ROBERT, lawyer; b. Chgo., Apr. 22, 1941; s. Henri and Ann (Sokolsky) W.; m. Katherine Slamski, Aug. 23, 1979; children: Josiah, Zoe. BA, U. Ill., 1963; JD, DePaul U., 1965. Bar: Ill. 1965, U.S. Supreme Ct. 1976, Mich. 1985. Staff atty. Argonne (Ill.) Nat. Lab., 1968-71; asst. U.S. Atty., Chgo., 1971-74; owner firm Shelly Waxman & Assocs., Chgo. and South Haven, Mich., 1976—. Author: In the Teeth of the Wind--Memoirs of a Libertarian Lawyer, 1995; editor-in-chief New Z Letter; contbr. articles to profl. jours. Founder Freedom Lawyers of Am., People for Simplified Tax Law, Nukes to the Sun. Office: PO Box 309 South Haven MI 49090-0309

WAXMAN, STEPHEN GEORGE, neurologist, neuroscientist; b. Newark, Aug. 17, 1945; s. Morris and Beatrice (Levitch) W.; m. Merle Applebaum, June 25, 1968; children: Matthew, David. AB, Harvard U., 1967; PhD, Albert Einstein Coll. Med., Yeshiva U., 1970, MD, 1972; MA (hon.), Yale U., 1986. Rsch. fellow in neurosci. Albert Einstein Coll. Medicine, Bronx, N.Y., 1970-72; clin. fellow Boston City Hosp., 1972-75; asst. prof. neurology Med. Sch. Harvard U., Boston, 1975-77, assoc. prof., 1977-78; prof. Stanford (Calif.) U., 1978-86; chief neurology unit Palo Alto (Calif.) VA Hosp., 1978-86; prof., chmn. dept. neurology Yale U., New Haven, 1986—; chief neurology Yale-New Haven Hosp., 1986—; vis. asst. prof. biology MIT, Cambridge, 1975-77, vis. assoc. prof., 1977-78; vice chmn. dept.neurology Stanford, 1981-86, chmn. neurosci. program, 1982-86; mem. adv. bd. Regeneration Programs VA, Washignton, 1982-86; mem. sci. adv. com. Nat. Spinal Cord Injury Assn., 1982-87, Paralized Vets Am., 1981-91; dir. Ctr. Rsch. Neurol. Disease, VA Med. Ctr., West Haven, Conn., 1986—; mem. corp. Marine Biol. Labs., Woods Hole, Mass., 1988; mem. sci. adv. coun. Am. Paralysis Assn., 1988-92, mem. bd. sci. counselors NINDB, 1990-92; mem. bd. neurosci. and behavior Inst. Medicine, 1990; Geschwind vis. prof. Harvard U., 1996; mem. Dana Alliance for Brain Initiatives, 1993. Author: Spinal Cord Compression, 1990, Correlative Neuroanatomy, 1995, The Axon, 1995; editor: Physiology and Pathobiology of Axons, 1978; editor-in-chief The Neuroscientist; assoc. editor Jour. Neurol. Scis.; mem. editl. bd. Brain Rsch., Muscle and Nerve, Internat. Rev. Neurobiology, Annals of Neurology, Jour. Neurol. Rehab., Glia, Devel. Neurosci., Jour. Neurotrauma, Neurobiology of Disease, Cerebrovascular Disease, Synapse. Recipient Trygve Tuve Meml. award NIH, 1973, Rsch. Career Devel. award NIH, 1975, Disting. Alumnus award Albert Einstein Coll. Medicine, 1990; rsch. fellow Univ. Coll., London, 1969; Nat. Multiple Sclerosis Soc. established investigator, 1987; numerous vis. lectureships. Fellow NAS, Inst. Medicine, Royal Soc. Medicine (Gr. Britain), Am. Heart Assn. (stroke coun.); mem. Am. Soc. Cell Biology, Am. Acad. Neurology, Internat. Brain Rsch. Orgn. (U.S. nat. com.), Soc. Neurosci., Am. Neurol. Assn. (counsillor 1980), World Fedn. Neurology, Assn. Rsch. in Nervous and Mental Diseases (trustee, pres. 1992), Assn. Univ. Profs. Neurology. Office: Yale U Sch Medicine 33 Cedar St New Haven CT 06519-2314

WAXSE, DAVID JOHN, lawyer; b. Oswego, Kans., June 29, 1945; s. I. Joseph and Mary (Poole) W.; m. Linda Schilling (div.); children: Rachel, Ryan, Rebecca; m. Judy Pfannenstiel, May 29, 1982; 1 child, Elayna. BA, U. Kans., 1967; teaching cert., Columbia U., 1968, JD, 1971. Bar: Kans. 1971, U.S. Ct. Appeals (10th cir.) 1971, U.S. Supreme Ct. 1975. Dean of students Intermediate Sch. 88, N.Y.C., 1968-70; spl. edn. tchr. Peter Cooper Sch., N.Y.C., 1970-71; assoc. Payne & Jones, Olathe, Kans., 1971-74, ptnr., 1974-84; of counsel Shook, Hardy & Bacon, Overland Park, Kans., 1984-86, ptnr., 1986-95; ptnr. Shook, Hardy & Bacon L.L.P., Overland Park, Kans., 1995—; shareholder Shook, Hardy & Bacon P.C., Overland Park, 1993-95, v.p., asst. gen. counsel, 1995—; mcpl. judge City of Shawnee, Kans., 1974-80; atty. City of DeSoto, Kans., 1972-79; adj. prof. U. Kans. Sch. Law, Lawrence, 1981-82; mem. juv. code adv. com. Kans. Jud. Coun., 1979-83, guardianship adv. com., 1982-83, atty. fees adv. com., 1986-87; mem. Civil Justice Reform Act Adv. Com., U.S. Dist. Ct. for Dist. Kans., 1991—; mem. Kans. Commn. on Jud. Qualifications, 1992-94, vice-chmn. 1994-97, chair, 1997—; v.p. Kans. Legal Svcs., Inc., 1980-82, pres., 1985-87; bd. advisors Kans. Coll. Advocacy, 1979-80. Author: (with others) Kansas Employment Law, 1985, Litigating Employment Law Cases, 1987, Kansas Employment Law Handbook, 1991, supplements, 1992, 95, Kansas Annual Survey, 1990—. Mem. Kan. Gov.'s Adv. Com. on Criminal Justice, 1974-77; gen. counsel Western Mo. Dist. ACLU, 1976-78, 86—, v.p., 1983-86, nat. bd. dirs., 1979-86, 91—, chmn. children's rights com., 1980-86; mem. AIDS Pol. Network, 1987—, med. treatment issues com., 1991—, constn. com., 1991—; mem. med./tech. com. AIDS Coun. Greater Kans. City, 1986—, ethics com. consortium Midwest Bioethics Ctr., 1990—; bd. dirs. Parents Anonymous Kans., 1978-83, pres., 1979; bd. dirs., mem. fin. com. Kans. Com. for Prevention Child Abuse, 1980-83. Mem. ABA (chmn. children's rights com. and family law sects. 1985-86), Am. Employment Law Coun., Kans. Bar Assn. (v.p. 1996-97, chmn. legal aid com. 1978-83, bd. govs. 1988—, Pres.' Outstanding Svc. award 1982, pres. elect 1997—), Johnson County Bar Assn. (chmn. legal aid com. 1975-82, 92—), Amnesty Internat. (legal com. Kansas City chpt.), Common Cause, Sierra Club. Home: 9976 Hemlock Dr Shawnee Mission KS 66212-3447 Office: Shook Hardy and Bacon LLP 40 Corporate Woods 6th flr 9401 Indian Creek Pky Overland Park KS 66210-2005

WAY, BARBARA HAIGHT, dermatologist; b. Franklin, N.J., Dec. 27, 1941; d. Charles Padley and Alice Barbara (Haight) Shoemaker; m. Anthony Biden Way; children: Matthew Shoemaker Way, Sarah Shoemaker Way. AB in Music cum laude, Bryn Mawr Coll., 1962, postgrad., 1963-64; MD, U. Pa., 1968. Diplomate Am. Bd. Dermatology. Systems engr. IBM, Balt., 1962-63; mem. dean's staff Bryn Mawr (Pa.) Coll., 1963-64; med. intern U. Wis. Hosps., Madison, 1968-69, resident in dermatology, 1969-72; physician emergency rm. St. Francis Hosp., La Crosse, Wis., 1969-72, founder dept. of dermatology, 1972; asst. prof. dept. dermatology Tex. Tech U. Sch. Medicine, Lubbock, 1972-73, from asst. clin. to assoc. clin. prof., 1973-74, asst. prof., assoc. chair, 1974-76, assoc. prof., chair, 1976-81; assoc. clin. prof. Tex. Tech U. Health Scis. Ctr. (formerly Tex. Tech U. Sch. Medicine), Lubbock, 1981-92; clin. prof. Tex. Tech. U. Health Scis. Ctr., Lubbock, 1995—; founder, dir. dermatology residency tng. program Tex. Tech U. Health Scis. Ctr. (formerly Tex. Tech U. Sch. Medicine), Lubbock, 1978-81; pvt. practice Lubbock, 1973-74, 81—; acting dir. Lubbock City Health Dept., 1982-83; active staff Meth. Hosp., Lubbock, subsection chief, 1992, 94; active staff St. Mary of Plains Hosp., Lubbock, mem. credentials com., 1990, 92, 94, 95, founding dir. phototherapy unit, 1990-91, 93, mem. exec. com., 1991, 93, chief dermatology sect., 1991, 93. Alumna admissions rep. Bryn Mawr Coll., 1972-75, 87-96; mem. selection com. outstanding physician Lubbock chpt. Am. Cancer Soc., 1991-94, chmn., 1991; bd. dirs. Tex. Tech. U. Med. Found., 1987-89, Double T. Connection, 1988-90. Fellow Am.

Acad. Dermatology (reviewer jour.); mem. Am. Soc. Dermatologic Surgery, Tex. Dermatol. Soc. (chmn. roster com. 1980), Tex. Med. Assn. (mem. sexually transmitted diseases com. 1986-90, mem. coun. pub. health 1990-92, vice councillor dist. III 1992—, chmn. reference com. fin. and orgnl. affairs ann. session 1992), Lubbock County-Garza County Med. Soc. (mem. various coms. 1980—, chmn. sch. and pub. health com. 1983, mem. bd. censors 1983-85, chair 1985, sec. 1986, v.p. 1987, liaison with Tex. Tech. U. Health Scis. Ctr. com. 1988-91, co-chmn. pub. rels. com. 1988-89, alt. Tex. Med. Assn. del. 1988-89, del. 1990-95, pres.-elect 1989, pres. 1990, chmn. ad hoc bylaws com. 1991-94, chmn. Hippocratic award 1991), Soc. Pediatric Dermatology, Women's Dermatologic Soc. (founding mem.). Office: 4102 24th St Ste 201 Lubbock TX 79410-1801

WAY, E(DWARD) LEONG, pharmacologist, toxicologist, educator; b. Watsonville, Calif., July 10, 1916; s. Leong Man and Lai Har (Shew) W.; m. Madeline Li, Aug. 11, 1944; children: Eric, Linette. BS, U. Calif., Berkeley, 1938, MS, 1940; PhD, U. Calif., San Francisco, 1942. Pharm. chemist Merck & Co., Rahway, N.J., 1942; instr. pharmacology George Washington U., 1943-46, asst. prof., 1946-48; asst. prof. pharmacology U. Calif., San Francisco, 1949-52; assoc. prof. U. Calif., 1952-57, prof., 1957-87, prof. emeritus, 1987—, chmn. dept. pharmacology, 1973-78; USPHS spl. rsch. fellow U. Berne, Switzerland, 1955-56, China Med. Bd.; rsch. fellow, vis. prof. U. Hong Kong, 1962-63; Sterling Sullivan disting. vis. prof. martin Luther King U., 1982; hon. prof. pharmacology and neurosci. Guangzhou Med. Coll., 1987; mem. adv. com. Pharm. Rsch. Mfrs. Assn. Found., 1968—; mem. coun. Am. Bur. for Med. Advancement in China, 1982; bd. dirs. Li Found., 1970—, pres., 1985—, bd. dirs. Haight Ashbury Free Clinics, 1986-93; Tsumura prof. neuropsychopharmacology med. sch. Gunma U., Maebashi, Japan, 1989-90; sr. staff fellow Nat. Inst. on Drug Abuse, 1990-91; researcher on drug metabolism, analgetics, devel. pharmacology, drug tolerance, drug dependence and Chinese materia medica. Editor: New Concepts in Pain, 1967, (with others) Fundamentals of Drug Metabolism and Drug Disposition, 1971, Endogenous and Exogenous Opiate Agonists and Antagonists, 1979; mem. editl. bd. Clin. Pharmacology, Therapeutics, 1975-87, Drug, Alcohol Dependence, 1976-87, Progress in Neuro-Psychopharmacology, 1977-91, Research Communications in Chem. Pathology and Pharmacology, 1978-91, Alcohol and Drug Dependence, 1986-91, Asian Pacific Jour. Pharm., 1985—, Jour. Chinese Medicine, 1993—; contbr. numerous articles and revs. to profl. publs. Recipient Faculty Rsch. Lectr. award U. Calif., San Francisco, 1974, San Francisco Chinese Hosp. award, 1976, Cultural citation and Gold medal Ministry of Edn., Republic of China, 1978, Nathan B. Eddy award Coll. on Problems in Drug Dependence, 1979, Chancellor's award for pub. svc. U. Calif., 1986, Disting. Alumnus award U. Calif., San Francisco, 1990, Asian Pacific Am. Systemwide Alliance award, 1993. Fellow AAAS, Am. Coll. Neuropsychopharmacology, Am. Coll. Clin. Pharmacology (hon.), Coll. on Problems of Drug Dependence (exec. com. 1978-92, chmn. bd. dirs. 1978-82); mem. Am. Soc. Pharmacology, Exptl. Therapeutics (bd. editors 1957-65, pres. 1976-77, Torald Sollman award 1992), Fedn. Am. Socs. Exptl. Biology (exec. bd. 1975-79, pres. 1977-78), Am. Pharm. Assn. (life, Rsch. Achievement award 1962), AMA (affiliate), Soc. Aid and Rehab. Drug Addicts (Hong Kong, life), Western Pharmacology Soc. (pres. 1963-64), Japanese Pharm. Soc. (hon.), Coun. Sci. Soc. Pres.' (exec. com. 1979-84, treas. 1980-84), Chinese Pharmacology Soc. (hon.), Academia Sinica. Office: U Calif Dept of Pharmacology San Francisco CA 94143-0450

WAY, JACOB EDSON, III, museum director; b. Chgo., May 18, 1947; s. Jacob Edson Jr. and Amelia (Evans) W.; m. Jean Ellwood Chappell, Sept. 6, 1969; children: Sarah Chappell, Rebecca Stoddard, Jacob Edson IV. BA, Beloit Coll., 1968; MA, U. Toronto, 1971, PhD, 1978. Instr. Beloit (Wis.) Coll., 1972-73, asst. prof., 1973-80, assoc. prof., 1980-85; dir. Logan Mus. Anthropology, Beloit, 1980-85, Wheelwright Mus. Am. Indian, Santa Fe, 1985-89; interim dir. N.Mex. Mus. Natural History, Albuquerque, 1990-91; exec. dir. Space Ctr. Internat. Space Hall of Fame, Alamogorgo, N.Mex., 1991-94; dir. N.Mex. Farm and Ranch Heritage Mus., 1994—; evaluator Nat. Park Service, Denver, 1986. Contbr. articles to profl. jours. Mem. Nuke Watch, Beloit, 1983-84. Research grants Wis. Humanities Com., 1984, NSF, 1981; grantee Cullister Found., 1978-84; fellow U. Toronto, 1971. Mem. Am. Assn. Mus., Am. Assn. Phys. Anthropology, Can. Assn. for Phys. Anthropology, N.Mex. Assn. Mus. (pres. 1994-96), Soc. Am. Archaeology, Wis. Fedn. Mus. (adv. bd. 1982-85). Mem. Soc. Friends. Avocations: camping, skiing, fishing, reading, horseback riding. Office: N Mex Farm & Ranch Heritage Mus PO Drawer 1898 Las Cruces NM 88004

WAY, JAMES LEONG, pharmacology and toxicology educator; b. Watsonville, Calif., Mar. 21, 1926; s. Wong Bung Wee and Wow Wee (Wong) W.; m. Diana Chen, Dec. 20, 1991; children: Lani, Jon, Lori. BA, U. Calif., Berkeley, 1951; PhD, George Washington U., 1955. Asst. prof. U. Wis., Madison, 1959-62; assoc. prof. Marquette Med. Sch., Milw., 1962-67; prof. Washington State U., Pullman, 1967-82; endowed Shelton prof. pharmacology Tex. A&M U., College Station, 1982—; mem. toxicology study sect. NIH, Bethesda, Md., 1974-78; mem. toxicology data bank peer rev. com., NIH-NLM, 1978-85; mem. environ. health sci. study sect. NIEHS, 1985-90; vis. prof. pharmacology Nat. Def. Med. Ctr., Taipei, Taiwan, 1981-82; mem. toxicology data bank NLM, 1976-85; vis. scientist Med. Rsch. Coun./Nat. Inst. Med. Rsch., London, 1973-75. Contbr. over 200 articles to profl. jours. Recipient rsch. career devel. award NIH, 1959-72; Greenwald scholar U. Calif., Berkeley, 1960, Disting. scholar of U.S. NAS, 1986-88; N.Am. Baxter fellow, 1954-55, fellow NIH, 1969-80, Nat. Cancer Inst., 1955-58, also others. Mem. Am. Soc. Pharmacology and Exptl. Therapeutics (treas. 1989-90), Soc. Toxicology, Western Pharmacology Soc. (pres. 1978-79, mem. editorial bd. Toxicology and Applied Pharmacology 1978-90, Ann. Rev. Pharmacology and Toxicology 1986-91, assoc. editor 1991-96), Internat. Soc. Resealed Erthrocyte (pres. 1994-96). Avocations: skiing, sky diving, windsurfing, scuba, handball. Office: Tex A&M U Health Sci Ctr Dept Med Pharmacology Med Sci Bldg College Station TX 77843-1114

WAY, KENNETH L., seat company executive; b. 1939. BS, Mich. State U., 1961, MBA, 1971. V.p. Lear Siegler, Inc., Southfield, Mich., 1966-88; chmn., chief exec. officer Lear Seating Co., Southfield, Mich., 1988—. With USAF, 1962-66. Office: Lear Corp 21557 Telegraph Rd Southfield MI 48034-4248*

WAY, WALTER LEE, anesthetist, pharmacologist, educator; b. Rochester, N.Y., June 27, 1931; s. Kenneth F. and Mary F. (Faulkner) W.; m. Elizabeth J. Folwell, July 9, 1955; children: Barbara, Jonathan, Jeffrey. BS in Pharmacy, U. Buffalo, 1953; MD, SUNY, Syracuse, 1957; MS, U. Calif., San Francisco, 1962. Intern Highland Hosp., Rochester, N.Y., 1957-58; resident U. Calif., San Francisco, 1958-60, trainee, 1960-62, instr. anesthesia and oral medicine, 1960-64, asst. prof. anesthesia, 1962-64, asst. prof. anesthesia and pharmacology, 1964-68, assoc. prof. anesthesia and pharmacology, 1968-74, prof. anesthesia and pharmacology, 1974-94; prof. emeritus anesthesia and pharmacology, 1994—; vis. prof. various univs.; cons. in field. Mem. Am. Soc. Anesthesiologists, Calif. Soc. Anesthesiologists, Assn. Univ. Anesthesiologists, Am. Soc. Pharmacology and Exptl. Therapeutics. Office: PO Box 191 Ross CA 94957-0191

WAYCASTER, BILL, chemicals executive; b. 1942. With Tex. Olefins Co., Houston, 1969—, CEO; with Tex. Petrochems., Houston, 1969—, CEO. Office: Tex Olefins Co 8707 Katy Fwy Ste 300 Houston TX 77024-1706 also: Tex Petrochems 8600 Park Place Blvd Houston TX 77017*

WAYLAND, J(AMES) HAROLD, biomedical scientist, educator; b. Boise, Idaho, July 2, 1909; s. Charles William and Daisy (McConnell) W.; m. Virginia Jane Kartzke, June 24, 1933; children—Ann Marie Peters, Elizabeth Jane (Mrs. Paul T. Barber). B.S., U. Idaho, 1931, D.Sc. (hon.), 1977; M.S., Calif. Inst. Tech., 1935, Ph.D., 1937. Am. Scandinavian Found. fellow U. Copenhagen, 1937; asst. prof. physics U. Redlands, 1938-41; mil. research in mine warfare and torpedo devel., 1941-48; assoc. prof. applied mechanics Calif. Inst. Tech., Pasadena, 1949-57; prof. Calif. Inst. Tech., 1957-63, prof. engring. sci., 1963-79, prof. emeritus, 1979—; U.S. coordinator U.S.-Japan Coop. Seminars on Peripheral Circulation, 1967, 70; mem. cardiovascular and renal study sect. NIH, 1973-77; vis. prof. Shinshu U., Matsumoto, Japan, 1973, U. Limburg, Maastricht, The Netherlands, 1979, U. New South Wales, Australia, 1980, U. Heidelberg, 1982, U. of Tsukuba, Japan, 1987; Disting. vis. prof. U. Del., 1985. Contbr. articles to profl. publs., also books and articles on history of playing cards. Recipient Ordnance Devel. award U.S. Navy, 1945, Cert. of Recognition, NASA, 1975, Humboldt Sr. Scientist Rsch. award U. Heidelberg, 1982, 91, Malpighi prize, 1988; named to Alumni Hall of Fame, U. Idaho, 1990; Guggenheim fellow, 1953-54; rsch. grantee NIH, NSF, John A. Hartford Found., Kroc Found. Fellow AAAS (chmn. med. scis. sect. 1976); founding fellow Am. Inst. Med. and Biol. Engring.; mem. AAUP, Microcirculatory Soc. (pres. 1971-72, Landis award 1981), Am. Phys. Soc., Am. Physiol. Soc., European Microcirculatory Soc. (hon.), German Microcirculatory Soc. (hon.), Internat. Soc. Biorheology, Am. Heart Assn., Am. Inst. Archeology, Am. Soc. Enologists, Playing Card Soc., Sigma Xi, Phi Beta Kappa, Sigma Tau. Democrat. Unitarian. Club: Athenaeum. Achievements include patents for scanning confocal microscopy; development of quantitative methods for measuring blood flow in microvessels and macromolecular diffusion in living tissues, of servo-microscope for maintaining focus on moving tissue. Home: 900 E Harrison Ave Apt B-21 Pomona CA 91767 Office: Calif Inst Tech Mail Code 104 # 44 Pasadena CA 91125

WAYLAND, NEWTON HART, conductor; b. Santa Barbara, Calif., Nov. 5, 1940; s. L.C. Newton and Helen Bertha (Hart) W.; m. Judith Anne Curtis, July 3, 1969 (div. 1986). MusB, New Eng. Conservatory Music, 1964, MusM, 1966. Host, composer, performer Sta. WGBH-TV, Boston, 1963-82; pianist, harpsichordist Boston Symphony Orch., 1964-71; music dir. Charles Playhouse, 1965-67; pianist, guest condr., arranger Boston Pops Orch., 1971-74; resident Pops condr. Midwest Pops Orch., South Bend, Ind., 1979-91, Oakland Symphony Orch., Calif., 1980-85, Houston Symphony Orch., 1986-93; prin. Pops condr. Denver Symphony Orch., 1987-89, Vancouver (B.C.) Symphony Orch., 1993—; guest condr. numerous orchs. U.S. and Canada, 1977—. Recs. include: Music for Zoom (PBS Emmy-winning TV show), 1971-78, Music for Nova (award-winning PBS-TV show), 1972-78, America Swings, 1987, Gershwin Plays Gershwin, 1987, Pop Go the Beatles, 1987, Classical Jukebox, 1988, Stompin' at the Savoy, 1988, Sophisticated Ladies, 1988, A Touch of Fiedler, 1989, Prime Time, 1989; arranger, performer: Jazz Loves Bach, 1968, Fiedler in Rags, 1974; arranger, condr.: Berlin to Broadway with Kurt Weill, 1972; condr. Oedipus Tex (Grammy award 1991); arranger, composer, performer (songs A&M Records) Come On and Zoom, Zoom Tunes. Recipient highest honors New Eng. Conservatory Music, 1974, Chadwick Disting. Achievement medal New Eng. Conservatory Music, 1966. Avocations: hiking, history, theatre. Home and Office: 2970 Hidden Valley Ln Santa Barbara CA 93108-1619

WAYLAND, ROBERT H., III, government official. Grad., George Washington U. Mem. U.S. Ho. of Reps., U.S. Senate; mem. congl. affairs staff Office Enforcement, Office Solid Waste & Emergency, U.S. EPA, 1974-86; spl. asst. to adminstr. and dep. adminstr. EPA, Washington, 1986-88, dep. asst. adminstr. Office Policy, Planning & Evaluation, 1988-89, dep. asst. adminstr. Office of Water, 1989-91, dir. Office Wetlands, Oceans and Watersheds, 1991—. Planning commr. City of Falls Church; mem. Archtl. Rev. Bd., Falls Church; mem. Nat. Transp. Safety Bd. Office: US EPA Wetlands Oceans & Watersheds Office 401 M St SW Washington DC 20460-0001

WAYLAND, RUSSELL GIBSON, JR., retired geology consultant, government official; b. Treadwell, Alaska, Jan. 23, 1913; s. Russell Gibson and Fanchon (Borie) W.; m. Mary Mildred Brown, 1943 (div. 1964); children: Nancy, Paul R.; m. Virginia Bradford Phillis, Dec. 24, 1965. B.S., U. Wash., 1934; A.M., Harvard, 1937; M.S., U. Minn., 1935, Ph.D., 1939. Engr., geologist Homestake Mining Co., Lead, S.D., summers 1930-39; with U.S. Geol. Survey, 1939-42, 1952-80, chief conservation div., 1966-78; research phys. scientist Office of Dir., 1978-80; energy minerals cons., 1980—; Washington rep. Am. Inst. Profl. Geologists, 1982-88; commr. VA Oil and Gas Conservation Bd., 1982-90; with Army-Navy Munitions Bd., 1942-45, Office Mil. Govt. and Allied High Commn., Germany, 1945-52; instr. geology U. Minn., 1937-39. Author sci. bulls. in field. Served to lt. col. AUS, 1942-46. Decorated Army Commendation medal; recipient Distinguished Service award Dept. Interior. Mem. AIME, Mineral Soc. Am., Geol. Soc. Am., Am. Inst. Profl. Geologists, Soc. Econ. Geologists, Assn. Engring. Geologists, Cosmos Club, Sigma Xi, Tau Beta Pi, Phi Gamma Delta, Sigma Gamma Epsilon, Gamma Alpha, Phi Mu Alpha Sinfonia. Episcopalian. Home and Office: 4660 35th St N Arlington VA 22207-4462

WAYLAND-SMITH, ROBERT DEAN, banker; b. Oneida, N.Y., July 2, 1943; s. Robert and Prudence Cragin (Skinner) W.-S.; m. Kathleen Anne Schultz, Aug. 24, 1968; children: Kristin, Debra. BA in Econs., U. Rochester, 1965. Mgr. equipment svc. Strong Meml. Hosp., Rochester, N.Y., 1965-67; mgmt. trainee Chase Lincoln First Bank, N.A., Rochester, 1967-68, mgr. mcpl. securities, 1968-81, mgr. portfolio mgmt. depart., 1981-84, mgr. fin. and investment svc. dept., 1984-87, mgr. trust and fin. svc. dept., 1987-88; pres. and CEO Rochester region Chase Manhattan Bank, N.A., 1988-93, upstate wealth segment exec., 1993—; mem. adv. bd. Roberts Wesleyan Coll., Rochester, 1989—; mem. adv. coun. J.W. Jones Sch. Bus. SUNY, Geneseo, 1990—. Trustee Ctr. for Govtl. Rsch., 1985—, Rochester Visitors Assn., 1990-93, Rochester Downtown Devel. Corp., 1991-93; dir. United Neighborhood Ctrs., Greater Rochester Found., 1992—; mem. fin. execs. adv. bd. Coll. Bus. Rochester Inst. Tech., 1994—; mem. adv. bd. Help Our World Found., 1990—. Fellow Assn. for Investment Mgmt. and Rsch.; mem. Internat. Assn. Fin. Planners, Rochester Soc. Security Analysts, Greater Rochester Met. C. of C. (dir. 1992-95), Genesee Valley Club, Oak Hill Country Club. Avocations: golf, gardening, reading. Office: Chase Manhattan Bank NA One Chase Sq Rochester NY 14643

WAYMAN, COOPER HARRY, environmental legal counsel; b. Trenton, N.J., Jan. 29, 1927; s. Cooper Ott and Helen Viola (Unverzagt) W.; m. Ruth Treier, June 16, 1951; children: Carol Beth Withers, Andrea Lee Daschbach. BS, Rutgers U., 1951; MS, U. Pitts., 1954; PhD, Mich. State U., 1959; JD, U. Denver, 1967. Bar: Colo. 1969, Tex. 1972; registered profl. engr., Colo.; cert. real estate broker, Colo. Rsch. chemist U.S. Geol. Survey, Lakewood, Colo., 1960-65; assoc. prof. chemistry Colo. Sch. Mines, Golden, 1965-70; regional counsel EPA, Dallas, 1971-74; asst. to regional adminstr. EPA, Denver, 1974-83; exec. asst. to mayor City of Denver, 1981-85; dir. environment compliance Cord Labs., Inc., Broomfield, Colo., 1986-88; environ. and permits mgr. Chem. Waste Mgmt. Inc., Port Arthur, Tex., 1988-92; regional regulatory mgr. Chem. Waste Mgmt., Inc., Houston, 1992-94; compliance branch mgr. Adv. Scis., Inc., Carlsbad, N.Mex., 1994-95; area office legal counsel Waste Isolation Project, Dept. Energy, Carlsbad, N.Mex., 1995—; dir. energy office EPA, Denver, 1974-78; adj. prof. law U. Denver, 1981-84; mem. State of Colo. Air Pollution Commn., Denver, 1969-70. Author: Detergents and Environment, 1965, Permits Handbook, 1981; contbr. articles to profl. jours. V.p. WE Lockwood Civic Assn., Lakewood, 1985-86. With USNR, 1945-46. Grantee U.S. Fish and Wildlife Svc., 1967; fellow, rsch. assoc. MIT, 1956-58. Fellow Am. Inst. Chemists, 1993. Avocations: skiing, golf, photography, art. Home: 901 Fountain Dr Carlsbad NM 88220 Office: US Dept Energy Carlsbad Area Office PO Box 3090 Carlsbad NM 88221

WAYMIRE, BONNIE GLADINE, nursing administrator; b. Williamsport, Ind., Dec. 16, 1954; d. Jackie Lee and Mary Lou (Jennings) W. LPN diploma, Danville Jr. Coll., 1978; diploma, Lakeview Sch. Nursing, 1986; BS in Bus. Mgmt., Ind. Inst. of Tech., 1996. RN, Ind., Ill., Tenn.; cert. vascular nurse, dir. nursing. Supr. evening shift Vermillion Manor, Danville, Ill., 1986; staff nurse, rsch. coord. VA Med. Ctr., Indpls., 1986-92; vis. nurse Vis. Nurse Svc., Indpls., 1992; charge nurse Eagle Valley Health Care, Indpls., 1992; DON Vinewood Health Care, Plainfield, Ind., 1992-93, Records Autumn Care, Franklin, Ind., 1993, Bloomfield (Ind.) Health Care, 1993-94, Shakamak Good Samaritan, Jasonville, Ind., 1994—. Co-author: Am. Jour. Vascular Surgery, 1992. Mem. Soc. Vascular Nursing (nursing standard and practice Acte com. 1988-92), Nat. Assn. Dirs. Nursing Adminstrn. in Long Term Care, VFW Aux., Women of the Moose (Acad. Friendship award 1992, Am. Legion Aux., Shakamak Women's Civic Club, Wednesday Rsch. Club. Roman Catholic. Avocations: collecting stamps, coins and Star Trek memorabilia. Home: 387 E Main St Bloomfield IN 47424-1458

WAYMIRE, JOHN THOMAS, principal; b. Rensselaer, Ind., June 10, 1949; s. John Frederick and Elizabeth Ann (Pettet) W.; m. Kristi Antoinette Cerny, Oct. 4, 1975; children: John Johanson, Thomas Joseph. BS, St. Joseph's Coll., 1971; MS, Ind. U., Gary, 1976; postgrad., U. Iowa, 1978-82. Cert. tchr., adminstr., Ind., Iowa, S.D. Tchr. Kankakee Valley Schs., DeMotte, Ind., 1971-73, South Ctrl. Schs., Union Mills, Ind., 1973-78; grad. asst. U. Iowa, Iowa City, 1978-79; tchr. sci. Lincoln Community Schs., Mechanicsville, Ind., 1979-80; test editorial asst. Riverside Pub. Co., Iowa City, 1980-82; prin. elem. edn. Sully Buttes Schs., Onida, S.D., 1982-86; asst. prin. Tippecanoe Valley Schs., Mentone, Ind., 1986-90; prin. Pioneer Regional Schs., Royal Center, Ind., 1990-94, Granville Wells Sch., Jamestown, Ind., 1994—. Mem. ASCD, NAESP, S.D. Assn. Elem. Sch. Prins. (dist. rep. 1985), Ind. Assn. Sch. Prins. (charter 1992), Ind. Prin.'s Acad. (grad.), Royal Center Lions (pres. 1992-94), Phi Delta Kappa (pres. 1989-90). Avocations: reading, model ship building, gardening, horseback riding. Home: 217 E Main St Jamestown IN 46147-9742 Office: 5046 S State Road 75 Jamestown IN 46147-9294

WAYMOUTH, JOHN FRANCIS, physicist, consultant; b. Barahona, Dominican Republic, May 24, 1926; came to U.S., 1936; s. John Francis and Margaret Logan (Postell) W.; m. Frances O'Bannon Pope, Sept. 3, 1949; children: John F., George L., Anne K., Mark D. BS, U. of South, 1947; PhD in Physics, MIT, 1950. From sr. engr. to sect. head Sylvania Electric Products Co., Salem and Danvers, Mass., 1950-69; lab. dir. GTE Products Corp., Danvers, 1969-88; cons. physicist Marblehead, Mass., 1988—; chmn. exec. com. Phys. Electronic Conf., 1969-72; mem. evaluation panel heat div. Nat. Bur. Standards, Gaithersburg, Md., 1972-74; mem. tech. elec. products radiol. saftey standards com. Bur. of Radiol. Health, Rockville, Md., 1977-79; mem. adv. com. for physics NSF, Washington, 1981-83. Author: Electric Discharge Lamps; contbr. articles to profl. jours.; patentee in field. With U.S. Army, 1944-46, PTO. Recipient Elenbaas prize Dutch Phys. Soc., 1973. Fellow Am. Phys. Soc., Illuminating Engring. Soc. N.Am. (medal 1991).

WAYNE, LOWELL GRANT, air pollution scientist, consultant; b. Washington, Nov. 27, 1918; s. Glenn Lytten and Bonnie Jean (Leming) W.; m. Martha Lee Dolson, June 21, 1942; children: Garth Lee, Randall Rush. BS, U. Calif., Berkeley, 1937; student, U. Calif., Davis, 1939-41, Harvard U., 1942; PhD, Calif. Inst. Technology, 1948. Diplomate Am. Bd. Indsl. Hygiene. Fellow Mellon Inst. for Indsl. Rsch., Pitts., 1949-52; phys. chemist Stanford Rsch. Inst., Menlo Park, Calif., 1953-54; occupational health engr. U. Calif., L.A., 1954-56; rsch. photochemist Air Pollution Control Dist., L.A., 1956-62; rsch. analyst Hancock Found. U. So. Calif., L.A., 1962-72, section head Air Pollution Control Inst., 1966-72; v.p., sr. scientist Pacific Environ. Svcs., Inc., Santa Monica, Calif., 1972-85; cons. L.A., 1985—; sr. scientist Valley Rsch. Corp., Van Nuys, Calif., 1987—. Lt. comdr. USNR, 1942-46. Fellow AAAS; mem. So. Calif. Fedn. Scientists, Air and Waste Mgmt. Assn., Am. Chem. Soc., Sigma Xi (chmn. Humboldt State U. chpt., 1995—). Unitarian. Avocation: chamber music. Home: 285 Bayside Rd Arcata CA 95521-6463

WAYNE, MARVIN ALAN, emergency medicine physician; b. Detroit, Dec. 11, 1943; s. Jack I. and Marian M. (Berk) W.; m. Joan A. Tobin, Dec. 30, 1971; children: Michelle, Dana. MD, U. Mich., 1968. Diplomate Am. Bd. Emergency Medicine. Fellow St. Bartholomew's Hosp., London, 1968, Virginia Mason Hosp., Seattle, 1973-74; resident in surgery U. Colo. Med. Ctr., Denver, 1968-71; pvt. practice Bellingham, Wash., 1974—; staff emergency dept. St. Joseph's Hosp. (merger St. Joseph's Hosp. and St. Luke's Hosp.), Bellingham, Wash., 1974—, vice chmn. dept. emergency medicine, 1980-83, chmn., 1984-86; med. dir. Emergency Med. Svcs., Bellingham, Wash., 1975—; assoc. clin. prof. sch. medicine U. Wash., Seattle, 1986—; vice chmn. emergency med. svcs. com. State of Wash., 1982-83, chmn., 1983-86; med. dir. Med-Flight Helicopter, 1980—, Inst. for Pre-Hosp. Medicine, 1980—; pres. Whatcom County Emergency Med. Svcs. Coun., 1979; med. advisor Mt. Baker Ski Patrol; spkr. nat. and internat. edn. programs; founder, owner Dr. Cookie Inc., Edmonds, Wash., 1985—. Contbr. articles to med. jours. Bd. dirs. YMCA, Bellingham, 1980-84. Maj. M.C., U.S. Army, 1971-73, Vietnam. Recipient Outstanding Achievement award Whatcom County Emergency Med. Svcs. Coun., 1980, Outstanding Ednl. Achievement award Abbott Labs., 1982, Outstanding Advanced Life Support System award State of Wash., 1983, Emergency Med. Svc. rsch. award Wash. Assn. Emergency Med. Technicians and Paramedics, 1983. Fellow Am. Coll. Emergency Physicians (bd. dirs. Wash. chpt. 1977-84, pres. 1978, sci. meetings com. 1984, Outstanding Ednl. Achievement award 1982), Royal Soc. Medicine (Eng.); mem. Wash. State Med. Soc. (emergency med. svc. adv. com. 1978--), Whatcom County Med. Soc., Univ. Assn. for Emergency Medicine, Soc. Critical Care Medicine, Am. Trauma Soc. (founding), Nat. Assn. Emergency Med. Svc. Physicians, Am. Soc. Automotive Medicine, Nat. Assn. Emergency Med. Technicians. Avocations: sailing, windsurfing, skiing, baking. Office: Emergency Med Svcs 1800 Broadway Bellingham WA 98225-3133

WAYNE, STEPHEN J., government educator, academic director, writer; b. N.Y.C., Mar. 22, 1939; s. Arthur G. and Muriel Wayne; m. Cheryl Beil, May 22, 1982; children: Jared B., Jeremy B. BA with honors, U. Rochester, 1961; MA, Columbia U., 1963, PhD, 1968. Instr. polit. sci. U.S. Naval Postgrad. Sch., 1963-65; instr. politics and govt. Ohio Wesleyan U., 1966-68; asst. prof. polit. sci. and pub. affairs The George Washington U., 1968-73, assoc. prof., 1973-79, prof., 1979-89; prof. govt. Georgetown U., Washington, 1989—; adviser Pres.-Elect Portillo and staff, Mexico City, 1976; dir. U.S. Studies program Ctr. Advanced Study of Am., 1985-87; presenter and lectr. in field. Author: The Legislative Presidency, 1978, The Road to the White House, 1980, post election edit., 1981, 5th post election edit., 1997, (with George C. Edwards) Presidential Leadership: Politics and Policy Making, 1985, 4th edit., 1997 (with Cal MacKenzie, David O'Brien and Richard L. Cole) The Politics of American Government, 1995, 2d edit., 1997; editor: Investigating the American Political System: Problems, Methods, and Projects, 1974, (with George C. Edwards) Studying the Presidency, 1983, (with Clyde Wilcox) The Quest for National Office, 1992; appeared on 3 one-hour programs on presidency Every Four Years, sta. WHYY-TV, PBS, 1980; election night analyst ARD-German TV, 1992; adv. editor Polit. Sci. McGraw Hill Coll. Divsn., 1982—; series editor Am. Political Institutions and Pub. Policy, M. E. Sharpe, Inc., 1990—; contbr. numerous articles, chpts. and book revs. to books and profl. jours. Office: Georgetown U Dept Govt 37th and O NW Washington DC 20057

WAYTE, (PAUL) ALAN, lawyer; b. Huntington Park, Calif., Dec. 30, 1936; s. Paul Henry and Helen Lucille (McCarthy) W.; m. Beverly A. Bruen, Feb. 19, 1959 (div. 1972); children: David Alan, Lawrence Andrew, Marcia Louise; m. Nancy Kelly Wayte, July 5, 1975. AB, Stanford U., 1958, JD, 1960. Bar: Calif. 1961, U.S. Dist. Ct. (so. dist.) Calif. 1961, U.S. Supreme Ct. 1984. Ptnr. Adams, Duque & Hazeltine, Los Angeles, 1966-85, Dewey Ballantine, Los Angeles, 1985—. Mem. L.A. County Bar Assn. (chmn. real property sect. 1981-82), Am. Coll. Real Estate Lawyers (bd. govs. 1989—, pres. 1994), Am. Coll. Mortgage Attys., Anglo-Am. Real Property Inst. (bd. govs. 1989-91), L.A. Philharm. Assn. (exec. com. bd. dirs. 1973—), Chancery Club, Calif. Club (L.A.), Valley Hunt Club (Pasadena). Home: 1745 Orlando Rd Pasadena CA 91106-4131 Office: Dewey Ballantine 333 S Hope St Los Angeles CA 90071-1406

WAZIR, TADAR JIHAD, chaplain, small business owner; b. Kansas City, Mo., Dec. 28, 1944; s. Roosevelt and Osceola (Moore) Byers; m. Kay Frances Kyle-Byers, May 17, 1969; children: Tarik, Ibrahim; 1 adopted child, Ajamu. AA in Adminstrn. of Justice, Penn Valley Community Coll., Kansas City, 1977. Ins. salesperson Western & So. Life Ins. Co., Kansas City, 1968-69, N.Y. Life Ins. Co., Kansas City, 1969; supr. check transit dept. First Nat. Bank, Kansas City, 1969-70, methods analyst, 1971-72; paramedic St. Joseph's Hosp., Kansas City, 1974-77; owner W. K. Enterprises, Kansas City, 1977-79; ins. salesperson Roosevelt Nat. Life, Independence, Mo., 1978-79; pvt. mcht., Kansas City, 1980-81, Marshall, Mo., 1989—; bd. dirs. Welcome Home, Inc. 1994—; real estate salesperson Mid-Western Realty, Kansas City, 1980-86; chaplain, hostage negotiator, Mo. Dept. of Corrections, Jefferson City, 1982—; speaker, cons. Masjid Omar, Inc., Kansas City, 1977-92, Islamic Life Mission, 1992-96; contract chaplain, cons. U.S. Med. Ctr. Fed. Prison, Springfield, Mo., 1979—; co-chmn. report the drug pusher Ad-Hoc Group Against Crime, Kansas City, 1978-82, pres. A.U. (African Unity, Inc.) 1994-95, (Qadi) spl. master of the Jackson County, Mo. cir. ct., 1992. Chaplain chpt. 393, Vietnam Vets. Assn. Am. Jefferson City, 1991; Mo. st. coun. of the Vietnam Vets. of Am. co-chaplain 1991, treas. 1992-94; With USMC, 1962-66; mem. U.S. affiliate Islamic African Relief Agy. Mem. Am. Corrections Assn., Mo. Corrections

Assn., Mo. Assn. Social Welfare, Nat. Assn. Muslim Chaplains, NAACP (pres. Marshall-Saline chpt. 1989-90, v.p., 1990-91, polit. action com. chmn. 1994—), Mid.-Am. Coun. Imams, Islamic Soc. N.Am., Optimists (chaplain Marshall 1990-91, chmn. community svcs. 1991-92, co-organizer ROTC program Ark. AM&N Coll.). Avocations: reading, horseback riding, swimming, selling. Home: 456 W Porter St Marshall MO 65340-1358 Office: Tipton Correction Ctr 619 Osage Ave Tipton MO 65081

WAZZAN, A(HMED) R(ASSEM) FRANK, engineering educator, dean; b. Lattakia, Syria, Oct. 17, 1935; married, 1959; 3 children. BS, U. Calif., Berkeley, 1959, MS, 1961, PhD in Engring. Sci., 1963. From asst. prof. to assoc. prof. engring. UCLA, 1962-69, prof. engring. and applied sci., 1974—, assoc. dean Sch. Engring. and Applied Sci., 1981-86, dean Sch. Engring. and Applied Sci., 1986—; cons. McDonnell Douglas Corp., 1962-71, Lawrence Radiation Lab., 1965-67, Westinghouse Electric Corp., 1974-76, N.Am. Aviation, 1975-78, Rand Corp., 1975—; Honeywell Corp., 1976-78; vis. scholar Electricité de France, Paris, Office of Commr. Atomic Energy, Saclay, France, 1973-79. Reviewer Applied Mech. Rev., 1971-87. Guggenheim fellow, 1966. Fellow Am. Nuclear Soc. Research in modeling of fuel elements for fast breeder reactor, stability and transition of laminar flows, thermodynamics of solids and of dense gases, and thermal hydraulics of pressurized water reactors. Office: UCLA Sch of Engring PO Box 951600 74 Boelter Hall Los Angeles CA 90095-1600

WEADON, DONALD ALFORD, JR., lawyer; b. Brisbane, Australia, Sept. 15, 1945; came to U.S., 1946; s. Donald Alford and Ellen Martha (Salisbury) W. BA, Cornell U., 1967; JD, U. Calif.-Hastings Coll. Law, 1975; MBA, Harvard U., Iran Ctr. for Mgmt. Studies, Tehran, 1976. Bar: Calif. 1976, D.C. 1988. Assoc. Hancock, Rothert & Bunshoft, San Francisco, 1977-80; jr. ptnr. Bryan, Cave, McPheeters & McRoberts, Washington, 1980-83; ptnr., head internat. dept. Anderson Baker Kill & Olick, Washington, 1983-84; sr. ptnr. Weadon, Dibble & Rehm, 1984-88, Weadon, Rehm and Assocs., 1988-89, Weadon, Rehm, Thomsen & Rehm, 1989-90, Weadon & Assocs., 1991— ; speaker, cons. U.S. Dept. Commerce, 1980-83; cons. Internat. Mktg. Assn., 1980—; Scientific Apparatus Mfg. Assn., 1983—, Valve Mfrs. Assn., 1983—; internat. counsel Am. Electronics Assn., 1986—; adj. prof. internat. law Golden Gate U., San Francisco, 1979-82, George Mason U., Arlington, Va., 1989—. Contbr. articles to profl. jours. Lt. comdr. USNR, 1968-72. Mem. ABA (chmn. China trade law com. 1982-84, chmn. software and tech. data com. 1983-85). Episcopalian. Clubs: Olympic, Savage, Knights Templar (grand officer), Press Club, Harvard Club.

WEAKLAND, ANNA WU, artist, art educator; b. Shanghai, China, May 1, 1924; came to the U.S., 1947; d. Tse-Chien and Kwei-Ying (Sze) Wu; m. John H. Weakland, Feb. 11, 1950; children: Alan Wade, Lewis Francis, Joan. BA, U. Shanghai, China, 1943; MA, Columbia U., 1948; postgrad., Stanford U., 1953-55. art instr. U. Calif., 1968, 72, 78, 82, 84, Stanford (Calif.) U., 1990; vis. art prof. Zhejiang Acad. Arts, Hangzhou, China, 1991. One-woman shows include De Young Mus., San Francisco, 1959, San Francisco Mus. Modern Art, 1961, Chathan Gallery, Hong Kong, 1963, Seattle Art Mus., 1964, Ashmolian Mus., Oxford, Eng., 1964, Sale Internat./Palacio De Bellas, Mexico City, 1966, Downtown Gallery, N.Y., 1967, Victoria (Can.) Art Mus., 1967, Heritage Gallery, L.A., 1971, Wells Fargo Bank Hdqs., San Francisco, 1973, Macy's, Palo Alto, 1976, I. Magnin, Palo Alto, 1981, Tresidor Union Gallery, Stanfor U., 1982, Palo Alto (Calif.) Med. Found., 1984, Stanford (Calif.) Mus. Art, 1988, Hewlett-Packard Co. Art Gallery, Palo Alto, 1989, Gump's Art Gallery, San Francisco, 1990, Marin County Civic Ctr., San Rafael, Calif., 1994; represented in permanent collections including Ashmolean Mus., Oxford, Eng., U. B.C., Vancouver, Fukuoka (Japan) U., Stanford U., Seattle (Wash.) Art Mus., IBM Corp., others. Named Artist of the Yr., Friends of The Libr. award, Palo Alto, Calif., 1979, Artist of the Month, No. Calif. Home and Garden Mag., Redwood City, Calif., 1992. Mem. Am. Women Caucas for Art, Asian Am. Women Artists Assn. Avocations: music, tennis, aerobic dancing, cooking, photography. Home: 4245 Manuela Ct Palo Alto CA 94306-3731

WEAKLAND, REMBERT G., archbishop; b. Patton, Pa., Apr. 2, 1927; s. Basil and Mary (Kane) W. AB, St. Vincent Coll., Latrobe, Pa., 1948, DD (hon.), 1963, LHD (hon.), 1987; MS in Piano, Juilliard Sch. Music, 1954; grad. studies sch. music, Columbia U., 1954-56; LHD (hon.), Duquesne U., 1964, Belmont Coll., 1964, Cath. U. Am., 1975, Loyola U., Chgo., 1986, Xavier U., Cin., 1988, DePaul U., 1989, Loyola U., New Orleans, 1991, Villanova U., 1992, Dayton U., 1993, Marian Coll., Fond du Lac, Wis., 1995, St. Anselm Coll., Manchester, N.H., 1996, St. Norbert Coll., De Pere, Wis., 1996; HHD (hon.), St. Ambrose U., Davenport, 1990, Aquinas Inst. Theology, St. Louis, 1991, St Mary's Coll., Notre Dame, Ind., 1994; LLD (hon.), Cardinal Stritch Coll., Milw., 1978, Marquette U., 1981, U. Notre Dame, 1987, Mt. Mary Coll., Milw., 1989, John Carroll U., Cleve., 1992, Fairfield U., 1994; D of Sacred Music (hon.), St. Joseph's Coll., Rensselaer, Ind., 1979; DST (hon.), Jesuit Sch. Theology, Berkeley, Calif., 1989, St. John's U., Collegeville, Minn., 1991, Santa Clara U., 1991, Yale U., 1993; DD (hon.), Lakeland Coll., Sheboygan, 1991, Ill. Benedictine Coll., Lisle, Ill., 1992, Regis Coll., Toronto, 1993, Trinity Coll., Hartford, 1996. Joined Benedictines, Roman Cath. Ch., 1945, ordained priest, 1951. Mem. faculty music dept. St. Vincent Coll., 1957-63, chmn., 1961-63, chancellor chmn. of bd. of Coll., 1963-67; elected co-adjutor archabbot, 1963; abbot primate Benedictine Confederation, 1967-77; archbishop of Milw., 1977—. Mem. Ch. Music Assn. Am. (pres. 1964-66), Am. Guild Organists. Office: PO Box 07912 Milwaukee WI 53207-0912

WEAN, BLANCHE MCNEELY, accountant; b. Monroe County, Ind., Jan. 28, 1901; d. Homer Clark and Ruth Jane (Tutterrow) McNeely; m. Francis Willard Wean, June 16, 1926 (dec.); children: Jane, Doris, Ruth. BA, Ind. U., 1923, MA, 1932, postgrad., 1945-46. CPA, Ind. Tchr. Mt. Carroll (Ill.) High Sch., 1918-19, Bloomington (Ind.) High Sch., 1923-26, Jefferson High Sch., Lafayette, Ind., 1923-26; head bus. dept. Cen. Normal Coll., Danville, Ind., 1931-47; acct. Wean Acctg., Danville, 1947-80, Wean, Andrews & Co., Danville, 1980—. Author: Blanche Accountant, 1996. Mem. Danville Pub. Libr. Bd., 1969-82, treas. Recipient John F. Jenner III Citizenship award, 1972. Mem. Nat. Assn. Pub. Accts., Ind. Pub. Accts. Assn. (pres. 1977-78, 89, Hall of Fame), Danville C. of C. (sec. 1950-75), Bus. and Profl. Womens Assn., Beta Gamma Sigma. Republican. First woman to be admitted to Sch. of Commerce, Ind. U., 1922. Home and Office: PO Box 128 Danville IN 46122-0128

WEAN, KARLA DENISE, middle school educator, secondary education educator; b. Lakewood, Ohio, Apr. 10, 1956. BS in Biology and Gen. Sci., Wheeling (W.Va.) Jesuit Coll., 1978, BA in Art, 1981; MA in Art Edn., Fla. State U., 1990; grad. Arts Mgm. Sch., N.C. State U., 1980. Art chairperson, art tchr. Mount De Chantal Acad., Wheeling, 1978-81; fine arts dir. Montverde (Fla.) Acad., 1981-83; coll. art instr. Lake Sumter C.C., Leesburg, Fla., 1981-82; art and sci. tchr. Santa Fe Cath. High Sch., Lakeland, Fla., 1983-85; art tchr. Kathleen (Fla.) Jr. High/Mid. Sch., 1985-95; instr. Polk Mus. Art, Lakeland, Fla., 1989—; musician, composer Nav Videos, Lakeland, 1990-91; art tchr. Bartow (Fla.) H.S., 1995—; bd. dirs. Arts on the Park, Lakeland, 1989—, performer original music in concert entitled Seasons of Time, 1993; children's choir dir. St. John Neuman's Ch., Mulberry, Fla., 1991-95, St. Matthews, Winter Haven, Fla., 1995-96; singer, violinist, guitarist, flutist Ch. of the Resurrection, Lakeland, 1989-90, St. John Neuman's Ch. Folk Choir, 1991—, Folkgroup-St. Matthews, Winter Haven, 1995-96; mem. Up With People, internat. song and dance group, 1978. Composer, performer videos Look and Draw, Faces and Figures; one woman show includes Wheeling Jesuit Coll.; exhibited in group shows at Lakeland Electric, 1990, Bartow Bloomin' Arts, 1990, Lakeland Art Guild Show, 1991. Goodwill ambassador State of W.Va., 1978; vol. sheltered workshop of handicapped, 1984-85. Recipient Disting. Leadership award in teaching, 1985, Jim Harbin Fame video award State of Fla., Tallahassee, 1991, Excellence in Edn. Bahai award Bahai Assn., Lakeland, 1991, Merit award Arts on the Park Mixed Media Show, 1995, awards in various art shows. Mem. Nat. Art Edn. Assn., Fla. Art Edn. Assn. Office: Bartow HS 1270 S Broadway Ave Bartow FL 33830-6429

WEARLY, WILLIAM LEVI, business executive; b. Warren, Ind., Dec. 5, 1915; s. Purvis Gardner and Ethel Ada (Jones) W.; m. Mary Jane Riddle, Mar. 8, 1941; children: Patricia Ann, Susan, William Levi, Elizabeth. B.S., Purdue U., 1937, Dr. Engring. (hon.), 1959. Student career engr. C.A. Dunham Co., Michigan City, Ind., 1936; mem. elec. design staff Joy Mfg. Co., Franklin, Pa., 1937-39; v.p., gen. sales mgr. Joy Mfg. Co., 1952-56, exec. v.p., 1956-57, pres., dir., 1957-62; v.p., dir. Ingersoll-Rand Co., 1964-66, exec. v.p., 1966-67, chmn., chief exec. officer, 1967-80, chmn. exec. com., 1981-85; dir. ASA Ltd., Med. Care Am.; trustee LMI; speaker engring. groups. Author tech. publs. relating to mining. Bd. dirs. Boys Clubs Am. Mem. NAE, IEEE, AIME, Nat. Acad. of Engring., C. of C., Sky Club N.Y.C., Blind Brook Golf Club, Desert Forest Golf Club, Ariz. Club, Masons, Shriners, Eta Kappa Nu, Tau Beta Pi, Beta Theta Pi. Republican. Methodist. Patentee in field. Home: One Milbank IIF Greenwich CT 06830 also: PO Box 1072 Carefree AZ 85377-1072

WEARN, WILSON CANNON, retired media executive; b. Newberry, S.C., Oct. 7, 1919; s. George F. and Mary (Cannon) W.; m. Mildred Colson, Feb. 21, 1948; children: Jean Wearn Held, Joan Wearn Gilbert, Wilson Cannon Jr. B.E.E., Clemson U., 1941. Engr. Westinghouse Electric Corp., Pitts., 1941, FCC, Washington, 1946-48; assoc. cons. electronic engr. firm Weldon & Carr, Washington, 1948-50; ptnr. Vandivere, Cohen & Wearn (cons. engrs.), Washington, 1950-53; with Multimedia Broadcasting Co., Greenville, S.C., 1953-68; organizer of corp. Multimedia Broadcasting Co., 1953, became corp. officer, 1960, pres., 1966-77; pres. Multimedia, Inc., Greenville, 1977-81; chief exec. officer Multimedia, Inc., 1978-84, chmn. bd., 1981-89; chmn. emeritus Multimedia, Inc., Greenville, 1989-95; instr. electronic engring. Clemson U., 1946. Mem. S.C. Hosp. Adv. Council, 1969-71; bd. dirs. Family and Children Service of Greenville County, 1967-69, pres., 1969; bd. dirs. Newspaper Advt. Bur., 1981-85; trustee Greenville Symphony Assn., 1960-62, 71-77, pres., 1977; trustee Greenville Hosp. System, 1964-70, chmn., 1968-70; trustee Broadcast Rating Council, 1969-73, chmn., 1971-73; trustee Clemson U. Found., 1973-79, pres., 1979; trustee Presbyn. Coll., F.W. Symmes Found. Served to capt. Signal Corps, AUS, 1941-45, PTO. Decorated Bronze Star; recipient Outstanding Alumni award Clemson U., 1972. Mem. Nat. Assn. Broadcasters (chmn. bd. 1975-77), S.C. Broadcasters Assn. (pres. 1967), Greater Greenville C. of C. (pres. 1972), Nat. Assn. Securities Dealers (bd. govs. 1985-88), Kiwanis (Greenville), Poinsett Club (Greenville), Green Valley Country Club (Greenville), Augusta (Ga.) Nat. Golf Club. Presbyterian (elder).

WEART, SPENCER RICHARD, historian; b. Detroit, Mar. 8, 1942; s. Spencer Augustus and Janet (Streng) W.; m. Carole Ege, June 30, 1971; children: Lara Kimi, Spencer Gen. BA, Cornell U., 1963; PhD, U. Colo., 1968. Postdoctoral fellow Calif. Inst. Tech., 1968-71, U. Calif., Berkeley, 1971-74; dir. Ctr. for History Physics, Am. Inst. Physics, College Park, Md., 1974—. Author: Scientists in Power, 1979, Nuclear Fear, 1988; contbr. articles to profl. jours. Recipient Andrew Gemant award Am. Inst. of Physics, 1994. Fellow AAAS. Home: 12 Buena Vista Dr Hastings On Hudson NY 10706 Office: Am Inst Physics One Physics Ellipse College Park MD 20740-3843

WEARY, PEYTON EDWIN, medical educator; b. Evanston, Ill., Jan. 10, 1930; s. Leslie Albert and Conway Christian (Fleming) W.; m. Janet Edsall Gregory, Aug. 23, 1952; children—Terry, Conway Christian, Carolyn Fielder. B.A., Princeton U., 1970; M.D., U. Va., 1955. Diplomate: Am. Bd. Dermatology (dir. 1978-88, pres. 1987-88). Intern, case Western Res. U. Hosps., Cleve., 1955-56; rotating intern Univ. Hosp. Cleve., 1955-56; asst. resident dermatology U. Va., Charlottesville, 1958-60; resident dermatology U. Va., 1960-61, instr. dept. dermatology, 1961-62, asst. prof., 1962-65, asso. prof., 1965-70, prof., chmn. dept. dermatology, 1970-93; mem. staff Univ. Hosp., mem. cancer com., 1979—, sec.-treas.; Univ. Hosp. house staff, 1960-61, clin. staff, 1965-66, pres. clin. staff, 1966-67. Mem. editorial bd. Jour. Am. Acad. Dermatology, 1978-87; editorial adv. bd. Skin and Allergy News, 1978—; contbr. articles to profl. jours. Bd. dirs. Lupus Found. Am., 1980-84; trustee, mem. exec. com. Dermatology Found., 1975-79; pres. Albermarle County unit Am. Cancer Soc., 1967-69. Served from 1st lt. to capt., M.C. U.S. Army, 1956-58. Mem. Nat. Assn. Physicians Environ. (pres. 1995—), Va. Dermatol. Soc. (sec.-treas. 1965-71), Am. Acad. Dermatology (hon. bd. dirs. 1973-76, Gold medal 1990, pres. 1993-95), Soc. Investigative Dermatology (bd. dirs. 1976-81, v.p.1985, hon. mem. 1996), Assn. Profs. Dermatology (sec.-treas. 1976-79), Am. Dermatol. Assn. (bd. dirs. 1987-93, pres. 1992-93), Dermatology Found., Albermarle County Med. Soc., Med. Soc. Va., So. Med. Assn., Raven Soc., Am. Bd. Med. Specialties (v.p. 1988, pres-elect 1989, pres. 1990-92), Coun. Med. Specialty Socs. (bd. dirs. 1989-92, sec. 1992-95), Alpha Omega Alpha, Sigma Xi. Republican. Presbyn. Club: Boar's Head Sports. Home: 110 Magnolia Dr Charlottesville VA 22901-2015 Office: Dept Dermatology Univ Va Hosp Charlottesville VA 22908

WEATHERBEE, DONALD EMERY, political scientist, educator; b. Portland, Maine, June 21, 1932; s. Perley Emery and Ruby Francis (Smith) W.; m. Mary Ellen Bailey, Sept. 4, 1954; children: Mercy Meria, Donald Bailey, Thais Elizabeth, Amy Francesca, Oliver Parks Emery. A.B. magna cum laude, Bates Coll., 1954; M.A., Johns Hopkins U. Sch. Advanced Internat. Studies, 1956, Ph.D. (Earhart dissertation fellow), 1968. Spl. lectr. Gajah Mada State U., Jogjakarta, Indonesia, 1957-61; Ford Found. fellow The Hague, Netherlands, 1962-64; asst. prof. to prof. U. S.C., 1964-74; Donald S. Russell prof. contemporary fgn. policy, 1981—; sr. Fulbright fellow Inst. Southeast Asian Studies, Singapore, 1981-82; asst. dean Coll. Social Scis., 1972; Henry L. Stimson prof. polit. sci. U.S. Army War Coll., 1974-77; vis. asst. prof. U. R.I., 1965; exchange prof. Free U. Berlin, 1969; vis. fellow Inst. Security and Internat. Studies, Chulalongkorn U., Bangkok, Thailand, 1988-89; panelist reviewer Nat. Endowment for Humanities; cons., lectr. for U.S. govt. agys. Author: Ideology in Indonesia, 1965, The United Front in Thailand, 1970, Ancient Indonesia, 1974, Indonesian Security Policy and Perceptions, 1978, Southeast Asia Divided: The Asean-Indochina Crisis, 1985; editorial bd.: Asian Survey; exec. editor: Asian Affairs; contbr. numerous articles, revs. to publs. on S.E. Asian politics and internat. relations. Recipient Disting. Civilian Service decoration Dept. of the Army, 1977. Fellow Inter-Univ. Seminar on Armed Forces and Soc.; mem. Assn. Asian Studies, Internat. Studies Assn., Koninklijke Instituut voor Taal, Land- en Volkenkunde (Leiden, Netherlands). Office: Dept Govt and Internat Studies U SC Columbia SC 29208

WEATHERBY, SUSAN MOORMANN, elementary school educator; b. Cin., Dec. 14, 1950; d. Ambrose Francis and Susan G. Moormann; 1 child, Shannon Rose Lydon Weatherby. BA, U. So. Fla., Tampa, 1974, MA, 1976, MEd, 1989. Cert. tchr., Fla. Tchr., reading coord. St. Cecelia Sch., Clearwater, Fla., 1974-81; tchr. Meadowlawn Middle Sch., St. Petersburg, Fla., 1981-82; vol. Pinellas County Schs., Clearwater, Fla., 1982-85; tchr. Ponce de Leon Elem., Clearwater, 1985-88; adj. instr. St. Petersburg Jr. Coll., Clearwater, 1987, mem. support team beginning tchrs., 1987—; clin. tchr. Suncoast Area Tchr. Tng., 1987; reading specialist North Ward Elem., Clearwater, 1988-92; tchr. Kings Hwy. Elem. Sch., Clearwater, 1992—; rep. Tchr. Edn. Coun., Pinellas County, Fla., 1988-91; mem. planning and writing coms. Profl. Edn. Ctr., 1991-96, mem. steering com., 1990-91, 92-93, mem. adv. coun., 1991-95, proed facilitator, 1993—; instr. adult edn. Seminole (Fla.) Community Sch., 1990; instr. computer component, 1990, 92; participant Pinellas Writing Project, 1992; Administrv. Insights and Methodologies, 1988, reading staff devel. com., 1988-89. Editorial adv. bd. The Reading Tchr., 1992-93; proposal and manuscript review bd. Internat. Reading Assn., 1993-96. Vol. Fla. Internat. Mus., 1995; mem. Pinellas County Juvenile Welfare Cmty. Coun., 1995-96. Fla. Ctr. Tchrs. Humanities fellow, 1995; recipient Teach for Excellence award Edn. Found., Largo, Fla., 1987; Poynter Inst. Media Studies Writers Camp fellow, St. Petersburg, 1988. Mem. Internat. Reading Assn., Fla. Reading Assn. (conf. sec. 1993), Pinellas Reading Coun. (bd. dirs. 1994—), Phi Kappa Phi, Kappa Delta Pi, Phi Delta Kappa. Avocations: reading, writing, speaking, scuba diving. Home: Villa 1922 14840 Shipwatch Trce Largo FL 33774-5724 Office: Pinellas County Sch 301 4th St SW Largo FL 33770-3536

WEATHERFORD, GEORGE EDWARD, civil engineer; b. Oakdale, Tenn., Jan. 8, 1932; s. Walter Clyde and Kathleen (Hinds) W.; m. Martha Jeannette Beck, July 9, 1960; children: Kathleen Jeannette Weatherford-Hommeltoft, Elizabeth Lynn. BSCE, Ind. Inst. Tech., Fort Wayne, 1957; BS Engr. in Constrn., U. Mich., 1959; MSBA, St. Francis Coll., 1975. Registered profl. engr., Ind., Ga., Ohio, Minn., Iowa, S.C., Pa., Ky., Ill., Md., La., Tenn., Mich. Plant engr. Cen. Soya Co., Inc., Decatur, Ind., 1959; civil engr. Cen. Soya Co., Inc., Decatur, 1959-64; county hwy. engr. Allen County Ind. Govt., Ft. Wayne, 1964-66; sr. civil engr. Cen. Soya Co., Inc., Fort Wayne, 1966-69, engring. mgr., 1969-77, prin. engr., 1977—; ind. cons. 1964—. Author book chpts.; contbr. articles to profl. jours. Trustee Ft. Wayne YWCA, 1973-76, North Christian Ch. and Endowment Trust. Sgt. USMC, 1950-54. Mem. ASCE (state treas. 1957), NSPE, Am. Concrete Inst., Am. Inst. Steel Constrn., Nat. Grain and Feed Assn. (fire and explosion rsch. and edn. com.), Ill. Assn. Structural Engrs., Grain Elevator and Processing Soc. (edn. programming com.). Republican. Home: 3617 Delray Dr Fort Wayne IN 46815-6012

WEATHERHEAD, LESLIE R., lawyer; b. Tacoma, Sept. 28, 1956; s. A. Kingsley and Ingrid A. (Lien) W.; m. Anali C. Torrado, June 24, 1985; children: Spencer, Madeleine, Audrey. BA, U. Oreg., 1977; JD, U. Wash., 1980. Bar: Wash. 1980, Oreg. 1996, U.S. Ct. Appeals (9th cir.) 1981, U.S. Dist. Ct. (ea. dist.) Wash. 1984, U.S. Ct. Internat. Trade 1984, Hawaii 1987, U.S. Dist. Ct. (we. dist.) Wash. 1989, Idaho 1989, U.S. Dist. Ct. Idaho 1989, U.S. Supreme Ct. 1994, Colville Tribal Ct. 1993, U.S. Ct. Apeals (10th cir.) 1995, U.S. Ct. Fed. Claims 1995. Asst. terr. prosecutor Territory of Guam, Agana, 1980-83; spl. asst. U.S. Atty. Dist. of Guam and No. Marianas, Agana, 1982-83; atty. Witherspoon, Kelley, Davenport & Toole, Spokane, 1984—; lawyer-rep. 9th cir. jud. conf., 1989-95, lawyer-rep. chmn., 1995; adj. faculty Gonzaga U. Sch. of Law, 1994-95. Contbr. articles on Indian law and administrv. investigations to profl. jours. Bd. dirs. Spokane Uptown Opera, 1989-96, pres., 1992-94. Mem. ABA, Fed. Bar Assn. (pres. ea. dist. 1997—), Hawaii Bar Assn., Idaho Bar Assn., Wash. State Bar Assn., Oreg. State Bar Assn. Avocations: sailing, scuba, skiing. Office: Witherspoon Kelley Davenport & Toole 428 W Riverside Ave Spokane WA 99201-0301

WEATHERLEY-WHITE, ROY CHRISTOPHER ANTHONY, surgeon, consultant; b. Peshawar, India, Dec. 1, 1931; S. Roy and Elfreda (Milward) Boehm, m. Dorian Jeanne Freeman Weatherley-White, Dec. 27, 1961; children: Carl Christopher, Matthew Richard, Larissa Chantal. MA, Cambridge U., 1953; MD, Harvard U., 1958. Surgeon Biomedical Cons., Denver, 1970—; pres., 1992—; chmn. Plastic Surgery Rsch. Coun., 1975-76; pres. Rocky Mountain Assn. Plastic Surgeons, 1973-74; v.p. Am. Cleft Palate Assn. Author: Plastic Surgeru of the Female Breast, 1982; contbr. over 45 articles to profl. jours. Cons. Colo. Biomedical Venture Ctr., Denver, 1993—. Recipient Rsch. award Am. Soc. Plastic Surgery, 1962, 64. Mem. Harvard Club of N.Y., Oxford-Cambridge Club, Denver Country Club, Denver Athletic Club. Episcopalian. Avocations: flying, skiing, scuba diving, archaeology. Home: 100 S Humboldt St Denver CO 80209-2516 Office: 4500 E 9th Ave Ste 470 Denver CO 80220-3923

WEATHERLY, ROBERT STONE, JR., banker; b. Birmingham, Ala., May 12, 1929; s. Robert Stone and Gladys (Manning) W.; m. Mary Anne Burr, May 1, 1955; children: Robert Stone, III, Henry, William. A.B., Princeton U., 1950; LL.B., Harvard U., 1953, grad. advanced mgmt. program, 1972. Bar: Ala. 1953. Assoc. firm Burr, McKamy Moore & Thomas, Birmingham, 1955-62; asst. gen. atty. Vulcan Materials Co., Birmingham, 1962-69; v.p. chems. div. Vulcan Materials Co., Wichita, Kans., 1969-71; treas. Vulcan Materials Co., 1971-74, v.p. and controller, 1974-77; pres. metals div. Vulcan Materials Co., Birmingham, Ala., 1977-87, pres. Middle East div., 1982-87; chmn., chief exec. officer Jefferson Fed. Savings, Birmingham, 1987-91; dir. All Seasons Travel, Birmingham, 1991—; disting. lectr.-practitioner U. Ga. Served with U.S. Army, 1953-55. Mem. Nat. Assn. Accts. (cert. mgmt. acct.), Beta Gamma Sigma. Presbyterian. Club: Country of Birmingham, Chattooga (Cashiers, N.C.). Home: 4608 Old Leeds Rd Birmingham AL 35213-1802 Office: All Seasons Travel 120 Office Park Dr Birmingham AL 35223-2422

WEATHERMON, SIDNEY EARL, elementary school educator; b. Abilene, Tex., Jan. 20, 1937; s. Sidney Elliot Weathermon and Evelyn Marie (Landreth) Parker. BA, U. Colo., 1962, MA, 1968, EdD, 1976. Cert. K-12 reading tchr., elem. edn. tchr., K-12 reading specialist. Tchr. Jefferson County (Colo.) Pub. Schs., 1963-66; grades 5-6 tchr. Boulder (Colo.) Valley Pub. Schs., 1962-63, reading tchr., 1968-71, consortium dir. right-to-read project Louisville Mid. Sch., 1974-75, comm. skills program coord. Vocat.-Tech. H.S., 1976, K-12 dist. reading specialist, 1971-85, chpt. 1 tchr. grades 1-6, 1985-89, chpt. 1 kindergarten project coord., 1985-89, grade 1 tchr., 1989—; instr. U. Colo., Boulder, 1971-72, U. No. Colo., Greeley, 1977; adj. faculty Regis U., Denver, 1972—, dept. edn. instr., 1982. Contbr. articles to profl. jours. Recipient Celebrate Literacy award, Boulder Coun. Internat. Reading Assn., 1986, IBM Corp. Tchr. of Yr. award, 1989, Colo./Nat. Educator, Milkin Family Found., 1990; NDEA fellow, 1966-68. Mem. NEA, Internat. Reading Assn., Colo. Edn. Assn., Boulder Valley Edn. Assn. (chair tchr. adv coun., assoc. rep., tchrs. rights and activities commn., negotiations team, profl. leave com.), Phi Delta Kappa (certs. of recognition 1987, 90), Kappa Delta Pi. Democrat. Avocation: Southwest Indian art. Home: 449 S Shore Dr Osprey FL 34229-9657 Office: 449 N Shore Dr Osprey FL 34229-9282

WEATHERS, MELBA ROSE, hospital utilization review coordinator; b. Ladonia, Tex., Mar. 31, 1940; d. E. Carl and Rosa Lee (Evans) W. BSN, Holy Family Coll., 1974; BS, Tex. Woman's U., 1989. Staff/charge nurse maternal and child health St. Paul Med. Ctr., Dallas, 1974-87; rev. coord. Tex. Med. Found., Austin, 1989-95; utilization review mgmt. coord. Marshall (Tex.) Meml. Hosp., 1995—. Mem. Am. Health Info. Mgmt. Assn., VFW Ladies Aux. Roman Catholic. Avocation: collecting nursing memorabilia. Home: 100 Stonecreek Dr #210 Marshall TX 75670-4580

WEATHERS, MILLEDGE WRIGHT, retired economics educator; b. Augusta, Ga., May 11, 1926; s. Robert Edward Lee and Margaret Elizabeth (Johnson) W.; m. Anna-Maria Helene von Bertrab; children: Helene Boehnlein, Martin, Margarete, Benjamin. BA, George Washington U., 1949, MA, 1957; Dr. oec. publ., U. Munich, 1961. Rsch. analyst U.S. Dept. Air Force, Washington, 1951-57, Gen. Electric Co., Santa Barbara, Calif., 1959-62; pvt. practice cons. Munich, 1962-64; cons. Gesellschaft fuer Anlagewerte, Munich, 1964-66; sr. staff analyst Lockheed-Ga. Co., Marietta, 1966-68; prof. econs. Adrian (Mich.) Coll., 1968-91. Contbr. articles to profl. jours. With U.S. Army, 1944-46. Mem. Am. Econs. Assn., Assn. for Evolutionary Econs., Nat. Tax Assn., Economists Allied for Arms Reduction, Kappa Sigma. Avocations: music, walking. Home: 930 Lincoln Ave Adrian MI 49221-3230

WEATHERS, WARREN RUSSELL, forester, appraiser, consultant; b. La Jolla, Calif., Feb. 17, 1947; s. Warren Obert and Cicely Joanne (Hawken) W.; m. Terri Ruth Pillette, May 5, 1988; children: Nathan, Stuart, Erik. BS in Forestry, Oreg. State U., 1970; MBA, U. Oreg., 1985. Chief forester Pacific Timber Products, Haines, Alaska, 1972-75; exec. v.p. Shee Atika, Inc., Sitka, Alaska, 1975-82; cons. forester, 1982—; commr. Alaska State Bd. Forestry, Juneau, 1979-80. Mem., pres. Lowell (Oreg.) City Coun., 1987-91, chmn. budget com., 1987-88; mayor City of Lowell, 1991—. 1st lt. U.S. Army Res., 1971-80. Mem. Nat. Trappers Assn., Am. Assn. Cert. Appraisers, Nat. Woodland Owners Assn., Soc. Am. Foresters (chpt. chair 1979-80), Assn. Consulting Foresters. Avocations: outdoor sports, volunteer work. Office: PO Box 39 1/2 Lowell OR 97452-0039

WEATHERSBY, GEORGE BYRON, investment management executive; b. Albany, Calif., Dec. 9, 1944; s. Byron and Fannie A. W.; m. Linda Rose Scheirer, June 29, 1979; children: Deborah Jane, Geoffrey Byron. BS, U. Calif., Berkeley, 1965, MS, 1966, MBA, 1967; MS, Harvard U., 1968, PhD, 1970; DHL (hon.), U. San Francisco, 1987; LLD (hon.), U. So. Ind., 1992. Mem. faculty, assoc. dir. analytical studies, dir. Ford Found. rsch. program U. Calif., Berkeley, 1969-72; spl. asst. to U.S. Sec. of State Washington, 1972-73; dir. rsch. Nat. Commn. on Financing Higher Edn., Washington, 1973-74; assoc. prof. mgmt. Harvard U., Cambridge, Mass., 1974-78; commr. higher edn. State of Ind., 1977-83; pres. Curtis Pub. Co., 1983-86, New UPI Inc., Washington, 1985-86; corp. v.p. fin. Ontario Corp., Muncie, Ind., 1986-88, pres., 1988-91, also bd. dirs.; ptnr. Founders Court Inc., Princeton, N.J., 1991-93; independant cons., 1975—; pres. Oxford Mgmt. Corp., 1994—, Cambridge Parallel Processing, 1994—; chmn. bd. dirs. Otis Conner Cos., 1984-86, Curtis Media Corp., 1984-86, Curtis Internat. Ltd., 1985-86, Prince Gardner, Inc., 1991-93, Alma Industries, 1992-93, Hanes Holding Co., 1992-93; bd. dirs. Holnam Inc., Farm Fans Inc., Delta Consol. Industries, Cambridge Parallel Processing, Advanced Retail Mktg., ERS, Inc. Author: (books) Financing Postsecondary Education in the U.S, 1974,

Colleges and Money, 1976; contbr. numerous articles to profl. jours., 1967—; cons. editor: Jour. Higher Edn., 1974—; exec. editor: Change mag., 1980-84. Bd. dirs. Nat. Ctr. for Higher Edn Mgmt. Sys., 1980-83, U.S.A. Group, 1989—; mem. steering com. Edn. Commn. of States, 1978-82; mem. Ind. Com. Humanities, 1981-87; trustee U. So. Ind., 1985-91, Park Tudor Sch. Indpls., 1986-91, Butler U., 1987-93. Calif. Regents scholar, 1963-65; NSF fellow, 1966-67; AEC fellow, 1966-67; Kent fellow, 1967-70; White House fellow, 1972-73; named 1 of 100 Outstanding Young Leaders in Higher Edn. Change Mag., 1978. Mem. Am. Coun. Edn., Ops. Rsch. Soc. Am., Inst. Mgmt. Scis., Econometrica, Young Pres. Orgn. Republican. Office: 660 Madison Ave Fl 18 New York NY 10021-8405

WEATHERSBY, JAMES ROY, lawyer; b. Pine Bluff, Ark., Aug. 28, 1935; s. Willard Alton and Francis (McCormick) W.; children: Jim, Brad; m. Lydia Huber, Jan. 20, 1990. BScE, U. Tenn., 1958; JD, Vanderbilt U., 1964. Bar: Ala. 1965, Tenn. 1965, Ga. 1971, U.S. Dist. Ct. (no. dist.) Ala. 1966, U.S. Dist. Ct. (no. dist.) Ga. 1971, U.S. Dist. Ct. (middle dist.) Ga. 1985, U.S. Dist. Ct. (so. dist.) Ga. 1990. Labor counsel Rust Engring. Co., Pitts., Birmingham, Ala., 1964-70; ptnr. Wilson & Wilson, Atlanta, 1971-76; ptnr., head labor sect. Powell Goldstein Fraser & Murphy, Atlanta, 1976-90; mng. ptnr. Ogletree Deakins Nash Smoak & Stewart, Atlanta, 1991-95, Littler, Mendelson, Fastiff, Atlanta, 1996—; dep. atty. gen. State of Ga., Atlanta, 1974—; gen. counsel Gen. Assocs. Ga. Associated Builders & Contractors, Atlanta, 1976—; bd. dirs. Kamtech Inc., Glen Falls, N.Y. Mem. ABA, Lawyers Club Atlanta, Ga. Bar Assn., Atlanta Bar Assn. Home: 510 Valley Rd Atlanta GA 30305 Office: Littler Mendelson Fastiff 1100 Peachtree St NE Ste 2000 Atlanta GA 30309-4520

WEATHERSTONE, SIR DENNIS, bank executive; b. London, Nov. 29, 1930; s. Henry Philip and Gladys (Hart) W.; m. Marion Blunsum, Apr. 4, 1959; children—Hazel, Cheryl, Gretel, Richard Paul. Student, Northwestern Poly., London, 1946-49. Sr. v.p. Morgan Guaranty Trust Co. N.Y., N.Y.C., 1972-77, exec. v.p., 1977-79, treas., 1977-79, vice chmn., 1979-80, chmn. exec. com., 1980-86; pres. J.P. Morgan & Co., Inc. (formerly Morgan Guaranty Trust Co. N.Y.), N.Y.C., 1987-90, chmn., chief exec. officer, 1990-95; bd. dirs. GM Corp., Merck & Co., Inc., L'Air Liquide; mem. bd. banking supervision Bank of Eng. Decorated Knight Comdr. Order Brit. Empire.

WEAVER, ALBERT BRUCE, university administrator; b. Mont., May 27, 1917; s. John B. and Myrtle (Dragstedt) W.; m. Adeline Okerberg, Sept. 1945; children: Janet, Gail, John. Student, Mont. Sch. Mines, 1935-37; AB, U. Mont., 1940; MS, U. Ida., 1941; postgrad., U. Minn., 1941-42; PhD, U. Chgo., 1951. Physicist Naval Ordnance Lab., 1942-45; research asso. U. Chgo., 1952, U. Wash., 1952-54; mem. faculty U. Colo., 1954-58, asso. prof., 1957-58, chmn. dept. physics, 1956-58; prof., head dept. physics U. Ariz., 1958-70, asso. dean, 1961-70, provost acad. affairs, 1970-72, exec. v.p., 1972-83, exec. v.p. emeritus, 1983—. Fellow Am. Phys. Soc., AAAS; mem. Am. Assn. Physics Tchrs., Ariz. Acad. Sci., Sigma Xi. Home: 5726 E Holmes St Tucson AZ 85711-2426

WEAVER, BARBARA FRANCES, librarian; b. Boston, Aug. 29, 1927; d. Leo Francis and Nina Margaret (Durham) Weisse; m. George B. Weaver, June 6, 1951; 1 dau., Valerie S. Clark. B.A., Radcliffe Coll., 1949; M.L.S., U. R.I., 1968; Ed.M., Boston U., 1978. Head libr. Thompson (Conn.) Pub. Libr., 1961-69; dir. Conn. State Libr. Svc. Ctr., Willimantic, 1969-72; regional adminstr. Cen. Mass. Regional Libr. System, Worcester, 1972-78; asst. commr. of edn., state libr. State of N.J., Trenton, 1978-91; dir. R.I. Dept. State Libr. Svcs., Providence, 1991-96; chief info. officer State of R.I., 1996—; lectr. Simmons Coll., Boston, 1976-78. Mem. ALA, R.I. Libr. Assn., Chief Officers State Libr. Agys. Office: Office Libr & Info Svcs 1 Capitol Hl Providence RI 02908-5803

WEAVER, CARLTON DAVIS, retired oil company executive; b. Grantsville, W.Va., May 27, 1921; s. Arley Ezra and Grace (Davis) W.; m. Nancy Mason McIntosh, Mar. 21, 1951; 1 child, Nancy Mason. B.S. Engr. Mines, W.Va. U., 1948. Office engr. E.I. du Pont de Nemours & Co., 1941-42, tech. service rep., 1948-51; with Ashland (Ky.) Oil, Inc., 1951-81, exec. asst., 1960-67, v.p., 1967-72, sr. v.p., 1972-81, group operating officer, 1976-81, pres. Ashland Resources Co. div., 1970-74; chmn. bd. Ashland Coal, Inc., 1981-84, Ven-Black, Inc., 1983-86; chmn. vis. com. Coll. Mineral and Energy Resources, W.Va. U., 1967-80. Served to maj. USMCR, 1942-46, 52-53. Mem. Nat. Coal Assn. (dir.). Home: PO Box 578 White Sulphur Springs WV 24986-6036 also: 64 Surfsong Rd Kiawah Island SC 29455 Office: 1409 Winchester Ave Ashland KY 41101-7555

WEAVER, CHARLES HENRY, business consulting executive; b. Phila., Aug. 10, 1914; s. Charles Henry and Isabel (Walker) W.; m. Louise Schildecker, Sept. 7, 1940 (dec. Nov. 1977); children—Patricia Ann Weaver Telkins, William Schildecker, Peter Charles; m. Lois S. Amper, May 20, 1979. B.S., U. Pa., 1936. With Westinghouse Electric Corp., 1936-79; beginning as trainee, successively sales dept. transp. and generator div., sales engr. marine sect., mgr. marine sect., mgr. marine dept. Westinghouse Electric Corp., Pitts., mgr. marine and aviation sales dept., mgr. ctrl. dist. sales office; mgr. atomic power div. Westinghouse Electric Corp., 1948-55, v.p. charge atomic power activities, 1955-62, group v.p. atomic, def. and space group, 1962-67, v.p. govt. affairs, 1967-71, pres. world regions, 1971-75, exec. v.p. corp. world relations, 1975-79; pres. Pitts. Cons. Group, Inc., 1979—; dir., vice chmn. IEM (S.A.), Mexico, 1973-78. Trustee Moore Sch. Elec. Engring. of U. Pa., also bd. overseers Sch. Engring. and Applied Sci.; chmn. Allegheny County Air Pollution Adv. Com., 1959-67; mem. Coun. on Fgn. Rels., Nat. Fgn. Trade Coun. (past dir.), World Affairs Coun. Pitts. (past pres.), trustee Pitts. Coun. Internat. Visitors; past trustee Bus. Coun. Internat. Understanding; adv. coun. Japan-U.S. Econ. Rels.; past vice chmn. U.S.-Korea; past chmn. U.S.-Yugoslav Econ. Coun., Polish-U.S. Econ. Coun. Recipient order of merit Westinghouse Elec. Corp., 1948; ann. Nat. Transp. award for outstanding contbns. transp. industry, 1955. Mem. IEEE, ASME, Atomic Indsl. Forum (past pres.), Soc. Naval Archs. and Marine Engrs., Am. Nuclear Soc., Nat. Security Indsl. Assn. (past chmn.), Coun. Def. and Space Industry Assn. (past chmn.), Internat. C. of C. (past dir. U.S. coun.), Duquesne Club, Concordia Club, River Forest Country Club. Home: 540 N Neville St Pittsburgh PA 15213

WEAVER, CHARLES HORACE, educator; b. Statesville, N.C., Nov. 11, 1927; s. Lucius Stacy and Elizabeth Roderick (Hallyburton) W.; m. Nancy Jane Veale, June 24, 1955; 1 child, Charles Horace. BA, Wofford Coll., Spartanburg, S.C., 1951; MA, Columbia U., 1956; PhD, U. N.C., 1961. Tchr. English Oak Ridge Mil. Inst., N.C., 1951-54, High Point (N.C.) Cen. High Sch., 1954-56; asst. prin. Ferndale Jr. High Sch., High Point, 1956-58; prin. N.E. Jr. High Sch., High Point, 1959-60, Ferndale Jr. High Sch., High Point, 1960-62; asst. supt. Asheboro (N.C.) City Schs., 1962-65; supt. Elizabeth City (N.C.) pub. schs., 1965-69, Burke County Pub. Schs., Morganton, N.C., 1969-79; with State Dept. Pub. Instrn., Raleigh, N.C., 1979—; asst. state supt. aux. svcs. State Dept. Pub. Instrn., 1989-96; educator Shook Design, Charlotte, N.C., 1996—; bd. dirs. We. Carolina Bank & Trust Co., Wilmington Food Sys., Inc., Greenville Food Sys., Inc. Contbr. articles to profl. ours. Bd. dirs. Burke County United Fund, Burke County Council on Alcoholism, We. Piedmont Mental Health Assn., We Piedmont Symphony. Mem. Am. Assn. Sch. Adminstrs., N.C. Assn. Sch. Adminstrs., Horace Mann League (pres. 1975-76), High Point Jr. C. of C. (bd. dirs.), Burke Country C. of C., Rotary, Asheboro Country Club, Raleigh Capital City Club. Democrat. Methodist. Avocations: reading, golf, antiques.

WEAVER, CHARLES LYNDELL, JR., educational facilities administrator; b. Canonsburg, Pa., July 5, 1945; s. Charles Lyndell and Georgia Lavelle (Gardner) W.; m. Ruth Marguerite Uxa, Feb. 27, 1982; children: Charles Lyndell III, John Francis. BArch, Pa. State U., 1969; cert. in assoc. studies U. Florence (Italy), 1968. Registered architect, Pa., Md., Mo., Va., Mass., Ky. With Celento & Edson, Canonsburg, Pa., part-time 1966-71; project architect Meyers & D'Aleo, Balt., 1971-76, corp. dir., v.p., 1974-76; ptnr. Borrow Assocs.-Developers, Balt., 1976-79, Crowley/Weaver Constrn. Mgmt., Balt., 1976-79; pvt. practice architecture, Balt., 1976-79; cons., project mgr. U. Md., College Park, 1979-80; corp. cons. architect Bank Bldg. & Equipment Corp., Am., St. Louis, 1980-83; dir. archtl. and engring. svcs. Ladue Bldg. & Engring. Inc., St. Louis, 1983-84; v.p., sec. Graphic Products Corp.; pres. CWCM Inc. Internat., 1987—; dir. K-12 Edn. Market Ctr. and sr. program mgr., Sverdrup Corp., 1989-95; prin. Benham Internat. Eurasia, 1995; v.p., dir. mktg. and bus. devel. The Benham Group, St. Louis, 1995-96; v.p. Chiodini Assocs., 1997—; vis. Alpha Rho Chi lectr. Pa. State U., 1983; vis. lectr. Washington U. Lindenwood Coll., 1987, Wentworth Inst., Boston, Am. Assn. Cost Engrs., So. Fla., 1994; panel mem. Assn. Univ. Architects Conv., 1983. Project bus. cons. Jr. Achievement, 1982-85; mem. cluster com., advisor Explorer Program, 1982-85. Recipient 5 brochure and graphic awards Nat. Assn. Indsl. Artists, 1973; 1st award Profl. Builder/Am. Plywood Assn., 1974; Honor award, 2 articles Balt. chpt. AIA, 1974; Better Homes and Gardens award Sensible Growth, Nat. Assn. Home Builders, 1975; winner Ridgely's Delight Competition, Balt., 1976. Mem. ASCD, BBC Credit Union (bd. dirs. 1983-85), AACE (conv. speaker So. Fla. sect. 1994), Vitruvius Alumni Assn., Penn State Alumni Assn., BOCA, NFPA, Am. Assn. Sch. Administrs. (nat. coun., panel moderator 1994), Coun. Ednl. Facilities Planners, Assn. Sch. Bus. Officials (Mehlville Mo. schs. program mgmt. 1992-94, Chelsea, Mass., 1993-95. Orange County, Fla., 1994-95), Alpha Rho Chi (nat. treas. 1980-82, dir. nat. found. treas. 1989-97). Office: 1318 Shenandoah Ave Saint Louis MO 63104-4123

WEAVER, CONNIE MARIE, foods and nutrition educator; b. LaGrande, Oreg., Oct. 29, 1950; d. Robert Chesley and Averil Jean (Harris) Shelton; m. Lloyd Rollin Weaver, Dec. 22, 1971; children: Douglas, Mark, Richard. BS, Oreg. State U., 1972, MS, 1974; PhD, Fla. State U., 1978. Teaching asst. Oreg. State U., Corvallis, 1973-74; instr. Grossmont Coll., El Cajon, Calif., 1974-75; rsch. assoc. U. R.I., Kingston, 1975; teaching asst. Fla. State U., Tallahassee, 1975-78, mem. adj. faculty, 1977-78; asst. prof. foods and nutrition Purdue U., West Lafayette, Ind., 1978-84, assoc. prof., 1984-88, prof., 1988—, head, 1991—; rsch. fellow Kraft, Inc., Glenview, Ill., 1988. Contbr. articles to profl. jours. Mem. Inst. Food Technologists (exec. com. 1991-94, Outstanding Svc. and Recognition award Ind. sect. 1984), Am. Chem. Soc., Am. Inst. Nutrition (treas. 1992-96), Soc. for Exptl. Biology and Medicine, Sigma Xi, Gamma Sigma Delta. Office: Purdue U Foods-Nutrition Stone Hall West Lafayette IN 47907

WEAVER, DAVID HUGH, journalism educator, communications researcher; b. Hammond, Ind., Dec. 23, 1946; s. David W. and Josephine L. Weaver; m. Gail Shriver, June 28, 1969; children: Quinn David, Lesley Jo. BA, Ind. U., Bloomington, 1968, MA, 1969; PhD, U. N.C., 1974. Copy editor The Post-Tribune, Gary, Ind., 1968; wire editor, reporter The Courier-Tribune, Bloomington, Ind., 1968; wire editor The Chapel Hill Newspaper, N.C., 1973; asst. prof. journalism Ind. U., Bloomington, 1974-78, assoc. prof., 1978-83, prof., 1983-88; Roy W. Howard prof. Ind. U., Bloomington, Ind., 1988—. Author: Videotex Journalism, 1983; co-author: Newsroom Guide to Polls and Surveys, 1980, 90, Media Agenda-Setting, 1981, The American Journalist, 1986 (award Soc. Profl. Journalists 1987), 2d edit., 1991, The Formation of Campaign Agendas, 1991, Contemporary Public Opinion, 1991, The American Journalist in the 1990's, 1996. Lt. U.S. Army, 1969-71. Fellow Midwest Pub. Opinion Rsch. (pres. 1986-87); mem. Assn. for Edn. in Journalism and Mass Comm. (pres. 1987-88, Krieghbaum award 1983), Soc. Prof. Journalists (award 1997), Internat. Comm. Assn. Avocations: guitar, music. Office: Ind U Sch of Journalism Ernie Pyle Hall Bloomington IN 47405-6201

WEAVER, DELBERT ALLEN, lawyer; b. Shoshone, Idaho, May 28, 1931; s. Arlo Irving and Kate Rosamond (McCarter) W.; m. Jeanne Carol Alford, June 1959; children: Tobin Elizabeth, Michael Andrew, Matthew Stewart, Edward Malcolm. BA, U. Oreg., 1953, LLB, 1956. Bar: Oreg. 1956, U.S. Dist. Ct. Oreg. 1956, U.S. Ct. Appeals (9th cir.) 1968. Ptnr. Weaver & Oram, Eugene, Oreg., 1956-59; dep. atty. City of Portland, Oreg., 1959-68; assoc. Winfree, Latourette, Murphy, et al., Portland, 1968-71; stockbroker Dupont Glore Forgan, Portland, 1971-73; securities examiner corp. div. State of Oreg., Salem, 1973-75, dep. commr. corp. div., 1975-80; pvt. practice Portland, 1980-87; counsel Schwabe, Williamson & Wyatt, Portland, 1987-90, sr. ptnr., 1991-96; pvt. practice Portland, 1996—. Office: 1207 SW 6th Ave Portland OR 97204-1001

WEAVER, DENNIS, actor; b. Joplin, Mo., June 4, 1924; s. Walter and Lenna Weaver; m. Gerry Stowell, Oct. 20, 1945; children: Rick, Robby, Rusty. BFA, U. Okla., 1948. Appeared on N.Y. stage, 1948-52; appeared in Streetcar Named Desire, Hollywood, Calif., 1953; under contract to Universal Internat., Hollywood, 1952-53, freelance actor, Hollywood, 1953-55; appeared on: TV series Gunsmoke, 1955-64, Kentucky Jones, 1964-65, Gentle Ben, 1967-69, McCloud, 1970-77, Stone, 1980, Buck James, 1985-87, Lonesome Dove, 1994; also TV movies: Duel, 1971, Forgotten Man, 1971, Rolling Man, 1973, Terror on the Beach, 1973, Female Artillery, 1973, Patty Hearst, 1979, Stolen Women-Captured Hearts, 1997, Seduction in a Small Town, 1997; spls. Intimate Strangers, 1977, Police Story-A Cry for Justice, 1977, Pearl, 1978, Ishi, 1978, Islander, 1978, Centennial-The Longhorns, 1978, Amber Waves, 1979, The Ordeal of Dr. Mud, 1979, The Day the Loving Stopped, 1981, Don't Go to Sleep, 1982, Cocaine: One Man's Seduction, 1983, Winners Never Quit, 1986, Bluffing It, 1987, Disaster at Silo 7, 1988, The Return of Sam McCloud, 1989, Mastergate, 1991, (pilot) Greyhounds, 1993, "Buffalo Bill" in Lonesome Dove, the series, 1994-95, (pilot) called "The Wolfe Pack" for CBS, 1996—. Mem. SAG (pres. 1973-75), AFTRA, Dirs. Guild. Office: care Alice Billings PO Box 257 Ridgway CO 81432

WEAVER, DONNA RAE, company executive; b. Chgo., Oct. 15, 1945; d. Albert Louis and Gloria Elaine (Graffis) Florence; m. Clifford L. Weaver, Aug. 20, 1966; 1 child, Megan Rae. BS in Edn., No. Ill. U., 1966, EdD, 1977; MEd, De Paul U., 1974. Tchr. H.L. Richards High Sch., Oak Lawn, Ill., 1966-71, Sawyer Coll. Bus., Evanston, Ill., 1971-72; asst. prof. Oakton Community Coll., Morton Grove, Ill., 1972-75; vis. prof. U. Ill., Chgo., 1977-78; dir. devel. Mallinckrodt Coll., Wilmette, Ill., 1978-80, dean, 1980-83; campus dir. Nat.-Louis U., Chgo., 1983-90, dean div. applied behavioral scis., 1985-89; dean Coll. Mgmt. and Bus., 1989-90; pres. The Oliver Group, Inc., Kenilworth, Ill., 1993—; mng. ptnr. Le Miccine, Gaiole-in-Chianti, Tuscany, Italy, 1996—; cons. Nancy Lovely and Assocs., Wilmette, 1981-84, North Ctrl. Assn., Chgo., 1982-90. Contbr. articles to Am. Vocat. Jour., Ill. Bus. Edn. Assn. Monograph, Nat. Coll. Edn.'s ABS Rev., Nat. View. Mem. Ill. Quality of Work Life Coun., 1987-90, New Trier Twp. Health and Human Svcs. Adv. Bd., Winnetka, Ill., 1985-88; bd. dirs. Open Lands Project, 1985-87, Kenilworth (Ill.) Village House, 1986-87. Recipient Achievement award Women in Mgmt., 1981; Am. Bd. Master Educators charter disting. fellow, 1986. Mem. Nat. Bus. Edn. Assn., Delta Pi Epsilon (past pres.). Avocations: reading, traveling, decorating. Office: 505 N Lake Shore Dr Apt 4010 Chicago IL 60611-6432

WEAVER, EDWARD T., foundation executive, educator; b. Beggs, Okla., Dec. 13, 1931; s. Thurmon Wesley and Thelma Cleo (Wright) W.; m. Judith A. DeVliegher; children: Mark E., Kirk B. Student, S.W. Mo. State U., 1958-59; BA, Cen. Bible Coll., Springfield, Mo., 1959; M Social Work, Washington U., 1961; MPA, U. So. Calif., 1981, D Pub. Adminstrn., 1985. Adminstr. Lake Bluff (Ill.) Children's Home, 1961-64; regional dir. Ill. Dept. Children and Family Services, Champaign, 1964-66, Chgo., 1966-68; dir. Ill. Dept. Children and Family Services, Springfield, 1968-72, Ill Dept. Pub. Aid, Springfield, 1971-73; sr. assoc. Booz, Allen & Hamilton, Washington, 1973-74; exec. dir. Am. Pub. Welfare Assn., Washington, 1974-85; v.p. Paramount Communications, Inc. (formerly Gulf & Western Inc.), N.Y.C., 1985-89; pres. Paramount Communications Found., N.Y.C., 1985-91; prof. Henry W. Bloch Sch. Bus. and Pub. Adminstrn. U. Mo.-Kansas City, 1989—; lectr. U. Ill., Champaign, 1966; vis. prof. Washington U., St. Louis, 1978-85, 90-92; bd. dirs. Independent Sector, Washington, 1987-92; trustee Lois and SamuelSilberman Fund, N.Y.C., 1988-91, Am. Humane Assn., 1990-94, Camp Fire Inc., 1992—, Mid-Am. Care Found., 1991—, Midwest Care Ctrs., Inc., 1995—. Mem. Internat. Council on Social Welfare (asst. treas. gen., treas. gen., v.p.). Presbyterian.

WEAVER, ELIZABETH A, judge; b. New Orleans; d. Louis and Mary Weaver. BA, Newcomb Coll.; JD, Tulane U. Elem. tchr. Glen Lake Cmty. Sch., Maple City, Mich.; French tchr. Leelanau Sch., Glen Arbor, Mich.; pvt. practice Glen Arbor, Mich.; law clk. Civil Dist. Ct., New Orleans; atty. Coleman, Dutrey & Thomson, New Orleans; atty., title specialist Chevron Oil Co., New Orleans; probate and juvenile judge Leelanau County, Mich., 1975-86; judge U.S. Ct. of Appeals (3d cir.), Mich., 1987-94, Mich. Supreme Ct., Lansing, 1995—; rep. Mich. com. on juvenile justice Nat. Conv. State Adv. Groups on Juvenile Judtice for U.S. Office Juvenile Justice and Deliquency Prevention; treas. Children's Charter of Cts. of Mich.; chair Task Force on Children's Justice, Mich. Trial Ct. Assessment Commn. Chairperson Western Mich. U. Continuing Legal Adv. Bd.; mem. steering com. Grand Traverse/Leelanau Commn. on Youth; mem. Glen Arbor Twp. Zoning Bd.; mem. chamber arts north Leelanau County; mem. citizen's adv. coun. Arnell Engstrom Children's Ctr.; mem. cmty. adv. com. Pathfinder Sch. Treaty Law Demonstration Project; active Grand Traverse/Leelanau Mental Health Found. Named one of five Outstanding Young Women in Mich., Mich. Jaycees. Fellow Mich. State Bar Found.; mem. ABA, Mich. Bar Assn. (chair continuing legal edn. adv. bd., chair crime prevention ctr., chair juvenile law com.), Nat. Coun. Juvenile and Family Judges, La. Bar Assn., Grand Traverse County Bar Assn., Leelanau County Bar Assn., Antrim County Bar Assn., Delta Kappa Gamma (hon.). Office: 2nd Fl Law Bldg PO Box 30052 Lansing MI 48909

WEAVER, ESTHER RUTH, medical and surgical, geriatrics and oncology nurse; b. Kansas City, Mo., Mar. 20, 1951; d. Fred Bicknell and Mary Elizabeth (Williams) Crigler; 1 child, Scott Lee McPhee; m. Charles Edward Weaver, June 10, 1995; stepchildren: Alan Bower, Ward. ADN, Eastern N.Mex. U., Roswell, 1989. Cert. chemotherapy nurse. Staff nurse med. floor St. Mary's Hosp., Roswell, Eastern N.Mex. Med. Ctr., Roswell; night nurse Sunset Villa Care Ctr., Roswell; nurse supr. Turtle Creek Health Care Ctr., Jacksonville, Fla.; oncology staff nurse, active with dept. corrections unit Meml. Med. Ctr., Jacksonville. Mem. Merrill Rd. Bapt. Ch.; dir. children's ch. Merrill Rd. Comty. Ch. Nursing Found. scholar. Mem. N.Mex. Nurses Assn. (publicity chmn. Dist. 5), Oncology Nurses Soc., Phi Theta Kappa (v.p.).

WEAVER, FRANKLIN THOMAS, newspaper executive; b. Johnstown, N.Y., Oct. 11, 1932; s. Edwin K. and Bertha J. (Wendt) W.; children: Thomas, James, Michael, David, Tammy, Kelly, Anna; m. Joyce W. Phelps, Oct. 23, 1991. B.A. with high honors in Journalism, Mich. State U., 1954. Advt. sales rep. Grand Rapids Press, Mich., 1955-64; controller Muskegon (Mich.) Chronicle, 1964-66; mgr. Bay City (Mich.) Times, 1966-73; mgr. Jackson (Mich.) Citizen Patriot, 1973-84, pub., 1984—. Mem. Newspapers Assn. Am., Mich. Press Assn. (pres. 1991), Ella Sharp Mus. (pres. 1995-96), Greater Jackson C. of C., Jackson Country Club. Office: Jackson Citizen Patriot 214 S Jackson St Jackson MI 49201-2213

WEAVER, HOWARD C., newspaper executive; b. Anchorage, Oct. 15, 1950; s. Howard Gilbert and Lurlene Eloise (Gamble) W.; m. Alice Laprele Gauchay, July 16, 1970 (div. 1974); m. Barbara Lynn Hodgin, Sept. 16, 1978. BA, Johns Hopkins U., 1972; MPhil, Cambridge U., 1993. Reporter, staff writer Anchorage Daily News, 1972-76, columnist, 1979-80, mng. editor, 1980-83, editor, 1983-95; editor, owner Alaska Advocate, Anchorage, 1976-79; asst. to pres., McClatchy Newspapers, 1995-97, editor of editl. pages, 1997—; internat. co-chair Northern News Svc., 1989-94; disting. lectr. journalism U. Alaska, Fairbanks, 1991. Pulitzer Prize juror, 1988, 89, 94, 95. Recipient Pulitzer prize, 1976, 89, Pub. Svc. award AP Mng. Editor's Assn., 1976, 89, Headliner award Press Club of Atlantic City, 1976, 89, Gold medal Investigative Reporters and Editors, 1989. Mem. Am. Soc. Newspaper Editors, Investigative Reporters and Editors, Sigma Delta Chi (Nat. award 1989), Alaska Press Club (bd. dirs. 1972-84), Upper Yukon River Press Club (pres. 1972). Avocations: ice hockey, foreign travel, opera.

WEAVER, JACQUELYN KUNKEL IVEY, artist, educator; b. Richmond, Ky., Mar. 14, 1931; d. Marion David and Margaret Tabitha (Brandenburg) Kunkel; m. George Thomas IveySr., 1951 (dec. 1989); children: George Thomas Ivey Jr., David Richard Ivey; m. Harrell Fuller Weaver, 1991. BFA, Wesleyan Coll., 1987. Owner J. K. Ivey Art, Macon, Ga., 1974-91, J.K. Ivey Bookkeeping and Tax Svc., Macon, Ga., 1976-84, Ivey-Weaver Art Studio, Macon, 1991—. Exhibited in galleries including Mid. Ga. Art Assn. Gallery, Macon, 1980—, Mus. Arts and Scis., Macon, 1987, 91, 94, 96, Attaway Cottage, Macon, 1990—, AAPL Salmungundi Club, N.Y.C., 1992, Frames and Art Gallery, Macon, 1995—, CLWAC Nat. Arts Club, N.Y.C., 1996, Jabberwocky, Macon, 1995—, Strozier Gallery, Macon, 1997—, Hilton Head Island Art League, Self Family Art Ctr., Hilton Head Island, 1997. Bd. dirs., treas. Mid. Ga. Art Assn., Macon, 1981-84, 92, publicity chmn., 1988-89, nom. com., 1991. Mem. Nat. Mus. of Women in the Arts (charter), Wesleyan Coll. Alumnae Assn., Mus. of Arts & Scis., Catherine Lorillard Wolf Art Club. Presbyterian. Avocations: ballroom dancing, reading, walking, music. Office: Ivey-Weaver Art Studio 6183 Hwy 87 Macon GA 31210

WEAVER, JO NELL, elementary school educator; b. Dallas, Apr. 22, 1941; d. Robert Glen and Lottie (Harris) Bryant; m. L. Ben Weaver, Sr., June 20, 1963 (div. Mar. 1968); children: Carolyn Cantrell, L. Ben Weaver, Jr. BA, So. Meth. U., Dallas, 1968; MEd, U. North Tex., 1974. Cert. elem. tchr., elem. supr. Tchr. Richardson (Tex.) Ind. Sch. Dist., 1968—. Curriculum writer Delta Edn., Inc., 1984-85; critic reader Silver Burdett & Ginn, 1989. Mem. Sch. Dist. edn. coun., Richardson, Ind., 1994-95; area communication coun. Richardson Ind. Sch. Dist., 1995-96, mem. lang. arts contact com., 1995—, area comm. coun., 1995—. Recipient Tex. Congress of Parents and Tchrs. scholarship/grant Tex. PTA, 1974, Ross Perot award for Excellence in Tchg., 1978; named one of Outstanding Elem. Tchrs. of Am., 1975. Mem. Richardson Edn. Assn., North Tex. Reading Assn., Assn. Tex. Profl. Educators, ASCD, TEx. State Tchrs.' Assn., Alpha Delta Kappa. Republican. Baptist. Avocations: travel, photography, reading. Home: 2210 Sylvan Dr Garland TX 75040 Office: Richardson Ind Sch Dist 2100 Copper Ridge Dr Richardson TX 75080-2312

WEAVER, KENNETH, gynecologist, researcher; b. Whitetop, Va., Dec. 4, 1933; s. Grover Cleveland and Violet Elaine (Baldwin) W.; children: Teresa Marie, Janice Eileen, Beverly Lynn, Pamela Jean, Cynthia Ann; m. Shelby Jean Davis, June 15, 1966. BA, U. N.C., 1957, MD, 1960. Diplomate Am. Bd. Ob-Gyn. Intern U.S. Pub. Health Svc., Boston, 1960-61; med. officer Cherokee (N.C.) Indian Hosp., 1961-64; gen. physician Haywood County Hosp., Waynesville, N.C., 1964-70; obstetrician, gynecologist Haywood County Hosp., Waynesville, N.C., 1974-77; resident U. Ark. Med. Ctr., Little Rock, 1970-74; asst. prof. U. Ark., Little Rock, 1977-78, acting chmn., dept. ob-gyn., 1978; pvt. practice Johnson City, Tenn., 1978—; mem. Gov. Com. on Cancer, Raleigh, N.C., 1970-71; dir. Maternity and Infant Care, Little Rock, 1977-78; assoc. prof. James H. Quillen Coll. Medicine, Johnson City, 1978-83. Contbr. articles to sci. jours. Fellow Am. Coll. Ob-Gyn., Am. Coll. Nutrition, Am. Asson. Gynecol. Laparoscopists, N.Y. Acad. Scis. Achievements include six patent devices having to do with laser surgery and other gynecol. and urol. uses; rsch. in magnesium and preeclampsia, in magnesium and migraine, in relationship between magnesium and blood platelet function. Home: 377 Tavern Hill Rd Jonesborough TN 37659-5026 Office: 1103 Jackson Blvd Jonesborough TN 37659

WEAVER, KENNETH NEWCOMER, geologist, state official; b. Lancaster, Pa., Jan. 16, 1927; s. A. Ross and Cora (Newcomer) W.; m. Mary Elizabeth Hoover, Sept. 9, 1950; children—Wendy Elaine, Matthew Owen. BS, Franklin and Marshall Coll., 1950; MA, Johns Hopkins U., 1952, PhD, 1954. Instr. geology Johns Hopkins, 1953- 54; ops. analyst Ops. Rsch. Office, Washington, 1954-56; chief geologist, then mgr. geology and quarry dept. Medusa Portland Cement Co., Wampum, Pa., 1956-63; dir., state geologist Md. Geol. Survey, Balt., 1963-92; chmn. Md. Land Reclamation Com., 1978-92; Gov.'s rep. Interstate Oil Compact Commn., Interstate Mining Compact Commn.; mem. outer shelf adv. com. U.S. Dept. Interior; chmn. Md. Topographic Mapping Com.; mem. com. on surface mining and reclamation NAS, 1978, vice chmn. com. on disposal of excess spoil, 1980-81, mem. com. on geologic mapping, 1983, liaison mem. bd. earth scis., 1982-88, mem. com. on water resources rsch., 1989-92, chmn. com. on abandoned minelands rsch. priorities, 1987; mem. subcom. on mgmt. of maj. underground constrn. projects Nat. Acad. Engring.; mem. Md. Commn. on Artistic Property, 1988-92. With AUS, 1954-56. Recipient John Wesley Powell award USGS, 1994; named hdqr. bldg. The Kenneth N. Weaver Bldg. Md. Geol. Survey, 1994. Fellow Geol. Soc. Am. (sec. N.E. sect. 1985—), AAAS; mem. Am. Assn. Petroleum Geologists (Ea. sect., George V. Cohee Pub. Svc. award 1991), Am. Inst. Mining Engrs., Am. Inst. Profl. Geologists (editor 1983-84, Martin Van Couvering Meml. award 1992), Am. Geol. Inst. (governing bd. 1973, exec. com. 1989-90), Am. Water Rsch. Assn., Geol. Soc. Washington, Assn. Am. State Geologists (pres. 1973, hon. mem. 1992),

Johns Hopkins Club (Balt.). Republican. Presbyterian (elder). Home: 14002 Jarrettsville Pike Phoenix MD 21131-1409 Office: Md Geol Survey 2300 St Paul St Baltimore MD 21218-5210

WEAVER, LEAH ANN, journalist, speech writer; b. Galion, Ohio, May 4, 1958; d. William Hiram and Virginia Louise (Reif) Weaver; m. Charles Lamont Hall, Jr., Apr. 14, 1990. BA, Malone Coll., Canton, Ohio, 1980; MA, Ohio State U., 1989. Program coord. editorial projects Ohio State U. Office of the Pres., Columbus, 1989-92, editorial coord., 1992-96, editor, 1996—; English tutor Creative Living, Columbus, 1987, 88. Author: (plays) Wilber and Wife, 1989, Dora Dodd, 1991; contbg. writer Univ. Comms., Columbus, 1993—; spl. assignment reporter The Lantern, Columbus, 1987-88; freelance scriptwriter Ctr. for Teaching Excellence, Columbus, 1989; contbr. articles to jours. Mem. Soc. Profl. Journalists, N.Y. Dramatists Guild (playwright and assoc. mem.), Authors League Am., Coun. for Advancement and Support of Edn., Kappa Tau Alpha, Phi Kappa Phi. Avocations: playwrighting, freelance feature writing. Home: 4077 Bimini Ct Columbus OH 43230-5136

WEAVER, LYNN EDWARD, academic administrator, consultant, editor; b. St. Louis, Jan. 12, 1930; s. Lienous E. and Estelle F. (Laspe) W.; m. JoAnn D., 1951 (div. 1981); children: Terry Sollenberger, Gwen, Bart, Stephen, Wes; m. Anita G. Gomez, Oct. 27, 1983. BSEE, U. Mo., 1951; MSEE, So. Meth. U., 1955; PhD, Purdue U., 1958. Devel. engr. McDonnell Aircraft, St. Louis, 1952-53; aerophysics engr. Convair Corp., Ft. Worth, 1953-55; instr. elec. engring. Purdue U., Lafayette, Ind., 1955-58; assoc. prof., then prof., dept. head U. Ariz., Tucson, 1959-69; assoc. dean coll. engring. U. Okla., Norman, 1969-70; exec. asst. to pres. Argonne Univs., Chgo., 1970-72; dir. sch. nuclear engring. and health physics Ga. Inst. Tech., 1972-82; dean engring., disting. prof. Auburn (Ala.) U., 1982-87; pres. Fla. Inst. Tech., Melbourne, 1987—; cons. Ga. Power; bd. dirs. Oak Ridge Associated Univs., 1984-87, DBA Systems, Inc., Melbourne, Fla.; chmn. pub. affairs coun. Am. Assn. Engring. Soc., Washington, 1984-87; bd. advisors Ctr. for Sci., Tech. & Media, Washington. Author: (textbook) Reactor Dynamics & Control, State Space Techniques, 1968; exec. editor Annals of Nuclear Energy; contbr. numerous articles to tech. jours. U.S. rep. World Fedn., Engring. Orgn. Energy Com., 1981-86. Served to lt. USAF, 1951-53. Recipient Mo. Honors award for disting. svc. in engring., 1996. Fellow Am. Nuclear Soc.; mem. IEEE (sr.), Am. Soc. Engring. Edn., Sigma Xi. Republican. Roman Catholic. Club: Eau Gallie Yacht. Avocations: tennis, jogging. Office: Fla Inst Tech 150 W University Blvd Melbourne FL 32901-6982

WEAVER, MARGUERITE MCKINNIE See WEAVER, PEGGY

WEAVER, MICHAEL JAMES, lawyer; b. Bakersfield, Calif., Feb. 11, 1946; s. Kenneth James and Elsa Hope (Rogers) W.; m. Valerie Scott, Sept. 2, 1966; children: Christopher James, Brett Michael, Karen Ashley. AB, Calif. State U., Long Beach, 1968; JD magna cum laude, U. San Diego, 1973. Bar: Calif., 1973, U.S. Dist. Ct. (so. dist.) Calif. 1973, U.S. Ct. Appeals (9th cir.) 1975, U.S. Supreme Ct. 1977. Law clk. to chief judge U.S. Dist. Ct. (so. dist.) Calif., San Diego, 1973-75; assoc. Luce, Forward, Hamilton & Scripps, San Diego, 1975-80, ptnr., 1980-86; ptnr. Sheppard, Mullin, Richter & Hampton, San Diego, 1986—; judge pro tem San Diego Superior Ct.; master of the Bench of the Inn, Am. Inns of Ct., Louis M. Welch chpt.; lectr. Inn of Ct., San Diego, 1981—, Continuing Edn. of Bar, Calif., 1983—, Workshop for Judges U.S. Ct. Appeals (9th cir.), 1990; mem. task force on establishment of bus. cts. sys. Jud. Coun. Calif., 1996-97. Editor-in-chief: San Diego Law Rev., 1973; contbr. articles to profl. jours. Bd. dirs., pres. San Diego Kidney Found., 1985-90; bd. dirs. San Diego Aerospace Mus., 1985—; trustee La Jolla (Calif.) Playhouse, 1990-91. Served to lt. USNR, 1968-74. Fellow Am. Coll. Trial Lawyers; mem. San Diego Assn. Bus. Trial Lawyers (founding mem., bd. govs.), San Diego Def. Lawyers Assn. (dir.), Am. Arbitration Assn., 9th Cir. Jud. Conf. (del. 1987-90), Safari Club Internat. (San Diego chpt.), San Diego Sportsmen's Club. Republican. Presbyterian. Avocations: reading, family activities, flying, skiing. Office: Sheppard Mullin Richter & Hampton 501 W Broadway Fl 19 San Diego CA 92101-3536

WEAVER, MOLLIE LITTLE, lawyer; b. Alma, Ga., Mar. 11; d. Alfred Ross and Annis Mae (Bowles) Little; m. Jack Delano Nelson, Sept. 12, 1953 (div. May 1970); 1 dau., Cynthia Ann; m. 2d, Hobart Ayres Weaver, June 10, 1970; stepchildren: Hobart Jr., Mary Essa, Robert. BA in History, U. Richmond, 1978; JD, Wake Forest U., 1981. Bar; N.C. 1982, Fla. 1983; Cert. profl. sec.; cert. adminstrv. mgr. Supr., Western Electric Co., Richmond, Va., 1952-75; cons., owner Cert. Mgmt. Assocs., Richmond, 1975-76; sole practice, Ft. Lauderdale, Fla., 1982-86, Emerald Isle, N.C., 1986-89, Richmond, 1989—. Author: Secretary's Reference Manual, 1973. Mem. adv. coun. to Bus. and Office Edn., Greensboro, N.C., 1970-73, adv. com. to bus. edn. Va. Commonwealth U., Richmond, 1977. Recipient Key to City of Winston-Salem, N.C., 1963; Epps award for scholarship, 1978. Mem. ABA, N.C. Bar Assn., Fla. Bar Assn., Word Processing Assn. (v.p., founder Richmond 1973-75), Adminstrv. Mgmt. Soc. (com. chmn. Richmond, 1973-75), Phi Beta Kappa, Eta Sigma Phi, Phi Alpha Theta. Republican. Home: 12301 Renwick Pl Glen Allen VA 23060-6959

WEAVER, PAMELA ANN, hospitality research professional; b. Little Falls, N.Y., July 7, 1947; d. Floyd Aron Weaver and Norma May (Putnam) Hoyer; m. Ken Ward McCleary, Mar. 2, 1947; children: Brian Wilson, Blake McCleary, Ryan McCleary. AA, Fulton Montgomery Community Co, Amsterdam, NY, 1968; BA, SUNY, 1970; MA, U. S. Fla., 1973; PhD, Mich. State U., East Lansing, 1978. Mem. Mathematics Dept., Riviera Jr. High Sch., Miami, Fla., 1970-72; grad. asst. Office of Med., Edn. Research and Devel., Mich. State U., East Lansing, 1973-74, Dept. of Mktg., Mich. State U., East Lansing, 1974-75; instr. mktg. Mich. State U., East Lansing; asst. prof. mktg., hospitality svcs. administrn. Cen. Mich. State U.,, Mt. Pleasant, 1978-79, Cen. Mich. U., 1982-86; chair acad. senate Cen. Mich. U., Mt. Pleasant, 1985-86, prof. mktg., hospitality svcs. administrn., 1986-89; prof. Dept. Hospitality and Tourism Mgmt. Va. Poly. Inst. and State U., Blacksburg, 1989—. Contbr. articles to profl. jours. Recipient John Wiley and Sons award for Lifetime Achievent to Hospitality Industry John Wiley & Sons, Inc., 1994. Mem. Coun. on Hotel, Restaurant and Instln. Edn., Acad. Mktg. Sci., So. Mktg. Assn. Office: Va Poly Inst and State U Wallace Hall Blacksburg VA 24061-0429

WEAVER, PEGGY (MARGUERITE MCKINNIE WEAVER), plantation owner; b. Jackson, Tenn., June 7, 1925; d. Franklin Allen and Mary Alice (Caradine) McKinnie; children: Elizabeth Lynn, Thomas Jackson III, Franklin A. McKinnie. Student, U. Colo., 1943-45, Am. Acad. Dramatic Arts, 1945-46, S. Meisner's Profl. Classes, 1949, Oxford U., 1990, 91. Actress, 1946-52; mem. staff Mus. Modern Art, N.Y.C., 1949-50; woman's editor radio sta. WTJS-AM-FM, Jackson, Tenn., 1952-55; editor, radio/TV Jackson Sun Newspaper, 1952-55; columnist Bolivar (Tenn.) Bulletin-Times, 1986—; chmn. Ho. of Reps. of Old Line Dist., Hardeman County, Tenn., 1985-91, 94—. Founder Paris-Henry County (Tenn.) Arts Coun., 1965; pres. Assn. Preservation of Tenn. Antiquities, Hardeman County chpt., 1991-95; charter mem. adv. bd. Tenn. Arts Commn., Nashville, 1967-74, Tenn. Performing Arts Ctr., Nashville, 1972—; chmn. Tenn. Libr. Assn., Nashville, 1973-74; regional chmn. Opera Memphis, 1979-91; mem. nat. coun. Met. Opera, N.Y.C., 1980-92, Tenn. Bicentennial Com., Hardeman County, 1993-96. Mem. DAR, Nat. Soc. Colonial Dames Am. (treas. Memphis chpt. 1996—), Oxford Alumni Assn. N.Y., Jackson Golf and Country, English Speaking Union (London chpt.), Summit (Memphis), Dilettantes (Memphis). Methodist. Avocations: horseback riding, travel, theatre.

WEAVER, RICHARD L., II, writer, speaker, educator; b. Hanover, N.H., Dec. 5, 1941; s. Richard L. and Florence B. (Grow) W.; m. Andrea A. Willis; children: R. Scott, Jacquelynn Michelle, Anthony Keith, Joanna Corinne. AB, U. Mich., 1964, MA, 1965; PhD, Ind. U., 1969. Asst. prof. U. Mass., 1968-74; assoc. prof. speech communication Bowling Green State U., 1974-79, prof., 1979-96, dir., basic speech communication course, 1974-96; vis. prof. U. Hawaii-Manoa, 1981-82, Bond U., Queensland, Australia, 1990, St. Albans, Melbourne, Australia, 1990, Western Inst., Perth, Australia, 1990. Author: (with Saundra Hybels) Speech/Communication, 1974, 2d edit., 1979, Speech/Communication: A Reader, 1975, 2d edit., 1979, Speech/Communication: A Student Manual, 1976, 2d edit., 1979, Understanding Interpersonal Communication, 1978, 2d edit., 1981, 3d edit., 1984, 4th edit., 1987, 5th edit., 1990, 6th edit., 1993, 7th edit., 1996, (with Raymond K. Tucker, Cynthia Berryman-Fink) Research in Speech Communication, 1981, Foundations of Speech Communication: Perspectives of a Discipline, 1982, Speech Communication Skills, 1982, Understanding Public Communication, 1983, Understanding Business Communication, 1985, Understanding Speech Communication Skills, 1985, Readings in Speech Communication, 1985, (with Saundra Hybels) Communicating Effectively, 1986, 2d edit., 1989, 3d edit., 1992, 4th edit., 1995, Skills for Communicating Effectively, 1985, 2d edit., 1988, 3d edit., 1991, 4th edit., 1993, rev. edit., 1995, (with Howard W. Cotrell) Innovative Instructional Strategies, 1987, 2d edit., 1988, 3d edit., 1989, 4th edit., 1990, 5th edit., 1992, 6th edit., 1993, (with Curt Bechler) Listen to Win: A Guide to Effective Listening, 1994, Study Guide to Accompany Communicating Effectively, 1995, Essentials of Public Speaking, 1996. Mem. Nat. Comm. Assn., Ctrl. States Speech Assn., Ohio Speech Assn. Home and Office: 9583 Woodleigh Ct Perrysburg OH 43551-2669

WEAVER, SARA LEE, sales executive; b. Jefferson City, Mo., Apr. 4, 1962; d. Thomas Henry and Majorie Gwendolyn (Jones) W. BJ, BA, BS, U. Mo., 1984; student, U. London, 1980, Université Laval, 1983. Sales asst. Katz Communications, Dallas, 1985-87, Chgo., 1987-88; media systems trainer Katz Communications, N.Y.C., 1988-90; sales exec. Katz Communications, Chgo., 1990-94, Sta. KGO-TV, San Francisco, 1994—. Bd. dirs. Art Span, San Francisco; v.p. bd. dirs. ArtSpan, San Francisco. Mem. AAUW (v.p. membership San Francisco br.),Omicron Delta Kappa, Sigma Rho Sigma, Kappa Epsilon Alpha, Pi Beta Phi. Democrat. Presbyterian. Avocations: bicycling, snow skiing, reading, golf, Scottish country dancing. Office: Sta KGO-TV 900 Front St San Francisco CA 94111-1427

WEAVER, SIGOURNEY (SUSAN ALEXANDRA WEAVER), actress; b. N.Y.C., Oct. 8, 1949; d. Sylvester (Pat) Weaver and Elizabeth Inglish; m. James Simpson, 1984; 1 child, Charlotte. BA in English, Stanford U., 1971; MA in Drama, Yale U., 1974. First profl. theater appearance in The Constant Wife, 1974; other roles in Beyond Therapy, Hurlyburly, 1984, The Merchant of Venice, 1987; films include: Annie Hall, 1977, Alien, 1979, Eyewitness, 1981, The Year of Living Dangerously, 1982, Deal of the Century, 1983, Ghostbusters, 1984, Aliens, 1986 (Acad. award nomination for best actress), Half Moon Street, 1986, One Woman or Two, 1987, Working Girl, 1988, Gorillas in the Mist, 1988 (Golden Globe award 1989), Ghostbusters II, 1989, Alien 3, 1992, 1492: Conquest of Paradise, 1992, Dave, 1993, Death and the Maiden, 1994, Jeffrey, 1995, Copycat, 1995, Snow White in the Black Forest, 1996, Ice Storm, 1996. Office: ICM 8942 Wilshire Blvd Beverly Hills CA 90211-1934

WEAVER, THOMAS HAROLD, health facility administrator; b. Asheville, N.C., July 21, 1943; s. Thomas Harold and Evelyn (Morris) W.; m. Marsha Va Fossen, Dec. 17, 1982; 1 child, Sallie Jayne. BA, Va. Mil. Inst., 1964; MEd, U. Ga., 1970; MAHA, George Washington U., 1973. Vol. EMS, various locations, 1965-94; mgmt. analyst VA Med. Ctr., Martinez, Calif., 1972-74; health planner VA Ctrl. Hdqs., Washington, 1974-76, sr. health sys. specialist, 1976-79; asst. dir. VA Med. Ctr., Lexington, Ky., 1979; COO, assoc. dir. VA Med. Ctr., Ft. Howard, Md., 1980-82; sr. exec. sys. specialist VA Med. Ctr., Durham, N.C., 1982-85; COO, assoc. med. dir. VA Med. Ctr., Pitts., 1985-89; CEO, med. ctr. dir. VA Med. Ctr., Martinsburg, W.Va., 1989-94; CEO, dir. VA Med. Ctr., Bay Pines, Fla., 1994—; v.p., bd. dirs. Berkeley County Emergency Ambulance Authority, Martinsburg, 1989-94; pres., chmn. bd. Bedington Vol. Fire and Rescue Dept., 1989-93; disting. vis. lectr. W.Va. U., 1992-94; adj. prof. U. Tampa. Contbr. articles to profl. jours. Emergency med. svcs. instr. various locations, 1967-94, W.Va., 1990-94; bd. dirs. Pinellas County EMS Med. Control Bd., 1995-96, Hurricanes and Health Care Consortium, 1994-96; mem. Pinellas County Disaster Adv. Com., 1996—. Recipient Nat. Cmty. Svc. award Sec. Vets. Affairs, Washington, 1975, Cert. of Merit, Geico Pub. Svc., Washington, 1985, Spl. Act Commendation award DVA and County Commn. for outstanding actions during cmty. disaster, 1993. Fellow Am. Coll. Healthcare Execs. (Fed. Exec. of Yr. W.Va. chpt. 1994); mem. Nat. Registry EMTs, Rotary. Office: Dept VA Affairs Med Ctr 10000 Bay Pines Blvd Saint Petersburg FL 33708

WEAVER, TIMOTHY ALLAN, lawyer; b. Elkhart, Ind., Nov. 30, 1948; s. Arthur and Joan Lucile (Yoder) W.; m. Catherine Anne Power, Nov. 23, 1974; children: Daniel Timothy, Christopher Matthew, David Colwell. AB, Brown U., 1971; JD, U. Ill., 1974. Bar: Ill. 1974, U.S. Dist. Ct. (no. dist.) Ill. 1975, U.S. Ct. Appeals (7th cir.) 1975, U.S. Dist. Ct. (no. dist. trial bar) Ill. 1982. Asst. pub. defender Cook County Pub. Defender, Chgo., 1974-75; trial atty. Chgo. Transit Authority, 1975-78; assoc. Philip E. Howard Ltd., Chgo., 1978; assoc. Pretzel & Stouffer, Chartered, Chgo., 1978-82, ptnr., 1982—. Editor: Medical Malpractice, 1989, 92, 96; contbr. chpts. to books. Mem. ABA, Ill. Bar Assn., Chgo. Bar Assn., Ill. Assn. Def. Trial Counsel, Am. Soc. Law and Medicine, The Law Club of Chgo. Office: Pretzel & Stouffer One S Wacker Dr #2500 Chicago IL 60606

WEAVER, VELATHER EDWARDS, small business owner; d. Willie and Ethel Edwards; m. Ellerson Weaver; children: Frank Mattox Jr., Terence Mattox, Christopher Williams, Sharon, Shelley, Stephanie. Student, Sonoma State Coll., 1972, U. Calif., Berkeley, 1972; BA, Calif. State U., Hayward, 1973; MBA, St. Mary's Coll., Moraga, Calif., 1989. Coach, counselor Opportunities Industrialization Ctr., Oakland, Calif., 1967-69; tchr. Berkeley Headstart, 1969-70; instr., cons. external degree program Antioch Coll.-West, San Francisco, 1971-74; market analyst World Airways, Inc., Oakland, 1972-75, affirmative action adminstr., 1975-78; cons. A.C. Transit, Oakland, 1982; owner, mgr. Val's Designs and Profl. Svcs., Lafayette, Calif., 1980—; mgr. adminstrn., tng. supr. North Oakland Pharmacy, Inc., 1970—, also bd. dirs.; adv. bd. The Tribune, Oakland, 1982-88. Author RAPRO Self Mgmt. Program, 1985. Program coord., mem. publicity com. Lafayette Arts and Sci. Found., 1982-83; mem. admission bd. St. Mary's Coll. Grad. Sch. Bus., 1990; bd. dirs. Acalanes H.S., Lafayette, 1980-82, Lafayette Elem. Sch., 1975-80; mem. Lafayette Econ. Devel. Task Force, 1994-95; vice chmn. Lafayette Econ. Devel. Commn., 1995—. Mem. Calif. State Pharmacists Assn. Aux. (pres. Contra Costa Aux. 1980, pres. state aux. 1986-88, recognition award 1987), Calif. Pharmacists Polit. Action Com. (appreciation award 1988), Diablo Valley Bus. and Profl. Women (pub. rels. com. 1986-87, best local orgn. award 1987, author yearbook 1987), No. Calif. Med., Dental and Pharm. Assn. Aux. (bd. dirs., com. chair 1975—, pres. elect 1991, pres. 1991-93), Internat. Platform Assn., Links, Inc. Avocations: reading, researching family businesses, travel, attending auctions. Office: North Oakland Pharmacy Inc 5705 Market St Emeryville CA 94608-2811

WEAVER, WAYNE, professional sports team executive; b. Columbus, Ga., Jan. 1, 1935; m. Delores Weaver; children: Bradley, Leigh. Past co-owner, pres., CEO Nine West Group, Inc., 1978-93; owner, chmn., CEO LC Footwear, L.L.C., 1995—; chmn. CEO Shoe Carnival, Inc., Evansville, Ind., 1985—; mng. gen. ptnr. Touchdown Jacksonville!, 1993; chmn., CEO Jacksonville Jaguars, 1993—. Active Weaver Family Found., Jacksonville Jaguars Found., Dana-Farber Cancer Inst./Harvard Med. Sch.; bd. dirs. Jacksonville Symphony Assn. Mem. Fashion Footwear Assn. of N.Y. (past chmn.), Two/Ten Internat. Footwear Found. (bd. dirs., exec. com.). Avocations: skiing, running (ran Boston Marathon in 1991 to support the Dana-Farber Cancer Inst.). Office: Jacksonville Jaguars One Stadium Pl Jacksonville FL 32202

WEAVER, WILLIAM CHARLES, retired industrial executive; b. Pitts., Nov. 10, 1941; s. Curtis D. and Mary (Yahres) W.; BS in Edn., Indiana U. of Pa., 1963; postgrad. in acctg. Tex. Christian U., 1964-65; m. Karla Lee Kottas, June 13, 1964; children: Michael, Kelli. With Price Waterhouse & Co., Pitts., 1965-73, audit mgr., 1970-73; corp. contr. Kennametal Inc., Latrobe, Pa., 1973-78, v.p., contr., 1978-83, v.p., treas., 1983-86, v.p., CFO, 1987-89; sr. v.p., CFO Oak Industries, Inc., Waltham, Mass., 1990-95; ret., 1995; bd. dirs. Gemini Precision Products. Trustee, Hampton United Presbyn. Ch., 1972-73; pres. Mountain View Parent Tchrs. Orgn., 1976-77; bd. dirs. East High Acres Civic Assn., 1976-77; treas. Greater Latrobe Hockey Club, 1982-87; chmn. bd. dirs., mem. adv. coun. Jr. Achievement, Latrobe, 1982-85; chmn. bd. trustees Latrob United Way, 1988-89. 1st lt. U.S. Army, 1963-65. CPA, Pa. Mem. AICPA, Pa. Inst. CPAs, Nat. Investors Rels. Inst., Fin. Execs. Inst., MAPI Fin. Coun.

WEAVER, WILLIAM CLAIR, JR. (MIKE WEAVER), human resources development executive; b. Indiana, Pa., Apr. 11, 1936; s. William Clair and Zaida (Bley) W.; m. Janet Marcelle Boyd, Sept. 18, 1963 (div. 1978); 1 child, William Michael; m. Donna June Hubbuch, Feb. 10, 1984. B Aero Engring., Rensselaer Poly. Inst., 1958; MBA, Washington U., St. Louis, 1971; postgrad., Rutgers U.; grad., Armed Forces Indsl. Coll. Registered profl. engr. Engr. aerodynamics N.Am. Aviation, Los Angeles, 1959-60; engr. flight test ops. Boeing/Vertol, Phila., 1963-66; engr. flight test project Lockhead Electronics, Plainfield, N.J., 1966-69; project engr. advanced systems, sr. staff engr. Emerson Electric Co., St. Louis, 1969-72; pres. Achievement Assocs., Inc., St. Louis, 1972—; founder, charter mem. Catalyst, 1978—; speaker in field. Author: Winning Selling, 1983, Winning Manager, 1997; contbr. articles to profl. jours. Mem. adv. com. Boy Scouts Am., Bridgeton, Mo., 1974. Served to capt. USAF, 1960-63, USAFR. Mem. Nat. Soc. Profl. Engrs.,Am. Soc. Bus. and Mgmt. Cons., Am. Ordnance Soc., Am. Inst. Aeronautics and Astrounautics, Assn. MBA Execs., Air Force Assn., Am. Helicopter Soc., Acacia Frat., St. Louis C. of C., Mensa, Beta Gamma Sigma. Republican. Lutheran. Avocations: photography, music, sports. Home and Office: 13018 Ray Trog Ct Saint Louis MO 63146-1802

WEAVER, WILLIAM MERRITT, JR., investment banker; b. Phila., Jan. 7, 1912; s. William Merritt and Frances (Jones) W.; m. Rosemary R. Fine, May 9, 1972; children by previous marriage: Judith (Mrs. Ross Campbell), Patricia (Mrs. Clarence Wurts), Wendy, Alison M. Grad., Phillips Exeter Acad., 1930; BA, Princeton, 1934. Ptnr. Nathan Trotter & Co., Phila., 1934-40; pres., dir. Frank Samuel & Co., Inc., Phila., 1945- 59, Haile Mines, N.Y.C., 1957-58; pres. Howmet Corp., N.Y.C., 1958-65; chmn. bd. dirs. Howmet Corp., 1965-66; ptnr. Alexander Brown & Sons, Balt., 1966-86, ltd. ptnr. emeritus, 1986—; dir. Allen Group, Inc. Served to col. AUS, 1941-45. Decorated Legion of Merit, Bronze Star, Croix de Guerre (France and Belgium).. Mem. Knickerbacker Club, River (N.Y.C.) Club, Lyford Cay (Nassau) Club, Country Club of Fairfield (Southport, Conn.), Phi Beta Kappa. Home: Lazy W Ranch Smith NV 89430

WEAVER, WILLIAM SCHILDECKER, electric power industry executive; b. Pitts., Jan. 15, 1944; s. Charles Henry and Louise (Schildecker) W.; m. Janet Kae Jones, Mar. 7, 1981. BA, Hamilton Coll., 1965; JD, U. Mich., 1968. Bar: Wash. 1968. Assoc. Perkins Coie, Seattle, 1968-74; ptnr. Perkins COIE, Seattle, 1975-91; exec. v.p., CFO Puget Sound Power & Light Co., Bellevue, Wash., 1991—; vice chmn., chmn. unregulated subsidiaries Puget Sound Energy, 1997—, also bd. dirs.; bd. dirs. Puget Sound Power & Light Co., Hydro Electric Devel. Co., Bellevue, Connex T, Inc., Seattle. Bd. dirs. Wash. Rsch. Coun., Seattle, 1991—, chmn., 1995—; trustee Seattle Repertory Theatre, 1992-95, Corp. Coun. Arts, 1995-97. Mem. ABA, Wash. State Bar Assn., Seattle Yacht Club, Rainier Club. Office: Puget Sound Power & Light Co PO Box 97034-obc- Bellevue WA 98009

WEBB, ALEXANDER, III, investment company executive; b. Raleigh, N.C., Aug. 19, 1945; s. Alexander Jr. and Mary (Hall) W.; m. Laura Lee Robinson; children: Alexander IV, William Robinson. BA, U. N.C., 1968; MBA, Columbia U., 1972. Investment analyst First Union Nat. Bank, Charlotte, N.C., 1968-69; investment officer New Eng. Life Ins. Co., Boston, 1972-73; exec. v.p., dir., chief investment officer State Street Research & Mgmt. Co., Boston, 1973-89; pres. Fidelity Mgmt. Trust Co. (Fidelity Investments), Boston, 1990-95, also bd. dirs.; vice chmn., chief investment officer The Boston Co. Asset Mgmt. Inc., 1995—; adv. com. Investment Counseling, Inc., 1995—. Investment com. Soc. Preservation New England Antiquities. Mem. Boston Security Analysts Soc., Fin. Anaylsts Fedn. Episcopalian. Avocations: running, hiking. Office: Boston Co Asset Mgmt Inc One Boston Pl Boston MA 02108

WEBB, ANTHONY ALLAN, banker; b. Lincoln, Nebr., May 24, 1943; s. Robert McGraw and Ruth Irene (Good) W.; m. Micheline Touchette, July 10, 1971; children—Annie, Christian. B.A., U. Colo., 1965; B.Internat. Mgmt., Am. Grad. Sch. Internat. Mgmt., 1970. Various positions Royal Bank Can., Montreal and London, 1970-77; assoc. mgr. Royal Bank Can., Toronto, Ont., Can., 1977-80; v.p. Royal Bank Can., Toronto, 1980-83, sr. v.p. merchant banking, 1983-84; dir. gen. Royal Bank Can., Geneva, 1984-88; sr. v.p. personal fin. svcs. Royal Bank Can., Montreal, 1988-93; chmn. Royal Bank Can. Suisse, Royal Bank Can., Channel Islands; pres., CEO Royal Trust, Toronto, 1993—. Served to lt. comdr. USNR, 1965-69. Home: 48 Suncrest Dr, Don Mills, ON Canada M3C 2L3 Office: PO Box 7500 Sta A, Toronto, ON Canada M5W 1P9

WEBB, BERNICE LARSON, writer, consultant, press owner, publisher; b. Ludell, Kans.; d. Carl Godfred and Ida Genevieve (Tongish) Larson; m. Ralph Raymond Schear, Aug. 9, 1942 (div. July 1956, dec. Aug., 1981); children: William Carl Schear, Rebecca Rae Schear Gentry; m. Robert MacHardy Webb, July 14, 1961 (dec. June 1983). BA, U. Kans., 1956, MA, 1957, PhD, 1961; postgrad., U. Aberdeen, Scotland, 1959-60. Cert. counseler Nat. Multiple Sclerosis Soc., peer counselor for cancer, ARC. Asst. instr. English U. Kans., Lawrence, 1958-59, 60-61; asst. prof. U. Southwestern La., Lafayette, 1961-67, assoc. prof., 1967-80, prof., 1980-87; owner, publisher Spider Press, 1991—; vis. assoc. prof. S.S. Universe Campus/World Campus Afloat, 1972; coord. Poetry in the Schs., Lafayette Parish, La., 1974; dir. grad. seminars NDEA Inst. Intellectual and Cultural History, Lafayette, summer 1966; poetry cons. Acadiana Arts Coun., 1976-87, Lafayette Parish Schs., 1976-87; bd. dirs. Deep South Writers Conf., 1978-87; acting dir. English reading-writing lab. U. Southwestern La., summers 1977, 78, 79, writing cons., 1987—; founder, coord. Webb's Writers, 1974—. Author: The Basketball Man, 1973, transl. to Japanese, 1981, new edit., 1994, Beware of Ostriches, 1978, Poetry on the Stage, 1979, Lady Doctor on a Homestead, 1987, Two Peach Baskets, 1991 (with J. Allan) Born to Be a Loser, 1993, Spider Web, 1993, Mating Dance, 1996; contbr. poetry and articles to various publs.; book reviewer Jour. Am. Culture, Jour. Popular Culture, 1980-87; actress Little Theater, La., 1969-83, off-off Broadway, 1980. Vol. Mayor's Commn. on the Needs of Women, City of Lafayette, 1976-86; vol. La. Talent Bank of Women, 1978-86; judge of writing contests for schs., clubs, profl. socs., La. and U.S., 1961—; newsletter editor Bayou Coun. Girl Scouts of Am., 1964-66; guest editor The New Laurel Rev., 1976. Mem. AAUW (bd. dirs. br. 1967-71, state editor 1967-71, grantee 1978-80, faculty rsch. grant U. Southwestern La. 1980-81, 85-86), Soc. for Values in Higher Edn. (Svc. award 1995), South Cen. Coll. English Assn. (pres. 1986-87), S.W. Br. Poetry (pres. 1988—), La. State Poetry Soc. (Disting. Lifetime mem., pres. 1978-79, 81-82, editor 1970-90), South Cen. MLA, Coll. English Assn. (life mem.), Am. Folklore Soc., Conf. on Christianity and Lit., Nat. Fedn. State Poetry Socs., Inc. (Queen of Poetry 1993), Phi Beta Kappa (regional pres. 1976-77, 83-84). Democrat. Roman Catholic. Avocations: acting, travel, collecting oral history. Home: 159 Whittington Dr Lafayette LA 70503-2741

WEBB, BRAINARD TROUTMAN, JR., lawyer, distribution company executive; b. Brooklyn, Conn., Feb. 13, 1943; s. Brainard Troutman and Loretta (Dwyer) W.; m. Leigh Wickersham, Apr. 6, 1968; children: Patrick Brewster, Elizabeth Ryan. B.S., Spring Hill Coll., 1965; J.D., Emory U., 1968. Bar: Ga. 1968. Assoc. Tarleton & Zion, Decatur, Ga., 1970-73; corp. counsel Barwick Industries, Inc., Chamblee, Ga., 1973-75; corp. counsel Genuine Parts Co., Atlanta, 1975—, sec. 1984-95, v.p. 1988—. Served to capt. AUS, 1968-70; Vietnam. Decorated Bronze Star, Air medal. Mem. Ga. Bar Assn., Greater Atlanta Corp. Counsels Assn., Lawyers Club Atlanta, Am. Soc. Corp. Secs. Roman Catholic. Home: 7990 Innsbruck Dr Dunwoody GA 30350-4308 Office: Genuine Parts Co 2999 Circle 75 Pky NW Atlanta GA 30339-3050

WEBB, CHARLES HAIZLIP, JR., university dean; b. Dallas, Feb. 14, 1933; s. Charles Haizlip and Marion (Gilker) W.; m. Kenda McGibbon, June 21, 1958; children: Mark, Kent, Malcolm, Charles Haizlip III. AB, So. Meth. U., 1955, MMus, 1955; DMus, Ind. U., 1964; DMus (hon.), Anderson. Coll., 1979. Asst. to dean Sch. Music, So. Meth. U., 1957-58; mem. faculty Sch. Music, Ind. U., 1960—, dean, 1973—. dir. Indpls. Symphony Choir, 1967-81; guest condr. chorus and orch. festivals throughout U.S.; duo-pianist with Wallace Hornibrook in U.S. and Australian tour, 1973; organist First Meth. Ch., Bloomington, 1961—, mem. hymnal revision com. Meth. Ch.; mem. jury Chopin competition; mem. jury internat. piano competitions in Munich, Budapest, South Africa, Paris, Chile, Warsaw, Bolzano, London,

Cologne, Japan; mem. adv. bd. Classical Insitea. Chmn. adv. bd. Internat. Music Festivals, Inc.; mem. Ind. Arts Commn., 1975-83, U.S.-USSR Commn. on Music Performance Edn., Am. Coun. Learned Socs./USSR Ministry of Culture; mem. adv. panel The Music Found.; mem. recommendation bd. Avery Fisher Prize Program; bd. dirs. Busoni Found.; mem. bd. advisors Van Cliburn Internat. Piano Competition; mem. nat. adv. bd. Am. Guild Organists; trustee Indpls. Symphony Orch. With U.S. Army, 1955-57. Decorated D.S.M.; recipient Disting. Alumni award So. Meth. U., 1980, Sagamore of Wabash Gov. award, 1987, 89, Thomas Hart Benton medal Ind. U., 1987, Disting. Alumni award Highland Park High Sch., Dallas, 1989, Ind. Gov. award for arts, 1989, Rocking Chair award, Ind. U., 1997; Rockefeller scholar Bellazio Study Ctr., 1997; named Disting. Prof. (hon.) Ind. U., 1997, Paul Harris fellow, Rotary Internat., 1997. Mem. Ind. Acad., Century Assn. of N.Y., Pi Kappa Lambda, Phi Mu Alpha, Phi Delta Theta. Home: 648 S Woodcrest Dr Bloomington IN 47401-5417 Office: Ind U Sch Music Bloomington IN 47405

WEBB, CHARLES RICHARD, retired university president; b. Berkeley, Calif., Oct. 4, 1919; s. Charles Richard and Adele (McDaniel) W.; m. Andrée Bonno; 1 child, Charles Richard III. AB, U. Calif., Berkeley, 1942, MA, 1944; MA, Harvard U., 1947, PhD, 1949. Faculty San Diego State Coll., 1949-64, prof., 1958-64, chmn. dept. history, 1956-58; dean acad. affairs Stanislaus State Coll., Turlock, Calif., 1964-66; prof. history San Diego State Coll., 1966-70; pres. Eastern Conn. State U., Willimantic, 1970-88; ret., 1988; former assoc. dean acad. planning Calif. State Colls., 1966-69, former dep. state coll. dean acad. planning. Author: Workbook in Western Civilization, 2 vols, 1959, Western Civilization vol. 1 (with Schaefer), vol. 2 (with Palm), 1958, (with Crosby) The Past as Prologue, 2 vols, 1973; contbr. articles to profl. jours. Mem. pers. com. Santa Rosa Symphony Assn., New Eng. Program, Windham Meml. Comty. Hosp., Sea Rsch. Found.; mem. Commn. on Conn.'s Future. With USNR, 1941-45. Mem. AAUP, Am. Hist. Assn., Am. Fedn. Musicians, Nat. Pks. and Conservation, Sonoma Land Trust, Sierra Club, Nature Conservancy, New Eng. Hist. Assn., Assn. Calif. State Coll. Profs. (v.p. 1958-60), Save the Redwoods League, Conn. Employees Assn., Am. Assn. State Colls. and Univs., Phi Alpha Theta, Kappa Delta Pi, Omicron Delta Pi, Alpha Delta Phi. Clubs: University (San Diego), Commonwealth of Calif., Willimantic Country, Saddle Club, Santa Rosa, Montecito Heights Health & Raquet Club, Santa Rosa. Home: 6495 Timber Springs Dr Santa Rosa CA 95409-5900

WEBB, CLIFTON ALAN, media consultant; b. New London, Conn., Nov. 3, 1950; s. Robert Lee Sr. and June Mildred (Hargrove) W.; m. Jacqueline Diana Gales, Oct. 14, 1988; children: Diana Rose, Joanna Joy. BA, So. Conn. State, 1972; postgrad., U. Conn., 1972-73. Lic. radiotelephoner. Announcer Sta. WSUB-AM/FM, Groton, Conn., 1974-78; program dir. Sta. WYBC-FM, New Haven, Conn., 1978-81; prodr. Conn. Radio Network, Hamden, 1981-82; news anchor Nat. Black Network, N.Y.C., 1982-83; editor UPI Radio Network, N.Y.C., 1983-85; correspondent NBC News, Washington, 1985-87; news anchor Media Gen. Cable, Fairfax, Va., 1987-91, News Channel 8, Springfield, Va., 1991-97; media cons. Ryan-McGinn, Arlington, Va., 1997—; dir. Wolf Trap Assocs., Vienna, Va., 1990-96. TV reporter Blacks & Koreans, 1992, Teen Moms, 1992, Election Diary, 1994. Spokesman No. Va. Mental health, Fair Oaks, 1994—, Alexandria (Va.) Valor Awards, 1994—, Urban League Ann. Dinner, Alexandria, 1994—. Baptist. Avocations: diving, swimming. Home: 805 W Tantallon Dr Fort Washington MD 20744 Office: Ryan McGinn 2300 Clarendon Blvd Ste 610 Arlington VA 22201-3367

WEBB, DAN K., lawyer; b. Macomb, Ill., Sept. 5, 1945; s. Keith L. and Phyllis I. (Clow) W.; student Western Ill. U., 1963-66; J.D., Loyola U., 1970; m. Laura A. Buscemi, Mar. 15, 1973; children—Jeffrey, Maggie, Michael, Melanie. Bar: Ill. 1970. Chief spl. prosecutions div. U.S. Atty.'s Office, Chgo., 1970-76; ptnr. firm Cummins, Decker & Webb, Chgo., 1976-79; dir. Ill. Dept. Law Enforcement, Chgo., 1979-80; ptnr. Pierce, Webb, Lydon & Griffin, Chgo., 1980-81; U.S. atty., Chgo., 1981-84; ptnr. Winston & Strawn, Chgo., 1984—; instr. John Marshall Law Sch., 1975—, Loyola U. Sch. Law, 1980—. Vice chmn. Met. Fair and Expn. Authority, 1978—; bd. advisers Mercy Hosp. and Med. Ctr.; mem. Chgo. Council on Arson. Recipient spl. commendation award U.S. Justice Dept., 1975; named 1 of 10 Outstanding Young Chicagoans, Chgo. Jaycees, 1979. Mem. ABA, Ill. Bar Assn., Chgo. Bar Assn., Fed. Bar Assn., Legal Club Chgo., Execs. Club Chgo. Republican. Home: 10020 S Damen Ave Chicago IL 60643-2004 Office: Winston & Strawn 35 W Wacker Dr Chicago IL 60601-1614

WEBB, DAVID OWEN, petroleum engineer, association executive; b. Matador, Tex., July 21, 1938; s. Owen Raby Webb and Mary Ernest (Echols) West; m. Jean S. Skidmore, May 6, 1967; children: William David, Jon Patrick. BS in Petroleum Engring., Tex. Tech. U., 1962. With Sun Oil Co., Houston, 1962-63, Kentron Hawaii Ltd., Honolulu, 1963-73, LTU Aerospace Corp., Washington, 1973-75; asst. dir., congressional liason for fossil energy U.S. Energy Rsch. & Devel. Adminstrn., Washington, 1975-77, sr. dir. energy rsch. ctrs., 1977; v.p. policy and regulatory affairs Gas Rsch. Inst., Washington, 1977-83, sr. v.p. policy and regulatory affairs, 1983—; pres., CEO Gas Tech. Info., Inc., Washington; operating agt. Internat. Energy Agy. Internat. Ctr. for Gas Tech. Info., Paris, 1993—. Home: 4804 Autumn Lake Way Annandale VA 22003-4401 Office: Gas Rsch Inst Ste 730N 1331 Pennsylvania Ave NW Washington DC 20004-1703

WEBB, DENNIS WAYNE, protective services official; b. Washington, Sept. 7, 1955; s. Clarence Edward and Henrietta Agnes (Rison) W.; m. Linda Faye Morgan, May 31, 1991; children: Shaun Dennis, Brian Patrick. BA, Bold Christian U., 1987. Dep. sheriff Price William County Sheriff Dept., Manassas, Va., 1977-79, supr., 1979-82; lt., asst. shift comdr. Prince William-Manassas Regional Adult Detention Ctr., 1982-83, lt., tng./staff devel. and security liaison, 1983-87, capt./ dir. tng., staff devel. and recruitment, 1987-89, dir. adminstrn., 1989—; cons., trainer Eppanhannock Regional acad., Fredericksburg, Va., 1985—; corrections sci. curriculum advisor No. Va. C.C., Arlington, 1983—; chmn. tng. subcom. Coun. Govts. Corrections Chiefs, 1990-91; chmn. spl. ops. and tactics workgroup, 1994; owner, pres. Commonwealth Tng. Cons. Contbr. articles to profl. jours. Bd. dirs. Prince William-Manassas Acad., 1987-89; mem. Manassas Dem. Com., 1989; chmn. spl. edn. adv. com. Manassas City Schs., 1991; instr. ARC, Manassas, 1984—. Recipient Cert. of Appreciation, ARC, 1991, 92, 93. Mem. Am. Criminal Justice Assn., Am. Jail Assn., Police Marksman Assn., Fraternal ORder Police (charter, treas. 1984-87, guard 1988, chaplain 1989, dir. 1994—), Nat. Tactical Officers Assn., Spl. Equipment and Tactics Assn., Internat. Assn. Chiefs of Police, Internat. Assn. Law Enforcement Firearms Instrs. Avocation: Hwardo (black belt), Dragon Kenpo, Dragon Kenpo instruction. Office: Adult Detention Ctr 9320 Lee Ave Manassas VA 20110-5517

WEBB, DONALD ARTHUR, minister; b. Wales, May 4, 1926; came to U.S., 1958; s. Arthur and Emily W.; m. Renee Mowbray, May 18, 1946; children—Cheryl, Marian, Christopher, Alison, Ian. Student, Queen's Coll., Cambridge (Eng.) U., 1944-45; BA, Ohio Wesleyan U., 1960; MDiv, Methodist Theol. Sch. in Ohio, 1963; PhD, Drew U., 1966; postdoctoral, Lincoln Coll., Oxford (Eng.) U., 1969, 72; LLD, Centenary Coll. La., 1991. Ordained to ministry Methodist Ch., 1960. Insp. Brit. Social Services, 1953-58; pastor various chs. Ohio and N.J., 1958-68; dean admissions, asst. prof. theology and lit. Meth. Theol. Sch. in Ohio, 1968-75, v.p. adminstrn., 1975-77; pres. Centenary Coll. La., Shreveport, 1977-91; sr. pastor First United Meth. Ch., Shreveport, 1991-92, scholar-in-residence, 1992—. Author: The Flame and Dusty Miller, 1970, We Hold These Truths, 1960; author: Dostoevsky and Christian Agnosticism, 1971; contbr. articles, revs. to profl. jours. With Brit. Royal Navy, 1945-53. Mem. Shreveport C. of C. (bd. dirs. 1978-80). Home: 5709 Lakefront Dr Shreveport LA 71119-3913 Office: Centenary Coll La 2911 Centenary Blvd Shreveport LA 71104-3335

WEBB, EDSEL PHILIP, retired textile engineer; b. Birmingham, Ala., May 18, 1928; s. Evan Hall and Mary Lee (Hough) W.; m. Mary Ann Pritchett, 1954; children: Phyllis Ann, Rebecca Hough Webb Campbell, Jeffery, Richard. BS in Textiles, Ga. Inst. Tech., 1954, MS in Indsl. Mgmt., 1955. Textile mfr. Callaway Mills, Manchester and LaGrange, Ga., 1954-59; devel. engr. Firestone Tire and Rubber Co., Akron, Ohio, 1959-62, tire and process engr. radial tires, 1962-65, mgr. internat. radial tire engring., 1965-68; sales engr., mgr. water mgmt. Firestone Coated Fabrics Co., Magnolia, Ark., 1968-70, product sales mgr. fuel cells and allied products worldwide, 1970-75, developer of rubber-coated fuel tank for GM Corvette, 1973-75, sales mgr. coated fabrics northern divsn. and internat., 1975-79, sales mgr. Ea. U.S., Can. and all exports, 1979-80, staff prodn., processing, testing and R & D engr., 1980-83; staff prodn., processing, testing and R & D engr. Am. Fuel Cell and Coated Fabric Co., Magnolia, 1983-92, ret., 1992; exec. v.p. TFR Financial Svcs., Magnolia, 1990-93; participant internat. conf. for radial tire devel. and engring. Firestone Tire & Rubber Co., London, Rome, Madrid, and Hamburg, Germany, 1965; served on team with reps. of Belgium, Sweden, Italy, Eng. and Germany for NATO, 1974. Asst. scoutmaster Troop 54 Boy Scouts Am., Anchorage, 1947-50; asst. scoutmaster and scoutmaster Troop and Post 24, Manchester, Ga., 1955-56, explorer advisor, 1956-58, explorer, scout commr., 1957-59, instl. rep., 1957-58; asst. scoutmaster, mem. troop com. Troop 50, Akron, Ohio, 1960-70; asst. scoutmaster Troop 49, Magnolia, Ark., 1971-73, scoutmaster, 1973-76, dist. chmn., dist. vice chmn., 1973-76, mem. coun. exec. bd., 1974—, dist. commr., 1976-79, 90-92, fin. chmn., 1977-78; numerous other positions Boy Scouts Am.; chmn. mfg. com. Am.'s Pub. Works Assn. 85th Congress FWPA, 1968-69; deacon Presbyn. Ch., Ohio and Ga., supt. Sunday Sch., Ohio and Ga., asst. supt. Sunday Sch., Ark.; pres. Men of Ch., Ohio, Ark. and Ga.; pres. Couples Club, Ohio; elder, trustee 1st Presbyn. Ch., Magnolia; tchr. Sunday Sch.; Stephen's min. Peachtree Presbyn. Ch., Atlanta, 1995—; mem. various chs. orgnl. coms.; mem. Vols. in Probation, Vols.-in-Drug-Abuse Edn. Program, Ohio and Ark.; mem. adv. bd. Magnolia Adult Drug Edn. Program; mem. DeSoto Area Coun. Exec. Bd., 1971-93; exec. bd. Atlanta Area coun., 1993—, v.p. camping com., 1993-96; asst. leader Boy Scouts Am. Atlanta group to 1st Russian Boy Scouts Am. Jamboree, Russia, 1994—; mem. internat. com. as ptnr. to World Scouting Program, Boy Scouts Am., Atlanta, 1990—, mem. Jamboree com. Atlanta area coun., 1997. Staff sgt. USAF, 1946-49, USAFR, 1949-52. Recipient Wood Badge award Boy Scouts Am., 1972, Scouter Trainer award and cert. Boy Scouts Am., 1977, Scouter Key Tng. Recognition award Boy Scouts Am., 1978, Silver Beaver award, 1978, cub scout cub master and dist. cub commr., 1978-90, Man of Achievement award, 1979, 17th edit., 1996, Vigil Honor Order of Arrow award, 1980, Dist. Merit award, 1993; recognized for 50 years in scouting as a vol., 1996—, Com. Nat. Jamboree Boy Scouts Am.; recipient Good Neighbor award City of Magnolia, 1993. Mem. Am. Assn. Textile Chemists and Colorists, Nat. Fire Protection Assn., So. Overseers Assn., Soc. Automotive Engrs. (mem. and cons. G9 and AE5 com.), Kiwanis, Jaycees, Rotary, Masons, Toastmasters Internat. (pres. club 151, dist. commr.), Scottish Rite, Akron Rubber Group, Sigma Nu, Alpha Phi Omega (pres., commr. of scouting). Avocations: camping, hiking, tennis, golf, photography. Home: 1631 Willow Way Woodstock GA 30188-4649

WEBB, EMILY, retired plant morphologist; b. Charleston, S.C., Apr. 10, 1924; d. Malcolm Syfan and Emily Kirk (Moore) W.; m. John James Rosemond, Apr. 23, 1942 (div. 1953); 1 child, John Kirk; m. Julius Goldberg, Sept. 9, 1954; children: Michael, Judith. AB in Liberal Arts and Sci. with honors, U. Ill., Chgo., 1968, MS in Biol. Scis., 1972, PhD in Biol. Scis., 1985. Undergrad. fellow in bacteriology Med. Coll. S.C., Charleston, 1952-54; teaching asst. U. Ill., Chgo., 1969-72, 77-84, rsch. asst., 1977; teaching fellow W.Va. U., Morgantown, 1974, instr., 1974-75; rsch. in N.Am. bot. needlework art, 1986—. Author: Studies in Several North American Species of Ophioglossum, 1986; translator Nat. Transl. Ctr., Chgo., 1976; contbr. articles to profl. jours. James scholar U. Ill., 1968-69. Mem. DAR. Democrat. Episcopalian. Avocations: garden design, writing, money management. Home and Office: 1356 Mandel Ave Westchester IL 60154-3433

WEBB, ERMA LEE, nurse educator; b. Hitchcock, Okla., Mar. 16, 1933; d. Edward B. and Annabelle G. (Schnell) Haffner; m. James M. Webb, Apr. 4, 1959; children: Scott, Sandee, Steve. BSN, Union Coll., 1957; MSN, Loma Linda (Calif.) U., 1976. Charge and staff nurse pediatrics and surg. units Porter Meml. Hosp., Denver, 1960-68; dir. LPN program Hialeah (Fla.) Hosp., 1969-72; asst. prof. Loma Linda U., 1972-76; assoc. prof. So. Coll. 7th Day Adventists, Orlando, Fla., 1976—, coord. BS program Fla. campuses, 1976—. Mem. Fla. Nurse's Assn., Fla. League Nursing, So. Regional Edn. Bd., Sigma Theta Tau. Home: 3233 Holiday Ave Apopka FL 32703-6635

WEBB, EUGENE, English language educator; b. Santa Monica, Calif., Nov. 10, 1938; m. Marilyn Teruko Domoto, June 4, 1964. B.A., U. Calif., Los Angeles, 1960; M.A., Columbia U., 1962, Ph.D., 1965. Asst. prof. Simon Fraser U., 1965-66; asst. prof. U. Wash., Seattle, 1966-70, assoc. prof., 1970-75, prof. comparative lit. and comparative religion, 1975—. Author: Samuel Beckett: A Study of His Novels, 1970, The Plays of Samuel Beckett, 1972, The Dark Dove: The Sacred and Secular in Modern Literature, 1975, Eric Voegelin: Philosopher of History, 1981, Philosophers of Consciousness: Polanyi, Lonergan, Voegelin, Ricoeur, Girard, Kierkegaard, 1988, The Self Between: From Freud to the New Social Psychology of France, 1993. Active Colloquium on Violence and Religion. Mem. Am. Acad. Religion, Phi Beta Kappa. Episcopalian. Home: 6911 57th Ave NE Seattle WA 98115-7834 Office: U Wash Thomson Hall Jackson Sch Intrnat Studies Box 353650 Seattle WA 98195-3650

WEBB, HOWARD WILLIAM, JR., retired humanities educator, university official; b. Dayton, Ohio, June 23, 1925; s. Howard William and Martha (Brown) W.; m. Joyce Moore Cooper, Nov. 20, 1947; children: Howard William (dec.), Amy Forrest, Sarah Winship. BA, Denison U., 1947; MA, State U. Iowa, 1950, PhD, 1953. Asst. prof. English Central Mo. State Coll., 1953-56, So. Ill. U., Carbondale, 1956-62; assoc. prof. So. Ill. U., 1962-67, prof., 1967-90, dir. grad. studies in English, 1961-67, acting chmn., 1968, chmn., 1968-72, acad. affairs officer on bd. trustees staff, 1974-79, system acad. officer on chancellor's staff, 1979-85, vice chancellor for acad. affairs, 1985-90; interim dir. SIU Press, 1993. Editor: Illinois Prose Writers: An Anthology, 1968; contbr. articles to profl. jours. With USNR, 1943-46. Mem. MLA, Melville Soc. Home: 904 S Oakland St Carbondale IL 62901-2557

WEBB, IGOR MICHAEL, academic administrator; b. Malacky, Czechoslovakia, Nov. 8, 1941; came to U.S., 1952; s. Michael and Josephine (Nash) W.; m. Catherine Lamb (div. 1989); 1 child, Kelly Webb-Lamb; m. Marianne F. Walters, 1990; children: Rebecca Alice, Sarah Elizabeth, Benjamin Oliver. BA, Tufts U., 1963; MA, Stanford U., 1966, PhD, 1971. Asst. prof. English Loyola U. Montreal, Can., 1968-70; asst. prof. English U. Mass., Boston, 1971-77, assoc. prof., 1977-78; chair div. humanities Richmond Coll., London, 1979-86; spl. asst. to pres. Adelphi U., Garden City, N.Y., 1986-87, acting provost, 1987-89, provost, 1989—, sr. v.p., 1992—. Author: From Custom to Capital, 1981, Against Capitulation, 1984. Creative Writing fellow Nat. Endowment for Arts, 1978. Mem. Phi Beta Kappa. Office: Adelphi U Executive Offices Garden City NY 11530

WEBB, JACK M., lawyer; b. Monroe, La., Feb. 23, 1936; s. Sam L. and Lillian Etta (McCowen) W.; m. Diane Adele Waterman, Aug. 22, 1964; children: Julia Lillian Pogue, Kathryn Joy, Samuel Logan. BS in Geology, Centenary Coll. La., 1957; JD, Tulane U., 1960. Bar: La. 1960, Tex. 1962. Atty. Standard Oil Co. Tex., Houston, 1961-66; staff atty. Trunkline Gas. Co., Houston, 1966-71; sr. atty. M.W. Kellogg Co., Houston, 1971-73; sec., asst. gen. counsel Gulf Resources & Chem. Corp., Houston, 1973-78, v.p. govt. rels., adminstrv. asst. to chmn. bd., 1978-82; pres. Jack M. Webb & Assocs., 1983—; U.S. spl. amb. Bolivia, 1985; spl. amb. Finland, 1986, Haiti, 1991, Angola, 1992, Ghana, 1993; hon. consul gen. of Ghana, 1996; bd. dirs. Houston Nat. Bank, Scotia Pacific Holding Co., Employers Indemnity Co. Bd. dirs. U.S. Peace Corps, 1985-86, Nat. Park Found., 1986-92. Capt. U.S. Army, 1960-61. Mem. Tex. Bar Assn., La. Bar Assn. Methodist. Home: 3434 Locke Ln Houston TX 77027-4139

WEBB, JAMES OKRUM, JR., insurance company executive; b. Cleve., Nov. 25, 1931; s. James Okrum and Bessie Ruth (Eubanks) W.; m. Frankie L. Lowe, Feb. 19, 1954; children: Pamela Ruth, Lisa Suzanne. B.A., Morehouse Coll., Atlanta, 1953; M.B.A. in Actuarial Sci, U. Mich., 1955-57. Actuarial asst. Mut. of N.Y., N.Y.C., 1957-62; asst. to pres., actuary Supreme Life Ins. Co. Am., Chgo., 1962-64; v.p., actuary Supreme Life Ins. Co. Am., 1964-66; asst. actuary Health Care Service Corp. (Blue Cross and Blue Shield), Chgo., 1966-68; asst. v.p. product devel. Health Care Service Corp. (Blue Cross and Blue Shield), 1968-69, v.p. product and project mgmt., 1969-73, v.p. finance, asst. treas., 1973-74, v.p. finance, treas., 1974-75, v.p. corp. planning and devel., 1975-79, sr. v.p. planning and devel., 1979-85; pres., chief exec. officer Effective Data Processing, Inc., Oakbrook Terrace, Ill., 1985-94; pres. Managed Dental Care of Can., Toronto, 1987-94; chmn., pres., CEO Dental Network Am., 1985-94; pres. Village of Glencoe, Ill., 1993—; dir. South Shore Nat. Bank Chgo., 1975-87, Harris Bank Glencoe/Northbrook, 1994—, Harris Bankcorp, 1995—, Harris Bankmont, 1995—, Harris Trust and Savings Bank, 1995—; Mem. Ill. Ins. Adv. Com., 1965-67; mem. Ill. Commn. Urban Area Govt., 1970-72. Mem. Glencoe (Ill.) Sch. Bd., 1970-77, pres., 1976-77; pres. Glencoe Human Relations Com., 1970-71; Bd. dirs., mem. budget and finance com. Mid-Am. chpt. ARC, 1974-75; v.p., mem. exec. com., chmn. devel. com. Chgo. Black United Fund, 1974-76; pres., bd. dirs. Chgo. Caucus; founder, past pres. bd. dirs. Home Investments Fund, 1968—; mem. Gov.'s Commn. on Health Assistance Programs; bd. dirs., v.p. Leadership Coun. for Met. Open Cmtys. Served with C.E. AUS, 1953-55. Mem. Am. Acad. Actuaries (dir., treas. 1975-78), Conf. Actuaries in Pub. Practice (assoc.), Alpha Phi Alpha. Clubs: Economics, Executives (Chgo.). Home: 260 Wentworth Ave Glencoe IL 60022-1932

WEBB, JERE MICHAEL, lawyer; b. Portland, Oreg., July 28, 1944; s. Jesse F. Webb and Olive Rea (Coble) Chin; m. Judith A. Hartmann, Sept. 11, 1966. AB with distinction, Stanford U., 1966; JD, U. Chgo., 1969. Law clk. to justice Oreg. Supreme Ct., Salem, 1969-70; with Stoel, Rives, Boley, Portland, 1970—; bd. dirs. Oreg. Law Inst., Pacific Computer Law Inst. Editor Advising Oreg. Businesses, 1994, Marketing and Trade Regulation Law News; contbr. articles to numerous profl. jours. Mem. Oreg. State Bar (bd. govs. 1986-89, chmn. continuing legal edn. com. 1984-85). Home: 5433 SW Vacuna St Portland OR 97219-7260 Office: Stoel Rives & Boley 900 SW 5th Ave Ste 2300 Portland OR 97204-1232

WEBB, JOHN, state supreme court justice; b. Rocky Mount, N.C., Sept. 18, 1926; s. William Devin and Ella (Johnson) W.; m. Martha Carolyn Harris, Sept. 13, 1958; children: Caroline Webb Smart, William Devin. Student, U. N.C., 1946-49; LLB, Columbia U., 1952. Judge Superior Ct., Wilson, N.C., 1971-77, N.C. Ct. Appeals, Raleigh, 1977-86; justice Supreme Ct. N.C., Raleigh, 1986—. Served with USN, 1944-46. Mem. N.C. Bar Assn. Democrat. Baptist. Home: 808 Trinity Dr W Wilson NC 27893-2131 Office: NC Supreme Ct PO Box 1841 Raleigh NC 27602-1841

WEBB, JOHN GIBBON, III, lawyer; b. Flint, Mich., June 1, 1944; s. John Gibbon Jr. and Martha Elizabeth (Sweet) W.; m. Fain Murphey, July 6, 1968; children: Jennifer, Philip, Andrew, Matthew. AB, Davidson Coll., 1966; JD, Vanderbilt U., 1970. Bar: N.Y. 1971, N.J. 1981. Assoc. Curtis, Mallet, Prevost, Colt & Mosle, N.Y.C., 1970-80; gen. counsel, sec. J.M. Huber Corp., Edison, N.J., 1980-95, v.p., 1991-95; ind. counsel Mt. Olive, N.J., 1996—. Lay eucharistic min. Episcopal chs., S.I., N.Y., Millburn, N.J., Rumson, 1972-80, 89-90; trustee Lunch Break, Red Bank, N.J., 1986-89, pres., 1988-89; chair standing com. on constn. and canons Diocese of N.J., 1996-97. Named Vol. of Yr., Jr. League of Monmouth County, Red Bank, 1990. Avocations: jogging, tennis, soccer.

WEBB, KARRIE, professional golfer. Profl. golfer, 1995—. Won Weetabix Women's Brit. Open, 1995, Healthsouth Inaugural, 1996, Sprint Titleholders Championship, 1996, SAFECO Classic, 1996; named Rolex Rookie of Yr., LPGA, 1996. Office: c/o LPGA 100 Internat Golf Dr Daytona Beach FL 32124

WEBB, LAMAR THAXTER, architect; b. Hapeville, Ga., Sept. 13, 1928; s. Eugene Garnette and Sara Ethel (Moore) W.; m. Bettye Jayne Jackson, Dec. 6, 1957; children: Mark Maynard, Robin Lynn. BBA in Fin., U. Ga., 1950; BS, Ga. Inst. Tech., 1959, BArch, 1960. Registered architect, Ga., Fla. Intern architect Abreu and Robeson, Inc., Brunswick, Ga., 1960-66; architect, pres. Webb & Baldwin, Inc., St. Simons Island, Ga., 1966-72; pres., owner Lamar Webb, Arch., Inc., St. Simons Island, 1972—. 1st lt. USAF, 1953-55. Mem. AIA (State bd. dirs. 1985—, v.p. Golden Isles chpt. 1988-89, pres. 1989-90), Am. Soc. Interior Designers, Am. Soc. Landscape Architects (assoc.), Audubon Soc., Nat. Hort. Soc., Humane Soc. (local bd. dirs. 1985-87), Smithsonian Assocs., Coastal Alliance for Arts, Nat. Trust for Hist. Preservation, Ga. Trust for Hist. Preservation, Coastal Ga. Hist. Assn., Met. Mus. Art, Golden Isles Gourmet Club (bd. dirs.) Chien de Rotessieurs, G.I. Chap. Avocations: cooking, drawing, painting, travel. Home: Marsh Oaks Saint Simons GA 31522 Office: 13 Retreat Pl Saint Simons GA 31522-2401

WEBB, LEWIS M., retail executive; b. 1934. Owner Webb's Texaco Svc., Los Alamitos, Calif., 1960-72; pres. Bargain Rent-A-Car Inc., Cerritos, Calif., 1960—, L.M. Webb & Sons, Inc., Mission Viejo, Calif., 1988—; pres., CFO Webb Automotive Group, Inc., Cerritos, Calif., 1989—; pres. Buick Mart Inc., Cerritos, Cerritos Body Works, Inc., Irvine, Calif., Kit Fit Inc., Buena Park, Calif., Lew Webb's Irvine Toyota, Mr. Wheels Inc., Cerritos. Office: Webb Automotive Group Inc 18700 Studebaker Rd Cerritos CA 90703-5335*

WEBB, LOUIS, automotive company executive. CEO Webb Automotive Group, Irvine, CA. Office: Webb Automotive Group 44 Auto Center Dr Irvine CA 92618-2802*

WEBB, MARTY FOX, principal; b. Des Moines, July 15, 1942; d. Joseph John and Jean (Way) Fox; m. Andrew H. Rudolph, Aug. 17, 1963 (div. Jan. 1988); children: Kristen Ann, Kevin Andrew; m. Eugene J. Webb, Nov. 23, 1991. BS, U. Mich., 1964; MEd, Houston Bapt. U., 1982; EdD, U. San Francisco, 1993. Cert. adminstr., Tex., elem. and spl. edn. educator, Mich., Tex. Tchr. spl. edn. Hawthorn Ctr., Northville, Mich., 1964-70; tchr. Bellaire (Tex.) Sch. for Children, 1977-80; dir., owner Ednl. Consulting, Houston, 1979-80; prin. Corpus Christi Sch., Houston, 1980-97; founding head The Monarch Sch., Houston, 1997—; cons. Hawthorn Ctr., Northville, 1970-72, Bellaire Sch. for Young Children, 1974-78; instr. Excellence in Edn. Seminars, Galveston, Houston, 1985—; speaker in field. Recipient Elem. Sch. Recognition award U.S. Dept. Edn., 1989-90, Blue Ribbon Sch. award, 1990, Outstanding Doctoral Student award, 1994. Mem. ASCD, Nat. Cath. Edn. Assn., Child Abuse Prevention Network, U. Mich. Alumni. Avocations: reading, flyfishing, camping, exercise, hiking. Home: 3531 Sun Valley Dr Houston TX 77025-4148 Office: The Monarch Sch 10400 S Post Oak Rd Ste E 328 Houston TX 77035-3304

WEBB, O. GLENN, farm supplies company executive; b. 1936; married. B.S., U. Ill., 1957; Ph.D., So. Ill. U., 1973. With Growmark, Inc., Bloomington, Ill., 1965—, sec., 1968-72, v.p., 1972-80, pres., from 1980, chmn., 1980—, also dir.; trustee, chmn. Am. Inst. Coop.; dir. St. Louis Farm Credit Banks, Farmers Export Co., Nat. Coop. Refinery Assn., Ill. Agr. Leadership Found.; trustee Grad. Inst. Coop. Leadership. Office: Growmark Inc Box 2500 1701 N Towanda Ave Bloomington IL 61701-2040*

WEBB, O(RVILLE) LYNN, physician, pharmacologist, educator; b. Tulsa, Aug. 29, 1931; s. Rufus Aclen and Berla Ophelia (Caudle) W.; m. Joan Liebenheim, June 1, 1954 (div. Jan. 1980); children—Kathryn, Gilbert, Benjamin; m. Jeanne P. Heath, Aug. 24, 1991. B.S., Okla. State U., 1953; M.S., U. Okla., 1961; Ph.D. in Pharmacology, U. Mo., 1966, M.D., 1968. Diplomate Nat. Bd. Med. Examiners, Am. Bd. Family Practice. Research assoc. in pharmacology U. Okla., 1959-61; research fellow NIH, 1962-66; instr. pharmacology U. Mo., Columbia, 1966-68, asst. prof., 1968-69; intern, U. Mo. Med. Center, 1968-69; family practice, New Castle, Ind., 1969-89, med. dir. VA Clinic, Lawton, Okla., 1989-94, Comanche County Hosp., 1994—; clin. assoc. prof. family medicine U. Okla. Coll. Medicine, 1989—; adj. assoc. prof. pharmacology U. Okla. Coll. Medicine, 1989—; mem. U. Okla. Coll. Medicine Admissions Bd., 1995—; mem. staff Henry County Meml. Hosp., New Castle, 1969-89; guest prof. pharmacy and pharmacology Butler U. Coll. Pharmacy, Indpls., 1970-75; owner, dir. Carthage Clinic, 1975-89; clin. assoc. prof. family medicine Ind. U. Coll. Medicine, 1986-89; county physician, jail med. dir. Henry County, Ind., 1976-89. Bd. dirs. Lawton Philharmonic, 1990-95. Recipient Cert. of merit in Pharmacol. and Clin. Med. Research, 1970; Med. Student Research Essay award Am. Acad. Neurology, 1968. Fellow Am. Acad. Family Physicians, Am. Coll. Physician Execs.; mem. AMA (ann. award recognition 1975—), Ind. State Med. Assn.,

Am. Coll. Sports Medicine, AAAS, N.Y. Acad. Sci., Am. Soc. Contemporary Medicine and Surgery, Festival Chamber Music Soc. (bd. dirs. Indpls. 1981-87), Nat. Fraternity Eagle Scouts, Mensa, Phi Sigma, Sigma Xi. Clubs: Columbia, Skyline (Indpls.), Country, Kiwanis. Lodge: Elks. Author: (with Blissitt and Stanaszek, Lea and Febiger) Clinical Pharmacy Practice, 1972; contbr. 30 articles to profl. jours. Home: 30 Quail Creek Dr NW Lawton OK 73501-9026

WEBB, PATRICIA DYAN W., speech and language pathologist, sign language educator; b. Anniston, Ala., July 16, 1948; d. Gary Gene and Jewell Frances (Billingsley) West; m. Thomas Elliott Webb, May 11, 1969; children: Amy Kristin, Michael Elliott. BA in Comm., Winthrop U., 1969, MS in Speech Pathology, 1974; MS in Speech Pathology, U. S.C., 1993, Specialist Cert., 1993. Cert. clin. competence-speech lang. pathologist; specialist in spl. edn. Speech/lang. pathologist York (S.C.) Sch. Dist. 1, 1974-76, St. Nicholas Speech and Hearing Ctr., Greenwood, S.C., 1980-81; speech pathologist Abbeville (S.C.) Sch. Dist. 60, 1981-88; speech/lang. pathologist Greenwood Sch. Dist. 51, Ware Shoals, S.C., 1988—; sign lang. instr. Piedmont Tech. Coll., Greenwood, S.C., 1990—; accents and dialects cons., Greenwood, 1993—; interpretor for deaf Self Meml. Hosp., Greenwood, 1990—; pres. bd. dirs. S.C. Ednl. Found., Columbia; owner/pres. Corp. Comm. Co-author Multi-age language and articulation screening test, 1986; author "How to Tame a Wild Accent" accent modification program; participant (video) Use of Cued Speech With Minimally Impaired Children", 1989. Fundraiser Greenwood County Women's Shelter, 1991—; past pres. Greenwood Bus. and Profl. Women. Mem. Am. Speech and Hearing Assn., S.C. Speech and Hearing Assn., Upper Savannah Consortium of Speech-Lang. Pathologists (co-chair 1991-94), Phi Delta Kappa, Phi Kappa Phi. Avocations: reading, gourmet cooking, playing bridge. Home: 123 Fawnbrook Dr Greenwood SC 29646-7531 Office: Greenwood Sch Dist 51 42 Sparks Ave Ware Shoals SC 29692-1626

WEBB, PATRICK MCIVOR, artist, educator; b. N.Y.C., July 20, 1955; s. Dwight Willson and Nancy Webb. BFA, Md. Inst., 1976; postgrad., Skowhegan Sch., 1977; MFA, Yale U., 1979. lectr. U. Wis. Oshkosh, 1979-81; asst. prof. Cornell U., Ithaca, N.Y., 1981-83; vis. artist Yale U., New Haven, 1985, Brandeis U., Waltham, Mass., 1988, Mpls. Coll. Art and Design, 1989, St. Mary's Coll., 1990, Truro Ctr. for the Arts at Castle Hill, Princetown Art Assn., 1992, R.I. Sch. Design, 1993, Fla. Internat. U., Miami, Cranbrook, Detroit, 1992, 94; instr. N.Y. Acad. Art, Grad. Sch. in Figurative Art, N.Y.C., 1992-94, Swarthmore Coll., 1996, Pratt Inst., 1995—. One man show includes Ripon (Wis.) Coll., 1980, Allen Priebe Gallery, 1981, Kendall Gallery, 1985-89, Alpha Gallery, Boston, 1987-95, Capricorn Galleries, Bethesda, 1988, Forum Gallery, Mpls., 1990, Amos Eno Gallery, N.Y.C., 1993, Mercer Gallery, N.Y.C., 1995; two person shows include East End Galleries, 1987-88, Provincetown Group Gallery, 1992, 93, 450 Broadway Gallery, 1994, Tatistcheff-Rogers Gallery, 1995; exhibited in group shows at Forum Gallery, Mpls., 1989, Robert I. Kahn Gallery, 1989-90, Minn. Mus. of Art, 1989-90, AMMO Exhbn. Space, 1989, Provincetown Art Assn. and Mus., 1990, 91, 92, Clocktowner Gallery, Longwood Gallery, 37 Gallery, 1990, 55 Mercer St., 1990, Claude Gallery, 1991, Daniel Quinn Gallery, 1991, Contemporary Realist Gallery, 1993, Marymount Coll., 1993, Open Space Gallery, 1993, Multi Media Gallery, N.Y.C., 1994, Lowe Art Gallery at the Hudson Guild, N.Y.C., 1994, Leslie-Lohman Gay Art Found., N.Y.C., 1995, Warren Street Gallery, Hudson, 1995, Peter Madero Gallery, 1995, Atrium at Park Avenue, N.Y.C., 1995, Julie Heller Gallery, Georgetown, Mass., 1996, Cortland Jessup Gallery, N.Y.C., 1996-97, Smith Coll., Mass., 1996, St. Mary's Coll., Md., 1996, Blue Mtn. Gallery, N.Y.C., 1996, Parsons Sch. Art, N.Y.C., 1997; work represented in permanent collections, Fred Alger & Co., Boston Pub. Libr., Chem. Bank, Horton & Calamifde, N.Y., Houstatonic Mus., Interneuron, Inc., Boston, Glickenhause & Co., Otis Elevator, Pier-Fine Assocs., Queensboro Coll. Mus., CUNY, Michelle Rosenfeld, Inc., Fine Arts, Sharf Mktg. Group, Shearson Lehman, U. Wis.-Oshkosh. Fellowship Art Matters Inc., 1992, Nat. Endowment for the Arts, 1984, 86, 88, Ford Matching grant, 1978, Skowhegan scholarship, 1977; recipient Ingram Merrill award, 1989, 95. Mem. Provincetown Art Assn., Art Group, Artists Equity, Coll. Art Assn. Avocation: running. Office: PO Box 903 New York NY 10011

WEBB, PAUL, physician, researcher, consultant, educator; b. Cleve., Dec. 2, 1923; s. Monte F. and Barbara (Webb) Bourjaily; m. Eileen Whalen, Mar. 13, 1948; children: Shaun P., Paul S. Webb Womacks. BA, U. Va., 1943, MD, 1946; MS in Physiol., U. Wash., 1951. Asst. prof. physiol. U. Okla. Sch. Medicine, Oklahoma City, 1952-54; chief environ. sect. Aeromed. Lab., Wrights-Patterson AFB, Ohio, 1954-58; prin. assoc. Webb Assocs., Yellow Springs, Ohio, 1959-82; vis. scientist INSERM, Paris, 1983; vis. prof. U. Limburg, Maastricht, The Netherlands, 1986, U. Uppsala, Sweden, 1988-89; clin. prof. Wright State U. Sch. Medicine, Dayton, Ohio, 1980—; cons. aerospace and undersea medicine, Yellow Springs, Ohio, 1958-90; cons. energy balance and thermal physiology, Yellow Springs, 1980—. Author: Human Calorimeters, 1985; contbr. articles to profl. jours. Village councilman Village of Yellow Springs, Ohio, 1969-75; mem. Air Force Scientific Adv. Bd., Washington, 1984-88. Recipient Ely award Human Factors Soc., 1972. Fellow Aerospace Med. Assn. (Aerospace Indsl. Life Scis. Assn. award 1969), Am. Inst. Med. and Biol. Enging.; mem. Am. Physiol. Soc., Am. Soc. for Clin. Nutrition, Undersea Med. Soc. (oceaneering internat. award 1979, pres. 1980-81). Home and Office: 370 Orton Rd Yellow Springs OH 45387-1321

WEBB, RALPH LEE, mechanical engineering educator; b. Parker, Kans., 1934; m. Sylvia Apple; children: Janet, Laura. BSME (with honors), Kans. State U., 1957; MME, Rensselaer Poly. Inst., 1962; PhD, U. Minn., 1969. Registered profl. engr., Wis. Instr. mech. engring. Kans. State U., 1957; engring. maintenance officer USAF, Nellis AFB, Nev., 1957-59; engr. Knolls Atomic Power Lab., Schenectady, N.Y., 1960-62; mgr. heat transfer rsch. Trane Co., La Crosse, Wis., 1963-77; assoc. prof. mech. engring. Pa. State U., University Park, 1977-81, prof., 1981—; lectr., cons. in field; condr. various workshops. Author: Principles of Enhanced Heat Transfer, 1994; contbr. articles to profl. jours. Recipient Hall-Thermotank gold medal Inst. Refrigeration, 1989; rsch. grantee NSF, 1978-80, 83-86, Dept. Energy, 1979-82, 90-92, Internat. Copper Assn., 1984—, EPRI, 1988-92, Improved Radiators Studies Assn., 1988—, Wolverine, 1988-89, York Internat., 1988-89, 94—, Olin Brass Corp., 1992—, Marlow Industries, 1994—, Showa Aluminum Corp., 1992—, Thermo King Corp., 1994—, LG Electronics, Inc., 1995—. Fellow ASME (chmn. heat transfer divsn., honors and awards com. 1987-90, nat. nominating com. 1983-86, heat transfer divsn. rep. to basic engring. group 1980-86, exec. com. heat transfer divsn. 1976-81, tech. editor Jour. Heat Transfer 1972-76, nat. heat transfer conf. coordinating com. 1972-77, Outstanding Svc. award 1973-76, 82, Heat Transfer Meml. award 1987); mem. AIChE, ASHRAE (tech. editor Heat Transfer Engring. 1978—, Jour. Heat Recovery 1981—, editor-in-chief Jour. Enhanced Heat Transfer 1992—, Jour. Paper award 1985). Office: Pa State Univ Dept Mech Engring University Park PA 16802

WEBB, RICHARD ALAN, physicist; b. L.A., Sept. 10, 1946; married; 2 children. BA, U. Calif., Berkeley, 1968; MS, U. Calif., San Diego, 1970, PhD, 1973. Rsch. assoc. U. Calif., San Diego, 1973-75; from asst. to assoc. rsch. physicist Argonne Nat. Lab., 1975-78; mem., mgr. rsch. staff T.J. Watson Ctr. IBM, Yorktown Heights, 1978-93; Alford Ward chaired prof. semicondr. physics, dept. physics Ctr. Superconductivity Rsch., Univ. Md., College Park, 1993—. Recipient Simon Mem prize, 1989. Fellow Am. Physics Soc. (Oliver E. Buckley condensed Malter Physics prize 1992); mem. Nat. Acad. Sci. Achievements include research in macroscopic quantum tunneling in Josephson junctions at low temperatures, investigations of the Aharonov-Bohm effect and universal conductance fluctuations in very small semiconducting and normal metal rings, measurement of temperature, magnetic field and Fermi Engery dependencies of the conduction process of very small Si MOSFET devices in both insulating and metallic regimes. Office: U Md Dept Physics College Park MD 20742

WEBB, RICHARD C., engineering company executive; b. Omaha, Sept. 2, 1915; m. Virginia; 1 son. B.S.E.E., U. Denver, 1937, DSc (hon.), 1996; M.S.E.E., Purdue U., 1944, Ph.D., 1951. Registered profl. engr., Colo. Traffic engr. Mountain States Telephone and Telegraph Co., Denver, 1937-39; research engr. RCA Labs. Div., Princeton, N.J., 1945-53; pres., founder, tech. dir. Colo. Research Corp. (subs. Carrier Corp.), Syracuse, N.Y., 1956-61; pres., founder. tech. dir. Colo. Instruments, Inc., Broomfield, Colo., 1961-71; pres., gen. mgr. Colo. Instruments div. Mohawk Data Scis. Corp., Utica, N.Y.C., 1971-73; pres. Webb Enging. Co. (name changed to Data Ray Corp.), Boulder, Colo., 1973-85; vis. lectr. U. Colo., 1962-82; prof. elec. engring. U. Denver, 1953-56, Iowa State Coll., 1950. Contbr. articles to profl. jours. Recipient Disting. Enging. Alumnus award Purdue U., 1970, Profl. Achievement award U. Denver Alumni Assn., 1983, Outstanding Elec. Engr. award Purdue U., 1992. Fellow IEEE; mem. Soc. Motion Picture and TV Engrs., Acoustical Soc. Am., Inst. Aerospace Scis., Am. Ordnance Assn., Western Electronics Mfrs. Assn. (past v.p., dir.), Sigma Xi, Tau Beta Pi, Eta Kappa Nu. Patentee in field. Home: PO Box 3078 Estes Park CO 80517-3078

WEBB, RICHARD GILBERT, financial executive; b. Tulsa, May 11, 1932; s. William Leslie and Cora (Kroshus) W.; m. Patricia S. Wagdin, Apr. 13, 1957 (div. Sept. 1974); children: Catherine, Andrea, Nicholas; m. Judith A. Burke, Jan. 12, 1980; stepchildren: Mara, Karen, Jennifer, Christopher. Student, U. Okla., 1950-52; BBA, So. Meth. U., 1954; MBA, Harvard U., 1956. CPA, Okla. Mgmt. cons. McKinsey & Co., N.Y.C., 1959-61; planning analyst Mobil Oil Co., N.Y.C., 1961-64; sub controller, treas. ITT, N.Y.C., 1964-66; v.p., mgr. corp. devel. Ill. Tool Works, Chgo., 1966-70; v.p. planning, treas., chief fin. officer Interstate Bakers, Kansas City, Mo., 1970-78; v.p., treas., chief fin. officer Gen. Host Corp., Stamford, Conn., 1979-81; v.p., treas., chief fin. officer Grolier, Inc., Danbury, Conn., 1981-89, fin. cons., 1989—; cons. to State Ill., Springfield, 1969; adj. prof. fin. dept. We. Conn. State U., 1984; adv. bd. Conn. Bank and Trust Co., Danbury, 1986-88. Fundraiser, bd. dirs. United Way, Danbury, Conn., 1982-86; bd. dirs. Danbury YMCA, 1983-89, treas., 1985-87, chmn. bd. dirs., 1987-89, chmn. bd. trustees, 1981-91, trustee, 1991—; mem. bd. advisors dept. fin. U. Conn., 1984-88; trustee Conn. Pub. Expenditure Coun., 1986-88. 1st lt. U.S. Army, 1956-59. Mem. AICPA, Okla. Soc. CPAs, Greater Danbury C. of C. (bd. dirs. 1985-89, treas. 1986-88, chmn. bd.dirs. 1988-89), Harvard Club (N.Y.C.). Republican. Avocations: swimming, reading, antiques, golf. Home and Office: 37 Saddle Ridge Rd Pound Ridge NY 10576-1111

WEBB, RICHARD STEPHEN, manufacturing executive; b. Nottingham, Eng., Aug. 3, 1944; came to U.S., 1988; s. Sydney and Kathleen Florence (Day) W.; m. Pamela Anne Fowlds, Sept. 3, 1966 (dec. July 1976); children: Jane, Simon, Elizabeth; m. Anne Hessel, Aug. 19, 1978 (div. 1997); children: Clare, Penelope. BSc, U. Sheffield, Eng., 1966, PhD, 1970. Rsch. scientist U. Sheffield, 1966-69; tech. asst. C.E. Ramsden & Co. Ltd., Stoke-on-Trent, Eng., 1969-74; mktg. exec. Magnesium Elektron Ltd., Manchester, Eng., 1974-80, mktg. mgr., 1980-84; bus. devel. mgr. Alcan Aluminium, Mont., Can., 1984-88; bus. mgr. Alanx Products Inc., Newark, Del., 1988-91; pres. Alanx Products Inc., Newark, 1992-95, Lanxide Coated Products divsn. Lanxide Performance Materials, Newark, Del., 1995-97; dir. sales and mktg. Electro-Sci. Labs., Inc., King of Prussia, Pa., 1997—; chmn. Del. Mfg. Alliance, 1993-95. Contbr. articles to profl. jours. Fellow Inst. Materials U.K.; mem. Am. Ceramic Soc., Can. Ceramic Soc., Am. Chem. Soc. Avocations: marathon and road running. Office: Electro-Sci Labs Inc 416 E Church Rd King Of Prussia PA 19406

WEBB, RICHMOND JEWEL, professional football player; b. Dallas, Jan. 11, 1967. BA in Indsl. Distbn., Texas A&M. Offensive tackle Miami Dolphins, 1990—. Named NFL Rookie of Yr., Sporting News, 1990, Sporting News All-Pro Team, 1992; selected to Pro Bowl, 1990-93, 96. Office: Miami Dolphins 7500 SW 30th St Miami FL 33314*

WEBB, ROBERT KIEFER, history educator; b. Toledo, Nov. 23, 1922; s. Charles Ellis and Melva Marie (Kiefer) W.; m. Patty Bradburn Shull, Dec. 28, 1957; children: Emily, Margaret. A.B., Oberlin Coll., 1947; A.M., Columbia U., 1948, Ph.D., 1951; postgrad., London Sch. Econs., 1949-51. Instr. history Wesleyan U., 1951-53; from asst. prof. to prof. history Columbia U., 1953-70; editor Am. Hist. Rev., Washington, 1968-75; prof. history U. Md. Baltimore County, 1975-89, Presdl. Rsch. prof., 1989-93, acting vice-chancellor for acad. affairs, 1978-79, prof. emeritus, 1993—; vis. professorial fellow Victorian Studies Ctr. U. Leicester, Eng., 1967; mem. Inst. Advanced Study, Princeton, 1982-83; vis. fellow Australian Nat. U., 1986, Humanities Rsch. Ctr. Australian Nat. U., 1996; fellow Ctr. for History of Freedom, Washington U., 1988; assoc. fellow Harris Manchester Coll. Oxford, Eng., 1988—; Sorenson rsch. fellow St. Catherine's Coll. Oxford, 1992; hon. fellow Australian Acad. Humanities, 1995—. Author: The British Working-Class Reader, 1790-1848: Literacy and Social Tension, 1955, Harriet Martineau, a Radical Victorian, 1960, Modern England, from the Eighteenth Century to the Present, 2d edit., 1980, (with Peter Gay) Modern Europe, 1973; editor: bull. AAUP, 1975-78, Academe, 1979-81. Served with AUS, 1943-46. Fulbright scholar, 1950-51; Guggenheim fellow, 1959-60, 73-74, Am. Coun. Learned Socs. fellow, 1966-67; NEH rsch. grantee, 1978-80, 85-88. Democrat. Club: Cosmos (Washington). Home: 3309 Highland Pl NW Washington DC 20008-3234

WEBB, RODNEY SCOTT, judge; b. Cavalier, N.D., June 21, 1935; s. Chester and Aylza (Martin) W.; m. Betty M. Lykken, Aug. 31, 1957; children: Sharon, Crystal, Todd, Wade, Susan. BS, U. N.D., 1957, JD, 1959. Bar: N.D. 1959, U.S. Dist. Ct. N.D. 1965, U.S. Ct. Appeals (8th cir.) 1981. Assoc. Ringsak, Webb, Rice & Metelman, Grafton, N.D., 1959-81; state's atty. Walsh County, Grafton, 1966-74; mcpl. judge City of Grafton, 1975-81; spl. asst. atty. gen. State of N.D., 1970-81; U.S. atty. Dist. of N.D., Fargo, 1981-87, judge U.S. Dist. Ct. N.D., 1987—, now chief judge. Col. JAG, N.D. Army N.G., ret. Mem. N.D. State Attys. Assn. (past pres.). Lutheran. Office: US Dist Ct PO Box 3164 Fargo ND 58108-3164*

WEBB, THEODORE STRATTON, JR., aerospace scientist, consultant; b. Oklahoma City, Mar. 4, 1930; s. Theodore S. and Helen (Klabzuba) W.; m. Cuba Evans, Sept. 2, 1952; children: Theodore S. III, Kelly Elizabeth. BS in Physics, Okla. U., 1951; PhD in Physics and Math., Calif. Inst. Tech., 1955. Engr. Ft. Worth div. Gen. Dynamics, 1955-62, program mgr., 1962-69, dir. aero. tech., 1969-75, v.p. rsch. and engring., 1975-80, v.p. F-16 programs, 1980-89; pvt. practice cons. Ft. Worth, 1989—; engring. adv. bd. U. Okla., Norman, 1983—; mem. aerospace coun. Soc. Automotive Engrs., 1975-81; bd. dirs. Lear Astronics Inc. Bd. mem. Engring. Found. U. Tex., Austin, 1975-81, Found. for Sci. and Engring. So. Meth. U., Dallas, 1974-81, Tarrant County Day Care Assn., Ft. Worth, 1975-80, 89-96; All Saints Episcopal Hosp., 1989—, Goodwill Industries of Tarrant Country, 1989-96. Mem. AAAS, Am. Phys. Soc., Rivercrest Country Club. Home: 4901 Westridge Ave Fort Worth TX 76116-8222 Office: 6100 Southwest Blvd Ste 250 Fort Worth TX 76109-3964

WEBB, THEORA GRAVES, public relations executive; b. Norfolk, Va., July 21, 1941; d. Lemuel and Theora (Weaver) Graves. BA, Wilson Coll., 1962. Chmn. modern langs. dept. William Henry High Sch., Dover, Del., 1962-64; abstractor-indexer, Rockville, Md., 1966-67; owner RML Translations, Acton, Mass., 1969-70; asst. dir. communications and pub. relations, acting dir. publs. br., spl. asst. to dep. supt., cons.-expert, instr. adult edn. pub. schs. D.C., 1971-78; regional coordinator, cons. Nat. Energy Edn. Day, Cedar Rapids, Iowa, 1979; projects mgr. U.S. Com. for Energy Awareness, Washington, 1980-83; dir. office pub. affairs Internat. Trade Adminstrn., U.S. Dept. Commerce, Washington, 1983-86; pres. HSW Comm., 1986-92; dir. pub. affairs Duracell North Atlantic Group, Bethel, Conn., 1992—; bd. dirs. U. Found. of Western Conn.; bd. advisors Ctr. for Corp. Cmty. Rels. Boston Coll., 1996—. Mem. energy and econ. devel. com. nat. NAACP, 1980-83, energy task force Nat. Conf. Black Mayors, 1982-83; adv. council vol. svcs. Dist. 7 Dept. Correctional Svcs., 1979-80; adv. bd. Linn County Jail Chaplaincy, 1979-80, Cedar Rapids YWCA, 1978-80; mem. bd. dirs. Wilson Coll., 1992-94; bd. dirs. Young Audiences of Conn., 1995—. Mem. Am. Assn. Blacks in Energy, Md. State Right to Read Task Force, Nat. Sch. Pub. Rels. Assn., Nat. Assn. Women's Bus. Owners. Coun. of 100, Nat. Press Club. Home: 2 Davis Ct Martinsville NJ 08836-2314 Office: Duracell Internat Inc Berkshire Corporate Park Bethel CT 06801

WEBB, THOMAS EVAN, biochemistry educator; b. Edmonton, Alta., Can., Mar. 4, 1932; came to U.S., 1970, naturalized, 1978; s. Donald John and Sarah Jane (McMinis) W.; m. Ellen Adair Armstrong, Sept. 4, 1961; children: Linda Carol, Sharon Laura. B.S., U. Alta., 1955, M.S., 1957; Ph.D., U. Toronto, 1961. Rsch. assoc. Nat. Rsch. Coun., Ottawa, Can., W. Wis., Madison, 1963-65; 1961-63; asst. prof. biochemistry U. Man. (Can.), Winnipeg, 1965-66; asst. prof. McGill U., Montreal, Que., Can., 1966-70, acting dir. cancer unit., 1969-70; assoc. prof. med. biochemistry Ohio State U., Columbus, 1970-74, prof., 1974-95, prof. emeritus, 1995—. Contbr. numerous articles on biochemistry of cancer to profl. jours. Grantee NIH/Nat. Cancer Inst., 1970-95; fellow Air Force Office Sci. Rsch., 1982. Mem. Am. Soc. Biol. Scientists, Am. Assn. Cancer Research, AAAS, Sigma Xi. Home: 270 Naples Cove Unit 3406 Naples FL 34110 Office: Ohio State U Dept Med Biochemistry 1645 Neil Ave Columbus OH 43210-1218

WEBB, THOMAS GEORGE, aircraft manufacturing engineer; b. N.Y.C., Oct. 5, 1944; s. Charles George and Mary-Louise (Hollaman) W.; m. Laurie Jean Dallmer. BS, N.Y. Inst. Tech., 1979; MA, Calif. State U., 1994. Prodn. control mgr. Bischoff Chem. Co. Inc., Hicksville, N.Y., 1968-71; fin. analyst Dun & Bradstreet, Rockville Centre, N.Y., 1971-74; instr. Human Resources Ctr., Albertson, N.Y., 1975-76; indsl. engr. Alarm Device Mfg. Co. Inc., Syosset, N.Y., 1977-80; sr. indsl. engr. Fairchild Republic Co. Inc., Farmingdale, N.Y., 1980-82; mfg. engr. Grumman Aerospace, Bethpage, N.Y., 1983-85; engring. cons. Brunswick Nuclear Project, Southport, N.C., 1985-86; pres. T&L Mgmt. Co. Inc., Holden Beach, N.C., 1987—; owner Tom Webb's Seminars; cons. Deknatel Inc., Floral Park, N.Y., 1977-78, U.S. Dept. Energy, Savannah River Site, Aiken, S.C., 1993; sr. indsl. engr. Grumman Electronics Systems, 1987; indsl. engring. cons. Wilson Concepts of Fla., 1987; engring. cons. McDonnell Douglas Astronautics Co., Huntington Beach, Calif., 1988-89, FL Aerospace, Greenwood, S.C., 1989, Douglas Aircraft Co., Long Beach, Calif., 1990. Served with U.S. Army, 1966-68, Vietnam. Mem. AIAA, Inst. Indsl. Engrs. (sr.), Wilmington Engrs. Club. Episcopalian. Avocations: swimming, boating, gardening, woodworking. Home: 151 Marlin Dr Supply NC 28462-1803

WEBB, THOMAS IRWIN, JR., lawyer; b. Toledo, Sept. 16, 1948; s. Thomas Irwin and Marcia Davis (Winters) W.; m. Polly S. DeWitt, Oct. 11, 1986; 1 child, Elisabeth Hurst. BA, Williams Coll., 1970; postgrad., Boston U., 1970-71; JD, Case Western Res. U., 1973. Bar: Ohio. Assoc. Shumaker, Loop & Kendrick, Toledo, 1973-79, ptnr., 1979—, chmn. corp. law dept., 1992-94, mgmt. com., 1994—; dir. Calphalon Corp., York Oldsmobile, Inc. Coun. mem. Village of Ottawa Hills, Ohio, Divsn. Securities, 1979—, adv. com.; trustee Kiwanis Youth Found. of Toledo, 1982—; dir. Toledo Area Regional Transit Authority, 1989-91; trustee Arts Commn. Greater Toledo, 1993—, exec. com., 1994—, v.p., 1994-96, pres., 1996—; trustee Jr. Achievement of Northwestern Ohio, Inc., 1992—, Lourdes Coll. Found., 1995—. Mem. ABA, Ohio Bar Assn. (corp. law com. 1989—), Toledo Bar Assn., Northwestern Ohio Alumni Assn. of Williams Coll. (pres. 1974-83), Toledo-Rowing Found. (trustee 1985—), Toledo Area C. of C. (trustee 1991—, exec. com. 1993—), Order of Coif, Crystal Downs Country Club, Toledo Country Club, The Toledo Club (trustee 1984-90, pres. 1987-90), Williams Club N.Y. Republican. Episcopalian. Office: Shumaker Loop & Kendrick 1000 Jackson St Toledo OH 43624-1515

WEBB, THOMPSON, geological sciences educator, researcher; b. L.A., Jan. 13, 1944; s. Thompson and Diana (Stimson) W.; m. Joan Moscovitch Webb, Aug. 10, 1969; children: Rosanna, Sarah. BS with honors, Swarthmore Coll., 1966; PhD, U. Wis., 1971. Rsch. assoc. U. Mich., Ann Arbor, 1970-72; asst. prof. geol. sci. Brown U., Providence, 1972-75, assoc. prof., 1975-84, prof., 1984—; vis. prof. U. Wis., Madison, summer 1976; chmn. paleoclimate adv. panel NOAA, 1994; chmn. terrestrial earth sys. history com. NSF, 1996. Author: (book chpt.) Late Quat. Environments of the US, vol. 2, 1983; editor: (book) Vegetation History, 1988 (publ.) Geographie Physique et Quat. v. 39, no. 2, 1985, Global Climates Since the Last Glacial Maximum, 1993. Interviewer Swarthmore Coll., Providence, 1972—, pres. 30th ReunionClass of 1966; sec. Seekonk Land Trust, 1995—. NSF postdoctoral fellow, 1970; vis. fellow Clare Hall, U. Cambridge, Eng., 1977; CIRES fellow U. Colo., Boulder, 1988; Bullard fellow Harvard U., 1995. Fellow AAAS; mem. Am. Meteorol. Soc. Office: Brown U Dept Geol Sci 324 Brook St Providence RI 02912-9019

WEBB, TODD (CHARLES CLAYTON WEBB), photographer, writer; b. Detroit, Sept. 15, 1905; s. Joseph Franklin and Bertha (Hollingshead) W.; m. Lucille Minqueau, Sept. 10, 1949. Student, U. Toronto, Ont., Can., 1924-25. Free-lance photographer Standard Oil, N.Y.C., 1947-48, Marshall Plan, Paris, 1948-52, UN, N.Y.C., Togoland, Ghana, Sudan, Italian Somaliland, Tanganyika, Kenya., Rhodesia, Zanzibar, 1956-60, Santa Fe, N.Mex., 1961-71, St. Restitut, Provence, France, 1971-74; free-lance photographer Avon, Eng., 1974-75, Bath, Maine, 1975—. Photographer Tex. Homes of 19th Century, 1968, Pub. Tex. Bldgs., 1974, Georgia O'Keeffe: The Artist and Her Landscape, 1986, photos of N.Y.C., 1986, Paris, 1987; author: (Western U.S. history) Gold Strikes and Ghost Towns, 1961, The Gold Rush Trail and the Road to Oregon, 1963; (memoirs) Looking Back, 1991; film Honest Vision, A Portrait of Todd Webb by Huey released 1996. With USN, 1942-45, PTO. Guggenheim fellow, 1955, 56; NEA grantee for Photography, 1979. Democrat. Mem. Soc. of Friends. Avocation: traveling. Home and Studio: 120 North St Bath ME 04530-2224 also: Betsy Evans Sea View Cape Elizabeth ME 04107

WEBB, VERONICA, fashion model, journalist; b. Detroit, Feb. 25, 1965; d. Leonard Douglas and Marion (Stewart) W. Student, New Sch. Social Rsch., 1983; signed with, Ford Models, Inc., N.Y.C., 1992—. Contbg. editor, columnist Paper Mag., 1989—; contbg. editor features column Interview Mag., 1990—; spokesmodel Revlon, 1992-96. First featured on cover of Vogue, 1988; appearances include (films) Jungle Fever, 1991, Malcolm X, 1992, For Love or Money, 1993, Catwalk, 1995. First African-Am. to receive exclusive cosmetics contract. Mem. Lifebeat (bd. dirs. 1994—). Office: NS Bienstalk 1740 Broadway Fl 24 New York NY 10019-4315 Address: 575 Broadway New York NY 10012*

WEBB, WATT WETMORE, physicist, educator; b. Kansas City, Mo., Aug. 27, 1927; s. Watt Jr. and Anna (Wetmore) W.; m. Page Chapman, Nov., 1950; children: Watt III, Spahr C., Bucknell C. BS, MIT, 1947, ScD, 1955. Rsch. engr., asst. dir. rsch. Union Carbide Metals Co., Niagara Falls, N.Y., 1947-52, 55-61; prof. applied physics Cornell U., Ithaca, N.Y., 1961—, dir. Sch. Applied and Enging. Physics, 1983-88; dir. NIH-NSF Resource Biophysical Imaging and Opto-electronics, 1988—, dir. Biophysics Program, 1991-94; NIH scholar-in-residence Fogarty Internat. Ctr. for Advanced Study, 1988-92; mem. adv. panels Materials Adv. Bd., 1958-59, 63-64, NSF, 1974—; co-chair NAS panel on sci. interfaces and tech. applications, Physics Through the 90s, 1983-86; bd. dirs., exec. com. Cornell Rsch. Found., 1983—. Mem. adv. com. Physics Today, 1991—; assoc. editor Phys. Rev. Letters, 1975-91; mem. editorial bd. Biophysics Jour., 1975-78, mem. publ. com., 1976-83; contbr. 200 articles to profl. jours. Guggenheim fellow, 1974-75. Fellow AAAS, Am. Phys. Soc. (chmn. 1988-89, exec. com. divsn. biol. physics 1975-77, Biol. Physics prize 1991), Am. Inst. Med. and Biol. Engrs. (founding 1992); mem. Nat. Acad. Engring., Biophys. Soc. (mem. coun. 1972-75, 82-85), Nat. Acad. Scis., Am. Soc. Cell Biology, Am. Soc. Gen. Physiology, Optical Soc. Am., Ithaca Yacht Club, N.Y. Yacht Club. Achievements include patents in optical instruments, two photon laser microscopy, fluorescent probes, microcrystals, welding technology. Office: Cornell U Clark Hall Ithaca NY 14853

WEBB, WATTS RANKIN, surgeon; b. Columbia, Ky., Sept. 8, 1922; s. Frank Elbert and Susie Josephine (Rankin) W.; m. Frances Luella Cooke, Aug. 19, 1944; children: Andrew Michael, Paul Alan, Harvey Elbert, Gordon Lewis. BA, U. Miss., 1942; MD, Johns Hopkins U., 1945. Diplomate Am. Bd. Surgery, Am. Bd. Thoracic Surgery, Am. Bd. Surg. Critical Care. Intern Barnes Hosp., St. Louis, 1945-48; resident in surgery VA Hosp., Biloxi, Miss., 1946-48; resident in gen. and thoracic surgery Barnes Hosp., 1948-52; chief surgeon Miss. State Sanatorium, 1952-63; instr. surgery U. Miss., 1955-56, asst. prof. surgery, 1956-58, prof., 1958-63; prof., chmn. div. thoracic and cardiovascular surgery U. Tex. Southwestern Med. Sch., Dallas, 1964-70; prof., chmn. dept. surgery SUNY Upstate Med. Center, Syracuse, 1970-77; prof. surgery Tulane U., New Orleans, 1977-93, La. State U., New Orleans, 1993—; chmn. dept. Tulane U., New Orleans, 1977-89. Author: Pulmonary Problems in Surgery, 1974, Surgery in Acute Coronary Problems, 1974, Aneurysms, 1983, Cardiovascular Emergencies, 1986, Atlas of Pulmonary Resections, 1988, (with others) Surgical Management for Chest Injuries, Vol. VII, 1990; editorial bd.: Annals of Thoracic Surgery, 1968-79, Surg. Rounds, 1978-82, Surgery Clinics, 1980-82, Microcirculation, 1983-84,

Brit. Jour. Surgery, 1981-89; contbr. over 450 articles to profl. jours. Recipient award Hadassah, 1965, Knockers Soc. Outstanding Tchr. award SUNY Upstate Med. Ctr., 1972, Owl Club Clin. Tchr. of Yr. award Tulane U. Med. Sch., 1978, 86, 88-93, Gloria P. Walsh award for best tchr. in Med. Sch., 1992, Aesculapian Tchr. of Yr. award La. State U., 1995, 96. Fellow ACS, Am. Coll. Chest Physicians; mem. AMA, Am. Assn. Thoracic Surgery, Am. Coll. Cardiology, Am. Fedn. Clin. Research, Am. Heart Assn. (Silver medal 1963), Am. Physiol. Soc., Am. Surg. Assn., Am. Thoracic Soc., Halsted Soc., La. Med. Soc., Orleans Parish Med. Soc., New Orleans Surg. Soc., Societe International de Chirurgie, Soc. Cryobiology, Soc. Thoracic Surgeons, Soc. Univ. Surgeons, Southeastern Surg. Congress, So. Med. Assn., So. Soc. Clin. Research, So. Surg. Assn. (Shipley medal 1961), So. Thoracic Soc., So. Thoracic Surg. Assn., Surg. Assn. La., Surg. Biology Club II, Internat. Soc. Heart Transplantation, Gulf Coast Vascular Soc., Sigma Xi, Alpha Omega Alpha, Pi Kappa Pi, Beta Beta Beta, Alpha Epsilon Delta. Methodist. Home: 21 Park Island Dr New Orleans LA 70122-1228 Office: La State U Dept Surgery 1542 Tulane Ave New Orleans LA 70112-2825

WEBB, WELLINGTON E., mayor; BA in Edn. Colo. State Coll., 1964, MA in Edn. Univ. No. Colo., 1970; teacher, 1964-76; elected Colo. House of Reps., 1972, 74, 76; regional dir. HEW, 1977-81, governor's cabinet, 1981-87; elected auditor City of Denver, 1987-91, mayor, 1991—. Chmn. U.S. Conf. of Mayor's Task Forces on Violence, 1993—. Office: Office of Mayor City & County Bldg Rm 350 1437 Bannock St Denver CO 80202-5308*

WEBB, WILLIAM DUNCAN, lawyer, investment executive; b. Dayton, Ohio, Feb. 14, 1930; s. Herbert Henry and Dorothy (Chamberlain) W.; m. Nancy Helen Regester, June 12, 1953; children: Joseph Chamberlain (dec.), Mary Helen, Nancy Katherine, Sarah Elizabeth, Lucy Ellen. AB, U. Mich., 1952, JD, 1956. Bar: Mo. 1956, Kans. 1958, U.S. Supreme Ct. 1969. Assoc. Stinson, Mag, Thomson, McEvers & Fizzell, Kansas City, Mo., 1956-58; sec. Kansas City (Mo.) Power & Light Co., 1960-78, asst. treas., 1969-78, asst. v.p. communications, 1978-79, asst. v.p. fed. affairs, 1979-84; legal counsel Fellowship of Christian Athletes. Mem. city coun. Roeland Park, Kans., 1960-62; chmn. Kansas City Myasthenia Gravis Found., 1965-67; bd. dirs. Boys Club of Kansas City, Mo., 1969-74, Greater Kansas City YMCA, Greater Kansas City chpt. ARC; chmn. bd. councilors Avila Coll., 1969-70; trustee, asst. sec., 1970-89; bd. dirs. Rural Water Dist. # 7, Johnson County, Kans., 1992-94. Mem. Internat. Maine-Anjou Assn. (dir., sec.-treas. 1969-76), Theta Delta Chi, Phi Alpha Delta. Presbyterian. Home: 37000 W 155th St Gardner KS 66030-9617 Office: 7500 College Blvd Ste 225 Overland Park KS 66210-4035

WEBB, WILLIAM JOHN, public relations counsel; b. Chgo., Jan. 9, 1922; s. Archibald Roy and Nina Spencer (Brown) W.; m. Madeline Betty Calkins, Oct. 24, 1989. BA, U. Calif., L.A., 1947; MA in Polit. Sci. and Pub. Adminstrn., Am. U., 1976. Spl. projects, plans and policy staff officer CIA, Washington, 1951-58; press sec., spl. asst. Senator William Knowland of Calif., Washington, 1958-59; spl. asst. pub. info. Army Chief R & D, 1959-63; spl. asst. Senator John Tower of Tex., Washington, 1963-64; spl. asst. to asst. dir. inspections and spl. projects OEO, 1965, spl. asst. regional rels., sr. pub. affairs officer, 1973-74; spl. asst. pub. affairs, chief public info. Navy Seabees Naval Facilities Engring. Command, Washington, 1966-69; dir. spl. projects Maritime Adminstrn., 1969-70; spl. asst. regional liaison-coordination Office of Sec. Dept. Transp., 1970-71; dir. congl. and pub. affairs Nat. Reading Ctr., 1972-73; spl. asst. communication liaison-coordination White House, Washington, 1974; regional and intergovtl. liaison officer Office of Adminstr. EPA, 1975; staff specialist in indsl. rels. communication Fed. Energy Adminstrn., Washington, 1976; sr. public affairs officer, dir. Pubs. Health Care Financing Adminstrn. HHS, 1976-79; sr. staff officer intergovt. and regional affairs Office of Sec. Dept. Energy, 1980-81; dep. spl. asst. public affairs to Sec. of Labor, 1981. Mem. Pub. Rels. Soc. Am. (Nat. Capital chpt. bd. dirs. 1963, 65-67, 69-70, 72, 74, 76-77, 79, Silver Anvil award 1968), Nat. Assn. Govt. Communicators (bd. dirs. 1977-78, pres. Nat. Capital chpt. 1977-78, Blue Pencil awards), Mensa, Nat. Press Club, Am. Legion, Kappa Sigma. Home: 2124 Powhatan St Falls Church VA 22043-1910

WEBB, WILLIAM LOYD, JR., army officer; b. Mineral Wells, Tex., Sept. 30, 1925; s. William Loyd and Francis (Mayer) W.; m. Muriel Emma Hinson, Dec. 27, 1947; children: George Sidney, William Loyd III, Lucinda Adrienne, Alicia Muriel. Student, Tex. A & M Coll., 1942-44; B.S., U.S. Mil. Acad., 1947; M.A., U. Pa., 1958. Commd. 2d lt. U.S. Army, 1947, advanced through grades to maj. gen., 1974; co. comdr. Korea, 1950, Ft. Riley, Kans., 1951-52, Germany, 1953-54; assoc. prof. English U.S. Mil. Acad. West Point, N.Y., 1958-61; regimental comdr., dep. comdt. of cadets U.S. Mil. Acad., 1969-71; squadron comdr. 14th Armored Cavalry Germany, 1963-64; mem. faculty U.S Army War Coll., 1965-68; comdr. support command 1st Inf. Div. Vietnam, 1969; dep. comdg. gen. Ft. Ord, Calif., 1971-73; ops. officer 8th Army, U.S. Forces Korea, UN Command Korea, 1973-75, sr. mem. UN Command Mil. Armistice Commn., 1975; comdr. 1st Armored Div., U.S. Army Europe W.Ger., 1975-78; dep. comdg. gen. V Corps, U.S. Army Europe W. Ger., 1978; asst. dep. chief of staff for personnel Dept. Army Washington, 1978-82. Decorated D.S.M., Legion of Merit with oak leaf cluster, D.F.C., Bronze Star medal with oak leaf cluster, Air medal with 5 oak leaf clusters, Army Commendation medal with 2 oak leaf clusters, Purple Heart. Mem. Assn. U.S. Army, Armor Assn. Episcopalian. Office: 10148 Hillington Ct Vienna VA 22182-2908

WEBBER, ANDREW LLOYD, composer; b. England, 1948. Composer (theater) Joseph and the Amazing Technicolor Dreamcoat, Jesus Christ Superstar, Jeeves, Evita, Variations, Tell Me On A Sunday, Song and Dance, Cats (longest running show in Broadway history 1997), Starlight Express, Requiem, The Phatom of the Opera, Aspects of Love, Sunset Boulevard (film) Gumshoe, The Odessa File. Recipient four Drama Desk awards, six Tony's, three Grammy's, five Laurence Olivier awards, Am. Soc. Composers, Authors, and Pubs. Triple Play award, Praemium Imperiale award for music, 1995; inducted Am. Songwriter's Hall of Fame, 1995. Fellow Royal Coll. Music. Office: PRS, 29/33 Berners St, London WIP4AA, England

WEBBER, CHRIS, III (MAYCE EDWARD CHRISTOPHER WEBBER), professional basketball player; b. Detroit, Mar. 1, 1973; s. Mayce and Doris Webber. Student, U. Mich., 1991-93. Drafted Orlando (Fla.) Magic, 1993; forward Golden State Warriors, San Francisco, 1993-94, Washington Bullets, 1994—. Founder Timeout Found. Drafted 1st round Orlando Magic, 1993; named Nat. H.S. Player of Yr., 1990-91, Mr. Basketball State of Mich., 1991, Coca-Cola Classic NBA Player of Yr., 1994, Brut Bullets Player of Yr., 1994-95, NBA All-Rookie 1st Team, 1994. Avocations: collecting signed historical documents of prominent African-Americans. Office: Washington Bullets US Air Arena Landover MD 20785*

WEBBER, HOWARD RODNEY, computer company executive; b. Berlin, N.H., Oct. 20, 1933; s. Robert Alfred and Amelia (Rousseau) W.; m. Helen Margaret McCubbin, May 6, 1959; children: Benjamin James, Adam Brooks, Holly Isabella. A.B., Dartmouth Coll., 1956; postgrad., Lehigh U., 1956-57. Editor in chief U. N.C. Press, Chapel Hill, 1960-63, Johns Hopkins Press, Balt., 1963-65; dir. Case Western Res. U. Press Cleve., 1965-70, MIT Press, Cambridge, 1970-74; v.p., gen. mgr., pub. Open Court Pub. Co., LaSalle, Ill., 1974-83; v.p., pub. Reference div. Houghton Mifflin Co., Boston, 1983-87; mgr. advanced devel. Groupware Systems Digital Equipment Corp., Nashua, N.H., 1987-95; chmn. FutureTense, Inc., Acton, Mass., 1995—. Served with AUS, 1957-59. Mem. Phi Beta Kappa. Democrat. Episcopalian. Home: 49 Wilson Rd Bedford MA 01730-1340 Office: FutureTense Inc 33 Nagog Park Acton MA 01720

WEBBER, JOHN BENTLEY, orthopedic surgeon; b. Morritown, N.J., Jan. 27, 1941; s. George Bentley and Gladys (Moody) W.; m. Mary Christina Thometz, Feb. 25, 1978; children: John Bentley, Edward Alan. B.A., Lehigh U., 1962; M.D., Temple U., 1966. Intern Rochester Gen. Hosp., N.Y., 1966-67; resident Temple U. Med. Ctr., Phila., 1967-70; Stelrling Bunnell fellow in hand surgery Pacific Med. Ctr., San Francisco, 1971; practice medicine specializing in orthopedic surgery and surgery of hand Phila., 1973—; assoc. prof. orthopedic surgery and rehab. Hahnemann Med. Coll. and Hosp., Phila., 1973—, chief sect. on hand surgery, 1973—; attending surgeon St. Christopher's Hosp. for Children, Phila., 1996—; cons. in hand surgery Mcpl. Med. Svcs., Phila., 1973-87, USPHS, Phila., 1973-76, burn ctr. St. Agnes Med. Ctr., Phila., 1973—, Phila. unit Shriners' Hosp. for Crippled Children, 1979-95. Served to maj. USAF, 1971-73. Fellow ACS (Pa. com. on trauma), Am. Acad. Orthopedic Surgeons; mem. AMA, Am. Soc. for Surgery of Hand, Bunnell Hand Club (pres. 1978-80), Assn. for Acad. Surgery, Eastern Orthopedic Soc., Pa. Med. Soc., Phila. Orthopedic Soc., Phila. Hand Soc. (pres. 1987-89), Phila. County Med. Soc., Phila. Coll. Physicians, Meigs Med. Assn., Rotary, Union Leauge, Riverside Yacht Club (fleet surgeon), Phila. Country Club, Delaware Valley Ducks Unltd. (chmn. 1983-88). Republican. Congregationalist. Home: 1139 Rock Creek Rd Gladwyne PA 19035-1439 Office: 221 N Broad St Philadelphia PA 19107-1511

WEBBER, RICHARD JOHN, lawyer; b. Mpls., July 27, 1948; s. Richard John and Mary Lee (Moore) W.; m. Susan Barbara Listerman, Jan. 8, 1972; children: Hillary, Joanna. BA, Princeton U., 1970; JD, U. Mich., 1973. Bar: D.C. Ct. Appeals 1974, U.S. Ct. Appeals (9th and D.C. cirs.) 1980, U.S. Dist. Ct. D.C. 1980, U.S. Claims Ct. 1974, U.S. Supreme Ct. 1980. Law clk. U.S. Ct. Claims, Washington, 1973-75; trial atty. U.S. Dept. Justice, Washington, 1975-80; assoc. Arent, Fox et al, Washington, 1980-85, ptnr., 1985—. Mem. ABA (chmn. fed. contract claims and remedies com. sect. pub. contract law 1986-91), Fed. Bar Assn. (chmn. ADP procurement com. govt. contracts sect. 1992-94, chmn. govt. contracts sect. 1994-96). Office: Arent Fox Washington Sq 1050 Connecticut Ave NW Washington DC 20036

WEBBER, ROSS ARKELL, management educator; b. New Rochelle, N.Y., July 18, 1934; s. Richard and Muriel (Arkels) W.; m. Mary Louise Foradora, Sept. 29, 1956; children: Sarah Ruth, Judith Mary, Gregory Ross, Jennifer Louise, Stephen Andrew. BSE, Princeton U., 1956; PhD, Columbia U., 1966; MS (hon.), U. Pa., 1972. Indsl. engr. Eastman Kodak Co., Rochester, N.Y., 1959-61; instr. Columbia U., New York, N.Y., 1961-64; lectr. Wharton Sch. U. Pa., Phila., 1964-65, asst. prof., 1965-70, assoc. prof., 1970-76, prof., 1976—; v.p. U. Pa., Phila., 1981-86; chmn. dept. mgmt. Wharton Sch. U. Pa., Phila., 1992-95; dir. Wharton-Industry Exec. Program, U. Pa., 1966-68, chmn. Wharton Internat. Bus. com., 1968-69, coord. Orgn. Behavior and Mgmt. Group, 1968-75, asst. dept. chmn., PhD com., 1972-75, coord. Orgnl. and Mgmt. Component, Advanced Mgmt. Program in Health Care Adminstrn., 1973-74, mem. Univ. Coun., 1975-77, adv. com. Pub. Mgmt. Unit, The Wharton Sch., 1977-81, chmn. Grad. Admissions com.; mem. editl. bd. The Wharton Mag.; bd. dirs. Heidemij N.V., Am. Water Works Co., N.J.-Am. Water Co.; owner, prin. Ross A. Webber Assocs., 1970—. Author: Organizational Behavior and the Practice of Management, 1968, 5th rev. eit., 1987; Spanish lang. edit., 1982, Culture and Management: Text and Reading in Comparative Management, 1969, Management: Basic Elements of Managing Organizations, 1979, 3rd rev. edit., 1984, Polish lang. edit., 1984, Management Pragmatics: Readings and Cases on Managing Organizations, 1979, Time is Money!: The Key to Managerial Success, 1980, Japanese lang. edit. 1983, Swedish edit. 1983, Spanish lang. edit., 1985, Portugese lang. edit., 1989, To Be a Manager, 1981, A Guide to Getting Things Done, 1984, Becoming a Courageous Manager: Overcoming Career Problems of New Managers, 1991, Breaking Your Time Barriers: Becoming a More Effective Strategic Time Manager, 1992; also over 55 articles to profl. jours. Past mem. bd. dirs. United Way Southeastern Pa.; coach youth athletics, fund raiser for church and religious educator. Lt. (jg) USN, 1956-59. Avocations: painting, tennis, skiing. Office: Univ Pa The Wharton Sch 2000 Steinberg Hall Philadelphia PA 19104

WEBBER, WILLIAM ALEXANDER, university administrator, physician; b. Nfld., Can., Apr. 8, 1934; s. William Grant and Hester Mary (Constable) W.; m. Marilyn Joan Robson, May 17, 1958; children—Susan Joyce, Eric Michael, George David. M.D., U. B.C., Can., Vancouver, 1958. Intern Vancouver Gen. Hosp., 1958-59; postdoctoral fellow Cornell U. Med. Coll., N.Y.C., 1959-61; asst. prof. medicine U. B.C., 1961-66, assoc. prof., 1966-69, prof., 1969—, dean faculty medicine, 1977-90, assoc. v.p. acad., 1990-96. Mem. B.C. Med. Assn., Can. Assn. Anatomists, Am. Assn. Anatomists. Research on renal structure and function. Home: 2478 Crown St, Vancouver, BC Canada V6R 3V8 Office: U BC, 2177 Westbrook Mall, Vancouver, BC Canada V6T 1Z3

WEBB-GROE, MARY CHRISTINE, special education educator; b. Ames, Iowa, Jan. 3, 1947; d. Howard Darrell and Lorena Faye (North) Webb; m. Harlen DuWayne Groe, Dec. 29, 1989. BS in Elem. Edn., Iowa State U., 1969, MS in Emotional Disabilities, 1980, MEd in Learning Disabilities, 1986. Cert. tchr. K-9, learning disabilities, behavioral disabilities, multicategorical, cons., Iowa. 1st grade tchr. Holy Spirit Sch., Carroll, Iowa, 1970; severe behavior disabilities tchr. Area Edn. Agy 7, Waterloo, Iowa, 1979-85; teaching and rsch. assistantship Iowa State U., Ames, 1985-86; multicategorical 3-8 self contained with integration tchr. Madrid Elem. and Jr. High Sch., 1986-87; behavior disability self contained with integration tchr. Des Moines Pub. Schs., 1987-88, resource rm. tchr., 1988-95; multicategorical self contained with integration tchr., 1995—. mem. People to People Spl. Edn. Delegation to Mainland China, 1993. Mem. ASCD, NEA, Des Moines Edn. Assn., Iowa State Edn. Assn., Coun. for Exceptional Children. Office: Perkins Elem School 4301 College Ave Des Moines IA 50311-2454

WEBEL, RICHARD KARL, landscape architect; m. Janet Darling, July 25, 1947 (dec.); 1 son, Richard Crawford; m. Pauline Dodge Pratt, Sept. 27, 1969. BA, Harvard U., 1923, M.Landscape Architecture, 1926; hon. degrees, Wofford Coll., 1979, Furman U., 1983. Fellow Am. Acad. in Rome, 1926-29; asst. prof. Harvard U. Sch. Design, Cambridge, Mass., 1929-39; pvt. practice landscape architecture, 1931—; mem. N.Y.C. Fine Arts Commn.; mem. vis. com. Grad. Sch. Design, Harvard U., 1962-68. Prin. works include, colls., univs., racetracks, clubs and redesign of Washington Mall and Lincoln Meml. areas, Washington. Recipient numerous awards Am. Assn. Nurserymen, 1955-81, Nat. Landscape award Am. Assn. Nurserymen, 1991, Mrs. Oakleigh Thorne medal Garden Club Am., 1970. Fellow Am. Soc. Landscape Architects (pres. N.Y. chpt. 1954); mem. NAD, Archtl. League N.Y. Clubs: Harvard; Century Assn. (N.Y.C.); Jupiter Island (Hobe Sound, Fla.); Piping Rock (Locust Valley, N.Y.). Home: Cedar Swamp Rd Glen Head NY 11545 Office: Innocenti & Webel 85 Forest Ave Box 506 Locust Valley NY 11560

WEBER, ADELHEID LISA, former nurse, chemist; b. Cottbus, Germany, June 1, 1934; came to the U.S., 1958; d. Johannes Gustav Paul and Johanna Katinka (Askevold) Haertwig; m. Joseph Cotrell Weber (dec. 1986), Oct. 25, 1957; children: Robert Andreas, Miriam Lisa. RN, Stadtisches Hosp., Dortmund, Germany, 1956; BS in Distributive Sci., Am. U., 1983; MBA, U. Md., 1991. RN. Nurse Krankenhaus, Wuppertal, Germany, 1956-57; pvt. nurse Wellesley, Mass., 1969-74; lab. tech. Microbiol. Assoc., Bethesda, Md., 1979-84; switchboard operator Best Products Co., Bethesda, 1983-87; lab. tech. Uniformed Svcs. U. Health Scis., Bethesda, 1984-90; info. rsch. tech. Info. Rsch. Internat. Inc., Bethesda, 1987; chemist USDA, Beltsville, Md., 1990-93; ret., 1993. Vol. Sibley Meml. Hosp., Washington, 1991. Recipient Cert. award County of Montgomery, Md., 1988, Whitman Walker Clinic, 1987. Mem. NAFE, Soc. for Rsch. Adminstrs., Am. Chem. Soc., Nat. Assn. for Amputees, Soc. for Applied Spectroscopy, Nat. Trust for Historic Preservation, Hemlock Soc. Nat. Capital Area, Nat. Mus. for Women in Arts, Wash. Performing Arts Soc. Avocations: stained glass, pottery, gardening, needlework, reading. Home: 23 Sunset Ln Osterville MA 02655-2036

WEBER, ALFONS, physicist; b. Dortmund, Germany, Oct. 8, 1927; s. Alexander and Ilona (Banda) W.; m. Jeannine K. Weber, Oct. 8, 1955; children: Karl, Louise, Paul. PhD, Ill. Inst. Tech., 1956. Instr. physics Ill. Inst. Tech., Chgo., 1953-56; from asst. prof. physics to prof. Fordham U., Bronx, N.Y., 1957-81, prof. physics and chemistry, 1976-81, chmn. dept. physics, 1964-70; rsch. physicist Nat. Inst. Stds. and Tech., Gaithersburg, Md., 1977—, acting chief molecular spectroscopy divsn., 1980-81, chief molecular physics divsn., 1982-95, sr. scientist physics lab., 1995—; with chem scis. divsn. U.S. Dept. Energy, 1991-92, chem. divsn. NSF, 1992-95. Editor: Raman Spectroscopy of Gases and Liquids, 1979; Structure and Dynamics of Weakly Bound Molecular Complexes, 1987, Spectroscopy of the Earth's Atmosphere and Interstellar Medium, 1992; mem. editorial bd. Jour. of Raman Spectroscopy, Jour. Chem. and Phys. Reference Data. V.p. Union Free Dist. # 1 Sch. Bd., Eastchester, N.Y., 1970-73. Postdoctoral fellow NRC Can., U. Toronto, 1956-57. Fellow Am. Phys. Soc. (councillor 1987-91); mem. AAAS, ASTM, Optical Soc. Am., Coblentz Soc., Soc. Applied Spectroscopy. Office: Nat Inst Stds and Tech Optical Tech Divsn Rm B208 Bldg 221 Gaithersburg MD 20899

WEBER, ARNOLD R., academic administrator; b. N.Y.C., Sept. 20, 1929; s. Jack and Lena (Smith) W.; m. Edna M. Files, Feb. 7, 1954; children: David, Paul, Robert. B.A., U. Ill., 1951; M.A., MIT, 1958, Ph.D. in Econs., 1958. Instr., then asst. prof. econs. MIT, 1955-58; faculty U. Chgo. Grad. Sch. Bus., 1958-69, prof. indsl. relations, 1963-69; asst. sec. for manpower Dept. Labor, 1969-70; exec. dir. Cost of Living Council; also spl. asst. to Pres. Nixon, 1971; Gladys C. and Isidore Brown prof. urban and labor econs. U. Chgo., 1971-73; former provost Carnegie-Mellon U.; dean Carnegie-Mellon U. (Grad. Sch. Indsl. Adminstrn.), prof. labor econs. and pub. policy, 1973-80; pres. U. Colo., Boulder, 1980-85; pres. Northwestern U., Evanston, Ill., 1985-95, chancellor, 1995—; vis. prof. Stanford U., 1966; cons. union, mgmt. and govt. agys., 1960—, Dept. Labor, 1965; mem. Pres.'s Adv. Com. Labor Mgmt. Policy, 1964, Orgn. Econ. Coop. and Devel., 1987; vice chmn. Sec. Labor Task Force Improving Employment Svcs., 1965; chmn. rsch. adv. com. U.S. Employment Svc., 1966; assoc. dir. OMB, Exec. Office of Pres., 1970-71; chmn. Presdl. R.R. Emergency Bd., 1982; trustee Com. for Econ. Devel.; bd. dirs. Aon Corp., Burlington No., Inc., Inland Steel Co., Pepsico Inc., Tribune Corp., Deere & Co. Author: Strategies for the Displaced Worker, 1966; Contbr. articles to profl. jours. Trustee com. econ. devel., U. Notre Dame; bd. dirs. Chgo. Coun. Fgn. Rels. Lt. (j.g.) USCGR, 1952-54. Laureate, Lincoln Acad. Ill.; Ford Found. Faculty Rsch. fellow, 1964-65. Mem. Am. Acad. Arts and Scis., Indsl. Rels. Rsch. Assn. (bus.-higher edn. forum), Nat. Acad. Pub. Adminstrn., Comml. Club Chgo. (pres., civic com.), Econ. Club Chgo. (pres.), Phi Beta Kappa. Jewish. Office: Northwestern U Office of Chancellor 555 Clark St Evanston IL 60208-0805

WEBER, ARTHUR, magazine executive; b. Chgo., Feb. 1, 1926; s. Philip and Mary (Arlinsky) W.; m. Sylvia Zollinger, Aug. 19, 1950; children—Randy, Lori. Student, Ill. Inst. Tech., 1943-44; BSEE, Northwestern U., 1946. Elec. design engr. Corn Products Refining Co., 1946-48, Naess & Murphy (architects & engrs.), Chgo., 1949-51, Ford Motor Co., 1952-53, Skidmore, Owings & Merill, Chgo., 1954-57, Shaw, Metz & Dolio, Chgo., 1958-59; pres. Consumers Digest mag., Chgo., 1959—; pub. Money Maker mag. (name changed to Your Money mag., 1991), 1979-91, U. Chgo. Better Health Letter, 1995-96. Served with USNR, 1944-46.

WEBER, BARBARA M., sales executive, consultant; b. Oneonta, N.Y., Apr. 27, 1945; d. Peter J. and Helen (Bettiol) Macaluso; m. Peter Biddle Weber, July 29, 1972 (div. July 1988). Student, SUNY, Cortland, 1963-67; AAS in Merchandising and Retail Mgmt., SUNY, Mohawk Valley. Service cons. N.Y. Telephone, Albany, N.Y., 1966-68; sr. service advisor N.Y. Telephone, Albany, 1970-73; data communications instr. AT & T, nationwide, 1968-70; equipment mgr. Rushmore & Weber, Albany, 1978-82; v.p. ops. Rushmore & Weber, 1983-92, gen. mgr., v.p., 1987-88, pres., chief exec. officer, 1988-92, also bd. dirs.; ind. cons. Orange Handling, Inc., Latham, N.Y., 1992-93; owner The Weber Group, Newtonville, N.Y., 1993—. Chmn. fin. com. Albany County Rep. Com., 1996—; bd. dirs. ARC Northeastern N.Y., 1994—. Mem. Schuyler Meadows Country Club. Roman Catholic. Avocations: skiing, tennis, golf, sailing, knitting. Home: PO Box 236 Newtonville NY 12128-0236

WEBER, CAROL MARTINEZ, physician; b. N.Y.C., May 5, 1950; d. Eduardo and JAcqueline Martinez; children: Julia, Andres. Student, Mt. Holyoke Coll., 1968-70; BA, Williams Coll., 1972; MD, Tufts U., 1981. House officer Mt. Sinai Hosp., N.Y.C., 1981-83; house officer St. Vincents Hosp., N.Y.C., 1983-84, chief resident, 1984-85, attending physician, 1985—; assoc. prof. N.Y. Med. Coll., Valhalla, 1986—; cons. in field. Contbr. articles to profl. jours. and chpts. to books. Bd. trustees Corlears Sch., N.Y.C., 1987. Grantee N.Y. State Dept Health, N.Y.C., 1993-94, 94-95, 95, McKinney Healthcare for Homeless, N.Y.C., 1993-94, USPHS, N.Y.C., 1995. Fellow Am. Coll. Physicians, Am. Coll. Preventive Medicine; mem. Am. Diabetes Assn., Physicians for Social Responsibility, Physicians for Prevention of Nuclear War, Alpha Omega Alpha. Office: St Vincents Hosp 41 E 11th St Fl 9 New York NY 10003-4602

WEBER, CHARLES L., electrical engineering educator; b. Dayton, Ohio, Dec. 2, 1937. BSEE, U. Dayton, 1958; MSEE, U. So. Calif., 1960; PhD, UCLA, 1964. Tech. staff Hughes Aircraft Co., Calif., 1958-62; from asst. prof. to prof. elec. engring. U. So. Calif., 1964—. Mem. IEEE. Office: U So Calif Comm Scis Inst Dept Elec Engring-Systems Los Angeles CA 90089-2565*

WEBER, CHARLES WALTER, nutrition educator; b. Harold, S.D., Nov. 30, 1931; s. Walter Earl and Vera Jean (Scott) W.; m. Marylou Merkel Adam, Feb. 3, 1961; children: Matthew, Scott. BS, Colo. State U., 1956, MS, 1958; PhD, U. Ariz., 1966. Research asst. U. Ariz., Tucson, 1963-66, asst. prof., 1966-68, assoc. prof., 1969-72, prof. nutrition, 1973-97, prof. emeritus, 1997—; cons. Hermosillo, Mex., 1970-74, Inst. of Health, Cairo, 1981-82, U. Fortaleza, Rio de Janiero, 1986. Contbr. articles to sci. jours. Served as cpl. U.S. Army, 1952-54. Mem. Am. Assn. Cereal Chemists, Am. Inst. Nutrition, Inst. Food Technologists, N.Y. Acad. Scis., Am. Soc. Clin. Nutrition, Poultry Sci. Assn., Ariz. Referees Assn., Sigma Xi. Club: Randolph Soccer (Tucson) (pres. 1976-79). Avocation: stamp collection. Home: 4031 E Calle De Jardin Tucson AZ 85711-3410 Office: U Ariz Dept Nutritional Sci 309 Shantz Bldg Tucson AZ 85721-0033

WEBER, DELBERT DEAN, academic administrator; b. Columbus, Nebr., July 23, 1932; s. Charles and Ella M. (Hueschen) W.; m. Lou Ann Ross, Dec. 29, 1954; children: William, Bethany, Kelly. BA, Midland Coll., Fremont, Nebr., 1954; MEd, U. Nebr., 1958, EdD, 1962; LittD (hon.), Shizuoka (Japan) U., 1982; LLD (hon.), U. City of Manila, 1984. Tchr. social studies and English, prin. Creston (Nebr.) High Sch., 1956-58; instr. ednl. founds. U. Nebr., Lincoln, 1958-60, instr. and coord. jr. high lab. sch., 1960-62; chancellor U. Nebr., Omaha, 1977—; from asst. to assoc. prof. edn. Ariz. State U., Tempe, 1962-65, dean and prof. edn., 1969-77; asst. to pres. and sec. to trustees Cleve. State U., 1965-69; chmn. commn. on culture and edn. to Pakistan, U.S. Dept. of State, 1984; bd. dirs. Norwest Bank, Omaha. Author: (with N.L. Haggerson, L.H. Griffith) Secondary Education Today, 1968; contbr. articles to profl. jours. trustee Nebr. Meth. Hosp., Omaha Home for Boys, Nebr. Meth. Hosp., 1980—; bd. dirs. Midlands region NCCJ, Omaha Community Playhouse, numerous others; gen. campaign chmn. United Way of Midlands, 1983; chmn. midlands region Nat. Conf. Christians and Jews, 1989-92; mem. consultation com. Strategic Command, 1988—, adv. bd. Salvation Army, 1991—, Nebr. state exec. bd. U.S. West Comm., Inc., 1992—, merit selection panel for Magistrate Judge, 1992. With U.S. Army, 1954-56. Named Citizen of Yr., United Way of Midlands, 1984, Disting. Educator N. Cen. Region Bosy Scouts Am., 1989, Outstanding Citizen, Woodmen of the World, 1990, King of Ak-Sar-Ben, 1990, Man of Yr. Omaha Club 1992, Merry Makers 1992; recipient Vision award Soc. Prevention of Blindness, 1991, Svc. to Mankind award Sertoma Club, 1994. Mem. Am. Assn. Colls. for Tchr. Edn. (bd. dirs. 1976-79, chmn. ann. conv. 1975, appeals bd. 1984-85, task force 1984-85), Am. Assn. State Colls. and Univs. (task force on excellence in edn. 1982-84, bd. dirs., exec. com. 1983-86, com. communications tech. 1984-86, resource ctr. bd. liaison 1985, com. acad. affairs, com. on internat. programs 1987, com. on urban affairs 1987), Assn. Urban Univs. (bd. dirs. 1980-85), Nat. Assn. State Univs. and Land Grant Colls. (mem. exec. com. 1982-83, chmn. urban affairs div. 1982-83), Nat. Assn. Colls. and Schs. of Edn. in State Univs. and Land Grant Colls. (bd. dirs. 1974-77, pres. 1977-78), Nat. Collegiate Athletic Assn. (pres. commn. 1984-89), Nat. Coun. for Accreditation of Tchr. Edn. (appeals bd. 1983), Omaha C. of C., Strategic Air Command (bd. dir. consultation com.). Lutheran. Avocation: golf. Home: 1307 N 97th Plz Omaha NE 68114-2101 Office: U Nebr Eppley 201 Omaha NE 68182

WEBER, DONALD B., advertising and marketing executive; b. Jersey City, Nov. 6, 1932; s. John William and Rose Ann (Saroshi) W.; m. Ann McDermaid, 1955 (div. 1975); children: Martha Elizabeth, Margaret Ann; m. Jean Host, 1980. BA, Rollins Coll., 1954; MBA, Northwestern U., 1959. Account exec. Leo Burnett Co., Inc., Chgo., 1958-63; sr. v.p., mgmt. supr. Foote, Cone & Belding, Chgo., 1963-76; pres. Blau Bishop Assocs., 1976-79; v.p. Russell Reynolds Assocs., Chgo., 1979-82; sr. v.p., regional mgr. MSL Internat., Chgo., 1982-85; exec. v.p. Rumrill-Hoyt, Inc., Rochester, N.Y.,

1985-88; sr. v.p. D'Arcy Masius Benton & Bowles, Chgo., 1988-95; sr. v.p. mgmt. dir. Cramer-Krasselt, Chgo., 1996—; lectr. Northwestern U. Chmn. bd. Am. Cancer Soc., Chgo., 1996—, chmn. Chgo. Area Crusade, 1994-96; bd. dirs. Am. Inst. of Wine and Food, 1995-97; chmn. Chgo. coun. Boy Scouts Am., 1991-95. Lt. comdr. USNR, 1955-58. Mem. Chgo. Advtg. Fedn. (bd. dirs. 1988-93), Oak Hill Country Club, Exmoor Country Club, Tavern Club. Republican. Episcopalian. Office: Cramer-Krasselt 225 N Michigan Ave Chicago IL 60601-7601

WEBER, EICKE RICHARD, physicist; b. Muennerstadt, Germany, Oct. 28, 1949; s. Martin and Irene (Kistner) W.; m. Magdalene Graff (div. 1983); m. Zuzanna Liliental , June 10, 1985. BS, U. Koeln, Fed. Republic of Germany, 1970, MS, 1973, PhD, 1976, Dr.Habil., 1983. Sci. asst. U. Koeln, 1976-82; rsch. asst. U. Lund, Sweden, 1982-83; asst. prof. Dept. Material Sci. U. Calif., Berkeley, 1983-87, assoc. prof., 1987-91, prof. materials sci., 1991—; prin. investigator Lawrence Berkeley Lab., 1984—; vis. prof. Tohoku U., Sendai, Japan, 1990; cons. in field; internat. fellow Inst. for Study of Defects in Solids, SUNY, Albany, 1978-79; chmn. numerous confs.; mem. founding com. CAESAR Found., Bonn, 1995—; lectr. in field. Editor: Defect Recognition and Image Processing in III-V Compounds, 1987, Imperfections in III-V Compounds, 1993; co-editor: Chemistry and Defects in Semiconductor Structures, 1989, others; series co-editor: Semiconductors and Semimetals, 1991—; contbr. over 300 articles to profl. jours. Recipient IBM Faculty award, 1984, Humboldt U.S. Sr. Scientist award, 1994; rsch. grantee Dept. of Energy, 1984—, Office Naval Rsch., 1985—, Air Force Office Sci. Rsch., 1988—, NASA, 1988-90, Nat. Renewable Energy Lab., 1992—. Mem. IEEE (sr.), Am. Phys. Soc., Materials Rsch. Soc. Achievements include first identification of point defects formed by dislocation motion in silicon; determination of the energy levels of antisite defects in GaAs, of 3d transition metal solubility and lattice site in silicon, of mechanism of internal gettering in silicon; research in defects formed in III/V thin films and interfaces; on lattice mismatched heteroepitaxial growth; in structure and electronic properties of metal GaAs heterostructures; in nature and electronic properties of defects in GaAs, GaN, and related compounds; in MBE prower of GaN and related compounds; in low-temperature MBE growth of As-nics GaAs; in transition metal gettering in silicon; polysilicon for photovoltaic applications; scanning tunneling microscopy of semiconductor thin films and interfaces; on electron paramagnetic resonance of defects in semiconductors. Office: 587 Evans Hall Dept Materials Sci U Calif Berkeley CA 94720

WEBER, ELLEN SCHMOYER, pediatric speech pathologist; b. Allentown, Pa., Oct. 6, 1952. BS in Speech Pathology, Kutztown State Coll., 1975; MS in Speech Pathology, U. So. Fla., 1982, MEd in Ednl. Leadership, 1991. Cert. tchr., ednl. adminstr., Fla. Itinerant therapist Schuylkill County Ind. Sch. Dist., Pottsville, Pa., 1975-76, Pinellas County Sch. Dist., Largo, Fla., 1979-95; pvt. therapist Pinellas County, Fla., 1982-87, 94—; owner, dir. Children's Speech and Lang. Svcs.; staffing team coord. Pinellas County Sch. Dist., Largo, Fla., 1986-91, 93-94, mem. sch. adv. coun., 1990-93, union rep., 1989-92. Computer grantee Pinellas County Sch. Dist., 1986-87, travel grantee, 1991-92. Mem. Am. Speech-Lang.-Hearing Assn., Fla. Speech-Lang.-Hearing Assn. Avocations: travel, skiing, cycling, hiking, computer. Home: 458 Richmond St Dunedin FL 34698-7934

WEBER, ERNESTO JUAN, counselor, educator, industrialist; b. Mexico City, Aug. 20, 1930; m. Vera Elisa Engels, Oct. 25, 1958; children: Frank, Ernesto Jr., Monica. BS in Mech. Engring., Calif. Inst. Tech., 1952; PhD in counseling, U. Iberoamericana, Mexico City, 1980. Gen. mgr. Schultz y Cia, S.A., Mexico City, 1961-68, owner, pres., 1968-76; prof. U. Iberoamericana, Mexico City, 1976-85, dean dept. human devel. and edn., 1982-84; gen. corp. dir. Grupo Indsl., Aloymex, Mex., 1987-84; dir. dept. psychology Centro Medico la Pascua, Mexico City, 1980-81; profl. counselor, Mexico City, 1976—; dir. Metron S.A., 1966-70, Sycmatica, S.A. de C.V., 1967-76, Ascomatica, S.A. de C.V., 1967-76 (all Mexico City); pres. Weber y Asociados, S.C. Author: Der Integrierte Mensch, 1988; patentee in automatic controls; contbr. articles to profl. jours. Recipient Achievement award United Inventors and Scientists, 1974; award Automatic Switch Co., 1976. Mem. Assn. de Profs. e Inv. de La U.I.A., Assn. Mex. de Terapia Familiar, Assn. Suiza de Mex., A.C. (pres.). Club: Assoc. Empresarial Mexicano-Suiza, A.C. Home and Office: Prol Hidalgo-Garcia Lorca 282-PB3 Cuajimalpa frente, Deportivo Cacalote, Mexico City 05270, Mexico

WEBER, EUGEN, historian, educator, author; b. Bucharest, Romania, Apr. 24, 1925; came to U.S., 1955; s. Emanuel and Sonia (Garrett) W.; m. Jacqueline Brument-Roth, June 12, 1950. Student, Inst. d'études politiques, Paris, 1948-49, 51-52; M.A., Emmanuel Coll., Cambridge U., 1954, M.Litt., 1956. History supr. Emmanuel Coll., 1953-54; lectr. U. Alta., 1954-55; asst. prof. U. Iowa, 1955-56; asst. prof. history UCLA, 1956, assoc. prof., 1959-63, prof., 1963—, Joan Palevsky prof. modern European history, 1984—, chmn. dept., 1965-68; dir. study center U. Calif., France, 1968-70; dean social scis. UCLA, 1976-77, dean Coll. Letters and Scis., 1977-82; Ford faculty lectr. Stanford U., 1965; Patten lectr. Ind. U., 1981; vis. prof. Collège de France, Paris, 1983; dir. d'ètudes Ecole des hautes ètudes, Paris, 1984-85; Christian Gauss lectr., Princeton U., 1990. Author: Nationalist Revival in France, 1959, The Western Tradition, 1959, Paths to the Present, 1960, Action Française, 1962, Satan Franc-Maçon, 1964, Varieties of Fascism, 1964; (with H. Rogger) The European Right, 1965, A Modern History of Europe, 1970, Europe Since 1715, 1972, Peasants into Frenchmen, 1976 (Commonwealth prize Calif. 1977), La Fin des Terroirs, 1983 (Prix de la Société des gens de lettres 1984), France Fin-de-siècle, 1986 (Commonwealth prize Calif. 1987), The Western Tradition (WGBH/PBS TV series), 1989, My France, 1990, Movements, Currents, Trends, 1991, The Hollow Years, 1994, La France des annèes trente (Prix littèraire Etats-Unis/France, 1995, Prix Maurice Baumont 1995, Prix de Jeux Floraux 1997), 1995; adv. editor Jour. Contemporary History, 1966—, French History, 1985—, French Cultural Studies, 1990—, Am. Scholar, 1992—. Served as capt. inf. Brit. Army, 1943-47. Recipient Luckman Disting. Teaching award UCLA Alumnae Assn., 1992; decorated Ordre Nat. des Palmes Academiques, France; Fulbright fellow, 1952, 82-83; research fellow Am. Philos. Soc., 1959, Social Sci. Research Council, 1959-61, Am. Council Learned Socs., 1962; Guggenheim fellow, 1963-64; NEH sr. fellow, 1973-74, 82-83. Fellow Netherlands Inst. Advanced Studies, Assn. française de science politique, Am. Acad. Arts and Scis.; mem. Am. Hist. Assn., Soc. d'histoire moderne, Soc. French Hist. Studies, Phi Beta Kappa (hon., Ralph Waldo Emerson prize 1977, senator 1988—).

WEBER, FRED J., retired state supreme court justice; b. Deer Lodge, Mont., Oct. 6, 1919; s. Victor N. and Dorothy A. (Roberts) W.; m. Phyllis M. Schell, June 2, 1951; children: Anna Marie, Donald J., Mark W., Paul V. B.A., U. Mont., 1943, J.D., 1947. Bar: Mont. 1947. Atty. Kuhr & Weber, Havre, Mont., 1947-55, Weber, Bosch & Kuhr, and successors, 1956-80; justice Supreme Ct. Mont., Helena, 1981-95. Served to capt. inf. U.S. Army, 1943-46. Fellow Am. Bar Found., Am. Coll. Probate Counsel; mem. ABA, Am. Judicature Soc.

WEBER, FREDRIC ALAN, lawyer; b. Paterson, N.J., July 31, 1948; s. Frederick Edward and Alida (Hessels) W.; m. Mary Elizabeth Cook, June 18, 1983. BA in History, Rice U., 1970; JD, Yale U., 1976. Bar: Tex. 1976, U.S. Dist. Ct. (so. dist.) Tex. Assoc. Fulbright & Jaworski, Houston, 1976-80, participating assoc., 1980-83, ptnr., 1983—. Dir. Houston Symphony Soc., 1993—. Recipient Benjamin Scharps prize Yale Law Sch., 1976, Ambrose Gherini prize Yale Law Sch., 1976. Mem. ABA, Am. Coll. Bond Counsel, Nat. Assn. Bond Lawyers (bd. dirs. 1988-89, treas. 1989-90, pres.-elect 1991, pres. 1991-92), Houston Bar Assn. Office: Fulbright & Jaworski LLP 1301 Mckinney St Ste 5100 Houston TX 77010-3095

WEBER, FREDRICK LOUIS, JR., hepatologist, medical researcher; b. Syracuse, N.Y., June 8, 1944; s. Fredrick L. and Jean (Caldwell) W.; m. Gayle Christine Freer; children: Luke, Laura, Nell, Charles, Andrew. BA, Wesleyan U., 1966; MD, Cornell U., 1970. Intern, resident in internal medicine Bellevue Hosp./NYU Med. Ctr., N.Y.C., 1970-73; fellow in gastroenterology Johns Hopkins Hosp., Balt., 1973-75; asst. prof. medicine U. Ky. Med. Ctr., Lexington, 1975-81; assoc. prof. medicine Case Western Res. U., Cleve., 1981-93; dir. liver unit U. Cin. Med. Ctr., 1993—. Achievements include research in hepatic encephalopathy and intestinal nitrogen metabolism. Office: U Cin Med Ctr Liver Unit ML 595 Cincinnati OH 45267

WEBER, GEORG FRANZ, immunologist; b. Erlangen, Germany, July 7, 1962; came to U.S., 1989; s. Otto and Margret (Hartung) W.; m. Chitra Edwin, Sept. 21, 1991; 1 child, Ramona Sara. BS, Ohm-Gymnasium, Erlangen, Germany, 1981; MD, Julius Maximilians U., Wuerzburg, Germany, 1988, PhD, 1988. Rsch. assoc. U. S. Ala., Mobile, 1989; rsch. fellow dept. biochemistry and Dana-Farber Cancer Inst. Harvard U., Boston, 1990-91, rsch. assoc. dept. pathology and Dana-Farber Cancer Inst., 1991-93, instr., 1993—. Contbr. articles to profl. jours. Mem. Amnesty Internat., N.Y.C., 1991--. Deutsche Forschungsgemeinschaft fellow, 1989-91. mem. AMA, Deutscher Aerzteverband, Oxygen Soc. Achievements include research into reactive oxygen species in medicine and 1991 link of enzyme defect to childhood seizures, cancer research, theory of chess, biomechanics. Office: Dana-Farber Cancer Inst 44 Binney St Boston MA 02115-6013

WEBER, GEORGE, oncology and pharmacology researcher, educator; b. Budapest, Hungary, Mar. 29, 1922; came to U.S., 1959; s. Salamon and Hajnalka (Arvai) W.; m. Catherine Elizabeth Forrest, June 30, 1958; children: Elizabeth Dolly Arvai, Julie Vibert Wallace, Jefferson James. BA, Queen's U., 1950, MD, 1952; MD (hon.), U. Chieti, Italy, 1979, Med. Faculty, Budapest, 1982, U. Leipzig, Fed. Republic of Germany, 1987, Tokushima (Japan) U., 1988; Kagawa (Japan) U., 1992. Rsch. assoc. Montreal Cancer Inst., 1953-59; prof. pharmacology Ind. U. Sch. Medicine, Indpls., 1959—; dir. Lab for Exptl. Oncology Sch. Medicine, Ind. U., Indpls., 1974—; Milan Panič prof. oncology Ind. U., Indpls., 1994—, Wellcome prof., 1995—; prof. Lab. for Exptl. Oncology Sch. Medicine, Ind. U., Indpls., 1974-90, disting. prof. Lab. for Exptl. Oncology, 1990—; chmn. study sect. USPHS, Washington, 1976-78; sci. adv. com. Am. Cancer Soc., N.Y.C., 1972-76, 94—, Damon Runyon Fund, N.Y.C., 1971-76; mem. U.S. Nat. Com., Internat. Union Against Cancer, Washington, 1974-80, 90-94, NAS, Washington, 1974-80, 90-94, U.S. Army Med. Rsch. & Breast Cancer Rsch. Program, 1996—. Editor: Advances in Enzyme Regulation, Vols. 1-38, 1962—; assoc. editor Jour. Cancer Rsch., 1969-80, 82-89. Recipient Alecce Prize for cancer rsch. Tiberine Acad., Rome, 1971, Best Prof. award Student AMA, Indpls., 1966, 68, G.F. Gallanti prize for enzymology Internat. Soc. Clin. Chemists, 1984, Outstanding Investigator award Nat. Cancer Inst., NIH, 1986-94. Mem. Am. Soc. for Pharmacology and Exptl. Therapeutics, Am. Assn. Cancer Rsch. (G.H.A. Clowes award 1982), Russian Acad. Sci. (hon.), Hungarian Cancer Soc. (hon.), Hungarian Acad. Scis. (hon.), Acad. Scis. Bologna (Italy) (hon.). Home: 7307 Lakeside Dr Indianapolis IN 46278-1618 Office: Ind U Sch Medicine Lab Exptl Oncology 699 West Dr Indianapolis IN 46202-5119

WEBER, GEORGE, international social welfare administrator; b. Montreal, Que., Can., Apr. 18, 1946; s. Harry and Johanna (Alexopoulos) W.; m. Mary Ellen Morris, May 8, 1976. BEd, McGill U., 1970, MA, 1974; postgrad., Harvard U., 1989. Vol. instr., examiner, mem. staff Canadian Red Cross, 1963-73; field del. with Indochina operational group Canadian Red Cross, Vietnam, 1973-74; nat. dir. internat. affairs Canadian Red Cross, 1976-81, nat. dir. programs, 1981-83, sec. gen., CEO, 1983-93, hon. v.p., 1993—; field del. with Indochina Operational Group Internat. Red Cross, Vietnam, 1973-74; chief del., disaster relief officer League of Red Cross Socs., Geneva, 1974-76; founder, chmn., CEO Nat. Charity Coun., 1990-92; sec. gen., CEO Internat. Fedn. Red Cross and Red Crescent Socs., Geneva, 1993—. Contbr. articles to sci. jours. Bd. dirs. Nat. Capital Harvard Bus. Sch. Alumni Club, Amundsen Found. Recipient Vanier award, 1984, Internat. Comm. and Leadership award Toastmasters, 1985, Friendship medal Turkish Red Crescent Soc., 1988, Exceptional Humanitarian Svc. award Portuguese Red Cross, 1989, hon. medal of merit Venezuelan Red Cross Soc., 1991. Mem. Am. Coll. Sports Medicine, Canadian Inst. Internat. Affairs, Canadian Soc. Assn. Execs. (mem. bd. dirs.), Canadian Comprehensive Auditing Found., Nat. Health Agy's. CEO Orgn., Canadian Cross Soc. (hon. v.p.), Internat. Devel. Execs. Assn. (founder), Rideau Club, Harvard Club, Five Lakes Club. Avocations: diving, tennis, squash, skiing. Office: PO Box 372, 1211 Geneva 19, Switzerland

WEBER, GEORGE RICHARD, financial consultant, writer; b. The Dalles, Oreg., Feb. 7, 1929; s. Richard Merle and Maud (Winchell) W.; m. Nadine Hanson, Oct. 12, 1957; children: Elizabeth Ann Weber Katooli, Karen Louise Weber Zaro, Linda Marie. BS, Oreg. State U., 1950; MBA, U. Oreg., 1962. CPA, Oreg. Sr. trainee U.S. Nat. Bank of Portland (Oreg.), 1950-51; jr. acct. Ben Musa, CPA, The Dalles, 1954; tax and audit asst. Price Waterhouse, Portland, 1955-59; sr. acct. Burton M. Smith, CPA, Portland, 1959-62; pvt. practice, Portland, 1962—, assoc. World Mktg. Alliance, 1996—; lectr. acctg. Portland State Coll.; expert witness fin. and tax matters. Sec.-treas. Mt. Hood Kiwanis Camp, Inc., 1965. Exec. counselor SBA; mem. fin. com., powerlifting team U.S. Powerlifting Fedn., 1984, amb. People to People, China, 1987. Arty. officer AUS, 1951-53. Decorated Bronze Star. Mem. AICPA, Internat. Platform Assn., Oreg. Hist. Soc.,Oreg. City Traditional Jazz Soc., Order of the Holy Cross Jerusalem, Order St. Stephen the Martyr, Order St. Gregory the Illuminator, Knightly Assn. St. George the Martyr., World Literary Acad., Portland C.S. Lewis Soc., Beta Alpha Psi, Pi Kappa Alpha. Republican. Lutheran. Clubs: Kiwanis, Portland Track, City (Portland); Multnomah Athletic; Sunrise Toastmasters. Author: Small Business Long-term Finance, 1962, A History of the Coroner and Medical Examiner Offices, 1963, CPA Litigation Service References, 1991, Letters to a Friend, 1995; contbr. to profl. publs. and poetry jours. Home: 2603 NE 32d Ave Portland OR 97212-3611 Office: 4380 SW Macadam Ave Ste 210 Portland OR 97201-6404 *My basic beliefs are in faith, family and freedom through limited government and personal responsibility, with personal responsibility including development and use of capabilities.*

WEBER, GLORIA RICHIE, minister, retired state representative; married; 4 children. BA, Washington U., St. Louis; MA, MDiv, Eden Theol. Sem., Webster Groves, Mo. Ordained to ministry Evang. Luth. Ch. Am., St. Louis, 1974;. Family life educator Luth. Family and Children's Svcs. Mo.; mem. Mo. Ho. of Reps., 1993-94; Mo. state organizer, dir. comm. Mainstream Voters C.A.R.E., 1995. Exec. dir. Older Women's League, 1990-95. Recipient Woman of Achievement award St. Louis Globe-Dem., 1977, Unselfish Cmty. Svc. award St. Louis Sentinel Newspaper, 1985, Faith in Action award Luth. Svcs. St. Louis, 1994, Outstanding Woman award Coalition of St. Louis Labor Women, 1994; named Woman of Yr., Variety Club, 1978, Woman of Worth, Older Women's League, 1993. Democrat. Home and Office: 4910 Valley Crest Dr Saint Louis MO 63128-1829

WEBER, HANNO, architect; b. Barranquilla, Colombia, Sept. 24, 1937; came to U.S., 1952; s. Hans and Ester (Oks) W. BA magna cum laude, Princeton U., 1959, MArch, 1961. Registered architect, Ill., Fla., Mo., Pa., N.J., Va. Urban designer, research assoc. Guayana project MIT and Harvard U., Caracas, Venezuela, 1961-63; project architect Paul Schweikher Assocs., Pitts., 1963-67; asst. prof. architecture Princeton U., 1967-73; assoc. prof. architecture Washington U., St. Louis, 1973-80; sr. design architect, studio head, assoc. Skidmore, Owings & Merrill, Chgo., 1980-83; prin. Hanno Weber & Assocs., Chgo., 1984—; vis. lectr. Escuela Nacional de Arquitectura Universidad Nacional de Mex., 1975; research assoc. Research Ctr. Urban and Environ. Planning, Princeton, N.J., 1967-70; project dir. The Community Design Workshop, Washington U. Sch. Architecture, St. Louis, 1973-78; assoc. prof. architecture U. Wis., Milw., 1983—. Contbr. articles to profl. jours. Mem. Pres.'s Commn. on Education of Women Princeton U., 1968-69. Fellow NEH, 1970, Graham Found., 1973; 1st prize winner Flagler Dr. Waterfront Master Plan design competition, West Palm Beach, Fla., 1984; 1st prize winner Mcpl. Ctr. design competition, Leesburg, Va., 1987; finalist Okla. City Meml. Internat. design competition, 1997; Chgo. AIA Disting. Bldg. award Citation of Merit, Altamira, Terrace, Highland Park, Fla., 1987. Mem. AIA (Urban Design award Mcpl. Govt. Ctr., Leesburg, Va., 1992, Chgo. AIA Interior Architecture award citation of merit, Mcpl. Govt. Ctr., Leesburg, 1992), The Arch. Assn., Phi Beta Kappa. Office: Hanno Weber & Assocs 417 S Dearborn St Chicago IL 60605-1120

WEBER, HARM ALLEN, college chancellor, former college president; b. Pekin, Ill., Sept. 28, 1926; s. Harm Allen and Hilda (Meyer) W.; m. Arlene Olson, Dec. 18, 1948; children: Jan Christine, Harm Allen III, Matthew Karl. B.A., Bethel Coll., St. Paul, 1950; B.D., Bethel Sem., 1954; M.R.E., Christian Theol. Sem., Indpls., 1959; postgrad., Ball State U., Muncie, Ind., 1961-62; D.D., Judson Coll., Elgin, Ill., 1964. Ordained to ministry Baptist Ch., 1953; pastorates at Isle (Minn.) Bapt. Ch., 1950-53, Central Bapt. Ch., Indpls., 1954-60, First Bapt. Ch., Muncie, 1960-64, Covenant Bapt. Ch., Detroit, 1964-69; pres. Judson Coll., Elgin, 1969-91; vice chmn. bd. trustees Judson Coll., chancellor, 1992—; chmn. Indpls. Fedn. Chs., 1955-59; pres. Delaware County (Ind.) Coun. Chs., 1963-64; chmn. evangelism Detroit Coun. Chs., 1967-69; v.p. Am. Bapt. Home Mission Soc., 1969—; mem. exec. com. Gt. Lakes Coun. on Ministry, 1969—; mem. Ministers and Missionaries Benefit Bd., 1974-75; mem. gen. bd. Am. Bapt. Chs./USA; mem. nat. adv. com. Ednl. Assistance Ltd., 1987—. Mem. Ind. Gov.'s Multiple Sclerosis Bd., 1957-60; bd. dirs. Camp Isongal, Delaware County Crippled Children's Assn.; chmn. bd. dirs. Galloway Meml. Youth Camp, Wahkon, Minn.; mem. state exec. bd. Vols. of Am.-Minn., 1976—; trustee Am. Bapt. Sem. of the West, 1984-86. Mem. Am. Assn. Pres. Ind. Colls. and Univs., Elgin Area C. of C. (dir. 1975-78), Am. Bapt. Assn. Colls. and Univs. (pres. 1986-89). Club: Rotary. Office: Judson Coll 1151 N State St Elgin IL 60123-1404

WEBER, HERMAN JACOB, federal judge; b. Lima, Ohio, May 20, 1927; s. Herman Jacob and Ada Minola (Esterly) W.; m. Barbara L. Rice, May 22, 1948; children: Clayton, Deborah. BA, Otterbein Coll., 1949; JD summa cum laude, Ohio State U., 1951. Bar: Ohio 1952, U.S. Dist. Ct. (so. dist.) Ohio 1954. Ptnr. Weber & Hogue, Fairborn, Ohio, 1952-61; judge Fairborn Mayor's Ct., 1956-58; acting judge Fairborn Mcpl. Ct., 1958-60; judge Greene County Common Pleas Ct., Xenia, Ohio, 1961-82, Ohio Ct. Appeals (2d dist.), Dayton, 1982-85, U.S. Dist. Ct. (so. dist.) Ohio, Cin., 1985—; chmn. Ohio Jud. Conf., Columbus, 1980-82; pres. Ohio Common Pleas Judges Assn., Columbus, 1975. Vice mayor City of Fairborn, 1955-57, council mem., 1955-59. Served with USNR, 1945-46. Office: US Dist Ct 801 Potter Stewart US Courthse 5th & Walnut Sts Cincinnati OH 45202

WEBER, JANET M., nurse; b. Lansdale, Pa., Mar. 12, 1936; d. Russell H. and Naomi (dec.) Moyer W. Diploma in nursing, Washington County Hosp. Sch. Nursing, 1959; B.S. in Nursing, Grace Coll., 1960; M.Ed., Duquesne U., 1969. Staff nurse, supr. Murphy Med. Ctr., Warsaw, Ind., 1959-60; coll. nurse Grace Coll., Winona Lake, Ind., 1959-60; med. surg. nursing instr. Washington County Hosp. Sch. Nursing, Hagerstown, Md., 1961-64; pvt. duty nurse Washington County Hosp., Hagerstown, 1964; chmn. found. of nursing Presbyn. Univ. Hosp. Sch. Nursing, Pitts., 1964-72; curriculum coordinator Albert Einstein Med. Ctr. Sch. Nursing, Phila., 1972-73; assoc. dir. Albert Einstein Med. Ctr. Sch. Nursing, 1973-74, acting dir., 1974, dir., 1974-87; staff nurse ARC Penn-Jersey Blood Drive Donor Services, Phila., 1988-92, asst. nurse mgr., 1992—; nurse mgr. ARC Penn-Jersey Blood Drivce Donor Svcs., Phila., 1992—; cons. Md. Bd. Higher Edn., 1981-82. Author: The Faculty's Role in Policy Development, 1981, Assisting Students with Educational Deficiencies, 1975. Mem. Washington County Hosp. Nurses Alumni Assn. (pres. 1962-64), Grace Coll. Alumni Assn., Duquesne U. Alumni Assn. Republican. Home: 5640 Arbor St Philadelphia PA 19120-2502 Office: ARC Blood Donor Svcs 700 Spring Garden St Philadelphia PA 19123-3508

WEBER, JEROME CHARLES, education and human relations educator, former academic dean and provost; b. Bklyn., Sept. 1, 1938; s. Meyer and Ethel (Shier) W.; m. Elizabeth Lynn Wiley, July 18, 1975; children: Amy Elizabeth, Jeffrey Glenn. B.S., Bklyn. Coll., 1960; M.A., Mich. State U., 1961, Ph.D., 1966. Mem. faculty U. Okla., Norman, 1964—, prof. edn., phys. edn., human rels. and social work, 1973—, Regents' prof. edn. and human rels., 1991—, asst. and acting dean, 1969-72, dean Univ. Coll., 1973-91, vice provost instructional svcs., 1979-91; chmn. ednl. leadership and policy studies, 1993. Author: (with D.R. Lamb) Statistics and Research in Physical Education, 1970, (with G. Henderson) College Survival for Student-Athletes, 1985, (with R. Cintron) Enduring Enigmas: Issues in Adult and Higher Education, 1997; contbr. articles to profl. jours. Bd. dirs. Univ. div. United Way, 1970; pres. Norman Kindergarten Assn., 1968; commr. Norman Bd. Parks, 1971-79. Fellow Am. Coun. Sports Medicine; mem. Am. Assn. Higher Edn., Coun. Sports Psychology, Am. Coun. on Edn. Democrat. Jewish. Home: 5 Pebble Creek Rd Norman OK 73072-2822 Office: 630 Parrington Oval Norman OK 73069-8813

WEBER, JOHN BERTRAM, architect; b. Evanston, Ill., Oct. 15, 1930; s. Bertram Anton and Dorothea W.; m. Sally Ann French; children: Suzanne French Roulston, Jane Marie McCarthy, Patricia Ann Blodgett, Nancy Brammer. AB in Architecture, Princeton U., 1953; postgrad., Ill. Inst. Tech., 1959. Lic. architect. Field engr. United Constrn. Co., Riverdale, N.D., 1952; draftsman Bertram A. Weber Architect, Chgo., 1947- 53, architect, 1958-1973; field engr. Atkinson United Constrn. Co., Greenup and Ashland, Ky., 1956-58; ptnr., proprietor Weber & Weber Architects, Chgo., Northbrook and Winnetka, Ill., 1973—; Mem. Ill. Architecture Act Revision task force, 1982-89. Prin. works include Prestwick Country Club, the 3175 Commercial Ave. Bldg., Northbrook, med. office bldg. and additions to Bi-county hospital, Warren, Mich., additions and alterations to Detroit Osteopathic Hosp., addition to Duraclean Internat. Bldg., Deerfield, additions to The Admiral (a retirement home in Chgo.), and numerous pvt. residences, churches, comml., ednl., and recreational bldgs. Active Winnetka (Ill.) Cmty. Caucus, 1965, 74; mem. Mayor's adv. com. on bldg. codes, Chgo., 1975-80; chmn. bldg. com. Winnetka Cmty. House, 1977-81; mem. Winnetka Zoning Bd. Appeals, 1983-88, chmn., 1987-88; mem. Winnetka Ad Hoc Zoning Com., 1995-96; deacon, elder Winnetka Presbyn. Ch. With USN, 1953-56. Fellow Ill. Soc. Architects (bd. dirs. 1969-84, 91—, pres. 1976-78); mem. AIA (health com. 1969-76), Ill. Architect-Engr. Coun. (chmn. 1981-82, del. 1976-87, 92-96), Northbrook C. of C., Architects Club Chgo. (pres. 1981, bd. dirs. 1976-86, 94), Builders Club Chgo. (bd. dirs. 1966—, pres. 1973-74), Am. Legion, Old Willow Club, Mchts. and Mfrs. Club, Dairymen's Country Club. Home: 415 Berkeley Ave Winnetka IL 60093-2109 Office: Weber & Weber Architects 415 Berkeley Ave Winnetka IL 60093-2109 *Do what you should do, not what you have to do. In the end, it is only the things that we do that impact on other people's and other living being's lives that have real meaning.*

WEBER, JOHN WALTER, insurance company executive; b. Rochester, N.Y., Jan. 10, 1959; s. Donald J. and Patricia M. (Mangon) W.; m. Tracy Ann Sitler, Nov. 4, 1989. BS, U. Conn., 1984. Claims supr. Hartford Ins. Group, Southington, Conn., 1986-90; regional claims mgr. Housing Authority Risk Retention Group, Cheshire, Conn., 1990—. Mem. U. Conn. Alumni Assn. Republican. Avocations: fishing, reading, bowling, softball, cooking.

WEBER, JOSEPH H., communications company executive; b. N.Y.C., Dec. 10, 1930; s. Sol and Minna (Hoffman) W.; m. Sophie Ruderman, Apr. 10, 1954 (div. 1973); m. J. V. Hammar, Jan. 10, 1976; children—Leslie, Jonathan, David. B.E.E., Rensselaer Poly. Inst., 1952; M.S.E., George Washington U., 1956. Engr. Hazeltine Electronics Co., Little Neck, N.Y., 1952-53; mem. tech. staff Bell Telephone Labs., N.Y.C., 1956-61; head network analysis dept. Bell Telephone Labs., Holmdel, N.J., 1961-72; dir. data services AT&T Long Lines, N.Y.C., 1972-75; dir. network services planning Bell Telephone Labs., Holmdel, 1975-80; dir. tech. standards and regulatory planning AT&T, Basking Ridge, N.J., 1980-84; dir. strategic planning AT&T, N.Y.C., 1984-85; dir. venture tech. AT&T, Berkeley Heights, N.J., 1985-87; v.p. tech. Global Transactions Services Co., Parsippany, N.J., 1987-88; ptnr. T.E.L.A. Group, 1989-94, Weber Temin & Co., 1995—. Vice-pres. Holmdel Twp. Bd. Edn., 1970-72; mem. Morris Twp. Planning Bd., 1988—, chmn. 1997—. Served with U.S. Navy, 1953-56. Mem. IEEE (sr.), IEEE Communications Soc. (chmn. switching com. 1972-73). Patentee in field. Home: Box 224 16 Canfield Rd Convent Station NJ 07961

WEBER, JULIAN L., lawyer, former publishing and entertainment company executive; b. Des Moines, July 19, 1929; s. Milton and Zelda (Robinson) W.; m. Idelle Feinberg, Apr. 17, 1957; children—Jonathan Todd, Suzanne. B.A., UCLA, 1951; J.D., Harvard U., 1955. Bar: N.Y. 1956. Partner Botein Hays & Sklar, 1964-79; pres. Nat. Lampoon, Inc., N.Y.C., 1979-84; pvt. practice law N.Y.C., 1984—; dir. Viaweb, Inc., 1995—. Mem. ABA, Assn. of Bar of City of N.Y.

WEBER, LARRY, public relations executive. Founder, pres. Weber Group, Inc., Cambridge, Mass., 1987—; chmn., CEO The Weber Group, Inc., Cambridge, Mass. Office: The Weber Group Inc 101 Main St Cambridge MA 02142-1519*

WEBER, LAVERN JOHN, marine science administrator, educator; b. Isabel, S.D., June 7, 1933; s. Jacob and Irene Rose (Bock) W.; m. Shirley Jean Carlson, June 19, 1959 (div. 1992); children: Timothy L., Peter J., Pamela C., Elizabeth T.; m. Patricia Rae Lewis, Oct. 17, 1992. AAS, Everett Jr. Coll., 1956; BA, Pacific Luth. U., 1958; MS, U. Wash., 1962, PhD, 1964. Instr. U. Wash., Seattle, 1964-67, asst. prof., 1967-69, acting state toxicologist, 1968-69; assoc. prof. Oreg. State U., Corvallis, 1969-75, prof., 1976—, asst. dean grad. sch., 1974-77; dir. Hatfield Marine Sci. Ctr. Oregon State U., Newport, 1977—, supt. Coastal Oreg. Marine Exptl. Sta., 1989—. Pres., trustee Newport Pub. Libr., 1991-92, Yaquina Bay Econ. Found., Newport, 1991-92; chmn. Oreg. Coast Aquarium, 1983-95. Recipient Pres. award Newport Rotary, 1984-85. Mem. South Slough Mgmt. Commn., Am. Soc. Pharm. and Exptl. Therapy, West Pharm. Soc., Soc. Toxicology, Soc. Exptl. Biol. Med. (n.w. divsn., pres. 1978, 82, 87), Pacific N.W. Assn. Toxicologists (chair 1985-86, coun. 1991-93), Western Assn. Marine Lab. (pres. 1993). Avocations: woodworking, reading, walking, scuba, gardening. Office: Oregon State Univ Hatfield Marine Sci Ctr Aquarium 2030 SE Marine Science Dr Newport OR 97365-5229

WEBER, MARY ELLEN HEALY, economist; b. San Francisco, May 28, 1943; d. Ignatius Bernard and Grace Marie (Hogan) Healy; B.A., Dominican Coll., 1965; postgrad. Nat. U. Mex., 1967, (vis. scholar) Stanford U., 1969-70, Cath. U. Chile, 1970-71, U. Chile, 1971-72; Ph.D., U. Utah, 1974; m. Stephen Francis Weber, Dec. 21, 1971. U. Utah teaching fellow, 1965-68; asst. prof. Smith Coll., 1972-75; country economist World Bank, IBRD, 1975-76; sr. economist Internat. Research & Tech. Corp., McLean, Va., 1976-78; dir. regulatory analysis, chief economist OSHA, U.S. Dept. Labor, Washington, 1979-84; pres. Weber Software Enterprises, 1984-86, Web-Wolf Data Systems, Inc., 1986-90; dir. econs., exposure and tech divsn. Office of Pollution Prevention & Toxics US EPA, Washington, 1990—. Social Sci. Research Council fgn. area fellow 1969-71. Mem. Sr. Execs. Assn., Exec. Women in Govt. Roman Catholic.

WEBER, MERRILL EVAN, lawyer, business executive; b. Chgo., Sept. 1, 1956; s. Robert and Mildred (Kurchitzer) W.; m. Mindy Kallus, Mar. 29, 1987; children: Stephanie Margalit, Sarah Abigail. BA, Columbia Coll., 1978, MS in Journalism, 1978, JD, 1984. Bar: N.Y. 1985, U.S. Dist. Ct. (so. and ea. dists.) N.Y. 1985. Assoc. Fried, Frank, Harris, Shriver & Jacobson, N.Y.C., 1984-85, Mayer, Brown & Platt, N.Y.C., 1985-87, Paul, Weiss, Rifkind, Wharton & Garrison, N.Y.C., 1987-91, D'Ancona & Pflaum, Chgo., 1991-92; CEO Merrill Weber & Co., Inc. (formerly Weber, Halpert & Co., Inc.), Northbrook, Ill., 1992—. Harlan Fiske Stone scholar, Columbia Law Sch., 1982-83, 1983-84. Mem. ABA, N.Y. State Bar Assn., Assn. of Bar of City of N.Y. Jewish. Office: Merrill Weber & Co Inc 95 Revere Dr Ste A Northbrook IL 60062-1585

WEBER, MICHAEL JAMES, conductor; b. Grand Forks, ND, Jan. 28, 1957; s. James Warren and Donna Jean (Christiansen) W. BS in Edn., U. N.D., 1980; MusM, Calif. State U., 1986; MusD, U. Ariz., 1990. Music tchr. Hillsboro (N.D.) Pub. Schs., 1980-84, Grand Forks (N.D.) Pub. Schs., 1990-92; choral conductor The Victoria (Tex.) Coll., 1992—; organist, choir master Trinity Episcopal Ch., Victoria, Tex., 1994—; conductor Victoria (Tex.) Master Chorale, 1995—. Arranger (choral music): I Wonder As I Wander, 1996. Mem. adv. bd. Hopkins Fine Arts Sch., Victoria, Tex., 1994—. Mem. Am. Choral Dirs. Assn., Victoria (Tex.) Symphony Soc. (bd. dirs. 1993—), Victoria Fine Arts Assn. (bd. dirs. 1992—), Music Educators Nat. Conf., Tex. Music Educators Nat. Conf., Tex. ACDA. Office: The Victoria Coll 2200 E Red River St Victoria TX 77901-4442

WEBER, MORTON M., microbial biochemist, educator; b. N.Y.C., May 26, 1922; s. Morris and Mollie (Scherer) W.; m. Phyllis Stern Levy, July 31, 1955; children—Stephen Abbott, Ethan Lenard. B.S., Coll. City N.Y., 1949; Sc.D., Johns Hopkins, 1953. Instr. microbiology Sch. Medicine, Johns Hopkins, 1951-55; Am. Cancer Soc. fellow in biochemistry McCollum-Pratt Inst., 1953-56; instr. bacteriology and immunology Med. Sch., Harvard, 1956-59; asst. prof. Sch. Medicine, St. Louis U., 1959-61, assoc. prof., 1961-63, prof., 1963—, chmn. dept. microbiology, 1964-87, chmn. emeritus, 1987—, prof. emeritus, 1992—; vis. scientist microbiology unit U. Oxford (Eng.) Dept. Biochemistry, 1970—; sr. mem. Linacre Coll. Oxford U., 1970—; mem. microbial chemistry study sect. NIH, USPHS, 1969-73. Served with USAAF, 1942-46. Fellow AAAS, Am. Acad. Microbiology, Infectious Disease Soc. Am., Johns Hopkins Soc. Scholars; mem. Am. Soc. Biol. Chemists, Am. Soc. Microbiology (sec. physiology div. 1964-65, vice chmn. 1965-66, chmn. 1966-67), Soc. Gen. Microbiology, N.Y. Acad. Scis., St. Louis Biochemistry Group (pres. 1968-69), Phi Beta Kappa (hon.), Sigma Xi. Research in biochemistry of microorganisms, with emphasis on pathways and mechanisms of electron transport, enzymatic regulatory mechanisms, and mode of action of antimicrobial drugs and antibiotics. Home: 7068 Waterman Ave Saint Louis MO 63130-4323 Office: St Louis U Sch Medicine Dept Microbiology Saint Louis MO 63104

WEBER, NANCY WALKER, charitable trust administrator; b. Adrian, W.Va., Aug. 26, 1936; d. James Everett and Wanna Virginia (Alderman) Walker; m. J. Raymond Jacob, Jr., June 12, 1955 (div. 1967); children: Paul M., Sharon L.; m. George Harry Weber, Apr. 27, 1983 (dec. Mar. 1995). Student, Peabody Prep. Mus., 1946-53, Peabody Conservatory Mus., 1954-56. Asst. buyer cosmetics Hutzler's Dept. Store, Balt., 1967-69; exec. sec. to exec. v.p. Martin Marietta Corp., Bethesda, Md., 1969-75; asst. exec. to exec. dir. hosp. U. Utah, Salt Lake City, 1976-80; dir. program adminstrn. Lucille P. Markey Charitable Trust, Miami, Fla., 1983—. Pianist, organist Middle River Bapt. Ch., Balt., 1953-61. Named Mrs. Del. in Mrs. Del./Am. Pagent, 1966. Avocations: piano, organ. Office: Lucille P Markey Charitable Trust 3250 Mary St Ste 405 Miami FL 33133-5232

WEBER, OWEN, broadcast executive; b. N.Y.C., Apr. 29, 1946; s. Francis and Margaret (Korn) W. BS in Broadcasting, U. Fla., 1968. Program dir. Sta. WLYH-TV, Lancaster, Pa., 1970-72; dir. affiliate rels. Mut. Radio Networks, Washington, 1972-77; account exec. Sta. WCBM, Balt., 1977-78; local sales mgr. Sta. WTOP, Washington, 1979-80; gen. sales mgr. Sta. WTOP-Radio Outlet Co., Washington, 1980-81; gen. sales mgr. Sta. WCBM-Radio Metromedia, Balt., 1981-83; gen. sales mgr. Sta. WPGC-AM-FM First Media Corp., Washington, 1983-85; v.p., gen. mgr. Stas. WCAO-Radio and WXYV-Radio Summit Broadcasting Corp., Balt., 1985-88; exec. v.p. Summit Broadcasting Corp., Atlanta, 1988-93; pres., CEO HMW Comm., Inc., Atlanta, 1993-95; v.p., gen. mgr. Sta. KIKK-AM-FM and Sta. KILT-AM-FM CBS-Radio, Houston, 1995—. Office: CBS Radio Houston 24 E Greenway Plz Ste 1900 Houston TX 77046-2419

WEBER, PAUL FREDERICK, physician, pharmacist, educator; b. Cleve., Mar. 21, 1960; s. Paul Henry and Anna (Papastathis) W.; m. Ann Marie Vinci, June 29, 1985. BS, Rutgers Coll. Pharmacy, 1983; MD, U. Med. Dental N.J., 1987. Diplomate Am. Bd. Internal Medicine; reg. pharmacist, N.J. Pharm. scientist Parke-Davis divsn. Warner-Lambert Co., Morris Plains, N.J., 1983; staff pharmacist Wallkill Valley Gen. Hosp., Sussex, N.J., 1984; rsch. asst. UMDNJ-Robert Wood Johnson Med. Sch., Piscataway, N.J., 1985; clin. asst. prof. medicine UMDNJ-Robert Wood Johnson Med. Sch., New Brunswick, N.J., 1990—; asst. med. dir. Health and Scis. Rsch., Inc., Englewood, N.J., 1990, assoc. med. dir., 1990-92, safety officer, 1991-92; dir. clin. rsch. Medicis Pharm. Co., Phoenix, 1992-93; v.p. med. affairs Girgenti, Hughes, Butler and McDowell, Inc., N.Y.C., 1993-95; med. dir. Roche Labs., Inc., Nutley, N.J., 1995-96, team leader, 1996—, team leader oncology/HIV/AIDS, 1997—. Recipient Roche Pharmacy Comm. award Rutgers U., 1983; Rotary Achievment scholar, 1981. Mem. ACP, AMA, Am. Coll. Physician Execs. Avocations: triathlon, marathons, music, travel. Office: Roche Labs Inc 340 Kingsland St Nutley NJ 07110-1150

WEBER, PHILIP JOSEPH, retired manufacturing company executive; b. Chgo., Mar. 15, 1909; s. Joseph and Theresa (Zollner); m. Esther P. White, Aug. 29, 1941; 1 child, Patricia G. B.B.A., Northwestern U., 1938. With Ernst & Ernst, Chgo., 1938-41; with Doall Co., Des Plaines, Ill., 1941—88; exec. v.p. Doall Co., 1969-80, pres., 1969-74, chmn. bd., 1974-88, ret. Clubs: Mason (Shriner), Elk, Park Ridge Country. Home: 709 N Merrill St Park Ridge IL 60068-2701 also: 4545 N Ocean Blvd Apt 9-d Boca Raton FL 33431-5344

WEBER, RAY EVERETT, engineering executive, consultant; b. Kenton, Ohio, Dec. 11, 1946; s. Mervin Clarence and Phylis Jean Weber; m. Carolyn Antinoro, Aug. 16, 1980; children: David Charles, Stephen Ray. BS in Physics, Ohio State U., 1973. lic. real estate agent, N.Y. Project engr. Erie Lackawanna R.R., Hoboken, N.J., 1974-75; nuclear engring. adminstr. ASME, N.Y.C., 1975-78; cognizant engr. Burns & Roe Inc., Oradell, N.J., 1978-80; supervising engr. Impell Corp., Melville, N.Y., 1980-88; pres. Webtor Inc., Northport, N.Y., 1988—; pres. Forest Ventures Inc., Northport, N.Y., 1987—. Author plans and codes. With USN, 1966-70. Mem. ASME (nuclear subcom.), Am. Legion, Northport Yacht Club. Avocations: boating, fishing, skiing, golf. Home: 115 Soundview Ter Northport NY 11768-1231 Office: Webtor Inc 115 Soundview Ter Northport NY 11768-1231

WEBER, ROBERT CARL, lawyer; b. Chester, Pa., Dec. 18, 1950; s. Robert Francis and Lucille (Nobili) W.; m. Linda Brediger, June 30, 1972; children: Robert F., Mary Therese, David P., Joseph T. BA cum laude, Yale U., 1972; JD, Duke U., 1976. Bar: Ohio 1976, U.S. Dist. ct. (no. dist.) Ohio 1976, U.S. Ct. Claims 1980, U.S. Ct. Appeals (6th cir.) 1981, U.S. Ct. Appeals (5th cir.) 1995. Assoc. Jones, Day, Reavis & Pogue, Cleve., 1976-83, ptnr., 1983—. Bd. dirs. United Way Svcs. of Cleve., 1992—. Fellow Am. Coll. Trial Lawyers; mem. Ohio Bar Assn., Am. Law Inst., Product Liability Adv. Coun., Cleve. Bar Assn. (chmn. jud. selection com. 1985-86, trustee 1990-93, pres.-elect 1994-95, pres. 1995-96), Jud. Conf. for 8th Jud. Dist. Ohio (life), Order of Coif. Roman Catholic. Office: Jones Day Reavis & Pogue 901 Lakeside Ave E Cleveland OH 44114-1116

WEBER, ROBERT MAXWELL, cartoonist; b. L.A., Apr. 22, 1924; p. Milton and Edith (Huston) W.; m. Marilyn Baum, Oct. 11, 1953 (div.); children—Peter, Lee; m. Debora Graves, Dec. 24, 1988. Student, Pratt Inst., 1945-48, Art Students League, 1948-50. Fashion illustrator, 1949-54; artist New Yorker mag., 1962—; work commd. by IBM, N.Y. Telephone, Am. Airlines, Mobil, Blue Cross/Blue Shield, U.S. Healthcare, Goodyear Co., J.C. Penney Co., Air Canada, Swissair, others; contbr. cartoons to nat. mags. Served with USCGR, 1942-45. Office: New Yorker 20 W 43rd St New York NY 10036-7400

WEBER, SAMUEL, editor, retired; b. N.Y.C., July 31, 1926; s. Bernard and Gertrude (Ellenberg) W.; m. Eileen Gloria Hornstein, Mar. 5, 1950; children—Bruce Jay, Robert Matthew. B.S. in Elec. Engring, Va. Poly. Inst., 1947. Engr. N.Y. Bd. Transp., 1948-50, U.S. Naval Shipyard, Bklyn., 1950-52, Barlow Engring. Co., N.Y.C., 1952-54; engring. supr. Curtiss Wright Corp., Woodridge, N.J., 1954-56; electronics engr. Loral Electronics Corp., N.Y.C., 1957-58; with Electronics mag., N.Y.C., 1958-67, assoc. mng. editor, 1968-70, exec. editor, 1970-79, editor in chief, 1979-84, exec. tech. editor, 1984-88, editor-at-large, 1988-92; editor in chief Electrotechnology mag., N.Y.C., 1968—; pres. Samuel Weber & Assocs., 1988-91, Samuel Weber & Assocs., Inc., 1991-96; contbg. editor Asic & Eda Magazine, 1991-94; spl. projects editor Electronic Engring. Times, 1992-96, ret., 1997. Author: Modern Digital Circuits, 1964, Optoelectronic Devices and Circuits, 1968, Large and Medium Scale Integration, 1974, Circuits for Electronics Engineers, 1977, Electronic Circuits Notebook, 1981. Served with AUS, 1944-46. Mem. IEEE (life). Home and Office: 4242 E Allison Rd Tucson AZ 85712-1039

WEBER, SAMUEL LLOYD, tap dancer, choreographer; b. Washington, Oct. 16, 1950; s. Abe Charles and Mary Louise (Walker) W.; m. Rosine Anne Bena, July 28, 1973 (div. May 1986); 1 child, Ananda Bena. Grad., Calif. State U., L.A. Prin. dancer Peninsula Ballet Theatre, San Mateo, Calif., 1972-86; ballet master, prin. dancer Sacramento Ballet, 1986; prin. dancer Jazz Tap Ensemble, L.A., 1986—; instr. dance artist-in-residence L.A. County H.S. for Arts, 1989-91, Calif. State U., Fullerton, 1990, 94. Tap dancer Joyce Theatre season, 1992 (Bessie award 1993), soloist with Lyon Symphony Biennial, 1991. Home: 1163 Guerrero St San Francisco CA 94110-2934 Office: 1433 Yale St # B1 Santa Monica CA 90404-3133

WEBER, STEPHEN LEWIS, university president; b. Boston, Mar. 17, 1942; s. Lewis F. and Catherine (Warns) W.; m. Susan M. Keim, June 27, 1965; children: Richard, Matthew. BA, Bowling Green State U., 1964; postgrad., U. Colo., 1964-66; PhD, U. Notre Dame, 1969; EdD (hon.), Capital Normal U., China, 1993. Asst. prof. philosophy U. Maine, Orono, 1969-75, assoc. prof., 1975-79, asst. to pres., 1976-79; dean arts and scis. Fairfield (Conn.) U., 1979-84; v.p. acad. affairs St. Cloud (Minn.) State U., 1984-88; pres. SUNY Oswego, 1988-95; interim provost SUNY, Oswego, 1995-96; pres. San Diego State U., 1996—; participant Harvard Inst. Ednl. Mgmt., Cambridge, Mass., 1985; cons. Sloan Found., 1981. Contbr. numerous articles on philosophy and acad. adminstrn. to profl. jours. Mentor Am. Coun. Edn. Fellowship Program; co-chair Minn. State Bd. Edn. Curriculum Task Force on Educating the Black Learner, 1988; mem. Minn. Tech. Alliance, 1987; mem. program adv. com. Minn. Higher Edn. Coordinating Bd., 1986-88; mem. Gov.'s Commn. on Internat. Edn., 1988. Named Outstanding Humanities Tchr., U. Maine, 1975; Rsch. fellow U. Notre Dame, 1968-69. Mem. Am. Philos. Assn., Am. Assn. Higher Edn. Democrat. Avocations: art, woodworking, swimming, boating. Office: Office of President San Diego State University San Diego CA 92182-0001

WEBER, STEVEN, actor. Appeared in films Single White Female, 1992, Jeffrey, 1995, Dracula: Dead and Loving It, 1995, Leaving Las Vegas, 1995. Office: Internat Creative Mgmt 8942 Wilshire Blvd Beverly Hills CA 90211*

WEBER, THOMAS WILLIAM, chemical engineering educator; b. Orange, N.J., July 15, 1930; s. William A. and Dorothy (Negus) W.; m. Marianne S. Hartmann, June 4, 1966; children—Anne Louise, William Alois. B.Chem. Engring., Cornell U., 1953, Ph.D., 1963; M.S. in Chem. Engring., Newark Coll. Engring., 1958. Registered profl. engr., N.Y. Chem. engr. econs. and planning Esso Research & Engring., Linden, N.J., 1955-58; instr. Cornell U., 1961-62; asst. prof. SUNY-Buffalo, 1963-66, assoc. prof. chem. engring., 1966-82, prof., 1982—, assoc. chmn. dept., 1980-82, chmn. dept., 1982-89. Author: An Introduction to Process Dynamics and Control, 1973. Named Prof. of Yr., Tau Kappa Chi, 1965; recipient Chancellor's award for excellence in teaching, 1981, Tchr. of Yr. award Tau Beta Pi, 1982. Fellow AIChE (chmn. western N.Y. sect. 1969-70, Profl. Achievement award western N.Y. sect. 1978), Am. Soc. Engring. Edn. (chmn. instrumentation divsn. 1975-77, chmn. St. Lawrence sect. 1979-80, 92-94, chmn. divsn. experimentation and lab.-oriented studies 1985-86, Outstanding Zone Campus Rep. award 1988, AT&T Found. award 1987-88); mem. Tech. Socs. Coun. Niagara Frontier (sec. 1973-75, pres. 1975-76, treas. 1978—), Swedish Club of Buffalo (pres. 1974-76), U.S. Masters Swimming Club, Sigma Xi, Phi Kappa Phi, Tau Beta Pi, Theta Xi. Presbyterian. Home: 52 Autumnview Rd Buffalo NY 14221-1602

WEBER, WALTER JACOB, JR., engineering educator; b. Pitts., June 16, 1934. Sc.B., Brown U., 1956; M.S.E., Rutgers U., 1959; A.M., Harvard, 1961, Ph.D., 1962. Registered profl. engr. Diplomate Am. Acad. Environ. Engrs. Engr. Caterpillar Tractor Co., Peoria, Ill., 1956-57; instr. Rutgers U., 1957-59; engr. Soil Conservation Service, New Brunswick, N.J., 1957-59; research, teaching asso. Harvard, 1959-63; faculty U. Mich., Ann Arbor, 1963—; prof., chmn. water resources program U. Mich., 1968-91, The Earnest Boyce Disting. Prof. of Engring., 1987-94; The Gordon Maskew Fair and Earnest Boyce Disting. U. Prof. U. Mich., Ann Arbor, 1994—; dir. Great Lakes & Mid-Atlantic Hazardous Substance Rsch. Ctr., Nat. Ctr. for Integrated Bioremediation R & D; Internat. cons. to industry, govt. Author: (with K.H. Mancy) Analysis of Industrial Wastewaters, 1971, Physicochemical Processes for Water Quality Control, 1972, (with F.A. DiGiano) Process Dynamics in Environmental Systems, 1996; editor, author: (with E. Matijevic) Adsorption from Aqueous Solution, 1968; contbr. numerous articles and chpts. to tech. and profl. jours. and books. Recipient Disting. Faculty awards U. Mich., 1967, 78, Rsch. Excellence award, 1980, Stephen S. Attwood award, 1977; Disting. Faculty award Mich. chpt. Assn. Gov. Bds. of State Univs., 1989; Disting. Scientist award U.S. EPA, 1991; Athalie Richardson Irvine Clarke prize Nat. Water Rsch. Inst., 1996. Mem. NAE, Am. Acad. Environ. Engrs. (Diplomate 1975, Gordon Maskew Fair award, 1995), Am. Chem. Soc. (cert. of merit 1962, F.J. Zimmerman award 1982), Am. Inst. Chem. Engrs., ASCE (Rudolph Hering medal 1980, Thomas R. Camp award 1982, Simon W. Freese award 1984, G. Brooks Earnest award 1985), Am. Water Works Assn. (life, Acad. Achievement awards 1981, 89, A.P. Black Rsch. award 1991), Assn. Environ. Engring. Profs. (Disting. Faculty award 1968, NALCO rsch. award 1979, Engring. Sci. rsch. award 1984, Outstanding Publ. award 1989, Disting. Lectr. award 1990), Internat. Assn. for Water Pollution Rsch. and COntrol (Founders Outstanding Publ. award 1987, 92), Water Pollution Control Fedn. (John R. Rumsey Meml. award 1975, Willard F. Shepard award 1980, Thomas R. Camp medal 1988, Gordon Maskew Fair medal 1990), Tau Beta Pi, Sigma Xi, Chi Epsilon, Delta Omega. Home: PO Box 7775 Ann Arbor MI 48107-7775 Office: U Mich Coll Engring Environ Engring Program Ste 181 EWRE Bldg Ann Arbor MI 48109-2125

WEBER, WENDELL WILLIAM, pharmacologist; b. Maplewood, Mo., Sept. 2, 1925; s. Theodore William and Flora Ann (Holt) W.; m. La Donna Tavis, Sept. 29, 1952; children—Jane Holt, Theodore Wendell. A.B., Central Coll., 1945; Ph.D. in Phys. Chemistry, Northwestern U., 1950; M.D., U. Chgo., 1959. Diplomate Am. Bd. Pediatrics; lic. Mich., N.Y., Calif. Asst. prof. chemistry U. Tenn., Knoxville, 1949-51; mem. ops. research staff U.S. Army Chem. Center, Edgewood, Md., 1951-55; successively instr., asst. prof., asso. prof., prof. pharmacology N.Y. U. Sch. Medicine, N.Y.C., 1963-74; prof. U. Mich., Ann Arbor, 1974—; Disting. Lectureship in Biomedical Rsch. U. Mich., 1993; mem. pharmacology-toxicology com. NIH, 1969-73, rev. coms., 1968—. Editorial bd. Bioessays, 1984-91, Pharmacogenetics, 1990—. NIH spl. fellow, 1962-65; research grantee, 1967—; recipient Career Scientist awards N.Y.C. Health Research Council, 1965-70, 70-74. Fellow N.Y. Acad. Scis.; mem. Am. Soc. Pharmacology and Therapeutics, Am. Chem. Soc., Am. Soc. Human Genetics, Soc. Toxicology (hon.), AAAS, Sigma Xi, Phi Lambda Upsilon. Research specialty in pharmacogenetics. Home: 14 Geddes Hts Ann Arbor MI 48104-1724 Office: Dept Pharmacology U Mich Ann Arbor MI 48109-0632

WEBERPAL, MICHAEL ANDREW, lawyer; b. Sycamore, Ill., Sept. 16, 1951; s. Michael Andrew Sr. and Mary Elizabeth (Egan) W.; m. Michelle Vinet, Aug. 20, 1971. BA in Econs., U. Wis., Milw., 1975; JD, U. Wis., Madison, 1978; LLM, So. Meth. U., 1992. Bar: Wis. 1978, Tex. 1980, U.S. Dist. Ct. (we. dist.) Wis. Assoc. LaRowe & Gerlach, Reedsburg, Wis., 1978-79; tax specialist Laventhol & Horwath, Dallas, 1980-81; sr. atty. Otis Engring. Corp. (subsidiary of Halliburton Co.), Dallas and London, 1983-88; sr. tax counsel Halliburton Co., Dallas, 1988-92, sr. atty., asst. sec., 1992-93; v.p., gen. counsel, sec. Highlands Ins. Co., Houston, 1993-97; sr. atty. Halliburton Co., 1997—. Mem. ABA, State Bar Tex., State Bar Wis., Houston Bar Assn. Republican. Roman Catholic. Avocations: skiing, jogging, golf. Home: 61 Ambleside Crescent Dr Sugar Land TX 77479-2528 Office: Brown & Root Inc 4100 Clinton Dr Houston TX 77020-6237

WEBER-ROOCHVARG, LYNN, English second language adult educator, communications consultant; b. Long Beach, Calif., Jan. 5, 1945; d. Bernard R. and Ruth M. (Oehler) Weber; m. Edward A. Birge (div.); 1 child, Colin E.; m. Alan C. Roochvarg. BA, U. Wis., 1966, MA in Libr. Sci., 1967; PhD, Ariz. State U., 1980. Teaching asst. U. Wis., Madison, 1966-67; libr. Madison Pub. Libr., 1967-70, New Haven Free Pub. Libr., 1970-72; ESL instr. Tempe (Ariz.) Adult Basic Education Program, 1972-77, supr., 1977-80; archival cons. Phoenix, 1980-82; libr. Phoenix Coll., 1982-84, Lansdale (Pa.) Sch. Bus., 1985-92; pres. LWR Assocs., Colmar, Pa., 1991—. Author: Serving Adult Learners, 1981; contbr. articles to profl. jours. Ford Found fellow, 1966; Ariz. Dept. Edn. grantee, 1978-80. Mem. ALA, Pa. TESOL, Phi Beta Kappa. Office: LWR Assocs PO Box 501 Colmar PA 18915-0501

WEBRE, SEPTIME, ballet company artistic director, choreographer; b. New Orleans, Dec. 7, 1961; s. Alfred L. and Juanita (Chisholm) W. BA, U. Tex., 1984. Dancer Merce Cunningham Dance Co., N.Y.C., 1991; dancer Am. Repertory Ballet/Princeton (N.J.) Ballet, 1987—, choreographer, 1988—, artistic dir., 1993—; freelance choreographer with Pacific N.W. Ballet, Sacramento Ballet, Columbia City Ballet, Ballet Austin, Dayton Ballet, Eglevsky Ballet, the Carslile Project, others, 1988—; guest master tchr. various ballet cos., 1990—. Former mem. exec. bd. Young Dems. Am., Austin. Choreographic fellow N.J. Coun. on Arts, 1992. Roman Catholic. Office: Am Repertory Ballet 80 Albany St New Brunswick NJ 08901-1227

WEBSTER, ARTHUR EDWARD, lawyer; b. Hartford, Conn., Dec. 2, 1956; s. Arthur Ellsworth and Carrie Mabel (Goodrich) W. BA summa cum laude, Bradley U., 1978; JD, Georgetown U., 1982. Bar: Conn. 1982, U.S. Dist. Ct. Conn. 1983. Assoc. Halloran, Sage, Phelan & Hagarty, Hartford, 1982-85; asst. atty. gen. Office of Atty. Gen., State of Conn., Hartford, 1986—; adj. faculty U. Conn. Sch. Law, Hartford, 1991—; faculty mem. Dept. Children & Families Tng. Acad., Bridgeport, Conn., 1989—; co-dir., instr. Conn. Bar Assn./State of Conn. Jud. Dept. CLE seminars, Hartford, 1992—, mem. faculty trial skills seminar for child protection lawyers, 1996; panelist (TV program) Child Abuse, 1992. Author: Child Protection in Connecticut Courts, 1992, rev. edit., 1996, The Art of the Deal: A Common Sense Approach to Settlement of Child Protection Cases, 1996. Pres. Middletown br. Am. Heart Assn., 1989-90, v.p., 1987-89; mem. steering com. March of Dimes, WalkAmerica, 1988-90. Nyaradi Meml. fellow Bradley U. Inst. Internat. Studies, 1978; law fellow Georgetown U. Law Ctr., Washington, 1981, Beaudry fellow, 1982; recipient Order of Lincoln from Gov. of Ill., 1978. Mem. Conn. Bar Assn. (chmn. juvenile justice com. 1983—). Home: 359 Main St Cromwell CT 06416-2308 Office: Office of Atty Gen 110 Sherman St Hartford CT 06105-2267

WEBSTER, DAVID ARTHUR, life insurance company executive; b. Downs, Ill., July 20, 1937; s. Harold Sanford and Carmen Mildred (Moore) W.; m. Anna Elizabeth Prosch, June 10, 1956; children: Theodore David, Elizabeth Anna, Arthur Lee, William Harold. B.S., U. Ill., 1960. Actuarial asst. Mass. Mut. Life Ins. Co., Springfield, 1960-64; cons. actuary George Stennes & Assocs., Mpls., 1964-68; v.p., actuary Piedmont Life Ins. Co., Atlanta, 1968-72, Pacific Fidelity Life Ins. Co., Los Angeles, 1972-74; v.p., chief actuary U.S. Life Corp., N.Y.C., 1974-76; exec. v.p. U.S. Life Corp., 1976-78, dir., 1976-78; pres., dir. Beneficial Pension Svcs, BPS Agy., Inc.; v.p., treas., dir. Beneficial Assurance Co., 1978-82; asst. sec., dir. Beneficial Computer Svcs., Inc.; treas. Tel-Assurance Corp.; exec. v.p., dir. Beneficial Standard Life, 1978-82; pres., dir. U.S. Life Ins. Co. of Calif., 1982-84, Western World Fin. Group Inc., 1984-86; exec. v.p., COO R.W. Durham and Co., 1987—. Fellow Soc. Actuaries; mem. Am. Acad. Actuaries. Clubs: Actuaries of Pacific States, Woodland Hills Country. Home: 5131 Encino Ave Encino CA 91316-2523

WEBSTER, DOUGLAS PETER, emergency physician; b. Chgo., July 4, 1957; s. David Ferguson and Margaret Webster; m. Mariruth K. Burkhart, Sept. 25, 1989. BA in Chemistry, BS in Psychology, Loyola U., Chgo., 1978; MS in Chem. Physics, Wayne State U., 1980; DO, Chgo. Coll. Osteo. Medicine, 1985. Diplomate in emergency medicine Am. Osteo. Bd. Emergency Medicine, Am. Bd. Forensic Examiners. Intern Chgo. Coll. Osteo Medicine, 1985-86; resident in gen. surgery Sinai Hosp. Detroit, 1986-87; resident in emergency medicine Chgo. Coll. Osteo Medicine, 1988-90; clin. asst. prof. emergency medicine Chgo. Coll. Osteo. Medicine, 1990-93, clin. assoc. prof., 1993—, assoc. chmn. dept. emergency medicine, 1995—; assoc. dir. emergency svcs. Olympia Fields (Ill.) Osteo Med./Trauma Ctr., 1990-91; dir. emergency svcs. St. Anthony Hosp., Chgo., 1991-93; sr. ptnr. Med. Rev. Assocs., S.C., 1992—; chmn., med. dir. emergency medicine Little Co. of Mary Hosp., Evergreen Park, Ill., 1993-95; med. dir. Trauma Ctr. Columbia Olympia Fields (Ill.) Osteo. Med. Ctr., 1996—; pres. Emergency Med. Assocs., Ill., Ind., 1996—; assoc. clin. coord., cons. Crescent Counties Found. for Med. Care, 1992—; pres. Emergency Med. Assocs. of Ill. and Ind., 1996—; speaker in field. Diplomate in emergency medicine Am. Osteo. Bd. Emergency Medicine, Am. Bd. Forensic Examiners, Am. Bd. Forensic Medicine. Recipient award Disting. Physicians Am., 1991, Family Medicine award Lemmon Pharm. Found., 1985, others; Univ. Grad. fellow Wayne State U., 1979. Fellow Am. Coll. Osteo. Emergency Physicians; mem. Am. Bd. Forensic Examiners, Am. Bd. Forensic Medicine, Am. Coll. Emergency Physicians, Am. Osteo. Assn., Phi Lambda Upsilon, Alpha Epsilon Delta. Avocations: music, computers, electronics, private pilot. Home: 4439 Cascara Ln Lisle IL 60532-4368 Office: Columbia Olympia Fields Osteo Med Ctr 20201 Crawford Ave Olympia Fields IL 60461-1010

WEBSTER, EDWARD WILLIAM, medical physicist; b. London, Apr. 12, 1922; came to U.S., 1949, naturalized, 1957; s. Edward and Bertha Louisa (Cornish) W.; m. Irene Ruth Henry, June 4, 1950 (dec. 1958); m. Dorothea

Anne Wood, June 24, 1961; children: John, Peter, Anne, Edward, Mark, Susan. BSc in Elec. Engring., U. London, 1943, PhD, 1946; postgrad., MIT, 1949-51, 65-66, Columbia U., 1966; AM (hon.), Harvard U., 1989. Diplomate: Am. Bd. Radiology in radiol. physics (examiner 1958-84, chmn. physics com. 1966-76), Am. Bd. Health Physics. Research engr. English Electric Co., Stafford, Eng., 1945-49; travelling fellow lab. for nuclear sci. MIT, 1949-50, staff scientist, 1950-51; lectr. U. London, 1952-53; physicist Mass. Gen. Hosp., Boston, 1953—, chief radiol. scis. div., 1970—; prof. radiology Harvard U. Med. Sch., Boston, 1975-92, prof. emeritus, 1992—; prof. radiology div. health scis. and tech. Harvard-MIT, 1978-86; Langham lectr. U. Ky. Coll. Medicine, 1989; mem. com. radiology NAS, 1962-68; mem. com. on planning radiotherapy facilities, WHO, Geneva, Switzerland, 1964, Radiological Health Study section, U.S. Environ. Control Adminstrn., 1969-72, biol. effects of ionizing radiation com. NAS, 1977-80, oversight com. on Radioepidemiologic Tables, NAS, 1983-84; adv. com. on environ. hazards VA, 1985-95, Med. Use of Isotopes, U.S. Nuclear Regulatory Commn., 1971-93; U.S. del. UN Sci. Com. on Effects of Atomic Radiation, 1987-97; sec.-gen. 2d Internat. Conf. Med. Physics, Boston, 1966-69; lectr. Harvard Sch. Pub. Health, 1971-86; Garland lectr. Calif. Radiol. Soc., 1980; cons. Radiation Effects Rsch. Found., Hiroshima, Japan, 1988; Adams lectr. U Okla. Med. Ctr., 1989; Taylor lectr. Nat. Coun. on Radiation Protection, 1992, mem., 1965-89, hon. mem., 1989—, cons. Presdl. Adv. Com. on Human Radiation Experiments, 1994-95. Author: A Basic Radioisotopes Course, 1959, Atlas of Radiation Dose Distributions, 1965, Physics in Diagnostic Radiology, 1970; co-author: Instrumentation and Monitoring Methods for Radiation Protection, 1978, Low-level Radiation Effects, 1982; co-editor: Advances in Medical Physics, 1971, Biological Risks of Medical Irradiations, 1980; inventor composite shields against low energy X-rays, 1970. Robert Blair travelling fellow London County Council, 1949; USPHS fellow, 1965; NIH grantee, 1958-80. Fellow Health Physics Soc. (Landauer award 1985, Failla award 1989), Am. Coll. Radiology (commn. mem. 1963-93, Gold medal 1991), Am. Assn. Physicists in Medicine (dir. 1958-65, pres. 1963-64, Coolidge medal 1983); mem. Soc. Nuclear Medicine (trustee 1973-77), Radiol. Soc. N.Am. (v.p. 1977-78), New Eng. Roentgen Ray Soc. (hon., exec. com. 1976-77), Radiation Rsch. Soc., Sigma Xi (nat. lectr. 1988-89). Office: Mass Gen Hosp Fruit St Boston MA 02114-2620 *My efforts have focused on increasing and spreading knowledge which will improve man's control over his environment, including his health.*

WEBSTER, GORDON VISSCHER, JR., minister; b. Huntington, N.Y., Oct. 2, 1947; s. Gordon Visscher and Marion Beatrice (French) W.; m. Gloria Marie Farwagi, May 31, 1975; children: David Gordon, Daniel Farwagi, Diana Alexandra. AB, Hamilton Coll., 1969; postgrad., St. Andrews Divinity Sch., 1970-71, McCormick Theol. Sem., 1982-87; MDiv, Union Theol. Sem., 1973. Ordained to ministry Presbyn. Ch. (USA), 1973. Staff assoc. Met. Ch. Bd., Syracuse, N.Y., 1973-75; assoc. pastor 1st Presbyn. Ch., Syracuse, 1975-83; missionary Middle East Coun. of Chs., Limassol, Cyprus, 1983-84; missionary-in-residence Presbyn. Ch. (USA), Stony Point Center, N.Y., 1984-86; interim pastor 1st Presbyn. Ch., Oneida, N.Y., 1988-89, United Presbyn. Ch., Cortland, N.Y., 1989-91; pastor Ogden Presbyn. Ch., Spencerport, N.Y., 1991—; exec. dir. Am. Coalition for Middle East Dialogue, Jamesville, N.Y., 1986-88; v.p. Greater Rochester Cmty. of Chs., 1992-93, pres., 1994-97; chairperson Interfaith Forum of Greater Rochester, 1995; mem. Mayor's Adv. Bd. for Comprehensive Planning, City of Rochester, 1996-97; mem. Martin Luther King Jr. Commn. of Monroe County, 1995-97; bd. dirs. N.Y. State Cmty. Chs., 1996—; mem. coun. Susquehanna Valley Presbytery, Bainbridge, N.Y., 1990-91; leader workshops on Middle East, 1983-89; moderator Syracuse Middle East Dialogue Group, 1981-83; mem. coun. Presbytery of Utica, 1988-89. Chaplain Internat. Mgmt. Assn., Liverpool, N.Y., 1982-83, Svc. Club-Oneidas Tribe, 1988-89. Grantee George Gund Found., 1987, Presbyn. Women's Opportunity Giving, 1987. Mem. Witherspoon Soc. (steering com. 1974-76), Presbyn. Peace Fellowship (bd. advisors, nat. com. 1972-83). Democrat. Office: Ogden Presbyn Ch 2400 S Union St Spencerport NY 14559-2226 *American cities and their suburbs today are destined to work within regional frameworks. Racial justice, educational opportunity, fair housing and metropolitan prosperity require collaborative community building. The human spirit desires nothing less, and religious communities are rising to the challenge.*

WEBSTER, HENRY DEFOREST, neuroscientist; b. N.Y.C., Apr. 22, 1927; s. Leslie Tillotson and Emily (deForest) W.; m. Marion Havas, June 12, 1951; children: Christopher, Henry, Sally, David, Steven. AB cum laude, Amherst Coll., 1948; MD, Harvard U., 1952. Intern Boston City Hosp., 1952-53, resident, 1953-54; resident in neurology Mass. Gen. Hosp., 1954-56, research fellow in neuropathology, 1956-59; prin. investigator NIH research grants for electron microscopic studies of peripheral neuropathy, 1959-69; mem. staffs Mass. Gen., Newton-Wellesley hosps.; instr. neurology Harvard Med. Sch., 1959-63, assoc. in neurology, 1963-66, asst. prof. neuropathology, 1966; assoc. prof. neurology U. Miami Sch. Medicine, 1966-69, prof., 1969; head sect. cellular neuropathology Nat. Inst. Neurol. Diseases and Stroke, Bethesda, Md., 1969-97; chief Lab. Exptl. Neuropathology, 1984-97; scientist emeritus Nat. Insts. Health, 1997—; disting. scientist, lectr. dept. anatomy Tulane U. Sch. Medicine, 1973; Royal Coll. lectr. Can. Assn. Neuropathologists, 1982; Saul Korey lectr. Am. Assn. Neuropathologists, 1992; chmn. Winter Conf. on Brain Rsch., 1985, 86; head neuropathology delegation to visit China in 1990, Citizen Amb. Program, People to People Internat.; mem. exec. com. rsch. group on neuromuscular disease World Fedn. Neurology, 1986-93. Author: (with A. Peters and S.L. Palay) The Fine Structure of the Nervous System, 1970, 76, 91; contbr. articles to sci. jours. Recipient Superior Svc. award USPHS, 1977, A. von Humboldt award Fed. Republic Germany, 1985, Sci. award Peripheral Neuropathy Assn., 1994; named hon. prof. Norman Bethune U. of Med. Scis., Chanchun, China, 1991. Mem. Am. Assn. Neuropathologists (v.p. 1976-77, pres. 1978-79, Weil award 1960), Internat. Soc. Neuropathology (councillor 1976-80, v.p. 1980-84, exec. com. 1980-84, 86-94, pres. 1986-90), Internat. Congress Neuropathology (sec. gen. VIII 1978), Peripheral Nerve Study Group (exec. com. 1975-93, chmn. 1977 meeting), Japanese Soc. Neuropathology (hon.), Am. Neurol. Assn., Am. Acad. Neurology, Am. Soc. Cell Biologists, Am. Assn. Anatomists, Soc. Neurosci., Rotary Internat., Washington Ctr. Photography, Ausable Club. Office: NIH Bldg 36 Rm 4A 29 Bethesda MD 20892

WEBSTER, JAMES RANDOLPH, JR., physician; b. Chgo., Aug. 25, 1931; s. James Randolph and Ruth Marian (Burtis) W.; m. Joan Burchfield, Dec. 28, 1954; children: Susan, Donovan, John. B.S., U. Chgo.-Northwestern U., 1953; M.D., M.S., Northwestern U., 1956. Diplomate: Am. Bd. Internal Medicine (sub bd. pulmonary disease and geriatrics). Resident in medicine, NIH fellow in pulmonary disease Phila. Gen. Hosp., 1956-57; resident in medicine and fellow in pulmonary disease Northwestern U., 1957-60, 62-64; asst. chief medicine Northwestern Meml. Hosp., Chgo., 1968-73; chief medicine Northwestern Meml. Hosp., 1973-88; prof. medicine Northwestern U. Med. Sch., 1977—, chief gen. med. sect. Dept. Medicine, 1987-88; chief exec. officer Northwestern Med. Group Practice, 1978-88; dir. ctr. on aging/geriatrics Northwestern U. Med. Ctr., 1988—; chief staff Northwestern Meml. Hosp., 1988-90. Contbr. chpts. to books, articles to med. jours. Served with U.S. Army, 1960-62. Recipient Outstanding Clin. tchr. award Northwestern U. Med. Sch., 1974, 77, 84, 86, Alumni Merit award Northwestern U., 1979. Mem. Am. Fedn. Clin. ACP (gov. for Ill. 1988-92, chair sub-com. on aging 1993—, Claypoole award 1994), Am. Thoracic Soc., Am. Geriatrics Soc., Ill. Geriatrics Soc. (pres. 1992-94), Soc. Rsch. and Edn. in Geriatrics. Home: 227 E Delaware Pl Chicago IL 60611-1713 Office: 750 N Lake Shore Dr Rm 601 Chicago IL 60611-4403 *Life should best be measured not by how long you live, but how.*

WEBSTER, JEFFERY NORMAN, technology policy analyst; b. Erie, Pa., Oct. 23, 1954; s. Norman A. and Betty B. (Bessetti) W.; m. Harriet Marie McGinley, Nov. 27, 1982; 1 child, Jessica Marie. BA, Pa. State U , 1980; MPA, U. So. Calif., 1985. Sr. evaluator, technologist U.S. Gen. Acctg. Office, L.A., 1981—. Co-author numerous technology assessment reports to the Congress, 1983—. Mem. AIAA (chmn. San Gabriel Valley sect.). Achievements include congl. testimony on tech. risks and scientific utility of NASA's space sta. design, congl. report on tech. risks of assembling and maintaining NASA's space sta., loss of irreproduceable space sci. data due to faulty archiving practices by NASA, improvements needed in NASA's spacecraft computer technology. Home: 1191 E Mendocino St Altadena CA 91001-2524 Office: US Gen Acctg Office 350 S Figueroa St Ste 1010 Los Angeles CA 90071-1306

WEBSTER, JILL ROSEMARY, historian, educator; b. London, Sept. 29, 1931; arrived in Can., 1965; d. Harold James and Dora Elena (Andreini) W. BA in Hispanic Studies with honors, U. Liverpool, Eng., 1962, postgrad. cert. in edn., 1965; PhD in Spanish, U. Toronto, Can., 1969; MA in Spanish, U. Nottingham, Eng., 1964; BA in History with honors, U. London, Eng., 1978. Prof. U. Toronto, 1968-94, assoc. dean, 1978-81, dir. Ctr. for Medieval Studies, 1979-94, grad. chair dept. Spanish and Portuguese, 1993-94; prof. emeritus, 1995—. Author: Els Menorets: The Franciscans in the Realms of Aragon from St. Francis to the Black Death (1348), 1993. Fellow Royal Soc. Can.; mem. Am. Hist. Assn., Am. Cath. Hist. Assn., Medieval Acad. Am., Am. Acad. Rsch. Historians of Medieval Spain (pres. 1990-95), Secció Històric-Arqueològica of the Inst. d"Estudis Catalans. Office: U Toronto St Michaels Coll, 81 St Mary St, Toronto, ON Canada M5S 1J4

WEBSTER, JOHN GOODWIN, biomedical engineering educator, researcher; b. Plainfield, N.J., May 27, 1932; s. Franklin Folger and Emily Sykes (Boody) W.; m. Nancy Egan, Dec. 27, 1954; children: Paul, Robin, Mark, Lark. BEE, Cornell U., 1953; MSEE, U. Rochester, 1965, PhD, 1967. Engr. North American Aviation, Downey, Calif., 1954-55; engr. Boeing Airplane Co., Seattle, 1955-59, Radiation Inc., Melbourne, Fla., 1959-61; staff engr. Mitre Corp., Bedford, Mass., 1961-62, IBM Corp., Kingston, N.Y., 1962-63; asst. prof. elec. engring. U. Wis.-Madison, 1967-70, assoc. prof. elec. engring., 1970-73, prof. elec. and computer engring., 1973—. Author: (with others) Medicine and Clinical Engineering, 1977, Sensors and Signal Conditioning, 1991; editor: Medical Instrumentation: Application and Design, 1978, 3d edit., 1997, Clinical Engineering: Principles and Practices, 1979, Design of Microcomputer-Based Medical Instrumentation, 1981, Therapeutic Medical Devices: Application and Design, 1982; Electronic Devices for Rehabilitation, 1985; Interfacing Sensors to the IBM-PC, 1988, Encyclopedia of Medical Devices and Instrumentation, 1988, Tactile Sensors for Robotics and Medicine, 1988, Electrical Impedance Tomography, 1990, Teaching Design in Electrical Engineering, 1990, Prevention of Pressure Sores, 1991, Design of Cardiac Pacemakers, 1995. Recipient Rsch. Career Devel. award NIH, 1971-76; NIH fellow, 1963-67. Fellow IEEE, Am. Inst. Med. and Biol. Engring., Instrument Soc. Am. (Donald P. Eckman Edn. award 1974), Am. Soc. Engring. Edn. (Western Electric Fund award 1978, Theo C. Pilkington Outstanding Educator award 1994), Assn. for Advancement Med. Instrumentation (Found. Laufman-Greatbatch prize 1996). Office: Univ Wis Dept Elec Computer Engring 1415 Engineering Dr Madison WI 53706-1607

WEBSTER, JOHN KIMBALL, investment executive; b. N.Y.C., June 7, 1934; s. Reginald Nathaniel and Lillian (McDonald) W.; m. Katherine Taylor Mulligan; children: John McDonald, Katherine Kimball. B.A., Yale U., 1956; postgrad., Wharton Sch., U. Pa., 1957-58. With Dominick & Dominick, N.Y.C., 1961-73; v.p. Dominick & Dominick, 1968-73; v.p., sec. Dominick Fund, Inc., also Barclay Growth Fund, N.Y.C., 1971-73; v.p. Dominick Mgmt. Corp., N.Y.C., 1971-73, Monumental Capital Mgmt., Inc., Balt., 1974-75, Bernstein-Macaulay, Inc., N.Y.C., 1975-78; v.p., dir. Penmark Investments, Inc., Chgo., 1978-79; sr. v.p. Penmark Investments, Inc., 1979-80, exec. v.p., 1980-84; exec. v.p. Trust Banking Group, Sun Banks, Inc., 1984-85; v.p. MPT Assocs., 1986-90, Value Line Asset Mgmt., N.Y.C., 1990-96, M&T Capital Advisors Group, 1996—; mem. no-load com. Investment Co. Inst., Washington, 1971-73; exec. com. No Load Mut. Fund Assn., N.Y.C., 1971-73; treas. No Load Mut. Fund Assn., 1972-73. Chmn. Nat. Telethon Com., Lawrenceville, Sch., 1986-88, chmn. Ann. Giving, 1988-89; vice chmn. Parents Fund Trinity Coll., Conn., 1987-90. Capt. USAF, 1958-61. Mem. Church Club (N.Y.C.), Yale Club (N.Y.C.), Rumson (N.J.) Country Club, Seabright (N.J.) Lawn Tennis Club, Baltusrol Golf Club, Summit Paddle Tennis Club. Episcopalian. Home: 46 Meadowview Ln Berkeley Heights NJ 07922-1308 Office: M&T Capital Adv Group 350 Park Ave Fl 6 New York NY 10022-6022

WEBSTER, JOHN KINGSLEY OHL, II, health administrator, rehabilitation manager; b. L.A., July 27, 1950; s. John Kingsley Ohl and Inez (Gilbert) W.; m. Marcia Lanier McKnight, June 16, 1977; children: David Lilly, Jason Kingsley McKnight. AA, Pasadena (Calif.) City Coll., 1973; BS, San Jose (Calif.) State U., 1975; MS, Calif. State U., L.A., 1989. Registered occupational therapist, Calif. Supervising occupational therapy cons. San Gabriel Valley Regional Ctr., 1976-79; supr. II occupational therapy cons. San Diego Regional Ctr., 1979-83; sr. occupational therapist Mesa Vista Hosp., 1983-84; pvt. practice Vista, Calif., 1983-85; occupational therapy cons. Calif. Children Svcs., State Dept. Health Svcs., L.A., 1985-86, regional adminstrv. cons., 1986-90; dir. occupational therapy Eureka Gen. Hosp., 1990; dir. ops. and mktg. Life Dimensions Inc., Newport Beach, Calif., 1990; occupational therapy cons., licensing and cert. Calif. Dept. Health Svcs., 1990-93; program dir. rehab. svcs. Scripps Meml. Hosp., Encinitas, Calif., 1993-94; dir. rehab. Vista (Calif.) Knoll, 1994; clin. dir. occupational therapy Sundance Rehab., San Diego, 1994-95; regional dir. ops. Quest Rehab, L.A., 1995-96; area mgr. Am. Therapy Svc., 1996; western divsn. dir. of ops. Accelerated Care Plus, L.A., 1996—; cons. Hopi and Navajo Tribes, Winslow, Ariz., 1978; dir. Imperial County SPRANS grant, El Centro, Calif., 1986-88; pres., owner Kingsley Constrn., Vista, 1988—. Artist (sculpture) Free Form (3d pl. award 1973), (oil painting) Jamaican Woman (3d pl. award 1979). Recipient Esquire title Lady Elliott of STOBS, Edinburough, Scotland, 1973, spl. dept. recognition Calif. State U., 1989. Mem. Am. Occupational Therapy Assn., Inst. Profl. Health Svc. Adminstrs., Student Assn. of Am. Coll. Health Care Execs. Avocations: oil painting, sculpting, producing films, woodworking, tennis.

WEBSTER, LARRY RUSSELL, artist; b. Arlington, Mass., Mar. 18, 1930; s. James Burpee and Ethel (Hughes) W.; m. Rosemary Siekman, June 13, 1953; children: Wendy Lyn, Ricky Stewart, Holly Jean. B.F.A., Mass. Coll. Art, 1952; M.S., Boston U., 1953. Package designer Union Bag & Paper Co., N.Y.C., 1953-54; art dir., graphic designer, v.p., dir. Thomas Todd Co., Boston, 1956-78; asst. prof. design Mass. Coll. Art, 1964-66. Paintings in permanent collections including, DeCordova Mus., Lincoln, Mass., Grand Rapids (Mich.) Art Mus., Springfield (Mo.) Art Mus., Davenport (Iowa) Municipal Gallery, Colby Coll. Art Mus., Waterville, Maine, Peabody Mus. Salem, Mass. Served with U.S. Army, 1954-56. Recipient Silver medal Am. Watercolor Soc., 1968, 72; recipient C.F.S. award, 1963, Ed Whitney award, 1973, High winds medal, 1983, Rhinehold award, 1967, Ranger Fund Purchase prize, 1965, Adolph and Clara Obrig prize in watercolor NAD, 1970, gold medal Allied Artists Am., 1971, Washington Sch. Art award, 1977, Lena Newcastle award, 1978, Colo. Watermedia award, 1978, Golden award Rocky Mountain Nat. Watermedia Exhbn., 1979, Lorraine Fetzer Meml. award, 2d prize N.Am. Open Competition, 1990. Mem. NAD, Soc. Printers Boston (past mem. council), Am. Watercolor Soc. (Dolphin fellow 1981), Boston Watercolor Soc. (pres. 1974-75), Guild of Boston Artists. Home: 116 Perkins Row Topsfield MA 01983-1923

WEBSTER, LESLIE TILLOTSON, JR., pharmacologist, educator; b. N.Y.C., Mar. 31, 1926; s. Leslie Tillotson and Emily (de Forest) W.; m. Alice Katharine Holland, June 24, 1955; children—Katharine White, Susan Holland Webster Van Drie, Leslie Tillotson III, Romi Anne. B.A., Amherst Coll., 1947, Sc.D. (hon.), 1982; student, Union Coll., 1944; M.D., Harvard U., 1948. Diplomate: Am. Bd. Internal Medicine. Rotating intern Cleve. City Hosp., 1948-49, jr. asst. resident in medicine, 1949-50; asst. resident medicine Bellevue Hosp., N.Y.C., 1952-53; research fellow medicine Harvard and Boston City Hosp. Thorndike Meml. Lab., 1953-55; from demonstrator to instr. Sch. of Medicine Western Res. U., 1955-60; research assoc. to sr. instr. biochemistry Case Western Res. U. Sch. Medicine, 1959-60, asst. prof. medicine, 1960-70, asst. prof. biochemistry, 1960-65, asst. prof. pharmacology, 1965-67, asso. prof., 1967-70, prof. pharmacology, 1976-92, chmn. pharmacology dept., 1976-91, prof. pharmacology dept. emeritus, 1992, prof. medicine, 1980-86; prof., chmn. pharmacology dept. Northwestern U. Med. and Dental Sch., 1970-76. Served to lt. USNR, 1950-52. Russell M. Wilder fellow Nat. Vitamin Found., 1956-59; Sr. USPHS Research fellow, 1959-61; Research Career Devel. awardee, 1961-69; Macy faculty scholar, 1980-81. Mem. ACP (life), Central Soc. Clin. Rsch. Coalition (emeritus), Am. Soc. Clin. Investigation (emeritus), Am. Soc. Biochemistry and Molecular Biology (emeritus), Assn. Med. Sch. Pharmacology (emeritus), Am. Soc. Pharmacology and Exptl. Therapeutics (emeritus), Alpha Omega Alpha (hon.). Home: 2728 Leighton Rd Shaker Heights OH 44120-1325 Office: Univ Hosps of Cleve Rainbow Babies and Childrens Hosp 2074 Abington Rd Cleveland OH 44106-2602

WEBSTER, LINDA JEAN, communication educator, media consultant; b. L.A., July 16, 1948; d. Stanley Stewart and Irene M. (Sabo) W. BS, So. Conn. State U., New Haven, 1981, MA, 1983; PhD, La. State U., Baton Rouge, 1987. CEO CBE Enterprises, Inc., Baton Rouge, 1984-89; rsch. fellow La. State U., Baton Rouge, 1983-87; instr. speech Southeastern La. U., Hammond, 1984-89, Hancock Coll., Santa Maria, Calif., 1989; curator of edn. Lompoc (Calif.) Mus., 1989; asst. prof. speech U. Ark., Monticello, 1990-95, assoc. prof. speech, 1995—, dir. honors program, 1995—; exec. dir. Drew County Hist. Mus., Monticello, 1992-95; media dir. Oasis Resources-Homeless Shelter, Warren, Ark., 1991—; bur. chief Pine Bluff (Ark.) Comml., 1992-94; media consulting WZXS-FM radio, Holly Ridge, N.C., 1995—; apptd. State Ark. Mus. Svcs. Rev. Panel, 1997-97. Editor Jour. Comm. Studies, 1997—; contbr. chpts. to books and articles to jours. in field. Apptd. mem. Ark. Mus. Svcs. Rev. Panel, 1997—; vol. media chair Oasis Transitional Shelter, Warren, 1991—, Boys/Girls Club, Monticello, 1992-93; campaign dir. Gloria Wright election, Monticello, 1995; campaign media dir. Ken Harper election-Dist. 82, 1996. Recipient Noel Ross Strader award Coll. Media Advisors, Inc., 1991, Coll. Tchr. of the Yr. award Ark. State Commn. Assn., 1993. Mem. Ark. Press Women (state pres. 1993-95, Communicator of Achievement award 1991), Ark. State Comm. Assn. (1st v.p. 1997, Stds. Bearer 1997—), So. State Comm. Assn. (chair honors session 1995, mem. constitutio com. 1997—), Internat. Comm. Assn., Oral History Assn., Speech Comm. Assn. (commn. chair 1993-96). Roman Catholic. Avocations: historic preservation, gardening, baseball, Boston Terriers, driving. Office: U Ark-Arts & Langs Monticello AR 71656

WEBSTER, MERLYN HUGH, JR., manufacturing engineer, information systems consultant; b. Beaver Falls, Pa., Nov. 7, 1946; s. Merlyn Hugh and Helen Ruth (Dillon) W.; m. Linda Jeanne Gundlach, June 14, 1969; children: Matthew Jason, Nathaniel Kevin. AA, Palomar Coll., San Marcos, Calif., 1975; BA, Chapman Coll., 1978. Registered profl. engr., Calif. Sr. cons., pres. WEB Internat. Corp., 1992—; mfg. analyst NCR Corp., Rancho Bernardo, Calif., 1968-72, indsl. engr., 1972-76, sr. indsl. engr., 1976-78; sr. project mgr. Tektronix, Beaverton, Oreg., 1978-83, corp. distbn. I.E. mgr., 1983-86; sr. info. systems cons. Intel Corp., Hillsboro, Oreg., 1986—; pres. WEB Internat. Corp., Tualatin, Oreg., 1992—; cons. material handling Intel Mfg., Puerto rico and Ireland, 1989-92; cons. info. systems M.I.S.I., N.Y.C., 1992-93. Chmn. United Way Hillsboro, Oreg., 1986. With USMC, 1964-68, Vietnam. Mem. NSPE, Inst. Indsl. Engrs. (cert.), Shelby Car Club Am. Republican. Office: WEB Internat Corp 5200 SW Joshua St Ste 101 Tualatin OR 97062-9792

WEBSTER, MICHAEL ANDERSON, experimental psychologist; b. Atlanta, Mar. 24, 1958; s. John Calvin and Evelyn Gayle (Cox) W.; m. Shernaaz Michael Irani, Aug. 6, 1983; children: Anjali Dianne, Menka Linda. Exch. student, Am. U., Cairo, 1978-79; BA in Psychology, U. Calif., San Diego, 1981; MA in Psychology, U. Calif., Berkeley, 1985, PhD in Psychology, 1988. Postdoctoral fellow dept. exptl. psychology U. Cambridge, Eng., 1988-94; asst. prof. dept. psychology U. Nev., Reno, 1994—. Contbr. articles to profl. jours. Nat. Rsch. Svc. Award fellow Nat. Eye Inst., Cambridge U., 1989-91, NATO fellow NSF, Cambridge U., 1988. Mem. Assn. for Rsch. in Vision and Ophthalmology, Optical Soc. Am. Achievements include research in psychophysical studies of human color vision. Office: Univ Nevada Dept Psychology Reno NV 89557

WEBSTER, MICHAEL LEE, academic administrator; b. Fulton, N.Y., Sept. 2, 1949; s. Fred Smith and Ida Josephine (Stewart) W.; m. Donna Eileen Turk, Aug. 16, 1969; children: Andrew Michael, Bethany Sarah. BS, Clarkson U., 1971; MDiv, Trinity Evangelical Div. Sch., 1974, DMin, 1981; student, Skyline Coll., San Bruno, Calif., 1981. Ordained to ministry Koinonia Ch., Elim Fellowship, 1975. Grad. asst. Trinity Evangelical Divinity Sch., Deerfield, Ill., 1971-74; pastor Koinonia Ch., Potsdam, N.Y., 1974-78; faculty Melodyland Sch. Theology, Anaheim, Calif., 1978; pastor Coastside Christian Ctr., Pacifica, Calif., 1979-82; instr. Elim Bible Inst., Lima, N.Y., 1982-84, acad. dean, 1984-88, pres., 1988-94, pres. emeritus, 1994—; dir. Believer's Chapel Bible Inst., Cicero, N.Y., 1997—; bd. adminstrn. Elim Fellowship, Lima, 1984-92; assoc. staff Mobilized to Serve, Lima, 1982-92; mem. NAE Commn. on Higher Edn., Network Christian Ministries; v.p. Crossroads Coun.; speaker in field. Bd. dirs. Ctr. for Theol. Studies, Newport Beach, Calif., 1978-81. Mem. Eta Kappa Nu, Tau Beta Pi. Republican. Avocations: amateur radio, music, electronics, chess, fishing. Office: Believers Chapel 7912 Thompson Rd Cicero NY 13039-9376 Home: M5 Cobblestone Dr Cicero NY 13039 *We all have the resources to effectively serve our needy world: our value as a human being in the image of God, our destiny as a person in the purposes of God and our woundedness as an individual forming a conduit for the Grace of God.*

WEBSTER, MURRAY ALEXANDER, JR., sociologist, educator; b. Manila, Philippines, Dec. 10, 1941; s. M.A. and Patricia (Morse) W.; A.B., Stanford U., 1963, M.A., 1966, Ph.D., 1968. Asst. prof. social relations Johns Hopkins U., Balt., 1968-74, assoc. prof., 1974-76; prof. sociology, adj. prof. psychology U. S.C., Columbia, 1976-86; vis. prof. sociology Stanford U., 1981-82, 85, 88-89; sr. lectr. San Jose State U., 1987-89; sociology program dir. NSF, 1989-91; prof. sociology U. N.C., Charlotte, 1993—; NIH fellow, 1966-68; grantee NSF, Nat. Inst. Edn. Mem. AAAS, Am. Sociol. Assn., So. Sociol. Soc., Am. Psychol. Assn., Am. Psychol. Soc., N.Y. Acad. Scis. Presbyterian. Author: (with Barbara Sobieszek) Sources of Self-Evaluation, 1974; Actions and Actors, 1975, (with Martha Foschi) Status Generalization: New Theory and Research, 1988; mem. editorial bd. Am. Jour. Sociology, 1976-79, Social Psychology Quar., 1977-80, 84-87, 93—, Social Sci. Research, 1975—. Office: Univ NC Dept Sociology Charlotte NC 28223

WEBSTER, NORMAN ERIC, journalist, charitable foundation administrator; b. Summerside, P.E.I., Can., June 4, 1941; s. Eric and Elizabeth (Paterson) W.; m. Pat Roop, 1966; children: David, Andrew, Derek, Gillian, Hilary. BA, Bishop's U., Que., Can.; MA, St. John's Coll., Oxford, Eng. Corr. Globe and Mail, Que. and Ottawa, Ont., Can.; editor Globe Mag., Toronto, Ont.; corr. Globe and Mail, Peking, China, 1969-71; columnist Ont. affairs Globe and Mail, Toronto; European corr. Globe and Mail, London; editor-in-chief Globe and Mail, Toronto, 1983-89, Montreal (Que.) Gazette, 1989-93; pres. R. Howard Webster Found., Montreal, 1993—. Chancellor U. P.E.I. Recipient Nat. Newspaper award for Peking corr., 1971, for editl. writing, 1988; Rhodes scholar; mem. Order of Can. Office: R Howard Webster Found Ste 2912, 1155 Rene Levesque Blvd W, Montreal, PQ Canada H3B 2L5

WEBSTER, OWEN WRIGHT, chemist; b. Devils Lake, N.D., Mar. 25, 1929; s. Daniel Milton and Maude May (Wright) W.; m. Lillian Brostek; children: Ellen, Anne, John, James, Mary. BS in Chemistry, N.D. U., 1951, DSc (hon.), 1986; PhD in Chemistry, Pa. State U., 1955. Research chemist E.I. Du Pont de Nemours, Wilmington, Del., 1955-74, group leader, 1974-79, research supr., 1979-84, research leader, 1984-95, Du Pont fellow, 1986-95; ret., 1995. Patentee in field; contbr. articles to profl. jours. Recipient Chem. Pioneer award Am. Inst. Chemists, 1995. Mem. AAAS, Am. Chem. Soc. (chmn. Del. sect. 1975-76, Excellence in Research award 1987, Applied Polymer Sci. award 1993), Sigma Xi. Republican. Roman Catholic. Avocations: chess, bridge, golf. Home: 2106 Navaro Rd Wilmington DE 19803-2310 Office: EI DuPont De Nemours Exptl Sta # 356 E Wilmington DE 19880

WEBSTER, ROBERT KENLY, lawyer; b. N.Y.C., May 16, 1933; s. Francis Kenly and Mary Louise (Rathbone) W.; m. Sally Irene Stratton, Apr. 16, 1960; children: Timothy Kenly, Kimberly Anne. AB, Princeton U., 1955; LLB, U. Va., 1960. Assoc. Cadwalader, Wickersham & Taft, N.Y.C., 1960-65; asst. U.S. atty. Dept. of Justice, Washington, 1965-68; prin. dep. gen. counsel Dept. of Army, Washington, 1968-73; ptnr. Kennedy & Webster, Washington, 1973-81, Shaw, Pittman, Potts & Trowbridge, Washington, 1981—; spl. investigator Iran FMS program Sec. of Def., Washington, 1977; advisor conflict of interest issues Watergate defendants Dept. Justice, Washington, 1977. Sec., gen. counsel, bd. dirs. Princeton (N.J.) Project 55, Inc., 1989—. Lt. (j.g.) USN, 1955-57. Mem. ABA, Fed. Bar Assn., Met. Club.

Avocations: pottery, reading, traveling, squash, tennis. Office: Shaw Pittman Potts 2300 N St NW Washington DC 20037-1122

WEBSTER, ROBERT LEE, accounting educator, researcher; b. Little Rock, Oct. 4, 1946; s. Daniel and Mildred LaNette (Patishall) W.; m. Mary Katherine Fiske, Aug. 26, 1967; children: Elizabeth Ashley, Jessica Lee. BA, Ouachita Bapt. U., 1968; MBA, Syracuse U., 1975; MS, L.I. U., 1986; DBA, La. Tech. U., 1993. Cert. govt. fin. mgr. Commd. 2d lt. U.S. Army, 1968, advanced through grades to lt. col., 1985; dep. contr. U.S. Army Electronics R&D Command, Adelphi, Md., 1975-80; chief of ops., comms. security NATO, Mons, Belgium, 1980-83; asst. prof. acctg. and fin. U.S. Mil. Acad., West Point, N.Y., 1983-86; prof. mil. sci. Henderson State U., Arkadelphia, Ark., 1986-88; ret. U.S. Army, 1988; asst. prof. acctg. Henderson State U., 1988-91, chair dept. acctg., econs. and bus. edn., 1991-93; chair dept. acctg. Ouachita Bapt. U., Arkadelphia, 1993—; George Young chair bus. Ouachita Bapt. U., 1995—; bd. dirs. Hospitality Care Ctr., Arkadelphia, 1992-93; speaker in field. Editor Jour. Bus. & Behavioral Scis., 1995; author articles. Army scholar Syracuse U., 1974-75; Exch. Educator to Republic of Kazakhstan, 1994-95; recipient Dean's award for acad. achievement L.I. U., 1986. Mem. Nat. Social Sci. Assn. (bd. govs. 1992—, Outstanding Conf. Paper award 1992), Am. Acctg. Assn., Assn. of Govt. Accts., Beta Gamma Sigma, Sigma Beta Delta. Avocations: coin collecting, exercising. Home: 205 Forrest Park Dr Arkadelphia AR 71923-2811 Office: Ouachita Bapt U PO Box 3689 Arkadelphia AR 71998-0001

WEBSTER, ROBERT LOUIS, insurance company executive; b. Beautfort, S.C., Nov. 27, 1959; s. Robert Lee and Audrey Joyce (Hays) W.; m. Denise Ann Distelrath, June 26, 1982; children: Megan, Katelyn, Sydney, Bobby, Chris. BS in Bus. Adminstrn., Fin., U. Akron, 1983. CLU; ChFC. Agt. The Prudential, Newport News, Va., 1983-84, mgr. sales, 1989-95; agt. Life of Va., Newport News, 1984-85; mgr. sales Jefferson Pilot Life, Newport News, 1985-89; v.p. Harwood & Garrett, Newport News, 1995-96; pres. Webster Ins. & Fin. Svs., Inc., Newport News, 1997—. Bd. mem. Richmond Diocesan Cath. Sch. Bd., 1997—. Fellow Life Underwriters Tng. Coun. (instr. 1986—); mem. Am. Soc. CLU-ChFC's (bd. dirs. 1995—), Nat. Assn. Life Underwriters (bd. dirs. 1990-92, Nat. Sales Achievement award 1990), Gen. Agts. and Mgrs. Assn., Kiwanis (bd. dirs. 1990-92, treas. 1992, v.p. 1993, pres.-elect 1994, pres. 1995), KC. Republican. Roman Catholic. Avocation: golf. Office: The Webster Insurance Agency 1769 Jamestown Rd Williamsburg VA 23185-2307

WEBSTER, RONALD B., lawyer; b. Cle Elum, Wash., June 11, 1942; s. Burnette O. and Lucille (Beck) W.; m. M. Gail Skinner, June 26, 1971; children: Noel, Michelle. BA, U. Wash., 1964; JD, Gonzaga U., 1969. Bar: Wash., U.S. Dist. Ct. (ea. and we. dists.) Wash., U.S. Ct. Appeals (9th cir.). Dep. pros. atty. Cowlitz County, Kelso, Wash., 1970-73; ptnr. Hickman, Webster, Ensley & Carpenter, Colfax, Wash., 1973-90, Hickman, Webster & Moulton, 1973-92, Hickman & Webster, P.S., 1992-95. Mem. Whitman County Bd. Mental Health, Pullman, Wash., 1973-83; chmn. civil svc. commn. Whitman County Sheriffs Office, Colfax, 1973—; pres. Colfax and Cmty. Fund, 1973-74; pres. Whitman Cmty. Concerts, 1990-93. Mem. Whitman County Bar Assn. (pres. 1981-82), Wash. State Bar Assn. (inter profl. com. 1986-89—, disciplinary com. 1986—). Club: Colfax Golf and Country. Lodge: Rotary (pres. Colfax club 1983-84). Home: 1801 N Oak St Colfax WA 99111-9705 Office: Hickman & Webster PS 302 N Mill St Colfax WA 99111-1865

WEBSTER, RONALD D., communications company executive; b. Richwood, W.Va., Aug. 9, 1949; s. Ralph D. and Victoria M. (Cisek) W.; m. Donna M. Falkenthal, Aug. 9, 1975; 1 child, Kathryn E. BSBA with high distinction, U. Ill., Chgo., 1971; MBA, U. Chgo., 1980. CPA, Ill. Sr. auditor Arthur Andersen & Co., Chgo., 1970-75; dir. corp. reporting Trans Union Corp., Lincolnshire, Ill., 1975-77; asst. group contr. Union Tank Car Co. (subs. of Trans Union Corp.), Chgo., 1977-83; treas. Telephone and Data Systems, Inc., Chgo., 1983-87, 88—, v.p., 1992—; v.p. Ideal Sch. Supply Corp., Oak Lawn, Ill., 1987-88. Bd. dirs., v.p. fin. Ivy Glen Homeowners Assn., Aurora, Ill., 1972-73. Staff sgt. USNG, 1970-76. Mem. Fin. Execs. Inst., Am. Soc. CPAs (Elijah Watt Sells nat. honorable mention 1973), Ill. CPA Soc., Beta Gamma Sigma. Home: 7637 Ridgewood Ln Burr Ridge IL 60525-5132 Office: Telephone & Data Systems Inc 30 N La Salle St Ste 4000 Chicago IL 60602-2507

WEBSTER, STEPHEN BURTIS, physician, educator; b. Chgo., Dec. 3, 1935; s. James Randolph Webster and Ruth Marion (Burtis) Holmes; m. Katherine Griffith Webster, Apr. 4, 1959; children: David Randolph, Margaret Elizabeth, James Lucian. BS, Northwestern U., 1957, MD, 1960. Diplomate Am. Bd. Dermatology. Intern Colo. Gen. Hosp., Denver, 1960-61; resident Walter Reed Gen. Hosp., Washington, 1962-65; staff physician Henry Ford Hosp., Detroit, 1969-71, Gundersen Clinic, La Crosse, 1971—; assoc. clin. prof. U. Wis., Madison, 1976—, U. Minn., Mpls., 1978—. Lt. col. U.S. Army, 1962-69. Fellow Am. Acad. Dermatology (sec.-treas. 1985-88, pres. 1991), Am. Bd. Dermatology (dir. 1992—); mem. AMA, Am. Dermatol. Assn. (pres. 1996-97), Wis. State Med. Soc., La Crosse County Med. Soc., Soc. Investigative Dermatology, Alpha Omega Alpha. Republican. Congregationalist. Avocations: bagpipes, model R.R. Home: 2062N Wedgewood Dr E La Crosse WI 54601 Office: Gundersen Clinic Ltd 1836 South Ave La Crosse WI 54601-5429

WEBSTER, THOMAS GLENN, psychiatrist; b. Topeka, Jan. 23, 1924; s. Guy Welland and Iva Amanda (Keefover) W.; m. Mary Tupper Dooly, June 27, 1948; children—Warnie Louise, Guy Weyman, David Michael. AB, Ft. Hays State Coll., 1946; MD, Wayne State U., 1949. Intern Los Angeles County Gen. Hosp., Calif., 1949-50; resident in psychiatry Mass. Mental Health Ctr., Boston, 1953-55, resident in child psychiatry, 1955-56; resident in child psychiatry James Jackson Putnam Children's Ctr., Boston, 1956-58; dir. presch. program for retarded children Greater Boston, 1958-62; coordinator 3d yr. med. student psychiatry clerkship Harvard U. Med. Sch.-Mass. Mental Health Ctr., Boston, 1960-63; practice medicine specializing in psychiatry Boston, 1953-62, Bethesda, Md., 1963-72, Washington, 1972—; tng. specialist psychiatry, then chief continuing edn. br. NIMH, Bethesda, Md., 1963-72; prof. psychiatry George Washington U., Washington, 1972-86, chmn. dept. psychiatry and behavioral scis., 1972-75, prof. emeritus, 1986-96; vis. prof. Harvard U. Med. Sch., 1980-83, McLean Hosp., 1980-86; U.S.-Poland exchange health scientist, 1981. Pres. Woodhaven Citizens Assn., 1971-72. Served with AUS, 1943-46; as sr. asst. surgeon USPHS, 1951-53. Fellow Am. Coll. Psychiatrists, Am. Coll. Psychoanalysts; mem. Assn. Acad. Psychiatry (pres. 1976-78), Group Advancement Psychiatry. Home: 8506 Woodhaven Blvd Bethesda MD 20817-3117 Office: 2112 F St NW Washington DC 20037-2715

WEBSTER, WILLIAM HEDGCOCK, lawyer; b. St. Louis, Mar. 6, 1924; s. Thomas M. and Katherine (Hedgcock) W.; m. Drusilla Lane, May 5, 1950 (dec. 1984); children: D silla Lane Busch, William Hedgcock, Katherine Hagee Roessle; m. Lynda Clugston, Oct. 20, 1990. AB, Amherst Coll., 1947, LLD, 1975; JD, Washington U., 1949, LLD, 1978; LLD (hon.), William Wood Coll., 1978, DePauw U., 1978, Drury Coll., Columbia Coll., U. Dayton, U. Notre Dame, Center Coll., Dickinson Coll., U. Miami, DePaul U., Am. U., John Jay Coll., Westminster Coll., Georgetown U., Rockhurst Coll., Pepperdine U. Bar: Mo. 1949, D.C. 1981. With Armstrong, Teasdale, Kramer and Vaughan (and predecessors), St. Louis, 1949-50, 52-59, 61-70; U.S. atty. U.S. Dist. Ct. (ea. dist.) Mo., 1960-61, judge, 1971-73; judge U.S. Ct. Appeals (8th cir.), 1973-78; dir. FBI, 1978-87, CIA, 1987-91; sr. ptnr. Milbank, Tweed, Hadley & McCloy, Washington, 1991—; mem. Mo. Bd. Law Examiners, 1964-69, mem. adv. com. on criminal rules, 1971-78, mem. ct. adminstrs. com., 1975-78; bd. dirs. Anhauser-Busch Cos., Maritz Inc., Pinkertons Inc., T.L.C. Beatrice Internat. Holdings Inc., Nextwave, Inc. Trustee Washington U., 1974—; bd. dirs. Atlantic Coun., Nat. Legal Ctr. for Pub. Interest, Nat. Symphony Assn., Coun. on Fgn. Rels.; bd. dirs., chmn. Police Found; hon. life pres. Big Bros. Orgn. St. Louis; bd. dirs. Big Bros. Am., 1966, hon. bd. dirs., 1978—. Lt. USNR, 1943-46, 50-52. Recipient Disting. Alumnus award Washington U., 1977, Stein award Fordham U., Law award U. Va., Nat. Svc. medal Freedoms Found., Theodore Roosevelt award, Presdl. medal of Freedom, Nat. Security medal, Silver Buffalo award Boy Scouts Am., Disting. Svc. award Am. Legion; named Father of Yr., 1986, Man of Yr., St. Louis Globe Dem., 1980. Fellow Am. Bar Found.; mem. ABA (chmn. sect. on corp. banking and bus. law 1977-78), FBA, Mo. Bar Assn., St. Louis Bar Assn., Am. Law Inst. (mem. coun. 1978—), Wash. U. Alumni Fedn. (pres. 1956-57), Rotary, St. Louis Country Club, Noonday Club (St. Louis), Met. Club, Chevy Chase Club, Alfalfa Club, St. Alban's Tennis Club, Order of Coif, Psi Upsilon, Delta Sigma Rho, Phi Delta Phi. Office: 1825 I St NW Ste 1100 Washington DC 20006-5417

WECHMAN, ROBERT JOSEPH, economist, educator; b. N.Y.C., Sept. 23, 1939; s. David Samuel and Blanche (Udell) W.; B.A., City U. N.Y., 1961, M.A., 1964; M.A., Columbia, 1966; Ph.D., Syracuse U., 1970; postdoctoral U. Pa., 1974; C.B.M., Am. Mgmt. Assn. Inst., 1980, C.M.M., 1981, C.F.M., 1982; m. Stephanie Helene Kellman, June 18, 1967; children: Craig Samuel, Evan Mitchell, Darren Max. Tchr. history and econs., N.Y.C., 1961-63, Dobbs Ferry (N.Y.) High Sch., 1963-66; instr. history and econs. Elmira (N.Y.) Coll., 1966-70; vis. lectr. history and econs. SUNY, Corning, summers 1967, 70—; asst. prof. social sci., coordinator urban studies Hartwick Coll., Oneonta, N.Y., 1970-74; asst. v.p. Beavertown Mills, 1976-80, v.p., 1980-90; pres. Robert J. Wechman, Cons., 1984-90, Verdin Assocs., Inc., 1982-88; pres. Robert J. Wechman Assocs., Inc., 1990-93; adj. prof. social sci. and bus. adminstrn. New Sch. for Social Research, also SUNY, Rockland Community Coll., 1974-80, Empire State Coll., 1974—, Bergen Community Coll., 1976-80, Berkeley Coll., 1979; adj. assoc. prof. mktg. Pace U., 1980-86; adj. prof. econs. and bus. adminstrn. and econs. St. Thomas Aquinas Coll., 1981-94, Dominican Coll., summer 1981; adj. assoc. prof. bus. mgmt. City U. N.Y., 1981—; adj. prof. econs. SUNY/Westchester C.C., 1996—; cons. urban affairs SUNY, Corning, 1969-70; prof. econs. & bus. adminstrn. Lehman Coll., CUNY, 1990—; cons. Choice Jour., 1972—. Mem. Oneonta Bd. Ethics, 1971-74, Oneonta Anti-Pollution Commn., 1972-74; committeeman and dist. chmn. Rockland County Republican Com., 1978—, Heritage Found. Served with U.S. Army, 1959, USAR, 1959-65. Recipient Marcus award for disting. teaching, 1972, Outstanding Educators Am. award, 1972, President's Appreciation award, 1989, 90, 91, Congl. Cert. Appreciation award, 1991, 93, Disting. Svc. award, Rockland County, 1992, Cert. of Merit award, N.Y. State Senate, 1992, Appreciation award City U. N.Y., 1993, Excellence in Teaching Econs. award Found. for Teaching Econs., 1994, Newsday, 1995. Mem. Phi Alpha Theta, Delta Tau Kappa, Delta Pi Epsilon. Republican. Club: K.P. Author: The Eager Immigrants, 1972, The Economic Development of the Italian-American, 1983, Encountering Management, 1987, Essentials of American Business, 1990, Aspects of German Nationalism, 1994, Dictionary of Economics and Business, 1997; editor: Critical Issues in Modern American Life, 1968; The Crisis in Population, 1969, Urban America: A Guide to the Literature, 1971. Reviewer for social sci. and bus. jours. Home: 9 Verdin Dr New City NY 10956-3707

WECHSLER, ALFRED ELLIOT, engineering executive, consultant, chemical engineer; b. Suffern, N.Y., Sept. 12, 1934; m. Nancy L. Lyons, Apr. 22, 1961; children: Charles, Elizabeth, Abigail. BS in Chem.Engring., MIT, 1955, MS, 1958; Sc.D. in Chem. Engring, M.I.T., 1961; ScD in Ghem. Engring., MIT. Registered profl. engr., Mass. Staff engr. Chevron Research Corp., 1957; asst dir. field sta. MIT Sch. Chem. Engring. Practice, Bangor, Maine, 1958; rsch. asst. chem. engring. MIT, Cambridge, 1959-61; sr. research engr. engring. div. Arthur D. Little, Inc., Cambridge, 1961-66, leader research and experiments group, 1966-73, mgr. bio/enviro systems sect., v.p., 1973-80, corp. staff v.p., 1980—, sr. v.p., mgr. profl. ops. bus. unit, 1980-83, sr. v.p., gen. mgr. profl. ops., 1983-85, sr. v.p., chief profl. officer, 1985—. Contbr. articles to profl. jours. Trustee Environ. Careers Orgn. With U.S. Army, 1956-57. Fellow AAAS; mem. NSPE, Am. Chem. Soc., Am. Inst. Chem. Engrs. (bd. dirs. 1991-93). Office: Arthur D Little Inc 25 Acorn Park Cambridge MA 02140-2301

WECHSLER, ANDREW STEPHEN, surgery educator; b. N.Y.C., July 19, 1939; s. James Erwin and Nina (Wander) W.; m. Donna Clare; children: Jennifer Lynn, Hollis Ann. AB, Brandeis U., 1960; MD summa cum laude, SUNY-Downstate Med. Ctr., 1964. Diplomate Am. Bd. Thoracic Surgery (bd. dirs. 1986—). Asst. prof. surgery Duke U. Med. Ctr., Durham, N.C., 1974-77, assoc. prof., 1977-80, prof., 1980-88; chmn. dept. surgery Med. Coll. Va., Richmond, 1988—; chmn. surgery and bioengring. study sect. NIH, 1989—. Mem. editorial bd. Annals Thoracic Surgery, 1980-88, Circulation, 1985—, Jour. Cardiac Surgery, 1985—, Jour. Cardiac Anesthesiology, 1985—; contbr. numerous articles to profl. jours. Comdr. USPHS, 1966-68. Fellow ACS, Am. Coll. Cardiology. Home: 8905 Brennan Rd Richmond VA 23229-8114 Office: Med Coll Va Sta Box 645 Richmond VA 23205-0645 also: Med Coll Va Hosp 401 N 12th St Richmond VA 23298

WECHSLER, ARNOLD, osteopathic obstetrician, gynecologist; b. N.Y.C., June 10, 1923; s. David and Eva (Kirsch) W.; m. Marlene Esta Jurnovoy, Sept. 11, 1955 (div. Sept. 1986); children: Diane, Paul, Stewart. Grad., Rutgers U.; DO, Phila. Coll. Osteo. Medicine, 1952. Diplomate Am. Bd. Osteo. Obstetricians and Gynecologists; lic. physician, Pa., N.Y., Fla. Intern Hosps. of Phila. Coll. Osteo. Medicine, 1952-53, resident in ob-gyn. and gen. surgery, 1953-56; lectr. in ob-gyn. Nursing Sch. Phila. Coll. Osteo. Medicine; founder, mem. staff Tri County Hosp., Delaware County, Pa., from 1960, chief staff, 1960-62, chief dept. ob-gyn. surgery, 1960-77, dir. med. edn., 1968-71; attending and cons. in ob-gyn. surgery Met. Hosp., Phila., 1956-60, 71-75; chief dept. ob-gyn. Humana Hosp.-South Broward, Hollywood, Fla., 1980-84; cons. and attending in gynecol. surgery Drs. Hosp. of Hollywood, 1982-86; insp. for intern and resident tng. programs Bur. Hosps. of Am. Osteo. Assn., 1965-66; founder, med. dir. Women's Med. Svcs., 1973-77, Nutrients Inc., Phila., 1977-79, Supplements Inc., Phila., 1979-80, Alternative Lifestyle Ctr., Fla., 1983-86; founder, dir. A.W. Profl. Consultants, Inc.; cons. Practice Mgmt. Group, Med Temps Plus, Plantation, Fla.; provider ambulatory gyn. surgery for multiple gyn ctrs. in Dade, Broward and Palm Beach Counties, Fla. Author: Dr. Wechsler's New You Diet, 1978. Staff Sgt. Signal Corps, USAF, 1942-46, PTO, Japan. Fellow Am. Coll. Osteo. Obstetricians and Gynecologists, Internat. Coll. Applied Nutrition; mem. Am. Osteo. Assn., Pa. Osteo. Med. Assn., Philadelphia County Osteo. Soc., Fla. Osteo. Med. Assn., Broward County Osteo. Med. Assn., Am. Soc. Bariatric Physicians, Assn. Maternal and Child Welfare, Internat. Acad. Preventive Medicine, Inst. Food Technologists, Coun. for Responsible Nutrition, Internat. Coll. Gynecologic Laparoscopists, Assn. Reproductive Health Profls. Avocations: photography, sculpture, woodworking.

WECHSLER, GIL, lighting designer; b. N.Y.C., Feb. 5, 1942; s. Arnold J. and Miriam (Steinberg) W. Student Rensselaer Poly. Inst., 1958-61; BS, NYU, 1964; MFA, Yale U., 1967. Lighting designer Harkness Ballet, N.Y.C., 1967-69, Pa. Ballet, Phila., 1969-70, Stratford Shakespeare Festival, Ont., Can., 1969-78, 97, Guthrie Theatre, Mpls., 1971, Lyric Opera Chgo., 1972-76, Met. Opera, N.Y.C., 1976-96; tchr. NYU; guest lectr. Teatro Colon, Buenos Aires, Argentina, 1985, Yale U., New Haven, 1980, Broadway Lighting Designers, 1994—; guest lighting designer Am. Ballet Theatre, N.Y.C., 1980, Paris Opera, 1983, Chatelet Theatre, Paris, 1991. Cons. editor Opera Quar., 1983-90. Recipient Emmy award nominations. Mem. U.S. Inst. for Theatre Tech., Illuminating Engring. Soc., United Scenic Artists. Avocations: collecting ocean liner memorabilia, gardening, kayaking. Home: 1 Lincoln Plz New York NY 10023-7129

WECHSLER, HENRY, research psychologist; b. Warsaw, Poland, Aug. 16, 1932; came to U.S., 1941, naturalized, 1953; s. William and Lucy (Fryd) W.; m. Joan Goldstein, Oct. 16, 1955; children: Stephen Bruce, Pamela Jane, Peter Thomas. AB summa cum laude, Washington and Jefferson Coll., 1953; M.A. (Harvard Found. Advanced Study fellow, resident fellow), Harvard U., 1955, PhD in Social Psychology, 1957. USPHS postdoctoral rsch. fellow, 1957; rsch. assoc. Joint Commn. Mental Illness and Health, 1957-58; rsch. assoc., asst. prof. Clark U., 1958-59; rsch. social psychologist Mass. Mental Health Ctr., 1959-65; rsch. assoc. in psychology Med. Sch., Harvard U., 1960-66; rsch. assoc. in psychology Harvard Sch. Pub. Health, 1963-66, lectr. social psychology, 1966—, dir. Youth Alcohol-Drug Program, dept. health & social behavior, 1988—; dir. rsch. and community health programs Med. Found., Inc., Boston, 1965-88; vis. lectr. Boston U., 1967-68; pres. SocioTech. Systems, 1969-74; lectr. in rsch. Simmons Coll. Sch. Social Work, 1969-80; dir. coll. alcohol study Harvard Sch. Pub. Health, 1992—; adj. prof. Simmons Coll. Sch. Social Work, 1981-84. Author, editor: The Threat of Impending Disaster; contbr. to books Psychology of Stress, 1964, Social Psychology and Mental Health, 1970, Emergency Medical Services: Behavioral and Planning Perspectives, 1973, Social Work Research in the Human Services, 1976, Handbook of Medical Specialties, 1976, The Horizons of Health, 1977, Explorations in Nursing Research, 1978, Handbook of Dental Specialties, 1979, Minimum Drinking Age Laws, 1980, The Social Context of Medical Research, 1981, Medical School Admissions, 1982; contbr. numerous articles to profl. jours. Fellow Am. Psychol. Assn., Am. Sociol. Assn., Am. Pub. Health Assn.; mem. Harvard Club, Phi Beta Kappa. Club: Harvard (Boston). Home: 148 Puritan Dr Quincy MA 02169-1739 Office: Harvard Sch Pub Health Dept Health & Social Behavior 677 Huntington Ave Boston MA 02115-6028

WECHSLER, HERBERT, retired legal educator; b. N.Y.C., Dec. 4, 1909; s. Samuel and Anna (Weisberger) W.; m. Elzie S. Stix, May 29, 1933 (div. 1957); m. Doris L. Klauber, Apr. 13, 1957. AB, CCNY, 1928; LLB, Columbia U., 1931, LLD (hon.), 1978; LLD (hon.), U. Chgo., 1962, Harvard U., 1967, Georgetown U., 1984, CUNY, 1988, Yale U., 1991. Bar: N.Y. 1933. Editor Columbia U. Law Rev., 1929-31; instr. law Columbia U., 1931-32, asst. prof., 1933-38, assoc. prof., 1938-45, prof., 1945—, Harlan Fiske Stone prof. constl. law, 1957-78, emeritus, 1978—; law sec. to Mr. Justice Harlan F. Stone, 1932-33; counsel to minority leader N.Y. State Constl. Conv., 1938; asst. atty. gen. of N.Y. (assigned Bklyn. investigation), 1938-40; exec. sec. U.S. Bd. Legal Examiners, 1941-42; mem. adv. com. on rules criminal procedure U.S. Supreme Ct., 1941-45; spl. asst. to atty. gen. of U.S., 1940-44; asst. atty. gen. of U.S., in charge war div. U.S. Dept. Justice, 1944-46; tech. adviser to U.S. mems. Internat. Mil. Tribunal, 1945-46; vis. prof. Harvard Law Sch., 1956-57, Oliver Wendell Holmes lectr., 1958-59; Am. Law Inst. reporter Model Penal Code, 1952-62; exec. dir. Am. Law Inst., 1963-84, mem. council, 1984—; dir. Social Sci. Research Council, 1953. Author: (with J. Michael) Criminal Law and Its Administration, 1940, The Federal Courts and the Federal System, (with H. Hart Jr.), 1953, 3d edit. (with others), 1988, Principles, Politics and Fundamental Law, 1961, The Nationalization of Civil Liberties and Civil Rights, 1969. Mem. Pres.'s Commn. on Law Enforcement and Adminstrn. of Justice, 1965-67, N.Y. Temporary Commn. Rev. Penal Law and Criminal Code, 1961-70; mem. permanent com. for Oliver Wendell Holmes Devise, 1966-74; mem. com. on rev. fed. ct. appellate system, 1973-75; chmn. N.Y. Jud. Nomination Commn., 1978-82. Recipient Henry J. Friendly medal Am. Law Inst., 1993. Fellow Am. Acad. Arts and Scis., Brit. Acad. (corr.); mem. ABA, Fed. Bar Coun., Assn. of Bar of City of N.Y. (past v.p., medal), Am. Philos. Soc., CCNY Alumni Assn. (Townsend Harris medal, Learned Hand award), Order of Coif (hon.). Democrat. Club: Century Assn. Home: 179 E 70th St New York NY 10021-5154 Office: 435 W 116th St New York NY 10027-7201

WECHSLER, MARY HEYRMAN, lawyer; b. Green Bay, Wis., Jan. 8, 1948; d. Donald Hubert and Helen (Polcyn) Heyrman; m. Roger Wechsler, Aug. 1971 (div. 1977); 1 child, Risa Heyrman; m. David Jay Sellinger, Aug. 15, 1981; 1 stepchild, Kirk Benjamin; 1 child, Michael Paul. Student, U. Chgo., 1966-67, 68-69; BA, U. Wash., 1971; JD cum laude, U. Puget Sound, 1979. Bar: Wash. 1979. Assoc. Law Offices Ann Johnson, Seattle, 1979-81; ptnr. Johnson, Wechsler, Thompson, Seattle, 1981-83; pvt. practice Seattle, 1984-87; ptnr. Mussehl, Rosenberg et al, Seattle, 1987-88, Wechsler, Besk, Erickson, Ross & Roubik, Seattle, 1988—; bd. dirs. U. Wash. Law Sch. Child Advocacy Clinic; mem. Walsh Commn. on Jud. Selection, 1995-96; mem. commn. on domestic rels. Wash. State Supreme Ct., 1996-97, mem. law-related edn. com., 1997; chair edn. com. Access to Justice Bd., 1996-97; presenter in field. Author: Family Law in Washington, 1987, rev. edit., 1988, Marriage and Separation, Divorce and Your Rights, 1994; contbr. articles to legal publs. Mem. Wash. State Ethics Adv. Com., 1992-95; bd. dirs. Seattle LWV, 1991-92. Fellow Am. Acad. Matrimonial Lawyers (trustee Wash. state chpt. 1994, sec.-treas. 1996, profl. com. 1996-97, v.p. 1997); mem. ABA (chmn. Wash. state 1987-88), Wash. State Bar Assn. (exec. com. family law sect. 1985-91, chair 1988-89, legis. com. 1991-96, Outstanding Atty. of Yr. family law sect. 1988), Wash. Women Lawyers, King County Bar Assn. (legis. com. 1985—, vice-chair 1990-91, chair family law sect. 1986-87, chair domestic violence com. 1986-87, trustee 1988-90, policy planning com. 1991-92, 2d v.p. 1992-93, 1st v.p. 1993-94, pres. 1994-95), Nat. Conf. of Bar Pres. (commn. com. 1994-95, long range planning com. 1996). Office: Wechsler Besk Erickson Ross & Roubik 701 5th Ave Seattle WA 98104-7016

WECHSLER, SUSAN LINDA, software design engineer; b. Burbank, Calif., Oct. 7, 1956; d. Robert Edward and Sharron Ilene Wechsler; m. Gary Daniel Grove, Aug. 24, 1975 (dec. Dec. 1980); m. Dane Bruce Rogers, Feb. 28, 1987; children: Shayna Marneen Rogers, Ayla Corinne Rogers. BA in Math., Calif. State U., Long Beach, 1979. R&D software engr. Hewlett-Packard Co., Corvallis, Oreg., 1980—, R&D project mgr. sys. integration of laptop computers; Presenter N.W. Software Quality Conf., 1984. Contbr. articles to profl. publs.; co-developer nine calculators and handheld computers; patentee in field; co-designer HP 200LX Palmtop PC/Organizer, 1994; writer user interface DMI and BIOS software for laptop computers, 1994-97. Pres. Gifts for a Better World, Corvallis, Oreg., 1994, bd. dirs. 1990-1995. Democrat. Avocations: sewing, hiking, camping, reading. Office: Hewlett-Packard 1000 NE Circle Blvd Corvallis OR 97330-4239

WECHTER, CLARI ANN, paint manufacturing company executive; b. Chgo., June 1, 1953; d. Norman Robert and Harriet Beverly (Golub) W.; m. Gordon Jay Siegel, Feb. 10, 1980; 1 child, Alix Jessica. BA, U. Ariz., 1975; BE, Loyola U., Chgo., 1977. Cert. tchr., Ill. Saleswoman, v.p. sales Federated Paint Mfg. Co., Chgo., 1979—. Republican. Jewish. Avocation: travel. Home: 25 E Cedar St Chicago IL 60611-1109 Office: Federated Paint Mfg Co 1882 S Normal Ave Chicago IL 60616-1013

WECHTER, IRA MARTIN, tax specialist, financial planner; b. Bkyn., June 26, 1947; s. Nathan Harris and Mollie (Bauer) W.; m. Myrna Ellen Rosenbaum, Dec. 22, 1968; 1 child, Megan Jill. BA, CCNY, 1969; MPA, Bernard Baruch Coll., 1973. CFP; cert. practitioner of taxation; accredited tax advisor; registered investment advisor; accredited tax advisor; enrolled to practice before IRS; lic. in gen. securities, life, health and disability ins., N.J., N.Y. Dir. adminstrv. svcs. N.Y.C. Dept. City Planning, 1971-77; dep. asst. budget dir. N.Y., N.Y.C. Office Mgmt. and Budget, 1977-81; dep. commr. N.Y.C. Dept. Environ. Protection, 1981-84; pres. Wechter Fin. Svcs., Inc., Parsippany, N.J., 1984—. Mem. Community Bd. No. 1 S.I., 1973-76, 1st v.p., 1976-77; treas. S.I. Coun. on Arts, 1974-75. Recipient Outstanding Citizenship award Borough Pres. of S.I., 1977. Mem. Nat. Assn. Enrolled Agts., Inst. Cert. Fin. Planners, Nat. Assn. Tax Practitioners, Nat. Soc. Tax Preparers, Nat. Soc. Pub. Accts. Republican. Jewish. Avocations: U.S. mint stamp collecting, organist. Office: Wechter Fin Svcs Inc 1719 State Rt 10 Ste 310 Parsippany NJ 07054-4507

WECHTER, VIVIENNE THAUL, artist, poet, educator; b. N.Y.C.; d. Samuel Joshua and Hilda (Thaul) Rosenthal; m. Nathan Wechter; 1 dau., Robyrta Joan Wechter Rapoport. B. Pedagogy, Jamaica Tchrs. Coll.; postgrad., Columbia U., N.Y. U., New Sch. for Social Research, Art Students League, Sculpture Center, Pratt Inst. Graphic Center; Ph.D. in Interarts and Psychology of Creativity, Union Inst. Artist in residence Fordham U., 1964—, asst. prof. art and esthetics, 1964, now prof. interdisciplinary creative arts, chmn. acquisitions and exhbns.; vis. poet-artist Kansas City Art Inst., 1975, Md. Inst. Coll. Art, 1975, New Sch., N.Y.C., 1976, Marist Coll., Poughkeepsie, N.Y., 1977; vis. prof. New Sch. for Social Rsch., spring 1986; past chmn. coll. liaison divsn. Bronx Coun. on Arts; vis. prof. creative devel. Miami (Fla.) Jewish Home and Hosp. for Aged, 1993; lect. Sch. Internat. Affairs U. Malta; sole U.S. rep. Internat. Brennale, Malta, 1995. Moderator: weekly radio broadcast Today's World, WFUV, 1951—, created 6 programs in South Pacific, 1986-87; illustrator: (Alfeo Marzi) book cover Park of Jonas, 1965; author: A View from the Ark, 1973; contbr. articles to profl. jours.; one-woman shows Castellane Gallery, East Hampton Gallery, N.Y.C., Cornell U., Ithaca, N.Y., Neville Pub. Mus., Green Bay, Wis., Nashville Fine Arts Ctr., Fairleigh Dickinson U., Rutgers U., Waterloo (Iowa) Mcpl. Galleries, Bodley Gallery, Gloria Cortella Gallery, N.Y.C., Manhattan Coll., N.Y.C., Kouros Gallery, N.Y.C., Everson Mus. Art, Syracuse, N.Y., CCNY, B.R. Kornblatt Gallery, Balt., New Sch. Social Research, N.Y.C., Arts Interaction, N.Y.C., 1993, Douglass Gardens, Miami, also Paris, Rejik, Yugoslavia, multimedia show, Everson Mus. Fine Art, Syracuse, 1979, Dyansen Gallery, N.Y.C., 1981, L.I. U., 1986, Schiller-Wapner, N.Y.C., Shapolsky Gallery, N.Y.C., 1989, New England Mus. Contemporary Arts, 1991, 92, Douglas Gardens, Miami, 1992, Nassau County Mus. Art, 1994; solo shows and poetry readings New Sch., N.Y.C.,

Arts Interaction, N.Y.C., L.I. U., 1988, Arts Interaction Gallery 12, N.Y.C., 1988, 93, Fordham U., N.Y.C., 1994; represented in permanent collections Corcoran Gallery, Washington, Houston Mus. Fine Arts, Jewish Mus. N.Y.C., Fordham U., N.Y.C., Univ. Art Museum Berkeley, Calif., Museum Art and Sci., Norfolk, Va., NYU, Mus. of Fine Arts, Moscow, Russia, Mus. of Fine Art, Newark, Ohio State U., Phoenix Mus. Fine Arts, Fairleigh Dickinson U., Madison, N.J., UN, Internat. Culture Ctr., Jerusalem, Mus. Modern Art Warsaw, Poland, Mus. Fine Arts Moscow, N.J. State Mus., Trenton, others; monumental outdoor sculpture The Emerging Sun commd. for Manhattan Psychiat. Ctr., Ward's Island, N.Y.C.; permanent sculpture installed George Meany Internat. Ctr. Labor Studies, Washington, 1981, Simple Justice on Columbus Ave. nr. Lincoln Ctr., N.Y.C., 1989; logo sculpture Miami Jewish Home & Hosp. for Aged; developer, curator, 1st Biennial of Outdoor Sculpture, Fordham U. Rose Hill Campus, 1983. Author: Art, Where Are We Today and Why?, 1985; solo exbn. and video presentation New Sch. for Social Research, Mar. and Apr., 1986, Wagner-Schiller Galleries, Sept., 1986; solo painting, sculpture, video presentation and poetry reading, Nov. Dec., 1986; sole exhbn. and poetry reading, The Silver Dream, Provincetown Art Assn. and Mus., July, 1987; chair, moderator Influences in Art (Italian Am. Roundtable Art & Lit., 1988, video on RAI TV, Rome, 1989; panelist St. Bartholomew's, N.Y.C., 1987; rep., exhbns. Leister Fine Arts, Ltd., London; prin. speaker annual cong. Arts Interaction, N.Y.C., 1993. Bd. dirs. Urban Arts Corps; founder, trustee, past pres. Bronx Mus. Art; v.p. U.S. Com. IAA-UNESCO; trustee Bronx Soc. Arts and Letters, 1988—. New England Ctr. Contemporary Arts, 1992—. Recipient awards Am. Acad. Arts and Letters, awards Am. Soc. Contemporary Art, Silver Malta Cross, 1996. Mem. Am. Abstract Artists, Univ. Council of Art Educators, Urban League Center Greater N.Y. (dir., mem. advisory bd. 1952—), United World Federalists (1st chmn.), Fedn. Modern Painters and Sculptors (v.p.), Alpha Mu Gamma, Kappa Pi. *To be an artist-poet who requires solitude in order to create yet has the urgent need to be actively involved in the human community is a frightening challenge. Yet I know that to live one without the other will be for me, neither.*

WECKER, WILLIAM A., preventive medicine physician, neuropsychiatrist; b. N.Y.C., Mar. 14, 1923; s. Philip and Ruth (Frumkin) W.; m. Norma Cairney (dec. 1993); 1 child, Lyle Jeffery. BA, NYU, 1943, MD, 1946; MPH in Adminstrn., Harvard U., 1950; diploma Sch. Aviation Medicine, USAF, 1953. Lic. physician, surgeon, psychiatrist, N.Y.; cert. treating physician N.Y. State Workmen's Compensation Bd.; qualified psychiatrist N.Y. State Dept. Mental Health. Intern Bellevue Hosp., N.Y.C., 1946, Bayonne Gen. Hosp., 1946-47; health officer N.Y.C. Health Dept., 1948-50; dist. health officer N.Y. State Health Dept., Albany, 1950-52; pvt. practice medicine N.Y.C., 1954-59; grad. Sch. Aviation Medicine USAF, 1953; resident in psychiatry U.S. VA Hosp., N.Y.C., 1959-62, psychiatrist, 1962-64; psychiatrist Riverside Hosp., N.Y.C. Hosp. Dept., 1964-65, Postgrad. Ctr. for Mental Health, N.Y.C., 1964-65; pvt. practice preventive medicine, neuropsychiatry N.Y.C., 1948—; advisor Pan Am. Med. Assn., N.Y.C., 1952-55; cons. World Med. Assn., N.Y.C., 1954-61; staff physician Meml. Hosp., Queens, N.Y., 1955-64, Springfield (Mass.) Hosp., 1970-71; civil def. lectr. N.Y.C. Dept. of Health, 1955-58; advisor, charter mem. Acad. Religion and Mental Health, N.Y.C., 1959-62; psychiatrist, mgmt. cons., advisor in staff devel. program Youth House, N.Y.C., 1963-71; psychiatrist, cons. Mahoney Health Ctr., N.Y.C. Dept. Health, Bklyn., 1964-71; psychiatrist N.Y. State Narcotic Addiction Control Commn., 1970-71; med. examining physician N.Y.C. Workers Compensation Bd., 1971-76. Author: 3rd World Economics, 1981, Psychology for Everybody, 1983, Comprehensive Psychenomics, 1983, American Confetti, 1990, Anatomy of an Asylum, 1968, The Story of "H", 1971, The Honduran Syndrome, 1973, Devil's Den, 1978, Growing Up in Honduras, 1980. Cons. Allen Haus, Zurich, 1990-91; advisor English Gentlemen's Club, Zurich, 1982-87, Centro Cultural, Honduras, 1978-82; corr. Harry Schulz Internat. Newsletter, Switzerland and monaco, 1983-91. 2d lt. U.S. Army, 1943-45, ATO, capt. MC-USAF, 1952-54, ETO. Fellow Nat. Poliomyelitis Found., 1949-50, U.S. VA, 1960-61, NIMH fellow Postgrad. Ctr. for Mental Health, N.Y.C., 1964-65; recipient 50th Anniversary cert. NYU, 1996; decorated Nat. Def. Svc. medal, WWII Victory medal, Am. Theatre medal, Occupation medal (Germany). Mem. VFW, Am. Legion, Acad. Medicine Bklyn. (life), Nat. Inst. Mental Health, N.Y. State Med. Soc. (life, citation for 50 yrs. of svc. 1996), N.Y. Coun. Child Psychiatry, Kings County Med. Soc. (life), Royal Soc. Health (London), VFW. Avocations: medical astrology and medical psychecology, writing science books, esperanto and languages. Home and Office: 52 Macdougal St # 1-a New York NY 10012-2961

WECKESSER, ELDEN CHRISTIAN, surgery educator; b. Marshallville, Ohio, Mar. 31, 1910; s. Christian and Ella Elizabeth (Long) W.; m. Kathryn Alice Tuttle, Mar. 17, 1937; children: Jane, Elizabeth, Nancy, Mary. Student, Duke U., 1928-29; AB, Western Reserve U., 1933, MD, 1936. Diplomate Bd. of Surgery, Am. Coll. Surgeons. Intern Cin. Gen. Hosp., 1936-37; sr. intern surgery Univ. Hosps., Cleve., 1937-38, asst. resident gen. surgery, 1938-39, resident, 1939-40; from demonstrator in surgery to clin. prof. surgery Case Western Res. U., Cleve., 1940-74, prof. surgery, 1974-81, prof. emeritus surgery, 1981—; asst. surgeon Lakeside Hosp., Cleve., 1940-61, assoc. surgeon, 1961—; assoc. surgeon Highland View Hosp., St. Lukes Hosp., Cleve., 1961—; cons. surgeon VA Hosp., 1961—. Author: (books) Treatment of Hand Injuries, 1974, The Department of Surgery, Case Western Reserve University, 1843-1986, His Name Was Mudd, 1991; co-author: Flynn's Hand Surgery, 1966, rev. edits., 1975, 82, 91; co-author: (chpts.) Medicine in Cleveland and Cuyahoga County 1810-1976, 1977; contbr. numerous articles to profl. jours. Lt. col. Med. Corps U.S. Army, 1942-46, Australia, New Guinea. Named Disting. Alumnus, Case Western Res. U., 1981. Mem. AMA, ACS (mem. trauma com.), Am. Bd. Surgery, Acad. Medicine Cleve. (v.p. 1965-66, pres. 1966-67), Ohio State Med. Assn., Cleve. Surg. Soc. (pres. 1964-65), Am. Assn. Surgery Trauma, Am. Soc. Surgery of Hand, Cen. Surg. Assn., Internat. Soc. Surgery, Cleve. Med. Libr. Assn. (v.p. 1973-74, pres. 1974-75), Western Res. Med. Alumni Assn. (pres. 1965-66), Alpha Omega Alpha. Republican. Presbyterian. Avocations: author. Home and Office: 129 Manorbrook Dr Chagrin Falls OH 44022-4163

WECKESSER, ERNEST PROSPER, JR., publisher, educator; b. Akron, Ohio, Mar. 23, 1933; s. Ernest Prosper and Sadie (Liken) W.; m. Mary B. Hunter, Jan. 12, 1959; children—Jeffrey, Franz, Kathleen, Lynne. B.A., Bowling Green State U., 1955, M.A., 1960; Ph.D., Mich. State U., 1963. Asst. prof. speech SUNY-Oneonta, 1962-63, Kent State U., 1963-64; mem. faculty Purdue U., 1964-70, assoc. prof., 1968-70; prof. speech Montclair (N.J.) Coll., 1970-71; assoc. prof. speech Pa. State U., 1971-72; dir. Ernest Weckesser Assos.; chmn. bd. dirs. Green Tree Press, Inc., Dunkirk, N.Y.; pres. Bierhaus Internat., Inc., Erie, Pa. Author: The Radio Rhetoric of John L. Lewis, 1963, How To Succeed in College, 1971, The 12,000 Housewife, 1975, Dollars in Your Mailbox, 1975, Alternatives: A Network of Small Business Opportunities, 1992; co-author: The Bradley-Cooper Smoke Cessation Program, 1995. Bd. dirs. Florerence Crittenden Home, Erie.; Mem. Pres.'s Council Gannon U.; Mem. adv. bd. Villa Maria Coll. Served to capt. USAF, 1955-59. Named Disting. Pennsylvanian William Penn Soc., 1983.

WECLEW, ROBERT GEORGE, lawyer, educator; b. Chgo., Oct. 30, 1911; s. Victor T. and Mary (Tadrowski) W.; m. Jean Helen Vinson, Jan. 5, 1942; children: Harlene Villio, Robert Vinson Weclew. B.S. in Law, Northwestern U., 1932, J.D., 1935. Bar: Ill. 1934, U.S. Dist. Ct. (no. dist.) Ill. 1937, U.S. Supreme Ct. 1966. Assoc. Case and Lynn, Chgo., 1935-40; atty. Employers of Wausau, Chgo., 1940-42, VA, Chgo., 1945-57; prof. Law Sch., DePaul U., Chgo., 1957-78; acting dean Law Sch., DePaul U., 1968-71, prof. emeritus, 1978—; sole practice Chgo., 1978—; Mem. Am. Law Inst., 1968-71; counsel, co-founder Acad. of Gen. Dentistry, 1952-70. Contbr. articles on constl. law to profl. jours. Mem. Ill. Constl. Study Commn., Chgo., 1968-69. Fellow Acad. Continuing Edn. (counsel, co-founder 1974—); mem. Ill. Bar Assn. (council legal edn. 1969-71), Advocates Soc., Phi Kappa Theta, Delta Theta Phi. Home and Office: 5766 N Kercheval Ave Chicago IL 60646-6610

WECLEW, VICTOR T., dentist; b. Chgo., Mar. 18, 1916; m. Gertrude David, 1945; 1 child, Victor T. III. B.S., U. Ill., 1939, D.D.S., 1943. Gen. practice dentistry Chgo., 1946—. Contbr. articles to profl. jours. Active Boy Scouts Am. Served to maj. AC, U.S. Army, 1943-46. Fellow Acad. Gen. Dentistry (co-founder 1952, bd. dirs., asst. editor jour. 21 yrs.), Acad. Continuing Edn. (co-founder 1974), Am. Coll. Dentists, Acad. of Dentistry Internat. (trustee); mem. ADA, Ill. State Dental Soc., Chgo. Dental Soc. (various coms., past. dir., pres. N.W. br. 1969-70), U. Ill. Dental Alumni Assn. (bd. dirs. 10 yrs., Disting. Alumnus award 1991), Omicron Kappa Upsilon, Psi Omega. Roman Catholic. Home: 5781 N Forest Glen Ave Chicago IL 60646-6610

WEDDELL, LINDA ANNE, speech and language pathologist; b. Pitts., Nov. 21, 1946; d. Gilbert Eugene and Anna Margaret (Duffer) Everett; m. Charles Michael Weddell, Aug. 7, 1971; children: Michael Everett, Allison Joanne. BS, Purdue U., 1970; postgrad., Butler U., 1987. Speech pathologist Clermont County Sch. System, Batavia, Ohio, 1970-71, MSD Decatur Twp., Indpls., 1971-76; asst. dir. Mom's Day Out program Calvary United Meth. Ch., Brownsburg, Ind., 1983-86; speech pathologist Brownsburg Community Schs., 1989—. Vol. Am. Heart Assn., Indpls., 1988; com. mem. Calvary United Meth. Ch., Brosnwburg, 1976—; dir. Brownsburg Tennis Tournament, 1988; leader Girl Scouts U.S.A., Brownsburg, 1987-89. Continuing edn. grantee Brownsburg Fellowship, 1990. Mem. Ind. Speech & Hearing Assn., Purdue Alumni Assn. (life). Avocations: watching Purdue basketball, bowling, swimming, spending time with family. Home: 3115 N 950th E Brownsburg IN 46112

WEDDIGE, EMIL ALBERT, lithographer, art educator; b. Sandwich, Ont., Can., Dec. 23, 1907; came to U.S., 1909; s. Carl Albert and Marie Emma (Boismier) W.; m. Juanita Gertrude Pardon, Aug. 18, 1919. BS (hon.), Ea. Mich. U., 1934, DFA (hon.), 1973; student, Art Students League, N.Y.C.; studies with Emil Ganso, Woodstock, N.Y.; M of Design, U. Mich., 1937; Dr. Fine Arts (hon.), Ea. Mich. U., 1973; D (hon.), Cleary Coll., 1992. Tchr. Dearborn (Mich.) Pub. Schs., 1934-35; supr. art Dearborn Sch. System, 1935-37; from instr. to prof. art Univ. Mich., Ann Arbor, 1937-73, ret., apptd. prof. emeritus, 1974; owner pvt. studio Paris, 1949—, Ann Arbor; Cons. to John Weiss, Detroit, 1969—, to Louis G. Basso, West Bloomfield Hills, Mich., 1980—. One-man shows include Fishy Whale Studio, 1975, Washtenaw Community Coll., Ann Arbor, Tokyo, Japan, numerous others; exhibited in Paris, 1986, 87, T'Marra Gallery, Japan, 1991, U. Mich. Mus. of Art, Tokyo, Japan, 1993; permanent collections at Met. Mus. Art, N.Y.C., Libr. of Congress, Washington, Bibliotheque Nationale, Paris, Nat. Gallery of Art, Washington, various worldwide U.S. Embassies, many colls. and univs., many others; commd. by Parke Davis & Co., Chrysler Corp., Dow Chem. Co., United Nergo S. F.; designer Mich. Artain; contbr. articles to profl. jours. Pres. Izaack Walton League, Ann Arbor, 1945—. Recipient Philip and Ester Klein prize Am. Color Print Soc., 1965, Print award Libr. of Congress, 1951, Print of Yr. award The Print Club, Phila., 1957, Eugene Power award for art work done for United Negro Found., 1993, United Meml. Coll. Found. award, numerous other awards. Mem. Internat. Soc. Appraisers, Mich. Water Color Soc. (founder, pres., charter organizer), Mich. Printmakers (founder, pres.), Ann Arbor Art Assn. (exhbn. dir. 1943-55). Republican. Congregational. Home and Studio: 870 Stein Rd Ann Arbor MI 48105-9216

WEDDING, CHARLES RANDOLPH, architect; b. St. Petersburg, Fla., Nov. 16, 1934; s. Charles Reid and L. Marion (Whitaker) W.; m. Audrey Whitsel, Aug. 18, 1956 (div. Apr. 1979); children: Daryl L., Douglas R., Dorian B.; m. Vonnie Sue Hayes, June 22, 1984 (div. Dec. 1991); stepchildren: Stephanie M., Brian E.; m. June A. Free, Mar. 31, 1993; stepchildren: Gregory, Kristine. BArch, U. Fla., 1957. Registered architect, Fla., Ga., N.C., S.C., Del., Va., Tex., Ill., Ind., Kans., La., Mo., Okla., Tenn. Architect in tng. Harvard & Jolly AIA, St. Petersburg, 1957-60; architect, prin., pres. Wedding & Assocs., St. Petersburg, 1960—. Mayor City of St. Petersburg, 1973-75; past chmn. Pinellas County Com. of 100, Bldg. Dept. Survey Team, City of St. Petersburg; trustee All Children's Hosp., 1968-70; sect. leader St. Petersburg United Fund, 1965-70; mem. city council Action Team for Pier Redevel., 1967-68; mem. exec. com. Goals for City of St. Petersburg, 1970-72; den. leader Weblos, Boy Scouts Am., 1971-72; chmn., trustee Canterbury Sch. YMCA, 1968-72; mem. adv. com. Tomlinson Vocat. Sch., 1969-79; past trustee Mus. Fine Arts; past bd. dirs. Neighborly Ctr., Jr. Achievement Pinellas County. Served to 1st lt. U.S. Army, 1958-60. Fellow AIA (5 Silver Spike awards, Merit of Honor, Medal of Honor); mem. Am. Soc. Landscape Architects, St. Petersburg Assn. Architects (past. pres.), Fla. Assn. Architects (8 Merit Design awards). Republican. Episcopalian. Clubs: Suncoasters; St. Petersburg Yacht. Avocations: sailing, hunting, golfing, tennis. Home: 6900 10th Ave N Saint Petersburg FL 33710-6152 Office: Wedding & Assocs Inc 300 1st Ave S Saint Petersburg FL 33701-4236

WEDDINGTON, ELIZABETH GARDNER (LIZ GARDNER), actress, editor; b. N.Y.C., Oct. 13, 1932; d. A. Adolph and Anne Mary (Gardner) Blank; m. George Lee Weddington, Jr., Oct. 23, 1965; 1 child, Georgiana Marie. Actress TV, radio, telephone, N.Y./Calif, 1957—; editor comml. scripts N.Y., 1969—; freelance writer N.Y. City Tribune, various other publs., N.Y., nat., 1984—. Columnist polit. commentary, 1984—; appeared in over 300 TV commls., also TV and radio voice-overs. Mem. County Com., Conservative Party, N.Y.C., 1988-90, 94-96, 17th Precinct Comty. Coun., N.Y.C., 1974-96; rep. Yorkville Area Cath. Coun., N.Y.C., 1986-93. Recipient Mayor's Vol. Action Ctr. award, N.Y.C., 1981-82, Cert. Recognition N.Y.C. Dept. Police Dep. Commr. Community Affairs, 1981. Mem. Screen Actors Guild, Am. Fedn. Radio and TV artists, Nat. League Am. Pen Women, Internat. Platform assn., Nat. Soc. Children of Am. Revolution - Fraunces Tavern Soc. (sr. pres. 1985-89), N.Y. State Soc. Children Am. Revolution (sr. historian 1988-90, sr. 2d v.p. 1990-92), Nat. Soc. DAR (assoc. mem. Washington colonial chpt. 1996—, Warren chpt., chmn. com. Mary Washington Colonial chpt., corr. sec. 1992-94, mem. Warren chpt. 1996—, assoc. mem. Mary Washington Colonial chpt. 1996—), Nat. Soc. U.S. Daughters of 1812 (organizing pres. Pres. James Madison Chpt. 360 1988—), N.Y. State Soc. Daughters 1812, N.Y. State Soc. Dames of Ct. of Honor (pres. 1984-88), United Daughters of Confederacy (pres. N.Y. div. 1988-90, nat. chmn. revision of gen. bylaws com. 1989-91, McMath Scholarship gen. com. 1991-92, nat. chmn. gen. bylaws com. 1992-96), Daus. Colonial Wars (N.Y. State chpt.), Nat. Geneal. Soc., Colonial Dames of Am. (parent chpt. N.Y. claims com. 1993-96). Republican. Roman Catholic. Avocations: genealogy, military, English, constitutional and religious history, opera, antiques, porcelains. Home and Office: 316 N Main St Warrenton NC 27589-1826

WEDDINGTON, SARAH RAGLE, lawyer, educator; b. Abilene, Tex., Feb. 5, 1945; d. Herbert Doyle and Lena Catherine (Morrison) Ragle. BS magna cum laude, McMurry Coll., 1965, hon. doctorate, 1979; JD, U. Tex., 1967; hon. doctorate, Hamilton Coll., 1979, Southwestern U., 1989, Austin Coll., 1993. Bar: Tex. 1967, D.C. 1980, U.S. Dist. Ct. (we., no. and ea. dists.) Tex., U.S. Ct. Appeals (5th cir.), U.S. Supreme Ct. Pvt. practice law Austin, 1967-77; gen. counsel Dept. Agr., Washington, 1977-78; spl. asst. to Pres., Washington, 1978-79, asst. to Pres., 1979-81; chmn. Interdepartmental Task Force on Women, 1978-81; mem. Pres.'s Commn. on Exec. Exchange, 1981; Carl Hatch prof. law and pub. adminstrn. U. N.Mex., Albuquerque, 1982-83; pvt. practice law Austin, Tex., 1985—; dir. Tex. Office State-Fed. Relations, Austin, 1983-85; vis. prof. govt. Wheaton Coll., Norton, Mass., 1980-81; sr. lectr. Tex. Woman's U., Denton, 1981-93, U. Tex., Austin, 1986—. Author: A Question of Choice, 1992; contbg. editor Glamour mag., 1981-83. Mem. Tex. Ho. of Reps., 1973-77. Recipient Woman of Yr. award Tex. Women's Polit. Caucus, 1973, Elizabeth Boyer award Equity Action League, 1978, Outstanding Woman award, 1979, Leadership awards Ladies Home Jour., 1979, spl. recognition Esquire mag., 1984, Woman Who Dares award Nat. Coun. Jewish Women, 1993, Woman of Distinction award Nat. Conf. for Coll. Women Student Leaders, 1993, Colby award for Pub. Svc. Sigma Kappa, 1996; named Lectr. of Yr. Nat. Assn. for Coll. Activities, 1990, 91. Mem. Tex. Bar Assn. Office: S Weddington Law Offices 709 W 14th St Austin TX 78701-1707

WEDE, RICHARD J., school superintendent; b. Cherokee, Iowa, Nov. 11, 1949; s. Robert C. and Beatrice I. (Albers) W.; m. Carol E. Teeter, Dec. 22, 1969; 1 child, Robert D.R. BA, U. No. Iowa, 1971; MS, Iowa State U., 1979; EdS, N.W. Mo. State U., 1985; D in Edn., Drake U., 1996. Drivers' edn. tchr. N.W. Webster Community Sch. Dist., Barnum, Iowa, 1971, Everly (Iowa) Community Sch. Dist., 1974-75; jr. high math tchr. Blessed Sacrament Sch., Waterloo, Iowa, 1973-75; high sch. math tchr. Council Bluffs (Iowa) Community Sch. Dist., 1975-80; assoc. mid. sch. prin. Lewis Cen. Community Sch. Dist., Council Bluffs, 1980-83; sec. prin. Bedford (Iowa) Community Sch. Dist., 1983-86; supt. schs. Everly Community Sch. Dist., 1986-89, Everly & Clay Cen. Community Sch. Dists., 1989-91, Prairie Community Sch. Dist., Gowrie, Iowa, 1991-93, Cedar Valley Community Sch. Dist., 1991-93, Praire Valley Community Sch. Dist., Gowrie, Iowa, 1993-94; supt. Dunkerton (Iowa) Cmty. Sch. Dist., 1994—. Bd. dirs. Regional Transit Authority, Spencer, Iowa, 1990-91. Mem. Am. Assn. Sch. Adminstrs., Sch. Adminstrs. Iowa, Am. Legion, Westend Optimists of Council Bluffs, Dunkerton Area C. of C., Delta Kappa. Roman Catholic. Home: Box 67 207 E Sycamore Dunkerton IA 50626 Office: Dunkerton Cmty Sch Dist PO Box 308 509 S Canfield Dunkerton IA 50626

WEDEEN, MARVIN MEYER, hospital executive; b. Perth Amboy, N.J., Jan. 3, 1926. BS, Cornell U., 1949; MSc in Hosp. Adminstrn., Columbia U., 1971. Rsch. asst. Sealtest divsn. Kraft Foods, Schenectady, N.Y., 1949-55, dir. work simplification, 1955-59; pers. mgr. Dellwood Foods, Yonkers, N.Y., 1959-63; asst. v.p. Dellwood Foods, Yonkers, 1964-69; cons. pers. N.Y. Infirmary, N.Y.C., 1971; asst. adminstr. Sewickley Valley Hosp., Sewickley, Pa., 1971-80, v.p., 1980-90, spl. advisor to pres., 1991, ret., 1992; cons. Exec. Svc. Corp., 1992—; bd. dirs. Valley Care Assn., Sewickley, pres., 1993-96; mem. Human Resources com., Hosp. Coun. Western Pa., 1987-89; cons. Sr. Med. Cons., N.Y.C., 1971. Chmn. oper. com. Health Sys. Agy., Pitts.; class fund rep. Cornell U. Alumni Fund, 1967-72; bd. dirs. United Jewish Fedn. Bd., 1991-94. Named Man of the Yr., Sewickley Hist. Soc. and Gateway Press, 1980. Fellow, Am. Coll. Health Care Execs.; mem. APHA, Am. Hosp. Assn., Hosp. Assn. (planning and mktg. sect. 1984-96), Edgeworth Club. Avocations: racket sports, music, theater art.

WEDEL, PAUL GEORGE, retired hospital administrator; b. Elizabeth, N.J., Jan. 1, 1927; s. Paul John and Helen (Cleary) W.; m. Jean Marie Martin, June 18, 1949; children: Dana Lyn Wedel, Laurie Ann Wedel Musser, Paul John II, Kurt Frederick. Grad., Peddie Sch., Hightstown, N.J., 1944; B.S. in Bus. Adminstrn., Am. U., 1952; M.S. in Hosp. Adminstrn., Northwestern U., 1955. Adminstrv. resident Harrisburg (Pa.) Polyclinic Hosp., 1953-54; asst. adminstr. Williamsport (Pa.) Hosp., 1954-59, adminstr., 1959-64; pres. Lancaster (Pa.) Gen. Hosp., 1964-89; pres. Lancaster Gen. Hosp. Found., 1989-92, pres. emeritus, 1992-94; ret., 1994. Bd. dirs. Inter-County Hospitalization Plan, Inc., 1966-84, James Buchanan Found., Preservation Wheatland, 1968-80, Linden Hall Sch., 1984-91; sr. warden St. Thomas Episcopal Ch., 1979-81; trustee Millersville U., 1991—. Served with USNR, 1944-46, 50-51. Named Outstanding Young Man, Williamsport Jr. C. of C., 1957. Fellow Am. Coll. Health Care Execs. (regent Pa. 1984-89); mem. Am. Hosp. Assn., Hosp. Assn. Pa. (bd. dirs. 1970-73, 84-89), Lancaster Assn. Commerce and Industry (bd. dirs.), Hamilton Club, Pirates Club, Rotary (pres. 1978-79), Masons. Home: Rock Rimmon Ridges 203 Riveredge Dr Leola PA 17540-9745

WEDEPOHL, LEONHARD MARTIN, electrical engineering educator; b. Pretoria, Republic of South Africa, Jan. 26, 1933; s. Martin Willie and Liselotte B.M. (Franz) W.; m. Sylvia A.L. St. Jean; children: Martin, Graham. B.Sc. (Eng.), Rand U., 1953; Ph.D., U. Manchester, Eng., 1957. Registered profl. engr., B.C. Planning engr. Escom, Johannesburg, Republic of South Africa, 1957-61; mgr. L.M. Erricson, Pretoria, Republic of South Africa, 1961-62; sect. leader Reyrolle, Newcastle, Eng., 1962-64; prof., head dept. Manchester U., 1964-74; dean engring. U. Man., Winnipeg, Can., 1974-79; dean applied sci. U. B.C., Vancouver, Can., 1979-85, prof. elec. engring., 1985—; mem. Sci. Rsch. Coun., London, 1968-74; dir. Man. Hydro, Winnipeg, 1975-79, B.C. Hydro, Vancouver, 1980-84, B.C. Sci. Coun., 1982-84; cons. Horizon Robotics, Saskatoon, 1986; chmn. implementation team Sci. Place, Can., 1985; cons. CEPEL, Rio de Janeiro; adv. Man. High Voltage D.C. Rsch. Ctr.; tech. advisor RTDS Techs., Inc., Winnipeg, 1994—; head protection devel. Rolls Royce Indsl. Power Group, 1995-96. Contbr. articles to sci. jours.; patentee in field. Named Hon. Citizen City of Winnipeg, 1979. Fellow Instn. Elec. Engrs. (premium 1967); mem. Assn. Profl. Engrs. B.C. Avocations: music; cross-country skiing; hiking. Office: 4321 Hoskins Rd, North Vancouver, BC Canada V7K 2P7

WEDGEWORTH, ANN, actress; b. Abilene, Tex., Jan. 21, 1935; m. Rip Torn (div.); 1 child, Danae; m. Ernest Martin; 1 child, Dianna. Attended, U. Tex.; B.A. in Drama, So. Methodist U. Broadway debut in Make A Million, 1958; other Broadway appearances Chapter Two (Tony award), Thieves, Blues for Mr. Charlie, The Last Analysis; off-Broadway appearances Line, Chapparal, The Crucible, Days and Nights of Beebee Fenstermaker, Ludlow Fair, The Honest to God Shnozzola, A Lie of the Mind; toured with nat. cos. of The Sign in Sidney Brustein's Window and Kennedy's Children; appeared: in TV series Three's Company, The Edge of Night, Another World, Somerset, Filthy Rich, Evening Shade; other TV appearances All That Glitters, The Equalizer, Bronk, Evening Shade, Twilight Zone, Trapper John, M.D.; TV film The War Between the Tates, Bogey, Right to Kill, Cooperstown, The War Between the Tates, Bogie, A Stranger Waits; movies Handle With Care (Nat. Soc. Film Critics award), Thieves, Bang the Drum Slowly, Scarecrow, Catamount Killing, Law and Disorder, One Summer Love, Dragon-Fly, Birch Intervals, Soggy Bottom, USA, No Small Affair, Sweet Dreams, Mens Club, A Tiger's Tale, Made in Heaven, Far North, Miss Firecracker, Green Card, Love and a 45, The Whole Wide World. Address: 4203 Colfax Ave #F Studio City CA 91604

WEDGEWORTH, ROBERT, dean, university librarian, former association executive; b. Ennis, Tex., July 31, 1937; s. Robert and Jimmie (Johnson) W.; m. Chung Kyun, July 28, 1972; 1 child, Cicely Veronica. AB, Wabash Coll., 1959, DHL (hon.), 1980; MS, U. Ill., 1961; LittD, Park Coll., 1973; LLD, Atlanta U., 1982; DHL, Western Ill. U., 1983, Coll. William & Mary, 1988. Cataloguer Kansas City Pub. Library, 1961-62; asst. librarian, then acting librarian Park Coll., Parkville, Mo., 1962-64; librarian Meramec Community Coll., Kirkwood, Mo., 1964-66; acquisitions librarian Brown U. Library, Providence, 1966-69; asst. prof. Rutgers U., New Brunswick, N.J., 1971-72; exec. dir. ALA, Chgo., 1972-85; dean Sch. Library Service Columbia U., N.Y.C., 1985-92; univ. libr., prof. libr. adminstrn. U. Ill., Urbana, 1992—; mem. Nat. Commn. on New Technol. Uses of Copyrighted Works, 1975-78, biomed. library rev. com. Nat. Library Medicine, 1975-78, chmn., 1978-79; mem. network adv. com. Library of Congress, 1977-78; nat. adv. bd., exec. com., council Ctr. for the Book, Library of Congress, 1978-82; bd. dirs. Newberry Library, Chgo., 1979—, Pub. Service Satellite Consortium, 1975-85; bd. visitors U. Miami Libraries, Air U.; mem. exec. bd. Internat. Fedn. Library Assns. and Instns., The Hague, 1985-91, pres. 1991-97; trustee Am. Library in Paris, 1986-92; trustee Wabash Coll., 1988—; alumni bd. Wabash Coll., pres. 1987-89; vis. prof. Sch. Library Sci. U. N.C., Chapel Hill, 1985; mem. adv. coun. Princeton U. Libraries, 1977-78, Stanford U. Librs., 1989-92, Harvard Coll. Libr. Vis. Com., 1994-97; mem. nat. adv. com. Gannett Ctr. for Media Services; mem. Accrediting Council on Edn. in Journalism and Mass Communication, 1989-97. Editor: Library Resources and Tech. Services, 1971-73; editor-in-chief: ALA Yearbook, 1976-85, World Encyclopedia of Library and Information Services, 3d edit., 1993. Chmn. U.S. Nat. Com. for UNESCO/PGI, 1976-81. Council on Library Resources fellow, 1969; recipient Medal of Honor Internat. Coun. Archives, 1996. Mem. ALA (life), NAACP (life), Am. Soc. Info. Sci., Grolier Club, Am. Antiquarian Soc. Home: 2008 Bentbrook Dr Champaign IL 61821-9204 Office: Univ of Illinois 1408 W Gregory Dr Rm 230 Urbana IL 61801-3607

WEDGWOOD, RUTH, law educator, international affairs expert; b. N.Y.C.; d. Morris P. and Anne (Williams) Glushien; m. Josiah Francis Wedgwood; May 29, 1982. BA magna cum laude, Harvard U., 1972; fellow, London Sch. Econs., 1972-73; JD, Yale U., 1976. Bar: D.C., N.Y. Law clk. to judge Henry Friendly U.S. Ct. Appeals (2d cir.), N.Y.C., 1976-77; law clk. to justice Harry Blackmun U.S. Supreme Ct., Washington, 1977-78; spl. asst. to asst. atty. gen. U.S. Dept. Justice, Washington, 1978-80; asst. U.S. atty. U.S. Dist. Ct. (so. dist.) N.Y., N.Y.C., 1980-86; prof. law Yale U., New Haven, 1986—, faculty fellow Inst. for Social and Policy Studies, 1989—, faculty fellow Berkeley Coll., 1989—, faculty mem. Yale Internat. Security program, 1992—; faculty Yale UN Studies program, 1992—; mem. Sec. of State's Adv. Com. Internat. Law, 1993—; dir. Yale UN Legal Studies, 1996—; dir., sr. fellow project internat. orgns. and law Coun. Fgn. Rels., 1994—. Exec. editor Yale Law Jour., 1975-76; author: The Revolutionary Martyrdom of Jonathan Robbins, 1990, The Use of Force in International Affairs, 1992, American National Interest and the United Nations, 1995; contbr. articles to profl. jours. Prin. rapporteur U.S. Atty. Gen.'s Guidelines on FBI Undercover Ops., Informant Use and Racketeering and Gen. Crime Investigations, 1980; bd. dirs. Lawyers Com. for Human Rights, N.Y.C., 1988-94. Recipient Israel Peres prize, 1976, Ford Found. rsch. grant; Rockefeller

Found. fellowship. Mem. ABA, Am. Law Inst., Am. Soc. Internat. Law (exec. com. 1995—, chmn. N.Y. Ctr. 1994—), Internat. Law Assn. (v.p. 1994—, program chmn. Am. br. 1992, exec. coun. 1992-94), Assn. Am. Law Sch. (chmn. sect. internat. law 1995-96), Assn. Bar City N.Y. (arms control and internat. security affairs com., chmn. 1989-92, chmn. internat. affairs coun. 1992-95, exec. com. 1995—), Union Internationale des Avocats, U.S.A. (chpt. bd. govs. 1993—, rep. to UN 1995—), Coun. on Fgn. Rels., Elizabethan Club, Mory's Assn., Yale Club (N.Y.C.). Office: Yale U Sch Law PO Box 208215 New Haven CT 06520-8215 also: Coun on Fgn Rels 58 E 68th St New York NY 10021-5984 *Notable cases include: U.S. vs. Kostadinov, which involved a Bulgarian spy traded for 25 East Bloc detainees; U.S. vs. Gold, Orosz, Egerhazi and Kompar, which involved a $1 million racketeering/landlord arson ring in N.Y.C. and defrauding Lloyd's of London Sasse Syndicate; U.S. vs. Kazemzadeh and DeVelasco, which involved pub. corruption in N.Y.C. health and hosp. corps. and in the fed. WIC program.*

WEDZICHA, WALTER, foreign language educator; b. Jezor, Poland, June 5, 1920; came to U.S., 1946; s. Wladyslaw and Maria (Kruczek) W.; m. Sabina Purzynska, Nov. 28, 1945; children: John M., Christine S. AB, U. Miami, 1965; MA, U. Pitts., 1966. Attaché Consulate Gen. of Poland, N.Y.C., 1946-49; acct. Miami, 1950-65; asst. prof. German and Russian Clarkson U., Potsdam, N.Y., 1967-86, prof. emeritus, 1986—. Author: Song of the City, 1957, From Love of God and All Creation, 1992. Fellow NDEA, U. Pitts., 1965-66; grantee NEH, Ohio State U., 1977, NEH, U. Ill., 1978. Mem. MLA. Democrat. Avocations: photography, music, gardening. Home: 2311 SE Bowie St Port Saint Lucie FL 34952-7317

WEED, EDWARD REILLY, marketing executive; b. Chgo., Jan. 25, 1940; s. Cornelius Cahill and Adelaide E. (Reilly) W.; student Fordham U., 1959-61, Loyola U., 1961-62; m. Lawrie Irving Bowes, Feb. 2, 1969. Account exec. Leo Burnett Co., Chgo., 1961-71; pres. GDC Ad Inc., corporate officer, Miami, Fla., 1971-74; v.p., account supr. D'Arcy Mac Manus & Masius, Chgo., 1975; group v.p. mktg. Hart Schaffner & Marx (Hartmarx), Chgo.; pres. Hart Services, Inc., 1975-82; v.p. mktg. Tishman, 1983-86; exec. v.p. Hannah Marine, 1986-87; exec. v.p., dir. U.S. Auction, 1988-92; v.p. mktg. Telemedia, 1992-95; mng. dir. Brochure Assoc., Lake Geneva, Wis., 1996—; dir. First Nat. Bank So. Miami; seminar instr. Grad. Sch. Notre Dame U., South Bend, Ill.; guest faculty Loyola U., Chgo. Contbr. articles to profl. jours. Trustee, Latin Sch. Found., 1976—; bd. dirs. North Ave. Day Nursery, 1969-73, Santa for Poor, 1975-87, Off-the-Street, 1982-87, Chgo. Boys' and Girls' Clubs, 1983-87, Map Inc., 1988—, Geneva Lake Conservancy, 1994—. Recipient Chi Ad Club award. Served with Ill. N.G. Republican. Roman Catholic. Tavern Club, Lake Geneva Country Club. Office: Brochure Assocs 3638 Snake Rd Lake Geneva WI 53147

WEED, ITHAMAR DRYDEN, life insurance company executive; b. Pomeroy, Ohio, Sept. 3, 1914; s. Ithamar B. and Besse (Smith) W.; m. Sally Lemert, July 5, 1941; children—Judith Lynne (Mrs. Lloyd Lindner), Charles Boyd, Donald Lemert. A.B., Ohio U., 1938; J.D. summa cum laude, Ohio State U., 1939. Bar: Ohio 1939. Clk. U.S. Dist. Ct. So. Dist. Ohio, Columbus, 1939-41; assoc. firm Vorys, Sater, Seymour and Pease, Columbus, 1946-54; assoc. counsel Western and So. Life Ins. Co., Cin., 1954-63; v.p., chief counsel Western and So. Life Ins. Co., 1963-73, sr. v.p., chief counsel, 1973-81; sec., dir Eagle Savs. Assn., Cin., 1970-81, West Ad, Inc., Cin., 1970-81; lectr. Coll. Law, Ohio State U., 1949-53. Served to lt. col. AUS, 1941-46. Mem. Order of Coif, Beta Theta Pi, Phi Delta Pi. Home: 5538 E Galbraith Rd Apt 34 Cincinnati OH 45236-2849

WEED, LAWRENCE L., pharmacology educator; b. Troy, N.Y., Dec. 26, 1923; married, 1952; 5 children. BA, Hamilton Coll., 1945; MD, Coll. Physicians & Surgeons, 1947. Asst. prof. medicine and pharmacology Sch. Medicine Yale U., 1954-56; dir. medicine edn. Eastern Maine Gen. Hosp., Bangor, 1956-60; asst. prof. microbiology Case Western Reserve U., 1961-64, assoc. prof., 1964-69; prof. cmty. medicine U. Vt., 1969-82, emeritus prof. Coll. Medicine, 1982—; pres. PKC Corp., 1984—; prof. medicine, dir. outpatient clinic Clv. Met. Gen. Hosp., 1964-69; dir. Promis Lab., 1969-81; chief scientist Promis Info. Sys., Inc., 1981-82. Recipient Gustav O. Lienhard award, 1995. Mem. Am. Coll. Physicians, Am. Soc. Microbiology. Achievements include research in problem oriented medical information system. Address: RR 1 Box 630 Cambridge VT 05444-9611 Office: U Vt Burlington VT 05405

WEED, MAURICE JAMES, composer, retired music educator; b. Kalamazoo, Oct. 16, 1912; s. Frank Eugene and Ella May (Britton) W.; m. Berneice Laverne Pope, Aug. 23, 1937; children: Allison Gilbert (Mrs. Walter D. Herrick), Laurice Ellen (Mrs. Samuel L. Rich). BA, Western Mich. U., 1934; MusB, Eastman Sch. Music, 1940, MusM, 1952, PhD, 1954. Supr. instrumental music pub. schs. Ionia, Mich., 1934-36, Three Rivers, Mich., 1937-43; asst. prof. music, dir. instrumental music, tchr. music theory Ripon Coll., 1946-51; tchr. Eastman Sch. Music, summer 1954; prof., head dept. music No. Ill. U., 1954-61, prof. music, 1961-74; adj. prof. music Western Carolina U., 1974-75; ret., 1975. Composer in residence, MacDowell Colony, 1961; performances include: Serenity for chamber orch. Eastman-Rochester Symphony, 1953, Symphony Number 1, Nat. Symphony Orch., Washington, 1956, Symphony of the Air, Carnegie Hall, 1957, Wonder of the Starry Night, 1st ann. symposium Contemporary Am. Music, U. Kans., 1959, Serenity and Fanfare for Two Trumpets and Organ, 8th ann. symposium Univ. Composers Exchange, Valparaiso, Ind., 1959; Sept Cinquains for Soprano Voice and chamber instrumental group, No. Ill. U., 1964, 67, Symphonie Breve, 6th ann. symposium Contemporary Am. Music U. Kans., 1967, Symphonie Breve, Oklahoma City Symphony Orch.; MBS broadcast, 1965, U. Redlands, 1964, Asheville (N.C.) Symphony Orch., 1979; condr. symposium of 8 sacred choral and 2 organ works by 6 coll., univ., high sch. and ch. choirs, Atlanta, 1975; Serenity, Asheville Symphony Orch., 1977; composer: over 65 works including Ships, Witchery (songs for soprano and piano), 1937, Rain, for contralto and piano, 1940, Three Preludes for Organ, 1945, Introduction and Scherzo, symphonic band, 1948, Gratitude, for contralto with organ, 1950, An After Easter Prayer, 1950, Serenity, for chamber orch., 1953, Wonder of the Starry Night, a capella choir, 1958, Symphonie Breve, 1959, Trio for violin, cello and piano, 1961, Concertino for cello and orch, 1962, Psalm XIII (mixed choir and organ), 1964, Hopkins Park, concert march, 1966, Triptych for Voices, a cappella choir, 1966, Vestigia Nulla Retrorsum, processional march, 1968, Praise Ye the Lord (mixed choir), 1968, A Wedding Song (soprano and organ), 1969, In the Midnight Hour (soprano and organ), 1970, In Te, Domini, Speravi (mixed choir), 1970, 4 Anthems for Mixed Choir, 1973, Postlude for Organ, 1974, The Catamounts, concert march for band, 1974, Duo for Viola and C Trumpet, 1977, Choral Fanfare No. 2, 1977, An Appalachian Celebration for Choir and Band, 1978; Celebration (hymn-anthem), 1981; 3 anthems for mixed voices Let All the People Praise Thee, 1980, Sing Praises to God, 1981, Praise Ye the Lord, 1982, The 3Bs-Brass Sextet, 1982, Voices of Appalachia, 1986; numerous others. Recipient 25th Anniversary award Nat. Symphony Orch., 1956, Ostwald award, 1959, J. Fisher & Bro. Centennial award, 1964, Pedro Paz award, 1966; Eastman Sch. Music teaching fellow, 1951-54. Mem. Nat. Assn. Composers U.S.A., Am. Music Ctr., Music Edn. Nat. Conf., N.C. Music Educators, Am. Soc. Univ. Composers, Phi Mu Alpha. Methodist. Home: Givens Estates Sweeten Creek Rd Wesley Dr N Villa 21-F Asheville NC 28803

WEED, ROGER OREN, rehabilitation services professional, educator; b. Bend, Oreg., Feb. 2, 1944; s. Chester Elbert and Ruth Marie (Urie) W.; m. Paula J. Keller; children: Nicholette, Andrew. BS in Sociology, U. Oreg., 1967, MS in Rehab. Counseling, 1969; PhD in Rehab. Counseling, U. Ga., 1986. Cert. rehab. counselor; cert. disability mgmt. specialist; lic. profl. counselor; cert. case mgr., cert. life care planner. Vocat. rehab. counselor State of Alaska, Anchorage, 1969-71; instr. U. Alaska, Anchorage, 1970-76; counselor Langdon Psychiat. Clinic, Anchorage, 1971-74; from asst. dir. to exec. dir. Hope Cottages, Anchorage, 1974-79; owner Profl. Resources Group, Anchorage, 1978-80; mng. ptnr. Collins, Weed & Assocs., 1980-84; assoc. dir. Ctr. for Rehab. Tech. Ga. Tech. U., Atlanta, 1986-87; catastrophic injury rehab. Weed & Assocs., Atlanta, 1984—; assoc. prof. Ga. State U., Atlanta, 1987—; adj. faculty Ga. Inst. Tech.; courtesy faculty U. Fla., 1996—. Co-author: Vocational Expert Handbook, 1986, Transferable Work Skills, 1988, Life Care Planning: Spinal Cord Injured, 1989, 94, Life Care Planning: Head Injured, 1994, Life Care Planning for the Amputee, 1992, Rehab Consultant Handbook, 1994; mem. editl. bd. Jour. of Pvt. Sector Rehab., Athens, Ga., 1986—; mem. Disting. Editl. Bd. Vanguard Series in Rehab., Athens, 1988—; contbr. articles to profl. publs. Recipient Gov.'s award Gov.'s Com. on Employment, Alaska, 1982, Goldpan Svc. award Gov.'s Com. on Employment, Alaska, 1978, Profl. Svcs. award Am. Rehab. Counselors Assn., 1993. Fellow Nat. Rehab. Assn. (chair legis. com., bd. dirs. met. Atlanta chpt. 1988—, pres. Pacific region 1983-85, pres.'s award Pacific region 1986), Nat. Assn. Rehab. Profls. in Pvt. Sector (chair resh. and tng. com. 1988-93, pres. 1994-95, Educator of the Yr. award 1991), Nat. Brain Injury Assn., Pvt. Rehab. Suppliers Ga., Rehab. Engring. Soc. N.Am., Anchorage Amateur Radio Club. Republican. Methodist. Avocations: sailing, skiing, bicycling, flying, computers. Office: 9th Fl College of Education Ga State U Dept Counseling Atlanta GA 30303

WEEDEN, DEBBIE SUE, early childhood education educator; b. Tenn., Nov. 7, 1952; d. Edward Jr. and Ann Arrants; m. Gordon H. Weeden, May 5, 1979; children: Lance Edward, Lindsey Brooke. BS in Early Child Edn. magna cum laude, Va. Intermont U., 1975; MA in Reading Rsch., East Tenn. State U., 1979. Cert. K-8 reading tchr., Tenn. Kindergarten tchr. Weaver Sch., Bristol, Tenn., 1975—. V.p. Weaver Sch. PTA; tchr. rep. Weaver Sch. Mem. Career Ladder Tchrs., Alpha Delta Kappa (historian). Methodist. Avocations: crafts, volleyball. Home: 328 Orchard Ln Bluff City TN 37618-1160 Office: Weaver Sch Rte 1 Bristol TN 37620

WEEDON, ALAN CHARLES, chemist, educator, university dean; b. Oxford, Eng., Mar. 29, 1951; arrived in Can., 1976; s. Charles Arthur Reginald and Marjorie Elsie (Cook) W. BSc, London U., 1973, PhD, 1976. Rsch. assoc. U. Western Ont., London, Can., 1976-80, asst. prof., 1980-86, assoc. prof., 1986-91, prof., 1991—, dean Faculty Grad. Studies, 1996—. Contbr. articles to sci. jours. Recipient Merck-Frosst award Can. Soc. Chemistry, 1991. Fellow Chem. Inst. Can.; mem. Am. Chem. Soc. Office: U Western Ont, Faculty of Grad Studies, London, ON Canada N6A 5B8

WEEKER, ELLIS, emergency physician; b. New Orleans, June 7, 1944; s. Harry and Marion W.; m. Gail Otis, July 3, 1982; children: Michael, Lisa, Elizabeth, Matthew. BS, Tulane U., 1966; MD, La. State U., 1970. Diplomate Am. Bd. Emergency Medicine. Intern Kaiser Found. Hosp., Oakland, 1970-71, resident in internal medicine, 1972-73; resident in internal medicine Highland Gen. Hosp., Oakland, 1972-73, assoc. chief emergency svcs., 1973-75; staff physician Calif. Emergency Physicians Med. Group, Oakland, 1975—, also bd. dirs.; med. dir. capitation svcs. Calif. Emergency Physicians/Medamerica, 1994—; med. dir. Calif. Emergency Physicians Med. Group, Oakland, 1976-95, regional med. dir., 1978—, chmn. bd. dirs., 1979-87; mem. staff Good Samaritan Hosp., San Jose, Calif., 1975—, chmn. emergency dept., 1977-82; mem. staff South Valley Hosp., Gilroy, Calif., 1990—. Commnr. Emergency Med. Care Commn., Santa Clara County, Calif., 1990-92. Mem. Am. Heart Assn. (chmn. bd. Santa Clara chpt. 1991-92, pres. 1988-89, nat. affiliate faculty ACLS 1982-91). Republican. Roman Catholic. Avocations: music, skiing, sailing. Office: Calif Emergency Physicians Med Group 588 Blossom Hill Rd San Jose CA 95123-3212

WEEKLEY, DAVID, real estate developer; b. 1954. Student, Trinity Univ., 1975. General Homes, Inc., Houston, 1975-76; CEO David Weekley Homes, Houston, 1976—. Home: 1300 Post Oak Blvd Ste 1000 Houston TX 77056*

WEEKLEY, FREDERICK CLAY, JR., lawyer; b. San Antonio, Aug. 29, 1939; s. F. Clay and Topsy (Stevens) W.; m. Lynda Freeman; children: Amber Lee, Caroline Lee. BBA, Baylor U., 1962, JD, 1963; LLM, NYU, 1969. Bar: Tex. 1963. Ptnr. Bracewell & Patterson, Houston, 1974-90; trust counsel Bank One, Tex., N.A., 1990—; mem. coun. real property, probate and trust law sect., State Bar of Tex., 1987-90; mem. trust divsn. Tex. Bankers Assn., 1992-95, chmn. legis. com., 1992-95. Editor: Texas Wills System, 1984. Mem. Commn. Probate Law Examiners, Tex. Bd. Legal Specialization, 1978-82. Fellow Am. Coll. Trust and Estate Counsel. Home: 1821 Mossy Oak St Arlington TX 76012-5619 Office: Bank One Texas NA Legal Dept 1717 Main St Fl 9 Dallas TX 75201-4605

WEEKLY, JOHN WILLIAM, insurance company executive; b. Sioux City, Iowa, June 21, 1931; s. John E. Weekly and Alyce Beatrice (Preble) Nichols; m. Bette Lou Thomas, Dec. 31, 1949; children: John William Jr., Thomas Patrick, Michael Craig, James Mathew, Daniel Kevin. Grad. high sch., Omaha. V.p. First Data Resources, Inc., Omaha, 1969-74; v.p. Mut. of Omaha/United of Omaha Ins. Co., Omaha, 1974-81, sr. exec. v.p., 1981-87, pres., COO, 1987-95, vice chmn., pres., COO, 1995—; vice chmn., pres., CEO Mut. of Omaha/United of Omaha Ins. Co., 1996—; chmn. bd. Mut. of Omaha Investor Svcs., Inc., Tele-Trip Co., Inc., United World Life Ins. Co.; vice chmn. bd. Companion Life Ins. Co.; bd. dirs. Midwest Express Airlines, Inc., Harbor Holdings, Inc., Kirkpatrick, Pettis, Omaha Property and Casualty Co., Mut. Asset Mgmt. Co., Omaha Airport Authority. Bd. dirs. Bellevue (Nebr.) U., 1986—. Mem. Am. Coun. Life Ins. (bd. dirs. 1995—), Greater Omaha C. of C. (bd. dirs. 1991-96). Avocations: hunting, fishing, golf. Office: Mut Omaha Ins Co Mutual Omaha Plz Omaha NE 68175

WEEKS, ALBERT LOREN, author, educator, journalist; b. Highland Park, Mich., Mar. 28, 1923; s. Albert Loren and Vera Grace (Jarvis) W. Student, U. Mich., 1942-43; MA, U. Chgo., 1949; PhD, Columbia U., 1965; cert., Russian Inst., 1960. Reporter Chgo. City News Bur., 1946; polit. analyst U.S. Dept. State, 1950-53, Free Europe Com., Inc., 1953-56; editorial asst. Newsweek mag., 1957-58; Russian tech. glossary compiler McGraw-Hill Book Co., 1960-61; prof. continuing edn. NYU, 1959-89; lectr. U.S. diplomatic history and soviet govt. Columbia U., 1951-52; mem. adv. coun. Nat. Strategy Info. Ctr., 1979-89; instr. Ringling Sch. Art and Design, 1991—; pub. spkr. S.W. Fla. Host: A Week's View of Red Press, Sta. WNBC, 1965-68; series Myths That Rule America, NBC-TV, 1979-82; author: Reading American History, 1963, The First Bolshevik: A Political Biography of Peter Tkachev, 1968, The Other Side of Coexistence: An Analysis of Russian Foreign Policy, 1970, Richard Hofstadter's The American Political Tradition and the Age of Reform, 1973, Andrei Sakharov and the Soviet Dissidents, 1975, The Troubled Detente, 1976, Solzhenitsyn's One Day in the Life of Ivan Denisovich, 1976, Myths That Rule America, 1980, War and Peace: Soviet Russia Speaks, 1983; editor/compiler Brassey's Soviet and Communist Quotations, 1987, The Soviet Nomenklatura, 1987-1991; internat. affairs editor Def. Sci. mag., 1982-85; columnist Def. Report, 1982-90; nat. sec., editor N.Y.C. Tribune, 1982-90; contbr. articles N.Y. Times, New Republic, New Leader, Annals, Russian, Slavic revs., Christian Sci. Monitor, Problems of Communism, Survey, Mil. Intelligence, Strategic Rev., World War II mag., Air Univ. Rev., L.A. Times, Washington Times, Orbis, Global Affairs, Panorama, Sarasota Herald-Tribune, Bradenton Herald, Defense and Diplomacy, Am. Intelligence Jour., USA Today, Rossiiskiye Vesti. Home: 4884 Kestral Park Cir Sarasota FL 34231-3369

WEEKS, ARTHUR ANDREW, lawyer, law educator; b. Hanceville, Ala., Dec. 2, 1914; s. A.A. and Anna S. (Seibert) W.; m. Carol P. Weeks; children: John David, Carol Christine, Nancy Anna. A.B., Samford U., 1936; LL.B., U. Ala., 1939, J.D., 1939; LL.M., Duke U., 1950; LL.D. (hon.), Widener U., 1980. Bar: Ala. 1939, Tenn. 1948. Sole practice Birmingham, Ala., 1939-41, 1946-47, 1954-61; dean, prof. law Cumberland U. Sch. Law, 1947-54; dean, prof. Samford U., 1961-72, prof. law, 1972-74; prof. law Cumberland Sch. Law, Samford U., 1984—; prof. law Del. Sch. Law of Widener U., Wilmington, 1974-82, dean, 1974-80, interim dean, 1982-83, dean emeritus, prof., 1983—. Served to capt. AUS, 1941-46. Mem. ABA, Tenn. Bar Assn., Ala. Bar Assn., Birmingham Bar Assn., Del. Bar Assn. (assoc.), Phi Alpha Delta, Phi Kappa Phi, Delta Theta Phi. Home: 1105 Water Edge Ct Birmingham AL 35244-1437

WEEKS, DAVID FRANK, foundation administrator; b. Salt Lake City, Sept. 9, 1926; s. Frank Harold and Myrtle June (Larsen) W.; m. Betty Alice Tellin, Aug. 14, 1949; children: David Rice, Clayton Frank. Student, So. Meth. U., 1945, U. Tex., 1946; B.S. (Union Pacific Carl Raymond Gray scholar), U. Idaho, 1949; HHD (hon.), U. Louisville, 1993. Pres. Assoc. Students U. Idaho, 1948-49; announcer Sta. KBIO, Burley, Idaho, 1949; Idaho rep. Nat. Found. for Infantile Paralysis, Boise, 1949-53; asst. to nat. dir. fund raising Nat. Found. for Infantile Paralysis, N.Y.C., 1953-57; asst. nat. dir. March of Dimes, N.Y.C., 1957-59; account exec. Kersting, Brown & Co., N.Y.C., 1959-61; exec. dir. Rsch. to Prevent Blindness, Inc., N.Y.C., 1961-70, exec. v.p., 1970-83, pres., 1983—; pres., trustee RPB Endowment Fund Inc., N.Y.C., 1988—; mem. borough coun. Borough of Ho-Ho-Kus, N.J., 1966-68; mayor Borough of Ho-Ho-Kus, 1968-75; consumer rep. subcom. ophthalmic prostheses HEW, 1976-79; cons. Bur. Med. Devices, FDA, 1977-80; mem. nat. adv. eye coun. NIH, HHS, 1985-90; trustee Okla. Eye Found., 1988-92. Mem. Ho-Ho-Kus Planning Bd., 1962-65, chmn., 1965; mem. Zoning Bd., 1975-85, Bergen County (N.J.) Ethics Bd., 1977-82; founder, pres. Ho-Ho-Kus Republican Club, 1983-86. Served with USN, 1944-46. Recipient Bronze Palm Eagle Scout award Boy Scouts Am., 1941, Disting. Pub. Svc. award Am. Acad. Ophthalmology and Otolaryngology, 1976, cert. of recognition Johns Hopkins U. Schs. Medicine, Hygiene and Pub. Health, 1984, Nat. Vision Rsch. Leadership award Assn. U. Profs. Ophthalmology, 1989, Disting. Svc. award Johns Hopkins Med. Instns.-Wilmer Ophthal. Inst., 1989, Disting. Svc. award Am. Acad. Ophthalmology, 1995; named Ky. col., 1969, U. of Idaho Alumni Hall of Fame award, 1992. Mem. Assn. Rsch. in Vision and Ophthalmology (hon.), Pan Am. Ophthalmol. Assn. (assoc.), Am. Soc. Assn. Execs., Internat. Assn. Eye Rsch., Bergen County Mayors Assn. (pres. 1975-77), Am. Tentative Soc. (treas. and trustee 1974-94, v.p. 1982-94), Assn. U. Profs. Ophthalmology (hon.), Met. Club. Home: 4058 NW Northcliff Bend OR 97701-8248 Office: Rsch Prevent Blindness 645 Madison Ave New York NY 10022-1010

WEEKS, GERALD, psychology educator; b. Morehead City, N.C., Nov. 20, 1948; s. Marion G. and Ada (Willis) W.; m. Kathleen Glass, Sept. 2, 1972. BA in Philosophy and Psychology, East Carolina U., 1971, MA in Gen. Psychology, 1973; PhD in Clin. Psychology, Ga. State U., 1979. Diplomate Am. Bd. Profl. Psychology (pres. 1987-88, bd. dirs. 1982-87), Am. Bd. Family Psychology, Am. Bd. Sexology; cert. marital and family therapist; lic. practicing psychologist, N.C., Pa.; registered Health Care Providers in Psychology. Intern in family therapy Harlem Valley Psychiatric Ctr., Wingdale, N.Y., 1978-79; assoc. prof. psychology U. N.C., Wilmington, 1979-85; dir. tng. Penn Coun. for Relationships, 1985—; clin. asst. prof. psychology Sch. Medicine U. Pa., Phila., 1985-87, clin. assoc. prof., 1988—; pvt. practice Carolina Ob-gyn Ctr., Wilmington, 1980-85. Author: Promoting Change Through Paradoxical Therapy, 1985, Treating Couples: The Intersystem Model of the Marriage Council of Philadelphia, 1989, Promoting Change through Paradoxical Therapy, 1991, (with L. L'Abate) Paradoxical Psychotherapy: Theory and Practice with Individuals, Couples, and Families, 1982, (with R. Sauber, L. L'Abate) Family Therapy: Basic Concepts and Terms, 1985, (with L. Hof) Integrating Sex and Marital Therapy: A Clinicians Guide, 1987, (with S. Treat) Couples in Treatment, 1992, Integrative Solutions: Treating Common Problems in Coupld Therapy, 1995; mem. editl. bd. Am. Jour. Family Therapy, Am. Jour. Family Psychology; contbr. articles to profl. jours. Fellow Am. Assn. Marital and Family Therapy (clin. mem., nat. adv. bd., approved supr.); mem. APA, Acad. Family Psychology, Interpersonal and Social Skills Assn. (founding mem.), Acad. Psychologists in Marital, Sex, and Family Therapy. Home: 210 Church St # D Philadelphia PA 19106-4519 Office: Penn Coun for Relationships 4025 Chestnut St Fl 2 Philadelphia PA 19104-3098

WEEKS, JEROME CHRISTOPHER, writer, drama critic; b. Detroit, Dec. 10, 1953; s. William Lawrence and Frances (Podgurski) W.; m. Sara Rankin; 1 child, Suzanna Beckett. Bachelor, U. Detroit, 1975; Master, U. Conn., 1977; postgrad., U. Tex., 1977-80. Rsch. asst. Detroit Free Press, 1973-75; columnist, editor Third Coast Mag., Austin, Tex., 1982-84; entertainment writer Houston Post, 1984-86; drama critic, book columnist Dallas Morning News, 1986—. Recipient Katy award Dallas Press Club, 1993. Mem. Am. Theatre Critics Assn., Nat. Book Critics Cir. Office: Dallas Morning News 508 Young St Dallas TX 75202-4808

WEEKS, JOHN ROBERT, geographer, sociology educator; b. Sacramento, June 1, 1944; s. Robert Louis and Thelma Hope (Evans) W.; m. Deanna Jean Hosea, May 16, 1965; children: John Robert, Gregory, Jennifer. AB, U. Calif., Berkeley, 1966, MA, 1969, PhD, 1972. Asst. prof. sociology Mich. State U., East Lansing, 1971-74; asst. prof. sociology San Diego State U., 1974-78, assoc. prof., 1978-81, prof., 1981-92; prof. geography, 1992—; chmn. dept. San Diego State U., 1978-85; adminstrv. dir. Internat. Population Ctr., 1985—; vis. research demographer U. Calif.-Berkeley, 1972; cons. Allied Home Health Assn., 1978-80, Area Agy. on Aging, San Diego, 1979-81, Los Angeles Regional Family Planning Council, 1986—, East County Econ. Devel. Coun., 1986—. Author: Teenage Marriages, 1976, Population, 6th edit., 1996, Aging, 1984, Demography of Islamic Nations, 1988, High Fertility Among Indochinese Refuges, 1989, Demographic Dynamics of the U.S.-Mexico Border, 1992. Grantee USPHS, 1983-84, 87-88, 88-89, 90—, U.S. Adminstrn. on Aging, 1979-80, U.S. Bur. of Census, 1988-89; trainee USPHS, 1967-71. Mem. Population Assn. Am., Am. Sociol. Assn., Internat. Union for Sci. Study Population, Am. Assn. Geographers. Democrat. Office: San Diego State U Dept Geography San Diego CA 92182

WEEKS, MARIE COOK, health and physical education educator; b. High Point, N.C., Jan. 21, 1949; d. Paul Hue Cook and Beulah Edna (Smith) Townsend; m. Lewis Tirey Weeks, June 5, 1970; children: Gina, Corby. BS in Edn., Western Carolina U., 1971. Tchr. grades 6,7,8, math. science, health, physical edn. Ramseur (N.C.) Elem. Sch., 1971-91; tchr. grades 6,7,8, health and physical edn. Archdale-Trinity Middle Sch., Trinity, N.C., 1991—; coach girls softball and volleyball Randolph County Schs., Asheboro, N.C., 1971—; mentor tchr. Randolph County Schs., Asheboro, 1989—; student tchr. supr. Archdale Trinity Middle Sch. 1993—, head of health and phys. edn. dept., 1993—. Coach girls' softball Hillsville (N.C.) Civitan's Youth Softball League, 1984—. Named Ramseur Sch. Tchr. of Yr., Ramseur Faculty, 1983, 89, Outstanding Young Educator Asheboro/Randolph County, Asheboro Jaycees, 1989. Mem. NEA, N.C. AAHPERD, Nat. Fedn. Coaches, N.C. Assn. Educators. Baptist. Avocations: arts and crafts, softball, family. Home: 3725 Lynn Oaks Dr Trinity NC 27370-9445 Office: Archdale-Trinity Mid Sch 5105 Archdale Rd Trinity NC 27370-9457

WEEKS, MARTA JOAN, priest; b. Buenos Aires, May 24, 1930; came to U.S., 1932; d. Frederick Albert and Anne (Newman) Sutton; m. Lewis Austin Weeks, Aug. 17, 1951; children: Kermit Austin, Leslie Anne. BA in Polit. Sci., Stanford U., 1951; MDiv, Episcopal Theol. Sem. S.W., 1991. Ordained priest Episcopal Ch., 1992. Legal libr., sec. Mene Grande Oil Co., Caracas, Venezuela, 1948; English tchr. Centro-Venezolano Americano, Caracas, 1948; sec. Household Fin. Corp., Salt Lake City, 1951; legal sec. McKelvey & McKelvey Attys., Durango, Colo., 1952; sec., dir. Weeks Air Mus., Miami, Fla., 1985—; chaplain Jackson Meml. Hosp., 1992-93; priest-at-large Episcopal Diocese of S.E. Fla., until 1997; interim asst. St. James Episcopal Ch., Salt Lake City, 1994-95. Trustee Beloit (Wis.) Coll., 1980-82, U. Miami, 1983-88, 95—, Bishop Gray Inns, Lake Worth and Davenport, Fla., 1992—. Mem. Am. Soc. Order St. John of Jerusalem. Address: 7350 SW 162nd St Miami FL 33157-3820

WEEKS, RICHARD RALPH, marketing educator; b. Champaign, Ill., Sept. 18, 1932; s. Frank Cook and B. Caroline (Pool) W.; m. Sue Ann Grunwald, Aug. 29, 1953; children: Kimberly Sue, Bret William. B.S., U. Ill., 1955; M.B.A., Washington U., St. Louis, 1960, D.B.A., 1966. Exec. sec., editor bull. Am. Assembly Collegiate Schs. Bus., St. Louis, 1960-64; exec. sec. Beta Gamma Sigma; also editor Beta Gamma Sigma Exchange, 1961-64; 1st ann. A.A.C.B.S. doctoral fellow in bus. adminstrn., 1964-65; dir. MBA program, asst. prof. mktg. Coll. Bus., Okla. State U., 1965-66, asst. dean, dir. MBA program, asso. prof. mktg., 1966-67; dean, prof. mktg. Walter E. Heller Coll. Bus. Adminstrn., Roosevelt U., 1967-70; dean Coll. Bus. Adminstrn. U. R.I., 1970-85, acting v.p. bus. and fin., 1976-77, provost for pub. policy, pub. service and mgmt., 1979-85, prof. mktg., 1970-92, prof. emeritus, dean emeritus, 1992—; dir. Potter Hazlehurst Inc., Providence Gas Co., Providence Energy Co., Newport Am. Corp., Daly & Walcott, Inc. Editor: Faculty Personnel, 9th edit, 1965; contbg. editor Ency. Bus. Information Sources, 1964; editorial adv. bd. Bus. and Soc. 1968-70. Bd. dirs. Chgo. Econ. Devel. Corp., 1968-70, v.p., 1969-70; bd. dirs. Chgo. Fin. Devel. Corp., 1970, Progress Assn. for Econ. Devel., 1972-73; bd. dirs. Coun. on Postsecondary Accreditation, 1974-83, mem. exec. com., 1977-82, chmn., 1979-81; bd. dirs. Friends of Jamestown Philomenian Library, 1972-77, pres., 1974-76; mem. adv. bd. Intercollegiate Case Clearinghouse, 1976-79; pres. Friends of URI Library, 1986-88. Served to capt. USAF, 1955-63. Fulbright grantee, 1986. Mem. Am. Mktg. Assn. (dir. acad. placement 1966, 68), Ea. Fin. Assn. (dir. 1974-77), Council Profl. Edn. Bus. (sec.-treas. 1960-64, exec. com. 1961-64), Nat. Assn. State Univs. and Land-Grant Colls., Commn. on Edn. for Bus. Professions (sec. 1973-76, chmn. 1976-78), New Eng. Assn. Schs. and Colls.

(sec.-treas. 1983-85), Am. Assn. Collegiate Schs. Bus. (various com., bd. dirs. 1976-85, pres. 1983-84), Greater Providence C. of C. (dir. 1979-82), Delta Sigma Pi, Alpha Kappa Lambda, Beta Gamma Sigma (various coms., pres. 1978-80), Mu Kappa Tau, Pi Sigma Epsilon, Phi Kappa Phi. Home: 2048 Imperial Cir Naples FL 34110-1089

WEEKS, ROBERT LEE, electronic engineer, program manager; b. Woonsocket, R.I., Mar. 8, 1957; s. Joseph Bernard and Claire Lorraine (Jolicoeur) W.; m. Christine Ann Bentley; children: Barbara Ann, Christopher Lee. BSEE, U. Ariz., 1985, postgrad., 1987; MBA, U. Phoenix, 1996. Laborer ASARCO Mine Inc., Sahuarita, Ariz., 1979-82; test engr. EMI and TEMPEST br. U.S. Army Electronic Proving Ground, Ft. Huachuca, Ariz., 1985-88, chief EMI and TEMPEST br., 1988-95; chief electromagnetics br. U.S. Army Electronic Proving Ground, Ft. Huachuca, 1995-96, mgr. R&D program, 1996—; mem. MIL-STD-461 Joint Working Group, 1989-94; mem. DOD and industry E3 standards com. Dept. Def., 1994—. Bd. dirs. Bristol Park Neighborhood Assn., Tucson, 1994—; vol. YMCA, 1994—. With USMC, 1975-79. Mem. IEEE (named Engr. of Yr. local chpt. 1994), Electromagnetic Compatibility Soc. of IEEE, Nat. Assn. Radio and Telecomms. Engrs. (cert. electromagnetic compatibility engr.). Democrat. Roman Catholic. Avocations: basketball, bowling, hiking. Office: US Army Electronic Proving Ground STEWS-EPG-TE Fort Huachuca AZ 85613

WEEKS, ROBERT ANDREW, materials science researcher, educator; b. Birmingham, Ala., Aug. 23, 1924; s. William Andrew and Annie Bell (Hammond) W.; m. Jane Sutherland, Mar. 20, 1948; children: Kevin Dale, Robin Dee, Loren Hammond, Kerry Andrew. BS, Birmingham-So. Coll., 1947; MS, U. Tenn., 1951; PhD, Brown U., 1966. Sr. physicist Union Carbide Corp., Oak Ridge, Tenn., 1951-84; rsch. prof. material sci. Vanderbilt U., 1984—; disting. vis. prof. Am. U. in Cairo, 1970-71; invited prof. Ecole Poly. Fed. de Lausanne, Switzerland, 1981; vis. prof. Cath. U., Leuven, Belgium, 1983; cons. numerous pvt. corps. and fed. agys.; prin. investigator lunar materials, 1968-74; co-prin. investigator expdn. Western desert of Egypt to desert glass site, 1981. Co-editor: Effects of Modes of Formation on Structure of Glass, 1985, 88, Editing the Refereed Scientific Journal, 1994; assoc. editor Jour. Geophys. Rsch., 1968-74; editor Jour. Noncrystalline Solids, 1988—; contbr. numerous articles to profl. jours. Served with U.S. Army, 1943-46. Union Carbide fellow, 1964; Fulbright lectr., 1980; research fellow Reading U., 1971. Fellow Am. Ceramic Soc. (R. A. Weeks Symposium on Sci. and Tech. Si02 and Related Materials named in his honor, Honolulu 1993); mem. AAAS, Am. Phys. Soc., Materials Rsch. Soc. Avocation: photography. Home: 331 Southshore Dr Greenback TN 37742-2301 Office: Vanderbilt U PO Box 1678 Nashville TN 37240

WEEKS, ROLAND, JR., newspaper publisher; b. Knoxville, Tenn., July 8, 1936. B.S., Clemson (S.C.) U., 1958. Sales engr. Metal Products, Inc., Greenville, S.C., 1961-63; mgmt. trainee, then bus. mgr. Columbia Newspapers, Inc.; pubs. The State and Columbia (S.C.) Record newspapers, 1963-68; pres., pub. Gulf Pub. Co., Inc.; pubs. Biloxi-Gulfport (Miss.) Sun Herald, 1968—; dir. Hancock Bank, Gulfport. Pres. Pine Burr area council Boy Scouts Am., 1980; chmn. Miss. Bd. Corrections, 1982-88. Served to 1st lt. USAF, 1958-61. Mem. Am. Newspaper Assn., So. Newspaper Pubs. Assn. (pres. 1981), Young Pres. Orgn., Gulf Coast C. of C. (pres. 1989). Presbyterian. Office: Gulf Pub Co Inc 205 DeBuys Rd PO Box 4567 Biloxi MS 39535-4567*

WEEKS, ROSS LEONARD, JR., museum executive; b. Jamestown, N.Y., Sept. 11, 1936; s. Ross Leonard and Cecile Forbes (Carrie) W.; AB, Colgate U., 1958; MS, George Washington U., 1971, cert. Fed. Exec. Inst., 1988; m. Patricia Ann Earley, June 10, 1951; children: Susan Woodall, Ross Leonard, III, William Andrew, David James. Reporter, Jamestown Post-Jour., 1958-60, Richmond (Va.) News Leader, 1960-65; dir. public info. Coll. William and Mary, Williamsburg, Va., 1965-71, asst. to exec. v.p. 1971-74, asst. to pres., dir. univ. communications, 1974-81; exec. dir. Jamestown (Va.)-Yorktown Found., 1981-91; exec. dir. Historic Crab Orchard Mus., Inc., Tazewell, Va., 1992—; grant reviewer U.S. Inst. Mus. Svcs., Va. Arts Commn. Editor William & Mary Alumni Gazette, 1966-81. Chmn. Williamsburg-James City Bicentennial, 1975-77; treas. Coalfield Regional Tourism Devel. Authority S.W. Va., 1993—; Va. Southwest Blue Ridge Highlands, Inc., 1993—, v.p., 1996-97, pres., 1997—; sec., treas. Frontier Culture Found., 1982-86; exec. dir. Va. Independence Bicentennial Commn., 1981-83; trustee council, Thirteen Original States, 1982-87; chair Tazewell County Tourism Devel. Commn., 1993—; mem. exhibition mine com. Town of Pocahontas, Gov.'s Va. History Initiative, 1995-97; lay reader Cluster Episc. Parishes, Tazewell. Mem. Am. Assn. Mus. (mus. assessment cons. 1988—), Am. Assn. State and Local History, St. Andrews Soc., Masons, Rotary (Paul Harris fellow 1987), Clan Ross Assn. U.S. Sigma Delta Chi, Kappa Delta Rho (Ordo Honora 1986). Avocations: travel, landscaping, antiquities, historical research. Home: Hemlock Ridge PO Box 82 Tazewell VA 24651-0082 Office: Hist Crab Orchard Mus Rt 1 Box 194 Tazewell VA 24651

WEEKS, SANDRA KENNEY, healthcare facilitator; b. Akron, Ohio; d. Robert and Virginia Kenney; m. Theron Weeks, Jr., 1963; children: Rebecca, Theron R. BSN, Stockton State Coll., 1990; MSN, The Coll. of N.J., 1996. RN, N.J., cert. rehab. registered nurse Assn. Rehab. Nurses. Staff nurse Akron (Ohio) Childrens Hosp., William Beaumont Hosp., Royal Oak, Mich.; elected pub. official Twp. of Cranford (N.J.); rehab. nurse Kessler Inst. Rehab., West Orange, N.J.; supr. HIP/HMO Ambulatory Care Ctr., Medford, N.J.; rehab. nurse mgr. Lourdes Rehab. Ctr., Camden, N.J.; rschr. in nursing. Contbr. articles to profl. jours. Bd. dirs. United Way; trustee pub. libr.; mem. Twp. Com. Bd. Health. Named Citizen of the Yr. Cranford C. of C., 1974; recipient B'nai B'rith award for Comm. Svc., 1980. Mem. Am. Nurses Assn., N.J. Nurses Assn., Assn. Rehab. Nurses, Sigma Theta Tau. Avocations: golf, bicycling. Home: 3 Dewberry Ct Medford NJ 08055-9159 Office: Lourdes Regional Rehab Ctr 1600 Haddon Ave Camden NJ 08103-3101

WEEKS, STEVEN WILEY, lawyer; b. Topeka, Mar. 7, 1950; s. Glen Wiley and Grace Aileen (West) W.; m. Lee Nordgren, Aug. 1, 1974 (div. 1985); 1 child, Kirstin Nordgren. BS summa cum laude, Washburn U., 1972; JD cum laude, Harvard U., 1977. Bar: Ohio. Project leader Nat. Sanitation Found., Ann Arbor, Mich., 1972; engr. Kans. Dept. Health and Environ., Topeka, 1972-74; ptnr. Taft, Stettinius & Hollister, Cin., 1977—; dir. The Myers Y. Cooper Co., Cin.; adj. faculty Chase Coll. Law, 1987-88. Mem. adv. com. prosecuting atty., Hamilton County, Cin., 1992; mem. Hamilton County Rep. Ctrl. Com., 1994—. Mem. Ohio State Bar Assn., Cin. Bar Assn. Republican. Methodist. Avocations: computers, golf. Home: 3641 Michigan Ave Cincinnati OH 45208-1411 Office: 425 Walnut St Cincinnati OH 45202

WEEKS, WILFORD FRANK, retired geophysics educator, glaciologist; b. Champaign, Ill., Jan. 8, 1929; married; 2 children. BS, U. Ill., 1951, MS, 1953; PhD in Geology, U. Chgo., 1956. Geologist mineral deposits br. U.S. Geol. Survey, 1952-55; glaciologist USAF Cambridge Research Ctr., 1955-57; asst. prof. Washington U., St. Louis, 1957-62; adj. prof. earth scis. Dartmouth Coll., Hanover, N.H., 1962-85; glaciologist Cold Regions Rsch. and Engring. Lab., Hanover, 1962-89; chief scientist Alaska Synthetic Aperture Radar Facility, Fairbanks, 1986-93; prof. geophysics Geophys. Inst. U. Alaska, Fairbanks, 1986-96; cons. in field, 1996—; vis. prof. Inst. Low Temperature Sci. Hokkaido U., Sapporo, Japan, 1973; chair Arctic marine sci. USN Postgrad. Sch., Monterey, Calif., 1978-79; mem. earth sys. sci. com. NASA, Washington, 1984-87; advisor U.S. Arctic Rsch. Commn., divsn. polar programs NSF, Washington, 1987-88; chmn. NAS Com. on Cooperation with Russia in Ice Mechanics, 1991-92; mem. environ. task force MEDEA Cons. Group, 1992—. Capt. USAF, 1955-57. Recipient Emil Usibelli Prize for Rsch., 1996. Fellow Arctic Inst. N.Am., Am. Geophys. Union; mem. NAE, Internat. Glaciological Soc. (v.p. 1969-72, pres. 1973-75, Seligman Crystal award 1989). Avocations: skiing, diving, contrabassist. Home and Office: 6533 SW 34th Ave Portland OR 97201-1077

WEEMS, JOHN EDWARD, writer; b. Grand Prairie, Tex., Nov. 2, 1924; s. J. Eddie and Anna Lee (Scott) W.; m. Jane Ellen Homeyer, Sept. 11, 1946; children: Donald (dec.), Carol, Mary, Barbara, Janet. BJ, U. Tex., 1948, M.Journalism, 1949; MA in Libr. Sci., Fla. State U., 1954. Tel. editor Temple (Tex.) Daily Telegram, 1950; instr. Calif. State Poly. Coll., San Dimas, 1950-51; night news editor San Angelo (Tex.) Standard-Times, 1951; copy editor Dallas Morning News, 1952-53; asst. prof., head cataloger main library Baylor U., 1954-57; asst. prof. U. Ala., also asst. mgr. Ala. Press Assn., 1957-58; asst. to dir. U. Tex. Press, 1958-68; prof. English, Baylor U., 1968-71, lectr. creative writing, fall 1979; reference librarian McLennan Community Coll., Waco, Tex., 1969-70; freelance writer, 1971—. With USNR, 1943-46, 51-52; lt. Res. (ret.). Am. Philos. Soc. grantee, 1964. Fellow Tex. State Hist. Assn., Tex. Inst. Letters; mem. PEN, Nat. Book Critics Circle, Authors Guild, Western Writers Am., Sigma Delta Chi, Beta Phi Mu. Author: A Weekend in September, 1957; The Fate of the Maine, 1958; Race for the Pole, 1960; Peary: The Explorer and the Man, 1967; Men Without Countries, 1969; Dream of Empire (Amon G. Carter award), 1971; To Conquer a Peace: The War Between the United States and Mexico (Richard Fleming award), 1974; Death Song, 1976; The Tornado, 1977; (with John Biggers and Carroll Simms) Black Art in Houston, 1978; "If You Don't Like the Weather," 1986; editor: A Texas Christmas: A Miscellany of Art, Poetry, Fiction, Vol. I, 1983, Vol. II, 1986; (San Antonio Conservation Soc. Spl. award), The Story of Texas, 1986, Austin (Texas): 1839-1989, 1989 (Tex. Inst. Letters Barbara McCombs Lon Tinkle award lifetime Writing achievement 1989). Address: 2012 Collins St Waco TX 76710-2626

WEEMS, ROBERT CICERO, economist, educator; b. Meridian, Miss., July 22, 1910; s. Robert Cicero and Susie (Vaughan) W.; m. Frances Dodds, Aug. 13, 1941; 1 dau., Susan. B.S. with honors, Miss. State U., 1931; M.B.A., Northwestern U., 1934; Ph.D. in Econs., Columbia U., 1951. Part-time staff Bank of Shubuta, Miss., 1924-33; teaching fellow econs. La. State U., 1933-34; instr. bus. adminstrn. Miss. State Coll., 1934-35, asst. prof. banking and finance, 1935-38, assoc. prof., 1938-40, acting dean Sch. Bus. and Industry, 1940-42; dean Miss. State Coll. Sch. Bus. and Industry, 1942-56; dir. Bus. Research Sta. of Coll. Miss. State Coll., 1940-56, asst. dir. engring. sci. and mgmt. War Tng. Program, 1941-43; dean Coll. Bus. Adminstrn., dir. Bur. Research U. Nev., 1956-77; adviser-cons. U. Nev. Endowment Fund, 1975—; chmn. Regional (Nev.) Export Expansion Council, 1960-74; mem. Nat. Export Expansion Council, U.S. Dept. Commerce, 1960-74; chmn. adv. council Miss. Employment Security Commn., 1952-56; mem. Western Indsl. Nev., Nev. Public Employees Retirement Bd., 1963-78, vice chmn., 1975-78; mem. employment security council Nev. Employment Security Dept.; mem. nat. adv. council SBA, 1975-77. Trustee U.S. Travel Data Center, 1973-76, Calif.-Nev. Meth. Found., 1980—; trustee Am. Inst. Econ. Research, 1964—, chmn. bd., 1972-76. Served to lt. comdr. USN, 1943-46. Recipient cert. of appreciation U.S. Dept. Commerce, 1968, 1973. Mem. Am. Hotel and Motel Assn. (trustee ednl. inst.), Travel Research Assn. (treas.), Western Econ. Assn., Nev. World Trade and Internat. Tourism Assn. (trustee 1974—, pres. 1976-77), Blue Key, Omicron Delta Kappa (hon.), Chi Lambda Rho, Delta Sigma Pi, Beta Gamma Sigma (nat. exec. com. 1970-74), Phi Kappa Phi, Pi Kappa Alpha, Kappa Kappa Psi. Methodist. Club: Rotary (Reno). Home: 1135 Williams Ave Reno NV 89503-2648

WEERTMAN, JOHANNES, materials science educator; b. Fairfield, Ala., May 11, 1925; s. Roelof and Christina (van Vlaardingen) W.; m. Julia Ann Randall, Feb. 10, 1950; children: Julia Ann, Bruce Randall. Student, Pa. State Coll., 1943-44; BS, Carnegie Inst. Tech. (now Carnegie Mellon U.), 1948, DSc, 1951; postgrad., Ecole Normale Superieure, Paris, 1951-52. Solid State physicist U.S. Naval Rsch. Lab., Washington, 1952-58, cons., 1960-67; sci. liaison officer U.S. Office Naval Rsch., Am. Embassy, London, 1958-59; faculty Northwestern U., Evanston, Ill., 1959—, prof. materials sci. dept., 1961-68, chmn. dept., 1964-68, prof. geol. scis. dept., 1963—, Walter P. Murphy prof. materials sci., 1968—; vis. prof. geophysics Calif. Inst. Tech., 1964, Scott Polar Rsch. Inst., Cambridge (Eng.) U., 1970-71, Swiss Fed. Inst. Reactor Rsch., 1986; cons. Cold Regions Rsch. and Engring. Lab., U.S. Army, 1960-75, Oak Ridge (Tenn.) Nat. Lab., 1963-67, Los Alamos (N.Mex.) Sci. Lab., 1967—; co-editor materials sci. books MacMillan Co., 1962-76. Author: Dislocation Based Fracture Mechanics, 1996, (with Julia Weertman) Elementary Dislocation Theory, 1964, 2d edit., 1992; mem. editorial bd. Metal. Trans., 1967-75, Jour. Glaciology, 1972—; assoc. editor Jour. Geophys. Rsch., 1973-75; contbr. articles to profl. jours. With USMC, 1943-46. Honored with naming of Weertman Island in Antarctica.; Fulbright fellow, 1951-52; recipient Acta Metallurgica gold medal, 1980; Guggenheim fellow, 1970-71. Fellow Am. Soc. Metals, Am. Phys. Soc., Geol. Soc. Am., Am. Geophys. Union (Horton award 1972, AIME Mathewson Gold medal 1977); mem. AAAS, Nat. Acad. Engring., Am. Inst. Physics, Internat. Glaciol. Soc. (Seligman Crystal award 1983), Arctic Inst., Am. Quaternary Assn., Explorers Club, Fulbright Assn., Sigma Xi, Tau Beta Pi, Phi Kappa Phi, Alpha Sigma Mu, Pi Mu Epsilon. Home: 834 Lincoln St Evanston IL 60201-2405 Office: Northwestern U Materials Sci Dept Evanston IL 60208

WEERTMAN, JULIA RANDALL, materials science and engineering educator; b. Muskegon, Mich., Feb. 10, 1926. BS in Physics, Carnegie-Mellon U., 1946, MS in Physics, 1947, DSc in Physics, 1951. Physicist U.S. Naval Rsch. Lab., Washington, 1952-58; vis. asst. prof. dept. materials sci. and engring. Northwestern U., Evanston, Ill., 1972-73, assoc. prof., 1978-82, prof., 1982—, Walter P. Murphy prof., 1989, chmn. dept., 1987-92, asst. to dean grad. studies and rsch. Tech. Inst., 1973-76; mem. various NRC coms. and panels. Co-author: Elementary Dislocation Theory, 1964, 1992, also pub. in French, Japanese and Polish; contbr. numerous articles to profl. jours. Mem. Evanston Environ. Control Bd., 1972-79. Recipient Creativity award NSF, 1981, 86; Guggenheim Found. fellow, 1986-87. Fellow Am. Soc. Metals Internat., Minerals, Metals and Materials Soc. (leadership award 1997); mem. ASTM, NAE, Am. Acad. Arts and Scis., Am. Phys. Soc., Materials Rsch. Soc., Soc. Women Engrs. (disting. engring. educator award 1989, achievement award 1991). Home: 834 Lincoln St Evanston IL 60201-2405 Office: Northwestern U Dept Material Sci & Engring 2225 N Campus Dr Evanston IL 60208-3108

WEESE, BENJAMIN HORACE, architect; b. Evanston, Ill., June 4, 1929; s. Harry Ernest and Marjorie (Mohr) W.; m. Cynthia Rogers, July 5, 1963; children: Daniel Peter, Catharine Mohr. B.Arch., Harvard U., 1951, M.Arch., 1957; cert., Ecole des Beaux Arts, Fontainebleau, France, 1956. Assoc., Harry Weese & Assocs., Architects, Chgo., 1957-77; prin. Weese Langley Weese, Chgo., 1977—; co-founder, pres. Chgo. Arch. Found., Glessner House, Chgo., 1966—. Trustee Graham Found. for Advanced Studies in Fine Arts, 1988—, pres. 1995—. Fellow AIA; mem. Nat. Council Archtl. Registration Bds. Home: 2133 N Hudson Ave Chicago IL 60614-4522 Office: Weese Langley Weese Ltd 9 W Hubbard St Chicago IL 60610-4605

WEESE, BRUCE ERIC, pharmaceutical industry lobbyist, human services manager; b. Chewelah, Wash., Mar. 22, 1942; s. Harry M. and Roberta B. (Carman) W.; m. Elaine M. Smith, June 18, 1962 (div. July 1972); children: Sandra G., Michael D.; m. Vera B. Reed, Mar. 22, 1975; stepchildren: Kevin E. Bayron, Kelly M. Bayron. BA in Edn., Ea. Wash. State U., Cheney, 1964; MBA, Pepperdine U., 1981. Tchr. Grant Joint Union High Sch. Dist., Sacramento, 1964-70; pharm. sales McNeil Labs., San Jose, Calif., 1970-77, Adria Labs., San Francisco, 1977-83, Serono Labs., San Francisco, 1983-84; pharm. sales Boehringer Ingelheim, Santa Rosa, Calif., 1984-91, mgr. govt. affairs (lobbyist) for western states, 1991-97, area mgr. managed care, 1997—. Bd. dirs. Russian River Health Ctr., Guerneville, Calif., 1994-95. Mem. United Anglers, Sequoia Paddlers, Santa Rosa Sailing Club, Sierra Club. Democrat. Avocations: kayaking, sailing, fishing. Home: 20303 NE 226th Cir Battle Ground WA 98604-4943 Office: Boehringer Ingelheim PO Box 368 Ridgefield CT 06877-0368

WEESE, CYNTHIA ROGERS, architect, educator; b. Des Moines, June 23, 1940; d. Gilbert Taylor and Catharine (Wingard) Rogers; m. Benjamin H. Weese, July 5, 1963; children: Daniel Peter, Catharine Mohr. B.S.A.S., Washington U., St. Louis, 1962; B.Arch., Washington U., 1965. Registered architect, Ill. Pvt. practice architecture Chgo., 1965-72, 74-77; draftsperson, designer Harry Weese & Assocs., Chgo., 1972-74; prin. Weese Langley Weese Ltd., Chgo., 1977—; design critic Ball State U., Muncie, Ind., Miami U., Oxford, Ohio, 1979, U. Wis.-Milw., 1980, U. Ill.-Chgo., 1981, 85, Iowa State U., Ames, 1982, Washington U., St. Louis, 1984, U. Ill., Champaign, 1987-92, Kans. State U., 1992; dean sch. architecture Washington U., St. Louis, 1993—. Bd. regents Am. Architecture Found., 1990-93. Recipient Alpha Rho Chi award Washington U., 1965, Met. Chgo. YWCA Outstanding Achievement award, 1990. Mem. AIA (bd. dirs. Chgo. chpt. 1980-83, v.p. 1983-85, 1st v.p. 1986-87, pres. 1987-88, regional dir. 1990-92, Disting. Bldg. awards 1977, 81-83, 86, 91, 95, Interior Architecture award 1981, 90, 92, nat. v.p. 1993), AIA/ACSA Coun. on Archtl. Rsch. (chair 1991-92), AIA Found. (pres. Chgo. chpt. 1988-89), Soc. Archtl. Historians (bd. dirs. 1992-94), Chgo. Women in Architecture, Chgo. Network, Nat. Inst. Archtl. Edn. (bd. dirs. 1988-90), Chgo. Archtl. Club (pres. 1988-89), Washington U. Sch. Architecture Alumni (nat. coun. 1988-93), Lambda Alpha. Democrat. Clubs: Arts, Chgo. Archtl. Office: Washington U Sch Architecture Campus Box 1079 Saint Louis MO 63130

WEESE, JOHN AUGUSTUS, mechanical engineer, educator; b. Topeka, Kans., July 24, 1933; s. Ray Augustus and Margaret Maureen (Richmond) W.; m. Betty Kay Dietrich, June 5, 1955; children: Carol Ann, Katherine Lynn. BSME, Kans. State U., 1955; MS, Cornell U., 1958, PhD, 1959. Asst. prof. USAF Acad., Colo., 1960-62; assoc. prof. mech. engring. U. Denver, 1963-67, prof., 1967-74, chmn. mech. sci. and environ. engring., 1968-70, dean engring., 1970-74; dean engring. Old Dominion U., Norfolk, Va., 1974-83; dir. mech. engring. and applied mechanics NSF, Washington, 1983-85, dir. mechanics structures and materials engring., 1985-86; prof. mech. engring. Tex. A&M U., College Station, 1986—, head dept. engring. tech., 1986-97, coord. accreditation, 1997—; rsch. specialist The Boeing Co., Whichita, Kans., 1962-63, structural dynamics engr., 1959-60; rsch. engr. Martin-Marietta Corp., Denver, 1963; grad. tng. engr. Allis-Chalmer, Milw., 1955; mem. accreditation bd. for engring. and tech. Engring. Accreditation Commn., 1983-88. Co-author: Mechanics of Materials, 4th edition, 1985; contbr. articles to profl. jours. Fellow Am. Soc. for Engring. Edn. (chmn. engring. rsch. coun. 1988-90, exec. com. 1984-90, chmn. publs. com. 1983-86, projects bd. engring. rsch. coun. 1982-85, Outstanding Educator mechanics div. 1989), ASME (ad hoc visitor 1977-83, Ben C. Sparks medal 1994); mem. Va. Soc. Profl. Engrs. (Engr. of Yr. award 1978), Kiwanis. Republican. Congregationalist. Avocations: fishing, photography. Home: 2802 Barwick Cir Bryan TX 77802-2101 Office: Tex A&M U Dept Mech Engring College Station TX 77843-3123

WEG, JOHN GERARD, physician; b. N.Y.C., Feb. 16, 1934; s. Leonard and Pauline M. (Kanzleiter) W.; m. Mary Loretta Flynn, June 2, 1956; children: Diane Marie, Kathryn Mary, Carol Ann, Loretta Louise, Veronica Susanne, Michelle Celeste. BA cum laude, Coll. Holy Cross, Worcester, Mass., 1955; MD, N.Y. Med. Coll., 1959. Diplomate: Am. Bd. Internal Medicine. Commd. 2nd lt. USAF, 1958, advanced through grades to capt., 1967; intern Walter Reed Gen. Hosp., Washington, 1959-60; resident, then chief resident in internal medicine Wilford Hall USAF Hosp., Lackland AFB, Tex., 1960-64; chief pulmonary sect. Wilford Hall USAF Hosp., 1964-66, chief inhalation sect., 1964-66, chief pulmonary and infectious disease service, 1966-67; resigned, 1967; clin. dir. pulmonary disease div. Jefferson Davis Hosp., Houston, 1967-71; from asst. prof. to assoc. prof. medicine Baylor U. Coll. Medicine, Houston, 1967-71; assoc. prof. medicine U. Mich. Med. Sch. Univ. Hosp., Ann Arbor, 1971-74; prof. U. Mich. Med. Sch. Univ. Hosp., 1974—; physician-in-charge pulmonary div., 1971-81, physician-in-charge pulmonary and critical care med. div., 1981-85; cons. Ann Arbor VA, 1971—, Wayne County Gen. hosps., 1971-84; mem. adv. bd. Washtenaw County Health Dept., 1973—; mem. respiratory and nervous system panel, anesthesiology Sect. Nat. Ctr. Devices and Radiol. Health, FDA, 1983—, chmn., 1985-88. Contbr. med. jours., reviewer, mem. editorial bds. Decorated Air Force Commendation medal; travelling fellow Nat. Tb and Respiratory Disease Assn., 1971; recipient Aesculpaius award Tex. Med. Assn., 1971. Fellow Am. Coll. Chest Physicians (chmn. bd. govs. 1976-79, gov. Mich. 1975-79, chmn. membership com. 1976-79, prof.-in-residence 1972—, chmn. critical care coun. 1982-85), Am. Coll. Chest Physicians and Internat. Acad. Chest Physicians (exec. council 1976-82, pres. 1980-81), ACP (chmn. Mich. program com. 1974); mem. AAAS, Am. Fedn. Clin. Rsch., AMA, Am. Thoracic Soc. (sec.-treas. 1974-76), Am. Assn. Inhalation Therapy, Air Force Soc. Internists and Allied Specialists, Soc. Med. Consultants to Armed Forces, Internat. Union Against Tb, Mich. Thoracic Soc. (pres. 1976-78), Mich. Lung Assn. (dir., Bruce Douglas award 1981), Am. Lung Assn., Rsch. Club U. Mich., Assn. Advancement Med. Instrumentation, Central Soc. Clin. Rsch., Am. Bd. Internal Medicine (subsplty. com. on pulmonary disease 1980-86, critical care medicine test com. 1985-87, critical care medicine policy com. 1986-87), N.Y. Med. Coll. Alumni Assn. (medal of honor 1990), Alpha Omega Alpha. Home: 3060 Exmoor Rd Ann Arbor MI 48104-4132 Office: B I H 245 Box 0026 1500 E Medical Center Dr Ann Arbor MI 48109-0005

WEGENER, MARK DOUGLAS, lawyer; b. Cedar Rapids, Iowa, Nov. 1, 1948; s. Virgil Albert and Jean Frances (Wilke) W.; m. Donna Chait, May 28, 1972; children: Tara, David, Marisa. BA cum laude, Cen. Coll., Pella, Iowa, 1970; JD, Rutgers U., 1973. Bar: D.C. 1974, U.S. Dist. Ct. D.C. 1974, U.S. Ct. Appeals (D.C. cir.) 1974. Assoc. Howrey & Simon, Washington, 1973-79, ptnr., 1979—. Mem. ABA (anti-trust sect., litigation sect.), The Metropolitan Club, Stage Harbor Yacht Club. Office: Howrey & Simon 1299 Pennsylvania Ave NW Washington DC 20004-2400

WEGENER, PETER PAUL, engineering educator, author; b. Berlin, Aug. 29, 1917; came to U.S., 1946; naturalized, 1953.; m. Annette Schleiermacher, Aug. 14, 1961; children: Paul, Christopher, Philip. Dr rer. nat., U. Berlin, 1943; MA (priv.), Yale U., 1960; Dr. Ing. (E.h.) (hon.), U. Karlsruhe, Germany, 1979. Researcher supersonic wind tunnels Kochel, Germany, 1943-45; researcher gasdynamics, hypersonic wind tunnels U.S. Naval Ordnance Lab., 1946-53, Jet Propulsion Lab. Calif. Inst. Tech., 1953-60; prof. applied sci. Yale U., New Haven, 1960-72, Harold Hodgkinson prof. engring. and applied sci., 1972—, chmn. dept. engring, applied sci., 1966-71, prof. emeritus, 1987—; sr. Am. scientist Humboldt Found., 1979;. Researcher and contbr. articles on hypersonics, condensation metastable state, chem. kinetics, flow systems real gases, bubbles to profl. jours. Inst. Advanced Study Berlin fellow, 1986. Fellow Am. Phys. Soc., Conn. Acad. Sci. & Engring. (charter). Home: 29 Montgomery Pky Branford CT 06405-5128 Office: Yale U PO Box 208286 New Haven CT 06520-8286

WEGER, WILLIAM JOHN, public relations executive; b. Washington, Nov. 11, 1960; s. Adolph John and Janet Virginia (Warren) W. BS in Journalism, U. Md., 1985; MA in Pub. Comm., Am. U., 1995. Reporter Daily Banner, Cambridge, Md., 1984-85; writer, media rels. asst. ARC Nat. Hdqs., Washington, 1985-87; publs. editor, writer Aspen Pubs., Inc., Rockville, Md., 1987-89; dir. comm. Hardwood, Plywood and Veneer Assn., Reston, Va., 1989-92; dir. pub. affairs Am. Trucking Assns., Inc., Alexandria, Va., 1992-94; mgr. media rels. for Mass. Transit Adminstrn. Md. Dept. Transp., Balt., 1994—; pres. Blue Chip Comms., Silver Spring, Md., 1995—; stringer AP, Easton, Md., 1984, Times Jour. Newspapers, Springfield, Va., 1985-87. Fundraiser, vol. Muscular Dystrophy Assn., Fairfax, Va., 1985—. Recipient 1st place best newspaper award for ARC news Soc. Nat. Assn. Publs., 1986, dedicated svc. award MADD, 1994. Mem. Pub. Rels. Soc. Am., Am. Soc. Assn. Execs. Avocations: writing, running, history. Home: 3304 Pendleton Dr Silver Spring MD 20902-2427 Office: Blue Chip Comms PO Box 2278 Silver Spring MD 20915

WEGGE, LEON LOUIS FRANÇOIS, economics educator; b. Breendonk, Antwerp, Belgium, June 9, 1933; came to U.S., 1959; s. Petrus Maria and Alberta (De Maeyer) W.; m. Beate Maria Teipel, Nov. 22, 1962; children: Simone, Robert, Elizabeth. B in Thomistical Philosophy, Cath. U. Louvain, Belgium, 1957, Licentiate in Econ. Sci., 1958; PhD in Indsl. Econs., MIT, 1963. Assoc. lectr. U. New S. Wales, Kensington, Australia, 1963-66; prof. econs. U. Calif., Davis, 1966—; vis. prof. U. Bonn, Fed. Republic Germany, 1980-81. Assoc. editor Jour. Internat. Econs., 1971-84; contbr. articles to profl. jours. Rsch. fellow Ctr. for Ops. Rsch. and Econometrics, 1972-73, fellow The Netherlands Inst. for Advanced Study, 1987-88. Mem. Econometric Soc., Am. Statistical Assn. Roman Catholic. Home: 26320 County Rd # 98 Davis CA 95616 Office: U Calif Davis Dept Econs Davis CA 95616

WEGMAN, HAROLD HUGH, management consultant; b. Cin., June 29, 1916; s. Clarence H. and Lillian (de Tellem) W.; m. Ruth Ellen Volk, May 1, 1937; children—Susan Ruth (Mrs. Michael Manning), Sally Ann (Mrs. Jerry Fine). B.B.A., U. Cin., 1941; M.B.A., Xavier U., 1954. Band leader, studio mgr. Rudolph Wurlitzer Co., 1946-50; Tng. supr., then asst. to v.p. Gruen Watch Co., 1950-55; personnel dir., asst. to pres. Bavarian Brewing Co., Covington, Ky., 1955-59; dir. indsl. relations, asst. to pres. Howard Paper

Co., Dayton, Ohio, 1959-62; v.p., gen. mgr. Elano Corp., Xenia, Ohio, 1962-64; v.p., dir. indsl. relations Champion Papers Inc., Hamilton, Ohio, 1964-67; v.p. U.S. Plywood Champion Papers, Inc., 1967-71, Champion Internat., 1971-72; pres. PEP Group, 1972—; dir. Mgmt. Center, Sacred Heart U., 1974—. Contbr. articles to profl. publs. Trustee Foreman Found., 1965-71. Served to lt. (j.g.) USNR, 1944-46. Mem. Am. Soc. Personnel Adminstrs. (bd. dirs. 1969—, treas. 1970), Am. Soc. for Tng. and Devel., NAM, Am. Paper Inst., Am. Mgmt. Assn., Conn. songwriters assn., Lambda Chi Alpha. Home: 3400 S Ocean Blvd Ste 7-d Highland Beach FL 33487

WEGMAN, MYRON EZRA, physician, educator; b. Bklyn., July 23, 1908; s. Max and Nettie (Finkelstein) W.; m. Isabel Howe, July 4, 1936 (dec. Jan. 1997); children: Judith (Mrs. John A. Hirst), David Howe, Jane (Mrs. David D. Dunatchik), Elizabeth Gooding (Mrs. Ralph A. Petersen). A.B., CCNY, 1928; M.D. cum laude, Yale U., 1932; M.P.H., Johns Hopkins U., 1938. Diplomate Am. Bd. Preventive Medicine, Am. Bd. Pediatrics (ofcl. examiner). Intern, asst. resident, resident in pediatrics New Haven Hosp., 1932-36; instr. pediatrics Yale U., 1933-36; cons. pediatrics Md. State Health Dept., 1936-41; asst. prof. child hygiene sch. Tropical Medicine, San Juan, P.R., 1941-42; dir. research and tng. in child health, dir. sch. health N.Y.C. Health Dept., 1942-46; instr. pediatrics and lectr. public health adminstrn. Johns Hopkins U., 1939-46; asst. prof. pediatrics and pub. health Cornell U., 1942-46; asst. prof. pub. health Columbia U., 1940-46; prof. pediatrics, head dept. La. State U., 1946-52; pediatrician-in-chief Charity Hosp., New Orleans, 1946-52; prof. public health Sch. Public Health, U. Mich., Ann Arbor, 1960-74; dean Sch. Public Health, U. Mich., 1960-74, dean emeritus, 1974—; prof. pediatrics U. Mich. Med. Sch., 1961-78, prof. emeritus, 1978—, chmn. div. health sci., 1970-74; John G. Searle prof. public health, 1974-78, emeritus, 1978—; vis. prof. U. Malaya, 1974, Centro Universitario de Salud Publica, U. Autónoma Madrid, 1990—, U Cin., 1993; external examiner Nat. U. Singapore, 1983; cons. Internat. Sci. and Tech. Inst., 1986—, Sch. Pub. Health U. Kinshasa, Zaire, 1987, Schs. Pub. Health Jakarta, Surabaya, Ujung Pandang, Medan, Semarang, Indonesia, 1988; coord. Mich.-Madrid Sch. Pub. Health collaboration, 1990—. Editor: Public Health in the People's Republic of China, 1973; author: also pediatrics and public health textbooks, articles in med. jours. Status of Pan American Centers; mem. editorial bd. Revista Mexicana de Salud Publica, 1990—. Chief divsn. edn. and tng. Pan-Am. San. Bur., Regional Office for Ams., WHO, 1952-56; sec. gen. Pan-Am. San Bur., WHO Regional Office, 1957-60; pres. Assn. Schs. Pub. Health, 1963-66; pres. Comprehensive Health Planning Coun., S.E. Mich., 1970-74; trustee Pan-Am. Health and Edn. Found., 1970-85, 86-92, 94—, pres., 1984-85, chmn. devel. com., 1991—, v.p., 1996—; trustee Nat. San. Found., 1969-84, emeritus trustee, 1984—; pres. Physicians for Social Responsibility, Ann Arbor, 1987-92; mem. com. on carcinogenesis of pesticides Nat. Acad. Sci., 1977-79, com. on advanced study in China, 1978-82; chmn. Task Force in Nat. Immunization Policy, HEW, 1975-76; adv. com. Kellogg Nat. Fellowship Program, 1982—; rsch. adv. com. Resources for Future, 1978-84, spl. cons. State U. System Fla., 1982-87; mem. com. on prevention ctrs. CDC, 1986-84. Recipient Man of Yr. award CCNY, 1955; Clifford G. Grulee award Am. Acad. Pediatrics, 1958; Townsend Harris medal CCNY, 1961; Bronfman prize Am. Public Health Assn., 1967; Disting. Service award Mich. Public Health Assn., 1974; Walter P. Reuther award for disting. service United Auto Workers, 1974; Sedgwick medal Am. Pub. Health Assn., 1974; Outstanding Alumnus award Johns Hopkins Sch. Hygiene, 1982; Disting. Service award Delta Omega Soc., 1982; Spes Hominum award Nat. Sanitation Found., 1986, Disting. Alumnus award Yale U. Med. Sch., 1987; Spl. award Korean Soc. Preventive Medicine, 1989. Fellow AAAS, Royal Soc. Health (hon.); mem. Am. PEdiatric Soc., Soc. Pediatric Rsch., Am. Acad. Pediatrics, Am. Assn. World Health (v.p. 1979-82, 85-88, pres. 1982-84), Am. Pub. Health Assn. (chmn. exec. bd. 1965-70, pres. 1971-72), Fedn. Assn. Schs. Health Professions (1st pres. 1968-70), Soc. Exptl. Biol. and Medicine, Peruvian, Eduadorian, Artentinian Pediatric Socs. (hon.), P.R. Pub. Health Assn. (hon.), Sigma Xi, Alpha Omega Alpha, Delta Omega, Phi Kappa Phi, Phi Beta Kappa (hon.). Club: Cosmos (Washington). Home: 2760 Overridge Dr Ann Arbor MI 48104-4049 Office: Sch Public Health U Mich Ann Arbor MI 48109-2029

WEGMAN, ROBERT B., food service executive; b. 1918; married. BBA, Niagara Univ. With Wegman's Food Markets, Inc., Rochester, pres., 1950—, chmn., 1969—, now CEO. With USMC, ret. Office: Wegmans Food Markets Inc PO Box 844 1500 Brooks Ave Rochester NY 14624-3512*

WEGMAN, WILLIAM GEORGE, artist; b. Holyoke, Mass., Dec. 2, 1943; s. George W. and Eleanor (Vezina) W. BFA in Painting, Mass. Coll. Art, 1965; MFA, U. Ill., 1967. One-man shows include Gallerie Sonnabend, Paris, 1971, Pomona Coll. Art Gallery, 1971, Sonnabend Gallery, N.Y.C., 1972, 77, Galerie Ernst, Hanover, Ger., 1972, Situation, London, 1972, Konrad Fischer Gallery, 1972, 75, 79, Courtney Sale Gallery, 1972, Tex. Gallery, Houston, 1973, 75, 79, L.A. County Mus. of Art, Calif., 1973, 112 Greene St., N.Y.C., 1974, Mayor Gallery, London, 1975, Galleria Alessandra Castelli, Milan, 1975, The Kitchen, N.Y., 1976, Bruna Soletti Gallery, Milan, 1977, 82, Rosamund Felsen Gallery, 1978, Holly Solomon Gallery, N.Y.C., 1979, 80, 82, 84, 86, 88, 90, 92, Arnolfini Gallery, Eng., 1979, U. Wis., Milw., 1979, U. Colo. Art Galleries, Boulder, 1980, Marianne Deson Gallery, Chgo., 1980, Vivianne Esders Gallery, Paris, 1981, Magnuson Lee Gallery, Boston, 1981, Robert Hull Fleming Mus., Burlington, Vt., 1981, Locus Solus, Genoa, Italy, 1982, Dart Gallery, Chgo., 1982, Fraenkel Gallery, San Francisco, 1982, 88, 90, 92, 93, James Corcoran Gallery, Los Angeles, 1982, 90, Nancy Drysdale Gallery, Washington, 1982, 87, 94, Walker Art Ctr, Mpls., 1982, Ft. Worth Art Mus., Tex., 1982, De Cordova & Dana Mus. & Park, Mass., 1982, Southeastern Ctr. for Contemporary Art, Winston-Salem, N.C., 1982, The Contemporary Arts Ctr., Ohio, 1982, Newport Harbor Mus., Calif., 1982, Inst. Contemporary Arts at Va. Mus., Richmond, 1983, Fine Arts Gallery, U. Mass., Amherst, 1983, Tex. Gallery, Houston, 1983, 86, Greenville County Mus. Art, 1984, Lowe Mus. Art, Miami, Fla, 1985, Cleve. Mus. Art, 1986, Honolulu Acad. Arts, 1987, Mass. Coll. Art, Boston, 1987, U. San Diego, La Jolla, Calif., 1988, Pace MacGill Gallery, N.Y., 1988, 90, 92, 93, San Francisco Mus. Modern Art, Calif., 1988, Galerie Durand-Dessert, Paris, 1989, Budoin Lebon, Paris, 1989, Maison de la Culture et de la Communication de Saint Etienne, France, 1989, Linda Cathcart Gallery, L.A., 1990, 92, 94, The Taft Mus. Cin., 1990, The Butler Inst., Ohio, 1990, Sperone Westwater Gallery, N.Y., 1992, Kunstmuseum, Lucerne, Switzerland, 1990, ICA, London, 1990, Stedelijk Mus., The Netherlands, 1990, Frankfurt Kunstverein, Germany, 1990, Pompidou Ctr., Paris, 1990, ICA, Boston, 1990, Ringling Mus., Fla., 1990, Whitney Mus., N.Y., Contemporary Arts Mus., Tex., 1990, Neuberger Mus., SUNY, 1991, Galerie Andreas Binder, Germany, 1992, Athenaeum Music & Arts Library, Calif., 1992, Lisa Sette Gallery, Phoenix, 1994, Greg Kucera Gallery, Seattle, 1994, George Eastman House: Internat. Mus. Photography and Film, 1995, Aspen Art Mus., ACC Galerie, Weimar, Germany, 1995, Pace Wildenstein, L.A., 1995, others; exhibited in group shows at Walker Art Ctr., Mpls., 1968, N.J. State Mus., Trenton, 1968, Detroit Inst. Art, 1969, Mus. Contemporary Art, Chgo., 1969, 77, Allen Meml. Mus., 1970, L.A. County Mus., Calif., 1971, Pasadena Art Mus., 1972, Contemporary Arts Mus., Houston, 1972, Whitney Mus. Am. Art, N.Y.C., 1973, 81, 89, Sonnabend Gallery, N.Y.C., 1974, Milw. Art Ctr., 1975, Sarah Lawrence Coll. Gallery, 1975, Phila. Mus. Art, 1976, San Francisco Mus. Modern Art, 1976, U. Calif.-Berkeley Art Mus., 1976, U. Chgo., 1976, Ringling Mus. Art, Sarasota, Fla., 1977, Walker Art Gallery, Eng., 1978, Holly Solomon Gallery, N.Y.C., 1978, 82, 87, Mus. Fine Arts, Houston, 1978, Aspen Ctr. Visual Arts, 1979, Santa Barbara Mus. Art, 1979, Mus. Modern Art, N.Y.C., 1980, 82, 83, Sidney Janis Gallery, 1981, Art Inst. Chgo., 1981, 82, Young Hoffman Gallery, Chgo., 1983, Inst. Contemporary Art, Boston, 1983, Castelli Graphics, N.Y.C., 1983, Queens Mus., N.Y., 1986, James. Madison U., Harrison, Va, 1987, Fay Gold Gallery, Atlanta, 1988, Hudson River Mus., 1989, Volcano Arts Ctr., 1989, Pace/MacGill, N.Y.C., 1990, The History of Travel, The Taft Museum, Cin., The Butler Inst. Youngstown, Ohio, 1990, William Wegman: Paintings, Drawings, Photographs, Videotapes, Kunstmuseum, Luzern, Stedelijk Museum, Amsterdam, Frankfurt Kunstverein Frankfurt, Centre Nat. d'Art et de Culture Georges Pompidou, Paris, Inst. of Contemporary Art, London, Inst. of Contemporary Arts, Boston, Contemporary Arts Mus., Houston, J.M. Ringling Mus., Sarasota, Whitney Mus., of American Art, N.Y., 1990-92, Outdoor Photographs, Neuberger Mus., State U. of N.Y. at Purchase, 1991, William Wegman: L'oeuvre photographique, 1969-76, Fonds Regional d'Art Contemporary, Limousin, France, 1991, New Polaroids, Holly Solomon Gallery, N.Y.C., Early Black and White Photographs, Pace/MacGill Gallery, N.Y.C., New Paintings, Sperone Westwater Gallery, N.Y.C., 1992, many others; contbr. articles to profl. jours.; videography: Reel 1, 1970-72, Reel 2, 1972, Reel 3, 1972-73, Reel 4, 1973-74, Reel 5, 1975, Reel 6, 1975-76, Reel 7, 1976-77, Spit Sandwich, 1970, Gray Hairs, 1974-75, Man Ray, Man Ray, 1978, The World of Photography, 1985, Sesame Street Videos, 1989, 92, 93; film: Dog Baseball, 1986; filmography; The Hardy Boys in Hardly Gold; publications: Man's Best Friend, 1982, Everyday Problems, 1984, William Wegman: Paintings, Drawings, Photographs, Videotapes, 1990, Cinderella, 1993, Little Red Riding Hood, 1993, ABC, 1994. Recipient Creative Artists Pub. Svc. award, 1979; Guggenheim Found. fellow, 1975, 86, Nat. Endowment for the Arts grantee, 1976, 82. Office: 431 W 18th St New York NY 10011-3817*

WEGNER, GARY ALAN, astronomer; b. Seattle, Dec. 26, 1944; s. Herbert Edward and Melba Jean (Gardner) W.; m. Cynthia Kay Goodfellow, June 25, 1966; children: Josef, Kurt, Christian, Peter-Jürgen, Emma. Student, Wash. State U., Pullman, 1963-65; BS, U. Ariz., 1967; PhD, U. Wash., Seattle, 1971. Fulbright fellow Mount Stromlo Obs., Camberra, A.C.T., 1971-72; departmental demonstrator in astrophysics Oxford U., Eng., 1972-75; sr. sci. rsch. officer South African Astron. Obs., Capetown, Republic of South Africa, 1975-78; Annie J. Cannon fellow U. Del., Newark, 1978-79; asst. prof. Pa. State U., State College, 1979-82; asst. prof. to assoc. prof. physics and astronomy Dartmouth Coll., Hanover, N.H., 1982-88, Margaret Anne and Edward Leede Disting. prof. physics and astronomy, 1988—; dir. Mich.-Dartmouth-MIT Obs., 1991—; vis. astronomer Cornell U., 1992. Editor: White Dwarfs, 1989; contbr. articles to jours. in field. Keeley fellow Wadham Coll., Oxford, 1992-93, vis. fellow in astrophysics Oxford U., 1992-93; vis. prof. Astron. Inst. Ruhr U. Bochum, Germany, 1993-94; recipient rsch. prize The Alexander von Humboldt Found., Germany, 1993-94, numerous grants NSF, NASA. Mem. Am. Astron. Soc., Internat. Astron. Union. Lutheran. Office: Dartmouth Coll Dept Physics & Astronomy Wilder Lab Hanover NH 03755

WEGNER, HELMUTH ADALBERT, lawyer, retired chemical company executive; b. Berlin, Germany, Feb. 5, 1917; came to U.S., 1936, naturalized, 1943; s. Leo Michael and Hertha Johanna (Erdmann) W.; m. Cordelia Elizabeth Claussen, Aug. 23, 1941 (wid. Nov. 1996); children: Harold C., Ruth Ellen Wegner Hennessey, Linda Ann Levinson. B.S., U. Ill., 1938; postgrad., U. Wis., 1939; J.D., Chgo.-Kent Coll. Law, 1950. Bar: Ill. 1950, Va. 1979, D.C. 1981. With G.D. Searle & Co., Skokie, Ill., 1939—; patent dir. G.D. Searle & Co., 1958-63, gen. counsel, 1963-78, sec., 1972-78, sr. counsel, 1978-79, 82-92; ptnr. Wegner, Cantor, Mueller and Player, Washington, 1992-94. Contbr. articles to profl. jours. Mem. ABA (past com. chmn.), Va. Bar Assn., Am. Intell. Property Law Assn. (past com. chmn.), Am. Chem. Soc. (past dir. Chgo. sect., exec. com.), Chgo. Chemists Club, Phi Delta Phi. Mem. United Ch. of Christ. Home: 5000 Fairbanks Ave Apt 275 Alexandria VA 22311-1234

WEGNER, JUDITH WELCH, law educator, dean; b. Hartford, Conn., Feb. 14, 1950; d. John Raymond and Ruth (Thulen) Welch; m. Warren W. Wegner, Oct. 13, 1972. BA with honors, U. Wis., 1972; JD, UCLA, 1976. Bar: Calif. 1976, D.C. 1977, N.C. 1988, U.S. Supreme Ct. 1980, U.S. Ct. Appeals. Law clk. to Judge Warren Ferguson, U.S. Dist. Ct. for So. Dist. Calif., L.A., 1976-77; atty. Office Legal Counsel and Land & Natural Resources Divsn. U.S. Dept. Justice, Washington, 1977-79; spl. asst. to sec. U.S. Dept. Edn., Washington, 1979-80; vis. assoc. prof. U. Iowa Coll. Law, Iowa City, 1981; asst. prof. U. N.C. Sch. Law, Chapel Hill, 1981-84, assoc. prof., 1984-88, prof., 1988—, assoc. dean, 1986-88, dean, 1989—; spkr. in field. Chief comment editor UCLA Law Rev., 1975-76; contbr. articles to legal publs. Mem. ABA (chmn. planning com. African Law Sch. Initiative 1994, co-chmn. planning com. 1994 mid-yr. deans meeting sect. on legal edn. and admission to bar), AAUP, N.C. Assn. Women Attys. (Gweneth Davis award 1989), N.C. State Bar Assn., Assn. Am. Law Schs. (mem. exec. com. sect. on law & edn. 1985-88, mem. exec. com. sect. on local govt. law 1989-92, mem. accreditation com. 1986-88, chmn. 1989-91, program chmn. 1992 ann. meeting, program chmn. 1994 ann. meeting, mem. exec. com. 1992-94, pres. 1995), Soc. Am. Law Tchrs., Nat. League Cities (coun.-mentor program 1989-91), Women's Internat. Forum, Order of Coif (nat. exec. com. 1989-91), Phi Beta Kappa. Democrat. Office: U NC Sch Law Van Hecke-Wettach Hall Campus Box 3380 Chapel Hill NC 27599-3380

WEGNER, KARL HEINRICH, physician, educator; b. Pierre, S.D., Jan. 5, 1930; s. Lester Fred and Nellie (Norbeck) W.; m. Mary Josephine Waddell, June 15, 1957; children: Madeleine Jean, Peter Norbeck, Mary Nell. B.A., Yale U., 1952; M.D., Harvard U., 1959. Intern, resident Mass. Gen. Hosp./Harvard U., 1959-62; pathologist Sioux Valley Hosp., Sioux Falls, S.D., 1962-90; pathologist, dir. Lab. Clin. Medicine, Sioux Falls, 1962-90; prof., chmn. dept. pathology U. S.D., 1968-73, v.p. health affairs, dean Sch. Medicine, 1973-79, Regents Disting. prof. emeritus, 1992—; owner, operator Meadowlark Farms, Montrose, S.D.; mem. Bd. of Regents for Higher Edn., State of S.D., pres. bd. regents, 1996-97. Bd. dirs. U. S.D. Found., Sioux Valley Hosp. Found., Sioux Falls Area Found. With USMC. Karl H. Wegner Endowed Professorship, Bd. of Regents for Higher Edn., 1979; recipient Disting. Svc. award S.D. State Med. Assn., 1984, Community Svc. award, 1975; inducted to S.D. Hall of Fame, 1987. Fellow Coll. Am. Pathologists, Internat. Acad. Pathologists, Am. Soc. Pathologists; mem. Am. Pathology Found. (pres. 1984-85, Am. pathologist of Yr award, 1989), Alpha Omega Alpha. Home: 5010 S Sunnymede Cir Sioux Falls SD 57108

WEGNER, SAMUEL JOSEPH, museum executive; b. Twin Falls, Idaho, Aug. 27, 1952; s. Albert Henry and Eleanor Esther (Wright) W.; m. Linda Louise Talley, May 27, 1972; children: Ethan, Elena. BA, U. Ariz., 1973; MA, U. Idaho, 1975. Curator Mansion Mus.-Oglebay Inst., Wheeling, W.Va., 1975-76; curator of edn. State Hist. Soc. Wis., Madison, 1976-78; asst. supt. Region I Mo. Dept. Nat. Resources, Brookfield, 1978-85; dir. ops. So. Oregon Hist. Soc., Jacksonville, Oreg., 1985-87; exec. dir. So. Oregon Hist. Soc., Medford, Oreg., 1987-96; dep. exec. dir. Jamestown-Yorktown Found., Williamsburg, Va., 1996—; mem. Nat. Adv. Com. Common Agenda for History Mus., 1990-92, Nat. Adv. Com. Phila. Documentation Project for Common Agenda, 1989-91; chmn. Region 11 Am. Assn. State and Local History Awards Program, 1989-90, chmn. Oregon State chpt., 1987-88; chmn. Western Region Assn. Living History Farms and Agrl. Mus., 1986-87; mem. Am. Assn. Mus. Ad Hoc Com. for Hist. Sites and Mus. in Pks., 1984-85. Mem. adv. com. Medford (Oreg.) Vis. and Conv. Bur., 1988-96; bd. dirs. Oreg. Trail Coordinating Coun., 1994-96, So. Oreg. Visitors Assn., 1995-96; bd. dirs., coord. Applegate Trail Coalition, 1993-96; mem. Jacksonville Transp. Com., 1993-95. Mem. Am. Assn. Mus., Nat. Trust for Hist. Preservation, Oreg. Mus. Assn., Rotary. Office: Jamestown-Yorktown Found PO Box 1607 Williamsburg VA 23187-1607

WEGNER, SANDRA SUE, library director; b. Hutchinson, Kans., July 30, 1938; d. John Wilbur and Evelyn Lucille (White) DeFore; m. Leroy Gene Wegner, Oct. 7, 1960; children: Ross Eugene, Barry John. BS in Journalism, Tex. Woman's U., 1960; MS in LS, North Tex. State U., 1985. Cert. county libr., Tex. Reporter oil sect. Midland (Tex.) Reporter-Telegram, 1960; libr. clk. Midland County Pub. Libr., Midland, 1974-82, spl. collections libr., 1982-85, asst. dir., 1985-90, dir., 1990—. Literacy tutor Midland Need To Read, 1987-90, bd. dirs., 1988—. Mem. ALA, Tex. Libr. Assn., Midland Geneal. Soc. (bd. dirs.), DAR (registrar Col. Theunis Dey chpt. 1993-95), Beta Phi Mu. Republican. Methodist. Avocation: genealogy. Home: 1502 Seaboard Midland TX 79705 Office: Midland County Pub Libr 301 W Missouri Ave Midland TX 79701-5108

WEHLAND, GRANVILLE WARREN PEARSON, lawyer, consultant; b. Sandy Spring, Md., Sept. 9, 1934; s. Henry Wadsworth and Ellen Alberta (Pearson) W.; m. Mary Constance Colbert, Aug. 21, 1963; children: Mary Jeanne McCabe, Matthew Henry Colbert. JD, U. Balt., 1959. Chief Bur. Highways Howard County Govt., Ellicott City, Md., 1960-93; cons Wehland Law Offices, Ellicott City, 1994—; cons. Greater Balt. Regional Planning Com., 1971-75, MD Motion Picture Commn., Howard County, Md., 1975-93; rep. Classic Realty, Ellicott City, 1993—, AFLAC Ins., Timonium, Md., 1994—; bd. dirs. County Engrs. Assn., Md., 1977-80, pres. 1980-81, hist., 1993—. Author: Howard County Road Code and Specifications, 1963. Bd. dirs. Howard County Hist. Soc., Ellicott City, pres. 1980-81; councillor Patpasco unit Boy Scouts Am., Ellicott City, 1993—. Mem. SAR (pres. 1986-87, nat. trustee, Patriots Award medal 1985, Silver Good Citizenship medal 1983), Order of Founders and Patriots of Am. (gov. gen. 1990, dep. gov. gen. 1996, Disting. Svc. award 1994), Nat. Gavel Soc. (sec. 1993—, Diamond Gavel 1994), Sons and Daus. of Pilgrims (gov. 1988-90). Democrat. Episcopalian. Avocations: genealogy, history, travel. Home: 3892 College Ave Ellicott City MD 21043-4609 Office: Order Founders & Patriots 3982 College Ave Ellicott City MD 21043-5502

WEHLING, ROBERT LOUIS, household products company executive; b. Chgo., Nov. 27, 1938; s. Ralph Joseph and Rita Helen (Casey) W.; m. Carolyn Thierry Harmon, July 5, 1958; children: Susan, Mary, Jennifer, Linda, Karen, Sandra. BA magna cum laude, Denison U., 1960. Brand asst. Procter & Gamble Co., Cin., 1960, 63-64, asst. brand mgr., 1964-66, br. mgr., 1966-70, assoc. advt. mgr., 1970-74, advt. mgr. bar soap and household cleaning products div., 1974-77, div. mgr. gen. advt., 1977-84, assoc. gen. advt. mgr., 1984-87, gen. mktg. svcs. mgr., 1987-88, v.p. mktg. svcs., 1988-90, v.p. pub. affairs, 1990-94, sr. v.p. advt., market rsch. and pub. affairs, 1994—, sr. v.p. advt., market rsch. and govt. rels., 1994—; mem. edn. task force Bus. Roundtable, 1990—. Pres. March of Dimes, Cin., 1981-84; mem. allocations com. Fine Arts Fund, Cin., 1987—; bd. dirs. Just Say No Internat., 1991-93; co-founder with USA Today, Coalition on Edn. Initiatives, 1991—; mem. Mayor's Commn. on Children, 1992—; vice chmn. Downtown Cin., Inc.; exec. com. Cin. Youth Collaborative; trustee United Way Cin., Ohio Schs. Devel. Corp.; bd. dirs. Edn. Excellence Partnership; participant Gov.'s Edn. Mgmt. Coun.; mem. Hamilton county Family and Children First Coun., 1993-94, numerous other civic activities. Named Citizen of Yr., City of Wyoming, 1986, One of 200 Greater Cincinnatians, Cin. Bicentennial Commn., 1988; recipient awards Nat. Coun. Negro Women, 1989, United Way, 1991, Madison Square Boys and Girls Club, 1991, Disting. Svc. award Ohio Assn. Colls. for Tchr. Edn., 1993, award Coun. for Acad. Excellence, 1994, U.S. Dept. Edn., 1994, The Seasongood Good Govt. award 1994, Nat. Vol. of Yr./Elaine Whitelaw award March of Dimes, 1994, Ohio Gov.'s award, 1995, Community Hero Torchbearer for the 1996 Olympic Torch Relay, 1996, numerous others. Mem. Assn. Nat. Advertisers (Robert V. Goldstein award for Disting. Svc. 1993), Advt. Coun. (campaign dir. 1988—), Greater Cin. C. of C. (trustee, exec. com.), Queen City Club, Commonwealth Club, Phi Beta Kappa. Republican. Methodist. Avocations: running, reading, education, children's issues. Office: Procter & Gamble Co 1 Procter And Gamble Plz Cincinnati OH 45202-3315

WEHLITZ, RALF, physicist; b. Berlin, Apr. 15, 1960; s. Diethelm and Erna Wehlitz. Diploma in physics, Tech. U., Berlin, 1985, D in Natural Sci., 1991. Teaching asst. Tech. U., Berlin, 1982-85, rsch. asst., 1985-90; rsch. assoc. Fritz-Haber-Inst., Berlin, 1990-93, U. Tenn., Knoxville, 1994—; sec. workshop IWP-92, Berlin, 1992. Feodor-Lynen fellow Alexander von Humboldt Found., 1993. Mem. German Phys. Soc., Am. Phys. Soc. Home: 3700 Sutherland Ave Apt A12 Knoxville TN 37919-3011 Office: U Tenn Dept Physics Knoxville TN 37996-1200

WEHMEIER, HELGE H., chemical, health care and imaging technologies company executive; b. Goettingen, Germany, 1943; married; 2 children. Attended, Internat. Mgmt. Devel. Inst., Switzerland, Inst. Europeen d'Adminstrn. des Affaires, France. With Bayer AG, 1965; mktg. synthetic fibers U.S. and Can. Mobay, N.Y.C., 1969; mktg. mgr. Leverkusen, Ger., 1974-78; gen. mgr. U.K., 1978-80; mgr. organic chem. divsn., 1981-84; head indsl. photographic divsn. Agfa-Gevaert AG subs. Leverkusen, 1984-89; pres., CEO Afga Corp., Ridgefield Park, N.J., 1989-91; also bd. dirs., exec. com. Agfa Corp., Ridgefield Park, N.J.; pres., CEO Bayer Corp. (formerly Miles Inc.), 1991—; bd. dirs. PNC Bank Corp. Bd. dirs. Pitts. Symphony Soc.; mem. exec. com., officer Allegheny Conf. Cmty. Devel., Pitts.; mem. Conf. Bd., Trilateral Commn. Mem. Chem. Mfrs. Assn. (exec. com., internat. com.). Office: Bayer Corp One Mellon Bank Ctr 500 Grant St Pittsburgh PA 15219-2502

WEHNER, HENRY OTTO, III, pharmacist, consultant; b. Birmingham, Ala., Mar. 3, 1942; s. Henry O. Jr. and Carolyn (Kirkland) W.; m. Sammye Ruth Murphy, June 8, 1974 (div. July 1989). AA, Daytona Beach Community Coll., 1967; BS in Biology, North Ga. Coll., Dahlonega, 1971; BS in Pharmacy, U. Ga., 1978. Registered pharmacist, Fla., Ga.; cert. sci. tchr. grades 7-12, Ga. Tchr. biology Irwin County High Sch., Ocilla, Ga., 1971-75; extern Eckerd Drugs, Athens, Ga., 1977; intern/extern St. Mary's Hosp., Athens, 1977; pharmacy intern Button Gwinnett Hosp., Lawrenceville, Ga., 1978; co-owner, mgr. Hiawassee (Ga.) Pharmacy, 1978-79; staff pharmacist Dyal's Pharmacy, Daytona Beach, Fla., 1979, Little Drug Co., New Smyrna Beach, Fla., 1979-80; staff pharmacist, mgr. Super X Drugs, New Smyrna Beach, 1980-81; staff pharmacist Fish Meml. Hosp., New Smyrna Beach, 1981-92, Halifax Med. Ctr., Daytona Beach, Fla., 1992—. With USAF, 1961-65. Mem. Am. Pharm. Assn., Fla. Soc. Hosp. Pharmacists, Volusia County Pharm. Assn., Ea. Shores Soc. Hosp. Pharmacists (charter, pres. 1995-96), Eastern Shores Fla. Soc. Hosp. Pharmacists, Phi Lambda Sigma, Phi Theta Kappa. Methodist. Avocations: painting, cycling, tennis. Office: Halifax Med Ctr PO Box 1350 303 N Clyde Morris Blvd Daytona Beach FL 32114-2709

WEHRENBERG, WILLIAM BUSSE, agricultural studies educator; m. Jane E. Kurhajec, May, 1973. BS in Chemistry, Valparaiso (Ind.) U., 1973; MS in Biol. Sci., Purdue U., Ft. Wayne, Ind., 1975; PhD in Endocrinology-Reproductive Phys., U. Wis., 1978. Postdoctoral rsch. fellow Internat. Inst. for Study Human Reprodn., Columbia U., N.Y.C., 1978-80; asst. prof. Labs. for Neuroendocrinology, Salk Inst., San Diego, 1980-82, Andrew W. Mellon asst. prof., 1982-85; assoc. prof. dept. health scis. U. Wis., Milw., 1985-87, chmn. dept. health scis., 1988-89, prof., 1987-96, assoc. dean for rsch. Sch. Allied Health Professions, 1989-96; affiliate scientist Wis. Regional Primate Rsch. Ctr., U. Wis., Madison, 1986-96; prof. dept. biol. sci., dean Coll. Agr., Forestry, Life Sci. Clemson (S.C.) U., 1996—; vis. prof. dept. medicine U. Geneva, Switzerland, 1986, 91; adj. prof. dept. physiology Med. Coll. Wis., Milw., 1988-96. Editl. bd. Trends in Endocrinology and Metabolism, 1993—, Growth, Devel. and Aging, 1988—, Endocrinology, 1987-90, 93—, Domestic Animal Endocrinology, 1994—, Neuroendocrinology, 1995—, Advances in Life scis.-Exptl. and Clin. Endocrinology, 1995—; reviewer for over 20 sci. jours. annually; contbr. over 150 articles to profl. jours. Sec. Watertower Landmark trust, Milw., 1988-94; mem. coun. Lake Park Luth. Ch., Milw., 1990-91; block watch capt. Milw. Police Dept. Recipient Andrew W. Mellon Found. award, 1982, U. Wis.-Milw. Found./Grad. Sch. Rsch. award, 1987, Rsch. Career Devel. award NIH, 1988, Rsch. Incentive award U. Wis.-Milw., 1989, Award for Tchg. Excellence, U. Wis.-Milw. Alumni Assn., 1989, Valparaiso U. Disting. Alumni award, 1992; Fulbright Rsch. scholar, U. Bordeaux, France, 1991; recipient numerous grants from The Upjohn Co., Eli Lilly & Co., Genentech, Inc., Monsanto Agrl. Co., Medialanum Farmaceutici, Milan, Italy, Europeptides, Inc., Paris, Intervet Am., Inc., U. Wis.-Milw., Wis. Dept. Agr., NIH, NIDDK, USDA. Mem. AAAS, Internat. Soc. Neuroendocrinology, Am. Assn. for Lab. Animal Sci., Wis. Endocrine Soc., Endocrine Soc., Soc. for Study of reprodn., Internat. Fur Animal Sci. Assn. (alt. mem. bd. dirs.), Wis. Assn. Biomed. Rsch. and Edn. (treas., mem. bd. dirs.), Wis. Soc. for Neursci. (organizing com. for regional midwest meeting), Sigma xi, Phi Kappa Phi. Office: Clemson Univ Coll Agr Forestry Life Sci 101 Barre Hall Box 340303 Clemson SC 29634-0303

WEHRER, CHARLES SIECKE, business and education educator; b. Norfolk, Nebr., July 13, 1914; s. Charles C. and Ella (Augusta) W.; m. May Winther Hansen, Aug. 21, 1982 (dec. Oct. 27, 1991). BA, Nebr. State Tchrs. Coll., 1940; MA in Sch. Adminstrn., U. Nebr., 1950, postgrad., 1950; postgrad., Columbia U., 1950, U. So. Calif., 1954-55; PhD without dissertation, Ohio State U., 1961; LHD (hon.), Sioux Empire Coll., 1967. Asst. commandant, basketball coach Black-Foxe Mil. Inst., Hollywood, Calif., 1945-46; coach, supt. local schs. Wood Lake, Nebr., 1947-49; prin. Scottsbluff (Nebr.) Jr. High Sch., 1950-51; grad. asst. in edn. U. Nebr., 1949-50, U. So. Calif., 1954-55; grad. asst. prof. elem. edn. Ohio State U., 1960; tchr. pub. schs. Paramount, Calif., 1953-54; tchr. Excelsior Adult Sch., Norwalk, Calif., 1953-57; supt. local schs. Shandon, Calif., 1956-57; assoc. prof. edn., supr. student teaching Ohio No. U., Ada, 1958-60; assoc. prof., supr. elem. student teaching Capital U., Columbus, Ohio, 1961-62; prin. Norwalk Iowa Elem. Jr. High Sch., 1962-63; prof. edn., dir. student affairs, asst. to pres. Grand View Coll., Des Moines, 1962-64; with depts. youth, TV, ednl. programming City of Des Moines, 1965; cons. program Iowa Civil Def./Health Dept., 1966; prof. edn. and psychology S.W. Community Coll.,

Creston, Iowa, 1967; acad. dean Sioux Empire Coll., Hawarden, Iowa, 1967-68; chmn. depts. edn., psychology, dir. tchr. edn. J.F. Kennedy Coll., Wahoo, Nebr., 1970-71; prodr., emcee youth radio/TV program Let's Listen to Youth, Lincoln, Nebr., 1971, Des Moines, Sioux City, Iowa, 1952-74, L.A., Columbus, Ohio, 1952-74; prof. edn. Concordia Coll., Seward, Nebr., 1973; tng. coord., dir. spl. tng. programs for mgmt. State of Nebr., 1974-75; prof. bus. Metro Tech., Omaha, 1976-82; prof. mgmt. tng. Bus. Devel. Ctr. U. Nebr., Omaha, 1976-82; prof. bus. Nebr. State Coll., Wayne, 1982-88, ret.; pres. Bus. Mgmt. Cons. Co., Wisner, Nebr., 1982-90; lectr. in field. Author: Keep in Touch, My Students, 1966; contbr. articles to profl. jours. Phys. dir. YMCA, Norfolk, 1934-36, McCook, Nebr., 1937-38, L.A. Downtown Y, 1940-41; counselor, adv. Nebr. Boys' State, 1949-50; Nebr. del. White House Conf. on Children and Youth, 1950; chmn. Nebr. Com. on Juvenile Delinquency; mem. Gov.'s Com. on Youth, Calif., Nebr.; spl. youth cons. radio program Art Linkletter House Party, Calif., 1952; dir. dept. guest rels. NBC, Hollywood, Calif., 1952; dir. spl. project Iowa Dept. Health, 1965-66; contbr. to sub-com. on poverty-youth programs U.S. Congress, 1964-65; chmn. youth sect. Iowa Congress Parents & Tchrs., 1966-67; lay min. Protestant Chs., 1967—, past ch. official First Cong. United Ch. of Christ, Norfolk, Elkhorn Valley Hist. Soc. Capt. USAAF, 1941-45. Decorated Bronze Star, Soldiers medal, 3 Battle Stars, 15th AF Unit citation, Pres. Unit citation, others; recipient spl. awards/commendations for radio/TV programs State PTA and other civic and youth groups, 1960-75, numerous awards for tchg. and youth work; named Outstanding Sch. Adminstr. in Nebr. dept. sch. adminstrn. U. Nebr., Nebr. Dept. Edn., 1948-50; named to Hall of Honor, Nebr. Softball Assn., 1993, Norfolk H.S. Students honor as Sr. Citizens of Yr., 1995, Spl. Proclamation for Edn. and Youth Svcs. State of Nebr., 1994; named to Norfolk H.S. Close Up Club Unanimous Spl. Honor Selection to Hall of Fame. Mem. NEA (Spl. Commendation for tchr. edn. programs), AAUP, Am. Assn. Ret. Persons (pres. 1997-98, Nebr. Sr. Citizen Spl. Commendation 1980-81), Assn. for Higher Edn., Nat. Assn. Sch. Adminstrs., Nat. Soc. for Study of Edn., Internat. Platform Assn. (spl. spkr. conv. 1970, spl. honors for Vets. Day), Am. Legion, VFW (spl. commendation for helping veterans, sr. citizens and youth 1997), SCORE, Lions (bd. dirs., past pres.), Kiwanis (past pres.), Rotary, Delta Sigma, Phi Delta Kappa (Spl. Recognition award 1992), Sigma Tau Delta (past pres.). Address: 1000 Village Green Dr Apt 1 Norfolk NE 68701-2279 *We are living in a dangerous world of unrest, a difficult time for all of us to adjust to the emotional and mental problems of this changing environmental world. If we can be of help to those who are in need of a friendly act then let us do our best to be of help and service to young and old alike as we may not pass this way again.*

WEHRING, BERNARD WILLIAM, nuclear engineering educator; b. Monroe, Mich., Aug. 3, 1937; s. Bernard Albert and Alma Christina (Graf) W.; m. Margaret Mary Robinson, Sept. 5, 1959; children: Mary Ann, James, Susan, Barbara. B.S.E. in Physics, U. Mich., 1959, B.S.E. in Math, 1959; M.S. in Physics, U. Ill., 1961, Ph.D. in Nuclear Engring, 1966. Asst. prof. nuclear engring. U. Ill., Urbana, 1966-70, assoc. prof., 1970-77, prof., 1977-84, asst. dean engring., 1981-82; prof. nuclear engring. N.C. State U., Raleigh, 1984-89, dir. nuclear reactor program, 1984-89; prof. mech. engring. U. Tex., Austin, 1989—, dir. Nuclear Engring. Teaching Lab., 1989—; cons. Argonne and Los Alamos nat. labs.; mem. crosssect. evaluation working group Brookhaven Nat. Lab. Contbr. sects. to books, articles to profl. publs. AEC fellow, 1963-65; NSF grantee, 1968—. Fellow Am. Nuclear Soc.; mem. Am. Soc. Engring. Edn., Am. Nuclear Soc. (standards com.), Am. Phys. Soc., IEEE. Achievements include contributing in the generation of basic nuclear data and development of new instruments and experimental techniques. Home: 8907 Spring Lake Dr Austin TX 78750-2932 Office: U Tex Nuclear Engring Teaching Lab J J Pickle Rsch Campus Austin TX 78712

WEHRLE, LEROY SNYDER, economist, educator; b. St. Louis, Feb. 5, 1932; s. Fred Joseph and Eleanor (Snyder) W.; m. JoAnn Griffith, Aug. 29, 1959; children—Chandra Lee, Lon Joseph. B.S., Washington U., St. Louis, 1953; M.A. in Econs, Yale, 1956, Ph.D. with honors, 1959. Asst. instr. Yale, 1958-59; with econ. sect. AID mission to Laos, 1960-61; sr. staff economist President's Council Econ. Advisers, 1961-62; spl. econ. adviser to U.S. Ambassador Unger, Vientiane, 1962; dep. dir. AID mission to Laos, 1963-64; asst. dir. AID mission, also econ. counsellor to U.S. ambassador, Saigon, 1964-67; asso. dir. AID Mission, Saigon, 1964-67; dept. asst. adminstr. Vietnam, AID, Dept. State, 1967-68; univ. fellow Harvard, 1968-69; sr. fellow Brookings Instn., 1969-70; dir. Ill. Inst. for Social Policy, Springfield, 1970-72; aide to Lt. Gov. Paul Simon, 1972; prof. economics Sangamon State U., 1972-88; founding ptnr., chief exec. officer Health Econs. and Mkt. Analysis Inc., Springfield, 1987-94; pres. Healthcare Cost Analysis, Inc., 1994—; chmn. bd. Tie Collar, Ltd. Mem. spl. study group Alliance Progress, 1962; mem. Rockefeller Latin Am. Mission, 1969; chmn. study team world food and nutrition study Nat. Acad. Sci., 1976-77. Served with AUS, 1953-55. Recipient William A. Jump meml. award, 1966. Home and Office: 2001 S Bates Ave Springfield IL 62704-3304

WEHRLI, JOHN ERICH, biotechnology executive; b. Bogota, Colombia, Dec. 1, 1963; came to U.S., 1969; s. Werner Freiderich and Graciela Wehrli; m. Vicki Lee Burnett, Aug. 18, 1991; children: Sophia Cristina, Sarina Darlene. BS summa cum laude in Mgmt. and Econs., Golden Gate U., 1993; Tax cert., Foothill Coll., 1994; postgrad., U. Calif., San Francisco, 1994—, U. Calif., Berkeley, 1995—. Analytical chemist dept. Chem. Analysis Syva Diagnostics Co., 1985-87; robotics specialist dept. Automation Tech. Syntex Rsch. Inc., 1987-89, rsch. chemist Inst. Pharm. Scis., dept. Pharm. Chemistry, 1987-91, sr. sci. analyst programmer, sys. mgr. Rsch. Info. Sys., 1991-93, sys. analyst, sr. sys. mgr., 1993-94; part-time fin. cons. assoc. Shearson Lehman Bros., San Francisco, 1989; v.p. Precision Instrument Design Inc., Tahoe City, Calif., 1989-96; legal intern patent and tech. licensing Lawrence Berkeley Nat. Lab., 1995-96; dir. Raptorgraphics, LLC, Mountain View, Calif., 1995-96; pres. Wehrli Tech. Cons., Mountain View, Calif., 1995-96; legal intern Cooley Godward LLP, 1996—; v.p. bus. devel. and intellectual property NaviCyte Inc., Reno, 1996—. Contbr. articles to profl. jours. Enterprise scholar Golden Gate U., 1992, Kanze scholar, 1993, Univ. Honors scholar, 1993, Pres.'s scholar Foothill Coll., 1993. Mem. AAAS, ABA (sci. and tech. sect.), Am. Chem. Soc. (chem. info. and computer scis. sect.), Assn. Univ. Tech. Mgrs., Licensing Execs. Soc., Am. Intellectual Property Law Assn., N.Y. Acad. Scis., Phi Alpha Delta. Avocations: wildlife preservation, animal cruelty prevention, fractal mathematics, nonlinear systems, Graeco Roman history. Home: 1879 Springer Rd Apt B Mountain View CA 94040-4052 Office: NaviCyte Inc Reno NV 89501

WEHRWEIN, AUSTIN CARL, newspaper reporter, editor, writer; b. Austin, Tex., Jan. 12, 1916; s. George S. and Anna (Ruby) W.; m. Judith Oakes, 1950; children: Sven Austin, Paul, Peter, Joanna Judith. A.B., U. Wis., 1937; LL.B., Columbia U., 1940; student, London Sch. Econs., 1948. Reporter Washington Bur., UP, 1941-43, 46-48; information specialist E.C.A., London, Copenhagen, Oslo, Stockholm, 1948-51; financial writer Milw. Jour., 1951-53; staff corr. Time, Inc., Chgo., 1953-55; reporter Chgo. Sun-Times, 1955-56, fin. editor, 1956-57; chief Chgo. bur. N.Y. Times, 1957-66; editorial writer Mpls. Star, 1966-82; contbr. London Economist, Collier's Year Book; corr. Chronicle of Higher Edn., Edn. Week. Editor The Observer, 1984-87. Served with USAAF, 1943-45; mem. staff Stars and Stripes 1945-46, Shanghai, China. Recipient Pulitizer prize for internat. reporting, 1953; Disting. Journalism award U. Wis., 1963; cert. of merit ABA Gavel competition, 1968, 80; Gavel award, 1969, 71. Home and Office: 2309 Carter Ave Saint Paul MN 55108-1640

WEHRWEIN-HUNT, JERI LYNN, elementary education educator; b. New Richmond, Wis., Aug. 13, 1952; d. Harlan Fredric and Olive Angeline (Steis) Wehrwein; 1 child, Katie Lynn. BS in Elem. Edn., St. Cloud State U., 1973, BS in Spl. Edn., 1973; MEd, U. Minn., 1990. cert. elem. and spl. edn. tchr., Minn. Coord. social studies curriculum Minneapolis Pub. Schs., 1977-78, tchr., 1973—, asst. spl. edn. camp program coord., 1982, coord. and tchr. gifted program, 1984-86. Recipient recognition for outstanding environmental activities in the classroom, Minn. Atty. Gen., 1994. Mem. Am. Fedn. Tchrs., Minn. Fedn. Tchrs. Roman Catholic. Avocations: interior decorating, singing, theater. Office: Jenny Lind Elem Sch 5025 Bryant Ave N Minneapolis MN 55430-3500

WEI, BENJAMIN MIN, engineering educator; b. Hebei, Hebei, China, Aug. 11, 1930; s. Fu Shun and Yuan Qing (Zhang) W.; m. Diana Yun Dee; children: Victor Mark, Jane Jiang. BSME, Chung Cheng Inst. Tech., 1954; MSME, Concordia U., 1970; PhD, Pa. State U., 1981. Mech. engr. Ordnance Corps Arsenal, Taipei, Taiwan, 1953-59; tchr. Wenshan High Sch., Taipei, 1960-61; teaching asst. New Brunswick (Can.) U., 1962-64; supr. Domtar Constrn. Materials Co., Can., 1964-66; computer programmer McGill U., Can., 1966-67, Montreal (Can.) U., 1967-68; tchr. Pierrefond Comprehensive High sch., Que., 1970-73; prof. Norfolk (Va.) State U., 1974—; hon. prof., cons. Taiyuan U. Polytech. Contbr. articles to profl. jours. Mem. Statistical Quality Control of China. Home: 1152 Janaf Pl Norfolk VA 23502-2631

WEI, FONG, nephrologist; b. Shanghai, May 2, 1941; came to U.S., 1941; s. Tseh Heen and Waling (Chung) W.; m. Theodora Mary Zopko, July 16, 1966; children: Christopher, Alexander. BA, Yale U., 1963; MD, Tufts U., 1967. Diplomate Am. Bd. Internal Medicine, Am. Bd. Nephrology. Intern Boston City Hosp., 1967-68, resident, 1968-69; resident Bronx (N.Y.) Mcpl., 1969-70; fellow in nephrology U. N.C., Chapel Hill, 1970-72; pvt. practice, Princeton, N.J., 1974—; clin. assoc. prof. Robert Wood Johnson Med. Sch., New Brunswick, N.J., 1975—; pres. med. staff Med. Ctr. Princeton, 1981-82; prin. investigator Bristol Myers Squibb, Princeton, 1984—, Merck and Co., Princeton, 1988—; cons. Princeton U., 1990—. Med. advisor Princeton Regional Homemakers Assn., 1975—. Fellow ACP; mem. Am. Soc. Nephrology, Internat. Soc. Nephrology, Am. Soc. Hypertension. Office: Princeton Med Group 419 N Harrison St Princeton NJ 08540-3521

WEI, I-YUAN, research and development consultant and director; b. Taipei, Taiwan, Republic of China, Nov. 1, 1940; came to U.S., 1967; s. Kun-Te and Kun (Lu) W.; m. Shirley Chen, Dec. 28, 1968; children: Jerray, Jiaying. BS, Nat. Taiwan Normal U., 1963; MS, Nat. Taiwan U., 1966; PhD, Tufts U., 1971. Rsch. assoc. U. N.C., Chapel Hill, 1972-75; scientist Sprague Electric Co., North Adams, Mass., 1976-77; mgr. R & D Republic Foil, Salisbury, N.C., 1977-81; sr. engr. AMP Inc., Harrisburg, Pa., 1981-86, mem. tech. staff, 1986-88, project mgr., 1988-90, mgr. plating rsch., 1990-93, dir. contacts materials, consulant tech., 1994—. Contbr. articles to Jour. Chinese Chem. Soc., Jour. Chem. Physics, Jour. Am. Chem. Soc., Inorganic Chemistry, Chem. Phys. Lett., Jour. Magna. Reson. Mem. Am. Electroplaters and Surface Finishers Soc. (chmn. electronics finishing com. 1991-94, advisor 1994—, chmn. meetings and symposia 1993—, dir. tech. edn. 1993—, Bd. Recognition award 1994), Electrochem. Soc., Ctrl. Pa. Chinese Assn. (pres. 1984, chmn. bd. 1985-93, 96—). Achievements include rsch. in deuteron quadrupole coupling constants in nitrobenzenes, hydrogen-bonded systems of aluminum hydroxides and anodic oxide films by deutron magnetic resonance, palladium and palladium-nickel as contact materials, electronic materials, electroplating; patentee in field. Home: 1046 W Areba Ave Hershey PA 17033-2203 Office: AMP Inc (MS106-11) PO Box 3608 Harrisburg PA 17105-3608

WEI, JAMES, chemical engineering educator, academic dean; b. Macao, China, Aug. 14, 1930; came to U.S., 1949, naturalized, 1960; s. Hsiang-chen and Nuen (Kwok) W.; m. Virginia Hong, Nov. 4, 1956; children: Alexander, Christina, Natasha, Randolph (dec.). B.S. in Chem. Engring, Ga. Inst. Tech., 1952; M.S., Mass. Inst. Tech., 1954, Sc.D., 1955; grad., Advanced Mgmt. Program Harvard, 1969. Research engr. to research assoc. Mobil Oil, Paulsboro, N.J., 1956-62; sr. scientist Princeton, N.J., 1963-68; mgr. corp. planning N.Y.C., 1969-70; Allan P. Colburn prof. U. Del., Newark, 1971-77; Sherman Fairchild distinguished scholar Calif. Inst. Tech., 1977; Warren K. Lewis prof. MIT, Cambridge, 1977-91, head dept. chem. engring., 1977-88; Pomeroy and Betty Smith prof. chem. engring., dean Sch. Engring. and Applied Sci. Princeton (N.J.) U., 1991—; vis. prof. Princeton, 1962-63, Calif. Inst. Tech., 1965; cons. Mobil Oil Corp.; cons. com. on motor vehicle emissions Nat. Acad. Sci., 1972-74, 79-80; mem. sci. adv. bd. EPA, 1976-79; mem. Presdl. Pvt. Sector Survey Task Force on Dept. Energy, 1982-83. Bd. editors Chem. Tech, 1971-80, Chem. Engring. Communications, 1972—; cons. editor chem. engring. series, McGraw-Hill, 1964—; editor-in-chief: Advances in Chemical Engineering, 1980; Contbr. papers, monographs to profl. lit., The Structure of Chemical Processing Industries, 1979. Recipient Am. Acad. Achievement Golden Plate award, 1966. Mem. AIChE (dir. 1970-72, Inst. lectr. 1968, Profl. Progress award 1970, Walker award 1980, Lewis award 1985, v.p. 1987, pres. 1988, Founders award 1990), Am. Chem. Soc. (award in petroleum chemistry 1966), Nat. Acad. Engring. (nominating com. 1981, 96, peer com. 1980-82, membership com. 1983-85, Draper award com. 1995-97), AAAS, Am. Acad. Arts and Scis., Academica Sinica of Taiwan, Sigma Xi. Home: 571 Lake Dr Princeton NJ 08540-5632 Office: Princeton U Engring Quadrangle Princeton NJ 08544-5263

WEIANT, WILLIAM MORROW, investment banking executive; b. Perth Amboy, N.J., Nov. 30, 1938; s. Monroe Alden and Lois May (Dayer) W.; m. Joan Claire Eberstadt, June 10, 1967; children: Clarissa Leigh, Pamela Anne. BA, Amherst Coll., 1960; MBA, NYU, 1964. Chartered fin. analyst. Ptnr. Blyth Eastman Dillon, N.Y.C., 1963-75; mng. dir. CS 1st Boston, N.Y.C., 1976-91, Dillon, Read & Co. Inc., N.Y.C., 1991-94, Morgan Stanley & Co., N.Y.C., 1994—. With USAF, 1960-61. Mem. Bank and Fin. Analysts (pres. 1976, 87). Avocations: tennis, golf, skiing, piano. Home: 46 Northover Pl Red Bank NJ 07701-6311

WEICHENTHAL, BURTON A., beef cattle specialist; b. Stanton, Nebr., Nov. 7, 1937; s. Arthur W. and Bertha M. (Topp) W.; m. Phyllis A. Bonner, June 12, 1960; 1 child, Susan. BS, U. Nebr., 1959; MS, S.D. State U., 1962; PhD, Colo. State U., 1967. Beef specialist U. Ill., Urbana, 1967-81; assoc. dir. U. Nebr. Panhandle Ctr., Scottsbluff, 1982-97, beef specialist, 1987—. Mem. Sugar Valley Singers (past pres., treas.), Lions (past pres.), Elks. Avocations: barbershop chorus singing. Office: U Nebr Panhandle Ctr 4502 Avenue I Scottsbluff NE 69361-4939

WEICHERT, DIETER HORST, seismologist, researcher; b. Breslau, Silesia, Germany, May 2, 1932; came to Can., 1954; s. Kurt Herman and Margarete Adelheid (Buresch) W.; m. Edith Struning (div. 1983), children: Thomas, Andreas. BASc, U. B.C., Vancouver, Can., 1961, PhD, 1965; MS, McMaster U., Hamilton, Ont., Can., 1963. Rsch. scientist earth physics br. Dominion Obs., Ottawa, Ont., 1965-78; rsch. scientist Pacific Geosci. Ctr., Sidney, B.C., 1978-81, head earthquake studies, 1981-88, assoc. dir., acting dir., 1988-90; head Pacific Geo. Sci. Ctr., Sidney, B.C., 1996-97; rsch. scientist Geol. Survey Can., Sidney, B.C., 1990-96, emeritus, 1997—; cons. U.K. Atomic Energy Authority, Blacknest, Eng., 1970; guest lectr. Fredericiana U., Karlsruhe, Germany, 1971; mem. Can. Earthquake Engring. Com., Ottawa, 1982—; supt. constrn. industry, Germany, 1951-57. Contbr. over 80 articles to profl. jours. Woodrow Wilson fellow, 1961; Inco fellow, 1962-64. Mem. Seismol. Soc. Am. Achievements include research on underground nuclear explosion detection and identification; seismic hazard and strong seismic ground motion. Office: Geol Survey Can, 9860 W Saanich Box 6000, North Saanich, BC Canada V8L 4B2

WEICHLER, NANCY KAREN, pediatric nurse; b. Pitts., Feb. 19, 1959; d. John James and Ruth Catherine (Miller) Janosko; m. Kevin William Weichler, June 4, 1983; children: Kara Lenore, Karleigh Josephine. BSN, Villanova U., 1981; MSN, U. Pitts., 1987. RN, Pa. Nurse's aide Negley House, 1978; nurse technician Shadyside, 1980; nurse's aide United Presbyn. Nursing Home, Wilkinsburg, Pa., 1979; surg./transplant staff nurse Children's Hosp. Pitts., 1981-87, clin. nurse facilitator, 1987-89, amb., 1988, renal clin. nurse specialist, 1989-95; pediatric ICU staff nurse, educator Brandon (Fla.) Hosp., Fla., 1995—; adj. faculty nursing care children grad. program U. Pitts., 1988-95; lectr. nursing Carlow Coll., Pitts., 1989-90; researcher and presenter in field. Contbr. articles to profl. and med. jours. March of Dimes scholar, 1977; Disting. Nursing Alumni award Villanova U., 1994. Mem. Am. Nephrology Nurses Assn., Soc. Pediatric Nephrology Nurses, Hosp. Asn. Pa. (Achievement award 1988), Villanova Sch. Nursing Alumni Assn. (recruiter 1987-89), Sigma Theta Tau. Roman Catholic. Avocations: reading, swimming, weight-lifting.

WEICKER, JACK EDWARD, educational administrator; b. Woodburn, Ind., June 23, 1924; s. Monald Henry and Helen Mae (Miller) W.; m. Janet Kathryn Thompson, May 29, 1946; children: John H., Kathryn Ann, Jane Elizabeth, Emily Jo. AB, Ind. U., 1947, MA, 1950. James Albert Woodburn fellow, All-Univ. fellow; tchr. history and English, Harrison Hill Sch., Ft. Wayne, Ind., 1947-48, South Side High Sch., Ft. Wayne, 1951-61; counselor, asst. prin. South Side High Sch., 1961-63, prin., 1963-90. Mem. Ind. State Scholarship Commn., 1969-77; mem. exec. com. Midwest regional assembly Coll. Entrance Exam. Bd., 1974-77, chmn. nominating com., 1976-77, mem. nat. nominating com., 1979; mem. Midwest Regional Coll. Access Svcs. Com., 1982-84. Chmn., Easter Seal Telethon, Allen County Soc. Crippled Children and Adults, 1982, 83. Recipient award for meritorious svc. Ball State U., 1980; Outstanding Prin. of Yr. award Ind. Secondary Sch. Adminstrs. Assn., 1981, Ind. Prin. Yr., Ind. Assn. Ednl. Secs., 1986, Disting. Service award Midwestern Regional Assembly of Coll. Entrance Examination Bd., 1987, Sagamore of the Wabash award Ind. Gov. Evan Bayh, 1989; Rotary Paul Harris fellow, 1985; South side High Sch. Prin. Emeritus,1996. Mem. Ft. Wayne Prins. Assn., Nat. Assn. Secondary Sch. Prins. (conf. speaker New Orleans 1985, 89), Ind. Secondary Sch. Adminstrs., PTA (life), Phi Beta Kappa, Phi Delta Kappa, Phi Alpha Theta. Mem. Christian Ch. (Disciples of Christ) (moderator of bd. trustees 1975-79). Clubs: Ft. Wayne Rotary (dir. 1973-76, 79-82, pres.-elect 1981-82, pres. 1982-83), Quest (dir. 1979-81, v.p. 1988-89, pres. 1989-90), Fortnightly (v.p. 1984-85, pres. 1985-86, 91-92). Author: (with others) Indiana: The Hoosier State, 1959, 63; (monographs) Due Process and Student Rights/Responsibilities: Two Points of View, 1975; Back to Basics: Language Arts, 1976; College Entrance Exams—Friend or Foe?, 1981; How the Effective Principal Communicates, 1983; Readin', Writin', and Other Stuff, 1984, The Last 25 Years in Education: One Educator's Perspective, 1988, The Power of Poetry: A Muse for All Seasons, 1988, American Political Humor: Mark Twain to Mark Russell, 1992. Home: 5200 N Washington Rd Fort Wayne IN 46804-1844

WEIDA, LEWIS DIXON, marketing analyst, consultant; b. Moran, Ind., Apr. 23, 1924; s. Charles Ray and Luella Mildred (Dixon) W.; student Kenyon Coll., 1943, Purdue U., 1946; B.S., Ind. U., 1948; M.S., Columbia U., 1950. Mgr. statis. analysis unit Gen. Motors Acceptance Corp., N.Y.C., 1949-55; asst. to exec. v.p. Am. Express Co., 1955-82. Served with USAAF, 1943-46; PTO. Mem. Internat. Platform Assn. Democrat. Club: Masons. Home: 25 Tudor City Pl New York NY 10017-6819

WEIDE, WILLIAM WOLFE, housing and recreational vehicles manufacturer; b. Toledo, Aug. 19, 1923; s. Samuel and Pearl Celia (Weide) W.; m. Beatrice Lieberman, June 4, 1950; children: Brian Samuel, Bruce Michael, Robert Benjamin. Student, U. Toledo, 1942, Marquette U., 1943-44; B.S., U. So. Calif., 1949. Asst. controller Eldon Mfg., 1950; mem. Calif. Franchise Tax Bd., 1951; controller Sutone Corp., 1951-53; contr., treas. Pacific Concessions Corp., 1953; treas. Descoware Corp., 1953-58; sr. v.p., dir. Fleetwood Enterprises, Inc., Riverside, Calif., 1958-73, pres., chief oper. officer, 1973-82, vice chmn., 1982—, dir.; treas. So. Eastern Manufactured Housing Inst., Atlanta., 1972-74; vice chmn. bd. dirs. Fleetwood Enterprises, Inc.. Mem. City of Riverside Housing Com.; mem. exec. com. of policy adv. bd. Joint Ctr. for Urban Studies, Harvard-MIT, Cambridge; trustee City of Hope Hosp., Duarte, Calif.; Orange County chmn. United Jewish Welfare Fund, 1982-83; mem. Pres.'s Circle of U. So. Calif.; pres. Orange County Jewish Community Found., 1986-88; chmn. Calif. Mfrs. Housing Inst. Polit Action Com., 1986-92; vice chmn., chmn. devel. Wellness Community of Orange County. With USNR, 1942-46. Recipient Jack E. Wells Meml. award for service to manufactured housing industry, 1976; named to Recreational Vehicle/Manufactured Housing Industry Hall of Fame Elkhart, Ind., 1981; named Man of Yr., City of Hope, 1986. Mem. Nat. Assn. Accts. (past v.p., dir. Los Angeles and Orange County chpt.), Manufactured Housing Inst. (chmn., founding com. Calif. chpt. 1986), Western Manufactured Housing Inst. (vice-chmn.), Trailer Coach Assn., NAM (public affairs com.), Riverside C. of C. Office: Fleetwood Enterprises Inc PO Box 7638 Riverside CA 92513-7638 *Love your family. Love your job. Give all you can for what you wish to achieve. Be a Jonathan Livingston Seagull.*

WEIDEMANN, CELIA JEAN, social scientist, international business and financial development consultant; b. Denver, Dec. 6, 1942; d. John Clement and Hazel (Van Tuyl) Kirlin; m. Wesley Clark Weidemann, July 1, 1972; 1 child, Stephanie Jean. BS, Iowa State U., 1964; MS, U. Wis.-Madison, 1970, PhD, 1973; postgrad. U. So. Calif., 1983. Advisor, UN Food & Agr. Orgn., Ibadan, Nigeria, 1973-77; ind. researcher, Asia and Near East, 1977-78; program coord., asst. prof., rsch. assoc. U. Wis., Madison, 1979-81; chief institutional and human resources U.S. Agy. for Internat. Devel., Washington, 1982-85, team leader, cons., Sumatra, Indonesia, 1984; dir. fed. econs. program Midwest Rsch. Inst., Washington, 1985-86; pres., CEO Weidemann Assocs., Arlington, Va., 1986—; cons. U.S. Congress, Aspen Inst., Ford Found., World Bank, Egypt, Nigeria, Gambia, Pakistan, Indonesia, AID, Thailand, Jamaica, Panama, Philippines, Sierra Leone, Kenya, Jordan, Poland, India, Egypt, Russia, Finnish Internat. Devel. Agy., Namibia, pvt. client, Estonia, Lativa, Russia, Japan, Internat. Ctr. Rsch. on Women, Zaire, UN Food and Agriculture Orgn., Ghana, Internat. Statis. Inst., The Netherlands, Global Exchange, 1986-87, Asian Devel. Bank, Mongolia, Nepal, Vietnam, Bangladesh, Indonesia, Philippines. Author: Planning Home Economics Curriculum for Social and Economic Development, Agricultural Extension for Women Farmers in Africa, 1990, Financial Services for Women, 1992, Egyptian Women and Microenterprise: The Invisible Entrepreneurs, 1992, Small Enterprise Development in Poland: Does Gender Matter?, 1994, Microenterprise and Gender in India, 1995; contbr. chpts. to books and articles to profl. jours.: Natl. Rsch. Counc., Natl. Acad. Scis. (peer reviewer), Am. Home Econs. Assn. fellow, 1969-73 (recipient research grant Ford Found. 1987-89). Mem. Soc. Internat. Devel., Am. Sociol. Assn., U.S. Dirs. of Internat. Agrl. Programs, Assn. for Women in Devel. (pres. 1989, founder, bd. dirs.), Internat. Devel. Conf. (bd. dirs., exec. com.), Am. Home Econs. Assn. (Wis. internat. chmn. 1980-81), Internat. Platform Assn., Pi Lambda Theta, Omicron Nu. Avocations: mountain trekking, piano/pipe organ, canoeing, photography, poetry. Home: 2607 24th St N Arlington VA 22207-4908

WEIDEMANN, JULIA CLARK, principal, educator; b. Batavia, N.Y., May 21, 1937; d. Edward Thomas and Grace Eloise (Kenna) Clark; m. Rudolph John Weidemann, July 9, 1960 (dec.); 1 child, Michael John (dec.). BA in English, Daemen Coll., 1958; MS in Edn., SUNY, Buffalo, 1961, MEd in Reading Edn., 1973, postgrad, 1985-86. Cert. sch. adminstr., supr. Tchr Buffalo Pub. Schs., 1958-61, 66-67; remedial reading tchr. West Seneca (N.Y.) Cen. Sch. Dist., 1972-79, coord. chpt. I reading program, 1974-79, reading coord., 1980-87; prin. Parkdale Elem. Sch. East Aurora (N.Y.) Union Free Sch., 1987—; adj. prof. edn. Canisius Coll., Medaille Coll.; tchr. cons. Scott Foresman Lang. Arts Textbooks; chmn. elem. com. staff devel. West Seneca Ctrl. Sch., 1985-87; mem. adv. coun. Medaille Coll.; chmn. various confs.; lectr. in field. Author numerous poems; invited poet Women's Impact Gallery, Buffalo, N.Y., 1996, 97. Mem. West Seneca Dist. Computer Adv. Com., 1980-87, East Aurora Hist. Soc., 1990—; mem. cmty. adv. coun. SUNY, Buffalo, 1994—, Women's Health Initiative, 1994—; mem. Women's Action Coalition of Buffalo, 1994; pres. Roycroft Wordsmiths; mem. steering com. Kids Voting N.Y., 1996—. Scholar Rosary Hill Coll., 1954, N.Y. State Regents, 1954; recipient Reading award Niagara Frontier Reading Coun., 1986. Mem. AAUW (life, pres. Buffalo br. 1994-95, exec. bd. dirs., named gift ednl. found., state bd. dirs. equity in edn. com. 1995—), Assn. Compensatory Edn. (pres. 1984-85, exec. bd. Region VI 1983-87, conf. chmn. Region VI 1985-87), Internat. Reading Assn. (acting chmn. 3d ea. regional reading conf. 1980), Niagara Frontier Reading Assn. (pres. 1979-80, fin. com. chmn., bd. dirs. 1973—), Daeman Coll. Alumni Assn. (bd. govs. 1987, chmn. alumni reunion weekend, chmn. sr. reception, Disting. Alumna 1989), Assn. Supervision and Devel., Assn. Tchr. Educators, Delta Kappa Gamma (pres., Ruth Fraser scholar 1986), Beta Zeta (pres.), Phi Delta Kappa (Buffalo-South chpt. 1989). Democrat. Roman Catholic. Home: 50 Boxwood Cir Hamburg NY 14075-4212 Office: Parkdale Elem Sch 80 Parkdale Ave East Aurora NY 14052-1615

WEIDEMEYER, CARLETON LLOYD, lawyer; b. Hebbville, Md., June 12, 1933. BA in Polit. Sci., U. Md., 1958; JD, Stetson U., 1961. Bar: Fla. 1961, D.C. 1971, U.S. Dist. Ct. (mid. dist.) Fla. 1963, U.S. Ct. Appeals (5th cir.) 1967, U.S. Ct. Appeals (D.C. cir.) 1976, U.S. Supreme Ct. 1966, U.S. Ct. Appeals (11th cir.) 1982. Research asst. Fla. 2d Dist Ct. Appeals, 1961-65; ptnr. Kalle and Weidemeyer, St. Petersburg, Fla., 1965-68; asst. pub. defender 6th Jud. Cir., Fla., 1966-69, 81-83; ptnr. Wightman, Weidemeyer, Jones, Turnbull and Cobb, Clearwater, Fla., 1968-82; pres. Carleton L. Weidemeyer, P.A. Law Office, 1982—; guest lectr., Stetson U., 1978-80; lectr. estate planning seminars; bd. dirs. 1st Nat. Bank and Trust Co., 1974-78, Fla. Bank of Commerce, 1973-77. Author: (handbook) Arbitration of

Entertainment Claims, Baltimore County's Second District, The Emerging Thirties, 1990, Area History, Baltimore County, 1990; editor: Ad Lib mag., 1978-81; contbr. numerous articles to profl. jours. & geneal. pubs.; performer This Is Your Navy Radio Show, Memphis, 1951-52; leader Polka Dots, The Jazz Notes, 1976—; mem. St. Paul Ch. Orch., Fla. Hist. Soc., 1973—, Md. Hist. Soc., 1990—, com. planned giving Upper Pinellas Assn. for Retarded Citizens, 1996—; performer Clearwater Jazz Holiday, 1980, 81, co-chmn., 1981. Bd. advisors Musicians Ins. Trust; trustee Francis G. Prasse Meml. Scholarship Trust, 1984—. Served with USN, 1951-54. Mem. SAR, Musicians Assn. Clearwater (pres. 1976-81), Fla.-Ga. Conf. Musicians (sec., treas. 1974-76), NRA, ABA (sr. bar sect.), Fed. Bar Assn., Fla. State Hist. Soc., Md. Hist. Soc., Greater St. Petersburg Musicians Assn., Clearwater Fla. Bar Assn. (probate divsn.), Am. Fedn. Musicians (internat. law com.; pres. so. conf. musicians 1979-80), Clearwater Genealogy Soc., Pinellas Genealogical Soc. (lectr. on genealogical rsch.), Md. Geneal. Soc., Pa. Geneal. Soc., Pinellas (Fla.) Geneal. Soc. (lectr. 1995—), Balt. County Geneal. Soc., Lancaster (Pa.) Mennonite Hist. Soc., Navy Hurricane Hunters, Sons Union Vets. Civil War, Md. Hist. Soc., Catonsville (Md.) Hist. Soc., Am. Legion, German Am. Geneal. Assn. D.A.V. Fleet Res., Masons, Egypt Temple Shrine, Scottish Rite, Moose, Sertoma (bd. dirs. Clearwater chpt. 1984-86, v.p. 1989-92), Phi Delta Phi, Sigma Pi, Kappa Kappa Psi. Home: 2261 Belleair Rd Clearwater FL 34624-2761 Office: 501 S Fort Harrison Ave Clearwater FL 33756

WEIDENAAR, DENNIS JAY, college dean; b. Grand Rapids, Mich., Oct. 4, 1936; s. John and Jennie (Beukema) W.; m. Kristin Andrews, July 14, 1943; children: Kaarin Jaye, John Andrews. AB, Calvin Coll., Grand Rapids, 1958; MA, U. Chgo., 1961; PhD, Purdue U., W. Lafayette, 1969. Asst. prof. of econs.. Purdue U., West Lafayette, 1966-72, assoc. prof. of econ., 1972-77, prof. of econ., 1977—; interim dean Krannert Sch. of Mgmt., West Lafayette, 1983-84, assoc. dean, 1984—; dean Krannert Grad. Sch. Mgmt., West Lafayette, Ind., 1990—; cons. TRW, B.F. Goodrich, Ea. Panhandle. Author: Economics. Contbr. articles to profl. jours. Bd. dirs. Ind. Coun. on Econ. Edn., Lafayette, 1974-83, St. Elizabeth Hosp., Lafayette, Lafayette Ins. Co. Recipient The Leavey Awd for Excellence in Pvt. Enterprise Edn., Freedom's Found., Valley Forge, 1983, Distinguished Service Awd., Joint Council on Econ. Edn., N.Y., 1986, Golden Key Nat. Honor Soc., 1985. Mem. Rotary, Delta Sigma Pi, Beta Gamma Sigma (bd. dirs. 1996—), Phi Delta Kappa (vice chmn. bd. dirs. Washington campus). Presbyterian. Home: 3703 Moss Hill Dr West Lafayette IN 47906-8885 Office: Purdue U Krannert Sch Mgmt West Lafayette IN 47907

WEIDENBAUM, MURRAY LEW, economics educator; b. Bronx, N.Y., Feb. 10, 1927; s. David and Rose (Warshaw) W.; m. Phyllis Green, June 13, 1954; children: Susan, James, Laurie. BBA, CCNY, 1948; MA, Columbia U., 1949; MPA, Princeton U., 1954, PhD, 1958; LLD, Baruch Coll., 1981, U. Evansville, 1983, McKendree Coll., 1993. chmn. rsch. adv. com. St. Louis Regional Indsl. Devel. Corp., 1965-69; exec. sec. Pres.'s Com. on Econ. Impact of Def. and Disarmament, 1964; mem. U.S. Fin. Investment Adv. Panel, 1970-72; cons. various firms and instns. Fiscal economist Bur. Budget, Washington, 1949-57; corp. economist Boeing Co., Seattle, 1958-62; sr. economist Stanford Rsch. Inst., Palo Alto, Calif., 1962-63; mem. faculty Washington U., St. Louis, 1964—, prof., chmn. dept. econs., 1966-69, Mallinckrodt prof., 1971—; dir. Ctr. for Study Am. Bus. Ctr. for Study Am. Bus., St. Louis, 1974-81, 82-95; chmn. Ctr. for Study Am. Bus. Washgnton U., St. Louis, 1995—; asst. sec. econ. policy Treasury Dept., 1969-71; chmn. Coun. of Econ. Advs., 1981-82. Author: Federal Budgeting, 1964, Modern Public Sector, 1969, Economics of Peacetime Defense, 1974, Economic Impact of the Vietnam War, 1967, Government-Mandated Price Increases, 1975, Business, Government, and the Public, 1990, The Future of Business Regulation, 1980, Rendezvous With Reality: The American Economy After Reagan, 1988, paperback edit., 1990, Small Wars, Big Defense, 1992, Business and Government in the Global Marketplace, 1995, The Bamboo Network, 1996; mem. editl. bd. Publius, 1971—, Jour. Econ. Issues, 1972-75, Challenge, 1974-81, 83—. With AUS, 1945. Recipient Alexander Hamilton medal U.S. Dept. Treasury, 1971, Disting. Writer award Georgetown U., award for disting. teaching Freedoms Found., 1980, award for best book in econs. Assn. Am. Pubs., 1992; named to Free Market Hall of Fame, 1983; Banbury fellow Princeton U., 1954. Fellow AIAA, Nat. Assn. Bus. Economists, City Coll. Alumni Assn. (Townsend Harris medal 1969), Assn. for Pvt. Enterprise Edn. (Adam Smith award 1986), Cosmos Club. Office: Washington Univ Ctr for Study Am Bus 1 Brookings Dr Saint Louis MO 63130-4862

WEIDENFELD, EDWARD LEE, lawyer; b. Akron, Ohio, July 15, 1943; s. Sam and Beatrice (Cooper) W.; m. Sheila Rabb, Aug. 11, 1968; children: Nicholas, Daniel. BS, U. Wis., 1965; JD, Columbia U., 1968. Bar: N.Y. 1968, U.S. Supreme Ct. 1972, D.C. 1973. Pvt. practice N.Y.C., 1969-71, 73-82, Washington, 1982—; counsel, dir. energy staff Com. on Interior and Insular Affairs, U.S. Ho. of Reps., 1971-73; mem. faculty Am. Law Inst.-Am. Bar Assn. Continuing Legal Edn. Programs; mem. Internat. del. to observe Philippine Election, 1986, internat. del. to observe Republic Korea Election, 1987, Pakistan Election, 1988, Chilean Election, 1989; lectr. to profl. groups; spl. cons. N.Y.C. Dept. Bldgs., 1967. Editor in chief Atomic Energy Law Jour., 1975-76. Mem. Pres.'s Commn. on White House Fellowships, 1977; nat. chmn. Lawyers for Reagan/Bush, 1980; chief dep. counsel Reagan/Bush Campaign, 1980; chmn. Reagan/Bush '84 Legal Adv. Bd., 1984; mem. D.C. Rep. Com., 1984-92, vice chmn., 1984-88; mem. Coun. Adminstrv. Conf. of U.S., 1981-92, sr. fellow, 1992-95; trustee Danny Kaye and Sylvia Fine Kaye Found. Mem. ABA, D.C. Bar Assn., Am. Law Inst., Assn. Bar City N.Y., D.C. Estate Planning Coun., Nat. Network Estate Planning Lawyers. Club: Met. (Washington). Office: 1899 L St NW Ste 500 Washington DC 20036-3814

WEIDENFELD, SHEILA RABB, television producer, author; b. Cambridge, Mass., Sept. 7, 1943; d. Maxwell M. and Ruth (Cryden) Rabb; BA, Brandeis U., 1965; m. Edward L. Weidenfeld, Aug. 11, 1968; children: Nicholas Rabb, Daniel Rabb. Assoc. producer Metromedia, Inc., WNEW-TV, N.Y.C., 1965-68; talent coord. That Show with Joan Rivers, NBC, N.Y.C., 1968-71; coord. NBC network game programs, N.Y.C., 1968-71; producer Metromedia, Inc., WTTG-TV, Washington, 1971-73; creator/producer Take It From Here, NBC (WRC-TV), Washington, 1973-74; press sec. to first lady Betty Ford and spl. asst. to Pres. Gerald R. Ford 1974-77; mem. Pres.'s Adv. Commn. on Historic Preservation, 1977-81; TV producer, moderator On the Record, NBC-TV, WRC-TV, Washington, 1978-79; pres. D.C. Prodns., Ltd., 1978; producer, host Your Personal Decorator, 1987; mem. Sec. State's Adv. Commn. on Fgn. Service Inst., 1972-74; founding mem. Project Censured Panel of Judges, 1976—. Author: First Lady's Lady, 1979. Mem. U.S. Holocaust Meml. Council, 1987—; corporator, Dana Hall Sch., Wellesley, Mass; bd. dirs. Wolf Trap Found., Women's Campaign Fund, 1978-79; bd. dirs. D.C. Contemporary Dance Theatre, 1986-88, D.C. Rep. Cen. Com., 1984—, D.C. Preservation League, 1987-90; chmn. C&O Canal Nat. Hist. Park Commn, 1988—; bd. dirs. Am. Univ. Rome, 1988—. Recipient awards for outstanding achievement in the media AAUW, 1973, 74, Silver Screen award A Campaign to Remember for the U.S. Holocaust Meml. Coun., 1989, Bronze medal Internat. Film and Video Festival N.Y., 1990; named hon. consul gen. of Republic of San Marino to Washington; knighted by Order of St. Agatha, Republic of San Marino, 1986. Mem. NATAS (Emmy award 1972), Washington Press Club, Am. Newspaper Women's Club, Am. Women in Radio and TV, Cosmos Club, Consular Corps, Sigma Delta Chi. Home and Office: 3059 Q St NW Washington DC 20007-3081

WEIDENFELLER, GERALDINE CARNEY, speech and language pathologist; b. Kearny, N.J., Oct. 12, 1933; d. Joseph Gerald and Catherine Grace (Doyle) Carney; BS, Newark State U., 1954; postgrad. Northwestern U., summer 1956, U. Wis., summer 1960; MA, NYU, 1962; m. James Weidenfeller, Apr. 4, 1964; children: Anne, David. Lic speech/language pathologist, N.J. Speech pathologist Kearny (N.J.) Public Schs., 1954-61, North Brunswick (N.J.) Public Schs., 1961-65, Bridgewater (N.J.) Public Schs., 1969-72; speech therapist Somerset County Ednl. Commn., 1983-88; real estate agt., N.J., 1982-89; pvt. practice speech therapy, Somerville, N.J., 1980-92; speech therapist no. br. Midland Sch., 1989, No. Plainfield, N.J., 1989-90. V.p. Rosary Soc., Hillsborough, N.J., 1986—; Rep. county com. woman, 1989-96, chmn. scholarship com.; chmn. fedn. of Rep. women program com., Somerset, program chmn., scholarship chmn. 1991—; dancer Hillsborough Rockettes, 1994—; tudor Literacy Vol. of Am., 1993-96; storyteller Cath. Charities, 1992-93. Mem. Am. Speech and Hearing Assn., N.J. Speech and Hearing Assn. Roman Catholic. Club: Toastmasters (winner dist. humorous speech contest 1984, sec. 1985, advanced Toastmaster 1986). Home: 3 Banor Dr Somerville NJ 08876-4501

WEIDENTHAL, MAURICE DAVID (BUD WEIDENTHAL), educational administrator, journalist; b. Cleve., Nov. 26, 1925; s. William and Evelyn (Kolinsky) W.; m. Grace Schwartz, Apr. 14, 1957; 1 child, Susan Elizabeth Weidenthal Saltzman. B.A., U. Mich., 1950. Mem. staff Cleve. Press, 1950-81, editorial writer, 1950-51, asst. city editor, 1956-58, edn. editor, 1958-81; v.p. public affairs Cuyahoga Community Coll. Dist., Cleve., 1981-88; dir. Urban Colls. Project RC-2000, Tempe, Ariz., 1989—. Editor The Urban Report, Cleve., 1989—. Mem. pub. affairs com. Greater Cleve. Growth Assn., 1981-88; mem. bd. advisors Coun. for Advancement and Support of Edn., 1981-88, Nat. Coun. Mktg. and Pub. Rels., 1981-84; alt. bd. dirs. St. Vincent Quadrangle, 1983-88; trustee Hebrew Free Loan Assn., 1975-86; mem. philanthropic adv. com. Jewish Community Fedn. Served with AUS, 1944-45. Decorated Air medal. Mem. Edn. Writers Assn., Soc. Profl. Journalists, (bd. dirs.), Edn. Press Assn., Cleve. City Club (bd. dirs. 1969-76), Cleve. Press Club. Home: 25858 Fairmount Blvd Cleveland OH 44122-2214 Office: 4250 Richmond Rd Cleveland OH 44122-6104

WEIDLINGER, PAUL, civil engineer; b. Budapest, Hungary, Dec. 22, 1914; came to U.S., 1944; s. Andrew and Juliete W.; m. Solveig Hojberg, Dec. 24, 1964; children—Thomas, Pauline, Jonathan. B.S., Tech. Inst., Brno, Czechoslovakia, 1934; M.S., Swiss Poly. Inst., Zurich, 1937. Registered profl. engr. 17 states. Chief engr. Atlas Aircraft Products, N.Y.C., 1944-46; chief tech. cons., dir. Nat. Housing Agy., Industrialization Program Div., Washington, 1946-47; dir. engring. div. United Indsl. Assocs., Washington, 1947-48; sr. ptnr. Weidlinger Assocs., cons. engrs., N.Y.C., 1948—; mem. seismic loads com. Am. Nat. Standards Inst., 1978-80; chmn. Nat. Acad. Scis. Evaluation Panel, Nat. Bur. Standards, 1978-80; mem. sci. adv. bd. to chief staff USAF, 1957-58; vis. lectr. Harvard U., 1955-64, MIT, 1952-64. Author: Aluminum in Modern Architecture, Vol. II, 1956; contbr. papers to profl. jours. Recipient award Engring. News-Record, 1966. Fellow ASCE (Ernest E. Howard award, Moisseiff award 1975, J. James R. Cross medal 1963), Franklin Inst. (Frank P. Brown medal 1987); mem. AIAA, Am. Concrete Inst., Nat. Acad. Engring., Earthquake Engring. Rsch. Inst., Internat. Assn. Bridge and Structural Engrs., N.Y. Acad. Scis., Nat. Bldg. Mus. (bd. dirs. 1982-88). Office: Weidlinger Assocs 375 Hudson St New York NY 10014-3658*

WEIDMAN, HAZEL HITSON, anthropologist, educator; b. Taft, Calif., Aug. 3, 1923; d. Frederick Dhu and Estell M. (Griesemer) Hitson; m. William H. Weidman, Sept. 9, 1960; children: William, Charles. B.S. in Social Anthropology, Northwestern U., 1951; A.M. (Thomas Dana Scholar in Social Anthropology), Radcliffe Coll., 1957; USPHS fellow, Burma, 1957-59; PhD, Radcliffe Coll., 1959. Staff anthropologist Mass. Dept. of Pub. Health, Boston, 1959-60; cons. social sci. USPHS, Washington, 1960, Calif. Dept. Pub. Health, 1964; asst. prof. sociology and anthropology Coll. of William and Mary, Williamsburg, Va., 1964-65; asst. prof. social anthropology dept. psychiatry U. Ala. Med. Center, Birmingham, 1965-67; asso. research fellow Social Sci. Research Inst., U. Hawaii, Honolulu, 1967-68; assoc. prof. social anthropology dept. psychiatry U. Miami Sch. Medicine, Miami, 1968-72; prof. U. Miami Sch. Medicine, 1972-89, prof. emerita, 1989—, staff anthropologist and sr. social scientist, 1979-81, dir. Office Transcultural Edn. and Research, 1981-89, ret., 1990; assoc. prof. dept. anthropology U. Miami, Coral Gables, 1968-72, prof., 1972-77; Cons. social sci. U. Ala. Hosps. and Clinics, Birmingham, 1965-67; cons. social anthropology Nat. Center for Health Services Research and Devel., 1970-71; social sci. cons. Am. Found. Blind, 1973-76; cons. to Miccosukee Indian tribe and sec. higher edn. exec. com. Miccosukee Corp., 1978-82; mental health research edn. rev. com. NIMH, 1980-84; mem. vis. com. So. Assn. Colls. and Schs., 1980; mem. med. adv. bd. Ednl. Film Prodn., Riverside, Calif., 1969-72; dir. programs in cross-cultural tng. health profls., 1981-89. Founding editor: Med. Anthropology Newsletter, 1968-71; Contbr. articles and book revs. on social anthropology to profl. jours.; contbr. book chpts. on social anthropology. Mem. nat. adv. com. for cross-cultural demonstration project, Epilepsy Found. Am., 1985-89; mem. nat. adv. council Transcultural Nursing Rsch. Inst. U. Miami, 1986-89. Am. Philos. Soc. research grantee, 1965; Commonwealth Fund research grantee, 1971-73; Continuation grantee, 1973-75; State of Fla. Community Hosp. Edn. Council research and tng. grantee, 1979-81. Fellow Soc. Applied Anthropology, Am. Anthrop. Assn. (chmn. steering com. group for med. anthropology 1967-69, mem. com. on membership 1968-70, chmn. organizing com. group for med. anthropology 1969-70); mem. So. Anthrop. Soc., Assn. for Behavioral Scis. and Med. Edn., Soc. for Med. Anthropology, Council on Anthropology and Edn., Soc. Anthropology of Visual Communication, Soc. Psychol. Anthropology (mem. bd. dirs. 1979-81), Assn. Anthropology and Gerontology, World Fedn. Mental Health, World Future Soc., Phi Beta Kappa. Home: 58 Park St Camden ME 04843-2012

WEIDMAN, JEROME, author; b. N.Y.C., Apr. 4, 1913; s. Joseph and Annie (Falkovitz) W.; m. Peggy Wright, 1943; children: Jeffrey, John Whitney. Ed., CCNY, 1930-33, Washington Sq. Coll., N.Y.C., 1933-34, N.Y.U. Law Sch., 1934-37. Author: (novel) I Can Get It for You Wholesale, 1937, (novel) What's in It for Me?, 1938; (short stories) The Horse that Could Whistle Dixie, 1939; (travel) Letter of Credit, 1940; (novel) I'll Never Go There Any More, 1941, (novel) The Lights Around the Shore, 1943, (novel) Too Early To Tell, 1946; (short stories) The Captain's Tiger, 1947; (novel) The Price is Right, 1949, (novel) The Hand of the Hunter, 1951, (novel) The Third Angel, 1953; (essays) Traveler's Cheque, 1954; (novel) Give Me Your Love, 1954, (novel) Your Daughter, Iris, 1955; (short stories) A Dime A Throw, 1957; (novel) The Enemy Camp, 1958; (play) Fiorello!, 1959; (novel) Before You Go, 1960; (play) Tenderloin, 1961; (short stories) My Father Sits In The Dark, 1961; (novel) The Sound of Bow Bells, 1962; (play) I Can Get It For You Wholesale, 1962; (essays) Back Talk, 1963; (short stories) Nine Stories, 1964; (novel) Word Of Mouth, 1964; (short stories) The Death of Dickie Draper, 1965; (novel) Other People's Money, 1968; (novel) The Center of The Action, 1969; (play) Ivory Tower, 1969, (play) Asterisk, 1969; (novel) Fourth Street East, 1971, (novel) Last Respects, 1972, (novel) Tiffany Street, 1974, (novel) The Temple, 1976, (novel) A Family Fortune, 1978; (novel) Counsellors-at-Law, 1980, (autobiography) Praying For Rain, 1986. Co-recipient Pulitizer prize in drama for play Fiorello!, 1960; recipient Antoinette Perry award, N.Y. Drama Critics Circle award. Mem. Authors League Am. (pres. 1969-74). Home: 1230 Park Ave New York NY 10128-1724

WEIDMAN, JOHN CARL, II, education educator, consultant; b. Ephrata, Pa., Oct. 3, 1945; s. John Carl and Mary Elizabeth (Grube) W.; m. Carla Sue Fassnacht, Aug. 20, 1967; children: Jonathan Scott, Rebecca Mary. AB in Sociology cum laude, Princeton U., 1967; AM, U. Chgo., 1968, PhD, 1974. Acting asst. prof. edn. U. Minn., Mpls., 1970-74, asst. prof. edn., sociology and Am. studies, 1974-77; sr. rsch. assoc. Bur. Social Sci. Rsch., Inc., Washington, 1977-78; assoc. prof. edn. and sociology U. Pitts., 1979-86, prof. edn. and sociology, 1986—, chmn. dept. adminstrv. and policy studies, 1986-93; cons. Nat. Ctr. Adminstrv. Justice, Youthwork, Inc., Upper Midwest Tri-Racial Gen. Assistance Ctr., Acad. for Ednl. Devel., Mongolia, Asian Devel. Bank, Laos; UNESCO chair higher edn. rsch. Maseno U. Coll., Kenya, 1993. Author: rsch. monographs; mem. editl. bd. Rev. of Higher Edn., 1984-88, Am. Ednl. Rsch. Jour., 1991-92, 96—; cons. editor Jour. Higher Edn., 1989—; contbr. chpts. to books, articles to profl. jours. Bd. dirs. Sch. Vol. Assn. Pitts., 1982-90, pres., 1984-87. Grantee, U.S. Office Edn., 1971-73, Spencer Found., 1973-76, Nat. Inst. Edn., 1976-79, NEH, 1985-86; Fulbright scholar U. Augsburg, Germany, 1986-87. Mem. Am. Ednl. Rsch. Assn. (sec. postsecondary divsn. 1987-89), Am. Sociol. Assn., Assn. Study of Higher Edn., Comparative and Internat. Edn. Soc. Office: U Pitts 5S01 Forbes Quadrangle 230 S Bouquet St Pittsburgh PA 15213-4015

WEIDNER, DONALD J., geophysicist educator; b. Dayton, Ohio, Apr. 26, 1945; s. Virgil Raymond and Aletha Winifred Weidner; m. Deborah Mary Ray, April 13, 1968; children: Raymond V., Jennifer L. AB in Physics cum laude, Harvard, 1967; PhD in Geophysics, Mass. Inst. Tech., 1972. Asst prof. SUNY, Stony Brook, N.Y., 1972-77, assoc. prof., 1977-82, prof. geophysics, 1982—; dir. Mineral Physics Inst., SUNY, 1988—, Ctr. for High Pressure Rsch, SUNY, 1991—. Am. Geophysical Union fellow, 1981; recipient James B. Macelwane award Am. Geophysical Union, 1981. Achievements include building (with others) the high pressure facility at Stony Brook SUNY; large volume high pressure studies with synchrotron radiation; determining the equation of state of earth materials; phase stability fields of minerals and has pioneered the use of this system to determine the yield strength of these materials; design team leader for the large volume experiments that the GeoCars program is preparing for the Advanced Photon Source. Office: SUNY Sci & Tech Ctr High Pressure Rsch Dept Earth & Space Scis Stony Brook NY 11794

WEIDNER, EDWARD WILLIAM, university chancellor, political scientist; b. Mpls., July 7, 1921; s. Peter Clifford and Lillian (Halbe) W.; m. Jean Elizabeth Blomquist, Mar. 23, 1944; children: Nancy Louise, Gary Richard, Karen, William. BA magna cum laude, U. Minn., 1942, MA, 1943, PhD, 1946; postgrad., U. Wis., 1943-45; LHD (hon.), No. Mich. U., 1969; PhD (hon.), Linköping U., Sweden, 1975. Staff mem. Nat. Mcpl. League, 1944, research assoc., 1944-45; cons. govts. div. U.S. Bur. Census, 1945; statistician U.S. Bur. Census, Washington, 1946; lectr. U. Wis., Madison, 1945; instr. U. Minn., Mpls., 1945-47, asst. prof., 1947-49, asst. dir. research in inter-govtl. relations, 1946-53; asst. prof. UCLA, 1949-50; faculty Mich. State U., East Lansing, 1950-62, from assoc. prof., dir. govtl. research bur., to prof. polit. sci., 1952-62, chmn. polit. sci. dept., 1952-57; coordinator, chief adviser Vietnam Project, 1955-57; dir. Inst. Research on Overseas Programs, 1957-61; vice chancellor E.W. Ctr., 1962-65; prof. polit. sci., dir. ctr. for devel. change U. Ky., Lexington, 1965-67; chancellor U. Wis., Green Bay, 1966-86, prof. polit. sci., 1966-89, chancellor emeritus, prof. emeritus, 1989—, dir. Cofrin Arboretum, 1986-89; project dir. Edward W. Weidner Ctr. for Performing Arts, U. Wis., Green Gay, 1987-92; bd. dirs. Univ. Bank, Green Bay; cons. Fgn. Ops. Adminstrn., Vietnam, 1954-55, Baltimore County (Md.) Reorgn. Commn., 1953-54, Ford Found., Pakistan, 1956, Nat. Assn. Fgn. Student Advisers, 1959-60, Pres.'s Task Force Fgn. Econ. Assistance, 1961, Dept. State, 1962-63, AID, 1964-65, Lees Coll., 1971-72, Mcpl. Clks. Edn. Found., 1992—; mem. Gov. Mich. Commn. Inter-Govtl. Rels., 1954-55, UN Univ. Coun., 1974-80. Author: (with William Anderson) American Government, 1951, State and Local Government, 1951, (with others) The International Programs of American Universities, 1958, Intergovernmental Relations as Seen by Public Officials, 1960, (with William Anderson, Clara Penniman) Government for the Fifty States, 1960, The World Role of Universities, 1962, Technical Assistance in Public Administration Overseas, 1964; editor: Development Administration in Asia, 1970. Mem. Wis. Gov.'s Commn. on UN, 1975-81; trustee Prairie Sch., 1969-91, mem. adv. bd., 1991—; bd. dirs. Inst. for Shipboard Edn., 1976-89, Lab. Ornithology, Cornell U., 1992—; chmn. adv. bd. Lakeland chpt. ARC, 1981-84; mem. N.Am. adv. group UN Environ. Programme, 1983-90; bd. advisers Nature Conservancy Wis., 1984-91; bd. dirs. Heritage Hill Found., 1987-92, 95—, pres. 1991-92; bd. dirs. Assn. Am. Colls., 1978-80, Family Svc. Assn., 1988-93; chmn. Brown County Cultural Coun., 1991-94; mem. nat. coun. ASPA, 1947-50; mem. internat. coun. UN U., 1974-80; bd. dirs. Am. Coun. on Edn., 1971-74, sec. bd., 1971-72; mem. nat. coun. Am. Polit. Assn., 1950-52. Recipient Outstanding Achievement award U. Minn., 1975. Mem. Internat. Assn. Mcpl. Clks. Found., Nature Conservancy, Audubon Soc., Am. Birding Assn., Phi Beta Kappa, Pi Sigma Alpha. Home: 5953 N Shore Acres New Franken WI 54229-9443

WEIDNER, RICHARD TILGHMAN, physicist, educator; b. Allentown, Pa., Mar. 31, 1921; s. Miles Percival and Mabel (Aichroth) W.; m. Jean Elizabeth Fritsch, June 28, 1947 (dec. 1995); children: Christopher, Allegra, Timothy. B.S. summa cum laude, Muhlenberg Coll., 1943; M.S., Yale U., 1943, Ph.D., 1948. Instr. physics Yale U., 1943-44; instr. Rutgers U., 1947-48, asst. prof., 1948-53, assoc. prof., 1953-63, prof. physics, 1963-88, prof. emeritus, 1988—; asst. dean Rutgers Coll., 1966-69, assoc. dean, 1969-77, acting dean, 1977-78; physicist U.S. Naval Research Lab., Washington, 1944-46. Author: (with R.L. Sells) Elementary Modern Physics, 3rd edit., 1980, Elementary Classical Physics, 2d edit., 1973, Elementary Physics, Classical and Modern, 1975, (with H.Y. Carr) Physics from the Ground Up, 1971, Physics, 1985, rev. edit., 1988 (transls. in German, Spanish, Vietnamese); also articles in field; contbr. Physics sect. Ency. Britannica, 15th edit., 1974; assoc. editor Jour. Internat. Trumpet Guild, 1984-96. Mem. Bd. Edn. Bridgewater Twp., N.J., 1957-63. Lt. (j.g.) USNR, 1944-45. Recipient Alumni Achievement award Muhlenberg Coll., 1994; Lindback award Rutgers U., 1984. Fellow Am. Phys. Soc.; mem. Internat. Trumpet Guild, Sigma Xi. Lutheran. Home: 1426 Calypso Ave Bethlehem PA 18018-4740

WEIDNER, ROSWELL THEODORE, artist; b. Reading, Pa., Sept. 18, 1911; s. Harry and Amelia (Hughes) W.; m. Marilyn Kemp, Dec. 1, 1957; children: Roslyn, Janice. Student, Pa. Acad. Fine Arts, 1930-36, Barnes Found., 1933-35. Works Progress Admnstrn. (WPA) Art Project, 1936-38; sr. instr. Pa. Acad. Fine Arts, 1938-96, Dawson Metal, 1965, 72. One-man shows include Pa. Acad. Fine Arts, 1940, 60, 65, Reading Mus., 1961, William Penn Meml. Mus., Harrisburg, Pa., 1966, McCleaf Gallery, Phila., 1970, Newman Galleries, Phila., 1978, 87, Marion Locks Gallery, 1981, So. Alleghenies Mus. Art, Loretto, Pa., 1991, F.A.N. Gallery, Phila., 1995; represented in permanent collections Pa. Acad. Fine Arts, Phila. Mus. Art, Met. Mus. Art, Libr. Congress, U. Pa., Conn. State Libr., Hahnemann Hosp., Phila., Temple U., Phila. Maritime Mus., Free Libr. Phila., Smith Kline, Berwin Corp., Price Waterhouse, Nat. Assn. Broadcasters, Washington, Bell Atlantic Corp., Phila., Dauphin Deposit Bank and Trust Co., Harrisburg, Phila. Conv. Ctr.; work represented by Art Communication Internat., Phila.; contbr. articles to profl. jours. Cresson Fgn. Travelling scholar, 1935-36; recipient Percy Owens award, 1975; recipient Dean's award for Disting. Svc. to Sch. of Pa. Acad. of Fine Arts, 1996. Fellow Pa. Acad. Fine Arts (pres. 1955-70).

WEIERSTALL, RICHARD PAUL, pharmaceutical chemist; b. Jersey City, N.J., Nov. 5, 1942; s. William August and Emily Lois (Haughey) W.; m. Gail Janet Thomsen, Aug. 17, 1968; children: Eric, Kurt, Karen. BS, Rutgers U., 1966, MS, 1969; PhD, U. Calif., San Francisco, 1973. Unit head drug metabolism Sandoz Pharm., East Hanover, N.J., 1973-74; dir. tech. svc. Banner Gelatin Products, Chatsworth, Calif., 1974-76; v.p. tech. svc. Banner Gelatin Prod., Chatsworth, Calif., 1976-81; dir. pharm. sci. Ayerst Labs Inc., Rouses Point, N.Y., 1981-87; asst. v.p. Wyeth Ayerst Rsch., Rouses Point, 1987—. Mem. Am. Assn. Pharm. Sci., Am. Pharm. Assn. Home: 7 Stewart St Rouses Point NY 12979-1511

WEIFBECKER, ROBERT T., healthcare administrator. BS in Nuclear Medicine Tech., U. Wis., LaCrosse, 1988; MBA, U. Minn., 1992, M in Hosp. and Health Care Adminstrn., 1992. Sr. nuclear medicine technologist St. Joseph's Hosp., Milw., 1988-90; adminstrv. resident HealthEast-St. Joseph's Hosp., St. Paul, summer 1991; adminstrv. fellow North Meml. Med. Ctr., Mpls., 1992-93; program coord. Ctr. for Women and Infant St. Joseph's Hosp.-Covenant Healthcare Inc., Milw., 1994—. Mem. Southeastern chpt. healthcare adv. bd. March of Dimes; mem. planning com. WAPC Shorten Length of Stay Seminar, 1995; mem. Jacob's Inst. Mem. AHA, Soc. for Healthcare Planning and Mktg., MHA (treas. class of 1992), Nat. Assn. Women Health Profls., Wis. Soc. Healthcare Mktg. and Planning, Wis. Assn. Perinatal Care. Office: St Joseph's Hosp 5000 W Chambers St Milwaukee WI 53210-1650

WEIGAND, WILLIAM KEITH, bishop; b. Bend, Oreg., May 23, 1937. Ed., Mt. Angel Sem., St. Benedict, Oreg., St. Edward's Sem. and St. Thomas Sem., Kenmore, Wash. Bishop Diocese Salt Lake City, 1980-93, Diocese Sacramento, 1993—; Ordained priest Roman Cath. Ch., 1963. Office: See of Sacramento 2110 Broadway Sacramento CA 95818-2518*

WEIGEL, JOHN J., lawyer; b. New Orleans, Feb. 4, 1932; s. George Edward and Marian Rose (Martin) W.; m. Barbara Ann Laporte, July 9, 1955; children: Leslie Ann, John J. Jr., Lynn Ann, Guy Edward. LLB, Tulane U., 1956. Bar: La. 1956, U.S. Dist. Ct. (ea., mid., we. dists.) La. 1959, U.S. Ct. Appeals (5th cir.) 1959, U.S. Supreme Ct. Law clk. La. Supreme Ct., New Orleans, 1958-59; from assoc. to sr. ptnr. Jones, Walker, Waechter, Poitevent, Carrere & Denegre, New Orleans, 1959—. Pers. bd. Jefferson Parish, La., 1974-83; bd. dirs. La. Civil Svc. League, New Orleans, 1975—. Fellow Am. Coll. Trial Lawyers; mem. ABA, Am. Bd. Trial Advocates, La. Bar Assn., New Orleans Bar Assn., Internat. Assn. Def. Counsel.

Office: Jones Walker Waechter Poitevent Carrere & Denegre 201 Saint Charles Ave New Orleans LA 70170-1000

WEIGEL, PAUL HENRY, biochemistry educator, researcher, consultant; b. N.Y.C., Aug. 11, 1946; s. Helmut and Jeanne (Wakeman) W.; m. Nancy Shulman, June 15, 1968 (div. Dec. 1987); 1 child, Dana J.; m. Janet Oka, May 17, 1992. BA in Chemistry, Cornell U., 1968; MS in Biochemistry, Johns Hopkins U., Balt., 1969, PhD in Biochemistry, 1975. NIH postdoctoral fellow Johns Hopkins U., Balt., 1975-78; asst. prof. U. Tex. Med. Br., Galveston, Tex., 1978-82, assoc. prof., 1982-87; prof. biochemistry and cell biology U. Tex. Med. Br., Galveston, 1987-94, vice chmn. dept. human biol. chemistry and genetics, 1990-93, acting chmn. dept. human biology, chemistry and genetics, 1992-93; prof., chmn. dept. biochemistry and molecular biology U. Okla. Health Scis. Ctr., Okalahoma City, 1994—; em. NIH Pathobiochemistry Study Sect., Washington, 1985-87; cons. Teltech, Mpls., 1985—. ontbr. articles to profl. jours.; patentee in field. reas. Bayou Chateau Neighborhood Assn., Dickinson, Tex., 1981-83, v.p., 1983-84, pres., 1984-86. With U.S. Army, 1969-71. rantee NIH, 1979—, Office Naval Rsch., 1983-87, Tex. Biotech., 1989-94; recipient Disting. Tchr. award U. Tex. Med. Br., 1989, Disting. Rsch. award, 1989. em. Am. Chem. Soc., Am. Soc. Cell Biology, Am. Soc. Biochemistry and Molecular Biology. emocrat. Lutheran. vocations: raquetball, basketball card collecting, poetry, camping. Home: 817 Hollowdale Edmond OK 73003-3022 Office: U Okla Health Scis Ctr Dept Biochem & Mol Biology BMSB Rm 860 Oklahoma City OK 73190

WEIGEL, STANLEY ALEXANDER, judge; b. Helena, Mont., Dec. 9, 1905; s. Louis and Jennie (Hepner) W.; m. Anne Kauffman, Apr. 21, 1940; children: Jane Anne, Susan Mary. AB, Stanford U., 1926, JD, 1928. Bar: Calif. 1928. Pvt. practice law San Francisco, 1928-62; judge U.S. Dist. Ct. (no. dist.) Calif., from 1962, now sr. judge; non-resident lectr. Stanford Law Sch., 1952—; mem. Jud. Panel on Multidist, Litigation, 1968-79; mem. temporary emergency Ct. Appeals of U.S., 1980—; now sr. judge; pres. Internat. Hospitality Ctr. Bay Area, 1959-68, Nat. Council for Community Services to Internat. Visitors, 1972-73; adv. gov. Calif. on Automobile Accident Commn., 1959; chmn. bd. visitors Stanford Law Sch., 1958-63; trustee World Affairs Council No. Calif., 1960—, pres., 1973-74; chmn. Ford Found. vis. com. to study behavioral sci. depts. Stanford U., 1956-57; mem. jud. conf. com. on jud. ethics, 1982-87. Served to lt. USNR, 1943-45. Decorated chevalier Order Leopold II (Belgium). Mem. Delta Sigma Rho, Phi Alpha Delta, Sigma Delta Chi. Office: US Ct Appeals PO Box 36060 Rm 15-6504 450 Golden Gate Ave San Francisco CA 94102-3400*

WEIGELE, RICHARD SAYRE, police officer; b. Passaic, N.J., Oct. 5, 1949; s. Louis Charles and Marjorie (Sayre) W. BA, Hope Coll., Holland, Mich., 1972; MPA, Kean Coll. N.J., Union, 1989. Police officer Summit (N.J.) Police Dept., 1973-80; mobile intensive care paramedic Overlook Hosp., Summit, 1977—; first response tng. coord. Union County Police acad., Scotch Plains, N.J., 1980—; police sgt., 911 mcpl. coord. Mountainside (N.J.) Police Dept., 1980—; paramedic preceptor Overlook Hosp., 1980—, pre-hosp. trauma life support instr., 1993—, pediatric prehosp. emergency care instr., 1995—; CPR instr. Am. Heart Assn., Summit, 1978; police instr. Union County Police Acad., 1980—; EMS text reviewer Brady Publishing, 1996. Officer Summit First Aid Squad, 1975-80; vol. Overlook Hosp., 1974-81; mem. Liberty Corner First Aid Squad, 1993—; instr. ARC, Somerville, N.J., 1992—. With N.J. Army NG, 1972-78. Recipient Award of Merit N.J. State Police Benevolent Assn., 1974, Award of recognition, Union County Police Acad., 1990. Mem. Nat. Assn. EMT/Paramedics (charter), N.J. Police Honor Legion, Internat. Police Assn. (reception officer 1989—), Mountainside Police Benevolent Assn. (Police Officer of the Yr. 1986), Pi Alpha Alpha. Ref. Ch. of Am. Avocations: skiing, biking, computers, community service. Home: 268 Crabtree Ct Basking Ridge NJ 07920-3154 Office: Mountainside Police Dept 1385 Rt 22 E Mountainside NJ 07092

WEIGEND, GUIDO GUSTAV, geographer, educator; b. Zeltweg, Austria, Jan. 2, 1920; came to U.S., 1939, naturalized, 1943; s. Gustav F. and Paula (Sorgo) W.; m. Areta Kelble, June 26, 1947 (dec. 1993); children: Nina, Cynthia, Kenneth. B.S., U. Chgo., 1942, M.S., 1946, Ph.D., 1949. With OSS, 1943-45; with mil. intelligence U.S. War Dept., 1946; instr. geography U. Ill., Chgo., 1946-47; instr. then asst. prof. geography Beloit Coll., 1947-49; asst. prof. geography Rutgers U., 1949-51, assoc. prof., 1951-57, prof., 1957-76, acting dept. chmn., 1951-52, chmn. dept., 1953-67, assoc. dean, 1972-76; dean Coll. Liberal Arts, Prof. geography Ariz. State U., Tempe, 1976-84, prof. geography, 1976-89; ret., 1989; Fulbright lectr. U. Barcelona, 1960-61; vis. prof. geography Columbia U., 1963-67, NYU, 1967, U. Colo., summer 1968, U. Hawaii, summer 1969; liaison rep. Rutgers U. to UN, 1950-52; invited by Chinese Acad. Scis. to visit minority areas in Chinese Cent. Asia, 1988; mem. U.S. nat. com. Internat. Geog. Union, 1951-58, 61-65; chmn. Conf. on Polit. and Social Geography, 1968-69. Author articles, monographs, bulls. for profl. jours.; contbr.: (4th edit.) A Geography of Europe, 1977; geog. editor-in-chief: Odyssey World Atlas, 1966. Bd. adjustment Franklin Twp., N.J., 1959; mem. Highland Park (N.J.) Bd. Edn., 1973-75, v.p., 1975; mem. Ariz. Coun. on Humanities and Pub. Policy, 1976-80; vice chmn. Phoenix Com. on Fgn. Rels., 1976-79, chmn., 1979-81; mem. exec. com. Fedn. Pub. Programs in Humanities, 1977-82; bd. dirs. Coun. Colls. Arts and Scis., 1980-83, Phoenix Chamber Music Soc., 1995—; commr. N. Cen. Assn. Colls. and Schs., 1976-80, bd. dirs. commn. on instns. of higher edn., 1980-83. Research fellow Office Naval Research, 1952-55, Rutgers Research Council, 1970-71; grantee Social Sci. Research Council, 1956, Ford Found., 1966, Am. Philos. Soc., 1970-71, German Acad. Exchange Service, 1984; Fulbright travel grantee Netherlands, 1970-71. Mem. Assn. Am. Geographers (chmn. N.Y. Met. divsn. 1955-56, editl. bd. 1955-59, mem. coun. 1965-66, chmn. N.Y.-N.J. divsn. 1965-66), Am. Geog. Soc., Phoenix Chamber Mus. Soc. (bd. dirs. 1995—), Sigma Xi (pres. Ariz. State U. chpt. 1989-91). Home: 2094 E Golf Ave Tempe AZ 85282-4046 Office: Ariz State U Dept Geography Tempe AZ 85287

WEIGER, JOHN GEORGE, foreign language educator; b. Dresden, Germany, Feb. 6, 1933; came to U.S., 1938, naturalized, 1945; s. Willy and Elisabeth (Prinz) W.; m. Leslie Lawrence Carpenter, Dec. 28, 1955; children: Robert Boyden, Mark Owen, Heidi Elaine. B.A., Middlebury Coll., 1955; M.A., U. Colo., 1957; Ph.D. (NDEA fellow), Ind. U., 1966. Instr. U. Colo., Boulder, 1955-57, Lawrence Coll., Appleton, Wis., 1957-58; instr. Romance langs. U. Vt., Burlington, 1958-62, asst. prof., 1964-67, assoc. prof., 1967-73, prof., 1973—, vice chmn. Romance lang. dept., 1964-68; chmn., 1994—; asst. dean Coll. Arts and Scis. U. Vt., Burlington, 1968-69; assoc. dean U. Vt. (Coll. Arts and Scis.), Burlington, 1969-71, dean, 1971-76; instnl. rep. for Rhodes scholarships, Danforth fellowships, Turrell Fund scholarships, 1971-76; program chmn. George Aiken lecture series, 1975; vis. lectr. U. Bologna, 1978, 87, U. Venice, Italy, 1987, U. Valencia, Spain, 1987; Cervantes lectr. Fordham U., 1990; cons. Eirik Borve, Inc., 1979—. Author: Introduction to the Youthful Deeds of the Cid, 1969, The Valencian Dramatists of Spain's Golden Age, 1976, Cristobal de Virues, 1978, Hacia la Comedia, 1978, The Individuated Self: Cervantes and the Emergence of the Individual, 1979, The Substance of Cervantes, 1985, In the Margins of Cervantes, 1988; editor: Las Hazañas del Cid, 1981, La Infelice Marcela, 1985; mem. editl. bd.: Bull. of Comediantes, 1978—; editl. bd.: Hispania, 1993-98; contbr. articles to profl. jours., also chpts. to books. U. Vt. Faculty Research fellow, 1967, 83, 86; Am. Council Learned Socs. grantee, 1978; U. Vt. Univ. scholar for the humanities, 1985-86. Mem. MLA (chmn. comedia sect. 1970-71), Renaissance Soc. Am., Am. Assn. Tchrs. Spanish and Portuguese (chmn. com. hon. mems. and fellows 1984), The Comediantes, Internat. Assn. Hispanists, Cervantes Soc. Am., Phi Beta Kappa, Phi Sigma Iota, Phi Eta Sigma (hon.). Home: 8 Woodbine Rd Shelburne VT 05482-7268 Office: U Vermont 506A Waterman Bldg Burlington VT 05405

WEIGERT, ANDREW JOSEPH, sociology educator; b. N.Y.C., Apr. 8, 1934; s. Andrew Joseph and Marie Teresa (Kollmer) W.; m. Kathleen Rose Maas, Aug. 31, 1967; children: Karen Rose, Sheila Marie. BA, St. Louis U., 1958, PhL, 1959, MA, 1960; BTh, Woodstock (Md.) Coll., 1964; PhD, U. Minn., 1968. NIMH trainee U. Minn., Mpls., 1965-67; asst. prof. sociology U. Notre Dame, Ind., 1968-72, assoc. prof., 1972-76, prof., 1976—, chmn. dept., 1980-84, 88-89; vis. assoc. prof. Yale U., New Haven, 1973-74; participant nat. and regional profl. meetings. Co-author: Family Socialization, 1974, Interpretive Sociology, 1978, Society and Identity, 1986; author: Everyday Life, 1981, Social Psychology, 1983, Life and Society, 1983, Mixed Emotions, 1991, Self, Interaction, and Natural Environment, 1997; adv. editor various sociology jours.; contbr. numerous articles to profl. jours., chpts. to books. Grantee NSF, 1969. Mem. Soc. for Study Symbolic Interaction, Soc. for Sci. Study Religion, Assn. for Sociology Religion. Avocation: woodlot management. Office: U Notre Dame Dept Sociology Notre Dame IN 46556

WEIGHT, DOUG, professional hockey player; b. Warren, Mich., Jan. 21, 1971. Student, Lake Superior State Coll., Mich. Selected 2d round NHL entry draft N.Y. Rangers, 1990; traded Edmonton Oilers, 1993, center, 1993—; named to CCHA All-Rookie team, 1989-90, NCAA All-Am. West 2d team, 1990-91, CHA All-Star 1st team, 1990-91; selected for NHL All-Star Game, 1996. Office: care Edmonton Oilers, Edmonton Coliseum, Edmonton, AB Canada T5B 4M9

WEIGHT, GEORGE DALE, banker, educator; b. Salt Lake City, Mar. 25, 1934; s. Sheldon J. and Florence (Noe) W.; m. Carilee Kesler, June 16, 1959; children: Camille, Kristene, Denise, Marcie, Nancy. BS, U. Utah, 1961; MS, U. Oreg., 1965, PhD, 1968. Instr. U. Oreg., Eugene, 1963-68; economist Fed. Res. Bank, Cleve., 1968-69; asst. v.p. fiscal ops. Fed. Res. Bank, Pitts., 1969-71; v.p. bank ops. Fed. Home Loan Bank Bd., Pitts., 1971-73; exec. v.p. Syracuse Savs. Bank, N.Y., 1972-73, pres., chief exec. officer, 1973-83; chmn., chief exec. officer Ben Franklin Fed. Savs. and Loan Assn., Portland, Oreg., 1983-90; dean Atkinson Grad. Sch. Mgmt. Willamette U., Salem, Oreg., 1990—; adj. prof. Oreg. Grad. Inst. Sci. & Tech., 1994—, Syracuse U., 1974; chmn. bd. Savs. Banks Life Ins. Fund, N.Y.C., bd. dirs. Onondaga County Indsl. Devel. Agy., Fed. Res. Bank San Francisco, Portland Br., State Accident Ins. Fund, Fed. Home Loan Bank Seattle; chmn. Oreg. State Bd. Edn., 1991; vis. prof. econ. and fin. Aomori (Japan) Pub. Coll., 1995—. Pres. Hiawatha coun. Boy Scouts Am., Syracuse, 1974-77; chmn. bd. Crouse-Irving Meml. Hosp., 1978-83; mem. Gov.'s Commn. Edn. Reforms, 1988, Oreg. State Bd. Edn., 1989-95, chmn., 1991-92; chmn. Associated Oreg. Industries Found., 1993-95; pres. Canal Mus.; bd. dirs. Oreg. Bus. Coun., York (Pa.) Graphic Svcs., 1997—. Recipient Silver Beaver award Boy Scouts Am., 1978; recipient Vol. of Yr. award Am. Heart Assn., 1980, Community Service award Rotary, Syracuse, 1982. Mem. Am. Fin. Assn., Arlington Club, Beta Gamma Sigma. Republican. Home: 16057 NW Claremont Dr Portland OR 97229-7841 Office: Willamette U Atkinson Grad Sch Mgmt 900 State St Salem OR 97301-3930

WEIGHTMAN, ESTHER LYNN, emergency trauma nurse; b. Tawas City, Mich., June 13, 1966; d. Garrie Lee and Naomi Ruth (Atwood) Schneller; m. Robert Thomas Weightman, Dec. 31, 1996. BS in Christian Secondary Edn., Ozark Bible Inst. & Coll., Neosho, Mo., 1988; BSN, Ind. Wesleyan U., Marion, 1991; MS in Cmty. Health Nursing, U. Colo. Health Scis. Ctr., Denver, 1995. RN, Colo.; CEN; cert. ACLS, pediatric advanced life support, trauma nurse core course; cert. type E cert. Colo. Dept. Edn. Staff nurse emergency dept. Marion Gen. Hosp., 1991-92, Penrose-St. Francis Healthcare Sys., Colorado Springs, Colo., 1992-95; staff nurse registry QS Nurses Corp., Colorado Springs, 1992—; staff devel. nurse 302d ASTS-USAFR, Peterson AFB, Colo., 1994—; mentor various healthcare instnl. facilities, 1991—; vol. tchr. health classes Knowledge is Power, Red Cross Shelter, Colorado Springs, 1995-96. Mem. orch. Living Springs Worship Centre, 1993—. Mem. Emergency Nurses Assn., Res. Officers Assn., Sigma Theta Tau. Avocations: tennis, French, cooking, aerobics, orchestra (trumpet).

WEIGHTMAN, JUDY MAE, lawyer; b. New Eagle, Pa., May 22, 1941; d. Morris and Ruth (Gutstadt) Epstein; children: Wayne, Randall, Darrell. BS in English, California U. of Pa., 1970; MA in Am. Studies, U. Hawaii, 1975; JD, U. Hawaii, 1981. Bar: Hawaii 1981. Tchr. Fairfax County Sch. (Va.), 1968-72, Hawaii Pub. Schs., Honolulu, 1973-75; lectr. Kapiolani Community Coll., Honolulu, 1975-76; instr. Olympic Community Coll., Pearl Harbor, Hawaii, 1975-77; lectr. Hawaii Pacific Coll., Honolulu, 1977-78; law clk. to atty. gen. Hawaii & Case, Kay & Lynch, Davis & Levin, 1979-81, to chief judge Intermediate Ct. Appeals State of Hawaii, 1981-82; dep. pub. defender Office of Pub. Defender, 1982-84; staff atty. Dept. Commerce & Consumer Affairs, State of Hawaii 1984-86; pres., bd. dirs. Am. Beltwrap Corp., 1986—; asst. prof. law, dir. pre-admission program, asst. prof. Richardson Sch. Law, U. Hawaii, 1987—, faculty senator; faculty senate exec. com. U. Hawaii Manoa. Author: Days of Remembrance: Hawaii Witnesses to the Holocaust; producer (documentary) The Panel: The First Exchange, Profile of An Aja Soldier, Profile of a Holocaust Survivor; prodr., dir. From Hawaii to The Holocaust: A Shared Moment in History; patentee in field; mem. Richardson Law Rev., 1979-81. Mem. neighborhood bd. No. 25 City and County Honolulu, 1976-77; vol. Legal Aid Soc., Honolulu, 1977-78; bd. dirs. Jewish Fedn., Protection and Advocacy Agy.; parent rep. Wheeler Intermediate Adv. Coun., Honolulu, 1975-77; trustee Carl K. Mirikitani Meml. Scholarship Fund, Arts Coun. Hawaii; membership dir. ACLU, 1977-78, bd. dirs., Hawaii, 1988—, treas. Amicus; founder Hawaii Holocaust Project; trustee Jewish Fedn. Hawaii. Community scholar, Honolulu, 1980; Internat. Rels. grant Chaminade U., 1976; recipient Hawaii Filmmakers award Hawaii Internat. Film Festival, 1993, Golden Eagle award CINE, 1995, Silver Apple Nat. Edn. Film & Video Festival, 1995, Bronze World medal N.Y. Festivals, 1996, CINDY Bronze medal, 1996, Lifetime Achievement award Jewish Fedn. Hawaii, Kansha award 442 Vets. Club. Mem. ABA, Afro-Am. Lawyers Assn. (bd. trustee), Hawaii Women Lawyers, Assn. Trial Lawyers Am., Hawaii State Bar Assn., Am. Judicature Soc., Richardson Sch. Law Alumni Assn. (alumni rep. 1981-82), Advocates for Pub. Interest Law, U. Hawaii Senate Faculty (senator), Phi Delta Phi (v.p. 1980-81), Hadassah Club, Women's Guild Club. Democrat. Jewish. Office: U Hawaii William S Richardson Sch Law 2515 Dole St Honolulu HI 96822-2328

WEIGLE, ROBERT EDWARD, civil engineer, research director; b. Shiloh, Pa., Apr. 27, 1927; s. William Edgar and Hilda Geraldine (Fans) W.; m. Mona Jean Long, Aug. 13, 1949; 1 child, Geoffrey Robert. BCE in Structures, Rensselaer Poly. Inst., 1951, MS in Mechanics, 1957, PhD in Mechanics, 1959. Registered profl. engr., N.Y., Pa. Assoc. rsch. scientist Rensselaer Poly. Inst., Troy, N.Y., 1955-59; chief scientist Watervliet Arsenal, 1959-77; technical dir. U.S. Army and Armament R & D Command, 1977-82; dir. U.S. Army Rsch. Office, 1982-88; dir. phys. sci. lab. N.Mex. State U., Las Cruces, 1988-96; dir. emeritus phys. sci. lab. N. Mex. State U., Las Cruces, 1996—; tech. dir., then dir. Benet Weapons Lab., 1959-77; chmn. numerous DoD and Army coms.; dir. emeritus Phys. Sci. Lab. N.Mex. State U., 1996. Contbr. articles to profl. jours. Recipient Meritorious Civilian Service award for cannon breech design U.S. Army, 1964, U.S. Army Materiel Command citation for engineering achievement in Vietnam, 1966, Presidential citation for development of cannon firing simulator, 1965, Exceptional Civilian Svc. medal U.S. Army, 1988, Rank of Meritorious Exec. Pres. Reagan, 1982; elected to Am. Acad. of Mechanics, 1972. Mem. NSPE, ASME, AAAS, ASTM, Soc. Exptl. Mechanics, Am. Def. Preparedness Assn. (Crozier prize 1985), Nat. Conf. Advancement Rsch. (program com. 1987, exec. coml. com., host rep. NCAR-46 ann. conf. 1992), Army Sci. Bd. (chmn. rsch. and new initiatives group 1992), Tau Beta Pi, Chi Epsilon, Sigma Xi.

WEIGLE, WILLIAM OLIVER, immunologist, educator; b. Monaca, Pa., Apr. 28, 1927; s. Oliver James and Caroline Ellen (Alsing) W.; m. Kathryn May Lotz, Sept. 4, 1948 (div. 1980); children—William James, Cynthia Kay; m. Carole G. Romball, Sept. 24, 1983. B.S., U. Pitts., 1950, M.S., 1951, Ph.D., 1956. Research assoc. pathology U. Pitts., 1955-58, asst. prof. immunochemistry, 1959-61; assoc. div. exptl. pathology Scripps Rsch. Inst., La Jolla, Calif., 1961-62, assoc. mem. div., 1962-63; mem. dept. exptl. pathology Scripps Rsch. Inst., La Jolla, 1963-74, mem. dept. immunopathology, 1974-82, chmn. dept. immunopathology, 1980-82, mem., vice chmn. dept. immunology, 1982-85, mem. dept. immunology, 1982—, chmn. dept. immunology, 1985-87; adj. prof. biology U. Calif., San Diego; McLaughlin vis. prof. U. Tex., 1977; mem. adv. bd. Immunetech Pharms., San Diego, 1988—; cons. in field. Author: Natural and Acquired Immunologic Unresponsiveness, 1967; assoc. editor: Clin. and Exptl. Immunology, 1972-79; Jour. Exptl. Medicine, 1974-84; Immunochemistry 1964-71; Procs. Soc. Exptl. Biology and Medicine, 1967-72; Jour. Immunology, 1967-71; Infection and Immunity, 1969-86, Aging: Immunology and Infectious Disease, 1987—; sect. editor: Jour. Immunology, 1971-75; editorial bd.: Contemporary Topics in Immunobiology, 1971-93; Cellular Immunology, 1984—; contbr. articles to profl. jours. Emeritus Coun. of the Trustees, Lovelace Inst., Albuquerque, 1996—. Pub. Health Research fellow, Nat. Inst. Neurol. Diseases and Blindness, 1956-59; NIH sr. research fellow, 1959-61, Research Career award, 1962. Mem. Am. Assn. Immunologists, Am. Soc. Exptl. Pathology (Parke Davis award 1967), Am. Soc. Microbiology, N.Y. Acad. Scis., Am. Assn. Pathologists, Soc. Exptl. Biology and Medicine. Home: 688 Via De La Valle Solana Beach CA 92075-2461 Office: Scripps Rsch Inst Dept Immunology IMM9 10666 N Torrey Pines Rd La Jolla CA 92037-1027

WEIGLEY, RUSSELL FRANK, history educator; b. Reading, Pa., July 2, 1930; s. Frank Francis and Meta Beulah (Rohrbach) W.; m. Emma Eleanor Seifrit, July 27, 1963; children: Jared Francis Guldin, Catherine Emma Rohrbach. BA, Albright Coll., 1952; MA, U. Pa., 1953, PhD, 1956; HLD (hon.), Albright Coll., 1978. Instr. history U. Pa., Phila., 1956-58; asst. prof. Drexel Inst. Tech., Phila., 1958-60, assoc. prof., 1960-62; assoc. prof. Temple U., Phila., 1962-64, prof. history, 1964-85, Disting. Univ. prof., 1985—; vis. prof. Dartmouth Coll., Hanover, N.H., 1967-68; U.S. Army vis. prof. mil. history rsch. U.S. Army War Coll., U.S. Army Mil. History Rsch. Collection, Carlisle Barrakcs, Pa., 1973-74; pres. Am. Mil. Inst., Washington, 1975-76. Author: Quartermaster General of the Union Army: A Biography of M.C. Meigs, 1959, Towards an American Army: Military Thought from Washington to Marshall, 1962, History of the United States Army, 1967, 84, The Partisan War: The South Carolina Campaign of 1780-82, 1970, The American Way of War, 1973, Eisenhower's Lieutenants, 1981 (Athenaem of Phila. Spl. award for Nonfiction by a Phila. Author, 1983), The Age of Battles: The Quest for Decisive Warfare from Breitenfeld to Waterloo, 1991; editor: The American Military: Readings in the History of the Military in American Society, 1969, New Dimensions in Military History, 1976, Philadelphia: A 300-Year History, 1982. Mem. hist. adv. commn. Dept. of Army, Washington, 1976-79, 88—, Pa. Hist. Records Adv. Com., Harrisburg, 1977-79; bd. dirs. Masonic Libr., Mus. of Pa., The Grand Lodge of Masons of Pa., Phila., 1990-95. Penrose Fund grantee Am. Philos. Soc., 1958; fellow John Simon Guggenheim Meml. Found., 1969-70; recipient Samuel Eliot Morison prize Am. Mil. Inst., 1989. Mem. Hist. Soc. Pa. (vice chmn. 1989-93, councilor 1983-89, 92—), Pa. Hist. Assn. (pres. 1975-78, v.p. 1967-75, coun. 1967—, editor jour. 1962-67), Am. Hist. Assn., Orgn. Am. Historians, Soc. Mil. Hist. (Disting. Book award 1992), So. Hist. Assn., Soc. Am. Historians Inc., Interuniv. Seminar on Armed Forces and Soc., Am. Philos. Soc. Democrat. Unitarian. Home: 327 S Smedley St Philadelphia PA 19103-6717 Office: Temple U Dept History Philadelphia PA 19122

WEIHAUPT, JOHN GEORGE, geosciences educator, scientist, university administrator; b. La Crosse, Wis., Mar. 5, 1930; s. John George and Gladys Mae (Ash) W.; m. Audrey Mae Reis, Jan. 28, 1961. Student, St. Norbert Coll., De Pere, Wis., 1948-49; BS, U. Wis., 1952, MS, 1953; MS, U. Wis.-Milw., 1971; PhD, U. Wis., 1973. Exploration geologist Am. Smelting & Refining Co., Nfld., 1953, Anaconda Co., Chile, S.Am., 1956-57; seismologist United Geophys. Corp., 1958; geophysicist Arctic Inst. N.Am., Antarctica, 1958-60, Geophys. and Polar Research Center, U. Wis., Antarctica, 1960-63; dir. participating Coll. and Univ. program, chmn. dept. phys. and biol. sci. U.S. Armed Forces Inst., Dept. Def., 1963-73; assoc. dean for acad. affairs Sch. Sci., Ind. U.-Purdue U., Indpls., 1973-78; prof. geology Sch. Sci., Ind. U.-Purdue U., 1973-78; asst. dean (Grad. Sch., prof. geoscis. Purdue U.), 1975-78; prof. geology, assoc. acad. v.p., dean grad. studies and research, v.p. Univ. Research Found., San Jose (Calif.) State U., 1978-82; vice chancellor for acad. affairs U. Colo., Denver, 1982-86, prof. geoscis., 1987—; Sci. cons., mem. sci. adv. bd. Holt Reinhart and Winston, Inc., 1967—; sci. editor, cons. McGraw-Hill Co., 1966—; hon. lectr. U. Wis., 1963-73; geol. cons., 1968—; editorial cons. John Wiley & Sons, 1968; editorial adv. bd. Dushkin Pub. Group, 1971—. Author: Exploration of the Oceans: An Introduction to Oceanography; mem. editorial bd. Internat. Jour. Interdisciplinary Cycle Research, Leiden; co-discoverer USARP Mountain Range (Arctic Inst. Mountain Range), in Victoria Land, Antarctica, 1960; discoverer Wilkes Land Meteorite Crater, Antarctic. Mem. Capital Community Citizens Assn.; mem. Madison Transp. Study Com., Found. for Internat. Energy Research and Tng.; U.S. com. for UN Univ.; mem. sci. council Internat. Center for Interdisciplinary Cycle Research; mem. Internat. Awareness and Leadership Council; mem. governing bd. Moss Landing Marine Labs.; bd. dirs. San Jose State U. Found. Served as 1st lt. AUS, 1953-55, Korea. Mt. Weihaupt in Antarctica named for him, 1966; recipient Madisonian medal for outstanding community service, 1973; Outstanding Cote Meml. award, 1974; Antarctic medal, 1968. Fellow Geol. Soc. Am., Explorers Club; mem. Antarctican Soc., Nat. Sci. Tchrs. Assn., Am. Geophys. Union, Internat. Council Corr. Edu., Soc. Am. Mil. Engrs., Wis. Alumni Assn., Soc. Study Biol. Rhythms, Internat. Soc. for Chronobiology, Marine Tech. Soc., AAAS, Univ. Indsl. Adv. Council, Am. Council on Edn., Expdn. Polaire France (hon.), Found. for Study Cycles, Assn. Am. Geographers, Nat. Council Univ. Research Adminstrs., Soc. Research Adminstrs., Man-Environ. Communication Center, Internat. Union Geol. Scis., Internat. Geog. Union, Internat. Soc. Study Time, Community Council Pub. TV, Internat. Platform Assn., Ind., Midwest assns. grad. schs., Western Assn. Grad. Schs., Council Grad. Schs. in U.S., Wis. Alumni Assn. of San Francisco, Kiwanis, Carmel Racquet Club (Rinconada), The Ridge at Hiwan (Evergreen, Colo., pres. 1991-93). Achievements include discoveryof the Wilkes Land Anomaly in Antarctica; also credited with revision of the discovery date of Antarctic continent by 3 centuries. Home: 23906 Currant Dr Golden CO 80401-9243 Office: U Colo Campus Box 172 PO Box 173364 Denver CO 80204-5310

WEIHING, JOHN LAWSON, plant pathologist, state senator; b. Rocky Ford, Colo., Feb. 26, 1921; s. Henry John and Clara Adele (Krull) W.; m. Shirley Ruth Wilkerson, Aug. 18, 1948; children: Lawson James, Martin Roy, Adell Ann, Warren John. BS in Agronomy, Colo. State U., 1942; MSc in Agronomy, U. Nebr., 1949, PhD in Botany and Plant Pathology, 1954. Instr. plant pathology U. Nebr., Lincoln, 1950-54, asst. prof., 1954-56, assoc. prof., 1956-60, prof., 1960-61, 62-64, 66-71, prof., interim chmn. plant pathology dept., 1961-62; prof., dir. Panhandle Rsch. and Extension Ctr. U. Nebr., Scottsbluff, 1971-84; with Alumni Office, Panhandle Found. U. Nebr., Scottsbluf, 1984-86; prof., chmn. plant sci. dept. Ataturk U., Erzurum, Turkey, 1964-66; mem. dist. 48 Nebr. Legislature, Lincoln, 1987-91; cons. Am. Hydrponics Systems, Inc., Grapevine, Tex., 1969-72. Creator U. Nebr. TV series Backyard Farmer, The Equation of Nature, 1959-60. Campaign chmn. United Way, Scottsbluff and Gering, Nebr., 1978. Lt. U.S. Army, 1942-46. Recipient Honor award Soil Conservation Soc. Am., 1982, Merit award Gamma Sigma Delta, 1977, Disting. Svc. award Nebr. Turfgrass Found., 1982, Nebr. Coop. Extension, 1970; named to Nebr. Hall Agrl. Achievement, 1987. Mem. Am. Phytopathol. Soc. (chmn. nat. extension com. 1963, pres. north cen. dir. 1971-72), AAAS, Am. Inst. Biol. Scis., Nebr. State Hist. Soc. (trustee 1992—), Scottsbluff/Gering United C. of C. (pres. 1980-81), Rotary (bd. dirs. 1977-80), Elks. Republican. Presbyterian. Avocation: archeology. Home: 1605 Holly Dr Gering NE 69341-1954

WEIHRICH, HEINZ, management educator; came to U.S., 1959; s. Paul and Anna Weihrich; m. Ursula Weihrich, Aug. 3, 1963. BS, UCLA, 1966, MBA, 1967, PhD, 1973. Assoc. Grad. Sch. Mgmt. UCLA, 1968-73; from asst. to assoc. prof. Ariz. State U., Tempe, 1973-80; prof. global mgmt. and behavioral sci. U. San Francisco, 1980—; internat. mgmt. cons. in field. Author: (with Harold Koontz and Cyril O'Donnell) Management, 7th edit., 1980, Japanese, Chinese and Indonesian edits., 8th edit., 1984, Singapore edit., 1985, Indonesian edit., 1986, Philippines edit., Bengali edit., 1989, Taiwan edit., 1985 (with Harold Koontz) 9th edit., 1988, Singapore edit., 1988, Chinese edit., 1989, Spanish edit., 1990, best-seller Spanish speaking world, Korean edit., 1988, 90, Pengurusan (Malaysian) edit., 1991, Management: A Global Perspective, 10th edit. (with Harold Koontz), 1993, Administracão Fundamentos da Teoriae da Cienca, Primeiro Volume 1986, Administracão Organizacão Planejamento e Controle, Segundo Volume, 1987, Administracão Recursos Humanos: Desenvolvimento de Administradores, Terceiro Volume, 1987, (with Harold Koontz and Cyril O'Donnell) Management: A Book of Readings, 5th edit., 1980, (with George Odiorne and Jack Mendleson) Executive Skills: A Management by Objectives Approach, 1980, (with Harold Koontz) Measuring Managers--A Double-Barreled Approach, 1981, (with Harold Koontz and Cyril O'Donnell) Essentials of Management, 3d edit. 1982, Taiwan, Philippines, Chinese and India edits., 4th edit., 1986, Singapore edit., 1986, 5th edit., 1990, (with Harold Koontz) Manajamen, Jilid 1, Indonesian edit., 1987, Manajamen, Jilid 2, 1986, Elementos de Administracion, 3d edit., 1983, 4th edit. 1988, Management

Excellence--Productivity through MBO, 1985, Singapore edit. 1986, Japanese edit., 1990, Greek edit., Produttivita con L' Italian edit. 1987, Administracion, 1985, Management Basiswissen, German edit., 1986, Excelencia Administrativa (Mex.), Spanish edit., 1987, (with Harold Koontz and Cyril O'Donnell) Adminstracion Moderna, Tomo 1, 1986, (with Harold Koontz) Management: A Global Perspective, internat. edit., 1993, Administración: Una Perspectiva Global, 1994, Korean edit., 1993, 96, Croatian edit., 1996, Czech edit., 1993, 96; editor: (with Jack Mendleson) Management: An MBO Approach, 1978; contbr. numerous articles and papers to profl. jours. Grantee Am. Mgmt. Assn., 1970. Fellow Internat. Acad. Mgmt., mem. Acad. Mgmt., Assn. Mgmt. Excellence (trustee 1985-87), Assn. Bus. Simulation Exptl. Learning, Acad. Internat. Bus., Beta Gamma Sigma, Sigma Iota Epsilon. Roman Catholic. Office: U San Francisco 2130 Fulton St San Francisco CA 94117-1080

WEIKART, DAVID POWELL, educational research foundation administrator; b. Youngstown, Ohio, Aug. 26, 1931; s. Hubert James and Catherine (Powell) W.; m. Phyllis Saxton, Aug. 24, 1957; children: Cynthia, Catherine, Jennifer, Gretchen. AB, Oberlin Coll., 1953, DSc (hon.), 1992; PhD, U. Mich., 1966. Cert. sch. psychologist, Mich. Dir. spl. svcs. Ypsilanti (Mich.) Pub. Schs., 1957-70; pres. High Scope Ednl. Rsch. Found., Ypsilanti, 1970—; dir. High Scope Inst., London, 1991—. Author: Young Children in Action, 1979, Changed Lives, 1984, Challenging the Potential, 1992, Significant Benefits, 1993, Educating Young Children, 1995, Lasting Difference, 1997; editor: How Nations Serve Young Children, 1991, Families Speak, 1994. Mem., Nat. Commn. on Children, 1990-93. 1st lt. USMC, 1953-55. Recipient Lela Rowland award Nat. Mental Health Assn., Washington, 1987. Mem. Nat. Assn. for Edn. of Young Children. Avocation: camping.

WEIKEL, MALCOLM KEITH, health care company executive; b. Shamokin, Pa., Mar. 9, 1938; s. Malcolm J. and Marian Eleanor (Faust) W.; m. Barbara Joan Davis, Dec. 17, 1960; children: Richard, Kristin. BSc, Phila. Coll. Pharmacy and Sci., 1960; MSc, U. Wis., 1962, PhD, 1966. Mgr. Roche Labs., 1966-70; commr. health svcs. HEW, Washington, 1970-77; v.p. Am. Med. Internat., 1978-82, pres., CEO, 1982-84; exec. v.p., COO, Manor Healthcare Corp., Silver Spring, Md., 1984-86; exec. v.p. Health Care & Retirement Corp., Toledo, 1986-88, sr. exec. v.p., COO, 1988—. Recipient sec.'s spl. citation HEW, 1975, 77. Mem. Am. Health Care Assn. (v.p. 1990—, chmn. multifacility group 1990-93). Office: Health Care & Retirement Corp One SeaGate Toledo OH 43604-2616

WEIKSNER, SANDRA S., lawyer; b. D.C., Nov. 9, 1945; d. Donald B. and Dick (Cutter) Smiley; m. George B. Weiksner, Aug. 19, 1969; children: Michael, Nicholas. BA in Psychology, Stanford U., 1966, JD, 1969. Teaching fellow Stanford U., Calif., 1969-70; assoc. Cleary, Gottlieb, Steen & Hamilton, N.Y.C., 1970-77, ptnr., 1978—; vis. lectr. Yale Law Sch., 1991-92. Bd. dirs. N.Y. Law Sch. Fellow Am. Bar Found., Am. Coll. Trusts and Estates Counsel, Internat. Acad. Estate and Trust Law; mem. ABA, N.Y. State Bar Assn., Assn. Bar of City of N.Y., Conn. Bar Assn., N.Y. Women's Found. (dir.), N.Y. Law Sch. (dir.). Democrat. Unitarian. Home: 164 E 81st St New York NY 10028-1804 Office: Cleary Gottlieb Steen & Hamilton 1 Liberty Plz New York NY 10006-1404

WEIL, ANDREW THOMAS, physician; b. Phila., June 8, 1942; s. Daniel Pythias and Jenny (Silverstein) W. BA, Harvard U., 1964, MD, 1968. Intern Mt. Zion Hosp. Med. Ctr., San Francisco, 1968-69; assoc. Harvard Bot. Mus., Cambridge, Mass., 1971-84; fellow Inst. Current World Affairs, N.Y.C., 1971-75; lectr. U. Ariz., Tucson, 1983—, dir. program in integrative medicine, 1996—; founder Ctr. for Integrative Medicine, Tucson, 1995—. Author: Natural Mind, 1972, Marriage of the Sun and Moon, 1980, Chocolate to Morphine, 1983, Health and Healing, 1984, Natural Health, Natural Medicine, 1990, Spontaneous Healing, 1995, 8 Weeks to Optimum Health, 1997. Served to lt. USPHS, 1969-70. Fellow Linnean Soc. London; mem. Sigma Xi. Democrat. Buddhist. Avocations: gardening, backpacking. Home: PO Box 900 Vail AZ 85641-0900 Office: Ariz Health Scis Ctr Coll Medicine Room 2211 1501 N Campbell Ave Tucson AZ 85724-0001

WEIL, D(ONALD) WALLACE, business administration educator; b. Cleve., July 20, 1923; s. Laurence J. and Carol S. (Wallace) W.; m. Jane A. Bittel, Dec. 29, 1947; children—John Wallace, Charles Andrew, Margaret Jane, Carol Wyn. B.A., Oberlin Coll., 1947; J.D., Willamette U., 1950. Pres. James Foundry Corp., Fort Atkinson, Wis., 1960-70; faculty bus. adminstrn. U. Wis., Eau Claire, 1971-74; chmn. dept. bus. adminstrn. U. Wis., 1974-77, prof., 1985—; pres. Diversified Industries, Inc., St. Louis, 1977-81, UHI Corp., Los Angeles, 1981-85; dir. U.H.I. Corp. Diversified Industries, Inc., St. Louis Sales Investments, Mgmt. Inc., Elmwood, Wis., Jane B. Inc., Eau Claire. Served with AUS, 1942-45. Mem. Am. Security Council, Nat. Council Small Bus. Mgmt. Devel., Phi Kappa Phi, Beta Gamma Sigma. Republican. Congregationalist. Home: 1530 Canfield St Eau Claire WI 54701-4018 Office: U Wis-Eau Claire Dept Bus Adminstrn Eau Claire WI 54701

WEIL, EDWARD DAVID, chemistry researcher, consultant, educator; b. Phila., June 13, 1928; s. Irving E. and Minna M. (Stainbrook) W.; m. Barbara Joy Hummel, Sept. 11, 1952; children: David L., Claudia E. BS in Chemistry, U. Pa., 1950; PhD in Organic Chemistry, U. Ill., 1953; MBA, Pace U., 1982. Chemist, supr. Hooker Chem. Co., Niagara Falls, N.Y., 1950-65; supr., sr. scientist Stauffer Chem. Co., Dobbs Ferry, N.Y., 1965-86; ind. cons., patent agt., propr. Intertech. Svcs., 1986—; dir. exploratory rsch. Adelphi Rsch. Ctr., Garden City, 1986-87; rsch. prof., Poly. U., Bklyn., 1987—; . Contbr. articles to Kirk-Othmer Ency., Ency. Polymer Sci., Rsch. Mgmt., others. Recipient IR-100 award Indsl. Rsch. Mag. Achievements include over 220 patents for commercial flame retardants, processes, agricultural chemicals, others. Mem. Am. Chem. Soc. (chmn. profl. rels. com. N.Y. sect. 1980-95), Assn. Cons. Chemists and Chem. Engrs., Sigma Xi. Home: 200 E 57th St Apt 5L New York NY 10022 Office: Polytechnic U 6 Metrotech Ctr Brooklyn NY 11201-3840

WEIL, FRANK A., investment banker, lawyer; b. Bedford, N.Y., Feb. 14, 1931; s. Sylvan and Ruth Alice (Norman) W.; m. Denie Sandison, Feb. 10, 1951; children: Deborah Weil Harrington, Amanda, Sandison, William. A.B. cum laude, Harvard U., 1953, LL.B., 1956. Bar: N.Y. 1956. Practiced in N.Y.C., 1957-60; gen. partner Loeb, Rhoades & Co., N.Y.C., 1960-71; pres. Abacus Fund, Inc., 1968-72; chief fin. officer, dir. Paine, Webber, Jackson & Curtis, N.Y.C., 1972-77; asst. sec. industry and trade Dept. Commerce, Washington, 1977-79; partner firm, bd. chmn., Ginsburg, Feldman, Weil & Bress, Washington, 1979-83, Wald, Harkrader & RossExxel/Altmos Inc., Washington, 1983-85; chmn., chief exec. officer, dir., Abacus and Assocs., Inc., 1985—; dir. Dorr-Oliver, Inc., Stamford, Conn., 1968-77, Hamburg Savs. Bank, N.Y.C., 1975-77, J.B. Lippincott Co., Phila., 1975-77, Govt. Research Corp., 1975-77, 79-85; dir., pres. Norman Found., 1953-77, 79, 92, chmn. bd. trustee, Ednl. Alliance. Trustee Tchrs. Coll., Columbia U., 1976-79, Montefiore Hosp., 1960-77; trustee, vice chmn. No. Westchester Hosp., 1971-77; past vice chmn. bd. govs. Atlantic Inst. Internat. Affairs; past pres. Ednl. Alliance, trustee, 1957-77; trustee, sec. Fedn. Jewish Philanthropies, N.Y.C., 1965-77; trustee, chmn. Harvey Sch., 1969-76; trustee Hurricane Island Outward Bound Sch., 1974—, Washington Opera, 1984-85, Asia Soc., 1993—; bd. dirs., pres., vice chmn., Hickrill Found., Inc., 1953-77, 79—; bd. dirs. Coun. Excellence in Govt., 1984—, chmn., 1988-93, Am. Assembly, 1992—, Smithsonian Inst., 1994—, vice chmn., 1997—; mem. vis. com. Kennedy Sch. Govt., Harvard U.; chmn. tax com., mem. N.Y. State Econ. Devel. Bd., 1975-77, mem. Appleseed Found. bd., 1995—; chmn., mem. N.Y. State Bd. Equalization and Assessment, 1976-77; adv. bd. Sch. Advanced Internat. Studies, Johns Hopkins U., 1979-88; mem. N.Y. State Council on Fiscal and Econ. Priorities, 1985-89, N.Y. Coun. Fgn. Rels.; mem. N.Y. State Adv. Commn. on Liability Ins., 1986. Mem. Century Assn., Harvard Club, The Links, River Club, Met. Club. Home: 1516 28th St NW Washington DC 20007-3058 Office: Abacus & Assocs Inc 147 E 48th St # 3fl New York NY 10017-1223

WEIL, GILBERT HARRY, lawyer; b. N.Y.C., Aug. 31, 1912; s. Alexis and Esther (Marks) W.; m. Louise Rhoda Cohen, Mar. 14, 1936; children: Allen Charles, Jeffrey Lee. B.S., NYU, 1933, J.D., 1937. Bar: N.Y. 1937, U.S. Dist. Ct. (so. dist.) N.Y. 1941, U.S. Ct. Appeals (2d cir.) 1949, U.S. Ct. Appeals (4th cir.) 1950, U.S. Dist. Ct. (ea. dist.) N.Y. 1952, U.S. Ct. Appeals (3d cir.) 1956, U.S. Dist. Ct. D.C. 1961, U.S. Supreme Ct. 1964, U.S. Ct. Appeals (9th cir.) 1968, U.S. Ct. Appeals (5th cir.) 1969, U.S. Ct. Appeals (7th cir.) 1976, U.S. Ct. Appeals (fed. cir.) 1982. Law clk. and assoc. to Isaac W. Digges, 1935-53; pvt. practice, 1953-65; partner Weil and Lee, N.Y.C., 1966-69, Weil, Lee & Bergin, N.Y.C., 1969-76, Weil, Guttman & Davis, N.Y.C., 1976-82, Weil, Guttman, Davis & Malkin, N.Y.C., 1982-86, Weil, Guttman & Malkin, N.Y.C., 1986—; lectr. in field, 1952—. Contbr. articles to profl. jours. Served to lt (j.g.) USNR, 1943-45. Office: Weil Guttman & Malkin 60 E 42nd St New York NY 10165

WEIL, IRWIN, Slavic languages and literature educator; b. Cin., Apr. 16, 1928; s. Sidney and Florence (Levy) W.; m. Vivian Weil, Dec. 27, 1950; children: Martin, Alice, Daniel. A.B., U. Chgo., 1948, M.A., 1951; Ph.D., Harvard U., 1960. Sr. social sci. research analyst Library of Congress, 1951-54; teaching fellow Harvard U., 1956-58; mem. faculty Brandeis U., 1958-65; mem. faculty dept. Slavic langs. and lit. Northwestern U., Evanston, Ill., 1966—; chmn. dept. Northwestern U., 1976-82; vis. prof. U. Moscow, Soviet Acad. Scis.; set up series of internat. symposia between Am. scholars and USSR Acad. Scis.; founder 1st Soviet-Am. TV Student Competition in Lit., 1988-89. Author books and articles pub. in field, pub. in U.S.A. and Russia. Recipient Pushkin Internat. gold medal for outstanding teaching and research, 1984, Outstanding Teaching award Northwestern U. Alumni Assn., 1987, Tempo All-Professor Team, Humanities, Chicago Tribune, 1993; Ford Found. fellow, 1954-55. Mem. Am. Assn. Tchrs. Slavic and East European Langs. (exec. sec. 1962-68, Excellence in Teaching award 1993), Am. Coun. Tchrs. Russian (v.p. 1975-79, pres. 1980-84), Internat. Assn. Profs. Russian (founding U.S. mem.). Jewish. Established TV competition on American and Russian literature between American and Russian high schoolers. Office: Northwestern U Slavic Dept Evanston IL 60208 *As a scholar and teacher trying hard to develop mutual understanding and cultural exchange with the USSR, I have discovered how important and fruitful it is to apply the normal standards of friendly discourse with people from an entirely different country and historical background.*

WEIL, JEFFREY GEORGE, lawyer; b. Allentown, Pa., Apr. 28, 1951; s. Russel G.E. and Irene Marie (Kozlowski) W.; divorced; children: Michael, Stephen, Brooke; m. Rachel Eisner, 1994. AB, Princeton U., 1973; JD, Harvard U., 1976. Bar: Pa. 1976, U.S. Dist. Ct. (ea. dist.) Pa. 1976, U.S. Ct. Appeals (3d cir.) 1976, U.S. Supreme Ct., 1988. Assoc. Dechert, Price & Rhoads, Phila., 1976-84, ptnr., 1984—, chmn. firm hiring com., 1987-89, mem. firm exec. com., 1990-94. Chmn. com. United Way Southeastern Pa., Phila., 1982-85, trustee, 1983-89, mem. funding policy com., 1987-90; participant Community Leadership Seminar Program, Phila., 1986; bd. dirs. Hawk Mountain Sanctuary, 1993—, Pa. Wildlife Fedn., 1996—. Mem. ABA (vice chmn. adminstrn. law com. on pub. advs. and pub. representation 1985-88, mem. antitrust sect. pvt. litigation subcom. 1991—), Pa. Bar Assn., Phila. Bar Assn. (fed. cts. com. 1985—), Princeton U. Alumni Schs. Com., Princeton Club Phila. Avocations: fly-fishing, reading. Home: 2 Esprit Ter Wayne PA 19087-5713 Office: Dechert Price & Rhoads 1717 Arch St Philadelphia PA 19103-2713

WEIL, JOHN DAVID, company executive; b. Chgo., Sept. 28, 1947; s. Leslie Joseph and Carlyne (Strauss) W.; m. Marcie Bornfriend, July 4, 1981; children: Jessica Lauren, Michael Brandon, Samantha Leigh. BS in Econs., U. Ill., 1969; MBA in Fin., Northwestern U., 1971. Asst. to chmn. bd. Stanwood Industries, Lake Forest, Ill., 1971-74; pres. Kent Paper Co., Ridgewood, N.Y., 1974-81; pres., CEO Am. Envelope Co., Chgo., 1982-94; dir. Sage Enterprises, Inc., 1995—; operating affiliate McCown De Leeuw & Co., 1995—; bd. dirs., chmn. bd. DEC Internat., Inc., Atlanta, 1995—; bd. dirs. Fibermark Corp., Tiara Motorcoach Corp., Internat. Data Response Corp. Mem. Envelope Mfrs. Am. (bd. dirs. 1986-94), Northmoor Country Club. Office: 5 Revere Dr Ste 200 Northbrook IL 60062-8000

WEIL, JOHN WILLIAM, technology management consultant; b. N.Y.C., Feb. 3, 1928; s. Frank Leopold and Henrietta Amelia (Simons) W.; m. Joan Leatrice Landis, June 15, 1950; children—Nancy Ellen, Linda Jill. B.S., MIT, 1948; Ph.D., Cornell U., 1953. Various positions in nuclear reactors and computers Gen. Electric Co. (various locations), 1953-70; v.p. advanced systems and tech. Honeywell Info. Systems, Inc., Waltham, Mass., 1970-74; v.p., chief tech. officer Bendix Corp., Southfield, Mich., 1974-77; sr. v.p., chief tech. officer Bendix Corp., Southfield, 1977-83; v.p. advanced tech. and engring. Allied Corp., Southfield, 1983; pres. Modular Bio Systems, Inc., 1983-85, Weil Assocs., Inc., Bloomfield Hills, Mich., 1985—; bd. dirs. Access Corp.; founder Met. Detroit Sci. and Engring. Coalition, 1977, sec., 1977-80, pres., 1980-82; chmn. Mich. Biotech. Inst., 1981-85, trustee, 1985-92; mem. Army Sci. Bd., 1982-84. Contbr. articles to prof. jours. AEC fellow, 1950-51. Home and Office: 218 Guilford Rd Bloomfield Hills MI 48304-2737

WEIL, LEON JEROME, diplomat; b. N.Y.C., June 15, 1927; m. Mabel Selig, Apr. 8, 1952; children: Leon Jerome Jr., Katherine A., Caroline E. A.B. cum laude, Princeton U. Ptnr. Herzfeld & Stern, N.Y.C., 1974-84, Steiner Rouse & Co., 1950-74; now with Gruntal & Co., N.Y.C.; U.S. ambassador to Nepal, 1984-87; cons. UN Devel. Programme, Financial Svcs. Vol. Corps., Internat. Found. for Electoral Systems; exch. ofcl. Am. Stock Exchange. Trustee Berkshire Sch., Sheffield, Mass., Outward Bound Inc., Greenwich, Conn., Robert Taft Inst. Govt., N.Y.C.; mem. Pres.'s Council on Phys. Fitness and Sports; bd. dirs. Media Rsch. Center of Alexandria, Va. Served with USN, 1945-46. Republican. Club: City Athletic (N.Y.C.). Home: 213 E 48th St New York NY 10017-1538

WEIL, LEONARD, banker; b. 1922; married. With U.S. Dept. State, Vienna, Austria, 1946; with Union Bank, Los Angeles, 1946-62; pres., CEO Mfrs. Bank, Los Angeles, 1962-86; pres. emeritus Mfrs. Bank, 1986—; adj. asst. prof. fin. Anderson Grad. Sch. Mgmt., UCLA. Trustee UCLA Found.; bd. visitors UCLA Grad. Sch. Mgmt.; past pres. Town Hall; bd. dirs. Braille Inst. Served with U.S. Army, 1943-45. Mem. Calif. Bankers Assn. (bd. dirs., past pres.), Am. Mgmt. Assn., Am. Econs. Assn., Am. Bankers Assn. Office: 233 Wilshire Blvd Fl 6 Santa Monica CA 90401-1205

WEIL, LOUIS ARTHUR, III, newspaper publishing executive; b. Grand Rapids, Mich., Mar. 14, 1941; s. Louis Arthur, Jr. and Kathryn (Halligan) W.; m. Mary Elizabeth Buckingham, Sept. 7, 1963 (div. June 1977); children: Scott Arthur, Christopher Davison, Timothy Buckingham; m. Daryl Hopkins Goss, Jan. 26, 1980. B.A. in English, Ind. U., 1963; DHL (hon.), Mercy Coll., Grand Valley State U. Various positions Times Herald, Port Huron, Mich., 1966-68; personnel dir., pub. Journal and Courier, Lafayette, Ind., 1968-73; gen. mgr., pub. Gannett Westchester Rockland Newspapers, White Plains, N.Y., 1973-74, pres., gen. mgr., 1974-77, pres., pub., 1977-79; v.p. devel. Gannett Co., Inc., N.Y.C., 1979-83, sr. v.p. planning and devel., 1982-86; chmn., pub. Gannett Westchester Rockland Newspapers, White Plains, 1984-86; pres. The Detroit News, 1986-89, pub., 1987-89; U.S. pub. Time Mag., 1989-91; pub., chief exec. officer, exec. v.p. Ariz. Republic, Phoenix Gazette, Ariz. Bus. Gazette, 1991-96; pres., CEO Central Newspapers, Inc., Phoenix, 1996—; bd. dirs. Ctrl. Newspapers, Inc., Prudential. Chmn. membership Trustee Found. for Am. Comm.; bd. trustees, adv. bd. Ariz. Cancer Ctr. at U. Ariz.; chmn. adv. bd. Kids Voting USA; bd. dirs. Ariz. Cmty. Found., Ariz. Cities in Schs., Ind. U. Found.; campaign chmn. Valley of the Sun United Way, 1992; past chmn. Greater Phoenix Leadership; past pres. bd. trustees Phoenix Art Mus. With USN. Office: Phoenix Newspapers Inc 200 E Van Buren St Phoenix AZ 85004-2238*

WEIL, MAX HARRY, physician, medical educator, medical scientist; b. Baden, Switzerland, Feb. 9, 1927; came to U.S., 1937, naturalized, 1944; s. Marcel and Gretl (Winter) W.; m. Marianne Judith Posner, Apr. 1955; children: Susan Margot, Carol Juliet. AB, U. Mich., 1948; MD, SUNY, N.Y.C., 1952; PhD, U. Minn., 1957. Diplomate Am. Bd. Internal Medicine and Critical Care Medicine, Nat. Bd. Med. Examiners. Intern in internal medicine U. Cin. Med. Ctr., 1952-53; resident U. Minn. Hosps., Heart Hosp., VA Hosp., Mpls., 1953-55; rsch. fellow U. Minn., Mpls., 1955-56; sr. fellow Nat. Heart Inst., Mayo Clinic, Rochester, Minn., 1956-57; chief cardiology City of Hope Med. Ctr., Duarte, Calif., 1957-59; asst. clin. prof. U. So. Calif. Sch. Medicine, L.A., 1957-59, asst. prof., 1959-63, assoc. prof., 1963-71, prof., 1971-81; chmn. L.A. Com. on Emergency Med. Svcs., 1968-73; prof., chmn. dept. medicine, chief divsn. cardiology Chgo. Med. Sch., Finch U. Health Scis., North Chicago, Ill., 1981-91, disting. univ. prof., 1992-94, disting. univ. prof. emeritus, 1994—; prof. clin. med. bioengring. U. So. Calif., 1972-91, adj. prof. medicine, 1981—, dir. Shock Rsch. Unit, 1961-81, Inst. Critical Care Medicine Ann. Symposium, 1963—, Ctr. Critically Ill., 1968-80; pres. Inst. Critical Care Medicine, Palm Springs, Calif. and Northbrook, Ill., 1974—; attending cardiologist children's divsn. L.A. County/U. So. Calif. Med. Ctr., 1958-65, attending physician, 1958-71, sr. attending cardiologist, 1968-73, sr. attending physician, 1971-81; vis. prof. anesthesiology/critical care medicine U. Pitts., 1972—; clin. prof. anesthesiology UCLA, 1981-95; adj. prof. Northwestern U. Med. Sch., Chgo., 1992—; clin. prof. anesthesiology U. So. Calif. Sch. Medicine, L.A., 1995—, Weil Internat. lectr. in critical care medicine, 1987; numerous vis. professorships and lectureships; cons. in field; prin. rschr. numerous grants and rsch. projects. Sect. editor Archives Internal Medicine, 1983-86, JAMA, 1969-72; guest editor Am. Jour. Cardiology, 1982, Critical Care Medicine, 1985; mem. editl. bd. Am. Jour. Medicine, 1971-79, Chest, 1980-95, Jour. Circulatory Shock, 1979-92, Clin. Engring. Newsletter, 1980—, Methods of Info. in Medicine, 1977-91, Jour. Clin. Illness, 1986—, Clin. Intensive Care, 1989—; mem. editl. adv. bd. Emergency Medicine, 1978—, Issues in Health Care Tech., 1983-86; assoc. editor Critical Care Medicine, 1973-74, mem. editl. bd., 1973-91, 94-96, sr. editor, 1997; editor-in-chief Acute Care, 1983-90; contbr. articles to profl. jours.; patentee in field. Pres. Temple Brotherhood, Wilshire Blvd. Temple, L.A., 1967-68; bd. dirs. Hollywood Presbyn. Med. Ctr., 1976-81, L.A. chpt. Met. Am. Heart Assn., 1962-67, Chgo. chpt. Met. Am. Heart Assn., 1982-88. With U.S. Army, 1946-47. Recipient prize in internal medicine SUNY, 1952, Alumni medallion SUNY, 1970; Disting. Svc. award Soc. Critical Care Medicine, 1984; numerous rsch. grants, 1959—; named Disting. Alumni Lectr., 1967, Oscar Schwindetzky Meml. Lectr. Internat. Anesthesia Rsch. Soc., 1978; recipient Lawrence R. Medoff award Chgo. Med. Sch., 1987, Morris L. Parker Rsch. award, 1989; Lilly scholar, 1988-89. Master ACP; fellow Am. Coll. Cardiology (chmn. emergency cardiac care com. 1974-81), Am. Coll. Chest Physicians (coun. clin. cardiology, coun. critical care medicine), Am. Coll. Clin. Pharmacology, Am. Coll. Critical Care Medicine (Disting. Investigator award 1990, 96), Am. Heart Assn. (coun. circulation, coun. basic sci., coun. cardiopulmonary and critical care, coun. clin. cardiology), N.Y. Acad. Sci., Chgo. Soc. Internal Medicine; mem. AMA (sect. editor jour. 1969-72), IEEE, L.A. County Med. Assn., Am. Physiol. Soc. Am. Soc. Pharmacology and Exptl. Therapeutics, Am. Soc. Echocardiography, Am. Soc. Nephrology, Am. Trauma Soc. (founding mem.), Assn. Computing Machinery, Assn. Am. Med. Colls., Ctrl. Soc. Clin. Rsch., Chgo. Cardiol. Group (sec.-treas. 1986-88, chmn. 1988-90), Chgo. Soc. Internal Medicine, Lake County Heart Assn. (bd. govs. 1983-86), Intensive Care Soc. U.K., L.A. Soc. Internal Medicine, Soc. Exptl. Biology and Medicine, Western Soc. Clin. Rsch., Fedn. Am. Socs. Exptl. Biology, Am. Soc. Parenteral and Enteral Nutrition, Nat. Acad. Practice (disting. practitioner), Skull and Dagger, Sigma Xi, Alpha Omega Alpha. Jewish. Avocations: swimming, tennis, photography, philosophy-economics. Office: Inst Critical Care Medicine Bldg 1695 N Sunrise Way # 3 Palm Springs CA 92262-5309

WEIL, MYRON, retired banker; b. Lincoln, Nebr., Apr. 17, 1918; s. Julius and Fannie (Livingston) W.; m. Pauline Clayton, Sept. 26, 1945; children—Michele Susan, Judy Lynn, Layla. B.S., Yale, 1939. Exec. v.p., dir. Nat. Bank Commerce, Lincoln, 1939-67; bd. dir. First Nat. Bank, Clinton, Iowa, 1967-91, chmn. bd. dirs., 1984-91; exec. v.p. Hawkeye Bancorp., Des Moines, 1967-83, bd. dirs., 1967-91; vice chmn. bd Hawkeye Bancorp., 1983-86. Served to maj., Q.M.C. AUS, 1939-45. Decorated Bronze Star. Home: 1025 Crescent Dr Clinton IA 52732-4739

WEIL, PETER HENRY, lawyer; b. N.Y.C., Nov. 20, 1933; s. Frank L. and Henrietta Amelia (Simons) W.; m. Helen Fay Kolodkin, Dec. 18, 1960; children: Karen W. Markus, Frank L. BA cum laude, Princeton U., 1954; LLB cum laude, Harvard U., 1957. Bar: N.Y. 1957, U.S. Dist. Cts. (so. and ea. dists.) N.Y. 1972. Assoc. Weil, Gotshal & Manges, N.Y.C., 1958-62; from assoc. to ptnr. Kaye Scholer, N.Y.C., 1962-95, ret., 1995; lectr. SMU Inst. on Comml. Financing, 1985-94, Banking Law Inst., 1987-89. Author: Asset Based Lending: An Introductory Guide to Secured Financing, P.L.I., 1989, 3d edit., 1996. Fellow Am. Coll. of Commercial Fin. Lawyers; former chmn. N.Y. bd. overseers, former bd. govs. Hebrew Union Coll., Jewish Inst. Religion, Cin., N.Y.C., Los Angeles, Jerusalem. With U.S. Army 1957-58. Mem. Ringwood Golden Master Volleyball Team, U.S. Nat. Champions, 1983. Mem. ABA, Assn. of Bar of City of N.Y. (banking law com. 1975-78).

WEIL, RAYMOND RICHARD, soil scientist; b. Detroit, May 27, 1948; s. Ulrich L. and Hilde C. (Levy) W.; m. Susan R. Boscov, Feb. 22, 1968 (div. Feb. 1982); children: Benjamin S., Joshua J.; m. Patricia Lynn Driggers, Feb. 5, 1983. BS, Mich. State U., 1970; MS, Purdue U., 1972; PhD, Va. Poly. Inst. and State U., 1977. Cert. profl. soil scientist. Vol. Peace Corps, Ethiopia, 1970; farm mgr. Nat. Sharecropper's Fund, Wadesboro, N.C., 1972-73; instr. Va. Poly. Inst. and State U., Blacksburg, 1975-77; lectr. U. Malawi, Lilongwe, 1977-79; from asst. prof. to assoc. prof. U. Md., College Park, 1979-91, prof., 1991—; cons. Forest Dept., Sri Lanka Govt., 1981; adv. bd. Com. on Agr. Sustainability for Developing Countries, Washington, 1988—; mem. task force Ecosystem Farm, Accokeek (Med.) Found., 1990—, chair medium size farm bd. Future Harvest Project, 1995—. Author: Lab Manual for Soil Science, 1993; co-author: Nature and Properties of Soil: A Study Guide, 1984; co-author: Nature and Properties of Soils, 11th edit., 1996; contbr. articles to profl. jours. Named Fulbright-Hayes Scholarship Exch. fellow, Zimbabwe, 1985, Fulbright-Hayes Africa Regional Rsch. scholar, Tanzania, 1994, Nat. Def. Edn. Act fellow, Ind., Md., 1991, Md. Agr. Exptl. Sta., 1991-94, U.S. AID, Malawi, 1988-92, USDA Agrl. Rsch. Edn., 1996—. Mem. Am. Soc. Agronomy (internat. div. chair 1993-94), Soil Sci. Soc. Am., Internat. Soil Sci. Soc. Achievements include development of new methods of matching fertilizer use to soil requirements in peasant farming sectors by mapping soil and plant nutrient status, of improved cropping system for sustainable production of cereals and legumes; development of new soil management system to reduce groundwater contamination by nitrates; contributions to understanding how best to manage organic wastes such as animal manure and sewage sludge in farming systems; development of new method for indigenous nutrient sources to enhance soil fertility, practical measures of soil quality. Office: U Md Dept Natural Resource Scis College Park MD 20742

WEIL, ROLF ALFRED, economist, university president emeritus; b. Pforzheim, Germany, Oct. 29, 1921; came to U.S., 1936, naturalized, 1944; s. Henry and Lina (Landauer) W.; m. Leni Metzger, Nov. 3, 1945; children: Susan Linda, Ronald Alan. B.A., U. Chgo., 1942, Ph.D., 1950; D. Hebrew Letters, Coll. Jewish Studies, 1967; L.H.D., Loyola U., 1970; D.H.L., Bowling Green State U., Ohio, 1986; LHD, Roosevelt U., 1988. Rsch. asst. Cowles Commn. for Rsch. in Econs., 1942-44; rsch. analyst Ill. Dept. Revenue, 1944-46; mem. faculty Roosevelt U., Chgo., 1946—, prof. fin. and econs., also chmn. dept. fin., 1954-65, dean Coll. Bus. Adminstrn., 1957-64, acting pres., 1965-66, pres., 1966-88, pres. emeritus, 1988—; past pres. Selfhelp Home for the Aged, Chgo.; cons. to non-profit orgns., 1988—. Author: Through these Portals-from Immigrant to College President, 1991; contbr. articles on fin. Bd. dirs. trustees Roosevelt U., Selfhelp of Chgo., Inc. Mem. Am. Econ. Assn., Cliff Dwellers Club.

WEIL, ROMAN LEE, accounting educator; b. Montgomery, Ala., May 22, 1940; s. Roman L. and Charlotte (Alexander) W.; children: Alexis Cherie, Charles Alexander Roman, Lacey Lorraine. BA, Yale U., 1962; MS in Indsl. Adminstrn, Carnegie-Mellon U., 1965, PhD in Econs., 1966. CPA. From instr. to prof. U. Chgo., 1965-93, Sigmund E. Edelstone prof. acctg., 1993—; Mills B. Lane prof. indsl. mgmt. Ga. Inst. Tech., 1974-76; mem. adv. com. replacement cost implementation SEC, 1976-77; prof. acctg. Stanford (Calif.) U., 1984, prof. econs., 1985, prof. law, 1990-96; prof. acctg. and law NYU Sch. Law, 1985; mem. adv. coun. Fin. Acctg. Stds., 1989-94; mem. task force on consolidations Fin. Acctg. Stds. Bd., 1984-89, mem. task force on discounting, 1989—, mem. task force on fin. instruments, 1994—, mem. adv. coun., 1989-94. Author: Fundamentals of Accounting, 1975, Financial Accounting, 8th edit., 1997, Accounting: The Language of Business, 9th edit., 1994, Inflation Accounting, 1976, Replacement Cost Accounting, 1976, Managerial Accounting, 1979, 6th edit., 1997, Litigation Svcs. Handbook, 1990-96; editor: Handbook of Modern Accounting, 1977, 3rd edit., 1983, Handbook of Cost Accounting, 1980, 4th edit., 1985, Acctg. Rev., 1974-79, Fin. Analysts Jour., 1980-88. NSF grantee, 1967-81. Mem. AICPA, Ill. Soc. CPAs, Am. Econ. Assn., Inst. Mgmt. Scis., Nat. Assn. Accts. (cert. mgmt. acct.), Am. Acctg. Assn., Inst. Managerial Acctg., Assembly Am. Collegiate Schs. Bus. (mem. acctg. accreditation com. 1987-88), Oenonomy

Soc. (co-chmn.). Home: 175 E Delaware Pl Apt 8302 Chicago IL 60611-1732 Office: U Chgo Grad Sch Bus 1101 E 58th St Chicago IL 60637-1511

WEIL, STEPHEN EDWARD, museum official; b. N.Y.C., June 24, 1928; s. Sidney and Beatrice (Sachs) W.; m. Rose Reicherson, Oct. 15, 1950 (div.); children: Rachel J., David N., Michael D.; m. Elizabeth Carbone, Sept. 7, 1974 (div.); m. Wendy Luke, Apr. 8, 1990. A.B., Brown U., 1949; LL.B., Columbia U., 1956. Bar: N.Y. 1956. Assoc. firm Rosenman, Colin, Kaye, Petschek & Freund, N.Y.C., 1956-63; v.p., gen. mgr. Marlborough-Gerson Gallery, N.Y.C., 1963-67; adminstr., sec., trustee Whitney Mus. Am. Art, N.Y.C., 1967-74; dep. dir., sec. Hirshhorn Mus. and Sculpture Garden, Smithsonian Instn., Washington, 1974-95; emeritus sr. scholar, 1995—; mem. cultural property adv. com. USIA, 1995—; chair adv. com. Museum Loan Network, 1995—. Co-author: Art Works - Law, Policy, Practice, 1974, Art Law - Rights and Liabilities of Creators and Collectors, 1986; author: Beauty and the Beast, 1983, Rethinking the Museum, 1990, A Cabinet of Curiosities, 1995; co-editor: Art Galleries and Museums, 1973. Mem. mus. adv. panel N.Y. State Coun. on Arts, 1974-78; mem. adv. panel Inst. for Mus. Scis.; trustee Brown U., 1989-95. Mem. Am. Assn. Mus. (treas., v.p., councilor), Am. Fedn. Arts (trustee 1988-95). Jewish. Home: 800 25th St NW Washington DC 20037 Office: Ctr for Museum Studies Smithsonian Instn Washington DC 20560

WEIL, THOMAS ALEXANDER, electronics engineer, retired; b. N.Y.C., Jan. 22, 1930; s. Frank Leopold and Henrietta Amelia (Simons) W.; m. Dianne Isaacs; children: Deborah, Elizabeth, Alexander. BSEE, MIT, 1951. Engr. modulator sect. Raytheon Co., Watertown, Mass., 1951-55, sect. mgr. transmitters, 1955-69, dept. mgr. transmitters, 1969-77, staff scientist equipment devel. labs., 1972-95, lab. mgr. radar systems, 1977-79, lab. mgr. advanced devel., 1979-80, program mgr. oil shale program, 1980-84; cons. in field, 1995—. Contbr. 33 articles to profl. jours., 3 chpts. to books; patentee (10) in field. Recipient Excellence in Tech. award Raytheon co., 1990; Raytheon Co. fellow, 1989. Fellow IEEE (tech. papers com. Modulator Symposia Microwave Tube Symposia, Germeshausen award 1994). Republican. Mem. Universalist-Unitarian Ch. Avocations: classical music, photography, mountain climbing. Home: 14 Lanark Rd Wellesley MA 02181-3029 *Evolution and survival of the fittest have left mankind aggressive and prone to make war. Peace depends on finding how to overcome this heritage. Shouldn't we be working on how to resteer mankind's instincts?.*

WEIL, THOMAS P., health services consultant; b. Mount Vernon, N.Y., Oct. 2, 1932; s. H.M. and Alice (Franc) W.; m. Janet Whalen, Feb. 13, 1965. BA, Union Coll., 1954; MPH, Yale U., 1958; PhD, U. Mich., 1964. S.S. Goldwater fellow Mount Sinai Med. Ctr., N.Y.C., 1957-58; assoc. cons. J.G. Steinle Assocs., Garden City, N.Y., 1958-61; asst. prof. UCLA, 1962-65; assoc. dir. Touro Infirmary, New Orleans, 1964-66; prof., dir. U. Mo., 1966-71; v.p. E.D. Rosenfeld Assocs., N.Y.C., 1971-75; pres. Bedford Health Assocs. Inc., N.Y., N.C., 1975—; chmn. Health Edn. & Applied Rsch. Found., Washington, 1981-83; bd. dirs. Albany (N.Y.) Med. Ctr., Inc., 1974-77; cons. to numerous hosps., med. schs., health related orgs., 1958—. Contbr. articles profl. jours. Named vis. prof. W.K. Kellogg Found., Sydney, Australia, 1969; recipient svc. award Am. Assn. Healthcare Cons., 1982; Weil Disting. Profl. in Health Svcs. Mgmt., U. Mo. established in 1991. Fellow APHA, Am. Assn. Healthcare Cons. (emeritus), Am. Coll. Healthcare Execs. (emeritus). Jewish. Avocations: mantrailing bloodhounds, quarter horses. Home: 1400 Town Mountain Rd Asheville NC 28804-2936 Office: Bedford Health Assocs Inc 1400 Town Mountain Rd Asheville NC 28804-2936

WEILAND, CHARLES HANKES, lawyer; b. Billings, Mont., Feb. 19, 1921; s. George Michael and Elizabeth (Hankes) W. A.B. cum laude, Johns Hopkins U., 1942; J.D., Harvard U., 1948. Bar: Ill. 1949, U.S. Dist. Ct. (no. dist.) Ill. 1949, U.S. Ct. Appeals (7th cir.) 1949, U.S. Supreme Ct. 1968. Assoc. Lord, Bissell & Brook, Chgo., 1948-55, ptnr., 1956-83; chmn. Cook County Inquiry Bd., Supreme Ct. Ill. Atty. Regis. and Disciplinary Commn., 1974-75. Served with AUS, 1942-46. Mem. Ill. Bar Assn., Chgo. Bar Assn. Republican. Clubs: Law; Legal (Chgo.).

WEILBACHER, WILLIAM MANNING, advertising and marketing consultant; b. Albany, N.Y., June 23, 1928; s. William Carl and Gladys (Manning) W.; m. Martha Ethel Meyer, May 19, 1962; children: Barbara Taylor, Elizabeth Manning. BS, Yale U., 1949; MS, Columbia, 1951. Supr. product analysis Nat. Biscuit Co., 1951-53; v.p., dir. rsch. Dancer-Fitzgerald-Sample, Inc., 1953-62, sr. v.p., 1971-73, exec. v.p., 1973-74, vice chmn., 1974-79; bd. dir., sr. v.p. McCaffrey & McCall, 1962-66; exec. dir. Ctr. for Advanced Practice, 1966; ptnr. Jack Tinker and Ptnrs., Interpub. Inc., 1966-69; v.p., dir. rsch. J. Walter Thompson Co., 1969-70; pres. Master Jazz Recs., Inc., 1967—, D-F-S Realty Inc., 1975-79, D-F-S Holdings Inc., 1974-79, Bismark Corp., 1979—, Second Mktg. Opinion, Inc., 1981—; lectr. advt. Grad. Sch. Bus., Columbia U., 1956-64, adj. prof. mktg., 1976-77, 81-82, 83; lectr. mktg. CCNY, 1955-57; adj. prof. mktg. Grad. Sch. Bus., NYU, 1965-70, 80-81, 88; Spencer vis. prof. S.I. Newhouse Sch. Pub. Comms., Syracuse U., 1982-86; mem. Radio-TV Ratings Rev. Com., 1958-65; bd. dirs. Audit Bur. Circulation, 1964-71, Broacast Rating Coun., 1963-67; mem. tech. adv. com. Robert Wood Johnson Found., 1994—. Author: (with L.O. Brown, R. S. Lessler) Advertising Media, 1957, (with H.C. Barksdale) Marketing Research; Selected Readings and Analytic Commentaries, 1966, (with R.A. Bauer, S.A. Greyser) Advertising in America: The Consumer View, 1968, Marketing Management Cases, 1970, 4th edit. 1986, Advertising, 1979, 2d edit. 1984, Cases in Advertising, 1981, Auditing Productivity, 1981, Choosing an Advertising Agency, 1983, Current Advertiser Practices in Compensating Their Advertising Agencies, 1983, 86, 89, 92, 95, Choosing and Working with Your Advertising Agency, 1991, Managing Agency Relations, 1991, Brand Marketing, 1993, contbg. editor: Marketing Handbook, 1965. Vice chmn. tech. com. Advt. Rsch. Found., 1960-63, chmn., 1963-65, bd. dirs., 1965-67. Mem. Am. Assn. Advt. Agys. (past vice chmn. rsch. com.), Market Rsch. Coun. (pres. 1970-71), Yale Club of N.Y.C., Eastward Ho Country Club, Alpha Kappa Psi, Beta Gamma Sigma. Home: Box 2002 30 Bismark Way Dennis MA 02638-2207

WEILER, JEFFRY LOUIS, lawyer; b. N.Y.C., Dec. 31, 1942; s. Kurt and Elaine (Kabb) W.; m. Susan Karen Goodman, June 8, 1964; children: Philip K., June M. BS, Miami U., Oxford, Ohio, 1964; JD, Cleve. State U., 1970. Bar: Ohio 1970, Fla. 1981; CPA, Ohio 1968. Acct. Meaden & Moore, CPAs, Cleve., 1964-65; IRS agt. U.S. Dept. Treasury, Cleve., 1965-70; assoc. Ulmer & Berne, Cleve., 1970-71; ptnr. Benesch, Friedlander, Coplan & Aronoff, Cleve., 1971—; adj. assoc. prof. Cleve.-Marshall Coll. Law, Cleve. State U., 1980-87. Contbr. to profl. pubs. Former trustee, Jewish Community Fedn., Cleve., 1978-83. Fellow Am. Coll. Trust and Estate Counsel; mem. ABA (sect. taxation, estate and gift tax subcom.), Cleve. Estate Planning Inst. (chmn. 1980), Cleve. Tax Inst. (chmn. 1983), Cleve. Bar Assn. (treas. 1993-96, trustee 1988-91), Tax Club of Cleve. (sec. 1996-97). Avocations: photography, sailboat racing, ice skating. Home: 24714 Maidstone Ln Cleveland OH 44122-1614 Office: Benesch Friedlander 2300 BP America Bldg 200 Public Sq Cleveland OH 44114-2301

WEILER, KURT WALTER, radio astronomer; b. Phoenix, Mar. 16, 1943; s. Henry Carl and Dorothy (Esser) w.; m. Geertje Stoelwinder, June 8, 1979; children: Corinn Nynke Yoon, Anil Erick Jivan, Sanna Femke Lee. BS, U. Ariz., 1964; PhD, Calif. Inst. Tech., 1970. Guest investigator Netherlands Found. for Radioastronomy, Groningen, 1970-74; sci. collaborator Inst. for Radioastronomy, Bologna, Italy, 1975-76; sr. scientist Max Planck Inst. for Radioastronomy, Bonn, W.Ger., 1976-79; program dir. NSF, Washington, 1979-85; radio astronomer Naval Rsch. Lab, Washington, 1985—; Halley steering com. NASA, Washington, 1981-85. Author: WSRT Users Guide, 1973, 75; editor Radio Astronomy from Space, 1987; editor: Low Frequency Astrophysics from Space, 1990; contbr. over 150 articles to profl. jours. and mags. Mem. Am. Astron. Soc., Royal Astron. Soc., Internat. Astron. Union, Internat. Sci. Radio Union, Nederlandse Astronomen Club, Jaguar Club, Nat. Capital Club. Home: 6232 Cockspur Dr Alexandria VA 22310-1504 Office: Naval Rsch Lab Code 7214 4555 Overlook Ave SW Washington DC 20375-0001

WEILER, SCOTT MICHAEL, machine tool manufacturing company executive; b. Fargo, N.D., Jan. 9, 1952; s. F.S. and Lorraine M. (Kopach) W.; m. Sandra L. Meyer, Aug. 28, 1971 (div. July 1986); 1 child, Kimberly. Application engr. Devlieg Machine Co., Royal Oak, Mich., 1973-84; project mgr. Devlieg Machine Co., 1984-89, Giddings & Lewis, Fraser, Mich., 1989-94; project mgr. Ingersoll CM Systems, Midland, Mich., 1994—, dir. engring. ops. & projects, 1997—. Mem. Soc. Mfg. Engrs., Am. Mgmt. Assn., Project Mgmt. Inst. Office: Ingersoll CM Systems Midland MI 48642

WEILER, TODD ALAN, army official; b. Texarkana, Tex., Oct. 7, 1964; s. Gerald and Mamie Ruth (Clements) Penny. BA, Tex. Christian U., 1987. Cert. comml. rated rotorcraft aviator. Mem. campaign staff Clinton for Pres., 1992; White House liaison Dept. Def., Washington, 1993; dep. asst. sec. U.S. Army, Washington, 1993—; Dept. of Army rep. Civil-Tiltrotor Commn., Washington, 1993-95; mem. Dept. of Def. Fed. Prison Industries, 1996—. With U.S. Army, 1987-91, Desert Storm. Decorated 2 Air medals. Mem. VFW, Am. Legion, 101st Airborne Assn., Clinton-Gore Adminstrn. Assn. Democrat. Avocations: boating, flying, skiing. Home: 326 Cloudes Mill Dr Alexandria VA 22304-3077 Office: OASA M&RA The Pentagon Rm 2E 580 Washington DC 20310

WEILERT, RONALD LEE, data processing executive; b. Alhambra, Calif., July 12, 1948; s. Edwin H. and Leona M. (Pierson) W.; m. Geri A. Ode, July 31, 1971; children: Jeff, Kathy, Joanna, Kristin, Jenny. BS in Engring. Mgmt., USAF Acad., 1971; MA in Indsl. Engring., Cen. Mich. U., 1974. Commd. 2d lt. USAF, 1971, advanced through grades to capt., 1974, resigned, 1978; salesman Scott Paper Co., L.A., 1978-79; salesman, dir. sales Consumer Systems Corp., Oakbrook, Ill., 1979-84; from salesman to v.p. Oracle Corp., Lisle, Ill., 1984-93; pres., CEO Baan Internat., Lisle, 1993-95; pres. bd. Oswego Found. for Ednl. Excellence, 1995—. Mem., v.p. sch. bd. Dist. 308, Oswego, Ill., 1987-91; dist. chmn. Meramech Hill dist. Three Fires coun. Boy Scouts Am., 1996—. Mormon. Home: 3838 E Plainfield Rd Oswego IL 60543-9642

WEIL-GARRIS BRANDT, KATHLEEN (KATHLEEN BRANDT), art historian; d. Kurt Hermann and Charlotte (Garris) Weil; m. Werner Brandt (dec. 1983). BA with honors, Vassar Coll., 1956; postgrad., U. Bonn, Germany, 1956-57; MA, Radcliffe U., 1958; PhD, Harvard, 1966. Asst. prof. NYU, N.Y.C., 1963-67, assoc. prof., 1967-72, prof., 1973—; asst. prof. NYU Inst. Fine Arts, N.Y.C., 1966-67, assoc. prof., 1967-72, prof., 1973—; vis. prof. Harvard U., Cambridge, Mass., 1980; editor in chief The Art Bulletin, N.Y.C., 1977-81; cons. on Renaissance art Vatican Mus., 1987—; vis. fellow Bibliotheca Hartziana (Max-Planck Inst.) Rome. Author: Leonardo and Central Italian Art, 1974, Problems In Cinquecento Sculpture, 1977; author: (with J. d'Amico) The Renaissance Cardinal's Ideal Palace, 1981; contbr. numerous articles to profl. jours.; editor: Michelangelo: la cappella Sistina: documentazione e interpretazione, vol. III, 1996. Mem. Am. com. Medici Archive Project, 1996—. Decorated officer Order of Merit (Italy); recipient rsch. award Humboldt Found., 1985, Disting. Tchg. award Lindback Found., 1967, Golden Dozen Tchr. award NYU, 1993, Alumni Great Tchr. award, 1996; Guggenheim fellow, 1976; grantee Henkel Found., 1987. Mem. Coll. Art Assn. (bd. dirs. 1973-74, 77-81), Renaissance Soc. Am. (editl. bd. 1992—), Soc. Archtl. Historians, N.Y. Acad. Scis., Phi Beta Kappa (v.p. NYU chpt. 1979-81). Avocations: art films, conservation, music, dance. Office: NYU Inst Fine Arts 1 E 78th St New York NY 10021-0102

WEILL, GEORGES GUSTAVE, mathematics educator; b. Strasbourg, France, Apr. 9, 1926; came to U.S., 1956; s. Edmond and Germaine (Falck) W. Ed., Ecole Polytechnique, Paris, 1950; E.N.S., Telecom., Paris, 1952; Licence de Mathematiques, U. Paris, France, 1954, D.Sc. in Physics, 1955; Ph.D. in Math, U. Calif. at Los Angeles, 1960. Research scientist Compagnie Generale de Telegraphie Sans Fil, France, 1952-56; research fellow dept. elec. engring. Calif. Inst. Tech., Pasadena, 1956-59; teaching asso. math. U. Calif. at Los Angeles, 1959-60; research fellow math. Harvard, 1960-62; lectr., research asso. Yale, 1962-64; vis. asst. prof. Belfer Grad. Sch. Sci., Yeshiva U., 1964-65; assoc. prof. math. Poly. U., Bklyn., 1964-65, prof., 1966-95, prof. math. emeritus, 1995—. Mem. Am. Math. Soc., Societe Mathematique de France, IEEE (sr. mem.), Sigma Xi, Pi Mu Epsilon. Office: Polytechnic Univ 333 Jay St Brooklyn NY 11201-2907

WEILL, HANS, physician, educator; b. Berlin, Aug. 31, 1933; came to U.S., 1939; s. Kurt and Gerda (Philipp) W.; m. Kathleen Burton, Apr. 3, 1958; children: Judith, Leslie, David. B.S., Tulane U., 1955, M.D., 1958. Diplomate: Am. Bd. Internal Medicine. Intern Mt. Sinai Hosp., N.Y.C., 1958-59; resident Tulane Med. Unit, Charity Hosp. La., New Orleans, 1959-60; chief resident Tulane Med. Unit, Charity Hosp. La., 1961-62, sr. vis. physician, 1972—; NIH research fellow dept. medicine and pulmonary lab. Sch. Medicine Tulane U., New Orleans, 1960-61; instr. medicine Sch. Medicine Tulane U., 1962-64, asst. prof. medicine, 1964-67, assoc. prof., 1967-71, prof. medicine, 1971—, Schlieder Found. prof. pulmonary medicine, 1985—; chief Environ. Medicine sect. Tulane Med. Center, 1980—; dir. univ. Ctr. for Bioenviron. Rsch., 1989-93; dir. interdisciplinary research group in occupational lung diseases Nat. Heart, Lung and Blood Inst., 1972-92, mem. nat. adv. council, 1986-90, chmn. pulmonary disease adv. com., 1982-84; active staff Tulane Med. Center Hosp., 1976—; program dir. Nat. Inst. for Environ. Health Sci., 1992—; cons. pulmonary diseases Touro Infirmary, New Orleans, 1962—; cons. NIH, Nat. Inst. Occupational Safety and Health, Occupational Safety and Health Adminstrn., USN, NAS, EPA; lectr., participant workshops and confs. profl. groups in U.S., France, Can., U.K.; dir. Nat. Inst. Environ. Health Scis Superfund. Basic Rsch. Program, 1992—. Mem. editorial bd. Am. Rev. of Respiratory Disease, 1980-85, CHEST, 1987-91; editor Respiratory Diseases Digest, 1981; guest editor Byssinosis conf. supplement, CHEST, 1981. Fellow Am. Acad. Allergy, Royal Soc. Medicine, ACP; mem. Am. Thoracic Soc. (pres. 1976), Am. Lung Assn. (bd. dirs. 1975-78), New Orleans Acad. Internal Medicine (sec., treas. 1973-75), Am. Coll. Chest Physicians (gov. for La. 1970-75), Am. Fedn. Clin. Research, So. Soc. Clin. Investigation, N.Y. Acad. Scis., Brit. Thoracic Assn., Internat. Epidemiol. Assn., Am. Heart Assn. (task force on environment and cardiovascular system 1978), Brit. Thoracic Soc., Phi Beta Kappa, Alpha Omega Alpha. Home: 755 Hearthstone Dr Basalt CO 81621 Office: Tulane U Sch Medicine Sect Environ Medicine 1430 Tulane Ave New Orleans LA 70112-2699

WEILL, RICHARD L., lawyer; b. Lincoln, Nebr., Jan. 28, 1943; s. Walter and Irma (Heineman) W.; m. Judy A. Brumm, July 11, 1965; children: David, John. BS, U. Nebr., 1964; LLB, NYU, 1967. Bar: N.Y. 1967, Nebr. 1969. Assoc. Proskauer Rose Goetz & Mendelsohn, N.Y.C., 1967-69; ptnr. Kutak Rock, Omaha, 1969-89; gen. counsel MBIA Inc., Armonk, N.Y., 1989-91, exec. v.p., 1991-94, pres., 1994—. Office: MBIA Inc 113 King St Armonk NY 10504-1611

WEILL, SAMUEL, JR., automobile company executive; b. Rochester, N.Y., Dec. 22, 1916; s. Samuel and Bertha (Stein) W.; student U. Buffalo, 1934-35; m. Mercedes Weil, May 20, 1939 (div. Aug. 1943); children: Rita and Eric (twins); m. Cléanthe Kimball Carr, Aug. 12, 1960 (div. 1982); m. Jacqueline Natalie Bateman, Jan. 5, 1983. Co-owner, Brayton Air Coll., St. Louis, 1937-42; assoc. editor, advt. mgr., bus. mgr. Road and Track Mag., Los Angeles, 1951-53; pres. Volkswagen Pacific, Inc., Culver City, Calif., 1953-73, Porsche Audi Pacific, Culver City, 1953-73; chmn. bd. Minto Inter., Inc., London; v.p. fin. Chieftain Oil Co., Ojai, Calif. Recipient Tom May award Jewish Hosp. and Research Center, 1971. Served with USAAF, 1943-45. Home: 305 Palomar Rd Ojai CA 93023-2432 Office: Chieftain Oil Co 214 W Aliso St Ojai CA 93023-2502 *Try to find a position that can utilitze whatever knowledge and abilities you have. Learn all you can about that company and its workings and then work as hard as you can, giving more than is expected of you, much more, but not more than you can capably handle.*

WEILL, SANFORD I., bank executive; b. N.Y.C., Mar. 16, 1933; s. Max and Etta (Kalika) W.; m. Joan Mosher, June 20, 1955; children: Marc P., Jessica M. B.A., Cornell U., 1955, student Grad. Sch. Bus. and Pub. Adminstrn., 1954-55. Chmn. bd., chief exec. officer Carter, Berlind & Weill (name changed to CBWL-Hayden, Stone, Inc. 1970, to Hayden Stone, Inc. 1972, to Shearson Hayden Stone 1974, to Shearson Loeb Rh, N.Y.C., 1960-84; dir., chmn. exec. com. Carter, Berlind & Weill (name changed to CBWL-Hayden, Stone, Inc. 1970, to Hayden Stone, Inc. 1972, to Shearson Hayden Stone 1974, to Shearson Loeb Rh, 1981-83, pres., 1983-85; chmn. Fireman's Fund, 1984-85; past pres., chmn. exec. com., mem. fin. com. Am. Express Co., until 1989; chmn., chief exec. officer Primerica Corp., N.Y.C., 1989—, pres., until 1992; chmn. Primerica Holdings Inc., N.Y.C.; chmn., pres., chief exec. officer Comml. Credit Co., Balt., 1986—; chmn., CEO Travelers Group, N.Y.C., 1996—; dir. IDS Mutual Funds Group; vice chmn. adv. council The Johnson Grad. Sch. of Mgmt.; founder Acad. of Fin. Mem. bd. overseers Cornell Med. Coll.; chmn. Carnegie Hall, N.Y.C.; mem. bus. com. Mus. of Modern Art, N.Y.C. Mem. N.Y. Soc. Security Analysts. Clubs: Cornell (N.Y.C.), Century Country (Purchase, N.Y.), Harmonie (N.Y.C.). Office: Travelers Group 388 Greenwich St New York NY 10013-2375

WEIMAN, ENRIQUE WATSON, lawyer; b. Rio de Janeiro, Jan. 1, 1946; came to U.S., 1947; BA, U. Tampa, 1968, JD, 1976; LLM, Atlanta Law Sch., 1976. Bar: Ga.1984. Staff atty. Eason Kennedy and Assocs., Atlanta, 1984-85; mng. ptnr. Hyatt Legal Svcs., Sandy Springs, Ga., 1985-90; pres. Weiman & Perry, P.C., Stone Mountain, Ga., 1990—. Contbr. to local newspaper. Capt. USMC, 1969-71, Res., 1972-80. Avocations: tennis, swimming, sailing. Home: 5575 S Pines Ct Stone Mountain GA 30087 Office: Weiman & Perry 739 Main St Ste 9 Stone Mountain GA 30083-3089

WEIMAN, HEIDI, early childhood education educator; b. Chgo., July 5, 1952; d. Edwin and Sandra (Cordell) W. AA, Kendall Coll., 1972; BA summa cum laude, Northeastern Ill. U., 1992, MA in Spl. Edn., 1995; postgrad., Loyola U., 1996—. Early interventionist Home Infant Stimulation Program, Chgo., 1976-78; tchr. aid, arts and crafts tchr. Ill. Deaf-Blind Svc. Ctr. and Sch., Chgo., 1978-80; head tchr. Lad and Lassie Pre-Sch., Evanston, Ill., 1981; child care worker Jewish Children's Bur., Chgo., 1981; tchr. pre-sch. Sunshine Pre-Sch., Chgo., 1982-83; tchr. kindergarten and primary sch. aged, program coord., spl. educator, interventionist Sunshine Sch., Chgo., 1982-93; dir. George's Sunshine Preschool & Kindergarten, Chgo., 1993-95; free lance tutor, Chgo., 1969-; adv. bd. Cook County Child Care Resource and Referral N. Satellit Dist., Chgo., 1991—; dir., head tchr., early internventionist state prekindergarten at-risk program Albany Park Comty. Ctr., Chgo., 1995; instr., acad. advisor early childhood edn. program Northeastern Ill. U., 1996; instr. child devel. program Truman Coll., City Colls. Chgo., 1997—; edn. cons., tchr. trainer, 1990—. Author, illustrator: Mother Goose Yesterday and Today; author, lyricist children's rhymes and lyrics; inventor: interactive learning materials and board games; choreographer adaptations of ethnic dances for young children; designer multicultural curriculum and costumes, 1990-95, Sunshine Sch., editor newsletter, 1991-95. vol. tchr.'s asst. Head Start P. Sheridan Sch., Chgo., 1968; tutor Avalon Park Tutoring Project, Chgo., 1968-69; food distributor Operation Breadbasket, Chgo., 1969-72; counselor Urban Gateways, Wilmette, Winnetka, Ill., 1969; child care worker Kibbutz Palmachim and Kibbutz Sarid, Rishon Le Zion and Afula, Israel, 1973-74; vol. hotline Parental Stress Svcs./Child Abuse Prevention Svcs., Chgo., 1993-94; child life worker Children's Meml. Med. Ctr., Chgo., 1995. Recipient Excellence in Child Care award Pre-Sch. Owners Ill. Assn., 1991, Disting. Accomplishment in Scientific Literacy Workshops, Chgo. Techr.'s Ctr., 1992, Outstanding Attendance and Contribution in Adminstrv. Tng. Jane Addams Hull House Acad. Achievement award Univ. Without Walls, 1992. Mem. Nat. Ill. and Chgo. Assns. for the Edn. Young Children, Assn. for Childhood Edn. Internat. (Hall of Excellence citation 1993), Assn. for Supervision and Curriculum Devel., Ill. Sch. Age Child Care Network, Ill. Assn. Infant Mental Health, World Assn. Infant Mental Health, Coun. Exceptional Children (divsn. early childhood). Avocations: writing poetry, interior decorating, intercultural studies and dancing, tennis. Home: 1432 W Elmdale Ave Chicago IL 60660-2406 Office: City Coll Chgo Truman Coll Dept Social Scis 1145 W Wilson Ave Chicago IL 60640-5616

WEIMAR, ROBERT HENRY, counselor, clinical hypnotherapist; b. Chgo., July 4, 1946. BA in Psychology, U. Ill., 1968; MS in Community Mental Health, No. Ill. U., 1971. Cert. med. hypnotherapist, cert. clin. mental health counselor. Cons., edn. coord. No. Community Mental Health Ctr., Ashland, Wis., 1978-79; pvt. practice counselor and cons. Ashland, 1981-88; alcohol prevention coord. Bad River Chippewa Tribe, Odanah, Wis., 1982-88; prodr. freelance radio programs Ashland, Wis., 1984-90, Lynchburg, Va., 1984-90; mental health counselor Ctrl. Health (Bridges), Lynchburg, 1988-90, mental health cons. 1990—; coord. Va. Divsn. Drug Abuse Control, Richmond, 1972-74; planner N.Y. State Drug Abuse Control Commn., N.Y.C., 1974-75. Contbr. numerous articles to profl. jours. Recipient Outstanding Svc. award Nat. Indian Bd. on Alcohol and Drug Abuse, 1987. Office: Hypnosis For Health 3313 Old Forest Rd Lynchburg VA 24501-2912

WEIMER, GARY W., academic administrator, consultant; b. Louisville, Mar. 28, 1944; s. G. Wilfred and Wanda Ruth (Green) W.; m. M. Elizabeth Enterline, Aug. 29, 1966; children: Inga Elizabeth, Kirk Ayleston. AB, Princeton U., 1966; M.T.S., Harvard U., 1971. Reporter, copy editor The Vindicator, Youngstown, Ohio, 1970; dir. devel. programs Oberlin (Ohio) Coll., 1971-78; dir. devel. U. Calif., Santa Barbara, 1978-82; v.p. Hiram (Ohio) Coll., 1982-87; sr. devel. officer Case Western Res. U., Cleve., 1987-90; dir. devel. U. Hosps. of Cleve., 1991—. Contbr. articles to profl. jours. Trustee U. Calif. Santa Barbara Found., 1979-82, Robert Maynard Hutchins Ctr. for the Study of Dem. Insts., Santa Barbara, 1979-81. With U.S. Army, 1968-69, Vietnam. James A. Garfield fellow Hiram Coll., 1982, Rockefeller Bros. Theol. fellow Rockefeller and Booth-Ferris Founds., Harvard Divinity Sch., 1966-67; decorated Bronze Star, Air medal, U.S. Army Am. Spirit Honor medal. Mem. Princeton Club N.Y.

WEIMER, JEAN ELAINE, nursing educator; b. Denver, June 8, 1932; d. John and Marquerite Christina (Friehauf) Jacoby; m. James David Weimer, Aug. 5, 1956; 1 dau., Lisa Marie. Diploma in nursing Children's Hosp. Sch. Nursing, Denver, 1953; BS in Nursing, U. Denver, 1954; MA, NYU, 1962. RN, Colo., S.D., N.Y., Ill. Staff nurse Children's Hosp., Denver, 1953-54, head nurse, 1954-56; dir. nursing edn. Yankton (S.D.) State Hosp., 1956-60; instr. Mt. Sinai Hosp. Sch. Nursing, N.Y.C., 1962-63, curriculum coord., 1964-67; asst. prof. nursing City Colls. Chgo., 1968-78, assoc. prof., 1978-85, prof., 1985—, Disting. prof., 1995-96, co-chmn. nursing dept. Truman Coll., 1984-93, chmn. 1993—; chmn. program com. RN Tutoring project, 1988-92. Deacon United Ch. of Christ, 1988-90. NIMH grantee, 1960-62. Mem. Am. Nurses Assn., Coun. Advanced Practioners Psychiat. Coun. of Dirs. of Assoc. Degree Nursing Programs, Nat. League Nursing, Truman Coll. Faculty Coun. (pres. 1996-97), City Coll. Faculty Coun., Kappa Delta Pi, Pi Lambda Theta. Home: 50 E Bellevue Pl Apt 904 Chicago IL 60611-1167 Office: Truman Coll 1145 W Wilson Ave # 184 Chicago IL 60640-5616

WEIMER, ROBERT JAY, geology educator, energy consultant, civic leader; b. Glendo, Wyo., Sept. 4, 1926; s. John L. and Helen (Mowrey) W.; m. Ruth Carol Adams, Sept. 12, 1948; children: Robert Thomas, Loren Edward (dec.), Paul Christner, Carl Scott. BA, U Wyo., 1948, MA, 1949; PhD, Stanford U., 1953. Registered profl. engr., Colo. Geologist Union Oil Co. Calif., 1949-54; cons. geologist U.S. and fgn. petroleum exploration, 1954—; prof. geology Colo. Sch. Mines, 1957-83, prof. emeritus, 1983—, Getty prof. geology, 1978-83; vis. prof. U. Colo., 1961, U. Calgary, Can., 1970, Inst. Tech., Bandung, Indonesia, 1975; Fulbright lectr. U. Adelaide, South Australia, 1967; disting. lectr. and continuing edn. lectr. Am. Assn. Petroleum Geologists, Soc. Expl. Geophysicists; ednl. cons. to petroleum cos., 1964—; mem. energy rsch. adv. bd. Dept. Energy, 1985-90, Bd. on Mineral and Energy Resources, NAS, 1988. Editor: Guide to Geology of Colorado, 1960, Symposium on Cretaceous Rocks of Colorado and Adjacent Area, 1959, Denver Earthquakes, 1968, Fossil Fuel Exploration, 1974, Studies in Colorado Field Geology, 1976. Trustee Colo. Sch. Mines Research Found., 1967-70; pres. Rockland Found., 1982-83. With USNR, 1944-46. Recipient Disting. Alumnus award U. Wyo., 1982, Mines medal Colo. Sch. Mines, 1984, Brown medal, 1990, Parker medal Am. Inst. Profl. Geologists. Fellow Geol. Soc. Am. (chmn. Rocky Mountain sect. 1966-67), AAAS; mem. Am. Assn. Petroleum Geologists (pres. 1992, Sidney Powers medal, Dist. Educator award 1996), Soc. Econ. Paleontologists and Mineralogists (hon., sec.-treas. 1966-67, v.p. 1971, pres. 1972, Twenhofel medal 1995), Colo. Sci. Soc. (hon., pres. 1981), Rocky Mountain Assn. Geologists (pres. 1969, hon. mem., Scientist of Yr. 1982), Wyo. Geol. Assn. (hon.), Colo. Sch. Mines Alumni Assn. (hon., Coolbaugh award), Am. Geol. Inst. Found. (sec., treas. 1984-88), Nat. Acad. Engring., Mt. Vernon Country Club (Golden, bd. dirs. 1956-59, 81-84, pres. 1983-84). Home: RR 3 25853 Mt Vernon Rd Golden CO 80401-9699

WEIN, ALAN JEROME, urologist, educator, researcher; b. Newark, Dec. 15, 1941; s. Isadore R. and Jeanette Frances (Abrams) W. AB cum laude, Princeton U., 1962; MD, U. Pa., 1966. Diplomate, trustee emeritus Am. Bd. Urology. Intern mixed surgery Hosp. U. Pa., Phila., 1966-67, resident surgery, 1967-68; resident urology U. Pa., Phila., 1969-72, fellow Harrison Dept. Surg. Rsch. Urology Sch. Medicine, 1968-69, asst. instr. surgery Sch. Medicine, 1967-68, asst. instr. urology, 1969-71, instr., 1971-72, asst. prof., 1974-76, assoc. prof., 1976-83, prof., 1983—, asst. chief urology, 1974-79, dir. Urodynamic Evaluation Ctr., 1974—, chmn. div. urology, 1981—, chief urology, 1981—; dir. resident edn. com. div. urology Sch. Medicine U. Pa., 1976—, coord. program urologics oncology, 1976—; chief urology VA Hosp., Phila., 1974-82, attending urologist, 1982—; asst. surgeon Children's Hosp. Phila., 1974—; cons. CDC Coun. Incontinence, 1990—; assoc. surgeon Pa. Hosp., Phila., 1977—; attending urologist Grad. Hosp., Phila., 1980—. Author: (with D.M. Barrett) Controversies in Neuro-Urology, 1984, Voiding Function and Dysfunction: A Logical and Practical Approach, 1988, 2d edit., 1995, (with A.R. Mundy and T.P. Stephenson) Urodynamics: Principles, Practice and Application, 1984, 2d edit., 1994, (with P.M. Hanno) A Clinical Manual of Urology, 1987, 2d edit., 1994, (with Hanno, Staskin and Krane) Interstitial Cystitis, 1990; editl. bd. asst. Urol. Survey, 1978-81; editl. bd. cons. Investigative Urology, 1978-81; mem. editl. bd. World Jour. Urology, 1982—, Am. Urol. Assn. Update series, 1983—, Urol. Survey, 1987—, Internat. Jour. Impotence Rsch.: Basic and Clin. Studies, 1989—, Urology, 1991—; ad hoc reviewer Cancer, 1985—; cons. editor Sexuality and Disability, 1985—; asst. editor Jour. Urology, 1980-89, ad hoc reviewer clin. sect., 1989—, editl. bd. investigative sect., 1989—; assoc. editor Neurourlogy and Urodynamics, 1982—; contbr. over 560 articles and abstracts to profl. jours. Mem. coun. urology Nat. Kidney Found., Inc.; mem lectrs. bur. Am. Cancer Soc., 1984—; mem. adv. panel Nat. Assn. for Incontinence, 1987—; mem. adv. bd. Simon Found., 1987—; mem. med. adv. bd. Institial Cystitis Assn., 1987—; chmn. bladder health coun. Am. Found. Urologic Disease, 1990—; trustee Am. Bd. Urology, 1990-96. Maj. MC, U.S. Army, 1972-74. Grantee VA, 1974-79, 79, 81, 81-84, 82-85, 85-88, 88-92, Eaton Labs., 1975-76, 78-80, McCabe Rsch. Fund, 1975-82, 87-88, Merrell Nat. Labs., 1979-82, 1980-82, Nat. Kidney Found., 1980-81, NIH, 1980-83, 83-88, 84-87, 87—, Roche Labs., 1981, Smith Kline and French Labs., 1982, 86-88, Eli Lilly Labs., 1986-88, 91, Found. Interstitial Cystitis, 1986-87, 87-88, Sterling Drug Co., 1991. Fellow ACS; mem. AAAS, AMA (cons. com. drug evaluation 1977—), Am. Acad. Clin. Neurophysiology, Am. Assn. Surgery of Trauma, Am. Assn. Clin. Urologists, Am. Assn. Genito-Urinary Surgeons, Am. Fertility Soc., Am. Inst. Ultrasound in Medicine, Am. Soc. Pharmacology and Exptl. Therapeutics, Am. Soc. Andrology, Am. Soc. Clin. Oncology, Am. Urol. Assn. (chmn. practical cases urology 1982—, rsch. com. 1985—, editl. com. mid-Atlantic sect. 1988—), Assn. Acad. Surgery, Can. Urol. Assn., Clin. Soc. Genito-Urinary Surgeons, Ea. Coop. Oncologic Group, Endourol. Soc., Internat. Continence Soc., Nat. Assn. VA Physicians, N.Y. Acad. Scis., Coll. Physicians Phila., John Morgan Soc., Pa. Med. Assn., Pa. Oncologic Soc., Phila. Acad. Surgery, Phila. County Med. Soc., Phila. Profl. Standards Rev. Orgn., Phila. Urologic Soc. (pres. 1990-91), Ravdin-Rhoads Surg. Soc., Urol. Assn. Pa., Radiation Therapy Oncology Group (genitourinary working com. 1980—), Royal Soc. Medicine, Soc. Internat. d'Urologie, Soc. Basic Urologic Rsch., Soc. Sex Therapy and Rsch., Soc. Govt. Svc. Urologists, Soc. Pelvic Surgeons, Soc. Univ. Surgeons, Soc. Univ. Urologists, Soc. Urologic Oncology, Univ. Urologic Forum, Urodynamics Soc. (exec. com. 1980—), Urologic Rsch. Soc., Urologist's Corr. Club, Home: 1224 Mirabeau Ln Gladwyne PA 19035 Office: Hosp U Pa 1 Rhoads Pavilion 3400 Spruce St Philadelphia PA 19104

WEINACHT, JOHN WILLIAM, lawyer; b. Orange, Tex., Nov. 13, 1963; s. Charles and Mary Ann W.; m. Luz Marina Lara, Aug. 21, 1985; children: Lara, Jake, Claire. BA, U. Tex., 1987; JD, Baylor U., 1989. Bar: Tex. 1989, N. Mex. 1994, U.S. Dist. Ct. (all dists.) Tex. 1993, U.S. Dist. Ct. N. Mex. 1994, U.S. Ct. Appeals (5th cir.) 1993, U.S. Ct. Appeals (10th cir.) 1995, U.S. Ct. Internat. Trade 1995; U.S. Supreme Ct. 1995. Atty. pvt. practice, Pecos, Tex., 1989—; county atty. Reeves County, Pecos, Tex., 1993-96; spl. counsel Reeves County Detention Ctr., Pecos, Tex., 1997—. Mem. ABA, Tex. Trial Lawyers Assn., Reeves County Bar Assn., Trans-Pecos Bar Assn. Democrat. Office: 420 S Cypress St Pecos TX 79772-4012

WEINBACH, ARTHUR FREDERIC, computing services company executive; b. Waterbury, Conn., May 3, 1943; s. Max and Winifred (Eckstein) W.; m. Joanne Kaplan, Nov. 20, 1970; children: Michael Scott, Jonathan David. BS in Econs., U. Pa., 1965, MS in Acctg., 1966. CPA. Various positions with Touche Ross & Co., N.Y.C., 1966-75; ptnr. Touche Ross & Co., Stamford, Conn., 1976-79; v.p. Automatic Data Processing, Inc., Roseland, N.J., 1980-81; sr. v.p. adminstrn. and fin. Automatic Data Processing, Inc., Clifton, N.J., 1982-91, exec. v.p., 1992-94, pres., 1994—, CEO, 1996—; also bd. dirs. Automatic Data Processing, Inc., Roseland, 1989—; bd. dirs. Decision One, 1996—, Health Plan Svcs., 1997—. Bd. dirs. Boys Hope, 1991—, Overlook Hosp. Found., 1991—, Metro N.J. U. Pa. Club, 1993—. Jewish. Home: One Twin Oak Rd Short Hills NJ 07078-1208 Office: ADP Inc 1 A D P Blvd Roseland NJ 07068-1728

WEINBACH, LAWRENCE ALLEN, financial executive; b. N.Y.C., Jan. 8, 1940; s. Max N. and Winifred E. Weinbach; m. Patricia Leiter, Dec. 1961; children: Wendy, Peter, Daniel. BS in Econs., U. Pa., 1961. CPA, Conn., N.Y., other states. With Arthur Andersen & Co. (CPA's), N.Y.C., 1961—; mng. ptnr. Arthur Andersen & Co. (CPA's), Stamford, Conn., 1974-80; ptnr.-in-charge N.Y. acctg. and audit practice Arthur Andersen & Co., N.Y.C., 1980-83, mng. ptnr. N.Y. and N.Y. Met. area, 1983-87, mem. bd. ptnrs., 1984-87, chmn. bd. ptnrs., 1986-87, mng. ptnr., COO, 1987-89, mng. ptnr., chief exec., 1989—; bd. dirs. Asia Soc., 1995—, U.S.-Japan Bus. Coun., 1989-94. With Hartman Regional Theatre, Stamford, 1976-80, chmn. bd. dirs., 1977-78; mem. bd. incorporators Stamford Hosp., 1976-84; bd. dirs. United Way, Stamford, 1976-78, Phoenix House Inc., 1984-92, Coun. on Fgn. Rels., 1986—, catalyst, 1991—; trustee Carnegie Hall, 1985—, Northwestern U., 1990—; mem. bd. overseers Wharton Sch., U. Pa., 1988—; mem. bd. Stern Sch., 1989—, Pub. Policy Inst., 1990—, Am. Bus. Conf., 1992—, YMCA-Greater N.Y., 1995—. Mem. AICPA, N.Y. Soc. CPAs, Conn. Soc. CPAs, Econs. Club N.Y., Asia Soc. (bd. dirs. 1995—), Chgo. Club, Harmonie Club, Univ. Club, Beta Gamma Sigma, Beta Alpha Psi. Office: Andersen Worldwide 1345 Avenue Of The Americas New York NY 10105-0302

WEINBAUM, SHELDON, biomedical engineer; b. Bklyn., July 26, 1937; s. Alexander Weinbaum and Frances Clare (Stark) Colby; m. Alexandra Tamara, June 10, 1962; children: Alys Eve, Daniel Eden. BAE, Rensselaer Polytech. Inst., Troy, 1959; MS, Harvard U., 1960, PhD, 1963. Mem. rsch. staff Sperry Rand Rsch. Lab., Sudbury, Mass., 1963-64; prin. rsch. scientist Avco Everett Rsch. Lab., Everett, Mass., 1964, G.E. Space Sci. Lab., Valley Forge, Pa., 1964-67; assoc. prof. CUNY, N.Y.C., 1967-72, H. Kayser Prof., 1980-85, CUNY Disting. Prof., 1986—, dir. Ctr. Biomed. Engring., 1994—; vis. prof. Imperial Coll. Sci. and Tech., London, 1973-74, MIT, 1980-81; Russell S. Springer vis. prof. U. Calif., Berkeley, 1979-80; sr. fellow scientific rsch. coun. of Gt. Britain, 1973-74. Chair legal action com. CUNY, 1992. Recipient Rsch. award European Soc. Biomechanics, 1994, Pub. Svc. award Fund for City of N.Y., 1988; Gordon McKay prize fellow Harvard U., 1959-60, NSF fellow Harvard U., 1961-63; spl. creativity grantee NSF, 1985-87. Fellow ASME (H.R. Lissner award 1994, Melville medal 1996), Am. Phys. Soc., Am. Inst. Med. Bio. Engring.; mem. NAE, Biomed. Engring. Soc. (bd. dirs. 1989-92). Achievements include contributions in the broad application of engineering principles to the understanding of biological and medical processes including water and solute transport in capillary interendothelial clefts, bioheat transfer, plasma skimmings and red cell screening in blood flow, leaky junction-cell turnover mechanism for LDL transport, intraocular fluid mechanics, convective transport in the arterial intima and atherogenesis and the mechano-sensory mechanism for bone growth. Office: City Coll City of New York Convent Ave & 137th St New York NY 10031

WEINBERG, ALVIN MARTIN, physicist; b. Chgo., Apr. 20, 1915; s. J.L. and Emma (Levinson) W.; m. Margaret Despres, June 14, 1940 (dec. 1969); children: David, Richard; m. Gene K. DePersio, Sept. 20, 1974. A.B., U. Chgo., 1935, A.M., 1936, Ph.D., 1939; LL.D., U. Chattanooga, Alfred U.; D.Sc., U. Pacific, Denison U., Wake Forest U., Kenyon Coll., Worcester Poly. Inst., U. Rochester, Stevens Inst. Tech., Butler U., U. Louisville, U. Bridgeport. Research assoc. math. biophysics U. Chgo., 1939-41, Metall. Lab., 1941-45; joined Oak Ridge Nat. Lab., 1945, dir. physics div., 1947-48, research dir. lab., 1948-55, dir. lab., 1955-74; dir. Office Energy R&D, Fed. Energy Adminstrn., 1974, Inst. Energy Analysis, Oak Ridge, 1975-85; disting. fellow Oak Ridge Associated Univs., 1985—; mem. Pres.'s Sci. Adv. Com., 1960-62, Pres.'s Medal of Sci. Com. Author: Reflections on Big Science, (with E.P. Wigner) Physical Theory of Neutron Chain Reactors, 1958, Continuing the Nuclear Dialogue, 1985, Nuclear Reactions: Science and Trans-Science, 1992, The First Nuclear Era: The Life and Times of a Technological Fixer, 1994; co-author: The Second Nuclear Era, 1985; co-editor: The Nuclear Connection, 1985, Strategic Defenses and Arms Control, 1987; editor: Eugene Wigner's Collected Works on Nuclear Energy. Recipient Atoms for Peace award, 1960, E.O. Lawrence award, 1960, U. Chgo. Alumni medal, 1966, Heinrich Hertz award, 1975, N.Y. Acad. Scis. award, 1976, Enrico Fermi award, 1980, Harvey prize, 1982, Eugene Wigner award in reactor physics, 1992. Mem. Nat. Acad. Scis. (applied sci. sect.), Am. Nuclear Soc. (pres. 1959-60, Alvin M. Weinberg award 1996), Nat. Acad. Engring., Am. Acad. Arts and Scis., Am. Philos. Soc., Royal Netherlands Acad. Sci. (fgn. asso.). Home: 111 Moylan Ln Oak Ridge TN 37830-5351 Office: Oak Ridge Associated Univs PO Box 117 Oak Ridge TN 37831-0117

WEINBERG, DAVID B., lawyer, investor; b. Chgo., Feb. 19, 1952; s. Judd A. and Marjorie (Gottlieb) W.; m. Lynne Ellen Mesirow, July 6, 1980; children: Julie, Jane, Jonathan. AB cum laude, Harvard U., 1974; JD, Georgetown U., 1977. Bar: Ill. 1977, U.S. Dist. Ct. (no. dist.) Ill. 1977, U.S. Ct. Appeals (7th cir.) 1978. Law clerk to Hon. William G. Clark Supreme Ct. Ill., 1977-79; assoc. Lord, Bissell & Brook, Chgo., 1979-84, ptnr., 1985-89; ptnr. Mayer, Brown & Platt, Chgo., 1989-96, sr. counsel, 1996—; chmn., CEO Judd Enterprises, Inc., Chgo., 1996—; pres. Digital BandWidth LLC, Chgo., 1996—; Ill. Supreme Ct. com. Profl. Responsibility, Chgo., 1984-94, chmn. subcom. lawyers certification; dir. Rubicon Ins. Co., Applied Lang. Tech., Inc., VIEWnet, In c. Founding mem. Friends of Prentice, Chgo., 1986-87; assocs. bd. Rush-Presbyn. St. Luke's Med. Ctr., 1989—; pres. Ravinia Festival Assn., Highland Park, Ill., 1997—; trustee Northwestern U., 1994—, chmn. com. on ednl. policies and appointments, 1996—; dir. Northwestern U./Evanston Rsch. Park, Inc., 1996—. Mem. ABA (sect. bus. law, com. fed. regulation securities), Harvard Club Chgo. (v.p. 1985-89, dir.), Chgo. Club, Standard Club Chgo. (dir. 1988-90), Econ. Club Chgo., Lake Shore Country Club, Arts Club Chgo. Office: Judd Enterprises Inc 1 First Natl Plz # 3148 Chicago IL 60603-2003

WEINBERG, EDWARD BRILL, lawyer; b. Louisville, Mar. 27, 1945; s. Manuel and Evelyn (Brill) W.; m. Elaine Ruth Yoffe, Feb. 27, 1972; children: Matthew, Reed. BS in Econs., U. Pa., 1967; JD, U. Mich., 1970. Bar: Ky. 1971. Mem. Greenebaum, Doll & McDonald, Louisville, 1970—; lectr. seminars U. Ky. Coll. Law, Ea. Mineral Law Found. Contbr. articles to profl. publs.; bd. editors Ky. Mineral Law Manual, Jour. Natural Resources and Environ. Law. Chmn. bd. dirs. Four Cts., Louisville, Inc., St. Francis H.S.; pres. The Temple, Louisville, 1990-92; chmn. bd. trustees City of Spring Green, Ky.; pres. Jewish Cmty. Fedn. Louisville, 1993-95; bd. trustees Jewish Hosp. Healthcare Svcs., Inc. Mem. ABA (lectr., mem. litigation subcom. natural resources sect.), Louisville Bar Assn., Ky. Bar Assn., Ea. Mineral Law Found. (trustee, mem. exec. com., pres.), Order of Coif. Office: Greenebaum Doll & McDonald 3300 Nat City Tower Louisville KY 40202

WEINBERG, EUGENE DAVID, microbiologist, educator; b. Chgo., Mar. 4, 1922; s. Philip and Lenore (Bergman) W.; m. Frances Murl Izen, Sept. 5, 1949; children—Barbara Ann, Marjorie Jean, Geoffrey Alan, Michael Benjamin. B.S., U. Chgo., 1942, M.A., 1948, Ph.D., 1950. Instr. dept. microbiology Ind. U., Bloomington, 1950-53; asst. prof. Ind. U., 1953-57, asso. prof., 1957-61, prof., 1961—, head microbiology sect., med. sci. program, 1978—. Served with AUS, 1942-45. Mem. AAAS, Am. Soc. Microbiology. Office: Ind U Biology Dept Jordan Hall Bloomington IN 47405

WEINBERG, GERHARD LUDWIG, history educator; b. Hannover, Germany, Jan. 1, 1928; came to U.S., 1940, naturalized, 1949; s. Max Bendix and Kate Sarah (Gruenebaum) W.; m. Janet Kabler White, Apr. 29, 1989. BA, N.Y. State Coll. Tchrs., Albany, 1948; MA, U. Chgo., 1949, PhD, 1951; LHD honoris causa, SUNY, Albany, 1989. Research analyst War Documentation project Columbia U., 1951-54; vis. lectr. history U. Chgo., 1954-55, U. Ky., Lexington, 1955-56; dir. project microfilming captured German documents Am. Hist. Assn., 1956-57; asst. prof. U. Ky., 1957-59; mem. faculty U. Mich., Ann Arbor, 1959-74; prof. history U. Mich., 1963-74, chmn. dept., 1972-73; William Rand Kenan, Jr. prof. history U. N.C., Chapel Hill, 1974—; acting chmn. dept., 1989-90; vis. prof. Bonn U., 1983, USAF Acad., 1990-91; bd. dirs. World War II Studies Assn., 1968—; cons. in field. Author: Guide to Captured German Documents, 1952, Germany and the Soviet Union, 1939-41, 1954, The Foreign Policy of Hitler's Germany, 1933-36, 1970, The Foreign Policy of Hitler's Germany, 1937-39, 1980, World in the Balance: Behind the Scenes of World II, 1981, A World at Arms: A Global History of World War II, 1994, Germany, Hitler and World War II, 1995; co-author: Soviet Partisans in World War II, 1964; editor: Hitlers zweites Buch, 1961, 95, Transformation of a Continent, 1975; bd. editors Jour. Modern History, 1970-72, Central European History, 1970-72, Kansas Humanities Series, 1987—, Internat. History Rev., 1990—. Chmn. Ann Arbor Democratic Com., 1961-63; mem. Mich. Dem. Central Com., 1963-67; mem. adv. com. on the air force history program Sec. of Air Force, 1987-90; mem. adv. com. army history program Sec. Army, 1996—; mem. dept. defence Hist. Records Declassification Adv. Panel, 1996—. Wwith AUS, 1946-47. Fellow Social Sci. Research Council, 1962-63; fellow Am. Council Learned Socs., 1965-66; fellow Guggenheim Found., 1971-72; fellow Nat. Endowment Humanities, 1978-79. Mem. Am. Hist. Assn. (George Louis Beer prize 1971, 95, v.p. rsch. 1982-84), So. Hist. Assn. (chmn. European sect. 1989), Conf. Group for Ctrl. European History (chmn. 1982), Coordinating Com. Women in Hist. Profession, German Studies Assn. (exec. com. 1989-92, Halverson prize 1981, v.p. 1994-96, pres. 1996—), World War II Studies Assn., Am. Acad. Arts and Scis., Phi Beta Kappa. Jewish. Home: 1416 Mount Willing Rd Efland NC 27243-9646 Office: Dept History Univ NC Chapel Hill NC 27599-3195

WEINBERG, H. BARBARA, art historian, educator, curator paintings and sculpture; b. N.Y.C., Jan. 23, 1942; d. Max and Evelyn Kallman; m. Michael B. Weinberg, Aug. 30, 1964. AB, Barnard Coll., 1962; MA, Columbia U., N.Y.C., 1964, PhD, 1972. From asst. prof. to prof. art history Queens Coll. and Grad. Sch., CUNY, 1972-94; curator dept. Am. paintings and sculpture Met. Mus. Art., 1990—. Author: The Decorative World of John La Farge, 1977, The American Pupils of Jean-Léon Gérome, 1984, The Lure of Paris: Nineteenth-Century American Painters and Their French Teachers, 1991, Thomas Eakins and the Metropolitan Museum of Art, 1994; co-author: American Impressionism and Realism: The Painting of Modern Life, 1885-1915, 1994; mem. editorial bd. Am. Art Jour., 1984—. Mem. Coll. Arts Assn., Gallery Assn. N.Y. State (bd. trustees), Phi Beta Kappa. Office: Met Mus Art 1000 5th Ave New York NY 10028-0113

WEINBERG, HARRY BERNARD, cardiologist; b. Fremont, Nebr., Apr. 29, 1913; s. Ephraim and Goldie (Levynsky) W.; m. Evelyn Waxenberg, Mar. 26, 1939; 1 son, Steven M. B.S. in Medicine, U. Nebr., 1935, M.D., 1936. Intern, Univ. Hosp., Omaha, 1936-37; resident cardiovascular disease Michael Reese Hosp., Chgo., 1938-40; pvt. practice internal medicine and cardiology Davenport, Iowa, 1940-69; coordinator Iowa Regional Med. Program, clin. prof. internal medicine U. Iowa Coll. Medicine, 1969-72; dir. med. edn. Meml. Hosp., Hollywood, Fla., 1972-74; pvt. practice medicine specializing in cardiology Hollywood, 1974-82; hon. med. staff Meml. Hosp., Hollywood, Fla., 1982—; physician utilization rev. cons., 1982-91; Bd. dirs. Iowa Heart Assn., 1953-64, pres., 1955-56. Bd. dirs. Davenport C. of C., 1958-61, v.p., 1961. Served to lt. col. AUS, 1940-46. Fellow ACP, Am. Coll. Cardiology; mem. AMA, Am. Heart Assn. (bd. dirs. 1956-69, fellow council clin. cardiology 1965—), Alpha Omega Alpha. Home: 2470 N Park Rd # 210 Hollywood FL 33021

WEINBERG, HELEN ARNSTEIN, American art and literature educator; b. Orange, N.J., June 17, 1927; d. Morris Jerome and Jeannette (Tepperman) Arnstein; m. Kenneth Gene Weinberg, Sept. 12, 1949; children: Janet Sue Weinberg Strassner, Hugh Benjamin, John Arnstein. BA in English Lit., Wellesley Coll., 1949; MA in English Lit., Western Res. U., 1953, PhD in English Lit., 1966. Teaching fellow Ohio State U., Columbus, 1949-51, Western Res. U., Cleve., 1953-57; instr. to prof. Cleve. (Ohio) Inst. Art, 1958—; standing officer Coll. English Assn. Ohio, 1987-90; vis. tchr. NYU, 1985, Sch. Visual Art's, 1981; lecture tours Israel, 1968, 70, 71. Author: The New Novel in America: The Kafkan Mode in Contemporary Fiction, 1970. Recipient fellowship in art history NEH, Columbia U., N.Y.C., 1977-78; Recipient Am. Culture grantee NEH/Vassar Coll., 1993. Mem. AAUP, Modern Lang. Assn., Coll. Art Assn. Democrat. Jewish. Home: 3015 Huntington Rd Shaker Hts OH 44120-2407 Office: Cleve Inst Art 11141 East Blvd Cleveland OH 44106-1710

WEINBERG, HERSCHEL MAYER, lawyer; b. Bklyn., Oct. 13, 1927; s. Jacob and Gertrude (Wernick) W. B.A., Bklyn. Coll., 1948; LL.B., Harvard U., 1952. Bar: N.Y. 1952. Atty. firm Payne & Steingarten, N.Y.C., 1952-57, Jacobs, Persinger & Parker, N.Y.C., 1957-61; partner firm Rubin, Rubin, Weinberg, & Di Paola, N.Y.C., 1961-78, Weinberg Tauber & Pressman, 1979-90; pvt. practice N.Y.C., 1990—. Served with AUS, 1946-47. Mem. Assn. of Bar of City of N.Y., N.Y. State Bar Assn. Club: Harvard (N.Y.C.). Home: 50 Sutton Pl S New York NY 10022-4167 Office: 110 E 59th St New York NY 10022-1304

WEINBERG, JOHN LEE, federal judge; b. Chgo., Apr. 24, 1941; s. Louis Jr. and Jane Kitz (Goldstein) W.; m. Sarah Kibbee, July 6, 1963; children: Ruth, Leo. BA, Swarthmore Coll., 1962; JD, U. Chgo., 1965. Bar: Ill. 1966, Wash. 1967, U.S. Dist. Ct. (we. dist.) Wash. 1967, U.S. Ct. Appeals (9th cir.) 1967. Law clk. to Hon. Henry L. Burman Ill. Appellate Ct., Chgo., 1965-66; law clk. to Hon. Walter V. Schaefer Ill. Supreme Ct., Chgo., 1966; law clk. to Hon. William T. Beeks U.S. Dist. Ct. Wash., Seattle, 1967-68; atty. Perkins Coie Law Firm, Seattle, 1968-73; magistrate judge U.S. Dist. Ct.; U.S. Magistrate judge Seattle, 1973—. Author: Federal Bail and Detention Handbook, 1988. Mem. ABA, Am. Judicature Soc., Wash. State Bar Assn., Seattle-King County Bar Assn., Fed. Magistrate Judges Assn. (nat. pres. 1982-83). Avocations: sports and physical fitness activities, bridge. Office: US Magistrate Judge 304 US Courthouse 1010 5th Ave Seattle WA 98104-1130

WEINBERG, JOHN LIVINGSTON, investment banker; b. N.Y.C., Jan. 5, 1925; s. Sidney James and Helen (Livingston) W.; m. Sue Ann Gotshal, Dec. 6, 1952; children: Ann K. (dec.), John, Jean. A.B. cum laude, Princeton U., 1948; M.B.A., Harvard U., 1950. With Goldman, Sachs & Co., N.Y.C., 1950—, ptnr., 1956-76, sr. ptnr., 1976-90, co-chmn. mgmt. com., 1976-84, chmn. mgmt. com., 1984-90; sr. chmn. Goldman, Sachs & Co., 1990—; bd. dirs. Knight-Rider, Inc., Champion Internat. Corp.; dir. emeritus Providian Fin. Corp.; mem. Conf. Bd. Bd. govs. N.Y. Hosp.-Cornell Med. Ctr. lt. USMCR, 1942-46, capt., 1951-52. Fellow AAAS; mem. Va. Neurol. Inst., Coun. on Fgn. Rels., Bus. Coun., DeWitt Wallace Fund for Meml. Sloan Kettering Cancer Ctr. Office: Goldman Sachs & Co 85 Broad St Fl 22 New York NY 10004-2434

WEINBERG, LAWRENCE, professional basketball team owner. Owner, formerly pres. Portland Trail Blazers, Nat. Basketball Assn., Oreg.; now pres. emeritus Portland Trail Blazers. Office: care Portland Trail Blazers One Ctr Ct Ste 200 Portland OR 97232-4109*

WEINBERG, LEONARD BURTON, political scientist; b. N.Y.C., Nov. 10, 1939; s. Max R. and Rose (Levin) W.; m. Ellen Bach, Aug. 23, 1966 (div.); 1 son, David; m. Sinikka Palomaki, June 4, 1986. B.A., Syracuse U., 1961, Ph.D., 1967; M.A., U. Chgo., 1963. Instr. polit. sci. U. Wis., Milw., 1966-67; asst. prof. polit. sci. U. Nev., Reno, 1967-71; assoc. prof. U. Nev., 1971-78, prof., 1978—, chmn. dept., 1979-82; vis. prof. U. Florence, Italy, 1992. Author: Comparing Public Policies, 1977, After Mussolini, 1979, The Rise and Fall of Italian Terrorism, 1987, Introduction to Political Terrorism, 1989; editor: Political Parties and Terrorist Groups, 1992, Revival of Right-Wing Extremism in the 1990s, 1996; co-editor: Encounters with the Radical Right, 1992, The Transformation of Italian Communism, 1994, Revival of Right-Wing Extremism in the 1990s, 1997. Recipient Fulbright Rsch. award, 1984; Italian Govt. Borsa di Studio, 1965-66; Fulbright grantee, 1965-66, Harry F. Guggenheim grantee, 1995-96. Mem. Am. Polit. Sci. Assn., Internat. Polit. Sci. Assn. (political sociology com.), Conf. Group on Italian Politics of Am. Polit. Sci. Assn., Phi Kappa Phi. Jewish. Office: Dept Political Science U Nevada Reno NV 89557

WEINBERG, LILA SHAFFER, writer, editor; d. Sam and Blanche (Hyman) Shaffer; m. Arthur Weinberg, Jan. 25, 1953; children: Hedy Merrill Cornfield, Anita Michelle Miller, Wendy Clare Rothman. Editor Ziff-Davis Pub. Co., 1944-53; assoc. chief manuscript editor jours. U. Chgo. Press, 1966-80, sr. manuscript editor books, 1980—; mem. faculty Sch. for New Learning DePaul U., Chgo., 1976-88; vis. faculty continuing edn. programs U. Chgo., 1984-92. Author: (with A. Weinberg) The Muckrakers, 1961 (selected for White House Library 1963), Verdicts Out of Court, 1963, Instead of Violence, 1963, Passport to Utopia, 1968, Some Dissenting Voices, 1970, Clarence Darrow: A Sentimental Rebel, 1980; contbr. articles and revs. to various publs. Bd. dirs. Hillel Found. U. Chgo. Recipient Friends of Lit. award Chgo. Found. Lit., 1980, Social Justice award Darrow Community Ctr., 1980, Disting. Body of Work award Friends of Midwest Authors, 1987. Mem. Soc. Midland Authors (dir. 1977-83, pres. 1983-85, Best Biography award 1980), ACLU, Clarence Darrow Commemorative Com., YIVO, Authors' League. Home: 5421 S Cornell Ave Chicago IL 60615-5646

WEINBERG, LOUISE, law educator, author; b. N.Y.C.; m. Steven Weinberg; 1 child, Elizabeth. AB summa cum laude, Cornell U.; JD, Harvard U., 1969, LLM, 1974. Bar: Mass. Sr. law clk. Hon. Chas. E. Wyzanski, Jr., Boston, 1971-72; assoc. in law Bingham, Dana & Gould, Boston, 1969-72; teaching fellow Harvard Law Sch., Boston, 1972-74; lectr. law Brandeis U., Waltham, Mass., 1974; assoc. prof. law Suffolk U., Boston, 1974-76, prof., 1977-80; vis. assoc. prof. law Stanford U., Palo Alto, Calif., 1976-77; vis. prof. law U. Tex., Austin, 1979; prof. law Sch. Law, U. Tex., Austin, 1980-84, Thompson prof. law, 1984-90, Andrews and Kurth prof. law, 1990-92; Fulbright and Jaworski regents rsch. prof. U. Tex., Austin, 1991-92, Angus G. Wynne, Sr. prof. civil jurisprudence, 1992-97, Fondren chair faculty excellence, 1995-96, Eugene R. Smith Centennial rsch. prof. law, 1993-97, William B. Bates chair adminstrn. justice, 1997—; vis. scholar Hebrew U., Jerusalem, 1989; Forum fellow World Econ. Forum, Davos, Switzerland, 1995—; lectr. in field. Author: Federal Courts: Judicial Federalism and Judicial Power, 1994, and ann. suppliments; co-author: Conflict of Laws, 1990; contbr. chpts. to books, articles to profl. jours. Bd. dirs. Ballet Austin, 1986-88, Austin Coun. on Fgn. Affairs, 1985—. Recipient Disting. Educator award Tex. Exes Assn., 1996. Mem. Am. Law Inst. (consultative com. complex litigation 1989-93, consultative com. enterprise liability 1990—, adv. group judicial code revision project 1996—), The Philos. Soc. Tex., Assn. Am. Law Schs.(chmn. com. on conflict laws 1991-93, exec. coun. 1989-90), Tex. Asian C. of C., Maritime Law Assn., Scribes, Phi Beta Kappa, Phi Kappa Phi. Office: U Tex Sch Law 727 E 26th St Austin TX 78705-3224 *The right thing is usually also the humane and liberal thing.*

WEINBERG, MARTIN HERBERT, retired psychiatrist; b. Bklyn., Sept. 3, 1923; s. Abe and Ida (Levine) W.; m. Elizabeth Carwardine, Sept. 20, 1951; children: Mark David, Sheila Ann, Keith Warren. B.S., CCNY, 1947; licentiate, Royal Coll. Surgeons, Edinburgh, Royal Coll. Physicians, Edinburgh, Royal Faculty Physicians and Surgeons, Glasgow. Diplomate: Am. Bd. Psychiatry and Neurology, certified mental hosp. adminstr. Intern Kings County Med. Center, Bklyn., 1952; resident psychiatry Essex County Overbrook Hosp., Cedar Grove, N.J., 1954-56; staff psychiatrist Ancora State Hosp., Hammonton, N.J., 1956; chief service Ancora State Hosp., 1957, clin. dir., 1958-60, asst. med. dir., 1960-62, dep. med. dir., 1962-67; med. dir. Trenton Psychiat. Hosp., 1967-73; dir. div. mental health and hosps. N.J. Dept. Instns. and Agys., 1973-74; med. dir. Trenton Psychiat. Hosp., 1974-79; surveyor psychiat. programs Joint Commn. Accreditation of Hosps., 1979-80; asst. supt. clin. services Phila. State Hosp., 1980-81; individual practice medicine specializing in psychiatry, 1981-86; staff psychiatrist Woods Sch., Langhorne, Pa., to 1986; cons. N.J. Neuropsychiat. Inst., 1981-83, New Lisbon State Sch., to 1985. Fellow Am. Psychiat. Assn., AAAS; mem. N.J. Psychiat. Assn. (past pres.). Home: 26 Diane Dr Trenton NJ 08628-2621

WEINBERG, MARYLIN LYNN, foreign language educator; b. Kansas City, Mo., June 26, 1940; d. Mildred Marie Goetsch; m. Richard Lee

Weinberg, Dec. 26, 1962 (div. Oct. 1988); children: Eric H., Kerstin I. BA, Cornell Coll., 1962; MA, Marycrest Coll., 1982. English tchr. Galesburg (Ill.) Community Schs., 1962-63, Grant Community Schs., Fox Lake, Ill., 1963-64, Saydel Community Schs., Des Moines, 1965-66; English instr. Grandview Coll., Des Moines, 1966-70; behavior disorders cons. Western Ill. Assn., Galesburg, Ill., 1976-77; prevocational coord. Knox-Warren Spl. Edn. Dist., Galesburg, 1977-78; Spanish tchr. Winola Community Schs., Viola, Ill., 1979-80; spl. edn. tchr. Pleasant Valley (Iowa) Community Schs., 1980-86; English instr. Ea. Iowa Community Coll. Dist., Davenport, 1983-86; spl. edn. tchr. Davenport Community Schs., 1986-94, fgn. lang. tchr., 1994—. Author: (with others) Parent Prerogatives, 1979. Recipient Tchr. Incentive award State of Iowa Dept. Edn., 1982; chpt. II grant U.S. Office of Edn., Williams Jr. High, 1988. Mem. NEA, Iowa State Edn. Assn., Am. Coun. Tchg. Fgn. Langs., Davenport Edn. Assn. Republican. Lutheran. Avocations: home decorating, bird watching. Home: 4614 Hamilton Dr Davenport IA 52807-3427

WEINBERG, MEYER, humanities educator; b. N.Y.C., Dec. 16, 1920; s. Charles and Anna (Palatnik) W.; m. Erica C. Mueller, Sept. 5, 1943; children: Rachel (dec.), David, Daniel, Carl, Benjamin. B.A., U. Chgo., 1942, M.A., 1945; A.A., Herzl Jr. Coll., 1940. Faculty history Wright br. City Coll. Chgo., 1945-67, coordinator master planning, 1968-69, coordinator innovations center, 1970-71; prof. history City Coll. Chgo. (Loop br.), 1971-78; dir. Ctr. for Equal Edn. Northwestern U., Evanston, Ill., 1972-78, prof. Sch. Edn., 1978-88; prof. Afro-Am. studies, dir. Horace Mann Bond Center for Equal Edn., U. Mass., Amherst, 1978-90, prof. emeritus, 1990-92, 94—; inaugural holder Veffie Milstead Jones chair in multicultural edn. Calif. State U., Long Beach, 1992-94; chmn. edn. com. Coordinating Council Community Orgns., 1963-67; cons. Howard U., 1964-65, Am. Inst. for Research, 1972, bds. of edn. various cities, univs., 1964-79; bds. of edn. various cities, univs. Fla. Desegregation Center, U. Miami, 1973, NAACP Legal Def. Fund, 1972, Ford Found., 1978, System Devel. Corp., 1975, Nat. Cath. Conf. on Interracial Justice, 1977-78, Stanford Research Inst., 1976, WTTW-TV, Chgo., 1975-78, Edn. Commn. of States, 1978, Cemrel, Inc., 1977, System Devel. Corp., 1979, ESAA Human Relations Study, 1977; mem. tech. adv. com. Ill. Bd. Edn., 1971-72. Author: (with O.E. Shabat) Society and Man, 1956, 65, TV in America-The Morality of Hard Cash, 1962, Race and Place-A Legal History of the Neighborhood School, 1968, Desegregation Research-An Appraisal, 1968, 70, Minority Students-A Research Appraisal, 1977, A Chance to Learn (A History of the Education of Black, Mexican American, American Indian and Puerto Rican Children), 1977, 95, In Search of Quality Integrated Education, 1983, Because They Were Jews: A History of Antisemitism, 1986; editor: Issues in Social Science, 1959, Learning Together, 1964, Integrated Education-A Reader, 1968, Education of the Minority Child-A Comprehensive Bibliography of 10,000 Selected Entries, 1970, W.E.B. DuBois-A Reader, 1970, The Education of Poor and Minority Children: A World Bibliography Supplement, 1986, America's Economic Heritage: A Documentary History, 2 vols., 1983, Racism in the United States, 1990, World Racism and Related Inhumanities: A Country-by-Country Bibliography, 1992, The World of W.E.B. DuBois, 1992, Racism in Contemporary America, 1996, Asian-American Education, 1997; editor Rsch. Rev. of Equal Edn., 1977-79, Integrateducation mag., 1963-86; contbr. chpts. to books, articles to profl. jours. Recipient Center for Human Relations award for creative leadership in edn. NEA, 1971, Human Relations award Mass. Tchrs. Assn., 1988. Mem. Am. Hist. Assn., Soc. for History of Tech., Am. Soc. for Legal History. Home: 5140 S Hyde Park Blvd Apt 7-d Chicago IL 60615

WEINBERG, MILTON, JR., cardiovascular, thoracic surgeon; b. Sumter, S.C., Aug. 8, 1924; s. Milton and Ethel (Harper) W.; m. Joan Ehrenstrom, Nov. 24, 1956; children: Caryl, Susan, Amy. Student, Duke U., 1941-43, MD, 1947. Diplomate Am. Bd. Surgery, Am. Bd. Thoracic Surgery. Attending surgeon Rush Presbyn.-St. Luke's Med. Ctr., Chgo., 1957-90, emeritus attending, 1990—; attending surgeon Cook County Hosp., Chgo., 1956—, Luth. Gen. Hosp., Park Ridge, Ill., 1986—; mem. governing coun., 1996—; assoc. prof. Rush Med. Coll., Chgo., 1969-78, prof. surgery, 1978-90, emeritus prof., 1990—; clin. prof. U. Chgo., 1990—; chmn. dept. surgery Luth. Gen. Hosp., Park Ridge, 1988-94, vice-chmn. dept. surgery, 1994—; pres. med. staff Rush Med. Ctr., Chgo., 1977-79; presenter movies at mtgs. ACS. Mem. editorial bd. Annals of Thoracic Surgery, 1968-79; contbr. articles to profl. jours., chpts. to surg. textbooks. Trustee The Presbyn. Home, Evanston, Ill., 1984-94; bd. dirs. Chgo. Symphony Orch., 1985-95; adv. Charitable Found., 1996—. Maj. U.S. Army, 1951-53. Decorated Bronze Star. Fellow ACS, Am. Coll. Chest Physicians, Am. Coll. Cardiology; mem. Am. Assn. Thoracic Surgery, Soc. Thoracic Surgeons, Soc. Vascular Surgery, Internat. Cardiovascular Soc., Ctrl. Surg. Soc. Avocations: fly fishing, fly rod building. Home: 2550 Princeton Ave Evanston IL 60201-4941 Office: Luth Gen Hosp 1775 Dempster St Park Ridge IL 60068-1143

WEINBERG, NORMAN LOUIS, electrochemist; b. Toronto, Ont., Can., May 6, 1936; s. Samuel and Helen (Wise) W.; m. Hannah Rita Cohen, Aug. 30, 1959; children: Eric, Laurie. BSc, U. Toronto, 1959, MSc, 1960; PhD, U. Ottowa, Can., 1963; postdoctoral studies, Technion, Israel, 1963-64. Sr. rsch. chemist Bristol Labs. Can., Candiac, Que., 1964-66, Am. Cyanamid Co., Stamford, Conn., 1966-70; group leader Hooker Chems. & Plastics Corp., Grand Island, N.Y., 1970-74, supr./program leader, 1974-77; pres. Berg Color-Tone, Inc., Lancaster, N.Y., 1977—, The Electrosynthesis Co., inc., Lancaster, 1977—, Benham Electrosynthesis Co., Inc., Lancaster, 1995—; lectr. electrochem. courses Buffalo, 1986, 87, 89; lectr. in-house course DuPont, 1987, 88; lectr./editor Internat. Forum on Electrolysis in the Chem. Industry, 1987-96. Editor: Technique of Electroorganic Synthesis, vol. 1, 1974, vol. 2, 1975, (with Tilak) Technique of Electroorganic Synthesis: Scale-Up, vol. 3, 1982, (with Little) Electroorganic Synthesis: Festschrift in Honor of Manuel Baizer, 1991; contbr. numerous articles to profl. jours. including Jour. Am. Chem. Soc., Can. Jour. Chemistry, Jour. Organic Chemistry, Jour. Applied Electrochemistry. Recipient Inventor of Yr. award Niagara Frontier Patent Law Assn., 1990. Mem. ECS, ISE, Am. Chem. Soc. (lectr. 1972-78). Achievements include 27 patents including for Radiographic Image Enhancement, Methods for the Electrosynthesis of Polyols, Fluorinated Carbons and Method of Manufacture, (with others) Modified Carbons and Electrochemical Cells Containing Same, (with others) Reactions in an Electrochemical Cell Including an Electrode Comprising Magneli Phase Titanium Oxide, (with others) Methods for Paired Electrosynthesis with Simultaneous Ethylene Glycol Formation, (with other) Membrane Divided Aqueous-Nonaqueous System for Electrochemical Cells, others; 9 patent applications for flourinated carbons and uses thereof, (with others) porous electrodes for use in electrochemical gas sensors, (with others) methods for purification of air, (with others) manufacture of flourinated carbons, (with others) high surface area electrodes. Office: Electrosynthesis Co Inc 72 Ward Rd Lancaster NY 14086-9779

WEINBERG, RICHARD ALAN, psychologist, educator; b. Chgo., Jan. 28, 1943; s. Meyer and Mollie I. (Soell) W.; m. Gail E. Blumberg Aug. 25, 1964; children: Eric, Brett. BS, U. Wis., 1964; MAT, Northwestern U., 1965; PhD, U. Minn., 1968. Lic. psychologist, Minn. Asst. prof. Tchrs. Coll., Columbia U., N.Y.C., 1968-70; prof. edn. psychology, psychology and child psychology U. Minn., Mpls., 1970—, Birkmaier professorship, 1994—; dir. Inst. Child Devel., former dir. Ctr. for Early Edn. and Devel., former chair adv. coun. Children, Youth & Family Consortium; cons. EPA; reviewer Office of Edn., NSF, NRC; guest speaker TV and radio shows. Former mem. adv. com. Children's Mus. Minn.; past pres. Am. Assn. State Psychol. Bds.; liaison Nat. Register for Health Care Providers in Psychology. Grantee Bush Found.; NSF; NIH. Fellow APA, Am. Psychol. Soc.; mem., Soc. Rsch. in Child Devel. (former chair pub. policy coun.), Behavior Genetics Assn., Am. Psychol. Soc. (bd. dirs.), Phi Beta Kappa, Phi Kappa Phi. Author: (with A. Boehm) The Classroom Observer: Developing Observation Skills in Early Childhood Settings, 1997; (with Scarr and Levine) Understanding Development, 1986; former assoc. editor Contemporary Psychology; editor: Applied Developmental Science. Office: U Minn 180 Child Devel 51 E River Rd Minneapolis MN 55455-0365

WEINBERG, ROBERT LESTER, lawyer, law educator; b. N.Y.C., May 23, 1931; s. Abraham Matthew and Beatrice (Kohn) W.; m. Patricia Wendy Yates, Aug. 19, 1956; children: Susan Clare, David Hal, Jeremy Michael. BA, Yale U., 1953, LLB, 1960; PhD in Econs., London Sch. Econs., U. London, 1960. Bar: D.C. 1961, Conn. 1960, U.S. Supreme Ct. 1963, U.S. Ct. Appeals (D.C. and 2d cirs.) 1961, U.S. Ct. Appeals (3d and 7th cirs.) 1965, U.S. Ct. Appeals (6th cir.) 1968, U.S. Ct. Appeals (9th cir.) 1976, U.S. Ct. Appeals (10th cir.) 1977, U.S. Ct. Appeals (5th cir.) 1978, U.S. Ct. Appeals (4th cir.) 1982. Assoc. Williams & Connolly and predecessors, Washington, 1960-66, ptnr., 1967-96, ret. founding ptnr., 1996; vis. lectr. U. Va. Sch. Law, Charlottesville, 1965—; adj. prof. U. Tex. Sch. Law, summer 1986; chmn. standing com. on pro bono matters D.C. Cir. Jud. Conf., 1980-96. Columnist No. Va. Sun, 1970s; contbr. articles to profl. jours. Pres. No. Va. Fair Housing, Inc., 1968-69; chmn. Arlington Pub. Utilities Commn. (Va.), 1968, Arlington County Dem. Com., 1969-71, 10th Congl. Dist. Dem. Com., No. Va., 1972-76; del. Dem. Nat. Conv., 1976; pres. Arlington County Civic Fedn., 1973-75; mem. governing coun. Am. Jewish Congress, 1984—. Served with U.S. Army, 1957-59. Recipient Outstanding Citizen of Yr. award Washington Evening Star and Arlington County Civic Fedn., 1975, Servant of Justice award Legal Aid Soc. of D.C., 1996. Mem. ABA (ho. of dels. 1977-82, 93-95), Bar Assn. D.C. (pres. 1994-95), Conn. Bar Assn., D.C. Bar (pres. 1977-79), D.C. Bar Found. (pres. 1988-89, 91-92), Internat. Assn. Jewish Lawyers & Jurors (bd. dirs.), Nat. Jewish Dem. Coun. (bd. dirs.). Home: 4 Quaintance Rd Sperryville VA 22740 Office: 262 Main St Washington VA 22747

WEINBERG, STEVEN, physics educator; b. N.Y.C., NY, May 3, 1933; s. Fred and Eva (Israel) W.; m. Louise Goldwasser, July 6, 1954; 1 child, Elizabeth. BA, Cornell U., 1954; postgrad., Copenhagen Inst. Theoretical Physics, 1954-55; PhD, Princeton U., 1957; AM (hon.), Harvard U., 1973; ScD (hon.), Knox Coll., 1978, U. Chgo., 1978, U. Rochester, 1979, Yale U., 1979, CUNY, 1980, Clark U., 1982, Dartmouth Coll., 1984, Columbia U., 1990, U. Salamanca, 1992, U. Padua, 1992; U. Barcelona, 1996, U. Barcelona, 1996; PhD (hon.), Weizmann Inst., 1985; DLitt (hon.), Washington Coll., 1985. Rsch. assoc., instr. Columbia U., 1957-59; rsch. physicist Lawrence Radiation Lab., Berkeley, Calif., 1959-60; mem. faculty U. Calif., Berkeley, 1960-69, prof. physics, 1964-69; vis. prof. MIT, 1967-69, prof. physics, 1969-73; Higgins prof. physics Harvard U., 1973-83; sr. scientist Smithsonian Astrophys. Lab., 1973-83; Josey prof. sci. U. Tex., Austin, 1982—; sr. cons. Smithsonian Astrophys. Obs., 1983—; cons. Inst. Def. Analyses, Washington, 1960-73, ACDA, 1973; Sloan fellow, 1961-65; chair in physics Coll. de France, 1971; mem. Pres.'s Com. on Nat. Medal of Sci., 1979-82, Coun. of Scholars, Libr. of Congress, 1983-85; sr. adv. La Jolla Inst.; mem. Com. on Internat. Security and Arms Control, NRC, 1981, Bd. on Physics & Astronomy, 1989-90; dir. Jerusalem Winter Sch. Theoretical Physics, 1983-94; mem. adv. coun. Tex. Superconducting Supercollider High Energy Rsch. Facility, 1987; Loeb lectr. in physics Harvard U., 1966-67, Morris Loeb vis. prof. physics, 1983—; Richtmeyer lectr., 1974; Scott lectr. Cavendish Lab., 1975; Silliman lectr. Yale U., 1977; Lauritsen Meml. lectr. Calif. Inst. Tech., 1979; Bethe lectr. Cornell U., 1979; de Shalit lectr. Weizman Inst., 1979; Cherwell-Simon lectr. Oxford U., 1983; Bampton lectr. Columbia U., 1983; Einstein lectr. Israel Acad. Arts and Scis., 1984; Hilldale lectr. U. Wis., 1985; Clark lectr. U. Tex., Dallas, 1986; Dirac lectr. U. Cambridge, 1986; Klein lectr. U. Stockholm, 1989; Brittin lectr. U. Colo., 1994; Sackler lectr. U. Copenhagen, 1994; Gibbs lectr. Am. Math. Soc., 1996; Sloan fellow, 1961-65; mem. Supercollider Sci. Policy Com., 1989-93. Author: Gravitation and Cosmology: Principles and Application of the General Theory of Relativity, 1972, The First Three Minutes: A Modern View of the Origin of the Universe, 1977, The Discovery of Subatomic Particles, 1982; co-author (with R. Feynman) Elementary Particles and the Laws of Physics, 1987, Dreams of a Final Theory, 1992, The Quantum Theory of Fields - Vol. I: Foundations, 1995, Modern Applications, Vol. II, 1996; rsch. and publs. on elementary particles, quantum field theory, cosmology; co-editor Cambridge U. Press, monographs on math. physics; mem. adv. bd. Issues in Sci. and Tech., 1984-87; mem. sci. book com. Sloan Found., 1985-91; mem. editl. bd. Jour. Math. Physics, 1986-88; mem. bd. editors Daedalus, 1990—; mem. bd. assoc. editors Nuclear Physics B. Bd. advisors Santa Barbara Inst. Theoretical Physics, 1983-86; bd. overseers SSC Accelerator, 1984-86; bd. dirs. Headliners Found., 1993—. Recipient J. Robert Oppenheimer meml. prize, 1973, Dannie Heineman prize in math. physics, 1977, Am. Inst. Physics-U.S. Steel Found. sci. writing award, 1977, Nobel prize in physics, 1979, Elliott Cresson medal Franklin Inst., 1979, Madison medal Princeton U., 1991, Nat. Medal of Sci. NSF, 1991. Mem. Am. Acad. Arts and Scis. (past councilor), Am. Phys. Soc. (past councilor at large, panel on faculty positions com. on status of women in physics), NAS (supercollider site evaluation com. 1987-88), Einstein Archivess (adv. bd. 1988—), Internat. Astron. Union, Coun. Fgn. Rels., Am. Philos. Soc., Royal Soc. London (fgn. mem.), Am. Mediaeval Acad., History of Sci. Soc., Philos. Soc. Tex. (pres. 1994), Tex. Inst. of Letters, Phi Beta Kappa. Clubs: Saturday (Boston); Headliners, Tuesday (Austin); Cambridge Sci. Soc.

WEINBERG, SYDNEY STAHL, historian; b. N.Y.C., Oct. 2, 1938; d. David Leslie and Berenice (Jarvis) Stahl; B.A., Barnard Coll., 1960; M.A., Columbia U., 1964; Ph.D., 1969; divorced; children: Deborah Sara, Elisa Rachel; m. Gerald Tenenbaum, Mar. 23, 1996. Instr. history N.J. Inst. Tech., 1967-69, asst. prof., 1969-72; assoc. prof. history Ramapo Coll. N.J., Mahwah, 1972-74, prof., 1974—; dir. Master of Arts Program in Liberal Studies, 1994—; dir. Garden State Immigration History Consortium, 1987-89. Nat. Endowment for Humanities fellow, 1977-78; sec./treas. Berkshire Conf. Women Historians, 1994—. Mem. Am. Hist. Assn., Orgn. Am. Historians, Am. Studies Assn., Jewish Studies Assn., Assn. of Graduate Liberal Studies Programs. Author: The World of Our Mothers: The Lives of Jewish Immigrant Women, 1988; contbr. articles to profl. jours. Home: 80 La Salle St Apt 19F New York NY 10027-4760 Office: Ramapo Coll MA Liberal Studies Program Office Mahwah NJ 07430

WEINBERG, SYLVAN LEE, cardiologist, educator, author, editor; b. Nashville, June 14, 1923; s. Abraham J. and Beatrice (Kottler) W.; m. Joan Hutzler, Jan. 29, 1956; children: Andrew Lee, Leslie. BS, Northwestern U., 1945, BM, 1946, MD, 1947. From intern to resident, fellow Michael Reese Hosp., Chgo., 1947-51; attending physician Good Samaritan Hosp., Dayton, Ohio, 1953—, chief of cardiology, 1966—, founding dir. coronary care unit, 1967—; clin. prof. medicine Wright State U., Dayton, 1975—; panelist Med. Affairs, nat. TV; pres. Weinberg Marcus Cardiomed. Group, Inc. Author: An Epitaph for Merlin and Perhaps for Medicine, 1983; founding editor Dayton Medicine, 1980—, Heart & Lung, 1972-87; contbr. articles to profl jours. Capt. U.S. Army, 1951-53, Korea. Recipient Army Commendation medal; Outstanding Pub. Svc. award Ohio State Senate, 1980. Fellow Am. Coll. Cardiology (editor in chief jour. ACCEL 1985—, pres. 1993-94, chmn. bd. Inst. for Study of Cardiovascular Medicine 1993—), Am. Coll. Chest Physicians (pres. 1984); mem. Montgomery County Med. Soc. (pres. 1980). Avocations: writing, travel, golf. Home: 4555 Southern Blvd Dayton OH 45429-1118 Office: Weinberg Marcus Cardiomed Group 9000 N Main St Ste 402 Dayton OH 45415-1165

WEINBERG, WILLIAM HENRY, chemical engineer, chemical physicist, educator; b. Columbia, S.C., Dec. 5, 1944; s. Ulrich Vivian and Ruth Ann (Duncan) W. BS, U. S.C., 1966; PhD in Chem. Engring, U. Calif., Berkeley, 1970; NATO postdoctoral fellow in phys. chemistry, Cambridge U., Eng., 1971. Asst. prof. chem. engring. Calif. Inst. Tech., 1972-74, assoc. prof., 1974-77, prof. chem. engring. and chem. physics, 1977-89, Chevron disting. prof. chem. engring. and chem. physics, 1981-86; prof. chem. engring. and chemistry U. Calif., Santa Barbara, 1989—, assoc. dean Coll. Engring., 1992-96; chief technology officer Symyx Technologies, Sunnyvale, Calif., 1996—; vis. prof. chemistry Harvard U., 1980, U. Pitts., 1987-88, Oxford U., 1991; Alexander von Humboldt Found. fellow U. Munich, 1982; cons. E.I. DuPont Co. Author: (with Van Hove and Chan) Low-Energy Electron Diffraction, 1986; editor 4 books in field; mem. editorial bd. Jour. Applications Surface Sci., 1977-85, Handbook Surfaces and Interfaces, 1978-80, Surface Sci. Reports, 1980—, gen. editor, 1992—, Applied Surface Sci., 1985—, Langmuir, 1990—, Surface Sci., 1992—; contbr. articles to profl. jours., chpts. to books. Recipient Giuseppe Parravano award Mich. Catalysis Soc., 1989, Disting. Teaching award Coll. of Engring., U. Calif. Santa Barbara, 1995, Arthur W. Adamson awardAm. Chem. Soc., 1995; fellow NSF, 1966-69, Alfred P. Sloan Found., 1976-78, Camille and Henry Dreyfus Found. fellow, 1976-81. Fellow AAAS, Am. Phys. Soc. (Nottingham prize 1972), Am. Vacuum Soc.; mem. AIChE (Colburn award 1981), Am. Chem. Soc. (LaMer award 1973, Kendall award 1991, Arthur W. Adamson award 1995), N.Am. Catalysis Soc., Nat. Acad. Engring., Phi Beta Kappa. Home: 25 Hidden Valley Ln Woodside CA 94062-1203 Office: U Calif Dept Chem Engr Santa Barbara CA 93106 Office: Symyx Technologies 420 Oakmead Pkwy Sunnyvale CA 94086-4708

WEINBERGER, ADRIENNE, artist; b. Washington, Apr. 28, 1948; d. Samuel Aaron and Marta (Barta) W.; m. Edward Herschel Egelman, Mar. 21, 1980; children: Serge Maurice, Liana Dora. BA, Goucher Coll., 1970; MEd, Johns Hopkins U., 1973; MA, Northwestern U., 1974; postgrad., Sch. of Mus. of Fine Arts, 1979-82. Lectr. Art Inst. Chgo., 1973-75; lectr., docent trainer Mus. of Fine Arts, Boston, 1978-82; mus. educator Yale Ctr. Brit. Art, Yale Art Gallery, New Haven, 1984-86; instr., coord. alumni coll. Albertus Magnus Coll., New Haven, 1987-89; instr. Mpls. C.C., 1989-94; propr. Studio 95, Edina, Minn., 1995—; panelist New England Regional Confs., Am. Assn. Muss., Mass., Conn., 1976-77; mem., workshop leader New Haven Green Found., New Haven 350 Com., 1987-88. Author, illustrator, pub.: New Haven Coloring Book, 1987, CulchaMan Visits New York City, 1988, CulchaMan Visits Washinton, D.C., 1988. Participant Edina Futures Forum, 1990; mem. adv. bd. gifted edn. svcs. Edina Pub. Schs., 1993-96; del. chair, mem. nominating com. Dem. State Conv., St. Paul, 1994, del. chair, Rochester, 1996; dir. Edina-Woodhill Assn., 1997; sec. Dem.-Farmer Labor Party, Edina, Eden Prairie, 1990-94, chair, 1994-96; mem. Dem. State Cen. Com., 1994—; mem. State Affirmative Action Commn., 1996—; treas. 3d Congl. Dist. Dem. Farmer Labor Party, 1997—. Recipient Juror's award Berkshire Mus., Pittsfield, Mass., 1981, New Haven Brush & Palette Club, 1985, Edina Art Ctr., 1991. Mem. Am. Soc. of Appraisers (sec. Twin Cities chpt. 1997). Avocations: travel, reading, politics, advising on education. Home: 6624 Brittany Rd Edina MN 55435-1531 Office: Studio 95 7104 Ohms Ln Ste 201 Minneapolis MN 55439-2140

WEINBERGER, ALAN DAVID, corporate executive; b. Washington, July 31, 1945; s. Theodore George and Shirley Sunshine (Gross) W.; m. Lauren Myra Kaminski, Dec. 2, 1979; children: Mark Henry, Benjamin Charles. BA, NYU, 1967, JD, 1970; LLM, Harvard U., 1973. Bar: N.Y. 1971, D.C. 1978, U.S. Supreme Ct. 1980. Assoc. White & Case, N.Y.C., 1970-72; founding law prof. Vt. Law Sch., South Royalton, 1973-75; atty. SEC and Fed. Home Loan Bank Bd., Washington, 1977-81; founder, chmn. bd. dirs., CEO The ASCII Group Inc., Washington, 1984—; founder, chmn. bd. dirs. Tech. Net, Inc., Bethesda, Md., 1995; mem. adv. bd. Ashton Tate Inc., Torrance, Calif., 1986-87; sponsor, agt. All Union Fgn. Trade Acad., Acad. Nat. Economy of USSR in U.S.A., 1988-90; chmn. U.S. adv. bd. Moscow State U. of Commerce, 1992—; chmn. govt. affairs com. Computer Tech. Industry Assn., 1993-95. Author: White Paper to Reform Business Education in Russia, 1996; law rev. editor NYU Sch. Law, 1970. Named one of Top 25 Most Influential Execs. in Computer Industry, Computer Reseller News, 1988. Mem. Nat. Orgn. on Disability (CEO coun.), D.C. Bar Assn., Order of Coif, Kenwood Country Club. Avocation: tennis. Office: ASCII Group Inc 7101 Wisconsin Ave Bethesda MD 20814-4805

WEINBERGER, ARNOLD, retired electrical engineer; b. Bardejov, Czechoslovakia, Oct. 23, 1924; came to U.S., 1939; s. Henry C. and Bina (Shapira) W.; widowed; children: Paul I., Ronda B., Keith A. BSEE, CCNY, 1950. Engr. Nat. Bur. Standards, Washington, 1950-60; rsch. staff mem. IBM, Yorktown Heights, N.Y., 1960-66; engr., Poughkeepsie, N.Y. IBM, 1966-91, ret., 1991. Contbr. articles on computer arithmetic, logic, large-scale integration, system organization, memories, design automation. Patentee in field. With U.S. Army, 1944-46, ETO. Fellow IEEE (Outstanding sect. award 1981). Avocation: table tennis.

WEINBERGER, CASPAR WILLARD, publishing executive, former secretary of defense; b. San Francisco, Aug. 18, 1917; s. Herman and Cerise Carpenter (Hampson) W.; m. Jane Dalton, Aug. 16, 1942; children: Arlin Cerise, Caspar Willard. AB magna cum laude, Harvard U., 1938, LLB, 1941; LLD (hon.), U. Leeds, Eng., 1989; LittD (hon.), U. Buckingham, 1995. Bar: Calif., 1941, U.S. Ct. Appeals (D.C. cir.) 1990. Law clk. U.S. Judge William E. Orr, 1945-47; with firm Heller, Ehrman, White & McAuliffe, 1947-69, ptnr., 1959-69; mem. Calif. Legislature from 21st Dist., 1952-58; vice chmn. Calif. Rep. Ctrl. Com., 1960-62, chmn., 1962-64; chmn. Com. Calif. Govt. Orgn. and Econs., 1967-68; dir. fin. Calif., 1968-69; chmn. FTC, 1970; dep. dir. Office Mgmt. and Budget, 1970-72, dir., 1972-73; counsellor to the Pres., 1973; sec. HEW, 1973-75; gen. counsel, v.p., dir. Bechtel Power Corp., San Francisco, 1975-80, Bechtel Inc., 1975-80, Bechtel Corp., 1975-80; sec. U.S. Dept. Def., Washington, 1981-87; counsel Law Firm of Rogers & Wells, Washington and N.Y.C., 1988-94; chmn. Forbes Magazine, New York, 1989—; formerly staff book reviewer San Francisco Chronicle; moderator weekly TV program Profile, Bay Area, sta. KQED, San Francisco, 1959-68; Frank Nelson Doubleday lectr., 1974. riter column on Calif. govt., 1959-68; author: Fighting for Peace: Seven Critic al Years in the Pentagon, 1990, (with Peter Schweizer) The Next War, 1996; co-author: The Next War, 1996. Chmn. Pres.'s Com. on Mental Retardation, 1973-75; former mem. Trilateral Commn.; former mem. adv. coun. Am. Ditchley Found.; former bd. dirs. Yosemite Inst.; former trustee St. Luke's Hosp., san Francisco, Mechanics Inst.; former chmn. nat. bd. trustees Nat. Symphony, Washington; former bd. govs. San Francisco Symphony; chmn. bd. USA-ROC Econ. Coun., 1991-94; co-chmn. Winston Churchill Travelling Fellowships Found., 1989—. Capt., inf. AUS, 1941-45; PTO. Decorated Bronze Star, Grand Cordon of Order of the Rising Sun (Japan), Hon. Knight Grand Cross Civil Div. Order of Brit. Empire; recipient Presdl. medal Freedom with distinction, 1987, George Catlet Marshall medal, 1988, Civil award Hilal-i-Pakistan, 1989. Mem. ABA, State Bar Calif., D.C. Ct. Appeals, Century Club (N.Y.), Bohemian Club (San Francisco), Pacific Union Club (San Francisco), Harvard Club (Washington). Episcopalian (former treas. Diocese of Calif.). Office: Forbes Mag Office of Chmn 1901 L St NW Ste 711 Washington DC 20036-3511

WEINBERGER, FRANK, information management consultant; b. Chgo., Sept. 18, 1926; s. Rudolph and Elaine (Kellner) W.; m. Beatrice Natalie Fixler, June 27, 1953; children: Alan J., Bruce I. BSEE, Ill. Inst. Tech., Chgo., 1951; MBA, Northwestern U., 1959; DBA, U.S. Internat. U., San Diego, 1996. Registered profl. engr., Ill, Calif. Engr. Admiral Corp., Chgo., 1951-53; sr. engr. Cook Rsch., Chgo., 1953-59; mem. tech. staff Rockwell Internat., Downey, Calif., 1959-80, info. systems advisor, 1980-95; info. mgmt. cons., 1995—. Pres. Temple Israel, Long Beach, Calif., 1985-87, bd. dirs. 1973-85. With USN, 1944-46. Mem. Assn. for Computer Machinery. Democrat. Jewish. Avocation: microcomputers. Home and Office: 3231 Yellowtail Dr Los Alamitos CA 90720-5253 *Don't ask "what can I do?" Instead, survey the needs, prepare the information, and give your best recommendation.*

WEINBERGER, HAROLD PAUL, lawyer; b. N.Y.C., Mar. 12, 1947; s. Fred and Elaine (Schonfeld) W.; m. Toby Ann Strassman, Dec. 15, 1968; children—James David, Karen Ellen. B.A., CCNY, 1967; J.D., Columbia U., 1970. Bar: N.Y. 1971, U.S. Dist. Cts. (so., ea. and no. dists.) N.Y. 1972, U.S. Ct. Appeals (2d cir.) 1972. Law clk. to presiding justice U.S. Ct. Appeals (2d cir.) N.Y.C., 1970-71; assoc. Kramer, Levin, Naftalis, Nessen, Kamin & Frankel, N.Y.C., 1971-77, ptnr., 1978—. Recipient John Ordronaux prize Columbia U. Law Sch., 1970. Mem. Assn. Bar City N.Y. (com. fed. legislation 1975-78, com. on products liability 1983-86, mem. com. on trademarks and unfair competition 1995—). Democrat. Jewish. Home: 336 Central Park W New York NY 10025-7111 Office: Kramer Levin Naftalis & Frankel 919 3rd Ave New York NY 10022

WEINBERGER, LEON WALTER, sanitary engineer; b. N.Y.C., Aug. 28, 1923; s. Nathan and Margaret (Feldman) W.; m. Greta Stovsky, Dec. 16, 1950; children: Jeffrey Howard, Paula Lynn, Gayle Ellen. BS in Civil Engring., Cooper Union Coll., 1943; MS, MIT, 1947, ScD, 1949. Diplomate, Am. Assn. Environ. Engrs. Rsch. assoc. MIT, Cambridge, Mass., 1947-49; assoc. prof. Case Inst. Tech., Cleve., 1949-63; asst. com. R&D water pollution Depts. Interior & HEW, Washington, 1963-68; group v.p. Zurn Industries, Erie, Pa., 1968-70; v.p. EnviroControl, Washington, 1970; prin. Leon W. Weinberger & Assocs., Berkeley Springs, W.Va., 1970-76, 96—; chief engr. Peer Cons., Rockville, Md., 1978-96. Contbr. articles to profl. jours., presentations to sci. meetings. Lt. US Navy 1943-46, PTO. Fellow ASCE; mem. Water Environment Fedn., Am. Water Works Assn., Sigma Xi. Jewish. Home: 14 Coolfont Berkeley Springs WV 25411

WEINBERGER, MILES M., physician, pediatric educator; b. McKeesport, Pa., June 28, 1938; divorced; 4 children; m. Leslie Kramer, Aug. 22, 1992. A.B., U. Pitts., 1960, M.D., 1965. Diplomate Am. Bd. Pediatrics, Am. Bd. Allergy and Immunology, Am. Bd. Pediatric Pulmonology. Intern U. Calif. Med. Ctr., San Francisco, 1965-66, pediatric resident, 1965-67;

research assoc NIH, Bethesda, Md., 1967-69; allergy and pulmonary fellow U. Colo., Denver, 1969-71; staff Ross Valley Med. Clinic, Greenbrae, Calif., 1971-73; clin. pharmacology fellow U. Colo., Denver, 1973-75; divsn. dir. U. Iowa, Iowa City, 1975—; cons. D.C.Hosp. for Sick Children, 1967-69, allergy and immunology Family Practice Program, Sonoma County Community Hosp., U. Calif. Sch. Medicine, 1972-73; clin. instr. pediatrics Georgetown U. Sch. Medicine, Washington, 1967-69; staff pediatrician part-time West Side Neighborhood Health Ctr., Denver, 1970-71; pediatric sr. staff mem. Nat.Jewish Hosp. and Research Ctr., 1973-75; clin. asst. U. Colo. Med.Ctr., 1974-75; assoc. prof. pediatrics, chmn. pediatric allergy and pulmonary div. U. Iowa Coll. Medicine, 1975-80, assoc. prof. pharmacology, 1975-79, dir. Cystic Fibrosis Ctr., 1977—, prof. pediatrics, 1980—, dir. pediatric allergy and pulmonary div., 1975—. Author: Managing Asthma, 1990; contbr. numerous articles to profl. jours., chpts. to books, also audio-visual materials, commentaries, pub. letters and presentations in field. Recipient Clemens von Pirquet award Am. Coll. Allergy, 1974; grantee NIH, 1980-85, Cystic Fibrosis Ctr., Pharm. Mfrs. Assn. Fellow Am. Acad. Pediatrics (allergy sect. 1972, sect. on clin. pharmacology and therapeutics 1978, diseases of chest 1978); mem. Am. Acad. Allergy, Am. Soc. Clin. Pharmacology and Therapeutics, Soc. for Pediatric Rsch., Am. Thoracic Soc. (pres. Iowa Thoracic Soc. 1992-93), Camp Superkids of Iowa (adv. bd. 1981—), Am. Lung Assn. (pediatric pulmonbary ctr. task force com. 1984-86). Home: 7 Cottage Grove Dr NE Iowa City IA 52240-9171 Office: U Iowa Dept Pediatrics Iowa City IA 52242

WEINBERGER, MYRON HILMAR, medical educator; b. Cin., Sept. 21, 1937; s. Samuel and Helen Eleanor (Price) W.; m. Myrna M. Rosenberg, June 12, 1960; children: Howard David, Steven Neal, Debra Ellen. BS, Ind. U., Bloomington, 1959, MD, 1963. Intern Ind. U. Med. Ctr., Indpls., 1963-64, resident in internal medicine, 1964-66, asst. prof. medicine, 1969-73, assoc. prof., 1973-76, prof., 1976—, dir. Hypertension Research Ctr., 1981—; USPHS trainee in endocrinology and metabolism Stanford U. Med. Ctr., Calif., 1966-68, USPHS spl. fellow in hypertension, 1968-69. Contbr. articles to profl. jours. Recipient Tigerstedt award Am. Soc. Hypertension, 1996. Fellow ACP, Am. Coll. Cardiology, Am. Coll. Nutrition, Am. Soc. for Clin. Pharmacology and Therapeutics; mem. AAAS, Am. Fedn. Clin. Research, AMA, Am. Heart Assn., Am. Soc. Nephrology, Internat. Soc. Nephrology, Central Soc. Clin. Research, Endocrine Soc., Internat. Soc. Hypertension, Soc. for Exptl. Biology and Medicine. Home: 135 Bow Ln Indianapolis IN 46220-1023 Office: Ind U Hypertension Research Ctr 541 Clinical Dr Indianapolis IN 46202-5233

WEINBERGER, SIEGBERT JACOB, food company executive; b. Berlin, Fed. Republic Germany, July 20, 1924; came to U.S., 1938; s. Adolf S. and Meta C. (Bettauer) W.; m. Violetta Elvin (div. 1955). BA, Ind. U., 1945; MA, NYU, 1947. Editorial asst. Middle Eastern Affairs Jour., N.Y.C., 1950-53; asst. concert mgr. S.A. Gorlinsky, London, 1953-54; concert mgmt. cons. London, 1953-55; sales mgr. Eastern Transatlantic Corp., N.Y.C., 1956-58, v.p., sales mgr., 1958-67, pres., 1967—; cons. N.Y. Commodities Corp., N.Y.C., 1986-89; cons. for internat. devel. WMS Industries; agent/cons. for U.S.A. Lothar Krüger Co., Munich, 1991—. Contbr. articles and book revs. on the Middle East to mags. V.p., trustee Kaliski Found. for Gifted Children, Inc., N.Y.C., 1985—. Served to sgt. U.S. Army, 1943-46, ETO. Decorated Purple Heart; Order of Merit (Poland). Republican.

WEINBRENNER, GEORGE RYAN, aeronautical engineer; b. Detroit, June 10, 1917; s. George Penbrook and Helen Mercedes (Ryan) W.; BS, M.I.T., 1940, MS, 1941; AMP, Harvard U., 1966; ScD (hon.), Mapua Inst. Tech., Manila, 1994; m. Billie Marjorie Elwood, May 2, 1955. Commd. 2d lt. USAAF, 1939, advanced through grades to col., 1949; def. attaché Am. embassy, Prague, Czechoslavakia, 1958-61; dep. chief staff intelligence Air Force Systems Command, Washington, 1962-68; comdr. fgn. tech. div. U.S. Air Force, Wright-Patterson AFB, Ohio, 1968-74; comdr. Brooks AFB, Tex., 1974-75; ret., 1975; exec. v.p. B.C. Wills & Co., Inc., Reno, Nev., 1975-84; lectr. Sch. Aerospace Medicine Brooks AFB, Tex., 1975-84; chmn. bd. Hispaño-Technica S.A. Inc., San Antonio, 1977—; adv. dir. Plaza Nat. Bank, San Antonio; cons. Def. Dept., 1981, Dept. Air Force, 1975-84. Decorated D.S.M., Legion of Merit, Bronze Star, Air medal, Purple Heart; Ordre National du Merite, Medaille de la Resistance, Croix de Guerre (France). Fellow AIAA (asso.); mem. World Affairs Council, Air Force Assn. (exec. sec. Tex. 1976-94), Assn. Former Intelligence Officers (nat. dir.), Air Force Hist. Found. (dir.), U.S. Strategic Inst., Nat. Mil. Intelligence Assn., Tex. Aerospace & Nat. Def. Tech. Devel. Coun., Am. Astronautical Soc., Aerospace Ednl. Found. (trustee), Disabled Am. Vets. (life), Mil. Order World Wars, Am. Legion, Assn. Old Crows, Kappa Sigma. Roman Catholic. Clubs: Army-Navy (Washington). Home: 7400 Crestway Dr Apt 903 San Antonio TX 78239-3094 Office: PO Box 139 Reno NV 89504-0139

WEINBROT, HOWARD DAVID, English educator; b. Bklyn., May 14, 1936; s. William and Rose (Shapiro) W. BA, Antioch Coll., Yellow Springs, Ohio, 1958; MA with honors (Woodrow Wilson fellow 1959, grad. fellow 1959-63), U. Chgo., 1959, PhD, 1963. Teaching fellow U. Chgo., 1962-63; instr. English Yale U., 1963-66; asst. prof., then assoc. prof. U. Calif., Riverside, 1966-69; mem. faculty U. Wis., Madison, 1969—, prof. English, 1972-84, Ricardo Quintana prof., 1984-87, Vilas prof., 1987—; Andrew Mellon vis. prof. Inst. Advanced Studies, Princeton, N.J., 1993-94. Author: The Formal Strain, 1969, Augustus Caesar in Augustan England, 1978, Alexander Pope and the Traditions of Formal Verse Satire, 1982, Essays on 18th-Century Satire, 1988, Britannia's Issue, 1993; also numerous articles, revs.; editor: New Aspects of Lexicography, 1972, Northrop Frye and 18th Century Studies; co-editor: The 18th Century: A Current Bibliography for 1973, 1975, Poetry in English, An Anthology, 1987. Fellow Inst. for Advanced Studies, Princeton, N.J, 1993-94; Guggenheim fellow, 1988-89. Mem. Am. Soc. 18th Century Studies (mem. editl. bd. 1977-80, exec. com. 96—), Johnson Soc. (sec.-treas. ctrl. region 1970-95), Johnsonians, Midwest Soc. 18th Century Studies (pres. 1980). Home: 1505 Wood Ln Madison WI 53705-1456 Office: U Wis Dept English 600 N Park St Madison WI 53706-1403

WEINER, ANDREW JAY, lawyer; b. Hartford, Conn., Dec. 19, 1950; m. Debra Lewin, May 29, 1977; children: Joshua Isaac, Hannah Leah. BA, Yale Coll., 1972; JD, Harvard U., 1976. Bar: N.Y. 1977. Planner N.Y.C. Dept. City Planning, 1972-73; assoc. Shearman & Sterling, N.Y.C., 1976-84; ptnr. Gordon Hurwitz Butowsky Weitzen Shalov & Wein, N.Y.C., 1984-89, Morrison & Foerster, N.Y.C., 1990—. Office: Morrison & Foerster 1290 Avenue Of The Americas New York NY 10104-0199

WEINER, ANDREW MARC, electrical engineering educator; b. Boston, July 25, 1958; s. Jason and Geraldine Hannah (Aronson) W.; m. Brenda Joyce Garland, Apr. 1, 1989. SB in Elec. Engring., MIT, 1979, SM, 1981, ScD, 1984. Mem. tech. staff Bellcore, Red Bank, N.J., 1984-89, dist. mgr., 1989-92; prof. elec. engring. Purdue U., West Lafayette, Ind., 1992—; assoc. editor IEEE Jour. Quantum Electronics, 1988-94; adv. editor Optics Letters, 1989-94, topical editor, 1995—; assoc. editor: IEEE Photonics Tech. Letters, 1994-95. Fannie and John Hertz Found. grad. fellow, 1979-84. Fellow Optical Soc. Am. (tech. coun. 1988-91, Adolph Lomb award 1990), IEEE (Traveling Lectr. award Lasers and Electro-optics Soc. 1988-89, bd. Govs. Lasers and Electro-optics Soc. 1997—), Am. Soc. Engring. Edn. (Curtis W. McGraw award 1997). Avocations include invention of techniques for manipulating the shapes of ultrashort laser pulses; pioneering studies of ultrafast nonlinear optics. Office: Purdue U Sch Elec & Computer Engring West Lafayette IN 47907-1285

WEINER, ANNETTE BARBARA, university dean, anthropology educator; b. Philadelphia, Pa., Feb. 14, 1933; d. Archibald W. and Phyllis M. (Stein-Goldman) Cohen; m. Martin Weiner, 1953 (div. 1973); children: Linda Matisse, Jonathan Weiner; m. Robert Palter, 1979 (div. 1982); m. William E. Mitchell, 1987. B.A., U. Pa., 1968; Ph.D., Bryn Mawr Coll., 1974. Vis. asst. prof. Franklin and Marshall Coll., Lancaster, Pa., 1973-74; assoc. prof. Clare Hall, Cambridge, Eng., 1976; asst. prof. anthropology U. Tex., Austin, 1974-80, assoc. prof., 1980-81; prof., chmn. dept. anthropology NYU, N.Y.C., 1981-91; David B. Kriser prof. NYU, 1985—; dean Grad. Sch. Arts and Scis. NYU, N.Y.C., 1991-96, dean Social Scis., 1993-96; mem. adv. com. NRC, 1993—; bd. dirs. Social Sci. Rsch. Coun. Author: Women of Value: Men of Renown: New Perspectives in Trobriand Exchange, 1976, The Trobrianders of Papua New Guinea, 1989; editor (with J. Schneider) Cloth and Human Experience, 1989, (film, with D. Wason) The Trobriand Islanders of Papua New Guinea, Bilan du Film Ethnographique, Paris, 1991 (Grand Prix award), Inalienable Possessions: The Paradox of Keeping-While-Giving, 1992. Guggenheim fellow, 1980; grantee Wenner-Gren Found. Anthrop. Rsch., 1982, 85, 86, NEH, 1976, 85, Am. Council Learned Socs., 1976, NIMH, 1972-73. Fellow Am. Anthrop. Assn. (pres. 1991-93), Royal Anthrop. Inst. Gt. Britain and Ireland, Assn. Social Anthropology in Oceania, Soc. Cultural Anthropology (bd. dirs. 1985-87, pres. 1988-89), N.Y. Inst. of the Humanities; mem. Cibola Anthrop. Assn. (pres. 1977-79), Commn. Visual Anthropology, Nat. Rsch. Coun. (adv. com. 1993-96), Social Sci. Rsch. Coun. (bd. dirs. 1993-95). Office: Dept of Anthropology Dean Grad Sch 25 Waverly Pl New York NY 10003-6701

WEINER, CARL DORIAN, historian; b. N.Y.C., Mar. 26, 1934; s. Alexander and Ann (Goodson) W.; m. Ruth Ann Feinglass, Sept. 6, 1959; children—Nicholas, Kevin, Daniel. B.A., Queens Coll., 1955; postgrad., U. Wis., 1958-61; M.A., Columbia U., 1959. Instr. U. Pitts., 1961-62; mem. faculty Carleton Coll., Northfield, Minn., 1964—, chmn. dept. history, 1974-77, 95—; prof. Carleton Coll., 1982—. Served with U.S. Army, 1957. Recipient 2d Century award Carleton Coll., 1968; Bush grantee, 1983-84. Jewish. Home: 403 Laurel Ave Saint Paul MN 55102-2015

WEINER, CHARLES R., federal judge; b. Phila., June 27, 1922; s. Max and Bessie (Chairney) W.; m. Edna Gerber, Aug. 24, 1947; children: William, Carole, Harvey. Grad., U. Pa., 1947, M.A., 1967, Ph.D., 1972; LL.B., Temple U., 1950. Bar: Pa. bar 1951. Asst. dist. atty. Philadelphia County, 1952-53; mem. Pa. Senate from Phila. County, 1952-67, minority floor leader, 1959-60, 63-64, majority floor leader, 1961-62; U.S. dist. judge Eastern Dist. Pa., 1967—; now sr. judge; Mem. Phila. County Bd. Law Examiners, 1959—. Mem. Pres.'s Adv. Commn. Inter-Govtl. Rels., Phila., Pub. Policy Com., Phila. Crime Prevention Assn., Big Bros. Assn.; mem. Pa. Bd. Arts and Scis.; trustee, exec. com. Fedn. Jewish Philanthropies of Phila., Allied Jewish Appeal of Phila.; bd. dirs. Mental Health Assn. of Pa., Phila. Psychiat. Ctr., Phila. Tribune Charities, Phila. Wharton Ctr. Parkside YMCA, Jewish Publ. Soc. Am., The Athenaeum, and others. Recipient Phila. Fellowship award; Founder's Day award Temple U.; Alumni award U. Pa.; Founder's award Berean Inst.; others. Mem. ABA, Pa. Bar Assn., Phila. Bar Assn., Am. Law Inst. Office: US District Ct 6613 US Courthouse Ind Mall W 601 Market St Philadelphia PA 19106-1713*

WEINER, EARL DAVID, lawyer; b. Balt., Aug. 21, 1939; s. Jacob Joseph and Sophia Gertrude (Rachanow) W.; m. Gina Helen Priestley Ingoglia, Mar. 30, 1962; children: Melissa Danis Balmain, John Barlow. A.B., Dickinson Coll., 1960; LL.B., Yale U., 1968. Bar: N.Y. 1969. Assoc. Sullivan & Cromwell, N.Y.C., 1968-76, ptnr., 1976—; adj. prof. Rutgers U. Sch. Law, 1987-88; bd. dirs. Solvay Techs. Inc., Hedwin Corp., The Acting Co., vice chair, 1992—, v.p., 1991-92. Gov. Bklyn. Heights Assn., 1980-87, pres., 1985-87, adv. com., 1987—; gov. The Heights Casino, 1979-84, pres., 1981-84; trustee Bklyn. Bot. Garden, 1985—, vice chmn., 1989—; trustee Green-Wood Cemetery, 1986—; bd. advisors Dickinson Coll., Carlisle, Pa., 1986-90, chmn., 1988-90, trustee, 1988—; mem. adv. com. East Rock Inst., 1988—. Lt. USN, 1961-65. Mem. ABA, N.Y. State Bar Assn., Assn. of Bar of City of N.Y. Office: Sullivan & Cromwell 125 Broad St New York NY 10004-2400

WEINER, FERNE, psychologist; b. N.Y.C., June 14, 1928; d. Irving Kapp and Peggy (Finkelstein) Hessberg; m. Howard Weiner, July 20, 1948; children: Irving Kenneth, Laurie. BA, Skidmore Coll., 1965; MA, Sarah Lawrence Coll., 1971; PhD, U. Hawaii, 1975. Lic. psychologist, Conn., Hawaii. Asst. prof. West Oahu Coll. U. Hawaii, Honolulu, 1975-77; staff psychologist Cmty. Guidance Clinic, Manchester, Conn., 1978-83; chief cons. psychologist Consultation and Evaluation Ctr., Meriden, Conn., 1984-85; psychologist cons. Disability Determination Svcs., Hartford, Conn., 1986-87, Honolulu, 1988—; police psychologist Honolulu Police Dept., 1988; pvt. practice, Greenwich, Conn., 1983-87, Honolulu, 1988—; cons. Adopt-A-Sch. Project, Honolulu, 1991-94; interviewer, therapist Sexual Abuse Treatment Team, Manchester, 1979-83; cons., trainer Conn. schs., day care, ch. groups, 1979-87. Contbr. articles to profl. jours. Active Disaster Assistance Mgmt. Team, Hawaii, 1994-95; v.p., sec. Queens Court at Kapiolani Bd., Honolulu, 1992-95; admissions rep. Hawaii Sarah Lawrence Coll., Honolulu, 1970-80; cons. to adoptees search Orphan Voyage, Conn., 1980-87; mentor Girl Scout Coun. Am., Oahu, 1993-94. Mem. Am. Psychol. Assn. (clin. psychotherapy and neuropsychology divsn.), Hawaii Psychol. Assn., Nat. Registry Health Svcs. Providers, Outrigger Canoe Club, Honolulu Club. Democrat. Jewish. Avocations: aerobics, interior design, property renovation, gourmet cooking, travel. Home: 3004 Hibiscus Dr Honolulu HI 96815-4725 Office: Behavior Therapy Clinic Kahala Office Ctr 4211 Waialae Ave Honolulu HI 96816-5319 also: Disability Determination Br 1580 Makaloa St Honolulu HI 96814-3237

WEINER, IRVING BERNARD, university administrator, psychologist, educator; b. Grand Rapids, Mich., Aug. 16, 1933; s. Jacob H. and Mollie Jean (Laevin) W.; m. Frances Shair, June 9, 1963; children: Jeremy Harris, Seth Howard. B.A., U. Mich., Ann Arbor, 1955, M.A., 1957, Ph.D., 1959. Diplomate: Am. Bd. Profl. Psychology. From instr. to prof. psychiatry and pediatrics U. Rochester, N.Y., 1959-72; head div. psychology U. Rochester Med. Center, 1968-72; prof. psychology, chmn. dept. Case Western Res. U., 1972-77, dean grad. studies, 1976-79; vice chancellor for acad. affairs U. Denver, 1979-83, prof. psychology, 1979-85; v.p. for acad. affairs Fairleigh Dickinson U., Teaneck, N.J., 1985-89; prof. psychology Fairleigh Dickinson U., 1985-89; prof. psychiatry U. South Fla., Tampa, 1989—; adv. editor John Wiley & Sons, 1967-93, Lawrence Erlbaum Assocs., 1993—; psychology edn. rev. com. NIMH, 1977-81. Author: Psychodiagnosis in Schizophrenia, 1966, Psychological Disturbance in Adolescence, 1970, rev. edit., 1992, Rorschach Handbook, 1971, Child Development, 1972, Principles of Psychotherapy, 1975, Development of the Child, 1978, Child and Adolescent Psychopathology, 1982, Rorschach Assessment of Children and Adolescents, 1982, rev. edit., 1995, Adolescence, 1985, rev. edit., 1995, Handbook of Forensic Psychology, 1987; editor: Readings in Child Development, 1972, Clinical Methods in Psychology, 1976, 83, Jour. Personality Assessment, 1985-93, Rorschachiana, 1989—; mem. editl. bd. Profl. Psychology, 1971-76, Jour. Adolescent Health Care, 1979-87, Children and Youth Svcs. Rev., 1979-91, Jour. Pediatric Psychology, 1981-87, Devel. and Behavioral Pediatrics, 1985-96, Studi Rorschachiani, 1985—, European Jour. Psychol. Assessment, 1985—, Jour. Adolescent Rsch., 1986-91, Jour. Personality Disorders, 1986-92, Psychol. Assessment, 1994—. Recipient Disting. Profl. Achievement award Genesee Psychol. Assn., 1974. Fellow APA, Am. Psychol. Soc., Acad. Clin. Psychology, Acad. Forensic Psychology; mem. Assn. Advancement Psychology, Soc. Personality Assessment (pres. 1976-78, Disting. Contbn. award 1983), Assn. Internship Ctrs. (exec. com. 1971-76), Soc. Rsch. in Adolescence, Soc. for Rsch. in Child and Adolescent Psychopathology, Soc. for Exploration Psychotherapy Integration, Soc. Pediat. Psychology, Am. Psychol. Law Soc., Phi Beta Kappa, Sigma Xi, Phi Kappa Phi. Home: 13716 Halliford Dr Tampa FL 33624-6903 Office: U South Florida Psychiatry Ctr 3515 E Fletcher Ave Tampa FL 33613-4706

WEINER, IRWIN M., medical educator, college dean, researcher; b. N.Y.C., Nov. 5, 1930; s. Samuel and Pearl (Levine) W.; m. Lois M. Fuxman, Apr. 18, 1961 (div. 1980); children: Stefanie F., Jeffrey N.; m. Lieselotte Roth, June 20, 1981. AB, Syracuse U., 1952; MD, SUNY-Syracuse, 1956. Postdoctoral fellow Johns Hopkins Sch. Medicine, Balt., 1956-58, instr., 1958-60, asst. prof., 1960-66; assoc. prof. SUNY, Upstate Med. Ctr., Syracuse, 1966-68, prof., chmn. dept., 1968-87, v.p. rsch., 1982-88, dean Coll. Medicine, 1987-91, v.p. for med. and biomed. edn., 1988-91; dean Coll. Medicine SUNY Health Sci. Ctr., Bklyn., 1991-96; emeritus prof. pharmacology SUNY Health Sci. Ctr., Syracuse, 1995—; vis. asst. prof. Albert Einstein Coll Medicine, Bronx, N.Y., 1964-65; cons. Sterling-Winthrop Rsch. Inst., N.Y., 1968-82, mem. rsch. bd., 1973-76; mem. study sect. Pharmacology and Exptl. Therapeutics "A", NIH, 1965-72, ad hoc com. on comparative pharmacology, Nat. Inst. Gen. Med. Scis., 1966-68, ad hoc com. rsch. career devel. awards and fellowships pharmacology, 1975-76; mem. consensus devel. panel analgesic associated kidney disease NIH, 1984; mem. pharmacology com. Nat. Bd. Med. Examiners, 1977-82; mem. rsch. com. Am. Heart Assn., 1969-74, chmn., 1969-74; mem. pharmacology adv. com. Pharm. Mfrs. Assn. Found., 1981—, chmn. basic pharmacology adv. com., 1987—; mem. N.Y. State Health Rsch. Coun., 1987—, chmn., 1991—. Field editor for renal pharmacology Jour. Pharmacology & Exptl. Theapeutics, 1965-72, editorial adv. bd., 1981-86; editorial bd. Life Scis. jour., 1973-79, renal, fluid and electrolyte physiology Am. Jour. Physiology, 1982-86; editorial com Ann. Rev. Pharmacology and Toxicology, 1982-86; contbr. over 90 articles to profl. jours., chpts. to books. Trustee Loretto Geriatric Ctr., 1989-91; bd. regents L.I. Coll. Hosp., 1993—; bd. dirs. Rsch. Found. SUNY, 1994—. Predoctoral fellow in physiology SUNY Upstate Med. Ctr., 1953-54; recipient numerous fed. fellowships, grants, 1956—, Rsch. Career Devel. award NIH, 1964-65. Mem. AAAS, Am. Soc. Pharmacology and Exptl. Therapeutics (bd. publs. trustees 1973-79), N.Y. Acad. Scis., Am. Soc. Nephrology, Internat. Soc. Biochem. Pharmacology, Internat. Soc. Nephrology, Assn. Med. Sch. Pharmacologists, N.Y. Acad. Medicine. Democrat. Jewish. Home: 39 Plaza St W Apt 10A Brooklyn NY 11217-3932 Office: State Univ NY Health Sci Ctr Bklyn Coll Med 450 Clarkson Ave # 97 Brooklyn NY 11203-2012

WEINER, JEROME HARRIS, mechanical engineering educator; b. N.Y.C., Apr. 5, 1923; s. Barnet and Dora (Muchar) W.; m. Florence Mensch, June 24, 1950; children: Jonathan David, Eric Daniel. B. Mech. Engring., Cooper Union U., 1943; A.M., Columbia U., 1946, Ph.D., 1952. Mem. faculty Columbia U., N.Y.C., 1952-68; prof. mech. engring. Columbia U., 1960-68, acting chmn. dept., 1961-62; L. Herbert Ballou Univ. prof. Brown U., Providence, 1968-93; L. Herbert Ballou Univ. prof. emeritus, 1993—. Author: (with B.A. Boley) Theory of Thermal Stresses, 1960, Statistical Mechanics of Elasticity, 1983. Fulbright research scholar Rome, Italy, 1958-59, Haifa, Israel, 1965- 66; Guggenheim fellow, 1965-66. Mem. Am. Phys. Soc., Am. Math. Soc., ASME. Home: 24 Taber Ave Providence RI 02906-4113 Office: Brown U 79 Waterman St Providence RI 02912-9079

WEINER, JOEL DAVID, retired consumer packaged goods products executive; b. Chgo., Aug. 27, 1936; m. Judith L. Metzger; children: Beth, David. BBA, Northwestern U. Dir. new products and household div. Alberto-Culver Co., Melrose Park, Ill., 1963-66; group mktg. mgr. Bristol Myers Co., N.Y.C., 1966-74; v.p. new products Carter Wallace Co., N.Y.C., 1974-78; exec. v.p. Joseph E. Seagram Corp., N.Y.C., 1979-84; exec. v.p. corp. mktg. Kraft, Inc., Glenview, Ill., 1984-89. Home: 550 Park Dr Kenilworth IL 60043-1005

WEINER, JONATHAN DAVID, writer; b. N.Y.C., Nov. 26, 1953; s. Jerome Harris and Ponnie (Mensch) W.; m. Deborah Heiligman, May 29, 1982; children: Aaron, Benjamin. BA cum laude, Harvard U., 1977. Asst. editor Moment, Boston, 1978; sr. editor The Sciences N.Y. Acad. of Scis., N.Y.C., 1978-84, contbg. editor, 1984—, columnist "Field Notes", 1984—; columnist "Quanta", The Sciences, "Tech Photo", Close-Up. Author: Planet Earth, 1986 (award Am. Geol. Inst. 1986), The Next One Hundred Years: Shaping the Fate of Our Living Earth, 1991, The Beak of the Finch: A Story of Evolution in Our Time, 1994 (L.A. Times Sci. Book prize 1994, Pulitzer prize for nonfiction 1995). Mem. Nat. Assn Sci. Writers. Office: care Victoria Pryor Arcadia 20A Old Neversink Danbury CT 06811-3337

WEINER, KATHY CAROLE, secondary educator; b. Ardmore, Okla., Sept. 24, 1952; d. Walter Norman Cross and Carole Pearl (Cottle) Gossett; children: Nicholas, Patrick. BS in Edn., Okla. State U., 1974; MEd, Cen. State U., 1976. Tchr. Putnam City Schs., Oklahoma City, 1975-90, Durant (Okla.) Schs., 1990—. Mem. NEA, ASCD, Okla. Edn. Assn., Durant Edn. Assn., Nat. Coun. Tchrs. English, Delta Kappa Gamma. Home: 902 Crooked Oak Dr Durant OK 74701-2218 Office: Durant High Sch 802 W Walnut St Durant OK 74701-3233

WEINER, LAWRENCE, lawyer; b. Phila., Aug. 20, 1942; s. Robert A. and Goldie Weiner; m. Jane M. Coulthard, Feb. 28, 1976; 1 child, Kimberly. BS in Econs., U. Pa., 1964, JD, 1967. Bar: Pa. 1967, U.S. Dist. Ct. (ea. dist.) Pa. 1967, Fla. 1970, U.S. Dist. Ct. (so. dist.) Fla. 1976, U.S. Ct. Appeals (5th cir.) 1976, U.S. Tax Ct. 1984. Assoc., ptnr. Blank, Rome, Klaus & Comisky, Phila., 1967-71, 1975-77; ptnr. Weiner & Weisenfeld, P.A., Miami Beach, Fla., 1971-73, Pettigrew & Bailey, Miami, Fla., 1973-75; pres. Lawrence Weiner, P.A., Miami, 1977-83; ptnr. Spieler, Weiner & Spieler, P.A., Miami, 1983-89, Weiner & Cummings, P.A., Miami, 1989-94, Weiner, Cummings & Vittoria, Miami, 1994—; lectr. Wharton Sch. U. Pa., Phila., 1968-70; instr. bus. law and acctg. Community Coll. Phila., 1967-70; lectr. estate planning various non-lawyer groups, Miami, 1972—. Mem. ABA (pension, profit sharing trust coms. 1976-77), Fla. Bar (liaison non-lawyers groups 1980-87), Pa. Bar Assn., Phila. Bar Assn., Dade County Bar Assn. (chmn. ins. com. 1977-78, probate law com. 1992—). Democrat. Jewish. Office: Weiner Cummings & Vittoria 1428 Brickell Ave Ste 400 Miami FL 33131-3436

WEINER, LAWRENCE CHARLES, sculptor; b. Bronx, N.Y., Feb. 10, 1942. One-man shows include Hirshhorn Mus. and Sculpture Garden, Washington, 1990, San Francisco Mus. Modern Art, 1992, Walter Art Ctr., Mpls., 1994, Städtische Galerie Chemnitz, Germany, 1994, Phila. Mus. Art, 1994, Radio Düsseldorf, Germany, 1994, Leo Castelli Gallery, N.Y., 1994; exhibited in group shows Mus. Modern Art, N.Y., 1970, Art Inst. Chgo., 1974, Tate Gallery, London, 1982, Mus. Contemporary Art, L.A., 1983; represented in permanent collections Mus. Modern Art, N.Y., Guggenheim Mus., N.Y., Vanabbe Mus., Eindhoven, The Netherlands, Staatiches Mus. Monchengladbach, Germany, Ctr. Georges Pompidou, Paris, Nat. Gallery Australia, Canberra, others. Recipient Arthur Kopcke prize, Copenhagen, 1991, Wolfgang Hahn prize, 1995; fellow Nat. Endowment Arts, 1976, 83; John Simon Guggenheim fellow, 1994. Home: 297 W 4th St New York NY 10014-2207

WEINER, LESLIE PHILIP, neurology educator, researcher; b. Bklyn., Mar. 17, 1936; s. Paul Larry and Sarah (Paris) W.; m. Judith Marilyn Hoffman, Dec. 26, 1959; children: Patrice, Allison, Matthew, Jonathan. BA, Wilkes Coll., 1957; MD, U. Cin., 1961. Diplomate Am. Bd. Psychiatry and Neurology. Intern in medicine SUNY, Syracuse, 1961-62; resident in neurology Johns Hopkins Hosp., Balt., 1962-65, fellow, 1967-69; resident Balt. City Hosp., 1962-63; fellow in virology Slow Virus Lab., Nat. Inst. Neurol and Communicative Disorders-Stroke, NIH, Balt., 1969; asst. prof. neurology Johns Hopkins U., 1969-72, assoc. prof., 1972-75; prof. neurology and microbiology U. So. Calif. Sch. Medicine, L.A., 1975—, chmn. dept. neurology, 1979—, Richard Angus Grant Sr. chair in neurology, 1987—; chief neurologist U. So. Calif. Univ. Hosp., 1991, mem. bd. govs.; chief neurologist L.A. county-U. So. Calif. Med. Ctr., 1979-94, chief U. So. Calif. U. Hosp., 1991-96; chmn. U. So. Calif. Gen. Clin. Res. Ctr., 1994-95; bd. dirs. John Douglas French Found., L.A., 1987—; mem. neurosci. tng. study sect. NIH, 1990-93, chmn., mem. sci. adv. bd. Hereditary Disease Found., 1992—, chmn., 1994-96. Contbr. over 120 articles on neurology, immunology and virology to med. jours., chpts. to books; assoc. editor: Neurobase, 1994-95, Neuronet; mem. editl. bd. Infectious and Geographic Neurol., 1994—; assoc. editor: Neurobase. Bd. dirs. Starbright Found., L.A., 1991. Capt. M.C., U.S. Army, 1965-67. Grantee NIH, 1995-99, Kenneth Norris Found., 1995-97, Conrad Hilton Found., 1995-97. Fellow Am. Acad. Neurology; mem. AAAS, Am. Health Assistance Found., Am. Neurology Assn., Soc. Neurosci., Johns Hopkins U. Soc. Scholars, L.A. Acad. of Medicine, Assn. of Univ. Profs. of Neurology, Alpha Omega Alpha. Democrat. Jewish. Avocations: collecting books, concerts, plays. Home: 625 S Rimpau Blvd Los Angeles CA 90005-3842 Office: U So Calif Sch Medicine 1510 San Pablo St Ste 646 Los Angeles CA 90033-4614

WEINER, LOUIS MAX, retired mathematics educator; b. Chgo., Nov. 11, 1926; s. Samuel and Lena (Adelman) W.; m. June Belmont, Aug. 18, 1957; children: Howard, Joel, Todd. BS, U. Chgo., 1947, MS, 1948, PhD, 1951. Examiner Civil Svc. Commn., Chgo., 1951-52; asst. prof. DePaul U., Chgo., 1952-58; rsch. engr. Gen. Am. Rsch. Divsn., Niles, Ill., 1958-64; prof. math. Northeastern Ill. U., Chgo., 1964-93, chmn. dept., 1968-74; ret., 1993; instr. Oakton C.C., Des Plaines, Ill., 1974-92. Assoc. editor Math. mag., 1968-72; author: Introduction to Modern Algebra, 1970, Basic Mathematical Concepts, 1972. Mem. Am. Math. Soc., Math. Assn. Am., Sigma Xi, Phi Beta Kappa. Avocation: photography.

WEINER, MAX, educational psychology educator; b. Hartford, Conn., May 7, 1926; s. Harry Sam and Gertrude (Cohen) W.; m. Gloria Sall, Feb. 24, 1960; children: William Ronald, Jennifer Sharon. BA, U. Conn., 1950; MA, Trinity Coll., 1953; PhD, Yale U., 1957. Sci. tchr. Meriden (Conn.) Pub. Schs., 1952-55; guidance dir. White Plains (N.Y.) Pub. Schs., 1956-59; assoc.

prof. Bklyn. Coll., CUNY, 1959-68; prof. Grad. Sch. CUNY, 1968-81, acting univ. dean, tchr. edn., 1973-74, exec. officer PhD program edn. psychology, 1970-76, dir. Ctr. for Advanced Study Edn., 1970-78, acting dean rsch. Grad. Sch., 1978-79; dean edn. Fordham U., N.Y.C., 1981-93, prof. ednl. psychology, 1981—; cons. psychologist SUNY Health Sci. Ctr., Bklyn., 1967-89; mem. nat. commn. on excellence in edn. adminstrn. Univ. Coun. for Edn. Adminstrn., 1985-87; mem. nat. adv. commn. Coll. Bd. Equity 2000, 1993—. Contbr. articles to profl. jours. Treas. N.Y. Alliance for Pub. Schs., N.Y.C., 1987-93; mem. Mayor's Commn. on Spl. Edn., N.Y.C., 1984-85; bd. dirs. Arthritis Found., Atlanta, 1974-76; trustee Beth El Synagogue, New Rochelle, N.Y., 1985—, La Scuola, N.Y., 1986—; mem. bd. visitors Sch. Edn., Scranton U., 1992—. Fellow Japan Soc. Promotion Scis., 1978. Fellow APA, Am. Psychol. Soc., N.Y. Acad. Scis.; mem. ACA (life), AAAS, Arthritis Health Professions Assn. (pres. 1974-75), Am. Ednl. Rsch. Assn., Assn. Colls. and Schs. Edn. in State Univs. and Land Grant Colls. and Affiliated Pvt. Univs. (mem. exec. com. 1986-89, 92-93), Assn. for Measurement and Evaluation in Guidance (senator 1966-72, sec. 1973-75), Nat. Coun. Measurement in Edn., Westchester Assn. Hebrew Schs. (pres. 1982-84), Sigma Xi, Phi Delta Kappa, Kappa Delta Pi. Office: Fordham U Grad Sch Edn 113 W 60th St New York NY 10023-7404

WEINER, MORTON DAVID, banker, insurance agent; b. Balt., Aug. 19, 1922; s. Max and Rose (Wolfe) W.; m. Joan M. Maggin; children: Bruce, Lori, Julie, Jeff. B.S., Towson State Coll., 1942; grad. exec. program, UCLA, 1959. Pres., dir. AVNET, Inc., N.Y.C., 1963-69; pres., owner Morton D. Weiner & Co., Inc., N.Y.C., 1969-70; dir. USLIFE Corp., 1968-77; chmn. bd. Nat. Investors Life Ins. Cos., 1970-78; exec. v.p. Norris Grain Co., 1971-78; pres., chief exec. officer Norin Corp., 1971-78; chmn. bd. Maple Leaf Mills, Ltd., Toronto, Ont., Can., 1974-78; chmn., dir. South Atlantic Fin. Corp., 1978-80, Atico Fin. Corp., 1980-81; chmn. Morton D. Weiner & Co., 1981—; bd. dirs. City Nat. Bank Fla. Served to capt. Signal Corps, U.S. Army, 1942-46, CBI. Office: 200 SE 1st St Miami FL 33131

WEINER, MYRON, political science educator; b. N.Y.C., Mar. 11, 1931; s. Hyman and Anna (Peretz) W.; m. Sheila Leiman, June 29, 1952; children: Beth, Saul Jeremy. B in Social Scis., CCNY, 1951; MA in Politics, Princeton U., 1953, PhD, 1955. Instr. Princeton (N.J.) U., 1951-52; asst. prof. U. Chgo., 1956-61; mem. faculty MIT, 1961—, prof. polit. sci., 1965—, Ford prof. polit. sci., 1977—, chmn. dept., 1974-77; sr. staff mem. Under Ctr. Internat. Studies, MIT, 1965—, dir., 1967-92, 95-96; mem. com. on comparative politics Social Sci. Rsch. Coun., 1961-71; NAS chmn. project population policy in less-developed countries, 1972-75; mem. Ctr. for Population Studies, Sch. Pub. Health, Harvard U., 1973—; co-chmn. joint Harvard-MIT faculty seminar on polit. devel.; vis. prof. Inst. Econ. Growth, Delhi (India) U., 1970; vis. scholar U. Paris, 1966-67, Harry S Truman Inst., Hebrew U., 1979; chmn. joint com. on South Asia, Am. Coun. Learned Socs./Social Sci. Rsch. Coun., 1980-84; vis. prof. Harvard U., 1984; vis. scholar Balliol Coll., Oxford, 1992; cons. to govt. and founds. Author: Party Politics in India, 1957, The Politics of Scarcity, 1962, Political Change in South Asia, 1963, Party Building in a New Nation: The Indian National Congress, 1967, Sons of the Soil, 1978, India at the Polls: The Parliamentary Elections of 1977, 1978, India at the Polls-1980, 1983, The Indian Paradox: Essays in Indian Politics, 1989, The Child and the State in India, 1993, The GLobal Migration Crisis: Challenge to States and to Human Rights, 1995; co-author: Politics of the Developing Areas, 1960, Rapid Population Growth: Consequences and Policy Implication, 1972, Crises and Sequences in Political Development, 1972, Policy Sciences and Population, 1975, India's Preferential Policies: Migrants, the Middle Classes and Ethnic Equality, 1981; editor: Modernization: The Dynamics of Growth, 1966, Political Parties and Political Development, 1966, State Politics in India, 1968, International Migration and Security, 1993; co-editor: Indian Voting Behavior, 1963, Electoral Politics in Indian States, 4 vols., 1974-77,The State, Religion and Ethnic Politics: Afghanistan, Iran and Pakistan, 1986, Understanding Political Development, 1987, Competitive Elections in Developing Countries, 1987, The Political Culture of Foreign Area and International Studies, 1991, The New Politics of Central Asia and Its Borderlands, 1995, Threatened Peoples, Threatened Borders: World Migration and U.S. Policy, 1995; editorial bd.: Global Political Assessment, Asian Survey, Jour. Commonwealth and Comparative Studies, Jour. Interdisciplinary History, Third World Quarterly. Chmn. external rsch. adv. com. UN High Commr. for Refugees. Named Fulbright 40th Anniversary Disting. fellow, 1986-87; fellow Fulbright Found., 1953, Ford Found., 1953, 87, Soc. Sci. Rsch. Coun., 1957, 79, Rockefeller Found., 1961, Guggenheim Found., 1961, Carnegie Found., 1966, NSF, 1969, Rockefeller-Ford Found. program population policy, 1975, Nat. Inst. Child Health and Human Devel. NIH, 1976, Smithsonian Instn., 1985, MacArthur Found., 1992, Japan Found., 1994. Mem. Assn. Asian Studies (dir. 1961-69, chmn. adv. com. rsch. and devel. 1966-69, chmn. Indian state politics com. 1960-70), New Eng. Assn. Asian Studies (pres. 1980), Am. Polit. Sci. Assn. (sec. 1986, chmn. nominating com. 1987, editl. bd. rev. 1966-70), Am. Acad. Arts and Scis. (dir. joint German-Am. project on migration and refugee policies 1993—), Internat. Union for Sci. Study of Population, Coun. Fgn. Rels. Office: MIT Dept Polit Sci E53-369 Cambridge MA 02142-1320

WEINER, MYRON FREDERICK, psychiatrist, educator, clinical investigator; b. Atlantic City, June 4, 1934; s. Jack and Eva (Friedman) W.; m. Jeanette Harmon; children: Daniel, Gary, Darrel, Holli. MD, Tulane U., 1957. Diplomate Am. Bd. Psychiatry, qualifications in geriatric psychiatry. Intern Parkland Hosp., Dallas, 1957-58, resident, 1960-63; fellow in geriatrics and adult devel. Mt. Sinai Med. Ctr., N.Y.C., 1984-85; clin. instr. to assoc. prof. U. Tex. Southwestern Med. Ctr., Dallas, 1963-77, prof. psychiatry, 1980—; head geriatric psychiatry U. Tex Southwestern Med. Ctr., Dallas, 1985—; assoc. prof. neurology U. Tex. Southwestern Med. Ctr., Dallas, 1997, head clin. core Alzheimer Disease Ctr., 1988—, vice-chair clin. affairs psychiatry, 1993—. Author: Techniques of Group Psychotherapy, 1984, Practical Psychotherapy, 1986; editor: The Dementias: Diagnosis and Management, 1991, 2d edit., 1996; co-author: The Psychotherapist Patient Privilege, 1987. Mem. Tex. Alzheimer's Coun., 1991—. Capt. USAF, 1958-60. Mem. AMA, Am. Psychiatric Assn., Am. Assn. Geriatric Psychiatry, Tex. Soc. Psychiatry Physicians (pres. 1985-86). Office: U Tex Southwestern Med Ctr 5323 Harry Hines Blvd Dallas TX 75235-7208

WEINER, PETER H., lawyer; b. N.Y.C., July 10, 1944. BA, Harvard U., 1966; MSc, London Sch. Econs., 1967; LLB, Yale U., 1970. Bar: Calif. 1971. Ptnr. Paul, Hastings, Janofsky & Walker, San Francisco. Mem. Phi Beta Kappa. Office: Paul Hastings Janofsky & Walker 345 California St San Francisco CA 94104-2806

WEINER, RICHARD, public relations executive; b. Bklyn., May 10, 1927; s. George M. and Sally (Kosover) W.; m. Florence Chaiken, Dec. 9, 1956; children: Jessica Weiner Lampert, Stephanie Weiner Iosbaker. B.S., U. Wis., 1949, M.S., 1950. Pres. Creative Radio Assocs., Madison, Wis., 1951-52, Weiner-Morton Assocs., Madison, 1952-53; sr. v.p. Ruder & Finn, Inc., N.Y.C., 1953-68; pres. Richard Weiner, Inc., N.Y.C., 1968-86; pres. N.Y. div. Porter/Novelli, N.Y.C., 1987-88, sr. counselor, 1988—. Author: Professional's Guide to Public Relations Services, 1968, New Bureaus in the U.S., 1970, Syndicated Columnists, 1972, Professional's Guide to Publicity, 1979, Military Publications, 1979, College Alumni Publications, 1980, Investment Newsletters, 1981, Webster's New World Dictionary of Media and Communications, 1996. Fellow Pub. Rels. Soc. Am. (accredited counselor, Silver Anvil award 1965, 84, 86, 87, John Hill award 1984, Gold Anvil award 1990), Am. Acad. Physician and Patient (bd. dirs.), Am. Arbitration Assn. Jewish. Office: Porter/Novelli 437 Madison Ave New York NY 10022-7001 *The essence of life is growth, adaptation, change. I hope to continue to succeed in living vigorously.*

WEINER, RICHARD DAVID, psychiatrist, researcher; b. N.Y.C., Nov. 25, 1945. BS, MIT, 1967; M of Systems Engring., U. Pa., 1969; MD, PhD, Duke U., 1973. Diplomate Am. Bd. Psychiatry and Neurology. Prof. psychiatry Duke U. Med. Ctr., Durham, N.C., 1984—, dir. electroconvulsive therapy program, 1991—; chief, psychiatry svc. VA Med. Ctr., Durham, N.C., 1993—. Recipient Merit award NIMH, 1988. Mem. Am. Psychiat. Assn. (chmn. electroconvulsive therapy task force 1987—). Office: Duke U Med Ctr PO Box 3309 Durham NC 27710-3309

WEINER, ROBERT MICHAEL, engineering design company executive, consulting engineer; b. N.Y.C., Jan. 20, 1936; s. Dudley John and Ruth Alice (McCormick) W.; m. Mary Carole Soetje, June 8, 1957; children: Michael, David, Therese, Paul, Kathryn, John, Thomas, James. BS in Chem. Engring. maxima cum laude, U. Notre Dame, 1957; grad., Bettis Reactor Engring. Sch., 1958; MS in Nuclear Engring., U. Md., 1965. Power systems engr. br. naval reactors AEC, Washington, 1957-62, sect. leader br. naval reactors, 1962-65; systems engr. MPR Assocs. Inc., Washington, 1965-68, sect. supr., 1968-87, prin. officer, 1987—. Contbr. articles to profl. jours. Parish rep., charter mem. Annandale (Va.) Christian Community for Action, 1967—; active Christian Family Movement, No. Va.); coach, leader youth activities Boys Sports Clubs, Boy Scouts Am., 1967-82. Served to lt. USN, 1957-61. Mem. K.C. Avocations: photography, camping, ch. related edn. and social action work. Home: 4820 Randolph Dr Annandale VA 22003-6222 Office: MPR Assocs Inc 320 King St Alexandria VA 22314-3230

WEINER, ROBERT STEPHEN, federal agency administrator; b. Paterson, N.J., Apr. 3, 1947; s. Jess Joseph Weiner and Dorothea Violet (Slavin) Tabor. BA, Oberlin Coll., 1969; MA, U. Mass., 1974. Student coord. Hampshire County, dir. telephone bank Kennedy for U.S. Senate, Amherst, Mass., 1970; dir. nat. voter registration Young Dems. Am., Washington, 1971-72; dir. voter registration, media dir. get out the vote Dem. Nat. Com., Washington, 1972; legis. asst. Congressman Edward Koch, Washington, 1974-75; staff dir. subcom. health and long-term care U.S. Ho. of Reps., Washington, 1975-76, staff dir. com. aging, 1976-80, media dir., press sec. com. narcotics, 1987-90, press sec./comms. dir. com. on govt. ops., 1990-95; nat. campaign aide Kennedy for Pres., Washington, 1980; sr. assoc. Mgmt. Recruiters Internat., Springfield, Mass., 1981-83; dir. Robert Weiner Assocs., Amherst, 1983-86; dir. comm. Ho. Judiciary com. Minority and Cong. John Conyers Jr., 1995; dir. pub. affairs White House Drug Policy Office, Washington, 1995—; dir. gen. press rm. Dem. Nat. Convention, Atlanta, 1988, N.Y.C, 1992, Chgo., 1996; cons. Carter-Mondale Transition, Washington, 1976-77, Congressman Claude Pepper, Washington, 1975-89. Represented in permanent exhbns. Nat. Mus. Am. History, Smithsonian Instn., Washington; contbr. numerous articles to profl. jours. Dem. nominee for U.S. Congress, Mass., 1986; chmn. Road Runners Am. Nat. 10 Mile Championship, Amherst, 1984; vice chmn. Dem. Town Com., Amherst, 1984-87; legis. chmn. Pioneer Valley Gray Panthers, Amherst, 1981-87. Named Communicator of Yr., Washington Crime News Svcs., 1988, 89, 90; 2d place U.S. Nat. 1500 Meter Masters Indoor Track Championship, 1994. Mem. Assn. House Dem. Press Assts., Congl. Staff Club, Nat. Dem. Club, Sugarloaf Mountain Athletic Club (pres. 1984-86), White House Athletic Ctr. (exec. bd. 1995—), Potomac Valley Track Club, Capitol Hill Runners (pres. 1991—). Avocations: running, attending performing arts. Home: 1104 Sanford Ln Accokeek MD 20607-2324 Office: Exec Office of Pres Office Nat Drug Control Pol Washington DC 20500

WEINER, RONALD GARY, accounting firm executive; b. Newark, N.J., Nov. 24, 1945; s. Seymour and Beatrice (Goldberg) W.; m. Vicki Miles, Sept. 8, 1973; children: Jennie, Maureen. BSBA, Babson Coll. (Mass.), 1966; postgrad. NYU, 1968-69; Harvard U., 1982. CPA, N.Y., N.J., Pa. Mgmt. cons., acct., pres. Perelson Weiner, N.Y.C., 1971—. Bd. dirs. Jewish Cmty. Rels. Coun. N.Y.; officer; trustee Babson Coll., Citizens Budget Com., N.Y.C.; treas., dir. Roundtable Polit. Action Com., N.Y.C.; officer, bd. govs. Am. Jewish Com.; dir. Irvington Inst.; mem. adv. com. Muehlenberg Coll., Nat. Polish Am. Jewish Am. Coun. Fellow Wexner Heritage Found., Adenauer Exch. Program; mem. AICPA, Accts. Club Am., Pa. State Soc. CPAs, N.J. State Soc. CPAs (dir.), N.Y. State Soc. CPAs., Chief Execs. Orgn., Young Pres.'s Orgn., Econ. Club, Harmonie Club, Harvard Club, Mt. Ridge Country Club, Pottsville Club. Office: Perelson Weiner One Dag Hammarskjold Plz New York NY 10017-2286

WEINER, SANDRA SAMUEL, critical care nurse, nursing consultant; b. N.Y.C., Jan. 12, 1947; d. Herbert A. and Ruth (Wallerstein) Samuel; m. Neil D. Weiner, June 15, 1969 (div. June 1980); 1 child, Jaime Michelle. BS in Nursing, SUNY, Buffalo, 1968; cert. in critical care, Golden West Coll., 1982; postgrad. UCLA, U. West L.A. Sch. of Law, 1992. RN, Pa., Calif. Staff nurse N.Y. Hosp.-Cornell Med. Ctr., 1968-69; head nurse med.-surg. nursing Abington (Pa.) Hosp., 1969; assoc. prof. Sch. Nursing, U. Pa., Phila., 1970; instr. nursing Coll. of Med. Assts., Long Beach, Calif., 1971-72; surg. staff nurse Med. Ctr. of Tarzana, Calif., 1978-79, Cedar-Sinai Med. Ctr., L.A., 1979-81; supr. recovery room Beverly Hills Med. Ctr., L.A., 1981-92; Post Anesthesia Care Unit nurse Westside Hosp., 1992-96, Midway Hosp., Beverly Hills, Calif., 1996—; med. cons. RJA & Assocs., Beverly Hills, Calif., 1984-92; instr. CPR, L.A., 1986-95. Mem. women's aux. Ctr. Theater Group Vols., L.A., 1986—, Maple Ctr., Beverly Hills, 1987-96. Mem. Am. Nursing Assn., Am. Soc. Post-Anesthesia Nursing, Am. Assn. Critical Care Nurses, Heart and Lung Assn., Post Anesthesia Nurses Assn., U.S. Ski Assn. Democrat. Jewish. Avocations: skiing, aerobics, travel, theater, ballet. Home: 12633 Moorpark St Studio City CA 91604-4537

WEINER, STEPHEN ARTHUR, lawyer; b. Bklyn., Nov. 20, 1933; s. Joseph Lee W. and Ruth Lessall (Weiner); m. Mina Rieur, Sept. 1, 1958; children: Karen, James. B.A. summa cum laude, Harvard U., 1954; J.D. cum laude, Yale U., 1957. Bar: N.Y. 1958, U.S. Supreme Ct. 1963. Assoc. Winthrop, Stimson, Putnam & Roberts, N.Y.C., 1958-65, ptnr., 1968—; vice chmn. mgmt. com., 1984-97; acting prof. law U. Calif., Berkeley, 1965-68. Contbr. articles to legal publs. Comment editor Yale Law Jour., 1956-57. Fellow Am. Coll. Trial Lawyers, Am. Bar Found.; mem. Assn. Bar City N.Y. (chmn. recruitment of lawyers com., chmn. com. on Stimson medal), Fed. Bar Coun. (chmn. com. on 2d cir. cts., trustee), Order of Coif, Phi Beta Kappa. Home: 190 Harbor Rd Port Washington NY 11050-2636 Office: Winthrop Stimson One Battery Park Pla New York NY 10004-1490

WEINER, STEPHEN L., lawyer; b. N.Y.C., Sept. 9, 1946; m. Nan E. Weiner. AB, Columbia Coll., 1967, JD cum laude, 1970. Bar: N.Y. 1971, U.S. Dist. Ct. (so. and ea. dists.) N.Y. 1971, U.S. Ct. Appeals (2d cir.) 1971. Assoc. Hughes Hubbard & Reed, N.Y.C., 1970-72; asst. dist. atty. N.Y. County Dist. Atty., N.Y.C., 1972-75; law sec. to Hon. Leon B. Polsky N.Y. Supreme Ct., N.Y.C., 1975-78; spl. counsel N.Y. State Commn. Investigation, N.Y.C., 1978-79; ptnr. Hoffinger Friedland, N.Y.C., 1979-96; pvt. practice N.Y.C., 1996—; chmn. and commr. N.Y. State Commn. Investigation, 1996—; mem. nat. evaluation team, assigned counsel plan, 1st jud. dept., sch. pub. affairs, Am. U., Washington, 1991. Mem. ind. jud. screening panel Supreme Ct. Dem. County Com., 1986, ind. jud. screening panel surrogates ct. and civil ct., 1990; mem. N.Y. Gov. George E. Pataki's transition team, 1994-95; bd. dirs. Legal Aid Soc., 1995—, Ctr. Cmty. Alternatives, 1995—; mem. N.Y. Unified Ct. Sys. Office Ct. Adminstrn. Adv. Com. Criminal Law and Procedure, 1994—; mem. appellate divsn. N.Y. Supreme Ct. First Jud. Dept. Disciplinary com., policy com., 1989-92, hearings panel, 1986—. Mem. ABA (criminal justice, family law, litigation sects.), Nat. Assn. Criminal Def. Lawyers (mem. ethics adv. com. 1989—), Fed. Bar Coun., N.Y. State Bar Assn. (del. ho. of dels. 1991—, mem. second century com., 1993—, mem. various coms. and sects.), N.Y. Criminal Bar Assn. (co-chair com. legislation 1981-84), N.Y. State Assn. Criminal Def. Lawyers (charter), Assn. Bar City of N.Y. (chair com. criminal justice ops. and budget 1987-90, com. criminal justice 1990—, mem. delegation to N.Y. State Bar Assn. ho. of dels. 1991—, mem. various coms. and couns.), Soc. of Columbia Grads., Phi Delta Phi. Avocations: fishing, sailing, boating, photography. Office: care White & Case 1155 Avenue Of The Americas New York NY 10036-2711

WEINER, STEPHEN MARK, lawyer; b. Boston, Mar. 20, 1943; s. Meyer and Esther (Lowenstein) W.; m. Roslyn G. Weiner, Dec. 19, 1967 (div. 1992); children: Jeremiah, Ben, Miriam, Isaac. AB magna cum laude, Harvard U., 1964; LLB, Yale U., 1968. Bar: Mass. 1968. Teaching fellow Boston Coll. Law Sch., Chestnut Hill, Mass., 1968-69; assoc. Goodwin, Proctor & Hoar, Boston, 1969-71; spl. asst. to Gov. Francis W. Sargent Commonwealth of Mass., Boston, 1971-74; chmn. Mass. Rate Setting Commn., Boston, 1972-78; assoc. prof. Boston U. Sch. Law, 1978-81, dir. Ctr. for Law and Health Scis.; mem. Goulston & Storrs, Boston, 1981-90, Mintz, Levin, Cohn, Ferris, Glovsky and Popeo, P.C., Boston, 1990—; co-chair and sect. mgr. health law sect. Mintz, Levin, Cohn, Ferris, Glovsky and Popeo, P.C.; adj. prof. law Boston U. Sch. Law, 1993-94; vis. lectr. Yale Law Sch., 1994-95. Mem. editorial bd. New Eng. Jour. Human Svcs., 1979-81; mem. adv. bd. Hosp. Risk Mgmt., 1979-83; contbr. articles to profl. jours. Mem. gov. task to evaluate Mass. Determination of Need Program, 1979-80; profl. adv. coun. Mass. Dept. Elder Affairs,1979-81; dir., treas. AIDS Action Com. Mass.; bd. dirs. Boston Film/Video Found.; del. Mass. Easter Seal Soc.; trustee Beth Israel Hosp., Boston, 1979-95, Spaulding Rehab. Hosp., Boston, 1979-95; corp. Ptnrs. HealthCare Sys., Inc., Boston. Mem. ABA, Nat. Health Lawyers Assn., Mass. Bar Assn., Boston Bar Assn. Home: 65 Heron St West Roxbury MA 02132-4115 Office: Mintz Levin Cohn Ferris Glovsky and Popeo PC 1 Financial Ctr Boston MA 02111-2621

WEINER, TIMOTHY EMLYN, newspaper journalist; b. June 20, 1956; s. Herbert and Dora B. Weiner. BA, Columbia U., 1978, MS in Journalism, 1979. Reporter, freelance writer N.Y.C., 1979-81; reporter Kansas City (Mo.) Times, 1981-82, Phila. Inquirer, 1982-93, N.Y. Times, Washington, 1993—. Author: Blank Check: The Pentagon's Black Budget, 1990. Recipient Pulitzer prize (with others) Kansas City Times, 1982, for nat. reporting, 1988. Office: NY Times 1627 I St NW Washington DC 20006-4007*

WEINER, WALTER HERMAN, banker, lawyer; b. Bklyn., Aug. 29, 1930; s. Harry and Sylvia (Freifeld) W.; m. Nina Ester Avidar, Oct. 11, 1966; children: Thomas Field, Jon Michael. BA, U. Mich., 1952, JD, 1953. Bar: N.Y. 1953. Sr. ptnr. Kronish, Lieb, Weiner & Hellman, N.Y.C., 1965-79; chmn. exec. com., chief exec. officer Republic N.Y. Corp., 1980-81, pres., chief exec. officer, 1981-83, chmn. bd., chief exec. officer, 1983—; chmn. exec. com., chief exec. officer Republic Nat. Bank of N.Y., 1980-82, pres., chief exec. officer, 1981-86, chmn. bd., chief exec. officer, 1986—, also bd. dirs.; bd. dirs. Republic N.Y. Corp., Republic Nat. Bank of N.Y. Assoc. editor U. Mich. Law Rev. Bd. dirs., treas. Bryant Park Restoration Corp., Internat. Sephardic Edn. Found.; trustee Guild Hall, East Hampton, N.Y.; mem. N.Y. Holocaust Meml. Commn.; bd. visitors U. Mich. Law Sch. Recipient Humanitarian award NAACP, 1987, Human Rels. award Accts., Bankers, Factors and Fin. divsn. Am. Jewish Com., 1988, Man of Yr. award Bklyn. Sch. for Spl. Children, 1988, Good Scout award Greater N.Y. Couns./Boy Scouts Am., 1994, Jewish Theol. Sem.'s Louis Marshall award, 1994, numerous others. Mem. ABA, N.Y. State Bar Assn., Assn. of Bar of City of N.Y., Am. Bankers Assn., N.Y. Clearing House Assn., Bankers Roundtable. Home: 876 Park Ave New York NY 10021-1832 Office: Republic Nat Bank of NY 452 5th Ave New York NY 10018-2706

WEINER-HEUSCHKEL, SYDELL, theater educator; b. N.Y.C., Feb. 18, 1947; d. Milton A. and Janet (Kay) Horowitz; children: Jason, Emily; m. Rex Heuschkel, Sept. 3, 1992. BA, SUNY, Binghamton, 1968; MA, Calif. State U., L.A., 1974; postgrad., Yale U., 1968-70; PhD, NYU, 1986; MS in Counseling, Calif. State U., Dominguez Hills, 1996. Prof. theater arts, chmn. dept., dir. honors program Calif. State U. Dominguez Hills, Carson, 1984—; guest lectr. Calif. Inst. Arts, 1988. Appeared in play Vikings, Grove Shakespeare Festival, 1988; dir. Plaza Suite, Brea (Calif.) Civic Theatre, 1982, Gypsy, Carson Civic Light Opera, 1990, Same Time Next Year, Muckehthaler, 1987, Slow Dance on the Killing Ground, Alternative Repertory Theatre, 1989; co-author: School and Community Theater Problems: A Handbook for Survival, 1978, (software) Public Speaking, 1991; contbr. Am. Jour. Psychotherapy, Jour. Clin. Psychology, 1997. Yale U. fellow, 1969; recipient Lyle Gibson Disting. Tchr. award, 1989. Mem. Screen Actors Guild, Am. Fedn. TV and Radio Artists, Calif. State U. Women's Coun. (treas. 1989-91), Phi Kappa Phi.

WEINERT, DONALD G(REGORY), association executive, engineer; b. Aberdeen, S.D., Sept. 16, 1930; s. McDonald Donnegan and Susan Mae (Mathis) W. B.S., U.S. Mil. Acad., 1952; M.S.E., Purdue U., 1958; grad., Northwestern U. Inst. for Mgmt., 1974, Command Staff Gen. Coll., 1965, Armed Forces Staff Coll., 1967, Army War Coll., 1969. Registered profl. engr., Tex. Commd. 2d lt. U.S. Army C.E., 1952, advanced through grades to brig. gen., 1977; troop comdr. Korea, 1953-54, Ger., 1958-60, 67-68; dist. engr. Little Rock, Ark., 1972-75; staff officer Hdqrs. Dept. Army, Washington, 1970-72; dir. Engr. Studies Group, Washington, 1975-77; spl. asst. to Chief Engrs., C.E., Washington, 1978, ret., 1978; exec. dir., sec. NSPE, 1978-95, exec. dir. emeritus, 1995; v.p. Jr. Engring. Tech. Soc.; bd. dirs. chmn. Nat. Mathcount. Vice chair engring. & tech. exploring com. Boy Scouts Am. Decorated Legion of Merit (3), Bronze Star medal (2), Army Commendation medal (4). Mem. NSPE (exec. dir. emeritus), Soc. Am. Mil. Engrs., Assn. U.S. Army. Republican. Home: 8121 Dunsinane Ct Mc Lean VA 22102-2719

WEINERT, HENRY M., biomedical company executive; b. Nordhausen, Kassel, Fed. Republic Germany, May 31, 1940; s. Heinrich V. Nennenstiehl and Martha H. Weinert; m. Helen Koopmans, Feb. 14, 1966 (div. June 1982); children: Jason C., Brian T.; m. Kerri V. Keaton, Sept. 25, 1989. BA in Sci., Columbia Coll., 1962; MBA, Harvard Grad. Sch. Bus., 1970. Med. rsch. assoc. Columbia Univ., N.Y.C., 1964-65; exec. v.p., founder Clin. Diagnostic Lab., New Haven, Conn., 1966-68; dir. planning, bus. devel. Lederle Labs./Am. Cyan., Pearl River, N.Y., 1970-73, mktg. dir., 1973-74; bus. devel. mgr. Corning (N.Y.) Glass Works, 1974-77; pres., founder Boston Biomed. Cons., Waltham, Mass., 1977—; spl. ltd. ptnr. MedVenture Assocs., San Francisco, 1965—, Interwest Ptnrs., San Francisco, 1989; presenter, lectr. in field. Patentee laser fabrication of microsuture needles; contbr. articles to profl. jours. Pres. Svc. Soc., Columbia Coll., 1959; chmn. Student Union Com., Columbia Coll., 1961; treas. Class 1962, Columbia Coll., 1962-64; others. Recipient Alumni Achievement award Columbia Coll., 1962; grantee NIH, 1964-66. Mem. Biomed. Mktg. Assn. (bd. dirs. 1978-86, Recognition award 1986), Am. Assn. Clin. Chemistry, Van Slyke Soc. (bd. mem. 1991—). Lutheran. Avocations: reading sci. fiction and mystery novels, sailing, cars, landscaping. Home: 86 Myles Standish Rd Weston MA 02193-2124 Office: Boston Biomed Cons 100 5th Ave Waltham MA 02154-8703

WEINGARTEN, JOSEPH LEONARD, aerospace engineer; b. N.Y.C., June 5, 1944; s. Herman H. and Irene Jane (Binzer) W.; 1 child, Toby. B of Mech. Engring., NYU, 1966; postgrad., Air War Coll., 1976. Chief engr. Air Transportability Test Loading Agy. Wright-Patterson AFB, Wright-Patterson AFB, Ohio, 1972-74; project engr. dept. engring. USAF, Wright-Patterson AFB, 1966-72, sr. project engr. dept. engring., 1974-76, planning and project engr. dept. engring., 1976-81, chief mgmt. ops. dept. engring., 1981-83, sr. tech. planner dept. engring., 1983-92; tech. asst. DCS Engring. and Tech. Mgmt. Air Force Material Command, Wright-Patterson AFB, 1992-93; founder, CEO Huffman Wright Inst., 1993—; CEO Weingarten Gallery, Dayton, Ohio, 1967—; pres., v.p., sec., treas., bd. dirs. Ohio Designer Craftsmen, Columbus; sec. Ohio Designer Craftsmen Enterprise, Columbus, 1982-90; chmn. continuing edn. design dept. Affiliate Socs. Coun., Dayton, 1971-74, chmn. edn. coord. com. Kettering Inst., Wright State U., 1974-76, chmn. scientist and engr. awards panel, 1990-91, mem., 1992-94. Contbr. articles on systems engring. to Aeronautical Sys. divsn. Mech. Engring. Jour. (1st place award nat. contest 1970), Procs. 4th Intersoc. Conf. on Transp., Air Force Sys. Command, USAF Spl. Purpose Report, Gems and Minerals, Friends Jour. USAF Mus., Ceramics Monthly, The Crafts Report, Macintosh Software. Scoutmaster Troop 81 Boy Scouts Am., Kettering, Ohio, 1985-91, com. mem., 1991-93, dist. chmn. Sequoia Dist. Miami Valley Coun., 1991-93, asst. coun. commr., 1993—; pres. Friends of Montessori Sch. South Dayton, 1978-94. Capt. USAF, 1967-71. Named Eagle Scout Boy Scouts Am., 1962; recipient Disting. Eagle award Boy Scouts Am., 1992, Silver Beaver award Boy Scouts Am., 1995. Mem. AIAA (sr. mem., air transport systems tech. com. 1976-78, 80-82, Lawrence Sperry award 1977), ASME (sr. mem.), Am. Nat. Standards Inst. (materials handling 5 com. 1968-70), Soc. Automotive Engrs. (aircraft ground support equipment com. 1969-75). Achievements include 11 patents for expendable air cargo pallet, mail container, collapsible air cargo container, process for reinforcing extruded articles, process for large scale extrusions, air flotation cargo handling system, integral aircraft barrier net, load distributive cargo platform, laminated plastic packaging material, computer printer paper support, and investment casting mold base; developments include 3g cargo restraint criteria used worldwide on aircraft/spacecraft/shuttles, rope extraction system for C-5A, system for large scale structural plastics extrusions, advanced planning documents for Air Force, report in new type of DOD procurement system; other achievements include the design and creation of jewelry sold in museums and retail stores.

WEINGARTEN, MURRAY, manufacturing executive; b. N.Y.C., Feb. 8, 1925; s. Ellis and Ethel (Gaies) B.; m. Shirley L. Bowersox, Apr. 30, 1955; children—Steven Ellis, Betsy Lori. E.E., Rensselaer Poly. Inst., 1947. With J.R. Rider, N.Y.C., 1947-48; engr. Bendix Radio, Towson, Md., 1948-50; with Bendix Field Engring. Corp., Columbia, Md.; became v.p. Bendix Field Engring. Corp., 1963; chmn. bd., pres., dir.; chmn. bd., pres., dir. Bendix Comml. Services Corp., Columbia, 1974; ret. Bendix Comml. Services Corp., 1989; chmn. bd., pres. Morrison & Knudsen Svcs. Inc., ret., 1992—; pres. United Geophys. Corp. (subs. Bendix Corp.); also dir.; pres. Skagit Corp. (subs. Bendix Corp.), Sedro-Woolley, Wash. Served with USNR, 1943-45. Mem. IEEE (sr.), Armed Forces Communication and Electronics Assn., Soc. Exploration Geophysicists (asso.), Engring. Soc. Balt. Home: 9442 Dunloggin Rd Ellicott City MD 21042-5148

WEINGARTEN, SAUL MYER, lawyer; b. Los Angeles, Dec. 19, 1921; s. Louis and Lillian Dorothy (Alter) W.; m. Miriam Ellen Moore, Jan. 21, 1949; children: David, Steven, Lawrence, Bruce. AA, Antelope Valley Coll., 1940; AB, UCLA, 1942; cert., Cornell U., 1943; JD, U. Southern Calif., 1949. Prin. Saul M. Weingarten, Inc., Seaside, Calif., 1954—; pres, CEO Quaestor Inc., Seaside, Calif., 1995—, also bd. dirs.; atty. City of Gonzales, Calif., 1954-74, City of Seaside, 1955-70; gen. counsel Redevel. Agy., Seaside, 1955-76, Security Nat. Bank, Monterey, Calif., 1968-74; bd. dirs., exec. com. Frontier Bank, Cheyenne, Wyo., 1984—, Mariposa Hall Inc., 1989—. Author: Practice Compendium, 1950; contbr. articles to profl. jours. Del. Internat. Union of Local Authorities, Brussels, Belgium, 1963, 73; candidate state legislature Dem. Com., Monterey County, 1958; counsel Monterey Peninsula Mus. of Art, Inc., 1972-80; gen. counsel Monterey County Symphony Assn., Carmel, Calif., 1974—, Mountain Plains Edn. Project, Glasgow, Mont., 1975-81; chmn. fund raising ARC, Monterey, 1964; chmn., bd. dirs. fund raising United Way, Monterey, 1962-63; pres., bd. dirs. Alliance on Aging, Monterey, 1968-82; bd. dirs. Family Svc. Agy., Monterey, 1958-66, Monterey County Cultural Coun., 1986—, Clark Found., 1982—; dir., mem. exec. com. Monterey Bay Performing Arts Ctr., 1990. Served to commdr. USN, 1942-46, 50-54, Korea. Grad. fellow Coro Found., 1949-50. Mem. Calif. Bar Assn., Monterey County Bar Assn., Monterey County Trial Lawyers Assn., Rotary (pres. 1970-71, 82-83), Commonwealth Club, Meadowbrook Club. Jewish. Avocations: tennis, travel. Home: 4135 Crest Rd Pebble Beach CA 93953-3008 Office: 1123 Fremont Blvd Seaside CA 93955-5759

WEINGARTNER, H(ANS) MARTIN, finance educator; b. Heidelberg, Germany, Apr. 4, 1929; came to U.S., 1939, naturalized, 1944; s. Jacob and Grete (Kahn) W.; m. Joyce Trellis, June 12, 1955; children—Steven M., Susan C., Eric H., Kenneth L. A.B., S.B., U. Chgo., 1950, A.M., 1951; M.S., Carnegie Mellon U., 1956, Ph.D., 1962. Economist Dept. Commerce, 1951-53; instr. Grad. Sch. Indsl. Adminstrn., Carnegie Mellon U., 1956-57; instr., then asst. prof. Grad. Sch. Bus., U. Chgo., 1957-63; assoc. prof. fin. Alfred P. Sloan Sch. Mgmt., Mass. Inst. Tech., 1963-66; prof. Grad. Sch. Mgmt., U. Rochester, N.Y., 1966-77; Brownlee O. Currey prof. fin. Owen Grad. Sch. Mgmt., Vanderbilt U., Nashville, 1977—; dir. Computer Consoles, Inc., 1974-89; cons. to industry. Author: Mathematical Programming and the Analysis of Capital Budgeting Problems, 3d edit, 1974, (with George Benston and Dan Horsky) An Empirical Study of Mortgage Redlining, 1978; also articles.; Deptl. editor: Mgmt. Sci, 1967-73. Served with AUS, 1951-53. Mellon fellow, 1954-55; Ford Found. fellow, 1955-56, recipient first prize Dissertation Competition, 1963. Mem. Inst. Mgmt. Scis. (v.p. fin. 1978-84, pres. 1985-86), Coun.Sci. Soc. Pres.s, Am. Econ. Assn., Am. Fin. Assn., Beta Gamma Sigma. Home: 1616 Ash Valley Dr Nashville TN 37215-4202 Office: Vanderbilt U Owen Grad Sch Mgmt 401 21st Ave S Nashville TN 37203

WEINGARTNER, RUDOLPH HERBERT, philosophy educator; b. Heidelberg, Germany, Feb. 12, 1927; came to U.S., 1939, naturalized, 1944; s. Jacob and Grete (Kahn) W.; m. Fannia Goldberg-Rudkowski, Dec. 28, 1952 (dec. Nov. 1994); children: Mark H., Eleanor C. A.B., Columbia U., 1950, M.A., 1953, Ph.D., 1959. Fellow Inst. Philos. Research, San Francisco, 1953-55; instr. philosophy Columbia, 1955-59; from asst. prof. to prof., chmn. dept. philosophy San Francisco State Coll., 1959-68; prof. philosophy Vassar Coll., Poughkeepsie, 1968-74, chmn. dept., 1969-74, Taylor prof. philosophy, 1973-74, dean Coll. Arts and Scis.; prof. philosophy Northwestern U., Evanston, Ill., 1974-87; provost U. Pitts., 1987-89, prof. philosophy, 1987-94, fellow Ctr. for the Philosophy of Sci., 1990-94, chmn. dept. philosophy, 1991-93. Author: Experience and Culture: The Philosophy of Georg Simmel, 1962, The Unity of the Platonic Dialogue: The Cratylus, The Protagoras, The Parmenides, 1973, Undergraduate Education, Goals and Means, 1992 (Frederick W. Ness book award 1993), Fitting Form to Function: A Primer on the Organization of Academic Institutions, 1996; editor: (with Joseph Katz) Philosophy in the West, 1965; exhibited sculptures in Mendelson Gallery, 1992, 94, UP Gallery, 1992; contbr. articles to profl. jours. Bd. dirs. Chamber Music Chgo., 1982-87, pres., 1986-87; mem. bd. advisors Pitts. Symphony, 1991—; mem. adv. bd. dept. music Carnegie Mellon U., Pitts., 1992—. Social Sci. Rsch. Coun. fellow, 1958-59; Guggenheim fellow, 1965-66; Am. Coun. Learned Socs. fellow, 1971-72; residency Rockefeller Found. Study and Conf. Ctr. in Bellagio, 1994. Mem. Am. Philos. Assn., Assn. Am. Colls. (bd. dirs. 1985-89, task force on gen. edn. 1985-88, editorial bd. liberal edn. jours. 1986-94), Assoc. Artists Pitts. (artist mem.), Phi Beta Kappa. Home: 5448 Northumberland St Pittsburgh PA 15217-1129

WEINGAST, MARVIN, laboratory executive; b. Bklyn., Jan. 1, 1943; s. Abe and Rose (Altein) W. BS, L.I. U., 1967, MS, 1971; postgrad., Poly. Inst., 1967-68. Analytic and pollution chemist Amerada Hess Corp., Pt. Reading, N.J., 1969-73; asst. lab. dir. Chem. Constrn., North Brunswick, N.J., 1973-74; dir. Indsl. Hygiene Lab. Nat. Starch and Chemical, Bridgewater, N.J., 1974—; grant com. mem. Ctr. for Hazardous and Toxic Substance Mgmt., Newark, 1988—; mem. Sourland Regional Citizens Planning Coun., Neshanic, N.J., 1989—. Contbr. to book: Small Business Programs, 1980; contbr. articles to profl. jours. Recipient Chemistry Dept. award L.I. U., 1967, Teaching fellowship Poly. Inst., 1967, L.I. U., 1968. Mem. MENSA, Am. Chem. Soc., Am. Conf. Chem. Labeling, Soc. Toxicology. Achievements include development of improved system for identification of hazardous chemicals; organization of first global monitoring of indsl. workers to hazardous workplace chemicals. Office: Nat Starch & Chem Co 10 Finderne Ave Bridgewater NJ 08807-3355

WEINGEIST, THOMAS ALAN, ophthalmology educator; b. N.Y.C., Jan. 28, 1940; s. Samson and Fausta (Haim) W.; m. Carol Perera, Mar. 19, 1963 (div. Aug. 1977); children: Aaron P., Rachel; m. Catherine McGregor, Aug. 18, 1977; children: Robert M., David M. BA, Earlham Coll., 1963; PhD, Columbia U., 1969; MD, U. Iowa, 1972. Resident in ophthalmology U. Iowa, 1972-75, fellow in retina, 1976; asst. prof. ophthalmology U. Iowa, Iowa City, 1976-80, assoc. prof., 1980-83, prof., 1983—, prof., head dept. ophthalmology, 1986—. Mem. editl. bd. Documenta Ophthalmologica, The Netherlands, 1989-94, Ophthalmology World News, vice chair, 1994-96; med. editor Argus/Ophthalmology's World News, 1996—. Fellow Am. Acad. Ophthalmology (editorial bd. jour. 1982—, Honor award 1979, Sr. Honor award 1989, assoc. sec. for self-assessment 1988-93, sec. continuing edn. 1993—, trustee 1993—, sr. sec. clin. edn. 1994—); mem. Macula Soc., Retina Soc., Vitreous Soc., Am. Medico-Legal Found., Assn. Univ. Profs. Ophthalmology (bd. dirs., pres.-elect. 1994, pres. 1995). Avocations: photography, tennis. Home: 3 Heather Ct Iowa City IA 52245-3226 Office: U Iowa Dept Ophthalmology Iowa City IA 52242

WEINGOLD, ALLAN B., obstetrician, gynecologist, educator; b. N.Y.C., Sept. 2, 1930; s. Irving and Evelyne (Gold) W.; m. Marjorie Nassau, Dec. 21, 1952; children: Beth, Roberta, Matthew, Daniel. B.A., Oberlin Coll., 1951; M.D., N.Y. Med. Coll., 1955. Diplomate Am. Bd. Ob-Gyn. Instr. N.Y. Med.Coll., N.Y.C., 1960-63, asst. prof., 1963-67, assoc. prof., 1967-70, prof., 1970-73; prof., chmn. dept. ob-gyn George Washington U., Washington, 1973-92, v.p. med. affairs and exec. dean, 1992—; cons. NIH, Bethesda, Md., 1974—, Walter Reed Army Med. Ctr., Washington, 1974—. Author: Principles and Practices of Clinical Gynecology, 1988; editor: Monitoring the Fetal Environment, 1969, Surgical Complications of Pregnancy, 1984. Bd. dirs. Mayor's Adv. Bd. Maternal Health, Washington, 1981-87; mem. host com. John Glenn Campaign Com., Washington, 1983-85. Maj. U.S. Army, 1957-66. Recipient Alumni award N.Y. Med. Coll., 1974. Fellow Am. Coll. Obstetricians and Gynecologists (program chmn. 1975-77), Am. Gyn.-Ob. Soc. (coun. 1988-90); mem. Assn. Profs. Ob-Gyn. (sec. 1981-84, pres. 1985-86), Soc. Perinatal Rsch. Republican. Office: George Washington U 2300 I St NW Washington DC 20037-2336

WEINGROW, HOWARD L., financial executive, investor; b. N.Y.C., Dec. 6, 1922; s. Nathan and Anna (Mintzes) W.; m. Muriel Corrine Franzblau, Nov. 24, 1946; children: Terry Vaccaro, Caron Abby Haim. Owner Legion Fluorescent Corp., N.Y.C., 1946-56; ptnr. Hechler & Weingrow, Inc., N.Y.C., 1956-58, Hechler, Lifton & Weingrow, Inc., N.Y.C., 1958-78; exec. v.p. Tanscontinental Investing Corp., N.Y.C., 1960-67; pres. Tanscontinental Investing Corp., 1967-70; prin. Lifton & Weingrow, N.Y.C., 1970—; co-chmn. Marcade Group, Inc., N.Y.C., 1986-91, bd. dirs., 1986-93; pres. Cell Diagnostics, Inc. and Medis Ltd., 1992—, Stanoff Corp., 1980—, Wesak Internat., 1992-94, PR Medis Inc., 1992—; chmn. Wesak Chrysler, 1992-94; bd. dirs. Preferred Health Care, N.Y.C., Four Winds Inc., N.Y.C.; founder Weingrow Family Pediatric Urology Lab., L.I.J. Hosp., 1990. Treas. Dem. Nat. Com., Washington, 1970-72; mem. bd. govs. Hofstra U. Law Sch., 1977-79; dep. fin. chmn. Pres. Carter, Washington, 1980; trustee Hofstra U., Hempstead, N.Y., 1973-76, James S. Brady Presdl. Found., 1982, Children's Med. Fund, L.I. Jewish Children's Hosp., Lake Success, N.Y., 1986—, Am. Jewish Congress, 1988—; treas. Nassau County Mus. Fine Arts, 1988—; advisor to Pres. Lyndon Johnson, OEO, Washington; fin. advisor to the Govt. of Grenada and Office of Prime Minister Garry, 1977-79; founder Howard and Muriel Weingrow Collection of Avant Garde Arts and Lit., Hofstra U. Libr., 1972; founder Weingrow Family Pediatric Urology Lab., L.I. Jewish Hosp., 1990. Decorated Air medal, DFC; recipient Presdl. medal Hofstra U., Presdl. citation. Office: Stanoff Corp 805 3rd Ave Fl 15 New York NY 10022-7513

WEINHAUER, WILLIAM GILLETTE, retired bishop; b. N.Y.C., Dec. 3, 1924; s. Nicholas Alfred and Florence Anastacia (Davis) W.; m. Jean Roberta Shanks, Mar. 20, 1948; children: Roberta Lynn, Cynthia Anne, Doris Jean. BS, Trinity Coll., Hartford, Conn., 1948; MDiv, Gen. Theol. Sem., 1951, STM, 1956, ThD, 1970. Ordained to ministry Episcopal Ch., 1951. Pastor Episcopal parishes Diocese N.Y., 1951-56; prof. N.T. St. Andrews Theol. Sem., Manila, Philippines, 1956-60; asst. prof. N.T. Gen. Theol. Sem., 1961-71; rector Christ Ch., Poughkeepsie, N.Y., 1971-73; bishop Episcopal Diocese of Western N.C., Black Mountain, 1973-90, ret., 1990; vis. prof. religion Western Carolina U., Cullowhee, N.C., 1991-96; adj. faculty Seabury-Western Theol. Sem., Evanston, Ill., 19991-94. Served with USN, 1943-46. Mem. Soc. Bibl. Lit.

WEINHOLD, LINDA LILLIAN, psychologist, researcher; b. Reading, Pa., Nov. 9, 1948; d. Aaron Zerbe Weinhold and Nancy Louise (Spotts) Weikel; m. Jack Wayne Prisk, Jan. 21, 1967 (div. 1969). Lic. practical nurse, AVTS, 1970; BS, Penn State U., 1975; MS, C.W. Post Ctr., 1982; PhD, Fordham U., 1986. LPN; cert. profl. counselor. Instr., asst. prof. Gettysburg (Pa.) Coll., 1985-86; post doc. fellow John Hopkins U., Balt., 1986-88; staff fellow NIH NIDA Addiction Rsch. Ctr., Balt., 1988-93; cons. NIH NIDA Medications Devel., Rockville, Md., 1993-94; sci. program coord. Med. Ctr. NIDA Rsch., Washington, 1994-95; cons. The Clin. Cons. Group Antech, Inc., Balt., 1995; substance abuse counselor Hope Village, Inc., Washington, 1996—. Various presentations. Mem. Am. Psychological Assn., Phi Kappa Phi, Sigma Xi. Democrat. Avocations: singing, dancing, painting, photography, reading. Home: Apt 104 210 Congressional Ln Rockville MD 20852-1507 Office: Hope Village Inc 2840 Langston Pl SE Washington DC 20020-3284

WEINHOLD, VIRGINIA BEAMER, interior designer; b. Elizabeth, N.J., June 21, 1932; d. Clayton Mitchell and Rosemary (Behrend) Beamer; divorced; children: Thomas Craig, Robert Scott, Amy Linette. BA, Cornell U., 1955; BFA summa cum laude, Ohio State U., 1969; MA in Design Mgmt., Ohio State U., 1982. Freelance interior designer, 1969-72; interior designer, dir. interior design Karlsberger and Assocs. Inc., Columbus, Ohio, 1972-82; assoc. prof. dept. design Ohio State U., 1982—, grad. studies chairperson, 1986-89, 1995-96; lectr. indsl. design Ohio State U., 1972, 79-80. Trustee Found. for Interior Design Edn. and Research. Mem. Inst. Bus. Designers (chpt. treas. 1977-79, nat. trustee 1979-81, nat. chmn. contract documents com. 1979-84, chpt. pres. 1981-83), Constrn. Specifications Inst., Interior Design Educator's Coun. (nat. treas. 1989-93), Interior Design Educator's Coun. Found. (nat. treas. 1992-94), Illuminating Engring. Soc. (chpt. v.p. 1997), AIA (assoc.), Internat. Interior Design Assn. (nat. dir. 1994-97). Prin. works include Grands Rapids (Mich.) Osteo. Hosp., Melrose (Mass.) Wakefield Hosp., Christopher Inn, Columbus, John W. Galbreath Hdqrs., Columbus, Guernsey Meml. Hosp., Cambridge, Ohio, Trinity Epis. Ch. and Parish House, Columbus, Hale Hosp., Haverhill, Mass., Ohio State U. Dept. Indsl. Design Lighting Lab., others. Author: IBO Forms and Documents Manual, Interior Finish Materials for Health Care Facilities, Subjective Impressions: Lighting Hotels and Resturants, 1989, Effects of Lighting on The Perception of Interior Spaces, 1993. Home: 112 Glen Dr Columbus OH 43085-4010 Office: Ohio State U Dept Design 128 N Oval Mall Columbus OH 43210-1318

WEINHOUSE, SIDNEY, biochemist, educator; b. Chgo., May 21, 1909; s. Harry and Dora (Cutler) W.; m. Sylvia Krawitz, Sept. 15, 1935 (dec. Aug. 1957); children: Doris Joan, James Lester, Barbara May; m. Adele Klein, Dec. 27, 1969. B.S., U. Chgo., 1933, Ph.D., 1936; D.M.S. (hon.), Med. Coll. Pa., 1973; D.Sc. (hon.), Temple U., 1976, U. Chieti, Italy, 1979, Jefferson Med. Coll., 1983. Eli Lilly fellow U. Chgo., 1936-38, Coman fellow, 1939-41; staff OSRD, 1941-44; with Houdry Process Corp., 1944-47; biochem. research dir. Temple U. Research Inst., 1947-50, prof. chemistry, 1952-77; emeritus prof. biochemistry Temple U. Med. Sch., 1977—; emeritus prof. Jefferson Med. Coll., 1991; sr. scientist Lankenau Med. Research Ctr., 1987—; head dept. metabolic chemistry Lankenau Hosp. Research Inst. and Inst. Cancer Research, 1950-57; chmn. div. biochemistry Inst. Cancer Research, 1957-61; assoc. dir. Fels Research Inst., Temple U. Med. Sch., Phila., 1961-64, dir., 1964-74; mem. bd. sci. advisers Inst. Environ. Health, NIH. Contbr. articles on original research to sci. jours.; editor: Jour. Cancer Research, 1969-79. Bd. dirs. Am. Cancer Soc. Mem. Am. Chem. Soc., Am. Soc. Biol. Chemists, Am. Assn. Cancer Research, Nat. Acad. Sci. Home: 1919 Chestnut St Phildelphia PA 19103-3401 Office: Lankenau Med Rsch Ctr 100 E Lancaster Ave Wynnewood PA 19096 also: Jefferson Cancer Inst Rm 1034 273 S 10th St Philadelphia PA 19107

WEINKAUF, MARY LOUISE STANLEY, clergywoman; b. Eau Claire, Wis., Sept. 22, 1938; d. Joseph Michael and Marie Barbara (Holzinger) Stanley; m. Alan D. Weinkauf, Oct. 12, 1962; children: Stephen, Xanti. BA, Wis. State U., 1961; MA, U. Tenn., 1962, PhD, 1966; MDiv Luth. Sch. Theology, Chgo., 1993. Grad. asst., instr. U. Tenn., 1961-66; asst. prof. English, Adrian Coll., 1966-69; prof., head dept. English, Dakota Wesleyan U., Mitchell, S.D., 1969-89; instr. Columbia Coll., 1989-91; pastor Calvary Evangelical Luth. Ch., Siloa Lutheran Ch., Ontonagon Faith, White Pine, Mich., Gowrie, Iowa. Mem. Mitchell Arts Council; bd. trustees, The Ednl. Found., 1986—; bd. dirs. Ontonagon County Habitat for Humanity, 1995—. Author: Hard-Boiled Heretic, 1994, Sermons in Science Fiction, 1994, Murder Most Poetic, 1996. Mem. Nat. Council Tchrs. English, S.D. Council Tchrs. English, Sci. Fiction Research Assn., Popular Culture Assn., Milton Soc., AAUW (div. pres. 1978-80), S.D. State Poetry Soc. (pres. 1982-83), Delta Kappa Gamma (pres. local chpt., mem. state bd. 1972-89 , state v.p. 1979-83, state pres. 1983-85), Sigma Tau Delta, Pi Kappa Delta, Phi Kappa Phi. Republican. Lutheran.

WEINKAUF, WILLIAM CARL, instructional media company executive; b. Fond du Lac, Wis., Apr. 7, 1934; s. Carl Alfred and Erma Gertrude (Lueck) W.; m. Carole Jean Hill, May 3, 1958 (div.); children: Carl William, Mary Gretchen, Donald Hill; m. Jean Boyne Hawks, Sept. 10, 1988. BA, Ripon (Wis.) Coll., 1955; postgrad. U. Wis., 1954, 57-58. Dir. Wis. Cen. Lumber Co., 1959-63; with Carlton Films, Beloit, Wis., 1965-68; founder, pres. IMCO Inc., Green Lake, Wis., 1968—; founder, pres. initiator of distribution of ednl. instructional materials catalogs, IMCO Pub. Co., 1978—; bd. dirs. The Peterson System, Inc.; co-founder, chmn. Affluence Unltd., Inc., Dallas, 1986; founder, pres. Weinkauf Technologies, LLC, Dallas, 1996; Chmn. council Cub Scouts Am., 1968-69; mem. exec. com. county Reps., 1970-71. Served to maj. AUS, 1955-57. Mem. Nat. Audio Visual Assn. (chmn. legis. com. Wis. 1975—), Nat. Sch. Supply and Equipment Assn. (bd. dirs. 1986-87), U.S. Res. Officers Assn. (chpt. pres. 1966-70), Green Lake C. of C., Sigma Nu. Mem. United Ch. Christ (bd. trustees Green Lake, Wis. 1965-66, mem. bd. deacons Dallas 1989-93, chmn. 1992-93). Lodges: Mason (32 degree), KT. Office: 2215 Commerce St Dallas TX 75201-4345

WEINKOPF, FRIEDRICH J., lawyer; b. Bautsch, Germany, Feb. 17, 1930. Referendar, U. Marburg, Germany, 1954; LLM, U. Pa., 1958; JD, Chgo.-Kent Coll. Law, 1967. Bar: Ill. 1967. Ptnr. Baker & McKenzie, Chgo. Office: Baker & McKenzie 1 Prudential Plz 130 E Randolph Dr Chicago IL 60601

WEINLANDER, MAX MARTIN, retired psychologist; b. Ann Arbor, Mich., Sept. 9, 1917; s. Paul and Emma Carol (Lindemann) W.; BA, Ea. Mich. Coll., 1940; MA, U. Mich., 1942, PhD, 1955; M.A., Wayne U., 1951; m. Albertina Adelheit Abrams, June 4, 1946; children: Bruce, Annette. Psychometrist, VA Hosp., Dearborn, Mich., 1947-51; sr. staff psychologist Ohio Div. Corrections, London, 1954-55; lectr. Dayton and Piqua Centers, Miami U., Oxford, Ohio, 1955-62; chief clin. psychologist Child Guidance Clinic, Springfield, Ohio, 1956-61, acting dir., 1961-65; clin. psychologist VA Center, Dayton, Ohio, 1964-79; cons. Ohio Divsn. Mental Hygiene; summer guest prof. Miami U., 1957, 58, Wittenberg U., 1958; adj. prof. Wright State U., Dayton, 1975-76; cons. State Ohio Bur. Vocat. Rehab., Oesterlen Home Emotionally Disturbed Children. Pres. Clark County Mental Health Assn., 1960, Clark County Health and Welfare Club, 1961; mem. Community Welfare Coun. Clark County, 1964; chmn. Comprehensive Mental Health Planning Com. Clark County, 1964; trustee United Appeals Fund, 1960. Mem. citizens adv. coun. Columbus Psychiat. Inst., Ohio State U. Served as sgt. AUS, 1942-46. Fellow Ohio Psychol. Assn. (chmn. com. on utilization of psychologists; treas., exec. bd. 1968-71); mem. Am. Psychol. Assn., Ohio Psychol Assn., Mich. Psychol. Assn., DAV, U. Mich. Pres. Club, Pi Kappa Delta, Pi Gamma Mu, Phi Delta Kappa. Republican. Lutheran. Lodge: Kiwanis. Contbr. 18 articles to psychology jours. Home: 17185 Valley Dr Big Rapids MI 49307-9523

WEINMAN, GLENN ALAN, lawyer; b. N.Y.C., Dec. 9, 1955; s. Seymour and Iris Rhoda (Bergman) W. BA in Polit. Sci., UCLA, 1978; JD, U. So. Calif., 1981. Bar: Calif. 1981. Assoc. counsel Mitsui Mfrs. Bank, Los Angeles, 1981-83; assoc. McKenna, Conner & Cuneo, Los Angeles, 1983-85, Stroock, Stroock & Lavan, Los Angeles, 1985-87; sr. counsel Buchalter, Nemer, Fields & Younger, Los Angeles, 1987-91; ptnr. Keck, Mahin & Cate, 1991-93; sr. v.p., gen. counsel Western Internat. Media Corp., L.A., 1993-96; gen. counsel Guess?, Inc., L.A., 1996—. Mem. ABA (corp. banking and bus. law sect., com. on savs. instns., com. on banking law corp. counsel sect.), Calif. Bar Assn. (bus. law sect., com. fin. instns. 1989-91, com. consumer svcs. 1991-94), L.A. County Bar Assn. (corp. legal depts. sect., bus. and corps. law sect., subcom. on fin. instns.), Calif. Fashion Assn. (legal com. 1997—), Am. Apparel Mfgs. Assn. (legal com. 1997—), Legion Lex., U. So. Calif. Law Alumni Assn., Phi Alpha Delta. Avocation: tennis. Office: Guess? Inc 1444 S Alameda St Los Angeles CA 90021-2448

WEINMAN, HOWARD MARK, lawyer; b. N.Y.C., May 6, 1947; s. Joseph and Kate (Dorn) W.; m. Pamela Eve Brodie, Jan. 6, 1980; children: David Lewis, Nathaniel Saul. B.A. magna cum laude, Columbia U., 1969; M.P.P., Harvard U, 1973, J.D. cum laude, 1973; LL.M. with highest honors in Taxation, George Washington U., 1981. Assoc., Fried, Frank, Harris, Shriver & Kampelman, Washington and N.Y.C., 1973-78; legis. atty. Joint Com. on Taxation, U.S. Congress, Washington, 1978-80; assoc. Sachs, Greenebaum, & Tayler, Washington, 1980-82; assoc. Crowell & Moring, Washington, 1982-84, ptnr., 1984—; adj. prof. internat. tax Georgetown U. Law Ctr., 1988-89. Contbr. articles to profl. jours. Mem. ABA (sect. on taxation), Kenwood Club, Phi Beta Kappa. Jewish. Home: 5404 Center St Bethesda MD 20815-7101 Office: Crowell & Moring 1001 Pennsylvania Ave NW Washington DC 20004-2505

WEINMAN, ROBERT ALEXANDER, sculptor; b. N.Y.C., Mar. 19, 1915; s. Adolph Alexander and Margaret Lucille (Landman) W.; m. Jane Morrison, July 14, 1945; children: Paul Alexander, Christopher Robert. Student, NAD, 1931-39, Art Students League, N.Y.C., 1939-40. Exhbns. include, NAD, 1937, 38, 49, 53, 71, 83, Pa. Acad. Fine Arts, 1939, N.Y. State Nature Assn., 1939, Nat. Arts Club, 1941, Georg Jensen, Inc., 1941, Allied Artists Am., 1946, 3d Sculpture Internat., Phila., 1949, Nat. Sculpture Soc., 1952, 64, 68, 69, 71, 79, 81, Soc. Animal Artists, 1970, 72; works include bronze doors, Baylor U., Tex.; bronze overdoor motif, U. Tenn. Ctr.; bronze dolphin fountain group, S.I. Community Coll.; small bronze, Bessie the Belligerent; study of an Indian rhinoceros, and a watercolor, Great Blue Heron, Brookgreen Gardens, Georgetown, S.C.; Stations of the Cross, chapel Manhattanville Coll. Sacred Heart, Purchase, N.Y., bronze airman, Tulsa Mcpl. Airport, granite eagle, Fed. Res. Bank, Buffalo, rood group and twelve apostles, Our Lady of Perpetual Help, Queens, N.Y., others; creator numerous medals for athletic, ednl., bus., mil., religious and cultural orgns. Served to sgt. U.S. Army 1942-45. Recipient Sanford Saltus medal award Am. Numis. Soc., 1964, Sculptor of Year award Am. Numis. Assn., 1975. Fellow Nat. Sculpture Soc. (pres. 1973-76, Bennett Prize 1952, Henry Hering medal 1985); mem. Nat. Acad. Design (academician). Address: 941 Old Post Rd Bedford NY 10506-1223

WEINMANN, JOHN GIFFEN, lawyer, diplomat; b. New Orleans, Aug. 29, 1928; s. Rudolph John and Mary Victoria (Mills) W.; m. Virginia Lee Eason, June 11, 1955; children: Winston Eason, Robert St. George Tucker, John Giffen Jr., Mary Virginia Lewis, George Gustafis. BA, Tulane U., 1950, JD, 1952. Bar: La. 1952. Pvt. practice law Phelps Dunbar and predecessor firm, New Orleans; ptnr. Phelps Dunbar and predecessor firm, 1955-80, of counsel, 1981-83, 85-89; of counsel, 1993—; gen. counsel Times-Picayune Pub. Corp., 1968-80; pres., dir. Waverly Oil Corp., 1981-89; amb. to Finland Am. Embassy, Helsinki, 1989-91; amb., chief of protocol of White House Dept. of State, Washington, 1991-93; lectr. bills and notes New Orleans chpt. Am. Inst. Banking, 1958-59; bd. dir. Eason Oil Co., 1961-81, chmn., 1977; bd. dir. 1st Nat. Bank of Oklahoma City, 1978-84, Am. Life Ins. Co. of N.Y., 1981-88, Allied Investment Corp., 1985-88; asst. sec. Am. Bar Endowment, 1971-74, bd. dirs., sec., 1975-80. Mem. adv. bd. Tulane Law Rev., 1965-92. Bd. govs. Tulane Med. Ctr., 1968-81; bd. adminstrs. Tulane Ednl. Fund, 1981—, chmn. devel. com., 1985-89, co-chmn. Tulane Parents Fund, 1980-81, bd. chmn., 1993—; nat. chmn. ann. giving Campaign for Tulane, 1983-85; bd. dirs. Coun. for Better La., 1987-89, Tulane Children's Ctr., 1981-84, WYES Ednl. TV Sta., 1981-82; trustee S.W. Legal Found., 1978-80, Metairie Park Country Day Sch., v.p., 1976-77, pres., 1978-80, U.S. commr. gen. for 1984 La. Workd Expn., 1983-85; U.S. del. Bur. Internat. Expositions, Paris, 1984-85, chmn. del., 1985; state fin. chmn. George Bush for Pres., and Victory La. '88, 1987-89. Named Outstanding Law Alumnus Tulane U., 1985; selected Rex, King of Carnival, New Orleans, 1996. Mem. ABA (chmn. jr. bar conf. 1963-64, mem. ho. dels. 1964-66, 70, 72-76, sec. com. ethics evaluation 1965, rep. to conv. Union des Jeunes Avocats de France, 1964, chmn. sect. bar activities 1969-70), La. Bar Assn. (sec. treas. 1965-67, Outstanding Young Lawyer award), La. Soc. Colonial Wars (gov. 1976), Swiss-Am. Cultural Exch. Found. (hon. com. 1994—), Phi Beta Kappa, Order of Coif, Delta Kappa Epsilon, Omicron Delta Kappa. Episcopalian. Home: 611 Hector Ave Metairie LA 70005-4415 Office: Waverly Enterprises 601 Poydras St Ste 2690 New Orleans LA 70130-6026

WEINMANN, JUDY MUNGER, nurse; b. Georgetown, Tenn., June 1, 1943; d. Paul and Martha Edith (Smith) Powell; m. David Finley Munger, Dec. 6, 1963 (div. June 1985); children: David Finley Jr., Robert Powell. Grad., Erlanger Hosp., Chattanooga, 1964; AS, Cleveland (Tenn.) State Coll., 1982; BS, U. Tenn., 1984. RN, Tenn.; cert. occupational health nurse, Tenn. Med. staff nurse Bradley Meml. Hosp., Cleveland, 1964; office nurse William I. Proffitt, M.D., Cleveland, 1964-65; occupational health nurse Singer-Cobble Co., Chattanooga, 1966-67, Burlington Woolens Co., Cleveland, 1967-68, Am. Uniform Co., Cleveland, 1972-73; sch. nurse Cleveland State Coll., 1968-72, Bradley High Sch., Cleveland, 1973-79; occupational health nurse M&M/Mars, Cleveland, 1979-91; dir. nursing Open Arms Care Corp., Ooltewah, Tenn., 1992-93, Tenn. Home Health, Hixson, Tenn., 1993; dir. cmty. edn./case mgmt. Med. Shares Home Care, Chattanooga, Tenn., 1994—; presenter in field. Nurse ARC, Cleveland, 1979—; chmn. Bradley County Substance Abuse Com., Cleveland, 1980-87; com. mem. Am. Cancer Soc., Chattanooga, 1984—. Recipient Schering award as Tenn. outstanding occupational health nurse Schering-Plough Co., 1989. Mem. Chattanooga,

Tenn. Nurses Assn., Tenn. Occupational Health Nurses Assn. (bd. dirs. 1986—), Chattanooga Occupational Health Nurses Assn. (v.p., bd. dirs., Pres.'s award 1989), Cleveland Area Safety Coun. (Safety award 1988). Democrat. Baptist. Avocations: dancing, reading, music, crafts. Home: 1200 King Arthur Rd Chattanooga TN 37421-4020

WEINMANN, ROBERT LEWIS, neurologist; b. Newark, Aug. 21, 1935; s. Isadore and Etta (Silverman) W.; m. Diana Weinmann, Dec. 13, 1980 (dec. Dec. 1989); children: Paul, Chris, Dana, Paige. BA, Yale U., 1957; MD, Stanford U., 1962. Diplomate Am. Bd. of EEG and Neurophysiology, v.p.; diplomate Am. Acad. Pain Mgmt., Am. Bd. Forensic Medicine. Intern Pacific Presbyn. Med. Ctr., San Francisco, 1962-63; resident in neurology Stanford U. Hosp., 1963-66, chief resident, 1965-66; pvt. practice San Jose, Calif., 1969—; former clin. instr. neurology, Stanford (Calif.) U. Chmn. editl. bd. Clin. EEG Jour.; mem. editl. bd. Jour. Am. Acad. Pain Mgmt.; formerly mem. editl. bd. Clin. Evoked Potentials Jour.; contbr. articles to various publs. Capt. M.C., U.S. Army, 1966-68, Japan. Award recipient State of R.I., Santa Clara County Med. Soc., Epilepsy Soc., other orgns.; fellow Univ. Paris, 1957-58. Union of Am. Physicians and Dentists (pres. 1990—, bd. dirs. 1972—, pres. Calif. fedn. 1990—). Avocations: softball, tennis, music, theater, martial arts. Office: Union Am Physicians & Dentists 1330 Broadway Ste 730 Oakland CA 94612-2506

WEINREB, LLOYD LOBELL, law educator; b. N.Y.C., Oct. 9, 1936; s. Victor and Ernestine (Lobell) W.; m. Ruth Plaut, May 5, 1963; children—Jennifer, Elizabeth, Nicholas. B.A., Dartmouth, 1957; B.A., U. Oxford, 1959, M.A., 1963; LL.B., Harvard, 1962. Bar: N.Y. 1963, Mass. 1969. Faculty Harvard Law Sch., Cambridge, Mass., 1965—; prof. law Harvard Law Sch., 1968—. Home: 119 Russell Ave Watertown MA 02172-3453 Office: Law Sch Harvard U Cambridge MA 02138

WEINREICH, GABRIEL, physicist, minister, educator; b. Vilnius, Lithuania, Feb. 12, 1928; came to U.S., 1941, naturalized, 1949; s. Max and Regina (Szabad) W.; m. Alisa Lourié, Apr. 19, 1951 (dec. 1970); m. Gerane Siemering Benamou, Oct. 23, 1971; children: Catherine, Marc, Daniel, Rebecca, Natalie. A.B., Columbia U., 1948, M.A., 1949, Ph.D., 1954. Ordained priest Episcopal Ch., 1986. Mem. staff Bell Telephone Labs., Murray Hill, N.J., 1953-60; mem. faculty U. Mich., Ann Arbor, 1960—; prof. physics U. Mich., 1964-95; prof. emeritus, 1995—; Collegiate prof. U. Mich., 1974-76; adj. min. St. Clare's Episcopal ch., Ann Arbor, 1986-90; rector St. Stephen's Episcopal Ch., Hamburg, Mich., 1993-96. Author: Solids: Elementary Theory for Advanced Students, 1965, Fundamental Thermodynamics, 1968, Notes for General Physics, 1972. Recipient Disting. Teaching award U. Mich., 1968, Klopsteg award Am. Assn. Physics Tchrs., 1992, Internat. medal French Acoustical Soc., 1992. Fellow Acoustical Soc. Am. (assoc. editor Jour. 1987-89). Home: 754 Greenhills Dr Ann Arbor MI 48105-2718 Office: Randall Lab U Mich Ann Arbor MI 48109-1120

WEINRIB, SIDNEY, retired optometric and optical products and services executive; b. N.Y.C., Sept. 29, 1919; s. David and Rose (Lichtig) W.; m. Ruth Lois Simon, Aug. 25, 1946 (dec. 1988); children: Irene Henry, Donna Acker, Jeri Taylor. BS in Optometry, Columbia U., 1941. Practice optometry Sterling Optical, N.Y.C., 1947-66, from sec. treas. to chmn. bd., 1966-87; v.p. Ipco Corp., White Plains, N.Y., 1971-87; tchr. Bernard Baruch Sch. Bus., N.Y.C., 1953-54. Served with U.S. Army Signal Corps, 1942-46. Recipient commendation U.S. War Dept., 1946. Mem. Nat. Assn. Optometrists and Opticians (pres. 1978-87), Am. Nat. Standards Inst. Pioneer in modern optical chain retailing. Home: 270 Grand Central Pky # 32D Floral Park NY 11005

WEINRICH, ALAN JEFFREY, occupational hygienist; b. Passaic, N.J., Aug. 24, 1953; s. Erwin Hermann and Ann Elizabeth (Gall) W.; m. Nina Kathryn Hooker, Jan. 14, 1983; 1 child, Sheena Elizabeth Rochelle. BS with high honors, Rutgers U., 1975; MS, U. Iowa, 1988, postgrad., 1988-89. Cert. Am. Bd. Indsl. Hygiene, cert. environ. trainer Nat. Environ. Tng. Assn. Indsl. hygienist Tenn. Dept. Labor, Nashville, 1975-78; health info. specialist occupl. health program U. Tenn., Memphis, 1980-82; vol. tchr. Internat. Sch. Moshi, Tanzania, 1982-84; sr. rsch. asst. agrl. medicine rsch. facility U. Iowa, Iowa City, 1985-89; sr. indsl. hygienist PSI Energy, Inc., Plainfield, Ind., 1989-92; asst. dir. health & safety programs environ. mgmt. and edn. Purdue U., West Lafayette, 1992-94; assoc. dir. tech. affairs Am. Conf. Govtl. Indsl. Hygienists, Cin., 1994-97, dir. tech. affairs, 1997—. Co-editor book supplement: Documentation of the Threshold Limit Values and Biological Exposure Indices, 1996. Mem. healthy cities com. Butler-Tarkington Neighborhood Assn., Indpls., 1992-94. Mem. Am. Acad. Indsl. Hygiene, Am. Conf. Govtl. Indsl. Hygienists (column editor newsletter 1995—), Am. Indsl. Hygiene Assn. (v.p. Mid-South sect. 1981-82, bd. dirs. Iowa-Ill. sect. 1987-89, bd. dirs. Ind. sect. 1991-94, pres. Ind. sect. 1994-95), Internat. Occupl. Hygiene Assn., Am. Soc. Assn. Execs. Avocations: bicycling, family, reading, walking, softball. Office: Am Conf Govtl Indsl Hygienists 1330 Kemper Meadow Dr Cincinnati OH 45240-4120

WEINRICH, GLORIA JOAN CASTORIA, retired elementary education educator; b. Bklyn., Dec. 12, 1930; d. Louis and Elsie (Doddato) Castoria; m. Robert L. Weinrich, Aug. 16, 1952 (dec. 1993); 1 child, Russell Louis. BA, Hofstra U., 1952, MS, 1962. Cert. tchr., N.Y. Tchr. Oceanside (N.Y.) Bd. Edn., 1952-53, Troy (N.Y.) Bd. Edn., 1953-56, Carle Place (N.Y.) Bd. Edn., 1956-60, 69-93; ret., 1993. Mem. nominating com. Western Garden City Property Owners, 1995, mem. bird sanctuary com., 1995-97; mem. dist. adv. com. to edn. Garden City Schs., 1996—. Mem. AAUW, N.Y. State Ret. Tchrs. Assn. (co-chairperson polit. action 1993-97), Carle Pl. Ret. Tchrs. Assn. (pres. 1993-95), Alpha Upsilon, Delta Kappa Gamma (pres. 1992-96). Roman Catholic. Avocations: travel, lit. groups, opera, piano, bridge. Home: 1 Hawthorne Rd Garden City NY 11530-1017

WEINS, LEO MATTHEW, retired publishing executive; b. Racine, Wis., Sept. 2, 1912; s. Leo Matthew and Lula (Vollman) W.; m. Margaret Killion, Oct. 19, 1955. Student, Loyola U., Chgo., 1935-36, Northwestern U., 1946-47, U. Chgo., 1937-38. Comptroller ALA, 1952-57; with H. W. Wilson Co., N.Y.C., 1957-95, pres., treas., 1967-95, retired, 1995, bd. dirs., 1996—; chmn. bd. Mansell Pub., Ltd., London, 1981-87, bd. dirs.; mem. editorial bd. Choice, 1963-70, 77-81; mem. govt. adv. com. book and library programs Dept. State, 1973-76; mem. Bronx adv. com. Chase Manhattan Bank, 1968-78; trustee Dollar Dry Dock Savs. Bank N.Y., 1969-87; trustee, treas. N.Y. Met. Reference and Research Library Agency, 1979-83. Mem. sci. info. coun. NSF, 1968-72; bd. dirs. Highbridge Conservation Program, Bronx, 1966-69; pres. H.W. Wilson Found., 1967-95; trustee Maritime Coll. at Ft. Schuyler Found., Bronx, 1978-90. Served with AUS, 1943-46. Mem. ALA, Am. Anitquarian Soc., Fgn. Policy Assn. (gov. 1981-94). Home: 20 Beekman Pl New York NY 10022-8032

WEINSCHEL, ALAN JAY, lawyer; b. Bklyn., Feb. 9, 1946; m. Barbara Ellen Schure, Aug. 20, 1967; children: Lawrence, Adam, Naomi. BA, Bklyn. Coll., 1967; JD, NYU, 1969. Bar: N.Y. 1970, U.S. Dist. Ct. (so. and ea. dists.) N.Y. 1973, U.S. Ct. Appeals (2d cir.) 1979, U.S. Ct. Appeals (9th cir.) 1986, U.S. Ct. Appeals (3d cir.) 1993, U.S. Ct. Appeals (7th cir.) 1996. Assoc. Breed, Abbott & Morgan, N.Y.C., 1969-74; assoc. Weil, Gotshal & Manges, N.Y.C., 1974-78, ptnr., 1978—; lectr. Practising Law Inst., Ohio Legal Ctr., Am. Mgmt. Assn., Law Jour. Seminars, Law and Bus. Seminars. Trustee N.Y. Inst. Tech., Old Westbury, N.Y., 1969-76, Temple Sinai, Roslyn, N.Y., 1981-87, 89-95. Capt. U.S. Army res., 1969-74. Mem. ABA (editl. bd. Antitrust Devels. 1981-87), N.Y. State Bar Assn. (chmn. antitrust sect. 1993-95), Assn. Bar of City of N.Y. Office: Weil Gotshal & Manges 767 5th Ave New York NY 10153-0001

WEINSCHEL, BRUNO OSCAR, engineering executive, physicist; b. Stuttgart, Germany, May 26, 1919; came to U.S., 1939; m. Shirley Kittredge; 6 children. BA in Physics, Technische Hochschule, Stuttgart, 1938; Dr. Engring., Technische Hochschule, Munich, Fed. Republic of Germany, 1966; DSc (hon.), Capitol Inst. Tech., 1984. Registered profl. engr., Md., D.C. Sr. engr. Western Electric, 1943-44; chief engr. Indsl. Instruments Co., Jersey City, 1944-48; group leader, rsch. scientist Nat. Bur. of Standards, 1949-52; chief engr., pres. Weinschel Engring. Co., Inc., Gaithersburg, Md., 1952-86, cons., 1987-88; pres., chief engr. Weinschel Rsch. Found., Gaithersburg, Md., 1987—; chief engr. Weinschel Assocs., Gaithersburg, 1988—. Contbr. over 50 articles to profl. jours.; inventor and co-inventor with 20 patents. Mem. Pres. Reagan's Com. Medal of Sci., 1986-87; bd. trustees Shady Grove Adventist Hosp., chair bus. and industry com., 1981-84, pres., 1984-86. Recipient William A. Wildhack award Nat. Conf. of Standards Labs., 1985. Fellow IEEE (pres. 1986, Richard M. Emberson award 1992), Instn. Elec. Engrs.-U.K.; mem. Annapolis Yacht Club, Cosmos Club, Univ. Club. Republican. Avocations: sailing, snow and water skiing.

WEINSHEIMER, WILLIAM CYRUS, lawyer; b. Chgo., Jan. 12, 1941; s. Alfred John and Coress (Searing) W.; m. Roberta Limarzi, June 5, 1965; children: William C. Jr., Kurt R., Robert L. BBA in Mktg., U. Notre Dame, 1962; JD, Northwestern U., 1965. Bar: Ill. 1965, U.S. Dist. Ct. (no. dist.) Ill. 1967, U.S. Tax Ct. 1968. Assoc. Hopkins & Sutter, Chgo., 1967-73, ptnr., chmn. trust and estates sect., 1973—; lectr. continuing legal edn. programs; mem. estate planning adv. coun. Northwestern U. Author: (with others) The New Generation Skipping Tax; Analysis, Planning & Drafting, 1987; Drafting Wills and Trust Agreements, 1990; contbr. articles to profl. jours. Bd. dirs. The Ragdale Found., Lake Forest, Ill., 1987—, Lawyers for Creative Arts, 1973-90, Winnetka United Way, 1989-92; pres. Family Svc. Winnetka-Northfield, Inc., 1978-79. Capt. U.S. Army, 1965-67. Fellow Am. Coll. Trust and Estate Coun. (bus. planning com. 1993—, internat. estate planning com., 1997—, chair Ill. chpt. 1989-92, editor Actec Notes 1991-92, bd. regents 1992—, chair edit. bd. 1993-96); mem. ABA (vice chmn. com. on generation-skipping tax 1988-92), Ill. Bar Assn., Chgo. Bar Assn. (chmn. probate practice com. 1989), Chgo. Bar Found. (bd. dirs. 1992—), Ill. Bar Found. (bd. dirs. 1985-91), Law Club, Econ. Club, Mid-Day Club, Skokie Country Club, Notre Dame Club Chgo. (bd. govs. 1984-90). Roman Catholic. Avocations: golf, visual arts, performing. Office: Hopkins & Sutter 3 First National Plz Chicago IL 60602

WEINSHIENK, ZITA LEESON, federal judge; b. St. Paul, Apr. 3, 1933; d. Louis and Ada (Dubov) Leeson; m. Hubert Troy Weinshienk, July 8, 1956 (dec. 1983); children: Edith Blair, Kay Anne, Darcy Jill; m. James N. Schaffner, Nov. 15, 1986. Student, U. Colo., 1952-53; BA magna cum laude, U. Ariz., 1955; JD cum laude, Harvard U., 1958; Fulbright grantee, U. Copenhagen, Denmark, 1959; LHD (hon.), Loretto Heights Coll., 1985; LLD (hon.), U. Denver, 1990. Bar: Colo. 1959. Probation counselor, legal adviser, referee Denver Juvenile Ct., 1959-64; judge Denver Mcpl. Ct., 1964-65, Denver County Ct., 1965-71, Denver Dist. Ct., 1972-79, U.S. Dist. Ct. Colo., Denver, 1979—. Precinct committeewoman Denver Democratic Com., 1963-64; bd. dirs. Crime Stoppers. Named one of 100 Women in Touch with Our Time Harper's Bazaar Mag., 1971, Woman of Yr., Denver Bus. and Profl. Women, 1969; recipient Women Helping Women award Soroptimist Internat. of Denver, 1983, Hanna G. Solomon award Nat. Coun. Jewish Women, Denver, 1986. Fellow Colo. Bar Found., Am. Bar Found.; mem. ABA, Denver Bar Assn., Colo. Bar Assn., Nat. Conf. Fed. Trial Judges (exec. com.), Dist. Judges' Assn. of 10th Cir. (past pres.), Colo. Women's Bar Assn., Fed. Judges Assn., Denver Crime Stoppers Inc. (bd.dirs.), Devner LWV, Women's Forum Colo., Harvard Law Sch. Assn., Phi Beta Kappa, Phi Kappa Phi, Order of Coif (hon. Colo. chpt.). Office: US Dist Ct US Courthouse Rm C-418 1929 Stout St Denver CO 80294-0001

WEINSIER, PHILIP DAVID, electronics educator; b. Orlando, Fla., May 16, 1953; s. Stanley Cecil and Ruth (Potsdamer) W. BS, Berry Coll., 1978; MEd, Clemson U., 1979, EdD, 1990. Instr. West Orange High Sch., Orlando, Fla., 1980-84; grad. teaching asst. Clemson (S.C.) U., 1985-89; lectr. Appalachian State U., Boone, N.C., 1990-91; asst. prof. No. Mich. U., Marquette, 1991-95; regional tng. dir. Centerpoint Techs. Inc., Orlando, Fla., 1995—; adj. prof. electronics U. Ctrl. Fla., 1995—; cons. Superior-Newco, Marquete, 1991, OHAB & Co., CPA, Orlando, 1995. Co-author: The Computer and Information Technology Attitude Inventory, 1988. Program dir. Fgn. Exchange Program, Orange County, Fla., 1982-84. Fulbright scholar, 1987-88; grantee Clemson U., 1989, German Sci. Found., 1989, No. Mich. U., 1992, 93. Mem. Internat. Fulbright Orgn. (life), European Assn. Rsch. on Learning and Instrn., Internat. Tech. Edn. Assn. (chmn. internat. rels. com. 1993-96, coun. tech. tchr. edn. rsch. com. 1995—), Nat. Assn. Indsl. Tech. (cert.), Nat. Assn. Indsl. and Tech. Tchr. Educators, Orange County Indsl. Arts Assn. (v.p. 1982-83, pres. 1983-84), Orange County Adult Comty. Edn. Assn. (bd. dirs. 1983-84), Epsilon Pi Tau. Avocations: international travel, foreign languages, tennis, scuba diving.

WEINSIER, ROLAND LOUIS, nutrition educator and director. MD, DPH, Harvard U., 1973. Prof. nutrition, chmn. U. Ala., Birmingham, 1975—. Office: U Ala at Birmingham Med Ctr Dept Nutrition Scis U Sta PO Box 188 Birmingham AL 35294-3360

WEINSTEIN, ALAN EDWARD, lawyer; b. Bklyn., Apr. 20, 1945; s. John and Matilda W.; m. Patti Kantor, Dec. 18, 1965; children: Steven R., David A. AA, U. Fla., 1964; BBA, U. Miami (Fla.), 1965, JD cum laude, 1968. Bar: Fla. 1968, U.S. Dist. Ct. (so. dist.) Fla. 1968, U.S. Ct. Appeals (5th cir.) 1969, U.S. Supreme Ct. 1973, U.S. Ct. Appeals (4th & 11th cirs.) 1981. Assoc. Cohen & Hogan, Miami Beach, Fla., 1968-71; pvt. practice Miami Beach, 1972-81; sr. ptnr. Weinstein & Preira, Miami Beach, 1981-92; prin. Law Offices of Alan E. Weinstein, Miami, 1992—; lectr. continuing legal edn. programs. Mem. ABA (criminal and family law sect. 1968—), Nat. Assn. Criminal Def. Lawyers, Fla. Bar Assn. (criminal and family law sect. 1968—, ethics com. 1987-88, bench/bar com. 1988-89), Fla. Criminal Def. Attys. Assn. (pres. 1978-79), Fla. Assn. Criminal Def. Lawyers (treas. 1989-90), Miami Beach Bar Assn., Soc. Wig and Robe, Phi Kappa Phi. Avocations: marlin fishing, reading, travel. Office: 1801 West Ave Miami FL 33139-1431

WEINSTEIN, ALLAN M., medical device company executive; b. Bklyn., June 25, 1945; s. Henry I. Weinstein and Hannah L. (Broidy) Glasser; m. Phyllis Fishman, Aug. 28, 1965; children: Craig, Brett, Danielle. BS, Poly. Inst., Bklyn., 1965, MS, 1966, PhD, 1972. Registered profl. engr. Postdoctoral fellow U. Pa., Phila., 1971-72; asst. prof. Clemson U., 1972-75; prof., dir. biomaterials Tulane U., New Orleans, 1975-81; v.p. tech. affairs Intermedics Orthopaedics, Dublin, Calif., 1981-83, also bd. dirs.; pres., chief exec. officer Harrington Arthritis Rsch. Ctr., Phoenix, 1983-87; co-founder, chmn., pres., CEO OrthoLogic Corp., Phoenix, 1987-96, chmn., CEO, 1987—. Editor: spl. publs. 472, 601, Nat. Bur. Stds., 1977, 81; contbr. numerous articles to profl. jours.; patentee (3) in field. Rsch. grantee NIH, 1973-91. Mem. Soc. for Biomaterials (charter mem., pres. 1985-86, Clemson Award for contbns. to biomaterials lit. 1995), Orthopaedic Rsch. Soc., Am. Soc. Metals, N.Y. Acad. Scis., Sigma Xi. Republican. Jewish. Avocations: tennis, skiing, golf. Home: 3177 East Sierra Vista Dr Phoenix AZ 85016 Office: OrthoLogic Corp 2850 S 36th St Phoenix AZ 85034-7239

WEINSTEIN, ALLEN, educator, historian, non-profit administrator; b. N.Y.C., Sept. 1, 1937; s. Samuel and Sarah (Popkoff) W.; m. Adrienne Dominguez, June 14, 1995; children: Andrew Samuel, David Meier. BA, CCNY; MA, Yale U., PhD, 1967. Prof. Smith Coll., Northampton, Mass., 1966-81, Georgetown U., Washington, 1981-83; pres. R.M. Hutchins CSDI, Santa Barbara, Calif., 1984; prof. Boston U., 1985-89; founder, pres. The Ctr. for Democracy, Washington, 1985—. Author: Prelude to Populism, 1970, Freedom and Crisis, 1974, 3d edit., 1981, Perjury, 1978 (NISC award 1978), new edit., 1996, Between the Wars, 1978; editor: Am. Negro Slavery, 1968, 3d edit., 1981, HST and Israel, 1981; mem. editorial bd. The Washington Post, 1981; exec. editor The Washington Quar., 1982-83. Exec. dir. The Democracy Program, Washington, 1982-83; acting pres. Nat. Endowment for Democracy, Washington, 1983-84; chmn. edn. com. U.S. Inst. Peace, Washington, 1986—; mem. U.S. Observer del., Feb., 1986 Philippines election, co-author report; vice chmn. U.S. del. UNESCO World Conf. on Culture, 1982, UNESCO/IPDC meeting, 1983. Recipient Meade prize in history CCNY, 1960, Egleston prize Yale U., 1967, Binkley-Stephenson prize Orgn. Am. Historians, 1968, UN Peace medal, 1986, Coun. of Europe silver medal, 1990, 96; Fulbright lectr., Australia, 1968, 71; Commonwealth Fund lectr. U.S. History, U. London, 1981; Fourth of July Orator Fanueil Hall, Boston, 1987. Fellow Woodrow Wilson Ctr., NEH; mem. Soc. Am. Historians. Democrat. Jewish. Office: The Ctr for Democracy 1101 15th St NW Ste 505 Washington DC 20005-5002*

WEINSTEIN, ANDREW H., lawyer; b. Pitts., Oct. 5, 1943; s. Adolph J. and Meta I. (Schwartz) W.; m. Susan Balber, Aug. 11, 1968; children: Jodi L., Toby M., Jamie M. BSBA, Duquesne U., 1965; JD, U. Pitts., 1968; LLM in Tax Law, NYU, 1969. Bar: Pa. 1969, U.S. Tax Ct. 1969, Fla. 1970, U.S. Dist. Ct. (so. dist.) Fla., U.S. Claims Ct. Trial atty. IRS, L.A., 1969-70, Miami, Fla., 1970-73; ptnr. Glass, Schultz, Weinstein & Moss, Coral Gables, Fla., 1973-80, Holland & Knight, Miami, 1980—. Contbr. articles to profl. jours. Bd. dirs. New World Symphony, Miami, Performing Arts Found., Zool. Soc. Fla. Fellow Am. Coll. Tax Counsel; mem. ABA (tax sect. com., chmn. subcom. 1981-87), The Fla. Bar Assn. Republican. Avocations: golf, swimming, travel. Office: Holland & Knight 701 Brickell Ave Ste 3000 Miami FL 33131-2847

WEINSTEIN, DAVID CARL, investment company executive, lawyer; b. Flushing, N.Y., Nov. 21, 1951; s. Philip and Molly (Rencoff) W.; m. Clare Villari, Aug. 14, 1988; 1 child, Matthew Charles. BA, Boston U., 1972; JD, Boston Coll., 1975. Bar: Mass. 1975. Assoc. gen. counsel Prucapital, Inc., Cambridge, Mass., 1976-84; v.p., corp. counsel Fidelity Investments, Boston, 1984-95, sr. v.p. adminstrn., 1995—; bd. dirs. Empire Fidelity Investments Life Ins. Co., N.Y.C. Trustee Hebrew Coll., Brookline, Mass., 1993—; bd. dirs. Goodwill Industries, Boston, 1990—. Mem. Am. Corp. Counsel Assn., Mass. Bar Assn. Office: Fidelity Investments 82 Devonshire St Boston MA 02109-3605

WEINSTEIN, DIANE GILBERT, federal judge, lawyer; b. Rochester, N.Y., June 14, 1947; d. Myron Birne and Doris Isabelle (Robie) Gilbert; m. Dwight Douglas Sypolt; children: Andrew, David. BA, Smith Coll., Northampton, Mass., 1969; postgrad., Stanford U., 1977-78, Georgetown U., 1978; JD, Boston U., 1979. Bar: D.C. 1979, Mass. 1979. Law clk. to judge D.C. Ct. Appeals, Washington, 1979-80; assoc. Peabody, Lambert & Meyers, Washington, 1980-83; asst. gen. counsel Office of Mgmt. and Budget, Washington, 1983-86; dep. gen. counsel U.S. Dept. Edn., Washington, 1986-88, acting gen. counsel, 1988-89; legal counselor to V.P. of U.S., White House; counsel Pres.'s Competitiveness Coun., Washington, 1989-90; judge U.S. Ct. Fed. Claims, Washington, 1990—. Recipient Young Lawyer's award Boston U. Law Sch., 1989. Mem. Fed. Am. Inn of Ct. (pres.), Federalist Soc., Univ. Club. Republican. Office: US Ct Fed Claims 717 Madison Pl NW Washington DC 20005-1011

WEINSTEIN, EDWARD MICHAEL, architect, consultant; b. Bklyn., May 5, 1947; s. Hyman and Freda (Rochkes) W.; m. Melanie Jane Ross, June 22, 1969; children: Valerie, David. BS, CCNY, 1969. Registered architect; lic. N.Y., N.J. Jr. architect N.Y.C. Dept. Ports and Terminals, 1970-72, architect, 1972-75, sr. urban designer, 1975-80, dir. waterfront devel., 1980-84, asst. commr., 1984-87; pres. EMW Assocs., Hastings-On-Hudson, N.Y., 1984—; ptnr. The Hastings Design Group, Hastings-On-Hudson, 1987—; adv. bd. Metro Marine Express Ltd., N.Y.C., 1989-91. Active Planning Bd., Hastings-on-Hudson, 1990—, Waterfront Ctr.; trustee Greenburgh Hebrew Ctr., Dobbs Ferry, N.Y., 1986-89, 92—; v.p. N.Y. Port Promotion Assn., N.Y.C., 1984-87; adv. com. on waterfront devel. N.Y. State Assembly. Recipient Gold Key award House Plan Assn., 1969. Mem. AIA, Am. Assn. Port Authority, N.Y. Soc. Architects, The Waterfront Ctr., CCNY Alumni Assn. Democrat. Jewish. Avocations: tennis, art. Office: The Hastings Design Group 14 Spring St Hastings Hdsn NY 10706-1511

WEINSTEIN, GEORGE WILLIAM, ophthalmology educator; b. East Orange, N.J., Jan. 26, 1935; s. Henry J. and Irma C. (Klein) W.; m. Sheila Valerie Wohlreich, June 20, 1957; children: Bruce David, Elizabeth Joyce, Rachel Andrea. AB, U. Pa., 1955; MD, SUNY, Bklyn., 1959. Diplomate Am. Bd. Ophthalmology (bd. dirs. 1981-89). Intern then resident in ophthalmology Kings County Hosp., Bklyn., 1959-63; asst. prof. ophthalmology Johns Hopkins U., Balt., 1967-70; head ophthalmology dept. U. Tex., San Antonio, 1970-80; prof., Jane McDermott Shott chmn. W.Va. U., Morgantown, 1980-95. Author: Key Facts in Ophthalmology, 1984; editor: Open Angle Glaucoma, 1986; editor Ophthalmic Surgery jour., 1971-81, Current Opinion in Ophthalmology jour., 1988—; contbr. articles to profl. jours. Served to lt. comdr. USPHS, 1963-65. Sr. Internat. fellow Fogarty Internat. Ctr. NIH, 1987. Mem. ACS (bd. govs. 1983-85, bd. regents 1987-92), Assn. Univ. Profs. Ophthalmology (pres. 1986-87, exec. v.p. 1994), Am. Acad. Ophthalmology (bd. dirs. 1980-92, chmn. long range planning com. 1986-89, pub. and profl. sec. 1983-89, pres.-elect 1990, pres. 1991, Honor award, Sr. Honor award), Alpha Omega Alpha (faculty 1987), Am. Ophthalmology Soc. (coun. 1992—). Jewish. Avocations: jazz, banjo, photography, tennis, basketball. Home: 104 Planters Row W Ponte Vedra Beach FL 32082

WEINSTEIN, GERALD D., dermatology educator; b. N.Y.C., Oct. 13, 1936; m. Marcia Z. Weinstein; children: Jeff, Jon, Debbie. BA, U. Pa., 1957, MD, 1961. Diplomate Am. Bd. Dermatology. Intern Los Angeles County Gen. Hosp., 1961-62; clin. assoc. dermatology br. Nat. Cancer Instn. NIH, Bethesda, Md., 1962-64; resident dept. dermatology U. Miami, Fla., 1964-65; asst. prof. Dept. Dermatology U. Miami, Fla., 1966-71, assoc. prof., 1971-74, prof., 1975-79; prof., chmn. dept. dermatology U. Calif., Irvine, 1979—, acting dean Coll. Medicine, 1985-87; attending staff VA Med. Ctr., Long Beach, Calif., 1979—, UCI Med. Ctr., Orange, Calif., 1979—, St. Joseph Hosp., Orange, 1980—. Contbr. articles to profl. jours., chpts. to books. Recipient Lifetime Achievement award Nat. Psoriasis Found., 1994; co-recipient award for psoriasis rsch. Taub Internat. Meml., 1971; NIH spl. postdoctoral fellow, 1965-67. Mem. Am. Acad. Dermatology (chmn. task force on psoriasis 1986—, bd. dirs. 1984-88). Office: U Calif Irvine Coll Medicine Dept Dermatology Irvine CA 92697-2400

WEINSTEIN, HARRIS, lawyer; b. Providence, May 10, 1935; s. Joseph and Gertrude (Rusitzky) W.; m. Rosa Grunberg, June 3, 1956; children: Teme Feldman, Joshua, Jacob. BS in Math., MIT, 1956, MS in Math., 1958; LLB, Columbia U., 1961. Bar: D.C. 1962. Law clk. to judge William H. Hastie U.S. Ct. Appeals (3d cir.), Phila., 1961-62; with Covington & Burling, Washington, 1962-67, 69-90, 1993—; chief counsel Office of Thrift Supervision U.S. Dept. of Treasury, Washington, 1990-92; asst. to solicitor gen. U.S. Dept. Justice, 1967-69; pub. mem. Adminstrv. Conf. of U.S., 1982-90; lectr. U. Va. Law Sch., 1996. V.p. Jewish Social Svc. Agy.; mem. MIT Corp., 1989-95. Mem. Nat. Press Club. Home: 7717 Georgetown Pike Mc Lean VA 22102-1411 Office: Covington & Burling PO Box 7566 1201 Pennsylvania Ave NW Washington DC 20004-2401

WEINSTEIN, HARVEY, film company executive. Co-chmn. Miramax Films Corp., L.A. Producer (with Robert Weinstein): Playing For Keeps (with Alan Brewer), 1986, Scandal (with Joe Boyd & Nik Powell), 1989, Strike It Rich, 1990, Hardware (with Nik Powell, Stephen Woolley & Trix Worrell), 1990, A Rage In Harlem (with Terry Glinwood, William Horberg & Nik Powell), 1991, The Night We Never Met (with Sidney Kimmel), 1993, Benefit Of The Doubt, 1993, True Romance (with Gary Barber, Stanley Margolis & James G. Robinson), 1993, Mother's Boys (with Randall Poster), 1994, Pulp Fiction (with Richard N. Gladstein), 1994, Ready To Wear/Pret-A-Porter (with Ian Jessel), 1994, Smoke (with Satoru Iseki, 1995, A Month By The Lake (with Donna Gigliotti), 1995, The Crossing Guard (with Richard Gladstein), 1995, The Journey Of August King (with Richard Gladstein), 1995, Things To Do In Denver When You're Dead (with Marie Cantin), 1995, The Englishman Who Went Up A Hill But Came Down A Mountain (with Sally Hibbin & Robert Jones), Blue In The Face (with Harvey Keitel), 1995, Restoration (with Donna Gigliotti), 1995. Office: Miramax Films Corp 375 Greenwich St New York NY 10013-2376*

WEINSTEIN, HERBERT, chemical engineer, educator; b. Bklyn., Mar. 10, 1933; s. Abraham and Pauline (Feldman) W.; m. Judith Cooper, Apr. 6, 1957; children: Michael Howard, Edward Marc, Ellen Rachel. B.Engring. in Chem. Engring, Coll. City N.Y., 1955; M.S. in Chem. Engring, Purdue U., 1957; Ph.D., Case Inst. Tech., 1963. Staff mem. Los Alamos Sci. Lab., 1956-58; research engr. NASA Lewis Research Center, Cleve., 1959-63; asst. prof. chem. engring. Ill. Inst. Tech., 1963-66, assoc. prof., 1966-72, prof., 1972-77; dir. Center for Biomed. Engring., 1973-77; prof. CUNY, 1977—; Herbert G. Kayser prof. of chem. engring., 1987—; vis. rsch. assoc., mem. Med. Rsch. Inst. Michael Reese Hosp. and Med. Ctr., Chgo., 1965-77; vis. prof. mech. engring. Technion-Israel Inst. Tech., 1972-73; vis. prof. biomed. engring. Rush Med. Coll., Chgo., 1973-76; summer prof. Exxon Rsch. and Engring. Co., annually, 1981-92; Lady Davis vis. prof. Technion-Israel Inst. Tech., 1985; cons. to industry, rsch. labs. Mem. Am. Inst. Chem. Engrs., Sigma Xi. Jewish. Research and publs. on fluidization, chem. reactor engring., fluid mechanics, biomed. engring. Office: CUNY Dept Chem Engring New York NY 10031

WEINSTEIN, I. BERNARD, oncologist, geneticist, research administrator; b. Madison, Wis., Sept. 9, 1930; married, 1952; 3 children. BS, U. Wis., 1952, MD, 1955, DSc (hon.), 1992. Nat. Cancer Inst. spl. rsch. fellow bacteriology/immunology Harvard Med. Sch./MIT, Boston, 1959-61; career scientist Health Rsch. Coun., City of N.Y., 1961-72; assoc. vis. physician Francis Delafield Hosp., 1961-66; from asst. attending physician to assoc. attending physician Presbyn. Hosp., 1967-81, attending physician, 1981—; from asst. to assoc. prof. medicine Columbia U. Coll. Phys. and Surg., N.Y.C., 1978-90; prof. medicine Columbia U., N.Y.C., 1973—, prof. pub. health, 1978—, prof. genetics and devel., 1990—, Frode Jensen prof. medicine, 1990-96, dir. comprehensive cancer ctr., 1985—; advisor Lung Cancer Segment, Carcinogenesis Program, Nat. Cancer Inst., 1971-74, Chem. and Molecular Biol. Segment, 1973-76; mem. interdisciplinary comm. program Smithsonian Inst., 1971-74, Pharmacology B Study ect., NIH, 1971-75, numerous sci. and adv. coms. Nat. Cancer Inst., Am. Cancer Soc., 1976-88; advisor Roswell Park Meml. Inst., Buffalo, Brookhaven Nat. Lab., Divsn. Cancer Cause and Prevention, Nat. Cancer Inst., Coun. on Analysis and Projects, Am. Cancer Soc., Internat. Agy. for Rsch. on Cancer, WHO, Lyon, France; Nakasone vis. prof., Tokyo, 1987; GM Cancer Rsch. Found. vis. prof. Internat. Agy. Rsch. Cancer, Lyon, 1988; mem. adv. coun. Nat. Inst. Environ. Health Scis., 1995—; chmn. Bristol-Myers Squbb Cancer Awards, 1993-96. Assoc. editor Cancer Rsch., 1973-76, 86—, Jour. Environ. Pathology and Toxicology, 1977-84, Jour. Cellular Physiology, 1982-89. Recipient Meltzer medal, 1964, Dlowes award Am. Assn. Cancer Rsch., 1987, Silvio O. Conte award Environ. Health Inst., 1990; Louise Weissberger lectr. U. Rochester, 1981, Mary Ann Swetland lectr. Case Western Res. U., 1983, Daniel Laszlo Meml. lectr. Montefiore Med. Ctr., 1983, Samuel Kuna Disting. lectr. Rutgers U., 1985, Ester Langer lectr. U. Chgo., 1989, Harris Meml. lectr. MIT, 1989; European Molecular Biology Orgn. travel fellow, 1970-71. Mem. AAAS (coun. del. 1985-88), Am. Assn. Cancer Rsch. (pres. 1990-91), Inst. Medicine/Nat. Acad. Sci., Am. Acad. Arts and Scis., Am. Assn. Physicians, Am. Soc. Microbiology, Internat. Soc. Quantum Biology, Am. Soc. Clin. Investigation, N.Y. Acad. Sci. Achievements include research in oncology, cellular and molecular aspects of carcinogenesis, environmental carcinogenesis, control of gene expression. Office: Cancer Ctr Columbia Univ 701 W 168th St New York NY 10032-2704

WEINSTEIN, IRA PHILLIP, advertising executive; b. Chgo., June 10, 1919; s. Phillip Marshall and Lillian (Greenblatt) W.; m. Norma Randall; children: Terri, Laura Temkin. Student, Crane Tech. Inst., 1937, Northwestern U., 1945-46. Chmn. bd. Schram Advt. Co., Chgo., 1945—. 1st lt. USAAF, 1942-45, ETO. Decorated D.F.C., Air medal, Purple Heart, Ex-Prisoner of War medal; recipient Presdl. citation, 1988. Mem. Chgo. Direct Mail Assn., Air Force Assn., Ex-POW Assn., Bombardiers Assn., Caterpillar Assn., Air Force Heritage League, 2d Air Divsn. Assn., Mil. Order of Purple HEart, 8th Air Force Hist. Soc. Office: The Schram Advt Co 450 Skokie Blvd Ste 800 Northbrook IL 60062-7916

WEINSTEIN, IRWIN MARSHALL, internist, hematologist; b. Denver, Mar. 5, 1926; m. Judith Braun, 1951. Student, Dartmouth Coll., 1943-44, Williams Coll., 1944-45; MD, U. Colo., Denver, 1949. Diplomate Am. Bd. Internal Medicine (assoc. bd. govs. hematology subcom.). Intern Montefiore Hosp., N.Y.C., 1949-50; jr. asst. resident in medicine Montefiore Hosp., 1950-51; sr. asst. resident in medicine U. Chgo., 1951-52, resident in medicine, 1952-53, instr. in medicine, 1953-54, asst. prof. medicine, 1954-55; vis. assoc. prof. medicine U. Calif. Center for Health Scis., L.A., 1955-56, assoc. clin. prof., 1957-60, clin. prof., 1970—; hon. prof., 1996—; sect. chief in medicine, hematology sect. Wadsworth Gen. Hosp., VA Center, L.A., 1956-59; pvt. practice medicine specializing in hematology and internal medicine Los Angeles, 1959—; mem. staff Cedars-Sinai Med. Center, L.A., 1959—; chief of med. staff Cedars-Sinai Med. Ctr., 1972-74, bd. govs., 1974—; mem. staff U. Calif. Ctr. Health Scis., Wadsworth Gen. Hosp., VA Ctr.; vis. prof. Hadassah Med. Ctr., Jerusalem, 1967; adv. for health affairs to Hon. Alan Cranston, 1971-92; mem. com. on space biology and medicine Space Sci. Bd.; active UCLA Comprehensive Cancer Ctr. Contbr. articles to profl. publs.; editor: (with Ernest Beutler) Mechanisms of Anemia, 1962. Master ACP (gov. So. Calif. Region I 1989-93); fellow Israel Med. Assn. (hon.); mem. AAAS, Am. Fedn. Clin. Rsch., Am. Soc. Hematology (exec. com. 1974-78, chmn. com. on practice 1978-87, mem. council 1974-78), Am. Soc. Internal Medicine, Assn. Am. Med. Colls., Internat. Soc. Hematology, Internat. Soc. Internal Medicine, L.A. Acad. Medicine, L.A. Soc. Nuclear Medicine, Inst. of Medicine NAS, N.Y. Acad. Sci., Reticulo-Endothelial Soc., Royal Soc. Medicine, Western Soc. Clin. Rsch., Alpha Omega Alpha. Office: 8635 W 3rd St Ste 665 Los Angeles CA 90048-6101

WEINSTEIN, JACK BERTRAND, federal judge; b. Wichita, Kans., Aug. 10, 1921; s. Harry Louis and Bessie Helen (Brodach) W.; m. Evelyn Horowitz, Oct. 10, 1946; children: Seth George, Michael David, Howard Lewis. BA, Bklyn. Coll., 1943; LLB, Columbia, 1948; LLD (hon.), Bklyn. Law Sch., Yeshiva U., Albany Law Sch., Hofstra Law Sch., L.I. U.; Yale U. Bar: N.Y. 1949. Assoc. Columbia Law Sch., 1948-49; law clk. N.Y. Ct. Appeals Judge Stanly H. Fuld, 1949-50; ptnr. William Rosenfeld, N.Y.C., 1950-52; mem. faculty Columbia Law Sch., 1952-67, prof. law, 1956-67, adj. prof., 1967—; U.S. judge (Eastern Dist. N.Y.), 1967-93, chief judge, 1980-88; sr. judge Ea. Dist. N.Y., 1993—; vis. prof. U. Tex., 1957, U. Colo., 1961, Harvard U., 1982, Georgetown U., 1991, Bklyn. Law Sch., 1988—, others; counsel N.Y. Joint Legis. Com. Motor Vehicle Problems, 1952-54, State Sen. Seymour Halpern, 1952-54; reporter adv. com. practice and procedure N.Y. State Temp. Commn. Cts., 1955-58; adv. com. practice N.Y. Judicial Conf., 1963-66; adv. com. rules of evidence U.S. Jud. Conf., 1965-75, mem. com. jurisdiction, 1969-75, mem., 1983-86; mem. 2d Cir. Jud. Coun., 1982-88, U.S. Jud. Conf., 1983-86, others in past. Author: (with Morgan and Maquire) Cases and Materials on Evidence, 4th edit., 1965, (with Maguire, Chadbourne and Mansfield, 5th edit.), 1971, 6th edit., 1975, (with Mansfield, Abrams and Bergen), 8th edit., 1988, (with Rosenberg) Cases and Materials on Civil Procedure, 1961, rev. edit, (with Smit), 1971, (with Smit, Rosenberg and Korn), 1976, (with Korn and Miller) New York Civil Procedure, 9 vols., rev. edit, 1966, Manual of New York Civil Procedure, 1967, Basic Problems of State and Federal Evidence, 1976, (with Berger) Weinstein's Evidence, 7 vols., 1967, rev. edit., 1993, Revising Rule Making Procedures, 1977, A New York Constitution Meeting Today's Needs and Tomorrow's Challenges, 1967, Disaster, A Legal Allegory, 1988, (with Greenawalt) Readings for Seminar on Equality and Law, 1979, (with Murphy) Readings for Seminar in Individual Rights in a Mass Society, 1990-91, (with Berger) Readings for Seminar in Science and Law, (with Feinberg) Mass Torts, 1992, 94, Individual Justice in Mass Litigation, 1995. Chmn. N.Y. Dem. adv. com. on Constl. Conv., 1955; bd. dirs. N.Y. Civil Liberties Union, 1956-62, Cardozo Sch. Law, Conf. on Jewish Social Studies, 1980-88; nat. adv. bd. Am. Jewish Congress, 1960-67, CARE, 1985-90, Fedn. Jewish Philanthropies, 1985-94; chmn. lay bd. Riverside Hosp. Adolescent Drug Users, 1954-55. Lt. USNR, 1943-46. Mem. ABA, N.Y. State Bar Assn., Assn. of Bar of City of N.Y., Nassau County Bar Assn., Am. Law Inst., Soc. Pub. Tchrs. Law (Eng.), Am. Acad. Arts and Scis. Jewish. Office: US Dist Ct US Courthouse 225 Cadman Plz E Brooklyn NY 11201-1818

WEINSTEIN, JAY A., social science educator, researcher; b. Chgo., Feb. 23, 1942; s. Lawrence E. and Jacqueline L. (Caplan) W.; m. Diana S. Staffin, Sept. 16, 1961; m. Marilyn L. Schwartz, Nov. 25, 1972; children—Liza, Bennett. A.B., U. Ill., 1963, Ph.D., 1973; M.A., Washington U., St. Louis, 1965. Teaching fellow U. Ill., Urbana, 1963-64; teaching asst. McGill U., Montreal, Que., Can., 1966-68; instr. Sir George Williams U., Montreal, Que., Can., 1967-68; lectr. Simon Fraser U., Vancouver, B.C., Can., 1968; asst. prof. North Central Coll., Naperville, Ill., 1970-71, U. Iowa, 1973-77; prof. social sci. Ga. Inst. Tech., Atlanta, 1977-86; head dept. sociology Eastern Mich U., 1986-90, faculty rsch. fellow, 1990-91; U.S. Info. Agy. and Soros Found. grantee ednl. devel. project, Bulgaria and Albania,, 1992—; dir. Applied Rsch. Unit, 1996—; researcher; cons. pub. and pvt. agys. Author: Madras: An Analysis of Urban Ecological Structure in India, 1974, Demographic Transition and Social Change, 1976, Sociology-Technology: Foundations of Postacademic Social Science, 1982, The Grammar of Social Relations: The Major Essays of Louis Schneider, 1984; editor: Paradox and Society, 1986; (with Vinod Tewari and V.L.S. Prakash Rao) Indian Cities: Ecological Perspectives, Social and Cultural Change: Social Science for a Dynamic World, 1997, 1987; Studies in Comparative International Development, 1978-88; mem. editorial bd. Social Development Issues, 1977-85; specialized contbr. Calcutta Mcpl. Gazette, 1979—; editor: Social and Cultural Change, 1974-75; editorial reviewer Jour. Asian Studies, Social Devel. Issues, Tech. and Culture, Am. Sociologist, Technol. Forecasting and Social Change; contbr. chpts. to book, articles to profl. jours. Fulbright prof. Ahmedabad, India, 1975-76, Hyderabad, India, 1981-82; grantee Ga. Tech. Found., 1981-82, World Order Studies Course, 1994-97, State of Mich. Rsch. Excellence Fund; Steinberg fellow, 1967. Mem. Am. Sociol. Assn., Soc. for Applied Sociology, Soc. South Indian Studies, Mich. Sociol. Assn. (pres. 1988-89, v.p. 1994-95), Sigma Xi. Jewish. Office: Eastern Mich U Sociology Dept Ypsilanti MI 48197

WEINSTEIN, JEFFREY ALLEN, consumer products company executive, lawyer; b. N.Y.C., Jan. 20, 1951; s. Herbert and Pearl (Linksman) W.; m. Kyle D. Jacobson, Mar. 30, 1996; children: Jamie Kate, Jonathan Alexander. BA, Pa. State U., 1972; JD, Villanova U., 1975. Bar: Pa. 1975, N.H. 1983, U.S. Dist. Ct. (ea. dist.) Pa. 1975, U.S. Dist. Ct. N.H. 1983. Litigator Arthur Alan Wolk Assocs., Phila., 1975-78; v.p. adminstrn., sec., gen. counsel Centronics Data Computer Corp., Hudson, N.H., 1978—; exec. v.p., sec., gen. counsel Ekco Group, Inc., also bd. dirs.; pres. Ekco Concumer Plastics, Inc. (a/k/a Frem Corp.); sec., bd. dirs. Ekco Housewares, Inc., Woodstream Corp.; sec. Ekco Can. Inc., Wright-Bennet, Inc.; asst. clk. Kellogg Brush Mfg. Co., B.VIA Internat. Housewares, Inc., Ekco Consumer Products Ltd.; asst. clk., bd. dirs. Ekco Consumer Plastics. Bd. dirs. Boys Club, Nashua, N.H., 1982-83; mem. N.H. Library Adv. Bd., Concord. Mem. Pa. Bar Assn., N.H. Bar Assn. Office: Ekco Group Inc 98 Spit Brook Rd Nashua NH 03062-5737

WEINSTEIN, JOSH, television producer; m. Lisa Weinstein. Student Stanford U. Co-writer Lampoon parodies USA Today, Time, also others; writer Spy, Nat. Lampoon America's Most Waanted. Writer The Simpsons, from 1992, also story editor, supervising prodr., now exec. prodr. (Emmy award 1995). Office: care Fox Publicity 10201 W Pico Blvd Los Angeles CA 90064-2606*

WEINSTEIN, JOYCE, artist; b. N.Y.C., June 7, 1931; d. Sidney and Rose (Bier) W.; student CCNY, 1948-50, Art Students League, 1948-52; m. Stanley Boxer, Nov. 28, 1952. Exhibited in one-women shows: Perdalma Gallery, N.Y.C., 1953-56, L.I. U., Bklyn., 1969, U. Calif.-Santa Cruz, 1969, T. Bortolazzo Gallery, Santa Barbara, Calif., 1972, Dorsky Gallery, N.Y.C., 1972, 74, Galerie Ariadne, N.Y.C., 1975, Gloria Cortella Gallery, N.Y.C., 1976, Meredith Long Contemporary Gallery, N.Y.C. 1978, 79, 88-90, Martin Gerard Gallery, Edmonton, Alta., Can., 1981, 82, 84, Galerie Wentzel, Cologne, W.Ger., 1982, Haber Theodore Gallery, N.Y.C., 1983, 85, Cologne, W.Ger., 1987, Gallery One, Toronto, Ont., Can., 1983, Paul Kuhn Gallery, Calgery, 1985, Eva Cohn Gallery, Highland Park, Chgo, Ill., 1985, Galerie Wentzell, Cologne, 1987, Meredith Long & Co., Houston, 1988, Alena Adlung Gallery, N.Y.C., 1989, Meredith Long & Co., Houston, 1990, Flanders Art Gallery, Mpls., 1997; group shows: Marlborough Gallery, N.Y.C., 1968, Bula Mus. Art, Calcutta, India, 1970, Phoenix Gallery, N.Y.C., 1988, 1988, Provident Nat. Bank, Phila., 1988, Alena Adlung Gallery, N.Y.C., 1989, 90, Edmonton Art Mus., 1989, Rose Fried Gallery, N.Y.C., 1970, Hudson River Mus., 1971, Dorsky Gallery, 1972, 94, Suffolk Mus., Stony Brook, N.Y., 1972, New York Cultural Center, 1973, Stamford (Conn.) Mus., 1973, Landmark Gallery, N.Y.C., 1974, Women's Interart Center, N.Y.C., 1974, 75, 78, New Sch. Social Research, N.Y.C., 1975, Bklyn. Mus., 1975, Galerie Areadne, N.Y.C., 1975, Edmonton Art Gallery Mus., Alta., Can., 1989, Mus. of Modern Art N.Y.C., 1981, The Queens Mus. N.Y., 1984, The Centre de Creacio Contemporania, Barcelona, Spain, 1987, Fairleigh Dickinson U., Hackensack, N.J., 1976, Gloria Cortella, Inc., 1976, Edmonton Art Gallery Mus., 1977, 77, 83, Northeastern U., Boston, 1977, Lehigh (Pa.) U., 1977, Meredith Long Contemporary Gallery, 1977, 78, 79, 80, Mus. Modern Art, N.Y.C., 1981, Galerie Wentzel, Cologne, W.Ger., 1981-85, Martin Gerard Gallery, Edmonton, 1981, Gallery One, Toronto, 1983, 84, Martin Girard Gallery, 1981-84, Haber Theodore Gallery, 1982-85, Queens Mus., N.Y.C., 1984, Jerald Melberg Gallery, Charlotte, N.C., 1984, Edmonton Art Gallery Mus., 1985, Richard Green Gallery, N.Y.C., Rosel Art Fair, Basel, Switzerland, 1986, Centre de Creacio, Barcelona, Spain, 1987, Meredith Long & Co. Gallery, Houston, 1988-90, Broome St. Gallery, N.Y.C., 1991, Andre Zarre Gallery, N.Y.C., 1990, Alena Adlung Gallery, N.Y.C., 1989-90, Cork Gallery, N.Y.C., 1990, Chgo. Internat. Art Expn., 1990, Queens Coll., N.Y.C., 1991, Miami Art Fair, 1993, Meredith Long & Co. Gallery, Houston, 1988, 89, 90, 93, Bklyn. Botanic Gardens, 1994, Flanders Contemporary Art Gallery, 1996; also numerous univs. and colls.; represented in permanent collections: Pa. Acad. Fine Arts, N.J. State Mus., Ciba-Geigy Corp., New Sch. Social Research, Bula Mus. Art, U. Calif., Mus. Modern Art, N.Y.C., McMullen Gallery, Edmonton, Ga., De Spisset Mus., U. Santa Clara, Edmonton Art Gallery Mus., Edmonton, The Hines Collection, Boston, others; represented by Hokin Gallery, Palm Beach and Miami, Fla., Galerie Wentzel, Cologne, W. Ger., Meredith Long and Co., Houston , Dorsky Gallery, N.Y.C., Gallery One, Toronto, Can., Smith Anderson Gallery, Palo Alto, Calif., Flanders Art Gallery, Mpls., 1996; exec. coordinator Women in Arts Found., Inc., 1975-79, 81-82, coordinating bd., 1983-87. Recipient Lambert Fund award Pa. Acad. Fine Arts, 1955; Susan B. Anthony award NOW, 1983. Home and Studio: 46 Fox Hill Rd Ancramdale NY 12503-5311

WEINSTEIN, LEONARD HARLAN, institute program director; b. Springfield, Mass., Apr. 11, 1926; s. Barney Willard Weinstein and Ida Pauline (Feinberg) Weinstein Clark; m. Sylvia Jane Sherman, Oct. 15, 1950; children: Beth Rachel, David Harold (dec.). BS, Pa. State U., 1949; MS, U. Mass., 1950; PhD, Rutgers U., 1953. Postdoctoral fellow Rutgers U., New Brunswick, N.J., 1953-55; plant physiologist Boyce Thompson Inst., Yonkers, N.Y., 1955-63; program dir. Boyce Thompson Inst., Ithaca, N.Y., 1963-91, bd. dirs., 1976-96; dir. ecosystem rsch. ctr. Cornell U., Ithaca, 1988-90; William Boyce Thompson scientist, emeritus, 1993; adj. prof. dept. natural resources Cornell U., Ithaca, 1979—; mem. rsch. adv. com. Oak Ridge Nat. Lab, 1985-87. Contbr. articles (150) to profl. jours. and chpts. to books. Mem. sci. adv. bd. EPA, Washington, 1988-91; mem. com. natural resources NASULGS, 1986-89. Grantee NIH, NSF, HEW, Am. Cancer Soc., NASA, EPA, DOE, USDA. Mem. Am. Soc. Plant Physiologists, Sigma Xi, Pi Alpha Xi, Gamma Sigma Delta. Home: 608 Cayuga Heights Rd Ithaca NY 14850-1424 Office: Cornell U 125 Boyce Thompson Inst Tower Rd Ithaca NY 14853

WEINSTEIN, MARK MICHAEL, lawyer; b. N.Y.C., Apr. 20, 1942; s. Nathan and Caroline (Levine) W.; m. Adrienne Peni Kuba, Aug. 15, 1965; children: Samantha Beth, Caleb Jonathan. AB, Columbia Coll., 1964; LLB, U. Pa., 1968. Assoc. Paul Weiss, Rifkind, Wharton and Garrison, N.Y.C., 1968-76; asst. v.p., dep. gen. counsel Warner Communications Inc., N.Y.C., 1976-78, v.p., 1978-85; v.p., gen. counsel Viacom Internat. Inc., N.Y.C., 1985-87, sr. v.p., gen. counsel and sec., 1987-93, sr. v.p. govt. affairs, 1993—. Office: Viacom Inc 1515 Broadway New York NY 10036 also: Viacom/DC 1501 M St NW Washington DC 20005-1700

WEINSTEIN, MARK S., finance company executive; b. N.Y.C., June 1, 1957; s. Martin and Betty Weinstein. BS in Acctg., Queens Coll., 1983. V.p. Am. Fire Extinguisher Co., L.I., 1980-85; 1st v.p. DH Blair Co., N.Y.C., 1985—. Avocations: trumpet, guitar, singing, baseball, basketball. Home: 191 E 76th St New York NY 10021 Office: DH Blair Co 44 Wall St New York NY 10005-2401

WEINSTEIN, MARTIN, aerospace manufacturing executive, materials scientist; b. Bklyn., Mar. 3, 1936; s. Benjamin and Dora (Lemo) W.; m. Sandra Rebecca Yaffie, June 5, 1961; children: Hilary Ann, Sarah Elizabeth, Joshua Aaron. BS in Metals Enginrg., Rensselaer Poly. Inst., 1957; MS, MIT, 1960, PhD, 1961. Mgr. materials sci. Tycolabs, Waltham, Mass., 1961-68; tech. dir. turbine support div. Chromalloy Am. Corp., San Antonio, 1968-71, v.p., asst. gen. mgr., 1971-74, pres. 1975-79; pres. Chromalloy Compressor Techs., San Antonio, 1979-82; group pres. Chromalloy Gas Turbine, San Antonio, 1982-86, chmn., chief exec. officer, N.Y.C., 1986—; supervisory mng. dir. Turbine Support Europe, Tilburg, Netherlands, 1975—; bd. dirs. Turbine Support Thailand, Bankok, Chromalloy U.K., Nottingham, Eng., Internat. Coating Co., Tokyo, Japan, Heurchrome, Paris, Malichaud Orleans, France. Bd. dirs. Jewish Fedn., 1981-85, Chamber Players of San Antonio, 1979-83, NCCJ, 1982-85; mem. vis. com. dept. metallurgy and materials sci. MIT, 1992—. Recipient Turner Meml. award Electrochem. Soc., 1963; Achievement award NASA, 1965; Am. Iron and Steel Inst. fellow, 1960. Mem. Am. Soc. Metals, Am. Inst. Metall. Engrs., N.Y. Acad. Sci., Sigma Xi. Patentee diffusion coating of jet engine materials. Contbr. articles to profl. jours. Home: 111 Sheffield San Antonio TX 78213-2626 Office: Chromalloy Gas Turbine Corp 200 Park Ave New York NY 10166-0005

WEINSTEIN, MICHAEL ALAN, political science educator; b. Bklyn., Aug. 24, 1942; s. Aaron and Grace (Sosin) W.; m. Deena Schneiweiss, May 31, 1964. B.A. summa cum laude, NYU, 1964; M.A. in Polit. Sci., Case Western Res. U., 1965, Ph.D., 1967. Asst. prof. polit. sci. Case Western Res. U., summer 1967, Va. Poly. Inst., 1967-68; asst. prof. Purdue U., 1968-70, assoc. prof., 1970-72, prof., 1972—; Milward Simpson disting. prof. polit. sci. U. Wyo., 1979. Author: (with Deena Weinstein) Living Sociology, 1974, The Polarity of Mexican Thought, 1976, The Tragic Sense of Political Life, 1977, Meaning and Appreciation, 1978, The Structure of Human Life, 1979, The Wilderness and the City, 1982, Unity and Variety in the Philosophy of Samuel Alexander, 1984, Finite Perfection, 1985, Culture Critique: Fernand Dumont and New Quebec Sociology, 1985, (with Helmut Loiskandl and Deena Weinstein) Georg Simmel's Scopenhauer and Nietzsche, 1986; (with Deena Weinstein) Deconstruction as Cultural History/The Cultural History of Deconstruction, 1990, La Déconstruction un Jeu Symbolique, 1990, (with Deena Weinstein) Georg Simmel: Sociological Flâmeur/Bricoleur, 1991, Photographic Realism as a Moral Practice, 1992, (with Deena Weinstein) Postmodern(ized) Simmel, 1993, (with Arthur Kroker) Data Trash: The Theory of the Virtual Class, 1994, Culture/Flesh: Explorations of Postcivilized Modernity, 1995; mem. editorial bd. Humanitas, Social Philosophy Rsch. Book Series. Recipient Best Paper prize Midwest Polit. Sci. Assn., 1969; Guggenheim fellow, 1974-75; Rockefeller Found. humanities fellow, 1976; fellow Center Humanistic Studies, Purdue U., 1981. Mem. Phi Beta Kappa. Home: 800 Princess Dr West Lafayette IN 47906-2038 Office: Dept Polit Sci Purdue U West Lafayette IN 47907 *And which is worse, to be arbitrary or to be contradictory? I have attempted to be the most consistent rationalist of all by refusing to harmonize what is irreconcilable in the name of reason.*

WEINSTEIN, MILTON CHARLES, health policy educator; b. Brookline, Mass., July 14, 1949; s. William and Ethel (Rosenbloom) W.; m. Rhonda Kruger, June 14, 1970; children: Jeffrey William, Daniel Jay. AB, AM, Harvard U., 1970, MPP, 1972, PhD, 1973. Asst. prof. John F. Kennedy Sch. Govt., Harvard U., Cambridge, Mass., 1973-76, assoc. prof., 1976-80; prof. policy and decision scis. Harvard Sch. Pub. Health, Boston, 1980-86, Henry J. Kaiser prof. health policy and mgmt., 1986—; prof. medicine Harvard Med. Sch., Boston, 1992—; adj. prof. community and family medicine Dartmouth Med. Sch., Hanover, N.H., 1981-87; cons. U.S. office Tech. Assessment, 1979-87, HHS, 1979—, VA, 1984-86, EPA, 1983—, Smith Kline and French, 1984-87, Ciba-Geigy, 1987—, New Eng. Med. Ctr., 1986-87, Intermountain Health Care, 1987—, Bristol Myers-Squibb, 1989-92, E.I. DuPont de Nemours Co., 1989-91, Schering-Plough Corp., 1991—,Hoechst Marion Roussel, 1992—; Pharmacia and Upjohn, Inc., 1993—, Berlex Corp., 1996—; mem. adult treatment panel Nat. Cholesterol Edn. Program, NIH; co-chair Panel on Cost-Effectiveness in Health and Med., USPHS, 1993-96. Author: Clinical Decision Analysis, 1980, Hypertension: A Policy Perspective, 1976, Cost-Effectiveness in Health and Medicine, 1996; mem. editl. bd. Med. Decision Making, 1981—, Jour. Environ. Econs. and Mgmt., 1986-88, Jour. Clin. Oncology, 1996—; assoc. editor Med. Decision Making, 1994—. NSF fellow, 1972. Mem. Inst. Ops. Rsch. Mgmt. Scis., Inst. Medicine of NAS (com. on priorities for new vaccine devel., com. to evaluate the NIH artificial heart program), Soc. Med. Decision Making (trustee 1980-82, pres. 1984-85), Internat. Health Econs. Assn., Soc. Risk Analysis, Internat. Soc. Tech. Assessment in Health Care, Am. Med. Joggers Assn., US Speedskating (bd. dirs. 1996—), Phi Beta Kappa. Office: Harvard U Sch Pub Health Dept Health Policy & Mgmt Boston MA 02115

WEINSTEIN, NORMAN JACOB, chemical engineer, consultant; b. Rochester, N.Y., Dec. 31, 1929; s. Sol. and Anne (Trapunsky) W.; m. Ann Francine Keiles, June 30, 1957; children: Maury S., Aaron S., Kenneth B. BChemE, Syracuse U., 1951, MChemE, 1953; PhD, Oreg. State Coll., 1956. Registered profl. engr.; diplomate Am. Acad. Environ. Engrs. Chem. engr. ESSO Rsch. Engring. Co., Linden, N.J., 1956-60; sr. engr. ESSO Rsch. Engring. Co., Baton Rouge, 1960-65; engring. assoc. ESSO Rsch. Engring. Co., Florham Park, N.J., 1965-66; asst. dir. engring. and devel. Princeton Chem. Rsch. Inc., 1966-67, dir. engring. and devel., 1967-69; pres. Recon Environ. Corp., Raritan, N.J., 1969-96. Author: Thermal Processing of Municipal Solid Waste for Resource and Energy Recovery, 1976; contbr. numerous articles to profl. jours. Fellow AIChE (chmn. air sect., environ. divsn.); mem. ASTM, Am. Chem. Soc., Assn. Cons. Chemists and Chem. Engrs., N.Y. Acad. Scis. Democrat. Achievements include 8 patents in chemical processing; expert in waste oil technology. Home and Office: 1005 Canal Rd Princeton NJ 08540-8431 Office: Recon Environ Corp 5 Johnson Dr Raritan NJ 08869-1651

WEINSTEIN, PETER M., lawyer, state senator; b. N.Y.C., Feb. 3, 1947; s. Moses and Muriel W.; m. Barbara Ann Forman; children: Andrew, Michael. BS, NYU; JD, Bklyn. Law Sch. Bar: N.Y., Fla. Asst. dist. atty. Queens County, N.Y.; asst. state's atty., Broward County, Fla.; pvt. practice, Tamarac, Fla.; mem. Fla. State Senate, Tallahassee, 1982-96, chmn. Broward County legis. del., 1985-86. Mem. Broward County Charter Rev. Commn.; mem. Coral Springs Planning and Zoning Bd. Capt. U.S. Army. Recipient Allen Morris award Fla. Senate; named Most Effective Freshman, Fla. Senate. Mem. Jewish War Vets., Coral Springs Dem. (pres. 1980-82). Avocation: photography. Office: 7880 N University Dr Ste 201 Tamarac FL 33321-2124

WEINSTEIN, RHONDA KRUGER, elementary mathematics educator, administrator; b. Boston, May 18, 1948; d. David Solomon and Henrietta Reina (Slocum) Kruger; m. Milton Charles Weinstein, June 14, 1970; children: Jeffrey William, Daniel Jay. AB, Mt. Holyoke Coll., 1970; MA, Suffolk U., 1973. Cert. supt./dir.; math. 7-12; elem. K-8; elem. prin.; supt., Mass. Tchr. grade 3 Brookline (Mass.) Pub. Schs., 1974-78, math. resource tchr. K-6, 1980-81, math. resource tchr. K-8, 1981-82, elem. curriculum coord. for math., 1982—; program evaluator Newton (Mass.) Pub. Schs., 1992-93; part-time instr. Suffolk U., Boston, 1976, 79; mem. math. adv. bd. Ency. Britannica, Chgo., 1993-95; cons. Mass. sch. sys. including Northborough/ Southborough, 1987-88, Sudbury, 1987, North Andover, 1993; spkr. profl. meetings Assn. Tchrs. Math. in New Eng., 1990, 94, 95, ASCD, Boston, 1988. Co-author: Calculator Activities, 1987; reviewer 2 books Arithmetic Teacher, 1991. Alumnae fund vol. Mt. Holyoke Coll., South Hadley, Mass., 1985-90; vol. Am. Heart Assn., Brookline, 1982-93; mem. PTO, Baker Sch., Brookline, 1983-95. Sarah Williston scholar Mt. Holyoke Coll., 1967; grantee Brookline Found., 1994, Tchrs. and Adminstrs. Tng. Fund, 1992, 96. Mem. Nat. Coun. Tchrs. Math. (nat. conv. com. chair 1995, speaker profl. meeting 1993), Nat. Coun. Suprs. of Math., Assn. Tchrs. of Math. in Mass., Boston Area Math. Specialists, Phi Beta Kappa. Avocations: cross-country skiing, gourmet cooking, walking, swimming, playing piano. Home: 50 Princeton Rd Chestnut Hill MA 02167-3061 Office: Brookline Pub Schs 88 Harvard St Brookline MA 02146-7349

WEINSTEIN, ROBERT, film company executive. Co-chmn. Miramax Films Corp., L.A. Producer (with Harvey Weinstein): Playing For Keeps (with Alan Brewer), 1986, Scandal (with Joe Boyd & Nik Powell), 1989, Strike It Rich, 1990, Hardware (with Nik Powell, Stephen Woolley & Trix Worrell), 1990, A Rage In Harlem (with Terry Glinwood, William Horberg & Nik Powell), 1991, The Night We Never Met (with Sidney Kimmel), 1993, Benefit Of The Doubt, 1993, True Romance (with Gary Barber, Stanley Margolis & James G. Robinson), 1993, Mother's Boys (with Randall Poster), 1994, Pulp Fiction (with Richard N. Gladstein), 1994, Ready To Wear/Pret-A-Porter(with Ian Jessel), 1994, Smoke (with Satoru Iseki), 1995, A Month By The Lake (with Danna Gigliotti), 1995, The Crossing Guard (with Richard Gladstein), 1995, The Journey Of The August King (with Richard Gladstein), 1995, Things To Do In Denver When You're Dead (with Marie Cantin), 1995, The Englishman Who Went Up A Hill But Came Down A Mountain (with Sally Hibbin & Robert Jones), 1995, Blue In The Face (with Harvey Keitel), 1995, Restoration (with Donna Gigliotti), 1995. Office: Miramax Films Corp 375 Greenwich St New York NY 10013-2376*

WEINSTEIN, RONALD S., physician, pathologist, educator; b. Schenectady, N.Y., Nov. 20, 1938; s. H. Edward and Shirley (Diamond) W.;

m. Mary Dominica Corabi, July 12, 1964; children: Katherine Eiliesh, John Benjamin. B.S., Union Coll., Schenectady, 1960; M.D., Tufts U., 1965. Diplomate: Am. Bd. Pathology; 1972. Chemist Marine Biol. Lab., Woods Hole, Mass., 1960-62; intern Mass. Gen. Hosp., Boston, 1965-66, clin. and research fellow, 1965-70, resident in pathology, 1966-70; dir. Mixter Lab., 1966-70; vice chmn. pathology Aerospace Med. Research Labs., Dayton, Ohio, 1970-72; asso. prof. pathology Tufts U., 1972-75; Harriet Blair Borland prof., chmn. dept. pathology Rush Med. Coll. and Rush-Presbyn.-St. Luke's Med. Center, Chgo., 1975-90; prof., head dept. pathology U. Ariz. and U. Med. Ctr., Tucson, 1990—; dir. Ariz. Telemedicine Program, Tucson, 1996—; teaching fellow Harvard Med. Sch., 1966-70; dir. Central Pathology Lab., Nat. Bladder Cancer Group, 1983-89, mem. editorial bd. Pathology, 1991—, J. Urologic Pathology, 1992—. Mem. editorial bd. Ultrastructural Pathology, 1979—, Human Pathology, 1980—, assoc. editor, 1983-92, mem. editorial bd. Lab. Investigation, 1983—; assoc. editor Advances in Pathology, 1985-91, editor, 1991—; contbr.: articles profl. jours. Served as maj. USAF, 1970-72. Ford Found. fellow, 1959; Congressional intern, 1959; USPHS fellow, 1965-68. Mem. AMa, Am. Soc. Cell Biology, Internat. Acad. pathology (councilor 1980-82, internat. councilor 1982-84), U.S. and Can. Acad. Pathology (pres. 1988-89), Assn. Pathol. (chmn., sec.-treas. 1989-90), Chgo. Pathol. Soc. (pres. 1979-80), Internat. Soc. Urologic Pathology (pres.-elect 1992-94, pres. 1995-96), Internat. Coun. Soc. Pathology (v.p. 1992-93). Office: U Ariz 1501 N Campbell Ave Tucson AZ 85724-0001

WEINSTEIN, ROY, physics educator, researcher; b. N.Y.C., Apr. 21, 1927; s. Harry and Lillian (Ehrenberg) W.; m. Janet E. Spiller, Mar. 26, 1954 (dec. 1995); children: Lee Davis, Sara Lynn; m. Gail Birdsell, July 26, 1996. B.S., MIT, 1951, Ph.D., 1954; Sc.D. (hon.), Lycoming Coll., 1981. Research asst. Mass. Inst. Tech., 1951-54, asst. prof., 1956-59; asst. prof. Brandeis U., Waltham, Mass., 1954-56; assoc. prof. Northeastern U., Boston, 1960-63, prof. physics, 1963-82, exec. officer, chmn. grad. div. of physics dept., 1967-69, chmn. physics dept., 1974-81; spokesman MAC Detector Stanford U., 1981-82; dean Coll. Natural Scis. and Math. U. Houston, 1982-88; prof. physics, 1982—; dir. Inst. Beam Particle Dynamics U. Houston, 1985-95; assoc. dir., spokesman Tex. Ctr. for Superconductivity, 1987-89; vis. scholar and physicist Stanford (Calif.) U., 1966-67, 81-82; bd. dirs. Perception Tech., Inc., Winchester, Mass., Omniwave Inc., Gloucester, Mass., Wincom Inc., Woburn, Mass.; cons. Visidyne Inc., Burlington, Mass., Houston Area Rsch. Ctr., Stanford U., Hodotector Inc., Houston Park Square Engring., Marietta, Ga., Harvard U., Cambridge, Mass., Cambridge Electron Accelerator, mem. adv. com., 1967-69; mem. adv. com. and portfolio evaluation com. Houston Venture Ptnrs., 1990—; chmn. bd. dirs. Xytron Corp., 1986-91; dir., mem. exec. com. Houston Area Rsch. Ctr., 1984-87; 3d ann. faculty lectr. Northeastern U., 1966; chmn. organizing com. 4th ann. Internat. Conf. on Meson Spectroscopy, 1974, chmn. program com. 5th ann., 1977, mem. organizing com. 6th ann., 1980, 83; chmn. mgmt. group Tex. Accelerator Ctr., Woodlands, 1985-90; chmn. Tex. High Energy Physicists, 1989-91; keynote spkr. MIT Alumni series, 1988; permanent mem. exec. com. Large Vol. Detector (Underground Neutrino Telescope, Italy), 1988—; organizer session High Temperature Superconducting Magnets 3d and 4th World Congress on Superconductivity, Munich, 1993, Orlando, 1994. Author: Atomic Physics, 1964, Nuclear Physics, 1964, Interactions of Radiation and Matter, 1964; editor: Nuclear Reactor Theory, 1964, Nuclear Materials, 1964; editor procs.: 5th Internat. Conf. on Mesons, 1977; contbr. numerous articles to profl. jours. Mem. Lexington (Mass.) Town Meeting, 1973-76, 77-84; vice chmn. Lexington Coun. on Aging, 1977-83. With USNR, 1945-46. Recipient Founders award World Congress Superconductivity, 1988, Materials/Devices award Internat. Superconductivity Technology Ctr. and Materials Rsch. Soc., 1995, Tex. Rsch. awards, 1986-87, 90—, U.S. Dept. Energy award 1974, 77, 87—, NASA award, 1990—, ARO award, 1994—, Elec. Power Rsch. Inst. award, 1990-95; NSF fellow Bohr Inst., Copenhagen, 1959-60, Stanford U. 1969-70, Guggenheim fellow Harvard U., 1970-71; NSF grantee, 1961—. Fellow Am. Phys. Soc. (organizer session SSC and High Energy Physics 1984); mem. Am. Assn. Physics Tchrs., Masons, Sigma Xi, Phi Kappa Phi (chpt. pres. 1977-79, Nat. Triennial Disting. Scholar prize 1980-83), Pi Lambda Phi. Unitarian. Achievements include measurement of fine structure of positronium; first measurement of rho meson coupling to gamma rays, of phi meson decay to two muons; early observation of break down in SU3 symmetry; demonstration of electron-muon universality, discovery of non-applicability of Lorentz contraction to length measured by a single observer; disproof of splitting of A2 meson; independent discovery of upsilon meson (bottom quark); achievement of highest magnetic field for any permanent magnet, in YBa2Cu307, 10.1 Tesla. Home: 4368 Fiesta Ln Houston TX 77004-6603 Office: U Houston IBPD Rm 632 SR1 Houston TX 77204

WEINSTEIN, RUTH JOSEPH, lawyer; b. N.Y.C., Mar. 26, 1933; d. David Arthur and Toby (Landau) Joseph; m. Marvin Walter Weinstein, June 3, 1962; children: Rosalyn S., Steven M., Barbara E. AB magna cum laude, Radcliffe Coll., 1954; LLB, Harvard U., 1957. Bar: N.Y. 1957, D.C. 1966. Assoc. Hale Russell & Gray and predecessor firms, N.Y.C., 1957-66, ptnr., 1966-85; ptnr. Winthrop Stimson Putnam & Roberts, N.Y.C., 1985—; chairperson Practising Law Inst. Forum, N.Y.C., 1978. Mem. sch. bd. Union Free Sch. Dist. 5, Rye Town, N.Y., 1976-79, pres., 1978-79. Mem. ABA, Assn. of Bar of City of N.Y. (com. on Aeronautics Assn. 1987-90), Harvard-Radcliffe Club of Westchester, The Wings Club Inc. Avocations: boating, skiing. Home: 21 Meadowlark Rd Rye Brook NY 10573-1209 Office: Winthrop Stimson 1 Battery Park Plz New York NY 10004-1405

WEINSTEIN, SHARON SCHLEIN, public relations executive, educator; b. Newark, Apr. 15, 1942; d. Louis Charles and Ruth Margaret (Franzblau) Schlein; m. Elliott Henry Weinstein, May 7, 1978. BA, U. Pa., 1964; MA, New Sch. for Social Rsch., N.Y.C., 1985. Researcher London Daily Express, N.Y.C., 1965-69; reporter Forbes mag., N.Y.C., 1969-72; sr. editor Merrill Lynch, N.Y.C., 1972-74; pub. rels. officer Chase Manhattan Bank, N.Y.C., 1974-79; mgr. corp. communication Sanford C. Berstein & Co., N.Y.C., 1980-83; v.p. corp. affairs Nat. Westminster Bancorp, N.Y.C., 1983-95; dir. corp. comms. Nat. Securities Cleaning Corp., N.Y.C., 1995—; adj. asst. prof. NYU, 1988—. Avocation: volunteer cook in soup kitchen. Home: 161 W 15th St New York NY 10011

WEINSTEIN, SIDNEY, university program director; b. N.Y.C., July 1, 1920; s. Jacob and Yetta W.; m. Celia Kahn, Mar. 6, 1943 (dec.); children: Risa, Jeri; m. Florence Landau, June 21, 1988. B.A., Bklyn. Coll., 1951; M.A., Columbia U., 1955; DPA, Indsl. Coll. Armed Forces, 1964. Contract adminstr. U.S. Corps Engrs., 1941-43; mgmt. analyst Dept. Army, N.Y.C., 1946-55; dir. data processing procurement GSA, 1956-68; dep. asst. commr. automated data mgmt. services GSA, Washington, 1968-72; asst. commr. automated data and telecommunications GSA, 1972-75; exec. dir. Assn. Computing Machinery, N.Y.C., 1975-85; assoc. prof., dir. affiliates program Ctr. Research Info. Systems, Leonard N. Stern. Sch. Bus. NYU, 1985—; cons. to chmn. U.S. CSC. Served with USAF, 1943-46. Recipient Exceptional service award U.S. Govt., 1975. Mem. ABA (arbitrator 1989—), Coun. Engring. and Sci. Soc. Execs. (dir.), N.Y. Soc. Assn. Execs., Assn. Indsl. Coll. Armed Forces, Assn. Fed. Execs. Inst., Assn. Computing Machinery, Soc. Info. Mgmt. Home: 360 E 72nd St New York NY 10021-4753 Office: 44 W 4th St New York NY 10012-1106

WEINSTEIN, SIDNEY, neuropsychologist; b. N.Y.C., Apr. 27, 1922; s. Celia (Schneider) W.; m. Margaret Carla Diamond, July 28, 1968; children—Ethan, Ari; children by previous marriage—Curt, Karen, Laura. B.S., CCNY, 1949; M.A. in Exptl. Psychology, NYU, 1950, Ph.D. in Physiol. Psychology, 1952. Lic. psychologist, N.Y., Conn. Dir. neuropsychol. lab., research assoc. prof. det. rehab. medicine Albert Einstein Coll. Medicine, N.Y.C., 1958-66, research assoc. prof. dept. neurology, 1960-66, research asst. prof., 1958-60; research assoc. neuropsychology Bronx Mcpl. Hosp. Ctr., 1958-66; pres. NeuroCommunication Research Labs., Inc., Danbury, Conn., 1974-77, chief exec. officer, 1977—; dir. Neuropsychol. Research Found., Danbury, 1974—; vis. assoc. prof. NYU, 1958-64, Yeshiva U., 1960-67; adj. prof. CUNY, 1966—; lectr. Mt. Sinai Sch. Medicine, 1966—; prof. dept. pediatrics N.Y. Med. Coll., N.Y.C., 1967-80, prof. dept. psychiatry, 1985—; prof., dir. neuropsychol. lab. N.Y. Med. Coll.-Flower and Fifth Ave. Hosps., 1967-73; adj. clin. prof. dept. neurology NYU Sch. Medicine, 1975—. Author: (with others) Somatosensory Changes after Penetrating Brain Wounds in Man, 1960; The Neuropsychology of Alcohol Ingestion, 1970; editor-in-chief Internat. Jour. Neurosci.; editor Neurosci. Monographs; contbr. articles to sci. jours. Decorated knight of honor and merit Imperial Order of St. John of Jerusalem Ecumenical. Fellow AAAS, Am. Psychol. Assn. (pres. div. physiol. and comparative psychology 1963), Internat. Council Psychologists; mem. Eastern Psychol. Assn., Soc. Cosmetic Chemists, Am. Acad. Neurology, N.Y. Acad. Scis., Psychonomic Soc. (charter), N.Y. State Psychol. Assn. (div. exec. com. 1965-68), Acad. Aphasia (bd. govs. 1966-70), Internat. Neuropsychol. Soc. (bd. govs. 1980-82), AAUP, N.Y. Brain Function Group (charter mem., scribe 1964), Soc. Research in Child Devel., Assn. Am. Med. Colls., European Brain and Behavior Soc. (charter mem.), Soc. Neurosci. (charter mem.), Soc. Psychophysiol. Research, Conn. Psychol. Assn., Internat. Soc. Bioengring. and the Skin, Dermal Clin. Evaluation Soc. (charter), Sigma Xi, Psi Chi. Address: NeuroCommunication Rsch Labs 36 Mill Plain Rd Ste 412 Danbury CT 06811-5114

WEINSTEIN, STANLEY, Buddhist studies educator; b. Bklyn., Nov. 13, 1929; s. Louis Arthur and Ruth (Appleson) W.; m. Lucie Ruth Krebs, Sept. 23, 1951; 1 son, David Eli. BA, Komazawa U., Tokyo, 1954-58; MA, U. Tokyo, 1960; PhD, Harvard U., 1966; MAH (hon.), Yale U., 1974. Lectr. Sch. Oriental and African Studies, London, 1962-68; assoc. prof. Buddhist studies Yale U., New Haven, 1968-74, prof., 1974—, chmn. council East Asian studies, 1982-85. Author: Buddhism under T'ang, 1987. Served with U.S. Army, 1952-54. Ford Found. fgn. area fellow, 1958-62; NEH sr. fellow, 1974-75. Mem. Am. Oriental Soc., Assn. Asian Studies. Home: 270 Ridgewood Ave Hamden CT 06517-1426 Office: Yale U Hall Grad Studies New Haven CT 06520

WEINSTEIN, STEPHEN BRANT, communications executive, researcher, writer; b. N.Y.C., Nov. 25, 1938; s. Max S. and Evelyn A. (Brandt) W.; m. Judith Louise Benham, June 10, 1961; children: Brant M., Anna M. SB, MIT, 1960; MS, U. Mich., 1962; PhD, U. Calif. at Berkeley, 1966. Mem. tech. staff Philips Rsch. Labs., Eindhoven, The Netherlands, 1967-68, Bell Labs., Holmdel, N.J., 1968-79; v.p. tech. strategy Am. Express Co., N.Y.C., 1979-84; exec. dir. subscriber systems rsch. Bellcore (formerly, Bell Communications Rsch.), Morristown, N.J., 1984-93; fellow C&C Rsch. Lab. NEC USA, Inc., 1994—. Author: Getting the Picture: A Guide to CATV and the New Electronic Media, 1986; co-author: Data Communication Principles, 1992; contbr. articles to profl. jours.; patentee in field. Fellow IEEE (editor-in-chief Comms. mag. 1984-89, chmn. press 1979-82, Centennial medal 1984), IEEE Comms. Soc. (pres. 1996-97, v.p. tech. affairs 1994-95, dir. publs. 1990-93). Avocations: skiing, woodworking, video editing. Home: 150 Woodland Ave Summit NJ 07901-2029 Office: NEC USA Inc C & C Res Lab 4 Independence Way Princeton NJ 08540-6634

WEINSTEIN, STEVEN DAVID, lawyer; b. Phila., May 3, 1946; s. Leon and Elizabeth (Evantash) W.; m. Karin Elkis, Feb. 16, 1986. BA, Rutgers U., 1968, JD, 1975. Bar: N.J. 1975, Pa. 1975, U.S. Dist. Ct. N.J. 1975, U.S. Dist. Ct. (ea. dist.) Pa. 1975, U.S. Supreme Ct. 1979, U.S. Ct. Appeals (3d cir.) 1981, U.S. Ct. Claims 1986. Assoc. Lewis Katz P.C., Cherry Hill, N.J., 1975-78; pvt. practice law Collingswood, N.J., 1978-84; ptnr. Blank, Rome, Comisky & McCauley, Cherry Hill, 1984—; atty. Camden (N.J.) County Counsel, 1982-84; v.p. N.J. County Counsels Assn. 1983. Trustee Camden County Coll., Blackwood, N.J., 1983, West Jersey Hosps. Found., Camden, 1984-96, chmn. 1989-91; trustee Rowan Coll., N.J., 1990-96, chmn. 1992-94, trustee devel. fund. bd., 1989-90; mem. N.J. Bus.-Higher Edn. Forum. Mem. ABA, N.J. Governing Bds. Assn. (sec. 1993-94, vice chmn. 1996, chair 21 Fund), Camden County Bar Assn. Democrat. Jewish. Office: Blank Rome Comisky & McCauley Woodland Falls Corporate Park 210 Lake Dr E Ste 200 Cherry Hill NJ 08002-1163

WEINSTEIN, WILLIAM JOSEPH, lawyer; b. Detroit, Dec. 9, 1917; s. Joseph and Bessie (Abromovitch) W.; m. Evelyn Ross, Apr. 5, 1942 (dec.); children: Patricia, Michael; m. 2d, Rose Sokolsky, Oct. 25, 1972. LL.B., Wayne State U., 1940. Bar: Mich. 1940, U.S. Dist. Ct. (ea. and so. dists.) Mich. 1940, U.S. Ct. Appeals (6th cir.) 1951, U.S. Ct. Appeals (9th cir.) 1972. Ptnr. Charfoos, Gussin & Weinstein, Southfield, Mich., 1951-54, Charfoos, Gussin, Weinstein & Kroll, Detroit, 1955-59, Gussin, Weinstein & Kroll, Detroit, 1959-65, Weinstein & Kroll, P.C., Detroit, 1965-73, Weinstein, Kroll & Gordon, P.C., Detroit, 1973-85; pvt. practice, Southfield, 1985—; apptd. to standard jury instrn. com. Mich. Supreme Ct. 1965-72. Maj. gen. USMCR, 1941-75. Decorated Bronze Star with Combat V, Legion of Merit (2), Purple Heart (2). Recipient Disting. Alumnus award Wayne State U., 1973. Mem. Mich. Bar Assn. (chmn. negligence sect. 1962-63), Am. Coll. Trial Lawyers, Internat. Acad. Trial Lawyers, USN League (nat. v.p. 1971-72), Tam-o-Shanter Club (Orchard Lake, Mich.), St. Andrews Country Club (Boca Raton, Fla.). Contbr. articles to legal jours. Home and Office: 3922 Wabeek Lake Dr E Bloomfield Hills MI 48302-1261 also: 2205 Gateside Boca Raton FL 33496

WEINSTEIN-BACAL, STUART ALLEN, lawyer, educator; b. Stuttgart, Germany, May 23, 1948; s. Marvin Stuart and Mae (Beal) W.; m. Holly Laurette Thompson, Aug. 7, 1982; children: Rachel Lee, Maximillian II, Sarah Nicole. BA, U. Va., 1970, MEd, 1973; JD cum laude, U. Miami, 1979. Bar: D.C. 1979, Va. 1981, V.I. 1985, P.R. 1988. Tchr., pvt. tutor various schs., Conn., Fla., Costa Rica, 1973-76; mem. prof. staff Merchant Marine and Fisheries Com. U.S. Ho. of Reps., Washington, 1977; assoc. Cameron, Hornbostel & Adelman, Washington, 1979-80, Burch, Kerns & Klimek, P.C., Washington, 1980, 81; staff atty. C.A.C.I., Washington, 1982, 83; sr. assoc. Dudley, Dudley & Topper, St. Thomas, U.S. Virgin Islands, 1984, 85; v.p. , gen. counsel Redondo Construction Corp., San Juan, P.R., 1985-89; pvt. practice law San Juan, 1989—; sr. ptnr. Indiano, Williams & Weinstein-Bacal; early neutral evaluator U.S. Dist. Ct. P.R.; dir. Caribbean Medi Bank. Contbr. articles to profl. jours. Bd. dirs. Bucaplaa Libr. Capt. USAR, 1970-85. Mem. ABA, Am. Arbitration Assn. (pres., adv. coun. 1988—, arbitrator 1989—), Res. Officers Assn., Colegio de Abogados de P.R., U. Va. Alumni Assn., Nature Conservancy, Sovereign Order of the Oak (knight comdr.), Rotary, Club of San Juan (bd. dirs. 1991-95), The Langley Club, Bankers Club P.R., Phi Alpha Delta. Avocations: scuba diving, golf, tennis, gourmet cooking, traveling. Home: 11 Vanda St Los Filtros Guaynabo PR 00969 also: 7829 Old Dominion Dr McLean VA 22302-2404 Office: Hato Rey Tower 21st Fl 268 Muñoz Rivera Ave San Juan PR 00918

WEINSTOCK, HAROLD, lawyer; b. Stamford, Conn., Nov. 30, 1925; s. Elias and Sarah (Singer) W.; m. Barbara Lans, Aug. 27, 1950; children—Nathaniel, Michael, Philip. B.S. magna cum laude, N.Y. U., 1947; J.D., Harvard, 1950. Bar: Conn. bar 1950, Ill. bar 1950, Calif. bar 1958. Atty. SEC, Washington, 1950-52, IRS, 1952-56; tax atty. Hunt Foods & Industries, Inc., Los Angeles, 1956-58; pvt. practice Beverly Hills, Calif., 1958-71, Los Angeles, 1971—; mem. Weinstock, Manion, Reisman, Shore & Neumann (and predecessor firms), 1958—; Lectr. extension div., estate planning courses U. Calif. at Los Angeles, 1959—; estate planning and taxation courses Calif. Continuing Edn. of the Bar, 1960—. Author: Planning An Estate, 4th edit., 1995; contbr. articles to profl. publs. Nat. trustee Union Am. Hebrew Congregations, 1976-79; bd. trustees Jewish Cmty. Found., L.A.; adv. bd. Estate Planning Inst. UCLE Law Sch., 1979-92, NYU Inst. on Fed. Taxation, 1986-95. Mem. ABA, Calif. Bar Assn., Beverly Hills Bar Assn. (chmn. probate and trusts com. 1967-68), Los Angeles Bar Assn., Beverly Hills Estate Planning Council (pres. 1968-69), Estate Counselors Forum of Los Angeles (pres. 1963-64). Jewish (pres. temple 1974-76). Office: Weinstock Manion 1888 Century Park E Los Angeles CA 90067-1702

WEINSTOCK, HERBERT FRANK, public relations executive; b. Los Angeles, July 26, 1913; s. Frank and Sarah (Mantel) W.; m. Evelyn June Hanson, July 27, 1940; children—Allan Herbert, William Jay, Joan Louise. A.A., Los Angeles City Coll., 1933. Financial editor Los Angeles Daily News, 1939-54; pub. relations assoc. H. F. Weinstock & Assocs., 1955-61, 80-91; public relations dir. Burton, Booth & Weinstock, Inc., 1961-63; with Eisamen, Johns & Laws (advt.), Los Angeles, 1964; v.p. charge corporate and financial pub. relations Kennett Pub. Relations Assos., 1966-71; pres. Conway/Weinstock/ Assos., Inc., 1971-80. Pres. Intercommunity Care Centers, Inc., Long Beach, Calif. Served with AUS, 1943-45; with 3d Army 1944-45. Home: 533 21st St Manhattan Beach CA 90266-2201

WEINSTOCK, JOEL VINCENT, immunologist; b. Detroit, Mar. 21, 1948; s. Herman and Esther B. (Frazein) W.; m. Allison Lee Rose, July 15, 1979; children: Lisa, Jeffrey, Andrew. BS, U. Mich., 1969; MD, Wayne State U., 1973. Diplomate Am. Bd. Internal Medicine, subspeciality gastroenterology; lic. physician, Mich., Iowa. Straight med. intern Univ. Hosp., Ann Arbor, Mich., 1973-74, resident internal medicine, 1974-76, fellow gastroenterology dept. internal medicine, 1976-78; asst. prof. internal medicine Wayne State U. Sch. Medicine, Detroit, 1978-83, assoc. prof., 1983-86, adj. assoc. prof. dept. immunology and microbiology, 1983-86, vice chief divsn. gastroenterology, 1984-86; assoc. prof., dir. gastroenterology divsn. U. Iowa, Iowa City, 1986-91, prof., dir., 1991—, dir. Ctr. Digestive Diseases, 1990—, dir. divsn. gastroenterology-hepatology, 1986—, dir. Ctr. Digestive Diseases, 1990—; mem. exec. bd. Crohn's and Colitis Found. Am., N.Y.C., 1993—, mem. tng. awards rev. com., 1991-93, chmn., 1993—; chief sect. gastroenterology Hutzel Hosp., Detroit, 1978-84, dir. endoscopy unit, 1978-84, dir. nutritional support svc., 1980-84; vice chief gastroenterology dept. medicine Wayne State U. Sch. Medicine, 1984-86; dir. gastroenterology subspecialty unit Harper Hosp., Detroit, 1984-86, vice-chief gastroenterology, 1984-86; mem. sci. adv. ang grant rev. com. Crohn's and Colitis Found. Am., 1987—; mem. NIH Task force for developing nat. agenda for IBD rsch., 1989; mem. Lederle award selection com., 1989; mem. study sect. NIH Core Ctr. Rev. Com., 1990, 92; mem. abstract rev. com. ASCI, 1990; vis. prof. Washington U., St. Louis, 1990, U. Tex., Houston, 1991, Cleve. Clinic, 1992, U. Md., Balt., 1993; participant various conferences and meetings; mem. Digestive Diseases Ctr. Planning Com., 19886—; mem. Adult TPN Subcom., 1986—; chmn. coord. com. Ctr. Digestive Diseases, 1986—; mem. grant rev. coms. NIH, 1980—; mem. gastroenterology subspecialty coun. CSCR, 1993—. Mem. editl. bd. Autoimmunity Forum: Gastroenterology Edit., 1989-92; mem. internat. adv. bd. Alimentary Pharmacology and Therapeutics, 1990—; sect. editor Jour. Inflammatory Bowel Disease, 1994; reviewer Am. Jour Gastroenterology, Jour. Clin. Investigation, Jour. Immunology, Jour. Clin. Immunology, Gastroenterology, Digestive Diseases and Scis.; contbr. articles to profl. jours., chpts. to books. Rsch. grantee NIH, 1982—, Sandoz Pharm., 1993, Marion Merrell Dow, 1994, Centocor, 1995. Mem. AAAS, Am. Inst. Nutrition, Am. Soc. Clin. Nutrition, Ctrl. Soc. Clin. Rsch., Am. Soc. Gastrointestinal Endoscopy, Am. Assn. Study Liver Disease, Am. Fedn. Clin. Rsch., Am. Assn. Immunologists, Ileitis and Colitis Found. Am., Am. Soc. Clin. Investigation, Clin. Immunology Soc., Am. Gastroenterological Assn. (rsch. com. 1987-90, chmn. task force rsch. fellowship awards 1989-90, program evaluation com. 1990—), Midwest Gut Club (councillor 1990—), Alpha Omega Alpha. Achievements include research in elucidaiton of immunoregulatory circuits that control granulomatous inflammation; characterization of how neurokines help control inflammatory responses; avocations: stamp collecting, reading, gardening, exercising, child rearing. Office: U Iowa College of Med Internal Medicine 4607JCP Iowa City IA 52242*

WEINSTOCK, LEONARD, lawyer; b. Bklyn., Aug. 18, 1935; s. Samuel Morris and Evelyn (Reiser) W.; m. Rita Lee Itkowitz, May 25, 1963; children—Gregg Douglas, Valerie Lisa, Tara Diane. B.S., Bklyn. Coll., 1956; J.D., St. John's U., Bklyn., 1959. Bar: N.Y. 1961, U.S. Supreme Ct. 1964, U.S. Ct. Appeals (2d cir.) 1963, U.S. Dist. Ct. (ea. and so. dists.) N.Y. 1963, U.S. Tax Ct. 1963. Assoc. Bernard Helfenstein law practice, Bklyn., 1962-63; supr. All State Ins. Co., Bklyn., 1963-64; atty. Hertz Corp., N.Y.C., 1964-65; ptnr. Nicholas & Weinstock, Flushing, N.Y., 1965-68; v.p., ptnr. Garbarini & Scher, P.C., N.Y.C., 1968—; lectr. Practicing Law Inst., N.Y.C., 1975—; arbitrator Nassau County Dist. Ct., Mineola, N.Y., 1979—, U.S. Dist. Ct. (ea. dist.) N.Y. 1986—; mem. Med. Malpractice Mediation Panel, Mineola, 1978—. Legal counsel Massapequa Soccer Club (N.Y.), 1981—; county committeeman Democratic Party, Massapequa Park, N.Y., 1979—. Served with U.S. Army, 1959-62. Mem. ABA, N.Y. State Bar Assn., Nassau County Bar Assn. (mem. med. jurisprudence ins. com. 1978), N.Y. Trial Lawyers Assn., Queens County Bar Assn. (mem. legal referral com. 1969). Avocations: stamp collecting, softball, racquetball. Home: 38 Barstow Rd Great Neck NY 11021-2218 Office: Garbarini and Scher PC Ste 1111 1114 Avenue Of The Americas Fl 35 New York NY 10036-7703

WEINSTOCK, RONALD JAY, research and development company executive; b. L.A., Mar. 14, 1960; s. Howard Frank and Anne Carol (Schneider) W.; m. Sigrid Lipsett, June 11, 1988; children: Rachel, Brent. Student, U. Calif., San Diego, 1978-80, U. Calif., Santa Barbara, 1980-81. CEO Magnetic Resonance Diagnostics Corp., Thousand Oaks, Calif., 1989—; vice chmn. Magnetic Resonance Rsch. Soc., Tokyo, 1991—; lectr. in field. Codeveloper Magnetic Resonance Analyzer; contbr. articles to profl. jours. CPR instr. Am. Heart Assn., Beverly Hills, 1981; EMT, UCLA, 1980; chmn. police dept. disaster response team City of Thousand Oaks, 1995—.

WEINSTOCK, WALTER WOLFE, systems engineer; b. Phila., Aug. 18, 1925; s. Abraham and Jeanne (Feldman) W.; m. Doris Alpert, Sept. 21, 1946; children—Steven Eric, Bruce Alan. B.S.E.E., U.Pa., 1946, M.S.E.E., 1954, Ph.D., 1964. Design engr. Philco, 1946-49; with RCA Corp., 1949-87; prin. scientist RCA Corp. (Missile and Surface Radar div.), Moorestown, N.J., 1979-87; cons., 1987—; mem. planning and steering adv. group Surface Ship Security Panel, Dept. Navy, 1979-82. Contbg. author: Modern Radar, 1965, Practical Phased Array Antenna Systems, 1991; contbr. articles to profl. jours. Recipient David Sarnoff award for Outstanding Achievement in Enrging. RCA, 1972. Fellow IEEE; mem. Tau Beta Pi, Eta Kappa Nu, Sigma Tau, Pi Mu Epsilon. Patentee in field. Home: 6 Beryl Rd Cheltenham PA 19012-1206

WEINTRAUB, DANIEL RALPH, social welfare administrator; b. N.Y.C., Apr. 23, 1939; s. Benjamin Zion and Ida (Barman) W.; BA in Biology, NYU, 1959; DDS, Columbia U., 1963; certificate pub. health U. Wash., 1963; m. Sally Ann Franco, Mar. 16, 1968; children—David Arlo, Jeremy Michael. Rural community devel. adviser AID, Dominican Republic, 1966-68, population and pub. health adviser, 1968-69; asso. planning dir. Alan Guttmacher Inst. (formerly Center for Family Planning Program Devel.), N.Y.C., 1969-74; dep. dir. Family Planning Internat. Assistance, N.Y.C., 1974-76, COO, 1977—; v.p. internat. programs Planned Parenthood Fedn. Am., N.Y.C., 1978—, mem. speaker's bur., 1982—; vol. leader, coordinator U.S. Peace Corps, Bolivia, 1964-65; cons. HEW, 1971-74, Nat. Center Health Statistics, 1974. Recipient Certificate of Honor, Dominican Republic, 1969; commendation Dept. Interior, Cochabamba, Bolivia, 1965. Mem. ACLU, Nat. Geog. Soc., Nature Conservancy, Choice in Dying. Author books and manuals on community devel. theory and practice, plans for area-wide family planning programs in met. areas, family planning tech. assistance in developing nations, nat. studies including Need for Subsidized Family Planning Services: United States, Each State and County, 1971. Home: 8 Dock Ln Port Washington NY 11050-1732 Office: FPIA 810 7th Ave New York NY 10019-5818

WEINTRAUB, JERRY, motion picture producer, executive; b. Sept. 26, 1937; m. Jane Morgan. Prodr.: (films) including Nashville, 1975, Oh God!, 1977, Cruising, 1980, All Night Long, 1981, Diner, 1982, The Karate Kid, 1984, The Karate Kid, Part II, The Karate Kid, Part III, 1989, Pure Country, 1992, The Next Karate Kid, 1994, The Specialist, 1994, Vegas Vacation, 1997 (also appeared in film); appeared in (film) The Firm, 1993, Vegas Vacation, 1997. Office: Weintraub Prodns Bungalow 1 4000 Warner Blvd Burbank CA 91522-0001*

WEINTRAUB, JOSEPH BARTON, publishing executive; b. Phila., Dec. 2, 1945; s. George and Edith (Lubner) W.; m. Denise Waters, June 14, 1974. BA, U. Pitts., 1966; MA, U. Chgo., 1967, PhD, 1973. Assoc. faculty U. Ind., Gary, Ind., 1970-74; mktg. specialist journalism div. U. Chgo. Press, 1974-75, sr. copywriter journalism div., 1975-78; periodical specialist ABA Press, Chgo., 1978-80, mktg. mgr., 1980-92, dir. publ. planning, 1992—; mktg. cons. Teachers Coll. Record, N.Y.C., 1977-79, Repertoire Internat. de la Litterature de l'Art, N.Y.C., 1977-79, Am. Lung Assn., 1980-82. Contbr. essays, translations, plays, poems, short fiction to lit. revs. and small press anthologies. Recipient award Ill. Art Coun., Barrington Art Coun. Mem. ABA (book publ. divsn.), Phi Beta Kappa. Avocations: writing, language study. Office: Am Bar Assn 750 N Lake Shore Dr Chicago IL 60611-4403

WEINTRAUB, KARL JOACHIM, history educator; b. Darmstadt, Fed. Republic Germany, Dec. 31, 1924; came to U.S., 1948; s. Micha B. Weintraub and Elizabeth (Hammel) Anders; m. D. Kathryn Lamphiear, Mar. 16, 1957 (div. 1980); m. Katy O'Brien, Apr. 23, 1983. BA, U. Chgo., 1949, MA, 1952, PhD, 1957; LHD (hon.), Knox Coll., 1986. Bibliographer U.

Chgo. Librs., 1953-60; instr. U. Chgo. Coll., 1954-57, asst. prof., 1957-63; assoc. prof. U. Chgo., 1963-70, prof., 1970—, Disting. Svc. prof., 1978—, dean humanities, 1973-83. Author: Visions of Culture, 1966, The Value of the Individual, 1978; contbr. articles to profl. jours. Trustee Knox Coll., Galesburg, Ill., 1978—, Art Inst., Chgo., 1984—; bd. govs. Sch. of the Art Inst., Chgo., 1981—. Recipient Quantrell award for Excellence in Teaching, 1960, 86, E. Harris Harbison award Danforth Found., 1967, Amoco Teaching award, 1995. Fellow Am. Acad. Arts and Scis.; mem. Am. Hist. Assn., Quadrangle Club (pres. 1960s). Mem. Soc. of Friends. Home: 5844 S Stony Island Ave Chicago IL 60637-2022 Office: U Chgo History Dept 1050 E 59th St Chicago IL 60637-1512

WEINTRAUB, MICHAEL IRA, neurologist; b. N.Y.C., Aug. 14, 1940; s. Abraham and Mildred Weintraub (Kuttner) W.; m. Anita Bellin, Aug. 2, 1964; children: Jeffrey Brian, Lisa Ellen. BA, NYU, 1962; MD, SUNY, Buffalo, 1966. Diplomate: Am. Bd. Psychiatry and Neurology, Am. Bd. EEG., Am. Acad. Pain Mgmt., Am. Bd. Prof. Disability Cons., Am. Soc. of Neurorehabilitation. Intern E. J. Meyer Hosp., Buffalo, 1966-67; fellow neurology State U. N.Y., Buffalo, 1967-68; fellow neurology Yale U.-New Haven Med. Center, 1968-70, chief resident, 1969-70; instr. neurology Boston U. Sch. Medicine, 1970-72; instr. Albert Einstein Sch. Medicine, Bronx, N.Y., 1972-73; asst. prof. neurology N.Y. Med. Coll., 1974-77, assoc. clin. prof., 1977-83, clin. prof. neurology, 1983—; chief pediatric neurology Westchester County Med. Center, Valhalla, N.Y., 1974-77; practice medicine specializing in neurology/pain mgmt. Briarcliff, N.Y., 1972—; adj. clin. prof. neurology Mt. Sinai Sch. Medicine, 1997—; attending neurologist Phelps Meml. Hosp., 1972—, chief of neurology, 1981—; sr. neurologist Putnam Community Hosp., 1981—. Contbr. articles to med. jours. Recipient Outstanding Young Men of Am. award U.S. Jr. C. of C., 1971. Fellow ACP, Am. Acad. Neurology, Am. Bd. Electroencephalography; mem. AMA, Westchester County Med. Soc. Home: Quaker Bridge Rd E Croton On Hudson NY 10520 Office: 325 S Highland Ave Briarcliff Manor NY 10510-2054

WEINTRAUB, RUSSELL JAY, lawyer, educator; b. N.Y.C., Dec. 20, 1929; s. Harry and Alice (Lieberman) W.; m. Zelda Kresshover, Sept. 6, 1953; children—Sharon Hope, Harry David, Steven Ross. BA, NYU, 1950; JD, Harvard U., 1953. Bar: N.Y. 1955, Iowa 1961, Tex. 1980. Teaching fellow Harvard U. Law Sch., 1955-57; asst. prof. law U. Iowa, 1957-61, prof., 1961-65; prof. U. Tex., 1965—, Marrs McLean prof. law, 1970-80, Bryant Smith chair, 1980-82, John B. Connally chair, 1982—; vis. prof. law U. Mich., 1965, UCLA, 1967, U. Calif., Berkeley, 1973-74, Bklyn. Law Sch., 1990, 95, Inst. Internat. Comparative Law, Paris, 1975, U. Houston, 1979-80, Inst. Internat. and Comparative Law, Oxford, Eng., 1982, 83, 86, 87, 92, Dublin, Ireland, 1991, La. State U., Aix-en-Provence, France, 1993, Florence, Italy, 1997; lectr. Hague Acad. Internat. Law, 1984; cons. in field. Author: International Litigation and Arbitration, 1994, 2d revised edit., 1997, (with Eugene Scoles) Cases and Materials on the Conflict of Laws, 1967, 2d rev. edit., 1972, supplement, 1978, Commentary on the Conflict of Laws, 1971, 3d rev. edit., 1986, supplement, 1991, (with Hamilton and Rau) Cases and Materials on Contracts, 1984, 2d rev. edit., 1992, (with Rosenberg and Hay) Cases and Materials on the Conflict of Laws, 10th rev. edit., 1996, supplement, 1997; contbr. articles to profl. jours. Trustee U. Iowa Sch. Religion, 1960-65. Served with U.S. Army, 1953-55. Recipient Disting. Prof. award U. Tex. Sch. Law, 1977, Teaching Excellence award, 1979, cert. of meritorious service Am. Bar Assn., 1977, cert. of meritorious service Tex. Bar Assn., 1978, Best Tchr. award U. Houston, 1980, Carl Fulda award scholarship in internat. law, 1993. Mem. Am. Law Inst., Am. Bar Found., Tex. Bar Found., Scribes. Jewish. Home: 7204 Sungate Dr Austin TX 78731-2141 Office: U Tex Sch Law 727 E 26th St Austin TX 78705-3224 *The only true happiness lies in useful work done to the best of your ability.*

WEINTRAUB, SIDNEY, economist, educator; b. N.Y.C., May 18, 1922; s. Reuben and Anna Weintraub; m. Gladys Katz, Aug. 11, 1946; children: Jeffrey, Marcia Weintraub Plunkett, Deborah Weintraub Chilewich. B.B.A., CCNY, 1943; B.J., M.A. in Journalism, U. Mo., 1948; M.A. in Econs., Yale U., 1958; Ph.D. in Econs, Am. U., 1966. Commd. fgn. service officer Dept. State, 1949; dep. asst. sec. of state for internat. fin. and devel. Dept. State, Washington, 1969-74; asst. adminstr. for interagy. devel. coordination AID, 1974-75, exec. dir. interagy devel. coordination com., 1974-75; ret., 1975; sr. fellow Brookings Instn., Washington, 1978-79; Dean Rusk prof. Lyndon B. Johnson Sch. Public Affairs, U. Tex., Austin, 1976-96; prof. emeritus, 1996; also co-dir. Program for U.S.-Mex. Policy Studies Lyndon B. Johnson Sch. Public Affairs, U. Tex.; William E. Simon chair in polit. economy Ctr. Strategic and Internat. Studies, 1993—; Disting. vis. scholar Ctr. for Strategic and Internat. Studies, Washington, 1990. Author: Free Trade with Mexico, 1984, A Marriage of Convenience: Relations Between Mexico and The United States, 1990, NAFTA: What Comes Next, 1994, NAFTA at Three: A Progress Report, 1997; contbr. articles to profl. jours. Served with U.S. Army, 1943-46. Recipient Disting. Career Service award AID, 1975. Mem. Coun. on Fgn. Rels., Am. Econ. Assn., Am. Fgn. Service Assn. Club: Cosmos (Washington). Office: Lyndon B Johnson Sch Pub Affairs Drawer Y University Sta Austin TX 78712 *Once having been thrust into the Second World War, my main intellectual interest has been in foreign affairs. I had concluded, as President Kennedy did later, that domestic issues can hurt but misplaced foreign policy can kill. My drive has been to understand what motivates nations, what stimulates people within different nations, what is the U.S. national interest, and to become as expert as my talents would allow about such crucial issues as domestic security, international economic interaction, social mobility, and human development generally. This remains my ambition.*

WEINTRAUB, STANLEY, arts and humanities educator, author; b. Phila., Apr. 17, 1929; s. Ben and Ray (Segal) W.; m. Rodelle Horwitz, June 6, 1954; children: Mark, David, Erica. BS, West Chester (Pa.) State Coll., 1949; MA, Temple U., 1951; PhD, Pa. State U., 1956. Instr. Pa. State U., University Park, 1953-59; asst. prof. Pa. State U., 1959-62, assoc. prof., 1962-65, prof. English, 1965-70, research prof., 1970-86, Evan Pugh prof. Arts and Humanities, 1986—; dir. Inst. for Arts and Humanistic Studies, 1970-90; Vis. prof. U. Calif. at Los Angeles, 1963, U. Hawaii, 1973, U. Malaya, 1977, Nat. U. Singapore, 1982. Author: Private Shaw and Public Shaw, 1963, The War in the Wards, 1964, Reggie, 1965, The Art of William Golding, 1965, Beardsley, 1967, The Last Great Cause, The Intellectuals and the Spanish Civil War, 1968, Evolution of a Revolt: Early Postwar Writings of T.E. Lawrence, 1968, The Literary Criticism of Oscar Wilde, 1968, Journey to Heartbreak, 1971, Whistler: A Biography, 1974, Lawrence of Arabia: the Literary Impulse, 1975, Four Rossettis, A Victorian Biography, 1977, Aubrey Beardsley: Imp of the Perverse, 1976, The London Yankees: Portraits of American Writers and Artists in England, 1894-1914, 1979, The Unexpected Shaw. Biographical Approaches to G.B. Shaw and His Work, 1982, A Stillness Heard Round the World: The End of the Great War, 1985, Victoria. An Intimate Biography, 1987, Long Day's Journey into War: December 7, 1941, 1991, Bernard Shaw: A Guide to Research, 1992, Disraeli: A Biography, 1993, The Last Great Victory-The End of World War II, July/August 1945, 1995, Shaw's People. Victoria to Churchill, 1996, Uncrowned King: The Life of Prince Albert, 1997; editor: An Unfinished Novel by Bernard Shaw, 1958, C.P. Snow: A Spectrum, 1963, The Yellow Book: Quintessence of the Nineties, 1964, The Savoy: Nineties Experiment, 1966, The Court Theatre, 1966, Biography and Truth, 1967, Evolution of a Revolt: Early Postwar Writings of T.E. Lawrence, 1968, The Literary Criticism of Oscar Wilde, 1968, Shaw: An Autobiography 1856-1898, 1969, Shaw: An Autobiography, The Playwright Years, 1898-1950, 1970, Bernard Shaw's Nondramatic Literary Criticism, 1972, Directions in Literary Criticism, 1973, Saint Joan Fifty Years After: 1923/24-1973/74, 1973, The Portable Bernard Shaw, 1977, (with Anne Wright) Heartbreak House. A Facsimile of the Revised Typescript, 1979, (with Richard Aldington) The Portable Oscar Wilde, 1981, Modern British Dramatists, 1900-1945, 1982, The Playwright and the Pirate. Bernard Shaw and Frank Harris: A Correspondence, 1982, British Dramatists Since World War II, 1983, Bernard Shaw, the Diaries, 1885-1897, 1986, Bernard Shaw on the London Art Scene, 1885-1950, 1989, also editor Comparative Literature Studies, 1987-92, Shaw, The Ann. of Bernard Shaw Studies, 1956-89. Pres. Jewish Community Council of Bellefonte (Pa.) State Coll., 1966-67. Served to 1st lt. AUS, 1951-53, Korea. Decorated Bronze Star medal.; Guggenheim fellow, 1968-69; recipient Disting. Humanist award Pa. Humanities Council, 1985. Mem. The Authors' Guild, PEN. Home: 840 Outer Dr State College PA 16801-8233 Office: Pa State U 202 Ihlseng Bldg University Park PA 16802-1705 *I subscribe to Bernard Shaw's declaration in the Preface to Man and Superman that "This is the true joy in life, the being used for a purpose recognized by yourself as mighty one; the being thoroughly worn out before you are thrown on the scrap heap; the being a force of Nature instead of a feverish selfish little clod of ailments and grievances complaining that the world will not devote itself to making you happy.".*

WEINTZ, CAROLINE GILES, non-profit association consultant, travel writer; b. Columbia, Tenn., Dec. 8, 1952; d. Raymond Clark Jr. and Caroline Higdon (Wagstaff) Giles; m. Walter Louis Weintz; children: Alexander Harwood, Elizabeth Pettus. AB, Princeton U., 1974; postgrad. diploma, U. London, 1976. Dir. advt. and promotion E.P. Dutton Pubs., N.Y.C., 1977-86; advt. cons. Assn. Jr. Leagues Internat., N.Y.C., 1986-91, advt. mgr., 1992-94, dir. of systems, 1994—. Author: The Discount Guide for Travelers over 55, 4th edit., 1988. Vol. researcher St. Paul's Nat. Hist. Site and Bill of Rights Mus., Westchester, N.Y., 1986—; treas. Soc. Nat. Shrine of The Bill of Rights; mem. Jr. League, Pelham, N.Y. Mem. Authors Guild, Nat. Soc. Colonial Dames, Huguenot Soc. Am., Daus. Cin., Mensa. Episcopalian. Home: 806 Pines Bridge Rd Ossining NY 10562

WEINTZ, JACOB FREDERICK, JR., retired investment banker; b. N.Y.C., June 27, 1926; s. Jacob Frederick and Grace (Cortelyou) W.; m. Elisabeth Hamlin Brewer, Nov. 26, 1955; children: Elizabeth Hunt Cerf, Polly Warren, Eric Cortelyou, Karl Frederick. Student, Norwich U., 1943-44; BA, Stanford U., 1948; MBA, Harvard U., 1951. Salesman Vick Chem. Co., N.Y.C., 1948-49; assoc. buying dept. Goldman, Sachs & Co., N.Y.C., 1951-54, assoc. new bus. dept., 1954-65, ptnr., 1965-84; ltd. ptnr. Goldman, Sachs Group L.P., 1984—. Pres., chmn. bd. dirs. Stonebridge Condominium Assn., Snowmass Village, Colo., 1978-85; trustee Pace U., 1981-97, Norwich U., Stanford U., 1985-95, Sierra Club Found., 1984-90, 92—, treas.; trustee Harbor Lights Found., N.Y.C.; mem. corp. Greenwich Hosp.; vice chmn. bd. dirs. Guiding Eyes for Blind, 1984-93; bd. dir. The Forum for World Affairs, Stanford, Conn., 1988-94; mem. Ctr. Internat. Security and Arms Control Stanford U.; pres. Harvard U. Bus. Sch. Alumni Assn., 1988-90; del. Coun. Governing Bds., Albany, N.Y.; chmn. bd. dirs. N.Y. Young Rep. Club, 1957-58; mem. exec. com. Greenwich Rep. Town Com., Conn., 1962-69, The Task Force on Def. Spending, The Economy and the Nation's Security, BENS-ED Commn. on Fundamental Def. Mgmt. Issues; mem. Stanford in Washington Coun.; mem. pres.'s coun. AmeriCares Found., New Canaan, Conn.; mem. vis. com. Inst. Internat. Studies Stanford U. With USAAF, 1944-45. Recipient La Medaille de la Ville de Paris, 1990, Stanford Gold Spike award, 1992. Mem. Ambs. Round Table (Stamford), Bond Club (N.Y.), Newcomen Soc. N.Am., Down Town Assn., Harvard Club, Riverside Yacht Club, Manhattan Yacht Club, Stanford (Calif.) Golf Club, Flying Scot Sailing Assn. (pres. 1968-69), Theta Chi. Republican. Episcopalian. Home: Harbor Lights 43 Jones Park Dr Riverside CT 06878-2205 Office: Goldman Sachs & Co 85 Broad St New York NY 10004-2434

WEINTZ, WALTER LOUIS, book publishing company executive; b. Westchester, N.Y., Apr. 19, 1952; s. Walter Henry and Helen (Bennett) W.; m. Caroline Harwood Giles, Aug. 31, 1974; children: Alexander Harwood, Elizabeth Pettus. AB, Princeton U., 1974; MPhil, U. London, 1976. Dir. sales and mktg. St. Martin's Press, N.Y.C., 1977-84; v.p., dir. mktg. Atlantic Monthly Press, N.Y.C., 1985-86; v.p. A.M.E. Pub., Ltd., N.Y.C., 1987-91; pres. Mondadori Pub. Co., N.Y.C., 1987-91; v.p., assoc. pub. Random House Inc., N.Y.C., 1991—; pres. random House Info. Group, 1997—; exec. v.p. Random House Trade Pub. Group, 1997—. Co-author: Discount Guide for Travellers Over 55, 1983. Avocation: fencing. Office: Random House Inc 201 E 50th St New York NY 10022-7703

WEIR, ALEXANDER, JR., utility consultant, inventor; b. Crossett, Ark., Dec. 19, 1922; s. Alexander and Mary Eloise (Field) W.; m. Florence Forschner, Dec. 28, 1946; children: Alexander III, Carol Jean, Bruce Richard. BSChemE, U. Ark., 1943; MChemE, Poly Inst. Bklyn., 1946; PhD, U. Mich., 1954; cert., U. So. Calif. Grad. Sch. Bus. Adminstrn., 1968. Chem. engr. Am. Cyanamid Co., Stamford Rsch. Labs., 1943-47; with U. Mich., 1948-58; rsch. assoc., project supr. Engring. Research Inst., U. Mich., 1948-57; lectr. chem. and metall. engring. dept. U. Mich., 1954-56, asst. prof., 1956-58; cons. Ramo-Woolridge Corp., L.A., 1956-57; mem. tech. staff, sect. head, asst. mgr. Ramo-Wooldridge Corp., Los Angeles, 1957-60, incharge Atlas Missile Captive test program, 1956-60; tech. adv. to pres. Northrop Corp., Beverly Hills, Calif., 1960-70; prin. scientist for air quality So. Calif. Edison Co., Los Angeles, 1970-76, mgr. chem. systems research and devel., 1976-86, chief research scientist, 1986-88; utility cons. Playa Del Rey, Calif., 1988—; rep. Am. Rocket Soc. to Detroit Nuclear Council, 1954-57; chmn. session on chem. reactions Nuclear Sci. and Engring. Congress, Cleve., 1955; U.S. del. AGARD (NATO) Combustion Colloquium, Liege, Belgium, 1955; Western U.S. rep. task force on environ. research and devel. goals Electric Research Council, 1971; electric utility advisor Electric Power Research Inst., 1974-78, 84-87; industry advisor Dept. Chemistry and Biochemistry Calif. State U., Los Angeles, 1981-88. Author: Two and Three Dimensional Flow of Air through Square-Edged Sonic Orifices, 1954; (with R.B. Morrison and T.C. Anderson) Notes on Combustion, 1955, also tech. papers; inventor acid rain prevention device used in 5 states. Sea scout leader, Greenwich, Conn., 1944-48, Marina del Rey, Calif., 1965-70; bd. govs., past pres. Civic Union Playa del Rey, chmn. sch., police and fire, nominating, civil def., army liaison coms.; mem. Senate, Westchester YMCA, chmn. Dads sponsoring com., active fundraising; chmn. nominating com. Paseo del Rey Sch. PTA, 1961; mem. L.A. Mayors Cmty. Adv. Com.; asst. chmn. advancement com., merit badge dean Cantinella dist. L.A. Area coun. Boy Scouts Am. Recipient Nat. Rsch. Coun. Flue Gas Desulfurization Industrials Scale Reliability award NAS, 1975, Power Environ. Achievement award EPA, 1980, Excellence in Sulfur Dioxide Control award EPA, 1985. Mem. AICE, Am. Geophys. Union, Navy League U.S. (v.p. Palos Verdes Peninsula coun. 1961-62), N.Y. Acad. Scis., Sci. Rsch. Soc. Am., Am. Chem. Soc., U.S. Power Squadron, St. Andrew Soc. So. Calif., Clan Macnachtan Assn., Clan Buchanan Soc. Am., Betty Washington Lewis Soc. of Children of Am. Revolution (past pres.), Ark. Soc. of Children of Am. Revolution (past pres.), Santa Monica Yacht Club, Sigma Xi, Phi Kappa Phi, Phi Lambda Upsilon, Alpha Chi Sigma, Lambda Chi Alpha. Office: 8229 Billowvista Dr Playa Del Rey CA 90293-7807

WEIR, BRYCE KEITH ALEXANDER, neurosurgeon, neurology educator; b. Edinburgh, Scotland, Apr. 29, 1936; came to U.S., 1992; s. Ernest John and Marion (Stewart) W.; m. Mary Lou Lauber, Feb. 25, 1976; children: Leanora, Glyncora, Brocke. BSc, McGill U., Montreal, Que., Can., 1958, MD, CM, 1960, MSc, 1963. Diplomate Am. Bd. Neurol. Surgery, Nat. Bd. Med. Examiners. Intern Montreal Gen. Hosp., 1960-61; resident in neurosurgery Neurological Inst., Montreal, 1962-64, 65-66, N.Y. Neurol. Inst., N.Y.C., 1964-65; neurosurgeon U. Alta., Edmonton, Can., 1967-92, dir. div. neurosurgery, 1982-86, Walter Anderson prof., chmn. dept. surgery, 1986-92; surgeon-in-chief U. Alta. Hosps., 1986-92; Maurice Goldblatt prof. surgery and neurology U. Chgo., 1992—, dir. Brain Rsch. Inst., 1993—; past pres. V Internat. Symposium on Cerebral Vasospasm; mem. neurology A study sect. NIH, 1991-93; invited speaker at over 100 profl. meetings; vis. prof. over 60 univs., including Yale U., Cornell U., Columbia U., Duke U., U. Toronto, U. Calif., San Francisco; over 10 named lectureships, including White lectr. Harvard U., Gainey lectr., Mayo Clinic. Author: Aneurysms Affecting the Nervous System, 1987, Subarachnoid Hemorrhage-Causes and Cures, 1997; co-editor Primer on Cerebrovascular Diseases, 1997; mem. editl. bd. Jour. Neurosurgery, chmn. bd., 1993-94; mem. editl. bd. Neurosurgery Quar., Jour. Ceberovascular Disease; contbr. over 250 articles to med. jours. Named Officer of the Order of Can., 1995. Fellow ACS, Royal Coll. Surgeons Can., Royal Coll. Surgeons Edinburgh (hon.); mem. Am. Surg. Assn., James IV Assn. Surgeons, Am. Acad. Neurol. Surgeons, Soc. Neurol. Surgeons (Grass gold medal 1992). Achievements include contributions to the understanding of cerebral vasospasm and the surgical management of intracranial aneurysms. Office: U of Chgo Pritzker Sch of Medicine 5841 S Maryland Ave Chicago IL 60637-1463

WEIR, EDWARD KENNETH, cardiologist; b. Belfast, No. Ireland, Jan. 7, 1943; came to U.S. 1973; s. Thomas Kenneth and Violet Hilda (ffrench) W.; m. Elizabeth Vincent Pearman, May 29, 1971; children: Fergus G., Conor K. BA, U. Oxford, U.K., 1964, MA, BM, BCh, U. Oxford, Eng., 1967, DM, 1976. Diplomate Am. Bd. Internal Medicine. Intern Churchill Hosp., Oxford, Eng., 1968; intern Radcliffe Infirmary, Oxford, 1968, resident, 1970-71; resident Hammersmith Hosp., London, 1969, Groot Schuur Hosp., Cape Town, South Africa, 1969-70; registrar in cardiology Groot Schuur Hosp., Cape Town, 1971-73; sr. house physician Nuffield Dept. Medicine, Radcliffe Infirmary, Oxford, 1970-71; postdoctoral rsch. fellow U. Colo., Denver, 1973-75; cons. pediatric cardiologist U. Cape Town Med. Sch., 1975-76; cons. cardiologist U. Natal Med. Sch., Durban, South Africa, 1976-77; assoc. prof. medicine U. Minn., Mpls., 1978-85, prof. medicine, 1985—; staff physician Va. Med. Ctr., Mpls., 1978—; dir. Grover Confs. on Pulmonary Circulation, 1984—. Co-editor: Pulmonary Hypertension, 1984, The Pulmonary Circulation in Health and Disease, 1987, Pulmonary Vascular Physiology and Pathophysiology, 1989, The Diagnosis and Treatment of Pulmonary Hypertension, 1992, Ion Flux in Pulmonary Vascular Control, 1993, The Pulmonary Circulation and Gas Exchange, 1994, Nitric Oxide and Radicals in the Pulmonary Vasculature, 1996, Pulmonary Edema, 1997. Fulbright scholar, 1973-75; Sr. Internat. Fogarty fellow, 1993. Fellow Am. Coll. Cardiology, Royal Coll. Physicians London; mem. Am. Heart Assn. (Minn. affiliate bd. dirs. 1989-93, Nat. Cardiopulmonary Coun. (exec. com. 1992—), Pulmonary Circulation Found. (treas. 1985—). Office: VA Med Ctr 1 Veterans Dr # 111C Minneapolis MN 55417-2300 *What you "achieve" in life is much less important than what you do for those around you. One hundred years after their death, very few people are remembered for what they achieved.*

WEIR, JOHN KEELEY, lawyer; b. New Haven, Jan. 27, 1947; s. John H. and Helen K. (Keeley) W.; m. Lucy P. Persico, May 21, 1977; children: John P., Keeley Anne. BA, Yale U., 1968; JD, Northwestern U., 1971. Bar: N.Y. 1972, U.S. Dist. Ct. (so. dist.) N.Y. 1973, U.S. Ct. Appeals (2d cir.) 1975, U.S. Supreme Ct. 1982, U.S. Ct. Appeals (4th cir.) 1989, U.S. Ct. Appeals (9th cir.) 1991, U.S. Dist. Ct. Conn. 1995, U.S. Ct. Internat. Trade 1995, U.S. Ct. Appeals (11th cir.) 1995. Assoc. Haight, Gardner, Poor & Havens, N.Y.C., 1971-80, ptnr., 1980—. Mem. ABA (del.), Internat. Bar Assn. (del.), Yale U. Alumni Assn., Yale Club (N.Y.C.). Roman Catholic. Avocations: tennis, golf, soccer coaching, reading. Home: 47 Winthrop Dr Riverside CT 06878-1911 Office: Haight Gardner Poor & Havens 195 Broadway New York NY 10007-3100

WEIR, KENNETH WYNN, marine corps officer, experimental test pilot; b. Sherman, Tex., Oct. 20, 1930; s. Kenneth Herbert and Berye Lee (Wynn) W.; m. Nancy Corr Mosher, Oct. 10, 1953; children—Kenneth Mosher, David Wynn, William Scott. B.S., U.S. Naval Acad., 1952; M.S., U. So. Calif., 1968. Commd. 2d lt. USMC, 1952, advanced through grades to maj. gen., 1977, comdg. gen. 65th Marine Amphibian Brigade, 1978, dep. comdg. gen. Fleet Marine Force Pacific, 1981, comdg. gen. 4th Marine Air Wing, 1985; chief U-2/TR 1 Test Pilot Lockheed Skunk Works, Burbank, Calif., 1966-93; ret., 1993. Fellow Soc. Exptl. Test Pilots (pres. 1980-81). Achievements include more flight test experience above 60,000 feet altitude in high performance airplanes than anyone else in the world.

WEIR, MORTON WEBSTER, retired academic administrator, educator; b. Canton, Ill., July 18, 1934; s. James and Frances Mary (Johnson) W.; m. Cecelia Ann Rumler, June 23, 1956; children: Deborah, Kevin, Mark. AB, Knox Coll., 1955; MA, U. Tex., 1958, PhD, 1959. Rsch. assoc., asst. prof. child devel. U. Minn., Mpls., 1959; asst. prof. child devel. U. Ill., Urbana, 1960-64, assoc. prof., 1964-68, prof., 1968-93, prof. emeritus, 1993—, head dept. psychology, 1969-71, vice chancellor acad. affairs, 1971-79, v.p. acad. affairs, 1982-88, chancellor, 1988-93, chancellor emeritus, 1993—, sr. found. rep., 1993—; dir. Boys Town Center Study Youth Development, 1979-80. Contbr. numerous articles to profl. jours. Chmn. bd. trustees Knox Coll., 1995—. With AUS, 1960. NSF Predoctoral fellow, 1957-59. Fellow AAAS; mem. Soc. Rsch. in Child Devel. (chmn. bd. publs. 1971, chmn. fin. com. 1993-95), Sigma Xi, Phi Beta Kappa, Phi Kappa Phi. Office: U Ill Found Harker Hall 1305 W Green St Urbana IL 61801-2945

WEIR, PETER FRANK, lawyer; b. Stuttgart, Germany, Mar. 26, 1933; s. Robert Henry and Ruth Sophie W.; m. Jean M., Sept. 27, 1958; children: Bradford F., Elizabeth A. BA, Williams Coll., 1955; LLB, Harvard U., 1958; MBA, N.Y.U., 1967. Bar: N.Y. 1959, Ga. 1957. Assoc. Winston & Strawn (formerly Cole & Deitz), N.Y.C., 1959-66, ptnr., 1966-92, ret. ptnr., 1992; pvt. practice, 1993—. Bd. dirs. Episc. Ch. Found., 1981-93, sec., 1989-93, also treas., chmn. fin. com., 1982-89, chmn. audit com., 1982-88; mem. exec. com. N.Y. Regional Coun., 1975-81, chmn. 1979-81, mem. steering com., 1981-93; mem. adv. bd. First Am. Title Ins. Co. of N.Y., Inc., 1984-95. Bd. dirs., counsel Point O'Woods Assn., N.Y., 1976-91, v.p., 1982-91; alt. bd. dirs. Fire Island Assn., 1976-86, 92—; sec. and dir. Elderworks Found., 1982-92; dir. Episc. Evangelism Found., 1995—. Served with Air N.G., 1958-63. Mem. ABA, Internat. Bar Assn., N.Y. State Bar Assn., Assn. of Bar of City of N.Y., Church Club (trustee 1988-91), Down Town Assn. Club, Williams Club, Club at Point O'Woods (v.p., gov. 1970-79), Hillsboro Club. Republican. Home: 530 E 86th St Apt 11C New York NY 10028-7535 Office: c/o Winston & Strawn 200 Park Ave Fl 41 New York NY 10166-4499

WEIR, PETER LINDSAY, film director; b. June 21, 1944, Sydney; s. Lindsay Weir and Peggy Barnsley; m. Wendy Stites, 1966; 2 children. Ed. Scots Coll., Sydney, Vaucluse Boys High Sch., Sydney U. Worked in real estate until 1965; worked as stagehand in TV, Sydney, 1967; dir. film sequences in variety show, 1968; dir. amateur univ. revs., 1967-69; dir. for Film Australia, 1969-73; made own short films, 1969-73, ind. feature film producer, dir. and writer, 1973—. Films include: Cars that Ate Paris, 1973, Picnic at Hanging Rock, 1975, The Last Wave, 1977, The Plumber (TV), 1978, Gallipoli, 1980, The Year of Living Dangerously, 1982, Witness, 1985, The Mosquito Coast, 1986, Dead Poets Society, 1989, Green Card, 1990, Fearless, 1993, The Truman Show, 1997. Mem. Australia A.M. Recipient various film awards. Office: CAA care John Ptak 9830 Wilshire Blvd Beverly Hills CA 90212-1804

WEIR, RICHARD DALE, elementary education educator; b. Diamond Springs, Calif., Oct. 2, 1940; s. Martin Gaines and Phyllis Lorene (Sargent) W.; m. Carol Jean Baker, Dec. 25, 1976; children:; David Richard, Barbara Anne, Susan Michelle, Roger Allen. BS in Elem. Edn., Oklahoma City U., 1976, MEd, 1988; BS in Mgmt. Info. Sys., Coleman Coll., LaMesa, Calif., 1987. Cert. tchr. K-8, Okla. Joined USCG, 1961, advanced through grades to chief warrant officer, 1976; adminstrv. officer USCG, Washington, 1976-82; ret. USCG, 1982; platform instr. IBM Corp., Oklahoma City, 1985-86; mid. sch. tchr. Archdiocese Oklahoma City, 1987-88; adj. prof. Oklahoma City U., 1988-91; elem. tchr. Oklahoma City Pub. Schs., 1988—, adminstrv. intern, 1997—; cons. in tng. math.-sci. tchrs.; trainer for Activities Integrating Math./Scis. Nat. Leadership Network. Recipient Presdl. award for excellence in sci. and math. teaching NSF, Washington, 1993, Okla. Outstanding Tchr. award Math. Assn. Am., Washington, 1996. Mem. ASCD, Nat. Sci. Tchrs. Assn., Nat. Coun. Tchrs. Math., Coun. Presdl. Awardees Math., Okla. Coun. Tchrs. Math. (advisor Metro Oklahoma City), Soc. Elem. Presdl. Awardees. Republican. Methodist. Avocation: golf. Home: 9109 NW 99th Pl Yukon OK 73099-8313 Office: PO Box 720226 Oklahoma City OK 73172-0226

WEIR, ROBERT H., lawyer; b. Boston, Dec. 7, 1922; s. Abraham and Beatrice (Stern) W.; A.B., Harvard U., 1944, LL.B., 1948; m. Ruth Hirsch, July 2, 1954 (dec. Nov. 1965); children—Anthony, David, Michael H.; m. 2d, Sylvia T. Frias; children—Nicole F., Daniella F. Admitted to Mass. bar, 1948, Wash. bar, 1952, Calif. bar, 1957; spl. asst. to atty. gen. U.S. Dept. Justice, Seattle, 1948-53, Washington, 1953-56; practiced in San Jose, also Palo Alto, Calif., 1957—. Instr. taxation of real estate U. Calif. at San Jose and San Francisco, 1957—; lectr. U. So. Calif. Tax Inst. Mem. prison com. Am. Friends Service Com. Bd. dirs. San Jose Light Opera Assn., Inc. Served with U.S. Army, 1942-45. Mem. Am., Santa Clara County bar assns., State Bar Calif., Am. Judicature Soc. Author: Advantages in Taxes, 1960. Tax columnist Rural Realtor, Chgo., 1959—. Speaker taxation annual meetings Nat. Assn. Real Estate Bds., 1958-60. Author: Taxes Working for You, 1966; How to Make the Most of Depreciation Write Off. Contbr. articles to profl. jours. Address: 27743 Via Ventana Los Altos CA 94022-3241

WEIR, STEPHEN JAMES, financial executive; b. Calgary, Alta., Can., Mar. 22, 1940; s. Jack W. and Elizabeth T. (Speirs) W.; m. Janet R Suggitt, July 1961; children: James, Jennifer. C.A., U. Man., 1962; M.B.A., U. Western Ont., Can., 1967. Accountant Winnipeg, Man., 1957-63; mgr. credit and control 3M Co. of Can., London, Ont., 1963-65; asst. credit mgr. corporate credit Bank of Montreal, 1967-72; treas. Dominion Textile Inc., Montreal, 1972-77; compt., 1977-81; v.p. internat. divsn. Dominion Textile Inc., 1981-83, v.p. consumer div., 1983-84, v.p. ops. service, 1984-85, v.p. APP/IND div., 1985-87, v.p. fin. ops., 1987-88; v.p. fin. Telemedia Inc., Montreal, 1988-90, exec. v.p., chief fin. officer, 1990—. Mem. Can. Inst. Chartered Accountants, Financial Execs. Inst.. Office: Telemedia Inc 1411 Peel St, Montreal, PQ Canada H3A 1S5

WEIR, THOMAS CHARLES, banker; b. Sandwich, Ill., Oct. 18, 1933; s. Glendon V. and Eleanor (Hoge) W.; m. Angela Di Giovanni. Grad., Pacific Coast Banking Sch., U. Wash., 1966. Mgr. consumer loans Barnett Nat. Bank, Cocoa, Fla., 1955-58; with 1st Interstate Bank Ariz., 1958-79; head retail banking div. 1st Nat. Bank Ariz., various locations, 1974-79, exec. v.p., 1975-79; chmn., chief exec. officer Home Fed. Savs., Tucson, 1979-87; chmn. Ariz. Commerce Bank, 1987-88; pres. Tucson Resources, Inc., 1988-89; pres., chief exec. officer Tucson Electric Power Co., 1989-90; fin. cons. Tucson, 1990—; pres. WD Enterprises, Inc., 1994—, Dependable Personnel, Inc., 1994—; bd. dirs. Apollo Group, Inc.; pres. Dependable Nurses, Inc., 1994—. With AUS, 1953-55. Republican. Episcopalian. Clubs: Tucson Country, White Mountain Country.

WEIRICH, RICHARD DENIS, government official; b. Aurora, Ill.. BS, U. Notre Dame, 1966; MBA, U. Chgo., 1968. Computer programmer/analyst Armour & Co., Chgo., 1966-68; software specialist NIMH, Washington, 1968-70; mgr. software support State of Ill., Springfield, 1970-73; dir. info. requirements U.S. Postal Svc., Washington, 1973-75, mgr. tech. support, 1975-80; dir. postal data ctr. U.S. Postal Svc., San Bruno, Calif., 1980-84; dir. comms. and tech. U.S. Postal Svc., Washington, 1984-88, asst. postmaster gen. tech. resources, 1988-89, asst. postmaster gen., v.p. info. systems, 1989—. Office: US Postal Svc Information Systems 475 Lenfant Plz SW Washington DC 20260-0004

WEIS, EDMUND BERNARD, JR., orthopaedist, educator, engineer, lawyer; b. Bismarck, N.D., Aug. 4, 1931; s. Edmund Bernard and Margaret Catherine (Rickert) W.; m. Annette Mary Fernandes, Nov. 19, 1972; children: John Paul, Giselle Anne, Susan Ellen, Melanie Elizabeth, Edmund Bernard III, Bronwyn Kristen. Attended, U. Utah, 1949-52; grad., U. Notre Dame, 1953; MD, U. Colo., 1957; MS in Bioengring., Drexel Inst. Tech., 1962; doctoral candidate, Ohio State U., 1968-71; JD, Newport U., 1994. Diplomate Am. Bd. Orthopaedic Surgery; Bar: Calif. 1994. Intern Good Samaritan Hosp., Phoenix, 1957-58; chief vibration and impact br. mercury astronaut crew selection Aerospace Med. Rsch. Labs., Wright-Patterson AFB, Ohio, 1958-66; resident in orthopaedics Ohio State U., Columbus, 1968-71; amputations tng. Dept. Vet. Affairs, Grossinger, N.Y., 1985; pedicle screw fixation tng. Cleve. Rsch. Inst., 1987; thermography tng. Acad. Neuromuscular Thermography, L.A., 1989; surg. lasers tng. Loma Linda (Calif.) U., 1992; rsch. med. officer USAF, Wright-Patterson AFB, Ohio, 1966-68; mem. staff Ohio Vets. Oupatient Ctr., Columbus, 1974-76, N.D. Vets. Hosp., Fargo, 1976-79; mem. staff VA Hosp., Omaha, 1979-85, acting chief rehab., 1983-85; mem. staff, chief orthopaedics VA Hosp., Loma Linda, 1985—; mem. staff Loma Linda Cmty. Hosp., 1985—, chief orthopaedics, 1989-90; mem. staff Loma Linda U. Med. Ctr., 1985—, Redlands (Calif.) Cmty. Hosp., 1986-94, San Bernardino (Calif.) Cmty. Hosp., 1990—, Moreno Valley (Calif.) Hosp., 1992-94, San Gorgonio Meml. Hosp., Banning, Calif., 1993-94; instr. to asst. prof. orthopaedics Ohio State U., 1971-76; assoc. prof. U. N.D., Grand Forks, 1976-79, asst. dean, 1977-79; prof. Creighton U., Omaha, 1979-85; clin. prof. Loam Linda U., 1985—; bioengring. cons. Cox Coronary Heart Inst., Dayton, Ohio, 1962-66, Battelle Meml. Inst., Columbus, 1970-76; orthopaedics cons. Grand Forks AFB Hosp., 1976-79, Ehrling-Berquist AFB Hosp., Omaha, 1979-84, Jour. Bone and Joint Surgery, Waltham, Mass., 1980—; com. mem. Am. Acad. Orthopaedics Emergency Svcs. Contbr. numerous articles to profl. jours.; inventor sonic surg. tool; patentee method and sys. for control of a powered prosthesis. Maj. USAF, Wright-Patterson AFB, 1957-66. Recipient R & D award USAF, 1966, Rsch. award Dept. Vet. Affairs, 1988, U.S. Svc. award, 30 Yr. pin, Jerry L. Pettis Vets. Hosp., 1993; rsch. fellow NIH, 1969-71, travelling fellow Am. Orthopaedics Assn., 1971. Fellow Am. Acad. Orthopaedic Surgeons (Rsch. and Edn. Found. award 1969), Am. Coll. Legal Medicine; mem. AMA, Orthopaedic Rsch. Soc., San Bernardino County Med. Soc., Calif. Med. Soc., Nat. Assn. Vet. Physicians, N.Am. Spine Soc., Phi Rho Sigma. Avocations: restoring old Fords. Home: 30555 7th Ave Redlands CA 92374-7619 Office: 1800 Western Ave Ste 300 San Bernardino CA 92411-1354

WEIS, JOSEPH FRANCIS, JR., federal judge; b. Pitts., Mar. 12, 1923; s. Joseph Francis and Mary (Flaherty) W.; m. Margaret Horne, Dec. 27, 1958; children: Maureen, Joseph Francis, Christine. BA, Duquesne U., 1941-47; J.D., U. Pitts., 1950; LLD (hon.), Dickinson Coll., 1989. Bar: Pa. 1950. Individual practice law Pitts., 1950-68; judge Ct. Common Pleas, Allegheny County, Pa., 1968-70, U.S. Dist. Ct. (we. dist.) Pa., 1970-73, U.S. Ct. Appeals (3d cir.), Pitts., 1973—; lectr. trial procedures, 1965—; adj. prof. law U. Pitts., 1986—; chmn. Fed. Cts. Study Com., Jud. Conf. Com. on Experiment to Videotape Trial Proceedings within the 3rd Cir., Internat. Jud. Conf. the Joint Am.-Can. Appellate Judges Conf., Toronto, 1986, London, 1985, futurist subcom. bicentennial com. Ct. Common Pleas, Allegheny County, Pa., 1988; participant programs legal medicine, Rome, London; mem. Am.-Can. Legal Exchange, 1987. Contbr. articles to legal jours. Mem. Mental Health and Mental Retardation Bd., Allegheny County, 1970-73; mem. Leukemia Soc., 1970-73, Knights of Malta, Am. Legion, 4th Armored Div. Assn., Disabled Am. Vets., Cath. War Vets., Mil. Order of the World Wars; mem. bd. adminstrn. Cath. Diocese Pitts., 1971-83; trustee Forbes Hosp. System, Pitts., 1969-74. Capt. AUS, 1943-48. Decorated Bronze Star, Purple Heart with oak leaf cluster; recipient St. Thomas More award, 1971, Phillip Amram award, 1991, Edward J. Devitt Disting. Svc. to Justice award, 1993, History Makers award, 1997. Fellow Internat. Acad. Trial Lawyers (hon.), Am. Bar Found.; mem. ABA (chmn. appellate judges' conf. 1981-83), Pa. Bar Assn., Allegheny Bar Assn. (past v.p.), Acad. Trial Lawyers Allegheny County (past pres), Am. Judicature Soc., Jud. Conf. U.S. (chmn. civil rules com. 1986-87, com. on adminstrn. bankruptcy system 1983-87, subcom. on jud. improvements 1983-87, chmn. standing com. rules of practice and procedure 1988), Inst. Jud. Adminstrn., KC. Home: 225 Hillcrest Rd Pittsburgh PA 15238-2307 Office: US Ct Appeals 513 US PO & Courthouse 7th & Grant St Pittsburgh PA 15219

WEIS, JUDITH SHULMAN, biology educator; b. N.Y.C., May 29, 1941; d. Saul B. and Pearl (Cooper) Shulman; m. Peddrick Weis; children: Jennifer, Eric. BA, Cornell U., 1962; MS, NYU, 1964, PhD, 1967. Lectr. CUNY, 1964-67; asst. prof. Rutgers U., Newark, 1967-71, assoc. prof., 1971-76, prof., 1976—; Congl. sci. fellow U.S. Senate, Washington, 1983-84; mem. grant rev. panel NSF, Washington, 1976-82, program dir., 1988-90; mem. rev. panel EPA, 1984-92; vis. scientist EPA Lab., Gulf Breeze, Fla., 1992. Mem. marine bd. NAS, 1991—. Grantee NOAA, 1977—, N.J. EPA Rsch., 1978-79, 81-83, N.J. Marine Scis. Consortium Rsch., 1987—; NSF fellow, 1962-64. Mem. Am. Inst. for Biol. Scis. (bd. dirs. 1986-88, 89-91, 97—), Soc. Environ. Toxicology and Chemistry (bd. dirs. 1990-93), Estuarine Rsch. Fedn., Ecol. Soc. Am., NOW (pres. Essex County 1972), Sierra Club (bd. dirs. N.J. chpt. 1986-88). Avocations: choral singing, swimming, jogging, light opera. Office: Rutgers U Dept Biol Scis Newark NJ 07102

WEIS, LAWRENCE FREDERICK, city official; b. Highland Park, Mich., Aug. 26, 1939; s. Howard Emanuel and Amelia Lansom (Morell) W.; children: Leonard, Daniel, Richard. BS, Purdue U., West Lafayette, Ind., 1962; MA, Wayne State U., Detroit, 1984. Hockey referee Detroit, 1956—; gen. mgr. Detroit Jr. Wings Hockey Club, 1970-72; ops. mgr. data processing Federal-Mogul Corp., Southfield, Mich., 1963-70; tchr. polit. sci. Bishop Gallagher H.S., Harper Woods, Mich., 1983-88; baseball mgr. ITM Corp., Detroit, 1969-87; referee-in-chief Internat. Hockey Referee Assn., Detroit, 1974—; cross country coach Wayne State U., Detroit, 1988-94; pres. World Pancratium Fedn., Detroit, 1989—; arena mgr. City of St. Clair Shores, Mich., 1988—; scout Detroit Red Wings Hockey Club, 1971-75. Author/editor: Cross Country Guide, 1994, Baseball Guide, 1985. Pres., chmn. bd. Mich. Amateur Sports Hall of Fame, Detroit, 1974—; mem. ground observers corp U.S. Dept. of Def., Detroit, 1953-56. Named U.S. Amateur Mgr. of Yr., Soc. Baseball Friends, 1973. Lutheran. Avocations: martial arts coaching, writing, bicycling. Home: 31671 Cindy Fraser MI 48026 Office: City of St Clair Shores 20000 Stephens Dr St Clair Shores MI 48080-3109

WEIS, MERVYN J., physician, gastroenterologist; b. Chgo., June 9, 1940; s. Theodore A. and Anita (Stavins) W.; m. Myra Rubenstein, Nov. 26, 1966 (dec. Nov. 1990); children: Jonathan Mandel, Sari Tova; m. Anita Kaplan Sherbet, Oct. 1992. BA, Northwestern U., 1961, MD, 1965. Diplomate Am. Bd. Internal Medicine. Intern in internal medicine Michael Reese Hosp. and Med. Ctr., Chgo., 1965-66, resident in internal medicine, 1966-67, 69-70, attending physician, 1972-78; fellow in gastroenterology Northwestern U. Med. Ctr., Chgo., 1970-72; attending physician Ravenswood Hosp., Chgo., 1979-83, St. Francis Hosp., Evanston, Ill., 1984-88, Rush North Med. Ctr., Skokie, Ill., 1985-91; attending physician Louis A. Weiss Meml. Hosp., Chgo., 1972—, chmn. divsn. medicine, 1987-89, pres. med. staff, 1989-93, mem. bd. govs., 1987—; cons. in gastroenterology VA Rsch. Hosp., Chgo., 1972-80. Contbr. articles to profl. jours. Capt. U.S. Army, 1967-69. Fellow ACP, Am. Coll. Gastroenterology; mem. AMA, Ill. State Med. Soc., Chgo. Soc. Gastroenterology, Chgo. Med. Soc. Avocations: golf, jogging, computers. Office: 4640 N Marine Dr Ste C 6100 Chicago IL 60640-5719

WEIS, ROBERT FREEMAN, supermarket company executive; b. Sunbury, Pa.; m. Patricia Ross; children: Jennifer, Colleen, Jonathan. Grad., Mercersburg Acad., 1937; BA, Yale U., 1941. With Weis Markets, Sunbury, Pa., 1946—; v.p., treas. Weis Markets, chmn. bd. dirs., treas., 1995—; chair steering com. capital campaign Susquehanna U., Selinsgrove, Pa., past vice chmn. bd. trustees; past pres. bd. trustees Sunbury Cmty. Hosp., trustee; bd. dirs. Lown Cardiovascular Rsch. Found., Brookline, Mass. Past pres. Sunbury C. of C.; past chmn. bd. dirs. First Nat. Trust Bank Sunbury, eneritus dir.; past dir. Susquehanna Bancshares; treas. Sunbury chpt. United Jewish Appeal. Office: Weis Markets Inc PO Box 471 Sunbury PA 17801

WEISBERG, ADAM JON, lawyer; b. Cocoa Beach, Fla., June 5, 1963; s. Melvin H. Weisberg and Joan Julie (Carney) Vargo; m. Cheryl Lynn Scupp, June 25, 1994. BS in Bus. Econs., Rider Coll., 1985; JD, N.Y. Law Sch., 1988. Bar: N.Y. 1989, N.J. 1989, U.S. Dist. Ct. 1989, Fla. 1991. Law clk., asst. prosecutor Middlesex County Prosecutors Office, New Brunswick, N.J., 1988-90; workers' compensation atty. Levinson Axelrod Wheaton, Edison, N.J., 1990-91; trial atty. workers compensation Richard J. Simon, Esq., New Brunswick, 1991-92; pvt. practice lawyer New Brunswick, 1992—; pres. Asbury Music Co., Belmar, N.J. Mem. ABA, N.J. Bar Assn., Middlesex County Bar Assn., Monmouth County Bar Assn., Assn. Criminal Def. Lawyers. Avocations: fishing, surfing. Office: Monmouth Exec Plz II 1300 Hwy 35 Ste 201 Ocean NJ 07712 Office: 46 Bayard St New Brunswick NJ 08901-2152

WEISBERG, HERBERT FRANK, political science educator; b. Mpls., Dec. 8, 1941; s. Nathan R. and Jean (Schlessinger) W.; m. Judith Ann Robinson, Dec. 16, 1979; 1 child, Bryan Bowen. BA, U. Minn., 1963; PhD, U. Mich., 1968. Asst. prof. polit. sci. U. Mich., Ann Arbor, 1967-73, assoc. prof. polit. sci., 1973-74; assoc. prof. polit. sci. Ohio State U., Columbus, 1974-77, prof. polit. sci., 1977—. Author: Central Tendency and Variation, 1992; coauthor: Theory Building and Data Analysis, 1984, Controversies in Voting Behavior, 1992, Survey Research Polling and Data Analysis, 1996; editor: Political Science: Science of Politics, 1985, Democracy's Feast: Elections in America, 1995; co-editor Am. Jour. Polit. Sci., 1979-82. Mem. Midwest Polit. Sci. Assn. (v.p. 1983-85), Am. Polit. Sci. Assn. (program chmn. 1983), Phi Beta Kappa, Pi Sigma Alpha, Phi Kappa Phi. Home: 742 Gatehouse Ln Columbus OH 43235-1732 Office: Ohio State U Dept Polic Sci 2140 Derby Hall 154 N Oval Mall Columbus OH 43210-1330

WEISBERG, JONATHAN MARK, public relations executive; b. Troy, N.Y., Dec. 5, 1943; s. David G. and Elizabeth (Cohn) W.; m. Pamela Crowe, Apr. 30, 1972; children: Zoe, Amanda. BA, Syracuse U., 1965; MA, Newhouse Communications Ctr., Syracuse U., 1968. V.p. Harshe, Rotman & Druck, N.Y.C., 1972-74, Rowland Co., N.Y.C., 1974-76; exec. v.p. Richard Weiner Inc., N.Y.C., 1976-84; dir. consumer, med. device and nutritional communications Bristol-Myers Squibb Co., N.Y.C., dir. corp. comms., 1984—; dir. internat. pub. affairs Bristol-Myers Squibb Co., 1994—; cons. Interbank Card Assn., N.Y.C., 1972-74, Ky. Fried Chicken, Louisville, 1974-76, Cigar Assn. Am., Washington, 1984, Am. Soc. Journalists and Authors, N.Y.C., 1980-84, Belgian Endive Mktg. Bd., Brussels, 1982-84. Office: Bristol Myers Squibb Co 345 Park Ave New York NY 10154-0004

WEISBERG, LEONARD R., retired research and engineering executive; b. N.Y.C., Oct. 17, 1929; s. Emanuel E. and Esther (Raynes) W.; m. Frances Simon, Mar. 23, 1980; children: Glenna Weisberg Andersen, Orren Weisberg Falk, Frances Weisberg Brookner. BA magna cum laude, Clark U., 1950; MA, Columbia U., 1952. Rsch. asst. Watson Labs. IBM, N.Y.C., 1953-55; with RCA Labs., Princeton, N.J., 1955-71; mem. tech. staff RCA Labs., 1955-66, head rsch. group, 1966-69, dir. semicondr. device rsch. lab., 1969-71; dir. materials rsch. lab. Itek Corp., Lexington, Mass., 1972-74; v.p., dir. ctrl. rsch. lab. Itek Corp., 1974-75; dir. electronics tech U.S. Dept. Def., Washington, 1975-79; v.p. rsch. and engring. Honeywell Inc., Mpls., 1980-94, ret., 1994; mem. adv. group on electron devices U.S. Dept. Def.; bd. dirs. SubMicron Sys. Corp. Contbr. articles to profl. jours. Recipient award for initiating VHSIC program U.S. Dept. Def., 1979. Fellow IEEE; mem. Am. Phys. Soc., Sigma Xi. Home: 30 Coonamessett Cir East Falmouth MA 02536-4032

WEISBERG, LOIS, arts administrator, city official. Commr. Chgo. Dept. Cultural Affairs, 1989—. Office: Chicago Cultural Center 78 E Washington St Chicago IL 60602-4801

WEISBERG, MORRIS L., retired lawyer; b. Phila., June 7, 1921; s. Alexander and Hilda (Lichtenstein) W.; m. Mildred Norma Lubich, July 7, 1948; children—Richard, James, John. B.A., U. Pa., 1943, LL.B., 1947; M.A., Yale U., 1944. Bar: Pa. 1950, U.S. Dist. Ct. (ea. dist.) Pa. 1950, U.S. Supreme Ct. 1962. Bigelow teaching fellow U. Chgo. Law Sch., 1947-48, Raymond grad. fellow, 1948-49; Gowen fellow U. Pa. Law Sch., Phila., 1948-49; ptnr. Harry Norman Ball, Phila., 1950-56; assoc. Blank, Rome, Comisky & McCauley, and predecessor, Phila., 1956-60, ptnr., 1960-93; permanent mem. Jud. Conf. 3d Cir. Fellow Am. Bar Found.; mem. Order of Coif, Phi Beta Kappa Assocs. Office: Blank Rome Comisky & McCauley 4 Penn Center Plz Philadelphia PA 19103-2521

WEISBERG, STUART ELLIOT, federal official, lawyer; b. Bklyn., Feb. 2, 1949; s. Julius and Esther Weisberg; m. Elizabeth Jane Kruckoff, June 24, 1979; children: Andrew Jonathan, Eric Nathaniel. BA, Brandeis U., 1971; JD, U. Pa., 1974. Bar: N.Y. 1976, D.C. 1976, U.S. Ct. Appeals (9th cir.) 1976, U.S. Supreme Ct. 1979. Assoc. NLRB, Washington, 1975-84; staff dir., counsel employment and housing subcom. U.S. Ho. of Reps., Washington, 1984-93; now chmn. Occupational Safety and Health Review Commission, Washington. Democrat. Jewish. Avocations: basketball, tennis. Office: Occupational Safety and Health Review Commission 1120 20th St NW Washington DC 20036-3406

WEISBERGER, BARBARA, choreographer, artistic director, educator; b. Bklyn., Feb. 28, 1926; d. Herman and Sally (Goldstein) Linshes; m. Sol Spiller, Sept. 3, 1945 (div. 1948); m. Ernest Weisberger, Nov. 15, 1949; children: Wendy, Steven. B.S. in Edn., Psychology, Pa. State U., 1945; L.H.D. (hon.), Swarthmore Coll., 1970; D.F.A. (hon.), Temple U., 1973, Kings Coll., 1978, Villanova U., 1978, U. New England, 1996. Founder, dir., tchr. Wilkes-Barre (Pa.) Ballet Theater, 1953-63; founder, dir. Pa. Ballet, Phila., 1962-82, Carlisle (Pa.) Project, 1984—; vice chmn. dance panel Nat. Endowment for the Arts, Washington, 1975-79. Performed with Met. Opera Ballet, N.Y.C., 1937, 38, Mary Binney Montgomery Co., Phila., 1940-42, ballet mistress, choreographer, Ballet Co. of Phila. Lyric Opera, 1961-62, ; choreographic works include Italian Concerto, Bach, Symphonic Variations, Franck; also operas for, Phila. Lyric Opera Co. Named Disting. Dau. of Pa., 1972, Disting. Alumna, Pa. State U., 1972; recipient 46th ann. Gimbel Phila. award, 1978. Mem. Psi Chi. Home and Office: 571 Charles Ave Kingston PA 18704-4711

WEISBERGER, JOSEPH ROBERT, state supreme court chief justice; b. Providence, Aug. 3, 1920; s. Samuel Joseph and Ann Elizabeth (Meighan) W.; m. Sylvia Blanche Pigeon, June 9, 1951; children: Joseph Robert, Paula Ann, Judith Marie. AB, Brown U., 1942; JD, Harvard U., 1949; LLD, R.I. Coll., Suffolk U., Mt. St. Joseph Coll.; DCL, Providence Coll.; DHL, Bryant Coll.; LLD, Roger Williams Coll., 1992, Brown U., 1992. Bar: Mass. 1949, R.I. 1950. With Quinn & Quinn, Providence, 1951-56; solicitor Glocester, R.I., 1953-56; judge Superior Ct. R.I., Providence, 1956-72; presiding justice R.I. Supreme Ct., Providence, 1972-78, chief justice, 1993—; adj. prof. U. Nev., 1986—; mem. faculty Nat. Jud. Coll.; vis. lectr. Providence Coll., Suffolk Law Sch., Roger Williams Coll.; Chmn. New Eng. Regional Conf. Trial Judges, 1962, 63, 65; chmn. New Eng. Regional Commn. Disordered Offender, 1968-71, R.I. Com. Adoption on Rules Criminal Procedure, 1968-72, chmn. of R.I. Adv. Com. Corrections, 1973, Nat. Conf. State Trial Judges ABA, 1977-78; exec. com. Appelate Judges Conf. ABA, 1979—, vice chmn., 1983-85, chmn., 1985-86; bd. dirs. Nat. Ctr. for State Cts., 1975-81. Chmn. editorial bd. Judges Jour., 1973-75. Pres. R.I. Health Facilities Planning Coun., 1967-70; chmn. Gov. R.I. Coun. Mental Health, 1968-73; moderator Town of East Providence, 1954-56; mem. R.I. Senate, 1953-56, minority leader, 1955-56; vice chmn. bd. trustee R.I. Hosp., 1968-92, St. Joseph's Hosp., trustee, 1962—. Lt. comdr. USNR, 1941-46. Recipient Erwin Griswold award Nat. Jud. Coll., 1989; named to R.I. Hall of Fame; Paul Harris fellow Rotary Internat. Fellow Am. Bar Found.; mem. ABA (ho. of dels., task force on criminal justice stds. 1977-79, exec. com. appellate judges' conf. 1979-95), R.I. Bar Assn., Am. Judges Assn. (gov.), Inst. Jud. Adminstrn., Am. Judicature Soc. (Herbert Harley award 1990), Am. Law Inst., KC, Order of St. Gregory (knight comdr. with star 1989, Goodrich award for Svc. 1995), Phi Beta Kappa (past pres. Alpha chpt. Brown U.). Home: 60 Winthrop St Riverside RI 02915-2624 Office: RI Supreme Ct 250 Benefit St Providence RI 02903-2719 *My professional life for the last 40 years has been occupied with judicial duties. I have been blessed with the opportunity to meet ever changing challenges and to attempt to solve a myriad of problems. These opportunities have been rewarding and absorbing. I consider judicial work to be a great privilege.*

WEISBIN, CHARLES RICHARD, nuclear engineer; b. Bklyn., Jan. 4, 1944; s. Alma (Schwartz) Lovitt; m. Alison Norma Weisbin, June 20, 1964; children: Daniel Mark, Amy Gayle. MS in Nuclear Engring., Columbia U., 1965, DSc in Nuclear Engring., 1969. Group leader Oak Ridge (Tenn.) Nat. Lab., 1977-80, section head, 1980-89, dir. Ctr. for Engring. Systems Advanced Rsch., 1982-89, dir. robotics and intelligence systems, 1986-89; mgr. telerobotics tech. Jet Propulsion Lab., Pasadena, Calif., 1991-92, mgr. robotic systems and advanced computer tech. sect., 1989-93; mgr. rover and telerobotic tech., 1993-95; Mars program technologist Jet Propulsion Lab., Pasadena, Calif., 1994—, mgr. robotics and Mars exploration tech., 1995—; mem. joint tech. panel on robotics DOD Joint Dirs. Labs., 1986-89; assoc. prof. computer sci. U. Tenn., Knoxville, 1984-89; program chmn. 2d Internat. Conf. on Artificial Intelligence, IEEE Computer Soc., 1985; co-chmn. U.S. NASA Telerobotics Working Group, robotics and telepresence Space Tech. Interagency Group, 1992—. Author: Sensitivity and Uncertainty Analysis of Reactor Performance Parameters, 1982; mem. editorial bd. Applied Intelligence, 1990-95; contbr. articles to profl. jours. Recipient NASA Exceptional Svc. medal, 1993. Mem. IEEE (Cert. Appreciation 1987), Am. Nuclear Soc. (program chmn. 1977-79), Robotics and Automation Soc., Sigma Chi, Tau Beta Pi. Republican. Jewish. Achievements include initiation of robotics and intelligent systems at Oak Ridge; rsch. on sensitivity analysis, non-destructive assay of spent nuclear fuel, supervised inspection, and emergency response robotics. Home: 775 Starlight Heights Dr La Canada Flintridge CA 91011-1854 Office: Jet Propulsion Lab 4800 Oak Grove Dr Pasadena CA 91109-8001

WEISBROD, CARL BARRY, lawyer, public official; b. N.Y.C., Oct. 5, 1944; s. Walter and Hilda (Pelzer) W.; m. Jody Adams, Jan. 21, 1979; 1 child, William. BS, Cornell U., 1965; JD, NYU, 1968. Bar: N.Y., 1968; U.S. Dist. Ct. (so. dist.) N.Y., 1969. Asst. commr. N.Y.C. Housing Dept., 1970-72; counsel, chief exec. officer Wildcat Svc. Corp., N.Y.C., 1972-77; gen. counsel Manpower Demonstration Rsch. Corp., N.Y.C., 1977-78; dir. Mayor's Office of Midtown Enforcement, N.Y.C., 1978-84; exec. dir. City Vol. Corps, N.Y.C., 1984-86, N.Y.C. Planning Commn., 1986-87; pres. 42d St. Devel. Project, N.Y.C., 1987-90; pres., chief exec. officer N.Y.C. Econ. Devel. Corp., 1990-94; pres. Alliance for Downtown N.Y., 1995—; chmn. N.Y.C. Loft Bd., 1982-84. Contbr. articles to profl. jours. Trustee The Ford Found., 1996; chmn. Nat. Income Realty Trust, 1995—. Office: Alliance for Downtown NY 120 Broadway New York NY 10271-0002

WEISBURD, STEVEN I., lawyer; b. Bklyn., Sept. 18, 1949; s. Walter Bennett Weisburd and Sandra (Goldstein) Schmidt; m. Irene Soohoo-Weisburd; children: Bryan Joshua, Amy Rebecca, Daniel Timothy. BSEE, U. Hartford, 1971; JD, Temple U., 1974. Bar: Pa. 1974, N.Y. 1977. Assoc. Seidel, Gonda & Goldhammer, Phila., 1974-76; assoc. Ostrolenk, Faber, Gerb & Soffen, N.Y.C., 1976-79, ptnr., 1980—. Mem. ABA, N.J. Patent Law Assn., N.Y. Patent, Trademark, and Copyright Law Assn., Inc. Home: 315 W 70th St New York NY 10023-3504

WEISBURGER, ELIZABETH KREISER, retired chemist, editor; b. Greenlane, Pa., Apr. 9, 1924; d. Raymond Samuel and Amy Elizabeth (Snavely) Kreiser; m. John H. Weisburger, Apr. 7, 1947 (div. May 1974); children: William Raymond, Diane Susan, Andrew John. BS, Lebanon Valley Coll., Annville, Pa., 1944, DSc (hon.), 1989; PhD, U. Cin., 1947, DSc (hon.), 1981. Rsch. assoc. U. Cin., 1947-49; col. USPHS, 1951-89; postdoctoral fellow Nat. Cancer Inst., Bethesda, Md., 1949-51, chemist, 1951-73, chief carcinogen metabolism and toxicology br., 1972-75, chief Lab. Carcinogen Metabolism, 1975-81, asst. dir. chem. carcinogenesis, 1981-89, ret.; cons. in field; lectr. Found. for Advanced Edn. in Scis., Bethesda, 1980-95; adj. prof. Am. U., Washington, 1982—. Asst. editor-in-chief Jour. Nat. Cancer Inst., 1971-87; mem. editl. adv. bd. Environ. Health Perspectives, 1993-96; mem. editl. bd. Chem. Health and Safety, 1994—, Jour. Applied Toxicology, 1996—; contbr. articles to profl. jours. Trustee Lebanon Valley Coll., 1970—, pres. bd. trustees, 1985-89. Recipient Meritorious Svc. medal USPHS, 1973, Disting. Svc. medal, 1985; Hillebrand prize Chem. Soc. Washington, 1981. Fellow AAAS (nominating com. 1978-81); mem. Am. Chem. Soc. (Garvan medal 1981), Am. Assn. Cancer Research, Soc. Toxicology, Am. Soc. Biochem. and Molecular Biology, Royal Soc. Chemistry, Am. Conf. Govtl. Indsl. Hygienists (Herbert Stokinger award 1996), Grad. Women in Sci. (hon.), Iota Sigma Pi (hon.). Lutheran.

WEISBURGER, JOHN HANS, medical researcher; b. Stuttgart, Germany, Sept. 15, 1921; came to U.S., 1943, naturalized, 1944; s. William and Selma (Barth) W.; children: William, Diane, Andrew. AB, U. Cin., 1947, MS, 1948, PhD, 1949; MD (hon.), U. Umeå, Sweden, 1980. Mem. staff Nat. Cancer Inst., NIH, Bethesda, Md., 1950-61, head carcinogen screening sect., 1961-72; dir. bioassay segment, Carcinogenesis Programs Nat. Cancer Inst., Bethesda, Md., 1971-72; v.p. rsch. Am. Health Found., Valhalla, N.Y., 1972-87; dir. Naylor Dana Inst. for Disease Prevention, Valhalla, 1972-87, dir. emeritus, sr. mem., 1987—; rsch. prof. pathology N.Y. Med. Coll., Valhalla, 1974—; pres. Weisburger Assocs., North White Plains, N.Y., 1987—; mem. biochemistry and nutrition study sect. NIH, 1957-58; mem. interdepartmental panel on carcinogens FDA, USDA, USPHS, 1962-71; chmn. subcom. Nat. Cancer Program Strategic Plan, 1971-74; chmn. carcinogenesis subcom. Nat. Large Bowel Cancer Project, 1972-75; mem. expert panel on nitrites and nitrosamines USDA, 1973-77; chmn. Workshop Colo-rectal Cancer, Unio Internat. Contra Cancrum, Geneva, 1975; mem. Nat. Cancer Inst. Clearinghouse on Environ. Carcinogens, 1976-78; co-chmn. organizing com. U.S.-Japan Coop. Workshop on GI Tract Cancer, 1979, Workshop on Dietary Fats and Fiber in Human Cancer, 1986; chmn. symposium on large bowel cancer 7th congress OMGE, 1982; mem. program com. Internat. Congress of Toxicology III, 1982-83; bd. dirs. Westchester div. Am. Cancer Soc., 1983-89; mem. pancreas cancer working group Nat. Cancer Inst., 1985-86; chmn. sci. rev. panel N.J. State Commn. Cancer Rsch., 1988-90; chmn. nutrition and cancer sect. 15th meeting Unio Internt. Contra Cancrum, Hamburg, Germany, 1990; chmn. internat. group Belgian Soc. Psychosocial Aspects of Cancer, Brussels, 1990; internat. lectr. on nutrition and cancer prevention, S.E. Asia, 1991; co-chmn. internat. symposium on health effects of tea, N.Y., 1991; chmn. nutrition and cancer sect. 3d anticarcinogenesis and antimutagenesis conf., Italy, 1991; chmn. study sect. NIH-Nat. Cancer Inst., Bethesda, Md., 1991; co-chmn. mechanisms nutrition cancer European Sch. Oncology, Venice, Italy, 1992; rsch. fellow Japanese Found. for Promotion of Cancer Rsch. Nat. Cancer Ctr. Rsch. Inst, Tokyo, 1992; advisor com. rev. RDA Food and Nutrition Bd. NAS, 1993; lectr. 2d conf. Internat. Fedn.

Socs. Toxicologic Pathol., Tours, France, 3d Internat. Symposium Green Tea, Seoul, Korea, 6th Internat. Conf. Carcinogenic Mutagenic N-Aryl Compounds, Internat. Conf. Food Factors, Hamamatsu, Japan, 4th Internat. Yakult Intestinal Flora Symposium, Tokyo, 1995; chmn. workshop tea and health 2d Internat. Congress, Food and Cancer, Ede, The Netherlands, 1996; internat. orgn. com. & lectr. 5th Internat. Conf. Mech. Antimutag. Anticarc, Okayama, Japan, 1996; chmn. Internat. Conf. Health Effects Tomatoes Lycopene, N.Y., 1997; vis. lectr. U. Pretoria, South Africa, 1997; lectr. Internat. Conf. Nutritional Cancer, Irvine, Calif., 1997, Internat. Seminar Tea and Health, Colombo, Sri Lanka, 1997. Assoc. editor Jour. Nat. Cancer Inst., 1960-62, Xenobiotica, 1971—, Archives of Toxicology, 1977-87, Jour. Am. Coll. Toxicology, 1982—, Preventive Medicine, 1988—; mem. internat. editl. adv. bd. Food and Chem. Toxicology, 1967—; assoc. editor Cancer Rsch., 1969-80, mem. cover editl. bd., 1987—; mem. editl. bd. Chemico-Biol. Interactions, 1969-88, Carcinogenesis, 1979-87, Inst. Sci. Info. Atlas of Sci., 1987-89, Cancer Epidemiology Biomarkers Prevention, 1991—, Cancer Detection Prevention, 1994—; mem. guest editl. bd. Japanese Jour. Cancer Rsch., 1987—. With AUS, 1944-46; col. USPHS, 1950-72. Decorated D.S.M., 1964; recipient Meritorious Svc. medal USPHS HEW, 1970, Outstanding Service award Westchester div. Am. Cancer Soc., 1984, Meyer and Anna Prentis award Mich. Cancer Ctr., 1987; named one of 1000 most cited scientists, ISI List, 1981. Leadership plaque N.J. State Commn. Cancer Rsch., 1990. Fellow N.Y. Acad. Scis., Am. Coll. Nutrition; mem. Am. Assn. Cancer Rsch. (rep. to European Assn. Cancer Rsch. 1985-89), Am. Chem. Soc. (com. environ. improvement 1992-94, chmn. lectr. chemistry and health 31st Middle Atlantic regional meeting 1997), Am. Gastroent. Assn., Am. Conf. Govt. Indsl. Hygienists, Am. Soc. Biochem. Molecular Biologists, Am. Soc. Preventive Oncology (founding mem., bd. dirs. 1983-90, Disting. Svc. award 1990), Biochem. Soc. (London, emeritus), Environ. Mutagen Soc., European Assn. Cancer Rsch. (coun. 1985-90), Japan Cancer Assn. (hon. life), Soc. Exptl. Biol. Medicine, Soc. Toxicology (chmn. bd. publs. 1968-71, councilor 1972-74, amb. toxicology Mid-Atlantic divsn. 1990, hon. mem. 1995, Award of Merit 1981), Westchester Chem. Soc. (Disting. Scientist 1996), Sigma Xi, Alpha Chi Sigma (pres. Washington profl. chpt. 1967-68), Phi Lambda Upsilon. Achievements include research and over 500 publs. on lifestyle and chronic disease prevention, relevant mechanisms, and medical care cost reduction. Home: 4 Whitewood Rd White Plains NY 10603-1137 Office: Am Health Found Naylor Dana Inst Valhalla NY 10595-1599 *In my lifetime a revolutionary change occurred in our knowledge of the causes and the mechanisms involved in the major premature killing diseases—heart disease, hypertension, stroke, many forms of cancer. These key advances stemmed from the partnership between the federal government, public-supported societies and academic institutions that encourage health research. The impact of these diseases can be reduced in virtually all countries of the world provided their political bodies can agree that peaceful endeavors and cooperation in fostering better health for their people can be made a high priority goal. Medical science now can implement successful prevention efforts. I am glad I have lived through this period and have played a role in this development.*

WEISE, CHARLES MARTIN, zoology educator; b. Bridgeville, Pa., July 8, 1926; s. Louis August and Alice (Martin) W.; m. Joan C. Spencer, July 18, 1951; children—Patricia, Carla, Christopher, Charles, Robert. B.S., Ohio U., 1950; M.S., U. Ill., 1951; Ph.D., 1956. Asst. prof. biology Fisk U., Nashville, 1953-56; asst. prof. zoology U. Wis., Milw., 1956-60, assoc. prof., 1960-66, prof., 1966-95, prof emeritus, 1995. Served with USMCR, 1945-46. Mem. Am., Brit. ornithologists unions, Wis. Soc. Ornithology, Am. Soc. Zoologists, Phi Beta Kappa. Research physiology of bird migration, population ecology of vertebrates. Home: 2314 E Stratford Ct Milwaukee WI 53211-2630 Office: U Wis-Milw Dept Biol Sci Milwaukee WI 53201

WEISE, GEORGE JAMES, commissioner; b. Scranton, Pa., Mar. 3, 1949; s. George Franklin and Rita Marie W.; m. Therese Lee Palmer, Oct. 20, 1984; children: Michelle Lyddane, Melissa Anne. BS, U. Md., 1971, JD with honors, 1975; MBA with honors, George Washington U., 1983. Bar: Md. 1975, Ct. Internat. Trade 1984. Import specialist U.S. Customs Svc., Dept. Treasury, Washington, 1972-75, commr., 1993—; atty. U.S. Internat. Trade Commn., Washington, 1975-83, IBM Corp., Armonk, N.Y., 1983-84; profl. staff mem. Subcom. on Trade, Ho. of Reps. Ways and Means Com., Washington, 1984-89, staff dir., 1989-93. Office: US Customs Svc Dept Treasury 1301 Constitution Ave NW Washington DC 20229-0001

WEISENBURGER, RANDALL, company executive; b. 1958. With Coopers & Lybrand, 1980-85, First Boston Corp., 1987-88; mng. dir. Wasserstein Perella & Co., 1988—; CEO Wickes Mfg. Co., Inc., Southfield, Mich., 1990-93; co-chmn. Collins & Aikman; vice-chmn. Maybelline, Inc.; chmn. Yardley of London; bd. dirs. Alliance Entertainment Corp. Office: Wasserstein Perella & Co 31 W 52nd St New York NY 10019-6118

WEISER, MARK DAVID, computer scientist, researcher; b. Chgo., July 23, 1952; s. David Warren and Audra Laverne (Hunsaker) W.; m. Victoria Ann Reich, Dec. 16, 1976; children: Nicole Reich-Weiser, Corinne Reich-Weiser. Student, New Coll., Sarasota, Fla., 1969-71; MS, U. Mich., 1976, PhD, 1979. V.p. Cerberus Video, Ann Arbor, Mich., 1972-75; programmer Omnitext, Ann Arbor, Mich., 1971-76; project leader MIS, Internat., Romulus, Mich., 1975-76; from asst. prof. to assoc. prof. computer sci. U. Md., College Park, 1979-87; prin. scientist Xerox Palo Alto (Calif.) Rsch. Ctr., 1987—, lab. mgr., 1988—, chief technologist, 1996—; founder Cerberus Video, Ann Arbor, 1972-75. Contbr. over 70 articles to profl. jours. Mem. IEEE, AAAS, Assn. for Computing Machinery. Avocations: existential philosophy, Go, drummer for rock band Severe Tire Damage. Office: Xerox PARC Office of Chief Technol 3333 Coyote Hill Rd Palo Alto CA 94304-1314

WEISER, PAUL DAVID, manufacturing company executive; b. N.Y.C., May 30, 1936; s. Irving Julius and Rose (Peckerman) W.; m. Paula Lee Block, June 19, 1960; children: Amy Helen, Deborah Susan. B.S. in Metallurgy, M.I.T., 1959; LL.B. (editor law rev.), U. Calif., Berkeley, 1963. Bar: Calif. 1963. Assoc. firm Mitchell, Silberberg & Knupp, Los Angeles, 1963-68; with Dataproducts Corp., Simi Valley, Calif., 1968—; sec., gen. counsel Dataproducts Corp., 1968—, sr. v.p., 1980—; chmn. adv. com. shareholder communications SEC, 1981. Contbr. articles legal publns. Served with USAR, 1959-60. Mem. Am. Bar Assn., Am. Soc. Corp. Secs. Jewish. Office: 1757 Tapo Canyon Rd Simi Valley CA 93063-3391

WEISER, RALPH RAPHAEL, business executive; b. N.Y.C., May 25, 1925; children: Jane, Jeffrey. BA, NYU, 1947; JSD, Harvard U., 1950. Bar: N.Y. 1950. Ptnr. Lotterman & Weiser, Esq., N.Y.C., 1955-64; pres. Dragor Shipping Inc., N.Y.C., 1964-65; chmn. Nat. Equipment Rental, N.Y.C., 1965-67; exec. v.p. Am. Export Industries, N.Y.C., 1967-69; pvt. practice investment, 1970-84; chmn. World Fuel Svcs. Corp., Miami, Fla., 1984—. Sgt. USAAF, 1943-45, PTO. Office: World Fuel Svcs Corp 700 S Royal Poinciana Blvd Miami FL 33166-6600

WEISER, SHERWOOD MANUEL, hotel and corporation executive, lawyer; b. Cleve., Mar. 9, 1931; s. Aaron A. and Helen (Scheiner) W.; m. Judith A. Zirkin, July 31, 1955; children: Douglas J., Warren P., Bradley A. BS, Ohio State U., 1952; LLB, Case Western Res. U., 1955. Bar: Ohio 1955. Ptnr. Weiser & Weiser, Attys., Cleve., 1955-65, Weiser & Lefton, Attys., Cleve., 1965-69; chmn., chief exec. officer TCC, Miami, Fla., 1970—; bd. dirs. United Nat. Bank, Miami, Carnival Cruise Lines, Miami. Trustee Fla. Internat. U. Found., Miami, 1984-94, U. Miami, 1988—, New World Symphony, Miami, 1987—; trustee, chmn. bd. Ransom-Everglades Sch., Miami, 1974-84; co-chmn. bd. advisors Coconut Grove Playhouse, 1986—. Mem. Am. Hotel and Motel Assn., Cleve. Bar Assn., Soc. of Benchers, Order of Coif. Jewish. Avocations: tennis, sailing, art. Office: CHC International Inc 3250 Mary St Miami FL 33133-5232

WEISFELDT, MYRON LEE, physician, educator; b. Milw., Apr. 25, 1940; s. Simon Charles and Sophia (Price) W.; m. Linda Nan Zaremski, Dec. 29, 1963; children—Ellyn Joy, Lisa Janel, Sara Michelle. Student, Northwester U., 1958-60; BA, Johns Hopkins U., 1962, MD, 1965. Intern and resident Columbia-Presbyn. Med. Ctr., N.Y.C., 1965-67; fellow in cardiology Mass. Gen. Hosp., Boston, 1970-72; asst. prof. medicine Johns Hopkins U., Balt., 1972-78, prof. medicine, 1978-91, Robert L. Levy prof. cardiology, 1979-91; Samuel Bard prof. medicine, chair dept. Columbia-Presbyn. Med. Ctr., N.Y.C., 1991—; dir. cardiology Johns Hopkins Med. Inst., Balt., 1975-91, Peter Belfer Lab. for Johns Hopkins, Ischemic Heart Disease Spl. Ctr. Rsch., 1977-91; nat. pres. Am. Heart Assn., 1989-90; cardiology adv. com. Nat. Heart, Lung and Blood Inst., 1986-90, chmn., 1988-90. Editor: The Aging Heart, 1980; editorial bd. Jour. Clin. Investigation, 1984-88, Circulation, 1980-86, 88—, Jour. Am. Coll. Cardiology, 1987-93, Jour. Molecular and Cellular Cardiology, 1975-80, 86-89, Circulation Rsch., 1988-94. Served with USPHS, 1967-69. NIH grantee, 1977-91. Fellow AAAS, ACP, Am. Coll. Cardiology; mem. Assn. Univ. Cardiologists, Am. Soc. Clin. Investigation, Assn. Am. Physicians, Assn. Prof. Medicine, Inst. of Medicine, Phi Beta Kappa, Alpha Omega Alpha, Interurban Clin. Club. Jewish. Home: 47 Havermeyer Rd Irvington NY 10533-2642 Office: Columbia Presbyn Med Ctr 630 W 168th St New York NY 10032-3702

WEISGALL, HUGO DAVID, composer, conductor; b. Ivancice, Czechoslovakia, Oct. 13, 1912; came to U.S., 1920, naturalized, 1926; s. Adolph Joseph and Aranka (Stricker) W.; m. Nathalie Shulman, Dec. 28, 1942; children: Deborah, Jonathan. Student, Johns Hopkins, 1929-31, Ph.D., 1940; musical edn., Peabody Conservatory, Baltimore, 1927-30, Curtis Inst., Phila., 1936-39; studied composition with, Roger Sessions. Instr. composition Cummington Sch. Arts, 1948-51; instr. Julliard Sch. Music Arts, 1957-69; Disting. prof. composition CUNY, 1960-83; disting. vis. prof. Penn State U., 1959-60; disting. prof. Peabody Inst., Balt., 1974-75; chmn. faculty Sem. Coll. of Jewish Music, Jewish Theol. Sem. of Am.; pres. Am. Music Ctr., 1964-73; assoc. Lincoln Ctr. Fund, 1965-68; dir. Hilltop Mus. Co., Balt., 1951-54. Condr. Har Sinai Temple Choir, 1931-42, Y-Alliance Orch., 1935-42, Balt. String Symphony, 1936-38, Md. N.Y.A. Orch., 1940-41; guest condr. London Symphony, London Philharmonic, BBC Symphony orchs., Orchestre de la Chapelle Musicale de la Reine Elizabeth, Belgium, Radio National Belge, dir. Balt. Inst. Mus. Arts, 1949, composer in residence Am. Acad. in Rome, 1966-67, 84; composer Songs, 1929, Quest; ballet, 1937, One Thing Is Certain, ballet, 1939, Hymn for chorus and orch, 1941; Overture in F, 1942, Soldier Songs, 1944-45, Outpost, 1947; opera The Tenor, 1949-50, The Stronger, 1952, Three Symphonic Songs for high voice and orch, 1952, Six Characters in Search of an Author, 1956, Purgatory, 1958, Athaliah, 1963, Nine Rivers from Jordan, 1968; song cycle Fancies and Inventions, 1970, Translations, 1971, End of Summer, 1974; cantata for soprano, tenor, chorus and orch. Song of Celebration, 1976; (opera) Jenny or the Hundred Nights, 1976, The Golden Peacock, 1976; song cycle Liebeslieder, 1979; opera The Gardens of Adonis, 1981, Piano Sonata, 1982, Prospect, 1983, 4 Birthday Cards, 1983, Lyrical Interval, song cycle for low voice and piano, 1984, Tekiatot: Rituals for Rosh Hashannah for orch., 1985, Tangents, 4 episodes for flute and marimba, 1985, Arioso and Burlesca for cello and piano, 1983, Loves Wounded 2 songs for baritone and orch., 1986, opera Will You Marry Me?, 1987, opera Esther, 1992, Evening Liturgies, 1994; Ditson Opera commn., Columbia, 1952, Koussevitzky commn., 1961, Psalm of the Distant Dove canticle for mezzo soprano and piano, 1992, Evening Liturgies for baritone, chorus and organ, 1995. Enlisted as pvt. AUS, 1942; asst. mil. attache to govts. in exile, London, later to Czechoslovakia cultural attache Am. embassy 1946-47, Prague. Awarded Bearns prize Columbia, 1931, William Schuman award, 1994; traveling fellow Curtis Inst., 1938; Ditson fellow Columbia, 1944; grantee Nat. Inst. Arts and Letters, 1952; Guggenheim fellow, 1955-56, 61-62, 66-67. Mem. Nat. Inst. Arts and Letters, Am. Acad.-Inst. Arts and Letters (pres. 1990-93), Phi Beta Kappa. Home: 81 Maple Dr Great Neck NY 11021-1909

WEISGERBER, DAVID WENDELIN, editor, chemist; b. Delphos, Ohio, May 20, 1938; s. Hubert Louis and Catherine Margaret (Laudick) W.; m. Carole Ann Friemoth, Oct. 23, 1965; children: Jason, Erik. B.S., Bowling Green State U., 1960; Ph.D., U. Ill., 1965. Research chemist E.I. duPont de Nemours & Co., Inc., Deepwater, N.J., 1964-69; indexer Chem. Abstracts Service, Columbus, Ohio, 1969-73, asst. to editor, 1973-77, mgr. chem. substance handling, 1977-79, dir. editorial ops., 1979-82, editor, 1982—. Mem. Am. Chem. Soc., N.Y. Acad. Sci., Am. Soc. Info. Sci. Roman Catholic. Home: 6178 Middlebury Dr E Worthington OH 43085-3375 Office: PO Box 3012 Columbus OH 43210-0012

WEISGERBER, JOHN SYLVESTER, provincial legislator; b. Barrhead, Alta., Can., June 12, 1940; s. Sylvester and Eva (Kilshaw) Harrison; m. Judith Muriel Janke, June 30, 1961; children: Joanne, Pamela. BBA, N. Alta. Inst. Tech., 1962. Owner Carland Ltd., 1975-81; econ. devel. commr. Peace River-Liard Regional Dist., Dawson Creek, 1982-84; sales mgr. Timberline Pontiac Buick GMC Ltd., Dawson Creek, 1984-86; mem. legis. assembly Govt. of B.C. (Can.), Victoria, 1986—, parliamentary sec. to atty. gen., 1987-88, min. of state for Nechako and N.E., 1988-89, min. native affairs, 1989—; chmn. Cabinet Com. on Native Affairs, Victoria, 1988-90; mem. Cabinet Com. on Sustainable Devel., Victoria, 1988-90; mem. Select Standing Com. of Forests and Lands, Victoria, 1988-90; mem. Select Standing Com. on Agr. and Fisheries, Victoria, 1988-90; interim leader B.C. Social Credit Party, 1992-93; leader Reform Party of B.C., 1995. Bd. dirs., pres. Dawson Creek and Dist. Fall Fair, 1980-86. Mem. Rotary (past pres.), Mile O Riding Club (bd. dirs., pres. 1976-81). Avocations: hunting, fishing, downhill skiing. Office: Parliament Bldgs, Rm 237, Victoria, BC Canada V8V 1X4

WEISINGER, RONALD JAY, economic development consultant, real estate developer; b. Youngstown, Ohio, Feb. 13, 1946; s. David S. and Sterna (Woolf) W.; married; children: Morgan, Megan. BS, Carroll Coll., 1968; MBA, U. Palm Beach, 1970. Dir. cash dept. Nat. United Jewish Appeal, 1975-77; exec. dir. Jewish Fedn. Pinellas County, Inc., Fla., 1978-80; prin. VIP Mortgage Trust Co., VIP Mgmt. and Realty, Inc., West Palm Beach, 1984-91; developer, builder affordable housing, 1991—; econ. devel. in Eastern Europe, former countries of Soviet Union and Mid. East. Jewish.

WEISKITTEL, RALPH JOSEPH, real estate executive; b. Covington, Ky., Jan. 1, 1924; s. Nelson I. and Hilda (Nieman) W.; m. Audrey Bushelman, June 19, 1948; children—Thomas, Carol Anne, Barbara Jane. Eve. student, Xavier U., Cin., 1946-47. Mem. staff Cin. Enquirer, 1942-43, 45—, home sect. editor, 1958-63, bus. editor, 1963-77; v.p. corp. markets Koetzle Corp. (Realtors), 1977-79; v.p. Devitt and Assocs. (Realtors), 1979-90; v.p. sales and mktg. Toebben Cos., 1990-91; sr. v.p. The Chelsea-Moore Co., 1991-94; v.p. sales Cline Realtors, 1994—; dir. New Comty. Developers, Inc. Mem. city council, Ft. Wright, Ky., 1960-68; mem. St. Agnes Parish Council, 1974-77; mem. bishop's adv. council Diocese of Covington. Served with AUS, 1943-46. Mem. Nat. Assn. Real Estate Editors, Soc. Am. Bus. Writers. Club: Cin. Athletic. Home: 1571 St Anthony Dr Covington KY 41011-3752 Office: The Federated Bldg 7 W 7th St Ste 1900 Cincinnati OH 45202-2417

WEISL, EDWIN LOUIS, JR., foundation executive, lawyer; b. N.Y.C., Oct. 17, 1929; s. Edwin L. and Alice (Todriff) W.; m. Barbara Butler, June 12, 1974; 1 child, by previous marriage, Angela Jane. A.B., Yale, 1951; LL.B., Columbia, 1956. Bar: N.Y. 1956, D.C. 1968. Assoc. Simpson Thacher & Bartlett, N.Y.C., 1956-64; mem. firm Simpson Thacher & Bartlett, 1964-65, 69-73; adminstr. parks, recreation and cultural affairs, commr. parks City of N.Y., 1973-75; asst. atty. gen. of U.S. in charge of land and natural resources division, 1965-67, asst. atty. gen. in charge civil div., 1967-69; asst. spl. counsel, preparedness investigating com. U.S. Senate, 1957-58; former pres. Internat. Found. for Art Research. Dir. N.Y. State Dem. campaign, 1964; mem. The 1001, World Wildlife Fund; mem. vis. com. dept. European paintings Met. Mus. Art; bd. dirs. Robert Lehman Found.; mem. corp. Presbyn. Hosp., N.Y.C.; bd. dirs. Old Master Exhbn. Soc. N.Y.; mem. Villa I Tatti Coun, Harvard Ctr. for Renaissance Studies. Lt. U.S. Navy, 1951-53. Mem. Explorers Club, Warrenton Hunt Club, Century Assn. Office: 50 E 77th St New York NY 10021-1836

WEISMAN, GARY ANDREW, biochemist; b. Bklyn., June 18, 1951; s. Joseph Herman and Elaine (Melman) W.; m. Sandra Kay Hille, Aug. 4, 1979; children: Laura Joanne, Pamela Michelle, Veronica Evelyn. BS, Polytechnic U., 1972; postgrad., U. Bordeaux, France, 1972-74; PhD, U. Nebr., 1980. Postdoctoral rsch. assoc. Cornell U., N.Y.C., 1980-85; asst. prof. U. Mo., Columbia, 1985-92, assoc. prof., 1992—; spl. reviewer NIH; reviewer NSF, Jour. Membrane Biology and Eur. Jour. Cancer, Am. Jour. Physiology. Contbr. articles to profl. jours. Grantee USDA, 1987—, NIH, 1988—, CF Found., 1994—, Am. Diabetes, 1995—. Mem. AAAS, Am. Chem. Soc., Am. Soc. Biochem. and Molecular Biology, Am. Diabetes Assn., Am. Heart Assn., N.Y. Acad. Scis. Home: 1804 University Ave Columbia MO 65201-6004 Office: U Mo Dept Biochemistry M121 Med Scis Bldg Columbia MO 65212

WEISMAN, HARLAN FREDERICK, pharmaceutical company executive; b. Bklyn., July 17, 1952; s. Herman Muni and Margaret Madeline (Cohen) W.; m. Sally Harowitz, June 7, 1981; children: Sara Rachel, Daniel Michael. BA, U. Md., 1975, MD, 1979. Cert. Nat. Bd. Med. Examiners, Am. Bd. Internal Medicine-Cardiovascular Disease. Resident internal medicine Mt. Sinai Hosp., N.Y.C., 1979-82; fellow cardiology Johns Hopkins Hosp., Balt., 1982-84; asst. in medicine Johns Hopkins Sch. Medicine, Balt., 1984-85, asst. prof. medicine, 1985-90; guest researcher Gerontology Rsch. Ctr., NIH, Balt., 1985-90; dir. cardiology Centocor, Inc., Malvern, Pa., 1990-93, sr. dir. cardiology, 1993-94, v.p. cardiology and immunology clin. rsch., 1994-95, v.p. clin. rsch. and biomed. ops., 1996—; cons. cardiologist Johns Hopkins Hosp., Balt., 1985-90. Guest reviewer Circulation, 1983—, Jour. of the Am. Coll. Cardiology, 1988—; contbr. articles to profl. jours. Samuel J. Katcef Meml. fellow Am. Heart Assn., 1989-90. Fellow Am. Coll. Cardiology, Am. Coll. Chest Physicians, Coun. on Clin. Cardiology Am. Heart Assn.; mem. Internat. Soc. for Thrombosis and Hemostasis, Internat. Soc. for Heart Rsch., Am. Fedn. for Clin. Rsch., Phi Beta Kappa, Alpha Omega Alpha. Home: 759 Applegate Ln Rosemont PA 19010 Office: Centocor Inc 200 Great Valley Pky Malvern PA 19355-1307

WEISMAN, IRVING, social worker, educator; b. N.Y.C., May 6, 1918; s. Max and Sadie (Berkowitz) W.; m. Cyrille Gold, May 1, 1941; children: Seth, Adam. B.S., CCNY, 1939; M.S., U. Buffalo, 1942; Ed.D., Columbia U., 1962. Cert. social worker N.Y. State. Caseworker Nat. Refugee Service, N.Y.C., 1941; warden's asst. Fed. Detention Hdqrs., Bur. Prisons, Dept. Justice, N.Y.C., 1942-43; psychiat. social worker to chief social worker VA, Camden and Union City, N.J., 1943-46, psychiatric social worker, 1946-47, chief social worker, 1947-49; case supr. Altro Health and Rehab. Service, N.Y., 1949-50; field instr., lectr. Columbia U. Sch. Social Work, 1950-57, assoc. prof., 1957-62, prof., 1962-84, prof. emeritus, 1984, adj. prof., 1984, acting dean, 1964-65; assoc. dean Hunter Coll. Sch. Social Work, 1967-69; exec. officer doctoral program social work Grad. Ctr. CUNY, 1975-78; clin. practice William Alanson White Inst., 1976-79; vis. prof. Sch. Social Work, Barry U., 1984-85; adj. prof. Sch. Social Work, San Diego State U., 1988—; UN adv. on social welfare to Ceylon Sri Lanka, 1963-64; sr. Simon research fellow U. Manchester (Eng.), 1970-71; cons. U.S. Office Juvenile Delinquency and Youth Devel., U.S. Children's Bur., NIMH, NIDA, HEW, N.Y.C. Dept. Personnel, Westchester County (N.Y.) Dept. Mental Health, Community Service Soc., Council Social Work Edn., Moblzn. for Youth, N.Y.C., Universidad Católica Madre y Maestra, Santo Domingo, Dominican Republic, 1983-84, United Jewish Appeal-Fedn. Jewish Philanthropies of N.Y.C., 1986-87, U. Puertorriqueña de los Antillas Aguadilla, P.R., 1993; condr. continuing edn. workshops, various univs. Contbr. articles to profl. jours., also monographs. Capt. U.S. Army Air Corps., 1943-46. HEW and HHS grantee, 1961-62, 64-76, 77-81. Home: 4612 Monongahela St San Diego CA 92117-2415

WEISMAN, JOEL, nuclear engineering educator, engineering consultant; b. N.Y.C., July 15, 1928; s. Abraham and Ethel (Marcus) W.; m. Bernice Newman, Feb. 6, 1955; 1 child, Jay (dec.). B.Ch.E., CCNY, 1948; M.S., Columbia U., 1949; Ph.D., U. Pitts, 1968. Registered profl. engr., N.Y., Ohio. Plant engr. Etched Products, N.Y.C., 1950-51; from jr. engr. to assoc. engr. Brookhaven Nat. Lab., Upton, N.Y., 1951-54; from engr. to fellow engr. Westinghouse Nuclear Energy Systems, Pitts., 1954-59, from fellow engr. to mgr. thermal and hydraulic analysis, 1960-68; sr. engr. Nuclear Devel. Assocs., White Plains, N.Y., 1959-60; assoc. prof. nuclear engring. U. Cin., 1968-72, prof. nuclear engring., 1972-96, dir. nuclear engring. program, 1977-86, dir. lab. basic and applied nuclear research, 1984-94, prof. emeritus nuclear engring., 1996—. Co-author: Thermal Analysis of Pressurized Water Reactors, 1970, 2d edit., 1979, 3rd edit., 1996, Introduction to Optimization Theory, 1973, Modern Power Plant Engineering, 1985; editor: Elements of Nuclear Reactor Design, 1977, 2d edit., 1983; contbr. tech. articles to profl. jours.; patentee in field. Mem. Cin. Environ. Adv. Council, 1976-78; mem. Cin. Asian Art Soc., 1977—, v.p., 1980-82, pres., 1982-84; mem. exec. bd. Air Pollution League Greater Cin., 1980-90. Sr. NATO fellow, Winfrith Lab., U.K. Atomic Energy Authority, 1972; sr. fellow Argonne Nat. Lab., Ill., 1982; NSF research grantee, 1974-78, 82-85, 86-89; recipient Dean's award U. Cin. Coll. Engring., 1987. Fellow Am. Nuclear Soc. (v.p. Pitts. sect. 1957-58, mem. exec. com. thermal-hydraulics div. 1989-92); mem. Am. Inst. Chem. Engrs., Sigma Xi. Democrat. Jewish. Avocation: Japanese art. Home: 3419 Manor Hill Dr Cincinnati OH 45220-1522 Office: U Cin Dept Mech Ind & Nuclear Engring Cincinnati OH 45221

WEISMAN, JOHN, author; b. N.Y.C., Aug. 1, 1942; s. Abner I. Weisman and Syde (Lubowe) Kremer; m. Susan Lee Povemire, Feb. 12, 1983. AB, Bard Coll., 1964. Mng. editor Coast mag., Los Angeles, 1969-70; staff writer Rolling Stone, San Francisco, 1971, Detroit Free Press, 1971-73; assoc. editor TV Guide, Radnor, Pa., 1973-77; bur. chief TV Guide, Washington, 1977-89; sr. fellow Annenberg Washington program Northwestern U., Washington, 1989-91; bd. dirs. Va. Writing mag. Author: (nonfiction) Guerrilla Theatre, 1973, Shadow Warrior, 1989, Rogue Warrior, 1992 (#1 bestseller N.Y. Times Book Rev.), (novels) Evidence, 1980, Watchdogs, 1983, Blood Cries, 1987, Rogue Warrior II, Red Cell, 1994 (bestseller N.Y. Times), Green Team, 1995 (bestseller N.Y. Times), Task Force Blue, 1996 (bestseller N.Y. Times), (anthology) Unusual Suspects, 1996, Designation Gold, 1997 (bestseller N.Y. Times). Mem. Bard Coll. Alumni Assn. (bd. govs. 1975-81, pres. 1981-83). Club: Army and Navy (Washington). Home: PO Box 170 Bluemont VA 20135-0170 Address: Ground Zero PO Box 170 Bluemont VA 20135-0170

WEISMAN, LORENZO DAVID, investment banker; b. Guatemala, Apr. 22, 1945; came to U.S., 1957; s. Eduardo Tobias and Suzanne (Loeb) W.; m. Danielle Maysonnave, June 22, 1971; children—Melissa Anne, Alexia Maria, Thomas Alexander. B.A. in History and Lit. cum laude, Harvard U., 1966; postgrad., Conservatoire Nat. D'Art Dramatique, Paris, 1966-71; M.B.A. in Fin., Columbia U., 1973. V.p. Dillon, Read & Co., Inc., N.Y.C., 1977-80, sr. v.p., 1980-82; mng. dir. Dillon, Read & Co., Inc., London, 1982-84; pres., chief exec. officer Dillon Read Ltd., London, 1984-93; head Internat. Dillon Read & Co., N.Y.C., 1993—; bd. dirs. Sudimer Buy-Out Fund, Spain, Corporacion Borealis, Spain, France Capital Devel., France, Dillon, Read & Co., Inc., N.Y.C., Dillon, Read, Ltd., London; com. univ. resources Harvard U., 1991, mem. adv. com. David Rockefeller Ctr. for L.Am. Studies, 1995—; mem. internat. bd. overseers Columbia Bus. Sch., 1992; mem. bd. overseers Institut Français/Alliance Française, N.Y., 1995—. Trustee Institut Français/Alliance Française, N.Y.C., 1995. Mem. Harvard Club (N.Y.C.), Travelers Club (Paris), RAC Club (London).

WEISMANN, DONALD LEROY, art educator, artist, filmmaker, writer; b. Milw., Oct. 12, 1914; s. Friedrich Othello and Stela Priscilla (Custer) W.; m. M. Virginia Stant; children: Anne Wilder, Christopher Thomas. B.S., U. Wis., Milw., 1935; Ph.M., U. Wis., Madison, 1940; Ph.D., Ohio State U., 1950. Asst. prof. art Ill. State U., Normal, 1940-42, 47-48, Wayne U., Detroit, 1949-51; prof., head dept. art U. Ky., Lexington, 1951-54; prof., chmn. dept. art U. Tex., Austin, 1954-58, Univ. prof. arts, 1959-81, prof. emeritus, 1981—; cons. Ford Found., N.Y.C., 1958, 66, U.S. Nat. Com. UNESCO, 1953, Rockefeller Found., 1956, Nat. Council Arts., 1966-72; spl. cons. USIS, Forence, Italy, 1961-62. Author: Language and Visual Form, 1968, Visual Arts as Human Experience, 1970, Duncan Phyfe & Drum, 1984, Follow the Bus with the Greek License Plates, 1981, Frank Reaugh, Painter to the Longhorns, 1985, The Stuff of Stories, 1997; contbr. articles, poems, stories and revs. to profl. jours.; painter, collagist one-man shows, Cushman Gallery, Houston, Nye Gallery, Dallas, Petite Gallery, N.Y.C., Art Mus. U. N. Mex., group shows, Bocur Gallery, N.Y.C., Chgo. Art Inst., Dallas Mus. Fine Arts, Rockefeller Ctr., N.Y.C., Vanucci Gallery, Pistoia, Italy, Villa Monte Carlo Chapala, Jalisco, Mexico; film-maker numerous productions. Served to lt. (j.g.) USN, 1942-45, PTO. Recipient Letter of Commendation Pres. U.S., 1972; recipient Teaching awards U. Tex., 1963, 65, 70, 77, honor for book Some Folks Went West 12th Annual Writers Conf., Austin, 1960; grantee U. Tex. Research Inst., Italy, Eng., 1961-62, 71, Pub. Broadcast Corp., 1970, 72; named fine arts scholar Harvard U., 1941. Mem. Nat. Humanities Faculty. Home: 1108 Yaupon Valley Rd Austin TX 78746-4329 Office: Am Studies U Tex Austin TX 78712

WEISMANTEL, GREGORY NELSON, management consultant and software executive; b. Houston, Sept. 8, 1940; s. Leo Joseph and Ellen Elizabeth (Zudis) W.; m. Marilyn Ann Fanger, June 18, 1966; children: Guy Gregory, Christopher Gregory, Andrea Rose. BA in English, U. Notre Dame, 1962; MBA in Internat. Bus., Loyola U., Chgo., 1979. With mgmt. staff Gen. Foods Corp., White Plains, N.Y., 1966-80; pres., chief exec. officer Manor House Foods, Inc., Addison, Ill., 1980-82, Weismantel & Assocs., Downers Grove, Ill., 1982-84; v.p. perishable div. Profl. Marketers, Inc., Lombard, Ill., 1984-86; group v.p. sales and mktg. services, dir. corp. strategy Profl. Marketers, Inc., Lombard, 1986-87; v.p. mng. prin. CPG Industry, Louis A. Allen Assoc. Inc., Palo Alto, Calif., 1987-88; pres., chief exec. officer The Vista Group, St. Charles, Ill., 1989—; bd. dirs. Epicurean Foods, Ltd., Chgo.; pres., CEO The Vista Tech. Group, Ltd., The Vista Mgmt. Group. Chmn. fin. St. Edward's High Sch. Jubilee, Elgin, Ill., 1982-85; bd. dirs. Dist. 301 Sch. Bd., Burlington, Ill., 1980-84, St. Edward's Found., Elgin, 1982—. Capt. U.S. Army, 1962-66. Recipient ICP/Chgo. Software Assoc. Re-Engring. award, 1994-96; State of Ill. grantee, 1989, Build Ill. Investment Fund. Mem. Grocery Mfg. Sales Execs., Chgo. Software Assn., Chg. C. of C. (small bus. com.). Roman Catholic. Clubs: Merchandising Execs., Food Products, Am. Mktg. (Chgo.). *Success can only occur when a person realizes that life is not a rehearsal.*

WEISMILLER, DAVID R., library administrator; b. Victoria, B.C., Can., Feb. 12, 1943. BA, U. B.C., 1967; B Library Sci., U. Toronto, 1968, MLS, 1972; MPA, Queen's U., Kingtson, Ont., Can., 1986. Cataloguer, MAP libr., acquisitions libr. Trent U., Peterborough, Ont., 1968-74; asst. dir. libr. Scarborough (Ont.) Pub. Libr., 1974-77; cons. Waterloo-Brazil-CIDA Programme in Engring., Brazil, 1977-79; chief libr. Belleville (Ont.) Pub. Libr., 1979-85, Nepean (Ont.) Pub. Libr., 1985-88; dir. librs. Winnipeg (Man., Can.) Pub. Libr., 1988—. Mem. ALA, Inst. Pub. Adminstrn. Can., Can. Library Assn. Office: Winnipeg Pub Libr, 251 Donald St, Winnipeg, MB Canada R3C 3P5*

WEISNER, MAURICE FRANKLIN, former naval officer; b. Knoxville, Tenn., Nov. 20, 1917; s. Clinton Hall and Adra Inez (Ogg) W.; m. Norma Holland Smith, May 30, 1942; children: Maurice Hall, Franklin Lee, Stewart Holland. B.S., U.S. Naval Acad., 1941; aviation tng., 1943; grad., Nat. War Coll., 1959. Commd. ensign U.S. Navy, 1941, advanced through grades to adm., 1972; assigned U.S.S. Wasp, 1941-42; various aircraft squadrons in PTO, 1942-46, (U.S.S. Badoeng Strait), 1947-48; comdr. Patrol Squadron 46, 1949-51; assigned Office Chief Naval Operations, 1951-53; comdr. Fighter Squadron 193, 1954-55; assigned air striking forces study sect. Office Chief Naval Operations, 1955-58; comdr. Fighter Squadron 101, 1959-60, U.S.S. Guadalupe, 1960-61, U.S.S. Coral Sea, 1961-62; assigned Bur. Naval Personnel, 1962-64; dir. air weapons systems analysis staff Office Chief Naval Operations, 1964-65; comdr. Carrier Div. 1, 1965-67; dep. chief naval personnel, 1967-69; comdr. Attack Carrier Striking Force 7th Fleet, 1969-70, 7th Fleet, 1970-71; dep. chief naval operations (air warfare), 1971-72, vice chief of naval operations, 1972-73; comdr. in chief U.S. Pacific Fleet, 1973-76, Unified Pacific, 1976-79. Decorated Def. D.S.M., Navy D.S.M. with 4 gold stars, Army D.S.M., Air Force D.S.M.; Legion of Merit with gold star; D.F.C. with gold star; Air medal with 5 gold stars; Navy Commendation medal. Home: 351 Woodbine Dr Pensacola FL 32503-3202

WEISS, ALAN, musician, educator; b. Boston, July 9, 1954; s. Daniel and Riva (Adlerstein) W.; m. Ann Marie Rosandich, Oct. 11, 1986. MusB, Boston U., 1977, MusM, 1986. Prin. flutist Va. Symphony, Norfolk, 1977-78; sub-prin. flutist Iceland Nat. Symphony, Rekjavik, 1978-79; co-prin. flutist State Orch. of Mex., Toluca, 1981-82, Mexico City Philharm., 1982-84, Boston Classical Orch., 1988—; prin. flutist Orch. for the Art of Music, 1996—; prof. flute, chamber music Boston U., 1987-96; from flute faculty to dir. Tanglewood Inst. Boston U., Lenox, Mass., 1987-94; artistic, exec. dir. Manchester (N.H.) Cmty. Music Sch., 1996—; artistic dir. Manchester Chamber Players, 1996—, Greater Manchester Youth Symphony. Solo flutist (world premier performances and on Nat. Pub. Radio) Fall of the House of Usher, 1988, Orphee by Phillip Glass, 1993; recitalist Sta. WGBH-FM, 1988—; soloist Romanian Radio Orch., 1995; soundtract (PBS movie) Edgar Allan Poe, 1995. Trustee Boston Classical Orch., 1989-93, founder youth competition, 1990—; bd. dirs. Orch. for Art of Music. Mem. Boston Musician's Assn., Pi Kappa Lambda. Republican. Jewish. Avocations: reading, travel.

WEISS, ALLAN JOSEPH, transport company executive, lawyer; b. Boston, Nov. 1, 1932; s. Mark and Eve S. (Kane) W.; m. Sherrill Roecker, Feb. 18, 1973; children: Stephanie Eve, Mark Allan. B.S., U.S. Mcht. Marine Acad., 1955; J.D., Cornell U., 1961. Bar: N.Y. 1961, D.C. 1962, Calif. 1965, U.S. Supreme Ct. 1965. Trial atty. admiralty and shipping U.S. Dept. Justice, 1961-67; chief trial atty. admiralty office U.S. Dept. Justice, San Francisco, 1967-74; Pacific counsel Sea-Land Service, Inc., Oakland, Calif., 1974-76; dep. gen. counsel Sea-Land Service, Inc., 1977-78, gen. counsel, 1978-82, sec., 1979-82; assoc. gen. counsel Sea-Land Industries, 1979-82; pres. Freights Unltd., Inc., 1982—; gen. counsel Toledo, Peoria & Western Rwy., 1994-96; adj. prof. law McGeorge Sch. Law, 1974-76. Served with U.S. Navy, 1956-57. Mem. Fed. Bar Assn., Calif. Bar Assn., D.C. Bar Assn., San Francisco Bar Assn., Maritime Law Assn. U.S., Cornell U. Law Assn., Kings Point Alumni Assn. Home: 126 Seney Dr Bernardsville NJ 07924-1818 Office: Freights Unlimited Inc PO Box 428 Peapack NJ 07977-0428

WEISS, ALVIN HARVEY, chemical engineering educator, catalysis researcher and consultant; b. Phila., Apr. 28, 1928; s. Louis and Helen F. (Wilinsky) W.; children: Linda S., Louis B.; m. Devorah Schwartz, June 10, 1979. BSChemE, U. Pa., 1949, PhD in Phys. Chemistry, 1965; MSChemE, Newark Coll. Engring., 1955. Registered profl. engr., Mass., Del. Chem. engr. Fiber Chem. Corp., Cliffwood, N.J., 1949-51, Colgate-Palmolive Co., Jersey City, 1953-55, Houdry Process and Chems. Co., Linwood, Pa., 1956-63; research assoc., lectr. U. Pa., Phila., 1963-66; prof. chem. engring. Worcester Poly. Inst., Mass., 1966-94, prof. emeritus, 1994—; NASA-ASEE summer faculty fellow Stanford U., Ames Research Ctr., 1967, 68; affiliate scientist Worcester Found. Exptl. Biology, 1972-74; Fulbright-Hays sr. faculty fellow to dept. chem. engring. Ben-Gurion U. of Negev, Beersheva, Israel, 1973-74, vis. prof. chem. engring., 1974; U.S. coord. U.S.-USSR Coop. Sci. Program in Chem. Catalysis, Topic IV, 1973-76, prin. investigator (with M.M. Sakharov), 1976-78; prin. investigator (with K.I. Ione) U.S.-USSR Coop. Sci. Program in Chem. Catalysis, Topic III, 1978-80; Fulbright-Hays vis. lectr. dept. chem. engring. Middle East Tech. U., Ankara, Turkey, 1974, vis. prof., 1991; vis. research scientist dept. organic chemistry Weizmann Inst., Rehovoth, Israel, 1974; vis. lectr. Inst. Isotopes and Central Inst. Chemistry, Hungarian Acad. Scis., Budapest, 1976; vis. prof. Inst. Cultural Relations and Inst. Isotopes, Hungarian Acad. Scis., 1978, 80; UNIDO chief tech. advisor to Petrochem. Complex of Bahia Blanca, Argentina, 1980; sr. research fellow chem. systems lab. Army Chem. Ctr., Md., 1981; UNIDO expert in chem. process devel. Rsch. Inst. for Chem. Industry, Beijing, Peoples Republic of China, 1982; UNIDO expert in catalysis to YARPET Petrochemical Complex, Yarimca, Turkey, 1986-87; bd. dirs. U.S. com. for sci. coop. with Vietnam; vis. lectr. Nat. Ctr. for Sci. Rsch., Hanoi, Inst. of Indsl. Chemistry, Ho Chi Minh City, 1986. translator: (with M. Delleo, G. Dembinski and J. Happel) Catalysis by Non-Metals (O.V. Krylov), 1970; contbr. articles to profl. jours.; patentee in field. With U.S. Army, 1951-53. Named Outstanding Researcher and Creative Scholar, Worcester Poly. Inst., 1984; recipient Sci. Achievement award Worcester Engring. Soc., 1984; research grantee NSF, PRF, NASA, DOD, DOE. Fellow Am. Inst. Chem. Engrs. (rsch. com. 1968-80, symposia chmn. 1973-84); mem.AAUP, ACS, Am. Inst. Chem. Engrs., Catalysis Soc. (bd. dirs., sec. 1968-88), Catalysis Soc. New England (founding pres. 1967-68, bd. dirs. 1968—), Am. Chem. Soc. (New England petroleum div. rep. 1970-88, session chmn. 1973—), Deutsche Gesellschaft für Chemische Apparatwesen. Office: Worcester Poly Inst 100 Institute Rd Worcester MA 01609-2247

WEISS, ANDREW RICHARD, lawyer; b. Hartford, Conn., Jan. 11, 1945; s. Irving and Clara E. (Miller) W.; m. Sara N. Brookwood, Apr. 3, 1981 (dec. June 1982); m. Avril M. Bell, Oct. 14, 1989. BA, Dartmouth Coll., 1967; MA, U. Wis., 1968; postgrad., Boston U., 1970; JD, Boston Coll., 1977. Bar: Mass. 1977, U.S. Dist. Ct. Mass. 1978, U.S. Supreme Ct. 1992. Tchr. English Saddle River (N.J.) County Day Sch., 1968-69; rsch. & writing asst. Soun-View Throg's Neck Cmty. Mental Health Ctr., Bronx, 1969-70; legal advocate Mass. Advocaty Ctr., Boston, 1975-77; atty. pvt. practice, Boston, 1978-89, RESOLUTION, Wellesley, Mass., 1989—. Trustee Thacher Montessori Sch., Milton, Mass., 1981—, Newbury Insight Meditation Ctr., 1995—; pres. Zaltho Found., Inc., Concord, Mass., 1994—. Mem. Mass. Bar Assn., Soc. Profls. Dispute Resolution, Internat. Alliance Holistic Lawyers. Avocations: music, motorcycles, hiking, pets. Home: 20 Elm St Maynard MA 01754 Office: RESOLUTION 40 Grove St Wellesley MA 02181-7702

WEISS, ARMAND BERL, economist, association management executive; b. Richmond, Va., Apr. 2, 1931; s. Maurice Herbert and Henrietta (Shapiro) W.; BS in Econs., Wharton Sch. Fin., U. Pa., 1953, MBA, 1954; D.B.A., George Washington U., 1971; m. Judith Bernstein, May 18, 1957; children: Jo Ann Michele, Rhett Louis. Cert. assn. exec. Officer, U.S. Navy, 1954-65; spl. asst. to auditor gen. Dept. Navy, 1964-65; sr. economist Center for Naval Analyses, Arlington, Va., 1965-68; project dir. Logistics Mgmt. Inst., Washington, 1968-74; dir. systems integration Fed. Energy Adminstrn., Washington, 1974-76; sr. economist Nat. Commn. Supplies and Shortages, 1976-77; tech. asst. to v.p. System Planning Corp., 1977-78; chmn. bd., pres., chief exec. officer Assns. Internat., Inc., 1978—; chmn. bd. dirs., chief fin. officer RAIL Digital Corp., 1988-91; v.p., treas. Tech. Frontiers, Inc., 1978-80; sr. v.p. Weiss Pub. Co., Inc., Richmond, Va., 1960—; v.p. Condo News Internat., Inc., 1981; v.p., bd. dirs. Leaders Digest Inc., 1987-88; sec., bd. dirs. Mgmt. Svcs. Internat. Inc., 1987-88; adj. prof. Am. U., 1979-80, 89-90; vis. lectr. George Washington U., 1971; assoc. prof. George Mason U., 1984; treas. Fairfax County (Va.) Dem. Com. 1992-94, assisted Pres. Clinton, v.p. Gore transition at White House, 1993, pres. Washington Mgnt. and Business Assn., 1993—; chmn. U.S. del., session chmn. NATO Symposium on Cost-Benefit Analysis, The Hague, Netherlands, 1969, NATO Conf. on Operational Rsch. in Indsl. Systems, St. Louis, France, 1970; pres. Nat. Council Assns. Policy Scis., 1971-77; chmn. adv. group Def. Econ. Adv. Council Dept. Def., 1970-74; resident asso. Smithsonian Instn., 1973—; expert cons. Dept. State, GAO; undercover agt. FBI, 3 yrs. Del. Pres.'s Mid-Century White House Conf. on Children and Youth, 1950; scoutmaster Japan, U.S., leader World Jamborees, France, Can., U.S., 1945-61; Eagle scout, 1947; U.S. del. Internat. Conf. on Ops. Rsch., Dublin, Ireland, 1972; organizing com. Internat. Cost-Effectiveness Symposium, Washington, 1970; speaker Internat. Conf. Inst. Mgmt. Scis., Tel Aviv, 1973, del., Mexico City, 1967. Mem. bus. com. Nat. Symphony Orch., 1968-70, Washington Performing Arts Soc., 1974-88; bus. mgr. Nat. Lyric Opera Co., 1983—; mem. mktg. com. Fairfax Symphony Orch., 1984-91; bd. dirs. Mc Lean (Va.) Orch., 1992-94; exec. com. Mid Atlantic council Union Am. Hebrew Congregations, 1970-79, treas., 1974-79, mem. nat. MUM com., 1974-79; mem. dist. com. Boy Scouts Am., 1972-75; bd. dirs. Nat. Council Career Women, 1975-79; Va. Acad. Scis., 1991—. Recipient Silver medal 50-yard free style and half mile swimming meet No. Va. Sr. Olympics, 1990. Fellow AAAS, Washington Acad. Scis. (gov. 1981-92, v.p. 1987-88, pres.-elect 1989-90, pres. 1990-91, past pres. 1991-92); mem. Ops. Research Soc. Am. (chmn. meetings com. 1969-71; chmn. cost-effectiveness sect. 1969-70, Moving Spirit award 1994), Washington Ops. Research/Mgmt. Sci. Council (editor newsletter 1969-93, sec. 1971-72, pres. 1973-74, trustee 1975-77, bus. mgr. 1976-93), Internat. Inst. Strategic Studies (London), Am. Soc. Assn. Execs. (membership com. 1981-82, assn. mgmt. co. sect. coun. 1995—, cert.), Inst. for Mgmt. Sci., Inst. for Ops. Rsch. and the Mgmt. Scis., Am. Econ. Assn., Wharton Grad. Sch. Alumni Assn. (exec. com. 1970-73), Am. Acad. Polit. and Social Sci., Nat. Eagle Scout Assn., Am. Legion, Navy League of the U.S., Greater Wash. Soc. Assn. Execs. (new ventures com. 1995—), Fairfax County C. of C., Vienna, Va. C. of C., Alumni Assn. George Washington U. (governing bd. 1974-82, chmn. univ. publs. com. 1976-78, Alumni Service award 1980), Alumni Assn. George Washington U. Sch. Govt. and Bus. Adminstrn. (exec. v.p. 1977-78, pres. 1978-79), George Washington U. Doctoral Assn. (sr. v.p. 1968-69), Nat. Assn. Acad. Sci. (del. 1991-93). Jewish. (pres. temple 1970-72). Club: Wharton Sch. Washington (sec. 1967-69, pres. 1969-70, exec. dir. 1987—, Joseph Wharton award 1991). Co-editor: Systems Analysis for Social Problems, 1970, The Relevance of Economic Analysis to Decision Making in the Department of Defense, 1972, Toward More Effective Public Programs: The Role of Analysis and Evaluation, 1975. Editor: Cost-Effectiveness Newsletter, 1966-70, Operations Research/Systems Analysis Today, 1971-73, Operation Research/Mgmt. Sci. Today, 1974-87; Feedback, 1969-93, Condo World, 1981, The Democrat, 1997—; assoc. editor Ops. Research, 1971-75; publisher: IEEE Scanner, 1983-89, Spl. and Individual Needs Tech. (SAINT) Newsletter, 1987-88, Jour. Parametrics, 1984-88. Home: 6516 Truman Ln Falls Church VA 22043-1821

WEISS, BARRY RONALD, education administrator; b. Superior, Wis., May 12, 1946; s. Harold Nathan and Frances Ann (Fergal) W.; m. Barbara McDaniel, Aug. 15, 1988; children: Angela Jeanette, Shauna Mikail, Ben Nathan. BS in Math. Edn., SUNY, New Paltz, 1969, MA in Math., 1975; postgrad., NYU, 1992—. Cert. tchr. N.Y., edn. adminstrn. N.Y. Tchr. elem. speech therapy Fed. Head Start Program, Middletown, N.Y., 1968-69; tchr. high sch. math. Newburgh (N.Y.) Enlarged City Sch. Dist., 1969-82, dir. edn. tech., 1982—; chmn. planning com. Mid-Hudson Tech. Fest, N.Y., 1986-91; mem. R&D tech. adv. coun. Mid-Hudson Regional Computer Ctr., N.Y., 1981—; presenter in restructuring learning and ednl. tech. Author of poems, short stories; contbr. articles to profl. jours. Mem. N.Y. State Computers and Tech. in Edn. Assn., Sch. Adminstrs. Assn. N.Y. State, Newburgh Suprs. and Adminstrs. Assn., Mega Soc., Triple Nine Soc., Four Sigma Soc. Avocations: reading, writing, outdoor adventures. Home: 51 Leslie Rd Newburgh NY 12550-1232

WEISS, BRUCE JORDAN, academic administrator; b. N.Y.C., Mar. 17, 1945; s. Robert and Margolith (Goldsmith) W.; m. Dianne Mary McConville, Sept. 1, 1968; children: Jenna Lynn, Evan Michael. BA in Psychology, CUNY, 1965; MA in Psychology, U. Toledo, 1967; PhD in Psychology, U. Md., 1971. Lic. psychologist, Mass. Counseling psychologist Am. U., Washington, 1970-71, U. Calif., Berkeley, 1971-72; clin. dir. Pedregal House, San Mateo, Calif., 1973-74; dir. Berkeley Day Treatment Ctr., 1974-77; program dir. Mass. Sch. Profl. Psychology, Newton, 1977-79; dean Dedham, 1979-86; pres., 1986—. Contbr. chpt. to book. Fellow Mass. Psychol. Assn.; mem. Am. Psychol. Assn. Jewish.

WEISS, CARL, aerospace company executive; b. Bklyn., Dec. 6, 1938; s. Morris Harold and Sonia B. (Botwinick) W.; m. Judith Fellner, Jan. 27, 1963; children: Daniel Oren, Jonathan Michael. BBA, CUNY, 1961, MBA, 1968; postgrad., Harvard U., Boston, 1971. CPA, N.Y. Acct. Joseph Warren & Co., N.Y.C., 1965-68; asst. contr. Fisher Radio Corp., L.I., N.Y., 1968-69; sr. v.p. Deutsch Relays, Inc., East Northport, N.Y., 1969-83; owner, exec. v.p. Logical Solutions, Inc., Melville, N.Y., 1983-92; owner, pres., COO G&H Tech., Inc., Camarillo, Calif., 1992—. Bd. dirs. Deutsch Dagan, Inc. With U.S. Army, 1961-67. Mem. AICPA (future issues com. 1985-88); N.Y. Soc. CPA. Office: G & H Tech Inc 750 W Ventura Blvd Camarillo CA 93010-5804

WEISS, CHARLES ANDREW, lawyer; b. Perryville, Mo., Jan. 24, 1942; s. Wallace Francis and Iola Frances Weiss; m. Marie Suzanne Desloge, June 10, 1972; children—Christopher, Robert, Julie, Anne. B.J. with highest honors, U. Mo., 1964, A.B. in History, 1965; J.D. cum laude, Notre Dame U., 1968. Bar: Mo. 1968, U.S. Dist. Ct. (ea. dist.) Mo. 1968, U.S. Ct. Appeals (8th cir.) 1968, U.S. Supreme Ct. 1972, U.S. Ct. Appeals (9th cir.) 1974, U. S. Ct. Appeals (2d cir.) 1977. Law clk. to chief judge U.S. Ct. Appeals (8th cir.), 1968-69, U.S. Ct. Appeals (5th cir.) 1992; ptnr. Bryan Cave, St. Louis, 1969—; lectr., researcher St. Louis U. Law Sch., 1970-73. Supr., Red Cross Water Safety Program, Perry County, Mo., 1962-64; dir. Neighborhood Youth Corps., Perry County, 1965-66; pres. Perry County Young Democrats Club, 1965-67; committeeman Boy Scouts Am., 1982-86. Fellow Am. Coll. Trial Lawyers; mem. ABA (ho. of dels. 1986—), Met. Bar Assn. St. Louis (pres. 1984-85), Mo. Bar Assn. (bd. govs. 1985, v.p. 1994-95, pres-elect 1995-96, pres. 1996-97). Roman Catholic. Clubs: Mo. Athletic (St. Louis), The Riverlands Assn., Inc. (pres. 1991-93), Jefferson Nat. Expansion Hist. Assn. (chmn. 1993—), Notre Dame of St. Louis (dir. 1983—). Office: Bryan Cave 211 N Broadway Saint Louis MO 63102-2733

WEISS, CHARLES MANUEL, environmental biologist; b. Scranton, Pa., Dec. 7, 1918; s. Morris and Fannie (Levy) W.; m. Shirley Friedlander, June 7, 1942. BS, Rutgers U., 1939, postgrad., 1939-40; postgrad., Harvard U., 1940; PhD, Johns Hopkins U., 1950. Fellow in marine microbiology, research assoc. in marine biology Woods Hole Oceanographic Instn., Mass., 1939-47; chemist, biologist Balt. Harbor Project, Johns Hopkins U. Dept. San Engring., 1947-50; basin biologist div. water pollution control USPHS, N.Y.C., 1950-52; biologist med. labs. Army Chem. Ctr., Edgewood, Md., 1952-56; prof. environ. biology U. N.C., Chapel Hill, 1956-89, prof. emeritus, 1989—, creator/sponsor C. & S. Weiss Urban Livability program, 1992—; cons. limnology Duke Power Co.; mem. ad hoc panel waste treatment Space Sci. Bd., Nat. Acad. Sci., 1966-68, chmn. panel mgmt. of spacecraft solid and liquid wastes, 1968-69, subcom. atmosphere and water contaminants of manned spacecraft, 1971; mem. triennial water quality standards rev. com. N.C. Dept. Natural Resources and Community Devel., 1982-83; cons. Nat. Health Service, Santiago, Chile, 1971. Author: Water Quality Investigations, Guatemala: Lake Atitlan 1968-70, 1971, Water Quality Investigations, Guatemala: Lake Amatitlan 1969-70, 1971, The Trophic State of North Carolina Lakes, 1976, The Water Quality of the Upper Yadkin Drainage Basin, 1981, Water Quality Study, B. Everett Jordan Lake, N.C., 1981-85, 87; editor N.C. Conf. AAUP Newsletter, 1985-91. Mem. Chapel Hill Planning Bd., 1969-76, chmn., 1970-72, 75-76; trustee Chapel Hill Preservation Soc., 1972; bd. dirs. Triangle Theatre Opera, 1986, 89, 91—; mem. adv. coun. Santa Fe Chamber Music Festival, 1990-91, trustee, 1991—. Bigelow fellow Woods Hole Oceanographic Instn., 1970—. Fellow AAAS, APHA, N.Y. Acad. Scis.; mem. AAUP (chpt. pres. 1980-81, pres. N.C. conf. 1982-83, William S. Tacey award Assembly of State Confs. 1992), Am. Chem. Soc., Am. Geophys. Union, Am. Fisheries Soc., Am. Soc. Limnology and Oceanography, Ecol. Soc. Am., Soc. Internat. Limnologie, Water Pollution Control Fedn. (chmn. rsch. com. 1966-71), Am. Water Works Assn. (chmn. subcom. water quality sampling for quality control in reservoirs 1978-80), Am. Soc. Microbiology, Sigma Xi, Delta Omega. Home: 155 N Hamilton Rd Chapel Hill NC 27514-5628 Office: U NC Sch Pub Health CB7400 Rosenau Chapel Hill NC 27599-7400

WEISS, CHRISTOPHER JOHN, lawyer; b. Oswego, N.Y., Sept. 1, 1952; s. Robert Leo and Flora Elizabeth Weiss; m. Corinne Fratt, Mar. 28, 1973; children: Allison Ardis, Natalie Elizabeth, Christine Corinne, Kathryn Creigh. BS, Fla. State U., 1970, JD, 1977. Bar: Fla. 1977, U.S. Dist. Ct. (mid. and so. dists.) Fla. 1977, U.S. Supreme Ct. Ptnr. Maguire, Voorhis & Wells, P.A., Orlando, Fla., 1979—; lectr., author various constrn. litigation issues, 1977—. Mem. Orlando Rep. Com., 1975—. Mem. Fla. Bar, Orange County Bar Assn. (jud. rels. com. 1987—), Am. Arbitration Assn. (nat. panelist 1982—), Assoc. Gen. Contractors, Assoc. Builders and Contractors. Presbyterian. Avocations: camping, fishing, reading. Office: Maguire Voorhis & Wells PA PO Box 633 Orlando FL 32802-0633

WEISS, DANIEL EDWIN, clergyman, educator; b. Kenosha, Wis., June 9, 1937; s. Edwin and Ruth J. (Stromquist) W.; m. Rachel A. Johnson, Aug. 9, 1958; children: Daniel E., Kristen R. BA, Wheaton Coll., 1959, MA, 1962; MDiv, Gordon Conwell Theol. Sem., South Hamilton, Mass., 1962; PhD, Mich. State U., 1964; DD (hon.), Judson Coll., 1976, Franklin Coll., 1990; DHL (hon.), Ottawa (Ontario) U., Can., 1997. Ordained to ministry Am. Bapt. Chs., 1962. Prof. ministry Gordon Div. Sch., Wenham, Mass., 1964-69; v.p. Gordon Coll., Wenham, 1969-73; pres. Eastern Coll., St. Davids, Pa., 1973-81, Eastern Bapt. Theol. Sem., Phila., 1973-81; exec. v.p. Pace U., N.Y.C., 1981-83; exec. dir. Am. Bapt. Bd. Edn. and Publ., Valley Forge, Pa., 1983-88; gen. sec. Am. Bapt. Chs. U.S.A., Valley Forge, 1988—; mem. ctrl. com. World Coun. Chs., Geneva, 1989—; mem. gen. bd. Nat. Coun. Chs., N.Y.C., 1989—; mem. gen. coun. Bapt. World Alliance, Washington, 1985—. Office: Am Bapt Chs USA PO Box 851 Valley Forge PA 19482-0851

WEISS, DAVID, religion educator; b. Sighet, Rumania, Dec. 21, 1928; came to U.S., 1947, naturalized, 1953; s. Callel and Fanny (Weiss) Wiederman; m. Tzipora Hager, Dec. 9, 1953; children—Baruch, Ephraim, Isaiah. BA, Bklyn. Coll., 1953; MA, NYU, 1956; MHL, Jewish Theol. Sem., 1957, DHL, 1958; PhD (hon.), Haifa U., Israel, 1993; DHL (hon.), Gratz Coll., 1994; DTh (hon.), U. Lund, Sweden, 1995. Instr. religion and Talmud Jewish Theol. Sem., 1957-62, asst. prof. Talmud, 1962-68, assoc. prof., 1968-86, prof. Rabbinics, 1970-86; lectr. religion Columbia U., N.Y.C., 1961-63, adj. asst. prof., 1963-65, adj. assoc. prof., 1965-68, adj. prof., 1968-86, prof., 1986—, Lucius N. Littauer prof. classical Jewish civilization, 1995—; vis. prof. Talmud Bar-Ilan U., Israel, 1974; Lady Davis vis. prof. Talmud Hebrew U., Israel, 1984; vis. prof. Harvard U. Law Sch., 1996. Author: (under name Halivni): Sources and Traditions: A Source Critical Commentary on the Talmud, Vol. I. on Seder Nashim, 1968; author: Vol. II on Seder Nashim, 1975, Vol. III on Tractate Shabbath, 1983, Vol. IV on Tracrate Erubin and Pesahim, 1983, Vol. V on Tractate Baba Qama, 1993, Midrash, Mishnah and Gemara, 1986, Peshat and Derash, 1991, The Book and the Sword: A Life of Learning in the Shadow of Destruction, A Memoir, 1996, Revelation Restored, 1997. Recipient Blalik prize City of Tel-Aviv, Israel, 1984; grantee Council Research Humanities Columbia, 1964; Guggenheim fellow, 1970-71; recipient L. Ginzberg award Jewish Theol. Sem., 1971-72; Nat. Endowment for Humanities fellow, 1980; fellow Inst. for Advanced Studies Hebrew U., Jerusalem, Israel, 1981. Mem. Am. Acad. Jewish Rsch. (past pres.), Am. Acad. Arts and Scis. Home: 435 Riverside Dr New York NY 10025-7743 Office: Columbia U 626 Kent Hall New York NY 10027

WEISS, DAVID ALAN, international economist; b. Washington, June 22, 1953; s. Leonard and Mary Louise (Barker) W.; m. Mamie Kresses, June 2, 1991. BA, Hamilton Coll., 1975; MS in Fgn. Svc., Georgetown U., 1978. Staff asst. Office of Senator Thomas F. Eagleton, Washington, 1970-71; rsch. fellow Carnegie Endowment for Internat. Peace, Washington, 1975-76; spl. asst. to dir. Peace Corps, Washington, 1978-80; fgn. svc. officer U.S. Dept of State, Washington, 1980-90; with econ. office Am. Embassy, Port-au-Prince, Haiti, 1981-83; with secretariat staff Office of Sec. of State, 1983-84; sr. spl. asst. to dep. sec. of state U.S. Dept. of State, 1985-87; dir. European Community high tech and east-west trade policy Office of European Affairs, U.S. Trade Rep., Washington, 1987-89; exec. dir. for policy coordination Exec. Office of The Pres., U.S. Trade Rep., Washington, 1989-92; dep. asst. U.S. Trade Rep. for North Am. Affairs, 1992-95, asst., 1995-97; dir. trade policy Verner, Liipfert, Bernhard, McPherson & Hand, Washington, 1997—. Mem. Am. Fgn. Svc. Assn., Diplomatic and Consular Officers Ret. Office: Verner Liipfert Bernhard McPherson & Hand 901 15th St NW Washington DC 20005

WEISS, DENIS ANTHONY, manufacturing executive, mechanical engineer; b. Cleve., July 25, 1942; s. William Richard and Mary Margaret (Ragazinskas) W.; m. Joan Hilda Hammink, Sept. 1, 1962; children: Eric, Mark, Alan, Lori. BMSE, Gen. Motors Inst. Engring., 1968; MS in Engring., U. Mich., 1967; MBA, Bowling Green (Ohio) State U., 1987. Plant engr. McLouth Steel, Detroit, 1973-74, supt. maintenance, 1974-75; with Rockwell Internat., 1975-87; plant mgr. Rockwell Internat., Kenton, Ohio, 1983-87; v.p. mfg. div. Huffy Bicycle Co., Celina, Ohio, 1987-89; v.p. mfg. Kirby Co., div. Scottfetzer Corp., Cleve., 1989-92; v.p. ops. Crown Leisure Products, Inc., Owosso, Mich., 1992-94, Taylor Bldg. Products, West Branch, Mich., 1994—; asst. prof. part-time Oakland Community Coll., Pontiac, Mich., 1971-72. Mem. Charter Study Commn., Pontiac, 1974, Pontiac Zoning Bd. of Appeals, 1974-75; mem. engring. adv. bd. Wright State U. Lake Campus, Celina, Ohio, 1988; co-founder Bay St. Block Club, Pontiac, 1971, Pontiac Citizens Watch, 1973. Recipient Resolution of Appreciation, Pontiac City Commn., 1975; named Boss of the Yr., Am. Bus. Women's Assn., 1981. Mem. Assn. Mfg. Excellence, Soc. Mfg. Engrs., Am. Mgmt. Assn., Home Owners Assn. (trustee Lima, Ohio chpt. 1988-89), Northeast Mich. Indsl. Assn. (pres. 1996—). Roman Catholic. Avocations: gunsmiths, stained glass, golf. Home: 2980 Arrowhead Trl West Branch MI 48661-9715 Office: Taylor Bldg Products PO Box 280 631 N 1st St West Branch MI 48861

WEISS, DONALD L(OGAN), retired sports association executive; b. Aurora, Ill., Aug. 22, 1926; s. Harry H. and Esther (Cook) W.; m. Charlene Thomas, Aug. 23, 1947; children: Deborah Lynn Weiss Geline, Barbara Jane Weiss Juckett, Pamela Sue Weiss Van der Lee. Student, Cornell Coll., Mt. Vernon, Iowa, 1943, 46; B.J., U. Mo., 1949. Newsman AP, Huntington, W.Va., 1949-51; sports writer-editor AP, N.Y.C., 1951-63; publs. editor, info. dir. U.S. Golf Assn., N.Y.C., 1963-65; dir. info. Nat. Football League, N.Y.C., 1965-68; dir. public relations Nat. Football League, 1968-77; exec. dir. Nat. Football League, N.Y.C., 1977-94. Contbr. articles on golf and football to profl. publs., 1963—. With submarine svc., USN, 1944-46. Recipient Journalistic Achievement awards Sigma Delta Chi, Kappa Tau Alpha, 1948-49, Trustees' award Ohio U., 1978, Nat. citation Nat. H.S. Athletic Coaches Assn., 1990. Methodist. Office: 280 Park Ave New York NY 10017-1216

WEISS, EARLE BURTON, physician; b. Waltham, Mass., Nov. 23, 1932; s. Murray E. and Ruth R. (Pill) W.; m. Ruth Lithwick, Dec. 1, 1963; children—Ilana, Joshua. BS with honors, Northeastern U., 1955; MS, M.I.T., 1957; MD, Albert Einstein Coll. Medicine, 1961. Intern King's County Hosp., Bklyn., 1961-62; resident Boston City Hosp., 1962-64, Nat. Heart Inst. fellow, 1964-66; assoc. dir. Tufts Med. Svc., 1969-71; dir. respiratory ICU, physician pulmonary svc. Boston City Hosp., 1964-71; dir. div. respiratory diseases St. Vincent Hosp., Worcester, Mass., 1971-89; also acting med. dir. St. Vincent Hosp., 1985-87; prof. medicine U. Mass. Med. Sch., 1977—; sr. pulmonary rsch. scientist, dept. anesthesia Rsch. Labs. Brigham and Womens Hosp., Boston, 1989—; lectr. Tufts Med. Sch.; assoc. affiliated prof. life scis. Worcester (Mass.) Poly. Inst.; vis. prof. Faculty of Medicine, dept. of anesthesia Harvard Med. Sch., 1990—; med. dir. Found. Rsch. in Bronchial Asthma and Related Diseases; Tb cons. Commonwealth of Mass., 1972-89; dir. regional inpatient Tv, Worcester County, 1989. Author: Bronchial Asthma, 2d edit., 1976, 3d edit., 1993, Status Asthmaticus, 1978; contbr. (with artist Frank H. Netter) Ciba Collection: The Respiratory System and Clinical Symposia, An Anthology of Medical Classics, 1997—. Served to capt. USAF, 1965-70. Recipient Dr. J. McKeever award for outstanding educator St. Vincent Hosp., 1970, Chadwick medal for meritorious contbn. thoracic diseases Mass. Thoracic Soc., 1990. Fellow ACP, Am. Coll. Chest Physicians, Royal Coll. Physicians (assoc.); mem. AAAS, AMA, Mass. Thoracic Soc. (pres. 1976-78, Chadwick medal for meritorious contbn. 1990), Mass. Med. Soc., Am. Thoracic Soc. (co-founder clin. assembly), Am. Assn. Clin. Scientists, Am. Soc. Internal Medicine, Soc. Free Radical Rsch., N.Y. Acad. Scis., Interasthma. Achievements include research in role of calcium and oxygen toxic products in asthma and airways reactivit. Avocations: oil painting, piano, family. Home: 57 South St Natick MA 01760-5526 Office: Brigham and Womens Hosp Dept Anesthesia Rsch L Boston MA 02115

WEISS, EDITH BROWN, law educator; b. Salem, Oreg., Feb. 19, 1942; d. Leon Michael and Edith E. Brown; A.B., Stanford U., 1963; J.D., Harvard U., 1966; Ph.D., U. Calif.-Berkeley, 1973; DDL (hon.) Chgo.-Kent Coll. Law, 1993; m. Charles Weiss, Jr., July 24, 1969; children—Jed, Tamara. Bar: D.C., 1967, U.S. Ct. Claims, 1967, U.S. Ct. Customs and Patent Appeals, 1967, U.S. Ct. Mil. Appeals, 1967; atty. adv. ACDA, Washington, 1966-68; rsch. assoc. Columbia U., N.Y.C., 1970-72, Brookings Instn., Washington, 1972-74; asst. prof. civil engring. and politics Princeton (N.J.) U., 1974-78; prof. law Georgetown U., Washington, 1978—, Francis Cabell Brown prof. internat. law, 1996—; cons. UN Environ. Program, 1974-78, 94—, UN U., 1983—; assoc. gen. coun. internatl law, EPA, 1990-92; chmn. Social Sci. Rsch. Coun. Com. on Rsch. on Global Environ. Change, 1989-94; spl. legal adv. North Am. Commn. Environ. Coop., 1996—. Bd. editors Am. Jour. Internat. Law, Internat. Legal Materials, Global Governance. Recipient Dinkelspiel award Stanford U., 1963, Leland T. Chapin award, 1962, Mellinkoff award, 1963; Harold and Margaret Sprout award, 1979, Elizabeth Haub prize, 1994; Woodrow Wilson fellow, 1968. Mem. ABA (standing com. world order), Am. Soc. Internat. Law (chmn. ann. meeting 1979, nominating com. 1979-80, exec. coun. 1981-85, v.p. 1983-85, pres. 1994-96, Cert. Merit 1990), Nat. Acad. Scis. (environ. studies bd. 1981-84, vice chmn. U.S. nat. com. for SCOPE 1984-85, water sci. and tech. bd. 1985-88, commn. on geoscis., environment and resources 1992-95), U.S. Dept. State adv. com. pub. internat. law 1994—, Coun. Fgn. Relations, Am. Law Inst., Internat. Coun. Environ Law, Cousteau Soc. (coun. advs.), Phi Beta Kappa, Sigma Xi. Club: Bannockburn Civic Assn. Author: (with Brown, Fabian, Cornell) Regimes for the Oceans, Outer Space and Weather, 1977, In Fairness to Future Generations: International Law, Common Patrimony and Intergenerational Equity, 1989, Environmental Change and International Law, 1992; contbr. articles to profl. jours. Office: Georgetown U Law Ctr 600 New Jersey Ave NW Washington DC 20001-2075

WEISS, EGON ARTHUR, retired library administrator; b. Vienna, Austria, June 7, 1919; Came to U.S., 1938; s. Arthur and Martha (Schrecker) W.; m. Renee Hansi Weiss, July 11, 1942; children—Helen Louise, Steven Arthur. Student, Berea Coll., Ky., 1938-40; A.B., Harvard U., 1947; M.A., Boston U., 1949; M.S.L.S., Simmons Coll., Boston, 1951. Prof. asst. Brookline (Mass.) Pub. Library, 1949-51, br. dir., 1951-58; asst. dir. library U.S. Mil. Acad., West Point, N.Y., 1958-62, libr., dir. libr., 1962-87, libr. emeritus, 1987—; libr. cons., 1987—; trustee Southeast N.Y. Libr. Rsch. Coun., Poughkeepsie, 1966—; mem. John Cotton Dana Com., N.Y.C., 1975-79; cons. Pergamon Press, McLean, Va., 1983—. Co-author: Catalog Military Science Coll., 4 vols., 1969; contbr. to Funk & Wagnalls Ency., 1965—; appraiser rare books and spl. collections. Chmn. Black Rock Forest Preservation Council, Cornwall, N.Y., 1981—; trustee Mus. Hudson Highlands, Cornwall-on-Hudson, N.Y., 1968; vice chmn. Citizens Adv. Com., Cornwall, 1963-64; pres. Friends of Cornwall (N.Y.) Pub. Libr., 1989—, chmn. gifts and bequests, 1984—; counsellor Friends of West Point Libr., 1987—; trustee David Libr. of Am. Revolution, Pa., 1986—; alt. del. The White House Conf. on Libr. and Info. Svcs., 1991. Served to lt. col. U.S. Army, 1942-46, ETO. Mem. ALA (pres. armed forces sect. 1966), Spl. Libraries Assn. (chmn. mil. library div. 1970), Archons of Colophon, Res. Officers Assn. (pres. Orange County 1965—), Assn. U.S. Army (bd. govs. 1984—). Club: Harvard (v.p. schs. and scholarship) (Poughkeepsie, N.Y.) Lodges: Toastmasters (edn. v.p. Newburgh, N.Y. 1968), Masons. Avocations: reading; swimming; tennis; playing violin. Home: 33 Spruce St Cornwall On Hudson NY 12520-1124

WEISS, ELAINE LANDSBERG, community development management official; b. N.Y.C.; d. Louis and Sadie Blossum (Schoenfeld); divorced. BA in Philosophy and Polit. Sci., Bklyn. Coll., 1960; postgrad., NYU Law Sch., 1960-62; MA in Sociology, Hunter Coll., N.Y.C., 1969. Social investigator N.Y.C. Dept. Social Services, 1963-64; intern, fellow Eleanor Roosevelt Meml. Found., Nat. Assn. Intergroup Relations Ofcls., 1964-65; asst. dir. housing and asst. project dir. Operation Equality, Nat. Urban League, 1965-67; program assoc. housing div. ch. missions Am. Bapt. Home Mission Socs., 1967-70; pres. E.L. Weiss Assocs., 1970-76; exec. dir. Suffolk Community Devel. Corp., Coram, N.Y., 1976-89, E.L. Weiss Assocs., East Quoque, N.Y., 1990—, Grenadier Realty Corp., 1990-92; COO Morningside Heights Housing Corp., 1992-95; exec. dir. Fairmont Housing Corp. (N.J.) subsidiary YWCA Hudson County, 1995-97, Westchester Residential Opportunities, Inc., N.Y.C., 1997—; mem. citizens adv. com. N.Y.C. Dept. Housing Preservation and Devel.; exec. com. L.I. Community Devel. Orgn.; past 2d v.p. Suffolk Housing Task Force; chmn. Suffolk County Citizens Adv. Com., 1981-82. Recipient cert. of commendation L.I. Council Chs., 1981, Woman of Yr. award Am. Biog. Inst., 1994. Mem. Nat. Assn. Housing Ofcls., N.Y. State Assn. Housing and Redevel. Ofcls., Am. Contract Bridge League (life master). Home: PO Box 1532 East Quogue NY 11942-1333

WEISS, ELLYN RENEE, lawyer; b. Phila., Aug. 11, 1947; d. Samuel J. and Ruth G. (Miller) Paul; m. Robert Lowell Weiss Jr., June 26, 1969; 1 child, Nora Caroline. BA cum laude, Smith Coll., Northampton, Mass., 1969; JD cum laude, Boston U., 1972. Bar: Mass. 1972, D.C. 1978, U.S. Dist. Ct., Mass., U.S. Dist. Ct., D.C., U.S. Ct. Appeals (D.C., 1st and 3d cirs.), U.S. Supreme Ct. Lectr. environ. law Boston U., 1976-77; asst. atty. gen. Mass. Atty. Gen., Boston, 1973-77; ptnr. Harmon & Weiss, Washington, 1977-88; mng. ptnr. Foley, Hoag & Eliot, Washington, 1988—; mem. Clinton/Gore Presdl. Transition Team, 1992; spl. counsel, dir. human radiation experiments investigation U.S. Dept. Energy, dep. asst. sec. Office of Environment, Safety and Health, 1994-95. Recipient Disting. Svc. Citation Mass. Atty. Gen., Boston, 1975. Mem. Union Concerned Scientists (dir. 1988—). Avocation: painting. Office: Foley Hoag & Eliot 1615 L St NW Washington DC 20036-5610

WEISS, ERNEST, federal agency administrator; b. Detroit, Oct. 28, 1918; s. Louis and Eugenie (Glick) W.; m. Gloria Caroline Hacker, Feb. 21, 1943; children: Lynn Carol, Gail Corynn. BBA, CUNY, 1942; postgrad., Am. U., 1948-54. With Gen. Svc. Adminstrn. VA, 1946-52; with ICC, Washington, 1952-67, asst. to mng. dir., 1955-63, asst. mng. dir., 1963-67; exec. dir. Nat. Transp. Safety Bd., Washington, 1967-72; sr. staff scientist George Washington U., Washington, 1973-78; commr. Montgomery County (Md.) Commn. on Health, 1990-94. Recipient Meritorious Achievement award Transp. Dept., 1968. Mem. Phi Sigma Alpha. Home: 3312 Brooklawn Ter Chevy Chase MD 20815

WEISS, GAIL ELLEN, legislative staff director; b. N.Y.C., Apr. 11, 1946; d. Joseph and Elaine (Klein) W.; m. John A. Kelly. BA, U. Md., 1967. Staff asst. U.S. Office Econ. Opportunity/Job Corps, Washington, 1967-69; legis. asst. Hon. William L. Clay, Mem. Congress, Washington, 1969-72; rsch. asst. Rt. Hon. Roy Hattersley, Mem. Parliament, London, 1972-73; legis. asst. various coms. U.S. Ho. of Reps., Washington, 1973-90, staff dir. Com. on P.O. and Civil Svc., 1991-94, Dem. staff dir. Com. on Econ. and Ednl. Opportunities, 1995&; mem. working group Pres.'s Task Force on Nat. Health Reform, 1993. Democrat. Jewish. Office: Com on Edn and the Workforce 2100 Rayburn Ho Office Bldg Washington DC 20515

WEISS, GEORGE HERBERT, mathematician, consultant; b. N.Y.C., Feb. 19, 1930; s. Morris and Violet (Mayer) W.; m. Delia Esther Orgel, Dec. 20, 1961; children: Miriam Judith, Alan Keith, Daniel Jonathan. BA, Columbia U., 1951; MA, U. Md., 1953, PhD, 1958. Physicist USN, White Oak, Md., 1951-61; asst. prof. U. Md., College Park, 1959-63; fellow Rockefeller U., N.Y.C., 1963-64, Weizmann Inst., Rehovot, Israel, 1958-59; mathematician NIH, Bethesda, Md., 1964—; cons. GM, IBM, GE. Author: Lattice Dynamics in the Harmonic Approximation, 1963, 2d edit., 1971, The Master Equation in Chemical Physics, 1977, Contemporary Problems in Statistical Physics, 1994, Aspects and Applications of the Random Walk, 1994, Introduction to Crystallographic Statistics, 1995. With U.S. Army, 1954-56. Recipient Disting. Svc. in Math. award Washington Acad. Sci., 1967, Disting. Svc. award NIH, 1970. Avocations: photography, music. Office: NIH Bethesda MD 20816

WEISS, GERHARD HANS, German language educator; b. Berlin, Aug. 6, 1926; came to U.S., 1946; s. Curt Erich and Gertrud (Grothus) W.; m. Janet Marilyn Smith, Dec. 27, 1953; children: John Martin, Susan Elizabeth Weiss Spencer, James David. BA, Washington U., St. Louis, 1950, MA, 1952; PhD, U. Wis., 1956. Prof. German U. Minn., Mpls., 1956—, assoc. dean, 1967-71, 79, chmn. dept. German, 1987-95; mem. German-Am. Textbook Commn., Braunschweig, Fed. Republic Germany, 1985-88. Author: Begegnung mit Deutschland, 1970; editor: Unterrichtspraxis, 1975-80, Minn. Monographs in the Humanities, 1964-70; contbr. articles to profl. jours. Served to lt. col. USAR, 1946-75. Recipient Cross Merit, Fed. Republic Germany, 1982. Mem. MLA, Am. Assn. Tchrs. German (pres. 1982-83, cert. of merit 1981, Disting. German Educator award 1991, elected hon. mem. 1995), German Studies Assn. (v.p. 1997—), Am. Coun. Tchg. Fgn. Langs. (Nelson Brooks award 1987). Methodist. Home: 4101 Abbott Ave S Minneapolis MN 55410-1004

WEISS, GERSON, physician, educator; b. N.Y.C., Aug. 1, 1939; s. Samuel and Lillian (Wolpe) W.; m. Linda Gordon, Dec. 24, 1959; children: Jonathan, David, Michele, Andrew. B.A., NYU, 1960, M.D., 1964. Diplomate Am. Bd. Ob-Gyn. (mem. div. reproductive endocrinology 1985-90). Intern, fellow dept. medicine Johns Hopkins Sch. Medicine, 1964-65; resident ob-gyn NYU Med. Center, 1964-69; research fellow physiology U. Pitts. Sch. Medicine, 1971-73; asst. prof. ob-gyn NYU Med. Center, 1971-76, asso. prof., 1976-80, prof., 1980-85, dir. div. reproductive endocrinology, 1975-85; prof. ob-gyn U. Med. and Dentistry N.J.-N.J. Med. Sch., 1986—, chmn. dept., 1986—. Mem. editl. bd. Fertility and Sterility Jour., 1986-93, Gyn.-Ob. Investigation; contbr. rsch. articles reproductive endocrinology and gynecology to med. jours. Served to maj. MC U.S. Army, 1969-71. Rsch. grantee NIH, 1975—, United Cerebral Palsy Found., 1977-83, Mellon Found., 1982-85; John Polachek Found. Med. Rsch. fellow. Mem. Am. Coll. Ob-Gyn., Am. Ob-Gyn. Soc., Am. Bd. Ob-Gyn. (bd. dirs., treas. 1997—, ob-gyn. residency rev. com. 1995—), Endocrine Soc. Gynecol. Investigation, N.Y. Obstet. Soc. (pres. 1990-91), N.Y. Gynecol. Soc. (pres. 1989-90), Soc. Study of Reprodn., Phi Beta Kappa, Sigma Xi, Alpha Omega Alpha. Home: 390 1st Ave Apt 11D New York NY 10010-4935 Office: UMDNJ NJ Med Sch Dept Ob-Gyn 185 S Orange Ave Newark NJ 07103-2714

WEISS, HEDY, theater critic. Theater critic Chgo Sun-Times. Office: Chgo Sun-Times Inc 401 N Wabash Ave Chicago IL 60611-5642

WEISS, HERBERT KLEMM, retired aeronautical engineer; b. Lawrence, Mass., June 22, 1917; s. Herbert Julius and Louise (Klemm) W.; m. Ethel Celesta Giltner, May 14, 1945 (dec.); children: Janet Elaine, Jack Klemm (dec.). B.S., MIT, 1937, M.S., 1938. Engr. U.S. Army Arty. Bds., Ft. Monroe, Va, 1938-42, Camp Davis, N.C., 1942-44, Ft. Bliss, Tex., 1944-46; chief WPN Systems Lab., Ballistic Research Labs., Aberdeen Proving Grounds, Md, 1946-53; chief WPN systems analysis dept. Northrop Aircraft Corp., 1953-58; mgr. advanced systems devel. mil. systems planning aeronutronic div. Ford Motor Co., Newport Beach, Calif., 1958-61; group dir., plans devel. and analysis Aerospace Corp., El Segundo, Calif., 1961-65; sr. scientist Litton Industries, Van Nuys, Calif., 1965-82; cons. mil. systems analysis, 1982-90; Mem. Sci. Adv. Bd. USAF, 1959-63, sci. adv. panel U.S. Army, 1965-74, sci. adv. commn. Army Ball Research Labs., 1973-77; advisor Pres.'s Commn. Law Enforcement and Adminstrn. Justice, 1966; cons. Office Dir. Def., Research and Engring., 1954-64. Contbr. articles to profl. jours. Patentee in field. Recipient Commendation for meritorious civilian service USAF, 1964, cert. appreciation U.S. Army, 1976. Fellow AAAS, AIAA (assoc.); mem. IEEE, Ops. Research Soc. Am. Republican. Presbyterian. Club: Cosmos. Home: PO Box 2668 Palos Verdes Peninsula CA 90274-8668 *The difference between having something to do and having to do something is a pain in the neck. Anything worth doing takes more doing than it is worth except for the fun of it.*

WEISS, HOWARD A., violinist, concertmaster, conductor, music educator; b. Chgo.; s. Morris X. and Rose (Weiner) W. B.Music, Chgo. Musical Coll. of Roosevelt U., 1960; M.Music with honors, Roosevelt U., 1966. Founder, music dir., condr. Rochester Philharm. Youth Orch., N.Y., 1970-89; prof. violin Eastman Sch. Music, Rochester, 1981—, Nazareth Coll., Rochester, 1983-85; mem. adv. bd. Young Audiences of Rochester, 1975—, Rochester Chamber Orch., 1981—. Concertmaster Rochester Philharm. Orch., 1967-87, concertmaster emeritus, 1987— , concertmaster Rochester Oratorio Soc., 1987—, Chgo. Chamber Orch., 1962-70, Va. Symphony, 1964, San Francisco Ballet Orch., 1962, Eastern Music Festival, Greensboro, N.C., 1976-80, Grand Teton Music Festival Seminar, Jackson Hole, Wyo., 1983-86, Bear Lake Mus. Festival, Utah, 1992-93; 1st violinist Cleve. Orch., 1965-67; violin soloist more than 45 concertos with Cleve. Orch., Rochester Philharm., New Orleans Philharm., Chgo. Grant Park Symphony, Cin. Chamber Orch., Chgo. Chamber Orch., Rochester Chamber Orch.; soloist in complete concerti, (5) of J.S. Bach for Violin and Orch. with Rochester Bach Festival; soloist in complete concerti, (3) of Haydn for Violin and orch. with Rochester Chamber Orch.; soloist rec. Amram Elegy for Violin and Orchestra, David Zinman, Rochester Philharm. Orch., on RCA Red Seal; performed chamber music with: Misha Dichter, Leonard Rose, Lynn Harrell, Yo-Yo Ma, Elly Ameling, Jaime Laredo, Walter Trampler, Lillian Fuchs, James Buswell, Gary Karr, Alan Civil, Lukas Foss; violinist of Brockport Piano Trio, 1971-74; leader of Hartwell String Quartet, 1975-78; asst. concertmaster, participant Casals Festival, P.R., 1975-80; as music dir. and condr. Rochester Philharm. Youth Orch. recorded 21 LPs including symphonies by Franck, Sibelius, Shostakovich, Dvorak, Borodin and Rachmaninoff, made 12 tours, including 4 abroad, Eng. and Scotland, 1984, Germany, Austria and Switzerland, 1986, Dominican Republic, 1987, Jamaica, 1989, and appears on Voice of Am. Named Outstanding Grad. of 1966, Roosevelt U., 1973; recipient Monroe County (N.Y.) Medallion, 1986. Home: 228 Castlebar Rd Rochester NY 14610-2914

WEISS, JAMES LLOYD, cardiology educator; b. Chgo., Jan. 15, 1941; s. Edward Huhner and Ruth (Wingerhoff) W.; m. Susan Forscher Weiss. July 23, 1967; children: Ethan James, Lisa Fleur. BA, Harvard Coll., 1963; MD, Yale U., 1968. Intern, resident U. Mich. Hosp., Ann Arbor, 1968-70; staff fellow NIH, Bethesda, Md., 1970-72; resident medicine Johns Hopkins Hosp., Balt., 1972-73; fellow cardiology, 1973-75, dir. Heart Station, 1976—, asst. prof. Medicine, 1975-81, assoc. prof. Medicine, 1981-90, prof. Medicine, Cariology, 1990—; Michael J. Cudahy prof. of cardiology Johns Hopkins Hosp., 1992—; editorial bd. Johns Hopkins Med. Ctr., 1991—. Contbr. 100 articles to profl. jours. Recipient Harvard Book prize, 1959. Fellow Am. Coll. Cardiology, AHA Coun. on Circulation; mem. Harvard Club N.Y.C., Ctr. Club. Office: Cardiology Div. Johns Hopkins Hosp. 600 N Wolfe St Baltimore MD 21205-2110

WEISS, JAMES MICHAEL, financial analyst, portfolio manager; b. Chgo., July 20, 1946; s. Harold Cornelius and Elizabeth Josephine (Jesse) W.; m. Kathleen Jane Postorino, July 18, 1970; children: Elizabeth, Ann, Jane, William. BA, Marquette U., 1968; MBA, U. Pa., 1972. CFA; chartered investment counselor. Credit analyst Provident Nat. Bank, Phila., 1972; ptnr., sr. portfolio mgr. Stein Roe & Farnham Investment Counsel, Chgo., 1972-87; 1st v.p., prin., sr. portfolio mgr. Stein Roe & Farnham Investment Counselors, Chgo., 1987-90, sr. v.p., prin., sr. portfolio mgr., 1991-92; exec. v.p., sr. portfolio mgr. IDS Adv. Group, Inc., Mpls., 1993-95; pres., chief investment officer IDS Equity Advisors, 1995; sr. v.p., dep. chief investment officer Equities, State St. Rsch. & Mgmt. Co., Boston, 1995—; bd. dirs. Colie & Harris, Inc., Tropp & Co., Chgo.; v.p. Stein Roe Cash Reserves Fund, Chgo., 1982-87. Author: (with others) Handbook of Cash Flow and Treasury Management, 1987; contbr. articles to profl. jours. Commr. Glenview (Ill.) Zoning Bd., 1978-80; trustee Glenview Village Bd. Trustees, 1980-86; chmn. Marquette U. Exec. Senate, Chgo., 1984-87; mem. Glenview Bus. Area Redevel. Com., 1990-93; mem. bus. adv. coun. Elmhurst (Ill.) Coll., 1986-93; founding bd. dirs. Glenview Edn. Found., 1990-93; bd. trustees The Fenn Sch., Concord, Mass., 1996—. With U.S. Army, 1968-70. Recipient Cert. Merit Village of Glenview, 1987. Mem. Investment Analysts Soc., Fin. Analysts Fedn., Investment Counsel Assn., Marquette U. Alumni Assn. (nat. bd. dirs. 1989-91, Nat. Svc. award 1995), North Shore Country Club (Glenview). Avocations: golf, travel, writing. Home: 251 Caterina Hts Concord MA 01742-4774 Office: 1 Financial Ctr Boston MA 02111-2621

WEISS, JAMES MOSES AARON, psychiatrist, educator; b. St. Paul, Oct. 22, 1921; s. Louis Robert and Gertrude (Simon) W.; m. Bette Shapera, Apr. 7, 1946; children: Jenny Anne Weiss Ford, Jonathan James. AB summa cum laude, U. Minn., 1941, ScB, 1947, MB, 1949, MD, 1950; MPH with high honors, Yale U., 1951. Diplomate: Am. Bd. Psychiatry and Neurology (examiner 1963-83). Teaching asst. psychology St. Thomas Coll., St. Paul, 1941-42; intern USPHS Hosp., Seattle, 1949-50; resident, fellow psychiatry Yale Med. Sch., 1950-53; from instr. to asst. prof. psychiatry Washington U., St. Louis, 1954-60; mem. faculty U. Mo., 1959—, First Prof. psychiatry, 1961—, founding chmn. dept., 1960-91, prof. community medicine, 1971—, univ. prof. emeritus, 1991—; vis. prof. Inst. Criminology, Cambridge (Eng.) U., 1968-69, All-India Inst. Med. Scis. and U. Malaya, 1984; internat. cons., 1958—; founding co-chmn. Asian-Am. Consortium on Psychiat. Disorders, 1986—; Kohler disting. lectr. St. Louis U., 1988. Author numerous articles in field; editor, co-author: Nurses, Patients, and Social Systems, 1968; corr. editor: Jour. Geriatric Psychiatry, 1967-93; founding editor, chmn. bd. Jour. Operational Psychiatry, 1970-90; editorial advisor Community Mental Health Jour., 1979-87; trustee Mo. Rev., 1982-83. Served with M.C., AUS, 1942-46, PTO; to capt. M.C., AUS, 1953-54. Decorated Philippine Liberation medal, 1945; recipient Sir Henry Wellcome award, 1955, Israeli bronze medal, 1963, Basic Books award, 1974, Disting. Service commendation Nat. Council Community Mental Health Ctrs., 1982, 83, 86, Guhleman award for Clin. Excellence U. Mo., 1987, Hon. Achievement award U.Mo., 1991, Disting. Svc. award VA, 1991; named Chancellor's Emissary U. Mo., 1979; faculty fellow Inter-Univ. Council, 1958, sr. research fellow Am. Council Edn. and NSF, 1984. Found. fellow Royal Coll. Psychiatrists; fellow Royal Soc. Medicine, Am. Psychiat. Assn. (life), Am. Pub. Health Assn. (life), Am. Coll. Preventive Medicine (emeritus), Royal Soc. Health, AAAS, Am. Coll. Psychiatrists (life), Am. Assn. Psychoanalytic Physicians (hon.); mem. Assn. Mil. Surgeons U.S. (hon. life), Assn. Western Profs. Psychiatry (chmn. 1970-71), Mo. Acad. Psychiatry (1st pres. 1966-67), Mo. Psychiat. Assn. (life, pres. 1987-88), Assn. de Methodologie et Documentation en Psychiatrie, Mil. Order World Wars, Phi Beta Kappa, Sigma Xi, Psi Chi, Alpha Omega Alpha, Alpha Epsilon Sigma, Gamma Alpha. Clubs: Scholars (Cantab.); Wine Label (London); Yale (St. Louis); Univ. (Columbia). Research on suicide, homicide, antisocial behavior, aging, social psychiatry. Home: Crow Wing Farm RR 2 Box 2 Columbia MO 65201-9802 Office: U Mo Dept Psychiatry Columbia MO 65212 *Only this endures: creativity, the pursuit of excellence, and continuing concern for human civilization.*

WEISS, JAY M(ICHAEL), psychologist, educator; b. Passaic, N.J., Mar. 20, 1941; s. Benjamin and Anne (Pearl) W.; m. Meryl Etta Levenson, June 9, 1963; children: Jennifer, Jason. BA, Lafayette Coll., 1962; PhD, Yale U., 1967. Asst. prof. Rockefeller U., N.Y.C., 1969-73, assoc. prof., 1973-84; prof. dept. psychiatry Med. Ctr., Duke U., Durham, N.C., 1984-92; prof. dept psychiatry behavioral scis. Emory U. Sch. Medicine, Atlanta, Ga., 1992-95, Jenny Culbreth Adams prof. psychiatry and behavioral scis., 1995—; adj. assoc. prof. NYU, 1973-84, CCNY, 1979-84. MacArthur Found. fellow, 1984-89. Fellow AAAS, Soc. for Behavioral Medicine. Office: Emory Univ Sch Medicine Ga Mental Health Inst 1256 Briarcliff Rd NE Atlanta GA 30306-2636

WEISS, JOANNE MARION, writer; b. Wayne, N.J., Mar. 16, 1960; d. Henry Daniel and Florence Frances (Zaratkiewicz) W. BA, Bennington Coll., 1982; MA, U. Cambridge, Eng., 1988. Prodn. mgr. The Suburban News, N.J., 1982-83; gardener Artistic Landscaping, N.J., 1983; case mgr. Mid-Bergan Mental Health Ctr., N.J., 1985-86; founder Isis Farm Writers, 1995—. Author, dir.; (play) The Gift, 1987, 88. Translator Solidarity, Poland, 1983; co-leader Vols. for Peace, 1986; mem., worker Pregnancy Adv. Svc., Cambridge, 1991-92. Recipient scholarship Inst. for Brit. and Irish Studies, Trinity Coll., Dublin, 1985, Chancellor's medal for poetry U. Cambridge, Eng., 1988, grants for Edinburgh, Sir John Gielgud, 1988, grant Judith Wilson Fund, U. Cambridge, Eng., 1988. Mem. People for Ethical Treatment of Animals. Avocations: dog and horse training, animal welfare, singing, classical Greek, organic farming. Home: Isis Farm 265 River Rd Suncook NH 03275-2364

WEISS, JOSEPH JOEL, consulting company executive; b. Newark, July 27, 1931; s. Harry H. and Belle (Sass) W.; m. Leah Kneller, Apr. 10, 1954 (div. 1961); children: Sara, Daniel; m. Carol Lynn Seegott, Sept. 29, 1967; children: Laura, John. BSBA, Rutgers U., 1953, MBA, 1958. Dist. mgr. N.J. Bell Telephone Co., 1955-61; asst. comptroller ITT P.R. Telephone Co., San Juan, 1964-68; sr. cons. N.Y.C., 1968-71; v.p. data services Rio De Janeiro, 1971-74; dir. ops. N.Y.C., 1975-80; v.p. Control Data Corp., Rio De Janeiro, 1974-75; exec. v.p., chief adminstrv. officer Burger King Corp., Miami, 1980-89; chief oper. officer Goode, Olcott, Knight & Assocs., Coral Gables, Fla., 1989-90; pres. Contraband Detection Internat., Miami, Fla., 1990-92, Seegott Inc., Streetsboro, Ohio, 1992—; sr. v.p., bd. dirs. Sta. WPBTV. Pres. Civic Betterment Assn., Franklin Twp., N.J., 1961; trustee U. Miami Citizens Bd., 1987—; bd. dirs. Boy Scouts Am., 1982—. Recipient Strategic Planning Achievement award Boy Scouts Am., 1985. Mem. Hist. Soc. Fla. (bd. dirs. 1986—). Republican. Presbyterian. Club: Fisher Island. Avocations: oil painting, tennis. Home: 8216 Chagrin Rd Chagrin Falls OH 44023-4746 Office: Seegott Inc 10040 Aurora Hudson Rd Streetsboro OH 44241-1621

WEISS, JUDITH MIRIAM, psychologist; b. Chgo., June 29, 1939; d. Louis and Annette (Frazin) Schmerling; m. Jon Howard Kaas, May 19, 1963 (div. Dec. 1984); children: Lisa Karen, Jon Michael; m. Stephen Fred Weiss, Dec. 22, 1988. AB in Liberal Arts, Northwestern U., 1961; PhD, Duke U., 1969. Lic. clin. psychologist, Tenn. Postdoctoral fellow U. Wis. Hosp., Madison, 1969-71; neuropsychologist Mental Health Assocs., Madison, 1971-72; asst. prof. George Peabody Coll., Nashville, 1972-77, Vanderbilt U., Nashville, 1972-77; neuropsychologist Comprehensive Clin. Svcs., Nashville, 1977—; advocate, cons. Tenn. Protection and Advocacy, Inc., Nashville, 1976—. Mem. CABLE, Nashville. Mem. APA, Tenn. Psychol. Assn., Internat. Neuropsychol. Assn., Nat. Acad. Neuropsychology, U.s.-China Peoples Friendship Assn., Tenn. Head Injury Assn., B.R.A.I.N., Tenn. Assn. for the Talented and Gifted, Tenn. Assn. Audiologists and Speech-Lang. Pathologists, Nashville Area Psychol. Assn., Coun. for Learning Disabilities, Assn. for Children with Learning Disabilities. Jewish. Home: 893 Stirrup Dr Nashville TN 37221-1918 Office: Comprehensive Clin Svcs 102 Woodmont Blvd Ste 215 Nashville TN 37205-2287

WEISS, JULIE, costume designer. Costume designer: (stage) The Elephant Man, 1979 (Tony award nomination best costume design 1979); (films) I'm

Dancing as Fast as I Can, 1982, Independence Day, 1983, Second Thoughts, 1983, Spacehunter: Adventures in the Forbidden Zone, 1983, Testament, 1983, The Mean Season, 1985, Creator, 1985, F/X, 1986, Masters of the Universe, 1987, The Whales of August, 1987, 1969, 1988, Tequila Sunrise, 1988, Steel Magnolias, 1989, Wicked Stepmother, 1989, The Freshman, 1990, Married to It, 1991, Honeymoon in Vegas, 1992, House of Cards, 1993, Searching for Bobby Fischer, 1993, Naked in New York, 1993, It Could Happen to You, 1994, 12 Monkeys, 1995 (Acad. award nominee for best costume design 1996); (TV movies) The Gangster Chronicles, 1981, The Elephant Man, 1982 (Emmy award nominee for best costume design 1982), Little Gloria...Happy at Last, 1982 (Emmy award nominee for best costume design 1983), The Dollmaker, 1984 (Emmy award for best costume design 1984), Do You Remember Love?, 1985, Evergreen, 1985 (Emmy award nominee for best costume design 1985), Conspiracy of Love, 1987, A Woman of Independant Means, 1994 (Emmy award for best costume design), Love She Sought, 1990, The Portrait, 1993; costume cons.: (films) Cherry 2000, 1988. Office: care Costume Designer's Guild 13949 Ventura Blvd Ste 309 Sherman Oaks CA 91423-3570*

WEISS, KENNETH ANDREW, lawyer, law educator; b. New Orleans, Jan. 16, 1951; s. Irving and Julia (Mayer) W.; m. Barbara Hollingsworth, June 30, 1979. BA, Tulane U., 1972, JD with honors, 1975; LLM in Taxation with highest honors, George Washington U., 1981. Bar: La. 1975, D.C. 1976. Edit. writer, Washington corr. The Times-Picayune, New Orleans and Washington, 1973-79; news editor Congl. Quarterly, Washington, 1979-81; mng. editor Reporters Com. for Freedom of the Press, Washington, 1981-82; assoc. atty. McGlinchey Stafford, New Orleans, 1982-84, dir., 1984—; prof. Tulane U. Law Sch., New Orleans, 1987—; mem. trust code com. La. Law Inst., Baton Rouge, 1993—, mem. successions and donations com., 1996—; mem. planning com. Tulane Tax Inst., 1996—. Co-author: Bankers' Guide to Establishing, Managing and Operating Common Trust Funds, 1986, Business Uses of Life Insurance, 1986, Executive Compensation, 1990; assoc. editor Tulane Law Rev., 1974-75, mem. bd. adv. editors, 1992—; contbr. articles to profl. jours. Bd. dirs. Longue Vue House and Gardens Adv. Corp., 1993-95, bd. dirs. Longue Vue Found., 1995—; trustee Greater New Orleans Ednl. TV Found., Sta. WYES-TV, 1994—; mem. profl. adv. com., Jewish Endowment Found., 1982—; mem. planned gifts adv. com. Tulane U., 1989—; active Met. Area Com. Leadership Forum, New Orleans, 1983; fellow Inst. Politics Loyola U., New Orleans, 1989-90; mem. devel. com. Greater New Orleans Found., 1995—. Recipient Addy award for polit. advt., 1989, awards for investigative reporting; Phi Delta Phi scholar, 1972-73. Fellow Am. Coll. Trust and Estate Counsel; mem. La. State Bar Assn. (taxation sect., bd. cert. tax atty., bd. cert. estate planning and adminstrn. specialist), New Orleans Bar Assn., Nat. Coun. Planned Giving (greater New Orleans chpt.), New Orleans Estate Planning Coun., Order of the Coif. Republican. Jewish. Office: McGlinchey Stafford 643 Magazine St New Orleans LA 70130-3405

WEISS, KENNETH JAY, education educator, reading specialist, administrator; b. N.Y.C., Mar. 26, 1950; s. Daniel and Ida (Berson) W.; m. Roberta Carol Ungar, June 10, 1973; children: Seth, Marc, Richard. BA, C.W. Post Coll., 1972; MBA, Long Island U., 1982; EdM, Rutgers U., 1989, EdD, 1993. Cert. tchr. reading specialist, adminstr., N.J. Tchr. Rabbi Pesach Raymon Yeshiva, Edison, N.J., 1988-92; ednl. cons. New Brunswick (N.J.) Tomorrow, 1992-93; teaching rsch. asst. Rutgers U. Grad. Sch. of Edn., New Brunswick, 1991-93; asst. prof. edn., dir. grad. reading program Nazareth Coll., Rochester, N.Y., 1993—; spkr., facilitator, Rutgers Annual Summer Inst. on Literature and Literacy, New Brunswick, N.J., 1991, 92, 93, IRA Confs. Editl. rev. bd. Reading Teacher, 1995—, NYS Lang. and Literacy Spectrum. Bd. dirs. IRA SIG Children's Reading and Lit. Named Holmes Group Scholar, 1992-93. Mem. NCTE, Internat. Reading Assn., N.Y. State Reading Assn., Nat. Reading Conf., Nat. Conf. Rsch. in Lit. & Lang. Arts, Kappa Kelta Pi (counselor Rho Psi chpt. 1996—).

WEISS, LAWRENCE N., lawyer; b. N.Y.C., Aug. 9, 1942; s. Joseph and Martha (Guggenheimer) W.; m. Osnat Gad. BA, CCNY, 1963; LLB summa cum laude, Columbia U., 1966. Bar: N.Y. 1966, U.S. Ct. Appeals (2d cir.) 1967, U.S. Dist. Ct. (so. and ea. dists) N.Y. 1968, U.S. Supreme Ct. 1971, U.S. Ct. Appeals (3d cir.) 1968, U.S. Ct. Appeals (6th cir.) 1980, U.S. Tax Ct. 1977. Assoc. Kaye, Scholer, Fierman, Hays & Handler, N.Y.C., 1966-67, 67-73; law clk. to judge N.Y. Ct. Appeals, Albany and N.Y.C., 1967; assoc. Botein, Hays, Sklar & Herzberg, N.Y.C., 1973-76; assoc. Weisman, Celler, Spett, Modlin & Wertheimer, N.Y.C., 1976, ptnr., 1977-79, counsel, 1979-81; prin. Lawrence N. Weiss, P.C., N.Y.C., 1981—; Pantaleoni & Weiss, N.Y.C., 1993—; arbitrator Am. Arbitration Assn., 1968—, Civil Ct., N.Y.C., 1985—, Better Bus. Bur., N.Y.C., 1987—; mediator U.S. Dist. Ct. (ea. dist.) N.Y. and N.Y. Supreme Ct. Mem. Assn. Bar of City of N.Y. (com. on legal edn. and admission to bar), N.Y. State Bar Assn. (chair com. on fed. judiciary, spl. com. on copyright, vice chair com. on UN, subcom. internat. cts., com. continuing legal edn. litig. sect., judiciary com.). Avocations: Shakespearean studies, equestrian, scuba. Home: 230 Central Park W New York NY 10024-6029

WEISS, LEONARD, senate staff director, mathematician, engineer; b. N.Y.C., Mar. 14, 1934; s. Max and Sadie (Albert) W.; m. Sandra Joyce Raynes, June 15, 1958; children: Madelyn, Eugene. B.E.E., CCNY, 1956; M.S., Columbia U., 1959; Ph.D., Johns Hopkins U., 1962. Lectr. CCNY, 1956-59; staff scientist Research Inst. for Advanced Studies, Balt., 1962-64; asst. prof. Brown U., Providence, 1964-66; assoc. prof. Brown U., 1966-68; prof. U. Md., College Park, 1968-78; legis. asst. to Senator John Glenn of Ohio, 1976-77; cons. Naval Research Lab., Washington, 1970-77; staff dir. Senate Subcom. on Energy, Nuclear Proliferation and Govt. Processes, 1977-86, Senate Com. Govtl. Affairs., 1987—. Editor: Ordinary Differential Equations, 1972; contbr. articles to profl. jours.; author legislation on nuclear proliferation, energy, govt. orgn., and govt. mgmt. Alfred P. Sloan research fellow, 1966-68; IEEE Congl. fellow, 1976. Mem. AAAS, IEEE, Sigma Xi. Home: 11701 Auth Ln Silver Spring MD 20902-1644 Office: 326 Dirksen Bldg Washington DC 20510-0010

WEISS, LIONEL EDWARD, geology educator; b. London, Eng., Dec. 11, 1927; came to U.S., 1956, naturalized, 1972; s. S. and E. (Carney) W.; m. Liv Mariane Nissen-Sollie, Dec. 27, 1964; children: Nicholas Erling, Elin Katrina. B.Sc. with 1st class honours, U. Birmingham, Eng., 1949, Ph.D., 1953; Sc.D., U. Edinburgh, Scotland, 1956. Commonwealth Fund fellow U. Calif. at Berkeley, 1951-53; sr. research fellow U. Edinburgh, 1953-56; mem. faculty U. Calif. at Berkeley, 1956—, prof. geology, 1964-89, emeritus prof. geology, 1989—, Miller research prof., 1965, 66; cons. in field. Author: (with F.J. Turner) Structural Analysis of Metamorphic Tectonites, 1963, (with others) The Earth, 1970, The Minor Structures of Deformed Rocks, 1972; also articles. Guggenheim fellow, 1962, 69; Fulbright scholar Norway, 1975. Home: 1954 Patricia Dr Pleasant Hill CA 94523-2930

WEISS, LOREN ELLIOT, lawyer, law educator; b. Cleve., Sept. 28, 1947; s. Harry and Gertrude (Rapport) W.; m. Gina Dalton. BA with honors, UCLA, 1969; JD cum laude, U. San Diego, 1972. Bar: Calif. 1972, U.S. Dist. Ct. (so. dist.) Calif. 1972, Utah 1983, U.S. Dist. Ct. (cen. dist.) Calif. 1983, U.S. Dist. Ct. Utah 1983, U.S. Ct. Appeals (9th cir.) 1972, U.S. Ct. Appeals (10th cir.) 1986. With various law firms, San Diego, 1972-80; owner, gen. mgr. Mid-Mountain Lodge, Park City, Utah, 1980-83; pvt. practice, Salt Lake City, 1983-89, 93—; of counsel Purser, Okazaki & Berrett, Salt Lake City, 1989-93; prin. Weiss Berrett Loyd Petty, Salt Lake City, 1996—; mem. Utah Com. Bar Examiners, Salt Lake City, 1989-93; mem. ann. meeting com. Utah State Bar, 1985-91, chmn., 1994-95; liaison, panel atty. rep. U.S. Jud. Conf.Com. on Defender Svc., 1992-95; mem. mandatory cont. legal edn. bd. Utah Judicial Conf., 1995—. Contbr. articles to legal jours. Trustee Utah Trout Found., Salt Lake City, 1988—. Mem. FBA, Calif. Bar Assn., Utah Bar Assn., Nat. Assn. Criminal Def. Lawyers (co-chmn. continuing legal edn. com. 1992-93, co-chair indigent svcs. com. 1994-95), Utah Assn. Criminal Def. Lawyers (pres. 1993), Am. Bd. Trial Advocates. Avocations: fly fishing, reading. Office: 170 S Main St Ste 1100 Salt Lake City UT 84101-1652

WEISS, MAREDA RUTH, dean; b. Chgo., Sept. 23, 1941; d. William Arthur and Ruth Emily (Schauble) W. BBA, U. Wis., 1963. Acct., then supr. rsch. adminstrn./fin. U. Wis. System, Madison, 1964-69; specialist, asst. dean, assoc. dean, dir. rsch. programs U. Wis., Madison, 1969—; univ. chair State Employees Combined Campaign, Madison, 1986. Treas. Wis. Cen. Ctr. Aux., Madison, 1971-73, 75-77, 79-81, Frineds of WHA-TV pub. tv, Madison, 1989-91; chair nominating com. U. Wis. Credit Union, 1982-88. Recipient Excellence in Leadership award Wis. Alumni Assn., 1997. Mem. Nat. Coun. Univ. Rsch. Adminstrs. (presenter workshops, program. coms. 1990, 95, sec.-treas. 1980-83, chair, vice-chair mid-Am. region 1989-91, Disting. Svc. award 1989), Univ. Ins. Assn. (bd. dirs. 1982—). Avocations: skiing, golf, photography, travel. Office: U Wis Grad Sch 500 Lincoln Dr Madison WI 53706-1314

WEISS, MARK, public relations executive; b. N.Y.C., Mar. 5, 1950. BA in Psychology, Queens Coll., 1972; MA om Social Psychology, New Sch. for Social Rsch., 1975. With Multimedia Advt./Pub. Rels., 1970-74; account rep. Edward Baker, Inc., 1974-78; account exec. Rowland Co., 1978-81, v.p., 1980-84, sr. v.p., 1984-86, exec. v.p., 1986-90, sr. exec. v.p., COO, 1991-92, pres., CEO, 1992—. Office: Rowland Worldwide Inc 1675 Broadway New York NY 10019-5820*

WEISS, MARK ANSCHEL, lawyer; b. N.Y.C., June 20, 1937; s. George and Ida (Galin) W.; m. Joan Roth, June 8, 1958; children—Rebecca, Sarabeth, Jonathan, Deborah. A.B., Columbia U., 1958; LL.B. magna cum laude, Harvard U., 1961; Bar: N.Y. 1961, D.C. 1962, U.S. Supreme Ct. 1965. Assoc. Covington & Burling, Washington, 1961-66, 69-70, ptnr., 1970—; spl. asst. to Under Sec. Treasury Dept., Washington, 1966-68, spl. asst. to sec., 1968-69. Mem. editl. adv. bd. Electronic Banking Law and Commerce Report. Mem. D.C. Bar, ABA, Fed. Bar Assn. (mem. exec. coun., banking law com.), City Club (Washington). Office: Covington & Burling PO Box 7566 1201 Pennsylvania Ave NW Washington DC 20044

WEISS, MARK LAWRENCE, anthropology educator; b. Bklyn., Nov. 1, 1945; s. Arthur A. and Ruth E. Heilbrunn W.; m. Linda K. Spangler, July 31, 1993; children: Evan M., Emily C. BA, SUNY, Binghamton, 1966; MA, U. Calif., Berkeley, 1968, PhD, 1969. Asst. prof. anthropology Wayne State U., Detroit, 1969-73, assoc. prof., 1973-87, prof., 1987—; program dir. phys. anthropology NSF, Washington, 1990-92, 95—. Co-author: Human Biology and Behavior, 1975; contbr. articles to Nature, Am. Jour. Primatology, Yearbook, Phys. Anthropology, Jour. Molecular Biology; mem. editorial bd. Human Biology, 1988—, Yearbook of Phys. Anthropology, 1992—, Jour. Human Evolution, 1994—. Recipient award in excellence in teaching and rsch. Probus Club, 1973. Fellow Am. Anthrop. Assn., Am. Assn. Phys. Anthropologists (exec. com. 1993-96). Jewish. Office: Dept Anthropology Wayne State Univ. Detroit MI 48202

WEISS, MARTIN HARVEY, neurosurgeon, educator; b. Newark, Feb. 2, 1939; s. Max and Rae W.; m. R. Debora Rosenthal, Aug. 20, 1961; children: Brad, Jessica, Elisabeth. AB magna cum laude, Dartmouth Coll., 1960, BMS, 1961; MD, Cornell U., 1963. Diplomate Am. Bd. Neurol. Surgery (bd. dirs. 1983-89, vice chmn. 1987-88, chmn. 1988-89). Intern Univ. Hosps., Cleve., 1963-64; resident in neurosurgery Univ. Hosps., 1966-70; sr. instr. to asst. prof. neurosurgery Case Western Res. U., 1970-73; asso. prof. neurosurgery U. So. Calif., 1973-76, prof., 1976-78, prof., chmn. dept., 1978—; chmn. neurology B study sect. NIH; mem. residency rev. com. for neurosurgery Accreditation Commn. for Grad. Med. Edn., 1989—, vice chmn., 1991-93, chmn., 1993-95, mem. appeals coun. in neurosurgery, 1995—; Courville lectr. Loma Linda U. Sch. Medicine, 1989; Edgar Kahn vis. prof. U. Mich., 1987; W. James Gardner lectr. Cleve. Clinic, 1993; Edwin Boldrey vis. prof. U. Calif., San Francisco, 1994; hon. guest San Francisco Neurol. Soc., 1994, Australian Neurosurg. Soc., 1996; Aurthur Ward vis. prof. U. Wash., 1988; John Raff vis. prof. U. Oreg., 1995; Afrox traveling prof. South African Congress Neurol. Surgeons, 1989; Loyal Davis lectr. Northwestern U., 1990; vis. prof. U. Melbourne, 1996, U. Sydney, 1996; Wagner lecr. U. Md., 1997. Author: Pituitary Diseases, 1980; editor-in-chief Clin. Neurosurgery, 1980-83; assoc. editor Bull. L.A. Neurol. Socs., 1976-81, Jour. Clin. Neurosci., 1981—; mem. editl. bd. Neurosurgery, 1979-84, Neurol. Rsch., 1980—, Jour. Neurosurgery, 1987—, chmn., 1995—, assoc. editor, 1996. Served to capt. USAR, 1964-66. Spl. fellow in neurosurgery NIH, 1969-70; recipient Jamieson medal Australasian Neurosurg. Soc., 1996. Mem. ACS (adv. coun. neurosurgery 1985-88), Soc. Neurol. Surgeons, Neurosurg. Soc. Am., Am. Acad. Neurol. Surgery (exec. com. 1988-89, v.p. 1992-93), Rsch. Soc. Neurol. Surgeons, Am. Assn. Neurol. Surgeons (bd. dirs. 1988-91, sec. 1994-97), Congress Neurol. Surgeons (v.p. 1982-83), Western Neurosurg. Soc., Neurosurg. Forum, So. Calif. Neurosurg. Soc. (pres. 1983-84), Phi Beta Kappa, Alpha Omega Alpha. Home: 357 Georgian Rd La Canada-Flintridge CA 91011-3520 Office: 1200 N State St Los Angeles CA 90033-4525

WEISS, MAX TIBOR, retired aerospace company executive; b. Hajduananas, Hungary, Dec. 29, 1922; came to U.S., 1929, naturalized, 1936; s. Samuel and Anna (Hornstein) W.; m. Melitta Newman, June 28, 1953; children: Samuel Harvey, Herschel William, David Nathaniel, Deborah Beth. BEE, CCNY, 1943; MS, MIT, 1947, PhD, 1950. Rsch. assoc. MIT, 1946-50; mem. tech. staff Bell Tel. Labs., Holmdel, N.J., 1950-59; assoc. head applied physics lab. Hughes Aircraft Co., Culver City, Calif., 1959-60; dir. electronics rsch. lab. The Aerospace Corp., L.A., 1961-63, gen. mgr. labs. div., 1963-67, gen. mgr. electronics and optics div., 1968-78, v.p., gen. mgr. lab. ops., 1978-81, v.p. engring. group, 1981-86; v.p. tech. and electronics system group Northrop Corp., L.A., 1986-91; v.p., gen. mgr. electronics systems div. Northrop Corp., Hawthorne, Calif., 1991-94; corp. v.p., dep. gen. mgr. electronics/systems integration Northrop Grumman Corp., Bethpage, N.Y., 1994-96, corp. v.p., 1996; asst. mgr. engring. ops. TRW Systems, Redondo Beach, Calif., 1967-68; mem. sci. adv. bd. USAF. Contbr. articles to physics and electronics jours.; patentee in electronics and communications. With USNR, 1944-45. Fellow Am. Phys. Soc., IEEE (Centennial medal, 1983, Fredrik Philips award, 1993), AIAA, AAAS; mem. NAE, Sigma Xi.

WEISS, MICHAEL JAMES, chemistry educator; b. N.Y.C., May 29, 1941; s. Irving and Florence (James) W.; m. Myra Lee Landau, June 10, 1967; 1 child, Amy Merril Weiss Musikar. BS in Chemistry, Bklyn. Coll., 1964; MS in Chemistry, Adelphi U., 1966; PhD in Biochemistry, N.Y. Med. Coll., 1971. Supr. clin. chemistry Queens Gen. Hosp., N.Y.C., 1971-77; dir. biochemistry Kingsborough Med. Ctr., N.Y.C., 1977-78; lab. dir. Nassau (N.Y.) Diagnostic Lab., 1978-86; chemistry educator N.Y. Bd. Edn., 1986—; lab. cons., N.Y., 1986—. Author: (chpt.) The Antigenic Nature of Mamalian Cell Membranes, 1976; contbr. articles to profl. jours. Trustee Village of Atlantic Beach, 1995. Maj. U.s. Army, 1978—. Decorated Army Achievement medal; recipient Conspicuous Svc. cross; Howard Hughes Med. Inst. fellow, 1994. Mem. AAAS, N.Y. Acad. Sci., Armed Forces Soc. Med. Lab. Scientists. Achievements include research in oneofetal antigens.

WEISS, MYRNA GRACE, business consultant; b. N.Y.C., June 22, 1939; d. Herman and Blanche (Stiftel) Ziegler; m. Arthur H. Weiss; children: Debra Anne Huddleston, Louise Esther. BA, Barnard Coll., 1958; MA, Hunter Coll., 1968; MPA, NYU, 1978; cert. in Mktg., U. Pa. Tchr. N.Y.C. and Vallejo, Calif., 1959-68; dir. admissions Columbia Prep. Sch., N.Y.C., 1969-72; dir. PREP counselling NYU, N.Y.C., 1973-74; dept. head Hewitt Sch., N.Y.C., 1974-79; mgr. Met. Ins. Co., N.Y.C., 1979-84; mktg. exec. Rothschild, Inc., N.Y.C., 1984-85; pres. First Mktg. Capital Group Ltd., N.Y.C., 1985—; mng. dir. Wrap Co. Internat. N.V., 1992—; advisor Lared Group, N.Y.C., 1987—; advisor Gov.'s Hwy. Safety Com., N.Y.C., 1985-88; pres. Fin. Women's Assn. N.Y., 1984-85. Bd. dirs. 92nd Y, N.Y.C., 1972-90, ARC, N.Y.C., 1989-96, asst. treas., 1993-96. Mem. Internat. Women's Forum (bd. dirs. 1990-92), Econ. Club N.Y., Women's Econ. Roundtable (bd. dirs. 1988-90). Office: 1st Mktg Capital Group Ltd 1056 Fifth Ave New York NY 10028-0112

WEISS, PAUL, philosopher, educator; b. N.Y.C., May 19, 1901; s. Samuel and Emma (Rothschild) W.; m. Victoria Brodkin, Oct. 27, 1928 (dec. Dec. 31, 1953); children: Judith, Jonathan. BS, CCNY, 1927; MA, Harvard U., 1928, PhD (Sears Travelling fellow), 1929; hon. degrees, Grinnell Coll., 1960, Pace Coll., 1969, Bellarmine Coll., 1973, Haverford Coll., 1974, Boston U., 1989. Instr., tutor philosophy Harvard U., also instr. Radcliffe Coll., 1930-31; assoc. in philosophy Bryn Mawr (Pa.) Coll., 1931-33, assoc. prof., 1933-40, prof., 1940-46, chmn. dept., 1944-46; Guggenheim fellow, 1938; vis. prof. Yale U., 1945-46, prof. philosophy, 1946-62, Sterling prof. philosophy, 1962-69, Sterling prof. emeritus, 1969—; fellow Ezra Stiles Coll.; vis. prof. philosophy Hebrew U., Jerusalem, 1951; Luce-Rabinowitz grantee for study, Israel and India, 1954; lectr. Aspen Inst., 1952, Chancellor's Forum, U. Denver, 1952; Orde Wingate lectr., 1954; Powell lectr. U. Ind., 1958; Gates lectr. Grinnell Coll., 1960; Matchette lectr. Purdue U., 1961, Wesleyan Coll., 1963; Aquinas lectr. Marquette U., 1963; Townsend Harris medalist, 1963; Rhoades lectr. Haverford Coll., 1964; Phi Beta Kappa lectr., 1968-69; resident scholar State U. N.Y., 1969, 70; vis. prof. U. Denver, spring 1969; Eliot lectr. Marquette U., 1970; William De Vane medalist Yale, 1971; Aquinas lectr. St. Mary's, 1971; medalist City Coll., 1973, Hofstra U., 1973; B. Means lectr. Trinity Coll.; lectr., Japan, 1981; Ann. McDermott Lectr. U. Dallas, 1983; vis. Heffer prof. Philosophy Cath. U. Am., 1969-91, 93-94. Author: Reality, 1938, Nature and Man, 1947, Man's Freedom, 1950 (Portugese transl., 1960), Modes of Being, 1958, Our Public Life, 1959, World of Art, 1961 (Hebrew transl., 1970), Nine Basic Arts, 1961, History: Written and Lived, 1962, Religion and Art, 1963, The God We Seek, 1964, Philosophy in Process, 12 vols., 1955-88, The Making of Men, 1967, Sport: A Philosophic Inquiry, 1969 (Japanese transl., 1985, Korean transl., 1993), Beyond All Appearances, 1974, Cinematics, 1975, First Considerations, 1977, You, I and The Others, 1980, Privacy, 1983, Toward a Perfected State, 1986, Creative Ventures, 1991, Being and Other Realities, 1995; co-author: Right and Wrong: A Philosophical Dialogue Between Father and Son, 1967, 71 (Hebrew transl., 1971), Approaches to World Peace, 1944, Perspectives on a Troubled Decade, 1950, Moral Principles of Action, 1952, Personal Moments of Discovery, 1953, Perspectives on Peirce, 1965, Dimensions of Job, 1969, Mid-Century American Philosophy, 1974, Philosophy of Baruch Spinoza, 1980, Existence and Actuality, 1984, When the Worst That Can Happen Already Has, 1992, The Philosophy of Paul Weiss: Autobiography, Replies to Critics, Drawings, and Bibliography, 1995; co-editor: Collected Papers of Charles S. Peirce, 6 vols.; founder, editor Rev. Metaphysics, 1947-63; mem. editl. bd. Judaism, Jour. Speculative Philosophy; contbr. articles to profl. jours. Mem. Assn. for Symbolic Logic (councillor 1936), Am. Philos. Assn. (co-pres. 1966), Conf. on Sci., Philosophy and Religion (founding), C.S. Peirce Soc. (founding, pres.), Metaphys. Soc. Am. (founder, pres. 1951-52, councillor 1953-58), Philos. Soc. for Study of Sport (co-founder, pres. 1973), Am. Friends Hebrew U., Philos. Edn. Soc. (founder), Washington Philosophic Club (C.S. Peirce award), European Soc. Culture, Internat. Acad. Philosophy of Art, Am. Assn. Mid. East Studies, Aurelian Club, Elizabethan Club, Phi Beta Kappa. Address: 2000 N St NW Washington DC 20036-2336

WEISS, PAUL THOMAS, management consultant; b. Bismarck, N.D., Nov. 18, 1944; s. Earl Paul and Hazel Lucretia (Baker) W.; children: Mark David, Clare Elizabeth. BS, U. N.D., 1967. Pers. mgmt. specialist Dept. Justice, Washington, 1970-72; labor employee relations specialist Dept. Treasury, Washington, 1972-77; assoc. dir. human resources Comptr. of Currency, Washington, 1977-80; dep. dir. pers. Dept. Treasury, Washington, 1980-83, dir. pers., 1984-85; assoc. adminstr. for adminstrn. GSA, Washington, 1985-89; assoc. dir. mgmt. and budget U.S. Action Agy., Washington, 1989-90; dep. asst. sec. for adminstrn. Dept. Transp., Washington, 1990-95; pvt. practice mgmt. cons., 1995—; mem. Pres. Coun. Mgmt. Improvement, 1985-89; mem. panel on pub. svc. Nat. Acad. Pub. Adminstrn., 1986—; v.p., mem. exec. com. Am. Consortium for Internat. Pub. Adminstrn., 1986—; bd. dirs. Worldwide Assurance for Employees of Pub. Agys., Inc., 1986—. Author (booklet) You and Your Employees, 1974; author, reviewer numerous reports and govt. manuals. With Med. Svc. Corps, U.S. Army, 1969-70, Vietnam. Decorated Bronze Star medal with 3 oak leaf clusters; recipient Pres. Rank Meritorious Svc. award Pres. U.S., 1987, awards U.S. Treas., 1979, 85, Govt. Exec. Mag. Leadership award, 1992. Mem. Am. Soc. Pub. Adminstrs. (bd. dirs. Nat. Capital area chpt., treas.). Roman Catholic. Avocations: bridge, jogging, reading. Office: Nat Acad Pub Adminstrn 800 N Capitol St NE Ste 110 Washington DC 20002-4244

WEISS, RANDALL A., television producer, supermarket executive; b. Gary, Ind., Sept. 3, 1952; s. Arthur and Sylvia (Mednick) W.; m. Adrienne J. Weiss, Feb. 5, 1973; children: Benjamin, Caleb, Joshua, James, Abigail, Emma. AA, Coll. DuPage, 1977; BA, Dallas Bapt. U., 1993; MA in Religious Studies, Greenwich U., 1994; diploma of practical theology, Christ for the Nations Inst., 1993; PhD, Greenwich U., 1995; MS in Jewish Studies, Spertus Inst. Jewish Studies, 1996; DMin, Faraston Theol. Sem., 1996. Ordained to Ministry, Ch. of Nations. Gen. mgr. We Care Food Stores, Inc., Knox, Ind., 1975-84; pres., CEO We Care Food Stores, Inc. subs. Five Star Foods, Knox, Ind., 1984—; prodn. mgr. Excellence in Christian Broadcasting; songwriter, pub. Lordship Music Pub., BMI; asst. prof. on adj. faculty ICI U.; dean Jewish studies dept. Faraston Theol. Sem.; chmn. acad. rev. bd. Gateway Coll. Program. Author: Jewish Sects of the New Testament Era, Does Jacob's Trouble Wear a Cross?: Christianity: A Jewish Religion, In Search of the Lost Jewish Atonement; writer, artist: (TV show) Crosstalk, 1994, 95, 96, 97. Internat. dir. Lesea Global Feed the Hungry, South Bend, Ind., 1988—; sr. pastor Grace Worship Ctr., Inc. Mem. Full Gospel Bus. Men's Fellowship Internat. (life, banquet spkr.), Soc. for Pentecostal Studies, Evang. Theol. Soc. Avocations: fishing, travel, reading, music. Office: Five Star Foods 1209 S Heaton St Knox IN 46534-2311

WEISS, RENÉE KAROL, editor, writer, musician; b. Allentown, Pa., Sept. 11, 1923; d. Abraham S. and Elizabeth (Levitt) Karol; m. Theodore Weiss. BA, Bard Coll., 1951; student, Conn. Sch. Dance; studied violin with, Sascha Jacobinoff, Boris Koutzen, Emile Hauser, Ivan Galamian. Mem. Miami U. Symphony Orch., 1941, N.C. State Sympnony, 1942-45, Oxford U. Symphony, Opera Orchs., Eng., 1953-54, Woodstock String Quartet, 1956-60, Bard Coll. Chamber Ensemble, 1950-66, Hudson Valley Philharmonic, 1960-66, Hudson Valley String Quartet, 1965, Princeton Chamber Orch., 1980-93; orchestral, chamber, solo work, 1966—; presenter Theodore and Renée Weiss poetry writing workshops Princeton U., 1985, Hofstra Coll., 1985, modern poetry workshop Cooper Union, 1988, Princeton Adult Edn.; tchr. modern dance to children Bard Coll., Kindergarten Tivoli, N.Y. Pub. Sch., 1955-58. Author: (children's books) To Win A Race, 1966, A Paper Zoo, 1968 (best books for children N.Y. Times, Book World 1968, N.J. Author's award 1968, 70, 88), The Bird From the Sea, 1970, Biography: David Schubert: Works and Days, 1984; co-editor, mgr. Quar. Rev. Lit., 1945—; author of poetry with Theodore Weiss; poetry readings (with Theodore Weiss) at various colls. in U.S. and abroad, including China. Mem. PEN (Nora Magid Lifetime Achievement award with Theodore Weiss 1997). Home and Office: Q R L Poetry Series 26 Haslet Ave Princeton NJ 08540-4914

WEISS, RICHARD RONALD, rocket propulsion technology executive; b. Detroit, Nov. 4, 1934; s. Charles Max and Edna May (Guard) W.; m. Sally Anita Sparkman, Aug. 10, 1957; children: Mark, Kevin, Todd, Scott. BS in Aero. Engring., U. Mich., 1957; MSME, U. So. Calif., 1964; PhD in Mech. Engring., Purdue U., 1970. Devel. engr. Jupiter Missile rocket engine Rocketdyne, 1957-58; unit chief, test condr. THOR Missile test program Air Force Rocket Prop. Lab., 1958-61, various tech. positions, 1961-65, various engring. mgmt. positions, 1965-74, chief scientist, 1974-89, 1st dir. Strategic Def. Initiative Tech. Office, 1985-87; chief scientist Air Force Rocket Prop. Lab. (renamed Astronautics Lab.), 1987-89; dir. Astronautics Lab., 1989-90; chief scientist, dir. Astronautics Lab. (merger Phillips Lab.), 1990-91; dir. Propulsion Directorate Phillips Lab. Operating Location, Edwards AFB, Calif., 1991-93; dep. dir. space launch systems and tech. Office of Under Sec. of Def., Strategic and Space Systems, Missiles and Space Systems, 1993-94; ret., 1994; past tech. panel chmn. Space Launch Modernization Plan, 1994; mem. Nat. Rsch. Coun. Aeronautics & Space Engring. Bd., Advanced Space Tech. Panel, Washington, 1992-94; U.S. rep. Agard Propulsion & Energetics Panel, Paris, 1987—; mem. ad hoc panel on space launch USAF Sci., 1993—; chmn. Joint Army, Navy, AF (JANNAF) Interagy. Chem. Propulsion Exec. Com.; contbr. to rocket propulsion devels. for most of the nation's space and missile sys. including Apollo, Space Shuttle, Titan, Atlas, Peacekeeper, Minuteman, Strategic Def. Initiative;. 1st lt. USAF, 1958-61. Co-recipient Air Force Sys. Command Aerospace Primus award, 1986. Fellow AIAA (assoc., AIAA Wyld Propulsion award 1994). Home: 5912 Walnut Way Palmdale CA 93551-2812

WEISS, ROBERT BENJAMIN, lawyer; b. Perth Amboy, N.J., Aug. 27, 1948; s. Denes and Patricia (Chazin) W.; m. Susan Stern, June 11, 1972; children: Elana, Shira, Danielle. BA, Yeshiva U., 1971; JD, Case Western U., 1975. Bar: Mich. 1977, U.S. Dist. Ct. (ea. dist.) Mich. 1978. Assoc. Ulmer, Berne, Laronge, Glickman & Curtis, Cleve., 1975-76; staff atty. Gen.

Motors Corp., Detroit, 1976-82; ptnr. Honigman Miller Schwartz & Cohn, Detroit, 1982—. Office: Honigman Miller Schwartz & Cohn 2290 1st National Bldg Detroit MI 48226

WEISS, ROBERT FRANCIS, former academic administrator, religious organization administrator, consultant; b. St. Louis, Aug. 27, 1924; s. Frank L. G. and Helen M. (Beck) W. B.A., St. Louis U., 1951, Ph.L., 1953, M.A., 1953, S.T.L., 1961; Ph.D., U. Minn., 1964. Joined Soc. of Jesus, 1946; ordained priest Roman Catholic Ch., 1959; tchr. Rockhurst High Sch., Kansas City, Mo., 1953-56; adminstrv. asst. to pres. St. Louis U., 1961-62; asst. dean Rockhurst Coll., Kansas City, Mo., 1964-66, dean, v.p., asst. prof. edn., 1966-72, pres., 1977-88; pres. St. Louis U. High Sch., 1973-77, interim pres., 1992; asst. for higher edn. and continuing formation Mo. Province S.J., St. Louis, 1989-92, treas., 1992—; mem. Commn. on Govtl. Rels., Am. Coun. Edn., 1985-87; bd. dirs. Kansas City Regional Coun. for Higher Edn., 1978-88, Boys Hope/Girls Hope, 1977—. Contbr. chpts. to books, articles to profl. jours. Trustee St. Louis U., 1973-87, 91—, Loyola U., New Orleans, 1973-82, 85-88, United Student Aid Funds, Inc., 1977-94, U. San Francisco, 1987—, Marymount Coll., Salina, Kans., 1986-88, St. Louis U. H.S., 1989—, Fontbonne Coll., St. Louis, 1973-77, Sacred Heart Program, Radio and TV Apostolate, St. Louis, 1990-96, pres., 1992-96; bd. dirs. Creighton U., Omaha, 1981—, Our Little Haven, 1992—. With U.S. Army, 1943-46. Decorated Bronze Star. Mem. Am. Assn. for Higher Edn., Rainbow Divsn. Vets. Assn. (nat. chaplain 1976-84, 88-90, pres.-elect 1990-91, pres. 1991-92, assoc. nat. chaplain 1992—), Alpha Sigma Nu, Alpha Phi Omega. Home and Office: 4511 W Pine Blvd Saint Louis MO 63108-2109 *The only way for me to look at life is in the light of faith, which I consider one of God's greatest gifts. Life for me is an opportunity to serve God and as many of my neighbors as I can. I am basically an optimist. There is so much beauty around us, so many good people, so many marvels to behold—that I thank the Lord for giving me the ability to know and experience this life and to look forward to eternal life with God, the Source of all life. Any success I have had I attribute to taking advantage of the opportunities that God has put in my path.*

WEISS, ROBERT JEROME, psychiatrist, educator; b. West New York, N.J., Dec. 9, 1917; s. Harry and Dora (Samuels) W.; m. Minnie Thompson Moore, Apr. 21, 1945; children—Scott Tillman, James Woodrow, Elizabeth Thompson. Student, Johns Hopkins, 1937; A.B., George Washington U., 1947; M.D., Columbia, 1951; M.A. (hon.), Dartmouth, 1964. Intern Columbia div. Bellevue Hosp., 1951, asst. resident medicine, 1953; resident psychiatry N.Y. Psychiat. Inst., 1954-56; asst. attending Vanderbilt Clinic, 1957-58, Presbyn. Hosp., N.Y.C., 1958-59; chief psychiatry Mary Hitchcock Meml. Hosp., 1959-70; career tchr. trainee Nat. Inst. Mental Health, 1956-58; tchr., research Columbia Coll. Phys. and Surg., 1956-59; prof. psychiatry, chmn. dept. Dartmouth Med. Sch., 1959-70; psychiatrist Beth Israel Hosp., 1988-90; attending physician Presbyn. Hosp., 1975-85, cons., 1985—; vis. prof. comty. medicine Harvard Med. Sch., 1970-75, assoc. dir. comty. health, 1970-95, assoc. dean health care planning; prof. psychiatry and social medicine Columbia Coll. Physicians and Surgeons, 1975-86, also dir. Ctrs. for Comty. Health, 1975-86; De Lamar prof. pub. health practice, dean Columbia U. Sch. Pub. Health, 1980-86, dean and De Lamar prof. of pub. health practice, prof. psychiatry, prof. social medicine, prof. emeritus, 1986—; vis. prof. comty. medicine U. N.Mex. Med. Sch., 1986-89; cons. Nat. Ctr. for Health Svcs. Rsch., 1975-86, NIMH, 1977-86; chmn. psychiatry tng. com. NIMH, 1967-68, mem. coord. panel, 1965-67, ad hoc com. interdisciplinary tng. program, 1966, mem. agenda com., 1966; cons. AT&T, 1990-92; chmn. bd. Academica, 1992, Employee Managed Care Corp., 1994—. Co-editor: Columbia U. Coll. Physicians and Surgeons Complete Home Medical Guide, 1986, editor emeritus 2d and 3d edits., 1989; contbr. articles to profl. jours., chpts. to books. Served to maj. AUS, 1941-46. Recipient Bi-Centennial medal Columbia Coll. Phys. and Surg., 1967. Fellow Am. Psychiat. Assn. (life); mem. Am. Assn. Chmn. Depts. Psychiatry (pres. 1979-80). Achievements include demonstrated social supports reduce disability due to mental illness; research in special health care delivery, health care preventive psychiatry. Home: 10 Cromwell Dr Orono ME 04473

WEISS, ROBERT M., urologist, educator; b. N.Y.C., Jan. 13, 1936; s. David and Laura W.; m. Ilana Shemer, May 20, 1973; children—Erik Daniel, Dana Alexandra. B.S. magna cum laude, Franklin and Marshall Coll., Lancaster, Pa., 1957; M.D., SUNY, Bklyn., 1960; M.A. (hon.), Yale U., 1976. Diplomate: Am. Bd. Urology, Nat. Bd. Med. Examiners. Intern Cornell Med. Div., Bellevue Hosp., N.Y.C., 1960-61; resident in gen. surgery Beth Israel Hosp., N.Y.C., 1961-62; resident in urology Squier Urol. Clinic, Presbyn. Hosp., N.Y.C., 1963-64, 65-67; vs. fellow Columbia U. Coll. Physicians and Surgeons, N.Y.C., 1964-65, adj. assoc. prof. pharmacology, 1975-77, adj. prof. pharmacology, 1977—; mem. faculty Yale U. M.ed. Sch., New Haven, 1967—, prof. urology, 1976-88, prof., chief sect. of urology, 1988—; attending urology Yale-New Haven Hosp., New Haven, 1967-88, head sect. of urology, 1988—; cons. West Haven VA Hosp., Waterbury (Conn.) Hosp. Contbr. articles to med. publs. Served with USAR, 1962-63. Fellow ACS, Am. Acad. Pediatrics; mem. Am. Assn. Genito-Urinary Surgeons, Am. Physiol. Soc., Soc. Gen. Physiologists, Assn. Univ. Urologists, Soc. Pediatric Urology, Am. Urol. Assn., Am. Soc. Clin. Pharmacology and Therapeutics, Internat. Urodynamics Soc., AAAS, Internat. Soc. Dynamics of Upper Urinary Tract, Clin. Soc. Genito-Urinary Surgeons, Phi Beta Kappa, Sigma Xi.

WEISS, ROBERT ORR, speech educator; b. Kalamazoo, Apr. 8, 1926; s. Nicholas John and Ruth (Orr) W.; m. Ann Lenore Lawson, Sept. 16, 1951; children: Elizabeth Ann, John Lawson, James Robert, Virginia Lenore. BA, Albion Coll., 1948; MA, Northwestern U., 1949, PhD, 1954. Instr. speech Wayne State U., Detroit, 1949-51; instr. pub. speaking Northwestern U., Evanston, Ill., 1954-55; mem. faculty DePauw U., Greencastle, Ind., 1955—, H.B. Gough prof. speech, 1965—, dir. forensics, head communication arts and scis., 1963-78, 85-86, 93. Author: Public Argument, 1995; editor: Speaker and Gavel, 1968-75; co-editor: Current Criticism, 1971; contbr. articles to profl. jours. Served with AUS, 1945-46. Recipient Fred C. Tucker Disting. Career award, 1995, Lifetime award, Nat. Ednl. Debate Assn., 1997. Mem. AAUP (pres. DePauw U. chpt. 1961-62), Speech Communication Assn. (legis. assembly 1966-68), Am. Forensic Assn. (sec.-treas. 1958-59), Cen. States Communication Assn., Internat. Communication Assn., Phi Beta Kappa, Delta Sigma Rho-Tau Kappa Alpha (nat. v.p. 1981-83, pres. 1983-85), Theta Alpha Phi, Omicron Delta Kappa, Sigma Nu. Home: 722 Highridge Ave Greencastle IN 46135-1402

WEISS, ROBERT STEPHEN, medical manufacturing and services company financial executive; b. Honesdale, Pa., Oct. 25, 1946; s. Stephen John and Anna Blanche (Lescinski) W.; BS in Acctg. cum laude, U. Scranton, 1968; m. Marilyn Annette Chesick, Oct. 29, 1970; children: Christopher Robert, Kim Marie, Douglas Paul. CPA, N.Y. Supr., Peat, Marwick, Mitchell & Co., N.Y.C., 1971-76; asst. corp. contr. Cooper Labs., Inc., Parsippany, N.J., 1977-78, v.p., corp. contr. Palo Alto, Calif., 1981-83; v.p., corp. contr. The Cooper Cos., Inc. (formerly CooperVision, Inc.), Palo Alto, Calif., 1984-89; v.p., treas., CFO The Cooper Cos., Inc., Pleasanton, Calif., 1989—, sr. v.p., 1992-95, exec. v.p., 1995—; v.p. fin., contr. CooperVision Pharms., Mountain View, Calif., 1979, v.p. fin., group contr., 1980; bd. dirs. The Cooper Cos., Inc., Ft. Lee, N.J., 1992-94, 96—. With U.S. Army, 1969-70. Decorated Bronze Star with oak leaf cluster, Army Commendation medal. Mem. AICPA, N.Y. State Soc. CPAs. Home: 446 Arlington Ct Pleasanton CA 94566-7708 Office: The Cooper Cos Inc 6140 Stoneridge Mall Rd Pleasanton CA 94588-3232

WEISS, SHIRLEY F., urban and regional planner, economist, educator; b. N.Y.C., Feb. 26, 1921; d. Max and Vera (Hendel) Friedlander; m. Charles M. Weiss, June 7, 1942. BA, Douglass Coll., Rutgers U., 1942; postgrad., Johns Hopkins U., 1949-50; M in Regional Planning, U. N.C., 1958; PhD, Duke U., 1973. Assoc. research dir. Ctr. for Urban and Regional Studies U. N.C., Chapel Hill, 1957-91, lectr. in planning, 1958-62, assoc. prof., 1962-73, prof., 1973-91, prof. emeritus, 1991—; joint creator-sponsor Charles and Shirley Weiss Urban Livability Program, U. N.C., Chapel Hill, 1992—; research assoc. Inst. for Research in Social Sci., U. N.C., 1957-73; research prof. U. N.C., Chapel Hill, 1973-91, acting dir. women's studies program Coll. Arts and Scis., 1985, faculty marshal, 1988-91; mem. tech. com. Water Resources Rsch. Inst., 1976-79; mem. adv. com. on housing for 1980 census Dept. Commerce, 1976-81; cons. Urban Inst., Washington, 1977-80; mem. rev. panel Exptl. Housing Allowance Program, HUD, 1977-80; mem. adv. bd. on built environ. Nat. Acad. Scis.-NRC, 1981-83, mem. program coordinating com. fed. constrn. coun. of adv. bd. on built environ., 1982-83; mem. Planning Accreditation Bd., Site Visitation Pool, Am. Inst. Cert. Planners and Assn. Collegiate Schs. Planning, 1985—; mem. discipline screening com. Fulbright Scholar awards in Architecture and City Planning, Coun. for Internat. Exchange of Scholars, 1985-88; mem. N.Mex. adv. bd. The Enterprise Found., Santa Fe, 1997—. Author: The Central Business District in Transition: Methodological Approaches to CBD Analysis and Forecasting Future Space Requirements, 1957, New Town Development in the United States: Experiment in Private Entrepreneurship, 1973; co-author: A Probabilistic Model for Residential Growth, 1964, Residential Developer Decisions: A Focused View of the Urban Growth Process, 1966, New Communities U.S.A., 1976; co-author, co-editor: New Community Development: Planning Process, Implementation and Emerging Social Concerns, vols. 1, 2, 1971, City Centers in Transition, 1976, New Communities Research Series, 1976-77; mem. editl. bd.: Jour. Am. Inst. Planners, 1963-68, Rev. of Regional Studies, 1969-74, 82-92, Internat. Regional Sci. Rev., 1975-81. Trustee Friends of Libr., U. N.C., Chapel Hill, 1988-94, Santa Fe Chamber Music Festival, adv. coun., 1990-91, trustee, 1991—; bd. dirs. Triangle Opera, 1986-89, 91—, Chamber Orchestra of the Triangle, 1997—. Recipient Cornelia Phillips Spencer Bell award in recognition of contbns. to life and success of U. N.C. at Chapel Hill, 1996, Disting. Alumni award in recognition of outstanding contbns. in field of city and regional planning Alumni Assn. Dept. City and Regional Planning, U. N.C. at Chapel Hill, 1996, Mary Turner Lane award Assn. Women Faculty, 1994; Adelaide M. Zagoren fellow Douglass Coll., Rutgers U., 1994. Fellow Urban Land Inst. (sr., exec. group, community devel. coun. 1978—); mem. Am. Inst. Planners (sec., treas. southeast chpt. 1957-59, v.p. 1960-61), Am. Inst. Cert. Planners, Am. Planning Assn., Am. Econ. Assn., So. Regional Sci. Assn. (pres. 1977-78), Regional Sci. Assn. (councillor 1971-74, v.p. 1976-77), Nat. Assn. Housing and Redevelopment Ofcls., Interamerican Planning Soc., Internat. Fedn. Housing and Planning, Town and Country Planning Assn., Internat. Urban Devel. Assn., Econ. History Assn., Am. Real Estate and Urban Econs. Assn. (regional membership chmn. 1976-82, 84-85, dir. 1977-80), AAUP (chpt. pres. 1976-77, pres. N.C. Conf. 1978-79, mem. nat. council 1983-86, William S. Tacey award Assembly of State Confs.), Douglass Soc., Order of Valkyries, Phi Beta Kappa. Home: 155 N Hamilton Rd Chapel Hill NC 27514-5628

WEISS, STANLEY C., electrical and electronics products wholesale distribution executive; b. Chgo., Apr. 20, 1929; s. Edward and Belle Rose (Heifler) W.; m. Fern Adrienne Dellheim, Feb. 26, 1956;children: Sharon Anne Maluth, Lisa Karen Forbess. BBA, So. Meth. U., 1951; postgrad., Northwestern U., Chgo., 1953. Asst. mgr. men's furnishings Gassman's, Chgo., 1951-53; restaurant and hotel supplies salesman Edward Don & Co., Chgo., 1953; sales trainee, mgr. EDP, Kuppenheimer Clothing, Chgo., 1954-56; with EESCO, Inc. (Englewood Electric), Chgo., 1956-96; exec. v.p. Wesco Distbn., Inc. (formerly EESCO), 1996—; bd. dirs. Cameron Ashley Bldg. Material Supply; speaker at profl. meetings; adv. cons. various elec. mfrs., 1980-92. Contbr. articles to profl. mags. Banquet co-chmn. Better Boys Found., Chgo., 1984-93; bd. dirs. Jewish Cmty. Ctrs. of Chgo., 1994—. Recipient Banquet Co-chmn.'s award Better Boys Found., 1984-92. Mem. Nat. Assn. Elec. Distbrs. (bd. dirs., chmn. 1991-92), Nat. Assn. Wholesalers (product liability com. Chgo. 1984, bd. dirs. 1991-92), Nat. Assn. Credit Mgmt. (chmn. WES group Chgo. 1970-74), Lake Michigan Club (chmn., bd. dirs. 1975-85), Twin Orchard Country Club (Longwood, Ill., bd. dirs. 1988-92), DuPage Club (Oak Brook Terrace, Ill.), B'nai Brith (officer Chgo. 1954-64, bd. dirs. 1962-64). Avocations: reading, travel, golf. Office: Wesco Distbn Inc 510 Lake Cook Rd Ste 350 Deerfield IL 60015-4943

WEISS, STEPHEN J., lawyer; b. N.Y.C., Sept. 12, 1938; s. Morris and Frances (Dinkin) W.; m. Madeline Adler, Aug. 12, 1962; children: Lowell Andrew, Valerie Elizabeth, Bradley Lawrence. B.S., Queens Coll., 1959; LL.B., Cornell U., 1962; LL.M., Georgetown U., 1966. Bar: N.Y. 1963, D.C. 1966, U.S. Supreme Ct. 1975. Atty. SEC, Washington, 1962-65; assoc. firm Arent Fox Kintner Plotkin & Kahn, Washington, 1965-70, ptnr., 1971-94; ptnr. Holland & Knight, Washington, 1994—; lectr. securities and corp. law and D&O liability and ins. Am. Law Inst., ABA, Fed. Bar Assn., Practicing Law Inst., Bur. Nat. Affairs, Exec. Enterprises, Aspen Law & Bus. Orgn. Mgmt., Inc., Inst. for Internat. Rsch. Mem. adv. bd.; Securities Regulation and Law Report, Bur. Nat. Affairs, 1980—; contbr. articles on securities, corp. dirs. and officers liability and ins. law to legal and bus. jours.; author: Regulation D-A Practical Guide, 1994. Mem. nat. com. Cornell Law Sch. Fund, 1987-88. Mem. ABA (fed. regulation securities com. 1970—, chmn. Rule 10b-5 subcom. 1976-78, chmn. civil liabilities subcom. 1978-81, chmn. ad hoc com. fgn. corrupt practices legislation 1976-77, Guiding Principles Task Force bus. ins. com. 1994-95, devels. in bus. financing com. 1982—), Fed. Bar Assn. (chmn. securities law comm. 1968-70, mem. exec. com. of securities law com. 1971—, chmn. coun. on financing and taxation 1971-72, chmn. publs. bd. 1977-78, nat. coun. 1972-80, Leadership commendation 1973, Disting. Svc. award). Club: Cornell Law (Washington) (pres. 1971-79). Office: Holland & Knight 2100 Pennsylvania Ave NW Washington DC 20037-3202

WEISS, STEPHEN MAX, health care administrator, surgeon, educator; b. Phila., Nov. 20, 1947; s. Walter and Rita (Griffin) W. BS, Ursinus Coll., 1969; MD, Temple U., 1973; postgrad., Allentown Coll., 1997—. Diplomate Am. Bd. Surgery, recert.; lic., Pa. Surgery resident Pa. Hosp., Phila., 1973-78; fellow in surg. oncology Thomas Jefferson U., Phila., 1978-79; from asst. prof. surgery to assoc. prof. surgery Jefferson Med. Coll., Phila., 1979-93; attending surgeon Thomas Jefferson Univ. Hosp., Phila., 1979-87; asst. surgeon Pa. Hosp., Phila., 1984-87; attending surgeon, chmn. dept. surgery, dir. surg. res. prg. Mercy Cath. Med. Ctr., Darby, Pa., 1987-93; chmn. dept. surgery, dir. surg. residence program Mercy Cath. Med. Ctr., Darby, 1987-93; attending surgeon Mercy Haverford Hosp., Havertown, Pa., 1991-93; clin. assoc. prof. surgery Coll. Medicine Pa. State U., 1993-95; chmn. dept. surgery, dir. surg. residency program Pinnacle Health Sys. (merger Polyclinic Med. Ctr. and Harrisburg Hosp.), Harrisburg, Pa., 1993—; gen. and oncologic surgeon Capital Area Surg. Assocs., P.C., Harrisburg, 1995—; cons. Wilmington (Del.) VA Hosp., 1979-86, Wills Eye Hosp., Phila., 1981-87; adj. asst. prof. surgery Sch. Medicine, U. Pa., 1984-88; mem. com. on sci. bus. Phila. Acad. Surgery, 1987-88, sec., 1989-92, 2d v.p., 1993, 1st v.p., 1994, pres., 1995; assoc. examiner Am. Bd. Surgery, 1992, 95. Contbr. numerous articles and abstracts to profl. jours. Bd. dirs. Phila. divsn. Am. Cancer Soc., 1983-92, chmn. profl. edn. com., 1986-88, pres., 1990-91, bd. dirs., 1994-95. Recipient Vol. Achievement award Phila. divsn. Am. Cancer Soc., 1987; jr. faculty clin. fellow Am. Cancer Soc., 1979-82, clin. fellow, 1976-77; grantee Am. Cancer Soc., 1988, Nat. Cancer Inst., 1993. Fellow ACS (mem. Phila. chpt. 1986-93, mem. cen. Pa. chpt. 1993-95, pres. cen. Pa. chpt. 1995, 97, field liaison commn. on cancer Thomas Jefferson Univ. Hosp. 1982-87); mem. AMA, Am. Coll. Radiology (mem. instnl. rev. bd. Radiation Oncology Study Ctr. 1982-85, 92, chmn. surg. com. Radiation Therapy Oncology Group 1982-88), Am. Soc. Parenteral and Enteral Nutrition, Assn. for Acad. Surgery, Am. Radium Soc., Soc. Surg. Oncology, Am. Coll. Physician Execs., Phila. County Med. Soc., Sigma Xi. Office: Pinnacle Health Sys at Polyclinic Hosp 2601 N 3rd St Harrisburg PA 17110-2004

WEISS, SUSAN, newspaper editor. Managing editor Life Section, USA Today, Arlington, Va. Office: USA Today 1000 Wilson Blvd Arlington VA 22209-3901*

WEISS, SUSETTE MARIE, technical consultant, specialist in imaging; b. New Orleans, June 14, 1957; d. Stanley and Dorothy Lee (Cambre) Weiss. AA in Photojournalism, No. La. U., Monroe, 1977; PhD in Religion, Universal Life Coll., Modesto, Calif., 1990. Cert. retinal angiographer; cert. ophthalmic asst.; cert. CPR. Prodn. supr., lab. mgr. Colorpix Custom Photogs., Inc., New Orleans, 1978-84; ophthalmic photographer Ochsner Clinic, New Orleans, 1984-85; dir. ophthalmic photography Omni/Medivision, Metairie, La., 1986-87; audiovisual meeting planner, technician and cons. New Orleans, 1988-89; tech. supr. Retina and Vitreous Assocs. of Ala., Mobile, 1989; dir. photography Dauphin West Eye, Ear, Nose and Throat Specialists, Mobile, 1989-91; tech. sales rep., tech. specialist Nikon, Inc., Melville, N.Y., 1992-95; contractual cons. Simply Susette, Inc., New Orleans, 1995—. Inventor stereo-imaging calibrator and quantitative stereopsis technique. Achievements include ongoing rsch. and devel. in new techniques and applications of teletronic comms. and imaging for the med. and comml. field. Home and Office: 5905 Colbert St New Orleans LA 70124

WEISS, THEODORE RUSSELL, poet, editor; b. Reading, Pa., Dec. 16, 1916; s. Nathan and Mollie T. (Weinberg) W.; m. Renée Karol, July 6, 1941. B.A., Muhlenberg Coll., 1938, Litt.D. (hon.), 1968; M.A., Columbia U., 1940, postgrad., 1940-41; Litt.D. (hon.), Bard Coll., 1973. Instr. English U. Md., 1941, U. N.C., 1942-44, Yale U., 1944-46; prof. English, Bard Coll., 1946-68; vis. prof. poetry MIT, 1961-62; resident fellow creative writing Princeton U., 1966-67, prof. English and creative writing, 1968-87, emeritus, William and Annie S. Paton prof. ancient and modern lit., 1977-87, emeritus; Fannie Hurst prof. lit. Washington U., St. Louis, 1978; prof. English poetry Cooper Union, 1988; poet-in-residence Monash U., Melbourne, Australia, 1982; lectr. New Sch. Social Research, 1955-56, N.Y.C. YMHA, 1965-67; lectr. for USIS in various countries; guest Inst. for Advanced Study, Princeton, N.J., 1986-87, 87-88, Villa Serbelloni, Bellagio, Italy, 1989; guest lectr. Peking U., Shanghai U., People's Republic China, 1991. Editor, pub. Quar. Rev. Lit., 1943—; editor poetry series Princeton U. Press, 1974-78; mem. poetry bd. poetry series Wesleyan U. Press, 1964-70; juror in poetry for poetry series, Bollingen Com., 1965, Nat. Book Awards, 1967, 77; author: Selections from the Note-Books of G.M. Hopkins, 1945; author: The Breath of Clowns and Kings: Shakespeare's Early Comedies and Histories, 1971, The Man from Porlock, Selected Essays, 1982; (poems) The Catch, 1951; Outlanders, 1960, Gunsight, 1962, The Medium, 1965, The Last Day and the First, 1968, The World Before Us: Poems, 1950-70, 1970, Fireweeds, 1976, Views and Spectacles, Selected Poems, 1978, Views and Spectacles, New and Selected Shorter Poems, 1979, Recoveries, 1982, A Slow Fuse, 1984, Collected Poems, 1987, paper back edit., 1988, A Sum of Destructions, 1994, Selected Poems, 1995; also articles and recs. Recipient Wallace Stevens award, 1956, Creative Arts award Brandeis U., 1977, Shelley Meml. award Poetry Soc. Am., 1989, Lifetime Achievement award Pen/Nora Magid, 1997; fellow Ford Found., 1953-54, Ingram Merrill Found., 1974-75, Guggenheim Found., 1986-87 hon. fellow Ezra Stiles Coll., Yale U.; grantee Nat. Found. Arts and Humanities, 1967-68; subject of films Living Poetry, 1988, Yes, With Lemon, 1996. Home: 26 Haslet Ave Princeton NJ 08540-4914

WEISS, THOMAS EDWARD, physician; b. New Orleans, June 15, 1916; s. Carl Adam and Viola Maine W.; m. Catherine Torres Edwards, June 29, 1950; children: Thomas Edward, Hampton Carl. Student, La. State U., 1933-34; M.D., Tulane U., 1940. Diplomate: Am. Bd. Internal Medicine. Intern Touro Infirmary, New Orleans, 1940-41; resident in pathology Touro Infirmary, 1940; fellow in internal medicine Alton Ochsner Med. Found., New Orleans, 1946-47; staff physician specializing in internal medicine Ochsner Clinic, New Orleans, 1947-50; head rheumatology sect. Ochsner Clinic, 1960-77, now mem. staff emeritus rheumatology sect., bd. mgrs. clinic, 1966-74; mem. staff Ochsner Found. Hosp.; sr. vis. physician Charity Hosp. La., New Orleans; mem. faculty Tulane U. Med. Sch., 1960-84, emeritus prof. clin. medicine, 1989—; chmn. vol. support com. Alton Ochsner Med. Found., 1984—, dir. alumni affairs, 1984-95. Contbr. articles to profl. jours. Bd. dirs. Vis. Nurses Assn., Alton Ochsner Med. Found., also trustee; founder, bd. govs. La. Arthritis Found.; nat. bd. govs. Arthritis Found., 1968-74. Maj. AUS, 1941-45, ETO and PTO. Fellow ACP (Laureate award 1991); mem. AMA, Orleans Parish Med. Soc. (dir.), La. Med. Soc., Soc. Med. Assn., Nat. Soc. Rheumatologists, Am. Coll. Rheumatology (master, pres. 1973-74, exec. com.), Vis. Nurses Assn., New Orleans Country Club, Sigma Chi, Alpha Kappa Kappa. Democrat. Roman Catholic. Home: 401 Metairie Rd Apt 625 Metairie LA 70005-4305 Office: 1514 Jefferson Hwy New Orleans LA 70121-2429

WEISS, THOMAS FISCHER, electrical engineering educator, biophysicist; b. Prague, Czechoslovakia, Oct. 17, 1934; came to U.S. 1941, naturalized citizen; s. Eugene and Erna (Frenkel) W.; m. Aurice B Vernon, June 10, 1962; children: Max Philip, Elisa Lane, Eric Radford. BSEE, CCNY, 1956; SM, MIT, 1959, PhD, 1963. Postdoctoral fellow Ford Found., 1963-65; engr. Douglas Aircraft Co., 1957; rsch. asst. dynamic analysis and control lab., rsch. lab. of electronics MIT, Cambridge, Mass., 1956-57, 57-63, cons., 1961-65, from asst. prof. to assoc. prof. electrical engring., 1963-1978, prof. electrical engring., 1978—; mem. many MIT coms.; rsch. assoc. dept. otolaryngology Mass. Eye & Ear Infirmary, 1964—; rsch. assoc. preventive medicine Harvard U. Med. Sch., 1964-69, instr. dept. preventive and social medicine, 1969-74; faculty Harvard-MIT divsn. health scis. and tech. Harvard U., 1980—; mem. bioelectric pheonmena com. Biomed. Engring. Group IEEE; cons. communicative disorders panel for nat. plan, NIH, 1978, mem. rev. com., 1978-83; participant multidisciplinary workshop on inner ear and hearing, NIH, 1974. Edit. bd. Hearing Rsch., 1986—; orgnr., chair workshops in field; contbr. numerous abstracts, articles to profl. jours.; invited lectr. in field. Recipient NIH Rsch. Career Devel. award, 1975-80, Javits Neurosci. Investigator award, 1984-91, Higher Edn. Software award best engring. software EDUCOM/NCRIPTAL, 1990; apptd. Thomas and Gerd Perkins prof. electrical and bioelectrical engring., 1992—. Home: 1607 Centre St Newton MA 02161-1256 Office: MIT 77 Massachusetts Ave Rm 36-857 Cambridge MA 02139-4301

WEISS, VOLKER, university administrator, educator; b. Rottenmann, Austria, Sept. 2, 1930; came to U.S., 1953, naturalized, 1960; s. Othmar and Pauline (Morianz) W.; m. Peg Hake, Sept. 14, 1957; children: Erick V., Christopher J. Dipl.Ing. Physics, Tech. U. Vienna; Dipl.Ing. Physics (Fulbright scholar), 1955; Ph.D. in Solid State Sci. and Tech, Syracuse U., 1957. Rsch. metallurgist DEMKA Steel, Utrecht, The Netherlands, 1952; asst. prof. metallurgy Syracuse U., 1957-60, prof. materials sci., 1965—, prof. engring. and physics, 1986—, chmn. solid state sci. and tech. program, 1960-77, assoc. dean sponsored programs, 1972-78; dir. Inst. Energy Rsch., 1976-80, v.p. rsch. and grad. affairs, 1978-86, dir. engring physics program, 1988—, chmn. dept. mechanical, aerospace, mfg. engring., 1992-94; U.S.-Can Prof., 1993—; cons. indsl. firms Dept. Transp.; bd. dirs., past pres. Syracuse Friends of Chamber Music, Tech. Club Syracuse; v.p., bd. dirs. Discovery Ctr. of Sci. and Tech., 1979—; NATO sr. scientist fellow, Germany and Gt. Britain, 1967-68. Editor: Sagamore Conf. Procs, 1962-86; contbr. articles on mech. behavior of materials and phys. metallurgy to profl. jours. Fellow Am. Soc. Metals; mem. ASME, ASTM, Am. Physical Soc., Sigma Xi. Home: 238 Scottholm Ter Syracuse NY 13224-1738 Office: Syracuse U 449 Link Hall Syracuse NY 13244

WEISS, WALTER STANLEY, lawyer; b. Newark, Mar. 12, 1929; s. Jack and Mollie (Orkin) W.; m. Misty M. Moore; children from previous marriage: Jack Stephen, Andrew Scott. A.B., Rutgers U., 1949, J.D., 1952. Bar: D.C. 1952, N.J. 1956, Calif. 1961. Trial atty. IRS, Phila., Los Angeles, 1957-62; asst. U.S. atty., chief tax div. Los Angeles, 1962-63; ptnr. firm Goodson & Hannam, Los Angeles, 1963-67; mng. ptnr. firm Long & Levit, Los Angeles, 1967-79; ptnr. firm Greenberg & Glusker, Los Angeles, 1979-81, Rosenfeld, Meyer and Susman, Beverly Hills, Calif., 1981-93; prin. Law Office of Walter S. Weiss, L.A., 1993—. Contbr. articles to legal jours. Served to capt. JAGC USAF, 1953-56. Named Arbitrator Nat. Assn. Securities Dealers, 1974. Fellow Am. Coll. Trial Lawyers; mem. Am., Los Angeles County, Beverly Hills, Century City bar assns. Home: 1805 Westridge Rd Los Angeles CA 90049-2215 Office: Law Office Walter S Weiss 9th Flr 12424 Wilshire Blvd Fl 9 Los Angeles CA 90025-1052

WEISS, WILLIAM, retired pulmonary medicine and epidemiology educator; b. Phila., July 30, 1919; s. William and Anna (Grossman) W.; m. Esther E. Sabul, June 22, 1941; children: Winifred A., Seth S., Deborah E. BA, U. Pa., 1940, MD, 1944. Clin. dir. pulmonary disease svc. Phila. Gen. Hosp., 1950-74; chest cons. Norristown (Pa.) State Hosp., 1951-60; dir. Pulmonary Neoplasm Rsch. Project, Phila., 1957-67; faculty U. Pa. Grad. Sch. Medicine, Phila., 1952-66, Med. Coll. Pa., Phila., 1952-86; from assoc. prof. to prof. medicine Hahnemann U. Med. Coll., Phila., 1966-84, prof. emeritus, 1984—; cons. to various indsl. cos., Pa., N.J., 1962—. Editor Phila. Medicine, 1976—; mem. editl. bd. Arch. Environ. Health, 1968-86; contbr. over 220 articles and over 120 editls. to profl. jours., 18 chpts. in books. Bd. dirs. Am. Cancer Soc., Phila., 1980-86; cons. on asbestos Bd. Edn., Phila., 1983—; mem. EPA Sci. Review Panel for Health Rsch., Washington, 1980-81, Toxics/Health Effects adv. com. Pa. Dept. Health, 1985-87. Capt. USAF, 1953-55. Recipient Ann. Sci. award Phila. divsn. Am. Cancer Soc., 1979, Cristol award Phila. County Med. Soc., 1989; picture on cover Cancer Rsch., Mar. 1, 1990 for lung cancer rsch. Fellow ACP, Coll.

Physicians Phila., Am. Coll. Occupl. and Environ. Medicine (merit in authorship award 1974, 85); mem. AMA, Laennec Soc. Phila. (pres. 1970), Phila. Occupl. Med. Assn. (pres. 1980-81), Am. Thoracic Soc., Pa. Med. Soc., Phila. County Med. Soc. (Strittmatter award 1991, Gold medal). Avocation: classical music. Home: 3912 Netherfield Rd Philadelphia PA 19129-1014

WEISSBACH, HERBERT, biochemist; b. N.Y.C., Mar. 16, 1932; s. Louis and Vivian (Ruhalter) W.; m. Renee Kohl, Dec. 27, 1953; children—Lawrence, Nancy, Marjorie, Robert. B.S., CUNY, 1953; M.S., George Washington U., 1955, Ph.D., 1957. Chemist Nat. Heart Inst., Bethesda, Md., 1953-68; acting chief NIH, Bethesda, Md., 1968-69; assoc. dir. Roche Inst. Molecular Biology, Nutley, N.J., 1969-83, dir., 1983-96; v.p. Hoffmann-La Roche, Nutley, N.J., 1983—; disting. rsch. prof. biol. scis. Fla. Atlantic U., Boca Raton, Fla.; adj. prof. George Washington U., 1964-69, Columbia U., 1969-85, U. Medicine and Dentistry N.J., Newark, 1981-93, Princeton U., 1984-85. Editor: Molecular Mechanisms of Protein Biosynthesis, 1977, Archives of Biochemistry and Biophysics; contbr. articles to profl. jours. Recipient Superior Svc. award NEW, 1968, Enzyme award Am. Chem. Soc., 1970, Disting. Alumni award George Washington U., 1994. Mem. Am. Soc. Biol. Chemists, Am. Soc. Pharmacology and Exptl. Therapeutics, Nat. Acad. Scis., AAAS. Home: 8008 Desmond Dr Boynton Beach FL 33437 Office: Fla Atlantic U 777 Glades Rd Boca Raton FL 33431-6424

WEISSBARD, DAVID RAYMOND, minister; b. Albany, N.Y., July 10, 1940; s. Alfred Henry and E. Ramona (Van Wie) W.; m. Mary Linda Roberts, Mar. 31, 1963 (dec. May 1987); children: Melissa Anne, Michele Lee Weissbard Burns, Andrew Van Wie (dec.), Meredith Lynn Weissbard Andrews; m. Karen Wells, Sept. 1, 1990; 1 child, Hilary Rebecca. BA, St. Lawrence U., 1962, MDiv., 1965; diploma in applied social studies, U. Southampton, Eng., 1973. Ordained to ministry Unitarian Universalist Assn., 1965; cert. social worker, Eng. Student min. 1st Universalist Ch., Dexter, N.Y., 1963-65, Henderson, N.Y., 1963-65; min. 1st Parish in Bedford (Mass.) Unitarian Universalist Ch., 1965-74; sr. min. Fairfax Unitarian Ch., Oakton, Va., 1974-79, The Unitarian Universalist Ch., Rockford, Ill., 1979—; v.p. Cen. Midwest Dist. Unitarian Universalist Assn., 1989-92. Producer, host weekly TV program Fusion, WIFR-TV, 1980—. Mem. religious policy com. Rockford Sch. Dist., 1991. Recipient Skinner award Unitarian Universalist Assn., 1979; named One of Rockford's 15 Most Interesting People, 1990. Mem. ACLU (co-pres. No. Ill. chpt.), Greater Rockford Clergy Assn., Unitarian Universalist Mins. Assn. (treas. 1976-78). Democrat. Home: 1805 Clinton St Rockford IL 61103-4805 Office: The Unitarian Ch 4848 Turner St Rockford IL 61107-5029

WEISSBARD, SAMUEL HELD, lawyer; b. N.Y.C., Mar. 3, 1947; children: Andrew Joshua, David S. BA, Case Western Res. U., 1967; JD with highest honors, George Washington U., 1970. Bar: D.C. 1970, U.S. Supreme Ct. 1974. Assoc. Fried, Frank, Harris, Shriver & Kampelman, 1970-73, Arent, Fox, Kintner, Plotkin & Kahn, 1973-78; prin. Weissbard & Fields, P.C., 1978-83; shareholder, v.p. Wilkes, Artis, Hedrick & Lane, Washington, 1983-86; ptnr. Foley & Lardner, Washington, 1986-97, L.A., 1997—; co-chair Creditors' Rights Workout and Bankruptcy Group, 1992-95. Editor in chief George Washington U. Law Rev., 1969-70. Bd. dirs. Luther Rice Soc., George Washington U., 1985-87, Atlanta Coll. Art, 1993, Nat. Learning Ctr., 1993—, Georgetown Arts Commn. and gen. counsel 1995-96; Chmn. steering com. of Lawyer's Alliance for Nat. Learning Ctr. and Capital Children's Mus., 1989-90; mem. steering com. DC/NLC Don't Drop Out Campaign, 1992,93, bd. dirs., 1994-96. Recipient John Bell Larner medal, 1970. Mem. ABA, D.C. Bar, Georgetown Bus. and Profl. Assn. (bd. dirs. 1993-96, sec., gen. counsel 1994-96), Order of Coif. Office: Foley & Lardner 2029 Century Park E Ste 3500 Los Angeles CA 90067-3021

WEISS-CORNWELL, AMY, interior designer; b. Mpls., Dec. 8, 1950; d. August Carl and Margaret Amelia (Wittman) Weiss; m. Dan Cornwell, July 31, 1995; 1 child, Emma Elizabeth. AA in Home Econs., Cerritos Coll.; student, Long Beach State U., Santa Ana Jr. Coll. Asst. to interior designer Pati Pfahler Designs, Canoga Park, Calif., 1974-75; interior designer B.A. Interiors, Fullerton, Calif., 1976-78, Birns Cos., Rancho Mirage, Calif., 1978-79, Carole Eichen Interiors, Fullerton, 1981, Sears, Roebuck and Co., Alhambra, Calif., 1982-84; staff interior designer Assoc. Design Studios, Costa Mesa, Calif., 1979-81; sr. corp. designer, mgr. design studio Barratt Am., Irvine, Calif., 1984-88; owner Amy Weiss Designs, Coronado, Calif., 1988—; designer in residence San Diego Design Ctr., 1990-94. Mem. Am. Soc. Interior Designers (Globe-Guilders steering com. 1989-92, chmn. Christmas party, co-chmn. Christmas on Prado 1989, 89, designer for ASID showcase house 1992, 93), Bldg. Industry Assn. (sales and mktg. coun. awards com. 1993, mem. sales and mktg. coun. 1986-88, mem. home builders coun. 1994, 2d place M.A.M.E. award 1987, 1st place M.A.M.E. award 1986, 2d place S.A.M. award 1987), Building Industry Assn. Remodeler's Coun., Nat. Kitchen and Bath Assn., Coronado C. of C., Coronado Rotary; participant in Pacific Design Ctr. Designer on Call program, L.A.. Coronado Cays Yacht Club (head entertainment and spl. events 1997). Home and Office: Amy Weiss Designs 10 Admiralty Cross Coronado CA 92118-3202

WEISSKOPF, BERNARD, pediatrician, child behavior, development and genetics specialist, educator; b. Berlin, Dec. 11, 1929; came to U.S., 1939, naturalized, 1944; s. Benjamin and Bertha (Loew) W.; m. Penelope Allderdice, Dec. 26, 1965; children: Matthew David, Stephen Daniel. BA, Syracuse U., 1951; MD, U. Leiden, Netherlands, 1958. Diplomate Am. Bd. Med. Mgmt. Intern Meadowbrook Hosp., East Meadow, N.Y., 1958-59; resident Meadowbrook Hosp., 1959-60, Johns Hopkins Hosp., Balt., 1962-64; fellow child psychiatry Johns Hopkins U. Sch. Medicine, Balt., 1962-64; asst. prof. pediatrics U. Ill. Coll. Medicine, Chgo., 1964-66; faculty U. Louisville, 1966—, prof. pediatrics, 1970—; also assoc. in psychiatry, pathology and Ob-gyn, dir. Child Evaluation Ctr., Louisville, 1966—; chmn. Gov.'s Adv. Com. Early Childhood, Gov.'s Council on Early Childhood, Ky., 1986-88. Contbr. articles to profl. jours. Trustee Jewish Hosp., Louisville, 1974-77. Served to capt. USAF, 1960-62. Fellow Am. Acad. Pediatrics, Am. Assn. Mental Deficiency; mem. Am. Soc. Human Genetics, So. Soc. Pediatric Rsch., Am. Soc. Law and Medicine, Am. Coll. Physician Execs. Home: 6409 Deep Creek Dr Prospect KY 40059-9422 Office: Child Evaluation Ctr 571 S Floyd St Louisville KY 40202-3818

WEISSMAN, EUGENE YEHUDA, chemical engineer; b. Bucharest, Romania, Sept. 23, 1931; came to U.S., 1958; s. Alfred A. and Paula D. (Braunstein) W.; children: Ian A., Michael L. BS, Israel Inst. Tech., 1953; MS, U. Mich., 1959; PhD in chem. engr., Case Western Reserve U., 1963; MBA, U. Chgo., 1972. Registered profl. engr. Mgr. Israel Atomic Energy Comm., 1953-58; process engr. Hercules Powder Co., 1960-61; sr. engr. Gen. Electric Co., 1963-65, mgr. R&D, 1965-68; head rsch. dept. Johnson Controls, 1968-73; dir. rsch. B.A.S.F. Corp., 1973-91; dir. technology transfer Nat. Ctr. for Mfg. Scis., 1991-92; exec. dir. Ctr. for Process Analytical Chemistry U. Wash., 1992-94; pres. Weissman Assocs., Seattle, 1994—; adv. coun. Coll. Engring. U. Akron; mem. editorial and tech. adv. bd. PI Quality. Contbr. articles to profl. jours.; patentee in field. Fellow USPHS, 1959, 62. Mem. AAAS, AIChE (dir. heat transfer and energy conversion divsn.), NRC (co. rep.), Catalysis Soc. New Eng. (dir.), Electrochem. Soc., Nat. Membership Com., Am. Soc. for Quality Control, Indsl. Rsch. Inst. (bd. dirs., chmn. bd. editors, chmn. nominating com., univ. rels. com., advanced study groups com., fin. com.), Am. Chem Soc. (corp. assocs. com.), Nat. Coun. Advancement Rsch. (conf. com.), Coun. Chem. Rsch. (Univ. Ind. interaction com.), Tech. Transfer Soc., Inst. Mgmt. Cons., Product Devel. and Mgmt. Assn., Am. Translators Assn. N.W. Translators and Interpreters Soc., Mich. Materials Processing Inst. (bd. dirs.), Internat. Forum Process Analytical Chemistry (sci. bd.). Home and Office: 4119 NE 142nd St Seattle WA 98125-3841

WEISSMAN, IRVING L., medical scientist; b. Great Falls, Mont., Oct. 21, 1939; married, 1961; 4 children. BS, Mont. State Coll., 1960, DSc (hon.), 1992; MD, Stanford U., 1965. NIH fellow dept. radiology Stanford U., 1965-67, rsch. assoc., 1967-68, from asst. prof. to assoc. prof. dept. pathology, 1969-81, prof. pathology Sch. Medicine, 1981—, prof. devel. biology dept. pathology, 1989—; James McGinnis Meml. lectr. Duke U., 1982; George Feigen Meml. lectr. Stanford U., 1987; Albert Coons Meml. lectr. Harvard U., 1987; Jame Stahlman lectr. Vanderbilt U., 1987; R. E. Smith lectr. U. Tex. Sys. Cancer Ctr., 1988; Chauncey D. Leake lectr. U. Calif., 1989; Harvey lectr. Rockefeller U., 1989; Rose Litman lectr., 1990; sr. Dernham fellow, Calif. divsn. Am. Cancer Soc., 1969-73; mem. immunobiology study sect. NIH, 1976-80; mem. sci. rev. bd. Howard Hughes Med. Inst., 1986—; mem. sci. adv. com. Irvington House Inst., 1987—; co-founder Systemix, Inc., 1988, bd. dirs., 1988—; Karel & Avice Beekhuis prof. cancer biology, 1987; 5th Ann. vis. prof. cancer biology U. Tex. Health Sci. Ctr., 1987; disting. lectr. Western Soc. Clin. Investment, 1990; chmn. U.S.-Japan Immunology Bd., 1992-94; chmn. sci. adv. com. of McLaughlin Rsch. Inst., 1992—, trustee, 1992—; bd. govts. Project Inform, 1995—. Recipient Pasarow award, 1989, Faculty Rsch. award Nat. Am. Cancer Soc., 1974-78, Mont. Conservationist of Yr. Mont. Land Reliance, 1994; named One of Top 100 Alumni Mont. State U., 1993; Josiah Macy Found. scholar, 1974-75. Fellow AAAS; mem. NAS (steering com. NIOM AIDS panel 1985-86), Am. Acad. Arts and Scis., Am. Assn. Immunologists (pres. 1994-95), Am. Assn. Univ. Pathologists, Am. Assn. Pathologists, Am. Soc. Microbiology, Am. Assn. Cancer Rsch., Inst. Immunology. Office: Stanford U Dept Pathology B257 Beckman Ctr Sch Medicine Stanford CA 94305

WEISSMAN, JACK (GEORGE ANDERSON), editor; b. Chgo., June 6, 1921; s. Ben and Ida (Meyerson) W.; m. Bernice Platt, Nov. 13, 1949; children: Bruce, David, Ellen Montgomery. B.A. in Edn., Northwestern U., 1943, M.S. in Journalism, 1944. Asst. editor Bankers Monthly, Chgo., 1944-45; mng. editor Practical Knowledge, Chgo., 1945-50; with pub. relations dept. Roosevelt U., Chgo., 1947-50; editor Opportunity Mag., Chgo., 1950-89, ret. Author: Make Money at Home, 1963, How to Make Correct Decisions, 1964, Money Making Businesses You Can Start for $500 Or Less, 1965, Making It Big in Selling, 1987. Served to cpl. USAAF, 1945-46. Mem. Sigma Delta Chi, Phi Delta Kappa. Jewish.

WEISSMAN, MICHAEL LEWIS, lawyer; b. Chgo., Sept. 11, 1934; s. Maurice and Sue (Goldberg) W.; m. Joanne Sherwin, Dec. 19, 1961; children: Mark Douglas, Greg Steven, Scott Adam, Brett Anthony. Student (White scholar), U. Chgo., 1951-52; BS in Econs, Northwestern U., 1954; MBA in Acctg., U. Pa., 1956; JD, Harvard U., 1958; postgrad. (Fulbright scholar), U. Sydney, Australia, 1958-59; postgrad., Hague Acad. Internat. Law, 1959. Bar: D.C. 1958, Ill. 1959. Asst. prof. bus. law Roosevelt U., Chgo., 1959-61; pvt. practice Chgo., 1959—; mem. firm Aaron, Aaron, Schimberg & Hess, 1969-78; sr. ptnr. Boorstein & Weissman, 1978-82, Weissman, Smolev & Solow, 1982-88, Foley & Lardner, 1988-92, McBride Baker & Coles, Chgo., 1992—; asst. prof. Roosevelt U., 1960-62; lectr. Lake Forest (Ill.) Coll., 1979-80; chmn. Banking Group, Union League Club Chgo.; mem. Com. on Bank Counsel Ill. Bankers Assn., 1987-88, vice chmn., 1988-89; panelist Robert Morris Assocs., Banking Law Inst., Midwest Fin. Conf., Greater O'Hare Assn., Miss. Law Inst., Bank Lending Inst., Chgo. Assn. Commerce and Industry, State of Art Seminars, Infocast Inc., SBA, Fed. Res. Bank Chgo., Lenders Ednl. Inst., Bank Adminstrn. Inst. Found., Lender's Forum. Author: Lender Liability, 1988, Commercial Loan Documentation and Secured Lending, 1990, How to Avoid Career-Ending Mistakes in Commercial Lending, 1996, The Lender's Edge, 1997; mem. editl. bd. Commercial Damages, 1985—; contbr. articles to profl. jours. Mem. adv. bd. Affective Disorders Clinic, U. Ill. Med. Sch., 1979-81. Mem. ABA, Ill. Bar Assn., Chgo. Bar Assn., Ill. Bankers Assn., Ill. Inst. Continuing Legal Edn. (bd. dirs. 1989-97), Assn. Comml. Fin. Attys. (bd. dirs.), Harvard Law Soc. Ill., Turnaround Mgmt. Assn. (steering com. Chgo. chpt.), Comml. Fin. Assn. Ednl. Found. (adv. bd.), Robert Morris Assn., Beta Alpha Psi. Home: 2067 Old Briar Rd Highland Park IL 60035-4245 Office: McBride Baker & Coles 500 W Madison St Ste 4000 Chicago IL 60661-2511

WEISSMAN, NORMAN, public relations executive; b. Newark, Apr. 12, 1925; s. Julius and Lenora (Schimmel) W.; m. Sheila Holtz, Dec. 12, 1950 (div. Dec. 1973); 1 son, Lee; m. Natalie Ruvell, Aug. 31, 1984. BA in English, Rutgers U., 1949; MA in Journalism, U. Wis., 1951. Asst. editor McGraw Hill Pub. Co., Inc., 1951-54; sec. to Dept. Air Pollution Control, N.Y.C., 1954-56; account exec. Ruder & Finn, N.Y.C., 1956-59, v.p., 1959-62, sr. v.p., 1962-68, pres., 1968-85, vice-chmn., 1983-85; vice-chmn. G.C.I. Group, Inc., N.Y.C., 1986-90; chmn. Edward Aycoth Worldwide, 1991-93, Citigate, Inc., N.Y.C., 1993—. Served with USN, 1943-46. Mem. Advt. Women N.Y. (hon.), Internat. Pub. Rels. Assn., Phi Beta Kappa, Sigma Delta Chi. Lodge: Rotary. Home: 162 E 93rd St New York NY 10128-3711 Office: Citigate Inc 850 3rd Ave New York NY 10022-6222

WEISSMAN, ROBERT EVAN, information services company executive; b. New Haven, May 22, 1940; s. Samuel and Lillian (Warren) W.; m. Janet Johl, Aug. 27, 1960; children: Gregory, Christopher, Michael. BSBA, Babson Coll., Wellesley, Mass., 1964. Exec. v.p. Rediffusion Inc., Saugus, Mass., 1972-73; dir. corp. devel. Nat. CSS, Wilton, Conn., 1973-74, chmn., 1975-81; exec. v.p. Dun & Bradstreet Corp., N.Y.C., 1981-84, pres., 1985-93, chmn., CEO, 1995-96; chmn., CEO Cognizant Corp., Westport, Conn., 1996—; bd. dirs. State St. Boston Corp.; mem. bus. roundtable com. econ. devel. U.S.-Japan Bus. Coun. Vice chmn. bd. trustees Babson Coll. Mem. IEEE, Info. Tech. Assn. Am., Inst. Mgmt. Accts., Soc. Mfg. Engrs. (sr.). Office: Cognizant Corp 200 Nyala Farms Rd Westport CT 06880-6267

WEISSMAN, WILLIAM R., lawyer; b. N.Y.C., Aug. 16, 1940; s. Emanuel and Gertrude (Halpern) W.; m. Barbra Phylis Gershman; 1 child, Adam; stepchildren: Eric, Jace, Julie Greenman. BA, Columbia U., 1962, JD cum laude, 1965. Bar: N.Y. 1965, D.C. 1969, U.S. Dist. Ct. (no. dist.) Tex. 1965, U.S. Dist. Ct. (so. and ea. dists.) N.Y. 1977, U.S. Ct. Appeals (5th cir.) 1966, U.S. Ct. Appeals (D.C. cir.) 1969, U.S. Ct. Appeals (9th cir.) 1973, U.S. Ct. Appeals (2d and 3d cirs.) 1974, U.S. Ct. Appeals (10th cir.) 1979, U.S. Ct. Appeals (11th cir.) 1981, U.S. Supreme Ct. 1968. News dir., program dir. WKCR-FM, N.Y.C., 1960-62; law clk. U.S. dist. judge, Dallas, 1965-66; trial atty. antitrust div. Dept. Justice, Washington, 1966-69; spl. asst. U.S. atty., Washington, 1967; assoc. Wald, Harkrader & Ross, Washington, 1969-72, ptnr., 1973-85; ptnr. Piper & Marbury, L.L.P., Washington, 1986—; instr. Georgetown U. Law Sch.-D.C. Bar Continuing Legal Edn. Program, 1980-89, environ. regulation course Exec. Enterprises, Inc., 1985-95. Mem. Arlington (Va.) County Tenant-Landlord Comm., 1973-77, chmn., 1975-77; parliamentarian Arlington County Dem. Com., 1971-75; sec. Columbia Law Sch. Alumni Assn. of Washington, 1982-84, pres., 1984-86, bd. dirs. 1984-88. Mem. editorial adv. bd. Jour. Environ. Regulation, 1991-95, Environ. Regulation & Permitting, 1995—. Recipient James Gordon Bennett prize Columbia U., 1962, E.B. Convers prize Columbia U., 1965. Mem. ABA, Fed. Bar Assn., D.C. Bar Assn. Jewish. Club: Columbia U. of Washington (bd. dirs. 1987-93). Home: 3802 Lakeview Ter Falls Church VA 22041-1313 Office: Piper & Marbury LLP 1200 19th St NW Washington DC 20036-2412

WEISSMANN, GERALD, medical educator, researcher, writer, editor; b. Vienna, Austria, Aug. 7, 1930; came to U.S., 1938; s. Adolf and Greta (Lustbader) W.; m. Ann Raphael, Apr. 1, 1953; children: Lisa, Andrew. BA with honors, Columbia U., N.Y.C., 1950; MD, NYU, 1954. Diplomate Am. Bd. Internal Medicine. Intern Mt. Sinai Hosp., N.Y.C., 1954-55, asst. resident medicine, 1957-58; chief resident medicine Bellevue Hosp., N.Y.C., 1959-60; fellow depts. biochemistry and medicine Arthritis and Rheumatism Fedn., NYU, 1958-59; rsch. asst. dept. medicine NYU Sch. Medicine, 1959-60, instr. medicine, 1959-62, asst. prof., 1962-65, assoc. prof., 1966-70, prof., 1970—, dir. div. cell biology, 1969-73, dir. div. rheumatology of dept. medicine, 1973—; USPHS spl. rsch. fellow dept. biophysics Strangeways Lab., Cambridge, Eng., 1960-61; sr. investigator Arthritis and Rheumatism Found., N.Y.C., 1961-65; career rsch. scientist Health Rsch. Coun. N.Y.C., 1966-71; instr. physiology Marine Biol. Lab., Woods Hole, Mass., 1973-77, investigator, 1970—, trustee, 1993—; vis. investigator ARC Inst. Animal Physiology, Babraham, Eng., 1964-69, Centre de Physiologie et d'Immunologie Cellulaires, Hosp. St. Antoine, Paris, 1973-74, William Harvey Rsch. Inst., London, 1987; mem. postdoctoral fellowships rev. com. Pfizer Internat., N.Y.C., 1983—; mem. scholarship selection com. Pew Scholars in Biomed. Scis., New Haven, 1984—; lectr. Johns Hopkins U., 1976, 89, Med. Coll. Ga., Augusta, 1980, Med. Coll. Pa., 1988, William Harvey Rsch. Inst., London, 1987, others; nat. adv. bd. Pew Scholars Biomed. Sci., 1984-95. Author: The Woods Hole Cantata, 1995, They All Laughed at Christopher Columbus, 1987, The Doctor With Two Heads, 1990, The Doctor Dilemma, 1992, Democracy and DNA, 1996; editor-in-chief Inflammation, 1975—, Advances in Inflammation Rsch., 1979—, MD Mag., 1989-94; mem. editl. bd. Clin. Immunology and Immunopathology, 1972-88, Advances in Prostaglandin, Thromboxane and Leukotriene Rsch., 1975—, Am. Jour. Medicine, 1976-88, Tissue Reactions, 1979, Immunopharmacology, 1982; contbr. over 300 articles to profl. jours. Capt. M.C., U.S. Army, 1955-57. Recipient Allesandro Robecchi prize Internat. League Against Rheumatism, 1972, Marine Biol. Lab. award, 1974, 1979, U. Bologna medal, Italy, 1978, Lila Gruber Cancer Rsch. award Am. Acad. Dermatology, 1979, Solomon A. Berson Med. Alumni Achievement award NYU, 1980, Merit award NIH, 1987, Centennial award Marine Biol. Lab., 1988, C.M. Plotz award N.Y. Arthritis Found., 1993, Paul Klemperer award N.Y. Acad. Medicine, 1997, others; Guggenheim Found. fellow, N.Y.C., 1973-74. Fellow AAAS; mem. Am. Coll. Rheumatology (pres. 1982-83, Disting. Investigator award 1992), Am. Fedn. Clin. Rsch., Am. Soc. Exptl. Biology and Medicine, Am. Soc. Pharmacology and Exptl. Therapeutics, Am. Soc. Exptl. Pathology, Assn. Am. Immunologists, Am. Soc. Cell Biology, Am. Soc. Clin. Investigation, Am. Soc. Biol. Chemistry and Molecular Biology, Assn. Am. Physicians, Harvey Soc. of N.Y. (pres. 1981-82), Interurban Clin. Club, PEN Am. Ctr., Phi Beta Kappa, Alpha Omega Alpha. Avocation: tennis. Office: NYU Med Ctr Dept Medicine 550 1st Ave New York NY 10016-6481

WEISS-SWEDE, FRANCES ROBERTA See **ZAMIR, FRANCES ROBERTA**

WEISSTEIN, ULRICH WERNER, English literature educator; b. Breslau, Germany, Nov. 14, 1925; came to U.S., 1950, naturalized, 1959; s. Rudolf and Berta (Wende) W.; m. Elisabeth Rieckh; children: Cristina, Cecily, Eric Wolfgang, Anton Edward. Student, Goethe-Universität, Frankfurt, 1947-50, 51-52, U. Iowa, 1950-51; MA, Ind. U., 1953, PhD, 1954; Doctorate (hon.), U. Lund, Sweden, 1993. Instr. Lehigh U., Bethlehem, Pa., 1954-58; asst. prof. Lehigh U., 1958; asst. prof. English and comparative lit. Ind. U., Bloomington, 1959-62; assoc. prof. Ind. U., 1962-66, prof. German and comparative lit., 1966-90, chmn. comparative lit. program, 1985-89; dir. Ind. U.-Purdue U. Studienprogramm U. Hamburg, 1981-82; vis. prof. U. Wis., summer 1966, Middlebury Sch. German, summer 1970, U. Hamburg (Germany), spring 1971, spring 1982, U. Vienna, 1976, Stanford U., 1979 , Graz U., Austria, 1985, 95, 96, U. Bologna, Italy, 1991, U. Antwerp, Belgium, 1992, U. Salzburg, 1997; external examiner comparative lit. U. Hong Kong, 1974-76. Author: Heinrich Mann, 1962, The Essence of Opera, 1964, Max Frisch, 1967, Einführung in die Vergleichende Literaturwissenschaft, 1968, English version: Comparative Literature and Literary Theory, 1973; Spanish version: Introducción a la Literatura Comparada, 1975, Chinese version, 1987, Japanese version, 1976, Korean version, 1979; Forschungsbericht zur Vergleichenden Literaturwissenschaft, 1968-1977, 1981, Links und links gesellt sich nicht: Gesammelte Aufsätze zum Werk Heinrich Manns und Bertolt Brechts, 1985; editor: Literatur und Bildende Kunst: Ein Handbuch zur Theorie und Praxis eines komparatistischen Grenzgebiets, 1992; editor German sect. Twayne World Authors series, 1964-86, Yearbook of Comparative and General Literature, 1960-90, Expressionism as an International Literary Phenomenon, 1973; co-editor: Literature and the Other Arts, 1981, Texte und Kontexte: Festschrift für Norbert Fuerst, 1973, Intertextuality: German Literature and Visual Art from the Renaissance to the Twentieth Century, 1993, Musico-Poetics Today Calvin S. Brown in Memoriam, 1997; translator: The Grotesque in Art and Literature (W. Kayser), 1963. Recipient Grosses goldenes Ehrenzeichen des Landes Steiermark, 1996; Guggenheim fellow, 1974-75; MLA grantee, 1958-59. Mem. MLA (exec. coun. 1983-86), Internat. Comparative Lit. Assn. (exec. coun. 1979-85, sec. 1985-89), Am. Comparative Lit. Assn., Coun. Internat. Exchange Scholars (area com. for W. Ger. and Austria 1983-85). Home: Baiernstrasse 54/IV, 8020 Graz Austria

WEISWASSER, STEPHEN ANTHONY, lawyer, broadcast executive; b. Detroit, Nov. 21, 1940; s. Avery and Eleanor (Sherman) W.; m. July 3, 1962 (div. 1985); children: Jonathan, Gayle; m. Andrea Timko, Apr. 19, 1986; children: Anne, Emily. BA, Wayne State U., 1962; student, Johns Hopkins U., 1962-63; JD, Harvard U., 1966. Bar: D.C. 1967, U.S. Supreme Ct. 1970. Law clk. to chief judge U.S. Ct. Appeals, Washington, 1966-67; assoc. Wilmer, Cutler and Pickering, Washington, 1967-74, ptnr., 1974-86; sr. v.p., gen. counsel Capital Cities/ABC, Inc., N.Y.C., 1986-91, sr. v.p., exec. v.p. ABC-TV network group, 1991, sr. v.p., exec. v.p. ABC News, 1991-93, sr. v.p., 1993; sr. v.p., pres. Multimedia Group, N.Y.C., 1993-95; pres., CEO Americast, L.A., 1995—; bd. dirs. Ctr. Comm.; pres. Internat. Radio and TV Soc. Found., Inc., 1995-97. Trustee Woodrow Wilson Found., 1994—. Mem. ABA, Fed. Comm. Bar Assn. Jewish. Home: 2718 32nd St NW Washington DC 20008 Office: Americast 10880 Wilshire Blvd # 1750 Los Angeles CA 90024

WEISZ, PAUL B(URG), physicist, chemical engineer; b. Pilsen, Czechoslovakia, July 2, 1919; naturalized, 1946; s. Alexander and Amalia (Sulc) W.; m. Rhoda A.M. Burg, Sept. 4, 1943; children: Ingrid B., P. Randall. Student, Tech. U. Berlin, 1938-39; BS, Auburn U., 1940; ScD, Swiss Fed. Inst. Tech., Zurich, 1965, ScD (hon.), 1980. Research physicist Bartol Research Found., Swarthmore, Pa., 1940-46; Research physicist Mobil Oil Corp. (formerly Socony Mobil Oil Corp.), 1958-61, sr. scientist, 1961-69, mgr. process research sect., 1967-69; mgr. Central Research Lab. Mobil Research & Devel. Corp., Princeton, N.J., 1969-82, sr. scientist and sci. adv., 1982-84; Disting. prof. chem. and bio-engring. sci. U. Pa., 1984-90, prof. emeritus, 1990—; adj. prof. Pa. State U., 1992—; cons. rsch. and tech. strategy, 1984—; vis. prof. Princeton U., 1974-76, mem. adv. council dept. chem. engring., 1973-78; mem. adv. and resource council Princeton U. Sch. Engring., 1974-78; chmn. center policy bd. Center for Catalytic Sci. and Tech., U. Del., 1977-81; mem. energy research adv. bd. U.S. Dept. Energy, 1985-90. Editor: Advances in Catalysis, 1956-93; edtl. bd. Jour. Catalysis, 1962-83, Chem. Engring. Comms., 1972-78, Heterogenous Chem. Reviews, 1993—; monthly columnist Sci. of the Possible, Chemtech, 1980-83; contbr. numerous articles to sci. jours.; holder 80 patents. Recipient ann. award Catalysis Club Phila., 1973, Lavoisier medal, Société Chimique de France, 1983, Perkin medal Soc. Chem. Industries, 1985, Nat. Medal of Tech., 1992. Fellow Am. Phys. Soc., Am. Inst. Chemists (Chem. Pioneer award 1974); mem. AIChE (R.H. Wilhelm award 1978), Am. Chem. Soc. (sci. award South Jersey sect. 1963, E.V. Murphree award 1972, Leo Friend award 1977, Chemistry of Contemporary Tech. Problems award 1986, Carothers award 1987), N.Y. Acad. Sci., Nat. Acad. Engring., Nassau Club (Princeton). Quaker. Office: Univ of Pa Dept Bio-Engring Philadelphia PA 19104

WEISZ, WILLIAM JULIUS, electronics company executive; b. Chgo., Jan. 8, 1927; m. Barbara Becker, Dec. 25, 1947; children: George, Terri, David. B.S. in Elec. Engring, MIT, 1948; D.B.A. (hon.), St. Ambrose Coll., 1976. With Motorola, Inc., Chgo., 1948-90, exec. v.p., 1969-70, pres., 1970-80, chief oper. officer, 1972-86, vice chmn., 1980-93, chief exec. officer, 1986-87, officer of bd., 1988-89, ret., 1990, chmn. bd. dirs., 1993-97; Pres. Motorola Communications Internat., 1966-69; Motorola Communications and Electronics, Inc., 1966-69; dir. (Motorola Israel.), Harris Bankcorp Harris Trust and Savs. Bank; mem. exec. com. land mobile adv. com. to FCC. Com. chmn. Cub Scout Pack Evanston coun. Boy Scouts Am., 1960-62; trustee MIT, 1975-85, 91—; mem. Def. Policy Adv. Com. on Trade, 1988-92. Recipient award of merit Nat. Electronics Conf., 1970; Freedom Found. of Valley Forge award, 1974; MIT Corp. Leadership award, 1976. Fellow IEEE (past nat. chmn. vehicular communications group, Ernst Weber engring. leadership recognition award 1997); mem. Electronic Industries Assn. (past chmn., bd. govs., past chmn. indsl. elec. div., medal of honor 1981), Bus. Roundtable, MIT Club (bd. dirs. Chgo.), Sigma Xi, Tau Beta Pi, Eta Kappa Nu. Office: Motorola Inc 1303 E Algonquin Rd Schaumburg IL 60196-4041

WEITKAMP, WILLIAM GEORGE, retired nuclear physicist; b. Fremont, Nebr., June 22, 1934; s. Alvin Herman and Georgia Ann (Fuhrmeister) W.; m. Audrey Ann Jensen, June 2, 1956; children—Erick, Jay, Gretchen, Laurie. B.A., St. Olaf Coll., 1956; M.S., U. Wis., 1961, Ph.D., 1965. Research asst. prof. U. Wash., Seattle, 1965-67; asst. prof. U. Pitts., 1967-68; tech. dir., research prof. Nuclear Physics Lab., U. Wash., Seattle, 1968-95; retired, 1995, rsch. prof. emeritus, 1995—. Served with USAF, 1956-59. Acad. guest Eidgenossische Technische Hochschule Zurich, Switzerland, 1974-75. Mem. Am. Phys. Soc. Home: 2019 E Louisa St Seattle WA 98112-2207 Office: Univ Wash Nuclear Physics Lab GL-10 Seattle WA 98195

WEITZ, JEANNE STEWART, artist, educator; b. Warren, Ohio, Apr. 30, 1920; d. William McKinley and Ruth (Stewart) Kohlmorgan; m. Loyal Wilbur Weitz, Aug. 1, 1940 (dec. 1986); children: Gail, Judith, John,

Marc. BS in Art and English, Youngstown U., 1944; MEd in Art, U. Tex., El Paso, 1964; postgrad., Tex. Tech U., 1976. Indsl. engr. Republic Iron & Steel, Youngstown, Ohio, 1942-43; art tchr. pub. schs., Bessemer, Pa., 1943-44; art tchr. El Paso (Tex.) Independent Sch. Dist., 1944-50, 54-78, art. cons., 1978-87; art tchr. Hermosa Beach (Calif.) Independent Sch. Dist., 1950-53, El Paso Mus. Art, 1960-65; lectr. in art U. Tex., El Paso, 1963-66; instr. El Paso Community Coll., 1970-78; free-lance artist, lectr. El Paso, 1987-91; supr. student tchr. U. Tex., El Paso, 1989-91. Represented in group exhibitions at Sun CarnivalExhbn., 1961, El Paso Mus. Art, 1962; author highsch. curriculum guide; exhibited at LVAA Shows, 1990 (5 First Places), Westside Art Guild, 1992, LVAA, 1992 (1st in Watercolor). Coordinator art edn. El Paso Civic Planning Coun., 1985-86; chmn. art edn., art resources dept. City of El Paso, 1982-83. Recipient Purchase award El Paso Art Assn. Spring Show, 1995, 1st Pl. award KCOS (PBS), 1996, 1st Pl. award Westside Art Guild, 1996. Mem. Tex. Art Edn. Assn. (conf. planner, local orgn. 1981, Hon. Mention award 1972), Nat. Soc. Arts and Letters (sec. El Paso chpt. 1988—), El Paso Mus. Art Guild, Lower Valley Art Assn. (Hon. Mention award 1988), Nat. Art Edn. Assn. (sec. 1988-93, two 1st Place award LVAA shows 1989), Westside Art Guild (pres. 1993-95), Nat. Soc. Am. Pen Women. Republican. Presbyterian. Avocations: printmaking, travel. Home and Studio: 890 Forrest Hills Dr El Paso TX 79932-3017

WEITZ, JOHN, fashion designer, writer; b. Berlin, May 25, 1923; came to U.S., 1940, naturalized, 1943; s. Robert and Hedy (Jacob) W.; m. Susan Kohner, Aug. 30, 1964; children: Paul John, Christopher John; children by previous marriage: Karen Weitz Curtis, Robert. Student, Hall Sch., London, 1936, St. Paul's Sch., London, 1936-39; certificate, Oxford-Cambridge Sch., 1938. Founder John Weitz Designs, Inc., N.Y.C., 1954—. Designer various cos., until 1954; author: Value of Nothing, Man in Charge (Best Seller list 1974), Friends in High Places, 1982, Hitler's Diplomat, 1992. Bd. dirs. emeritus The Allen-Stevenson Sch., N.Y.C.; bd. dirs. Phoenix House, William J. Donovan Found., Vets. of OSS, Am. Coun. n Germany; mem. pres.'s coun. Mus. City of N.Y. Capt. M.I. AUS, 1942-46, ETO. Decorated First Class Cross Order of Merit (Fed. Republic Germany), 1988, Comdr.'s Cross (Fed. Republic Germany), 1995; recipient Sports Illustrated award, 1959, NBC Today award, 1960, Phila. Mus. award, 1960, Caswell Massey awards 1963-66, Harpers Bazaar medallion, 1966, Moscow diploma, 1967, Coty award, 1974, Cartier Design award, 1981, Mayor's Liberty medal, N.Y.C., 1986, Cutty Sark Career Achievement award, 1986, Dallas Menswear Mart award, 1990, Pres.'s award of Fashion Inst. of Tech., 1990, Ellis Island medal of Honor, 1992; named to Internat. Best Dressed List Hall of Fame, 1971. Mem. The Pilgrims, Union Club, Century Assn., Spl. Forces Club, Old Pauline Club (v.p., London), The Naval Club (London), Beach Club (Palm Beach), Vintage Sports Car Club Am., Sports Car Club Am., Road Racing Drivers Club, USN Acad. Sailing Squadron, Sag Harbor Yacht Club. Office: 600 Madison Ave New York NY 10022-1615

WEITZEL, JOHN PATTERSON, lawyer; b. Pitts., Aug. 24, 1923; s. Albert Philip and Elizabeth (Patterson) W.; m. Elisabeth Swan, Mar. 20, 1965; children: Mary Middleton, Paul Patterson. Student, Deerfield (Mass.) Acad., 1937-40; A.B., Yale U., 1946; LL.B., Harvard U., 1949. Bar: Mass. 1949, U.S. Supreme Ct. 1960. Asso. Herrick, Smith, Donald, Farley & Ketchum (now Herrick & Smith), Boston, 1949-53, ptnr., 1961-86; ptnr. Palmer & Dodge, Boston, 1986-93; of counsel, 1993—, spl. asst. to asst. sec. treasury, 1953-55, asst. to under sec. treas, 1955-56; asst. gen. counsel Treasury Dept., 1956-59, dep. to sec. treasury, 1959-60, asst. sec. treasury, 1960-61; U.S. exec. dir. World Bank, 1960-61; mem. planning bd. NSC, 1959-61; cons. to sec. def., 1973. Mem. Mass. Council Arts and Humanities, 1966-71; overseer, dir. sec. Boys and Girls Clubs, Boston; mem. corp. Mass. Gen. Hosp., Boston Mus. Sci.; trustee Roxbury Latin Sch. Served with USAAF, 1943-45. Mem. Am., Boston bar assns., Am. Law Inst. Clubs: Harvard (Boston), Union Boat (Boston). Home: 45 Devon Rd Chestnut Hill MA 02167-1851 Office: Palmer & Dodge 1 Beacon St Boston MA 02108-3107

WEITZEL, JOHN QUINN, bishop; b. Chgo., May 10, 1928; s. Carl Joseph and Patricia (Quinn) W. BA, Maryknoll (N.Y.) Sem., 1951, M of Religious Edn., 1953; PMD, Harvard U. Ordained priest Roman Cath. Ch., 1955. With ednl. devel. Cath. Fgn. Mission Soc. of Am., Maryknoll, 1955-63, nat. dir. vocations for Maryknoll, dir. devel. dept. and info. services, 1963-72, mem. gen. council, 1972-78; asst. parish priest Cath. Ch., Western Samoa, 1979-81, pastor, vicar gen., 1981-86; consecrated bishop, 1986; bishop Cath. Ch., Am. Samoa, 1986—. Office: Diocese Samoa-Pago Pago Fatuoaiga PO Box 596 Pago Pago AS 96799-0596

WEITZEL, WILLIAM CONRAD, JR., lawyer; b. Washington, Feb. 6, 1935; s. William Conrad and Pauline Lillian (Keeton) W.; m. Loretta LeVeck, Mar. 10, 1978; children: William Conrad III, Richard S., Sarah L., Andrew K. AB, Harvard U., 1956, LLB, 1959; postgrad., MIT, 1974. Bar: D.C. 1961. Law clk., chief judge U.S. Cts. Md., Balt., 1959-60; asst. U.S. atty., Washington, 1961-66; atty. Texaco, Inc., White Plains, N.Y., 1966-73; assoc. gen. counsel Texaco, Inc., 1973-76, gen. counsel, 1977-82, v.p., gen. counsel, 1982-84, sr. v.p., gen. counsel, 1984-90; Pres. Texaco Philanthropic Found., Inc., 1980-90; ptnr., chmn. bus. clients dept. Cummings & Lockwood, Stamford, Conn., 1991-95. Trustee Southwestern Legal Found.; bd. dirs. Forum for World Affairs, 1995—. With USN, 1960-61. Fellow Ctr. for Pub. Resources; mem. ABA, Am. Law Inst., Conn. Bar Assn., D.C. Bar Assn., Assn. Gen. Counsel (v.p., bd. dirs. 1988-90), Westchester-Fairfield Corp. Counsel Assn. (pres. 1981, chmn., chief legal officers com. 1982-90), Am. Petroleum Inst. (gen. com. on law, chmn. 1983-84), Darien (Conn.) Country Club, Harvard Club (dir. Harvard Alumni Assn. for Conn. 1990-93, pres. Fairfield County club 1987—). Republican. Episcopalian. Office: Cummings & Lockwood 4 Stamford Plz PO Box 120 Stamford CT 06904

WEITZER, BERNARD, telecommunications executive; b. Bronx, N.Y., Sept. 22, 1929; s. Morris R. and Eva (Kurtz) W.; m. Anne DeHaven Jones, Nov. 5, 1982. BS, CCNY, 1950; MS, NYU, 1951, postgrad., 1951-54. Mgr., asst. v.p. systems engring and analysis Western Union Telegraph Co., Upper Saddle River, N.J., 1966-71, v.p. engring. and computer systems, 1976-85, sr. v.p. ops., 1985-90; cons. pvt. practice, Fort Lee, N.J., 1990—; exec. v.p., gen. mgr. Western Union Teleprocessing Industries, Inc., Mahwah, N.J., 1971-76; dir. U.S. Telecomm. Tng. Inst.; mem. adv. com. TV comm. U.S. Info. Agy. Pres. Ft. Lee Bd. Edn.; pres., bd. trustees Ft. Lee Pub. Libr. Served to lt. U.S. Army, 1954-57. Mem. Chaines des Rotisseurs, Internat. Wine Food Soc. Home: 6 Horizon Rd Apt 2509 Fort Lee NJ 07024-6622

WEITZMAN, ALLAN HARVEY, lawyer; b. Balt., Feb. 22, 1949; s. Harry and Freida (Caplan) W.; m. Joan Parker, July 19, 1970 (div. Sept. 1980); m. Regina Anne Kilcullen, Jan. 19, 1984. BS, Cornell U., 1970, JD, 1973. Bar: N.Y. 1971, U.S. Dist. Ct. (so. dist.) N.Y. 1975, U.S. Ct. Appeals (2d cir.) 1975, U.S. Dist. Ct. (ea. dist.) N.Y. 1977, U.S. Supreme Ct. 1982, U.S. Ct. Appeals (11th cir.) 1982, U.S. Ct. Appeals (6th cir.) 1987. Atty. Proskauer Rose Goetz & Mendelsohn, N.Y.C., 1973—; instr. Cornell U. Sch. Indsl. & Labor Rels., N.Y.C., 1986-94, adj. prof., 1976-81; mem. adv. bd. Cornell U. Labor Rels. Studies Program, N.Y.C., 1988-94. Mem. Am. Arbitration Assn. (labor adv. com. 1988-94), Fla. Bar Assn. (continuing edn. com. 1995—). Avocations: jogging, marathons, wine collecting, golf. Office: Proskauer Rose Goetz & Mendelsohn 2255 Glades Rd Boca Raton FL 33431

WEITZMAN, ARTHUR JOSHUA, English educator; b. Newark, Sept. 13, 1933; s. Louis I. and Cecele W.; m. Catherine Ezell, Aug. 8, 1982; children: Peter A., Anne E. B.A., U. Chgo., 1956, M.A., 1957; Ph.D., NYU, 1964. Instr. English, Bklyn. Coll., 1960-63; asst. prof. Temple U., Phila., 1963-69; assoc. prof. Northeastern U., Boston, 1969-72; prof. Northeastern U., 1972—; field editor G.K. Hall (Macmillan Pub.). Editor: Letters Writ by a Turkish Spy (G.P. Marana), 1970; founder, co-editor: The Scriblerian, 1968—; co-editor: Milton and the Romantics, 1980-81; contbr.: revs. and articles to profl. jours. and newspapers including Los Angeles Times, Boston Globe, Miami Herald. NEH fellow, 1972-73; Mellon fellow, 1976; research grantee Temple U.; research grantee Northeastern U. Mem. MLA, Am. Soc. 18th Century Studies, Conf. Editors Learned Jours. Jewish. Home: 4 Bellis Ct Cambridge MA 02140-3240 Office: Northeastern U Dept English 406 Holmes Boston MA 02115

WEITZMAN, ROBERT HAROLD, investment company executive; b. Chgo., July 15, 1937; s. Nathan and Selma Weitzman; m. Marilynn Beth Felzer, Sept. 5, 1965; children—Joshua C., Eliza S. B.A. in Bus., Econs., Grinnell Coll., 1959; J.D., DePaul U., 1963. Bar: Ill 1963. Vice pres. Weitzman Enterprises, Chgo., 1955-63; assoc. Lissner, Rothenberg, Reif & Barth, Chgo., 1963-68; real estate counsel Continental Ill. Nat. Bank and Trust Co., Chgo., 1968-74; v.p., group head Continental Ill. Investment Trust, Chgo., 1974-76; founding ptnr. Group One Investments, Chgo., 1977—; lectr. in field. Editor: Real Estate Finance Handbook, 1979. Contbr. articles to profl. jours. Trustee, advisor Weitzman Found., 1963-77, mng. trustee, 1978—; cons., advisor Ill. chpt. Big Bros. Am. Orgn., 1969-72; trustee The Wis. Real Estate Investment Trust, 1980, 81. Recipient Outstanding Young Man Am. award U.S. Jaycees, 1973. Mem. Ill. Bar Assn., Chgo. Bar Assn., Nat. Assn. Rev. Appraisers and Mortgage Underwriters (charter mem. cert. rev. appraiser designation), Real Estate Securities and Syndication Inst. (bd. dirs. Ill. chpt. 1982-90, pres. 1984, regional v. p. 1988, specialist in real estate securities designation 1988, chmn. nat. com. on continuing edn. 1989, 90). Real Estate Investment Assn. (founding mem., Nat. bd. dirs. 1990—, exec. com. nat assn. and Ill. chpt. 1990—, chmn. nat. com. for advanced edn., 1990—, nat. pres. 1996—, specialist in real estate investment designation 1990), Am. Inst. Banking, Internat. Coll. Real Estate Cons. Profls., Internat. Real Estate Bd. Home: 535 Carriage Way Deerfield IL 60015-4554 Office: Group One Investments Suite 1005 77 W Washington St Ste 1005 Chicago IL 60602-2805

WEITZNER, HAROLD, mathematics educator; b. Boston, May 19, 1933; s. Morris and Alice Savitz W.; m. Lois S. Friedlander, June 12, 1962; children: Daniel J., Henry D. AB, U. Calif., Berkeley, 1954; AM, Harvard U., 1955, PhD, 1958. Assoc. rsch. scientist Courant Inst. NYU, N.Y.C., 1959-60, rsch. scientist, 1960-62, asst. prof., 1962-65, assoc. prof., 1965-69, prof., 1969—; assoc. dir. Magneto-Fluids div. Courant Inst. NYU, N.Y.C., 1988—, dir., 1973-79, 84-88; chmn. Math. Dept. Courant Inst. NYU, N.Y.C., 1989-91; cons. Oak Ridge Nat. Labs., Oak Ridge, Tenn., 1980—; mem. magnetic fusion adv. com. U.S. Dept. Energy, 1986-89, fusion energy adv. com., 1991-93; mem. adv. com. Gen. Atomics Corp., 1994-96. Contbr. articles to sci. jours. Fellow Am. Phys. Soc.; mem. Soc. for Indsl. and Applied Math., Univ. Fusion Assn. (exec. com. 1993-96). Home: 10 Cedar Ave Larchmont NY 10538-4121 Office: NYU Courant Inst 251 Mercer St New York NY 10012-1110

WEKSLER, MARC EDWARD, physician, educator; b. N.Y.C., Apr. 16, 1937; s. Jacob J. and Lillian W.; m. Babette Barbash; children: David J., Jennifer Lee. B.A., Swarthmore Coll., 1958; M.D., Columbia U., 1962. Intern Bronx (N.Y.) Mcpl. Hosp., 1962-63, resident in medicine, 1963-64; asst. prof. medicine Cornell U. Med. Coll., N.Y.C., 1970-75; asso. prof. Cornell U. Med. Coll., 1975-78, Wright prof. medicine, 1978—, dir. div. geriatrics and gerontology, 1978—; attending physician N.Y. Hosp., Meml. Hosp., N.Y.C.; vis. prof. Pasteur Inst., Paris; cons. NIH, VA, N.Y.C., WHO, Pontifical Acad. Scis., Nat. Acad. Scis.; James Day lectr. Cornell U., 1980; pres. bd. trustees Am. Fedn. Aging Rsch., 1992-94. Editorial bd.: Jour. Clin. Immunology, Annals of Internal Medicine, Proc. Soc. Exptl. Biology and Medicine; asso. editor: Exptl. Aging Research. Founder, pres. Graphic Arts Coun. N.Y.; pres. Am. Fedn. Aging Rsch. Fellow Morgan Libr., Frick Collection. Fellow ACP; mem. Am. Soc. Clin. Investigation, N.Y. Acad. Medicine (chmn. geriatric sect.), Gerontol. Soc. (humanities and arts com.), Assn. Am. Physicians, Interurban Clin. Club, Alpha Omega Alpha. Office: Cornell U Med Coll 1300 York Ave New York NY 10021-4805

WELBORN, JOHN ALVA, former state senator, small business owner; b. Kalamazoo, Mich., Dec. 20, 1932; s. H. Sterling and Elizabeth Catherine (Dougherty) W.; m. Dorothy Yeomans, Aug. 15, 1952; children: Kayla, John, Kami. Grad. high sch., Richland, Mich. Previously supr. Cooper Twp., Mich.; Mich. state rep. Lansing, 1972-74, Mich. sen., 1974-82, 85-94; dairy farmer Kalamazoo area, 1985-94; agt. Welborn Ins. Agy., Kalamazoo area; owner Welborn's Yesteryear Antiques; cons. Rehabilitation and Corrections Corp., U.S. Corrections Corp. Candidate for gov. Mich., 1982; past chmn. Kalamazoo Rep. Exec. Com.; past mem. Gull Lake (Mich.) Sch. Bd.; past bd. suprs. Kalamazoo County, dir. Kalamazoo Soil Conservation Dist.; vol. fireman Cooper Twp. Fire Dept. Named Legislator of Yr. Police Officers Assn. Mich., 1988; recipient Golden Eagle Nat. Fedn. Police. Home: 6304 N Riverview Dr Kalamazoo MI 49004-9649

WELBORN, REICH LEE, lawyer; b. Winston-Salem, N.C., Nov. 1, 1945; s. Bishop M. and Hazel (Weatherman) W.; m. Martha Huffstetler, Aug. 27, 1966; children: Judson Allen, Spencer Brooks. AB, U. N.C., 1968, JD with honors, 1971. Bar: N.C. 1971. Assoc. Moore & Van Allen, PLLC and predecessor Powe Porter & Alphin, P.A., Durham, N.C., 1971-76; ptnr. Moore & Van Allen and predecessor Powe Porter & Alphin, P.A., Durham, N.C., 1976—; v.p. Family Counseling Svc., Durham, 1978-79. Recipient Order of Long Leaf Pine award Gov. of N.C., 1981, Spl. Citation, 1983. Mem. ABA, N.C. Bar Assn., Durham County Bar Assn. (v.p. 1987-89, pres. 1989-90), N.C. State Bar, Croasdaile Club (pres. 1989-90), Sertoma (pres. Durham chpt. 1987-88), N.C. Jaycees (pres. 1981-82), Durham C. of C. (bd. dirs. 1992-93). Home: 7 Lanecrest Pl Durham NC 27705-1854 Office: Moore & Van Allen PLLC 2200 W Main St Ste 800 Durham NC 27705-4677

WELCH, ARNOLD DEMERRITT, pharmacologist, biochemist; b. Nottingham, N.H., Nov. 7, 1908; s. Lewis H. and Stella M. (Batchelder) W.; m. Mary Grace Scott, June 15, 1933 (dec.); children: Michael Scott, Stephen Anthony, Gwyneth Jeanne Sinizer; m. Erika Petrová, Mar. 15, 1966. B.S., U. Fla., 1930, M.S., 1931, D.Sc. (hon.), 1973; Ph.D., U. Toronto, 1934; M.D., Washington U., 1939. Research asst. U. Fla., 1929-31; fellow pharmacology U. Toronto, 1931-35; asst. pharmacology Washington U., 1935-36, instr., 1936-40; dir. pharmacol. research Sharp and Dohme, Inc., Phila., 1940-44, dir. research, 1943-44; prof. pharmacology, dir. dept. Sch. Medicine, Western Res. U., 1944-53; Fulbright sr. research scholar Oxford U., 1952; prof. pharmacology, chmn. dept. Sch. Medicine, Yale U., 1953-67, Eugene Higgins prof. pharmacology, 1957-67; dir. Squibb Inst. Med. Research, 1967-72; v.p. R&D E.R. Squibb & Sons, Inc.; pres. Squibb Inst. Med. Research, Princeton, N.J., 1972-74; chmn. dept. biochem. and clin. pharmacology St. Jude Children's Research Hosp., Memphis, 1974-81, rschr., mem. emeritus, 1981-83; cancer expert Nat. Cancer Inst., 1983-86, acting dep. dir. divsn. of cancer treatment, 1984; scientist emeritus and rschr. NIH, 1986-88; mem. com. on growth NRC, chmn. panel mech. action, 1946-48, chmn. sect. chemotherapy, 1948-52, chmn. com. on growth, 1952-54; mem. sci. adv. bds. Leonard Wood Meml., 1947-53, Nat. Vitamin Found., 1953-56, St. Jude Children's Rsch. Hosp., Memphis, 1968-71; mem. divsn. biology and medicine NSF, 1953-55; mem. study sect. pharmacology and exptl. therapeutics USPHS, 1952-56, 1959-63, chmn., 1960-63, chmn. study sect. chemotherapy, 1963-65; mem. coordinating com. cancer chemotherapy Nat. Cancer Svc. Ctr., USPHS, 1955-57; mem. rsch. adv. coun. Am. Cancer Soc., 1956-59; mem. adv. coun. biol. sci. Princeton U., 1969-75; mem. working cadre Nat. Large Bowel Cancer program Nat. Cancer Inst., 1975-80; sci. adv. bd. La Jolla Cancer Rsch. Found., 1978-81; mem. Memphis Med. Seminar, 1977-83, pres., 1981-82. Assoc. editor: Cancer Research, 1950-58, Pharmacological Revs., 1962-66, Ann. Rev. Pharmacol., 1965-69; Am. editor: Biochem. Pharmacology, 1958-62, vice chmn. internat. bd. editors, 1962-83, chmn., 1983-93; mem. adv. bd. Advances in Pharmacology and Chemotherapy, 1962-85; mem. bd. editors Handbuch der experimentellen Pharmakologie, 1966-85; contbr. articles to profl. jours., chpts. in books. Recipient alumni award U. Fla., 1953, Washington U., 1957, Torald Sollmann award Am. Soc. Pharmacology and Exptl. Therapeutics, 1966, Chester Stock award Meml. Sloan-Kettering Cancer Ctr., 1987, J. Heyrovský gold medal Czechoslovak Acad. Scis., 1990; Commonwealth fellow Inst. für Therapeutische Biochemie, U. Frankfurt, Germany, and Acad. Scis., Prague, Czechoslovakia, 1964-65. Fellow AAAS; mem. Am. Soc. Pharmacol. and Exptl. Therapeutics, Assn. Am. Physicians, Am. Assn. Cancer Rsch., Am. Soc. Biol. Chemistry and Molecular Biology, Am. Soc. Clin. Pharmacology and Therapeutics, Am. Soc. Hematology, Am. Chem. Soc., Soc. Exptl. Biology and Medicine, Biochem. Soc. Gt. Britain, Cosmos Club (Washington), Fairbanks Ranch Country Club, Phi Beta Kappa, Phi Kappa Phi, Sigma Xi, Alpha Omega Alpha, Delta Tau Delta. Home: 5333 Renaissance Ave San Diego CA 92122-5634

WELCH, ASHLEY JAMES, engineering educator; b. Ft. Worth, May 3, 1933; married, 1952; 3 children. BS, Tex. Tech U., 1955; MS, So. Meth. U., 1959; PhD in Elec. Engring., Rice U., 1964. Aerophys. engr. Gen. Dynamics, Ft. Worth, 1957-60; instr. elec. engring. Rice U., 1960-64, from asst. to assoc. prof., 1964-68, dir. engring. computing facility, 1970-75, dir. biomed. engring. program, 1971-75, 95-96; prof. elec. and biomed. engring. U. Tex., Austin, 1975—, Marion E. Forsman Centennial prof. engring., 1985—. Fellow IEEE, Am. Soc. Lasers Surg. Medicine (bd. dirs. 1989-92). Research in laser-tissue interaction, application of lasers in medicine. Office: U Tex at Austin Dept Elec & Computer Engring Austin TX 78712

WELCH, BYRON EUGENE, communications educator; b. Kansas City, Mo., Mar. 3, 1928; s. Paul C. and Lucile Irene (Sherman) W.; m. Mabel Holmberg, May 18, 1947; 1 son, Byron Eugene, II. Ed., Swarthmore Coll., Tex. Christian U., U. Tex., Austin. Dir. devel. and planning Atlantic Christian Coll., Wilson, N.C., 1956-58; dir. devel. Chapman Coll., Orange, Calif., 1958-59; asst. to pres. Calif. Western U., San Diego, 1959-60, William Woods Coll., Fulton, Mo., 1960-62; pres. Welch Assocs., Inc.; fund raising and devel. cons. Welch Assocs., Inc., Houston, 1962-94; adj. prof. communication U. Tex., Austin, 1968—. Mem. exec. bd. Sam Houston Area coun. Boy Scouts Am., 1974-91; bd. dirs. population program Baylor U. Coll. Medicine, 1975—; sec., mem. exec. com. U. Amas., Pueblo, Mex., 1978—; chmn. bd. elders, chmn. ch. bd. Bethany Christian Ch., Houston, 1972-79, mem. pension fund bd., 1979-86; pers. Houston Community Found., 1980-91; chmn. bd. Excape Ctr., 1989-91. With USNR, 1945-46. Recipient Silver Beaver award Boy Scouts Am., 1981. Mem. Nat. Soc. Fund Raisers (pres. 1975-77, chmn. bd. 1977-78, mem. cert. bd. 1981-86), Southwest Soc. Fund Raisers (pres. 1968-70), U. Tex. Southwest Inst. Fund Raising (dean 1974-85, dean Rice U. fund raising 1986-91), Nat. Soc. Fund Raising Execs. Found. (pres. 1980-83). Home: 4515 W Alabama St Houston TX 77027-4803 *The supreme satisfaction is to give without counting the cost. I have tried to make it a rule of my life never to remember what I do for others, but never to forget what others do for me.*

WELCH, CAROL MAE, lawyer; b. Rockford, Ill., Oct. 23, 1947; d. Leonard John and LaVerna Helen (Ang) Nyberg; m. Donald Peter Welch, Nov. 23, 1968 (dec. Sept. 1976). BA in Spanish, Wheaton Coll., 1968; JD, U. Denver, 1976. Bar: Colo. 1977, U.S. Dist. Ct. Colo. 1977, U.S. Ct. Appeals (10th cir.) 1977, U.S. Supreme Ct. 1981. Tchr. State Hosp., Dixon, Ill., 1969, Polo Cmty. Schs., Ill., 1969-70; registrar Sch. Nursing Hosp. of U. Pa., Phila., 1970; assoc. Hall & Evans, Denver, 1977-81, ptnr., 1981-92, spec. counsel, 1993-94; mem. Miller & Welch, L.L.C., Denver, 1995—. mem. Colo. Supreme Ct. Jury Inst., Denver, 1982—; vice chmn. com. on conduct U.S. Dist. Ct., Denver, 1982-83, chmn., 1983-84; lectr. in field. Pres. Family Tree, Inc. Named to Order St. Ives, U. Denver Coll. Law, 1977. Mem. ABA, Am. Coll. Trial Lawyers (state com.), Internat. Soc. Barristers, Internat. Assn. Def. Counsel, Am. Bd. Trial Advs. (treas. Colo. chpt. 1991-92, pres. 1992-93), Colo. Def. Lawyers Assn. (treas. 1982-83, v.p. 1983-84, pres. 1984-85), Denver Bar Assn., Colo. Bar Assn. (mem. litigation sect. coun. 1987-90), Colo. Bar Found. (trustee 1992—, pres. 1995—), Def. Rsch. Inst. (chmn. Colo. chpt. 1987-90, regional v.p. 1990-93, bd. dirs. 1993-96), William E. Doyle Inn. Office: Miller & Welch LLC 730 17th St Ste 925 Denver CO 80202-3520

WELCH, CHARLES DAVID, diplomat; b. Munich, Germany, Dec. 25, 1953; s. Donald Mansel and Jackie (Brown) W.; m. Gretchen Anne Gerwe, May 14, 1983; children: Emma Frances, Margaret Elizabeth, Hannah Alice. Student, London Sch. Econs., 1973-74; BS in Fgn. Svc., Georgetown U., 1975; MA in Law and Diplomacy, MA, Tufts U., 1977. Staff asst. office of undersecretary U.S. State Dept. Security Assistance, Washington, 1977-79; polit. officer U.S. Embassy, Islamabad, Pakistan, 1979-81; country officer Syria desk U.S. State Dept. Bur. of Near Ea. and South Asian Affairs, Washington, 1981-82, country officer Lebanon desk, 1982-83; polit. sect. chief U.S. Embassy, Damascus, Syria, 1984-86; polit. counselor U.S. Embassy, Amman, Jordan, 1986-88; mem. sr. seminar fgn. policy U.S. State Dept. Fgn. Svc. Inst., Washington, 1988-89; dir. near Ea. and South Asian affairs Nat. Security Coun., White House, Washington, 1989-91; exec. asst. to undersec. for polit. affairs Dept. of State, Washington, 1991-92; dep. chief mission U.S. Embassy, Riyadh, Saudi Arabia, 1992-95; prin. dep. asst. sec. for near ea. affairs Dept. of State, Washington, 1995—. Mem. Coun. Fgn. Rels., Am. Fgn. Svc. Assn., Phi Beta Kappa, Phi Alpha Phi. Presbyterian. Avocations: sports, books, music, history. Home and Office: Rm 6242 Dept State Washington DC 20520

WELCH, CLAUDE (RAYMOND), theology educator; b. Genoa City, Wis., Mar. 10, 1922; s. Virgil Cleon and Deone West (Grenelle) W.; m. Eloise Janette Turner, May 31, 1942 (div. 1970); children—Eric, Thomas, Claudia; m. Theodosia Montigel Blewett, Oct. 5, 1970 (dec. 1978); m. Joy Neuman, Oct. 30, 1982. BA summa cum laude, Upper Iowa U., 1942; postgrad., Garrett Theol. Sem., 1942-43; BD cum laude, Yale U., 1945, PhD, 1950; DD (hon.), Ch. Div. Sch. of Pacific, 1972, Jesuit Sch. Theology, 1982; LHD (hon.), U. Judaism, 1976. Ordained to ministry Meth. Ch., 1947. Instr. religion Princeton (N.J.) U., 1947-50, asst. prof., 1950-51, vis. prof., 1962; asst. prof. theology Yale U. Div. Sch., New Haven, 1951-54, assoc. prof., 1954-60; Berg prof. religious thought, chmn. dept. U. Pa., Phila., 1960-71, assoc. dean Coll. Arts and Scis., 1964-68, acting chmn. dept. philosophy, 1965-66; prof. hist. theology Grad. Theol. Union, Berkeley, Calif., 1971—, dean, 1971-87, pres., 1972-82; vis. prof. Garrett Theol. Sem., 1951, Pacific Sch. Religion, 1958, Hartford Sem. Found., 1958-59, Princeton Theol. Sem., 1962-63, U. Va., 1987; Fulbright sr. lectr. U. Mainz, Germany, 1968; Sprunt lectr. Union Theol. Sem., Richmond, Va., 1958; Willson lectr. Southwestern U., Georgetown, Tex., 1994; dir. study of grad. edn. in religion Am. Coun. Learned Socs., 1969-71; del. World Conf. on Faith and Order, 1963. Author: In This Name: the Doctrine of the Trinity in Contemporary Theology, 1952, (with John Dillenberger) Protestant Christianity, interpreted through its Development, 1954, 2d rev. edit., 1988, The Reality of the Church, 1958, Graduate Education in Religion: A Critical Appraisal, 1971, Religion in the Undergraduate Curriculum, 1972, Protestant Thought in the 19th Century, vol. 1, 1799-1870, 1972, vol. 2, 1870-1914, 1985; Editor, translator: God and Incarnation in Mid-19th Century German Theology (Thomasius, Dorner and Biedermann), 1965; Contbr. to publs. in field. Recipient decennial prize Bross Found., 1970; Guggenheim fellow, 1976; NEH research fellow, 1984, Fulbright research fellow, 1956-57. Mem. Am. Acad. Religion (pres. 1969-70), Coun. of Socs. for Study of Religion (chmn. 1969-74, 85-90), Soc. for Values in Higher Edn. (pres. 1967-71), Am. Soc. Ch. History, Am. Theol. Soc., Phi Beta Kappa. Home: 123 Fairlawn Dr Berkeley CA 94708-2107

WELCH, DOUGLAS LINDSAY, physics educator; b. Karamursel, Turkey, Oct. 8, 1958; s. Gene Armour and Katharin (Lindsay) W.; m. Carol Marie Gibbons, Aug. 28, 1982. BSc, U. Toronto, Ont., Can., 1981, MSc, 1983, PhD, 1985. Rsch. assoc. Nat. Rsch. Coun. Dom Astrophys. Obs., Victoria, B.C., Can., 1986-88; from asst. prof. to assoc. prof., univ. rsch. fellow McMaster U., Hamilton, Ont., 1988-97, prof., 1997—. Office: McMaster U Dept Physics & Astron, 1280 Main St W, Hamilton, ON Canada L8S 4M1

WELCH, EDWIN HUGH, academic administrator; b. Balt., Apr. 11, 1944; s. Lester Kenneth and Catherine (Dodrer); m. Janet Gail Boggess, Nov. 22, 1977. BA, Western Md. Coll., 1965; STB, Boston U. Sch. Theology, 1968; postgrad., London Sch. Econs. and Polit. Sci., 1968-69; PhD, Boston U., 1971. Assoc. prof., chmn. W.Va. Wesleyan Coll., Buckhannon, 1971-75; assoc. prof., chmn. Lebanon Valley Coll., Annville, Pa., 1975-79, dir. weekend coll., 1979-80; dean Lakeland Coll., Sheboygan, Wis., 1980-81; provost Wartburg Coll., Waverly, Iowa, 1981-89; pres. U. Charleston, W.Va., 1989—; chmn. Iowa Deans Confs., Des Moines, 1984-89; title III evaluator Iowa Wesleyan Coll., Mt. Pleasant, 1983-85; pres. W.Va. Intercollegiate Athletic Conf., 1994-96. Contbr. articles to edn. jours. Bd. dirs. Bus. and Indsl. Devel. Corp., One Valley Bank, Charleston Area Med. Ctr.; v.p. Nat. Inst. Chem. Studies; creator, dir. Community Leadership Devel. Program, Waverly, 1986-88; bd. dirs., pres. Lebanon (Pa.) Family Planning Assn., 1976-81. Named Tchr. of Yr., W.Va. Wesleyan Coll., 1974. Mem. Nat. Assn. Ind. Colls. and Univs., Balt. Conf. United Meth. Ch. (ordained), Appalachian Coll. Assn. (treas.), Coun. Ind. Colls., Rotary Internat. (bd. dirs. Charleston, pres. 1997—). Democrat. Methodist. Office: U Charleston Office of Pres Charleston WV 25304-1099

WELCH, GARTH LARRY, chemistry educator, retired; b. Brigham City, Utah, Feb. 14, 1937; s. Samuel and Minnie Jane (Hughes) W.; m. Melba Lael Coombs, Sept. 9, 1960; children: Larry Kent, Kathryn Louise, Richard Samuel, Garth Edward, Robert Irvine, David Jonathan. B.S., U. Utah, 1959, Ph.D., 1963. Teaching asst. U. Utah, 1959-62; postdoctoral research fellow UCLA, 1962-64; asst. prof. Weber State U., Ogden, Utah, 1964-68; assoc. prof. Weber State U., 1968-72; prof. Weber State U., Ogden, 1972-97, dean Sch. Natural Sci., 1974-83, exec. dir. bus. affairs, 1983-89, assoc. v.p. phys. facilities, 1990-91, prof. emeritus, 1997—; mem. Utah State Council on Sci. and Tech., 1980-84. Mem. Mormon Tabernacle Choir, Salt Lake City, 1958-62, Jay Welch Chorale, 1983-93, Pleasant View Planning Commn., 1988-91, chmn., 1990-91, sci. adv. com. Salt Lake C.C., 1994-96. Mem. LDS Ch. (bishop 1966-74). Home: 3910 N 800 W Ogden UT 84414

WELCH, HARRY SCOVILLE, lawyer, retired gas pipeline company executive; b. Hugo, Okla., Nov. 14, 1923; s. John Calvin and Gaynell (Potts) W.; m. Peggy Joyce Weis, Dec. 18, 1954; children—Marshall Porter, Gay, Harry Scoville, Mary Margaret, Anne. B.B.A., U. Tex. at Austin, 1947, LL.B., 1949. Bar: Tex. 1948. Atty. Am. Republics Corp., Houston, 1949-51; ptnr. Turner, White, Atwood, McLane & Francis, Dallas, 1951-59; exec. asst., then v.p. Tenneco Inc., Houston, 1959-73; v.p., gen. counsel Panhandle Ea. Corp., Houston, 1973-74, sr. v.p., gen. counsel, 1975-85; v.p., gen. counsel Tex. Ea. Corp., Houston, 1987-89; mem. bd. adjustment Hunter's Creek Village, Tex., 1970-77, chmn., 1973-77; mem. adv. bd. Internat. Oil and Gas Ednl. Ctr., Southwestern Legal Found., Dallas, 1975-85; bd. dirs. Barrett Resources Corp. Served with USNR, 1943-46. Fellow Tex. Bar Found.; mem. Am., Houston Bar Assns., State Bar Tex., Phi Kappa Sigma, Phi Alpha Delta. Presbyterian. Club: Ramada (Houston). Home: 10611 Twelve Oaks Dr Houston TX 77024-3135

WELCH, JOE BEN, academic administrator; b. Amite County, Miss., May 18, 1940; s. H.A. Joe and Mildred Pill (Bean) W.; m. Dorothy Louise Rostron, June 2, 1962; children: Wendi Jo Welch Sands, Robin Clare Welch Peveto, Sandra Tres Welch Dobbs, Roxana Merry Welch Blackwell. BS, La. Tech. U., 1963; MEd, Lamar U., 1967; EdD, McNeese State U., 1974. Instr. math., sci. Clinton (La.) High Sch., 1963-64; instr. math. Port Neches (Tex.) Groves High Sch., 1964-67; acting head math. and sci. dept. Trinity Christian Coll., Baton Rouge, 1967-68; head math. and sci. dept. Mid-City Bapt. Jr. Coll., New Orleans, 1968-69; instr. math. Orange (Tex.) Extension Ctr., Lamar U., 1969-70, dir., 1970-75; dean Lamar U. Ctr.-Orange, 1975-81, provost, 1981-83, pres., 1983-89; pres. Middle Ga. Coll., Cochran, 1989—. Mem. adv. bd. dirs. Bleckley Meml. Hosp., 1989—. Recipient Grateful Appreciation award West Orange-Cove Consol. Sch. Dist., 1976-82, Outstanding and Dedicated Svc. award ARC, Orange, 1985; named Citizen of Yr. C. of C., Orange, 1985. Mem. Am. Assn. Community and Jr. Colls., Cochran (Ga.) Bleckley C. of C., Macon City Club (bd. dirs. 1991—), Phi Delta Kappa. Baptist. Office: Mid Ga Coll 1100 2nd St SE Cochran GA 31014-1564

WELCH, JOHN DANA, urologist, performing arts association executive; b. Canton, Ill., Mar. 14, 1938; m. Myrna Lee Loring, Dec. 23, 1962; children: Timothy Lance, Christina Dawn. BS, U. Ill., 1960, MD, 1963. Diplomate Am. Bd. Urology, Nat. Bd. Med. Examiners, Fla. Bd. Med. Examiners. Rotating intern Tampa (Fla.) Gen. Hosp., 1963-64, resident in urology, 1964-68; pvt. practice, Sarasota, Fla., 1970—; bd. dirs. Bay Area Renal Stone Ctr.; chief surgery HCA Doctors Hosp., 1981, chief of staff, 1983, trustee, 1988-91. Bd. dirs. Asolo Ctr. for Performing Arts, 1982-95, sec., 1989-90, v.p., 1990-93, pres., 1993-94. Maj. USAF, 1968-70. Mem. Fla. Med. Assn., Sarasota County Med. Soc., Am. Urological Assn. (SE sect.), Fla. Urological Soc. (pres. 1986), Am. Lithotripsy Soc. Home: 650 Mourning Dove Dr Sarasota FL 34236-1926 Office: 1921 Waldemere St Sarasota FL 34239-2943

WELCH, JOHN FRANCIS, JR. (JACK WELCH), electrical manufacturing company executive; b. Peabody, Mass., Nov. 19, 1935; s. John Francis and Grace (Andrews) W.; m. Carolyn B. Osburn, Nov. 1959 (div. 1987); children: Katherine, John, Anne, Mark; m. Jane Beasley, Apr. 1989. B.S. in Chem. Engring, U. Mass., 1957; M.S., U. Ill., 1958, Ph.D., 1960. With Gen. Electric Co., Fairfield, Conn., 1960—, v.p., 1972, v.p., group exec. components and materials group, 1973-77, sr. v.p., sector exec., consumer products and services sector, 1977-79, vice chmn., exec. officer, 1979-81, chmn., chief exec. officer, 1981—; also dir. Gen. Electric Capital Services; chm National Broadcasting Corporation. Patentee in field. Mem. NAE, The Bus. Coun. (former chmn.), Bus. Roundtable. Office: Gen Electric Co 3135 Easton Tpke Fairfield CT 06431-0002

WELCH, JOSEPH DANIEL, lawyer; b. University City, Mo., Feb. 1, 1952; s. Robert Joseph and Mary Virginia (Church) W.; m. Sharon Susan Filipek, Mar. 16, 1973; children: Eric Ryan, Christopher Joseph, Colin Andrew, Maria Nicole, Theresa Katherine. BA cum laude, St. Louis U., 1974, JD, 1977. Bar: Mo. 1977, U.S. Dist. Ct. (ea. and we. dists.) Mo. 1977, U.S. Ct. Appeals (8th cir.) 1984, U.S. Supreme Ct. 1994. Assoc. Ely & Cary, Hannibal, Mo., 1977-79; ptnr. Ely, Cary & Welch, Hannibal, Mo., 1979-82, Ely, Cary, Welch & Hickman, Hannibal, Mo., 1982—; mem. Mississippi River Pky. Commn., St. Paul, 1988-95, head Mo. del., 1988; mem. Nat. Heritage Corridor Commn., Washington, 1990-96; prof. bus. law Hannibal-LaGrange Coll.; speaker various orgns. Editor: Year in Review-Bankruptcy, 1991-94, co-author, 1988-90; speaker various profl. orgns.; contbr. articles to profl. jours. Bd. dirs. Mark Twain Area Physician's Recruitment Assn., Hannibal, 1984-85, Hannibal Free Pub. Libr., 1980-82, Hannibal C. of C., 1978-80; pres. Hannibal Ctrl. Bus. Devel., Inc., 1982-85; mem. Mo. Right-to-Life, 1977—; community adv. bd. St. Elizabeth Hosp., 1985-86; Birthright of Hannibal, Inc., 1980—, Holy Family Sch. Bd., 1990-95. Recipient acad. scholarship St. Louis U., 1970-74, recognition for Significant Contribution to Bush Administrn., Dept. Interior, 1993. Mem. ATLA, Mo. Assn. Trial Lawyers., Mark Twain Astron. Soc. (co-founder). Roman Catholic. Avocations: parenting, basketball, tennis, boating, creative writing. Home: 601 Country Club Dr Hannibal MO 63401-3033 Office: Ely Cary Welch and Hickman 1000 Center St Hannibal MO 63401-3449

WELCH, LLOYD RICHARD, electrical engineering educator, communications consultant; b. Detroit, Sept. 28, 1927; s. Richard C. and Helen (Felt) W.; m. Irene Althea Main, Sept. 12, 1953; children: Pamela Irene Towery, Melinda Ann Bryant, Diana Lia Worthington. BS in Math., U. Ill., 1951; PhD in Math., Calif. Inst. Tech., 1958. Mathematician NASA-Jet Propulsion Lab., Pasadena, Calif., 1956-59; staff mathematician Inst. Def. Analyses, Princeton, N.J., 1959-65; prof. elec. engring. U. So. Calif., L.A., 1965—; cons. in field of elec. comms. Contbr. articles to profl. jours. Served with USN, 1945-49, 51-52. Fellow IEEE; mem. Nat. Acad. Engring., Am. Math. Soc., Math. Assn. Am., Soc. for Indsl. and Applied Math., Phi Beta Kappa, Sigma Xi, Phi Kappa Phi, Pi Mu Epsilon, Eta Kappa Nu. Office: U So Calif Elec Engring Bldg 500A Los Angeles CA 90089

WELCH, MICHAEL JOHN, chemistry educator, researcher; b. Stoke-on-Trent, Staffordshire, Eng., June 28, 1939; came to U.S., 1965; s. Arthur John W. and Mary (Welch); m. Teresa Jean Conocchiolli, Apr. 22, 1967 (div. 1979); children: Colin, Lesley. B.A., Cambridge U., Eng., 1961; M.A., Cambridge U., 1964; Ph.D., London U., 1965. Asst. prof. radiation chemistry in radiology Washington U. Sch. Medicine, St. Louis, 1967-70, assoc. prof., 1970-74; assoc. prof. dept. chemistry Washington U. Sch., St. Louis, 1971-75, prof. dept. chemistry, 1978—; prof. radiology Washington U. Sch. Medicine, St. Louis, 1991—, prof. molecular biology and pharmacology, 1993—; dir. radiol. scis. dept. Washignton U., 1990—; mem. diagnostic radiology study sect. NIH, 1986-89, chmn., 1989-91; mem. sci. adv. com. Whitaker Found., 1995—. Author: Introduction to the Tracer Methods, 1972; editor: Radiopharmaceuticals and Other Compounds Labeled with Shortlived Radionuclides, 1977; assoc. editor Jour. Nuclear Medicine, 1989—; contbr. chpts. to books, more than 400 articles to profl. jours. Recipient Georg Charles de Hevesy Nuclear Medicine Pioneer award, 1992; scholar St. Catharine Coll. Cambridge U., 1958-61. Mem. Soc. Nuclear Medicine (trustee, pres. 1984, Paul C. Aebersold award 1980), Radiopharm. Sci. Coun. (pres. 1980-81), Am. Chem. Soc. (St. Louis award 1988, award for nuclear chemistry 1990, Mid-West award 1991), Chem. Soc. London, Radiation Rsch. Soc., Sigma Xi. Home: 1 Spoede Ln Saint Louis MO 63141-7708 Office: Washington U Sch Medicine Edward Mallinckrodt Inst Radiology 510 S Kingshighway Blvd Saint Louis MO 63110-1016

WELCH, OLIVER WENDELL, retired pharmaceutical executive; b. Jacksonville, Tex., Jan. 9, 1930; s. Jackson Andrew and Annie Laura (Trapp) W.; m. Wanda Virginia Urrey, Nov. 14, 1948. BA, Tex. Tech U., 1952; MA, Columbia U., 1958. Pharm. rep., supr. mktg. rsch., manpower devel. Warner Lambert Co., Morris Plains, N.J., 1962-72; mgr. corp. devel. Boehringer Mannheim Corp., N.Y.C., 1972-75; v.p. Biomed. Data Co., N.Y.C., 1975-77; assoc. dir., dep. dir. regulatory affairs Sterling Winthrop Inc., N.Y.C., 1977-94; ret., 1994; cons. Sanofi Winthrop, Inc., N.Y.C., 1995. Mem. Regulatory Affairs Profls. Soc., Drug Info. Assn., Order St. John of Jerusalem. Republican. Episcopalian. Avocations: music, travel, theatre. *Pursue excellence. Pay attention to detail. Expect a positive result.*

WELCH, PHILIP BURLAND, electronics and office products company executive; b. Portland, Maine, Nov. 15, 1931; s. Philip Gerald Welch and Clara Jenny (Berry) Hawxwell; children: Jahna Holly Welch Roth, Victoria Preston Welch Johnsen. Student, Berklee Coll., 1955-58. Nat. sales mgr. Akai Am. Ltd., Anaheim, Calif., 1970-73, BSR, USA, Blaupunkt, N.Y., 1973-76; nat. sales and mktg. mgr. Philips High Fidelity Labs, Ft. Wayne, Ind., 1976-79; dir. mktg. Pioneer Electronics, Moonachie, N.J., 1979-82; pres. Schneider N.Am. Ltd., Dayton, N.J., 1982-83; v.p. Lyons Assn., Indpls., 1986-88; pres. Nat. Electric Mktg. Co., Jacksonville, Fla., 1975—, Hemisphere Enterprises Corp., Jacksonville, 1988-91, Phil Welch Enterprises, Jacksonville, 1989—; cons. ContraTech Corp., Portland, Preg., 1986-87, Kukje Internat., N.Y.C., 1986, FCI Inc., N.J., 1985, Multiform Products, Inc., Jacksonville, 1989-90, gen. mgr., v.p., 1990-96; pres. Atlantic Office Sources, Inc., Jacksonville, 1996—. Contbr. articles to profl. jours. With USAF, 1950-54. Named Man of Decade Audio/Video Cons. USA, 1982, Man of Yr. Soc. of Audio Cons., 1974. Republican. Avocations: flying, golf. Office: 10991 San Jose Blvd Ste 141 Jacksonville FL 32223-6675

WELCH, RHEA JO, special education educator; b. Jacksonville, Ill., Jan. 26, 1957; d. James Daniel and Bobbye Jo (Weatherford) W. BA, William Woods Univ. for Women, Fulton, Mo., 1980; secondary teaching cert., Sangamon State U., Springfield, Ill., 1981; postgrad., MacMurray Coll., 1985, 86, 88, So. Ill. U., 1990, 91. Cert. 6-12 tchr., spl. edn., Ill. Tchr. recreational skills Ill. Sch. for Visually Impaired, Jacksonville, 1984; cross categorical tchr. Sangamon Area Spl. Edn. Dist., Springfield, 1988-89; tchr.'s aid Four Rivers Spl. Edn. Dist., Jacksonville, 1981, substitute tchr. spl. edn., 1982-86, tchr. learning disabilities, 1987, tchr. students with severe behavioral disorders, 1989—; mem. human rights com. Jacksonville Devel. Ctr., 1992—; pub. speaker; project dir. for community svc. programs Garrison Sch., Ill. Adv. Coun. on Voluntary Action-Serve Ill.; originator Class Time Community Svc. Volunteerism Four Rivers Spl. Edn. Dist.; coord. Spl. Olympics Ivan K. Garrison Sch., 1992-93; speaker Ill. Coun. Children With Behavior Disorders, 1997. Vol. ARC, instr. HIV-AIDS, CPR, First Aid. Named Staff Mem. of Month, Ivan K. Garrison Alternative Sch., 1992; recipient 2 Disting. Svc. citations, 1992; grantee Kraft Food Co., 1991-92. Mem. Coun. for Exceptional Children, Nat. Soc. for Experiential Edn. Office: Four Rivers Spl Edn Dist 936 W Michigan Ave Jacksonville IL 62650-3113

WELCH, ROBERT BOND, ophthalmologist, educator; b. Balt., May 24, 1927; s. Robert S.G. and Sally (Bond) W.; m. Elizabeth Truslow, May 30, 1953. A.B., Princeton U., 1949; M.D., Johns Hopkins U., 1953. Diplomate: Am. Bd. Ophthalmology. Intern in internal medicine Duke U. Hosp., 1953-54; resident in ophthalmology Wilmer Inst., Johns Hopkins U., 1954-57, chief resident in ophthalmology, 1959, co-dir. retina service, 1959-84, dir. retina service, 1984-85; retinal cons. in ophthalmology Walter Reed Army Hosp., 1961—, Bethesda Naval Hosp, 1976—; assoc. prof. ophthalmology Johns Hopkins U.; chmn. dept. ophthalmology Greater Balt. Med. Ctr., 1985-91. Author: (with others) The Wilmer Institute 1925-1975, 1976; editor Transactions Am. Ophthal. Soc., 1984-91; mem. editorial staff Retina mag., 1980-86. Served with USNR, 1945-47. Mem. Am. Ophthal. Soc. (v.p. 1992-93, pres. 1993-94, editor 1984-90), Retina Soc. (pres. 1981-83), Pan. Pacific Surg. Assn. (v.p. 1972-80), Md. Soc. Eye Physicians and Surgeons (pres. 1963-64), Md. Club., Elkridge Club, South River Club. Democrat. Episcopalian. Home: 4409 Atwick Rd Baltimore MD 21210-2811 also: 86 State Cir Annapolis MD 21401-1906

WELCH, ROBERT MORROW, JR., lawyer; b. Wichita Falls, Tex., Dec. 17, 1927; s. Robert Morrow and Sue (Hays) W.; children: Catherine C., Robert Morrow III, Candice C. LLB, Baylor U., 1951. Bar: Tex. 1951, Colo. 1989. Briefing clk. Supreme Ct. Tex., Austin, 1951-52; from assoc. to ptnr. Fulbright & Jaworski, Houston, 1952-92, ret. sr. ptnr., 1992—. Sgt. USMC, 1946-48. Fellow Tex. Bar Found.; mem. ABA, Am. Acad. Matrimonial Lawyers (cert. matrimonial arbitrator), Internat. Acad. Matrimonial Lawyers, Houston Bar Assn. Home: PO Box 10000 Silverthorne CO 80498 Office: Fulbright & Jaworski 1301 Mckinney St Houston TX 77010-3031

WELCH, ROBERT W., production designer, art director. Prodn. designer: (TV movies) Heart of Steel, 1983, Slow Burn, 1986, Stark: Mirror Image, 1986, (films) The Lost Boys, 1987, The Accidental Tourist, 1988, Beetlejuice, 1988, Ghostbusters II, 1989, Joe Versus the Volcano, 1990, Edward Scissorhands, 1990, Grand Canyon, 1991, Batman Returns, 1992, Wolf, 1994; art dir.: (films) The Star Chamber, 1983, Deal of the Century, 1983, Swing Shift, 1984, Best Defense, 1984, The Color Purple, 1985 (Academy award nomination best art direction 1985). Office: 7869 Fareholm Dr Los Angeles CA 90046-2110*

WELCH, (WILLIAM) ROGER, artist; b. Westfield, N.J., Feb. 10, 1946; s. Herbert Russell and Yvonne (Miller) W.; m. Carla M. Stellweg. BFA, Miami U., Oxford, Ohio, 1969; MFA, Chgo. Art Inst., 1971. visiting artist Univ. of Tex., Austin, 1988, 90, Univ. Tenn., Knoxville, 1989. One-man shows include Miami U., Oxford, Ohio, 1984, Whitney Mus. of Am. Art, N.Y.C., 1982, Museo Nacional, Havana, Cuba, 1981, Museo De Arte Moderno, Mex. City, 1980, Albright Knox Art Gallery, Buffalo, 1977, Milw. Art Ctr., 1974, Sonnabend Gallery, Paris and N.Y.C., 1972, Ewing Gallery, U. Tenn., Knoxville, 1990, Liverpool Gallery, Brussels, 1991. Grantee Nat. Endowment for the Arts, 1980, 74, N.Y. State Coun. on the Arts, 1976, 73. Democrat. Methodist. Home: 87 E Houston St New York NY 10012-2805

WELCH, RONALD J., actuary; b. Luling, Tex., June 26, 1945; s. Billie C. and Irene (Anton) W.; m. Leslie Ann Herman, Oct. 9, 1971; children: Kelley, Stephen. BBA, U. Tex., 1966; MS, Northeastern U., 1968. V.p., actuary Am. Nat. Ins. Co., Galveston, Tex., 1975-80, sr. v.p., actuary, 1980-86, sr. v.p., chief actuary, 1986-95, exec. v.p., chief actuary, 1995-96; bd. dirs. Standard Life & Accident Ins. Co., Oklahoma City, Am. Nat. Property & Casualty Ins., Springfield, Mo., Am. Nat. Life Ins. Co. of Tex., Galveston; chmn. bd. Garden State Life Ins. Co., Newark. Fellow Soc. of Actuaries; mem. Am. Acad. Actuaries. Office: Am Nat Ins Co 1 Moody Plz Galveston TX 77550-7948

WELCH, ROSS MAYNARD, plant physiologist, researcher, educator; b. Lancaster, Calif., May 8, 1943; s. Lloyd C. and Theda W. (Slane) W.; m. Jill Susanne Varley, Aug. 22, 1965; children: Renell Cherie, Brent Ross. BS, Calif. Poly. U., 1966; MS, U. Calif., Davis, 1969, PhD, 1971. Plant physiologist USDA Agrl. Rsch. Svc., Ithaca, N.Y., 1971—; rsch. assoc. Cornell U., Ithaca, 1971-75, asst. prof. plant physiology, 1975-81, assoc. prof., 1981-87, prof., 1987-94; co-organizer food sys. for improved health program Coll. Agr. and Life Scis., Cornell U., Ithaca, 1994—; disting. vis. scientist Murdoch U., Perth, Australia, 1980-81; vis. disting. scholar and lectr. U. Adelaide, Australia, 1991—; coord. food systems for health program coll. agriculture and life sci. Cornell U., 1994—. Editor: Crops as Sources of Nutrients for Humans, 1984; co-editor: Micronutrients in Agriculture, 2d edit., 1989; contbr. over 100 rsch. articles and 20 rev. articles to profl. jours. Fellow Am. Soc. Agronomy (Rsch. award N.E. br. 1992), Soil Sci. Soc. Am.; mem. Am. Soc. Plant Physiologists, AAAS, N.Y. Acad. Scis., Masons (master 1984-85), Sigma Xi. Republican. Mem. United Ch. of Christ. Achievements include discovery that nickel is an essential element for all higher plants; discovery that zinc plays a role in maintaining the integrity of root-cell plasma membranes. Home: 24 Hickory Cir Ithaca NY 14850-9673 Office: US Plant Soil & Nutrition Lab Tower Rd Ithaca NY 14853

WELCH, S(TEPHEN) ANTHONY, university dean, Islamic studies and arts educator; b. Phila., Apr. 29, 1942; s. Arnold DeMerritt and Mary Scott Welch; m. Hyesoon Kim; children: Nicholas, Bronwen, Emily. Student, U. Munich, Free U. of Berlin; BA in German Lit. with honors, Swarthmore Coll., 1965; MA, Harvard U., 1967, PhD (Fine Arts) History of Islamic Art and Architecture, 1972. Lectr. dept. history in art U. Victoria, B.C., 1971-72, asst. prof., 1972-75, assoc. prof., 1975-80, prof., 1980—, assoc. dean, 1982-85, Dean of Faculty of Fine Arts, 1985—; vis. prof. U. Minn., U. Wash., U. Chgo.; specialist in Iranian painting, Mughal painting in India, Islamic calligraphy and Sultanate architecture in medieval India; v.p., bd. dirs. McPherson Found.; mem., bd. dirs. Innovation and Devel. Corp., U. Victoria. Author: Shah 'Abbas and the Arts of Isfahan, 1973, Artists for the Shah, 1976, Collection of Islamic Art, Prince Sadruddin Aga Khan, 4 Vols., 1972-78, Calligraphy in the Arts of the Muslim World, 1979, Arts of the Islamic Book, 1982, Treasures of Islam, 1985; contbr. articles to scholarly and profl. jours. Office: Dean Faculty Fine Arts, Univ Victoria, Victoria, BC Canada V8W 2Y2

WELCH, THOMAS ANDREW, retired lawyer, arbitrator; b. Lincoln, Nebr., Dec. 22, 1936; s. Lawrence William and Edna Alberta (Tangeman) W.; m. Ann Reinecke, Sept. 12, 1959; children: Jonathan Thomas, Michael Andrew, Susan Jennifer. Student, Stanford U., 1955-56; BA, UCLA, 1959; JD, Harvard U., 1965. Bar: Calif. 1966, U.S. Dist. Ct. (no. dist.) 1966, U.S. Ct. Appeals (9th cir.) 1966, U.S. Supreme Ct. 1976. Assoc. Brobeck, Phleger & Harrison, San Francisco, 1965-71, ptnr., 1972-96; ret., 1996; exec. com. Asia/Pacific Ctr. Resolution Internat. Disputes, San Francisco; bd. dirs. Ctr. Internat. Dispute Resolutions, Honolulu. Chmn. bd. dirs. Youth Law Ctr., San Francisco, 1990—. Lt. USNR, 1959-66. Mem. ABA, Calif. Bar Assn., Am. Law Inst., Am. Arbitration Assn. (large complex case panel of neutrals). Republican. Presbyterian. Club: World Trade (San Francisco). Home: 38 Irving Ln Orinda CA 94563-1108 Office: Brobeck Phleger & Harrison 1 Market Pla 2800 Spear Tower San Francisco CA 94105

WELCH, WILLIAM BEN, emergency physician; b. Maryville, Mo., June 29, 1954; s. William Verne and Mary Lou (Steins) W.; m. Peggy Patricia Allen, Mar. 24, 1985; children: Jesse Lee, John Michael. BA in Biosci. cum laude, U. Mo., 1976, MD, 1980. Bd. cert. in family practice and emergency medicine. Resident in family practice U. Iowa Hosps. and Clinics, Iowa City, 1980-83; emergency staff physician Fransiscan Sisters Health Care, Danville, Ill., 1983-89; emergency staff physician Level II Trauma Ctr. St. Elizabeth Hosp., Danville, 1983-89; emergency staff physician Level I Trauma Ctr. Carle Found. Hosp., Urbana, Ill., 1989—; clin. asst. prof. U. Ill. Sch. Medicine, Champaign-Urbana, 1989—. Dir. ACLS Ill. chpt. Am. Heart Assn., 1983—, affiliate faculty ACLS Activities, East Cen. Ill., 1986—. Recipient Physician Recognition award AMA, 1984, 87, 90, 93, 96. Fellow Am. Coll. Emergency Physicians. Office: Carlo Clinic Assn 602 W University Ave Urbana IL 61801-2530

WELCH, WILLIAM HENRY, oil service company executive, consultant; b. Pharr, Tex., Nov. 24, 1929; married. AA, Edinburg (Tex.) Jr. Coll., 1949; BS, Trinity U., 1951. Sales engr. NL Baroid div. NL Industries, Inc., Liberty, Tex., 1955-58; dist. mgr. NL Industries, Inc., Liberty, Alvin (Tex.), New Orleans, Ardmore (Okla.), 1958-65; gen. mgr. Baroid de Venezuela NL Industries, Inc., Marcaibo, 1965-69; mgr. Latin Am. ops. Baroid Internat. NL Industries, Inc., Houston, 1969-71; mgr. Latin Am. ops. NL Industries, Inc., 1971-74, dir. internat. drilling svcs. NL Baroid div., 1974-77, pres. NL Atlas Bradford, 1977-81; sr. v.p. NL Ind., 1981; pres. NL Oilfield Svcs. NL Industries, Inc., 1981-83, pres. NL Baroid, 1983-86, pres., chief operating officer NL Petroeum Svcs., 1986-87, cons., 1987; retired, 1987—; chmn. Valley Shamrock Inc., 1987—; chmn. bd. dirs. Cottonwood Ctrs., 1993. Bd. dirs. Jr. Achievement Southeast Tex., Houston, 1985-86; fund raiser United Way, Houston, 1985-86. 1st lt. U.S. Army, 1952-55. Mem. Petroleum Equipment Suppliers Assn. (1st v.p. 1988-89), Nat. Oilfield Material and Del. Soc. (pres. 1984-85), Am. Petroleum Inst., Soc. Petroleum Engrs., Nat. Oil-Equipment Mfrs. and Dels. Soc., Petroleum Club, Sugar Creek Country Club. Avocations: golf, fishing, travel. Home: 115 Cattle Tr Way Georgetown TX 77628

WELCHERT, STEVEN JOSEPH, public affairs consultant; b. Davenport, Iowa, June 16, 1956; s. Richard Marshall and Norma Jean (Waters) W.; m. Kathleen Ann Agnitsch, June 13, 1981; children: Sarah Elizabeth, Matthew Joseph. BGS, U. Iowa, 1979. Nat. field staff Ted Kennedy for President, 1979-80; polit. dir. Lucero for U.S. Senate, Denver, 1984; legis. dir. for Gov. Richard Lamm, Denver, 1984-87, sr. edn. advisor for, 1985-87; issues dir. for Mayor Federico Peña, Denver, 1987; v.p. Bonham/Shlenker & Assocs., Denver, 1988-90; pres. The Welchert Co., Denver, 1990—; staff chmn. Nat. Govs. Assn., Washington and Denver, 1986; on-air analyst Sta. KMGH-TV, Denver, 1987-94; Wis. dir. Gore for Pres., Milw., 1988; floor whip Dem. Nat. Platform Com., 1988; dir. Western Hemisphere Trade and Commerce Forum Hosting Trade Mins. and Bus. Leaders, 1995. Writer radio series Ind. Thinking, 1987-88. Advisor Cultural Facilities Dist., Denver, 1988; bd. dirs. Citizens for Denver's Future, 1989-90; mem. Denver Baseball Commn., 1986-89, also chmn. govt. com., Rocky Mt. chpt. Am. Ireland Fund. Named Rising Leader for 90's Colo. Bus. Mag., 1990. Mem. Am. Assn. Polit. Cons. (Pollie awards 1st pl. Best Free Media, 2d pl. Print Graphics and Collateral Material 1995). Democrat. Roman Catholic. Avocations: hiking, mountain biking, youth coaching. Office: The Welchert Co 1525 Market St # 200 Denver CO 80202-1607

WELCH-MCKAY, DAWN RENEE, legal assistant; b. Lincoln, Nebr., Jan. 21, 1965; d. David Eugene and Helen Bessie (Hypes) W. BA in Pre-Law, Hawaii Pacific U., 1988; postgrad., U. Alaska, Anchorage, 1995—. Cert. Emergency Med. Tech., Alaska, 1994. Supr. Sizzler Family Steakhouse, Anchorage, 1981; dept. mgr. sales Jay Jacobs, Anchorage, 1982-83; resident asst. Hawaii Pacific U., Kaneohe, 1987-88; legal asst., intern Atkinson, Conway & Gagnon, Anchorage, 1988; contract paralegal Anchorage, 1989—; legal asst. Bogle & Gates, Anchorage, 1989, Bradbury, Bliss & Riordan, Anchorage, 1990-91; owner Welch's Ind. Paralegal Svc., Anchorage, 1991-94; ind. contractor, Anchorage, 1991-94. Vol. Rep. Party of Alaska, 1987, State of Alaska Cmty. Clean-Up, 1981-82, Concerned Citizens of Anchorage, 1981-82; med. asst., EMT II British Petroleum, 1993-96. Hawaii Pacific U. grantee, 1987-88; named to Outstanding Young Women Am., 1987. Mem. NAFE, Nat. Fedn. Paralegal Assns., Alaska Assn. Legal Assts., Nat. Assn. Legal Assts. Avocations: hiking, body surfing, biking, softball. Home and Office: PO Box 112552 Anchorage AK 99511-2552

WELD, JONATHAN MINOT, lawyer; b. Greenwich, Conn., Feb. 25, 1941; s. Alfred White and Sally (Duggan) W.; m. Jane Paige, June 19, 1965; children: Elizabeth, Eric. A.B. in History cum laude, Harvard U., 1963; J.D., Cornell U., 1967. Bar: N.Y. 1967, U.S. Ct. Appeals (2d cir.) 1969, U.S. Dist. Ct. (ea. and so. dist.) N.Y. 1970. Assoc. Shearman & Sterling, N.Y.C., 1967-75, ptnr., 1976—; ptnr. Shearman & Sterling, London, 1982-85; bd. dirs. Bank of N.S. Internat. Bd. dirs. Bklyn. Hosp., St. Ann's Sch.; former bd. dirs. Bklyn. Home for Children, Harvard Coll. Fund, Winant and Clayton Vols. Mem. ABA, N.Y. State Bar Assn. Office: Shearman & Sterling 599 Lexington Ave New York NY 10022-6030

WELD, ROGER BOWEN, clergyman; b. Greenfield, Mass., Dec. 1, 1953; s. Wayland Mauney and Luvycie (Bowen) W.; m. Patricia Ann Kaminski, June 7, 1978 (div. 1979); m. Cynthia Lou Lang, Apr. 15, 1995. Grad., Sacred Acad. Jamilian U. of the Ordained, Reno, 1976-77, Seminary, 1978-82; student, U. Nev., 1983-85; postgrad., Sacred Coll. Jamilian Theology, 1988-90. Ordained to ministry, Internat. Comty. of Christ Ch. of Second Advent, 1977; appointed Rabban priest Internat. Comty. of Christ, 1993. Adminstrv. staff Internat. Community of Christ Ch. of Second Advent, Reno, 1977—, exec. officer dept. canon law, 1985—, exec. officer advocates for religious rights and freedoms, 1985—, exec. officer speakers bur., 1985—, exec. officer office pub. info., 1986—, mgr. Jamilian Univ. Press, 1987—, dir. advt. prodns., 1988—; founder, pres. Crown Rsch. Found., 1992—. Author: Twelve Generations of the Family of Weld: Edmund to Wayland Mauney, 1986; dir. photography, supervising editor: (video documentary) Gene Savoy's Royal Roads to Discovery, 1993, The Gran Vilaya Expeditions, Reclaiming a Legendary Lost City From the High Jungles of Peru, 1996. Staff sgt. USAF, 1971-75. Named Life Mem., Sacred Oversee, 1991. Mem. Nev. Clergyman's Assn., Andean Explorers Found. (Explorer's medal 1990), Ocean Sailing Club (exec. sec. 1988-94, v.p. 1994—, Participant's Silver Medallion 1989). Avocations: photography, cinematography, videography, print media. Office: Internat Cmty Christ Ch Second Advent 643 Ralston St

Reno NV 89503-4436 *In the volatile arena of international politics, mankind's hope rests upon the acceptance of its spiritual destiny, not dwelling on its material past.*

WELD, WILLIAM FLOYD, governor, lawyer; b. Smithtown, N.Y., July 31, 1945; s. David and Mary Blake (Nichols) W.; m. Susan Roosevelt, June 7, 1975; children: David Minot, Ethel Derby, Mary Blake, Quentin Roosevelt, Frances Wylie. A.B. summa cum laude, Harvard U., 1966, J.D. cum laude, 1970; diploma with distinction, Oxford (Eng.) U., 1967. Bar: Mass. 1970. Law clk. to Hon. R.A. Cutter, Supreme Jud. Ct. Mass., 1970-71; ptnr. firm Hill & Barlow, Boston, 1971-81; assoc. minority counsel U.S. Ho. of Reps. Judiciary Com. Impeachment Inquiry, 1973-74; U.S. atty. for the Dist. of Mass., 1981-86; asst. atty. gen., criminal div. U.S. Justice Dept., Washington, 1986-88; sr. ptnr. Hale & Dorr, Boston, Washington, 1988-90; gov. Commonwealth of Mass., 1990—. Republican nominee for atty. gen., Mass., 1978. Republican. Office: Office of Gov Executive Office 360 State House Boston MA 02133*

WELDEN, ARTHUR LUNA, biology educator; b. Birmingham, Ala., Jan. 27, 1927; s. Arthur Luna and Mary Woodson (Smith) W.; m. Frances Merkl Colvin, Aug. 19, 1950; children: Charles Woodson, Arthur Frederick. AB, Birmingham-So. Coll., 1950; MS, U. Tenn., 1951; PhD, U. Iowa, 1954. Asst. prof. Millikin U., Decatur, Ill., 1954-55; instr. in botany Tulane U., New Orleans, 1955-59, asst. prof., 1959-63, assoc. prof., 1963-68, prof. biology, 1968-79, Ida Richardson prof. botany, 1979-93, chmn. dept. biology, 1979-83, prof. emeritus, 1994—; panel chmn. So. Assembly, Biloxi, Miss., 1970-71; program dir. Mesoam. Ecology Inst., New Orleans, 1982-87. Assoc. editor Tulane Studies in Zoology and Botany, 1966-78; contbr. articles to profl. jours. Served with U.S. Army, 1945-47. Grantee Am. Philos. Soc., 1957, NSF, 1960-75, NSF and Consejo Nacional de Mex., 1976-79, fellow AAAS, 1992; named to Socio Honorario, Sociedad Mexicana de Mex., 1982. Mem. Mycol. Soc. Am. (councilor 1967-69), Assn. for Tropical Biology, Swiss Mycol. Soc., Orgn. for Tropical Studies (life), Sigma Xi. Democrat. Home: 7826 Willow St New Orleans LA 70118-4056 Office: Tulane U Dept Biology 6823 Saint Charles Ave New Orleans LA 70118-5665

WELDON, DAVID BLACK, financial executive; b. London, Ont., Can., June 27, 1925; s. Douglas Black and Margaret (Black) W.; m. Ina G. Perry, July 7, 1951; children: Susan, Douglas, Anthony, Mardie, Kate. BA with honors, U. Western Ont., London, 1947, LLD (hon.). With Midland Doherty Fin. Corp. and predecessor cos., Toronto, Ont., 1950—, ret., 1989; chancellor U. Western Ont., 1984-88, chancellor emeritus, 1994—; dir. Dover Industries Ltd., Toronto, Emco Ltd., London, Goderich Elevators Ltd., Ont. Trustee Ont. Jockey Club; bd. dirs. Royal Agrl. Winter Fair, Toronto, 1970—, pres., 1980-82. Served with inf. Can. Army, 1944-45. Progressive Conservative. Anglican. Clubs: Toronto (bd. mgrs. 1983-85), York, Toronto Golf; London Hunt, London; Ristigouche Salmon (Quebec, Que., Can.); Griffith Island. Avocations: breeding and racing standardbred horses; fishing; hunting. Home: Prospect Farms, Arva, ON Canada N0M 1C0 also: 18A Hazelton Ave Apt 408, Toronto, ON Canada M5R 2E2 Office: Denison Mines Ltd, 40 Dundas St W Ste 320, Toronto, ON Canada M5G 2C2

WELDON, DAVID JOSEPH, JR., congressman, physician; b. Amityville, N.Y., Aug. 31, 1953; s. David Joseph and Anna (Mallardi) W.; m. Nancy Sourbeck, Nov. 26, 1956; 1 child, Kathryn. BS, SUNY, Stony Brook, 1978; MD, SUNY, Buffalo, 1981. Elder Zion Christian Fellowship, Palm Bay, Fla., 1991—; mem. 104th Congress from 15th Fla. dist., Washington, DC, 1995—; pvt. practice, Melbourne, Fla., 1987—; pres. Space Coast Family Forum, Melbourne, 1988-91. Maj. USAR, 1981—. Mem. AMA, Am. Coll. Physicians, Fla. Med. Assn. Office: US House of Reps 216 Cannon Bldg Washington DC 20515-3807

WELDON, JEFFREY ALAN, lawyer; b. Billings, Mont., May 6, 1963; s. Richard Allen and Monica (Michaud) W.; m. Leslie Helen Boileau, July 7, 1990. BA, U. Mont., 1986, MPA, 1994, JD, 1997. Rsch. analyst Heritage Rsch. Ctr., Missoula, Mont., 1989-91, v.p., 1991—; state senator Mont., 1993-97. Democrat.

WELDON, NORMAN ROSS, financial company executive; b. Greencastle, Ind., July 21, 1934; s. David M. and Lenora F. (Evens) W.; m. Carol J. Warne, Oct. 2, 1954; children: Thomas D., Cynthia M. B.S., Purdue U., 1956, M.S. in Indsl. Mgmt, 1962, Ph.D., 1964. With CTS Corp., Elkhart, Ind., 1964-79; exec. v.p. CTS Corp., 1970-76, pres., 1976-79, chief exec. officer, 1977-79, also dir.; pres. Cordis Corp., Miami, Fla., 1979-87; also chief exec. officer Cordis Corp.; pres., dir. Corvita Corp., Miami, 1987-96; mng. dir. Partisan Mgmt. Corp., 1996—; mem. adv. bd. Investment Co. Am., Inc.; trustee New Economy Fund; bd. dirs. SMALLCAP World Fund, Inc., Novoste Corp., Enable Med. Corp., Hemo Cleanse, Inc., Rx Kinetrix, Inc. Trustee Fla. Internat. U. Served to capt. USAF, 1956-60. Recipient Disting. Alumnus award Krannert Grad. Sch. Mgmt., Purdue U., 1979; NSF fellow, 1962-63; Ford Found. fellow, 1963-64. Mem. Tau Kappa Epsilon, Phi Eta Sigma, Alpha Zeta. Presbyterian. Club: Royal Palm Tennis, Weston Hills Country Club. Address: 7026 Timbers Dr Evergreen CO 80439 Office: Partisan Mgmt Group 15600 NW 67th Ave Ste 310 Miami Lakes FL 33014-2175

WELDON, THEODORE TEFFT, JR., retail company executive; b. Evanston, Ill., July 19, 1932; s. Theodore Tefft and Dorothe Galbraith (Stover) W.; m. Barbara Ann Eskilson, Aug. 17, 1957; children: Lisa Courtney Weldon LeFevre, Theodore Tefft III, Margaret Helen. BA, Dartmouth Coll., 1954. Retail store salesman Sears Roebuck & Co., Gary, Ind., 1954-58; retail store mgr. Sears Roebuck & Co., Kankakee, Ill., 1958-62; sales mgr. Craftsman Sears Roebuck & Co., Chgo., 1962-69, advt. mgr. Craftsman, 1969-70, mktg. mgr. tires, 1970-81, sr. buyer sporting goods, 1981-82, nat. gen. catalog mgr., 1982-86; dir. home TV shopping Sears/QVC, Chgo., 1986-92; cons. Drake, Beam, Morin, Inc., Chgo., 1992-94, Focus Media, Inc., L.A., 1993-96, Std. Mktg. Corp., Naperville, Ill., 1993—, King World Direct, L.A., 1993-97, Sears Roebuck and Co., 1997—, Ovation Group, 1997—, Home Depot, 1997—. Mem. Jr. Achievemnt, Chgo., 1966-68; rep. Winnetka (Ill.) Village Caucus, 1972-74; advisor Children's Theatre of Winnetka, 1972—; pres. Sunset Improvement Assn., Winnetka, 1975—. Avocations: internat. travel, theatre, swimming, biking, golf. Home: 426 Sunset Rd Winnetka IL 60093-4232

WELDON, VIRGINIA V., corporate executive, physician; b. Toronto, Sept. 8, 1935; came to U.S., 1937; d. John Edward and Carolyn Edith (Swift) Verral; children: Ann Stuart, Susan Weldon Mohart. A.B. cum laude, Smith Coll., 1957; M.D., SUNY-Buffalo, 1962; L.H.D. (hon.), Rush U., 1985. Diplomate Am. Bd. Pediatrics in pediatric endocrinology and metabolism. Intern Johns Hopkins Hosp., Balt., 1962-63, resident in pediatrics, 1963-64; fellow pediatric endocrinology Johns Hopkins U., Balt., 1964-67, instr. pediatrics, 1967-68; instr. pediatrics Washington U., St. Louis, 1968-69, asst. prof., 1969-73, assoc. prof. pediatrics, 1973-79, prof. pediatrics, 1979-89, v.p. Med. Ctr., 1980-89, dep. vice chancellor med. affairs, 1983-89; v.p. sci. affairs Monsanto Co., St. Louis, 1989, v.p. pub. policy, 1989-93, sr. v.p. pub. policy, 1993—; mem. gen. clin. rsch. ctrs. adv. com. NIH, Bethesda, Md., 1976-80, mem. rsch. resources adv. coun., 1980-84; bd. dirs. Gen. Am. Life Ins. Co., Security Equity Life Ins. Co.; bd. dirs., advisor Monsanto Co., 1989—. Contbr. articles to sci. jours. Trustee Calif. Inst. Tech., 1996—; commr. St. Louis Zool. Park, 1983-92; bd. dirs., vice chmn. St. Louis Symphony Orch.; bd. dirs. United Way Greater St. Louis, 1978-90, St. Louis Regional Health Care Corp., 1985-91; mem. risk assessment mgmt. commn. EPA, 1992-97; mem. Pres.'s Com. of Advisors on Sci. and Tech., 1994—. Fellow AAAS, Am. Acad. Pediatrics; mem. Inst. Medicine, Assn. Am. Med. Colls. (del., chmn. coun. acad. socs. 1984-85, chmn. assembly 1985-86), Am. Pediatric Soc., Nat. Bd. Med. Examiners (bd. dirs. 1987-89), Endocrine Soc., Soc. Pediatric Rsch., St. Louis Med. Soc., Equestrian Order of Holy Sepulchre, Knights of Malta, Sigma Xi, Alpha Omega Alpha. Roman Catholic. Home: 242 Carlyle Lake Dr Saint Louis MO 63141-7544 Office: Monsanto Co DIA 800 N Lindbergh Blvd Saint Louis MO 63141-7843

WELDON, W(AYNE) CURTIS, congressman; b. Marcus Hook, Pa., July 22, 1947; m. Mary Gallagher; children: Karen, Kristin, Kimberly, Curt, Andrew. BA in Humanities, West Chester State Coll., 1969; AAS in Fire Sci., Del. County Community Coll., Media, Pa., 1972; state instrn. cert., Cheyney State Coll.; postgrad., Cabrini Coll., Temple U., St. Joseph's U. Lic. tchr. Pa. From tchr. to head tchr. Walnut St. Sch., Darby-Colwyn-William Penn Sch. Dist., Pa., 1972-76; dir. tng. and manpower CIGNA (INA Corp.), Del. County, 1976-87; mayor City of Marcus Hook, 1977-81; councilman Del. County Council, 1981-87, vice chmn. then chmn., 1984-87; mem. 100th-103rd Congresses from 7th Pa. dist., Washington, D.C., 1987—; former chmn. Del. Valley Regional Planning Commn.; asst. dir. Elem. Secondary Edn. Act Title I Program, 1972-76; environ. specialist Project KARE, 1972-76; chmn. R&D House Nat. Security Com. Readiness; mem. Com. on Sci. Energy and Environ. Basic Rsch.; co-chmn. Congl. Fire Svcs. Caucus, The Empowerment Caucus, Globe Ocean Protection Task Force, Congl. Missil Def. Caucus, US-FSU Energy Caucus. Named Man of Yr. Chester Bus. and Profl. Assn., Most Effective Freshman Legislator Am. Security Coun., Citizen of the Yr. Del. County C. of C., Clean Air Champion Sierra Club, Man of Yr. Internat. Soc. Fire Protection Engrs., 1988, taxpayers hero Citizen's Against Government Waste; recipient Outstanding Govt. Leadership award Nat. Recycling Coalition, Fed. Legis. award Pa. Dirs. Assn. Community Action Agys., Spirit of Enterprise award U.S. C. of C., Golden Bulldog Watchdogs of Treasury award. Office: US Ho of Reps Office Ho Mems 2452 Rayburn Bldg Washington DC 20515-0915

WELDON, WILLIAM FORREST, electrical and mechanical engineer, educator; b. San Marcos, Tex., Jan. 12, 1945; s. Forrest Jackson and Rubie Mae (Wilson) W.; m. Morey Sheppard McGonigle, July 28, 1968; children: William, Embree, Seth Forrest. BS in Engring. Sci., Trinity U., San Antonio, 1967; MSME, U. Tex., 1970. Registered profl. engr., Tex. Engr. Cameron Iron Works, Houston, 1967-68; project engr. Glastron Boat Co., Austin, Tex., 1970-72; chief engr. Nalle Plastics Co., Austin, 1972-73; rsch. engr. U. Tex., Austin, 1973-77, tech. dir. Ctr. Electromechanics, 1977-85, dir. Ctr. Electromechanics, 1985-93, prof., 1985—, Josey Centennial prof. in energy resources, 1992—; mem. permanent com. Symposium on Electromagnetic Launch Tech., 1978—, vice chair, 1995-97, naval rsch. adv. com., 1992-97; cons. numerous cos. and govts., 1973—. Contbr. over 285 articles to profl. publs. Bd. dirs. Water Control & Improvement Dist. No. 10, Travis County, Tex., 1984—. Recipient Peter Mark medal Electromagnetic Launch Symposium, 1986, IR 100 award Indsl. Rsch. mag., 1983. Fellow ASME; mem. IEEE (sr.), NSPE. Achievements include 34 patents for rotating electrical machines, pulsed power, and electromagnetic propulsion.

WELFELD, JOSEPH ALAN, healthcare consultant; b. Bklyn., May 8, 1948; s. Morris Welfeld and Shirley Schachner; m. Blossom Yablon, June 15, 1969; children: Robyn Elise, Michael Evan. BE, The Cooper Union, 1970; MBA, Baruch Coll., 1975. Asst. dir. Kings County Hosp., Bklyn., 1972-75; exec. dir. L.I. Cancer Coun., Inc., Melville, N.Y., 1975-78, Nassau Physicians Rev. Orgn., Inc., Westbury, N.Y., 1978-82; CEO Ocean State Physicans Health Plan, Providence, 1982-86; regional v.p. United Healthcare Corp., Providence, 1986-87; pres. Managed Care Resources, Inc., Miami, Fla., 1987-93; regional dir. healthcare cons. The Hay Group, N.Y.C., 1993-96; prin. assoc. McManis Assocs., Ft. Lee, N.J., 1996—; pres., CEO Affiliated Physicians Network, Inc., Ft. Lee, 1997—. Author: Contracting with Managed Care Organizations: A Guide for the Health Provider, 1996. Fellow Am. Coll. Healthcare Execs. (chmn. managed care execs. com. 1994-95), Metro N.Y. Healthcare Fin. Mgmt. Assn. (chmn. managed care com. 1992-96). Office: McManis Assocs Inc Parker Plz Ste 1500 400 Kelby St Fort Lee NJ 07024

WELFER, THOMAS, JR., utility company executive; b. Pitts., Sept. 21, 1936; s. Thomas and Gertrude (Myers) W.; m. Kathleen Ward, Aug. 25, 1962; children: Karen A. Welfer Rapp, Sharon A., Thomas III, Gary, Jeff, Kathy Welfer Dlugonski. BSBA cum laude, Duquesne U., 1961; postgrad., U. Pitts., 1962, C.C. Allegheny County, 1977. Lic. real estate salesman, Pa. Union relations statistician Duquesne Light Co., Pitts., 1965-68, union relations analyst, 1968-70, mgr. office of pres., 1970-80, corp. sec., 1980-84, coordinator human resources, 1984-85, benefits compliance coordinator, 1985—. Com. chmn. troop 670 Boy Scouts Am., 1975-87, mem.-at-large Seneca dist. Allegheny Trails coun., 1983-92; coach Westview-Ross Athletic Assn., Pitts., 1985-86; chmn. adminstrv. bd. McKnight United Meth. Ch., Pitts., 1976-77, mem. fin. com., 1978—, chmn., 1986—, mem. bldg. com. and bldg. fund steering com., 1995—. Mem. Pa. Electric Assn. (mem. econ. survey com. 1972-80, supr. ann. conv. registration 1975, 77, 79), Beta Alpha Phi. Republican. Avocations: travel; camping; fishing; photography; bowling. Office: Duquesne Light Co PO Box 1930 411 Seventh Ave Pittsburgh PA 15230-1930

WELGE, DONALD EDWARD, food manufacturing executive; b. St. Louis, July 11, 1935; s. William H. and Rudelle (Fritze) W.; m. Mary Alice Childers, Aug. 4, 1962; children: Robert, Tom. B.S., La. State U., 1957. With Gilster-Mary Lee Corp., Chester, Ill., 1957—, pres., gen. mgr., 1965—; dir. Buena Vista Bank of Chester; pres. Buena Vista Bankcorp. Former chmn. St. John's Luth. Bd. Edn. 1st lt. Transp. Corp, U.S. Army, 1958-63. Named So. Ill. Bus. Leader of Yr. So. Ill. U., 1988. Mem. Perryville C. of C. (pres. 1989), Chester, Ill. C. of C. (past pres.), Alpha Zeta, Phi Kappa Phi. Republican. Lutheran. Home: 5 Knollwood Dr Chester IL 62233-1416 Office: Gilster Mary Lee Co 1037 State St Chester IL 62233-1657

WELHAN, BEVERLY JEAN LUTZ, nursing educator, administrator; b. Phila., Dec. 7, 1950; d. Winfield E. and Mary Helen (James) Lutz; m. Robert John LeBar, Aug. 28, 1971 (div. July 1978); m. Joseph Welhan, Jan. 7, 1984; children: James Benjamin, Jillian Grace. Diploma, Montgomery Hosp. Sch. Nursing, 1971; B.S.N., Gwynedd Mercy Coll., 1974; M.Ed., Lehigh U., 1977; M.S.N., Villanova U., 1983; postgrad., Widener U. Staff nurse recovery room Montgomery Hosp., Norristown, Pa., 1971-72; charge nurse North Penn Convalescent Residence, Lansdale, Pa., 1972-74; instr. med./surg. nursing Episcopal Hosp., Phila., 1974-78; staff nurse Montgomery Hosp., Norristown, Pa., 1978-79; asst. dir. nursing edn. Episcopal Hosp., Phila., 1979-85, assoc. dir. nursing edn., 1985-89, dir. nursing edn., 1989—; adj. instr. Pa State U., 1983-84. Author: Testing Program for Scherer's Introductory Medical/Surgical Nursing, 1986. Mem. Nat. League Nursing (program evaluator 1990—, bd. rev. 1993-96), Southeastern Pa. League for Nursing (mem. nominating com. 1982-83, bd. dirs. 1983-85), Northeast Coalition of Hosp. & Diploma Schs. of Nursing (bd. dirs., 1993-94, chair nominating com., 1993-94, nominating com. 1991-92, mem. mktg. com. 1995—), Montgomery Hosp. Alumni Assn., Nurses' Alumni Assn. of Episcopal Hosp. (hon.), Sigma Theta Tau, Phi Kappa Phi. Republican. Home: 607 Overbrook Ln Oreland PA 19075-2403 Office: Episc Hosp Sch Nursing 100 E Lehigh Ave Philadelphia PA 19125-1012

WELIKSON, JEFFREY ALAN, lawyer; b. Bklyn., Jan. 8, 1957; s. Bennet Joseph and Cynthia Ann Welikson; m. Laura Sanders, Aug. 19, 1979; children: Gregory Andrew, Joshua Stuart. BS, U. Pa., 1976, MBA, 1977; JD, Harvard U., 1980. CPA, N.Y.; bar: N.Y. 1981. Assoc. Shearman & Sterling, N.Y.C., 1980-83; staff counsel Reliance Group Holdings Inc., N.Y.C., 1983-84, dir. legal dept., 1984-85, asst. v.p., corp. counsel, 1985-88, v.p., asst. gen. counsel, asst. sec., 1988-94; exec. v.p., gen. counsel, sec. Reliance Nat. Ins. Co., N.Y.C., 1994—. Contbg. editor Harvard U. Internat. Law Jour., 1979-80. Mem. ABA, N.Y.C. Bar Assn., Am. Corp. Counsel Assn. Office: Reliance Nat Ins Co 77 Water St New York NY 10005-4401

WELIN, WALTER, financial advisor; b. Lund, Sweden, Sept. 20, 1908; s. Lars and Adele (Hellegren) W.; m. Ulla Olsson, Nov. 25, 1950; 1 child, Lars. Grad. Econs. and Fin., U. Lund, MA in Polit. Sci. 1943, grad. law sch. 1945. Dir. dept. The Royal Swedish Patent Office, Stockholm, 1948-74; fin. advisor/cons. in pvt. practice, Lund. Club: St. Knut Guild. Mem. AAAS, N.Y. Acad. Scis., Nat. Geographic Soc., Planetary Soc. Address: Siriusgatan 25 S-224, 57 Lund Sweden

WELKE, ELTON GRINNELL, JR., publisher, writer; b. Berkeley, Calif., June 15, 1941; s. Elton Grinnell and Elsie Maud (Shattuck) W.; m. Anna Lange, July 28, 1963 (div. 1980); children: Allison Espy, Erik Grinnell; m. Bonnie Jean Lum, Jan. 24, 1981; 1 child, Erica Irene. BA in Zoology, U. Calif., Berkeley, 1962. Staff writer Sunset mag., Menlo Pk., Calif., 1962-65, assoc. editor, 1965-69, sr. editor, 1978-80; travel editor Better Homes & Gardens, Des Moines, 1969-71; mng. editor Apt. Life mag., Des Moines, 1971-72; exec. editor Sunset Spl. Interest mags., Menlo Pk., 1972-78; freelance editorial cons. San Francisco and Seattle, 1981-84; v.p., dir. Livingston & Co., Seattle, 1984-89; publisher Microsoft Press, 1989—; chmn. North Wave Comms., Inc., Alaska, 1996—; cons. Holland Am. Line, Seattle, 1983-84, Livingston & Co. Advt., Seattle, 1983-84. Author: How to Survive Being Alive, 1977, Place's to go With Children Around Puget Sound, 1987. Bd. dirs. Olympic Nat. Pk. Assocs., Washington, 1965-69, March of Dimes, Western Washington, 1987-92, chmn. campaign com., 1989-92. Recipient 1st Pl. award Washington Press Assn., 1985, 86, 88, WPA award, 1987. Mem. Soc. A. Travel Writers, PRSA, Internat. Assn. Bus. Communicators (Golden Quill award 1985), Washington Athletic Club, Safari Club, Sierra Club, Alpha Delta Phi. Republican. Avocations: gardening, plant collecting, fly fishing, cattle ranching, Asian art. Home: 11329 NE 103rd St Kirkland WA 98033-5178 Office: Microsoft Corp 1 Microsoft Way Redmond WA 98052-8300

WELKER, WALLACE IRVING, neurophysiologist, educator; b. Batavia, N.Y., Dec. 17, 1926. Ph.D. in Psychology, U. Chgo., 1954. Mem. faculty U. Wis. Med. Sch., 1957—, prof. neurophysiology, 1965-90, emeritus prof., 1990—. Served with AUS, 1945-47. Sister Kenny Found. scholar, 1957-62; recipient NIH Career Devel. award, 1962-67. Mem. Am. Anat. Soc., Neurosci. Soc. Office: 1802 Fordem Ave Apt 14 Madison WI 53704-7116

WELKER, WILLIAM ANDREW, reading specialist; b. Shamokin, Pa., Apr. 26, 1947; s. William Howard and Dorothy Irene (Bertolette) W.; m. Margaret Jean Bainbridge, Mar. 1, 1969; children: William, Richard, Tiffany, Daniel. BS, U. Pitts., 1969, MEd, 1970; EdD, W.Va. U., 1989. Cert. tchr. health, phys. edn. K-12, Pa., W.Va., reading specialist K-12, Pa., W.Va., secondary prin. 5-12, W.Va., elem. prin. K-5, Pa., lang. arts 7-9, W.Va. Tchr. health phys. edn. Philip Murray Elem. Sch., Pitts., 1969-70, Swissvale (Pa.) Elem. Sch., 1970; tchr. 6th grade Edgington Lane Elem. Sch., Wheeling, W.Va., 1970-72; tchr. reading and English Ctrl. Cath. H.S., Wheeling, 1972-76; tchr. reading Warwood Mid. Sch., Wheeling, 1976—; adj. asst. prof. W.Va. U., Morgantown, 1991—; mem. steering com. Rschrs. In-Sch. Environ, Ohio County Schs., Wheeling, 1990-94. Contbr. articles to profl. jours. Commr. Wheeling Human Rights Commn., 1990-93. Minigrantee W.Va. Edn. Fund, Charleston, 1987, 89, 90. Mem. Internat. Reading Assn. (Columnist Svc. award 1991), Wheeling Island Lions Club. Avocations: writing, sports officiating, wrestling clinician, interpreter. Home: 110 N Huron St Wheeling WV 26003-2226 Office: Warwood Mid Sch 150 Viking Dr Wheeling WV 26003-7028

WELKOWITZ, WALTER, biomedical engineer, educator; b. Bklyn., Aug. 3, 1926; s. Samuel and Shirley (Rosenblum) W.; m. Joan Horowitz, June 17, 1951; children: David, Lawrence, Julie. BS, The Cooper Union, N.Y.C., 1948; MS, U. Ill., 1949, PhD, 1954. Profl. engr., N.J. Rsch. assoc. U. Ill., Urbana, 1948-54, Columbia U., N.Y.C., 1954-55; asst. to pres., gen. mgr. Gulton Industries, Inc., Metuchen, N.J., 1955-64; prof., chmn. elec. engring. Rutgers U., Piscataway, N.J., 1964-86, prof. biomed. engring., 1986—, chmn. biomedical engring., 1986-90; cons. Gulton Industries, Metuchen, N.J., 1964-74. Author: Engineering Hemodynamics: Application to Cardiac Assist Devices, 1977, 2d edit., 1987; co-author: Biomedical Instruments: Theory and Design, 1976, 2d edit., 1992; author numerous chpts. in books; contbr. more than 100 articles to profl. jours. With U.S. Navy, 1944-46. Rutgers U. Rsch. Coun. fellow, 1974-75; recipient Centennial medal IEEE, 1984, Excellence in Rsch. award Rutgers Bd. Trustees, 1985, IEEE Career Achievement award Soc. Engring. Med. Biology, 1991; Llewellyn Thomas vis. prof. U. Toronto, Can., 1989. Fellow IEEE (engring. in medicine and biol. soc. career achievement award 1991), N.Y. Acad. Medicine, Am. Inst. of Medicine and Biol. Engring. Achievements include 26 patents for Electron Tube, Ultrasonic Flowmeter, Ultrasonic Transducer, Piezoelectric Heart Assist Apparatus, Method and Apparatus for Non-Invasive Monitoring Dynamic Cardiac Performance, and others. Home: PO Box 2289 Lenox MA 01240 Office: Rutgers U Biomed Engring PO Box 909 Piscataway NJ 08855-0909

WELL, IRWIN, language educator; b. Cin., Apr. 16, 1928; s. Sidney and Florence (Levy) W.; m. Vivian Max, Dec. 27, 1950; children: Martin, Alice, Daniel. BA, U. Chgo., 1948, MA, 1951; PhD, Harvard U., 1960. Teaching fellow Harvard U., Cambridge, Mass., 1955-58; asst. prof. Brandeis U., Waltham, Mass., 1958-65; assoc. prof. Northwestern U., Evanston, Ill., 1966-70, prof. Russian, Russian Lit., 1970—; pres., mem. bd. dirs. Am. Coun. Tchrs. of Russian., Washington, 1967—. Author numerous books in field; contbr. articles to scholarly jours. Recipient Pushkin medal Internat. Assn. of Russian Profs. Jewish. Avocations: music, singing. Office: Northwestern U Slavic Dept Evanston IL 60208

WELLBERG, EDWARD LOUIS, JR., insurance company executive; b. Eagle Pass, Tex., June 5, 1945; s. Edward L. Wellberg and Nell L. (Kownslar) Walker; children: Elizabeth, Ashley, Jennifer; m. Yvonne Hill, Feb. 4, 1989. Student, St. Mary's U., San Antonio, 1978. CLU, Life Underwriters Tng. Coun. Fellow. Sales agt. Washington Nat. Ins. Co., San Antonio, 1969-82; ptnr. Mazur Bennett Wellberg Assocs., San Antonio, 1982-91; mktg. exec. Wellberg Assocs., San Antonio, 1991—; bd. dirs. Tex. State Ins. Bd. Adv. Coun., Austin, 1988-94. Contbr. articles to trade publs. Mem. Am. Soc. CLU's, Tex. Assn. Life Underwriters (bd. dirs. 1983-86, 92-93, pres. 1996), Tex. Life Underwriters Polit. Action Com. (vice chmn. 1981-83, 88-90, chmn. 1990-92), San Antonio Assn. Life Underwriters (pres. 1982). Home: 1707 Ashley Cir San Antonio TX 78232-4710 Office: 14400 Northbrook Dr Ste 200 San Antonio TX 78232-5038

WELLBORN, CHARLES IVEY, science and technology licencing company executive, lawyer; b. Houston, Dec. 9, 1941; s. Fred W. and Emily R. (Gladu) W.; m. JD McCausland, Aug. 14, 1965; children: Westly O., Kerry S. BA in Econs., U. N.Mex., 1963, JD, 1966; LLM, NYU, 1972. Bar: N.Mex. 1966, U.S. Dist. Ct. N.Mex. 1966. Assoc. Neal & Matkins, Carlsbad, N.Mex., 1966-68; Robinson & Stevens, Albuquerque, 1969-71; ptnr. Schlenker, Parker, Payne & Wellborn, Albuquerque, 1971-76, Parker & Wellborn, Albuquerque, 1976-82; ptnr. Modrall, Sperling, Roehl, Harris & Sisk, Albuquerque, 1982-95; pres., CEO Sci. and Tech. Corp. at U. N.Mex., Albuquerque, 1995—. Bd. dirs. N.Mex. Symphony Orch., 1988-91; bd. dirs. U. N.Mex. Anderson Schs. Mgmt. Found., 1989-94; vice chair U. N.Mex. Found., Inc., 1990-94; mem. Gov.'s Bus. Adv. Coun., 1989—; Small Bus. Adminstrn. Fin. Svcs. Adv., N.Mex., 1989; mem. venture capital mgmt. adv. com. N.Mex. State Investment Coun., 1991—; mem. Econ. Forum, vice-chair, 1993-94, chmn., 1995—; chmn. Roots & Wings Found., 1989—; v.p. N.Mex. Dem. Bus. Coun., 1992-96; bd. dirs. Accion N.Mex., 1994-97. Contbr. articles to law revs. Sgt. USAF, 1968-69, Korea. Fellow Am. Bar Found.; mem. ABA (ho. of dels. 1984-91), Albuquerque Bar Assn. (pres. 1977-78), N.Mex. Bar Found. (pres. 1980-82), State Bar N.Mex. (pres. 1982-83). Democrat. Roman Catholic. Office: Sci & Tech Corp at U NMex 851 University Blvd SE Ste 200 Albuquerque NM 87106-4341

WELLBORN, OLIN GUY, III, law educator; b. Galveston, Tex., Oct. 21, 1947; s. Olin Guy Jr. and Betty Jean (Merriman) W.; m. Jodi Boston, July 1, 1983; children: Olivia Boston, Olin Guy IV. AB in English magna cum laude, Harvard U., 1970, JD magna cum laude, 1973. Law clk. U.S. Ct. Appeals, San Francisco, 1973-74; asst. prof. Sch. Law U. Tex., 1974-77, prof. Sch. Law, 1977—, William C. Liedtke sr. prof. Sch. Law, 1985—, assoc. dean acad. affairs Sch. Law, 1987-91; vis. prof. Harvard Law Sch., 1978, U. Mich. Law Sch., summer 1987; co-reporter liaison com. rules evidence State Bar Tex., 1981-83, adv. com. subcom. on criminal matters Tex. Senate-House Select Com. on Judiciary, 1984, standing com. adminstrn. rules of evidence State Bar Tex., 1983-88, 94—, faculty Tex. Ctr. for Judiciary, 1992-97. Author: (with John F. Sutton Jr.) Cases and Materials on Evidence, 6th edit., 1987, 7th edit., 1992, 8th edit., 1996, Teacher's Manual to Accompany Cases and Materials on Evidence, 1992, 96, (with Steven Goode and M. Michael Sharlot) Guide to the Texas Rules of Evidence: Civil and Criminal, 1988, 2d edit., 1993, Courtroom Handbook on Texas Evidence, 1994, 4th rev. edit. 1997, Courtroom Evidence Handbook, 1995, Courtroom Handbook on Federal Evidence, 1995, 3d rev. edit., 1997; contbr. articles to profl. jours. Mem. Phi Beta Kappa. Office: U Tex Sch Law 727 E 26th St Austin TX 78705-3224

WELLBURN, TIMOTHY, film editor. Editor: (films) The Irishman, 1978, Cathy's Child, 1979, Chain Reaction, 1980, Caddie, 1981, (with Michael Balson and David Stiven) The Road Warrior, 1982, The Killing of Angel Street, 1983, The Coolangatta Gold, 1984, Burke and Wills, 1985, The

Fringe Dwellers, 1987, Dangerous Game, 1989, Judgment Night, 1993, Blown Away, 1994. Office: The Lyons/Sheldon Agency 8344 Melrose Ave Ste 20 Los Angeles CA 90069-5496*

WELLEK, RICHARD LEE, business executive; b. Chgo., Dec. 2, 1938; s. William I. and Mae (Silbert) W.; m. Susan Lee Pollack, Aug. 20, 1960; children: Jeffrey Alan, Marcia Rae, Deborah Lynn. BS, U. Ill., 1960. Material mgr. National Metalwares Inc., Aurora, Ill., 1963-65, sales mgr., 1968-73, exec. v.p. ops., 1977-80, pres., 1980-83; sales mgr. Decar Corp., Middleton, Wis., 1965-68; group exec. Varlen Corp., Naperville, Ill., 1983, pres., chief exec. officer, 1983—, also bd. dirs.; bd. dirs. AMCO Corp. Bd. dirs. Ill. Math. & Sci. Acad., Bus. Adv. Coun., Coll. Commerce & Bus. U. Ill., 1986—; bd. trustees Temple Bnai Israel, 1983—. Served to capt. USAF, 1960-63. Club: Economic (Chgo.). Avocations: motor sports, tennis. Office: Varlen Corp 55 Schuman Blvd PO Box 3089 Naperville IL 60566

WELLEN, ROBERT HOWARD, lawyer; b. Jersey City, Aug. 19, 1946; s. Abraham Louis and Helen Rose (Krieger) W.; m. Anita Fass, June 16, 1968; children: Elizabeth, Judith Maria. BA, Yale Coll., 1968; JD, Yale U., 1971; LLM in Taxation, Georgetown U., 1975. Bar: Conn. 1971, D.C. 1972, Colo. 1982. Assoc. Fulbright & Jaworski, Washington, 1975-76, participating assoc., 1976-79, ptnr., 1979-93; ptnr. Ivins, Phillips & Barker, Washington, 1993—; adj. prof. law Georgetown U. Law Ctr., 1982-85. Mem. lawyers com. Democratic Nat. Com., Washington, 1988. Served to lt. JAGC, USNR, 1971-75. Mem. ABA (asst. sec., past chmn. com. on corp. tax, sect. taxation, past supr. editor sect. taxation newsletter), Fed. Bar Assn. (council taxation), Phi Beta Kappa. Jewish. Contbr. articles to legal publs. Office: Ivins Phillips & Barker 1700 Pennsylvania Ave NW Washington DC 20006-4704

WELLER, ELIZABETH BOGHOSSIAN, child and adolescent psychiatrist; b. Aug. 7, 1949; m. Ronald A. Weller, Feb. 18, 1978; children: Andrew, Christine. BS, American U., Beirut, Lebanon, 1971, MD, 1975. Lic. psychiatrist, Lebanon, Mo., Kans., Ohio. Intern Am. U. of Beirut, 1974-75; resident Renard Hosp./Washington U., St. Louis, 1975-78; fellow U. Kans. Med. Ctr., Kansas City, 1978-79; asst. prof. psych. U. Kans. Med. Sch., Kansas City, Kans., 1979-84; chief child/adolescent psychiatry Ohio State U., Columbus, 1985-94, assoc. chair dept. psychiatry, 1994—; cons. Am. Psychiat. Assn. Task Force; Fred Allen chair dept. psychiatry Children's Hosp. of Phila., med. dir. Child Guidance Ctr.; vice chair dept. psychiatry U. Pa. Co-author: Psychiatric Disorders in Child/Adolescent, 1990, Current Perspectives on Major Depression Disorders in Children, 1984. Fellow APA, Am. Acad. Child/Adolescent Psychiatry; mem. Kans. Med. Soc., World Federation for Mental Health, Central Ohio Psychiat. Assn., Ohio Psychiat. Assn.,Soc. of Biological Psychiatry. Office: 34th St and Civic Ctr Blvd Philadelphia PA 19104-4399

WELLER, GERALD C., congressman; b. Streator, Ill., July 7, 1957. Degree in Agriculture, U. Ill., 1979. Aide to U.S. Congressman Tom Corcoran, 1977-78, aide to U.S. Sec. of Agriculture John R. Block, 1981-85; active family farm, 1985-88; rep. State of Ill., 1988-94; mem. 104th-105th Congresses from 11th Ill. dist., 1994—; asst. majority whip, mem. ways and means com.; rep. House Republican steering com.; mem. Newt Gingrich's policy com.; exec. com. NRCC, House Banking Com., House Veterans Affairs Com., House Transp. and Infrastructure Com. Mem. 1st Christian Ch. of Morris, Ill. Mem. Nat. Republican Legis. Assn. (nominated Legislator of Yr.). Office: US House Reps 130 Cannon Washington DC 20515-3012*

WELLER, GUNTER ERNST, geophysics educator; b. Haifa, June 14, 1934; came to U.S., 1968; s. Erich and Nella (Lange) W.; m. Sigrid Beilharz, Apr. 11, 1963; children: Yvette, Kara, Britta. BS, U. Melbourne, Australia, 1962, MS, 1964, PhD, 1968. Meteorologist Bur. Meteorology, Melbourne, 1959-61; glaciologist Australian Antarctic Exps., 1964-67; from asst. prof. to assoc. prof. geophysics Geophys. Inst., U. Alaska, Fairbanks, 1968-72, prof., 1973—, dep. dir., 1984-86, 90—; project dir. NASA-UAF Alaska SAR Facility, Fairbanks, 1983-93; program mgr. NSF, Washington, 1972-74; pres. Internat. Commn. Polar Meteorology, 1980-83; chmn. polar rsch. bd. NAS, 1985-90, Global Change Steering Com. Sci. com. on Antarctic Rsch., 1988-92; chmn. Global Change Working Group Internat. Arctic Sci. Com., 1990—; dir. Ctr. for Global Change and Arctic Sys. Rsch., U. Alaska, 1990—; dir. Coop. Inst. Arctic Rsch., 1994—. Contbr. numerous articles to profl. jours. Recipient Polar medal Govt. Australia, 1969; Mt. Weller named in his honor by Govt. Australia, Antarctica; Weller Bank named in his honor by U.S. Govt., Arctic. Fellow AAAS (exec. sec. arctic divsn. 1982-93), Arctic Inst. N.Am.; mem. Internat. Glaciological Soc., Am. Meteorol. Soc. (chmn. polar meteorology com. 1980-83), Am. Geophys. Union. Home: PO Box 81024 Fairbanks AK 99708-1024 Office: U Alaska Geophys Institute Fairbanks AK 99775

WELLER, JANE KATHLEEN, emergency nurse; b. Balt., May 26, 1948; d. Donald Boyd and Jane Lee (Collins) Sealing; m. Richard Earl Weller, Oct. 20, 1973 (div. Dec. 1978); 1 child, Jennifer Lee. AA in Nursing, Essex Community Coll., Balt., 1971; BS in Health, U. Md., 1983. RN, Md. Nurse, clin. dir. Liberty Med. Ctr., Balt., 1971—. Mem. Nat. Emergency Nurses Assn., Md. Emergency Nurses Assn., Md. Accident Injury Prevention Network. Lutheran. Avocations: symphony, cooking, reading. Home: 8737 Sicklebar Way Ellicott City MD 21043-6569 Office: Liberty Med Ctr 2600 Liberty Heights Ave Baltimore MD 21215-7804

WELLER, JANET LOUISE, lawyer; b. Boston, Sept. 17, 1953; d. Thomas Huckle and Kathleen (Fahey) W.; m. John Lee Holloway; children: Kelly Brianna, Janine Fahey. BA, Harvard U., 1975; JD, U. Mich., 1978. Bar: D.C. 1978, U.S. Dist. Ct. D.C. 1978, U.S. Ct. Appeals (D.C. cir.) 1979. Assoc. Cleary, Gottlieb, Steen & Hamilton, Washington, 1978-86, ptnr., 1986—. Office: 1752 N St NW Washington DC 20036-2907

WELLER, MICHAEL, playwright, screenwriter; b. Sept. 26, 1942; s. Paul and Rosa (Rush) W. BA, Brandeis U.; student, Manchester U. Author: plays Cello Days at Dixon's Place, 1965, How Ho-Ho Rose and Fell in Seven Short Scenes, 1966, Happy Valley, 1969, The Bodybuilders, 1969, Open Space, 1969, Poison Come Poison, 1970, Cancer, 1970, Moonchildren, 1972, Grant's Movie, 1971, Tira Tells Everything There is to Know About Herself, 1971, Twenty Three Years Later, 1973, Fishing, 1975, Alice, 1976, Split, 1978, Loose Ends, 1979, Dwarfman, 1980, The Ballad of Soapy Smith, 1983-84, Ghost On Fire, Broadway, 1985, Spoils of War, 1988, Lake No Bottom, 1990, Help!, 1995, Buying Time, 1996, Dogbrain, 1996, The Heart of Art, 1996-97; lyricist (with Jim Steinman) More Than You Deserve, 1973; screenwriter Hair, 1979, Ragtime, 1980 (Academy award nomination for best adapted screenplay 1981), Lost Angels, 1989, Writing on the Wall, God Bless You Mr. Rosewater, 1991, Getting Rid of Alex, 1995, The Sixteen Pleasures, 1996 (TV) Spoils of War, 1994, Stranger at the Gate, 1996; adapter, composer: Fred, 1965, The Making of Theodore Thomas, Citizen, 1968. Recipient Drama Desk award for most promising playwright, 1971; Rockefeller fellowship, 1973; Creative Artists Pub. Svc. grantee, 1976. Office: McNaughton Lord Representation Ltd, 200 Fulham Rd, London SW10 9PN, England

WELLER, ROBERT N(ORMAN), hotel executive; b. Harrisburg, Pa., Feb. 1, 1939; s. Charles Walter and Martha Ann (MacPherson) W.; m. Nancy M. Wood, June 21, 1975; children—Wendi Elizabeth, Terrie Lynn, Nikki Ann. B.S., Cornell U., 1969. Mgr. Hall's Motor Transit Co., Harrisburg, Pa., 1961-65; market research analyst Carrolls Devel. Corp., Syracuse, N.Y., 1970-72; asst. to pres. Econo-Travel Motor Hotel Corp., Norfolk, Va., 1972-74; dir. franchise sales Econo-Travel Motor Hotel Corp., 1975, pres., dir., 1976-84; pres., dir. Econo-Travel Devel. Corp., Norfolk, 1977-84; pres. Internat. Data Bank Ltd., 1985-86; pres., dir. Econo Lodges of Am., 1986-90; group pres., exec. v.p. Choice Hotels Internat., Silver Spring, Md., 1990-91; with Hospitality Ventures, Virginia Beach, 1991—; pres. Super 8 Motels, Inc. divsn. Hospitality Franchise Systems, Parsippany, N.J., 1993—. Served in USMC, 1957-60. Home: 3027 Lynndale Rd Virginia Beach VA 23452-6233 Office: 339 Jefferson Rd Parsippany NJ 07054-3707

WELLER, SOL WILLIAM, chemical engineering educator; b. Detroit, July 27, 1918; s. Ira and Bessie (Wieselthier) W.; m. Miriam Damick, June 11, 1943; children—Judith, Susan, Robert, Ira. B.S., Wayne State U., 1938; Ph.D., U. Chgo., 1941. Asst. chief coal hydrogenation U.S. Bur. Mines, Pitts., 1945-50; head fundamental rsch. Houdry Process Corp., Linwood, Pa., 1950-58; mgr. propulsion rsch. Ford Aeronutronic Co., Newport Beach, Calif., 1958-61; dir. chem. lab. and materials rsch. lab. Philco-Ford Co., Newport Beach, 1961-65; prof. chem. engring. SUNY-Buffalo, 1965—; emeritus, 1989; C.C. Furnas prof. SUNY-Buffalo, 1983—; vis. fellow Oxford U., 1989. Author numerous sci. papers, book chpts., ency. entries. Fulbright lectr. Madrid, 1975, Istanbul, 1980. Mem. Am. Chem. Soc. (chmn. Orange County sect. 1964, H.H. Storch award 1981, E.V. Murphree award 1982, Schoellkopf medal 1984, Dean's award 1991), ASTM (founder com. D32 on catalysts). Achievements include patents in field. Office: SUNY Buffalo 305 Furnas Hall Buffalo NY 14260

WELLER, THOMAS HUCKLE, physician, former educator; b. Ann Arbor, Mich., June 15, 1915; s. Carl V. and Elsie A. (Huckle) W.; m. Kathleen R. Fahey, Aug. 18, 1945; children: Peter Fahey, Nancy Kathleen, Robert Andrew, Janet Louise. A.B., U. Mich., 1936; M.S., 1937, LL.D. (hon.), 1956; M.D., Harvard, 1940; Sc.D., Gustavus Adolphus U., 1975, U. Mass., 1985; L.H.D., Lowell U., 1977. Diplomate Am. Bd. Pediatrics. Teaching fellow bacteriology Harvard Med. Sch., 1940-41, research fellow tropical medicine, pediatrics, 1947-48, instr. comparative pathology, tropical medicine, 1948-49, asst. prof. tropical pub. health Sch. Pub. Health, 1949-50, assoc. prof., 1950-54, Richard Pearson Strong prof. tropical pub. health, 1954-85, prof. emeritus, 1985—, head dept., 1954-81; intern bacteriology and pathology Children's Hosp., Boston, 1941; intern medicine Children's Hosp., 1942, asst. resident medicine, 1946, asst. dir. research div. infectious diseases, 1949-55; mem. commn. parasitic diseases Armed Forces Epidemiol. Bd., 1953-72, dir., 1953-59. Author sci. papers. Served to maj. M.C. AUS, 1942-46. Recipient E. Mead Johnson award for devel. tissue culture procedures in study virus diseases Am. Acad. Pediatrics, 1953, Kimble Methodology award, 1954, Nobel prize in physiology and medicine, 1954, George Ledlie prize, 1963, Weinstein Cerebral Palsy award, 1973, Stern Symposium honoree, 1972, Bristol award Infectious Diseases Soc. Am., 1980, Gold medal and diploma of honor U. Costa Rica, 1984, First Sci. Achievement award VZV Rsch. Found., 1993. Fellow Am. Acad. Arts and Scis.; mem. Harvey Soc., AMA, Am. Soc. Parasitologists, Am., Royal Socs. Tropical Medicine and Hygiene (Walter Reed medal Am. chpt. 1996), Am. Pub. Health Assn., AAAS, Am. Epidemiological Soc., Nat. Acad. Scis., Am. Pediatric Soc., Assn. Am. Physicians, Soc. Exptl. Biology and Medicine, Am. Assn. Immunologists. Soc. Pediatric Research, Phi Beta Kappa., Sigma Xi, Alpha Omega Alpha. Home and Office: 56 Winding River Rd Needham MA 02192-1025

WELLES, ERNEST I., chemical company executive; s. Henry and Lena (Halberg) W.; BS cum laude, Coll. City N.Y., 1946, BS, Sch. Edn., 1949, MS, 1953; ScD (hon), London Inst., 1973. Chemist, Lucius Pitkin, Inc., N.Y.C., 1944-45; rsch. chemist Nuodex Products Co., Elizabeth, N.J., 1946-50; group leader Foster D. Snell, Inc., N.Y.C., 1950-51; asst. tech. dir. Permatex, Inc., Bklyn., 1951-52; chief chemist Dexter Chem. Corp., N.Y.C., 1952-67; product mgr. textile chem. sales Quaker Chem. Corp., Conshohocken, Pa., 1967-74; dir. mktg., textile chem. sales Hart Products Corp., Jersey City, 1974; mktg. dir. Leatex Chem. Co., Phila., 1974-78; v.p. mktg. Eaton Labs., Inc., 1978-85; pres. Pure-Kem, Inc., Paterson, N.J., 1985—. Mem. Am. Chem. Soc. (sr.), Am. Assn. Textile Chemists and Colorists. C-lub: Masons. Patentee in field. Home: PO Box 1140 Bryn Mawr PA 19010-7140 Office: 295 Governor St Paterson NJ 07501-1320

WELLES, JAMES BELL, JR., lawyer; b. Schenectady, N.Y., Aug. 27, 1918; s. James Bell and Grace E. (Frazer) W.; m. Ann Bouton Thom, Apr. 26, 1946; children—Ann, James Bell, III, William (dec.), Thomas, Amy. A.B., Columbia U., 1939, J.D., 1942. Bar: N.Y. 1943. Assoc. Mitchell, Capron, Marsh, Angulo & Cooney, N.Y.C., 1946-56; mem. firm. Angulo, Cooney, Marsh & Ouchterloney, N.Y.C., 1956-59, Debevoise & Plimpton, N.Y.C., 1960-93. Bd. visitors Columbia Law Sch., N.Y.C., 1974-94; bd. dirs. Burke Found., White Plains, N.Y., 1959—, pres.; trustee Emma Willard Sch., Troy, N.Y., 1974-82. Maj. USAAF, 1942-45. Fellow Am. Coll. Trust and Estate Counsel; mem. ABA, N.Y. State Bar Assn., Assn. of Bar of City of N.Y., Delta Phi, Phi Delta Phi. Republican. Episcopalian. Club: University (N.Y.C.). Home: 25 Ivy Hill Rd Chappaqua NY 10514-1805 Office: Debevoise & Plimpton 875 3rd Ave New York NY 10022-6225

WELLES, JOHN GALT, museum director; b. Orange, N.J., Aug. 24, 1925; s. Paul and Elizabeth Ash (Galt) W.; m. Barbara Lee Chrisman, Sept. 15, 1951; children: Virginia Chrisman, Deborah Galt, Barton Jeffery, Holly Page. BE, Yale U., 1946; MBA, U. Pa., 1949; LHD (hon.) U. Denver, 1994. Test engr. Gen. Electric Co., Lynn, Mass., 1947; labor relations staff New Departure div. Gen Motors Corp., Bristol, Conn., 1949-51; mem. staff Mountain States Employers Coun., Denver, 1952-55; head indsl. econs. div. U. Denver Research Inst., Denver, 1956-74; v.p. planning and devel. Colo. Sch. Mines, Golden, 1974-83; regional adminstr. EPA, Denver, 1983-87; exec. dir. Denver Mus. Natural History, 1987-94, exec. dir. emeritus, 1994—. Sr. cons. Secretariat, UN Conf. Human Environment, Geneva, 1971-72; cons. Bus. Internat., S.A., Geneva, 1972; trustee Tax Free Fund of Colo., N.Y., 1987—, Denver Pub. Libr. Friends Found., 1996—; mem. Rocky Mountain regional adv. bd. Inst. Internat. Edn., 1996—; exec. com. Denver Com. on Fgn. Rels., 1987—; bd. dirs Gulf of Maine Found., 1995—; chmn. Colo. Front Range Project, Denver, 1979-80. Contbr. articles to profl. jours., newspapers. Recipient Disting. Svc. award Denver Regional Coun. Govts., 1980, Barnes award EPA, 1987. Mem. AAAS, Am. Assn. Museums (ethics commn. 1991-94, v.p. 1992-95), Sustainable Futures Soc. (nat. adv. bd. 1994—), Met. Denver Exec. Club (pres. 1967-68), World Future Soc., Univ. Club (Denver) Denver Athletic Club, Tau Beta Pi, Blue Key. Republican. Episcopalian.

WELLES, JUDITH, public affairs executive; b. N.Y.C., Jan. 15, 1946; d. John and Millicent (Richman) Welles; m. Alan M. Bekelman, June 26, 1966 (div. Sept. 1994); children: David B., Justin E. BA, Vassar Coll., 1963. Speechwriter, editor U.S. Dept. Interior, Washington, 1965-66; asst. to dir. VISTA, Washington, 1967-70; speechwriter to sec. HHS, Washington, 1971-76, mgr. pub. affairs, 1977-86; dir. comm. and pub. affairs Pension Benefit Guaranty Corp., Washington, 1987—. Chmn. County Health Planning Commn., Md., 1986-88. Recipient 1st place ann. report competition Fin. World, 1991, 92. Mem. Nat. Assn. Govt. Communicators (Gold Screen award 1992, award of Excellence 1994). Office: Pension Benefit Guaranty Corp 1200 K St NW Washington DC 20005-4025

WELLES, MELINDA FASSETT, artist, educator; b. Palo Alto, Calif., Jan. 4, 1943; d. George Edward and Barbara Helena (Todd) W. Student, San Francisco Inst. Art, 1959-60, U. Oreg., 1960-62; BA in Fine Arts, UCLA, 1964, MA in Spl. Edn., 1971, PhD in Ednl. Psychology, 1976; student fine arts and illustration Art Ctr. Coll. Design, 1977-80. Cert. ednl. psychologist, Calif. Asst. prof. Calif. State U., Northridge, 1979-82, Pepperdine U., L.A., 1979-82; assoc. prof. curriculum, teaching and spl. edn. U. So. Calif., L.A., 1980-89; prof. liberal studies Art Ctr. Coll. Design, 1978—; mem. acad. faculty Pasadena City Coll., 1973-79, Otis Coll. Art and Design, L.A., 1986—, UCLA Extension, 1980-84, Coll. Devel. Studies, L.A., 1978-87, El Camino C.C., Redondo Beach, Calif., 1982-86; cons. spl. edn.; pub. adminstrn. analyst UCLA Spl. Edn. Rsch. Program, 1973-76; exec. dir. Atwater Park Ctr. Disabled Children, L.A., 1976-78; coord. Pacific Oaks Coll. in svc. programs for L.A. Unified Schs., Pasadena, 1978-81; mem. Southwest Blue Book, The Blue Ribbon, Friends of Robinson Gardens, Freedom's Found. at Valley Forge; bd. dirs. The Mannequins, Costume Coun. L.A. County Mus. of Art., Assistance League of So. Calif. Author: Calif. Dept. Edn. Tech. Reports, 1972-76; editor: Teaching Special Students in the Mainstream, 1981, Educating Special Learners, 1986, 88, Teaching Students with Learning Problems, 1988, Exceptional Children and Youth, 1989, Left Brain Right Brain, 1997; group shows include: San Francisco Inst. Art, 1960, U. Hawaii, 1978, Barnsdall Gallery, L.A., 1979, 80; represented in various pvt. collections. HEW fellow, 1971-72; grantee Calif. Dept. Edn., 1975-76, Calif. Dept. Health, 1978. Mem. Am. Psych. Assn., Calif. Learning Disabilities Assn., Am. Council Learning Disabilities, Calif. Scholarship Fedn. (life), Alpha Chi Omega. Office: 700 Levering Ave Apt 1 Los Angeles CA 90024-2795

WELLFORD, HARRY WALKER, federal judge; b. Memphis, Aug. 6, 1924; s. Harry Alexander and Roberta Thompson (Prothro) W.; m. Katherine E. Potts, Dec. 8, 1951; children: Harry Walker, James B. Buckner P., Katherine T., Allison R. Student, U. N.C., 1943-44; BA, Washington and Lee U., 1947; postgrad. in law, U. Mich., 1947-48; LLD, Vanderbilt U., 1950. Bar: Tenn. 1950. Atty. McCloy, Myar & Wellford, Memphis, 1950-60, McCloy, Wellford & Clark, Memphis, 1960-70; judge U.S. Dist. Ct., Memphis, 1970-82; judge U.S. Ct. Appeals (6th cir.), Cin. and Memphis, 1982-92, sr. judge, 1992—; mem. pres.' adv. coun. Rhodes Coll. Chair Senator Howard Baker campaigns, 1964-66; chair Tenn. Hist. Commn., Tenn. Constnl. Bicentennial Commn., 1987-88; mem. charter drafting com. City of Memphis, 1967, Tenn. Am. Revolution Bicentennial Commn., 1976, com. on Adminstrn. Fed. Magistrates Sys., Jud. Conf. Subcom. Adminstrn. of Criminal Law Probation; clk. session, commr. Gen. Assembly; elder Presbyn. Ch.; moderator Memphis Presbytery, 1994. Recipient Sam A. Myar award for svc. to profession and community Memphis State Law U., 1963. Mem. Phi Beta Kappa, Omega Delta Kappa. Home: 91 N Perkins Rd Memphis TN 38117-2425 Office: US Ct Appeals 1176 Federal Bldg 167 N Main St Memphis TN 38103-1816

WELLIN, KEITH SEARS, investment banker; b. Grand Rapids, Mich., Aug. 13, 1926; s. Elmer G. and Ruth (Chamberlin) W.; m. Carol D. Woodhouse, Sept. 5, 1951 (dec. 1970); children: Cynthia Wellin Plum, Peter, Marjorie Wellin King; m. Nancy Brown Negley, Aug. 2, 1985. B.A., Hamilton Coll., 1950; M.B.A., Harvard U., 1952. With E.F. Hutton & Co., Inc., Chgo., 1952-71; regional v.p., dir. E.F. Hutton & Co., Inc., 1962-66; pres. E.F. Hutton & Co., Inc., N.Y.C., 1967-71; vice chmn. E.F. Hutton & Co., Inc., 1970-71; sr. v.p., treas., dir. Reynolds Securities Inc., 1971-74, pres., dir., 1974-78; exec. v.p., dir. Dean Witter Reynolds Orgn., from 1978; chmn. Dean Witter Reynolds Inter-Capital, from 1978; former vice chmn. Dean Witter Reynolds Inc.; chmn. bd. Moorco Internat., Houston; former gov., mem. exec. com. Assn. Stock Exchange Firms; mem. governing council Securities Industry Assn. Mem. investment com., trustee Hamilton Coll. Served to 2d lt., inf. AUS, 1945-47. Clubs: Knickerbocker (N.Y.C.); Clove Valley Rod and Gun (La Grangeville, N.Y.); Round Hill (Greenwich, Conn.); River Club. Home: El Tule Ranch Drawer C Falfurrias TX 78355 Office: c/o Dean Witter Reynolds 1345 Avenue Of The Americas New York NY 10105-0302

WELLING, KATHRYN MARIE, editor; b. Ft. Wayne, Ind., Feb. 4, 1952; d. Arthur Russell Sr. and Genevieve (Disser) W.; m. Donald Robert Boyle, Oct. 21, 1978; children: Brian Joseph, Thomas Arthur. BS in Journalism, Northwestern U., 1974. Copy reader Dow Jones News Retrieval, N.Y.C., 1974-75; copy reader/reporter AP-Dow Jones, N.Y.C., 1975-76; copy editor Wall Street Jour., N.Y.C., 1976; reporter Barron's, N.Y.C., 1976-81, asst. to editor, 1981, mng. editor, 1982-92, assoc. editor, 1992—. Charter mem. Northwestern U. Coun. of One Hundred. Avocations: sailing, skiing. Office: Barron's 200 Liberty St New York NY 10281-1003

WELLINGTON, CAROL STRONG, law librarian; b. Altadena, Calif., Jan. 30, 1948; d. Edward Walters and Elizabeth (Leonards) Strong; m. David Heath Wellington, May 27, 1978; 1 child, Edward Heath. BA, Lake Forest (Ill.) Coll., 1969; MLS, Simmons Coll., 1973. Libr. Hill & Barlow, Boston, 1973-88, Peabody & Arnold, Boston, 1988—. Mem. Am. Assn. Law Librs., Assn. Boston Law Librs. (v.p. 1979-80, pres. 1980-81), Spl. Librs. Assn., Law Librs. New England. Office: Peabody & Arnold 50 Rowes Wharf Boston MA 02110-3339

WELLINGTON, HARRY HILLEL, lawyer, educator; b. New Haven, Aug. 13, 1926; s. Alex M. and Jean (Ripps) W.; m. Sheila Wacks, June 22, 1952; children: John, Thomas. AB, U. Pa., 1947; LLB, Harvard U., 1952; MA (hon.), Yale U., 1960. Bar: D.C. 1952. Law clk. to U.S. Judge Magruder, 1953-54, Supreme Ct. Justice Frankfurter, 1955-56; asst. prof. law Stanford U., 1954-56; mem. faculty Yale U., 1956—, prof. law, 1960—, Edward J. Phelps prof. law, 1967-83, dean Law Sch., 1975-85, Sterling prof. law, 1983-92, Sterling prof. emeritus law, 1992—, Harry H. Wellington prof. lectr., 1995—; pres., dean, prof. law N.Y. Law Sch., N.Y.C., 1992—; Ford fellow London Sch. Econs., 1965; Guggenheim fellow; sr. fellow Brookings Instn., 1968-71; Rockefeller Found. fellow Bellagio Study and Conf. Ctr., 1984; faculty mem. Salzburg Seminar in Am. Studies, 1985; John M. Harlan disting. vis. prof. N.Y. Law Sch., 1985-86; review person ITT-SEC; moderator Asbestos-Wellington Group; cons. domestic and fgn. govtl. agys.; trustee N.Y. Law Sch.; bd. govs. Yale U. Press; mem. jud. panel, exec. com. Ctr. Public Resources Legal Program; Harry H. Wellington lectr., 1995—. Author: with Harold Shepherd) Contracts and Contract Remedies, 1957, Labor and the Legal Process, 1968, (with Clyde Summers) Labor Law, 1968, 2d edit., 1983, (with Ralph Winter) The Unions and the Cities, 1971, Interpreting the Constitution, 1990; contbr. articles to profl. jours. Mem. ABA, Bar Assn. Conn., Am. Law Inst., Am. Arbitration Assn., Am. Acad. Arts and Scis., Common Cause (nat governing bd.). Office: NY Law Sch 57 Worth St New York NY 10013-2926 also: Yale U Sch Law New Haven CT 06520

WELLINGTON, JEAN SUSORNEY, librarian; b. East Chicago, Ind., Oct. 23, 1945; d. Carl Matthew and Theresa Ann Susorney; m. Donald Clifford Wellington, June 12, 1976; 1 child, Evelin Patricia. BA, Purdue U., 1967; MA in LS, Rosary Coll., River Forest, Ill., 1969; MA, U. Cin., 1976. Head Burnam Classical Libr. U. Cin., 1970—. Compiler: Dictionary of Bibliographic Abbreviations Found in the Scholarship of Classical Studies and Related Disciplines, 1983. Mem. Art. Librs. Soc. N.Am. (chair Ohio br. 1984-85). Office: U Cin Classics Libr Box 210191 Cincinnati OH 45221-0191

WELLINGTON, JUDITH LYNN, cultural organization administrator; b. Yonkers, N.Y., Feb. 4, 1947; d. James William Wellington and Ardath (Sweet) Longden; m. Charles L. Lerman (div.); 1 child, Michael J. BA, Wheaton Coll., Norton, Mass., 1969; MA, Harvard U., 1971, PhD, 1975. Asst. prof. Juniata Coll., Huntingdon, Pa., 1974-76; asst. dir., assoc. mem. Monell Chem. Senses Ctr., Phila., 1976-86; v.p. Zool. Soc. Phila., 1986-92; pres., CEO N.J. Acad. for Aquatic Scis., Camden, N.J., 1992-95; pres. N.J. Aquarium Found., Camden, 1995—. Bd. dirs. South Jersey Performing Arts Ctr., Camden, N.J., 1989—. Office: Thomas H Kean NJ State Aquarium 1 Riverside Dr Camden NJ 08103-1037 Home: 18 Allendale Rd Wynnewood PA 19096

WELLINGTON, ROBERT HALL, manufacturing company executive; b. Atlanta, July 4, 1922; s. Robert H. and Ernestine V. (Vossbrinck) W.; m. Marjorie Jarchow, Nov. 15, 1947; children: Charles R., Robert H., Christian J., Jeanne L. BS, McCormack Sch. of Engring. and Applied Scis. (formerly Northwestern Tech. Inst.), 1944; MSBA, MBA, U. Chgo., 1958. With Griffin Wheel Co., 1946-61; v.p. parent co. Amsted Industries, Inc., Chgo., 1961-74, exec. v.p., 1974-80, pres., chief exec. officer, 1981-88, chmn. bd., chief exec. officer, 1988-90. Served to lt. USN, 1943-46. Mem. Chgo. Athletic Club, Mid-Am. Club. Office: Amsted Industries Inc 205 N Michigan Ave Fl 44 Chicago IL 60601

WELLINGTON, SHEILA WACKS, foundation administrator, psychiatry educator; b. N.Y.C., Feb. 24, 1932; d. Louis and Rose Feldman; m. Harry Hillel Wellington, June 22, 1952; children: John, Thomas. BA in Polit. Sci., Wellesley Coll., 1952; traineeship, USPHS, 1966-68; MUS, Yale U., 1968, MPH, 1968. Lectr. dept. psychiatry Sch. Medicine Yale U., New Haven, 1974-93; dir. Hill-West Haven div. Conn. Mental Health Ctr., 1977-80, Greater Bridgeport Community Mental Health Ctr., 1980-86; sec. Yale U., New Haven, Conn., 1987-93; pres. Catalyst, N.Y.C., 1993—; mem. plan and rev. pnel Pres.'s Com. Mental Health; mem. exec. com. Conn. conf. Ind. Colls., Am. Coll. Mental Health Adminstrn.; fellow Berkeley Coll.; trustee Nuveen Select Portfolios. Contbr. articles to profl. jours. Bd. dirs. N.Y. Women's Agenda, Bus. Coun. N.Y. State, Inst. for Women's Policy Rsch. Recipient New Haven Mayoral Citation for Cmty. svc., 1981, Conn. Gov.'s Com. to Employ Handicapped Outstanding Svc. award, 1984, Ofcl. Citation Gen. Assembly of Conn., 1985, Spl. Citation for Pub. Svc. Gov. William O'Neill, 1986, New Haven YWCA Women in Leadership award, 1990, Marrakech Founders award, 1990, Elm Ivy award, 1993. Mem. Phi Beta Kappa. Home: 55 Huntington St New Haven CT 06511-1332 Office: Pres Catalyst 250 Park Ave S New York NY 10003-1402

WELLINGTON, WILLIAM GEORGE, plant science and ecology educator; b. Vancouver, B.C., Can., Aug. 16, 1920; s. George and Lilly (Rae) W.; m. Margret Ellen Reiss, Sept. 22, 1959; children: Katherine Jean, Stephen Ross. B.A., U. B.C., 1941; M.A., U. Toronto, 1945, Ph.D., 1947.

Meteorol. officer Can. Meteorol. Service, Toronto, 1942-45; research entomologist Can. Dept. Agr., Sault Ste. Marie, Ont., 1946-51; head bioclimatology sect. Can. Dept. Forestry, Sault Ste. Marie, Ont., Victoria, B.C., 1951-67; prin. scientist Can. Dept. Forestry, Victoria, 1964-68; prof. ecology U. Toronto, 1968-70; dir. Inst. Animal Resource Ecology, U. B.C., Vancouver, 1973-79; prof. plant sci. and resource ecology Inst. Animal Resource Ecology, U. B.C., 1970-86, hon. prof. dept. plant sci., 1986—, prof. emeritus, 1986—; Killam sr. research fellow U. B.C., 1980-81; inaugural lectr. C.E. Atwood Meml. Seminar Series, Dept. Zoology, U. Toronto, 1993. Contbr. articles to profl. jours. Named Prof. of Yr., Faculty Agrl. Sci., U. B.C., 1986. Fellow Entomol. Soc. Can. (Gold medal 1968), Royal Soc. Can., Explorers Club; mem. Am. Meteorol. Soc. (award 1969), Entomol. Soc. Am. (C. J. Woodworth award 1979), Japanese Soc. Population Ecology, Entomol. Soc. Ont. Anglican. Club: Am. Philatelic Soc. Home: 2350 130A St, Surrey, BC Canada V4A 8Y5 Office: U BC, ARE and Dept Plant Sci, Vancouver, BC Canada V6T 1W5

WELLISCH, WILLIAM JEREMIAH, social psychology educator; b. Vienna, Austria, July 3, 1938; came to U.S., 1940; s. Max and Zelda (Schanser) W.; m. Geraldine Eve Miller (dec. Feb. 1970); children: Garth Kevin, Miriam Rhoda; m. Claudine Abbey Truman, Sept. 5, 1971; children: Rebecca Colleen, Marcus Joshua, Gabriel Jason. MA in Sociology, U. Mo., 1965, PhD in Sociology, 1968. Researcher urbanization Hemispheric Consultants, Columbia, Mo., 1968-69; cons. to local govt. ofcl. on L.Am. Bicultural Consultants, Inc., Denver, 1969-70; prof. Red Rocks Coll., Lakewood, Colo., 1970-76, 77—. Author: Bi-Cultural Development, 1971, Honduras: A Study in Sub-Development, 1978. Mem. citizen's adv. bd. Sta. KCFR Pub. Radio, Denver, 1989—. Republican. Mem. Unification Ch. Avocations: still-life photography, landscape gardening. Home: 2325 Clay St Denver CO 80211-5123 Office: Red Rocks CC 13300 W 6th Ave Golden CO 80401-5357

WELLIVER, CHARLES HAROLD, hospital administrator; b. Wichita, Kans., Feb. 14, 1945; married. BA, Wichita State U., 1972; MHA, U. Mo., 1974. Asst. dir. St. Luke's Hosp., Kansas City, 1974-79, assoc. dir., 1979-80; adminstr. Spelman Meml. Hosp., Smithville, Mo., 1980-82; sr. adminstr., COO Good Samaritan Med. Ctr., Phoenix, 1982-86, v.p., CEO, 1989—; v.p., CEO Thunderbird Samaritan Hosp., Glendale, Ariz., 1986-89. Office: Good Samaritan Regional Med Ctr 1441 N 12th St Phoenix AZ 85006-2837*

WELLIVER, WARREN DEE, lawyer, retired state supreme court justice; b. Butler, Mo., Feb. 24, 1920; s. Carl Winfield and Burdee Marie (Wolfe) W.; m. Ruth Rose Galey, Dec. 25, 1942; children: Gale Dee (Mrs. William B. Stone), Carla Camile (Mrs. Dayton Stone), Christy Marie. BA, U. Mo., 1945; JD, U. Mo., 1948. Bar: Mo. 1948. Asst. pros. atty. Boone County, Columbia, 1948-54; sr. ptnr. Welliver, Atkinson and Eng, Columbia, 1960-79; tchr. law Law Sch. U. Mo., 1948-49; mem. Mo. Senate, 1977-79; justice Supreme Ct. Mo., Jefferson City, 1979-89; mem. Gov. Mo. Adv. Coun. Alcoholism and Drug Abuse, chmn. drug coun., 1970-72; chmn. Task Force Revision Mo. Drug Laws, 1970-71; liaison mem. coun. Nat. Inst. Alcoholism and Alcohol Abuse, 1973-76; mem. Cen. Regional Adv. Coun. Comprehensive Psychiat. Svcs., 1990-92. Bd. dirs. Nat. Assn. Mental Health, 1970-76, regional v.p., 1973-76; pres. Mo. Assn. Mental Health, 1968-69, Stephens Coll. Assocs., 1965-79; pres. Friends of Libr., U. Mo., 1976, bd. dirs., 1979-92; chmn. Dem. Com., 1954-64; hon. fellow Harry S. Truman Libr. Inst., 1979—; bd. dirs. Supreme Ct. Hist. Soc., 1982—; vice chair adv. bd. U. Mo. Multiple Sclerosis Inst., 1992—; bd. curators Stephen's Coll., 1980-92. With USNR, 1941-45. Recipient Disting. Alumni medal and award U. Mo., 1994. Fellow Am. Coll. Trial Lawyers, Am. Bar Found.; mem. ABA, Mo. Bar Assn. (pres. 1967-68), Boone County Bar Assn. (pres. 1970), Am. Judicature Soc., Am. Legion (past post comdr.), Multiple Sclerosis Soc. (Gateway chpt. bd. dirs. 1986-92), Order of Coif, Country Club of Mo., Columbia Country Club (past pres.). Home: 3430 Woodrail Ter Columbia MO 65203-0926

WELLMAN, BARCLAY ORMES, furniture company executive; b. Jamestown, N.Y., May 13, 1936; s. Albert Austin and Leona (Greenlund) W.; m. Diane Taylor, July 2, 1960; children: Barclay Ormes Jr., Taylor A., Alexandra C. BA, Dartmouth Coll., 1959; grad., U.S. Army War Coll., 1982. Interior designer Wellman Bros., Inc., Jamestown, 1963-64, treas., 1964—, pres., 1978—. Trustee Lakeview Cemetery Assn., Jamestown, 1978—, Sheldon Found., Jamestown, 1981—. Maj. gen. U.S. Army, ret. Mem. Am. Soc. Interior Designers (v.p. 1972-74), Am. Appraisers Assn., Am. Legion, Res. Officers Assn., Sr. Army Res. Comdrs. Assn., Sportsmens Club, Moon Brook Country Club, Delta Kappa Epsilon. Republican. Presbyterian. Avocation: fishing. Home: 1235 Prendergast Ave Jamestown NY 14701-3146 Office: Wellman Bros Inc 130 S Main St Jamestown NY 14701-6623

WELLMAN, CARL PIERCE, philosophy educator; b. Lynn, Mass., Sept. 3, 1926; s. Frank and Carolyn (Heath) W.; m. Farnell Parsons, June 20, 1953; children: Timothy, Philip, Lesley, Christopher. B.A., U. Ariz., 1949; M.A., Harvard U., 1951, Ph.D., 1954; postgrad., U. Cambridge, Eng., 1951-52. Instr. Lawrence U., Appleton, Wis., 1953-57; asst. prof. Lawrence U., 1957-62, assoc. prof., 1962-66, prof., chmn. dept. philosophy, 1966-68; prof. philosophy Washington U., St. Louis, 1968-88, Hortense and Tobias Lewin Disting. prof. humanities, 1988—; Mem. rev. panel research grants NEH, 1968-71. Author: The Language of Ethics, 1961, Challenge and Response: Justification in Ethics, 1971, Morals and Ethics, 1975, Welfare Rights, 1982, A Theory of Rights, 1985, Real Rights, 1995, An Approach to Rights, 1997. Recipient Uhrig Distinguished Teaching award Lawrence U., 1968; Am. Council Learned Socs. fellow, 1965-66; NEH sr. fellow, 1972-73; Nat. Humanities Center fellow, 1982-83. Mem. Am. Philos. Assn., Internat. Assn. for Philosophy Law and Social Philosophy. Home: 625 S Skinker Blvd # 902 Saint Louis MO 63105-2301

WELLMAN, GERALD EDWIN, JR., safety and fire inspector; b. Steubenville, Ohio, Feb. 27, 1948; s. Gerald Edwin Sr. and Rose Marie (Bonacci) W.; 1 child, Jerad Anthony. AS Data Processing, West Liberty State Coll., 1974, BSBA, 1974; MS in Safety Mgmt., W.Va. U., 1991, cert. of advanced study, 1995. With production, mechanical Wheeling and Pitts. Steel Corp., Beech Bottom, W.Va., 1966-76; with production, mechanical, safety Wheeling and Pitts. Steel Corp., Steubenville, Ohio, 1976—, also safety and fire insp., safety coord.;, 1993, 95; mem. wellness com. Wheeling and Pitts. Steel Plant; safety coord. Wheeling and Pitts. Steel Corp. Hazardous Material Team; safety chmn., trustee local 1190 United Steel Workers Am.; mem. Am. Iron and Steel Inst. R.R. Com. Contbr. articles to profl. jours. With U.S. Army, 1967-69, Vietnam. Mem. Am. Iron and Steel Inst. (railroad com.), West Liberty State Coll. Alumni Club, West Liberty State Coll Hilltops Club, W.Va. U. Alumni Club, Mountaineer Athletic Club, Dapper Dan Club Upper Ohio Valley, Brooke High Sch. Boosters Club, W.Va. Sheriffs Assn., Follansbee Blue Waves Boosters Club, Nat. Fire Protection Assn., Nat. Safety Coun., W.Va. Safety Coun., Western Pa. Safety Coun., U.S. Steel Workers Am., Eagles Club, Am. Soc. Safety Engrs. (nominating com. 1989—), Alpha Kappa Psi. Avocations: golf, swimming, basketball, baseball, coaching youth football. Home: 311 Hillcrest Dr Wellsburg WV 26070-1943

WELLMAN, RICHARD VANCE, legal educator; b. Worthington, Ohio, Sept. 10, 1922; s. Burton Singley and Blanche (Gardner) W.; m. Louise Dewey Laylin, Oct. 18, 1944 (dec. Dec. 1982); children: Martha, Anne, Jane, Sarah, Peter Burton, Charles Dewey; m. Natalie Lancaster Robertson, Dec. 12, 1983. A.B., U. Mich., 1947; J.D., 1949. Bar: Ohio 1949, Mich. 1960. Practice in Cleve., 1949-51, Mt. Vernon, Ohio, 1951-54; mem. faculty U. Mich. Law Sch., 1954-74; Alston prof. law U. Ga. Sch. Law, 1974-90, prof. emeritus, 1990—. Engaged in nat. effort to encourage state probate code revisions, 1965—; commr. Mich. Uniform State Laws, 1970-73, Ga. Uniform State Laws, 1974—; exec. dir. Joint Editorial Bd. Uniform Probate Code, 1990—. Served to 1st lt. AUS, 1943-46. Mem. Am. Bar Assn., Mich. Bar Assn., Am. Law Inst., Am. Coll. Trust and Estate Counsel. Home: 190 Tipperary Rd Athens GA 30606-3833

WELLMAN, THOMAS PETER, lawyer; b. Farrell, Pa., Feb. 25, 1932; s. Peter Michael and Bessie Thomas (George) W.; m. Jeanne Ann Harding, July 9, 1971; children: Elizabeth Thomas, Katherine Thomas. BA, Miami U., Oxford, Ohio, 1956; JD, Ohio State U., 1959. Bar: Ohio 1959, U.S. Dist. Ct. (no. dist.) Ohio 1961. Asst. atty. gen. State of Ohio, Columbus, 1959-60; sr. atty. Wellman & Jeren Co., L.P.A., Youngstown, Ohio, 1960—; mng. ptnr. Tablack, Wellman, Jeren, Hackett & Skoufatos Co., L.P.A., Youngstown, 1973—. Mem. Canfield (Ohio) Income Tax Rev. Bd., 1981—. With U.S. Army, 1952-54. Mem. ABA, Ohio Bar Assn., Mahoning County Bar Assn. (chmn. unauthorized practice of law wcom. 1984-85, mem. inquiry com. 1990—). Presbyterian. Avocation: sailing. Office: 67 Westchester Dr Youngstown OH 44515-3902

WELLNER, MARCEL NAHUM, physics educator, researcher; b. Antwerp, Belgium, Feb. 8, 1930; came to U.S., 1949; s. Jules and Lucie (Rapoport) W.; m. Magdeleine Misselyn, Apr. 7, 1961; children: Pierre, Lucie. BS, MIT, 1952; PhD, Princeton U., 1958. Instr. Brandeis U., Waltham, Mass., 1957-59; mem. Inst. Advanced Study, Princeton, N.J., 1959-60; rsch. assoc. Ind. U., Bloomington, 1960-63; vis. scientist Atomic Energy Rsch. Establishment, Harwell, Eng., 1963-64; from asst. prof. to prof. Syracuse (N.Y.) U., 1964-95, prof. emeritus, 1995—; rsch. prof. Health Sci. Ctr. SUNY, Syracuse, 1995—. Author gen. physics textbook; contbr. numerous articles on quantum field theory to profl. jours. Mem. Am. Phys. Soc. Office: Syracuse U Dept Physics Syracuse NY 13244

WELLNITZ, CRAIG OTTO, lawyer, English language educator; b. Elwood, Ind., Dec. 5, 1946; s. Frank Otto and Jeanne (Albright) W.; m. Karen Sue Thomas, Apr. 13, 1974 (div. Sept. 1987); children: Jennifer Suzanne, Anne Katherine; m. Carol L. Hinesley, Jan. 23, 1988. BA, Purdue U., 1969; MA, Ind. U., 1972; JD, Ind. U.-Indpls., 1978. Bar: Ind. 1978, U.S. Dist. Ct. (so. dist.) Ind. 1978, U.S. Supreme Ct. 1983, U.S. Ct. Appeals (7th and Fed. cirs.) 1984, U.S. Dist. Ct. (no. dist.) 1990; registered mediator, Ind. Instr. Danville Jr. Coll., Ill., 1972-74, S.W. Mo. State U., Springfield, Mo., 1974-75; ptnr. Coates, Hatfield, Calkins & Wellnitz, Indpls., 1978—; pub. defender criminal div. Marion Superior Ct., Marion County, 1979-88, master commr. criminal div., 1988-96; instr. U. Indpls., 1981-82; mem. adj. faculty dept. English Butler U., Indpls., 1982—; instr. English Ind. U.-Purdue U., Indpls., 1987-90; pres. Ind. Account Mgmt., Inspls., 1985-94; v.p. Carol Craig Assocs., Indpls., 1987—; lectr. in field. Columnist A Jury of Your Peers, 1984-86. Vice committeeman Indpls. Rep. precinct, 1978; chmn. fin. com. St. Luke's United Meth. Ch., 1985-87; sponsor Christian Children's Fund, 1990—; active Am. Mus. Nat. History, Indpls. Zoo, Children's Mus. Indpls. Postgrad. study grantee S.W. Mo. State U., Springfield, 1975. Mem. ABA, AAUP, MLA, ATLA, Nat. Lawyers Assn., Nat. Assn. Retail Collection Attys., Am. Collectors Assn., Ind. Bar Assn., Ind. Trial Lawyers Assn., Indpls. Bar Assn., Nat. Coun. Tchrs. English, Smithsonian Assocs., Libr. Congress Assocs., Internat. Platform Assn., Nat. Spkrs. Assn., Spkrs. U.S.A., Internat. Spkrs. Network, Broad Ripple Village Assn., Columbia Club, Rivera Club Indpls., Elks. Home: 6248 N Meridian St Indianapolis IN 46260-4226 Office: 1 Indiana Sq Ste 2335 Indianapolis IN 46204-2012

WELLON, ROBERT G., lawyer; b. Port Jervis, N.Y., Apr. 18, 1948; s. Frank Lewis and Alice (Stephens) W.; m. Jan Montgomery, Aug. 12, 1972; children: Robert F., Alice Wynn. AB, Emory U., 1970; JD, Stetson Coll. Law, 1974. Assoc. Turner, Turner & Turner, Atlanta, 1974-78; ptnr. Ridley, Wellon, Schwieger & Brazier, Atlanta, 1978-86; of counsel Wilson, Strickland & Benson, Atlanta, 1987—; adj. prof. Atlanta Law Sch., 1981-94; adj. prof. law Emory U. Sch. of Law, 1995—. Gov.'s task force chmn. Atlanta 2000, 1978; exec. com., treas., 2d v.p. Atlanta Easter Seals Soc., 1983-88; rep. Neighborhood Planning Unit, 1981-83; adminstrv. bd. Northside United Meth. Ch.; bd. dirs. Atlanta Found. for Psychoanalysis, Inc. Served with USAR, 1970-76. Recipient Judge Joe Morris award Stetson Coll. Law, St. Petersburg, 1974, Charles E. Watkins svc. award 1995). Mem. Fla. Bar, State Bar. Ga. (professionalism com. 1994—), Atlanta Bar Assn. (bd. dirs. 1978-88, pres. 1986-87, bd. trustees CLE), Lawyers Club Atlanta, Old War Horse Lawyers Club. Methodist. Office: 1100 One Midtown Pla 1360 Peachtree St NE Atlanta GA 30309-3214

WELLS, ANNIE, photographer; b. 1954. B in Sci. Writing, U. Santa Cruz; past postgrad., San Francisco State U. Past photographer Herald Jour., Logan, Utah, Greeley (Colo.) Tribune, Associated Press, San Francisco; photographer Press Dem., Santa Rosa, Calif., 1989—. Represented in permanent collections Nat. Mus. Women Arts, Washington. Recipient Pulitzer prize spot news photography, 1997. Office: Press Dem 427 Mendocino Ave Santa Rosa CA 95401*

WELLS, ARTHUR STANTON, retired manufacturing company executive; b. Kingsport, Tenn., Jan. 8, 1931; s. Arthur Stanton and Blanche Welch (Duncan) W.; m. Ellen N. Blackburn, June 15, 1957; children: Arthur S., Thomas B., Emily B., Richard R. B.S., Yale U., 1953; M.B.A., Harvard U., 1957. Fin. analyst Eastman Kodak Co., Kingsport, Tenn., 1957-65; mgr. profit analysis Xerox Corp., Rochester, N.Y., 1966-68; asst. treas. Xerox Corp., Stamford, Conn., 1969-76, treas., 1976-79; v.p. fin. Barnes Group Inc., Bristol, Conn., 1979-86, exec. v.p. fin., 1987-93, pres., CEO, 1994-96, also dir., 1994-96; bd. dirs. Nash Engring. Co., Trumbull, Conn., 1995—. Trustee, treas. Wilton (Conn.) Libr. Assn., 1972-78; bd. dirs. New Eng. Opera Assn., 1972-78; assoc. bd. dirs. Conn. Bank and Trust Co., Hartford, 1984-90; chmn. bd. trustees, exec. com. Conn. Pub. Expenditure Coun., Inc., 1990-93. With AUS, 1953-55. Mem. Fin. Execs. Inst. Democrat. Home: 4 CCIA Rd South Bristol ME 04568 Office: Barnes Group Inc 123 Main St Bristol CT 06010-6307

WELLS, BENJAMIN GLADNEY, lawyer; b. St. Louis, Nov. 13, 1943; s. Benjamin Harris and Katherine Emma (Gladney) W.; m. Nancy Kathryn Harpster, June 7, 1967; children: Barbara Gladney, Benjamin Harpster. BA magna cum laude, Amherst (Mass.) Coll., 1965; JD cum laude, Harvard U., 1968. Bar: Ill. 1968, Tex. 1973, U.S. Tax Ct. 1973, U.S. Ct. Claims 1975, U.S. Ct. Appeals (5th cir.) 1981, U.S. Dist. Ct. (so. dist.) Tex. 1985, U.S. Dist. Ct. (we. dist.) Tex. 1993. Assoc. Kirkland & Ellis, Chgo., 1968-69; assoc. to ptnr. Baker & Botts, L.L.P., Houston, 1973—; mem. Harvard Legal Aid Bur., 1966-68. Contbr. articles to profl. jours. Mem. devel. com. St. John's Sch., Houston, 1987—, chmn. planned giving com., 1987—; active Harvard Legal Aid Bureau, 1966-68. Capt. U.S. Army, 1969-72. Fellow Am. Coll. Tax Counsel; mem. Houston Tax Roundtable (pres. 1994-95), The Forest Club, The Houston Club, Phi Beta Kappa. Presbyterian. Office: Baker & Botts LLP One Shell Plaza 910 Louisiana St Houston TX 77002-4916

WELLS, CAROLYN CRESSY, social work educator; b. Boston, July 26, 1943; d. Harris Shipman Wells and Marianne Elizabeth (Monroe) Glazier; m. Dale Reed Konle, Oct. 11, 1970 (div. Sept. 3, 1982); m. Dennis Alan Loefler, Sept. 29, 1990. BA, U. Calif., Berkeley, 1965; MSW, U. Wis., 1968, PhD, 1973. Cert. ind. clin. social worker, marriage and family therapist. Vol. VISTA, Espanola, N.Mex., 1965-66; social worker Project Six Cen. Wis. Colony, Madison, 1968, Milw. Dept. Pub. Welfare, 1969, Shorewood (Wis.) Manor Nursing Home, 1972; sch. social worker Jefferson (Wis.) County Spl. Edn., 1977-78; lectr. sociology and social work Marquette U., Milw., 1972-73, dir. social work program, 1973-90, 93—, assoc. prof. social work, 1981-94, prof. social work, 1994—; social work therapist Lighthouse Counseling Assocs., Racine, Wis., 1989-91, The Cambridge Group, 1991-92; Achievement Assocs., 1992-95; vis. lectr. social work U. Canterbury, Christchurch, N.Z., 1983. Author: Social Work Day to Day, 1982, rev. edit., 1988, Social Work Ethics Day to Day, 1986; co-author: The Social Work Experience, 1991, rev. edit., 1996. Mem. Wis. Coun. on Social Work Edn., pres., 1980-82, sec., 1985-87, mem. exec. com., 1993-96. Mem. NASW, Am. Assn. Profl. Hypnotherapists, Coun. on Social Work Edn. (mem. publs. and media com. 1989-91, site visitor for accreditation 1987—), Acad. Cert. Social Workers, Assn. Baccalaureate Program Dirs. Democrat. Avocations: writing, silent sports. Home: 4173 Sleeping Dragon Rd West Bend WI 53095-9296 Office: Marquette U Social Work Program 526 N 14th St Milwaukee WI 53233-2211

WELLS, CHARLENA RENEE, editor, writer; b. Cleve., Oct. 2, 1964. BA in Comm., Cleve. State U., 1988. Libr. asst./typist John Carroll U., University Heights, Ohio, summer 1982; asst. sociology dept., registration asst. Cleve. State U., 1985-88; project asst. Jones, Day, Reavis & Pogue, Cleve., 1988-94; asst. writer Righteousness Newsletter, Cleve., 1990—; editor-in-chief, writer Holiness Inc., Cleve., 1993—; project asst. Jones, Day, Reavis & Pogue, 1988-94; adminstrv. exec. USA Mobile Comms., 1994; file adminstrv. clk. Pioneer Stds. Electronics Inc., 1994; mktg. rep. APT Publs., 1996—; adminstrv./registration asst. MBA degree program Case Western Res. U., Cleve., 1996—; switchboard operator Roetzel & Andress, 1996—; radio asst. Sta. WABQ, Cleve., spring 1987. Nursing asst. St. Vincent Charity Hosp., Cleve., 1987; co-hostess Sta. WCIN, Cin., 1991; guest speaker AME Zion Ch., Cleve., 1993, Assembly Missionary Bapt. Ch., Cleve., 1994; facilitator/exhibit guide Cleve. Children's Mus., summer 1986. Acad. scholar John Carroll U., 1982. Avocations: tennis, chess, singing, reading, writing. Office: Case Western Res U Enterprise Hall # 310 10900 Euclid Ave Cleveland OH 44106-1712

WELLS, CHARLES ROBERT, secondary education educator; b. Chgo., Jan. 11, 1952; s. Samuel and Wanda Jean (Few) W. BA, Harris Tchrs. Coll., St. Louis, 1978; MS in Edn., Ind. U., 1992. Cert. tchr., Ind., Mo. Tchr. social studies Gary (Ind.) Cmty. Schs., 1984—; mem. adv. com. Ind. Dept. Edn., Indpls. Mem. Ind. Social Studies Coun., Gary Reading Coun. Lutheran. Home: PO Box 6563 Gary IN 46406-0563

WELLS, CHARLES TALLEY, judge. Bar: Fla. 1965, U.S. Dist Ct. (middle dist. of Fla.), U.S. Ct. Appeals,(5th cir.) now (11th cir.) 1966, U.S. Supreme Ct., 1969, U.S. Dist. Ct., U.S. Dist. Ct. (So. dist), Fla., 1976, U.S. Ct. of Claims, 1990. Trial atty. U.S. dept justice Washington, 1969; pvt. practice maguire, Voohris and Wells, PA, Orlando, Fla., 1965-68, 1970-75, Wells, Gattis, Hollowes & Carpenter, PA, Orlando, Fla., 1976-94; justice Fla. Supreme Ct., Tallahassee. Methodist. Office: Fla Supreme Ct Supreme Ct Bldg 500 S Duval St Tallahassee FL 32399-6556

WELLS, CHRISTINE, foundation executive; b. Grayling, Mich., Aug. 6, 1948; d. Chester John and Mary W. BA, Mich. State U., 1970, MLIR, 1972; MLS, U. Mich., 1976. Head libr. Lansing State Jour., E. Lansing, Mich., 1973-82; mng. editor libr. svcs. USA TODAY, Washington, 1982-87; libr. dir. Gannett Co., Inc., Washington, 1985-87, chief staff, chmn. and CEO office, 1988-89; v.p. adminstrn. Gannett Found., Washington, 1989-90; v.p. internat. The Freedom Forum, Washington, 1991—; exec. dir. The Newseum, 1993-94; sr. v.p. internat. The Freedom Forum, 1994—. Mem. bd. overseers Internat. Press Ctr. and Club, Moscow; mem. bd. visitors Coll. Sci., Mich. State U. Recipient Disting. Alumni award U. Mich., 1991. Mem. ALA, Spl. Librs. Assn. (Profl. award 1994). Office: The Freedom Forum 1101 Wilson Blvd Arlington VA 22209-2248

WELLS, CHRISTOPHER BRIAN, lawyer; b. Belleville, Ill., Jan. 23, 1948; s. Frederick Meyers and Ethel Pauline (Morris) W.; m. Gaynelle Vansandt, June 6, 1970; 1 child, Deva Marie. BA in Econs., U. Kans., BS in Bus., 1970, JD, 1973. Enforcement atty. SEC, Seattle, 1977-82; ptnr. Lane, Powell, Spears , Lubersky, LLP, Seattle, 1982—. Capt. U.S. Army, 1973-77. Mem. ABA, Wash. State Bar Assn., King County Trial Lawyers Assn., Wash. Soc. CPA's., Kans. Bar Assn. Democrat. Office: Lane Powell Spears Lubersky LLP 1420 5th Ave Ste 4100 Seattle WA 98101-2333

WELLS, CLYDE KIRBY, Canadian provincial government official; b. Buchans Junction, Newfoundland, Nov. 9, 1937; s. Ralph and Maude (Kirby) W. B.A. in polit. sci., Meml. U., 1959; LL.B., Dalhousie U. Law Sch., 1962. Bar: N.S. 1963, Nfld. 1964. Pvt. practice, 1964-66; rep. dist. Humber East Nfld. Ho. of Assembly, 1966; mem. cabinet Premier Joseph R. Smallwood, 1966-68; pvt. practice, 1968-77; rep. from Nfld. Can. Bar Assn. com. constitutional changes, 1977-79; counsel to fed. govt. and Nfld. Supreme Ct., 1979-87; elected leader Liberal Party of Nfld. and Labrador, 1987; mem. Ho. of Assembly for dist. Windsor-Buchans, 1987; premier Nfld. and Labrador, 1987—; mem. Bay of Islands, 1989—. Liberal. Office: Office of Premier, Confederation Bldg 8th Fl, Saint Johns, NF Canada A1B 4J6

WELLS, DAMON, JR., investment company executive; b. Houston, May 20, 1937; s. Damon and Margaret Corinne (Howze) W.; BA magna cum laude, Yale U., 1958; BA, Oxford U., 1964, MA, 1968; PhD, Rice U., 1968. Owner, CEO Damon Wells Interests, Houston, 1958—, pres.,Damon Wells Found., 1993—. Bd. dirs. Child Guidance Ctr. of Houston, 1970-73; trustee Christ Ch. Cathedral Endowment Fund, 1970-73, 84-88, chmn., 1987-88, Kinkaid Sch., 1972-86, Kinkaid Sch. Endowment Fund, 1981-86; hon. friend of Somerville Coll., Oxford U., 1988—; mem. Sr. Common Room, Pembroke Coll., Oxford U., 1972—; trustee Camp Allen retreat of Episc. Diocese of Tex., 1976-78; founding bd. dirs. Brit. Inst. U.S., 1979-80; mem. pres.'s coun. Tex. A&M U., 1983-89. Named Hon. Comdr. Most Excellent Order of Brit. Empire by Her Majesty Queen Elizabeth II, 1991, Outstanding Alumnus Yr. by Kinkaid Sch., 1994. Fellow Jonathan Edwards Coll. (assoc.), Yale U., 1982—; hon. fellow Pembroke Coll., Oxford U., 1984—. Mem. English-Speaking Union (nat. dir. 1970-72, v.p. Houston br. 1966-73), Coun. Fgn. Rels., Phi Beta Kappa, Pi Sigma Alpha. Episcopalian. Clubs: Houston Country, Houston, Yale (N.Y.C.), United Oxford and Cambridge U. (London); Cosmos (Washington), Buck's (London), Coronado (Houston), Little Ship Club (London) . Author: Stephen Douglas: The Last Years, 1857-1861, 1971 (Tex. Writer's Roundup prize 1971), paperback edit., 1990. Home: 5555 Del Monte Dr Houston TX 77056-4116 Office: 2001 Kirby Dr Ste 806 Houston TX 77019-6033

WELLS, DANIEL RUTH, physics educator; b. N.Y.C., May 2, 1921; s. Daniel R. and Charlotte T. (Danziger) W.; m. Mary E. O'Connell, 1944; children: Donna Mary, Christina Mary. BME, Cornell U., 1942; MS, NYU, 1953; PhD, Stevens Inst. Tech., 1963. Instrument rated comml. pilot. Aero. engr. Chance-Vought Aircraft, Stratford, Conn., 1942-43; aero. engr. Sunsdet Aircraft, N.Y.C., 1943; engr. Indsl. Tng. Co., N.Y.C., 1946-50; design engr. Republic Aircraft, L.I., N.Y., 1950-52; physicist Plasma Physics Lab. Princeton U., 1955-63; assoc. prof. physics U. Miami, Fla., 1963-66, prof. physics, 1966-92, prof. emeritus; nuclear physicist rsch. div. NYU, N.Y.C., 1952-53; assoc. prof. physics Seton Hall U., South Orange, N.J., 1962-63; cons. U.S. Army Piccatiny (N.J.) Arsenal, 1968-70, Sandia Labs. (N.Mex.), 1972-73, various Fla. cos., 1973—. Contbr. numerous articles to profl. jours.; patentee in field. 1st. lt. U.S. Army Air Force, 1943-46. Recipient AFOSR (1964-73) and NSF (1973-78) grants for plasma rsch. Mem. Am. Phys. Soc., Sigma Xi, Theta Chi, Sigma Pi Sigma. Avocations: flying, boating, tennis, golf. Home: 6950 SW 62nd St Miami FL 33143-1842 Office: U Miami Physics Dept PO Box 248046 Miami FL 33124-8046

WELLS, DAVID JOHN, program director, academic administrator, mechanical engineer; b. Ithaca, N.Y., Jan. 4, 1949; s. Arthur John and Dorothy Helen (Edwards) W.; m. Jane Baran, July 10, 1971; children: Jacob David, Abbe Grace, Anastasia Catherine. BS in Interdisciplinary Engring. and Mgmt., Clarkson U., 1972, MSME, 1980, PhD in Engring. Sci., 1985. Lic. profl. engr., Conn., Wyo. Planning engr. Newport News (Va.) Shipbuilding, 1973-76, Stone & Webster Engring., Boston, 1976-78; instr., counselor Clarkson U., Potsdam, N.Y., 1978-81, dir., 1986—86; project mgr., mgr. Combustion Engring., Windsor, Conn., 1981-86; dir. engring. and mgmt. program, mem. adminstrv. coun. Clarkson U., Potsdam, N.Y., 1986—, mem. exec. com., 1986—; cons. prin. Line-up directions, 1994—; cons. in field; cons. Excellence in Edn. Action Plan, Potsdam Pub. Schs. Author: Managing Your First Years in Industry, 1994; editor Engring. Mgmt. Rev., 1994; contbr. articles to profl. jours. Bd. dirs. Windsor Pub. Schs., 1985-86. Mem. ASME, IEEE (pres. editl. bd.), Engring. Mgmt. Soc. (bd. govs. 1994—). Home: RR 1 Box 368A Potsdam NY 13676-9758 Office: Clarkson U Engring And Mgmt Progr Potsdam NY 13699

WELLS, DAVID LEE, professional baseball player; b. Torrance, Calif., May 20, 1963. Grad. high sch., San Diego. Pitcher Toronto Blue Jays, 1987-92, Detroit Tigers, 1993-95, Cin. Reds, 1995, Balt. Orioles, 1996, N.Y. Yankees, 1997—. Named Am. League All-Star Team, 1995. Achievements include mem. Am. League East Divsn. Champions, 1989, 91, 92, World Series Champions, 1992, Cin. Reds Nat. League Ctrl. Divsn. Champions. Office: NY Yankees E 161st St and River Ave Bronx NY 10451*

WELLS, DEWEY WALLACE, lawyer; b. Raleigh, N.C., Oct. 14, 1929; s. B.C. and Alma (Blanchard) W.; m. Ann D. Wells, Aug 25, 1951; children: Robert, Betty W., Daniel, Brady, Jeff. AA, Mars Hill Coll., 1950; BS, Wake Forest U., 1952, JD, 1954. Bar: N.C. 1954, U.S. Dist. Ct. (ea. dist.) N.C. 1960, U.S. Ct. Appeals (4th cir.) 1961, U.S. Dist. Ct. (mid. dist.) N.C. 1985. Exec. sec. N.C. Jud. Council, Raleigh, 1954-55; trust officer Planter's Nat. Bank & Trust Co., Rocky Mt., N.C., 1955-57; ptnr. LeRoy, Wells, Shaw, Hornthal & Riley, Elizabeth City, N.C., 1958-85, Womble, Carlyle, Sandridge & Rice, Winston Salem, N.C., 1985-95; judge Superior Ct., 1st Jud. Dist. N.C., 1974. Trustee N.C. Natural Heritage Trust, 1990-95, chmn.

1995—. 1st lt. USAR, 1954-58. Fellow Am. Coll. Trial Lawyers, Am. Bar Found.; mem. ABA, N.C. Bar Assn. (pres. 1980-81), Rotary. Republican. Baptist. Home: 1890 Pilot Ridge Rd Collettsville NC 28611 Office: Womble Carlyle Sandridge & Rice PO Drawer 84 1600 Southern Nat Fin Ctr Winston Salem NC 27102-0084

WELLS, EDWARD PHILLIPS, radiologist; b. Hanover, N.H., Oct. 4, 1916; s. Harry Artemas and Madeleine Roberta (Lucky) W.; m. Barbara Mix, Jan. 25, 1941; children: James C., Phyllis L. Fahey, Lucinda W. Graves, Patricia Wells-Bogue, Kenneth R. BA, Dartmouth Coll., 1939; MD, NYU, 1942. Diplomate Am. Bd. Radiology. Intern rotating Mary Hitchcock Hosp., Hanover, N.H., 1942-43; maj. U.S. Army Med. Corps, 1943-46; resident in radiology Mary Hitchcock Hosp., Hanover, 1946-48; radiologist Rutland (Vt.) Hosp., 1949-51, North Shore Radiol. Assoc., Danvers, Mass., 1951-82; adj. radiologist Hitchcock Hosp., Hanover, 1982-82; intermittent radiologist V.A. Hosp., White River Junction, Vt., 1984-94. Named to U.S. Olympic Ski Team, 1940. Mem. AMA, New Eng. Med. Assn., Vt. Med. Assn., N.H. Med. Assn., Lake Mitchell Trout Club, Black Brook Salmon Club. Avocations: trout and salmon fishing. Home: Old Farm Rd HCR 63 Box 502 Grantham NH 03753

WELLS, EVERETT CLAYTON, JR., marketing professional; b. Hopkinsville, Ky., May 11, 1954; s. Everett Clayton and Lois Gertrude (Aday) W.; m. Suzanne Walden. BS, Murray State U., 1977; postgrad., Memphis State U., 1978. Credit mgr. Dunlap Sales, Hopkinsville, 1979-85; asst. exec. dir. Hopkinsville C. of C., 1985-86; exec. dir. Hopkinsville Christian County C. of C., 1986-87; sr. econ. devel. coord. Mcpl. Electric Authority of Ga., Atlanta, 1987-96; bus. developer pub. sector Beers Constrn. Co., Atlanta, 1996—; bd. dirs., vice-chmn. of promotions Ky. Western Waterways, Grand Rivers, 1986-87. Pres. Murray State U. Alumni Assn., 1985-86; mem. High Mus. Mem. Nat. Assn. Corp. Real Estate Execs., Am. Econ. Devel. Coun. (editorial rev. com. 1996), Ga. C. of C. Execs. Assn., Ga. Ind. Developers (chmn. Vol. of Yr. com. 1991), So. Econ. Devel. Coun. (alt. state bd. dirs. 1993, bd. dirs. 1992-95, exec. com. 1995, chair constn. and bylaws 1996, 97), Rotary (chmn. pub. rels. 1981-82, chmn. youth com. 1986-87, chmn. free enterprise 1986-87), Little River Road Runners Club (co-founder, pres. 1981-83, state rep. 1983-88), Atlanta Track Club. Republican. Baptist. Avocations: running, basketball, reading, weight lifting. Home: 455 Amberidge Tr NW Atlanta GA 30328 Office: Beers Constrn Co 70 Ellis St Atlanta GA 30303

WELLS, HERMAN B, university chancellor; b. Jamestown, Ind., June 7, 1902; s. Joseph Granville and Anna (Harting) W. Student, U. Ill., 1920-21; BS, Ind. U., 1924, AM, 1927, LLD, 1962; postgrad., U. Wis., 1927-28, LLD (hon.), 1946; LLD (hon.), Butler U., Rose Poly. Inst., DePauw U., 1939, Wabash Coll., 1942, Earlham, 1948, Valparaiso U., 1953, Miami U., Tri-State Coll., 1959, U. Louisville, 1961, Franklin Coll., Anderson Coll., 1962, Ball State Tchrs. Coll., Washington U., 1963, U. Notre Dame, St. Joseph's Coll., U. Calif., Ind. State Coll., 1964, Drury Coll., 1968, Columbia, 1969, Chgo. Circle Campus U. Ill., 1973, Howard U., 1976, U. S.C., 1980, L.H.D., 1963, Marian Coll., 1970; hon. doctorate in edn., Coll. Edn., Bangkok, 1968. Asst. cashier First Nat. Bank, Lebanon, Ind., 1924-26; asst. dept. econs. U. Wis., 1927-28; field sec. Ind. Bankers Assn., 1928-31; sec., research dir. Study Commn. for Ind. Fin. Instns., 1931-33; instr. econs. Ind. U., 1930-33, asst. prof., 1933-35, prof. adminstrn. sch. bus. adminstrn., 1935-72, dean sch. bus. adminstrn., 1935-37, acting pres. sch. bus. adminstrn., 1937-1938, pres. sch. bus. adminstrn., 1938-62, univ. chancellor, 1962—, interim pres., 1968; supr. div. of banks and trust cos., div. of research and statistics Ind. Dept. Fin. Instns., 1933-35; sec. Commn. for Ind. Fin. Instns., 1933-36; chmn. Ind. U. Found., 1937-62, 69-72, vice chmn., 1975—, pres., 1962-69, chmn. exec. com., 1969—; chmn. Fed. Home Loan Bank of Indpls., 1940-71; dir. Ind. Bell Telephone Co., 1951-72, Chemed Corp., 1970—, Lilly Endowment, Inc., 1973—; Spl. adviser on Liberated Areas, U.S. Dept. State, 1944; cons. U.S. delegation San Francisco Conf. for Am. Council on Edn., 1945; Mem. Allied Missions for Observation Greek elections, rank of Minister, 1946; adviser on cultural affairs to mil. gov. U.S. Zone, Germany, 1947-48; del. 12th Gen. Assembly of UN, 1957; adviser Ministry Edn., Pakistan, 1959; head U.S. delegation SEATO Prep. Commn. on Univ. Problems, Bangkok, 1960; mem. UN com. experts to rev. activities and orgn. UN Secretariat, 1960-61, Nat. Citizen's Commn. Internat. Cooperation, Com. Econ. Devel., 1958-61; chmn. legislature's cons. higher edn. State N.Y., 1963-64; mem. Pres.'s Com. U.S. Soviet Trade Relations, 1965; mem. rev. com. on Haile Sellassie I U., Addis Ababa, 1966-75; mem. pres.'s Spl. Com. on Overseas Vol. Activities, 1967; mem. Nat. Commn. on U.S.-China Relations, 1969; tech. adv. bd. Milbank Meml. Fund, 1973-78; Ex-pres. Nat. Assn. State Univs., State U. Assn.; exec. com. Am. Council on Edn. (chmn. council), 1944-45; mem. 1st bd. regents Am. Savs. & Loan Inst. Grad. Sch. Savs. and Loan; Trustee Edn. and World Affairs, 1963-71, chmn., 1963-70; trustee Howard U., 1956-75, Am. U. at Cairo, 1957-75, Ind. Inst. Tech. (emeritus), Earlham Coll. (hon.), Carnegie Found. for Advancement Teaching, 1941-62; former mem. adv. council Am. Sch. of Madrid; mem. nat. com. on govt. fin. Brookings Instn.; bd. visitors Tulane U.; chmn. Aerospace Research Applications Center, Ind. U., 1962-72; nat. bd. dirs. Goodwill Industries Am., 1962-69; bd. dirs. James Whitcomb Riley Meml. Assn. (hon. chmn.), Sigma Nu Ednl. Found., 1946—, Arthur R. Metz Foundation (v.p.), Learning Resources Inst., 1959-65, Council on Library Resources, Historic Landmarks Found. Ind., 1974—; chmn. adv. com. Acad. in Pub. Service, 1976-83; founder, active mem. Ind. Acad., 1971—. Author: (with others) Report of Study Commission for Indiana Financial Institutions, 1932, Being Lucky: Reminiscences and Reflections, 1980, articles in mags. Recipient Distinguished Service award Ind. Jr. C. of C., 1938; 1st ann. award N.Y. Alumni chpt. Beta Gamma Sigma, 1939; Gold medal award Internat. Benjamin Franklin Soc., 1959; Comdrs. Cross of Order of Merit Germany, 1960; Radio Sta. WHAS Ind. Man of Year, 1960; Man of Year awards Indpls. Times, 1961; Man of Yr. awards Ind. Optometric Assn., 1961; comdr. Most Exalted Order White Elephant, Thailand, 1962; knight comdr. 2d class Most Noble Order White Crown, 1968, Most Exalted Order of White Elephant, Thailand, 1986; Nat. Interfrat. Conf. award, 1962; Hoosier of Yr. award Sons of Ind. in N.Y., 1963; Interfrat. Service award Lambda Chi Alpha, 1964; Robins of Am. award, 1964; Distinguished Service Sch. Adminstrn. award Am. Assn. Sch. Adminstrs., 1965; Ind. Arts award, 1977; Liberty Bell award, 1978, Lifetime Achievement award Ind. Coun. Fund-Raising Execs., 1985; Disting. award for Lifetime Achievement Am. Coun. on Edn., 1985; Diamond Jubilee award Kappa Alpha Psi, 1986; Hon. mem. United Steelworkers Am., Dist. 30, Nat. Exchange Clubs, DeMolay Legion of Honor, 1975; hon. v.p. AM. Sunday Sch. Union; recipient Ind. U. medal, 1989; Great Am. Traditions award B'nai B'rith Internat., 1991, Lifetime Achievement award Entrepreneur of Yr., 1992, Maynard K. Hine medal Ind. U.-Purdue U. Indpls., 1993. Fellow Internat. Coll. Dentists (hon.), Am. Coll. Dentists (hon.), Am. Acad. Arts and Scis.; mem. NEA (ex. pres. div. higher edn.), AAUP, Am. Philos. Soc., Am. Assn. Sch. Adminstrs., Royal Soc. Art London (Benjamin Franklin fellow), Am. Econ. Assn., Internat. Assn. Univs. (v.p. 1955-60), Am. Research Inst. for Arts (chmn. bd. 1975-77), Nat. Commn. on Humanities (vice chmn. 1964-65), Ind. Acad. Social Scis. (past pres.), Ind. Soc. of Chgo., Ind. Soc. Pioneers, Ind. Hist. Soc. (dir. 1968—), Ind. Tchrs. Assn., Mortar Bd., Blue Key, Phi Beta Kappa, Phi Mu Alpha, Kappa Delta Pi, Beta Gamma Sigma, Alpha Kappa Psi, Kappa Kappa Psi, Sigma Nu (regent 1968-70). Methodist (trustee). Clubs: Mason (33 deg.), Kiwanian (hon.), Rotarian (hon.), Athenaeum; Columbia (Indpls.), Athletic (Indpls.); Century Assn. (N.Y.C.), University (N.Y.C.); University (Chgo.); Cosmos (Washington). Home: 1321 E 10th St Bloomington IN 47408-3964 Office: Ind U Owen Hall Office of Chancellor Bloomington IN 47405*

WELLS, HERSCHEL JAMES, physician, former hospital administrator; b. Kirkland, Ark., Feb. 23, 1924; s. Alymer James and Martha Thelma (Cross) W.; m. Carmen Ruth Williams, Aug. 5, 1946; children: Judith Alliece Wells Jarecki, Pamela Elliece Wells McKinven, Joanne Olivia Wells Bennett. Student, Emory U., 1941-42, U. Ark., 1942-43; MD, U. Tenn., 1946. Rotating intern, then resident internal medicine Wayne County Gen. Hosp. (and Infirmary), Eloise, Mich., 1946-50; dir. infirmary div. Wayne County Gen. Hosp. (and Infirmary), 1955-65, gen. supt., 1965-74; dir. Wayne County Gen. Hosp. (Walter P. Reuther Meml. Long Term Care Facility), 1974-78; rev. physician DSS, SSA, Traverse City, Mich., 1978—. Served to maj. M.C. AUS, 1948-55. Mem. AMA, Mich. Med. Soc., Am. Fedn. Clin. Rsch., Masons (32 deg.), Alpha Kappa Kappa, Pi Kappa Alpha. Home and Office: 9651 N 3 Rd Copemish MI 49625-9608

WELLS, JOEL FREEMAN, editor, author; b. Evansville, Ind., Mar. 17, 1930; s. William Jackson and Edith (Strassell) W.; m. Elizabeth Louise Hein, June 5, 1952; children: William, Eugenia, Susan, Steven, Daniel. A.B. in Journalism, U. Notre Dame, 1952; Litt.D. (hon.), Rosary Coll., 1980. Advt. and promotion dir. Thomas More Assn., Chgo., 1955-64; v.p. Thomas More Assn., 1967—, dir., 1968—; editor The Critic, Chgo., 1964-80; editor-in-chief Thomas More Press, Chgo., 1975-94; lectr. grad. dept. library sci. Rosary Coll., River Forest, Ill., 1964-67; mem. assoc. grad. faculty Loyola U., Chgo., 1984—. Author: Grim Fairy Tales for Adults: Parodies of the Literary Lions, 1967, A Funny Thing Happened To The Church, 1969, Under the Spreading Heresy, 1971, The Bad Children's Book, 1972, Second Collection, 1973, Here's to the Family, 1977, How To Survive with Your Teenager, 1982, Coping in the 80s: Eliminating Needless Stress and Guilt, 1986, No Rolling in the Aisles, 1987, Who Do You Think You Are?, 1989, The Manger Mouse, 1990; also articles. revs.; editor: Pilgrim's Regress, 1979; co-editor: anthologies Bodies and Souls, 1961, (with Dan Herr) Blithe Spirits, 1962, Bodies and Spirits, 1964, Through Other Eyes, 1965, Moments of Truth, 1966, Contrasts, 1972; contbr. to: Ann Landers Ency., A to Z, 1978. Served to lt. (j.g.) USNR, 1952-55. Home: 1500 Oak Ave # 5D Evanston IL 60201-4217 Office: Thomas More Assn 205 W Monroe St Chicago IL 60606-5013

WELLS, JOHN CALHOUN, federal agency administrator; b. N.J., Aug. 17, 1945. BA in English and Polit. Sci., U. Ky., 1966; MS in Planning and Devel., Rutgers U., 1971, PhD in Planning and Policy Devel., 1977. Sr. rsch. fellow JFK Sch. of Govt., Harvard U., Cambridge, Mass., 1987-89; with Sec. of Labor, Labor Cabinet, Commonwealth of Ky., Frankfort, 1989-91; pres. John Gray Inst., Lamar U. Sys., Beaumont, Tex., 1988-91; dir. rsch. John Grey Inst., Beaumont, 1991-92; cons. Beaumont, 1991-93; dir. Fed. Mediation and Conciliation Svc., Washington, 1994—. Office: Fed Mediation Concilation Svc 2100 K St NW Washington DC 20427-0001

WELLS, JUDEE ANN, lawyer; b. Claremont, Okla., June 10, 1951. BS, S.W. Mo. State Coll., 1972; JD, U. Tex., 1977; LLM, NYU, 1985. Bar: Tex. 1977, Wash. 1978. Assoc. Strassburger & Price, Dallas, 1977-78; assoc. prof. Pacific Luth. U., Tacoma, Wash., 1978-79; tax atty. Exxon, Houston, 1979-81; assoc. Atlantic Richfield, Dallas, 1981-84; ptnr. Foster, Pepper & Shefelman, Seattle, 1985—; bd. dirs., officer Harrison Pub., Bellevue, Wash. Author: Real Estate Excise Tax, 1991. Mem. ABA, Wash. State Bar Assn., Tex. State Bar Assn. Office: Foster Pepper & Shefelman 1111 3rd Ave Ste 3400 Seattle WA 98101-3299

WELLS, KITTY (MURIEL DEASON WRIGHT), country western singer; b. Nashville, Aug. 30, 1919; d. Charles Carey and Murtle Bell (Street) Deason; m. Johnnie Robert Wright, Oct. 30, 1937; children: Ruby Jean Wright Taylor, Bobby, Carol Sue Wright-Sturdivant. Grad. high sch. Country music singer; sang gospel in chs. as a child; performed on radio, early 1930s; with John and Jack and the Tenn. Mountain Boys, late 1930's-early 1940's, regular on Grand Ole Opry, from 1952, now with Johnny Wright, Bobby Wright and the Tennessee Mountain Boys; songs include: Release Me, It Wasn't God Who Made Honky Tonk Angels, Making Believe; albums include Kitty Wells & Roy Drusky, Vol. 1 & 2, Back to Back Patsy Kline, 1995, (with Red Foley, Webb Pierce, others) Duets, 1995; author: Kitty Wells Cookbook. Bd. dirs. Nashville Meml. Hosp. Recipient award as number 1 female singer Cashbox Mag., 1953-62, Billboard 1954-65, award of yr. for top female country vocalist Record World mag. 1965, award for highest artistic achievement in rec. arts 1964, various awards Downbeat mag., award as all-time queen of country music Music Bus. mag. 1964, Woman of Yr. award 1974, named Top Female Artist of Decade, Record World mag. 1974, named to Country Music Hall of Fame 1976. Mem. Country Music Assn., Nat. Assn. Rec. Arts and Scis. Mem. Ch. of Christ. First woman to hit No. 1 on the country charts with "It Wasn't God Who Made Honky Tonk Angels." Office: 240 Old Hickory Blvd Madison TN 37115 also: Pair Records Inc Essex Entertainment Inc 560 Sylvan Ave Englewood NJ 07632*

WELLS, LEONARD NATHANIEL DAVID, JR., lawyer; b. Akron, Ohio, Aug. 24, 1914; s. Leonard Nathaniel David and Lida Holmes (Carr) W.; m. Louise Cauker, July 31, 1937; children—Leonard Nathaniel David III, Sarah Ann (Bennett), Lida Louise (Angione), Joe Cauker. B.A., Tex. Christian U., 1934; LL.B., Columbia U., 1937. Bar: Tex. 1937. Regional atty. for NLRB Ft. Worth, 1937-39, NLRB, St. Louis, 1939-41; sr. atty. NLRB, Washington, 1941-44; assoc. dir. field div. NLRB, 1944-46; founding ptnr. Mullinax, Wells, Baab & Cloutman (and predecessors), Dallas, 1947-89; gen. counsel Tex. State Fedn. Labor, 1947-57; counsel So. Conf. Teamsters, 1956-92; monitor Internat. Brotherhood Teamsters, 1958-59; bd. dirs. lawyers coordinating com. AFL-CIO, 1984-93. Trustee Gulf Coast Trades Ctr., 1990—. Fellow Coll. Labor and Employment Lawyers (emeritus); mem. ABA (ho. of dels. 1959-60, chmn. labor law sect. 1954-55), Tex. State Bar (chmn. labor law sect. 1951-52). Democrat. Home: 7525 Fisher Rd Dallas TX 75214-2908 Office: 3301 Elm St Dallas TX 75226-1637

WELLS, LESLEY BROOKS, judge; b. Muskegon, Mich., Oct. 6, 1937; d. James Franklin and Inez Simpson W.; m. Arthur V.N. Brooks, June 20, 1959; (div.); children: Lauren Elizabeth, Caryn Alison, Anne Kristin, Thomas Eliot. BA, Chatham Coll., Pitts., 1959; JD cum laude, Cleve. State U., 1974; cert. Nat. Jud. Coll., Reno, 1983, 85, 87, 89. Bar: Ohio 1975, U.S. Dist. Ct. (no. dist.) Ohio 1975. Pvt. practice, Cleve., 1975; ptnr. Brooks & Moffet, Cleve., 1975-79; dir., atty. ABAR Litigation Ctr., Cleve., 1979-80; assoc. Schneider, Smeltz, Huston & Ranney, Cleve., 1980-83; judge Ct. of Common Pleas Cleve., 1983-94; judge, U.S. District Ct. (no. Ohio)6th Cir., Cleveland, 1994—; adj. prof. law and urban policy Cleve. State U., 1979-82. Editor, author: Litigation Manual, 1980. Past pres. Cleve. Legal Aid Soc.; legal chmn. Nat. Women's Polit. Caucus, 1981-82; chmn. Gov.'s Task Force on Family Violence, Ohio, 1983-87; mem. biomedical ethics com. Case Western Res. U. Med. Sch., 1985-94; master Inns of Ct., 1989—, Northwest Ordinance U.S. Constitution Commn., Ohio, 1986-88; trustee Miami U., 1988-92, Urban League of Clevel., 1989-90, Rosemary Ctr., 1986-92, Chatham Coll., 1989-94. Recipient Disting. Alumna award Chatham Coll., 1988, Superior Jud. award Supreme Ct. of Ohio, 1983; J. Irwin award Womenspace, Ohio, 1984, award Womens City Club, 1985, Alumni Civic Achievement award Cleve. State U., 1992, Golden Gavel award Ohio Judges Assn., 1994, Outstanding Alumi award Cleve. Marshall Law Alumni Assn., 1994, Greater Cleve. Achievement award YWCA, 1995. Mem. ABA (sect. litigation coun. 1996—), Am. Law Inst., Ohio Bar Assn., Cleve. Bar Assn. (Merit Svc. award 1983), Cuyahoga County Bar Assn., Nat. Assn. Women Judges, Philosophical Club of Cleve. Office: 338 US Courthouse 201 Superior Ave E Cleveland OH 44114-1201

WELLS, LINDA ANN, editor-in-chief; b. N.Y.C., Aug. 9, 1958; d. H. Wayne and Jean (Burchell) W.; m. Charles King Thompson, Nov., 1993. BA in English, Trinity Coll., 1980. Edit. asst. Vogue Mag., N.Y.C., 1980-83, assoc. editor beauty, 1983-85; style reporter New York Times, N.Y.C., 1985, beauty editor, food editor, 1985-90; founding editor, editor-in-chief Allure Mag., N.Y.C., 1990—; speaker Am. Womens' Econ. Devel., N.Y., 1988-89. Contbr. numerous articles to N.Y. Times Mag., Allure Mag., 1985—. Chmn. N.Y. Shakespeare Festival, 1993, 94. Recipient Fragrance Found. award, 1991, Nat. Mag. Design award, 1994, Legal Def. and Edn. Fund Equal Opportunity award NOW, 1994. Mem. Am. Soc. Mag. Editors (bd. dirs. 1993—). Office: Allure Mag Condé Nast Publs 360 Madison Ave New York NY 10017-3136*

WELLS, LINTON, II, federal official; b. Luanda, Angola, Apr. 7, 1946; s. Linton and Helen Fay (Gillis) W.; m. Linda Marie Motta; children: Linton III, Frank. BS in Physics and Oceanography, U.S. Naval Acad., 1967; MSE in Math. Scis., PhD in Internat. Rels., Johns Hopkins U., 1975; student, Boueikeushusho (Japanese Nat. Def. Coll.), Tokyo. Commd. ensign USN, 1967; commdr. USS Joseph Strauss, 1984-86, Destroyer Squadron 21, 1989-91; advanced through grades to capt. USN, 1994, ret., 1994; asst. to under sec. for policy Dept. Def., The Pentagon, Washington, 1991-93, dept. to under sec. for policy, 1993—. Decorated Def. Superior Svc. medal, Legion of Merit (2), others; recipient C.N.G. Hendrix award for excellence in oceanography, 1967, Arleigh Burke Leadership award, 1975, Silver medal Naval Inst. Prize Essay Contest, 1985, Def. award for outstanding pub. svc. Mem. Nat. Space Soc., Army and Navy Club, U.S. Naval Inst., Soc. Physics Students, Tau Beta Pi (hon.). Avocations: flying, scuba diving, reading, travel. Office: Dep to Under Sec Def for Policy The Pentagon Rm 2E812 Washington DC 20301-2200

WELLS, LIONELLE DUDLEY, psychiatrist; b. Winnsboro, S.C., Nov. 22, 1921; s. Lionelle Dudley and Mary Wells; m. Mildred Wohltman, June 28, 1945 (dec. 1986); children: Lucia, Lionelle, John, Diane; m. Eilene Bromfield, Sept. 23, 1989. BS, U. S.C., 1943; MD, Med. U. S.C., 1945; grad., Boston Psychoanalytic Inst., 1960. Diplomate Am. Bd. Psychiatry and Neurology; lic. physician, S.C., Mass.; cert. in psychoanalysis. Intern Met. Hosp., N.Y.C., 1945-46; psychiatry resident VA Hosp., North Little Rock, Ark., 1948-50; asst. resident in Psychiatry Graylyn, Bowman-Gray Sch. Medicine, Winston-Salem, 1950-51; instr. psychiatry U. Ark., 1949-51, Mass. Gen. Hosp./Harvard Med. Sch., Boston, 1955-69; clin. instr. psychiatry Harvard Med. Sch., Boston, 1969-78; lectr. psychiatry Boston U. Sch. Medicine, 1977—; asst. clin. prof. psychiatry Harvard Med. Sch., 1978-93; lectr. psychiatry Tufts U. Med. Sch., Boston, Mass., 1981—; cons. staff Newton-Wellesley Hosp., Newton, Mass., 1983-95, hon. staff, 1995—; assoc psychiatrist Mass. Gen. Hosp., Boston, 1975-82, psychiatrist, 1982-96, sr. psychiatrist, 1996—; courtesy staff Waltham Deaconess Hosp. and Med. Ctr., 1977—; cons. Edith Nourse Rogers Meml. VA Med. Ctr., Bedford, Mass., 1966—; cons. in psychiatry VA Outpatient Clinic, Boston, 1959—, others in past; chmn. bd., chief exec. officer Bay State Health Care, 1984-91; nominating com. Am. Managed Care and Rev. Assn., 1988-89, others. Contbr. articles to profl. jours. Recipient Robert Wilson award, Med. U. S.C., 1943, 44. Fellow Am. Coll. Physician Execs., Am. Psychiat. Assn. (life); mem. AMA, Am. Psychoanalytic Assn., Am. Assn. Geriatric Psychiatry, Internat. Gero-Psychiatry Assn., Mass. Psychiat. Soc., Mass. Med. Soc., Boston Psychoanalytic Soc. and Inst., Boston Soc. for Gerontologic Psychiatry (mem. chmn. and dir. 1974-76). Home and Office: 73 Rolling Ln Weston MA 02193-2474

WELLS, MERLE WILLIAM, historian, state archivist; b. Lethbridge, Alta., Can., Dec. 1, 1918; s. Norman Danby and Minnie Muir (Huckett) W.; student Boise Jr. Coll., 1937-39; A.B., Coll. Idaho, 1941, L.H.D. (hon.), 1981; M.A., U. Calif., 1947, Ph.D., 1950; L.H.D., U. Idaho, 1990. Instr. history Coll. Idaho, Caldwell, 1942-46; assoc. prof. history Alliance Coll., Cambridge Springs, Pa., 1950-56, 58, dean students, 1955-56; cons. historian Idaho Hist. Soc., Boise, 1956-58, historian and archivist, 1959—; hist. preservation officer, archivist State of Idaho, Boise, 1968-86. Treas., So. Idaho Migrant Ministry, 1960-64, chmn., 1964-67; nat. migrant adv. com. Nat. Council Chs., 1964-67, gen. bd. Idaho council, 1967-75; bd. dirs. Idaho State Employees Credit Union, 1964-67, treas., 1966-67; mem. Idaho Commn. Arts and Humanities, 1966-67; mem. Idaho Lewis and Clark Trail Commn., 1968-70, 84-88; mem. Idaho Bicentennial Commn., 1971-76; bd. dirs. Sawtooth Interpretive Assn., 1972—, dept. history United Presbyn. Ch., 1978-84; v.p. Idaho Zool. Soc., 1982-84, bd. dirs., 1984-94, treas., 1988-90, historian, 1990—. State Hist. Preservation Officers (dir. 1976-81, chmn. Western states council on geog. names 1982-83), Am. Hist. Assn., Western History Assn. (council 1973-76), AAUP, Am. Assn. State and Local History (council 1973-77), Soc. Am. Archivists, Assn. Idaho Historians (pres., 1994), others. Author: Anti-Mormonism in Idaho, 1978, Boise: An Illustrated History, 1982, Gold Camps and Silver Cities, 1984, Idaho: Gem of the Mountains, 1985. Office: Idaho State Hist Soc 210 Main St Boise ID 83702-7264 *Those of us in government positions need to focus upon helping people: when reviewing projects that may be harmful, we should help make them acceptable, rather than simply express opposition or reject them.*

WELLS, PALMER DONALD, performing arts executive; b. Keokee, Va., Jan. 31, 1937; s. Lon S. Wells and Ada Mae (Russell) Craft. BA in Journalism, U. Ky., 1960. Founder, mng. dir. Theatre in the Square, Marietta, Ga., 1982—; v.p. IBM Drama Club, White Plains, N.Y., 1976. Appeared in The Three Penny Opera, 1963; director plays The Glass Menagerie, 1965, Dark of the Moon, 1966, The Little Foxes, 1983, Tobacco Road, 1985, Mary Shelly's Frankenstein, 1988; director musicals The 1940's Radio Hour, 1987. Founder Lonesome Pine Players, Cumberland, Ky., 1960; mem. Cobb Landmarks Soc., Marietta, 1990. With U.S. Army, 1961-63. Democrat. Avocations: pottery, Spanish. Home: 43 Mcdonald St Marietta GA 30064-3217 Office: Theatre in the Square 11 Whitlock Ave Marietta GA 30064-2321

WELLS, RAYMOND O., JR., mathematics educator, researcher; b. Dallas, June 12, 1940; s. Raymond O. and Hazel (Rand) W.; m. Rena Schwarze, Aug. 1, 1963; children: Richard Andrew, René Michael. BA, Rice U., 1962; MS, NYU, 1964, PhD, 1965. Asst. prof. math. Rice U., Houston, 1965-69, assoc. prof., 1969-74, prof. math., 1974—, prof. edn., 1993—, chmn. dept. edn., 1994—, dir. sch. math. project, 1987—, dir. computational math. lab., 1990—; vis. asst. prof. Brandeis U., Waltham, Mass., 1967-68; vis. prof. U. Göttingen, Germany, 1974-75, U. Colo., Boulder, 1983-84, U. Bremen, Germany, 1995-96; adj. prof. cmty. medicine Baylor Coll. Medicine, 1994—; active Inst. for Advanced Study, Princeton, N.J., 1970-71, 79-80; exch. visitor NAS, Sofia, Bulgaria, 1984. Author: Differential Analysis on Complex Manifolds, 1973, Mathematics in Civilization, 1973, Twister Geometry and Field Theory, 1990; editor: Mathematical Heritage of Herman Weyl, 1989; contbr. numerous articles to sci. jours. Pres. Stages Repertory Theater, Houston, 1989-90. Recipient Alexander von Humboldt Sr. U.S. Scientist award U. Göttingen, 1974-75; Fulbright fellow, 1968, Guggenheim fellow, 1974. Fellow AAAS (coun. 1989—); mem. Am. Math. Soc. (coun., editor 1978-88), Cosmos Club Washington. Home: 5000 Montrose Blvd Apt 21B Houston TX 77006-6564 Office: Rice U Dept Math PO Box 1892 Houston TX 77251-1892

WELLS, RICHARD H., gaming research executive; b. Stillwater, Okla., June 24, 1940; s. James R. and Edna Ruth (McKnight) W.; m. Peggy P. Puyear, Aug. 7, 1988; children: Shanley Renne, Richard Carlyle, Amy Luru. BS in Gen. Bus., Okla. State U., 1964; postgrad. sys. dynamics, MIT, 1985-86. Sr. fin. analyst Conoco, Houston, 1964-69; v.p. planning Union Planters Nat. Bank, Memphis, 1969-75; v.p. fin. planning Inn devel. Holiday Inns, Memphis, 1975-78, v.p. corp. adminstrn., 1979-80; sr. v.p. planning-adminstrn. Harrah's, Reno, 1980-86; v.p. Bally's Casino Hotels, Reno, 1986-90; co-owner Pennington & Assocs., Reno, 1990—; founder, owner Casino Player Count Svc., Reno, 1990—; founder, pres. Wells Gaming Rsch., Reno, Nev., 1995—. Mem. Reno Downtown Redevel. Com., 1983-84, Reno Task Force for Econ. Diversification, 1984, Nev. Gov.'s Econ. Adv. Com., 1983-84, Reno-Sparks Conv. Authority Rsch. Coun., 1990; chmn. Washoe Med. Found. Project Mgmt. Group, 1990; mem. dir. Econ. Devel. Authority Western Nev., 1992-96. Served with U.S. Army, 1958-61. Mem. Reno C. of C. (dir. 1983-84), Fin. Execs. Inst. (pres. 1974-75). Home: PO Box 3781 Reno NV 89505-3781

WELLS, RICHARD LEWIS, insurance company executive. Pres. Farmers Ins. Columbus, Columbus, Ohio. Office: Farmers Ins Columbus 2400 Farmers Dr Columbus OH 43235-2762

WELLS, ROBERT ALFRED, lawyer; b. Louisiana, Mo., Dec. 1, 1942; s. Harry Armstrong and Irene Jacobson W.; m. Binney Kitchel, Dec. 21, 1968; children: Hylah, Theodore. BA with honors, DePauw U., 1964; JD cum laude, Univ. Mich., 1967. Bar: U.S. Tax Ct. 1973, U.S. Supreme Ct. 1976, U.S. Mil. Ct. Appeals 1978. Assoc. Dewey, Ballantine, Bushby, Palmer & Wood, N.Y.C., 1967-68, McLane, Graf, Raulerson & Middleton, Manchester, N.H., 1971—. Bd. dirs. N.H. Lung Assn., pres., 1980-81; bd. dirs. Am. Lung Assn., 1982—, mem. exec. com., 1987—; active St. Andrew's Episc. Ch., Hopkinton, N.H., 1971—, vestry mem., 1974-77, warden, 1979-85; trustee Protestant Episc. Ch. of N.H., 1985—; mem. Town of Hopkinton Planning Bd., 1977-79; co-chmn. Hopkinton Master Plan Revision Com., 1986-88; chmn. State Adv. Com. to the U.S. Civil Rights Commn., 1985-89; bd. dirs. Pat's Peak Ednl. Found., Inc., 1982-87, bd. dirs. Youth Soccer Assn.; trustee Heritage Heights/Homewood, 1994—, Soc. for Protection of N.H. Forests, 1988-94, 95-96, sec., 1995-96. Lt. USN, 1968-70. Mem. Am Coll. Trust & Estate Counsel, N.H. Bar Assn. (chmn. elderly legal devel. Program 1978-81, continuing legal education program 1981-85, fee dispute resolution com. 1986-88), Internat. Assn. of Fin. Planners (edn. com. 1985—), Phi Beta Kappa. Episcopalian. Office: PO Box 326 900 Elm St Manchester NY 03105

WELLS, ROBERT HARTLEY, chemistry professional; b. Springfield, Mass., Mar. 23, 1926; s. Cecil and Anna (Coates) W.; m. Mary G. Frinzi,

May 30 1952 (wid. May 1969); children: Michael J., Brian H., Donald L.; m. Alice G. Asplund, June 20, 1970. BS in Chemistry, U. Maine, 1948, MS in Chemistry, 1950. Instr. in chemistry Lafayette Coll., Easton, Pa., 1950-51; rsch. chemist Celanese Corp., Summit, N.J., 1952-56, S.D. Warren, Westbrook, Maine, 1956-58; epoxy rsch. engr. CIBA Corp., Toms River, N.J., 1958-66; sect. head Foundry Products Borden Chem., Bainbridge, N.Y., 1966-70; sr. rsch. engr. Amoco Chem., Naperville, Ill., 1970-73; product mgr. epoxies Wilmington (Del.) Chem., 1973-76; product mgr. epoxy resins AZS Corp., Lakeland, Fla., 1976-83; cons. chemist Lakeland, 1983—. Patentee in field; contbr. articles to profl. jours.; photographer exhibits in field. Mem. Toms River Sch. Bd., 1962-66, Garden State Symphony, Toms River, 1963-66; pres. Toms River Jaycees, 1962; photographer SPCA, Lakeland, 1993—. Sgt. U.S. Army, 1944-46. Mem. AAAS, Am. Chem. Soc., Photographic Soc. (mem. chmn. 1993-95, Merit Svc. award 1994), Am. Contract Bridge League, Bartow Camera Club (pres. 1988-91), Sigma Xi, Kappa Phi Kappa. Republican. Methodist.

WELLS, ROBERT STEVEN, law association executive; b. Pitts., July 7, 1951; s. Richard H. and Mary J. (Kimball) W. BS, Purdue U., 1972; JD, Ohio State U., 1976. Bar: Ohio 1977, U.S. Dist. Ct. (so. dist.) Ohio 1977, Ill. 1980, U.S. Dist. Ct. (no. dist.) Ill. 1981, U.S. Supreme Ct. 1983. Pvt. practice, Columbus, Ohio, 1977-78; rsch. counsel ABA Ctr. for Profl. Responsibility, Chgo., 1979-84, ethics counsel, 1985; exec. dir. S.C. Bar, 1985—. Editor: ABA/BNA Lawyers' Manual on Profl. Conduct, 1984, ABA Disciplinary Law and Procedure Rsch. System, 1979. Mem. S.C. Bar, Am. Judicature Soc., Nat. Assn. Bar Execs. (past chmn. long-range planning com., past chmn. bylaws com., chmn. membership records com.). Office: SC Bar 950 Taylor St Columbia SC 29201-2745

WELLS, ROBIN DENISE, nurse; b. Ft. Oglethorpe, Ga., Jan. 16, 1955; d. Marvine Eugene and Opal Evelyn (Edmonds) Wells; m. Dennis Ray Hicks, Nov. 19, 1976 (div. 1994); 1 child, Amy Nicole. Diploma in nursing, J.F. Drake Tech., 1974; degree in nursing, John C. Calhoun, Decatur, Ala., 1979; BSN magna cum laude, U. Ala., 1991. RN, Ala.; ACLS. Office nurse Cromeans Clinic, Scottsboro, Ala., 1974-76; charge nurse Huntsville (Ala.) Nursing Home, 1976-78; operating rm. nurse Huntsville Hosp., 1980-81, Jackson County Hosp., Scottsboro, 1981-85; hemodialysis charge nurse BMA Dialysis, Scottsboro, 1985-90; asst. dir. blood svc. No. Ala. ARC, Huntsville, 1991-97; ret., 1997; part-time charge nurse Jackson County Nursing Home, Scottsboro, 1978-80. Vol. Madison chpt. ARC, Huntsville, EMT, Woodville, Ala. Democrat. Avocations: travelling, camping. Home: PO Box 24 462 Kimberly Dr Woodville AL 35776-0024

WELLS, ROGER STANLEY, software engineer; b. Seattle, Apr. 13, 1949; s. Stanley A. and Margaret W. BA, Whitman Coll., 1971; postgrad., U. Tex., Austin, 1973-74; BS, Oreg. State U., 1977. Software evaluation engr. Tektronix, Beaverton, Oreg., 1979-83; computer engr. Aramco, Dhahran, Saudi Arabia, 1983-84; software engr. Conrac Corp., Clackamas, Oreg., 1984-85, Duarte, Calif., 1985; software analyst Lundy Fin. Systems, San Dimas, Calif., 1986-89; contract software analyst for various orgns. Seattle, 1989-92; software engr. Illuminet (formerly U.S. Intelco. Networks), Olympia, Wash., 1993—. Bd. dirs. The Sci. Fiction Mus., Salem, Oreg., 1993—; co-founder, bd. dirs., pres. Oreg. Sci. Fiction Conv., 1979-81. Mem. IEEE, Am. Philatelic Soc., Nat. Assn. Parliamentarians, Am. Inst. Parliamentarians (chpt. v.p. 1996-97), Nat. Assn. Parliamentarians, Portland Sci. Fiction Soc., N.W. Sci. Fiction Soc., Internat. Platform Assn., Mensa, Assn. Computing Machinery, L.A. Sci. Fantasy Soc., Melbourne (Australia) Sci. Fiction Club, Toastmasters Internat. (pres. 1980, v.p. edn. 1994-95, area gov. 1994-95, dist. 32 parliamentarian 1996-97). Avocations: travel, public speaking, science fiction, stamp collecting. Home: 4820 Yelm Hwy SE Apt B-102 Lacey WA 98503-4903

WELLS, SAMUEL ALONZO, JR., surgeon, educator; b. Cuthbert, Ga., Mar. 16, 1936; s. Samuel Alonzo and Martha (Steele) W.; m. Barbara Anne Atwood, Feb. 13, 1964; children: Sarah, Susan. Student, Emory U., 1954-57, M.D., 1961. Diplomate: Am. Bd. Surgery (bd. dirs., exec. com. 1986-89, vice chmn. 1987-88, chmn. 1988-89). Intern Johns Hopkins Hosp., Balt., 1961-62, resident in internal medicine, 1962-63; asst. resident in surgery Barnes Hosp., St. Louis, 1963-64; resident in surgery Duke U., Durham, N.C., 1966-70; guest investigator dept. tumor biology Karolinska Inst., Stockholm, 1967-68; asst. prof. surgery Duke U., Durham, N.C., 1970-72, assoc. prof., 1972-76, prof., 1976-81; clin. assoc. surgery br. Nat. Cancer Inst., NIH, Bethesda, Md., 1964-66, sr. investigator surgery br., 1970-72, cons. surgery br., 1975—; prof., chmn. dept. surgery Washington U., St. Louis, 1981—; dir. Duke U. Clin. Rsch. Ctr., 1978-81. Mem. editl. bd. Annals of Surgery, 1975-93, Surgery, 1975-93, Jour. Surg. Rsch., 1981-93; editor in chief World Jour. Surgery, 1983-92, Current Problems in Surgery, 1989—. Pres. GM Cancer Rsch. Found., 1996—. Lt. comdr. USPHS, 1964-66. Mem. ACS (bd. regents 1989—, residency rev. com. for surgery 1987-93, chmn. 1991-93, vice chmn. 1995—; mem. editl. bd. Current Problems in Surgery 1988—, editor-in-chief 1989—), Am. Surg. Assn. (recorder, mem. coun. 1986-91, pres. 1995-96), Soc. Univ. Surgeons (exec. coun. 1976-78), Soc. Clin. Surgery (treas. 1980-86, v.p. 1986-88, pres. 1988-90), Am. Soc. Clin. Investigation, Inst. of Medicine of NAS, Am. Bd. Surgery (vice chmn. 1987-88, chmn. 1988-89), Nat. Cancer Adv. Bd., Halsted Soc. (pres. 1987), Soc. Surg. Oncology (pres. 1993-94), Alpha Omega Alpha. Home: 46 Westmoreland Pl Saint Louis MO 63108-1244 Office: Washington U Sch Medicine 660 S Euclid Ave Saint Louis MO 63110-1010

WELLS, SAMUEL FOGLE, JR., research center administrator; b. Mullins, S.C., Sept. 13, 1935; s. Samuel Fogle and Mildred Inez (Meeks) W.; m. Novella R. Cloninger, June 15, 1957 (div. 1969); children: Lauren, Anthony (dec.), Jeffrey (dec.); m. Sherrill Perkins Brown, June 7, 1969; 1 child, Christopher Wentworth. AB, U. N.C., 1957; MA, Harvard U., 1961, PhD, 1967. Instr. Wellesley (Mass.) Coll., 1963-65; asst. prof. U. N.C., Chapel Hill, 1965-70, assoc. prof., 1970-78; dir. internat. security studies program Woodrow Wilson Ctr., Washington, 1977-87, assoc. dir., 1985-88, dep. dir., 1988—; cons. Office of Sec. of Def., Washington, 1974-77; trustee Z. Smith Reynolds Found., Winston-Salem, 1977-83. Author: The Challenges of Power: American Diplomacy, 1900-1921, 1990; editor and contbr. to books: Economics and World Power: An Assessment of American Diplomacy Since 1789, 1984, Limiting Nuclear Proliferation, 1985, Strategic Defenses and Soviet-American Relations, 1987, Security in the Middle East: Regional Change and Great Power Strategies, 1987, Superpower Competition and Security in the Third World, 1988, The Helsinki Process and the Future of Europe, 1990, New European Orders, 1919 and 1991, 1996; contbr. articles to profl. jours. Capt. USMC, 1957-60. Woodrow Wilson fellow, 1957, Danforth Found. fellow, 1957, Peace fellow Hoover Instn., 1972-73, Woodrow Wilson Internat. Ctr. for Scholars fellow, 1976-77. Mem. Am. Hist. Assn., Internat. Inst. for Strategic Studies, Orgn. Am. Historians, Soc. for Historians of Am. Fgn. Rels., Internat. Studies Assn., Coun. on Fgn. Rels. Avocations: hiking, soccer. Home: 1509 Woodacre Dr Mc Lean VA 22101-2538 Office: Woodrow Wilson Internat Ctr 1000 Jefferson Dr SW Washington DC 20560-0008

WELLS, THOMAS B., federal judge; b. 1945. BS, Miami U., 1967; JD, Emory U., 1973; LLM, NYU, 1978. Atty. Graham & Wells, Vidalia, Ga., Hurt, Richardson, Garner, Todd & Cadenhead, Vidalia, Ga., Shearer & Wells, Vidalia, Ga.; city atty. City of Vidalia; county atty. Toombs County, Ga.; judge U.S. Tax Ct., Washington, 1986—. With USNR, 1970. Mem. ABA. Office: US Tax Ct 400 2nd St NW Washington DC 20217-0001*

WELLS, TONI LYNN, accountant; b. Lexington, Ky., June 24, 1959; d. George Andrew and Noreta Florence (Collins) W. AA, Hinds Jr. Coll., 1979; BSBA in Fin., U. So. Miss., 1982, M in Profl. Accstancy, 1984. Internal auditor First Nat. Bank Co., New Orleans, 1984; staff auditor Touche Ross & Co., Jackson, Miss., 1984-85, semi-sr., 1985-87; staff auditor Occidental Petroleum Corp., L.A., 1987-88, sr. auditor, 1988, audit supr., 1988-92; gen. acctg. supr. Occidental Petroleum Corp., Corpus Christi, Tex., 1992-95; regional accounts payable supr. Occidental Petroleum Corp., Houston, 1995-96, sr. ops. analyst, 1996-97; contr. Laurel Industries (subs. of Occidental Petroleum Corp)., Houston, 1997—. Vol. jr. achievement Calallen High Sch.; alt. del. West Tex. Diocese, Episcopal. Ch. Coun., 1995. Mem. Am. Soc. Women Accts., U. So. Miss. Alumni Assn., U. So. Miss. Golden Eagles, Corpus Christi Plant Recreation Club (sec. bd. dirs.), Internat. Order of St. Luke, Scottish Heritage Soc. (advisor to treas.). Episcopalian. Avocations: hiking, bicycling, antiques, travel.

WELLS, VICTOR HUGH, JR., advertising agency executive; b. Bloomington, Ill., Apr. 19, 1924; s. Victor Hugh and Wilma Julia (Codlin) W.; m. Jacqueline L. Wade, Nov. 25, 1949; children—Victor Hugh, III, Polly Jo, Ken Douglas. B.S., Bradley U., 1948. Copywriter Chgo. Tribune, 1949-54; copywriter Earle Ludgin & Co., Chgo., 1954-58, creative dir., 1959-64; group creative dir. Tatham-Laird, Chgo., 1958-59; founder, creative dir., pres. Rink Wells & Assos. (advt. agy.), Chgo., 1964-72; exec. v.p., dir. creative services N.W. Ayer Inc., Chgo., 1972-84; exec. v.p., dir. creative services N.W. Ayer Inc., N.Y.C., 1984-86, also bd. dirs.; cons. N. W. Ayer Inc., N.Y.C., 1986—. Served to 2d lt. AC U.S. Army, 1943-45. Recipient various advt. creative awards, including Clio, Andy awards. Office: One Worldwide Plaza 825 8th Ave New York NY 10019-7416

WELLSTONE, PAUL, senator; b. Washington, July 21, 1944; s. Leon and Minnie W.; m. Sheila Wellstone, 1963; children: David, Marcia, Mark. BA, U. N.C., 1965, PhD Polit. Sci., 1969. Tchr. Carleton Coll., Minn.; U.S. senator from Minn., 1991—, mem. coms. on small bus., energy and natural resources, Indian affairs, labor and human resources, sen. dem. policy com., chmn. subcom. rural economy and family farming. Author: How the Rural Poor Got Power, Powerline. Dir. Minn. Community Energy Program. Office: US Senate 717 Hart Senate Office Bldg Washington DC 20510*

WELNA, CECILIA, mathematics educator; b. New Britain, Conn., July 15; d. Joseph and Sophie (Roman) W. B.S., St. Joseph Coll., 1949; M.A., U. Conn., 1952, Ph.D., 1960. Instr. Mt. St. Joseph Acad., 1949-50; asst. instr. U. Conn., 1950-55; instr. U. Mass., Amherst, 1955-56; prof., chmn. dept. math. and physics U. Hartford, 1957-82, dean Coll. Edn., Nursing and Health Professions, 1982-91, prof. math., 1991—. Mem. Math. Assn. Am., Nat. Council Tchrs. Math., Assn. Tchrs. Math. Conn., Sigma Xi. Office: U Hartford Dana 295A Bloomfield Ave West Hartford CT 06117

WELNETZ, DAVID CHARLES, human resources executive; b. Antigo, Wis., Apr. 12, 1947; s. Francis P. and Marquette A. (Stengl) W.; m. Mary L. McCulley, Aug. 25, 1973; children: Andrew, Timothy. BS in Biology, U. Wis., Stevens Point, Wis., 1969; MS in Indsl. Rels., U. Wis. Madison, 1975. Mgr. coll. recruitment tng. Rexnord Inc., Milw., 1975-77; personnel mgr. Rexnord Inc., Sarasota, Fla., 1977-80; corp. dir. employee rels. Rexnord Inc., Milw., 1980-83; sr. cons. The Thompson Group, Brookfield, Wis., 1983-87; v.p. The Thompson Group, Brookfield, 1987-91; pres. Thompson Cons., Brookfield, 1991—; adv. bd. SUNY, Buffalo, 1982-88; bd. dirs. Matarah Industries. Mem. adv. bd. Am. Cancer Soc., 1994—; bd. dirs. Matarah Ind., 1994—, Lutheran Social Svcs., Milw. Ctr. for Independence. Recipient Bronze Star U.S. Army, 1972. Mem. Pers. Indsl. Rels. Assn. (program com. 1988-91, chmn. pers. rsch. 1980-82), Human Resources Planning Soc., Human Resources Mgmt. Assn. Roman Catholic. Home: 1918 Forest St Wauwatosa WI 53213-2153 Office: Thompson Cons Ltd 17700 W Capitol Dr Brookfield WI 53045-2006

WELPOTT, JACK WARREN, photographer, educator; b. Kansas City, Kans., Apr. 27, 1923; s. Ray Calvert and Dolores (Davenroy) W.; m. Doris Jean Franklin, June 12, 1949; children—Jan Marie, Matthew David; m. Judy Dater, May 22, 1969; m. Wendy Brooke Gray, May 11, 1986. B.S., Ind. U., 1949, M.S., 1954, M.F.A., 1959. Mem. acad. staff Ind. U., 1949-59; mem. faculty San Francisco State U., 1959-93, ret., 1993; artist in residence RISD, 1984; workshop leader Columbia Coll., 1985, Friends of Photo, 1985, Humboldt State U., 1985, Parsons Sch. Design, Paris, 1985, Volcano Hawaii, 1986, numerous others in France, England, Switzerland, Japan and Mexico. One man shows include, U. Calif., Davis, Art Inst. Chgo., 1972, Wall Street Gallery, Spokane, 1973, Gallery 113, Santa Cruz, Calif., 1974, San Francisco Mus. Art, 25 year retrospective, 1976, U. So. Calif., 25 year retrospective, 1977, Ind. U., 25 year retrospective, 1977, Silver Image Gallery, Seattle, 1977, Ohio State U., 1978, Center for Creative Photography, U. Ariz., 1979, Colo. Mountain Coll., 1980, Bard Coll., 1981, Jehu Gallery, San Francisco, 1981, Galerif Voor Fotografie, Antwerp, Belgium, 1983, R.I. Sch. Design, 1984, La Photographie Creative, Pavillon des Arts, Paris, 1984, New Sch. Social Research, N.Y.C., 1984, Foto Biennale Enschede, Netherlands, 1984, Vision Gallery, San Francisco, 1984, Min Gallery, Tokyo, 1987, Osaka (Japan) Cultural Ctr., 1989, Retrospective Vision Gallery, San Francisco, 1992; two man shows include Musee Reattu, Arles, France, 1976, Photographers Gallery, Palo Alto, Calif., 1986, group exhbns. include Santa Barbara Mus., Mus. Modern Art, Mexico City, Photography in Am, Whitney Mus., N.Y.C., Photography in the 20th Century, George Eastman House, California Photography, Oakland Mus., San Francisco Mus. Art, U. Oreg. Commitment to Vision, 1986, U. Colo. Photographics, 1986, numerous others, Met. Mus. Art, N.Y.C., De Cordova Mus., Lincoln, Mass.; represented in permanent collections Graham Nash Collection, Mus. Modern Art, N.Y.C., Whitney Mus. Art, N.Y.C., Art Inst. Chgo., Biblioteque Nat, Paris, Tokyo Coll. Photography, Open U., London, Internat. Mus. Photography, Rochester, N.Y., San Francisco Mus. Art, Musee Reattu, Arles, Frances, Oakland (Calif.) Mus., U. Colo., Center Creative Photography, Tucson, U. N.Mex., Pasadena Art Mus., Australian Nat. Gallery, Houston Mus. Fine Arts, Fogg Art Mus., Cambridge, Mass., Gallery Van Haarlem, Netherlands; author: The Halide Conversion, 1989; contbr. photos to books. Served with USAAF, 1943-46. NEA fellow, 1979; grantee Polaroid, 1983, Marin Arts Coun., 1991. Home: PO Box 496 Inverness CA 94937-0496

WELSCH, GLENN ALBERT, accounting educator; b. Woodward, Okla., Apr. 1, 1915; s. George Franklin and Minnie Melissa (Bowers) W.; m. Irma Richards, Apr. 5, 1942; children: Glenn Andrew, Linden Richards, Mary Ann Welsch Williamson. B.S., Northwestern State Coll., Alva, Okla., 1935; grad., Army Staff and Command Sch., 1943; M.S., Okla. State U., 1949; Ph.D., U. Tex., 1952. CPA, Okla., Tex. Comml. tchr. pub. high sch. Alva, Okla., 1937-40; mem. faculty Coll. Bus. Adminstrn., U. Tex., 1952-85, prof. acctg., 1956-85, chmn. dept., 1959-62, assoc. dean grad. studies, 1962-67, John Arch White prof. acctg., 1968-78, Peat, Marwick, Mitchell prof. acctg., 1978-83, Bayless chair in free enterprise, 1984-85, Bayless chair emeritus, 1985—; instr. Exec. Devel. Program, 1956-72; vis. prof. Carman G. Blough Disting. prof. U. Va., 1970-71; Prickett Disting. vis. prof. Ind. U., 1975; cons. various companies on fin. acctg. and profit planning and control; expert witness. Author: (with Ronald W. Hilton and Paul Gordon) Budgeting: Profit Planning and Control, 5th edit., 1988, (with B.H. Sord) Business Budgeting: A Survey of Management Planning and Control Practices, 1958, (with C.T. Zlatkovich) Intermediate Accounting, 8th edit., 1989, (with C.H. Griffin and T.H. Williams) Advanced Accounting, 1966, (with Daniel G. Short) Fundamentals of Financial Accounting, 6th edit., 1987, (with R.N. Anthony) Fundamentals of Management Accounting, 4th edit., 1984. Served to maj. AUS, 1940-46. Recipient numerous awards for teaching excellence and service to acctg. profession, including Outstanding Educators award Amn. Acctg. Assn., 1985; named to Hall of Fame, Coll. and Grad. Coll. of Bus. Adminstrn., U. Tex., 1988. Mem. Tex. Soc. CPA's (v.p. 1959-60), Am. Acctg. Assn. (pres. 1963), Am. Inst. CPA's (council 1968-73, acctg. prins. bd. 1970-73), Nat. Assn. Accts., Fin. Execs. Inst., Planning Execs. Inst., Beta Alpha Psi, Beta Gamma Sigma. Home: 3405 Taylors Dr Austin TX 78703-1047

WELSCH, ROY ELMER, statistician; b. Kansas City, Mo., July 31, 1943. AB, Princeton U., 1965; MS, Stanford U., 1966, PhD in math., 1969. Dir. Stats Ctr. MIT, Cambridge, Mass., asst. prof. ops. rsch. Sloan Sch. Mgmt., 1969-73, assoc. prof., 1973-79, prof. mgmt. sci. and stats., 1979—. Assoc. editor: Jour. Am. Statist. Assn. Fellow Am. Statis. Assn., Inst. Math. Stats. Office: MIT-Sloan Sch of Mgmt Bldg E53 Rm 383 Cambridge MA 02139-4301 Office: MIT Dept Mgmt & Stats 77 Massachusetts Ave Cambridge MA 02139-4301*

WELSH, ALFRED JOHN, lawyer, consultant; b. Louisville, May 10, 1947; s. Elvin Alfred and Carol (Kleymeyer) W.; m. Lee Mitchell, Aug. 1, 1970; children: Charles Kleymeyer, Kathryn Thomas. BA, Centre Coll., 1969; JD, U. Ky., 1972; LLM in Internat. Law cum laude, U. Brussels, 1973. Bar: Ky. 1972, U.S. Dist. Ct. (we. and ea. dists.) Ky. 1972, U.S. Ct. Appeals (6th cir.) 1972. Atty. Ky. Atty. Gen. Office, Frankfort, 1973-74; legis. counsel to congressman Ho. of Reps., Washington, 1974-77; mng. ptnr. Nicolas Welsh Brooks & Hayward, Louisville, 1977—, Boone Welsh Brooks and Hayward Internat. Law; hon. counsel of Belgium, 1983—; econ. devel. advisor Kimgdom of Belgium; mem. Ky. Econ. Adv. Coun.; pres. Transcontinental Trading Cons., Ltd.; participant in North African Mideast Econ. Summit Conf., Morocco, 1994. Bd. dirs. Greater Louisville Swim Found., 1983-94, exec. com., 1994—, Louisville com. Coun. Fgn. Rels., 1993—, Jefferson County Alcohol and Drug Abuse Found., Louisville, 1986—. Decorated knight Order of the Crown (Belgium). Mem. ABA (internat. law sect., commn. on impairment), Ky. Bar Assn. (bd. dirs. 1981-82, pres. young lawyers divsn. 1981-82), Am. Judicature Soc., Louisville C. of C. Democrat. Presbyterian. Avocations: swimming, water polo, soccer. Office: Barristers Hall 1009 S 4th St Louisville KY 40203-3207

WELSH, DIANE M., judge. BA in Polit. Sci. magna cum laude, Villanova U., 1976, JD, 1979. Bar: Pa. 1979, U.S. Dist. Ct. (ea. dist.) Pa. 1981, U.S. Ct. Appeals (3rd cir.) 1984, U.S. Supreme Ct. 1985. Legal counsel Pa. Senate Judiciary Com., 1980-81; dep. dist. atty. Bucks County Dist. Atty.'s Office, Pa., 1981-84; ptnr. Gold-Bikin Welsh & Assocs., 1984-94; magistrate judge U.S. Dist. Ct. (ea. dist.) Pa., Phila., 1994—; spkr. in field. Contbr. articles to legal jours. Trustee Manor Jr. Coll., 1981-83, Norristown State Hosp., 1987-90. Mem. ABA, Fed. Bar Assn., Fed. Magistrate Judge Assn., Nat. Assn. Women Judges, Pa. Bar Assn., Montgomery County Bar Assn., Phila. Bar Assn., Brehon Law Soc. Office: US Courthouse 601 Market St Rm 4613 Philadelphia PA 19106-1713

WELSH, DONALD EMORY, publisher; b. Youngstown, Ohio, Oct. 6, 1943; s. Edward Francis and Clevelle Rose W.; m. Elizabeth Bourne Floyd, June 25, 1966; children: Leah Bourne, Emory Philip. A.B., Columbia U., 1965; J.D., Cleveland Marshall Sch. Law, 1969. Bar: Ohio 1969. Trust devel. officer Cleve. Trust Co., 1968-70; advt. sales rep. Fortune mag., Time, Inc., N.Y.C., 1970-75; advt. dir. Rolling Stone mag., N.Y.C., 1975-77; v.p., assoc. pub. Rolling Stone mag., 1977-78; pub. Outside mag., N.Y.C., 1978-82; pub. Muppet mag. and pres. Lorimar Pub. Group (formerly Telepictures Publs., Inc.), 1982-87; pres. Welsh Pub. Group, Inc., 1987-94; exec. v.p. Marvel Comics Group, N.Y.C., 1994-96; chmn. Group XXVII Comms., N.Y.C., 1997—. Trustee Outward Bound, U.S.A.; bd. dirs. Big Apple Circus. Mem. ABA, Mag. Pubs. Assn. (past bd. dirs.), Ohio Bar Assn., Cleve. Bar Assn., Century Assn., Racquet and Tennis Club, Sharon Country Club (Conn.), Ocean Reef Club (Fla.). Home: 501 E 79th St New York NY 10021-0735 Office: Group XXVII Comms 230 Park Ave Rm 1450 New York NY 10169-1499

WELSH, JAMES JOHN, computer consultant; b. Huntington, N.Y., Nov. 4, 1966; s. Brian James and Alice Theresa (Weiler) W.; m. Diane Romano, July 9, 1988; children: Matthew James, Daniel Joseph, Jake Alexander. AS, Champlain Coll., 1990. Programmer Whalstrom & Co., Inc., Stamford, Conn., 1990-91; cons. software WELCON, Port Chester, N.Y., 1991-92; dir. mktg. Dancik-On-Disk Internat., Ltd., Raleigh, N.C., 1993—; pres. Weller Enterprises, Inc., Wilson, 1995—. Republican. Lutheran. Avocations: cycling, oil painting, weight lifting, music. Home: 202 Raleigh Rd Wilson NC 27893 Office: Weller Enterprises Inc 202 Raleigh Rd Wilson NC 27893

WELSH, JOHN RICHARD, state official; b. Neillsville, Wis., May 27, 1938; s. Francis Richard and Bernice Margaret (Schneider) W.; m. Carol Kay Ableidinger, Sept. 30, 1961; children: Tony, Becky, Cathy, Michael, Chelley. BBA, Loyola U., Chgo., 1977; MEd, No. Ariz. State U., 1996. Benefit mgr. George F. Brown & Sons, Chgo., 1968-69, Marsh & McLennon, Chgo., 1969-71; adminstrv. mgr. Kemper Ins. Group, Long Grove, Ill., 1971-73; benefits mgr. 1st Nat. Bank of Chgo., 1973-79, The Arizona Bank, Phoenix, 1979-81; cons. Phoenix, 1981-84; benefits mgr., arbitrator Frontier Airlines, Inc., Denver, 1984-85; benefits mgr. Dept. Adminstrn., State of Ariz., Phoenix, 1985-91; retirement officer, seminar facilitator Ariz. State Retirement Sys., Phoenix, 1991—; team leader, benefits adv. Total Quality Mgmt. Ariz. State Retirement System, Phoenix, 1995. High sch. football ofcl. Ariz. Interscholastic Assn., Phoenix, 1980-93; football coach Portage Park Sports, Chgo., 1969-79; baseball coach, 1969-79; basketball coach K.C., Durand, Wis., 1966-68. With USN, 1956-59. Mem. Nat. Assn. for Pre-Retirement Edn., Loyola U. Alumni Assn. (Phoenix chpt.), Notre Dame Club of Phoenix, Bellaire Men's Golf Assn. Roman Catholic. Avocations: golf, snow skiing, reading, walking, swimming. Home: 4141 W Hayward Ave Phoenix AZ 85051-5751 Office: Ariz State Retirement Sys 3300 N Central Ave Phoenix AZ 85012-2501

WELSH, KELLY RAYMOND, lawyer, telecommunications company executive; b. Chgo., July 6, 1952; s. Raymond J. and Mary Jane (Kelly) W.; m. Ellen S. Alberding, June 28, 1985; children: Katherine A., Julia S. AB cum laude, Harvard U., 1974, JD magna cum laude, 1978; MA, Sussex U., Eng., 1975. Assoc. Mayer, Brown & Platt, Chgo., 1979-85, ptnr., 1985-89; corp. counsel City of Chgo., 1989-93; v.p., assoc. gen. counsel Ameritech Corp., Chgo., 1993-96, exec. v.p., gen. counsel, 1996—. Chmn. Met. Pier and Exposition Authority, Chgo., 1994—. Mem. ABA, Chgo. Bar Assn., Chgo. Coun. Lawyers, Chgo. Coun. Fgn. Rels. (mem. Chgo. com.), Legal Club Chgo. Office: Ameritech Corp 38th Fl 30 S Wacker Dr Fl 38 Chicago IL 60606-7402

WELSH, MICHAEL LOUIS, business executive; b. Clayton, Ga., June 14, 1959; s. John F. and Mary Ann (Casimes) W.; m. Susie Googe, June 5, 1982; children: Sarah Alex, Daniel. BBA magna cum laude, U. Ga., 1981, MACC, 1986. Consolidation acct. Tex. Instruments, Dallas, 1981-82, fin. analyst, 1982-84; v.p. cons. MISA, Atlanta, 1986-87; consolidation analyst Coca-Cola Enterprise, Atlanta, 1987-88; mid-Atlantic supr., mgr. Coca-Cola Bottling Co., Columbia, Md., 1988-90; div. mgr. Coca-Cola Enterprises-North, Columbia, 1990-91; ops. controller Cott Beverages USA, Columbus, Ga., 1993-95; sr. v.p. adminstrn. Thompson Hardwoods, Inc., Hazlehurst, Ga., 1995—; acctg. and system implementation cons., Dallas and Athens, Ga., 1982-86. Youth leader Ascension Ch., Dallas, 1982-83, St. Michael's Ch., Stone Mountain, Ga., 1986-88, St. John's Episc. Ch., Ellicott City, Md., 1988-91; pres., co-founder Youth Soccer Assn., 1996; leader Approved Workers Are Not Ashamed (AWANA), 1995-96, Altamaha Youth Soccer Assn., pres. 1996-97, co-founder. Mem. U. Ga. Alumni Soc. (pres. Dallas chpt. 1983-84), Blue Key, Golden Key, Phi Kappa Phi, Beta Gamma Sigma, Phi Eta Sigma, Beta Alpha Psi, Phi Kappa Psi. Baptist. Avocations: sports, reading, rapelling. Home: PO Box 1067 Hazlehurst GA 31539 Office: Thompson Hardwoods Inc PO Box 646 Hazlehurst GA 31539

WELSH, PETER CORBETT, museum consultant, historian; b. Washington, Aug. 28, 1926; s. Arthur Brinkley and Susan Jane (Putney) W.; m. Catherine Beatrice Allen, Nov. 27, 1951 (div. 1969); children—Susan Jane, Peter Corbett; m. Caroline Levert Mastin, Sept. 8, 1970; 1 child, James Munson Corbett. BA, Mt. Union Coll., Alliance, Ohio, 1950; postgrad., U. Va., 1950-51; M.A. (Hagley fellow), U. Del., 1956. Research asst., fellowship coordinator Eleutherian Mills-Hagley Found., Wilmington, Del., 1956-59; assoc. curator dept. civil history Mus. History and Tech., Smithsonian Instn., 1959-61; curator Growth U.S., 1962-64, curator dept. civil history, 1964-69, asst. dir. gen. mus. of instn., 1969-70, dir. Office Mus. Programs, 1970-71; dir. N.Y. State Hist. Assn., Cooperstown, 1971-74; vis. prof. Cooperstown Grad. Program, N.Y. State Hist. Assn.; dir. Cooperstown Grad. Programs, 1971-74; dir. spl. projects N.Y. State Mus., Albany, 1975-76; dir. Bur. Mus., Pa. Hist. and Mus. Commn., 1976-84; pres. The Welsh Group, 1984-86; curator The Adirondack Mus., Blue Mountain Lake, N.Y., 1986-88, sr. historian, 1988-89; mus. cons., lectr., 1989—; adj. prof. SUNY; cons. FDR Mus. and Little White House, Warm Springs, Ga., 1968-72; trustee Landon Sch., Bethesda, Md., 1964-70; bd. dirs., mem. exec. com. Ctr. for Conservation of Hist. Art and Artifacts, 1979-83; bd. dirs. Lake Placid Ctr. for the Arts, 1992-96. Author: Tanning in the United States: A Brief History, 1964, American Folk Art: The Art and Spirit of the People, 1967, Track and Road: The American Trotting Horse, 1820-1990, 1968, The Art of Enterprise: A Pennsylvania Tradition, 1983, Jacks, Jobbers and Kings: Logging the Adirondacks, 1850-1950, 1996; contbr. articles to profl. publs.; editor Smithsonian Jour. History, 1967-70. Served to 1st lt. AUS, 1951-54. Mem. Am. Hist. Assn., Am. Studies Assn., Am. Assn. Mus., N.Y. State Assn. Mus. (council 1971-75), Am. Assn. State and Local History (publ. com.), Soc. History of Tech., Sigma Nu. Democrat. Roman Catholic. Club: Country of Harrisburg. Office: 34 2nd St Tupper Lake NY 12986-2011

WELSH, ROBERT K., relgious organization executive. Pres. Ch. Fin. Coun. Office: Ch Fin Coun PO Box 1986 Indianapolis IN 46206*

WELSH, RONALD ARTHUR, physician, educator; b. Houston, Oct. 13, 1926; s. Leo Arthur and Octavia Virginia (Franssen) W.; m. Mary Jeanne Duncan, June 24, 1950; children: Mary Jeanne, William, James. A.B., U. Tex., 1947, M.D., 1950. Intern USPHS, Hosp., New Orleans, 1950-51; resident in pathology USPHS, Balt., 1951-55; chief pathology USPHS Hosp., Galveston, Tex., 1955-57; asst. prof. pathology L. Tex. Med. Br., Galveston, 1955-57, La. State U., New Orleans, 1957-59; assoc. prof. La. State U., 1959-61, prof., 1961-95; chief surg. pathology Charity Hosp., New Orleans, 1975-93; cons. forensic pathology Orleans Parish Coroner, 1961-79; cons. path. Va. Hosp., New Orleans, 1971—; Mem. La. Commn. on Narcotics and Rehab., 1970-72; Bd. dirs. La. div. Am. Cancer Soc., 1960-89, La. div. Am. Cancer Soc. (nat. div.), 1966-68, nat. del. dir., 1980-86. Served with USNR, 1944-46; Served with USPHS, 1950-57. Recipient Distinguished Prof. award La. State U. Alumni Assn., 1973-74, Asclepian award Am. Cancer Soc., New Orleans unit, 1992. Mem. AMA, Internat. Acad. Pathology, Am. Soc. Clin. Pathologists, Coll. Am. Pathologists, Assn. Pathologists, La., Orleans Parish med. socs., Phi Beta Kappa, Alpha Omega Alpha, Nu Sigma Nu. Republican. Episcopalian. Home: 2429 Octavia St New Orleans LA 70115-6533 Office: 1901 Perdido St New Orleans LA 70112-1328

WELSH, THOMAS J., bishop; b. Weatherly, Pa., Dec. 20, 1921. Grad., St. Charles Borromeo Sem., Phila., Cath. U. Am. Ordained priest Roman Cath. Ch., 1946. Ordained titular bishop of Scattery Island and aux. bishop of Phila., 1970-74; 1st bishop of Arlington Va., 1974-83; bishop of Allentown Pa., 1983—. Office: Bishop of Allentown PO Box F 202 N 17th St Allentown PA 18105*

WELSH, WILLIAM DANIEL, family practitioner,; b. Balt., May 18, 1950; s. Joseph Leo and Bessie Mary (Tangires) W.; m. Loraine Lynn Barkhaus, July 11, 1985; children: Sean William, Ryan Daniel. Student, Johns Hopkins U., 1971; BS in Biology cum laude, Fairleigh Dickinson U., 1972; DO, Coll. Osteo. Medicine-Surgery, Des Moines, 1975. Diplomate Nat. Bd. Osteo. Physicians. Intern Martin Place Hosp., Madison Heights, Mich., 1975-76, resident in internal medicine, 1976-77; pvt. practice, Detroit, 1976-79, Whittier, Calif., 1979—; instr. ACLS, L.A., 1980-92; dir. Family Asthma Forum, L.A., 1982-88; bd. dirs. Whittier Hosp. Med. Ctr., 1981, vice chief staff, 1982-84, med. dir. family asthma forum, 1979-88, med. dir. Summit Place alcohol treatment program, 1983-88; med. dir. Mirada Hills Rehab. Hosp., La Mirada, Calif., 1980-88; former clin. preceptor Coll. Osteo. Med. Pacific, Pomona, Calif., clin. assoc. prof. internal medicine; mem. dept. family practice, physician rev. com. Friendly Hills Regional Med. Ctr., La Habra, Calif.; mem. staff Presbyn. Intercmty. Hosp., Whittier. Participant Calif. Beach Clean Up Day, 1996. Mem. Am. Osteo. Assn., Am. Coll. Osteo. Family Physicians (bd. cert.), Osteo. Physicians and Surgeons Calif., Am. Coll. Osteopathic Family Practitioners (bd. cert. 1991). Avocations: boating, skiing, reading, tennis. Home: 16871 Marina Bay Dr Huntington Beach CA 92649-2913 Office: Friendly Hills HealthCare Network 12291 Washington Blvd Whittier CA 90606

WELSHANS, MERLE TALMADGE, management consultant; b. Murphysboro, Ill., June 17, 1918; s. Arthur Isaac and Martha Ellen (Blair) W.; B.Ed., So. Ill. U., 1940; M.A., Washington U., St. Louis, 1947, Ph.D., 1951; m. Mary Katherine Whitenbaugh, June 2, 1942; children: Elizabeth Margaret Van Steenbergh, Arthur Edmund, Janice Ann. Asst. v.p. Merc. Mortgage Co., Olney, Ill., 1940; exec. officer, dept. bus. adminstrn. George Washington U., 1950-54; prof. fin. Grad. Sch. Bus. Adminstrn., Washington U., 1954-69; v.p. fin. Union Electric Co., St. Louis, 1969-83; mgmt. cons., 1983—; dir. Prudential Mutual Funds, Hotchkis & Wiley Funds. Trustee United Meth. Found. Served to capt. U.S. Army, 1942-45. Decorated Bronze Star medal. Mem. Fin. Mgmt. Assn. (dir.), Am. Econ. Assn., Am. Fin. Assn., Am. Soc. Fin. Analysis, Fin. Analysts Assn. St. Louis (trustee), Alpha Kappa Phi, Beta Gamma Sigma, Artus. Methodist. Author: (with R.W. Melicher) Finance, 9th edit., 1992; cons. economist, editor Fin. Newsletter, 1965-69. Address: 14360 Ladue Rd Chesterfield MO 63017-2524

WELSOME, EILEEN, journalist; b. N.Y.C., Mar. 12, 1951; d. Richard H. and Jane M. (Garity) W.; m. James R. Martin, Aug. 3, 1983. BJ with honors, U. Tex., 1980. Reporter Beaumont (Tex.) Enterprise, 1980-82, San Antonio Light, 1982-83, San Antonio Express-News, 1983-86, Albuquerque Tribune, 1987-94. Recipient Clarion award, 1989, News Reporting award Nat. Headliners, 1989, John Hancock award, 1991, Mng. Editors Pub. Svc. award AP, 1991, 94, Roy Howard award 1994, James Aronson award, 1994, Gold Medal award Investigative Reporters and Editors, 1994, Sigma Delta Chi award, 1994, Investigative Reporting award Nat. Headliners, 1994, Selden Ring award, 1994, Heywood Broun award, 1994, George Polk award, 1994, Sidney Hillman Found. award, 1994, Pulitzer Prize for nat. reporting, 1994; John S. Knight fellow Stanford U., 1991-92.

WELT, PHILIP STANLEY, lawyer, consultant; b. Freeport, N.Y., July 5, 1959; s. Morris and Rose (Offenberg) W.; m. Karen Teresa Gault, May 22, 1994. BBA summa cum laude, Hofstra U., 1983; MBA, Columbia U., 1988; JD cum laude, NYU, 1995. Bar: N.J. 1995, N.Y. 1995; U.S. Dist. Ct. N.J. 1995, U.S. Dist. Ct. (so. and ea. dists.) N.Y. 1996, U.S. Ct. Appeals (2d cir.), 1997; CPA. Sr. mgr. Deloitte & Touche, N.Y.C., 1983-92; assoc. Reboul MacMurray Hewitt Maynard & Kristol, N.Y.C., 1993, Davis Polk & Wardwell, N.Y.C., 1994, 96—; jud. clk. U.S. Dist. Ct. N.J., Newark, 1995-96; pres. Louis Michael Coins & Jewelry, Inc., Woonsocket, R.I., 1993-95, also bd. dirs.; bd. dirs., treas. Pub. Interest Law Found., N.Y.C., 1993-94; guest spkr. Boy Scouts Am., Nassau County, 1984-91, Nat. Assn. Accts., N.Y./N.J., 1988-92, others. Sr. editor Columbia Jour. World Bus., 1986-88; sr. exec. editor Ann. Survey Am. Law, 1993-95; contbr. articles to profl. jours. Vol. income tax asst. Dept. Treasury, IRS, N.Y.C., 1981-87; vol. Variety-The Children's Charity, N.Y.C., 1985-87; advisor Friends of Jon Kaiman, Nassau County, 1995. Provost's scholar Hofstra U., 1981-83, Deloitte & Touche fellow Columbia U., 1986-88; recipient Appreciation cert. Dept. Treasury, IRS, 1981-87, Variety, 1985-87, Bovenaan Outstanding Cmty. Svc. award Hofstra U., 1983, moot ct. advocacy award Orison S. Marden; named Best Oralist, NYU Sch. Law, 1993, recipient Seymore A. Levy meml. award, 1995. Mem. ABA, ATLA, AICPAs, N.Y. State Soc. CPAs, Beta Alpha Psi, Beta Gamma Sigma. Avocations: golf, rock climbing, photography, philately, amateur radio. Home: 157 Mountain Wood Rd Stamford CT 06903-2107 Office: Davis Polk and Wardwell 450 Lexington Ave New York NY 10017-3911

WELTER, WILLIAM MICHAEL, marketing and advertising executive; b. Evanston, Ill., Nov. 18, 1946; s. Roy Michael and Frances (DeShields) W.; m. Pamela Bassett, June 11, 1971; children: Barclay, Robert Michael. BS, Mo. Valley Coll., 1966. Account exec. Leo Burnett Co., Inc., Chgo., 1966-74; v.p., account supr. Needham Harper Worldwide, Chgo., 1974-80; v.p. mktg. Wendy's Internat., Inc., Dublin, Ohio, 1981, sr. v.p. mktg., 1981-84, exec. v.p., 1984-87; owner, chief exec. officer Haunty & Welter Advt. Agy., Worthington, Ohio, 1987-91; sr. exec. v.p. mktg. Rax Restaurants Inc., Dublin, 1992; exec. v.p. mktg. Metromedia Steakhouses, Inc., Dayton, 1992-93; sr. v.p. mktg. Metromedia Co., Dayton, 1993-95; exec. v.p., chief mktg. officer Heartland Foods Inc., Dublin, Ohio, 1995-96; exec. v.p. brand mgmt. Late Nite Magic, Inc., Las Vegas, Nev., 1996—. Founder Santa's Silent Helpers, Columbus, Ohio, 1985. Mem. Advt. Fedn. Las Vegas, Scioto Country Club, Lakes Golf and Country Club, T.P.C. Golf Club. Avocations: golf, fishing. Home: 1517 Angelberry St Las Vegas NV 89117 Office: Late Night Magic Inc 1081 S Cimarron Rd Ste B-5 Las Vegas NV 89128-2454

WELTMAN, DAVID LEE, lawyer; b. Springfield, Mass., Jan. 12, 1933; s. Sol Walter and Esther (Ziskind) W.; m. Lois Handmaker, Sept. 2, 1956; children: John, Elizabeth, Herman, Sally. AB, Yale U., 1954; LLB, Harvard U., 1957. Bar: Mass. 1957. Assoc. Mintz, Levin & Cohn, Boston, 1957-60; v.p. Ansonia Mills, Inc., Taunton, Mass., 1960-63; assoc. Foley, Hoag & Eliot, Boston, 1963-67, ptnr., 1967—; sec., clk. Charles River Assocs., Boston, 1965—, Brigham Med. Group Found., 1972—, Siemens-Nixdorf Info. Systems, Burlington, Mass., 1979—, Am. Brush Co., Clairmont, N.H., 1982-92. Chmn. leadership devel. coun. Jewish Fedn. and Welfare Funds, 1966-68; trustee New Eng. Med. Ctr., Boston, 1970-82, Combined Jewish Philanthropies, Boston, 1970—, Hebrew Coll., Boston, 1995—; chmn. Newbury Coll., Boston, 1972—, Lown Cardiovasc. Rsch. Found., 1993—; incorporator Mus. Sci., Boston, 1972-92, Boston U. Med. Ctr., 1965-96; pres. Beaver Country Day Sch., Chestnut Hill, Mass., 1975-80, Jewish Cmty. Ctr., Brookline and Newton, 1968-71; bd. overseers South Shore Hosp. Found., Weymouth, Mass., 1990—; trustee, dir. Hebrew Coll., Brookline, 1995—. Recipient Young Leadership award Combined Jewish Philanthropies, 1968, Class of 1954 award Yale U., 1989, Founders Day award Beaver Country Day Sch., 1991. Mem. ABA, Boston Bar Assn., Nat. Health Lawyers Assn., Cohasset Golf Club, Cohasset Yacht Club (Mass.), Downtown Club. Avocations: tennis, sailing. Home: 90 Gammons Rd Cohasset MA 02025-1406 Office: Foley Hoag & Eliot 1 Post Office Sq Boston MA 02109

WELTON, ALICE GORDON (GUILFOY), artist; b. Balt., May 26, 1948; d. John Berryman and Helen (Gaddy) Guilfoy; m. James Frank Welton, Nov. 23, 1968; children: Jaime Alan, Eric Grahame. Student, No. Ill. U., 1966-67, Elgin C.C., 1976-79, 87-89; studied sculpture and pottery with Dale Raddatz and Michael Brown, 1972-74; studied watercolor with Alan Yau, 1981-83. Lic. commodities broker, series 3, 1997. Draftsperson Western Electric, Rolling Meadows, Ill., 1968-69; tech. illustrator Hallicrafters, Palatine, Ill., 1969-70; advt. mgr. ABC Records & Tapes, Elk Grove, 1970-71; performer, studio singer Chgo., 1972-76; fine artist Welton Fine Arts, Elgin, Ill., 1977—; instr. gifted art program U46 Sch. Dist. Coleman Sch., Elgin, 1982; presenter watercolor workshop U. Wis., Whitewater, 1982, Des Plaines (Ill.) Art Guild, 1987, handmade paper workshop Mary Bell Galleries, Chgo., 1989, Lincoln Coll., 1990; guest artist Artist to Artist, 1990. One-woman shows include Ill. Inst. Tech., Chgo., 1987, Mary Bell Galleries, Chgo., 1983, 84, 85, 86-87, 88, 89, 90, 92, 95, Judith Posner Gallery, Milw., 1989, 93, Mary Bell Galleries, 1995; exhibited in group shows at Mazur-Mazur Gallery, Deerfield, Ill., 1982, Mary Bell Galleries, 1983, 84, 86, 88, 93, 94, 95, 96, No. Ill. U. Swen Parson Gallery, DeKalb, 1986, Art Expo, N.Y.c., 1988, Katy Gingrass Galleries, Milw., 1993, Corp. Artworks, Schaumburg, Ill., 1993, 94; juried and nat. competitions House Gallery Mus., Oklahoma City, 1981, Westmoreland County Mus. Art, Greensburg, Pa., 1982, others; corp. collections include United Airlines, Arthur Young, Amoco, Prudential Ins. of Chgo., OCE USA, Chgo. Title and Trust, La Salle Internat. Group, Inc., Marshall Field and Co., Nat. Assn. Ind. Insurers; represented by Mary Bell Galleries, Chgo., Boritzer, Gray, Hamano Gallery, L.A., Corp. Art Works, Schaumburg, Katie Gingrass Gallery, Windsor Gallery, Dania, Fla. 2d degree Black Belt instr. Kwon's Taekwondo, Bloomingdale, Ill., 1992-93. Recipient Sparring Gold medal Wis. State Champion World Taekwondo Fedn., exec. sr. div. 1991, Forms Gold medal, Sparring Bronze medal Ill. State Champion, 1992, Forms Gold medal, Sparring Silver medal Nat. Champion World Taekwondo Fedn. Hampton (Va.) Coliseum, 1992. Mem. Am. Watercolor Soc. (assoc.), Midwest Watercolor Soc., Ill. Watercolor Soc., Ga. Watercolor Soc., Chgo. Artist Coalition. Avocations: martial arts, reading, commodities trading, writing, designing Japanese gardens and landscaping.

WELTON, CHARLES EPHRAIM, lawyer; b. Cloquet, Minn., June 23, 1947; s. Eugene Frances and Evelyn Esther (Koski) W.; m. Nancy Jean Sanda, July 19, 1969, (div.); children: Spencer Sanda, Marshall Eugene. BA, Macalester Coll., 1969; postgrad., U. Minn., 1969-70; JD, U. Denver, 1974. Bar: Colo. 1974, U.S. Dist. Ct. Colo. 1974, U.S. Supreme Ct. 1979, U.S. Ct. Appeals (10th cir.) 1980. Assoc. Davidovich & Assocs., and predecessor firm, Denver, 1974-77, Charles Welton and Assocs., Denver, 1978-80, 1984-88; ptnr. Davidovich & Welton, Denver, 1981-84, OSM Properties, Denver, 1982—; prin. Charles Welton, P.C. and predecessor firms, 1988—; grievance com., panelist, arbitrator Colo. Supreme Ct., 1996—; adj. prof. Inst. Advanced Legal Studies U. Denver, 1991—; lectr. in field. Author of instructional materials; author study; contbr. articles to profl. jours. Sch. pres. PTSA, Denver, 1983-84; coach Colo. Jr. Soccer League, 1980-85; coach Odessey of the Mind (formerly Olympics of the Mind), 1986-88; bd. dirs. Virginia Vale Swim Club, officer, 1989-91, Pioneer Jr. Hockey Assn., 1990-92. Served alt. mil. duty Denver Gen. Hosp., 1970-72. Mem. Denver Bar Assn. (facilitator bench/bar retreat 1995, 96, legal fee arbitration com.), Colo. Bar Assn. (legal fee arbitration com.), Assn. Trial Lawyers Am., Colo. Trial Lawyers Assn. (bd. dirs. 1985-90, chmn. seminar com. 1986-88, exec. com. 1987-88, legis. com. 1988-94, case assistance com. 1995—), Am. Bldg. a Lasting Earth (founder), Exec. Ventures Group of Am. Leadership Forum (adv. bd. 1987-90). Democrat. Lutheran. Home: 680 Vista Ln Lakewood CO 80215-6037 Office: Old Smith Mansion 1751 Gilpin St Denver CO 80218-1205

WELTON, THEODORE ALLEN, retired theoretical physics educator, consultant; b. Saratoga Springs, N.Y., July 4, 1918; s. William Edwin and Mathilde (Hatton) W.; m. Jean Elizabeth Malloy, June 10, 1943 (dec. Dec. 1976); children: William Edwin, Caroline Elizabeth, Mary Louise, John Edward; m. Regina Bogden, Oct. 29, 1977; stepchildren: Melisande Regina, James Courtney. BS, MIT, 1939; PhD, U. Ill., 1943. Physics instr. U. Ill., Urbana, 1943-44; jr. scientist Los Alamos (N.Mex.) Sci. Lab., 1944-46; rsch. assoc. physics MIT, Cambridge, 1946-48; asst. prof. physics U. Pa., Phila., 1948-50; prin. physicist Oak Ridge (Tenn.) Nat. Lab., 1950-59, mem. sr. rsch. physics staff, 1959-82, cons., 1983—; ret.; adj. prof. physics U. Tenn., Knoxville, 1963-83; cons. Westinghouse Atomic Power Divsn., Pitts., 1949-50; vis. scientist Lawrence Radiation Lab., Berkeley, Calif., 1959-60. Author: (with others) Fast Neutron Physics, 1963, Bright Field Electron Microscopy, 1979. Reader, marking books in preparation for reading Recording for the Blind, Oak Ridge, 1982—; sec., bd. dirs. Oak Ridge Civic Music Assn., 1970-72, mem. guild, 1989—. Recipient Alexander von Humboldt Found. award, 1980. Fellow Am. Phys. Soc. Avocations: history, travel, computer programming, cosmological theory.

WELTS, RICK, sports association executive. V.p. comms. Nat. Basketball Assn., N.Y.C., 1984-88, dir. nat. promotions, then v.p. mktg.; exec. v.p., chief mktg. officer NBA, N.Y.C., 1988—; pres. Nat. Basketball Assn. Properties. Office: N B A Properties Inc 645 5th Ave New York NY 10022-5910 Office: Nat Basketball Assn 645 5th Ave New York NY 10022-5910*

WELTY, EUDORA, author; b. Jackson, Miss.; d. Christian Webb and Chestina (Andrews) W. Student, Miss. State Coll. for Women; B.A., U. Wis., 1929; postgrad., Columbia Sch. Advt., 1930-31. Author: A Curtain of Green, 1941, The Robber Bridegroom, 1942, The Wide Net, 1943, Delta Wedding, 1946, Music From Spain, 1948, Short Stories, 1949, The Golden Apples, 1949, The Ponder Heart, 1954 (William Dean Howells medal Am. Acad. Arts and Letters 1955), The Bride of the Innisfallen, 1955, Place in Fiction, 1957, The Shoe Bird, 1964, Thirteen Stories, 1965, A Sweet Devouring, 1969, Losing Battles, 1970 (Nat. Book award nomination 1971), One Time, One Place, 1971 (Christopher Book award 1972), The Optimist's Daughter, 1972 (Pulitzer prize in fiction 1973), The Eye of the Story, 1978, The Collected Stories of Eudora Welty, 1980 (Notable Book award ALA 1980, Am. Book award 1981), One Writer's Beginnings, 1985 (Am. Book award 1984, Nat. Book Critics Circle award nomination 1984), Eudora Welty Photographs, 1989, A Writer's Eye: Collected Book Reviews, 1994, Monuments to Interruption: Collected Book Reviews, 1994, The Shoe Bird, 1993; editor: (with Ronald A. Sharp) The Norton Book of Friendship, 1991; contbr.: New Yorker. Recipient O. Henry award, 1942, 43, 68, Creative Arts medal for fiction Brandeis U., 1966, Nat. Inst. Arts and Letters Gold Medal, 1972, Nat. Medal for Lit., 1980, Presdl. Medal of Freedom, 1980, Commonwealth medal MLA, 1984, Nat. Medal of Arts, 1987; Lit. grantee Nat. Inst. Arts and Letters, 1944; Guggenheim fellow, 1942; Chevalier de l'Ordre des Arts et Lettres (France), 1987. Mem. Am. Acad. Arts and Letters. Home: 1119 Pinehurst Pl Jackson MS 39202-1812*

WELTY, GAIL ANN HARPER, physical education educator; b. Allentown, Pa., Feb. 19, 1956; d. James Adam and Doris (Bachman) Harper; 1 child, Peter Frederick. BS in Health, Phys. Edn., Lock Haven State Coll., 1978; MS in Edn., Syracuse U., 1980. Cert. tchr., Pa., Md. Asst. athletic trainer Syracuse (N.Y.) U., 1978-80; elem. tchr., then secondary tchr. Allentown Sch. Dist., 1980-83, head athletic trainer, coach, 1980-83; tchr. elem. sch. Howard County Pub. Schs., Ellicott City, Md., 1984—, coach, 1986; coop. tchr. for student tchrs., Howard County Schs., 1989—; presenter at profl. confs. Mem. AAHPERD, Md. Assn. Health, Phys. Edn., Recreation and Dance. Avocations: swimming, gardening, crafts. Office: Atholton Elem Sch 6700 Seneca Dr Columbia MD 21046-1130

WELTY, JOHN DONALD, academic administrator; b. Amboy, Ill., Aug. 24, 1944; s. John Donald and Doris (Donnelly) W.; m. Sharon Welty; children: Anne, Elisabeth. B.S., Western Ill. U., 1965; M.A., Mich. State U., 1967; Ed.D., Ind. U., 1974. Asst. v.p. for student affairs SW State U., Marshall, Minn., 1973-74; dir. residences SUNY-Albany, 1974-77, assoc. dean for student affairs, 1977-80; v.p. for student and univ. affairs Indiana U. of Pa., 1980-84, pres., 1984-91; pres. Calif. State U., Fresno, 1991—; lectr. in field. Contbr. articles to profl. jours. Chmn. Small Bus. Incubator of Indiana, 1985-91; bd. dirs. Open Door Crises and Counseling Ctr., Indiana, Big Bros./Big Sisters, Indiana, 1980-84. Recipient Chancellor's award SUNY, 1977. Mem. Fresno Bus. Coun., Fresno Econ. Devel. Commn., Sunnyside Country Club. Roman Catholic. Lodge: Rotary. Office: Calif State U 5241 S Maple Ave Fresno CA 93725-9739

WELTY, JOHN RIDER, lawyer; b. Waynesboro, Pa., Nov. 5, 1948; s. Richard Samuel and Mary Catherine (Rider) W.; m. Susan Eileen Mescall, Aug. 7, 1970; children: John R. II, David Richard, Brian James. BA in Econs., Shippensburg State U., 1970; JD, Am. U., 1975. Bar: Pa. Economist bur. econ. analysis U.S. Dept. of Commerce, Washington, 1970-76; staff atty. to sr. atty. Carpenter Tech. Corp., Reading, Pa., 1976-82; assoc. gen. counsel Carpenter Tech. Corp., Reading, 1982-89, dir. law, 1989-90, dir. law, asst. sec., 1990-91, gen. counsel, asst. sec., 1991-92, gen. counsel, sec., 1993—, v.p., gen. counsel, sec. Founder Drexelwood Cmty. Assn., Wyomissing, Pa., 1981-82; bd. dirs. Cornwall Terr. Cmty. Assn., Sinking Spring, Pa., 1977-79; pres. Sch. Bd., Conrad Weiser Area Sch. Dist., 1992-97; asst. commr. Hawk Mountain coun. Boy Scouts Am., 1991-96. Mem. ABA, Pa. Bar Assn., Am. Corp. Counsel Assn., Pa. Self Insurers Assn. (bd. dirs. 1978-81), Phi Alpha Delta, Alpha Phi Omega. Republican. Avocations: tennis, golf, reading. Office: Carpenter Tech Corp PO Box 14662 101 Bern St Reading PA 16901-1203

WELU, JAMES A., art museum director; b. Dubuque, Iowa, Dec. 15, 1943; s. Andrew L. and Anna E. (Riley) W. BA, Loras Coll., 1966; MA, U. Notre Dame, 1967, MFA, 1968; PhD, Boston U., 1977. Instr. St. Mary-of-the-Woods (Ind.) Coll., 1968-70; asst. curator Worcester (Mass.) Art Mus., 1974-76, assoc. curator, 1976-80, instr., 1977-78, 80-81, chief curator, 1980-86, dir., 1986—; instr. Clark U., Worcester, 1980. Panelist Mass. Coun. on Arts and Humanities, Boston, 1981-82, 90, Utilization of Mus. Resources Nat. Endowment for the Arts, 1988; trustee Williamstown Regional Art Conservation Lab., Inc., Mass., 1981-86; mem. panel Utilization Mus. Resources, NEA, 1988. Boston U. grantee, 1973, NEA Mus.' Profl. grantee, 1976-81; Samuel H. Kress Found. fellow, 1973; recipient Netherland-Am. Found. award Netherland Found., 1973, Disting. Alumni award Boston U. Grad. Sch., 1986. Mem. Assn. Art Mus. Dirs. (trustee), Am. Fedn. Arts (trustee), Coll. Art Assn. Am., Am. Assn. Mus., New Eng. Mus. Assn., Historians Netherlandish Art. Home: 16 Rutland Ter Worcester MA 01609-1664 Office: Worcester Art Mus 55 Salisbury St Worcester MA 01609-3123

WEMPLE, JAMES ROBERT, psychotherapist; b. Hardin, Mont., May 31, 1943; s. Charles Clifford and Lillian Louise (Smith) W.; m. Sarah Ann House, May 7, 1983; children: Brian Matthew, Laura Ashley. BA, U. Mont., 1966, MA, 1970, postgrad., 1970-71; PhD, Wash. State U., 1979. Diplomate Am. Acad. Pain Mgmt. Tchr., coach Custer County High Sch., Miles City, Mont., 1966-67; sch. psychologist Missoula, Mont., 1970-71; grad. asst. U. Mont., Missoula, 1970-71; dir. counseling Medicine Hat (Alberta) Coll., Canada, 1971-73; counselor Lethbridge (Alberta) C.C., 1973-76; head resident Wash. State U., Pullman, 1976-79; mental health specialist Missoula Rehab., 1979-82; clin. mental health counselor Missoula, 1982—. With U.S. Army, 1960-69, Korea. Fellow Am. Bd. Med. Psychotherapists; mem. Am. Psychol. Assn., Soc. for Clin. and Exptl. Hypnosis, Am. Soc. for Clin. Hypnosis, Internat. Soc. for Hypnosis, Nat. Acad. Cert. Clin. Mental Health Counselors, Soc. for Personality Assessment, AACD, Phi Kappa Phi. Avocations: fishing, hunting. Home: 2410 Clydesdale Ln Missoula MT 59804-9297 Office: 255 W Front St # B Missoula MT 59802-4301

WEMPLE, WILLIAM, lawyer; b. N.Y.C., Nov. 3, 1912; s. William Lester and Dorothy (Gunnels) W.; m. Dorothea Dutcher, Nov. 1, 1941; children: Littlepaige, Katharine Holland, William Barent, Leslie, Wendy, Stephanie, Liana Ashley. AB, Harvard U., 1934; LLB, Columbia U., 1937. Bar: N.Y. 1938. Assoc. Cravath, deGersdorff, Swaine & Wood, N.Y.C., 1937-42; civilian with Office Gen. Counsel, Navy Dept., 1942-43, 45-46; assoc. Dewey, Ballantine, Bushby, Palmer & Wood, N.Y.C., 1946-52, ptnr., 1952—. Mem. planning commn. Village of Scarsdale, N.Y., 1957-64; bd. dirs. Scarsdale Community Fund and Council, 1955-60. Served to lt. comdr. USNR, 1943-45. Fellow Am. Bar Found.; mem. ABA (council corp., banking and bus. law sect. 1976-80), Am. Law Inst., N.Y. State Bar Assn. (chmn. banking, corp. and bus. law sect. 1969-70). Republican. Club: Town (Scarsdale) (gov. 1959-62, 75-76, chmn. edn. com. 1976-77). Home: 36 Old Farm Rd Charlottesville VA 22903-4723 Office: Dewey Ballantine 1301 Avenue Of The Americas New York NY 10019-6022

WEMPNER, GERALD ARTHUR, engineering educator; b. Waupun, Wis.; s. Paul Christian and Thekla Nelda (Jung) W.; m. Lorraine Bischel, Sept. 6, 1952 (div. Apr. 1983); children: Susan K., Paul J. BS, U. Wis., 1952, MS, 1953; PhD, U. Ill., 1957. Instr. U. Ill., Urbana, 1953-57, asst. prof., 1957-59; assoc. prof. U. Ariz., Tucson, 1959-62; prof. U. Ala., Huntsville, 1964-73; prof. Ga. Inst. Tech., Atlanta, 1973-91, prof. emeritus, 1991—; vis. prof. U. Calif., Berkeley, 1962-63. Author: Mechanics of Solids, 1973; co-author: Mechanics of Deformable Bodies, 1961, Mechanics of Solids, 1995; contbr. articles to profl. jours. With U.S. Army, 1946-48. NSF fellow, Stanford (Calif.) U., 1963-64, Sr. fellow Alexander von Humboldt Found., Germany, 1973, Killam fellow U. Calgary, Can., 1983. Fellow ASME (assoc. editor 1976-83), Am. Acad. Mechanics. Avocations: art, sculpture, photography, woodwork. Home and Office: 3397 Hidden Acres Dr Doraville GA 30340-4445

WEN, SHIH-LIANG, mathematics educator; came to U.S., 1959; s. S.W. and C.F. (Hsiao) W.; children: Dennis, Andy, Jue. BS, Nat. Taiwan U., Taipei, 1956; MS, U. Utah, 1961; PhD, Purdue U., 1968. Assoc. research engr. The Boeing Co., Seattle, 1961-63; with dept. math. Ohio U., Athens, 1968—, successively asst. prof., assoc. prof. and prof., chmn. dept. math., 1985-93; rsch. analyst Applied Math Rsch. Lab. USAF, Wright-Patterson AFB, Ohio, summer, 1972; vis. rsch. scientist Courant Inst. Math. Scis. NYU, 1978-79; hon. prof. Jiangxi U., People's Republic of China, 1985; disting. vis. prof. Lanzhou U., People's Republic of China, 1989. Mem. Am. Math. Soc., Soc. for Indsl. and Applied Math., Math. Assn. Am. Avocations: fishing, bridge, music. Office: Ohio Univ Dept Of Math Athens OH 45701

WENDEBORN, RICHARD DONALD, retired manufacturing company executive; b. Winnipeg, Man., Can.; came to U.S., 1976; naturalized, 1988; s. Curtis and Rose (Lysecki) W.; m. Dorothy Ann Munn, Aug. 24, 1957; children: Margaret Gayle, Beverley Jane, Stephen Richard, Peter Donald, Ann Elizabeth. Diploma, Colo. Sch. Mines, 1952; grad. advanced mgmt. program, Harvard U., 1974. With Can. Ingersoll-Rand Co., Montreal, 1952—, gen. mgr., v.p., dir., 1968, pres., 1969-74, chmn. bd., 1976—; exec. v.p. Ingersoll-Rand Co., Woodcliff Lake, N.J., 1976-89; ret., 1989; mem. Can Govt. Oil and Gas Tech. Exch. Program with former USSR, 1972—, Minerals and Metals Mission to China, 1972—. Mem. Resource Fund Colo. Sch. Mines; past pres., dir. Town and River Civic Assn. Mem. Machinery and Equipment Mfrs. Assn. Can. (bd. dirs. 1974—, past chmn.), Royal Palm Yacht Club (commodore 1994), Internat. Order of Blue Gavel (past Commodore's Club, pres. Royal Palm br. dist. 8), Useppa Island Club, Tau Beta Pi. Home: 9990 Cypress Lake Dr Fort Myers FL 33919-6020

WENDEL, CHARLES ALLEN, lawyer; b. Lockport, N.Y., Aug. 13, 1942; s. Harold Henry and Doris Lillian (Gardner) W.; m. Helen W. Roberts, June 23, 1973; children: William Charles, Jonathan David. BChem. Engring., Rensselaer Poly. Inst., 1964; JD, Am. U., 1968. Bar: N.Y. 1969, Va. 1971, D.C. 1980, U.S. Supreme Ct., U.S. Ct. Appeals (fed. and 4th cirs.), U.S. Dist. Ct. (ea. and we. dists.) Va. Patent examiner U.S. Patent and Trademark Office, Washington, 1964-66; patent trainee Union Carbide Corp, Washington, 1966-68, patent atty., N.Y.C., 1968-70; assoc., then ptnr. Stevens, Davis, Miller & Mosher, Arlington, Va., 1970-83; ptnr. firm Wegner & Bretschneider, Washington, 1983-85, assoc. solicitor U.S. Patent and Trademark Office, 1985-88; assoc. Lyon & Lyon, Washington, 1988-90; founding ptnr. Parkhurst, Wendel & Rossi, Alexandria, Va., 1990-95. Contbr. articles to profl. jours. Mem. Va. State Bar (patent trademark copyright sect., chmn. 1977-78), Am. Intellectual Patent Law Assn., Patent Lawyers Club Washington (pres. 1982-83), Delta Theta Phi. Republican.

Office: Parkhurst Wendel & Burr LLP 1421 Prince St Ste 210 Alexandria VA 22314-2805

WENDEL, MARTIN, lawyer; b. Elizabeth, N.J., Sept. 30, 1944; s. Henry H. and Catherine (McGovern) W.; m. Louise A. Damasiewicz, Oct. 19, 1968; children: Martin Jr., Andrew. BS with honors, Rutgers U., 1974; JD, N.Y. Law Sch., 1978. Bar: N.J. 1978, U.S. Dist. Ct. N.J. 1978, N.Y. 1979, U.S. Dist. Ct. (so. and ea. dists.) N.Y. 1979, U.S. Ct. Appeals (2d cir.) 1979, Supreme Ct. of U.S. 1988. Assoc. Costello & Shea, N.Y.C., 1979-81; assoc. Curtis Mallet Prevost Colt & Mosle, N.Y.C., 1981-87, ptnr. Atty. mcpl. planning bd., Rahway, N.J., 1979-87; mem. com. Union County N.J., 1981-88; bd. dirs. Make-a-Wish Found., N.J., 1983-85; mem. malpractice mediation panel 1st Jud. Dept., 1980-87. With USN, 1962-66. Mem. ABA (sect. of litigation, com. on product liability 1992—), Fed. Bar Coun., N.Y. State Bar Assn. (com. cert. specialization), N.J. State Bar Assn. (mem. civil bar sect.), N.Y. County Lawyers Assn., Assn. Trial Lawyers Am., N.Y. State Trial Lawyers Assn., Def. Rsch. Inst., Masons, Univ. Club. Home: 1071 Midwood Dr Rahway NJ 07065-1716 Office: Curtis Mallet Prevost Colt & Mosle 101 Park Ave New York NY 10178

WENDEL, RICHARD FREDERICK, economist, educator, consultant; b. Chgo., Apr. 29, 1930; s. Elmer Carl and Victoria Matilda (Jeffrey) W.; m. Leslie Jane Travis, June 15, 1957; children: John Travis, Andrew Stewart. A.B., Augustana Coll., 1951; M.B.A., U. Pa., 1957, Ph.D. (fellow 1962-64), 1966. Asst. to pres. Flexonics Corp., Maywood, Ill., 1957-59; sales rep., product mgr. Kordite div. Nat. Distillers Corp., Macedon, N.Y., 1959-62; instr. Wharton Sch., U. Pa., 1964-65; asst. prof. mktg. Grad. Sch. Bus. Adminstrn., Washington U., St. Louis, 1965-69; assoc. prof. U. Conn., 1969-74, prof., 1974-90, prof. emeritus, 1990; mem. U.S. Census Field Adv. Commn., 1967-69; mem. acad. adv. commn. Bur. Labor Stats., U.S. Bur. Census Survey of Consumer Expenditures, 1971-76; mem. Conn. Export Devel. Council, Dept. Commerce, 1972-76; dir. Neon Software Inc. Author: (with M.L. Bell) Economic Importance of Highway Advertising, 1966; (with W. Gorman) Selling: Preparation. Persuasion. Strategy., 1983, 88; editor: Readings in Marketing, 1973-74, 75-76, 77-78, 78-79, 79-80, 80-81, (with C.L. Lapp) Add to Your Selling Know-How, 1968; editorial staff: jour. Mktg., 1965-74. Bd. dirs. Roper Center. Served with USAF, 1951-55. Center for Real Estate and Urban Econs. grantee, 1969-70. Mem. Am. Mktg. Assn., N.Y. Acad. Scis. Republican. Episcopalian. Home: 106 S Queen St Chestertown MD 21620

WENDELBURG, NORMA RUTH, composer, pianist, educator; b. Stafford, Kans.; d. Henry and Anna Louise (Moeckel) W.; MusB, Bethany Coll., 1943; MusM, U. Mich., 1947; MusM, Eastman Sch. Music, 1951, postgrad., 1964-65, 66-67, PhD in Composition, 1969; postgrad. Mozarteum, 1953-54, Vienna Acad. Music, 1955. Teaching music edn., piano Wayne (Nebr.) State Coll., 1947-50; asst. prof. Bethany Coll., Lindsborg, Kan., 1952-53, U. Iowa, 1956-58; asst. prof. composition, theory, piano Hardin-Simmons U., Abilene, Tex., 1958-66, chmn. grad. com. Sch. Music, 1960-66, founder ann. univ. festival contemporary music, 1959, chmn., 1959—; assoc. prof. music Dallas Bapt. Coll., 1973-75; research asst. to dir. grad. studies Eastman Sch. Music, 1966-67; former assoc. prof., chmn. dept. theory, composition Southwest Tex. State U., 1969-72; mem. faculty Friends Bible Coll., Haviland, Kans., 1977-83; guest composer several colls. including U. Ottawa, 1984; performed in Eng., Am. Conservatory Mus., Chgo., Charles Ives Ctr. for Am. Mus., Conn., 1990—; various solo recitals, festivals. Recipient Meet the Composer award N.Y. State Council of Arts, 1979; Composition scholar Composers' Conf. Middlebury (Vt.), 1950, Berkshire Center, 1953; Fulbright award, 1953-55; Residence fellow Huntington Hartford Found., 1955-56, 58, 61; MacDowell Colony, 1958, 60, 70; fellow Nat. Festival of Performing Arts, 1989. Mem. Music Tchrs. Nat. Conf., Am. Music Center, MacDowell Colonists, ASCAP (Composition awards 1988-90, 91, 92, 93, 94, 95, 96), Am. Soc. Univ. Composers, Minn. Composers Forum, Am. Women Composers, Sigma Alpha Iota. Composer numerous works including Symphony, 1967, Suite for Violin and Piano, 1965, Song Cycle for Soprano, Flutes, Piano, 1974, Music for Two Pianos, 1985, Affirmation, 1982, Interlacings (organ), 1983, (recorded) Suite No. 2 for Violin and Piano, 1989, Fantasy for Trumpet and Piano, 1990, Sonata for Clarinet and Piano, Sinfonietta, 1994, Concerto for Clarinet and Orch., others. Republican. Club: Music (Hutchinson). Avocations: traveling, photography, gardening. Address: 2206 N Van Buren St Hutchinson KS 67502-3738

WENDELL, EARL W., entertainment company executive; b. 1928. Grad., Wooster Coll., 1950. Officer Opryland USA Inc. and affiliates and predecessors, Nashville, 1950—, pres., 1983—, pres., CEO Gaylord Entertainment Co., 1991—. Office: Opryland USA Inc 2802 Opryland Dr Nashville TN 37214-1200

WENDELN, DARLENE DORIS, English language educator; b. Indpls., July 18, 1956; d. Robert Edward and Doris Mae (Brabender) W. BS, U. Indpls., 1978; MS, Ind. U., 1986. Lic. tchr., Ind. Secondary English tchr., coach Centerville (Ind.)-Abington Sch. Corp., 1978—; coach girls' tennis regional and sectional championships. Mem. NEA, Nat. Coun. Tchrs. English, Ind. H.S. Tennis Coaches Assn., U.S. Tennis Assn. Lutheran. Avocations: bicycling, tennis, golf, reading. Office: Centerville High Sch Willow Grove Rd Centerville IN 47330

WENDELSTEDT, HARRY HUNTER, JR., umpire; b. Balt., July 27, 1938; m. Cheryl Maher, Nov. 2, 1970; children: Harry III, Amy. Student, Essex Community Coll.; BS in Edn., U. Md. Profl. baseball umpire, 1962—; with minor leagues, Ga.-Fla., 1962, (Northwest), 1963, Tex., 1964, (Internat.), 1965; with maj. leagues (Nat.), 1966—; umpire All-Star Game, 1968, 76, 83, 92, Nat. League championship series, 1970, 72, 77, 80, 82, 84, 88, 90, 96, World Series, 1973, 80, 86, 91, 95; owner, operator Harry Wendelstedt Umpire Sch. Named Top Umpire in Maj. League Baseball Md. Profl. Baseball Players Assn., 1975, Best Umpire in Nat. League Chgo. Tribune, 1982, Best Ball and Strike Umpire Sports Illustrated, 1982, Major League Umpire of Yr., 1992, Fla. Diamond Club, 1993. Mem. Major League Umpires Assn. (4 term past pres.). Office: Major League Umpires Assn 88 S St Andrews Dr Ormond Beach FL 32174-3857

WENDER, HERBERT, title company executive; chmn. CMAC Investment Corp.; chmn. and CEO Commonwealth Land Title Ins. Co.; Office: CMAC Investment Corp 1700 Market St Philadelphia PA 19103-3913

WENDER, IRA TENSARD, lawyer; b. Pitts., Jan. 5, 1927; s. Louis and Luba (Kibrick) W.; m. Phyllis M. Bellows, June 24, 1966; children: Justin B., Sarah T.; children by previous marriage: Theodore M., Matthew G., Abigail A., John B. Student Swarthmore Coll., 1942-45; JD, U. Chgo., 1948; LLM, NYU, 1951. Atty. Lord, Day and Lord, N.Y.C., 1950-52, 54-59; asst. dir. internat. program in taxation Harvard U. Law Sch., 1952-54; lectr. N.Y. U. Sch. Law, N.Y.C., 1954-59; ptnr. Baker and McKenzie, Chgo., 1959-61, founding ptnr. N.Y.C. office, 1961-71; sr. ptnr. Wender, Murase & White, 1971-82, of counsel, 1982-86; chmn. C. Brewer and Co., Ltd., Honolulu, 1969-75; pres., chief exec. officer A.G. Becker Paribas Inc., 1978-82; chmn., chief exec. officer Sussex Securities Inc., 1983-85; of counsel Patterson, Belknap, Webb & Tyler, N.Y.C., 1986-87, ptnr., 1988-93, of counsel, 1994—; chmn. Perry Ellis Internat., Inc., N.Y.C., 1994; bd. dirs. REFAC Tech. Devel. Corp., N.Y.C., United Dominion Realty Trust, Inc., Richmond, Dime Bancorp, N.Y.C.. Bd. mgrs. Swarthmore Coll.. 1978-89; pres., bd. mgrs. PARC Vendome Condominium, 1990-94; trustee Brearley Sch., N.Y.C., 1980-85, Putney (Vt.) Sch., 1985—; active Council on Fgn. Relations. Mem. Am., N.Y. State bar assns., Assn. of Bar of City of N.Y. Author: (with E.R. Barlow) Foreign Investment and Taxation, 1955. Home: 340 W 57th St New York NY 10019 Office: Patterson Belknap Webb & Tyler 1133 Avenue Of The Americas New York NY 10036-6710

WENDER, PAUL ANTHONY, chemistry educator. BS, Wilkes Coll., 1969; PhD, Yale U., 1973; PhD (hon.), Wilkes U., 1993. Asst. prof., assoc. prof. Harvard U., 1974-81; prof. chemistry Stanford U., 1981—; Bergstrom prof. chemistry, 1994—; cons. Eli Lilly & Co., 1980—, lectr. Am. Chem. Soc.. Recipient ICI Am. Chem. award Stuart Pharm., merit award NIH, Pfizer rsch. award, 1995, Pfizer Rsch. award, 1995. Mem. AAAS, Am. Chem. Soc. (Arthur C. Cope Sholan award 1990, Guenther award). Office: Stanford U Dept Chemistry Stanford CA 94305

WENDER, PHYLLIS BELLOWS, literary agent; b. N.Y.C., Jan. 6, 1934; d. Lee and Lillian (Frank) Bellows; m. Ira Tensard Wender, June 24, 1966; children: Justin Bellows, Sarah Tensard. B.A., Wells Coll., 1956. Asst. advt dir. Book Find Club, N.Y.C., 1957-58; publicity dir. Grove Press, N.Y.C., 1958-61, Dell Pub. Co., N.Y.C., 1961-63; theatrical agt. Artists Agy. Inc., N.Y.C., 1963-68; agt. Wender & Assocs., N.Y.C., 1968-81; writers' agt. Rosenstone/Wender, N.Y.C., 1981—. Bd. dirs. Just Women Inc., Bklyn., 1982, mem. adv. com., 1983-87; bd. dirs. Fortune Soc., N.Y.C., 1977-80; trustee Wells Coll., Aurora, N.Y., 1981-90. Mem. Women's Media Group (dir. 1988-90). Club: Cosmopolitan (N.Y.C.). Office: Rosenstone Wender 3 E 48th St New York NY 10017-1027

WENDERS, WIM, motion picture director; b. Dusseldorf, Germany, Aug. 14, 1945. Dir. films including Summer in the City, 1970, The Goalie's Anxiety at the Penalty Kick, 1972, The Scarlet Letter, 1974, Alice in the Cities, 1974, The Wrong Move, 1975, Kings of the Road, 1976, The American Friend, 1977, Lightning Over Water (Nick's Movie) (with Nicholas Ray), 1980, The State of Things, 1982, Hammett, 1982; Paris, Texas, 1984 (Palme d'Or, Cannes Internat. Film Festival), Tokyo-Ga, 1985, Wings of Desire, 1987 (Best Dir., Cannes Internat. Film Festival), Aufzeichnungen zu Kleiderund Stadten, 1989, Until the End of the World, 1991, Far Away, So Close, 1993 (Cannes Internat. Film Festival Grand Prize), The End of Violence, 1997; co-dir. Par Dela' Les Nuages, 1995, Lumiere et Compagnie, 1995, A Trick of The Light, 1996. Author: Emotion Pictures,1986, Written in the West, 1987, Die Logik de Bilder, 1988, The Act of Seeing, 1992, Office: Road Movies Filmproduktion Gmbh, Potsdamer Strasse 199, 1000 Berlin 30, Germany*

WENDLER, WALTER V., dean. B in Environ. Design, Texas A&M U.; MArch, U. Calif., Berkeley; PhD, U. Tex. Cert. Nat. Coun. Archtl. Registration Bd. Lic. Tex., La. Pvt. practice, 1977-81; faculty Tex. A&M U. Coll. Architecture, College Sta., 1981—, assoc. dean acad. affairs, 1988-89, head dept. architecture, 1989-92, dean, 1992—. Contbr. articles to profl. jours. Office: Texas A&M U College of Architecture College Station TX 77843-3137

WENDORF, DENVER FRED, JR., anthropology educator; b. Terrell, Tex., July 31, 1924; s. Denver Fred and Margaret (Hall) W.; m. Anna Christy Bednar, Apr. 27, 1996; children: Frederick Carl, Michael Andrew, Gail Susan, Cynthia Ann, Kelly Peta, Scott Frederick. B.A., U. Ariz., 1948; M.A., Harvard U., 1950, Ph.D., 1953. Research assoc. Mus. N.Mex., Santa Fe, 1950-56; assoc. dir. Mus. N.Mex., 1958-64; assoc. prof. Tex. Tech U., Lubbock, 1956-58; prof. anthropology So. Meth. U., Dallas, 1964—; chmn. dept. anthropology So. Meth. U., 1968-74, Henderson-Morrison prof. prehistory, 1974—; dir. Ft. Burgwin Research Ctr., Taos, N.Mex., 1957-76. Author: numerous books including The Prehistory of Nubia, 1968, The Midland Discovery, 1955, Paleoecology of the Llano Estacado, 1961, A Guide to Salvage Archaeology, Prehistory of the Eastern Sahara, 1980; also articles. Chmn. Tex. State Antiquities Com., 1969-82; mem. Nat. Park System Adv. Bd., 1983-87, chmn., 1985-87; mem. Cultural Properties Adv. Bd., 1984-90. Served with AUS, 1943-47. Decorated Purple Heart; decorated Bronze Star. Mem. Soc. for Am. Archaeology (treas. 1974-77, pres. 1979-81), Nat. Acad. Scis., Soc. of Profl. Archaeologists (pres. 1995-97). Home: 401 S Centre Ave Lancaster TX 75146-3830

WENDORF, HULEN DEE, law educator, author, lecturer; b. West, Tex., Oct. 29, 1916; s. Reinhardt and Laura (Blume) W.; m. Mary Jane Pfeffer, June 13, 1939; children: Robert Joseph, Donald Joseph, Florence Ann. BS, U.S. Mil. Acad., 1939; JD, Yale U., 1951. Bar: Conn. 1951, Tex. 1961, U.S. Ct. Mil. Appeals 1952, U.S. Supreme Ct. 1958, U.S. Dist. Ct. 1960. Commd. 2d lt. U.S. Army, 1939, advanced through grades to col., ret. as chief of adminstrv. law div. Office Judge Adv. Gen., 1959; practice El Paso, Tex., 1959-61; prof. law Baylor U. Law Sch., 1961-86, prof. emeritus, 1986—; former chmn. and long-time mem. Citizens Adv. Com. to Juvenile Judge; former dir. Heart of Tex. Legal Aid Assn. Author: Texas Law of Evidence Manual, 1983, 4th rev. edit., 1995, also 3 law sch. casebooks; columnist United Retirement Bull.; contbr. various articles to law revs. Rsch. dir. Texans War on Drugs, 1980-81; chmn. Food For People, 1981—. Decorated Legion of Merit, Bronze Star, Army Commendation medal. Mem. Waco-McLennan County Bar Assn. (former dir., former v.p.), Phi Delta Phi. Home: 2808 Cumberland Ave Waco TX 76707-1324 *Enjoying the work you do, the support of a good family, and a strong religious faith are the cornerstones of a good life. Do your best work when the boss is not looking.*

WENDORF, RICHARD HAROLD, library director, educator; b. Cedar Rapids, Iowa, Mar. 17, 1948; s. Harold Albert and Jeanne Ellen (Hamblin) W.; m. Barbara Hilderman, 1970 (div. 1983); m. Diana Thanet French, 1984 (div. 1995); children: Reed Thanet Wendorf-French, Carolyn Thanet Wendorf-French. BA, Williams Coll., 1970; PhB, U. Oxford, Eng., 1972; MA, Princeton U., 1974, PhD, 1976. From asst. prof. English to assoc. prof. English Northwestern U., Evanston, Ill., 1976-86, assoc. dean, 1984-88, prof. English and art history, 1986-89; libr. dir. Houghton Libr., Harvard U., Cambridge, Mass., 1989-97; dir., libr. Boston Athenaeum, 1997—; sr. lectr. fine arts Harvard U., 1990-97, acting libr. Fine Arts Libr., 1991-92; lectr. Phi Beta Kappa Assocs., 1992—; dir. NEH summer seminars for coll. tchrs. Northwestern U., 1987, Harvard U., 1990, 92, 96; Robert Sterling Clark vis. prof. art history Williams Coll., 1993. Author: William Collins and Eighteenth-Century English Poetry 1981, The Elements of Life: Biography and Portrait Painting in Stuart and Georgian England, 1990, paperback edit., 1991, Sir Joshua Reynolds: The Painter in Society, 1996; editor: Articulate Images: The Sister Arts from Hogarth to Tennyson, 1983, Rare Book and Manuscript Libraries in the Twenty-First Century, 1993, (eith Charles Ryskamp) The Works of William Collins, 1979; contbr. essays in field; mem. editl. bd. Studies in 18th Century Culture, 1985-89, Word and Image, 1992-95, Yale edit. Writings of Samuel Johnson, Old-Time New Eng. Rsch. grantee Folger Shakespeare Libr., Washington, 1976, Am. Philos. Soc., Phila., 1977, 82, Henry E. Huntington Libr., 1979, Yale Ctr. for Brit. Art, 1983; jr. rsch. fellow Am. Coun. Learned Socs., 1978-79; summer stipend NEH, 1979; sr. rsch. fellow Am. Coun. Learned Socs., 1981-82; NEH rsch. fellow Newberry Libr., Chgo., 1988-89; fellow John Simon Guggenheim Meml. Found., 1989-90. Mem. Signet Soc. (assoc.), Keats-Shelley Assn. Am. (bd. dirs. 1993—), Am. Antiquarian Soc., Am. Soc. for 18th Century Studies (pres. Midwest regional soc. 1986), Coll. Art Assn., Soc. Brit. Art Historians, Colonial Soc. Mass., Nat. Com. on Stds. in Arts, The Johnsonians (chmn. 1994-95), Harvard Faculty Shop Club, Saturday Club, Cambridge Sci. Club, Club of Odd Volumes, Grolier Club, Phi Beta Kappa (exec. bd. Chgo. 1984-87). Office: Boston Athenaeum 10 1/2 Beacon St Boston MA 02108-3703

WENDT, CHARLES WILLIAM, soil physicist, educator; b. Plainview, Tex., July 12, 1931; s. Charles Gottlieb and Winnie Mae (Bean) W.; m. Clara Anne Diller, Oct. 15, 1955; children: Charles Diller, John William, Elaine Anne, Cynthia Lynne. B.S. in Agronomy, Tex. A&M U., 1951, Ph.D. in Soil Physics, 1966; M.S. in Agronomy, Tex. Tech U., 1957. Research asst. Tex. Tech Coll., 1953-55, instr. agronomy, 1957-61, asst. prof., 1961-63; research asst. soil physics Tex. A&M U., 1963-65, research assoc., 1965-66; asst. prof. Tex. A&M U. (Agrl. Research and Extension Center), Lubbock, 1966-69; assoc. prof. Tex. A&M U. (Agrl. Research and Extension Center), 1969-74, prof., 1974-91, prof. emeritus, 1991—; cons. cotton prodn. Ministry of Agr. Sudan, summer 1960; cons. Irrigation Assn., 1977-81, Office of Tech. and Assessment, 1982, S.E. Consortium for Internat. Devel., 1989, Rhone Poulenc Agrl. Co., 1992-93; prin. backstop scientist U.S. AID West African Rsch. Program on Soil-Plant0Water Mgmt., 1982-91; chmn. agrl. sect. Southwestern and Rocky Mountain divsn. AAAS, 1982-83. Contbr. articles to profl. jours., chpt. to book. Del. Lubbock County Rep. Conv., 1978; elder Westminster Presbyn. Ch.; Tex. rep. to Great Plains Coun. 1 com. on evapotranspiration. 1st lt. U.S. Army, 1951-53. Named Outstanding Researcher High Plains Research Found., 1982; recipient Superior Achievement award for rsch., soil and crop scis. dept. Tex. A&M Univ., 1987; grantee industry and water dists. Dept. Interior, U.S. AID, EPA. Mem. Soil Sci. Soc. Am., Am. Soc. Agronomy, Brit. Plant Growth Regulator Soc., Optimist Club (1st v.p., bd. dirs.), Sigma Xi, Phi Kappa Phi. Home: 4518 22nd St Lubbock TX 79407-2515 Office: Texas Agrl Expt Station RR 3 Lubbock TX 79401-9703

WENDT, GARY CARL, finance company executive; b. Portage, Wis., Mar. 13, 1942; s. Walter Carl and Dorothy Mae (Neesam) W.; m. Lorna Joyce Jorgenson, July 31, 1965; children: Sarah, Rachel. B.S. in Civil Engring., U. Wis., 1965; M.B.A., Harvard U., 1967. V.p. La. Co. Inc., Houston, 1967-71, Diversified Advisor, Miami, 1971-75; v.p. GE Credit Corp., Stamford, Conn., 1975-84, COO, 1984-86; pres., CEO GE Capital Svcs. (formerly Gen. Electric Credit Corp.), Stamford, 1986—. Trustee Boy's and Girl's Club of Stamford, past campaign chmn. capital fund campaign; past chmn. Stamford United Way; chmn. Conn. Bus. Edn. Coun.; trustee Outward Bound USA; chmn. corp. adv. com. Fairfield County Community Found. Recipient of His Royal Highness Prince Philips award, 1996, Corporate award for Outstanding Svs., to Outward Bound, Stamford Vol. Ctr Heart of Gold Soc. award, Herbert Hoover Humaniarian award, The Boys and Girl Club of Am., 1994, Recipirnt of The Nat. Ethnic Coalition Org. Ellis Island Medal, 1993, Recipient of the SACIA Walter H. Wheeler Jr. Business Leadership award, 1993, Disting Svs. Citation from The Coll. Engring. at U. Wis., Recipient of The Nat. Conf. of Christian and Jews Nat. Human Rels. award, 1990, Recipient of The Outward Bound Corp. Leadership award, 1990, The SACIA Excalibur Leadership award, 1990, Regional Plan Assn. Leadership award, 1990. Mem. Southwestern Area Commerce and Industry Assn. of Conn. (bd. dirs., past chmn.), The Regional Plan Assn. (mem. bd., past chmn.), mem nat. bd of governors, Boys and Girls Club of Am., mem. bd., of govs. for United Way of Tri State. Office: GE Capital Svcs 260 Long Ridge Rd Stamford CT 06927-1600

WENDT, HANS W(ERNER), life scientist; b. Berlin, July 25, 1923; s. Hans O. and Alice (Creutzburg) W.; m. Martha A. Linger, Dec. 23, 1956 (div. 1979); children: Alexander, Christopher, Sandra; m. Judith A. Hammer, June 25, 1988. MSc, U. Hamburg, Germany, 1949; PhD in Psychopharmacology, U. Marburg, Germany, 1953. Diplomate in psychology. Rsch. asst. U. Marburg, 1949-53; rsch. assoc. Wesleyan U. and Office Naval Rsch., Middletown, Conn., 1952-53; asst. prof., field dir. internat. project U. Mainz, Germany, 1955-59; engrng. psychologist to prin. human factors scientist Link Aviation, Apollo Simulator Systems, Binghamton, N.Y., 1959-61; assoc. to prof. psychology Valparaiso (Ind.) U., 1961-68; prof. psychology Macalester Coll., St. Paul, 1968-93; sr. rsch. fellow Chronobiology Labs. U. Minn., 1980—; prin. investigator A.v. Humboldt Geomedicine Collaboration, 1994—; cons. and reviewer, 1961—; hon. prof. sci. U. Marburg, Germany, 1971—; vis. prof. U. Victoria, B.C., Can., U. Marburg, U. Bochum, U. Bielefeld, U. Goettingen, all Germany, 1966-89. Contbr. articles to profl. jours., chpts. to books. Recipient Disting. Sr. Scientist award, Alexander von Humboldt Found., 1976. Mem. Internat. Soc. Biometeorology, Internat. Soc. Chronobiology, Bioelectromagnetics Soc., Soc. Sci. Exploration, Planetary Soc., others. Home: 2180 Lower Saint Dennis Rd Saint Paul MN 55116-2831

WENDT, LINDA M., educational association administrator; b. Garmisch Partenkirchen, Germany; m. Martin J. Wendt; 1 child, Angelica. BS, Western Mich. U., 1967. Cert. fund raising exec., Va. Tchr. Mich. (Tex.) Pub. Schs., 1968-80; small bus. owner Battle Creek, Mich., 1980-85; supr. Allied Stores, Battle Creek, Mich., 1985-86; pres. Jr. Achievement, Battle Creek, Mich., 1986—; steering com. Ctr. for Workforce Excellence, Battle Creek, 1991—; edn. subcom. Econ. Devel. Forum, Battle Creek, 1991—; v.p. Volunteerism in Action, Battle Creek, 1988-91; chair Oper. GRAD Oversight, Battle Creek, 1995—. Com chair Cereal Fest, Battle Creek, 1986-91; campaign divsn. chair United Arts Coun., Battle Creek, 1990; campaign vol. United Way, Battle Creek, 1986—; bd. dirs. Thornapple Arts Coun., Downtown Battle Creek Assn. U.S.-China Ednl. Inst. fellow, 1995. Mem. AAUW, Rotary (com chair 1993—), Battle Creek C. of C. Avocations: tennis, boating. Office: Jr Achievement S Ctrl Mich Four Riverwalk Ctr Ste B Battle Creek MI 49017

WENDT, LLOYD, writer; b. Spencer, S.D., May 16, 1908; s. Leo L. and Marie (Nylen) W.; m. Helen Sigler, June 16, 1932 (dec. Jan. 1980); 1 child, Bette Joan; m. Martha Toale, 1981. Student, Sioux Falls Coll., 1928-29; S.B., Northwestern U., 1931, MS, 1934. Reporter, later columnist, drama reviewer Sioux Falls (S.D.) Press, 1927-28; publicity dir. S.D. Democratic Central Com., 1928; reporter Daily Argus-Leader, 1929, telegraph editor, 1932-33; also tchr. journalism Sioux Falls Coll.; joined staff Chgo. Tribune, 1934; as reporter, becoming spl. feature writer mag. sect., later editor Grafic mag., Sunday editor, until 1961, asso. Sunday editor, asso. editor, 1975-77; editor Chgo.'s Am. newspaper, 1961-69; pub., editor Chgo. Today, 1969-74, also pres.; lectr. fiction writing Northwestern U., 1946; chmn. fiction div. Medill Sch. Journalism, 1950-53. Free lance writer, 1977—; author: (with Herman Kogan) Lords of the Levee, 1943, Gunners Get Glory, 1944, Bright Tomorrow, 1945, Bet a Million, 1948, Give the Lady What She Wants, 1952, Big Bill of Chicago, 1953, Chicago: A Pictorial History, 1958, Chicago Tribune, the Rise of a Great American Newspaper, 1979, The Wall Street Journal, the Story of Dow Jones and the Nation's Business Newspaper, 1982, Swift Walker, Informal Biography of Gurdon Saltonstall Hubbard, 1986 (non-fiction award Chgo. Found. for Lit. 1986), Dogs: A Historical Journey, 1996. Pres. Soc. Midland Authors, 1947-50. Served to lt. comdr. USNR, 1942-46. Recipient Disting. Svc. award Nat. Soc. Journalists, 1980, award of merit Northwestern U. Alumni Assn., 1953. Home: 2332 Harrier Way Nokomis FL 34275-5339

WENDT, MARILYNN SUZANN, elementary school educator, principal; b. Bay City, Mich., Oct. 6, 1939; d. Clarence Henry and Margaret Viola (Rugenstein) W. AA, Bay City Jr. Coll., 1959; BA, Ctrl. Mich. U., 1962, MA, 1964; EdD, Wayne State U., 1971. Cert. elem. adminstr., Mich. Tchr., teaching prin. Baxman Sch., Bay City, 1959-62; tchr., guidance counselor, dir. elem. edn. Essexville (Mich.)-Hampton Schs., 1962-66; tchr., dir. elem. edn., dir. curriculum rsch. Bloomfield Hills (Mich.) Schs., 1966-78; elem. prin., staff development trainer, learning improvement ctr. supr. Waterford (Mich.) Schs., 1978—; consortium facilitator Mich. Dept. Edn. Exptl. & Demonstration Ctr., Lansing, 1975-76; part time faculty mem. Wayne State U., Detroit, 1972-78. Co-author: Rational Basis for Planning School Accountability, 1976; contbr. articles to profl. jours. Trustee, v.p. Waterford Twp. Libr., 1990-95; trustee St. Mark's Bd. Edn., West Bloomfield, Mich., 1991-95. Recipient Outstanding Educator award U.S. Office of Edn.-Harold Howe II, 1968, Disting. Svc. award Bloomfield Hills Schs., 1980. Mem. ASCD, Nat. Coun. Tchrs. English, Internat. Reading Assn., Mich. Reading Assn. (Celebrate Literacy award 1989, Adminstr. of Yr. 1991), Mich. ASCD (editor newsletter, conf. planner), Oakland County Reading Assn., Oakland County State & Fed. Program Specialists, Delta Kappa Gamma (v.p. 1990-93, Woman of Distinction 1982). Avocations: reading, swimming.

WENDT, RICHARD L., manufacturing executive; b. 1931. From mgr. of frame factory to mgr. ops. Caradco; CEO Jeld-Wen Inc., Klamath Falls, Oreg. Office: Jeld-Wen Inc PO Box 1329 Klamath Falls OR 97601-1017 Office: 3250 Lakeport Blvd Klamath Falls OR 97601-1036*

WENDTLAND, MONA BOHLMANN, dietitian, consultant; b. Schulenburg, Tex., Mar. 30, 1930; d. Willy Frank and Leona A. (Bruns) Bohlmann; m. Charles William Ewing, Mar. 8, 1953 (div. Sept. 1975); children: Charles William Jr., Deborah Susan Ewing Richmond; m. William Wolters Wendtland, Jan. 12, 1991 (dec.). BS in Home Econs., U. Tex., 1952, postgrad., 1952-57. Registered dietitian, Tex. Dietitian sch. lunch program Port Arthur (Tex.) Ind. Sch. Dist., 1952-53; elem. tchr. Portsmouth (Va.) Sch. Dist., 1953-54; dietitian, mgr. lunch room E.M. Scarbrough Dept. Store, Austin, Tex., 1955-57; asst. chief adminstrv. dietitian John Sealy HOsp., Galveston, Tex., 1957-59; chief therapeutic dietitian USPHS Hosp., Galveston, 1959-60, asst. chief dietitian, 1960-62; cons. dietitian Sinton (Tex.) Nursing Home, 1963-65; dietary cons. Deaton Hosp., Galena Park, Tex., 1966-68; dir. food svcs. Nat. Health Enterprises, Houston, 1975-76; dietary cons. to nursing homes and retirement ctrs. Drug Abuse Ctr., Houston, 1976—. Del. Internat. Congress Arts & Comm., 1993. Mem. Am. Dietetic Assn. (registered), Tex. Dietetic Assn., South Tex. Dietetic Assn. (chmn. cons. interest group 1978-79), U. Tex. Home Econs. Assn., Dietitians in Bus. and Industry (nat. rep. to mgmt. practices group 1980-83, treas. Houston chpt. 1980-81, pres. 1981-82, advisor 1983-84), Tex. Gerontol Nutritionists (sec. 1994-95), Tex. Cons. Dietitians in Healthcare Facilities, Tex. Nutrition Coun., Dietary Mgrs. Assn. (advisor Houston dist. 1979-92). Republican. Methodist. Avocations: cooking, gardening, interior decorating, genealogy. Home and Office: PO Box 186 221 N Ave D Shiner TX 77984-0186

WENDZEL, ROBERT LEROY, political science educator; b. May 28, 1938; married; 3 children. BA in Polit. Sci. magna cum laude, Kalamazoo Coll., 1960; PhD in Polit. Sci., U. Fla., 1965. Assoc. prof. polit. sci. U. Maine, Orono, 1977-81, 82-83; prof. internat. affairs U.S. Air War Coll., Maxwell AFB, Ala., 1981-82; asst. dean arts & scis., prof. polit. sci., coord. internat. affairs program U. Maine, 1984-86; prof. internat. politics U.S. Air War Coll., Maxwell AFB, 1986-87, ednl. advisor to the Commandant, 1987—; mem. internat. affairs com., U. Maine, 1970-86, budget adv. com., 1983-86, coord. internat. affairs program, 1984-86. Author: International Relations: A Policymaker Focus, Thai edit., 1989, Relacoes Internacionais, 1985, International Politics: Policymakers and Policymaking, 1981, International Relations: A Policymaker Focus, 1977, 2d edit., 1980; co-author: American's Foreign Policy in a Changing World, 1994, Defending America's Security, 1988, 2d edit., 1990, To Preserve the Republic: The Foreign Policy of the United States, 1985, Games Nations Play, 9th edit., 1996; contbr. articles to profl. jours. Mem. Phi Beta Kappa. Home: 160 Oldfield Dr Montgomery AL 36117-3938 Office: Air War Coll Maxwell AFB AL

WENEGRAT, SAUL S., arts administrator, art educator, consultant; b. Jersey City, Mar. 28, 1933; s. John and Tillie (Freeman) W. BA, Rutgers U., 1960; MPA, Harvard U., 1962; cert., London U., 1975. Dir. art program Port Authority of N.Y. & N.J., N.Y.C., 1962-95; prof. grad. divsn. Fashion Inst. Tech., N.Y.C., 1987-95; v.p. Forums Internat., 1995—; pub. art panelist N.J. State Com. Arts, Trenton, 1985-95, Conn. State Com. Arts, Hartford, 1988, N.Y.C. Cultural Affairs, 1980-88, Met. Transit Authority, N.Y.C., 1994-95. Editor: Art for the Public, 1985. Capt. USAF, 1953-57. Recipient Doris Freedman award Mayor of N.Y.C., 1984, Merit cert. Mcpl. Art Soc., 1980, 85; Carnegie fellow, 1960, Fels fellow, 1960. Mem. Nat. Assn. Corp. Art Adminstrn. (chmn. bd. 1985-95), Harvard Club. Avocations: bridge, walking, museums. Home: 2 Beekman Pl New York NY 10022

WENG, CHUAN, mechanical engineer; b. Guang Zhou, China, July 13, 1963; came to U.S., 1986; B of Engring., Changsha (China) Ry. U., 1983; MSME, Ohio U., 1990. Registered profl. engr., N.C. Asst. engr. Guang Zhou Railway Adminstrn., Guang Zhou, 1983-86; rsch. asst. Ohio U./Forma Sci., Athens, Ohio, 1988-90; project engr. Revco/Lindberg, Asheville, N.C., 1990—. Patentee in field. Mem. NSPE, N.C. Soc. Profl. Engrs. Avocations: biking, hiking, tennis. Home: 3 Dorman Dr Weaverville NC 28787

WENG, JOHN JUYANG, computer science educator, researcher; b. Shanghai, Apr. 15, 1957; came to U.S., 1983; m. Min Guo, 1985; children: Colin S., Rodney D. BS in Computer Sci., Fudan U., Shanghai, 1982; MS in Computer Sci., U. Ill., 1985, PhD in Computer Sci., 1989. Rsch. asst. U. Ill., Urbana, 1984-88; rschr. Computer Rsch. Inst. Montreal, Can., 1989-90; vis. asst. prof. U. Ill., 1990-92; asst. prof. Mich. State U., East Lansing, 1992—; mem. com. Internat. Conf. Computer Vision and Pattern Recognition, 1997, Internat. Conf. Automatic Face and Gesture Recognition, Killington, Vt., 1996, Internat. Symposium on Computer Vision, Coral Gables, Fla., 1995, 12th Internat. Conf. Pattern Recognition, Jerusalem, 1994, Conf. on Computer Vision and Pattern Recognition, 1997, Internat. Conf. on Automatic Face and Gesture Recognition, 1996. Author: (chpt.) Early Visual Learning, 1996; co-author: (chpt.) Handbook of Pattern Recognition and Computer Vision, 1993, Motion and Structures from Image Sequences, 1993, Visual Navigation, 1997. Mem. IEEE (Computer Soc., assoc. editor IEEE Transactions on Image Processing 1994—), Am. Soc. Engring. Edn., Sigma Xi, Phi Beta Delta. Achievements include contributions to understanding and computation of estimation of motion and structure from image sequences; co-inventor of Cresceptron, an experimental system for recognizing and segmenting objects from natural images; introducer of the concept of comprehensive visual learning for intelligent sensor-based machines; inventor of SHOSLIF, a general framework for visual learning by computers. Office: Mich State Univ 3115 Engring Bldg East Lansing MI 48824

WENGER, LARRY BRUCE, law librarian, law educator; b. Everett, Wash., Dec. 21, 1941; s. Lester Edwin Wenger and Selma Marie (Norberg) W. Saterstrom; m. Marilyn Diane Watt, June 26, 1965; children: Bruce Daniel, Kathleen Marie. BA, U. Wash., 1964, JD, 1967; MLS, Simmons Coll., 1969. Reference libr. Sch. Law Harvard U., Cambridge, Mass., 1967-69; asst. law libr. SUNY, Buffalo, 1969-71, law libr., assoc. prof. law, 1971-76; law libr., prof. law U. Va., Charlottesville, 1976—; cons. to law librs.; bd. dirs. Nat. Ctr. for Preservation Law. Mem. Am. Assn. Law Librs., Internat. Assn. Law Librs. (pres.), Bibliog. Soc., Bibliog. Soc. Am. Home: 2630 Meriwether Dr Charlottesville VA 22901-9513 Office: U Va Law Libr N Grounds Charlottesville VA 22901

WENGER, LUKE HUBER, educational association executive, editor; b. Ephrata, Pa., Oct. 23, 1939; s. Luke Martin and Elva B. (Huber) W. B.A., Eastern Mennonite Coll., Harrisonburg, Va., 1962; postgrad., U. Gottingen, W.Ger., 1962-63, U. Munich, W.Ger., 1967-78; Ph.D., Harvard U., 1973. Editor, asst. exec. dir. Medieval Acad. Am., Cambridge, Mass., 1973-81, exec. dir., 1981—. Editor: Speculum: A Jour. of Medieval Studies, 1981—. Fulbright fellow, 1962-63; Woodrow Wilson fellow, 1963-64; German Acad. Exchange fellow, 1967-68. Office: Medieval Academy of America 1430 Massachusetts Ave Cambridge MA 02138-3810

WENGER, VICKI, interior designer; b. Indpls., Aug. 30, 1928. Ed., U. Nebr., Internat. Inst. Interior Design, Parsons in Paris. Pres. Vicki Wenger Interiors, Bethesda, Md., 1963-71, Washington, 1982-95; pres. Beautiful Spaces Inc., Washington, 1982-95; chief designer Creative Design, Capitol Heights, Md., 1969-84; lectr. Nat. Assn. Home Builders, 1983-88; mem. programs com. D.C. Assn. Home Builders, 1983-88. Author-host: (patented TV interior design show) Beautiful Spaces 1984; producer, host (cable TV show) Design Edition, 1988—. Designer Gourmet Gala, March of Dimes, Washington, 1986-88; decorator showhouse Nat. Symphony Orch., Washington, 1983-94, 96, 97, chmn. women's com., 1991-92; decorator showhouse Am. Cancer Soc., Washington, 1983, Alexandria Comty. YWCA, 1990. Mem. Am. Soc. Interior Designers (profl., nat. bd. dirs. 1973-75, nat. examining com. 1977-78, pres. Md. chpt. 1976, bd. dirs. Washington Metro chpt. 1989-91, pres. 1995-96, past pres. 1996-97, mem. pres.'s barrier free com. 1980), Nat. Trust Hist. Preservation, Smithsonian Instn. (sponsor), Nat. Press Club. Democrat. Presbyterian.

WENGERT, NORMAN IRVING, political science educator; b. Milw., Nov. 7, 1916; s. Eugene F. and Lydia (Semmann) W.; m. Janet Mueller, Oct. 9, 1940; children: Eugene Mark, Christine Ann, Timothy John. B.A., U. Wis., 1938, J.D., 1942, Ph.D., 1947; M.A., Fletcher Sch., 1939. With TVA, 1941-48; faculty City Coll. N.Y., 1948-51; mem. program staff Office Sec. Dept. Interior, 1951-52; prof., chmn. social sci. dept. N.D. State U., Fargo, 1952-56; research asso. Resources for Future, Inc., 1956; prof. pub. adminstrn. U. Md., 1956-59; dep. dir. Nat. Outdoor Recreation Resources Rev. Com., 1959-60; prof., chmn. dept. polit. sci. Wayne State U., Detroit, 1960-68; vis. prof. pub. adminstrn. Pa. State U., 1968-69; prof. polit. sci. Colo. State U., Ft. Collins, 1969-87, prof. emeritus; mem. policy analysis staff Office of Chief, U.S. Forest Service, 1978-79; vis. rsch. prof. U.S. Army Engr. Inst. Water resources, 1969-70; Royer lectr. U. Calif., Berkeley, 1975; lectr. U. Sarajevo, Yugoslavia, summer 1978, NATO Adv. Study Inst., Sicily, summer 1981; lectr. U. Linkoping, Sweden, summer, 1984; spl. adviser Govt. of India on food, agr., 1959; cons. U.S. Army Corps Engrs., 1968, Thorne Ecol. Inst., 1972-75, FAA, 1963, Atlantic Richfield Oil Corp., 1973-74, Nat. Water Quality Commn., 1974—, Office Water Resources and Tech., USDI, 1973-75, and states Colo., Md., Ga., Mich., also Western Interstate Nuclear Bd.; summer fellow Fonds für Umweltstudien, Bonn, Germany, 1973; cons. No. Colo. Water Conservancy Dist., 1988—; mem. com. NAS/NRC. 1990. Author: Valley of Tomorrow: TVA and Agriculture, 1952, Natural Resources and the Political Struggle, 1955, Administration of Natural Resources, 1961, (with George M. Walker, Jr.) Urban Water Policies and Decision Making in Detroit Metro Region, 1970, Urban-Metropolitan Institutions for Water Planning, Development and Management, 1972, Impact on the Human Environment of Proposed Oil Shale Development in Garfield County, 1974, Property Rights in Land: A Comparative Exploration of German and American Concepts and Problems, 1974, Public Participation in Water Resources Development, 1974, The Political Allocation of Burdens and Benefits: Externalities and Due Process in Environmental Protection, 1976, Regional Factors in Siting and Planning Energy Facilities in the Eleven Western States, 1976, The Purposes of the National Forests, 1979; also chpts. in other books.; editor: (with others) Institutions for Urban-Metropolitan Water Management, 1972, Natural Resources Jour. issue, 1979; co-editor: (with others) The Energy Crisis: Reality or Myth, 1973; contbg. author: Planning the Use and Management of Land, 1979, Unified River Basin Management, 1981, Encyclopedia of Policy Studies, 1983, Operation of Complex Water Systems, 1983. Served as ensign USNR, 1944-45. Mem. Western Polit. Sci. Assn., Am. Soc. Pub. Adminstrn., State Bar Wis. (emeritus), Forest Hist. Soc., Soil Conservation Soc. Am. (Nat. Honor award 1982), Order of Coif, Sigma Xi, Phi Kappa Phi.

WENGLOWSKI, GARY MARTIN, economist; b. Rochester, N.Y., Sept. 2, 1942; s. Henry Bernard and Isabelle (Franc) W.; m. Joyce Richards, Oct. 3, 1964; children: Gary Martin, Catherine Jean. B.S. in Econs., U. Pa., 1964, M.A. (NDEA fellow), 1965, Ph.D. in Econs. (NDEA fellow), 1967. With Goldman Sachs & Co., N.Y.C., 1967—, v.p., economist, 1972-78, ptnr., dir. econ. research, 1978-86, ltd. ptnr., 1986—; adj. prof. NYU, Pace U.; tech. cons. The Bus. Coun., 1982-85; chmn. vis. com. econ. dept. U. Pa., 1985—. Author: Industry Profit Forecasting, 1972, Industry Profit Forecasting—Progress Report, 1975. Trustee CARE Found., 1991—, Haystack Mountain Sch., 1993—. Named Best Economist on Wall St., Ann. Instnl. Investor Mag. Polls, 1976-86. Fellow Nat. Assn. Bus. Economists; mem. Am. Econ. Assn., Deer Isle Yacht Club (vice commodore 1993-94, commodore 1994—). Office: Goldman Sachs & Co 85 Broad St Fl 2 New York NY 10004-2434

WENIG, MARY MOERS, law educator; b. N.Y.C.; d. Robert and Celia Lewis (Kauffman) Moers; m. Jerome Wenig, Dec. 19, 1946; children: Margaret Moers Wenig Rubenstein, Michael M. Wenig. BA, Vassar Coll., 1946; JD, Columbia U., 1951. Bar: N.Y. 1952, U.S. Ct. Appeals (2d cir.) 1954, U.S. Dist. Ct. (so. dist.) N.Y. 1956, Conn. 1977. Assoc. Cahill, Gordon, Reindel & Ohl, N.Y.C., 1951-57; assoc. Greenbaum, Wolff & Ernst, N.Y.C., 1957-60, Skadden, Arps, Slate, Meagher & Flom, N.Y.C., 1960-71; asst. prof. sch. law St. John's U., N.Y.C., 1971-75, assoc. prof. sch. law, 1975-78; rsch. affiliate Yale Law Sch., New Haven, 1978-79; prof. sch. law U. Bridgeport, Conn., 1978-82, Charles A. Dana prof. law, 1982-92; prof. sch. law Quinnipiac Coll., Bridgeport, 1992-95, Hamden, 1995—; cons. The Merrill Anderson Co., Stratford, Conn., 1982—, Conn. Permanent Commn. on Status of Women, 1978-79; vis. prof. sch. law Pace U., White Plains, N.Y., 1979; commr. State of Conn. Permanent Commn. on Status of Women, 1985-91; mem. Conn. Gen. Assembly's Adv. Commn. to Study the Uniform Marital Property's Act., 1985-86; lectr. in field; bd. dirs. Tax Analysts. Author: Tax Management Portfolio on Disclaimer, 1992; editor: PLI Tax Handbooks, 1978-86; co-editor: Bittker, Fundamentals of Federal Income Taxation, student edit., 1983; co-author: (with Douthwaite) Unmarried Couples and the Law, 1979; contbr. tax, estate planning, trust and estates and marital property articles to profl. jours.; editorial adv. bd. Estate Planning for the Elderly & Disabled, 1987-90, Community Property Jour., 1986-88, Estate Planning, 1975—, Estates, Gifts & Trusts Jour., 1976—; assoc. editor: Encyclopedia of Marriage and the Family, 1996. Mem. probate com. Conn. Law Revision Commn., 1985—, com. to study the probate system Conn. Probate Assembly, 1988-91, task force on the legal rights of women in marriage NOW, 1987-91; 2nd cir. rep. Fedn. of Women Lawyers Jud. Screening Panel, 1979; bd. govs. Radcliffe Club N.Y., 1975-77; mem. 1st selectman's com. on taxation relief for the elderly Town of Westport, 1974-75; pres. bd. dirs. Conn. Women's Ednl. and Legal Fund, Inc., 1975-79, bd. dirs., 1973-79. Named Salute to Women honoree Outstanding Women of Conn., Greater Bridgeport YWCA, 1990, Women in Leadership honoree New Haven YWCA, 1979, honoree U. Bridgeport Sch. Law Women's Law Assn., 1990; Harlan Fiske Stone scholar Columbia U. Sch. Law, 1949; recipient Award for Equality United Nations Assn.-USA of Conn., 1987; Summer Stipend grantee NEH, 1984, rsch. grantee Conn. Bar Found., 1980. Fellow Am. Coll. Trust & Estate Counsel (bd. regents 1985-91); mem. ABA (advisor to NCCUSL 1980-84, sect. coun. mem. 1970-72), Internat. Acad. Estates & Trust Law (academician, exec. coun. mem. 1992-94), Conn. Bar Assn. (sects.' exec. coun., Disting. Svc. commendation 1977), Assn. Am. Law Schs., Assn. of Bar of City of N.Y., N.Y. State Bar Assn., Am. Law Inst. (hon.), Am. Coll. Tax Counsel (hon.). Democrat. Jewish. Home: 5 Lamplight Ln Westport CT 06880-6106 Office: Quinnipiac Coll School of Law 275 Mt Carmel Ave New Haven CT 06518-1961

WENK, EDWARD, JR., civil engineer, policy analyst, educator, writer; b. Balt., Jan. 24, 1920; s. Edward and Lillie (Heller) W.; m. Carolyn Frances Lyford, Dec. 27, 1941; children: Lawrence Shelley, Robin Edward Alexander, Terry Allan. BE, Johns Hopkins U., 1940, DEng, 1950; MSc, Harvard U., 1947; DSc (hon.), U. R.I., 1968; LHD (hon.), Johns Hopkins U., 1989. Registered profl. engr. Head structures div. USN David Taylor Model Basin, Washington, 1942-56; chmn. dept. engring. mechanics S.W. Research Inst., San Antonio, 1956-59; sr. specialist sci. and tech. Legis. Reference Service, Library of Congress, Washington, 1959-61; chief sci. policy research div. Legis. Reference Service, Library of Congress, 1964-66; tech. asst. to U.S. President's sci. adviser and exec. sec. Fed. Council for Sci. and Tech., White House, Washington, 1961-64; exec. sec. Nat. Council on Marine Resources and Engring. Devel., Exec. Office of Pres., Washington, 1966-70; prof. engring. and pub. affairs U. Wash., Seattle, 1970-83, prof. emeritus, 1983—; dir. program in social mgmt. tech. U. Wash., 1973-79; tech. advisor to gov. State of Wash., 1993-96; lectr. numerous univs.; cons. in pub. policy for environ. and tech. affairs, risk assessments, human and orgnl. error, futures, ocean engring., decision theory; Nat. Adv. Com. on Oceans and Atmosphere, 1972-73; vice chmn. U.S. Congress Tech. Assessment Adv. Coun., 1973-79; adviser Congress, GAO, NSF, EPA, NOAA, White House, UN Secretariat, Wash. State, Alaska, U.K., Australia, Sweden, The Philippines, Alaska Oil Spill Commn., 1989, Wash. State Marine Oversight Bd., 1992, pub. interest groups, 1997, Dept. Transportation; vis. scholar Woodrow Wilson Internat. Ctr. for Scholars, 1970-72, Harvard U., 1976, Woods Hole Oceanographic Instn., 1976, U. Sussex, 1977. Author: The Politics of the Ocean, 1972, Margins for Survival, 1979, Tradeoffs-Imperatives of Choice in a High-Tech World, 1986, Making Waves--Engineering, Politics and the Social Management of Technology, 1995; editor: Engring. Mechs. Jour., 1958-60, Exptl. Mechs. Jour., 1954-56; mem. editl. bd. Tech. Forecasting, Tech. in Soc.; contbr. articles to profl. jours.; designer Aluminaut submarine, 1959; author of concept of tech. assessment, 1964. Bd. dirs. Human Interaction Rsch. Inst., 1980-90, Smithsonian Sci. Info. Exch., 1977-82, URS Corp., 1973-88; mem. Interfaith Alliance. Ensign USNR, 1944-45. Recipient Navy Meritorious Civilian Svc. award, 1946, authors prize Gov. Wash., 1974, ann. prize Edn. Press Assn., 1997; named Disting. Alumnus Johns Hopkins U., 1979, Tchr. of Yr., Wash. State Engrs., 1980, Tchr. of Yr., Students in Pub. Adminstrn., 1986, Disting. Alumnus, Balt. Poly. Inst., 1991; Ford Found. grantee, 1970; Rockefeller Found. Belagio fellow, 1976, 90; 1st Stuckenburg lectr. Wash. U., 1988; Regents lectr. U. Calif., Berkeley, 1989. Fellow ASME (exec.), AAAS; mem. ASCE, NSPE, Soc. Exptl. Stress Analysis (past pres. and William M. Murray lectr.), Internat. Assn. Impact Assessment (pres. 1981-82), NAE (chmn. com. on pub. policy 1970-75), Nat. Acad. Pub. Adminstrn., Am. Soc. for Pub. Adminstrn. (chmn. com. on sci. and tech. in govt. 1974-78), Assembly Engring. and Marine Bd. NRC, Nat. Oceanography Assn. (v.p. pub. affairs 1979-72), Cousteau Soc. (chmn. adv. bd.), USA Club of Rome (bd. dirs.), Explorers Club, Sigma Xi (nat. lectr.), Tau Beta Pi, Chi Epsilon. Club: Cosmos (Washington). Home: 111 Lake Ave W #302 Kirkland WA 98033-6155 *Each of us has the opportunity, indeed responsibility, to contribute to the human experience and to enrich the lives of future generations. In a world of change, cultural diversity and uncertainty, we must be ourselves and not merely slaves of conventional thought. We must act on the basis of what we believe to be right rather than only from the desire to be loved.*

WENNER, CHARLES RODERICK, lawyer; b. New Haven, Jan. 10, 1947; s. Charles Bellew and Joan Rhoda (Morrison) W. BS, Coll. Charleston, 1969; JD, U. Conn., 1973. Bar: Conn. 1974, D.C. 1977. Law clk. Conn. Superior Ct., Hartford, 1973-74; staff atty. SEC, Washington, 1974-76, spl. counsel to chmn., 1976-77; assoc. Fulbright & Jaworski, Washington, 1977-81, ptnr., 1981—; lectr. law Sch. Law U. Conn., 1973-74. Trustee Calvary United Meth. Ch., Arlington, Va., 1993-95; counselor Gospel Mission of Washington, 1991—; bd. dirs. Operation Friendship Internat., Inc., Washington, 1993—. Recipient Am. Hist. award DAR, Charleston, 1969. Mem. ABA, D.C. Bar Assn. Methodist. Avocations: running. Home: 1101 S Arlington Ridge Rd Arlington VA 22202-1951 Office: Fulbright & Jaworski 801 Pennsylvania Ave NW Washington DC 20004-2615

WENNER, GENE CHARLES, arts management executive; b. Catasauqua, Pa., Dec. 21, 1931; s. Clinton G. and Bertha (Taggert) W.; m. Carole Brunner, Aug. 15, 1953; children: Robert Larren, Laurel E. Wenner Carsell. B.S. in Music, West Chester (Pa.) State Coll., 1953; M.Ed. in Music, Pa. State U., 1954. Tchr. music Phila. pub. schs., 1945-55, 56-60; assoc. prof. Kutztown (Pa.) State Coll., 1960-66, dir. coll. choir, 1960-66; fine arts adv. Pa. Dept. Edn., 1966-69, U.S. Office Edn., 1969-71; asst. dir. arts in edn. program John D. Rockefeller 3d Fund, 1971-78; arts edn. coordinator Office Commr., U.S. Office Edn., 1978-79; pres. Am. Music Conf., Wilmette, Ill., 1979-81; v.p. for programs Nat. Found. Advancement in Arts, Miami, Fla., 1983-87; pres. Arts and Edn. Cons., Inc., Reston, Va., 1987-91; sr. cons. Bus. & Industry for Arts Edn., 1990-91; exec. dir. Charlotte (N.C.) Community Sch. for the Arts, 1991-96; pres. Arts & Edn. Cons., Inc., Charlotte, 1996—; fund raising cons. Nat. Pub. Radio, Funding Ctr., S.C. Gov. Sch.; sr. cons. Spl. Kids in Pub., 1991; master tchr. Inst. Arts; guest lectr. U. N.C., U. Tex., Loyola U.; mus. dir. Allentown (Pa.) Mcpl. Opera, 1962-63, Allentown Civic Little Theatre, 1964, Little Theatre Alexandria, Va., 1971; dir. Hershey (Pa.) Little Theatre, 1967-68, Hershey Community Chorus, 1967-69. Composer: I'll Never Forget You, 1968, Chorale of Dedication, 1974, Turn Thou to Me, 1975, Are You Nobody, Too?, 1976, Great Things God Hath Done, 1986, In My Father's House, 1986; original music and script Adventures in the Arts, Hershey, 1968; also original TV music, I Am the Way, 1985, When You Remember, 1985; author papers, reports in field. Served with AUS, 1955-56. Named Best Mus. Dir. Little Theatre Alexandria. Mem. Music Educators Nat. Conf., Nat. Guild of Community Schs. of the Arts. Club: Masons. Home and Office: 4100 B Bannockburn Pl Charlotte NC 28211-4532

WENNER, HERBERT ALLAN, pediatrician; b. Drums, Pa., Nov. 14, 1912; s. Herbert C. and Verna (Walp) W.; m. Ruth I. Berger, June 27, 1942; children—Peter W., James M., Susan T., Thomas H. B.S., Bucknell U., 1933; M.D., U. Rochester, 1939. Diplomate: Am. Bd. Microbiology, Am. Bd. Pediatrics. Intern in pathology Sch. Medicine, U. Colo., Denver, 1939-40; intern in pediatrics Yale Sch. Medicine, 1940-41, asst. resident and fellow in pediatrics, 1941-43, instr. preventive medicine, 1944-46; NRC fellow Yale U.-Johns Hopkins U., 1943-44; asst. prof. pediatrics and bacteriology Sch. Medicine, U. Kans., Kansas City, 1946-49; asso. prof. Sch. Medicine, U. Kans., 1949-51, research prof. pediatrics, 1951-69, adj. prof., 1975—; Joyce C. Hall Disting. prof. pediatrics U. Mo. Sch. Med., Kansas City, 1969-83; emeritus adj. prof. U. Mo. Sch. Med. (Sch. Dentistry), 1970—; formerly cons. epidemiology Kans. Bd. Health, Mo. Bd. Health. Asso. editor: Am. Jour. Epidemiology, 1967-79; mem. editorial bd.: Intervirology, 1972-79; past mem. editorial adv. bd.: Archives of Virology, 1975-79; contbr. articles to med. books and jours. NIH Research Career awardee, 1962. Fellow AAAS, Am. Public Health Assn., Am. Coll. Epidemiology, Am. Acad. Pediatrics; mem. Soc. Pediatric Research, Am. Pediatric Soc., Soc. Exptl. Biology and Medicine, Biometrics Soc., Mo. Med. Assn., AMA, Royal Soc. Health, AAUP, N.Y. Acad. Scis., Am. Epidemiology Soc., Infectious Disease Soc. Am. Episcopalian. Home: 9711 Johnson Dr Shawnee Mission KS 66203-3147 *Good parents, a devoted family, superb teachers and hard work have contributed to my career, and the rewards therein.*

WENNER, JANN SIMON, editor, publisher; b. N.Y.C., Jan. 7, 1946; s. Edward and Ruth N. (Simmons) W.; m. Jane Ellen Schindelhiem, July 1, 1968; children: Alexander Jann, Theodore Simon, Edward Augustus. Student, U. Calif.-Berkeley, 1964-66. Editor, pub. Rolling Stone mag., N.Y.C., 1967—, Record, N.Y.C., 1981-86, Look mag., N.Y.C., 1979, Men's Jour., 1992—; editor in chief Outside Mag., San Francisco, 1977-78, US Mag., N.Y.C., 1985—, Men's Jour., 1992—; exec. v.p. Rock & Roll Hall of Fame. Author: Lennon Remembers, 1971, Garcia, 1972. Bd. dirs. Robinhood Found. Recipient Disting. Achievement award U. So. Calif. Sch. Journalism and Alumni Assn., 1976, Nat. Mag. award, 1970, 77, 86, 87, 88, 89. Mem. Am. Soc. Mag. Editors. Office: Rolling Stone Wenner Media Inc 1290 Avenue Of The Americas New York NY 10104-0199*

WENNERSTROM, ARTHUR JOHN, aeronautical engineer; b. N.Y.C., Jan. 11, 1935; s. Albert Eugene and Adele (Trebus) W.; m. Bonita Gay Westenberg, Sept. 6, 1969 (div. Jan. 1989); children: Bjorn Erik, Erika Lindsay; m. Vicki Lynn Merrick, Feb. 17, 1990. BS in Mech. Engring., Duke U., 1956; MS in Aero. Engring., MIT, 1958; DSc of Tech., Swiss Fedn. Inst. Tech., Zurich, 1965. Sr. engr. Aircraft Armaments, Inc., Cockeysville, Md., 1958-59; rsch. engr. Sulzer Bros., Ltd., Winterthur, Switzerland, 1960-62; project engr. No. Rsch. and Engring. Corp., Cambridge, Mass., 1965-67; rsch. leader Air Force Aerospace Rsch. Lab., Dayton, Ohio, 1967-75, Air Force Aero Propulsion Lab., Dayton, 1975-91; dir. NATO Adv. Group for Aerospace R & D, Paris, 1991-94; engring. cons. Hillsborough, N.C., 1994-95, Hot Springs Village, Ark., 1995—; mem. tech. adv. com., von Karman Inst. for Fluid Dynamics, Rhode-St-Genese, Belgium, 1988-94, bd. dirs.; lectr. in field. Contbr. articles to profl. jours. 1st lt., USAF, 1962-65. Recipient Cliff Garrett Turbo Machinery award Soc. Automotive Engrs., 1986; named Fed. Profl. Employee of Yr. Dayton C. of C., 1975; fellow Air Force Wright Aeronautical Labs., 1987. Fellow AIAA (assoc. editor 1980-82, Air Breathing Propulsion award 1979), ASME (chmn. turbomachinery com. gas turbine divsn. 1973-75, mem. exec. com. 1977-82, chmn. 1980-81, program chmn. internat. gas turbine conf. 1976, Beijing internat. gas turbine symposium 1985, mem. nat. nominating com. 1985-87, mem. TOPC bd. on rsch. 1985-88, mem.-at-large energy conversion group 1986-88, mem. bd. comm. 1989-91, editor Jour. Engring. for Gas Turbines and Power 1983-88, chmn. bd. editors 1989-91, founder, editor Jour. Turbomachinery 1986-88, mem. internat. adv. com. 1995-96, R. Tom Sawyer award 1993). Achievements include introduction of wide-chord integrally-bladed fan, introduction of swept blading into mil. aircraft turbine engines; 5 patents in field. Home and Office: 5 Sosegado Ln Hot Springs Village AR 71909-7744

WENRICH, JOHN WILLIAM, college president; b. York, Pa., June 8, 1937; s. Ralph Chester and Helen Louise (McCollam) W.; m. Linda Larsen, June 23, 1961 (dec. Sept. 1966); 1 child, Thomas Allen; m. Martha Gail Lofberg, Sept. 1, 1967; 1 child, Margaret Ann. A.B., Princeton U., 1959; M.A., U. Mich., 1961, Ph.D., 1968. Fgn. service officer Dept. State, Washington, 1962-65; rep. Internat. Devel. Found., N.Y.C., 1965-66; project dir. U. Mich., Ann Arbor, 1966-69; asst. to pres. Coll. San Mateo, Calif., 1969-71; v.p. Ferris State U., Big Rapids, Mich., 1971-75, pres., 1984-88; pres. Canada Coll., Redwood City, Calif., 1975-79, Santa Ana Coll., Calif., 1979-84; chancellor San Diego Community Coll. Dist., 1988-90, Dallas County Community Coll., 1990—. Co-author: Leadership in Administration of Technical and Vocational Education, 1974, Administration of Vocational Education. Recipient Meritorious Service medal Dept. State, 1966; Hinsdale scholar Sch. Edn. U. Mich., 1968. Avocations: bridge; tennis; travel. Home: 1520 Wyndmere Dr De Soto TX 75115-7808 Office: 701 Elm St Dallas TX 75202-3201

WENSINGER, ARTHUR STEVENS, language and literature educator, author; b. Grosse Pointe, Mich., Mar. 9, 1926; s. Carl Franklin and Suzanne (Stevens) W. Grad., Phillips Acad. Andover, 1944; BA, Dartmouth Coll., 1948; MA, U. Mich., 1951; postgrad., U. Munich, 1948, 50-51, U. Innsbruck, 1953-54; PhD, U. Mich., 1958. Instr., asst. prof., assoc. prof. Wesleyan U., Middletown, Conn., 1955-68, prof. German and humanities, 1968-93, Marcus Taft prof. German and humanities, 1977-93, prof. emeritus, 1994—, chmn. dept. German lang. and lit., 1971-93, also sr. tutor Coll. Letters; pres. Friends of Davison Art Ctr.; mem. selection com. German Acad. Exch. Svc., 1980-92. Author: Hogarth on High Life, 1970, Plays by Arthur Schnitzler, 1982-83, 95; translator, editor: The Theater of the Bauhaus, 1961, rev. edit., 1996, The Letters and Journals of Paula Modersohn-Becker, 1983, 2d edit., 1990; translator, editor: Querelle: The Film Book, 1983; translator: Franz Kafka: Pictures of a Life, 1984, The Sons, 1989, Marlene Dietrich: Portraits, 1984, Shabbat (Peter Stefan Jungk), 1985, (reprinted 1994), Hanna Shygulla and R.W. Fassbinder, 1986, Kaethe Kollwitz: The Work in Color, 1988, Niklas Frank, In the Shadow of the Reich, 1991, selected plays Arthur Schnitzler; co-translator: Günter Grass, Two States-One Nation?, 1990; contbr. to R.W. Fassbinder, The Anarchy of the Imagination, 1992; editor: Stone Island (Peter S. Boynton), 1973; co-editor: Hesse's Siddhartha, 1962; continuing editor: Correspondence of Norman Douglas, 1868-1952; contbr. to Columbia U. Database CD-ROM for quotations, aphorisms, 1995—; contbr. articles to profl. jours.; translator in field. Wesleyan Ctr. for Humanities fellow, 1974, Reynolds fellow, 1950-51, Fulbright fellow, 1954-55, Danforth fellow, 1959, Ford Found. fellow, 1970-71; Inter Nations grantee, 1978, 82, NEH rsch. grantee, 1993. Mem.

MLA, Am. Assn. Tchrs. German, Heinrich von Kleist Gesellschaft, Internat. Brecht Soc., Kafka Soc. Am., Auden Soc., Soc. Preservation New Eng. Antiquities, Conn. Acad. Arts and Scis., Yale Libr. Assocs., Haddam, Conn. Land Trust, Phi Beta Kappa, Phi Kappa Phi, Delta Tau Delta. Home: Candlewood Farm 95 Jacoby Rd Higganum CT 06441-4225 Office: Wesleyan U Fisk Hall Middletown CT 06459-6082

WENSITS, JAMES EMRICH, newspaper editor; b. South Bend, Ind., Oct. 8, 1944; s. John Andrew and Melva Mae (Betz) W.; m. Wendy Anne Reygaert, June 12, 1965; children: Cheryl Wensits Lightfoot, John, Kristin Wensits Hough, Amy; m. Catherine Marie Palmer Pope, Nov. 27, 1987 (dec. Sept. 1996); 1 stepchild, Christina Pope. BA in Journalism, Purdue U., 1966. Reporter South Bend Tribune, 1966-92, assoc. editor, 1992—. Office: South Bend Tribune 225 W Colfax Ave South Bend IN 46626-1000

WENSTROM, FRANK AUGUSTUS, state senator, city and county official; b. Dover, N.D., July 27, 1903; s. James August and Anna Petra (Kringstad) W.; student public schs., Carrington, N.D.; LLD (hon.), U. N.D., 1990. m. Mary Esther Pickett, June 10, 1938. In oil bus., Carrington, 1932-38, Williston, N.D., 1938-45; mgr. Williston C. of C., 1945-51; pub. rels. officer 1st Nat. Bank, Williston, 1951-53, mng. officer real estate mortgage dept., 1953-60; exec. officer Northwestern Fed. Savs. and Loan Assn. Williston, 1964-68; spl. cons. Am. State Bank Williston, 1968-73; mem. N.D. Senate, 1957-60, 67—, pres. pro tem, 1973-74; lt. gov. State of N.D., 1963-64; dir., sec. Williston Cmty. Hotel Co., 1950—; chmn. subscriber's com. N.W. dist. N.D. Blue Cross-Blue Shield, 1972—. Mem. Williston Public Housing Authority, 1951—, Williams County Park Bd., 1951—, N.D. Yellowstone-Ft. Union Commn., 1957-64, Legis. Rsch. Coun., 1957-60, Legis. Coun., 1969-70; del. N.D. 2d Constl. Conv., 1970, pres., 1971-72; Williams County chmn. U.S. Savs. Bonds Com., 1958-69; creator Frank A. Wenstrom Libr. for Student Rsch., Grank Forks, N.D., 1984; co-chair N.D. Constitution subcom. for developing and displaying hist. papers pertaining to U.S. constitution; mem. Constitutional Celebration com., 1985; pres. N.D. 2d Constitutional Conv., 1971-72; co-chair archives search com. N.D. Const. Conv., 1971-72; bd. dirs. N.D. Easter Seals Soc., 1960-75, state pres., 1970-71; bd. advisors Salvation Army, 1960-75; bd. dirs. Univ. Found., U. N.D., Williston Center, 1965—; mem. joint legis. com. Nat. Assn. Ret. Tchrs.-Am. Assn. Ret. Persons, 1975—, chmn., 1979-80. Recipient Liberty Bell award N.D. Bar Assn., 1977, Disting. Svc. award Bismarck Jr. Coll., 1981; award Nature Conservancy, 1982; Svc. award Greater N.D. Assn., 1983, C.P. Lura award Disting. Service to Edn. Minot State Coll., 1986, Award of Excellence Com. of Gov.'s Council on Human Resources, 1986. Mem. Upper Missouri Purebred Cattle Breeders Assn. (sec.-treas. 1947-62), N.D. Wildlife Fedn. (state pres. 1947-48), Greater N.D. Assn. (dir. 1955-56, mem. Roosevelt Nat. Meml. Park com. 1957-63), U.S. Savs. and Loan League (legis. com. 1965-67). Republican. Congregationalist. Clubs: Rotary, Elks, Masons (hon. grand master), Shriners, Order Eastern Star. Office: PO Box 187 Williston ND 58802-0187

WENSTRUP, H. DANIEL, chemical company executive; b. Cin., Sept. 27, 1934; s. Carl D. and Lucille (Cahill) W.; m. Eileen O'Brien, Nov. 24, 1956; children: Gary, Julie, Patrick, Kevin, Katy, Greg. BSBA, Xavier U., 1956. Sales rep. Chemcentral Corp., Cin., 1958-66; sales mgr. Chemcentral Corp., Detroit, 1966-72, gen. mgr., 1972-75, v.p. regional mgr., 1975-82; v.p. dir. mktg. Chemcentral Corp., Chgo., 1982-86, pres., 1986—, pres., chief exec. officer, 1988—, bd. dirs.; bd. dirs. Prove Quim S.A. de C.V. Mem., supporter Mus. Sci. Industry, Chgo., 1991—, Ravinia Chgo. Symphony, 1991—, adv. com. Gov. Edgar. 1st lt. U.S. Army, 1956-58. Mem. Chem. Mfrs. Assn. (dir. 1990-92), Chem. Industry Coun. Ill. (dir. 1989-93, pres., chmn.), Nat. Paint & Coatings Assn., Nat. Petroleum Refiners Assn., Ill. Mfrs. Assn., Ill. C. of C., Medinah Country Club, Oak Brook Tennis Club, Am. Cancer Soc., NACD Edn. Found. (trustee). Republican. Roman Catholic. Avocations: golf, tennis, jogging, reading, theatre. Office: Chemcentral Corp 7050 W 71st St Bedford Park IL 60638-5902

WENTSLER, GERTRUDE JOSEPHINE, secondary school educator; b. Campbell, Ohio, July 16, 1943; d. John Tofil and Irene S. (Glass) Wallace; m. Lawrence L. Murray, Dec. 29, 1967 (div. 1978); 1 child, Carolyn Murray Joyce; m. Wm. Scott Wentsler, Mar. 4, 1989. BA, Miami U., Oxford, Ohio, 1964; MEd, Xavier U., Cin., 1967. Cert. secondary tchr., Ohio. Tchr. history Cin. Pub. Schs., 1964-71, Northwest Sch. Dist., Cin., 1974—. Dist. dir. College Hill Forum, Cin., 1972, mem. edn. com., 1970-73. Jennings scholar, 1986-87; recipient Journalism awards, 1987-89, Outstanding Tchr. award U. Chgo., 1989, Tchr. award Friends of Wm. Howard Taft Birthplace, 1992. Mem. NOW, N.W. Tchrs. Assn. (bldg. rep. 1975-77), Nat. Coun. Social Studies, Cin. Fedn. Tchrs. (membership chair 1968, bldg. rep. 1966-69). Avocations: needlework, reading, travel. Home: 2075 Connecticut Ave Cincinnati OH 45224-2368

WENTWORTH, ANDREW STOWELL, lawyer; b. Boston, Mar. 3, 1938; s. Walter Adams and Helen (Goodrich) W.; m. Natalie Cobb, Mar. 3, 1968 (div.); children: Michelle, Nicole; m. Mary Ellen O'Brien, May 30, 1992. BA, Mich. State U., 1960; LLB, JD, Ohio State U., 1966. Bar: Ohio 1967, U.S. Dist. Ct. (so. dist.) Ohio 1968. Auditor U.S. Audit Agy., Paris, 1962-63; asst. pros. atty. Franklin County Prosecutor's Office, Columbus, Ohio, 1967-69; ptnr. Freda & Wentworth, Columbus, 1969-71, Schwenker, Reeves, Wentworth, Stridsberg & Perrin, Columbus, 1971-75, Connor & Wentworth, Columbus, 1975-79; pvt. practice Andrew S. Wentworth, LPA, Columbus, 1979-95, Las Vegas, Nev., 1995—; law dir. Village of Thurston, Ohio, 1992-95. Lectr. Maryhaven Hosp., Columbus, 1985-95; fundraiser Mich. State U., East Lansing, 1989-91. 1st lt. Q.M.C., U.S. Army, 1960-62, capt. USAR, 1962-66. Mem. Ohio Acad. Criminal Def. Lawyers, Ohio Acad. Trial Lawyers, State Bar Nev., Nev. Acad. Trial Lawyers, Delta Tau Delta. Republican. Episcopalian. Avocations: Civil War, reading history and biography, travel, competitive amateur tennis. Home: 6128 Sandstone Mesa Dr Las Vegas NV 89130-1995 Office: 501 S High St Columbus OH 43215-5601

WENTWORTH, DIANA VON WELANETZ, author; b. L.A., Mar. 4, 1941; d. Eugene and Marguerite (Rufi) Webb; m. Frederic Paul von Welanetz, Nov. 2, 1963 (dec. Mar. 19, 1989); 1 child, Lisa Frances von Welanetz; m. Theodore S. Wentworth, Dec. 9, 1989; stepchildren: Christina Linn, Kathryn Allison. Student, UCLA, 1958-60. Ptnr. von Welanetz Cooking Workshop, L.A., 1968-85; host New Way Gourmet, 1983-86; founder Inside Edge Found. Edn., Calif., 1985-93; spkr. in field. Author: The Pleasure of Your Company, 1976 (Cookbook of Yr.), With Love from Your Kitchen, 1976, The Art of Buffet Entertaining, 1978, The Von Welanetz Guide to Ethnic Ingredients, 1983, L.A. Cuisine, 1985, Celebrations, 1985, Chicken Soup for the Soul Cookbook, 1995. Treas. Louise L. Hay Found., Carson, Calif., 1988—; advisor Women of Vision, Calif., 1995—. Mem. Internat. Food, Wine & Travel Writers Assn., Internat. Assn. Cooking Profls., Angels of Arts/Orange County Performing Arts Ctr., Ctr. Club. Avocations: painting, fine art, travel writing, design. Home: 3 Malibu Cir Corona Del Mar CA 92625-1014 Office: 4631 Teller Ave Ste 100 Newport Beach CA 92660-8105

WENTWORTH, JACK ROBERTS, business educator, consultant; b. Elgin, Ill., June 11, 1928; s. William Franklin and Elizabeth (Roberts) W.; m. Rosemary Ann Pawlak, May 30, 1956; children—William, Barbara. Student, Carleton Coll., 1946-48; BS, Ind. U., 1950, MBA, 1954, DBA, 1959. Coord. displays Cadillac divsn., Gen. Motors Corp., Detroit, 1954-56; asst. prof. bus., assoc. dir. research Sch. of Bus. Ind. U., Bloomington, 1957-60, assoc. prof., dir. rsch., 1960-70, prof., 1970-93, chmn. MBA program, 1970-76, chmn. dept., faculty rep. NCAA, 1978-85, dean Sch. of Bus., 1984-93, Arthur M. Weimer prof., 1993-97, Arthur M. Weimer prof. emeritus, 1997—; mktg. cons., Bloomington, 1960—; bd. dirs. Kimball Internat., Jasper, Ind., Market Facts Inc., Chgo., Lone Star Industries, Stamford, Conn. Editor: (monograph) Marketing Horizons, 1965; exec. editor Bus. Horizons, 1960-70. Served to 1st lt. USAF, 1950-53. Recipient Teaching award MBA Assn., 1973, 78, 81, 84, 85, Svc. award Assn. for Bus. and Econ. Rsch., 1983. Mem. Am. Mktg. Assn. (v.p. 1971-73), Grad. Mgmt. Admissions Coun. (chmn. bd. trustees 1977-78), Univ. Club, Masons, Beta Gamma Sigma (pres. Alpha of Ind. chpt. 1971-72, bd. govs. 1986—, nat. pres. 1994-96). Republican. Episcopalian. Avocations: athletic events; travel; bicycling; model railroading; magic. Office: Indiana Univ Sch Bus Bloomington IN 47405

WENTWORTH, MALINDA ANN NACHMAN, former small business owner, real estate broker; b. Greenville, S.C.; d. Mordecai and Frances (Brown) Nachman; m. William A. Wentworth, June 22, 1964; children: William Allen Jr., Linda Ann. BBA, U. Miami, 1960. Registered rep. brokerage, real estate broker. Personnel Mgrs. Asst. Jordan March, Miami, 1960-61; stock broker Barron & Co., Inc., Greenville, 1961-64; real estate agt. Par Realty, Inc., Conyers, Ga., 1969-72; real estate broker Par Realty, Inc., Conyers, 1972-83; owner/ops. Rockdale Cablevision, Conyers, 1979-83; real estate broker Coldwell Banker, Conyers, 1983-85; owner, operator Wentworth's Gym & Fitness Ctr., Conyers, 1981-90; real estate broker First Realty, Conyers, 1981-89; ptnr. and dir. Santa Barbara (Calif.) Cellular Systems, Inc., 1986-89; v.p. Santa Barbara Cellular Systems, Inc., Atlanta, 1986-87; investor Cocoa Beach, Fla., 1990—. Producer and dir.: local sport events on cable to sta., 1979, 80, 81, 87. Founding dir., past pres. Porterdale PTO, 1972-79; mem. Nat. Cable TV Assn., 1979-83, pres. Unity Ch. of Rockdale, Conyers, 1984-85, dir., 1984-89. Named Lt. Col.--Aide-De-Camp, Gov. Staff, state of Ga., Gov. George Busbee, 1979, Appreciation Plaque award, Rockdale County High Sch. Football, 1987. Mem. Nat. Health & Strength Assn., Rockdale County Bd. of Realtors, Cellular Telephone Industry Assn., Rockdale County C. of C. Avocations: scuba diving, weight lifting.

WENTWORTH, MICHAEL JUSTIN, curator; b. Detroit, June 15, 1938; s. Harold Arnold and Marian (Jones) W. MFA, U. Mich., 1962; PHD, Harvard U., 1976. Curator, acting dir. Smith Coll. Mus. Art, Northhampton, Mass., 1968-69; dir. Rose Art Mus., Brandies U., Waltham, Mass., 1970-74; assoc. prof. Wellesley Coll., Mass., 1976; curator Boston Athenaeum, Mass., 1985—. Author: Tissot: Catalogue Raisonné of Prints, 1976, James Tissot, 1984, Tissot, 1988, 50 Books in the Collection of the Boston Athenaeum, 1994, The Boston Library Society, 1995. Office: Boston Athenaeum 10 1/2 Beacon St Boston MA 02108-3703

WENTWORTH, MURRAY JACKSON, artist, educator; b. Boston, Jan. 18, 1927; s. Harold Squires and Mary Louise (Murray) W.; m. Elaine Magnuson, June 16, 1953; 1 child, Janet Louise. Diploma, Art Inst. Boston, 1950. Advt. artist Agy. Art Svcs., Boston, 1950-58; instr. Art Inst. Boston, 1958-78; artist, instr. Norwell, Mass., 1968—. Group shows, Allied Artists Am., 1980, 82 (Silver medal 1980), Allied Art Am., 1982 (Obrig prize 1982), Am. Watercolor Soc., 1980 (Dolphin fellow 1980), Rocky Mount Nat. Exhibition, 1982 (Grumbacher award 1982). Cpl. U.S. Army, 1945-47. Recipient Hudson Valley Art Assn. award, 1991, Whitney Meml. award, 1996, Guild Boston Artists award, 1992, Watercolor award Acad. Artists' Assn., 1997. Mem. Allied Artists Am., Nat. Acad. Design (Pike Meml. award 1986), Am. Watercolor Soc., New England Watercolor Soc. (Grumbacher Gold medal award 1989). Home: 132 Central St Norwell MA 02061-1306

WENTWORTH, RICHARD LEIGH, editor; b. Concord, N.H., July 6, 1930; s. Leigh Mayhew and Yvonne Regina (Wilcott) W.; m. Marlene McClenning, June 9, 1950; children—Douglas, John, Elizabeth, James. B.A., U. Okla., 1956. Editorial asst. U. Okla. Press, 1957-58; asst. editor U. Wis. Press, 1958-59; mgr. sales and promotion La. State U. Press, 1959-62, asst. dir., 1962-63, dir., 1963-70; assoc. dir., editor U. Ill. Press, Urbana, 1970-79; dir. U. Ill. Press, 1979—. Contbr. articles to pub. and sports jours. Served with USAF, 1948-52. Mem. Assn. Am. Univ. Presses (dir. 1966, 77-79), Orgn. Am. Historians, Ill. Hist. Assn., Abraham Lincoln Assn. Democrat. Home: 808 W Springfield Ave Champaign IL 61820-4725 Office: U Ill Press 1325 S Oak St Champaign IL 61820-6903

WENTWORTH, THEODORE SUMNER, lawyer; b. Bklyn., July 18, 1938; s. Theodore Sumner and Alice Ruth (Wortmann) W.; AA, Am. River Coll., 1958; JD, U. Calif., Hastings, 1962; m. Sharon Linelle Arkush, 1965 (dec. 1987); children: Christina Linn, Kathryn Allison; m. Diana Webb von Welanetz, 1989; 1 stepchild, Lexi von Welanetz. Bar: Calif. 1963, U.S. Dist. Ct. (no., ctrl. dists.) Calif., U.S. Ct. Appeals (9th cir.), U.S. Supreme Ct.; cert. civil trial specialist; diplomate Nat. Bd. Trial Advocacy; assoc. Am. Bd. Trial Advocates. Assoc. Adams, Hunt & Martin, Santa Ana, Calif., 1963-66; ptnr. Hunt, Liljestrom & Wentworth, Santa Ana, 1967-77; pres. Solabs Corp.; chmn. bd., exec. v.p. Plant Warehouse, Inc., Hawaii, 1974-82; prin. Law Offices of Wentworth & Faoli, specializing in personal injury, product liability, profl. malpractice, bus. fraud, fire loss litigation, human rights issues, Newport Beach and Temecula, Calif.; judge pro tem Superior Ct. Attys. Panel, Harbor Mcpl. Ct.; owner Eagles Ridge Ranch, Temecula, 1977—. Pres., bd. dirs. Santa Ana-Tustin Community Chest, 1972; v.p., trustee South Orange County United Way, 1973-75; pres. Orange County Fedn. Funds, 1972-73; bd. dirs. Orange County Mental Health Assn. Mem. ABA, Am. Bd. Trial Advocates (assoc.), State Bar Calif., Orange County Bar Assn. (dir. 1972-76), Am. Trial Lawyers Assn., Calif. Trial Lawyers Assn. (bd. govs. 1968-70), Orange County Trial Lawyers Assn. (pres. 1967-68), Lawyer-Pilots Bar Assn., Aircraft Owners and Pilots Assn., Bahia Corinthian Yacht Club, Balboa Bay Club, Corsair Yacht Club, The Center Club, Pacific Club, Newport. Research in vedic prins., natural law, quantum physics and mechanics. Office: 4631 Teller Ave Ste 100 Newport Beach CA 92660-8105 also: Wells Fargo Bank Bldg 41530 Enterprise Cir S Temecula CA 92590-4816

WENTWORTH, WILLIAM EDGAR, journalist; b. Newton, N.H., Nov. 4, 1931; s. Charles Bertrand and Mildred Frances (Ingalls) W. BA in Journalism, U. Tenn., Knoxville, 1958. Reporter Rochester (N.H.) Courier, 1959; reporter, copy editor Foster's Daily Democrat, Dover, N.H., 1959-68; copy editor Florida Today, Melbourne, Fla., 1968-93; ret., 1993. Author: (book) Vital Records, 1790-1829, 1995; editor: (periodical) Genealogical Record, 1995—. Data entry-online Dover Pub. Libr., N.H., 1993-97. Sgt. USAF, 1950-54. Mem. Strafford County Genealogical Soc., Citizens Against Government Waste, Accuracy in Media. Republican. Baptist. Avocation, genealogy research. Home: 13 Olde Madbury Ln Dover NH 03820-5440

WENTZ, BILLY MELVIN, JR., finance executive; b. Charlotte, N.C., Aug. 11, 1953; s. Billy M. Wentz and Betty Jane (Harper) Bass; m. Cynthia Gardner, Aug. 2, 1975; children: Jessica, Kyle. BSBA, U. of N.C., 1975; MBA, U. of Tampa, 1979. CPA, N.C. Contr. Kerley and Edwards, Charlotte, N.C., 1975-76; plant acct. Rexham Corp., Charlotte, 1976-77; acctg. mgr. Rexham Corp., Sarasota, Fla., 1977-79, div. controller, 1979-80, group controller, 1980-82; corp. cost mgr. Rexham Corp., Charlotte, 1982-86, corp. dir. acctg., 1986-87, corp. contr., 1987-89, fin. dir., 1989—. Bd. dirs. YMCA, Charlotte. Mem. AICPA, N.C. Assn. CPA's. Office: 4201 Congress St Ste 340 Charlotte NC 28209-4621

WENTZ, CHARLES ALVIN, JR., environmentalist, chemical engineer; b. Edwardsville, Ill., Oct. 12, 1935; s. Charles Alvin and Frances Margaret (Bohm) W.; m. Sandra Niederecker, Dec. 11, 1961 (div. Jan. 1982); children: Sharon, Christopher, Suzanne, Sheila; m. Joan Domigan, Aug., 1983. BSChemE, U. Mo., 1957, MSChemE, 1959; PhDChemE, Northwestern U., 1961; MBA, So. Ill. U., 1985. Cert. safety profl.; registered profl. engr. Various exec. positions Phillips Petroleum Co., Bartlesville, Okla., 1961-82; pres. New Park Waste Treatment, Inc., New Orleans, 1982-83, ENSCO, Inc., El Dorado, Ark., 1983-84; pres., CEO Wentz Healthcare, Inc., Lebanon, Ill., 1984—; CEO Internat. Sci. Mgmt., Inc., Edwardsville, Ill., 1985—; mgr., waste and safety Argonne (Ill.) Nat. Lab., 1988-91; assoc. dean Chulalongkorn U., Bangkok, 1994; vis. prof. So. Ill. U., Edwardsville, 1984-86. Author: Hazardous Waste Management, 1989, 2d edit., 1995, (with others) Occupational and Environmental Safety, 1990, Encyclopedia of Environmental Control Technology, vol. 5, 1992; editor spl. issues Environ. Progress, 1988, 89; patentee in field; contbr. articles to profl. jours. Mem. adv. bd. Ill. Hazardous Waste Rsch. and Info. Ctr., 1989-91. Mem. Am. Chem. Soc., Am. Inst. of Chem. Engrs., Am. Inst. for Pollution Prevention, Nat. Safety Coun., Acad. Chem. Engrs., Water Pollution Control Fedn., Air and Waste Mgmt. Assn., Sigma Xi. Avocations: hunting, fishing, gardening, cooking. Home and Office: Internat Sci Mgmt Inc 5953 Old Poag Rd Edwardsville IL 62025-7341

WENTZ, JEFFREY LEE, information systems consultant; b. Philippi, W.Va., Nov. 29, 1956; s. William Henry and Edith Marie (McBee) W. AS in Data Processing, BS in Acctg., Fairmont (W.Va.) State Coll., 1978. Programmer/analyst U.S. Dept. Energy, Morgantown, W.Va., 1978-79; analyst Middle South Svcs., New Orleans, 1979-81; sr. analyst Bank of Am., San Francisco, 1981-83; pres., cons. Wentz Cons. Inc., San Francisco, 1983—. Office: Wentz Consulting Inc 1378 34th Ave San Francisco CA 94122-1309

WENTZ, SIDNEY FREDERICK, insurance company executive, foundation executive; b. Dallas, Mar. 27, 1932; s. Howard Beck and Emmy Lou (Cawthon) W.; m. Barbara Strait, Sept. 9, 1961; children: Eric, Jennifer, Robin. AB, Princeton U., 1954; LLB, Harvard U., 1960. Bar: N.Y. 1961. Atty. White & Case, N.Y.C., 1960-65, Western Electric Co., 1965-66, AT&T Corp., 1966-67; with Crum & Forster Inc., Morristown, N.J., 1967—, v.p., gen. counsel, 1967-71, sr. v.p., gen. counsel, 1971-72, exec. v.p., 1972, pres., 1972-87, chmn. bd., 1987-88, chmn. exec. com., 1988-90, also bd. dirs.; chmn. bd. Robert Wood Johnson Found., Princeton, N.J., 1989—. Trustee Morristown Meml. Hosp., 1974-96, Drew U., 1991—. Served to lt. (j.g.) USNR, 1954-57. Mem. Morris County Golf Club, Morristown Field Club, Sakonnet (R.I.) Golf Club, Baltusrol Golf Club, Jupiter Hills (Fla.) Golf Club, Loblolly Pines (Fla.) Golf Club. Office: Robert Wood Johnson Found PO Box 2316 College Rd E Princeton NJ 08540-6672

WENTZ, WALTER JOHN, health administration educator; b. Newburgh, Ohio, June 17, 1928; s. Walter John and Gladys Marjory W.; m. Lynne E. Putnam; children: Marcia, Sharon, Diane, Courtney, Richard, Jerry, Rick. B.A., U. Iowa, 1949, M.A., 1950, Ph.D., 1963. Pres. Meml. Hosp., Saulte Ste Marie, Mich., 1965-71; assoc. prof. Central Mich. U., Mt. Pleasant, 1977-78; prof. health adminstrn. Wichita State U., 1978-87, chmn. dept. health adminstrn. Coll. Health Professions., 1978-87; prof. div. health adminstrn. Gov's State U., Univ. Pk., Ill., 1987—. Contbr. articles to profl. jours., chpts. to books.; Mem. editorial bd.: Jour. Hosp. and Health Services Adminstrn. Fellow Am. Pub. Health Assn., AAAS, Royal Soc. Health, Am. Coll. Healthcare Execs.; mem. Phi Kappa Phi, Sigma Iota Epsilon, Omicron Delta Kappa, Beta Gamma Sigma, Alpha Eta. Republican. Methodist. Club: Rotary (dir.). Office: Governors State U Divsn Health Adminstrn University Park IL 60466

WENTZ, WILLIAM HENRY, JR., aerospace engineer, educator; b. Wichita, Kans., Dec. 18, 1933. BS in Mech. Engring. cum laude, Wichita State U., 1955, MS in Aeronautical Engring., 1961; PhD in Engring. Mechanics, U. Kans., 1969. Lic. profl. engr., Kans. Liaison engr. Beech Aircraft, 1952-53; propulsion engr. Boeing Co., Wichita, Kans., 1955; instr. mech. engring. Wichita State U., 1957-58; aerodynamicist Boeing Co., Wichita, 1958-63; from asst. prof. to assoc. prof. aeronautical engring. Wichita State U., 1963-75, prof. aeronautical engring., 1975-83, Gates-Learjet prof. aeronautical engring., 1983-86, disting. prof. aerospace engring., 1986—, dir. Ctr. Basic and Applied Rsch. Inst. Aviation Rsch., 1986-89, exec. dir. Nat. Inst. Aviation Rsch., 1988-97; sr. fellow Nat. Inst. Aviation Rsch., 1997—; dir. rsch. projects Boeing Co., 1960, 61, NASA, 1964-66, 66-68, 70-71, 71-83, 86-87, 86-88, 82-87, Dept. of Def., 1986-88, Kans. Tech. Enterprise Corp., 1988—, FAA, 1986—. Contbr. articles to profl. jours. With USAF, 1955-57. Sci. Faculty fellow NSF, 1967-68. Fellow AIAA (assoc., past chmn. Wichita sect., Outstanding advisor student chpt. 1964, 65, 70, Gen. Aviation award 1981, Engr. of Yr. award Wichita sect. 1992, Engr. of Yr. award Region V 1991-92; mem. Soc. Automotive Engrs. (Ralph R. Teeter award 1973), Sigma Gamma Tau, Tau Beta Pi. Office: Wichita State U Nat Inst Aviation Rsch Campus Box 93 Wichita KS 67260-0093

WENZEL, JAMES GOTTLIEB, ocean engineering executive, consultant; b. Springfield, Minn., Oct. 16, 1926; s. Gottlieb Henry and Elvira Wilhemina (Runck) W.; m. Elaine Joyce Abrahamson, June 17, 1950; children: Lori Lynn, Jodi Ann, Sheri Lee, James G. II. BA in Aero Engring. with high distinction, U. Minn., 1948, MS, 1950; DHL (hon.), Calif. Luth. U., Thousand Oaks, 1985. Mgr. aerodynamics Convair, San Diego, 1950-56, asst. to v.p engring., 1956-58; asst. to sr. v.p. engring. Gen. Dynamics Corp., N.Y.C., 1958-60, mgr., govt. planning, 1960-62; v.p. ocean systems Lockheed Missiles & Space Co., Sunnyvale, Calif., 1962-84; pres., chmn. Ocean Minerals Co., Sunnyvale, 1977-84, Marine Devel. Assocs. Inc, Saratoga, Calif., 1984—; chmn. Oreg. Resource Exploration Co., Portland, 1985—; pres. Centry Systems Inc., Saratoga, 1994—; bd. dirs. Yr. of the Ocean Found., Washington, 1984-8; pres., chmn. Sea/Space Symposium, Phila., 1971—. Author (with others) Ocean Engineering, 1968; author 58 published papers on ocean engring., 1966-88; patentee in field. Regent Calif. Luth. U., Thousand Oaks, 1975-78, 85-87; pres., chmn. Jr. Achievement, Santa Clara County, Calif., 1976-81; chmn. Luth. Lay Renewal, No. Calif., 1975-81, 88—; pres. Immanuel Luth. Trusts, Saratoga, Calif., 1989-94. With USN, 1944-46. Recipient Mayor's award for Oceanology City of L.A., 1967, Japan Govt. Contbns. award Marine Facilities Panel, 1992. Fellow Marine Tech. Soc. (ocean sci. and engring. award 1988); mem. NAE (life) , NRC Marine bd. 1978-84), Cosmos Club (Washington), Saratoga Mens Club, Tau Beta Pi, Tau Omega. Republican. Lutheran. Avocations: scuba diving, wood working, fishing. Office: Marine Devel Assocs Inc PO Box 3409 Saratoga CA 95070-1409

WENZEL, JOAN ELLEN, artist; b. N.Y.C., July 23, 1944; d. Irwin S. and Pearl (Silverman) Rever; m. Allen Jay Wenzel, June 12, 1966 (div. June 1987); 1 child, Kimberly Anne; m. Robert Harold Messing, July 23, 1987 (dec.). Student, Syracuse U., 1962-64; BS in Painting, NYU, 1966, MA in Painting, 1976; postgrad., Harvard U., 1967. One-woman shows include Coplan Gallery, Boca Raton, Fla., 1997, Esperante Sculpture Ctr., 1996, Lighthouse Sch. and Gallery, Tequesta, Fla., 1996, Helander Gallery, Palm Beach, Fla., 1985, 89, 95, Adamar Fine Art, Miami, 1993, Gallery Contemporena, Jacksonville, Fla., 1993, Alexander Brest Mus., Jacksonville, 1993, Albertson Peterson Gallery, Winter Park, Fla., 1992, Amerifest, Miami, 1991, Gallery Yves Arman, N.Y.C., 1982, Palm Beach County Court House, West Palm Beach, Fla., 1991, One Brickall Square, Miami, 1992; exhbns. include Aldrich Mus., Ridgefield, Conn., 1977, Queens Mus., N.Y.C., 1981. Democrat. Jewish. Home: 2275 Ibis Isle Rd W Palm Beach FL 33480-5307

WENZEL, LEONARD ANDREW, engineering educator; b. Palo Alto, Calif., Jan. 21, 1923; s. Robert N. and Frances A. (Browne) W.; m. Mary E. Leathers, Oct. 21, 1944; children: Frances B., Alma L., Jesse R., Sara V. BSChemE, Pa. State U., 1943; MSChemE, U. Mich., 1948, PhD in Chem. Engring., 1950. Registered profl. engr., Pa. Jr. rsch. engr. Phillips Petroleum Co., Bartlesville, Okla., 1943-44; jr. rsch. scientist Mellon Inst., Pitts., 1944; rsch. engr. Colgate-Palmolive, Jersey City, 1949-51; asst. prof. engring. Lehigh U., Bethlehem, Pa., 1951-56—, assoc. prof., 1956-60, prof., 1960-88, chmn. dep. chem. engring., 1962-83, prof. emeritus, 1988—; project dir. UNESCO, Bucaramanga, Colombia, 1969-70, cons. in chem. engring., Maracaibo, Venezuela,, 1970-73; cons. Air Products and Chems., Allentown, Pa., 1951-80, Exxon, Baytown, Tex., 1983-86; chief scientist Arencibia Techs., Inc., Allentown, 1987-93; pres. L.A. Wenzel, Inc., Bethlehem, 1988—; dir. of tech. Eco-Gen Techs., Inc., Bethlehem, 1993—. Co-author: Principles of Unit Operations, 1960, Introduction to Chemical Engineering, 1961, Chemical Process Analysis: Mass and Energy Balances, 1987. Bd. dirs. South Bethlehem Neighborhood Assn., 1986—, Bethlehem Housing Authority, 1988—. Lt. (j.g.) USN, 1944-46, PTO. Fellow Am. Inst. Chem. Engrs.; mem. Am. Chem. Soc., Am. Soc. for Engring. Edn. Avocations: stamps, gardening, travel. Home: 517 15th Ave Bethlehem PA 18018-6429 Office: Lehigh Univ Bldg #111 Bethlehem PA 18015

WENZEL, RICHARD PUTNAM, internist; b. Phila., Jan. 8, 1940; m. Jo Gail Wenzel; children: Amy, Richard. BS, Haverford (Pa.) Coll., 1961; MD, Jefferson Med. Coll., 1965; MSc, London U., 1986. Diplomate Am. Bd. Internal Medicine. Intern Phila. Gen. Hosp., 1965-66; resident in internal medicine U. Md. Hosp., Balt., 1966-68, fellowship infectious diseases, 1968-69, chief resident in internal medicine, 1969-70; asst. in medicine U. Md. Med. Sch., Balt., 1969-70; hosp. epidemiologist U. Va. Med. Ctr., Charlottesville, 1972-86; asst. prof. internal medicine U. Va. Sch. of Medicine, Charlottesville, 1972-76, assoc. prof., 1976-81, prof. internal medicine, 1981-86; dir. divsn. clin. epidemiology U. Iowa Coll. Medicine, Iowa City, 1986-89, prof. medicine, preventive medicine, 1986—, dir. hosp. epidemiology and statewide epidemiology svcs., 1986—, dir. divsn. gen. medicine, clin. epidemiology and health svcs. rsch., 1989—; MD MSC Med. Coll. Va., Richmond, 1995; founding chair dept. epidemiology MS degree granting program Grad. Sch. Arts and Scis., U. Va., Charlottesville, 1981-86; pres. ho. staff assn. of interns, residents and fellows U. Md. Hosp., 1968-69; cons. U.S. HO. Reps. Ethics Adv. Bd. Ethics Regarding Freedom of Info. and Infection

Surveillance Data, Washington, 1979-80, NIH small bus. innovation rsch, 1988; infection control cons. U. Calif. Systemwide Task Force on AIDS, 1987; spl. cons. NIH Study Sect. Epidemiology and Disease Control (#2), 1987-92. Author: Assessing Quality Care: Perspective for Clinicians, 1992, Prevention and Control of Nosocomial Infections, 1987, Handbook on Hospital Acquired Infections, 1981; founding editor Infection Control and Hospital Epidemiology, 1979—, Clinical Performance and Quality Health Care, 1993—; editorial bd. Jour. of Hosp. Infection, London, 1984—, Enfermedades Infecciosas y Microbiologia Clinica, 1990—, New England Jour. of Medicine, 1992—, others; contbr. numerous articles to profl. jours. Recipient Sir Henry S. Wellcome medal prize, 1971, Major Louis Livingston Seaman prize, 1974, Burlington No. Found. Faculty Achievement award, 1990; Sr. Internat. fellowship, NIH, 1985-86. Fellow ACP, Infectious Diesease Soc. of Am. (coun. mem. 1988-91), Am. Coll. Epidemiology, Am. Acad. of Microbiology; sr. internat. fellow NIH, 1985-86; mem. Am. Assn. of Physicians, Am. Soc. for Clin. Investigation, Am. Clin. and Climatological Assn., Am. Epidemiological Soc., So. Soc. for Clin. Investigation, Cen. Soc. for Clin. Investigation, Am. Fedn. for Clin. Rsch., Am. Soc. for Microbiology, Assn. for Practitioners in Infection Control, Surg. Infection Soc., Soc. for Epidemiologic Rsch., Hosp. Infections Soc. (Europe). *

WENZEL, SANDRA LEE ANN, pediatrics nurse; b. Peoria, Ill., July 4, 1940; d. Henry M. and Gertrude R. (Burchell) W. Diploma, St. Mary's Sch. Nursing, Kankakee, Ill., 1962; BSN, Bradley U., Peoria, 1966; cert. PNP, Wilford Hall Med. Ctr., San Antonio, 1972. RN, Ill., Tex.; cert. sch. health nurse. Asst. clin. instr. pediatrics St. Francis Sch. Nursing, Peoria, 1962-66; commd. 1st lt. USAF, 1966, advanced through grades to lt. col., 1981; staff nurse cardiology, ICU and pediatrics units, PNP, Wilford Hall Med. Ctr., 1966-68, 72-74; ret., 1986; charge nurse newborn nursery USAF Hosp., Lakenheath Air Base, Eng., 1968-72; PNP USAF Hosp., Goodfellow AFB, Tex., 1974-77; dir. nursing, part-time PNP USAF Clinic, Vance AFB, Okla., 1978-86; PNP USAF Hosp., Scott AFB, Ill., 1987-88; sch. health nurse Marissa, Ill., 1987-88; PNP Family Care Ctr. Corondolet, St. Louis, 1989—. Fellow Nat. Assn. Pediatric Nurse Assocs. and Practitioners (cert.); mem. Am. Diabetic Assn., Uniformed Mil. Practitioners Assn., Sigma Theta Tau.

WEPFER, JULIA M., psychologist; b. El Dorado, Ark., May 12, 1936; d. Joseph Gottlieb and Julia Witherspoon (Fletcher) W.; m. Harry Ames Metcalf, June 1, 1957 (div.); 1 child, Holly Kinyon. BS in Bus. Adminstrn., U. Ark., 1958, MA in Psychology, 1965; PsyD, Fla. Inst. Tech., 1980. Lic. psychologist, Ark. Market analyst Am. Investment Advisors, Little Rock, 1958; office mgr. to orthodontist Little Rock, 1958-60, office mgr. to psychiatrist, 1961-64; psycholog. examiner U. Ark. for Med. Scis. Dept. Psychiatry, Little Rock, 1966-67, tchg. asst., 1967-69, instr., 1969-75, asst. prof., 1975-85; pvt. practice Little Rock, 1985—; mem. Ark. Bd. Examiners in Psychology, Little Rock, 1973-78. Ark. coord. Deaf-Blind Project, Little Rock, 1971-72; mem. Regional AIDS Interfaith Network Care Team, Little Rock, 1992—; mem. commn. on ministry Episcopal Diocese of Ark., Little Rock, 1994—; vol. Stewpot Free Kitchen, Little Rock; v.p. bd. dirs. Columbia Land & Timber Co., Beauregard Parish, La. Fellow Ark. Psychol. Assn. (pres. 1982-83); mem. APA, Assn. for Study of Dreams, Chi Omega (Psi chpt.). Democrat. Avocations: water aerobics, gardening, computers, scuba diving. Home and Office: 13001 Ridgehaven Rd Little Rock AR 72211-2211

WEPNER, SHELLEY BETH, education educator, software developer; b. Phila., Oct. 23, 1951; d. Bernard and Carole Frances (Abramson) Markovitz; m. Roy Henry Wepner, Aug. 3, 1974; children: Leslie Marcia and Meredith Susan (twins). BS magna cum laude, U. Pitts., 1972; MS, U. Pa., 1973, EdD, 1980. Cert. reading specialist, prin., supr., elem. tchr., N.J. Reading tchr. West Deptford (N.J.) Sch. Dist., 1973-74; reading resource tchr. Middletown (N.J.) Sch. Dist., 1974-75, Title I tchr., 1975-76; reading specialist Marlboro (N.J.) Sch. Dist., 1976-78, curriculum cons., 1978-80, supr. curriculum and instrn., 1980-82; prof. edn. William Paterson Coll., Wayne, N.J., 1989, chair dept. curriculum and instrn., 1991-94; asst. to dean William Paterson Coll., Wayne, 1994-97; dir. ctr. edn., assoc. dean, prof. edn. Widener U., 1997—; cons. Tchr. Support Software, Gainesville, Fla., 1988—, East Brunswick (N.J.) Sch., 1989. Co-author: Using Computers in the Teaching of Reading, 1987, Moving Forward with Literature: Basals, Books, and Beyond, 1993; co-editor: The Administration and Supervision of Reading Programs, 1989, 2d edit., 1995, Process Reading and Writing: A Literature Based Approach, 1992; author software Read-A-Logo, 1987 (Methods and Media award 1989), Reading Realities, 1989 (Top Five award, Methods and Media award), Reading Realities Elem. Series, 1990 (Top 36 award, Methods and Media award). Chmn. gifted and talented Coles Sch. PTA, Scotch Plains, N.J., 1989-90. Mem. Am. Assn. Colls. Tchr. Edn., N.J. Assn. Colls. Tchr. Edn., Coll. Reading Assn., Internat. Soc. for Tech. in Edn., Internat. Reading Assn., N.J. Reading Assn. (bd. dirs. 1982-85), Phi Delta Kappa. Avocations: computer applications, walking, aerobics, reading. Home: 3 Hacklorn Ln Scotch Plains NJ 07076-2836 Office: William Paterson Coll 300 Pompton Rd Wayne NJ 07470-2103

WERBA, GABRIEL, public relations consultant; b. Paris, Feb. 28, 1930; came to U.S., 1941; s. Aron and Dina (Lewin) W.; m. Barrie Celia Sakolsky, June 1, 1952; children: Dean Steffen, Annmarie Alexandra. BA in Journalism, U. Tex., 1948; postgrad., NYU Grad. Sch. Bus., 1948-49, NYU Sch. Law, 1961-62. Account exec. Harold C. Meyers & Co., N.Y.C., 1959-61; dir. pub. rels. and advt. Yardney Electric Corp., N.Y.C., 1961-63; sr. assoc. Shiefman & Assocs., Detroit, 1963-66; account exec. Merrill Lynch, Detroit, 1966-70; exec. v.p. Shiefman Werba & Assocs., Detroit, 1970-73; sr. v.p., exec. v.p., pres., chief oper. officer Anthony M. Franco, Inc., Detroit, 1973-88; pres., chief exec. officer The Werba Group, Inc. and Gabriel Werba and Assocs., Inc., Detroit, 1988-94; prin. Durocher, Dixson, Werba, L.L.C., Detroit, 1994—; bd. dirs. Environ. Recovery Technologies, Inc., Troy, Mich., Intrepid World Comm., Inc., Birmingham, Mich. Contbr. articles to profl. jours. Bd. dirs. Oakland Citizens League, Detroit, 1970-93, Detroit Symphony Orch. Hall, Detroit Chamber Winds, 1985-91, Common Ground, Royal Oak, Mich., The Attic Theatre, Detroit, 1989-93, The Children's Ctr., Detroit, mem. strategic planning com., chmn. comm. com., bd. dirs., 1989-95, adv. bd., 1995-96, bd. dirs., 1996—; bd. dirs. NATAS, Detroit, The Jewish Cmty. Coun. Met. Detroit, 1989-95, Margaret W. Montgomery Hosp., 1993-95, adv. bd. 1988-93; mem. comm. com. Detroit Inst. Arts, 1986—, exhibits com., 1990—. Mem. Nat. Investor Rels. Inst. (past dir., pres. Detroit chpt., spkr., panelist), Pub. Rels. Soc. Am. (bd. dirs. Detroit chpt. 1988-94, pres. 1992-93, past treas. Detroit Counselors' sect., nat. membership com., nat exec. com. fin. sect., spkr., panelist), Fin. Analysts Soc. Detroit (past chmn. pub. info. com.), Am. Mensa (bd. dirs. 1975-91, nat. chmn. 1979-83), Internat. Mensa (bd. dirs. 1979-83, 85-93). Avocations: art collecting, concerts, theater. Home: 20775 Indian Creek Dr Farmingtn Hls MI 48335-5503 Office: Durocher Dixson Werba LLC 400 Renaissance Ctr Ste 2250 Detroit MI 48243-1602

WERBITT, WARREN, gastroenterologist, educator; b. Phila., Jan. 29, 1939; s. Saull Boris and Pearl (Weiner) W.; m. Drue Natalie Engman Werbitt, Aug. 30, 1964; children: Julie Michele, Jeffrey Brian. BS in Pharmacy, Temple U., 1960; D in Osteopathy, U. Osteopathic Med. and Health Scis., Des Moines, 1966; MD, Allegheny U. Hosps.- Med. Coll. Pa. divsn., 1973. Diplomate Am. Osteo. Bd. Internal Medicine, also sub-splty. bd. Gastroenterology; diplomate Am. Bd. Internal Medicine, also sub-splty. bd. Gastroenterology. Internship Doctor's Hosp., Columbus, Ohio, 1966-67; residency in internal medicine Doctor's Hosp., Columbus, 1967-68, Kennedy Meml. Hosps., Cherry Hill, N.J., 1968-69, Mercy Catholic Med. Ctr., Phila., 1969-70; residency in internal medicine Allegheny U. Hosps.- Med. Coll. Pa. divsn., Phila., 1971-72, fellow in gastroenterology, 1970-71, 72-74, instr., 1971—; instr. Allegheny U. Hosps.- Med. Coll. Pa. divsn., 1973-75; attending physician and cons. in gastroenterology Allegheny U. Hosps.- Med. Coll. Pa. divsn., Phila., 1974—; chmn. div. gastroenterology Phila. Coll. Osteopathic Medicine, 1975-77; clin. assoc. prof. medicine U. Medicine and Dentistry, N.J., 1977—; attending physician and cons. in gastroenterology Vet. Adminstrn. Hosp., Phila., 1972-75; chmn. Div. Gastroenterology, Dept. Medicine Phila. Coll. Osteopathic Medicine, 1975-77; chmn. Dept. Medicine Kennedy Meml. Hosp. U. Med. Ctr., Cherry Hill, 1979-81, chmn. subsect. Gastroenterology, 1979-87. Contbg. editor The N.J. Jour. for Osteopathic Physicians and Surgeons, 1980—; mem. scientific adv. com. Phila. chpt. Nat. Found. Ileitis & Colitis, Inc., 1982—; contbr. articles to profl. jours. Recipient Profl. Svc. award Med. Soc. N.J., 1991. Fellow Am. Coll. Physicians, Am. Coll. Gastroenterology, Acad. Med. N.J.; mem. AMA, Am. Soc. Gastrointestinal Endoscopy, Am. Gastroenterology Assn., Am. Soc. Parenteral and Enteric Nutrition, Am. Inst. Ultrasound in Medicine, Am. Assn. Gynecologic Laparoscopists, Phila. Gastrointestinal Rsch. Forum, State Med. Soc. N.J., Camden County Med. Soc., N.J. Endoscopic Soc., Del. Valley Soc. for Gastrointestinal Endoscopy, South Jersey Gastroenterological Soc., Am. Osteopathic Assn., N.J. Soc. Osteopathic Physicians and Surgeons, Am. Coll. Osteopathic Internists, Camden County Osteopathic Assn., Am. Cancer Soc. (bd. dirs. N.J. chpt.), Pres.'s Circle Am. U., N.Y. Acad. Scis., John Sherman Myers Soc., Med. Club Phila., Lambda Omicron Gamma. Avocations: golf, running, music, reading, American History. Office: Profl Gastroenterology Assn 1939 Route 70 E Ste 250 Cherry Hill NJ 08003-4505

WERBOS, PAUL JOHN, neural net research director; b. Darby, Pa., Sept. 4, 1947; s. Walter Joseph and Margaret Mary (Donohue) W.; m. Lily Fountain, July 13, 1979; children: Elizabeth, Alexander, Maia. BA magna cum laude, Harvard U., 1967; MSc, London Sch. Econs., 1968; MA, Harvard U., 1969, PhD, 1974. Rsch. assoc. MIT, Cambridge, Mass., 1973-75; asst. prof. U. Md., College Park, 1975-78; math. statistician U.S. Census Bur., Suitland, Md., 1978-79; energy analyst U.S. Dept. Energy, Washington, 1979-88, 89; program dir. NSF, Washington, 1988, 89—. Author: The Roots of Backpropagation: From Ordered Derivatives to Neural Network & Political Forecasting, 1993; contbr. chpt. to Handbook of Intelligent Control, 1992. Regional dir., Washington rep. L-5 Soc. (merged with Nat. Space Soc.), Washington, 1980s. Mem. Internat. Neural Network Soc. (pres. 1991-92, sec. 1990). Quaker-Universalist. Achievements include patent for elastic fuzzy logic and associated adaptation techniques; devised theory of intelligence; created alternative formulation of quantum theory. Home: 8411 48th Ave College Park MD 20740-2403 Office: NSF 4201 Wilson Blvd Rm 675 Arlington VA 22230-0001

WERBOW, STANLEY NEWMAN, language educator; b. Phila., Apr. 19, 1922; s. Morris and Sadie (Newman) W.; m. Naomi Esther Ecker, June 1, 1952; children: Susan Linda, Emily Frances, Carol Martha. B.A., George Washington U., 1946; postgrad., Middlebury Coll., 1946, 47, U. Mich., 1948; Ph.D., Johns Hopkins, 1953. Tchr. Ea. High Sch., Washington, 1946-47; research analyst specialist U.S. Dept. Def., Washington, 1952-53; mem. faculty U. Tex., Austin, 1953—, prof., 1965-69, 78—, chmn. dept. Germanic langs., 1969-71, dean Coll. Humanities, 1971-78, acting dean Coll. Fine Arts, 1980-81; vis. prof. U. Marburg, 1963, U. N.Mex. German Summer Sch., 1984, 87, 89. Author: Martin von Amberg, 1957, (with Lehmann, Rehder, Shaw) Review and Progress in German, 1959; Editor: Formal Aspects of Medieval German Poetry, 1970. Served with Signal Corps AUS, 1943-45. Decorated Bronze Star medal; Bundesverdienstkreuz erster klasse W. Ger.; recipient Fulbright award to Netherlands, 1950-51; Guggenheim fellow, 1960; Fulbright research scholar Germany, 1960-61. Mem. Modern Lang. Assn. (pres. South Central assn. 1976—), Medieval Acad., Internat. Assn. Germanists, Phi Beta Kappa, Phi Kappa Phi, Delta Phi Alpha. Home: 4205 Prickly Pear Dr Austin TX 78731-2017 Office: Univ Texas Dept Germanic Langs Austin TX 78712

WERCKMEISTER, OTTO KARL, art historian and educator; b. Berlin, Apr. 26, 1934; came to U.S., 1965; s. Karl and Rose (Petzold) W.; m. Maria Eugenia Lacarra, July 3, 1965 (div. 1985); children: Christina, Robert, Veronica. PhD, Freie U., Berlin, 1958. Research assoc. German Archeol. Inst., Madrid, Spain, 1962-65; assoc. prof. to prof. UCLA, 1965-84; Mary Jane Crowe Disting. prof. Northwestern U., 1984—. Author: Ende der Ästhetik, 1971, 1972, Ideologie und Kunst bei Marx und andere Essays, 1974, Versuche über Paul Klee, 1981, Zitadellenkultur, 1989, Eng. edit., 1991, The Making of Paul Klee's Career, 1914-20, 1989, Linke Ikonen, 1997. Guggenheim fellow, 1981, Wissenschaftskolleg (Berlin) fellow, 1986. Office: Northwestern U Dept Art Hist Evanston IL 60208

WERDEGAR, KATHRYN MICKLE, judge; b. San Francisco; d. Benjamin Christie and Kathryn Marie (Clark) Mickle; m. David Werdegar; children: Maurice Clark, Matthew Mickle. Student, Wellesley Coll., 1954-55; AB with honors, U. Calif., Berkeley, 1957; JD with distinction, George Washington U., 1962; JD, U. Calif., Berkeley, 1990. Bar: Calif. 1964, U.S. Dist. Ct. (no. dist.) Calif. 1964, U.S. Ct. Appeals (9th cir.) 1964, Calif. Supreme Ct. 1964. Legal asst. civil rights divsn. U.S. Dept. Justice, Washington, 1962-63; cons. Calif. Study Commn. on Mental Retardation, 1963-64; assoc. U. Calif. Ctr. for Study of Law and Soc., Berkeley, 1965-67; spl. cons. State Dept. Mental Hygiene, 1967-68; cons. Calif. Coll. Trial Judges, 1968-71; atty., head criminal divsn. Calif. Continuing Edn. of Bar, 1971-78; assoc. dean acad. and student affairs, assoc. prof. Sch. Law, U. San Francisco, 1978-81; sr. staff atty. Calif. 1st Dist. Ct. Appeal, 1981-85, Calif. Supreme Ct., 1985-91; assoc. justice Calif. 1st Dist. Ct. Appeal, 1991-94, Calif. Supreme Ct., San Francisco, 1994—. Author: Benchbook: Misdemeanor Procedure, 1971, Misdemeanor Procedure Benchbook, 1975, 83; contbr. California Continuing Education of the Bar books; editor: California Criminal Law Practice series, 1972, California Uninsured Motorist Practice, 1973, I California Civil Procedure Before Trial, 1977. Recipient Charles Glover award George Washington U., J. William Fulbright award for disting. pub. svc. George Washington U. Law Sch. Alumni Assn., award of excellence Calif. Alumni Assn., also 5 Am. Jurisprudence awards. Mem. Nat. Assn. Women Judges, Calif. Judges Assn., Nev./Calif. Women Judges Assn., Boalt Hall Alumni Assn. (bd. dirs.), Order of the Coif. Office: Calif Supreme Court South Tower 303 2nd St San Francisco CA 94107

WERKING, RICHARD HUME, librarian, historian, academic administrator; b. Charleston, S.C., Sept. 29, 1943; s. F. Woody and Mary S. (Prissinger) W. BA, U. Evansville, 1966; MA in Am. History, U. Wis., 1967, PhD in Am. History, 1973; MA in Librarianship, U. Chgo., 1975. Instr. history Northland Coll., Ashland, Wis., 1967-68; pers. staffing specialist U.S. Civil Svc. Commn., Indpls., 1968-69; reference libr. Lawrence U., Appleton, Wis., 1975-77; head reference dept., asst. prof. history U. Miss., Oxford, 1977-79, asst. libr. dir., asst. prof. history, 1979-80, acting libr. dir., asst. prof. history, 1980-81; assoc. libr. dir., asst. prof. history Trinity U., San Antonio, Tex., 1981-83, libr. dir., assoc. prof. history, 1983-91; libr. dir., assoc. dean, prof. history U.S. Naval Acad., Annapolis, Md., 1991—; With OCLC Adv. Com. on Coll. and Univ. Librs., Dublin, Ohio, 1986-92; sr. fellow Grad. Sch. Libr. & Info. Sci., UCLA, 1989. Author: The Master Architects: Building the U.S. Foreign Service, 1977; contbr. articles to profl. jours., chpts. to books, also papers, monographs and revs. With U.S. Army, 1962. Sparks fellow Phi Kappa Phi, 1966, postdoctoral fellow Coun. on Libr. Resources, 1974. Mem. ALA (chmn. coll. librs. sect. 1987-88), Orgn. Am. Historians. Office: US Naval Acad Nimitz Libr 589 Mcnair Rd Annapolis MD 21402-1323

WERKMAN, ROSEMARIE ANNE, past public relations professional, civic worker; b. Washingtonville, N.Y., Apr. 21, 1926; d. Alexander and Michelina (Russo) Di Benedetto; m. Henry J. Werkman, June 29, 1947; children: Elizabeth, Kristine, Hendrik. Student, U. Miami, Fla. Billing clk. Stern's Dept. Store, N.Y.C., 1945; clk., typist Doubleday-Doran Book Pub., N.Y.C., 1945-46; receptionist Moser & Cotins Advt. Agy., Utica, N.Y., 1947-48, Washingtonville Sch., N.Y., 1960-75. Author: (biography/autobiography) Love, War and Remembrance, 1992; author short stories; poetry pub. in several anthologies. Mem. Dem. Com., Blooming Grove; bd. dirs. Blooming Grove Hist. Assn.; mem. com. Update: Blooming Grove Master Plan; mem. Orange County Coun. Disabled; bd. dirs. Rehab. Support Svcs. Named Poet of Merit, Am. Poetry Assn., 1989; recipient Notable Civic Contbns. award Blooming Grove/Washingtonville C. of C., 1996. Mem. Blooming Grove C. of C. (v.p.), Orange County Classic Choral Soc., Clearwater (Fla.) Chorus. Democrat. Roman Catholic. Avocations: reading, gardening, furniture refinishing, singing.

WERKMAN, SIDNEY LEE, psychiatry educator; b. Washington, May 3, 1927. A.B., Williams Coll., 1948; M.D., Cornell U., 1952. Diplomate Am. Bd. Psychiatry and Neurology, Am. Bd. Child Psychiatry. Intern U. Va. Hosp., Charlottesville; resident in psychiatry Yale U., 1953-55, St. Elizabeth's Hosp., Washington, 1955-56; assoc. prof. psychiatry George Washington U., Washington, 1960-69; prof. U. Colo. Sch. Medicine, Denver, 1969-87; dir. div. adolescent psychiatry Children's Hosp. of Washington, 1965-69; clin. prof. Georgetown U. Sch. Medicine, Washington, 1989—; psychiatrist Capital Area Permanente Med. Group, Washington, 1990—; cons. grants NIMH, Washington, 1982—, guest researcher, 1984-85. Author: The Role of Psychiatry in Medical Education, 1966, Only a Little Time: A Chronicle of Dying, 1972, Bringing Up Children Overseas, 1977. Bd. dirs. Med. U. So. Africa, Performing Arts Soc., Washington Concert Operas. Master sgt. U.S. Army. Fellow Commonwealth Fund, Florence, Italy, 1963-64, NEH, 1979. Mem. Am. Psychiat. Assn., Am. Acad. Child Psychiatry, Group for Advancement Psychiatry, Am. Orthopsychiat. Assn. (bd. dirs. 1970-73), Colo. Psychiat. Soc. Office: Ste AG 29 3636 16th St NW Apt Ag 29 Washington DC 20010-1127

WERLEIN, EWING, JR., federal judge, lawyer; b. Houston, Sept. 14, 1936; s. Ewing and Ruth (Storey) W.; m. Kay McGibbon Werlein, June 29, 1963; children: Ewing Kenneth, Emily Kay. BA, So. Meth. U., 1958; LLB, U. Tex., 1961. Bar: Tex. 1961, U.S. Dist. Ct. (so. dist.) Tex. 1965, U.S. Dist. Ct. (ea. dist.) Tex. 1990, U.S. Ct. Appeals (5th cir.) 1970, U.S. Ct. Appeals (10th cir.) 1980, U.S. Claims Ct. 1985, U.S. Tax Ct. 1985, U.S. Supreme Ct. 1983. Ptnr. Vinson & Elkins, Houston, 1964-92; dist. judge U.S. Dist. Ct. (so. dist.) Tex., 1992—. Trustee So. Meth. U., Dallas, 1976-92, Asbury Theol. Sem., Wilmore, Ky., 1989—; mem. gen. bd. pub. United Meth. Ch., Nashville, 1974-84, chmn., 1980-84, chancellor Tex. ann. conf., 1977—; mem. exec. com. World Meth. Counh., 1981-96, treas, 1991-93. Capt. USAF, 1961-64. Fellow Am. Coll. Trial Lawyers, 1984, Internat. Soc. Barristers, 1987; recipient Disting. Alumni award SMU Alumni Assn., 1994. Fellow Am. Bar Found., Tex. Bar Found., Houston Bar Found.; mem. State Bar Tex. (dir. 1990-93), Nat. Conf. Bar Pres., Houston Bar Assn. (pres. 1988-89), Houston C. of C. (life), SAR, Order of Coif, Ramada Club (Houston), Houston Club, Phi Beta Kappa. Office: US Dist Ct Tex US Courthouse 515 Rusk St Ste 9136 Houston TX 77002-2605

WERLING, DONN PAUL, environmental educator; b. Ft. Wayne, Ind., Oct. 14, 1945; s. Paul Henry and Lydia Sophia (Rebber) W.; m. Diane Mueller, July 11, 1970; 1 child, Benjamin Paul. BS, Valparaiso U., 1967; MS, Mich. State U., 1968; MEd, Loyola U., 1970; Ph.D., U. Mich., 1979. Dir. nature project Raymond Sch., Chgo. Bd. Edn., 1969-72; dir. Evanston Environ. Assn., Ill., 1973-81; dir. Henry Ford Estate, U. Mich.-Dearborn, 1983—, adj. asst. prof. edn., 1984-95, adj. assoc. prof., 1996—; founder N.Am. Voyageur Conf., 1977. Author: Environmental Education and Your School Site, 1973; A School-Community Stewardship Model, 1979; Lake Michigan and Its Lighthouses, 1982, Lakes and Lighthouses, 1989, Lighthouse Library of the Great Lakes, 1993, Lore and Legacy, 1994. Mem. state master plan com. on environ. edn. State of Ill., Springfield, 1970; mem. adv. com. Ill. Coastal Zone, Chgo., 1978; bd. dirs. Ill. Shore council Girl Scouts U.S., 1978-82, Chgo. Maritime Soc., 1982. Recipient Mayor's award City of Evanston, 1976, Russell E. Wilson award U. Mich. Sch. Edn., 1979, Service award Ill. Shore council Girl Scouts U.S., 1978, J. Lee Barrett award Met. Detroit Tourist & Conv. Bur., 1986, award for interpretative excellence Nat. Assn. for Interpretation, 1989; named to Outstanding Young Men Am., Jaycees, 1975. Mem. Nat. Assn. Interpretation (founder), Am. Assn. Mus., Great Lakes Lighthouse Keepers Assn. (founder, pres. 1982-86), Tourist and Travel Assn. Southeast Mich. (chmn. 1984-86), Kiwanis. Avocations: historic restoration, gardening, writing, composing, singing Christian and bluewater music. Address: Henry Ford Estate-Fair Lane U of Michigan-Dearborn Evergreen Rd Dearborn MI 48128

WERMAN, DAVID SANFORD, psychiatrist, psychoanalyst, educator; b. N.Y.C., Jan. 1, 1922; s. Morris and Blanche (Heftel) W.; m. Marjolijn R. de Jager, Oct. 25, 1958 (div. 1975); children: Marco W., Claudia J. B.A., Queens Coll., 1942; postgrad., Columbia U., 1946-47; M.D., Cert. d'Etudes Medicales, U. Lausanne, Switzerland, 1952. Diplomate Am. Bd. Obstetrics and Gynecology, Am. Bd. Psychiatry and Neurology. Intern Beth Israel Hosp., N.Y.C., 1953-54, resident, 1954-57; resident Montefiore Hosp., Bronx, N.Y., 1964-67; pvt. practice specializing in ob-gyn. N.Y.C., 1957-64; faculty acad. psychiatry U. N.C., Chapel Hill, 1967-76, assoc. prof., instr. psychoanalytic tng. program, 1974—; prof. psychiatry Duke U. Med. Ctr., Durham, N.C., 1976—, supervising and tng. analyst psychoanalytic tng. program, 1981—, Honored prof. psychiatry, 1990—, prof. emeritus, 1992—; cons. Durham VA Hosp. Author: The Practice of Supportive Psychotherapy, 1984. Contbr. chpts. to books, articles to profl. jours. With AUS, 1943-45. Named Outstanding Tchr. psychiatry U. N.C., 1975, honored tchr. psychiatry Duke U., 1978, hon. prof., 1990. Fellow ACS, Am. Psychiat. Assn., Am. Coll. Psychoanalysts, others. Home: 1503 Michaux Rd Chapel Hill NC 27514-7637 Office: Duke Univ Med Ctr Dept Psychiatry PO Box 3812 Durham NC 27702-3812

WERMAN, THOMAS EHRLICH, record producer; b. Newton, Mass., Mar. 2, 1945; s. Lester and Ruth (Ehrlich) W.; m. Susan Lynne Gould, Aug. 25, 1968; children—Julia Gould, Nina Eve, Daniel Lester. B.A., Columbia U., 1967, M.B.A., 1969. Asst. account exec. Grey Advt., N.Y.C., 1969-70; asst. to dir. Epic Records Artistes and Repertoire, 1970-73; dir. talent acquisition Epic Records, 1973-76, staff producer, 1976-80; v.p., exec. producer CBS Records, Inc., L.A., 1980-81; sr. v.p. Elektra Records, 1981-82; pres. Julia's Music Inc., 1981—; v.p. artists and repertoire EMI-Capitol Entertainment Properties. Recipient N.Y.C. Civilian Commendation award for heroism, 1968, 14 platinum records awards Rec. Industry Assn. Am., 1977—, 8 Gold Record awards, 1977—. Mem. Nat. Assn. Recording Arts and Scis. Democrat. Jewish.

WERMUTH, PAUL CHARLES, retired English educator; b. Phila., Oct. 28, 1925; s. Paul C. and Susan (Manga) W.; m. Barbara Ethel Braun, Aug. 26, 1951; children—Geoffrey Paul, Paul Charles, Alan John, Stephen Mark. A.B., M.A., Boston U., 1951; Ph.D., Pa. State U., 1955. Instr. Clarkson Coll., Potsdam, N.Y., 1951-52; part-time instr., grad. asst. Pa. State U., 1952-55; asst. prof. Coll. William and Mary, 1955-57; mem. faculty Central Conn. State Coll., New Britain, 1957-68; asso. prof. English Central Conn. State Coll., 1966-68; prof. English Northeastern U., 1968-90, prof. emeritus, 1990—, chmn. dept., 1968-75; vis. prof. Middlebury Coll., 1963-64. Author: Modern Essays on Writing and Style, 2d edit, 1969, Essays in English, 1967, Bayard Taylor, 1974, also articles. Served with USAAF, 1943-46. Danforth summer study grantee, 1961. Mem. Modern Lang. Assn., AAUP, Mensa. Home: 73 Mostyn St Swampscott MA 01907-1616 Office: English Dept Northeastern Univ Boston MA 02115

WERNER, ELIZABETH HELEN, librarian, Spanish language educator; b. Palo Alto, Calif., June 21, 1944; d. Fielding and Lucy Elizabeth (Hart) McDearmon; m. Michael Andrew Werner, Aug. 21, 1976. BA, Mills Coll., 1966; MA, Ind. U., 1968; MLS, U. Md., 1973. Instr. Spanish, Western Md. Coll., Westminster, 1968-72; libr., assoc. prof. Clearwater (Fla.) Christian Coll., 1975—; sec. Sunline Libr. users group Tampa Bay Libr. Consortium, Tampa, Fla., 1993-94. Contbr. book revs. to profl. jours. Com. mem. Upper Pinellas County Post Office Customers' Adv. Coun., Clearwater, 1992—. Mem. Fla. Libr. Assn., Assn. Christian Librs., Fla. Assn. Christian Librs. (pres. 1991-94, sec. 1987-90, 95-96), Friends of the Clearwater Libr., Am. Assn. Tchrs. Spanish and Portuguese. Avocations: reading, choir, travel, language study. Office: Clearwater Christian Coll 3400 Gulf To Bay Blvd Clearwater FL 33759-4514

WERNER, GERHARD, pharmacologist, psychoanalyst, educator; b. Vienna, Austria, Sept. 28, 1921; came to U.S., 1957, naturalized, 1965; s. Rudolf and Elizabeth (Lukas) W.; m. Marion E. Hollander, July 25, 1958; children—Philip Ralph, Karen Nicole. M.D., U. Vienna, 1945. With dept. pharmacology U. Vienna, 1945-50; prof. pharmacology, head dept. U. Calcutta (India) Sch. Tropical Medicine, 1952-54, U. Sao Paulo (Brazil) Med. Sch. of Ribeirao Preto, 1955-57; assoc. prof. Cornell U. Med. Sch., 1957-61; assoc. prof. pharmacology and physiology Johns Hopkins U. Med. Sch., 1963-65; v.p. prof. affairs Univ. Health Ctr., Pitts., 1975-78; prof. pharmacology, head dept. U. Pitts. Med. Sch., 1965-75, dean, 1975-78, prof. psychiatry, 1978-89, F.S. Cheever Disting. prof., emeritus prof., 1990; pres. Med. Comp, Inc., 1990—; assoc., chief of staff Dept. Vets. Affairs Med. Ctr. Highland Drive, Pitts., 1991; cons. Ctr. for Emergent Technology, Motorola, Inc., 1995—; cons. psychobiology program NSF, 1970-75, mem. adv. panel regulatory biology div. biology and med. sci., 1969-70, mem. primate ctr. rev. com., 1973-79; mem. chem. biol. info. panel NIH, 1967-70, mem. study sect. pharmacology and exptl. therapeutics, 1964-68; mem. study sect. Pitts. Psychoanalytic Inst., 1973-79; external examiner for Ph.D (med. scis.) U. Calcutta, 1953—; mem. adv. bd. Indian Coun. Med. Rsch., 1952-54. Mem. editorial bd. Jour. Neurophysiology, 1970-78, Internat. Jour. Neuropharmacology, Jour. Clin. Pharmacology; asso. editor Pharmacol. Revs, 1969-70; contbr. articles to profl. jours. Recipient Humboldt prize,

1984. Fellow N.Y. Acad. Sci.; mem. Soc. Neuroscis., AAAS, Harvey Soc., Am. Soc. Pharmacology and Exptl. Therapeutics, Am. Physiol. Soc., Soc. Gen. Systems Research, Internat. Union for Psychobiology, Soc. for Artificial Intelligence, Assn. for Computing Machinery, Internat. Brain Research Orgn., Am. Psychoanalytic Assn., Indian Soc. Biochemistry and Physiology, German Pharmacol. Soc., Sigma Xi. Home: PO Box 161178 Austin TX 78716

WERNER, GLORIA S., librarian; b. Seattle, Dec. 12, 1940; d. Irving L. and Eva H. Stolzoff; m. Newton Davis Werner, June 30, 1963; 1 son, Adam Davis. BA, Oberlin Coll., 1961; ML, U. Wash., 1962; postgrad. UCLA, 1962-63. Reference librarian UCLA Biomed Library, 1963-64, asst. head pub. services dept., 1964-66, head pub. services dept., head reference div., 1966-72, asst. biomed. librarian public services, 1972-77, asso. biomed. librarian, 1977-78, biomed. librarian, assoc. univ. librarian, dir. Pacific S.W. regional Med. Library Service, 1979-83; asst. dean library services UCLA Sch. Medicine, 1980-83; assoc. univ. librarian for tech. services, 1983-89, dir. libraries, acting univ. librarian, 1989-90, univ. librarian, 1990—; adj. lectr. UCLA Grad. Sch. Library and Info. Sci., 1977-83. Editor, Bull. Med. Library Assn., 1979-82, asso. editor, 1974-79; mem. editorial bd. Ann. Stats. Med. Sch. Libraries U.S. and Can., 1980-83; mem. accrediting commn. Western Assn. Schs. and Colls., N.W. Assn. Schs. and Colls. Mem. ALA, Assn. Rsch. Librs. (bd. dirs. 1993—, v.p./pres.-elect 1995-96, pres. 1996-97). Office: UCLA Rsch Libr Libr Adminstrv Office 405 Hilgard Ave Los Angeles CA 90095-9000

WERNER, MARLIN SPIKE, speech pathologist and audiologist; b. Portland, Maine, Aug. 15, 1927; s. Leonard Matthews and Margaret (Steele) W.; m. Caroline Emma Paul, Dec. 23, 1985; children: Leo Hart, Joseph Hart. BA in Sociology and Social Work, U. Mo., 1950; ScM in Audiology and Speech Pathology, Johns Hopkins U., 1957; PhD in Speech and Hearing Sci., Ohio State U., 1966. Lic. in audiology, hearing aid dispensing, speech pathology, Hawaii; lic. in audiology and speech pathology, Calif. Audiologist/speech pathologist, dir. Speech and Hearing Ctr. Asheville (N.C.) Orthopedic Hosp., 1960-64; assoc. prof. speech pathology and audiology We. Carolina U., Cullowhee, N.C., 1965-69; assoc. prof. speech pathology, audiology and speech sci. Fed. City Coll. (now U. D.C.), Washington, 1969-73; pres. Friends of Nepal's Hearing Handicapped, Oakland, Calif., 1979-84; audiologist, speech pathologist pvt. practice, Oakland and Lafayette, Calif., 1973-85; pvt. practice Lafayette, 1985-87; pvt. practice speech pathology and audiology Hilo, Hawaii, 1987—; speech and hearing cons. VA Hosp., Oteen, N.C., 1960-64; clin. cons. Speech and Hearing Clinic, Asheville Orthopedic Hosp., 1966-67; lectr., presenter in field. Contbr. articles to profl. jours.; contbr. to Ency. Brit., Am. Heritage Book of Natural Wonders, others. 16602435ring impaired svcs. task force State of Hawaii Dept. Health, 1987-88; mem. Hawaii County Mayor's Com. for Persons with Disabilities, 1988-94; adv. bd. Salvation Army, 1992; bd. dirs. Hawaii chpt. Am. Arthritis Found.; past pres. Big Island Safety Assn.; mem. Hawaii Gov.'s Bd. Hearing Aid Dealers and Fitters; mem. adv. com., pres. Older Adult Resource Ctr., Laney Coll., Oakland, Calif.; v.p. Hawaii Speleol. Survey; chmn. Hawaii Grotto of Nat. Speleol. Soc., others; mem. adv. bd. Hilo Bay Clinics. MCH fellow Johns Hopkins U., 1954, Pub. Health fellow Ohio State U., 1964. Fellow Nat. Speleological Soc.; mem. AAAS, Am. Speech and Hearing Assn., Acoustical Soc. Am., Calif. Speech and Hearing Assn., Calif. Writers Club (bd. dirs., past pres.), Hawaii Speech/Lang. Hearing Assn. Avocations: collecting and making musical instruments, graphic arts, photography, cave exploring, writing. Home: PO Box 11509 Hilo HI 96721-6509 Office: 400 Hualani St Ste 191-a Hilo HI 96720-4378

WERNER, PATRICE (PATRICIA ANN WERNER), college president; b. Jersey City, May 31, 1937; d. Louis and Ella Blanche (Smith) W. BA in French, Caldwell Coll., 1966; MA in French, McGill U., 1970; PhD in French, NYU, 1976; postgrad. Inst. Ednl. Mgmt., Harvard U., 1991. Joined Dominican Sisters of Caldwell, 1954. Sch. tchr. Archdiocesan Sch. Systems, N.J., Ala., 1954-62; tchr. French, Latin Jersey City, Caldwell, N.J., 1962-72; instr. French Caldwell Coll., 1973-76; dir. continuing edn. Caldwell Coll., Caldwell, 1976-79, chair dept. fgn. langs., assoc. prof. French, 1979-85, acad. dean, prof. French, 1985-94; pres. Caldwell Coll., 1994—; cons. Dept. of Higher Edn. Grant Program, 1986; bd. trustees Caldwell Coll., Providence Coll. Mem. NAICU (chair com. on financing higher edn. 1997), Am. Assn. Higher Edn., Assn. Ind. Colls. and Univs. N.J., N.J. Presidents Coun. (new program rev. com.), Coun. of Ind. Colls. Avocations: tennis, reading, avid sports fan, travel. Office: Caldwell Coll 9 Ryerson Ave Caldwell NJ 07006-6109

WERNER, R(ICHARD) BUDD, retired business executive; b. Lorain, Ohio, Aug. 27, 1931; s. Paul Henry and Bessie Marie (Budd) W.; m. Janet Sue Kelsey, Aug. 28, 1932; children: Richard Budd, David Kelsey, Mary Paula. BS in Commerce, Ohio U., 1953. CPA, Ohio. Sr. auditor Arthur Andersen & Co., Cleve., 1955-59; various fin. positions Glidden Co., Cleve., 1959-65; v.p., asst. treas. Harshaw divsn. Kewanee Oil Co., Cleve., 1965-72; v.p. fin., treas. Weatherhead Co., Cleve., 1973-77; v.p. finance, treas. Hauserman, Inc., Cleve., 1977-81; v.p. fin., CFO SPX Corp., Muskegon, Mich., 1981-94, sr. v.p. planning and devel., 1994-95; exec. in residence coll. of bus. Ohio U., Athens, 1995—. Mem. Lakewood (Ohio) City Coun., 1972-73; mem. North Muskegon (Mich.) Sch. Bd., 1981-85. Lt. Q.M.C., U.S. Army, 1953-55. Mem. Fin. Execs. Inst., Fin. Execs. Rsch. Found., Athletic Club Columbus, Ohio. Office: Ohio U Copeland Hall Athens OH 45701

WERNER, ROBERT JOSEPH, college dean, music educator; b. Lackawanna, N.Y., Feb. 13, 1932; s. Edward Joseph and Marian L. (Gerringer) W.; m. Sharon Lynne Mohrfeld, June 22, 1957; children: Mark J., Kurt M., Erik J. BME, Northwestern U., 1953, MusM, 1954, PhD, 1967. Dir. instrumental music Evanston (Ill.) Twp. High Sch., 1956-66; assoc. prof. mus. Harpur Coll. SUNY, Binghamton, 1966-68, dir. Contemporary Music Project, 1968-73; dir. Sch. Mus. U. Ariz., Tucson, 1973-85, deanfine arts, 1981-82; dean Coll.-Conservatory of Music U. Cin., 1985—. Editor: Comprehensive Musicianship: An Anthology of Evolving Thought, 1971; contbtr. articles to profl. jours. Mem. exec. bd. Tucson Symphony Orch., 1974-85; bd. dirs. Cultural Commn. Tucson, 1974-75, Cin. Symphony Orch., 1985—, Cin. Opera, 1985—, Cin. Ballet, 1985—. With U.S. Army, 1954-56. Mem. Nat. Assn. Schs. Music (pres. 1989-91), Coll. Music Soc. (pres. 1977-78), Internat. Soc. for Music Edn. (pres. 1984-86, treas. 1986-97), Music Educators Nat.Conf., McDowell Soc., Coll. Music Soc., Psi Upsilon, Phi Mu Alpha Sinfonia. Office: U Cin Coll Conservatory of Music Cincinnati OH 45221-0003

WERNER, ROBERT L., lawyer; b. N.Y.C., Feb. 28, 1913; s. Abraham L. and Elsa (Ludwig) W.; m. Raye Davies, Oct. 13, 1945; children: William, John. A.B., Yale U., 1933; L.L.B., Harvard U., 1936. Bar: N.Y. 1936, U.S. Supreme Ct. 1936, also various fed. cts. and adminstrv. agys. 1936. Spl. asst. to U.S. atty. So. Dist. N.Y., 1936, asst. U.S. atty, 1937-40, confidential asst., 1940-42; 1st asst. civil div. U.S. Dept. Justice, Washington, 1946-47; spl. asst. to atty. gen. U.S., 1946-47; mem. law dept. RCA, N.Y.C., 1947; v.p., gen. atty. RCA, 1951-62, exec. v.p., gen. atty., 1962-66, exec. v.p., gen. counsel, 1966-78, dir., 1963-79, cons., 1978-83; mem. adv. bd. Internat. and Comparative Law Ctr. Southwestern Legal Found., Dallas, 1966—, treas., 1970-72, vice chmn., 1972-73, chmn. advisory bd., 1974-76, found. trustee 1976-88, hon. trustee 1988—; lectr. Conf. Bd., Practicing Law Inst., others; mem. nat. adv. council corp. law depts. Practising Law Inst., 1974-78; com. on restrictive bus. practices U.S. council Internat. C. of C., 1973-78; N.Y. Lawyers' Com. for Civil Rights under Law, 1972-78. Trustee Ithaca Coll., N.Y., 1968-88, hon. trustee, 1988—, chmn. bd., 1976-78; trustee Salisbury (Conn.) Sch., 1975-77, N.Y. Chiropractic Coll., 1986-89; bd. dirs. Midtown Arts Common at St. Peter's Ch., 1983-89. Capt. U.S. Army, 1942-44; to lt. col. USAAF, 1944-46, ETO. Recipient Disting. Service award Ithaca Coll., 1988. Fellow Am. Bar Found.; mem. Internat., Fed., Am., N.Y. State, City N.Y., FCC bar assns., IEEE (sr.), Am. Legion, Harvard Law Sch. Assn., Assn. Gen. Counsel (emeritus), U.S. Naval Inst., Internat. Law Assn. (Am. br.), Nat. Legal Aid and Defender Assn. (dir. 1974-79), Am. Judicature Soc., Newcomen Soc., N.Y. County Lawyers' Assn., Am. Soc. Internat. Law, Yale Club, Harvard Club N.Y., The Rockefeller Ctr. Club, Nat. Lawyers Club, Army and Navy Club (Washington), Coral Beach Club (Bermuda). Home: 116 E 68th St New York NY 10021-5905

WERNER, SETH MITCHELL, advertising executive; b. N.Y.C., Sept. 23, 1954; s. Michael M. and Helen (Barasch) W.; children: Zachary Michael, Harry Dean. BS in Pub. Rels., Boston U., 1976. Writer Monett Media, Atlanta, Ga., 1976-77; writer, copy chief Goldberg/Marchesano, Washington, 1977-79; writer The Marshalk Co., N.Y.C., 1979-86, Foote, Cone & Belding, San Francisco, 1986-87; then pres., exec. creative dir. Bloom FCA! (now Publicis/Bloom), Dallas, now co-chmn., exec. creative dir. Allstar Writer of Yr. Adweek mag., 1984, 87, Advt. Exec. of Yr., 1988. Office: Publicis Bloom 3500 Maple Ave Ste 450 Dallas TX 75219-3931

WERNER, STUART LLOYD, computer services company executive; b. N.Y.C., June 2, 1932; s. Leroy Louis and Frances Werner; m. Davideen Price, Jan. 6, 1990; children by previous marriage: Joan Leslie, Susan Lyn, Richard Wayne. BArch, Rensselaer Poly. Inst., 1954. Cert. FilePro/Unix instr. Ptnr. in charge architecture Werner-Dyer & Assos., Washington, 1959-68; v.p. Rentex Corp., Phila., 1968-70; pres. Werner & Assos., Inc., Washington, 1970-81; v.p. spl. projects ARA Svcs., Inc.; v.p. ARA, 1981-83; chmn. STN, Inc., Falls Church, Va., 1982-83; pres. Werner & Monk, Inc., 1983-90; pres. STN, Inc., 1981—; nat. instr. file prodatabase programming; mem. indsl. engring. terminology U.S. Stds. Inst. Bd. dirs. Watergate South, Washington Opera Soc., Friends of the Corcoran Gallery, Washington. With AUS, 1955-57. Mem. AIA, Am. Inst. Indsl. Engrs., Marinette Yacht Club, Masons,Tau Beta Pi. Republican. Contbr. articles to tech. jours. Home: 700 New Hampshire Ave NW Washington DC 20037-2406 Office: STN Inc 5113 Leesburg Pike Falls Church VA 22041-3204

WERNER, TOM, television producer, professional baseball team executive; m. Jill Werner; 3 children, Teddy, Carolyn, Amanda. BA, Harvard Univ., 1971. With ABC Television, Inc., 1972-82; co-owner Carsey-Werner Co., Studio City, Calif., 1982—; chmn. San Diego Padres, 1991-94; mem. bd. dirs.: Old Globe Theatre; Sharp Hospital. Co-exec. producer TV series: Oh, Madeline, 1983; exec. producer: The Cosby Show, (Emmy awd. Outstanding Comedy Series-1985), 1984-92, A Different World, 1987-93, Roseanne, 1988—, Chicken Soup, 1989-90, Grand, 1990, Davis Rules, 1991, You Bet Your Life, 1992-93, Frannie's Turn, 1992. Office: Carsey Werner Productions 4024 Radfoed Ave Studio City CA 91604*

WERNER, WILLIAM ARNO, architect; b. San Francisco, Dec. 11, 1937; s. William Arno and Sophie (Menutis) W.; m. Wendy Rolston Wilson, Feb. 3, 1963 (div. Jan. 1983); 1 child, Christa Nichol. BA with honors, Yale U., 1959, BArch, 1962, MArch, 1963. Drafter Serge Chermayeff, Paul Rudolph and Charles Brewer, New Haven, 1961-63; project designer Johnson, Poole & Storm, San Francisco, 1963-64; project designer Leo S. Wou & Assocs., Honolulu, 1965-66, v.p. of design, 1971-72; project architect John Tatom Assocs., Honolulu, 1965-66; sr. designer Skidmore, Owings & Merrill, San Francisco, 1968-71, assoc./project architect, 1972-76; prin. W.A. Werner Assocs., San Francisco, 1976-80; ptnr. Werner & Sullivan, San Francisco, 1980—; mem. planning commn. City of Sausalito, Calif.; bd. govs. Yale U., New Haven; visitorship in architecture U. Auckland Found., New Zealand, 1994. Prin. works include Alameda Mcpl. Credit Union, Lane Pub. Co., Menlo Park, Calif., Pacific Data Images, Mountain View, Calif., Saga Corp., Menlo Park, Tiffany & Co., Union Square, San Francisco, Somerset Collection, Troy, Mich., Touche Ross & Co., Oakland, U.S. Post Office, San Francisco, (renovations) Fed. Express Co., San Francisco, KD's Grog N' Grocery, San Francisco, Jessie Street. Substation, San Francisco, Lakeside Tower Health Ctr./Mt. Zion Hosp., Qantas Bldg, San Francisco, Women's Care, San Francisco, Moon Residence, Dillon Beach, Calif., Shenkar Residence, San Francisco, Tacker Residence, Denver, Lasky Residence, San Francisco, Starring Residence, San Francisco, Whitehead Residence, Monte Rio, Calif., various laboratories, theatres and rsch. facilities, urban design. Recipient Progressive Architecture Design award Jessie St. Substation, 1980, DuPont Co. Design award Touche Ross & Co., 1983, award of Excellence Woodwork Inst. of Calif., 1989, USPS/NEA Nat. Honor award for Design Excellence, 1990, Tucker Design Excellence award Bldg. Stone Inst., Tiffany & Co., 1992. Mem. AIA (San Francisco chpt.), Found. for San Francisco's Architectural Heritage (hon.). Home: 213 Richardson St Sausalito CA 94965-2422 Office: Werner & Sullivan 207 Powell St Ste 800 San Francisco CA 94102-2209

WERNER-JACOBSEN, EMMY ELISABETH, developmental psychologist; b. Eltville, Germany, May 26, 1929; came to U.S., 1952, naturalized, 1962; d. Peter Josef and Liesel (Kunz) W. B.S., Johannes Gutenberg U., Germany, 1950; M.A., U. Nebr., 1952, Ph.D., 1955; postgrad., U. Calif., Berkeley, 1953-54. Research asso. Inst. Child Welfare, U. Minn., 1956-59; vis. scientist NIH, 1959-62; asst. prof. to prof. human devel., rsch. child psychologist U. Calif., Davis, 1962-94, rsch. prof., 1995—. Sr. author: The Children of Kauai, 1971, Kauai's Children Come of Age, 1977, Cross-Cultural Child Development: A View from the Planet Earth, 1979, Vulnerable, but Invincible, 1982, 2d edit., 1989, Child Care: Kith, Kin and Hired Hands, 1984, Overcoming the Odds, 1992, Pioneer Children on the Journey West, 1995, Reluctant Witnesses: Children's Voices From the Civil War, 1997; contbr. articles to profl. jours. Mem. Am. Psychol. Soc., German Acad. Social Pediats. (hon.), Soc. for Rsch. in Child Devel.

WERNICK, EDWARD RAYMOND, company executive, computer consultant; b. Irvington, N.J., Mar. 11, 1955; s. Edward Joseph and Ann (Czech) W.; m. Ione Sharon Greenbaum, Nov. 2, 1984; 1 child, Elissa Ann. BS in Computer Sci., Kean Coll., 1977. Computer analyst N.Y. Life Ins., N.Y.C., 1978-81; computer cons. Horizons, N.Y.C., 1981-84; data base adminstr. oracle Standard & Poors, N.Y.C., 1984-88; tchr. sybase Sybase, N.Y.C., 1988-89; data base adminstr. sybase Merrill Lynch, N.Y.C., 1989-91, Paramount Comms., Old Tappan, N.J., 1991-95; v.p. Crossmar, Parsippany, N.J., 1995—; computer, fin. cons., pvt. practice, Oradell, N.J., 1981—. Designer stage lighting for more than 80 plays, 1978-84; writer relational scripts for Australian govt., 1994; exhibited sculpture in India, 1991, Brazil, 1992, Oslo, Norway, 1994. Mem. Rep. Nat. Com.; sec. Stockton (N.J.) Rifle Club, 1974; pres. Irvington (N.J.) Masquers, 1978. Named Outstanding Young Rep. Union, N.J., Rep. Com., 1976; Best of Show sculpture Art Assoc., Irvington, N.J., 1979; 100 yd. standing rifle champion Stockton (N.J.) Rifle Club, 1974. Mem. Assn. for Computing Machinery, Sybase Internat. Users Group, Relational Database Users Group, Oradell Arts Com., Internet Users Group. Roman Catholic. Avocations: lighting design, theater, logic. Home: 920 Oradell Ave Oradell NJ 07649-1925 Office: Crossmar 4 Sylvan Way Parsippany NJ 07054-3801

WERNICK, JACK HARRY, chemist; b. St. Paul, May 19, 1923; s. Joseph and Eva (Legan) W.; B.Met.E., U. Minn., 1947, M.S., 1948; Ph.D., Pa. State U., 1954; m. Sylvia Katz, Dec. 20, 1947 (dec.); children—Phyllis Roberta Wernick Lauer, Rosanne Pauline; m. 2d, Charlotte Adler, 1983. Staff, Manhattan Project, Los Alamos, 1944-46; mem. staff Bell Labs., Murray Hill, N.J., 1954-84, head solid state chemistry research dept., 1963-81, head device materials research dept., 1981-83; div. mgr. Bell Comm. Rsch., 1983-92; cons. U.S. Office Sci. and Tech., Nat. Bur. Standards, NSF; mem. steering com. div. nuclear fusion ERDA, 1977-79; mem. Gov.'s Roundtable on Superconductivity, N.J., 1989-90. Served in U.S. Army, 1944-46. Fellow N.Y. Acad. Scis., Am. Phys. Soc., AIME, Am. Soc. Metals (McFarland award 1969); mem. Nat. Acad. Engring., AAAS, IEEE, Electrochem. Soc., Sigma Xi, Phi Lambda Upsilon. Jewish. Author: (with E.A. Nesbitt) Rare Earth Permanent Magnets, 1973, (with J.L. Shay) Chalcopyrite Crystals, 1975; editor: Materials and Energy: Selected Topics, 1977; Materials Letters; contbr. articles to profl. jours. Home: 21 Haran Cir Millburn NJ 07041-1403 Office: AT&T Bell Labs New Providence NJ 07974

WERNICK, RICHARD FRANK, composer, conductor; b. Boston, Jan. 16, 1934; s. Louis and Irene (Prince) W.; m. Beatrice Messina, July 15, 1956; children: Lewis, Adam, Peter (dec.). BA, Brandeis U., 1955; MA, Mills Coll., 1957. Instr. music U. Buffalo, 1964-65; asst. prof. music, dir. univ. symphony U. Chgo., 1965-68; conductor Pa. Contemporary Players, 1968-93; prof. music U. Pa., 1968-96, prof. emeritus, 1996—; co-founder Community Youth Orch. of Delaware County; cons. Contemporary Music, The Phil. Orch., 1983-89, spl. cons. to the music dir., 1989-93; bd. dirs. Theodore Presser Co. Music dir. Royal Winnipeg Ballet Can., 1957-58; composer: Haiku of Basho, 1967, A Prayer for Jerusalem, 1971 (Naumburg award 1975), Moonsongs from the Japanese, 1972, Kaddish Requiem, 1973, String Quartet 2, 1973, Songs of Remembrance, 1974, Visions of Terror and Wonder, 1976 (Pulitzer prize 1977), Contemplations of the Tenth Muse, Book I, 1976, Book II, 1978, Introits and Canons, 1977, A Poison Tree, 1979, Concerto for Cello and Ten Players, 1980, In Praise of Zephyrus, 1981, Piano Sonata: Reflections of a Dark Light, 1982, Sonata for cello and piano: Portraits of Antiquity, 1982, The Oracle of Shimon bar Yochai, 1983, Concerto for Violin and Orch., 1983-84 (Friedheim 1st prize 1986); Oracle II for soprano, oboe and piano, 1985, Concerto for Viola and Orch., 1985-86, Musica Ptolemeica brass quintet, 1987, Symphony #1, 1988, String Quartet #3, 1988, Concerto for Piano and Orch. (Friedheim award 1992), 1989-90, Fragments of Prophecy, 1990, String Quartet #4, 1991 (Friedheim 1st prize 1991), Concerto for Saxophone Quartet and Orch., 1991, Cello Concerto #2, 1992, Symphony #2, 1993, ...and a time for peace, 1994, String Quartet #5, 1995, Cassation music Tom Jefferson Knew, 1995, trio for violin, cello, piano, 1996, Da'are for solo guitar, 1996, closed synapses for solo basoon, 1997. Recipient music award Nat. Inst. Arts and Letters, 1976, Nat. Endowment Arts grantee, 1975, 79, 82; Fellow Ford Found., 1962-64, Guggenheim Found., 1976. Mem. ASCAP. Democrat. Office: 201 S 34th St Philadelphia PA 19104-6313

WERNICK, SANDIE MARGOT, advertising and public relations executive; b. Tampa, Sept. 13, 1944; d. Nathan and Sylvia (Bienstock) Rothstein. BA in English, U. Fla., 1966. Tchr. English Miami Beach (Fla.) Sr. High Sch., 1967; adminstrv. asst. pub. rels. Bozell & Jacobs, Inc., N.Y.C., 1968-69; asst. to dir. pub. rels. Waldorf-Astoria, N.Y.C., 1969-70; dir. advt. and pub. rels. Hyatt on Union Square, San Francisco, 1974-82; pres. Wernick Mktg. Group, San Francisco, 1982—. Bd. mem. Nat. Kidney Assn., San Francisco, 1985-87; advisor Swords to Plowshares, San Francisco, 1988-89. Recipient Award of Merit, San Francisco Advt. and Cable Car Awards, 1979, Award of Excellence, San Francisco Art Dirs. 1978, Disting. Mktg. award Sales and Mktg. Internat., 1997, awards Am. Hotel and Motel Assn., 1981, 1982, awards of excellence San Francisco Publicity Club, 1990, 1994, 1995, 1996. Mem. Women in Comms. (bd. dirs. 1987-89), Am. Women in Radio and TV (bd. dirs. 1989-90), Pub. Rels. Soc. Am., San Francisco Publicity Club (pres. 1989), Variety Club, Profl. Bus. Women's Assn., Calif. Pacific Med. Ctr. (aux. 1988-95). Democrat. Jewish. Home: 1690 Broadway San Francisco CA 94109-2417 Office: Wernick Marketing Group 444 Market St Ste 1125 San Francisco CA 94111-5328

WERNTZ, CARL WEBER, physics educator; b. Washington, Aug. 7, 1931; s. Walter Hartman and Elizabeth Katherine (Weber) W.; m. Margaret Anne Bjerke, Aug. 23, 1958; children: Heidi, Paul. BS, George Washington U., 1953; PhD, U. Minn., 1960. Postdoctoral fellow U. Wis., Madison, 1960-62; asst. prof. Cath. U. Am., Washington, 1962-65, assoc. prof., 1965-70, prof. physics, 1970—, chmn. physics dept., 1974-77, 92—; vis. prof. Calif. Inst. Tech., Pasadena, 1969-70. Nat. Rsch. Ctr. fellow, 1975-76. Office: Catholic U Physics Dept Cardinal Sta Washington DC 20064

WERRIES, E. DEAN, food distribution company executive; b. Tescott, Kans., May 8, 1929; s. John William and Sophie E. Werries; m. Marjean Sparling, May 18, 1962. B.S., U. Kans., 1952. With Fleming Foods Co., Topeka, 1955-89, exec. v.p., 1973-76; exec. v.p. Eastern ops. Fleming Foods Co., Phila., 1976-78; pres. Fleming Foods Co., Oklahoma City, 1978-81; pres., chief operating officer Fleming Cos., Inc., Oklahoma City, 1981-88, also dir.; pres., chief exec. officer Fleming Cos., Inc., 1988-89, chmn., CEO, 1989-93; chmn. bd. Sonic Corp., 1995—. Sec. of Commerce State of Okla., 1995. With U.S. Army, 1952-54, Korea. Mem. Nat. Am. Wholesale Grocers Assn. (bd. dirs. 1979-93), Food Mktg. Inst. (bd. dirs. 1984—, chmn. 1989-91), Ind. Grocers Alliance (bd. dirs. 1984-94). Republican. Presbyterian. Office: Fleming Cos Inc PO Box 26647 6301 Waterford Blvd Oklahoma City OK 73126-0647

WERT, BARBARA J. YINGLING, special education educator; b. Hanover, Pa., May 18, 1953; d. Richard Bruce and Jacqueline Louise (Myers) Yingling; m. Barry Thomas Wert, Aug. 23, 1975; children: Jennifer Allison, Jason Frederick. BS in Elem. Edn., Kutztown (Pa.) U., 1975; MS in Spl. Edn., Bloomsburg (Pa.) U., 1990. Cert. in elem. edn., spl. edn., Pa. Dir. children's program Coun. for United Ch. Ministries of Reading, Reading, Pa., 1975-76; instr. Berks County Vo-Tech., Oley Valley, Pa., 1976-77; asst. tchr. Ostrander Elem. Sch., Wallkill, N.Y., 1982-85; spl. needs surp., instrnl. support tchr., cons. Danville (Pa.) Child Devel. Ctr., 1986—; dir. Little Learners Pre-Sch., Northumberland, Pa., 1991-94, ednl. cons., 1991—; pvt. cons. Families with Spl. Needs, Northumberland, 1991—; adj. prof. spl. edn., Bloomsburg U., 1995. Recipient Parent Profl. Partnership award 1993. Mem. ASCD, Coun. for Exceptional Children (exec. bd. dirs. divsn. early childhood 1991—, sec. 1991-93, newsletter editor, v.p. 1993-94, pres. 1995-96), Nat. Assn. for Edn. Young Children (v.p. Pa. divsn. for early childhood 1993—, tchr. edn. divsn., coun. for behavior disorders divsn., learning disabilities divsn.), Local Autism Support and Advocacy Group. Avocations: photography, needlework, hiking, reading. Home: RR 1 Box 372-n Northumberland PA 17857-9717 Office: Danville Child Devel Ctr PO Box 183 Danville PA 17821-0183

WERT, CHARLES ALLEN, metallurgical and mining engineering educator; b. Battle Creek, Iowa, Dec. 31, 1919; s. John Henry and Anna (Spotts) W.; m. Lucille Vivian Mathena, Sept. 5, 1943; children: John Arthur, Sara Ann. B.A., Morningside Coll., Sioux City, 1941; M.S., State U. Iowa, 1943, Ph.D., 1948. Mem. staff Radiation Lab., Mass. Inst. Tech., 1943-45; instr. physics U. Chgo., 1948-50; mem. faculty U. Ill. at Urbana, 1950—, prof., 1955, head dept. metall. and mining engring., 1967-86, prof. emeritus, 1989; cons. to industry. Author: Physics of Metals, 1970, Opportunities in Materials Science and Engineering, 1977; also articles.; Cons. editor, McGraw Hill Book Co. Recipient sr. scientist award von Humboldt-Stiftung. Fellow Am. Phys. Soc., Am. Soc. Metals, AAAS, AIME; mem. Sigma Xi. Home: 1708 W Green St Champaign IL 61821-3721 Office: U Ill Metallurgy & Mining Bldg Urbana IL 61801

WERT, JAMES JUNIOR, materials scientist, educator; b. Barron, Wis., Jan. 9, 1933; s. James Lewis and Bernice Janet (Walker) W.; m. Jane Alice Thornton, Aug. 16, 1958; children: Thaddeus Thornton, Melissa Jane. B.S., U. Wis., 1957, M.S., 1958, Ph.D., 1961; postgrad., Carnegie Tech. Inst., 1958-59. Assoc. engr. Westinghouse Electric Corp., Pitts., 1958-60; rsch. scientist A.O. Smith Corp., Milw., 1961-62; mem. faculty Vanderbilt U., Nashville, 1962—; prof. material sci. and engring. Vanderbilt U., 1967—, chmn. dept., 1969, chmn. materials, mechanics and structures div., 1969-72, chmn. materials sci. dept., 1975-82, chmn. dept. mech. and materials engring., 1976-82, George A. Sloan prof. metallurgy, 1976—; mayor City of Forest Hills, Tenn., 1990-95; dir. Ctr. for Coatings Sci. and Tech., Vanderbilt U., 1969-74; co.-dir. Ctr. for Materials Tribology, 1987—; vis. prof. Cambridge U., 1974; sr. Fulbright lectr. Mid. East; cons. Avco, 1964-71, Temco, 1964-71, Arnold Engring. Ctr., Tullahome, Tenn., 1966-71, Nat. Acad. Scis., 1969-70; pres. Technology Assocs., Inc., Nashville, 1975-85; pres. James Wert & Assocs., 1985—. Contbr. articles to profl. jours. Served with AUS, 1953-55. Ampco fellow, 1957-58; Westinghouse-Bettis fellow, 1958-59; Foundry Edn. fellow, 1952-57; recipient Adams award Am. Welding Soc., 1969, Teaching award Tau Beta Pi, 1970, 78. Fellow ASME, ASM Internat.; mem. ASTM, AIME, Am. Welding Soc., Am. Soc. Metals, Hillwood Country Club, Vines Golf and Country Club, Sigma Xi, Tau Beta Pi, Phi Eta Sigma, Alpha Sigma Mu, Pi Kappa Alpha, Pi Tau Sigma, Omicron Kappa Delta. Methodist. Patentee nuclear fuels and cladding materials. Home: 2510 Ridgewood Dr Nashville TN 37215-4518

WERT, JONATHAN MAXWELL, II, management consultant; b. Port Royal, Pa., Nov. 8, 1939; s. Jonathan Maxwell I and Helen Leona (Leonard) W.; m. Monica Kay Manbeck; children: Jonathan Maxwell III, Kimberly Dee, Jon Adam, Justin Tyler, Amanda Elizabeth. B.S. in Biology, Austin Peay State U., 1966, M.S. in Biology, 1968; Ph.D. in Adminstrn., U. Ala., 1974. Park supt., chief interpretive services Bur. State Parks Pa. Dept. Environ. Resources, Harrisburg, 1968-69; chief naturalist Bays Mountain Park Environ. Edn. Ctr., Kingsport, Tenn., 1969-71; environ. and energy edn. specialist TVA, Knoxville, 1971-75; cons. energy, environment, conservation U. Tenn., Knoxville, 1975; sr. assoc.-energy Energy Extension Svc., Coop. Extension Svc., Pa. State U., 1977-80; pres. Energy-Environ. Consultants, Port Royal, Pa., 1981-85, Mgmt. Diagnostics, Inc., Port Royal, 1985—. Author: Writing Environmental Education Grant Proposals, 1974, Environmental Education Study Projects for High School Students, 1974, Environmental Education Study Projects for College Students, 1974, Developing Environmental Study Areas, 1974, Developing Environmental

Education Curriculum Material, 1974, Finding Solutions to Environmental Problems . . . A Process Guide, 1975, Assessing an Issue in Relation to Environmental, Economic, and Social Impact . . . A Process Guide, 1976, Energy Conservation Measures for Mobile Home Dwellers, 1978, Selected Energy Conservation Options for the Home, 1978, Selected Energy Management Options for Small Business and Local Government, 1978, Life Lines: A Book of Poetry, Prose, and Axioms, 1983, Survivorship and Growth in Employment: A Question and Answer Guide, 1983; mem. adv. bd.: Environ. Edn. Report, 1974—; cons. editor: Jour. Environ. Edn, 1975; contbr. articles to profl. jours. Counselor Boy Scouts Am., 1975. Served with USMC, 1958-61. Recipient Conservation award Am. Motors Co., 1976. Mem. U.S. Energy Assn., Inst. Mgmt. Cons., Orgn. Devel. Inst., Inst. of Mgmt. Cons. (cert. mgmt. cons.), The Cons. Bur. (profl. mgmt. cons.). Lutheran. Office: Mgmt Diagnostics Inc PO Box 240 Port Royal PA 17082-0240

WERTH, ANDREW M., telecommunications executive; b. Saarbruck, Germany, Mar. 2, 1934; came to U.S., 1944; s. Steven S. and Margot Werth; m. Eileen B. Pighini, Jan. 30, 1954; children: Gregory, Jeffrey, Karen. BS, Columbia U., 1955, MS, 1961. Project engr. ITT Labs., Nutley, N.J., 1959-64; mem. tech. staff Comsat Corp., Washington, 1964-68; br. mgr. Comsat Labs., Clarksburg, Md., 1968-72; pres. Hughes Network Systems Internat., Germantown, Md., 1972—. Patentee in field. Capt. USAF, 1955-57. Fellow IEEE; mem. AIAA, Cosmos Club. Roman Catholic.

WERTH, JEAN MARIE, biology educator; b. Rochester, N.Y., Jan. 21, 1943; d. Henry Richard and Marjorie Frances (Vrooman) W. BS, Nazareth Coll., 1964; MS, Syracuse U., 1968, PhD, 1973. Asst. prof. William Paterson Coll., Wayne, N.J., 1972-75, assoc. prof., 1975-83, prof. biology, 1983—, chmn. dept., 1984-87; vis. scientist Roche Inst. Molecular Biology, Nutley, N.J., 1980-81; NIH trainee Syracuse U., 1966-71. Contbr. articles to profl. jours. Pres. Lake Reality Homeowners Assn., Kinnelon, N.J., 1983. Mem. AAAS, N.Y. Acad. Scis., Sigma Xi. Avocations: hiking, camping, music, reading, computing. Home: 24 Reality Dr Kinnelon NJ 07405 Office: William Paterson Coll 300 Pompton Rd Wayne NJ 07470-2103

WERTHAMER, N. RICHARD, physicist; b. Milw., Feb. 9, 1935. BS, Harvard Coll., 1956; PhD in physics, U. Calif., 1961. Rsch. assoc. U. Calif., San Diego, 1961-62; mem. tech. staff Bell Labs, 1962-75; mem. corp. planning dept. AT&T, 1975-76; chmn. N.Y. State Energy Rsch. and Devel. Authority, 1976-78; sr. advisor sci. and tech. dept. Exxon Corp., 1978-83; dir. Becton Dickinson Devel. Corp., 1983-89; exec. officer Am. Phys. Soc., 1990-93; mgmt. cons. Chelsea Technols, N.Y.C., 1993—. Fellow AAAS, Am. Phys. Soc. Office: Chelsea Technols 43 W 16th St Ste 7-d New York NY 10011-6322

WERTHEIM, MARY DANIELLE, elementary education coordinator; b. N.Y.C.; d. Daniel Leo and Helen Loretta (Sudimick) Conroy; m. Stanley Claude Wertheim, Mar. 9, 1963. BA in English with honors, CCNY, 1960, MA, 1979. Coord. English and lang. arts Horace Mann Lower Sch., Riverdale, N.Y., 1969—; pvt. investor Wertheim Trust, N.Y.C., 1985—; pres. Horace Mann Investment Club, Riverdale, 1989—. Founder, advisor Horace Mann Lower Sch. Cmty. Svc. Group, Riverdale, 1980—; active Rep. nat. Com., 1980—. Mem. ASCD, The Grolier Club, Zonta, Mensa. Avocations: desk top publishing, manuscript collecting, frogs, Sherlock Holmes. Home: 180 Cabrini Blvd New York NY 10033 Office: Horace Mann Lower Sch 4440 Tibbett Ave Bronx NY 10471-3416

WERTHEIM, MITZI MALLINA, technology company executive; b. N.Y.C.; d. Rudolf and Myrtle B. (McGraw) Mallina; m. Ronald P. Wertheim, Feb. 25, 1965 (div. July 1988); children: Carter, Christiana. B.A., U. Mich., 1960. Asst. dir. div. research Peace Corps, Washington, 1961-66; sr. program officer Cafritz Found., Washington, 1970-76; dep. undersec. navy, 1977-81; with Fed. Sector Div. IBM, 1981-94; v.p. enterprise solutions Systems Rsch. and Applications Corp., 1994—; Woodrow Wilson vis. fellow, 1979, 80. Bd. dirs. Nat. Coalition for Sci. and Tech., 1983—, Youth Policy Inst., 1986-91, VITA, 1990—; mem. vis. com. MIT, 1983-89. Recipient Federally Employed Women award Def. Dept., 1980; Disting. Pub. Svc. medal Navy Dept., 1981; fellow Maxwell Sch. Syracuse U., 1996—. Mem. Coun. on Fgn. Rels. Episcopalian. Home: 3113 38th St NW Washington DC 20016-3726

WERTHEIM, ROBERT HALLEY, security consultant; b. Carlsbad, N.Mex., Nov. 9, 1922; s. Joseph and Emma (Vorenberg) W.; m. Barbara Louise Selig, Dec. 26, 1946; children: Joseph Howard, David Andrew. Student, N.Mex. Mil. Inst., 1940-42; B.S., U.S. Naval Acad., 1945; M.S. in Physics, M.I.T., 1954; postgrad., Harvard U., 1969. Commd. ensign U.S. Navy, 1945, advanced through grades to rear adm., 1972; assigned Spl. Projects Office, Washington, 1956-61, Naval Ordnance Test Sta., China Lake, 1961-62, Office Sec. Def., Washington, 1962-65; head Missile br. Strategic Systems Project Office, Washington, 1965-67; dep. tech. dir. Missile br. Strategic Systems Project Office, 1967-68, tech. dir., 1968-77, dir., 1977-80; sr. v.p. Lockheed Corp., 1981-88; cons. nat. def., 1988—; emeritus mem. Draper Lab., Inc.; mem. U. Calif. Pres. Adv. Coun.; mem. sci. adv. group Dept. Def., Dept. Energy, Inst. for Def. Analysis, Ctr. for Naval Analysis, U.S. Strategic Command; mem. nat. security adv. Los Alamos Nat. Lab., Lawrence Livermore Nat. Lab. Decorated D.S.M. with cluster, Legion of Merit, Navy Commendation medal, Joint Svc. Commendation medal; recipient Rear Adm. William S. Parsons award Navy League U.S., 1971, Chmn. Joint Chiefs of Staff Disting. Pub. Svc. award, 1996, Sec. of Def. medal for outstanding pub. svc., 1996. Fellow AIAA; mem. Am. Soc. Naval Engrs. (hon. mem., Gold medal 1972), Nat. Acad. Engring., U.S. Naval Inst., Nat. Acad. Scis. (com. on internat. security and arms control), Bernardo Heights Country Club, Masons, Sigma Xi, Tau Beta Pi. Home: 17705 Devereux Rd San Diego CA 92128-2084 Office: Sci Applications Internat Corp 1200 Prospect St La Jolla CA 92037-3608

WERTHEIM, STEVEN BLAKE, orthopedist; b. Apr. 1, 1956; m. Melinda Mitchell; children: Meredith, Julia, Eve. BA, Northwestern U., 1977; MD, Case Western Reserve U., 1981. Cert. Am. Bd. orthopaedic Surgery, Ga., 1989. Intern in Surgery Univ. Hosp. Cleve., 1981-82; resident in orthopaedics, 1982-86; fellow in Sports Medicine U. Pa., 1986-87; asst. prof. Orthopaedic Surgery U. Pa. Sch. Medicine, 1987-88; faculty U.S. Sports Acad., 1995—; clin. asst. prof. Orthopaedics Emory U. Sch. Medicine, 1989—; bd. trustees Atlanta Jewish Fedn.,; com. Am. Israeli Pub. Affairs; regional v.p. Macabah USA/Sports for Israel; team physician East Paulding H.S., 1993-94 Atlanta Fire Ants U.S. Profl. roller Hockey League, 1993-94; chmn. Promina Windy Hill Bd. Dirs. 1993, 94, Kennestone Hosp at Windy Hill, 1992, 93; chief of staff elect Kennestone Hosp. at Windy Hill, 1991, 92; chief of Orthopaedics Kennestone Hosp. at Windy Hill, 1989, 91; Ambulatory Care Com., Cobb Hosp. and Med. Ctr., 1989, 91; O.r. Com. Kennestone Hosp. at Windy Hill, 1989-92. Numerous lectures and exhibits in field; contbr. articles to profl. jours. Recipient Jesse T. Nicholson award, U. Pa. Dept. Orthopaedics, 1988, James Scholar award Psychology, 1977, Bus. Atlanta Forty Under Forty award, 1993. Mem. AMA, Am. Acad. Orthopaedic Surgeons, Arthroscopy Assn. N.Am., U.S. Olympic Com. Sports Medicine Soc., Nat. Athletic Trainers Assn., Southern Orthopaedic Assn., Southern Med. Assn. Office: C/O Resurgens Orthopaedics Ste 900 5671 Peachtree Dunwoody Rd NE Atlanta GA 30342-5009*

WERTHEIMER, FRANC, retired corporate executive; b. Nuremberg, Germany, Sept. 26, 1927; came to U.S., 1938; s. Erich Z. and Sophie (Prager) W.; m. Sidelle Shaiken, Sept. 2, 1951; children: Laura S., David F. BA summa cum laude, Bklyn. Coll., 1950; MA, Columbia U., 1951. Head dept. systems analysis Vitro Labs., West Orange, N.J., 1952-68; pres., chief exec. officer ManTech Internat. Corp., Alexandria, Va., 1968-91; vice chmn. Forensic Techs. Internat. Corp., Annapolis, Md., 1968-92; adj. prof. math. Bklyn. Coll., CUNY, 1951-53, Fairleigh Dickinson U., Rutherford, N.J., 1954-58, Kean Coll., Union, N.J., 1968-72; instr. math., dir. Emeritus Found., program dir. Emeritus Scientists, Mathematicians and Engrs. Program, 1991—; instr. math. Project Apply, AAAS, 1991—; mentor Dingman Ctr., U. Md. Sch. Bus. and Mgmt., 1991-96, adj. prof. mgmt., 1995-96. Contbr. over 500 reports, monographs, position papers, concept documents pub. and submitted to U.S. Govt. and pvt. sector clients, articles to profl. jours.; guest editor Technical Jour., 1969; session chmn. tech. seminar, 1980. Bd. dirs. Washington Urban League, 1979-84; bd. dirs., pres., v.p., sec., treas. Sumner Village Condominium, Bethesda, Md., 1988—; mem. Com. on Coms., Montgomery County, Md., 1991-93; docent Nat. Archives and Records Adminstrn., 1991-93; docent Phillips Collection, 1991—, mgr. vols., 1994—; cons. Nat. Inst. Stds. and Tech., 1996; asst. to dir. men's group OASIS, 1993-95. With U.S. Army. Grad. scholar Columbia U., 1950. Mem. Ops. Rsch. Soc. Am., Navy League U.S. (life), Bklyn. Coll. Alumni Assn. (pres. D.C. chpt. 1989), Cosmos Club, B'nai B'rith, Phi Beta Kappa, Pi Mu Epsilon. Home: 4956 Sentinel Dr Bethesda MD 20816-3594

WERTHEIMER, FREDRIC MICHAEL, public policy advocate; b. Bklyn., Jan. 9, 1939; s. Irving Wertheimer and Mildred (Klein) Van Brink; m. Linda Cozby, June 15, 1969. B.A., U. Mich., 1959; LL.B., Harvard U., 1962. Bar: N.Y. bar 1963. Atty. SEC, 1963-66; legis. counsel Congressman Silvio Conte, 1967-68; counsel House Small Bus. Com., 1969-70; lobbyist, legis. dir., v.p. Common Cause, Washington, 1971-81; pres. Common Cause, 1981-95; news polit. analyst CBS News, Washington, 1996; pres. Democracy 21, 1997—; fellow Press Politics and Policy Ctr. Harvard U., 1996; J. Skelly Wright fellow, vis. lectr. Yale Law Sch., 1997. Author: Common Cause Manual on Money and Politics. With U.S. Army, 1962-63. Fellow Inst. Politics Harvard U., 1972. Jewish. Home: 3502 Macomb St NW Washington DC 20016

WERTHEIMER, ROBERT E., paper company executive; b. 1928; married. BSME, U. Wash., 1950; MBA, Harvard U., 1952. With Longview (Wash.) Fibre Co., 1952—, package engr., 1955-59, asst. mgr. container ops., 1959-60, asst. mgr. container sales, 1960-63, v.p. container sales West, 1963-75, v.p. prodn., 1975, group v.p. containers, now exec. v.p., dir. Office: Longview Fibre Co 120 Montgomery St Ste 2200 San Francisco CA 94104-4325 Office: Longview Fiber Co Longview WA 98632*

WERTHEIN, JORGE R., diplomat; b. Buenos Aires, Argentina, Sept. 20, 1941; s. Abraham and Sara (Savloff) W.; m. Miriam Abramovay; children: Claudio, Paulo, Rodrigo, Gustavo, Lucas. BA, U. Calif., Berkeley, 1971; MA on Edn., Stanford (Calif.) U., 1972, MA in Comms., 1974, PhD in Edn., 1977. V.p. Cordex S.A., Buenos Aires, 1966-69; specialist in edn. IICA, Rio de Janeiro, 1977-86; dir. external rels. IICA, San Jose, Costa Rica, 1986-94; rep. to U.N., dir. UNESCO, N.Y., 1994—. Co-author: (book) Education and Participation, 1986; editor: (book) Adult Education in Latin America, 1986. Avocations: tennis, soccer. Office: UNESCO 2 UN Plz New York NY 10017

WERTS, MERRILL HARMON, management consultant; b. Smith Center, Kans., Nov. 17, 1922; s. Mack Allen and Ruth Martha (Badger) W.; BS, Kans. State U., 1947; MS, Cornell U., 1948; m. Dorothy Wilson, Mar. 22, 1946; children: Stephen M., Riley J., Todd J., Kelly M. Beef sales mgr. John Morrell & Co., Topeka and Memphis, 1948-53; dir. mktg. Kans. Dept. Agr., Topeka, 1953-55; sec.-treas. Falley's Markets, Inc., Topeka, 1955-58; v.p. S.W. State Bank, Topeka, 1958-65; pres. First Nat. Bank, Junction City, Kans., 1965-78; pvt. practice mgmt. cons., Junction City, 1978—; mem. Kans. Senate, 1978-88; mem. Kans. Pub. Employee Rels. Bd., 1989-94, Kans. Comsn. on Future of Health Care, 1991-94; chmn. Kans. WWII Commemoration Com. 1995-96, Kans. Commn. on Vets. Affairs, 1995—, Geary County Pub. Bldg. Commn., 1996—; dir. Stockgrowers State Bank, Maple Hill, Kans., J.C. Housing & Devel., Inc., Kans. State Hist. Soc., Transformer Disposal Specialists, Inc. Mem. Kans. Bank Mgmt. Commn., 1967-71; mem. adv. com. U.S. Comptroller of Currency, 1971-72. Mem. Topeka Bd. Edn., 1957-61; pres. Junction City-Geary County United Fund, 1967-68; pres. Junction City Indsl. Devel., Inc., 1966-72. Trustee Kans. State U. Endowment Assn., Kans. Pub. Policy Inst., Kans. Synod Presbyn. Westminster Found., 1965-72. 1st lt., inf., AUS, 1943-46. Decorated Bronze Star medal, Purple Heart, Combat Inf. badge; named to Inf. Officer Candidate Hall Fame, 1981, Civilian Aide to Sec. of Army for Kans., 1991-95; named Outstanding State Legis. Am. Legis. Exchange Coun., 1988. Mem. Kans. State U. Alumni Assn. (pres. 1957), Am. Legion, VFW, Kans. Bankers Assn., Assn. U.S. Army, U.S., Kans. (bd. dirs., v.p. 1979-84), Junction City (pres. 1975-76) chambers commerce, Kans. Farm Bur., Kans. Livestock Assn., DAV, Junction City Country Club (past pres.), Masons, Shriners, Jesters, Rotary (dist. gov. 1973-74), Sigma Phi Epsilon. Republican. Presbyterian. Address: 1228 Miller Dr Junction City KS 66441-3312 *I believe that parents have no greater responsibility than that of being positive role models for their children, whether it be in their private, vocational or public pursuits.*

WERTSMAN, VLADIMIR FILIP, librarian, information specialist, author, translator; b. Secureni, Romania, Apr. 6, 1929; came to U.S., 1967; s. Filip and Anna Wertsman. LLM summa cum laude, U. A.I. Cuza, Romania, 1953; MLS, Columbia U., 1969. Judge lower and appellate cts. Romania, 1953-67; examiner stock certs. 1st Nat. City Bank, N.Y.C., 1967-68; reference libr. sci. div. Bklyn. Pub. Libr., N.Y.C., 1969-74, sr. libr. Canarsie br., 1974-77, sr. libr. Greenpoint br., 1977-80, sr. libr. Leonard br., 1980-82; sr. libr., Slavic and Romanian specialist Donnell Libr. Ctr. N.Y. Pub. Libr., 1982-86; sr. libr. Learner's Adv. and Job Info. Ctr., 1987-93. Author, editor: The Romanians in America, 1748-1974, 1974, The Ukrainians in America, 1608-1975, 1976, The Russians in America, 1727-1970, 1977, The Armenians in America, 1618-1976, 1978, The Romanians in America and Canada, 1980, Librarian's Companion: A Handbook of Thousands of Facts and Figures on Libraries/Librarians, 1987, 2d edit., 1996, Career Opportunities for Bilinguals and Multilinguals: A Directory of Resources in Education, Employment and Business, 1991, 2d eidt., 1994, What's Cooking in Multicultural America, 1996, New York: The City in Over 500 Memorable Quotations From American & Foriegn Sources, 1996, Directory of Ethnic and Multicultural Publishers, Distributors and Resource Organizations, 3d edit., 1995; co-author: Ukrainains in Canada and United States, 1981, Free Voices in Russian Literature, 1950s-1980s, 1986; editl. cons. Harvard Ency. Am. Ethnic Groups, 1980; contbr. Books, Libraries and Information in Slavic and East European Studies, 1986, Immigrant Labor Press in North America, 1840s-1970s, 1987, Through American Eyes, 1989, Ency. of N.Y.C., 1995; mem. adv. bd., contbr.: Gale Ency. Multicultural Am., 1995; contbr. articles, book revs. to profl. jours. Recipient Disting. Lit. Achievement award Am. Soc. Writers, 1977. Mem. ALA (chair multilingual libr. materials and svcs. com. 1976-88, spl. merit award 1988, chair Gale Rsch./Ethnic Materials Info. Exchange Round Table Multicultural Award Com. 1989—), Am. Assn. Advancement of Slavic Studies, Am. Romanian Acad. Arts & Scis., Delta Tau Kappa. Avocations: chess playing, travel, stamp collecting, dancing. Home: Unit 96 60 Babcock St Brookline MA 02146 *America is by its very nature of historical formation and development a multiethnic, multicultural and multilingual society. And if variety is the spice of life then American ethno-linguistic and cultural mosaique is the spice of our society. America's pluralism is also a microcosm of the entire world its citizens representing virtually all continents.*

WERTZ, JOHN ALAN, secondary school educator; b. Mpls., May 28, 1945; s. John Edward and Florence (Carlson) W.; m. Margaret M. Schlangen, 1993. BS, Hamline U., 1967; MS, St. Cloud State Coll., 1973; postgrad., George Washington U., 1985. Tchr. social sci. St. Cloud (Minn.) Community Schs., 1967—; trainer and field rep. New Games Found., San Francisco, 1980-83; tchr.-coach Apollo H.S. Mock Trial team, 1987—. Mem. com. social action Minn. Synod, Luth. Ch. Am., 1971-74; chair social action com. Salem Luth. Ch. Coun., St. Cloud, 1974-76; mem. affirmative action com. St. Cloud Cmty. Schs., 1975-78, co-chair student assistance com., 1982-83, mem. site coun. Apollo H.S., 1994-96, co-chair site coun. Apollo H.S., 1995-96; chair St. Cloud Human Rights Commn., 1979-86; adv. Ctrl. Minn. Sexual Assault Ctr., 1981-83; bd. dirs. St. Cloud Area Tenants' Assn., 1975-77, St. Cloud Area Spl. Olympics, 1982-83, United Way St. Cloud Area, 1996—, Minn. Edn. Assn., 1996—; bd. dirs. Great River Roundtable, 1997—. Recipient Merit award St. Cloud Area Coun. for Handicapped, 1976; grad. St. Cloud Area Leadership Program, 1995. Mem. ASCD, NEA, Minn. Edn. Assn., St. Cloud Edn. Assn. (chair govtl. rels. coun. 1978-83, 88-96), Am. Hist. Soc. of Germans from Russia, St. Cloud Area C. of C. (edn. divsn. 1992-97, vice-chmn. PreK-12 com. 1993-94, chair edn. recognition com. 1994-96, Thayer Youth Leadership steering com. 1995—). Avocations: theatre arts, camping, computing. Home: 816 Rilla Rd Saint Cloud MN 56303-1037 Office: Apollo High Sch 1000 44th Ave N Saint Cloud MN 56303-2037

WERTZ, KENNETH DEAN, real estate executive; b. Oklahoma City, July 14, 1946; s. Walter K. and Kathryn L. (Moore) W.; children: Adam Troy, Kirsten Paige. B.S. in Acctg., Okla. State U., 1968, M.S. in Acctg. and Econs., 1969; JD, U. San Francisco, 1978. CPA, Okla., Calif; lic. real estate broker, Okla. Sr. acct. Deloitte, Haskins & Sells, San Francisco, 1969-70, 71-75; v.p. acquisitions, mng. dir. Landsing Corp., Menlo Park, Calif., 1975-86; pres. Detrick Salsberry Mgmt. Inc., Tulsa, 1987-88; v.p. asset mgmt. Corporex Co., Cin., 1989-90; exec. v.p. real estate Brunner Cos., Dayton, Ohio, 1990-92; pres. Pillar Real Estate Advisors, Dayton, Ohio, 1992—. Lt. col. Med. Svc. corps U.S. Army, 1968—. Decorated Army Commendation medal with three oak leaf clusters. Mem. Am. Inst. CPA's, Okla. Soc. CPA's, Calif. Soc. CPA's, Nat. Assn. Securities Dealers (fin. prin., registered sales rep.). Republican. Methodist. Avocations: running, snow and water skiing, racquetball, camping, fishing. Home: 835 Hunterskoll Ln Cincinnati OH 45230-4343 Office: Pillar Real Estate Advisors 5335 Far Hills Ave Ste 318 Dayton OH 45429-2317

WERTZ, SPENCER K., philosophy educator; b. Amarillo, Tex., Oct. 27, 1941; s. Ralph E. and Pauline (Tressler) W.; m. Linda Loflin, Aug. 12, 1967. BA, Tex. Christian U., 1965, MA, 1966; PhD, U. Okla., 1970. Instr. Austin Coll., Sherman, Tex., 1969; from instr. to full prof. philosophy Tex. Christian U., Ft. Worth, 1969—, chmn. dept. philosophy, 1983-92; instr. Tex. Christian U. Div. Extended Edn., Ft. Worth, 1975—. Author: Talking a Good Game, 1991; co-editor: Sport Inside Out, 1985; contbr. over 60 articles to profl. jours. and mags. Mem. N.Mex.-West Tex. Philos. Soc. (pres. 1980-81), Southwestern Philos. Soc. (pres. 1985-86), Philos. Soc. Study Sport (pres. 1985-86), North Tex. Philos. Assn. (pres. 1987-88), Phi Sigma Tau, Phi Beta Kappa. Avocations: tennis, gardening, wilderness travel. Home: 303 Mini Ranch Rd Weatherford TX 76088-8410 Office: Tex Christian Univ Dept Of Philosophy Fort Worth TX 76129

WERZBERGER, ALAN, pediatrician; b. Toronto, Dec. 4, 1954; came to U.S., 1985; s. Bernard and Clara (Hilman) W.; m. Sabina Fischman, June 18, 1978; children: Samuel, Moshe, Yehuda, Jacob Joseph, Mayer, Joel, Susan, Henry, Rochelle, David, Menachem. MD, U. Toronto, 1981. Intern, resident Hosp. for Sick Children, Toronto, 1981-85; pvt. practice Monroe, N.Y., 1985—; attending dept. pediatrics Good Samaritan Hosp., Suffern, N.Y., 1985—; assoc. attending dept. pediatrics St. Agnes Hosp., White Plains, N.Y., 1992—; clin. asst. prof. pediatrics N.Y. Med. Coll., Valhalla, 1991—; asst. prof. pediatrics NYU Med. Ctr., N.Y.C., 1994—, dir., 1994—; vlin. asst. dept. Pediatrics Bellevue Hosp. Ctr., N.Y.C., 1995—; pres. Kiryas Joel Med. Rsch. Inst., Monroe, 1991—. Fellow Am. Acad. Pediatrics; mem. Med. Group Mgmt. Assn. Achievements include publication of the first demonstration of efficacy of a vaccine against Hepatitis A. Office: 43 Van Buren Dr Monroe NY 10950-3810

WESBERRY, JAMES PICKETT, JR., financial management consultant, auditor, international organization executive; b. Columbia, S.C., Sept. 22, 1934; s. James P. and Ruby L. (Perry) W.; m. Lea Esdras Casteneda, June 13, 1975; children: Jonathan Jesse, Perry Latimer, Ruby Lee Nilda; children by previous marriage: James Pickett III, Elisa Marie, Lillian Sue, Paul Armand. BBA, Ga. State U., 1955; LLD (hon.), Atlanta Law Sch., 1967; MPA, Am. U., 1983. CPA, Ga.; cert. internal auditor; cert. fraud examiner; cert. govt. fin. mgr., cert. fin. svcs. auditor. Page, U.S. Ho. of Reps., 1949-51; acct., mgmt. cons., Atlanta, 1956-67; v.p. fin. and adminstrn. Computer Tech. South, Atlanta, 1969-70; sr. cons. Inst. Pub. Adminstrn., N.Y.C., 1967-69, 70-76; cons. to comptroller gen. of Peru, 1970-74, of Ecuador, 1974-78; adv., prof. Latin Am. Inst. Auditing Scis., Peruvian and Ecuadorean Sch. Govtl. Auditing, 1971-78; pres. Internat. Profl. Devel. Inst., 1976-78; condr. seminars; dir. systems, standards and procedures Days of Inns Am., Inc., 1979-80; chief auditor OAS, Washington, 1980-82; cons. World Bank, 1982-83, prin. advisor acctg. and auditing pub. sector modernization divsn. Latin Am. and Caribbean region, 1994—; sr. adv. to comptroller gen. U.S., 1983-85; dir. internat. ops. Price Waterhouse, 1985-88; sr. fin. adviser AID, 1988-93, pres., CEO, Inst. Pub. Adminstrn., 1993-94, trustee, 1993-94; dir. N.Y. Bur. Mcpl. Rsch., 1993-94; mem. panel of experts in acctg. and auditing UN, 1972—; adj. prof. Am. U., Washington, 1981-85; founding dir. Internat. Consortium Govtl. Fin. Mgmt., 1977-88, 94—, pres., 1984-87; cons./tchr., all Spanish-speaking Western Hemisphere nations, Brazil,, Haiti, Jamaica, The Netherlands Antilles, Guyana, Peoples Republic of China, The Philippines, Can., U.S. Co-author: UN Handbook on Government Auditing for Developing Countries, editor: Latin American Manual of Professional Auditing in the Public Sector; editor Spanish lang. newsletter Pistas de Auditoria, 1985-92; mem. editorial bd. Pub. Budgeting and Fin. Mgmt.; mem. editorial bd., 1982-92. The Govt. Accts. Jour.; contbr. articles to profl. jours. Mem. Ga. Senate, 1962-67; mem. Fulton County Democratic Exec. Com. (Ga.), 1962-66. Decorated Order of Merit (Peru), 1972; recipient Outstanding Career Achievement award USAID, 1993. Mem. AICPA (chmn. interam. com. 1988-95), Interam. Acctg. Assn. (cert. assoc., bd. dirs. 1989-95, chmn. pub. sector com. 1989-91, mem. exec. com. 1994-95, Vet. Acct. Am. award 1987, lifetime acct. of Am. 1995), Am. Acctg. Assn., Assn. Govt. Accts. (Authors award 1981-82, 89-90); chmn. internat. affairs com. 1981-82, 89-91), Inst. Internal Auditors (v.p. Latin Am. 1978-79, internat. relations com. 1977-82, 84-88, regional dir. Latin Am. 1986-88, chpt. bd. govs. 1981-87, v.p. 1982-84, pres. 1984-85, vice chmn. internat. membership com. 1989-90, chpt. Disting. Svc. award 1987, Bradford Cadmus Meml. award internat. orgn. 1989, Outstanding Contbr. Author's award 1990), Honduras CPA Soc. (hon. award 1990), Jr. Chamber Internat. (life senator), Quito (Ecuador) Inst. Internal Auditors (life bd. dirs.), Lima (Peru) Coll. Pub. Accts. (hon.), Lima Jr. C. of C. (hon.), Pinchicha Coll. Pub. Accts. (hon.), Ecuador Fedn. Pub. Accts. (hon.), No. Va. Inst. Internal Auditors (hon.). Baptist. Home: 4004 Franconia Rd Alexandria VA 22310-2136 Office: World Bank Pub Sector Modernization Divsn Rm I-8383 Washington DC 20433 *Accountability to a higher authority is the cornerstone of human existence. Those who do not recognize this in their personal lives have great difficulty being accountable and responsible in their business and professional lives.*

WESBURY, STUART ARNOLD, JR., health administration and policy educator; b. Phila., Dec. 13, 1933; s. Stuart Arnold and Jennie (Glazewska) W.; m. June Carol Davis, Feb. 23, 1957; children: Brian, Brent, Bruce, Bradford. BS, Temple U., 1955; MHA, U. Mich., 1960; PhD, U. Fla., 1972. Commd. pharmacist USPHS, 1955, served as adminstrv. officer, hosp. and clinic pharmacist, resigned, 1958; adminstrv. asst. Del. Hosp., 1960-61; asst. adminstr. Bronson Meth. Hosp., 1961-66; assoc. dir., asst. prof. U. Fla. Tchg. Hosp., 1966-67, dir., assoc. prof., 1967-69; v.p. Computer Mgmt. Corp., Gainesville, Fla., 1969-72; dir., prof. grad. studies in health svcs. mgmt. U. Mo., Columbia, 1972-78; pres. Am. Coll. Healthcare Execs., Chgo., 1979-91; sr. v.p. TriBrook Group, Inc., Westmont, Ill., 1992-94; prof. Sch. of Health Adminstrn. and Policy Ariz. State U., Tempe, 1994—, dir., exec. edn. programs Coll. Bus., 1996—. Co-author: Why We Spend Too Much on Health Care; contbr. articles to profl. jours. Bd. dirs. Health Task, Inc., Atlanta, Blood Sys., Inc., Scottsdale, Ariz., Boys Clubs, Gainesville, Heartland Inst.; chmn. bd. dirs. Mid-Am. chpt. ARC, 1988-91, DuPage County Dist., 1984-87; active Boy Scouts Am.; chmn. adminstrv. bd. Meth. Ch.; trustee Nat. Blood Found.; Rep. Congl. candidate Dist. 13, Ill. Fellow Am. Coll. Health Care Adminstrs. (hon.), Am. Coll. Healthcare Execs. (Silver Medal award 1991); mem. APHA, Am. Hosp. Assn., Hosp. Mgmt. Sys. Soc., Assn. Univ. Programs in Health Adminstrn. (chmn. 1977-78), Am. Assn. Healthcare Cons. (hon.), Rotary (past pres.). Home: 6711 E Camelback Rd Unit 25 Scottsdale AZ 85251-2064 Office: Ariz State Univ Sch Health Adminstrn Policy PO Box 874506 Tempe AZ 85287-4506

WESCHLER, ANITA, sculptor, painter; b. N.Y.C.; d. J. Charles and Hulda Eva (Mayer) W.; widow. del. U.S. Com. Internat. Assn. Art, Fine Arts Fedn., N.Y. Exhibited in group shows at Met. Mus. Art, Mus. Modern Art, Art Inst. Chgo., Phila. Mus. Internat., Am. Acad., Inst. Arts and Letters, Bklyn. Mus., Newark Mus., Hofstra Mus., U. Conn., Carnegie Inst. Internat., Whitney Mus. Annuals, Storm King Art Ctr., mus. and galleries throughout U.S.; represented in permanent collections U. Pa., Michael Wolfson Found., Miami, Fla., Met. Mus. Art, Syracuse U.,Lehigh U., Butler Art Inst., Whitney Mus., Norfolk Mus., Brandeis U., Wharton Sch., Middlebury Coll., Amherst Coll., Yale U., Wichita State Mus., SUNY-Binghamton, U. Iowa, N.Y. Design Ctr., Pa. Acad. Fine Arts, Insts. for Achievement of Human Potential in Pa., Italy, and Brazil, Art Students League; one-man shows include Birmingham (Ala.) Mus. Art, Main Libr., Horace Mann-Barnado, Winston-Salem, N.C., U. Wis., Milw., Miami Beach Art Ctr., Tel Fair Acad., Savannah, Ga., Columbia (S.C.) Mus., U. N.C.-

Chapel Hill, Stover Mill Gallery, Erwinna, Pa., Suffolk Art Mus., Stony Brook, N.Y., L.A. County Mus., Montgomery Mus. of Art, Coryell Gallery, N.J., Cast Iron Gallery, N.Y., 1994, Wichita Art Mus., 1995, Nat. Acad. Design, 1996, Kyoto Japan, also 50 traveling and stationary shows in N.Y.C. and nationwide, 1993; exhibited in over 500 shows; creator plastic resins and fiberglass as sculpture medium (bonded bronze), synthetic glazes as painting medium; author; (poetry) Nightshade, A Sculptor's Summary. Recipient prizes Corcoran Gallery, San Francisco Mus., Am. Fedn. Arts Traveling Show, Montclair Art Mus.; fellow MacDowell Colony, Yaddo. Mem. Archtl. League Sculptors Guild (past bd. dirs., treas.), Nat. Assn. Women Artists, Nat. Mus. Women in the Arts, Artist Craftsmen N.Y., Fedn. Modern Painters and Sculptors. Address: 136 Waverly Pl New York NY 10014 *Imposed overall are multiple work hours. The deliberate shift is in periods, to another form—a contrasting medium. A life can be won or lost for work. The focus of attention remains entirely on the creative project. It is replenished by travel and forays into the outer world, a cultural and human renascence.*

WESCHLER, LAWRENCE MICHAEL, writer, journalist; b. Van Nuys, Calif., Feb. 13, 1952; s. Irving R. and Franzi (Toch) W.; m. Joanna S. Wegrzynowicz, Feb. 22, 1984; 1 child, Sara Alice. BA in Philosophy and Cultural History, U. Calif., Santa Cruz, 1974. Interviewer, editor Oral History Program UCLA, 1974-78; freelance writer L.A., 1978-80; staff writer The New Yorker mag., N.Y.C., 1981—. Author: Seeing is Forgetting the Name of the Thing One Sees: A Life of Contemporary Artist Robert Irwin, 1982, The Passion of Poland, 1984 , David Hockney's Cameraworks, 1986 (Kodakpreis 1986), Shapinsky's Karma, Boggs's Bills and Other True-Life Tales, 1988 (George Polk award 1988), A Miracle, A Universe: Settling Accounts with Torturers, 1990, Mr. Wilson's Cabinet of Wonder, 1995; contbr. to Village Voice, L.A. Times, Internat. Herald Tribune, L.A. Weekly, Rolling Stone, N.Y. Times, Artforum, ArtNews, The Nation, others. Co-dir. Ernst Toch Archive & Soc., L.A., 1972—. Recipient Hemingway prize Overseas Press Club, 1982, Sidney Hillman award, 1989, George Polk award for best mag. reporting, 1992; Pointer fellow Yale U., 1982, Guggenheim fellow, 1986-87, N.Y. Inst. for Humanities fellow, 1991—, Bard Ctr. fellow, 1992—. Mem. PEN, Nat. Writers Union. Jewish. Office: The New Yorker 20 W 43rd St New York NY 10036-7400*

WESCOE, W(ILLIAM) CLARKE, physician; b. Allentown, Pa., May 3, 1920; s. Charles H. and Hattie G. (Gilham) W.; m. Barbara Benton, Apr. 29, 1944; children: Barbara, William, David. BS, Muhlenberg Coll., 1941; ScD, 1957; MD, Cornell U., 1944. Intern N.Y. Hosp., 1944-45, resident, 1945-46; asst. prof. pharmacology Med. Coll., Cornell U., 1949-51; prof. pharmacology and exptl. medicine U. Kans. Med. Center, from 1951, dir., 1953-60; dean U. Kans. Med. Center (Sch. Medicine), 1952-60; chancellor U. Kan., 1960-69; v.p. med. affairs Sterling Drug Inc., N.Y.C., 1969-71; exec. v.p. Sterling Drug Inc., 1971-72, vice chmn., 1972-74, chmn., 1974-85. Editor: Jour. Pharmacol. and Exptl. Therapeutics, 1953-57. Chmn. China Med. Bd. N.Y., N.Y.C., 1960-90; bd. dirs. N.Y. Stock Exch., 1986-92, Tinker Found., 1968-93, Minn. Opera; trustee emeritus Samuel Kress Found., Columbia U.; chmn. John Simon Guggenheim Meml. Found., 1983-91, Muhlenberg Coll. Markle scholar med. scis., 1949-54. Fellow ACP; mem. Am. Soc. Pharmacology and Exptl. Therapeutics, Phi Beta Kappa, Sigma Xi, Alpha omega Alpha, Alpha Tau Omega, Nu Sigma Nu. Home: 8935 N Shore Dr Spicer MN 56288-9514

WESCOTT, ROGER WILLIAMS, anthropologist; b. Phila., Apr. 28, 1925; s. Ralph Wesley and Marion (Sturges-Jones) W.; m. Hilja J. Brigadier, Apr. 11, 1964; children: Walter, Wayne. Grad., Phillips Exeter Acad., 1942; B.A. summa cum laude, Princeton U., 1945, M.A., 1947, Ph.D., 1948; M.Litt., Oxford U., 1953. Asst. prof. history and human relations Boston U. and Mass. Inst. Tech., 1953-57; assoc. prof. English and social sci., also dir. African lang. program Mich. State U., 1957-62; prof. anthropology and history So. Conn. State Coll., 1962-66; prof., chmn. anthropology and linguistics Drew U., Madison, N.J., 1966-91; Presdl. prof. Colo. Sch. Mines, 1980-81; first holder endowed Chair of Excellence in Humanities U. Tenn., 1988-89; shipboard lectr., 1980—; fgn. lang. cons. U.S. Office Edn., 1961; pres. Sch. Living, Brookville, Ohio, 1962-65; exec. dir. Inst. Exploratory Edn., N.Y.C., 1963-66; Korzybski lectr. Inst. Gen. Semantics, N.Y.C., 1976; forensic linguist N.J. State Cts., 1982-83; host Other Views, N.J. Cable TV, Trenton, 1985-87. Author: A Comparative Grammar of Albanian, 1955, Introductory Ibo, 1961, A Bini Grammar, 1963, An Outline of Anthropology, 1965, The Divine Animal, 1969, Language Origins, 1974, Visions, 1975, Sound and Sense, 1980, Language Families, 1986, Getting It Together, 1990; also poems and articles; host, program dir. Other Views, N.J. Cable TV, 1985-87; co-author: Sorokin and Civilization, 1996. Rhodes scholar, 1948-50; Ford fellow, 1955-56; Am. Council Learned Socs. scholar, 1951-52. Fellow AAAS, Am. Anthrop. Assn., African Studies Assn.; mem. Acad. Ind. Scholars (life mem.), Assn. for Poetry Therapy, Internat. Soc. Comparative Study Civilizations (co-founder, pres. 1992—), Linguistic Assn. Can. and U.S. (pres. 1976-77), Internat. Linguistic Assn., Com. for Future, Soc. for Hist. Rsch. (v.p.), Internat. Orgn. for Unification Terminological Neologisms (1st .p.), World Hist. Assn., Assn. for Study of Lang. in Prehistory (v.p., co-editor), Phi Beta Kappa. Home: 16A Heritage Crest Southbury CT 06488-1370 *Since our lives are short, it seems appropriate that our reflections on them should be comparably brief. Success is transient and high regard, relative. Though my occupational classification is that of a teacher and administrator, I have rarely been able seriously to picture myself as an educational careerist. I have thought of myself, rather, as an intellectual explorer, perennially fascinated by the inadequately explained aspects of man and his world and powerfully impelled to share that sense of fascination with fellow explorers.*

WESCOTT, WILLIAM BURNHAM, oral pathologist, educator; b. Pendleton, Oreg., Nov. 10, 1922; s. Merton Girard and Josephine (Creasey) W.; m. Barbara L., Dec. 31, 1944 (dec. June 12, 1969); children: William Douglas, Diane Elizabeth; m. Gloria Greer-Collins, Aug. 28, 1989. DMD, U. Oreg., Portland, 1951, MS, 1962. Asst. prof. to assoc. dean admin. U. Oreg. Dental Sch., Portland, 1953-72; co-dir. oral disease rsch. VA, Houston, 1972-75; dir. dental edn. ctr. VA, L.A., 1980-85; acting dir. Reg. Med. Edn. Ctr., Birmingham, Ala., 1978-80; chief dental svc. Dept. of Veteran's Affairs, San Francisco, 1985-94; clin. prof. U. Calif., San Francisco, 1994—; dental surgeon, Oreg. Air N.G., Portland, 1954-68; cons. Madigan Army Med. Ctr., Ft. Lewis, W. Va., 1971-74, VA Med. Ctrs., No. Calif., 1985—, prof. pathology Duke U. Med. Sch., 1977-79. Contbr. articles to profl. jours. Dist. chmn. Boys Scouts Am., Portland, 1965-67; bd. dirs. Am. Cancer Soc., Portland, 1964-67; sr. vice comdr. Veterans Foreign Wars Post 5731, Gridley, Calif., 1994-95, comdr., 1996-98. Lt. Col. U.S. Army, 1942-68. Decorated DFC, USAF, Oreg. N.G. Merit Svc. Medal, Portland. Fellow Am. Acad. Oral and Maxillofacial Pathology, Omicron Kappa Upsilon, Sigma Xi. Avocations: woodworking, fishing. Home: 437 Justeson Ave Gridley CA 95948-9434 Office: U Calif Sch of Dentistry S 512 San Francisco 3rd & Parnassus San Francisco CA 94143-0424

WESELI, ROGER WILLIAM, lawyer; b. Cin., Dec. 23, 1932; s. William Henry and Margaret Antoinette (Hoffman) W.; m. Sue Ann Daggett, Sept. 1, 1956; children: Erin, Stacey, Vincent. BA in Polit. Sci, U. Cin., 1955; MS in Hosp. Adminstrn, Northwestern U., 1959; D Tech. Letters (hon.), Cin. Tech. Coll., 1985; JD, No. Ky. U., 1995. Bar: Ohio 1995. Adminstrv. asst. Good Samaritan Hosp., Cin., 1959-61, asst. adminstr., 1961-70, assoc. adminstr., 1970-75, v.p., adminstr., 1975-78, exec. v.p., adminstr., 1978-79, pres., 1979-91, cons., 1991-93; cons. healthcare practice Deloitte & Touche, Cin., 1991-93; sec. Greater Cin. Hosp. Council, 1978-80, chmn. bd., 1983-84; assoc. Copeland & Brown Co., L.P.A., Cin., 1995—. Chmn. legis. com. health dept. Ohio Cath. Conf., 1978-83, 86; bd. dirs. Friars Boys Club, 1978-94. Recipient Praestans Inter Omnes award Purcell High Sch., 1984, Laura Jackson award Northwestrern U. Program in Health Svcs. Mgmt., 1987, Preceptor of Yr. award Xavier U. Program Hosp. and Health Svcs. Adminstrn., 1990. Fellow Am. Coll. Healthcare Execs. (regent for Ohio 1983-90, bd. govs. 1990-94); mem. ABA, Am. Hosp. Assn. (coun. on fedn. rels. 1983-84, coun. on patient svcs. 1984-86, ho. of dels. 1989-91), Ohio Bar Assn., Cin. Bar Assn., Ohio League for Nursing (v.p. 1977-79, cert. of appreciation 1978), Ohio Hosp. Assn. (chmn. govt. liaison com. 1978-83, 86, trustee 1981-83, sec.-treas. 1987, chmn.-elect 1988, chmn. 1989), Cath. Health Assn. (trustee 1983-86), Alpha Mu Sigma. Democrat. Roman Catholic. Home: 3615 Clifton Ave Cincinnati OH 45220-1703 Office: 119 E Court St Ste 510 Cincinnati OH 45202-1203

WESELY, DONALD RAYMOND, state senator; b. David City, Nebr., Mar. 30, 1954; s. Raymond Ely and Irene (Sabata) W.; m. Geri Williams, 1982; children: Sarah, Amanda, Andrew. BA, U. Nebr., 1977; LLD (hon.), Kirksville Coll. Osteopathic Medicine, 1989. Mem. Nebr. Legislature, Lincoln, 1978—; exec. assoc. Selection Rsch., Inc., Lincoln, 1984-86; sr. rsch. assoc. Lincoln Telephone Co., 1985—. Del., Dem. Nat. Conv., 1984, 88, 92, 96; chair Assembly on Legislature, Nat. Conf. State Legislatures., 1992-93, 96-97, exec. com., 1992-97; del. Am. Coun. Young Polit. Leaders, 1993. Recipient Friend of Edn. award Nebr. State Edn. Assn., 1982, Disting. Svc. award Nebr. Pub. Health Assn., 1984, Disting. Alumni award Lincoln Northeast High Sch., 1991, Disting. Health Care award Nebr. Nurse Anesthetists Assn., 1992, Leadership award for Quality in Health Care, Nebr. League Nursing, 1992, Pres.'s award Nebr. Acad. Physicians Assts., 1993, U. Nebr.- Lincoln Outstanding Young Alumni award, 1994; named Mental Health Citizen of Yr., Nebr. Mental Health Assn., 1984, Outstanding Young Man, Nebr. Jaycees, 1985, Pub. Official of Yr., Nebr. Assn. Retarded Citizens, 1992, Advocate of Yr, Nebr. Family Day Care Assn., 1993. Roman Catholic. Office: State Capitol Lincoln NE 68509

WESELY, EDWIN JOSEPH, lawyer; b. N.Y.C., May 16, 1929; s. Joseph and Elizabeth (Peles) W.; children: Marissa Celeste, Adrienne Lee; m. Marcy Brownson, Sept. 23, 1992. Ed., Deep Springs Coll., 1945-47; AB, Cornell U., 1949; JD, Columbia U., 1954. Bar: N.Y. 1954, D.C. 1985, U.S. Supreme Ct. 1960, others. Law clk. to judge U.S. Dist. Ct. (so. dist.) N.Y., 1954-55; asst. U.S. atty. So. Dist. N.Y., 1955-57; assoc. Winthrop, Stimson, Putnam & Roberts, N.Y.C., 1957-63, ptnr., 1964—; spl. master numerous cases; chmn. spl. com. on effective discovery in civil cases U.S. Dist. Ct. (ea. dist.) N.Y., 1982-84, com. on civil caseflow, 1985-88, com. on civil litigation, 1988—, civil justice reform adv. group, 1990-95; com. on pretrial phase civil cases Jud. Coun. 2d Cir., 1984-86, standing com. on improvement civil litigation, 1986-89; ex-officio Civil Justice Reform Act adv. group U.S. Dist. Ct. (so. dist.) N.Y.; pres. CARE, 1986-89, chmn., 1978-86, 89-90, internat. bd. dirs., 1981-90, pres., 1987-90; bd. dirs. Internat. Rescue Com.; bd. dirs., exec. com. Internat. Ctr. in N.Y., 1990—. Trustee Deep Springs Coll., 1991—. Decorated Order of Civil Merit (Republic of Korea); recipient World Humanitarian award Fgn. Press Assn., 1988, Commendation Bd. Judges U.S. Dist. Ct. (ea. dist.) N.Y., 1993. Fellow Am. Coll. Trial Lawyers (internat. com. 1990—); mem. ABA (spl. adv. com. on internat. activities 1990-93, litigation sect. chmn. com. on discovery 1977-78, spl. com. study discovery abuse 1977-82, chmn. task force on liaison with internat. profl. assns. on matters of mutual concern 1989-93, Civil Justice Reform Act task force 1991-93, task force on the state of the justice sys. 1993-95, fed. initiatives task force 1995—), UN Assn. U.S.A. (bd. govs. 1991—), Assn. of Bar of City of N.Y. (com. mem., organized demostration observation panel), Coun. on Fgn. Rels., India House. Office: Winthrop Stimson One Battery Park Pla New York NY 10004-1490

WESELY, MARISSA CELESTE, lawyer; b. N.Y.C., Apr. 25, 1955; d. Edwin Joseph and Yolanda Teresa (Pyles) W.; 1 child, Emma Elizabeth Wesely Allen. BA magna cum laude, Williams Coll., 1976; JD cum laude, Harvard U., 1980. Bar: N.Y. 1981. Assoc. Simpson Thacher & Bartlett, N.Y.C., 1980-82, 84-88, ptnr., 1989—; assoc. Simpson Thacher & Bartlett, London, 1982-84; lectr., cons. Harvard Inst. Internat. Devel., Beijing, 1981, Jakarta, Indonesia, 1982; guest lectr. Yale Law Sch., New Haven, 1991; spkr. Am. Conf. Inst., Practicing Law Inst., Bankers Assn. for Fgn. Trade, N.Y. State Bar Assn. confs., 1993—. Bd. dirs. City Lore, N.Y.C. Mem. N.Y.C. Bar Assn., N.Y. State Bar Assn. (mem. exec. com. sect. internat. law and practice), Internat. Bar Assn., Phi Beta Kappa.

WESENBERG, JOHN HERMAN, professional society administrator; b. Davenport, Iowa, Jan. 16, 1927; s. Herman B. and Nell (Watterson) W.; m. Alice Jane McMahill, Sept. 10, 1949; children: Anne, John, Sue, James. Student, Iowa State U., 1944-45, 47, Amherst Coll., 1946; B.A., U. Iowa, 1951, M.A., 1952; postgrad., Northwestern U., 1952-55, Mich. State U., 1956-67. Research asso. Bur. Bus. and Econ. Research, U. Iowa, 1949-52; asst. mgr. Danville (Ill.) C. of C., 1952-54; exec. v.p. Belleville (Ill.) C. of C., 1954-57; sec. Retail Mchts. and Central Dist. Bur., Des Moines, 1957-62; exec. v.p. Greater Des Moines C. of C., 1963-80; sec. Greater Des Moines Com., 1963-80; sr. exec. v.p. Greater Albuquerque C. of C., 1980-82, Met. Tulsa C. of C., 1982-91; dir. mgmt. adv. program Okla. State C. of C. and Industry, Tulsa, 1992—; sr. exec. counselor U.S. C. of C., 1993—; trustee Employee Stock Ownership Plan, Internat. Bank, Washington, 1977-80, 83-84; lectr. Inst. Orgn. Mgmt., Mich. State U., 1959-67, 69-70, U. Colo., 1970, 75, 78, 79, 81, 85, 87, 90, 91, Syracuse U., 1971, U. Santa Clara, Calif., 1972, 74-75; lectr. Tex. Christian U., 1971, 73, U. Del., 1973-76, 80, 82, U. Ga., 1973, 82, 86, U. Notre Dame, 1975, 81, So. Meth. U., 1975-76, 81, 84, 85, 87, 88, 89, 90, 91, Mills Coll., 1976, San Jose Coll., 1981, U. Okla., 1984, 86, 88, 90-91, Stanford U., 1990, Econ. Devel. Inst. U. Okla., 1994; cons. Met. Tulsa C. of C., 1997—. Co-chmn. Des Moines Mail Users Council, 1963-68; sec.-treas. Des Moines Housing Corp., Baseball, Inc., 1963-80; sec. Des Moines Devel. Corp., Des Moines Industries, Inc., 1963-80, Community Improvement, Inc., 1968-80, Greater Des Moines Community Found., 1968-80; treas. Greater Des Moines Shippers Assn., 1971-80; trustee Fringe Benefits, Inc., Washington, 1969-82; mem. exec. com. Iowa Council on Econ. Edn., 1978-80; mem. planning com. Grand View Coll., 1976-80; mem. adv. council, region VIII SBA, 1973-80; Memb. bd. regents Inst. Orgn. Mgmt., Mich. State U., 1962-67, chmn., 1965-66; bd. regents U. Colo., 1977-80, So. Meth. U., 1980-81; vice chmn. nat. bd. regents Inst. for Orgn. Mgmt., 1978-79, chmn., 1979-80; trustee U. Albuquerque, 1980-82. Served with USAAF, 1944-46. Recipient Outstanding Community Leadership award Religious Heritage of Am., 1978. Mem. Am. Arbitration Assn., Am. Retail Execs. Assn. (dir. 1962-63), Am. C. of C. Execs. (dir. 1965-73, 84-91, hon. life dir./mem. 1992—, pres. 1971-72), U.S. C. of C. (dir. 1979-81, liaison officer 1989-91), Iowa C. of C. Execs. (dir. 1960-66, pres. 1964), Okla. C. of C. Execs. (dir. 1983-86, pres. 1986), Ill. Mfrs. Assn. (exec. com. So. div. 1955-57), St. Louis Indsl. Coun. (v.p. 1957), Okla. C. of C. and Industry (mem. exec. com. bd. dirs. 1986, fin. com. 1986-94), Industries for Tulsa (sec. 1986-91), Beta Theta Pi (gen. sec. 1974-81, adv. coun. former trustees 1981—), Mtn. States Assn. (v.p. 1980-81—), Des Moines Club, Petroleum Club. Home: 6718 E 65th Pl Tulsa OK 74133-4007 Office: Met Tulsa C of C 616 S Boston Ave Tulsa OK 74119-1208

WESLER, KEN, theater company manager; b. Phila., Apr. 3, 1964; s. Irwin Harvey and Marcia Elaine (Trilling) W.; m. Deborah Lee Rader, Nov. 2, 1986; children: Alexander, Samantha. BA, Temple U., 1994. Prodn. mgr. The Wilma Theatre, Phila., 1983-89; gen. mgr. Gretna Prodns., Inc., Mt. Gretna, Pa., 1989, 90, Walnut St. Theatre, Phila., 1989-95; exec. dir. The Grand Opera House, Wilmington, 1995—; guest lectr. Cabrini Coll., Phila., 1988, Temple U., Phila., 1988—. Bd. dirs. MBNA Excellence in Edn. Found., Downtown Visions, Best of Broadway. Mem. Stage Mgr.'s Assn., Actor's Equity, Del. Assn. Non-Profit Agys. (bd. dirs.). Office: The Grand Opera House 818 N Market St Wilmington DE 19801-3011

WESLER, OSCAR, mathematician, educator; b. Bklyn., July 12, 1921; s. Israel Edward and Sarah (Hartman) W. B.S., Coll. City N.Y., 1942; M.S., N.Y. U., 1943; postgrad., Princeton U., 1943-46; Ph.D., Stanford U., 1955. Mem. faculty Stanford U., 1952-56, vis. prof. stats., 1978; mem. faculty U. Mich., 1956-64; prof. stats. and math. N.C. State U., Raleigh, 1964—; cons. Inst. Sci. and Tech., U. Mich., 1957-64, IBM, 1966; vis. prof. statistics Stanford, 1962-63, 73, 74, 78, U. Calif., Berkeley, 1972-73; vis. lectr. NSF Program vis. lectrs. in statistics, 1963—. Author: Solutions to Problems in Theory of Games and Statistical Decisions, 1954; also articles in profl. jours. Recipient Outstanding Tchr. award N.C. State U., 1966. Mem. Inst. Math. Statistics, Am. Math. Soc., Sigma Xi, Phi Kappa Phi. Research in statis. decision theory, probability, stochastic processes. Home: 1926 Smallwood Dr Raleigh NC 27605-1302

WESLEY, JOHN MERCER, artist; b. Los Angeles, Nov. 25, 1928; s. Ner Wesley and Elsa Marie (Patzwaldt) W.; m. Hannah Allen Green, Dec. 18, 1971; children: Christine Alice, Ner. Student, Los Angeles City Coll., UCLA, 1947-50. One-man shows include, Robert Elkon Gallery, N.Y.C., 1963-80, 84, Premio Internat., Instituto Torcuato di Tella, Buenos Aires, 1967, Documenta 5, Kassel, 1972, Carl Solway Gallery, Cin., 1972, 85, 89, Galerie Rudolf Zwirner, Cologne, 1973, Rush Rhees Gallery, U. Rochester, 1974, PS 1, N.Y.C., 1978, Reinhard Onnasch Ausstellungen, Berlin, 1982-83, 101 Spring St. Gallery, N.Y.C., 1987, fiction/non fiction, N.Y.C., 1990, 91, Chinati Found., Marfa, Tex., 1990, Daniel Weinberg Gallery, Santa Monica, Calif., 1992, Portikus, Frankfurt, 1993, Stedelijk Mus., Amsterdam, 1993, Kunstverein, Ludwigsburg, Germany, 1993, daad-Galerie, Berlin, 1993, Galerie Rolf Ricke, Cologne, 1994, José Freire Gallery, N.Y.C., 1994, Jessica Fredericks Gallery, N.Y.C., 1996, Galerie Haus Schneider, Karlsruhe, Germany, 1996; group exhbns. include, Whitney Mus., 1968, 69, 76, Indpls. Mus., 1976, Bonnefantenmuseum, Maastricht, 1977, Royal Academy, London, 1991, Mus. Contemporary Art, L.A., 1992-93, Mus. Beaux Arts, Montreal, 1992-93, Deichtorhallen, Hamburg, 1997, Kunsthaus, Zürich, 1997; represented in permanent collections, Albright-Knox Mus., Buffalo, Mus. Modern Art, N.Y.C., U. Tex., Austin, Mpls. Soc. Fine Arts., Chinati Found., Marfa, Tex., Rose Art Gallery, Brandeis U., Waltham, Mass., U. Kentucky, Lexington, Kunstmuseum, Basel, Switzerland, Dayton (Ohio) Mus. Art, Portland (Oreg.) Art Mus., Whitney Mus., Stedelijk Mus., Speed Mus., Louisville, Ky. Guggenheim fellow, 1976; grantee Nat. Endowment Arts, 1989. Address: 52 Barrow St New York NY 10014-3723

WESLEY, ROBERT COOK, dental educator; b. Jamestown, Ky., Aug. 19, 1926; s. Hulen Harrison and Bertie Marie (Cook) W.; m. Betty Jean Coffey, Feb. 21, 1953; children: Robert Cook II, Leigh Ann. BA, Berea Coll., 1950; DMD, U. Louisville, 1954. Dentist Berea (Ky.) Hosp., 1954-55; pvt. practice, Berea, 1955-65, Lexington, Ky., 1965-67; vis. prof. U. So. Calif., L.A., 1970-71; mem. faculty U. Ky. Dental Sch., Lexington, 1967—, asst. prof., 1967-72, assoc. prof., 1972—; assoc. prof. Univ. Hosp., Lexington, 1972-93; prof. emeritus, 1993—; vis. prof. U. So. Calif., 1970-71; cons. VA, Lexington, 1971-76. Contbr. articles to dental jours., chpts. to book. With USN, 1944-46, PTO. Mem. ADA, Ky. Dental Assn., Bluegrass Dental Soc., Am. Prosthodontic Soc., Southeastern Acad. Prosthodontics (pres. 1984-85, Fedn. Prosthodontic Orgns. (pres. 1988-89). Avocations: sport fishing, framing art works, golf. Office: U Ky Med Pla Lexington KY 40536

WESLING, DONALD TRUMAN, English literature educator; b. Buffalo, May 6, 1939; s. Truman Albert and Helene Marie (Bullinger) W.; m. Judith Elaine Dulinawka, July 28, 1961; children: Benjamin, Molly, Natasha. BA, Harvard U., 1960, PhD, 1965; BA, Cambridge U., Eng., 1962. Asst. prof. U. Calif. at San Diego, La Jolla, 1965-67, assoc. prof., 1970-80, prof., 1981—; lectr. U. Essex, Colchester, Eng., 1967-70. Author: Wordsworth and Landscape, 1970, Chances of Rhyme, 1981, The New Poetries, 1985, The Scissors of Meter, 1996, (with T. Slawek) Literary Voice, 1995. Mem. Amnesty Internat. Home: 4968 Foothill Blvd San Diego CA 92109-2234 Office: U Calif Lit # 0410 La Jolla CA 92093

WESSEL, DENNIS JAMES, mechanical engineering administrator; b. Pitts., Mar. 31, 1949; s. Elmer Herman and Fern (Staley) W.; m. Karen Dudziak, Jan. 1970; children: Eric, Heidi, Dana. BME, Cleve. State U., 1972. Registered profl. engr., Ohio, Pa., N.Y., Calif., Ariz., R.I., S.C., R.I., S.C., Az. Designer Avery Engring., Cleve., 1968-71; sales engr. Met-Chem Inc., Cleve., 1971-73; engr. Byers Engring., Cleve., 1973-78; assoc. URS Corp., Cleve., 1978-87; v.p. Bacik, Karpinski Assocs., Cleve., 1987—; instr. continuing edn. bldg. maintenance, Cleve. State U., 1982-84. Chmn. Hudson (Ohio) H.S. Career Night Com., 1987-91; mem. fin. com. St. Marys Ch., Hudson, 1986-96, bldg. com. 1986—. With USAR, 1972-78. Mem. ASHRAE (local pres. 1984-85, regional vice chmn. 1986-90, tech. com. chmn. 1991-93, vice chmn. task group 1989-93, 94-96, handbook com. 1993—, chmn. 1996-2000, Region V Energy award 1983, 86, Merit award 1990, Disting. Svc. award, 1996), Am. Cons. Engrs. Assn., Nat. Fire Protection Assn., Bldg. Ofcls. and Code Adminstrs, Mech. Engrs. and Constrn. Assn. (steering com., 1994—). Roman Catholic. Avocations: woodworking, leaded glass, photography, golf, skiing. Office: Bacik Karpinski Assocs 3135 Euclid Ave Cleveland OH 44115-2524

WESSEL, HENRY, photographer; b. Teaneck, N.J., July 28, 1942; s. Henry and Jennie (Cincotta) W.; children by previous marriage: Nicholas, Rider. B.A., Pa. State U., 1966; M.F.A., SUNY, Buffalo, 1972. Propr., mgr. comml. photog. studio State Coll., Pa., 1966-68; cinematographer for documentary film Dept. HEW, 1967; instr. dept. art Pa. State U., Phila., 1967-69; prof. dept. photography San Francisco Art Inst., 1973-96, chmn. grad. program photography, 1977-78, chmn. dept. photography, 1987-93; asst. prof. San Francisco State U., 1974-75; vis. lectr. photography various colls. and art schs., 1967-81; propr., dir. Photographic Resources, Point Richmond, Calif., 1977—; vis. artist Mills Coll., 1987-88;. One-man show at Mus. Modern Art, N.Y.C., 1973; represented in permanent collections, Mus. Modern Art, N.Y.C., Phila. Mus. Art, Boston Mus. Fine Arts, Library of Congress, Am. Arts Documentation Center, Exeter, Eng., Nat. Gallery of Can., Ottawa; author: Henry Wessel, 1987, House Pictures, 1992. Guggenheim fellow, 1971, 78; Nat. Endowment Arts fellow, 1975, 77, 78. Home: PO Box 475 Richmond CA 94807-0475 Office: Photographic Resources PO Box 475 Richmond CA 94807-0475

WESSEL, MORRIS ARTHUR, pediatrics educator; b. Providence, Nov. 1, 1917; s. Morris Jacob and Bessie (Bloom) W.; m. Irmgard Rosenzweig, June 1, 1952; children: David, Bruce, Paul, Lois. BA, Johns Hopkins U., 1939; MD, Yale U., 1943. Diplomate Am. Bd. Pediatrics. Intern Babies Hosp., N.Y.C., 1943-44; asst. dir. pediatric outpatient clinic Yale New Haven (Conn.) Hosp., 1951-52, dir. pediatric outpatient clinic, 1952-57; staff pediatrician, collaboration project Yale U. Sch. Medicine, 1957-62, instr. in pediatrics, 1950-53, clin. asst. prof., 1963-61, clin. assoc. prof. of pediatrics, 1961-75, clin. prof. pediatrics, 1975—; cons. pediatrician Clifford Beers Child Guidance Clinic, 1967—; bd. dirs. Clifford Beers Guidance Clinic, New Haven, 1950-55, Women's Health Svc., New Haven, 1992—, Child Welfare League, N.Y.C., 1979-91. Author: Parents Book on Raising a Healthy Child, 1987. Maj. AUS, 1944-47, ETO. Mem. Am. Acad. Pediat. (Practitioner Rsch. award 1994), Soc. Adolescent Medicine, Conn. Med. Soc., New Haven County Med. Soc.

WESSEL, PETER, lawyer; b. N.Y.C., N.Y., Feb. 2, 1952; s. Harry Nathan Jr. and Charlene (Freimuth) W.; married Vicki Brodsky; children: Daniel, Elizabeth. BS, Syracuse U., 1974, MPA, JD, 1980. Bar: N.Y. 1981, U.S. Dist. Ct. (no., so., ea. and we. dists.) N.Y. 1981, Fla. 1984, U.S. Ct. Mil. Appeals, 1988, U.S. Ct. Appeals (2d cir.) 1988, U.S. Supreme Ct. 1988. Confidential law clk. to Hon. David F. Lee Jr. N.Y. Supreme Ct., 1980-82; sr. atty. criminal def. div. The Legal Aid Soc., N.Y.C., 1982-87; pvt. practice N.Y.C., 1987—. Notes and comments editor Syracuse Law Rev., 1979-80; contbr. articles to profl. jours. Robert M. Anderson award for Writing and Legal Scholarship, 1980, Neal Brewster scholar, 1977-78, Syracuse U. Coll. Law scholar 1978-79, Louis Waters Meml. scholar, 1979-80, Hiscock, Cowie, Bruce & Lee scholar, 1979-80. Mem. ABA, N.Y. State Bar Assn., Assn. of Bar of City of N.Y., Fla. Bar Assn., Nat. Assn. Criminal Def. Lawyers, N.Y. State Assn. Criminal Def. Lawyers, N.Y. State Defender Assn., N.Y. State Trial Lawyers Assn., N.Y. County Lawyers Assn., N.Y. Criminal Bar Assn.

WESSELINK, DAVID DUWAYNE, finance company executive; b. Webster City, Iowa, Sept. 5, 1942; s. William David and Lavina C. (Haahr) W.; m. Linda R. DeWitt, Dec. 27, 1971; children: Catherine, Bill. BA in Bus., Cen. Coll., 1964; MBA, Mich. State U., 1970. Tchr. Peace Corps, Turkey, 1964-66, Karabuk Koleji, Turkey, 1967-68, Robert Koleji, Turkey, 1969-70; research analyst Household Fin. Corp., Chgo., 1971-73, asst. dir. research, 1973-77; asst. treasurer Household Fin. Corp., Prospect Heights, Ill., 1977, v.p., dir. research, 1977-82, group v.p., chief fin. officer, 1982-86, sr. v.p., chief fin. officer, 1986—; v.p., treas. Household Internat., Prospect Heights, 1988-93; sr. v.p., CFO Advanta Corp., 1993—. Bd. dirs. ARC, Phila., 1996—, Summerbridge Germantown, Phila., 1996—, Ctrl. Coll., Pella, Iowa, 1990—, CFC Internat., Chgo. Heights, Ill., 1992—. Mem. Fin. Execs. Inst., Chgo. Coun. on Fgn. Rels., Econ. Club Chgo., Conf. Bd. on Fin. Svc. CFO's. Office: Advanta Corp 300 Welsh Rd Horsham PA 19044-2248

WESSELLS, NORMAN KEITH, biologist, educator, university administrator; b. Jersey City, May 11, 1932; s. Norman Wesley and Grace Mahan Wessells; m. Catherine Pyne Briggs; children: Christopher, Stephen, Philip, Colin, Elizabeth. B.S., Yale U., 1954, Ph.D., 1960. Asst. prof. biology Stanford (Calif.) U., 1962-65, asso. prof., 1965-70, prof., 1971—, chmn. biol. sci., 1972-78; acting dir. Hopkins Marine Sta., 1972-75, asso. dean humanities and scis., 1977-81, dean, 1981-88; prof. biology, provost, v.p. acad. affairs U. Oreg., Eugene, 1988—. Author: (with F. Wilt) Methods in Developmental Biology, 1965, Vertebrates: Adaptations, 1970, Vertebrates: A Laboratory Text, 1976, 81, Tissue Interactions and Development, 1977,

Vertebrates; Adaptations; Vertebrates: Physiology, 1979, (with S. Subtelny) The Cell Surface, 1980, (with J. Hopson) Biology, 1988, (with Hopson) Essentials of Biology, 1990. Served with USNR, 1954-56. Am. Cancer Soc. postdoctoral fellow, 1960-62; Am. Cancer Soc. scholar cancer research, 1966-69; Guggenheim fellow, 1976-77. Mem. Soc. Devel. Biology (pres. 1979-80), Am. Soc. Zoologist. Office: U Oreg Office of Provost Johnson Hall Eugene OR 97403

WESSELMANN, GLENN ALLEN, retired hospital executive; b. Cleve., Mar. 21, 1932; s. Roy Arthur and Dorothy (Oakes) W.; m. Genevieve De Witt, Sept. 6, 1958; children: Debbie, Scott, Janet. A.B., Dartmouth, 1954; M.B.A. with distinction, Cornell U., 1959. Research aide Cornell U., Ithaca, N.Y., 1958-59; adminstrv. resident Meml. Hosp., N.Y.C., 1957-58; adminstrv. asst. Meml. Hosp., 1959-61, asst. adminstr., 1961-65, asst. v.p., 1965-68; v.p. for adminstrn. Meml. Hosp. for Cancer and Allied Diseases, N.Y.C., 1968-79; exec. v.p., chief operating officer St. John Hosp., Detroit, 1979-84; pres., CEO St. John Health System, 1984-95, vice chmn., 1995—; chmn., pres., CEO St. John Hosp. & Med. Ctr., 1984-94; mem. bus. adv. bd. City of Detroit, 1991-95, chmn., 1993-94; mem. exec. com. Greater Detroit Area Health Coun.; bd. dirs. Caymich Ins. Co. Ltd., Mich. Health Care Alliance, SelectCare, Detroit Econ. Growth Corp. Trustee Sisters of St. Joseph Health System 1981-94, Sisters of St. Joseph Health Svc., 1983—, St. John Hosp. and Med. Ctr., 1979-95, St. John Health System, 1984—, The Oxford Inst., 1984-95, Eastwood Clinics, 1992-95; mem. bus. adv. bd., City of Detroit, 1991—, chmn. 1993-94. Served with MC AUS, 1955-57. Fellow ACHE; mem. Am. Hosp. Assn., Internat. Hosp. Fedn., Mich. Hosp. Assn. (trustee, chmn. 1994—, mem. exec. com.), Assn. Am. Med. Colls. (Coth rep.), Am. Cancer Soc. (regional adv. bd. 1994—), Med. Group Mgmt. Assn., Soc. Health Service Adminstrs., Sigma Phi Epsilon. Home: 63 Big Woods Dr Hilton Head Island SC 29926

WESSELS, BRUCE W., materials scientist, educator; b. N.Y.C., Oct. 18, 1946; m. Beverly T. Wessels; children: David, Kirsten. BS in Metallurgy and Materials Sci., U. Pa., 1968; PhD in Materials Sci., MIT, 1973. Mem. tech. staff GE R&D Ctr., 1972-77, acting branch mgr., 1976; from asst. prof. to assoc. prof. Northwestern U., Evanston, Ill., 1977-83, prof. materials sci. and engring., 1984—; vis. sci. Argonne Nat. Lab., 1978; mem. program com. 3d Internat. Conf. Superlattices, Microdevices and Microstructures, 1987. Editor 4 books including (with G.Y. Chin) Advances in Electronic Materials, 1986; mem. editl. bd. Jour. Electronic Materials, 1982-88; contbr. numerous articles to profl. jours.; patentee in field. Fellow ASM; mem. The Minerals, Metals and Materials Soc.-AIME (chmn. electronic materials com. 1987-89, conf. program chmn. 1986-87, key reader Trans. of AIME 1985—, bd. dirs. 1993—, vice chmn. exec. coun. electronic, magnetic and photonic materials divsn. 1991-92, chmn. 1993—, v.p. 1995, pres. 1996, bd. trustees AIME), Electrochem. Soc. Materials Rsch. Soc. (symposium organizer 1993, 95), Sigma Xi, Tau Beta Pi. Office: Materials Science & Engring Northwestern U 2225 N Campus Dr Evanston IL 60208

WESSINGER, W. DAVID, management consultant; b. Leesville, S.C., Aug. 8, 1924; s. Noah F. and Willye W. (Quattlebaum) W.; m. Virginia Lou Hinsch, June 30, 1945; children: David, Clifford, Carol, Virginia Anne. BS in Bus., George Washington U., 1962; MS in Mgmt., U.S. Navy Postgrad. Sch., 1963. Cert. mgmt. cons. Ensign USN, 1943, advanced through grades to capt., 1964; cons. Orgn. Resources Counselors, Inc., N.Y.C., 1968-78, v.p., 1978-85, sr. v.p., 1985-93, sr. counselor, 1993—. Mem. Am. Arbitration Assn., Am. Compensation Assn., Inst. Mgmt. Cons. Presbyterian. Avocations: woodworking, fishing, tennis, golf. Office: Organization Resources Counselors Inc 1211 6th Ave New York NY 10036-8701

WESSLER, MARY HRAHA, marketing and management executive; b. Des Moines, Nov. 4, 1961; d. Francis M. and Shirley A. (Malone) Hraha; 1 child, Nick. BA in Mass Communications, Iowa State U., 1984; postgrad., U. Denver, 1990. Asst. mktg. dir. Des Moines Ballet Co.; asst. press sec. Governor State of Iowa, Des Moines; dir. mktg. Real Estate Mgmt. Corp., Scottsdale, Ariz., 1984-87; v.p. Great West Mgmt. and Realty, Ltd., Denver, 1987—; instr., spkr. for apt. assns., Multi-Housing World and IREM. Mem. Nat. Apt. Assn., Colo. Apt. Assn. (treas. bd. dirs. 1997—), Apt. Assn. of Metro Denver (sec., bd. dirs., treas., pres.-elect, pres. 1997—, Owner of Yr. 1992-93, 95, Woman of Yr. 1989-90), Met. Club. Home: 2685 S Dayton Way # 187 Denver CO 80231

WESSLER, MELVIN DEAN, farmer, rancher; b. Dodge City, Kan., Feb. 11, 1932; s. Oscar Lewis and Clara (Reiss) W.; grad. high sch.; m. Laura Ethel Arbuthnot, Aug. 23, 1951; children: Monty Dean, Charla Cay, Virgil Lewis. Farmer-rancher, Springfield, Colo., 1950—; dir., sec. bd. Springfield Co-op. Sales Co., 1964-80, pres. bd., 1980—. Pres., Arkansas Valley Co-op. Council, SE Colo. Area, 1965-87, Colo. Co-op. Council, 1969-72, v.p. 1974, sec. 1980-86; community com. chmn. Baca County, Agr. Stablzn. and Conservation Svc., Springfield, 1961-73, 79—, vice chmn. Baca County Com., 1980-90; mem. spl. com. on grain mktg. Far-Mar-Co.; mem. adv. bd. Denver Bapt. Bible Coll., 1984-89; chmn., bd. dirs. Springfield Cemetery Bd., 1985—; apptd. spl. com. Farmland Industries spl. project Tomorrow, 1987—. Recipient The Colo. Cooperator award The Colo. Coop Coun., 1990. Mem. Colo. Cattlemen's Assn., Colo. Wheat Growers Assn., Southeast Farm Bus. Assn. (bd. dirs. 1991-95), Big Rock Grange (treas. 1964-76, master 1976-82), Southwest Kans. Farm Bus. Assn. (dir. 1996—). Address: 18363 County Road Pp Springfield CO 81073-9210

WESSLER, RICHARD LEE, psychology educator, psychotherapist; b. St. Louis, Sept. 11, 1936; s. Harry Edward and Lorraine Grace (Hoffman) W.; m. Sheenah Hankin, Mar. 28, 1984; 1 child, Lisa. Student, U. Mo., 1954-55; A.B., Washington U., 1958, Ph.D., 1966. Research assoc. St. Louis U., 1962-66, asst. prof. sociology, 1966-69; assoc. prof. psychology Parsons Coll., Farifield, Iowa, 1969-73; prof. psychology Pace U., Pleasantville, N.Y., 1974—; postdoctoral fellow, dir. tng. Inst. for Rational-Emotive Therapy, N.Y.C., 1973-75, 76-82; pvt. practice psychotherapy N.Y.C., 1976—; vis. prof. Rijksuniversiteit te Leiden, Netherlands, 1981-82, U. Aston, Eng., 1982; cons. govt. agys., hosps., bus. Author: (with R.A. Wessler) The Principles and Practice of Rational Emotive Therapy, 1980, (with S.R. Wolen and R.D. Giuseppe) A Practioner's Guide to Rational-Emotive Therapy, 1980; editor: Rational Living, 1974-83; assoc. editor: Brit.. Jour. Cognitive Psychotherapy. Mem. Am. Psychol. Assn., Assn. for Advancement Behavior Therapy.

WESSLER, SHEENAH HANKIN, psychotherapist, consultant; b. Tamworth, England, Nov. 4, 1939; came to U.S., 1982; d. Alexander Rolfe Mackenzie and Irene May Richards; m. Philip Raymond Hankin, Apr. 16, 1962 (div. Mar. 1984); children: Stuart, James, Robin, Nicholas; m. Richard L. Wessler, Mar. 28, 1984. BA with honors, Birmingham Univ., 1961, diploma in sr. edn., 1963; diploma in counseling psychology, Aston Univ., 1979; PhD, Internat. U., 1995. Dir. Irish Pregnangy Counseling Clinic, Dublin, Ireland, 1979-81; counselor trainer Well Woman Clinic, Dublin, Ireland, 1979-81; pvt. practice Dublin, Ireland, 1979-81; co-dir. Cognitive Psychotherapy Assocs., N.Y.C., 1983—; cons. Coolemine Therapeutic Cmty., Dublin, 1983—; expert presenter Fox TV Network, 1994—. Contbr. articles to profl. jours. Mem. AFTRA, Am. Counseling Assn. Office: Cognitive Psychotherapy Svcs 18 E 93rd St New York NY 10128-0610

WESSLER, STANFORD, physician, educator; b. N.Y.C., Apr. 20, 1917; S. Hugo and Minerva (Miller) W.; m. Margaret Barnet Muhlfelder, Dec. 17, 1942; children—John Stanford, Stephen Lawrence, James Hugh. Grad., Fieldston Sch., N.Y.C., 1934; B.A., Harvard, 1938; M.D., N.Y.U., 1942. From fellow to asst. prof. medicine Harvard U. Med. Sch., 1946-64; from resident to assoc. chief med. svc. Beth Israel Hosp., Boston, 1946-64; prof. medicine Washington U. Sch. Medicine, St. Louis, 1964-74; John L. and Adalaine Simon prof. Washington U. Sch. Medicine, 1966-74; prof. medicine, assoc. dean postgrad. programs NYU Sch. Medicine, 1974-90; physician in chief Jewish Hosp., St. Louis, 1964-74; assoc. physician Barnes Hosp., St. Louis, 1964-74; attending physician NYU Med. Center, Univ. Hosp., N.Y.C., 1974-90, Bellevue Hosp. Center, N.Y.C., 1974-90, Manhattan VA Hosp. Med. Ctr., 1974-90; Mem. coms. NRC, Inst. of Medicine, Nat. Heart, Lung and Blood Inst.; bd. dirs. N.Y. Heart Assn., 1980-86; pres. Council Continuing Med. Edn., N.Y., 1979-85. Contbr. articles on vascular disease.; mem. editorial bds. jours. in field. Served with M.C. AUS, 1943-46. Recipient James A. Mitchell award, 1972. Mem. Am. Physiol. Soc., Am. Soc. Clin. Investigation, Assn. Am. Physicians, Am. Heart Assn. (investigator 1955-59, bd. dirs. 1971-76, chmn. publs. com. 1972-76, chmn. coun. on thrombosis 1974-76, v.p. 1974-76, mem. sci. adv. com. 1986-90, Merit award 1978, Disting. Achievement award 1989), Alpha Omega Alpha. Home: 60 Rye Rd Rye NY 10580-2228

WESSLING, ROBERT BRUCE, lawyer; b. Chgo., Oct. 8, 1937; s. Robert Euans and Marguerite (Rickert) W.; m. Judith Ann Hanson, Aug. 26, 1961; children: Katherine, Jennifer, Carolyn. BA, DePauw U., 1959; JD, U. Mich., 1962. Bar: Calif. 1963, U.S. Dist. Ct. (cen. dist.) Calif. 1963, U.S. Ct. Appeals (9th cir.) 1965. Assoc. Latham & Watkins, L.A., 1962-70, ptnr., 1970-94, of counsel, 1995-97; bd. govs. Fin. Lawyers Conf., Los Angeles, 1974—. Mem. World Affairs Coun., L.A., Town Hall, L.A.; trustee DePauw U. Mem. ABA, Los Angeles Bar Assn., Phi Beta Kappa, Phi Delta Phi, Phi Eta Sigma, Order of Coif. Democrat. Methodist. Avocations: tennis, travel. Office: 633 W 5th St Ste 4000 Los Angeles CA 90071-2005

WESSNER, DEBORAH MARIE, telecommunications executive, computer consultant; b. St. Louis, Aug. 15, 1950; d. John George and Mary Jane (Beetz) Eyerman; m. Brian Paul Wessner, Sept. 15, 1972; children: Krystin, David. BA in Math. and Chemistry, St. Louis U., 1972; M Computer Info. Sci., U. New Haven, 1980. Statistiian Armstrong Rubber Co., New Haven, 1972-74; programmer analyst Sikorsky div. United Techs., Stratford, Conn., 1974-77; project engr. GE, Bridgeport, Conn., 1977-79; software mgr. GE, Arlington, Va., 1979-8l; mgr. software ops. Satellite Bus. Systems, McLean, Va., 1981-83; v.p. ops. DAMA Telecommunications, Rockville, Md., 1983-87; dir. network ops. and adminstrn. Data Gen. Network Svcs., Rockville, 1987-91; dir. bus. ops. Sprint Internat., Reston, Va., 1991-92; v.p. network adminstrn. Citicorp, Washington, 1992-93; v.p. telecomm. product mgmt. Citicorp, Reston, Va., 1994-95, v.p. product mgmt., 1996—; assoc., cons. KDB Assocs., Columbia, Md., 1986—. Mem. Am. Bus. Women's Assn., NAFE. Avocations: sailing, windsurfing, tennis. Office: 1900 Campus Commons Dr Reston VA 20191-1535

WEST, ANN LEE, clinical nurse specialist, educator, trauma nurse coordinator; b. Terre Haute, Ind., Aug. 11, 1943; d. Paul Everette and Margaret Alice (Roush) Corbin; m. Donald J. West, Aug. 29, 1964; children: Lee Ann, Kevin, Brian, Christopher. Diploma in nursing, St. Vincent's Hosp., 1964; BS, St. Joseph's Coll., 1983; MSN, Med. Coll. Ohio, 1992. RN, Ohio; ACLS, Advanced Cardiac Life Support provider instr.; cert. pediatric advanced life support, emergency nurse, trauma nurse core curriculum, basic life support; emergency nursing pediatric course provider, instr. Staff nurse St. Vincent Med. Ctr., Toledo, Ohio, 1964-67; office nurse Dr. Richard Leahy, Tiffin, Ohio, 1976-77; project nurse, relief nurse Clinicas Migrantes Reg., Fremont, Ohio, 1977-79; head nurse emergency dept. Bellevue Hosp., 1979-81; relief charge nurse Fireland's Cmty. Hosp., Sandusky, Ohio, 1981-95; staff devel. educator Med. Coll. Hosps., Toledo, 1993-96; trauma nurse coord. Med. Coll. Hosps., 1995-97, clin. nurse specialist Ambulatory Clinic Edn., 1997—; med. and nursing educator Firelands Cmty. Hosp., Sandusky, 1987-95; trauma prevention/outreach, patient educator Med. Coll. Hosp., Toledo, 1994-96; disting. lectr. Am. Acad. Allergy and Immunology, 1993. Author booklet for Am. Lung Assn.; contbr. articles to profl. jours. Mem. Am. Trauma Soc., Am. Lung Assn. (bd. dirs., sec., sch. edn. chair 1984-96), Ohio State Coun. Emergency Nurses (pres.-elect 1997), Seagate Emergency Nurse Assn. (pres. 1996), Rolls Royce Owner's Club, Lion's Club Internat. (pres.). Roman Catholic. Avocations: travel, camping, oil painting, Rockwell Foundation. Home: 320 Douglas Dr Bellevue OH 44811-1305 Office: Med Coll Ohio 3000 Arlington Ave Toledo OH 43614-2595

WEST, A(RNOLD) SUMNER, chemical engineer; b. Phila., Jan. 12, 1922; s. Arnold and Mary (Sumner) W.; m. Beverly Helen Lehman, Oct. 5, 1946; children: Barbara Ann, Richard Sumner. BSChemE, U. Pa., 1943; MS, Pa. State U., 1946. With Rohm and Haas Co., Phila., 1946-87, rsch. engr., 1946-62, rsch. supr., 1962-72, mgr. research dept., 1972-77, sr. tech. specialist govt. and regulatory affairs, 1978-87; owner, prin. A.S. West Assocs., Huntingdon Valley, Pa., 1987—; cons. dept. chem. engring. U. Pa., 1952-72; mem. indsl. and profl. adv. com. Coll. Engring., Pa. State U., 1978-84, chmn. chem. engring. div., 1980-81, chmn. com., 1982-83. Mem. Lower Moreland Twp. (Montgomery County) Authority, 1970, sec., 1971—; vice-chmn. bd. dirs. Chemical Heritage Found., 1984-92; pres. United Engring. Trustees, 1986-87. Fellow Am. Inst. Chem. Engrs. (dir. 1964-66, treas. 1973-75, v.p. 1976, pres. 1977); mem. Engrs. Joint Council (dir. 1976-79), Am. Assn. Engring. Socs. (vice chmn. public affairs council 1981, chmn. council 1982-83), Am. Chem. Soc., Nat. Soc. Profl. Engrs., Soc. Automotive Engrs., Water Environ. Fedn. Club: The Valley (Huntingdon Valley). Home and Office: 3896 Sidney Rd Huntingdon Valley PA 19006-2347

WEST, ARTHUR JAMES, II, biologist; b. Boston, Dec. 14, 1927; s. Arthur James and Lillian (Laming) W.; BS, Suffolk U., 1951, MA in Edn., 1956; MS, U. N.H., 1962, PhD in Zoology, 1964; m. Carolyn Barbara Ross, June 4, 1948 (div. May 1972); children: Arthur James, Gregory Thomas, Donald Robert; m. Linda Jean Cummings, July 21, 1985 (div. Sept. 1993); children: Melissa Ida, Benjamin Cummings. Faculty, Suffolk U., Boston, 1952-68, asso. prof. biology, 1964-65, prof., 1965-68, co-chmn. biology, 1964-68; dean, prof. div. natural sci. New Eng. Coll., Henniker, N.H., 1968-70; prof. chmn. dept. biology Suffolk U., 1970-72, 78-88; assoc. program dir. Pre-coll. Edn. in Scis., NSF, 1972-73; prof. dept. biology Suffolk U., 1973-89, prof. emeritus, 1989—; acad. v.p. for curriculum devel. U. San Juan Capistrano, 1992-93; owner, operator Subway of Farmington and Skowhegan, Maine, chmn.adv. coun. 1993-94; treas. Dahl Assocs., Inc., Lamb Assocs., Inc.; dir. R.S. Friedman Cobscook Bay Lab., 1975-88; exec. com. M.I.T./Sea Grant Consortium Program, 1979-85; asst. prof., chmn. biology Mass. Coll. Optometry, 1957-60; instr., chmn. sci. Emerson Coll., 1956-59; staff Norwich U., 1960; cons. Ginn & Co. Sci. Pubs., 1967-70; hon. cons., parasitologist Akvapatologisk Lab., 1987; civil svc. examiner Mass. Dept. Natural Resources, 1965-72. Founding pres. Keltown Civic Assn., 1954; chmn. Woburn United Fund, 1958; mem. Woburn Sch. Com., 1955-60, chmn. 1957; chmn. Woburn YMCA, 1958, Woburn Rep. City Com., 1959, New Vineyard Town Com., 1990; vice chmn. Franklin County Rep. Com.; mem. commn. on ocean mgmt. Mass. Served with USN, 1946-47, with Res., 1947-52. NSF grantee, 1968-71, 70-71, 75-82. Mem. Mass. Bay Marine Studies Consortium (pres. 1982-85), Mass. Marine Educators, Inc. (com. 1978-86), AAAS, Am. Inst. Biol. Scis., Nat. Marine Edn. Assn. (dir. 1976-78, pres. 1985-86), Ea. Star, Rotary, Masons, Sigma Xi (Suffolk U. club pres. 1972), Sigma Zeta, Phi Beta Chi (pres. 1951), Beta Beta Beta, Phi Sigma. Research and publs. on Acanthocephala and undergrad. marine edn. Home: PO Box 104 New Vineyard ME 04956-0104 *To live with conscience is to live a life in grace. Helping others find and achieve their goals is the greatest reward a teacher may achieve.*

WEST, BOB, pharmaceutical company executive; b. Ellenville, N.Y., Mar. 7, 1931; s. Harry and Elsie May Wicentowsky; m. Betty Parker, May 9, 1957 (div.); children: Debra Ellen, Elizabeth Ann, Sharon Lynn; m. Jacqueline Cutler, Jan. 3, 1982. BS, Union U., 1952; MS, Purdue U., 1954, PhD, 1956; postgrad. mgmt. seminar, U. Chgo., 1972. Pres., dir. research Food, Drug, Chem. Svcs., Stamford, Conn., 1975—; pres., dir. research Bob West Assocs., Inc., Stamford, 1975—; pres. Drug Info. Assn., Phila., 1974-75; sci. adv. bd. Fountain Pharms., Inc., Largo, Fla., 1993—, Dovetail Techs., Inc., College Park, Md., 1996—. Editorial bd. Drug Info. Assn. Jour., Phila., 1977-85; contbr. articles to profl. jours. Mem. ASPET, Am. Soc. Toxicology, Acad. Pharm. Scis., Assn. Rsch. Dirs., Drug Info. Assn., Assn. Univ. Tech. Mgrs. Home and office: Food Drug Chem Svcs 3771 Center Way Fairfax VA 22033-2602

WEST, BURTON CAREY, physician; b. Pitts., Feb. 21, 1941; s. Pemberton Burton and Maree (Van Scoyoc) W.; m. Katherine Ann Young, Dec. 27, 1963; children: Amy Fay Chandler, Holly Katherine Brewer, John Pemberton, Abigail Coleman, Emily Van Scoyoc. AB, AMherst Coll., 1963; MD, Cornell U., 1967. Diplomate Am. Bd. Internal Medicine and Infectious Diseases. Resident U. Hosps., Seattle, 1967-69; clin. assoc., sr. staff fellow NIAID, NIH, Bethesda, Md., 1969-72; resident, chief resident Vanderbilt Hosp., Nashville, 1972-74; from asst. prof. to prof. medicine La. State U. Sch. Medicine, Shreveport, 1974-89, chief sect. infectious diseases, 1974-89; chmn. dept. medicine Meridia Huron Hosp., Cleve., 1989—. Contbr. articles to profl. jours. Lt. comdr. USPHS, 1969-71. Fellow ACP (chmn. program dirs. Ohio chpt. 1995—), Infectious Diseases Soc. Am. (pres. Ohio chpt. 1996-97). Office: Meridia Huron Hosp 13951 Terrace Rd Cleveland OH 44112-4308

WEST, CHARLES CONVERSE, theologian, educator; b. Plainfield, N.J., Feb. 3, 1921; s. George Parsons and Florence (Farish) W.; m. Ruth Floy Carson, Sept. 6, 1944; children: Russell Arthur, Walter Lawrence, Glenn Andrew. B.A., Columbia U., 1942; B.D., Union Theol. Sem., N.Y.C., 1945; Ph.D., Yale U., 1955. Ordained to ministry Presbyterian Ch. U.S.A., 1946; missionary, fraternal worker Bd. Fgn. Missions Presbyn. Ch. U.S.A., 1946-56; instr., chaplain Cheeloo U., Hangchow, China, 1948-49; instr. Nanking Theol. Sem., 1949-50; indsl. mission work Gossner Mission, Mainz-Kastel, Germany, 1950-51; lectr. Kirchliche Hochschule, Berlin, 1951-53; Lectr. Hartford Sem. Found., 1955-56; asso. dir. Ecumenical Inst., Bossey, Switzerland under World Council Chs., 1956-61; chargé de cours U. Geneva, 1956-61; instr. Peking Nat. U., 1948; assoc. prof. Christian ethics Princeton Theol. Sem., 1961-63, Stephen Colwell prof. Christian ethics, 1963-91, prof. emeritus, 1991—, acad. dean, 1979-84; mem. Commn. to Form Statement Faith U.P. Ch. U.S.A., 1961-67, chmn. internat. affairs adv. com., 1963-66; Chmn. U.S. Com. for Christian Peace Conf., 1965-72; chmn. working com. Dept. Studies in Mission, Evangelism World Council Chs., 1967-68; member Commn. on Internat. Affairs, Nat. Council Chs., 1968-73. Author: Communism and the Theologians, 1958, Outside the Camp, 1959, Ethics, Biolence and Revolution, 1969, The Power to be Human, 1971, Perspective on South Africa, 1985; editor: The Sufficiency of God, Essays in Honor of Dr. W.A. Visser't Hooft, 1963; assoc. editor: Religion in Eastern Europe, 1985—; translator: J. Hamel-A Christian in East Germany, 1960. Mem. Am. Soc. Christian Ethics (v.p. 1972-73, pres. 1973-74), Am. Theol. Soc. (v.p. 1982-83, pres. 1983-84), Presbytery N.Y.C., Ams. for Dem. Action., Christians Associated for Rels. with Eastern Europe (pres. 1988-92). Home: 157 Mountain Rd Ringoes NJ 08551-1402 Office: Princeton Theological Seminary CN821 Princeton NJ 08542

WEST, CLARK DARWIN, pediatric nephrologist, educator; b. Jamestown, N.Y., July 4, 1918; s. Clark Darwin and Frances Isabel (Blanchard) W.; m. Ruthann Asbury, Apr. 12, 1944 (div.); children: Charles Michael, John Clark, Lucy Frances; m. Dolores Lachenman, Mar. 1, 1986. A.B., Coll. of Wooster, 1940; M.D., U. Mich., 1943. Intern Univ. Hosp., Ann Arbor, Mich., 1943-44; resident in pediatrics Univ. Hosp., 1944-46; fellow in pediatrics Children's Hosp. Research Found., Cin., 1948-49; research asso. Children's Hosp. Research Found., 1951-89, asso. dir., 1963-89, dir. div. immunology and nephrology, 1958-89; with cardiopulmonary lab. chest service Bellevue Hosp., N.Y.C., 1949-51; attending pediatrician Children's Hosp., 1951-89; asst. prof. pediatrics U. Cin., 1951-55, asso. prof., 1955-62, prof., 1962-89; mem. coms. NIH, 1965-69, 1972-73. Mem. editorial bd.: Jour. Pediatrics, 1960-79, Kidney Internat., 1977-89, Clin. Nephrology, 1989-96; contbr. articles to profl. jours. Served to capt. M.C., AUS, 1946-47. Decorated Army commendation medal; recipient recognition award Cin. Pediat. Soc., 1980, Mitchell Rubin award, 1986, Henry L. Barnett award, 1995, Daniel Drake medal, 1996, John P. Peters award, 1996. Mem. Soc. Pediatric Research (sec.-treas. 1958-62, pres. 1963-64), Am. Pediatric Soc., Am. Soc. Pediatric Nephrologists (pres. 1973-74), Am. Physiol. Soc., Am. Assn. Immunologists, Am. Soc. Nephrology, Internat. Pediatric Nephrology Assn., Sigma Xi, Alpha Omega Alpha. Research on immunopathogenesis and treatment of glomerulonephritides and in the complement system. Home: 11688 Aristocrat Dr Harrison OH 45030-9753 Office: Children's Hosp Med Ctr Cincinnati OH 45229

WEST, DANIEL CHARLES, lay worker, dentist; b. Trenton, N.J., July 23, 1955; s. Harry E. and Alma R. (Washburn) W.; m. Deborah L. Scott, May 28, 1977; children: Lauren Elizabeth, Colin Jeffrey. BS, Ea. Nazarene Coll., 1977; DMD, U. Pitts., 1982. Min. youth/music South Hills Ch. of the Nazarene, Bethel Park, Pa., 1977-82; pvt. practice specializing in family dentistry Terre Hill, Pa., 1982-95; pvt. practice specializing in cosmetic, implant and reconstructive dentistry New Holland, Pa., 1995—; mem. Internat. Gen. Bd., Ch. of the Nazarene, Kansas City, Mo., 1989—, lay mem. dist. adv. bd. Phila. dist., Frazer, Pa., 1985—, coord. work and witness program, 1988-90, dir. compassionate ministries, 1990—; dir. Phila. dist. IMPACT, 1982-89; trustee Ea. Nazarene Coll., Wollaston, Mass., 1984—, mem. exec. com., chmn. dept. fin.; mem. clin. faculty U. Pa. Sch. Dental Medicine, Med. U. Ukraine, Kiev, Pediat. Med. U. Russia, Moscow. Contbr. articles to jours. Bd. dirs. Garden Spot Village Retirement Comty., 1996—. Lt. USPHS, 1982-85. Fellow Am. Acad. Gen. Dentistry; mem. ADA (Cert. Recognition for Internat. Svc. in a Fgn. County 1996), Am. Acad. Cosmetic Dentistry, Pa. Dental Assn., Lancaster County Dental Soc. Republican. Home: 1442 Hay Field Dr East Earl PA 17519-9685 Office: 650 E Main St New Holland PA 17557-1410 *The greatest joy I have is in serving others through ministry in the church, my dental practice, and especially in my home.*

WEST, DANIEL JONES, JR., hospital administrator, rehabilitaton counselor, health care consultant, educator; b. Coaldale, Pa., Sept. 19, 1949; s. Daniel J. and Mildred Elizabeth (Kreiger) W.; m. Linda Jean Werdt, Sep. 18, 1971; children: Jeffrey Bryan, Christopher Jones, Danielle K. BS cum laude, Pa. State U., 1971, EdM summa cum laude, 1972, PhD in Counseling Psychology summa cum laude, 1982; postgrad., Montgomery County Community Coll., 1973, Rutgers U., 1974. Diplomate Am. Acad. Behavioral Medicine, Am. Acad. Med. Adminstrs. Adminstr. Good Samaritan Hosp., Pottsville, Pa., 1975-78, asst. v.p. ambulatory svcs., 1978-83; adminstr. MEDIQ, Inc., Scranton (Pa.) State Hosp., 1983-85; pres., CEO HTC Consulting Group, Inc., Gouldsboro, Pa., 1986—; dir., assoc. prof. U. Scranton, 1990—; adj. prof. Pa. State U., 1974-83, U. Scranton, 1983-90, Wilkes Coll., 1986; CEO Medi-Group, Inc., Penn Health Care, Inc., A.I.R., Inc., Med. Sci. Lab., Inc., Lackawanna Med. Group, P.C., Scranton, 1986-91; stockholder, ptnr. Penn Health Care, Inc., 1987—, Health Care Support Svcs., Scranton, 1993—; stockholder, bd. dirs. Northeast Women's Diagnostic Ctr., Scranton, 1989—; regional dir. ops. HCP Consulting Group, Inc., Willow Grove, Pa., 1990—; moderator First Ann. Conf. on Drug and Alcohol Abuse, Bedford, Pa., 1977; mem. adv. com. to rehab. counseling programs Pa. State U., 1983—; numerous positions State Bd. of Medicine, Commonwealth of Pa., 1991-95—; mem. departmental review bd. for rsch. U. Scranton, 1991—; me. Scranton Temple residency program instnl. rev. bd. Mercy Hosp., 1991—; mem. Fedn. of State Med. Bd. of U.S., Inc., 1994—, mem. editl. adv. bd., 1984-85, voting del. from Pa. for osteopathic bd.; bd. dirs. comm. com. Midwest Regional Med. Bd., 1994-95; mem. task force on health care Econ. Devel. Coun. Northeast Pa., 1994-95; bd. dirs. Friendship House, 1995-96; bd. dirs. Robert Charles Zaloga Found, 1994—; spkr. in field. Author manuals on mgmt. and health care; contbr. articles to profl. jours. Chmn. planning and implementation coun. Schuylkill County Gov.'s Coun. on Drug and Alcohol Abuse, State of Pa., 1973-74; mem. Drug Adv. Task Force, 1973-74, Task Force Child and Family Resource Devel. Program, Schuylkill County, 1973—, Criminal Justice Sys. Task Force, Schuylkill County, 1975—; mem. adv. bd. Holy Family Home Health Care Agy., Schuylkill County, 1977—, chmn. bd. edn. com., 1977—; bd. dirs. St. David's Soc. Schuylkill and Carbon Counties, 1976—, Health Sys. Agy., Northeast Pa., 1977—; mem. instnl. review bd. Cmty. Med. Ctr., 1986—; bd. dirs. Scranton Counseling Ctr., 1990—; mem. long range planning com. and personnel com.; bd. dirs. Telespond Sr. Svcs., Inc., 1991—; mem. Diocesan health care com. Diocese of Scranton, 1992—; mem. steering com. Citizen Advocacy Ctr., AARP Health Advocacy Svcs., 1992—; bd. dirs., v.p. Citizen Advocacy Ctr., Arlington, Va., 1994-95; mem. ad hoc com. on children health United Way, 1995—. Recipient Rsch. award Am. Edni. Rsch. Assn., 1983, Svc. and Leadership award Schuylkill County Drug and Alcohol Exec. Comm., 1982, Dedication and Leadership award Gov.'s Coun. Drug and Alcohol Abuse Drug Adv. Task Force, 1978; Fellow Accrediting Commn. Edn. for Health Svcs. Adminstrn., 1994-95. Fellow Am. Acad. Med. Adminstrs. (editl. com. 1993—, diplomate 1995), Internat. Acad. Behavioral Medicine, Counseling and Psychotherapy, Inc., Am. Coll. Healthcare Execs. (regents adv. bd. Pa. Area B 1995—, regents award 1997), Fedn. State Med. Bds. US, Inc. (editl. com. 1994—), Coll. Osteo. Healthcare Execs. (editl. com. 1991—), Am. Coll. Med. Practice Execs., Am. Coll. Health Care Adminstr., Assn. Mental Health Adminstrs. (cert., editl. com. 1992—); mem. APHA, AAAS, Nat. Rehab. Assn., Nat. Rehab. Adminstrn. Assn., Am. Hosp. Assn., Med. Group Mgmt. Assn., Hosp. Assn. Pa., Pa. Rehab. Assn., Pa. Med. Group Mgmt. Assn., Phi Kappa Phi, Iota Alpha Delta. Address: RD # 1 Skyline Acres 101 Birch St Gouldsboro PA 18424

WEST, DOE, bioethicist, social justice activist; b. Tucson, July 14, 1951; d. George Oliver and Dorothy Marie (Watson) W.; m. Bruce Malcolm Gale, Feb. 1, 1980. AA, Dutchess C.C., 1975; BS, SUNY, New Paltz, 1977; BA, Logos Bible Coll., 1986, MDiv, 1993; MS, Boston U., 1980; PhD, Northeastern U., 1998. Dir. 504/compliance officer dept. health and hosps. City of Boston, 1979-81, commr. handicap affairs, 1981-84; pres. Myth Breakers, Inc., 1984—; writer, photographer; exec. dir. Social Action Ministries of Gtr. Boston, 1996—; lectr. Northeastern U., Mt. Ida Coll., 1982—; dir. chaplaincy svcs. Quincy (Mass.) Hosp., 1991-92; chief of staff State House Boston, 1992-94; project coord. task force on human subject rsch. Fernald State Sch., 1994. Home: PO Box 2006 Brookline MA 02146

WEST, DOROTHY, writer; b. Boston, 1910; d. Isaac Christopher and Rachel Pease (Benson) W. Founder literary mag., editor Challenge, N.Y.C., 1934-37, New Challenge, N.Y.C., 1937; with Fed. Writers' Project New Deal's Work Project Adminstrn., N.Y.C., 1937-43. Author: The Living Is Easy, 1948, The Wedding, 1995, The Richer, The Poorer, 1995; (story) Promise and Fulfillment, 1920, The Typewriter, 1926, award; contbr. articles and columnist in Daily News and Vineyard Gazette. Office: Doubleday Publishing 1540 Broadway New York NY 10036-4039

WEST, E. JOSEPH, financial analyst, investment portfolio manager; b. Kingston, Pa., Nov. 24, 1940; s. David Dimon and Elizabeth Irene (Emery) W.; m. Darla Jean Payne, Oct. 13, 1962 (div. Aug. 1972); 1 child, Emery Joseph II; m. Karen Marie Rowlands, Jan. 1, 1981. Grad., Mercersburg Acad., 1959, U.S. Air Force Acad., 1962; cert., Northwestern U., Evanston, Ill., 1964, U. Windsor, Ont., 1972, 73, 79, Rockford Coll., Ill., 1982; cert. investment mgmt., Princeton U., 1984; MBA, Coll. William & Mary, 1990. Chartered fin. analyst. Jr. investment analyst Tech. Stock Rev., Inc., N.Y.C., 1962-63; analyst, broker Grant, Jones & Co., Inc., Washington, 1963-64; sr. account exec. W.E. Hutton & Co., Washington, 1964-74; investment exec. E.F. Hutton & Co., Inc., Washington, 1974-78; 1st v.p. investments and portfolio mgr. Drexel Burnham Lambert, Inc., Washington, 1978-89; 1st v.p., portfolio mgr. Smith Barney Inc., Washington, 1989—; bd. dirs. Fairfax Cable Channel 10, 1985-88; trustee and chmn. investment com. Fairfax County Retirement System, 1985-89. Active Fairfax County (Va.) Rep. Com., 1983—, Fairfax County Econ. Adv. Commn., 1992—, Fairfax County Com. 100, 1984—, No. Va. Tech. Coun. Recipient Award Appreciation County of Fairfax Retirement System, 1989. Fellow Fin. Analysts Fedn., Inst. Chartered Fin. Analysts, Internat. Soc. Fin. Analysts; mem. Assn. for Investment Mgmt. and Rsch., Washington Soc. Investment Analysts, Nat. Assn. Bus. Economists, Nat. Economists Club, Washington Assn. Money Mgrs., Soc. Profl. Forecasters Fed. Res. Bank of Phila., Mercersburg Acad. Alumni Coun., Fairfax County C. of C., Belle Haven Country Club, The Tower Club. Republican. Lutheran. Avocations: golf, crossword puzzles, backgammon, bridge. Office: Smith Barney Inc 1776 I St NW Washington DC 20006-3700

WEST, FELTON, retired newspaper writer; b. Houston, May 9, 1926; s. Felton Eber and Clara Viola (Ross) W.; m. Jean Frances Osborn, Oct. 27, 1945; children—Felton Dale, Bruce Eugene, Wade Osborn, Barbara Jean. Student, U. N.Mex., 1944-46; B.S., U. Houston, 1952, M.Litt., 1957. Mem. staff Houston Post, 1943-95, Washington corr., 1961-65, chief Austin (Tex.) capitol bur., 1966-85, columnist, 1985-93, editorial writer, 1993-95, ret., 1995. Served with USNR, World War II. Mem. Soc. Profl. Journalists, Phi Kappa Phi. Home and Office: 2251 CR 284 Liberty Hill TX 78642-9761

WEST, GAIL BERRY, lawyer; b. Cin.; d. Theodore Moody and Johnnie Mae (Newton) B.; m. Togo D. West, Jr., June 18, 1966; children: Tiffany Berry, Hilary Carter. B.A. magna cum laude, Fisk U., 1964; M.A., U. Cin., 1965; J.D., Howard U., 1968. Bar: D.C. 1969, U.S. Supreme Ct. 1978. Staff atty. IBM, 1969-76; spl. asst. to sec. HUD, 1977-78; staff asst. to spl. asst. to Pres., Washington, 1978-80; dep. asst. sec. for manpower res. affairs installations Dept. Air Force, 1980-81; atty. AT&T, Washington, 1983-84; exec. dir. govt. affairs Bell Comms. Rsch. Inc., Washington, 1984-95; dir. govt. rels. Armstrong World Industries, Inc., Washington, 1995—. Mem. exec. com. ARC, Washington, 1974-85; bd. dirs. Family and Child Svcs., Washington, 1974-87; bd. trustees Corcoran Gallery Art, Arena Stage, Decatur House, WETA, Fisher House Found., Inc.; bd. dirs. Meridian House. Ford Found. fellow, 1965-68. Mem. ABA, D.C. Bar Assn., Unified Bar D.C. Democrat. Episcopalian. Home: 4934 Rockwood Pky NW Washington DC 20016-3211 Office: 1025 Connecticut Ave NW Washington DC 20036

WEST, GAIL MARCIA WEISS, special education educator; b. Queens, N.Y., Sept. 22, 1955; d. Martin Albert and Syra (Hamburg) Weiss; m. Gregg David West, Aug. 17, 1978; children: Rachel Leah, Dana Lindsay, Sasha Lynne. BS in Elem. Edn., . Wis., 1977; MS in Spl. Edn., Pepperdine U., 1980. Cert. tchr., spl. edn. tchr., Calif., Md. Asst. dir. Human Rels. Dept., Madison, Wis., 1977; tchr. La Tijera Elem. Sch., Inglewood, Calif., 1978-82; tchr. spl. edn. 153d St Sch., Gardena, Calif., 1980; tchr., tutor Specific Diagnostics, Rockville, Md., 1983-88, coord. svcs. and programs, 1985-87, ednl. diagnostician, 1987-88; ednl. cons., advocate A Helping Hand, Brookeville, Md., 1988—; speaker at parent orgn. meetings; tutor children with learning difficulties, 1980—. Contbr. articles to profl. jours. Exec. bd. Greenwood Elem. Sch. PTA, 1988—, pres., 1991-93; exec. bd. Hadassah, 1989-91; Sherwood Cluster coord. County Level of PTA's. Mem. Wash Ind. Svcs. Ednl. Resources, Children with Attention Deficit Disorders, Parents of Gifted/Learning Disabled Children, Phi Kappa Phi. Democrat. Jewish. Avocations: aerobics, arts and crafts, reading. Home and Office: A Helping Hand 18636 Tanterra Way Brookeville MD 20833-2832

WEST, GLENN EDWARD, business organization executive; b. Kansas City, Mo., Nov. 19, 1944; s. Ernest and Helen Cecil (Johnson) W.; m. Vicki Lynn Knox, May 22, 1970; children: Keele Kay, Kollen Chandler, Ashley Knox. BS in Acctg. and Mktg. cum laude, Northwest Mo. State U., 1966; student U. Colo. Inst. Orgn. Mgmt., 1974; student Notre Dame U. Acad. Orgn. Mgmt., 1977. Auditor Arthur Young & Co., Kansas City, Mo., 1966-68; sales mgr. Procter & Gamble, Kansas City, Mo., 1968-69; mgr. pub. relations St. Joseph Area C. of C., Mo., 1969-71, mgr. econ. devel., 1971-74; exec. v.p. Lawrence C. of C., Kans., 1974-81, Greater Macon C. of C., Ga., from 1981; now pres. Austin C. of C.; mem. bd. dirs. Tex. Assn. Bus. and C. of C., 1995, U.S. C. of C., 1995. Contbr. articles to profl. jours. Chmn. chpt. ARC, Macon, 1984; pres. Quality of Life Found. Austin, Greater Austin Sports Found.; cen. campaign chair Capital Area United Way, 1995. Recipient Leadership award Kiwanis Club, St. Joseph, Mo., 1974. Served with USNG, 1967-73. Mem. Kans Assn. Commerce and Industry (bd. dirs. 1977-79, leadership award 1981), Kans. C. of C. Execs. (bd. dirs. 1977-80, pres. 1979), Ga. C. of C. Execs. (bd. dirs. 1982—), Am. C. of C. Execs. (bd. dirs. 1979-81, 83-84, vice chmn. 1989—, chmn.-elect 1990, chmn. 1991, cert. chamber exec. 1980), C. of C. of U.S. (adv. com. 1981-89, bd. dir. 1995), Rotary, Barton Creek Country Club. Republican. Methodist. Office: Greater Austin C of C PO Box 1967 111 Congress Ave Plz Austin TX 78767-1967

WEST, GREGORY ALAN, physician; b. Houston, Aug. 1, 1950; s. Wayne Garland and Frankie Onalita (Russell) W.; m. Catherine Ann Sharp, June 18, 1976 (div. Oct. 1980); 1 child, Benjamin M.; m. Linda French Lucas, Apr. 13, 1985 (div. 1994); children: Robert, Scott; m. Cynthia Lee Swainston, Apr. 30, 1997. BA, Austin Coll., 1972; PhD, U. Louisville, 1980, MD, 1982; MDiv, 1981. Diplomate Am. Bd. Pediatrics, Am. Bd. Emergency Medicine. EMT Louisville Emergency Med. Svc., 1977-79; intern in pediatrics U. Louisville Affiliated Hosps., 1982-83, resident in pediatrics, 1983-85; staff physician emergency dept. St. Anthony Hosp., Louisville, 1985-86; staff physician emergency dept. King's Daus. Hosp., Madison, Ind., 1985-95, med. dir. emergency med. svcs., 1989-91; staff physician emergency dept. Tri-County Cmty. Hosp., La Grange, Ky., 1991-92, Hardin County Meml. Hosp., Elizabethtown, Ky., 1995—. Contbr. articles to profl. jours. Recipient pediatric radiology award and chmn.'s achievement award U. Louisville Affiliated Hosps. Fellow Am. Acad. Emergency Physicians, Am. Acad. Pediatrics; mem. Omicron Delta Kappa. Episcopalian. Avocations: tae kwon do karate, scuba diving, travel.

WEST, HUGH STERLING, aircraft leasing company executive; b. Kansas City, Kans., Apr. 5, 1930; s. Gilbert Eugene and Dorothy (Johnson) W.; BS, U. Va., 1952; BS in Aero., U. Md., 1959; grad. U.S. Naval Test Pilot Sch., 1959; m. Willa Alden Reed, Jan. 16, 1954; children: Karen, Phillip, Susan. Commd. 2d lt. U.S. Marine Corps., 1948, advanced through grades to maj., 1961; exptl. flight test pilot, U.S. Naval Air Test Center, Patuxent River, Md.; resigned, 1961; program mgr. Boeing Aircraft Co., Seattle and Phila., 1961-66, dir. airworthiness, comml. airplane divsn., 1969-71; dir. aircraft sales Am. Airlines, Tulsa, 1971-76; v.p. equipment mgmt. GATX Leasing Corp., San Francisco, 1976-80; v.p. tech., partner Polaris Aircraft Leasing Corp., San Francisco, 1980-85; v.p., co-founder U.S. Airlease, Inc. divsn. Ford Motor Co., 1986-96, ret., 1996; pres. Hugh S. West & Assocs., Comml. Aircraft Cons. Mem. Soc. Exptl. Test Pilots, Army Navy Country Club. Republican. Episcopalian. Home and Office: 387 Darrell Rd Hillsborough CA 94010-6763

WEST, JAMES HAROLD, accounting company executive; b. San Diego, Oct. 11, 1926; s. Robert Reed and Clara Leona (Moses) W.; m. Norma Jean, 1953 (div.); 1 son, Timothy James; m., Jerel Lynn Smith, Nov. 16, 1976; 1 child, James Nelson. BS, U. So. Calif., Los Angeles, 1949. CPA, Calif. Ptnr., McCracken & Co., San Diego, 1950-61; mgr. Ernst & Ernst, San Diego, 1961-64; ptnr. West Turnquist & Schmitt, San Diego, 1964—. Bd. govs. ARC, Washington, 1981-87; pres., bd. dirs. Combined Arts and Edn. Coun., San Diego, 1980-83; pres. Francis Parker Sch., 1988-90; bd. dirs. San Diego Hosp. Assn., 1981-95, San Diegans Inc., 1989-92, Mus. Photographic Arts, 1990-92; trustee Calif. Western Sch. Law, 1985—; mem. bd. advisors U. So. Calif. Sch. Acctg., 1985—; treas. San Diego Nat. Sports Tng. Found., 1988-92; mem. acctg. exec. bd. U. San Diego, 1992—. With AUS, 1945-46; PTO. Mem. AICPA, Calif. Soc. CPAs (bd. dirs. 1963-64), University Club (San Diego), Capital Hill Club (Washington), Masons. Republican. Home: 3311 Lucinda St San Diego CA 92106-2931 Office: West Turnquist & Schmitt 2550 5th Ave Fl 10 San Diego CA 92103-6612

WEST, JAMES JOSEPH, lawyer; b. Tarentum, Pa., Nov. 26, 1945; s. Samuel Elwood and Rose (McIntyre) W.; m. Kathleen Geslak, Aug. 19, 1967; children: Joseph Allen, Yvonne Michelle, KaiLynn Ann. BS in Econs., St. Vincent Coll., 1967; JD, Duquesne U., 1970. Bar: Pa. 1971, U.S. Dist. Ct. (we. dist.) Pa. 1971, U.S. Ct. Appeals (3d cir.) 1971, U.S. Dist. Ct. (mid. dist.) Pa., 1980. Law clk. to presiding justice U.S. Dist. Ct., Pa., 1970-74; asst. U.S. atty. chief appellate sect. U.S. Atty.'s Office, Pitts., 1974-79; dep. dir. criminal law Pa. Atty. Gen.'s Office, Harrisburg, 1979-82; 1st asst. U.S. atty. U.S. Dist. Ct. (mid. dist.) Pa., Harrisburg, 1982-84, U.S. atty., 1984-93; assoc. Sprague & Sprague, Phila., 1993-95; pvt. practice Harrisburg, Pa., 1995—. Mem. Nat. Environ. Enforcement Council. Recipient Outstanding Performance award U.S. Dept. Justice, 1974-78, Commendation Gov. of Pa., 1981. Mem. Pa. Bar Assn., Allegheny County Bar Assn., Dauphin County Bar Assn. Republican. Roman Catholic. Home: 129 Oxford Ln North Wales PA 19454-4402 Office: James West 105 N Front St Harrisburg PA 17011

WEST, JERRY ALAN, professional basketball team executive; b. Chelyan, W.Va., May 28, 1938; s. Howard Stewart and Cecil Sue (Creasey) W.; m. Martha Jane Kane, May 1960 (div. 1977); children: David, Michael, Mark; m. Karen Christine Bua, May 28, 1978; 1 son, Ryan. BS, W.Va. Coll.; LHD (hon.), W.Va. Wesleyan Coll. Mem. Los Angeles Lakers, Nat. Basketball Assn., 1960-74, coach, 1976-79, spl. cons., 1979-82, gen. mgr., 1982-94; exec. v.p. basketball operations L. A. Lakers, 1994—; mem. first team Nat. Basketball Assn. All-Star Team, 1962-67, 70-73, mem. second team, 1968, 69; mem. NBA champion L.A. Lakers, 1972. Author: (with William Libby) Mr. Clutch: The Jerry West Story, 1969. Capt. U.S. Olympic Basketball Team, 1960; named Most Valuable Player NBA Playoff, 1969, All-Star Game Most Valuable Player, 1972; named to Naismith Meml. Basketball Hall of Fame, 1979, NBA Hall of Fame, 1980; mem. NBA 35th Anniversity All-Time Team, 1980; named NBA Exec. of Yr. Sporting News, 1994-95. Office: LA Lakers 3900 W Manchester Blvd PO Box 10 Inglewood CA 90305*

WEST, JOHN BURNARD, physiologist, educator; b. Adelaide, Australia, Dec. 27, 1928; came to U.S., 1969; s. Esmond Frank and Meta Pauline (Spehr) W.; m. Penelope Hall Banks, Oct. 28, 1967; children: Robert Burnard, Joanna Ruth. M.B.B.S., Adelaide U., 1951, M.D., 1958, D.Sc., 1980; Ph.D., London U., 1960; Dr. honoris causa, U. Barcelona, Spain, 1987. Resident Royal Adelaide Hosp., 1952, Hammersmith Hosp., London, 1953-55; physiologist Sir Edmund Hillary's Himalayan Expdn., 1960-61; dir. respiratory research group Postgrad. Med. Sch., London, 1962-67; reader medicine Postgrad. Med. Sch., 1968; prof. medicine and physiology U. Calif. at San Diego, 1969—; Wiltshire lectr., London, 1977, Schwidetzky lectr., 1975, Fleischner lectr., 1977, Robertson lectr. Adelaide U., 1978, McClement lectr. NYU, 1996; leader Am. Med. Rsch. Expdn. to Mt. Everest, 1981; U.S. organizer China-U.S. Conf. on respiratory failure, Nanjing, 1986; mem. life scis. adv. com. NASA, 1985-88, task force sci. uses of space sta., 1984-87, aerospace med. adv. com., 1988-89, chmn. sci. verification com. Spacelab SLS-1, 1983-92; prin. investigator Spacelabs SLS 1, 2, LMS, Neurolab, 1983—; co-investigator European Spacelabs, D2, Euromir, 1987—; mem. commn. on respiratory physiol., 1985—; mem. commn. on clin. physiol., 1991—, mem. commn. gravitation physiol., 1986—; mem. U.S. nat. com. Internat. Union Physiol. Scis., 1984-87; mem. study sect. NIH, chmn., 1973-75; external examiner Nat. U. Singapore, 1995. Author: Ventilation/Blood Flow and Gas Exchange, 1965, Respiratory Physiology-The Essentials, 1974, Translations in Respiratory Physiology, 1975, Pulmonary Pathophysiology-The Essentials, 1977, Translations in Respiratory Physiology, 1977, Bioengineering Aspects of the Lung, 1977, Regional Differences in the Lung, 1977, Pulmonary Gas Exchange (2 vols.), 1980, High Altitude Physiology, 1981, High Altitude and Man, 1984, Everest-The Testing Place, 1985, Best and Taylor's Physiological Basis of Medical Practice, 1985, 91, Study Guide for Best and Taylor, 1985, High Altitude Medicine and Physiology, 1989, The Lung: Scientific Foundations, 1991, 2d edit., 1997, Lung Injury, 1992, Respiratory Physiology: People and Ideas, 1996. Recipient Ernest Jung prize for medicine, Hamburg, 1977, Presdl. citation Am. Coll. Chest Physicians, 1977, Reynolds Prize for history Am. Physiol. Soc., 1987; I.J. Flance lectr. Washington U., 1978; G.C. Griffith lectr. Am. Heart Assn., 1978; scholar Macy Found., 1974; Kaiser teaching award 1980; W.A. Smith lectr. Med. Coll. S.C., 1982; S.C., 1982; S. Kronheim lectr. Undersea Med. Soc., 1984; D.W. Richards lectr. Am. Heart Assn., 1980, E.M. Papper lectr. Columbia U., 1981, I.S. Ravdin lectr. ACS, 1982, Burns Amberson lectr. Am. Thoracic Soc., 1984, Harry G. Armstrong lectr. Aerospace Med. Assn., 1984, Annual Space Life Scis. lectr. Federation Associated Socs. of Exptl. Biology, 1991, Hermann Rahn lectr. SUNY Buffalo, 1992, Menkes lectr. Johns Hopkins, 1992, Jeffries Med. Rsch. award AIAA, 1992; Macallum lectr. U. Toronto, Can., 1989, Macleod lectr. Southampton U., U.K., 1990, Bulatto lectr. U. Philippines, Manila, 1990, Mohaideen lectr. L.I. Coll., Bklyn., 1992, Bullard lectr. Uniformed Svcs. U., Bethesda, Md., 1993, Raven lectr. Am. Coll. Sports Medicine, Dallas, 1995; external examiner Nat. U. Singapore, 1995. Fellow Royal Coll. Physicians (London), Royal Australasian Coll. Physicians, Royal Geog. Soc. (London), AAAS (med. sci. nominating com. 1987-93, coun. del. sect. med. scis.), Am. Inst. for Med. and Biol. Engring. (founder fellow 1992), Internat. Soc. for Mountain Medicine (pres. 1991-94); mem. NAS (com. space biology and medicine 1986-90, subcom. on space biology 1984-85, com. advanced space tech. 1992-94, panel on small spacecraft tech. 1994), Nat. Bd. Med. Examiners (physiology test com. 1973-76), Am. Physiol. Soc. (pres. 1984-85, coun. 1981-86, chmn. sct. on history of physiology 1984-92, hist. pubs. adv. com.), Am. Soc. Clin. Investigation, Physiol. Soc. Gt. Britain, Am. Thoracic Soc., Assn. Am. Physicians, Western Assn. Physicians, Russian Acad. Sci. (elected fgn. mem.), Explorers Club, Fleischner Soc. (pres. 1985), Harveian Soc. (London), Royal Instn. Gt. Britain, Royal Soc. Medicine (London), Hurlingham Club (London), La Jolla Beach & Tennis Club. Home: 9626 Blackgold Rd La Jolla CA 92037-1110 Office: U Calif San Diego Sch Medicine 0623 Dept Medicine La Jolla CA 92093

WEST, JOHN CARL, lawyer, former ambassador, former governor; b. Camden, S.C., Aug. 27, 1922; s. Shelton J. and Mattie (Ratterree) W.; BA, The Citadel, 1942; LB magna cum laude, U.S.C., 1942; D. (hon.) The Citadel, U. S.C., Davidson Coll., Presbyn. Coll., Francis Marion Coll., Wofford Coll., Coll. Charleston; m. Lois Rhame, Aug. 29, 1948; children: John Carl Jr., Douglas Allen, Shelton West Bosley. Bar: S.C. 1947. Ptnr. West, Holland, Furman & Cooper, Camden, S.C., 1947-70; state senator Kershaw County State of S.C., 1954-66; lt. gov. State of S.C., 1966-70; gov. State of S.C., 1971-75; ptnr., West, Cooper, Bowen, Beard & Smoot, Camden, S.C., 1975-77; amb. to Saudi Arabia, 1977-81; sr. ptnr. West & West, P.A., Hilton Head Island and Camden, S.C., 1981-88; prin., pvt. practice John C. West, P.A., Hilton Head Island and Camden, 1981—; disting. prof. Middle East Studies U. S.C., 1981—; of counsel McNair Law Firm, Hilton Head Island, S.C., 1988-92, of counsel, Bethea, Jordan & Griffin, P.A., Hilton Head Island and Camden, S.C., 1993—; bd. dirs., chmn. Seibels Bruce Group, Inc., Donaldson, Lufkin & Jenrette, Inc. Trustee So. Ctr. Internat. Studies. Maj. AUS, 1942-46. Decorated Army Commendation medal; comdr. Order of Merit (W. Ger.), Freedom award S.C. C. of C. Mem. Phi Beta Kappa. Democrat. Presbyterian. Address: PO Box 13 Hilton Head Island SC 29938-0013

WEST, JOHN MERLE, retired physicist, nuclear consultant; b. Stilwell, Okla., Jan. 18, 1920; s. James M. and Maude B. (Bacon) W.; m. Navlion F. Farmer, Oct. 5, 1945; children: J. Cornel, L. Clark. BS in Phys. Sci. and Math. with highest honors, Northeastern State U., 1939; MS in Physics, U. Iowa, 1941. Physicist, supr. Du Pont Co., Carney's Point, N.J., 1941-42, Pryor, Okla., 1942-43; physicist, supr. U. Chgo. Manhattan Project, 1943-44, Hanford Works Manhattan Project, 1944-46, GE, Hanford Works, Richland, Wash., 1946-49; asst. dir. reactor engring., project mgr. Argonne Nat. Lab., Lemont, Ill., 1949-57; exec. v.p. Gen. Nuclear Engring. Corp., Dunedin, Fla., 1957-65; v.p. nuclear activities Combustion Engring. Inc., Windsor, Conn., 1965-84; sr. v.p. Nuclear Combustion Engring. Inc., Windsor, Conn., 1984-85; nuclear cons., Cape Coral, Fla., 1985—. Contbr. numerous articles to profl. jours., papers at profl. meetings; holder numerous patents. Recipient Charles Coffin award GE, 1949. Fellow Am. Nuclear Soc. (charter mem., Walter Zinn award 1983); mem. NAE, Engrs. Club. Republican. Presbyterian. Home and Office: 1608 SE 40th Ter Cape Coral FL 33904-7467

WEST, JOHN THOMAS, surgeon; b. Live Oak, Fla., June 23, 1924; s. James Whitaker and Lelah Eulalia (Moore) W.; m. Ruth Marit Blakely, June 18, 1948; children: Phyllis Ann, Rebecca Ruth, James Carl, Jeffrey Moore, Paul Blakely. BS, U. Mich., 1946; MD, Vanderbilt U., 1951. Diplomate Am. Bd. Surgery. Commd. officer USPHS, 1951, advanced through grades to capt., 1963; rotating intern USPHS Hosp., Seattle, 1951-52; chief surgery USPHS Alaska Native Hosp., Anchorage, 1957-60, resident gen. surgery, 1954-57; chief surgery USPHS Hosp., Seattle, 1963-69, USPHS Indian Hosp., Phoenix, 1969-71; sr. investigator surg. br. Nat. Cancer Inst., USPHS, Bethesda, Md., 1960-63; ret., 1971; clin. assoc. prof. Tex. Tech U., Lubbock, 1974-77; pvt. practice La Grange, Ga., 1971-74, 77-94; ret., 1994; mem. active staff West Ga. Med. Ctr., La Grange, 1971-74, 77-94. Bd. dirs. Ga. divsn. Am. Cancer Soc., 1972-77, 77-92. Recipient Meritorious Svc. medal USPHS, 1968. Fellow ACS, Soc. Surg. Oncology. Presbyterian. Achievements include report of facilitation of major hepatic resection by an innovation in the surgical exposure of the liver. Home: 134 Hickory Ln La Grange GA 30240-8622

WEST, KATHLEEN SHEA, special education educator, reading specialist; b. Boston, Aug. 24, 1946; d. Everett W. and Catherine (Lally) Shea; m. William S. West, Sept. 4, 1966; children: Carl, Adam. BS, SUNY, Albany, 1983; MS, Russell Sage Coll., 1989, postgrad., 1989-90. Cert. permanent K-6, spl. edn., reading tchr., N.Y. Substitute tchr. pub. schs., N.Y., 1980-84; tchr. spl. edn. Glens Falls (N.Y.) City Sch. Dist., 1984—; speaker spl. edn. dept. Russell Sage Coll., Troy, N.Y., 1989-92. Vol. United Cerebral Palsy, Queensbury, N.Y., 1982-84; tutor Literacy Vols. Am., Glens Falls, 1992. Roman Catholic. Avocations: writing, sketching, reading, travel.

WEST, KENNETH EDWARD, lawyer; b. Phila., June 30, 1963; s. Edward Brown and Delores Ann (Brooks) W.; m. Cheryl Y. Tolerico; 1 child, Jessie Marie. BS, Pa. State U., 1985; JD, Villanova U., 1988. Bar: Pa. 1988, U.S. Dist. Ct. (ea. dist.) Pa. 1990, U.S. Dist. Ct. N.J. 1988. Assoc. Pachtman, Douglas & Assocs., Folsom, Pa., 1988-90; ptnr. Douglas, West & Riley, Drexel Hill, Pa., 1990-93, Douglas, West & Assocs., Drexel Hill, Pa., 1993—; Mem. bancruptcy conf. U.S. Dist. Ct. (ea. dist.) Pa. Avocations: squash, raquetball. Home: 608 S Elmwood Ave Glenolden PA 19036-2321 Office: Douglas West & Assocs 830 N Landsdowne Ave Drexel Hill PA 19026-1526

WEST, LEE ROY, federal judge; b. Clayton, Okla., Nov. 26, 1929; s. Calvin and Nicie (Hill) W.; m. MaryAnn Ellis, Aug. 29, 1952; children: Kimberly Ellis, Jennifer Lee. B.A., U. Okla., 1952, J.D., 1956; LL.M. (Ford Found. fellow), Harvard U., 1963. Bar: Okla. 1956. Individual practice law Ada, Okla., 1956-61, 63-65; faculty U. Okla. Coll. Law, 1961-62; Ford Found. fellow in law teaching Harvard U., Cambridge, Mass., 1962-63; judge 22d Jud. Dist. Okla., Ada, 1965-73; mem. CAB, Washington, 1973-78; acting chmn. CAB, 1977; practice law Tulsa, 1978-79; spl. justice Okla. Supreme Ct., 1965; judge U.S. Dist Ct. (we. dist.) Okla., 1979-94; sr. judge U.S. Dist. Ct. (we. dist.), Okla., 1994—. Editor: Okla. Law Rev. Served to capt. USMC, 1952-54. Mem. U. Okla. Alumni Assn. (dir.), Phi Delta Phi (pres. 1956), Phi Eta Sigma, Order of Coif. Home: 6500 E Danforth Rd Edmond OK 73034-7601 Office: US Dist Ct 3001 US Courthouse 200 NW 4th St Oklahoma City OK 73102-3026

WEST, LINDA LEA, administrator; b. Sparta, Wis., Oct. 5, 1943; d. Larry C. and Florance M. (Haskell) Lomax; m. Thomas C. West, Aug. 29, 1964; children: Timothy C., Daniel H., Deborah R. AB magna cum laude, Occidential Coll., 1965; MLS, UCLA, 1966. Cert. profl. adminstrv. svcs.; cert. tchr. Calif. Libr. young adult L.A. Pub. Libr., 1966-67; libr. edn., psychology Humbolt State Coll. Libr., Arcata, Calif., 1967-68; reference libr. Monterey (Calif.) Bay Area Coop. Libr., 1969-70; instr. Hacienda La Puente & El Monte (Calif.) Adult Edn., 1976-78; instr., curriculum writer Indochinese RAP, Hacienda La Puente (Calif.) Sch. Dist., 1978-81, coord. refugee project, 1981-88; instr. adult edn. UCLA Extension, 1988—; resource tchr. Baldwin Park (Calif.) Adult Sch., 1988-90; archives mgr. Outreach & Tech. Assistance Network Hacienda La Puente Sch. Dist., 1990-94; asst. dir. Outreach and Tech. Asst. Network, Sacramento County Office of Edn., Sacramento, 1994—; cons. in field. Contbr. articles to profl. jours. Jr. troop leader Girl Scouts Am., West Covina, Calif., 1985-88. Mem. ALA, AAUW, Am. Assn. Adult Continuing Edn., Am. Vocat. Assn., Calif. Tchrs. English to Speakers Other Langs. (asst. adult level chmn. 1985-86, adult level chmn. 1986-87), Calif. Coun. Adult Edn., Calif. Libr. Assn., Tchrs. English to Speakers Other Languages, Phi Beta Kappa, Beta Phi Mu, Phi Alpha Theta. Democrat. Episcopalian. Avocations: tennis, tropical fish, choral singing. Home: 912 S Coral Tree Dr West Covina CA 91791-3330 Office: Sacramento County Office Edn 9738 Lincoln Village Dr Sacramento CA 95827-3302

WEST, MARJORIE EDITH, elementary education educator; b. Lawrence, Kans., Aug. 18, 1940; d. Merwin Hales and Helen Aletha (Fellows) Wilson Polzin; m. Hammond Dean Watkins, Feb. 17, 1968 (div. 1971); 1 child, Michele Dawn; m. Merlin Avery West, Apr. 2, 1975 (div. 1984). BA in Elem. Edn., U. No. Colo., 1962, MA in Reading, 1970; postgrad., La. State U., 1981-82, U. New Orleans, 1981-82. Cert. tchr., Colo. Tchr. Sch. Dist. 11, Colorado Springs, Colo., 1962-64, Nat. Def. Overseas Teaching Program, Wiesbaden, Fed. Republic Germany, 1964-65, Alaska On-Base Schs., Fairbanks, 1965-66, Great Bend (Kans.) Sch. Dist., 1966-67, Killeen (Tex.) Sch. Dist., 1967-68, Jefferson County Schs., Lakewood, Colo., 1969—. Recipient Alumni Trail Blazer award U. No. Colo., 1988; named Colo. Tchr. of Yr., 1994, finalist Nat. Tchr. of Yr., 1994; inductee into Nat. Tchrs.' Hall of Fame, 1995. Mem. NAFE, AAUW, NEA, PTA (by-laws com. 1989-90, hon. life mem.), Colo. Edn. Assn. (del. to assembly 1985-90), Jefferson County Edn. Assn. (spl. svcs. com. 1989-90), Internat. Reading Assn., Phi Delta Kappa, Pi Lambda Theta, Epsilon Sigma Alpha (edn. chair 1989-90, chair ways and means com. 1990-91, publicity chair 1991-93). Democrat. Avocations: football, travel, golf, reading. Home: 10810 W Exposition Ave Lakewood CO 80226-3818*

WEST, MARSHA, elementary school educator; b. DeQueen, Ark., Sept. 1, 1950; d. Marshall T. and Mildred L. (Davis) Gore; m. Larry T. West, May 19, 1972; 1 child, Zachary. BS in Edn., So. State Coll., Magnolia, Ark., 1971; MEd, U. Ark., 1975; postgrad., Henderson State Coll., Arkadelphia, Ark., Purdue U.; specialist's degree, U. Ga., 1991. Cert. elem. and spl. edn. tchr., Tex., elem. tchr., early childhood, mid. sch. tchr., media specialist, Ga. Spl. edn. resource tchr. Gatesville (Tex.) Ind. Sch. Dist.; tchr. early childhood spl. edn. Bryan (Tex.) Ind. Sch. Dist.; elem. tchr. Tippecanoe Sch. Corp., Lafayette, Ind.; elem. tchr. Clarke County Sch. Dist., Athens, Ga., media specialist. Mem. ALA, NEA, Am. Assn. Sch. Librs., Ga. Assn. Educators, Ga. Assn. Instrnl. Tech., Ga. Libr. Media Assn. (dist. V chair),

N.E. Ga. Reading Coun., Clarke County Assn. Educators, Kappa Delta Pi. Office: David C Barrow Elem Sch 100 Pinecrest Dr Athens GA 30605-1459

WEST, MARVIN LEON, managing editor; b. Knoxville, May 1, 1934; s. Alvin Leon and Alma Oneta (Bishop) W.; m. Sarah Jane Blackburn, July 24, 1954; children: Michael, Gary, Jayne, Donna. BA in Journalism, U. Tenn., 1955. Sports writer Knoxville News-Sentinel, Tenn., 1955-80, sports editor, 1980-83, mng. editor, 1983-85; nat. sports editor Scripps Howard News Svc., Washington, 1985-95, mng. editor, 1995—. Named Sportswriter of Yr., Tenn. Nat. Broadcasters and Sports Writers Assn., Salisbury, N.C., 1967, 1974. Mem. U.S. Basketball Writers Assn. (pres. 1983-84). Presbyterian. Avocation: fishing. Home: PO Box 327 Mount Vernon VA 22121-0327 Office: Scripps Howard News Svc 1090 Vermont Ave NW Washington DC 20005-4905

WEST, MARY ELIZABETH, psychiatric management professional; b. Spartanburg, S.C., Aug. 27, 1939; d. Thomas Benjamin and Virginia Milster (Smith) Anderson; m. William Duane West, Sept. 13, 1960; children: William Kevin, Walter Duane, Litia Allyn West Harrison, Thomas Anderson. Diploma in nursing, Ga. Bapt. Hosp., 1960; BS in Nursing Leadership, Tift Coll., 1966; MS in Counseling, U. Scranton, 1972; EdD, Nova U., 1979. RNC, Tenn.; cert. profl. counselor, Tenn., nurse adminstr. advanced. Staff nurse pub. health Fulton County Health Dept., Atlanta, 1960-61; instr. in nursing Macon (Ga.) Hosp. Sch. Nursing, 1965-66, Western Piedmont C.C., 1973-74; dir. nursing Tyler Meml. Hosp., Tunkhannock, Pa., 1967-70; assoc. dir. nursing Nesbitt Meml. Hosp., Kingston, Pa., 1971; assoc. adminstr. Home Health Svcs. Luzerne County, Wilkes-Barre, Pa., 1972; cons. nursing Hosp. Affiliates Internat., Nashville, 1974-76, v.p. nursing, 1976-78, v.p. quality assurance, 1978-80; v.p. nursing cons. svc. Advanced Mgmt. Sys., Nashville, 1981; sr. v.p. planning Hosp. Affiliates Devel. Corp., Nashville, 1982-83; v.p. ops. Winter Haven (Fla.) Hosp., 1986-90; pres. Hope Psychiat. Mgmt., Inc., Winter Haven, 1994—. Contbg. author: Political Action Handbook for Nurses, 1985 (Am. Jour. Nursing Book of Yr. 1986); co-author, editor manual Hosp. Affiliates International, 1978; contbr. articles to mags., chpt. to book. V.p. part time svcs. Winter Haven Hosp., 1987-90; insvc. tng. dir. Rotary Internat., Winter Haven, 1989-91; v.p. Winter Haven C. of C., 1988-90; pres. Polk County Nurse Exec. Orgn., Lakeland, Fla., 1989-90; bd. dirs. Women's Resource Ctr., Inc., Winter Haven, 1989-91; bd. dirs., founder Mothers Alone, Haines City, Fla., 1991—; nat. chair Sunhealth Nursing Coun., Charlotte, N.C., 1990; founder, bd. chmn. Hope Christian Counseling Inc., 1994; state bd. dirs., dir. profl. edn. Bapt. Nursing Fellowship, 1995—. Mem. ANA, Fla. Nursing Assn., Am. Orgn. Nurse Execs., Inner Wheel (v.p., treas., bd. dirs. 1992—), Theta Chi Omega. Republican. Baptist. Avocations: piano, reading, travel, walking, hiking. Home: 3208 Lake Breeze Dr Haines City FL 33844-9333 Office: HOPE Psychiat Mgmt Ste 5013 5665 Cypress Gardens Blvd Winter Haven FL 33884-2273

WEST, MICHAEL ALAN, hospital administrator; b. Waseca, Minn., Aug. 4, 1938; s. Ralph Lel and Elizabeth Mary (Brann) W.; m. Mary Thissen, Jan. 21, 1961; children—Anne, Nancy, Douglas. B.A., U. Minn., 1961, M.H.A., 1963. Sales corr. Physicians and Hosps. Supply Co., Mpls., 1959-60; adminstrv. resident R.I. Hosp., Providence, 1962-63; adminstrv. asst. R.I. Hosp., 1963-65, asst. dir., 1965-68; exec. asst. dir. Med. Center U. Mo., Columbia, 1968-70; assoc. dir. Med. Center U. Mo., 1970-74, asst. prof. community health and med. practice, 1968-74; v.p. for adminstrn. Luth. Gen. Hosp., Park Ridge, Ill., 1974-80; exec. v.p. Luth. Gen. Hosp., 1980-84; pres., CEO Akron Gen. Med. Ctr., Ohio, 1984—; bd. dirs. Vol. Hosps. Am. Inc.; chair VHA-Ctrl., Inc. Bd. dirs. Great Trais Coun. Boy Scouts Am. Mem. Am. Coll. Healthcare Execs., Akron Regional Hosp. Assn. (chmn.), Portage Country Club, Akron City Club, Catawba Island Club. Home: 495 Woodbury Dr Akron OH 44333-2780 Office: Akron Gen Med Ctr 400 Wabash Ave Akron OH 44307-2433

WEST, MORRIS LANGLO, novelist; b. Melbourne, Australia, Apr. 26, 1916; s. Charles Langlo and Florence Guilfoyle (Hanlon) W.; m. Joyce Lawford, Aug. 14, 1952. BA, U. Melbourne, Australia, 1937; DLitt. (hon.), Santa Clara U., 1968, Mercy Coll., Dobbs Ferry, N.Y., 1982, U. Western Sydney, 1993; DLitt (hon.), Australian Nat. U., Canberra, 1995. Tchr. modern langs. and math New South Wales, Australia and Tasmania, 1933-39; sec. to William Morris Hughes, Prime Minister Australia, 1943; mng. dir. Australian Radio Prodns., 1943-53; publicity mgr. Mudroch Newspaper Chain, Melbourne, Australia, 1945-46; film, drama writer Shell Co. and Australian Broadcasting Network, from 1954. Author: Moon in My Pocket, 1945, Gallows on the Sand, 1955, Kundu, 1956, Children of the Shadows (English title: Children of the Sun), 1957, The Crooked Road (English title: The Big Story), 1957, McCreary Moves In, 1958, Backlash (English title: The Second Victory), 1958, The Devil's Advocate, 1959 (Nat. Brotherhood award Nat. Coun. Christians and Jews, 1960, James Tait Black Meml. award 1960, William Heinemann award Royal Soc. 1959), The Naked Country, 1960, Daughter of Silence, 1961, The Shoes of the Fisherman, 1963 (Bestsellers Paperback of Yr. award 1965), The Ambassador, 1965, Tower of Babel, 1967, (with R. Francis) Scandal in the Assembly, 1970, The Heretic, A Play in Three Acts, 1970, Summer of the Red Wolf, 1971, The Salamander, 1973, Harlequin, 1974, the Navigator, 1976, Proteus, 1979, The Clowns of God, 1981 (Universe Lit. prize 1981), The World is Made of Glass, 1983, Cassidy, 1986, Masterclass, 1988, Lazarus, 1990, The Ringmaster, 1991, The Lovers, 1993, Vanishing Point, 1996, A View From the Ridge, 1996. Served to lt. Australian Imperial Forces, 1939-43, PTO. Recipient Internat. Dag Hammarskjold prize Diplomatic Acad. of Peace (grand collar of merit), 1978. Fellow Royal Soc. Lit., World Acad. Arts and Sci., Order of Australia. Clubs: Royal Prince Alfred Yacht (Sydney, Australia), Australian (Sydney). Office: PO Box 102, Avalon NSW 2107, Australia

WEST, PAUL NODEN, author; b. Eckington, Derbyshire, Eng., Feb. 23, 1930; came to U.S., 1961, naturalized, 1971; s. Alfred Massick and Mildred (Noden) W. Student, Oxford U., 1950-53; MA, Columbia U., 1953. Asst. prof. English Meml. U. Nfld., Can., 1957-58; assoc. prof. Meml. U. Nfld., 1958-60; faculty Pa. State U., 1962-95, prof. English and comparative lit., 1968-95; prof. emeritus, 1995—; Crawshaw prof. Colgate U., 1972; Melvin Hill disting. vis. prof. Hobart and William Smith Colls., 1973; vis. English prof. Cornell U., 1986; disting. writer in residence Wichita State U., 1982; vis. prof. English Brown U., 1992; fiction judge Creative Artists Pub. Svc. Program, N.Y.C., 1974, 81; writer-in-residence U. Ariz., 1984; judge Katherine Ann Porter Prize for Fiction, 1984, Artists Found. Author: Byron and the Spoiler's Art, 1960, rev. edit., 1990, I Said the Sparrow, 1963, The Snow Leopard, 1965, Tenement of Clay, 1965, The Wine of Absurdity, 1966, Alley Jaggers, 1967, I'm Expecting to Live Quite Soon, 1970, Words for a Deaf Daughter, 1970, Caliban's Filibuster, 1972, Colonel Mint, 1973, Gala, 1976, The Very Rich Hours of Count von Stauffenberg, 1980, Out of My Depths: A Swimmer in the Universe, 1983, Rat Man of Paris, 1986, Sheer Fiction, 1987, The Universe and Other Fiction, 1988, The Place in Flowers Where Pollen Rests, 1988, Lord Byron's Doctor, 1989, Portable People, The Women of Whitechapel and Jack the Ripper, 1991, Sheer Fiction: II, 1991, James Ensor, 1991, Love's Mansion, 1992, Tenement of Clay, 2d edit., 1993, Sheer Fiction, III, 1994, A Stroke of Genius, 1995, The Tent of Orange Mist, 1995 (memoir) My Mother's Music, 1996 (novel) Sporting with Amaryllis, 1996, Terrestrials, 1997; contbr. Washington Post and N.Y. Times, 1962—, Harper's Mag., GQ Mag., Paris Rev., Yale Rev., Parnassus, Bookpress; fiction judge N.Y. Found. for the Arts, Nat. Book award, 1990. Served with RAF, 1954-57. Recipient Aga Khan Fiction prize, 1973, Hazlett Meml. award for Excellence in Arts (lit.), 1981, Lit. award Am. Acad. and Inst. Arts and Letters, 1985, Pushcart prize 1987, 91, The Best Am. Essays award, 1990, Outstanding Achievement medal Pa. State U., 1991, Grand Prix Halpérine Kaminsky award 1992, Lannan Fiction award 1993, Tchg. award Northeastern Assn. Grad. Schs. 1994; named Lit. Lion N.Y. Pub. Libr. 1987; Guggenheim fellow, 1963; Nat. Endowment for Arts Creative Writing fellow, 1979, 84; nominated for Médicis, Femina and Meilleur Livre Etranger prizes, France, 1991, Lannan Lit. Videos # 35, Nat. Book Critics award for Fiction, 1996; named to Honor Roll The Yr. in Fiction, DLB Yearbook, 1996; decorated Chevalier de l'Ordre des Arts et des Lettres, France, 1996. Mem. Authors Guild. Office: Elaine Markson Agy 44 Greenwich Ave New York NY 10011-8347 *The unexamined life may not be worth having, but the examined life is endurable only to an open mind, through which life holistically flows, keeping that mind as incomplete as our knowledge of the universe itself.*

WEST, PHILIP WILLIAM, chemistry educator; b. Crookston, Minn., Apr. 12, 1913; s. William Leonard and Anne (Thompson) W.; m. Tenney Constance Johnson, July 5, 1935 (dec. Feb. 1964); children: Dorothy West/Farwell, Linda West Gueho (dec.), Patty West Elstrott; m. Foymae S. Kelso, July 1, 1964. B.S., U. N.D., 1935, M.S., 1936, D.Sc. (hon.), 1958; Ph.D., State U. Iowa, 1939; postgrad., Rio de Janeiro, 1946. Chemist N.D. Geol. Survey, 1935-36; research asst. san. chemistry U. Iowa, 1936-37; asst. chemist Iowa Dept. Health, 1937-40; research microchemist Econ. Lab., Inc., St. Paul, 1940; faculty La. State U., 1940-80, prof. chemistry, 1951-80, Boyd prof., 1953-80, emeritus, 1980—, chmn. ann. symposium modern methods of analytical chemistry, 1948-65, dir. Inst. for Environmental Scis., 1967-80; co-founder, chmn. bd. West-Paine Labs. Inc., Baton Rouge, 1980-93; O. M. Smith lectr. Okla. State U., 1955; vis. prof. U. Colo., 1963, Rand Afrikaans U., 1980; adj. prof. EPA, 1969-80; founder Kem-Tech. Labs., Inc., Baton Rouge, 1954, chmn. bd., 1965-74; co-founder West-Paine Labs., Inc., Baton Rouge, 1978, pres., 1978-93, chmn. bd., lab dir., 1990; mem. 1st working party sci. com. on problems of environment, 1971-74; pres. analytical sect. Internat. Union Pure and Applied Chemistry, 1965-69, mem. sect. indsl. hygiene and toxicology, 1971-73, mem. air quality sect., 1973-75; mem. tech. adv. com. La. Air Pollution Control Com., 1979—; mem. Gov.'s Task Force Environ. Health, 1983-85; mem. sci. adv. bd. EPA, 1983-84; cons. WHO; tech. expert Nat. Bur. Standards Nat. Vol. Lab. Accreditation Program, 1988—; chmn. bd., CEO West & Assoc., Inc., 1992—; mem. adv. com. Coll. Basic Sci. La. State U. Author: Chemical Calculations, 1948, (with Vick) Qualitative Analysis and Analytical Chemical Separations, 2d edit., 1959, (with Bustin) Experience Approach to Experimental Chemistry, 1975; editor: (with Hamilton) Science of the Total Environment, 1973-78, (with Macdonald) Analytica Chimica Acta, 1959-78, Reagents and Reaction for Qualitative Inorganic Analysis; co-editor: Analytical Chemistry, 1963; asst. editor: Mikrochemica Acta, 1952-78, Microchem. Jour, 1957-75; adv. bd.: Analytical Chemistry, 1959-60; publ. bd.: Jour. Chem. Edn, 1954-57; contbr. articles to profl. jours. Recipient Honor Scroll award La. sect. Am. Inst. Chemistry, 1972. Fellow AAAS; mem. Am. Chem. Soc. (Southwest award 1954, Charles E. Coates award 1967, Analytical Chemistry award 1974, award for Creative Advances in Environ. Sci. and Tech.), La. Acad. Sci., Air Pollution Control Assn., Am. Indsl. Hygiene Assn., Austrian Microchem. Soc. (hon.), Soc. of Analysts Eng. (hon.), Internat. Union Pure and Applied Chemistry (pres. commn. I, pres. analytical div.), Japan Soc. for Analytical Chemistry (hon.), La. Cancer and Health Found., Sigma Xi, Phi Lambda Upsilon, Phi Kappa Phi, Alpha Epsilon Delta, Alpha Chi Sigma, Tau Kappa Epsilon. Office: West-Paine Labs Inc 7979 G S R I Rd Baton Rouge LA 70820-7402

WEST, RALPH LELAND, veterinarian; b. Grand Rapids, Minn., Apr. 23, 1915; s. Ralph Leland and Elsie (Wardall) W.; m. Mary Elizabeth Brann, June 14, 1937; children: Michael Alan, Janet Lee West Friedrich, Thomas James. DVM, Iowa State U., 1936; MS, Purdue U., 1972. Pvt. practice Waseca, Minn., 1936-42, 46-70; grad. asst. Sch. Vet. Medicine Purdue U., West Lafayette, Ind., 1970-72; asst. dir. sci. activities Am. Vet. Med. Assn., Schaumburg, Ill., 1972-77, dir. sci. activities, 1977-87. Contbr. articles to jours. in field. Mem. Pk. Bd., Waseca, 1948-50, Youth Commn., 1948-52; mem., chmn. Waseca Hosp. Bd., 1954-64; trustee Sunny Acres Village Inc., Denver, 1988-95. Maj. U.S. Army, 1942-46, ETO. Recipient Stange award Iowa State U., 1983. Mem. AMVA (award 1990), Am. Assn. Ret. Vets. (dir. 1987-90), Am. Vet. History Soc., Colo. Vet. Med. Assn., Minn. Vet. Med. Assn., Iowa State U. Vet. Alumni Assn., Phi Zeta. Republican. Avocations: reading, bridge, stock market. Home: 1719 E Bijou St Apt 611 Colorado Springs CO 80909-5732

WEST, REXFORD LEON, banker; b. Syracuse, N.Y., Feb. 18, 1938; s. Rexford A. and Nina (Crysler) W.; m. Pamela Hanlon, June 1, 1995; children from previous marriage: Lisa, Julie, Gregory, Kristen. AAS, Auburn C.C., N.Y., 1957; BS magna cum laude, Syracuse U., N.Y., 1972; Advanced Mgmt. Program, Harvard Bus. Sch., Boston, 1984. Accountant Marine Midland Bank, Syracuse, N.Y., 1959-67, v.p., asst. treas., 1967-72; v.p., contr. Marine Midland Services Corp., Buffalo, N.Y., 1972-76; v.p. ops. divsn. Marine Midland Bank, N.A., Buffalo, N.Y., 1976-77, sr. v.p., sr. ops. officer, 1977-79, exec. v.p., sr. ops. officer 1979-85, divsn. exec. ops., 1985-87, sector exec. ops. and fin. mgmt., 1987-90, sr. exec. v.p. corp. engring., 1990-92; exec. v.p. adminstrv. svc. Fleet Bank, Melville, N.Y., 1992-94; exec. v.p. loan servicing Fleet Mortgage Group, Columbia, S.C., 1994-96; ret., 1996. Served with U.S. Army, 1957-61.

WEST, RICHARD LUTHER, military association executive, defense consultant, retired army officer; b. Ithaca, N.Y., Jan. 8, 1925; s. Luther W. and Beatrice E. (Ryan) W.; m. June D. Kirby, June 5, 1945; children—John R., Lesley A., Peter L. Student, No. Mich. Coll., 1941-42; B.S., U.S. Mil. Acad., 1945; M.S., Princeton U., 1954; M.S. in Bus. Adminstrn, George Washington U., 1965. Commd. 2d lt. U.S. Army, 1945, advanced through grades to lt. gen., 1977; comptr. of the Army Washington, 1977-81, ret., 1981, cons. def., 1982—; dir. Inst. Land Warfare Assn. U.S. Army, 1988-97, v.p. Spl. Projects Assn., 1997—. Decorated D.S.M., Legion of Merit with 3 oak leaf clusters, Bronze Star, Air medal with 2 oak leaf clusters, Army Commendation medal with oak leaf cluster. Mem. Assn. U.S. Army (v.p. 1992—), Am. Mil. Engrs., Am. Soc. Mil. Comptrs., Am. Def. Preparedness Assn., Sigma Xi. Home: 1509 Laurel Hill Rd Vienna VA 22182-1713

WEST, RICHARD VINCENT, art museum official; b. Prague, Czechoslovakia, Nov. 26, 1934; came to U.S., 1938, naturalized, 1947; s. Jan Josef and Katherine Frieda (Mayer) Vyslouzil; 1 child, Jessica Katherine. Student, UCLA, 1952-55, Music Acad. of the West, 1958-60; BA with highest honors, U. Calif., Santa Barbara, 1961; postgrad., Akademie der Bildenden Kuenste, Vienna, 1961-62, Hochschule fur Musik und darstellende Kuenste, Vienna, 1961-62; MA, U. Calif., Berkeley, 1965. Curatorial intern Cleve. Art Mus., 1965-66, Albright-Knox Art Gallery, Buffalo, 1966-67; curator Mus. Art Bowdoin Coll., Brunswick, Maine, 1967-69, dir., 1969-72; dir. Crocker Art Mus., Sacramento, Calif., 1973-82, Santa Barbara Mus. Art, Calif., 1983-91; pres. Artmuse Assocs., Benicia, Calif., 1991-92; dir. Newport (R.I.) Art Mus., 1992-94, Frye Art Mus., Seattle, 1995—; mem. Joint Yugoslav-Am. Excavations at Sirmium, 1971; bd. dirs. Sacramento Regional Art Coun., 1973-77; bd. overseers Strawbery Banke, 1993—. Author: Painters of the Section d'Or, 1967, Language of the Print, 1968; The Walker Art Building Murals, 1972, Munich and American Realism in the 19th Cen., 1978, An Enkindled Eye: The Paintings of Rockwell Kent, 1985, Standing in the Tempest: Painters of the Hungarian Avant-Garde, 1991, America in Art, 1991, A Significant Story: American Painting and Decorative Arts from the Karolik Collection, 1993; editor: Contemporary American Marine Art, 1997; exhbn. catalogues, also various revs. and articles. Active Newport Reading Room; founding mem. New England Community Mus. Consortium; active USCG Aux., 1989—. Served with USN, 1956-57. Ford Found. fellow, 1965-67; Smithsonian fellow, 1971. Mem. Am. Assn. Mus., Coll. Art Assn., Internat. Coun. Mus., Western Assn. Art Mus. (pres. 1975-78), Calif. Assn. Mus. (bd. dirs. 1980-82, v.p. 1986-91), Newport Reading Rm., Rotary, Rainier Club. Office: Frye Art Mus 704 Terry Ave Seattle WA 98104-2019

WEST, ROBERT COOPER, geography educator; b. Enid, Okla., June 30, 1913; s. George Washington and Elva A. (Cooper) W.; m. Phyllis Devereaux, May 11, 1968. A.B., U. Calif. at Los Angeles, 1935, M.A., 1938; Ph.D., U. Calif. at Berkeley, 1946. Cartographer OSS, Washington, 1941-45; geographer Smithsonian Instn. (Mexico City office), 1946-48; asst. prof. to prof. La. State U. at Baton Rouge, 1948—, Boyd prof., 1970-80, prof. emeritus, 1980—; vis. prof. U. Wis. at Madison, 1966, U. Calif. at Los Angeles, 1968, U. Ariz. at Tucson, 1972, 76. Co-author: Middle America: Its Lands and Peoples, 3d edit., 1989, others; co-editor: Handbook of Middle American Indians, vol. 1, Nat. Environment and Early Cultures, 1964, Sonora: It's Geographical Personality, 1993, In Quest of Mineral Wealth, 1994. Recipient Alumni Faculty award La. State U., 1965; Guggenheim fellow, 1955. Mem. A.A.A.S., Assn. Am. Geographers (citation for meritorious contbn. 1964, Outstanding Achievement award 1973), Latin Am. Studies Assn., Conf. Latin Amercanist Geographers, Sigma Xi. Home: 4815 Tulane Dr Baton Rouge LA 70808-4762 Office: Dept Geography and Anthropology La State U Baton Rouge LA 70803

WEST, ROBERT CULBERTSON, chemistry educator; b. Glen Ridge, N.J., Mar. 18, 1928; s. Robert C. and Constance (MacKinnon) W.; children: David Russell, Arthur Scott, Derek. B.A., Cornell U., 1950; A.M., Harvard U., 1952, Ph.D., 1954; ScD (hon.), G. Asachi Tech. U., Iasi, Romania, 1995. Asst. prof. Lehigh U., 1954-56; mem. faculty U. Wis.-Madison, 1956—, prof. chemistry, 1963—, Eugene G. Rochow prof., 1980; indsl. and govt. cons., 1961—; Fulbright lectr. Kyoto and Osaka U., 1964-65; vis. prof. U. Würzburg, 1968-69, Haile Selassie I U., 1972, U. Calif.-Santa Cruz, 1977, U. Utah, 1981, Inst. Chem. Physics Chinese Acad. Sci., 1984, Justus Liebigs U., Giessen, Fed. Republic Germany, U. Estadual de Campinas, Brazil, 1989; Abbott lectr. U. N.D., 1964, Seydel-Wooley lectr. Ga. Inst. Tech., 1970, Sun Oil lectr. Ohio U., 1971, Edgar C. Britton lectr. Dow, Midland, Mich., 1971, Jean Day Meml. lectr. Rutgers U., 1973; Japan Soc. for Promotion Sci. vis. prof. Tohoku U., 1976, Gunma U., 1987; Lady Davis vis. prof. Hebrew U., 1979; Cecil and Ida Green honors prof. Tex. Christian U., 1983; Karcher lectr. U. Okla., 1986; Broberg lectr. N.D. State U., 1986; Xerox lectr. U. B.C., 1986, McGregory lectr. Colgate U., 1988; George Watt lectr. U. Tex., 1992; David Ginsburg meml. lectr. Technion, 1993; rsch. scholar lectr. Drew U., 1995; Reed lectr. Rensselaer Poly. Inst., 1997; Lady Davis vis. prof. Technion-Israel Inst. Tech., 1990; Humboldt prof. Tech. U. Munich, 1990; vis. prof. U. Estadual de Campinas, Brazil, 1993; Dozor vis. fellow Ben Gurion U. of Negev, Israel, 1993. Co-editor: Advances in Organometallic Chemistry, Vols. I-XXXVI, 1964—, Organometallic Chemistry--A Monograph Series, 1968—; contbr. articles to profl. jours. Pres. Madison Community Sch., 1970-81; founder, bd. dirs. Women's Med. Fund, 1971—; nat. bd. dirs. Zero Population Growth, 1980-86; bd. dirs., v.p. Protect Abortion Rights Inc., 1980; lay minister Prairie Unitarian Universalist Soc., 1982. Recipient F.S. Kipling award, 1970, Outstanding Sci. Innovator award Sci. Digest, 1985, Chem. Pioneering award Am. Inst. Chemists, 1988, Wacker Silicon prize, 1989, Humboldt U.S. Scientist award, 1990. Mem. Am. Chem. Soc., Chem. Soc. (London), Japan Chem. Soc., AAAS, Wis. Acad. Sci. Home: 305 Nautilus Dr Madison WI 53705-4333

WEST, ROBERT MACLELLAN, science education consultant; b. Appleton, Wis., Sept. 1, 1942; s. Clarence John and Elizabeth Ophelia (Moore) W.; m. Jean Sydow, June 19, 1965; 1 child, Christopher. BA, Lawrence Coll., 1963; SM, U. Chgo., 1964, PhD, 1968. Rsch. assoc. Princeton (N.J.) U., 1968-69; asst. prof. Adelphi U., Garden City, N.Y., 1969-74; curator of geology Milw. Pub. Mus., 1974-83; dir. Carnegie Mus. Natural History, Pitts., 1983-87, Cranbrook Inst. Sci., Bloomfield Hills, Mich., 1987-91; prin. RMW Sci. Action, Washington, 1992-95; pres. Informal Sci., Inc., Washington, 1993—; adj. prof. U. Wis., Milw., 1974-83; com. mem. Indo-U.S. Subcom., 1990-96. Contbr. articles to profl. jours. Bd. dirs. Friends of the New Zoo, Pitts., 1984-87; treas. East Mich. Environ. Action Coun., Birmingham, Mich., 1987-92. Recipient Arnold Guyot prize Nat. Geographic Soc., 1982; named Man of Yr. in Sci. by Vectors Pitts., 1988; NSF fellow, 1965-68, NSF rsch. grantee, 1970-82, Nat. Geographic Soc. rsch. grantee, 1973, 76, 77, 79, 80, 82. Mem. Nat. Ctr. Sci. Edn. (bd. dirs. 1984-88, 92—), Nepal Natural History Soc. (advisor 1992—), Soc. Vertebrate Paleontology, Geol. Soc. Am., Paleontology Soc., Am. Soc. Mammalogists, Am. Assn. Mus., Nepal Geol. Soc., Rotary. Avocations: nature, history, sports. Office: Informal Sci Inc PO Box 42328 Washington DC 20015-0928

WEST, ROBERT SUMNER, surgeon; b. Bowman, N.D., Nov. 20, 1935; s. Elmer and Minnie (DeBode) W.; m. Martha W. Hopkins, Mar. 23, 1957; children: Stephen, Christopher, Anna Marie, Catherine, Sarah. BA, U. N.D., 1957, BS in Medicine, 1959; MD, Harvard U., 1961. Diplomate Am. Bd. Surgery. Intern U.S. Naval Hosp., Chelsea, Mass., 1961-62; resident in surgery U. Vt. Med. Ctr. Hosp., 1965-69; pvt. practice Coeur d'Alene, Idaho, 1969—; coroner Kootenai County, Coeur d'Alene, 1984—. Trustee, pres. Coeur d'Alene Sch. Dist. 271 Bd. Edn., 1973-77. Lt. M.C., USN, 1960-65. Fellow ACS (pres. Idaho chpt. 1985, gov. at large); mem. Idaho Med. Assn. (pres. 1989-90, trustee), Kiwanis. Republican. Methodist. Avocation: sailing. Office: 920 W Ironwood Dr Coeur D Alene ID 83814-2643

WEST, ROBERTA BERTHA, writer; b. Saline County, Mo., Sept. 7, 1904; d. Robert and Amanda Melvina (Driver) Baur; m. Harold Clinton West, Aug. 27, 1932; children: Arle Faith W. Lohof, Lydia Ann (Lyda) F H. Hyde, Danna Rose F H. Burns. AB, William Jewell Coll., 1928; AM, U. Mo., 1930. Cert. tchr., Mo., Mont. Elem. and secondary sch. tchr. Mo. and Mont. Schs., 1922-47; supt. schs. Hogeland (Mont.) Schs., 1947-48, 55; prof. fgn. langs. Will Mayfield Coll., Marble Hill, Mo., 1930; columnist Quad County Star, Viburnum, Mo., 1982—; writer and researcher ch. history, 1964-91; cons. hist. com. Yellowstone Conf. Meth. Ch., 1971-84; compiler Mont. list of Meth. Mins. 1784-1984. Author: Northern Montana Methodist History, 3 vols., 1974, Faith, Hope and Love in the West, 1971; editor: Brother Van by Those Who Knew Him, 1975, reprinted, 1989,; also contbr. articles. Recipient 1st John M. Templeton prize, 1959. Mem. Alpha Zeta Pi. Democrat. Avocation: crocheting. Home: PO Box 583 Viburnum MO 65566-0583 Office: Quad County Star Viburnum MO 65566

WEST, STEPHEN ALLAN, lawyer; b. Salt Lake City, Mar. 23, 1935; s. Allan Morrell and Ferne (Page) W.; m. Martha Sears, Mar. 21, 1960; children: Stephen Allan, Jr., Page, Adam. JD, U. Utah, 1961, BS in Philosophy, 1962. Law clk. to judge U.S. Dist. Ct., Utah, 1961-62; assoc. Marr, Wilkins & Cannon, Salt Lake City, 1962-65; ptnr. Marr, Wilkins & Cannon, 1965-67; atty. Jennings, Strouss, Salmon & Trask, Washington, 1967-68; atty. Marriott Corp., Washington, 1968-71, asst. gen. counsel, 1971-74, v.p. and assoc. gen. counsel, 1974-87, v.p. and dep. gen. counsel, 1987-93; sr. v.p., gen. counsel Marriott Internat., Inc., Washington, 1993-94; pres. Tex. San Antonio mission Ch. of Jesus Christ of Latter-day Saints, 1995—. Bishop LDS Ch., 1977-81; mem. exec. bd. Interfaith Conf. Met. Washington, 1989-93, vice chmn., 1992-93; mem. exec. bd. Christa McAuliffe Inst. Task Force of Nat. Found. for Improvement Edn. Mem. ABA (exec. coun. young lawyers sect. 1964-65), Utah Bar Assn. (exec. com. young lawyers sect. 1962-67), D.C. Bar Assn., Utah Profl. Rels. Com., U. Utah Alumni Assn. (Disting. Alumni award 1971), Skull and Bones, Owl and Key, Phi Delta Phi, Sigma Chi. Office: Ch Jesus Christ Latter-day Saints Tex San Antonio Mission 404 E Ramsey Rd Ste 105 San Antonio TX 78216-4665 Home: 15818 Mission Rdg San Antonio TX 78232-2792

WEST, THOMAS LOWELL, JR., insurance company executive; b. Cedar Bluff, Va., June 7, 1937; s. Thomas Lowell and Kathleen (Bowling) W.; m. Katharine Thompson, Feb. 13, 1960; children: Thomas Lowell III, John Gardner, Katharine Covington. BS in Indsl. Engring., U. Tenn., 1959. CLU, 1967; chartered fin. cons., 1987. Asst. supr. Aetna Life Ins. Co., Memphis, 1960-62, supr., 1962-67, asst. gen. agt., 1967-69; gen. agt. Aetna Life Ins. Co., Jackson, Miss., 1969-80; regional v.p. Aetna Life & Casualty, Hartford, Conn., 1980-85; v.p. Aetna Life Ins. and Annuity Co., Hartford, 1985-88, sr. v.p. exec. com. and investment com., 1988-94, also bd. dirs.; v.p. Aetna Fin. Services, Hartford, 1986-87; pres., bd. dirs. Structured Benefits, Inc., Hartford, 1985-94, Systemized Benefits Adminstrn., Inc., SBFI, 1988; pres., dir. exec. com., mgmt. com., investment com. The Variable Annuity Life Ins. Co., 1994—; exec. v.p., dir. Am. Gen. Series Portfolio Co.; mem. bd. dirs. Houston Symphony. Named to Hall of Fame, Jackson Assn. Life Underwriters, 1977. Mem. Am. Soc. CLU's and CHFC, Am. Soc. Pension Actuaries (assoc.), Assn. for Advanced Life Underwriters (assoc.), Nat. Assn. Life Underwriters, Internat. Assn. Fin. Planners, Nat. Assn. Variable Annuities (bd. dirs.). Republican. Presbyterian. Avocations: tennis, running, E-type Jaguars, Mercedes Benz. Home: 2120 Brentwood Dr Houston TX 77019-3512 Office: The Variable Annuity Life Ins Co 2929 Allen Pky Houston TX 77019-2197

WEST, THOMAS MEADE, financial services strategic consultant; b. Owensboro, Ky., Aug. 15, 1940; s. Frank Thomas and Vivian (Brown) W.; children: Thomas Meade, Alexandra, Theodora. B.A. cum laude, Vanderbilt U., 1962; M.A. magna cum laude, U. Mich., 1964. Various mgmt. positions Lincoln Nat. Life Ins. Co., Fort Wayne, Ind., 1964-75, v.p., 1975-78, sr. v.p., 1978-81, exec. v.p., 1981-94; pres., CEO Lincoln Nat Reins. Cos.; prin. West Cons. Corp.; bd. dirs. Union Fed. Savs. Bank of Indpls., Union Acceptance Corp. Area pres. Boy Scouts Am., Ind.; dir. Jr. Achievement, Ft. Wayne. With U.S. Army, 1964-66. Fellow Soc. of Actuaries; mem. Am. Acad. Actuaries, Fort Wayne C. of C. (bd. dirs.). Presbyterian. Home: 2201 Turnberry Ln Fort Wayne IN 46804-9354

WEST, TOGO DENNIS, JR., secretary of Army, former aerospace executive; b. Winston-Salem, N.C., June 21, 1942; s. Togo Dennis and Evelyn (Carter) W.; m. Gail Estelle Berry, June 18, 1966; children: Tiffany Berry, Hilary Carter. BSEE, Howard U., 1965, JD cum laude, 1968. Bar: D.C.

1968, N.Y. 1969, U.S. Ct. Mil. Appeals 1969, U.S. Supreme Ct. 1978, U.S. Ct. Claims 1981. Elec. engr. Duquesne Light and Power Co., 1965; patent researcher Sughrue, Rothwell, Mion, Zinn and McPeak, 1966-67; legal intern U.S. EEOC, 1967; law clk. firm Covington & Burling, Washington, 1967-68; summer assoc. Covington & Burling, 1968, assoc., 1973-75, 76-77; law clk. to judge U.S. Dist. Ct. for So. Dist. N.Y., 1968-69; assoc. dep. atty. gen. U.S. Dept. Justice, Washington, 1975-76; gen. counsel Dept. Navy, Washington, 1977-79; spl. asst. to sec. and dep. sec. Dept. Def., Washington, 1979-80, gen. counsel, 1980-81; ptnr. Patterson, Belknap, Webb & Tyler, Washington, 1981-90; sr. v.p. govt. rels. Northrop Corp., Washington, 1990-93; sec. of Army, Washington, 1993—; adj. prof. Duke U. Sch. Law, 1980-81; bd. cons. Riggs Nat. Bank, Washington, 1990-93. Mng. editor: Howard Law Jour, 1968. Commr. D.C. Law Rev. Comm., 1982-89, chmn., 1985-89; mem. Nat. Council of Friends of John F. Kennedy Ctr. for Performing Arts, 1984-91, treas., 1987-91; bd. govs. Antioch U. Sch. Law, 1983-87, vice chmn., 1986-87; chmn. Greater Washington Bd. Trade, legis. bur., 1987-89, bd. dirs., 1987-93, mem. exec. com. 1987-92; mem. fed. legis. com., 1990-93; chmn. Kennedy Ctr. Community and Friends Bd., 1991—; mem. Washington Lawyers' Com. Civil Rights Under Law, 1987-93, D.C. Com. on Pub. Edn., 1988-93, chmn., 1990-91; trustee The Aerospace Corp., 1983-90, Ctr. for Strategic and Internat. Studies, 1987-90, Nat. Lawyers Com. for Civil Rights Under Law, 1987-93, Inst. for Def. Analyses, 1989-91, Protestant Episcopal Cathedral Found., 1989—, Shakespeare Theatre at The Folger, 1990-93, N.C. Sch. Arts, 1990—, Aerospace Edn. Found. of Air Force Assn., 1991-93; bd. dirs. D.C. Law Students in Ct. Program, 1986-92, World Affairs Coun., 1991-93, Atlantic Coun., 1991-93; mem. fin. com. Episcopal Diocese of Washington, 1989—, mem. standing com., 1990-92; sr. warden St. John's Ch., Lafayette Sq.; chmn. trustee coun. YMCA Metro. Wash., 1990-92; mem. nat. adv. com. UN Assn. USA, 1991-93; D.C. Ct. Appeals Admissions Com., 1990-93.. Served to capt. Judge Adv. Gen. Corps U.S. Army, 1969-73. Decorated Legion of Merit; recipient Disting. Pub. Svc. medal Dept. Def., 1981, Eagle Scout award with Bronze Palm Boy Scouts Am., 1957, Disting. Eagle Scout award 1995, Svc. to Howard U. award, 1965. Mem. ABA, Nat. Bar Assn., Washington Coun. Lawyers (dir. 1973-75), Sigma Pi Phi, Phi Alpha Delta, Omega Psi Psi, Alpha Phi Omega, Met. Club, Univ. Club (Washington), F St. Club. Democrat. Episcopalian. Clubs: Metropolitan, University (Washington). Democrat. Episcopalian. Office: Office of Sec Army 101 Army Pentagon Washington DC 20310-0101

WEST, W. RICHARD, museum director; b. San Bernardino, Calif., Jan. 6, 1943; s. W. Richard Sr. and Maribelle (McCrea) W.; m. Mary Beth Braden, June 29, 1968; children: Amy Elizabeth, Benjamin Braden. BA magna cum laude in Am. History, U. Redlands, 1965; AM in Am. History, Harvard U., 1968; JD, Stanford U., 1971; LHD (hon.), Bacone Coll., 1992, Ottawa U., 1994, U. Okla., 1995. Bar: Calif., D.C., U.S. Ct. Appeals (8th cir.), U.S. Supreme Ct. Clk. to Hon. Benjamin C. Duniway U.S. Ct. Appeals (9th cir.), 1971-72; assoc. Fried, Frank, Harris, Shriver & Jacobson, Washington, 1973-79, ptnr., 1979-88; dir. direct support component Am. Indian Lawyer Tng. Program, Inc., 1976-77; ptnr. Gover, Stetson Williams & West P.C., Albuquerque, 1988-90; founding dir. Smithsonian Instn's Nat. Mus. Am. Indian, Washington, 1990—; treas. Am. Indian Lawyer Tng. Program, Inc., 1973—; adj. prof. Indian law Stanford U., 1977. Mem. edit. bd. Am. Indian Historian, 1969-71; note editor Stanford Law Review, 1970-71; contbr. articles to profl. jours. Coord., treas. Native Am. Coun. Regents Inst. Am. Indian Arts, 1975-80; bd. visitors Stanford Law Sch., 1978-81; trustee Phelps Stokes Fund, 1981-87, Bush Found., 1991—, Bacone Coll., 1986-89, chmn., 1988-89, Morning Star Found., 1987-93, U. Redlands, 1991—, alumni bd., 1987-89, Ednl. Found. Am., 1993-96; bd. dirs. Amerindian Circle, Inc., 1981-88, Nat. Indian Justice Ctr., 1982-89; cultural edn. com. Smithsonian Inst., 1987-90; nat. support com. Native Am. Rights Fund, 1990—; adv. com. Winslow Found., 1991—; hon. coun. Wings Am., 1993—; mem. Environ. Def. Fund, bd. trustees, 1986—. Recipient Career Achievement award U. Redlands, 1987, Disting. Svc. award, 1992, award Appreciation and Recognition, Cheyenne and Arapaho Tribes Okla., 1990, Spirit of the People award Okla. Inst. Indian Heritage, 1990; named (with another) Amb. of Yr. Red Earth Indian Ctr. Okla., 1993. Mem. Am. Indian Bar Assn. (charter pres. 1976-77). Mem. Cheyenne and Arapaho Tribes Okla. Home: 3311 Rowland Pl NW Washington DC 20008-3226 Office: Nat Mus of Am Indian 470 Lenfant Plz SW Ste 7102 Washington DC 20024-2124

WEST, WALLACE MARION, cultural organization administrator; b. N.Y.C., Aug. 30, 1921; s. Florian and Mary (Wziatek) Wesolowski. BSBA, L.I. U., 1966; cert. mus. mgmt., Columbia U. Estimating engr. Sperry Rand Corp., Lake Success, N.Y., 1957-65; sys. analyst Grumman Aerospace, Bethpage, N.Y., 1965-71; exec. dir. Queens Coun. on Arts, Jamaica, N.Y., 1971-76, Hall of Sci. of City of N.Y., Flushing, 1976-79; pres. Am. Inst. Polish Culture, Pinellas Park, Fla., 1982—; cons. arts mgmt. N.Y. State Coun. on Arts, 1968-71. Author: Handbook for Directors of Non-Profit Corporations, 1974; editor: Sharing Our Heritage, 1996; contbr. articles to profl. jours. Recipient Order of Merit Republic of Poland, 1992; named Notable Am. of Bicentennial Era Am. Biog. Inst., 1976. Mem. Am. Inst. Polish Culture (pres., Polonian of Yr. 1985), Am. Coun. Polish Culture (bd. dirs., Founders award 1992, editor 1985—), Polish Am. Soc., Polish Inst. Arts/Scis. in Am., Polish Am. Pulaski Assn., Kosciuszko Found. Republican. Roman Catholic. Avocations: photography, crafts, electronics, swimming. Home: 6507 107th Ter N Pinellas Park FL 33782 Office: Am Inst Polish Culture 9190 49th St Pinellas Park FL 33782-5228

WEST, WILLIAM BEVERLEY, III, lawyer; b. Ft. Worth, Feb. 5, 1922; s. William Beverley Jr. and Ella Louise (Moore) W. B.A., U. Tex., 1942, LL.B., 1948; Indsl. Adminstr., Harvard Grad. Sch. Bus. Adminstrn., 1943; LL.M., Columbia, 1949; grad., Command and Gen. Staff Sch. Bar: Tex. 1949. Practice in Ft. Worth; asst. U.S. atty. No. Dist. Tex., 1953, 1st asst. U.S. atty., 1957-58, U.S. atty., 1958-61; exec. asst. to asst. atty. gen., lands div. Dept. Justice, 1961-63; ptnr. Clark, West, Keller, Butler & Ellis, Dallas, 1963-89, of counsel, 1989—; mem. adv. bd. Southwestern Law Enforcement Inst., Dallas, 1959-82; mem. adv. com. on criminal rules U.S. Jud. Conf., 1973-77; mem. lawyers adv. com. U.S. Ct. Appeals, 5th Cir., 1985-87. Bd. dirs. prison ministry Kairos, Inc. of Tex., 1990-96, chmn., 1992; mem. nat. bd. Kairos Inc., 1991-96, sec., 1992-96; lay eucharistic min. Episc. Ch. Capt. AUS, 1942-46. Decorated Bronze Star. Fellow Tex. Bar Found., Southwestern Legal Found.; mem. ABA (chmn. sect. jud. adinstrn. 1970-71, ho. dels. 1971-74, sect. litigation, co-editor Antitrust Litigator 1988-92), Inst. Jud. Adminstrn. N.Y.C., Nat. Assn. Former U.S. Attys. (bd. dirs. 1990-93), Nat. Inst. for Trial Advocacy (dir. 1970-83), Fed. Bar Assn., Am. Judicature Soc., Ft. Worth Club, City Club (Dallas), Delta Tau Delta, Phi Alpha Delta, Pi Sigma Alpha. Home: 3701 Turtle Creek Blvd Apt 8H Dallas TX 75219-5530 Office: Clark West Keller Butler & Ellis 4800 Renaissance Tower Dallas TX 75270-2146

WESTALL, SANDRA THORNTON, special education educator; b. Rochester, N.Y., Jan. 31, 1940; d. William Heldrith and Janice (King) Thonrton; m. Thomas Keith Westall, Jan. 10, 1965 (div. 1980); children: William Thornton, Robert Theodore. AS in Bus., So. Va. Coll. Women, 1962; BA in Early Childhood Edn., Mars Hill Coll., 1982; MA in Spl. Edn., Appalachian State U., 1989; MA in Behavioral Emotional Edn., Western Carolina U., 1990. Cert. tchr. spl. edn., learning disabilities, emotional handicapped, N.C., Fla. Tchr.'s asst. spl. edn. Mitchell County Sch., Spruce Pine, N.C., 1964-70; tchr. Pine Ridge Sch. for Learning Disabilities, Williston, Vt., summer 1985, 88, Summit Acad. for Learning Disabled Students, Waynesville, N.C., 1986-88; resource tchr. Ire B. Jones Elem. Sch. and Asheville Jr. High Sch., N.C., 1988-89; tchr. Irene Worthem Sch. for Severe/Profound Mentally Retarded, Asheville, 1989-90; resource tchr. G. Holmes Braddock High Sch., Miami, Fla., 1990-91, Kelsey L. Pharr Elem. Sch., Miami, 1991-94; tchr. severely emotionally disturbed Lakewood Elem. Sch., St. Petersburg, Fla., 1994—; night tchr. Nova U., Ft. Lauderdale, Fla., 1992—, Fla. Meml. Coll., Miami, 1992—; tchr. learning disabilities St. Leo (Fla.) Coll., 1995; tutor, counselor Black Mountain (N.C.) Correctional Ctr. for Women, 1988-90; trainer behavior disorders No. Colo. U., Breckenridge, 1989, Willie M. Workshop, Asheville, 1989; condr. workshops on left and right brain teaching, 1980-87; speaker on learning disabled adults Harvard U., 1989; tchr. day camps for handicapped students, 1983, 84; advocate for learning disabled students and adults; del. Citizen Amb. Program field of learning disabilities, Diagnostic Ctr., various schs., Vilnius, Siauliai Pedagogical Inst., Dept. Spl. Pedagogics, Lithuania, Inst. Defectology, Russian Acad. Pedagogical, Moscow, City Coun., Inst. Econ. Problem Studies, St. Petersburg, Russia, 1993. Vol. Dade County Helpline and Dade County Schs. (in aid of Hurricane Andrew victims), swimming courses for ARC, 1980—; bd. dirs. N.C. Advocacy Ctr. for Children's Edn. and Parent Tng., 1986-90. Grantee Creative Learning for Behavior Handicapped Students, 1989; honoree ARC, 1980. Mem. Am. Coun. on Rural Spl. Edn., Assn. for Children and Adults with Learning Disabilities, The Orton Dyslexia Soc., Coun. for Exceptional Children, Coun. for Behavior Emotionally Handicapped Children. Episcopalian. Avocations: teaching, swimming, drawing, attending flea markets. Home: 751 Pinellas Bayway S Apt 205 Tierra Verde FL 33715-1946 Office: Lakewood Elem Sch 4151 6th St S Saint Petersburg FL 33705-3909

WESTBERG, JOHN AUGUSTIN, lawyer; b. Springfield, Mass., Oct. 12, 1931; s. Carl Joseph and Elizabeth Rebecca (Glassmire) W.; BA, Coll. William and Mary, 1955; JD, U. Va., 1959; m. Mina Lari, Aug. 21, 1976; children: Christine, Steven, Jennifer, Saman. Bar: N.Y. 1960, D.C. 1969, U.S. Supreme Ct. 1968. Assoc. Lord, Day and Lord, N.Y.C., 1959-64; legal adv. AID, Washington, 1964-65, regional legal adv. for Mid. East, Am. Embassy, Teheran, Iran, also AID affairs officer, 1965-68; founder John A. Westberg & Assocs., Inc., Teheran, 1968, pres., 1968-79; ptnr. Wald, Harkrader & Ross, London and Washington, 1981-87; pvt. practice, Washington, 1987-89; ptnr. Westberg & Johnson, Washington, 1989-96; of counsel Pepper, Hamilton and Scheetz, Washington, 1996—. Bd. dirs. Damavand Coll.; mem. N.Y. County Dem. Com., 1963. 1st lt. U.S. Army, 1955-57, Korea. Mem. ABA, Internat. Bar Assn., Am. Soc. Internat. Law, D.C. Bar, Fed. Bar Assn., Iran Am. C. of C. (bd. govs. 1973-77), Shaybani Soc. (v.p.), Cosmos Club. Author: International Transactions and Claims Involving Government Parties--Case Law of the Iran-United States Claims Tribunal, 1991; contbr. articles to bus. and law jours. Avocations: tennis, skiing. Home: 4296 Massachusetts Ave NW Washington DC 20016-5548 Office: 1300 19th St NW Washington DC 20036-1609

WESTBERRY, BILLY MURRY, lawyer; b. Georgetown, La., Nov. 5, 1926; s. Iley Donley and Julia Frances (Thornton) W.; m. Nancy Elizabeth Kent, Aug. 7, 1953; children—Robert Kent, William Bishop. Student, Murray (Ky.) State U., 1946-48; LL.B., U. Louisville, 1950. Bar: Ky. 1950. Since practiced in Marion; county atty. Crittenden County, 1954-62, 1967-73; city atty. Marion, 1965-67; partner firm Westberry & Roberts, 1968—; chmn. Jud. Ethics Com. Ky., 1979—; mem. Ky. Commn. Law Enforcement and Crime Prevention, 1968—. Served with USAAF, 1944-45; Served with USAF, 1951-53. Mem. Am. Bar Assn., Ky. Bar Assn. (pres. 1978-79), Crittenden County Bar Assn., Am. Legion. Republican. Episcopalian. Clubs: Rotary, Shriners. Home: 125 Brookfield Dr Paducah KY 42001-5380 Office: Citizens Bank Bldg Ste 921 Paducah KY 42001-0761

WESTBO, LEONARD ARCHIBALD, JR., electronics engineer; b. Tacoma, Wash., Dec. 4, 1931; s. Leonard Archibald and Agnes (Martinson) W.; B.A. in Gen. Studies, U. Wash., 1958. Electronics engr. FAA, Seattle Air Route Traffic Control Center, Auburn, Wash., 1961-72; asst. br. chief electronics engring. br. 13th Coast Guard Dist., Seattle, 1972-87. Served with USCG, 1951-54, 1958-61. Registered profl. engr., Wash. Mem. Aircraft Owners and Pilots Assn., IEEE, Am. Radio Relay League. Home and Office: 10528 SE 323rd St Auburn WA 98092-4734

WESTBROOK, BILL, advertising executive. Pres., creative dir. Fallon-McElligott, Mpls. Office: Fallon-McElligott 901 Marquette Ave Ste 3200 Minneapolis MN 55402-3205

WESTBROOK, DON ARLEN, minister; b. Clinton, N.C., June 2, 1941; s. Ennis and Geneva (Gainey) W.; m. Carrol Ann Holder, Sept. 15, 1963; children: Felisha Ann, Neal Vance. Student, Logos Bible Coll./Grad. Sch., 1989, Duke Univ. Ordained to ministry Full Gospel Fellowship Chs. and Mins. Internat., 1965. Pastor Bethel Christian Ctr., Durham, N.C., 1969—; v.p. Full Gospel Fellowship Chs. and Mins. Internat., Dallas, 1982—; missionary to India, Nicaragua and Haiti, 1990. Chmn. Concerned Citizens for Moral Govt., Durham, 1989. Home: 5311 Emeraldwod Dr Durham NC 27705 Office: Bethel Christian Ctr 3518 Rose Of Sharon Rd Durham NC 27712-3306

WESTBROOK, JAMES EDWIN, lawyer, educator; b. Camden, Ark., Sept. 7, 1934; s. Loy Edwin and Helen Lucille (Bethea) W.; m. Elizabeth Kay Farris, Dec. 23, 1956; children: William Michael, Robert Bruce, Matthew David. BA with high honors, Hendrix Coll., 1956; JD with distinction, Duke U., 1959; LLM, Georgetown U., 1965. Bar: Ark. 1959, Okla. 1977, Mo. 1982. Assoc. Mehaffy, Smith & Williams, Little Rock, 1959-62; asst. counsel, subcom. of U.S. Senate Jud. Com., Washington, 1963; legis. asst. U.S. Senate, Washington, 1963-65; asst. prof. law U. Mo., Columbia, 1965-68, asst. dean, 1966-68, assoc. prof., 1968-70, prof., 1970-76, 80—, James S. Rollins prof. law, 1974-76, 80—, Earl F. Nelson prof. law, 1982—, interim dean, 1981-82; dean U. Okla. Coll. Law, Norman, 1976-80; George Allen vis. prof. law, U. Richmond, 1987; vis. prof. law Duke U., 1988, Washington U., St. Louis, 1996; arbitrator on roster of Fed. Mediation and Conciliation Service, 1974—; reporter Mid-Am. Assembly on Role of State in Urban Crisis, 1970; dir. Summer Internship Program in Local Govt., 1968; cons. various Mo. cities on drafting home-rule charters; mem. Gov.'s Adv. Council on Local Govt. Law, 1967-68, Fed. Practice Com. U.S. Dist. Ct. (we. dist.) Mo., 1986-90; chmn. Columbia Charter Revision Commn., 1973-74; mem. spl. com. labor relations Mo. Dept. Labor and Indsl. Relations, 1975; mem. Task Force on Gender and Justice, Mo. Jud. Conf., 1990-93; mem. com. to rev. govtl. structure of Boone County, Mo., 1991. Author: (with L. Riskin) Dispute Resolution and Lawyers, 1987, supplement, 1993, 2d edit., 1997; contbr. articles to profl. jours. Chair search com. for chancellor U. Mo., Columbia, 1992. Kemper fellow for tchg. excellence, 1997. Mem. ABA, Nat. Acad. Arbitrators, Assn. Am. Law Schs. (chmn. local govt. law round table coun. 1972), Ctrl. States Law Sch. Assn. (pres. 1982-83), Mo. Bar Assn. (vice chmn. labor law com. 1986-87, chmn. 1987-88, Spurgeon Smithton award 1995), Order of Coif, Blue Key, Alpha Chi. Roman Catholic. Home: 3609 S Woods Edge Rd Columbia MO 65203-6606 Office: U Mo Sch Law Columbia MO 65211

WESTBROOK, JAY LAWRENCE, law educator; b. Morristown, N.J., Dec. 11, 1943; s. Joel W. and Elaine Frances (Summers) W.; m. Pauline June Travis, Feb. 15, 1969; 1 child, Joel Mastin. BA in Polit. Sci./Philosophy, U. Tex., 1965, JD, 1968. Bar: Tex. 1968, D.C. 1969, U.S. Ct. Appeals (D.C. cir.) 1969, U.S. Supreme Ct. 1976, U.S. Ct. Appeals (4th cir.) 1978, U.S. Ct. Appeals (2d cir.) 1979. Assoc. Surrey & Morse (name now Jones, Day, Reavis, Pogue), Washington, 1969-74; ptnr. Surrey & Morse (name now Jones, Day, Reavis, Pogue, Surrey & Morse), Washington, 1974-80; mem. law faculty U. Tex., Austin, 1980—, Benno C. Schmidt Chair Bus. Law, 1991—; vis. prof. U. London, 1990, Harvard Law Sch., 1991-92; advisor Tex. Internat. Law Jour., 1985-91; reporter Am. Law Inst. Transnat. Insolvency Project, 1994—; co-leader U.S. delegation to UN Commn. on Internat. Trade Law Working Group on Model Law Internation Insolvency, 1995—. Co-author: As We Forgive Our Debtors: Bankruptcy and Consumer Credit in America, 1989 (Silver Gavel award ABA 1989), The Law of Debtors and Creditors: Text, Cases and Problems, 3d edit., 1996, Teacher's Manual, The Law of Debtors and Creditors, 3d edit., 1996; contbr. articles to profl. jours. Grantee U. Tex. Law Sch. Found., 1982, U. Rsch. Inst., 1982-83, NSF, 1983-86, Policy Rsch. Inst., Lyndon Johnson Sch. Pub. Affairs, 1984, Tex. Bar Found., 1985, Nat. Inst. Child Health and Human Devel., 1986, Nat. Conf. Bankruptcy Judges, 1991, 93. Mem. ABA (bus. bankruptcy com., internat. bankruptcy subcom., internat. sect., Meyer rsch. grant 1986), Am. Law Inst., Am. Coll. Bankruptcy, Nat. Bankruptcy Conf., State Bar Tex. (governing coun. internat. sect. 1987-89), Internat. Bar Assn., Internat. Bankruptcy Com. (com. J), Internat. Acad. Comml. and Consumer Law, Order of Coif. Office: U Tex Sch Law 727 E 26th St Austin TX 78705-3224

WESTBROOK, NICHOLAS KILMER, museum administrator, historian; b. Boston, July 10, 1948; s. Jack Hall and Elizabeth (Kirkland) W.; m. Virginia Lee Macleod, June 12, 1971; children: Benjamin Macoun, Samuel Farley. AB cum laude, Amherst Coll., 1971; MA, U. Conn., 1973; postgrad., U. Pa., 1973-76. Seasonal ranger-historian Nat. Park Svc., Stillwater, N.Y., 1969-71; asst. to v.p. for interpretation Old Sturbridge Village, Sturbridge, Mass., 1972-75; ednl. materials developer Uni-Coll Corp., Phila., 1975-76; exhibits coord. Minn. Hist. Soc., St. Paul, 1976-78, curator of exhibits, 1978-88; exec. dir. Ft. Ticonderoga, Ticonderoga, N.Y., 1989—; panelist NEH, Washington, 1985—, Inst. Mus. Svcs., Washington, 1991—; bd. dirs. N.Y. State Mil. Heritage Mus. Editor: Industrial Archeology of the Twin Cities, 1983, Bull. Ft. Ticonderoga Mus., 1991—; book rev. editor Indsl. Archeology, 1983-89; curator several exhibits. Trustee Fedn. for Hist. Svcs., 1990-94, treas., 1992-94; bd. dirs. Mohican coun. Boy Scouts Am. Winston Churchill travelling fellow Gt. Britain, 1981, Andrew W. Mellon fellowship, 1995. Mem. Soc. for Indsl. Archaeology (bd. dirs. 1983-85, sec. 1986-91), Am. Assn. for State and Local History, Am. Assn. Mus., Soc. for History of Tech., Am. Printing History Assn., Mus. Assn. N.Y. (councillor 1995-98), Ticonderoga C. of C. (v.p. 1989-94, bd. dirs. 1995—), Antiquarian Soc., Kiwanis. Presbyterian. Avocation: letterpress printing. Home: Creek Rd Box 8 Crown Point NY 12928 Office: Ft Ticonderoga Fort Rd Ticonderoga NY 12883

WESTBROOK, SUSAN ELIZABETH, horticulturist; b. Canton, Ohio, Sept. 27, 1939; d. Walter Simon and Rosella Hunt Tolley; m. Edward D. Westbrook, July 2, 1966 (div. 1980); 1 child, Tyler Hunt. Student, Smithdeal-Massey, Richmond, Va., 1958-59; student in Spanish, U. Honduras, 1960; student biology/geology, Mary Washington Coll., 1960, 72, 73; student hort., Prince Georges Community Coll., 1987-88. Farm owner Spotsylvania, Va., 1972-83; office mgr. Tolley Investments, Inc., Fredericksburg, Va., 1980-83; real estate agt. Cooper Realty, Fredericksburg, Va., 1981-83; salesperson Meadows Farms Nursery, Chantilly, Va., 1986-93; student Geology Dept. Mary Washington Coll., Fredericksburg, Va., 1993—; master gardener Va. Poly. Inst., 1993. Author booklets: Japanese Maples, 1990, Fruit Trees, 1989; author radio format: Gardening in Virginia, 1960; co-author computer program: Plantscape, 1990. Sec. Rep. Party, Spotsylvania, 1972-83, Elko County, Nev., 1968; judge Bd. Elections, Spotsylvania, 1980-83, cand. bd. suprs., 1979. Named Master Gardener Va. Poly. Inst., Blacksburg, Va., 1993. Mem. Nat. Wildlife Fedn., Md. Nurserymen's Assn., Friends of the Nat. Arboretum. Avocations: travel, gardening, plant research and identification. Home: 6110 S Virginia Ln PO Box 8 Dahlgren VA 22448

WESTBROOK, T. L., bishop. Bishop of Wash. Ch. of God in Christ, Spanaway. Office: Ch of God in Christ 1256 176th St S Spanaway WA 98387-9208*

WESTBROOK, WALTER WINFIELD, minister; b. Chattanooga, Sept. 15, 1955; s. Robert Stanley and Ruth Louise (Fisher) W.; m. Betty Blevins, June 3, 1978; 1 child, Cassandra Noel. BA, Emory (Va.) and Henry Coll., 1977; MDiv, Drew U., 1980; postgrad., Asbury Theol. Sem., 1991—, Ruah, 1993-95. Ordained to ministry United Meth. Ch., 1980. Min. Dahlgren (Va.) United Meth. Ch., 1980-87, Highland Springs (Va.) United Meth. Ch., 1987-95, Bethany United Meth. Ch., Reedville, Va., 1995—; dir. health and welfare ministries Ashland dist. United Meth. Ch., Va., 1989-90, dir. spiritual formation, 1990-92, chmn. spiritual formation com., 1993—, spiritural formation rep. Rappahannock dist.; mem. bd. comm. Va. Conf. United Meth. Ch., 1990, mem. bd. discipleship, chmn. divsn. spiritual formation, 1995—; creator, facilitator Monday Morning Meditation Group, Ashland Dist. Clergy; trainer for clergy, laity and mixed groups in 8 districts. Author: Two Sermons in Verse, 1994, Two More Sermons in Verse, 1994; creator, host, producer weekly radio program Tell Me Why, 1987-93; religion columnist The King George Jour., weekly newspaper, 1986-87; contbr. adult Sunday sch. lessons to Va. Adv., 1990; contbr. to Lenten Devotional Books, 1993-97. Bd. dirs. The Haven, battered women shelter, Fredericksburg, Va., 1983-86, The Bethlehem Ctr., Richmond, Va., 1989-90, Richmond Hill, Christian Retreat Ctr., Richmond, 1990-95; coordinating coun. Interfaith Svcs. Henrico County, Richmond, 1987-89; active Habitat for Humanity, 1986-90, Bread for World, 1986-90; vol. reader for Virginia Voice, 1989-90; vol. reading ptnr. Northumberland Elem. Sch., 1997; participant Blessing of the Fleet, Reedville, Va., 1996, 97. Co-recipient Couple of Yr. award Rappahannock Big Bros.-Big Sisters, 1985. Mem. Disciplined Order of Christ, Pathways Network, Internat. Jugglers Assn., Renovaré, United Meth. Vols. in Mission (mission trip to Haiti 1977, to Charleston, S.C. 1989). Address: PO Box 77 Reedville VA 22539 *The healing of our troubled world will begin when people of every religion discover the way to take their spiritual journey more seriously while, at the same time, taking themselves less seriously.*

WESTBY, TIMOTHY SCOTT, lawyer; b. Fargo, N.D., Apr. 16, 1957; s. Joseph Arlo and Dorothy Mae (Nye) W.; m. Holli Leigh Huber, Mar. 17, 1987; 1 child, Katherine Elizabeth. SBChemE, MIT, 1979; PhDChemE, U. Tex., 1984; JD, U. Houston, 1994. Bar: U.S. Dist. Ct. (so. dist.) Tex. Researcher Energy Lab., MIT, Cambridge, 1976-79; rsch. asst. U. Tex., Austin, 1979-84, teaching asst., 1981-83; assoc. rsch. engr. Shell Devel. Co., Houston, 1984-87, rsch. engr., 1987-91, sr. rsch. engr., 1991-94; assoc. Conley, Rose & Tayon, P.C., 1994—; mem. adv. com. Ohio Combustion Rsch., Columbus, 1985-90, Pa. Coal Rsch. Coop., University Station, 1986-89. Contbr. articles to profl. jours.; patentee method for in situ coal drilling, patentee coal blends having improved ash viscosity. Campaigner United Way, Houston, 1989-91. Scholar MIT, 1975-79; fellow U.S. dept. Energy, 1979-82, Getty Oil Co., 1983-84. Mem. ABA, ASTM (com. D-5 1989-94), ASME (advisor rsch. com. on corrosion and deposits from flue gases 1988—), Am. Intellectual Property Law Assn., Fed. Cir. Bar Assn., State Bar of Tex., Houston Bar Assn., Houston Intellectual Property Law Assn. Avocations: golf, gardening, racquet sports, Italian food, old sports cars. Office: Conley Rose & Tayon PC Ste 1850 600 Travis Houston TX 77002-2912

WESTCOTT, BRIAN JOHN, manufacturing executive; b. Rexford, N.Y., June 19, 1957; s. John Campbell and Norma (Cornell) W.; m. Andrea Belrose, Apr. 23, 1988; children: Sarah Katharine, Paul Brian. BS, Lehigh U., 1979; MS, Stanford U., 1980, PhD, 1987. Engr. Combustion Engring., Windsor, Conn., 1980-81; rsch. engr. Gen. Electric Corp. Rsch., Niskayuna, N.Y., 1981-83; rsch. fellow Stanford (Calif.) Grad. Sch. Bus., 1987-88; mgr. Gen. Electric Corp. Mgmt., Bridgeport, Conn., 1988-89; prin. A.T. Kearney Tech. Inc., Redwood City, Calif., 1989—; chief exec. officer Westt, Inc., Menlo Park, Calif., 1990—. Author: (with others) Paradox and Transformation, 1988; contbr. articles to profl. jours.; inventor, patentee in field. Mem. Menlo Park Vitality Task Force, 1993-94. Recipient Tech 500 award Westt, Inc., 1996; postdoctoral rsch. fellow Stanford U. Grad. Sch. Bus., 1987, 88; rsch. fellow Electric Power Rsch., Stanford, 1983-87. Mem. ASME.$Doc. Mfg. Engrs. Avocations: sports, politics. Office: Westt Inc 1090 Obrien Dr Menlo Park CA 94025-1409

WESTER, KEITH ALBERT, film and television recording engineer, television executive; b. Seattle, Feb. 21, 1940; s. Albert John and Evelyn Grayce (Nettell) W., m. Judith Elizabeth Jones, 1968 (div. Mar. 1974); 1 child, Wendy Elizabeth. AA, Am. River Coll., Sacramento, 1959; BA, Calif. State U., L.A., 1962; MA, UCLA, 1965. Lic. multi-engine rated pilot. Prodn. asst. Sta. KCRA-TV, Sacramento, 1956; announcer Sta. KSFM, Sacramento, 1960; film editor, sound rec. technician Urie & Assocs., Hollywood, Calif., 1963-66; co-owner Steckler-Wester Film Prodns., Hollywood, 1966-70; owner Profl. Sound Recorders, Studio City, Calif., 1970—, Aerocharter, Studio City, 1974—; owner Wester Devel., Sun Valley, Coeur d'Alene, Idaho, 1989—, also Studio City, 1989—; majority stockholder Channel 58 TV, Coeur d'Alene/Spokane, Idaho, 1993—. Prodn. sound mixer: (films) Mouse Hunt, 1997, Air Force One, 1996, Shadow Conspiracy, 1996, G.I. Jane, 1996, The Rock, 1996 (Acad. award co-nominee for best sound, 1997), Waterworld, 1995 (Acad. award co-nominee for best sound 1996), The Shadow, 1994, Wayne's World II, 1993, Coneheads, 1993, Body of Evidence, 1992, Indecent Proposal, 1992, School Ties, 1991, Frankie and Johnny, 1991, Another You, 1991, Thelma and Louise, 1990, Shattered, 1990, Desperate Hours, 1989, Joe vs. the Volcano, 1989, Black Rain, 1989, Sea of Love, 1988, Real Men, 1985, Mask, 1984, Thief of Hearts, 1983, Young Doctors in Love, 1982, First Monday in October, 1981. Mem. NATAS (Emmy award An Early Frost 1986, Emmy nominations in 1982, 84, 85, 87), SAG, Acad. Motion Picture Arts and Scis. (Acad. award nomination for best sound Black Rain 1990, Waterworld 1996, The Rock 1997), Brit. Acad. Film and TV Arts (award nomination for The Rock 1997), Cinema Audio Soc. (sec. 1985-91, Sound award 1987), Soc. Motion Picture and TV Engrs., Internat. Sound Technicians, Local 695, Assn. Film Craftsmen (sec. 1967-73, treas. 1973-76), Aircraft Owners and Pilots Assn. (Confederate Air Force col.), Am. Radio Relay League. Home: 4146 Bellingham Ave Studio City CA 91604-1601 Office: Profl Sound Recorders 22440 Clarendon St Woodland Hills CA 91367-4467

WESTERBECK, KENNETH EDWARD, retired insurance company executive; b. Des Moines, Sept. 5, 1919; s. Joseph David and Florence Alice (King) W.; m. Miriam M. Martens, Jan. 24, 1942; children: Kent E., Marcia M. Westerbeck Waltersheide. D.B.A., Upper Iowa U., 1979. With Equitable Life Ins. Co. of Iowa, 1938-84; v.p., chief fin. officer Equitable of Iowa Cos., 1977-84, v.p., treas., 1980-84; v.p., sec. Equitable Life Ins. Co. of Iowa, 1973-84; ret., 1984; pres. Equitable Investment Svcs. Inc., Des Moines, 1982-84. Bd. Trustees Upper Iowa U.; bd. dirs. A.R.C.; mem. West Des Moines City Council, 1976-93. Mem. Des Moines Soc. Fin. Analysts. Republican. Presbyterian. Home: 715 10th St West Des Moines IA 50265-3506

WESTERBERG, ARTHUR WILLIAM, chemical engineering educator; b. St. Paul, Oct. 9, 1938; s. Kenneth Waldorf and Marjorie Claire (Darling) W.; m. Barbara Ann Dyson, July 14, 1963; children: Kenneth, Karl. B.S., U. Minn., 1960; M.S., Princeton U., 1961; Ph.D., Imperial Coll., London, 1964. Pres. Farm Engring. Sales Inc., Savage, Minn., 1964-65; sr. analyst Control Data Corp., San Diego, Calif., 1965-67; asst. prof., assoc. prof., prof. U. Fla., Gainesville, 1967-76; prof. chem. engring. Carnegie-Mellon U., Pitts., 1976—, chmn. dept., 1980-83, Swearingen prof., 1982—, dir. Design Research Ctr., 1978-80, Univ. prof., 1992—; dir. Engring. Design Research Ctr., 1986-89. Co-author: Process Flowsheeting, 1979, Systematic Methods of Chemical Process Design, 1997. Recipient Murphree award Am. Chem. Soc., 1997. Fellow AIChE (lectr. 1989, Computers and Systems Tech. divsn. award 1983, Walker award 1987, McAfee award 1990, Founders Outstanding Contbns. Chem. Engring. award 1995); mem. NAE, Am. Soc. Engring. Edn. (chem. engring. divsn. lectr. 1981). Home: 5564 Beacon St Pittsburgh PA 15217-1972 Office: Engring Dept Carnegie Mellon U Pittsburgh PA 15213

WESTERDAHL, JOHN BRIAN, nutritionist, health educator; b. Tucson, Dec. 3, 1954; s. Jay E. and Margaret (Meyer) W.; m. Doris Mui Lian Tan, Nov. 18, 1989. AA, Orange Coast Coll., 1977; BS, Pacific Union Coll., 1979; MPH, Loma Linda U., 1981. Registered dietitian; chartered herbalist; cert. nutrition specialist. Nutritionist, health educator Castle Med. Ctr., Kailua, Hawaii, 1981-84, health promotion coord., 1984-87, asst. dir. health promotion, 1987-88, dir. health promotion, 1988-89; dir. nutrition and health rsch. Health Sci., Santa Barbara, Calif., 1989-90; sr. nutritionist, project mgr. Shaklee Corp., San Francisco, 1990-96; dir. nutrition Dr. McDougall's Right Foods, Inc., S. San Francisco, 1996—; mem. faculty staff, dir. continuing edn. Am. Acad. Nutrition, 1996—; talk show host Nutrition and You, Sta. KGU Radio, Honolulu, 1983-89; nutrition com. mem. Hawaii div. Am. Heart Assn., Honolulu, 1984-87; mem. nutrition study group Govs. Conf. Health Promotion and Disease Prevention for Hawaii, 1985. Editor: Nourish Mag., 1995-96; nutrition editor: Veggie Life Mag., 1995—. Mem. AAAS, Am. Coll. Sports Medicine, Am. Dietetic Assn. (Calif. coord. vegetarian nutrition practice group), Am. Nutritionists Assn., Am. Coll. Nutrition, Soc. for Nutrition Edn., Nat. Wellness Assn., Nutrition Today Soc., Am. Soc. Pharmacognosy, Inst. Food Technologists, Hawaii Nutrition Coun. (v.p. 1983-86,m pres.-elect 1988-89, pres. 1989), Hawaii Dietetic Assn., Calif. Dietetic Assn., N.Y. Acad. Scis., Seventh-day Adventist Dietetic Assn., several other profl. assns. Republican. Seventh-Day Adventist. Avocations: swimming, scuba diving. Office: Dr McDougall's Right Foods 101 Utah Ave South San Francisco CA 94080-6711 *Personal philosophy: "Beloved, I wish above all things that thou mayest prosper and be in health, even as thy soul prospereth." 3 John 2.*

WESTERFIELD, HOLT BRADFORD, political scientist, educator; b. Rome, Italy, Mar. 7, 1928; s. Ray Bert and Mary Beatrice (Putney) W.; m. Carolyn Elizabeth Hess, Dec. 17, 1960; children: Pamela Bradford, Leland Avery. Grad., Choate Sch., 1944; BA, Yale U., 1947; MA, Harvard U., 1951, PhD, 1952. Instr. govt. Harvard U., 1952-56; asst. prof. polit. sci. U. Chgo., 1956-57; mem. faculty Yale U., 1957—, prof. polit. sci., 1965—, chmn. dept., 1970-72, Damon Wells prof. internat. studies, 1985—; research asso. Washington Center Fgn. Policy Research, Johns Hopkins Sch. Advanced Internat. Studies, 1965-66; vis. prof. Wesleyan U., Middletown, Conn., 1967, 71. Author: Foreign Policy and Party Politics: Pearl Harbor to Korea, 1955, The Instruments of America's Foreign Policy, 1963; editor: Inside CIA's Private World: Declassified Articles from the Agency's Internal Journal, 1955-92, 1995. Sheldon traveling fellow Harvard, 1951-52; Henry L. Stimson fellow Yale, 1962, 73; sr. Fulbright-Hays scholar, 1973; hon. vis. fellow Australian Nat. U., 1973. Mem. Am. Polit. Sci. Assn. (Congl. fellow 1953-54), Internat. Polit. Sci. Assn., Internat. Studies Assn. Home: 115 Rogers Rd Hamden CT 06517-3541 Office: Yale Univ Dept Polit Sci PO Box 208301 New Haven CT 06520-8301

WESTERFIELD, PUTNEY, management consulting executive; b. New Haven, Feb. 9, 1930; s. Ray Bert and Mary Beatrice (Putney) W.; m. Anne Montgomery, Apr. 17, 1954; children: Bradford, Geoffrey, Clare. Grad., Choate Sch., 1942-47; B.A., Yale, 1951. Co-founder, v.p. Careers, Inc., N.Y.C., 1950-52; mgr. S.E. Asia Swen Publs., Inc., Manila, Philippines, 1952; mem. joint adv. commn. Korea, 1953-54; polit. officer Am. embassy, Saigon, Vietnam, 1955-57; asst. to pub. Time mag., N.Y.C., 1957-59, asst. circulation dir., 1959-61; circulation dir. Time mag., 1961-66, asst. pub., 1966-68; asst. pub. Life mag., N.Y.C., 1968; pub. Fortune mag., N.Y.C., 1969-73; pres. Chase World Info. Corp., N.Y.C., 1973-75; v.p. Boyden Assocs. Internat., San Francisco, 1976-80, sr. v.p., western mgr., 1980-84; pres., chief exec. officer Boyden Assocs. Internat., N.Y.C. and San Francisco, 1984-90, mng. dir., 1990—; chmn. bd. dirs. Upside Media Inc. Bd. dirs. Urban League, N.Y.C., 1969-71, Children's Village, 1968-71, Mediterranean Sch. Found., 1969-71, Nat. Boys Club, 1970-73, U.S. -S. Africa Leaders Exch. Program, 1971—, Bus. Coun. for Internat. Understanding, 1974-76, Yale-China Assn., 1975-78, East Meets West Found., 1991—; trustee Choate Sch., Wallingford, Conn., 1967-76, Westover Sch., Middlebury, Conn., 1975-79, Watch Hill Chapel Soc., 1963-77, Assn. Yale Alumni, 1972-75, 80-83. Mem. Burlingame Country Club, Pacific Union Club, Bohemian Club. Home: 10 Greenview Ln Hillsborough CA 94010-6424 Office: Boyden Internat 275 Battery St Ste 420 San Francisco CA 94111-3331

WESTERGAARD, PETER TALBOT, composer, music educator; b. Champaign, Ill., May 28, 1931; s. Harald Malcolm and Rachel (Talbot) W.; m. Barbara Jay, Sept. 11, 1955; children: Elizabeth, Margaret. BA, Harvard U., 1953; MFA, Princeton (N.J.) U., 1956. Fulbright guest lectr. Staatliche Hochschule, Freiburg, Germany, 1957-58; instr. Columbia U., N.Y.C., 1958-63, asst. prof., 1963-66; vis. lectr. Princeton U., 1966-67; assoc. prof. Amherst Coll., Mass., 1967-68; from assoc. prof. music to prof. Princeton U., 1968—, chmn. dept. music, 1974-78, 83-86, William Shubael Conant prof. music, 1995—, acting chmn. dept., 1995-96; vis. prof. U. B.C., 1987; lectr. internat. music seminar Univ. Bahia, Brazil, 1992; endowed prof. U. Ala., 1995. Condr. Princeton U. Orch., 1968-73; dir. Princeton U. Opera Theater, 1970—, June Opera Festival of N.J., 1983-86; composer: Cantata I (The Plot Against the Giant, 1956, Five Movements for Small Orchestra, 1958, Cantata II (A Refusal to Mourn the Death, by Fire, of a Child in London), 1958, Quartet for Violin, Vibraphone, Clarinet and Violoncello, 1960, Spring and Fall, To a Young Child, 1960, 64, Cantata III (Leda and the Swan), 1961, Trio for Flute, Violoncello and Piano, 1962, Variations for Six Players, 1963, Mr. and Mrs. Discobbolos, 1965, Divertimento on Discobbolic Fragments, 1967, Noises, Sounds and Sweet Airs, 1968, Tuckets and Sennets, 1969, Moto Perpetuo for Six Wind Industruments, 1976, Alonso's Grief, 1977, There Was a Little Man, 1979, Ariel Music, 1987, Two Fanfares, 1988, Ariel Songs, 1988, Ode, 1989, The Tempest, 1990, (for percussion ensemble) All 4s, 1996, (for chamber chorus) anyone lived in a pretty how town, 1996, (for soprano and violin) There Was a Lady, 1997; author: Introduction to Tonal Theory, 1975; translator operas: The Magic Flute, 1977, Don Giovanni, 1979, Der Freischutz, 1980, Fidelio (original version of 1805), 1982, Cosi fan tutte, 1983, The Marriage of Figaro, 1984, Cinderella, 1986. Guggenheim fellow, 1964-65, N.J. State Council on the Arts fellow, 1986-87, 89-90; grantee Nat. Endowment for Arts, 1990-91. Office: Princeton U Dept Music Princeton NJ 08544

WESTERHAUS, CATHERINE K., social worker; b. Corydon, Ind., Oct. 13, 1910; d. Anthony Joseph and Permelia Ann (Mathes) Kannapel; m. George Henry Westerhaus, Apr. 15, 1950. BEd in Music, Kans. U., 1934; MSW, Loyola U., Chgo., 1949. Cert. Acad. Cert. Social Workers. Clin. social worker Friendly Acres Home of Aged, Newton, Kans.; county welfare dir., state adult svcs. supr. Newton-Harvey County, State of Kans.; vol. cert. social worker Newton. Project dir.: Memories of War Years, 1995, The War Years Including Veterans of Harvey County, Kansas, 1995; contbr. articles to profl. jours. With USNR, 1945-46. Named Kans. Social Worker of Yr., 1975. Mem. NASW (cert.), Kans. Soc. Cert. Social Work, Am. Legion (comdr. Wayne G. Austin post 1981-82). Home: 313 W Broadway St Newton KS 67114-2631

WESTERHOFF, GARRET PETER, environmental engineer, executive; b. Fairlawn, N.J., Oct. 12, 1935; s. Garret Peter and Elizabeth (Ullmer) W.; m. Helga Ann Kasch, May 31, 1958; children: Garret Peter, Eric John, Paul Keith. BS in Civil Engring., N.J. Inst. Tech., 1957, MS in Sanitary Engring., 1967. Registered profl. engr., N.J., N.Y., Ohio, Va., Ariz., Calif., Md., Fla., Ala., La., Maine, Mass., Nebr., N.Mex., Nev., N.C., Pa., Wash.; cert. profl. planner; diplomate Am. Acad. Environ. Engrs. Loss prevention engr. Factory Mutual Engring. Co., 1960-64; project engr. Jersey Engring. Assocs., 1964-65; from v.p. to exec. v.p. Malcolm Pirnie, Inc., White Plains, N.Y., 1967—; mem. rsch. adv. coun. Nat. Water Rsch. Inst.; internat. rapporteur on water quality and treatment in U.S. Internat. Water Supply Assn., World Congress, Budapest, 1993, Durban, S. Africa, 1995; tech. cons. Office Drinking Water U.S. EPA; presenter in field. Contbr. articles to profl. jours. 1st lt. USAF, 1957-60. Mem. Am. Water Works Assn. (former stds. coun., chmn. Internat. Water Supply Assn. N.Am. com., former chmn. water supply planning and coord. com., former trustee engring. and constrn. divsn., former chmn. water reuse coom., former chmn. water treatment plant wastes disposal com., former chmn. alum recovery rsch. adv. com., rsch. adv. coun. Rsch. Found.), Am. Soc. Civil Engrs., NSPE, Water Environment Fedn. Avocations: fishing, photography, writing. Office: Malcolm Pirnie Inc 104 Corporate Park Dr White Plains NY 10604-3804

WESTERHOFF, JOHN HENRY, III, clergyman, theologian, educator; b. Paterson, N.J., June 28, 1933; s. John Henry and Nona Celia (Walsh) W.; m. Alberta Louise Barnhart, Dec. 27, 1955 (div. 1991); childen: Jill Louise, John Jeffrey, Beth Anne; m. Caroline Askew Hughes, Oct. 27, 1991. BS, Ursinus Coll., 1955; STB, Harvard U., 1958; EdD, Columbia U., 1974; DD, Ursinus Coll., 1990. Ordained to ministry United Ch. of Christ, 1958, Episcopal Ch., 1978; pastor Congl. Ch., Presque Isle, Maine, 1958-60; assoc. pastor Congl. Ch., Needham, Mass., 1960-64; pastor 1st Congl. Ch., Williamstown, Mass., 1964-66; edn. sec., editor Colloquy (United Ch. Bd. for Homeland Ministries), N.Y.C., 1966-73; Lentz lectr. Harvard U. Div. Sch., 1973-74; prof. Duke U. Div. Sch., Durham, N.C., 1974-94; dir. Inst. Pastoral Studies, Atlanta, 1992—; interim rector St. Bartholomew Episcopal Ch., Atlanta, 1993-94; assoc. rector St. Lukes Episcopal Ch., Atlanta, 1994—. Author: Values for Tomorrows Children, 1970, A Colloquy on Christian Education, 1972, Generation to Generation, 1974, Tomorrow's Church, 1976, Will Our Children Have Faith?, 1976, McGuffey and His Readers, 1978, Who Are We?, 1978, Learning Through Liturgy, 1978, Inner Growth-Outer Change, 1979, The Church's Ministry in Higher Education, 1979, Liturgy and Learning Through the Life Cycle, 1980, Christian Believing, 1980, Bringing Up Children in The Christian Church, 1980, A Faithful Church, 1981, The Spiritual Life: Learning East and West, 1981, Building God's People, 1983, A Pilgrim People, 1984, Living the Faith Community, 1985, On the Threshold of God's Future, 1986, Living Into Our Baptism, 1990, Schooling Christians, 1992, The Spiritual Life: Foundation for Preaching and Teaching, 1994; A People Called Episcopalians, 1995, Holy Baptism: A Guide for Parents and Godparents, 1996; editor: Religious Edn, 1979-89. Mem. Assn. Profs. and Researchers in Religious Edn., Religious Edn. Assn. Democrat. Episcopalian. Office: Saint Luke's Episcopal Ch 435 Peachtree St NE Atlanta GA 30308-3219

WESTERHOUT, GART, retired astronomer; b. The Hague, The Netherlands, June 15, 1927; came to U.S., 1962, naturalized, 1969; s. Gerrit and Magdalena (Foppe) W.; m. Judith Mary Monaghan, Nov. 14, 1956; children: Magda C., Gart T., Brigit M., Julian C., Anthony K. Drs., Leiden U., Netherlands, 1954, Ph.D., 1958. Asst. Leiden U. Observatory, 1952-56, sci. officer, 1956-59, chief sci. officer, 1959-62; prof., dir. astronomy U. Md., 1962-73, chmn. div. math. and phys. scis. and engring., 1972-73, prof. astronomy, 1973-77; sci. dir. U.S. Naval Observatory, Washington, 1977-93; vis. astronomer Max Planck Inst. Radio Astronomy, Bonn, Germany, 1973-74, mem. adv. bd., 1976-79; vice chmn. divsn. phys. sci. NRC, 1969-73; mem. com. on radio frequencies, 1971-92; trustee Assoc. Univs. Inc., 1971-74; mem. Intern Union Commn. on Allocation of Frequencies, 1974-82; mem. sci. coun. Stellar Data Ctr., Strasbourg, France, 1978-84, chmn., 1981; chmn. working group on astrometry, astronomy survey com. NAS, 1979-81; mem. adv. bd. Haystac-N.E. Radio Obs. Consortium, 1974-77; mem. Arecibo adv. bd. Nat. Astronomy and Ionosphere Ctr., 1977-80, chmn., 1979-80. Contbr. on radio astronomy, spiral structure of our galaxy and astrometry to profl. jours. Recipient citation for teaching excellence Washington Acad. Scis., 1972; U.S. Sr. Scientist award Alexander von Humboldt Stiftung, Ger., 1973; NATO fellow, 1959. Mem. Internat. Astron. Union (chmn. working group on astron. data 1985-91), Internat. Sci. Radio Union (pres. commn. on radio astronomy 1975-78), Am. Astron. Soc. (councilor 1975-78, v.p. 1985-87), Royal Astron. Soc. Roman Catholic. Home: 811 W 38th St Baltimore MD 21211-2203

WESTERMAN, ROSEMARY MATZZIE, nurse, administrator; b. Sewickley, Pa., May 20, 1949; d. Joseph Edward and Martha (Aquino) Matzzie; m. Philip M. Westerman, Aug. 7, 1971. BSN, Duquesne U., 1971, MSEd, 1975. RN, Pa. Head nurse Dept. Vet. Affairs VA Med. Ctr., Pitts.; assoc. chief, nursing svc., edn. W. S. Middleton Meml. VA Hosp., Madison, Wis.; assoc. chief, nursing svc., edn. Dept. VA Affairs VA Med. Ctr., Chilicothe, assoc. chief nursing svc., long term. care; assoc. chief nurse VA Med. Ctr., Augusta, Ga.; chief nurse VA Med. Ctr., Muskogee, Okla. Active Literacy Vol. of Am. Mem. ANA (cert. nursing adminstrn. advanced), Assoc. Am. Coll. Health Care Execs., Okla. Orgn. Nurse Execs., Okla. Nurses Found., Nursing Orgn. of VA, Okla. Nurses Assn., VA Nurse Execs., Sigma Theta Tau. Home: 1409 E Concord St Broken Arrow OK 74012-9259

WESTERN, KARL AUGUST, physician, epidemiologist; b. Trenton, N.J., July 6, 1940; s. August Earl and Lillian Theresa (Murphy) W.; m. Aileen Martin Worthington, May 2, 1964; children: Ann Worthington, Mark August. AB, Georgetown U., 1961, MD, 1965; diploma of tropical pub. health, London Sch. Tropical Medicine & Hygiene, 1972. Intern Bellevue Hosp.-Cornell Meml.-Sloan Kettering Joint Program, N.Y.C., 1965-66, resident, 1966-67; medical epidemiologist Ctr. Disease Control, Atlanta, 1967-70; resident supr. infectious diseases L.A. County-USC Med. Ctr., 1971-72; medical epidemiologist Va. State Health Dept., Richmond, 1972-74; dept. head Pan Am. Health Orgn., Washington, 1975-79; asst. dir. Nat. Inst. Allergy & Infectious Diseases, Bethesda, Md., 1979—; adj. assoc. prof. Uniformed Services U. Health Scis., Bethesda, 1981—, Tulane U., New Orleans, 1986—. Served as med. dir. USPHS, 1967—. Recipient Okeke award U. London, 1972, Meritorious Service award, 1970, Commendation award, 1983, Outstand. Service award, 1987, USPHS. Mem. AMA, Am. Soc. Tropical Medicine & Hygiene (editor Tropical Med. news, 1987—), Am. Pub. Health Assn. (sec. epidemiology sect. 1973-78), Nat. Council Internat. Health (chair annual meeting 1986). Republican. Roman Catholic. Home: 6436 31st St NW Washington DC 20015-2342 Office: Nat Inst Allergy Infectious Diseases/NIH 9000 Rockville Pike Bethesda MD 20814-1436

WESTERVELT, JAMES JOSEPH, insurance company executive; b. Bklyn., July 8, 1946; s. Cornealius V. and Regina Elizabeth (May) W.; m. Sue Jane Brubaker, Aug. 5, 1972; children: Kevin K., Natalie M. BBA, Manhattan Coll., 1967. Mgr. auditing Peat, Marwick & Mitchell, N.Y.C., 1967-78; dir. auditing City Investing, N.Y.C., 1978-81; asst. v.p., asst. contr. The Hartford Financial Svcs. Group, Inc., Conn., 1981-89, v.p., group contr., 1989-94; sr. v.p., group contr. The Hartford Financial Svcs. Group, Inc., Hartford, Conn., 1994—. With U.S. Army, 1968-69. Mem. AICPA, Hawaii Soc. CPAs, Conn. Soc. CPAs, Am. Ins. Assn. Roman Catholic. Avocations: skiing, wine tasting, tennis, chess, electronics. Office: Hartford Fire Insurance Co Hartford Plz Hartford CT 06115

WESTERVELT, PETER JOCELYN, physics educator; b. Albany, N.Y., Dec. 16, 1919; s. William Irving and Dorothy (Jocelyn) W.; m. Alice Francis Brown, June 2, 1956; children: Dirck Edgell, Abby Brown. B.S., MIT, 1947, M.S., 1949, Ph.D., 1951. Mem. staff radiation lab. MIT, 1940-41, underwater sound lab., 1941-45, asst. in physics, 1946-47, rsch. assoc., 1948-50; asst. prof. physics Brown U., 1951-58, assoc. prof., 1958-63, prof., 1963-90, prof. emeritus, 1990—; mem. subcom. aircraft noise NASA, 1954-59; mem. com. hearing and bio-acoustics NRC, 1957-83, exec. council, 1960-61, 78-83, chmn., 1967-68, 80-83; mem. sonic boom com. Nat. Acad. Sci., 1968-71; mem. R.I. Atomic Energy Commn., 1968-73; cons. applied research lab. U. Tex., Austin, 1973-83. Recipient Rayleigh medal Inst. Acoustics U.K., 1985. Fellow Am. Physics Soc., Acoustical Soc. Am. Home: 16 John St Providence RI 02906-1008 Office: Brown U Dept Physics Providence RI 02912

WESTFALL, CARROLL WILLIAM, architectural historian; b. Fresno, Calif., Dec. 23, 1937; s. Carroll W. and Alice Margaret (DeVore) W.; m. Cheryl Ludwig, June 6, 1964 (div. 1971); m. Relling Rossi, June 26, 1982; children: Nicholas William, John Salvatore. BA, U. Calif., Berkeley, 1961; MArch, U. Manchester, Eng., 1963; PhD, Columbia U., 1967. Asst. prof. Amherst (Mass.) Coll., 1966-72; asst. prof. U. Ill., Chgo., 1972-75, assoc. prof., 1975-82; assoc. prof. U. Va., Charlottesville, 1982-88, prof. archtl. history, 1988—, chmn. dept., 1983-89; cons. in field. Author: In This Most Perfect Paradise, 1974, Italian edit., 1984, (with Robert Jan van Pelt) Architectural Principles in the Age of Historicism, 1991; contbr. articles to profl. jours. Bd. dirs. Landmarks Preservation Coun., Chgo., 1973-82, pres., 1974-76. Mem. Soc. Archtl. Historians, Coll. Art Assn., Nat. Trust Historic Preservation, Cliffdwellers (Chgo.), Congress for the New Urbanism. Republican. Avocation: travel. Home: 1 Cottage Ln Charlottesville VA 22903 Office: Univ Va Sch Architecture Charlottesville VA 22903

WESTFALL, DAVID, lawyer, educator; b. Columbia, Mo., Apr. 16, 1927; s. Wilhelmus David A. and Ruth (Rollins) W.; children: Elizabeth Stewart, William Beatty, Thomas Curwen, Katharine Putnam. AB, U. Mo., 1947; LLB magna cum laude, Harvard U., 1950. Bar: Ill. 1950, Mass. 1956. Assoc. Bell, Boyd, Marshall & Lloyd, Chgo., 1950-55; asst. prof. law Harvard Law Sch., 1955-58, prof., 1958—, John L. Gray prof., 1983—, Carl F. Schipper Jr. prof., 1996—. Author: Estate Planning Cases and Text, 1985, Every Woman's Guide to Financial Planning, 1984, Family Law, 1993; co-author: Estate Planning Law and Taxation, 3rd edit., 1994; co-editor: Readings in Federal Taxation, 1983. Served as 1st lt. JAGC, AUS, 1951-53. Fellow Am. Coll. Trust and Estate Counsel (acad.); mem. ABA, Mass. Bar Assn., Am. Law Inst., Phi Beta Kappa, Phi Delta Theta. Home: Unit 801 199 Coolidge Ave Watertown MA 02172 Office: Law Sch Harvard U Cambridge MA 02138

WESTFALL, MORRIS, state legislator; b. Apr. 5, 1939; s. Raymond Earl and Ethel Faye (Neill) W.; m. Sharon Kay Douglas, Dec. 19, 1964; children: Craig Lin, Christi Dawn. BS, U. Mo., 1962. Rep. State of Mo., 1971-81; asst. minority floor leader, minority whip Mo. Ho. of Reps., 1995—; senator dist. 28 State of Mo.; state exec. dir. agrl. stabilization conservation svc. USDA, Mo., 1981-93. Bd. dirs. Polk County Fair, 1967-71, Polk Soil and Water, 1970-71. Mem. Mo. Vocation Assn., U. Mo. Alumni Assn., Saddle Club. Office: State Capitol Building Jefferson City MO 65101-1556

WESTFALL, STEPHEN DONALD, accountant, small business owner; b. Moscow, Idaho, Sept. 20, 1953; s. Donald Eugene and Elizabeth Ann (Morgan) W.; m. Joyce Beck, Aug. 29, 1976; children: Erin Kay, Corey Stephen. BS, U. Idaho, 1975. CPA, Idaho. Ptnr. Westfall & Westfall, C.P.A's, Burley, Idaho, 1975—; bd. dirs. Cassia Meml. Hosp. and Med. Ctr., Burley, 1983—, vice-chmn. 1994-96, chmn., 1996—; bd. dirs. First Fed. Savings Bank, Twin Fall, Idaho, 1992—; bd. dirs., pres. Burle Racquet and Health Corp., 1982—; bd. dirs., treas. Burley Regatta, Inc., Craters of the Moon Devel.; bd. dirs. ARC Mini Cossia chpt. 1994-96. Mem. AICPA, Idaho Soc. CPAs, Burley Area C. of C. (bd. dirs. 1986-91, pres. 1989), Elks Club. Republican. Presbyterian. Avocations: golf, racquetball, biking, travel. Home: 17 Granada Pl Burley ID 83318-2703 Office: Westfall & Westfall CPAs 1329 Albion Ave Burley ID 83318-1817

WESTFIELD, FRED M., economics educator; b. Essen, Germany, Nov. 7, 1926; came to U.S., 1940; s. Dietrich and Grete (Stern) W.; m. Joyce A. Horwitz Nochlin, Nov. 15, 1968; stepchildren: Steven Nochlin, Keith Nochlin. BA magna cum laude, Vanderbilt U., 1950; PhD in Indsl. Econs., MIT, 1957. Teaching asst., instr. MIT, Cambridge, 1952-53; lectr. Northwestern U., Evanston, Ill., 1953-57, asst. prof., 1957-60, assoc. prof., 1960-65; prof. econs. Vanderbilt U., Nashville, 1965—, mem. faculty coun. Coll. Arts and Sci., 1974-76, mem. faculty senate, 1979-82, 94-95, dir. undergrad. studies dept. econs. and bus. adminstrn., 1984-87, mem. grad. faculty coun., 1991; vis. prof. U. Colo., summers 1973-74; condr. seminars, lectr., participant univs. and rsch. orgns.; Fulbright sr. lectr. U. Nac. del Sur, Argentina, 1986; cons. Coun. Econ. Advisers, Exec. Office Pres., 1968, World Bank and Water and Power Devel. Authority, Pakistan, 1970-72, World Bank and East African Power and Light Co., Kenya, 1975, NSF, 1975, FTC, 1976-78, World Bank, UN Devel. Program and Econ. Planning Bd. South Korea, 1975-76; expert witness Tenn. Pub. Svc. Commn., 1980-89, Consumer Advocate Tenn. Atty. Gen., 1994; also others. Mem. editorial bd. Utilities Policy, 1990—; mem. bd. editors So. Econ. Jour., 1973-75; editorial referee Am. Econ. Rev., Jour. Polit. Economy, Econometrica, So. Econ. Jour., Econ. Inquiry; contbr. articles and book revs. to profl. jours. With U.S. Army, 1945-46. Fellow Gen. Edn. Bd., MIT, Ford Found., 1958-59. Mem. Am. Econ. Assn., Econometric Soc. (program com. 1967, chmn. conf. sessions), So. Econ. Assn. (v.p. 1976-77, chmn. conf. sessions), Phi Beta Kappa. Home: 1097 Lynnwood Blvd Nashville TN 37215-4540 Office: Vanderbilt U PO Box 1681 Sta B Nashville TN 37235

WESTHAVER, LAWRENCE ALBERT, electronics engineer, consultant; b. Washington, Oct. 24, 1936; s. James Waldo and Hattie Virginia (Bush) W.; m. Jo Ann Turner, Jan. 5, 1957; children: Lawrence Albert Jr., Wendy Jo Westhaver Burke, Bonnie Jo. Cert. engring., U. Va., 1966. Electronic design, cons. Westhaver Assocs., Inc., Laurel, Md., 1971—; engring. draftsman Office Rsch. and Devel. Nat. Security Agy., Arlington Hall, Va., 1955-57; engring. technician Office Rsch. and Engring. Nat. Security Agy., Ft. G.G. Meade, Md., 1958-66, electronic engr. Office Rsch. and Engring., 1967-82, sr. engr. Office of Rsch. and Engring., 1982-84; sr. engr. Communications Systems Support Group, Laurel, Md., 1984-93. Patentee method for photographic aperture control, photographic light integrator, switching current regulator, photographic test equipment, electronic tuner for stringed musical instruments, microcomputer-based Ni-Cd battery charger, and color-correcting filter for underwater photography. Avocations: scuba diving, snorkeling, biking, hiking, bird watching. Home: 8609 Portsmouth Dr Laurel MD 20708-1819

WESTHEIMER, DAVID KAPLAN, novelist; b. Houston, Apr. 11, 1917; s. Adolf and Esther (Kaplan) W.; m. Doris Gertrude Rothstein, Oct. 9, 1945; children: Fred, Eric. B.A., Rice Inst., Houston, 1937. Successively asst. amusement editor, radio editor, mag. editor, TV editor Houston Post, 1939-41, 45-46, 50, 53-60, columnist, 1984-88. Author: Summer on the Water, 1948, The Magic Fallacy, 1950, Watching Out for Dulie, 1960, Von Ryan's Express, 1964, My Sweet Charlie, 1965, Song of the Young Sentry, 1968, Lighter Than a Feather, 1971, Over the Edge, 1972, Going Public, 1973, Tha Avila Gold, 1974, The Olmec Head, 1974, Rider on the Wind, 1979, Von Ryan's Return, 1980, (with John Sherlock) The Amindra Gamble, 1982, Sitting It Out, 1992, Death Is Lighter Than a Feather, 1995, (with Karen Westheimer) LoneStar Zodiac, 1995, (play) My Sweet Charlie, 1966, (TV films) Trouble Comes to Town, 1972, A Killer Among Us, 1990. Served to capt. USAAF, 1941-45, ETO; served to capt. USAF, 1950-53; lt. col. USAF; ret. Decorated Air medal, D.F.C. Mem. ACLU, NAACP, PEN, Writer's Guild Am. West. Author's Guild, Ret. Officer Assn., Calif. Writers Club. Democrat. Avocation: travel. Home and Office: 11722 Darlington Ave Apt 2 Los Angeles CA 90049-5525

WESTHEIMER, FRANK HENRY, chemist, educator; b. Balt., Jan. 15, 1912; s. Henry Ferdinand and Carrie (Burgunder) W.; m. Jeanne Friedmann, Aug. 31, 1937; children: Ruth Susan, Ellen. AB, Dartmouth Coll., 1932, ScD (hon.), 1961; MA, Harvard U., 1933, PhD, 1935; ScD (hon.), U. Chgo., 1973, U. Cin., 1976, Tufts U., 1978, U. N.C., 1983, Bard Coll., 1983, Weizmann Inst., 1987, U. Ill. at Chgo., 1988. Rsch. assoc. U. Chgo., 1936-37, instr., 1937-41, asst. prof., 1941-44, assoc. prof., 1946-48, prof. chemistry, 1948-53; vis. prof. Harvard U., 1953-54, prof. chemistry, 1954-82, sr. prof., 1982-83, prof. emeritus, 1983—, chmn. dept., 1959-62; Overseas fellow Churchill Coll., U. Cambridge, Eng., 1962-63; mem. Pres.'s Sci. Adv. Com.,

1967-70; research supr. Explosives Research Lab., Nat. Def. Research Com., 1944-45; chmn. com. survey chemistry Nat. Acad. Scis., 1964-65. Assoc. editor Jour. Chem. Physics, 1942-44, 52-54; editorial bd. Jour. Am. Chem. Soc. 1960-69, Procs. Nat. Acad. Scis., 1983-89; contbr. articles to profl. jours. Recipient Naval Ordnance Development award, 1946, Army-Navy cert. of appreciation, 1946, James Flack Norris award in phys.-organic chemistry, 1970, Willard Gibbs medal, 1970, Theodore W. Richards medal, 1976; award in chem. scis. Nat. Acad. Sci., 1980, Richard Kokes award, 1980, Charles Frederick Chandler medal, 1980, Rosenstiel award, 1981, Nichols medal, 1982, Robert A. Welch award, 1982, Ingold medal, 1983, Cope award, 1982, Nat. Medal of Sci., 1986, Paracelsus medal, 1988, Priestley medal, 1988, Repligen award, 1992, Nakanishi award, 1997; fellow Columbia U. NRC, 1935-36, Guggenheim Found., 1962-63, Fulbright-Hays Found., 1974, NAS Exch. fellow, China, 1982, Japan Soc. Promotion of Sci., 1982. Mem. Nat. Acad. Sci. (council 1971-75, 76-79), Am. Philos. Soc. (council 1981-84), Am. Acad. Arts and Scis. (sec. 1985-90), Royal Soc. (fgn. mem.). Home: 3 Berkeley St Cambridge MA 02138-3409

WESTHEIMER, GERALD, optometrist, educator; b. Berlin, Germany, May 13, 1924; naturalized, 1944, came to U.S., 1951; s. Isaak and Ilse (Cohn) W. Optometry diploma, Sydney (Australia) Tech. Coll., 1943, fellowship diploma, 1950; BSc, U. Sydney, 1947; PhD, Ohio State U., 1953; DSc (hon.), U. NSW, Australia, 1988; ScD (hon.), SUNY, 1990. Practice optometry Sydney, 1945-51; research fellow Ohio State U., 1951-53; prof. physiol. optics U. Houston, 1953-54; asst. prof., then assoc. prof. physiol. optics Ohio State U., 1954-60; postdoctoral fellow neurophysiology Marine Biol. Lab., Woods Hole, Mass., 1957; vis. researcher Physiol. Lab., U. Cambridge, Eng., 1958-59; mem. faculty U. Calif. at Berkeley, 1960—, prof. physiol. optics, 1963-68, chmn. group physiol. optics, 1964-67, prof. physiology, 1968-89, prof. neurobiology, 1989—, head div. neurobiology, 1987-92; adj. prof. Rockefeller U., N.Y., 1992—; Sackler lectr. Tel Aviv U. Med. Sch., 1988, D.O. Hebb lectr. McGill U., 1991, Grass Found. lectr. U. Ill., 1991; mem. com. vision NRC, 1957-72; mem. visual scis. study sect. NIH, 1966-70, chmn. visual scis. B study sect., 1977-79; mem. vision, research and tng. com. Nat. Eye Inst., NIH, 1970-74, chmn. bd. sci. counselors, 1981-83; mem. exec. council com. vision NAS-NRC, 1969-72; mem. communicative scis. cluster Pres.'s Biomed. Rsch. Panel, 1975. Author rsch. papers; editor: Vision Rsch., 1972-79; editl. bd. Investigative Ophthalmology, 1973-77, Exptl. Brain Rsch., 1973-89, Optics Letters, 1977-78, Spatial Vision, 1985—, Ophthalmic and Physiological Optics, 1985—, Vision Rsch., 1985-92, Jour. of Physiology, 1987-94; editor: procs. of Royal Soc. London, 1990-96. Recipient Von Sallman prize Columbia U., 1986; Prentice medal Am. Acad. Optometry, 1986, Bicentennial medal Australian Optometric Assn., 1988. Fellow AAAS, Royal Soc. London (Ferrier lectr. 1992), Am. Acad. Arts and Scis., Optical Soc. Am. (Tillyer medal 1978, assoc. editor jour. 1980-83), Am. Acad. Optometry; mem. Royal Soc. New So. Wales, Soc. Neurosci., Assn. Rsch. in Vision and Ophthalmology (Proctor medal 1979), Internat. Brain Rsch. Orgn., Physiol. Soc. Gt. Britain, Sigma Xi. Home: 582 Santa Barbara Rd Berkeley CA 94707-1746

WESTIN, ALAN FURMAN, political science educator; b. N.Y.C, Nov. 11, 1929; s. Irving and Etta (Furman) W.; m. Beatrice Patricia Shapoff, June 20, 1954; children: David, Debra, Jeremy, Carla. BA, U. Fla., 1948; LLB, Harvard U., 1951; PhD tchg. fellow, 1965. Bar: D.C. 1951. Sr. fellow Yale U. Law Sch., New Haven, 1956-57, vis. prof. polit. sci., 1960-61; asst. prof. govt. Cornell U., Ithaca, N.Y., 1957-59; assoc. prof. pub. law and govt. Columbia U., N.Y.C., 1959-66; prof. Columbia U., 1966-96; dir. Ctr. Rsch. and Edn. in Am. Liberties, 1965-71; founder, pres. Ednl. Fund Individual Rights, N.Y.C., 1978-86; pres. Changing Workplaces, Englewood, N.J., 1982-87; program assoc. Harvard U., 1968-72; cons. IBM, 1973-75, U.S. Office Tech. Assessment, 1973—; pres. Ctr. Social and Legal Rsch., 1987—, Ref. Point Found., 1987—; ptnr. Privacy and Legis. Assocs., Washington, 1993—; chmn., CEO Toolkit Software, 1996—; cons. on privacy to Equifax, Citicorp, IBM, Am. Express, U.S. Social Security Adminstrn., Chrysler, Health Data Exch., N.Y. State Identification and Intelligence Sys., Bell Atlantic, Glaxo Wellcome, Eli Lilly; cons. on employee rights Fed. Express, Aetna Life and Casualty, Citicorp, IBM, 1980-86; acad. advisor nat. pub. surveys on privacy Louis Harris and Assocs., 1979, 90, 91, 92, 93, 94, 95, 96, nat. pub. surveys on cons. privacy, Can., 1992, 94; dir. privacy and human genome project U.S. Dept. Energy, 1992-95; chmn. emm. adv. panels U.S. Office Tech. Assessment, 1975-92; chmn. Res. Coun. Healthy Cos., 1991-95; spkr. nat. bus., profl., govt. confs., 1960—. Author: The Anatomy of a Constitutional Law Case, 1958, reprinted, 1990 (put in Notable Trials Libr. 1995), Privacy and Freedom, 1967 (George Polk award, Sidney Hillman award, Melcher award, Van Am. Soc. award 1967), (with Barry Mahoney) The Trial of Martin Luther King, 1975, (with Michael A. Baker) Databanks in a Free Society, 1972; editor: Whistle Blowing! Loyalty an Dissent in the Corporation, 1980, Information technology in a Democracy, 1971 (with Alfred Feliu) Resolving Employment Disputes Without Litigation, 1988, (with John D. Aram) Managerial Delemmas: Cases in Social, Legal, and Technological Change, 1988; editor-in-chief: The Civil Liberties Rev., 1973-79; polit. sci. editor: Casebook Series, 1960-66; contbr. numerous chpts. to books, articles to legal and popular publs.; mem. editl. bd. Employee Rights and Responsibilities Jour., Information Age, Jour. Computing and Society, Transnational Data Report: writer-narrator: CBS-TV Series, The Road to the White House, 1964; cons. spl. programs: ABC-TV; advisor Off Limits: Your Health, Your Job, Your Privacy, PBS Network, 1994; pub. editor-in-chief Privacy and American Business, 1993—. Mem. Nat. Wiretapping Commn., 1973-76; vice-chmn. N.J. Commn. Individual Liberty, 1977-81; sr. cons. U.S. Privacy Protection Study Commn., 1975-77. Recipient Mark Van Doren award Columbia U., 1972; recipient Disting. Alumnus award Delta Sigma Rho-Tau-Kappa Alpha, 1965; grantee Rockefeller Found., 1983, Russell Saga Found., 1969-71, 81-82. Mem. Nat. Acad. Scis. (computer sci. and engring. bd. 1969-72), Am. Polit. Sci. Assn., Assn. Computing Machinery (chmn. task force privacy 1972-73). Home: 1100 Trafalgar St Teaneck NJ 07666-1928 Office: Polit Sci Dept Coll U 118th St And Amsterdam Ave New York NY 10027 also: Ref Pt & Ctr Social Legal Rsch 2 University Plaza Dr Ste 414 Hackensack NJ 07601-6202 *As fast as technological and social changes are in our age, the enduring matters are how we try to live our personal lives, how we relate to the people we work with, and how strongly we support civility and democratic values in our communities and nation.*

WESTIN, DAVID, broadcast executive. Pres. ABC TV Network, N.Y.C. Office: ABC TV Network 77 W 66th St New York NY 10023-6201

WESTIN, DAVID LAWRENCE, lawyer; b. Flint, Mich., July 29, 1952; s. Lawrence Rae and Mary Louise (Holman) W.; m. Victoria Peters; children: Victoria, Elizabeth, Matthew. BA, U. Mich., 1974, JD, 1977. Bar: D.C. 1979. Law clk. U.S. Ct. Appeals (2d cir.), N.Y.C., 1977-78, U.S. Supreme Ct., Washington, 1979; assoc. Wilmer, Cutler & Pickering, Washington, 1979-84, ptnr., 1985-91; sr. v.p., gen. counsel Capital Cities/ABC, Inc., N.Y.C., 1991-93; pres. of prodn. ABC TV Network, N.Y.C., 1993-94, pres., 1994—; lectr. Harvard U. Law Sch., Cambridge, Mass., 1986; adj. prof. Georgetown U. Law Ctr., Washington, 1989-91. Bd. dirs. Lincoln Ctr. Film. Soc., 1994—, Am. Arbitration Assn., 1991—. Democrat. Presbyterian. Club: Chevy Chase (Md.). Home: 1717 Desales St NW Washington DC 20036-4401 Office: ABC TV Network 77 W 66th St New York NY 10023-6201

WESTLAKE, ROBERT ELMER, SR., physician; b. Jersey City, Oct. 2, 1918; s. Henry Ebenezer and Bertha (Fowle) W.; m. Agnes Vivian Kumpf, Oct. 1, 1944; children—Robert Elmer, Barbara Elizabeth, Richard Louis. Grad., Lawrenceville Sch., 1936; A.B., Princeton, 1940; M.D., Columbia, 1943. Diplomate: Am. Bd. Internal Medicine. Intern Englewood (N.J.) Hosp., 1944, 46-47; resident Univ. Hosp., Syracuse, N.Y., 1947-49; instr. medicine State U. N.Y. Med. Center, Syracuse, 1949-50; asst. prof. State U. N.Y. Med. Center, 1950-52, clin. asso. prof., 1956-67, clin. prof., 1967-81, clin. prof. emeritus, 1981—; pvt. practice internal medicine Syracuse, 1952-81; mem. staff State Univ., Crouse-Irving-Meml. VA hosps.; dir. profl. services Community Gen. Hosp., 1967-81; cons. USPHS, 1966-72, Social Security Adminstrn., 1968-71; mem. Com. Rev. Regional Med. Programs, NIH, 1966-67; med. adv. council Dept. Def., 1969-74; pres. Profl. Standards Rev. Orgn. Central N.Y., 1974-77. Contbr. articles to profl. jours. Pres. Onondaga Found. Med. Care, 1961-68; v.p. Blue Shield Central N.Y., 1965-73, chmn. bd., 1973-81. Served to lt. (j.g.) M.C. USNR, 1944-46. Fellow A.C.P.; mem. Am. Soc. Internal Medicine (pres. 1965-66), Onondaga County Heart Assn. (pres. 1963-64). Home: 5056 SE Bent Wood Dr Stuart FL 34997-1603

WESTLEY, JOHN RICHARD, foreign service officer; b. Fairmont, Minn., Feb. 25, 1939; s. Richard and Margaret (Kindschi) W.; m. Sidney Kathryn Bohanna, Mar. 26, 1966(div. Sept. 1977); children: Elizabeth Laura, Karen Margaret, Marian Bohanna; m. Joan Nancy Ehrlich, Apr. 12, 1980; 1 child, Katherine Matthea. BA in Philosophy, Yale U., 1961; MA in Econs., Columbia U., 1966; PhD in Econs., Am. Univ., 1983. Internat. economist U.S. Dept. Treasury, Washington, 1966-69; loan officer U.S. AID, Addis Ababa, Ethiopia, 1970-72; economist U.S. AID, Nairobi, Kenya, 1973-75, Washington, 1976-78; program officer U.S. AID, New Delhi, India, 1979-84; dir. mission to Bangladesh U.S. AID, Dhaka, 1985-87; assoc. asst. adminstr. bur. Africa U.S. AID, Washington, 1987-90; dir. mission to Kenya U.S. AID, Nairobi, 1990-94; dir. Mission to Egypt US AID, Cairo, 1994—. Author: Agriculture and Equitable Growth, 1986. With U.S. Army, 1961-64. Mem. Am. Econ. Assn., Soc. for Internat. Devel., Phi Beta Kappa. Presbyterian. Home and Office: Unit 64902 APO AE 09839-4902

WESTLING, JON, university administrator; b. Yakima, Wash., June 7, 1942; s. Norman L. and Jean R. (Bergamini) W.; m. Elizabeth A. Wüthrich, Oct. 14, 1977; children: Emma E., Matthew R., Andrew N. BA, Reed Coll., 1964; postgrad., St. John's Coll. Oxford (Eng.) U., 1964-67, UCLA, 1971-74. Instr. history Centre Coll., Danville, Ky., 1967-68; asst. prof. history and humanities Reed Coll., Portland, Oreg., 1968-71; assoc. dir. Boston Univ. Prodns., 1974-76; asst. to pres. Boston U., 1976-79, assoc. provost, 1979-83, provost ad interim, 1983-84, provost, 1984-88, exec. v.p., 1988-90, interim pres., 1990, exec. v.p., provost, 1991-95, provost, pres.-elect, 1995-96, pres., 1996—; bd. dirs. Century Bank. Bd. dirs. Mass. Corp. for Ednl. Telecomms., 1990—; trustee Boston Mus. Sci., 1990—, WGBH Ednl. Found., 1996—. Gen. Motors Nat. scholar, 1960-64, Rhodes scholar, 1964-67. Home: 135 Ivy St Brookline MA 02146 Office: Boston U Office Pres 147 Bay State Rd Boston MA 02215-1708

WESTMAN, CARL EDWARD, lawyer; b. Youngstown, Ohio, Dec. 12, 1943; s. Carl H. and Mary Lillis (Powell) W.; m. Carolyn J., July 17, 1965; children: C. Forrest, Stephanie A. BBA, Sam Houston State U., 1966; JD, U. Miami, 1969, LLM in Taxation, 1972. Bar: Fla. 1969. Ptnr. Frost & Jacobs, 1983-93, Roetzel & Andress, Naples, Fla., 1993—. S.W. Fla. coun. Boy Scouts Am. Eagle Bd. of Review, 1987—; trustee David Lawrence Found. for Mental Health, Inc., 1976-86, chmn. 1985-86; trustee Pikeville Coll., 1993—, Naples Cmty. Hosp., 1992—, Comty. Health Care, Inc. (NCH Healthcare Sys.), 1996—; past pres. bd. trustees, elder Moorings Presbyn. Ch. Mem. ABA, Fla. Bar, Collier County Bar Assn., Estate Planning Coun, Coral Reef Yacht Club, Useppa Island Club. Home: 1952 Crayton Rd Naples FL 34102-5070 Office: Roetzel & Andress 850 Park Shore Dr Naples FL 34103-3587

WESTMAN, JACK CONRAD, child psychiatrist, educator; b. Cadillac, Mich., Oct. 28, 1927; s. Conrad A. and Alice (Pedersen) W.; m. Nancy K. Baehre, July 17, 1953; children—Daniel P., John C., Eric C. M.D., U. Mich., 1952. Diplomate: Am. Bd. Psychiatry and Neurology. Intern Duke Hosp., Durham, N.C., 1952-53; resident U. Mich. Med. Center, 1955-59; dir. Outpatient Services, Children's Psychiatric Hosp., Ann Arbor, Mich., 1961-65; assoc. prof. U. Mich. Med. Sch., 1964-65; coordinator Diagnostic and Treatment Unit, Waisman Center, U. Wis., Madison, 1966-74; prof. psychiatry, 1965—; cons. Joint Commn. on Mental Health of Children, 1967-69, Madison (Wis.) Pub. Schs., 1965-74, Children's Treatment Center, Mendota Mental Health Inst., 1965-69. Author: Individual Differences in Children, 1973, Child Advocacy, 1979, Handbook of Learning Disabilities, 1990, Who Speaks for the Children?, 1991, Licensing Parents, 1994; editor: Child Psychiatry and Human Development; contbr. articles to profl. jours. Vice-pres. Big Bros. of Dane County, 1970-73; v.p. Wis. Assn. Mental Health, 1968-72; co-chmn. Project Understanding, 1968-75. Served with USNR, 1953-55. Fellow Am. Psychiat. Assn., Am. Coll. Psychiatrists, Am. Acad. Child and Adolescent Psychiatry, Am. Orthopsychiat. Assn. (bd. dirs. 1973-76); mem. Am. Assn. Psychiat. Svcs. for Children (pres. 1978-80), Multidisciplinary Acad. Clin. Edn. (pres. 1992—). Home: 1234 Dartmouth Rd Madison WI 53705-2214 Office: 600 Highland Ave Madison WI 53792-0001

WESTMORE, MICHAEL GEORGE, make-up artist; b. Hollywood, Calif., Mar. 22, 1938; s. Montague George and Edith Adeline W.; m. Marion Christine Bergeson, Dec. 4, 1966; children: Michael George, Michele, McKenzie. BA, U. Calif., Santa Barbara, 1961. Apprentice make-up artist Universal City Studios, Universal City, Calif., 1961-63, staff make-up artist, 1964, asst. head dept. make-up lab., 1965-71; freelance make-up artist various studios, Hollywood, Calif., 1971-87; make-up supr. and designer Paramount Studios, Hollywood, 1987—; instr. theatre arts dept. Los Angeles Valley Coll., 1966-71; pres. Cosmetic Control Ctrs., Inc., 1971-76; pres. Hollywood Magic Cosmetics, 1985-87; rsch. cons., lectr. therapeutic cosmetics for med. assns. Author: The Art of Theatrical Make-Up for Stage and Screen, 1971, also chpts. in books; co-author: Star Trek Makeup FX Journal; make-up artist for TV spls. Eleanor and Franklin (emmy award NATAS 1976), Why Me? (Emmy award 1984), Three Wishes of Billy Grier (Emmy award 1985), Star Trek (Emmy award 1988, 92, 93, 95, 96), Amazing Stories (Emmy award 1987), (films) 2010 (Acad. award nomination Acad. Motion Picture Arts and Scis. 1985), Mask (Acad. award 1986), Clan of the Cave Bear (Acad. award nomination 1987), Star Trek First Contact (Acad. award nomination 1996). Served with AUS, 1956. Mem. Internat. Alliance Theatrical Stage Employees, Soc. Make-up Artists, Vikings of Scandia, Lambda Chi Alpha (life). Address: 4616 Balboa Ave Encino CA 91316

WESTMORELAND, BARBARA FENN, neurologist, electroencephalographer, educator; b. N.Y.C., July 22, 1940; d. Robert Edward and Wanda Helen (Zabawski) Westmoreland. BS in Chemistry, Mary Washington Coll., 1961; MD, U. Va., 1965. Diplomate Am. Bd. Psychiatry and Neurology and certification of added qualification in clin. neurophysiology. Intern Vanderbilt Hosp., Nashville, 1965-66; resident in neurology U. Va. Hosp., Charlottesville, 1966-70; fellow in electroencephalography Mayo Clinic, Rochester, Minn., 1970-71, assoc. cons. neurology, 1971-73; asst. prof. neurology Mayo Med. Sch., Rochester, 1973-78, assoc. prof., 1978-85, prof., 1985—. Co-author: Medical Neurosciences, 1978, rev. edit., 1986, first author 3d edit., 1994. Mem. Am. Epilepsy Soc. (treas. 1978-80, pres. 1987-88), Am. EEG Soc. (sec. 1985-87, pres. 1991-92), Cen. Assn. Electroencephalographers (sec.-treas. 1976-78, pres. 1979-80, chair neurology resident in-svc. tng. exam 1994—), Mayo History of Medicine Soc. (pres. 1990-91), Sigma Xi (pres. chpt. 1987-88).

WESTMORELAND, THOMAS DELBERT, JR., chemist; b. near Vivian, La., June 2, 1940; s. Thomas Delbert and Marguerite Beatrice (Moore) W.; BS, N. Tex. State U., 1963, MS, 1965; PhD, La. State U., 1971, postdoctoral fellow, 1971-72; m. Martha Verne Beard, Jan. 1, 1966; children: Anne Laura, Kyle Thomas. Chemistry tchr., rsch. dir. Lewisville (Tex.) H.S., 1964; summer devel. program student Tex. Instruments, Inc., Dallas, 1966; sr. exptl./analytical engr. Power Systems div. United Technologies, South Windsor, Conn., 1972-76; sr. research chemist Pennzoil Co., Shreveport, La., 1976-82, rsch. assoc., 1983-93, sr. environ. engr. Pennzoil Products Co. Tech. Ctr., The Woodlands, Tex., 1993-96, chem. cons., 1996—. Recipient E.I. du Pont tching. award La. State U., 1968-69. Mem. Am. Chem. Soc. (treas. 1978-79, chmn. 1979-80), Assn. Rsch. and Enlightenment, Soc. Automotive Engrs., Sigma Xi (sec.), Phi Eta Sigma (pres. 1959-60), Alpha Chi Sigma, Kappa Mu Epsilon. Clubs: Jaycees (state dir. Conn. 1976, gov.'s civic leadership award Conn. 1975-76, C. William Brownfield Meml. award 1976), Masons (Scottish Rite, 32d degree). Contbr. sci. articles to profl. jours; patentee in field. Home and Office: 143 Melmont Ln Conroe TX 77302-1022

WESTOFF, CHARLES FRANCIS, demographer, educator; b. N.Y.C., July 23, 1927; s. Frank Barnett and Evelyn (Bales) W.; m. Joan P. Uszynski, Sept. 11, 1948 (div. Jan. 1969); children: David, Carol; m. Leslie Aldridge, Aug. 1969 (div. Feb. 1993). AB, Syracuse U., 1949, MA, 1950; PhD, U. Pa., 1953. Instr. sociology U. Pa., 1950-52; research assoc. Milbank Meml. Fund, N.Y.C., 1952-55; research assoc. Office Population Research Princeton U., 1955-62, prof. sociology, 1962—, Maurice P. During '22 prof. demographic studies and sociology, 1972—, chmn. dept. sociology, 1965-70, assoc. dir. Office Population Research, 1962-75, dir., 1975-92; assoc. prof. sociology N.Y.U., also chmn. dept. sociology Washington Sq. Coll., 1959-62; vis. sr. fellow East-West Population Inst., Honolulu, 1979, 81; Disting. vis. prof. Am. U., Cairo, 1979; mem. vis. com. Harvard-M.I.T. Joint Center for Urban Studies, 1980-83; exec. dir. Commn. Population growth and Am. Future, 1970-72; mem. adv. com. on population stats. U.S. Bur. Census, 1973-79; chmn. Nat. Com. for Rsch. on 1980 Census, 1981-88; bd. dirs. Alan Guttmacher Inst., 1977-88, 89—; sr. tech. advisor Demographic Health Surveys, 1984—; bd. dirs. Population Resource Ctr., 1985—, Population Ref. Bur., 1988-94, Population Comms. Internat., 1992—; com. on population NAS, 1983-88. Co-author: Family Growth in Metropolitan America, 1961, The Third Child, 1963, College Women and Fertility Values, 1967, The Later Years of Childbearing, 1970, From Now to Zero, 1971, Reproduction in the United States, 1965, 71, Toward the End of Growth: Population in America, 1973, The Contraceptive Revolution, 1976, Demographic Dynamics in America, 1977, Age at Marriage, Age at First Birth and Fertility in Africa, 1992, Unmet Need: 1990-1994, 1994; contbr. articles on demography and sociology to profl. jours. Recipient Irene Taeuber award for Outstanding Contbns., 1995. Fellow Am. Sociol. Assn., Am. Acad. Arts and Scis.; mem. Inst. Medicine Nat. Acad. Sci., Planned Parenthood Fedn. Am. (dir. 1978-81), Population Assn. Am. (bd. dirs. 1960-62, 68-70, 1st v.p. 1972-73, pres. 1974-75), Internat. Union Sci. Study Population. Home: 537 Drakes Corner Rd Princeton NJ 08540-7515

WESTON, ARTHUR WALTER, chemist, scientific and business executive; b. Smith Falls, Ont. Can., Feb. 13, 1914; came to U.S., 1935, naturalized, 1952; s. Herbert W. and Alice M. (Houghton) W.; m. V. Dawn Thompson, Sept. 10, 1940; children: Roger L., Randall K., Cynthia B. BA, Queen's U., Kingston, Ont., 1934, MA, 1935; PhD, Northwestern U., 1938. Postdoctoral fellow Northwestern U., Evanston, Ill., 1938-40; with Abbott Labs., North Chgo., Ill., 1940-79, dir. rsch. and devel., 1959-61, v.p. rsch. and devel., 1961-68, dir. company, 1959-68, v.p. sci. affairs, 1968-77, v.p. corp. licensing, 1977-79; v.p., dir. San-Abbott, Japan, 1976-79; cons. Abbott Labs., North Chgo., Ill., 1979-85; pres. Arthur W. Weston & Assocs., Lake Forest, Ill., 1979—. Contbr. profl jours. and books. Patentee in field. Mem. Office Sci. Rsch. and Devel., War Manpower Commn., 1942-45; mem. exec. com. indsl. chemistry, div. chemistry and chem. tech. NRC, 1961-65; mem. indsl. panel on sci. and tech. NSF, 1974-80; mem. ad hoc com. chem. agts. Dept. Def., 1961-65. Mem. Rsch. Dirs. Assn. Chgo. (pres. 1965-66), Am. Chem. Soc. (trustee Chgo. 1965—, dir. Chgo. sect. 1952-59, nat. com. corp. assocs. 1967-72), Dirs. Indsl. Rsch., Indsl. Rsch. Inst. (bd. dirs. 1970-73), Phi Beta Kappa, Sigma Xi, Phi Lambda Upsilon. Home and Office: 349 Hilldale Pl Lake Forest IL 60045-3031

WESTON, FRANCINE EVANS, secondary education educator; b. Mt. Vernon, N.Y., Oct. 8, 1946; d. John Joseph and Frances (Fantino) Pisaniello. BA, Hunter Coll., 1968; MA, Lehman Coll., 1973; cert., Am. Acad. Dramatic Arts, N.Y.C., 1976; PhD, NYU, 1991. Cert. elem., secondary tchr., N.Y. Tchr. Yonkers (N.Y.) Bd. Edn., 1968—; aquatic dir. Woodlane Day Camp, Irvington-on-Hudson, N.Y., 1967-70, Yonkers Jewish Community Ctr., 1971-75; creative drama tchr. John Burroughs Jr. H.S., Yonkers, 1971-77; stage lighting designer Iona Summer Theatre Festival, New Rochelle, N.Y., 1980-81, Yonkers Male Glee Club, 1981-89, Roosevelt H.S., 1980—; rsch. specialist Scholarship Locating Svc., 1992-94, Yonkers Civil Def. Police Aux., 1994—; master electrician NYU Summer Mus. Theatre, 1979-80. Actress in numerous comty. theater plays including A Touch of the Poet, 1979; dir. stage prodns. including I Remember Mama, 1973, The Man Who Came to Dinner, 1975; author: A Descriptive Comparison of Computerized Stage Lighting Memory Systems With Non-Computerized Systems, 1991, (short stories) A Hat for Louise, 1984, Old Memories: Beautiful and Otherwise, 1984; lit. editor: (story and poetry collection) Beautifully Old, 1984; editor: Command Post Dispatch quar., 1997—. Steering com. chairperson Roosevelt H.S.-Middle States Assn. of Schs. and Colls. Self-Evaluation, 1985-88; mem. Yonkers Civil Def. Police Aux., 1994—, adminstrv. asst. to commanding officer, 1996—. Named Tchr. of Excellence, N.Y. State English Coun., 1990; recipient Monetary award for Teaching Excellence, Carter-Wallace Products, 1992, Educator of Excellence award N.Y. State English Coun., 1995; named to Arrid Tchrs. Honor Roll, 1992. Mem. U.S. Inst. for Theatre Tech., Nat. Coun. Tchrs. English, N.Y. State English Coun., N.Y. State United Tchrs. Assn., Westchester Coun. English Educators, Yonkers Fedn. Tchrs., Port Chester Obedience Tng. Club, Inc., Kappa Delta Pi. Republican. Roman Catholic. Avocations: swimming, target shooting, animal related activities, anything theatrical. Office: Roosevelt High Sch Tuckahoe Rd Yonkers NY 10710

WESTON, I. DONALD, architect; b. Bklyn., Feb. 16, 1928; s. Martyn N. and Betty (Lash) W.; m. Sylvia Stone, Oct. 23, 1952; children: Suzanne, Pamela. BArch, MIT, 1950; MArch, Pratt Inst., 1959, M in City and Regional Planning, 1981. Cert. Nat. Coun. Archtl. Regis. Bd.; lic. architect N.Y., Mass. Ptnr., prin. Martyn & Don Weston Architects, Bklyn., 1956—. Co-authored 2 studies for determining methods of reducing the cost of pub. housing, 1960. Mem. Mayor's Blue Ribbon Panel to Investigate the Bldg. Process in N.Y.C., 1987-88; pro bono pub. mem., sec. Cadman Plz. Co-op., Bklyn., 1972-78. Fellow AIA (mem. Bklyn. chpt. 1954—, pres. 1964-65); mem. Architects Coun. of N.Y.C. (pres. 1970-72), N.Y.C. Art Commn.; mem. Nat. Sculpture Soc. (v.p. 1990—), Fine Arts Fedn. N.Y. (v.p. 1981—, pres. 1984-87, 90-91), Art Commn. Assocs. (pres. 1991-92). Avocations: tennis, golf, community activism. Office: Martyn & Don Weston Arch 100 Remsen St Brooklyn NY 11201-4256

WESTON, JOAN SPENCER, production director, communications executive; b. Barton, Vt., Aug. 11, 1943; d. Rolfe Weston and Dorothy Lena (Spencer) Schoppe. BA magna cum laude, U. Mass., 1965. Tchr. high sch. Gorham (Maine) Schs., 1965-66; tchr. Sherwood Hall Sch., Mansfield, Eng., 1966-67; tchr. middle sch. Meden Sch., Warsop, Eng., 1967-68; dept. head high sch. Goffstown (N.H.) Schs., 1968-82; dir. circulation T.H.E. Jour., Acton, Mass., 1982-83; prodn. mgr. The Robb Report, Acton, 1983-87, prodn. dir., 1988; prodn. cons. Spencer Weston Assocs., Portland, Maine, 1988-93; prodn. dir. New Age Pub. Inc., Watertown, Mass., 1993-97, Carnegie Comms., Inc., Westford, Mass., 1996—. Mem. Boston Prodn. Mgrs. Group, Phi Beta Kappa. Avocations: travel, music, psychology, antiques. Office: Carnegie Comms 239 Littleton Rd Ste 8A Westford MA 01886-3500

WESTON, JOHN FREDERICK, business educator, consultant; b. Ft. Wayne, Ind., Feb. 6, 1916; s. David Thomas and Bertha (Schwartz) W.; children: Kenneth F., Byron L., Ellen J. B.A., U. Chgo., 1937, M.B.A., 1943, Ph.D., 1948. Instr. U. Chgo. Sch. Bus., 1940-42, asst. prof., 1947-48; prof. The Anderson Sch. UCLA, 1949—, Cordner prof. The Anderson Sch., 1981-94, prof. emeritus recalled The Anderson Sch., 1986—, dir. rsch. program in competition and bus. policy, 1969—, dir. Ctr. for Managerial Econs. and Pub. Policy, 1983-86; econ. cons. to pres. Am. Bankers Assn., 1945-46; disting. lecture series U. Okla., 1967, U. Utah, 1972, Miss. State U., 1972, Miami State U., 1975. Author: Scope and Methodology of Finance, 1966, International Managerial Finance, 1972, Impact of Large Firms on U.S. Economy, 1973, Financial Theory and Corporate Policy, 1979, 2d edit., 1983, 3d edit., 1988, Mergers, Restructuring and Corporate Control, 1990, Managerial Finance, 9th edit, 1992; assoc. editor: Jour. of Finance, 1948-55; mem. editorial bd., 1957-59; editorial bd. Bus. Econs., Jour. Fin. Rsch., Managerial and Decision Econs.; manuscript referee Am. Econ. Rev., Rev. of Econs. and Statistics, Engring. Economist, Bus. Econs., Fin. Mgmt. Bd. dirs. Bunker Hill Fund. Served with Ordnance Dept. AUS, 1943-45. Recipient Abramson Scroll award Bus. Econs., 1989-94; McKinsey Found. grantee, 1965-68; GE grantee, 1967; Ford Found. Faculty Rsch. fellow, 1961-62. Fellow Nat. Assn. Bus. Economists; mem. Am. Finance Assn. (pres. 1966, adv. bd. 1967-71), Am. Econ. Assn., Western Econ. Assn. (pres. 1962), Econometric Soc., Am. Statis. Assn., Royal Econ. Soc., Fin. Analysts Soc., Fin. Mgmt. Assn. (pres. 1979-80). Home: 258 Tavistock Ave Los Angeles CA 90049-3229 Office: UCLA Anderson Sch Los Angeles CA 90095-1481

WESTON, JOSH S., data processing company executive; b. Bklyn., Dec. 22, 1928; married. B.S., CCNY, 1950; M.A., U. New Zealand, 1951. Exec. v.p. Popular Services, Inc., 1955-70; v.p. planning adminstrn. Automatic Data Processing, Inc., Roseland, N.J., 1970-75, exec. v.p., 1975-77, pres., 1977—, CEO, 1982—, former COO, now also chmn. bd. dirs.; bd. dirs. Shared Med. Sys., Pub. Svc. Electric and Gas Co., Olsten Corp., Vanstar Corp. Office: ADP Inc 1 A D P Blvd Roseland NJ 07068-1728*

WESTON, M. MORAN, II, real estate developer, banker, clergyman, educator; b. Tarboro, N.C., Sept. 10, 1910; s. Milton Moran and Catharine C. (Perry) W.; m. Miriam Yvonne Drake, June 27, 1946; children: Karann Christine, Gregory. BA, Columbia U., 1930, PhD, 1954, STD (hon.), 1968; DD (hon.), Va. Theol. Sch., 1964; DHL (hon.), Fordham U., 1988. Bus. mgr. St. Philips Episcopal Ch., N.Y.C., 1948-51; exec. sec. Christian Citizenship Nat. Council, Episcopal Ch., N.Y.C., 1951-57; rector, chief executive officer St. Philips Ch. and Community Svc. Council, N.Y.C., 1957-82; sr. prof. SUNY, Albany, 1959-77, prof. emeritus, 1977—; pvt. housing developer, 1982—; pres., founder M. Moran Weston Ctr. for Hope, N.Y.C., 1996—; vis. prof. U. Ife, Ile-Ife, Nigeria, 1977; founding bd. mem. Carver Fed. Savs. Bank, N.Y.C., 1948-58, pres., 1958-59, chmn. bd., 1980-95, vice chmn., 1995—; pres. 6 housing corps., providing over 1,200 rental apts.; co-developer 2 24-story, 600 apts. condominium bldgs. Towers-on-the-Park, N.Y.C., 1986; founding developer, pres. Greater Harlem Nursing Home, 1978. Author: Social Policy, 1964. Founder, pres. Weston United for Cmty. Renewal, N.Y.C., 1985—, Tri-Continental Assn., M. Moran Weston Ctr. for Hope, N.Y.C., 1996; trustee Columbia U., 1969-81, trustee emeritus, 1981—; trustee St. Augustine Coll., Raleigh, N.C., 1970—, Mt. Sinai Hosp. Med. Sch. and Ctr., N.Y.C., 1971—, NAACP Legal Def. Fund, N.Y.C., 1965—, Fgn. Policy Assn., N.Y.C., 1980-89, Phelps Stokes Fund, N.Y.C., 1970-80; founder com. One Million for Self Liberation of Black Am, Inc., 1972; cons. 3d Internat. UN Conf. Against Apartheid, 1977; founder, incorporator Bonds for Africa, Inc., 1987; founder, pres. M. Moran Weston Ctr. for Hope, N.Y.C., 1994—. Recipient St. Augustine's Cross, Archbishop of Canterbury, London, 1981, Excellence award Columbia Grad. Sch., N.Y.C., 1982, Humanitarian awards N.Y. Urban League, N.Y.C., 1982, N.Y. YMCA, 1982, Mickey Leland award Hope for the Homeless, 1989, Lifetime of Excellence in Pub. Svc. award Nat. Housing Assn., 1991, Phoenix award Abyssinian Devel. Corp. Mem. Housing for People (founder, pres. 1980—), Nat. Assn. for Affordable Housing (founder, pres. 1987—), Lotos Club (N.Y.C.), Sigma Pi Phi (pres. Zeta chpt. 1983-86). Club: Lotos (N.Y.C.). Lodge: Elks (Hon. Supreme Exalted Ruler 1946-50). Home: 228 Promenade Cir Heathrow FL 32746-4379 Office: Carver Fed Savs Bank 75 W 125th St New York NY 10027-4512 also: M Moran Weston Ctr for Hope AC Powell Jr Blvd 2262 66 7th Ave New York NY 10030

WESTON, MICHAEL C., lawyer; b. Asheville, N.C., Aug. 13, 1938; m. May Ann Damme; two children. AB in English, Brown U., 1960; JD, U. Mich., 1963. Bar: Mich. 1964, Ill. 1973. Assoc. Hill, Lewis, Detroit, 1963-68; from sec. to pres. corp. and indsl. consortium Econ. Devel. Corp. of Greater Detroit, 1969-73; chief staff atty. Northwestern U., Evanston, Ill., 1973-81, v.p. legal affairs, 1981-89; v.p. and gen. counsel, 1990—; lectr. minority bus. devel. Inst. Continuing Legal Edn., conflicts of interest Nat. Coun. Univ. Rsch. Adminstrs. Contbr. articles to profl. jours. Chmn. Univ. Gallery Com., 1982-85; bd. dirs. Northwestern U. Press. Mem. ABA (sec. taxation, com. on exempt orgns., lectr. Inst. on Minority Bus. Devel.), Chgo. Coun. Lawyers, Nat. Assn. Coll. and Univ. Attys. (lectr. fed. tax matters, outside activities faculty mems. univ.-cmty. rels., med. risk mgmt., bd. dirs. 1985-88, 92-97, pres. 1995-96). Office: Northwestern U 633 Clark St Evanston IL 60208-0001

WESTON, RANDY (RANDOLPH EDWARD WESTON), pianist, composer; b. Bklyn., Apr. 6, 1926; s. Frank Edward and Vivian (Moore) W.; children: Cherryl, Pamela, Niles, Kim. Student, Parkway Music Inst., Bklyn., 1950-52. lectr. on African music UN. Pianist Am. Soc. African Culture tour, Lagos, Nigeria, 1961, 63; toured with Randy Weston's sextet for State Dept., North and West Africa, 1967; appearances include Newport Festival, 1958, Monterey Festival, 1966, Carnegie Hall, 1973, Philharm. Hall, N.Y.C., 1973; appearances maj. jazz clubs in N.Y.C.; also numerous UN concerts, Billie Holiday Theatre, N.Y.U.; European tours include Kingsberg Jazz Festival, Oslo, 1974, Montreux (Switzerland) Jazz Festival, 1974, Festival de Costa del Sol, Marbella, Spain, 1974, Ahus Jazz Festival, Kristianstad, Sweden, 1974, Festival at Antibes, 1974; Tour of Brazil, 1981, Festival de Vienne, France, 1985, Pompeii Jazz Festival, Italy, 1985, Internat. Festival Marrahesh, Marocco, 1986, 1st Festival Gnaoua Culture, Marocco, 1987, Lygano Festival Jazz, Switzerland, 1988, Jazzaldia, San Sebastian, Spain, 1988; Caribbean Cultural Ctrs. Expressions Festival, N.Y.C., 1988, Roots Festival, Lagos, Nigeria, 1988; featured quest artist One Hundred Yrs. of Jazz, Amsterdam, The Netherlands, 1989; lecture-concerts in Europe including Bern, Basel, Zurich, Lyons, 1975; recs. include Blue Moses, 1972 (number 1 in Record World's jazz chart), Volcano Blues, 1993, Monterey '66, 1994; compositions include Pam's Waltz, 1950, Little Niles, 1950, Hi Fly, 1958, Portrait of Vivian, 1959, Berkshire Blues, 1960, Uhruru Africa suite, 4 movements, 1960, African Cook Book, 1965, The Last Day, 1966, The Ganawa, 1971, Portrait of F.E. Weston, 1974, Carnival, Blues to Africa, Nuits Americani, Blue, Trilogy: Portraits of Ellington; Portraits of Monk; Self-Portrait of Weston, Verve, The Spirits of Our Ancestors, 1992, The Splendid Master Gnawa Musicians of Morocco, 1995, Saga, 1996, (with Vinshu Bill Wood, Lennie McBrowne) Berkshire Blues, 1996; concert artist for radio-TV and maj. U.S. museums including Smithsonian Instn.; performed benefit concerts for anti-apartheid com. at UN through African-Am. Musicians Soc., 1961; appeared in film Jamboree, 1966; commd. The Africans, Spoleto Festival, U.S.A., 1981, The African Queens, Boston Pops, 1981, Portrait of Billie Holiday, Orch. Symphonique de Lyons and Ensemble Instrumental et Big Band de Grenoble, France, 1985, African Sunrise, City of Chicago, 1985; Spanish TV films: Jazz Entre Amigos, 1987, Randy in Tangier; Randy Weston, African Rhythms, Boston TV, 1989. Recipient New Star Pianist award Down Beat Internat. Critics Poll 1955, Pianist Most Deserving of Wider Recognition award, 1972, Broadway award Hollywood Advt. Club 1965, Premier prix de l'Academie du Jazz, France 1975; named World's Best Jazz Pianist Internat. Roots Festival, Lagos, Nigeria, 1988; Randy Weston Week declared in his honor Bklyn. Borough Pres.'s Office/ Bklyn. Acad. Music, 1986; French Office Nationale de Diffusion Artistique grantee, 1976; Nat. Endowment for Arts grantee, 1974. Mem. ASCAP (Composers awards), Am. Fedn. Musicians. Sufi. Address: PO Box 749 Maplewood NJ 07040-0749 also: care Louise Billotte 595 Connecticut St San Francisco CA 94107-2832 also: Verve 825 8th Ave New York NY 10019*

WESTON, ROGER LANCE, banker; b. Waukegan, Ill., Mar. 2, 1943; s. Arthur Walter and Vivian Dawn (Thompson) W.; m. Kathleen Plotzke, Sept. 15, 1979; children: Cynthia Page, Kent Andrew, Arthur Eladio, Rebecca Dawn, Alice Sinclair, Elliot Churchill, Evan Walter, Spencer Lance. BS, MacMurray Coll., 1965; MBA, Washington U., St. Louis, 1967. Investment adviser Harris Trust & Savs. Bank, Chgo., 1967-69; sr. investment counselor Security Suprs., Chgo., 1969-70; exec. v.p., treas., chief fin. officer Telemed Corp., Hoffman Estates, Ill., 1971-79; vice chmn. Bank Lincolnwood, Ill., 1979-85; pres., chief exec. officer GSC Enterprises, Lincolnwood, 1979-85, EVCO, Inc., Itasca, Ill., 1985-87; vice chmn., chief exec. officer Evanston (Ill.) Bank, 1985-88; chmn. bd. dirs., pres., chief exec. officer GreatBanc, Inc., Aurora, Ill., 1986—. Mem. Barrington Hills (Ill.) Zoning Bd. Appeals, 1987, com. Asian art Art Inst. Chgo., 1987. Mem. Washington U. Eliot Soc. (Chgo. nat. com., chmn. membership com. 1996-92), Univ. Club, John M. Olin Sch. Bus. (nat. coun., Hatchery devel. com.). Republican. Presbyterian. Office: Great Banc Inc 2300 Barrington Rd Hoffman Est IL 60195-2082

WESTON, ROY FRANCIS, environmental consultant; b. Reedsburg, Wis., June 25, 1911; s. Charles Frederick and Hattie (Jensen) W.; m. Madeleen Elizabeth Kellner, Dec. 31, 1934; children: Susan Weston Thompson, Katherine Weston Swoyer Fittipaldi. B.C.E., U. Wis., 1933; M.C.E., NYU, 1939; D.Engring. (hon.), Drexel U., 1981; DSc (hon.), U. Wis. Madison, 1995. Registered profl. engr., 18 states; diplomate Am. Acad. Environ. Engrs. (pres. 1973-74). Jr. hwy. engr. Wis. Hwy. Dept., 1934-36; dist. engr. Wis. Dept. Health, 1936-37; san. engring. research fellow NYU, N.Y.C., 1937-39; san. engr. Atlantic Refining Co., Phila., 1939-55; chmn. bd. Roy F. Weston, Inc., West Chester, Pa., 1955-91, chmn. emeritus, 1991—; environ. cons. Contbr. numerous articles on environ. control and sustainable devel. to profl. publs. vis. com. dept. civil and urban engring. U. Pa., Phila., also Ctr. for Marine and Environ. Studies, Lehigh U.; bd. overseers Sch. Engring., Pa. State U., former mem. indsl. and profl. adv. com. Pa. State U.; past bd. overseers Duke U. Sch. Engring.; past trustee Phila. Coll. Pharmacy and Sci.; former mem. Pa. Gov.'s Energy Coun. Recipient Disting. Svc. citation U. Wis., 1975, George Washington medal Phila. Engrs., 1973, Samuel S. Baxter Meml. award Water Resources Assn. of Delaware River Basin, 1994, Nat. Engring. award Am. Assn. Engring. Socs., 1994, Gordon Maskew Fair award Am. Acad. Environ. Engrs., 1977. National Engineering Award, 1994; American Assn of Engineering Societies. Mem. ASCE (Simon W. Freese Environ. Engrng. award and lecture 1995, Hon. Mention award 1994), APHA, NSPE (Engr. of Yr. award 1973), NAE, AIChE (environ. divsn. Lawrence K. Cecil award 1993), Am. Assn. Engring. Socs. (nat. engring. award 1994), Am. Chem. Soc., Air Pollution Control Assn., Cons. Engrs. Coun., Water Resources Assn., Pa. Soc. Profl. Engrs. (Engr. of Yr. 1970, 73), Water Pollution Control Fedn. (Arthur Sidney Bedell award 1959, Indsl. Wastes medal 1950, hon.), Delaware River Assn. (pres. 1976-77), Overbrook Golf Club, Phila. Engrs. Club. Office: Roy F Weston Inc 1 Weston Way West Chester PA 19380-1469

WESTON, W. GALEN, diversified holdings executive; b. Eng., Oct. 29, 1940; s. W. Garfield Weston and Reta L. Howard; m. Hilary Frayne, 1966; 2 children. BA, U. Western Ont., LLD (hon.). Chmn. bd. Wittington Investments, Ltd., George Weston Ltd., Toronto, Ont., Can., Holt, Renfrew & Co. Ltd., Loblaw Cos. Ltd., Weston Foods Ltd., Weston Resources Ltd.; vice chmn. bd. dirs. Fortnum and Mason PLC (U.K.); bd. dirs. Assoc. Brit. Foods PLC (U.K.), Can. Imperial Bank Commerce, Brown Thomas Group Ltd. (Ireland). Pres. United World Colls.; bd. dirs. Lester B. Pearson Coll. Pacific; life mem. Royal Ont. Mus., Art Gallery Ont.; hon. trustee The Upper Can. Coll. Found. Officer Order of Can. Mem. Badminton and Racquet Club, York Club, Toronto Club, Guards Polo Club, Lyford Cay Club, Windsor Club (Fla.), The Brook Club (N.Y.), White's Club (U.K.), Sunningdale Golf. (U.K.), Toronto Lawn Tennis, Windsor Club (Fla.). Avocations: polo, tennis, golf. Office: George Weston Limited, 22 Saint Clair Ave E Ste 1900, Toronto, ON Canada M4T 2S7

WESTON, WILLIAM LEE, dermatologist; b. Grand Rapids, Minn., Aug. 13, 1938; s. Eugene and Edith Kathryn (Lee) W.; m. Janet J. Atkinson, June 9, 1964; children: Elizabeth Carol, William Kemp. AB, Whitman Coll., 1960; B in Med. Sci., U. S.D., 1963; MD, U. Colo., 1965. Resident in pediatrics U. Calif., San Francisco, 1967-68; intern, then resident in pediatrics U. Colo., Denver, 1965-67, resident in dermatology, 1970-72, asst. prof. dermatology and pediatrics, 1972-76, prof., 1976—, chmn. dept. dermatology, 1976—. Author: Practical Pediatric Dermatology, 1979, rev. edit., 1985, Color Textbook of Pediatric Dermatology, 1991, rev. edit., 1996; editor-in-chief Current Problems in Dermatology, 1988-93. With AUS, 1968-70. Mem. Soc. Pediatric Dermatology (founder, sec.-treas. 1975-80, pres. 1984-85), Colo. Dermatol. Soc. (pres.), Soc. Investigative Dermatology (bd. dirs.), Am. Acad. Dermatology (bd. dirs.). Methodist. Home: 8550 E Ponderosa Dr Parker CO 80134-8233 Office: 4200 E 9th Ave Denver CO 80220-3706

WESTOVER, BECKE KARL, advertising executive. BA in Econs., Denison U. From account exec. to sr. v.p. Ogilvy & Mather Direct, N.Y.C., 1984-94, sr. ptnr., client svcs. dir., 1994—. Avocations: skiing, fishing, beach combing. Office: Ogilvy & Mather Direct 309 W 49th St New York NY 10019-7316

WESTPHAL, DEBORAH LOUISE, retail executive, choreographer; b. Des Moines; d. John Chester (stepfather) and Betty Hill Swander; 1 child, John Andrew. BA in English with honors, U. No. Iowa, 1970; MBA with honors, Drake U., 1979. Cert. tchr., Iowa. Tchr. lang. arts Holmes Jr. High Sch., Cedar Falls, Iowa, 1970-72, dir. CORE program, 1972-75; tchr. English Valley High Sch., West Des Moines, Iowa, 1975-78; instr. mktg. Drake U., Des Moines, 1979-85; tchr., choreographer Betty Hill Dance Studios, Inc., Des Moines, 1975—, pres., 1985—; cons. Valley Junction and Des Moines Theatrical Shop, West Des Moines, 1978—; co-dir., co-creator The Boys Club, Des Moines, 1988—. Choreographer numerous children and teen dance numbers, 1975—, Dancersize Fitness, 1976-87, Peace Child and Peace Child Great Plains Tour, Des Moines, 1987-88. Probation aide vol. Blackhawk County, Waterloo, Iowa, 1972-75; mem. adv. bd. Gifted and Talented Coun., Des Moines, 1982-84; dir. Iowa del. Nat. Dance Festival, 1987, 88, 92 (gold medals in ballet, tap, jazz, variety, duet). Drake U. fellow, 1978-79. Mem. Dance Masters Am. (chpt. sec.), Dance Educators Am., Mensa. Avocations: reading, theatre, music. Office: Betty Hill Dance Studios Inc 1233 73rd St Des Moines IA 50311-1315

WESTPHAL, JAMES ADOLPH, planetary science educator; b. Dubuque, Iowa, June 13, 1930; s. Henry Ludwig and Nancy Kathryn (Wise) W.; m. Lois Jean, Apr. 17, 1956 (div. 1966); 1 child, Andrew Johnathan; m. Barbara Jean Webster, Nov. 2, 1967. BS, U. Tulsa, 1954. Team leader Sinclair Rsch. Labs., Tulsa, 1955-61; sr. engr. Calif. Inst. Tech., Pasadena, 1961-66, sr. rsch. fellow, 1966-71, assoc. prof., 1971-76, prof., 1976—; dir. Palomar Observatory, Pasadena, 1994-97; prin. investigator Hubble space telescope NASA, Calif. Inst. Tech., Pasadena, 1977—. Fellow MacArthur Found., 1991; recipient Space Science award Am. Inst. Aeronautics and Astronautics, 1995. Mem. Am. Astron. Soc. Office: Calif Inst Tech MS 150-21 Pasadena CA 91125

WESTPHAL, KLAUS WILHELM, university museum administrator; b. Berlin, Mar. 20, 1939; came to U.S., 1969; s. Wilhelm Heinrich and Irmgard (Henze) W.; m. Margaret Elisabeth Dorothea Wagner, May 16, 1969; children: Barbara, Marianne, Christine. BS in Geology, Eberhard-Karls Universität, Tübingen, Germany, 1960, MS, 1964, PhD in Paleontology, 1969. Dir. geology mus. U. Wis. Madison, 1969—; bd. dirs. natural history coun. U. Wis. Madison, 1973—, Friends of Geology Mus., Inc., 1977—; nat. speaker on paleontology Outreach, 1977—; instr. paleontology U. Wis., 1977—; leader expeditions fossil vertebrates including dinosaurs, 1977—. Participant various tchr.-tng. projects Wis. Pub. Schs. Lutheran. Home: 3709 High Rd Middleton WI 53562-1003 Office: U Wis Geology Mus 1215 W Dayton St Madison WI 53706-1600

WESTPHAL, LEONARD WYRICK, health care executive, consultant; b. Kansas City, Mo., Sept. 28, 1946; s. Leonard Henry and Elizabeth (Wyrick) W.; m. Sandra Sanders, Aug. 13, 1972; children: Michael Weston, Margaret Elizabeth. BFA, So. Meth. U., 1969; MA, S.W. Mo. State U., 1972; post-grad., U. Mich., Cen. Mo. State U., Lincoln U. of Mo., Century U. Lic. nursing home adminstr., Mo., Ark. Exec. dir. Dist. III Area Agy. on Aging, Warrensburg, 1972-83; state dir. Mo. Div. of Aging, Jefferson City, Mo., 83-85; spl. asst. to dir. Mo. Dept. Mental Health, Jefferson City, 1985-86; exec. dir. Missouri River Health Care, Jefferson City, 1986-88; health care adminstr., cons., 1988—; continuing edn. instr., mem. adv. coun. continuing edn. SW Mo. State U., 1993—; adj. instr., internship supr. Cen. Mo. State U., Warrensburg, 1974-83; mem. rev. panel State of Mo., 1974-76, HHS, 1984-85; cons. Adminstrn. on Aging, Fed. Emergency Mgmt. Agy., 1977-83; bd. dirs. Mid-Am. Congress on Aging, 1975; chmn. Mo. Gov.'s Task Force, Hearings and Conf. on Alternative Care for Elderly, 1982-83; mem. Mo. Bd. Nursing Home Adminstrs., 1983-85; founder, coord. Older Missourians Craft Festival, 1978-83; pres., v.p. Mo. Alliance Area Agys. on Aging, 1974-76; host radio programs Sta. Kmos-TV, Sta. KCMW-FM, Sta. KWTO, 1993—; mem. adv. com. health care adm. program S.W. Mo. State U.; presenter in field. Author articles in disaster assistance. Mem. Mo. Rep. Com., 1970—, rev. panel United Way, Warrensburg, 1978; mem. coun. ministries 1st United Meth. Ch., Warrensburg, 1979-83, mem. adminstrv. coun., 1981-83, pres. Meth. Men, 1982-83; mem. commn. on missions, Wesley United Meth. Ch., Jefferson City, 1984-86, liturgist, 1985-89; mem. ch. and soc. commn. Wesley United Methodist Ch., Springfield, 1989—; pres. PTA, Warrensburg, 1982; coach Little League Football and Basketball, Warrensburg, 1981-82; bd. dirs. Warrensburg Community Betterment, 1976-78; mem. adminstrv. coun., mem. chancel choir Grace United Meth. Ch., Springfield, 1993—. Recipient Boss of Yr. award Warrensburg Jaycees, 1976, svc. recognition Mo. Office Aging, 1977, Mo. Alliance Area Agys. on Aging, 1977, Older Adult Transp. Svc., Columbia, Mo., 1983, Mo. State Fair, 1983, Mo. Dept. Mental Health, 1986; Exceptional Svc. in Disaster Assistance award City of Sedalia, 1977, 80; Outstanding Contbns. award Ret. Sr. Vol. Programs, 1977, 79, Excellence in Adminstrn. award Mo. Office Aging, 1977, Outstanding Svcs. award Hickory County, Mo., 1984, also others. Fellow Am. Coll. Healthcare Adminstrs. (cert.); mem. Am. Coll. Healthcare Execs., Gerontol. Soc. Am., Am. Soc. Pub. Adminstrn., Mo. Alliance for Homecare, Mo. League Nursing Home Adminstrs., Am. Coll. Healthcare Profls., Jefferson City C. of C., Springfield C. of C. (mem. retirement and devel. coms.), Optimists (v.p. Warrensburg 1979-81), Rotary, Elks, Delta Sigma Rho-Tau Kappa Alpha, Delta Chi (alumni advisor, alumni bd. trustees, achievement award). Avocations: political activities, hiking, travel, literature, canoeing. Home: 13476 W Farm Rd 128 Bois D Arc MO 65612-8148

WESTPHAL, WILLIAM HENRY, staff nurse; b. Pt. Washington, Wis., Oct. 29, 1946; s. Henry Vernon and Milda Emma (Sudbrink) W.; m. R. Elaine Stumreiter, Dec. 14, 1974. Cert. oper. rm. technician, Brook Army Med. Ctr., 1967; LPN with honors, Lakeshore Tech. Coll., 1971, ADN with honors, 1979; BBA, Lakeland Coll., 1993. LPN, RN, Wis. Staff nurse, surg. nurse orthopedics, gen. surgery, urology St. Nicholas Hosp., Sheboygan, Wis., 1969-79; surg. asst. orthopedics Sheboygan Clinics, 1979-89; staff nurse Sheboygan County Instns., 1989-95, Flambeau Med. Ctr., Park Falls, 1996—; owner, operator Edge of Town Motel, Park Falls, Wis., 1995—; treas. LPN state chpt. Wis. Fedn. LPN, Sheboygan, 1971-79. Mem. Park Falls planning comm., 1995—. Sgt. 1st class U.S. Army, 1967-77, Vietnam, 1968-69. Mem. Am. Fedn. Nurses and Health Profls. (Wis. nurses union 1989-95), , Wis. Innkeepers Assn., Price County C. of C., KC (1st degree knight). Roman Catholic. Avocations: world travel, photography, woodcraft, golf. Home: North Hwy 13 900 4th Ave N Park Falls WI 54552-1727

WESTWATER, JAMES WILLIAM, chemical engineering educator; b. Danville, Ill., Nov. 24, 1919; s. John and Lois (Maxwell) W.; m. Elizabeth Jean Keener, June 9, 1942; children: Barbara, Judith, David, Beverly. B.S., U. Ill., 1941; Ph.D., U. Del., 1948. Mem. faculty U. Ill., Urbana, 1948—; prof. chem. engring. U. Ill., 1962—, head dept., 1962-80; papers chmn. 5th Nat. Heat Transfer Conf., Buffalo, 1960; chmn. 3d Internat. Heat Transfer Conf., Chgo., 1966; Reilly lectr. Notre Dame U., 1958; Donald L. Katz lectr. U. Mich., 1978. Contbr. articles profl. jours. Recipient Conf. award 8th Nat. Heat Transfer Conf., 1965. Fellow AIChe (dir., past divsn. chmn., inst. lectr. 1964, named eminent chem. engr., William H. Walker award 1966, Max Jakob award with ASME 1972, Founders award 1984, heat transfer and energy conversion award 1989, Ernest Thiele award 1994); mem. ASME, NAE, Am. Chem. Soc., Am. Soc. Engring. Edn. (Vincent Bendix award 1974). Home: 116 W Iowa St Urbana IL 61801-5035

WESTWICK, CARMEN ROSE, retired nursing educator, consultant; b. Holstein, Iowa, Feb. 2, 1936; d. J. Alfred and Hazel C. (Lage) Armiger; m. Richard A. Westwick, Dec. 28, 1957; children: Timothy, Ann. BS in Nursing, U. Iowa, 1958; MS, U. Colo., 1960; PhD, Denver U., 1972. RN, Tenn. Instr. Sch. Nursing West Suburban Hosp., Oak Park, Ill., 1958-59, 60-62; nurse Navajo Presch., Carson's Trading Post, N.Mex., 1967; lectr. then prof. U. Colo., Denver, 1968-69, 72-77; program dir. Western Coun. on Higher Edn. in Nursing, Boulder, Colo., 1976-77; prof. nursing, dean U. N.Mex, Albuquerque, 1977-81, Boston U., 1982-85, S.D. State U., Brookings, 1988-91; NHC chair of excellence in nursing NHC, Murfreesboro, 1993-96; ret.; exec. dir. N.H. Bd. Nursing, Concord, 1986-87; case reviewer Joint Underwriters Assn., Boston, 1983-92; mem. publs. and rsch. com. Aberdeen (S.D.) Area Indian Health Svc., 1989-91; manuscript reviewer Midwest Alliance in Nursing, Indpls., 1989-92, Holistic Nursing Jour.; mem. adv. coun. S.D. Office Rural Health, Pierre, 1989-91. Contbr. articles to profl. jours. Nurse trainee fellow Nursing div. Dept. Health and Human Svcs., 1959-60, Predoctoral fellow, 1969-72; Nat. Merit scholar, 1954-56. Fellow Am. Acad. Nursing; mem. Sigma Theta Tau (nat. 1st v.p. 1968, disting. lectr. 1996—), Phi Kappa Phi, Kappa Delta Phi. Lutheran. Avocations: antiques, quilting. Office: Mid Tenn State U Dept Nursing Box 81 Murfreesboro TN 37132

WESTWOOD, ALBERT RONALD CLIFTON, engineer; b. Birmingham, Eng., June 9, 1932; came to U.S., 1958, naturalized, 1974; s. Albert Sydney and Ena Emily (Clifton) W.; m. Jean Mavis Bullock, 1956; children: Abigail, Andrea. B.S. with honors, U. Birmingham, 1953, Ph.D. in Phys. Metallurgy, 1956, D.Sc. in Materials Sci., 1968. Chartered engr. and physicist, U.K. Tech. officer research dept., metals div. Imperial Chem. Industries, Birmingham, 1956-58, successively scientist, sr. scientist, assoc. dir., head materials sci. dept., dep. dir., 1958-74; dir. Martin Marietta Labs., Balt., 1974-84, corp. dir. R & D, 1984-87; v.p. R & D Martin Marietta Corp., Bethesda, Md., 1987-90, v.p. sci., 1990, v.p. rsch. and tech., 1990-93; v.p. rsch. and exploratory tech. Sandia Nat. Labs. div. Lockheed Martin Corp., Albuquerque, 1993-96; mem. various govt. and univ. adv. coms. including Office Sci. and Tech. Policy, NASA, NRC, NAE, NSF, Nat. Inst. Standards and Tech., U. Md., U. Fla., MIT, Ga. Inst. Tech., Coun. on Competitiveness; dir. Martin Marietta Energy Systems. Bd. dirs. U.S. Civilian Rsch. and Devel. Found. for Former Soviet Union. Chmn. Md. Humanities Coun.; chmn. N.Mex. Symphony Orch.; bd. dirs. Santa Fe Opera; mem. N.Mex. Endowment for Humanities. Recipient disting. young scientist award Md. Acad. Scis., 1966, centennial award U. Md., 1994, Beilby gold medal Royal Inst. Chemistry, 1970, Herbert J. Holloman award Acta Metallurgica, 1996, Tewksbury lectr. U. Melbourne, 1974. Fellow AAAS (chmn. indsl. sci. sect.), Am. Soc. Metals Internat. (Burgess lectr. 1984, Campbell meml. lectr. 1987, disting. lectr. materials and soc. 1995), the Minerals, Metals and Materials Soc. (dir., fin. officer, pres. 1990, Krumb lectr. 1988, leadership award 1992); mem. NRC (chmn. com. engring. and tech. sys.), ASME (disting. lectr. 1989), NAE (elected), Royal Swedish Acad. Engring. Scis. (elected), Russian Acad. Engring. (elected), Royal Acad. Engring. (U.K.), Md. Acad. Scis. (coun.), Md. Inst. Metals (pres.), Indsl. Rsch. Inst. (bd. dirs., pres. 1989-90). Home: 1413 Pinnacle View Dr NE Albuquerque NM 87112-6558

WESTWOOD, JAMES NICHOLSON, lawyer; b. Portland, Oreg., Dec. 3, 1944; s. Frederick Alton and Catherine (Nicholson) W.; m. Janet Sue Butler, Feb. 23, 1980; children: Laura, David. BA, Portland State U., 1967; JD, Columbia U., 1974. Bar: Oreg. 1974, U.S. Dist. Ct. Oreg. 1974, U.S. Ct. Appeals (9th cir.) 1978, U.S. Supreme Ct. 1981, U.S. Ct. Appeals (fed. cir.) 1984. Assoc. Miller, Anderson, Nash, Yerke & Wiener, Portland, 1974-76, 78-81; asst. to pres. Portland State U., 1976-78; ptnr. Miller, Nash, Wiener, Hager & Carlsen, Portland, 1981—. Recipient Disting. Svc. award Portland State U. Found., 1984, Outstanding Alumni award Portland State U., 1992. Mem. ABA (chmn. forest resources com. 1987-89), Oreg. Bar Assn. (chmn. appellate practice sect. 1996-97), Am. Acad. Appellate Lawyers, Univ. Club (bd. govs. 1994), City Club (pres. 1991-92). Republican. Unitarian. Home: 3121 NE Thompson St Portland OR 97212-4908 Office: Miller Nash Wiener Hager & Carlsen 111 SW 5th Ave Portland OR 97204-3604

WESTWOOD, MELVIN NEIL, horticulturist, pomologist; b. Hiawatha, Utah, Mar. 25, 1923; s. Neil and Ida (Blake) W.; m. Wanda Mae Shields, Oct. 12, 1946; children: Rose Dawn, Nancy Gwen, Robert Melvin, Kathryn Mae. Student, U. Utah, 1948-50; BS in Pomology, Utah State U., 1952; PhD in Pomology, Wash. State U., 1956. Field botanist Utah State U., Logan, 1951-52, supt. Howell Field Sta., 1952-53; rsch. asst. State Coll. Wash., 1953-55; rsch. horticulturist Agrl. Rsch. Svc. USDA, Wenatchee, Wash., 1955-60; assoc. prof. Oreg. State U., Corvallis, 1960-67, prof., 1967-80, prof. emeritus, 1986—; rsch. dir. Nat. Clonal Germplasm Repository, Corvallis, 1980-83, nat. tech. advisor, 1984-86. Author: Deciduous Fruit and Nut Production, 1976, Temperate-Zone Pomology: Physiology and Culture, 1978, 3d edit., 1993, Contract Military Air Transport: From the Ground Up, 1995, Pear Varieties and Species, 1996; co-author: Cherry Nutrition, 1966, Pear Rootstocks, 1987, Management and Utilization of Plant Germplasm, 1988, Maintenance and Storage: Clonal Germplasm, 1989, Genetic Resources of Malus, 1991; contbr. more than 200 articles to profl. jours. With USAAF, 1946-47. Grantee NSF, 1966; recipient Hartman Cup award Oreg. Hort. Soc., 1989. Fellow Am. Soc. Hort. Sci. (bd. dirs. 1974-75, chmn. com. environ. quality 1971, adv. coun. 1974-79, mem. pomology sect. 1967-74, publs. com. 1971-74, pres. western region 1974, Joseph Harvey Gourley award for Pomology 1958, 77, Stark award for Pomology 1969, 77, Outstanding Researcher award 1986); mem. AAAS, Am. Soc. Plant Physiologists, Am. Pomological Soc. (adv. bd. 1970-75, exec. bd. 1980-84, Paul Howe Shepard award 1968, 82, Wilder medal 1980), UN Assn. USA, Ams. United for Separation of Ch. and State, Amnesty Internat., Phi Kappa Phi, Gamma Sigma Delta. Baptist. Achievements include patent for Autumn Blaze ornamental pear; research on Pyrus (pear), Malus (apple) and Prunus (plum, cherry, peach) and on the physiology of rootstock genera. Office: Oreg State U Dept Horticulture Corvallis OR 97331

WETHERILL, EIKINS, lawyer, stock exchange executive; b. Phila., Oct. 3, 1919; s. A. Hecksher and Edwina (Brunner) W. LL.B., U. Pa., 1948. Practiced in Phila., 1948-55, Norristown, 1955—; assoc. firm Evans, Bayard & Frick, 1948-50; ptnr. Reilly, Hepburn, Earle & Wetherill, 1950-55; firm Henderson, Wetherill, O'Hey & Horsey, 1955—; pres. Phila. Stock Exchange, Inc., 1965-81; bd. dirs. Germantown Savs. Bank; fin. commentator CBS-TV News, 1966-68; chmn. bd. Sta. WHYY-TV, 1970-76, dir., 1976-90;

dir. 1st Pa. Corp., 1st Pa. Bank, solicitor to lt. gov. Pa., 1951-55, asst. U.S. atty. gen., 1953-55, treas., Montgomery County, 1956-59; pres. Montgomery County Bd. Commrs., 1960-63; chmn. Pa. Securities Commn., 1963-65; commr. Delaware Valley Regional Planning Commn., 1965—, chmn., 1968-69, 70-71, 78-79. Former bd. dirs. Greater Phila. Partnership; chmn. Phila. Drama Guild, 1975-80, dir., 1980-87; trustee Davis and Elkins Coll., 1973-91. Served to capt., cav. Signal Corps, OSS, AUS, 1941-45. Mem. Am., Phila. bar assns., Delta Psi. Episcopalian. Clubs: Phila. (Phila.), Racquet (Phila.). Office: 1 Montgomery Ave Ste 902 Norristown PA 19401-1948

WETHERILL, GEORGE WEST, geophysicist, planetary scientist; b. Phila., Aug. 12, 1925; s. George West and Leah Victoria (Hardwick) W.; m. Phyllis May Steiss, June 17, 1950 (wid. 1995); children: Rachel, George, Sarah. Ph.B., U. Chgo., 1948, S.B. in Physics, 1949, S.M., 1951, Ph.D. in Physics, 1953. Mem. staff dept. terrestrial magnetism Carnegie Inst., Washington, 1953-60; prof. geophysics and geology UCLA, 1960-75, chmn. dept. planetary and space sci., 1968-72; dir. dept. terrestrial magnetism Carnegie Inst., Washington, 1975-91, mem. sci. staff, 1991—; cons. NASA, NSF, Nat. Acad. Sci. Editor Ann. Rev. of Earth and Planetary Sci., 1981-96, assoc. editor, 1972-80; assoc. editor, Meteoritics and Planetary Sci., Icarus; contbr. articles to profl. jours. With USN, 1943-46. Recipient G.K. Gilbert award Geol. Soc. Am., 1984, Profl. Achievement Citation U. Chgo. Alumni Assn., 1985. Fellow Am. Acad. Arts and Scis., Am. Geophys. Union (pres. planetology sect. 1970-72, recipient H.H. Hess medal, 1991), Meteoritical Soc. (v.p. 1971-74, 81-83, pres. 1983-85, Leonard medal 1981); mem. NAS, Geochem. Soc. (v.p. 1973-74, pres. 1974-75), Internat. Assn. Geochem. and Cosmochemistry (pres. 1977-80), Internat. Astron. Union, Am. Astron. Soc. Div. Planetary Scis. and Div. Dynamic Astronomy (G.P. Kuiper prize 1986), Religious Soc. Free Quakers, Internat. Soc. for Study of Origin of Life. Episcopalian. Office: Carnegie Inst 5241 Broad Branch Rd NW Washington DC 20015-1305 *Seek him that maketh the Pleiades and Orion, and turneth the shadow of death into morning. Amos 5:8.*

WETHERINGTON, ROGER VINCENT, journalism educator, newspaper copy editor; b. Jacksonville, Fla., Mar. 12, 1942; s. Roger Vincent and Ruby Estelle (Jones) W.; m. Andra Marie Miller, Aug. 31, 1972; 1 child, Brady Miller. BA in English Lit., Columbia U., 1965; MA in Journalism (with hons.), U. So. Calif., 1979, PhD in Comm., 1986. Copyboy, reporter, asst. city editor Daily News, N.Y.C., 1963-76; lectr. journalism Calif. State U., Long Beach, 1976-78, 87-90; asst. prof. Calif. State U., Northridge, 1979-84; asst. prof. comm. St. John's U., Jamaica, N.Y., 1990-93, assoc. prof., 1993—; copy editor N.Y. Times, N.Y.C., 1992—. Recipient media award for incisive reporting Cancer Care, Inc., 1974, faculty devel. award Calif. State U.-Northridge, 1983; teaching fellow Gannett Found., 1977. Mem. AAUP, Assn. for Edn. in Journalism and Mass Comm., Soc. Profl. Journalists, Investigative Reporters and Editors, Newspaper Guild, Deadline Club. Avocation: opera. Office: St John's U 8000 Utopia Pkwy Jamaica NY 11432-1335

WETHERUP, DANIELLE V., metal manufacturing executive; b. Montreal, Que., Can., Jan. 3, 1941; d. Alexandre and Viola (Dame) Binette; children: Marcia, Sylvie. BA in Polit. Sci., Mt. St. Vincent U., Halifax, N.S. V.p. profl. svcs. br. Can. Internat. Devel. Agy., Ottawa, Ont., 1988-93; chmn. bd. Internat. Ctr. for Oceans Devel., Ottawa, 1992; assoc. dep. minister Environment Canada, Ottawa, 1993-94; pres., master Royal Can. Mint, Ottawa, 1994—. Office: Royal Canadian Mint, 320 Sussex Dr, Ottawa, ON Canada K1A 0G8

WETHINGTON, CHARLES T., JR., academic administrator. AB, Ea. Ky. U., 1956; postgrad., Syracuse U., 1958-59; MA, U. Ky., 1962, PhD, 1965. Instr. ednl. psychology U. Ky., Lexington, 1965-66; dir. Maysville (Ky.) C.C., 1967-71; asst. v.p. c.c. system U. Ky., Lexington, 1971-81, v.p. c.c. system, 1981-82, chancellor c.c. system, 1982-88, chancellor c.c. system and univ. rels., 1988-89, interim pres., 1989-90, pres., 1990—; chmn. legis. com. State Dirs. Community and Jr. Colls., 1983-85, chmn. nat. coun., 1985-86; mem. commn. on colls. So. Assn. Schs. and Colls., 1978-84, vice chmn. exec. coun., 1984, trustee, 1986-89; mem. So. Regional Edn. Bd., 1988—, mem. exec. com., 1989-93, vice chmn., 1991-93. Bd. dirs. Bluegrass State Skills Corp., 1984-91, vice-chmn. bd. dirs., 1986-87; bd. visitors Community Coll. of Air Force, 1986-90; mem. Ky. Ednl. TV Adv. Com., 1984—; mem. jud. nominating commn. 22nd Jud. Dist., Fayette County, Ky., 1988-91; mem. Ky. Coal Authority, 1990—, So. Growth Policies Bd., 1990—; served with sec. svc. USAF, 1957-61. Home: Maxwell Pl 471 Rose St Lexington KY 40508 Office: U Ky 104 Administration Bldg Lexington KY 40506-0032*

WETHINGTON, JOHN ABNER, JR., retired nuclear engineering educator; b. Tallahassee, Apr. 18, 1921; s. John Abner and Mary McQueen (Hale) W.; m. Kathryn Kemp Greene, Aug. 19, 1943; 1 son, John Abner III. A.B., Emory U., 1942, M.A., 1943; Ph.D., Northwestern U., 1950. Vis. research asst. Princeton, 1943-44; chemist Fercleve Corp., Oak Ridge, 1944-46; chemist to sr. chemist Oak Ridge Nat. Lab., 1949-53; asst. prof. to prof. nuclear engrng. U. Fla., 1953-85, prof. emeritus, 1985—; on leave as fellow Lawrence Livermore Lab., Calif., 1971-72; vis. scientist P.R. Nuclear Center, 1962-63, Oak Ridge Nat. Lab., 1979-80; U.S. del. to Radiation Congress, Haregate, Eng., 1963, 2d Internat. Conf. Peaceful Uses of Atomic Energy, Switzerland, 1958; faculty participant Oak Ridge Sch. Reactor Tech., 1957-58. Contbr. articles to profl. jours. Fellow AAAS; mem. Am. Chem. Soc., Am. Nuclear Soc., Phi Beta Kappa, Sigma Xi, Alpha Chi Sigma. Democrat. Methodist. Home: 109 NW 22nd Dr Gainesville FL 32603-1426

WETHINGTON, NORBERT ANTHONY, medieval scholar; b. Dayton, Ohio, Sept. 14, 1943; s. Norbert and Sophie Lillian W.; m. Martha M. Vannice, Aug. 13, 1966. BA, U. Dayton, 1965; MA, John Carroll U., 1967; postgrad. Baldwin Wallace Coll., 1968-70, PhD, U. Toledo, 1997. Grad. asst., teaching assoc. John Carroll U., Cleve., 1965-67; English tchr. Padua Franciscan H.S., Parma, Ohio, 1967-70; instr., chmn. dept. tech. writing and speech N. Central Tech. Coll., Mansfield, Ohio, 1970-74; dir. evening divsn. Terra Tech. Coll., Fremont, Ohio, 1974-80, dir. public and cmty. svc. technologies, 1980-94; dir. humanities Terra State C.C., 1994-96, assoc. dean of instrn. 1996-97; cons. in field. V.p. Sandusky County Bd. Health, 1979-80. Mem. MLA, Am. Vocat. Assn., Ohio Vocat. Assn. (pres. tech. edn. divsn. 1985-86, Disting. Svc. award 1987), Nat. Council Tchrs. English. Democrat. Roman Catholic. Contbr. articles to profl. jours. Home: 1036 Hazel St Fremont OH 43420-2115

WETLAUFER, DONALD BURTON, biochemist, educator; b. New Berlin, N.Y., Apr. 4, 1925; s George C. and Olga (Kirckhoff) W.; m. Lucille D. Croce, May 5, 1950; children—Lise, Eric. B.S. in Chemistry, U. Wis., Madison, 1946, M.S. in Biochemistry, 1952, Ph.D., 1954. Chemist Argonne (Ill.) Nat. Lab., 1944, 46-47, Bjorksten Lab., Madison, 1948-50; Carlsberg Lab., Copenhagen, 1955-56; research asso. Harvard U., 1956-61, tutor biochem. sci., 1958-61; asst. prof. biochemistry Ind. U. Med. Sch., 1961-62; asso. prof., then prof. biochemistry U. Minn. Med. Sch., 1962-75; DuPont prof. chemistry U. Del., Newark, 1975-96, chmn. dept., 1975-85, prof. emeritus, 1996—; vis. investigator Max Planck Inst. Ernahrungsphy., 1974-78; mem. fellowship rev. com. NATO, 1970; cons. Nat. Inst. Gen. Med. Sci., 1964—, NSF, 1980—. Author rsch. papers in field of protein biochemistry, protein folding and high performance protein purification; severl editl. positions; indsl. cons. NSF predoctoral fellow, 1952-54; Nat. Found. Infantile Paralysis postdoctoral fellow, 1955-56; Am. Heart Assn. postdoctoral fellow, 1956-58; grantee USPHS, 1961—; grantee NATO, 1974-77; grantee NSF, 1977—; grantee AEC, 1962; recipient Career Devel. award USPHS, 1961-62. Mem. AAAS, Am. Chem. Soc. (councilor, alt. councilor divsn. biol. chemistry 1975-87), Am. Soc. Biochemistry and Molecular Biology, The Protein Soc., Chromatography Forum, Phi Beta Kappa. Office: U Del Dept Chemistry & Biochemistry Newark DE 19716

WETSCH, JOHN ROBERT, information systems specialist; b. Dickinson, N.D., Aug. 27, 1959; s. Joseph John and Florence Mae (Edwards) W.; m. Laura Jean Johnson, Aug. 29, 1981; children: Julie Elizabeth, Katherine Anne, John Michael. BS, U. State of N.Y.-Regents Coll., Albany, 1984; MA, Antioch U., 1989; PhD, Nova S.E. U., 1994. Radiation physics instr. Grand Forks (N.D.) Clinic, 1983-85; sr. programmer PRC, Inc., Cavalier Air Force Sta., N.D., 1987-91, PARCS project-SAFEGUARD sys.; pres. Dakota Sci. Inc., Langdon, N.D., 1988-95; instr. U. N.D.-Lake Region Devils Lake, 1988-91; systems adminstr. U.S. Courts Nat. Fine Ctr., Raleigh, N.C., 1991-94; bus. project leader Raleigh (N.C.) Info. Sys. Svc. Ctr., 1994—; v.p. R & D HYTEC Consulting, Inc., 1997—; cons. on Wave Obs./N.D. Proposal, Gov.'s Office, Bismarck, 1991; founder, developer Dakota Sci., Inc., Langdon, 1988-95; instr. divsn. continuing edn. Wake Tech. C.C., 1993—; Webmaster cons. on comml. applications, 1996—; prin. tech. advisor Litton/ PRC, 1997—; mem. adj. faculty computer info. systems N.C. Wesleyan Coll., 1997—. Author: (with others) COMPUTE!'s 2nd Book of Amiga, 1988; contbr. articles to COMPUTE! Jour. of Progressive Computing, 1987, other profl. jours. Mem. coll. scholarship selection com. Cavalier Air Force Sta., N.D., 1990; program coord. Lake Region Outreach, U. N.D., Cavalier Air Force Sta., 1988-91; mem. Bd. Alumni Trustees, SUNY-Regents Coll., Albany, 1995—, v.p., 1996-97, pres., 1997—, ex-officio mem. regents coll. bd.overseers, 1997—; pres. Zeta Rho chpt. Pi Kappa Alpha, Grand Forks, 1981. SMITS scholar N.D. Acad. Sci., 1990; Larimore-Mathews scholar U. N.D., Grand Forks, 1978, N.D. Acad. Sci. scholar, 1978; recipient Westinghouse Sci. Talent Search award, 1978; Sr. Tech. fellow Litton/PRC, 1997. Mem. AAAS, IEEE, IEEE Computer Soc., N.Y. Acad. Scis., Regents Coll. Degrees (grad. resource network), Assn. for Computing Machinery, Dakota Astron. Soc. (co-founder, pres. 1987-91). Republican. Roman Catholic. Achievements include missile simulation; microcomputer short range weather forecasting algorithm, model of the motion of freely falling bodies in 3 dimensions as an elliptic paraboloid, study in astronomy and culture, and astronomy's impact on devel. on Western civilization, system administration assessment of U.S. Courts and establishment and assessment of information control systems for the U.S. Courts National Fine Center. Office: RAISSC 4200 Wake Forest Rd Raleigh NC 27668-9000

WETSCHLER, ED, editor; b. N.Y.C., Nov. 3, 1946; s. Herman and Elsie (Singer) W.; m. Carol M. Loftus, Jan. 24, 1988. AB, U. Rochester, 1968; MA, CUNY, 1973. Tchr. Ersmns Hall High Sch., Bklyn., 1968-84; freelance writer, theatre critic Entertainment, N.Y., 1980-84; assoc. editor Diversion Mag. (Hearst), N.Y.C., 1984-89, sr. editor, 1989-92, exec. editor, 1992—. Contbg. author: Berlitz Guide to New York. Mem. Am. Soc. Mag. Editor. Avocations: gardening, cooking, music. Office: Diversion 1790 Broadway Fl 6 New York NY 10019-1412

WETTACK, F. SHELDON, academic administrator. AB, San Jose State U., 1960, MA, 1962; PhD, U. Tex., Austin, 1967. From asst. prof. to prof. Hope Coll., Holland, Mich., 1967-82, dean nat. and social scis., 1974-82; dean faculty arts and scis. U. Richmond, 1982-89; pres. Wabash Coll., Crawfordsville, Ind., 1989-93; v.p., dean of faculty Harvey Mudd Coll., Claremont, Calif., 1993—. Office: Harvey Mudd Coll 301 E 12th St Claremont CA 91711-5901

WETTELAND, JOHN KARL, professional baseball player; b. San Mateo, Calif., Aug. 21, 1966. Ed., Coll. of San Mateo. With L.A. Dodgers, 1989-91, Montreal Expos, 1992-94; pitcher N.Y. Yankees, 1995-96, Texas Rangers. Named Am. League Fireman of the Year, The Sporting News, 1996, named Most Valuable Player of World Series, 1996. Office: Texas Rangers 1000 Ballpark Way Arlington TX 76011*

WETTER, EDWARD, broadcasting executive; b. Hoboken, N.J., Feb. 2, 1919; s. Edward and Ottilie (Steup) W.; m. Alice Kornat, Nov. 6, 1940 (div. 1946); 1 son, Robert Edward; m. Ruth Lowenstein, Oct. 26, 1954 (div. 1971); 1 dau., Karen Deborah; m. Virginia F. Pate, Apr. 7, 1972. B.A., U. Mich., 1939, M.S., 1941. Dir. spl. ops. Office Sec. Def., 1946-57; bus. broker Allen Kander & Co., N.Y.C., 1957-59; pres. Edward Wetter & Co., Inc., Havre de Grace, Md., 1959—, Harford Enterprises, Havre de Grace, 1978—; v.p. Edwin Tornberg and Co., Inc., N.Y.C., 1959-73; sec-treas. Radio One Five Hundred, Inc., Indpls., 1964—, Radio 900, Inc., Louisville, 1966-90, Radio 780, Inc., Arlington, Va., 1977—. Contbr. to: Biol. Scis., Vol. 2, 1955. Chmn. Zoning Appeals Bd., Havre de Grace, 1982. Served to capt. AUS, 1941-46. Lodge: Rotary. Home and Office: 1000 Chesapeake Dr Havre De Grace MD 21078-3902

WETTERHAHN, KAREN ELIZABETH, chemistry educator; b. Plattsburgh, N.Y., Oct. 16, 1948; d. Gustave George and Mary Elizabeth (Thibault) W.; m. Leon H. Webb, June 19, 1982; children—Leon Ashley, Charlotte Elizabeth. B.S., St. Lawrence U., 1970; Ph.D., Columbia U., 1975. Chemist, Mearl Corp., Ossining, N.Y., 1970-71; research fellow Columbia U., N.Y.C., 1971-75, postdoctoral fellow, 1975-76; asst. prof. chemistry Dartmouth Coll., Hanover, N.H., 1976-82, assoc. prof., 1982-86, prof., 1986—, Albert Bradley 3rd Century prof. in the scis., 1996—; assoc. dean faculty scis., 1990-94, acting dean faculty, 1995. Contbr. articles to profl. jours. A.P. Sloan fellow, 1981. Mem. Am. Chem. Soc., Am. Assn. Cancer Research, AAAS, N.Y. Acad. Scis. Office: Dartmouth Coll Dept Chemistry 6128 Burke Lab Hanover NH 03755-3564

WETTIG, PATRICIA, actress; b. Cin., Dec. 4, 1951; m. Ken Olin, 1982; children: Clifford, Roxanne. Student, Ohio Wesleyan U., U. Aberdeen, Scotland; grad. in drama, Temple U.; studies with Bill Esper, Neighborhood Playhouse, N.Y.C. Personal dresser to Shirley MacLaine; mem. Circle Repertory Co. Appeared in theater prodns. including The Woolgatherer, 1980, The Diviners, 1981, Talking With, 1984, TV series St. Elsewhere, 1986-88, thirtysomething, 1987-91 (Emmy award for best supporting actress in drama 1988, for best lead actress in drama 1990, 1991), Courthouse, 1995—; guest appearances on L.A. Law, Hill Street Blues; appeared TV movies Silent Motive, 1992, Taking Back my Life: The Nancy Ziegenmeyer Story, 1992, Parallel Lives, 1994, The Langoliers, 1995; appeared in motion pictures, Guilty by Suspicion, 1991, City Slickers, 1991, City Slickers II: The Legend of Curley's Gold, 1994. *

WETZEL, DONALD TRUMAN, engineering company executive; b. Thayer, Mo., June 22, 1937; s. Ralph Noel and Jane Stiles (Hoyt) W.; m. Betty Ann Benbenek, June 20, 1959; children: James Douglas, Kathleen, Margaret. BS in Engring., U. Mo., 1959; postgrad., London Sch. Bus. Studies, 1981. Registered profl. engr., Mo., Ohio, Pa. Project engr. Ralston Purina Co., St. Louis, 1965-73; mgr. engring., Europe Ralston Purina Co., Brussels, 1973-75; project mgr. A.G. McKee Co., Chgo., 1976-80, v.p. ops., 1980-82; sr. v.p., gen. mgr. Davy-McKee Corp., Chgo., 1982-88; v.p., dep. div. mgr. Sverdrup Corp., St. Louis, 1989-90, v.p., ops. mgr., 1990-93, v.p., prin., 1993—. Capt. USAF, 1959-65, Europe. Decorated Air Force Commendation medal, Pres.'s Unit citation. Mem. NSPE, Nat. Inst. Food Technologists. Avocations: upland bird and water fowl hunting, fishing.

WETZEL, EDWARD THOMAS, investment company executive; b. Indpls., Apr. 16, 1937; s. Edward George and Sarah Catherine Wetzel; children from previous marriage: Raymond, Cynthia; m. Christine E. Healy. BA, Bethany (W.Va.) Coll., 1959; MBA, U. Mass., Amherst, 1963. Market research analyst Gen. Electric Co., Pittsfield, Mass., 1960-63; editor, spl. projects dir., asst. v.p. DMS, Inc., Greenwich, Conn., 1964-70; pres. Industry News Service, Inc., Wilton, Conn., 1970-92; v.p. Wright Investor's Svc., Bridgeport, Conn., 1992—. Pres. Wilton Vol. Ambulance Corps, 1976-81, 83-87. Served to 2d lt. USAFR, 1959-65. Recipient Disting. Citizen award Town of Wilton, 1986. Mem. Strategic Leadership Forum, Info. Industry Assn., Kiwanis (pres. bd. dirs. Wilton chpt. 1991-92). Office: Wright Investor's Svc 1000 Lafayette Blvd Bridgeport CT 06604-4725

WETZEL, FRANKLIN TODD, spinal surgeon, educator, researcher; b. Wilmington, Del., Mar. 7, 1955; s. Franklin Huff and Jean Hartman (Clouser) W.; m. Patricia Ann Cassanos, May 23, 1981 (div. June 1993); m. Cathleen Ann Myers, Nov. 21, 1993; 1 child, Colin Todd. AB, Harvard Coll., 1977; MD, U. Pa., 1981. Diplomate Am. Bd. Orthop. Surgery. Resident Yale U., New Haven, 1981-86, instr. Med. Sch., 1986-87; fellow S. Henry LaRocca, MD, New Orleans, 1987-88; asst. prof. Pa. State U., Hershey, 1988-91, assoc. prof., 1991-93; assoc. prof. U. Chgo., 1993—, dir. Spine Ctr., 1993—; reviewer Clin. Orthops., Phila., 1993—. Assoc. editor Spine, 1990—; contbr. articles to profl. jours. Physician Armenian Gen. Benevolent, Hershey, 1988; mem. alumni coun. Wilmington Friends Sch., 1991—. Fellow Am. Acad. Orthop. Surgery; mem. Cervical Spine Rsch. Soc., N.Am. Spine Soc., Am. Neuromodulation Soc. (bd. dirs. 1994—), Acad. Orthop. Soc., Am. Pain Soc., Harvard Club (interviewer 1995—), Sigma Xi. Presbyterian. Avocations: vertebrate palentology, vintage cars, military history, baseball, tennis, squash. Office: U Chgo Spine Ctr 4646 N Marine Dr Chicago IL 60640-5714

WETZEL, HEINZ, foreign language educator; b. Ziesar, Germany, May 11, 1935; immigrated to Can., 1965; s. Ernst and Katharina (Jentzsch) W.; m. Marianne Dummin, Mar. 19, 1957; children: Andreas, Susanne, Claudia. Staatsexamen, Free Univ., Berlin, 1960; Dr. phil., U. Göttingen, Fed. Republic Germany, 1967. Asst. prof. German dept. Queen's U., Kingston, Can., 1965-69; assoc. prof., grad. sec. German dept. U. Toronto, Can., 1969-72, prof. German dept., 1972—; chmn. German dept. U. Toronto, 1984-89; vis. prof. U. Calif., San Diego, 1973, Technische U. Braunschweig, Germany, 1973, Humboldt U. Berlin, 1995. Author: (book) Konkordanz zu den Dichtungen Georg Trakls, 1971, Klang und Bild in den Dichtungen Georg Trakls, 2d edit., 1972, Banale Vitalitaet und laehmendes Erkennen, Drei vergleichende Studien zu T.S. Eliots, The Waste Land; editor: Seminar: A Journal of Germanic Studies, 1980-85; contbr. 50 articles to German and comparative lit. to profl. jours. Fellowships and grants from Social Scis. and Humanities Rsch. Coun. of Can. Mem. MLA of Am., Can. Assn. Univ. Tchrs. German. Office: U Toronto, Univ College, Toronto, ON Canada M5S 3H7

WETZEL, JODI (JOY LYNN WETZEL), history and women's studies educator; b. Salt Lake City, Apr. 5, 1943; d. Richard Coulam and Margaret Elaine (Openshaw) Wood; m. David Nevin Wetzel, June 12, 1967; children: Meredith (dec.), Richard Rawlins. BA in English, U. Utah, 1965, MA in English, 1967; PhD in Am. Studies, U. Minn., 1977. Instr. Am. studies and family social sci. U. Minn., 1973-77, asst. prof. Am. studies and women's studies, 1977-79, asst. to dir. Minn. Women's Ctr., 1973-75, asst. dir., 1975-79; dir. Women's Resource Ctrs. U. Denver, 1980-84, mem. adj. faculty history, 1981-84, dir. Am. studies program, dir. Women's Inst., 1983-84; dir. Women in Curriculum U. Maine, 1985-86, mem. coop. faculty sociology, social work and human devel., 1985-86; dir. Inst. Women's Studies and Svcs. Met. State Coll. Denver, 1986—, assoc. prof. history, 1986-89, prof. history, 1990—; speaker, presenter, cons. in field; vis. prof. Am. studies U. Colo., 1985. Co-author: Women's Studies: Thinking Women, 1993; co-editor: Readings Toward Composition, 2d edit., 1969; contbr. articles to profl. publs. Del. at-large Nat. Women's Meeting, Houston, 1977; bd. dirs. Rocky Mountain Women's Inst., 1981-84; treas. Colo. Women's Agenda, 1987-91. U. Utah Dept. English fellow, 1967; U. Minn. fellow, 1978-79; grantee NEH, 1973, NSF, 1981-83, Carnegie Corp., 1988; named to Outstanding Young Women of Am., 1979. Mem. Am. Hist. Assn., Nat. Assn. Women in Edn. (Hilda A. Davis Ednl. Leadership award 1996, Sr. Scholar 1996), Am. Assn. for Higher Edn., Am. Studies Assn., Nat. Women's Studies Assn., Golden Key Nat. Honor Soc. (hon.), Alpha Lambda Delta, Phi Kappa Phi. Office: Met State Coll Denver Campus Box 36 PO Box 173362 Denver CO 80217-3362

WETZEL, KARL JOSEPH, physics educator, university official and dean; b. Waynesboro, Va., May 29, 1937; s. Mark Ernest and Margaret K. (Jungbluth) W.; m. Barbara Carol Damutz, Aug. 3, 1968; children: Sebastian P., Christopher M. BS in Physics, Georgetown U., 1959; MS in Physics, Yale U., 1960, PhD in Physics, 1965. Physicist Nat. Bur. Standards, Washington, 1959; postdoctoral fellow Inst. Nuclear Physics, Darmstadt, Germany, 1965-67, Argonne (Ill.) Nat. Lab., 1967-69; asst. prof. physics U. Portland, Oreg., 1969-72, assoc. prof., 1972-80, prof., 1980—, chmn. sci. dept., 1980-86, dean Grad. Sch., 1987—; cons. in field; adj. prof. State of Oreg. Dept. Continuing Edn., Portland, 1976-96. Contbr. articles to profl. publs. Bd. dirs. Friendly House Ctr., Portland, 1979-82, Choral Arts Ensemble, Portland, 1988-95. NSF fellow, 1965, 76-77; recipient Pres.' award Oreg. Mus. Sci. and Industry, 1972, Outstanding Advisor award Am. Coll. Test/Nat. Academic Advising Assn., 1984. Mem. Am. Phys. Soc., AAUP. Achievements include first to describe experiments using germanium detectors with neutron-capture gamma-ray spectroscopy; first measurement of Delbrück effect in photon scattering. Office: U Portland 5000 N Willamette Blvd Portland OR 97203-5743

WETZEL, ROBERT GEORGE, botany educator; b. Ann Arbor, Mich., Aug. 16, 1936; s. Wilhelm and Eugenia (Wagner) W.; m. Carol Ann Andree, Aug. 9, 1959; children: Paul Robert, Pamela Jeanette, Timothy Mark, Kristina Marie. BS, U. Mich., 1958, MS, 1959; PhD, U. Calif. at Davis, 1962; PhD (hon.), U. Uppsala, Sweden, 1984. Research assoc. Ind. U., Bloomington, 1962-65; asst. prof. botany Mich. State U., Hickory Corners, 1965-68; assoc. prof. Mich. State U., 1968-71, prof., 1971-86; prof. U. Mich., Ann Arbor, 1986-90; Bishop prof. biology U. Ala., Tuscaloosa, 1990—; cons. Internat. Biol. Program, London, 1967-75; chmn. Internat. Seagrass Commn., 1974-75; founding mem. Internat. Lake Environment Com., 1986—. Author: Limnology, 1975, 2d rev. edit., 1983, Limnological Analyses, 1979, 2d rev. edit., 1990, To Quench Our Thirst: Present and Future Freshwater Resources of the United States, 1983, Freshwater Ecosystems: Revitalizing Educational Programs in Limnology, 1996; editor: Periphyton of Freshwater Ecosystems, 1983, Wetlands and Ecotones, 1993, Recent Studies on Ecology and Management of Wetlands, 1994, Wetland Ecology, 1995, Lake Okeechobee: A Synthesis, 1995, Limnology of Developing Countries, vol. 1 1995; contbr. numerous articles on ecology and freshwater biology sys. to profl. jours.; mem. editl. bd. Aquatic Botany, 1975—, Jour. Tropical Freshwater Ecology, 1987—, Internat. Jour. Salt Lake Resources, 1991—, Biogeochemistry, 1993—, Lakes and Reservoirs, 1995—, Aquatic Ecology, 1996—, Boreal Environ. Rsch., 1996—, Aquatic Ecology, 1996—, Boreal Environment Rsch., 1996—; N.Am. editor Archiv fü Hydrobiologie, 1989—. Served with USNR, 1954-62. Recipient First T. Erlander Nat. professorship Swedish Nat. Research Council and U. Uppsala, 1982-83, award of Distinction U. Calif. at Davis, 1989; AEC grantee, 1965-75; NSF grantee, 1962—; ERDA grantee, 1975-77; Dept. Energy grantee, 1978—. Fellow AAAS; mem. Royal Danish Acaad. Scis. (elected fgn. mem. 1986), Am. Acad. Arts and Scis. (elected 1993), Am. Inst. Biol. Scis., Am. Soc. Limnology and Oceanography (editl. bd. 1971-74, v.p. 1979-80, pres. 1980-81, G.E. Hutchinson medal 1992), Aquatic Plant Mgmt. Soc., Ecol. Soc. Am., Internat. Assn. Ecology, Freshwater Biol. Assn. U.K., Internat. Assn. Theoretical and Applied Limnology (gen. sec. treas. 1968—, Baldi Meml. award 1989, Naumann-Thienemann medal 1992), Internat. Phycological Soc., Mich. Acad. Scis., N.Am. Benthological Soc., Phycological Soc. Am., Internat. Assn. Great Lakes Rsch., Internat. Consortium Salt Lake Rsch. (edtl. bd. 1991—), Japanese Soc. Limnology, Mich. Bot. Soc., Internat. Assn. Aquatic Vascular Plant Biologists (founder, pres. 1979—), Water Assn. Finland (editl bd. 1990—), Asociacion Argentina de Limnologia (hon.), Brazilian Soc. Limnology, Finnish Limnological Soc. (edtl. bd. 1989—), Internat. Lake Environ. Comm. Found. (exec. bd. 1986—), Netherlands Soc. Aquatic Ecology, Soc. Wetland Scientists, Sigma Xi, Phi Sigma. Home: 16 Dunbrook Tuscaloosa AL 35406-1962 Office: U Ala Dept Biol Scis Tuscaloosa AL 35487-0206

WETZLER, JAMES WARREN, economist; b. N.Y.C., Dec. 27, 1947; s. Benjamin and Deborah (Rabinowitz) W. B.S., U. Pa., 1969; Ph.D., Harvard U., 1973. Economist Joint Com. on Taxation, U.S. Congress, Washington, 1973-76; chief economist Joint Com. on Taxation, U.S. Congress, 1976-83, dep. chief staff, 1983-84; investment banker Bear Stearns and Co., Inc., N.Y.C., 1985-88; commr. N.Y. State Dept. Taxation and Finance, Albany, 1988-94; dir. Deloitte & Touche LLP, N.Y.C., 1995—. Office: Deloitte & Touche LLP 2 World Fin Ctr New York NY 10281

WETZLER, MONTE EDWIN, lawyer; b. N.Y.C., May 7, 1936; s. Alvin and Sally (Epstein) W.; m. Sally Jane Elsas, Dec. 19, 1963; 1 child, Andrew Elsas. AB, Brown U., 1957; LLB, U. Va., 1960; LLM in Taxation, NYU, 1966. Bar: N.Y. 1960, Calif. 1979. Assoc. Regan Goldfarb Heller Wetzler & Quinn, N.Y.C., 1960-66, ptnr., 1966-73, mng. ptnr., 1973-81; sr. v.p., gen. counsel Damson Oil Corp., N.Y.C., 1981-86, exec. v.p., CFO, 1986-88; pres. B&D Equities Inc., 1986-88; ptnr. Breed, Abbott & Morgan, N.Y.C., 1988-93, mng. ptnr., 1992-93; ptnr., exec. com. Whitman Breed Abbott & Morgan, N.Y.C., 1993-96; ptnr. Brown Rayman, Millstein Felder & Stein, 1997—. Editor: Selected Problems in Securities Law, 1972, Joint Ventures and Privatization in Eastern Europe, 1991-92. Counsel, N.Y. State Senate Com. on Housing, N.Y.C. Recipient Svc. award Practicing Law Inst., N.Y.C., 1973. Mem. ABA, N.Y. State Bar Assn. (exec. com. bus. law sect. 1993-94, securities law com.), Bar Assn. City N.Y., Corp. Law com.; Harmonie Club (gov. 1983-84, 86-88), Cedar Point Yacht Club, Essex Yacht Club, Phi Delta Phi, Order of Coif. Republican. Jewish. Home: 8 River

Road Dr Essex CT 06426-1377 Office: Whitman Breed Abbott & Morgan 200 Park Ave New York NY 10166-0005

WEVERS, JOHN WILLIAM, retired Semitic languages educator; b. Baldwin, Wis., June 4, 1919; emigrated to Can., 1951; s. Bernard and Wilemina (Te Grootenhuis) W.; m. Grace Della Brondsema, May 22, 1942; children: Robert Dick, John William, Harold George, James Merritt. A.B., Calvin Coll., Grand Rapids, Mich., 1940; Th.B., Calvin Sem., 1943; Th.D., Princeton Theol. Sem., 1945; D.D. (hon.), Knox Coll., Toronto, 1973; D.H.C. (hon.), Leiden U., 1985. Lectr., then asst. prof. O.T. and Semitic langs. Princeton Theol. Sem., 1946-51; mem. faculty U. Toronto, Ont., Can., 1951—, prof. Near Eastern studies, 1963—, prof. emeritus, 1984—, grad. chmn., 1972-75, chmn. dept., 1975-80; chmn. adminstrv. council Presbyn. Ch. Can., 1960-65. Author: Commentary on the Book of Ezekiel, 1969, Septuaginta Vetus Testamentum Graecum: Genesis, 1974, Deuteronomium, 1977, Numeri, 1981, Leviticus, 1986, Exodus, 1991; also text histories, 1974, 78, 83, 86, 92, Notes on the Greek Text of Exodus, 1990, Genesis, 1993, Deuteronomy, 1995, Leviticus, 1997. Bd. govs. Ctrl. Hosp., Toronto, 1963-96, chmn., 1967-80; chmn. Hosp. Coun. Met. Toronto, 1974-75; bd. govs. Ont. Hosp. Assn., 1974-84, pres., 1978-79. Recipient Queen's Jubilee medal, 1978. Fellow Royal Soc. Can.; mem. Oriental Club Toronto, Internat. Orgn. Septuagint and Cognate Studies (pres. 1972-80, hon. pres. 1989—), Can. Bibl. Studies (hon. life), Akademie Wissenschaften Goettingen (corr.), Arts and Letters Club (Toronto). Home: 116 Briar Hill Ave, Toronto, ON Canada M4R 1H9 Office: U Toronto, Dept Near & Middle Eastern, Civilizations, Toronto, ON Canada M5S 1A1

WEXELBAUM, MICHAEL, lawyer; b. Bklyn., Aug. 12, 1946; s. Joseph and Beatrice (Skurnick) W.; m. Cynthia Debra Schorr, Apr. 15, 1973 (dec. 1984); children: Joshua David, Stephanie Faye; m. Joan Brenda Math, Aug. 21, 1994; stepchildren: Jonathan David Kaye, Matthew Lawrence Kaye, Julie Dana Kaye. BA in Econs., Bucknell U., 1968; JD, NYU, 1971. Bar: N.Y. 1972, U.S. Dist. Ct. (so. and ea. dists.) N.Y. 1973. Assoc. Sherman, Citron & Karasik, P.C., N.Y.C., 1972-80; ptnr., head litigation dept. Sherman, Citron & Karasik, P.C., 1980—. Arbitrator Am. Arbitration Assn. and Gen. Arbitration Coun. of Textile and Apparel Industries, N.Y.C., 1982—. Mem. Bankruptcy Lawyers Bar Assn., Lawyers Assn. Textile and Apparel Industries (bd. govs.), Am. Arbitration Assn. (arbitrator). Democratic. Jewish. Avocations: tennis, skiing, biking, theatre. Home: 85 Norrans Ridge Dr Ridgefield CT 06877-4237 Office: Sherman Citron & Karasik PC Carnegie Hall Tower 152 W 57th St New York NY 10019-3301

WEXLER, ANNE, government relations and public affairs consultant; b. N.Y.C., Feb. 10, 1930; d. Leon R. and Edith R. (Rau) Levy; m. Joseph Duffey, Sept. 17, 1974; children by previous marriage: David Wexler, Daniel Wexler. B.A., Skidmore Coll., 1951, LL.D. (hon.), 1978; D.Sc. in Bus. (hon.), Bryant Coll., 1978. Assoc. pub. Rolling Stone mag., 1974-76; personnel adviser Carter-Mondale transition planning group, 1976-77; dep. undersec. regional affairs Dept. Commerce, 1977-78; asst. to Pres. of U.S., Washington, 1978-81; pres. Wexler and Assocs., Washington, 1981-82; govt. relations and pub. affairs cons., chmn. Wexler, Reynolds, Harrison & Schule, Inc., Washington, 1981-90; vice chmn. Hill and Knowlton PA Worldwide, Washington, 1990-92; chmn. The Wexler Group, div. Hill & Knowlton, Washington, 1992—; bd. dirs. Alumax, Inc., NOVA, Nat. Park Found., New Eng. Electric System, Comcast Corp., Dreyfus Index Funds; mem. vis. com. J.F. Kennedy Sch. Govt., Harvard U. Mem. bd. advisors Carter Ctr., Emory U.; mem. bd. visitors U. Md. Sch. Pub. Affairs. Named Outstanding Alumna Skidmore Coll., 1972, recipient most disting. alumni award, 1984, Bryce Harlow award, 1989. Mem. Coun. on Fgn. Rels., Nat. Women's Forum. Jewish. Office: Wexler Group 1317 F St NW Ste 600 Washington DC 20004-1105*

WEXLER, HASKELL, film producer, cameraman; b. Chgo., 1922; s. Simon Wexler; m. Nancy Ashenhurst (div.); two children; m. Marian Witt (div.); 1 son, Mark; m. Rita Taggart. Ednl. documentaries, Chgo., for eleven years; cinematographer films: The Hoodlum Priest, The Best Man, America America, The Loved One, In the Heat of the Night, Who's Afraid of Virginia Woolf? (Acad. award), The Thomas Crown Affair, American Graffiti, One Flew Over the Cuckoo's Nest, Introduction to the Enemy, Bound for Glory (Acad. award), Coming Home, Colors, Three Fugitives, 1988, Blaze, 1989, Lookin' to Get Out, Matewan, Other People's Money, The Babe, Mulholland Falls, 1995, Rich Man's Wife, 1995, (with others) Days of Heaven, (with others) Rolling Stones-IMAX, The Secret of Roan Inish, Canadian Bacon; writer, dir., photographer: Medium Cool, 1969; wrote and directed Latino, 1985. Received star on Hollywood's Walk of Fame, 1996. Mem. Acad. Motion Picture Arts and Scis. (bd. govs. cinematographers br.). Address: 626 Santa Monica Blvd # 111 Santa Monica CA 90401-2538 Agent: Spyros Skouras Skouras Agy 725 Arizona Ave Ste 406 Santa Monica CA 90401

WEXLER, HERBERT IRA, retail company executive; b. Newark, Sept. 6, 1916; s. Irving and Jeanette (Lesser) W.; m. Elaine L. Ellis, Oct. 10, 1948; children: Susan, Peter, Toni. Student, Rutgers U., 1939-41; student advanced mgmt. program, Harvard U., 1956. Stock boy, salesman, asst. buyer L. Bamberger & Co., 1935-41, asst. buyer, 1946-47; buyer appliances R.H. Macy & Co., N.Y.C., 1947-48, TV radio buyer, 1949-54, mdse. adminstr., v.p., 1955-67, sr. v.p., mem. exec. com., dir., 1968-73; pres., CEO, chmn. bd. dirs. Marcade Group Inc., N.Y.C., 1973-86, cons., bd. dirs., 1987-97. Vice chmn. Greater N.Y. coun. Boy Scouts Am.; organizer, fundraiser Yale Grace New Haven Hosp.; mem. Gov. Harriman's Com. to Investigate Fraud and Misrepresentation in Consumer Products; mem. adv. coun. to bd. trustees Greens Farms Acad., Westport, Conn.; gen. chmn. State of Israel Bond Drive, 1980, testimonial, 1978; gen. chmn. N.Y. Cmty. Svc. Soc.; chmn. N.Y. sect. for fundraising Denver Jewish Hosp; dir. Children's Blood Found. N.Y. Hosp. Capt. AUS, 1941-46. Named Key Man of Yr. Am. Jewish Com. and B'nai B'rith, 1957; named B'nai B'rith Man of Yr., 1976; recipient Disting. Service award Am. Jewish Com. and Anti-Defamation League, 1960, Award of Honor Fedn. Jewish Philanthropies of N.Y., 1961, Scroll of Honor United Jewish Appeal of Greater N.Y., 1964, Man of Yr. award Conn. Digestive Disease Soc., 1973. Mem. Harvard Club, Harmonie Club, Birchwood Country Club. Home: Box 2390 Westport CT 06880-3817

WEXLER, JACQUELINE GRENNAN (MRS. PAUL J. WEXLER), former association executive and college president; b. Sterling, Ill., Aug. 2, 1926; d. Edward W. and Florence (Dawson) Grennan; m. Paul J. Wexler, June 1, 1969; stepchildren: Wendy, Wayne. A.B., Webster Coll., 1948; M.A., U. Notre Dame, 1957; LL.D., Franklin and Marshall Coll., 1968, Phila. Coll. Textiles and Sci., 1987; D.H.L., Brandeis U., 1968; LL.D., Skidmore Coll., 1967, Smith Coll., 1975; HHD, U. Mich., 1967, U. Ohio, 1976; D.H.L., Carnegie Inst., 1966, Colo. Coll., 1967, U. Pa., 1979, U. South Fla., 1991; HHD (hon.), U. Hartford, 1987; DH, St. Ambrose Coll., 1981; DD, Lafayette Coll., 1990. Tchr. English and math. Loretto Acad., El Paso, Tex., 1951-54; tchr. English and math. Nerinx Hall, St. Louis, 1954-59; tchr. English Webster Coll., 1959-60, asst. to pres., 1959, v.p. devel., 1960, exec. v.p., 1962-65, pres., 1965-69; v.p., dir. internat. univ. studies Acad. for Ednl. Devel., N.Y.C., 1969; pres. Hunter Coll., City U. N.Y., 1969-79, Acad. Cons. Assoc., N.Y.C., 1982-90; ret., 1990; pres. NCCJ, 1982-90; writer, commentator, cons.; mem. Am. Council on Edn., Commn. on Internat. Edn., 1967; mem. adv. com. to dir. NIH, 1978-80; mem. exec. panel chief naval ops. U.S. Navy, 1978-81; bd. examiners Fgn. Service, Dept. State, 1981-83; mem. Pres.'s Adv. Panel on Research and Devel. in Edn., 1961-65; mem. Pres.'s Task Force on Urban Edn. Opportunities, 1967. Author: Where I Am Going, 1968; contbr. articles to profl. jours. Trustee U. Pa. Recipient NYU Sch. Edn. Ann. award for creative leadership in edn., 1968, Elizabeth Cutter Morrow award YWCA, 1978, Abraham L. Sachar Silver medallion Brandeis U.'s Nat. Women's Com., 1988, The Albert Einstein award Am. Soc. Technion, 1989; named One of Six Outstanding Women of St. Louis Area St. Louis chpt. Theta Sigma Phi, 1963, Woman of Achievement in Edn. St. Louis Globe-Democrat, 1964, Woman of Accomplishment Harpers Bazaar, 1967, one of Am.'s Most Important 100 Women Ladies Home Jour., 1988; Kenyon lectr. Vassar Coll., 1967. Mem. Mo. Acad. Squires, Kappa Gamma Pi.

WEXLER, LEONARD D., federal judge; b. Bklyn., Nov. 11, 1924; s. Jacob and Bessie (Herman) W.; m. Barbara Blum, Mar. 1953; children: Allison Wexler Smeitanka, Robert, William. BS, Ind. U., 1947; JD, NYU, 1950. Bar: N.Y. 1983, U.S. Dist. Ct. (ea. dist.) N.Y. 1983. Assoc. Siben & Siben Esqs., Bay Shore, N.Y., 1950-56; ptnr. Meyer & Wexler Esqs., Smithtown, N.Y., 1956-83; judge U.S. Dist. Ct. (eastern dist.) N.Y., 1983—; now sr. judge; atty. Suffolk County Police Conf., 1956-83; 1st atty. Suffolk County Patrolmen's Benevolent Assn., 1960-75; 1st atty. Suffolk County Detectives Assn., 1964-70; temporary state chmn., legal counsel Com. for Rev. Juvenile Justice System, N.Y. State Bar Assn.; speaker, lectr.; 1st adminstr. Assigned Counsel Plan N.Y. State, 1966-83. Served with U.S. Army, 1943-45. Mem. Suffolk County Criminal Bar Assn. (founder 1965, dir. 1956-60). Republican. Jewish. Avocations: travelling; sailing. Home: 94 W Bayberry Rd Islip NY 11751-4905 Office: US Dist Ct Rm 122 300 Rabro Dr Hauppauge NY 11788-4256*

WEXLER, PETER JOHN, producer, director, set designer; b. N.Y.C., Oct. 31, 1936; s. S. David and Berda (Sarnoff) W.; m. Constance Ann Ross, Nov. 30, 1962. BS in Design, U. Mich., 1958; student, Yale Sch. Drama, 1958. Designs include White House stage, 1961, War and Peace, 1964, The White Devil, 1965, A Joyful Noise, 1966, The Happy Time, 1967, In the Matter of J. Robert Oppenheimer, 1968, Merv Griffin TV show, 1965, Terra Nova, 1979 (L.A. Dramalogue Critics award); prin. designer, Center Theatre Group, L.A., 1967-70, designer, N.Y. Philharmonic Promenades, 1965-78; play and film The Trial of the Catonsville 9, 1971-72; Leonard Bernstein's Mass, L.A., 1973, N.Y. Philharmonic Rug Concerts, 1973-77, Les Troyens, Met. Opera Co., 1973, Le Prophète, Met. Opera Co., 1977, Un Ballo in Maschera, Met. Opera Co., 1980, Theatre Space Prodns., Pitts. Pub. Theatre, 1975-77; mem. design team for Frank O. Gehry & Assocs., redesign Hollywood Bowl; designer: Albert Herring, Savonlinna Opera Festival, Finland, 1981; centennial prodn. Les Troyens, Met. Opera, 1983; directed: Cold Storage, Ariz. Theatre Co., 1978, Terra Nova, Pitts. Public Theatre, 1981; producer, Dallas Symphony Orch.'s Star Fest 80; producer Rocky Mountain Music Festival, Denver Symphony Orch., 1983-84, Star Spangled Banner, Permanent Exhibition U.S. Nat. Emblem, Smithsonian Instn., Washington, 1982; producer, design exhbn. Am. Anthem, LTV Ctr., Dallas/Smithsonian Instn., 1985; designer, broker exhbn. Liberties with Liberty, Trammell Crow Co./Mus. Am. Folk Art, 1985; designer Horizons '86, N.Y. Philharmonic, 1986; co-producer, designer video, exhbn. and space Albany Urban Cultural Park, Albany, N.Y., 1986; producer, dir. Pletka, multimedia theatre piece for orch., Dallas Symphony Orch., 1987; programmer, designer Trans-Hudson Ferry for the Port Authority of N.Y. and N.J., 1987-88; producer The Search for Life, Smithsonian Inst., 1987; producer Mstislav Rostropovich 60th Anniv. Gala Concert, Nat. Symphony Orch., Kennedy Ctr., Washington, 1987, Navy 87, Navy 89, USN multi-media orchestral prodn., Washington, 1987; producer, artistic dir. Spring Creek Music Festival, Garland, Tex. Dallas Ft. Worth Metroplex, 1992-94; dir. Lost in the Stars, A.C.O., Carnegie Hall, 1989; visual cons. Lifetime Med. (cable TV), 1989-90; design cons. Reebok River Stage - Radio City Music Hall Prodns, 1989; program designer Mega-Mall, Oxford Devel. Co., Pitts.; designer Unfinished Stories, 1994; prodr. A Salute to Slava, Kennedy Ctr., Washington, 1994, (TV series) Music in America Nat. Symphony Orch., Kennedy Ctr., Washington, 1997; creator Boston Pops invironment, 1995-97, Boston Symphony Hall Sys. Update Plan, 1995-97. Project leader Outdoor Performance Facility, Met. Opera Co., N.Y. Philharmonic Symphony, Dept. Cultural Affairs City of N.Y., 1980-91; cons. Temp. Quarters Project San Francisco Ballet, 1994. Recipient Internat. Theatre Inst. competition award ANTA, 1965, most imaginative use of scene design award Saturday Rev., 1965, Drama Desk-Joseph Maharam award for The Happy Time as best designer of mus., 1968, L.A. Drama Critics Circle award, 1971, Bard award for Excellence in Architecture & Urban Design, 1996. Address: 277 W End Ave New York NY 10023-2604

WEXLER, RICHARD LEWIS, lawyer; b. Chgo., June 19, 1941; s. Stanley and Lottie (Pinkert) W.; m. Roberta Seigel, June 13, 1962; children: Deborah (Mrs. Jonathan Sokobin), Joshua, Jonathan. Student, U. Mich., 1959-1962; JD cum laude, John Marshall Law Sch., 1965. Bar: Ill. 1965, US. Dist. Ct. (no. dist.) Ill. 1967. Gen. counsel Metro. Planning Council, Chgo., 1965-67; ptnr. Wexler, Kane, Rosenzweig & Shaw, Chgo., 1967-71, Taussig, Wexler & Shaw, Chgo., 1971-78, Wexler, Siegel & Shaw, Ltd., Chgo., 1978-83; ptnr. Sachnoff & Weaver, Ltd., Chgo., 1983-91, chair real estate dept., 1985-91, mng. ptnr., 1985-90; ptnr., co-chairperson real estate dept. Lord Bissell & Brook, Chgo., 1991—, mem. compensation com., 1995—; legal cons. Zoning Laws Study Commn., Ill. Gen. Assembly, Springfield, 1969-71, Urban Counties Study Commn., Springfield, 1971-72; legal counsel Ill. Coastal Zone Mgmt. Program, Springfield, 1979-81, Northeastern Ill. Planning Commn., Chgo., 1969—. Contbr. numerous articles to profl. jours. Pres. Jewish Fedn. Met. Chgo., 1986-88, mem. numerous coms., also bd. dirs., 1978-90; pres. Jewish United Fund, 1986-88; bd. dirs. Coun. Jewish Fedns., 1980, mem. exec. com., 1985—, v.p., 1988—, chmn. planning steering com., 1990-95, chmn. fedn./agy. rels. com., 1988-90; co-chmn. Task Force on Poverty and Low Income, 1985-87; nat. vice-chmn. United Jewish Appeal, 1988—, nat. chmn., 1996—, regional allocations chmn., 1987-88, chmn. region II, 1988-90, budget com., 1989-92, allocations com., 1990-91, campaign exec., 1991—; chmn. Operation Exodus II, 1993-94, chmn. nat. mktg. com., 1994-95, chmn. 1997 campaign planning and budget com., 1995—; bd. dirs. Jewish Edn. Soc. N.Am., 1982-85, Hebrew Immigrant Aid Soc., 1988—, Nat. Conf. on Soviet Jewry, 1989—, vice chmn., 1989-92, nat. chmn., 1992—; bd. dirs. Nat. Jewish Cmty. Rels. Adv. Coun., 1988-90, vice chmn., 1988-92; chmn. Jewish Com. Rels. Coun. Chgo., 1988-89. Fellow Eta Lambda; mem. ABA, Ill. State Bar Assn. (Lincoln award, Legal Writing, 1966). Avocations: tennis, reading, travel. Office: Lord Bissell & Brook 115 S La Salle St Ste 3400 Chicago IL 60603-3801

WEXLER, ROBERT, university administrator. Pres. U. of Judaism, L.A. Office: University of Judaism 15600 Mulholland Dr Bel Air CA 90077-1519

WEXLER, ROBERT, congressman; b. Queens; m. Laurie Wexler; children: Rachel, Zachary, Hannah. BA in Polit. Scis., U. Fla.; JD, George Washington U. Law Sch. Mem. 105th Congresses from 19th Fla. dist., 1996—, Fla. State Senate, 1990-96; subcom. on crime, immigration, Asia and Internat. Ops.; com. internat. rels., jud.; chair Criminal Justice com. Recipient Senatorial Leadership award Fla. Prosecutor's Assn.; named Legis. of the Year Palm Beach Police Benevolent Assn., Top Environ. Senator Fla. Leagues Conservation Voters, 1996. Office: Congress of the US House of Reps Washington DC 20515-0919

WEXNER, LESLIE HERBERT, retail executive; b. Dayton, Ohio, 1937. BSBA, Ohio State U., 1959, HHD (hon.), 1986; LLD (hon.), Hofstra U., 1987; LHD (hon.), Brandeis U., 1990; PhD (hon.), Jewish Theol. Sem. Founder, pres., chmn. bd. The Limited, Inc., fashion chain, Columbus, 1963—; dir., mem. exec. com. Banc One Corp., Sotheby's Holdings Inc., vis. com. Grad. Sch. Design Harvard U.; mem. bus. adminstrn. adv. coun. Ohio State U.; chmn. Retail Industry Trade Action Coalition. Bd. dirs. Columbus Urban League, 1982-84, Hebrew Immigrant Aid Soc., N.Y.C., 1982—; co-chmn. Internat. United Jewish Appeal Com.; nat. vice chmn., treas. United Jewish Appeal; bd. dirs., mem. exec. com. Am. Jewish Joint Distbn. Com., Inc.; trustee Columbus Jewish Fedn., 1972, Columbus Jewish Found., Aspen Inst., Ohio State U., Columbus Capital Corp. for Civic Improvement; former trustee Columbus Mus. Art, Columbus Symphony Orch., Whitney Mus. Am. Art, Capitol South Community Urban Redevel. Corp.; former mem. Governing Com. Columbus Found.; founding mem., first chair The Ohio State U. Found; exec. com. Am. Israel Pub. Affairs Com. Decorated cavaliere Republic of Italy. Named Man of Yr. Am. Mktg. Assn., 1974. Mem. Young Presidents Orgn., Sigma Alpha Mu. Club: B'nai B'rith. Office: Limited Inc PO Box 16000 3 Limited Pky Columbus OH 43230-6000*

WEY, JONG-SHINN, research laboratory manager; b. Kaohsiung, Taiwan, Oct. 26, 1944; came to U.S. 1968; s. Tan-Ding and Chao (Lee) W.; m. Hseh-Yi Su, 1965; children: John, Nancy. BS in Chem. Engring., Nat. Taiwan U., 1967; PhD, Clarkson U., 1973. Sr. rsch. chemist Eastman Kodak Co., Rochester, N.Y., 1973-80, rsch. assoc., 1980-84, lab. head, 1984-91, sr. lab. head, 1991—. Co-author: Preparation and Properties of Solid State Materials, 1981, Handbook of Industrial Crystallization, 1992. Recipient Jour. award Photographic Sci. and Engring. Fellow Soc. Photographic Scientists and Engrs.; mem. AIChE. Achievements include patents in field; published papers on crystallization, precipitation, nucleation, growth, size distribution control and photographic emulsion. Home: 259 Hillary Ln Penfield NY 14526-1646 Office: Eastman Kodak Co Rsch Labs Bldg 59 Rochester NY 14650-1736

WEYANDT, DANIEL SCOTT, naval officer, engineer; b. Altoona, Pa., Dec. 26, 1962; s. Blair Sherwood and Madolyn Rae (Dunmire) W. BS, Juniata Coll., Huntingdon, Pa., 1984; MS in Physics, Pa. State U., 1992; MBA, U. R.I., 1995. Commd. USN, 1984, advanced through grades to lt. comdr., 1996; divsn. officer USS John C. Calhoun, Charleston, S.C., 1987, USS Simon Bolivar, Charleston, 1986-89; rsch. officer Naval Undersea Warfare Ctr. Divsn., Newport, R.I., 1992-95; sr. engr., countermeasures mgr. Electronic Sensors and Sys. divsn. Northrop Grumman corp., Sykesville, Md., 1995—. Decorated Navy achievement medal, Navy commendation medal. Mem. Altoona Horseshoe Chorus (assoc. dir. 1978—), Sigma Pi Sigma. Republican. Methodist. Avocations: music, water sports, fitness. Home: PO Box 89 Hesston PA 16647-0089 Office: Northrop Grumman Corp 7301 Sykesville Rd Sykesville MD 21784-7404

WEYANDT, LINDA JANE, anesthetist; b. Altoona, Pa., Nov. 5, 1948; d. Charles Leroy and Edna Pearl (Schaefer) W. RN, Phila. Gen. Hosp. Sch. Nursing, 1970; BA, Stephens Coll., 1978; MD, UNAM-Noreste, Mex., 1983; PhD candidate, So. Calif. U., 1995. Cert. trauma resolutionist Am. Inst. Med. and Psychotherapeutic Hypnosis; cert. hypnotherapist Am. Bd. Hypnotherapy. Pvt. practice anesthesia J.L. Med. Svcs., McAllen, Tex., 1986-92; staff anesthetist MD Anderson Hosp., Houston, 1992, VA Hosp., Houston, 1994—; dir., owner Hypnosis and Pain Mgmt. Svcs. of Tex., Houston, 1993—; sr. disabilty analyst, diplomate Am. Bd. Disability Analysts; dir. Associated Hypnotherapy and Pain Mgmt., Houston, 1991; clin. instr. dept. anesthesia Baylor Coll. Medicine, Houston. Contbr. articles to profl. jours. Fellow Am. Bd. Med. Psychotherapists & Psychodiagnosticians (diplomate); mem. Am. Acad. Pain Mgmt. (diplomate), Am. Assn. Behavior Therapists, Biofeedback Soc. Tex., Am. Soc. Clin. Hypnosis, Am. Psychotherapy and Med. Hypnosis Assn. (Advance Med. Hypnosis award 1994), Internat. Soc. Hypnosis Assn. (Australia), Am. Soc. Clin. Hypnosis, Houston Soc. Clin. Hypnosis, Alumna Assn. Stephens Coll., Alumna Assn. Phila. Gen. Hosp., NOW. Avocations: ballooning, fishing, clown collecting. Office: Associated Hypnotherapy and Pain Mgmt Svcs Tex 6300 West Loop S Ste 333 Bellaire TX 77401-2913

WEYENBERG, DONALD RICHARD, chemist; b. Glenvil, Nebr., July 11, 1930; s. Clyde H. and Elva I. (Hlavaty) W.; m. Barbara Ann Oppenheim, Dec. 26, 1955; children: Ann Louise, Thomas Richard. B.S. in Chemistry, U. Nebr., 1951; Ph.D., Pa. State U., 1958; P.M.D. Program, Harvard U., 1968. Research chemist Dow Corning Corp., Midland, Mich., 1951-65, research mgr., 1965-68, dir. corp. devel., 1968-69, dir. silicone research, 1969-71, bus. mgr., 1971-76, dir. research, 1976-79, v.p. research and devel., 1979-86, chief sci. and sr. v.p. research and devel., 1987-93, sci. emeritus, 1993—; bd. dirs. Dendritech; Hurd lectr. Northwestern U., 1992—. Bd. editors Organometallics Jour., 1980-86; contbr. articles to sci. jours., chpts. to books; patentee silicone materials. Bd. visitors Memphis State U., 1981-87; mem. indsl. bd. advisors U. Nebr., 1988. Named Alumni fellow Pa. State U., 1988. Mem. Am. Chem. Soc. (chmn. Midland sect. 1967, Outstanding Achievement in Promotion Chem. Scis. award Midland sect.), Indsl. Rsch. Inst., Sigma Xi. Lodge: Rotary. Home: 4601 Arbor Dr Midland MI 48640-2644 Office: Dow Corning Corp PO Box 994 2200 Salzburg St Midland MI 48640-8594

WEYERHAEUSER, GEORGE HUNT, forest products company executive; b. Seattle, July 8, 1926; s. John Philip and Helen (Walker) W.; m. Wendy Wagner, July 10, 1948; children: Virginia Lee, George Hunt, Susan W., Phyllis A., David M., Merrill W. BS with honors in Indsl. Engring., Yale U., 1949. With Weyerhaeuser Co., Tacoma, 1949—, successively mill foreman, br. mgr., 1949-56, v.p., 1957-66, exec. v.p., 1966-88, pres., chief exec. officer, 1988, chmn. bd., chief exec. officer, 1988-91, chmn. bd., past CEO, also bd. dirs.; bd. dirs. Boeing Co., SAFECO Corp., Chevron Corp.; mem. Bus. Coun., Bus. Roundtable, Wash. State Bus. Roundtable. Office: Weyerhaeuser Fin Svcs CH 5B Tacoma WA 98477-0001*

WEYERS, LARRY L., energy executive. BA, Doane Coll.; ME, Columbia U.; MBA, Harvard U. Registered profl. engr. With Commonwealth Edison, Chgo.; mgmt. cons. Cresap, Inc., Chgo.; sr. v.p. Power Supply and Engring. Wis. Pub. Svc. Resources Corp., Green Bay, pres., COO. Office: Wis Pub Svc Resources Corp 700 N Adams St PO Box 19001 Green Bay WI 54307-9001

WEYGAND, ROBERT A., congressman; b. Attleboro, Mass., May 10, 1948. BA in Fine Arts, U. R.I., 1971, BS in Civil and Environ. Engring., 1976. Project mgr. R.I. Dept. Nat. Resources, 1973-82; owner Weygand, Orciuch & Christie, Inc., 1982-92; mem. R.I. Ho. of Reps. from 84th dist., 1984-92; lt. gov. State of R.I., 1993-97; mem. 105th Congress from 2d R.I. dist., 1997—; mem. budget com., small bus. com.; chmn. house com. on corps., 1990; chmn. E. Providence Planning Bd., 1978-84, R.I. Small Bus. Advocacy Coun., 1992—, R.I. Long Term Care Coord. Coun., 1992—, R.I. Delegation/White House Conf. on Aging, 1995; bd. dirs. R.I. Scenic Hwy., 1988-92; presdl. appointee White House Conf. on Small Bus., 1995. Bd. dirs. Save the Bay, 1984-87, United Way, 1993—, Meeting St. Ctr., 1993—; pres., bd. dirs. R.I. Parks Assn., 1983-92; chmn. R.I. Land Use Commn., 1987-92. Recipient Legislator of Yr. award R.I. League Cities and Towns, 1988, Exceptional Pub. Svc. award FBI, 1992, Disting. Svc. Star State of R.I., 1992. Mem. Am. Soc. Landscape Architects; Am. Planning Assn. (Outstanding Pub. Svc. award New Eng. chpt. 1992). Office: US Ho of Reps 507 Cannon Providence RI 20515*

WEYHER, HARRY FREDERICK, lawyer; b. Wilson, N.C., Aug. 19, 1921; s. Harry Frederick and Laura Gray (Carter) W.; m. Barbara Dore McCusker, Sept. 9, 1950 (div. May 1971); children: Barbara Brandon, Harry Frederick III, Laura Carter; m. Laura Hyman Harvey, Oct. 17, 1971 (div. Sept. 1986); m. Michelle Eimers, Dec. 29, 1989. B.S., U. N.C., 1946; student, U. Glasgow, Scotland, 1946; LL.B. magna cum laude, Harvard U., 1949. Bar: N.Y., 1950. Assoc. Cravath, Swaine & Moore, N.Y.C., 1949-54; sr. assoc. counsel N.Y. State Crime Commn., 1950-52; ptnr., counsel Olwine, Connelly, Chase, O'Donnell & Weyher, N.Y.C., 1954-91; adj. assoc. prof. N.Y.U. Sch. Law, 1952-62; bd. dirs. AFA Protective Systems, Inc., The Pioneer Fund, Inc. Author: (with Hiram Knott) ESOP--Employee Stock Ownership Plan, 2d ed., 1985, Hanging Out a Shingle, 1987; contbr. articles to profl. jours. Mem. ABA, N.Y. State Bar Assn., Assn. of Bar of City of N.Y., Phi Beta Kappa, Beta Gamma Sigma, Zeta Psi. Clubs: Harvard, Racquet and Tennis (N.Y.C.), Lyford Cay (Nassau), Boone & Crockett. Home: 211 E 70th St Apt 17B New York NY 10021-5207 Office: 551 5th Ave Fl 27 New York NY 10176-2799

WEYHER, HARRY FREDERICK, III, metals company executive; b. N.Y.C., Mar. 9, 1956; s. Harry F. and Barbara (McCusker) W.; m. Anda Gailitis, July 7, 1984; children: Harry F. IV, Jesse D. BA, Middlebury Coll., 1977. Treas. Bunge Corp., N.Y.C., 1977-90; v.p. fin. Gerald Metals Inc., Stamford, Conn., 1990-96; ptnr. Littlejohn & Co., LLC, Greenwich, Conn., 1996—. Mem. Racquet & Tennis Club. Home: 215 Ridgefield Rd Wilton CT 06897-2432 Office: Littlejohn & Co LLC 115 E Putnam Ave Greenwich CT 06830-5643

WEYLAND, DEBORAH ANN, learning disabilities teacher consultant; b. Fayetteville, N.C., Aug. 19, 1959; d. William Frederick Louis and Carol Joyce (Varhall) W. BA, Fairleigh Dickinson U., 1981; MA, Montclair (N.J.) State U., 1994. Cert. tchr. nursery sch., K-8, tchr. of handicapped; cert. learning disabilities tchr. cons. Permanent substitute tchr. Franklin Jr. H.S., Nutley, N.J., 1981-82, asst. tchr. SCE program, 1982-83; tchr. grade 2 and kindergarten Saint Peter's Sch., Belleville, N.J., 1983-85; tchr. grade 5 and kindergarten Belleville Pub. Schs., 1985-91, tchr. pre-sch. handicapped program, 1991-95; learning cons. Belleville Pub. Schs., 1994—; adv. bd. Belleville Alliance for Substance Edn., 1993—, exec. bd. 1994—; cons. Assn. of Learning, State of N.J., 1994—; cons. in field. Mem. Spl. Edn. Parent and Profls. Orgn., Belleville Edn. Assn., Women's Club Belleville, Phi Zeta Kappa, Phi Omega Epsilon. Avocations: arts and crafts, reading, walking. Office: Belleville Pub Schs 100 Passaic Ave Belleville NJ 07109-1807

WEYRAUCH, PAUL TURNEY, retired army officer; b. Alpine, Tex., July 22, 1941; s. Paul Russell and Margaret Fischer (Fletcher) W.; m. Nancy Virginia Haight, Dec. 18, 1965; children: Julie Lynn, Paul C. BS, U.S. Mil. Acad., West Point, N.Y., 1963; MBA, Tulane U., 1976; Tchg. Cert., S.W. Tex. State U., 1995. Commd. 2d lt. U.S. Army, 1963, advanced through grades to brig. gen.; bn. comdr. 1st Bn., 5th F.A., Ft. Riley, Kans., 1978-80; asst. chief of staff 1st Inf. Div., Ft. Riley, 1980-81; comdr. 1st Cav. Div. Arty., Ft. Hood, 1982-85; chief of staff U.S. Army F.A. Ctr., Ft. Sill, Okla., 1985-86; asst. chief of staff for plans and policy Allied Forces So. Europe, Naples, Italy, 1986-89; chief of staff III Corps and Ft. Hood, 1989-91; ret., 1991; tchr. math. Richarte H.S., Georgetown, Tex., 1995—; planning and zoning commr. City of Georgetown, 1994-96, chmn. planning and zoning commn., 1995-96. Tchr. Sunday sch. local Protestant chs., pres. chapel couns., leader, coord. Bible studies. Decorated D.S.M., Def. Superior Svc. Medal, Legion of Merit, Bronze Star medal with V. device, Bronze Star medal with 1 oak leaf cluster, Meritorious Svc. medal with 3 oak leaf clusters. Mem. 1st Cav. Div. Assn. Avocations: running, collecting military insignia. Home: 320 S Ridge Cir Georgetown TX 78628-8213

WEYRAUCH, WALTER OTTO, law educator; b. Lindau, Germany, Aug. 27, 1919; came to U.S., 1952; s. Hans Ernst Winand and Meta Margarete (Lönholdt) W.; m. Jill Carolyn White, Mar. 17, 1973; children from previous marriages—Kurt Roman, Corinne Harriet Irene, Bettina Elaine (dec.). Student, U. Freiburg, 1937, U. Frankfurt Main, Germany, 1940-43; Dr. iur, U. Frankfurt Main, Germany, 1951; LL.B., Georgetown U., 1955; LL.M., Harvard, 1956; J.S.D., Yale, 1962. Referendar Frankfurt, Germany, 1943-48; atty. German cts. U.S. Ct. Appeals, Allied High Commn., Frankfurt, 1949-52; expert on trade regulations, visit in U.S. under auspices Dept. State, 1950; Harvard U. Dumbarton Oaks Library and Collection, Washington, 1953-55; asst. in instrn. Law Sch., Yale, 1956-57; assoc. prof. law U. Fla., Gainesville, 1957-60, prof., 1960-89, Clarence J. TeSelle prof. law, 1989-94, Stephen C. O'Connell chair, 1994—; hon. prof. law Johann Wolfgang Goethe U., Frankfurt Main, 1980—; vis. cons. U. Calif. at Berkeley, Space Scis. Lab., 1965-66; vis. prof. law Rutgers U., 1968; vis. prof. polit. sci. U. Calif. at Berkeley, 1968-69; vis. prof. law U. Frankfurt, 1975; cons. Commn. of Experts on Problems of Succession of the Hague Conf. on Pvt. Internat. Law, U.S. Dept. State, 1968-71; Rockefeller Found. fellow, Europe, 1958-59. Author: The Personality of Lawyers, 1964, Zum Gesellschaftsbild des Juristen, 1970, Hierarchie der Ausbildungsstätten, Rechtsstudium und Recht in den Vereinigten Staaten, 1976, Gestapo V-Leute: Tatsachen und Theorie des Geheimdienstes, 1989, 2d edit., 1992; co-author (with Sanford N. Katz) American Family Law in Transition, 1983, (with Katz and Frances E. Olsen) Cases and Materials on Family Law: Legal Concepts and Changing Human Relationships, 1994; contbr. to: Clinical Law Training—Interviewing and Counseling, 1972, Law, Justice, and the Individual in Society—Psychological and Legal Issues, 1977, Marriage and Cohabitation in Contemporary Societies: Areas of Legal, Social and Ethical Change—An International and Interdisciplinary Study, 1980, Dutch transl., 1981, Group Dynamic Law: Exposition and Practice, 1988, The Living Law of Nations: Essays on Refugees, Minorities, Indigenous Peoples and the Human Rights of Other Vulnerable Groups, 1996, Law, Morality, and Religion: Global Perspectives, 1996. Mem. Law and Soc. Assn., Internat. Soc. on Family Law, Assn. Am. Law Schs. (chmn. com. studies beyond 1st degree in law 1965-67), Order of Coif. Home: 2713 SW 5th Pl Gainesville FL 32607-3113 Office: U Fla Coll Law Gainesville FL 32611

WEYRICH, PAUL MICHAEL, political organizations executive; b. Racine, Wis., Oct. 7, 1942; s. Ignatius A. and Virginia M. (Wickstrom) W.; m. Joyce Anne Smigun, July 6, 1963; children: Dawn, Peter, Diana, Stephen, Andrew. AA, U. Wis., 1962. Ordained deacon Melkite Greek Eparchy, 1990. News dir. Service Broadcasting, Kenosha, Wis., 1962-63; reporter Milw. Sentinel, 1963-64; polit. reporter, newscaster CBS, Milw., 1964-65; news dir. Sta. KQXI, Denver, 1966; asst. U.S. Sen. Gordon Allott of Colo., 1966-73; asst. to Sen. Carl T. Curtis, Nebr., 1973-77; founder, pres. Heritage Found., 1973-74; nat. chmn. Free Congress PAC, Coalitions for Am., BOD, AMTRAK, 1987-93; pres. Free Congress Found., Krieble Inst. of Free Congress Found., NET-Polit. Newstalk Network; Washington editor The Wanderer, 1969-71; nat. editor Transport Central, 1968-73; treas. Coun. Nat. Policy, 1981-92; bd. dirs. All News Radio WEEI, Boston, 1984-90, Krieble Inst. Russia; vice chmn. Com. for Effective State Govt. Host (TV) Direct Line, 1993—. Recipient Youth of Yr. award Racine Optimist Club, 1960, Excellence in Reporting citation Milw. Common Council, 1964, Documentary of Yr. award for Wis. TV, 1965, Crystal Ball award for predicting outcome 1996 presdl. election Washington Post, 1996, Thomas Jefferson award for servant leadership Coun. Nat. Policy, 1997. Mem. Central Electric Railroaders Assn., Internat. Policy Forum (chmn. 1983-94); former mem. HUD Adv. Commn. on Regulatory Barriers to Affordable Housing. Greek Catholic. Author: The Role of Rails series, 1964; pub. Polit. Report, 1975-89, The New Electric Rwy. Jour., 1988—, Spotlight on Congress, 1989-93; host (daily talk show) Direct Line, 1993—; co-host The New Electric Railway Jour., 1994—, Ways & Means, 1994—. Home: 12615 Lake Normandy Ln Fairfax VA 22030-7262 Office: Free Congress Found 717 2nd St NE Washington DC 20002-4368

WHALE, ARTHUR RICHARD, lawyer; b. Detroit, Oct. 28, 1923; s. Arthur B. and Orpha Louella (Doak) W.; m. Roberta Lou Donaldson, Oct. 29, 1949; children: Richard Donaldson, Linda Jean. BSChemE, Northwestern U., 1945; LLB, George Washington U., 1956. Bar: D.C. 1957, Mich. 1957, Ind. 1977, Office of U.S. Patent and Trademark 1957. Chem. engr. Ansul Chem. Co., Marinette, Wis., 1946-47, Parke, Davis & Co., Detroit, 1947-50; writer med. lit. Parke, Davis & Co., 1950-52; chem. engr. Bur. Ships, U.S. Dept. Navy, Washington, 1952-55; dep. sect. head, indsl. gas sect. Bur. Ships, U.S. Dept. Navy, 1954-55; patent engr. Swift & Co., Washington, 1955-56; patent atty. Upjohn Co., Kalamazoo, 1956-65; asst. mgr. organic chems. sect. patent dept. Dow Chem. Co., Midland, Mich., 1965-66; mgr. Dow Chem. Co., 1967-73, mng. counsel, 1973-75; asst. sec., gen. patent counsel Eli Lilly & Co., Indpls., 1975-86; of counsel Miller, Morriss, & Pappas, Lansing, Mich., 1986-89, Baker & Daniels, Indpls., 1987—; bd. dirs. Wyckoff Chem. Co., South Haven, Mich.; lectr. Practicing Law Inst., John Marshall Law Sch. Contbr. articles to profl. jours. Pres. Nat. Inventors Hall of Fame Found., 1978-79; bd. dirs. Holcomb Rsch. Inst., INdpls, 1982-86. Served to lt. (j.g.) USNR, 1943-46. Mem. State Bar Mich. (chmn. patent trademark copyright sect. 1967-69), D.C. Bar Assn. (mem. patent trademark copyright div.), Midland County Bar Assn. (pres. 1974-75), Am. Bar Assn. (mem. patent trademark copyright sect.), Assn. Corp. Patent Counsel, Nat. Coun. Patent Law Assns. (chmn. 1979-80), Am. Intellectual Property Law Assn. (pres. 1974-75), Ashlar Lodge, Masons, Shriners. Republican. Presbyterian. Avocation: golf. Home: 3513 Admiralty Ln Indianapolis IN 46240-3568 also: 2363 Gulf Shore Blvd N Naples FL 34103-4356 Office: Baker & Daniels 300 N Meridian St Ste 2700 Indianapolis IN 46204-1750

WHALEN, CHARLES WILLIAM, JR., author, business executive, educator; b. Dayton, Ohio, July 31, 1920; s. Charles William and Colette (Kelleher) W.; m. Mary Barbara Gleason, Dec. 27, 1958; children—Charles E., Daniel D., Edward J., Joseph M., Anne E., Mary B. B.S., U. Dayton, 1942, H.H.D. (hon.), 1980; M.B.A., Harvard U., 1946; postgrad., Ohio State U., 1959-60; LL.D., Central State U., Ohio, 1966. Vice pres. Dayton Dress Co., 1946-52; faculty U. Dayton, 1952-66; mem. 90th-95th Congresses 3d Dist. Ohio; pres. New Directions, Washington, 1978-79; fellow Woodrow Wilson Internat. Center for Scholars, 1980; adj. prof. Sch. Internat. Service, Am. U., 1981. Mem. Ohio Ho. of Reps., 1954-60, Ohio Senate, 1960-66; mem. Internat. Vol. Svcs., Inc., 1985-95; v.p. Washington Inst. Fgn. Affairs; mem. U. Dayton adv. bd. Ctr. for Internat. Studies; bd. dirs. Harvard Bus. Sch., Washington, 1982-84, 91-94. 1st lt. AUS, 1943-46. Recipient Disting. Alumnus award U. Dayton Alumni Assn., 1975;. Roman Catholic. Clubs: Capitol Hill, Kenwood Country, Dayton Bicycle.

WHALEN, JAMES JOSEPH, college president; b. Pottsville, Pa., Mar. 6, 1927; s. Frank Leo and Mary M. (McCusker) W.; m. Gillian Stuart Hamer, Sept. 29, 1956. AB, Franklin and Marshall Coll., 1950; MS (VA fellow), Pa. State U., 1952, PhD in Clin. Psychology (VA fellow), 1955; LLD (hon.), Newton (Mass.) Coll., 1975; DHL (hon.), Ithaca Coll., 1997. Lic. psychologist, Mass. VA tng. intern clin. psychology Roanoke (Va.) VA Hosp., 1951-52, Wilkes-Barre (Pa.) VA Hosp., 1954-55; clin. psychologist VA Hosp., Pitts., 1955-58; asst. dean, psychologist European div. U. Md., Munich, Germany, 1958-60; prof. psychology, lectr. European div. U. Md., Heidelberg, Germany, 1960-63; asst. dir., asst. prof. psychology U. Md., European Div., 1963-64; assoc. prof., prof. psychology Ohio U., 1964-69, dir. ctr. for psychol. services, 1964-65, dean students, 1965-66, adminstrv. v.p., 1966-67, exec. v.p., 1967-69; pres., prof. Newton Coll., 1969-75; pres. Ithaca (N.Y.) Coll., 1975—, prof., 1975—; past chmn. Am. Coun. Edn., chmn. nominating com., 1994, Ad Hoc study com., Commn. on Ednl. Credit and Credentials, 1992—, chmn. membership com., 1988-90, bd. dirs., 1984-91, chmn. constn. and by-laws rev. com., 1991-92; past mem. pres.'s commn. NCAA, past chmn. div. III subcom., mem. com. on rev. and planning, 1990—; co-chair NCAA Gender Equity Task Force, 1992-93; mem. Edn. Commn. States Task Force on State Policy and Ind. Higher Edn.; past chmn. bd. visitors Air U. USAF; cons., chmn. Joint Chiefs of Staff Profl. Mil. Edn. Rev. Panel, mem. exec. com. Joint Chiefs of Staff Process for Accreditation of Joint Edn., 1991—, chair bd. visitors Army War Coll., 1997—; mem. Knight Found. Commn. on Intercoll. Athletics, 1989-93; mem. bd. visitors U. N.C., Asheville, 1986-89; past chmn. Nat. Assn. Ind. Colls. and Univs., bd. dirs., 1982-85, mem. pub. rels. adv. com., 1989-90, mem. govt. rels. com., 1985-89, chmn. govt. rels. com. on state rels., 1988-89; mem. Commn. on Ind. Colls. and Univs. in N.Y. State, past chmn. bd., past chmn. fed. rels. Com., trustee, 1978-84, 89-92, chmn. fin. com., 1990-92, treas. CICU/NYSCICU bd. 1991-92; mem. regents adv. coun. for Planning in Higher Edn., State of N.Y.; mem. nat. adv. com. Ctr. for Study of Sports in Soc.; mem. commr. edns. adv. coun. State N.Y., mem. commrs. edns. task force to reorganize state edn. dept.; chmn. adv. bd. Fleet Bank, Ithaca; bd. dirs. Fleet Investment Svcs., Rochester, N.Y. Contbr. articles on exec. leadership and ednl. adminstrn. to profl. jours. Served with USNR, 1945-46. Recipient Keiper award Franklin and Marshall Coll., 1948, medal USAF, 1990; Pa. State U. scholar, 1950-52, Henry Paley Meml. award, 1997. Mem. Am. Psychol. Assn., Mass. Psycho. Assn., Internat. Assn. Univ. Pres., N.Y. Acad. Scis., N.Y. State C. of C. (edn. com.), Ind. Coll. Fund N.Y. State (past mem. exec. com.), Assn. Colls. and Univs. N.Y. State (past mem. exec. com., bd. trustees), Oracle Soc., Univ. Club, Royal Auto Club, Ithaca Garden Club, Rotary, Phi Kappa Phi (editorial adv. bd. Nat. Forum 1989-94), Phi Delta Kappa, Psi Chi, Phi Kappa Tau, Phi Mu Alpha, Delta Phi Alpha. Home: 2 Fountain Pl Ithaca NY 14850-4428 Office: Ithaca Coll 953 Danby Rd Ithaca NY 14850-7000

WHALEN, JEROME DEMARIS, lawyer; b. Portland, Oreg., Feb. 9, 1943; s. William F. and Rose (Demaris) W. BA, U. Wash., 1965; JD, Harvard U., 1969. Bar: Wash. 1969. Assoc. Foster Pepper & Shefelman, Seattle, 1969-74, ptnr., 1974-91, mng. ptnr., 1982-85; ptnr. Whalen, Firestone, Landsman, Fleming & Dixon, Seattle, 1991—; adj. prof. corps. Law Sch., U. Puget Sound, Tacoma, 1976-77; instr. securities regulation Law Sch., U. Wash., Seattle, 1979; bd. dirs. Wright Runstad & Co., Seattle. Author: Commercial Ground Leases, 1988. Mem. Port of Seattle Ctrl. Waterfront Devel. Panel, 1988-90; trustee Corp. Coun. for Arts, Seattle, 1989—; trustee Pratt Fine Arts Ctr., Seattle, 1989-94, pres., 1991-93, Seattle Internat. Music Festival, 1992—. Mem. Wash. State Bar Assn. (chmn. corp. bus. and banking law sect. 1980-81), Phi Beta Kappa. Office: Whalen Firestone Landsman Fleming & Dixon 1191 2nd Ave Seattle WA 98101-2933

WHALEN, JOHN PHILIP, retired educational administrator, clergyman, lawyer; b. Troy, N.Y., Jan. 4, 1928; s. Philip Joseph and Mary Catherine (Doyle) W.; B.A. summa cum laude, St. Mary's Sem. and Univ., Balt., 1949; S.T.L., Cath. U., 1953, M.A., 1954, S.T.D. summa cum laude, 1965; J.D., George Washington U., 1976; postgrad. Johns Hopkins U., 1959-60, U. Md., College Park, 1958-59, Fordham U., 1953-54; LHD (hon.), Marymount U., 1987. Ordained priest Roman Cath. Ch., 1953. Instr. Mater Christi Sem., Albany, N.Y., 1953-58; asst. prof. Mt. St. Mary's Coll., Emmitsburg, Md., 1959-61; assoc. prof. Cath. U. Am., Washington, 1961-67, acting pres., 1968-69; pastor St. Mary's Ch., Oneonta, N.Y., 1970-72; pres. Consortium of Univs. of Washington area, 1972-88; mng. editor New Cath. Ency., 1963-67; pres., editor-in-chief Corpus Publs., 1967-94; ret. 1994. cons. 12 colls. and univs.; chmn. Univ. Support Services Inc., 1986-94, pres., chief exec. officer; cons. student loans, capital access trust, capital loans to colls.; bd. dirs. U.S. Fund for Improvement Postsecondary Edn., 1988-91. Bd. dirs. Sta. WETA-TV, 1968-69, Washington Ctr. for Met. Studies, 1968-69, Met. Bd. Trade, D.C., 1975-90, sec. bd. dirs., 1983-85; bd. dirs. Cath. U. Am., 1968-69, Nat. Shrine of Immaculate Conception, 1968-69, Dumbarton Coll., 1970-72, Trinity Coll., 1969-72, St. Mary's Coll. (South Bend, Ind.), 1970-74, St. Anselm's, 1979-85, Mt. Vernon Coll., 1982-84; pres. Univ. Extension Ednl. Corp., 1974-94; mem. Fed. City Council, 1982—; mem. Council for Ct. Excellence, 1984-90; chmn. Ctr. Advanced Studies of the Ams., 1984-90. Named Man of the Yr. 1984; recipient Disting. Alumnus award George Washington U., 1988. Mem. Nat. Cath. Edn. Assn., Cath. Theol. Soc. Am. (dir. 1966-68), Higher Edn. Group Washington (pres. 1974-75). Clubs: Tired Hands (pres. 1982-84), Cosmos (Washington), City Club; Rotary. Editorial bd. Law and Edn.; weekly columnist Evangelist, Albany; contbr. to Nat. Geog. mag.; contbr. articles to ednl. and theol. jours. Office: 1614 Parham Rd Silver Spring MD 20903-2256

WHALEN, JOHN SYDNEY, management consultant; b. Moncton, N.B., Can., Sept. 26, 1934; s. Harry Edward and Sarah Maude (Bourgeois) W.; m. Margaret Joan Carruthers, May 3, 1958; children: Bradley Graham, Elizabeth Ann. Grad., Can. Inst. Chartered Accts., 1959. Chartered acct. Coopers & Lybrand (formerly McDonald, Currie & Co.), St. John, N.B., 1954-63; with Kaiser Services, Oakland, Calif., 1963-75; telecommunications mgr. Kaiser Services, 1966-69, asst. controller, 1969-70, controller, 1970-74; mgr. corp. acctg. Kaiser Industries Corp., Oakland, 1975; controller Kaiser Engrs., Inc., Oakland, 1975-76; v.p. fin. and adminstrn. Kaiser Engrs., Inc., 1976-82; mgmt. cons., owner Whalen & Assocs., Inc., Alamo, Calif., 1983—; prin. Corp. Restructuring Group, Inc., Alamo, Calif., 1989—; pres. Round Hill Holdings, Inc., 1993—. Mem. Fin. Execs. Inst., Turnaround Mgmt. Assn. Club: Round Hill Golf and Country; Commonwealth. Home: 2216 Nelda Way Alamo CA 94507-2004 Office: 3191 Danville Blvd Alamo CA 94507-1920

WHALEN, LAURENCE J., federal judge; b. 1944. BA, Georgetown Coll., 1967; JD, Georgetown U., 1970, LLM in Taxation, 1971. Judge U.S. Tax Ct., Washington, 1987—; atty. Crowe & Dunlevy, Oklahoma City, Hamel & Park, Washington; spl. asst. to Asst. Atty. Gen.; trial atty., tax div. U.S. Dept. Justice. With USAR, 1971. Mem. ABA (taxation, litigation and bus. law sects.), Fed. Bar Assn. Office: US Tax Ct 400 2nd St NW Washington DC 20217-0001*

WHALEN, LORETTA THERESA, religious educational administrator; b. Bklyn., May 21, 1940; d. William Michael and Loretta Margaret (Malone) Whalen; children: Ann Lindsay, Margaret Force. RN, St. Vincent's Hosp., N.Y.C., 1960; BSN, U. Pa., 1965; MA in Edn., Fordham U., 1971; cert. in sociology religion, Louvain U., Belgium, 1974; PhD in Global Edn., The Union Grad. Sch., 1994. Staff nurse Holy Family Hosp., Atlanta, 1967-69; Latin Am. communication dir. Med. Mission Sisters, Maracaibo, Venezuela, 1969-71; intensive care nurse St. Vincent's Hosp., N.Y.C., 1971-72; mem. ministry team Med. Mission Sisters, various locations, 1972-74; dir. communications Med. Mission Sisters, Phila., 1974-77; asst. to exec. Interreligious Peace Colloquium, Washington, 1977; freelance writing, photography Ch. World Svc., N.Y.C., 1978-79; dir. Office Global Edn. Nat. Council Chs., N.Y.C., 1980—. Co-author: Make a World of Difference: Creative Activities for Global Learning, 1990, Tales of the Heart: Affective Approaches to Global Education, 1991; mem. editorial bd., rev. editor Connections Mag., 1984-87; contbr. articles to profl. jours. Mem. Peace and Justice Commn., Archdiocese of Balt., 1985-89. Mem. Amnesty Internat., Bread for the World, NOW, World Wildlife Fund, Greenpeace, Sigma Theta Tau. Democrat. Roman Catholic. Avocations: photography, writing, racquetball, interior design, travel.

WHALEN, LUCILLE, academic administrator; b. Los Angeles, July 26, 1925; d. Edward Cleveland and Mary Lucille (Perrault) W. B.A. in English, Immaculate Heart Coll., Los Angeles, 1949; M.S.L.S., Catholic U. Am., 1955; D.L.S., Columbia U., 1965. Tchr. elem. and secondary parochial schs. Los Angeles, Long Beach, Calif., 1945-52; high sch. librarian Conaty Meml. High Sch., Los Angeles, 1950-52; reference/serials librarian, instr. in library sci. Immaculate Heart Coll., 1955-58; dean Immaculate Heart Coll. (Sch. Library Sci.), 1958-60, 65-70; assoc. dean, prof. SUNY, Albany, 1971-78, 84-87; prof. Sch. Info. Sci. and Policy SUNY, 1979-83; dean grad. programs, libr. Immaculate Heart Coll. Ctr., Los Angeles, 1987-90; ref. libr. (part-time) Glendale Community Coll., 1990—; dir. U.S. Office Edn. Instn. Author, editor: (with others) Reference Services in Archives, 1986. author: Human Rights: A Reference Handbook, 1989. Mem. ACLU, Common Cause, Amnesty Internat. Democrat. Roman Catholic. Home: 320 S Gramercy Pl Apt 101 Los Angeles CA 90020-4542 Office: Glendale Community Coll 1500 N Verdugo Rd Glendale CA 91208-2809

WHALEN, PHILIP GLENN, poet, novelist; b. Portland, Oreg., Oct. 20, 1923; s. Glenn Henry and Phyllis Bush W. B.A., Reed Coll., 1951. Ordained Zen Buddhist priest, 1973. Head monk Dharma Sangha, Santa Fe, 1984-87; abbot Hartford St. Zen Ctr., San Francisco, 1991-96; lectr., tchr., 1955—. Author: poetry Three Satires, 1951, Self-Portrait, From Another Direction, 1959, Like I Say, 1960, Memoirs of an Inter-Glacial Age, 1960, Every Day, 1965, Highgrade, 1966, On Bear's Head, 1969, Severance Pay, 1971, Scenes of Life at the Capitol, 1971, The Kindness of Strangers, 1975, Enough Said, 1980, Heavy Breathing, 1983, Canoeing Up Cabarga Creek, 1996; novels You Didn't Even Try, 1967, Imaginary Speeches for a Brazen Head, 1972; interviews Off the Wall, 1978; prose text The Diamond Noodle, 1980; juvenile The Invention of the Letter, 1967; Recipient Poet's Found. award 1962, V.K. Ratcliff award 1964; By & Large, tape cassette reading his own poems, 1987. Served with USAAF, 1943-46. Am. Acad. Arts and Letters grantee-in-aid, 1965, 91, Morton Dauwen Zabel award for Poetry, 1986, Fund for Poetry award, 1987, 91; Com. on Poetry grantee, 1968, 70, 71. Office: 57 Hartford St San Francisco CA 94114-2013

WHALEN, THOMAS EARL, psychology educator; b. Toledo, June 26, 1938; s. T. Mylo and Alice E. (Tallman) W.; m. Carolyn Margaret Lapham, Dec. 24, 1960; children: Jennifer Susan, Holly Elizabeth. BA, UCLA, 1960; MA, San Diego State U., 1967; PhD, U. Conn., 1970. Cert. secondary tchr., Calif. Secondary tchr. San Diego City Schs., 1964-68; rsch. assoc. Southwest Regional Lab., Inglewood, Calif., 1969; prof. Calif. State U., Hayward, 1970—, chair ednl. psychology dept., 1977-79, assoc. dean sch. edn., 1987-89, 95-96, prof. emeritus, 1997; rsch. con. Evaluation Assocs., San Sanfrancisco Bay Area Schs., 1971-88, Lawrence Livermore (Calif.) Nat. Lab., 1982-83. Author: (text book) Ten Steps to Behavioral Research, 1989; contbr. articles to profl. jours. Lt. USN, 1960-63. U.S. Office of Edn. fellow U. Conn., 1968-70, post doctoral scholar Am. Edn. Rsch. Assn., U. Iowa, 1972. Mem. Am. Ednl. Rsch. Assn., APA, Calif. Ednl. Rsch. Assn. (bd. dirs. 1982-84), Bay Area Coun. on Measurement and Evaluation in Edn. (pres. 1976-77), United Profs. of Calif. (exec. bd. Calif. State U. Hayward 1975-76). Avocations: golf, travel, gardening. Home: 325 Conway Dr Danville CA 94526-5511 Office: Calif State U 25800 Carlos Bee Blvd Hayward CA 94542-3001

WHALEN, WAYNE W., lawyer; b. Savanna, Ill., Aug. 22, 1939; s. Leo R. and Esther M. (Yackley) W.; m. Paula Wolff, Apr. 22, 1970; children: Amanda, Clementine, Antonia, Nathaniel. BS, U.S. Air Force Acad., 1961; JD, Northwestern U., 1967. Bar: Ill. 1967, U.S. Ct. Appeals (7th cir.) 1968, U.S. Supreme Ct. 1972. Commd. 1st lt. USAF, 1961, ret., 1964; assoc. Mayer, Brown & Platt, Chgo., 1967-74, ptnr., 1974; ptnr. Skadden, Arps, Slate, Meagher & Flom (Ill.), Chgo., 1984—; bd. dirs. Van Kampel Am. Capital Family Mut. Funds, Oak Brook, Ill. Author: Annotated Illinois Constitution, 1972. Del. 6th Ill. Constitutional Conv., 1969-70, chmn. style drafting and submission com. Named Outstanding Young Lawyer, Chgo. Bar Found., 1970. Mem. Chgo. Club. Home: 4920 S Greenwood Ave Chicago IL 60615-2816 Office: Skadden Arps Slate (Ill) 333 W Wacker Dr Chicago IL 60606-1220

WHALEN-BLAAUWGEERS, HERMA-JOZÉ, financial analyst; b. Lichtenvoorde, Gelderland, The Netherlands, Dec. 14, 1944; arrived in U.S., 1988; d. Hermanus Jozeph Blaauwgeers and Henrica Everdina Dute; m. Helmut Gueth, Jan. 3, 1968 (div. May 1983); m. Frank Whalen, Mar. 29, 1988 (div. Dec. 1994); children: Mariëtte, Joerg-Peter. BA, Lyceum Fons Vitae, Amsterdam, 1964. Cert. translator, Fed. Govt. of The Netherlands, 1971. Dir. resource mgmt. U.S. Army, Schweinfurt, Germany, 1981-88; project mgr. ARS, Alexandria, Va., 1988-90; group mgr. internat. mktg. ARS, Alexandria, 1990-92; sr. ptnr. Herold & Assocs., Arlington, Va., 1992—; sr. fin. analyst IBES, Inc., Falls Church, Va., 1993—. Contbr. articles to European newspapers. pres. Club Der Jungen Hausfauen, Schweinfurt, 1971-75, Kind Im Krankenhaus, Schweinfurt, 1977-81; founder Legal Aid for Abused Women and Children, Arlington, 1994—. Mem. Nat. Assn. Women Bus. Owners (internat. chair Capital Area chpt. 1996—), Am. Soc. Mil. Comptrollers, Nat. Female Execs. Assn., Nat. Women's Political Caucus, Am. Assn. Univ. Women, Zonta Club of Alexandria (pres. 1995—), Zonta Internat. (mem. ad hoc com. domestic violence, 1996—). Roman Catholic. Avocations: swimming, reading, travelling, writing.

WHALEY, CAROLYN LOUISE, primary school educator; b. Jackson, Tenn., Apr. 4, 1952; d. James M. and Allie L. (Williams) Brown; m. Roy Lynn Whaley, Aug. 13, 1978. BA, Union U., 1974; M of Music, Southwestern Bapt. Sem., Ft. Worth, 1976, MA, 1979; EdD, Tex. Woman's U., 1996. Cert. elem., early childhood, music tchr. Preschool tchr. Naval Acad. Primary Sch., Annapolis, Md., 1983-87; kindergarten tchr. Bosqueville Ind. Sch. Dist., Waco, Tex., 1987-94, mulit-age primary tchr., 1994-95, music tchr., 1995-96; music tchr. Waco Ind. Sch. Dist., 1996—. Guest columnist Waco Tribune Herald, 1994. Vol. Prison Fellowship, Waco, 1988-94, Habitat for Humanity, Waco, 1990-94. Mem. Assn. for Childhood Edn. Internat., Nat. Assn. for Edn. of Young Children, Moo Duk Kwan Fedn. (Tae Kwon Do), Internat. Reading Assn. Home: 708 N 15th St Waco TX 76707-3513

WHALEY, CHRISTOPHER DAVID, manufacturing engineer; b. Fulton, N.Y., Feb. 21, 1965; s. Lawrence Arthur and Shirley May (Beebe) W.; m. Nina Terresa Barucco (div.); children: Stefan, Aric. BS in Physics, SUNY, Oswego, 1986; BS in Polit. Sci., SUNY, Cortland, 1991; AAS in Mech. Engring. Tech., Onondaga C.C., Syracuse, N.Y., 1988. Rsch. and devel. toolmaker The Eraser Co., Syracuse, 1983-85; design engr. Greno Industries, Scota, N.Y., 1985-87; mfg. and design engr. Majestic Mold, Phoenix, N.Y., 1987-89; mfg. engr. GE Co., Syracuse, 1989-92; v.p. mfg. engr. Display Prodrs., Bronx, N.Y., 1992-95; v.p. engring. and ops. Viz Mold & Die Ltd., Northvale, N.J., 1995-96; pres. Merlin Mold & Mfg., Port Chester, N.Y., 1995—, CW Assocs., Port Chester, N.Y., 1995—; cons. Viz Plastics & Mold, Northvale, N.J., 1992—, Shar-Jo Industries, Fulton, N.Y., 1989—; tooling designer GTS Industries, Clifton, N.J., 1992—. Author: U.S. Naval Repair Manual, 1986. Asst. wrestling coach Mexico (N.Y.) Acad. Schs., 1983-85. Mem. Soc. Plastic Engrs. Republican. Avocations: formula style road racing, motorcross racing, remote control gas car racing. Home: 31 Reservoir Rd North White Plains NY 10603 Office: 49 Townsend St Port Chester NY 10573-4309

WHALEY, FRANK, actor; b. Syracuse, N.Y., July 20, 1963. film appearances include: Ironweed, 1987, Field of Dreams, 1989, Little Monsters, 1989, Born on the Fourth of July, 1989, The Freshman, 1990, JFK, 1991, The Doors, 1991, Career Opportunities, 1991, Back in the U.S.S.R., 1992, A Midnight Clear, 1992, Hoffa, 1992, Swing Kids, 1993, Pulp Fiction, 1994, Swimming With Sharks, 1995, Homage, 1995, Cafe Society, 1995, The Winner, 1996, Broken Arrow, 1996; TV movies include: Unconquered, 1989, Flying Blind, 1990, To Dance with the White Dog, 1993, Fatal Deception: Mrs. Lee Harvey Oswald, 1993, Dead Man's Gun, 1997; stage appearances include: Tigers Wild, 1986, The Years, 1993. Office: ICM 8942 Wilshire Blvd Beverly Hills CA 90211*

WHALEY, ROSS SAMUEL, academic administrator; b. Detroit, Nov. 7, 1937; s. Lyle John and Margaret Nielson (Semple) W.; m. Beverly Mae Heemstra, June 14, 1958; children—Heather Jean, Susan Lesli, Lindsay John. B.S., U. Mich., 1959, Ph.D., 1969; M.S., Colo. State U., 1961. Asst. prof., assoc. prof., prof. Utah State U., Logan, 1965-70, dept. head, 1967-70; assoc. dean Colo. State U., Ft. Collins, 1970-73; dept. head U. Mass., Amherst, 1973-76, dean, 1976-78; dir. econ. research USDA Forest Service, Washington, 1978-84; pres. SUNY Coll. Environ. Scis. and Forestry, Syracuse, 1984—; cons. UN FAO, Rome, 1983-84, UN, Budapest, Hungary, 1974, U.S. Peace Corps, South Am., 1972, Geddes, Brecher, Qualls & Cunningham, Denver, 1971-72. Contbr. articles to profl. jours. Bd. dirs. Hiawatha coun. Boy Scouts Am., 1985—; bd. dirs. Pinchot Inst. Conservation, 1985—, ARC, 1994—, Au Sable Inst. Environ. Studies. Fellow Soc. Am. Foresters (pres. 1991). Mem. Christian Ref. Ch. Avocations: reading, swimming, hiking, fly fishing, cross-country skiing. Home: 2

Bradford Heights Rd Syracuse NY 13224-2158 Office: SUNY Office of Pres Coll Environ Sci & Forestry Syracuse NY 13210

WHALEY, STORM HAMMOND, retired government official, consultant; b. Sulphur Springs, Ark., Mar. 15, 1916; s. Storm Onus and Mabel Etta (Prater) W.; m. Jane Florence Bucy, Oct. 6, 1935; children: Carroll Jean Whaley Anderson, Ann Marie Whaley Adams, Rebecca Glenn Whaley Dyess. B.A., John Brown U., 1935; LL.D. (hon.), 1959; postgrad., Am. U. Law Sch., 1954; D.Sc. hon., U. Ark. for Med. Scis., 1983. Mgr. Sta. KUOA, Siloam Springs, Ark., 1935-53, Sta. KGER, Long Beach, 1948-53, KOME, Tulsa, 1951-53; asst. to Congressman J.W. Trimble, 1953-54; asst. to pres. U. Ark., 1954-59, acting pres., 1959-60, v.p. health scis., 1960-70; assoc. dir. communications NIH, Bethesda, Md., 1970-92; retired, 1992; mem. U.S. del. World Health Assembly, 1962, 63, 64; mem. nat. adv. health council USPHS, 1963-66; chmn. ad hoc com. Report to Pres. and Congress Regional Med. Programs, 1967; mem. U.S. Sr. Exec. Service, 1979. Author: They Call It, 1951. Del. Democratic Nat. Conv., 1940, 44, 48, 52. Recipient Superior Service award HEW, 1974, SES Performance award, 1982, Superior Service award USPHS, 1987. Fellow AAAS; mem. Broadcast Pioneers, Ark. Broadcasters Assn., Internat. Sci. Writers Assn., NIH Alumni Assn. (bd. dirs. 1992—, sec. 1995—), KT, Masons (33 deg.), Nat. Press Club, Omicron Delta Kappa, Lambda Chi Alpha. Home and Office: 4400 E West Hwy Bethesda MD 20814-4524

WHALEY-BUCKEL, MARNIE, social service administrator; b. Madison County, Ohio, July 16, 1946; d. H. John and Frances (Kramer) Hostetler; m. John Benjamin Whaley, Sept. 14, 1974 (wid. Mar. 1977); 1 child, Monica Anne; m. Raymond J. Buckel, May 17, 1991; 1 adopted child, Dimitri R.A. Buckel. BA in Social Work, Bluffton Coll., 1969; MSW, Ohio State U., 1983. Lic. ind. social worker, Ohio. Counselor Family Counseling, Lima, Ohio, 1969-70; social worker psychiat. unit St. Rita's Hosp., Lima, 1970-74; emergency counselor Northwest Ctr. for Human Resources, Lima, 1975-78, outpatient therapist, 1977-80, coord. emergency svcs., 1979-82; intern coord. pub. rels. Northwest Couseling, Columbus, Ohio, 1982-83; coord. community rels. Madison County Hosp., London, Ohio, 1983-85; assoc. dir. Madison County Health Ctr Inc., London, 1985-89; exec. dir. Bd. Alcohol, Drug Addiction and Mental Health Svcs., London, 1989-94; chmn. Allen County Welfare Adv. Bd., Lima, 1979-82; vice chmn. Act. Inc., Columbus, 1989-91, chmn., 1991-93; Ohio Hospice Adv. Bd., London, 1990-91, pvt. cons., agy. adminstrn., mediation, 1995—. Chmn. bd. ch. edn. Big Darby Bapt. Ch., Plain City, Ohio, 1987, clk., 1989—, sec.-treas., 1988, 89,, chmn. constitution com., 1990. Mem. NASW, Mental Health Adminstrs., Phi Kappa Phi, Delta Sigma Mu. Avocations: sewing, crafts, gardening, flowers.

WHALLON, EVAN ARTHUR, JR., orchestra conductor; b. Akron, Ind., July 24, 1923; s. Evan Arthur and Katharine (Kistler) W.; m. Jean Borgman, Aug. 28, 1948 (dec. 1977); children: Paul Evan, Eric Andrew; m. Rachael Shumate, Dec. 29, 1983 (div. 1992. MusB, Eastman Sch. Music, 1948, MusM, 1949; MusD (hon.), Denison U., 1963, Otterbein U., 1969, Ohio Dominican U., 1970. Debut with Phila. Orch., 1948; condr.: opera The Consul, 1949-50, Springfield (Ohio) Symphony, 1951-56, Columbus (Ohio) Symphony, 1956-82, guest condr., Spoleto (Italy) Festival, Phila. Orch., Cleve. Orch., San Francisco Symphony, Buffalo Philharmonic, Boston Arts Festival, N.Y.C. Opera, San Francisco Spring Opera, Balt. Symphony, Prague Symphony Orch., Budapest Mav Symphony, condr., mus. dir., Chatauqua (N.Y.) Opera Assn., 1966-81; mus. dir. Merola program and Western Opera Theater, San Francisco Opera, 1982-87, Ohio Light Opera, 1988-93. Lt. (j.g.) USNR, WWII. Recipient citation Columbus City Council, 1963, Ohio citation Ohioana Assn., 1983. Mem. Condrs. Guild (bd. dirs., pres. 1988-90). Home: 95 Orchard Dr Gaithersburg MD 20878-2223

WHALLON, WILLIAM, literature educator; b. Richmond, Ind., Sept. 24, 1928; s. Arthur J. and Adelaide (Wheeler) W.; m. Joanne Holland, Aug. 22, 1957; children: Andrew, Nicholas. B.A., McGill U., 1950; Ph.D., Yale U., 1957. Prof. Mich. State U., East Lansing, 1963—. Author: Formula, Character, and Context, 1969, Problem and Spectacle, 1980, Inconsistencies, 1983, (poetry) A Book of Time, 1990, (scenarios) The Oresteia / Apollo & Bacchus, 1997. Fellow Center for Hellenic Studies, 1962-63; Fulbright prof. comparative lit., U. Bayreuth, 1984-85. Home: 1655 Walnut Heights East Lansing MI 48823-2943

WHAM, DOROTHY STONECIPHER, state legislator; b. Centralia, Ill., Jan. 5, 1925; d. Ernest Joseph and Vera Thelma (Shafer) Stonecipher; m. Robert S. Wham, Jan. 26, 1947; children: Nancy S. Wham Mitchell, Jeanne Wham Ryan, Robert S. II. BA, MacMurray Coll., 1946; MA, U. Ill., 1949; D of Pub. Adminstrn. (hon.), MacMurray Coll., 1992. Counsellor Student Counselling Bur. U. Ill., Urbana, 1946-49; state dir. ACTION program, Colo./Wyo. U.S. Govt., Denver, 1972-82; mem. Colo. Ho. of Reps., 1986-87; mem. Colo. Senate, 1987—, chair jud. com., 1988—; with capital devel. com., health, environ., welfare, instns., appropriations, legal svcs. Mem. LWV, Civil Rights Commn. Denver, 1972-80; bd. dirs. Denver Com. on Mental Health, 1985-88, Denver Symphony, 1985-88. Mem. Am. Psychol. Assn., Colo. Mental Health Assn. (bd. dirs. 1986-88), Colo. Hemophilia Soc., Civitan. Republican. Avocations: travel, furniture refinishing. Home: 2790 S High St Denver CO 80210-6352 Office: State Capitol Rm 342 Denver CO 80203

WHAM, GEORGE SIMS, publishing executive; b. Laurens, S.C., Jan. 27, 1920; s. George Sims and Nellie (Melette) W.; m. Beth Keeler, Sept. 13, 1947; children—Norman Brent, Bonnie Beth, Barry Keeler. B.S., Clemson U., 1941; M.S., U. Tenn., 1947; Ph.D., Pa. State U., 1951. Textile technologist USDA, 1947-49; research assoc. Sch. Chemistry and Physics, Pa. State U., 1949-51; prof., asst. dean Tex. Women's U., 1951-54; sr. editor Good Housekeeping mag., N.Y.C., 1954-60; v.p., tech. dir. Good Housekeeping mag., 1961-87; tech. cons., 1987—; disting. vis. prof. U. N.C., 1987-88; dir. R&D, Phillips Van Heusen, Inc., 1960-61; guest lectr. Purdue U., U. Md., Ariz. State U., U. Conn., U. Del., Clemson U., U. R.I., Mich. State U.; leader U.S. del. Internat. Standards Confs., 1968, 71, 86, 87. Contbr. articles to profl. jours. Pres. Governing Council, Hightstown, N.J., 1960-62; mem. Bd. Edn., Hightstown, 1959-61. Served to maj. AUS, 1941-46. Decorated Silver Star, Purple Heart. Mem. Am. Assn. Textile Chemists and Colorists (past pres., Harold C. Chapin award), Am. Nat. Standards Inst. (chmn. bd. dirs. 1986-88, chmn. textile standards bd. 1966-68, Howard Coonley medal 1985, George S. Wham Leadership medal 1990), Consumer Coun. (chmn. 1985), Sigma Xi, Phi Psi, Omicron Nu. Home: 201 E Ward St Hightstown NJ 08520-3313 Office: 959 8th Ave New York NY 10019-3737

WHAM, WILLIAM NEIL, publisher; b. N.Y.C., Dec. 28, 1934; s. William and Jessie (Neill) W.; m. Lynn McCorvie, Mar. 6, 1966; children: McCorvie, Avery. B.S., Syracuse U., 1956. Salesman Mut. N.Y., N.Y.C., 1959-61; regional sales mgr. Doubleday Pub. Co., N.Y.C., 1961-64, Reinhold Pub. Co., N.Y.C., 1964-68; sales mgr. United Bus. Publs., N.Y.C., 1968; pres., pub. jours. Internat. Scientific Communications, Inc., Shelton, Conn., 1968—. Founder: sci. jours. Am. Lab., Internat. Lab., Am. Biotech. Lab., Am. Clin. Lab., Internat. Biotech. Lab., Lab. Products Tech., Am. Lab. News, European Clin. Lab., Internat. Lab. News, Internat. Biotech. News, European Clin. Lab. News, Am. Environ. Lab. Served with AUS, 1956-58. Home: 157 Pinewood Trl Trumbull CT 06611-3312 Office: Internat Sci Communications Inc 30 Control Dr Shelton CT 06484-6111

WHANG, YUN CHOW, space science educator; b. Foochow, China, Dec. 13, 1931; came to U.S., 1955; s. Ta Chun and Wenlun (Lin) W.; m. Yeong-Ping Chu, Aug. 29, 1959; children: Ruth, Joyce, Kenneth. Ph.D., U. Minn., 1961. Asst. prof. U. Fla., 1961-62; asst. prof. The Cath. U. Am., 1962-63, assoc. prof., 1963-67, prof., 1968—, chmn. dept., 1971-83; sr. research assoc. Nat. Acad. Scis., 1967-68; vis. prof. Royal Inst. Tech., Stockholm, Sweden, 1972-73. Mem. Am. Geophys. Union, ASME. Research on slow shocks, solar wind theory, termination shock and heliopause, interaction solar wind with moon and planets. Home: 8003 Grand Teton Dr Potomac MD 20854-4073

WHARE, WANDA SNYDER, lawyer; b. Columbia, Pa., Nov. 5, 1959; d. William Sylvester and Dorothy Jacqueline (Luttman) W.; m. James Robert Snyder, Nov. 14, 1987; 1 child, Eric James. BA, Franklin & Marshall Coll., 1981; JD, Dickinson Sch. Law, 1984. Bar: Pa. 1984. Asst. counsel Pa. Dept. Labor and Industry, Harrisburg, 1984-87; assoc. Gibbel, Kraybill & Hess, Lancaster, Pa., 1987-89; corp. counsel Irex Corp., Lancaster, 1990—. Mem. parish-staff rels. com. 1st Meth. Ch., Lancaster, 1987-92, mem. com. on status and role of women, 1989-95, chair, 1992-95; chair commn. on status and role of women Ea. Pa. Conf. of United Meth. Ch., 1996—; mem., chair awareness subcom. Irex Continuous Improvement Coun. Democrat. Office: Irex Corp 120 N Lime St Lancaster PA 17602-2951

WHARTON, BEVERLY ANN, utility company executive; b. St. Louis, Nov. 17, 1953; d. Lawrence A. and Helen M. Bextermueller; m. James R. Wharton, March 30, 1974; 1 child, Laura. BS, So. Ill. U., 1975; MBA, U. of S.D., 1980. Tax acct. supr. Iowa Pub. Service Co., Sioux City, Iowa, 1978-84; asst. sec. Iowa Pub. Service Co., Sioux City, 1981-84, sec., 1984-88, v.p. staff services, 1985-88, sr. v.p. support group, 1988-91; corp. sec. Midwest Energy Co., Sioux City, 1984-88, v.p., 1986-88, sr. v.p., 1988-90; gen. mgr. Midwest Gas, Sioux City, 1991-95, group v.p., gen. mgr., 1992-95; pres. Gas divsn. Mid-American Energy Co., Sioux City, 1995-96, sr. v.p. energy delivery, 1996—; bd. dirs. Am. Gas Assn. Bd. dirs. Security Nat. Bank, Briar Cliff Coll. Mem. Midwest Gas Assn. (bd. dirs. 1992-96), Rotary (Sioux City club). Roman Catholic. Office: Mid American Energy Co 401 Douglas St Sioux City IA 51101-1443

WHARTON, DANNY CARROLL, zoo biologist; b. Ontario, Oreg., Mar. 13, 1947; s. Carroll Curtis and Norma (Grigg) W.; m. Marilyn Christine Hoyt, Sept. 22, 1973; children: Amanda, Catherine, Margaret, Arcadio. BA in Psychology, Coll. Idaho, 1969; MA in Internat. Adminstrn., Sch. for Internat. Tng., 1975; PhD in Biology, Fordham U., 1990. Rsch. assoc. Foresta Inst., Carson City, Nev., 1973-74; curatorial asst. Woodland Park Zool. Garden, Seattle, 1974-79; asst. curator N.Y. Zool. Soc./The Wildlife Conservation Soc., Bronx, 1979-85; assoc. curator N.Y. Zool. Soc., Bronx, 1985-89, curator, 1989—; dir. Ctrl. Pk. Wildlife Ctr., N.Y.C., 1994—; adjunct faculty Columbia U.; chmn. Internat. Advisors Internat. Snow Leopard Trust, Seattle, 1986; mem. US-USSR Environ. Agreement of U.S. Fish and Wildlife Svc., 1983. Contbr. articles to profl. jours.; editor Jour. Zoo Biology, 1996—. Vol. U.S. Peace Corps., Ecuador, 1969-71. Fulbright scholar, U. Münster, Fed. Republic Germany, 1976-77. Fellow Am. Assn. Zool. Parks and Aquariums (chmn. gorilla species survival plan 1992—, chmn. snow leopard species survival plan 1986—, co-chmn. marsupial and monotre,e taxon adv. group 1990-94; mem. Soc. for Conservation Biology, Internat. Union for Conservation of Nature/Species Survival Commn. (mem. captive breeding specialist group). Office: Wildlife Conservation Soc Ctrl Park Wildlife Ctr 830 5th Ave New York NY 10021-7001

WHARTON, JOHN JAMES, JR., research physicist; b. Warrensburg, Mo., May 28, 1949; s. John James and Carol Jean (West) W.; m. Anne Elizabeth Connolly, Sept. 21, 1985; children: Elizabeth, Angela, J.J., Eric. BSEE, U. Mo., 1971; MS, Air Force Inst. Tech., 1977; PhD, U. Ariz., 1984. Asst. prof. physics U.S. Air Force Acad., Colorado Springs, Colo., 1978-80; assoc. prof. physics, dep. dept. head Air Force Inst. Tech., Dayton, 1983-87; program mgr. Def. Advanced Rsch. Projects Agy., Rosslyn, Va., 1987-91; dir. Tech. Applications Ctr. ERIM Internat., Inc., Ann Arbor, 1991—; adj. assoc. prof. Coll. Engring., U. Mich., 1996—. Mem. IEEE, Optical Soc. Am. (bd. dirs. 1990-92), Am. Phys. Soc., Mensa, Tau Beta Pi. Home: 7409 Steeple Chase Ct Saline MI 48176-9031 Office: ERIM Internat Inc PO Box 134001 Ann Arbor MI 48113-4001

WHARTON, KAY KAROLE, special education educator; b. Butler, Pa., Nov. 19, 1943; d. Clarence Henry Jr. and Alberta Elizabeth (Yost) Gilkey; m. David Burton Wharton, Nov. 28, 1975 (dec. May 1987). BS in Edn., Geneva Coll., 1965. Cert. spl. edn. tchr., Md. Tchr. 2d grade Butler Area Sch., 1965-71; resource tchr. Queen Anne County Bd. of Edn., Centreville, Md., 1971—; facilitator sch. improvement team Centreville Mid. Sch., 1992-95. Music dir. Diocese of Easton (Md.) Mid. Convocation Episcopal Cursillo, Old St. Paul's, Kent, 1989-91, St. Paul's, Hillsboro, 1993—; Sunday sch. supt. primary dept. St. Mark's Luth. Ch., 1966-71, St. Paul's Episcopal Ch., 1985-87; program dir. Queen Anne's County chpt. Am. Cancer Soc., Centreville, 1981-85; mem. PTA; Episcopal lay min. Meridian Nursing Home, 1978—. Mem. NEA, Queen Anne County Edn. Assn., Md. State Tchrs. Assn., Coun. for Exceptional Children, Internat. Reading Assn., Upper Shore Reading Assn. (sec. 1985-91, 93—), Learning Disabled Am., Guardians Learning Disabled (sec. 1991-92), Smithsonian Assocs., Order Ea. Star (worthy matron Centreville 1977, sec. 1982-93), Nat. Geographic Soc., Town and Country Women's Club (pres. 1977, 79), Delta Kappa Gamma (Nu chpt. pres. 1992—, rsch. com. chairperson Alpha Beta State 1993-95, membership chairperson 1995-97). Republican. Avocations: piano, embroidery, handicrafts. Home: PO Box 237 Centreville MD 21617-0237 Office: Centreville Mid Sch 231 Ruthsburg Rd Centreville MD 21617-9702

WHARTON, LENNARD, engineering company executive; b. Boston, Dec. 10, 1933; s. Nathaniel Philip and Deeda (Levine) W.; m. Judith R. Gordon, Dec. 26, 1957; children: Ruth, Rebecca, Nathaniel. B.S. in Chem. Engring, MIT, 1955; B.A., Cambridge U., 1957, M.A., 1957; A.M., Harvard U.; A.M. (NSF fellow 1957-60), 1960, Ph.D. (Jr. fellow Soc. of Fellows 1960-63), 1963. Registered profl. engr., N.J., Ill. Prof. dept. chemistry U. Chgo., 1963-80; v.p. engring. ITE Imperial Corp., 1972-73; v.p. tech. Studebaker-Worthington, Barrington, Ill., 1979-78, McGraw Edison Co., Rolling Meadows, Ill., 1979-80; v.p. engring. and tech. Worthington group McGraw Edison Co., Mountainside, N.J., 1980-85; corp. v.p. tech. Material Research Corp., Pearl River, N.Y., 1985-87; v.p. Packer Engring. Inc., Naperville, Ill., 1987-95, chmn. bd., 1994-95; pres. Evidentia Engring. Inc., Short Hills, N.J., 1995—. Sloan fellow, 1964-66; named Outstanding Young Man of Chgo. Chgo. Jr. Assn. Commerce and Industry, 1968. Mem. IEEE (sr.), Nat. Fire Protection Assn., Am. Inst. Chem. Engrs. Office: 10 Park Pl Short Hills NJ 07078-2826

WHARTON, MARGARET AGNES, artist; b. Portsmouth, Va., 1943. BS, U. Md., 1965; MFA, Sch. of Art Inst. Chgo., 1975. vis. artist Sch. of Art Inst. of Chgo., 1978, 89, 90, Columbia Coll., Chgo., 1994. One women shows include Phyllis Kind Gallery, Chgo., 1976, 80, 85, 88, 91, N.Y.C., 1977, 78, 79, 81, 83, 87, 90, Mus. Contemporary Art, Chgo, 1981-82, Laguna Gloria Art Mus., Austin, Tex., 1981-82, Zolla/Lieberman Gallery, Inc., Chgo., 1992, 94, Evanston Art Ctr., 1994; exhibited in group shows at The Cinn. Art Mus., 1988-90, U. Wis. Art Mus., Milw., 1991, The Chgo. Cultural Ctr., 1992, Rockford (Ill.) Art Mus., 1994, and numerous others; represented in permanent collections Am. Med. Assn., Art Inst. of Chgo., Dallas Mus., Seattle Art Mus., State Ill. Collection, Whitney Mus. Am. Art, and others; comms. include Mus. of Contemporary Art, Chgo., 1985, Chgo. Pub. Libr., West Lawn Branch, Chgo., 1986. Founding mem. Artemesia Cooperative Gallery, Chgo., Ill. Recipient NEA grant 1979, 88, 93, Visual Arts award, 1984.

WHARTON, THOMAS WILLIAM, mining executive; b. St. Louis, Nov. 20, 1943; s. Thomas William and Elaine Margaret (Bassett) w.; divorced; children: Thomas William, Christopher John. BSc in Econs., U. Mo., 1967; M in Health Adminstrn., U. Ottawa, Ont., Can., 1978. Asst. to exec. dir. Ottawa Civic Hosp., 1978-80; exec. dir. Caribou Meml. Hosp., Williams Lake, B.C., Can., 1980-83; dir. clinic and rehab. services Workers' Compensation Bd., Vancouver, B.C., 1983-89; dir. Conquistador Gold Mines, Vancouver, 1989—; pres. Diagnostic and Health Cons., Vancouver, 1989—; dir. Citrine Holdings, Ltd., Vancouver, B.C., Can., 1994—; bd. dirs. Corona Goldfields, Inc., Vancouver, USV Telemanagement, Inc., Vancouver, Leopardus Resources, Inc., Vancouver. Recipient Founder award Cariboo Musical Soc., 1983; named Lord of the Manors of Wharton and Kirkby Stephen (Eng.), 1991. Avocations: music, art.

WHARTON, WILLIAM POLK, consulting psychologist, retired educator; b. Hopkinsville, Ky.; s. William Polk and Rowena Evelyn (Wall) W.; m. Lillian Marie Andersen, Mar. 11, 1944; 1 child, Christine Evelyn Wharton Leonard. BA, Yale U., 1934; MA, Tchrs. Coll., 1949; PhD, Columbia U., 1952. Diplomate Am. Bd. Profl. Psychology; lic. psychologist, Pa. Rsch. advt. promotion, advt. sales Esquire Inc., N.Y.C., 1934-40; dir. counseling, prof. edn., counseling psychologist Allegheny Coll., Meadville, Pa., 1952-74, emeritus dir. and prof. edn., 1974—; prof., dir. The Ednl. Guidance Clinic, Meadville, 1958-74; pvt. practice cons. psychologist Meadville, 1974—; cons. U.S. Army Edn. Ctr., Ft. Meade, Md., 1960-61; rsch. adv. coun. Ednl. Devel. Ctr., Berea, Ohio, 1971-72; cons. to pres. Alliance Coll., Cambridge Springs, Md., 1975-76. Mem. editorial bd. Psychotherapy, 1966-68; reviewer Jour. Coll. Student Personnel, 1984-88; contbr. articles to profl. jours. Chmn. MH/MR Bd. Crawford County Pa., Meadville, 1970-73; com. chmn., Drug and Alcohol Coun. Crawford County Pa., Meadville, 1973-76; ethics com. chmn. North West Pa. Psychol. Assn., 1975-78; del. Pa. Mental Health Assn. Crawford County, 1978-79. Served U.S. Army, 1940-46; from pvt. to lt. col. USAR, 1964. Psychotherapy Research Group vis. fellow, 1961-62; Romiett Stevens scholar, 1951. Fellow Pa. Psychol. Assn.; mem. Am. Psychol. Assn. (Disting. Contbn. award 1985), Am. Assn. for Counseling and Devel., Nat. Vocat. Guidance Assn., Pa. Coll. Personnel Assn. (chmn. 1956-57), Phi Beta Kappa. Phi Delta Kappa, Kappa Beta Pi, Pi Gamma Mu. Home and Office: 415 N Main St Meadville PA 16335-1510

WHATCOTT, MARSHA RASMUSSEN, elementary education educator; b. Fillmore, Utah, Mar. 29, 1941; d. William Hans and Evangelyn (Robison) Rasmussen; m. Robert LaGrand Whatcott, Sept. 14, 1961; children: Sherry, Cindy, Jay Robert, Justin William. Assoc., So. Utah State U., 1962; BS, Brigham Young U., 1968. Cert. tchr. early childhood, Utah. Tchr. 1st grade Provost Elem. Sch., Provo, Utah, 1968-84, kindergarten tchr., 1984-91, tchr. 3d grade, 1991—; music specialist Provost Elem., 1984-87, 91-92, 93-94, art specialist, 1984-85, math. specialist, 1988-89, sci. specialist, 1994-95, 96, 97, 98; del. Utah Edn. Assn., 1989-90; bldg. rep. Provo Edn. Assn., 1993-94, 94-95. Mem. polit. action com. Provo Sch. Dist., 1982, 90, mem. profl. devel. com. Bonniville Uniserve (Provo, Alpine and Nebo Sch. Dist.), 1994-95. Recipient Millard County Utah PTA scholarship, 1959-62, Golden Apple award Provo City PTA, 1984, Recognition Disting. Svc. in Edn. award Utah State Legis., 1992; named Outstanding Educator in Utah Legis. Dist. # 64, 1992. Mem. Utah Edn. Asn. (del. 1989-90), Provo Edn. Assn. (bldg. rep. 1993-94, 94-95), Bonneville Uniserve (profl. devel. com.). Mem. LDS Ch. Avocations: music, gardening, art, drama, crafts. Office: Provost Elem Sch 629 S 1000 E Provo UT 84606-5204

WHEALEY, LOIS DEIMEL, humanities scholar; b. N.Y.C., June 20, 1932; d. Edgar Bertram Deimel and Lois Elizabeth (Hatch) Washburn; m. Robert Howard Whealey, July 2, 1954; children: Richard William, David John, Alice Ann Whealey Dediu. BA in History, Stanford U., 1951; MA in Edn., U. Mich., 1955; MA in Polit. Sci., Ohio U., 1975. Tchr. 5th grade Swayne Sch., Owyhee, Nev., 1952-53; tchr. 7th grade Ft. Knox (Ky.) Dependent's Sch., 1955-56; tchr. adult basic edn. USAF, Oxford, 1956-57; tchr. 6th grade Amerman Sch., Northville, Mich., 1957-58; tchr. 8th grade English, social studies Slauson Jr. High Sch., Ann Arbor, Mich., 1958-59; adminstrv. asst. humanities conf. Ohio U., Athens, 1974-76, 83; part-time instr. Ohio U., Athens, 1966-68, 75, VISTA with Rural Action, 1996—. Contbr. articles to profl. jours. Mem. Athens County Regional Planning Commn., 1974-78, treas., 1976-78; bd. dirs. Ohio Meadville Dist. Unitarian-Universalist Assn., 1975-81, Ohio Women Inc., 1995—; mem. Ohio coord. com. Internat. Women's Yr., 1977; v.p. Black Diamond Girl Scout Coun., 1980-86; chair New Day for Equal Rights Amendment, 1982; mem. Athens City Bd. Edn., 1984-90, v.p., 1984, pres., 1985; mem. Tri-County Vocat. Sch. Bd., Nelsonville, Ohio, 1984-90, v.p., 1988-89; mem. adv. com. Ohio River Valley Water Sanitation Commn., 1986-95; bd. dirs. Ohio Environ. Coun., 1984-90, sec., 1986-90; bd. dirs. Ohio Alliance for Environ., 1993—, Ohio Women, Inc., 1995—. Recipient Unsung UU award Ohio-Meadville Dist. Unitarian Universalist Assn., 1984, Thanks badge Black Diamond Girl Scout Coun., 1986, How to award Ednl. Press Assn. Am., 1990, Donna Chen Women's Equity award Ohio U., 1994; named Woman of Achievement, Black Diamond Girl Scout Coun., 1987. Mem. AAUW (pres. Athens br. 1969-70, 89-90, 93—, nat. pub. policy chair AAUW/Ohio 1995—), LWV (pres. 1975-77), Phi Lambda Theta (life). Democrat. Avocations: classical music, square dancing, choral singing. Home: 14 Oak St Athens OH 45701-2605

WHEAT, FRANCIS MILLSPAUGH, retired lawyer; b. L.A., Feb. 4, 1921; s. Carl Irving and Helen (Millspaugh) W.; m. Nancy Loring Warner, Oct. 14, 1944; children—Douglas Loring, Carl Irving, Gordon Warner. A.B., Pomona Coll., 1942; LL.B. cum laude, Harvard U., 1948. Bar: Calif. 1949. With firm Gibson, Dunn & Crutcher, Los Angeles, 1948-64; partner Gibson, Dunn & Crutcher, 1955-64, 69-89; commr. SEC, 1964-69. Contbr. articles to profl. jours. Trustee S.W. Mus., L.A., 1964, Pomona Coll., 1967-95, vice chmn., 1972-95, Ralph Parson Found., 1995—; bd. dirs. UN Assn. L.A., 1963-64, Assn. Governing Bds. Univs. and Colls., 1968-70, Ctr. for Law in Pub. Interest, 1974—, Alliance for Children's Rights (pres. 1992-94), Calif. Commn. on Campaign Fin. (co-chmn. 1985—), Sierra Club Legal Def. Fund, 1978—. Lt. USNR, 1942-45. Mem. Am. Law Inst., Los Angeles County Bar Assn. (chmn. com. corps. 1963-64, com. juvenile cts. 1957, trustee 1971-76, pres. 1975-76), Alumni Assn. Pomona Coll. (pres. 1964-65), Nat. Assn. Securities Dealers (bd. govs. 1973-76), Phi Beta Kappa. Democrat. Congregationalist (pres. 1961). Home: 2130 Lombardy Rd San Marino CA 91108-1302 Office: 333 S Grand Ave Fl 46 Los Angeles CA 90071-1504

WHEAT, JOE BEN, anthropologist; b. Van Horn, Tex., Apr. 21, 1916; s. Luther Peers and Elizabeth (Wellborn) W.; m. Frances Irene Moore, Apr. 6, 1947 (dec. Nov. 1987); m. Barbara K. Zernickow, Mar. 18, 1992. B.A., U. Calif.-Berkeley, 1937; M.A., U. Ariz., 1947, Ph.D. (Fund for Advancement Edn. fellow), 1953. Field dir. W.P.A. Archaeol. Project, Tech. Tech. Coll., Lubbock, 1939-41; archaeologist Smithsonian Instrn. River Basin Survey, Houston, 1947; fellow U. Ariz., Tucson, 1947-48; instr. anthropology U. Ariz., 1949-51; ranger, archaeologist Grand Canyon Nat. Park, U.S. Nat. Park Service, 1952-53; co-dir. Nubian Expdn., U. Colo., 1962-67; curator anthropology, prof. natural history Univ. Mus., 1953-87, prof. emeritus, 1987—; cons. to numerous profl. publs.; mem. anthropology rev. bd. NSF, 1978-79. Contbr. numerous articles to profl. jours. Served with USAAF, 1941-45. Recipient Colo. State Archeologists award, 1981, Robert L. Stearns award, 1982, Clarence T. Hurst award, 1990, Byron S. Cummings award, 1991; NSF grantee, 1968, 70-71; Graham Found. grantee, 1976-79; Smithsonian Instn. grantee, 1962-66, 70. Fellow Am. Anthrop. Assn., AAAS; mem. Soc. Am. Archaeology (pres. 1966-67, 50th Anniversary award), Council Mus. Anthropology (pres. 1977-78), Internat. Congress Americanists, Am. Ethnol. Soc. Club: Town and Gown. Home: 1515 Baseline Rd Boulder CO 80302-7650 Office: U Colo Museum Boulder CO 80309

WHEAT, MYRON WILLIAM, JR., cardiothoracic surgeon; b. Sapulpa, Okla., Mar. 24, 1924; s. Myron William and Mary Lee (Hudiburg) W.; m. Erlene Adele Plank, June 12, 1949 (div. June 1970); children: Penelope Louise, Myron William III, Pamela Lynn, Douglas Plank; m. Carol Ann Karmgard, June 18, 1970 (div. Apr. 1996); 1 child, Christopher West. AB, Washington U., St. Louis, 1949; MD cum laude, Washington U., 1951. Diplomate Am. Bd. Surgery, Am. Bd. Thoracic Surgery. Instr., clin. fellow Washington U., St. Louis, 1956-58; asst. prof. surgery U. Fla., Gainesville, 1958-65, prof. surgery, 1965-72; dir. profl. svcs., chief clin. physician U. Fla. Shands Teaching Hosp., Gainesville, 1968-72; prof. surgery, dir. thoracic and cardiothoracic surgery U. Louisville Sch. Medicine, 1972-75; clin. prof. surgery U. Louisville Sch. of Medicine, 1975—; cardiothoracic surgeon Cardiac Surg. Assocs., P.A., St. Petersburg, Fla., 1975-91; cons., thoracic surgery Bay Pine VA Hosp., St. Petersburg, Fla., 1994—; clin. prof. surgery U. So. Fla. Sch. Medicine, Tampa, 1995—; cardiothoracic surgeon Cardiac Surg. Assocs., P.A., Clearwater, Fla., 1991—; clin. prof. surger U. South Fla., 1995—; cons. Bay Pines VA Hosp., St. Petersburg, Fla., 1991—. Author (with others) 14 books; contbr. over 100 articles to profl. jours.; developed drug therapy for acute dissecting aneurysms of the aorta. 1st lt. USAF, 1943-46, ETO. Named First Howard W. Lillenthal Meml. lectr. Mt. Sinai Hosp., 1963; recipient DFC Air medal, Presdl. Citation. Fellow Am. Coll. Cardiology (chmn. bd. govs. 1968-69), Am. Coll. Surgeons (gov.); mem. Am. Surg. Assn., Am. Assn. for Thoracic Surgery, So. Surg. Assn., So. Thoracic Surg. Assn., Soc. Thoracic Surgeons, Soc. Thoracic Surgeons Great Britain and Ireland, Alpha Omega Alpha. Republican. Avocation: field trials-bird dogs. Home and Office: 1772 Long Bow Ln Clearwater FL 34624-6402

WHEAT, WILLIS JAMES, retired university dean, management educator; b. Oklahoma City, Feb. 28, 1926; s. Willis R. and Aubyn (Roach) W.; m. Julia Francis Maguire, July 4, 1946; children—Willis J., Chatham James. B.S., Okla. State U.-Stillwater, 1949, M.S., 1950; DPA in Pub. Adminstrn., U. Pacific, 1968; LL.D., Tex. Wesleyan Coll., 1962; Dr. Comml. Sci., Oklahoma City U., 1980. Prof. mgmt., dean Sch. Bus., Oklahoma City U., 1954-64; exec. v.p., dir. mktg. Liberty Nat. Bank & Trust Co., Oklahoma City, 1964-87; mem. faculty Stonier Grad Sch. Banking, Rutgers U., New

Brunswick, N.J., 1975-87; pres. Oklahoma City U., 1979-80, dean Meinders Sch. Bus., 1987-89, T.K. Hendricks prof. mktg. and mgmt, 1987-96; mem. faculty Essentials of Banking Sch., Norman, Okla., 1980-82, Grad. Sch. Banking of South, Baton Rouge, 1981-83. Contbr. articles to profl. jours. Chmn. Oklahoma City Plan Adv. Com., 1974-81, Okla. Employment Security Commn., Oklahoma City, 1981-89; trustee, mem. exec. com. Oklahoma City U., 1975-87; bd. dirs., chmn. United Bank Okla., 1987-95; bd. dirs. Pace Co., Baldor Electric Co. Served with U.S. Army, World War II. Recipient Disting. Service citation U.S. SBA, 1978; Disting. Service award Oklahoma City U., 1980, Okla. Council on Econ. Edn., 1982. Mem. Am. Bankers Assn., Soc. Advancement of Mgmt. (past pres.), Nat. Council for Small Bus. Mgmt. Devel., Okla. Polit. Sci. Assn., Okla. Council on Econ. Edn., Delta Sigma Pi, Beta Gamma Sigma. Methodist. Lodges: Masons, Shriners, Jesters. Office: PO Box 60804 Oklahoma City OK 73146-0804

WHEATER, ASHLEY, dancer; b. Cutler, Scotland. Student, Royal Ballet Sch. Mem. Royal Ballet, London Festival Ballet, Australian Ballet, Joffrey Ballet; soloist San Francisco Ballet, 1989-90, prin. dancer, 1990—. Performances with the San Francisco Ballet include The Sleeping Beauty, Swan Lake, Romeo and Juliet, Menuetto, Valses Poeticos (Love Letters), Handel-a Celebration, Forevermore, Bugaku, Who Cares?, The Four Temperaments, Duo Concertant, Symphony in C, Company B, In G Major, In the Night, In the middle, somewhat elevated, New Sleep, Maelstrom, Tagore, The End, La Fille mal gardée, La Sylphide, Nutcracker, Forgotten Land, Pulcinella, Connotations, Job, The Son of Horus, The Wanderer Fantasy; with other cos. include La Fille mal gardée, Monotones II, The Dream, Wedding Bouquet, Romeo and Juliet, La Sylphide, Love Songs, Remembrances, Return to the Strange Land, Etudes, Echoing of Trumpets, Sphinx, Greening; performed at Reykjavik Arts Festivals, Iceland, 1990, Jacob's Pillow, 1990. Office: San Francisco Ballet 455 Franklin St San Francisco CA 94102-4438*

WHEATLAND, RICHARD, II, fiduciary services executive, museum executive; b. Boston, Nov. 25, 1923; s. Stephen and Dorothy (Parker) W.; m. Cynthia McAdoo, Feb. 13, 1954; 1 child, Sarah Wheatland Fisher. AB, Harvard U., 1944, postgrad., 1946-47; JD, Columbia U., 1949. Various positions with Marshall Plan adminstrn. Office Spl. Rep. in Europe, Dept. State, Paris, 1950-53; v.p. N.Y. Airways, N.Y.C., 1953-68; pres. Acadia Mgmt. Co., Inc., Boston, 1968-93, chmn., 1993—; bd. dirs., v.p. Pingree Assocs., Bangor, Maine. Mem. Mayor's Com. Insl. Leaders for Youth, N.Y.C., 1963-66; mem. corp. New Eng. Forestry Found.; mem., former chmn. Fund for Preservation of Wild Life and Natural Areas, Boston, 1980-92, bd. dirs. 1980-91; trustee Penobscot Marine Mus., Searsport, Maine, 1968-90, hon. trustee, 1990—, ; bd. dirs. Friends of Pub. Garden, Boston, 1972-89, 90-96, 97—, Beacon Hill Civic Assn., Boston, 1985-89, Boston Natural Areas Fund, 1987—, asst. treas., 1993-94, treas. 1994-96, bd. dirs. 1997; treas. Frank Hatch for Gov. com., Boston, 1977-78; chmn., bd. trustees & overseers Peabody Essex Mus., Salem, Mass., 1992—, trustee, 1972-92, pres., 1983-92. Lt. (j.g.) USN, 1943-46, PTO. Mem. Am. Assn. Mus. (bd. dirs. trustee com. 1976-86, govt. affairs com. 1985—), Mus. Trustee Assn. (founder, bd. dirs. 1986—, sec. 1986-92), City Club Corp. (former bd. mgrs., former treas.). Avocations: jogging, sailing, travel. Office: Acadia Mgmt Co Inc 31 Milk St Boston MA 02109-5104

WHEATLEY, GEORGE MILHOLLAND, medical administrator; b. Balt., Mar. 21, 1909; s. William Francis and Teresa Genevieve (Milholland) W.; m. Eleanor Dodge, June 28, 1933 (dec. June 1969); children: George Milholland, Jr., Mary Ellen Rausch, Sarah Grinnell Nichols, William Bradford; m. Virginia Connelly Garling, Feb. 21, 1970 (dec. 1997). BS, Cath. U., 1929; MD, Harvard U., 1933; MPH, Columbia U., 1942. Diplomate Am. Bd. Pediatrics, Am. Bd. Preventive Medicine. Intern Hartford Hosp., Conn., 1933-35; house officer pediatrics Johns Hopkins Hosp., Balt., 1935-36; rsch. fellow N.Y. Post. Grad. Hosp., N.Y.C., 1936-37; prin. pediatrician Health Dept., N.Y.C., 1937-40; asst. med. dir. Met. Life Ins. Co., N.Y.C., 1940-45, asst. v.p., 1945-69, v.p., chief med. dir., 1969-74; med. dir. Dept. Social Svcs., Hauppauge, N.Y., 1974-95; ret., 1995; founder, 1st chmn. com. for joint action with Am. Coll. Surgeons and Assn. Surgery of Trauma Nat. Safety Coun. Author: Health Observation of School Children, 3d edit., 1965; contbr. articles to profl. jours. Bd. dirs. Med. Alert Found. Internat., Calif., 1974-84. Recipient Disting. Svc. award Am. Heart Assn., 1968. Fellow Am. Acad. Pediatrics (pres. 1960-61, trustee Partnership for Child Health 1987—, Clifford Grulee award 1964, Injury and Poison Prevention award 1993); mem. Union League Club, Piping Rock Club. Avocations: civil war history, water-color painting.

WHEATLEY, JOSEPH KEVIN, physician, urologist; b. N.Y.C., Jan. 5, 1946; s. Patrick Owen and Catherine (Malloy) W.; m. Anne Johanna Foody, Aug. 22, 1970; children: Joseph, Thomas. BSChemE, Manhattan Coll., 1967; MSChemE, U. Del., 1969; MD, N.J. U. of Medicine, 1974. Diplomate Am. Bd. Urology. Rsch. engr. NASA, Houston, 1965, 66, Exxon, Florham Park, N.J., 1968-69; urology resident Emory Univ., Atlanta, 1975-79, assoc. prof. urology, 1979—; clin. urology practice Urology Assocs., Atlanta, 1986—; chief of urology Kennestone Hosp., Marietta, Ga., 1990-93; medicare care cons. Ga. Found. med. Care, Atlanta, 1982—; tchr. Atlanta VA Med. Ctr., Atlanta, 1979—; mem. hosp. exec. com. Kennestone Hosp., Marietta, 1990-93. Contbr. chpts. to books and articles to profl. jours. Active various Rep. actitives, 1992—. Named Top Drs. in Atlanta Atlanta Mag., 1995-96. Fellow ACS; mem. AMA, Urol. Assn., Urodynamics Soc., Am. Fertility Soc., Soc. of Reproductive Surgeons, Lithotripsy Soc. Roman Catholic. Avocations: skiing, hiking, biking trips, tennis, computers. Home: 692 N Saint Mary's Ln Marietta GA 30064 Office: Urology Assocs 833 Campbell Hill St NW Ste 300 Marietta GA 30060-1137

WHEATLEY, MELVIN ERNEST, JR., retired bishop; b. Lewisville, Pa., May 7, 1915; s. Melvin Ernest and Gertrude Elizabeth (Mitchell) W.; m. Lucile Elizabeth Maris, June 15, 1939; children: Paul Melvin, James Maris, John Sherwood. AB magna cum laude, Am. U., 1936, DD, 1958; BD summa cum laude, Drew U., 1939; DD, U. of Pacific, 1948. Ordained to ministry Meth. Ch., 1939. Pastor area Meth. ch., Lincoln, Del., 1939-41; assoc. pastor First Meth. Ch., Fresno, Calif., 1941-43; pastor Centenary Meth. Ch., Modesto, Calif., 1943-46, Cen. Meth. Ch., Stockton, Calif., 1946-54, Westwood Meth. Ch., L.A., 1954-72; bishop Denver Area, 1972-84, ret., 1984; instr. philosophy Modesto Jr. Coll., 1944; summer session instr. Hebrew-Christian heritage U. of Pacific; instr. Homiletics U. So. Calif., So. Calif. Sch. Theology, Claremont; lectr. St. Luke's Lectures, Houston, 1966; mem. Bd. of Ch. and Soc., Commn. on Status and Role of Women, United Meth. Ch., 1976-84; condr. European Christian Heritage tour, 1961, Alaska and Hawaii Missions, 1952, 54. Author: Going His Way, 1957, Our Man and the Church, 1968, The Power of Worship, 1970, Family Ministries Manual, 1970, Christmas Is for Celebrating, 1977; contbr. articles to profl. jours. Chmn. Community Rels. Conf. So. Calif., 1966-69; pres. So. Calif.-Ariz. Conf. Bd. Edn., 1960-68; hon. trustee Iliff Sch. Theology; hon. dir., active mem. Parents and Friends of Lesbians and Gays, 1980—. Recipient Disting. Alumnus award Am. U., 1979, Ball award Meth. Fedn. Social Action, 1984, Prophetic Leadership award The Consultation on Homosexuality, Tolerance and Roman Cath. Theology, 1985, Human Rights award Universal Fellowship of Met. Community Congregations, 1985. Home: 859A Ronda Mendoza Laguna Hills CA 92653-5940

WHEATLEY, SHARMAN B., art educator, artist; b. N.Y.C., Nov. 21, 1951; d. Norman Alexander and Marjorie Grace (Biggs) Johnson; m. Simon J. Wheatley, June 21, 1975; children: Gregory Drew, Justin West. BA in Art Edn., Wagner Coll., 1973; MA in Art Edn., Coll. of New Rochelle, 1979. Cert. art educator, N.Y.; provisional cert. art educator, Conn. Art educator for multi-handicapped students Bd. Coop. Edn. Svcs., New City, N.Y., 1973-75; art educator Ardsley Pub. Schs., N.Y., 1975-76; art and humanities educator The Ursuline Sch., New Rochelle, N.Y., 1976-83; owner, dir. of tour co. Big Apple Enrichment Tours, Larchmont, N.Y., 1981-83; libr. publicist Monroe Pub. Libr., Conn., 1987-88; newspaper editor Trumbull Times, Conn., 1988; art educator Trumbull Pub. Schs., Conn., 1989-91; theatrical prodr. Little Theatre Prodns., Wilton, Conn., 1993-96; art educator Wilton Pub. Schs., Conn., 1991—; summer crafts supr. Ardsley Pub. Schs., N.Y., 1971-79. Artist, illustrator cover design for Street Bagel mag., 1982; exhibited in group shows at Larchmont Libr., 1982, Union Trust Bank, Darien, Conn., 1983; cover illustrator Litton Pubs., N.Y.C., 1980. 1st v.p., treas., corr. sec. mem. parents coun. Monroe PTO, Conn., 1985—. Recipient 2d prize Darien Arts Coun., 1983, Adams Interior Design Ctr. award Darien Arts Coun., 1983. Mem. NEA, Conn. Edn. Assn., Met. Mus. Art, N.Y. Mus. Modern Art. Avocations: writing, dancing, sculpting, drawing, reading. Home: 44 Oakwood Dr Monroe CT 06468-2134

WHEATLEY, WILLIAM ARTHUR, architect, musician; b. Knoxville, Tenn., Sept. 23, 1944; s. Arthur Cornwallis and Inda Mary (Benway) W.; m. Celeste Ann George, Mar. 25, 1970 (div.); children: Charles Arthur, James Harris Giddings; m. Rosaria Giovanna Cilia, June 10, 1995. Student, Rice U., 1962-66; BA, U. St. Thomas, 1972. Registered architect, Pa., Md., N.J. Design draftsman W.W. Alexander, Houston, 1966-70; chief of prodn. W.W. Scarborough, Houston, 1970-74; project architect Ronald H. Waldie & Assocs., Houston, 1972-74; pres. Wheatley & Assocs., Houston, 1974-81; project architect Brooks Assn., Houston, 1977-79; mgr. design Stone Bldg. Systems, Inc., Houston, 1979-81; project architect Bechtel, Houston, 1981-84; prin. Wheatley & Assocs., Houston, 1984-87; project mgr. STV/Sanders & Thomas, Pottstown, Pa., 1987-88, MDC Sys. (divsn. Day & Zimmerman Internat., Inc.), Phila., 1988—. Composer piano solos, chorales, oratorio and cantata, 1961—; co-contbr. articles to profl. jours. Del. Tex. Rep. Convs., 1980, 82, 84. Mem. AIA (Phila. chpt.), Royal Archtl. Inst. of Can., Am. Arbitration Assn., Pa. Soc. Architects, Bldg. Ofcls. and Code Adminstrs. Internat., Forest Products Soc., The Mastersingers (bd. dirs. 1989-92, treas. 1990-91), Choral Soc. Montgomery County (bd. dirs. 1990-96, pres. 1992-95). Episcopalian. Avocations: writing poetry and fiction, drawing, painting, sculpture. also: MDC Systems Inc 1818 Market St Philadelphia PA 19103-3672

WHEATON, DAVID, professional tennis player; b. Mpls., Minn., June 2, 1969; s. Bruce and Mary Jane W. Student, Stanford U. 9th in U.S. Tennis Assn. rankings, 1992, 95. U.S. Jr. Titles: Open Jr. Singles, 1987, 19 Clay Singles, 1987, 18 Natl. Doubles (with Jeff Tarango) 1987, 18 Hard Court Doubles (with Tarango) 1985; Career Pro Tour Singles Titles, 1990, U.S. Clay Courts, 1991, Grand Slam Cup, 1994, Newport. Office: US Tennis Assn 70 W Red Oak Ln White Plains NY 10604-3602*

WHEATON, PERRY LEE, management consultant; b. Corning, N.Y., Jan. 31, 1942; s. Raymond Elmer and Beatrice Estella (Rose) W.; A.B., Hamilton Coll., 1963; M.B.A., Rutgers U., 1964; m. Diane Lynn Mathewson, Sept. 18, 1971; children: James Gardner, William Bard, Lynley Mathewson. Mgr., mgmt. cons. services Coopers & Lybrand, Boston, 1964-76; prin., regional mgr. Theodore Barry & Assocs., 1976-81; sr. v.p., Putnam Fin. Services, Inc., 1981-85; dir. Theodore Barry & Assocs., 1985-90; mng. dir. Barrington Wellesley Group, Inc., 1990—. Served with N.G., 1965-71. C.P.A.; cert. mgmt. cons. Mem. AICPA, N.Y. Soc. C.P.A.s, Inst. Mgmt. Cons. Republican. Unitarian. Home: 23 Poor Rd New London NH 03257 Office: Barrington Wellesley Group Inc PO Box 2390 New London NH 03257-2390

WHEDON, GEORGE DONALD, medical administrator, researcher; b. Geneva, N.Y., July 4, 1915; s. George Dunton and Elizabeth (Crockett) W.; m. Margaret Brunssen, May 12, 1942 (div. Sept. 1982); children: Karen Anne, David Marshall. AB, Hobart Coll., 1936, ScD (hon.), 1967; MD, U. Rochester, 1941, ScD (hon.), 1978. Diplomate Am. Bd. Internal Medicine, Am. Bd. Nutrition. Intern in medicine Mary Imogene Bassett Hosp., Cooperstown, N.Y., 1941-42; asst. in medicine U. Rochester Sch. Medicine; also asst. resident physician medicine Strong Meml. Hosp., Rochester, 1942-44; instr. medicine Cornell U. Med. Coll., 1944-50, asst. prof. medicine, 1950-52; chief metabolic diseases br. Nat. Inst. Arthritis, Diabetes, Digestive and Kidney Diseases, NIH, Bethesda, Md., 1952-65, asst. dir., 1956-62, dir., 1962-81, sr. sci. adv., 1981-82; sr. assoc., dir. conf. program Kroc Found., Santa Ynez, Calif., 1982-84; adj. prof. medicine (endocrinology) UCLA Sch. Medicine, 1982-84; dir. med. rsch. programs Shriners Hosps. for Crippled Children, Tampa, 1984-91; mem. subcom. on calcium, com. dietary allowances Food and Nutrition Bd., NRC, 1959-64; cons. to office manned space flight NASA, 1963-78, chmn. Am. Inst. Biol. Scis. med. program adv. panel to, 1971-75, chmn. NASA life scis. com., 1974-78, mem. space program adv. coun., NASA, 1974-78; cons. on endocrinology and metabolism adv. com. Bur. Drugs, FDA, 1977-82; mem. subcommn. on gravitational biology Com. on Space Rsch., Internat. Union Physiol. Scis., 1979-85; mem. rsch. adv. bd. Shriners Hosps., 1981-84; mem. subcom. spacecraft maximum allowable concentrations, com. toxicology, bd. on environ. studies and toxicology Commn. on Life Scis. NRC, 1989—; cons. in medicine Wadsworth Gen. Hosp. VA Ctr., L.A., 1982-84; mem. U.S. Del. of U.S.-Japan Coop. Med. Sci. Program, 1984-93; mem. Internat. Soc. Gravitational Physiol., 1991—. Mem. editorial bd. Jour. Clin. Endocrinology and Metabolism, 1960-67; adv. editor Calcified Tissue Rsch., 1967-76; contbr. articles to profl. publs. Mem. med. alumni coun. Sch. Medicine, mem. trustees' coun. U. Rochester, 1971-76, vice chmn. trustees' coun., 1973-74, chmn., 1974-75; trustee Dermatology Found., 1978-82; bd. dirs. Osteogenesis Imperfecta Found., 1991—, med. adv. coun., 1993-96. Recipient Superior Svc. award USPHS, 1967, Alumni citation U. Rochester, 1971, Alumni citation Hobart Coll., 1986, Exceptional Sci. Achievement medal NASA, 1974, NASA award of Merit, 1996. Fellow Royal Soc. Medicine; mem. AAAS, Am. Fedn. Med. Rsch. Assn., Am. Physicians, Aerospace Med. Assn. (Arnold D. Tuttle Meml. award 1978), Internat. Bone and Mineral Soc., Internat. Soc. Gravitational Physiology, Md. Acad. Scis. (sci. coun. 1964-70, 81-82), Endocrine Soc. (Robert H. Williams Disting. Leadership award in endocrinology 1982, Ayerst award 1974), Am. Physiol. Soc., Am. Inst. Nutrition, Am. Acad. Orthopaedic Surgeons (hon.), Am. Soc. Bone and Mineral Rsch., Orthopaedic Rsch. Soc., Am. Soc. Gravitational/Space Biology (Founders award 1994), Theta Delta Chi. Episcopalian. Home: 880 Mandalay Ave Apt 1002S Clearwater FL 34630-1230

WHEDON, RALPH GIBBS, manufacturing executive; b. Elizabeth, N.J., Aug. 10, 1949; s. Ralph Gibbs and Jane (MacMaster) W.; m. Lorna Jean Neebe, June 3, 1972; children: Deborah, David. Student, Clarkson Coll., 1968-70; BS, St. Lawrence U., 1972; student, Rensselaer Polytech. Inst., 1978; MBA, De Paul U., 1985. CPA, Ohio. Credit rep. Internat. Harvester Credit Corp., Albany, N.Y., 1972-75, ops. supr., 1975-79; mgr. export ops. Internat. Harvester Co., Chgo., 1979-86; treas. Pettibone Corp., Des Plaines, Ill., 1986-91; mgr. cash resources Bailey Controls Co., Wickliffe, Ohio, 1991—, acting dir. treas., 1992—, mgr. adminstrn., 1993—; dir. MIS HMI Industries, Cleve., 1995—; sec. Tube Form, 1995—; sec. Bliss Mgg., 1995—; sec. Newton Falls Holding Co., 1995—. Bd. dirs. Naperville (Ill.) Cmty. Chorus, 1985-87; trop leader Boy scouts Am., Naperville, 1985—; mem. adv. coun. United Way, 1993—; mem. adv. coun. Cleve. Treas. Club, 1992—, bd. dirs., 1994—; v.p. Brightwood Lakes Assn., 1996—; treas. S.J.E.C. Found., 1996—. Episcopalian. Avocations: sailing, flying. Home: 7066 Brightwood Dr Concord OH 44077-2167 also: Branchview Dr N Ellsworth ME 04605

WHEELAN, R(ICHELIEU) E(DWARD), lawyer; b. N.Y.C., July 10, 1945; s. Richard Fairfax and Margaret (Murray) W. BS, Springfield (Mass.) Coll., 1967; MS, Iona Coll., 1977; JD, Pace U., 1981. Bar: N.Y. 1982, Minn. 1983, Colo. 1989, Tex. 1990, U.S. Dist. Ct. (no dist.) Calif. 1982, (so. dist.) Tex. 1991, U.S. Internat. Trade 1982, U.S. Ct. Appeals (2d cir.) 1982, (9th cir.) 1983, (5th cir.) 1993, U.S. Supreme Ct. 1994; bd. cert. criminal law, trial advocacy. Lt. of detectives White Plains (N.Y.) Police Dept., 1969-81; area counsel IBM, Armonk, N.Y., 1981-89; gen. counsel Kroll Assocs. (Asia), Hong Kong, 1989-91; pvt. practice, Houston, 1991—. Mem. ABA (mem. sentencing guidelines com.), Nat. Assn. Criminal Def. Lawyers (life mem., mem. death penalty com.), Houston Bar Assn., Coll. of State Bar Tex., Pro Bono Coll. State Bar Tex., Tex. Assn. Criminal Def. Lawyers, Harris County Criminal Def. Lawyers Assn. (treas. 1993). Office: 602 Sawyer St Ste 480 Houston TX 77007-7510

WHEELAND, D. A., church administrator. V.p. gen. svcs. The Christian and Missionary Alliance, Colorado Springs. Office: The Christian & Missionary Alliance PO Box 35000 Colorado Springs CO 80935-3500*

WHEELER, ALBIN GRAY, U.S. Army career officer, educator, retail executive, law firm executive; b. Huntington, W.Va., Mar. 16, 1935; s. Harvey Gray and Hattie Benson (Weddle) W.; m. Beatrice Thomas, May 17, 1958; children: Dianne, Michelle, Patrice. BA, Marshall U., 1958; MBA, Pepperdine U., 1975; postgrad., Army War Coll., Carlisle Barracks, Pa., 1976, Harvard U., 1990. Enlisted U.S. Army, 1952, commd. 2nd lt., 1959, advanced through grades to maj. gen., 1985; comdr. divsn. spt. command, chief of staff 1st Inf. Divsn., Ft. Riley, Kans., 1978-80; dep. comdr. U.S. Army Logistics Ctr., Ft. Lee, Va., 1980-81; chief exec. officer Army AF Exch. Svc.-Europe, Munich, 1981-83; comdr. 2d Spt. Command, VII U.S. Corps, Germany, 1983-85; pres. Indsl. Coll. Armed Forces, Washington, 1985-89; dir. human resources Army Materiel Command, Washington, 1989-91; CEO Army and Air Force Exch. Svc., Dallas, 1991-93; ret. U.S. Army, 1993; exec. dir. Arent Fox Kintner Plotkin & Kahn, Washington, 1993-96. Mem. Yeager Scholars Bd., Marshall U., 1986-96; bd. advisors Army Quartermaster Found. Decorated Def. and Army D.S.M., Bronze Star with two oak leaf clusters. Mem. Marshall U. Alumni Assn.

WHEELER, BEVERLY (BARNES), cardiology nurse specialist; b. St. Stephens, N.B., Can., Nov. 9, 1946; parents Am. citizens; d. Robert George and Elizabeth B. (Rideout) Barnes; divorced; children: Jeffrey, Tami. AA, Mohegan C.C., Norwich, Conn., 1981; BSN and cert. in gerontology, George Mason U., 1989, MSN, 1991. RN, Va.; cert. and registered clin. nurse specialist, Va.; cert. ACLS. Various civilian adminstrv. positions U.S. Navy, Groton, Conn., Arlington, Va., 1974-87; vis. nurse Comprehensive Health Agy., Springfield, Va., 1984-86; nursing agy. pers. SRT Med.-Staff Internat., Springfield, 1982-88; legal asst. Office of Asst. Sec. of Navy for Rsch., Engring. and Sys., Washington, 1987-89; staff nurse Arlington Hosp., 1986-90, Fairfax Hosp., Falls Church, Va., 1991—; cardiology nurse specialist Nat. Naval Med. Ctr., Bethesda, Md., 1989—; mem. test devel. com. ANCC; textbook cons., 1994, 96; legal cons. and expert witness; rschr. in field. Contbr. articles to profl. nursing jours. Vol. Am. Heart Assn., 1994-96. Mem. ANA, NAFE, ANCC, TDC, Va. Nurses Assn. Episcopalian. Avocations: aerobics, reading, gardening, crocheting. Home: 10302 Annaberg Ct Burke VA 22015-2833 Office: Nat Naval Med Ctr 8901 Wisconsin Ave Bethesda MD 20814-3708

WHEELER, BURTON M., literature educator, higher education consultant, college dean; b. Mullins, S.C., Mar. 12, 1927; s. Paul and Elizabeth (Cleveland) W.; m. Jacquelyn Mulkey, Aug. 20, 1950; children—Paul, Geoffrey, Kristin. A.B., U. S.C., 1948, M.A., 1951; Ph.D., Harvard U., 1961. Teaching fellow Harvard U., Cambridge, Mass., 1953-56; mem. faculty Washington U., St. Louis, 1956-96, prof., 1974-96; prof. emeritus, 1996—; dean Coll. Arts and Scis. Washington U., St. Louis, 1966-78, interim dean univ. librs., 1988-89; cons., panelist Danforth Found., St. Louis, 1958-82; mem. GPEP panel Assn. Am. Med. Colls., Washington, 1981-84; cons.-evaluator North Cen. Assn., Chgo. Contbr. articles to profl. jours. Eli Lilly Found. fellow, 1965-66. Mem. Soc. Values in Higher Edn., Kent Fellow, Phi Beta Kappa (senator, chmn. qualifications com.).

WHEELER, C. HERBERT, architect, consultant, educator; b. Merchantville, N.J., June 6, 1915; s. Clarence Herbert and Louise Emma (Pennell) W.; m. Cicely Pointer, Aug. 29, 1940; children—Pamela, Janet, Betsy. B.Arch., U. Pa., 1937; M.Arch., MIT, 1940, postgrad. in acoustics and creative engring., 1953, 56; postgrad. bus. program, Alexander Hamilton Inst., 1947. Registered architect N.Y., N.J., Pa., Mich.; cert. Nat. Council Archtl. Registration Bds. Archtl. designer Austin Co., N.Y.C., 1938-41; architect, then chief architect J.G. White Engring. Co., N.Y.C., 1941-55; mgr. engring. Stran Steel Corp., Detroit, 1955-58; mgr. environ. systems Curtiss-Wright Corp., Quehanna, Pa., 1958-64; prof. archtl. engring. Pa. State U., University Park, 1964-80, prof. emeritus, 1980—. author: Public Organizations and Public Architecture, 1987; co-author: Emerging Techniques of Architectural Practice, 1966, Emerging Techniques of Architectural Programming, 1969. Served to maj. C.E., U.S. Army, 1942-46. Decorated Commendation Ribbon U.S. Army CE, 1945. Fellow AIA (emeritus, internat. relations com. 1981-84, v.p. Central Pa. chtp. 1984), Union Internat. des Architects Paris (permanent sec. profl. devel. work group 1980-85, coll. dels. 1981-85), mem. Am. Soc. Engring. Edn. (emeritus, chmn. archtl. engring. div. 1970), constrn. Specifications Inst., Ret. Officers Assn., Theta Xi (v.p. St. Louis 1953-54). Republican. Episcopalian/Methodist. Avocations: travel; precanceled stamp collecting; geography; literature. Home: 638 Franklin St State College PA 16803-3459 Office: Pa State U 104 Engring A Unit University Park PA 16802

WHEELER, CLARENCE JOSEPH, JR., physician; b. Dallas, Sept. 25, 1917; s. Clarence Joseph Sr. and Sadie Alice (McKinney) W.; m. Alice Mary Freels, Dec. 6, 1942; deceased; m. Patsy Lester Butler, Sept. 2, 1995; children: Stephen Freels, C.J. III, Robert McKinney, Thomas Michael, David Ritchey. BS in Math., So. Meth. U., 1941, BA in Psychology, 1946; MD, John Hopkins U., 1950. Diplomate Am. Bd. Surgery; cert. provider ACLS and advanced trauma life support, Am. Heart Assn. Intern John Hopkins Hosp., Balti., 1950-51; resident in surgery Barnes Hosp., St. Louis, 1951-54; fellow thoracic surgery U. Wis. Hosp., Madison, 1954-56, instr. surgery, 1955-56; attending surgeon Welborne Clinic Baptist Hosp., Evansville, Ind., 1956-57; mem. consulting staff Tex. Children's Hosp., 1957-70; courtesy and consulting staffs Pasadena Hosp., Spring Br. Hosp., others, Houston, 1957-70; mem. active staff Hermann Hosp., Houston, 1957-70, St. Luke's Hosp., Houston, 1957-70, Meth. Hosp., Houston, 1957-70, St. Joseph's Hosp., Houston, 1957-70, Meml. Hosp., Houston, 1957-70, Ben Taub Gen. City/County Hosp., Houston, 1957-70, Diagnostic Hosp., &, 1957-70; attending surgeon Lindley Hosp., Duncan, Okla., 1970-71; sr. attending, chief surgery Gordon Hosp., Lewisburg, Tenn., 1971-73; chief thoracic surgery Lewisburg Community Hosp., 1973-75; mem. active med. staff, med. dir. Carver Family Health Clinic, 1975-82; dir. emergency dept. Meth. Med. Ctr. Ill., Peoria, 1975-82; mem. staff Contract Emergency Med. Care, Houston and Dallas, 1982-88; med. dir. substance abuse unit Terrell (Tex.) State Hosp., 1988-90; med. dir. Schick-Shadel Hosp., Dallas-Ft. Worth, 1991—; med. dir., chief of staff Schick-Shadel Hosp., Ft. Worth, 1991-93; med. dir. Skillman Med. Ctr., Dallas, 1993-95, Centers for Preventative Medicine, Dallas, 1996—; instr. surgery U. Wis. Med. Sch., 1955-56; clin. instr. Baylor Coll. Medicine, Houston, 1959-70; lectr. U. Tex. Postgrad. Sch., Houston, 1957-70; clin. asst. prof. U. Ill. Sch. Medicine, Peoria, 1977-82; sr. med. advisor Thue Tien Province, So. Vietnam, 1968-69; chief of surgery Bien Vien Hué So. Vietnam, 1968-69. Treas. Samuel Clark Red Sch. PTA, Houston, 1959-61; bd. dirs. Salvation Army Boys Club, Houston; mem. Am. Mus. of Nat. History, Met. Mus. Art, Smithsonian Inst., Dallas Symphony Assn., Dallas Opera Soc., Dallas Theatre Ctr., Theatre Three Assn. Capt. USMCR, 1942-45, PTO. Decorated DFC with three stars, Air medal with four stars, Pacific Combat Theatre Ribbon with three stars, Purple Heart, Vietnamese Medal of Health (1st class), Vietnamese Medal Social Welfare, Navy Commendation medal, Presdl. Unit citation medal, Meritorious Bronze Star. Fellow ACS, Am. Coll. Angiology, Am. Coll. Chest Physicians, Royal Soc. Medicine, Internat. Coll. Surgeons, Am. Coll. Gastroenterology, Southea. Surg. Congress, Southwestern Surg. Congress, Internat. Assn. Proctologists; mem. AAAS, AMA, Am. Thoracic Soc., Nat. Tb Assn., Am. Assn. History of Medicine, Am. Soc. Contemporary Medicine and Surgery, Am. Soc. Addiction Medicine (cert.), Am. Heart Assn., Am. Cancer Soc., Am. Soc. Abdominal Surgeons, Marine Corps Officer's Assn., Naval Res. Officer's Assn., Nat. Geog. Soc., Mil. Order of the World Wars, Navy League, Indsl. Med. Assn., So. Med. Assn., Tex. Med. Assn., Tex. Thoracic Soc., Tex. Heart Assn., Tex. Anti-Tb Assn., Postgrad. Med. Assembly So. Tex., St. Louis Med. Soc., Dallas County Med. Soc., Marshall County Med. Soc. (pres.), Harris County Med. Soc., Houston Heart Assn., Houston Gastroent. Soc., Houston Surg. Soc., Greater Dallas Res. Officers Assn., Sierra Club, Rotary, Kappa Sigma, Phi Eta Sigma, Kappa Mu Epsilon, Psi Chi. Episcopalian. Address: 7111 Chipperton Dr Dallas TX 75225-1708

WHEELER, CLAYTON EUGENE, JR., dermatologist, educator; b. Viroqua, Wis., June 30, 1917; s. Clayton Eugene and Vista Beulah (Heal) W.; m. Susie Brooks Overton, Oct. 11, 1952; children: Susan Brooks, Margaret Ann, Elizabeth Clayton. B.A., U. Wis., 1938, M.D., 1941. Diplomate Am. Bd. Internal Medicine, Am. Bd. Dermatology (vice pres. 1977-78, pres. 1978-79). Intern Cin. Gen. Hosp., 1941-42; resident in internal medicine U. Mich. Hosps., 1942-44, research fellow endocrinology and metabolism, 1947-48, resident in dermatology, 1948-51; from asst. prof. to prof. dermatology U. Va. Med. Sch., 1951-62; prof. dermatology U. N.C. Med. Sch., Chapel Hill, 1962—, chmn. div., 1962-72, chmn. dept., 1972-87, chmn., exec. com. Med. Faculty Practice Plan, 1986-90; Clayton E. Wheeler Jr. prof. dermatology Sch. Medicine, U. N.C., 1991. Author: Practical Dermatology, 3d edit, 1967, also articles. Served to maj. M.C. AUS, 1944-47. Recipient U. N.C. Med. Alumni Disting. faculty award, 1986, honored with establishment of Clayton E. Wheeler Jr. Professorship of Dermatology position, 1991. Mem. Soc. Investigative Dermatology (pres. 1974-75, Rothman award 1979, hon. mem. 1993), Assn. Profs. Dermatology (pres. 1975-76), Am. Dermatol. Assn. (pres. 1982-83), Am. Acad. Dermatology (past dir., pres.-elect 1983-84, pres.

1984-85, past pres. 1985-86, hon. mem. 1988, masters in dermatology 1993, Gold medal 1993), Phi Beta Kappa, Alpha Omega Alpha. Methodist. Home: 2120 N Lakeshore Dr Chapel Hill NC 27514-2027 Office: NC Meml Hosp Manning Dr Chapel Hill NC 27514

WHEELER, DANIEL SCOTT, management executive, editor; b. Richmond, Va., Apr. 23, 1947; s. Arthur Bruce Jr. and Lavinia (Akers) W.; m. Kathy E. Wheeler; children: Matthew, Beth Marie, Jennifer Lynne, Brandy, Jennifer Ann. Student, Va. Commonwealth U., 1966-69, Butler U., 1981, Ind. U., 1984-85. Spl. agt. Northwestern Mut. Life, Richmond, 1969-71; enlisted USN, 1971, resigned, 1979; editor Am. Legion Mag., Indpls., 1979-85, pub., editor-in-chief, 1985-95; exec. dir. The Am. Legion, 1995—; bd. dirs. HPC/PM Direct. pres. Citizens Flag Alliance, Inc. Mem. Am. Legion, Mensa. Republican. Avocation: oil painting. Home: 4518 Fairhope Dr Indianapolis IN 46237-2951 Office: The American Legion Mag PO Box 1055 Indianapolis IN 46206-1055

WHEELER, DAVID LAURIE, university dean; b. Saginaw, Mich., July 30, 1934; s. Clayton Final and Blanche Beatrice (Hunt) W.; m. Jane Louise Manchester, Sept. 6, 1958; children: Elizabeth, Anne. AB, U. Mich., 1956, AM, 1958, Ph.D., 1962. Asst. dean student service Ill. State U., Normal, 1967-68, assoc. dean, 1968-69, assoc. dean grad. sch., 1969-72; dean grad. sch. West Tex. State U., Canyon, 1972-79; dean grad. sch. Ball State U., Muncie, Ind., 1979-96, dean emeritus, 1996—; cons. McGraw-Hill Pub. Co., N.Y.C., Van Nostrand Reinhold Pub. Co., N.Y.C. Editor: The Human Habitat: Contemporary Readings, 1971. Woodrow Wilson fellow, 1961; recipient Commdrs. Pub. Svc. award Dept. of Army, 1996. Mem. Assn. Am. Geographers, Nat. Coun. Univ. Rsch. Adminstrs., Western History Assn., Tex. State Hist. Assn., U.S. Army War Coll. Found., Sigma Xi, Phi Kappa Phi. Republican. Presbyterian.

WHEELER, DOUGLAS PAUL, conservationist, government official, lawyer; b. Bklyn., Jan. 10, 1942; s. Robert S. and Lottie (Neubauer) W.; m. Heather A. Campbell, Aug. 28, 1965; children—Clay Campbell, Christopher Campbell. AB in Govt. with honors, Hamilton Coll., Clinton, N.Y., 1963; LLB, Duke U., 1966. Bar: N.C. 1966. Assoc. Levine, Goodman & Murchison, Charlotte, N.C., 1966-69; legis. atty. to asst. legis. counsel U.S. Dept. Interior, Washington, 1969-72, dep. asst. sec. Fish and Wildlife and Pks., 1972-77; exec. v.p. Nat. Trust for Hist. Preservation, Washington, 1977-80; pres. Am. Farmland Trust, Washington, 1980-85, now life mem.; exec. dir. Sierra Club, San Francisco, 1985-86; v.p. Conservation Found., Washington, 1986-88, exec. v.p., 1989-91; sec. for resources State of Calif., 1991—. Bd. visitors Duke U. Sch. of Law; bd. dirs. Calif. Nature Conservancy, Calif. Environ. Forum; candidate N.C. Ho. of Reps., 1968; mem. D.C. Rep. Ctrl. Com., 1984-85. Lt. JAGC, USNR, 1969-75. Recipient commendation U.S. Dept. Interior, 1976, Achievement award, 1980, Conservation award Gulf Oil Corp., 1985, Charles S. Murphy award for pub. svc, 1995, Presdl. award for sustainable devel., 1996. Mem. N.C. Bar Assn., Sierra Club (life), Am. Farmland Trust (life). Episcopalian. Home: PO Box 3164 El Macero CA 95618-0764

WHEELER, ED RAY, mathematics educator; b. Bowling Green, Ky., June 13, 1947; m. Claire Mosteller; children: Aaron, Jodi. BA, Samford U., 1969; PhD, U. Va., 1973. Instr. Lynchburg (Va.) Coll., 1969-70; teaching asst. U. Va., Charlottesville, 1970-73; asst. prof. No. Ky. U., Highland Heights, 1973-77, assoc. prof., 1977-80; dept. head Meredith Coll., Raleigh, N.C., 1980-87, Armstrong State Coll., Savannah, Ga., 1987—. Author: (with others) Mathematics: An Every Day Language, 1979, Modern Mathematics, 1995, Activity Manual for Elementary School Teachers, 1995; contbr. articles to profl. jours. Woodrow Wilson Found. fellow, 1969. Mem. Maths. Assn. Am., Am. Math. Soc., Am. Sci. Affiliation. Baptist. Avocations: tennis, jogging, reading. Office: Armstrong State Coll 11935 Abercorn St Savannah GA 31419-1909

WHEELER, GEORGE CHARLES, materials and processes engineer; b. Balt., Oct. 9, 1923; s. George Charles and Julia Elizabeth (Watrous) W.; m. Dorothy W. Whittemore, Sept. 13, 1947; children: Scott, Craig, Mark, Matthew, Tracy, Bruce; m. Clare Frances Weiner, Jan. 21, 1978. BS in Metall. Engring., Lehigh U., 1944. Various engring. and supervisory positions GE, Mass. and N.Y., 1944-62; mgr. materials, welding and nondestructive test engring. Knolls Atomic Power Lab., G.E., Schenectady, N.Y., 1962-68; mgr. nondestructive testing G.E. Power Sys., Schenectady, N.Y., 1968-85; pres., chief exec. officer Wheeler Nondestructive Testing, Inc., Schenectady, 1985-95; pres. Materials and Processes Cons., Schenectady, 1995—; mgr. tech. svcs. Am. Soc. for Nondestructive Testing (ASNT), Columbus, Ohio, 1993-94; cons. UN, N.Y.C., 1985—, IAEA, Vienna, Austria, 1985—, numerous others; guest lectr. Rensselaer Poly. Inst., Troy, N.Y., Union Coll., Schenectady, 1978-87; mem. math. sci. and tech. com. Schenectady County C.C., 1978-85, adj. prof., 1987—; U.S. del. Internat. Stds. Orgn., com. TC 135/SC7 NDT Pers. Qualification, 1987—, convenor working group #2, ISO-9712; mem. ASNT Cert. Mgmt. Bd., 1994—, chmn. 1976-80, 86-89. Author: Guide to Developing Certification Exams, 1992; Guide to Personnel Cert., 1990; contbg. editor Jour. of ASNT; tech. editor Nondestructive Testing Handbook, 3d edit., vol. 3. Fellow Am. Soc. Nondestructive Testing (hon. life mem., bd. dirs. 1976-85, pres. 1983-84, chmn. cert. com. 1976-80, 86-89); mem. ASTM (com. internat. stds., com. nondestructive testing), NRA (life), Am. Soc. Metals (life), Nature Conservancy (life), Adirondack Mountain Club, Adirondack Forty-Sixers. Avocations: mountaineering, flying, firearms, photography.

WHEELER, GEORGE WILLIAM, university provost, physicist, educator; b. Dedham, Mass., Dec. 23, 1924; s. John Brooks, Jr. and Alice (Chamberlin) W.; m. Margaret C. Pirie, Oct. 27, 1957; children: William Cameron, Alice Chamberlin. BS in Physics, Union Coll., Schenectady, 1949; PhD, Yale U., 1953. Research assoc. Woods Hole (Mass.) Oceanographic Inst., 1953-54; asst. prof. physics, sr. research assoc. Yale U., 1954-64; physicist, div. head accelerator dept. Brookhaven Nat. Lab., Upton, N.Y., 1964-72; br. chief high energy physics program, div. phys. research AEC, Washington, 1972-74; dean natural and social sci., prof. physics Herbert H. Lehman Coll., CUNY, Bronx, 1974-79; prof. physics Temple U., Phila., 1979-83; dean Coll. Arts and Scis. Temple U., 1979-83; provost, prof. physics U. Tenn., Knoxville, 1984-90, ret., 1990; Trustee Southeastern Univs. Research Assn., 1984-92, chmn. 1985-89; dir. Oak Ridge Associated Univs., 1985-91; cons. in field; mem. bd. overseers Super Conducting Super Collider, 1988-91. Author papers on physics, particle accelerators. Mem. Branford (Conn.) Bd. Edn., 1961-64; trustee Village of Belle Terre, N.Y., 1967-69, bd. dirs. Southeastern Libraries Network, 1992-95; trustee Webb Sch. of Knoxville, 1985-94. Decorated Bronze Star. Mem. IEEE (sr.), AAAS, Am. Phys. Soc., Phi Beta Kappa, Sigma Xi. Home: 4909 Scenic Point Channel Louisville TN 37777-3221

WHEELER, HEWITT BROWNELL, surgeon, educator; b. Louisville, July 21, 1929; s. Arville and Lois (Vance) W.; m. Elizabeth Jane Maxwell, July 21, 1956; children: Stephen, Elizabeth, Jane, Mary. Student, Vanderbilt U., 1945-48; M.D., Harvard U., 1952. Diplomate Am. Bd. Surgery (bd. dirs. 1984-90). Cushing fellow Harvard Med. Sch., Boston, 1953, Peters fellow, 1956, research fellow, 1959-60, instr. surgery, 1961-64, clin. assoc. surgery, 1964-67, asst. clin. prof. surgery, 1967-70, assoc. prof. surgery, 1970-71; asst. in surgery Peter Bent Brigham Hosp., Boston, 1959-60, jr. assoc. surgery, 1961-64, assoc. surgery, 1964-69, sr. assoc. surgery, 1969-71; asst. chief surgery Roxbury VA Hosp., Boston, 1961-62, chief surgery, 1962-71, chief of staff, 1968-71; cons. surgery U. Mass. Med. Sch. at Worcester, 1966-71, prof., chmn. dept. surgery, 1971-96, Harry M. Haidak disting. prof. surgery, 1985—; chief staff U. Mass. Hosp., 1974-76, surgeon-in-chief, 1976-96; exec. dir. Ctr. for Advanced Clin. Tech., 1995—; affiliate prof. biomed. engring. Worcester Poly. Inst., 1974—; lectr. surgery Harvard Med. Sch., 1974-96; chief surgery St. Vincent Hosp., Worcester, 1971-75; cons. Meml. Hosp., Worcester City Hosp., 1970—, Worcester Hagnemann Hosp., 1974-94, Peter Bent Brigham Hosp., 1973—; chmn. surg. research program com. VA, Washington, 1965-67, nat. participant surg. cons., 1965-69, chmn. ad hoc adv. com. surgery, 1969-71. Trustee Cen. Mass. Health Care Found., 1975-77, Worcester Found. for Biomed. Rsch., 1996—, Boston Med. Libr., 1996—. Served to 1st lt., M.C. AUS, 1953-55. Mem. ACS (bd. govs. 1984-90, coun. Mass. chpt. 1973-76, pres. 1980), AAAS, AMA, Am. Surg. Assn., Soc. Univ. Surgeons, Internat. Cardiovascular Soc., Soc. Surg. Chairmen, New Eng. Surg. Soc. (treas. 1977-84, v.p. 1986-87, pres. 1989-91), Boston Surg. Soc. (pres. 1995-96), Worcester Surg. Soc. (pres. 1973-75), Transportation Soc., Mass. Med. Soc. (100th Shattuck lectr. 1990), Worcester Dist. Med. Soc., New Eng. Vascular Spc. (v.p. 1985-86, pres. 1988-89), Internat. Chirurg. Soc. Research exptl. transplantation, blood vessel surgery, method to detect blood clots. Home: 10 Old English Rd Worcester MA 01609-1306

WHEELER, JACK COX, army officer; b. Canton, Ga., Feb. 2, 1939; s. Clinton Alfred and Juanita I. (Cox) W.; m. Marjorie Gunn, May 5, 1962; children: Leigh Ann, Clinton Alan. BA in History, North Ga. Coll., 1961; MA in Pub. Adminstrn., Shippensburg State U., 1979; postgrad., Harvard U., 1988. Commd. 2d lt. U.S. Army, 1961, advanced through grades to maj. gen., 1989; chief, officer mgmt. br. Mil. Assistance Command Vietnam, Tan Son Nat, 1969-70; pers. staff officer Dep. Chief of Staff for Pers., Washington, 1971-75; asst. to dir. army staff Office U.S. Army Chief of Staff, Washington, 1975-76; adj. gen. 1st Armored Div., Ansbach, Fed. Republic Germany, 1976-78; student Army War Coll., Carlisle Barracks, Pa., 1979; chief structure br. Dep. Chief of Staff for Pers., Washington, 1979-80, chief enlisted div., 1980-82, chief profl. devel., 1982-84; comdr. 8th Pers. Command-Korea, Youngsan, Seoul, 1984-86; dir. Enlisted Pers. Mgmt., Alexandria, Va., 1986-88; dep. comdg. gen. U.S. Army Recruiting Command, Ft. Sheridan, Ill., 1988-89, comdg. gen., 1989-93; sales dir. Citizen Newspapers, Fayetteville, Ga., 1995—. Decorated D.S.M., Legion of Merit, Bronze Star. Mem. Assn. U.S. Army. Methodist. *

WHEELER, JOCK R., dean. Dean Ea. Va. Med. Sch. Med. Coll. Hampton Rds. Office: Ea Va Med Sch Med Coll Norfolk Va PO Box 1980 Norfolk VA 23501-1980*

WHEELER, JOHN CRAIG, astrophysicist, writer; b. Glendale, Calif., Apr. 5, 1943; s. G.L. and Peggy Wheeler; m. Hsueh Lie, Oct. 29, 1967; children: Diek Winters, J. Robinson. BS in Physics, MIT, 1965; PhD in Physics, U. Colo., 1969. Asst. prof. astronomy Harvard U., Cambridge, Mass., 1971-74; assoc. prof. U. Tex., Austin, 1974-80, prof., 1980—, Samuel T. and Fern Yanagisawa Regents prof. astronomy, 1985—, chmn. astronomy dept., 1986-90; vis. fellow Joint Inst. Lab. Astrophysics, Boulder, Colo., 1978-79, Japan Soc. for Promotion of Sci., 1983; 1st vis. prof. Assn. Univs. for Rsch. in Astronomy, 1990; mem. exec. com. Aspen (Colo.) Ctr. for Physics, Tex. Symposium on Relativistic Astrophysics. Author: The Krone Experiment, 1986; editor: Accretion Disks in Compact Stellar Systems, 1993. Recipient undergrad. teaching award Coll. Natural Scis., U. Tex., 1984, teaching award Bd. Visitors, Dept. Astronomy, U. Tex., 1986; Fulbright fellow, Italy, 1991. Mem. Internat. Astron. Union, Am. Astron. Soc., Sigma Xi. Avocations: running, writing, reading. Office: U Tex Dept Astronomy Austin TX 78712

WHEELER, JOHN HARVEY, political scientist; b. Waco, Tex., Oct. 17, 1918; m. Norene Burleigh; children: David Carroll, John Harvey III, Mark Jefferson. B.A., Ind. U., 1946, M.A., 1947; Ph.D., Harvard U., 1950. Instr. dept. govt., asst. dir. Summer Sch., Harvard U., 1950; asst. prof. Johns Hopkins U., 1950-54; assoc. prof. Washington and Lee U., 1954-56, prof. polit. sci., 1956-60; fellow in residence Ctr. for Study Dem. Instns., 1960-69, program dir., 1970-75; chmn., pres. Inst. Higher Studies, Carpinteria, Calif., 1975—; Martha Boaz rsch. prof. in acad. info. systems U. So. Calif. Libr. Systems, 1986—, Martha Boaz disting. rsch. prof., 1987—; cons. Fund for Republic, 1958-61; adj. prof. New Sch., 1986—, ISIM, 1989—; founder, bd. dirs. The Virtual Acad., 1987; mem. faculty Western Behavioral Scis. Inst., 1990—; mem. BESTnet, Nat. Rsch. and Edn. Network; pres. C-Mode Inst., 1992—; bd. dirs. Silicon Beach Comm. Author: The Conservative Crisis, 1958, (with Eugene Burdick) Fail-Safe, 1962, Democracy in a Revolutionary Era, 1968, The Politics of Revolution, 1971, The Virtual Library, 1987, The Virtual Society, 1988, 2d edit., 1992, (with E.M. Nathanson) The Rise of the Elders, 1996; editor, contbg. author: Beyond Punitive Society, 1973, Structure of Ancient Wisdom, 1983, Bioalgebra of Judgment, 1986, Fundamental Structures Human Reflexion, 1990; editor: (with George Boas) Lattimore, The Scholar, 1953; co-founder, joint chief editor: (with James Danielli) Jour. Social and Biol. Structures, 1973—; joint editor Goethe's Science, 1986; developed computer-mediated "Freshman Academy", 1993; contbr. articles to profl. jours. Served with AUS, 1941-46. Office: Inst Higher Studies PO Box 704 Carpinteria CA 93014-0704

WHEELER, JOHN OLIVER, geologist; b. Mussoorie, India, Dec. 19, 1924; s. Edward Oliver and Dorothea Sophie (Danielsen) W.; m. Nora Jean Hughes, May 17, 1952; children: Kathleen Anna Wheeler Hunter, Jennifer Margaret Wheeler Crompton. B.A.Sc. in Geol. Engring, U. B.C., 1947; Ph.D. in Geology, Columbia U., 1956. Geologist Geol. Survey Can., Ottawa, Ont., 1951-61, Vancouver, B.C., 1961-65; rsch. scientist Geol. Survey Can., 1965-70; rsch. mgr. Geol. Survey Can., Ottawa, 1970—; chief regional and econ. geology div. Geol. Survey Can., 1970-73, dep. dir. gen., 1973-79; rsch. scientist Geol. Survey Can. (Cordilleran div.), 1979-90, rsch. scientist emeritus, 1990—. Compiler of regional geol. maps of we. Can., Can. and no. N.Am. and Greenland; contbr. articles to profl. jours. Recipient Earth Sci. Sector award Nat. Resources Can., 1996. Fellow Royal Soc. Can., Geol. Assn. Can. (pres. 1970-71, Logan medal 1983, Disting. fellow 1996), Geol. Soc. Am. (councillor 1971-74), Can. Geosci. Council (pres. 1981); mem. Can. Inst. Mining and Metallurgy., Can. Geol. Found. (pres. 1974-79). Anglican. Clubs: Can. Alpine, Am. Alpine. Office: Geol Survey Can, 101-605 Robson St, Vancouver, BC Canada V6B 5J3

WHEELER, JOHN WATSON, lawyer; b. Murfreesboro, Tenn., Sept. 11, 1938; s. James William and Grace (Fann) W.; m. Dorothy Anita Pressgrove, Aug. 5, 1959; children: Jeffrey William, John Harold. BS in Journalism, U. Tenn., 1960, JD, 1968. Bar: Tenn. 1968, U.S. Dist. Ct. (ea. dist.) Tenn. 1968, U.S. Supreme Ct. 1974, U.S. Ct. Appeals (6th cir.) 1975. Editor The Covington (Tenn.) Leader, 1963-65; adminstrv. asst. to lab. dir. UT-AEC Rsch. Lab., Oak Ridge, Tenn., 1965-68; assoc. Hodges, Doughty & Carson, Knoxville, Tenn., 1968-72; ptnr. Hodges, Doughty & Carson, Knoxville, 1972—; mem. commn. to study Appllelate Cts. in Tenn.; chair U.S. Magistrate Merit Selection Panel, Ea. Dist., Tenn., 1991; mem. Bankruptcy Judge Merit Selection Panel, Ea. Dist. Tenn., 1992-94; chmn. Hist. Soc., U.S. Dist. Ct. (ea. dist.) Tenn. Mem. organizing com. Tenn. Supreme Ct. Hist. Soc. Lt. U.S. Army, 1961-63, capt. Res. Fellow Am. Bar Found. (life), Tenn. Bar Found.; mem. ABA (ho. of dels. 1986—), Tenn. Bar Assn. (pres. 1989-90, bd. govs. 1981-91), Nat. Conf. Bar Pres., Am. Inns. of Ct. (master of bench), Internat. Assn. Def. Counsel, So. Conf. Bar Pres., Fox Den Country Club. Republican. Lutheran. Avocations: golf, travel. Home: 12009 N Fox Den Dr Knoxville TN 37922-2540 Office: Hodges Doughty & Carson PO Box 869 Knoxville TN 37901-0869

WHEELER, KATHERINE FRAZIER (KATE WHEELER), writer; b. Tulsa, July 27, 1955; d. Charles Bowen and Jan Nette (Moses) W. BA in English Fine Arts, Rice U., 1977; MA in Creative Writing, Stanford U., 1981. News reporter The Miami (Fla.) Herald, 1977-79; tchr. English composition Middlesex C.C., Lawrence, Mass., 1991; tchr. meditation Insight Meditation Soc., Barre, Mass., 1991—. Author: (short stories) Not Where I Started From, 1993; editor: (essays) In This Very Life, 1990; translator: (poems) Borrowed Time/Lo Esperady Lo Vivido, 1987; contg. editor: Tricycle Mag. Buddhist nun Mahasi Sasana Yeiktha, Rangoon, Burma, 1988; vol. Pet Share, Somerville (Mass.) Hosp., 1994. Recipient Pushcart Press prize, 1983-84, Best Am. Short Stories award Houghton Miflin, 1992, O'Henry award Doubleday, Inc., 1982, 93; nominee PEN/Faulkner award, 1994, Whiting Found. award, 1994; named one of Best 20 U.S. Novelists under 40, Granta Mmag., 1996; NEA grantee, 1994. Avocations: travel, dog training, sky gazing. Home: 72 Rev Nazareno Properzi Way Somerville MA 02143-3707

WHEELER, KATHERINE WELLS, state legislator; b. St. Louis, Feb. 8, 1940; d. Benjamin Harris and Katherine (Gladney) Wells; m. Douglas Lanphier Wheeler, June 13, 1964; children: Katherine Gladney, Lucille Lanphier. BA, Smith Coll., 1961; MA, Washington U., St. Louis, 1966. Founder auction N.H. Pub. TV, Durham, 1973-76; pub. mem. N.H. Pub. Broadcasting Coun., Durham, 1975-80; founding mem. bd. govs. N.H. Pub. TV, 1980-88; elected N.H. Ho. of Reps., Concord, 1988, 90, 92,94; mem. N.H. Senate, 1996—; coord. internat. visitors program N.J. Coun. World Affairs, 1981-95. Bd. dirs. Planned Parenthood No. New England, 1989-95, Gt. Bay Sch. and Tng. Ctr., Newington, N.H., 1989-97, Devel. Svcs. Strafford County, Inc., 1991—; vice chairperson Strafford County Legis. Del., 1993-94; active Commn. on Health, Human Svcs. and Elderly Affairs N.H. Ho. of Reps., Concord, 1988-96; bd. mem. N.H. Pub. Health Assn., 1996—, N.E. Citizen Action Resource Coun., 1996; pres. elect N.H. Order of Women Legislators, 1997—. Named Woman of Yr., Union Leader Newspaper, 1984, Citizen of Yr., Homemakers of Strafford County, 1990, N.H. sect. NASW, 1993, Legislator of Yr., N.H. Nurses Assn., 1996, N.H. Acad. Pediat., 1996; recipient Elizabeth Campbell Outstanding Pub. TV Vol. award Nat. Friends Pub. Broadcasting, 1984, Meritorious Svc. award N.H. Women's Lobby, 1992, Dist. Contbn. award N.H. Psychol. Orgn., Inc., 1994, Cert. of Achievement for Outstanding Legis. Leadership N.H. Citizen Action, 1994. Mem. AAUW, LWV, Am. Assn. Ret. Persons, Order of Women Legislators, N.H. Smith Coll. Club (v.p. 1974-76, pres. 1976-78, v.p. class of 1961, 1991-96), N.H. Assn. Social Workers (Legislator of Yr. 1993), N.H. Psychol. Orgn. Inc. (Disting. Contbn. award 1994). Democrat. Mem. United Ch. of Christ. Home and Office: 27 Mill Rd Durham NH 03824-3006

WHEELER, KENNETH WILLIAM, history educator; b. Amarillo, Tex., Mar. 7, 1929; s. Homer N. and Bertha (Campbell) W.; children: Amanda, Philip, David. B.A., U. Tex., 1951; diplome D'etudes Degré Superieur, Sorbonne, Paris, 1956; Ph.D., U. Rochester, 1963. Lectr., instr. history and city planning, asst. dean Grad. Sch. Ohio State U., 1960-66; asso. dean Met. Coll.; acting dean, dir. MetroCenter; assoc. prof. history Boston U., 1967-69; prof. history, dean Univ. Coll., Rutgers U., 1969-72, provost, 1972-87; sr. v.p. acad. affairs Rutgers U., 1987-91, Univ. prof. history, 1974—; mem. vis. com. Harvard U., 1972-80, adv. com. Lahey Clinic, 1989—, Planned Parenthood, 1988—. Author: To Wear a City's Crown, 1968, Women, The Arts, and The 1920's in New York and Paris, 1982; editor: For the Union, 1968. Trustee New Brunswick Tomorrow, George Street Theatre, Rutgers Prep. Sch. Served with AUS, 1951-53. Recipient award Am. Philos. Assn., 1966; fellow Am. Council Edn., 1966-67. Mem. Am. Hist. Assn., Orgn. Am. Historians, Soc. des amis des Univs. de Paris, Urban League, Lotos Club, Phi Kappa Psi, Delta Sigma Pi. Clubs: Century Assn. (N.Y.C.), Palo Duro (Tex.). Office: Rutgers U 7 W 43rd St New York NY 10036-7402

WHEELER, LAWRENCE JEFFERSON, art museum administrator. BA cum laude in History and French, Pfeiffer Coll., 1965; MA in European History, U. Ga., 1969, PhD in European History, 1972; cert., Fed. Execs. Inst., Charlottesville, Va., 1977, U. N.C., 1982. Asst. prof. European history Pfeiffer Coll., Misenheimer, N.C., 1970-74; dep. sec. N.C. Dept. Cultural Resources, Raleigh, 1977-85; asst. dir. mus. and dir. devel. Cleve. Mus. Art, 1985-94; staff liaison for bldg. and staffing N.C. Mus. Art, Raleigh, 1977-83, dir., 1994—; cons. on fundraising and pub. rels. N.C. Mus. History, Raleigh; coord. 400th anniversary celebration Sir Walter Raleight's voyages festival, 1984. Bd. dirs. Am. Arts Alliance, 1991-92. Mem. Am. Assn. Mus. (chmn. dvel. and membership profl. com. 1990-92, sr. reviewer mus. assessment program 1992—), Inst. Mus. Svcs. (reviewer 1988—), Art Mus. Devel. Assn. (pres. 1987-88). Home: 507 North St Chapel Hill NC 27514 Office: NC Mus Art 2110 Blue Ridge Rd Raleigh NC 27607-6433

WHEELER, M. CATHERINE, organization executive; b. Plainfield, N.J., May 31, 1942; d. William R. and Josephine S. (Ford) W. BA in Politics, Hollins Coll., 1964; MA in Theatre, U. Kans., 1966. Asst. mgr. South Shore Music Circus, Cohasset, Mass., 1967; pub. rels. asst. Trinity Square Repertory Co., Providence, 1967-68; co. mgr. Acad. Playhouse, Wilmette, Ill., 1968; adminstrv. asst. Am. U. Theatre, Washington, 1968-71; pub. rels. asst. Winterthur Mus. and Gardens, Wilmington, Del., 1972-76, dir. pub. rels., 1976-84; dir. Del. Tourism Office, Dover, 1984-93; pub. rels. coord. New Castle County Bd. of Realtors, Wilmington, 1994-95, dir. polit. affairs and comm., 1995—; pub. rels. cons. Historic Deerfield, Mass., 1983, Tourism Coun. Frederick County, Md., Bristol Riverside Theatre, Pa., 1994; bd. dirs. U.S. Travel Data Ctr., 1989-93. Editor Winterthur Newsletter, 1972-84. Mem. Del. Heritage Commn., 1984-93, Del. Coastal Heritage Greenways Coun., 1991-93. Mem. Nat. Coun. State Travel Dirs. (chmn. nominating com. 1987-89, chmn. edn. com. 1989-91, chmn. rsch. task force 1991-92), Travel Industry Assn. (bd. dirs. 1990-94, chmn. Mid-Atlantic U.S.A (1989-92). Avocations: theatre, music, museums, travel, writing. Office: New Castle Cty Bd Realtors 3615 Miller Rd Wilmington DE 19802-2523

WHEELER, MALCOLM EDWARD, lawyer, law educator; b. Berkeley, Calif., Nov. 29, 1944; s. Malcolm Ross and Frances Dolores (Kane) W.; m. Donna Marie Stambaugh, July 21, 1981; children: Jessica Ross, M. Connor. SB, MIT, 1966; JD, Stanford U., 1969. Bar: Calif. 1970, Colo. 1992, U.S. Dist. Ct (cen. dist.) Calif. 1970, U.S. Ct. Appeals (9th cir.) 1970, U.S. Ct. Appeals (10th cir.) 1973, U.S. Dist. Ct. (no., so., ea. and cen. dists.) Calif. 1975, U.S. Ct. Appeals (11th cir.) 1987, U.S. Ct. Appeals (D.C. cir.) 1987, U.S. Supreme Ct. 1976, U.S. Ct. Appeals (3d cir.) 1989, (4th cir.) 1992. Assoc. Howard, Prim, Smith, Rice & Downs, San Francisco, 1969-71; assoc. prof. law U. Kans., Lawrence, 1971-74; assoc. Hughes Hubbard & Reed, Los Angeles, 1974-77, ptnr., 1977-81, 83-85, cons., 1981-83; ptnr. Skadden, Arps, Slate, Meagher & Flom, Los Angeles, 1985-91; dir. Parcel, Mauro, Hultin & Spaanstra P.C., Denver, 1991—; vis. prof. U. Iowa, 1978, prof., 1979; prof. U. Kans., Lawrence, 1981-83; chief counsel U.S. Senate Select Com. to Study Law Enforcement Undercover Activities, Washington, 1982-83. Mem. editorial bd. Jour. Products Liability, 1984—; bd. editors Fed. Litigation Guide Reporter, 1986—; contbr. articles to profl. jours. Mem. ABA, Calif. Bar Assn., Colo. Bar Assn., Am. Law Inst. Office: Parcel Mauro Hultin & Spaanstra PC 1801 California St Denver CO 80202-2658

WHEELER, MARK ANDREW, SR., lawyer; b. Pitts., Feb. 14, 1963; s. Andrew Mote Murdock and Anna Ruth (Whitfield) W.; m. Darla Jo Fusselman, May 10, 1993; children: Mark Andrew Jr., Lauren Anna. BA in Philosophy, Hampden-Sydney Coll., 1985; JD, W.Va. U., 1991. Bar: Pa. 1993, U.S. Dist. Ct. (we. dist.) Pa. 1993. Staff litigator W.Va. U. Coll. Law Legal Clinic, Morgantown, 1991-92; jud. clk. Mahoning County, Youngstown, Ohio, 1992-93; pvt. practice Reynoldsville, Pa., 1993—, Clarion, Pa., 1994—; legal cons. S.T. & E., Inc., Punxsutawney, Pa., 1993—, Jefferson County Gun Owners Assn., Brookville, Pa., 1994—, Crimestoppers of Jefferson County, Brookville, 1993-94, Five Star Homes, Inc., 1995—, Bembeng Cons., Inc., 1994—. Bd. dirs. Reynoldsville Area Indsl. Bd., 1993-96; mem. exec. dist. com. Boy Scouts Am., Dubois, Pa., 1993—; bd. dirs. Reynoldsville Pub. Libr. Assn., 1993-96; mem. Dubois Christian and Missionary Alliance Ch., mem. choir, 1995—. Mem. ABA, ATLA, Pa. Bar Assn. (young lawyers divsn., chair zone 7), Am. Ctr. for Law and Justice, Pa. Trial Lawyers Assn., Pa. Assn. Notaries, Jefferson County Bar Assn., Western Pa. Trial Lawyers Assn., Clarion County Bar Assn., Masons, Nat. Eagle Scout Assn. Republican. Avocations: songwriting, public speaking, home renovation, car restoration. Office: PO Box 176 512 Main St Reynoldsville PA 15851 also: 8 Grant St Clarion PA 16214

WHEELER, MARSHALL RALPH, zoologist, educator; b. Carlinville, Ill., Apr. 7, 1917; s. Ralph Adelbert and Hester May (Ward) W.; m. Edna Vivian Cronquist, July 3, 1944; 1 dau., Sandra Wheeler King; m. Linda Carol Lackner, May 10, 1966; children: Karen, Carson. Student, Blackburn Coll., 1935-37; B.A., Baylor U., 1939; postgrad., Tex. A&M U., 1939-41; Ph.D. (NRC fellow), U. Tex., 1947. Mem. faculty U. Tex., Austin, 1947—, assoc. prof. zoology, 1955-61, prof., 1961-78, emeritus prof., 1978—; Gosney fellow Calif. Inst. Tech.; former dir. Nat. Drosophila Species Resources Ctr.; mem. Nat. Wildflower Rsch. Ctr. Editor: Studies in Genetics, 1960-72. Served with USN, 1941-45. NSF grantee; NIH grantee. Mem. Entomol. Soc. Am. (editor Annals 1970-75), S.W. Assn. Naturalists (pres. 1961), Southwestern Entomol. Soc. (pres. 1978), Am. Hemerocallis Soc., Wilderness Soc., Nature Conservancy, Sierra Club. Home: 1313 Ardenwood Rd Austin TX 78722-1105 Office: U Tex Dept Zoology Austin TX 78712

WHEELER, ORVILLE EUGENE, university dean, civil and mechanical engineering educator; b. Memphis, Dec. 31, 1932; s. Eugene Lloyd and Sarah Josephine (Craig) W.; m. Mary Bea Rychlik, June 6, 1956; 1 dau., Lynnette Layne. B.Engring. cum laude, Vanderbilt U., 1954; M.S. in Civil Engring, U. Mo., 1956; Ph.D., Tex. A&M U., 1966. Registered profl. engr., Ala., Tenn., Wis. With Chance Vought Co., Dallas, 1959-60, Hayes Aircraft Co., Birmingham, Ala., 1960-61, Brown Engring. Co., Huntsville, Ala., 1961-62, NASA, Huntsville, 1962-66; design specialist Gen. Dynamics Co., Ft. Worth, 1966-72; chief structures engr. Bucyrus Erie Co., Milw., 1972-78; prof. civil and mech. engring., dean Herff Coll. Engring. Memphis State U., 1978-87, Herff prof. structural mechanics, 1987—. Served with USN, 1956-59. Mem. ASCE, ASTM, Assn. for Computing Machinery, Am. Inst. Steel

Constrn., Memphis Engrs. Club. Methodist. Home: 3307 E Monticello Cir Memphis TN 38115-0640 Office: Dept of Engring U Memphis Memphis TN 38152

WHEELER, OTIS BULLARD, academic administrator, educator emeritus; b. Mansfield, Ark., Feb. 1, 1921; s. Clarence Charles and Georgia Elizabeth (Bullard) W.; m. Doris Louise Alexander, Jan. 17, 1943; children: Ann Carolyn, Ross Charles; m. Anne Carol Loveland, Mar. 23, 1991. B.A., U. Okla., 1942; M.A., U. Tex., 1947; Ph.D., U. Minn., 1951. Faculty La. State U., Baton Rouge, 1952—; prof. English La. State U., 1965-81, prof. emeritus, 1981—, chmn. dept., 1974, asst. dean grad. sch., 1962-67, vice chancellor for acad. affairs, 1974-80, acting chancellor, 1981; Fulbright-Hayes lectr. U. Innsbruck, Austria, 1968-69. Author: The Literary Career of Maurice Thompson, 1965; photographer: (with R.W. Heck) Religious Architecture in Louisiana, 1995. Served with U.S. Army, 1942-46, 51-52. Decorated Bronze Star medal. Mem. Phi Kappa Phi, Omicron Delta Kappa. Democrat. Methodist. Home: 162 Clara Dr Baton Rouge LA 70808-4709

WHEELER, OTIS V., JR., public school principal; b. Silex, Mo., Oct. 1, 1925; s. Otis V. and Pearla F. (Howell) W.; m. Virginia Rogers, June 7, 1947; children: Jan Leigh, Mark Patrick. BBA, U. Mo., 1948, MEd, 1965, EdD, 1971. USN, 1948-52, Bus. mgr., 1952-61; sci. tchr. Columbia (Mo.) Pub. Schs., 1961-63, principal, 1963-91; supt. Boone County Sch. Dist., Mo., 1971; instr. U. Mo., Columbia, 1970-72, asst. prof. 1972-75, 78-79; cons. Midwest Ctr for Equal Ednl. Opportunities, 1972-75. Served to lt. USNR, 1943-85, World War II, Korea. Mem. Nat. Assn. Elem. Sch. Prins. (U.S. Dept. Edn., Nat. Disting. Prin. award 1985, Excellence in Edn. award 1986), Mo. Assn. Elem. Sch. Prins. (Disting. Service award 1984, editor jours. 1967-88), Mo. State Tchrs. Assn., Retired Officers Assn., U. Mo. Columbia Coll. Edn. Alumni (Citation of Merit award 1987), Nat. Soc. of the SAR. Methodist. Club: Lake Ozark Yachting Assn. (Mo.). Avocations: boating, dancing, travel, scuba diving. Home: 916 W Ash St Columbia MO 65203-2636 Office: Ridgeway IGE Sch 107 E Sexton Rd Columbia MO 65203-4082

WHEELER, PAUL JAMES, real estate executive; b. Mpls., Jan. 8, 1953; s. Philip James and Phyllis Lavonne (Holmquist) W.; m. Marianne Marie Stanton, June 3, 1978; children: Allison, Nathan, Kathryn. BA in Econs., DePauw U., 1975; MBA in Mgmt., Northwestern U., 1977. CPA, Ill. Acct. Deloitte, Haskins & Sells, Chgo., 1976-79; v.p. fin. Quinlan & Tyson, Inc., Evanston, Ill., 1979-82; sr. v.p. The Inland Group, Inc., Oakbrook, Ill., 1982—; bd. dirs. Westbank of Westchester, Inland Property Sales Inc., Inland Am. Ins. Co., Inland Securities Corp., Oak Brook, Ill. Mem. Ill. Soc. CPA's, Nat. Assn. Real Estate Investment Trusts, Nat. Multi Housing Coun., Investment Program Assn., Libertyville Sunrise Rotary. Republican. Evangelical Free. Home: 255 Ridgeway Ln Libertyville IL 60048-2457 Office: The Inland Group Inc 2901 Butterfield Rd Oak Brook IL 60523-1106

WHEELER, PETER MARTIN, federal agency administrator; b. Bronx, N.Y., Nov. 10, 1939; s. James and Mary A. (Doyle) W.; m. Mary Gaffey, Aug. 7, 1982; children: Bernadette, Peter, Mary Beth, James, Sam, Andrea. BA, Iona Coll., New Rochelle, N.Y., 1961; MPA, U. So. Calif., 1985, DPA (Dr. Pub. Administrn.), 1992. Claims rep., field rep. Social Security Adminstrn., Bronx, 1961-64; claims authorizer Social Security Adminstrn., Balt., 1964-65, comms. specialist, 1965-70, dep. assoc. commr., 1973-91, assoc. commr., 1992—; asst. exec. sec. Office of Sec. Dept. of Health, Edn. and Welfare, Washington, 1970-73; rep. Internat. Conf. on Social Welfare, Holland, 1972, Kenya, 1974; cons. Can. helath and Welfare Agy. Ottawa, 1989; adj. prof. George Washington U., Washington, 1994—. Mem. U.S. study team Benefits & Svcs. for Poor Children Eng., 1973; vol. City Jail, Balt., 1988—. Recipient Nat. Inst. Pub. Affairs award U. So. Calif., 1969-70. Mem. Internat. Social Security Assn. (social security adminstrn. rep., mem. adv. com. rsch. Geneva, Vienna). Roman Catholic. Achievements include Social Security rsch., rebuilding Social Security Adminstrn.'s quality assurance systems. Home: 3238 Birchmede Dr Ellicott City MD 21042 Office: Social Security Adminstrn Rm 4-C-15 Ops 6401 Security Blvd Baltimore MD 21235-0001

WHEELER, RAYMOND LOUIS, lawyer; b. Ft. Sill, Okla., Feb. 10, 1945; s. Raymond Louis and Dorothy Marie (Hutcherson) W.; m. Priscilla Wheeler, July 1, 1966 (div. 1982); children: Jennifer, Hilary; m. Cynthia Lee Jackson, July 14, 1984 (div. 1994); children: Matthew Raymond, Madeline Elizabeth; m. Freddie Kay Park, June 10, 1995. BA, U. Tex., 1967; JD, Harvard U., 1970. Bar: Calif. 1972, U.S. Dist. Ct. (no., cen., ea. dists.) Calif., U.S. Ct. Appeals (9th cir.), U.S. Supreme Ct. Law clk. to hon. Irving L. Goldberg U.S. Ct. Appeals 5th cir., 1970-71; assoc. Morrison & Foerster, San Francisco, 1971-76, ptnr., 1976-90; ptnr. Morrison & Foerster, Palo Alto, Calif., 1990—; chmn. labor and employment law dept. Morrison & Foerster, San Francisco, 1984-88, 92—; lectr. labor and EEO law. Exec. editor Harvard Law Rev., 1969-70; editor in chief The Developing Labor Law; mem. nat. adv. bd. Indsl. Rels. Law Jour., 1980—; contbr. articles to law jours. Mem. ABA (chmn. com. on law devel. under labor rels. act 1990-93, coun. mem. sect. labor and employment 1994—). Republican. Office: Morrison & Foerster 755 Page Mill Rd Palo Alto CA 94304-1018

WHEELER, R(ICHARD) KENNETH, lawyer; b. Washington, July 25, 1934; s. Nathaniel Dudley and Ruth Lee (Matthews) W.; m. Christine Kandris, Jan. 11, 1990; children by previous marriage: Jennifer L., Ruth E. BA, Emory and Henry Coll., U. Richmond, 1957; LLB, U. Richmond, 1964. Bar: Va. 1963, D.C. 1977, U.S. Tax Ct. 1978. Assoc., then ptnr. Hunton, Williams, Gay, Powell & Gibson and successor firms, Richmond, 1963-88; sr. ptnr. Kane, Wheeler, Fenderson & Jeffries, Richmond, 1988-90; counsel Durrette, Irvin, Lemons & Fenderson, P.C., Richmond, 1990-94; sr. ptnr. Wallace, Harris & Wheeler, Richmond, 1994-95; adj. prof. law T.C. Williams Sch. Law, U. Richmond, 1966, 83, bd. dirs., 1977-79; adj. prof. law Va. Commonwealth U., 1970; lectr. trial practice U. Va., 1981-82, 85, 87; arbitrator Am. Arbitration Assn. Served to capt. USMCR, 1957-61. Williams scholar U. Richmond, 1961-63. Mem. ABA, Fed. Bar Assn., Nat. Assn. R.R. Trial Counsel, Am. Judicature Soc., Am. Law Inst., Va. State Bar (chmn. com. liaison with law schs. 1977-78, chmn. com. legal edn. and admission to bar 1978-80, spcl. com. on professionalism 1987-88), Va. Bar Assn., Bar Assn. D.C., Richmond Trial Lawyers Assn., Va. Trial Lawyers Assn., Richmond Bar Assn., Chesterfield-Colonial Heights Bar Assn., Henrico Bar Assn., Web Soc., McNeill Law Soc., Supreme Ct. Hist. Soc., Marine Corps League (life), Rector's Club (U. Richmond, life), Pi Sigma Alpha, Phi Delta Phi, Omicron Delta Kappa (hon.).

WHEELER, RICHARD WARREN, banker; b. Boston, Feb. 8, 1929; s. Wilfrid and Sybil Constance (Leckenby) W.; m. Betty Ann Owens, Sept. 9, 1950; children: Emily, Susan Knight, Thomas Adams, Alice Owens, Sarah Bennett. BA, Williams Coll., 1952; cert. mgmt. devel., Harvard U., 1962. With Citibank, N.A., 1952-82; assigned to Citibank, N.A., Hongkong, Manila and Tokyo, 1953-69, v.p., 1967-69, head Asia Pacific div., 1969-75, dep. overseas div., 1975-77; sr. v.p. Citibank, N.A., N.Y.C., 1969-82; head internat. relations unit Citibank, N.A., 1977-82; exec. v.p. Asia Soc., 1982-84; pres. Asia Internat. Bank, 1984-85; sr. v.p., gen. mgr. Bank of the Philippine Islands, N.Y.C., 1985-90; internat. fin. cons., 1991—. Chmn. Concord (Mass.) Bd. Assessors; bd. dirs., v.p. Am. Australian Assn., 1972-88; organizing dir. Nat. Coun. U.S.-China Trde; bd. dirs., chmn. exec. com. Presiding Bishop's Fund for World Relief, 1976-82; mem. standing com. on stewardship Episcopal Ch., 1978-84; mem. spl. refugee adv. panel Dept. State, 1982; mem. adv. bd. Ctr. for Contemporary Arab Studies, Georgetown U., 1977-79; chmn. adv. coun. Ctr. for Study World Religions, Harvard U., 1974-89, mem. adv. bd. Ctr. for East Asian Studies, 1971-76, mem. adv. bd. Ctr. for Strategic and Internat. Studies, 1970-80, v.p. exec. coun. Harvard Bus. Sch., 1971-75; chmn. bus. and industry adv. coun. com. on capital markets and capital movements OECD, 1980-82; mem. exec. com. ASEAN-U.S. Bus. Coun., 1976-82, Sudan-U.S. Bus. Coun., India-U.S. Bus. Coun., 1976-82; bd. dirs., pres. Philippine-Am. Found., 1987-92; chmn. adv. coun. Episc. Migration Ministries; pres., bd. dirs. U.S.-Korea Econ. Coun., mem. exec. com., 1978-82; trustee Cambridge Sch., Weston, Mass. With AUS, 1946-47. Mem. Japan Soc. (chmn. exec. com., bd. dirs. 1970-82), Nat. Planning Assn. (trustee, treas. 1976-82), Nat. Fgn. Trade Coun. (bd. dirs., mem. exec. com. 1976-82), Internat. C. of C. (vice chmn., trustee U.S. coun. 1976-82), Philippine Am. C. of C. (v.p., bd. dirs. 1987-92), U.S. Assn. for Internat. Migration (pres., bd. dirs., mem. exec. com. 1987-92), Univ. Club, Bronxville Field Club, Hodegaya Golf Club, Tokyo Law Tennis Club. Episcopalian. Home: 99 Sudbury Rd Concord MA 01742-2421 Office: Wheeler Realty Trust 150 Wheeler Rd Marstons Mills MA 02648-1138

WHEELER, STEVE DEREAL, neurologist; b. Chgo., Sept. 15, 1951; s. Clarence and Tommie L. (Andrews) W.; m. Debra B. Buckingham; children: Winter N., Ryan S., Gabrielle S. Student, Mich. State U., 1970-73; MD, Dartmouth Coll., 1976. Diplomate Am. Bd. Psychiatry and Neurology, Nat. Bd. Med. Examiners; lic. Mich., Ohio, Fla. Intern Thomas Jefferson U., Phila., 1976-77; emergency physician River Dist. Hosp. Emergency Cons., Inc., St. Clair, Mich., 1977-78; fellow Dartmouth Med. Sch., 1978; resident U. Miami, Fla., 1978-81; fellow Washington U., St. Louis, 1981-82; instr. in neurology Med. Coll. Pa., Phila., 1982-83; electroencephalograph reader, attending neurologist VA Med. Ctr., Phila., 1982-83; asst. neurologist, attending neurologist Muscle Clinic U. Hosps. Cleve., 1983-86; electromyographer Rainbow Babies and Children's Hosp., U. Hosps. Cleve., 1983-86; chief neuromuscular diseases divsn., asst. prof. neurology Case Western Res. U., Cleve., 1983-86, co-dir. muscle disease ctr. and lab., 1985-86; clin. assoc. prof. of neurology U. Miami, 1987-89; pvt. practice Miami, 1987—; lectr. Myasthenia Gravis Found., Vermillion, Ohio, 1984, Student Nat. Med. Assn., Cleve., 1983-86; vol. assoc. prof. U. Miami Sch., 1992—, vis. lectr., 1983—; neurology cons. Low Back Pain Team U. Hosps. Cleve., 1984-86; mem. quality assurance com. Coral Reef Hosp., Miami, 1987-88; cons. dir. planning Bapt. Headache Clinic Bapt. Hosp., Miami, 1993—; mem. adminstrv. com. Deering Hosp. Pain Mgmt. Ctr., Miami, 1993-94; mem. sleep diagnostic ctr. com. Bapt. Hosp., 1990-92, 94—, advisor to headache support group, 1995—; lectr. in field. Author (chpt.) Intensive Care For Neurological Trauma and Disease, 1982; contbr. articles to profl. jours. Named Internat. Man Yr., 1991-92; recipient Celebration Excellence Black Achiever award Family Christian Assn. Am., 1992. Fellow Royal Soc. Medicine, Am. Acad. Neurology; mem. Am. Acad. Clin. Neurophysiology, Am. Soc. Internal Medicine, Am. Assn. Study of Headache, Am. Coll. Physicians, Nat. Headache Found., Nat. Chronic Pain Outreach Program, Nat. Stroke Assn., Internat. Headache Soc., Fla. Med. Assn., Fla. Soc. Neurology, Fla. Soc. Internal Medicine, N.Y. Acad. Scis., Muscular Disease Soc. Northeastern Ohio (bd. trustees 1984-86), Dade County Med. Assn., So. Pain Soc., Internat. Assn. Study of Pain, Dartmouth Club Greater Miami, Am. Coun. for Headache Edn. Achievements include research in plasmapheresis in treatment of acute Guillain-Barre Syndrome; repeat neuroimaging in headache when first study normal. Office: 8950 N Kendall Dr Ste 501 Miami FL 33176-2132

WHEELER, STEVEN M., lawyer; b. Evanston, Ill., Jan. 5, 1949. AB, Pricneton U., 1971; JD with distinction, Cornell U., 1974. Bar: Ariz. 1974. Mem. Snell & Wilmer, Phoenix. Mng. editor Cornell Law Review, 1973-74; contbr. articles to profl. jours. Mem. ABA, Order Coif, Phi Kappa Phi. Office: Snell & Wilmer 1 Arizona Ctr Phoenix AZ 85004-0001

WHEELER, SUSIE WEEMS, retired educator; b. Cassville, Ga., Feb. 24, 1917; d. Percy Weems and Cora (Smith) Weems-Canty; m. Dan W. Wheeler Sr., June 7, 1941; 1 child, Dan Jr. BS, Fort Valley (Ga.) State U., 1945; MEd, Atlanta U., 1947, EdD, 1978; postgrad., U. Ky., 1959-60; EdS, U. Ga., 1977. Tchr. Bartow County Schs., Cartersville (Ga.) City Schs., 1938-44, Jeanes supr., 1946-58; supr., curriculum dir. Paulding Sch. Sys.-Stephens Sch., Calhoun City, 1958-64; summer sch. tchr. Atlanta U., 1961-63; curriculum dir. Bartow County Schs., 1963-79; ret., 1979; pres., co-owner Wheeler-Morris Svc. Ctr., 1990—; mem. Ga. Commn. on Student Fin., 1985-95. Coord. Noble Hill-Wheeler Meml. Ctr. Project, 1983—. Recipient Oscar W. Canty Cmty. Svc. award, 1991, Woman in History award Fedn. Bus. and Profl. Women, 1994-95. Mem. AAUW (v.p. membership 1989-91, Ga. Achievement award 1993), Ga. Assn. Curriculum and Supervision (pres.-elect 1973-74, pres. 1974-75, Johnnye V. Cox award 1975), Delta Sigma Theta (pres. Rome alumnae chpt. 1978-80, mem. nat. bd. 1984, planning com. 1988—, Dynamic Delta award 1967, 78), Ga. Jeanes Assn. (pres. 1968-70). Home: 105 Fite St Cartersville GA 30120-3410

WHEELER, THOMAS BEARDSLEY, insurance company executive; b. Buffalo, Aug. 2, 1936; s. William Henry and Ruth (Matthews) W.; m. Anne Tuck Robertson, Nov. 25, 1961; children: Elizabeth Wheeler Soule, Wendy Bennett. BA, Yale U., 1958. CLU. Sales rep. IBM, White Plains, N.Y., 1961-62; sales rep., asst. gen. agt. Mass. Mut. Life Ins. Co., Boston, 1962, gen. agt., 1972-83; exec. v.p. Mass. Mut. Life Ins. Co., Springfield, 1983-86, pres., 1987-88, pres., chief exec. officer, 1988-96; chmn., CEO, 1996—; chmn. bd. dirs. Oppenheimer Acquisition Corp., DLB Acquisition Corp.; bd. dirs. Bank of Boston Corp., Textron, Inc., Mass. Bus. Roundtable; pres. Jobs for Mass. Co-author: Managing Sales Professionals, 1984. Trustee Springfield Coll., 1985—, chmn., 1995—; trustee Am. Coll., Bryn Mawr, Pa., 1987-90, Baystate Health Systems, Inc., Springfield, 1983-92, Springfield Orch. Assn., Basketball Hall of Fame, Springfield; Mass. state chmn. U.S. Olympic Com., 1995-96. Lt. USNR, 1958-60. Mem. Springfield Life Underwriter's Assn., Am. Soc. C.L.U.'s (Pioneer Valley chpt., pres. Boston chpt. 1980-81), Boston Underwriter's Assn. (pres. 1972-73), Mass. Assn. Life Underwriters (pres. 1976-77), Health Ins. Assn. Am. (bd. dirs. 1990-93), Million Dollar Round Table, Yale Club of N.Y., Colony Club (Springfield), Longmeadow Country Club, Boca Grande, Chapoquoit Yacht Club (sec. 1973-75), The Links (N.Y.C.). Republican. Avocations: skiing, boating, art, antiques, music. Office: Mass Mut Life Ins Co 1295 State St Springfield MA 01111-0001

WHEELER, THOMAS EDGAR, communications technology executive; b. Redlands, Calif., Apr. 5, 1946; s. Charles Taylor and Martha (Edgar) W.; married; children: Nicole Pierce, David Maxwell. B.S., Ohio State U., 1968. Asst. dir. Ohio State U. Alumni Assn., Columbus, 1968-69; v.p. Grocery Mfrs. Am., Inc., Washington, 1969-76; exec. v.p. Nat. Cable TV Assn., Washington, 1976-79, pres., chief exec. officer, 1979-85; pres., chief exec. officer NABU: The Home Computer Network, 1985-86; chmn., chief exec. officer NuCable Resources Corp., Washington, 1986-94; pres., dir. Media Enterprises Corp., 1982-95; pres., chief exec. officer Cellular Telecommunications Industry Assn., 1992—. Bd. trustees John F. Kennedy Ctr. for Performing Arts; bd. dirs. Cibernet Corp. Democrat. Office: Cellular Telecom Ind Assn 1250 Connecticut Ave NW Washington DC 20036-2603

WHEELER, VALERIE A. SYSLO, credit analyst; b. New Brunswick, N.J., Nov. 16, 1958; d. Joseph Jr. and Florence (Kulesa) Syslo; m. Ray J. Wheeler, Oct. 7, 1978. AAS in Acctg., Middlesex County Coll., 1979; BA in Acctg. and Econs., Rutgers U., 1993. Prodn. acctg. technician E. I. DuPont, Sayreville, N.J., 1981-86; import acctg. clk. Jeri-Jo Knitwear, Inc., Edison, N.J., 1986-87; cost acctg. clk. Neilson & Brainbridge, Edison, 1987-88; tax clk. Johnson & Johnson-CPI, Skillman, N.J., 1988-92; acct. mil. sales divsn., assoc. credit analyst Johnson & Johnson-CPI, New Brunswick, 1992—. Fundraising chair Rugters U. Coll., 1990-91. Mem. Inst. Mgmt. Accts., Univ. Coll. Governing Assn. Roman Catholic. Avocations: travel, singing, dancing. Home: 12 Oxford Rd East Brunswick NJ 08816-4335

WHEELER, WARREN G(AGE), JR., retired publishing executive; b. Boston, Dec. 6, 1921; s. Warren Gage and Helen (Hoagl) W.; m. Jean Frances Moseley, Feb. 22, 1945; children: Richard, Michael, Ann, Duncan. B.S., Bowdoin Coll., 1943; B.J., U. Mo., 1947, M.A., 1948. With South Bend (Ind.) Tribune (name changed to Schurz Communications, Inc. 1976), 1948-82, gen. mgr., 1964-71, exec. v.p., 1971-75, pres., 1975-82. Campaign chmn. United Cmty. Svcs., South Bend, 1960, pres., 1964; treas. South Bend Urban League, 1962-63; trustee St. Joseph's Hosp., South Bend, 1969-77; gen. chmn. St. Joseph County (Ind.) Hosp. Devel., 1969-71; deacon, elder, pres. session 1st Presbyn. Ch., South Bend; chmn. bd. trustees United Ch. Marco Island, 1992-93, ch. pres., 1996-97. With USN, 1943-46. Protestant recipient Brotherhood award South Bend-Mishawaka chpt. NCCJ, 1970. Mem. Am. Newspaper Pubs. Assn., Am. Mgmt. Assn., Newspaper Personnel Relations Assn. (pres. 1955-56), Hoosier State Press Assn. (dir. 1967-70), Inland Daily Press Assn. (pres. 1972, pres. found. 1974-78), South Bend Press Club, Hideaway Beach Club, Sigma Delta Chi, Kappa Tau Alpha, Kappa Mu. Home: 6000 Royal Marco Way Apt 657 Marco Island FL 34145-1886

WHEELER, WILLIAM EARL, general surgeon; b. Fort Benning, Ga., Feb. 23, 1952; s. Thomas Harvey and Martha (Donaldson) W.; m. Rebecca Sue Shafer, May 6, 1984; children: Thomas Andrew, William Matthew. AA, East Ctrl. C.C., 1972; BS, Millsaps Coll., 1974; MD, U. Miss., 1977. Diplomate Am. Bd. Surgery. From asst. prof. to assoc. prof. Marshall Univ., Huntington, W.Va., 1983-91; staff surgeon Upstate Carolina Med. Ctr., Gaffney, S.C., 1991—; staff surgeon VA Med. Ctr., Huntington, 1983-91; chief surgical svc., 1985-91; staff and burn surgeon, Cabell Huntington Hosp, 1983-91; staff surgeon St. Mary's Hosp., Huntington, 1983-91; chief surg. sect. Upstate Carolina Med. Ctr., 1994-95; staff surgeon Mary Black Meml. Hosp., Spartanburg, S.C., 1992—; asst. clin. prof. surgery Med. Coll. S.C., Charleston, 1994—. Camp physician, committeeman Boy Scouts Am., Huntington, 1986-91; water safety instr. ARC, Decatur, Miss., 1971-80; elder Limestone Presbyn. Ch., Gaffney, 1994-96, fin. com., 1993-96. Recipient Eagle Scout award, Boy Scouts Am., 1967. Fellow Am. Coll. Surgeons; mem. AMA, Am. Burn Assn., S.C. Med. Assn., So. Med. Assn., Kiwanis (pres. Gaffney chpt. 1997-98). Avocations: golf, swimming, skiing. Home: 118 Greenbriar Dr Gaffney SC 29341 Office: 117 E Montgomery St Gaffney SC 29340-3058

WHEELER, W(ILLIAM) SCOTT, composer, conductor, music educator; b. Washington, Feb. 24, 1952; s. Malcolm Frederick and Aurora Dorothy (Anas) W.; m. Christen Struthers Frothingham, Jan. 5, 1985; children: Margaret Lee, Catherine Elizabeth. BA, Amherst Coll., 1973; MFA, Brandeis U., 1978, PhD, 1984. Artistic dir. Dinosaur Annex Music Ensemble, Boston, 1975—; dir. Cambridge (Mass.) Chorale, 1976-78; tchr. music, condr. Emerson Coll., Boston, 1978—. Composer (choral) A Babe is Born, , 1979, (chamber) Winter Hills, 1987 (Somerville Arts Coun. Commn.), (symphony) Northern Lights, 1987 (Koussevitzky commn.), (opera) The Construction of Boston (libretto by Kenneth Koch), 1989, (choral) The Angle of the Sun, 1994 (Nat. Endowment for the Arts). Guggenheim fellow, 1988-89. Mem. Am. Music Ctr., ASCAP. Episcopalian. Home: 85 Haverhill St North Reading MA 01864-2816 Office: Emerson Coll Div Performing Arts 100 Beacon St Boston MA 02116-1501

WHEELER, WILMOT FITCH, JR., diversified manufacturing company executive; b. Southport, Conn., June 5, 1923; s. Wilmot Fitch and Hulda Day (Chapman) W.; m. Barbara Rutherfurd, Sept. 30, 1944 (dec. Sept. 1971); children: Wilmot Fitch III, James Alexander, John R. (dec.), Susan; m. Nonnye Landers, Dec. 20, 1973; children: Tracy Lynne, Alexa Margaret. BA, Yale U., 1945; postgrad., NYU, 1947-48. Staff engr. Stevenson, Jordan & Harrison, Inc. (mgmt. cons.), 1946-51; with Am. Chain & Cable Co., Inc., N.Y.C., 1951-76; pres., chmn., chief exec. officer Am. Chain & Cable Co., Inc., 1966-76; chmn., dir. Jelliff Corp., Southport, Conn., 1976—; prin. Case & Co. Inc. (mgmt. cons.), 1977-82; trustee Dollar Savs. Bank, 1974-83, chmn., chief exec. officer, 1982-83; chmn., trustee, chief exec. officer Dollar Dry Dock Savs. Bank, 1983-84; vice chmn., chmn., bd. dirs., CEO Manhattan Nat. Corp., 1986-90; v.p. William T. Morris Found., 1976—; bd. dirs. Am. Mutual Liability Ins. Co., 1969-89, Am. Policyholders Ins. Co., 1969-89, Am. Dist. Telegraph Co., 1968-88, Bristol Co. of Canada Ltd., 1955-76, British Wire Products Ltd. (Eng.), 1955-76, Cables Automotrices, S.A. (Mexico), 1955-76, Dominion Chain Co. Ltd., 1955-76, FATA, SpA (Italy), 1975-76, Hersey Products Corp., 1976-86, Instrumentos Bristol, S.A. (Mexico), 1955-76, Manhattan Life Ins. Co., 1972-93, Arthur G. McKee & Co., 1972-79, Parsons Controls Ltd., 1955-76, People's Bank, 1988—, People's Mutual Holdings, 1975—, Pratt-Read Corp., 1978-85, Pujol y Tarrago S.A. (Spain), 1969-85, Sormir Petroleum, Inc., 1994—, Union Ctrl. Life Ins. Co., 1990-93, Wilmot F. Wheeler Found., 1944—. Trustee Am. Farm Sch., 1981-93, Bridgeport Hosp., 1977-94, U. Bridgeport, 1978—. With AUS, 1943-46. Decorated Bronze Star. Episcopalian. Clubs: Yale (N.Y.C.), Sky (N.Y.C.), Country of Fairfield. Home: PO Box 429 Southport CT 06490-0429 Office: Jelliff Corp PO Box 758 354 Pequot Ave Southport CT 06490-0758

WHEELOCK, ARTHUR KINGSLAND, JR., art historian; b. Worcester, Mass., May 13, 1943; s. Arthur Kingsland and Anne (Kneass) W.; m. Susan Hoffman, June 13, 1964 (div. June 1988); children: Arthur Tobey, Laura, Matthew; m. Perry Carpenter Swain, Aug. 24, 1991. BA, Williams Coll., 1965; PhD, Harvard U., 1973. Instr. Bement Sch., Deerfield, Mass., 1965-66; asst. prof. art history U. Md., College Park, 1974-84, assoc. prof., 1984-88, prof., 1988—; David E. Finley fellow Nat. Gallery Art, Washington, 1971-74; research curator Nat. Gallery Art, 1974-75, curator Dutch and Flemish painting, 1976-84, curator No. Baroque painting, 1984—; cons. Centraal Laboratorium voor Onderzoek van Voorwerpen van Kunst en Wetenschap, Amsterdam, 1969-70. Author: Perspective; Optics and Delft Artists around 1650, 1977, Jan Vermeer, 1981, 2d rev. edit., 1988, Dutch Painting in the National Gallery of Art, 1984, Dutch Paintings of the Seventeenth Century, 1995, Vermeer and the Art of Painting, 1995; exhbn. catalogue Gods, Saints and Heroes: Dutch Painting in the National Gallery of Art, 1987, Masterworks from Munich: Sixteenth-to-Eighteenth-Century Paintings from the Alte Pinakothek, 1988, Still Lifes of the Golden Age: Northern European Paintings from the Heinz Family Collection, 1989, Anthony Van Dyck, 1990, Jan Steen: Painter and Storyteller, 1996; co-author/editor: Johannes Vermeer, 1995; co-editor: Van Dyck 350, 1995; contbr. exhbn. catalogue Leonardo's Last Supper: Precedents and Reflections, 1984, Images of Reality, Images of Arcadia: Seventeenth-century Netherlandish Paintings from Swiss Collectins, Art for the Nation: Gifts in Honor of the 50th Anniversary of the National Gallery of Art, 1989; contbr. articles and revs. to profl. jours. and encys. Decorated Knight officer Order Orange-Nassau (Netherlands); NDEA fellow, 1967-70; Nat. Endowment Arts grantee, 1979-80; Nat. Gallery Art curatorial fellow Ctr. Advanced Study Visual Arts, 1983-84, 87-88, Robert H. Smith curatorial rsch. fellow, 1990; Nat. Endowment Arts grantee, 1979-80; recipient Dutch-Am. Achievement award Netherlands Am. Amity Trust, 1996. Mem. Coll. Art Assn. Democrat. Episcopalian. Office: National Gallery Art Washington DC 20565

WHEELOCK, KEITH WARD, retired consulting company executive, educator; b. Phila., Oct. 17, 1933; s. Ward and Margot Trevor (Williams) W.; m. Susan Bowen Kimball, June 15, 1956 (div. Nov. 1975); children: Helen Fraser, James Voorhees; m. Bente Lorentzen Ott, July 1978 (div. June 1988). BA, Yale U., 1955; MA, U. Pa., 1957; MS, MIT, 1972. Fgn. svc. officer Dept. State, Washington, 1960-69; dir. programs and policy div. N.Y.C. Housing and Devel. Adminstrn., 1970-71; devel. officer Moody's Investors Svc., Inc., N.Y.C., 1972-74, v.p. internat. ops., 1974-75, exec. v.p., 1975-76; pres. The Fantus Co., Millburn, N.J., 1976-83; mem. Sr. Dun & Bradstreet Mgmt. Group, 1979-83; prin. Wheelock Cons., 1983-88; project dir. Mng. Growth in N.J., 1986-90; asst. prof. Raritan Valley C.C., 1992—. Mem. Montgomery (N.J.) Twp. Com., 1986-88. Author: Nasser's New Egypt, A Critical Analysis, 1960, New Jersey Growth Management, 1989. Sloan fellow MIT, 1972. Home: 325 Mountain View Rd Skillman NJ 08558

WHEELOCK, LARRY ARTHUR, engineer, consultant; b. Chgo., Nov. 20, 1938; s. Preston J. and Rozella (Schonert) W.; m. Ruth E. Pruess (div. Sept. 1975); children: John P., J. Robert, William D., Thomas K.; m. Norma Jane Fair, Oct. 22, 1984. BSEE, U. Evansville, 1962. Registered profl. engr., Ind.; cert. instrument rated comml. pilot, airframe and powerplant mechanic with inspection authorization, FAA. Co-op student engr. Naval Avionics Facility, Indpls., 1958-59; co-op student engr. Naval Weapons Support Ctr., Crane, Ind., 1959-62, elec. engr., 1963-78; elec. engr. Delco Electronics, Kokomo, Ind., 1962-63; sr. mfg. eng. Ford Aerospace & Comm., Bedford, Ind., 1979-80; plant engr. Ethyl Corp., Terre Haute, Ind., 1980-81; plant mgr. Tredegar Industries/Ethyl Corp., Terre Haute, 1981-91. Patentee in field. Bd. dirs. Hulman Regional Airport Authority, 1991-95, pres., 1992; pres. Greene County Airport Bd. Commrs., Bloomfield, Ind., 1972-81. Mem. IEEE, NSPE, Aircraft Owners & Pilots Assn., Exptl. Aircraft Assn., Antique Aircraft Assn., Internat. Flying Farmers, Flying Engrs. Internat. (pres. 1994, 95), Mensa, Internat. Assn. Flying Rotarians, Rotary Internat. Avocations: aviation, agriculture, mechanics, amateur radio, computers. Home: 7480 State Road 42 Terre Haute IN 47803-9778 also: PO Box 309 Raymondville TX 78580

WHEELOCK, MAJOR WILLIAM, JR., health care adminstrator; b. Fall River, Mass., Dec. 12, 1936; s. Major William and Mildred Mary (Rogers) W.; m. Rita Pauline Gauthier, Feb. 22, 1962; children: Major William III, Nancy Beth. B.S., Providence Coll., 1958. Budget examiner, spl. asst. to asst. sec. of Navy Washington, 1963-66; legis. analyst, budget examiner Bur. of Budget, Exec. Office of Pres., Washington, 1966-71; exec. asst. to the gov. State of N.H., 1971-73; supt. N.H. Hosp., Concord, 1973-77; preceptor George Washington U. Sch. Hosp. Adminstrn.; exec. dir. N.H. Charitable Fund, Concord, 1977-78; pres. Rumford Nat. Graphics, Inc., Concord, 1978-

82; sr. v.p. N.H. Savs. Bank, 1982-85; exec. v.p. Franklin Pierce Coll., Rindge, N.H., 1985-95; pres. Crotched Mountain Found., Greenfield, N.H., 1995—; trustee N.H. Savs. Bank, 1981-83; bd. dirs. Yankee Pub. Co. Inc. Pres. Young Rep. Club, Fall River, Mass., 1957-58; bd. dirs. N.H. Indsl. Devel. Authority, 1972-75; bd. dirs. Community Health Care Assn., 1974-75, v.p., 1976; bd. dirs. N.H. Mental Health Assn., 1979-82, pres., 1980-82; bd. dirs. Crotched Mountain Found., 1980—; bd. dirs. N.H. Coun. for Humanities, 1980-86, chmn., 1984-86; bd. dirs. N.H. Social Welfare Coun., 1983, 90—, pres., 1986-90; bd. dirs. New Eng. Found. Humanities, 1990-95, Monadnock Family Svcs., 1990—, Monadnock Comm. Day Care Ctr., 1992—. Served with U.S. Army, 1959-61. Named N.H. Citizen of Yr., 1977; recipient Bancroft award N.H. Psychiat. Soc., 1977, Granite State award Plymouth State Coll., 1987. Mem. N.H. Hosp. Assn., Am. Coll. Hosp. Adminstrs., Concord Country (pres. 1976-77), Keene Country Club (v.p. 1993-94, pres. 1995—), Rotary (v.p. 1982-83, pres. 1983-84). Roman Catholic. Clubs: Concord Country (pres. 1976-77), Keene Country (pres. 1995-96); Lodge: Rotary (v.p. 1982-83, pres. 1983-84). Office: Crotched Mountain Foundation 1 Verney Dr Greenfield NH 03047-5000

WHEELON, ALBERT DEWELL, physicist; b. Moline, Ill., Jan. 18, 1929; s. Orville Albert and Alice Geltz (Dewell) W.; m. Nancy Helen Hermanson, Feb. 28, 1953 (dec. May 1980); children—Elizabeth Anne, Cynthia Helen; m. Cicely J. Evans, Feb. 4, 1984. B.Sc., Stanford U., 1949; Ph.D., Mass. Inst. Tech., 1952. Teaching fellow, then rsch. assoc. physics MIT, Boston, 1949-52; with Douglas Aircraft Co., 1952-53, Ramo-Wooldridge Corp., 1953-62; dep. dir. sci. and tech. CIA, Washington, 1962-66; with Hughes Aircraft Co., L.A., 1966-88, chmn., chief exec. officer, 1987-88; vis. prof. MIT, 1989; mem. Def. Sci. Bd., 1986-76; mem. Pres.'s Fgn. Intelligence, 1983-88; mem. Presdl. Commn. on Space Shuttle Challenger Accident, 1986; trustee Aerospace Corp., 1990-93, Calif. Inst. Tech., Rand Corp. Author 30 papers on radiowave propagation and guidance systems. Recipient R.V. Jones Intelligence award, 1994. Fellow IEEE, AIAA (Von Karman medal 1986, Goddard Astronautics award 1997); mem. NAE, Am. Phys. Soc., Sigma Chi. Republican. Episcopalian. Address: 181 Sheffield Dr Montecito CA 93108-2242

WHELAN, ELIZABETH ANN MURPHY, epidemiologist; b. N.Y.C., Dec. 4, 1943; d. Joseph and Marion (Barrett) Murphy; m. Stephen T. Whelan, Apr. 3, 1971; 1 child, Christine B. BA, Conn. Coll., 1965; MPH, Yale U., 1967; MS, Harvard U., 1968, ScD, 1971. Coordinator County study Planned Parenthood, 1971-72; research assoc. Harvard Sch. Pub. Health, Boston, 1975-80; exec. dir. Am. Council Sci. and Health, N.Y.C., 1980-92, pres., 1992—; mem. com. on pesticides and toxics EPA; mem. U.S. Com. of Vital Stats., HHS; mem. Nat. Adv. Com. on Meat and Poultry Inspection USDA; guest lectr. Queen Elizabeth 2 (Cunard Line). Author: Sex and Sensibility, 1973, Making Sense Out of Sex, 1974, Panic in the Pantry, 1975, 92, A Baby?...Maybe, 1975, Boy or Girl?, 1976, The Pregnancy Experience, 1977, Preventing Cancer, 1978, The Nutrition Hoax, 1983, A Smoking Gun, 1984, Toxic Terror, 1984, 86, 93, Balanced Nutrition, 1988; contbr. articles to profl. jours. and consumer pubs. Bd. dirs. Food and Drug Law Inst., Nat. Agrl. Legal Fund, Media Inst., N.Y. divsn. Am. Cancer Soc. Recipient Disting. Achievement medal Conn. Coll., 1979, award Am. Pub. Health Assn. Environ., 1992, Disting. Alumnus award Yale U., 1994-95, Ethics award Am. Inst. Chemists, 1996. Mem. APHA (Early Career award 1982, Homer Calver award 1992), Am. Inst. Nutrition, Am. Med. Writers Assn. (Walter Alvarez award 1986), U.S. Com. Vital Stats. Office: Am Council Sci and Health 1995 Broadway Fl 2 New York NY 10023-5882

WHELAN, JAMES ROBERT, communications executive, international trade and investment consultant, author, educator, mining executive, writer; b. Buffalo, July 27, 1933; s. Robert and Margaret (Southard) W.; children from previous marriage: Robert J., Heather Elizabeth; m. Guadalupe Aguirre, 1990. Student, U. Buffalo, 1951-53, U. R.I., 1955-57; BA, Fla. Internat. U., 1974. Staff corr., fgn. corr., country mgr., divsn. mgr. UPI, Buffalo, 1952-53; staff corr., fgn. corr., country mgr., div. mgr. UPI, Providence, 1955-57, Boston, 1957-58, Buenos Aires, Argentina, 1958-61, Caracas, Venezuela, 1961-66, San Juan, P.R., 1966, 68; regional dir. corp. rels., then v.p. ops. ITT World Directories, ITT, San Juan, 1968-70; Latin Am. corr. Scripps-Howard Newspaper Alliance, Washington, 1970-71; mng. editor Miami (Fla.) News, 1971-73; free-lance writer, 1973-74; pres., editor, pub. Hialeah (Fla.) Pub. Co., 1975-77; v.p., editl. dir. Panax Corp., Washington, 1977-80; v.p., editor Sacramento Union, 1980-82; editor, pub. Washington Times, 1982-84; mng. dir. CBN News, 1985-86; pres. Capital Comm. Internat., 1986—; editor-in-chief Conservative Digest, 1988-89; vice chmn. Inter-Am. Found., Arlington, Va., 1991-94; cons. external affairs advisor Inter-Am. Investment Corp., 1992-93; dir. strategic planning Cocetel Holding, Santiago, Chile, 1993-94; pres. Minera Silver Standard S.A., 1994—, Silver Std., Mex., 1995—; free-lance writer; vis. prof. Polit. Sci. Inst., U. Chile, 1993-95; assoc. prof. Finis Terrae U., 1993—; adj. prof. U. Md., 1993; guest lectr. ednl. instns., including Boston U., U. Miami, Ctrl. U. Venezuela, Cath. U., Andrés Bello U., Chile, U. Chile, U. Tex., Austin, U. Concepcion, U. Santiago; guest prof. U. Fla., 1973. Author: Through the American Looking Glass; Central America's Crisis, 1980, Allende: Death of a Marxist Dream, 1981, Catastrophe in the Caribbean: The Failure of America's Human Rights Policy in Central America, 1984, The Soviet Assault on America's Southern Flank, 1988, Out of the Ashes: Life, Death and Transfiguration of Democracy in Chile, 1833-1988, 1989, Hunters in the Sky, 1991, Desde las Cenizas: Vida, Muerte y Transfiguracion de la Democracia en Chile, 1833-1988, 1993, 2d edit., 1995. Bd. dirs. Christian Community Service Agy., Miami, 1973, Hialeah-Miami Springs (Fla.) C. of C., 1976-77, Wolf Trap Found., 1984-87; bd. dirs. Nat. Council for Better Edn.; chmn. print media div. United Way campaign, Sacramento, 1981; bd. govs. Council on Nat. Policy, Washington, 1981-87; del. Commn. of Californias, 1981; chmn. Council for Inter-Am. Security Ednl. Inst., 1986-90; mem. spl. task force on pub. safety Greater Washington Bd. Trade; mem. Nat. Commn. on Free and Responsible Media, 1983-84; bd. dirs. Nat. Bus. Consortium for Gifted and Talented Children, 1985-87; bd. govs. Internat. Policy Forum, 1985—; mem. Presdl. Bd. Fgn. Scholarships (Fulbright Commn.), 1986-92, exec. planning com., 1987-92. With Signal Corps U.S. Army, 1953-55. Nieman fellow Harvard U., 1966-67; recipient citation of excellence Overseas Press Club, 1971, Unity award Lincoln U., 1976, Golden Press award Am. Legion Aux., 1977, Freedom award Valley Forge Found., 1981, Bernardo O'Higgins award Chilean Govt., 1990, presented at Chilean Embassy by Amb. Octavio Errazuriz. Mem. Nat. Press Club, Overseas Press Club, Univ. Club (Washington), Georgetown Club, Cosmos Club, Harvard Club (N.Y.C.), Club de Ofcls. de Fuerza Aerea (Santiago), Club Militar Lo Curro (Santiago), Instituto O'Higginiano de Chile. Home: Orquideas 163-Bugambilias, Saltillo, Coahuila 25296, Mexico also: V Carranza 4120-13 D Europlaza Mall, 25230 Saltillo Coahuila Mexico

WHELAN, JOHN WILLIAM, lawyer, law educator, consultant; b. Cleve., Apr. 23, 1922; s. Walter Edmund and Stacia Miriam W.; m. Maryrose Shields, May 29, 1947; children: Moira Ann Whelan Dykstra, Thomas M. AB, John Carroll U., 1943; JD, Georgetown U., 1948. Assoc. prof. law Columbus U., Washington, 1948-50; asst. prof. law U. Va., Charlottesville, 1955-56; asso. prof. law U. Wis., Madison, 1956-59; prof. law Georgetown U., Washington, 1959-67, U. Calif., Davis, 1967-75, Hastings Coll. Law U. Calif., San Francisco, 1975-91; prof. emeritus Hasting Coll. Law U. Calif., San Francisco, 1991—; vis. prof. Nihon U. Coll. Law, Tokyo, summer 1989; cons. to atty. gen. Trust Ty. Pacific Islands, 1976-78; mem. atomic energy com. Bd. Contract Appeals, 1965-73; hearing examiner Medi-Cal Fiscal Intermediary Contract, 1979-82; adminstrn. law judge constrn. contracts Trust Ter. Pacific Island, 1984-86; cons. on govt. contracts to Polish govt., 1992. Author: (with R.S. Pasley) Federal Government Contracts, 1975; (with K.H. York) Insurance, 1983, 2d edit., 1988, Federal Government Contracts, 1985, Supplement, 1989, 3d edit., 1997, Understanding Government Contracts, 1994; (with K.H. York, Leo Martinez) Insurance, 3d edit., 1994; editor: Yearbook of Procurement Articles, 1965-90; mem. editl. bd. Pub. Procurement Law Rev. (U.K. pub.), 1991—; contbr. articles to profl. jours. Served with inf. AUS, 1943-45; served with J.A.G., 1950-55. Decorated Bronze Star; Ford Found. grantee, 1958-59, 63-64, summer 1970. Mem. ABA, Fed. Bar Assn., D.C. Bar Assn., Nat. Contract Mgmt. Assn., Bds. of Contract Bar Assn., Fed. Cir. Bar Assn. Home: 306 Bristol Pl Mill Valley CA 94941-4005 Office: U Calif Hastings Coll Law 200 Mcallister St San Francisco CA 94102-4707

WHELAN, JOSEPH L., neurologist; b. Chisholm, Minn., Aug. 13, 1917; s. James Gorman and Johanna (Quilty) W.; m. Gloria Ann Rewoldt, June 12, 1948; children: Joe, Jennifer. Student, Hibbing Jr. Coll., 1935-38; BS, U. Minn., 1940, MB, 1942, MD, 1943. Diplomate Am. Bd. Psychiatry and Neurology. Intern Detroit Receiving Hosp., 1942-43; fellow neurology U. Pa. Hosp., Phila., 1946-47; resident neurology U. Minn. Hosps., Mpls., 1947-49; chief neurology svc. VA Hosp., Mpls., 1949; spl. fellow electroencephalography Mayo Clinic, Rochester, Minn., 1951; practice medicine specializing in neurology Detroit, 1949-73, Petoskey and Gaylord, Mich., 1973-87; asst. prof. Wayne State U., 1957-63; chief neurology svcs. Grace Hosp., St. John's Hosp., Bon Secour Hosp., Detroit; cons. neurologist No. Mich. Hosps., Charlevoix Area Hosp.; instr. Med. Sch. U. Minn., 1949; cons. USPHS, Detroit Bd. Edn. Contbr. articles to profl. jours. Founder, mem. ad hoc Com. to Force Lawyers Out of Govt. Fellow Am. Acad. Neurology (treas. 1955-57), Am. Electroencephalography Soc.; mem. AMA, AAAS, Assn. Rsch. Nervous and Mental Diseases, Soc. Clin. Neurologists, Mich. Neurol. Assn. (sec.-treas. 1967-76, Disting. Physician award 1988), Mich. Med. Soc., No. Mich. Med. Soc., Grosse Pointe (Mich.) Club. Address: 9797 N Twin Lake Rd Mancelona MI 49659-9203

WHELAN, RICHARD J., director special education and pediatrics programs, academic administrator; b. Emmett, Kans, June 23, 1931; s. Richard Joseph and Margaret Alma (Cox) W.; m. Carol Ann King, Nov. 21, 1959; children—Mark Richard, Cheryl Lynne. B.A., Washburn U., 1955; Ed.D., U. Kans., 1966. Dir. edn. Menninger Clinic, Topeka, Kans., 1959-62; dir. edn. children's rehab. unit U. Kans. Med. Ctr., Kansas City, Kans., 1966—; prof. spl. edn. and pediatrics, chmn. dept. spl. edn. U. Kans., Lawrence, 1966-72, 78-80, 83-88, assoc. dean grad. studies and outreach, 1988-94, Ralph L. Smith disting. prof. child devel., 1968—, dean sch. edn., 1992-94; div. dir. U.S. Office Edn., Washington, 1972-74; cons. colls. and univs., state and fed. agys.; chmn. policy bd. Evaluation Tng., Kalamazoo, 1975-81. Author, editor: Promising Practices..., 1983; cons. editor Ednl. Research Ency., 1982; contbr. articles to profl. jours., chpts. to books. Chmn. adv. bd. Kans. Bd. Edn., Topeka, 1982-92; mem. adv. bd. Shawnee Mission Sch. Dist., Kans., 1984-92; mem. Gov.'s Task Force on Early Childhood, 1984-92; hearing officer various sch. dists. Served with U.S. Army, 1952-54. Mem. Soc. for Learning Disabilities (pres. 1980-81), Council for Exceptional Children, Assn. for Persons with Severe Handicaps (bd. dirs. 1975-79), Kans. Council for Exceptional Children (pres. 1963-64, Service award 1978), Phi Kappa Phi. Avocations: reading, music, golf, running, flying. Home: 7204 High Dr Shawnee Mission KS 66208-3355 Office: U Kans Med Ctr 39th and Rainbow Sts Kansas City KS 66160-7335

WHELAN, ROGER MICHAEL, lawyer, educator; b. Montclair, N.J., Nov. 12, 1936; s. John Leslie and Helen Louise (Callahan) W.; m. Rosemary Bogdan, Aug. 26, 1961; children: Helen, Theresa, John, James, Kathleen (dec.), Julie, Jennifer. AB cum laude, Georgetown U., 1959, JD, 1962. Bar: D.C. 1962, U.S. Dist. Ct. D.C. 1962, U.S. Ct. Appeals (D.C. cir.) 1962, U.S. Supreme Ct. 1968, U.S. Dist. Ct. Md. 1985. Assoc. Fried, Rogers & Ritz, Washington, 1961-66; ptnr. Doctor & Whelan, Washington, 1967-72; judge U.S. Bankruptcy Ct., Washington, 1972-83; sr. mem. Verner, Liipfert, Bernhard, McPherson & Hand, Chartered, Washington, 1984-89; sr. counsel Shaw, Pittman, Potts & Trowbridge, Washington, 1989—; dir. Lincoln Ctr. for Legal Studies, Arlington, Va., 1974-84; disting. lectr. Columbus Sch. Law, Cath. U. Am., Washington, 1975—. Sec. local campaign com., Alexandria, Va., 1964; trustee YMCAA, Silver Spring, Md., 1972-74. Recipient award D.C. Cir. Jud. Conf., 1984. Fellow Am. Coll. Bankruptcy (bd. regents 1989-95, bd. dirs. 1995—); mem. FBA (chmn. bankruptcy subcom. 1988, exec. com. 1993—), Am. Bankruptcy Inst. (bd. dirs. 1991—, exec. com. 1993-95, chmn. legis. com. 1991—), Walter Chandler Inn of Ct. (master emeritus 1990—). Republican. Roman Catholic. Avocations: fishing, hunting, boating. Home: 17908 Ednor View Ter Ashton MD 20861-9757 Office: Shaw Pittman Potts & Trowbridge 2300 N St NW Washington DC 20037-1122

WHELAN, STEPHEN THOMAS, lawyer; b. Phila., July 28, 1947; s. Stephen Thomas and Virginia King (Ball) W.; m. Elizabeth Ann Murphy, Apr. 3, 1971; children: Christine Barrett. BA magna cum laude, Princeton U., 1968; JD, Harvard U., 1971. Bar: N.Y. 1972, U.S. Dist. Ct. (so. dist.) N.Y. 1975. Assoc. Mudge Rose Guthrie & Alexander, N.Y.C., 1971-75; assoc. Thacher Proffitt & Wood, N.Y.C., 1975-77, ptnr., 1978—; chmn. corp. dept. Thacher Proffitt & Wood, 1992—. Author: The ABCs of the UCC: Article 2A (Leases), 1997, New York's Uniform Commercial Code Article 2A, 1994; contbr. articles to profl. jours. Bd. dirs. Sons Revolution, N.Y., 1979—; active N.Y. County Rep. Com., 1985—; active Princeton U. Alumni Coun., 1993—; trustee The Cloister Inn of Princeton U., 1996—. Fellow Am. Coll. Investment Counsel; mem. ABA (chmn. subcom. on leasing 1994—), N.Y. State Bar Assn., Equipment Leasing Assn. Am. (mem. fed. govt. rels. com. 1992—, legal com. 1995—). Roman Catholic. Avocations: road racing, secondary sch. students mentor, golf. Office: Thacher Proffitt & Wood 2 World Trade Ctr New York NY 10048-0203

WHELAN, WAYNE LOUIS, higher education administrator; b. Colonial Heights, Va., Jan. 10, 1939; s. Clarence Roscoe and Ruby Elizabeth (Farris) W.; m. Carlton Harville Whelan, Aug. 25, 1961; children: Karen Lynne Smith, Whitney Hoffman Whelan. BA in History, U. Va., 1960, M. in Edn. Adminstrn., 1967; EdD, Pacific States U., L.A., 1977. Tchr., administr. Hopewell (Va.) H.S., 1961-64; dir. guidance Colonial Heights (Va.) H.S., 1964-68; dir. evening and summer sessions Richard Bland Coll. Coll. William and Mary, 1968-72; assoc. dean evening and summer sessions Va. State U., 1972-78; dir. confs. and non-credit programs U. Tenn., 1978-86; assoc. v.p. continuing edn. and econ. devel. Trident Tech. Coll., Charleston, 1986—. Outstanding Young Man Colonial Heights, Va. Jaycees, 1977. Mem. Assn. Continuing Higher Edn. (exec. v.p., meritorious svc. award, 1989), N. Charleston Breakfast Rotary, Trident Metro C. of C. Avocations: sailing, naval history. Home: 553 Planter's Loop Mount Pleasant SC 29464 Office: Trident Tech Coll PO Box 118067 Charleston SC 29423-8067*

WHELAN, WENDY, ballet dancer; b. Louisville; d. Rich and Kay Whelan. Student, Louisville Ballet Acad., Sch. Am. Ballet. Apprentice N.Y.C. Ballet, 1984-86, mem. corps de ballet, 1986-89, soloist, 1989-91, prin., 1991—. Appeared in feature roles in George Balanchine's ballets such as Apollo, Raymonda Variations, Swan Lake, Who Cares?, Symphony in Three Movements, Danses Concertantes, Episodes, Cortege Hongrois, The Four Temperaments, Brahms-Schoenberg Quartet, Divertimento # 15, A Midsummer Night's Dream, Bournonville Divertissements, The Nutcracker, Walpurgisnacht Ballet, Brahms-Schoenberg Quartet Pieces, Union Jack, The Cage; in Jerome Robbins' Antique Epigraphs and Glass Pieces; in Peter Martins' Ash, Jazz, Les Petits Riens, Sleeping Beauty; in William Forsythe's Behind the China Dogs and Herman Scherman; in Christopher D'Amboise's The Bounding Line in Richard Tanner's A Schubert Sonata; and performed in N.Y.C. Ballet's Balanchine Celebration, 1993. Office: NYC Ballet NY State Theater 20 Lincoln Center Plz New York NY 10023-6913*

WHELCHEL, BETTY ANNE, lawyer; b. Augusta, Ga., Dec. 22, 1956; d. John Davis and Charnell (Ramsey) W.; m. Douglas Charles Kruse, June 20, 1987. AB, U. Ga., 1978; JD, Harvard U., 1981. Bar: D.C. 1981, N.Y. 1984, gaikokuho-jimu-bengoshi (fgn. lawyer) Japan, 1988-89. Atty.-advisor U.S. Dept. Treasury, Washington, 1981-84; assoc. Shearman & Sterling, N.Y.C., 1984-87, 89-90, Tokyo, 1987-89; dep. gen. counsel Deutsche Bank N.Am., N.Y., 1990—; staff atty. Depository Instns. Deregulation Com., Washington, 1983-84. Mem. Am. Soc. Internat. Law, Assn. of the Bar of the City of N.Y. (com. on fgn. and comparative law, chmn. 1996—), Harvard Law Sch. Assn. Office: Deutsche Bank AG 31 W 52nd St New York NY 10019-6118

WHELEN, ANDREW CHRISTIAN, microbiologist, army officer; b. El Paso, Tex., July 17, 1959; s. Henry James and Frances Annette (Lasiter); m. Jaclyn Kay Cunningham, Sept. 21, 1991. BS, S.D. State U., 1981; PhD, U. N.D., 1985. Grad. asst. S.D. State U., 1980-82, U. S.D., 1982-83; from grad. asst. to sr. grad. asst. U. N.D., 1983-85; commd. 2d lt. U.S. Army, 1982, advanced through grades to maj., 1993; chief virology Letterman Army Med. Ctr., San Francisco, 1986-88; chief microbiology Landstuhl (Germany) Army Regional Med. Ctr., 1989-93; postdoctoral fellow in microbiology Mayo Clinic, Rochester, Minn., 1993-94; asst. prof. lab. medicine and pathology Mayo Med. Sch., Rochester, Minn., 1994—; dir. microbiology Brooke Army Med. Ctr., San Antonio, Tex., 1995—; adj. faculty San Francisco State U., 1987-88, U. Md., European div., 1989-90, Uniformed Svcs. U. Health Scis., European divsn., 1991-93, 96—. Pres. Jr. Officers Assn., Landstuhl, 1990-91; commr. Installation Softball League, Landstuhl, 1990-91; vol. Spl. Olympics, San Antonio, 1988. Decorated 2 Meritorious Svc. medals. Mem. Am. Soc. Microbiology, German-Am. Med. Soc., Soc. Armed Forces Med. Lab. Scientists (bd. dirs. 1997—), Order of Mil. Med. Merit, Sigma Xi. Home: 1811 E Robinson Ave El Paso TX 79902-2219 Office: Dept Pathology & Area Lab Svcs Brooke Army Med Ctr San Antonio TX 78234

WHELESS, JAMES WARREN, neurologist; b. Glens Falls, N.Y., Apr. 18, 1956; s. True and Ada Adelphine (Bump) W.; m. Annette Carolyn Hyland, Apr. 7, 1982; children: Catherine Elizabeth, Margaret Caroline. BS, U. Okla., Oklahoma City, 1978, MD, 1982. Diplomate Am. Bd. Pediatrics, Am. Bd. Psychiatry and Neurology with spl. qualification in child neurology, with spl. qualification in clin. neurophysiology. Intern, then pediatric resident U. Okla.-Tulsa Med. Coll., 1982-85; fellow in child neurology Northwestern U., Chgo., 1985-88; fellow in clin. neurophysiology/epilepsy Med. Coll. Ga., Augusta, 1988-89; asst. prof. neurology and pediatrics U. Tex., Houston, 1989-95, dir. epilepsy monitoring unit, 1989—, assoc. prof. neurology and pediatrics, 1995—. Contbr. articles, editl. to profl. jours., chpt. to book. Camp physician Kamp Kleidoscope, Livingston, Tex., 1995—. Pres.'s Fund grantee U. Tex.-Houston, 1990, Children's Miracle Network Telethon grantee Hermann Children's Hosp. Fellow Am. Acad. Neurology, Child Neurology Soc.; mem. AMA, Am. Epilepsy Soc., Am. Acad. Pediatrics, Epilepsy Assn. of Houston/Gulf Coast (chmn. profl. adv. bd. 1992-94). Avocations: running, camping, hiking, travel, reading. Office: U Tex-Houston Dept Neurology 6431 Fannin St Ste 7044 Houston TX 77030-1501

WHELPLEY, DENNIS PORTER, lawyer; b. Mpls., Feb. 16, 1951; s. John Olsen and Harriet Marie (Porter) W.; m. Patricia Jan Adamy, Nov. 27, 1976; children: Heather Nicolle, Christopher Eric. BA, U. Minn., 1973, JD magna cum laude, 1976. Bar: Minn. 1976. Assoc. Oppenheimer Wolff & Donnelly, St. Paul, 1976-83, ptnr., 1983—. Mem. Order of Coif (Minn. chpt.), Phi Beta Kappa (Alpha of Minn. chpt.), Psi Upsilon (Mu chpt.), Dellwood Hills Golf & Country Club. Avocations: golf, tennis, squash, bridge. Home: 49 Locust St Mahtomedi MN 55115-1542 Office: Oppenheimer Wolff & Donnelly 45 S 7th St Ste 3400 Minneapolis MN 55402-1632

WHETTEN, JOHN D., food products executive; b. Chgo., June 8, 1940; s. Lester and Kate (Allred) W.; m. Becky Pearse; children: Carma, Rebecca, Mary Coza. BS, Brigham Young U., 1965; MBA, U. Calif., Berkeley, 1967. Advt. and mktg. mgr. The Clorox Corp., Oakland, Calif., 1967-79; pres., CEO Challenge Dairy Products, Inc., Dublin, Calif., 1982—; CEO Dairy-America, Inc., Dublin, Calif., 1995—; U.S. rep. Internat. Dairy Mktg. and Promotion Ann. Meeting, 1996. Co-chair U.S. Butter Task Force, 1990—; bd. dirs. U.S. Diry Export Coun., 1995—, Epidermolysis Bullosa Med. Rsch. Found., 1991—; mem. nat. steering com. Brigham Young U. Sch. Mgmt., 1992-95. Mem. Am. Butter Inst. (bd. dirs. 1982—, v.p. 1995—, Pres.'s Disting. Svc. award 1991), Am. Dairy Products Inst. (bd. dirs. 1982—), Dairy Export Incentive Program Coalition (pres. 1994—), Dairy Mktg. Coop. Fedn. (pres. 1992—), Barbecue Industry Assn. (dir. 1974-79, pres. 1977-78). Office: Challenge Dairy Products Inc 11875 Dublin Blvd Ste B230 Dublin CA 94568-2842

WHETTEN, JOHN THEODORE, geologist; b. Willimantic, Conn., Mar. 16, 1935; s. Nathan Laselle and Theora Lucille (Johnson) W.; m. Carol Annette Jacobsen, July 14, 1960; children—Andrea, Krista, Michelle. A.B. with high honors, Princeton U., 1957; Ph.D., 1962; M.S., U. Calif., Berkeley, 1959. Mem. faculty U. Wash., Seattle, 1963-81; research instr. oceanography U. Wash., 1963-64, asst. prof., 1964-68, assoc. prof., 1968-72, prof. geol. scis. and oceanography, 1972-81, chmn. dept. geol. scis., 1969-74; assoc. dean Grad. Sch., 1968-69; geologist U.S. Geol. Survey, Seattle, 1975-80; asst. div. leader geoscis. div. Los Alamos Nat. Lab., 1980-81, dep. div. leader earth and space scis. div., 1981-84, div. leader earth and space scis. div., 1984-86, assoc. dir. energy and tech., 1986-92, assoc. dir. quality, policy and performance, 1992-93; lab. affiliate, 1994—; cons. in nat. lab. partnerships and tech. transfer Motorola Corp., 1994—; bd. dirs. Quality N.Mex.; mem. bd. judges N.Mex. Quality Award, 1993—. Contbr. articles to profl. jours. Fulbright fellow, 1962-63. Home: 154 Piedra Loop Los Alamos NM 87544-3837 Office: Los Alamos Nat Lab MS J-591 Los Alamos NM 87545

WHETTEN, LAWRENCE LESTER, international relations educator; b. Provo, Utah, June 12, 1932; s. Lester B. and Kate (Allred) W.; m. Gabriele Indra, Oct. 28, 1974 (dec. May 1985). B.A., Brigham U., 1954, M.A., 1955; Ph.D. with honors, NYU, 1963. Sr. polit. analyst Hdqrs. USAFE, Wiesbaden, Fed. Republic Germany, 1963-70; resident dir. grad. program in internat. relations U. So. Calif., Munich, Fed. Republic Germany, 1971-78, dir. studies USC/SIR grad. program in Germany, 1978-86; Erich Voegelin Gast prof. Munich U., 1987-88; lectr. Boston U., 1988—; lectr. Profl. Assoc. Ctr. Def. and Strategic Studies S.W. Mo. State U., Springfield, 1991—; cons. Fgn. Policy Inst., Phila., 1969-71, 76-79, R & D Assocs., Munich, 1977; prof. Hochschule für Politik, Munich U.; adj. prof., profl. assoc. Ctr. for Def. and Strategic Studies, S.W. Mo. State U., 1991—. Author: Germany's Ostpolitik, 1971, Contemporary American Foreign Policy, 1974, The Canal War: Four Power Conflict, 1974, Germany East and West, 1981. Author, editor: Present State Communist Internationalism, 1983, The Interaction of Political Reforms Within the East Block, 1989. Served to capt. USAF, 1960-63. Penfield fellow NYU, 1957-59; grantee Ford Found., 1970, Royal Inst. Internat. Affairs, London, 1970, Thyssen Found., Cologne, Germany, 1974-82, 89, Volkswagen Found., 1982-85. Mem. Am. Acad. Polit. and Social Scis., Internat. Inst. Strategic Studies, Am. Assn. Advancement of Soviet Studies, Gesellschaft für Auslandskunde, German Am. Assn. Home: Widenmayerstrasse 41, 80538 Munich Germany

WHICHARD, WILLIS PADGETT, state supreme court justice; b. Durham, N.C., May 24, 1940; s. Willis Guilford and Beulah (Padgett) W.; m. Leona Irene Paschal, June 4, 1961; children: Jennifer Diane, Ida Gilbert. AB, U. N.C., 1962, JD, 1965; LLM, U. Va., 1984, SJD, 1994. Bar: N.C. 1965. Law clk. N.C. Supreme Ct., Raleigh, 1965-66; ptnr. Powe, Porter, Alphin & Whichard, Durham, 1966-80; assoc. judge N.C. Ct. Appeals, Raleigh, 1980-86; assoc. justice N.C. Supreme Ct., Raleigh, 1986—; instr. grad. sch. bus. adminstrn. Duke U., 1978; vis. lectr. U. N.C. Sch. Law, 1986—. Contbr. articles to profl. jours. Rep. N.C. Ho. of Reps., Raleigh, 1970-74; senator N.C. Senate, 1974-80, chair numerous coms. and commns.; N.C. legis. rsch. commn., 1971-73, 75-77, land policy coun., 1975-79; bd. dirs. Sr. Citizens Coordinating Coun., 1972-74; chair local crusade Am. Cancer Soc., 1977, state crusade chair, 1980, chair pub. issues com., 1980-84; pres., bd. chmn. Downtown Durham Devel. Corp., 1980-84; bd. dirs. Durham County chpt. ARC, 1971-79; Durham county campaign dir. March of Dimes, 1968, 69, chmn., 1969-74, bd. dirs. Triangle chpt., 1974-79; bd. advisors Duke Hosp., 1982-85, U. N.C. Sch. Pub. Health, 1985-96, U. N.C. Sch. Social Work, 1989—; bd. visitors N.C. Ctrl. U. Sch. Law, 1987—; mem. law sch. dean search com. U. N.C., 1978-79, 88-89, self-study com., 1985-86; pres. N.C. Inst. Justice, 1984-94; bd. dirs. N.C. Ctr. Crime and Punishment, 1984-94. Staff sgt. N.C. Army NG, 1966-72. Recipient Disting. Service award Durham Jaycees, 1971, Outstanding Legis. award N.C. Acad. Trial Lawyers, 1975, Outstanding Youth Service award N.C. Juvenile Correctional Assn., 1975, Citizen of Yr., Eno Valley Civitan Club, Durham, 1982, Faith Active in Pub. Life award N.C. Council of Churches, 1983, Outstanding Appellate Judge award N.C. Acad. Trial Lawyers, 1983, inducted Durham High Sch. Hall of Fame, 1987. Mem. ABA, N.C. Bar Assn. (v.p. 1983-84), Durham County Bar Assn., U. N.C. Law Alumni Assn. (pres. 1978-79, bd. dirs. 1979-82), Nat. Guard Assn. (judge advocate 1972-73, legis. com. 1974-76), Order of Golden Fleece, Order of Grail, Order of Old Well, Amphoterothen Soc., Order of Coif, Phi Alpha Theta, Phi Kappa Alpha. Democrat. Baptist. Clubs: Durham-Chapel Hill Torch (pres. 1984-85), Watauga (Raleigh, pres. 1994-95). Home: 5608 Woodberry Rd Durham NC 27707-5335 Office: NC Supreme Ct 2 E Morgan St Raleigh NC 27601-1445

WHIDDEN, ROBERT LEE, JR., health care consultant; b. Beverly, Mass., Oct. 10, 1943; s. Robert Lee and Phyllis Alma (Patch) W.; A.B. in English, Harvard U., 1965; m. Lois Ann Lapeza, Mar. 4, 1972. div. dir. Lowell (Mass.) Gen. Hosp., 1970-75; asst. adminstr. Union Hosp., Lynn, Mass., 1975-85; pres. Surgi/1 div., 1984-86, R.L. Whidden and Co., Andover, Mass., 1986—, Query, 1986—, hon. consul, Boston, St. Lucia, 1993—; prin. cons. Charlton Meml. Hosp., Fall River, Mass., 1987—, Boston Regional Med. Ctr., Stoneham, Mass., 1988—; hosp. rep. delegated rev. com. Eastern

Mass. Profl. Standards Rev. Orgn., bd. dirs., 1984—; ex-officio mem. Integrated Data Demonstration Grant Com. Blue Cross Mass., 1982—; health care advisor Govt. of Anguilla, Brit. West Indies, 1989-91; cons. health affairs Brit. Dept. Territories, 1990—. Bd. dirs. Lowell Area Continuing Edn. Ctr., Nat. Found. Environ. Control, 1971, Hospice of North Shore, Inc.; bd. dirs., chmn. Northshore Manpower Coalition; mem. corp. edn. adv. bd. North Shore Community Coll., 1981—; mem. North Shore Econ. Coun., 1981—; mem. Mass. Health Data Adv. Council. Nat. Merit scholar, 1960-61. Mem. Am. Coll. Health Care Execs. (diplomate), Mass. Hosp. Assn. (mem. program rev. com. 1982—, chmn. mgmt. com. 1984—, mem. facilities and service com. class of 1987), New Eng. Hosp. Assembly, Am. Soc. Law and Medicine, Health Care Mgmt. Assn., Am. Mgmt. Assn., Phi Beta Kappa. Episcopalian. Clubs: Myopia Polo (patron), Hasty Pudding, Andover Tennis. Home and Office: 3 Spruce Cir Andover MA 01810-4020

WHIDDEN, STANLEY JOHN, physiologist, physician; b. N.Y.C., Oct. 10, 1947; s. Stanley Graham and Maybell (Van Houten) W.; m. Jan Venable Whidden, 1987. AS, Delgado Coll., 1969; BS, Southeastern La. U., 1971, MS, 1973; PhD, Auburn U., 1979; MD, U. Auto. De Ciudad Juarex, Mex., 1984; postgrad. Hyperbaric Physicians Ctr., NOAA, Nat. Def. U., 1986, Naval War Coll., 1995. Asst. head ops. Nuclear Sci. Ctr., Auburn U., Ala., 1976-78; lectr. physiology U. Wis.-Madison, 1978-79; asst. prof. U. New Orleans, 1979-80; postdoctoral fellow shock physiology La. State U. Med. Ctr., New Orleans, 1980-82; rsch., med. staff JESM Baromed. Inst., New Orleans, 1984-86; asst. prof. rsch. physiology dept., La. State U. Med. Ctr., New Orleans, 1988-89; mgr. program Dept. of Justice, Nat. Inst. Justice; fellow Naval War Coll., Preventive Medicine U.S. Army Ctr. Health. Contbr. chpt. to books: Handbook of Shock and Trauma, 1983, Physiological Basis of Decompression Sickness, 1987, Active Duty Army Combat Operation "Just Cause" Panama, 1990. Lt. col. USAR, 1966—, Desert Storm/Shield, Saudia Action, 1991, Op. Provide Hope, Somalia, 1993. Decorated Bronze Star; recipient Meritorious Svc. medal, Acom medal, UN medal, 1994; named to Hon. Col., La. Gov. Staff, 1985; named one of Outstanding Young Men of Am., 1986; USAF fellow, Sch. Aero. Medicine, Brooks AFB, Tex., 1986, 87, NASA fellow, Johnson Space Ctr., 1987; named Outstanding Young Men in Am., 1986; recipient Md. Gov.'s Citation, 1991. Mem. AAUP, AAAS, Am. Physiology Soc., Soc. Neurosci. Am. Chem. Soc., Aerospace Med. Assn., Aerospace Physiol. Soc., Am. Vet. Physiology and Pharmacology Soc., Am. Burn Assn., N.Y. Acad. Sci., Shock Soc., Undersea Med. Soc. Republican. Club: Spl. Forces Assn. (New Orleans) (pres. 1983-84). Current work: Underlining preventive medical requirements during complex disaster with resources and from the government and non-goverment agencies. Subspecialties: Physiology (medicine); Space medicine. Office: US Army Ctr for Health Promotion & Preventive Medicine PO Box 1252 Temple Hills MD 20757-1252 also: Health Promotion & Preventive Medicine US Army Ctr Aberdeen Proving Ground MD 21010-5422

WHIDDON, CAROL PRICE, writer, editor, consultant; b. Gadsden, Ala., Nov. 18, 1947; d. Curtis Ray and Vivian (Dooly) Price; m. John Earl Caulking, Jan. 18, 1969 (div. July 1987); m. Ronald Alton Whiddon, Apr. 13, 1988. Student, McNeese State U., 1966-68; BA in English, George Mason U., 1984. Flute instr. Lake Charles, La., 1966-68; flutist Lake Charles Civic Symphony, 1966-69, Beaumont (Tex.) Symphony, 1967-68; freelance editor The Washington Lit. Rev., 1983-84, ARC Hdqrs., Washington, 1984; writer, editor Jaycor, Vienna, Va., 1985-87; writer, editor Jaycor, Albuquerque, 1987-90, publs. mgr., 1990-91; writer, editor Proteus Corp., Albuquerque, 1991-92; owner Whiddon Editorial Svcs., Albuquerque, 1989—; mem. S.W. Writer's Workshop, 1991—. Co-author: The Spirit That Wants Me: A New Mexico Anthology, 1991; contbr. various articles to Albuquerque Woman and mil. dependent pubs. in Fed. Rpublic Germany. Bd. dirs. Channel 27-Pub. Access TV, 1991-93, exec. bd. sec., 1992, v.p., 1993; dep. mgr. Fed. Women's Program, Ansbach, Fed. Republic Germany, 1980-81; pres. Ansbach German-Am. Club, 1980-82; sec. Am. Women's Activities, Fed. Republic Germany, 1980-81, chairwoman, 1981-82. Recipient cert. of appreciation from Am. amb. to Germany Arthur T. Burns, 1982, medal of appreciation from comdr. 1st Armored Div., Ansbach, Germany, 1982. Mem. NAFE, Women in Comm. (newsletter editor 1989-90, 91-92, 94-95, v.p. 1990-91, pres.-elect 1992-93, pres. 1993-94, chair programs com. Nat. Profl. Conf. 1994, sr. mem. 1994), Soc. Tech. Comm. (sr. mem., membership dir. 1993-94), Nat. Assn. Desktop Pubs., Am. Mktg. Assn., Greater Albuquerque C. of C., N.Mex. Cactus Soc. (historian 1989-94, sec. 1991, newsletter editor 1992—, various show ribbons 1989-91). Republican. Avocations: reading, writing, gardening, camping, music. Home: 1129 Turner Dr NE Albuquerque NM 87123-1917

WHIDDON, FREDERICK PALMER, university president; b. Newville, Ala., Mar. 2, 1930; s. Samuel Wilson and Mary (Palmer) W.; m. June Marie Ledyard, June 14, 1952; children: Charles Wilson, John Tracy, Karen Marie and Keith Frederick (twins). AB, Birmingham So. Coll., 1952; BD cum laude, Emory U., 1955, PhD in Philosophy, 1963, LittD (hon.), 1991. Asst. prof. philosophy, dean of students Athens (Ala.) Coll., 1957-59; dir. Mobile Ctr. U. Ala., 1960-63; pres. U. South Ala., Mobile, 1963—; mem. presdl. adv. com. Fed. Home Loan Bank, Atlanta. Contbr. articles to profl. jours. Chmn. Marine Environ Scis. Consortium. Named Outstanding Adminstr. in Ala., Am. Assn. Univ. Adminstrs., 1981. Mem. Am. Assn. Univ. Adminstrs., Phi Kappa Phi. Lodge: Kiwanis (Mobile). Office: U South Alabama AD 122 Pres Office Mobile AL 36688

WHIFFEN, JAMES DOUGLASS, surgeon, educator; b. N.Y.C., Jan. 16, 1931; s. John Phillips and Lorna Elizabeth (Douglass) W.; child from a previous marriage, Gregory James; m. Sally Vilas Runge, Aug. 21, 1993. B.S., U. Wis., 1952, M.D., 1955. Diplomate: Am. Bd. Surgery. Intern Ohio State U. Hosp., 1955-56; resident U. Wis. Hosp., 1956-57, 59-61; instr. dept. surgery U. Wis. Med. Sch., 1962-64, asst. prof., 1964-67, asso. prof., 1967-71, prof., 1971-96, vice chmn. dept., 1970-72, acting chmn., 1972-74; asst. dean Med. Sch., 1975-96; prof. emeritus U. Wis. Med. Sch., 1996—; mem. exam. council State of Wis. Emergency Med. Services, 1974-77. Bd. dirs. Wis. Heart Assn. Served to lt. comdr. USNR, 1957-59. John and Mary R. Markle scholar in acad. medicine, also; Research Career Devel. award NIH, 1965-75. Fellow A.C.S., Am. Soc. Artificial Internal Organs. Club: Maple Bluff Country. Research, publs. on biomaterials, thrombo-resistant surfaces and the physiology of heart-lung bypass procedures. Home: 17 Cambridge Ct Madison WI 53704-5906 Office: 600 Highland Ave Madison WI 53792-0001

WHINERY, MICHAEL ALBERT, physician; b. Watsford, Eng., June 30, 1951; s. Leo Howard and Doris Eileene W. and Alma Piper; m. Tatijana Dunnebier, 1976 (dec. Jan. 1981); m. Judy Renee Wright, Apr. 30, 1982; children: Rhiannon Daire Eileene, Terron Rae Lee. BS, Okla. U., 1976; D of Osteopathy, Okla. State U., 1980. Bd. cert. physician in gen. practice & family practice. Intern Hillcrest Health Ctr., Oklahoma City, Okla., 1980-81; with McLoud Clinic, McLoud, Okla.; house physician McLoud Nursing Ctr., 1988—; med. examiner Pottawatomie County Health, McLoud, 1983—. Author: Poetic Voices of America, 1991; composer (recorded song) At Stella Gospel, 1993. Mem. Presdl. Order Merit Nat. Repub. Senatorial Com., Washington, 1991, Presdl. Task Force, 1983—, Senatorial Commn. Repub. Senatorial Inner Circle, Washington, 1991; mem. U.S. Congrl. Adv. Bd., 1993. With USMC, Vietnam. Recipient Acknowledgement of Outstanding Contbn. in Clin. Rsch. award SANDOZ Labs., 1992, Rep. Presdl. Legion of Merit, 1994. Mem. Am. Legion, C. of C., Jr. C. of C., U.S. Senatorial Club (preferred mem.), U.S. Congressional Act Bd. (state advisor 1990-91). Baptist. Avocations: fishing, music, composing. Office: McLoud Clinic PO Box 520 107 S Main Mc Loud OK 74851

WHINNERY, JOHN ROY, electrical engineering educator; b. Read, Colo., July 26, 1916; s. Ralph V. and Edith Mable (Bent) W.; m. Patricia Barry, Sept. 17, 1944; children—Carol Joanne, Catherine, Barbara. B.S. in Elec. Engring, U. Calif. at Berkeley, 1937, Ph.D., 1948. With GE, 1937-46; part-time lectr. Union Coll., Schenectady, 1945-46; asso. prof. elec. engring. U. Calif., Berkeley, 1946-52, prof., vice chmn. div. elec. engring., 1952-56, chmn., 1956-59, dean Coll. Engring., 1959-63, prof. elec. engring., 1963-80, Univ. prof. Coll. Engring., 1980—; vis. mem. tech. staff. Bell Telephone Labs., 1963-64; research sci. electron tubes Hughes Aircraft Co., Culver City, 1951-52; disting. lectr. IEEE Microwave Theory and Technique Soc., 1989-92. Author: (with Simon Ramo) Fields and Waves in Modern Radio, 1944, 3d edit. (with Ramo and Van Duzar), 1994, (with D.O. Pederson and J.J. Studer) Introduction to Electronic Systems, Circuits and Devices; also tech. articles. Chmn. Commn. Engring. Edn., 1966-68; mem. sci. and tech. com. Manned Space Flight, NASA, 1963-69; mem. Pres.'s Com. on Nat. Sci. Medal, 1970-73, 79-80; standing com. controlled thermonuclear research AEC, 1970-73. Recipient Lamme medal Am. Soc. Engring. Edn., 1975, Centennial medal, 1993, Engring. Alumni award U. Calif.-Berkeley, 1980, Nat. Medal of Sci. NSF, 1992; named to Hall of Fame Modesto High Sch. (Calif.), 1983, ASEE Hall of Fame, 1993.; Guggenheim fellow, 1959. Fellow IRE (bd. dirs. 1956-59), IEEE (life, bd. dirs. 1969-71, sec. 1971, Edn. medal 1967, Centennial medal 1984, Medal of Honor 1985), Optical Soc. Am., Am. Acad. Arts and Scis.; mem. NAS, NAE (Founders award 1986), IEEE Microwave Theory and Techniques Soc. (Microwave Career award 1977), Phi Beta Kappa, Sigma Xi, Tau Beta Pi, Eta Kappa Nu. Congregationalist. Home: 1804 Wales Dr Walnut Creek CA 94595-2472 Office: U Calif Dept Electrical Engineering Berkeley CA 94720-1770

WHINSTON, ARTHUR LEWIS, lawyer; b. N.Y.C., Feb. 5, 1925; s. Charles Nathaniel and Charlotte (Nalen) W.; m. Melicent Ames Kingsbury, Mar. 19, 1949; children: Ann Kingsbury, James Pierce, Melicent Ames, Louise Ellen, Patricia Kingsbury. B.C.E., Cornell U., 1945; M.S.E., Princeton U., 1947; J.D., N.Y. U., 1957. Bar: N.Y. 1957, Oreg. 1964, U.S. Supreme Ct 1966, U.S. Patent Office 1958, U.S. Ct. Appeals (fed. cir.) 1959; registered profl. engr., N.Y., Oreg. Engr. Chas. N. & Selig Whinston, N.Y.C., 1947-50; lectr. Coll. City N.Y., 1950-51; structures engr. Republic Aviation Corp., Farmingdale, N.Y., 1951-57; practice in N.Y.C., 1957-64, Portland, Oreg., 1964—; patent lawyer Arthur, Dry & Kalish, 1957-64; partner Klarquist, Sparkman, Campbell, Leigh & Whinston, 1964—; chmn. Oreg. Bar com. on patent, trademark and copyright law, 1968-69, 77-78, mem. com. unauthorized practice law, 1970-73, chmn., 1972-73, com. on profl. responsibility, 1973-75. Served as ensign, C.E. USNR, 1945-46. Recipient Fuertes medal Cornell U. Sch. Civil Engring., 1945. Mem. ABA, Oreg. Bar Assn., N.Y. Bar Assn., Multnomah County Bar Assn., Am. Intellectual Property Law Assn., N.Y. Intellectual Property Law Assn., Oreg. Patent Law Assn. (pres. 1977-78), Profl. Engrs. Oreg. (past state legis. chmn.), Sigma Xi, Chi Epsilon, Phi Kappa Phi. Republican. Unitarian. Club: Multnomah Athletic. Home: 3824 SW 50th Ave Portland OR 97221-2112 Office: One World Trade Ctr Ste 1600 Portland OR 97204

WHIPPLE, DAVID DOTY, professional society administrator; b. Akron, Ohio, Dec. 26, 1923; s. Hugh Scott and Helene Eleanore (Doty) W.; m. Carolyn Terhune Decker, Feb. 28, 1953; children: Susan Casselman, Marc Evan, Tim Decker, Scott Adams Montgomery. BA, Dartmouth Coll., 1949; postgrad., Johns Hopkins U., 1949-50, The Nat. War Coll., Washington, 1966-67. From ops. officer to chief of various stations overseas CIA, Washington, 1950-85; with The Nat. Intelligence Officer for Counterterrorism, Washington, 1983-85; cons. internat. terrorism, 1985-89; exec. dir. Assn. Former Intelligence Officers, McLean, Va., 1989—; exec. v.p. Pagan Internat., Washington, 1987-89. Vol. Brit. 8th Army, 1944-45, Italy; sgt. U.S. Army, 1945-46, Italy, Philippines. Mem. Assn. Former Intelligence Officers (exec. dir. 1989—), Nat. War Coll. Alumni Assn., CIA Retirees Assn. Office: Assn Former Intel Officers 6723 Whittier Ave Ste 303A Mc Lean VA 22101-4533

WHIPPLE, DEAN, federal judge; b. 1938. BS, Drury Coll., 1961; postgrad., U. Tulsa, 1961-62; JD, U. Mo., Kansas City, 1965, postgrad., 1965. Pvt. practice Lebanon, Mo., 1965-75; cir. judge div. II 26th Jud. Cir. Mo., 1975-87; dist. judge U.S. Dist. Ct., Kansas City, Mo., 1987—; prosecuting atty. Laclede County, Mo., 1967-71. Mem. Cen. United Meth. Ch., Kansas City. With Mo. N.G., 1956-61; USAR, 1961-66. Mem. Mo. Bar Assn. (mem. pub. info. com. 1971-72, mem. judiciary com. 1971-72, mem. bd. govs. 1975-87, mem. exec. com. 1983-84, 86-87, mem. planning com. for ann. meeting 1985, 87, chmn. 1986, mem. selection com. for Lon Hocker award 1986), Mo. Trial Judges Assn., 26th Jud. Bar Assn., Laclede County Bar Assn. (pres. 1968-69, 72-73), Kansas City Met. Bar Assn., Kansas City Inn of Ct. (instr. 1988-93), Mo. Hist. Soc., Phi Delta Phi. Office: US Dist Ct US Courthouse 811 Grand Ave Rm 613 Kansas City MO 64106-1909

WHIPPLE, FRED LAWRENCE, astronomer; b. Red Oak, Iowa, Nov. 5, 1906; s. Harry Lawrence and Celestia (MacFarl) W.; m. Dorothy Woods, 1928 (div. 1935); 1 son, Earle Raymond; m. Babette F. Samelson, Aug. 20, 1946; children: Dorothy Sandra, Laura. Student, Occidental Coll., 1923-24; AB, UCLA, 1927; PhD, U. Calif., 1931; AM (hon.), Harvard, 1945; ScD, Am. Internat. Coll., 1958; DLitt (hon.), Northeastern U., 1961; DSc (hon.), Temple U., 1961, U. Ariz., 1979; LLD (hon.), C.W. Post Coll., L.I. U., 1962. Teaching fellow U. Calif. at Berkeley, 1927-29, Lick Obs. fellow, 1930-31; instr. Stanford U., summer 1929, U. Calif., summer 1931; staff mem. Harvard Obs., 1931-77; instr. Harvard U., 1932-38, lectr., 1938-45; research asso. Radio Research Lab., 1942-45, asso. prof. astronomy, 1945-50, prof. astronomy, 1950-77, chmn. dept., 1949-56, Phillips prof. astronomy, 1968-77; dir. Smithsonian Astrophys. Obs., 1955-73, sr. scientist, 1973—; mem. Rocket Rsch. Panel U.S., 1946-57; U.S. subcom. NASA, 1946-52, U.S. Rsch. and Devel. Bd. Panel, 1947-52; chmn. Tech. Panel on Rocketry; mem. Tech. Panel on Earth Satellite Program, 1955-59; other coms. Internat. Geophys. Year, 1955-59; mem., past officer Internat. Astron. Union; cons. missions to U.K. and MTO, 1944; del. Inter-Am. Astrophys. Congress, Mexico, 1942; active leader project on Upper-Atmospheric Rsch. via Meteor Photog. sponsored by Bur. Ordnance, U.S. Navy, 1946-51; b. Bur. Ordnance, U.S. Navy (Office Naval Rsch.), 1951-57, USAF, 1948-62; mem. com. meteorology, space sci. bd., com. on atmospheric scis. Nat. Acad. Scis.-NRC, 1958-65; advisor Sci. Adv. Bd., USAF, 1963-67; spl. cons. com. Sci. and Astronautics U.S. Ho. Reps., 1960-73; chmn. Gordon Rsch. Confs., 1963; dir. Optical Satellite Tracking Project, NASA, 1958-73; project dir. Orbiting Astron. Obs., 1958-72; dir. Meteorite Photography and Recovery Program, 1962-73, cons. planetary atmospheres, 1962-69; mem. space scis. working group on Orbiting Astron. Observatories, 1959-70; chmn. sci. coun. geodetic uses artificial satellites Com. Space Rsch., 1965-70. Author: Earth, Moon and Planets, rev. edit, 1968, Orbiting The Sun: Planets and Satellites of The Solar System, The Mystery of Comets, 1985; co-author: Survey of the Universe; Contbr.: sci. papers on astron. and upper atmosphere to Ency. Brit; mags., other publs.; Asso. editor: Astronomical Jour, 1954-56, 64-71; editor: Smithsonian Contributions to Astrophysics, 1956-73, Planetary and Space Science, 1958-83, hon. editor, 1983—, Science Revs, 1961-70; editorial bd.: Earth and Planetary Sci. Letters, 1966-73; inventor tanometer, meteor bumper; a developer window as radar countermeasure, 1944. Decorated comdr. Order of Merit for rsch. and invention, Esnault-Pelerie award France; recipient Donohue medals for ind. discovery of 6 new comets, Presdl. Cert. of Merit for sci. work during World War II, J. Lawrence Smith medal Nat. Acad. Scis. for rsch. on meteors, 1949, medal for astron. rsch. U. Liege, 1960, Space Flight award Am. Astronautical Soc., 1961, Disting. Fed. Civilian Svc. award, 1963; Space Pioneers medallion for contbns. to fed. space program, 1968, Pub. Svc. award for contbns. to OAO2 devel. NASA, 1969, Leonard medal Meteoritical Soc., 1970, Kepler medal AAAS, 1971, Career Svc. award Nat. Civil Svc. League, 1972, Henry medal Smithsonian Instn., 1973, Alumnus of Yr. Achievement award UCLA, 1976, Golden Plate award Am. Acad. Achievement, 1981, Gold medal Royal Aston. Soc., 1983, Bruce medal Astron. Soc. Pacific, 1986, Benjamin Franklin fellow Royal Soc. Arts, London, 1968—; depicted on postal stamp of Mauritania, 1986, St. Vincent, 1994. Fellow Am. Astron. Soc. (v.p. 1962-64, 1987 Russell lecturer), Am. Rocket Soc., Am. Geophys. Union (Fred L. Whipple yearly lectr. estab. in honor planetary div. 1990), Royal Astron. Soc. (assoc.); mem. AAAS, Nat. Acad. Scis., AIAA Astronautics (aerospace tech. panel space physics 1960-63), Astronautical Soc. Pacific, Solar Assos., Internat. Sci. Radio Union (U.S.A. nat. com. 1949-61), Am. Meteoritical Soc., Am. Standards Assn., Am. Acad. Arts and Scis., Am. Philos. Soc. (councillor sect. astronomy and earth scis. 1966-70), Royal Soc. Scis. Belgium (corr.), Internat. Acad. Astronautics (sci. advisory com. 1962-65), Internat. Astronautical Fedn., Am. Meteorol. Soc., Royal Astron. Soc. (assoc.), Phi Beta Kappa, Sigma Xi, Pi Mu Epsilon. Clubs: Examiner (Boston); Cosmos (Washington). Office: 60 Garden St Cambridge MA 02138-1516

WHIPPLE, HARRY M., newspaper publishing executive; b. Tulsa, June 30, 1947; m. Mary Jane Whipple; children: Garth, Erin. Student, Ind. U., 1965-68; U. Evansville, 1965-68, Ark Poly. Coll., 1965-68. Gen. mgr. Mt. Vernon (Ind.) Pub. Co., 1972-75; asst. pub. Pioneer Newspapers (formerly Scripps League Newspapers), Monongahela, Pa., 1975-77; advt. dir. Rockford (Ill.) Morning Star and Register Republic, 1977-81; pres., pub. Valley News Dispatch, The Herald, North Hills News Record, Tarentum, Pa., 1981-84; v.p., regional mgr. Midwest Gannett Media Sales/Gannett Nat. Sales, Chgo., 1984-87; pres. TNI Ptnrs., Tucson, 1987-92; pres., pub. The Cincinnati Enquirer, 1992—. Bd. trustees Cin. Symphony Orch., Jewish Hosp. Cin., Zool. Soc. Cin., NCCJ, Greater Cin. Region; co-chair, steering com. Nat. Underground R.R. Freedom Ctr.; bd. dirs. Greater Cin. Ctr. for Econ. Edn., Downtown Cin., Inc. Mem. Greater Cin. C. of C. (bd. trustees). Office: Cincinnati Enquirer 312 Elm St Cincinnati OH 45202-2739

WHIPPLE, JUDITH ROY, book editor; b. N.Y.C., May 14, 1935; d. Edwin Paul and Elizabeth (Levis) Roy; m. William Whipple, Oct. 26, 1963. AB, Mount Holyoke Coll., 1957. Head libr. Am. Sch. Lima (Peru), S.A., 1957-59; asst. editor children's books G.P. Putnam's Sons, N.Y.C., 1959-62; assoc. editor W.W. Norton & Co., Inc., N.Y.C., 1962-68; editor Four Winds Press, 1968-75; editor-in-chief Scholastic Gen. Book Divsn., 1975-77; pub. Four Winds Press subs. Scholastic Inc., N.Y.C., 1977-82; pub., v.p. Macmillan Pub. Co., N.Y.C., 1982-89, exec. editor, 1989-94; editl. dir. Benchmark Books and Cavendish Children's Books, Tarrytown, N.Y., 1994—. Mem. PEN, Children's Book Coun. (pres. 1977, bd. dirs. 1970-79), Women's Nat. Book Assn., Soc. Children's Book Writers and Illustrators. Avocations: gardening, swimming, piano, travel. Office: Marshall Cavendish Corp 99 White Plains Rd Tarrytown NY 10591-5502

WHIPPS, EDWARD FRANKLIN, lawyer; b. Columbus, Ohio, Dec. 17, 1936; s. Rusk Henry and Agnes Lucille (Green) W.; children: Edward Scott, Rusk Huot, Sylvia Louise, Rudyard Christian. B.A., Ohio Wesleyan U., 1958; J.D., Ohio State U., 1961. Bar: Ohio 1961, U.S. Dist. Ct. (so. dist.) Ohio 1962, U.S. Dist. Ct. (no. dist.) Ohio 1964, U.S. Ct. Claims 1963, U.S. Supreme Ct. 1963, Miss. 1965, U.S. Ct. Appeals (6th cir.) 1980. Assoc. George, Greek, King & McMahon, Columbus, 1961-66; ptnr. George, Greek, King, McMahon & McConnaughey, Columbus, 1966-79, McConnaughey, Stradley, Mone & Moul, Columbus, 1979-81, Thompson, Hine & Flory, Columbus, 1981-93; prin. Edward F. Whipps & Assocs., Columbus, 1993-94; ptnr. Whipps & Wistner, Columbus, 1995—; founder, trustee Creative Living, Inc., 1969—; trustee, v.p. Unverferth House, Inc., 1989; trustee Eagle Scholarship Trust. Host: TV programs Upper Arlington Plain Talk, 1979-82; TV program Briding Disability, 1981-82, Lawyers on Call, 1982—, U.A. Today, 1982-86, The Ohio Wesleyan Experience, 1984—. Mem. Ohio Bd. Psychology, 1992—; mem. Upper Arlington (Ohio) Bd. Edn., 1971-80, pres., 1978-79; mem. bd. alumni dirs. Ohio Wesleyan U., 1975-79; trustee Walden Ravines Assn., 1992-96, pres. 1993-96. Mem. ABA, Columbus Bar Assn., Ohio State Bar Assn., Assn. Trial Lawyers Am., Ohio Acad. Trial Lawyers, Franklin County Trial Lawyers Assn., Am. Judicature Soc., Columbus Bar Found., Ohio Bd. Pscyhology, Columbus C. of C., Upper Arlington Area C. of C. (trustee 1978—), Lawyers Club, Barrister Club, Columbus Athletic Club, Columbus Touchdown Club, Downtown Quarterback Club, Ohio State U. Faculty (Columbus) Club, Ohio State U. Golf Club, Highlands Country Club, Delta Tau Delta (nat. v.p. 1976-78). Republican. Home: 3111 Walden Ravines Columbus OH 43221-4640 Office: Whipps & Wistner 500 S Front St Columbus OH 43215-7619 *Personal philosophy: Commitment to personal growth, the development of interpersonal communication skills, the rule of law and a firm belief in the unique value of every individual are the primary factors seen in my approach to life.*

WHISENHUNT, DONALD WAYNE, history educator; b. Meadow, Tex., May 16, 1938; s. William Alexander Whisenhunt and Beulah (Johnson) King; m. Betsy Ann Baker, Aug. 27, 1960; children: Donald Wayne Jr., William Benton. BA, McMurry Coll., 1960; MA, Tex. Tech U., 1962, PhD, 1966. Tchr. Elida (N.Mex.) High Sch., 1961-63; from asst. to assoc. prof. history Murray (Ky.) State U., 1966-69; assoc. prof., chmn. dept. Thiel Coll., Greenville, Pa., 1969-73; Dean Sch. Liberal Arts and Scis., Ea. N.Mex. U., Portales, 1973-77; v.p. acad. affairs U. Tex., Tyler, 1977-83; v.p., provost Wayne (Nebr.) State Coll., 1983-91, interim pres., 1985; prof. history, chmn. dept. Western Wash. U., Bellingham, 1991—; Fulbright lectr. Peoples Republic of China, 1995. Author: Environment and American Experience, 1974, Depression in the Southwest, 1979, Chronological History of Texas, Vol. 1, 1982, Vol.2, 1987, Texas: Sesquicentennial Celebration, 1984; editor: Encyclopedia USA, 1988—, Poetry of the People: Poems to the President, 1929-1945, 1996. Democrat. Methodist. Office: Western Wash U Dept History Bellingham WA 98225

WHISLER, JAMES STEVEN, lawyer, mining and manufacturing executive; b. Centerville, Iowa, Nov. 23, 1954; s. James Thomas and Betty Lou (Clark) W.; m. Ardyce Dawn Christensen, Jan. 20, 1979; children: James Kyle, Kristen Elyse. BS, U. Colo., Boulder, 1975; JD, U. Denver, 1978; MS, Colo. Sch. Mines, Golden, 1984. Bar: Colo. 1978; CPA, Ariz. Assoc. gen. counsel, sec. Western Nuclear, Inc., Denver, 1979-81; exploration counsel Phelps Dodge Corp., N.Y.C., 1981-85; legal and adminstrv. mgr. Phelps Dodge Corp., Phoenix, 1985-87, v.p., gen. counsel, 1987-88, sr. v.p., gen. counsel, 1988-91; pres. Phelps Dodge Mining Co., Phoenix, 1991—; bd. dirs. Phelps Dodge Corp., Unocal Corp., Burlington No. Santa Fe Corp., So. Peru Copper Corp. Trustee Heard Mus., Phoenix, 1989-94, Rocky Mountain Mineral Law Found., 1989-92; mem. Dean's Coun. of 100, Ariz. State U., 1992—; mem. nat. bd. advs. Coll. Bus. and Pub. Adminstrn., U. Ariz., 1992—; bd. dirs. Met. Phoenix YMCA, 1989-92, Copper Bowl Found., Tucson, 1990-91, Ariz. Town Hall, 1991-96, We. Regional Coun., 1991—, Mont. Tech. Found., 1996—. Mem. AICPA, AIME, Soc. Mining Engrs., Colo. Bar Assn., Phoenix Thunderbirds, Phoenix Country Club. Office: Phelps Dodge Corp 2600 N Central Ave Phoenix AZ 85004-3050

WHISNAND, REX JAMES, housing association executive; b. Van Nuys, Calif., Jan. 2, 1948; s. Harold Theodore and Laura Fay (Brigham) Whisnand; m. Cathy Ladeane Bennett, Apr. 1, 1978; 1 child, Bryce James. BS in Agrl. Bus. Mgmt., Calif. Poly State U., San Luis Obispo, 1970; BSBA, Calif. State U., Sacramento, 1976; MPA in Housing Adminstrn., U. San Francisco, 1985; grad., U.S. Naval Submarine Sch., New London, Conn., 1972; C. of C. of U.S. grad. Inst. Orgn. Mgmt., Stanford U., 1994; adjunct faculty mem., U. San Francisco; cust. svc. rep., Oakland Athletic Baseball Club. Generalist W & W Hardware Store, Orcutt, Calif., 1964-70; state park ranger Calif. Dept. Parks and Recreation, Lompoc and Sacramento, 1969-75; exec. asst. Constrn. Industry Legis. Coun., Sacramento, 1974-75; dir. assn. svcs. Bldg. Industry Assn. Superior Calif., Sacramento, 1976-79; exec. v.p. West Bay divsn. Bldg. Industry Assn. No. Calif., Redwood City, 1980-84; exec. v.p. Bldg. Industry Assn., Tacoma/Pierce County, 1984-86; supr. Lumberjack Store, Lodi, Calif., 1988-90; exec. v.p. Rental Housing Owners Assn. of So. Alameda County, Hayward, Calif., 1990-96; mem. com. Calif. Bldg. Industry Assn., Sacramento, 1976-84; mem. exec. officers coun., local govt. com. Calif. Apt. Assn., 1991-96; mem. Alameda County Housing Rsch. Adv. Bd., Hayward, Calif., 1990-93; bd. dirs. Pacific Bay Fed. Credit Union, Credit Union Execs. Soc., Internat. Credit Assn., Pronet. Editor Pierce County Builder, 1984-86 (Assn. Achievement awards Nat. Assn. Home Builders 1984, 85), Superior California Builder Mag., 1978-80. Active 20-30 Club Internat. #1, Sacramento, 1976-80, officer, 1981-82; mem. South Sacramento Area Cmty. Planning Adv. Bd., 1978-79; grad. Pleasanton Leadership, 1995; chmn. Coastside Coalition for Safe Hwys., Half Moon Bay, 1983-84; bd. congregations Family Emergency Shelter Coalition Alameda County, 1995—; mem. Pleasanton Gen. Plan Econ./Fiscal Growth Com., 1994-96, Bay Area Indsl. Edn. Coun., 1995-96, Hayward Coalition for Youth, 1995-96; officer Half Moon Bay C. of C., 1982-84; cert. basketball coach Nat. Youth Sports Assn., 1994—. With USNR, 1970-76, U.S. Army, N.G., 1990-92. Named Outstanding Young Man. in Am., Jr. C. of C., Foster City, Calif., 1983. Mem. Internat. Assn. Bus. Communicators (pres. Sacramento chpt. 1979, pres. Peninsula chpt. 1981), Am. Soc. Assn. Execs. (cert.), No. Calif. Soc. Assn. Execs. (bd. dirs. 1994-97, com. chmn. 1993-95), Pleasanton C. of C. (econ. devel. com. 1990-96), Wash. State Home Builders Assn. (pres. exec. officers coun. 1985), Western Conf. Assn. Execs. (mem. com. 1995-96), So. Alameda County Assn. Realtors, Hayward C. of C. (govt. rels. coun. 1990-95), Calif. Vocat. Indsl. Clubs Am. (bd. dirs. 1977-80), Nat. Apt. Assn., Calif. Polytech. Alumni Assn., Alpha Gamma Rho (charter, com. chair 1969-96). Episcopalian. Avocations: YMCA Indian guides, little league baseball coach, dog training, genealogy. Home: 5435 Black Ave # 3 Pleasanton CA 94566

WHISNANT, JACK PAGE, neurologist; b. Little Rock, Oct. 26, 1924; s. John Clifton and Zula I. (Page) W.; m. Patricia Anne Rimmey, May 12, 1944; children: Elizabeth Anne, John David, James Michael. B.S., U. Ark.,

1948, M.D., 1951; M.S., U. Minn., 1955. Intern Balt. City Hosp., 1951-52; resident in medicine and neurology Mayo Grad. Sch. Medicine, Rochester, Minn., 1952-55; instr. neurology Mayo Grad. Sch. Medicine, 1956-60, asst. prof., 1960-64, asso. prof., 1964-69, prof., 1969—; Meyer prof. neurosci. Mayo Med. Sch.; chmn. dept. neurology Mayo Clinic, Mayo Med. Sch., Mayo Grad. Sch. Medicine, 1971-81; chmn. dept. health scis. research Mayo Clinic and Mayo Med. Sch., 1987-93; cons. neurology Mayo Clinic, 1955-96, head sect. neurology, 1963-71; dir. Mayo Cerebrovascular Clin. Research Center, 1975-96. Contbr. articles on neurology and cerebrovascular disease to med. jours. Trustee YMCA, Rochester. With USAAF, 1942-45. Decorated Air medal. NIH grantee, 1958, 75—. Fellow Am. Heart Assn., Am. Acad. Neurology (pres. 1993-95); mem. Am. Neurol. Assn. (pres. 1981-82), Am. Bd. Psychiatry and Neurology (bd. dirs. 1983-90, pres. 1989), Zumbro Valley Med. Soc., Minn. Med. Assn., Minn. Soc. Neurol. Scis., Ctrl. Soc. Neurol. Rsch., Nat. Adv. Neurol. Disease and Stroke Coun., Alumni Assn. Mayo Found. Presbyterian. Home: 1005 7th Ave NE Rochester MN 55906-7074 Office: Mayo Found Dept Health Scis Rsch 201 1st St SW Rochester MN 55902-3001

WHISTLER, ROY LESTER, chemist, educator, industrialist; b. Morgantown, W.Va., Mar. 31, 1912; s. Park H. and Cloe (Martin) W.; m. Leila Anna Barbara Kaufman, Sept. 6, 1935 (dec. 1994); 1 child, William Harris. B.S., Heidelberg Coll., 1934, D.Sc. (hon.), 1957; M.S., Ohio State U., 1935; Ph.D., Iowa State U., 1938; D.Litt. (hon.), St. Thomas Inst., 1982; D.Agr., Purdue U., 1985. Instr. chemistry Iowa State U., 1935-38; research fellow Bur. Standards, 1938-40; sect. leader dept. agr. No. Regional Rsch. Lab., 1940-46; prof. biochemistry Purdue U., 1946-76, Hillenbrand distinguished prof., asst. dept. head, 1974-82; Hillenbrand disting. prof. emeritus Purdue U., Lafayette, Ind., 1982—; chmn. Inst. Agrl. Utilization Research, 1961-75; pres. Lafayette Applied Chemistry Inc., 1980—; vis. lectr. U. Witwatersrand, 1961, 65, 77, 85, Czechoslovakia and Hungary, 1968, 85, Japan, 1969, Taiwan, 1970, Argentina, 1971, New Zealand, Australia, 1967, 74, Acad. Sci., France, 1975, Vladivostock Acad. Sci., 1976, Brazil, 1977, Egypt, 1979; lectr. Bradley Polytech. Inst., 1941-42, People's Republic of China, 1985; adviser Whistler Ctr. for Carbohydrate Chemistry; indsl. cons. dir. Pfanstiehl Lab., Inc., Greenwich Pharm. Inc., FruteTec; mem. NRC subcom. nomenclature biochemistry; pres. Lafayette (Ind.) Applied Chemistry; bd. dirs. Banproco Corp., Amaranth Resources. Author: Polysaccharide Chemistry, 1953, Industrial Gums, 1959, 2d rev. edit., 1976, 3d rev. edit., 1992; rev. edit.: Methods of Carbohydrate Chemistry, series, 1962—; co-author: Guar, 1979, Carbohydrates for Food Scientists, 1997; editor: Starch-Chemistry and Technology, 2 vols., 1965, 67, rev. edit., 1984; editorial bd. Jour. Carbohydrate Research, 1960-91, Starchs Chemistry and Technology, 1985; bd. advisors: Advances in Carbohydrate Chemistry, 1950-96, Organic Preparations and Procedures Internat., 1970—, Jour. Carbo-Nucleosides-Nucleotides, 1973-77, Starke, Starch, 1979—; contbr. over 500 articles to profl. jours. Recipient Sigma Xi rsch. award Purdue U., 1953, Medal of Merit, Japanese Starch Tech. Soc., 1967, German Saare medal, 1974, Thomas Burr Osborne award Am. Assn. Cereal Chemists, 1974, Sterling Henricks award USDA, 1991, 93, Nicholas Appert award Inst. Food Technologists, 1994; Roy L. Whistler internat. award in carbohydrates named in his hon.; Fred W. Tanner lectr., Chgo., 1994. Fellow AAAS, Am. Chem. Soc. (chmn. Purdue sect. 1949-50, carbohydrate divsn. 1951, cellular divsn. 1962, nat. councilor 1953-87, bd. dirs. 5th dist. 1955-58, chmn. com. edn. and students, chmn. sub-com. polysaccharide nomenclature, symposium dedicated in his honor 1979, hon. fellow award cellulose divsn. 1983, Hudson award 1960, Anselme Payen award 1967, Carl Lucas Alsburg award 1970, Spencer award 1970, 75, Disting. Svc. award 1983, named one of 10 outstanding chemists Chgo. sect. 1948), Am. Inst. Chemists (pres. 1982-83, Gold medal 1992), Am. Assn. Cereal Chemists (pres. 1978), Internat. Carbohydrate Union (pres. 1972-74); mem. Lafayette Applied Chemistry (pres. 1970—), Argentine Chem. Soc. (life), Rotary (pres. 1966), Sigma Xi (pres. Purdue sect. 1957-59, nat. exec. com. 1958-62, hon. life mem. 1983—), Phi Lambda Upsilon, Rotary (pres. 1966).

WHISTON, RICHARD MICHAEL, lawyer; b. N.Y.C., Mar. 1, 1944; s. Michael W. and Dorothy M. (Kussman) W. BS in Econs. cum laude, U. Pa., 1964; JD, Harvard U., 1968. Bar: N.Y. 1968, Conn. 1978, Fla. 1979, D.C. 1992, U.S. Dist. Ct. (so. and ea. dists.) N.Y. 1977, U.S. Dist. Ct. Conn. 1978, U.S. Ct. Claims 1979, U.S. Tax Ct. 1977, U.S. Ct. Appeals (5th cir.) 1979, U.S. Supreme Ct. 1977. Assoc. Kelley, Drye, Warren, N.Y.C., 1970-77; dep. div. counsel Hamilton Standard, Windsor Locks, Conn., 1977-78; asst. gen. counsel United Techs. Corp., Hartford, Conn., 1980-82; div. counsel Latin Am. ops. Otis Elevator Co., West Palm Beach, Fla., 1978-80; div. counsel European ops. Otis Elevator Co., Paris, 1982-83; v.p. counsel No. Am. ops. Otis Elevator Co., Farmington, Conn., 1983-85, v.p., gen. counsel, sec., 1985-90; v.p., gen. counsel, sec. Carrier World Hdqs., Farmington, 1990-92; sr. v.p., gen. counsel United Techs. divsn. Pratt & Whitney, East Hartford, Conn., 1993-96, exec. v.p., gen. counsel, 1996—. Served to capt. U.S. Army, 1968-70. Mem. Alpha Beta Psi, Beta Gamma Sigma. Episcopalian. Avocations: comml. pilot. Office: Pratt & Whitney M/S 101-10 400 Main St East Hartford CT 06108-0968

WHITACRE, CAROLINE CLEMENT, immunologist, researcher; b. Cin., Nov. 4, 1949; d. Richard Soteldo and Rosalyn (Wilson) W.; m. Michael Francis Para, June 28, 1975: 1 child, Alexander. BA, Ohio State U., 1971, PhD, 1975. Postdoctoral fellow Northwestern U., Chgo., 1975-78, instr., 1978-81; asst. prof. Ohio State U., Columbus, 1981-87, assoc. prof., 1987-92, prof. of microbiology and immunology, 1992—, interim chair, 1992-94, chair, 1994—. Contbr. articles to profl. pubs. NIMH grantee, 1988-91, Nat. Insts. for Allergy and Infectious Diseases grantee, 1987—, 90-91, 94—, NIH-Nat. Insts. for Neurol. Disorders and Stroke grantee, 1991—, Nat. Multiple Sclerosis grantee, 1991—. Mem. AAAS, NIH (spl. study sect. 1987-91, neurol. disorders com. 1991-95), Am. Assn. Immunologists, N.Y. Acad. Scis. Presbyterian. Achievements include discovery that experimental autoimmune encephalomyelitis can be suppressed by the oral administration of myelin basic protein due to the anergy or deletion of myelin basic protein specific T lymphocytes; research on multiple sclerosis and the animal model, experimental autoimmune encephalomyelitis, human immunodeficiency virus specific T lymphocyte responses, and effects of stress on immune function. Office: Ohio State U 2078 Graves Hall 333 W 10th Ave Columbus OH 43210-1239*

WHITACRE, EDWARD E., JR., telecommunications executive; b. Ennis, Tex., Nov. 4, 1941. BS in Indsl. Engring., Tex. Tech U., 1964. With Southwestern Bell Telephone Co., 1963-85; various positions in ops. depts. Tex., Ark., Kans.; pres. Kans. div. Topeka, 1984-85; group pres. Southwestern Bell Corp., 1985-86; v.p. revenues and pub. affairs, vice-chmn., chief fin. officer Southwestern Bell Corp., St. Louis, 1986-88, pres., chief oper. officer, 1988-89, chmn., chief exec. officer, 1990—, also bd. dirs.; bd. dirs. Anheuser-Busch Cos., Inc., May Dept. Stores Co., Emerson Electric Co., Burlington No. Santa Fe, Inc.; with Learning Nat. Adv. Bd. Bd. regents Tex. Tech. U. and Health Scis., Lubbock; mem. exec. bd. nat. coun. and so. region Boy Scouts Am.; trustee com. econ. devel. State N.Y., S.W. Rsch. Inst.; bd. govs. S.W. Found. Biomed. Rsch. Mem. Bus. Roundtable, Conf. Bd. Presbyterian. Office: SBC Communications Inc 175 E Houston St Rm 6u40 San Antonio TX 78205-2233

WHITACRE, JOHN, apparel executive; b. 1953. Student, U. Wash. With Nordstrom Inc., 1976—; co-chmn. Nordstrom Inc., Seattle, 1995—. Office: Nordstrom Inc 1501 5th Ave Seattle WA 98101-1603*

WHITAKER, A(LBERT) DUNCAN, lawyer; b. Ft. Wayne, Ind., Jan. 3, 1932; s. Robert Lynn and Rhoda Irene (Duncan) W.; m. Adelaide B. Saccone, Aug. 13, 1955; children: Brent Robert, Alene G., Karen E. B.A., Yale U., 1954; J.D., U. Mich., 1957. Bar: Mich. 1957, U.S. Ct. Appeals D.C. 1959, U.S. Supreme Ct. 1961. Atty. antitrust div. U.S. Dept. Justice, 1957-59; assoc. Howrey & Simon, Washington, 1959-65, ptnr., 1965—; lectr. George Washington U., George Mason U. Law Sch. Contbr. articles to profl. jours. Mem. ABA, Fed. Bar Assn., D.C. Bar Assn., Order of Coif, Phi Beta Kappa. Clubs: Metropolitan. Office: Howrey & Simon 1299 Pennsylvania Ave NW Washington DC 20004-2400

WHITAKER, BRUCE EZELL, college president; b. Cleveland County, N.C., June 27, 1921; m. Esther Adams, Aug. 22, 1947; children: Barry Eugene, Garry Bruce. BA, Wake Forest U., 1944; BD, So. Bapt. Theol. Sem., 1947, ThM, 1948, PhD, 1950; postgrad., George Peabody Coll., 1952; DL, Wake Forest U., 1987. Ordained to ministry Bapt. Ch., 1945; pastor Smithfield, Ky., 1945-49; instr. sociology and philosophy Ind. U., 1947-50; prof. religion Cumberland U., Lebanon, Tenn., 1950-51, Belmont Coll., Nashville, 1951-52; prof. sociology, asst. to pres. Shorter Coll., Rome, Ga., 1952-53; asso. pastor, minister edn. Atlanta, 1953-54; state sec., student dept. Bapt. State Conv., N.C., 1954-57; pres. Chowan Coll., Murfreesboro, N.C., 1957-89, pres. emeritus, 1989—; mem. adv. com. to Nd. Higher Edn., 1962-66; to N.C. Commn. Higher Edn. Facilities, 1964—; pres. N.C. Conf. Social Svc., 1965-67, Assn. Governing Bds., 1973-82, Assn. So. Baptist Colls. and Schs., 1967-68, Assn. Eastern N.C. Colls., 1968-69; bd. dirs. Regional Edn. Lab. for Carolinas and Va. Pres. bd. trustees N.C. Found. Church-Related Colls., 1970-74; bd. dirs., v.p. Nat. Coun. Ind. Jr. Colls., 1974-75, pres., 1975-76; mem. adv. coun. presidents Assn. Governing Bds., from 1973; mem. N.C. Bd. Mental Health, from 1966; bd. dirs. Am. Assn. Cmty. and Jr. Colls., 1976-82; pres. N.C. Assn. Colls. and Univs., 1977-78; chmn. N.C. Commn. Mental Health/Mental Retardation Sers., 1978-81; mem. N.C. Commn. on Mental Health, Developmental Disabilities, and Alcohol and Drug Svcs., 1995—. V.p. Bapt. State Conv. N.C., 1989-91. Named Tarheel of Week Raleigh News and Observer, 1962, Boss of Year N.C. Jaycees, 1972; tribute paid in Congl. Record, 1962, 89; Whitaker Libr. at Chowan Coll. named for him; Whitaker Sch. at Butner, N.C. named for him; selected one of nation's 18 most effective coll. pres. in 1985, funded study Exxon Found.; featured in We the People of North Carolina, 1989. Mem. N.C. Lit. and Hist. Assn. (pres. 1970-71), Am. Acad. Polit. and Social Scis., NEA, Am. Assn. Community and Jr. Colls. (dir. 1976-82, Leadership Recognition award 1989), Nat. Assn. Ind. Colls. and Univs. (dir. 1977-78, 81-85), Am. Assn. Higher Edn., Am. Coun. Edn. (bd. dirs. 1985-89), Internat. Platform Assn., Omicron Delta Kappa. Clubs: Capital City (Raleigh, N.C.), Capitol Club (Raleigh); Rotary (chmn. dist. student exchange com. 1969-72, Paul Harris fellow); Optimist; Beechwood Country (Ahoskie, N.C.); Harbor (Norfolk, Va.). Office: PO Drawer 40 Murfreesboro NC 27855-0040

WHITAKER, CHARLES F., journalism educator; b. Chgo., Oct. 28, 1958; s. Andrew L. and Marjorie Whitaker; m. Stephanie J. Sanders, Oct. 1, 1988; children: Joshua, Christopher. BS in Journalism, Northwestern U., 1980, MS in Journalism, 1981. Suburban edn. writer N.E. Dade County Bur., Miami (Fla.) Herald, 1981-82, staff writer, 1982-84; staff writer Louisville Times, 1984-85; assoc. editor Ebony Mag., Chgo., 1985-87, sr. assoc. editor, 1987-89, sr. editor, 1989-92; mem. adj. faculty Northwestern U. Medill Sch. Journalism, Evanston, Ill., 1990-92, asst. prof. journalism, 1992—; dir. Gertrude Johnson Williams Lit. Contest, 1989—; assoc. fellow Joint Ctr. for Polit. and Econ. Studies, Urban Policy Inst., Chgo., 1992—; advisor, faculty editor Passport Africa, 1992. Contbr. to various publs. Bd. dirs. Chocolate Chips Theatre Co., 1987—. Recipient 1st place award for mag. writing Nat. Assn. Edn. Writers, 1982; 1st place award for feature writing Louisville Assn. Black Communicators, 1984, for commentary or criticism, 1984. Mem. Nat. Assn. Black Journalists, Chgo. Assn. Black Journalists (faculty Exposure satellite program 1988—), Phi Beta Sigma (editor-in-chief Crescent 1989-93). Office: Northwestern U Medill Sch Journalism 1845 Sheridan Rd Evanston IL 60208-0815*

WHITAKER, CLEM, JR., advertising and public relations executive; b. Sacramento, Aug. 30, 1922; s. Clem and Harriett (Reynolds) W.; 1 child, Isabella Alexandra. Student, Sacramento Jr. Coll., 1942, U. Calif.-Berkeley, 1943. Reporter, Sacramento Union, 1938-40; staff mem. Campaigns, Inc.-Whitaker & Baxter, San Francisco, 1946-50; partner Campaigns, Inc.-Whitaker & Baxter, 1950-58, pres., 1958—; partner Whitaker & Baxter Advt. Agy., San Francisco, 1950-58; pres. Whitaker & Baxter Advt. Agy., 1958—; co-pub. Calif. Feature Svc., San Francisco, 1950—; chmn. Wye Energy Group. Bd. dirs. San Francisco Opera Assn. With USAAF, 1942-46, ETO. Mem. Cercle de L'Union. Home: 2040 Broadway St San Francisco CA 94115-1500 Office: Box 334 2443 Fillmore St San Francisco CA 94115-1825

WHITAKER, CYNTHIA ELLEN, nurse; b. Dearborn, Mich., June 15, 1948; d. John Harold and Marion Violet (Malmsten) Fields; m. Elbert Charles Whitaker, Sept. 7, 1968; children: Shannon Kaye, Kaycee Susan. ADN, Oakland C.C., Union Lake, Mich., 1982; BSN, U. Mich., 1985. RN, Calif.; cert. case mgr. Nurse Wheelock Meml. Hosp., Goodrich, Mich., 1982-86; clin. nursing instr. Oakland C.C., Union Lake, Mich., 1985-86; rehab. nurse Continental Ins.-UAC, Southfield, Mich., 1987-88; med. mgmt. cons. Continental Rehab. Resources, Sacramento, 1988-89; pres. RNS Healthcare Cons., Inc., Sacramento, 1989—; CFO, v.p. Strategic Health Alliances, Inc., Sacramento, 1993-97. Co-author: (book) Infectious Disease Handbook, 1981, (booklet) Standards of Practice for Case Management, 1995. Mem. adv. bd. grad. sch. nursing San Francisco State U., 1994—; mem. cmty. adv. bd. Mercy Healthcare Sacramento, 1993-95, Kentfield (Calif.) Rehab. Hosp., 1993—, North Valley Rehab. Hosp., Chico, Calif., 1991-93. Dean's Fellow Scholarship awardee U. Mich., 1986. Mem. ANA, AOHN, Am. Assn. Legal Nurse Cons., Case Mgmt. Soc. Am. (co-founder No. Calif. chpt., affiliate dir. 1993-95, affiliate pres. 1992-93, nat. sec. 1995-96, nat. pres. 1997—). Republican. Avocations: swimming, snow skiing, reading, hiking, fishing. Home: 800 Elmhurst Cir Sacramento CA 95825

WHITAKER, EILEEN MONAGHAN, artist; b. Holyoke, Mass., Nov. 22, 1911; d. Thomas F. and Mary (Doona) Monaghan; m. Frederic Whitaker. Ed., Mass. Coll. Art, Boston. Annual exhibits in nat. and regional watercolor shows; represented in permanent collections, Charles and Emma Frye Mus., Seattle, NAD, Hispanic Soc., N.Y.C., High Mus. Art, Atlanta, U. Mass., Norfolk (Va.) Mus., Springfield (Mass.) Mus. Art, Reading (Pa.) Art Mus., Nat. Acad. Design, U. Mass., Okla. Mus. Art, St. Lawrence U., Wichita State U., Retrospective show, Founders Gallery U. San Diego, 1988, invitational one-person show Charles and Emma Frye Art Mus., 1990; included in pvt. collections; featured in cover article of American Artist mag., Mar. 1987, in article Art of Calif. mag., July 1991; invitational Am. Realism Exhbn. Cir. Gallery, San Diego, 1992; author: Eileen Monaghan Whitaker Paints San Diego, 1986. Recipient numerous major awards, including Allied Artists Am., Am. Watercolor Soc., 1st prize Providence Water Color Club, Wong award Calif. Watercolor Soc., De Young award Soc. Western Artists, 1st award Springville (Utah) Mus., Ranger Fund purchase prize, Orbrig prize NAD, Walter Biggs Meml. award, 1987; silver medal Am. Watercolor Soc., Watercolor West; fellow Huntington Hartford Found., 1964. Academician NAD (William P. and Gertrude Schweitzer prize for excellence in watercolor 171st Annual Exbhn. 1996); mem. Am. Watercolor Soc. (Dolphin fellow), Watercolor West (hon.), San Diego Watercolor Soc. (hon.). Home and Studio: 1579 Alta La Jolla Dr La Jolla CA 92037-7101

WHITAKER, GILBERT RILEY, JR., academic administrator, business economist; b. Oklahoma City, Oct. 8, 1931; s. Gilbert Riley and Melodese (Kilpatrick) W.; m. Ruth Pauline Tonn, Dec. 18, 1953; children: Kathleen, David Edward, Thomas Gilbert. BA, Rice U., 1953; postgrad., So. Methodist U., 1956-57; MS in Econs., U. Wis., Madison, 1958, Ph.D. in Econs. (Ford Found. dissertation fellow), 1961. Instr., Sch. of Bus. Northwestern U., 1960-61, asst. prof. bus. econs., Sch. of Bus., 1961-64, asso. prof., Sch. of Bus., 1964-66, research assoc. Transp. Center, Sch. of Bus., 1962-66; asso. prof. Washington U., St. Louis, 1966-67; prof. Washington U., 1967-76, adj. prof. econs., 1968-76, asso. dean Sch. Bus. Adminstrn., 1969-76; dean, prof. bus. econs. M.J. Neeley Sch. Bus., Tex. Christian U., 1976-79; dean U. Mich., 1979-90; prof. Sch. Bus. Adminstrn. U. Mich., 1979—; provost, v.p. acad. affairs U. Mich., Ann Arbor, 1990-93, provost, exec. v.p. acad. affairs, 1993-95; sr. advisor Andrew W. Mellon Found., 1996—; dean Jesse Jones Graduate Sch. of Adminstrn./Rice U., Houston, 1997—; dir. Am. Assembly of Collegiate Schs. of Bus., 1984-91, v.p., pres.-elect, 1988-89, pres., 1989-90, dir. Washington campus, 1980-89, chmn., 1985-88; bd. dirs. Lincoln Nat. Corp., Johnson Controls, Inc., Structural Dynamics Rsch. Corp., Handleman Co.; sr. economist banking and currency com. U.S. Ho. of Reps., 1964; mem. Grad. Mgmt. Admissions Coun., 1972-75, chmn., 1974-75; bd. dirs. Washtenaw County United Way, 1990-96. Author: (with Marshall Colberg and Dascomb Forbush) books including Business Economics, 6th edit., 1981, (with Roger Chisholm) Forecasting Methods, 1971. Bd. trustees, sec.-treas. JSTOR, 1995—. With USN, 1953-56. Mem. Am. Econ. Assn., Ft. Worth Boat Club. Home: 2360 Londonderry Rd Ann Arbor MI 48104-4014 Office: Jesse Jones Grad Sch of Adminstrn Rice Univ 6100 Main St Houston TX 77005-1827

WHITAKER, GLENN VIRGIL, lawyer; b. Cin., July 23, 1947; s. Glenn M. and Doris (Handlon) W.; m. Jennifer Lynn Angus, Oct. 22, 1990. BA, Denison U., 1969; JD, George Washington U., 1972. Bar: Md. 1972, D.C. 1973, Ohio 1980. Law clk. to judge U.S. Dist. Ct., Balt., 1972-73; assoc. O'Donoghue and O'Donoghue, Washington, 1973-76; trial atty. civil div. U.S. Dept. Justice, Washington, 1976-78, spl. litigation counsel, 1978-80; ptnr. Graydon, Head & Ritchey, Cin., 1980-92, Voyrs, Sater, Seymour & Pease, Cin., 1992—; emeritus master of bench Potter Stewart Inn of Ct., Cin., 1985—; adj. prof. law Coll. Law U. Cin.; mem. Am. Bd. Trial Advocates. Fellow Am. Coll. Trial Lawyers; mem. ABA, ATLA, Ohio Bar Assn., D.C. Bar Assn., Md. Bar Assn., Cin. Bar Assn. Avocations: hiking, exploring. Office: Vorys Sater Seymour & Pease 221 E 4th St Ste 2100 Cincinnati OH 45202-4146

WHITAKER, JOEL, publisher; b. Indpls., May 27, 1942; s. Quincy Myers and Sigur Elizabeth (Moore) W.; m. Donna Kay, Apr. 27, 1986. BS in Bus. Journalism, Ind. U., 1964, MA in Journalism, 1971; JD, Temple U., 1979. Reporter St. Petersburg (Fla.) Times, 1964, copy editor, 1966-68; copy editor Wall St. Journal, N.Y.C., 1968-73; bus. news editor Phila. Evening and Sunday Bull., 1973-78; law clk. Fellheimer, Krakower & Eicen, Phila., 1978-79; mng. editor Bank Letter, N.Y.C., 1979-80; editor, pres. Whitaker Newsletters Inc., Fanwood, N.J., 1980—. Chmn. Fanwood Planning Bd., 1981-85; mem. Downtown Redevel. Commn., Fanwood, 1983-85; mem. Union County (N.J.) local adv. commn. on alcoholism and drug abuse, 1993—, chmn., 1994-95, vice chmn. 1997—. Major USAR, 1964-85. Mem. Newsletter Publishers Assn. (bd. dirs. 1983-92, found. trustee 1986—, treas. 1989-93), Soc. Profl. Journalists, Nat. Press Club (Washington), Rotary (bd. dirs. Fanwood-Scotch Plains club 1996—). Republican. Roman Catholic. Office: Whitaker Newsletters Inc 313 South Ave Fanwood NJ 07023-1350

WHITAKER, JOHN KING, economics educator; b. Burnley, Lancashire, Eng., Jan. 30, 1933; came to U.S., 1967; s. Ben and Mary (King) W.; m. Sally Bell Cross, Aug. 24, 1957; children: Ann Elizabeth, Jane Claire, David John. B.A. in Econs, U. Manchester, 1956; A.M., Johns Hopkins U., 1957; Ph.D., Cambridge U., 1962. Lectr. U. Bristol, Eng., 1960-66; prof., 1966-69; vis. prof. U. Va., Charlottesville, 1967-68; prof. econs. U. Va., 1969-86, chmn. dept. econs., 1979-82, Paul Goodloe McIntire prof. of econs., 1986-92; Georgia Bankard prof. of econs. U. Va., Charlottesville, 1992—. Author: The Early Economic Writings of Alfred Marshall, 1867-1890, 2 vols., 1975, The Correspondence of Alfred Marshall, Economist, 3 vols., 1996. Mem. Am. Econ. Assn., Royal Econ. Soc., Econometric Soc., History of Econs. Soc. Home: 1615 Yorktown Dr Charlottesville VA 22901-3046 Office: U Va Dept Econs Rouss Hall Charlottesville VA 22901

WHITAKER, LINTON ANDIN, plastic surgeon; b. Navasota, Tex., Nov. 16, 1936; s. Ira Andin and Lena Rivers (Stedman) W.; m. Renata Grasmanis, Dec. 20, 1963; children: Derek Andin (dec.), Ingrid Marlena, Brandon Andrew. BA, U. Tex., 1958; MD, Tulane U., 1962. Diplomate Am. Bd. Surgery, Am. Bd. Plastic Surgery. Intern Montreal Gen. Hosp., 1962-63; resident in gen. surgery Dartmouth Affiliated Hosps., Hanover, N.H., 1965-69; resident in plastic surgery U. Pa. Hosp., Phila., 1969-71; chief plastic surgery Grad. Hosp., 1971-77; chief plastic surgery U. Pa. Hosp., Phila., 1987—, attending surgeon, 1971—; chief plastic surgery Children's Hosp. Phila., 1981—, attending surgeon, 1971—; v.p. med. staff Children's Hosp., Pitts., 1992-94, pres. med. staff, 1994-96; attending physician VA Hosp., 1971—, Phila. Gen. Hosp., 1971-77; assoc. in plastic surgery Sch. Medicine, U. Pa., Phila., 1971-73, asst. prof. in plastic surgery, 1973-76, assoc. prof., 1976-81, prof., 1981—; founder, dir. ctr. human appearance U. Pa. Med. Ctr., Phila., 1988—; vis. prof. Walter Reed Army Med. Ctr., Washington, 1976, Ohio State U. Med. Ctr., Columbus, 1977, Cleve. Clinic, 1980, Wilmington Med. Ctr., 1980, South Australia Craniofacial Unit, Adelaide, Australia and New Zealand, 1981, U. Hawaii, 1983, Brown U., Providence, 1983, Mass. Gen. Hosp., Boston, 1984, U. Utah, Salt Lake City, 1984, U. B.C., Vancouver, 1986, U. Pitts., 1988, U. Calif., San Diego, 1992, Ohio Valley Soc. for Plastic and Reconstructive Surgery, 1992, N.Y. U., 1994; Curts vis. prof. Dartmouth U. Med. Ctr., Hanover, N.H., 1990, Kazanjian vis. prof. Mass. Gen. Hosp., Boston, 1990; First Seiichi Ohmori Meml. lectr. All Asiatic Congress on Aesthetic Surgery, Tokyo, 1988; vis. speaker Inst. Cosmotology and Inst. Stomatology, Moskow, Russia, 1985, vis. prof. Seoul Nat. U. and vis. speaker Korean Soc. for Plastic Surgeons, 1994; hon. vis. spkr. Chinese Plastic Surgery Soc., Beijing, 1996; lectr., speaker at univs., assns. in field. Co-author: Atlas of Cranio-maxillofacial Surgery, 1982, Aesthetic Surgery of the Facial Skelton, 1992; editor: (with P. Randall) Symposium on the Reconstruction of Jaw Deformity, Clinics in Plastic Surgery, 1987, 91; co-editor: Yearbook of Plastic and Reconstructive Surgery, 1980-97; mem. editorial bd. Jour. Cutaneous Aging and Cosmetic Dermatology, 1988—; contbr. articles to profl. jours. Capt. U.S. Army Med. Corps, 1963-65. Foederer fellow Foederer Fund for Excellence, 1985-88; NIH grantee, 1976-79, 81-87, 82-85, 89, Plastic Surgery Edn. Found. Rsch. grantee, 1980-82; recipient James IV Surg. Traveller award, 1979. Fellow Am. Coll. Surgeons, Am. Soc. Ophthalmic Plastic and Reconstructive Surgery (hon.); mem. AMA (mem. coun. sci. affairs, diagnostic and therapeutic tech. assessment reference panel 1982), Am. Assn. Plastic Surgeons (mem. program com. 1988, chmn. 1989, Rsch. grantee 1984-85), Am. Surg. Assn., Am. Alpine Workshop in Plastic Surgery (founding mem.), Am. Cleft Palate Assn. (chmn. com. classification craniofacial anomalies 1976-80, mem. program com. for 1978 mtg. 1977, mem. long-range planning com. 1980, mem. coun. 1981-84, chmn. internat. rels. com. 1981-83), Am. Cleft Palate Ednl. Found. (bd. dirs. 1975-84, chmn. rsch. com. 1975-78, chmn. instrl. courses 1980-81), Am. Soc. Aesthetic Plastic Surgery, Am. Soc. Craniofacial Surgery (mem. coun. 1992—), Am. Soc. Maxillofacial Surgeons, Am. Soc. Plastic and Reconstructive Surgeons (mem. pub. rels com. 1974-76, mem. plastic surgery speakers bur. 1977—), Am. Soc. Plastic and Reconstructive Surgeons Ednl. Found. (chmn. ednl. assessment com., maxillofacial truama and craniofacial anomalies 1975-78, mem. clin. symposia com. 1978-82, chmn. clin. symposia com. 1981-82), Internat. Cleft Palate & Related Craniofacial Anomalies Soc. (mem. program com. 1981, 89), Internat. Soc. Aesthetic Surgery, Internat. Soc. Craniofacial Surgeons (founding mem., organizer, mem. exec. com. 1987—, sec and treas. 1993-95, pres. 1995-97), Phila. Med. Soc., Phila. Acad. Surgery, Coll. Physicians Phila., Assn. Acad. Surgery, Northeastern Soc. Plastic Surgeons N.Y. (chmn. program com. 1987, mem. programcom. 1988), Plastic Surgery Rsch. Coun., John Morgan Soc., Robert H. Ivy Soc., The Columbian Soc. Plastic, Maxillofacial and Hand Surgery (hon.), Academia Medica Lombarda (Italy, hon.). Sociedad Jamie Planas de Cirugia Plastica (Spain, hon.), Mt. Kenya Safari Club (hon.), Soc. Former Residents and Assocs. Plastic Surgery (hon.), Japan Soc. Craniomaxillofacial Surgeons (hon.), asian Pacific Cranofacial Assn., Phila. Club, Merion Cricket Club. Avocations: mountaineering, skiing, wines. Office: U Pa Med Ctr 10 Penn Tower 3400 Spruce St Philadelphia PA 19104

WHITAKER, MARY FERNAN, lawyer; b. Kansas City, Mo., May 29, 1958; d. James Paul and Mildred Louise (Connor) Fernan; m. Mark Dwight Whitaker, May 28, 1983; children: Paul Connor, James Sullivan, Helen Foster. BSN, George Mason U., 1982, JD, 1987. Bar: Va. 1987, Pa. 1995. Nurse George Washington Med. Ctr., Washington, 1980-82, Mt. Vernon Hosp., Alexandria, Va., 1982-84; atty. Legal Svcs. No. Va., Arlington, 1987, Office Rev. and Appeals, EEOC, Falls Church, Va., 1987-88; pvt. practice Annadale, Va., 1988-93, Pottsville, Pa., 1993-95, Coopersburg, Pa., 1995-96, Solomons, Md., 1996—; adj. faculty paralegal program No. Va. C.C., 1992; counselor, mem. legal com. My Sister's Pl., Washington, 1987-93. Vol. ARC, Alexandria, 1987; vol. atty. Women's Legal Def. Fund, Washington, 1989-91; mem. Shelter Outreach Program, 1990-93; v.p. Ravensworth Bristow Civic assn., 1990-93; head makeup design for cmty. theatre troupe Camelot Players, 1990-91; tchr. 3d grade religious edn. St. Michael's Ch. Choir, 1991-92, tchr. 8th grade religious edn., 1992-93, choir, 1992-93; tchr. 7th grade religious edn. St. Joseph Ch., 1995-96. Mem. ABA, Va. State Bar Assn., Fairfax Bar Assn., Phi Delta Phi. Roman Catholic. Avocations: bicycling, swimming. Office: PO Box 881 Solomons MD 20688-0881

WHITAKER, PERNELL (SWEET PEA WHITAKER), professional boxer. Olympic Gold Medalist, boxing, lightweight divsn. L.A., 1984; lightweight champion Internat. Boxing Fedn., 1989; jr. lightweight champion World Boxing Coun., welterweight champion, 1993-97; lightweight champion World Boxing Assn., 1990, middleweight champion, 1995. Recipient Gold medal boxing lightweight divsn. Olympics, 1984; named pound for pound best boxer in the world Ring Mag., 1995, winner record 6 world championship titles in 4 weight classes, 1995. Office: World Boxing Coun, Genova 33 Colonia Juarez, Cuauhtemoc Mexico City Mexico

WHITAKER, SUSANNE KANIS, veterinary medical librarian; b. Clinton, Mass., Sept. 10, 1947; d. Harry and Elizabeth P. (Cantwell) Kanis; m. Daniel Brown Whitaker, Jan. 1, 1977. A.B. in Biology, Clark U., 1969; M.S. in Library Sci., Case Western Res. U., 1970. Regional reference librarian Yale Med. Library, New Haven, 1970-72; med. librarian Hartford Hosp., Conn., 1972-77; asst. librarian Cornell U., Ithaca, N.Y., 1977-78; vet. med. librarian Coll. Vet. Medicine, Cornell U., 1978—; sec. SUNY Council Head Librarians, 1981-83. Mem. Med. Libr. Assn. (sec.-treas. vet. med. librs. sect. 1983-84, chmn. 1984-85), Med. Libr. Assn. (upstate N.Y. and Ont. chpt.), Acad. Health Info. Profls. Home: 23 Wedgewood Dr Ithaca NY 14850 Office: Cornell U Coll Vet Medicine Flower-Sprecher Libr Ithaca NY 14853-6401

WHITAKER, THOMAS PATRICK, lawyer; b. Washington, Sept. 22, 1944; s. Thomas J. and Mary K. (Finn) W.; m. Donna Mae Brenish, Feb. 16, 1974; children: Laura, Kevin. BA, George Washington U., 1966, MPA, 1973, JD, 1979; postgrad., Naval War Coll., 1984. Bar: Va. 1979. Staff asst. Adminstrn. Office of U.S. Cts., Washington, 1972-73, analyst, 1975-77; cons. Planning Research Corp., McLean, Va., 1973-75; mgmt. analyst CAB, Washington, 1977-82; program analyst Social Security Adminstrn., Falls Church, Va., 1982—. Served to lt. (j.g.) USNR, 1966-71, Vietnam, capt. with Res. 1983—. Mem. ABA, Am. Soc. Pub. Adminstrn. (sect. chmn. 1974-76), U.S. Naval Inst., Naval Res. Assn., Res. Officers Assn. Home: 9817 Days Farm Dr Vienna VA 22182-7306

WHITAKER, THOMAS RUSSELL, English literature educator; b. Marquette, Mich., Aug. 7, 1925; s. Joe Russell and Sarah Genevieve (Houk) W.; m. Dorothy Vera Barnes, June 17, 1950; children: Thomas O'Hara, Sarah Mae, Mary Beth, Gwendolyn Anne. BA summa cum laude, Oberlin Coll., 1949; MA, Yale U., 1950, PhD, 1953. Instr. English Oberlin (Ohio) Coll., 1952-55, asst. prof., 1955-59, assoc. prof., 1959-63, prof., 1963-64; tchr. lit. Goddard Coll., Plainfield, Vt., 1964-66; prof. English U. Iowa, Iowa City, 1966-75; prof. English Yale U., New Haven, Conn., 1975-95, prof. theater studies, 1986-95, chmn. dept. English, 1979-85, Frederick W. Hilles prof. English, 1989-95; Frederick W. Hilles prof. emeritus English, 1995—. Author: Swan and Shadow: Yeats's Dialogue with History, 1964, 2d edit. with new preface, 1989, William Carlos Williams, 1968, rev. edit., 1989, Fields of Play in Modern Drama, 1977, Tom Stoppard, 1983, augmented edit., 1984; editor: Twentieth Century Interpretations of the Playboy of the Western World, 1969, Teaching in New Haven: The Common Challenge, 1991; editor Iowa Rev., 1974-77; chmn. editorial bd. On Common Ground, 1993—; author video script: Excellence in Teaching: Agenda for Partnership, 1997. Served with C.E. U.S. Army, 1944-46. Recipient Harbison award for gifted teaching Danforth Found., 1972; Am. Council Learned Socs. fellow, 1969-70; NEH-Huntington fellow, 1981. Mem. MLA. Home: 882 Moose Hill Rd Guilford CT 06437-2303

WHITAKER, VON BEST, nursing educator; b. New Bern, N.C.; d. Cleveland W. and Lillie (Bryant) Best; m. Roy Whitaker Jr., Aug. 9, 1981; 1 child, Roy Whitaker III. BS, Columbia Union Coll., 1972; MS, U. Md., 1974; MA, U. N.C., 1980, PhD, 1983. Lectr. U. N.C., Chapel Hill, 1981-82; asst. prof. U. Mo., Columbia, Mo., 1982-85; asst. prof. grad. sch. Boston Coll., Newton, Mass., 1985-86; asst. prof. U. Tex. Health Sci. Ctr., San Antonio, 1986-94; assoc. prof. Ga. So. U., Statesboro, 1994—; mem. cataract guideline panel Agy. for Health Care Policy Rsch., 1990-93; rsch. coord. glaucoma svc. Georgia Eye Inst., Savannah. Contbr. articles to profl. jours., chpts. to textbooks; presenter in field. Vol. to prevent blindness. Bush fellowship, 1979-81; recipient Cert. of Appreciation, Prevent Blindness South Tex., 1988, 89. Mem. ANA (cert. community health nurse), APHA, Am. Soc. Ophthalmic Nursing (chair rsch. com.), Assn. Black Faculty in Higher Edn., Nat. Black Nurses Assn., Sigma Theta Tau. Home: 1 Chelmsford Ln Savannah GA 31411

WHITBREAD, THOMAS BACON, English educator, author; b. Bronxville, N.Y., Aug. 22, 1931; s. Thomas Francis and Caroline Nancy (Bacon) W. B.A., Amherst Coll., 1952; A.M., Harvard U., 1953, Ph.D., 1959. Instr. English, U. Tex. at Austin, 1959-62, asst. prof., 1962-65, asso. prof., 1965-71, prof., 1971—; Vis. asso. prof. Rice U., 1969-70; mem. lit. adv. panel Tex. Commn. on Arts and Humanities, 1972-76. Author (poetry): Four Infinitives, 1964, Whomp and Moonshiver, 1982; contbg. author: Prize Stories, 1962, The O. Henry Awards, 1962; editor: Seven Contemporary Authors, 1966. Recipient third Aga Khan prize for fiction Paris Rev., 1960, Lit. Anthology Program award Nat. Endowment for Arts, 1968, Outstanding Freshman Tchr. award Phi Eta Sigma, 1972-73. Mem. AAUP, Tex. Inst. Letters (Poetry award 1965, 83), Nat., Am. amateur press assns., Phi Beta Kappa. Democrat. Home: 1014 E 38th St Austin TX 78705-1835 Office: U Tex Dept English Austin TX 78712

WHITBURN, GERALD, insurance company executive; b. Wakefield, Mich., July 12, 1944; s. Donald and Ruby E. (Nichols) W.; m. Charmaine M. Heise, May 3, 1969; children: Bree, Luke. BS, U. Wis., Oshkosh, 1966; MA, U. Wis., Madison, 1968; postgrad., Harvard U., 1988, U. Pa., 1997—. Aide Gov. Warren P. Knowles, Wis., 1966-69; personal asst. USN sec. John H. Chafee, Washington, 1969-72; automobile dealer, real estate developer Merrill, Wis., 1973-80; exec. asst. to Senator Robert W. Kasten U.S. Senate, Washington, 1981-87; dep. sec. Wis. Dept. Adminstrn., Madison, 1987-89; sec. Wis. Dept. Industry, Labor and Human Rels., Madison, 1989-91, Wis. Dept. Health and Social Svcs., Madison, 1991-95; sec. exec. office of health and human svcs. Commonwealth of Mass., Boston, 1995-96; v.p. adminstrn. Ch. Mut. Ins. Co., Merrill, Wis., 1996—; Mem. U.S. Labor Sec.'s Commn. on Achieving Necessary Skills, Washington, 1990-92. Contbr. articles to newspapers. Del. Rep. Nat. Conv., 1988, 92. Recipient Disting. Alumni award U. Wis., Oshkosh, 1991. Home: 1949 Sunset Dr Tomahawk WI 54487 Office: Ch Mut Ins Co 300 Schuster Ln Merrill WI 54452

WHITBURN, MERRILL DUANE, English literature educator; b. Mpls., Apr. 29, 1938; s. George and Marie Ellen (Carlstedt) W.; m. Diane Robertson, June 15, 1960; children: Stephen, Mark, Elizabeth. AB, U. Mich., 1960, AM, 1968; PhD, U. Iowa, 1973. With Western Electric Co., N.Y.C. and Indpls., 1965-67; asst. prof. Tex. A&M U., College Station, 1973-77, assoc. prof., 1977-79; assoc. prof. English Rensselaer Poly. Inst., Troy, N.Y., 1979-83, prof., 1983-89, Louis Ellsworth Laflin prof., 1989—, chmn. dept., 1979-85, 88-95; co-owner Pride and Prejudice Books, Ballston Lake, N.Y., 1985—. Co-author: (booklet) Guide for Departments of English, 1985; contbr. articles to profl. publs. Recipient Disting. Svc. award Tex. A&M U., 1976, Disting. Teaching award, 1979, Jay R. Gould award for excellence in tchg. tech. comm. Soc. Tech. Comm., 1995; grantee Fund for the Improvement of Postsecondary Edn., 1983. Mem. MLA, Soc. for Tech. Communication, Nat. Coun. Tchrs. English (best article in tech. writing award 1981), Coun. for Programs in Tech. and Sci. Communication, Assn. Depts. English. Office: Rensselaer Poly Inst Troy NY 12180

WHITCOMB, CARL ERVIN, horticulturist, researcher; b. Independence, Kans., Oct. 26, 1939; s. Albion Carlyle and Marie V. (Burck) W.; m. LaJean C. Carpenter, June 2, 1963; children: Andrew Carl, Benjamin Dwight. BS, Kans. State U., Manhattan, 1964; MS, Iowa State U., 1966, PhD, 1969. Asst. prof. horticulture U. Fla., Gainesville, 1967-72; prof. horticulture Okla. State U., Stillwater, 1972-85; pres. Lacebark Inc, Stillwater, 1985—; cons. Sierra Chem. Co., Milpitas, Calif., 1987-90. Author: Know It and Grow It, 1975, rev., 1978, 80, 85, 95, Plant Production in Containers, 1984, rev., 1990, Establishment and Maintenance of Landscape Plants, 1989, Production of Landscape Plants, 1991. Recipient Chadwick award Am. Assn. Nurserymen, 1983, Wight award So. Nurserymens Assn., 1986. Fellow Internat. Plant Propagators Soc.; mem. Am. Soc. Hort. Sci., Am. Soc. Agronomy, Weed Sci. Soc. Am. Achievements include 12 patents on products relative to horticulture, numerous patents other countries; avocations: photography, fishing. Office: Lacebark Inc PO Box 2383 Stillwater OK 74076

WHITCOMB, DARREL DEAN, pilot; b. Santa Ana, Calif., Oct. 27, 1947; s. George E. and June Delores (Miller) W.; m. Christine J. Sienicki, Dec. 28, 1974; children: Jennifer, Matthew, Sarah. BS, Air Force Acad., 1969; postgrad., Army Command/Gen. Staff Coll., 1987, Nat. War Coll., 1991. Commd. 2d lt. USAF, 1969; advanced through grades to col. USAFR, 1997; combat pilot USAF, 1970-74; fighter pilot USAF, La., Mo., 1978-89; pilot Delta Airlines, Atlanta, 1977—; capt. Delta Airlines, Cin., 1995—. Author: The Rescue of Bat 21, 1997; contbr. articles to profl. jours. Decorated Silver Star, USAF, 1973, 2 Disting. Flying Crosses, USAF, 1973, Meritorious Svc. medals, 1995. Mem. Res. Officers Assn., Air Force Assn. (mem. res. adv. coun.), Airline Pilots Assn., Am. Legion Post #1 Daedalians. Avocation: writing. Home: 5311 Lindsay St Fairfax VA 22032

WHITCOMB, JAMES HALL, geophysicist, foundation administrator; b. Sterling, Colo., Dec. 10, 1940; s. Clay Thane and Julia Melvina Whitcomb; m. Sandra Lynn McMurdo, July 13, 1965 (div. 1978); m. Teresa R. Idoni, Feb. 3, 1989; 1 child, Lisa M. Geophysics engring. degree, Colo. Sch. of Mines, 1962; MS in Oceanography, Geophysics, Oreg. State U., 1964; PhD in Geophysics, Calif. Inst. Tech., 1973. Grad. rsch. asst. dept. oceanography Oreg. State U., Corvallis, 1962-64; geophysicist ctr. astrogeology U.S. Geol. Survey, Flagstaff, Ariz., 1964-66; Fullbright-Hayes program rsch. fellow seismol. inst. U. Uppsala, Sweden, 1966-67; grad. rsch. asst. seismol. lab. Calif. Inst. Tech., Pasadena, 1967-73, sr. rsch. fellow seismol. lab., 1973-79; assoc. prof. attendant rank dept. geol. scis. U. Colo., Boulder, 1979-82, fellow Coop. Inst. Rsch. in Environ. Scis., 1979-84; v.p. technical applications and mktg. ISTAC, Inc., Pasadena, 1984-88; program dir. seismology NSF, Washington, 1989—; expert witness U.S. Ho. Reps. Com. on Sci. and Tech., 1977; mem. geodynamics rev. bd. Jet Propulsion Lab., 1980-82, com. on geodesy Nat. Acad. Scis., 1982-85; pres. Boulder Systems, Inc., Pasadena, 1987-88. Recipient Outstanding Achievement award U.S. Geol. Survey, 1964, Dir.'s award for mgmt. excellence NSF, 1995; scholar State of Colo., 1958-62, Mobil Oil Co., 1960; fellow Sweden-Am. Found., 1966. Mem. AAAS, Am. Geophysical Union, Seismol. Soc. Am., Soc. Exploration Geophysicists (scholar 1963), Tau Beta Pi, Phi Kappa Phi, Sigma Xi. Office: Nat Sci Found Geosciences 4201 Wilson Blvd Arlington VA 22230-0001

WHITCOMB, JAMES STUART, videographer, photographer, production company executive; b. Buffalo, May 7, 1957; s. C. Stuart and Helen Nancy (O'Reilly) W. BA in Journalism/Broadcasting, SUNY, Buffalo, 1983. Pres., owner Ad Astra Prodns., Williamsville, N.Y., 1987—; co-owner, videographer, photographer STB Prodns., Williamsville, N.Y., 1989—. Videographer, editor nature/stress reduction Videos A Celebration of the Four Seasons, 1991, Autumn on Cape Code and Martha's Vineyard, 1993, Gardens, Blossoms & Blooms, 1994, A Walk Through St. Francis Woods, 1994, Nantucket Noel: Christmas on Nantucket, 1994, Reflections: Nature's Watercolors, 1995, Autumn in Vermont, 1995, A Day On the Farm, 1995, Window Shopping, 1995, Singalong with your Old Favorites, 1997, A Celebration of the Four Seasons II: Seasons of the Seashore, 1997; videographer, writer promotion video Internat. Modeling and Talent Assn., 1990; videographer numerous prodns. for modelling, fashion, and spl. interest. Mem. People for Ethical Treatment of Animals, Wilderness Soc., Am. Hiking Soc., Nat. Audubon Soc., Farm Sanctuary. Avocations: skiing (former instr.), hiking (former mountain guide). Home: 71 Rinewalt St Williamsville NY 14221-5736 Office: Ad Astra and STB Prodns PO Box 1725 Williamsville NY 14231-1725

WHITCOMB, ROBERT BASSETT, journalist, editor; s. Robert B. and Alberta (Gillette) W.; m. Nancy Davison Spears, July 26, 1975; children: Lydia D., Elizabeth T. BA, Dartmouth Coll., 1970; MS, Columbia U., 1972. Cert. Am. Press Inst. Writer Boston Herald Traveler, 1970-71; editor, writer Wall Street Jour., N.Y.C., 1972-75; fin. editor Internat. Herald Tribune, Paris, 1983-87; news and bus. editor Providence Jour., 1976-82, news editor, 1987-89, editorial writer, 1989-92, editorial page editor, 1992—; mng. editor Brown World Bus. Adv., Providence, 1987-91; consulting editor, chmn. editorial adv. bd. Manisses Comm., Providence, 1987—; mem. exec. bd. Com. Fgn. Rels., Providence, 1989-92; trustee Am. Libr. Paris, 1984-87; co-moderator Truman Taylor Show, Providence, 1994—; columnist Primary Care Weekly, 1995—. Clapp-Poliak fellow Columbia U., 1972. Mem. Providence Art Club, Appalachian Mountain Club. Episcopalian. Office: Providence Jour Co 75 Fountain St Providence RI 02902-0050

WHITCOMB, VANESSA LIDE, editor; b. Washington, Apr. 29, 1961; d. David Reynolds Lide and Mary Ruth (Lomer) Clayton; m. David Chappell Whitcomb Jr., Oct. 19, 1991; 1 child, David Austell. BA in Govt. cum laude, Cornell U., 1983; MSc in Internat. Rels., London Sch. Econs., 1984. Publs. coord. Fedn. Am. Scientists, Washington, 1985-86; program assoc. Internat. Inst. for Energy Efficiency, Washington, 1987-90; assoc. editor China Bus. Rev., Washington, 1990-95, editor, 1995—. Office: China Bus Rev 1818 N St NW Ste 200 Washington DC 20036-2470

WHITCRAFT, EDWARD C. R., investment banker; b. Lutherville, Md., 1914; s. Franklin Pierce and Louise Virginia (Regester) W. B.A., Yale, 1936. With Bank of New York, 1936-58, v.p. investment research, trust investment com., 1952-58; with Clark, Dodge & Co., N.Y.C., 1958-74; sr. v.p. Kidder, Peabody & Co., Inc., 1974-87; assoc. Shields & Co., 1987—. With USNR, 1944-46. Mem. N.Y. Soc. Security Analysts. Home: PO Box 486 Locust Valley NY 11560-0486 Office: 140 Broadway New York NY 10005-1101 also: Box 566 230 Birch Hill Rd Locust Valley NY 11560-1832

WHITE, ADRIAN MICHAEL STEPHEN, financial executive; b. Erith, Eng., Aug. 15, 1940; s. Malcolm Royston and Joan May (Richards) W.; m. Elaine M. Dorion, 1966; children: Malcolm, Catherine. Grad., McGill U., Montreal, 1964. Chartered accountant, Que., Ont. With Coopers & Lybrand, chartered accountants, 1962-66; acting treas. Rothesay Paper Corp., 1965; asst. treas. Genstar Ltd., 1967-71; treas. Brinco Ltd.; also Churchill Falls (Labrador) Corp., 1971-75; treas. Algoma Steel Corp., Ltd., Sault Ste. Marie, Ont., 1975-80; v.p., chief fin. officer Little Long Lac Gold Mines Ltd., Toronto, Ont., 1980-81; v.p. Bank of Montreal, Toronto, 1981-88; exec. v.p., CFO, bd. dirs. Curragh Inc., Toronto, 1988-93; also bd. dirs. Curragh Resources Group, Toronto; fin. columnist Indsl. Mgmt. mag.; Curragh Inc.; chmn. White-Maven Corp., 1993—; mng. ptnr. Hannibal Group, 1996—; bd. dirs. Anvil Range Mining Corp., exec. v.p., CFP, 1994-96; bd. dirs. Doctors Hosp. Bd. dirs., chmn. Doctors Hosp. Found., 1986. Mem. Fin. Execs. Inst (past pres. Toronto chpt.), Can. Tax Found. Address: 72 Sir Williams Ln, Islington, ON Canada M9A 1V3

WHITE, ALICE ELIZABETH, physicist, researcher; b. Glen Ridge, N.J., Apr. 5, 1954; d. Alan David and Elizabeth Joyce (Jones) W.; m. Donald Paul Monroe, Oct. 13, 1990; children: Ellen Elizabeth White Monroe, Janet Clare White Monroe. BA in Physics, Middlebury (Vt.) Coll., 1976; MA in Physics, Harvard U., 1978, PhD in Physics, 1982. Postdoctoral mem. tech. staff AT&T Bell Labs., Murray Hill, N.J., 1982-84, mem. tech. staff, 1984-88, dept. head, 1988—. Contbr. over 100 articles to profl. pubs.; patentee in field. Recipient Alumni Achievement award Middlebury Coll., 1994. Fellow Am. Phys. Soc. (Maria Goeppert-Mayer award 1991); mem. Optical Soc. of Am., Materials Rsch. Soc., Phi Beta Kappa. Office: Bell Labs Lucent Technol PO Box 636 New Providence NJ 07974-0636

WHITE, ALLEN JORDAN, nursing home adminstrator, consultant; b. Boston, Mass. BSBA, Boston U.; PhD, Walden U., 1991. Adminstr., owner Whitehall Manor Nursing Home, Hyannis, Mass., 1975-85, Whitehall Pavillion, Hyannis, 1983—, Eagle Pond Nursing Home, Dennis, Mass., 1984-85; pres. Health Mgmt. Assn., Hyannis, 1985—; treas. Am. Aero Med. Transport, Hyannis, Mass., 1985—; mem. Boston Stock Exch.; del. 10th dist. White House Conf. on Aging, 1995. Exec. dir. Combined Action for Health Care Reform. Capt. U.S. Army, 1945-49. Fellow Am. Coll. Health Care Adminstrs. (cert., expert witness), Rotary. Office: Health Mgmt Assn 405 South St Hyannis MA 02601-5429

WHITE, ALVIN MURRAY, mathematics educator, consultant; b. N.Y.C., N.Y., June 21, 1925; s. Max and Beatrice White; m. Myra Goldstein, Dec. 4, 1946; children: Louis, Michael. BA, Columbia U., 1949; MA, UCLA, 1951; PhD, Stanford U., 1961. Acting instr. Stanford (Calif.) U., 1950-54; asst. prof. U. Santa Clara, Calif., 1954-61; postdoctoral fellow U. Wis., Madison, 1961-62; prof. Harvey Mudd Coll., Claremont, Calif., 1962—; vis. scholar MIT, 1975; initiator-facilitator humanistic math. network of over 2000 mathematicians worldwide; cons. coop. learning tutorial program Claremont Unified Sch. Dist. Author: Interdisciplinary Teaching, 1981; pub., editor: Humanistic Mathematics Network Jour.; contbr. articles to profl. jours. Served with USN, 1943-46, PTO. Grantee Fund for Improvement of Postsecondary Edn., Exxon Found. Mem. Am. Math. Soc., Math. Assn. Am., Nat. Coun. Tchrs. Math., Profl. Organizational Developers Network, Fedn. Am. Scientists, AAUP, Sigma Xi. Office: Harvey Mudd Coll 1250 N Dartmouth Ave Claremont CA 91711

WHITE, ALVIN SWAUGER, aerospace scientist, consultant; b. Berkeley, Calif., Dec. 9, 1918; s. Harold Hubbard and Ruth Amelia (Winkleman) W.; m. Betty Tomsett, Apr. 6, 1991; children: Stephen Alan, Cathie Lee, Leslie Ann. Student, U. Calif., Davis, 1936-37, U. Calif., Berkeley, 1937, 39-41; BME, U. Calif., Berkeley, 1947. Engr., test pilot N.Am. Aviation, Inc., L.A., 1954-61, chief test pilot L.A. divsn., 1961-66; mgr. flight ops., R & D TWA, N.Y.C., 1967-69; aerospace cons. Tuscon, 1969—. With USAAF, 1941-46; with USAF, 1948-54. Decorated D.F.C., Air medal with 9 oak leaf clusters; recipient Warsaw Uprising Cross, Republic of Poland, 1944, Iven C. Kincheloe award Soc. Exptl. Test Pilots, 1965, Golden Plate award Am. Acad. Achievement, 1966, Harmon Internat. trophy, 1967, Richard Hansford Burroughs Jr. award Flight Safety Found., 1969, Aerospace Walk of Honor, 1994. Fellow AIAA (assoc., Octave Chanute award 1965), Soc. Exptl. Text Pilots (pres. 1960-61): mem. Delta Upsilon. Republican. Episcopalian. Home and Office: 14254 N Fawnbrooke Dr Tucson AZ 85737 *As I grow older I look more and more for honesty in my associates. Without it you don't have much. An honest person probably knows better than anyone else how much courage it takes to be honest in some situations; so when you find honesty you find courage and character as well. And since I look for that in other people, I try very hard to be honest myself; I said, I try very hard!.*

WHITE, ANN STEWART, language educator, consultant; b. Petersburg, Va., July 24, 1960; d. John Carroll and Agnes Cordelia (Glunt) W. BA in Spanish and internat. studies, Willamette U., 1983; MA in Spanish, lang. and lits., U. Pitts., 1986, PhD Spanish, Linguistics, tchg. methods, 1988. Cert. Latin Am. studies, 1988. Asst. prof. spanish & teaching asst. coord. Mich. State U., East Lansing, Mich., 1988-94; asst. prof. hispanic studies Conn. Coll., New London, Conn., 1994-97; asst. prof. Spanish Va. Commonwealth Univ., Richmond, 1997—; adv. coun. mem. Ctrl. States Conf. Fgn. Langs., Indpls., 1991-92; manuscript cons., reviewer McGraw-Hill, Heinle & Heinle, John Wiley Publs., 1989—. Contbr. articles to profl. jours., book reviews. Recipient grants, 1989, 91. Mem. Mich. Fgn. Lang. Assn. (pres. 1992-93), Am. Assn. Tchrs. Spanish & Portuguese, Modern Lang. Assn., Phi Sigma Iota (pres. 1982-83, officer), Sigma Delta Pi (hon.), Golden Key Nat. Honor. Soc. (hon.). Democrat. Presbyterian. Avocations: painting, photography, calligraphy, travel. Office: Va Commonwealth Univ Dept Fgn Lang PO Box 842021 Richmond VA 23284-2021

WHITE, ANN WELLS, community activist; b. Kansas City, Mo., Mar. 16, 1927; d. William Gates and Annie Loretta (Morton) Wells; m. Norman E. White, Oct. 2, 1949 (div. Dec. 1977); children: Thomas Wells, Norman Lee. BJ, U. Mo., 1948. Asst. to pres. Cities in Schs., 1978-79. Lobbyist Common Cause, Atlanta, 1972-73; vol. Jimmy Carter's Peanut Brigade, 1976, Carter/Mondale campaign, 1980; bd. dirs., vice chair Atlanta Area Svcs. for the Blind, 1973-81; Gov.'s Commn. on the Status of Women, Atlanta, 1974-76; office mgr. Carter/Mondale Transition Office, Atlanta, 1976; chair evaluation com. United Way Met. Atlanta, 1980-90; bd. dirs. Mems. Guild, The High Mus. of Art, Atlanta, 1982-83, Hillside Hosp., Atlanta, 1989-94, Ga. Forum, Atlanta, 1988-91; bd. dirs. Planned Parenthood of Atlanta area, 1975-89, pres., 1978-81; bd. dirs. Planned Parenthood Fedn. Am., N.Y.C., 1980-86, chair ann. meeting, New Orleans, 1986; legis. chair, lobbyist Ga. Women's Polit. Caucus, 1984-90; convenor, founding chair Georgians for Choice, 1989. Democrat. Presbyterian. Home: Colony House 1237 145 Fifteenth St Atlanta GA 30309

WHITE, ANNETTE JONES, early childhood education administrator; b. Albany, Ga., Aug. 29, 1939; d. Paul Lawrence and Delores Christine (Berry) Jones; m. Frank Irvin White, Nov. 13, 1964; children: Melanie Francine, Sharmian Lynell. BA, Spelman Coll., 1964; MEd, Va. State U., 1980. Tchr. Flint Ave Child Devel. Ctr., Albany, 1966-67; tchr., supr. Flintside Child Devel. Ctr., Albany, 1967-68; tchr., dir. Albany Ga. Community Sch., 1968-69; tchr. Martin Luther King Community Ctr., Atlanta, 1975-77, The Appleton Sch., Atlanta, 1977-78; sec., proofreader The Atlanta Daily World, 1978-80; tchr. kindergarten Spelman Coll., Atlanta, 1981-88, dir. nursery and kindergarten, lectr. in edn., 1988—; cons., presenter child devel. assoc. program Morris Brown Coll., Atlanta, 1991; presenter ann. child care conf. Waycross (Ga.) Coll., 1993. Contbr. articles to profl. jours. including Am. Visions, Sage, So. Exposure, S.W. Georgian, Atlanta Tribune, Atlanta Daily World, Double Stitch. Mem. Peace Action, Washington, 1990—, Children's Def. Action Coun., Washington, 1990—; mem. Native Am. Rights Fund, Am. Indian Rights Coun. Mem. AAUW, ASCD, NOW, Acad. Am. Poets, Assn. Childhood Edn. Internat., Nat. Asn. Edn. Young Children, Nat. Black Child Devel. Inst., Ga. Assn. Young Children (cons., presenter 1992), Nat. Coun. Negro Women, Atlanta Assn. Edn. Young Children, Sierra Club. Avocations: cane weaving, crocheting, cooking, drawing, reading, creative writing. Office: Spelman Coll Nursery-Kinder 350 Spelman Ln SW # 89 Atlanta GA 30314-4346

WHITE, ARTHUR CLINTON, physician; b. Williamsburg, Ky., Aug. 1, 1925; s. Herman Roya and Ethel Margaret (Goins) W.; m. Mary Katherine Pope, Dec. 27, 1949; children: Anne Litton White, Arthur Clinton Jr., Herman Roy II. BS, U. Ky., 1948; MD, Harvard U., 1952. Intern, then resident in medicine Vanderbilt U. Hosp., Nashville, 1952-57; asst. prof. medicine U. Louisville Med. Sch., 1958-63; assoc. prof. Med. Coll. Ga., 1963-67; prof. medicine, dir. infectious disease div. Ind. U. Med. Sch., 1967—; mem. drug efficacy study com. Nat. Acad. Scis., 1967. Contbr. articles med. publns. Served with USAAF, 1944-45. John and Mary R. Markle scholar, 1958-63. Mem. Infectious Disease Soc. Am., Cen. Soc. Clin. Rsch., Am. Clin. and Climatol. Assn., Med. Benevolence Found. (trustee 1986—), Meridian Hills Country Club, Skyline Club. Republican. Presbyterian. Home: 6363 Glen Coe Dr Indianapolis IN 46260-4736 Office: 1100 W Michigan St Indianapolis IN 46202-5208

WHITE, AUGUSTUS AARON, III, orthopedic surgeon; b. Memphis, June 4, 1936; s. Augustus Aaron and Vivian (Dandridge) W.; m. Anita Ottemo; children: Alissa Alexandra, Atina Andrea, Annica Akila. AB in Psychology cum laude, Brown U., 1957; MD, Stanford U., 1961; D in Med. Sci., Karolinska Inst., Sweden, 1969; Advanced Mgmt. Program, Harvard U., 1984; DHL (hon.), U. New Haven, 1987; DMS (hon.), Brown U., 1997. Diplomate Nat. Bd. Examiners, Am. Bd. Orthopaedic Surgery. Intern U. Mich. Hosp., Ann Arbor, 1961-62; asst. resident in gen. surgery Presbyn. Med. Center, San Francisco, 1962-63; asst. resident in orthopaedic surgery Yale Med. Center, New Haven, 1963-65, sr. instr., resident orthopaedic surgery, 1965-66; asst. prof. orthopaedic surgery Yale Med. Sch., 1969-72, assoc. prof., 1972-76, prof., 1977-78, dir. biomech. research dept. orthopedics, 1978-89; prof. orthopedic surgery Harvard Med. Sch., 1978—; orthopedic surgeon-in-chief Beth Israel Hosp., Boston, 1978-96, chief spine surgery divsn., orthopedic surgeon-in chief, 1991-92, emeritus, 1996—; sr. assoc. orthopedic surgery Children's Hosp. Med. Ctr., Boston, 1979-89; assoc. in orthopedic surgery Brigham & Women's Hosp., Boston, 1980-89; cons. div. surgery Sidney Farber Cancer Inst., Boston, 1980—; rschr. biomechanics lab. Beth Israel Hosp.; chair sci. adv. bd., dir. OrthoLogic, Inc., Phoenix; bd. dirs. Am. Shared Hosp. Svcs., San Francisco; cons. orthopaedic surgery West Haven (Conn.) VA Hosp., 1970—, Hill Health Ctr., New Haven, 1970—; chief orthopedic surgery Conn. Health Care Plan, 1976-78; mem. adv. coun. Nat. Inst. Arthritis, Metabolism and Digestive Disease, NIH, 1979-82; mem. admission scom. Yale Med. Sch., 1970-72; presenter, moderator Symposium on Cervical Myelopathy, San Francisco, 1987; chmn. grant rev. com. NIH, 1985; founding mem., bd. overseers Brown U. Sch. of Medicine, 1996—; bd. overseers WGBH Radio/TV, Boston, 1996—. Author: (monograph) Analysis of the Mechanics of the Thoracic Spine in Man, Leprosy, The Foot and The Orthopaedic Surgeon at Am. Acad. Orthopaedic Surgeons, 1970; book Clinical Biomechanics of the Spine, 1978, 2d edit., 1990; Symposium on Idiopathic Low Back Pain, 1982, Your Aching Back-A Doctor's Guide to Relief, 1983, rev. and updated edit., 1990, translated in German, 1992; prin. editor Time/Life Med. Video Back Pain; contbr. articles to profl. jours., chpts. to sci. books. Trustee Brown U., Providence, 1971-76, bd. fellows, 1981-92, chmn. corp. com. on minority affairs, 1981-86, chmn. corp. com. on med. edn., 1989-96; trustee Northfield Mt. Hermon Sch., Northfield, Mass., 1976-81; bd. dirs. The Partnership, Boston, 1984—. Capt. AUS, 1966-68. Decorated Bronze Star medal; named

1 of 10 Outstanding Young Men U.S. Jr. C. of C., 1969, Selected for Exceptional Black Scientist poster series CIBA-GEIGY Corp., 1982; recipient Martin Luther King, Jr. Med. Achievement award, 1972, Kappa Delta award, nat. prize for outstanding research in orthopaedics field, 1975; nat. award for spinal research Eastern Orthopaedic Assn., 1980; Disting. Service award Northfield Mt. Hermon Sch. Alumni Assn., 1983; William Rogers award Associated Alumni Brown U., 1984; Outstanding Achievement award Delta Upsilon, 1986; Am.-Brit.-Canadian Travelling fellow Am. Orthopedic Assn., 1975. Fellow Am. Acad. Orthopaedic Surgeons, Scoliosis Rsch. Soc.; mem. Orthopaedic Rsch. Soc., Cervical Spine Rsch. Soc., Am. Acad. Orthopaedic Surgeons (chmn. com. on diversity), Internat. Soc. for Study Lumbar Spine, Internat. Soc. Orthopaedic Surgery and Traumatology, Nat. Med. Assn. (Orthopaedic Scholar award 1994), Cervical Spine Rsch. Soc. (pres. 1988), N.Am. Spine Soc., Acad. Orthopaedic Soc., Sigma Xi, Sigma Pi Phi.

WHITE, BARRY BENNETT, lawyer; b. Boston, Feb. 13, 1943; s. Harold and Rosalyn (Schneider) W.; m. Eleanor Greenberg; Joshua S., Adam J., Benjamin D. AB magna cum laude, Harvard U., 1964; JD magna cum laude, Harvard U., 1967. Bar: Mass. 1967, U.S. Dist. Ct. Mass.1967, U.S. Ct. Appeals, (1st cir.) 1967. Assoc. Foley Hoag & Eliot, Boston, 1969-74, ptnr., 1975—, mem. exec. com., 1981-92, 93—, chmn. exec. com., 1987-91, mng. ptnr., 1991-92, 93—, mem. exec. com. 1991—, sec. 1992-93; chmn. Lex Mundi, 1994. Secretary, General Counsel, Executive Committee, Greater Boston Chamber of Commerce. bd. dirs., exec. com. Mass. Assn. Mental Health, 1985—, pres., 1993-95; bd. dirs. Boston Mcpl. Rsch. Bureau, Vol. Lawyers Project, 1987-93, Support Ctr. of Mass., 1988-95; mem. Jewish Family and Children's Services, Boston, 1979-87; bd. visitors Boston U. Grad. Sch. Dentistry, 1981—; bd. trustees Jewish Community Relations Council, 1988-92; chmn. com. for Clinton/Gore New Eng. Lawyers, 1992-96,chmn. Tsongas for Pres. Com., 1991—. With USPHS, 1967-69. Mem. ABA, Mass. BarAssn., Boston Bar Assn., Internat. Bar Assn., Am. Acad. Hosp. Attys., Am. Hosp.Assn. (adj. task force on health planning, 1982-84, contbg. editor hosp. law manual, 1981-84). Democrat. Clubs: Harvard of Boston, Badminton & Tennis. Editor: Harvard Law Rev., 1965-67. Office: Foley Hoag & Eliot 1 Post Office Sq Boston MA 02109

WHITE, BENJAMIN VROOM, III, lawyer; b. Hartford, Conn., Nov. 25, 1941; s. Benjamin Vroom and Charlotte (Conover) W.; m. Elizabeth Dodge, Sept. 6, 1969; children: Constance Atwood, Charles Conover. AB, Harvard U., 1964; MAT, Harvard Grad. Sch. of Edn., 1970; JD, Boston U., 1974. Law clk. to Hon. Alfred H. Joslin R.I. Supreme Ct., Providence, 1974-75; assoc., ptnr. Hinckley, Allen, Salisburg & Parsons, Providence, 1975-81; ptnr. Vetter & White, Providence, 1981—; mem. faculty MCLE and Nat. inst. Trial Advocacy, Boston, 1983—. Editor Note and Case, Boston U. Law Rev., 1993-94; contbr. articles to profl. jours. Bd. govs. Gordon Sch., East Providence, 1981-87, 1st v.p., 1984—; bd. dirs. Lipptt Hill Tutorial, Providence, 1978-82, Westport River Watershed Alliance, 1989-95. lt. USNR, 1964-68. Mem. ABA (litigation sect.), R.I. Bar Assn. (fed. ct. bench and bar com. 1982—, chmn. 1993—), Boston Bar Assn., R.I. Fed. Ct. Bd. of Bar Examiners, New Bedford Yacht Club, Harvard (R.I. and N.Y.C.) Club, Hope (Providence) Club, Acoaxet (Westport, Mass.) Club. Republican. Episcopalian. Office: Vetter & White Inc 20 Washington Pl Providence RI 02903-1328

WHITE, BETTY, actress, comedienne; b. Oak Park, Ill., Jan. 17, 1922; m. Allen Ludden, 1963 (dec.). Student pub. schs., Beverly Hills, Calif. Appearances on radio shows This Is Your FBI, Blondie, The Great Gildersleeve; actress: (TV series) including Hollywood on Television, The Betty White Show, 1954-58, Life With Elizabeth, 1953-55, A Date With The Angels, 1957-58, The Pet Set, 1971, Mary Tyler Moore Show, 1974-77, The Betty White Show, 1977, The Golden Girls, 1985-92 (Emmy award for best actress 1986), The Golden Palace, 1992-93, Maybe This Time, 1995—; (TV miniseries) The Best Place to be, 1979, The Gossip Columnist, 1980, (film) Advise and Consent, 1962; guest appearances on other programs; summer stock appearances Guys and Dolls, Take Me Along, The King and I, Who Was That Lady?, Critic's Choice, Bells are Ringing. Recipient Emmy award NATAS, 1975, 76, 86; L.A. Area Emmy award, 1952. Mem. AFTRA, Am. Humane Assn., Greater L.A. Zoo Assn. (dir.). Office: care William Morris Agy care Tony Fantozzi 151 S El Camino Dr Beverly Hills CA 90212-2704*

WHITE, BEVERLY JANE, cytogeneticist; b. Seattle, Oct. 9, 1938. Grad., U. Wash., 1959, MD, 1963. Diplomate Nat. Bd. Med. Examiners, Am. Bd. Pediatrics, Am. Bd. Med. Genetics; lic physician and surgeon, Wash., Va., N.J. Rsch. trainee dept. anatomy Sch. Medicine U. Wash., Seattle, 1960-62, pediatric resident dept. pediatrics, 1967-69; rotating intern Phila. Gen. Hosp., 1963-64; rsch. fellow med. ob-gyn. unit Cardiovascular Rsch. Inst. U. Calif. Med. Ctr., San Francisco, 1964-65; staff fellow lab. biomed. scis. Nat. Inst. Child Health and Human Devel. NIH, Bethesda, Md., 1965-67, sr. staff fellow, attending physician lab. exptl. pathology Nat. Inst. Arthritis, Metabolism and Digestive Diseases, 1969-74, acting chief sect. cytogenetics, 1975-76, rsch. med. officer, attending physician sect. cytogenetics lab. cellular biology and genetics, 1974-86, dir. cytogenetics unit, interinstitute med. genetics program clin. ctr., 1987-95; dir. cytogenetics Corning Clin. Labs., Teterboro, N.J., 1995-96; assoc. med dir. cytogenetics Nichols Inst.-Quest Diagnostics, San Juan Capistrano, Calif., 1996—; vis. scientist dept. pediat. divsn. genetics U. Wash. Sch. Medicine, 1983-84; intramural cons. NIH, 1975-95; cons. to assoc. editor Jour. Nat. Cancer Inst., 1976; cons. dept. ob-gyn. Naval Hosp., Bethesda, 1988-89; lectr., presenter in field. Recipient Mosby Book award, 1963, Women of Excellence award U. Wash. and Seattle Profl. chpt. Women in Comm., 1963, Reuben award Am. Soc. for Study Sterility, 1963. Fellow Am. Coll. Med. Genetics (founding), Am. Acad. Pediatrics; mem. AMA. Am. Soc. Human Genetics, Assn. Genetic Technologists (program com. 1989). Home: One St Maxime Laguna Niguel CA 92677 Office: Nichols Inst/Quest Diagnostics Inc Dept Cytogenetics San Juan Capistrano CA 92690-6130

WHITE, BURTON LEONARD, educational psychologist, author; b. Boston, June 27, 1929; s. Jack J. and Evelyn S. W.; m. Janet Hodgson-White; children—Laura, Emily, David, Daniel. B.S.M.E., Tufts Coll., 1949; B.A., Boston U., 1956, M.A., 1957; Ph.D., Brandeis U., 1960. Research assoc. Brandeis U., 1960-62, M.I.T., 1962-65; sr. research assoc. Harvard Grad. Sch. Edn., 1965-78; head Center Parent Edn., Newton, Mass., 1978—. Author: books including Human Infants, 1971, Experience and Environment, Vol. I, 1973, Vol. II, 1978, The First Three Years of Life, 1975, latest edit. 1995, The Origins of Competence, 1979, Educating the Infant and Toddler, 1988, Raising A Happy, Unspoiled Child, 1994, The New First Three Years of Life, 1995; contbr. articles to profl. jours. Served with AUS, 1951-53. Home: 115 Pine Ridge Rd Newton MA 02168-1616

WHITE, BYRON R., former United States supreme court justice; b. Ft. Collins, Colo., June 8, 1917; m. Marion Stearns; children: Charles, Nancy. Grad., U. Colo., 1938; Rhodes scholar, Oxford (Eng.) U.; grad., Yale Law Sch. Clk. to chief justice U.S., 1946-47; atty. firm Lewis, Grant & Davis, Denver, 1947-60; dep. atty. gen. U.S., 1961-62; assoc. justice Supreme Ct., U.S., 1962-93; ret., 1993. Served with USNR, World War II, Pacific. Mem. Phi Beta Kappa, Phi Gamma Delta, Order of Coif. Address: US Supreme Ct Supreme Ct Bldg 1 First St NE Washington DC 20543

WHITE, C. THOMAS, state supreme court justice; b. Humphrey, Nebr., Oct. 5, 1928; s. John Ambrose and Margaret Elizabeth (Costello) W.; m. Joan White, Oct. 9, 1971; children: Michaela, Thomas, Patrick. JD, Creighton U., 1952. Bar: Nebr. County atty. Platte County (Nebr.), Columbus, 1955-65; judge 21st Dist. Ct. Nebr., Columbus, 1965-77; justice Nebr. Supreme Ct., Lincoln, 1977—, chief justice, 1995—. Served with U.S. Army, 1946-47. Roman Catholic. Clubs: Elks, KC. Office: Nebr Supreme Ct 2413 State Capitol Bldg Lincoln NE 68509*

WHITE, CALVIN JOHN, zoo executive, financial manager, zoological association executive; b. Twillingate, Nfld., Can., Feb. 28, 1948; s. Harold and Meta Blanche (Abbott) W.; m. Lorna Joan Maclachlan; children: Chelsea Elizabeth, Evan Alexander. B in Commerce, U. Toronto, Ont., Can., 1971. Fin. analyst Can. GE Co. Ltd., Toronto, 1971-72, Ford Motor Co. Can., Oakville, Ont., 1972-74; sr. fin. analyst Municipality of Met. Toronto, 1974-77, asst. dir. budget and ops. analysis, 1977-81, dir. budget analysis and internal control, 1981-86; gen. mgr. Met. Toronto Zoo, 1986—; pres. Zool. Soc. Met. Toronto, 1994—; bd. dirs. Met. Toronto Conv. and Visitors Assn., Can. Assn. Zool. Parks and Aquariums. Fellow Am. Zoo and Aquarium Assn.; mem. Am. Assn. Zoo Keepers, Inst. Pub. Adminstrn. Can. (bd. dirs. 1989-91), Zool. Soc. Met. Toronto (bd. dirs. 1991—, pres. 1994—), World Conservation Union, Internat. Union Dirs. Zool. Gardens, Toronto Sportmen's Assn., Mensa. Office: Met Toronto Zoo, 361A Old Finch Ave, Scarborough, ON Canada M1B 5K7

WHITE, CARL EDWARD, JR., pharmaceutical adminstrator; b. Huntington, W.Va., Apr. 4, 1955; s. Carl Edward Sr. and Peggy Joan (Church) W.; m. Denise Karen McDaniel, May 26, 1979; children: Daniel Aaron, David Kenton, Caitlin Ruth. BS, Purdue U., 1977; MBA, Ga. State U., 1996. Profl. sales rep. Ciba-Geigy Pharms., Huntington, 1977-85, dist. sales mgr., 1985-93; area bus. dir Ciba-Geigy Pharms., Atlanta, 1993-94; dist. bus. mgr. Atlanta, 1994—. Bd. dirs. Coventry Homeowners' Assn., Peachtree City, Ga., 1991, Park Brooke Homeowners' Assn., Alpharetta, Ga., 1996; chmn. deacons First Bapt. Ch., Peachtree City, 1992. Republican. So. Bapt. Avocations: computers, singing, gardening. Home: 3905 Brookline Dr Alpharetta GA 30202

WHITE, CHARLES ALBERT, JR., medical educator, obstetrician-gynecologist; b. San Diego, Aug. 1, 1922; s. Charles Albert and Helen (Hardy) W.; m. Suzan A. Alikadi, Dec. 6, 1960; children: Craig, Scott, Jennifer. D.V.M., Colo. State U., 1945; M.D., U. Utah, 1955. Diplomate: Am. Bd. Ob-Gyn. Intern Salt Lake County Hosp., 1955; resident in ob-gyn U. Iowa, 1959-61, mem. faculty ob-gyn, 1961-74; chmn. dept. ob-gyn W. Va. U., Morgantown, 1974-80; prof., chmn. dept. ob-gyn La. State U. Med. Ctr., New Orleans, 1980-92. Served to lt. comdr. USNR, 1957-59. Fellow ACS, Am. Gyn-Ob Soc.; mem. Am. Coll. Ob-Gyn, Central Assn. Ob-Gyn. Home and Office: 33 Chateau Du Jardin Kenner LA 70065

WHITE, CHARLES H., food science and technology educator; b. Birmingham, Ala., Mar. 15, 1943. BS, Miss. State U., 1965, MS, 1969; PhD, U. Mo., 1971. Sr. foods scientist Archer Daniels Midland Co., 1971-72; asst. prof. U. Ga., 1972-76; dir. quality assurance Dean Foods Co., 1976-80; prof. La. State U., 1980-85; E.W. Custer prof. dairy foods Miss. State U., 1985—, head dept. food sci. and tech., 1991—; mem. sci. adv. com. Dairy Rsch. Found.; mem. sci. adv. com. Nat. Dairy Promotion and Rsch. Bd., 1987-90; mem. task force on dairy tech., bd. on agr. NAS, 1988—; cons. with dairy food plants throughout U.S. and Can. Mem. editorial bd. Cultured Dairy Products Jour., Jour. Dairy Sci.; contbr. chpts. to books, articles to profl. jours. Served to col. U.S. Army Res., 1982-87. Recipient numerous grants. Mem. Am. Cultured Dairy Products Inst. (sec. 1988-89, tech. coun. 1979—), Am. Dairy Sci. Assn. (bd. dirs. 1984-87, v.p. So. div. 1988-89, pres. 1989-90), Internat. Assn. Milk, Food, and Environ. Sanitarians (pubs. com. 1979-82), Am. Men and Women of Sci., Inst. Food Technologists (microbiology sect., quality assurance sect.), Environ. Mgmt. Assn. Office: Miss State U Drawer NH Dept Food Sci and Tech Mississippi State MS 39762

WHITE, CHARLES OLDS, aeronautical engineer; b. Beirut, Apr. 2, 1931; s. Frank Laurence and Dorothy Alice (Olds) W.; m. Mary Carolyn Liechty, Sept. 3, 1955; children—Charles Cameron, Bruce Blair. B.S. in Aero. Engring., MIT, 1953, M.S., 1954. Aero. engr. Douglas Aircraft Long Beach, 1954-60, aero. engr. Ford Aerospace & Communication Corp., Calif., 1960-79, sr. engr. specialist, 1979-80, staff office of gen. mgr. DIVAD div., 1980-81, tech. mgr. DIVAD Fuzes, 1981-82, supr. design and analysis DIVAD div., 1982-85; tech. mgr. Advanced Ordnance Programs, 1985-87, PREDATOR Missile, 1987-90, cons. 1990-93; engring. tech. prin. Aerojet Corp., 1993-94; tech. prin. OCSW Ammunition Olin Ordinance, 1994-97, cons., 1997—. Mem. AIAA, Nat. Mgmt. Assn., Am. Aviation Hist. Soc., Sigma Gamma Tau. Republican. Presbyterian. Clubs: Masters Swimming, Newport Beach Tennis. Contbr. articles to profl. jours.

WHITE, CHRISTINE, physical education educator; b. Taunton, Mass., Apr. 1, 1905; d. Peregrine Hastings and Sara (Lawrence) W. Cert., Boston Sch. Phys. Edn.; BS, Boston U., 1935, MEd, 1939. Instr. Winthrop Coll., Rock Hill, S.C., 1927-29; instr., asst. prof. The Woman's Coll. U. N.C., Greensboro, N.C., 1929-41; assoc. prof., head dept. physical edn. Meredith Coll., Raleigh, N.C., 1941-43; assoc. prof., prof. chair dept. physical edn. Wheaton Coll., Norton, Mass., 1943-70, prof. emerita, 1970—. co-editor Taunton Architecture: A Reflection of the City's History, 1981, 89. Chmn. Hist. Dist. Study Com., 1975-78, Recreation Commn., 1972-81; mem. Hist. Dist. Commn., 1979—, sec., 1979-86, acting chair, 1992-94; mem. Park and Recreation Commn., 1982—; bd. dirs. Star Theatre for the Arts, Inc., 1993—. Fellow AAHPERD; mem. AAUP (pres. Wheaton Coll. chpt. 1960-61), AAUW, LWV, Nat. Assn. Phys. Edn. in Higher Edn., Pi Lambda Theta. Avocations: travelling, historic preservation, theatre, music. Home: 40 Highland Ter Taunton MA 02780-4729

WHITE, CLEVELAND STUART, JR., architect; b. Norwalk, Conn., Jan. 10, 1937; s. Cleveland Stuart and Helen Thurston (Stephenson) W.; m. Matilda Bowen Romaine, Sept. 14, 1963; children: Cleveland Stuart III, Laura Brewster. AB, Princeton U., 1959; BArch, Columbia U., 1963. Registered architect, Vt., N.H., N.Y., Mass., Conn. Draftsman, designer Hill & Assocs., Cambridge, Mass., 1964-68, Roy W. Banwell, Jr., Hanover, N.H., 1968-71; prin. Banwell White & Arnold, Hanover, N.H., 1968-84, Banwell White Arnold Hemberger & Ptnrs., Hanover, N.H., 1984—; cons. Brookhaven (N.Y.) Nat. Lab., 1979-83; adj. prof. environ. studies Dartmouth Coll., Hanover, 1981; lectr. MIT Summer Inst., Cambridge, 1979, 80, 81. Author, editor: Case Study: 424 W 33rd Street Apartment Conversion, 1981; prin. works include Dartmouth Coll. Boathouse, Madbury (N.H.) Elem. Sch., Pinckney Boathouse, Wolfeboro, N.H., Addition to Barton Hall-U. N.H., Durham, Soc. for Protection of N.H. Forests Conservation Ctr., Concord, Whitetail Ski and Summer Resort, Franklin County, Pa., Center Moriches (N.Y.) Free Pub. Libr. Recipient Merit award Am. Wood Coun., 1981, 2 Energy Innovation award U.S. Dept. Energy, 1984, 87, 1st Honor award New Eng. Reg. Coun. Architects, 1978, Internat. Solar Energy Soc./ Progressive Architecture Mag., 1982. Mem. AIA (chmn. environ. task force N.H. chpt. 1993-95, honor awards 1990, 92). Democrat. Avocations: sailing, skiing, music, gardening, art. Home: PO Box 40 Norwich VT 05055-0040

WHITE, CONSTANCE BURNHAM, state official; b. Odgen, Utah, July 2, 1954; d. Owen W. and Colleen (Redd) Burnham; m. Wesley Robert White, Mar. 18, 1977. BA in English magna cum laude, U. Utah, 1976, postgrad., 1977; postgrad., Boston Coll., 1979; JD, Loyola U., 1981. Law clerk Kruse, Landa, Zimmerman & Maycock, Salt Lake City, 1979; law clerk legal dept. Bell & Howell, Lincolnwood, Ill., 1980; clerk, assoc. Parsons, Behle & Latimer, Salt Lake City, 1981-82; assoc. Reynolds, Vance, Deason & Smith, Salt Lake City, 1982-83; chief enforcement sect. Utah Securities Divsn., Salt Lake City, 1984-87, chief licensing sect., 1988, asst. dir., 1989-90; legal counsel Utah Dept. Commerce, Salt Lake City, 1990-92, exec. dir., 1993-95, commsr pub service div, 1995; mem. Gov.'s Securities Fraud Task Force, 1984; spl. asst. atty. gen., 1986-88; spl. asst. U.S. atty., 1986—. Mem. North Am. Securities Adminstrs. Assn. (vice chair market manipulation com. 1988-89, penny stock/telecom. fraud com. 1989-90, chair uniform examinations com. 1990-92, chair forms revision com. 1992), Utah State Bar (securities adv. com. 1991—, task force on community-based mediation 1991—, chair securities sect. 1992-93). Office: Utah Pub Svc Commn 160 S 300 E Salt Lake City UT 84111-2005

WHITE, CRAIG MITCHELL, lawyer; b. Phoenixville, Pa., Aug. 12, 1952. BA, Dartmouth Coll., 1974; JD, Ind. U., 1977. Bar: Ill. 1977, U.S. Dist. Ct. (no. dist.) Ill. 1977, U.S. Dist. Ct. (cen. dist.) Ill. 1980, U.S. Dist. Ct. (no. dist.) Ind. 1983. Ptnr. Wildman, Harrold, Allen & Dixon, Chgo., 1977—. Mem. Order of the Coif, Phi Beta Kappa. Office: Wildman Harrold Allen & Dixon 30th Fl 225 W Wacker Dr Fl 30 Chicago IL 60606-1224

WHITE, DALE ANDREW, journalist; b. Jacksonville, Fla., Feb. 17, 1958; s. John Andrew and Jeannelle Corinne White. B in Journalism, U. Fla., 1983. Reporter UPI, Miami, Fla., 1980, Orlando (Fla.) Sentinel Star, 1981; corr. Fla. Times-Union, Gainesville, 1982; reporter, columnist, editorial writer Sarasota Herald-Tribune, Bradenton, Fla., 1983—. Contbr. short stories to profl. publs. Recipient Chmn.'s award N.Y. Times, 1987, 3d place Editorial Writing award Fla. Soc. Newspaper Editors, 1993, 1st place Ind. Reporter Media award Fla. Sch. Bds. Assn., 1996. Office: PO Box 1695 Bradenton FL 34206-1695

WHITE, DAVID CALVIN, electrical engineer, energy educator, consultant; b. Sunnyside, Wash., Feb. 18, 1922; s. David Calvin Sr. and Leafie Eloise (Scott) W.; m. Glorianna Guilii, July 30, 1949 (dec. Dec. 1965); 1 child, Julie Anne White Coman (dec.); m. Margot Ann Fuller, June 4, 1966; 1 child, Constance Anne. B.S., Stanford U., 1946, M.S., 1947, Ph.D., 1949. Registered profl. engr. Elec. engr. Kaiser Industries, Vancouver, Wash., 1941-42, 43-45; assoc. prof. elec. engring. U. Fla., Gainesville, 1949-52; asst. prof. elec. engring. MIT, Cambridge, 1952-54, assoc. prof., 1954-58, prof., 1958-62, Ford prof. engring., 1962-92, dir. energy lab., 1972-89, Ford prof. engring. emeritus, 1992—; pres., dir. Energy Conversion, Inc., 1961-64; cons. Gulf Oil, 1976-84, Johnson Controls, 1980—; sr. advisor and vis. prof. Birla Inst., India, 1968-70; mem. council U. Benin, Nigeria, 1972; trustee Lowell Tech. Inst., Mass., 1972-74; mem. corp. Woods Hole Oceanographic Inst., Mass., 1977-84; mem. research coordinating panel Gas Research Inst., Chgo., 1977-85; chmn. adv. council Electric Power Research Inst., Palo Alto, Calif., 1984-86, mem., 1980-87. Author: (with others) Electromechanical Energy Conversion, 1959. Commr. Electric Light Plant, Concord, Mass., 1959-64, Kalmia Woods Water Dist., Concord, 1960-63. Named hon. prof. Instituto Politecnico Nacional, Mex., 1961. Fellow IEEE; mem. Nat. Acad. Engring., Am. Acad. Arts and Scis., Am. Soc. Engring. Edn. (George Westinghouse award 1961), Phi Beta Kappa, Sigma Xi, Tau Beta Pi, Eta Kappa Nu. Republican. Clubs: New Seabury Country, Woodfield Country. Avocations: golf; boating. Home: 8 Chart Way Popponesset Island New Seabury MA 02649 also: 799 E Jeffery St Apt 314 Boca Raton FL 33487 Office: MIT 77 Massachusetts Ave Rm E40-473 Cambridge MA 02139-4301

WHITE, DAVID CLEAVELAND, microbial ecologist, environmental toxicologist; b. Moline, Ill., May 18, 1929; s. Frederick Berryhill and Dorothy (Cleaveland) W.; m. Sandra Jean Shoults, July 7, 1957; children: Winifred Shoults, Christopher Cleaveland, Andrew Berryhill. AB magna cum laude, Dartmouth Coll., 1951; MD, Tufts U., 1955; PhD, Rockefeller U., 1962. Rotating intern Hosp. of U. Pa., 1955-56; asst. prof., assoc. prof., then prof. biochemistry U. Ky., Lexington, 1962-72; prof. biol. sci. Fla. State U., Tallahassee, 1972-86; disting. scientist U. Tenn./Oak Ridge Nat. Lab., Knoxville, 1986—; prof. microbiology, ecology U. Tenn., Knoxville, 1986—; prin. investigator Oak Ridge (Tenn.) Nat. Lab., 1988—; mem. adv. com. Ctr. Theol. Inquiry, Princeton (N.J.) U., 1986-91; former dir. Ctr. for Environ. Biotech., 1991—; founder Inst. Applied Microbiology, Knoxville, 1986-91; mem. sci. adv. panel Mich. State Ctr. Microbial Ecology, Lansing, 1989-92, Mont. State Ctr. for Biofilm Engring., Bozeman, Mont., 1991-95; mem. sci. adv. bd. Nat. Water Rsch. Inst., 1993—; mem. Naval Rsch. Adv. Commn., 1995—; dir. Microbial Insights, Inc., Knoxville, 1992-95; Wellcome vis. prof. U. Okla., Norman, 1984-85; spkr. profl. confs. Author: Sex, Drugs and Pollution, 1983, 2d edit., 1985; founding editor-in-chief Jour. Microbiol. Methods, 1985—; author numerous refereed sci. publs. Lt. M.C. USN, 1956-58. Recipient P.R. Edwards award S.E. br. Am. Soc. Microbiology, 1981, Procter & Gamble Applied and Environ., Microbiology award Am. Soc. Microbiology, 1993, Applied and Environ. Microbiol. award ASM, 1993, Antarctic Svc. medal USN/NSF, 1984, Sci. and Tech. Achievement award EPA, 1987, Athalie Richardson Clarke prize in water sci. and tech. Nat. Water Rsch. Inst., 1995. Presbyterian. Achievements include discovery of signature biomarker technique for microbial biomass, community structure and nutritional status from environmental samples, microbial ecology of deep subsurface, tropical and antarctic sediments, microbial biofilms in microbial influenced corrosion, biosensors environmental biotechnology. Office: Ctr for Environ Biotech 10515 Research Dr Ste 300 Knoxville TN 37932-2572

WHITE, DAVID HYWEL, physics educator; b. Cardiff, Wales, June 4, 1931; came to U.S., 1959, naturalized, 1966; s. William Richard and Bessie (Morgan) W.; m. Frances Mary Shearman, July 23, 1954; children: Richard Gerwyn, Christopher David. B.S., U. Wales, 1953; Ph.D., Birmingham U., 1956. Asst. lectr. Birmingham U., 1958-59; asst. prof. U. Pa., 1961-64; asso. prof. Cornell U., Ithaca, N.Y., 1964-69; prof. Cornell U., 1969-78; sr. physicist, head exptl. facilities div. Isabelle Project, Brookhaven Nat. Lab., Upton, L.I., N.Y., 1978-82; group leader nuclear and particle physics rsch. P divsn. Los Alamos (N.Mex.) Nat. Lab., 1986-94; cons., 1967-69, 76-78. Author: Elementary Electronics, 1967; Editor: Scintillation Counters, 1966. NSF sr. postdoctoral fellow, 1970; JSPS fellow, 1981. Fellow Am. Phys. Soc., AAAS. Home: 913 Calle Vistoso Santa Fe NM 87501-1031

WHITE, DAVID LEE, journalist; b. Cleve., Nov. 17, 1946; s. Royden Lee and Loretta Elizabeth (Wolf) W.; m. Sandra Jean Sweet, Aug. 25, 1983. Student, Cuyahoga C.C., 1965-67. Sports corr. The Cleve. Plain Dealer, 1966-67; sports reporter The Willoughby (Ohio) News Herald, 1968, asst. sports editor, 1968-69; editor sports makeup Cleve. Press, 1969-70, sports reporter, 1970-73, editor night news, 1973-78, asst. community weekly editor, 1978-80, asst. editor world news, 1980-81, editor page makeup, PM edits., 1981-82, weekend chief copy desk, 1981-82, editor weekend news, 1981-82, asst. Sunday editor, 1981-82; editor prodn. The Charlotte (N.C.) Observer/Charlotte News, 1982-84, asst. editor features/lifestyles, 1984-86, editor TV week, 1986—; asst. coverage Ky. Derby United Press Internat., 1970, 71, 72, 74, 75, U.S. Open Golf Tournament, 1971. Copy editor: (book) Cleveland-Yesterday, Today and Tomorrow, 1976. Office: Charlotte Observer/Knight Pub Co PO Box 32188 600 S Tryon St Charlotte NC 28232

WHITE, DAVID OLDS, researcher, former educator; b. Fenton, Mich., Dec. 18, 1921; s. Harold Bancroft and Doris Caroline (Olds) W.; m. Janice Ethel Russell, Sept. 17, 1923; children: John Russell, David Olds Jr., Benjamin Hill. BA, Amherst Coll., 1943; MS, U. Mass., 1950; PhD, U. Oreg., 1970. Tchr. human physiology Defiance (Ohio) Coll., summer 1950; sci. tchr. Roosevelt Jr. High Sch., Eugene, Oreg., 1951-52; prin. Glide (Oreg.) High Sch., 1952-56; tchr. Munich Am. Elem. Sch., 1957-69; prin. Wurzburg (Fed. Republic Germany) Am. High Sch., 1959-60, Wertheim (Fed. Republic Germany) Am. Elem. Sch., 1960-61; tchr. Dash Point Elem. Sch., Tacoma, 1961-63, Eugene (Oreg.) Pub. Schs., 1963-81; internat. rschr. in field. Contbr. articles to profl. publs.; patentee electronic model airplane. Staff sgt. U.S. Army, 1942-45, PTO. Fulbright grantee, 1956-57, 72-73. Mem. NEA, Fulbright Alumni Assn., Phi Delta Kappa. Avocations: skiing, camping, tennis, hunting, piano. Home: 4544 Fox Hollow Rd Eugene OR 97405-3904

WHITE, DAVID OLIVER, museum executive; b. Phila., Mar. 3, 1938; s. Thomas Morton and Bernice Lorraine (Twist) W.; B.A., Glassboro State Coll., 1969; M.A., U. Conn., 1970; m. Lorraine Carolyn Wilt, June 19, 1965; children—Kristin Leigh, Andrew David. Acctg. clk. Penn Mut. Life Ins. Co., Phila., 1955-65; mus. dir. Conn. Hist. Commn., Hartford, 1970-74, 1992—; dir. Mus. Conn. History, State Library, Hartford, 1974-92; liaison to Conn. Hist. Commn., 1977-86, Conn. Film Festival com., 1977-80. Vice pres. Tolland Hist. Soc., 1972, 73, 79, pres., 1974, 75, 80, bd. dirs., 1977-79, 84—. Served with U.S. Army, 1961-63. Mem. Conn. Humanities Coun., N.E. Mus. Assn., Assn. for Study of Conn. History, Conn. Hist. Soc. Methodist. Author: Connecticut's Black Soldiers 1775-83, 1973. Office: Conn Hist Comm 59 S Prospect St Hartford CT 06106-1901

WHITE, DEAN, advertising executive; b. Norfolk, Nebr., 1923; m. Barbara White; 4 children. Student, U. Nebr.; grad., U.S. Merchant Marine Acad. Pres. Whiteco Industries, Inc., Merrillville, Ind., 1953—. Chief officer Merchant Marines, Navy. Office: Whiteco Outdoor Advt 1000 E 80th Pl Ste 600N Merrillville IN 46410-5604

WHITE, DEVON MARKES, professional baseball player; b. Kingston, Jamaica, Dec. 29, 1962. With Calif. Angels, 1981-90, Toronto Blue Jays, 1990-95, Florida Marlins, Miami, 1996—; player Am. League All Star Team, 1989, 93. Recipient Gold Glove award, 1988-89, 91-94; named Am. League leader put outs by outfielder, 1987, 91-92. *

WHITE, DIRK BRADFORD, printing company executive; b. St. Joseph, Mo., Aug. 18, 1955; s. John Paul and Sandra Sue (Dedmon) W.; m. Julie Maureen Eisenreich, June 30, 1979; children: Kristen Elizabeth, Paul Aaron. BS in Mktg., Southwest Mo. State U., 1977. Estimator I.J. Eagle Printing Co., Inc., Kansas City, Mo., 1978-83; customer svc. mgr. Eagle Lithographing Co., Kansas City, Mo., 1983-88, v.p. prodn., 1988-90, sr. v.p., gen. mgr., 1990-92; mgr. prodn. control Spangler Inc., Kansas City, Kans., 1992-96; mgr. Banta Publs.-Kansas City, Liberty, Mo., 1996—. Mem.

Printing Industries Am., Graphic Arts Tech. Found., Kappa Alpha. Avocations: fly fishing, bicycling, wilderness camping and hiking, mountaineering, photography. Home: 8309 Mullen Rd Lenexa KS 66215-4133

WHITE, DONALD FRANCIS, financial planner, insurance agent; b. Everett, Mass., Oct. 28, 1955; s. Donald Francis Sr. and Joan Frances (Cannatelli) W.; m. Grace Restrepo, May 10, 1975. MS in Fin. Svcs., Am. Coll., 1994. CLU, ChFC. Agt. N.Y. Life, Hollywood, Fla., 1976-79; sales mgr. Pacific Mutual Life, Coral Springs, Fla., 1979-82; owner Treasure Coast Fin. Svcs. former Donald F. White & Assocs., Ft. Lauderdale and Stuart, Fla., 1982—; speaker in field. Author: Legacy Leadership, Legacy Planning; broadcaster radio program Your Money From God's Perspective, 1993—. Bd. dirs. Martin County Estate Planning Coun., Stuart, 1988-95, pres., 1993-94; mem. Treasure Coast Planned Giving Coun., speaker liaison, 1993-94; bd. dirs., founder Treasure Coast Cmty. Ch., 1992—; active Leadership Martin County, 1995, bd., 1996. Named Agt. of Yr., Gen. Agt. and Mgrs. Assn. of the Palm Beaches, 1990. Mem. Am. Soc. CLU and ChFC, Am. Messianic Mission (bd. dirs. 1986-94), Nat. Assn. Life Underwriters (legis. liaison 1993-96, nat committeeman 1995—), Treasure Coast Assn. Life Underwriters (founder, bd. dirs. 1992—, nat. committeeman 1995—), Stuart/Martin County C. of C. (stategovt. affairs committeeman 1993-94, grad. leadership Martin County 1995-96), Assn. for Advanced Life Underwriting (polit. involvement committeeman 1994-96), Million Dollar Round Table (life, qualifying mem. 1986—, mem. productivity com. 1994—). Republican. Avocations: snow skiing, golfing, traveling, boating, fishing. Office: Treasure Coast Fin Svcs Inc Ste 300 901 SE Monterey Commons Stuart FL 34996-3339

WHITE, DONALD HARVEY, physics educator emeritus; b. Berkeley, Calif., Apr. 30, 1931; s. Harvey Elliott and Adeline White; m. Beverly Evalina Jones, Aug. 8, 1953; children: Jeri, Brett, Holly, Scott, Erin. AB, U. Calif., Berkeley, 1953; PhD, Cornell U., 1960. Rsch. physicist Lawrence Livermore (Calif.) Nat. Lab., 1960-71, cons., 1971-90; prof. physics Western Oreg. U., Monmouth, 1971-95; ret.; vis. rsch. scientist Inst. Laue-Langevin, Grenoble, France, 1977-78, 84-85, 91-92. Author: (with others) Physics, an Experimental Science, 1968, Physics and Music, 1980. Pres. Monmouth-Independence Cmty. Arts, 1983. DuPont scholar, 1958; Minna-Heineman Found. fellow, Hannover, Fed. Republic Germany, 1977. Mem. Am. Phys. Soc., Am. Assn. Physics Tchrs. (pres. Oreg. sect. 1974-75), Oreg. Acad. Sci. (pres. 1979-80), Phi Kappa Phi (pres. West Oreg. chpt. 1989-90). Democrat. Presbyterian. Home: 411 S Walnut Dr Monmouth OR 97361-1948

WHITE, DORIS GNAUCK, science educator, biochemical and biophysics researcher; b. Milw., Dec. 24, 1926; d. Paul Benjamin and Johanna (Syring) Gnauck; m. Donald Lawrence White Sr., Oct. 9, 1954 (div. Jan. 1986); children: Stanley, Dean, Victor, Donald Lawrence Jr. BS with honors, U. Wis., 1947, MS, 1949, PhD, 1956. Cert. tchr., Wis. Tchr. agr. U.S. Army Disciplinary Barracks, Milw., 1946-50; chairperson dept. sci. Waunakee (Wis.) High Sch., 1950-51; 4-H leader extension div. USDA, Wis., 1950-56; tchr. prof. U. Wis. Lab. High Sch., Madison, 1951-56; grad. teaching asst. health, rural, adult edn. U. Wis., Madison, 1951-56; prof. sci. edn., curriculum and instrn. William Paterson Coll., Wayne, N.J., 1957—; sci. teaching specialist Frankford (N.J.) Twp. Schs., 1962; steering com. N.J. Sci. Conv., 1977—; coll. liaison N.J. Sci. Suprs., 1979—; sr. faculty and grand marshal William Paterson Coll., 1992—; Eisenhower grant participant Belleville (N.J.) Pub. Schs., 1992-94; participant N.J. Sci. and Math. Coalition NSF grant, 1993—; judge Seiko Youth Challenge, 1994, Hudson Co. Sci. Fair, 1995—; R&D judge 100 top internat. inventions, 1994; mentor for handicapped scientists AAAS, 1995. Mem. nat. sci. tchrs. manuscript rev. panel Jour. Coll. Sci. Teaching, 1991-94. Active 4-H Club Leadership, Morristown, N.J., 1968— (N.J. Alumni award 1991), Geraldine Rockefeller Dodge Found. Animal Shelter, Madison, N.J., 1968—, St. Hubert's Giralda; vol. for poor and homeless of Paterson, N.J., 1971—; lic. blood tester for salmonella/fowl typhoid USDA, 1987—; mem. panel on curriculum improvement N.J. Commr. Edn., 1990-91, program com. N.J. Sci. Conv., 1978—, sex equality com. N.J. Dept. Edn., 1987, sci. core proficiencies panel, N.J. Sci. Coalition, 1989-90; judge presdl. candidates for N.J. schs. N.J. Dept. Edn., Trenton, 1985-88; judge sci. fairs Carteret, N.J., 1991, N.J. Sci. Olympiad, 1993—, SEER Morristown, 1986-92, Haledon, N.J., 1957-60, Atlantic County 4-H, N.J., 1995-96, Hudson County Sci. Fair, N.J., 1994-96; trustee N.J. Sci. Suprs. Assn.; handicapped mentor AAAS, 1995—. Recipient Educator award Am. Cancer Soc., 1967, Meth. Layleader award, 1995; Dyes Rsch. grantee William Paterson Coll. Alumni Found., 1989-90; grantee NSF. Fellow N.J. Sci. Tchrs. Assn. (exec. bd. 1978—, indsl. liaison com. 1990-92); mem. Am. Poultry Assn. (life, lic. judge 1948—), Am. Chem. Soc. (Poster Contest judge 1993-95), Am. Minor Breeds Assn., Nat. Sci. Tchrs. Assn., Nat. Sci. Suprs. Assn., Nat. Sci. Leadership Assn., N.J. Acad. Sci. (chair sci. edn. divsn. 1990-95, liaison to sci. tchrs. 1992—, judge 1990—), N.J. Sci. Suprs. Assn. (exec. bd. 1979—, pres. 1981, Outstanding Sci. Supr. award 1986, Pres.'s award 1992), N.J. Physics Tchrs. Assn., N.J. Sci. and Tech. Assn., Liberty Sci. Mus. (charter). Republican. Methodist. Achievements include research in chromosome mapping of domestic fowl, development of 2 new varieties of winter squash which are now commercial varieties, development of penguin-like ducks, research in poultry genetics, genetics of Cucurbitaceae, ultrasound treatment of seeds concerning effects on seed germination and plant growth, using helium-neon lasers for holographic interferometry to measure plant growth occurring in seconds measured in wavelengths of light, growth regulators on flowers for parthenogenesis and for polyploidy, development of new variety of cat, herpes virus research with fowl, experiments with leaf berms for highway sound barriers, recycling waste tires stuffed with grass clippings for highway median strips covered with leaf compost, investigation of turkey head ornament colors as indicators of contentment or stress, turkey head color ornament color changes during courtship and copulation, catatonic effects in domestic fowl, design of portable methane generator, design of wave action and tidal pumps to transport glacial melt, suggested uses for incinerator ash, pollution caused by fireworks, Bernoulli's theorem as applied to bird flight, plausibility of human virgin births by cloning. Home: 7 Beaver Brook Rd Annandale NJ 08801-2018 Office: William Paterson Coll 408 Raubinger Hall 300 Pompton Rd Wayne NJ 07470-2103

WHITE, DOUGLAS JAMES, JR., lawyer; b. N.Y.C., Mar. 20, 1934; s. Douglas James and Margaret (Stillman) W.; m. Denise Beale, May 28, 1960; children: Brian Douglas, James Roderick. BA, U. Oreg., 1955; LLB, Willamette U., 1958. Bar: Oreg. 1958. Law clk. to assoc. justice Oreg. Supreme Ct., Salem, 1958-59; assoc. Schwabe, Williamson & Wyatt (formerly known as Mautz, Souther, Spaulding, Kinsey & Williamson), Portland, Oreg., 1959-69; shareholder, gen. ptnr. Schwabe, Williamson & Wyatt, P.C. (formerly known as Schwabe, Williamson, Wyatt, Moore & Roberts), Portland, Oreg., 1969-79, sr. ptnr., 1979-93; shareholder, 1994—; bd. dirs. Portland Iron Works and Affiliates; gen. outside counsel Oreg. Grad. Inst. Sci. Tech., Beaverton. Trustee Jesuit H.S., Beaverton, 1991-94; bd. dirs. St. Vincent de Paul Child Devel. Ctr., Portland, 1979-90, Portland Coun., Soc. St. Vincent de Paul, 1989-92, Portland House of Umoja, 1995—; bd. dirs., officer Maryville Nursing Home, Beaverton, 1993—, St. Vincent de Paul Conf. of St. Thomas More, Portland, 1966—; active Saturday Acad. Beaverton, 1982—. Mem. ABA, Oreg. State Bar Assn. (real estate and land use sect. exec. com. 1984-85), Multnomah County Bar Assn., Multnomah Athletic Club (Portland), Arlington Club (Portland), Flyfisher Club of Oreg. Republican. Roman Catholic. Avocations: fly-fishing, cross-country skiing, bridge, hiking. Home: 6725 SW Preslynn Dr Portland OR 97225-2668 Office: Schwabe Williamson & Wyatt 1211 SW 5th Ave Portland OR 97204-3713

WHITE, DOUGLAS R., anthropology educator; b. Mpls., Mar. 13, 1942; s. Asher Abbott and Margaret McQuestin (Richie) W.; m. Jayne Chamberlain (div. Feb. 1971); m. Lilyan Amdur Brudner, Mar. 21, 1971; 1 child, Scott Douglas. BA, U. Minn., 1964, MA, 1967, PhD, 1969. Asst. prof. U. Pitts., 1967-72, assoc. prof., 1972-76; assoc. prof. U. Calif., Irvine, 1976-79, prof., 1979—; dep. dir. Lang. Attitudes Rsch. Project, Dublin, Ireland, 1971-73; vis. prof. U. Tex., Austin, 1974-75; chmn. Linkages: World Devel. Res. Coun., Md., 1986—, pres. 1986-90. Co-editor: Research Methods in Social Networks, 1989, Anthropology of Urban Environments, 1972; founder, gen. editor World Cultures Jour., 1985-90; author sci. software packages; contbr. articles to profl. jours. Fellow Ctr. for Advanced Studies, Western Behavioral Sci. Inst., La Jolla, Calif., 1981-84; recipient Sr. Scientist award Alexander von Humboldt Stiftung, Bonn, Germany, 1989-91, Bourse de Haute Niveau award Ministry of Rsch. and Tech., Paris, 1992. Mem. Social Sci. Computing Assn. (pres. elect 1991, pres. 1992.). Democrat. Home: 8888 N La Jolla Scenic Dr N La Jolla CA 92037 Office: U Calif Irvine School of Social Sci Irvine CA 92697

WHITE, DURIE NEUMANN, federal agency administrator; b. Westerly, R.I., June 19, 1950; d. Reed Maurice Neumann and Alice M. (Victoria) Quinn; m. Donald L. White, Oct. 6, 1979; 6 stepchildren. BA, U. R.I., 1972. Supply clk. USAF/Europe, Mainz Kastel, Germany, 1972-73; adminstrv. asst. Pearson's Travel, Providence, 1973; contracting officer GSA, Washington, 1973-77; contract specialist AID, Washington, 1977-80; procurement analyst A/SDBU Dept. State, Washington, 1980-91, ops. dir. A/SDBU, 1991—; mem. Interagy. Small Bus. Dirs. Group, Washington, 1993—, White House Conf. on Small Bus., 1995. Roman Catholic. Avocations: skiing, photography. Office: Small/Disadvantaged Bus 2201 C St NW Washington DC 20520-0001*

WHITE, EDMUND WILLIAM, chemical engineer; b. Phila., July 8, 1920; s. Edmund Britten and Grace Salome (Faunce) W.; m. Kathrine Nathalie Cadwallader, Apr. 24, 1948; children: Christine Louise, William Cadwallader, Thomas Edmund, James Christopher. BA, Columbia Coll., 1940; BS, Columbia Sch. Engring., 1941, MChemE, 1942; PhD, Lehigh U., 1952. Registered profl. engr., Ohio. Jr. chemist Westvaco Chlorine Products Corp., South Charleston, W.Va., 1942-44; chem. engr. C.L. Mantel, N.Y.C., 1946-47, Diamond Alkali Co., Painesville, Ohio, 1947-49; grad. asst. Lehigh U., Bethlehem, Pa., 1949-51; sr. chemist Cities Svc. R & D Co., various cities, 1951-59, Athabasca Inc., Edmonton, Alberta, Canada, 1960-64; project mgr. U.S. Dept. Navy, Washington, 1965-66; rsch. chem. engr. Naval Surface Warfare Ctr., Annapolis, Md., 1966-95; ret., 1995; cons. in field; mem. U.S. del. to ISO TC 28 mtgs. in Budapest, 1990, Phila., 1992, Paris 1994; mem. U.S. tech. adv. group in ISO TC 28; mem. Quadripartite Navies group on Fuels, Lubricants and Allied Products, mem. U.S. del. and co-chair mtg., 1993. Contbr. articles to profl. jours. Treas., v.p., pres. sch. PTAs, Silver Spring, Md., 1968-79; den father, mem. troop com. Boy Scouts Am., Silver Spring, 1966-75. Lt. (j.g.) USN, 1944-46. Fellow ASTM (chairperson sect. subcom., com. 1967—, Award of Merit 1990, Scroll of Honor 1993); mem. AIChE (50 Yr. award), Am. Chem. Soc. (50 Yr. award), Potomac Curling Club (bd. dirs., pres. 1982-84), Internat. Assn. for Stability and Handling of Liquid Fuels (mem. steering com. 1985-95), Sigma Xi. Republican. Achievements include 4 patents and 2 Canadian patents; research in consensus standardization, fuel stability testing, fuel stability, synthetic fuels, separation processes, wax oxidation, mixing and chlorine-caustic electrolytic cell. Home: 908 Crest Park Dr Silver Spring MD 20903-1307

WHITE, EDWARD ALFRED, lawyer; b. Elizabeth, N.J., Nov. 23, 1934. BS in Indsl. Engring., U. Mich., 1957, JD, 1963. Bar: Fla. 1963, U.S. Ct. Appeals (5th cir.) 1971, U.S. Supreme Ct. 1976, U.S. Ct. Appeals (11th cir.) 1981. Assoc. Jennings, Watts, Clarke & Hamilton, Jacksonville, Fla., 1963-66, ptnr., 1966-69; ptnr. Wayman & White, Jacksonville, 1969-72; pvt. practice, Jacksonville, 1972—; mem. aviation law com. Fla. Bar, 1972-94, chmn., 1979-81, bd. govs., 1984-88, admiralty com., 1984—, chmn., 1990-91, chmn. pub. relations com., 1986-88, exec. coun. trial lawyers sect., 1986-91, chmn. admiralty cert. com., 1995-97. Fellow Am. Bar Found.; mem. ABA (vice chmn. admiralty law com. 1995—), Fla. Bar Assn. (bd. cert. civil trial lawyer, bd. cert. admiralty lawyer), Jacksonville Bar Assn. (chmn. legal ethics com. 1975-76, bd. govs. 1976-78, pres. 1979-80), Assn. Trial Lawyers Am. (sustaining mem. 1984—), Acad. Fla. Trial Lawyers (diplomate), Fla. Coun. Bar Assn. Pres.'s, Lawyer-Pilots Bar Assn., Am. Judicature Soc., Maritime Law Assn. (proctor in admiralty), Southeastern Admiralty Law Inst. (bd. dirs. 1982-84, chmn./pres. 1994). Home: 1959 Largo Rd Jacksonville FL 32207-3926 Office: 610 Blackstone Bldg 233 E Bay St Jacksonville FL 32202-3452

WHITE, EDWARD ALLEN, electronics company executive; b. Cambridge, Jan. 1, 1928; s. Joseph and Bessie (Allen) W.; m. Joan Dixon, Dec. 22, 1949 (div. Aug. 1978); children: Dixon Richard, Leslie Ann White Lollar; m. Nancy Rhoads, Oct. 6, 1979. B.S., Tufts U., 1947. Chmn. Bowmar Instrument Corp., Phoenix, Mass., 1951—, White Technology Inc., Phoenix, 1980-86; pres. Ariz. Digital Corp., Phoenix, 1975-91; chmn., chief exec. officer AHI, Inc., Ft. Wayne, Ind., 1970-88; pres. EBH Corp., Ft. Wayne, 1994—, Interactive Digital Corp., Phoenix, 1992—; mem. World Pres's. Orgn., Washington D.C., 1978—. Patentee in field. Bd. dirs. Gov.'s Council Children, Youth and Families, Phoenix, 1982-84, Planned Parenthood Fedn. Am., 1984-88; pres., bd. dirs. Planned Parenthood Central and No. Ariz., 1984-88; trustee Internat House, N.Y.C., 1973-75, Tufts U., 1973-83. Mem. Tau Beta Pi. Club: Paradise Valley Country. Home: 5786 N Echo Canyon Cir Phoenix AZ 85018-1242 Office: Bowmar Instrument Corp 5080 N 40th St Ste 475 Phoenix AZ 85018-2150

WHITE, ERSKINE NORMAN, JR., management company executive; b. N.Y.C., July 21, 1924; s. Erskine Norman and Catharine (Putman) W.; m. Eileen E. Lutz, Nov. 5, 1949; children: Erskine Norman III, Carol Putnam White Wolfe, Catharine Lutz. BE, Yale U., 1947; MS, MIT, 1949. Staff mem. rsch. devel. bd. Dept. Def., 1949; plant mgr. Gorham Mfg. Co. (became Gorham Corp. 1961, Gorham div. Textron Inc. 1968), Asheville, N.C., 1956-57, 1956-57, exec. v.p., 1964-68, pres., 1968-69, dir., 1960-69; group v.p. Textron Inc., Providence, 1969-71; exec. v.p. ops. Textron Inc., 1971-75, exec. v.p., 1975-79, exec. v.p. corp. affairs, 1979-81; pres. E.N. White Mgmt. Corp., Providence, 1981-95; v.p., treas. Cadwagan Assoc. Trustee Women and Infants Hosp., R.I., 1974-93, R.I. Sch. Design, 1966-72, 82-95, chmn. fin. com., 1988-95, treas., 1990-95; bd. dirs., exec. com. New Eng. Coun., 1979-81; chmn. NCCJ, 1987-89. With USN, 1944-46, PTO. Mem. NAM (bd. dir. 1974-80, regional v.p. 1975, div. vice chmn. 1978-80, exec. com.), Urban League (bd. dir. R.I. chpt. 1989-97), Greater Providence C. of C. (bd. dir., pres. 1978), R.I. C. of C. Fedn. (pres. 1979), Sigma Xi, Tau Beta Pi.

WHITE, EUGENE VADEN, pharmacist; b. Cape Charles, Va., Aug. 13, 1924; s. Paul Randolph and Louise (Townsend) W.; m. Laura Juanita LaFontaine, Aug. 28, 1948; children: Lynda Sue, Patricia Louise. BS in Pharmacy, Med. Coll. Va., 1950; PharM (hon.), Phila. Coll. Pharmacy and Sci., 1966. Pharmacist McKim & Huffman Drug Store, Luray, Va., 1950, Miller's Drug Store, Winchester, Va., 1950-53; pharmacist, ptnr. Shiner's Drug Store, Front Royal, Va., 1953-56; pharmacist, owner Eugene V. White, Pharmacist, P.C., Berryville, Va., 1956—; Sturmer lectr. Phila. Coll. Pharmacy and Sci., 1979; Lubin vis. prof. U. Tenn. Sch. Pharmacy, Memphis, 1974; mem. bd. visitors Sch. Pharmacy, U. Pitts., 1969. Author: The Office-Based Family Pharmacist, 1978; created first office practice in community pharmacy, 1960, developed patient medication profile record, 1960. 2d lt. USAAC, 1943-45. Recipient Nat. Leadership award Phi Lambda Sigma, 1979, Outstanding Pharmacy Alumnus award Med. Coll. Va. Sch. Pharmacy Alumni Assn., 1989; Eugene V. White scholarship named in his honor Shenandoah U. Sch. Pharmacy, 1996. Fellow Am. Coll. Apothecaries (J. Leon Lascoff award 1973); mem. Am. Pharm Assn. (Daniel B. Smith award 1965, Remington Honor medal 1978), Va. Pharm. Assn. (Pharmacist of Yr. award 1966, Outstanding Pharmacist award 1992). Methodist. Avocations: reading, woodworking, computer. Office: 1 W Main St Berryville VA 22611-1340

WHITE, FAITH, sculptor; b. N.Y.C., Apr. 7, 1950; d. Edward and Faith-Hope (Green) Kahn. BA summa cum laude, L.I. U., 1971; studied woodcarving, with Nathaniel Burwash, Cambridge, Mass., 1976, with Joseph Wheelwright, Boston, 1977-94. Freelance sculptor Boston, 1971—, N.Y.C., 1995—; adminstrv. asst. to dean of students Grahm Jr. Coll., Boston, 1972-74; exec. sec. to New Eng. regional mgr. Bur. of Nat. Affairs, Inc., Boston, 1974-77; asst. to dir. New Eng. Aquarium, Boston, 1977-80, dir. pers., 1980-82; guest juror for travel grant Boston Visual Artists Union, 1994; show mgr. Sculpture and Large Works, The Copley Soc. of Boston, 1992; instr. woodcarving The Eliot Sch., Jamaica Plain, Mass., 1992-94; tchg. artist Very Spl. Arts program Mus. of Sci., Boston, 1992, 93; project coord. First Night, Boston, 1986, 87, 88; judge Sr. Panel Carving competition Belmont (Mass.) Hill Sch., 1985; docent Hands-On Sculpture show New Eng. Sculptors Assn. at Mus. of Sci., Boston, 1984. One-woman show at Mills Gallery, Boston, 1987; two-person invitational show at The Copley Soc. of Boston, 1994; other exhbns. include Boston Ctr. for Arts, 1984, 85, Boston Visual Artists Union Gallery, 1985, Concord Art Assn., 1985, Cambridge Art Assn., 1986, The Copley Soc. of Boston, 1984, 85, 88, 89, 91, 92, 93, 94, 95, 96 (including holiday invitationals for award winners 1988, 91, 92), Fed. Res. Bank of Boston Gallery, 1989, with Copley Masters, 1984, Howard Yezerski Gallery, 1989, 90, 91, 92, 93, 94, 95, 96, Libr. Ctr., Newport, Mass., 1990, Landau Gallery, Belmont Hill Sch., 1991, Attleboro (Mass.) Mus., 1992, Gallery NAGA, Boston, 1992, others; represented in permanent collection Sherrill House, Boston. Liaison between mission com. Trinity Ch., Boston and vol. program Sherrill House Nursing Home, 1987-94. Mem. Copley Soc. of Boston (Copley Master 1992), New Eng. Sculptors Assn. (bd. dirs., mem.-at-large 1985-86, 88-89), Nat. Sculpture Soc. Episcopalian. Avocations: fitness training, sailing. Studio: 300 E 34th St New York NY 10016-4912

WHITE, FREDERICK ANDREW, physics educator, physicist; b. Detroit, Mar. 11, 1918; s. Andrew Bracken and Mildred (Witzel) W.; m. Dorothy Janet Sibley, Nov. 7, 1942 (dec.); children: Wendell William, Lawrence Sibley, Eric Sibley, Roger Randolph (dec.). B.S., Wayne State U., 1940; M.S., U. Mich., 1941; postgrad., U. Rochester, 1943-46; Ph.D., U. Wis., 1959. Insp. U.S. Army Ordnance, Rochester, N.Y., 1941-43; research asst. Manhattan project U. Rochester, 1943-45, grad. instr. in research, 1946; research asst., research asso., cons. physicist Gen. Electric Co. Knolls Atomic Power Lab., Schenectady, 1947-62; adj. prof. nuclear sci. Rensselaer Poly. Inst., Troy, N.Y., 1961-62; prof. nuclear engring. and environmental engring., indsl. liaison scientist Rensselaer Poly. Inst., 1962-81, prof. emeritus, 1981—; mem. staff Bell Telephone Labs., 1969; research and liaison scientist Rochester Gas & Electric Co., N.Y., 1978—; adj. prof. physics SUNY, Albany, 1981-88; cons. NASA, 1965—; organist and acoustic cons., 1952—. Author: American Industrial Research Laboratories, 1961, Mass Spectrometry in Science and Technology, 1968, Our Acoustic Environment, 1975; Mass Spectrometry: Applications in Science and Engineering, 1986. Mem. AIAA, IEEE, Optical Soc. Am., Am. Guild Organists. Developer mass spectrometric instrumentation and its uses in measurements relating to nuclear and atomic physics; co-discoverer last naturally-occurring stable isotope. Home: 2456 Hilltop Rd Niskayuna NY 12309-2405 Office: Rensselaer Poly Inst Linac Lab Troy NY 12181

WHITE, GAYLE COLQUITT, religion writer, journalist; b. Lamar County, Ga., Nov. 4, 1950; d. Albert Candler and Ethel Eugenia (Moore) Colquitt; m. Robert Eugene White, Jr., Apr. 9, 1972; children: Margaret Candler, Robert Eugene III. AB in Journalism, U. Ga., 1972. Reporter Atlanta Jour. & Constn., 1972—. Named Templeton Reporter of Yr., Religion Newswriters Assn., 1992. Presbyterian. Office: Atlanta Journal & Constitution 72 Marietta St NW Atlanta GA 30303-2804*

WHITE, GEORGE, government official, physical scientist; b. Bklyn., Dec. 19, 1937; s. Samuel Louis and Mollie (Telson) W.; m. Susan Jane Doppelhammer, Apr. 13, 1969; 1 child, Jeffrey Steven. BS, CUNY, 1960; MS, NYU, 1964; postgrad. Am. U., 1966-68. Rsch. asst. Rockefeller Inst., N.Y.C., 1960, NYU, N.Y.C., 1961-64; rsch. scientist Atlantic Research Corp., Alexandria, Va., 1965-72; sr. staff officer Nat. Acad. Scis., Washington, 1973-80; div. chief, asst. to dir. U.S. Bur. Mines, Dept. Interior, Washington, 1981-96; lectr. chemistry, No. Va. C.C., Alexandria, Va., 1972-78, Bronx C.C., 1961-64; spl. asst. to congressman Ed Pastor, 1995—. Staff editor: Chemistry of Coal Utilization, 1980, Minerals and Materials, 1983-87, Minerals Position of the U.S., 1985-90. Named Presdl. Sci. Intern, Nat. Sci. Found., Dept. Transp., 1972; Legis. fellow U.S. Congress, 1992. Mem. Am. Chem. Soc., AAAS, Am. Inst. Mining Engrs., Washington Chem. Soc. Democrat. Jewish. Home: 3903 Forest Grove Dr Annandale VA 22003-1961 Office: Ho of Reps 2465 Rayburn Bldg Washington DC 20515-0302

WHITE, GEORGE COOKE, theater director, foundation executive; b. New London, Conn., Aug. 16, 1935; s. Nelson Cooke and Aida (Rovetti) W.; m. Elizabeth Conant Darling, July 5, 1958; children: George Conant, Caleb Ensign, Juliette Darling. Student, U. Paris, 1956; BA, Yale U., 1957, MFA, 1961; student, Shakespeare Inst., 1959; ArtsD (hon.), Conn. Coll., 1994. Stage mgr. Imperial Japanese Azumakabuki Co., 1955; asst. mgr. Internat. Ballet Festival, Nervi, Italy, 1955; prodn. coordinator Talent Assos., 1961-63; adminstrv. v.p. score prodns. Paramount Pictures, 1963-65; founder, pres. Eugene O'Neill Meml. Theatre Found., 1965—; adviser, dir. Theatre One, Conn. Coll. Women, 1967-70; regional theater cons. Nat. Ednl. TV Network; guest lectr. Wagner Coll., 1970; acting dir. Hunter Coll. Hunter Arts, 1972-73; adj. prof. U. N.C.; prof. theater adminstrn. program Yale U., 1978-91; co-chmn. Yale Drama Sch.; mem. exec. com. Theatre Library Assn., 1967; bd. govs. Am. Playwrights Theatre; mem. bd. ANTA, 1967-68; mem. Mayor N.Y.C.'s. Theatre Adv. Com.; advisory bd. Internat. Theatre Inst.; panel mem. Exptl. Theatre; U.S. State Dept. cultural exchange grantee to Australia; guest adminstr. Australian Nat. Playwrights Conf., 1973; U.S. del. Internat. Theatre Inst. Congress, Moscow, 1973; mem. Conn. Commn. on Arts, 1978-93, mem. exec. com., 1979-83, vice chair, 1992-93; co-founder Caribbean-U.S. Theatre Exchange; dir. Actors Theatre St. Paul, 1979, 80, 82, 83, 86, Hartman Repertory Theatre, 1980; guest dir. Chinese Theater Assn., Beijing, 1984, 87, Hedgerow Theatre, 1986; mem. nominating com. Antoinette Perry Awards, 1984-86, 88, 94; dir. Anna Christie Beijing Cen. Dramatic Theater, 1984, 87. Appeared in TV series Citizen Soldier, 1959-61; appeared in off-Broadway prodn. John Brown's Body. Trustee Goodspeed Opera House, 1966-68, Nat. Theatre Conf., 1973—, Eastern Conn. Symphony, Dance Arts Coun., Conn. Opera Assn., Conn. Pub. TV, 1973-83, Mitchell Coll., 1994—, Arts & Bus. Coun., 1994—; Trustee Conn. Edn. Telecommunications Corp., 1973-83, chmn., 1982; mem. planning bd. Op. Rescue; bd. dirs. Rehearsal Club, Centre for Inter-Am. Rels., Theater of Latin Am., Manhattan Theatre Club, 1970-80, Met. Opera Guild; Performance mag.; exec. com. Yale Drama Alumni, 1963-73; mem. Yale Alumni Bd.; bd. overseers drama dept. Brandeis U.; adv. bd. Am. Musical Theatre Program, Hartford Conservatory, Bd. Arts & Bus. Coun., Brandeis Creative Arts Award Jury, Theater and New Music Theatre Works Panel, NEA; mem. Waterford (Conn.) Rep. Town Meeting, 1975-77; presdl. appointment to Nat. Coun. NEA, 1992; mem. Coast Guard Auxillary, Crew mem. U.S. Coast Guard Barque Eagle. Served with AUS, 1957-59. Recipient spl. citation New Eng. Theatre Conf., 1968, Margo Jones award, 1968, Pub. Svc. award New London County Bar Assn., 1975, Disting. Citizen's award Town of Waterford, 1976, Disting. Service award Conn. mag., Contbns. to State award, 1981, Lifetime Contbn. to Theatre award Am. Theater Assn., Contbn. to Conn. Arts award Quinnipiac Coll., 1989; Internat. Communications Agy. cultural exch. grantee to People's Republic of China, 1980; Officer first class Royal Swedish Order of Polar Star; Chevalier des artes et des lettres (France). Fellow Royal Soc. Arts, Coll. of Am. Theatre; mem. Chinese Theatre Assn. (hon.). Clubs: Century; Cosmos (Washington); Thames (New London); White's Point Yacht. Office: O'Neill Theater Ctr 305 Great Neck Rd Waterford CT 06385-3825

WHITE, GEORGE EDWARD, legal educator, lawyer; b. Northampton, Mass., Mar. 19, 1941; s. George LeRoy and Frances Dorothy (McCafferty) W.; m. Susan Valre Davis, Dec. 31, 1966; children: Alexandra V., Elisabeth McC. BA, Amherst Coll., 1963; MA, Yale U., 1964, PhD, 1967; J.D., Harvard U., 1970. Bar: D.C. 1970, Va. 1975, U.S. Supreme Ct. 1973. Vis. scholar Am. Bar Found., 1970-71; law clk. to Chief Justice Warren, U.S. Supreme Ct., 1971-72; asst. prof. law U. Va., 1972-74, assoc. prof., 1974-77, prof., 1977-86, John B. Minor prof. law and history, 1987-92, Disting. Univ. prof., John B. Minor prof. law and history, 1992—; vis. prof. Marshall-Wythe Law Sch. spring 1988, N.Y. Law Sch., fall 1988. Mem. Am. Acad. Arts and Scis., Am. Law Inst., Am. Soc. Legal History (bd. dirs. 1978-81), Soc. Am. Historians. Author books, including The American Judicial Tradition, 1976, 2d edit., 1988, Tort Law in America: An Intellectual History (Gavel award ABA 1981), 1980, Earl Warren: A Public Life (Gavel award ABA 1983), 1982, The Marshall Court and Cultural Change, 1988, 2d edit. 1991 (James Willard Hurst prize 1990), Justice Oliver Wendell Holmes: Law and the Inner Self, 1993 (Gavel award ABA 1994, Scribes award 1994, Littleton-Griswold prize 1994, Triennial Order of the Coif award 1996), Intervention and Detachment: Essays in Legal History and Jurisprudence, 1994; Creating the National Pastime: Baseball Transforms Itself, 1903-1953, 1996—, editor Studies in Legal History, 1980-86, Delegate in Law, 1986-96—, Oxford U. Press. Office: U Va Law Sch Charlottesville VA 22903-1789

WHITE, GEORGE EDWARD, pedodontist; b. Jamestown, N.Y., July 31, 1941; s. Gordon Ennis and Margaret (Appleyard) W. AB, Colgate U., 1963; DDS, SUNY, Buffalo, 1967; PhD, MIT, 1973; DBA, Century U., 1982. Intern, then resident Children's Hosp., Buffalo, 1967-69; prof., chmn. dept.

pediat. dentistry Tufts U. Sch. Dental Medicine, Boston, 1973—; chief dept. oral pediat. New Eng. Med. Center Hosp., Boston, 1973-80; pvt. practice pedodontics, Boston, 1974—; lectr. MIT, 1975-80; cons. Abcor, Inc.; nat., internat. lectr. Nat. Inst. Dental Rsch. grantee, 1973—. Author: Dental Caries: A Multifactorial Disease, 1975, To Stand Alone, 1979; co-author: Maxillofacial Orthopedics: For the Growing Child, 1983; founder, editor-in-chief Jour. Pedodontics, 1976, now named Jour. Clin. Pediat. Dentistry; editor: Clin. Oral Pediatrics, 1979, founder, editor-in-chief Mastering Clin. Pediat. Dentistry, 1993; editor-in-chief Protocols for Clin. Pediat. Dentistry; contbr. articles to profl. jours. Master Acad. Gen. Dentistry; fellow Am. Acad. Pediat. Dentistry, Internat. Coll. Dentistry, Am. Coll. Dentistry; mem. Am. Assn. Functional Orthodontist, Northeast Craniomandibular Soc., Platform Soc., Fedn. Dentaire Internationale, Sigma Xi, Omicron Kappa Upsilon. Office: Tufts U Sch Dental Medicine Dept Pediat Dentistry 1 Kneeland St Boston MA 02111-1527

WHITE, GEORGE MALCOLM, architect; b. Cleve., Nov. 1, 1920; m. Susanne Neiley Daniels, Apr. 21, 1973; children: Stephanie, Jocelyn, Geoffrey, Pamela. B.S., MIT, 1942, M.S., 1942; M.B.A., Harvard, 1948; LL.B., Case Western Res. U., 1959. Design engr. Gen. Electric Co., Schenectady, 1942-47; practice architecture and law Cleve., 1948-71; Architect of Capitol, Washington, 1971-95; vice chmn. Leo A. Daly, Washington, 1996—; bd. dirs. 3D Internat. Works include First Unitarian Ch., Cleve., 1959, Preformed Line Products Co. Office Bldg., Cleve., 1960, Mentor Harbor Yacht Club, 1968, restoration, Old Senate and Supreme Ct. Chambers, U.S. Capitol, 1975, Libr. of Congress James Madison Meml. Bldg., 1979, U.S. Capitol Power Plant Extension, 1979, master plan for U.S. Capitol, 1981, Hart Senate Office Bldg., 1982, restoration of the west cen. front U.S. Capitol Bldg., 1987, Thurgood Marshall Fed. Judiciary Bldg., 1992, U.S. Capitol west terr. restoration and courtyard addt., 1993. former mem. D.C. Zoning Commn., U.S. Capitol Police Bd., U.S. Capitol Guide Bd., U.S. Ho. of Reps. Page Bd., Adv. Coun. on Hist. Preservation, Internat. Ctr. Com., Nat. Conservation Adv. Coun., Nat. Capital Meml. Commn., art adv. com. Washington Met. Area Transit Auth.; former acting dir. U.S. Bot. Garden; former mem. bd. dirs., chmn. design com. Pennsylvania Ave. Devel. Corp.; former bd. dirs. Nat. Bldg. Mus.; former trustee Fed. City Coun.; mem. bd. regents Am. Archtl. Found; former chmn. archtl. adv. com. Restoration of Statue of Liberty; chmn. com. for Statue of Liberty Mus.; mem. nat. panel arbitrators Am. Arbitration Assn.; former mem. vis. com. dept. architecture and planning MIT; mem. bd. cons. Nubian monuments at Philae, Egypt; mem. internat. com. cons. for Egyptian Mus., Cairo; chmn. rev. com. Nat. Capital Devel. Commn. for Canberra, Australia. Recipient Gold medal Archtl. Soc. Ohio, 1971, Burton award for Disting. Pub. Svc. Cleve. Club, 1991. Fellow AIA (Thomas Jefferson award 1992), ASCE (hon.), Nat. Soc. Profl. Engrs., Nat. Acad. Forensic Engrs.; mem. Sigma Xi, Eta Kappa Nu, Lambda Alpha, Tau Beta Pi. Office: Leo A Daly 1201 Connecticut Ave NW Washington DC 20036-2605 Address: 3337 N St NW Washington DC 20007

WHITE, GEORGE W., federal judge; b. 1931. Student, Baldwin-Wallace Coll., 1948-51; J.D., Cleveland-Marshall Coll. Law, 1955. Sole practice law Cleve., 1956-68; judge Ct. Common Pleas, Ohio, 1968-80; judge U.S. Dist. Ct. (no. dist.) Ohio, 1980-95, chief judge, 1995—; referee Ct. Common Pleas, Cuyahoga County, 1957-62. Councilman, Cleve., 1963-68. Mem. ABA, Fed. Bar Assn., 6th Circuit Jud. Coun. (exec. com. 1995—). Office: US Dist Ct 300 US Courthouse 201 Superior Ave E Cleveland OH 44114-1201*

WHITE, GERALD ANDREW, retired chemical company executive; b. L.I., N.Y., Aug. 2, 1934; s. Charles Eugene and Grace Mary (Trojan) W.; m. Mary Alice Turvey, June 8, 1957; children—Kevin, Patricia, Timothy, Megan. B in Chem. Engring., Villanova U., 1957; cert. advanced mgmt. program, Harvard Bus. Sch., 1975. Staff engr. Air Products and Chems., Inc., Allentown, Pa., 1962-65, mgr. systems devel., 1965-66, group controller, 1969-72, corp. controller, 1974-76, v.p. planning, 1977-82, v.p. fin., chief fin. officer, 1982-92, sr. v.p. fin., chief fin. officer, 1992-95. Pres. United Way in Lehigh County, 1981; bd. dirs. Pa. Coun. on Econ. Edn., 1981-95, Lord Corp., 1994; trustee, treas. Allentown Art Mus., 1984; trustee, chmn. bd. trustees Allentown Coll. St. Francis de Sales, Center Valley, 1983. Lt. USN, 1957-62. Recipient J. Stanley Morehouse Meml. award Villanova U. Coll. Engring., 1983. Mem. AICE, Fin. Execs. Inst. (pres. northeastern Pa. chpt. 1974-75), Fin. Execs. Rsch. Found. (trustee 1992-96), Tau Beta Pi. Avocation: squash.

WHITE, GILBERT F(OWLER), geographer, educator; b. Chgo., Nov. 26, 1911; s. Arthur E. and Mary (Guthrie) W.; m. Anne Elizabeth Underwood, Apr. 28, 1944; children: William D., Mary, Frances. BS, U. Chgo., 1932, SM, 1934, PhD, 1942; LLD (hon.), Hamilton Coll., 1951, Swarthmore Coll.; LL.D. (hon.), Earlham Coll., Richmond, Ind., Mich. State U., Augustana Coll.; ScD (hon.), Haverford Coll.; hon. degree, Northland Coll. Geographer Miss. Valley Com. of P.W.A., 1934, Nat. Resources Bd., 1934-35; sec. land and water com. Nat. Resources Com. and Nat. Resources Planning Bd., 1935-40; with Exec. Office Pres., Bur. Budget, 1941-42; asst. exec. sec. Am. Friends Service Com., 1945-46; relief adminstr. in France, 1942-43; interned Baden-Baden, 1943-44; sec. Am. Relief for India, 1945-46; pres. Haverford Coll., 1946-55; prof. geography U. Chgo., 1956-69; prof. geography, dir. Inst. Behavioral Sci., U. Colo., Boulder, 1970-78; Gustavson disting. prof. emeritus Inst. Behavioral Sci., U. Colo., 1979—; dir. Natural Hazards Info. Ctr., 1978-84, 92-94; exec. editor Environment mag., 1983-93; vis. prof. Oxford U., 1962-63; cons. Investigations Lower Mekong Basin, 1961-62, 70; U.S. mem. UNESCO adv. com. on arid zone research, 1954-55; mem. mission Am. Vol. Agys. Relief Germany, 1946; vice chmn. Pres.'s Water Resources Policy Commn., 1950; mem. com. natural resources Hoover Commn., 1948; chmn. UN Panel Integrated River Basin Devel., 1956-57; chmn. Task Force Fed. Flood Control Policy, 1965-66; sci. adv. to adminstr. UN Devel. Program, 1966-71; chmn. adv. bd. Energy Policy Project, 1972-74; chmn. Am. Friends Service Com., 1963-69; chmn. com. on man and environment IGU, 1969-76; chmn. steering com. High Sch. Geography com., 1964-70; mem. Tech. Assessment Adv. Council, 1974-76; chmn. environ. studies bd. NRC, 1975-77; pres. Sci. Com. on Problems of Environment, 1976-82; chmn. bd. Resources for Future, 1973-79; co-chmn. U.S.-Egypt Joint Consultative Com. on Sci. and Tech., 1981-86; mem. adv. group on greenhouse gases World Meteorol. Orgn., Internat. Council of Scientific Unions, UN Environ. Program, 1986-90; chmn. tech. rev. com. Nev. Nuclear Waste Project, 1987-93; mem. adv. group on water UN Environ. Program, 1989-93, working group for Action Plan for Aral Sea Basin, USSR, 1990-93; chmn. nat. rev. com. Status U.S. Floodplain Mgmt., 1989; bd. dirs. Am. Soc. Flood Plain Mgrs. Found., 1996—. Author: Human Adjustment to Floods, 1942, Science and Future of Arid Lands, 1960, Social and Economic Aspects of Natural Resources, 1962, Choice of Adjustment to Floods, 1964, Strategies of American Water Management, 1969; co-author: Drawers of Water, 1972, Assessment of Research on Natural Hazards, 1975, Flood Hazard in the United States, 1975, The Environment as Hazard, 1978, also various govt. reports, 1937-45; editor: Natural Hazards: Local, National and Global, 1974, Environmental Aspects of Complex River Development, 1977; co-editor: Environmental Issues, 1977, The World Environment, 1972-1982, 1982, Environmental Effects of Nuclear War, 1983. Reicpient Daly medal Am. Geog. Soc., 1971, Eben award Am. Water Resources Assn., 1972, Caulfield medal, 1989, Alumni medal U. Chgo., 1979, Outstanding Achievement award Nat. Coun. for Geog. Edn., 1981, Sasakawa UN Evniron. prize, 1985, Tyler prize, 1987, Laureat d'Honneur award Internat. Geog. Union, 1988, Vautrin Lud Internat. Geog. prize, 1992, Hubbard medal Nat. Geog. Soc., 1994, Volvo Environment prize, 1995. Mem. AAAS, NAS (mem. commn. on natural resources 1973-80, chmn. 1977-80, chmn. com. on water 1964-68, chmn. com. on sustainable water supplies of Middle East 1996—, Environ. award 1980), Assn. Am. Geographers (pres., Outstanding Achievement award 1955, 74, Anderson medal 1986), Internat. Coun. Sci. Unions (mem. steering com. on study of environ. consequences of nuclear war 1983-87, mem. adv. com. on environ. 1990-96), Russian Geog. Soc. (hon.), Royal Geog. Soc. (hon.), Russian Acad. Scis. (fgn.), Am. Philos. Soc., Cosmos Club (Washington, award 1993), Sigma Xi,. Mem. Soc. Friends. Home: 624 Pearl St Apt 302 Boulder CO 80302-5072

WHITE, GORDON ELIOT, historian; b. Glen Ridge, N.J., Oct. 25, 1933; s. Maurice Brewster and Sarah Fullove (Gordon) W.; m. Nancy Johnson, 1955 (div. 1957); m. Mary Joan Briggs, Aug. 6, 1960 (dec. Nov. 1987); children: Sarah Elizabeth and Gordon O'Neal Brewster (twins), David McIntyre; m. Francis C. Barrineau, 1989. B.A., Cornell U., 1955; M.S. in Journalism, Columbia U., 1957. Lic. master mariner USCG; lic. pilot FAA. Stringer Nassau Daily Rev.-Star, Rockville Centre, L.I., N.Y., 1948-50; stringer Freeport (N.Y.) Leader, 1949-50; sports writer Morris County (N.J.) Citizen, 1950-51; stringer Ithaca (N.Y.) Evening News, 1951-55; photo editor, editorial writer Cornell Daily Sun, 1951-55; copy editor Am. Banker, N.Y.C., 1958; Washington corr. Chgo. Am., 1958-61; chief Washington bur. Deseret News, Salt Lake City, 1961-88; also corr. in Europe, U.S. and Antarctic for WJR, Detroit; KSL-KSL-TV, Salt Lake City, also KGMB, Honolulu; free lance writer with U.S. Navy, Army and Air Force, 1959; cons. Nat. Air and Space Mus.; auto racing, mil. aviation electronics historian. Author: Offenhauser, the Legendary American Racing Engine and the Men Who Built It, 1996. Advisor auto racing Nat. Mus. Am. History, Smithsonian Instn., 1989—. Recipient 1st prize for newsphoto Sigma Delta Chi, 1954; Raymond Clapper Meml. award White House Corrs. Assn., 1978; award for excellence in reporting Exec. Dept. and White House; award for excellence in reporting Nat. Press Club, 1979; award for investigative reporting Utah-Idaho-Spokane Regional AP; Nat. Sigma Delta Chi award for disting. work as Washington Corr., 1979; Roy W. Howard award for outstanding public service by a newspaper corr., 1979; award for disting. investigative reporting Investigative Reporters and Editors, 1980; Disting. Public Service Reporting Service Scripps Howard Found., 1980; Mark E. Peterson award, 1980; Reser-Tuthill award for writing on history of automobile racing, Indpls., 1985. Mem. Sigma Delta Chi, Pi Kappa Phi, Pi Delta Epsilon. Episcopalian. Club: Nat. Press (Washington). Home and Office: Box 3067 Alexandria VA 22302

WHITE, H. BLAIR, lawyer; b. Burlington, Iowa, Aug. 2, 1927; s. Harold B. and Harriet E. (St. Clair) W.; m. Joan Van Alstine, Oct. 2, 1954; children—Blair W., Brian J. B.A., U. Iowa, 1950, J.D., 1951. Bar: Ill. 1951. Assoc. Sidley & Austin and predecessor firms, 1951-61, ptnr., 1962-95; dir. DeKalb Energy Corp., 1967-95, Kimberly-Clark Corp., 1971-95, R.R. Donnelley & Sons Co., 1979—, Bankmont Fin. Corp., 1986-92, DeKalb Genetics Co., 1988—. Pres., bd. dirs. Cook County (Ill.) Sch. Nursing, 1966-71; bd. dirs. Rush-Presbyn.-St. Lukes Med. Ctr., 1986-93, life trustee; bd. dirs. Children's Meml. Hosp., Chgo., 1980—, chmn. bd. dirs., 1993—. Mem. ABA, Ill. Bar Assn., Chgo. Bar Assn., Am. Coll. Trial Lawyers, 7th Fed. Cir. Bar Assn., Commercial Club, Legal Club, Law Club, Chgo. Club, Econ. Club (Chgo.), Skokie Country Club, Old Elm Country Club, Lost Tree Club. Office: Sidley & Austin 1 First Natl Plz Chicago IL 60603-2003

WHITE, HALBERT LYNN, JR., economist, educator, consultant; b. Kansas City, Mo., Nov. 19, 1950; s. H. Lynn and Emily (Roach) W.; m. Kim A. Titensor, Oct. 25, 1986; children: Richard H. Weeks, Rachel A. Weeks. AB, Princeton U., 1972; PhD, MIT, 1976. Asst. prof. U. Rochester, N.Y., 1976-80; assoc. prof. U. Calif., San Diego, 1980-84, prof., 1984-95, prof. above scale, 1995—; vis. asst. prof. MIT, Cambridge, 1984; mem. adv. bd. Merrill Lynch Acad., 1994-95; chmn. LaJolla (Calif.) Data Sys., 1988-91, Neural Net R&D Assocs., 1992—; commodity trading advisor, 1993—; cons. in field. Author: Asymptotic Theory for Econometricians, 1984, Estimation, Inference and Specification Analysis, 1994; co-author: Artificial Neural Networks - Approximation and Learning Theory, 1992: A Unified Theory of Estimation and Inference for Nonlinear Dynamic Models, 1988; editor: Abstracts of Working Papers in Economics, 1985—; contbr. articles to profl. jours. Guggenheim fellow Guggenheim Found., 1988-89; NSF grantee, 1980—; Jour. Econometrics fellow, 1995. Fellow Econometric Soc. (Multa Scripsit award on Econometric Theory 1997); mem. IEEE, Am. Math. Soc., Am. Statis. Assn., Internat. Neural Network Soc., Nat. Futures Assn., Jazz Soc. L.A., Jazz Soc. Lower So. Calif. (treas. 1988). Avocations: music performance and composition, antiques. Office: U Calif San Diego Dept Econs # 0508 La Jolla CA 92093

WHITE, HAROLD F., bankruptcy judge, retired federal judge; b. Hartford, Conn., Apr. 29, 1920; s. Harry and Maude C. (Strainge) W.; m. Edna Jeanette Murie, 1943; children: Francis James, Susan, Harold. BSc, Ohio U., 1946; JD, U. Akron, 1952. Bar: Ohio 1952. Chief police prosecutor City of Akron, Ohio, 1953; asst. prosecutor Summit County, Akron, 1957-58; bankruptcy referee, bankruptcy judge U.S. Cts., Akron, 1958-94; on recall as sr. bankruptcy judge U.S. Cts., 1994—. Trustee Summit County Kidney Found; elder Westminster Presbyn. Ch., Akron. Named Disting. Alumni Ohio U., 1979, Outstanding Alumni U. Akron Sch. Law, 1983; recipient John Quine adj. lectr. of law award U. Akron Sch. Law, 1991. Mem. Akron Bar Assn., Ohio State Bar Assn., Nat. Conf. Bankruptcy Judges (twice gov. 6th cir.), Commercial Law League, Am. Bankruptcy Inst. Office: US Bankruptcy Ct Fed Bldg Rm 260 2 S Main St Akron OH 44308

WHITE, HAROLD JACK, pathologist; b. Bklyn., Jan. 4, 1920; s. Abraham and Jennie (Warshawsky) W.; m. Lucette Darby, July 19, 1962; children: Elizabeth, Darby, Matthew, Esther. BS, Harvard U., 1941; MD, U. Geneva, 1952. Diplomate Am. Bd. Pathology. Intern, resident in pathology Yale U. Sch. Medicine, New Haven, 1953-58, fellow, 1957-58; assoc. pathologist Brigham and Women's Hosp., Boston, 1962-66; chief lab. svc. VA Hosp., West Roxbury, Mass., 1962-66, Little Rock, 1966-80; sr. scientist, acting head biomed. sci. dept. GM Rsch. Labs., Warren, Mich., 1980-85, cons., 1985—; prof. pathology, microbiology U. Ark. Med. Sch., Little Rock, 1966—; vis. scientist dept. comparative medicine, MIT, Cambridge, 1988—. Contbr. over 100 articles, abstracts in pathology, microbiology, immunology, toxicology, biomedicine to profl. jours. 1st lt. USAAF, 1942-46. Fellow Coll. Am. Pathologists, Internat. Coll. Pathology. Home: 24 Bass Rocks Rd Gloucester MA 01930-3276 Office: 35 Main St Gloucester MA 01930-5730

WHITE, HAROLD TREDWAY, III, management consultant; b. Stamford, Conn., Nov. 3, 1947; m. Elizabeth Phillips. BA in History, Northwestern U., 1970; MBA, Darmouth U., 1974. Asst. to dir. urban affairs Am. Bankers Assn., Washington, 1972-73; sr. assoc. Cresap, McCormick & Paget Cons., 1974-75; dir. planning and devel. Tilton (N.H.) Sch., 1975-78; dir. alumni affairs Amos Tuck Sch. Dartmouth U., Hanover, N.H., 1978-82; chief devel. officer Manhattanville Coll., Purchase, N.Y., 1982-84; cons., 1985; pres. Resource Dynamics Group, White Plains, N.Y., 1987—; adj. asst. prof. Iona Coll., New Rochelle, N.Y., 1989-93; assoc. mem. cons. bd. Nat. Ctr. Nonprofit Bds., Washington, 1991—. Contbr. articles to profl. jours. Trustee, v.p., chmn. planning, devel. and mktg. coms. Tilton Sch., 1978—, pres. bd., 1992-96; bd. dirs. Legal Awareness of Westchester, 1990-96, Westchester Ctr. for Tng. and Devel., 1992-96; pres. bd. Sci. Ctr. N.H., 1979-82, Nat. Coun. on Alcoholism and Other Drug Addictions/Westchester, 1985-89, Middle Patent Assn., 1988—; trustee Millbrook (N.Y.) Sch., 1981-87; mem. vestry St. Mary's Ch. of Bedford, 1996—. Avocations: cross-country running, skiing, hiking, sailing. Office: Resource Dynamics Group 215 Katonah Ave Katonah NY 10536-2138

WHITE, HARRY EDWARD, JR., lawyer; b. Menominee, Mich., Apr. 26, 1939; s. Harry Edward and Verena Charlotte (Leisen) W.; m. Mary P.A. Sheaffer, June 7, 1980. BS in Fgn. Svc., Georgetown U., Washington, 1961; LLB, Columbia U., 1964. Bar: N.Y. 1965, U.S. Supreme Ct. 1970, U.S. Dist. Ct. (so. dist.) N.Y. 1979, U.S. Tax Ct. 1980. Assoc. Milbank, Tweed, Hadley & McCloy, N.Y.C., 1964-65, 67-73, ptnr., 1974—. Contbr. chpts. to books, articles to legal jours. Served with M.I., U.S. Army, 1965-66, Vietnam. Decorated Bronze Star. Mem. ABA, Internat. Bar Assn., N.Y. State Bar Assn. (chmn. taxation com. internat. law practice sect. 1987-90, co-chmn. exempt orgns. com. tax sect. 1987-88), Internat. Law Assn., Am. Soc. Internat. Law, Assn. Bar of City of N.Y., Internat. Fiscal Assn. Republican. Roman Catholic. Home: 333 E 55th St New York NY 10022-8316 Office: Milbank Tweed Hadley & McCloy 1 Chase Manhattan Plz New York NY 10005-1401

WHITE, HERBERT CHARLES, psychiatrist; b. Madison, Wis., Nov. 16, 1937; s. Charles Gilbert and Marjorie (Spelman) W.; m. Darlene Rose Kramer, Dec. 17, 1961 (div. Apr. 1976); children: Claire Herdeman, Lesley Nelson, Gwenn White; m. Ardis June, July 11, 1977. BS, Denison U., 1959; DO, Chgo. Coll. Osteo. Medicine, 1964. Bd. cert. Am. Osteo. Bd. Gen. Practice; cert. Am. Med. Soc. on Alcoholism and Other Drug Dependencies, 1987. Intern Traverse City (Mich.) Osteo. Hosp., 1964-65; resident in psychiatry Med. Coll. Wis., Milw., 1991-95; med. dir. addiction program Elmbrook Hosp., Brookfield, Wis., 1972-90, Waukesha (Wis.) Meml. Hosp., 1975-85; med. dir. Kettle Moraine Hosp., Ocondmorool, Wis., 1985-87; med. dir. addiction program Greenbriar Hosp., Greenfield, Wis., 1990-95; dir. behavioral medicine St. Lukes South Shore, Cudahy, Wis., 1995—; med. dir. addiction program Milw. Psychiat. Hosp., 1995—; chair com. on edn. of com. on alcoholism Wis. State Med. Soc., Madison, 1980-90, chair com. alcoholism, 1988-89; asst. clin. prof. psychiatry Med. Coll. Wis., 1980—. Contbr. chpt. to book. Bd. dirs. Waukesha (Wis.) Coun. Alcoholism, 1975-83; trustee Prairie Hill Waldberg Sch., Delafield, Wis., 1995—. Mem. AMA, Am. Psychiat. Assn., Am. Osteo. Assn., Am. Med. Soc. Alcoholism. Avocations: outdoors sports. Office: 1220 Dewey Ave Wauwatosa WI 53213-2504

WHITE, HERBERT LAVERNE, meterologist, federal agency administrator; b. Waverly, N.Y., Oct. 28, 1950; s. Howard Chauncey and Edith Baylis (Soper) W.; m. Gayle Maureen Shannon, Dec. 28, 1975. BS in Meteorology, Pa. State U., 1972; postgrad., Marine Forecasting Naval, Postgrad. Sch., 1980. Meteorologist-student trainee Nat. Weather Svc., Charleston, S.C., 1970-71; meteorologist intern Nat. Weather Svc., Pitts., 1972-76, meteorologist, 1976-77; forecaster Nat. Weather Svc., Raleigh, N.C., 1977-80, evaluations officer, computer mgr., 1980-94; warning coordination meteorologist Nat. Weather Svc., Binghamton, N.Y., 1994-96; pub. safety meteorologist Nat. Weather Svc., Silver Spring, Md., 1996—. Asst. scoutmaster Boy Scouts Am., 1969-72, neighborhood commr. 1973-74. Recipient Gold Medal award U.S. Dept. Commerce, 1993; Modernization award Nat. Oceanic and Atmospheric Adminstrn., 1995. Mem. Am. Meteorol. Soc. (vice chmn. cen. N.C. chpt. 1993-94, newsletter editor Pitts. chpt. 1976-77), Nat. Weather Assn. (charter), Nat. Weather Svc. Employees Orgn. (sec. ea. region 1987-88, chmn. 1988-91, dir. legis. and pub. affairs 1991-94, mem. nat. negotiating com. 1988-94), Pa. State U. Alumni Assn. (life). Methodist. Avocations: travel, stamp collecting, matchbook cover collecting, gardening, walking. Office: National Weather Svc Headqtrs OM11 SSMC 2 #14394 1325 E West Hwy Silver Spring MD 20910-3280

WHITE, HERBERT SPENCER, research library educator, university dean; b. Vienna, Austria, Sept. 5, 1927; came to U.S., 1938, naturalized, 1944; s. Leon and Ernestine (Lichteneger) Hochweis; m. Mary Virginia Dyer, Feb. 19, 1953; 1 son, Jerome. BS in Chemistry, CCNY, 1949; MSLS, Syracuse U., 1950. Intern Libr. of Congress, Washington, 1950, mem. tech. info. divsn., 1950-53; tech. libr. AEC, Oak Ridge, Tenn., 1953-54; organizer, mgr. corp. libr. Chance Vought Aircraft, Dallas, 1954-59; mgr. engring. libr. IBM Corp., Kingston, N.Y., 1959-62; mgr. tech. info. ctr. IBM Corp., Poughkeepsie, N.Y., 1962-64; exec. dir. NASA Sci. and Tech. Info. Facility, College Park, Md., 1964-68; v.p. info. mgmt. Leasco Systems & Rsch. Corp., Bethesda, Md., 1968-70; sr. v.p. Inst. Sci. Info., Phila., 1970-74, corp. dir., 1971-74; pres. Stechert-Macmillan, Inc., Pennsaucken, N.J., 1974-75; prof., dir. Rsch. Ctr. Grad. Libr. Sch. Ind. U., Bloomington, 1975-80, dean Sch. Libr. and Info. Scis., 1980-90, disting. prof., 1991-95; prof. emeritus, 1995—; adj. prof. U. Ariz. Sch. Libr. Scis., 1995—; vis. prof. Alberta, San Jose State, Hawaii; cons., lectr. Author books; contbr. articles to profl. pubs.; columnist Libr. Jour. Mem. Pres.'s Adv. Com. for Adminstrn. Title II-B Higher Edn. Act, 1965-68, Libr. Rsch. Planning Com. for 1980s, U.S. Dept. Edn., v.p. Green Valley Cmty. Coordinating Coun., 1997—. Spl. honoree, U. of Essen (Germany) Conf., 1992. Fellow Spl. Libraries Assn. (pres. 1969-70, J.C. Dana award 1985, Hall of Fame 1994); mem. ALA (councillor 1988—, planning com. 1989-91, Dewey medal 1987), Am. Soc. Info. Sci. (pres. 1973-74, W. Davis award 1977, award of merit 1981, named Pioneer, 1987), Assn. Libr. and Info. Sci. Edn. (chmn. govtl. rels. com. 1980-88), Am. Fedn. Info. Processing Socs. (dir. 1972-78), Federation Internationale de Documentation (Netherlands, bd. dir. 1976-78, treas. 1978-82), Soc. for Scholarly Pub. (bd. dirs. 1981-82), Assn. Rsch. Libraries (com. on libr. edn, 1983-85), Coun. Libr. Resources (rsch. priorities task force 1984-88, Ind. Libr. Lifetime Achievement award 1990), Beta Phi Mu (Svc. award 1995). Address: 330 E El Viento Green Valley AZ 85614-2246

WHITE, HUGH VERNON, JR., lawyer; b. Suffolk, Va., July 24, 1933; s. Hugh Vernon and Mary Lois (Claud) W.; m. Mary Margaret Flowers, Nov. 25, 1961; children: Hunter, William, John. BS in Civil Engring., Va. Mil. Inst., 1954; LLB, Washington & Lee U., 1961. Bar: Va. 1961. Engr. E.I. DuPont de Nemours & Co., Parlin, N.J., 1954-55; exec. dir. Va. Legis. Study Commn., Richmond, Va., 1961-63; assoc. Hunton & Williams, Richmond, 1963-69, ptnr., 1969—; bd. dirs. Pulaski Furniture Corp., Pulaski, Va. Mem. Richmond First, 1966—, pres., 1971; bd. trustees Va. Hist. Soc., 1997—, Randolph-Macon Woman's Coll., 1997—. Mem. ABA, Va. Bar Assn., Richmond Bar Assn., Phi Beta Kappa, Omicron Delta Kappa. Presbyterian. Clubs: Commonwealth, Country (Richmond). Home: 512 Gaskins Rd S Richmond VA 23233-5710 Office: Hunton & Williams Riverfront Plaza East Tower 951 E Byrd St Richmond VA 23219-4040

WHITE, JAMES BARR, lawyer, real estate investor, consultant; b. Haverhill, Mass., June 13, 1941; s. Ned and Shirlee (Euster) W.; m. Carol Klein, June 23, 1963; children: Michael Andrew, Laurie Alison, Elizabeth Ellen. BS, Tufts U., 1962; LLB, Columbia U., 1965; MPA, Harvard U., 1988. Bar: Mass. 1965. Assoc. Goulston & Storrs, Boston, 1965-71, ptnr., 1971-74; ptnr. Palmer & Dodge, Boston, 1974-89; pvt. practice cons. Boston, 1989—; pres. ELAW Corp., Concord, Mass., 1992—; mem. adv. com. MIT Ctr. for Real Estate Devel., Cambridge, 1987-89; dir. Nat. Realty Com., Washington, 1987-89. Chmn., mem. Town of Wayland (Mass.) Planning Bd., 1974-78; mem. Route 128 Area Com., Lincoln, Mass., 1985-87; mem. Town of Lincoln Planning Bd., 1991—, Town of Lincoln Hist. Dist. Commn., 1992—; bd. overseers New Eng. Conservatory, 1995—. Mem. Boston Bar Assn., Handel and Haydn Soc. (gov. 1985-90, overseer 1990-94), Bostonian Soc. (bd. dirs. 1990—). Home: 38 Bedford Rd Lincoln MA 01773-2037 Office: ELAW Corp Office of Pres 175 Sudbury Rd Concord MA 01742-3419

WHITE, JAMES BOYD, law educator; b. Boston, July 28, 1938; s. Benjamin Vroom and Charlotte Green (Conover) W.; m. Mary Louise Fitch, Jan. 1, 1978; children: Emma Lillian, Henry Alfred; children by previous marriage: Catherine Conover, John Southworth. A.B., Amherst Coll., 1960; A.M., Harvard U., 1961, LL.B., 1964. Assoc. Foley, Hoag & Eliot, Boston, 1964-67; asst. prof. law U. Colo., 1967-69, assoc. prof., 1969-73, prof., 1973-75; prof. law U. Chgo., 1975-83; Hart Wright prof. law and English U. Mich., Ann Arbor, 1983—; vis. assoc. prof. Stanford U., 1972. Author: The Legal Imagination, 1973, (with Scarboro) Constitutional Criminal Procedure, 1976, When Words Lose Their Meaning, 1981, Heracles' Bow, 1985, Justice as Translation, 1990, "This Book of Starres", 1994, Acts of Hope, 1994. Sinclair Kennedy Traveling fellow, 1964-65; Nat. Endowment for Humanities fellow, 1979-80, 92; Guggenheim fellow, 1993. Mem. AAAS, Am. Law Inst. Office: U Mich Law Sch 625 S State St Ann Arbor MI 48109-1215

WHITE, JAMES CLAIBORNE, manufacturing engineer executive; b. Xenia, Ohio, May 6, 1962; s. John Delano and Janice Claire (Ingram) W.; m. Janna Unger, Aug. 24, 1985; children: Dakota James, Tristan Garrett, Colton Laramy. BS in Mech. Engring., Tenn. Tech. U., Cookeville, 1987; MS in Indsl. Engring., Purdue U., 1993. Registered profl. engr., Ky., Tenn. Quality assurance analsyt Johnson Controls, Inc., Greenfield, Ohio, 1987-88; mech. engr. Big Rivers Electric Corp., Henderson, Ky., 1988-95; sr. mfg. engr. Calsonic N.Am.-Tenn. Ops., Shelbyville, 1995-96, mfg. engring. supr., 1996—. Pres. Collegiate Bowling League, Cookeville, Tenn., 1984-85, U. Christian Student Ctr., Cookeville, 1984-85; fin. dir. local non-profit orgn., Evansville, Ind., 1993-95. Mem. ASME (assoc.), NSPE (engr. amb. 1989—, mathcounts co-chair 1989). Republican. Mem. Ch. of Christ. Achievements include design of modified sulfuric acid storage tanks; development and teaching of AutoCAD course at Henderson Community College; development of joint-venture contract between local electric utility and municipal wastewater treatment plant to provide water and waste services to newly located industry. Office: Calsonic NAM-Tenn Ops One Calsonic Way PO Box 350 Shelbyville TN 37160

WHITE, JAMES EDWARD, geophysicist; b. Cherokee, Tex., May 10, 1918; s. William Cleburne and Willie (Carter) W.; m. Courtenay Brumby, Feb. 1, 1941; children: Rebecca White Vanderslice, Peter McDuffie, Margaret Marie White Jamleson, Courtenay White Forte. B.A., U. Tex., 1941, M.A., 1946; Ph.D., MIT, 1949. Dir. Underwater Sound Lab., MIT, Cambridge, 1941-45; scientist Def. Research Lab., Austin, Tex., 1945-46; research assoc. MIT, 1946-49; group leader, field research lab. Mobil Oil Co., Dallas, 1949-55; mgr. physics dept. Denver Research Center, Marathon Oil Co., 1955-69; v.p. Globe Universal Scis., Midland, Tex., 1969-71; adj. prof. dept. geophysics Colo. Sch. Mines, Golden, 1972-73, C.H. Green prof., 1976-87, prof. emeritus, 1986—; L.A. Nelson prof. U. Tex., El Paso, 1973-76; Esso vis. prof. U. Sydney, Australia, 1975; vis. prof. MIT, 1982, U. Tex.-Austin, 1985, Macquarie U., Sydney, 1988; del. U.S.-USSR geophysics exchange Dept. State, 1965; mem. bd. Am. Geol. Inst., 1972; mem. space applications bd. Nat. Acad. Engring., 1972-77; exchange scientist Nat. Acad. Sci., 1973-74; del. conf. on oil exploration China Geophys. Soc.-Soc. Exploration Geophysicists, 1981; cons. world bank Chinese U. Devel. Project II, 1987. Author: Seismic Waves: Radiation, Transmission, Attenuation, 1965, Underground Sound: Application of Seismic Waves, 1983, (with R.L. Sengbush) Production Seismology, 1987; editor: Vertical Seismic Profiling (E.I. Galperin), 1974; contbr. articles to profl. jours.; patentee in field. Recipient Halliburton award, 1987, Kapitsa Gold medal Russian Acad. Natural Scis., 1996. Fellow Acoustical Soc. Am.; mem. NAE, Soc. Exploration Geophysicists (hon., Maurice Ewing medal 1986), Cosmos Club, Sigma Xi. Unitarian. Office: Colo Sch Mines Dept Geophysics Golden CO 80401

WHITE, JAMES FLOYD, theology educator; b. Boston, Jan. 23, 1932; s. Edwin Turner and Madeline (Rinker) W.; m. Marilyn Atkinson, Aug. 23, 1959 (div. 1982); children: Louise, Robert, Ellen, Laura, Martin; m. Susan Jan Waller, Oct. 28, 1982 (div. 1993); m. Claire Duggan, Mar. 2, 1997. Grad., Phillips Acad., Andover, Mass., 1949; AB, Harvard U., 1953; BD, Union Theol. Sem., 1956; PhD, Duke U., 1960. Ordained to ministry United Meth. Ch., 1955. Instr. Ohio Wesleyan U., Delaware, 1959-61, Meth. Theol. Sch. in Ohio, Delaware, 1960-61; prof. Perkins Sch. Theology, So. Meth. U., Dallas, 1961-83, U. Notre Dame, Ind., 1983—. Author: Cambridge Movement, 1962, New Forms of Worship, 1971, Introduction to Christian Worship, 1980, Protestant Worship, 1989, Roman Catholic Worship (1st place award Cath. Press Assn. 1996), Christian Worship in North America, 1997, also others; mem. editl. bd. Religious Book Club, 1980-93. Named one of 100 Most Influential People in Am. Religion, Christian Century mag., 1982; honored by book published in his honor: The Sunday Service of the Methodists: Studies in Honor of James F. White, 1996. Mem. N.Am. Acad. Liturgy (pres. 1979, Berakah award 1983), Am. Soc. Ch. History, Liturgical Conf., Societas Liturgica. Avocations: hiking, travel, book and antiques collecting. Office: U Notre Dame Dept Theology Notre Dame IN 46556

WHITE, JAMES PATRICK, law educator; b. Iowa City, Sept. 29, 1931; s. Raymond Patrick and Besse (Kanak) W.; m. Anna R. Seim, July 2, 1964. BA, U. Iowa, 1953, JD, 1956; LLM, George Washington U., 1959; LLD (hon.), U. Pacific, 1964, John Marshall Law Sch., 1989, Weidner U., 1989, Campbell U., 1993; Jur D (hon.), Whittier Coll., 1992; LLD (hon.), Campbell U., 1993; Southwestern U., 1995; LLD (hon.), Quinnipiac U., 1995, Calif. Western Law Sch., 1997. Bar: Iowa 1956, D.C. 1959, U.S. Supreme Ct. 1959. Teaching fellow George Washington U. Law Sch., 1958-59; asst. prof. U. N.D. Law Sch., Grand Forks, 1959-62; asso. prof., acting dean U. N.D. Law Sch., 1962-63, prof., asst. dean, 1963-67; dir. agrl. law rsch. program, prof. law Ind. U. Law Sch., Indpls., 1967—, also dir. urban legal studies program, 1971-74; dean acad. devel. and planning, spl. asst. to chancellor Ind. Univ., Indpls., 1974-83; mem. for N.D., Commn. on Uniform State Laws, 1961-66; cons. legal edn. ABA, Indpls., 1974—. Contbr. papers to tech. lit. 1st lt. JAGC, USAF, 1956-58. Carnegie postdoctoral fellow U. Mich. Ctr. for Study Higher Edn., 1964-65. Fellow Am. Bar Found.; mem. ABA, Am. Law Inst., Order of Coif. Roman Catholic. Home: 7707 N Meridian St Indianapolis IN 46260-3651 Office: Ind U 550 W North St Indianapolis IN 46202-3162

WHITE, JAMES RICHARD, lawyer; b. McKinney, Tex., Jan. 22, 1948; s. James Ray and Maxine (Brown) W.; m. Marian Olivia Gates, Feb. 3, 1979; children: Nicole Olivia, Mandi Leigh, James Derek. BBA, So. Meth. U., 1969, MBA, 1970, JD, 1973, LLM, 1977. Bar: Tex. 1973, U.S. Tax Ct. 1975, U.S. Supreme Ct. 1989, U.S. Ct. Appeals (5th cir.) 1989); cert. Comml. Real Estate Law Tex. Bd. Legal Specialization. Assoc. Elliot, Meer, Vetter, Denton & Bates, Dallas, 1973-74, Atwell, Cain & Davenport, Dallas, 1974-75; atty. Sabine Corp., Dallas, 1975-77; assoc. Brice & Barron, Dallas, 1977-79; ptnr. Millard & Olson, Dallas, 1979-82, Johnson & Swanson, Dallas, 1982-83, Winstead, Sechrest & Minick P.C., Dallas, 1983—; mem. staff Southwestern Law Jour., Dallas, 1971-73; mem. So. Meth. U. Moot Ct. Bd., Order Barristers, Dallas, 1972-73; prof. North Lake Coll., Dallas, 1985; bd. dirs. Tex. Assn. Young Lawyers, Austin, 1980-82; sec. bd. dirs. Dallas Assn. Young Lawyers, 1976-80. Contbr. articles to profl. jours. Chmn. bd. dirs. Tex. Lawyers Credit Union, Austin, 1980-82; pres. North Tex. Premier Soccer Assocs., Dallas, 1979-81; v.p. Lake Highlands Soccer Assn., 1995-96, pres., 1996—; mem. regional mobility task force Real Estate Coun., City of Dallas, 1991-92, mem. downtown revitalization com., 1995—; mem. Dallas Indsl. Devel. Bd., 1992-93, Dallas Higher Edn. Authority Bd., 1994-96; spkr.'s bur. and accreditation divsn. World Cup USA '94. Mem. ABA (mem. survey, accreditation and opinion coms.), Tex. Bar Assn. (cert. 1973, mem. mortgage loan opinion com.), Tex. Coll. Real Estate Attys., Coll. State Bar Tex. Methodist. Avocations: soccer, golf, skiing, racquetball. Home: 8003 Hundley Ct Dallas TX 75231-4728 Office: Winstead Sechrest & Minick 5400 Renaissance Tower 1201 Elm St Dallas TX 75270-2102

WHITE, JANE SEE, journalist; b. St. Louis, Aug. 26, 1950; d. Robert Mitchell and Barbara Whitney (Spurgeon) W.; 1 child, Laura Mitchell. BA in History and Am. Studies, Hollins Coll., 1972. Reporter Roanoke (Va.) Times, 1972-73, Kansas City (Mo.) City Star, 1973-76, AP, N.Y.C., Hartford, 1976-78; spl. writer AP, N.Y.C., 1978-81; sr. writer, chief news and bur., chief profl. div. Med. Econs. Mag., Oradell, N.J., 1981-87; dep. city editor, city editor Roanoke Times World News, 1987-91; asst. metro. editor Phoenix Gazette, 1991-93; asst. city editor Ariz. Rep., Phoenix, 1993, features editor, 1993-95; asst. mng. editor adminstrn. Ariz. Rep. and Phoenix Gazette, Phoenix, 1995-96; staff devel. and tng. editor Ariz. Rep. & Phoenix Gazette, 1996-97; freelance journalist Tucson, 1997—. Editor: Medical Practice Management, 1985; contbr. articles to profl. jurs. Avocations: golf, reading, cooking.

WHITE, JEAN TILLINGHAST, former state senator; b. Cambridge, Mass., Dec. 24, 1934; d. James Churchill Moulton and Clara Jean (Carter) Tillinghast; m. Peregrine White, June 6, 1970. B.A., Wellesley Coll., 1956. Supr., programmer Lumber Mut. Ins. Co., Cambridge, 1964-70; selectman, chmn. Town of Rindge (N.H.), 1975-80; clk. regulated revenues N.H. Ho. of Reps., Concord, 1978-80, vice chmn. regulated revenues, 1980-82; mem. N.H. Senate, 1982-88, chmn. fin. com.; commr., Cheshire County, 1995—; v.p., treas. Perry White, Inc., Rindge, N.H., 1970—; dir. Peterborough Savings Bank (N.H.). Chmn., Rindge Friends of Library, 1972; pres. Nat. Order Women Legislators, 1990-91. Trustee Univ. System of N.H., 1989-92, Jaffrey/Rindge Sch. Bd., 1989—; commr. Cheshire County, 1995—. Republican. Unitarian. Office: Hampshire Rd Rindge NH 03461

WHITE, JEFFERY HOWELL, lawyer; b. Tyler, Tex., Aug. 4, 1959; s. Bluford D. and Tempie R. (Tunnell) W.; m. Michael Anne Mackley, May 21, 1989; children: Kristin, Alex. BS in History, So. Ark. U., 1983; JD, Oklahoma City U., 1986. Bar: Tex. 1987. Assoc. Dean White, Canton, Tex., 1986-90; asst. dist. atty. Van Zandt Co., Canton, 1991-94; ptnr. Elliott Elliott & White, Canton, 1994—. Mem. Van Zandt County Bar Assn., Tex. Criminal Def. Lawyers Assn. Democrat. United Methodist. Avocations: golf, tennis, spectator sports. Home: PO Box 102 Canton TX 75103-0102 Office: Elliott Elliott & White 166 N Buffalo St Canton TX 75103-1338

WHITE, JEFFREY GEORGE, healthcare consultant, educator; b. Lawrence, Mass., Apr. 16, 1944; s. Alfred James and Ruth Virginia (Maylum) W.; children: Jennifer L., Tracy E. AB in Econs., Bowdoin Coll., 1966; MBA, U. N.H., 1985. Asst. pers. dir., then asst. adminstr. Maine Med. Ctr., Portland, 1967-71; asst. adminstr. Regional Meml. Hosp., Brunswick, Maine, 1971, adminstr., 1971-74; assoc. dir. Elizabeth Ann Seton Hosp. (now Mid-Maine Med. Ctr.), Waterville, 1974-75; assoc. adminstr. Mid-Maine Med. Ctr., 1975-79, v.p. ops., 1979-83; asst. dir. Wentworth-Douglass Hosp., Dover, N.H., 1983-85; exec. v.p. Frisbie Meml. Hosp., Rochester, N.H., 1985-89, pres., 1989-92; sr. cons., prin. Helms & Co., Inc., Concord, N.H., 1992—; preceptor dept. health mgmt. and policy U. N.H., Durham, 1985-92, adj. asst. prof., 1991-93, asst. prof., 1993—; mem. instrnl. conf. coun. New Eng. Healthcare Assembly, 1992—. Vol. pub. TV sta.; bd. dirs. Greater Seacoast United Way, 1991-94, chmn. comty. campaign, 1993; pres. Greater Rochester C. of C., 1990. Fellow Am. Coll. Healthcare Execs. (past regent for N.H.); mem. N.H. Hosp. Assn. (trustee emeritus). Republican. Avocations: running, skiing, reading, travel. Home: 37 Mill Pond Rd Durham NH 03824-2722 Office: Helms & Co Inc 14 South St Concord NH 03301-3744

WHITE, JEFFREY M., lawyer; b. Lewiston, Maine, Jan. 16, 1948. BS, Tufts U., 1970; JD, Boston Coll., 1975. Bar: Maine 1975, U.S. Ct. Appeals (1st cir.) 1979. Atty. Pierce, Atwood, Portland, Maine. Mem. ABA (mem. antitrust, intellectual property and litigation sects.), Maine State Bar Assn. (co-chmn. com. continuing legal edn. 1981-83), Maine Trial Lawyers Assn., Cumberland County Bar Assn. Office: Pierce Atwood Monument Sq Portland ME 04101

WHITE, JILL CAROLYN, lawyer; b. Santa Barbara, Calif., Mar. 20, 1934; d. Douglas Cameron and Gladys Louise (Ashley) W.; m. Walter Otto Weyrauch, Mar. 17, 1973. BA, Occidental Coll., L.A., 1955; JD, U. Calif., Berkeley, 1972. Bar: Fla. 1974, Calif. 1975, D.C. 1981, U.S. Dist. Ct. (no. and mid. dists.) Fla., U.S. Ct. Appeals (5th and 11th cirs.), U.S. Supreme Ct. Staff mem. U.S. Dept. State, U.S. Embassy, Rio de Janeiro, Brazil, 1956-58; with psychol. rsch. units Inst. Human Devel., Inst. Personality Assessment and Rsch., U. Calif., Berkeley, 1961-68; adj. prof. U. Fla. Criminal Justice Program, Gainesville, Fla., 1976-78; pvt. practice immigration and nationality law Gainesville, 1976—; appointed mem. Fla. Bar Inaugural Immigration and Nationality Law Certification Com., 1994—, chair certification com., 1997, mem. bd. cert. in immigration and nationality law, 1995—. Contbr. articles to profl. jours. Mem. ABA, Am. Immigration Lawyers Assn. (chair Ctrl. Fla. chpt. 1988-89, co-chmn. So. Regional Liaison com. 1990-92, nat. bd. dirs. 1988-89)), Bar Assn. 8th Jud. Cir. Fla., Gainesville Area C. of C., Gainesville Area Innovation Network, Altrusa Club Gainesville. Democrat. Office: 2830 NW 41st St Ste C Gainesville FL 32606-6667

WHITE, JOE LLOYD, soil scientist, educator; b. Pierce, Okla., Nov. 8, 1921; s. Claud Amos and Alta Maurice (Denney) W.; m. Wanita Irene Robertson, May 29, 1945; children—Lerrill, Darla, Ronna, Bren, Janeil. Student, Connors State Agrl. Coll., 1940-42; B.S., Okla. State U., 1944, M.S., 1945; Ph.D., U. Wis., 1947. Asst. prof. agronomy Purdue U., West Lafayette, Ind., 1947-51, assoc. prof., 1951-57, prof., 1957-88; cons. Bancroft Co., William H. Rorer Co., Chattem Chem. Co., Merck Sharp & Dohme Rsch. Lab. Patentee in field. Fellow NSF, 1965-66, Guggenheim Found., 1972-73; Fulbright scholar, 1973; recipient Sr. U.S. Scientist award Alexander von Humboldt Found., 1980-81. Fellow AAAS, Am. Soc. Agronomy, Am. Inst. Chemists, Soil Sci. Soc. Am., Mineral Soc. Am., Royal Soc. Chemistry; mem. Am. Chem. Soc., Clay Minerals Soc. (disting.), Am. Pharm. Assn., Coblentz Soc., Geochem. Soc., Internat. Soil Sci. Soc., Internat. Assn. Colloid and Interface Scientists, N.Y. Acad. Sci., Royal Soc. Chemists (chartered chemist), Soc. Petroleum Engrs. of AIME, Internat. Zeolite Assn., Soc. Applied Spectroscopy, Sigma Xi, Phi Kappa Phi, Phi Lambda Upsilon. Mem. Ch. of Christ. Achievements include patents for use of zeolites in ruminant nutrition, for stable dried aluminum hydroxide gel, for method and composition for treatment of hyperphosphatemia; establishment of the role of carbonate in inhibiting crystallization of aluminum hydroxide; definitive characterization of aluminum-containing adjuvants used in vaccines. Home: 2505 Roselawn Ave Lafayette IN 47904-2319 Office: Purdue U Dept Agronomy West Lafayette IN 47907

WHITE, JOHN, federal agency administrator. BS in Indsl. and Labor Rels., Cornell U.; MA in Econs., Syracuse U., PhD in Econs. Sr. v.p. nat. security rsch. programs Rand Corp., 1968-77; asst. sec. Def. Manpower, Res. Affairs, and Logistics, 1977-78; dep. dir. Office Mgmt. and Budget, 1978-81; CEO, chmn. bd. dirs. Interactive Sys. Corp., 1981-88; gen. mgr. integration and sys. products divsn., v.p. Eastman Kodak Co., 1988-92; dep. sec. Dept. of Def., Washington, 1995—. Officer USMC. Office: Office of the Sec Def 1000 Defense Pentagon Washington DC 20301-1000*

WHITE, JOHN ARNOLD, physics educator, research scientist; b. Chgo., Jan. 30, 1933; s. Maxwell Richard and Dorothy Edith (Arnold) W.; m. Rebecca Anne Cotten, June 20, 1964; children: Lauren, Thomas, Julia. B.A., Oberlin Coll., 1954; M.S., Yale U., 1955, Ph.D., 1959. Instr. physics Yale U., 1958-59, Harvard U., 1959-62; research assoc. Yale U., 1962-63; research physicist Nat. Bur. Standards, Washington, 1963-64; research assoc. U. Md., College Park, 1965-66; assoc. prof. Am. U., Washington, 1966-68; prof. Am. U., 1968—; cons. Nat. Bur. Standards, 1965-72; mem. tech. staff Bell Telephone Labs., summers 1954, 60-62; vis. scientist MIT, fall 1972, Nat. Bur. Standards, Washington, summer 1981; vis. prof. Inst. for Phys. Sci. and Tech., U. Md., College Park, fall 1993. Author sci. papers on atomic structure and fluorescence, magnetism, lasers, speed of light, thermodynamic fluctuations, critical point phenomena, extended renormalization group theory of fluids. Recipient (with Zoltan Bay) Boyden Premium Franklin Inst., Phila., 1980; honor scholar, 1950-54; Noyes Clark fellow, 1954-57; NSF fellow, 1957-58; grantee NSF, 1966, 67, 69, 71; grantee Office Naval Research, 1973, 74; Am. Soc. Engring. Edn. faculty fellow Naval Research Lab., Washington, summer 1985; Dept. Energy Office Basic Energy Scis. grantee, 1986, 88, 90. Fellow Am. Phys. Soc.; mem. AAUP, Washington Philos. Soc., Phi Beta Kappa, Sigma Xi. Home: 7107 Fairfax Rd Bethesda MD 20814-1234 Office: Am U Dept Physics Washington DC 20016-8058

WHITE, JOHN AUSTIN, JR., engineering educator, dean, consultant; b. Portland, Ark., Dec. 5, 1939; s. John Austin and Ella Mae (McDermott) W.; m. Mary Elizabeth Quarles, Apr. 13, 1963; children: Kimberly Elizabeth White Brakmann, John Austin III. BS in Indsl. Engring., U. Ark., 1962; MS in Indsl. Engring., Va. Poly. Inst., 1966; PhD, Ohio State U., 1969; PhD (hon.), Cath. U. of Leuven, Belgium, 1985, George Washington U., 1991. Registered profl. engr., Va. Indsl. engr. Tenn. Eastman Co., Kingsport, 1961-63, Ethyl Corp., Baton Rouge, 1965; instr. Va. Poly. Inst. and State U., Blacksburg, 1963-66, asst. prof., 1970-72, assoc. prof., 1972-75; teaching assoc. Ohio State U., Columbus, 1966-70; assoc. prof. Ga. Inst. Tech., Atlanta, 1975-77, prof., 1977-84, Regents' prof., 1984—, Gwaltney prof., 1988—, dean engring., 1991-97; disting. prof. indsl. engring., chancellor U. Ark., Fayetteville, 1997—; asst. dir. engring. NSF, 1988-91; founder, chmn. SysteCon Inc., Duluth, Ga., 1977-84; exec. cons. Coopers & Lybrand, N.Y.C., 1984-93; mem. mfg. studies bd. NRC, Washington, 1986-88; bd. dirs. CAPS Logistics, Russell Corp., Eastman Chem. Co., Motorola Corp.; pres. Nat. Consortium for Grad. Degrees for Minorities in Engring. and Sci., Inc., 1993-95; bd. dirs. Southeastern Consortium for Minorities in Engring., 1992—; apptd. U.S. del. to the Internat. Steering Com. of the Intelligent Mfg. System, 1995-97; mem. Nat. Sci. Bd., 1994—. Co-author: Facility Layout and Location: An Analytical Approach, 1974 (Book of Yr. award Inst. Indsl. Engrs. 1974), 2d edit., 1991, Analysis of Queueing Systems, 1975, Principles of Engineering Economic Analysis, 3d edit., 1989, Capital Investment Decision Analysis for Management and Engineering, 1980, 2d edit., 1996, Facilities Planning, 1984 (Book of Yr. award Inst. Indsl. Engrs. 1984), 2d edit., 1996; editor: Production Handbook, 1987; co-editor: Progress in Materials Handling and Logistics, Vol. 1, 1989; also numerous articles to profl. jours., chpts. to books and handbooks in field, conf. procs. Recipient Outstanding Tchr. award Ga. Inst. Tech., 1982, Disting. Alumnus award Ohio State U. Coll. Engring., 1984, Disting. Indsl. Engring. alumnus award Va. Polytech. Inst. and State U., 1993, Reed-Apple award Material Handling Edn. Found., 1985, Disting. Svc. award NSF, 1991, Rodney D. Chipp Meml. award Soc. Women Engrs., 1994. Fellow Am. Inst. Indsl. Engrs. (pres. 1983-84, facilities planning and design award 1980, outstanding indsl. engr. award region III 1974, region IV 1984, Albert G. Holzman disting. educator award 1988, outstanding pub. award 1988, David F. Baker disting. rsch. award 1990, Frank and Lillian Gilbreth award 1994), Am. Assn. Engring. Socs. (bd. govs., chmn. 1986, Kenneth Andrew Roe award 1989); mem. Nat. Acad. Engring., Ark. Acad. Indsl. Engring., Am. Soc. Engring. Edn. (Donald E. Marlowe award 1994), Coun. Logistics Mgmt. Internat. Material Mgmt. Soc. (material mgr. of yr. 1989), Soc. Mfg. Engrs. (mfg. educator award 1990), Nat. Soc. Profl. Engrs. Inst. for Ops. Rsch. and the Mgmt. Scis. (hon.), Golden Key, Sigma Xi, Alpha Pi Mu, Omicron Delta Kappa, Phi Kappa Phi, Tau Beta Pi, Omega Rho. Baptist. Avocations: reading, golf, writing. Office: Ga Inst Tech Coll Engring Office of Dean Atlanta GA 30332

WHITE, JOHN CHARLES, historian; b. Washington, Apr. 14, 1939; s. Bennett Sexton, Jr. and Mary Elizabeth (Wildman) W.; m. Carolyn R. West, July 6, 1963. A.B. magna cum laude with exceptl. distinction in History (Robert E. Lee scholar), Washington and Lee U., 1960; M.A. (So. fellow), Duke U., 1962, Ph.D. (So. fellow), 1964. Asst. prof. U. Ala., Huntsville, 1967-70, assoc. prof., 1970-76, prof., 1976-91, chmn. dept. history, 1970-91, dir., acting chmn. dept. langs. and lits., 1988-91, ret., 1991; dir., sec.-treas. Consortium on Revolutionary Europe, 1972-86; European travel cons., 1991—. Editor: Procs. Consortium on Revolutionary Europe, 1977, 81; contbr. articles on French adminstrv. history to profl. jours. Bd. dirs Ala. Preservation Alliance, 1989-95, Ala. com. humanities NEH, 1979-82, mem. exec. com., 1980-81; vice chmn. bd. Ala. Constn. Hall, 1979-81, chmn. bd. dirs., 1982-84; bd. dirs. Ala. Humanities Found., 1985-89, vice chmn. bd. 1988-89; assoc. Ala. Humanities, 1982-85; pres. Alliance Francaise, 1970; active Huntsville Lit. Assn., Huntsville Mus. Assn. Served to capt. Recipient Chalons and Dunkirk City medals, 1964-65, Ala. Hist. Commn. award of merit, 1978, Multi-Cultural Svcs. Recognition award U. Ala., Huntsville, 1991, appreciation award U. Ala. Alumni Assn., 1991, cert. of appreciation Gov. of Ala., 1991, Ala. Senate, 1991, award of merit Ala. Preservation Alliance, 1994, others; Woodrow Wilson summer grantee, 1961-62, U. Ala. rsch. grantee, 1969, 70, 74. Mem. Ala. Assn. Historians (pres. 1978-80), Ala. Hist. Soc., Consortium on Revolutionary Europe, Phi Alpha Theta (Nat. Scholarship medal 1991), Phi Kappa Phi, Omicron Delta Kappa (Founder's Day Leadership award 1991), Phi Sigma Iota (Nat. Svc. award 1991). Club: Rotary. Home: 220 Longwood Dr Huntsville AL 35801

WHITE, JOHN DAVID, composer, theorist, cellist; b. Rochester, Minn., Nov. 28, 1931; s. Leslie David and Millie (Solum) W.; m. Marjorie Manuel, Dec. 27, 1952; children: Jeffrey Alan, Michele Kay, David Eliot. BA magna cum laude, U. Minn., 1953; MA, U. Rochester, 1954, PhD, 1960. Mem. faculty Kent (Ohio) State U., 1956-58, 60-63, 65-73, prof. music, asso. dean Grad. Sch., 1967-73; asst. prof. U. Mich., 1963-65; dean Sch. Music, Ithaca (N.Y.) Coll., 1973-74; vis. prof. U. Wis., 1975-78; chmn. music dept. Whitman Coll., 1978-80; prof. U. Fla., 1980-97; prof. emeritus, 1997—. Prin. cellist, Eastman Philharmonia, 1959, Akron Symphony Orch., 1969-73; cellist Fla. Baroque Ensemble, 1980-97, Fla. Arts Trio, 1986-93; dir. Fla. Musica Nova, 1991-97; author: (with A. Cohen) Anthology of Music for Analysis, 1965, Understanding and Enjoying Music, 1968 (pub. in Japanese 1978), Music in Western Culture, 1972, The Analysis of Music, 1976, 2d edit., 1984, Guidelines for College Teaching of Music Theory, 1981, Comprehensive Musical Analysis, 1994, Theories of Musical Texture in Western History, 1995, Gothic Looking Glass, The Blue Dog and Other Stories; editor: Music and Man; editl. Jour. for Musicological Research, Jour. Music Theory Pedagogy; contbr. articles to profl. jours.; Composer: Symphony No. 2, 1960, Blake Songs, 1961, Divertimento for Flute, Violin and Viola, 1961; opera The Legend of Sleepy Hollow, 1962; Three Choruses From Goethe's Faust, 1965, Three Joyce Songs, 1966, Ode to Darkness, 1967, Cantos of the Year, 1969, Variations for Clarinet and Piano, 1971, Whitman Music, 1970, Three Madrigals for Chorus and Orchestra, 1971, Russian Songs for Voices and Winds, 1972, Prayer (Solzhenytsin), 1973, String Quartet 1, 1975, Variations for Piano, 1976, Ode on the Morning of Christ's Nativity (Donne), 1977, Music for Oriana for violin, cello and piano, 1978, Pied Beauty, 1980, Sonata for Cello and Piano, 1981, Zodiac, 1981, Music for Violin and Piano, 1982, The Soft Voice, 1983, Concerto for Flute and Wind Ensemble, 1983, Dialogues for Trombone and Piano, 1984, Symphony for Wind Band (3rd Symphony), 1985, Concerto da Camera for Cello and Orch., 1985, Symphony for a Saint (4th Symphony), 1986, The Heavens are Telling, 1988, Music for Cello and Percussion, 1988, Songs of the Shulamite, 1989, Mirrors for Piano and Orchestra, 1990, But God's Own Descent (5th Symphony), 1991, Music of the Open Road, 1993, Daylight and Moonlight, 1993, O Sing to the Lord a New Song, 1993, Illusions for Three, 1994, Music for Trumpet and Cello, 1994, Colors of Earth and Sky (6th Symphony), 1995, Summer Storm Madrigals, 1996, Time and the Water for Horn and Piano, 1996, O Sing to the Lord a New Song, 1997; recs. on Advent, Mark, Capstone and Opus One Labels. Served with AUS, 1954-56. Recipient Benjamin award, 1960, award Nat. Fedn. Music Clubs, 1962, internat. composition award U. Wis.-Oriana Trio, 1979, composition award Am. Choral Dirs. Assn., 1984; grantee NEA; Fulbright rsch. fellow, 1995-96. Fellow Am. Scandinavian Found.; mem. ASCAP (awards 1965—), Soc. Composers (nat. coun. 1987-89, 93-96), Soc. Music Theory, Pi Kappa Lambda, Delta Omicron, Phi Mu Alpha, Phi Beta Delta. Home: 29896 Troutdale Pk Pl Evergreen CO 80439-7730

WHITE, JOHN DOUGLAS, emergency physician; b. N.Y.C., Jan. 20, 1951. BA, Yale U., 1973, MD, 1977; M in Pub. Health, Johns Hopkins U., 1990. From clin. dir. to vice chair Georgetown U., Washington, 1981-95; chmn. dept. emergency medicine Med. Coll. Va., Richmond, 1995—. Office: Med Coll Va 401 N 12th St Richmond VA 23298-5035

WHITE, JOHN JOSEPH, III, lawyer; b. Darby, Pa., Nov. 23, 1948; s. John J. Jr. and Catherine (Lafferty) W.; m. Catherine M Staley, Dec. 9, 1983. BS, U. Scranton, 1970; MPA, Marywood Coll., 1977; JD, Loyola U., New Orleans, 1983. Bar: Pa. 1983, U.S. Dist. Ct. (ea. dist.) Pa. 1983, N.J. 1984, U.S. Ct. Appeals (3d cir.) 1983, U.S. Dist. Ct. N.J. 1984, U.S. Tax Ct. 1984, D.C. 1985, U.S. Supreme Ct. 1987. Exec. dir. Scranton (Pa.) Theatre Libre, Inc., 1973-77; pub. Libre Press Inc., Scranton, 1977-83; pvt. practice Phila., 1983—; pres. Washington Franklin Investment Corp., 1992—; owner Mercury Transp. Co., Inc., Lansdowne, Pa., 1987—; N.Am. agt. Palacky U. Med. Sch., Olomouc, Czech Republic, 1995—. Founder, pub. Metro Mag., 1977-83. Founder, Scranton Pub. Theatre, 1976; dir. Scranton Theatre Libre, Inc., 1973. Capt. USAF, 1970-73; lt. col. Res., 1973—. Mem. ABA, Pa. Trial Lawyers Assn., Phila. Bar Assn., Phila. Trial Lawyers Assn., Air Force Assn. (chpt. pres. 1975—), Phi Delta Phi Internat. Legal Frat. Democrat. Roman Catholic. Avocations: jogging, art collecting. Office: 1334 Walnut St Fl 5 Philadelphia PA 19107-5311

WHITE, JOHN KIERNAN, lighting company executive; b. Dallas, Nov. 11, 1939; s. John Kiernan and Anna Elizabeth (Hartnett) W.; 4 children. BS in Indsl. Engring., So. Meth. U., 1965, MBA, 1968. V.p. mktg. Conti Industries, 1970-71; v.p. mktg. Semco (merged into United Chair), Leeds, Ala., 1971-73, pres., 1973-75; pres. United Chair, Leeds, 1975-83; group chmn., CEO Office Group Am. United Chair/Anderson Hickey, Leeds, 1983-89; chmn., CEO Hanson Office Products Group, Atlanta, 1989-91, Weber Aircraft, Fullerton, Ga., 1991-92, Hanson Lighting Group (now Lighting Group Am., Atlanta and Birmingham, Ala., 1992—; bd. dirs. United Pacific Industries, Hong Kong. With USN, 1956-62. Mem. Birmingham C. of C., Bus. Coun. Ala., Nat. Elec. Mfg. Assn., Sigma Tau, Sigma Iota Epsilon.

WHITE, JOHN LINDSEY, lawyer; b. Camden, N.J., Apr. 1, 1930; s. John R. and Jean L. (Lord) W.; m. Jane V. Evans, Dec. 27, 1952; children: Linda White McFadden, John Lindsey Jr., Douglas A., Karen R. Ulmer. AB, Franklin and Marshall Coll., 1952; LLB, Temple U., 1955. Bar: N.J. 1955, U.S. Dist. Ct. N.J. 1955, U.S. Supreme Ct. 1960, U.S. Ct. Appeals (3d cir.) 1984. Of counsel George, Korin, Quattrone, Blumberg & Chant, Woodbury, N.J. Mem. N.J. Assembly, Trenton, 1964-68, N.J. State Senate, Trenton, 1968-72; trustee Underwood-Meml. Hosp., Woodbury, chmn. bd., 1994—. Recipient Disting. Svc. award Woodbury Jaycees, 1966. Fellow Am. Bar Found., Am. Coll. Trial Lawyers; mem. ABA, N.J. Bar Assn. (pres. 1985-86), Internat. Assn. Def. Counsel, N.J. Def. Assn. (pres. 1992-93), Trial Attys. N.J. (Trial Bar award 1991), Gloucester County Bar Assn. (pres. 1979-80), Masons, Shriners. Republican. Presbyterian. Avocations: hunting, fishing, boating. Home: 4 Mullray Ct Deptford NJ 08096 Office: George Korin Quattrone Blumberg & Chant 307 S Evergreen Ave Woodbury NJ 08096-2739

WHITE, JOHN MICHAEL, chemistry educator; b. Danville, Ill., Nov. 26, 1938; married, 1960; 3 children. BS, Harding Coll., 1960; MS, U. Ill., 1962, PhD in Chemistry, 1966. From asst. to assoc. prof. U. Tex., Austin, 1966-77, prof. chemistry, 1977—, now Hackerman prof. chemistry, dir. Sci. and Tech. Ctr. Mem. Am. Chem. Soc., Am. Phys. Soc. Research in surface and materials chemistry. Office: U Tex Dept Chemistry Welch Hall #3 310 Austin TX 78712

WHITE, JOHN PATRICK, lawyer; b. Boston, Oct. 14, 1946; s. John Marion and Margaret Patricia (Gannon) W.; m. Gemma Mary Flattly, Feb. 9, 1980; 1 son, John Myles. B.S. in Chem. Engring., Columbia U., 1968, M.A. in Biochemistry, 1971, M.Ph. in Molecular Biology, 1975; J.D., Fordham U., 1977. Bar: N.Y. 1978, U.S. dist. ct. (ea. and so. dists.) N.Y. 1978, U.S. Ct. Customs and Patent Appeals 1979, U.S. Ct. Appeals (Fed. cir.) 1982. Legis.

dir. Community Council Greater N.Y., 1971-77; assoc. Cooper, Dunham, Clark, Griffin & Moran, N.Y.C., 1977-81, ptnr., 1981-88; ptnr. Cooper & Dunham, LLP, N.Y.C., 1988—; owner Shallow Brook Farm, Stillwater, N.J.; breeder Reg Angus Cattle, Ringneck Pheasants and Carriage Horses; dir. Oncogene Sci., Inc., BioTech. Gen. Corp.; instr. Practicing Law Inst. Democratic dist. leader, 1975-81; vice chmn. Dem. Com. N.Y. County, 1977-81; jud. del. 1st jud. dept., 1975, 76, 77, 79; adminstr. screening panel 2d Mcpl. Ct. Dist.; pub. mem. Columbia U. Recombinant DNA Biosafety Com. Columbia U. faculty fellow, 1969-71; NIH grantee, 1969-71. Mem. ABA, Am. Chem. Soc., Am. Intellectual Property Law Assn., N.Y. Intellectual Property Law Assn., Assn. Bar City N.Y., Fed. Bar Coun. (com. patents). Club: Columbia of N.Y.C. Contbr. articles to sci. and legal jours. Home: 824 Hudson St Hoboken NJ 07030-5004 Office: Cooper & Dunham 1185 Avenue Of The Americas New York NY 10036-2601

WHITE, JOHN WESLEY, JR., university president; b. Nashville, Oct. 20, 1933; s. John W. and Ernestine (Engle) W.; m. Martha Ellen Bragg, June 24, 1956; children: Marcus Wesley, Michelle Suzanne. Student, Martin Jr. Coll., 1952-54; BA, Vanderbilt U., 1956, BD, 1959; MA, George Peabody Coll., 1966, PhD, 1968; LHD, U. Nebr., 1983; LLD, Kwansai Gakuin U., Japan, 1991. Dean admissions, dir. student affairs Martin Coll., 1960-65; asst. to acad. v.p. George Peabody Coll., 1965-67; assoc. dean for humanities Oklahoma City U., 1968-70, dean Coll. Arts and Scis., 1970-77, assoc. prof. English, 1968-73, prof., 1973-77; pres. Nebr. Wesleyan U., 1977—; cons., spkr. in field; bd. dirs. Norwest Bank, Woodmen Accident and Life Co.; chmn. Nebr. Ednl. Temecom. Commn., 1996-97. Immediate past pres. U. Senate, United Meth. Ch. Eli Lilly Sr. scholar Vanderbilt U., 1959. Mem. Nat. Assn. Ind. Colls. and Univs. (bd. dirs. 1989-93, 95—), Newcomen Soc. N.Am., Lincoln C. of C. (bd. dirs. 1990-93), Rotary (pres. West Oklahoma City sect. 1976), Kappa Delta Pi, Phi Kappa Phi, Alpha Mu Gamma, Blue Key. Office: Nebr Wesleyan U 5000 St Paul Ave Lincoln NE 68504-2760 *Two principles have been paramount in my life: One, related to the attitude toward myself, is that we can help to shape life, not simply endure it. We are "creative" creatures, not just "surviving" creatures. The second principle, related to the attitude toward others, is that communication is essential to coexistence; and only as we make a real effort to hear what is meant, rather than simply what is said or written, are we able to communicate effectively.*

WHITE, JOSEPH B., reporter; b. N.Y.C., July 7, 1958. Attended, Harvard U. Reporter The Wall Street Journal. Author: (with Paul Ingrassia) Comeback: The Fall and Rise of the American Automobile Industry, 1994. Recipient Pulitzer Prize for beat reporting, 1993. Office: The Wall Street Journal Detroit Bureau 500 Woodward Ave Ste 1950 Detroit MI 48226-3423

WHITE, JOSEPH CHARLES, manufacturing and retailing company executive; b. Toronto, Ont., Can., Aug. 14, 1922; s. Joseph Cleveland and Edith Parker (Johnson) W.; m. G. Evelyn Vipond, July 15, 1944; children—Ronald, Richard, JoAnne. Chartered acct., Queens U., Kingston, Ont.; B.Commerce, U. Toronto. Vice-pres., dir. Agnew-Surpass, Inc., Brantford, Ont., Can., 1964-78; v.p., dir. Genesco Can., Inc., Cambridge, Ont., Can., 1978-82, exec. v.p., dir., 1982-87; pres., gen. mgr. retail op. Genesco Can., Inc., Cambridge, Ont., 1986-87; dir., v.p. Genesco Group Inc.; dir. Genesco Fin. Ltd.; pres. Brantford Art Gallery, 1994-95, Brantford Probus Club, 1995-96. Chmn. Ross MacDonald Found., Brantford, Ont., 1983-86; pres. YMCA, Brantford, 1968-69; chmn. Brant County Post-Secondary Edn. Corp., Brantford, 1973-76. Served with Royal Can. Air Force, 1943-45. Mem. Ont. Inst. Chartered Accts., Can. Council Distbn. (pres. 1972-73), Brant County C. of C. (treas. 1966-68). Mem. United Ch. of Can. Avocations: downhill skiing; tennis. Home: 47 Golfdale Rd, Brantford, ON Canada N3T 5H6 Office: Genesco Can Inc, 401 Fountain St, Cambridge, ON Canada N3H 4V5

WHITE, JULIE ANN, foundation executive; b. Providence, R.I., Sept. 25, 1946; arrived in Can., 1969; d. Kenneth I. and Mima H. (McCreaner) Hunt; m. James . Floyd, Jan. 16, 1988. MBA, York U., 1984. Exec. implementation Min. Cmty. & Social Svcs., Govt. Ont., Toronto, Can., 1975-81; nat. mgr. pub. affairs Levi Strauss & Co., Markham, Ont., Can., 1981-93; CEO Trillium Found., Toronto, 1993—; mem. adv. bd. York U., Toronto, 1994—, Sch. of Policy Studies Queen's U., 1997; hon. chair Campaign for Centre for Women's Studies York U. Bd. dirs. Scotts Hospality Found., Toronto, 1993-96, Policy Ctr. Children, Family & Youth, Toronto, 1992-94; founding pres. Can. Women's Found., Toronto, 1987—. Recipient Gold award Race Rels., Human Rights & Race Rels. Ctr., Toronto, 1996; named Women of Distinction, YWCA, Toronto, 1990. Avocation: gardening.

WHITE, KAREN RUTH JONES, information systems executive; b. Ft. Meade, Md., Oct. 8, 1953; d. Frank L. Jones and Inge H. Lesser; m. M. Timothy Heath, Apr. 23, 1973 (div. Aug. 1976); m. Carl W. White, May 30, 1993. AS in electronic data processing, N.H. Tech. Inst., Concord, 1977; BS in MIS with high honors, Northeastern U., Boston, 1984, MS in Info. Sys., 1997. Programmer Chubb Life Ins. Co., Concord, Mass., 1977-79, Retailers Electronics Account Processing, Woburn, Mass., 1979-82; sr. programmer, analyst N.H. Ins. Group, Manchester, 1982-84; prin. systems analyst Wang Labs., Inc., Lowell, Mass., 1984-89; project mgr. TASC, Inc., Reading, Mass., 1989—. Bd. dirs. Brandywyne Common Assn., Derry, N.H., 1991-94; mem. St. Paul's Sch. Advanced Studies Pgm Alumni Assn., Concord, N.H. With U.S. Army Res., 1974-84. Decorated Army Commendation medal, 1980. Mem. IEEE (computer soc., tech. com. in software engring., program chair 5th reengring. forum 1996, mem. exec. adv. bd. 1996—), Engring. Mgmt. Soc., Project Mgmt. Inst. (Mass. Bay chpt. program dir. 1992-93, project chair PMI '96 1994-96, dir. seminars/symposium 1996—), Sigma Epsilon Rho. Home: 10 Brandywyne Common Derry NH 03038 Office: TASC 55 Walkers Brook Dr Reading MA 01867-3238

WHITE, KATE, editor-in-chief. Former editor-in-chief Child mag.; editor-in-chief Working Woman mag., N.Y.C., 1989-91, McCall's mag, N.Y.C., 1991-94, Redbook, N.Y.C., 1994—. Office: Redbook Hearst Magazines 224 W 57th St New York NY 10019-3212*

WHITE, KATHERINE ELIZABETH, retired pediatrician; b. Syracuse, N.Y., Mar. 23, 1920; d. Rufus Macandie and Marguerite Mary (Eselin) W.; m. Nicholas V. Oddo, Feb. 27, 1947 (dec. 1966); 1 child, Sandra S. Qualls. BA, Syracuse U., 1941, MD, 1943. Intern Syracuse U. Med. Ctr., 1944-45; asst. resident Buffalo Children's Hosp., 1945-46, chief resident, 1946-47; instr. pediatrics L.A. Children's Hosp., 1947; pvt. practice Long Beach, Calif., 1947—; mem. med. staff Miller Children's Hosp., Long Beach, 1966—; mem. bd. trustees Miller Children's Hosp., 1970—. Bd. dirs. Children's Clinic, Long Beach, 1968-87. Recipient Meml. Med. Ctr. Found., 1984; Cert. of Recognition, Children's Clinic, 1987, Found. for Children's Health Care, 1987; Humanitarian award Kiwanis, 1990. Fellow Am. Acad. Pediatrics; mem. Calif. Med. Assn., L.A. County Med. Assn., Long Beach Med. Assn., Soroptimist (Woman of Distinction 1989, Hall of Fame award 1990), Phi Beta Kappa. Republican. Roman Catholic. Home: 6354 Riviera Cir Long Beach CA 90815-4767

WHITE, KATHLEEN MERRITT, geologist; b. Long Beach, Calif., Nov. 19, 1921; d. Edward Clendenning and Gladys Alice (Merritt) White; m. Alexander Kennedy Baird IV, Oct. 1, 1965 (dec. 1985); children: Pamela Roberts, Peter Madlem, Stephen Madlem, Mari Afify. Attended, Sch. Boston Mus. Fine Arts, 1939-40, Art Students League, 1940-42; BS in Geology, Pomona Coll., 1962; MS in Geochemistry, Claremont Grad. Sch., 1964. Rsch. asst. geology Pomona Coll., Claremont, Calif., 1962-66, rsch. assoc. geology, 1966-75; cons. geology Claremont, Calif., 1975-; sr. scientist Jet Propulsion Lab./NASA, Pasadena, 1977-79, mem. tech. staff, 1979-86; ind. rschr. Claremont, 1986—; owner Kittie Tales, Claremont, 1992—. Contbr. Geosat Report, 1986; contbr. articles to profl. jours.; author, illustrator children's books. Grantee NASA, 1984, 85; Pomona Coll. scholar, 1963. Fellow Am. Geophys. Union; mem. Geol. Soc. Am. (invited paper 1994), Pomona Coll. Alumni Assn. Republican. Avocations: painting, piano playing, weaving, hiking, swimming. Home: 265 W 11th St Claremont CA 91711-3804

WHITE, KENNETH RAY, health administration educator, consultant; b. Okmulgee, Okla., June 28, 1956; s. Miles Delano and Ollie Jane (Roberts) W. BS, Oral Roberts U., 1979; MPH, U. Okla., Oklahoma City, 1980; BS in Nursing, Va. Commonwealth U., 1995, MS in Nursing, 1995, PhD in Health Svcs. Orgn. and Rsch., 1996. Dir. planning Mercy Health Ctr., Oklahoma City, 1980-81, adminstrv. asst., 1981-86, v.p. mktg., 1987-89; v.p. ops. Harris Hosp.-HEB, Bedford, Tex., 1986-87; sr. cons. Mercy Internat., Farmington Hills, Mich., 1989-93; instr. health adminstrn. Va. Commonwealth U., Richmond, 1993-95, asst. prof., assoc. dir. profl. grad. programs dept. health, 1995—. Contbr. articles to profl. jours. Bd. dirs., officer March of Dimes, Oklahoma City, 1980-89, Am. Heart Assn., Oklahoma City, 1984-89. Named Outstanding Alumni, U. Okla., 1983. Fellow Am. Coll. Healthcare Execs., Sigma Theta Tau, Phi Kappa Phi. Avocations: travel, home renovation, foreign films. Office: Va Commonwealth U Med Coll Va PO Box 980203 Richmond VA 23298-0203

WHITE, KERR LACHLAN, retired physician, foundation director; b. Winnipeg, Man., Can., Jan. 23, 1917; s. John Alexander and Ruth Cecelia (Preston) W.; m. Isabel Anne Pennefather, Nov. 26, 1943; children: Susan Isabel, Margot Edith. BA with honors (Oliver Gold medal), McGill U., 1940, M.D., C.M., 1949; M.D. (hon.), U. Leuven, 1978; postgrad., London Sch. Hygiene and Tropical Medicine, 1960; DSc (hon.), McMaster U., 1983. Intern, resident in medicine Mary Hitchcock Meml. Hosp., Hanover, N.H., 1949-52; Hosmer fellow McGill U. and Royal Victoria Hosp., Montreal, Que., Can., 1952-53; asst. prof. medicine U. N.C. Sch. Medicine, Chapel Hill, 1953-57, assoc. prof. medicine and preventive medicine, 1957-62; Commonwealth advanced fellow Med. Rsch. Coun., Social Medicine Rsch. unit London Hosp., 1959-60; chmn., prof. epidemiology and community medicine U. Vt., Burlington, 1962-64; prof. Sch. Hygiene and Pub. Health Johns Hopkins U., Balt., 1965-76, chmn. dept. health care orgn., 1965-72; dir. Inst. Health Care Studies United Hosp. Fund N.Y., 1977-78; dep. dir. health scis. Rockefeller Found., N.Y.C., 1978-97, ret., 1997; chmn. U.S. Nat. Com. Vital and Health Stats., 1975-79; mem. health adv. panel Office of Tech. Assessment, U.S. Congress, 1975-82; cons. Nat. Ctr. Health Stats., 1967-83, WHO, 1967—. Editor: Manual for Examination of Patients, 1960, Medical Care Research, 1965, Health Care: An International Study, 1976, Epidemiology as a Fundamental Science, 1976, Task of Medicine, 1988, Healing the Schism, 1991; contbr. articles to profl. jours., chpts. to books in field; mem. editl. bd. Med. Care, 1962-73, Inquiry, 1967-79, Internat. Jour. Epidemiology, 1971-81, Internat. Jour. Health Svcs., 1971—. Bd. dirs. Found. for Child Devel., 1969-80; trustee Case-Western Res. U., 1974-79. With Can. Army, 1942-45. Recipient Pew Primary Care Achievement award, 1995, Baxter award, 1996. Fellow ACP, AAAS, NAS (Inst. Medicine coun. 1974-76, chmn. membership com. 1975-77), APHA (gov. coun. 1964-68, 71-73, coun. med. care sect. 1962-65), Am. Acad. Preventive Medicine, Am. Heart Assn., Royal Soc. Medicine (hon.); mem. AMA, Internat. Epidemiol. Assn. (hon. life, pres. 1974-77, treas., exec. com. 1964-71, 74-77, coun. 1971-81), Assn. Tchrs. Preventive Medicine (coun. 1963-68), Am. Hosp. Assn. (adv. coun. ednl. and rsch. trust 1965-68), Kerr L. White Inst. Health Svcs. Rsch. (hon. dir. 1995—), Cosmos Club (Washington), Century Club (N.Y.C.), Sigma Xi, Alpha Omega Alpha.

WHITE, LAWRENCE J., economics educator; b. N.Y.C., June 1, 1943; s. Martin H. and Florence M. (Meiman) W. AB, Harvard U., 1964, PhD, 1969; MS in Econs., London Sch. Econs., 1965. Econ. adviser Harvard Devel. Adv. Svc., Pakistan and Indonesia, 1969-70; asst. prof. econs. Princeton U., N.J., 1970-76; mem. faculty Stern Sch. Bus., NYU., 1976—; prof. econs. Stern Sch. Bus., NYU, 1979—, chmn. dept., 1990-95; sr. staff economist U.S. Council Econ. Advisers, 1978-79; dir. econ. policy office, antitrust div. Dept. Justice, Washington, 1982-83; mem. Fed. Home Loan Bank Bd., 1986-89; cons. in field. Author: The Automobile Industry Since 1945, 1971, Industrial Concentration and Economic Power in Pakistan, 1974, Reforming Regulation: Processes and Problems, 1981, The Regulation: Processes and Problems, 1981, The Regulation of Air Pollutant Emissions from Motor Vehicles, 1982, The Public Library in the 1980s: The Problems of Choice, 1983, International Trade in Ocean Shipping Services: The U.S. and the World, 1988, The S&L Debacle: Public Policy Lessons for Bank and Thrift Regulation, 1991; N.Am. editor Jour. Indsl. Econs., 1984-87, 90-95. NSF fellow, 1965-69. Mem. Am. Econ. Assn., Phi Beta Kappa. Office: NYU Stern Sch Bus 44 W 4th St New York NY 10012-1106

WHITE, LEE CALVIN, lawyer; b. Omaha, Sept. 1, 1923; s. Herman Henry and Ann Ruth (Ackerman) W.; m. Cecile R. Zorinsky, Nov. 19, 1989 (dec. Apr. 1996); children: Bruce D., Rosalyn A., Murray L., Sheldon R., Laura H., Lori J. B.S. in Elec. Enging., U. Nebr., 1948, LL.B., 1950. Bar: Nebr. 1950, D.C. 1958. Atty. legal div. TVA, 1950-54; legis. asst. to Senator John F. Kennedy, 1954-57; asst. to Joseph P. Kennedy; mem. Hoover Commn., 1954-55; counsel U.S. Senate Small Bus. Com., 1957-58; adminstrv. asst. to Senator John S. Cooper, 1958-61; asst. spl. counsel to Pres. Kennedy, 1961-63; assoc. counsel to Pres. Johnson, 1963-65, spl. counsel, 1965-66; chmn. Fed. Power Commn., 1966-69; campaign mgr. R. Sargent Shriver (Democratic candidate v.p. U.S.), 1972; dir. Central Hudson Gas and Electric Corp., 1984-88. Bd. govs. N.Y. Merc. Exchange, 1980-84, 87-91. Served with AUS, 1943-46. Mem. D.C. Bar (gov. 1977-80). Home: 435 N St SW Washington DC 20024-3701 Office: 1350 New York Ave NW Ste 1100 Washington DC 20005-4709

WHITE, LEONARD, motion picture company executive. Pres., chief exec. officer Orion Pictures Corp., a Metromedia Entertainment Group Co. Office: Orion Pictures Corp 1888 Century Park E Ste 6 Los Angeles CA 90067-1702

WHITE, LESLIE MARY, epidemiologist; b. Huntington, N.Y., July 22, 1954; d. John B. and Inez M. (Montecalvo) W. BS, Mary Washington Coll., 1976; MPH, Johns Hopkins U., 1990; postgrad., U. Md., 1993-95. Microbiologist II Am. Type Culture Collection, Rockville, Md., 1980-83; analyst InterAm. Assocs., Rockville, Md., 1984-86; sr. assoc. Triton Corp., Washington, 1986-87; health analyst Row Scis., Inc., Rockville, 1987-88; rsch. analyst Nat. BioSystems, Rockville, 1988-90; sr. assoc. Clement International., Fairfax, Va., 1990-92; project dir. epidemiology Consultants in Epidemiology and Occupational Health, Washington, 1992-93; dir. epidemiology Scis. Internat., Inc., Alexandria, Va., 1993-94; pres. Epidemiology and Health Rsch., Inc., Bethesda, Md., 1994—, Dist. Nuskin/IDN Internat., Bethesda, 1996—; realtor Weichert Realtors, Potomac, Md., 1997—. Mem. APHA, U.S. Tennis Assn. (umpire coun.), Soc. Epidemiologic Rsch., Soc. Occupl. and Environ. Health, Am. Indsl. Hygiene Assn., Montgomery Assn. Realtors, Nat. Assn. Realtors, Bethesda Country Club, Assn. Md. Tennis Ofcls. Avocations: tennis, ballet, reading, public health. Home: 7401 Westlake Ter Apt 512 Bethesda MD 20817-6566 Office: Epidemiology and Health Rsch Inc 7401 Westlake Ter Apt 512 Bethesda MD 20817-6566

WHITE, LESLIE MILES, parochial school educator. BS in Gen. Studies, So. Oreg. Coll., 1965; MS in Edn., Portland State U., 1971; EdD, Pacific Western U., 1988; postgrad. in Ednl. Policy and Mgmt., U. Oreg. Cert. standard adminstr., K-12, elem./secondary tchr., Oreg., elem./secondary tchr., Wash. Tchr. Saint Cecilia Sch., Beaverton, Oreg., 1966-75; prin. St. Anthony Sch., Tigard, Oreg., 1975-78; chmn. social sci. dept. St. Mary of Valley High Sch., Beaverton, 1978-87, dean of acad., 1987-89; chmn. computer sci. dept. Valley Cath. High Sch., Beaverton, 1989—. Contbg. author: Archdiocese School Policy Handbook, others.

WHITE, LINDA DIANE, lawyer; b. N.Y.C., Apr. 1, 1952; d. Bernard and Elaine (Simons) Schwartz; m. Thomas M. White, Aug. 16, 1975; 1 child, Alexandra Nicole. AB, U. Pa., 1973; JD, Northwestern U., 1976. Bar: Ill. 1976. Assoc. Walsh, Case, Coale & Brown, Chgo., 1976-77, Greenberger & Kaufmann (merged into Katten, Muchin), Chgo., 1977-82; ptnr. Greenberger & Kaufmann (merged into Katten, Muchin), 1982-85, Sonnenschein Nath & Rosenthal, Chgo., 1985—. Mem. ABA (real property fin. com., comml. leasing com., real property, probate and trust law sect. 1987—), Ill. Bar Assn., Chgo. Bar Assn., Internat. Assn. Corp. Real Estate Execs. Office: Sonnenschein Nath & Rosenthal 8000 Sears Tower 233 S Wacker Dr Chicago IL 60606-6306

WHITE, LORAY BETTY, public relations executive, writer, actress, producer; b. Houston, Nov. 27, 1934; d. Harold White and Joyce Mae (Jenkins) Mills; m. Sammy Davis Jr., 1957 (div. 1958); 1 child, Deborah R. DeHart. Student, UCLA, 1948-50, 90-91, Nichiren Shoshu Acad., 1988-92; AA in Bus., Sayer Bus. Sch., 1970; study div. mem. dept. L.A., Soka U., Japan, 1970-86. Editor entertainment writer L.A. Community New, 1970-81; exec. sec. guest rels. KNBC Prodns., Burbank, Calif., 1969-75; security specialist Xerox X10 Think Tank, L.A., 1975-80; exec. asst. Ralph Powell & Assocs., L.A., 1980-82; pres., owner, producer LBW & Assocs. Pub. Rels., L.A., 1980—; owner, producer, writer, host TV prodn. co. Pub. Pub. Rels., L.A., 1987—; dir., producer L.B.W. Prodn. "Yesterday, Today, Tomorrow, L.A., 1981—. Actress (film) Ten Commandments, 1956, (Broadway) Joy Ride; appeared in the following endorsements including Budweiser Beer, Old Gold Cigarettes, Salem Cigarettes, TV commls. including Cheer, Puffs Tissue, Coca Cola, Buffern, others; entertainment editor L.A. Community News, 1970-73; writer (column) Balance News, 1980-82. Vol. ARC, 1995; mem. Habitat for Humanity Internat. Recipient award ARC, 1955, 84, Cert. of Honor, Internat. Orgn. Soka Gakkai Internat. of Japan, Cmty. Vols. of Am. award, 1994; named Performer of Yr. Cardella Demillo, 1976-77. Mem. ARC (planning, mktg., prodn. event com. 1995), UCLA Alumni Assn., Lupus Found. Am. (So. Calif. chpt.), Nat. Fedn. Blind, Myohoji-Hokkeko Internat., Libr. of Congress Assocs. (charter). Buddhist. Avocations: singing, acting, TV writing and producing. *Accepting challenges in life is a choice. The choice is always yours. I've chosen never to give up-to always give my best, to constantly keep a growing and open mind. To remember to strengthen and reinforce the quality of my integrity no matter what- be a winner to yourself.*

WHITE, LOWELL E., JR., medical educator; b. Tacoma, Wash., Jan. 16, 1928; s. Lowell E. and Hazel (Conley) W.; m. Margie Mae Lamb, June 21, 1947; children: Henry, Leanna White Maynes, Inger-Britt White Peterson. BS in Pharm., U. Wash., 1951, MD, 1953. Diplomate Am. Bd. Neurol. Surgery. Intern N.C. Meml. Hosp., Chapel Hill, 1953-54; resident neurosurgery, asst. to instr. U. Wash., 1954-60, asst. prof., 1960-64, assoc. prof., 1964-70; asso. dean U. Wash. Sch. Medicine, 1965-68; prof., chief divsn. neurol. surgery U. Fla., 1970-72; prof. U. South Ala., 1972-94, chmn. divsn. neurosci., 1972-77, ret., 1994; adj. prof. Ala. Sch. of Math. and Sci., 1993-94; chmn. nat. adv. com. Animal Resources NIH, 1966-70; cons. rsch. facilities and resources NIH; cons. divsn. hosp. and med. facilities USPHS; cons. grants adminstrn. policy U.S. Dept. HEW. Contbr. articles profl. jours. Bd. dirs. Mobile County Emergency Med. Svcs. Coun., 1973-82, Epilepsy chpt. Mobile, 1973-89, Mobile cpt. Myasthenia Gravis Found. Am., 1974-90, Mobile Mental Health Assn., 1979-89, Spl. Edn. Action Com., 1985—, pres. 1996. With USN, 1946-47, USNR, 1948-66. Guggenheim fellow, 1958-59. Mem. AMA, Am. Assn. Neurol. Surgeons, Am. Assn. Neuropathologists, Am. Acad. Neurol. Surgeons, Soc. for Neurosci., Assn. Am. Med. Colls., Am. Assn. Anatomists, Rsch. Soc. Neurol. Surgeons, Neurosurg. Soc. Ala. (pres. 1975), Am. Physicians Poetry Assn., Odyssey U. South Ala., Skyline Country Club (pres. 1986), Cajal Club. Home: 5750 Huffman Dr N Mobile AL 36693-3013

WHITE, LUTHER WESLEY, lawyer; b. Norfolk, Va., Aug. 29, 1923; s. Luther Wesley White Jr. and Edith Prettyman; m. Patricia Bowers; children: Luther, John P., Nell White King, Mary Dix. BA, Randolph-Macon Coll., 1947, LLD (hon.), 1989; LLB, Washington & Lee U., 1949, LLD, 1969; LHD (hon.), Bridgewater Coll., 1979; HHD (hon.), Ky. Wesleyan Coll., 1988. Bar: Va. 1949. Pvt. practice law Norfolk, 1949-67; pres. Randolph-Macon Coll., Ashland, Va., 1967-1979, Ky. Wesleyan Coll., Owensboro, 1979-88; atty. Eggleston & Thelen, Lovingston, Va., 1989-95; pres. Nat. Assn. Colls. and Univs. of United Meth. Ch., 1977-78. Pres. Norfolk Symphony Orch., 1966, Owensboro Symphony Orch., 1987. Lt. (j.g.) USN, 1943-46, PTO. Recipient Liberty Bell award Daviess County (Ky.) Bar Assn., Owensboro, 1983. Mem. Rotary (pres. Owensboro club 1982-83). Republican. Methodist. Avocations: music, tennis, gardening. Home: 31 Ashlawn Blvd Palmyra VA 22963-3329

WHITE, MARGITA EKLUND, television association executive; b. Linköping, Sweden, June 27, 1937; came to U.S., 1948; d. Eyvind O. and Ella Maria (Erikkson) Eklund; m. Stuart Crawford White, June 24, 1961 (div. 1987); children: Suzanne Margareta Morgan, Stuart Crawford Jr. B.A. magna cum laude in Govt, U. Redlands, 1959, LL.D. (hon.), 1977; M.A. in Polit. Sci. (Woodrow Wilson fellow), Rutgers U., 1960. Asst. to press sec. Richard M. Nixon Presdl. Campaign, Washington, 1960; adminstrv. asst. Whitaker & Baxter Advt. Agy., Honolulu, 1961-62; minority news sec. Hawaii Ho. of Reps., 1963; research asst. to Senator Barry Goldwater and Republican Nat. Com., 1963-64; research asst., writer Free Society Assn., 1965-66; research asst. to syndicated columnist Raymond Moley, 1967; asst. to Herbert G. Klein, White House dir. communications, 1969-73; asst. dir. USIA, 1973-75; asst. press sec. to Pres. Gerald R. Ford, 1975; asst. press sec. to Pres., dir. White House Office of Communications, Washington, 1975-76; commr. FCC, 1976-79; dir. Radio Free Europe-Radio Liberty Inc., 1979-82, vice chmn., 1982; dir. Taft Broadcasting Co., 1980-87, Armtek Corp., 1987-88, Rayonier Forest Resources Co., 1985-93; pres. Assn. Maximum Svc. Television; chmn. model HDTV sta. project; bd. dirs. ITT Corp., ITT Edn. Svcs., Inc., Washington Mut. Investors Fund, Growth Fund Washington, Leitch Tech. Corp., Mitretek Sys.; U.S. del. Internat. Telecom. Union Plenipotentiary Conf., Nairobi, 1982; coord. TV Operators Caucus, Inc., 1985-88; chmn. Model HDTV Sta. Project. Mem. George Foster Peabody Adv. Bd., 1979-86. Recipient Disting. svc. award U. Redlands Alumni Assn., 1974, Superior Honor award USIA, 1975, Dir.'s Choice award Nat. Women's Econ. Alliance, 1995, Disting. Svc. to Broadcasting award Broadcast Pioneers, 1995. Mem. Exec. Women in Govt. (founding mem., sec. 1975), Women's Forum of Washington. Home: 1533 28th St NW Washington DC 20007-3059 Office: 1776 Massachusetts Ave NW Washington DC 20036-1904

WHITE, MARILYN DOMAS, information science educator; b. Franklin, La., Aug. 16, 1940; d. George Julian and Norma Edwina (Melancon) Domas; m. Roger Stuart White, Aug. 31, 1968; 1 child, Joshua Stuart. BA, Our Lady of the Lake Coll., San Antonio, 1962; MS, U. Wis., 1963; PhD, U. Ill., 1971. Dir. Commerce Libr. U. Wis., Madison, 1963-65; head Social Sci./Bus. Libr. So. Ill. U., Edwardsville, 1965-67; cons. So. Ill. U./U.S. AID Adv. Team, South Vietnam, 1967; asst. prof. SUNY, Buffalo, 1972-74; lectr., vis. asst. prof. U. Md., College Park, 1976-77, asst. prof. info sci., 1977-82, assoc. prof. info. sci., 1982—; cons. USIA, Washington and abroad, 1977-83, Inst. for Def. Analyses, Bowie, Md.,Supercomputing Rsch. Ctr., 1990-91, Am. Health Care Assn., Washington, 1990-92, Am. Coun. on Edn., 1995. Contbr. articles to Libr. Quar., Drexel Libr. Quar., Reference Libr., others. James Lyman Whitney grantee ALA, 1983, Spl. Libr. Assn. rsch. grantee, 1993-94, Coun. Libr. Resources grantee, 1995-96. Mem. Am. Soc. for Info. Sci., Spl. Libr. Assn. Roman Catholic. Office: U Md Coll Libr and Info Svcs Hornbake 4117F South Wing College Park MD 20742

WHITE, MARTHA VETTER, allergy and immunology physician, researcher; b. Richmond, Va., Oct. 23, 1951; d. Robert Joseph and Miriam Ernestine (Thomas) Vetter; m. Frederick Joseph Kozub, Oct. 11, 1975 (div. June 1982); m. John Irving White, Feb. 18, 1984; children: Josh, Christie. Student, Vanderbilt U., Nashville, 1969-71; BA, U. Richmond, 1973; MD, Va. Commonwealth U., Richmond, 1978. Cert. m. Bd. Pediatrics, Am. Bd. Allergy and Immunology. Pediatric intern and resident Va. Commonwealth U., Richmond, 1978-81; locum tenans Pub. Health, Richmond, Va., 1981-82; fellow Allergy and Immunology U. Southern Calif., L.A., 1983-84, Georgetown U., 1983-84; sr. staff fellow Food and Drug Adminstrn., Bethesda, Md., 1984-85; NSRA fellow Nat. Inst. Allergy and Infectious Diseases, Bethesda, Md., 1985-88; sr. staff fellow, 1988-93; rsch. dir. Inst. for Asthma and Allergy, Washington, 1993—; cons. Sandoz Pharms., Marion Merrell Dow, Glaxo, Boehringer Ingleheim, Ciba-Geigy, Miles Genentech; rsch. Walsh, Glaxo, Abbott, Pfizer, Marion Merrell Dow, Miles, Rhône Poulenc Rhoen, Sanofi, Adams, Astra, Merck, Neurbiol. Techs., 3M, Zeneca, Wyeth, Smith-Kline Beecham; bd. dirs. Allery & Asthma Network/Mothers of Asthmatics, 1987—; med. editor MA Report, 1986—; assoc. editor Allergy, Asthma and Immunology Guide, 1989-90. Contbr. numerous scientific papers, abstracts, chpts. and reviews in field. Recipient Norwich Eaton Rsch. award, 1987; Merrell Dow scholar in allergy, 1989; Geigy fellow, 1984. Mem. Am. Assn. Immunologists, Am. Acad. Pediatrics, Adm. Acad. Allergy and Immunology, Am. Coll. Allergy and Immunology, Am. Thoracic Soc., Beta Beta Beta, Psi Chi, Gamma Sigma Epsilon. Office: Inst Asthma and Allergy 106 Irving St NW Ste 108 Washington DC 20010-2927

WHITE, MARTIN CHRISTOPHER, academic administrator; b. Anderson, S.C., Oct. 16, 1943; s. Jesse Martin and Christine Freida (Powell) W.; m. Linda Ann Fleming, July 31, 1965; children: Martin Lynn, Andrew

Christopher. AB, Mercer U., 1965; MDiv, So. Bapt. Theol. Sem., 1968; PhD, Emory U., 1972. Prof. Elon Coll. (N.C.), 1972-76, dean acad. affairs, 1976-82, v.p. for acad. and student affairs, 1982-86; pres. Gardner-Webb U., Boiling Springs, N.C., 1986—; cons. So. Assn. Colls. and Schs., Atlanta, 1982—. Contbr. articles in field. Bd. dirs. United Way, Shelby, N.C., 1987. Woodrow Wilson fellow, 1971. Mem. Soc. Bibl. Lit., Nat. Assn. Bapt. Profs. of Religion, N.C. Ind. Coll. Assn., Alpha Chi, Omicron Delta Kappa. Democrat. Baptist. Lodge: Rotary (bd. dirs. Burlington, N.C. chpt. 1986). Avocations: golfing, tennis, music, traveling. Home: 303 W Marion St Shelby NC 28150-5335 Office: Gardner-Webb U Campus Mail Dept Boiling Springs NC 28017

WHITE, MARTIN FRED, lawyer; b. Warren, Ohio, Nov. 12, 1952; s. Benjamin and Bella Dorothy (Bernstein) W. BA, Ohio State U., 1973; JD, 1977. Bar: U.S. Dist. Ct. (no. dist.) Ohio, 1981, Pa., 1993. Atty. pvt. practice, Warren, Ohio, 1977—; spl. counsel Ohio Atty. Gen., Columbus, Ohio, 1991—. Mem. Am. Trial Lawyers Assn., Ohio Acad. Trial Lawyers, Mahoning-Trumbull Trial Lawyers Assn., Ohio Acad. Criminal Def. Attys., Ohio Bar Assn., Trumbull County Bar Assn. Office: PO Box 1150 Warren OH 44482-1150

WHITE, MARY LOU, fundraiser, writer, educator; b. Davenport, Iowa, Feb. 17, 1939; d. Edward Joseph and Madeleine (Levart) Briglia; m. Morton Bartho White, Dec. 6, 1965 (dec. Jan. 1973). Cert. d'etudes francaises, U. Grenoble, France, 1959; BA, Gettysburg Coll., 1960; postgrad., Sorbonne, Paris, 1961; MA, Middlebury Coll., 1962; MS, U. Bridgeport, 1972. Writer CIA, N.Y.C., 1962-64; tchr. French Miss Porter's Sch., Farmington, Conn., 1964-66; fundraiser N.Y. Philharm., N.Y.C., 1966-72; tchr. French Fairfield (Conn.) Country Day Sch., 1973-77, Greens Farms (Conn.) Acad., 1977-79; spl. events coord. N.Y. Philharm., N.Y.C., 1979-80; econ. devel. Broward C.C., Ft. Lauderdale, Fla., 1989-91; programming grants writer Broward Ctr. for the Performing Arts, Ft. Lauderdale, 1992—. Vol. Polit. Party, Ft. Lauderdale, 1990-93. Mem. Hereditary Register of U.S. Avocations: chess, piano, breeding dachshunds. Home: 888 Intracoastal Dr Fort Lauderdale FL 33304-3638

WHITE, MARY RUTH WATHEN, social services administrator; b. Athens, Tex., Dec. 27, 1927; d. Benedict Hudson and Sara Elizabeth (Evans) W.; m. Robert M. White, Nov. 10, 1946; children: Martha Elizabeth, Robert Miles, Jr., William Benedict, Mary Ruth, Jesse Wathen, Margaret Fay, Maureen Adele, Thomas Evan. BA, Stephen F. Austin State U., Nacogdoches, Tex., 1948. Chmn. Regional Drug Abuse Com., San Antonio, 1975-81, Met. Youth Coun., San Antonio, 1976-78; state chmn. Citizens United for Rehab. Errants, San Antonio, 1978-91; sec. Bexar County Detention Ministries, San Antonio, 1979-88; chmn. Bexar County (Tex.) Jail Commn., 1980-82; chmn. com. on role of family in reducing recidivism Tex. Dept. Criminal Justice, Austin, 1985—; chmn. Met. Cmty. Corrections Com., San Antonio, 1986-90; bd. dirs. Tex. Coalition for Juvenile Justice, 1975-93, Target 90 Youth Coordinating Coun., San Antonio, 1986-89; local chmn. vol. adv. bd. Tex. Youth Commn., 1986-87. Pres. San Antonio City Coun. PTA, 1976-78, Rep. Bus. Women Bexar County, San Antonio, 1984-86, North Urban Deanery, San Antonio Alliance Mental Illness, 1995-96, also legis. chmn.; bd. dirs. CURE, 1978-92; legis. chmn. Archdiocese of San Antonio Coun. Cath. Women; mem. allocation com. United Way, San Antonio, 1986-91; founder chmn. South Tex. Consumer and Family Support Consortium, 1996-97. Named Today's Woman, San Antonio Light newspaper, 1985, Outstanding Rep. Woman, Rep. Bus. Women Bexar County, 1987; honoree Rep. Women Stars over Tex., 1992. Mem. Am. Corrections Assn., Assn. Criminal Justice Planners, LWV (pres. San Antonio chpt. 1984-86), Conservation Soc., Fedn. Women (bd. dirs. 1984-90), DAR (regent), Colonial Dames (pres.), Cath. Daus. Am. (profl. registered parliamentarian, past regent Ct. of St. Anthony), Tex. Cath. Daus. Am. (state legis. chair), San Antonio Alliance for Mentally Ill (pres. 1996-97). Home: 701 E Sunshine Dr San Antonio TX 78228-2516 Office: 5372 Fredericksburg Rd Ste 114 San Antonio TX 78229-3559

WHITE, MICHAEL LEE, lawyer; b. Dilley, Tex., Mar. 27, 1953; s. Deryl and Ruby Alice (Gillis) W. BA, Tex. A&M U., 1975; JD, U. Houston, 1978. Bar: Tex. 1979. Briefing atty. 14th Ct. Appeals, Houston, 1979; contracts analyst Texaco Inc., Houston, 1979-80, legis. coord., 1980-82; mgr. state govt. rels. Pennzoil Co., Houston, 1982-85, mgr. employee comms., pub. affairs liaison, 1985-87, mgr. media comms., 1987-88; dir. govt. affairs Met. Transit Authority Harris County, Houston, 1988-90; v.p. C. of C. divsn. Greater Houston Partnership, 1990-94; legis. cons. Austin, Tex., 1994—. Fellow Houston Bar Found.; mem. ABA, State Bar Tex., Houston Bar Assn., Tex. Lyceum Assn. (bd. dirs., exec. com. 1984-89), Travis County Bar Assn. Avocations: golf, tennis, skiing, reading. Office: PO Box 1667 Austin TX 78767-1667

WHITE, MICHAEL REED, mayor; b. Cleve., Aug. 13, 1951; s. Robert and Audrey (Silver) W. BA, Ohio State U., 1973, MPA, 1974. Spl. asst. Columbus (Ohio) Mayor's Office, 1974-76; adminstrv. asst. Cleve. City Coun., 1976-77; sales mgr. Burks Electric Co., Cleve., 1978-84; state senator Ohio Senate, Columbus, 1984-89; mayor Cleve., 1990—; minority whip Ohio Senate Dems., 1987-89. City councilman City of Cleve., 1978-84; bd. dirs. Glenville Devel. Corp., Cleve., 1978—, Glenville Festival Found., Cleve., 1978—, United Black Fund, Cleve., 1986, Greater Cleve. Dome Corp., 1986; trustee U.S. Conf. Democratic Mayors. Named one of Outstanding Young Men Am., 1985, Outstanding Svc. award Cleve. chpt. Nat. Assn. Black Vets., 1985, Cmty. Svcs. award East Side Jaycees, Pres.'s award, 1993, named Black Profl. of Yr., 1993, Humanitarian award, 1994, Pub Svc. award Am. Pub. Power Assn., 1995. Mem. Nat. Conference Dem. Mayors. Democrat. Home: 1057 East Blvd Cleveland OH 44108-2972 Office: Office of Mayor 601 Lakeside Ave E Cleveland OH 44114-1015

WHITE, MICHELLE JO, economics educator; b. Washington, Dec. 3, 1945; d. Harry L. and Irene (Silverman) Rich; m. Roger Hall Gordon, July 25, 1982. AB, Harvard U., 1967; MSc in Econs., London Sch. Econs., 1968; PhD, Princeton U., 1973. Asst. prof. U. Pa., Phila., 1973-78; from assoc. prof. to prof. NYU, N.Y.C., 1978-83; prof. econs. U. Mich., Ann Arbor, 1984—; dir. PhD program in econs. U. Mich., 1992-94; vis. asst. prof. Yale U., New Haven, 1978; vis. prof. People's U., Beijing, 1986, U. Warsaw, 1990, U. Wis., Madison, 1991, U. Munich, Germany, 1992, Tilburg U., The Netherlands, 1993, 95, U. Chgo., 1993, Copenhagen Bus. Sch., 1995, Uppsala U., Sweden, 1997; cons. Pension Benefit Guaranty Corp., Washington, 1987; chmn. adv. com. dept. econs. Princeton U., 1988-90. Editor: The Nonprofit Sector in a Three Sector Economy, 1981; contbr. numerous articles to profl. jours. Bd. dirs. Com. on Status of Women in Econs. Profession, 1984-86. Resources for Future fellow, 1972-73; grantee NSF, 1979, 82, 88, 91, 93, 96, Sloan Found., 1984, Fund for Rsch. in Dispute Resolution, 1989; Fulbright scholar, Poland, 1990. Mem. Am. Econ. Assn., Am. Law and Econ. Assn. (bd. dirs. 1991-92), Am. Real Estate and Urban Econs. Assn. (bd. dirs. 1992-95), Social Scis. Rsch. Coun. (bd. dirs. 1994—, treas. 1996—), Midwest Econs. Assn. (1st v.p. 1996-97). Office: Univ Mich Dept Economics 611 Tappan Ave Ann Arbor MI 48109-1220

WHITE, MIKE, professional sports team executive; b. Berkeley, Calif., Jan. 4, 1936. Offensive coord. Stanford U., 1964-71; offensive line coach San Francisco 49ers, 1978, adminstrv. asst. coach, 1979; cons. World League of Am. Football, 1989; quarterbacks coach Oakland (Calif.) Raiders, 1990-92, offensive line coach, 1993-94, head coach, 1995—. Named Coll. Football Coach of Yr., The Sporting News, 1975. Office: Oakland Raiders 1 Hegenberger Rd Oakland CA 94621-1405

WHITE, MORTON GABRIEL, philosopher, author; b. N.Y.C., Apr. 29, 1917; s. Robert and Esther (Levine) Weisberger; m. Lucia Perry, Aug. 29, 1940; children: Nicholas Perry, Stephen Daniel. B.S., CCNY, 1936; L.H.D., CUNY, 1975; A.M., Columbia U., 1938, Ph.D., 1942. Instr. philosophy Columbia U., 1942-46; instr. physics CCNY, 1942-43; asst. prof. philosophy U. Pa., 1946-48; asst. prof. philosophy Harvard U., 1948-50, asso. prof., 1950-53, prof., 1953-70, chmn. dept., 1954-57, acting chmn. dept., 1967-69; prof. Inst. Advanced Study, 1970-87; prof. emeritus, 1987—; Guggenheim research fellow, 1950-51; vis. prof. Tokyo U., 1952, 60, 66, U. Oslo, 1977-78; Neesima lectr. Doshisha U., Kyoto, 1985, CUNY, 1968-69, Rutgers U., 1987-88, 88-89; mem. Inst. Advanced Study, 1953-54, 62-63, 67-68, 68-69. Author: The Origin of Dewey's Instrumentalism, 1943, Social Thought in America, 1949, The Age of Analysis, 1955, Toward Reunion in Philosophy, 1956, Religion, Politics, and the Higher Learning, 1959, (with Lucia White) The Intellectual Versus the City, 1962; Editor: (with Arthur M. Schlesinger, Jr.) Paths of American Thought, 1963, Foundations of Historical Knowledge, 1965, Science and Sentiment in America, 1972, Documents in the History of American Philosophy, 1972, Pragmatism and the American Mind, 1973, The Philosophy of the American Revolution, 1978, What Is and What Ought to Be Done, 1981, (with Lucia White) Journeys to the Japanese, 1952-79, 1986, Philosophy, The Federalist and the Constitution, 1987, The Question of Free Will, 1993. Fellow Center Advanced Study Behavioral Scis., 1959-60; fellow Am. Council Learned Socs., 1962-63. Mem. Am. Acad. Arts and Scis., Am. Antiquarian Soc., Am. Philos. Soc. Office: Inst for Advanced Study Princeton NJ 08540

WHITE, NANCY G., journalism educator; b. N.Y.C., Oct. 21, 1923; d. John C. and Mamie (Comparetto) Giunta; m. Paul Michael White, June 16, 1946; children: Paul Michael Jr., Nancy Melissa. BA, U. Tampa, 1944; MEd, U. Fla., 1954; Advanced Masters Degree, Fla. State U., 1956. Tchr. journalism, dir. student publs. Hillsborough High Sch., Tampa, Fla., 1952-55; tchr. journalism, newspaper advisor Chamberlain High Sch., Tampa, Fla., 1956-68; tchr. journalism, head English dept., newspaper advisor Plant High Sch., Tampa, Fla., 1968-69; prof. journalism, dir. student publs. Hillsborough C.C., Tampa, Fla., 1969—; chair profl. devel. Coll. Media Advisors, Inc., 1993-95, chair awards com., 1990-93, pub. rels. chair, 1988-90; mem. U. West Fla. Adv. Coun., Pensacola, 1984—; mem. State Dept. Edn. Common Course Numbering System Com., 1974—. Contbr. articles to profl. jours.; reporter Tallahassee Dem., 1955-57. Newsletter editor Ybor City Mus. Soc., Tampa, 1990-95; pres., newsletter editor Suncoast Aux. U.S. Submarine Vets. WWII, Tampa, 1986-92; mem., newsletter editor Tampa Women's Club, 1973—. Recipient Columbia U. Gold Key, Columbia Scholastic Press Assn., 1971, Disting. Svc. award Kappa Tau Alpha, 1984, Gold medallion Fla. Scholastic Press Assn., 1989, Disting. Newspaper Adviser award Coll. Media Advisers, 1983, also Disting. Mag. Adviser award, 1988; named to Acad. Hall of Fame, Fla. C.C. Activities Assn., 1995, Hall of Fame, Fla. C.C. Press Assn., 1991. Mem. Nat. C.C. Journalism Assn. (pres. 1992-94), Fla. C.C. Press Assn. (pres. 1971-73, Hall of Fame 1997), Pan Am. Univ. Women (pres.-elect 1996, pres. 1997—), Fla. Scholastic Press Assn. (pres. 1954-57), Alpha Delta Kappa (pres. 1976-78), Phi Kappa Phi, Kappa Delta Pi, Sigma Delta Chi, Alpha Psi Omega. Democrat. Methodist. Avocations: sailing, travel, reading. Home: 5105 W Homer St Tampa FL 33629-7522 Office: Hillsborough C C 2001 N 14th St Tampa FL 33605-3662

WHITE, NATHAN EMMETT, JR., judge, lawyer; b. Dallas, Nov. 28, 1941; s. Nathan Emmett and Martha Eleanor (Scogin) W.; m. Wanda Joyce Cason, Feb. 28, 1964; children: Steven Kelly, Russell Bradley. BBA, So. Meth. U., 1964, JD, 1972; postgrad., George Washington U., 1969-71. Bar: Tex. 1972, U.S. Dist. Ct. (no. dist.) Tex. 1976. Sole practice, Plano, Tex., 1972-89; county judge, Collin County, McKinney, Tex., 1975-82, county treas., 1983-85; state dist. judge 366th dist. Ct., Collin County, Tex., 1989—. Chmn. Collin County Rep. Party, 1972-74; mem. exec. com. State Rep. Party, 1982-84. Served to lt. USNR, 1966-71. Named Citizen of Yr., Plano C. of C., 1982. Mem. State Bar Tex. (chmn. sch. law sect. 1981-82), Plano Bar Assn. (pres. 1988-89), Collin County Bar Assn. (pres. 1990-91). Mormon. Lodges: Rotary (pres. 1975-76, dist. gov. 1979-80), Masons. Home: 2406 Forest Ct Mc Kinney TX 75070 Office: PO Box 808 Mc Kinney TX 75070-0808

WHITE, NERA, retired basketball player; b. Macon County, Tenn., Nov. 15, 1935. Student, George Peabody Coll., Nashville, 1954-58. Named Most Valuable Player, Amateur Athletic Union (10 times), World Basketball Championships, 1957-58, Hall of Fame, 1992. Achievements include member ten-time Championship Team, Amateur Athletic Union, fifteen-time All-Am.; member World Basketball Championship Team, 1957-58. Office: c/o Basketball Hall of Fame PO Box 179 Springfield MA 01101

WHITE, NICK, retail executive; b. Alameda, Calif., Mar. 12, 1945; s. Melvin J. and Dorothy May (Van Cleve) W.; m. Connie White, June 1, 1968; children: Nichole White Williams, Michele White Hudson. Student, Mo. So. Coll., 1968, Ctrl. Mo. State Coll., 1969-73. Store mgr. Wal*Mart, Bentonville, Ark., 1973-77; dist. mgr. Wal*Mart, Bentonville, 1977-80, regional mgr., 1980-81, v.p., 1981-86, sr. v.p., 1986-97, exec. v.p., 1988—; spkr. in field. With USMC, 1963-67, Viet Nam. Avocations: tennis, golf. Home: 81 Champions Blvd Rogers AR 72758 Office: Wal*Mart Stores 702 SW 8th St Bentonville AR 72716-6209

WHITE, NORVAL CRAWFORD, architect; b. N.Y.C., June 12, 1926; s. William Crawford and Caroline Ruth (Taylor) W.; m. Joyce Leslie Lee, May 24, 1958 (div.); children: William Crawford, Thomas Taylor, Gordon Crawford, Alistair David; m. Camilla Cecilia Crowe, June 7, 1992. B.S., Mass. Inst. Tech., 1949; student, Sch. Fine Arts, Fontainbleau, 1954; M.F.A., Princeton, 1955. Designer, assoc. Lathrop Douglass (Architect), 1955-59; prin. Norval C. White (Architect), N.Y.C., 1959-62, 66-67; partner Rowan & White (Architects), N.Y.C., 1962-66, Gruzen & Partners, N.Y.C., 1967-70; prin. Norval C. White & Assos., N.Y.C., 1970-74; ptnr. Levien, Deliso & White, 1974-80, Levien Deliso White Songer, 1980-86; asst. prof. architecture Cooper Union, 1961-67; prof. architecture City Coll., CUNY, 1970-95, prof. emeritus, 1995—, chmn. dept. 1970-77. Author: (with E. Willensky) AIA Guide to New York City, 1968, 2d edit., 1978, 3d edit., 1988, The Architecture Book, 1976, New York: A Physical History, 1987, The Guide to the Architecture of Paris, 1991; prin. works include Seiden House, Tenafly, N.J., 1960, Essex Terrace (housing), Bklyn., 1970, N.Y.C. Police Hdqrs., 1973, Brookhaven Parks (L.I.) Sanitary Landfill, 1971, Forsgate Indsl. Park, South Brunswick, N.J., 1978-86, Del Vista Condominiums, Miami, 1981, 61 Christopher Street, Greenwich Village, 1987. Trustee Bklyn. Inst. Arts and Scis., 1973-82, Bklyn. Pub. Libr., 1993-96; gov. Bklyn. Mus., 1973-82, adv. com., 1982—; mem. N.Y.C. Art Commn., 1975-86, sec., 1975-77, v.p., 1978-80. Served with USNR, 1944-46. Fellow AIA; mem. Soc. Archtl. Historians, N.Y. State Assn. Architects. Democrat. Club: Century Assn. (N.Y.C.). Home and Office: 4 Bostwick St PO Box 1986 Lakeville CT 06039

WHITE, PAMELA JANICE, lawyer; b. Elizabeth, N.J., July 13, 1952; d. Emmet Talmadge and June (Howlett) W. BA, Mary Washington Coll., 1974; JD, Washington and Lee U., 1977. Bar: Md. 1977, U.S. Dist. Ct. Md. 1978, D.C. 1979, U.S. Dist. Ct. D.C. 1979, U.S. Ct. Appeals (4th cir.) 1979, U.S. Ct. Appeals (D.C. cir.) 1981, U.S. Ct. Claims 1981, U.S. Ct. Appeals (2d cir.) 1983, N.Y. 1983, U.S. Dist. Ct. (so. dist.) N.Y. 1983, U.S. Ct. Appeals (9th cir.) 1988, U.S. Supreme Ct. 1981. Assoc. Ober, Grimes & Shriver, Balt., 1977-84; ptnr. Ober, Kaler, Grimes & Shriver, Balt., 1985—; mem. Md. Bd. Law Examiners, 1986-94; mem. select com. on Gender Equality, 1989—, chair, 1997—; fed. dist. ct. adv. group, Civil Justice Reform Act, 1990. Note and comment editor Washington and Lee Law Rev. 1976-77, Washington and Lee Law Council 1983-87, emeritus mem., 1988-97, pres. 1991-92. Mem. Fed. Ct. Bicentennial Com., 1988-90; vol. Profl. Gov.'s Drug-Free Workplace Initiative, 1990-93; bd. trustees Washington and Lee U., 1995—. Named Disting. Alumna, Washington and Lee U., 1994, Hon. mem. Order of the Coif, 1994. Fellow Am. Bar Found., Md. Bar Found. (award for excellence in the advancement of profl. competence 1996); mem. ABA, Fed. Bar Assn., Nat. Conf. Lawyers Corp. Fiduciaries, N.Y. State Bar Assn., Md. Bar Assn. (coun. legal edn. sect. 1987-96, chmn. 1992-93, labor sect. coun. 1992-96, professionalism com. 1991—, chmn. 1994—, bd. govs. 1993-95, exec. com. 1994-95, task force on professionalism chair 1996-97), D.C. Bar Assn., Balt. City Bar Assn. (exec. coun. 1995-96, 1997—), Women's Bar Assn. Md. (treas. 1986-87, v.p. 1987-88, pres.-elect 1988-89, pres. 1989-90, bd. dirs. 1984-86), Md. Assn. Def. Counsel. Presbyterian. Avocation: baseball. Office: Ober Kaler Grimes & Shriver 120 E Baltimore St Baltimore MD 21202-1674

WHITE, PERRY MERRILL, JR., orthopedic surgeon; b. Texarkana, Ark., Oct. 11, 1925; s. Perry Merrill and Mary Gladys (Shelton) W.; m. Lucy Katherine Freeman, Dec. 23, 1947; children: Perry Merrill III, Georgia Lynette, Katherine Landis White Long, John David. B.S., Baylor U., 1948, M.D., 1953; postgrad., Vanderbilt U., 1948-49. Diplomate Am. Bd. Orthopedic Surgery. Intern VA Hosp., Houston, 1953-54; gen. practice medicine Spearman, Tex., 1955-57; resident orthopedic surgery Eugene Talmadge Meml. Hosp., Augusta, Ga., 1957-61; pvt. practice orthopedic surgery Atlanta, 1961-83; chief Ga. Adult Amputee Clinic, 1965-79; active staff Scottish Rite Hosp. for Crippled Children, Decatur, Ga., 1965-73; instr. orthopedic surgery residency program Ga. Bapt. Hosp., 1965-83; orthopedic panelist Ga. Dept. Vocat. Rehab.; cons. Ga. Crippled Children's Service, 1965-76. Former mem. bd. dirs. Haggai Inst., Atlanta, London, Singapore. Served with USNR, 1944-46. Fellow ACS, Am. Acad. Orthopedic Surgeons; mem. So., Ga., Atlanta med. assns., Eastern Orthopedic Assn., Ga., Atlanta orthopedic socs., Alpha Kappa Kappa. Republican. Baptist (deacon). Home: 1547 Cave Rd NW Atlanta GA 30327-3119

WHITE, PHILIP BUTLER, artist; b. Chgo., Jan. 23, 1935; s. Ralph Gerald and Mary (Butler) W.; m. Anita Malisani; children—David, Daniel. B.F.A., U. So. Calif., 1957. juror 71st annual exhbn. Nat. Water Soc., 1991, 24th ann. exhbn. Tenn. Watercolor Soc., 1995. One-man show, Oehlschlaeger Art Gallery, Chgo., 1976, 78, 80; exhibited in group shows 2d, 3d, ann. nat. art round-ups, Las Vegas, 1957, 58, Union League Club, Chgo., 1959, 63, 65, 67, 69, 72, 74, 76, Ill. State Fair, 1959, 60, 61, 62, 63, 64, 65, 66, 67, 68, Brotherhood Week Art Exhbn., Chgo., 1960, N. Miss. Valley Arts exhibit, Ill. State Mus., Springfield, 1961, 63, 65, 67, 69, 70, Magnificent Mile, Chgo., 1961, ann. midyear shows, Butler Inst. Am. Art, Youngstown, Ohio, 1962, 63, 64, ann. Chgo. Sun Times exhbns., 1962, 63, 21st ann. exhbn. Audubon Artists, N.Y.C., 1963, ann. exhbns., Nat. Acad. Design, N.Y.C., 1963, 64, 65, 67, 68, 69, 70, 74, 75, 76, Okla. Mus. Art, 1969, 70, Ball State U., 1970, Am. Watercolor Soc. ann., 1970-71, one-man show, Oak Park (Ill.) High Sch., 1968; subject of cover story, Am. Artist mag., 1978. Served with AUS, 1958-59. Recipient John Deluca medal Las Vegas, 1957, Henry Ward Ranger Fund Purchase prize Nat. Acad. Design, 1963, Julius Hallgarten award, 1964, 67, 69, Thomas B. Clark award, 1965, 68, 70, Helen H. Chambers Purchase prise Union League Club, 1959, 1st prize in oils Union League Club, 1963, 67, 1st prize in oils Ill. State Fair, 1960, 65, Emily Goldsmith award Am. Watercolor Soc., 1971, Mcpl. Art League Chgo. award of Excellence, 1995, Flora Exhbn. award of merit, 1986. Address: 710 Clinton Pl River Forest IL 60305-1914

WHITE, R. QUINCY, lawyer; b. Chgo., Jan. 16, 1933; s. Roger Q. and Carolyn Jane (Everett) W.; m. Joyce Caldwell, Aug. 4, 1962; children: Cleaver Layton, Annelia Everett. BA, Yale U., 1954; JD, Harvard U., 1960. Bar: Ill. 1960, U.S. Dist. Ct. (no. dist.) Ill. 1960, U.S. Ct. Appeals (9th cir.) 1989. Assoc. Leibman, Williams, Bennett, Baird & Minow, Chgo., 1960-67, ptnr., 1967-73; ptnr. Sidley & Austin, Chgo., 1973-93, of counsel, 1994—; sec., dir. W.F. McLaughlin Co., Chgo., 1964-68; hon. consul gen. Islamic Republic Pakistan, Chgo., 1978-92; designated mem. U.S. Trademark Assn., 1985-94. Bd. dirs. Off the Street Club, Chgo., 1974-84; sec. nat. governing bd. Ripon Soc., 1971-72; mem. exec. com. 43-44th ward Regular Rep. orgn., Chgo., 1970-73, mem. Coun. Fgn. and Domestic Affairs, 1970-76; v.p., bd. dirs. Juvenile Protective Assn., 1965-87. Recipient Sitara-i-Quaid-i-Azam Pakistan, 1982. Mem. ABA, Chgo. Coun. Lawyers, Chgo. Bar Assn., Harvard Law Soc. of Ill. (dir. 1988-93). Home: PO Box 178 10947 Marquette Rd New Buffalo MI 49117-0178 Office: Sidley & Austin 1 First Natl Plz Chicago IL 60603-2003

WHITE, RALPH DAVID, retired editor and writer; b. Cleve., Mar. 10, 1931; s. Ralph Davis and Mildred Eva (Stein) W.; m. Lucy Margaret Sturm, Aug. 20, 1960; children: Randall, Eric, Karen, Kathleen. BA, Hamilton Coll., 1953; postgrad., SUNY, Buffalo. With Buffalo Evening News, 1956-89, reporter, 1956-61, successively copy editor, asst. city editor, feature editor, to, 1974, picture editor and dir. editorial art dept., 1974-83, gen. features editor, 1983-89, antiques columnist, 1983-89; guest lectr. SUNY, Buffalo. Served with U.S. Army, 1953-55, Far East. Recipient local awards Buffalo Newspaper Guild. Home: 1389 Whitehaven Rd Grand Island NY 14072-1915

WHITE, RALPH PAUL, automotive executive, consultant; b. Watertown, Mass., Aug. 1, 1926; s. Irving William and Margaret Sarah (McGowan) W.; m. Shirley Irene Christie, Nov. 22, 1947; children: Karin Ann, Eric John. BS in Indsl. Engring., Columbia U., 1951; postgrad., Yale U., 1958-59. Instr. engring. mechanics U. Conn., Torrington, 1956-57; mgr. data processing. B.F. Goodrich Co., Shelton, Conn., 1958-61; ptnr., mgmt. cons. Bavier, Bulger & Goodyear, New Haven, 1961-66; v.p. Davidson Rubber Co., Dover, N.H., 1966-69; pres. Davidson Rubber Co., Dover, 1969-80; group v.p. parent co. Ex-Cell-O, Troy, Mich., 1980-83; pres. Troy (N.H.) Mills Inc., 1983-86, chief exec. officer, 1983-89, chmn., 1987-89, also bd. dirs.; cons., 1989—; bd. dirs. J.A. Wright Co., Keene, N.H., J.D. Cahill Co., Hampton, N.H., Exeter Trust Co. Mem. N.H. Indsl. Devel. Authority, 1972-80, 85-88, Pease Devel. Authority, State of N.H., N.H. Bus. and Fin. Authority, 1992—; exec. bd. Whittemore Sch. Bus., U. N.H., Durham, 1984—. Mem. Am. Inst. Indsl. Engrs., Soc. Automotive Engrs., N.H. Bus. and Industry Assn. (bd. dirs. 1970-80, pres. 1972-73, vice chmn. 1984-86), Abenaqui Country Club, Rye Beach Club, Coral Beach Club. Republican. Roman Catholic. Avocations: skiing, golf. Home: 70 Woodland Rd # 667 North Hampton NH 03862-2234

WHITE, RAYMOND PETRIE, JR., dentist, educator; b. N.Y.C., Feb. 13, 1937; s. Raymond Petrie and Mabel Sarah (Shutze) W.; m. Betty Pritchett, Dec. 27, 1961; children—Karen Elizabeth, Michael Wood. Student, Washington and Lee U., 1955-58; D.D.S., Med. Coll. Va., 1962, Ph.D., 1967. Diplomate: Am. Bd. Oral and Maxillofacial Surgery. Postdoctoral fellow anatomy Med. Coll. Va., Richmond, 1962-67; resident in oral surgery Med. Coll. Va., 1964-67; asst. prof. U. Ky., Lexington, 1967-70; asso. prof. U. Ky., 1970-71, chmn. dept. oral surgery, 1969-71; prof., asst. dean adminstrn. Va. Commonwealth U., Richmond, 1971-74; prof. Sch. Dentistry U. N.C., Chapel Hill, 1974—, Dalton L. McMichael disting. prof., 1993—; dean Sch. Dentistry, U. N.C., Chapel Hill, 1974-81, assoc. dean Sch. Medicine, 1981-92; mem. staff U.N.C. Hosps., mem. exec. com., 1974—, sec., 1977-78, assoc. chief staff, 1981-92; mem. adv. panel on dentistry U.S. Pharmacopeial Conv., 1985—; sr. program cons. The Robert Wood Johnson Found., 1982-90. Author: (with E.R. Costich) Fundamentals of Oral Surgery, 1971, (with Bell and Proffit) Surgical Correction of Dentofacial Deformities, 1980, (with W.R. Proffit) Surgical Orthodontic Treatment, 1990, (with M.R. Tucker, B.C. Terry, J.E. Van Sickels) Rigid Fixations for Maxillofacial Surgery, 1991; coeditor Internat. Jour. Adult Orthodontics and Orthodontic Surgery, 1985—; asst. editor Jour. Oral and Maxillofacial Surgery, 1993—; contbr. sci. articles to profl. jours. Bd. dirs. Am. Fund for Dental Health, 1978-86, v.p., 1982-85. Recipient Outstanding Tchr. award U. Ky., 1971, Disting. Service award Am. Fund Dental Health, 1987. Mem. ADA, AAAS, N.C. Dental Soc., Internat. Assn. Dental Rsch. (pres. Ky. sect. 1970), Inst. Medicine of NAS, Chalmers J. Lyons Acad. Oral Surgery, Am. Assn. Oral and Maxillofacial Surgeons (gen. chmn. sci. sessions com. 1974-76, Outstanding Svc. award as committeeman 1976, chmn. strategic planning com. 1990-96), N.C. Soc. Oral and Maxillofacial Surgeons, Sigma Xi, Psi Omega, Delta Tau Delta, Alpha Sigma Chi, Sigma Zeta, Psi Omega (Scholarship award 1962), Omicron Kappa Upsilon. Roman Catholic. Home: 1506 Velma Rd Chapel Hill NC 27514-7601 Office: U NC Sch Dentistry Dept Oral/Maxillofacial Surgery Chapel Hill NC 27599-7450

WHITE, REGGIE (REGINALD HOWARD WHITE), professional football player; b. Chattanooga, Dec. 19, 1961; m. Sara Copeland; children: Jeremy, Jecolia. Student, U. Tenn. With Memphis Showboats, 1984-85, Phila. Eagles, 1985-93; NFC Defensive Rookie of the Year, 1985; MVP Pro Bowl, 1986; NFL/NFC Defensive Player of the Year, 1987; Defensive Lineman of the Year NFL Players' Assn., 1990; NFL Defensive Player of the Year, 1991; with Green Bay Packers, 1993—. Established the Reggie & Sara White Maternity Home to aid unwed mothers. Named to Sporting News Coll. All-Am. team, 1983, Sporting News United States Football League All-Star team, 1985, Pro Bowl team, 1986-96, Sporting News All-Pro team, 1987, 88, 91, 93; recipient 1992 NFL Players' Assn. Byron 'Whizzer' White Humanitarian Awd. Holds NFL career record for sacks, 157. Office: Green Bay Packers 1265 Lombardi Ave Green Bay WI 54304-3927*

WHITE, RENEE ALLYN, judge; b. Bronx, N.Y., Sept. 22, 1945; d. Lawrence and Ann (Kaufman) W.; m. Michael W. Moore, Oct. 23, 1993. BA, Hofstra U., 1966, JD, Bklyn. Law Sch., 1969. Bar: N.Y. 1969, U.S. Dist. Ct. (ea. and so. dists.) N.Y. 1977, U.S. Supreme Ct. 1978. Trial atty. Criminal Def. div. The Legal Aid Soc. N.Y.C., 1969-74; atty. in charge Criminal Justice sect. Office of Projects Devel. Appellate div. First Dept., N.Y.C., 1974-78; adminstrv. law judge City N.Y. Office Adminstrv. Trials and Hearings, 1978-84; judge N.Y.C. Civil Ct., 1984, Criminal Ct. City of N.Y., 1985-88; acting supreme ct. justice,, supervising judge of N.Y. County Criminal Ct., 1988-90, acting supreme ct. justice, criminal term, 1990—; lectr. in field, mem. criminal procedure law com. of the office of ct. adminstrn. Editor: Criminal Trial Advocacy, 1977; contbr. in field. Mem. ABA, N.Y. State Bar Assn. (chmn. criminal justice sect. 1985-87, mem. house of dels. 1985-88, 91-95, elected nominating com. 1989-90, co-chair, spl. com. on AIDS and the law 1992-95, chair continuing legal edn. com. of judicial sect., 1994-96), Assn. of Bar of City of N.Y. (coun. on judicial adminstrn. 1990-94) , N.Y. Women's Bar Assn.

WHITE, RICHARD A., congressman; b. Bloomington, Ind., Nov. 6, 1953; m. Vikki; 4 children. BA in Govt., Dartmouth Coll., 1975; JD, Georgetown U., 1980. Law clk. to Hon. Charles Clark U.S. Ct. Appeals (5th dist.), 1980-81; assoc. Covington & Burling, 1981-83; assoc. Perkins Coie, 1983-88, ptnr., 1988—; mem. 104th-105th Congresses from 1st Wash. dist., 1994—; mem. commerce com. Del. to dist. county, State GOP Convs., 1984—; founder Farm Team; founder, trustee Books for Kids. Office: US House Reps 116 Cannon Bldg Ofc Bldg Washington DC 20515-4701*

WHITE, RICHARD BOOTH, management consultant; b. N.Y.C., Aug. 26, 1930; s. Frank K. and Doris (Booth) W.; m. Mary Kane Russell, Dec. 9, 1961; children: Katherine Learned, Richard Booth (dec.), Anne Tristram, Leslie Russell. B.A., Yale U., 1952. Asst. account exec. Batten, Barton, Durstine & Osborn, N.Y.C., 1955; account exec. Batten, Barton, Durstine & Osborn, 1956-58, account supr., 1958-63, v.p., 1959-70, mgmt. supr., 1963-76, sr. v.p., 1970-76, exec. v.p., 1976-83, also dir., chmn. exec. com.; dir. BBDO Internat. Inc.; sr. dir., ptnr. Spencer Stuart & Assocs., N.Y.C., 1984—. Pres. bd. Waveny Care Ctr., New Canaan, Conn. 1st lt. USMCR, 1952-54. Mem. Beta Theta Pi. Presbyterian. Clubs: Yale, Racquet and Tennis (N.Y.C.); Country of New Canaan. Home: 774 Oenoke Rdg New Canaan CT 06840-3125 Office: Spencer Stuart & Assocs 695 Main St Stamford CT 06901-2141

WHITE, RICHARD CLARENCE, lawyer; b. Sioux City, Iowa, Oct. 31, 1933; m. Beverly Frances Fitzpatrick, Feb. 22, 1955; children—Anne, Richard, William, Christopher. B.A.; LL.B., Stanford U., 1962. Bar: Calif. 1963, U.S. Supreme Ct. 1970, N.Y. 1983. Assoc. O'Melveny & Myers, L.A., 1962-70, ptnr., 1970-94; lectr. in field. Bd. dirs. Equal Employment Adv. Coun., Washington, 1976-80, 83, Performing Arts Ctr. of Orange County 1983-86. Capt. USMC, 1954-59; Mem. ABA (co-chmn. com. on practice and procedure labor and employment law sect. 1977-80, mem. equal opportunity law com. 1980-85, co-chmn. com. on insts. and meetings 1985-87, coun. 1987—), Coll. Labor and Employment Lawyers (founding fellow, gov.).

WHITE, RICHARD EDMUND, marketing executive; b. Reading, Pa., June 8, 1944; s. Carl Marshall and Miriam Elizabeth (Curry) W.; m. Kristen Margaret Lloyd, June 17, 1967; children: Ross, Peter, Andrew. BS in Econs., U. Pa., 1967; MBA with distinction, U. Mich., 1968. Gen. mgr. mktg. H. J. Heinz Co., Pitts., 1970-81; dir. mktg. Seven Up Co., St. Louis, 1981-83; v.p. mktg. & sales Herr Foods, Inc., Nottingham, Pa., 1984—; bd. dirs. Conard-Pyle Co. Chmn. fin. com. Sewickley Borough Coun., Pa., 1977-81; pres. So. Chester County Devel. Found., Jennersville, Pa., 1988-94; chmn., bd. govs. So. Chester County Med. Ctr., 1988—; pres., bd. mgrs. So. Chester County YMCA, West Grove, Pa., Avon Grove United Way, 1988-93; bd. dirs. Brandywine YMCA Assn. Mem. Am. Mgmt. Assn. (mktg. coun.). Republican. Avocations: physical fitness, reading. Home: 7 Sullivan Chase Dr Avondale PA 19311-9347 Office: Herr Foods Inc PO Box 300 Nottingham PA 19362-0300

WHITE, RICHARD MANNING, electrical engineering educator; b. Denver, Apr. 25, 1930; s. Rolland Manning and Freeda Blanche (Behny) W.; m. Chissie Lee Chamberlain, Feb. 1, 1964 (div. 1975); children: Rolland Kenneth, William Brendan. AB, Harvard U., 1951, AM, 1952, PhD in Applied Physics, 1956. Rsch. assoc. Harvard U., Cambridge, Mass., 1956; mem. tech. staff GE Microwave Lab., Palo Alto, Calif., 1956-63; prof. elect. engring. U. Calif., Berkeley, 1963—; chmn. Grad. Group on Sci. and Math. Edn., U. Calif. at Berkeley, 1981-85; co-dir. Berkeley Sensor and Actuator Ctr., 1986—. Co-author: Solar Cells: From Basics to Advanced Systems, Microsensors, 1991, Electrical Engineering Uncovered, 1997, Acoustic Wave Sensors, 1997; editor ElectroTechnology Rev.; patentee in field. Guggenheim fellow, 1968. Fellow AAAS, IEEE (Cledo Brunetto award 1986, Achievement award 1988, Disting. lectr. 1989); mem. Nat. Acad. Engring., Acoustical Soc. Am., Am. Phys. Soc., Phi Beta Kappa, Sigma Xi. Avocations: photography, hiking, skiing, running, music. Office: U Calif Sensor & Actuator Ctr EECS Dept Berkeley CA 94720

WHITE, RICHARD NORMAN, civil and environmental engineering educator; b. Chetek, Wis., Dec. 21, 1933; s. Norman Lester and Lorna Elwilda (Robinson) W.; m. Margaret Claire Howell, Dec. 28, 1957; children—Barbara Ann, David Charles. BSCE, U. Wis.-Madison, 1956, MS, 1957, PhD, 1961. Registered profl. engr., N.Y. Staff assoc. Gulf Gen. Atomic, San Diego, 1967-68; assoc. prof. civil and environ. engring. Cornell U., 1965-72, prof. structural engring., 1972—, dir. Sch. Civil and Environ. Engring., 1978-84, assoc. dean for undergrad. programs, 1987-89, James A. Friend Family prof. engring., 1988—; vis. prof. U. Calif.-Berkeley, 1974-75, U. P.R., Mayaguez, 1982; cons. Def. Nuclear Agy., Washington, 1983-84, Sandia Nat. Lab., Albuquerque, 1981—, Stone & Webster Engring., 1983-87, SRI Internat., Palo Alto, Calif., 1979-83 , Bakhtar Assoc., 1988—, Kamtech, 1994-95, numerous others. Author: Structural Engineering, vols. I and II, 1976, Vol. III, 1974; Structural Modeling and Experimental Techniques, 1982, Building Structural Design Handbook, 1987; contbr. numerous articles to tech. jours. Served with AUS, 1957. Fellow ASCE (Collingwood prize, 1967), Am. Concrete Inst. (Kelly award 1992, Wason medal 1993, Structural Rsch. award 1994, pres. 1997); mem. NAE, NSPE, Precast/Prestressed Contrete Inst., Earthquake Engring. Rsch. Inst., Sigma Xi, Tau Beta Pi, Chi Epsilon. Republican. Presbyterian. Office: Hollister Hall Cornell U Ithaca NY 14853

WHITE, ROBERT BROWN, medical educator; b. Ennis, Tex., Jan. 5, 1921; s. Robert Brown and Willia Elizabeth (Latimer) W.; m. Jimmie Estelle Sims, Oct. 18, 1942; children: Robert B., Canelia White Layton, Margaret White Gilbert. BS, Tex. A & M Coll., 1941; MD, U. Tex., 1944; cert., Western New Eng. Psychoanalytic Inst., 1959. Intern Phila. (Pa.) Gen. Hosp., 1944-45; psychiat. residency John Sealy Hosp., Galveston, Tex., 1945-46, 48-49; psychiatry fellow Austen Riggs Ctr., Stockbridge, Mass., 1949-51; staff psychiatrist Austen Riggs Ctr., Stockbridge, 1951-62; assoc. prof. U. Tex. Med. Br., Galveston, 1962-67, prof., 1967—, Marie Gale prof. of psychiatry, 1981-93; prof. emeritus, 1993—; tng. analyst New Orleans (La.) Psychoanalytic Inst., 1966-76; tng. analyst Houston-Galveston Psychoanalytic Inst., 1974-94; analyst emeritus, 1994—. Author: Elements of Psychopathology, 1975; contbr. chpts. to books and articles to profl. jours. Capt. U.S. Army, 1946-48. Recipient David Rapaport prize Western New Eng. Psychoanalytic Inst., New Haven, 1959; Ohio State award Ohio State Univ., 1976. Fellow Am. Psychiat. Assn., Am. Coll. Psychiatrists, Am. Coll. Psychoanalysts (bd. regents 1988-91); mem. Am. Psychoanalytic Assn., Alpha Omega Alpha. Democrat. Avocations: photography, carpentry. Home: 1013 Harbor View Dr Galveston TX 77550-3109 Office: Univ Tex Med Br Galveston TX 77550

WHITE, ROBERT DENNIS, pediatrician; b. South Bend, Ind., Dec. 29, 1949; s. Alfred Butler and Mary Ruth (Gibbens) W.; m. Kathy Lynn Samuels, Aug. 15, 1970; children: Luke Alfred, James Samuels, Kieran Claire, Benjamin Robert. Student, U. Notre Dame, 1967-69; BA, John Hopkins U., 1969-70, MD, 1970-74. Diplomate Am. Bd. Pediatrics. Resident in pediatrics Johns Hopkins Hosp., Balt., 1974-76; fellow in neonatology Johns Hopkins Hosp., Balt., 1976-77; sr. rsch. scientist Wellcome Rsch. Labs., London, 1980; dir. regional newborn program Mem. Hosp., South Bend, Ind., 1981—; adj. prof. psychology U. Notre Dame, 1989—, clin. asst. prof. pediatrics Ind. U. Sch. Med., 1983—. Co-author: Manual of Clinical Problems in Pediatrics, 1995, Recommended Standards for Newborn ICU Design, 1996. Co-chair Child Abuse Task Force, So. Bend, Ind., 1991—. Fellow Am. Acad. Pediatrics. Avocations: landscaping, outdoor sports. Office: Meml Hosp 615 N Michigan St South Bend IN 46601-1033

WHITE, ROBERT GORDON, research director, biology educator; b. Lithgow, NSW, Australia, Jan. 17, 1938; s. Richard Robert and Francis Elsie (Schubert) W.; m. Sandra Elizabeth Ferrier, Dec. 9, 1961 (dec. May 1995); children: Robert Ian, Andrew Douglas. B. in Agrl. Sci., Melbourne U., Australia, 1962; M in Rural Sci./Physiology, U. New Eng., Australia, 1968, PhD, 1974. Rsch. asst. Melbourne U., 1962-63; demonstrator U. New Eng., Armidale, Australia, 1963-66, teaching fellow, 1966-69; asst. prof. zoophysiology and nutrition Inst. Arctic Biology, U. Alaska, Fairbanks, 1970-75; assoc. prof. U. Alaska, Fairbanks, 1975-81, prof., 1981—; acting dir. Inst. Arctic Biology, U. Alaska, Fairbanks, 1985, 92, dir., 1993—; dir. Large Animal Rsch. Sta., 1979—. Co-editor: (with Hudson) Bioenergetics of Wild Herbivores, 1985; editor: (proceedings, with Klein, Keller) First International Muskox Symposium, 1984 (proceedings, with Luick, Lent, Klein) First International Reindeer and Caribou Symposium, 1975; editorial bd.: Rangifer/Biol. Papers U. Alaska; contbr. over 100 papers to profl. jours. Pipe major Fairbanks Red Hackle Pipe Band, 1975-90; pres. Fairbanks Nordic Ski Club, 1973-75. NATO Rsch. fellow, Trondheim, Norway, 1975-76. Fellow AAAS (Alaska chmn. 1985, 94), Arctic Inst. N.Am.; mem. Am. Physiol. Soc., Wildlife Soc., Am. Soc. Mammologists, Australasian Soc. Wildlife Mgmt., Australian Soc. Animal Prodn., Australian Soc. Biochemistry and Molecular Biology, Sigma Xi. Avocations: cross country skiing, river boating, hunting, playing bagpipes. Office: U Alaska Inst Arctic Biology Fairbanks AK 99775

WHITE, ROBERT JAMES, newspaper columnist; b. Mpls., Nov. 6, 1927; s. Robert Howard and Claire Lillian (Horner) W.; m. Adrienne Hoffman, Sept. 24, 1955; children: Claire, Pamela, Sarah. BS, U.S. Naval Acad., 1950. V.p. White Investment Co., Mpls., 1957-67; editl. writer Mpls. Tribune, 1967-73, assoc. editor, 1973-82; editor editl. pages Mpls. Star Tribune, 1982-93, columnist, 1993-95, contbg. columnist, 1996—. Recipient cert. of excellence Overseas Press Club, 1981. Mem. Coun. Fgn. Rels., Refugee Policy Group (mem. bd. trustees), Mpls. Club. Presbyterian. Home: 4721 Girard Ave S Minneapolis MN 55409-2212

WHITE, ROBERT JOEL, lawyer; b. Chgo., Nov. 1, 1946; s. Melvin and Margaret (Hoffman) W.; m. Gail Janet Edenson, June 29, 1969 (div. Dec. 1982); m. Penelope K. Bloch, Dec. 22, 1985. BS in Accountancy, U. Ill., 1968; JD, U. Mich., 1972. Bar: Calif. 1972, N.Y. 1985, U.S. Dist. Ct. (cen., ea., so. dists.) Calif. 1972, U.S. Ct. Appeals (9th cir.) 1978, U.S. Ct. Appeals (5th cir.) 1983, U.S. Ct. Appeals (6th cir.) 1984, U.S. Supreme Ct. 1977. Staff auditor Haskin & Sells, Chgo., 1968-69; assoc. O'Melveny & Myers, L.A., 1972-79, ptnr., 1980—; vis. lectr. U. Mich. Law Sch., Ann Arbor, 1986; lectr. Profl. Edn. Sys., Inc., Dallas, 1987, L.A., 1987, 89, Phoenix, 1990, Practicing Law Inst., San Francisco and N.Y.C., 1989-93, Southwestern Legal Found., Dalalas, 1991, UCLA Bankruptcy Inst., 1993, UCLA, 1993; mem. L.A. Productivity Commn., 1993-96. Contbr. articles to profl. jours. Active Constl. Rights Found., 1980—; active Am. Cancer Soc., 1989—, mem. L.A. bd. dirs., 1995—; mem. Nat. Bankruptcy Conf. With U.S. Army, 1968-74. Fellow Am. Coll. Brankruptcy; mem. ABA (litigation sect., mem. comml. law and bankruptcy com. 1972—), L.A. County Bar Assn. (comml. law and bankruptcy sect., chmn. fed. cts. com. 1981-82, exec. com. 1982—), Assn. Bus. Trial Lawyers (bd. govs. 1983-85), Fin. Lawyers Conf. (bd. govs. 1986—, pres. 1990-91), Am. Bankruptcy Inst. Avocations: skiing, running, U.S. history. Office: O'Melveny & Myers 400 S Hope St Los Angeles CA 90071-2801

WHITE, ROBERT JOHN, journalist; b. Cin., Mar. 12, 1953; s. Robert John and Jean W.; m. Mary C. Cupito, Apr. 26, 1986. BA in English & Journalism, Miami U., 1975. Intern Cin. Enquirer, 1975-76; reporter, photographer Franklin (Ind.) Daily Jour., 1976-79; reporter Charleston (S.C.) News and Courier, 1979-80, Evansville (Ind.) Courier, 1981; reporter Cin. Post, 1981-83, asst. met. editor, 1983-86, statehouse bur. chief, 1986-92, editorial page editor, 1993—. Recipient Investigative Reporters and Editors, Inc. award, 1988, ABA cert. merit, 1988. Mem. Nat. Conf. Editorial Writers, Cin. Assn., Leadership Cin., Cin. Hist. Soc. Office: Cin Post 125 E Ct St Cincinnati OH 45202

WHITE, ROBERT L. G., JR., aerospace company executive; b. Orange, N.J., Dec. 20, 1941; s. Robert L.G. and Gertrude Marie (Wilson) W.; m. Joan Adam, May 9, 1970; children: Robert L.G. III, Sonya Lynn. BS in Metallurgical Engring., Lafayette Coll., 1964. Sr. engr. Crucible Steel Co., 1964-68; various positions Curtiss-Wright Corp., Woodridge, N.J., 1968-76, plant mgr. nuclear facility, 1976-80, dir. gas turbine overhaul, 1980-83; v.p., gen. mgr. Curtiss-Wright/Marquette, Inc., Fountain Inn, S.C., 1983-87; pres. GEC-Marconi Aerospace Inc., Whippany, N.J., 1987-94, Breeze-Eastern, Union, N.J., 1994—. Office: Breeze-Eastern 700 Liberty Ave Union NJ 07083-8107

WHITE, ROBERT LEE, electrical engineer, educator; b. Plainfield, N.J., Feb. 14, 1927; s. Claude and Ruby Hemsworth Emerson (Levick) W.; m. Phyllis Lillian Arlt, June 14, 1952; children: Lauren A., Kimberly A., Christopher L., Matthew P. BA in Physics, Columbia U., 1949, MA, 1951, PhD, 1954. Assoc. head atomic physics dept. Hughes Rsch. Labs., Malibu, Calif., 1954-61; head magnetics dept. Gen. Tel. and Electronics Rsch. Lab., Palo Alto, Calif., 1961-63; prof. elec. engring., materials sci. and engring. Stanford U., Palo Alto, 1963, chmn. elec. engring. dept., 1981-86; William E. Ayer prof. elec. engring. Stanford U., 1985-88; exec. dir. The Exploratorium, San Francisco, 1987-89; dir. Inst. for Electronics in Medicine, 1973-87, Stanford Ctr. for Rsch. on Info. Storage Materials, 1991—; initial ltd. ptnr. Mayfield Fund, Mayfield II and Alpha II Fund, Rainbow Co-Investment Ptnrs., Halo Ptnrs.; vis. prof. Tokyo U., 1975; cons. in field. Author: (with K.A. Wickersheim) Magnetism and Magnetic Materials, 1965, Basic Quantum Mechanics, 1967; Contbr. numerous articles to profl. jours. With USN, 1945-46. Fellow Guggenheim Oxford U., 1969-70, Canton Hosp., Swiss Fed. Inst. Tech., Zurich, 1977-78, Christensen fellow Oxford U., 1986; Sony sabbatical chair, 1994. Fellow Am. Phys. Soc., IEEE; mem. Sigma Xi, Phi Beta Kappa. Home: 450 El Escarpado Stanford CA 94305-8431 Office: Stanford U Dept Material Sci Engr Stanford CA 94305

WHITE, ROBERT M., II, newspaper executive, editor, columnist; b. Mexico, Mo., Apr. 6, 1915; s. L. Mitchell and Maude (See) W.; m. Barbara Whitney Spurgeon, Aug. 19, 1948 (dec. Feb., 1983); children: Barbara Whitney, Jane See, Laura L., Robert M. III; m. Linda Hess Grimsley, July 11, 1992. Grad., Mo. Mil. Acad., 1933; A.B., Washington and Lee U., 1938, LL.B. (hon.), 1972. Writer of newspaper articles Australia, Africa, S.Am., Europe, USSR, 1966, 86, People's Republic China, 1972, 77; reporter Mexico (Mo.) Eve. Ledger, 1938-39, editor, pub., 1945; vis. prof. Sch. Journalism, Mo. U., 1968-69; reporter UP Bur., Kansas City, 1939-40; pres. Ledger Newspapers, Inc., Mexico, Mo., 1945-86; spl. cons. to pub. Chgo. Sun-Times, 1956-58; pres. See TV Co., Mexico, 1966-81; editor, pres., bd. dirs. N.Y. Herald Tribune, 1959-61; juror Pulitizer prize journalism, 1964-65; bd. dirs. World Press Freedom Com. Co-author: A Study of the Printing and Publishing Business in the Soviet Union. President Gen. Douglas MacArthur Found., 1981—. Lt. col. AUS, 1940-45. Decorated Bronze Star; recipient nat. disting. service award for editorials Sigma Delta Chi, 1952, 68; editorial award N.Y. Silurians, 1959; Disting. Service to Journalism award U. Mo., 1967; Pres. award of merit Nat. Newspapers Assn., 1967; Ralph D. Casey Minn. award disting. service in journalism, 1983; finalist Journalist in Space 1986—. Mem. Am. Soc. Newspaper Editors (dir. 1968-69, chmn. freedom of info. com. 1970-72), Am. Newspaper Pubs. Assn. (nat. treas. 1963, dir. 1955-63, chmn. internat. group 1982-86), Washington Inst. Fgn. Affairs, Inland Daily Press Assn. (chmn. bd. 1958-59, pres., past sec., v.p.), Mo. Press Assn. (dir., v.p. 1981-83, pres. 1983-84), Mo. Press-Bar Commn. (chmn. 1972-74), Internat. Press Inst. (chmn. Am. com. 1982-85), Nat. Press Club, Bohemian Club, Dutch Treat Club, Burning Tree Club, Cosmos Club, Internat. Club, Masons, Rotary, Sigma Delta Chi (nat. pres. 1967, pres. found. 1968), Beta Theta Pi. Office: 4871 Glenbrook Rd NW Washington DC 20016-3245

WHITE, ROBERT MARSHALL, physicist, government official, educator; b. Reading, Pa., Oct. 2, 1938; s. Carl M. and Miriam E. White; m. Sara Tolles; children: Victoria, Jonathan. BS in Physics, MIT, 1960; PhD, Stanford U., 1964. Vis. scientist Osaka U., Japan, 1963; NSF postdoctoral fellow U. Calif., Berkeley, 1965-66; asst. prof. physics Stanford U., 1966-70; NSF postdoctoral fellow, Cambridge, Eng., 1970-71; mgr. solid state research area Xerox PARC, 1971-78, mgr. storage technology, 1978-83, prin. scientist, 1983-84; v.p. research and tech. Control Data Corp. Data Storage Products Group, Mpls., 1984-86, chief tech. officer, v.p. research and engring, 1986-89; v.p., dir. advanced computer techs. Microelectronics & Computer Tech. Corp., Austin, Tex., 1989-90; under-sec. of commerce for tech., Dept. Commerce, Washington, 1990-93; prof., head dept. electrical and computer engring. Carnegie Mellon U., Pitts., 1993—, Univ. prof., 1997; lectr. dept. applied physics Stanford U., 1971-81; vis. scientist Ecole Polytechnique, Paris, 1976-78, U. Pernambuco, Brazil, 1978; cons. prof. applied physics, prin. investigator Magnetic Thin Film Program, Stanford U., 1982-93; adj. prof. dept. physics U. Minn., 1987-89; guest Chinese Acad. Scis., 1982. Author: Quantum Theory of Magnetism, 1970 (Russian transl., 1972, Polish transl., 1979); Long Range Order in Solids, 1979 (Russian transl., 1982); Quantum Theory of Magnetism, 1983; Introduction to Magnetic Recording, 1985. Contbr. articles to profl. jours. Bd. advisors Inst. Tech. U. Minn., 1987; mem. State Minn. Com. on Sci. and Tech. Research and Devel., 1987-90; mem. adv. bd. U. Ill. Coll. Engring. Recipient Alexander von Humboldt Prize, Fed. Republic of Germany, 1981. Fellow AAAS, IEEE (disting. lectr. Magnetics Soc., mem. editorial bd. SPECTRUM, IEEE Disting. Pub. Svc. award 1993), Am. Phys. Soc.; mem. NAE, NRC (mem. nat. materials adv. bd., chmn. com. magnetic materials 1984, material sci. and engring., nat. steering com. advanced steady state neutron source, vice chmn. IUPAP commn. on magnetism), Conf. Magnetism and Magnetic Materials (adv. com. 1976-78, 80-95, program com. 1973-75, chmn. 1981, chmn. Intermag Conf. 1991), Internat. Conf. Magnetism (program chmn. 1985), Found. Nat. Medals Sci. and Tech. (bd. dirs. 1993—), Ontrack Computer Systems (bd. dirs. 1994—), Zilog (bd. dirs. 1995—), SGS-Thompson Microelectronics (bd. dirs., 1996—); mem. Panel on Advanced Computing of the Japanese Tech. Evaluation Ctr.; mem. Nat. Adv. Com. on Semiconductors, 1990-92, Mfg. Forum, 1991, Nat.Critical Techs. Panel, 1990-91. Office: Carnegie Mellon U Elec & Computer Engring Dept Pittsburgh PA 15213-3890

WHITE, ROBERT MAYER, meteorologist; b. Boston, Feb. 13, 1923; s. David and Mary (Winkeller) W.; m. Mavis Seagle, Apr. 18, 1948; children—Richard Harry, Edwina Janet. B.A., Harvard, 1944; M.S., Mass. Inst. Tech., 1949, Sc.D., 1950; D.Sc. (hon.), L.I. U., 1976, Rensselaer Poly. Inst., 1977, U. Wis., Milw., 1978; ScD (hon.), U. Bridgeport, 1984, U. R.I., 1986, Clarkson U.; PhD (hon.), Johns Hopkins U., 1982, Drexel U., 1985, Ill. Inst. Tech., 1994. Project scientist Air Force Cambridge Research Center, 1950-58, chief meteorol. devel. lab., 1958-59; asso. dir. research dept. Travelers Ins. Co., 1959-60; pres. Travelers Research Center, Inc., 1960-63; chief U.S. Weather Bur., 1963-65; adminstr. Environ. Sci. Services Adminstrn., 1965-70, NOAA, 1970-77; pres. Joint Oceanographic Inst., Inc., 1977-79; chmn. Climate Research Bd., exec. officer Nat. Acad. Scis., 1977-79; Washington; adminstr. Nat. Research Council, 1979-80; pres. Univ. Corp. Atmospheric Research, 1980-83, Nat. Acad. Engring., 1983-95; Karl T. Compton lectr. MIT, Cambridge, 1995-96; sr. fellow Univ. Corp. Atmospheric Rsch., 1995—; sr. fellow H. John Heinz III Ctr. for Sci., Econs. and Environ., 1996—; pres. Wash. Adv. Group, 1996—. Author articles in field; mem. editorial bd. Am. Soc. Engring. Edn. jour. Bd. overseers Harvard U., 1977—; vis. com. meteorology and planetary sci. Mass. Inst. Tech.; Mem. vis. com. Kennedy Sch. Govt., Harvard U.; bd. dirs. Resources for Future, 1980—. Served to capt. USAAF, World War II. Decorated Legion of Honor France; recipient Jesse L. Rosenberger medal U. Chgo., 1971; Cleveland Abbe award Am. Meteorol. Soc., 1969; Godfrey L. Cabot award Aero Club Boston, 1966; Rockefeller Pub. Service award, 1974; David B. Stone award New Eng. Aquarium, 1975; Neptune award Am. Oceanic Orgn., 1977; Matthew Fontaine Maury award Smithsonian Instn., 1976; Internat. Conservation award Nat. Wildlife Fedn., 1976; Internat. Meteorol. Orgn. prize, 1980, Tyler prize for Environ. Achievement U. Calif., 1992. Fellow AAAS, Am. Meterol. Soc. (coun. 1965-67, 77—, Charles Franklin Brooks award 1978, pres. 1980), Am. Geophys. Union, World Acad. Art and Scis., Australian Acad. Tech. Scis. and Engring., Am. Acad. Arts and Scis., UCAR (sr.); mem. NAE (coun. 1977, pres. 1983-95), Marine Tech. Soc., Coun. Fgn. Rels., Nat. Action Coun. Minorities in Engring. Inc., Finnish Acad. Tech. (fgn. mem. 1991—), Am. Philos. Soc., Nat. Commn. on the Environment World Wildlife Fund, Engring. Acad. Japan (fgn. assoc. 1988—), Internat. Acad. Astronautics (Paris), Russian Acad. Engring., Royal Acad. Engring. (U.K.) (hon.), Cosmos Club (Washington). Home: Somerset House II 5610 Wisconsin Ave Apt 1506 Bethesda MD 20815-4419 Office: 1200 New York Ave NW Ste 410 Washington DC 20005-3929

WHITE, ROBERT ROY, chemical engineer; b. Bklyn., Mar. 1, 1916; s. Laurance S. and Grace A. (Diffin) W.; m. Elizabeth R. Clark, July 2, 1940; children: Robert Roy, William Wesley, Elizabeth Ann, Margaret. BS, Cooper Union Inst. Tech., 1936; postgrad., Bklyn. Poly. Inst., 1936-37; M.S. (Horace H. Rackham predoctoral fellow 1938), U. Mich., 1938; PhD, 1941; postgrad., DePaul U. Law Sch., 1940-41, MIT, 1962. Jr. chem. engr. Calco Chem. Co., Bound Brook, N.J., 1936-37; rsch. chem. engr. Dow Chem. Co., 1937-38; chem. engr. Stnd. Oil Co. Calif., 1940, Universal Oil Products Co., 1940-42; faculty U. Mich., 1942-60, prof. chem. engring., 1945-60, assoc. dean Horace H. Rackham Sch. Grad. Studies, 1958-60; assoc. dean U. Mich. Coll. Engring., 1958-60; dir. U. Mich. Inst. Sci. and Tech., 1959-60; v.p., gen. mgr. R & D Atlantic Refining Co., Phila., 1960-62; sr. staff mgmt. svc. divsn. Arthur D. Little, Inc., 1962; v.p. devel. Champion Papers, Inc., Hamilton, Ohio, 1962-66; pres. rsch. divsn. W.R. Grace & Co., 1966-67; dean Sch. Mgmt., Case Western Res. U., Cleve., 1967-71; mng. dir. Karl Kroyer S.A., Denmark, 1970; spl. asst. to pres., dir. forum Nat. Acad. Sci., Washington, 1971-1981; adj. prof. chem. engring. U. Md., 1982-85, Cath. U. Am., Am. U.; v.p. JC Tech., 1986—; cons. in field. Author: (with others) Unit Operations, 1950; Contbr. articles to profl. jours. Recipient Henry Russell award U. Mich., 1945; teaching award Phi Lambda Upsilon chpt. U. Mich., 1949; sesquicentennial award U. Mich., 1967; prof. award Cooper Union Inst., 1975; McCormack-Freud hon. lectr. Ill. Inst. Tech. Mem. AAAS, AIChE (jr. award 1945, presentation award 1951, profl. progress award 1956), SAR, Am. Chem. Soc., Am. Soc. Engring. Edn. (George Westinghouse award 1955), St. Andrews Soc., Order Crown of Charlemagne, Baron Magna Charta, Cosmos Club, Sigma Xi, Alpha Chi Sigma, Phi Lambda Upsilon, Phi Kappa Phi, Tau Beta Pi, Iota Alpha. Office: 2440 Virginia Ave NW Washington DC 20037-2601

WHITE, ROBERT STEPHEN, physics educator; b. Ellsworth, Kans., Dec. 28, 1920; s. Byron F. and Sebina (Leighty) W.; m. Freda Marie Bridgewater, Aug. 30, 1942; children: Nancy Lynn, Margaret Diane, John Stephen, David Bruce. AB, Southwestern Coll., 1942, DSc hon., 1971; MS, U. Ill., 1943; PhD, U. Calif., Berkeley, 1951. Physicist Lawrence Radiation Lab., Berkeley, Livermore, Calif., 1948-61; head dept. particles and fields Space Physics Lab. Aerospace Corp., El Segundo, Calif., 1962-67; physics prof. U. Calif., Riverside, 1967-92, dir. Inst. Geophysics and Planetary Physics, 1967-92, chmn. dept. physics, 1970-73, prof. emeritus physics dept., rsch. physicist, 1992—; lectr. U. Calif., Berkeley, 1953-54, 57-59. Author: Space Physics, 1970; contbr. articles to profl. jours. Officer USNR, 1944-46. Sr. Postdoctoral fellow NSF, 1961-62; grantee NASA, NSF, USAF, numerous others. Fellow AAAS, Am. Phys. Soc. (exec. com. 1972-74); mem. AAUP, Am. Geophys. Union, Am. Astron. Soc. Home: 5225 Austin Rd Santa Barbara CA 93111-2905 Office: U Calif Inst Geophysics & Planetary Physics Riverside CA 92521

WHITE, RONALD LEON, financial management consultant; b. West York, Pa., July 14, 1930; s. Clarence William and Grace Elizabeth (Gingerich) W.; m. Estheranne Wieder, June 16, 1951; children: Bradford William, Clifford Allen, Erick David. BS in Econs, U. Pa., 1952, MBA, 1957. Cost analysis supr. Air Products & Chem. Corp., Allentown, Pa., 1957-60; cost control mgr. Mack Trucks, Inc., Allentown, 1960-64; mgmt. cons. Peat, Marwick, Mitchell & Co., Phila., 1964-66; mgr. profit planning Monroe, The Calculator Co. (divsn. Litton Industries), Orange, N.J., 1966-67, contr., 1967-68; v.p. fin. Bus. Sys. Group of Litton Industries, Beverly Hills, Calif., 1968-70; pres. Royal Typewriter Co. divsn., Hartford, Conn., 1970-73; exec. v.p., COO, treas. Tenna Corp., Cleve., 1973-75, pres., dir., 1975-77; v.p. fin. Arby's, Inc., Youngstown, Ohio, 1978-79; exec. v.p., dir. Roxbury Am., Inc., 1979-81; v.p. fin., treas. Royal Crown Cos., Inc., Atlanta and Miami Beach, Fla., 1981-86, TDS Healthcare Sys. Corp., Atlanta, 1987-88; v.p. Corp. Fin. Assocs., Atlanta, 1988-90; prin. The Janelle Co., Atlanta, 1991—; instr. acctg. Wharton Sch. U. Pa., 1952-53, instr. industry, 1953-54. Deacon area United Ch. of Christ. Lt. USNR, 1954-57. Mem. Am. Mgmt. Assn., Inst. Mgmt. Accts., Nat. Assn. Corp. Dirs., Fin. Execs. Inst., Acacia, Masons, Rotary. Home: 2362 Kingsgate Ct Atlanta GA 30338-5931 Office: The Janelle Co 2362 Kingsgate Ct Atlanta GA 30338-5931

WHITE, ROSANNE TERESA, educational association executive; b. Allentown, Pa., Aug. 29, 1954; d. Hugh Dennis and Helen Anne (McCoog) McClafferty; m. Thomas Alexander White, June 19, 1976; children: Maureen, Douglas. BS, Radford (Va.) U., 1976; MEd, George Mason U., 1982. Tchr. Child Devel. Ctr., Falls Church, Va., 1977-80; instr. adult edn. Fairfax County Pub. Schs., Fairfax, Va., 1981-83; exec. dir. Childbirth Edn. Assn., Annandale, Va., 1982-83; program mgr. George Mason U., Fairfax, 1983-85, asst. dir., 1985-87; exec. dir. Tech. Student Assn., Reston, Va., 1987—; chmn. Nat. Coordinating Coun. Vocat. Student Orgns., Reston, 1989—. Mem. Va. Rep. Com., 1989—. Recipient Chmn.'s award Vienna (Va.) C. of C., 1987; named Ky. Col., Gov. of Ky., 1990, Tenn. Col., Gov. of Tenn., 1990. Mem. Am. Soc. Assn. Execs., Am. Vocat. Assn., Fairfax County C. of C., AAUW. Roman Catholic. Office: Tech Student Assn 1914 Association Dr Reston VA 20191-1538*

WHITE, ROY BERNARD, theater executive; b. Cin.; s. Maurice and Anna (Rudin) W.; m. Sally Lee Ostrom, June 17, 1951; children: Maurice Ostrom, Barbara Dee, Daniel Robert. B.A., U. Cin., 1949. Formerly mem. sales staff Twentieth Century Fox Films, Cin.; now pres. Mid-States Theatres; dir. Nat. Assn. Theatre Owners, nat. pres., exec. com., chmn. bd.; Mem. film adv. panel Ohio Arts Coun.; bd. dirs. Will Rogers Meml. Fund, Found. Motion Picture Pioneers, Inc.; mem. media arts panel Nat. Endowment for Arts. Served with USAAF, 1944-45. Named Exhibitor of Year Internat. Film Importers and Distbrs. Am. Mem. Nat. Assn. Theater Owners (pres.), Am. Film Inst. (trustee 1972-75, exec. com. 1972-75), Fedn. Motion Picture Pioneers (v.p.), Masons, Queen City Racquet, Crest Hills Country, Amberley Village (Ohio) Tennis Club (pres. 1972-73), Bankers Club, Quail Creek Country Club (Naples, Fla.), Alpha Epsilon Pi, Phi Eta Sigma. Home: 8171 Bay Colony Dr Apt 1904 Naples FL 34108-7567

WHITE, ROY MARTIN, engineering manager; b. Manchester, Conn., Sept. 10, 1947; s. Roy Henry and Elizabeth Mary (Mayer) W.; m. Jane Marie Pencek, Dec. 18, 1971; children: Rebecca Marie, Mary Elizabeth. BS, U.S. Air Force Acad., 1969; MPA, Golden Gate U., 1976. Commd. 2d lt. USAF, 1969, advanced through grades to lt. col., retired, 1989; systems engr. Systems Control Tech., Washington, 1989-94, sr. area mgr., engring., 1992—; bd. dirs. Vietnam Vets. of Am., No., Va.; mem. Advanced Automation Task Force, FAA, Washington, 1994. Author reports in field. Named to Outstanding Young Men of Am., 1976; decorated Disting. Flying Cross, USAF, Vietnam. Mem. AIAA, Air Force Acad. Soc., No. Va. Corvettes, K.C. Roman Catholic. Avocations: auto racing, zymurgist, mechanics, flying. Home: 13903 Quietway Ct Chantilly VA 22021-2829 Office: Nat Airspace Sys Implement Support Contract 400 Virginia Ave SW Washington DC 20024-2730

WHITE, SHARON ELIZABETH, lawyer; b. Galveston, Tex., July 5, 1955; d. Edward and Clara Adelia (Haden) W. BA, Baylor U., 1977; JD, So. Meth. U., 1981. Bar: Tex. 1981, U.S. Dist. Ct. (no. dist.) Tex. 1983, U.S. Ct. Appeals (5th cir.) 1985. Assoc. Underwood, Wilson, Berry, Stein & Johnson, Amarillo, Tex., 1981-86, ptnr., 1987-89, shareholder, 1990—. Asst. editor-in-chief Southwestern Law Rev., Dallas, 1980-81. Bd. dirs., sec. council Amarillo Girl Scout U.S., 1983-85, 3d v.p., 1985, 1st v.p. 1985-88, pres., 1988-90; bd. dirs. Amarillo Little Theatre, 1984-91, treas., 1985-89, 91; grants chmn. Don Harrington Discovery Ctr., 1984-86, future planning and devel. chmn., 1986-87; active Amarillo Symphony Guild (bd. dirs. 1994-95), Amarillo Art Alliance (bd. dirs. 1993-97), Panhandle Plains Hist. Soc.; mem. Jr. League Amarillo, 1987—, bd. dirs., 1993-94; chair Amarillo Race for the Cure , 1993, Devel. Coun. of Don & Sybil Harrington Cancer Ctr., 1995—. Fellow Tex. Bar Found.; mem. State Bar Tex. (dist. 13 grievance com. 1995—), Amarillo Bar Assn. (sec.-treas. 1989-90, bd. dirs. 1994-96), Amarillo Area Estate Planning Coun., Phi Delta Phi, Delta Delta Delta. Republican. Presbyterian. Office: Underwood Wilson PO Box 9158 Amarillo TX 79105-9158

WHITE, STANLEY ARCHIBALD, research electrical engineer; b. Providence, Sept. 25, 1931; s. Clarence Archibald White and Lou Ella (Givens) Arford; m. Edda María Castaño-Benítez, June 6, 1956; children: Dianne, Stanley Jr., Paul, John. BSEE, Purdue U., 1957, MSEE, 1959, PhD, 1965. Registered profl. engr., Ind., Calif. Engr. Rockwell Internat., Anaheim, Calif., 1959-68, mgr., 1968-84, sr. scientist, 1984-90; pres. Signal Processing and Controls Engring. Corp., 1990—; adj. prof. elec. engring. U. Calif., 1984—; cons. and lectr. in field; bd. dirs. Asilomar Signals, Systems and Computers Conf. Corp. Publisher, composer music; contbr. chpts. to books; articles to profl. jours.; patentee in field. With USAF, 1951-55. Fellow N.Am. Aviation Sci. Engring., 1963-65; recipient Disting. Lectr. award Nat. Electronics Conf., Chgo., 1973, Engr. of Yr. award Orange County (Calif.) Engring. Coun., 1984, Engr. of Yr. award Rockwell Internat., 1985, Leonardo Da Vinci Medallion, 1986, Sci. Achievement award, 1987, Disting. Engring. Alumnus award Purdue U., 1988, Meritorious Inventor's award Rockwell Internat. Corp., 1989, Outstanding Elec. Engr. award Purdue U., 1992. Fellow AAAS, AIAA, IEEE (Centennial medalist chair of ICASSP and ISCAS, Signal Processing Soc. disting. lect. and founding chmn. L.A. coun. chpt., Circuits and Sys. Soc. Tech. Achievement award 1996), Inst. for Advancement Engring., N.Y. Acad. Scis.; mem. Choral Condrs. Guild and Saddleback Master Chorale; mem. Air Force Assn. (life), Am. Legion (life), Sigma Xi (founding pres. Orange County chpt.), Eta Kappa Nu (disting. fellow, internat. dir. emeritus), Tau Beta Pi. Avocation: choral music. Home: 433 E Avenida Cordoba San Clemente CA 92672-2350

WHITE, STEPHEN HALLEY, biophysicist, educator; b. Wewoka, Okla., May 14, 1940; s. James Halley and Gertrude June (Wyatt) W.; m. Buff Ertl, Aug. 20, 1961 (div. 1982); children: Saill, Shell, Storn, Sharr, Skye, Sunde; m. Jackie Marie Dooley, Apr. 14, 1984. BS in Physics, U. Colo., 1963; MS in Physics, U. Wash., 1965, PhD in Physiology and Biophysics, 1969. USPHS postdoctoral fellow biochemistry U. Va., Charlottesville, 1971-72; asst. prof. physiology and biophysics U. Calif., Irvine, 1972-75, assoc. prof. physiology and biophysics, 1975-78, prof. physiology and biophysics, 1978—, vice chmn. physiology and biophysics, 1974-75, chmn. physiology and biophysics, 1977-89; guest biophysicist Brookhaven Nat. Lab., Upton, L.I., N.Y., 1977—. Contbr. numerous articles to profl. jours. Served to capt. USAR, 1969-71. Recipient Research Career Devel. award USPHS, 1975-80, Kaiser-Permanente award, 1975, 92; grantee NIH, 1971—, NSF, 1971—. Mem. NSF (adv. panel for molecular biology 1982-85, mem. nat. steering com. advanced neutron source 1992-95), Biophys. Soc. (chmn. membrane biophysics subgroup 1977-78, acting sec., treas. 1979-80, coun. 1981-84, exec. bd. 1981-83, program chmn. 1985, ann. meeting sec. 1987-95, pres. 1996-97), Am. Physiol. Soc. (editl. bd. 1981-93, membership com. 1985-86, publ. com. 1987-91), Assn. Chmn. Depts. Physiology (rep. to coun. acad. scos. 1981-82, councilor 1982-83, pres. 1986-87), Soc. Gen. Physiologists (treas. 1985-88, The Protein Soc. (electronic pub. coord. 1993—). Avocations: skiing, cooking, travel. Office: Univ of Calif Dept of Physiology & Biophysics Irvine CA 92697-4560

WHITE, STEVE ALLEN, health facility administrator; b. Harrisonburg, Va., Nov. 21, 1954. BS in Acctg., So. Coll., Collegedale, Tenn., 1977; MBA in Fin., Ind. U., 1984. Supr. acctg. Uniroyal Corp., Maryville, Mo., 1978-79; sr. auditor Uniroyal Corp., Detroit, 1979-80; fin. contr. Adventist Health Systems, Hinsdale, Ill., 1980-83; mgmt. cons. Touche Ross & Co., Atlanta, 1984-85; dir. devel. Ptnrs. Nat. Health Plans, Irving, Tex., 1985-87; dir. network mgmt. Aetna Health Plans, Atlanta, 1987-93, v.p. health svcs., 1993-95; CEO Healthsource, Inc., Hooksett, N.H., 1995—. Home: 818 Coxboro Dr Brentwood TN 37027

WHITE, SUSAN VICTORIA, nursing administrator; b. Ocala, Fla., Oct. 7, 1951; d. George and Agnes Victoria (Toffaletti) Spontak. BS in Nursing, U. Fla., 1973, MS in Nursing, 1982, PhD, 1997. Cert. critical care nurse. Asst. head nurse ICU Orlando (Fla.) Regional Med. Ctr., 1976-78, patient care coord., 1978-85; quality assurance mgr. Sand Lake Hosp., Orlando, 1985-88, assoc. exec. dir., dir. nursing, 1990-94; bus. sys. analyst Orlando Regional Healthcare Sys., 1995-97; v.p. quality mgmt. Fla. Hosp. Assn., 1997—. Mem. AACN, ANA (cert. nursing adminstrn.), Am. Hosp. Assn., Fla. Nurses Assn., Am. Orgn. of Nurse Execs., Fla. Orgn. Nurse Execs., Ctrl. Fla. Orgn. Nurse Execs., Nat. Quality Assurance Profession, Fla. Utilization Rev. Assn., Am. Coll. Healthcare Execs., Sigma Theta Tau (award for rsch.), Phi Kappa Phi. Home: PO Box 681133 Orlando FL 32868-1133

WHITE, SYLVIA FRANCES, gerontology home care nurse, consultant; b. Dayton, Ohio, May 2, 1952; d. Arthur Francis and Eleanor Ida (Beach) Scarpelli; m. Alan Bruce White, Nov. 28, 1981. BSN, Loyola U., 1975; MPH, U. Ill., Chgo., 1984. Cert. gerontl. nurse; lic. nursing home adminstrn., Ill. Staff nurse Vis. Nurse Assn., Chgo., 1975-80, team leader, 1980-81, supr., 1981-83, dist. adminstr., 1984-86, mgr. North side, 1986-87, dir. patient svcs., 1987; dir. clin. svcs. Kimberly Quality Care, Evanston, Ill., 1987-89; pub. health nurse City of Evanston, Ill., 1989-90; geriatric nurse assoc. City of Evanston, 1990—; cons. surveyor Joint Commn. on Accreditation of Healthcare Orgns., Oakbrook Terrace, Ill., 1988—; vol. Hospice, literacy. Trainer The Arthritis Found., Chgo., 1991-92; mem. Panel Rev. State of Ill. Continuing Edn.; mem. profl. edn. com. Arthritis Found.; hospice vol. Mem. APHA, Ill. Pub. Health Assn., Ill. Home Health Coun., Ill. Alliance for Aging, Zonta, Arthritis Profl. Edn. Com., Nat. Assn. Home Care. Roman Catholic. Avocations: reading, golf, racquetball, walking, quilting. Home: 222 Sunset Dr Wilmette IL 60091-3027 Office: Evanston Health Dept 2100 Ridge Ave Evanston IL 60201-2796

WHITE, TERRENCE HAROLD, academic administrator, sociologist; b. Ottawa, Ont., Canada, Mar. 31, 1943; s. William Harold and Shirley Margaret (Ballantine) W.; m. Susan Elizabeth Hornaday; children: Christine Susan, Julie Pamela. Ph.D., U. Toronto, 1972. Head dept. sociology and anthropology U. Windsor, Ont., Can., 1973-75; prof., chmn. dept. sociology U. Alta., Edmonton, 1975-80, dean faculty of arts, 1980-88; pres. Brock U., St. Catharines, Ont., 1988-96, T.H. White Orgn. Research Services Ltd., Edmonton, 1975—; dir. Labatt's Brewing Alta., Edmonton, 1981-88; pres. U. Calgary, 1996—. Author: Power or Pawns: Boards of Directors, 1978, Human Resource Management, 1979; editor: Introduction to Work Science, 1981, QWL in Canada: Case Studies, 1983. Bd. dirs. Progressive Conservative Assn., Edmonton South, 1976-81, 1st v.p., 1981-85, pres., 1985-87; bd. dirs. Tri-Bach Festival Found., Edmonton, 1981-88, Alta. Ballet Co., 1985-88, Edmonton Conv. and Tourism Authority, Arch Enterprises, 1984-88, Niagara Symphony Soc., YMCA, St. Catharines, 1988-92; chair United Way Campaign St. Catharines, 1992, Fox Found., 1990-96, Canada Summer Games 2001 Bid Com.; bd. dirs. Edmonton Symphony Soc., v.p., 1986-88; bd. govs. U. Alta., 1984-88, Brock U., 1988-96, Ridley Coll., 1990—, Atlanta Heridate Found. for Med. Rsch.; divsn. chair Calgary R&D Authority, 1997; vol. Calgary United Way Campaign. Recipient Can. 125 Commemorative medal, Govt. of Can. Mem. Calgary Petroleum Club, Ranchmen's Club, Rotary (pres. Edmonton South 1981-82), Delta Tau Kappa, Alpha Kappa Delta. Home: 4528 Varsity Green NW, Calgary, AB Canada T3B 3A5 Office: U Calgary, 2500 University Dr NW, Calgary, AB Canada T2N 1N4

WHITE, TERRY EDWARD, physician; b. Springfield, Mo., May 30, 1954; s. Roy Edward and Eselean (Moffis) W.; m. Susan Marie Peters, Aug. 16, 1981. BA, Drury Coll., 1976; MD, U. Mo., 1980. Diplomate Am. Bd. Physical Medicine and Rehab. Staff physician Lakeshore Hosp., Birmingham, Ala., 1983-86; clin. instr. U. Ala., Birmingham, 1984-86; staff physician Thomas Rehab., Asheville, N.C., 1986—, chief staff, 1987-88, 91-92, 94—, vice chief staff, 1992-94; alternate Medicare State Carrier adv. com., Greensboro, N.C., 1993; bd. dirs. Nationwide Post Polio Support Group, Dallas, N.C., 1992-94; vice chmn. Western N.C. Health Care Provider Coun., 1995-96, chmn., 1996-97; mem. editl. adv. com. Stroke Rehabilitation. Author: A Patient's and Physician Guide to Late Effects of Polio, 1995; mem. editl. staff Stroke Rehabilitation-Patient Education Guide, 1995. Named Rehab. Physician Yr., N.C. Med. Soc., 1993. Fellow Am. Acad. Phys. Medicine and Rehab.; mem. N.C. Soc. Phys. Medicine and Rehab. (v.p. 1989-91, pres. 1991-93). Republican. Mem. Christian Ch. Avocations: gardening, woodwork, metal work, reading, music. Office: Thomas Rehab Hosp 68 Sweeten Creek Rd Asheville NC 28803-2318

WHITE, THOMAS DAVID, II, academic administrator; b. Pittsburg, Kans., Sept. 19, 1946; s. Thomas David and Audrey Marie (Parrish) W.; children: Thomas David III, Phillip Edward. AA, Valley Forge Mil. Coll., 1967, BA, North Ga. Coll., 1969; postgrad., Pa. State U., 1978-82. Cert. adminstr., Vol. Svcs., Assn. Vol. Adminstrs., 1976. Dist. scout exec. Boy Scouts Am., Phila., 1969-72; vol. resource coord. Norristown (Pa.) State Hosp., 1972-74; assoc. dir. vol. resources Pennhurst Ctr., Spring City, Pa., 1974-79; dir. vol. resources Embreeville State Hosp., Coatesville, Pa., 1979-81; dir. alumni affairs and constituent rels. Valley Forge Mil. Acad., Wayne, Pa., 1981-85; assoc. univ. dir. alumni rels. Rutgers, The State Univ. N.J., Newark, 1985-90; exec. dir. alumni rels. George Washington U., Washington, 1990-93; exec. dir. Nat. Assn. for Artisans and Craftsmen, Audubon, Pa., 1993—; dir. bus. and industry devel. Montgomery County C.C., 1997—; adj. faculty Pa. State U., 1975-76; sr. cons., co-founder Cons. Community, Phila., 1976-82; founder, pres. AADM Assocs., Wayne, Pa., 1983-90; pres. Colonial Yard Garden Design, 1994—. Contbr. articles to profl. publs.; author profl. manuals; designer 19th century garden designs, Early Am. Homes Mag., 1997. Sec., Roboda Community Assn., Royersford, Pa., 1981-83. Mem. Internat. Platform Assn., Coun. for Advancement and Support of Edn., Assn. Vol. Adminstrn., Nat. Assn. Ind. Schs., Assn. Vocat. Action Scholars, S.E. Region Vol. Coords. Assn., Valley Forge Mil. Acad. Alumni Assn. (bd. dirs. exec. com.), VFMA Soc. of the Golden Sword (knight), Rutgers Club (bd. trustees), George Washington U. Club (adv. com.). Republican. Avocations: American antiques, wood carving, 19th century landscaping, folk art, antique weapons. Home: 500 S Park Ave Audubon PA 19403-1921 Office: MCCC-West 100 College Dr Pottstown PA 19464-5439

WHITE, THOMAS EDWARD, lawyer; b. N.Y.C., July 11, 1933; s. Thomas Aubrey and Gladys Mary (Piper) W.; m. Joan Carolyn Olsen, Dec. 2, 1967 (dec.); children: Charles Garret, Nancy Carolyn, Linda Marie, Penelope Lindsay, Elizabeth Ann. A.B., Princeton U., 1955; LL.B., Columbia U., 1960. Bar: N.Y. 1961. Atty. Seward & Kissel, N.Y.C., 1960-69; gen. counsel Howmet Corp., N.Y.C., 1969-70; v.p., gen. counsel, sec. Howmedica, Inc., N.Y.C., 1970-74; sr. v.p., dir. Howmedica, Inc., 1974-83; pvt. practice N.Y.C., 1983—; ptnr. Westmed Venture Ptnrs. (formerly Integrated Med. Venture Ptnrs.), N.Y.C., 1987—; chmn. Shoreside Cons. Ltd., Miami, Fla., 1987—. Mem. Mamaroneck Town Council, 1971-75; vestry Episcopalian Ch., 1987-90. Served to lt. U.S. Army, 1955-57. Republican. Clubs: Larchmont (N.Y.) Yacht; Princeton (N.Y.C.). Home: 260 Barnard Rd Larchmont NY 10538-1941

WHITE, THOMAS EDWARD, retired government park official; b. Bozeman, Mont., Dec. 29, 1936; s. James Henry and Louesa (Coon) W.; m. Sylvia Moon Young, July 17, 1965 (dec. Aug. 1974); children—James Allen, Edward Paul; m. Patricia Lee Swanson, Mar. 1, 1975; 1 child, Andrew Todd. B.S., Mont. State U., 1959, M.S., 1963. Cert. tchr., Mont. Tchr. pub. schs. Mont., 1959-62; park historian Manassas Nat. Battlefield Park, Nat. Park Service, Va., 1964-66, Central Nat. Capital Parks, Nat. Park Service, Washington, 1966-68; supervisory park historian Fort Laramie Nat. Hist. Site, Nat. Park Service, Wyo., 1968-73; interpretive specialist So. Ariz. Group, Nat. Park Service, Phoenix, 1973-83; chief park interpreter Hawaii Volcanoes Nat. Park, 1983-87; interpretive planner Harpers Ferry (W.Va.) Ctr., Nat. Park Svc., 1987-97; interpretive planner, internat. exchange assignment Can. Nat. Hist. Sites Service, Ottawa, Ont., 1969. Author: Garrison Life Trail: An Illustrated Guide to Fort Laramie, 1972 (Fed. Editors Assn. Blue Pencil award 1973). Adult adviser Order DeMolay, Mont., Va., Wyo., Ariz., 1960-83; Cub Scout and Boy Scout leader Theodore Roosevelt (Ariz.), Aloha (Hawaii), Shenandoah Area (W.Va.) coun. Boy Scouts Am., 1978—; adminstrv. bd. chmn. Hilo United Meth. Ch., 1985-87; scouting coord. New St. United Meth. Ch., 1988—, del. to ann. conf., 1996—; vol. Interfaith Caregivers. Recipient Chevalier Degree Order DeMolay, 1954, Legion of Honor award Order DeMolay, 1968; named Father of Yr., 1st Bapt. Ch., Scottsdale, Ariz., 1978, Statuette award Shenandoah Area coun. Boy Scouts Am., 1994, Cross and Flame Religious award for adult scout leaders Boy Scouts Am., 1995. Mem. Nat. Assn. Interpreters, Nat. Assn. United Meth. Scouters, NPS Employees and Alumni Assn., Sigma Nu. Lodge: Masons. Avocations: collecting stamps, hiking, model railroading, singing in church choir, genealogy.

WHITE, THOMAS RAEBURN, III, law educator, consultant; b. Phila., Aug. 18, 1938; s. Thomas Raeburn Jr. and Charlotte (Gerhard) W.; m. Margaret Bardwell, Dec. 12, 1960 (div. June 1975); children: Elizabeth Krusenstjerna, Kathleen Harris, Thomas Ray IV; m. Maria Llanes, Oct. 19, 1975. BA, Williams Coll., 1960; LLB, U. Pa., 1963. Bar: Pa. 1964, Va. 1971. Assoc. White and Williams, Phila., 1963-65; atty.-advisor TLC U.S. Treasury Dept., Washington, 1965-67; assoc. prof. U. Va., Charlottesville, 1967-70, prof. law, 1970-96, John C. Stennis prof., 1996—; legis. atty. Joint Com. on Tax U.S. Congress, Washington, 1973-75; cons. adminstrn. conf. IRS Project, Washington, 1975-76; vis. prof. NYU Law Sch., N.Y.C., 1978-79. Mem. ABA (com. chmn. tax sect. 1987-87, 96-98), Am. Coll. Tax Counsel, Va. Bar Assn., Va. State Bar Assn., Phila. Bar Assn., Charlottesville-Albemarle Bar Assn. Home: 12 Deer Path Charlottesville VA 22903-4707 Office: U Va Sch Law 580 Massie Rd Charlottesville VA 22903-1738

WHITE, TIMOTHY OLIVER, newspaper editor; b. Albany, N.Y., June 29, 1948; s. Oliver C. and Yvonne (Letourneau) W.; 1 child, Eric B. BA in English, Siena Coll., 1971. Reporter Cape Cod Times, Hyannis, Mass., 1971-72, asst. Sunday editor, 1972-75, news editor, 1975-79, asst. editor, 1979-83, mng. editor, 1983-97, editorial page editor, 1997—. Mem. AP Mng. Editors, New Eng. AP News Exec. Assn. (v.p. 1992, 93, pres. 1994), New Eng. Soc. Newspaper Editors, Nat. Coun. Editl. Writers. Avocations: community TV producer, photography, wilderness travel, bicycling, cooking, sailing. Home: PO Box 1187 56 Jolly's Crossing Rd Brewster MA 02631 Office: Cape Cod Times 319 Main St Hyannis MA 02601-4037

WHITE, TIMOTHY PAUL, brokerage house executive; b. Ft. Sill, Okla., Jan. 9, 1963; s. Paul R. and Lucille (Mattison) W.; m. Susan Gertrude Foreman, Dec. 29, 1984; children: Jessica Lynn, Rebecca Anne, Kathleen Marie. BS in Fin., Pa. State U., 1985. Cert. fin. planner, Colo. Assoc. planner, agt. Pa. Fin. Group, Harrisburg, Pa., 1988-92; mgr. mktg. and sales Meridian Securities, Inc., Reading, Pa., 1992-96; v.p. products and sales mgr. Core States Securities Corp., Reading, 1996—; spkr. Nat. Mut. Fund Conf., 1995, Cmty. Bank Investment Program Symposium, 1996, Nat. Investment Products Conf., 1996. Contbg. editor Bank Securities Jour.; contbr. articles to profl. jours. Program cons. Jr. Achievement, Lancaster, Pa., 1990-91; pres. Adamstown Recreation Bd., 1996. 1st lt. U.S. Army, 1985-88, with Res. 1989-92. Recipient George C. Marshall award U.S. Army, 1985; decorated Commendation medal, Achievement medal; U.S. Army ROTC scholar, 1980-84. Mem. Inst. CFP, U.S. Cavalry Assn. (fundraising com. 1994-96), Ctrl. Pa. Soc. Inst. CFP (bd. dirs. 1996—). Republican. Lutheran. Avocations: military and political history, reading, gardening, wood-working. Office: Core State Securities Corp 601 Penn St Reading PA 19601-3544

WHITE, TIMOTHY THOMAS ANTHONY, writer, editor, broadcaster; b. Paterson, N.J., Jan. 25, 1952; s. John Alexander and Gloria Marie (Thomas) W.; m. Judith Anne Garlan, June 28, 1987; children: (twins) Alexander and Christopher. BA, Fordham U., 1972. Copyboy, sports and entertainment writer AP, N.Y.C., 1972-76; mng. editor Crawdaddy mag., N.Y.C., 1976-77, sr. editor, 1977-78; assoc. editor Rolling Stone mag., N.Y.C., 1978-79, sr. editor, 1979-82; host, co-producer Timothy White's Rock Stars/The Timothy White Sessions nationally syndicated radio series ABC Radio Network, 1986; LBS Radio Network, 1987, Westwood One Radio Network, 1988—; editor in chief Billboard mag., N.Y.C., 1991—. Author: Catch a Fire: The Life of Bob Marley, 1983, rev. enlarged edit., 1989, meml. edit., 1991, rev. edit., 1996, (Brit., Italian, German, Brazilian, Czech and Japanese edits.), Rock Stars, 1984, Rock Lives: Profiles and Interviews, 1990, rev. edit., 1996 (Brit. and Japanese edits.), The Nearest Faraway Place: Brian Wilson, The Beach Boys and The Southern California Experience, 1995, rev. edit., 1995 (Brit. and Japanese edits.), Music To My Ears, 1996 (Brit. edit.); co-author: Rolling Stone Visits Saturday Night Live, 1979, (with others) Roadside Food, 1986; contbg. author: The Best of the Music Makers, 1979, The 80s: A Look Back at the Tumultuous Decade, 1979, The Rolling Stone Interviews, 1981, Reggae International, 1982, Suddenly Poor! A Guide for Downwardly Mobile, 1983, Twenty Years of Rolling Stone, 1987, A & M Records: The First 25 Years, 1987; contbr. articles to various mags. Recipient ASCAP-Deems Taylor award, 1991, 93. Democrat. Avocations: drums, dancing, Caribbean history, folklore, music. Office: Billboard Mag 1515 Broadway New York NY 10036

WHITE, WARREN WURTELE, retired retailing executive; b. McKeesport, Pa., Feb. 29, 1932; s. Jay Leonard and Elizabeth Katherine (Fehr) W.; m. Marjorie Ada Shuman, Mar. 20, 1954; 1 dau., Laura Lynn. B.S., Duquesne U., 1954; M.Retailing, U. Pitts., 1957. With Strawbridge & Clothier, Phila., 1957-97; buyer Strawbridge & Clothier, 1960-67, budget store divisional mdse. mgr., 1968-70, Clover Div. gen. mdse. mgr., 1970-76, v.p. for mdse. and sales promotion, 1977-79, exec. v.p., 1979-96, also dir., 1981-97; gen. mgr. Strawbridge & Clothier (Clover Div.), 1979-96; pvt. retailing cons. Haddonfield, N.J., 1997—. Bd. dirs. Ea. Star Charity Found. N.J., 1978-83. Served to 1st lt. arty. U.S. Army, 1954-56. Mem. Internat. Mass Retail Assn. (officer 1987-93, bd. dirs. 1981-96, chmn. bd. 1991-93), South Jersey C. of C. (bd. dirs. 1991-96), Am. Lung Assn. (bd. dirs. Phila. chpt. 1991-94). Republican. Methodist. Club: Kensington Golf and Country. Lodge: Masons. Home and Office: 1 Heritage Rd Haddonfield NJ 08033-3405

WHITE, WILL WALTER, III, public relations consultant, writer; b. Glen Ridge, N.J., July 3, 1930; s. Will Walter and Miriam Chandler (Milburn) W.; m. Phyllis Marcia DuFlocq, Dec. 28, 1951 (div. 1971); children: Will Walter IV, Scott, Alan; m. Anne Elizabeth Levenson, Nov. 21, 1971 (div. 1992); children: Duncan, Christopher; stepchildren: Michael, Susan; m. Catherine Laur, Aug. 26, 1992. B.A., Cornell U., 1952. Supr. Union Carbide Corp., N.Y.C., 1954-59; account exec. Ketchum, MacLeod & Grove, N.Y.C., 1959-62; sr. v.p. Wilson, Haight & Welch, Hartford, Conn., 1962-72; chmn., chief exec. officer Lowengard & Brotherhood, Hartford, 1972-83; pres., chief exec. officer Harland & Tine & White, Hartford, 1983-87; chmn. Donahue Inc., Hartford, 1987-89; ptnr. Laur White & White, Sarasota, Fla., 1992—; owner Omega Cubed Press, 1996—; exec. com. Conn. Dist. Export Council, 1979-88. Author: The Sunfish Book, 1983, 96; contbg. editor Mid-Gulf Sailing mag., 1994-95. Mem. exec. com. Hartford Stage Co., 1982-86; pres. Vis. Nurse Assn., Hartford, 1979; fin. chmn. Vis. Nurse and Home Care, Inc., Hartford and Waterbury, 1982-91; mem. pub. rels. com. Fairfield County Rep. Com., 1961; chmn. S.W. Fla. Regional Harbor Bd., 1995—. 1st lt. U.S. Army, 1952-54. Nat. champion Sunfish Racing Class, 1966, 68. Mem. Pub. Rels. Soc. Am. (accredited, chmn. investor rels. sect. 1983, charter mem. Hall of Fame 1990), Bus. Profl. Advt. Assn. (cert. bus. communicator), Nat. Investor Rels. Inst., U.S. Sunfish Class Assn. (pres. 1985-88, charter mem. Hall of Fame 1991), Boaters Action and Info. League (vp. edn. 1992—), Hist. Soc. Sarasota County (bd. dirs. 1995—), Sarasota Sailing Squadron. Address: 7362 Palomino Ln Sarasota FL 34241-9779

WHITE, W(ILLIAM) ARTHUR, geologist; b. Sumner, Ill., Dec. 9, 1916; s. Millard Otto and Joy Olive (Atkins) W.; m. Alma Evelyn Simonton McCullough, June 21, 1941. B.S., U. Ill., 1940, M.S., 1947, Ph.D., 1955. With Ill. Geol. Survey, Urbana, 1943-79, geologist, 1955-58, head clay resources and clay mineral tech. sect., 1958-72, geologist, 1972-79, geologist emeritus, 1979—; pvt. cons. geologist Urbana, 1979-88; prof. geology Fed. U. Rio Grande do Sul, Brazil, 1970. Contbr. articles to profl. jours. Fellow Geol. Soc. Am., Mineral Soc. Am., AAAS; mem. Internat. Clay Mineral Soc., Am. Clay Mineral Soc., Ill. Acad. Sci., Mus. Natural History (assoc.), Nat. Geog. Soc., Am. Chem. Soc., Colloid Chem. Soc., Soc. Econ. Paleontologists and Mineralogists, Inter-Am. Soc., Farm Bur., AARP, Order United Comml. Travelers Am., U. Ill. Alumni Assn., Sigma Xi. Home: 603 E Colorado Ave Urbana IL 61801-5923

WHITE, WILLIAM BLAINE, geochemist, educator; b. Huntingdon, Pa., Jan. 5, 1934; s. William Bruce and Eleanor Mae (Barr) W.; m. Elizabeth Loczi, Mar. 27, 1959; children: Nikki Elizabeth White McCurry, William Brion (dec.). BS, Juniata Coll., 1954; PhD, Pa. State U., 1962. Rsch. assoc. Mellon Inst., Pitts., 1954-58; asst. prof. Pa. State U., University Park, 1963-67; asso. prof. Pa. State U., 1967-72, prof. geochemistry, 1972—, chmn. grad. program in materials, 1990-93. Assoc. editor: Am. Mineralogist, 1972-75, Materials Rsch. Bull., 1979-93, Jour. Am. Ceramic Soc., 1985-93, Water Resources Bull., 1992-93; editor earth scis. Nat. Speleol. Soc. Bull., 1964-94; author: Geomorphology and Hydrology of Karst Terrains, 1988, (with Elizabeth L. White) Karst Hydrology: Concepts from the Mammoth Cave Area, 1989, (with Susan Barger) Daguerreotype: Nineteenth-Century Technology and Modern Science, 1991; contbr. articles to profl. jours. Home: Miller Rd RR 1 Box 527 Petersburg PA 16669-9211 Office: Pa State U Materials Rsch Lab University Park PA 16802

WHITE, WILLIAM DUDLEY, safety engineer; b. Birmingham, Mich., June 11, 1958; s. Paul Richard and Annetta Carole (Manhart) W.; m. Tamara Jean Wishon, Mar. 13, 1992; 1 child, Stacy Michelle; 1 stepchild, Royce Edward Vorel. BS cum laude, U. Ctrl. Okla., 1994. Chief maintenance engr. First Union Mgmt., Oklahoma City, 1984-89; safety rep., chmn. safety and suggestion coms. E-Systems, Inc., Greenville, Tex., 1994—; creator curriculum for various safety programs, 1994, 96. Pack master Boy Scouts Am., Edmond, Okla., 1991-92; CPR instr., std. first aid instr. ARC, Hunt County, Tex., 1993—. Mem. Am. Soc. Safety Engrs., Alpha Chi. Roman Catholic. Achievements include development of safety certification/O-J-T checklist tng. program to meet OSHA, Air Force Occupational Safety and Health and Department of Defense standards regarding task proficiency for aircraft servicing, maintenance and daily ops. powered aircraft ground and mobile equipment; restructured indsl. hygiene program in accordance with American Conference of Governmental Industrial Hygienists guidelines. Home: 2507 Hillcrest St Greenville TX 75402-8050 Office: Raytheon E-Sys Airborne Divsn PO Box 6056 CBN072 Greenville TX 75403

WHITE, WILLIAM FREDRICK, lawyer; b. Elmhurst, Ill., Sept. 30, 1948; s. William Daniel and Carol Ruth (Laier) W.; m. Kathie Jean Nichols, May 27, 1979; children: Nicholas Roland, Andrew William. BA, U. Ill., 1970; JD, Antioch Sch. of Law, 1976. Bar: U.S. Ct. Appeals (D.C. cir.) 1976, Wis. 1982, U.S. Dist. Ct. (we. dist.) Wis. 1982, U.S. Dist. Ct. D.C. 1976, U.S. Ct. Claims 1978, U.S. Ct. Appeals (7th and 10th cirs.) 1982. With U.S. Dept. Labor, Washington, 1976; interim exec. dir. Common Cause, Washington, 1977; asst. counsel Nat. Treasury Employees Union, Washington, 1977-79, assoc. gen. counsel, 1979-81, dir. litigation, 1981-82; assoc. Michael, Best & Friedrich, Madison, Wis., 1982-88, ptnr., chmn. assoc. devel. com., 1988—; bd. dirs. Med. Physics Publ. Co. Treas. The Lufler com., Madison, 1984—; chmn. Pub. Health Commn., Madison, 1983-89; bd. dirs. exec com. Dane County Mediation Program, Madison, 1983-90, Perinatal Found., Madison, 1984—, Arthritis Found., Madison, 1986-92, chmn., 1991-92; bd. dirs. Dane County Natural Heritage Found., 1988-91; mem. Dane County Regional Airport Commn., 1991—, chmn. 1994—; chancellor Wis. Conf. United Meth. Ch., 1992—, gen. coun. Fin. and Adminstrn., 1991—, chmn. Legal Svcs. Com.; bd. dirs. Downtown Madison Inc.; mem. Dane County Transferrable Devel. Rights Task Force, Team Terrace Transp. Com., 1996—, chair. Mem. ABA, D.C. Bar Assn., Med. Physics Found. (bd. dirs. 1987—), Dane County Bar Assn., State Bar Assn. (sec. Health Law sect.). Democrat. Methodist. Avocations: cycling, skiing, volleyball, softball. Office: Michael Best & Friedrich 1 S Pinckney St Madison WI 53703-2808

WHITE, WILLIAM JAMES, information management and services company executive; b. Kenosha, Wis., May 30, 1938; s. William H. and Dorothy Caroline White; m. Jane Schulte, Aug. 13, 1960; children: James N., Thomas G., Maria, Gretchen S. BS, Northwestern U., 1961; MBA, Harvard U., 1963. Mech. planning engr. Procter & Gamble Corp., 1961-62; bd. dirs. TJ Internat., Boise, Idaho; corp. v.p. Hartmarx Corp., Chgo., 1963-74; group v.p. Mead Corp., Dayton, Ohio, 1974-81; pres., COO, dir. Masonite Corp., Chgo., 1981-85; exec. v.p., dir. USG Corp., 1985-88, pres., CEO Whitestar Enterprises, Inc., 1989-90; pres., CEO Bell & Howell Co., 1990-95, chmn., 1990-95, 97—; chmn. Bell & Howell Holdings Co., 1995—. Author: (with Henderson et al) Creative Collective Bargaining, 1965. Vice chmn. adv. coun. McCormick Sch. Engring. and Applied Scis.; mem. bus. adv. coun. U. Ill., Chgo., 1981—; bd. dirs. TJ Internat., IMSA Fund for Advancement Edn., Aurora; past chmn. bd. Ill. div. Am. Cancer Soc. Mem. Econ. Club, The Chgo. Com., Chgo. Club, Glen View Country Club. Office: Bell & Howell Co 5215 Old Orchard Rd Skokie IL 60077-1035

WHITE, WILLIAM NELSON, lawyer; b. Balt., Sept. 8, 1938; s. Nelson Cardwell and Ellen Atwell (Zoller) W.; m. Mary Kathleen Bitzel, Sept. 2, 1960 (div. 1971); children: Craig William, Jeffrey Alan, Colin Christopher; m. Christine Lewin Hanna, July 8, 1978. LLB, U. Md., 1968, JD, 1969. Bar: Md. 1972, U.S. Ct. Appeals (4th cir.) 1975, U.S. Dist. Ct. Md. 1976, U.S. Spreme Ct. 1976. Asst. state's atty. Balt., 1972; assoc. Brooks & Turnbull, Balt., 1973-76; pvt. practice Balt., 1977—; counsel St. Andrews Soc. Balt., 1989—; former counsel, bd. dirs. St. George's Soc. Elder, former pres. of deacons, former trustee Roland Park Presbyn. Ch. Mem. ABA, Md. Bar Assn., Baltimore County Bar Assn., U. Md. Alumni Assn. for Greater Balt. (pres. 1977), Internat. Platform Assn., Supreme Ct. Hist. Soc. Avocations: history, philosophy, classical music, tennis, sailing. Office: 305 W Chesapeake Ave Ste Ll-3 Baltimore MD 21204-4421

WHITE, WILLIAM NORTH, chemistry educator; b. Walton, N.Y., Sept. 16, 1925; s. George Fitch and Frances (Peck) W.; m. Hilda R. Sauter, Sept. 8, 1951; children: Carla Ann, Eric Jeffrey. A.B., Cornell U., 1950; M.A., Harvard U., 1951, Ph.D., 1953. NRC postdoctoral fellow Calif. Inst. Tech., Pasadena, 1953-54; asst. prof. Ohio State U., Columbus, 1954-59; asso. prof. Ohio State U., 1959-63; prof. chemistry U. Vt., Burlington, 1963-76, 77-95, prof. emeritus, 1995—; chmn. dept. U. Vt., 1963-70, acting chmn. dept., 1975-76; prof. chemistry U. Tex. at Arlington, 1976-77, chmn. dept., 1976-77; NSF sr. postdoctoral fellow Brookhaven Nat. Lab., Upton, N.Y., 1963-64, Harvard U., 1965; vis. scholar Brandeis U., 1974-75; chmn. arrangements com. Nat. Organic Chemistry Symposium, 1965-67. Contbr. articles on organic chemistry profl. jours. Selectman Town of Shelburne, Vt., 1968-74, water commr., 1973-74, justice of the peace, 1981—, sewer commr., 1991-93; mem. Chittenden County Regional Planning Commn., 1983-91. Served with AUS, 1943-46. Mem. Am. Chem. Soc. (chmn. Western Vt. sect. 1966-67), Royal Soc. Chemistry, New Eng. Assn. Chemistry Tchrs., AAAS, N.Y. Acad. Scis., Phi Beta Kappa, Sigma Xi, Phi Kappa Phi, Phi Lambda Upsilon. Home: Pierson Dr Shelburne VT 05482-7224 Office: U Vt Dept Chemistry Burlington VT 05405-0125

WHITE, WILLIAM SAMUEL, foundation executive; b. Cin., May 8, 1937; s. Nathaniel Ridgway and Mary (Loundes) W.; m. Claire Mott, July 1, 1961; children: Tiffany Loundes, Ridgway Harding. BA, Dartmouth Coll., 1959, MBA, 1960; LL.D. (hon.), Eastern Mich. U., 1975; hon. degree, GMI Engring. & Mgmt. Inst., 1996. With Barrett & Williams, N.Y.C., 1961-62; sr. assoc. Bruce Payne & Assos., N.Y.C., 1962-71; v.p. C. S. Mott Found., Flint, Mich., 1971-75; pres. C. S. Mott Found., 1976—, trustee, 1971—, also chmn. bd. dirs.; bd. dirs. Continental Water Corp; chmn. bd. dirs. U.S. Sugar Corp. Mem. exec. com. Daycroft Sch., Greenwich, Conn., 1966-70; bd. dirs. Flint Area Conf., 1971-84, Coun. on Founds., 1985-90, Independent Sector, 1994—, European Found. Centre, 1994—, Civicus, 1995—; mem. citizens adv. task force U. Mich., Flint, 1974-79; chmn. Coun. of Mich. Founds., 1979-81, Flint Area Focus Coun., 1988—; mem. Pres.'s Task Force on Pvt. Sector Initiatives, 1982; trustee GMI Engring. and Mgmt. Inst., 1982-86. Served with U.S. Army, 1960-62. Office: C S Mott Foundation 1200 Mott Foundation Bldg Flint MI 48502-1807

WHITE, WILLIS SHERIDAN, JR., retired utilities company executive; b. nr. Portsmouth, Va., Dec. 17, 1926; s. Willis Sheridan and Carrie (Culpepper) W.; m. LaVerne Behrends, Oct. 8, 1949; children: Willis Sheridan III, Marguerite Louise White Spangler, Cynthia D.W. Haight. B.S., Va. Poly. Inst., 1948; M.S., Mass. Inst. Tech., 1958. With Am. Electric Power Co. Inc., 1948-91; chmn., chief exec. officer Am. Electric Power Co. Inc. and its subs., N.Y.C., 1976-90, chmn., 1991, mem. bd. dirs., 1972-92; pres., bd. dirs. Ohio Valley Electric Corp., Ind.-KTV Electric Corp., 1977-91; bd. dirs. Bank of N.Y. Trustee Battellle Meml. Inst., Grant/Riverside Meth. Hosp., Columbus. With USNR, 1945-46. Sloan fellow, 1957-58. Mem. IEEE, NAE, Eta Kappa Nu, Omicron Delta Kappa. Methodist.

WHITE, WILLMON LEE, magazine editor; b. Lamesa, Tex., Mar. 10, 1932; s. Aubrey F. and Jewel (Henderson) W.; m. Carol A. Nelson, Nov. 2, 1957 (div.); children: Tracy, Wrenn, Gehrig, Bob; m. Barbara K. Kelly, Sept. 16, 1977; 1 child, Theresa. BA, McMurry Coll., Abilene, Tex., 1953; MA, U. Tex., 1956. Reporter Abilene Reporter-News, 1953-54; pub. rels. writer Tex. Ins. Adv. Assn., Austin, 1955-56; asst. editor Humble Way mag. Humble Oil & Refining Co. (Exxon), Houston, 1956-65; assoc. editor, news editor Together mag. Methodist Ch., Park Ridge, Ill., 1965-69; sr. editor World Book Ency., Chgo., 1969-70; asst. editor, then asso. editor Rotarian mag. (publ. Rotary Internat.), Evanston, Ill., 1970-74, editor, 1974—, mgr. communications and pub. rels. div., 1979-95; asst. gen. sec. Rotarian mag. (publ. Rotary Internat.), Evanston, 1995-96; gen mgr. Rotary Found. Svcs., 1996—; editor-in-chief Rotarian Mag., 1996—; intern Newsweek mag., 1954. Mem. Am. Soc. Mag. Editors, Am. Soc. Assn. Execs., Rotary, Sigma Delta Chi. Office: Rotarian 1560 Sherman Ave Evanston IL 60201

WHITEFIELD, ANNE C., secondary school principal. Prin. Hum-Fogg High Sch., Nashville. Recipient Elem. Sch. Recognition award U.S. Dept. Edn., 1989-90. Office: Hum-Fogg High Sch 700 Broadway Nashville TN 37203-3937*

WHITEFORD, ANDREW HUNTER, anthropologist; b. Winnipeg, Man., Can., 1913; came to U.S., 1923, naturalized, 1928; s. John and Janet Carduff (Hunter) W.; m. Marion Bonneville Salmon, Sept. 2, 1939; children: John Hunter, Michael Bonneville, Linda McMillan Whiteford Uzzell, Laurie Andrea Whiteford Richards. BA, Beloit (Wis.) Coll., 1937, LLD (hon.), 1981; MA, U. Chgo., 1943, PhD, 1950. Archaeologist N.Mex., 1938; supr. U. Tenn.-WPA, 1938-42; mem. faculty Beloit Coll., 1942-74, prof. anthropology, 1955-74, George L. Collie prof., 1955-74, chmn. dept., 1944-73, emeritus, 1974—; vis. prof. Mich. State U., 1975, 76, 79; vis. prof. art history U. N.Mex., 1980; Faye Laverne Bumpass lectr. Tex. Tech. U., 1981; rsch. fellow com. human rels. U. Chgo., 1945-46; dir. Logan Mus. Anthropology, Beloit Coll., 1946-74; urban rschr., Mex., Colombia, Spain; rsch. curator Indian Art Rsch. Ctr., Sch. Am. Rsch., Santa Fe, 1980-84, 90—, interim adminstrv. dir., 1981-84 ; rsch. assoc. Wheelwright Mus. Am. Indian, Santa Fe, 1980—, trustee, 1979-85; mem. adv. bd. Florence H. Ellis Mus., Ghost Ranch Conf. Ctr., Abiquiu, N.Mex., 1979—; guest curator, rsch. assoc. N.Mex. Mus. of Indian Arts and Culture, 1987—. Author: Two Cities of Latin America, 1964, North American Indian Arts, 1970, An Andean City at Mid-Century, 1977, Southwestern Indian Baskets: Their History and Makers, 1988, (chpts.) The Thaw Collection of Indian Art, 1997; mem. editl. adv. bd. Am. Indian Art mag.; contbr. articles to profl. jours., encys. and festschrifts. NSF faculty fellow, 1960-61; Social Sci. Rsch. Coun.-ACLS fellow, 1961-62; grantee Wenner Gren Found., Social Sci. Rsch. Coun., NSF, USPHS, Am. Philos. Soc.; recipient Lifetime Achievement Honor award Native Am. Art Studies Assn., 1995-96. Fellow Am. Anthrop. Assn.; mem. Coun. for Mus. Anthropology, Soc. for Latin Am. Anthropology, Phi Beta Kappa, Sigma Xi, Beta Theta Pi, Omicron Delta Kappa. Address: 447 Camino Monte Vis Santa Fe NM 87501-4585

WHITEHEAD, BARBARA ANN, secondary school educator; b. Shreveport, La., Apr. 25, 1941; d. Clifton John and Leona Elizabeth (Lemoine) W. BA, McNeese State U., 1963, MEd, 1967; postgrad., Centenary Coll., 1982-83, La. Tech. U., 1983. Cert. secondary edn. tchr., La. Tchr. Calcasieu Parish Sch. System, Lake Charles, La., 1963-68, Caddo Parish Sch. System, Shreveport, 1968—; chair social studies dept. C.E. Byrd Math./Sci. Magnet High Sch., Shreveport, 1987—. Author: Teaching the Historical Origins of Nursery Rhymes and Folk Tales, 1982. Named La. Tchr. of Yr. DAR, 1983. Mem. NEA, La. Assn. Educators, Caddo Assn. Educators, Sigma Tau Delta. Roman Catholic. Avocations: writing, travel. Office: CE Byrd Math Sci Magnet High Sch 3201 Line Ave Shreveport LA 71104-4241

WHITEHEAD, E. DOUGLAS, urology educator; b. Galashiels, Scotland, Aug. 24, 1939; 1 child, Robin Stacey. BA, Vanderbilt U., 1961; MD, Ind. U., 1965; postgrad., U. London, 1972. Diplomate Am. Bd. Urology; med. lic. Ind., Ill., N.Y., Calif., N.J. Intern. surgery Mount Sinai Hosp., N.Y.C., 1965-66; resident in surgery Presbyn.-St. Luke's Hosp., Chgo., 1966-67; resident in urology N.Y.U. Med. Ctr., 1969-73; clin. assoc. urology Mount Sinai Sch. Medicine, N.Y.C., 1973-77, sr. clin. instr. urology, 1977-80, asst. clin. prof. urology, 1980-92; pvt. practice, N.Y.C., 1973—; assoc. clin. prof. urology Mount Sinai Sch. Medicine, 1992-94, Albert Einstein Coll. of Medicine, 1994—; assoc. attending Beth Israel Med. Ctr., N.Y.C.; mem. advisor Impotence Anonymous & Jr., Diabetes Self-Mgmt., 1983-85, Jour. Urol. Nursing; editl. adv. bd. The Female Patient, Med. Aspects of Human Sexuality; mem. med. adv. bd. Colostomy Soc., N.Y., Inc.; cons. and speaker in field. Editor: Current Operative Urology, 1975, 2d rev. edit., 1984, ann. edits., 1989-92, Mgmt. Impotence and Infertility, 1994, Sex Over Forty, 1990—; contbr. articles to profl. jours.; patentee in field. Grantee U.S.P.H., Clin. Research Ctr. Fellow ACS, Clin. Soc. Am. Diabetes Assn., N.Y. Diabetes Affiliate; mem. AMA, AAAS, Am. Urol. Assn., Soc. Internat. Urology (diplomate), Soc. for the Study of Impotence, Am. Assn. Clin. Urologists, N.Y. State Urol. Assn., Am. Acad. of Phalloplasty Surgeons (pres.-elect), Am. Acad. of Male Sexual Health (bd. dirs.), Internat. Soc. for Artificial Organs, Am. So. Nephrology, Med. Soc. State N.Y., Med. Soc. County N.Y., Am. Assn. Sex Educators, Counselors and Therapists, Soc. for the Sci. Study of Sex, Sex Info. and Edn. Coun. of the U.S. Coalition on Sexuality and Disability, Am. Cancer Soc., Nat. Kidney Found., Am. Geriatric Soc., N.Y. Acad. Sci., N.Y. Acad. Medicine, N.Y. Urodynamic Soc., Internat. Continence Soc. Office: 24 E 12th St Ste 2-1 New York NY 10003-4403

WHITEHEAD, GEORGE WILLIAM, retired mathematician; b. Bloomington, Ill., Aug. 2, 1918; s. George William and (Christine) Mary (Gutschlag) W.; m. Kathleen Ethelwyn Butcher, June 7, 1947. SB, U. Chgo., 1937, SM, 1938, PhD, 1941. Instr. math. Purdue U., West Lafayette, Ind., 1941-45, Princeton (N.J.) U., 1945-47; asst. prof. Brown U., Providence, 1947-48, assoc. prof., 1948-49; asst. prof. MIT, Cambridge, 1949-51, assoc. prof., 1951-57, prof., 1957-85, prof. emeritus, 1985—. Author: Homotopy Theory, 1966, Elements of Homotopy Theory, 1978, Recent Advances in Homotopy Theory, 1970. Fellow Guggenheim Found., 1955-56, sr. post-doctoral fellow NSF, 1965-66; Fulbright Rsch. scholar, 1955-56. Fellow Am. Acad. Arts & Scis.; mem. NAS, Am. Math. Soc. (v.p.), Math. Assn. Am. Avocations: archeology, bridge, genealogy. Home: 25 Bellevue Rd Arlington MA 02174-7919

WHITEHEAD, IAN, insurance company executive. CEO, pres. London PCF Lf & Annuity Co., Raleigh, N.C. Office: London PCF Lf & Annuity Co 3109 Poplarwood Ct Raleigh NC 27604-1011

WHITEHEAD, J. RENNIE, science consultant; s. William and Beatrice Cora (Fenning) W.; m. Nesta Doone James, Jan. 11, 1944; children—Valerie Lesley (dec.), Michael James Rennie. B.Sc. in Physics, Manchester U., Lancashire, Eng., 1939; Ph.D. in Phys. Chemistry, Cambridge U., Eng., 1949. Cert. profl. engr., Ont.; chartered engr., U.K. Sci. officer TRE (UK Radar), Eng., 1939-51; assoc. prof. McGill U., Montreal, P.Q., Can., 1951-55; dir. research RCA Victor Co Ltd., Montreal, 1955-65; prin. sci. adviser Govt. of Can., Ottawa, Ont., 1965-75; sr. v.p. Philip A. Lapp Ltd., Ottawa, 1975-82; pvt. practice sci. cons. Ottawa, 1982—; bd. dirs. Hancock-Lapp Assocs., Ottawa, 1986-89; bd. dirs. Found. for Internat. Tng., Toronto, 1976-86. Author: Superregenerative Receivers, 1949. Fellow Royal Soc. Can., Inst. Physics, Instn. Elec. Engrs., Can. Aeronautics and Space Inst., Can. Assn. for Club of Rome (chmn. 1976-81). Anglican. Avocations: automobiles; philately; carpentry; computers. Home and Office: 1368 Chattaway Ave, Ottawa, ON Canada K1H 7S3

WHITEHEAD, JAMES FRED, III, lawyer; b. Atlanta, July 3, 1946; s. James Fred Jr. and Jessie Mae (Turner) W.; m. Joanne Christina Mayo, June 21, 1969 (div. Feb. 1992); children: Matthew Nicholas, Rebecca Catherine; m. Nancy Karean Hatley, May 28, 1992; stepchildren: Brandon, Madison. AB with distinction, Stanford U., 1968; JD, U. Mich., 1975. Bar: Wash. 1975, U.S. dist. Ct. (we. dist.) Wash. 1975, U.S. Ct. Appeals (9th cir.) 1975, U.S. Supreme Ct. 1976, U.S. Dist. Ct. (ea. dist.) Wash. 1994, Alaska 1995, U.S. Dist. Ct. Alaska 1995. Assoc. LeGros, Buchanan, Paul & Madden, Seattle, 1975-79; dir., officer LeGros, Buchanan, Paul & Whitehead, Seattle, 1979-92; ptnr. McGee, Reno & Whitehead, Seattle, 1993; of counsel Faulkner, Banfield, Doogan & Holmes, Seattle, 1993-97, shareholder, 1997—; organizer, lectr. Pacific Northwest Admiralty Law Inst., Seattle, 1981—; chmn. Internat. Maritime Law Conf., Seattle, 1996. Assoc. editor Am. Maritime Cases, 1991—; contbr. articles to profl. jours. Mem. ABA, Maritime Law Assn. of U.S. Avocations: tennis, golf, birding. Office: Faulkner Banfield Doogan Holmes First Interstate Center Ste 2600 Seattle WA 98104

WHITEHEAD, JOHN C., state judge; b. Loup City, Nebr., Mar. 4, 1939; s. Cyrus C. and Regina (Costello) W.; m. Linda L. Lykins, Sept. 11, 1965; children: Sarah, Amy. AB in History, Benedictine Coll., 1961; LLB, Washburn U., 1964, JD, 1964. Bar: Nebr. 1964, Kans. 1964. Mem. firm Snell & Whitehead, Columbus, Nebr., 1965-66, Walker Luckey & Whitehead, Columbus, 1966-71, Walker, Luckey, Whitehead & Sipple, Columbus, 1971-77; judge Nebr. State Dist. Ct., Columbus, 1977—; dep. county atty. Platte County, Nebr., 1965-67; atty. City of Columbus, 1967-72. Bd. dirs. Lower Loup Natural Resource Dist., 1971-74, vice chmn., 1975-76; bd. dirs. Columbus Family YMCA, 1974-80, pres., 1978-80; bd. dirs. Platte County Playhouse, 1972-74. Mem. ABA (regional rep. Nat. Assn. State Trial Judges 1994—), Nebr. Bar Assn., Platte County Bar Assn. (pres. 1976-77), Nebr. Dist. Judges Assn. (sec.-treas. 1988-90, v.p. 1990, pres. 1991-92), Columbus C. of C. (bd. dirs. 1977-81, pres. 1979), Elks, Optimists (pres. 1971-72, lt. gov. Nebr. dist. 1972-73), Toastmasters (pres. 1968—), Am. Vets. (comdr. 1994—, state judge advocate 1995-96). Roman Catholic. Home: 3365 Pershing Rd Columbus NE 68601-8117 Office: State Dist Ct PO Box 445 Columbus NE 68602-0445 *What bothers me about America today is that we have become a nation of spectators, not just in sports, but in life itself. Life, like sports, provides the most rewards and enjoyment to the participant. The spectators only gain from the association, and when it's over find they have only the memories and no tangible benefits.*

WHITEHEAD, JOHN CUNNINGHAM, investment executive; b. Evanston, Ill., Apr. 2, 1922; s. Eugene C. and Winifred W.; m. Helene E. Shannon, Sept. 28, 1946 (div. Dec. 1971); children: Anne Elizabeth, John Gregory; m. Jaan W. Chartener, Oct. 22, 1972 (div. 1986); 1 child, Sarah; m. Nancy Dickerson, 1989. BA, Haverford Coll., 1943; MBA, Harvard U., 1947; LLD (hon.), Pace. U., Rutgers U., Haverford Coll., Harvard U., Amherst Coll. With Goldman, Sachs & Co., N.Y.C., 1947-84, ptnr., 1956-76, sr. ptnr., co-chmn., 1976-84; dep. sec. Dept. State, Washington, 1985-89; now chmn. AEA Investors Inc., N.Y.C., 1989—; chmn. Fed. Res. Bank of N.Y. Trustee Haverford Coll., Rockefeller U., Lincoln Ctr. Theater; past pres. bd. overseers Harvard U.; past chmn. trustees coun. Nat. Gallery Art; co-chmn. greater N.Y. coun. Boy Scouts Am.; chmn. Internat. Rescue Com., UN Assn. U.S.A., Internat. House; chmn. emeritus Brookings Inst., Youth for Understanding, Andrew Mellon Found. With USNR, 1943-46. Mem. Coun. on Fgn. Rels., Links Club, Univ. Club, F Street Club. Office: AEA Investors Inc 65 E 55th St New York NY 10022-3219

WHITEHEAD, JOHN JED, healthcare and biotech company executive; b. N.Y.C., June 1, 1945; s. Edwin Carl and Constance Rosemary (Raywid) W.; m. Christina Juillet, Sept. 24, 1985. B.A., Williams Coll., 1967; postgrad., Case Western Res. U., 1967-68. Dir. chem. mktg., chem. divsn. Technicon Corp., Tarrytown, N.Y., 1969-70; sr. v.p., gen. mgr. indsl. divsn. Technicon Corp., 1970-71, sr. v.p. clin. divsn., 1971-74, sr. v.p. corp. planning, 1974-75, sr. v.p. R&D, 1975-81, sr. v.p. bus. devel. and market planning, 1981-83, pres. diagnostic systems divsn., 1983-85; pres., dir., CEO TDS Corp., 1985-92, chmn., CEO, dir., 1992-93; bd. dirs. Digene Corp., Rsch. Am.; mem. adv. coun. Nat. Inst. Environ. Health Scis., NIH, 1971-73. Mem. Rockefeller adv. group to Pres.'s 1976 Bicentennial Planning Commn., 1971-72; bd. dirs. Westchester Urban League, 1973-74, Whitehead Biomed. Rsch. Inst., 1974—, Primary Care Network, 1985-87, i-Stat Corp., 1987-95, dir. emeritus, 1995—; bd. dirs. Friends Nat. Libr. Medicine, 1992—, Sci. and Tech. Mus. of Atlanta (SciTrek), 1992—, Ams. Med. Progress, 1993—, Atlanta Internat. Sch. Atlanta, 1995—; trustee Nat. Mus. Health and Medicine Found., 1991—. Home: Park Place on Peachtree 2660 Peachtree Rd NW Atlanta GA 30305-3673

WHITEHEAD, JOHN WAYNE, law educator, organization administrator, author; b. Pulaski, Tenn., July 14, 1946; s. John M. and Alatha (Wiser) W.; m. Virginia Carolyn Nichols, Aug. 26, 1967; children: Jayson Reau, Jonathan Mathew, Elisabeth Anne, Joel Christofer, Joshua Benjamen. BA, U. Ark., 1969, JD, 1974. Bar: Ark. 1974, U.S. Dist. Ct. (ea. and we. dists.) Ark. 1974, U.S. Supreme Ct. 1977, U.S. Ct. Appeals (9th cir.) 1980, Va. 1981, U.S. Ct. Appeals (7th cir.) 1981, U.S Ct Appeals (4th and 5th cirs.). Spl. counsel Christian Legal Soc., Oak Park, Ill., 1977-78; assoc. Gibbs & Craze, Cleve., 1978-79; sole practice law Manassas, Va., 1979-82; pres. The Rutherford Inst., Charlottesville, Va., 1982—, also bd. dirs.; frequent lectr. colls., law schs.; past adj. prof. O.W. Coburn Sch. Law. Author: The Separation Illusion, 1977, Schools on Fire, 1980, The New Tyranny, 1982, The Second American Revolution, 1982, The Stealing of America, 1983, The Freedom of Religious Expression in Public High Schools, 1983, The End of Man, 1986, An American Dream, 1987, The Rights of Religious Persons in Public Education, 1991, Home Education: Rights and Reasons, 1993, Religious Apartheid, 1994, several others; contbr. numerous articles to profl. jours.; contbr. numerous chpts. to books. Served to 1st lt. U.S. Army, 1969-71. Named Christian Leader of Yr. Christian World Affairs Conf., Washington, 1986; recipient Bus. and Profl. award Religious Heritage Am., 1990, Hungarian Freedom medal, Budapest, 1991. Mem. ABA, Ark. Bar Assn., Va. Bar Assn. Office: The Rutherford Inst PO Box 7482 Charlottesville VA 22906-7482

WHITEHEAD, KENNETH DEAN, author, translator, retired federal government official; b. Rupert, Idaho, Dec. 14, 1930; s. Clarence Christian and May Bell (Allen) W.; m. Margaret Mary O'Donohue, Aug. 2, 1958; children: Paul Daniel, Steven Francis, Matthew Patrick, David Joseph. BA in French, U. Utah, 1955; postgrad., U. Paris, 1956-57; cert. in Arabic and Middle East studies, Fgn. Service Inst., Beirut, 1962. Instr. English U. Utah, Salt Lake City, 1955-56; fgn. service officer Dept. State, Rome, Beirut and Tripoli, Libya, 1957-65; chief Arabic service Voice of Am., Washington, 1965-67; dep. dir. fgn. currency program Smithsonian Instn., Washington, 1967-72; exec. v.p. Caths. United for Faith Inc., New Rochelle, N.Y., 1972-81; dir. Ctr. for Internat. Edn. U.S. Dept. Edn., Washington, 1982-86, dep. asst. sec. for higher edn. programs, 1986-88, asst. sec. for postsecondary edn., 1988-89. Author: Respectable Killing: The New Abortion Imperative, 1972, Agenda for the Sexual Revolution, 1981, Catholic Colleges and Federal Funding, 1988, DOA: The Ambush of the Universal Catechism, 1993; co-author: The Pope, The Council and the Mass, 1981, Flawed Expectations: The Reception of the Catechism of the Catholic Church, 1996; sr. editor: World Almanac Book of Dates, 1982, Macmillan Concise Dictionary of World History, 1983; translator 20 books from French, German, Italian, 1980—. Bd. dirs. Notre Dame Inst. for Advanced study, Arlington, Va., 1986-95. Fulbright scholar U.S. Dept. State, 1956-57. Mem. Fellowship Cath. Scholars (bd. dirs. 1990—), Brent Soc. Cath. Profls. (bd. dirs. 1992—), Cath. League for Religious and Civil Rights (bd. dirs. 1992—), KC. Republican. Home: 809 Ridge Pl Falls Church VA 22046-3631

WHITEHEAD, LUCY GRACE, health facility administrator; b. Jacksonville, Fla., Jan. 12, 1935; d. William Alexander and Hester Grace (Gray) Fisackerly; m. John Vernon Whitehead, Sept. 4, 1957; children: Marilyn Ruth, John Vernon Jr., James Andrew. BA, Fla. So. Coll., 1956; M of Christian Edn., Emory U., 1957; BSN, U. North Fla., 1990. RN, Fla. Staff nurse Venice (Fla.) Hosp., 1977, Med. Personnel Pool, Largo, Fla., 1978; charge nurse/nurse educator Gadsden Nursing Home, Quincy, Fla., 1979-85; primary nurse Meml. Regional Rehab. Hosp., Jacksonville, Fla., 1990-92; staff nurse, nurse mgr. Nassau Gen. Hosp., Fernandina Beach, Fla., 1992-94; clin. coord. Integrated Health Svcs., Ft. Pierce, Fla., 1994, dir. nursing, 1994-95. Mem. ANA, Fla. Nurses Assn., Order Ea. Star (worthy matron), Sigma Theta Tau. Methodist. Avocations: singing, theater/drama, clowning. Home: 1083 Tallavana Trail Havana FL 32333

WHITEHEAD, MARVIN DELBERT, plant pathologist; b. Paoli, Okla., Dec. 18, 1917; s. Chester Arthur and Lola Elizabeth (Donnell) W.; 1 child, James Mark. BS, Okla. State U., 1939, MS, 1946; PhD (fellow), U. Wis., 1949. Seed analyst Soil Conservation Svc. USDA, Stillwater, Okla., 1936-38; asst. in agronomy Okla. State U., 1939-40; sr. seed analyst Fed. State Seed Lab., Montgomery, Ala., 1940-42; asst. plant pathologist U. Wis., Madison, 1946-48; asst. prof. plant pathology Tex. A&M U., College Station, 1949-55; assoc. prof. U. Mo., Columbia, 1955-60; prof. botany Edinboro State Coll., Pa., 1960-63; prof. plant pathology Ga. So. Coll., Statesboro, Ga., 1963-68; prof. botany and plant pathology Ga. State U., Atlanta, 1968-75; owner, dir. Marvern Plant Health, Inc., Atlanta, 1978—; cons. control of plant diseases. Editor Ga. Jour. Sci., 1969-75; contbr. 59 articles to rsch. jours. and publs.; developer fungicide Phyton 27 for control of Dutch Elm Disease. With USAAF, 1941-46, PTO. Mem. AAAS, VFW, Am. Phytopathol. Soc., Mycol. Soc. Am., Bot. Soc. Am., Am. Inst. Biol. Scis., Crop Sci. Soc. Am., Am. Soc. Agronomy, Ofcl. Seed Analysts N.Am., Ga. Acad. Sci., Wis. Acad. Sci., Druid Hills Golf Club (Atlanta). Democrat. Home and Office: 3260 College Pl Apt 81 Lemon Grove CA 91945-1456

WHITEHEAD, MICHAEL ANTHONY, chemistry educator; b. London, June 30, 1935; emigrated to Can., 1962; s. Francis Henry and Edith Downes (Rotherham) W.; 1 son, Christopher Mark. B.Sc. in Chemistry with honors, Queen Mary Coll., U. London, 1956, Ph.D., 1960, D.Sc., 1974. Asst. lectr. Queen Mary Coll., U. London, 1958-60; postdoctoral fellow U. Cin., 1960, asst. prof., 1961; asst. prof. theoretical chemistry McGill U., Montreal, Que., Can., 1962-66; asso. prof. McGill U., 1966-74, prof., 1974—; vis. prof. U. Cambridge, Eng., 1971-72, U. Oxford, Eng., 1972-74; vis. professorial fellow Univ. Coll. Wales, Aberystwyth, 1980, U. Oxford, 1990-91; invited prof. U. Geneva, 1983-84; life guest prof. Nat. U. Def. Tech., Changsha, People's Republic of China; mem. Internat. Com. on Nuclear Quadrupole Resonance.; co-chmn. 7th Internat. Symposium on Nuclear Quadrapole Resonance, Kingston, Ont., Can., 1983. Author more than 220 rsch. publs. in field of quantum chemistry and radio spectroscopy. Fellow Royal Chem. Soc., Chem. Inst. Can., Royal Soc. Arts; mem. Am. Chem. Soc., Am. Phys. Soc., James McGill Soc. (pres. 1993-95), Sigma Xi (pres. McGill chpt. 1971-72, 81-82, 92-95, 97—), Phi Lambda Upsilon. Anglican. Office: McGill U Dept Chemistry, 801 Sherbrooke St W, Montreal, PQ Canada H3A 2K6 *My faith in God and belief in Christ.*

WHITEHEAD, ROBERT, theatrical producer; b. Montreal, Can., Mar. 3, 1916; s. William Thomas and Lena Mary (Labatt) S.; m. Zoe Caldwell, 1968. Student, Trinity Coll. Sch., Port Hope, Can. Comml. photographer, 1936-38, actor, 1938-42, producer, 1946—; Dir ANTA Am. Shakespeare Festival. Producer: plays include Medea (Robinson Jeffers), starring Judith Anderson, 1947, Crime and Punishment, starring John Gielgud, 1947, Member of the Wedding (Carson McCullers), 1950 (N.Y. Times Drama Critics Circle award), Waltz of the Toreadors, 1957 (N.Y. Times Drama Critics Circle award), Separate Tables (Terrence Rattigan), 1956-57, A Touch of the Poet (Eugene O'Neill), 1958, The Visit (Friedrich Durrenmatt), 1958 (N.Y. Times Drama Critics Circle award 1958), Much Ado About Nothing (Shakespeare), 1959, A Man for All Seasons (Robert Bolt), 1961-62 (Tony award 1962, N.Y. Times Drama Critics Circle award 1961), The Physicists (Durrenmatt), 1964, The Price (Arthur Miller), 1968, The Prime of Miss Jean Brodie (Jay Presson Allen), 1968, Sheep On The Runway, 1970, Bequest to the Nation, 1970, The Creation of the World and Other Business (Miller), 1972, Finishing Touches, 1973-74, A Matter of Gravity, 1976, A Texas Trilogy, 1976, No Man's Land (Harold Pinter), 1976, The Prince of Grand Street, 1979, Betrayal (Harold Pinter), 1979, Lunch Hour, 1980-81, The West Side Waltz, 1980-81, Death of a Salesman (Miller), 1983-84, The Petition, 1986, The Speed of Darkness, 1991, Park Your Car in Harvard Yard (Israel Horowitz), 1991-92, Broken Glass (Miller), 1994, Master Class (Terrence McNally), 1995; co-producer: Artist Descending a Staircase (Tom Stoppard), 1989; dir. plays: Medea, N.Y.C., 1982, Melbourne, Australia, 1984, Lillian, 1986. Served Am. Field Service AUS, 1942-45. Recipient Sam S. Shubert Found. award, 1973, Edwin Booth award, 1990, United Jewish Appeal/Fedn. Lifetime Achievement award, 1991. Clubs: Century (N.Y.C.), Players (N.Y.C.). Office: 1501 Broadway New York NY 10036-5601

WHITEHILL, ANGELA ELIZABETH, artistic director; b. Leeds, Yorkshire, Eng., Oct. 21, 1938; came to U.S., 1952; became American citizen, Sept. 1995; d. Donald Paul and Audrey May (Clayforth) Warner; m. Norman James Whitehill, Dec. 16, 1928; children: Norman James III, Pamela Elizabeth. Student, Arts Ednl. Sch., London, 1955-59. With Corps de Ballet, Paris, 1958-59; dir. London Sch. Ballet, St. Thomas, V.I., 1960-63; asst. dir. Ocean County Ballet Co., Toms River, N.J., 1965-68; founder, dir. Shore Ballet Sch., Toms River, 1968-76; artistic dir. Shore Ballet Co., Toms River, 1971-76; artist in residence Castleton State Coll., Rutland, Vt., 1977-79; founder, artistic dir. Burklyn Ballet Theatre, Johnson, Vt., 1977—; vis. prof. Colby Sawyer Coll., New London, N.H., 1978-79; resident designer Atlanta Ballet Co., 1982-83; designer, pub. relations N.J. Ballet Co., Orange, 1983-85; artistic dir. Vt. Ballet Theatre, Burlington, 1985-94. choreographer Arensky dances, 1983, A Deux, 1984, 4 Plus 2, 1986, Twins From A Time Gone By, 1987; co-author: Parent's Book of Ballet, 1988, The Young Professional's Book of Ballet, 1990. Dir. Vt. Ballet Theatre Found., Caledonia County, 1993-96. Recipient Francis Hopkins award Ocean County, N.J., 1976, Woman of Achievement award Vt. Woman, 1989, Author's award N.J. Inst. Tech., 1989. Mem. Vt. Council on the Arts, Regional Dance Am. Quaker. Home: 218 Ocean Ave Island Heights NJ 08732 Office: Burklyn Ballet Theatre PO Box 5069 Burlington VT 05402-5069

WHITEHILL, JULES LEONARD, surgeon, educator; b. N.Y.C., Mar. 7, 1912; s. Karl and Jenny (Abrahams) W.; m. Muriel Jeannette Berry, Sept. 21, 1943 (dec.); children: Jonathan Robert (dec.), David Carl Evan, Jules Leonard II (dec.). BS magna cum laude, CCNY, 1931; MD, NYU, 1935. Diplomate Am. Bd. Surgery. Intern, resident, fellow Mt. Sinai Hosp., N.Y.C., 1935-40; assoc. Dr. John Garlock, Dr. Leon Ginzburg, N.Y.C., 1940-42; pvt. practice surgery, chief of surgery Pima County Hosp., Tucson, 1946-60; prof., chair dept. surgery Chgo. Med. Sch., 1960-70, prof. emeritus, 1970—; chief of surgery, med. dir. Mt. Sinai Med. Ctr., Chgo.; cons. in field San Diego, 1970—; trustee Chapman Coll., Orange, Calif., 1971-76; chmn. bd. dirs. World Campus Afloat, Orange, 1971-76; bd. visitors, steering com. exec. bd. U. Calif. San Diego Med. Sch., 1996—; vis. prof. surgery U. Zagreb, Yugoslavia, 1969; chmn. bd., pres. Equidyne Systems Inc., 1996—. Col. USAF, 1942—, Africa, Italy, France, 3rd gen. hosp. comdr. gen. surg. team 5th Aux. Surg. Group. Stroock scholar, N.Y. Regents scholar; Gallatin fellow NYU; Jules Leonard Whitehill chair in surgery named in his honor NYU; recipient citation Surgeon Gen. USAF. Fellow Am. Coll. Surgeons; mem. N.Y. Acad. Sci., Chgo. Surg. Soc., AMA, Internat. Coll. Surgeons (regent, bd. govs.), Royal Soc. Medicine (England), Phi Beta Kappa, Alpha Omega Alpha. Avocations: books, history of medicine. Home: 5238 Renaissance Ave San Diego CA 92122-5602

WHITEHOUSE, ALTON WINSLOW, JR., retired oil company executive; b. Albany, N.Y., Aug. 1, 1927; s. Alton Winslow and Catherine (Lyda) W.; m. Helen MacDonald, Nov. 28, 1953; children: Alton, Sarah, Peter. B.S., U. Va., 1949, LL.B., 1952. Bar: Ohio 1953. Asso. partner firm McAfree, Hanning, Newcomer, Hazlett & Wheeler, Cleve., 1952-68; v.p., gen. counsel Standard Oil Co., Ohio, 1968-69; sr. v.p. Standard Oil Co., 1969-70, pres., chief operating officer, 1970-77, vice chmn. bd., 1977-78, chmn. bd., chief exec. officer, 1978-86; bd. dirs. Timken Co., Canton, Ohio, McGean-Rohco, Cleve., Cleve.-Cliffs Inc., Orvis, Inc. Trustee Cleve. Clinic Found., Holden Arboretum; mem. Cleve. Mus. Art. Mem. Am. Petroleum Inst. Republican. Episcopalian.

WHITEHOUSE, DAVID BRYN, museum director; b. Worksop, Nottinghamshire, Eng., Oct. 15, 1941; came to U.S., 1984; s. Brindley Charles and Alice Margaret (Dobson) W.; m. Ruth Delamain Ainger, 1963; children: Sarah, Susan, Peter; m. Elizabeth-Anne Ollemans, 1975; children: Julia, Simon, Nicola. BA, Cambridge U., 1963, MA, 1965, PhD, 1967. Wainwright fellow Oxford U., Eng., 1966-73; dir. Brit. Inst. Afghan Studies, Kabul, Afghanistan, 1973-74, Brit. Sch., Rome, 1974-84; chief curator Corning Mus. of Glass, N.Y., 1984-87, dep. dir., 1988-92, dir., 1992—; dir. Siraf expdn. Brit. Inst. Persian Studies, Tehran, Iran, 1966-73. Author: (with Ruth Whitehouse) Archaeological Atlas of the World, 1975; (with David Andrews and John Osborne) Aspects of Medieval Lazio, 1982, (with Donald B. Harden and others) Glass of the Caesars, 1987, Glass of the Roman Empire, 1988; (with Richard Hodges) Mohammed, Charlemagne and the Origins of Europe, 1983, Glass: A Pocket Dictionary, 1993, English Cameo Glass, 1994. Contbr. numerous articles and revs. to profl. jours. Fellow Soc. Antiquaries (London), Royal Geog. Soc., Pontificia Accademia Romana di Archeologia; mem. Accademia Fiorentina delle Arti del Disegno, Accademia di Archeologia, Lettere e Belle Arti di Napoli, Deutsches Archaologisches Inst., Internat. Assn. for the History of Glass (pres. 1991-95), Athenaeum Club (London). Office: Corning Mus of Glass One Museum Way Corning NY 14830-2253

WHITEHOUSE, DAVID REMPFER, physicist; b. Evanston, Ill., Nov. 13, 1929; s. Horace and Emma (Rempfer) W.; m. Ruth Agnes Walker, June 23, 1956; children—Walker Philip, Laura Lees, Sanford Davis. B.S., Northwestern U., 1952; M.S., M.I.T., 1954, Sc.D., 1958. Assoc. prof. elec. engring. M.I.T., 1958-65; prin. research scientist Raytheon Co., Waltham, Mass., 1965-67; mgr. laser center Raytheon Co., Burlington, Mass., 1967-85; pres. Whitehouse Assocs., Weston, Mass., 1985—; co-founder, dir. Magnion Inc., Burlington, 1960-63; co-founder, chm. bd. DYMED Corp., Marlboro, Mass., 1989-91. Bd. dirs. New Eng. Bapt. Hosp., Boston, 1976—. Fellow Laser Inst. Am. (pres. 1981, bd. dirs. 1977—); mem. IEEE, Am. Inst. Physics. Episcopalian. Patentee in plasma physics, laser engring. Home and Office: 1 Whitehouse Ln Weston MA 02193-2324

WHITEHOUSE, FRED WAITE, endocrinologist, researcher; b. Chgo., May 6, 1926; s. Fred Trafton Waite and Grace Caroline (Peters) W.; m. Iris Jean Dawson, June 6, 1953; children: Martha, Amy, Sarah. BS, Northwestern U., 1947; MD, U. Ill., Chgo., 1949. Diplomate Am. Bd. Internal Medicine; cert. endocrinology and metabolism. Intern, then resident Henry Ford Hosp., Detroit, 1949-53, staff physician, 1955—, chief div. metabolism, 1962-88; chief div. endocrinology and metabolism Henry Ford Hosp., 1988-95; divsn. head emeritus, 1995—; fellow Joslin Clinic, Boston, 1954-55; cons. FDA, Washington, 1980—; mem. Coalition on Diabetes Edn. and Minority Health, 1989-91. Contbr. articles to profl. jours. Bd. dirs. Wheat Ridge Found., 1984-93. Lt. USNR, 1951-53. Fellow ACP; mem. NIH (nat. diabetes adv. bd. 1984-88), Am. Diabetes Assn. (pres. 1978-79, Banting medal 1979, Outstanding Clinician award 1989, Outstanding Physician Educators award 1994), Detroit Med. Club (pres. 1976), Detroit Acad. Medicine (pres. 1991-92). Lutheran. Avocations: bicycling, gardening. Home: 1265 Blairmoor Ct Grosse Pointe MI 48236-1230 Office: Henry Ford Hosp 2799 W Grand Blvd Detroit MI 48202-2608

WHITEHOUSE, JOHN HARLAN, JR., systems software consultant, diagnostician; b. Lakewood, Ohio, Sept. 12, 1951; s. John Harlan and Frances Elizabeth (Nation) W.; divorced; 1 child, John Harlan III. BA magna cum laude, Ohio Wesleyan U., 1973; MBA, Cleve. State U., 1976; PhD, Columbia Pacific U., San Rafael, Calif., 1988; postgrad., U. Chgo., 1974, Vedic U. of Am., 1996—. Cert. computing profl.; cert. info. sys. auditor. Programmer San Antonio Express-News, 1977; programming mgr. S.W. Info. Mgmt. Systems, San Antonio, 1977, Utility Data Corp., Houston, 1978; sr. data systems auditor Nat. City Corp., Cleve., 1978-81; sys. programmer Standard Oil Co., Cleve., 1981-84; adv. systems engr. IBM, Cleve., 1984-92; pres. Semiotica Corp., 1992—; mem. exams. editorial coun. Inst. for Cert. Computer Profls., Des Plaines, 1990—, test devel. mgr., 1996—. Author: CICS Problem Determination Workshop, 1990; co-author: ICCP Guidelines for Recertification, 1990, ICCP Official Study Guide, 1991-95; also numerous articles, columnist. Mem. Assn. for Computing Machinery (chmn. Greater Cleve. chpt. 1982-83, Svc. Recognition award 1984), Assn. of Inst. for Cert. Computer Profls. (regional dir. 1989-93, nominating com. 1991, test deployment mgr. 1996—), Masons, Philalethes Soc., Scottish Rite, Phi Beta Kappa. Unitarian. Home: 22291 Berry Dr Rocky River OH 44116-2013 Office: Semiotica Corp 25935 Detroit Rd Ste 241 Westlake OH 44145-2453

WHITEHURST, MARY TARR, artist, poet, writer; b. Norfolk, Va., Nov. 20, 1923; d. Henry Bennitt and Martha Ida Tarr; m. Jerry Rutter Whitehurst, Dec. 24, 1943; children: Henry Armistead, Jeffrey Tarr, Martha W. Bryant. Student, Coll. William & Mary, 1940-42, Wytheville C.C., 1968, Sullins Coll., 1976-80, Va. Western C.C., 1988. Docent Mus. Fine Arts, Roanoke, Va., 1973-75; dir., endowing mem. Fine Arts Ctr. of New River Valley, Pulaski, Va., 1980-93; charter, endowing mem. Bristol Mus. Fine Arts, Va./Tenn., 1975-80; benefactor, mem. Arts Found. Radford U., Va., 1991—. One-woman shows include Mus. Fine Arts, Roanoke, Va., 1977, Emory & Henry Coll., Emory, Va., 1982, Radford U. Art Gallery, Va., 1991, Ashland Area Art Galery, Ky., 1993, Va. Polytech. Inst. & State U., Blacksburg, 1985—, New River C.C. Found., 1985—, Coll. William & Mary, Williamsburg, 1995. Endowing mem. Va. Polytech. Inst. & State U., Blacksburg, 1985—, New River C.C. Found., 1985—, Coll. William & Mary, Williamsburg, 1995. Recipient Clement Gueenberg award of distinction Mus. Fine Arts, Roanoke, 1976, Grumbacher Gold medal Soc. Water Color Artists, 1995; art dept. named in honor New River C.C., Dublin, Va., 1994. Mem. Catharine Lorillard Wolfe Art Club (Joyce Williams water color award 1985), Midwest Transparent Water Color Soc. (signature mem.), Va. Water Color Soc. (dir. 1994), Ala. Water Color Soc., Blacksburg Regional Artists Assn., Allied Artists (assoc.), So. Water Color Soc. (two awards 1997). Avocations: travel abroad, art collection, history, philanthropy. Home: Painters Wood Rte 1 Box 356-E Draper VA 24324

WHITEHURST, WILLIAM WILFRED, JR., management consultant; b. Balt., Mar. 4, 1937; s. William Wilfred and Elizabeth (Hogg) W.; B.A., Princeton, 1958; M.S. with distinction, Carnegie Inst. Tech., 1963; m. Linda Joan Potter, July 1, 1961; children—Catherine Elizabeth, William Wilfred, III. Mathematician Nat. Security Agy., Fort George G. Meade, Md., 1961-63; mgmt. cons. McKinsey & Co., Inc., Washington, 1963-66; partner L.E. Peabody & Assos., Washington, 1966-69, exec. v.p., dir. L.E. Peabody & Assos., Inc., Lanham, Md., 1969-82, pres., dir., 1983-86, pres. W.W. Whitehurst & Assoc., Inc., Cockeysville, Md., 1986—. Contbr. to Code of Fed. Regulations 49 C.F.R. Sect. 1157. Served to comdr. USNR, 1958-65. Recipient Diploma De Honor 14th Pan Am. Rwy. Congress. Mem. Am. Railway Engring. Assn., Transportation Rsch. Forum, Assn. for Investment Mgmt. and Rsch., Ops. Rsch. Soc. Am., Inst. Mgmt. Scis., Washington Soc. Investment Analysts. Episcopalian. Clubs: University, Princeton (Washington); Princeton (N.J.) Quadrangle. Home and Office: 12421 Happy Hollow Rd Cockeysville Hunt Valley MD 21030-1711

WHITEKER, ROY ARCHIE, retired chemistry educator; b. Long Beach, Calif., Aug. 22, 1927; s. Ewing Harris and Mabel Mary (Williams) W.; m. Jean Fiske MacLean, June 3, 1960; 1 son, Scott MacLean. BS, UCLA, 1950, MS, 1952; PhD, Calif. Inst. Tech., 1956. Instr. chemistry M.I.T., 1955-57; asst. prof. Harvey Mudd Coll., Claremont, Calif., 1957-61; asso. prof. Harvey Mudd Coll., 1961-67, prof. chemistry, 1967-73; assoc. dir. fellowships Nat. Acad. Scis., Washington, 1967-68; dep. exec. sec. Council Internat. Exchange Scholar, Washington, 1971-72; exec. sec. Council Internat. Exchange Scholar, 1972-75; dir. Coun. Internat. Exchange Scholar, 1975-76; prof. chemistry U. Pacific, Stockton, Calif., 1976-92, dean Coll. Pacific, 1976-89. Bd. dirs. Stockton Symphony Assn., 1978-80; dir. cmty. adv. bd. Sta. KUOP, 1981-89; bd. dirs. Stockton Chorale, 1989—; pres. U. of the Pacific Emeriti Soc., 1992-94. With USNR, 1945-46. Recipient Dow Chem. Co. fellowship, 1953-54; DuPont Teaching fellowship, 1954-55; NSF Sci. Faculty fellowship Royal Inst. Tech., Stockholm, Sweden, 1963-64. Mem. Am. Chem. Soc., Alpha Chi Sigma, Phi Beta Kappa, Phi Kappa Phi, Sigma Xi. Home: 3734 Portsmouth Cir N Stockton CA 95219-3843

WHITELEY, BENJAMIN ROBERT, insurance company executive; b. Des Moines, July 13, 1929; s. Hiram Everett and Martha Jane (Walker) W.; m. Elaine Marie Yunker, June 14, 1953; children—Stephen Robert, Benjamin Walker. B.S., Oreg. State U., 1951; M.S., U. Mich., 1952; postgrad. advanced mgmt. program, Harvard U. Clk. group dept. Standard Ins. Co., Portland, Oreg., 1956-69, asst. actuary group dept. then asst. actuary acturial dept., 1959-63, asst. v.p., asst. actuary, 1963-64, asst. v.p., assoc. actuary, 1964-70, v.p. group ins. adminstrn., 1970-72, v.p. group ins. div., 1972-80, exec. v.p. group ins., 1980-81, exec. v.p., 1981-83, pres., CEO, 1983-92, chmn. bd. dirs., CEO, 1993-94, chmn. bd. dirs., 1994—; bd. dirs. Gunderson, Inc., Portland, U.S. Bancorp., N.W. Natural Gas Co., Willamette Industries, Inc., Canor Energy Ltd., The Greenbrier Cos. Past pres. Columbia Pacific coun. Boy Scouts Am.; past chmn. bd., trustee Pacific U., Forest Grove, Oreg.; past chmn. Oreg. Health Scis. Found., Oreg. Trail Coordinating Coun. 1st lt. USAF, 1952-55. Recipient Silver Beaver award Cascade Pacific coun. Boy Scouts Am., 1993, Harvey and Emiline Clark medal Pacific U., 1991, Alumni fellow award Oreg. State U., 1991, Aubrey R. Watzek award Lewis and Clark Coll., 1994, Lifetime Achievement award Bus. Youth Exch., Portland, Oreg., 1995. Fellow Soc. Actuaries; mem. Am. Acad. Actuaries (bd. dirs. 1984-86), Am. Council of Life Ins. (bd. dirs. 1986-89), Internat. Congress Actuaries, Portland C. of C. (bd. dirs. 1983-89). Republican. Methodist. Clubs: Arlington, Waverley Country, Multnomah Athletic (Portland, Oreg.). Office: Standard Ins Co PO Box 711 Portland OR 97207-0711

WHITELEY, HAROLD LEE, director; b. Graham, Tex., Aug. 5, 1948; s. Arthur Wiley and Cecilia Elizabeth (Boisclair) W.; m. Linda Sue Day, Dec. 27, 1969; children: Michael Kevin, Jason Lee, Christopher Brian, Kristen Michelle. BS, N. Tex. State U., 1970, MS, 1972; PhD, U. North Tex., 1995. Tchr. math., coach Newcastle (Tex.) Ind. Sch. Dist., 1970-71; tchr. biology, head football, basketball, track & field coach Munday (Tex.) Ind. Sch. Dist., 1971-73; asst. prin., athletic dir., head coach football, basketball and track, tchr. Argyle (Tex.) Rural H.S., 1973-77; mgr. southeast mktg. Turbo Refrigerating Co., Denton, Tex., 1977-82; pres., owner ICE Sys. Internat. Inc., Marietta, Ga., 1982-85, Whiteley & Assocs., Lewisville, Tex., 1983—; transp. rep. Spl. Programs for Assisting the Needy, Inc., Lewisville, 1992-97; pres., owner So. Developers, Inc., Marietta, 1980-84; aerial crop photo technician Agrl. Stabilization and Conservation Svc. Denton, 1991—; instr. golf, tennis, raquetball U. North Tex., Denton, 1989-90; ind. rep. Destiny Telecom. Internat., Inc., 1997—. Inventor (game boards) Bass Classic, 1986, Golf Classic, 1986; developer Amateur Sports Network, 1991, Amateur Team Golf Assn., 1991; contbr. articles on HIV issues in athletics to profl. jours. Grantee Bertha Found., 1991. Mem. Nat. Athletic Trainers Assn., Nat. Assn. Acad. Advisors for Athletes, Am. Assn. Wellnes Edn. Counseling and Rsch., Nat. Assn. Coll. Dirs. of Athletics, Am. Med. Athletic Assn., Golden Key Soc. Baptist. Avocations: tennis, softball, refinishing antiques, writing, recreational activities. Home and Office: 531 W Main St Ste 100 Lewisville TX 75057

WHITELEY, SANDRA MARIE, librarian, editor; b. May 24, 1943; d. Samuel Smythe and Kathryn Marie (Voigt) Whiteley; m. R. Russell Maylone, Jan. 8, 1977; 1 child, Cybele Elizabeth. BA, Pa. State U., 1963; MLS, Columbia U., 1970; MA, U. Pa., 1975; postgrad., Northwestern U., 1985—. Tchr. Amerikan Kiz Koleji, Izmir, Turkey, 1967-69; reference libr. Yale U., New Haven, Conn., 1970-74; head reference dept. Northwestern U., Evanston, Ill., 1975-80; asst. editor Who's Who in Libr. and Info. ALA, Chgo., 1980-81, editor Reference Books Bull., 1985-96; lectr. Grad. Libr. Sch. U. Chgo., 1982-83; assoc. exec. dir. Assn. Coll. and Rsch. Librs., Chgo., 1981-85; editor Chase's Calendar of Events NTC/Contemporary Pub., 1997—. Author: Purchasing an Encyclopaedia, 5th edit., 1996, The American Library Association Guide to Information Access, 1994. Mem. ALA (various coms. 1977-81), Beta Phi Mu. Democrat. Congregationalist. Avocations: reading, hiking, travel. Home: 1205 Noyes St Evanston IL 60201-2635 Office: NTC/Contemporary Pub 4255 W Touhy Ave Lincolnwood IL 60646-1933

WHITEMAN, DOUGLAS E., publisher; b. Emporia, Kans., Mar. 4, 1961; s. Floyd E. and Phyllis E. (Troyer) W.; m. Susan R. Anderson, Sept. 14, 1985; 1 child, Aaron Anderson Douglas. BS in Bus. Adminstrn., U. Kans., 1983. With Putnam Pub. Group, Denver and N.Y.C., 1983—; dir. trade sales and mktg., internat. sales mgr. Putnam Pub. Group, N.Y.C., 1987-89, v.p. sales and mktg., 1989-94; sr. v.p., pub. Putnam and Grosset Book Group, 1994-95, pres., pub., 1995—; exec. v.p. Penguin Putnam, Inc., 1997—; exec. v.p. Penguin Putnam Inc., 1997—. Methodist. Avocations: literature, tennis, golf, fantasy baseball. Office: Putnam Pub Group 200 Madison Ave New York NY 10016-3903

WHITEMAN, JOSEPH DAVID, lawyer, manufacturing company executive; b. Sioux Falls, S.D., Sept. 12, 1933; s. Samuel D. and Margaret (Wallace) W.; m. Mary Kelly, Dec. 29, 1962; children: Anne Margaret, Mary Ellen, Joseph David, Sarah Kelly, Jane. B.A., U. Mich., 1955, J.D., 1960. Bar: D.C. 1960, Ohio 1976. Assoc. Cox, Langford, Stoddard & Cutler, Washington, 1959-64; sec., gen. counsel Studebaker group Studebaker Worthington, Inc., N.Y.C., 1964-71; asst. gen. counsel. United Telecommunications, Inc., Kansas City, Mo., 1971-74; v.p., gen. counsel, sec. Weatherhead Co., Cleve., 1974-77, Parker Hannifin Corp., Cleve., 1977—. Immediate past chmn. bd. dirs. St. Lukes Med. Ctr. Served as lt. USNR, 1955-57. Mem. ABA, Beta Theta Pi, Phi Delta Phi. Republican. Roman Catholic. Home: 23349 Shaker Blvd Cleveland OH 44122-2670 Office: Parker Hannifin Corp 17325 Euclid Ave Cleveland OH 44112-1209

WHITEMAN, RICHARD FRANK, architect; b. Mankato, Minn., Mar. 24, 1925; s. Lester Raymond and Mary Grace (Dawald) W.; m. Jean Frances Waite, June 20, 1948 (dec. May 1980); children: David, Sarah, Lynn, Ann, Carol, Frank, Marie, Steven; m. Mavis Patricia Knutsen, May 30, 1982. BArch, U. Minn., 1945; MArch, Harvard U., 1948. Registered architect, Minn. Designer Ellerbe Co., St. Paul, Minn., 1946; architect Thorshov and Cerny, Mpls., 1948-53; ptnr. Jyring and Whiteman, Hibbing, Minn., 1953-62; pres. AJWM Inc., Hibbing and Duluth, Minn., 1963-72, Architects Four, Duluth, 1972-83; owner Richard Whiteman, Duluth, 1983-95; sr. architect U. Minn., Duluth, 1993—; chmn. Architect Sect. Registration Bd., Minn., 1972-80. Prin. works include Washington Sch., Hibbing, 1957 (Minn. Soc. Architects Design award 1957), Whiteman Summer Home, Pengilly, Minn. (Minn. Soc. Architects Design award 1959), Bemidji State Coll. Phys. Edn. Bldg. (Minn. Soc. Architects Design award 1960), Whiteman Residence, Griggs Hall UMD, 1990. Pres. U. for Srs., 1993-94; bd. govs. St. Louis County Hist. Soc.; mem. adv. com. Glensheen, U. Minn. Duluth. With USN, 1943-46, PTO. Mem. Minn. Soc. Architects (pres. 1972), Northeast Minn. Architects (pres. 1962), Service Corps Retired Execs. (chmn. Northeast Minn. chpt. 1986), Minn. Designer Selection Bd. (chmn. 1990). Democrat. Roman Catholic. Club: Kitchi Gammi (Duluth). Lodge: Kiwanis. Avocations: photography, fishing, cross-country skiing, travel. Home: 3500 E 3rd St Duluth MN 55804-1812

WHITENER, LAWRENCE BRUCE, political consultant, consumer advocate, educator; b. Alexandria, Va., Mar. 5, 1952; s. Ralph Verly and Alice Lee (Beard) W.; m. Deborah Susan Koons, Dec. 7, 1985; 2 foster children. BA in History and Polit. Sci., Va. Commonwealth U., 1975; diploma, Nat. Inst. Real Estate, 1986; AA in Sci., No. Va. C.C., Annandale, 1987, student, 1995—. Tchr. Fairfax (Va.) County Pub. Schs., 1975-96; wholesaler Consignment Auto, Falls Church, Va., 1975-77; coach Groveton High Sch. Wrestling Team, Alexandria, 1975-77; senate aide Va. Gen. Assembly, Richmond, 1978; pres. Whitener Cons., Springfield, Va., 1977-86, Real Estate Fin. Svcs., Springfield, 1986-90; U.S. Postal Svc., 1989—; pres. Amicus Curiae & Co., Springfield, 1992—; coach wrestling team Langley H.S., McLean, 1991-93, J.E.B. Stuart H.S., Falls Church, 1993-95; panelist Am. Arbitration Assn., Washington; automotive and banking specialist, 1994—. Author poetry, 1975, 76, 94, 97, screenplays Sorrow, 1993, Saro, 1996; photographer landscapes; subject of article in The Postal Record, 1996. Mem. Athletic Coun., Fairfax County, 1975-84; appointee Housing Assistance Adv. Com., Fairfax County, 1990; commr. Indsl. Devel. Authority, Fairfax County, 1985-93; candidate Fairfax County Bd. Suprs., Springfield Dist., 1991, Fairfax County Sch. Bd., 1995; chmn. vol. rev. com. Fairfax County Access Cable Ch. 10, 1994—; chmn. W.T. Woodson High Sch.'s Class of '70 25th Reunion, 1995; umpire Am. Softball Assn., 1996—. Recipient Cert. of Appreciation, Fairfax County Bd. of Suprs., 1990, Cert. of Appreciation, Nat. Ctr. for Missing and Exploited Children, 1990. Mem. Am. Arbitration Assn. (panel 1994—), Mortgage Bankers Assn. (legis. com. 1985-90, edn. com. 1986-89), No. Va. Bd. Realtors (pub. rels. com. 1985-90, Cert. of Appreciation, Am. Home Week 1986, 90). Avocations: Tae Kwon Do (Black Belt), scuba diving, skydiving, mountaineer, skiing. Office: Amicus Curiae PO Box 611 Springfield VA 22150-0611

WHITENER, WILLIAM GARNETT, dancer, choreographer; b. Seattle, Aug. 17, 1951; s. Warren G. and Virginia Louise (Garnett) W. Student, Cornish Sch. Allied Arts, Seattle, 1958-69. Dancer N.Y.C. Opera, 1969, Joffrey Ballet, N.Y.C., 1969-77, Twyla Tharp Dance, N.Y.C., 1978-87; asst. to choreographer Jerome Robbins for Robbins' Broadway, N.Y.C., 1988; artistic dir. Les Ballets Jazz de Montréal, 1991-93, Royal Winnipeg Ballet, 1993-95, State Ballet of Mo., 1996—; coord. dance dept. Concord Acad., Mass., 1988; vis. artist U. Wash., 1989-91; tchr. Harvard U. Summer Dance, 1989-90, NYU, 1985. Appeared in original Broadway cast Dancin', 1978; choreographer for Princeton Ballet, Joffrey II, John Curry Ice Theatre, Ballet Hispanico of N.Y., Boston Ballet Internat. Choreography Competition, Tommy Tune, Martine Van Hamel/Kevin McKenzie, Ann Reinking, Seattle Repertory Theatre, Am. Ballroom Theater, N.Y.C., Hartford (Conn.) Ballet, On the Boards, (with Bill Irwin) Alive From Off Center (PBS-TV), (opera ensemble of N.Y.) A Little Night Music, Pacific Northwest Ballet, (Seattle Opera) Rusalka, Aida; dancer (films) Amadeus, Zelig, (TV shows) The Catherine Wheel, Dance in America; performer Garden of Earthly Delights, 1988. Mem. Actor's Equity, Am. Guild Mus. Artists. Office: State Ballet of Missouri 706 W 42nd St Kansas City MO 64111-3120

WHITESELL, DALE EDWARD, retired association executive, natural resources consultant; b. Miamisburg, Ohio, Oct. 12, 1925; s. Harry Parker and Carmen Lucille (Holtzman) W.; m. Alma Irene Wells, Mar. 24, 1945; children: Catherine Elizabeth, Kimberly Lynn. B.S., Ohio State U., 1950, M.S. in Wildlife Mgmt., 1951. Game mgmt. supr. Ohio Div. Wildlife, Xenia, 1951-63, author farmer attitude survey, 1951-58; chief Ohio Div. Wildlife, Columbus, 1963-65; sr. exec. v.p. Ducks Unltd., Inc., Long Grove, Ill., 1965-

87; ret. Ducks Unltd., Inc., 1987; bd. dirs. Safari Club Internat. Conservation Found., Tucson, 1982-83. Served as 2d lt. USAAF, 1943-46. Fellow Ohio State U., 1950; recipient Conservation award Gulf Oil Co., 1985. Mem. Ohio Wildlife Mgmt. Assn. (pres.), Internat. Assn. Fish, Game and Conservation Commrs. Office: Ducks Unltd Inc 1 Waterfowl Way Memphis TN 38120-2350 *Natural resource conservation means wise use—anything more or less will be manifested in additional zoos, museums, junk yards and the bone yards of fertilizer plants.*

WHITESELL, JOHN EDWIN, motion picture company executive; b. DuBois, Pa., Feb. 23, 1938; s. Guy Roosevelt and Grace Ethlyn (Brisbin) W.; m. Amy H. Jacobs, June 12, 1960; 1 child, Scott Howard; m. Martha Kathlyn Hall, Sept. 3, 1975; m. Phyllis Doyle, May 8, 1993. B.A., Pa. State U., 1962. Asst. mgr. non-theatrical div. Columbia Pictures Corp., N.Y.C., 1963-66; with Warner Bros., Inc., 1966—; nat. sales mgr. non-theatrical div. Warner Bros., Inc., Burbank, Calif., 1968-75; v.p. Warner Bros., Inc., 1975-76; v.p. internat. sales adminstrn. Warner Bros. Internat. TV Distbn., 1976—; bd. dirs. Mastermedia Internat. Inc.; past bd. dirs. Found. Entertainment Programming in Higher Edn.; mem. self-study com. Nat. Entertainment Conf., 1974-75. Served with USNR, 1956-58. Recipient Outstanding Alumnus award Pa. State U. DuBois Campus, 1995, Founders award Nat. Entertainment Conf., 1975. Mem. Nat. Audio-Visual Assn. (motion picture coun. 1973-76, exec. com. film coun. 1969-76, ednl. materials producers coun. 1970-76), Acad. TV Arts and Scis., Nat. Assn. Media Educators (adv. com. 1973-76).

WHITESIDE, CAROL GORDON, state official, former mayor; b. Chgo., Dec. 15, 1942; d. Paul George and Helen Louise (Barre) G.; m. John Gregory Whiteside, Aug. 15, 1964; children: Brian Paul, Derek James. BA, U. Calif., Davis, 1964. Pers. mgr. Emporium Capwell Co., Santa Rosa, 1964-67; pers. asst. Levi Strauss & Co., San Francisco, 1967-69; project leader Interdatum, San Francisco, 1983-88; with City Coun. Modesto, 1983-87; mayor City of Modesto, 1987-91; asst. sec. for intergovtl. rels. The Resources Agy., State of Calif., Sacramento, 1991-93; dir. intergovtl. affairs Gov.'s Office, Sacramento, 1993—. Trustee Modesto City Schs., 1979-83; nat. pres. Rep. Mayors and Local Ofcls., 1990. Named Outstanding Woman of Yr. Women's Commn., Stanislaus County, Calif., 1988, Woman of Yr., 27th Assembly Dist., 1991; Toll fellow Coun. of State Govts., 1996. Republican. Lutheran. Office: Governor's Office 1400 10th St Sacramento CA 95814-5502

WHITESIDE, LOWELL STANLEY, seismologist; b. Trinidad, Colo., Jan. 7, 1946; s. Paul Edward and Carrie Belle (Burgess) W. BS, Hamline U., 1968; postgrad., Oswego State U. of N.Y., 1970-72; MS, U. Nebr., 1985; postgrad., Ga. Inst. of Tech., 1986-88, U. Colo., 1990-94. Instr. U.S. Peace Corps, Mhlume, Swaziland, 1968-71; rsch. assoc. CIRES, U. Colo., Boulder, 1988-90; geophysicist in charge of internat. earthquake data base NOAA, Nat. Geophys. Data Ctr., Boulder, 1990—; vis. rschr. Nuclear and Geol. Scis. Inst., Wellington, New Zealand, 1997. Scoutmaster Boy Scouts Am., St. Paul, Lincoln, Nebr., 1968-80, camp counselor, 1968-76. Recipient Eagle Scout award Boy Scouts Am., 1968, NGDC/DOAA Customer Svc. award, 1995. Mem. AAAS (chmn. 1986-87, vice chmn. 1985-86, Geology-Geography, Rocky Mountain sect., Outstanding Articles Referee 1992, Best Student Paper award 1984, 85), Seismol. Soc. of Am., Am. Geophys. Union, Sierra Club, Planetary Soc. Presbyterian. Avocations: hiking, camping, music, biking, running. Home: PO Box 3141 Eldorado Springs CO 80025-3141 Office: NOAA/NGDC/NESOIS 325 Broadway St Boulder CO 80303-3337

WHITESIDE, WILLIAM ANTHONY, JR., lawyer; b. Phila. Feb. 23, 1929; s. William Anthony and Ellen T. (Hensler) W.; m. Eileen Ann Ferrick, Feb. 27, 1954; children: William Anthony III, Michael P., Eileen A., Richard F., Christopher J., Mary P. BS Notre Dame U., 1951; LLB U. Pa., 1954. Bar: Pa. 1955. Assoc. Speiser, Satinsky, Gilliland & Packel, Phila., 1956-58, ptnr., 1958-61; ptnr. Fox, Rothschild, O'Brien & Frankel, Phila., 1961—. Served to 1st lt. USAF, 1954-56; chmn. bd. of trustees & chmn. exec. comm., Rochester Inst. Tech.; mem. pres. adv. coun. U. Notre Dame; bd. dirs. PAL, mem. exec. com.; emeritus trustee Germantown Acad (past pres.). Named Man of Yr., Notre Dame Club Phila., 1967. Mem. ABA, Pa. Bar Assn., Phila. Bar Assn., mem. Genesee Valley Club, Rochester, N.Y., Union League Club, Pyramid Club, Wissahickon Skating Club, Pa. Soc. (Phila.), Atlantic City (N.J.) Country Club. Republican. Roman Catholic. Home: 7808 Cobden Rd Laverock PA 19038 also: 901 Gardens Pkwy Ocean City NJ 08226-4719 Office: Fox Rothschild O'Brien 2000 Market St Ste 10 Philadelphia PA 19103-3201

WHITESIDES, GEORGE MCCLELLAND, chemistry educator; b. Louisville, Kty., Aug. 3, 1939; m. Barbara Breasted; children: George Thomas, Benjamin Haile. AB, Harvard U., 1960; PhD, Calif. Inst. Tech., 1964. Asst. prof. dept. chemistry MIT, Cambridge, 1963-69, assoc. prof., 1969-71, prof., 1971-75, Arthur C. Cope prof., 1975-80, Haslam and Dewey prof., 1980-82; prof. dept. chemistry Harvard U., Cambridge, 1982-86, Mallinckrodt prof., 1986—. Recipient Pure Chemistry award Am. Chem. Soc., 1975, Harrison Howe award Rochester sect., 1979, Arthur C. Cope award, 1995, James Flack Norris award, 1994, Remsen award, 1983, Arthur C. Cope scholar award, 1989, Disting. Alumni award Calif. Inst. Tech., 1980; Alfred P. Sloan fellow, 1968. Fellow AAAS; mem. NAS, Am. Acad. Arts and Scis. Office: Harvard U Dept of Chemistry 12 Oxford St Cambridge MA 02138-2902

WHITESIDES, JOHN LINDSEY, JR., aerospace engineering educator, researcher; b. San Antonio, Feb. 27, 1943; s. John Lindsey and Florene Lyndelle (Wheelis) W.; m. Sheila LaVerne Beadle, May 30, 1964 (div. 1975); children: Lisa Diane, John Gregory; m. Andrea Martina Chavez Lewis, Mar. 26, 1994. BS in Aerospace Engring., U. Tex., 1965, PhD, 1968. Asst. prof. George Washington U., Hampton, Va., 1968-74, assoc. prof., 1974-80, prof., 1980—; assoc. dir. Joint Inst. for Advancement of Flight Scis., Hampton, 1986—. Contbr. articles to profl. jours. Mem. Simga Series Lectures, Hampton, 1990—. Recipient disting. pub. svc. medal NASA, 1993, Malina medal Internat. Astronautical Fedn., 1995. Mem. AIAA (assoc. fellow, dir. 1987-93, nat. faculty advisor 1989), Am. Soc. Engring. Edn., Soc. Engring. Sci. (organizing com. 1975, 76, 77), Tau Beta Pi, Phi Eta Sigma, Sigma Gamma Tau. Avocations: sports, art. Home: 218 Cheadle Loop Rd Seaford VA 23696 Office: George Washington U-JIAFS Ms 269 Nasa Lrc Hampton VA 23665

WHITE-THOMSON, IAN LEONARD, mining company executive; b. Halstead, Eng., May 3, 1936; came to U.S., 1969; s. Walter Norman and Leonore (Turney) W-T.; m. Barbara Montgomery, Nov. 24, 1971. B.A. with 1st class honors, New Coll., Oxford U., 1960, M.A., 1969. Mgmt. trainee Borax Consol. Ltd., London, 1960-61; asst. to sales mgr. Borax Consol. Ltd., 1961-64, asst. to sales dir., 1964; comml. dir. Hardman & Holden Ltd., Manchester, Eng., 1965-67; joint mng. dir. Hardman & Holden Ltd., 1967-69; v.p. mktg. dept. U.S. Borax Inc., Los Angeles, 1969-73; exec. v.p. mktg. U.S. Borax Inc., 1973-88, pres., 1988—, also dir., chmn., 1996—; group exec. Pa. Glass Sand Corp., Ottawa Silica Co., U.S. Silica Co., 1985-87; bd. dirs. Canpotex Ltd., chmn. bd., 1974-76; bd. dirs. KCET. Served with Brit. Army, 1954-56. Mem. Can. POtash Prodrs. Assn. (v.p. 1976-77, dir. 1972-77), Chem. Industry Coun. of Calif. (bd. dirs. 1982-85, chmn. 1984), Am. Mining Congress (bd. dirs. 1989), RTZ Borax and Minerals (bd. dirs. 1992, chief exec. 1995—), Oryx Energy Co. (bd. dirs. 1993), Calif. Club, Annandale Golf Club. Home: 851 Lyndon St South Pasadena CA 91030-3712

WHITFIELD, EDWARD (WAYNE WHITFIELD), congressman; b. Hopkinsville, Ky., May 25, 1943; m. Constance Harriman; 1 child, Kate. BS in Bus., U. Ky., 1965, JD, 1969. Mem. Ky. Ho. of Reps., 1974-75; pvt. practice law, 1970-79; govt. affairs counsel Seaboard Sys. R.R. subs. CSX Corp., 1979-83, counsel to pres., 1983-85; v.p. state rels. CSX Corp., 1986-88, v.p. fed. r.r. affairs, 1988-91; legal counsel to chmn. Interstate Commerce Commn., 1991-93; mem. 104th Congress from 1st Ky. dist., 1995—. 1st lt. USAR. Republican. Office: US Ho of Reps 236 Cannon Bldg Washington DC 20515-1701

WHITFORD, DENNIS JAMES, naval officer, meteorologist, oceanographer; b. York, Pa., Nov. 21, 1950; s. Richmond Ordway and Kathryn W.; m. Dorothy Lee Bundy, Aug. 7, 1976; children: Scott, Bradley. BS, U.S. Naval Acad., 1972; MS, Naval Postgrad. Sch., 1979, PhD, 1988. Commd. ensign USN, 1972, advanced through grades to capt., 1994; officer-in-chg., staff oceanographer Naval Oceanography Cmd Detachment, Moffett Field, Calif., 1982-84; comdg. officer Oceanographic Unit Four aboard USNS Chauvenet, 1985; dir. numerical models dept. Fleet Numerical Oceanography Ctr., Monterey, Calif., 1988-89; comdg. officer Naval Oceanography Command Facility, San Diego, 1989-91; dir. Operational Oceanography Ctr., Stennis Space Ctr., Miss., 1991-93; exec. officer Naval Oceanographic Office, Stennis Space Ctr., Miss., 1993-95; chmn. dept. oceanography U.S. Naval Acad., Annapolis, Md., 1995—; Contbr. articles to profl. jours. Named to Outstanding Young Men of Am., 1982; Adam Burke PhD fellow, 1972. Mem. Am. Geophys. Union, Sigma Xi. Office: US Naval Academy 572 Holloway Rd Annapolis MD 21402-1314

WHITFORD, JOSEPH P., lawyer; b. N.Y.C., Apr. 30, 1950. BA, Union Coll., 1972; JD, Syracuse U., 1975; LLM in Taxation, George Washington U., 1978. Bar: N.Y. 1976, D.C. 1977, Wash. 1979. Staff atty. divsn. corp. fin. SEC, Washington, 1975-78; assoc. Foster, Pepper & Shefelman, Seattle, 1978-83, ptnr., 1983—; chmn. bd. dirs. MIT Forum on the Northwest, 1992-93. Office: Foster Pepper & Shefelman 1111 3rd Ave Fl 34 Seattle WA 98101-3207

WHITHAM, GERALD BERESFORD, mathematics educator; b. Halifax, Eng., Dec. 13, 1927; came to U.S., 1956; s. Harry and Elizabeth (Howarth) W.; m. Nancy Lord, Sept. 1, 1951; children—Ruth H., Michael G., Susan C. BS, Manchester U., Eng., 1948, MS, 1949, PhD, 1953. Lectr. Manchester U., 1953-56; assoc. prof. NYU, N.Y.C., 1956-59; prof. math. MIT, Cambridge, 1959-62; prof. aeros. and math. Calif. Inst. Tech., Pasadena, 1962-67, prof. applied math., 1967-83, Charles Lee Powell prof. applied math., 1983—. Author: Linear and Nonlinear Waves, 1974; also research papers on applied math. and fluid dynamics. Recipient Wiener prize in applied math., 1980. Fellow Royal Soc., Am. Acad. Arts and Scis. Home: 1689 E Altadena Dr Altadena CA 91001-1855 Office: Calif Inst Tech Applied Math 217-50 Pasadena CA 91125

WHITHAM, KENNETH, science and technology consultant; b. Chesterfield, Derbyshire, Eng., Nov. 6, 1927; emigrated to Can., 1948; s. Joseph and Evelyn (Murphy) W.; m. Joan Dorothy Glasspool, Nov., 1953; children—Melanie Judith, Katherine Hilary, Stephanie Frances. B.A. with honors, Cambridge U., Eng., 1948, M.A., 1952; M.A., Toronto U., 1949, Ph.D., 1951. Research scientist Dominion Observatory, Ottawa, Ont., 1951-59, 60-64; mem. UN Tech. Assistance Adminstrn., Nairobi, Kenya, 1959-60; dir. div. seismology and geothermal studies Earth Physics Br., Dept. Energy, Mines and Resources, Ottawa, 1964-73, dir. gen., 1973-80, asst. dep. minister conservation and non-petroleum energy, 1980-81, asst. dep. minister research and tech., 1981-87, chief sci. advisor, 1987; cons. in sci. and tech. Ottawa, 1987—. Contbr. articles to profl. jours. Recipient Outstanding Achievement award Public Service of Can., 1970. Fellow Royal Soc. Can. Anglican. Home and Office: 1367 Morley Blvd, Ottawa, ON Canada K2C 1R4

WHITING, ALBERT NATHANIEL, former university chancellor; b. Jersey City, July 3, 1917; s. Hezekiah Oliver and Hildegarde Freida (Lyons) W.; m. Charlotte Luck, June 10, 1950; 1 dau., Brooke Elizabeth. A.B., Amherst Coll., 1938; student, Columbia, summer 1938, U. Pitts., 1938-39; M.A. in Sociology, Fisk U., 1941, L.H.D. (hon.), 1980; Ph.D. in Sociology, Am. U., 1952; LL.D., Amherst Coll., 1968, Western Mich. U., 1974, Duke, 1974, Kyung Hee U., Seoul, Korea; L.H.D., N.C. Central U., 1983. Research and teaching asst. Fisk U., 1939-41; instr. sociology, dir. rural community study Bennett Coll., Greensboro, N.C., 1941-43, 46-47; asst. prof. sociology Atlanta U., 1948-53; dean coll., prof. sociology Morris Brown Coll., Atlanta, 1953-57; asst. dean coll. Morgan State Coll., Balt., 1957-59; dean of college Morgan State Coll., 1960-67; pres. N.C. Central U., Durham, 1967-72; chancellor N.C. Central U., 1972-83; mem. bd. regents U. Md. Sys., 1988-95. Contbr. articles profl. jours. Bd. dirs. Am. Coun. Edn., Ednl. Testing Svc.; bd. dirs., past pres. Assn. State Colls. and Univs.; v.p. Internat. Assn. Univ. Pres.; bd. dirs. Research Triangle (N.C.) Inst.; mem. Md. Higher Edn. Commn., 1995—. 1st lt. AUS, 1943-46. Episcopalian. Home: 11253B Slalom Ln Columbia MD 21044-2810

WHITING, ALLEN SUESS, political science educator, writer, consultant; b. Perth Amboy, N.J., Oct. 27, 1926; s. Leo Robert and Viola Allen (Suess) W.; m. Alice Marie Conroy, May 29, 1950; children: Deborah Jean, David Neal, Jeffrey Michael, Jennifer Hollister. B.A., Cornell U., 1948; M.A., Columbia U., 1950, cert. Russian Inst., 1950, Ph.D., 1952. Instr. polit. sci. Northwestern U., 1951-53; asst. prof. Mich. State U., East Lansing, 1955-57; social scientist The Rand Corp., Santa Monica, Calif., 1957-61; dir. Office Research and Analysis Far East U.S. Dept. State, Washington, 1962-66; dep. consul gen. Am. Consulate Gen., Hong Kong, 1966-68; prof. polit. sci. U. Mich., Ann Arbor, 1968-82; prof. U. Ariz., Tucson, 1982-93, Regents prof., 1993—, dir. Ctr. for East Asian Studies, 1982-93; cons. U.S. Dept. State, 1968-88; dir. Nat. Com. on U.S.-China Relations, N.Y.C., 1977-94; assoc. The China Council, 1978-88; pres. So. Ariz. China Coun., Tucson, 1983-95; fellow Woodrow Wilson Ctr., Washington, 1995-96. Author: Soviet Policies in China: 1917-1924, 1954, China Crosses the Yalu, 1968, Chinese Calculus of Deterrence, 1975, Siberian Development and East Asia, 1981, China Eyes Japan, 1989, others; contbr. articles to profl. jours.; spl. commentator McNeill-Lehrer Program; CBS and NBC Spls. on China. Served with U.S. Army, 1945. Social Sci. Rsch. Coun. fellow, 1950, 74-75; Ford Found. fellow, 1953-55; Rockefeller Found. fellow, 1978; Woodrow Wilson Ctr. fellow, 1995-96. Mem. Assn. Asian Studies. Home: 125 E Canyon View Dr Tucson AZ 85704-5901 Office: U Ariz Dept Polit Sci Tucson AZ 85721

WHITING, HENRY H., state supreme court justice. LLB, Univ. Va., 1949. Former judge 26th Jud. Cir. of Va.; sr. justice Va. Supreme Ct., Richmond, 1987—. Office: Va Supreme Ct 100 N 9th St Richmond VA 23219-2335*

WHITING, RICHARD ALBERT, lawyer; b. Cambridge, Mass., Dec. 2, 1922; s. Albert S. and Jessie (Coleman) W.; m. Marvelene Nash, Feb. 22, 1948 (div. 1984); children—Richard A. Jr., Stephen C., Jeffrey D., Gary S., Kimberly G.; m. Joanne Sherry, Oct. 14, 1984. A.B., Dartmouth Coll., 1944; J.D., Yale U., 1949. Bar: D.C. 1949. Assoc. Steptoe & Johnson, Washington, 1949-55, ptnr., 1956-86, of counsel, 1987—; adj. prof. Vt. Law Sch., South Royalton, 1985-90; mem. exec. com. Yale Law Sch. Assn., New Haven, 1985-88; mem. adv. bd. The Antitrust Bull., N.Y.C., 1975—. Contbr. articles to profl. jours. Trustee Colby-Sawyer Coll., 1987—. Served to 1st lt. U.S. Army, 1945-46. Mem. ABA (council mem. Antitrust Law sect. 1977-85, del. to Ho. Dels. 1982-83, chmn. 1984-85). Presbyterian. Home: PO Box 749 Grantham NH 03753-0749 Office: 1330 Connecticut Ave NW Washington DC 20036-1704

WHITING, STEPHEN CLYDE, lawyer; b. Arlington, Va., Mar. 20, 1952; s. Richard A. Whiting; m. Patrice Quinn, May 24, 1980; children: Kelsey, Daniel, Seth, Samuel. BA magna cum laude, Dartmouth Coll., 1974; JD, U. Va., 1978. Bar: Maine 1978, U.S. Dist. Ct. Maine 1978. Ptnr. Douglas, Whiting, Denham & Rogers, Portland, Maine, 1978—. Co-author: Trying the Automobile Injury Case in Maine, 1993, Premises Liability: Preparation and Trial of a Difficult Case in Maine, 1994, Trying Soft Tissue Injury Cases in Maine, 1995. Mem. ATLA, Maine Bar Assn., Maine Trial Lawyers Assn., Phi Beta Kappa. Office: Douglas Whiting Denham & Rogers 103 Exchange St Portland ME 04101-5001

WHITIS, GRACE RUTH, nursing educator; b. San Antonio, Sept. 14, 1942; d. Allan and Jewel (Conlee) Richardson; m. Robert E. Whitis, Mar. 6, 1965; children: Jay, Jennifer. PhD, U. Tex., 1981; BS, U. Mary Hardin - Baylor, 1968; MS, Baylor U., 1970; MS in Nursing, U. Tex., 1972. Staff nurse Providence Hosp., Waco, Tex., 1965-67; faculty U. Mary Hardin-Baylor, Belton, Tex., 1970-79, prof., dean, 1979-83; prof. nursing Ark. State U., Jonesboro, 1993—, chmn. dept., 1985-93; vis. prof. La. Tech. U., Ruston, 1982-84. Contbr. articles to profl. jours. Mem. ANA, Nat. League for Nursing, Ark. Nurses Assn., Soc. Pediatric Nurses, Sigma Theta Tau. Home: 2403 Paula Dr Jonesboro AR 72404 Office: Ark State U PO Box 69 State University AR 72467-0069

WHITKO, JEAN PHILLIPS, academic administrator; b. Dover, Del., Oct. 31, 1940; d. Albert Leroy and Helen (Busch) Phillips; m. Donald A. Whitko, July 1, 1972; children: Lenore Ann, Wayne P., Donna J., Sheri L. BS, U. Del., 1962; MEd, Pa. State U., 1968, postgrad., 1968-72. Cert. tchr., Del., Pa. Tchr. Newcastle (Del.) Spl. Sch. Dist., 1962-68; rsch. asst. Pa. State U., University Park, 1969, instr. edn., grad. asst., 1969-72; substitute tchr. Jerusalem Lutheran Nursery Sch. and Day Care, Schwenksville, Pa., 1983-85; supr. student teaching Pa. State U., 1988—; evaluator fed. title I and III projects Pa. Dept. Edn., Harrisburg, 1970-72. Officer Women's Civ. Club Schwenksville, 1972—; vol. tchr. Perkiomen Valley Schs., Schwenksville, 1976-86; bd. dirs. Jerusalem Lutheran Nursery Sch. and Day Care, 1983-85. Named Friend of Edn., Perkiomen Valley Edn. Assn., 1983; recipient Commendation from Gov. Richard Thornburg, 1985. Mem. ASCD, Pa. Assn. Colls. and Tchr. Educators. Avocations: reading, photography. Home: 623 Main St Schwenksville PA 19473-1012 Office: Pa State Univ 182 Chambers Bldg University Park PA 16802-3205

WHITLEY, ARTHUR FRANCIS, retired international consulting company executive, engineer, lawyer; b. Bklyn., Apr. 14, 1927; s. John Boyd and Ellen (Walls) W.; m. Isabella Mary Passidomo, Apr. 9, 1950; children: Brent John, Scott Michael, Todd Joseph. B.E.E., Poly. Inst. N.Y., 1951; J.D., Seton Hall U., 1955; LL.M., Bklyn. Law Sch., 1958. Bar: N.J. 1960, U.S. Customs Ct. 1967, U.S. Patent Office 1972. Sales engr., atty. Pub. Service E&G, Newark, 1951-60; mgmt. cons. Nelson Walker Assocs., N.Y.C., 1961; atty. assoc. gen. counsel Engelhard Industries, Iselin, N.J., 1962-75, v.p., group v.p., 1976-80, sr. v.p., 1981, exec. v.p., 1982-83; pres. Bro-Whit Assocs. Inc., 1983-89. Pres. World Trade Assn. N.J., 1965. Served with USN, 1945-46. Republican. Roman Catholic. Home: 24 Puddingstone Way Florham Park NJ 07932-2625

WHITLEY, DAVID SCOTT, archaeologist; b. Williams AFB, Ariz., Mar. 5, 1953; s. Edgar Duer and Yvonne Roca (Wightman) W.; m. Tamara Katherine Koteles, Feb. 13, 1987; 1 child, Carmen. AB in Anthrop. & Geog. (magna cum laude), U. Calif., 1976, MA in Geography, 1979, PhD in Anthropology, 1982. Soc. Profl. Archeology. Chief archeologist Inst. Archeology UCLA, L.A., 1983-87; rsch. fellow Archeology Dept. U. Witwatersrand, Johannesburg, S. Africa, 1987-89; pres. W&S Cons., Simi Valley, Calif., 1989—; U.S. rep. internat. com. rock art Internat. Coun. Monuments and Sites, 1992—, exec. com., 1997-99. Author: A Guide to Rock Art Sites: Southern California and Southern Nevada, 1996, L'Art des chamanes: art rupestre en Californie, 1997; editor: archeological monographs; contbr. articles to profl. jours. Prehistoric Archeologist, State of Calif. Hist. Resources Commn., 1986-87; mem. rsch. adv. com. Chauvet Cave, France, 1996—. Recipient post doctoral fellowship, Assn. for Field Archeology, 1983, tech. specialist grant, U.S. Aid, 1986. Fellow Am. Anthrop. Assn.; mem. Soc. Am. Archeology, SAR, Sons of the Indian Wars, Mayflower Soc. Home: 447 3rd St Fillmore CA 93015-1413 Office: W&S Consultants 2422 Stinson St Simi Valley CA 93065

WHITLEY, JOE DALLY, lawyer; b. Atlanta, Nov. 12, 1950; s. Thomas Youngie and Mary Jo (Dally) W.; m. Kathleen Pinion, Sept. 27, 1975; children: Lauren Jacqueline, Thomas McMillan. BA, U. Ga., 1972, JD, 1975. Bar: Ga. 1975, U.S. Supreme Ct. 1989. Assoc. Kelly, Denney, Pease & Allison, Columbus, Ga., 1975-78; asst. dist. atty. Chattahoochee Jud. Cir., Columbus, 1978-79; assoc. Hirsch, Beil & Partin, P.C., Columbus, 1979-81; U.S. atty. Dept. Justice, Macon, Ga., 1981-87; dep. asst. atty. gen., Criminal Div. Dept. Justice, Washington, 1987-88, dep. assoc. atty. gen., 1988-89, acting assoc. atty. gen., 1989; ptnr. Smith, Gambrell & Russell, Atlanta, 1989-90; U.S. atty. Dept. of Justice, Atlanta, 1990-93; ptnr. Kilpatrick Stockton, Atlanta, 1993-97, Alston & Bird, Atlanta, 1997—; mem. atty. gen.'s adv. com. Dept. Justice, Washington, 1982-85; chmn. organized crime and violent crime subcom. Atty. Gen.'s Adv. Com., 1990-93, mem. investigative subcom., 1990-93, chmn. white collar crime subcom., 1993. Treas. Muscogee County Young Reps., Columbus, 1979-80. Mem. Ga. Bar Assn., Macon Bar Assn., Young Lawyers Club (pres. Columbus chpt. 1980-81), Lawyers Club of Atlanta. Republican. Presbyterian. Office: Alston & Bird 1201 W Peachtree St Atlanta GA 30309-3424

WHITLEY, NANCY O'NEIL, retired radiology educator; b. Winston-Salem, N.C., Feb. 21, 1932; d. Norris Lawrence and Thelma Mae (Hardy) O'Neil; m. J.E. Whitley, Dec. 20, 1958; children—John O'Neil, Catherine Anne. Student, Duke U., 1950-53; M.D., Bowman Gray Sch. Medicine, 1957. Fellow in cardiology Bowman Gray Sch. Medicine, Winston-Salem, 1958-60; intern Jefferson Davis Hosp., Houston, 1957-58; resident in radiology Bowman Gray Sch. Medicine, 1966-69, instr., 1969-70, asst. prof., 1970-74, assoc. prof., 1974-78; prof. radiology U. Md. Sch. Medicine, Balt., 1978-92; prof. oncology U. Md. Cancer Ctr., Balt., 1988-92; prof. radiology Med. U. S.C., Charleston, 1992-94; ret., 1994. Author: (with J.E. Whitley) Angiopgraphy, Techniques and Procedures, 1971.

WHITLOCK, BENNETT CLARKE, JR., retired association executive; b. Charleston, S.C., June 10, 1927; s. Bennett C. and Isabel Price (Beckman) W.; m. Elizabeth Darley Marshall, July 18, 1959; children: Mary Elizabeth, Bennett C. III. A.B., Presbyn. Coll., 1946; LL.B., U. S.C., 1949. With Am. Trucking Assns., Inc., Washington, 1949-89, asst. to mng. dir., 1961-70, asst. to pres., 1970-73, v.p., 1973-75, exec. v.p., chief oper. officer, 1975-76, pres., 1976-84, spl. adviser, pres., 1984-89; ret., 1989. Bd. dirs Braddock Road Boys Club; bd. visitors Mary Washington Coll., 1985-93, vice rector, 1986-88, rector, 1990-92. Mem. Hwy. Users Fedn. for Safety and Mobility (dir.), Country Club of Fairfax, Kiawah Island Club, Blue Key, Pi Kappa Alpha. Episcopalian.

WHITLOCK, CHARLES PRESTON, former university dean; b. Highland Park, N.J., June 19, 1919; s. Frank Boudinot and Rosena Craig (Foster) W.; m. Patricia Hamilton Hoey, Mar. 10, 1960; children: Carol Foster, Adam Hoey, Susan Boudinot, Matthew Fitzsimmons, Beth Brewer. BA, Rutgers U., 1941; MA, Harvard U., 1947. Asso. dir. Bur. Study Counsel Harvard U., 1948-52, Allston Burr sr. tutor, 1952-58, lectr. social psychology, 1955-72, asst. to pres., 1958-70, assoc. dean of coll., 1970-72, dean of coll., 1972-76, asso. dean faculty, 1976-82, master Dudley House, 1976-82; Dir. Cambridgeport Savs. Bank.; Mem. Mass. Higher Edn. Facilities Commn. Co-author: Harvard University Reading Films. Trustee Charity of Edward Hopkins, Lesley Coll.; bd. corporators New Eng. Deaconess Hosp. Col. USAF. Decorated Silver Star, D.F.C., Air medal. Home: 9 Barberry Heights Rd Gloucester MA 01930-1201 Office: Harvard U Cambridge MA 02138

WHITLOCK, DAVID C., retired military officer; b. Little Rock, Ark., Jan. 24, 1935; m. Rosemarie Binik (dec.); children: D. Patrick, David D. B Bus., U. Nebr., 1962; grad., Squadron Officer Sch., 1965; MA Speech and Drama, U. Colo., 1966, PhD Communication, 1970; grad., Air Command and Staff Coll., 1978, Air War Coll., 1983. With USAF, 1952-62, tech. sgt., 1962; audiovisual tng. officer, 2d lt., 1st lt. Hdqs. N. Am. Air Defense Command USAF, Colo., 1962-67; from English, speech intr., asst., dir. forensics, capt. to prof., major USAF Acad., 1967-74, prof. English, Speech, dir. Forensics, lt. col., 1979, pres. Tenure Coun., 1981-82; dir. Disting. Visitors Bureau Hdqs. USAF, Ramstein AFB, Germany, 1982-84; assoc. dean Civilian Inst. programs, col. AF Inst. Tech., Ohio, 1984-86; base comdr. 26th Combat Support Group Zweibrucken AFB, Germany, 1986-88; dean Civilian Inst. Programs Wright Patterson AFB, Ohio, 1989, commandant emeritus AF Inst. Tech. Air U., 1992-93. Recipient Legion of Merit, Meritorious Svc. medal with four oak leaf clusters, Air Force Commendation medal with two oak leaf clusters. Achievements include qualified parachutist. Home: 441 Green Vista Dr Enon OH 45323-1340 Office: Air Force Institute of Tech Dayton OH 45433

WHITLOCK, JOHN JOSEPH, museum director; b. South Bend, Ind., Jan. 7, 1935; s. Joseph Mark and Helen Marcella (Cramer) W.; m. Sue Ann Kirkman, June 10, 1956; children—Kelly Ann, Michele Lynn, Mark. BS in Art, Ball State U., 1957, MA in Art, 1963; EdD, Ind. U., 1971. Tchr. art Union City (Ind.) Pub. Schs., 1957-59; tchr. art, art dir. Madison (Ind.) City Schs., 1959-64; prof. art, dir. gallery Hanover (Ind.) Coll., 1964-69; dir. Burpee Art Mus., Rockford, Ill., 1970-72; prof. arts and humanities Elgin (Ill.) Community Coll., 1970-72; dir. Brooks Meml. Art Gallery, Memphis, 1972-78; prof. mus. studies Southwestern Coll., Memphis, 1973-78; adj. asst. prof. art and museology Memphis State U., 1976-78; dir. Univ. Mus., mem.

grad. faculty So. Ill. U., Carbondale, 1978—, also dir. mus. studies, adj. assoc. prof. anthropology, 1978—, adj. assoc. prof. polit. sci., 1988—, adj. assoc. prof. history, 1994—, dir. mus. studies, 1989—, mem. ROTC acad. avc. coun., 1988—, mem. president's coun., 1988-93, adj. assoc. prof. art Univ. Mus., 1978-88; chmn. bd. Nat. Coal Mus., 1983-85; mem. Newsfront adv. bd. NC Broadcast News, Washington, 1982-85; sr. cons. Marine Mil. Acad. Mus., 1988—, mem. bd. advisors, 1991-97. Mem. Rockford Human Rels. Commn., 1971-72; mem. president's coun. Southwestern Coll., 1973-78. Mem. Am. Assn. Mus., Internat. Coun. Mus., Midwest Assn. Mus., Assn. Art Mus. Dirs., Marine Corps League (commandant Shawnee detachment 1994-96, comdr. USCG Aux. 1994-95), Dept. Ill. Marine Corps League (trustee rank and file 1994—), Semper Fi Soc. (faculty adviser So. Ill. U. 1995—). Office: So Ill U Univ Mus Carbondale IL 62901-4508

WHITLOCK, JOHN L., lawyer; b. New Orleans, Oct. 24, 1946; s. John Bert and Virginia Katherine (Marzolf) W.; m. Dorothy Florence Oeste, Sept. 13, 1969; children: Sarah Katherine, Thomas John. AB, Harvard U., 1968, JD, 1973. Bar: Mass. 1973, U.S. Dist. Ct. Mass. 1974, U.S. Ct. Appeals (1st cir.) 1975. Assoc. Herrick & Smith, Boston, 1973-80, ptnr., 1981-86; ptnr. Palmer & Dodge, Boston, 1986—. Bd. dirs., sec. Harvard-Radcliffe Collegiate Mus. Found., Inc., 1978—; treas. The Cecilia Soc., 1974-85, bd. dirs., 1974-86, 94—, pres., 1994—. With U.S. Army, 1968-70. Mem. Boston Bar Assn. (coun. 1996—). Lutheran. Avocation: singing. Office: Palmer & Dodge 1 Beacon St Boston MA 02108-3107

WHITLOCK, LUDER GRADICK, JR., seminary president; b. Jacksonville, Fla., June 20, 1940; s. Luder G. and Juanita O. (Nessmith) W.; m. Mary Louise Patton, Aug. 29, 1959; children: Frank Christopher, Alissa Ann, Beth LaVerne. BA, U. Fla., 1962; MDiv, Westminster Theol. Sem., 1966; D of Ministry, Vanderbilt U., 1973. Ordained to ministry Presbyn. Ch. in Am., 1966. Pastor Sharon Presbyn. Ch., Hialeah, Fla., 1966-69, West Hills Presbyn. Ch., Harriman, Tenn., 1969-75; prof. Reformed Theol. Sem., Jackson, Miss., 1975—, acting pres., 1978-79, pres., 1979—; bd. dirs. Barna Inst. Editorial adv. bd. Leadership, Wheaton, 1992—. Trustee Westminster Theol. Sem., Phila., 1973-76, Covenant Coll., Chattanooga, 1973-80; bd. dirs. Internat. Grad. Sch. Theology, Seoul, Republic of Korea, 1985-96, Ligonier Ministries, 1988-96; dir. Greater Orlando Leadership Found., 1989-92, Found. for Reformation, Orlando, Fla., 1990—, Key Life, 1995—, World Evang. Fellowship N.Am. Region, Wheaton, Ill., 1992-96, Internat. Christian Leadership Univ., Campus Crusade for Christ, exec. com., 1992—, Internat. Reformed Fellowship, co-pres., 1993—. Mem. Evang. Theo. Soc., Nat. Assn. Evangs. (bd. administrn. 1992—, dir. 1995, chmn. theology com. 1994—, nat. commn. higher edn. 1995—), Asns. Theol. Schs. (chair nominating com. 1995, exec. com. 1994—, v.p. 1995—), Fellowship of Evang. Sem. Pres. (chmn. 1990-93, 94-96), Citrus Club. Republican. Office: Reformed Theol Sem 1015 Maitland Center Common Bl Maitland FL 32751-7130

WHITLOCK, WILLIAM ABEL, retired lawyer; b. Faribault, Minn., Feb. 6, 1929; s. William Abel and Alice Eleanor (Bartel) W.; m. Shirley Rae Olhausen; children: Anne, William, Justin, Jane, Thomas. BSL, U. Minn., 1951, LLB, 1953. Law clk. to justice Minn. Supreme Ct., St. Paul, 1952-53; law clk. to presiding justice U.S. Dist. Ct. Minn., 1953-54; assoc. Dorsey & Whitney, Mpls., 1957-62, ptnr., 1962-95, of counsel, 1995—. Served to capt. USAR, 1954-57. Mem. Order of the Coif.

WHITLOW, JAMES ADAMS, lawyer; b. Mayfield, Ky., Jan. 29, 1968; s. Charles William and June (Hawkens) W. BA, Transylvania U., 1990; JD, Harvard U., 1993. Bar: N.C. 1994. Assoc. Parker Poe Adams & Bernstein, L.L.P., Charlotte, N.C., 1993-95, Akin, Gump, Strauss, Hauer & Feld, L.L.P., Dallas, 1995-97, Rubin, Baum, Levin, Constant, Friedman & Bilzin, Miami, 1997—. Office: Rubin Baum Levin Constant Friedman & Bilzin Friedman & Bilzon 2500 First Union Fin Ctr Miami FL 33131

WHITMAN, ALAN MORRIS, mechanical engineering educator; b. Phila., Jan. 26, 1937; s. Irwin Morris and Sybil (Garfinkel) W.; m. Matilda Sbar, June 21, 1959 (div. Mar. 1978); children: Karen Lynn Whitman Berman, Phyllis Ruth; m. Rachel Ariella Bregman, May 25, 1978; children:Noam Hillel, Roy Zipstein. BSME, U. Pa., 1958, MSME, 1959, PhD, 1965. Mech. engr. Air Proving Ground Ctr., Eglin AFB, Fla., 1959-62; sr. rsch. engr. power transmission divsn. GE Co., Phila., 1965-67; asst. prof. mech. engring U. Pa., Phila., 1967-72, assoc. prof. mech. engring, 1972-80; assoc. prof. interdisciplinary studies and mechanics Tel Aviv U., 1980-83, prof. interdisciplinary studies and mechanics, 1983-88, chmn. dept. interdisciplinary studies, 1986-88; prof., chmn. mech. engring Villanova (Pa.) U., 1988—; vis. prof. Tel Aviv U., 1975-76, 78-79, Villanova U., 1984-85. Contbr. articles to profl. publs. Fellow Optical Soc. Am.; mem. ASME, Am. Soc. Engring. Edn., Sigma Xi, Tau Beta Pi, Sigma Tau. Office: Villanova U Dept Mech Engring Villanova PA 19010

WHITMAN, CHRISTINE TODD, governor; b. Sept. 26, 1946; d. Webster Bray and Eleanor Schley Todd; m. John Whitman, 1974; children: Kate, Taylor. BA in Govt., Wheaton Coll., 1968. Former freeholder Somerset County, N.J.; former pres. State Bd. Pub. Utilities; host radio talk show Sta. WKXW, Trenton, N.J.; gov. State of N.J., 1994—; chmn. Com. for an Affordable N.J. Columnist newspapers. Bd. freeholders Somerset County, N.J., 1982-87; bd. pub. utilities, 1988-89; Rep. candidate for senator State of N.J., 1990. First female governor in N.J.; delivered Republican response to President Clinton's 1995 State of the Union address. Office: State House CN 001 Office of Governor Trenton NJ 08625-0001*

WHITMAN, DALE ALAN, lawyer, university professor; b. Charleston, W.Va., Feb. 18, 1939; m. Marjorie Miller; 8 children. Student, Ohio State U., 1956-59; BES, Brigham Young U., 1963; LLB, Duke U., 1966. Bar: Calif. 1967, Utah 1974. Assoc. O'Melveny & Myers, Los Angeles, 1966-67; asst. prof., then assoc. prof. Sch. Law, U. N.C., Chapel Hill, 1967-70; vis. prof. law N.C. Cen. U., Durham, 1968, 69; vis. assoc. prof. law UCLA, 1970-71; dep. dir. Office Housing and Urban Affairs, Fed. Home Loan Bank Bd., Washington, 1971-72; sr. program analyst FHA, HUD, Washington, 1972-73; prof. law Brigham Young U., 1973-78, 92—; vis. prof. law U. Tulsa, 1976, U. Mo., Columbia, 1976; prof. law, assoc. dean U. Wash., Seattle, 1978-82; prof., dean U. Mo. Sch. Law, Columbia, 1982-88, prof., 1988-91; cons., lectr. in field. Co-author: Cases and Materials on Real Estate Finance and Development, 1976, Real Estate Finance Law, 1979, 3d edit., 1994, Cases and Materials on Real Estate Transfer, Finance and Development, 1981, 3d edit., 1992, Land Transactions and Finance, 1983, 3d edit., 1997, The Law of Property, 1984, 2d edit., 1993, Basic Property, 1996; contbr. articles to profl. jours. Fellow Am. Bar Found.; mem. Am. Law Inst., Am. Coll. Real Estate Lawyers. Home: 480 E 450 S Orem UT 84058-6449 Office: BYU Law Sch Provo UT 84602

WHITMAN, HOMER WILLIAM, JR., investment counseling company executive; b. Sarasota, Fla., Jan. 8, 1932; s. Homer William and Phoebe (Corr) W.; m. Anne Virginia Sarran, May 8, 1954; children: Burke William, Michael Wayne. BA in Econs. optime merens, U. South, 1953; grad., U.S. Naval Officer Candidate Sch., 1953; postgrad., Emory U., 1969. Served to group v.p. 1st Nat. Bank Atlanta, 1956-72; pres., dir. Palmer 1st Nat. Bank & Trust Co., Sarasota, 1973-74, Hamilton Bank & Trust Co., Atlanta, 1974-76; v.p. Lionel D. Edie & Co., Atlanta, 1976-78, Mfrs. Hanover Trust Co., Atlanta, 1978-85; sr. v.p. Montag & Caldwell, Inc., Atlanta, 1985—. Dir. Asolo State Theatre. Trustee Selby Found., 1973-74, West Paces Ferry Hosp., Ringling Sch. Art, St. Stephens's Sch.; bd. vis. Emory U.; mem. Leadership Atlanta. Lt. j.g. USNR, 1953-56. Named Hon. French Consul, Atlanta, Atlanta's Outstanding Young Man of Yr., 1963. Mem. Govt. Fin. Officer's Assn., Gla. Govt. Fin. Officers Assn., Ga. Govt. Fin. Officers Assn., Assn. Investment Mgmt. Sales Execs., Atlanta Soc. Fin. Analysts, Healthcare Fin. Mgmt. Assn., Fla. Pub. Pension Trustees Assn., Assn. Pvt. Pension and Welfare Plans (regional chmn.), Am. Cancer Soc. (dir. Atlanta city unit), Newcomen Soc., 300 Club, Atlanta C. of C. (life mem.), Piedmont Driving Club, Peachtree Golf Club, Commerce Club, Buckhead Club (bd. govs.), Union League Club (N.Y.), Breakfast Club, Sarasota U. Club (bd. dirs.), Rotary. Episcopalian. Home: 77 E Andrews Dr NW Apt 353 Atlanta GA 30305-1344 Office: Montag & Caldwell Inc 1100 Atlanta Fin Ctr 3343 Peachtree Rd NE Atlanta GA 30326-1022

WHITMAN, KATHY VELMA ROSE (ELK WOMAN WHITMAN), artist, sculptor, jeweler, painter, educator; b. Bismarck, N.D., Aug. 12, 1952; d. Carl Jr. and Edith Geneva (Lykken) W.; m. Robert Paul Luger, Feb. 21, 1971 (div. Jan. 1982); children: Shannon, Lakota, Cannupa, Palani; m. Dean P. Fox (div. 1985); 1 child, Otgadahe. Student, Standing Rock C.C., Ft. Yates, N.D., 1973-74, Sinte Gleska Coll., Rosebud, S.D., 1975-77, U. S.D., 1977, Ariz. State U., 1992-93. Instr. art Sinte Gleska Coll., 1975-77, Standing Rock C.C., 1977-78; co-mgr. Four Bears Motor Lodge, New Town, N.D., 1981-82; store owner Nux-Baga Lodge, New Town, 1982-85; artist-in-residence N.D. Coun. on Arts, Bismarck, 1983-84, bd. dirs., 1985; artist-in-residence Evanston Twp. H.S., Ill., 1996; cultural cons. movie prodn., Phoenix, Ariz., 1994. One woman shows include Mus. of Am. Indian, N.Y.C., 1983, Charleroi Internat. Fair, Belgium, 1984, Heard Mus., Phoenix, 1987-92, Phoenix Gallery, Nurnburg, Germany, 1990-96, Lovena Ohl Gallery, Phoenix, 1990-94, Phoenix Gallery, Coeur d'Alene, Idaho, 1992, Turquoise Tortoise Gallery, Tubac, Ariz., 1992-93, Yah-ta-hey Gallery, New London, Conn., 1992-93, Silver Sun Gallery, Santa Fe, N.Mex., 1992-96, Tribal Expessions Gallery, Arlington Heights, Ill., 1994-96, others; represented in permanent collections at Mus. of the Am. Indian, N.Y.C., Mesa (Ariz.) C.C. Bd. dirs. Ft. Berthold C.C., New Town, 1983-85; pres. Cannonball (N.D.) Pow-Wow Com., 1978; parent rep. Head Start, Ft. Yates, 1974. Recipient best craftsman spl. award Bullock's Indian Arts and Crafts, 1986, best of fine arts award No. Plains Tribal Arts, Sioux Falls, S.D., 1988, best of show award Pasadena Western Relic and Native Am. Show, 1991, 2 1st place awards Santa Fe Indian Market, 1993, 2 2nd place awards, 1994, 2 3rd place awards, 1994, 74th Ann. SWAIA Santa Fe Indian Mkt. 1st place award, 1995, 2d place award, 1995, 2 3rd place awards, 1995, 2 Honorable Mentions in sculpture N.Mex. State Fair, 1996. Mem. Indian Arts and Crafts Assn., S.W. Assn. on Indian Affairs (life, 1st and 2nd place awards Santa Fe Indian Market 1995, 2 3rd place awards 1995, 1st place and 2nd place awards Santa Fe Indian Market 1996). Avocations: native American crafts, furniture building, running and hiking, dancing, singing. Home and Studio: 2717 E Victor Hugo Ave Phoenix AZ 85032

WHITMAN, MARINA VON NEUMANN, economist; b. N.Y.C., Mar. 6, 1935; d. John and Mariette (Kovesi) von Neumann; m. Robert Freeman Whitman, June 23, 1956; children: Malcolm Russell, Laura Mariette. BA summa cum laude, Radcliffe Coll., 1956; MA, Columbia U., 1959, PhD, 1962; LHD (hon.), Russell Sage Coll., 1972, U. Mass., 1975, N.Y. Poly Inst., 1975, Baruch Coll., 1980; LLD (hon.), Cedar Crest Coll., 1973, Hobart and William Smith Coll., 1973, Coe Coll., 1975, Marietta Coll., 1976, Rollins Coll., 1976, Wilson Coll., 1977, Allegheny Coll., 1977, Amherst Coll., 1978, Ripon Coll., 1980, Mt. Holyoke Coll., 1980; LittD (hon.), Williams Coll., 1980, Lehigh U., 1981, Denison U., 1983, Claremont U., 1984, Notre Dame U., 1984, Eastern Mich. U., 1992 . Mem. faculty U. Pitts., 1962-79, prof. econs., 1971-73, disting. pub. svc. prof. econs., 1973-79; v.p., chief economist Gen. Motors Corp., N.Y.C., 1979-85, group exec. v.p. pub. affairs, 1985-92; prof. bus. adminstrn. & pub. policy U. Mich., Ann Arbor, 1992-94, prof. bus. adminstrn. and pub. policy, 1994—; mem. U.S. Price Commn., 1971-72, Coun. Econ. Advisers, Exec. Office of Pres., 1972-73; bd. dirs. Chase Manhattan Corp., ALCOA, Procter & Gamble Co., Browning-Ferris Industries, UNOCAL; mem. Trilateral Commn., 1973-84, 88-95; mem. Pres. Adv. Com. on Trade Policy and Negotiations, 1987-93; mem. tech. assessment adv. coun. U.S. Congress Office of Tech. Assessment, 1990-95, Dept. Treasury, from 1977; mem. Consultative Group on Internat. Econs. and Monetary Affairs, from 1979; trustee Nat. Bur. Econ. Rsch., 1993—. Bd. dirs. Inst. for Internat. Econs, 1986, Salzburg Seminar, 1994—, Eurasia Found, 1992-95; bd. overseers Harvard U., 1972-78, mem. vis. com. Kennedy Sch., 1992—; trustee Princeton U., 1980-90. Fellow Earhart Found., 1959-60, AAUW, 1960-61, NSF, 1968-70, also Social Security Rsch. Coun.; recipient Columbia medal for excellence, 1973; George Washington award Am. Hungarian Found., 1975. Mem. Am. Econ. Assn. (exec. com. 1977-80), Am. Acad. Arts & Scis., Coun. Fgn. Rels. (dir. 1977-87), Phi Beta Kappa. Author: Government Risk-Sharing in Foreign Investment, 1965; International and Interregional Payments Adjustment, 1967; Economic Goals and Policy Instruments, 1970; Reflections of Interdependence: Issues for Economic Theory and U.S. Policy, 1979; also articles; bd. editors Am. Econ. Rev., 1974-77; mem. editorial bd. Fgn. Policy. Office: U Mich Sch Pub Policy 411 Lorch Hall Ann Arbor MI 48109-1220

WHITMAN, MARLAND HAMILTON, JR., lawyer; b. Balt., Oct. 13, 1947; s. M. Hamilton and Josephine Lee (Chatard) W.; m. Susan Zimmerman, Mar. 21, 1976; children: Elizabeth Miles, Hannah Minor. AB, Princeton U., 1969; JD, U. Va., 1976. Bar: Md. 1976, U.S. Supreme Ct. 1982, U.S. Ct. Appeals (3d cir.) 1986, (4th cir.) 1979 , U. S. Ct. Internat. Trade 1985, U.S. Dist. Ct. Md. 1977. From assoc. to ptnr. Ober, Kaler, Grimes & Shriver, Balt., 1976—. Contbr. chpt. (book) Construction Litigation: Strategies and Techniques, 1990. Lt. USN, 1969-73. Mem. ABA, Maritime Law Assn. of U.S. (proctor 1977—), Md. State Bar Assn., Bar Assn. of Balt. City, Propeller Club of U.S. Pt. of Balt.

WHITMAN, MARTIN J., investment banker; b. N.Y.C., Sept. 30, 1924; s. Irving and Dora (Cukier) W.; B.S. magna cum laude, Syracuse U., 1949; M.A., New Sch. for Social Research, 1956; postgrad. Princeton U., 1949-50; m. Lois M. Quick, Mar. 10, 1956; children—James Q., Barbara E., Thomas I. Research analyst, buyer Shearson Hammill & Co., N.Y.C., 1950-56; analyst William Rosenwald Co., N.Y.C., 1956-58; head research Ladenburg, Thalmann & Co., N.Y.C., 1958-60; gen. partner Gerstley Sunstein & Co., Phila., 1960-67; v.p., dir. Blair & Co., Inc., N.Y.C., 1967-68; pres. M.J. Whitman & Co. (now Inc.), N.Y.C., 1969—; pres., chief exec. officer Equity Strategics Fund, Inc., 1984—; dir. Nabors Industries, Inc.; chmn. bd. Danielson Holding Corp.; adj. prof. fin. Yale U., New Haven, 1972-83, 92; adv. bd. Yale Sch. Mgmt., New Haven, 1994-96; cons. disclosure study SEC, 1968; cons. Pres.'s Commn. on Accident at Three Mile Island, 1979. Bd. dirs. Ctr. for Humanities, 1987—; chmn. 3d Ave. Fund, 1991. Served with USNR, 1942-46. Chartered fin. analyst. Mem. N.Y. Soc. Security Analysts, Phila. Econ. Soc. Jewish. Author: (with M. Shubik) The Aggressive Conservative Investor, 1979; contbr. numerous articles to profl. publs., also booklets. Home: 285 Central Park W New York NY 10024

WHITMAN, ROBERT VAN DUYNE, civil engineer, educator; b. Pitts., Feb. 2, 1928; s. Edwin A. and Elsie (Van Duyne) W.; m. Elizabeth Cushman, June 19, 1954; children: Jill Martyne Whitman Marsee, Martha Allerton (dec.), Gweneth Giles Whitman Kaebnick. BS, Swarthmore Coll., 1948, DSc (hon.), 1990; SM, MIT, 1949, ScD, 1951. Faculty MIT, 1953—, prof. civil engring., 1963-93, head structural engring., 1970-74, head soil mechanics divsn., 1970-72; prof. emeritus, 1993—; vis. scholar U. Cambridge, Eng., 1976-77; cons. to govt. and industry, 1953—; mem. adv. com. for nat. earthquake hazard reduction program Fed. Emergency Mgmt. Agy., 1991-94, mem. commn. engring. and tech. systems NRC, 1992—. Author: (with T. W. Lambe) Soil Mechanics. Mem. Town Meeting Lexington, Mass., 1962-76, 85—, mem. permanent bldg. com., 1968-75, mem. bd. appeals, 1979-81, 84—. Lt. (j.g.) USNR, 1954-56. Recipient U.S. Scientist award Humboldt Found., 1984-90; Norwegian Geotech. Inst. Rsch. fellow, 1984. Mem. NAE, ASCE (Rsch. award 1962, Terzaghi Lecture 1981, Terzaghi award 1987, C. Martin Duke Lifeline Earthquake Engring. award 1992, James Croes medal 1994), Boston Soc. Civil Engrs. (Structural Sect. prize 1963, Desmond Fitzgerald medal 1973, Ralph W. Horne Fund award 1977), Internat. Soc. Soil Mechanics and Found. Engrs., Earthquake Engring. Rsch. Inst. (dir. 1978-81, 84-88, v.p. 1979-81, pres. 1985-87, Disting. lectr. 1994, hon. 1997—). Research in soil mechanics, soil dynamics and earthquake engring. Home: 5 Hancock Ave Lexington MA 02173-3412 Office: MIT Dept Civil & Environ Engring Cambridge MA 02139

WHITMAN, RUSSELL WILSON, lawyer; b. Phila., Feb. 20, 1940; s. Russell W. Whitman and Amelia M. (Schauer) Richard; m. Mary Carol Tyson, Sept. 16, 1961; children: Russell Whitman III, Douglas W. BS, Drexel Inst. Tech., 1964; LLB, U. Pa., 1967. Bar: N.Y. 1968, Pa. 1969, N.J. 1990. Ptnr. Dechert Price & Rhoads, Phila., 1969-93. Office: Ste 200 Box 5072 1322 Hooper Ave Toms River NJ 08754

WHITMAN, RUTH, poet, educator, translator; b. N.Y.C., May 28, 1922; d. Meyer David and Martha Harriet (Sherman) Bashein; m. Cedric Whitman, Oct. 13, 1941; children: Rachel Claudia, Leda Miriam; m. Firman Houghton, July 22, 1959; 1 child, David Will; m. Morton Sacks, Oct. 6, 1966. B.A., Radcliffe Coll., 1944; M.A., Harvard, 1947. Editor Harvard U. Press, 1947-60; dir. poetry workshop Cambridge Ctr. Adult Edn., 1964-68; fellow poetry and translation Bunting Inst., Radcliffe Coll., 1968-70; instr. Radcliffe Seminars, 1969—; faculty Harvard U., 1979-84; vis. poet Tufts U., 1972, 73; vis. poet in Israel, 1974, 77, 79, 81; poet-in-residence Hamden Sydney Coll., 1974, Trinity Coll., 1975, U. Denver, 1976, Holy Cross Coll., 1978, MIT, 1979, 1989, U. Mass., 1980, Centre Coll., Ky., 1980, 87, Ky. Arts Commn., 1981; founder, pres. Poets Who Teach, Inc., 1974—; dir. poetry writing program Mass. Council Arts, 1970-73; vis. prof. poetry MIT, 1989-92. Author: Selected Poems of Alain Bosquet, 1963, Anthology of Modern Yiddish Poetry, 1966, Blood and Milk Poems, 1963, Marriage Wig and other poems, 1968, Selected Poems of Jacob Glatstein, 1972, The Passion of Lizzie Borden: New and Selected Poems, 1973; editor: Poemmaking: Poets in Classrooms, 1975, Tamsen Donner: A Woman's Journey, 1977, Permanent Address: New Poems, 1973-80, 1980, Becoming a Poet: Source, Process and Practice, 1982, The Testing of Hanna Senesh, 1986, The Fiddle Rose, 1990, Laughing Gas: Poems New and Selected, 1963-90, 91, Hatshepsut, Speak to Me, 1992, An Anthology of Modern Yiddish Poetry, 3d edit., 1995. Recipient Alice Fay di Castagnola award, 1968, Kovner award, 1968, Chanin award, 1972, Guiness Internat. award, 1973; John Masefield award, 1976; grantee Nat. Found. Jewish Culture, 1968; Nat. Endowment Arts, 1974-75; Tananbaum Found. grantee, 1979, 80; R.I. Council grantee in lit., 1980; sr. Fulbright writer-in-residence fellow Hebrew U., Jerusalem, 1984-85. Mem. Authors League, P.E.N., Poetry Soc. Am., New Eng. Poetry Club, Phi Beta Kappa. Address: 40 Tuckerman Ave Middletown RI 02842-6044

WHITMER, FREDERICK LEE, lawyer; b. Terre Haute, Ind., Nov. 5, 1947; s. Lee Arthur and Ella (Diekhoff) W.; m. Valeri Cade; children: Caitlin Margaret, Meghan Connors, Christian Frederick. BA, Wabash Coll., 1969; JD, Columbia U., 1973. Bar: N.Y. 1975, U.S. Dist. Ct. (so. dist.) N.Y. 1975, N.J. 1976, U.S. Dist. Ct. N.J. 1976, U.S. Ct. Appeals (3d cir.) 1977, U.S. Ct. Appeals (fed. cir.) 1983, U.S. Ct. Appeals (2d cir.) 1987, U.S. Supreme Ct. 1988, U.S. Ct. Appeals (7th cir.) 1994. Assoc. Kaye, Scholer, Fierman, Hays & Handler, N.Y.C., 1973-76, Pitney, Hardin & Kipp, Morristown, 1976-78; ptnr. Pitney, Hardin, Kipp & Szuch, Morristown, 1979—. Mem. ABA, N.J. Bar Assn., Phi Beta Kappa. Republican. Lutheran. Home: 190 Hurlbutt St Wilton CT 06897-2706 Office: Pitney Hardin Kipp & Szuch Park Ave at Morris Co PO Box 1945 Morristown NJ 07962-1945

WHITMER, JOSEPH MORTON, benefits consulting firm executive, retired; b. Sacramento, Apr. 29, 1942; s. Carlos Raymond and Elizabeth Ellen (McDonald) W.; m. Judith Leigh Johnson, Aug. 11, 1963 (dec. Jan. 1985); children: Karen L., Brian D., Julia A.; m. Paula Ann Thurman, Mar. 19, 1986. BS in Acctg., U. Ky., 1964, JD, 1967. Ptnr. Veal & Whitmer, Nicholasville, Ky., 1967-68; v.p., sec., gen. counsel and dir. Consol. Mgmt. Svcs., Eagles Nat. Life Ins. Co., First Mut. Ins. Co., First Mut. Life Ins. Co., Lexington, Ky., 1970-75; pvt. practice Lexington, 1975-89; exec. v.p., dir. Profl. Adminstrs. Ltd., Lexington, 1968-86, pres. chief exec. officer, 1987-90, dir., 1990-93. Mem. bd. overseers Duke U. Comprehensive Cancer Ctr., Durham, N.C., 1987—, co-chair Melanoma Consortium, 1987-90. Named one of Outstanding Young Men Am., 1975. Mem. ABA, Ky. Bar Assn. Democrat. Methodist. Avocation: computers.

WHITMORE, CHARLES HORACE, utility executive, lawyer, management consultant; b. Atlantic, Iowa, June 29, 1914; s. Tom Cornell and Adda Maria (Baldwin) W.; m. Millicent Stahly, May 3, 1935; children: Jacqueline, Tom Cornell. B.A., Grinnell Coll., 1935; J.D., State U. Iowa, 1940; LL.D., St. Ambrose U., 1960. Bar: Iowa bar 1937, Ill. bar 1939. Asst. counsel United Light & Power Co., 1937-41, exec. operating asst., 1942-43; asst. to pres. Iowa-Ill. Gas & Electric Co., Davenport, Iowa, 1946-47; gen. counsel Iowa-Ill. Gas & Electric Co., 1948-54, v.p., 1950-54, dir., 1950-80, pres., 1954-75, chmn. bd., 1956-79, chmn. exec. com., 1979-80; v.p., dir. Overseas Adv. Assos., Inc., Riyadh, Saudi Arabia, 1979-80; pres. Quad-City Devel. Group, 1971-73; chmn. Mid-Am. Interpool Network; also founding mem. Nat. Elec. Reliability Council, 1968-69. Served as lt., aviation supply officer USNR, 1944-45. Mem. Rock Island Arsenal Golf Club (Ill.). Presbyterian. Home: Steepmeadow Rock Island IL 61201-4411 Office: 1800 Third Ave Rm 507 Rock Island IL 61201-8019

WHITMORE, DONALD CLARK, retired engineer; b. Seattle, Sept. 15, 1932; s. Floyd Robinson and Lois Mildred (Clark) W.; m. Alice Elinor Winter, Jan. 8, 1955; children: Catherine Ruth, William Owen, Matthew Clark, Nancy Lynn, Peggy Ann, Stuart John. BS, U. Wash., 1955. Prin. engr. The Boeing Co., Seattle, 1955-87, ret., 1987; developer, owner mobile home pk., Auburn, Wash., 1979—. Author: Towards Security, 1983, (monograph) SDI Software Feasibility, 1990, Characterization of the Nuclear Proliferation Threat, 1993, Rationale for Nuclear Disarmament, 1995. Activist for arms control, Auburn, Wash., 1962—; chmn. Seattle Coun. Orgns. for Internat. Affairs, 1973, Auburn Citizens for Schs., 1975; v.p. Boeing Employees Good Neighbor Fund, Seattle, 1977, Spl. Svc. award, 1977; bd. dirs. 8th Congl. Dist. Sane/Freeze, 1992—; pres., founder Third Millennium Found., 1994—. Avocations: hiking, travel, collecting. Home and Office: 16202 SE Lake Moneysmith Rd Auburn WA 98092-5274

WHITMORE, DOUGLAS MICHAEL, physician; b. Boston, Oct. 2, 1982; s. Donald Herbert and Marcia (Klein) W.; m. Ann Marie Lopez. BS, MS, U. Ill., Champaign Urbana, 1969; MS, PhD, Stanford U., Palo Alto, 1970, 74; MD, U. Miami, 1978. Physician U. Miami, 1983—; pres. med. staff Holy Cross Hosp., 1996-97. Mem. Am. Coll. Chest Physicians, 1983—, Catucean Med. Soc. (pres. 1996-97). Office: Medical Complex West 1930 NE 47th St Ste 205 Fort Lauderdale FL 33308-7728

WHITMORE, FRANK CLIFFORD, JR., geologist; b. Cambridge, Mass., Nov. 17, 1915; s. Frank Clifford and Marion Gertrude (Mason) W.; m. Martha Burling Kremers, June 24, 1939; children: Geoffrey, John, Katherine, Susan. B.A., Amherst Coll., 1938; M.S., Pa. State U., 1939; M.A., Harvard U., 1941, Ph.D., 1942. Tchg. fellow Harvard U., Cambridge, Mass., 1940-42; instr. geology R.I. State Coll., Kingston, 1942-44; geologist U.S. Geol. Survey, Washington, 1944-84, scientist emeritus, 1984—; mem. com. on rsch. and exploration Nat. Geog. Soc., 1970-96, vice chmn., 1990-96, emeritus, 1997—; rsch. assoc. dept. Paleobiology Smithsonian Instn., Washington, 1967—; mem. adv. bd. Ctr. for Study of Early Man, U. Maine, Orono, 1985-90. Editor: Resources for 21st Century, 1982. Contbr. articles on geology and vertebrate paleontology to profl. jours. Bd. dirs. Prince Georges County Boys Clubs, Md., 1954-56; mem. program com. Nat. Capital coun. Girl Scouts U.S.A., Washington, 1967-69; pres. Thornton Soc., Washington, 1977-84. Recipient Medal of Freedom, U.S. Army, 1946; spl. achievement award, U.S. Geol. Survey, 1980; Meritorious Svc. award, U.S. Dept. Interior, 1981, Arnold Guyot Meml. award Nat. Geographic Soc., 1993. Fellow AAAS, Geol. Soc. Am.; mem. Soc. Vertebrate Paleontology (hon. life, exec. com. 1960-62). Democrat. Clubs: Midriver, Harvard. Avocations: architectural history. Home: 20 Woodmoor Dr Silver Spring MD 20901-2447 Office: US Geol Survey Nat Mus Natural History MRC NHB 137 Washington DC 20560

WHITMORE, GEORGE MERLE, JR., management consulting company executive; b. Tarrytown, N.Y., Jan. 1, 1928; s. George Merle and Elizabeth Helen (Knodel) W.; m. Priscilla Elizabeth Norman, Mar. 30, 1963; children: Elizabeth Whitmore Lippincott, George Norman, Stephen Bradford. BE, Yale U., 1949; MBA, Harvard U., 1951. Test engr. Gen. Electric Co., Bridgeport, Conn., Erie, Pa., 1949; rsch. assoc. Harvard Bus. Sch., Boston, 1951-52; assoc. Cresap, McCormick and Paget Inc., N.Y.C., 1954-59, prin., 1959-61, ptnr., 1961-69, v.p., dir., 1969-79, mng. dir., CEO, 1979-81; mng. dir. Ayers, Whitmore & Co. Inc., N.Y.C., 1981-88, Ayers, Whitmore div. A.T. Kearney, Inc., N.Y.C., 1988-90; mng. dir. Whitmore & Co., Greenwich, Conn., 1990—; chmn. bd. dirs. Philo Smith & Co., Inc., Stamford, Conn.; bd. dirs. Carroll Enterprises, Inc., Worcester, Mass., RTI Inc., Rockaway, N.J. Hon. trustee, former bd. pres. Hackley Sch., Tarrytown, N.Y.; former trustee, bd. chmn. Greenwich (Conn.) Acad.; former trustee, treas. Salisbury (Conn.) Sch. With USAF, 1952-53. Mem. Inst. Mgmt. Cons. (founding mem.), Newcomen Soc., Tau Beta Pi. Presbyterian. Clubs: Stanwich (former dir.) (Greenwich); Yale (N.Y.C.). Home and Office: 4 Cedarwood Dr Greenwich CT 06830-3905

WHITMORE, JAMES ALLEN, actor; b. White Plains, N.Y., Oct. 1, 1921; s. James Allen and Florence Belle (Crane) W.; m. Nancy Mygatt, Mar. 24, 1978 (div.); m. Audra Lindley; children: James, Steven, Daniel. B.A., Yale

U., 1942; postgrad., Am. Wing Theatre Sch. Performances include: (Broadway plays) debut in Command Decision, 1947, Elba, Manhattan Theatre Club, Winesburg, Ohio, 1956, Inquest, 1970, Will Rogers U.S.A., Give 'Em Hell Harry, 1974, The Magnificent Yankee, Washington, 1976, Bully, 1977, Handy Dandy, 1985, (films) Battleground, 1949, Next Voice You Hear, 1950, Asphalt Jungle, 1950, Mrs. O'Malley and Mr. Malone, 1950, Outsiders, 1950, Please Believe Me, 1950, Across de Vide Missouri, 1951, It's a Big Country, 1951, Because You're Mine, 1952, Above and Beyond, 1952, Girl Who Had Everything, 1953, All the Brothers Were Valiant, 1953, Kiss Me Kate, 1953, The Command, 1954, Them!, 1954, Oklahoma, 1955, Battle Cry, 1955, McConnell Story, 1955, Eddy Duchin Story, 1956, Face of Fire, 1959, Who Was That Lady?, 1960, Black Like Me, 1964, Chuka, 1967, Waterhole 3, 1967, Nobody's Perfect, 1968, Planet of the Apes, 1968, Madigan, 1968, The Split, 1968, Guns of the Magnificent Seven, 1969, Chato's Land, 1972, Where the Red Fern Grows, 1974, Give 'Em Hell Harry, 1974 (Acad. award nomination 1975), Bully, 1978, The Serpent's Egg, 1978, First Deadly Sin, 1980, Nuts, 1987, Old Explorers, 1990, The Shawshank Redemption, 1994, The Relic, 1997, numerous others, (TV appearances) including The Law and Mr. Jones, 1960-61, My Friend Tony, 1969, Temperature Rising, 1972-73, Will Rogers U.S.A., 1973, (TV miniseries) Celebrity, 1986, Favorite Son, 1988, (TV movies) Glory! Glory!, 1989, Sky High, 1990. Served with USMCR, 1942-46. Nominated Acad. award, 1949; recipient Antoinette Perry award, 1947, Comedy award Am. Acad. Humor, Ace award, 1989; named Most Promising Newcomer, 1947. *

WHITMORE, JON SCOTT, university official, play director; b. Seattle, Mar. 22, 1945; s. Walter James and Eurma (Thody) W.; m. Jennifer Gean Gross, Aug. 17, 1985; children: Ian Scott, Amy Lee. BA in Speech and Theatre, Wash. State U., 1967, MA in Speech and Theatre, 1968; PhD in Dramatic Arts, U. Calif., Santa Barbara, 1974. Instr. theatre Highline Coll., Seattle, 1968-71; grad. asst. U. Calif., Santa Barbara, 1971-74; asst. prof. theatre W.Va. U., Morgantown, 1974-78, assoc. prof., 1978-82, prof., 1979-85, chmn. dept., 1979-84, interim dean, 1984-85; prof., dean faculty arts and letters SUNY, Buffalo, 1985-90; dean Coll. Fine Arts, U. Tex., Austin, 1990-96; provost U. Iowa, Iowa City, 1996—. Dir. plays including Suddenly Last Summer, The Miracle Worker, Equus, Romeo and Juliet, Long Days Journey Into Night, The Sea Gull, The Comedy of Errors, The Glass Menagerie, Blithe Spirit, The Tavern, Black Comedy, You're a Good Man Charlie Brown, Vanities, The Effect of Gamma Rays on Man-In-The-Moon Marigolds, Epiphany, Endgame, The Miser, J.B., The Mousetrap, Knapp's Last Tape, Miss Julie, Servant of Two Masters, Before We Were; actor various classical, modern and contemporary plays, and performance pieces; author: Directing Postmodern Theater, 1994, William Saroyan, 1994. Mem. Erie County (N.Y.) Cultural Resources Adv. Bd., 1986-89, long range planning com. Studio Arena Theatre, Buffalo, 1986-90, trustee, 1987-90; mem. coun. fellows Am. Coun. Edn., 1984—; pres. W.Va. Theater Conf., 1978-80, pres.-elect, 1977-78, founding mem., bd. dirs., 1975-81. Recipient ACE Fellow award Am. Council Edn., 1983-84; fellow U. Calif., Santa Barbara, 1973-74, Lilly Found., 1976-77; Maynard Lee Daggy scholar Wash. State U., 1967. Mem. Internat. Council Fine Arts Deans, Am. Council Arts, Assn. Theatre in Higher Edn. (v.p. adminstrn. 1991—, chmn. nat. conf. planning com. chief adminstrs. program, 1987), Assn. Communication Adminstrn. (elected to exec. com. 1982-85, chmn. task force theatre adminstrn., 1982-84), Speech Communication Assn., Council Colls. Arts and Scis., Assn. Coll., Univ. and Community Arts Adminstrs., Nat. Assn. State Univs. and Land-Grant Colls. (chair elect commn. arts, 1990-92, chair 1992—). Home: 461 Butternut Ln Iowa City IA 52246 Office: U Iowa Office of Provost 111 Jessup Hall Iowa City IA 52242-1316*

WHITMORE, SHARP, lawyer; b. Price, Utah, Apr. 26, 1918; s. Leland and Anne (Sharp) W.; m. Frances Dorr, Aug. 15, 1940; children: Richard, William, Ann. A.B., Stanford U., 1939; J.D., U. Calif.-Berkeley, 1942; LL.D., U. Pacific, 1982. Bar: Calif. 1944. Asso. Gibson, Dunn & Crutcher, Los Angeles, 1946-50; partner Gibson, Dunn & Crutcher, 1951—; chmn. Calif. Com. Bar Examiners, 1956-58. Bd. dirs. Nat. Jud. Coll., 1989-92. Fellow Am. Bar Found. (chmn. 1982-83); mem. L.A. County Bar Assn. (pres. 1970-71), Nat. Conf. Bar Examiners (chmn. 1957-58), State Bar Calif. (bd. govs. 1962-65, v.p. treas. 1964-65), ABA (ho. of dels. 1957-58, 68-93, bd. govs. 1985-88, editl. bd. jour. 1994—), Order of Coif (hon.). Republican. Clubs: Bohemian, Sunset, Chancery (pres. 1962-63). Home: 2005 Gird Rd Fallbrook CA 92028-8892 Office: 750 B St Ste 3300 San Diego CA 92101-8105

WHITNEY, ALISON See MOVIUS, ALISON WHITNEY BURTON

WHITNEY, BARRY LYN, religious studies educator; b. Cornwall, Ont., Can., Dec. 10, 1947; s. Earl Stanley Whitney and Gwendolyn Grace (Meldrum) Whitney. BA with honors, Carleton U., 1971; PhD in Religious Studies, McMaster U., Hamilton, Ont., 1977. Prof. religious studies U. Windsor, Ont., 1976—, rsch. prof., 1992-93; prof. pastoral edn. Southwestern Regional Ctr., Cedar Springs, Ont., 1977-79; mem. Anglican commn. Canterbury Coll., London and Windsor, 1977-79, tutor of admissions, Windsor, 1979-82, fellow, 1979-82; regional coord. Ctr. for Process Studies, 1979—. Author: Evil and the Process God, 1985, What are They Saying About God and Evil?, 1989, Theodicy, 1993; contbr. articles to profl. jours. Scholar Carleton U., 1967-71, McMaster U., 1971-76, Can. Coun. scholar McMaster, U., 1972-75; rsch. grantee Social Sci. and Humanities Rsch. Coun., 1988-90. Mem. Soc. for Study Process Philosophies, Coll. Theology, Soc. Am. Acad. Religion, Coun. for Study Religion, others. Home: 601-1385 Riverside Dr W, Windsor, ON Canada N9B3R9 Office: U Windsor Religious Studies, 401 Sunset Ave, Windsor, ON Canada N9B 3P4 *Committed to the process vision of reality (Whitehead, Hartshorne) as a viable vision of God and a major advance in dealing with the terrible agony of suffering and injustice.*

WHITNEY, EDWARD BONNER, investment banker; b. Glen Cove, N.Y., June 6, 1945; s. Edward Farley and Millicent Bonner (Bowring) W.; m. Martha Congleton Howell, Aug. 17, 1974; children: William Howell, John Howell. B.A., Harvard U., 1966, M.B.A., 1969. Systems engr. IBM, Cambridge, Mass., 1966-67; assoc. Dillon, Read & Co. Inc., N.Y.C., 1969-74, v.p., 1975-79, sr. v.p., 1980-83, mng. dir., 1984—, also bd. dirs.; bd. dirs. Investor Responsibility Rsch. Ctr., IRRC PubCo. Mem. Heights Casino Club (Bklyn.). Office: Dillon Read & Co Inc 535 Madison Ave New York NY 10022-4212

WHITNEY, JANE, foreign service officer; b. Champaign, Ill., July 15, 1941; d. Robert F. and Mussette (Cary) W. BA, Beloit Coll., 1963; CD, U. Aix, Marseille, France, 1962. Joined Fgn. Service, U.S. Dept. State, 1965, vice consul, Saigon, Vietnam, 1966-68, career counselor, 1968-70, spl. asst. Office of Dir. Gen., 1970-72, consul, Stuttgart, Fed. Republic Germany, 1972-74, Ankara, Turkey, 1974-76, spl. asst. Office of Asst. Sec. for Consular Affairs, 1976-77, mem. Bd. Examiners Fgn. Service, 1977-78, 79-81, consul, Munich, Germany, 1978-79, Buenos Aires, Argentina, 1981-82, ethics officer Office of Legal Adviser, 1982-85, advisor Office of Asst. Sec. for Diplomatic Security, 1985-86, dep. prin. officer, consul, Stuttgart, 1986-90, prin. officer, consul gen., Perth, Australia, 1990-91. Recipient awards U.S. Dept. State, 1968, 70, 81, 85, 87, 90. Mem. Presbyterian Ch.

WHITNEY, JOHN FREEMAN, JR., political science educator; b. Balt., Feb. 14, 1944; s. John Freeman and Agnese Jay (Taliaferro) W.; m. Carolyn Nordyke, Aug. 5, 1966; children: Cristina Elizabeth Whitney Waits, John Freeman III, William David. BA, Baylor U., 1967; MS, Tex. A&M U., 1968; PhD, Fla. State U., 1970. Instr. polit. sci. Fla. State U., Tallahassee, 1968-70, Tex. A&I U., Kingsville, 1967-68, Lamar U., Beaumont, Tex., 1970-71; adminstrv. asst. mgr. Ill. State Fair Agy., Springfield, Ill., 1973-77; mayor Chatham, Ill., 1977-85; exec. dir. Ill. Soc. Opticianry, Springfield, 1982-86; prof. polit. sci. Lincoln Land Community Coll., Springfield, 1971—; mem., chmn. Ill. Comptr. Merit Commn., Springfield, 1981-97; Ford found. legis. staff intern Fla. State U., 1970; cons. in field. Author (instrs. manual) Irony of Democracy, 1984, Uniform Welfare Systems and the State of Florida, 1970. Precinct committeeman Sangamon County Dem. Orgn., Springfield, 1974-80; del. Dem. Nat. Conv., N.Y.C., 1976, Dem. Nat. Midterm Conf., Phila., 1982; Ill. state steering com., campaign dir. Carter for Pres., 1976-80, Dukakis for Pres., 1986-88. Recipient Disting. Achievement award VFW, 1978, Tchg. Excellence award cmty. coll. leadership program dept. ednl. adminstrn. Nat. Inst. for Staff and Orgnl. Devel., U. Tex., Austin, 1995. Fellow Am. Polit. Sci. Assn.; mem. Nat. Assn. Civil Svc. Commrs. (cen. region pres. 1988-91), Internat. Pers. Mgmt. Assn., Soc. for Human Resource Mgmt., Am. Polit. Sci. Assn. Democrat. Methodist. Home: 18 Pheasant Run Dr Chatham IL 62629-1029 Office: Lincoln Land C C Shepherd Rd Springfield IL 62708

WHITNEY, PHYLLIS AYAME, author; b. Yokohama, Japan, Sept. 9, 1903; d. Charles J. and Lillian (Mandeville) W.; m. George A. Garner, July 2, 1925; m. Lovell F. Jahnke, 1950 (dec. 1973). Grad., McKinley High Sch., Chgo., 1924. Instr. dancing San Antonio, 1 yr; tchr. juvenile fiction writing Northwestern U., 1945; children's book editor Chgo. Sun, 1942-46, Phila. Inquirer, 1947, 48; instr. juvenile fiction writing N.Y.U., 1947-58; leader juvenile fiction workshop Writers Conf., U. Colo., 1952, 54, 56. Author: A Place for Ann, 1941, A Star for Ginny, 1942, (vocat. fiction for teenage girls) A Window for Julie, 1943, (mystery novel for adults) Red Is for Murder, 1943, The Silver Inkwell, 1945, Willow Hill, 1947, Writing Juvenile Fiction, 1947, Ever After, 1948, Mystery of the Gulls, 1949, Linda's Homecoming, 1950, The Island of Dark Woods, 1951, Love Me, Love Me Not, 1952, Step to the Music, 1953, A Long Time Coming, 1954, Mystery of the Black Diamonds, 1954, The Quicksilver Pool, 1955, Mystery on the Isle of Skye, 1955, The Fire and The Gold (Jr. Lit. Guild), 1956, The Highest Dream (Jr. Lit. Guild), The Trembling Hills (Peoples Book Club), 1956, Skye Cameron, 1957, Mystery of the Green Cat (Jr. Lit. Guild), 1957, Secret of the Samurai Sword (Jr. Lit. Guild), 1958, The Moonflower, 1958, Creole Holiday, 1959, Thunder Heights, 1960, Blue Fire, 1961, Mystery of the Haunted Pool, 1961 (Edgar award Mystery Writers Am.), Secret of the Tiger's Eye, 1961, Window on the Square, 1962, Mystery of the Golden Horn, 1962, Seven Tears for Apollo, 1963, Mystery of the Hidden Hand, 1963 (Edgar award Mystery Writers Am. 1964), Black Amber, 1964, Secret of the Emerald Star, 1964, Sea Jade, 1965, Mystery of the Angry Idol, 1965, Columbella, 1966, Secret of the Spotted Shell, 1967, Mystery of the Strange Traveler, 1967, Silverhill, 1967, Hunter's Green, 1968, Secret of Goblin Glen, 1968, Mystery of the Crimson Ghost, 1969, Winter People, 1969, Secret of the Missing Footprint, 1970, Lost Island, 1970, The Vanishing Scarecrow, 1971, Listen for the Whisperer, 1971, Nobody Likes Trina, 1972, Snowfire, 1973, Mystery of the Scowling Boy, 1973, The Turquoise Mask, 1974, Spindrift, 1975, Secret of Haunted Mesa, 1975, The Golden Unicorn, 1976, Secret of the Stone Face, 1977, The Stone Bull, 1977, The Glass Flame, 1978, Domino, 1979, Poinciana, 1980, Vermilion, 1981, Guide to Fiction Writing, 1982, Emerald, 1983, Rainsong, 1984, Dream of Orchids, 1985, Flaming Tree, 1986, Silversword, 1987, Feather on the Moon, 1988, Rainbow in the Mist, 1989, The Singing Stones, 1990, Woman Without a Past, 1991, The Ebony Swan, 1992, Star Flight, 1993, Daughter of the Stars, 1994, Amethyst Dream, 1997; sold first story to Chgo. Daily News; later wrote for pulp mags., became specialist in juvenile writing, now writing entirely in adult field. Pres. Authors Round Table, 1943, 44; pres. exec. bd. Fifth Annual Writers Conf., Northwestern U., 1944; spent first 15 years of life in Japan, China and P.I. (father in shipping and hotel bus.). Recipient Friends of Lit. award for contbns. to children's lit., 1974; Reynal and Hitchcock prize in Youth Today contest for book Willow Hill; Today's Woman award Coun. Cerebral Palsy Auxs., 1983, Agatha award Malice Domestic, 1990, Rita award Romance Writers Am., 1990, Lifetime award Romance Writers Am., 1990, Midland Authors award for a lifetime of literary achievement, 1995. Mem. Mystery Writers Am. (pres. 1975, Grandmaster award for lifetime achievement 1988), Am. Crime Writers League, Sisters in Crime, Authors League of Am. Address: c/o McIntosh and Otis 310 Madison Ave New York NY 10017-6009 *A learning period must be allowed for any talent. The accidental success is unfortunate because the person who achieves it doesn't really know how it happened. This does not mean that it ever becomes easy, even with learning. There is always work involved-long hours and dedication to that work-before a book is ready for publication. Any success demands a price, and the time and effort, and sometimes anguish a successful person gives to his work is that price. For me, the satisfactions have been worth it.*

WHITNEY, RALPH ROYAL, JR., financial executive; b. Phila., Dec. 10, 1934; s. Ralph Royal and Florence Elizabeth (Whitney) W.; m. Fay Wadsworth, Apr. 4, 1959; children: Lynn Marie, Paula Sue, Brian Ralph. BA, U. Rochester, 1957, MBA, 1972. Spl. agt. Prudential Ins. Co., Rochester, N.Y., 1958-59, divsn. mgr., 1959-63; gen. agt. Nat. Life Vt., Syracuse, 1963-64; contr. Wadsworth Mfg. Assocs. Inc., Syracuse, 1964-65, v.p., 1965-68, pres., 1968-71; pres. Warren (Pa.) Components Corp., 1968-72; pres., mng. prin. ptnr. Hammond Kennedy Whitney & Co., N.Y.C., 1972—; chmn. IFR Sys., Inc., Seneca Printing Inc., Control Devices Inc.; chmn., CEO Holbrook Patterson Inc., Globe Ticket & Label Co., Grobot File Co., Am. Maine Rubber Co., Miltco Inc.; bd. dirs. Excel Industries, Inc., Baldwin Tech. Corp., Selas Corp. Am., M. Mossberg & Son, Inc., Adage Inc., MedTek Inc. Bd. trustees U. Rochester. Mem. N.Y. Yacht Club, Lotus Club (N.Y.C.), Century Club (Syracuse), Merion Cricket Club, Princeton Club. Episcopalian. Home: 3441 Highway 34 Wheatland WY 82201-8714

WHITNEY, RICHARD BUCKNER, lawyer; b. Corpus Christi, Tex., Mar. 1, 1948; s. Franklin Loren and Betty Wolcott (Fish) W.; m. Chantal Marie Gindt, Aug. 18, 1972; children: Jennifer L., James R., Katherine E. BA in Polit. Sci., Union Coll., 1970; JD, Case Western Res. U., 1973. Bar: Ohio 1973, U.S. Dist. Ct. (no. dist.) Ohio 1974, U.S. Ct. Appeals (6th cir.) 1974, U.S. Ct. Appeals (3d cir.) 1987. From assoc. to ptnr. Jones, Day, Reavis & Pogue, Cleve., 1973—. Mem. ABA, Ohio Bar Assn., Cuyahoga County Bar Assn., Cleve. Bar Assn. (grievance com., unauthorized practice of law com.), Order of the Coif. Roman Catholic. Home: 2750 Southington Rd Shaker Heights OH 44120-1603 Office: Jones Day Reavis & Pogue 901 Lakeside Ave E Cleveland OH 44114-1116

WHITNEY, ROBERT MICHAEL, lawyer; b. Green Bay, Wis., Jan. 29, 1949; s. John Clarence and Helen (Mayer) W. Student, U. Wis., 1967-70, JD, 1974. Bar: Wis. 1974, U.S. Dist. Ct. (we. dist.) Wis. 1979, U.S. Ct. Appeals (7th cir.) 1980, U.S. Dist. Ct. (ea. dist.) Wis. 1984, U.S. Supreme Ct. 1990, U.S. Ct. Appeals (9th cir.) 1992. Legal counsel Wis. State Election Bd., Madison, 1976-78; ptnr. Walsh, Walsh, Sweeney & Whitney, S.C., Madison, 1979-86, Foley & Lardner, Madison, 1986—; counsel Advocacy Assn. for Retarded Citizens, Madison, 1977-79, Dane County Advocates for Battered Women; instr. torts I, U. Wis. Labor Sch., 1996; adj. prof. U. Wis. Law Sch., 1996-97. bd. dirs. Community TV, Inc., Madison, 1984-87. Mem. Assn. Trial Lawyers Am., Wis. Acad. Trial Lawyers, Wis. Bar Assn., Dane County Bar Assn., Rugby Club of Madison. Home: 5325 Lighthouse Bay Dr Madison WI 53704-1113 Office: Foley & Lardner PO Box 1497 Madison WI 53701

WHITNEY, RODGER FRANKLIN, university housing director; b. Dallas, Feb. 2, 1948; s. Roger Albert and Genevieve Mae (Mohr) W. Cert. higher studies, U. Lausanne, Switzerland, 1970; BA, So. Meth. U., 1971, M Liberal Arts, 1973; EdD, Harvard U., 1978. Dir. upperclass residences So. Meth. U., Dallas, 1971-73, mem. faculty, 1973-75; dir. Mohr Chevrolet Edn. Found., Dallas, 1975-77; dir. North Park East, Raymond D. Nasher Co., Dallas, 1977-79; dir. Stanford Housing Ctr., asst. dean student affairs Stanford (Calif.) U., 1979-91, assoc. dir. housing and dining, 1991—; dir. Camp Grady Spruce, YMCA, Dallas, 1971-76, bd. dirs., 1976-80. Bd. dirs. Kentfield Commons, Redwood City, Calif., 1989-91. Mem. APPA, Assn. Coll. and Univ. Housing Officers, Harvard Club San Francisco, Phi Beta Kappa. Avocations: swimming, travel, history, reading, music. Home: 861 Whitehall Ln Redwood City CA 94061-3685 Office: Stanford U Housing Ops 565 Cowell Ln Stanford CA 94305-8512

WHITNEY, RUTH REINKE, magazine editor; b. Oshkosh, Wis., July 23, 1928; d. Leonard G. and Helen (Diestler) Reinke; m. Daniel A. Whitney, Nov. 19, 1949; 1 son, Philip. BA, Northwestern U., 1949. Copywriter edn. dept. circulation div. Time, Inc., 1949-53; editor-in-chief Better Living mag., 1953-56; assoc. editor Seventeen magazine, 1956-62, exec. editor, 1962-67; editor-in-chief Glamour mag., N.Y.C., 1967—. Recipient Nat. Mag. award gen. excellence, 1981, 91; Pub. Interest, 1992, Cosmetic Executive Women Achiever award, 1993, honor award Women's City Club N.Y.; honoree Gala 11 Birmingham, So. Coll., 1993. Mem. Fashion Group, Am. Soc. Mag. Editors (pres. 1975-77, exec. com. 1989-92), Women in Communication (Matrix award 1980), Women in Media, U.S. Info. Agy. (mag. and print com. 1989-93), Alpha Chi Omega. Office: Glamour Condé Nast Bldg 350 Madison Ave New York NY 10017-3704*

WHITNEY, WILLIAM CHOWNING, retired banker, financial consultant; b. Fullerton, Nebr., June 28, 1920; s. Barlow N. and Lena C. (Price) W.; m. Joan F. Whitney; children—William H., David M., Terri Lynn, Sherri Lee, Jonathan P., Laura Louise. B.S. cum laude, Loyola U., Chgo., 1949. Asst. bank examiner Fed. Res. Bank, Chgo., 1938-41; asst. auditor South Side Bank and Trust Co., Chgo., 1946-49; comptroller Peoples Nat. Bank, Bay City, Mich., 1949-52; asst. v.p., comptroller Tex. Bank and Trust Co., Dallas, 1952-54; with Old Kent Bank and Trust Co., Grand Rapids, Mich., 1954-86; sr. v.p., CFO, sec. bd., dir. Old Kent Fin. Corp., 1965-86; cons. Amway Corp., 1986—. Chmn. Met. Hosp., 1986-93, Met. Health Corp., 1987-95; treas. Keswick United Meth. Ch. Capt. AUS, 1941-46. Mem. Fin. Execs. Inst. (past pres.), Mich. Banks Assn., Bank Adminstrn. Inst., Grand Rapids C. of C., Rotary, Peninsular Club, Cascade County Club, Univ. Club, Ada Lodge, Masons (fin. com. Grand Lodge), Econ. Club, VFW, Am. Legion. Home: 742 Apple Tree Dr Suttons Bay MI 49682-9778

WHITNEY, WILLIAM ELLIOT, JR., advertising agency executive; b. Albany, N.Y., Feb. 22, 1933; s. William Elliot and Louise E. (Goldsmith) W.; m. Nancy B. Bivings, Mar. 1, 1958; children—Susan, James, Douglas. B.A. cum laude, Amherst Coll., 1954; M.B.A., Harvard U., 1956. Account exec. McCann-Erickson, N.Y.C., 1956-58, Marschalk Co., N.Y.C., 1958-60; v.p., then sr. v.p. Ogilvy & Mather, N.Y.C., 1960-80; sr. v.p., mng. dir. Ogilvy & Mather, Chgo., 1980-85, exec. v.p., 1985-87, pres., 1987-89, chmn., 1990-91; cons. ptnr. Redirections, Inc., 1991—; lectr. U. Chgo. Grad. Sch. Bus., 1991—. Bd. dirs., v.p. Chgo. Coun. Boy Scouts Am., 1978-81, 88—, Off-the-St. Club, Chgo., 1979—, pres., 1988-89; bd. dirs. Hinsdale (Ill.) Cmty. House, 1981, King-Bruwaert House, 1988—; v.p. civic adv. bd. Hinsdale Hosp., 1989-93; bd. dirs. Exec. Svc. Corps of Chgo., 1996—; trustee Village of Hinsdale, 1993—, pres., 1997. Mem. Chgo. Advt. Club (pres.), Econs. Club, Hinsdale Golf Club. Home: 736 S Park Ave Hinsdale IL 60521-4646

WHITSEL, RICHARD HARRY, biologist, entomologist; b. Denver, Feb. 23, 1931; s. Richard Elstun and Edith Muriel (Harry) W.; children by previous marriages: Russell David, Robert Alan, Michael Dale, Steven Deane. BA, U. Calif., Berkeley, 1954; MA, San Jose State Coll., 1962. Sr. rsch. biologist San Mateo County Mosquito Abatement Dist., Burlingame, Calif., 1959-72; environ. program mgr., chief of watershed mgmt., chief of planning Calif. Regional Water Quality Control Bd., Oakland, 1972—; mem. grad. faculty water resource mgmt. U. San Francisco, 1987-89. Served with Med. Service Corps, U.S. Army, 1954-56. Mem. Entomol. Soc. Am., Entomol. Soc. Wash., Am. Mosquito Control Assn., Calif. Alumni Assn., The Benjamin Ide Wheeler Soc., Nat. Parks and Conservation Assn. (life), Sierra Club. Democrat. Episcopalian. Contbr. articles to profl. jours. Home: 4331 Blenheim Way Concord CA 94521-4258 Office: Calif Regional Water Quality Control Bd 2101 Webster St Oakland CA 94612-3027 *Any success that I have achieved probalby is the result of my fortune to have been exposed to some outstanding educators and scientists as well as being somewhat imaginative by nature. Working with young professional people keeps me young in spirit and seems to renew my enthusiasm in whatever I do.*

WHITSEL, ROBERT MALCOLM, retired insurance company executive; b. Lafayette, Ind., Dec. 30, 1929; s. Earl Newton and Elizabeth (Bader) W.; m. Marilyn Katherine House, Oct. 15, 1955; children—Rebecca Sue, Cynthia Ann. BS, Ind. U., 1951, MBA, 1954; hon. D of Mgmt., Purdue U. With Lafayette Life Ins. Co., 1954-95, mem. exec. com., 1968-95, exec. v.p., 1973, pres., 1973-95, also bd. dirs., ret., 1995; mem. adv. bd. NBD, Bank. Elder, trustee, deacon Presbyn. Ch., 1965-74; dir., past pres. Jr. Achievement Greater Lafayette, Inc., 1976-77, Ctrl. Presbyn. Found., Edgelea PTA; past pres., bd. dirs., past campaign chmn. United Way Greater Lafayette; past v.p., bd. dirs. Wabash Sch. for Mentally Retarded; past mem. adv. bd. Purdue Ctr. for Econ. Edn.; past pres., bd. dirs. Capital Funds Found. Greater Lafayette; bd. dirs. Lafayette Home Hosp., 1972—, mem. fin. com., 1976—, past pres.; trustee YWCA Found.; past chmn. Greater Lafayette Progress Inc., North Ctrl. Health Svcs., Inc.; chmn. West Lafayette Found., Inc., Westminster Village Retirement Ctr.; past pres. Greater Lafayette Cmty. Found.; bd. dirs., mem. exec. com. purdue Rsch. Found. 1st lt. USAF, 1951-53. Recipient Nat. Bus. Leadership award Jr. Achievement, 1977. Mem. Soc. Residential Appraisers, Ind. Mortgage Bankers Assn. (past pres.), Am. Coun. Life Ins. (past bd. dirs., chmn. Forum 500 sect.), Soc. Fin. Analysts, Assn. Ind. Life Ins. Cos. (past pres.), Ind. C. of C. (past dir.), Greater Lafayette C. of C. (past pres.), Ind. Soc. of Chgo., Lafayette Country Club (past pres., dir.), Sagamore of the Wabash (designated), Town and Gown Club, Masons, Beta Gamma Sigma. Republican. Home: 541 Old Farm Rd Lafayette IN 47905-3515 Office: Lafayette Life Ins Co 1905 Teal Rd # 7007 Lafayette IN 47905-2225

WHITSELL, DORIS BENNER, retired educator; b. Poplar Grove, Ill., Mar. 17, 1923; d. Ralph Erwin and Sarah McKay (Mulligan) Wheeler; m. Robert M. Benner, Dec. 1945 (div. 1955); 1 child, Geoffrey Mark Benner (dec.); m. Eugene B. Whitsell, Feb. 1969 (dec. 1972). BS, No. Ill. U., 1944, MS in Edn., 1967; postgrad., Rockford Coll., 1964. Tchr. English and home econs. Lee (Ill.) High Sch., 1944-45; tchr. English Ashton (Ill.) Cmty. H.S., 1945-46; tchr. Morris Kennedy Sch., Rockford, Ill., 1952-55, William Nashold Sch., Rockford, 1955-56; tchr. English, drama Jefferson Jr. H.S., Rockford, 1956-69; tchr. English Richwoods H.S., Peoria, Ill., 1969-71; tchr. Calvin Coolidge Sch., Peoria, 1972-81; mem. textbook selection com. Dist. 150, Peoria, 1973-75, curriculum planning com., 1974-75, tutor for homebound, 1982-83, cons. competency test seminar; cons. textbook divsn. Harcourt, Brace, Jovanovich, 1981-83; evaluator North Ctrl. Accreditation Team, Jefferson H.S., Rockford, 1980. Counselor Operation Sr. Security, Peoria, 1986-89; treas. Rockford Women's Club Fortnighty Dept., 1961-62; past deaconess 1st Federated Ch., Peoria; pres. Willow Heights Homeowner's Assn., Peoria, 1979-81; bldg. rep. Rockford Edn. Assn., 1954-56, 3d v.p., 1968-70; vol. Rockford Midway Village and Mus. Ctr., 1992, 95-96; bd. dirs. Forest Vale Estate Condominiums, Meadows Assn., Rockford, 1994-96, treas., 1995-96. Named for Significant Svc. to the Community, Ret. Sr. Vol. Program, Peoria, 1986. Mem. Ill. Ret. Tchrs. Assn. (life, sec. 1982-90, bd. dirs. Found. Inc., 1985-93, moderator conv. panel 1990, Outstanding Svc. award 1989), Peoria Area Ret. Tchrs. Assn. (2d v.p. 1987-88, pres. 1989-90, chmn. state bldg. fund. com. 1987-88), AAUW (program v.p. 1988-89), Nat. Ret. Tchrs. Assn. (life), No. Ill. U. Alumni Assn., Delta Kappa Gamma (chmn. ins. com. Beta Gamma chpt. 1956-60, v.p. 1962-64, pres. 1964-66, mem. profl. affairs com. 1992-96, mem. lit. com. 1997—, Winnebago County ret. tchrs. unit 1992-97, chmn. personal growth and svc. com. Nu chpt. 1988-90, mem. program com. Lambda state chpt. 1978-80, mem. literacy com. 1997—). Avocations: reading, traveling, interior decorating, theatre. Home: 1283 Aarons Ct Rockford IL 61108-1536

WHITSELL, JOHN CRAWFORD, II, general surgeon; b. St. Joseph, Mo., Dec. 21, 1929; s. Ora Earl and Lorena (Spratt) W. AB, Grinnell Coll., 1950; MD, Washington U., St. Louis, 1954. Diplomate Am. Bd. Surgery, Am. Bd. Thoracic Surgery. From instr. to clin. prof. surgery Cornell U. Med. Ctr., N.Y.C., 1963-70; from asst. attending to attending in surgery N.Y. Hosp., N.Y.C., 1964-70; surg. dir. Rogosin Kidney Ctr. N.Y. Hosp.-Cornell Med. Ctr., N.Y.C., 1973-75; attending in surgery N.Y. Hosp., 1970—; clin. prof. surgery Cornell Med. Coll., 1970—; surg. cons. Rogosin Kidney Ctr., 1975—, Sharon (Conn.) Hosp., 1976—. Contbr. articles to profl. jours. Capt. USAF, 1961-63, Eng. Fellow ACS; mem. Transplantation Soc., N.Y. Surg. Soc., Am. Soc. Transplant Surgeons, N.Y. Soc. for Thoracic Surgery, Soc. Thoracic Surgeons, N.Y. Acad. Medicine, N.Y. Soc. Cardiovascular Surgery, Harvey Soc., Union Club of N.Y., Phi Beta Kappa. Avocations: golf, fishing, auto racing, antique cars. Office: 449 E 68th St New York NY 10021-6310

WHITSITT, ROBERT JAMES, professional basketball team executive; b. Madison, Wis., Jan. 10, 1956; s. Raymond Earl and Dolores June (Smith) W.; m. Jan Leslie Sundberg; children: Lillian Ashley, Sean James. BS, U. Wis., Stevens Point, 1977; MA, Ohio State U., 1978. Intern Indiana Pacers, Inpls., 1978, bus. tickets mgr., 1979, dir. bus. affairs and promotions, 1980, asst. gen. mgr., 1981-82; v.p. mktg. Kansas City (Mo.) Kings, 1982-84, v.p., asst. gen. mgr., 1984-85; v.p., asst. gen. mgr Sacramento Kings, 1985-86; pres. Seattle Supersonics, 1986-97, Portland Trail Blazers, 1997—. Mem. Nat. Basketball Assn. (alternate gov., mem. competition and rules com.). Republican. Lutheran. Lodge: Rotary. Avocations: skiing, jogging, reading, music. Office: Portland Trailblazers 1 Center Court Ste 200 Portland OR 97227*

WHITSON, JAMES NORFLEET, JR., diversified company executive; b. Clinton, Okla., Mar. 14, 1935; s. James Norfleet and Georgia (Webb) W.; m. Lyda Lee Gibson, Apr. 19, 1956; 1 child, James Mark. BBA, Tex. Tech U., 1957. With LTV, Inc., Dallas, 1960-70; v.p. fin. Omega-Alpha, Inc., 1970-73; pres. Sammons Communications, Inc., Dallas, 1973-89; exec. v.p., chief operating officer Sammons Enterprises, Inc., Dallas, 1989—; bd. dirs. Sammons Enterprises, Inc., C-Span, Tri-Continental Corp. Mem. Alpha Tau Omega. Home: 6606 Forestshire Dr Dallas TX 75230-2856 Office: Sammons Enterprises Inc 300 Crescent Ct Dallas TX 75201-1876

WHITT, GREGORY SIDNEY, molecular phylogenetics, evolution educator; b. Detroit, June 13, 1938; s. Sidney Abram and Millicent (Ward) W.; m. Dixie Lee Dailey, Aug. 25, 1963. B.S., Colo. State U., 1962, M.S., 1965; Ph.D., Yale U., 1970. Asst. prof. zoology U. Ill., Urbana, 1969-72; asso. prof. genetics and devel. U. Ill., 1972-77, prof., 1977-87, prof. ecology, ethology and evolution, 1987—; affiliate Ill. Natural History Survey, 1981—; mem. NIH study sect., 1975-76. Co-editor: Isozymes: Current Topics in Biological and Medical Research, 1977-87; editor: Isozyme Bull., 1978-81; mem. editorial bd. Biochem. Genetics, 1975—, Devel. Genetics, 1978-83, Jour. Molecular Evolution, 1979—, Molecular Biology and Evolution, 1983-93, Molecular Phylogenetics and Evolution, 1992—; contbr. articles to profl. jours. Fellow AAAS; mem. Am. Genetics Assn., Am. Soc. Ichthyologists and Herpetologists, Soc. for Protection of Old Fishes, Internat. Soc. Molecular Evolution, Soc. Systematic Biologists. Home: 1510 Trails Dr Urbana IL 61802-7052 Office: U Ill Dept Ecol Ethol/Evol 515 Morrill Hall 505 S Goodwin Ave Urbana IL 61801-3707

WHITT, MARY F., reading educator, consultant; b. Montgomery, Ala.; d. Clarence D. Whitt Sr. and Georgia Arms. BS, Ala. State U., 1958; MEd, U. Ariz., 1971; EdD, U. Ala., 1980; postgrad., various colls. ongoing. Camp counselor N.Y.C. Mission Soc., Port Jervis, summer 1956; recreation counselor Dayton (Ohio) Parks and Recreation Dept., summer 1963; adminstrv. asst. Wiley Coll./NDEA Inst., Marshall, Tex., summer 1965; tchr. Montgomery (Ala.) County Schs., 1958-62; coordinator sci. and math. Dayton (Ohio) pub. schs., 1962-67; reading and spl. edn. tchr. Vacaville (Calif.) Unified Sch. Dist., 1967-70; coord. reading Dallas Pub. Schs., 1971-72; prof. reading Ala. State U., Montgomery, 1972—. Contbr. articles to profl. jurs. U.S. Office Edn. fellow, 1970, 76, 77, NSF fellow, 1961, 62, 64, 66. Mem. Internat. Reading Assn., Capstone Coll. of Edn. Soc., AAUW, Phi Delta Kappa, Kappa Delta Pi. Home: 717 Genetta Ct Montgomery AL 36104-5701

WHITT, RICHARD ERNEST, reporter; b. Greenup County, Ky., Dec. 15, 1944; s. Walter Charles and Irene (Hayes) W.; m. Terri Bellizzi; children: Hayes Chadwick, Emily. Student, Ashland (Ky.) Community Coll., 1966-68; B.A. in Journalism, U. Ky., 1970. Reporter Middlesboro (Ky.) Daily News, 1970-71; asst. state editor Waterloo (Iowa) Courier, 1971-72; city editor Kingsport (Tenn.) Times, 1972-76; No. Ky. bur. chief Courier-Jour., Louisville, 1977; Frankfort bur. chief Courier-Jour., 1977-80, spl. projects reporter, 1980-89; investigative reporter Atlanta Jour. & Constn., 1989—. Served with USN, 1962-66. Decorated Air medal; recipient Pulitzer prize for coverage of Beverly Hills Supper Club fire, 1978; named Outstanding Ky. Journalist, 1978; recipient John Hancock award for excellence, 1983; named to U. Ky. Journalism Hall of Fame, 1995. Democrat. Office: Atlanta Jour & Constn 72 Marietta St NW Atlanta GA 30303-2804

WHITT, ROBERT AMPUDIA, III, advertising executive, marketing professional; b. San Antonio, Oct. 15, 1930; s. Robert and Alice (Whitt) Ampudia; m. Mary Jane Kothmann, June 2, 1951; children: April Whitt Horner, Robert IV, Roxanne Seaman. BA in Internat. Trade, U. of the Ams., Mexico City, 1955; postgrad., Am. Grad. Sch. Internat. Mgmt., Phoenix, 1991, 92. Sales mgr. Sinclair & Valentine Co., Cali, Colombia, 1956-59; CEO for L.Am. Vision, Inc., Mexico City, 1960-74; pres., CEO Tex. Parade, Inc., Austin, 1974-77; CEO world ops. Novedades Editores, Mexico City, 1977-82; chmn., CEO Mktg. Mercadeo Internat., San Antonio, 1982-96, Ampudia Whitt & Assocs., Inc., Dallas, 1996—; bd. dirs. Robea, S.A., Mexico City, Poliform, S.A., Mexico City, Tex. Bus. Hall of Fame Foundation, Dallas; mem. Alliance for Progress Task Force, 1963-67; dir. gen. Disal Publicidad, Mexico City, 1996—, bd. dirs. Co-author: How to Market and Distribute in Mexico, 1995; editor: (Spanish lang.) Dallas Cowboys mag., 1979, 80, 91 (Best Content award), Bienestar mag., 1978 (Best Content award); contbr. articles to profl. jours. Sgt. U.S. Airborne, 1950-53. Recipient Nat. Winner award Silver Microphone, 1991, Nat. Finalist award, 1991, Addy award Am. Advt. Fedn., 1992, Nat. Winner award Telly awards (4), 1993, 95; named Speaker of the Year Toastmasters Internat., 1980. Mem. Fgn. Corr. Club, 11th Airborne Div. Assn. (life), Brookhaven Country Club (Dallas), Univ. Club (Dallas), Univ. Club (Mexico City), Metropolitan Soc. of Clubs. Office: Ampudia Whitt & Assocs Inc 15303 Dallas Pkwy Dallas TX 75248-4678 *Only oneself can truly measure one's achievements. My greatest achievement is that I have no regrets and wouldn't change a minute, day or year of my life...including the downtimes.*

WHITTAKER, BILL DOUGLAS, minister; b. Bowling Green, Ky., June 14, 1943; s. Ewing A. and Lois (Jenkins) W.; m. Rebecca Kaye Howard, June 18, 1966; children: John, Karen, Mary. BA, Western Ky. U., 1965; MDiv, So. Bapt. Theol. Sem., Louisville, 1969, D of Ministry, 1974. Ordained to ministry So. Bapt. Conv., 1964. Pastor 1st Bapt. Ch., Sturgis, Ky., 1969-76, Murray, Ky., 1976-82; missionary Internat. Mission Bd., So. Bapt. Conv., The Philippines, 1983-86; pastor Downtown Bapt. Ch., Orlando, Fla., 1986-88; pres. Clear Creek Bapt. Bible Coll., Pineville, Ky., 1988—. Author: Preparing to Preach, 1986; columnist Western Recorder newspaper, 1988—, Pineville Sun, 1993—. Bd. dirs. Coalition for the Homeless, Cen. Fla. YMCA, Orlando, 1986-88. Mem. Am. Assn. Bible Colls. (del. 1988), Assn. So. Bapt. Colls. and Schs. (del. 1988—), Ky. Bapt. Hist. Soc., Kiwanis (pres. Pineville chpt. 1994-95, dist. 6 lt. gov. 1997—), Ky. Bapt. Conv. (pres. 1980). Home and Office: 300 Clear Creek Rd Pineville KY 40977-9752

WHITTAKER, DOUGLAS KIRKLAND, school system adminstrator; b. Westfield, N.J., July 14, 1949; s. Alfred Albert and Marion I. (Crocket) W.; m. Susan Kay Helsing, Aug. 9, 1969; children: Jessica Erin, Angela Gaye. BS, Taylor U., 1971; MA, Ball State U., 1975; EdD, Nova U., 1981. Cert. elem. educator, elem. and middle adminstrn. Tchr. Marion (Ind.) Community Schs., 1971-73, Lee County Schs., Ft. Myers, Fla., 1973-80; asst. prin. Lee County Schs., Ft. Myers, 1980-81, elem. prin., 1981-86, middle sch. prin., 1986-90, elem. prin., 1990-92, dir. curriculum svcs., 1993-95; exec. dir. curriculum and sch. improvement James A. Adams Pub. Edn. Ctr., Ft. Myers, 1995-97, asst. supt. instrn., 1997—; adj. prof. Nova U., Ft. Lauderdale, Fla., 1983—; trainer in field. Contbr. articles to profl. jours. Mem. ASCD, NEA, Phi Delta Kappa. Republican. Avocations: golf, travel, reading, singing. Home: 3931 Hidden Acres Cir Fort Myers FL 33903-7120 Office: Dr James A Adams Pub Edn Ctr 2055 Central Ave Fort Myers FL 33901-3916

WHITTAKER, JEANNE EVANS, former newspaper columnist; b. Detroit, Jan. 1, 1934; d. Alfred Heacock and Margaret (Evans) W.; m. Charles Martin Hines Jr., Sept. 29, 1962 (div. Feb. 1970); children: Charles M. Hines III, Margaret Helen Whittaker. Student, Northwestern U., 1952-53; BS in History, U. Mich., 1956. Clubmobile worker UN forces ARC, Korea, 1956-58; staff programmer ARC, Chaumont, Evreux, France, 1958-61; dir. Bexar County chpt. youth ARC, San Antonio, 1961-62; staff writer/columnist Detroit Free Press, 1970-75; editor Mich. Social Register, 1975-77; Lifestyle editor Observer and Eccentric newspapers, Birmingham, Mich., 1977-87; staff writer, columnist Detroit News, 1987-91. Contbr. articles to mags. Bd. dirs. Detroit chpt. ARC, 1989-92, Detroit Hist. Soc. Recipient Penney-Mo. award U. Mo., 1984; 1st place lifestyles/Family award Mich. Press Assn., 1982, 84, Gen. Excellence award 1982, 86; Gen. Excellence award Suburban Newspaper Assn., 1979. Mem. Detroit Hist. Soc. (bd. dirs. 1986-91), Southeastern Mich. Chpt. ARC (bd. dirs. 1987-93). Episcopalian. Avocations: writing, reading, travel. Home: 552 Cadieux Rd Grosse Pointe MI 48230-1508

WHITTAKER, JUDITH ANN CAMERON, lawyer; b. N.Y.C., June 12, 1938; d. Thomas Macdonald and Mindel (Wallman) Cameron; m. Kent E. Whittaker, Jan. 30, 1960; children: Charles Evans II, Catherine Cameron. BA, Brown U., 1959; JD, U. Mo., 1963. Bar: Mo. 1963, U.S. Dist. Ct. (we. dist.) Mo. 1963, U.S. Ct. Appeals (8th cir.) 1965, U.S. Supreme Ct. 1980, D.C. 1987. Assoc. and ptnr. Sheffrey, Ryder & Skeer, Kansas City, Mo., 1963-72; asst. and assoc. gen. coun., v.p. gen. coun. Hallmark Cards, Inc., Kansas City, 1972—; dir., v.p., gen. coun. Univision Holdings, Inc., Kansas City, 1988-92; dir. MCI Comm. Corp., 1985—, Harmon Industries, 1993—; dir. Am. Arbitration Assn., 1996—. Trustee Brown U. Providence, 1977-83, U. Mo. Law Found., Kansas City, 1977-90; dir. Kansas City (Mo.) Indsl. Devel. Authority, 1981-84, Legal Aid Kansas City, 1971-77, De La Salle Sch., 1993—. Mem. Internat. Soc. Barristers. Episcopalian. Avocations: reading, skiing, hiking, piano. Office: Hallmark Cards Dept 339 PO Box 419126 Kansas City MO 64141-6126

WHITTELL, POLLY (MARY) KAYE, editor, writer; b. Washington, Oct. 20; d. Alfred Whittell Jr. and Mary Halsey (Patchin) Hopper. BA in English, U. Calif., Berkeley; postgrad., Radcliffe Coll., Columbia U. Rschr. Nat. Rev. Mag., N.Y.C., 1970-71; asst. to presdl. speech writer The White House, Washington, 1971-72; asst. editor Travel Age Mag., Dunn & Bradstreet Publs., N.Y.C., 1973-75; copy editor Ski Mag. Skier's Guides, Times-Mirror Mags. and Am. Express, N.Y.C., 1975-76; asst. editor to sr. editor Hearst Mags., Motor Boating & Sailing Mag., N.Y.C., 1977—. Contbr. articles to nat. and internat. consumer mags. Mem. charity benefit com. Youth Counseling League, N.Y.C., 1975-85, and others; v.p. Knickerbocker Rep. Club, N.Y.C., 1979-80; elected mem. N.Y. Rep. County Com., N.Y.C., 1980-84. Mem. Boating Writers Internat. (award for environ. article 1995), Soc. Profl. Journalists, Social Register Assn., SandBar Beach Club (v.p. membership 1980-82). Episcopalian. Avocations: photography, travel, boating, skiing. Home: 240 Central Park S New York NY 10019-1413 Office: Motor Boating & Sailing Hearst Mags 250 W 55th St New York NY 10019-5201

WHITTEMORE, EDWARD REED, II, poet, retired educator; b. New Haven, Sept. 11, 1919; s. Edward Reed and Margaret Eleanor (Carr) W.; m. Helen Lundeen, Oct. 3, 1952; children: Catherine Carr, Edward Reed III, John Lundeen, Margaret Goodhue. A.B., Yale U., 1941; postgrad., Princeton U., 1945-46; Litt.D., Carleton Coll., 1971. Mem. faculty Carleton Coll., 1947-67, prof. English, 1962-67, chmn. dept., 1962-64; program assoc. Nat. Inst. Pub. Affairs, 1966-68; editor Carleton Miscellany, 1960-64; cons. in poetry Libr. of Congress, 1964-65, 84-85; Bain-Swiggett lectr. Princeton, 1967; prof. U. Md., 1968-84, prof. emeritus, 1984—; poet laureate State of Md., 1985-88; lit. editor New Republic, 1969-74. Author: Heroes and Heroines, 1947, An American Takes a Walk, 1956, The Self-Made Man, 1959, The Boy From Iowa, 1962, The Fascination of the Abomination, 1963, Poems, New and Selected, 1967, From Zero to the Absolute, 1967, 50 Poems 50, 1970, The Mother's Breast and the Father's House, 1974, William Carlos Williams: Poet from Jersey, 1975, The Poet as Journalist, 1976, The Feel of Rock, 1982, Pure Lives, 1988, Whole Lives, 1989, The Past, the Future, the Present, 1990, Six Literary Lives, 1993; editor: Furioso, 1939-53, Browning, 1960, Delos mag., 1988-91. Capt. USAAF, 1941-45. Recipient award merit AAAL, 1971. Home: 4526 Albion Rd College Park MD 20740-3610

WHITTEMORE, FRANK BOWEN, environmental, energy and management consultant; b. Worcester, Mass., Dec. 16, 1916; s. Frank Bowen and Blanche (Barney) W.; m. Marjorie Usher, Jan. 24, 1943; children: Suzanne Blanche, David Chandler. Student, Roanoke Coll., 1937-38, Franklin Tech. Coll., 1941, Worcester Polytech. Inst., 1942; diploma, Inst. of Childrens Lit., 1996. Various positions Norton Co., Worcester, 1942-79; exec. dir. Providence Engring. Soc., 1978-79; pres. Rhode Islanders Saving Energy office of Gov., Providence, 1979-81; vice chmn. Narragansett Bay Commn., Providence, 1980-86; mgmt. cons. Barrington, R.I., 1980—. Contbr. numerous articles to mags., newspapers. Vice chmn. Barrington Zoning Bd., 1964-65; founder, exec. dir. Bar-Zap Litter Program, Barrington, 1966—; founder, chmn., trustee Save the Bay, Providence, 1973—; mem. Gov's. Task Force for Clean Water, Providence, 1981-82, Justice Assistance Corp., Providence, 1982-83; mem. Common Cause (coord. Nat. Issues), Providence, 1980—; dir. mktg. R.I. Parks Assn., 1985-86, Barrington Juvenile Hearing Bd., 1988—, Barrington Substance Abuse Task Force, 1988—, R.I. Earth Day State Com.; chair State Fund Raising; chmn. bd. dirs. Bristol County (R.I.) Citizens for Better Water Mgmt., 1990; mem. Save the Runnins River Task Force Barrington Land Conservancy. With USAF, 1943. Recipient citations from R.I. Senate, 1978, Ho. Reps., 1979, Gov., 1981, N.E. Environ. Network Leadership award Tufts U., Medford, Mass., 1984, Outstanding Environmentalist award Save The Bay, Providence, 1983, Outstanding Citizen, Town of Barrington, R.I., 1994, Outstanding Vol. award Ipswich River Wildlife Soc., 1995. Mem. Audubon Soc. of R.I. (bd. dirs., vol.), Police Athletic League. Unitarian. Avocations: cross-country and downhill skiing, tennis, hiking, canoeing. Home and Office: 123 Cherry St Wenham MA 01984-1101

WHITTEMORE, LAURENCE FREDERICK, private banker; b. Bangor, Maine, Mar. 7, 1929; s. John Cambridge and Elizabeth Payson (Prentiss) W.; m. Sarah Lee Arnold, Aug. 9, 1958; children—Arianna, Gioia, Lia, Nike. B.A., Yale U., 1951; M.B.A., Harvard U., 1953; student, Balliol Coll., Oxford U., Eng., 1950. Account mgr. Brown Bros. Harriman, N.Y.C., 1956-72; gen. mgr. Brown Bros. Harriman, 1972-74; ptnr. Brown Bros. Harriman & Co., 1974—; dir. Manhattan Life Ins. Co., N.Y.C., Otto Wolff US Holding Co., 1982-86, Hurricane Industries, Houston, 1982-85, Albany Ins. Co., N.Y.C., Atlas Assurance Co. of Am., N.Y.C., 1984-86; mem. investment adv. com. Union Investment GmbH, Frankfurt, West Germany, 1973—; mem. Chgo. Stock Exch., 1975—. Trustee Sarah Lawrence Coll., 1988—, Am. Inst. Contemporary German Studies, 1994—; mem. Nat. Com. on U.S. China Rels., N.Y.C., 1982—, Chgo. Coun. on Fgn. Rels., 1980—; del. Assn. Yale Alumni, New Haven, 1982-86; chmn. Yale 35th Reunion Gift Drive, 1983-86; gov. Opportunity Internat., 1996—; co-chair Asia Soc. Pres.'s Coun., 1996—; mem. Bus. Execs. for Nat. Security, 1996—. Mem. Econ. Club of Chgo., N.Y. Soc. Security Analysts, Investment Analysts Soc. Chgo., Assn. for Investment Mgmt. and Rsch. Republican. Episcopalian. Clubs: Links, Yale, India House (N.Y.C.); Chicago; Minneapolis (Mpls.). Office: Brown Bros Harriman & Co 59 Wall St New York NY 10005-2808

WHITTEMORE, PAUL BAXTER, psychologist; b. Framingham, Mass., Apr. 11, 1948; s. Harry Ballou and Margaret (Brown) W.; m. Jane L. Manson, Apr. 22, 1995. BA in Religion, Ea. Nazarene Coll., 1970; MDiv., Nazarene Theol. Sem., 1973; MA in Theology, Vanderbilt U., 1975, PhD in Theology, 1978; PhD in Clin. Psychology, U. Tenn., 1987. Lic. psychologist, Calif. Asst. prof. philosophy and edn. Trevecca Nazarene Coll., Nashville, Tenn., 1973-76; asst. prof. philosophy and theology Point Loma Coll., San Diego, Calif., 1976-80; asst. prof. philosophy Middle Tenn. State U., Murfreesboro, 1980-83; clin. psychology intern. LAC/U. So. Calif. Med. Ctr., L.A., 1986-87; coord. behavior health ctr. Calif. Med. Ctr., L.A., 1987-88; clin. asst. prof. family medicine sch. medicine U. So. Calif., L.A., 1988—; pvt. practice psychologist Newport Beach, Calif., 1989-; mem. behavioral sci. faculty Glendale Adventist Family Practice Residency Program, Glendale, Calif., 1989-90; inpatient group therapist Ingleside Hosp., Rosemead, Calif., 1990-92; founder, pres. The Date Coach, 1992—. Contbr. articles to profl. jours. Recipient Andrew W. Mellon Postdoctoral Faculty Devel. award Vanderbilt U., 1981. Mem. APA, Am. Acad. Religion, Am. Philos. Assn., AAUP (chpt. v.p. 1982-83), Calif. Psychol. Assn. (media divsn. sec.-treas. 1997—), Orange County Employee Assistance Profl. Assn. (bd. dirs. 1993—), Orange County Psychol. Assn. (bd. dirs. 1996—). Achievements include discovery of link between phenylthiocarbamide tasting and depression. Office: 3901 Macarthur Blvd Ste 200 Newport Beach CA 92660-3011

WHITTEMORE, RONALD P., hospital administrator, retired army officer, nursing educator; b. Saco, Maine, Aug. 10, 1946; s. Ronald B. and Pauline L. (Larson) W.; m. Judy D. McDonald, Feb. 17, 1967; 1 child, Leicia Michelle. BGS, U. S.C., 1974, MEd, 1977; BSN, Med. Coll. Ga., 1975. Enlisted U.S. Army, 1968, advanced through ranks to maj., 1985, ret., 1991; adult/oncology nurse practitioner Martin Army Community Hosp.; asst. head nurse SICU, infection control practitioner Moncrief Army Community Hosp.; infection control practitioner U.S. Army Hosp., Seoul, Korea; chief nurse 2d Combat Support Hosp., Ft. Benning, Ga.; community health nurse Brooke Army Med. Ctr., Ft. Sam Houston, Tex.; comty. health nurse Giessen (Fed. Republic Germany) Mil. Comty.; clin. instr. Eisenhower Army Med. Ctr., Ft. Gordon, Ga.; chief nursing adminstrn. E/N Frankfurt (Germany) Army Med. Ctr.; adminstr., dir. quality improvement Gracewood (Ga.) State Sch. and Hosp., 1995—; instr. Augusta (Ga.) Tech. Inst.; nurse epidemiologist Med. Coll. Ga., Augusta. Mem. ANA, Ga. ANA (3d Dist. honoree, pres. 1983-85), Am. Holistic Nurses Assn., Nat. Assn. Health Care Quality Profls., Sigma Theta Tau. Home: 352 Stagecoach Way Martinez GA 30907 Office: Gracewood State Sch & Hosp Gracewood GA 30812

WHITTEN, CHARLES ALEXANDER, JR., physics educator; b. Harrisburg, Pa., Jan. 20, 1940; s. Charles Alexander and Helen (Shoop) W.; m. Joan Emann, Nov. 20, 1965; 1 son, Charles Alexander III. B.S. summa cum laude, Yale U., 1961; Ph.D. in Physics, Princeton U., 1966. Research asso. A.W. Wright Nuclear Structure Lab., Yale U., 1966-68; asst. prof. physics UCLA, 1968-74, assoc. prof., 1974-80, prof., 1980—, vice chmn. physics dept., 1982-86; vis. scientist Centre d'Etudes Nucléaires de Saclay-Moyenne Energie, 1980-81, 86-87. Contbr. articles to profl. jours. Mem. Am. Phys. Soc., Sigma Pi Sigma, Phi Beta Kappa. Home: 9844 Vicar St Los Angeles CA 90034-2719

WHITTEN, DAVID GEORGE, chemistry educator; b. Washington, Jan. 25, 1938; s. David Guy and Miriam Deland (Price) W.; m. Jo Wright, July 9, 1960; children: Jenifer Marie, Guy David. A.B., Johns Hopkins U., 1959; M.A., Johns Hopkins U., 1961, Ph.D., 1963. Asst. prof. chemistry U. N.C., Chapel Hill, 1966-70, assoc. prof., 1970-73, prof., 1973-80, M.A. Smith prof., 1980-83; C.E. Kenneth Mees prof. U. Rochester, N.Y., 1983—, chair dept. chemistry, 1988-91, 95—; dir. Ctr. for Photoinduced Charge Transfer U. Rochester, N.Y., 1989-95; mem. adv. com. for chemistry NSF; cons. Eastman Kodak Co.; Rochester, N.Y. Alfred P. Sloan fellow, 1970; John van Geuns fellow, 1973; recipient special U.S. scientist award Alexander von Humboldt Found., 1975; Japan Soc. for Promotion of Sci. fellow, 1982. Mem. AAAS, Am. Chem. Soc. (award in colloid and surface chemistry 1992), Internat. Union of Pure and Applied Chemistry (commn. on photochemistry), Interam. Photochem. Soc. Democrat. Episcopalian. Home: 100 Gilbert Hall Rochester NY 14607-3405 Office: U Rochester Dept Chemistry 404 Hutchinson Hall Rochester NY 14627

WHITTEN, DOLPHUS, JR., former university administrator, educational consortium executive; b. Hope, Ark., June 20, 1916; s. Dolphus and Annie Tyree (Logan) W.; m. Marie Braden, May 1, 1939; 1 dau., Suzanne (Mrs. H. Robert Guy). B.A., Ouachita Coll., 1936; M.A., U. Tex., 1940, Ph.D., 1961; postgrad., Western Res. U.; LL.D., McMurry Coll., Abilene, Tex., 1964. High Sch. tchr. and prin., Ark. pub. schs., 1936-42; prin. Hope Jr.-Sr. High Sch., 1945-47; dir. extension and placement services, asso. prof. history Henderson State Tchrs. Coll., Arkadelphia, Ark., 1947-58; adminstrv. dean Oklahoma City U., 1958-61, adminstrv. v.p., 1961-70, acting pres., 1962-63, 69-70, pres., 1970-79, pres. emeritus, 1979—; adj. prof. history Elon Coll., 1979-80; exec. dir. Joint Ednl. Consortium, Arkadelphia, Ark., 1980-90. Bd. dirs. Ark. Humanities Coun., 1992—. Served with USAAF, 1942-45; lt. col. ret. Inducted into Okla. Hall of Fame, 1975. Mem. Am. Hist. Assn., Ark. Hist. Assn., Okla. Heritage Assn., Rotary (gov. local dist. 1991-92), Alpha Chi (past pres. region II), Pi Gamma Mu, Phi Alpha Theta, Sigma Alpha Iota. Methodist.

WHITTEN, JERRY LYNN, chemistry educator; b. Bartow, Fla., Aug. 13, 1937; s. John Graves and Dorothy Iola (Jordan) W.; m. Mary Hill (div. Sept. 1977); 1 child, Jerrard John; m. Adela Chrzeszczyk, June 21, 1980; 1 child, Christina. BS in Chemistry, Ga. Inst. Tech., 1960, PhD, 1964. Cert. chemist. Rsch. assoc. to instr. Princeton (N.J.) U., 1963-65; asst. prof. chemistry Mich. State U., East Lansing, 1965-67; asst. prof. chemistry SUNY, Stony Brook, 1967-68, assoc. prof., 1968-73, prof., 1973-89, chmn. chemistry dept., 1985-89; prof. chemistry, dean Coll. Phys. and Math. Scis. N.C. State U., Raleigh, 1989—; vis. prof. Centre Europèen de Calcul Atomique et Molèculaire, Orsay, France, 1974-75, Univ. Bonn and Wuppertal, Fed. Republic Germany, 1979-80, Eidgenossische Technische Hochschule, Zurich, Switzerland, 1984. Contbr. more than 140 articles to profl. jours. Bd. dirs. N.C. Sch. Sci. and Math Found., Burroughs Wellcome Fund. Recipient Alexander von Humboldt U.S. Sr. Scientist award, 1979; grantee Petroleum Rsch. Fund, 1966-67, 74-76, 77-81, NSF, 1967-72, U.S. Dept. Energy, 1977—; SDIO/ONR grantee, 1991-92; Alfred P. Sloan fellow, 1969-71. Mem. AAAS, Am. Phys. Soc., Am. Chem. Soc., N.Y. Acad. Scis., Sigma Xi. Democrat. Episcopalian. Avocations: boating, tennis, skiing. Office: NC State U Coll Dept Phy and Math Scis Box 8201 Raleigh NC 27695-8201

WHITTEN, LESLIE HUNTER, JR., author, newspaper reporter, poet; b. Jacksonville, Fla., Feb. 21, 1928; s. Leslie Hunter and Linnora (Harvey) W.; m. Phyllis Webber, Nov. 11, 1951; children: Leslie Hunter III, Andrew, Daniel, Deborah Wilson Gordon. B.A. in Journalism and English magna cum laude, Lehigh U., 1950, LHD, 1989. Newsman Radio Free Europe, 1952-57, I.N.S., 1957-58, U.P.I., 1958, Washington Post, 1958-63; with Hearst Newspapers, 1963-66; asst. bur. chief Hearst Newspapers, Washington, 1966-69; sr. investigator Jack Anderson's Washington Merry-Go-Round, 1969-92; pres. Athanor Inc., 1977-93; vis. assoc. prof. Lehigh U., 1967-69; adj. prof. So. Ill. U., 1984. Author: Progeny of the Adder, 1965, Moon of the Wolf, 1967, Pinion the Golden Eagle, 1968, The Abyss, 1970, F. Lee Bailey, 1971, The Alchemist, 1973, Conflict of Interest, 1976, Washington Cycle, 1979, Sometimes a Hero, 1979, A Killing Pace, 1983, A Day Without Sunshine, 1985, The Lost Disciple, 1989, The Fangs of Morning, 1994; contbr. numerous poems to anthologies and other publs. Served with AUS, 1946-48. Recipient hon. mention pub. service Washington Newspaper Guild, 1963, Edgerton award ACLU, 1974. Home and Office: 114 Eastmoor Dr Silver Spring MD 20901-1507

WHITTERS, JAMES PAYTON, III, lawyer, university administrator; b. Boston, Oct. 23, 1939; s. James P. Jr. and Norene (Jones) W.; m. Elizabeth Robertson, July 19, 1969; children: James P. IV, Catharine A. BA in History, Trinity Coll., Hartford, Conn., 1962; JD, Boston Coll., 1969; postgrad. U. Mass., Boston. Bar: Mass. 1969, U.S. Dist. Ct. Mass. 1970, U.S. Ct. Appeals (1st cir.) 1972. Assoc. Ely, Bartlett, Brown & Proctor, Boston, 1969-74; assoc. Gaston Snow & Ely Bartlett, Boston, 1974-79, ptnr., 1979-88; ptnr. Gaston & Snow, Boston, 1988-91; of counsel Peabody & Brown, Boston, 1991-95; dir. Office Career Svcs. Suffolk U. Law Sch., Boston, 1995—; adj. prof. Am. legal history Suffolk U. Law Sch., 1997—; bd. dirs., sec. Robertson Factories, Inc., Taunton, Mass., 1979—; v.p. Alkalol Co., Taunton, 1976-97, sr. v.p., 1997—; vis. tchr. Groton (Mass.) Sch., 1993-94; mem. Mass. Conflict Intervention Mediation Team, 1995—. Bd. dirs. New Eng. com. NAACP Legal Def. Fund, 1982—, Beacon Hill Nursery Sch., 1976-78, Mass. Applied Ctr. Law and Justice, 1997—; chmn. Mass. Outdoor Advt. Bd., Boston, 1975-81; vice chmn. Mass. Jud. Nominating Coun., Boston, 1983-87; trustee Trinity Coll., 1983-95; trustee, sec. Hurricane Island Outward Bound Sch., 1977-87; vice chmn., bd. dirs. Mass. affiliate Am. Heart Assn., 1979—, chmn., 1989-91; bd. dirs. Greater Boston Legal Svcs., 1982-84, 93—, Mass. Assn. Mediation Programs and Practitioners, 1993—. Lt. (j.g.) USN, 1962-65. Recipient Alumni Excellence award Trinity Coll., 1987. Mem. Boston Bar Assn., Mass. Bar Assn., ABA, The Country Club (Brookline, Mass.). Democrat. Unitarian. Avocations: reading history, mountain climbing & jogging. Home: 44 Mount Vernon St Boston MA 02108-1302

WHITTIER, MONTE RAY, lawyer; b. Pocatello, Idaho, June 28, 1955; s. Raymond Max and Marjorie Lucille (Pea) W.; m. Denise Womack, May 29, 1982; children: Jason Dennis, Sarah Michell, Sadie Mckenzie. BS in Acctg., U. Utah, 1976; JD, U. Idaho, 1978. Bar: U.S. Dist. Ct. Idaho, 1979, U.S. Supreme Ct. 1985, U.S. Tax Ct. 1989, U.S. Ct. Appeals (9th cir.) 1991, Idaho, 1979. Ptnr., shareholder Whittier & Souza, Pocatello, 1979-89; head pub. defender 6th jud. dist. State Idaho, 1989-95; shareholder, mng. atty. Whittier, Souza & Naftz, Pocatello, 1989-97, head pub. defender, 1989-95; asst. gen. counsel Maleleuca, Inc., Pocatello, 1997—. Vol. Internat. Spl. Olympics, South Bend, Ind., 1987, Mpls., 1991; mem. Magistrate Commn. 6th Jud. Dist., Pocatello, 1989-91; bd. dirs. Bannock Baseball, Inc., 1996—. Mem. ATLA, Idaho Trial Lawyers Assn. (bd. dirs. 6th Jud. Dist. Pro Bono award 1994), Civitan (pres. Bannock chpt. 1983-84, bd. dirs. 1981-87, 92-93, lt. gov. Intermountain chpt. 1986-87, Outstanding Pres. award 1984, Outstanding Svc. award 1982-83, 86-88, 91), Rotary. Avocations: bicycling, skiing, golfing, Spl. Olympics vol. activities. Office: Maleleuca Inc PO Box 4833 3910 S Yellowstone Hwy Idaho Falls ID 83402

WHITTINGHAM, CHARLES ARTHUR, library administrator, publisher; b. Chgo., Feb. 11, 1930; s. Charles Arthur and Virginia (Hartke) W.; m. Jean Bragger Whittingham, June 4, 1955; children: Mary Elizabeth, Charles Arthur III, Philip Alexander, Leigh Ann. B.S. in English Lit. cum laude, Loyola U., Chgo., 1951. With McCall Corp., Chgo., 1956-59, Time, Inc., Chgo., 1959-62; pub.'s rep. Fortune mag., Time, Inc., N.Y.C., 1962-65; mgr. Fortune mag., Time, Inc. (San Francisco Office), 1965-69; asst. to pub. Fortune, N.Y.C., 1969-70, asst. pub., 1970-78; pub. Life mag., N.Y.C., 1978-88; sr. v.p. N.Y. Pub. Libr., 1989-92; exec. prodr. Kunhardt Prodns., Inc., 1995—. Served to lt. (j.g.) USNR, 1951-55. Named to Athletic Hall of Fame Loyola U. Mem. Century Assn., Brook Club. Home and Office: 11 Woodmill Rd Chappaqua NY 10514-1128 also: 5584 Bartram St Boca Raton FL 33433

WHITTINGHAM, CHARLES EDWARD, thoroughbred race horse owner and trainer; b. San Diego, Apr. 13, 1913; s. Edward and Ellen (Taylor) W.; m. Peggy Boone, Oct. 12, 1944; children: Michael Charles, Charlene. T-trainer thoroughbred horses, Calif., 1930-42; asst. trainer Luro Pub. Stable, N.Y., 1945-49; owner, trainer Whittingham Pub. Stable, Sierra Madre, Calif., 1949—; winner Ky. Derby with Ferdinand, 1986, with Sunday Silence, 1989. Mem. Rep. Senatorial Inner-Circle, Washington, 1983—, nat. advisor bd. Am. Security Council, Washington, 1976—; campaigner mem. Rep. Nat. Com., Washington, 1976—. Served to master sgt. USMC, 1942-45, PTO. Recipient Eclipse awards Thoroughbred Race Track Assn./Daily Racing Form/Nat. Turf Writers Assn., 1971, 82, 89; named to Nat. Racing Hall of Fame, 1974, Brietbard Hall of Fame/Hall of Champions, San Diego, 1993. Mem. Horsemens Benevolent & Protective Assn. (v.p 1976—). Republican. Roman Catholic. Avocation: anything related to thoroughbred race horses. Home: 88 Lowell Ave Sierra Madre CA 91024-2510 Office: Charles Whittingham Inc 19 Suffolk Ave Ste E Sierra Madre CA 91024-2570

WHITTINGHAM, HARRY EDWARD, JR., retired banker; b. Albany, N.Y., Dec. 25, 1918; s. Harry E. and Mary (Baer) W.; m. Gladys D. Willstaedt, Sept. 2, 1942; children: Jeffrey A., Neal E. Grad., Stonier Grad. Sch. Banking, 1961. With Schenectady Trust Co., 1947-84, pres., chief exec. officer, 1974-82, chmn., chief exec. officer, 1982-84. Author: (with Purdy, Schneider, Aldom) Automation in Banking, 1962. Served with AUS, 1941-46. Episcopalian (vestryman). Clubs: Mohawk Golf (Schenectady). Home: 2314 Brookshire Dr Niskayuna NY 12309-4838

WHITTINGHAM, M(ICHAEL) STANLEY, chemist; b. Nottingham, Eng., Dec. 22, 1941; came to U.S., 1968, naturalized, 1980; s. William Stanley and Dorothy Mary (Findlay) W.; B.A. in Chemistry, Oxford U., 1964, M.A. (Gas Council scholar 1964-67), D.Phil., 1968; m. Georgina Judith Andai, Mar. 23, 1969; children: Jenniffer Judith, Michael Stanley. Rsch. asso., head solid state electrochemistry group Materials Center, Stanford U., 1968-72; mem. staff Exxon Research Co., Linden, N.J., 1972—, group head solid state chem. physics, 1975-78, dir. solid state scis., 1978-80, mgr. chem. engrng. tech., 1980-84; dir. phys. scis. Schlumberger Co., Ridgefield, Conn., 1984-88; prof. chemistry, dir. The Inst. for Materials Rsch., SUNY, 1988—, vice provost for rsch. SUNY, 1994—, vice-chair bd. dirs. Rsch. Found., 1995—; cons., lectr. in field. JSPS fellow U. Tokyo; mem. Electrochem. Soc. (Young Author award 1971, N.Y. chmn. 1980-81), Am. Chem. Soc. (chmn. solid state sect. 1987, chmn. Binghamton sect. 1991), Am. Phys. Soc., Materials Rsch. Soc. Author, editor papers in field; author 5 books. Achievements include patents in field; reversible (rechargeable) lithium batteries and methods for making intercalation batteries; method for making TiS2 mixed material cathodes, high briteness luminescent displays. Home: 396 Meeker Rd Vestal NY 13850-3230 Office: SUNY Dept Chemistry Binghamton NY 13902

WHITTINGTON, BERNARD WILEY, electrical engineer, consultant; b. Charleston, W.Va., July 19, 1920; s. Owen Wiley and Ethel Parker (Thaxton) W.; m. Jean Wilhelm, Feb. 2, 1950; children: David Brian, Ann Leslie, Brenda Wiley. B.S. in Elec. Engring., W.Va. U., 1951. Registered profl. engr., W.Va. Elec. engr. Appalachian Power Co., Charleston, W.Va., 1951-56; mgr. sales Virginian Electric Co., Charleston, W.Va., 1956-59; engring. cons. Union Carbide Corp., Charleston, W.Va., 1959-82; pres. Whittington Engring., Inc., Charleston, W.Va., 1983—; chmn. bd. dirs. Bank of Sissonville, Pocatalico, W.Va.; pres. W.Va. Assn. Pub. Svc. Dists., 1983-86; mem. U.S. nat. com. Internat. Electrotech. Commn. Chmn. Water and Sewage Bd., Pocatalico, W.Va., 1958-89. With U.S. Army, 1942-45. Fellow IEEE (Standards Medallion award 1976, Outstanding Achievement award 1978, Centennial medal 1984, Richard Harold Kaufman award 1989); mem. Industry Applications Soc. (pres. 1982), Acad. Elec. Engring. Republican. Methodist. Lodge: Lions. Home and Office: 100 Whittingshire Ln Charleston WV 25312-9554

WHITTINGTON, FLOYD LEON, economist, business consultant, retired oil company executive, foreign service officer; b. Fairfield, Iowa, May 27, 1909; s. Thomas Clyde and Ora E. (Trail) W.; m. Winifred Carol McDonald, July 31, 1933; children: Susan Whittington West, Thomas Lee. A.B., Parsons Coll., 1931; M.A., U. Iowa, 1936; student, U. Minn., 1940, Northwestern U., 1941-42. Econs., speech instr. Fairfield High Sch., 1931-36, Superior (Wis.) High Sch., 1936-40; supr. tchr. tng. Superior State Tchrs. Coll., 1936-40; econs., finance instr. Carroll Coll., Waukesha, Wis., 1940-42; price exec. OPA, Wis. and Iowa, 1942-46; indsl. relations mgr. Armstrong Tire & Rubber Co., Des Moines, 1946-48; dir. price and distbn. div. SCAP, Tokyo, Japan, 1948-51; Far East economist ODM, Washington, 1951-52; asst. adviser to sec. on Japanese financial and econ. problems Dept. State, Washington, 1952-53; chief Far Eastern sect. Internat. Finance div.; bd. govs. FRS, Washington, 1953-56; officer charge econ. affairs Office S.E. Asian Affairs, Dept. State, 1956-57, dep. dir., 1957-58; became counselor of embassy Am. embassy, Bangkok, 1958; counselor, polit. officer Am. embassy, Djakarta, Indonesia, 1962-65; counselor of embassy for econ. affairs Seoul, Korea, 1965-66; v.p. Pacific Gulf Oil, Ltd., Seoul, 1966—; exec. v.p. S.E. Asia Gulf Co., Bangkok, 1967-72, Gulf Oil Co. Siam, Ltd., Bangkok, 1967-72; v.p. Gulf Oil Co.-South Asia, Singapore, 1970-72; now Asian bus. cons. Recipient Meritorious Civilian Service citation Dept. Army, 1950. Mem. Am. Econ. Assn., Am. Acad. Polit. Sci., World Affairs Council Seattle (pres.), Seattle Com. Fgn. Relations, Pi Kappa Delta, Theta Alpha Phi. Presbyterian. Clubs: Royal Bangkok (Thailand); Sports; Lakes (Sun City, Ariz.). Lodges: Masons; Shriners; Rotary. Home: 1 Towers Park Ln Apt 515 San Antonio TX 78209-6421

WHITTINGTON, FREDERICK BROWN, JR., business administration educator; b. Sept. 22, 1934; m. Marjorie Ann Babington; children: Frederick Brown III, Marjorie Ellen, Lisa Anne. SB, MIT, 1958; MBA, Tulane U., 1965; PhD, La. State U., 1969. Staff economist Miss. Rsch. Commn., Jackson, 1961-64; sr. assoc. econ. rsch. Gulf South Rsch. Inst., Baton Rouge, 1966-69; asst. prof. bus. adminstrn. Emory U., Atlanta, 1969-73, assoc. prof., 1973-79, prof., 1979-96, prof. emeritus, 1997—, dir. customer bus. devel. track, 1991—; bd. dirs. Gwinnett Industries, Inc.; mem. forecasting panel Fed. Res. Bank Atlanta; vis. prof. Johannes Kepler U., Linz, Austria, 1983, 84, 85, 89, 95, 96; guest lectr. Austrian Univs., Linz, Vienna, Innsbruck and Klagenfurt; presenter workshops; cons. in field. Contbr. articles and reports to profl. jours. Mktg. plan, mgmt. audit State of Miss., Park Commn.; past chmn., bd. deacons Decatur Presbyn. Ch.; mem. adv. bd. DeKalb/Rockdale Svc. Ctr., ARC. Capt. USNR, ret. Recipient Trauner prize for ednl. innovation Upper Austrian Econ. Chamber, 1997; Sears, Roebuck Found. fellow, 1965-66. Mem. Am. Mktg. Assn., Nat. Assn. Purchasing Mgmt., So. Mktg. Assn., Coun. for Logistics Mgmt., Warehousing Edn. and Rsch. Coun., Omicron Delta Kappa, Beta Gamma Sigma, Delta Tau Delta. Office: Emory U Goizueta Bus Sch Atlanta GA 30322

WHITTINGTON, ROBERT BRUCE, retired publishing company executive; b. Oakland, Calif., Mar. 5, 1927; s. Edward and Loretta (Edalgo) W.; m. Marie D. Sanguinetti, June 18, 1950; children: Mark, Lynn. Student, Stockton Jr. Coll., 1946-48; B.A. in Journalism and Polit. Sci. (Friend W. Richardson fellow), U. Calif., Berkeley, 1950. Reporter Stockton (Calif.) Record, 1950-60, exec. news editor, 1965-68, asso. pub., 1968-69, pub., 1969-72; v.p., dir. Speidel Newspapers, Reno, 1972-77; regional pres., dir. Gannett Co., Inc., 1977-82; publ. Reno (Nev.) newspapers, 1980-82; v.p., trustee Gannett Found., 1982-85; dir. Sierra Pacific Resources; pres. Speidel Newspapers Charitable Found. Served with USNR, 1944-46, PTO. Roman Catholic. Home: 2432 Pheasant Run Cir Stockton CA 95207-5212

WHITTINGTON, ROBERT WALLACE, corporate professional, pianist; b. Birmingham, Ala., Sept. 25, 1967; s. Dorsey and Frances (Kohn) W.; m. Karen Smith, Dec. 10, 1967 (dec. 1984). BS, Auburn U., 1955; BA, U. Miami, Fla., 1956; MS, Cornell U., 1958. Chief exec. officer Travel Ctrs., Inc., Chgo.; pres. Svc. Ctrs., Inc., Sarasota, Fla., 1970-88, Exotics S.A., 1988—. Served to lt. U.S. Intelligence, 1960-62, Korea. Mem. Fla. Hort. Soc., Am. Landscape Assn., Fly Fisherman Assn., Can. Salmonoid Assn., Fla. Turf Assn., Am. Soc. Travel Agts. (bd. dirs. 1961-63). Avocations: angling, cooking, photography, boating, bee keeping. Home and Office: PO Box 025292 Miami FL 33102-5292

WHITTINGTON, STUART GORDON, chemistry educator; b. Chesterfield, England, Apr. 16, 1942; came to Can., 1967; s. Frank and Eva May (Gretton) W.; m. Ann Fretwell, Aug. 3, 1964; children: Graeme, Megan. BA, U. Cambridge, Eng., 1963, PhD, 1972. Scientist Unilever Research, Welwyn, U.K., 1963-66, 68-70; postdoctoral fellow U. Calif., La Jolla, 1966-67; postdoctoral fellow U. Toronto, Can., 1967-68, asst. prof., 1970-75, assoc. prof., 1975-80, prof. chemistry, 1980—, chmn. dept. chemistry, 1985-88. Contbr. 150 articles to profl. jours. Mem. Am. Math. Soc., Internat. Soc. Math. Chemistry, Can. Assn. Theoretical Chemists. Mem. New Democratic Party. Avocations: music, natural history. Home: 173 Airdrie Rd, Toronto, ON Canada M4G 1M7 Office: U of Toronto, Dept Chemistry, Toronto, ON Canada M5S 1A1

WHITTINGTON-COUSE, MARYELLEN FRANCES, education administrator; b. Waverly, N.Y., June 16, 1957; d. Philip John and Sheila (Dewey) Whittington; m. Daniel Couse, May 18, 1985; children: Kristen, Benjamin. BA, SUNY, Empire, 1983; M of Internat. Adminstrn., Sch. for Internat. Tng., Brattleboro, Vt., 1992. Adj. faculty Rockland C.C., 1983-85; cons. UN Non-Govtl. Liaison Svc., N.Y.C., 1987; adminstrv. asst. Manitoga Nature Ctr., Garrison, N.Y., 1987-88; coord. Intensive Tchr. Inst. Manhattanville and Coll. of New Rochelle Satellites, New Paltz, N.Y., 1990-92; dir. bilingual edn. tech. assistance ctr. Ulster BOCES, New Paltz, 1988—; adj. faculty SUNY, New Paltz, 1994—; co-chair PROSPAN; mem. Parent Edn. Adv. Coun., Ulster County, 1988—; local coord. World Learning Inc., 1993—. Editor: (curriculum) Teacher's Guide and Content Activities for Limited English Proficient Students, 1992; co-author video script for N.Y. State Edn. Dept., 1992. Mem. ASCD, Nat. Assn Bilingual Edn., N.Y. TESOL, TESOL Internat., N.Y. State Assn. Bilingual Edn. (conf. chair 1996). Avocations: running, hiking, reading. Home: PO Box 262 Tillson NY 12486-0262 Office: BETAC Ulster Bd Coop Ednl Svcs 175 State Route 32 N New Paltz NY 12561-1019

WHITTLE, CHARLES EDWARD, JR., consultant, lecturer; b. Brownsville, Ky., Mar. 8, 1931; s. Charles Edward and Lillian (Skaggs) W.; m. Suzanne Lee Miller, June 22, 1952; children: Charles, Jane, Jessica, Gayl, Tamara, Thomas, David, Jeffrey, Mary, Michael. AB, Centre Coll., Ky., 1949; PhD, Washington U., St. Louis, 1953; postgrad., U. Leiden, Netherlands, 1953-54, U. Tenn., 1975. Registered land surveyor, Ky. Engr. Union Carbide Corp., N.Y.C., 1954-56; physicist Western Ky. U., Bowling Green, 1956-62; prof., dean Centre Coll., Danville, Ky., 1962-74; researcher Inst. Energy Analysis-Oak Ridge Associated Univs., 1974-85, divsn. dir., 1985-88; v.p. C & S Assocs., Oak Ridge, Tenn., 1988-93; dean Pikeville (Ky.) Coll., 1988-93; v.p. M.W. Garay Assocs., Oak Ridge, 1993—; bd. dirs. Ky. World Trade Ctr.; cons. and lectr. in field. Author: Nuclear Moratorium, 1977; contbr. articles to profl. jours. Life mem. Ky. Hist. Soc. Fulbright scholar, 1953-54; Danforth Found. grantee, 1970. Mem. Am. Phys. Soc., East Tenn. Hist. Soc., Oak Ridge C. of C. (indsl. recruitment com. 1984-89), Rotary (bd. dirs. Oak Ridge 1980-86, 89-90, pres. 1984-85, dist. 6780 group study exch. team leader to Mex. 1986, chmn. dist. group study exch. com. 1987-89, 95-96, gov. 1997—), Phi Beta Kappa, Sigma Xi. Avocation: genealogy. Home: 109 Trevose Ln Oak Ridge TN 37830-5454 Office: MW Garay Assocs Trevose Ln Oak Ridge TN 37830-5454

WHITTLESEY, DIANA, surgeon; b. Alexandria, Va., Jan. 31, 1951; d. John Williams and Barbara (Baur) W.; m. John Walton Tomford, June 15, 1974 (div. Jan. 1980); m. Robert John Salamon, May 28, 1983; children: Matthew, Andrea. AB, Harvard U., 1972; MD, Johns Hopkins U., 1975. Diplomate Am. Bd. Thoracic Surgery. Assoc. staff Cleve. Clinic, 1982-83; staff surgeon UAMC, Cleve., 1983-87, sect. chief thoracic surgery, 1987—. Fellow ACS. Home: 21249 Shaker Blvd Shaker Heights OH 44122 Office: UAMC 10701 East Blvd Cleveland OH 44106-1702

WHITTLESEY, JUDITH HOLLOWAY, public relations executive; b. Bartlesville, Okla., Dec. 28, 1942; d. Harry Haynes and Suzanne (Arnote) Holloway; m. Dennis Jeffrey Whittlesey, Aug. 3, 1968; children: Kristin Arnote, Kevin Jeffrey. BA, U. Okla., 1964; postgrad., Tulsa U., 1965, U. Va., 1971-72. Staff aide Office of the V.P. of U.S., Washington, 1979-81, Com. for Future of Am., Washington, 1981-82; dep. dir. scheduling and advance Mondale-Ferraro Campaign, Washington, 1982-84; dir. media rels. The Susan Davis Cos., Washington, 1986-87, v.p., 1987-88, exec. v.p., 1988—. Bd. dirs. Cultural Alliance of Greater Washington, 1983-93, Washington Project for the Arts, 1987-93, Levine Sch. Music, 1993—, Food Rsch. and Action Ctr., 1993—; mem. Decatur house coun. Chevy Chase Presbyn. Ch., Washington. Recipient numerous Mercury and Anvil awards. Avocations: dance, art/contemporary and craft. Office: Susan Davis Internat 1000 Vermont Ave NW Washington DC 20005-4903

WHITWAM, DAVID RAY, appliance manufacturing company executive; b. Stanley, Wis., Jan. 30, 1942; s. Donald R. and Lorraine (Stoye) W.; m. Barbara Lynne Peterson, Apr. 13, 1963; children: Mark, Laura, Thomas. B.S., U. Wis., 1967. Gen. mgr. sales So. Calif. div. Whirlpool Corp., Los Angeles, 1975-77; mdse. mgr. ranges Whirlpool Corp., Benton Harbor, Mich., 1977-79, dir. builder mktg., 1979-80, v.p. builder mktg., 1980-83, v.p. whirlpool sales, 1983-85, vice chmn., chief mktg. officer, 1985-87, chmn., pres., chief exec. officer, 1987—, also bd. dirs.; bd. dirs. Combustion Engring. Inc., Stamford, Conn. Pres. bd. dirs. The Soup Kitchen, Benton Harbor, 1980—; mem. Nat. Council Housing Industry, Washington. Served to capt. U.S. Army. Fellow Aspen Inst. Republican. Lutheran. Club: Point O'Woods (Benton Harbor). Office: Whirlpool Corp 2000 M63 North Benton Harbor MI 49022*

WHITWORTH, ELAINE ATKINS, counselor; b. Carrollton, Ga., June 16, 1945; d. Dewey D. and Estelle (Lovvorn) Atkins; m. William Lee Whitworth, June 11, 1966 (div. Apr. 1985); children: Kim, Lee. BS in Edn., West Ga. Coll., 1966, Ed. Specialist, 1993; BS in Psychology, Kennesaw State Coll., 1986; MSW, U. Ga., 1988. Cert. sch. counselor; lic. master social worker; lic. profl. counselor; nat. bd. cert. counselor. Practicum case mgr. Ga. Mental Health Inst., 1987-88, mental health technician, 1988-89; Devereaux therapist North Met. Counseling, Marietta, Ga., 1988-90; spl. edn. tchr. Cobb County Schs., Kennesaw, 1990; counselor New Dawn Counseling, Kennesaw, 1990—, Cobb County Schs., Acworth, Ga., 1991—. Vol. group leader Ga. Coun. on Child Abuse, Atlanta, 1994. Recipient hon. award Kennesaw Alumni Assn., 1987. Mem. Psi Chi. Democrat. Episcopalian. Avocations: gardening, dogs, reading, movies. Office: New Dawn Counseling 2931 Lewis St Kennesaw GA 30144-2718

WHITWORTH, HALL BAKER, forest products company executive; b. St. Paul, N.C., Feb. 15, 1919; s. A. Frederick and Maude Ethel (Baker) W.; m. Mary Margaret Mease, May 18, 1946; children: Hall Baker, Laura Ellen, David Allen. Student, Miss. So. Coll., 1942, U. N.C., 1957. With Champion Internat., Canton, N.C., 1936-62; mgr. materials Champion Internat., Canton, 1956-62; dir. materials packages div. Champion Internat., Chgo., 1962-65; dir. purchase U.S. Plywood-Champion Papers, Inc. (now champion Internat. Corp.) Champion Internat., Hamilton, Ohio, 1965-68, dep. dir. corporate materials services, 1966, v.p., dir. purchase, 1968-75; v.p. materials Champion Internat., Stamford, Conn., 1975—, dir., 1975—, now ret.; v.p., dir. So. Agrl. Co., 1985—; pres., dir. H. Whitworth Enterprises, Cin., 1985—; dir. Pathfork-Harlan Coal Co. Served with U.S. Army, 1942-46. Recipient Thomas award Carolina-Va. Purchasing Agts. Assn., 1963. Mem. Am. Paper Inst. (chmn. energy subcom.), Am. Mgmt. Assn. (v.p. purchasing, transp. and phys. distbn. div. council). Methodist. Club: Canton Toastmakers (founder, 1st pres.). Lodges: Elks; Lions. Home and Office: 858 Lullwater Dr Oviedo FL 32765-8512

WHITWORTH, KATHRYNNE ANN, professional golfer; b. Monahans, Tex., Sept. 27, 1939; d. Morris Clark and Dama Ann (Robinson) W. Student, Odessa (Tex.) Jr. Coll., 1958. Joined tour Ladies Profl. Golf Assn., 1959—; mem. adv. staff Walter Hagen Golf Co., Wilson Sporting Goods Co. Named to Hall of Fame Ladies Profl. Golf Assn., Tex. Sports Hall of Fame, Tex. Golf Hall of Fame, World Golf Hall of Fame; Capt. of Solhiem Cup, 1990-92. Mem. Ladies Profl. Golf Assn. (sec. 1962-63, v.p. 1965, 73, 88, pres. 1967, 68, 71, 89, 1st mem. to win over $1,000,000). Office: care Ladies Profl Golf Assn 2570 Volusia Ave Daytona Beach FL 32114-1119

WHITWORTH, THOMAS C., neonatologist; b. Murfreesboro, Tenn., Apr. 24, 1944; s. James Leonard and Lillian (Alsup) W.; m. Ann McKnight, Sept. 2, 1967; children: James, Laura, David. BA, David Lipscomb Coll., Nashville, 1966; MD, Vanderbilt U., 1970. Pediatric intern Vanderbilt U. Hosp., Nashville, 1970-71, resident in pediatrics, 1971-73, asst. prof. pediatrics, 1975-81, asst. clin. prof., 1981-97, assoc. clin. prof. pediatrics, 1997—; fellow in neonatology Los Angeles County-U. So. Calif. Med. Ctr., L.A., 1973-75; dir. nurseries Bapt. Hosp., Nasvhille, 1976—. Contbr. poetry to anthologies. Sunday sc. tchr. Western Hills Ch. of Christ, Nashville, 1975—, elder, 1989—. Fellow Am. Acad. Pediatrics; mem. Tenn. Pediatric Soc., Nashville Acad. Medicine, Tenn. Med. Assn., Am. Acad. Pro-Life Pediatricians. Avocations: philately, writing poetry, gardening. Office: Bapt Hosp 200 Church St Nashville TN 37201-1606

WHITWORTH, WILLIAM A., magazine editor; b. Hot Springs, Ark., Feb. 13, 1937; s. William C. and Lois Virginia (McNabb) W.; m. Carolyn Hubbard, Dec. 27, 1969; children—Matthew, Katherine. B.A., U. Okla., 1960. Reporter Ark. Gazette, Little Rock, 1960-63; reporter N.Y. Herald Tribune, 1963-65; staff writer The New Yorker, 1966-72, assoc. editor, 1973-80; editor-in-chief The Atlantic Monthly, Boston, 1981—. Office: Atlantic Monthly 77 N Washington St Boston MA 02114-1908

WHORISKEY, ROBERT DONALD, lawyer; b. Cambridge, Mass., May 9, 1929; s. John Joseph and Katherine Euphemia (MacDonald) W.; m. Martha Beebe Poutas, Apr. 16, 1966; children: Alexandra, Jonathan, Eliza. AB, Harvard U., 1952; JD, Boston Coll., 1958; LLM, NYU, 1960. Bar: Mass. 1958, N.Y. 1963, U.S. Tax Ct. 1961, U.S. Claims Ct. 1969, U.S. Dist. Ct. (so. dist.) N.Y. 1969, U.S. Ct. Customs 1971, U.S. Ct. Appeals (2d cir.) 1972, U.S. Ct. Appeals (3d cir.) 1983, U.S. Ct. Appeals (D.C. cir.) 1991, U.S. Supreme Ct. 1974. Sr. trial atty. Office Chief Counsel, IRS, N.Y.C., 1960-67; assoc. Curtis, Mallet-Prevost, Colt & Mosle, N.Y.C., 1967-70, ptnr., 1970—, mem. exec. com., 1978-82, chmn. tax dept., 1982-87; bd. dirs. Internat. Tax Inst., v.p., lectr., 1980-84, chmn. bd., pres., lectr., 1985-87; lectr. Practicing Law Inst., World Trade Inst., Tax Execs. Inst., Am. Mgmt. Assn., Coun. for Internat. Tax Edn.; bd. dirs. Life Ins. Co. of Boston and N.Y., Inc. Author: Foreign Trusts, 1977, Annual Institute on International Taxation, 1966, 80, 81, (with Sidney Pine, Ralph Seligman) Tax and Business Benefits of the Bahamas, 1986; contbg. author: International Boycotts, Bender's Federal Service, 1988, Third Party Information, John Wiley and Sons, Inc.'s Transfer Pricing, 1993, Transfer Pricing Under IRC & 482: Overview and Planning, Part I, 1996, Accuracy Related Penalty Regulations for Transfer Pricing, Part II, 1997, Third Party Information, Part III, 1997, U.S. Taxation of International Operations. Trustee, treas. Montessori Sch. Westchester, 1974-77; mem. bd. ethics Village of Larchmont, N.Y., 1988—. Served with U.S. Army, 1952-54. Mem. ABA (com. on value added tax tax sect. 1994—), N.Y. State Bar Assn. (com. on practice and procedure tax sect. 1990—), Assn. of the Bar of the City of N.Y., Harvard Club, Larchmont Yacht Club. Democrat. Roman Catholic. Office: Curtis Mallet-Prevost Colt & Mosle 101 Park Ave New York NY 10178

WHORTON, M. DONALD, occupational and environmental health physician, epidemiologist; b. Las Vegas, N.Mex., Jan. 25, 1943; s. R.H. and Rachel (Siegal) W.; m. Diana L. Obrinsky, Apr. 9, 1972; children: Matthew Richard, Laura Elizabeth, Julie Hannah. Student, U.S. Naval Acad., 1961-62; B of Biology, N.Mex. Highlands U., 1964; MD, U. N.Mex., 1968; MPH, Johns Hopkins U., 1973. Intern Boston City Hosp., 1968-69; resident in pathology U. N.Mex., Albuquerque, 1969-71; instr., resident in medicine Balt. City Hosp., 1972-74; asst. prof. Johns Hopkins U., Balt.; assoc. dir. divsn. emergency medicine Balt. City Hosps., 1974-75; clin. asst. prof. divsn. ambulatory and cmty. medicine U. Calif. Sch. Medicine, San Francisco, 1975-77; lectr. sch. pub. health program Inst. Indsl. Rels., Ctr. for Labor Rsch. and Edn., 1975-79, med. dir. labor occupational program, 1975-79, assoc. clin. prof. occupational medicine, 1979-88; prin. Environ. Health Assocs., Inc., Oakland, 1978-88; v.p. ENSR Health Scis., 1988-94; pvt. practice Alameda, Calif., 1994—; chmn. adv. com. for hazard evaluation service and info. system Indsl. Relations Dept. State of Calif., 1979-84; cons. in field; chmn., statewide adv. com. U. Calif. Ctrs. on occupational and environmental health, 1996—. Contbr. articles to profl. jours. Recipient Upjohn Achievement award, 1968; Robert Wood Johnson Found. clin. scholar, 1972-74. Fellow Am. Coll. Epidemiology, Am. Coll. Occupational and Environ. Medicine; mem. Am. Pub. Health Assn., Soc. for Occupational and Environ. Health, Calif. Med. Assn. (adv. panel on occupational and environmental medicine), Inst. Medicine, Nat. Acad. Sci., Alpha Omega Alpha. Office: 1135 Atlantic Ave Alameda CA 94501-1145

WHYBARK, DAVID CLAY, educational educator, researcher; b. Tacoma, Wash., Sept. 18, 1935; s. Clay Alfred and Irene (Stanton) W.; m. Neva Jo Richardson, July 6, 1957; children: Michael David, Suzanne Marie (dec.). BS, U. Washington, 1957; MBA, Cornell U., 1960; PhD, Stanford U., 1967. Rsch. assoc. Stanford (Calif.) U., 1962-67; asst. prof. Ariz. State U., Tempe, 1965-66; assoc. prof. Purdue U., West Lafayette, Ind., 1967-76; prof. Ind. U., Bloomington, 1976-90; Macon G. Patton disting. prof. U. N.C., Chapel Hill, 1990—; vis. prof. Shanghai Inst. Mech. Engring., 1986-87, Chinese U. of the Hong Kong, 1996, Victoria U., New Zealand, 1996, Canterbury U., New Zealand, 1996; adj. prof. Inst. for Mgmt. Devel., Lausanne, Switzerland, 1981-82, 85-90; dir., founder Global Mfg. Rsch. Group, 1990—; cons. in field. uthor: Master Production Scheduling: Theory and Practice, 1979, Manufacturing P lanning Control Systems, 1984, 4th edit., 1997, International Operations Management, 1989, Integrated Production and Inventory Management, 1993; editor: Global Manufacturing Practices, 1993; editor Internat. Jour. Prodn. Econs., 1991-95. Recipient Lilly Alumni MBA Teaching Excellence award, 1990. Fellow Decision Scis. Inst. (past pres., disting. svc. award 1984), Pan Pacific Bus. Assn. (mem. coun.); mem. Ops. Mgmt. Assn. (pres. 1992-93), Am. Prodn. Inventory Control Soc., Internat. Soc. Inventory Rsch. (mem. coun., chair mgmt. sect.), Coun. Logistics Mgmt., Assn. Mfg. Excellence. Avocations: travel, winemaking. Office: U NC Kenan-Flagler Sch Global Mfg Rsch Ctr Chapel Hill NC 27599-3490

WHYBROW, PETER CHARLES, psychiatrist, educator; b. Hertforshire, Eng., June 13, 1939; came to U.S., 1964, naturalized, 1975; s. Charles Ernest and Doris Beatrice (Abbott) W.; children: Katherine, Helen. Student, Univ. Coll., London, 1956-59; MB BS, Univ. Coll., 1962; diploma psychol. medicine, Conjoint Bd., London, 1968; MA (hon.), Dartmouth Coll., 1974, U. Pa., 1984. House officer endocrinology Univ. Coll. Hosp., 1962, sr. house physician psychiatry, 1963-64; house surgeon St. Helier Hosp., Surrey, Eng., 1963; house officer pediatrics Prince of Wales Hosp., London, 1964; resident psychiatry U. N.C. Hosp., 1965-67, instr., research fellow, 1967-68; mem. sci. staff neuropsychiat. research unit Charshalton, Surrey, 1968-69; dir. residency tng. psychiatry Dartmouth Med. Sch., Hanover, N.H., 1969-71; prof. psychiatry Dartmouth Med. Sch., 1970-84, chmn. dept., 1970-78, exec. dean, 1980-83; prof., chmn. dept. psychiatry U. Pa., Phila., 1984-96; Ruth Meltzer prof. psychiatry, 1992; psychiatrist-in-chief Hosp. U. Pa., 1984-96; prof. psychiatry and biobehavioral scis., chmn. dept. psychiatry Sch. Medicine UCLA, 1996—, dir. Neuropsychiatric Inst., 1996—, physician-in-chief Neuropsychiatric Hosp., 1996—; dir. psychiatry Dartmouth Hitchcock Affiliated Hosp., 1970-78; vis. scientist NIMH, 1978-79; cons. VA, 1970—, NIMH, 1972— ; chmn. test com. Nat. Bd. Med. Examiners, 1977-84; researcher psychoendrocrinology. Author: Mood Disorders: Toward a New Psychobiology, 1984, The Hibernation Response, 1988, A Mood Apart, 1997; editor: Psychosomatic Medicine, 1977; mem. editl. bd. Cmty. Psychiatry, Psychiat. Times, Directions in Psychiatry, Neuropsychopharmacology;

contbr. articles to profl. jours. Recipient Anclote Manor award psychiat. rsch. U. N.C., 1967, Sr. Investigator award nat. Alliance for Rsch. into Schizophrenia and Depression, 1989; Josiah Macy Jr. Found. scholar, 1978-79; fellow Cen. for Advanced Studies in Behavioral Sci., Stanford, 1993-94; recipient Lifetime Investigator award NDMDA, 1996; decorated Knight of Merit, Sovereign Order of St. John of Jerusalem, 1993. Fellow AAAS, Am. Psychiat. Assn., Royal Coll. Psychiatrist (founding mem.), Am. Coll. Psychiatrists, Ctr. Advanced Study of Behavioral Scis.; mem. Assn. Am. Med. Colls., Soc. Psychosomatic Rsch., Am. Assn. Chmn. Depts. Psychiatry (pres. 1977-78), Royal Soc. Medicine, Am. Psychopath Assn., Am. Coll. Neuropsychopharmacology, Soc. Biol. Psychiatry, N.Y. Acad. Scis., Soc. Neurosci., Sigma Xi, Alpha Omega Alpha, Cosmos Club (Washington). Club: Cosmos (Washington). Office: UCLA Sch Medicine Dept Psychiatry Biobehavioral Sci 760 Westwood Plz Los Angeles CA 90024-8300

WHYTE, GEORGE KENNETH, JR., lawyer; b. Waukegan, Ill., Oct. 10, 1936; s. George K. and Ella Margaret (Osgood) W.; m. Ann B. Challoner, June 20, 1964; children: Mary, Douglas. AB in Polit. Sci., Duke U., 1958; LLB, U. Wis., 1965. Bar: Wis. 1965. Law clk. to chief justice Wis. Supreme Ct., Madison, 1965-66; assoc. Quarles & Brady, Milw., 1966-73, ptnr., 1973—. Lt. USN, 1958-62. Mem. ABA (employment law sect.), Wis. Bar Assn. (former chmn. labor and employment law sect.), Rotary. Congregationalist. Clubs: The Town, Milw. Athletic, Milw. Country. Home: 906 E Circle Dr Milwaukee WI 53217-5361 Office: Quarles & Brady 411 E Wisconsin Ave Milwaukee WI 53202-4409

WHYTE, JAMES PRIMROSE, JR., former law educator; b. Columbus, Miss., Aug. 25, 1921; s. James P. and Mary (Savage) W.; m. Martha Ann Jones, Sept. 11, 1948; children—James Jones, Stuart Ward, Wilson Scott. A.B., Bucknell U., 1943; M.A., Syracuse U., 1948; J.D., U. Colo., 1951. Bar: Okla. 1951, Mo. 1957, Va. 1961. With firm Gordon & Whyte, McAlester, Okla., 1951-55; county atty. Pittsburg County, Okla., 1955-56; atty. Great Lakes Pipe Line Co., Kansas City, Mo., 1957; prof. law Coll. William and Mary, 1958-82, asst. dean, 1958-68, asso. dean, 1969-70, dean, 1970-75; ad hoc arbitrator Fed. Mediation and Conciliation Svc., Va. Dept. Labor, also industry and govt. panels. Contbr. profl. jours.; Mem. editorial adv. bd.: John Marshall Papers, 1966-77. Mem. Bd. Zoning Appeals, Williamsburg, 1971-77, chmn., 1977; trustee, pres. Williamsburg Regional Libr., 1965; trustee Williamsburg Area Meml. Community Ctr., 1963-68, pres., 1966-67. Served with USNR, 1943-46. Mem. Va. State Bar, Phi Beta Kappa, Tau Kappa Alpha, Sigma Tau Delta. Home and Office: 5626 Boatwright Cir Williamsburg VA 23185-3799

WHYTE, MICHAEL PETER, medicine and pediatrics educator, research director; b. N.Y.C., Dec. 19, 1946; s. Michael Paul and Sophie (Dziuk) W.; m. Gloria Frances Golenda, Oct. 26, 1974; 1 child, Catherine Alexandra. BA in Chemistry, NYU, 1968; MD, SUNY, N.Y.C., 1972. Diplomate Am. Bd. Internal Medicine, Nat. Bd. Med. Examiners. Intern, 1st yr. resident dept. medicine NYU Sch. Medicine Bellevue Hosp., N.Y.C., 1972-74; clin. assoc. devel. and metabolic neurology br. Nat. Inst. Neurol. and Communicative Disorders and Stroke NIH, Bethesda, Md., 1974-76; fellow divsn. bone and mineral metabolism dept. medicine Wash. U. Sch. Medicine, 1976-79, instr. dept. medicine, 1979-80, asst. sci. dir. Clin. Rsch. Ctr., 1979—; asst. physician Barnes Hosp., 1979—; dir. Metabolism Clinic Shriners Hosp. Crippled Children, St. Louis, 1979—; staff physician St. Louis Children's Hosp., 1979—; NIH clin. assoc. physician Clin. Rsch. Ctr. Wash. U. Sch. Medicine, 1980-82, asst. prof. medicine dept. medicine, 1980-86, assoc. prof. medicine dept. medicine, 1986-91, asst. prof. pediatrics Edward Mallinckrodt dept. pediatrics, 1982-89, assoc. prof. pediatrics Edward Mallinckrodt dept. pediatrics, 1989-92, prof. medicine dept. medicine, 1991—, prof. pediatrics Edward Mallinckrodt dept. pediatrics, 1992—; med. dir. Metabolic Rsch. Unit Shriners Hosp. Crippled Children, St. Louis, 1982—, mem. staff., 1983—; assoc. attending physician Jewish Hosp. St. Louis, 1983—; staff cons. Shriners Hosp. Crippled Children, St. Louis, 1979-83, Mexico City, 1991—; editl. bd. Calcified Tissue Internat., 1995, Jour. Bone and Mineral Rsch., 1994—; med. adv. bd. Osteogenesis Imperfecta Found., 1986—, med. adv. panel Paget's Disease Found., 1986—; chmn. med. adv. coun., bd. dirs. Osteogenesis Found., 1995—. Assoc. editor: Primer on Metabolic Bone Diseases and Disorders of Mineral Metabolism, 1990, 93, 96; assoc. editor Calcified Tissue Internat., 1989—; contbr. chpts. to books, articles to profl. jours. Lt. comdr. USPHS, 1974-76. Mem. Am. Soc. Cell Biology, Am. Soc. Clin. Investigation, Am. Coll. Physicians (assoc.), Am. Fedn. Clin. Rsch., Am. Soc. Advancement Sci., Am. Soc. Bone and Mineral Rsch. (ednl. com. 1987—, Fuller Albright award 1987, Young Investigator award 1983), Am. Soc. Human Genetics, Endocrine Soc., Soc. Exptl. Biology and Medicine, Japanese Soc. Inherited Metabolic Disease (hon.). Office: Barnes-Jewish Hosp 216 S Kings Hwy Saint Louis MO 63110

WHYTE, RONALD M., federal judge; b. 1942. BA in Math., Wesleyan U., 1964; JD, U. So. Calif., 1967. Bar: Calif. 1967, U.S. Dist. Ct. (no. dist.) Calif. 1967, U.S. Dist. Ct. (cen. dist.) Calif. 1968, U.S. Ct. Appeals (9th cir.) 1986. Assoc. Hoge, Fenton Jones & Appel, Inc., San Jose, Calif., 1971-77, mem., 1977-89; judge Superior Ct. State of Calif., 1989-92, U.S. Dist. Ct. (no. dist.) Calif., San Jose, 1992—; judge pro-tempore Superior Ct. Calif., 1977-89; lectr. Calif. Continuing Edn. of Bar, Rutter Group, Santa Clara Bar Assn., State Bar Calif.; legal counsel Santa CLara County Bar Assn., 1986-89; mem. county select com. Criminal Conflicts Program, 1988. Bd. trustees Santa Clara County Bar Assn., 1978-79, 84-85. Lt. Judge Advocate Gen.'s Corps, USNR, 1968-71. Recipient Judge of Yr. award Santa Clara County Trial Lawyers Assn., 1992, Am. Jurisprudence award. Mem. Calif. Judges Assn., Assn. Bus. Trial Lawyers (bd. govs. 1991-93), Santa Clara Inn of Ct. (exec. com. 1993—), San Francisco Bay area Intellectual Property Inn of Ct. (exec. com. 1994—). Office: US Courthouse 280 S 1st St Rm 4156 San Jose CA 95113-3002

WHYTE, WILLIAM FOOTE, industrial relations educator, author; b. Springfield, Mass., June 27, 1914; s. John and Isabel (VanSickle) W.; m. Kathleen King, May 28, 1938; children: Joyce, Martin, Lucy, John. A.B., Swarthmore Coll., 1936, L.H.D. (hon.), 1984; mem., Soc. of Fellows, Harvard U., 1936-40; Ph.D., U. Chgo., 1943. Asst. prof. sociology, acting chmn. dept. anthropology U. Okla., 1942-43; asst., then assoc. prof. sociology U. Chgo., 1944-48, exec. sec. Com. Human Relations in Industry, 1946-48; prof. indsl. relations N.Y. State Sch. Indsl. and Labor Relations, Cornell U., 1948-79; dir. Social Sci. Research Center, 1956-61; rsch. dir. Programs for Employment and Workplace Systems Sch. Indsl. and Labor Rels., 1984—; dir. O & O Investment Fund, 1983. Author: Street Corner Society, 1943, Human Relations in the Restaurant Industry, 1948, Pattern for Industrial Peace, 1951, Money and Motivation, 1955, Man and Organization, 1959, Men at Work, 1961, Organizational Behavior, 1969, Organizing for Agricultural Development, 1975, Learning from the Field, 1984, Participatory Action Research, 1990, Participant Observer: An Autobiography, 1994; co-author: Action Research for Management, 1965, Toward an Integrated Theory of Development, 1968, Dominación y Cambios en el Peru Rural, 1969, Power, Politics, and Progress, 1976, Worker Participation and Ownership, 1983, Higher Yielding Human Systems for Agriculture, 1983, Making Mondragón, 1988, 91, Social Theory for Action, 1991; editor: Industry and Society, 1946, Human Organization, 1956-61, 62-63, Street Corner Society (4th expanded edit. 50th anniversary), 1993. Trustee Found. Research Human Behavior, 1960-67; bd. dirs. Nat. Ctr. for Employee Ownership, 1981-88.. Fulbright fellow Peru, 1961-62; recipient Career Research award NIMH. Mem. Am. Sociol. Assn. (pres. 1981), Am. Acad. Arts and Scis., Soc. Applied Anthropology (pres. 1964), Indsl. Rels. Rsch. Assn. (pres. 1963). Home: 223 Savage Farm Dr Ithaca NY 14850-6501 *In social research, I have been as much concerned with practical applications as with scientific knowledge, and I have always sought to express findings in simple and clear prose.*

WIANT, SARAH KIRSTEN, law library administrator, educator; b. Waverly, Iowa, Nov. 20, 1946; s. James Allen and Eva (Jorgensen) W.; m. Robert E. Akins. BA, Western State Coll., 1968; MLS, U. North Tex., 1970; JD, Washington & Lee U., 1978. Asst. law librarian Tex. Tech. U., 1970-72; asst. law librarian Washington & Lee U., 1972—, dir., 1978—, asst. prof. law, 1978-83, assoc. prof. law, 1984-92, prof. law, 1993—; participant Conf. on Fair Use, NII, 1995-96. Co-author: Copyright Handbook, 1984, Libraries and Copyright: A Guide to Copyright Law in the 1990s, 1994 Legal Research In the District of Columbia, Maryland and Virginia, 1995; contbr. chpts. to books; mem. adv. bd. Westlaw, 1990-93. Mem. ABA (com. on libraries 1987-93), Am. Assn. Law Libraries (program chmn. for ann. meeting 1987, copyright office rep.), Am. Law Sch. (chmn. sec. on librs. 1990-92, accreditation com. 1991-94), Spl. Libraries Assn. (chair copyright com. 1990-96), Maritime Law Assn., U.S. Trademark Assn. Office: Washington & Lee U Law Libr Lewis Hall Lexington VA 24450

WIATER, TERESA VERONICA, writer; b. Trenton, Nov. 17, 1949; d. John Michael and Lottie Mary (Kupiec) W. Student, Worcester (Eng.) Coll., 1969-70; BA magna cum laude, Trenton State Coll., 1971, MA, 1988. Cert. tchr., N.J. Singer, songwriter Duke Williams and the Extremes, 1974-76, United Artists Records Am., L.A., Chgo., N.Y.C., 1976-80; songwriter ETA, Inc., N.Y.C., 1980-84; tchr. English and t.v. prodn. Trenton Ctrl. H.S., 1986-96; playwright, screenwriter Global Intelligence Media Corp., L.A., 1995—. Author: (plays) A Cross-Eyed View Up a Blind Alley, 1987, Charity, 1989, Level Six, Crypto Twenty One, 1993, Pearl Harbor, 1994, Chronic Thinking, 1995, The Garbage Play, 1995, Point Panic in the Postbiological, 1996, Plan E.T. The Chronetics of Duke Williams, 1997, (screenplays) The Awareness Factor, 1992, Arrested, 1997, (anthology) The Reality Factor, 1996; albums include For The First Time Out, 1977, Undo Me, 1979; feature writer: Enterprize, 1975-76, US-1, 1983-85. Active Geraldine Rockefeller Dodge Found., N.J. Theatre Group, Playwrights Theatre N.J. Mem. N.J. Edn. Assn., N.J. Theatre Educators Coalition (founding mem.). Avocations: NASA. Office: 2743 Princeton Pike Lawrenceville NJ 08648-3220

WIATR, CHRISTOPHER L., microbiologist; b. Chgo., Jan. 5, 1948; s. Joseph Thomas and Beatrice Harriet (Kaminski) Wiatr; m. Jeanne Lynn Malecki, Oct. 20, 1978; children: Kelli Jean, Christopher Joseph, Kaycee Lynn, Kirby Ann, Nicholas Aloysius. BS, Ill. Benedictine Coll., 1969; MS, IIT, 1974; PhD, U. Ill., Chgo., 1985. Cert. tchr. Tchr., coach St. Rita High Sch., Chgo., 1969-74; rsch. microbiologist Swift & Co./Esmark/Beatrice Foods, Chgo., 1974-75, lab. mgr., 1975-76, tech. dir. rsch. and quality assurance, 1976-79; sr. microbiologist Nalco Chem. Co. Water and Waste Treatment R & D, Naperville, Ill., 1985-87, sr. rsch. microbiologist, 1988, group leader water rsch., 1989-91; group leader Pulp & Paper Chems. R & D, Naperville, Ill., 1991-94; mgr. microbiology and biochemistry R&D Calgon Corp.-ECCI, Pitts., 1994—; reviewer Nat. Assn. Corrosion Engrs; chmn. biocide and biofilms session Internat. Water Conf., 1996-97. Co-author: (book chpt.) Food Preservation by Irradiation, 1978; contbr. articles to profl. jours. Eagle scout, merit badge counselor Boy Scouts Am., 1963—; com. Maplebrook I Swim Club, Naperville, 1990-94; football coach St. Raphael, Naperville, 1993-94. Named Researcher of Yr., Nalco Chem. Co., 1987. Mem. TAPPI (microbiology and microbiol tech. and water quality com. 1993—), Am. Chem. Soc., Nat. Assn. Corrosion Engrs., Soc. Indsl. Microbiology, Am. Soc. for Microbiology, Am. Men and Women in Sci., Sigma Xi (pres. Nalco chpt. 1991-92). Roman Catholic. Achievements include 7 patents and 2 European patent applications; enzyme applications for controlling bacterial adhesion on equipment and surfaces; nontoxic biocontrol; recognition as expert on biofilms and molecular biology.

WIATT, JAMES ANTHONY, theatrical agency executive; b. L.A., Oct. 18, 1946; s. Norman and Catherine (Sonners) W.; m. Randie Laine. BA, U. So. Calif., 1969. Campaign coord. Tunney for Senate, L.A., 1969-71; adminstrv. asst. Senator John V. Tunney, L.A., 1972-75; agt. FCA, L.A., 1976-78; lit. agt. Internat. Creative Mgmt., L.A., 1978-81, motion picture agt., 1981-83, head of motion picture dept., 1983-85, pres., COO, 1985—; now pres., co-CEO Internat. Creative Mgmt., Beverly Hills, Calif. *

WIBERG, DONALD MARTIN, electrical engineering educator, consultant; b. Battle Creek, Mich., Sept. 20, 1936; s. Martin and Lina (Havstein) W.; children: Erik M., Kristin A., Kenneth C. B.S., Calif. Inst. Tech., 1959, M.S., 1960, Ph.D., 1965. Registered profl. engr., Calif. Sr. design engr. Convair, San Diego, 1964-65; asst. prof. system sci. UCLA, 1965-71, assoc. prof., 1971-77, prof., 1977-94, prof. anesthesiology, 1979-94, vice chmn. dept. elec. engring., 1985-86, prof. Emeritus, 1994—; cons. in field; vis. prof. German Rsch. Orgn. for Air and Space Flight, Munich, 1969-70, dept. elec. engring. and computer sci. U. Newcastle, Australia, 1989-90, Inst. for Systems Rsch., U. Md., College Park, 1994. Author: State Space and Linear Systems, 1971; co-editor: Regulation of Breathing, 1983. Mem. adv. bd. Parthenia Sch., Los Angeles, 1971-74. Sr. NATO research fellow KFZ Karlsruhe, W.Ger., 1973; sr. Fulbright fellow, Copenhagen, 1976-77, Trondheim, Norway, 1983-84. Fellow IEEE (applications assoc. editor Trans. on Automatic Control 1983, assoc.. editor-at-large 1987-89, 92-94, legis. asst. office Senator Tom Harkin, D-IA 1995), Am. Physiol. Soc. (assoc. editor Modelling Methodology Forum 1980-91), Sigma Xi. Home: 5959 Naples Plz # 307 Long Beach CA 90803-5020

WIBERG, LARS-ERIK, human resources consultant; b. Wakefield, Mass., June 1, 1928; s. Sverker Claesson and Ingrid (Heurlin) W.; m. Elizabeth Margaret Allenbrook, Oct. 18, 1957; children: Kirsten, Margaret, Brenda. BS in Geology, MIT, 1950; MA in Teaching, Harvard U., 1952. From engr. to dir. corp. communications EG&G Inc., Boston and Bedford, Mass., 1956-69; from asst. v.p. to v.p. compensation and orgnl. planning First Nat. Bank of Boston, 1969-81; cons. Rockport, Mass., 1981—; lectr. human resources mgmt. Boston U., 1988-92; lectr. job search and career planning U. Karlstad, Sweden, 1992. Author: It's Your Move, 1991; inventor in field. Mem. Gov. John A. Volpe's Mgmt. Engring. Task Force, 1965; mem. Planning Bd., Rockport, 1965-72, chmn., 1969-72; pres. ch. coun. Swedenborg Chapel, Cambridge, Mass., 1984—; dir. Mass. New Ch. Union, 1990—; mem. Zoning Bd. Appeals, Rockport, 1986—. 1st lt. USAF, 1953-55. Mem. Affiliated New Eng. Cons. (founder Lexington, Mass. 1985-95), Heritage Found., Internat. Platform Assn., Swedenborg Sci. Assn. Republican. Avocations: church work, home repairs, music, cooking, reading. Home and Office: 156 South St Rockport MA 01966-1916 *Most of us are well-motivated at heart. We really want to do good work. We are capable of strong, personal commitment. Nevertheless, indifferent motivation and weak commitment too often prevail. The main culprit is the wrong job!.*

WIBERLEY, STEPHEN EDWARD, chemistry educator, consultant; b. Troy, N.Y., May 31, 1919; s. Irving Charles and Ruth (Stanley) W.; m. Mary Elizabeth Bartle, Feb. 21, 1942; children: Stephen Edward, Sharon Elizabeth. B.A., Williams Coll., 1941; M.S., Rensselaer Poly. Inst., 1948, Ph.D., 1950. Sr. chemist Congoleum Nairn, Inc., Kearny, N.J., 1941-44; prof. chemistry Rensselaer Poly. Inst., Troy, N.Y., 1946—, chmn. dept. chemistry, 1984-88; dean Rensselaer Poly. Inst. (Grad. Sch.), 1964-79, vice provost, 1969-79; vis. sr. physicist Brookhaven Nat. Lab., Upton, N.Y., 1950; cons. Imperial Paper & Color Corp., Glens Falls, N.Y., 1957—, Socony Mobil Oil Co., Bklyn., 1957—, Huyck Felt Co., Rensselaer, N.Y., 1958—, Schenectady Chems. Inc., 1961—, U.S. Gypsum Co., Buffalo, 1962—. Author: Instrumental Analysis, 1954, Laboratory Manual for General Chemistry, 1963, Introduction to Infrared and Raman Spectroscopy, 1964. Served with AUS, 1944-46. Mem. Am. Chem. Soc., AAUP, Sigma Xi, Phi Lambda Upsilon. Home: 1676 Tibbits Ave Troy NY 12180-3726

WICE, PAUL CLINTON, news director, educator; b. West Branch, Mich., Sept. 30, 1944; s. Clinton Harold and Viola Ruth (Potratz) W.; m. Dolores Ann Janovec, Sept. 30, 1967. BA, Kearney State Coll., 1966; MA, U. Nebr., Kearney, 1989. News anchor Sta. KHGI-TV, Kearney, Nebr., 1965-66; news editor Sta. KWBE Radio, Beatrice, Nebr., 1966-67; city editor Kearney Hub, 1968-69; news dir. Sta. KGFW-AM, Kearney, 1967-68, 69—; adj. faculty speech communication U. Nebr., Kearney, 1981—. Bd. dirs. Buffalo County Crimestoppers, Kearney Area Habitat for Humanity, Luth. Family Svcs. of Nebr., Cmty. Concert Assn., Kearney Literacy Coun. Mem. Soc. Profl. Journs. (bd. dirs. Nebr. chpt.). Home: Box 1754 #2 Sycamore Pl Kearney NE 68848-1754 Office: Sta KGFW-AM PO Box 666 Kearney NE 68848-0666

WICHERN, DEAN WILLIAM, business educator; b. Medford, Wis., Apr. 29, 1942; s. Arthur William and Rebecca Ann (Ambler) W.; m. Dorothy Jean Rutkowski, Dec. 7, 1968; children: Michael, Andrew. B.S. in Math., U. Wis., 1964, M.S. in Stats., 1965, Ph.D. in Stats., 1969. Instr. Sch. Bus. U. Wis.-Madison, 1967-69, asst. prof., 1969-72, assoc. prof., 1972-76, prof., 1976-84, chmn. quantitative analysis dept., 1975-78; prof. Coll. Bus. Adminstrn. Tex. A&M U., 1984—, head bus. analysis and research dept., 1984-88, assoc. dean, 1988-95, John E. Pearson prof. bus. adminstrn., 1985—; vis. prof. Math. Research Ctr., 1978-79. Co-author: Intermediate Business Statistics, 1977, Applied Multivariate Statistical Analysis, 3d edit., 1992, Business Statistics: Decision Making With Data, 1997; assoc. editor Jour. Bus. and Econ. Stats., 1983-91. Mem. Royal Statis. Soc., Am. Statis. Assn., Inst. Mgmt. Sci., Beta Gamma Sigma, Phi Kappa Phi. Home: 9217 Riverstone Ct College Station TX 77845-8333 Office: Tex A&M U Coll Bus Adminstrn Dept Bus Analysis College Station TX 77843

WICK, HILTON ADDISON, lawyer; b. Mt. Pleasant, Pa., Feb. 11, 1920; m. Barbara G. Shaw; children: James H., William S., B. Jane, Ann W. Julia A. BA, Maryville Coll., 1942; LLB, Harvard U., 1948. Bar: Vt. 1948. Practiced in Burlington; ptnr. Wick, Dinse & Allen, 1949-72; of counsel Dinse, Allen & Erdmann, Burlington, 1972-80, Wick & Maddocks, Burlington, 1980—; state senator Vt., 1989-91; COO Gifford Med. Ctr., Inc., Randolph, 1993-95; bd. dirs. Blue Cross/Blue Shield Vt., Beach Properties, Inc., Vt. Pub. Radio, chmn., 1990-96. Trustee Middlebury Coll., 1969-85, Champlain Coll., 1974-94, Maryville Coll., 1981-86, Shelburne Mus., 1985-94, Ethan Allen Homestead, 1989-96, Vt. Assn. for Blind and Visually Impaired, 1992—; pres. Coll. St. Congl. Ch., 1996—; bd. dirs. Vt. divsn. Am. Cancer Soc., 1979-93, Intervale Found., 1995—; pres. bd. trustees Vt. Law Sch., 1975-95; chmn. bd. trustees Vt. Cmty. Found., 1985-91; chancellor Vt. State Colls., 1984-85; chmn. bd. dirs. Middlebury Coll., 1981-84. Mem. ABA, Vt. Bar Assn. (pres. 1967-68), Chittenden County Bar Assn. (pres. 1963-64), Internat. Soc. Barristers, Am. Bankers Assn. (bd. dirs. 1975-76), Vt. Bankers Assn. (pres. 1973-74), Ethan Allen Club, Harvard Club (Boston and N.Y.C.), Phi Kappa Delta. Home: Two Appletree Point Ln Burlington VT 05401 Office: 308 College St Burlington VT 05401-8319

WICK, LAWRENCE SCOTT, lawyer; b. San Diego, Oct. 1, 1945; s. Kenneth Lawrence and Lorrayne (Scott) W.; m. Beverly Ann DeRoss, Aug. 26, 1972 (div.); children: Ryan Scott, Andrew Taylor, Hayley Lauren. BA, Northwestern U., Evanston, Ill., 1967; JD, Columbia U., 1970. Atty. Leydig, Voit & Mayer Ltd., Chgo., 1978-84, ptnr., 1984-92, shareholder, 1984—. Contbr. articles to profl. jours. and encys. Vice pres. Northwestern Young Reps., Evanston, 1965-66; bd. govs. Brand Names Edn. Found., 1994-95; exec. dir. Lefkowitz Internat. Trademark Moot Ct., 1994-95. Mem. ABA (young lawyers exec. coun. 1976-78), Internat. Intellectual Property Assn., Internat. Trademark Assn. (assoc. rep.), Copyright Soc. U.S., Pharm. Trade Marks Group (London), Chgo. Bar Assn. (bd. mgrs. 1981-83, chmn. young lawyers sect. 1975-76), Law Club Chgo., Winter Club Lake Forest (bd. dirs. 1988-92). Republican. Presbyterian. Avocations: international travel, swimming, cycling. Home: 317 Rothbury Ct Lake Bluff IL 60044-1927 Office: Leydig Voit & Mayer Ltd Two Prudential Plaza Ste 4900 Chicago IL 60601-6780

WICK, SISTER MARGARET, college administrator; b. Sibley, Iowa, June 30, 1942. BA in Sociology, Briar Cliff Coll., 1965; MA in Sociology, Loyola U., Chgo., 1971; PhD in Higher Edn., U. Denver, 1976. Instr. sociology Briar Cliff Coll., Sioux City, Iowa, 1966-71, dir. academic advising, 1971-72, v.p., acad. dean, 1972-74, 76-84, pres., 1987—; pres. Colls. of Mid-Am., 1985-87; mem. adv. bd. Nations Bank, Sioux City. Bd. dirs. Mary J. Treglia Cmty. House, 1976-84, Marian Health Ctr., 1987—, Iowa Pub. TV, 1987-95. Mem. North Ctrl. Edn. Assn. (cons.-evaluator for accrediting teams 1980-84, 89—), Siouxland Initiative (adv. bd.), Quota Internat., Rotary. Home: 75 W Clifton Ave Apt 113 Sioux City IA 51104-2132 Office: Briar Cliff Coll Office of the President 3303 Rebecca St Sioux City IA 51104-2324

WICK, PHILIP, wholesale distribution executive. CEO Les Schwab Tire Ctrs., Prineville, Oreg. Office: PO Box 667 Prineville OR 97754-0667*

WICK, ROBERT THOMAS, retired supermarket executive; b. St. Louis, Nov. 26, 1927; s. Robert Berninger and Katherine (Burke) W.; m. Virginia Rose Allen, Sept. 6, 1952; children: Susan, Patrick, Nancy, Robert J. BS, St. Louis U., 1955; cert. in food distbn., Mich. State U., 1956. Sales mgr. Nat. Tea Co., St. Louis, 1966-68, asst. div. mgr., 1968-69; div. mgr. Nat. Tea Co., Sioux City, Iowa, 1969-71, Milw., 1971-73, Chgo., 1973-74; v.p., gen. mgr. A&P Food Stores, Indpls., 1975-77; div. v.p. Colonial Food Stores- Grand Union, Norfolk, Va., 1977-79; pres., chief exec. officer Bonnie Be-Lo Markets, Inc., Norfolk, 1979-90, ret., 1990. Bd. dirs. Virginia Beach (Va.) Community Svcs. Bd., 1985-89; mem. adv. bd. Straight, Inc., Chesapeake, Va., 1987-91; dir. Community Alternatives, Inc., Virginia Beach, 1991-92. Tech. sgt. U.S. Army, 1946-48. Recipient Citizen of Yr. award St. Louis Argus Newspaper, 1968. Mem. Food Mktg. Inst. (bd. dirs. 1982-89), Va. Food Dealers Assn. (bd. dirs. 1981-87), Tidewater Retail Mchts. Assn. (pres., bd. dirs. 1981-91). Conservative. Roman Catholic. Avocations: travel, stamp collecting, golf, cycling. Home: 801 Winthrope Dr Virginia Beach VA 23452-3940

WICK, WILLIAM DAVID, lawyer; b. Dayton, Ohio, Aug. 18, 1949; s. Wilhelm Palmer and Esther (Brehm) W.; m. Barbara Helene Maco; children: Chelsea Maco, Jenna Maco. BA, Northwestern U., 1971; JD, Georgetown U., 1974. Bar: Calif. 1974. Legis. asst. U.S. Rep. Charles Whalen, Washington, 1971-75; assoc. McCutchen, Doyle, Brown & Enersen, San Francisco, 1975-78; atty. Office Regional Counsel U.S. EPA, San Francisco, 1978-85, chief hazardous waste br. Office Regional Counsel, 1985-91; ptnr. Crosby, Heafey, Roach & May, Oakland, Calif., 1991—; adj. prof. law Golden Gate U., San Francisco, 1981—. Editor Shepard's Calif. Environ. Law and Regulation Reporter, 1992-95. Mem. ABA, San Francisco Bar Assn. Office: Crosby Heafey Roach & May 1999 Harrison St Oakland CA 94612-3520

WICK, WILLIAM SHINN, clergyman, chaplain; b. West Chester, Pa.; s. William R. and Barbara (Shinn) W.; m. Debra R. Smith, Apr. 1, 1989; 1 child, Christopher R. BA, Trinity Coll., Deerfield, Ill., 1975; MDiv, Trinity Evang. Div. Sch., Deerfield, 1978. Ordained to ministry Evang. Free Ch. Am., 1978. Pastor Bradford (Vt.) Evang. Free Ch., 1978-85, Evang. Free Ch. Newport, Vt., 1985-89, Grace Evang. Free Ch., Northfield, Vt., 1989-96; chaplain Norwich U., Northfield, 1989—; bd. dirs. Evang. Free Ch. Am., Mpls., 1991—. Avocations: alpine skiing, racquetball, tennis, scuba diving, sailing. Home: 92 S Main St Northfield VT 05663-1438 Office: White Chapel Norwich U 65 S Main St Northfield VT 05663-1000*

WICKENS, DONALD LEE, engineer executive, consultant, rancher; b. Oklahoma City, Aug. 11, 1934; s. Claude Preston and Idora Bell (Wainscott) W.; m. Sylvia Ann Knopp, Aug. 25, 1957; children: Julia Ann, Donna Sue. BS, Okla. State U., 1957, MS, 1962. Engr. HTB Inc., Oklahoma City, 1961-65; chief structural engr. The Benham Group, Oklahoma City, 1965-70, prin. structural engr., 1970-75, sr. v.p. indsl., 1975-80; pres. Houston div. The Benham Group, 1980-82, pres. St. Louis div., 1982-88; pres. The Benham Group, Oklahoma City, 1988—, chmn., chief exec. officer, pres., 1991—; chmn., chief exec. officer, pres. The Benham Cos., Oklahoma City, Benham Real Estate & Devel., Oklahoma City, Benham Internat., Oklahoma City; chmn. bd. dirs. Roberts-Schornick & Assocs., Norman, Okla., Stewart and Bottomley, Tulsa, Benham-OPUS, Mexico City, Benham-Electrosynthesis, Oklahoma City, Benham Internat.-Far East, Benham Internat. U.K.; bd. dirs. Dynalogic, Detroit; chmn. Benham Internat. Eurasia Moscow, Stainless Equipment and Sys. Co., Atlanta, Benham Constructors; chmn. Gov.'s Internat. Team. Bd. visitors Sch. Arch., U. Okla. Mem. NSPE, ASCE, Am. Soc. Mil. Engrs., So. U.S. Japan Assn., Phi Delta Theta, Sigma Tau, Chi Epsilon. Republican. Lutheran. Home: 2604 Charleston Rd Edmond OK 73003-1623 Office: The Benham Group 9400 N Broadway Ext Oklahoma City OK 73114-7401

WICKER, DENNIS A., state official; b. Sanford, N.C., 1952; s. J. Shelton and Clarice (Burns) W.; m. Alisa O'Quinn; children: Quinn Edward, Jackson Dennis, Harrison Lee. BA in Econs. with honors, U. N.C., 1974; JD, Wake Forest U., 1978. Atty. Love & Wicker, 1978-92; mem. N.C. Ho. of Reps., 1981-92; lt. gov. State of N.C., 1993—; chmn. law enorcement com., 1983, house com. cts. and adminstrn. justice, 1985, house jud. com., 1987; chmn. N.C. Small Bus. Coun., 1993—, N.C. State C.C. Bd., 1993—, N.C. State Health Purchasing Alliance Bd., 1993—, Gov.'s Task Force on Driving While Impaired, 1994—, N.C. Local Govt. Partnership Coun.; mem. N.C. Capitol Planning Com., 1993—, N.C. Coun. of State, 1993, N.C. Commn. on Bus. Laws and The Economy. Chmn. N.C. Local Govt. Partnership Coun.; chmn. Gov.'s Task Force on Driving While Impaired. Named Legis. of Yr., Children's Learning Disability Assn. N.C.; recipient Jane Alexander Pub. Svc. award MADD, 1993, Pres.'s award N.C. Assn. Educators, Legis.

Leadership award Nat. Commn. Against Drunk Driving, 1994; listed among 10 most effective legis. N.C. Ctr. Pub. Policy Rsch. Mem. Phi Beta Kappa. Democrat. Methodist. Office: Office of Lt Gov 116 W Jones St Raleigh NC 27603-1300*

WICKER, MARIE PEACHEE, civic worker; b. Detroit, July 9, 1925; d. Charles Andrew and Bessie Louise (Sullivan) Peachee; m. Warren Jake Wicker, July 31, 1948; children: Beth Wicker Walters, Jane Fields Wicker-Miurin, Thomas Alton. BA, Westhampton Coll., 1946; MA, U. N.C., 1950. Test technician N.C. Merit System Coun., Durham, 1950-51; classification analyst N.C. Personnel Dept., Raleigh, 1951-52; engring. placement dir. N.C. State U., Raleigh, 1952-57. Author: You Can Make It Yourself, 1988, First Women of Orange County, N.C., 1994, 2d edit., 1995, 3d edit., 1997, A History of the Chapel Hill Woman's Club, 1910-1995, 1995. Chmn. Chapel Hill Recreation Commn., 1961-62; legis. chmn. N.C. Congress Parents and Tchrs., 1972-73; mem. Chapel Hill-Carrboro Bd. Edn., 1973-75, Historic Hillsborough (N.C.) Commn., 1987-93. Recipient Dist. Conservation award N.C. Wildlife Resources Commn., 1987. Mem. N.C. Fedn. Women's Clubs (dist. pres. 1984-86, dist. chmn. conservation dept. 1992-94, state chmn. conservation dept. 1992-94, sec.-treas. past dist. pres. club 1992-94, Sallie Southall Cotten scholarship com. 1994—), N.C. Coun. Women's Orgns. (bd. dirs. 1990, 1st v.p. 1992-93), Chapel Hill Women's Club (pres. 1985-87, 1st v.p. 1996-98), Orange County Commn. for Women. Democrat. Avocations: cooking, crafts, family history research. Home: 1024 Highland Woods Rd Chapel Hill NC 27514-4410

WICKER, ROGER F., congressman; b. Pontotoc, Miss., July 5, 1951; m. Gayle Wicker; children: Margaret, Caroline, McDaniel. BA in Polit. Sci. and Journalism, U. Miss., 1973; JD, Ole Miss Law Sch., 1975. Judge advocate USAF, 1975-79; mem. staff rules com. Staff of U.S. Rep. Trent Lott, 1980-82; pvt. practice, 1982—; mem. Miss. State Senate, 1988-94, 104th-105th Congress from 1st Miss. dist., 1995—; mem. house appropriation com. Republican. Office: US House Reps 206 Cannon Bldg Washington DC 20515-2401

WICKER, THOMAS CAREY, JR., judge; b. New Orleans, Aug. 1, 1923; s. Thomas Carey and Mary (Taylor) W.; children: Thomas Carey III, Catherine Anne; m. Jane Anne Trepanier, Dec. 29, 1995. BBA, Tulane U., 1944, LLB, 1949, JD, 1969. Bar: La. 1949. Law clk. La. Supreme Ct., New Orleans, 1949-50; asst. U.S. Atty., 1950-53; practiced in New Orleans, 1953-72; mem. firm Simon, Wicker & Wiedemann, 1953-67; partner firm Wicker, Wiedemann & Fransen, 1967-72; dist. judge Jefferson Parish (La.), 1972-85, judge, Court of Appeals 5th cir., 1985—, mem. faculty Nat. Jud. Coll., 1979-93, Tulane U. Sch. Law, 1978-83. Past bd. visitors Tulane U.; bd. dirs. La. Jud. Coll.; past pres. Sugar Bowl. Author: (with others) Judicial Ethics, 1982, (with others) Modern Judicial Ethics, 1992; editor Tulane Law Review, 1949. Lt. (j.g.), USNR, 1944-46. Mem. ABA (jud. div. council), La. (chmn. jr. bar sect. 1958-59, gov. 1958, mem. ho. of dels. 1960-72), Jefferson Parish, bar assns., Tulane U. Alumni Assn. (past pres.), Am. Judicature Soc., La. Dist. Judges Assn. (past pres.), Order of Coif, Beta Gamma Sigma, Pi Kappa Alpha. Republican. Episcopalian. Clubs: Rotary (pres. 1971-72), Metairie (La.) Country. Avocations: golf, photography, military history. Home: 500 Rue St Ann #127 Metairie LA 70005 Office: La Ct Appeal 5th Cir Gretna Courthouse Fl 4 Gretna LA 70053

WICKER, THOMAS GREY, retired journalist; b. Hamlet, N.C., June 18, 1926; s. Delancey David and Esta (Cameron) W.; m. Neva Jewett McLean, Aug. 20, 1949 (div. 1973); children: Cameron McLean, Thomas Grey; m. Pamela Abel Hill, Mar. 9, 1974. AB in Journalism, U. N.C., 1948. Exec dir. Southern Pines (N.C.) C. of C., 1948-49; editor Sandhill Citizen, Aberdeen, N.C., 1949; mng. editor The Robesonian, Lumberton, N.C., 1949-50; pub. info. dir. N.C. Bd. Pub. Welfare, 1950-51; copy editor Winston-Salem (N.C.) Jour., 1951-52, sports editor, 1954-55, Sunday feature editor, 1955-56, Washington corr., 1957, editorial writer, city hall corr., 1958-59; assoc. editor Nashville Tennessean, 1959-60; mem. staff Washington bur. N.Y. Times, 1960-71, chief bur., 1964-68; assoc. editor N.Y. Times, 1968-85, columnist, 1966-91. Author: (novels) The Kingpin, 1953, The Devil Must, 1957, The Judgment, 1961, Facing the Lions, 1973, Unto This Hour, 1984, Donovan's Wife, 1992, (non-fiction) Kennedy without Tears, 1964, JFK and LBJ: The Influence of Personality upon Politics, 1968, A Time to Die, 1975, On Press, 1978, One of Us: Richard Nixon and the American Dream, 1991, Tragic Failure: Racial Integration in America, 1996. Served to lt. (j.g.) USNR, 1952-54. Nieman fellow Harvard, 1957-58, fellow Joan Shorenstein Barone Ctr. on the Press, Politics and Pub. Policy Harvard, 1993. Mem. Soc. Nieman Fellows, Century Assn., Soc. Am. Historians, Writers guild of Am. East.

WICKERHAM, RICHARD DENNIS, lawyer; b. Plainfield, N.J., Oct. 9, 1950; s. Richard Frame and Margaret Theresa (Waldron) W.; m. Margaret Ann Music, June 29, 1989. BS in Fgn. Svc., Georgetown U., 1972; JD, Fordham U., 1975. Bar: N.Y. 1976, U.S. Dist. Ct. (no. dist.) N.Y. 1977. Pvt. practice atty., counsellor at law Schenectady, N.Y., 1976—; law guardian Schenectady, 1976-85; atty., Office of Aging County of Schenectady, N.Y., 1981—; mem., Com. on Profl. Stds. N.Y. Supreme Ct., Appellate Divsn. (3rd. jud. dept.), Albany, N.Y., 1996—. Mem. St. Clare's Hosp. Found. Leadership, Schenectady, 1990—. Recipient Cert. of Appreciation and Merit, The Lawyers' Fund for Client Protection of the State of N.Y., Albany, 1994. Mem. Rotary Internat., Schenectady County C. of C. Roman Catholic. Avocations: rowing, salt water fishing. Home: 484 Hutchinson Rd Glenville NY 12302 Office: PO Box 1167 28 Jay St Schenectady NY 12301-1167

WICKES, GEORGE, English language educator, writer; b. Antwerp, Belgium, Jan. 6, 1923; came to U.S., 1923; s. Francis Cogswell and Germaine (Attout) W.; m. Louise Westling, Nov. 8, 1975; children by previous marriage: Gregory, Geoffrey, Madeleine (dec.), Thomas, Jonathan. BA, U. Toronto, Ont., Can., 1944; MA, Columbia U., 1949; PhD, U. Calif., Berkeley, 1954. Asst. sec. Belgian Am. Ednl. Found., N.Y.C., 1947-49; exec. dir. U.S. Ednl. Found. in Belgium, 1952-54; instr. Duke U., Durham, N.C., 1954-57; from asst. prof. to prof. Harvey Mudd Coll. and Claremont Grad. Sch., Calif., 1957-70; prof. English and comparative lit. U. Oreg., Eugene, 1970—; dir. comparative lit. U. Oreg., 1974-77, head English dept., 1976-83; lectr. USIS, Europe, 1969, Africa, 1978, 79; vis. prof. U. Rouen, France, 1970, U. Tübingen, Germany, 1981, U. Heidelberg, Germany, 1996. Editor: Lawrence Durrell and Henry Miller Correspondence, 1963, Henry Miller, Letters to Emil, 1989, Henry Miller and James Laughlin: Selected Letters, 1995; Author: Henry Miller, 1966, Americans in Paris, 1969, The Amazon of Letters, 1976: translator: The Memoirs of Frederic Mistral, 1986. Served with U.S. Army, 1943-46. Fulbright lectr. France, 1962-63, 66, 78; sr. fellow Ctr. for Twentieth Century Studies, U. Wis.-Milw., Milwaukee, 1971, Creative Writing fellow Nat. Endowment Arts, 1973, Camargo fellow, 1991. Mem. PEN. Office: U Oreg English Dept Eugene OR 97403

WICKES, R(ICHARD) PAUL, lawyer; b. Camden, N.J., June 11, 1948; s. Richard Gordon and Nancy Elizabeth (Roy) W.; m. Jane Avis Hunter, June 8, 1970, (div. Feb. 1978); m. Gail Thain Parker, Apr. 9, 1978. BA, Williams Coll., 1970; JD, Harvard U., 1973. Bar: Vt. 1973, U.S. Supreme Ct. 1976, Okla. 1982, Tex. 1985, N.Y. 1991. Ptnr. Williams & Wickes, Bennington, Vt., 1973-77; commr. Vt. Dept. Taxes, Montpelier, 1977-78; assoc. Gravel, Shea & Wright, Burlington, Vt., 1978-80; counsel to Gov. State of Vt., Montpelier, 1980-82; ptnr. Watson & McKenzie, Oklahoma City, 1982-84, Thompson & Knight, Dallas, 1984-90, Sherman & Sterling, N.Y.C., 1990—. Office: 153 E 53rd St New York NY 10022-4611

WICKESBERG, ALBERT KLUMB, retired management educator; b. Neenah, Wis., Apr. 2, 1921; s. Albert Henry and Lydia (Klumb) W.; m. Dorothy Louise Ahrensfeld, Oct. 28, 1944; children—Robert, William, James. B.A., Lawrence Coll., 1943; M.B.A., Stanford U., 1948; Ph.D., Ohio State U., 1955. Staff accountant S.C. Johnson & Son, Inc., Racine, Wis., 1948-50; asst. prof. Sacramento State Coll., 1950-51; prof. U. Minn., Mpls., 1953-86; prof. emeritus U. Minn., 1987—, chmn. dept. bus. adminstrn., 1959-62, dir. grad. studies, 1963-66, chmn. dept. mgmt. and transp., 1971-77. Author: Management Organization, 1966. Served with AUS, 1943-46, 51-52. Soc. Advancement Mgmt. fellow, 1972. Mem. Acad. Mgmt., Soc. Advancement Mgmt. (pres. Twin Cities chpt. 1961-62), Am. Assn. for Study Mental Imagery. Congregationalist. Home: 4501 Roanoke Rd Minneapolis MN 55422-5268 Office: U Minn Sch Mgmt Minneapolis MN 55455

WICKFIELD, ERIC NELSON, investment company executive; b. Bryn Mawr, Pa., Feb. 14, 1953; s. Paul Gilbert Jacobs and Patricia Ruth (Nelson) Davies; m. Kristine Margaret Erickson, June 21, 1974 (div. 1976); m. Sara Lou Datt, July 23, 1977 (div. 1990); 1 child, Eric N. Jr.; m. Leslie Walsh Willingham, June 8, 1990; 1 child, Douglas N. BS, Rochester Inst. Tech., 1974; MBA, Boston U., 1990. Project mgr. Flight Safety Internat., Wichita, Kans., 1976-82; v.p. Aufleger-Garrett, Stillwater, Okla., 1982-86; demonstration pilot citation div. Gen. Dynamics, Wichita, 1986-87; pres. Prompt Fin. Inc., Concord, Mass., 1987—; bd. dirs. Prompt Fin. Inc., Concord; bd. dirs. The Cleaning Solution, Inc., Boston. Co-author: Sustaining High Performance, 1990; editor: 421 Pilot's Training Manual, 1981. Bd. dirs. Groton Ctr. for The Arts. Mem. Internat. Operator's Coun., Aircraft Owner's & Pilot's Assn., Aero Club New Eng. (bd. dirs.). Republican. Methodist. Avocation: snow skiing. Office: Prompt Fin Inc 30 Monument Sq Concord MA 01742-1857

WICKHAM, JOHN ADAMS, JR., retired army officer; b. Dobbs Ferry, N.Y., June 25, 1928; s. John Adams and Jean Gordon (Koch) W.; m. Ann Lindsley Prior, June 18, 1955; children: Lindsley, John Adams, Matthew. B.S., U.S. Mil. Acad., 1950; M.A., Harvard U., 1955, M.P.A., 1956; grad., Nat. War Coll., 1967. Commd. 2d lt. U.S. Army, 1950, advanced through grades to gen., 1979; asst. prof. social scis. U.S. Mil. Acad., 1956-60; bn. comdr. 1st Cavalry Div., Republic of Vietnam, 1967; brigade comdr., chief of staff 3d Inf. Div., Fed. Republic of Germany, 1969-70; army mem. chmn.'s staff group Office of Chmn. Joint Chiefs of Staff, Washington, 1970-71; dep. chief of staff for econ. affairs Mil. Assistance Command, Republic of Vietnam, 1971-73; dep. chief, negotiator U.S. del. Four Party Joint Mil. Commn., Republic of Vietnam, 1973; sr. mil. asst. to Sec. Def. Washington, 1973-76; comdr. 101st Airborne Div. (Air Assault), Ft. Campbell, Ky., 1976-78; dir. Joint Staff Orgn. Washington, 1978-79; comdr. in chief UN Command, Republic of Korea-U,S. Combined Forces Command, Korea, 1979-82; vice chief of staff U.S. Army, Washington, 1982-83, chief of staff, 1983-87, ret., 1987; pres., chief exec. officer Armed Forces Communications and Electronics Assn., Fairfax, Va., 1987-92; bd. dirs. Cooper Inst. for Aerobic Rsch., Xsirius, Inc., Honeywell Fed. Sys., Advanced Photonics, Nortel Inc. Decorated D.S.M. (8), Silver Star (2), Legion of Merit (4), Bronze Star with V device, Air medal (11), Purple Heart, Legion of Honor (France), Order of Mil. Merit (Rep. of Korea), Royal Order of Polar Star (Sweden). Mem. Assn. U.S. Army, 101st Airborne Assn. Home: 13590 N Fawnbrooke Dr Tucson AZ 85737

WICKHAM, KENNETH GREGORY, retired institute official, army officer; b. Hayti, Mo., Apr. 8, 1913; s. Charles Lawrence and Nell (Lively) W.; m. Helen Wickham, July 12, 1938 (dec.); 1 dau., Mary Harvey Wickham Anderson.; m. Norma A. Newcomb, Aug. 21, 1982. B.S., U.S. Mil. Acad., 1938; M.A., George Washington U., 1963; grad., Armed Forces Staff Coll., 1948, Army War Coll., 1956. Commd. 2d lt. U.S. Army, 1938, advanced through grades to maj. gen., 1964; assigned arty. U.S. and Hawaii, 1938-42; with inf. in PTO, ETO, 1942-45; various staff and command assignments, 1945-54; assigned Korea, 1954-55; comdt. (Adj. Gen.'s Sch.), 1959-61; comdg. gen. (Combat Service Support Group, Combat Devel. Command), 1964-66; adj. gen. U.S. Army, 1966-71; with Bus. Mgmt. Inst., Western Assn. Coll. and Univ. Bus. Officers, Stanford, Calif., 1975-80; Area dir. in Korea ARC campaign, 1955; bd. dirs. Army Emergency Relief Assn., U.S. Olympic Com., Army Mut. Aid Assn., Internat. Mil. Sports Council; pres., 1969-70; mem. exec. com. Council Internat. Mil. Sports, 1967-71; pres. Calif. Assn. Mil. Personnel, 1972-78, U.S. Mil. Sports Assn., 1982-84. Decorated D.S.M., Legion of Merit with 2 oak leaf clusters, Bronze Star with oak leaf cluster, Purple Heart, Commendation medal; Legion of Honor (France); 2 Croix de Guerre (France); Cross of Haakon VII (Norway); Ulchi Disting. Svc. medal (Korea). Home: 15 Sunkist Ln Los Altos CA 94022-2334

WICKHAM, M(ARVIN) GARY, optometry educator; b. Ft. Morgan, Colo., Dec. 23, 1942; s. Marvin Gilbert W. and Dorothy Mae (Frazell) West; m. Irene Mary Wilhelm, Mar. 20, 1965. BS, Colo. State U., 1964, MS, 1967; PhD, Wash. State U., 1972. Rsch. physiologist VA, Gainesville, Fla., 1971-74; asst. prof. U. Fla., Gainesville, 1972-74; rsch. physiologist VA, San Diego, 1974-79; asst. rsch. biologist morphology of the eye U. Calif., San Diego, 1974-79; assoc. prof. histology, ocular anatomy and physiology Northeastern State U., Tahlequah, Okla., 1979-85, prof. histology, gen. biology, 1986-88, prof. optometry, histology, human genetics and immunology, 1988-93, prof. ocular anatomy and physiology, molecular biology and immunology, and gen. biology, 1993—; ad hoc reviewer vision scis. study sects. nat. rsch. grants NIH, 1990—. Contbr. articles to profl. jours. Recipient Glaucoma Studies grant VA, 1975, Core Em Facility grant, 1977-79, Focal Argon Laser Lesions grant, 1979; Morphology of Mammal Eyes grant NIH, 1980, Computer-Based Image Analysis grantee Nat. Eye Inst., 1990. Mem. AAAS, Soc. Integrative Comparative Biology, Am. Inst. Biol. Scis., Assn. for Rsch. in Vision and Ophthalmology. Achievements include co-development of first argon laser treatment for glaucoma; first co-documentation of movement of silicone away from clinically implanted breast prosthesis devices using EDXA; co-application of vitreous carbon as a knife-making material; confirmation of generality of occurrence of encapsulated receptors inside cetacean eyes. Office: Northeastern State U Coll Optometry Tahlequah OK 74464

WICKIZER, MARY ALICE See BURGESS, MARY ALICE

WICKLAND, J. AL, JR., petroleum product executive, real estate executive. CEO Wickland. Office: Wickland Corp 3640 American River Dr Sacramento CA 95864-5901 Office: PO Box 13648 Sacramento CA 95853-4648

WICKLEIN, JOHN FREDERICK, journalist, educator; b. Reading, Pa., July 20, 1924; s. Raymond Roland and Parmilla Catherine (Miller) W.; m. Myra Jane Winchester, July 31, 1948; children: Elizabeth, Peter, Joanna. Litt.B., Rutgers U., 1947; M.S. in Journalism, Columbia, 1948. Reporter Newark (N.J.) Evening News, 1947-51; news mng. editor Elec. World (McGraw-Hill weekly), N.Y.C., 1951-54; reporter, editor N.Y. Times, 1954-62; news dir. Sta. WNET-TV, N.Y.C., 1962-64; exec. producer news Sta. WABC-TV, N.Y.C., 1964-67; exec. producer Washington Bur. chief Pub. Broadcast Lab. (Nat. Ednl. TV), 1967-70; mng. news and pub. affairs broadcasts Sta. WCBS-TV, N.Y.C., 1970-71; gen. mgr. Sta. WRVR, N.Y.C., 1971-74; prof. journalism and broadcasting Boston U., 1974-80; dean Sch. Public Communication Boston U., 1974-78; vis. prof. communication Meth. U., São Paulo, Brazil, 1979; program officer for news and pub. affairs programs Corp. for Pub. Broadcasting, 1980-84; Willard M. Kiplinger chair in pub. affairs reporting, dir. Kiplinger mid-career program for journalists Ohio State U., 1984-89; Fulbright rsch. scholar Charles Sturt Univ., Bathurst, NSW, Australia, 1990; lectr., cons. to Rutgers U. Media Resources Ctr., Warsaw, Poland, 1992; Ayers vis. prof. of Journalism, Jacksonville (Ala.) State U., 1992-93; producer news documentaries for public and comml. TV; ind. writing, reporting and editing coach for newspapers 1994—; lectr., cons. in field; coord. Working Group for Pub. Broadcasting, 1987-89; spl. com. on regulation of media Am. Civil Liberties Union, 1988-92; adj. faculty, Poynter Inst. for Media Studies, 1988; adj. prof. journalism for rsch. Ohio State U., 1991-93; at-large mem., media ethics com. Nat. Coun. Chs., 1975-92; fellow Inst. Democratic Communication Boston U., 1975-78; lectr. journalism Columbia Grad. Sch. Journalism, 1966-67; Danforth lectr. Barnard Coll., 1960-61; cons. Dept. Journalism, Jagiellonian U., Krakow, Poland, 1994. Author: (with Monroe Price) Cable Television: A Guide for Citizen Action, 1972, Electronic Nightmare: The New Communications and Freedom, 1981; editor: Investigative Reporting: The Lessons of Watergate, 1975; contgb. editor The Washington Monthly, 1969-72; contbr. to Am. Journalism Review, The Progressive, TV Quar., Atlantic Monthly, Columbia Journalism Rev., Archeology, Quill, Australian Journalism Rev., others. Recipient Polk award, 1963, documentary award Venice Film Festival, 1968, Dupont award, 1973, Brechner Freedom Info. prize, 1987. Mem. ACLU, Investigative Reporters and Editors, Amnesty Internat. U.S.A., Soc. Prof. Jours., Phi Beta Kappa. Democrat. Home and Office: 23200 Wilderness Walk Ct Gaithersburg MD 20882-2732

WICKLIFFE, JERRY L., lawyer; b. Dallas, Jan. 12, 1941; s. John A. and Ola (Kirk) W.; m. Lynda Hart, Aug. 26, 1961; children: Lisa Schmalhausen, Jeffrey, Mark. BBA, U. Tex., 1963, JD, 1965. Bar: Tex. 1965. Assoc. Fulbright & Jaworski, Houston, 1965-73, ptnr., 1973—. Office: Fulbright & Jaworski 1301 Mckinney St Fl 51 Houston TX 77010-3031

WICKLINE, SAMUEL ALAN, cardiologist, educator; b. Huntington, W.Va., Oct. 23, 1952. BA in Philosophy cum laude, Pomona Coll., 1974; MD, U. Hawaii, 1980. Diplomate Am. Bd. Internal Medicine, Am. Bd. Cardiology. Intern, resident in internal medicine Barnes Hosp. Barnes/ Washington U. Sch. Medicine, St. Louis, 1980-83, clin. fellow in cardiology, 1983-85, rsch. fellow in cardiology, 1985-87; asst. prof. medicine Sch. Medicine Washington U. Sch. Medicine, St. Louis, 1987-93, assoc. prof., 1993—, adj. asst. prof. physics, 1990, adj. assoc. prof. physics, 1994, attending cardiologist, dir. echocardiology Jewish Hosp., 1992—, dir. divsn. cardiology, 1993—. Reviewer Jour. Clin. Investigation, Circulation, Arteriosclerosis and Thrombosis, Hypertension, Ultrasound in Medicine and Biology; contbr. over 80 articles to med. and sci. jours., chpts. to books on topics related to basic rsch. in cardiovascular biophysics and acoustics/ ultrasonics. Grantee NIH, 1990—, 92—, (two grants), 1995—, Whitaker Found., 1996. Fellow Am. Coll. Cardiology (reviewer jour.); mem. IEEE Soc. Ultrasonics, Ferroelectrics and Frequency Control (tech. program com. ultrasonics symposium), Am. Heart Assn. (coun. on radiology and clin. cardiology, Clinician-Scientist award 1988-93, Established Investigator award 1993—), Am. Soc. Clin. Investigation, Am. Inst. Ultrasound in Medicine, Acoustical Soc. Am., Alpha Omega Alpha. Home: 11211 Pointe Ct Saint Louis MO 63127-1741 Office: Jewish Hosp Cardiology 216 S Kingshighway Blvd Saint Louis MO 63110-1026

WICKLUND, DAVID WAYNE, lawyer; b. St. Paul, Aug. 7, 1949; s. Wayne Glenwood and Elna Katherine (Buresh) W.; m. Susan Marie Bubenko, Nov. 17, 1973; children: David Jr., Kurt, Edward. BA cum laude, Williams Coll., 1971; JD cum laude, U. Toledo, 1974. Bar: Ohio 1974. Assoc. Shumaker, Loop & Kendrick, Toledo, 1974-80, ptnr., 1981—; adj. instr. law, U. Toledo, 1988. Editor-in-chief U. Toledo Law Rev. 1973-74. Mem. ABA, Ohio State Bar Assn. (mem. bd. govs. antitrust sect.), Toledo Bar Assn., Inverness Club. Office: Shumaker Loop & Kendrick N Courthouse Sq 1000 Jackson St Toledo OH 43624-1515

WICKMAN, HERBERT HOLLIS, physical chemist, condensed matter physicist; b. Omaha, Sept. 30, 1936. AB, Mcpl. U. Omaha, 1959; PhD, U. Calif., Berkeley, 1965. Mem. tech. staff Bell Telephone Labs., Murray Hill, N.J., 1964-71; prof. phys. chemistry and biophysics Oreg. State U., Corvallis, 1971-87; program dir. condensed matter physics NSF, Washington, 1987—. Contbr. over 60 articles to profl. jours. Fellow Am. Phys. Soc.

WICKMAN, JOHN EDWARD, librarian, historian; b. Villa Park, Ill., May 24, 1929; s. John Edward and Elsie (Voss) W.; m. Shirley Jean Swanson, Mar. 17, 1951; children—Lisa Annette, Eric John. A.B., Elmhurst Coll., 1953; A.M., Ind. U., 1958, Ph.D., 1964; LL.D., Lincoln Coll., 1973. Instr. history Hanover (Ind.) Coll., 1959-62, Southeast Campus, Ind. U., Jeffersonville, 1962; asst. prof. history Northwest Mo. State Coll., Maryville, 1962-64; asst. to Gov. William H. Avery of Kans., Topeka, 1964-65; asst. prof. history Regional Campus, Purdue U., Fort Wayne, Ind., 1965-66; dir. Dwight D. Eisenhower Libr., Abilene, Kans., 1966-89; ret., 1989. Contbr. articles on Am. West, archival mgmt., adminstrv. history, oral history to profl. publs. Served with U.S. Army, 1953-55. Nat. Ctr. for Edn. in Politics faculty fellow, 1964-65; Am. Polit. Sci. Assn. Congl. fellow, 1975-76. Mem. Oral History Assn. (v.p. 1971-72, pres. 1972-73), Western History Assn. (coun. 1972-75), Kans. Hist. Soc. (2d v.p. 1974-75, pres. 1976-77, dir.). Home: 411 W 4th St PO Box 325 Enterprise KS 67441-0325

WICKS, EUGENE CLAUDE, college president, art educator; b. Coleharbor, N.D., Oct. 7, 1931; s. Claude Edward and Grace Ann (Wilkinson) W.; m. Lavonne Maureen Yineman, June 21, 1953; children: Christopher Edwin, Louis Eugene, James Edward. B.F.A., U. Colo., 1957, M.F.A., 1959. Mem. faculty U. Ill., Urbana, 1959-94; assoc. head U. Ill., 1961-76, head Sch. Art and Design, 1977-80, dir., 1981-89; also prof. art U. Ill. (Sch. Art and Design); pres. Burren Coll. Art, Newtown Castle, Ireland, 1994—; cons. in field. Represented in permanent collections at, Phila. Print Club, Art Inst. Chgo., Am. Fed. Arts, others. Served with USN, 1951-54. U. Ill. research grantee, 1960, 61, 67, 68, 69, 74, 75; Fulbright grantee, 1988-89. Mem. Coll. Art Assn., Nat. Assn. Schs. Art and Design (dir. commn. on accreditation 1978-81, v.p. 1981-84, pres. 1984-87). Home: Tigín, Ballyvaughan Co Clare, Ireland Office: Burren Coll Art, Newtown Castle, Ballyvaughan Ireland

WICKS, FREDERICK JOHN, research mineralogist, museum curator; b. Winnipeg, Can., Nov. 22, 1937; divorced; 1 child, Claire E. BSc, U. Manitoba (Can.), 1960, MSc, 1965. Geologist Giant Yellowknife Mines Ltd., 1960, 61; cons. mineralogist various govt. and pvt. industry cos., 1967; asst. curator Royal Ont. Mus., 1970-75, curator minerals, 1980—; assoc. prof. geology U. Toronto (Can.), 1980—. Fellow Geol. Assn. Can., Mineral Soc. Am., Clay Minerals Soc.; mem. Mineral Assn. Can. (sec. 1973-75, v.p. 1992-93, pres. 1994-95, past pres. 1996-97). Office: Royal Ontario Mus Dept Earth Scis, 100 Queens Park, Toronto, ON Canada M5S 2C6

WICKS, JOHN R., lawyer; b. Ottumwa, Iowa, Dec. 8, 1937; m. Nedra Morgan, Mar. 27, 1940; children: Catherine, John. BSC, U. Iowa, 1959, JD, 1964. Bar: Iowa 1964, Minn. 1966. Assoc. Dorsey & Whitney, Mpls., 1966-71; ptnr. Dorsey & Whitney LLP, Rochester, Minn., 1972-97. Fellow Am. Coll. Trusts and Estates Counsel; mem. Minn. State Bar Assn. (probate and trusts law coun. 1989-92), Olmsted County Minn. Bar Assn. Office: Dorsey & Whitney 201 1st Ave SW Ste 340 Rochester MN 55902-3155

WICKS, WILLIAM WITHINGTON, retired public relations executive; b. Chgo., Dec. 20, 1923; s. William and Alice (Withington) W.; m. Frances M. Horner, Nov. 29, 1947; children: Barbara Anne, Christine Frances. BNS, U. Notre Dame, 1944, AB in Journalism magna cum laude, 1947. Staff corr. United Press Assn., Milw., 1947; pub. rels. mgr. Internat. Harvester Co., Louisville, 1948-58; mgr. field svcs. pub. rels. Standard Oil Co. (Ind.), Chgo., 1959-60; v.p. pub. rels. Griswold-Eshleman Co., Chgo., 1961-68; dir. pub. rels. G. D. Searle & Co., Chgo., 1968-74; dir. pub. rels./investor rels. Kimberly-Clark Corp., Neenah, Wis., 1974, staff v.p., 1974-80; v.p. Kimberly-Clark Corp., Neenah (hdqrs. relocated to Dallas in 1985), 1980-89; v.p. and asst. to chmn. bd. Kimberly-Clark Corp., Irving, Tex., 1989-92; chmn. pub. relations sect. Pharm. Mfrs. Assn., Washington, 1974. Pres. Jr. Achievement Neenah-Menasha, 1978-81. Served to lt. (j.g.) USNR, 1942-46, PTO. Recipient Silver Anvil award Pub. Rels. Soc. Am., 1963, 79. Mem. PRSA (founder, pres. Bluegrass chpt. 1957-58), Optimist (pres. South End Club in Louisville 1957), Publicity Club of Chgo. (pres. 1967-68). Republican. Roman Catholic. Home: 1312 S Travis Cir Irving TX 75038-6243

WICKSER, JOHN PHILIP, lawyer; b. Buffalo, Oct. 14, 1922; s. Philip John and Margaretta Melissa (Fryer) W.; m. Frances M. Halsey, July 2, 1949; children: Margaretta Melissa, Philip John, Gaius Halsey. B.A., Yale U., 1945; J.D., Columbia U., 1949. Bar: N.Y. 1949. Since practiced in Buffalo; mem. firm Palmer, Houck & Wickser, 1949-50; ptnr. Palmer, Heffernan Wickser & Beyer, 1950-94; of counsel Magavern, Magavern & Grimm, 1994; pres. Main-Pearl Corp., 1963-82; dir. Union-Am. Re-Ins. Co., 1975-77; pres. Kleinhans Music Hall Mgmt., Inc. Life mem. adv. bd. Salvation Army, Internat. Inst., 1951-54; council State Tchrs. Coll., Buffalo, 1954-55; bd. dirs. Greater Buffalo Devel. Found., Grosvenor Soc.; chmn. bd. trustees Buffalo and Erie County Pub. Library; bd. dirs. Buffalo Fine Arts Acad., 1954-77. Served to lt. (j.g.) USNR, World War II. Mem. Johnson Soc. London, Sons of Revolution, Buffalo Hist. Soc. (trustee), N.Y. State, Erie County bar assns., Am. Judicature Soc. Republican. Episcopalian. Clubs: Buffalo Country (Buffalo), Pack (Buffalo), Saturn (Buffalo); Yale (N.Y.C.); Elizabethan (New Haven); Pacific, Nantucket Yacht. Home: 22 Oakland Pl Buffalo NY 14222-2009 Office: Rand Bldg Buffalo NY 14203

WICKSTROM, JON ALAN, telecommunications executive, consultant; b. San Antonio, Apr. 17, 1949; s. Stanley Alan and Louise (MacMillan) W.; m. Mary Carmen Sparkman, Jan. 25, 1969 (div. Jan. 1978); children: Dana Marie, Jon Alan Jr.; m. Jane Bielbey Slawson, June 19, 1988. BS, Tex. Tech.

U., 1975. Ptnr. Hensley & Assocs., Albuquerque, 1976-78; dealer svcs. mgr. Gulf States Toyota, Houston, 1978-80; comms. mgr. Hughes Tool Co., Houston, 1980-85; network svcs. mgr. Tenneco Oil Co., Houston, 1986-89; comms. mgr. Clarke Am., San Antonio, 1989-94; info/technology planner USAA, San Antonio, 1994-96; mgr. MMC Ernst & Young LLP, San Antonio, 1996—; prin. Comm. Tech. Cons., Houston, 1980-89; cons. Comms. Consulting Group, Inc., San Antonio, 1989-96. Author: (reference) 1976 Population Estimates for Bernallio County, New Mex., 1976. Rep. precinct chmn. Bexar County, Tex., 1992-94; cons. Houston Symphony Orch., 1988. Mem. Alamo Area Telecomms. Assn. (bd. dirs 1990-94, pres., 1992-93), S.W. Comms. Assn. (bd. dirs. 1981-85, pres. 1982-84), Tex. Telecomms. Conf. (bd. dirs. 1982-84, chmn. 1983). Avocations: sailing, golf, music, investing. Office: Ernst & Young LLP 100 W Houston St Ste 1900 San Antonio TX 78205

WICKSTROM, KARL YOUNGERT, publishing company executive; b. Moline, Ill., Sept. 20, 1935; s. George Washington and Harriet L. (Youngert) W.; m. Patricia Pinkerton, 1959 (div.); children: Eric, Blair, Drew, Holly; m. Sheila Zehner, June 9, 1979. B.S.J., U. Fla., 1957. Writer, editor Orlando (Fla.) Sentinel-Star, 1958-60; writer Miami (Fla.) Herald, 1960-67; adminstrv. asst. Fla. Senate, Tallahassee, 1968; founder, pres., publisher Wickstrom Pubs. Inc., mags., books, Miami, 1968—. Original pub.: Aloft Mag., for Nat. Airlines passengers, 1968-80; pub.: Fla. Sportsman, 1969—, Ryder World for Ryder System, Inc, 1980—. Bd. dirs. Nat. Coalition for Marine Conservation; v.p. Fla. Conservation Assn. Served with USAF, 1967-68. Recipient 1st Pl. award for pub. svc. Fla. AP, 1967; named Man of Yr., Am. Sportfishing Assn., 1995, Conservationist of Yr., Fla. Wildlife Fedn., 1995. Mem. Sigma Delta Chi (nat. 1st pl. award for investigative reporting Miami area crime, corruption 1967). Home: 745 S Alhambra Cir Miami FL 33146-3801 Office: Florida Sportsman 5901 SW 74th St Miami FL 33143-5165

WICKWIRE, PATRICIA JOANNE NELLOR, psychologist, educator; b. Sioux City, Iowa; d. William McKinley and Clara Rose (Pautsch) Nellor; m. Robert James Wickwire, Sept. 7, 1957; 1 child, William James. BA cum laude, U. No. Iowa, 1951; MA, U. Iowa, 1959; PhD, U. Tex., Austin, 1971; postgrad. U. So. Calif., UCLA, Calif. State U., Long Beach, 1951-66. Tchr., Ricketts Ind. Schs., Iowa, 1946-48; tchr., counselor Waverly-Shell Rock Ind. Schs., Iowa, 1951-55; reading cons., head dormitory counselor U. Iowa, Iowa City, 1955-57; tchr., sch. psychologist, adminstr. S. Bay Union High Sch. Dist., Redondo Beach, Calif., 1962-82, dir. student svcs. and spl. edn.; cons. mgmt. and edn.; pres. Nellor Wickwire Group, 1981—; mem. exec. bd. Calif. Interagency Mental Health Coun., 1968-72, Beach Cities Symphony Assn., 1970-82; chmn. Friends of Dominguez Hills (Calif.), 1981-85. Lic. ednl. psychologist, marriage, family and child counselor, Calif.; pres. Calif. Women's Caucus, 1993-95. Mem. APA, AAUW (exec. bd., chpt. pres. 1962-72), Nat. Career Devel. Assn. (media chair 1992—), Am. Assn. Career Edn. (pres. 1991—), L.A. County Dirs. Pupil Svcs. (chmn. 1974-79), L.A. County Personnel and Guidance Assn. (pres. 1977-78), Assn. Calif. Sch. Adminstrs. (dir. 1977-81), L.A. County SW Bd. Dist. Adminstrs. for Spl. Edn. (chmn. 1976-81), Calif. Assn. Sch. Psychologists (bd. dirs. 1981-83), Am. Assn. Sch. Adminstrs., Calif. Assn. for Measurement and Evaluation in Guidance (dir. 1981, pres. 1984-85), ACA (chmn. Coun. Newsletter Editors 1989-91, mem. com. on women 1989-92, mem. com. on rsch. and knowledge, 1994—, chmn. 1995—, chmn. 1996—), Assn. Measurement and Eval. in Guidance (Western regional editor 1985-87, conv. chair 1986, editor 1987-90, exec. bd. dirs. 1987-91), Calif. Assn. Counseling and Devel. (exec. bd. 1984—, pres. 1988-89, jour. editor 1990—), Internat. Career Assn. Network (chair 1985—), Pi Lambda Theta, Alpha Phi Gamma, Psi Chi, Kappa Delta Pi, Sigma Alpha Iota. Contbr. articles in field to profl. jours. Office: The Nellor Wickwire Group 2900 Amby Pl Hermosa Beach CA 90254-2216

WIDDEL, JOHN EARL, JR., lawyer; b. Minot, N.D., Nov. 17, 1936; s. John Earl Sr. and Angela Victoria (Gefroh) W.; m. Yvonne J. Haugen, Dec. 21, 1973; children: John P., James M., Susan N., Andrea K. B in Philosophy, BS in Bus. Adminstrn., U. N.D., 1966, BSBA, 1971. Bar: N.D. 1971, U.S. Dist. Ct. N.D., 1971, U.S. Ct. Appeals (8th cir.) 1989. Ptnr. Thorsen & Widdel, Grand Forks, N.D., 1971—; mcpl. judge City of Grand Forks, 1972—; ct. magistrate Grand Forks County, 1975. Mem. N.D. Foster Parent Program, 1974-87, Nat. Conf. of Bar Pres., 1986—; bd. dirs. YMCA, Grand Forks, 1982; dist. chmn. Boy Scouts Am., 1987-88; corp. mem. United Hosp. Served with U.S. Army, 1960-62. Mem. Am. Acad. Estate Planning Attys., State Bar Assn. N.D. (bd. govs. 1983-88, pres. 1986-87), Greater Grand Forks County Bar Assn. (pres. 1982), N.E. Cen. Jud. Dist. (pres. 1983), Grand Forks Cemetery Assn. (bd. dirs. 1984—, pres. 1989-94), Grand Forks Hist. Soc. (pres. 1983), Grand Forks Jaycees, Antique Automobile Club Am. (nat. bd. dirs. 1984—, v.p. 1985—), sec.-treas. 1989, pres. N.D. region 1977-78, 83-84), Sertoma (bd. dirs. 1994—), Elks (exalted ruler 1985-86), Masonic Bodies (Kem Temples Potentate 1995), Nat. Assn. Estate Planning Coun. (accredited estate planner, 1994), N.D. Mcpl. Judges Assn. (dir. 1993—). Roman Catholic. Home: Box 5624 Grand Forks ND 58206-5624 Office: Thorsen & Widdel 215A S 4th St Grand Forks ND 58206-5624

WIDDICOMBE, RICHARD PALMER, librarian; b. Paterson, N.J., Apr. 12, 1941; s. Robert Lord and Elvira Barbara (Guttilla) W.; m. Martha Elizabeth Bruyn, Feb. 26, 1972. B.A., Alfred U., 1963; M.S. L.S., Syracuse U., 1964. Asst. librarian Yonkers Pub. Library, N.Y., 1964-65; asst. librarian Cooper Union, N.Y.C., 1965-66; asst. librarian Stevens Inst., Hoboken, N.J., 1966-72, dir. library, 1973—. Episcopalian. Home: Castle Point Sta PO Box S-1342 Hoboken NJ 07030-5991 Office: SC Williams Libr Stevens Inst Hoboken NJ 07030

WIDDRINGTON, PETER NIGEL TINLING, environmental and energy company executive; b. Toronto, Ont., Can., June 2, 1930; s. Gerard and Margery (MacDonald) W.; m. Betty Ann Lawrence, Oct. 12, 1956; children: Lucinda Ann, Andrea Stacy. BA with honors, Queen's U., Kingston, Ont., 1953; MBA, Harvard, 1955. Salesman Labatt's Co., London, Ont., 1955-57; regional mgr. Ont. Labatt's Co., 1957-58, gen. mgr. Man., 1958-61, gen. mgr. B.C., 1962-65; gen. mgr. Kiewel & Pelissiers, Winnipeg, 1961-62; pres. Lucky Breweries Inc., San Francisco, 1968-71; v.p. corp. devel. John Labatt Ltd., 1971-73, sr. v.p., 1973-87, pres., chief exec. officer, 1973-89, chmn., 1987-91; pres., CEO Cuddy Internat. Corp., 1996—; chmn. Talisman Energy Inc., 1996—, Laidlaw Inc., 1990—; bd. dirs. Chief Execs. Orgn., Inc., CEC Resources Ltd., Cuddy Internat. Corp., Dialysis Ctrs. Am., Talisman Energy Inc., Can. Imperial Bank Commerce, Laidlaw Inc., The SNC-Lavalin Group, Inc. Office: 248 Pall Mall St Ste 400, London, ON Canada N6A 5P6

WIDEMAN, JOHN EDGAR, English literature educator, novelist; b. Washington, DC, June 14, 1941; married, 3 children. BA, U. Pa., 1963; BPhil, Oxford U., Eng., 1966; postgrad., U. Iowa Writers Workshop, 1967; DLitt (hon.), U. Pa., 1985, Rutgers U. Mem. faculty U. Wyo., Laramie; prof. English U. Wyo., 1974-85, U. Mass., Amherst, 1986—; USIS lectr. in Eastern Europe. Author: A Glance Away, 1967, Hurry Home, 1969, The Lynchers, 1973, Hiding Place, 1981, Damballah, 1981, Sent for You Yesterday, 1983 (PEN/Faulkner award for fiction 1984), Brothers and Keepers, 1984, Reuben, 1987, Fever, 1989, Philadelphia Fire, 1990 (PEN/Faulkner award for fiction 1991), The Homewood Books, 1992, The Stories of John Edgar Wideman, 1992, All Stories Are True, 1993, Fatheralong, 1994, The Cattle Killing, 1996; contbr. numerous articles and revs. to profl. jours., mags. Ben Franklin scholar; Lannan award, 1991; Kent fellow; Rhodes scholar; Nat. Endowment for Humanities grantee; MacArthur fellow 1993. Mem. Am. Assn. Rhodes Scholars (dir.), Am. Studies Assn. (council 1980-81), MLA, Am. Acad. Arts Scis. (elected), (Phi Beta Kappa). Office: Univ Mass Dept English Amherst MA 01003

WIDENER, HIRAM EMORY, JR., federal judge; b. Abingdon, Va., Apr. 30, 1923; s. Hiram Emory and Nita Douglas (Peck) W.; children: Molly Berendt, Hiram Emory III. Student, Va. Poly. Inst., 1940-41; B.S., U.S. Naval Acad., 1944; LL.B., Washington and Lee U., 1953, LL.D., 1977. Bar: Va. 1951. Pvt. practice law Bristol, Va., 1953-69; judge U.S. Dist. Ct. Western Dist. Va., Abingdon, 1969-71; chief judge U.S. Dist. Ct. Western Dist. Va., 1971-72; judge U.S. Ct. Appeals 4th Circuit, Abingdon, 1972—; U.S. commr. Western Dist. Va., 1963-66; mem. Va. Election Laws Study Commn., 1968-69. Chmn. Rep. party 9th Dist. Va., 1966-69; mem. Va. Rep. State Ctrl. Com., 1966-69, state exec. com., 1966-69. Served to lt. (j.g.) USN, 1944-49; to lt. USNR, 1951-52. Decorated Bronze Star with combat V. Mem. Am. Law Inst., Va. Bar Assn., Va. State Bar, Phi Alpha Delta. Republican. Presbyterian. Home and Office: 180 Main St Rm 123 Abingdon VA 24212-0868

WIDENER, PERI ANN, business development executive; b. Wichita, Kans., May 1, 1956; d. Wayne Robert and LuAnne (Harris) W. BS, Wichita State U., 1978; MBA, Fla. Tech., 1992. Advt. intern Associated Advt., Wichita, 1978; pub. rels. asst. Fourth Nat. Bank, Wichita, 1978-79; mktg. communications rep. Boeing Co., Wichita, 1979-83, pub. rels. rep., Huntsville, Ala., 1983-85, pub. rels. mgr., 1985-92; sr. pub. rels. mgr. Boeing Mil. Airplanes, Seattle, 1992-95; bus. devel. mgr. Boeing Defense & Space Group, Washington, D.C., 1995—. mem. exec. devel. program Boeing Def. & Space Group, 1993—. Preston Huston scholar, Wichita State U., 1978; recipient Best Electronic Ad award Def. Electronics mag., 1982, Best Total Pub. Rels. Program award Huntsville Press Club, 1985, Huntsville Media awards, 1986, 87, 88, 89, 90, 91, Huntsville Advt. Fedn. Addys, 1988. Mem. Pub. Rels. Soc. Am. (Seattle chpt.), Women in Communications, Pub. Rels. Coun. Ala. (bd. dirs. 1985-92, state pres. 1992, officer Huntsville chpt. 1984-91, pres. No. Ala. chpt. 1989, Excellence award 1986-91, Achievement award 1986-91, Pres.'s award Huntsville chpt. 1985, State Practitioner of Yr. 1989, PRCA Medallion award excellence, numerous others), Internat. Assn. Bus. Communicators (D2 Silver Quills award 1985, 91, D6 Silver Quills 1993, 94), Pub. Rels. Soc. Am. (accredited 1989—), So. Pub. Rels. Fedn. (practitioner of yr. 1991, Excellence award 1986-91, Lantern award 1991), Huntsville-Madison County C. of C. (pub. rels. adv. com. 1987-92), Huntsville Press Club (bd. dirs. 1989-92), Sigma Delta Chi (pres.'s award 1991). Methodist. Office: The Boeing Co 1700 N Moore St Fl 20 Arlington VA 22209-1903

WIDERA, GEORG ERNST OTTO, mechanical engineering educator, consultant; b. Dortmund, Germany, Feb. 16, 1938; came to U.S., 1950; s. Otto and Gertrude (Yzermann) W.; m. Kristel Kornas, June 21, 1974; children: Erika, Nicholas. BS, U. Wis., 1960, MS, 1962, PhD, 1965. Asst. prof., then prof. materials engring. dept. U. Ill.-Chgo., 1965-82, prof. mech. engring., 1982-91, head dept., 1983-91, acting head indsl. systems engring. dept., 1985-86, dir. off-campus engring. programs, 1987-88; prof., chairperson mech. and indsl. engring. dept. Marquette U., Milw., 1991— dir., Ctr for Indsl. Processes and Productivity, Marquette U., 1995—; Gastdozent U. Stuttgart, Fed. Republic of Germany, 1968; vis. prof. U. Wis.-Milw., 1973-74, Marquette U., Milw., 1978-79; cons. Ladish Co., Cudahy, Wis., 1967-76, Howmedica, Inc., Chgo., 1972-75, Sargent & Lundy, 1970-88, Nat. Bur. Standards, 1980, bd., dirs., Engrs and Scientists of Milw., 1996—; vis. sci. Argonne Nat. Lab., Ill., 1968. Editor: Procs. Innovations in Structural Engring., 1974, Pressure Vessel Design, 1982; assoc. editor: Pressure Vessel Tech., 1977-81, Applied Mechanics Revs., 1987-94, Manufacturing Review, 1991-95; editorial adv. bd. Acta Mechanica Sinica, 1990—; mem. editorial bd. Pressure Vessels and Piping Design Technology, 1982; tech. editor Jour. Pressure Vessel Technology, 1982-93; co-editor: SME Handbook of Metalforming, 1985, 94, Design and Analysis of Plates and Shells, 1986. Standard Oil Co. Calif. fellow, 1961-63; NASA fellow, 1966; NSF travel grantee, Russia, 1972; von Humboldt fellow, Fed. Republic Germany, 1968-69. Fellow ASME (v.p. materials and structures 1993-96, chmn. pressure vessel rsch. com. 1982-87, chmn. design and analysis com. pressure vessel and piping divsn. 1980-83, chmn. jr. awards com. applied mechanics divsn. 1973-76, chmn. machine design divsn. of Chgo. sect., 1967-68, editor newsletter Chgo. sect. 1971-73, exec. com. Chgo. sect. 1970-73, honors and awards chmn. Milw. sect. 1992-95, mem. exec. com. and program chmn. pressure vessel and piping divsn. 1985-89, vice-chmn., sec. pressure vessel and piping divsn., 1989-90, chmn. pressure vessel and piping divsn., 1990-91, historian, senate pressure vessel and piping divsn., 1991-92, pres. senate pressure vessel and piping divsn., 1992-93, bd. editors, 1983-93, mem. materials and structures group, 1990-91, mem. coun. on engring. 1992-96, mem. bd. on pressure tech. codes and standards, 1989-94, soc. rep. to Fedn. Materials Socs. 1994-95, mem. tech. execs. com. 1993-96, Pressure Vessel and Piping award 1995 and medal), ASCE (sec.-treas. structural divsn. of Ill. sect. 1972-73, chmn. divsn. 1976-77, chmn. peer review com., tech. coun. on rsch. 1984, coun. on structural plastics), Soc. Mfg. Engrs. (sr. mem.), Am. Soc. for Engring. Edn., French Preesure Vessel Assn., So. Plastics Engrs., Gesellschaft für Angewandte Mathematik und Mechanik, WRC (pressure vessel rsch. coun., chmn. subcom. on design procedures for shell intersections, 1983-87, chmn. com. on reinforced openings and external loads, 1987-91, vice chmn. com. on polymer pressure components 1991—, chmn. com. shells and ligaments 1994-97), Internat. Coun. on Pressure Vessel Tech. (chmn. Am. regional com. 1988—, internat. chmn. 1992-96), 2nd China Nat. Standards Com. for Pressure Vessels (hon. cons.), Wis. Club. Research on mechanics of composite materials, plate and shell structures, stress analysis (incl. FEM), pressure vessels, mechanics of deformation processing. Home: 19440 Killarney Way Brookfield WI 53045-4810 Office: Marquette U Dept Mech & Indsl Engring 1515 W Wisconsin Ave PO Box 1881 Milwaukee WI 53201-1881

WIDES, BURTON V., lawyer; b. Englewood, N.J., June 14, 1941. BA magna cum laude, Harvard U., 1962, LLB, 1965. Bar: N.Y. 1968, U.S. Supreme Ct. 1972, D.C. 1976. Clk. to Hon. James A Coolahan U.S. Dist. Ct. N.J., Newark, 1965-66; legis. coun. to Sen. Philip A. Hart, 1970-76, legis. dir., adminstrv. asst. to Sen. Paul Sarbanes, 1976-77; coun. Pres.' Intelligence Oversight Bd., 1977-79; legis. coun. U.S. Senate Com. Judiciary, 1979-80, coun., 1981-84, coun. to Sen. Edward Kennedy, 1984—; ptnr. Arent Fox Kinter Plotkin & Kahn, Washington. Office: Arent Fox Kintner Plotkin & Kahn Washington Sq 1050 Connecticut Ave NW Washington DC 20036

WIDGOFF, MILDRED, physicist, educator; b. Buffalo, Aug. 24, 1924; d. Leo Widgoff and Rebecca Shulimson; children—Eve Widgoff Shapiro, Jonathan Bernard Widgoff Shapiro. B.A., U. Buffalo, 1944; Ph.D., Cornell U., 1952. Rsch. assoc. Brookhaven Nat. Lab., Yaphank, N.Y., 1952-54; rsch. fellow Harvard U., Cambridge, Mass., 1955-58; asst. prof. rsch. Brown U., Providence, 1959-66, assoc. prof. rsch., 1966-74, prof. physics, 1974-95; prof. rsch., 1995—. Fellow Am. Phys. Soc.; mem. Sigma Xi, Phi Beta Kappa, Phi Kappa Phi. Office: Brown U Dept Physics PO Box 1843 Providence RI 02912-1843

WIDISS, ALAN I., lawyer, educator; b. L.A., Sept. 28, 1938; s. Al and Rose H. (Sobole) W.; m. Ellen Louise Magaziner, June 28, 1964; children: Benjamin L., Deborah Anne, Rebecca Elizabeth. BS, U. So. Calif., 1960, LLB, 1963; LLM, Harvard U., 1964. Bar: Calif. 1963. Teaching fellow Harvard U., 1964-65; asst. prof. law U. Iowa, Iowa City, 1965-68; asso. prof. U. Iowa, 1968-69, prof., 1969-78, Josephine R. Witte prof., 1978—; vis. prof. U. So. Calif., U. San Diego; dir. CLRS Mass. No-Fault Automobile Ins. Study, 1971-76. Author: A Guide to Uninsured Motorist Coverage, 1969; (with others) No-Fault Automobile Insurance in Action: The Experiences in Massachusetts, Florida, Delaware and New York, 1977, Uninsured and Underinsured Motorist Insurance (revised edit.), Vol. 1, 1991, Vol. 2, 1992, Vol. 3, 1995; author, editor: (with others) Arbitration: Commercial Disputes, Insurance and Tort Claims, 1979; (with Judge Robert E. Keeton) Insurance Law, 1988 and Course Supplement, 1988; Insurance: Materials on the General Principles, Legal Doctrines and Regulatory Acts, 1989; contbr. articles to law jours. Bd. fellows U. Iowa Sch. Religion, 1976, v.p., 1991-93, pres., 1993-95; chmn. Johnson County Citizens Adv. Com. for Regional Transp. Study, 1971-75; pres. Agudas Achim Synagogue, 1983-85, Iowa City Youth Orch., 1991-92. Mem. ABA, Am. Law Inst., Calif. Bar Assn., Assn. Am. Law Schs., Order of Coif, Phi Kappa Phi, Delta Sigma Rho. Avocations: tennis, theater. Home: 316 Kimball Rd Iowa City IA 52245-5825 Office: U Iowa Coll Law Iowa City IA 52242

WIDLUND, OLOF BERTIL, computer science educator; b. Stockholm, Feb. 11, 1938; s. Sten O. and Dagmar W.; m. Nadine H. Taub, June 13, 1972. M.S. in Engring., Royal Inst. Tech., Stockholm, 1960, Ph.D., 1964; Sc.D., Uppsala U., Sweden, 1966. Asst. prof. NYU, N.Y.C., 1968-72, assoc. prof., 1972-75, prof. computer sci., 1975—, chmn. dept. computer sci., 1980-86. Contbr. articles to various publs. Office: NYU Courant Inst 251 Mercer St New York NY 10012-1110

WIDMAN, GARY LEE, lawyer, former government official; b. Fremont, Nebr., June 1, 1936; s. Benjamin H. and Alice C. (Negley) W.; m. Mary Margaret Donnelly, Mar. 5, 1972(div. 1988); children: Andrew Scott, Natalie Claire. BS, U. Nebr., 1957; JD, Hastings Coll. Law U. Calif., 1962; LLM, U. Mich., 1966. Bar: Calif. 1962, D.C. 1982. Assoc. Thelen, Marrin, Johnson & Bridges, San Francisco, 1962-65; assoc. prof. law U. Denver, 1966-69; prof., dir. resource and environ. law program Hastings Coll. Law, U. Calif., San Francisco, 1969-80; gen. counsel Coun. Environ. Quality, Exec. Office Pres., Washington, 1974-76; lectr. U. Calif. at Davis, 1978, Boalt Hall, 1977-79; assoc. solicitor Dept. Interior, Washington, 1980-81; of counsel Fulbright & Jaworski, 1981-85; dir. staff attys. U.S. Ct. of Appeals (9th cir.), San Francisco, 1985-87; atty. Bronson, Bronson & McKinnon, San Francisco, 1988-95; chief counsel State Dept. Parks and Recreation, Sacramento, 1995-96; trustee Rocky Mountain Mineral Law Found., 1969-74, 77-80; apptd. by gov. P. Wilson to Bay-Delta Oversight Coun., 1993-95. Author and project dir.: Legal Study of Oil Shale on Public Lands, 1969. Served with U.S. Army, 1957-59. Mem. ABA (council sect. natural resources 1975-77, spl. com. energy law 1977-82, council lawyers and scientists 1984-90), Fed. Bar Assn. (chmn. com. natural resources 1977), Calif. Bar Assn., D.C. Bar Assn., Trout Unlimited Calif. (pres. 1986-90). Home: 28 Marinero Cir Apt 31 Belvedere Tiburon CA 94920-1644

WIDMAN, PAUL JOSEPH, insurance agent; b. DeSmet, S.D., Dec. 18, 1936; s. Warren Clay and Lorraine (Coughlin) W.; m. Elizabeth Ann Healy, July 30, 1959; children: Cynthia, Susan, Shelly, Richard, Mark. BS, Dakota State Coll., Madison, 1959; M in Comm., S.D. State U., 1968. Tchr. Clark (S.D.) Pub. Sch., 1959-60, Henry (S.D.) Pub. Sch., 1960-64, Custer (S.D.) Pub. Sch., 1964-66; ins. agt. Horace Mann Ins., Mitchell, S.D., 1966-77, Universal Underwriters, Mitchell, S.D., 1980-87, NGM Ins. Assn., Mitchell, S.D., 1987-91, Reginald Martin Agy., Mitchell, S.D., 1991—; state rep. State of S.D., 1993—. City coun. mem. Mitchell City Coun., 1972-76; state legislator S.D. Ho. of Reps., 1993-94. Sgt. U.S. Army N.G., 1955-61. Mem. Elks, Mitchell Jaycees (pres., v.p. 1968-70, Outstanding Jaycee 1970), S.D. Jaycees (v.p., regional dir. 1969-70). Democrat. Roman Catholic. Avocations: golf, bowling, hunting. Office: Reginald Martin Agy 510 W Havens St Mitchell SD 57301-3935

WIDMAN, RICHARD GUSTAVE, engineering and construction company executive; b. Detroit, Jan. 28, 1922; s. Edward J. and Lena E. (Hurrle) W.; m. Barbara Jean Roehm, Sept 7, 1946; children: Richard Thomas, Linda Widman Wyer, Jeanne Widman Overby. B.C.E., U. Mich., 1947. Various positions Arthur G. McKee & Co. and McKee Corp., 1948-65, gen. mgr. petroleum and chems. div., 1966-68, v.p., 1968-69, exec. v.p., dir., 1969, pres., 1970-71, pres., chief exec. officer, chmn. bd., 1971-79, also dir.; chmn. bd., dir. Am. Automobile Assn.; bd. dirs. Ohio Motorists Assn. Served with C.E. AUS, 1943-46. Mem. Royal Polinciana Golf Club (Naples, Fla.), Tau Beta Pi. Home: 2901 Gulf Shore Blvd N Naples FL 34103-3937

WIDMANN, GLENN ROGER, electrical engineer; b. Newark, Jan. 8, 1957; s. Elmer and Ellen (Eccles) W. BSEE, Rutgers U., 1979; MSEE, Purdue U., 1981, PhDEE, 1988. Engr. N.J. Bell Telephone Co., Hopelawn, 1979; instr. Purdue U., West Lafayette, Ind., 1979-81, 83-88; prof. elec. engring. Colo. State U., Ft. Collins, 1988-91; engr. Hughes Aircraft Co., Canoga Park, Calif., 1980-83; scientist, project mgr., automotive controls engring. dir. GM Hughes Electronics Corp., Canoga Park, Calif., 1991-94; sr. sci. automotive elecs. devel. dir. Hughes Rsch. Labs. GM Hughes Electronics Corp., Malibu, Calif., 1994-96; dept. mgr. GM Hughes Electronics Corp., Malibu, 1996-97; mgr. Delco Electronics GM Hughes Electronics Corp., Troy, Mich., 1997—; cons. Bur. Reclamation, Denver, 1989, Benjamin Cummings Pub. Co., Ft. Collins, 1989; mem. program com. Internat. Symposium Robotics and Mfg., Santa Fe, N.Mex., 1991—. Contbr. articles to tech. jours.; patentee in robotics field. Recipient presentation award Am. Controls Conf., 1990. Mem. IEEE, Soc. Automotive Engrs., Tau Beta Pi, Eta Kappa Nu. Avocation: coin collecting. Home: 3370 Crestwater Ct Apt 2011 Rochester Hills MI 48309 Office: Delco Electronics 500 Stephenson Hwy Troy MI 48083

WIDMARK, RICHARD, actor; b. Sunrise, Minn., Dec. 26, 1914; s. Carl H. and Ethel Mae (Barr) W.; m. Ora Jean Hazlewood, Apr. 5, 1942; 1 dau., Anne Heath. B.A., Lake Forest (Ill.) Coll., 1936, D.F.A. (hon.), 1973. Instr. drama dept. Lake Forest Coll., 1936-38; Pres. Heath Prodns., 1955—; v.p. Widmark Cattle Enterprises, 1957—. Actor various radio networks, N.Y.C., 1938-47; Broadway appearances include Kiss and Tell, 1943, Get Away Old Man, 1943, Trio, 1944, Kiss Them for Me, 1944, Dunnigan's Daughter, 1945, Dream Girl, 1946-47; summer stock appearances include The Bo Tree, 1939, Joan of Lorraine, 1947; motion picture appearances include Kiss of Death, 1947, Street with No Name, 1948, Yellow Sky, 1948, Roadhouse, 1948, Down to the Sea in Ships, 1949, Night and the City, 1949, No Way Out, 1949, Panic in the Streets, 1950, Slattery's Hurricane, 1949, Halls of Montezuma, 1950, The Frogmen, 1950, Price of Gold, 1954, Co Blue, 1954, Broken Lance, 1954, Backlash, 1955, St. Joan, 1956, Time Limit, 1957, Warlock, 1958, The Alamo, 1959, Judgement at Nuremberg, 1961, Flight from Ashiya, 1962, How the West Was Won, 1962, The Long Ships, 1963, Cheyenne Autumn, 1963, Bedford Incident, 1964, Alvarez Kelly, 1965, The Way West, 1966, Madigan, 1967, Patch, 1968, Talent for Loving, 1968, The Moonshine War, 1969, When the Legends Die, 1971, Murder on the Orient Express, 1974, The Sellout, 1975, To the Devil, A Daughter, 1975, The Twilight's Last Gleaming, 1976, The Domino Principle, 1976, Roller Coaster, 1976, Coma, 1978, The Swarm, 1977, Hanky Panky, 1982, The Final Option, 1983, Against All Odds, 1984, True Colors, 1990; NBC TV appearance in Vanished, 1971, TV series Madigan, 1972; TV appearance in Benjamin Franklin, 1974, Mr. Horn, 1979, Bear Island, 1979, All God's Children, 1980, A Whale for the Killing, 1981, Blackout, 1985, A Gathering of Old Men, 1986, Once Upon a Texas Train, 1987, Cold Sassy Tree, 1989. True Colors, 1990. Bd. dirs. Hope for Hearing. Named Comdr. of Arts and Letters (France), 1987. Mem. Valley Club (Montecito, Calif.), Century Club (N.Y.C.).

WIDMER, CHARLES GLENN, dentist, researcher; b. Daytona Beach, Fla., Jan. 8, 1955; s. Ernest Clyde and Martha Elizabeth (Hunter) W.; m. Alyson Lynn Byrd, Jul. 11, 1981; children: Kathryn Michelle, Elizabeth Ann. BS, Emory Univ., 1977, DDS, 1981; MS, SUNY, 1983. Asst. prof. Sch. Dentistry Emory Univ., Atlanta, 1983-91; assoc. prof. Coll. Dentistry Univ. Fla., Gainesville, 1991—, acting assoc. dean for rsch., 1996-97; reviewer NIH, Washington, 1988-89, 93-94, NIH Reviewer's Res., 1995-99. Contbr. articles to profl. jours. Contbr. Atlanta Zoo, 1985-91. NIH grantee for utilization of Trigeminal Evoked Potentials in dentistry, 1986-92, for orgn. and function of human masseter muscles, 1991—, for methods for conducting temporomandibular joint imaging using MRI, 1988-89, Rsch. Career Devel. award, 1991-96. Mem. ADA, Internat. Assn. Dental Rsch. (sec., treas., v.p., then pres., councilor neurosci. group 1989-95), Assn. Univ. Temporomandibular Disorders and Orofacial Pain Programs (sec., treas., v.p., then pres. 1990-95), Soc. Neurosci., Internat. Brain Rsch. Orgn., N.Y. Acad. Scis. Office: Univ Fla Dept Oral & Maxillofacial Surgery & Diagnostic Scis PO Box 100416 Gainesville FL 32610-0416

WIDMER, KEMBLE, geologist; b. New Rochelle, N.Y., Feb. 26, 1913; s. George Ellis and Beth (Kemble) W.; m. Virginia Maiers, Mar. 10, 1939; children—Kemble II, Katharine. A.B., Lehigh U., 1937; postgrad., Stanford, 1937-39; M.A., Princeton, 1947, Ph.D., 1950. Geologist Newfoundland Geol. Survey, summers 1937-41, 46, 47; asst. prof. geology Rutgers U., 1949-51; asso. prof. geology Chaplain Coll., State U. N.Y., 1951-53; prin. geologist N.J. Bur. Geology, 1953-58; state geologist N.J., 1958-81; seminar assoc. Columbia U., 1967-83; N.J. nuclear indsl. officer, 1964-74; mem. fed. adv. com. on water data for public use U.S. Geol. Survey, 1978-81; ret., 1981; cons. U.S. Mil. Acad., 1964-83. Served to lt. col. AUS, 1941-46; col. Res. (ret.). Recipient Outstanding Civilian Svc. medal Dept. Army, 1983. Fellow Geol. Soc. Am., N.J. Acad. Sci., AAAS, Company Mil. Historians; mem. Sigma Xi. Club: Explorers (N.Y.C.). Home: 228 King George Rd Pennington NJ 08534-2324

WIDNALL, SHEILA EVANS, secreatry of the airforce, former aeronautical educator, former university official; b. Tacoma, July 13, 1938; d. Rolland John and Genievieve Alice (Krause) Evans; m. William Soule Widnall, June 11, 1960; children: William, Ann. BS in Aero. and Astronautics, MIT, 1960, MS in Aero. and Astronautics, 1961, DSc, 1964; PhD (hon.), New Eng. Coll., 1975, Lawrence U., 1987, Cedar Crest Coll., 1988, Smith Coll., 1990, Mt. Holyoke Coll., 1991, Ill. Inst. Tech., 1991, Columbia U., 1994, Simmons Coll., 1994, Suffolk U., 1994, Princeton U., 1994. Asst. prof. aeros. and astronautics MIT, Cambridge, 1964-70, assoc. prof., 1970-74, prof., 1974-93, head divsn. fluid mechanics, 1975-79; dir. Fluid Dynamics Rsch. Lab., MIT, Cambridge, 1979-90; chmn. faculty MIT, Cambridge, 1979-80, chairperson com. on acad. responsibility, 1991-92, assoc. provost, 1992-93; sec. USAF, 1993—; bd. dirs. Chemfab Inc., Bennington, Vt., Aerospace Corp., L.A., Draper Labs., Cambridge; past trustee Carnegie Corp., 1984-92, Charles Stark Draper Lab. Inc.; mem. Carnegie Commn. Sci., Tech. and Govt. Contbr. articles to profl. jours.; patentee in field; assoc. editor AIAA Jour. Aircraft, 1972-75, Physics of Fluids, 1981-88, Jour. Applied Mechanics, 1983-87; mem. editorial bd. Sci., 1984-86. Bd. visitors USAF Acad., Colorado Springs, Colo., 1978-84, bd. chairperson, 1980-82; trustee Boston Mus. Sci., 1989—. Recipient Washburn award Boston Mus. Sci., 1987. Fellow AAAS (bd. dirs. 1982-89, pres. 1987-88, chmn. 1988-89), AIAA (bd. dirs. 1975-77, Lawrence Sperry award 1972), Am. Phys. Soc. (exec. com. 1979-82); mem. ASME, NAE (coun. 1992—), NAS (panel on sci. responsibility), Am. Acad. Arts and Scis., Soc. Women Engrs. (Outstanding Achievement award 1975), Internat. Acad. Astronautics, Seattle Mountaineers. Office: USAF Office of Sec 1670 AF Pentagon Washington DC 20330-1670*

WIDNER, RALPH RANDOLPH, civic executive; b. Phila., Oct. 21, 1930; s. Ralph Litteer and Viola (Cunningham) W.; m. Joan Sundelius Ziegler, July 9, 1955; children: Jennifer Anne, Wendy Rowe. BA, Duke U., 1952; student, Georgetown U., 1958; DHL (hon.), Union Coll., Ky., 1970, Capital U., Columbus, Ohio, 1971. Journalist Paterson (N.J.) Evening News, 1955-56, N.Y. Times, 1956-58; Congressional fellow Am. Polit. Sci. Assn., 1958; dir. pub. affairs Pa. Dept. Forests and Waters, 1959-60; asst. dir. Pa. Planning Bd., 1960-62; legis. asst. to U.S. Senator Clark, 1962-65; exec. dir. Appalachian Regional Commn., 1965-71; pres. Acad. for State and Local Govt., 1971-82; adj. prof. pub. adminstrn. and city planning Ohio State U., 1971-82; pres. Nat. Tng. and Devel. Service for State and Local Govt., 1979-81; staff v.p. Urban Land Inst., 1982-83; exec. dir. Greater Phila. First Corp., 1983-88; chmn. Fairfax House Internat., Alexandria, Va., 1988—; dir. Civic TN Network. Bd. dirs. Internat. Soc. Panetics, Ptnrs. for Democratic Change; dir. Internat. Coun. Lyon. Lt. (j.g.) USN, 1952-55. Fellow Nat. Acad. Pub. Administrn. Democrat. Methodist. Home: 2210 Belle Haven Rd Alexandria VA 22307-1100 Office: PO Box 7517 Alexandria VA 22307-0517

WIDOM, BENJAMIN, chemistry educator; b. Newark, Oct. 13, 1927; s. Morris and Rebecca (Hertz) W.; m. Joanne McCurdy, Dec. 21, 1953; children: Jonathan, Michael, Elisabeth. AB, Columbia U., 1949; PhD, Cornell U., 1953; DSc (hon.), U. Chgo., 1991. Rsch. assoc. U. N.C., Chapel Hill, 1952-54; instr. chemistry Cornell U., Ithaca, N.Y., 1954-55, asst. prof., 1955-59, assoc. prof., 1959-63, prof., 1963-83, Goldwin Smith prof., 1983—; van der Waals prof. U. Amsterdam, The Netherlands, 1972; vis. prof. Harvard U., Cambridge, Mass., 1975; IBM vis. prof. Oxford (Eng.) U., 1978; Lorentz prof. U. Leiden, The Netherlands, 1985; vis. prof. Cath. U. Louvain, Belgium, 1988. Author: (with J.S. Rowlinson) Molecular Theory of Capillarity, 1982. With U.S. Army, 1946-47. Recipient Clark disting. tchg. award Cornell U., 1973, Dickson prize for sci. Carnegie-Mellon U., 1986, Hirschfelder Prize in Theoretical Chemistry U. Wis., 1991, Bakhuis Roozeboom medal Royal Netherlands Acad. Arts & Scis., 1994, Onsager medal U. Trondheim, Norway, 1994. Fellow Am. Phys. Soc., Am. Acad. Arts and Scis., N.Y. Acad. Scis. (Boris Pregel award for chem. physics rsch. 1976); mem. NAS, Am. Philos. Soc., Am. Chem. Soc. (Langmuir award in chem. physics 1982, Hildebrand award in theoretical and exptl. chemistry of liquids 1992). Home: 204 The Parkway Ithaca NY 14850-2247 Office: Cornell U Chemistry Dept Ithaca NY 14853

WIDYOLAR, SHEILA GAYLE, dermatologist; b. Vancouver, B.C., Can., June 11, 1939; d. Walter Herbert and Olive Louise (O'Neal) Roberts; Kithi K. Widyolar, 1960 (div. 1979); 1 child, Keith. BS, Loma Linda U., 1962; MD, Howard U., 1972. Resident U. Calif., Irvine, 1973-76; dermatologist pvt. practice, Laguna Hills, Calif., 1976—; clin. instr. U. Calif. Sch. Medicine, 1978-86. Chmn. bd. dirs. Opera Pacific, Costa Mesa, Calif., 1996-97. Fellow Am. Acad. Dermatology, Am. Soc. Dermatophthology; mem. AMA, Calif. Med. Assn., Dermatological Soc. Orange County (pres. 1983), Alpha Omega Alpha. Avocations: music, travel. Office: Ste 403 23911 Calle de Mag Dalena Laguna Hills CA 92653

WIDZER, STEVEN J., pediatric gastroenterologist; b. Cleve., Jan. 11, 1950; s. Ben And Lillian Widzer; m. Helen M. Widzer, June 19, 1971; children: Joshua, Rebecca, Noah. BS, Northwestern U., 1972, MD, 1974. Diplomate Am. Bd. Pediat. Gastroenterology. Resident in pediats. Children's Hosp. of Phila., 1974-76, fellow in pediat. gastroenterology, 1976-78; mem. sect. pediat. gastroenterology St. Christopher's Hosp. for Children, Phila., 1978-84; acting chief St. Christopher's Hosp. of Children, Phila., 1984-85, chief, 1985-86; founding ptnr. Widzer and Kelly, Bryn Mawr, Pa., 1986—; asst. prof. pediats. Temple U. Sch. Medicine, Phila., 1978-86, adj. assoc. prof. pediats., 1991—; clin. assoc. prof. pediats. Med. Coll. Pa., Phila., 1987—; assoc. attending staff Bryn Mawr Hosp., 1986—. Contbr. articles to profl. jours. Fellow Am. Acad. Pediats.; mem. N.Am. Soc. for Pediat. Gastroenterology, Crohns and Colitis Found. Am., Am. Gastroent. Assn., Am. Soc. for Parenteral and Enteral Nutrition, Phila. Pediat. Soc. Avocations: swimming, biking. Office: Widzer and Kelly 864 County Line Rd Bryn Mawr PA 19010-2516

WIEBE, J. E. N., province official. Lt. gov. Govt. Saskatchewan, Regina, Can. Office: Office of the Lieutenant Gov, Govt House 4607 Dewdney Ave, Regina, SK Canada S4P 3V7*

WIEBE, LEONARD IRVING, radiopharmacist, educator; b. Swift Current, Sask., Can., Oct. 14, 1941; s. Cornelius C. and Margaret (Teichroeb) W.; m. Grace E. McIntyre, Sept. 5, 1964; children: Glenis, Kirsten, Megan. BSP, U. Sask., 1963, MS, 1966; PhD, U. Sydney, Australia, 1970. Pharmacist Swift Current Union Hosp., 1963-64; sessional lectr. U. Sask., Can., 1965-66; asst. prof. U. Alta., Can., 1970-73, assoc. prof., 1973-78, prof., 1978—, dir. Slowpoke Reactor Facility, 1975-89, asst. dean rsch., 1984-87; assoc. dean U. Alta., 1990—; sessional lectr. U. Sydney, Australia, 1973; pres. Internat. Bionucleonics Cons. Lts., 1991—; dir. BMH, Australian Nuclear Sci. Tech. Org., 1990, Noujaim Inst. Pharm. Oncology, 1994—; rsch. assoc. Cross Cancer Inst., Edmonton, 1978—, Med. Rsch. Coun. Can.; vis. prof. Royal P.A. Hosp., Sydney, 1983-84, Searle vis. prof., 1986; MRC vis. prof., Toronto, 1987; PMAC vis. prof., 1988; McCalla prof. U. Alta, 1993-94; radiopharmacy cons. Australian Atomic Energy Commn., Sydney, 1983-84; mem. MRC standing com. on sci. and rsch., 1995—; hon. liason prof. Peoples U. Bangladesh. Editor: Liquid Scintillation: Science and Technology, 1976, Advances in Scintillation Counting, 1983; guest editor Jour. of Radioanalytical Chemistry, 1981; editor Internat. Jour. Applied Radiation Instrumentation Sect. A, 1988-90; regional editor Internat. Jour. Nuclear Biology and Medicine, 1992-95; mem. editl. bd. Can. Jour. Pharm. Sci. Commonwealth Univs. Exchange grantee, 1966; Alexander von Humboldt fellow, 1976-79, 82. Mem. Pharm. Bd. of New South Wales, Sask. Pharm. Assn., Soc. Nuclear Medicine, Assn. Faculties of Pharmacy of Can. (McNeil Rsch. award 1988), Can. Radiation Protection Assn., Can. Assn. Radiopharm. Scientists, Am. Pharm. Assn., Am. Assn. Pharm. Sci., Australian Nuclear Sci. Tech. Orgn. (dir., biomedicine and health 1990), Internat. Assn. Radiopharmacy (exec. sec. 1991-95), Can. Assn. Pharm. Scis. (founding), Univ. Club (Edmonton) (pres. 1985). Mem. Mennonite Ch.

WIEBE, RICHARD HERBERT, reproductive endocrinologist, educator; b. Herbert, Sask., Can., Dec. 28, 1937; came to U.S., 1971; s. Herbert and Olga Maragratha (Jahnke) W.; m. Jacquelyn Dee Yancy, Aug. 30, 1975; 1 child, Richard Herbert, Jr. MD, U. Sask., 1962. Resident Queen's Univ., Kingston, Ont., Can., 1970; asst. to assoc. prof. Duke U., Durham, N.C., 1972-81; assoc. prof. to prof. U. So. Ala., Mobile, 1981-88; chmn. and prof. Dept. Ob-Gyn. U. S.D., Sioux Falls, 1988-95; chmn., prof. dept. ob-gyn. East Tenn. State U., Johnson City, 1996—; editorial cons., Fertility/Sterility, Birmingham, Ala., 1978—; sec., Univ. Physicians, Sioux Falls, 1991—. Contbr. numerous articles to profl. jours. Recipient, Rsch. Grant, NIH, Ala., 1981-89, Edn./Svc. Grant, USPHS, S.D., 1989—. Mem. ACOG, Assn. Profs. of Ob-Gyn., Am. Soc. Primatologists, Soc. for Gynecol. Investigation, Soc. for Study of Reproduction, Am. Soc. Reproductive Medicine, Endocrine Soc. Home: 4319 Summerfield Dr Piney Flats TN 37686-4561 Office: James H Quillen Sch Med East Tenn State U Dept Ob-Gyn Box 70569 Johnson City TN 37614

WIEBENSON, DORA LOUISE, architectural historian, educator, author; b. Cleve., July 29, 1926; d. Edward Ralph and Jeannette (Rodier) W. BA, Vassar Coll., 1946; MArch, Harvard U., 1951; MA, NYU, 1958, PhD, 1964. Architect N.Y., 1951-66; lectr. Columbia U., 1966-68; assoc. prof. U. Md., 1968-72, prof., 1972-77; vis. prof. Cornell U., 1974; prof. U. Va., Charlottesville, 1977-92, prof. emerita, 1992—, chmn. div. archtl. history, 1977-79, assoc. fellow U. Va. Ctr. Advanced Studies, 1982-83; pres. Archtl. Publs., N.Y.C., 1982—. Editor: Marsyas XI: 1962-64, 1965, Essays in Honor of Walter Friedlaender, 1965; Architectural Theory and Practice from Alberti to Ledoux, 1982, rev., 1983, Spanish transl., 1988; Guide to Graduate Degree Programs in Architectural History, 1982, rev., 1984, 86, 88, 90; author: Sources of Greek Revival Architecture, 1969, Tony Garnier: The Cité Industrielle, 1969, Japanese transl., 1983, The Picturesque Garden in France, 1978, Mark J. Millard Architectural Collection, Vol. I: French Books: Sixteenth through Nineteenth Centuries, 1993; contbr. articles to profl. jours. Student fellow Inst. Fine Arts, 1961-62, 62-63; grantee Am. Philos. Soc., 1964-65, 70, Samuel H. Kress Found., 1966, Gen. Rsch. Fund, U. Md., 1969, 74, 76, NEH, 1972-73, Samuel H. Kress Found., 1972-73, Am. Coun. Learned Socs., 1976, 81, 85, Ctr. Advanced Studies, U. Va., 1980, 81, Graham Found. Advanced Studies Fine Arts, 1982, 93, Archtl. History Found., 1996; fellow Yale Ctr. Brit. Art, 1983; sr. rsch. fellow NEH, 1986-87, Archtl. History Found., 1996. Mem. Soc. Archtl. Historians (bd. dirs. 1974-77, 80-83, chair edn. com. 1976-90), Coll. Art Assn., Am. Soc. Eighteenth Century (mem. exec. bd. 1991-94).

WIECEK, BARBARA HARRIET, advertising executive; b. Chgo., Mar. 30, 1956; d. Stanley Joseph and Irene (Zagajewski) W. AA, Am. Acad. of Art, Chgo., 1977. Illustrator Clinton E. Frank Advt., Chgo., 1977-78, art dir., 1978-80, assoc. creative dir., 1980-84, v.p.; instr. Am. Acad. of Art, Chgo., 1977-80; assoc. creative dir. Tatham, Laird & Kudner, 1984—; ptnr. Tatham, Laird & Kudner, Chgo., 1986—, creative dir., 1987—, sr. ptnr., 1995—, exec. creative dir., 1996. Recipient Silver Awd. Internat. Film Festival of N.Y., 1981, Gold Awd. Internat. Film Festival of N.Y., 1981. Roman Catholic. Avocations: painting, writing, gardening, remodeling, cycling. Office: Tatham Euro RSCG 980 N Michigan Ave Chicago IL 60611-4501

WIECEK, WILLIAM MICHAEL, law educator; b. Cleve., Jan. 31, 1938; s. Michael Frank and Mary (Kotecki) W.; m. Maryann Pickarski, June 17, 1961 (div. 1979); children: Michael, Sophie, Kristen. BA, Cath. U., 1959; LLB, Harvard U., 1962; PhD, U. Wis., 1968. Bar: N.H., 1962. Atty. Snierson & Chandler, Laconia, N.H., 1962-64; prof. history U. Mo., Columbia, 1968-84; prof. law. Syracuse (N.Y.) U., 1985—. Author: The Guarantee Clause of the U.S. Constitution, 1972, The Sources of Antislavery Constitutionalism in America, 1760-1848, 1977, Constitutional Development in a Modernizing Society: The United States, 1803-1917, 1985, (with Harold M. Hyman) Equal Justice Under Law: Constitutional Development, 1835-1875, 1982, (with Gerard H. Clarfield) Nuclear America: Military and Civilian Nuclear Power in the United States, 1940-1980, 1984, Liberty Under Law: The Supreme Court in American Life, 1988, (with Kermit Hall and Paul Finkelman) American Legal History: Cases and Materials, 1991 (with Kermit Hall, James Ely and Joel Grossman) The Oxford Companion to the Supreme Court of the United States, 1992; contbr. numerous articles, chpts. and papers on law to profl. books, jours. and confs. Vol. emergency med. technician, firefighter Fayetteville (N.Y.) Fire Dept. Mem. ABA, Am. Law Inst., Am. Soc. for Legal History (bd. dirs. 1987-90), Orgn. Am. Historians, Selden Soc., Am. Hist. Assn., Supreme Ct. Hist. Soc. (mem. editorial bd. 1984-86), Phi Beta Kappa. Democrat. Roman Catholic. Home: 137 Stanwood Ln Manlius NY 13104-1411 Office: Syracuse U Coll Of Law Syracuse NY 13244

WIECHA, JOSEPH AUGUSTINE, linguist, educator; b. Chorzów II, Poland, Sept. 20, 1926; came to U.S., 1955, naturalized, 1958; s. Karol and Gertruda (Rudzki) W.; m. Mary Ruth Moore, 1953; children: Joseph Damian, Charles Francis, John Moore. BA with 1st class honors, Nat. U. Ireland, 1950; PhD with highest distinction, NYU, 1963. Instr. fgn. langs. U.S. Third Air Force, London, 1951-55; instr. German and Spanish U. Md., London, 1951-55; tchr. Spanish and math. Bklyn. Friends Sch., 1955-56; instr. German N.Y. U., N.Y.C., summer, 1958; lectr. German and humanities Harvard U., Boston, 1959-63; lectr. German lit. Colby Coll., summer 1963; prof. German SUNY, Oswego, 1963-69; chmn. dept. fgn. langs. and lit. SUNY, 1963-69, chmn. dept. Germanic and Slavic langs. and lit., 1969-72, Disting. Teaching prof., 1973-92, disting. tchg. prof. emeritus, 1992—; chmn. SUNY (Fgn. Studies Center), 1972-73; lectr. and cons. methodology of tchg. fgn. langs., 1959—; condr. seminars tchg. methodology fgn. langs. Nat. U. of Pedro Enriquez Ureña, Santo Domingo, 1973, U. Pisa, Italy, 1974, Moscow State Pedagogical Inst.; Fgn. Langs., USSR, 1976; vis. prof. U. Wroctaw, Poland, 1977. Developed Wiecha Progressive-Reflex method of teaching fgn. langs. Served as officer 2d Polish Corps Brit. Army, 1944-47. Decorated Bronze medal Polish Army, also; Brit. Def. medal; French Star; Star of Italy; recipient diploma of spl. recognition Universidad Nacional de Pedro Enriquez Ureña, 1973; Galileo medal U. Pisa, 1974; Ogden Butler fellow, 1958-59; Fels fellow, 1956-59; Kosciuszko Found. fellow, 1959. Mem. MLA, N.Y. State Assn. Fgn. Lang. Tchrs. (dir. 1975-78, Disting. Tchr. award 1975, Disting. Bd. Dirs. award 1978, Spl. Contbn. to Teaching Fgn. Langs. award 1979), Am. Assn. Tchrs. of German, Polish Inst. Arts and Scis. in Am., Nat. Spanish Honors Soc. (hon.), Am. Coun. on Edn. (nat. honor roll), Delta Phi Alpha (hon.), Dobro Slovo (hon.). Home: 710 Copa De Oro Marathon FL 33050-5406 also: 22 Bayside Rd Northport ME 04849-4435

WIECHERT, ALLEN LEROY, educational planning consultant, architect; b. Independence, Kans., Oct. 25, 1938; s. Norman Henry and Serena Johanna (Steinke) W.; BArch, Kans. State U., 1962; m. Sandra Swanson, Aug. 19, 1961; children: Kirstin Nan, Brendan Swanson, Megan Ann. Architect in tng. McVey, Peddie, Schmidt & Allen, Wichita, Kans., 1962-63; architect Kivett & Myers, Kansas City, Mo., 1963-68; asst. to vice chancellor plant planning and devel. U. Kans., Lawrence, 1968-74, asso. dir. facilities planning, 1974-78, univ. dir. facilities planning, 1978-92; univ. architect, 1993-95; campus planner Gould Evans Assocs., Lawrence, Kans., 1995-96; mem. long range phys. planning com. Kans. Bd. Regents, 1971-95; designer, archtl. programmer of ednl. facilities; bd. dirs. Kans. U. Fed. Credit Union, 1972-81, pres. bd., 1974. Chmn. horizons com. Lawrence Bicentennial Commn.; designer Kaw River Trail, 1976; mem. Action 80 Com., 1980-81, Lawrence-Douglas County Horizon 2020 Task Group, 1993-95; mem. standing com. Kans. Episcopal Diocese, 1976-80, pres. com., 1981, mem. diocesan council, 1982-84, chmn. coll. work com., 1982-84, commn. on ch. architecture and allied arts, 1986—, long range planning com., 1988; sr. warden Trinity Episc. Ch., Lawrence, 1978-80; trustee Kans. Sch. Religion, 1973-80, 82-95, v.p., 1984-85, pres., 1986-92, trustee friends of the dept. of relig. studies, 1995—; mem. adv. bd. Salvation Army, 1990—; bd. dirs. Trinity Group Care Home, 1973-79; advancement chmn. troop com. Boy Scouts Am., 1981-87, dist. com. Pelathe dist., 1984—, vice chmn., 1984; chmn., 1985-87, exec. bd. Heart of Am. council, 1985-87. Recipient Dist. Award of Merit Boy Scouts Am., 1988, Silver Beaver award, 1991. 1st lt. Kans. Air N.G., 1961-67. Lic. architect, Kans.; cert. Nat. Council Archtl. Registration Bds. Mem. AIA, Assn. Univ. Architects (sec./treas. 1986-87, v.p. 1987-88, pres. 1988-89), Nat. Hist. Trust, Kans. U. Endowment Assn. (sec. 1981-85, founder, exec. bd. Hist. Mt. Oread Fund. div.), Nat. Cathedral Assn. (regional co-chairperson 1993—). Editor, contbr. to Physical Development Planning Work Book, 1973. Home: 813 Highland Dr Lawrence KS 66044-2431 Office: U Kans Office Of Capital Prog Lawrence KS 66045

WIECHMANN, ERIC WATT, lawyer; b. Schenectady, N.Y., June 12, 1948; s. Richard Jerdone and Ann (Watt) W.; m. Merrill Metzger, May 22, 1971. BA, Hamilton Coll., 1970; JD, Cornell U., 1974. Bar: Conn. 1975, U.S. Dist. Ct. (so. and ea. dists.) N.Y. 1975, U.S. Dist. Ct. Conn. 1975, U.S. Ct. Appeals (2d cir.) 1975, U.S. Supreme Ct. 1978, U.S. Ct. Appeals (9th cir.) 1980, D.C. 1981, U.S. Dist. Ct. D.C. 1981, U.S. Ct. Appeals D.C. 1982, U.S. Ct. Appeals (5th cir.) 1986, U.S. Ct. Appeals (10th cir.) 1989. Assoc., Cummings & Lockwood, Stamford, 1974-82, ptnr., 1982—, ptnr. in charge, 1996—; spl. pretrial master U.S. Dist. Ct. Conn. 1984—; state atty. trial referee, 1986—, mem. law revision commn., evidence code drafting com.; faculty Def. Counsel Trial Acad.; mem. civil task force, civil jury instrn. com. Conn. Superior Ct. Contbr. articles to profl. jours. Mem. Zoning Bd. Appeals, New Canaan, Conn., 1984-85. Mem. ABA, Def. Rsch. Inst., Internat. Assn. Def. Counsel (mem. faculty Def. Trial Acad. 1996), Conn. Bar Assn. (exec. com. antitrust sect. 1982—, ct. rules adv. com., chmn. 1991-93), Fed. Bar Coun., Hartford Club, Golf Club Avon. Republican. Episcopalian. Home: 21 Foxcroft Run Avon CT 06001-2509

WIECZOREK, RAYMOND J., mayor; b. New Britain, Conn., Dec. 9, 1928; m. Susan Wieczorek; 6 children. Founder RJW Assocs., Manchester, N.H., 1964; mayor City of Manchester, 1990—. Bd. dirs. Boys Club; trustee Manchester Girls and Boys Club; pres. Greater Manchester United Way, Greater Manchester Scholarship Found., Greater Manchester Human Svcs. Coun., Bradford Young Halfway House, Manchester Exchange Club; chmn., commr. Manchester Housing Authority; chmn. Manchester Rep. City Com.; mem. Rep. Nat. Com.; mem. com. Pulaski Day Celebration. With Armed Forces, Korea. Mem. VFW, Hundred Club N.H., Am. Legion, Henry J. Sweeney Post #2, Greater Manchester C. of C. Office: 908 Elm St Manchester NH 03101-2018

WIED, GEORGE LUDWIG, physician; b. Carlsbad, Czechoslovakia, Feb. 7, 1921; came to U.S., 1953, naturalized, 1960; s. Ernst George and Anna (Travnicek) W.; m. Daga M. Graaz, Mar. 19, 1949 (dec. Aug. 1977); m. Kayoko Y. Yamauchi, Nov. 1, 1990. MD, Charles U., Prague, 1945, Hon. Med. Degree, 1995. Intern County Hosp., Carlsbad, Czechoslovakia, 1945; intern U. Chgo. Hosps., 1955; resident in ob-gyn U. Munich, Fed. Republic Germany, 1946-48; practice medicine specializing in ob-gyn West Berlin, 1948-53; asst. ob-gyn Free U., West Berlin, 1948-52; assoc. chmn. dept. ob-gyn Moabit Hosp., Free U., West Berlin, 1953; asst. prof., dir. cytology U. Chgo., 1954-59, assoc. prof., 1959-65, prof., 1965-91, mem. bd. adult edn., 1964-68, prof. pathology, 1967-91, Blum-Riese prof. ob-gyn, 1968-91, acting chmn. dept. ob-gyn, 1974-75. Editor-in-chief Jour. Reproductive Medicine, Acta Cytologica, Analytical and Quantitative Cytology, Clinical Cytology; editor: Introduction to Quantitative Cytochemistry, Automated Cell Identification and Cell Sorting, Compendium on Clinical Cytology, Compendium on the Computerized Cytology and Histology Laboratory, Compendium on Quality Assurance in Clinical Cytology; sr. editor Gen. and Diagnostic Pathology. Hon. dir. Chgo. Cancer Prevention Ctr., 1959-83; chmn. jury Maurice Goldblatt Cytology award, 1963-92. Recipient Cert. of Merit, U.S. Surgeon Gen., 1952, Maurice Goldblatt Cytology award, 1961, George N. Papanicolaou Cytology award, 1970. Mem. Am. Soc. Cytology (pres. 1965-66), Mex. Soc. Cytology (hon.), Spanish Soc. Cytology (hon.), Brazilian Soc. Cytology (fgn. corr.), Indian Acad. Cytology (hon.), Latin-Am. Soc. Cytology (hon.), Japanese Soc. Cytology (hon.), Internat. Acad. Cytology (pres. 1977-80), German Soc. Cytology (hon.), Ctrl. Soc. Clin. Rsch., Chgo. Path. Soc., Chgo. Gynecol. Soc. (hon.), Am. Soc. Cell Biology, German Soc. Ob-Gyn, Bavarian Soc. Ob-Gyn, German Soc. Endocrinology, Russian Assn. Cytologists (hon.), Swedish Soc. Medicine (hon.), Austrian Soc. Clin. Cytology (hon.), Sigma Xi. Home and Office: 1640 E 50th St Chicago IL 60615-3161

WIEDEMAN, GEOFFREY PAUL, physician, air force officer; b. London, Eng., Mar. 9, 1917; came to U.S., 1934, naturalized, 1942; s. Julius William Paul and Fanny (Poile) W.; m. Carolyn Sterling, Feb. 2, 1947; 1 son, Geoffrey Paul. B.S., U. Vt., 1938, M.D., 1941. Diplomate: Am. Bd. Preventive Medicine. Commd 1st lt. USAAF, 1942; advanced through grades to brig. gen. USAF, 1970; surgeon Eastern Transport Air Force, McGuire AFB, N.J., 1958-61; comdr. USAF Hosp., Tachikawa, Japan; surgeon 315th Air Div., Japan; also surgeon Kanto Base Command, Japan, 1962-65; comdr. USAF Sch. Health Care Scis., 1965-69; command surgeon Air Tng. Command, Randolph AFB, Tex., 1969-74; retired USAF, 1974; physician Brooks AFB Clinic, Tex., retired, 1989. Decorated D.S.M., Legion of Merit, Bronze Star, Air medal, Air Force Commendation medal with oak leaf cluster, 1972; named outstanding grad. Nat. War Coll. Class of 1961-62. Fellow Am. Coll. Preventive Medicine; mem. Aerospace Medicine Assn., Assn. Mil. Surgeons, Am. Pub. Health Assn., Air Force Assn. Home: 6134 Windrock Dr San Antonio TX 78239-2707

WIEDEMAN, JOHN HERMAN, civil engineer; b. Atlanta, Oct. 31, 1935; s. Herman F. and Annie (Crum) W.; m. Joan B. Denson, May 10, 1959; children: Harold, Jonna, Justin. BCE, Ga. Inst. Tech., 1957, M in Pub. Health Engring., 1957. Registered profl. engr., 12 states. With Wiedeman & Singleton, Atlanta, 1959—; ptnr., civil engr. Wiedeman & Singleton, 1962—. Lt. (j.g.) USN, 1957-59. Mem. ASCE (pres. 1982-83), NSPE, Am. Water Works Assn., Water Pollution Control Fedn., Atlanta Athletic Club (bd. dirs. 1979-81). Methodist. Office: Wiedeman & Singleton 1789 Peachtree St NE Atlanta GA 30309-2300

WIEDEMANN, HERBERT PFEIL, physician; b. New Haven, Conn., May 9, 1951; s. Herbert Paul and Henrietta (Pfeil) W.; m. Patricia Barz, Feb. 12, 1983; children: Sarah, Andrew. BS, Yale U., 1973; MD, Cornell U., 1977. Diplomat Am. Bd. Internal Medicine, Am. Bd. Pulmonary Disease, Am. Bd. Critical Care Medicine. Med. resident U. Wash., Seattle, 1977-80; chief med. resident Harborview Med. Ctr., Seattle, 1980-81; postgrad. fellow in pulmonary and critical care medicine Yale U., New Haven, 1981-84; staff physician Cleve. Clinic Found., 1984—, chmn. dept. of pulmonary and critical care medicine, 1991—; pres. med. staff Cleve. Clinic Hosp., 1995-96, bd. trustees, 1994-96; prof. medicine Cleve. Clinic Found. Health Scis. Ctr. of Ohio State U., Cleve., 1993—; spkr. in field. Editor-in-chief Cleveland Clinic Jour. of Medicine, 1993-96; editor: Ann. Rev. of Pulmonary and Critical Medicine, 7 edits., 1986-93. Grantee NIH, 1994—. Fellow ACP, Am. Coll. Chest Physicians, Am. Coll. of Critical Care Medicine; mem. Am. Thoracic Soc., Alpha Omega Alpha. Achievements include rsch. on surfactants decrease release of cytokines from stimulated macrophages. Home: 18040 S Woodland Rd Shaker Hts OH 44120-1773 Office: Cleve Clinic Found 9500 Euclid Ave Cleveland OH 44195-0001

WIEDEMANN, JOSEPH ROBERT, insurance company executive; b. Chgo., June 18, 1928; s. Joseph Matthew and Ann Elizabeth (Zittman) W.; m. Ree McClure, Dec. 26, 1950; children: Sue Wiedemann Evans, Patti Wiedemann Podziomek, Jane Wiedemann Candela, Mary Wiedemann Darling, Julie Wiedemann Gotsch, Joseph, Thomas. BBA, Loyola U., Chgo., 1950. Sr. v.p. CNA Ins. Co., Chgo., 1952-77; v.p. Frank B. Hall Co., N.Y.C., 1977-79; pres., dir. Union Indemnity Ins. Co., N.Y.C., 1977-79, BCS Fin. Corp., Chgo., 1979-83; pres. C.V. Starr & Co., San Francisco, 1983-84, Lexington Ins. Co., Boston, 1985-87, Landmark Ins. Co., Los Angeles, 1986-87; pres. Am. Home Assurance Co., N.Y.C., 1987-92, chmn., 1992-93;, 1992-93; v.p. Am. Internat. Group, N.Y.C., 1986-93; sr. v.p. Starr Excess Liability Ins. Co. Ltd., 1993—; ret., 1996. City parking commr. Reading, Pa., 1970-73. Served to sgt. U.S. Army, 1950-52, Korea. Mem. Riddell's Bay Golf and Country Club (Bermuda), Royal Bermuda Yacht Club. Republican. Roman Catholic. Home: PO Box 341, Mangrove Bay Sandys MABX, Bermuda Office: Starr Excess Liability Ins Co Ltd, 29 Richmond Rd, Pembroke HM 08, Bermuda

WIEDEMANN, RAMONA DIANE, occupational therapist; b. Topeka, Kans., Oct. 1, 1962; d. John Daniel Fay and Sue Ann (Strotman) Fuller; m. William Newell Wiedemann, Aug. 9, 1986; children: William Jr., Meaghan, Nathaniel, Emily. BS in Occupl. Therapy, Tex. Woman's U., 1988. Occupl. therapist Healthcare Staff Resources, Dallas, 1988-91, Associated Rehab. Svcs., Greenville, Tex., 1991-96, 1st Rehab., Ft. Worth, 1996, Community Rehab. Svcs., Dallas, 1996-97; with Associated Rehab. Svcs., Greenville, Tex., 1997—. Mem. Am. Occupl. Therapy Assn. Republican. Methodist. Avocations: reading, travel, bicycling. Home: 210 Winding Creek Dr Highland Village TX 75067

WIEDEN, DAN G., advertising executive; b. 1945. With Georgia-Pacific Corp., Portland, Oreg., 1967-72; free-lance writer, 1972-78; with McCann-Erickson, Portland, 1978-80, William Cain, Portland, 1980-82; pres. Wieden & Kennedy, Portland, 1982—. Office: Wieden & Kennedy Inc 320 SW Washington St Portland OR 97204-2640*

WIEDENMAYER, CHRISTOPHER M., writing instrument manufacturer, distributor; b. Orange, N.J., May 16, 1941; s. Gustave E. and Margaret W.; m. Anne Iselin Morgan, June 18, 1966; children: Amanda, Elizabeth, Christopher. BA, Dartmouth Coll., 1963; MBA, Columbia U., 1968. Gen. mgr. Faber-Castell Corp., Parsippany, N.J., 1970-72, pres., chief exec. officer, 1972-84, chmn., chief exec. officer, 1984—; bd. dirs. DSG Internat. Ltd., Chem. Bank New Jersey N.A. Treas. Newark Mus., 1983—; bd. govs. Fairmount Cemetery Assn., Newark, 1978—; bd. dirs. Morristown YMCA, 1975-77. Mem. Writing Instrument Mfg. Assn. (bd. dirs. 1973—, v.p. 1989-

93, pres. 1993-95). Office: Faber-Castell Corp Box 338P Bernardsville NJ 07924

WIEDLE, GARY EUGENE, real estate management company executive; b. San Antonio, July 28, 1944; s. Eugene Wiley and Melba Frances (Keeney) W.; m. Regena Zokosky, July 7, 1977 (div. June 1983); children: Ana Lauren, Aric Brandt. AA, Coll. of the Desert, Palm Desert, Calif., 1975; BA, Calif. State U., Long Beach, 1967; MA, U. So. Calif., 1973. Lic. real estate broker, Calif.; cert. profl. community assn. mgr. Adminstrv. asst. City of Inglewood, Calif., 1967-68, asst. city mgr., 1970-74; exec. dir. Coachella Valley Assn. of Govts., Palm Desert, 1974-84; mgr. The Springs Country Club, Rancho Mirage, Calif., 1984-87; prof. polit. sci. Coll of the Desert, Palm Desert, 1987-90; owner Fortune West Mgmt., Palm Desert, 1990—; cons. polit. orgns., bus. and community groups, Riverside County, Calif., 1984—. State comdr. DAV, Dept. Calif., 1982. 1st lt. U.S. Army, 1968-70, Vietnam. Decorated Bronze Star for valor, Purple Heart, Commendation of valor. Mem. Am. Inst. Cert. Planners (cert. planner), Cmty. Assns. Inst. (pres. 1986-89), Calif. Assn. Cmty. Mgrs., Real Estate Educators Cert. Inst., Bd. Realtors Palm Desert, Am. Planning Assn., Western Govtl. Rsch. Assn., Gideons Internat. Republican. Lutheran. Avocation: reading history. Home: 82-362 Gable Dr Indio CA 92201-7439 Office: Fortune West Mgmt GE Wiedle Co 73-900 El Paseo Rear Palm Desert CA 92260-4336

WIEDMAN, TIMOTHY GERARD, management educator; b. Detroit, Nov. 3, 1951; s. Charles Albert and Doris Gertude (Kreager) W.; m. Lisa Kyle Mattimore, Mar. 24, 1987. BA, Oakland U., 1976; MS, Ctrl. Mich. U., 1978; cert. profl. fin. planning, Old Dominion U., 1995. Gen. mgr. Burger Chef Sys., Inc., Detroit, 1969-75; area mgr. Fotomat Corp., Cleve., Columbus, Ohio, 1978-85; instr. bus. mgmt. Ctrl. Ohio Tech. Coll., Newark, 1986-88, Ohio U., Lancaster, 1988-92; asst. prof. Thomas Nelson C. C., Hampton, Va., 1992-95; assoc. prof. Thomas Nelson C.C., Hampton, Va., 1995—; workshop leader Va. Peninsula Total Quality Inst., Hampton, 1994—; quality trainer Quality Union of Bus., Industry and Cmty. Program, Lancaster, 1991-92; invited spkr. Svc. Corps. Ret. Execs., Newark, 1988, USCGR Tng. Ctr., Yorktown, Va., 1994, USMCR, Hampton, 1994, So. Assn. Coll. and Univ. Bus. Officers, Memphis, 1996. Contbg. author: Great Ideas for Teaching Marketing, 1992, Great Ideas for Teaching Introduction to Business, 1994; contbr. articles to profl. jours.; author: (newsletter) The Quality Management Forum, 1993. Judge regional competition Future Bus. Leaders Am., Hampton, 1993—; judge team excellence competition Ohio Mfrs. Assn., Lancaster, 1991; county rep. UNICEF, Fairfield County, Ohio, 1988-91. Mem. Am. Soc. for Quality Control (invited speaker 1993, cert. quality mgr. 1997), Nat. Assn. Profl. Fin. Planners, Va. Educator's Quality Network. Avocations: photography, travel, skiing, swimming, sailing. Office: Thomas Nelson CC 99 Thomas Nelson Dr Hampton VA 23666-1433

WIEDRICK-KOZLOWSKI, JAN BARBARA, communications executive; b. Rochester, N.Y., Feb. 21, 1958; d. Sidney George and Mary Jane (Dunn) Wiedrick; m. Scott Anthony Kozlowski, Oct. 19, 1985. AAS, Monroe C.C., Rochester, N.Y., 1977; BA, SUNY, Brockport, 1991; lic., New Sch. Contemporary Radio. Reporter, producer, anchor WWCN, WGNA, WWOM Radio, Albany, N.Y., 1978-85, WXXI Radio, Rochester, 1985-90; media cons. Rochester, 1990-91; pub. info. officer Monroe County Legis., Rochester, 1991-93; pub. rels. and mktg. dir. DiMarco & Riley, Rochester, 1993-94; comm. cons. Manning & Napier Advisors Inc., Rochester, 1994-95, Upstart Comm., Rochester, 1996—; guest lectr. We. N.Y. Child Care Coun., Rochester, 1994, SUNY, Brockport, 1988, Union Coll., Schnectady, N.Y., 1984. Contbr. (book) Camp Good Days Joke Book, 1994. Bd. dirs. Monroe ARC, Rochester. Recipient Media award Monroe County Bar Assn., 1988, 89, Best News Program award AP, 1986, 89, Best Investigative Report award, 1989, 90, N.Y. State Pub. Broadcasting Assn., 1989. Mem. Pub. Rels. Soc. Am., Women in Radio and TV. Avocations: skiing, swimming, travel, crafts. Office: Upstart Comm 905 Monroe Ave Rochester NY 14620-1707

WIEGAND, SYLVIA MARGARET, mathematician, educator; b. Cape Town, South Africa, Mar. 8, 1945; came to U.S., 1949; d. Laurence Chisholm and Joan Elizabeth (Dunnett) Young; m. Roger Allan Wiegand, Aug. 27, 1966; children: David Chisholm, Andrea Elizabeth. AB, Bryn Mawr Coll., 1966; MA, U. Wash., 1967; PhD, U. Wis., Madison, 1972. Mem. faculty U. Nebr., Lincoln, 1967—, now prof. math.; vis. assoc. prof. U. Conn., Storrs, 1978-79, U. Wis., Madison, 1985-86; vis. prof. Purdue U., 1992-93. Editor Communications in Algebra jour., 1990, Rocky Mountain Jour. Math., 1991—; contbr. rsch. articles to profl. jours. Troop leader Lincoln area Girl Scouts U.S., 1988-92. Grantee NSF, 1985-88, 90-93, 94-96, 97—; Vis. Professorship for Women, 1992, Nat. Security Agy., 1995-97. Mem. AAUP, Assn. Women in Math (pres.-elect 1995-96, pres. 1997—), London Math. Soc., Math. Assn. Am., Can. math. Soc. (bd. mem. at large 1997—). Avocations: running, family activities. Office: U Nebr Dept Math Lincoln NE 68588-0323

WIEGEL, ROBERT LOUIS, consulting engineering executive; b. San Francisco, Oct. 17, 1922; s. Louis Henry and Antionette L. (Decker) W.; m. Anne Pearce, Dec. 10, 1948; children: John M., Carol E., Diana L. BS, U. Calif. at Berkeley, 1943, MS, 1949. Mem. faculty U. Calif. at Berkeley, 1946—, prof. civil engring., 1963-87, prof. emeritus, 1987—, asst. dean Coll. Engring., 1963-72, acting dean, 1972-73; dir. state tech. svcs. program for Calif. U. Calif., 1965-68, sec. acad. senate, 1988-89; vis. prof. Nat. U. Mex., summer 1965, Polish Acad. Sci., 1976, 88, U. Cairo, 1978; sr. Queen's fellow in marine sci. Australia, 1977; cons. to govt. and industry, 1946—; chmn. U.S. com. for internat. com. oceanic resources, mem. marine bd. Nat. Acad. Engring., 1975-81; pres. Internat. Engring. Com. on Oceanic Resources, 1972-75, hon. mem., 1988; mem. coastal engring. research bd. Dept. Army, 1974-85; mem. IDOE adv. panel NSF, 1974-77, Gov. Calif. Adv. Commn. Ocean Resources, 1967, Calif. Adv. Commn. on Marine and Coastal Resources, 1967-73, Tsunami Tech. Adv. Council, Hawaii, 1964-66; U.S. del. U.S.-Japan coop. sci. programs, 1964, 65. Author publs. in field; editor Shore and Beach jour., 1988-96; patentee in field. V.p., bd. dirs. Am. Shore and Beach Preservation Assn., 1988-95, dir. emeritus, 1995—; mem. Nat. Rsch. Coun. com. on Beach Nourishment and Protection, 1992-95. Recipient Outstanding Civilian Svc. medal Dept. Army, 1985, Berkeley citation U. Calif., 1987, Joe W. Johnson Outstanding Beach Preservation award Calif. Shore and Beach Preservation Assn., 1993, Coastal Zone Found. award, 1993, Morrough P. O'Brien award Am. Shore and Beach Preservation Assn., 1995. Fellow AAAS; mem. NAE, ASCE (hon., chmn. exec. com. waterways, harbors, coastal engring. div. 1974-75, vice chmn. coastal engring. rsch. coun. 1964-78, chmn. 1978-92, chmn. task com. wave forces on structures 1960-67, chmn. com. on coastal engring. 1970-71, Rsch. prize 1962, Moffatt-Nichol Coastal Engring. award 1978, Internat. Coastal Engring. award 1985), Japan Soc. Civil Engrs. (hon.), Sigma Xi. Home: 1030 Keeler Ave Berkeley CA 94708-1404

WIEGENSTEIN, JOHN GERALD, physician; b. Fredericktown, Mo., June 22, 1930; s. John Joseph and Dorothy Faye (Mulkey) W.; m. Dorothy Iris Scifers, Dec. 27, 1952; children: Mark, Barbara, Paula, Cynthia. BS, U. Mich., 1956, MD, 1960. Intern Tripler Army Gen. Hosp., Honolulu, 1960-61; dir. dept. emergency medicine Mich. Capital Med. Ctr., Lansing, 1975—, pres. profl. staff, 1996—; prof. emergency medicine Mich. State U., 1982—; founder Internat. Rsch. Inst. for Emergency Medicine, pres., 1983-85; pvt. practice, Lansing, 1963-96; founder Am. Bd. Emergency Medicine, 1982-83; pres. Physician Assocs., P.C., 1976-96; chmn. bd. Occupl. Medicine Assocs., P.C., 1989—; owner Health Care Info. Svcs., Inc., 1989—. With USAF, 1951-53; M.C., U.S. Army, 1960-63. Mem. AMA, Am. Coll. Emergency Physicians (founder, pres., chmn. bd. 1968-71, bd. dirs. 1968-76), Mich. State Med. Soc. (award 1971, 82), Ingham County Med. Soc., Galens Hon. Med. Soc., Soc. Acad. Emergency Medicine. Office: Mich Capital Med Ctr Dept Emergency Medicine 401 W Greenlawn Ave Lansing MI 48910-2819

WIEGERSMA, NAN, economics educator; b. Grafton, Mass., July 16, 1942; d. Oscar John and Esther Marie (Polson) Wiegersma; 1 child, Chandra Hancock. BS, U. Md., 1966, MA, 1969, PhD, 1976. Economist U.S. Dept. Agr., Washington, 1969-72; vis. asst. prof. econs. Antioch Coll., Yellow Springs, Ohio, 1972-73, San Diego State U., 1973-74; assoc. prof. econs. No. Va. Community Coll., Annandale, Va., 1974-79; prof. econs. Fitchburg (Mass.) State Coll., 1979—, chair all-coll. com., 1996-97; cons. UN, 1987, FAO, 1994. Author: Vietnam: Peasant Land, Peasant Revolution, 1988; co-author: Agriculture in Vietnam's Economy, 1973; co-editor: The Women, Gender and Development Reader: Decades of Crisis and Change, 1997; editl. bd. Vietnam Generation, 1988-93; contbr. articles to profl. jours., chpts. to books. Recipient Disting. Svc. award USDA, 1973; Joiner Ctr. grantee, 1987; Grad. Assoc. Faculty rsch. fellow Fitchburg State Coll., 1989-90; Fulbright fellow, 1991. Mem. NEA, Am. Econs. Assn., New Eng. Women and Devel. Group, N.E. Feminist Scholars, Women's Work Project (coord. 1974-79), Mass. Tchrs. Assn. (chpt. treas. 1986-90, pres. 1992-94), Women for Economic Justice (econ. literacy compaign 1982-86). Democrat. Avocations: photography, hiking. Office: Fitchburg State Coll Pearl St Fitchburg MA 01420

WIEGLEY, ROGER DOUGLAS, lawyer; b. Buffalo, Dec. 8, 1948; s. Richard John and Georgianna (Eggleston) W.; m. Susan Carol Straus, Nov. 22, 1969; children: John William, Douglas James, Jennifer Jeanne. BA, SUNY, Buffalo, 1970; JD magna cum laude, U. Wis., 1977. Bar: Wis. 1977, Hawaii 1978, N.Y. 1982, D.C. 1982, Calif. 1986. Spl. asst. U.S. atty. U.S. Justice Dept., Honolulu, 1978-81; spl. asst. to gen. counsel Dept. of the Navy, Washington, 1981-82; assoc. Sullivan & Cromwell, Washington, 1982-85, 86-88; ptnr. Sidley & Austin, Washington, 1988-94, Winthrop, Stimson, Putnam & Roberts, Washington, 1994-97; v.p. Strategic Planning and Gen. Counsel, MIC Industries, Inc., 1997—; gen. counsel Benson, Inc. and Sentry, San Jose, Calif., 1985-86; arbitrator nat. panel Am. Arbitration Assn., 1988—. Author: Trade and Export Finance, 1997; contbr. numerous articles to profl. jours. Mem. pvt. sector study on cost control, Washington, 1982-83. Served with USN, 1973-82. Mem. ABA, Order of Coif. Office: MIC Industries Inc 11911 Freedom Dr Ste 1000 Reston VA 20190-5602

WIEGMAN, EUGENE WILLIAM, minister, former college administrator; b. Fort Wayne, Ind., Oct. 27, 1929; s. A. Henry and E. Catherine (McDonald) W.; m. Kathleen Wyatt, Apr. 26, 1952; children: Kathryn, Rose Marie, Mark, Jeanine, Gretchen, Matthew. BS, Concordia Coll., 1953; MS, U. Kans., 1956, EdD, 1962; grad., Pacific Luth. Theol. Sem., 1985. Tchr., coach Trinity Luth. Sch., Atchison, Kans., 1954-58; prin. tchr. St. John's Coll., Winfield, Kans., 1958-61; prof. Concordia Coll., Seward, Nebr., 1961-65; adminstrv. asst. to Rep. Clair Callan, Lincoln, Nebr., 1965-66; asst. to adminstr. fed. extension service Dept. Agr., Washington, 1966-67; dean community edn. Fed. City Coll., Washington, 1967-69; pres. Pacific Luth. U., Tacoma, 1969-75, Independent Colls. Wash., 1975-76; dir. Wash. Office Community Devel., 1977-78; commr. Dept. of Employment Security, 1978-81; exec. dir., pres., CEO emeritus Family Counseling Service of Tacoma and Pierce County, Wash., 1987-97; assoc. pastor Luther Meml. Ch., Tacoma, 1987-90; pastor Gethsemane Luth. Ch., Tacoma, 1990—; dean clin. pastoral edn. Grad. Sch. of Korea, 1992—; mem. Wash. State Employment and Tng. Council; mem. cabinet Gov. of Wash., 1977-81. Candidate for U.S. Congress from 6th dist. Wash., 1976; mem. Council on Washington's Future; exec. bd. dirs. Pacific Harbors Coun. Boy Scouts Am.; bd. dirs. Tacoma Area Urban Coalition; past chmn. Wash. Friends Higher Edn.; bd. dirs. Tacoma Urban League, Bellarmine Prep. Sch., Tacoma, Camp Brotherhood; trustee Tacoma Gen. Hosp., Pacific Sci. Center; mem. Commn. on Children, Youth and Families for Tacoma and Pierce County; mem. com. Faith Homes for Young Women; pres. Second City chamber of Tacoma. Recipient Disting. Teaching award City Winfield, Kans., 1960, Freedom Found. Teaching award, 1961, Disting. Eagle Scout award, 1982, Pres. award St. Martins Coll., 1980. Mem. Kiwanis, Phi Delta Kappa. Home: 405 N Stadium Way Tacoma WA 98403-3228

WIEGNER, ALLEN WALTER, biomedical engineering educator, researcher; b. Bethlehem, Pa., July 22, 1947; s. Howard Jay and Anna (Strouse) W.; m. Sandra A. Waddock, Aug. 26, 1978; 1 child, Benjamin Waddock. SB, SM, MIT, 1970, PhD, 1978. Rsch. assoc. Harvard U. Med. Sch., Boston, 1978-87, asst. prof. neurology (biomed. engring.), 1987—; asst. biomed. engr. Mass. Gen. Hosp., Boston, 1980—; cons. rsch. svc. VA Med. Ctr., 1984—, biomed. engr., 1987-96, computer specialist, 1996—. Contbr. articles, book chpts. to profl. publs. Lt. USPHS, 1970-72. Mem. IEEE (sr.), Biomed. Engring. Soc. (sr.), Soc. for Neurosci. Office: VA Med Ctr IRM Svc 940 Belmont St Brockton MA 02401-5596

WIEGNER, EDWARD ALEX, multi-industry executive; b. Waukesha, Wis., Dec. 13, 1939; s. Roy Edward and Margaret (Kuehnlein) W.; m. Cathryn J. Mullens, Oct. 16, 1970; children: Carlin, Ryan; 1 child from previous marriage, Christine. BBA, U. Wis., 1961, MS in Econs., 1965, PhD in Econs., 1969. Asst. prof. bus. adminstrn. Marquette U., Milw., 1965-71; assoc. prof U. Wis., Madison, 1972-73; sec. Wis. Dept. Revenue, Madison, 1971-74; sr. v.p. fin., bd. dirs. Wis. Power and Light Co., Madison, 1974-76, sr. v.p. consumer, pub. and fin. affairs, dir., 1976-80, exec. v.p., bd. dirs., 1980-82; sr. v.p., chief fin. officer, bd. dirs. Am. Natural Resources Co., 1982-85, exec. v.p., chief adminstrv. officer, bd. dirs., 1985-86; sr. v.p. Coastal Corp., 1985-86; sr. v.p., chief fin. officer Household Internat., Inc., 1986-88; exec. v.p., chief fin. officer The Progressive Corp., Mayfield Heights, Ohio, 1988-91, pres. fin. svcs. div., 1989-93; gen. ptnr. Aurora Ptnrs., 1994—; vice chmn. 1st Am. Ins. Co., Kansas City, Mo., 1994-97; chmn., CEO First Am. Fin. Corp., 1997—. Contbr. articles to Northwestern Law Rev., others. Mem. Grand Harbor Country Club. Home: 1330 N Saint Davids Ln Vero Beach FL 32967-7247 Office: 3100 Broadway Ste 1000 Kansas City MO 64111

WIELAND, PAUL OTTO, environmental control systems engineer; b. Louisville, Apr. 9, 1954; s. Otto George and Flora Carolyn (Wolf) W. BS in Botany, U. Louisville, 1982, BS in Applied Sci., 1985, M. in Engring., 1987. Lic. profl. engr., Ala., Va.; cert. environ. insp. Paper carrier Courier-Jour., Louisville, 1976-77; youth program dir. UNICORN, Louisville, 1978; recreation worker Met. Parks Dept., Louisville, 1978-80; retail sales clk. Lose Bros. Lawn and Garden, Louisville, 1980-82; trainee engr. Sealand Svc., Inc., Elizabeth, N.J., 1982; engr. NASA Marshall Space Flight Ctr., Huntsville, Ala., 1983-96; pres. Wiseland Svcs., 1996—. Author: Designing for Human Presence in Space: An Introduction to Environmental Control and Life Support Systems, 1994, Living Together in Space: The Design and Operation of the Life Support Systems on the International Space Station, 1996; contbr. articles to profl. jours. Vol. advocate R.A.P.E. Relief Ctr., Louisville, 1977-80; vol. tutor Adult Basic Edn. Program, Huntsville, 1988-89; vol. projectionist Film Co-op., Huntsville, 1990-91; vol. tech. advisor Am. Lung Assn. Health House '96, Huntsville. Mem. ASME, ASHRAE, AIAA (chmn. student chpt. 1984-85), NSPE (mathcounts vol. 1990-91), Environ. Assessment Assn., Inst. for Advanced Studies in Life Support (treas. 1990-92). Avocations: appreciation of nature, creating visual arts, dancing. Home: 4219 Hawthorne Ave SW Huntsville AL 35805-3423 Office: NASA/MSFC/ED62 Marshall Space Flight Ctr Huntsville AL 35812

WIELGUS, CHARLES JOSEPH, information services company executive; b. Hadley, Mass., Jan. 2, 1923; s. Joseph John and Anna Mary (Armata) W.; m. Irene Helen Graham, Jan. 1, 1949; children: Charles, Paul, Martha Jane. B.S. summa cum laude in Bus. Adminstrn, Bryant Coll., 1947, D.S. in Bus. Adminstrn. (hon.), 1977. With Bigelow-Sanford Carpet Co., Enfield, Conn. and N.Y.C., 1947-56; with Reuben H. Donnelley Corp. (subs. Dun & Bradstreet Corp.), Chicago and N.Y.C., 1956-71; v.p. personnel Dun & Bradstreet, Inc. (subs.), 1971-73; v.p. personnel Dun & Bradstreet Corp., 1973-76, sr. v.p. human resources, 1976-82, exec. v.p. human resources and communications, 1983-88, ret., 1988; nature photographer, 1989—; adj. faculty New Sch. Social Research, 1977-88, mem. adv. com. Masters program in human resources, 1977-88, ret., 1988; mem. adv. council on mgmt. edn. N.Y.C. C. of C., 1975-80; mem. bus. edn. adv. com. N.Y.C. Bd. Edn., 1977-88; dir. Nat. Ctr. Career Life Planning, 1986—; mem. adv. council on human resources mgmt. Nat. Conf. Bd., 1987-88. Bd. dirs. United Cerebral Palsy Assn. Westchester, 1966-75; trustee Operation Hope, Inc., 1966-75, active local and state Republican orgns., 1965-75. Served in USAF, 1943-46. Mem. Am. Arbitration Assn. (arbitrator 1988—), Nat. Alliance Bus. (dir., steering com.). Clubs: Univ, Larchmont Shore. Home: 151 Rockingstone Ave Larchmont NY 10538-1512 also: 7 Hummingbird Ct Hilton Head Island SC 29926-2551

WIEMAN, CARL E., physics educator; b. Corvallis, Oreg., Mar. 26, 1951; m. Sarah Gilbert. BS, MIT, 1973; PhD, Stanford U., 1977. Asst. rsch. physicist dept. physics U. Mich., Ann Arbor, 1977-79, asst. prof. physics, 1979-84; assoc. prof. physics U. Colo., Boulder, 1984-87, prof., 1987—, disting. rsch. lectr., 1996; fellow Joint Inst. for Lab. Astrophysics, Boulder, 1985—; Loeb lectr. Harvard U., 1990-91; Rosenthal Meml. lectr. Yale U., Columbia U., 1988. Recipient Ernest Orlando Lawrence Mem. award U.S. Dept. Energy, 1993, Einstein medal for laser sci. Soc. Optical and Quantum Electronics, 1995, Fritz London prize for low temperature physics, 1996, Newcomb Cleveland prize AAAS, 1996, King Faisal Internat. Prize for Sci., 1997. Fellow Am. Phys. Soc. (Davisson-Germer prize 1994); mem. NAS, Optical Soc. Am., Am. Assn. Physics Tchrs. (Richtmyer lectr. award). Office: U Colo PO Box 390 Boulder CO 80309-0390

WIEMANN, JOHN MORITZ, communications educator, executive, consultant; b. New Orleans, July 11, 1947; s. John M. and Mockie (Oosthuizen) W.; m. Mary Eileen O'Loghlin, June 7, 1969; children: Molly E., John M. BA, Loyola U., New Orleans, 1969; postgrad., NYU, 1970-71; MS, Purdue U., 1973, PhD, 1975. With employee comm. dept. IBM, East Fishkill, N.Y., 1969-71; asst. prof. comm. Rutgers U., New Brunswick, N.J., 1975-77; from asst. prof. to prof. U. Calif., Santa Barbara, 1977—, prof., 1988—, prof. comm. and Asian Am. studies, 1994—, acting vice chancellor instnl. advancement, 1994-95; vice chancellor instnl. advancement, 1995—; bd. dirs. Santa Barbara (Calif.) Econ. Forecast Project, Santa Barbara Industry-Edn. Coun., Santa Barbara Econ. Cmty. Project.$Dultidisciplinary adv. bd. Ctrl. Coast Regional Tech. Alliance, 1996—. Editor: Nonverbal Interaction, 1983, Advancing Communication Science, 1988, Communication, Health and the Elderly, 1990, Miscommunication and the Problematic Talk, 1991, Strategic Interpersonal Communication, 1994, Interpersonal Communication in Older Adulthood, 1994; author: Competent Communication, 1995, 2nd edit., 1997; series editor Sage Ann. Rev. Comm. Rsch., 1988-94. Bd. dirs. Goleta Youth Basketball Assn., 1987-92; mem. sch. site coun. Foothill Elem. Sch., 1987-88; mem. budget adv. com. Goleta Union Sch. Dist., 1982-84. David Ross fellow Purdue U., 1975, W.K. Kellogg Found. fellow, 1980-83; Fulbright-Hayes sr. rsch. scholar U. Bristol, Eng., 1985. Mem. APA, Internat. Comm. Assn. (bd. dirs. 1988-90), Speech Comm. Assn. (bd. dirs. 1984-86), Western States Comm. Assn., Internat. Network on Personal Rels., Internat. Pragmatics Assn., Sigma Xi, Phi Kappa Phi. Democrat. Roman Catholic. Avocations: cooking, squash, golf. Office: U Calif Instnl Advancement Santa Barbara CA 93106-2030

WIEMER, DAVID ROBERT, plastic surgeon; b. Houston, Sept. 16, 1940; m. Beverly Biggs, Feb. 20, 1966; children: D. Robert Jr., J. Bradley. BS in Natural Sci., Okla. State U., 1961; MD, Baylor U., 1965. Intern Ben Taub Gen. Hosp., Houston, 1965-66; resident in gen. surgery Baylor Univ. Coll. Medicine Affiliated Program, Houston, 1966-69, resident in plastic surgery, 1971-74; pvt. practice Wiemer Plastic Surgery, Houston, 1974—; active staff Meth. Hosp., Houston, 1975—, dep. chief divsn. plastic surgery, 1977—, sec. med. staff, 1990-92, pres., 1994-96, bd. dir., 1990-96; bd. dirs. The Meth. Hosp. Sys., 1996—; dep. chief divsn. plastic surgery VA Med. Ctr., 1977—. Contbr. articles to profl. jours., chpts. to books. Maj. U.S. Army, 1969-71. Mr. Ting Chao grant to Baylor Coll. Medicine, 1993. Mem. ACS, Am. Soc. Plastic and Reconstructive Surgeons, Am. Soc. Aesthetic Plastic Surgery, Assn. Acad. Chmn. and Plastic Surgeons, Am. Hosp. Assn. (ho. of dels. 1997—), Tex. Med. Soc. (sec. 1980), Houston Soc. Plastic Surgeons (sec., v.p., pres.), Houston Surg. Soc. (sec., pres.). Presbyterian. Office: Wiemer Plastic Surgery Inc 6560 Fannin St Ste 1760 Houston TX 77030-2735

WIEMER, ROBERT ERNEST, film and television producer, writer, director; b. Highland Park, Mich., Jan. 30, 1938; s. Carl Ernest and Marion (Israelian) W.; m. Rhea Dale McGeath, June 14, 1958; children: Robert Marshall, Rhea Whitney. BA, Ohio Wesleyan U., 1959. Ind. producer, 1956-60; dir. documentary ops. WCBS-TV, N.Y.C., 1964-67; ind. producer of television, theatrical and bus. films N.Y.C., 1967-72; exec. producer motion pictures and TV, ITT, N.Y.C., 1973-84; pres. subs. Blue Marble Co., Inc., Telemontage, Inc., Alphaventure Music, Inc., Betaventure Music, Inc. ITT, 1973-84; founder, chmn., chief exec. officer Tigerfilm, Inc., 1984—; chmn., bd. dirs. Golden Tiger Pictures, Hollywood, Calif., 1988—; pres, CEO Tuxedo Pictures Corp., Hollywood, Calif., 1993—. Writer, prodr., dir.: (feature films) My Seventeenth Summer, Witch's Sister, Do Me a Favor, Anna to the Infinite Power, Somewhere, Tomorrow, Night Train to Kathmandu; exec. prodr.: (children's TV series) Big Blue Marble (Emmy and Peabody awards); dir. (TV episodes) seaQuest DSV, Star Trek: The Next Generation, Deep Space Nine, The Adventures of Superboy; composer (country-western ballad) Tell Me What To Do. Recipient CINE award, 1974, 76, 77, 79, 81, Emmy award, 1978. Mem. NATAS, ASCAP, Info. Film Producers Assn. (Outstanding Producer award), Nat. Assn. TV Programming Execs., Am. Women in Radio and TV, N.J. Broadcasters Assn., Dirs. Guild Am. Office: Golden Tiger Pictures 3896 Ruskin St Las Vegas NV 89117-1097

WIEN, STUART LEWIS, retired supermarket chain executive; b. Milw., Sept. 11, 1923; s. Julius and Mildred (Rosenberg) W.; m. Charlotte Jean Milgram, June 4, 1949; children: Steven, John, William, Thomas.; m. Sheila B. Davis, July 25, 1982; stepchildren: Andrew, Stephen, Laurence, Geoffrey. B.S., UCLA, 1947. Chmn. bd. Milgram Food Stores, Inc., Kansas City, Mo., 1979-84; bd. dirs. UMB Scout Funds. Trustee Menorah Med. Ctr.; bd. regents Rockhurst Coll. Mem. Oakwood Country Club.

WIENER, DANIEL NORMAN, psychologist; b. Duluth, Minn., Feb. 6, 1921; s. Joseph Baxter and Fannie (Winer) W.; m. Phyllis Eileen Zager, Dec. 9, 1971; children: Jonathan Marc, Paul Aaron, Sara Ruth Wiener Pearson. BA, U. Minn., 1941, MA, 1942, PhD, 1950. Diplomate in Clin. Psychology Am. Bd. Profl. Psychology; lic. psychologist, Minn. Psychologist State of Conn., Hartford, 1943-44; chief psychologist VA Rehab. and Mental Hygiene Clinic, St. Paul and Mpls., 1944-76; Comty. Clinic, Two Harbors, Minn., 1968-89; pvt. practice psychology Mpls., 1952—; clin. prof. psychiatry and psychology U. Minn., Mpls., 1952—; cons. Hennepin County Dist. Ct., Mpls., 1982—. Author: Discipline, Achievement and Mental Health, 1960, Dimensions of Psychotherapy, 1965, Short-Term Psychotherapy and Structured Behavior Change, 1966, Training Children, 1968, Practical Guide to Psychotherapy, 1968, Classroom Management, 1972, Consumers Guide to Psychotherapy, 1975, Albert Ellis: Passionate Skeptic, 1988, B.F. Skinner: Benign Anarchist, 1996; book reviewer: Star-Tribune, Mpls. With USAF, 1942-43. Mem. Fellow APA, Am. Psychol. Soc.; mem. PEN, Minn. Psychol. Assn. (life, exec. coun.), Nat. Book Critics Cir. Avocations: tennis, squash. Home and Office: 1225 Lasalle Ave Apt 801 Minneapolis MN 55403-2329

WIENER, HARRY, pharmaceutical company executive, physician; b. Vienna, Austria, Oct. 29, 1924; s. Joseph and Beile W.; m. Charlotte Baran, May 1, 1982. BS, Bklyn. Coll., 1945; MD, L.I. Coll. Medicine, 1949. With Pfizer Inc., N.Y.C., 1958-95, dir. profl. info., 1958-95. Author: Generic Drugs—Safety and Effectiveness, 1973, Schizophrenia and Anti-Schizophrenia, 1977, Findings in Computed Tomography, 1979. Served with M.C., AUS, 1953-55, Korea. Mem. AMA, N.Y. Acad. Medicine, Am. Med. Writers Assn. Developer Wiener numbers for calculation of phys. properties of hydrocarbons, 1947, proposer theory of human pheromones, 1966, genetics-environment symmetry in schizophrenia, 1976. Home and Office: 429 E 52nd St New York NY 10022-6430

WIENER, HESH (HAROLD FREDERIC WIENER), publisher, editor, consultant; b. Bklyn., July 20, 1946; s. Jesse Leonard and Regina (Rappaport) W. B.S. in Polit. Sci., MIT, 1969. Mem. staff systems devel. Data Gen. Corp., Southboro, Mass., 1969-70; dir. computer edn. project U. Calif., Berkeley, 1970-72; editor Computer Decisions Mag., Rochelle Park, N.J., 1973-78; editor, pub. Tech. News Am., N.Y.C., 1976-88; pres. Tech. News of Am. Co., Inc., N.Y.C., 1982—; mng. dir. Tech. News Ltd., London, 1992—; pub. Computer and Communications Buyer Newsletter, 1979-95, Mainstream Newsletter, 1980-82, Infoperspectives Newsletter, 1982—, Storage Tech. Monitor, 1984-87, Infoperspectives Internat. (U.K.), 1989—, (Mid. East), 1991—, The Four Hundred Newsletter (U.K.), 1990—, The Four Hundred Newsletter (U.S.), 1990—; editor Infoperspectives Internat. (Italy), 1991—, The Four Hundred Newsletter (Italy), 1995—; pub. U.S. edit. Computergram Internat. Newsletter, 1985-90; corr. Processeurs mag., 1989—; cons. Hewlett-Packard Co. (Paris), 1971-72, Xerox Corp., 1972-73; advisor NSF, 1975. Author: Big Blue and You, The IBM Atlas, The Mainframe; corr. Computer Weekly, U.K., 1975-81, Computable, Amsterdam, 1976-87, Computing Can., 1977-78, Ordinateurs, Paris, 1977-89, Data News, Brussels, 1979-86, Informatics, U.K., 1981-85, Datanytt, Copenhagen, 1982-89, Mgmt. Tech. mag., 1983-85; editor BusinessWeek Newsletter for Info. Execs., 1987-90, Datamation Mag., 1983-90, Infoperspectives Internat. (Milan), 1991—; contbg. editor Bus. and Soc. Rev., 1978-85; contbr. N.Y. Times Syndicate, Los Angeles Times Syndicate, N.Am. Newspaper Alliance Wireservice, Newsday, Manhattan, Inc., Rom Mag., Informatique (Paris), The Economist (London), Dun's Bus. Month, Software News, Intermedia, Digital News, Data Communications, Bus. Week Newsletter for Info. Execs., Bus. Strategy Internat., Nikkei Watcher on IBM (Tokyo), 1989-96. Club: Overseas Press. Home: 246 6th Ave Brooklyn NY 11215-2103 Office: Tech News Am 110 Greene St New York NY 10012-3813

WIENER, JACQUES LOEB, JR., federal circuit judge; b. Shreveport, La., Oct. 2, 1934; s. Jacques L. and Betty (Eichenbaum) W.; children: Patricia Wiener Shifke, Jacques L. III, Betty Ellen Wiener Spomer, Donald B. BA, Tulane U., 1956, JD, 1961. Bar: La. 1961, U.S. Dist. Ct. (we. dist.) La. 1961. Ptnr. Wiener, Weiss & Madison, Shreveport, 1961-90; judge U.S. Ct. Appeals (5th cir.), Shreveport, 1990—; mem. coun. La. State Law Inst., 1965—; master of the bench Am. Inn of Ct., 1990—. Pres. United Way N.W. La., 1975, Shreveport Jewish Fedn., 1969-70. Fellow Am. Coll. Trust & Estates Counsel, Am. Bar Found., La. Bar Found.; academician Internat. Acad. Trust & Estate Law; mem. ABA, La. State Bar Assn., Shreveport Bar Assn. (pres. 1982), Am. Law Inst. Avocations: fly fishing, upland game bird hunting, photography, travel. Office: US Ct Appeals 5th Cir US Ct House 300 Fannin St Ste 5101 Shreveport LA 71101-3121

WIENER, JERRY M., psychiatrist; b. Baytown, Tex., May 11, 1933; s. Isidore and Dora L. (Lerner) W.; m. Louise W. Weingarten, Apr. 12, 1964; children—Matthew, Ethan, Ross, Aaron. Student, Rice U., 1952; M.D., Baylor U., 1956; tng. in psychoanalysis, Columbia U. Psychoanalytic Center, 1968. Resident in psychiatry Mayo Clinic, Rochester, Minn., 1957-61, Columbia U. Coll. Physicians and Surgeons, N.Y.C., 1961-62; dir. child and adolescent psychiatry St. Luke's Hosp., N.Y.C., 1962-71; dir. child psychiatry Emory U., Atlanta, 1971-75; chmn. dept. psychiatry Children's Hosp., Washington, 1976-77; prof., chmn. dept. psychiatry George Washington U., 1977—; mem. faculty Washington Psychoanalytic Inst. Editor: Textbook of Child and Adolescent Psychiatry, 1991, 96, Psychopharmacology in Childhood and Adolescence, 1977, Diagnosis and Psychopharmacology in Childhood and Adolescence, 1995; contbr. articles to profl. jours., chpts. to books. Fellow Am. Psychiat. Assn. (past pres.), Am. Coll. Psychiatrists; mem. Am. Psychoanalytic Assn., Am. Assn. Chmn. Depts. Psychiatry (past pres.), Am. Psychiat. Press, Inc. (chmn. bd. dirs.), Am. Acad. Child and Adolescent Psychiatry (past pres.). Office: George Washington Univ Dept Psychiatry 2150 Pennsylvania Ave NW Washington DC 20037-3201

WIENER, JON, history educator; b. St. Paul, May 16, 1944; s. Daniel N. and Gladys (Aronsohn) Spratt. BA, Princeton U., 1966; PhD, Harvard U., 1971. Vis. prof. U. Calif.-Santa Cruz, 1973; acting asst. prof. UCLA, 1973-74; asst. prof. history U. Calif.-Irvine, 1974-83, prof., 1984—; plaintiff Freedom of Info. Lawsuit against FBI for John Lennon Files, 1983—. Author: Social Origins of the New South, 1979; Come Together: John Lennon in His Time, 1984, Professors, Politics, and Pop, 1991; contbg. editor The Nation mag.; contbr. articles to profl. jours. including The New Republic and New York Times Book Review. Rockefeller Found. fellow, 1979, Am. Coun. Learned Socs.-Ford Found. fellow, 1985. Mem. Am. Hist. Assn., Nat. Book Critics Circle, Orgn. Am. Historians, Nat. Writers' Union, Liberty Hill Found. (bd. of dirs.). Office: U Calif Dept History Irvine CA 92697-3275

WIENER, JOSEPH, pathologist; b. Toronto, Can., Sept. 21, 1927; came to U.S., 1949, naturalized, 1960; s. Louis and Minnie (Salem) W.; m. Judith Hesta Ross, June 20, 1954; children: Carolyn L., Adam L. M.D., U. Toronto, 1953. Intern Detroit Receiving Hosp., 1953-54; resident to chief resident pathology Mallory Inst. Pathology, 1954-55, 57-60; from asst. to assoc. prof. pathology Columbia U., N.Y.C., 1960-68; prof. pathology N.Y. Med. Coll., N.Y.C., 1968-78; prof. pathology Wayne State U., Detroit, 1978—, chmn. dept., 1978-90; cons. NIH, 1970—. Served to capt. M.C. U.S. Army, 1955-57. Grantee: Heart, Lung and Blood Inst., 1971-93; named fellow Coun. for High Blood Pressure Rsch., 1982—. Mem. AAAS, Am. Soc. Investigative Pathology, Am. Soc. Cell Biology, Mich. Path. Soc., Internat. Acad. Pathology, Am. Heart Assn., U.S./Can. Acad. Pathology, Mich. Heart Assn., Alpha Omega Alpha. Research on exptl. cardiovascular pathology and hypertension. Office: 540 E Canfield St Detroit MI 48201-1928

WIENER, MALCOLM HEWITT, foundation executive; b. Tsingtao, China, July 3, 1935; (parents Am. citizens); s. Myron and Ethel (Zimmerman) W.; m. Carolyn Talbot Seely, June 8, 1990; children: Catherine Diktynna Talbot, Elizabeth Ariadne Seely. BA, Harvard U., 1957, JD, 1963. Bar: N.Y. 1964. Atty. N.Y.C., 1963-71, pvt. practice investing, 1971—; chmn. Millburn Corp., N.Y.C., 1977—, Millburn Ridgefield Corp., Ridgefield, Conn., 1982—, ShareInVest, Ridgefield, 1982—; chmn. bd. trustees Malcolm Hewitt Wiener Found., N.Y.C., 1984—; lectr. in field; fellow faculty of govt., John F. Kennedy Sch. Govt., Harvard U., 1985; advisor U.S. Dept. State on Internat. Conv. on Illicit Traffic in Antiquities, 1970-75. Columnist Newsday; contbr. articles to profl. publs. Co-dir. Aegean Bronze Age Colloquium, NYU Inst. Fine Arts, 1975—; founder, exec. dir. Inst. Aegean Prehistory, 1982-89, pres., 1990—; trustee Am. Classical Studies in Athens; founder Wiener Lab. Am. Sch. Classical Studies, Athens; bd. trustees, co-chmn. vis. com. Dept. Egyptian Art, mem. vis. com. Dept. Painting Conservation, Prints and Drawings, Greek and Roman, chmn.'s coun.; vice chmn. bus. com. Met. Mus. Art; mem. adv. bd. Malcolm Wiener Ctr. for Social Policy, Kennedy Sch. Govt. Harvard U.; mem. vis. com., paintings Boston Mus. Fine Arts, 1985-91, drawings and prints Frick Collection; sponsor Malcolm and Carolyn Wiener Lab. for Aegean and Near East Dendochronology Cornell U. With USN, 1957-60. Fellow Archaeol. Inst. Am. (hon. life); mem. ABA, Coun. on Fgn. Rels. (ind. task force on non-lethal weapons). Office: 1270 Avenue Of The Americas New York NY 10020

WIENER, MARTIN JOEL, historian; b. Bklyn., June 1, 1941; s. Harold H. and Eva (Richter) W.; m. Carol Ann Zisowitz, Sept. 22, 1964 (div. 1977); children: Wendy, Julie; m. Meredith Anne Skura, May 17, 1981; children: Rebecca, Vivian. BA, Brandeis U., 1962; MA, Harvard U., 1963, PhD in History, 1967. Asst. prof. Rice U., 1967-72, assoc. prof., 1972-80, prof. history, 1980-82, Mary Gibbs Jones prof., 1982—; chair dept. history, 1990-94. Author: Between Two Worlds: The Political Thought of Graham Wallas, 1971, English Culture and the Decline of the Industrial Spirit, 1850-1980, 1981 (Schuyler prize Am. Hist. Assn. 1981), Reconstructing the Criminal, 1990. Research fellow NEH, 1973, 86, Am. Council Learned Socs., 1982. Fellow Royal Hist. Soc.; mem. Am. Hist. Assn., Am. Soc. Legal History, Coun. for European Studies (steering com. 1985-90), Conf. on Brit. Studies (nominating com. 1982-84, coun. 1992-96), Social History Soc. (U.K.), Am. Hist. Assn. (coun. 1987-90). Jewish. Home: 5510 Yarwell Dr Houston TX 77096-4012 Office: Rice U Dept of History 6100 Main St Houston TX 77005-1827

WIENER, MARVIN S., rabbi, editor, executive; b. N.Y.C., Mar. 16, 1925; s. Max and Rebecca (Dodell) W.; m. Sylvia Bodek, Mar. 2, 1952; children: David Hillel, Judith Rachel. B.S., CCNY, 1944, M.S., 1945; B.H.L., Jewish Theol. Sem. Am., 1947, M.H.L., Rabbi, 1951, D.D. (hon.), 1977. Registrar, sec. faculty Rabbinical Sch., Jewish Theol. Sem. Am., 1951-57; cons. Frontiers of Faith TV Series, NBC, 1951-57; dir., instr. liturgy Cantors Inst.-Sem. Coll. Jewish Music, Jewish Theol. Sem. Am., 1954-58; faculty coordinator Sem. Sch. and Women's Inst., 1958-64; dir. Nat. Acad. for Adult Jewish Studies, United Synagogue Am., N.Y.C., 1958-78; editor Burning Bush Press, 1958-78, United Synagogue Rev., 1978-86; dir. com. congregational standards United Synagogue Am., 1976-86, cons. community relations and social action, 1981-82, editor, exec. joint retirement bd., 1986—; mem. Joint Commn. on Rabbinic Placement, 1951-57, Joint Prayer Book Commn., 1957-62; mem. exec. coun. Rabbinical Assembly, 1958-86; editl. cons. N.Y. Bd. Rabbis, 1987-89; trustee joint retirement bd. Jewish Theol. Sem. Am. Rabbinical Assembly and United Synagogue Am., 1959-86, sec. 1968-76, 84-85, vice chmn., 1976-82, 85-86, chmn. 1982, treas., 1983-84; co-chmn. Jewish Bible Assn., 1960-64; chmn. bd. rev. Nat. Coun. Jewish Audio-Visual Materials, 1968-69; mem. exec. com. Nat. Coun. Adult Jewish Edn., 1966—; mem. exec. bd., editl. adv. bd., v.p. Jewish Book Couns., 1976-96; chmn. Internat. Conf. Adult Jewish Edn., Jerusalem, 1972. Editor: Nat. Acad. Adult Jewish Studies Bull., 1958-78, Past and Present: Selected Essays (Israel Friedlaender), 1961, Jewish Tract Series, 1964-78 (15 titles), Adult Jewish Edn., 1958-78, Talmudic Law and the Modern State (Moshe Silberg), 1973. Mem. Am. Acad. Jewish Research, Assn. Jewish Studies, N.Y. Bd. Rabbis, Rabbinical Assembly. Home: 67-66 108th St Apt D-46 Forest Hills NY 11375-2974 Office: Joint Retirement Bd 7 Penn Plz Ste 720 New York NY 10001-3900

WIENER, NORMAN JOSEPH, lawyer; b. Portland, Oreg., Sept. 10, 1919; s. Peter and Anna Wiener; m. Elizabeth Bentley, Jan. 26, 1945; children: Jane, Jon, Lisa. BA, U. Oreg., 1941, JD, 1947. Bar: Oreg. 1947. Assoc. King, Wood, Miller & Anderson, Portland, 1947-51; ptnr. Miller, Nash, Wiener, Hager & Carlsen, Portland, 1952—. Pres. United Way, Portland, 1977, Rehab. Inst. Oreg., Portland; trustee U. Oreg. Found. 1st lt. U.S. Army, 1942-46, World War II, 1951-52, Korea. Mem. ABA, Oreg. Bar Assn., Am. Bar Found. (life), Arlington Club (pres.), Portland Golf Club (pres.). Republican. Avocations: golf, swimming. Office: Miller Nash Wiener Hager & Carlsen 111 SW 5th Ave Ste 3500 Portland OR 97204-3638

WIENER, ROBERT ALVIN, accountant; b. N.Y.C., Jan. 9, 1918; s. George and Rose Vivian (Fink) W.; m. Annabelle Kalbfeld, Jan. 1, 1941; children—Marilyn Wiener Grunewald, Marjorie Wiener Petit, Mark. B.C.S., NYU, 1938. CPA, N.Y., Ill.; cert. insolvency and reorgn. acct. Sr. ptnr. Robert A. Wiener & Co. (CPAs), N.Y.C., 1946-71; ptnr. Grant Thornton & Co. (CPAs), N.Y.C., 1971-73; v.p., gen. auditor Seeburg Industries, Inc., N.Y.C., 1973-77; pvt. practice acctg., 1978—; asst. prof. Pace Coll., 1956-77; lectr. Baruch Coll., 1947-77; acctg. cons. Unistar Programme UN Devel. Programme, 1991. Author: Insolvency Accounting, 1977. Served with AUS, 1943-46. Decorated Bronze Star. Mem. AICPA, N.Y. State Soc. C.P.A.s, Accts. Club Am., Fin. Execs. Inst., Inst. Internal Auditors, Assn. Insolvency Accts., Am. Arbitration Assn. (arbitration panel), Pi Lambda Phi. Home: 30 Waterside Plz New York NY 10010-2622

WIENER, RUSSELL WARREN, environmental scientist, researcher; b. N.Y.C., June 23, 1952; s. Max and Rhoda (Bruntil) W.; m. Martha E. Smith, Sept. 5, 1982; children: Benjamin, Victoria. Student, Rensselaer Poly. Inst., 1970-71; BS in Biology, Emory U., 1974, MS in Environ. Sci., 1978; PhD in Environ. Health, U. Cin., 1987. Rsch. technician U. N.C., Chapel Hill, 1978-79; aerosol tech. GE, Cin., 1984-86; chief atmospheric methods and monitoring br. U.S. EPA, Research Triangle Park, N.C., 1987—; adj. asst. prof. U. N.C., Chapel Hill, 1989—, N.C. State U., Raleigh, 1994—. Mem. Am. Assn. for Aerosol Rsch. (chair indoor air 1988-94), Am. Indsl. Hygiene Assn., Am. Acad. Indsl. Hygiene. Avocations: swimming, tennis. Office: US EPA 79 Alexander Dr MD-77 Research Triangle Park NC 27711

WIENER, SOLOMON, author, consultant, former city official; b. N.Y.C., Mar. 5, 1915; s. Morris David and Anna (Pinchuk) W.; m. Gertrude Klings, Feb. 24, 1946; children: Marjorie Diane Wein, Willa Kay Ehrlich. BS, Cornell, 1936; MPA, NYU, 1946. Exam. asst. N.Y.C. Dept. Personnel, 1937-42, civil service examiner, 1946-55, asst. div. chief, 1955-59, div. chief, 1959-67, asst. dir. exams., 1967-70, dir. exams., 1970-72, asst. personnel dir. exams., 1972-75; author, cons., 1975—; tchr. Washington Irving Evening Adult Sch., N.Y.C., 1949-60, tchr.-in-charge, 1960-67. Served with AUS, 1942-46, PTO. Decorated Bronze Star. Mem. Am. Soc. Pub. Adminstrn., Internat. Personnel Mgmt. Assn., Authors Guild, Res. Officers Assn., Ret. Officers Assn., Assn. of U.S. Army, Am. Def. Preparedness Assn. Author: A Handy Book of Commonly Used American Idioms, rev. edit., 1981, Manual de Modismos Americanos Más Comunes, rev. edit., 1981, A Handy Guide to Irregular Verbs and the Use and Formation of Tenses, 1959, Guia Completa de Los Verbos Irregulares en Inglés y el Uso y Formación de los Tiempos, 1959, Questions and Answers on American Citizenship, rev. edit., 1982, Clear and Simple Guide to Business Letter Writing, rev. edit., 1978, The College Graduate Guide for Scoring High on Employment Tests, 1981, The High School Graduate Guide for Scoring High on Civil Service Tests, 1981, How to Take and Pass Simple Tests for Civil Service Jobs, 1981, Officer Candidate Tests, 3d edit., 1993, Military Flight Aptitude Tests, 2d edit., 1994; co-author Practice for the Armed Forces Test, ASVAB, 14th edit., 1994, Practica para el Examen de las Fuerzas Armadas, ASVAB En Español, 1989; contbr. to ARCO ROTC Coll. Guide, 1988. Home: 523 E 14th St New York NY 10009-2927

WIENER, THOMAS ELI, lawyer; b. Dallas, Nov. 29, 1940; s. Samson and Fan (Gardner) W.; m. Felice Gloria Goodwin, Jan. 24, 1970; children: Gary Allen, Debra Roslyn, Allison Beth, Todd David. B.A., U. Tex., 1962, J.D. with honors, 1968. Bar: Tex. 1968, D.C. 1969, Pa. 1972, U.S. Supreme Ct. 1972. Atty.-advisor office chief counsel IRS, Washington, 1968-72; assoc. Pepper Hamilton & Scheetz, Phila., 1972-74, Abrahams & Loewenstein, Phila., 1974-76, Goodis, Greenfield, Henry & Edelstein, Phila., 1976-77, Mesirov, Gelman, Jaffe, Cramer & Jamieson, Phila., 1977-78; prin. Franklin, Margulies & Huntington,, 1978-91, Riley & DeFalice, P.C., Phila., 1991-92, Wiener & Caplan, P.C., 1992-95; sole practitioner, 1995—; Dir. Lufkin (Tex.) Inds., Inc., Wiener Lumber Co., Dallas. Author: (with others) Tax Problems of Fiduciaries, 1977. Trustee Golden Slipper Club; pres. Main Line Reform Temple, 1992-94, pres. brotherhood 1981-83; pres. Rotary Gundaker Found., 1986-87; v.p. Nat. Fedn. Temple Brotherhoods, 1994—, N.Am. Bd. World Union Progressive Judaism, Phila. Fedn. Reform Synagogues, 1993—; chair Synagogue Fedn. Coun. of Phila., 1994-97; bd. trustees Union of Am. Hebrew Congregation, 1995—. Mem. ABA, D.C. Bar Assn., Pa. Bar Assn., Tex. Bar Assn., Phila. Bar Assn., Am. Law Inst., Order of Coif. Lodges: Masons (32 degree K.C.C.H., past master), Rotary (pres. chpt. 1985-86). Home: 1233 Remington Rd Wynnewood PA 19096-2329 Office: One Belmont Ave Ste 605 Bala Cynwyd PA 19004-1609

WIENER, VALERIE, communications consultant, state senator; b. Las Vegas, Nev., Oct. 30, 1948; d. Louis Isaac Wiener and Tui Ava Knight. BJ, U. Mo., 1971, MA, 1972; MA, U. Ill., Springfield, 1974; postgrad., McGeorge Sch. Law, 1976-79. Producer TV show "Checkpoint" Sta. KOMU-TV, Columbia, Mo., 1972-73; v.p., owner Broadcast Assocs., Inc., Las Vegas, 1972-86; pub. affairs dir. First Ill. Cable TV, Springfield, 1973-74; editor Ill. State Register, Springfield, 1973-74; producer and talent "Nevada Realities" Sta. KLVX-TV, Las Vegas, 1974-75; account exec. Sta. KBMI (now KFMS), Las Vegas, 1975-79; nat. traffic dir. six radio stas., Las Vegas, Albuquerque and El Paso, Tex., 1979-80; exec. v.p., gen. mgr. Stas. KXKS and KKJY, Albuquerque, 1980-81; exec. adminstr. Stas. KSET AM/FM, KVEG, KFMS and KKJY, 1981-83; press sec. U.S. Congressman Harry Reid, Washington, 1983-87; adminstrv. asst Friends for Harry Reid, Nev., 1986; press sec. U.S. Senator Harry Reid, Washington, 1987-88; owner Wiener Comm. Group, Las Vegas, 1988—; senator State of Nev., 1996-. Author: Power Communications: Positioning Yourself for High Visibility (Fortune Book Club main selection 1994), Gang Free: Friendship Choices for Today's Youth, 1995, The Nesting Syndrome: Grown Children Living at Home, 1997; contbg. writer The Pacesetter, ASAE's Comm. News. Sponsor Futures for Children, Las Vegas, Albuquerque, El Paso, 1979-83; mem. El Paso Exec. Women's Coun., 1981-83; mem. VIP bd. Easter Seals, El Paso, 1982; media chmn. Gov.'s Coun. Small Bus., 1989-93, Gov.'s Commn. on Aging, 1997—, Clark Coun. Sch. Dist. and Bus. Cmty. PAYBAC Spkrs. and Partnership Programs, 1989—; med. dir. 1990 Conf. on Women, Gov. of Nev.; media chmn. Congl. Awards Coun., 1989-93; vice chmn. Gov.'s Commn. on Postsecondary Edn., 1992-96; bd. dirs. BBB So. Nev. Named Outstanding Vol., United Way, El Paso, 1983, SBA Nev. Small Bus. Media Adv. of Yr., 1992; recipient Woman of Achievement in Media award, 1992, Outstanding Achievement award Nat. Fedn. Press Women, 1991, Disting. Leader award Nat. Assn. for Cmty. Leadership, 1993, over 106 other comm. awards. Mem. Nev. Press Women (numerous 1st place media awards 1990—), Nat. Spkrs. Assn., Nat. Assn. Women Bus. Owners (media chmn., nat. rep. So. Nev. 1990-91, Nev. Adv. of Yr. award 1992), Dem. Press Secs. Assn., El Paso Assn. Radio Stas., U.S. Senate Staff Club, Las Vegas C. of C. (Circle of Excellence award 1993), Soc. Profl. Journalists. Democrat. Avocations: reading, writing, fitness training, pub. speaking, community involvement. Office: 1500 Foremaster Ln Ste 2 Las Vegas NV 89101-1103

WIENS, ARTHUR NICHOLAI, psychology educator; b. McPherson, Kans., Sept. 7, 1926; s. Jacob T. and Helen E. (Kroeker) W.; m. Ruth Helen Avery, June 11, 1949; children: Barbara, Bradley, Donald. B.A., U. Kans., 1948, M.A., 1952; Ph.D., U. Portland, 1956. Diplomate: Am. Bd. Examiners Profl. Psychology. Clin. psychologist Topeka State Hosp., 1949-53; sr. psychologist outpatient dept. Oreg. State Hosp., Salem, 1954-58; chief psychologist Oreg. State Hosp., 1958-61, dir. clin. psychology internship program, 1958-61; clin. instr. U. Oreg. Med. Sch., Portland, 1958-61; asst. prof. U. Oreg. Med. Sch., 1961-65, asso. prof., 1965-66, prof. med. psychology, 1966—; clin. asso. prof. psychology U. Portland, 1959-61; field assessment officer Peace Corps, 1965; cons. psychologist Portland Center for Hearing and Speech, 1964-67, Dammasch State Hosp., 1967-69, Raleigh Hills Hosp., 1968-84, Oreg. Vocat. Rehab. Div., 1973—, mem. state adv. com., 1976-93; cons. William Temple Rehab. House, Episcopal Laymen's Mission Soc., 1968-88; chmn. State Oreg. Bd. Social Protection, 1971-84, State Oreg. Bd. Psychologist Examiners, 1974-77; v.p. bd. dirs. Raleigh Hills Research Found., 1974-80. Contbr. articles to profl. jours. Fellow AAAS, APA (chmn. com. on vis. psychologist program 1972-76, chmn. accreditation com. 1978, mem. task force edn. and credentialing 1979-84); mem. Am. Assn. State Psychology Bds. (pres. 1978-79), Nat. Register Health Svc. Providers in Psychology (bd. dirs. 1985-92), Profl. Exam. Svc. (bd. dirs. 1982-88, 90-96, chmn. 1986-88), Sigma Xi. Home: 74 Condolea Way Lake Oswego OR 97035-1010 Office: Oreg U-Health Sci Dept Sci Dept Portland OR 97201

WIER, PATRICIA ANN, publishing executive, consultant; b. Coal Hill, Ark., Nov. 10, 1937; d. Horace L. and Bridget B. (McMahon) Norton; m. Richard A. Wier, Feb. 24, 1962; 1 child, Rebecca Ann. B.A., U. Mo., Kansas City, 1964; M.B.A., U. Chgo., 1978. Computer programmer AT&T, 1960-62; lead programmer City of Kansas City, Mo., 1963-65; with Playboy Enterprises, Chgo., 1965-71; mgr. systems and programming Playboy Enterprises, 1971; with Ency. Britannica, Inc., Chgo., 1971—; v.p. mgmt. svcs. Ency. Britannica USA, 1975-83, exec. v.p. adminstrn., 1983-84; v.p. planning and devel. Ency. Britannica, Inc., 1985, pres. Compton's Learning Co. div., 1985; pres. Ency. Britannica (USA), 1986-91, Ency. Britannica N.A., 1991-92; exec. v.p. Ency. Britannica, Inc., 1986-94; pres. Ency. Britannica N.Am., 1991-94; mgmt. cons. pvt. practice, Chgo., 1994—; lectr. mktg. U. Chgo. Grad. Sch. Bus., 1995—; cons. pvt. practice, Chgo., 1994—; bd. dirs. NICOR, Inc., Golden Rule Ins., Alcas Corp., Hurley State Bank; mem. coun. Northwestern U. Assocs. Mem. fin. Coun. Archdiocese of Chgo., Coun. of Grad. Sch. of Bus. U. of Chgo. Mem. Direct Selling Assn. (bd. dirs. 1984-93, chmn. 1987-88, named to Hall of Fame 1991), Women's Coun. U. Mo. Kansas City (hon. life) Com. 200, The Chgo. Network. Roman Catholic. Office: Patricia A Wier Inc 175 E Delaware Pl Apt 8305 Chicago IL 60611-7748

WIER, RICHARD ROYAL, JR., lawyer, inventor; b. Wilmington, Del., May 19, 1941; s. Richard Royal and Anne (Kurtz) W.; m. Anne E. Edwards, Nov. 25, 1978; children—Melissa Royal, Emma Kurtz; children from previous marriage: Richard Royal, III, Mimi Poole. BA in English, Hamilton Coll., 1963; LLB, U. Pa., 1966; postgrad. in labor law, Temple U., 1981-82. Bar: D.C. 1967, Del. 1967, Pa. 1980, U.S. Dist. Ct. Del., U.S. Ct. Appeals (3d cir.), U.S. Supreme Ct. Assoc. Connolly, Bove & Lodge, Wilmington, 1966-68; dep. atty. gen. State of Del., Wilmington, 1968-70; state prosecutor Del. Dept. Justice, Wilmington, 1970-74; atty. gen. State of Del., Wilmington, 1975-79; ptnr. Prickett, Jones, Elliott, Kristol & Schnee, Wilmington, 1979-92; sole practice lawyer Wilmington, 1993—; lectr. criminal and labor law various instns. Active United Way campaign, 1976, 77; mem. supervisory bd. Gov.'s Commn. on Criminal Justice; bd. dirs. Del. Coun. Crime and Justice, 1982-89; mem. adv. coun. Diabetes Control, 1990-92; dir. Project Assist, 1992-95, Commn. on Cutreach, 1994—. Recipient Law Enforcement award Newark Police Dept., 1974; Law Enforcement Commendation medal Nat. Soc. SAR, 1976; Ideal Citizen award Am. Found. for Sci. Creative Intelligence, 1976; Commendation Del. Gen. Assembly Senate, 1976, 77, 80; Outstanding Achievement award, 1976. Mem. ABA, Nat. Dist. Attys. Assn. (state dir.), Del. Bar Assn. (chmn. criminal law sect. 1987-91, co-chmn. on drug crisis 1993—, vice chmn. labor law sect. 1987-88, chmn. 1989-90), Pa. Bar Assn., D.C. Bar Assn., Nat. Assn. Attys. Gen. (hon. life, exec. com.), Am. Judicature Soc., Am. Del. Trial Lawyers Assn., Nat. Assn. Extradition Ofcls. (hon. life, regional v.p., exec. dir.), Italian Radio/TV Assn. (hon., Outstanding Achievement award), Internat. Platform Assn., Pi Delta Epsilon. Office: Richard R Wier Jr PA 1220 N Market St Ste 600 Wilmington DE 19801-2598

WIERMAN, JOHN CHARLES, mathematician, educator; b. Prosser, Wash., June 30, 1949; s. John Nathaniel and Edith Elizabeth (Ashley) W.; m. Susan Shelley Graupmann, Aug. 13, 1971; 1 child, Adam Christopher. BS in Math., U. Wash., 1971, PhD in Math., 1976. Asst. prof. math. U. Minn., Mpls., 1976-81; asst. prof. Johns Hopkins U., Balt., 1981-82, assoc. prof., 1982-87, prof., 1987—, chmn. math. scis. dept., 1988—; sr. rsch. fellow Inst. Math. and Its Applications, Mpls., 1987-88. Co-author: First-Passage Percolation on the Square Lattice, 1978; contbr. articles to profl. jours. Grad. fellow NSF, 1971-74; NSF rsch. grantee, 1976-93. Fellow Inst. Math. Stats. (organizer spl. session on percolation theory 1982, organizer spl. session on probability and math. stats. 1986); mem. Am. Soc. Quality Control, Bernoulli Soc., Am. Math. Soc., Am. Statis. Assn., Math. Assn. Am., Sigma Xi, Phi Beta Kappa. Office: Johns Hopkins U Dept Math Scis 34th & Charles Sts Baltimore MD 21218

WIERNIK, PETER HARRIS, oncologist, educator; b. Crocket, Tex., June 16, 1939; s. Harris and Molly (Emmerman) W.; m. Roberta Joan Fuller, Sept. 6, 1961; children: Julie Anne, Lisa Britt, Peter Harrison. B.A. with distinction, U. Va., 1961, M.D., 1965; Dr. h.c., U. of Republic, Montevideo, Uruguay, 1982. Diplomate Am. Bd. Internal Medicine, Am. Bd. Med. Oncology (mem. writing com. 1981-87). Intern Cleve. Met. Gen. Hosp., 1965-66, resident, 1969-70; resident Osler Svc. Johns Hopkins Hosp., Balt., 1970-71; sr. asst. surgeon USPHS, 1966, advanced through grades to med. dir., 1976; sr. staff assoc. Balt. Cancer Rsch. Ctr., 1966-71, chief sect. med. oncology, 1971-76, chief clin. oncology br., 1976-82, dir., 1976-82; assoc. dir. div. cancer treatment Nat. Cancer Inst., 1976-82; asst. prof. medicine U. Md. Sch. Medicine, Balt., 1971-74, assoc. prof., 1974-76, prof., 1976-82; Gutman prof., chmn. dept. oncology Montefiore Med. Ctr., 1982-94; head divsn. med. oncology Albert Einstein Coll., 1982-94; assoc. dir. for clin. rsch. Albert Einstein Cancer Ctr., 1982-94, 95—; prof. medicine Albert Einstein Coll. Medicine, 1982—; cons. hematology and med. oncology Union Meml. Hosp., Greater Balt. Med. Ctr., Franklin Sq. Hosp.; bd. dirs. Balt. City unit Am. Cancer Soc., 1971-78; chmn. patient care com., 1972-75, mem. profl. edn. and grants com., N.Y.C. divsn., 1983-90, mem. nat. clin. fellowship com., 1984-96; mem. med. adv. com. Nat. Leukemia Assn., 1976-88, chmn. med. adv. com., 1989—; chmn. adult leukemia com. Cancer and Leukemia Group B, 1976-83; prin. investigator Ea. Coop. Oncology Group, 1982-94, 96—; chmn. gynecol. oncology com., 1986-88, chmn. leukemia com., 1988-94; sci. cons. Vt. Regional Cancer Ctr., 1987—. Editor: Controversies in Oncology, 1982, Supportive Care of the Cancer Patient, 1983, Neoplastic Diseases of the Blood, 1985, 2d edit., 1991, 3d edit. 1996; assoc. editor Medical Oncology and Tumor Pharmacotherapy, 1987-91, sr. editor, 1991—; assoc. editor oncology Am. Jour. Therapeutics, 1994—; co-editor: Year Book of Hematology, 1986—, Handbook of Hematologic and Oncologic Emergencies, 1988, Bone Marrow Transplantation (textbook), 1995, Am. Jour. Med. Scis., 1976-81; N.Am. editor Jour. Cancer Rsch. and Clin. Oncology, 1986-89; mem. editorial bd. Cancer Treatment Reports, 1972-76, Leukemia Rsch., 1977-86, 91—, Leukemia, 1986—, Cancer Clin. Trials, 1977—, Jour. Therapeutic Rsch., 1994—, Hosp. Practice, 1979—, Jour. Clin. Oncology, 1989-91, PDQ Nat. Cancer Inst., 1987-94; sect. editor antineoplastic drugs Jour. Clin. Pharmacology, 1985—; editor-in-chief Medical Oncology, 1993—; also articles, chpt. in books. Recipient Z Soc. award U. Va., 1961, Byrd S. Leavell Hematology award U. Va. Sch. Medicine, 1965. Fellow AAAS, ACP, Am. Coll. Clin. Pharmacology, Internat. Soc. Hematology, Royal Soc. Medicine (London), N.Y. Acad. Medicine; mem. Am. Soc. Clin. Investigation, Am. Soc. Clin. Oncology (chmn. edn. and tng. com. 1976-79, 84, subcom. on clin. investigation 1980-82, program com. 1990, pub. issues com., 1990-95, com. on rsch. awards 1996—), Am. Assn. Cancer Rsch., Am. Soc. Hematology, Am. Fedn. Clin. Rsch., Am. Acad. Clin. Toxicology, Internat. Soc. Exptl. Hematology, N.Y. Acad. Sci., Am. Soc. Hosp. Pharmacy, Am. Soc. Clin. Pharmacology and Therapeutics, Am. Radium Soc. (program com. 1987-93, exec. com. 1988-95, publ. com. 1988-92, sec. 1990-91, pres.-elect, 1992-93; pres. 1993-94, Janeway medalist, 1996), Polish Oncology Soc. (hon.), Harvey Soc., Uruguan Hematology Soc. (hon.), European Assn. Cancer Rsch., European Soc. for Hematology, Phi Beta Kappa (assoc. 1991—), Sigma Xi, Alpha Omega Alpha, Phi Sigma (award 1961). Home: 43 Longview Ln Chappaqua NY 10514-1304 Office: Montefiore Med Ctr 111 E 210th St Bronx NY 10467-2401 *Always* *remember why you entered a profession in the first place. Leave the politics to those who have forgotten.*

WIERSBE, WARREN WENDELL, clergyman, author, lecturer; b. East Chicago, Ind., May 16, 1929; s. Fred and Gladys Anna (Forsberg) W.; m. Betty Lorraine Warren, June 20, 1953; children: David, Carolyn, Robert, Judy. B.Th., No. Baptist Sem., 1953; D.D. (hon.), Temple Sem., Chattanooga, 1965, Trinity Ev-Div. Sch., 1986; LittD (hon.), Cedarville Coll., 1987. Ordained to ministry Bapt. Ch., 1951; pastor Central Bapt. Ch., East Chicago, 1951-57; editorial dir. Youth for Christ Internat., Wheaton, Ill., 1957-61; pastor Calvary Bapt. Ch., Covington, Ky., 1961-71; sr. minister Moody Ch., Chgo., 1971-78; bd. dirs. Slavic Gospel Assn., Wheaton, 1973-78; columnist Moody Monthly, Chgo., 1971-77; author, conf. minister, 1978-80; vis. instr. pastoral theology Trinity Div. Sch., Deerfield, Ill.; gen. dir. Back to the Bible Radio Ministries, Lincoln, Nebr., 1984-89; writer-in-residence Cornerstone Coll., Grand Rapids, Mich.; disting. prof. preaching Grand Rapids Bapt. Sem.; sr. contbg. editor Baker Book House, Grand Rapids. Author: over 100 books including William Culbertson, A Man of God, 1974, Live Like a King, 1976, Walking with the Giants, 1976, Be Right, 1977, (with David Wiersbe) Making Sense of the Ministry, 1983, Why Us? Why Bad Things Happen to God's People, 1984, Real Worship: It Can Transform Your Life, 1986, Be Compassionate, 1988, The Integrity Crisis, 1988, Be What You Are, 1988, The New Pilgrim's Progress, 1989, Be Courageous, 1989. Home and Office: 441 Lakewood Dr Lincoln NE 68510-2419

WIERSMA, G. BRUCE, dean, forest resources educator; b. Paterson, N.J., Oct. 26, 1942; s. George and Marjorie (Zeedyk) W.; m. Ann Becker, Aug. 15, 1964; children: Heather, Robin, Jennifer, Joshua. BS, U. Maine, 1964; MF in Forestry, Yale U., 1965; PhD Coll. Environ. Sci. & Forestry, SUNY, 1968. Teaching asst., 1965-66; rsch. biologist Coll. Environ. Sci. and Forestry SUNY, 1968; combat devels. staff officer U.S. Army Inst. Land Combat, Alexandria, Va., 1968-70; head monitoring sect. EPA, Washington, 1970-72, chief ecol. monitoring branch, 1972-74; chief pollutant pathways br. EPA, Las Vegas, Nev., 1974-79, sr. ecologist, 1979-80; mgr. environ. earth scis. group, Idaho Nat. Engring. Lab. EG&G Idaho, Inc., 1980-87; instr. Idaho Falls Campus of Higher Edn. U. Idaho, 1981-90, affiliate grad. faculty Coll. Forestry Wildlife and Range Scis., 1988-90; mgr., dir. Ctr. Environ. Monitoring and Assesment Environ. Sci. and Tech. Group, 1989-90; dir. Ctr. Environ. Monitoring and Assesment Idaho Nat. Engring. Lab., EG&G Idaho, Inc., Idaho Falls, 1988-90; dean Coll. Forest Resources, assoc. dir. Maine Agrl. Experiment Sta., prof. Forest Resources U. Maine, Orono, 1991-93, dean Coll. Natural Resources, Forestry & Agrl., dir. Maine Agrl. and Forest Experiment Sta., prof. Forest Resources, 1993—; dir. Ctr. Environ. Monitoring and Assessment, Idaho Falls, Idaho, 1980-90; mem. ad-hoc task force to plan global environ. monitoring sys., 1993-95; trustee Nature Conservancy, 1993-95; mem. UN ad hoc task force to plan global terrestrial observing sys., 1993-95; bd. dirs. Maine Forest Products Coun., 1993—; U.S. Nat. Com. on Data for Sci. and Tech., 1990-92, others. Contbr. chpts. to books, articles to profl. jours; editor, founder Jour. Environ. Monitoring and Assesment. Capt. U.S. Army, 1968-70. Recipient numerous rsch. grants from various orgns. Mem. NRC (chair com. on databases, 1990-94, com. on marine monitoring, 1986-90, Nat. Assn. Profl. Forestry Schs. (exec. com. 1993—), Assn. of Experiment Sta. Dirs. (exec. com. N.E. region 1996—). Avocations: jogging, swimming, cross country skiing, backpacking, mountain climbing. Home: 30 Wildwood Dr East Holden ME 04429-9708 Office: Univ of Maine/Coll Natural Scis Forestry and Agr 5782 Winslow Hall Orono ME 04469-5782

WIERZBICKI, JACEK GABRIEL, physicist, researcher; b. Lódz, Poland, Oct. 27, 1948; came to U.S., 1986; s. Gabriel Wiktor and Jadwiga Krystyna (Skarzynska) W.; m. Grazyna Maria Chawrona, Aug. 31, 1974; children: Grazyna, Przemystaw, Danuta, Kinga. MS in Physics, U. Lódz, 1971, MS in Math., 1973, PhD in Physics, 1981. Researcher U. Lódz, 1971-75; reseacher Joint Inst. for Nuclear Rsch., Dubna, USSR, 1975-79; med. physicist Oncological Ctr., Lódz, 1980-83; lectr. Fed. U. Tech., Bauchi, Nigeria, 1983-86; rsch. fellow Ohio U., Athens, 1986-88; asst. prof. U. Ky., Lexington, 1988-92; assoc. prof. Wayne State U., Detroit, 1993—; Russian translator Am. Inst. Physics, N.Y., 1987. Contbr. over 100 articles to sci. jours. Mem. Am. Phys. Soc., Am. Assn. Physicists in Medicine, Radiation Rsch. Soc., Sigma Xi. Roman Catholic. Achievements include rsch. in interactions of neutrons with light nuclei, in devel. of radium treatment in gynecology and radiation protection in the hospital, in interactions of 24 MeV neutrons with nuclei and optical model analysis, in use of Cf-252 in therapy of cancer, clinical radiobiology. Home: 3422 Shakespeare Dr Troy MI 48084-1489 Office: Wayne State U Radiation Oncology Ctr 3990 John R St Detroit MI 48201-2018

WIES, BARBARA, editor, publisher; b. Dec. 5, 1939; m. Norman W. Bassett. BA, U. Conn., 1961; student, New Sch. for Social Rsch., 1961-62. Product devel. Fearn Soya, Melrose Park, Ill., 1973-75; product devel. Modern Products, Milw., 1973-75; editor, pub. Bestways Mag., Carson City, Nev., 1977-89; pub. The Healthy Gourmet Newsletter, 1989-91, Fine Wine-Good Food Newsletter, 1991—; publicity dir. Nev. Artists Assn., 1994—; owner Gualala (Calif.) Galleries, 1989-90; owner, operator cooking sch. Greensboro N.C. 1969-73; instr. Very Spl. Arts Nev., 1997. Author: Natural Cooking, 1968, Wok and Tempura, 1969, Japanese Home Cooking, 1970, The Wok, 1971, Super Soy, 1973, The Health Gourmet, 1981, International Healthy Gourmet, 1982; one-woman show paintings Dolphin Gallery, Gualala, Calif., 1990, River Gallery, Reno, 1994; 2 women show 1992, 94, 96, Dolphin Gallery, Calif., 1994, solo exhbn. Nev. Artists Assn. Gallery, 1993, 95, 96, 97; featured artist Nev. State Libr., 1996, West Nev. C.C., 1996, art show judge, 1997; restaurant critic Reno Gazette Jour., 1995—. Recipient First Place adult fiction Nev. State Lit. Co., 1995. Mem. Nat. League Am. Pen Women (chair 1st ann. lit. competition Reno br., chairperson 1st Nat. Lit. award), Inst. Food Technologists, Pastel Soc. of the West Coast, Inst. Am. Culinary Profls.

WIESCHAUS, ERIC F., molecular biologist, educator; b. June 8, 1947. BS, U. Notre Dame, 1969; PhD in Biology, Yale U., 1974. Rsch. fellow Zool. Inst., U. Zurich, Switzerland, 1975-78; group leader European Molecular Biol. Lab., Germany, 1978-81; from asst. prof. to assoc. prof. Princeton (N.J.) U., 1981-87, prof. biology, 1987—; fellow Lab. de Genetique Moleculaire, France, 1976; vis. rschr. Ctr. Pathobiology, U. Calif., Irvine, 1977; mem. sci. adv. coun. Damon Runyon-Walter Winchell Cancer Fund, 1987-92. Contbr. articles to profl. jours. Recipient Nobel Prize in Medicine, 1995. Fellow Am. Acad. Arts and Scis.; mem. NAS. Office: Princeton U Dept Molecular Biology Princeton NJ 08544*

WIESCHENBERG, KLAUS, chemical company executive; b. Hannover, Germany, Mar. 2, 1932; came to U.S., 1959; s. Heinz and Ruth (Wilke) W.; Abitur, Hermann Billung Gymnasium, Celle, Ger., 1951; BA, Fairleigh Dickinson U., Madison, N.J., 1974, MBA, 1977; m. Nona Bodareva, June 7, 1958; children: Michael, Axel, Natasha. Export/import corr. Deutsche Bank, Hannover, 1953; export corr. Hoechst AG, Frankfurt, Germany, 1954-55; various mktg. positions Am. Hoechst Corp., 1956-68, various fin. positions, 1969-78; v.p. planning corp. div., Somerville, N.J., 1978-85; v.p. Office of Pres. and Corp. Devel., 1985-87; v.p. corp. devel. Hoechst Celanese Corp., 1987-95; strategic mgmt. concepts, principle, 1995—; mem. conf. bd. coun. planning execs., 1990-95. Mem. editorial bd. Bus. 2000, 1990-91. Mem. Comml. Devel. Assn. (chmn. membership com. 1984-86), Am. Mgmt. Assn., Planning Forum (internat. bd. dirs. 1990—, exec. com. 1991-92, chmn. internat. com. 1990-95, chmn. res. & edn. found. 1995—, v.p. N.Y. met. chpt. 1986-91), Somerset County C. of C. (bd. dirs. 1990-96). Republican. Eastern Orthodox. Home: 494 Steele Gap Rd Bridgewater NJ 08807-2339

WIESE, DOROTHY JEAN, business educator; b. Chgo., Sept. 20, 1940; d. Charles Ennis Chapman and Evelyn Catherine Flizikowski; m. Wallace Jon Wiese, Oct. 10, 1959; children: Elizabeth Jean Wiese Christensen, Jonathan Charles. BS in Edn., No. Ill. U., 1970, MS in Edn., 1976, EdD, 1994. Tchr. bus. Hampshire (Ill.) High Sch., 1970-78; prof. bus. Elgin (Ill.) C.C., 1978—; cons. Gould, Inc., Rolling Meadows, Ill., 1984; instr. vocat. practicum McDonald's Hamburger U., Ofcl. Airline Guides, Oak Brook, Ill., 1986; spkr. SIEC, Sweden and Austria, 1987-88, Czech Republic, 1995, North Ctrl. Bus. Edn. Assn./Wis. Bus. Edn. Assn. Conv., 1992, Chgo. Area Bus. Edn. Assn., 1992, AAUW, Batavia and Geneva, 1993, Elgin, 1996; 1995 Internat. Bus. Inst. for Cmty. Coll. faculty Mich. State U., 1995. Presented paper 34th annual Adult Edn. Rsch. Conf., Pa. State U., 1993. Mem., sec. N.W. Kane County (Ill.) Airport Authority, 1987-94; bd. dirs. St. Joseph Hosp. Found., 1995—, mem. adv. bd. Cancer Wellness and Resource Ctr., 1995—; host family Am. Intercultural Student Exch., 1989-90; presenter women's seminar Trinity Luth. Ch., Roselle, Ill., 1992; mem. Leadership Ill., 1996. Mem. AAUW, Am. Women of Internat. Understanding (bd. dirs.), Nat. Bus. Edn. Assn. (internat. task force), Internat. Soc. Bus. Edn. (North Ctrl. Bus. Edn. Assn. rep. 1989-90, rep.-elect 1996), Societe Internat. pour l'Enseignment Commercial, Ill. Bus. Edn. Assn., Ill. Vocat. Assn., Women in Mgmt. (spkr., co-chair membership No. Fox Valley chpt. 1996-97), Delta Pi Epsilon (past historian Alpha Phi chpt.), Kappa Delta Pi. Lutheran. Office: Elgin CC 1700 Spartan Dr Elgin IL 60123-7189

WIESE, JOHN PAUL, federal judge; b. Bklyn., Apr. 19, 1934; s. Gustav and Margaret W.; m. Alice Mary Donoghue, June 1961; 1 child, John Patrick. BA cum laude, Hobart College, Geneva, NY, 1962; LLB, U. of Va., Charlottesville, 1965. With Cox, Langford & Brown, Washington, DC, 1967-1969, Hodson & Creyke, 1969-74; trial commr. U.S. Claims Court, Washington, DC, 1974-1986, judge, 1986—. Mem. Phi Beta Kappa. Office: US Ct of Federal Claims 717 Madison Pl NW Washington DC 20005-1011*

WIESE, NEVA, critical care nurse; b. Hunter, Kans., July 23, 1940; d. Amil H. and Minnie (Zemke) W. Diploma, Grace Hosp. Sch. Nursing, Hutchinson, Kans., 1962; BA in Social Sci., U. Denver, 1971; BSN, Met. State Coll., 1975; MS in Nursing, U. Colo., Denvr, 1978; postgrad., U. N.Mex., 1986—. RN, N.Mex.; CCRN. Cardiac ICU nurse U. N.Mex. Hosp., Albuquerque; coord. critical care edn. St. Vincent Hosp., Santa Fe, charge nurse CCU, clin. nurse III intensive and cardiac care. Recipient Mary Atherton Meml. award for clin. excellence St. Vincent Hosp., 1986. Mem. ANA (cert. med. surg. nurse), AACN (past pres., sec. N.Mex. chpt., Clin. Excellence award 1991), N.Mex. League Nursing (past v.p., bd. dirs., sec., membership com. 1992-97).

WIESE, WOLFGANG LOTHAR, physicist; b. Tilsit, Fed. Republic Germany, Apr. 21, 1931; came to U.S., 1957; naturalized, 1965; s. Werner Max and Charlotte (Donath) W.; m. Gesa Ladehoff, Oct. 12, 1957; children: Margrit, Cosima. BS, U. Kiel, Fed. Republic Germany, 1954, PhD, 1957, PhD (hon.), 1993. Rsch. assoc. U. Md., College Park, 1958-59; rsch. physicist Nat. Bur. Standards, Gaithersburg, Md., 1960-62; chief plasma spectrosc. sect. Nat. Bur. Standards, Gaithersburg, 1962-77, chief atomic and plasma radiation div., 1978-91, chief atomic physics div., 1991—; lectr. U. Calif., 1963, 64. Author: Atomic Transition Probabilities, Vol. I., 1966, Vol. II, 1969, Vol. III, 1988, Vol. IV, 1988, Atomic Transition Probabilities for C, N, and O, 1996. Recipient Silver Medal award Dept. Commerce, 1962, Gold Medal award, 1971, Humboldt award, 1986, A.S. Fleming award U.S. C. of C., 1971, Disting. Career in Sci. award Wash. Acad. Sci., 1992; Guggenheim fellow, 1966. Fellow Am. Phys. Soc., Optical Soc. Am., Wash. Acad. Sci.; mem. Internat. Astron. Union, Sigma Xi. Lutheran. Home: 8229 Stone Trail Dr Bethesda MD 20817-4555 Office: Nat Inst Standards and Tech Gaithersburg MD 20899

WIESEL, ELIE, writer, educator; b. Sighet, Romania, Sept. 30, 1928; arrived in Paris, 1945; came to U.S., 1956, naturalized, 1963; s. Shlomo and Sarah (Feig) W.; m. Marion Erster, 1969; 1 child, Shlomo Elisha. Student, The Sorbonne, Paris, 1948-51; LittD (hon.), Jewish Theol. Sem., N.Y.C., 1967, Marquette U., 1975, Simmons Coll., 1976, Anna Maria Coll., 1980, Yale U., 1981, Wake Forest U., 1985, Haverford Coll., 1985, Capital U., 1986, L.I. U., 1986, U. Paris, 1987, U. Conn., 1988, U. Cen. Fla., 1988, Wittenberg U., 1989, Wheeling Jesuit Coll., 1989, Fairleigh Dickinson U., 1993; LHD (hon.), Hebrew Union Coll., 1968, Manhattanville Coll., 1972, Yeshiva U., 1973, Boston U., 1974, Coll. of St. Scholastica, 1978, Wesleyan U., 1979, Brandeis U., 1980, Kenyon Coll., 1982, Hobart/William Smith Coll., 1982, Emory U., 1983, Fla. Internat. U., 1983, Siena Heights Coll., 1983, Fairfield U., 1983, Dropsie Coll., 1983, Moravian Coll., 1983, Colgate U., 1984, SUNY, Binghamton, 1985, Lehigh U., 1985, Coll. of New Rochelle, 1986, Tufts U., 1986, Georgetown U., 1986, Hamilton Coll., 1986, Rockford Coll., 1986, Villanova U., 1987, Coll. of St. Thomas, 1987, U. Denver, 1987, Walsh Coll., 1987, Loyola Coll., 1987, Ohio U., 1988, Concordia Coll., 1990, N.Y.U., 1990, Fordham U., 1990, Conn. Coll., 1990, Upsala Coll., 1991, Duquesne U., 1991, Roosevelt U., 1991; PhD (hon.), Bar-Ilan U., 1973, U. Haifa, 1986, Ben Gurion U., 1988; LLD (hon.), Hofstra U., 1975, Talmudic U. Fla., 1979, U. Notre Dame, 1980, La Salle U., 1988, Bates Coll., 1995; HHD (hon.), U. Hartford, 1985, Lycoming Coll., 1987, U. Miami, 1988, Brigham Young U., 1989; D of Hebrew Letters, Spertus Coll. Judaica, 1973; DSc (hon.), U. Health Scis./Chgo. Med. Sch., 1989; ThD, U. Åbo Akadem, 1990; LHD (hon.), Hunter Coll., 1992, Susquehanna U., 1992, Am. U., 1992, Millersville U., 1993; hon. degree, U. Dayton, 1993, U. Mich., 1993; LHD (hon.), U. Bordeaux, 1993, Gustavus Adolphus Coll., 1994, McGill U., 1994, Mt. Sinai Med. Sch., 1994, Spelman Coll., 1995. Disting. prof. Judaic studies CCNY, 1972-76; prof. religious studies and univ. prof. Boston U., 1976—, prof. philosophy, 1988—; Disting. vis. prof. Henry Luce, 1982-83, Eckerd Coll., 1994; chmn. U.S. Pres.'s Commn. on the Holocaust, 1979-80, U.S. Holocaust Meml. Coun., 1980-86; founder Elie Wiesel Found. for Humanity, 1987; founding pres. Paris-based Universal Acad. Cultures; hon. chmn. Nat. Jewish Resource Ctr., N.Y.C. Holocaust Meml. Commn., Am. Friends of Ghetto Fighter's House; hon. pres. Am. Gathering of Jewish Holocaust Survivors; bd. dirs. Nat. Com. on Am. Fgn. Policy, 1983—, Elaine Kaufman Cultural Ctr., adv. bd. The Raoul Wallenberg Commn. of U.S., 1981—, Humanitas, Am. Assocs. Ben-Gurion U. of the Negev, Mut. of Am., France Libertés; v.p. Internat. Rescue Com., 1985—; bd. trustees Annenberg Rsch. Inst., 1983-89, Am. Jour. World Svc., 1985—; Haifa U., Tel-Aviv U.; bd. trustees Yeshiva U., 1977—; colleague Cathedral St. John the Divine, 1975—; mem. adv. bd. Boston U. Inst. for Philosophy & Religion, Nat. Inst. Against Prejudice & Violence, Internat. Ctr. in N.Y., Friends of Akim USA, Friends of LeChambon; mem. jury Neustadt Internat. Prize Lit., 1984; lectr. Andrew W. Mellon Ann. Lecture Series Boston U., 92d St. YMHA, YWHA Ann. Lectr. Series, ann. radio broadcast series Eternal Light for Jewish Theol. Sem. Am., advisory bd. Rena Costa Ctr. for Yiddish Studies at Bar-Ilan U., 1994, advisory Coun. Carnegie Commn. on Preventing Deadly Conflict, 1994. Author: Night, 1960, Dawn, 1961, The Accident, 1962, The Town Beyond the Wall, 1964, The Gates of the Forest, 1966, The Jews of Silence, 1966, Legends of Our Time, 1968, A Beggar in Jerusalem, 1970, One Generation After, 1970, Souls on Fire, 1972, The Oath, 1973, Ani Maamin, 1973, Zalmen, or the Madness of God, 1974, Messengers of God, 1976, A Jew Today, 1978, Four Hasidic Masters, 1978, The Trial of God, 1979, The Testament, 1980, Le Testament D'Un Poète Juif Assassiné (France's Prix Livre-Inter 1980, Bourse Goncourt, 1980, Prix des Bibliothécaires, 1981), 1985, Images from the Bible, 1980, Five Biblical Portraits, 1981, Somewhere A Master, 1982, Paroles d'Étranger, 1982, The Golem, 1983, The Fifth Son (Grand Prix de la Littérature, City of Paris), 1985, Signes d'Exode, 1985, Against Silence (3 vols., ed. Irving Abrahamson), 1985, Job ou Dieu dans la Tempête, 1986, A Song for Hope, 1987, The Nobel Address, 1987, Twilight, 1988; (essays) Silences et Mémoire d'hommes, 1989, L'Oublié, 1989, From the Kingdom of Memory, 1990, Célébration Talmudique, 1991, Sages and Dreamers, 1991, The Forgotten, 1992, (with John Cardinal O'Connor) A Journey of Faith, 1990, (with Albert Friedlander) The Six Days of Destruction, 1988, (dialogues with Philippe-Michaël Saint-Cheron) Evil and Exile, 1990; commentaries to A Passover Haggadah, 1993, All Rivers Run To The Sea (a memoir), 1994; editorial and adv. bds. Midstream, Religion and Lit. (U. Notre Dame), Sh'ma: Jour. of Responsibility, Hadassah Mag., Acad. of the Air for Jewish Studies, Holocaust and Genocide Studies: An Internat. Jour.; subject of 29 books; journalist Israeli, French and Am. newspapers. Chmn. adv. bd. World Union Jewish Students, 1985—; comité d'Honneur Ligue International Contre le Racisme et l'Antisemitisme, 1985—; founder Nat. Jewish Ctr. Learning and Leadership, 1974; mem. soc. fellows Ctr. Judaic Studies, U. Denver, 1980, bd. overseer Bar-Ilan U., 1970—. Recipient Prix Rivarol, 1963, Prix de l'Universite de la langue Francaise, 1963, Ingram Merrill award, 1964, Jewish Heritage award, Haifa U., 1975, Remembrance award, 1965, Prix du Souvenir, 1965, Nat. Jewish Book Council award, 1965, 73, Prix Médicis, 1968, Prix Bordin French Acad., 1972, Eleanor Roosevelt Meml. award, N.Y. United Jewish Appeal, 1972, Am. Liberties medallion Am. Jewish Com., 1972, Martin Luther King Jr. medallion, CCNY, 1973, Annual award for Disting. Service to Am. Jewry, Nat. Fedn. of Jewish Men's Clubs, 1973, Faculty Disting. Scholar award Hofstra U., 1974, Rambam award Am. Mizrachi Women, 1974, Meml. award N.Y. Soc. Clin. Psychologists, 1975, First Spertus Internat. award, 1976, Myrtle Wreath award Hadassah, 1977, King Solomon award, 1977, Liberty award HIAS, 1977, Jewish Heritage award, B'nai B'rith, 1966, Avodah award, Jewish Tchrs. Assn., 1972, Humanitarian award, B'rith Sholom, 1978, Joseph Prize for Human Rights, Anti-Defamation League, 1978, Zalman Shazar award State of Israel, 1979, Presdl. Citation, NYU, 1979, Inaugural award for Lit., Israel Bonds Prime Minister's Com., 1979, Jabotinsky medal, State of Israel, 1980, Rabbanit Sarah Herzog award Emunah Women of Am., 1981, Le Grand Prix Littéraire du Festival Internat. Deauville, 1983, Internat. Lit. prize for Peace, Royal Acad. Belgium, 1983, Lit. Lions award N.Y. Pub. Library, 1983, Jordan Davidson Humanitarian award Fla. Internat. U., 1983, Anatoly Scharansky Humanitarian award, 1983, Grand Officer, Legion of Honor, France, Congressional gold medal, 1985, Voice of Conscience award Am. Jewish Congress, 1985, Remembrance award, Israel Bonds, 1985, Anne Frank award, 1985, 4 Freedoms award FDR 4 Freedoms Found., 1985, Medal of Liberty award Statue of Liberty Presentation, 1986, Nobel Peace Prize, 1986, First Herzl Lit. award, First David Ben-Gurion award, Nat. UJA, Gov.'s award, Shaarei Tzedek, Internat. Kaplun Found. award Hebrew U. Jerusalem, Scopus award, 1974, Am.-Israeli Friendship award, Disting. Writers award Lincolnwood Library, 1984, First Chancellor Joseph H. Lookstein award Bar-Ilan U., 1984, Sam Levenson Meml. award Jewish Community Relations Council, 1985, Comenius award Moravian Coll., 1985, Henrietta Szold award Hadassah, 1985, Disting. Community Service award Mut. Am., 1985, Covenant Peace award Synagogue Council Am., 1985, Jacob Pat award World Congress Jewish Culture, 1985, Humanitarian award Internat. League Human Rights, 1985, Disting. Foreign-Born Am. award Internat. Ctr. N.Y., Inc., 1986, Freedom Cup award Women's League Israel, 1986, First Jacob Javits Humanitarian award UJA Young Leadership, 1986, Boston City Coun. Commendation, 1986, medal of Jerusalem, 1986, Freedom award Internat. Rescue Com., 1987, Achievement award Artist and Writers for Peace in the Middle East, 1987, La Grande Médaille de Vermeil de la Ville de Paris, 1987, La Médaille de la Chancellerie de l'Université de Paris, 1987, La Médaille de l'Université de Paris, 1987, First Eitinger Prize, U. Oslo, 1987, Lifetime Achievment award Present Tense mag., 1987, Spl. Christopher award The Christophers, 1987, Achievement award State Israel, 1987, Sem. medal Jewish Theol. Sem. Am., 1987, Metcalf Cup and Prize for Excellence in Teaching, Boston U., 1987, Spl. award Nat. Com. on Am. Fgn. Policy, 1987, Grã-Cruz da Ordem Nacional do Cruzeiro do Sul, Brazil's highest distinction, 1987, Profiles of Courage award B'nai B'rith, 1987, Centennial medal U. Scranton, 1987, Citation from Religious Edn. Assn., 1987, Golda Meir Sr. Humanitarian award, 1987, Presdl. medal Hofstra U., 1988, Human Rights Law award Internat. Human Rights Law Group, 1988, Bicentennial medal Georgetown U., 1988, Janus Korczak Humanitarian award NAHE, Kent State U., 1989, Count Sforza award in Philanthropy Interphil, 1989, Lily Edelman award for Excellence in Continuing Jewish Edn. B'nai B'rith Internat., 1989, George Washington award Am. Hungarian Found., 1989, Bicentennial medal N.Y.U., 1989, Humanitarian award Human Rights Campaign Fund, 1989, Internat. Brotherhood award C.O.R.E., 1990, Frank Weil award for Disting. Contbn. to Adv. of N.Am. Jewish Culture Jewish Community Ctrs. Assn. N.Am., 1990, 1st Raoul Wallenberg medal U. Mich., 1990, Award of Highest Honor Soka U., 1991, Facing History and Ourselves Humanity award, 1991, La Medaille de la Ville de Toulouse, 1991, 5th Centennial Christopher Columbus medal City of Genoa, 1992, 1st Primo Levi award, 1992, Lit. Arts award Nat. Found. for Jewish Culture, 1992, Ellis Island Medal of Honor, 1992, Guardian of the Children award AKIM USA, 1992, Bishop Francis J. Mugavero award for religious and racial harmony Cath. Newman Ctr. Queens Coll., 1994, Golden Slipper Humanitarian award, 1994, Interfaith Coun. on the Holocaust Humanitarian award, 1994, Crystal award Davos World Economic Forum, 1995, First Niebuhr award, Elmhurst Coll., 1995; named Humanitarian of the Century Coun. Jewish Orgns., Presdl. medal Freedom, 1992; Beth Hatefutsoth hon. fellow, 1988; honors established in his name: Elie Wiesel award for Holocaust Rsch., U. Haifa, Elie Wiesel Chair in Holocaust Studies, Bar-Ilan U., Elie Wiesel Endowment Fund for Jewish Culture, U. Denver, 1987, Elie Wiesel Disting. Svc. award, U. Fla., 1988, Elie Wiesel awards for Jewish Arts and Culture B'nai B'rith Hillel Founds., 1988, Elie Wiesel Chair in Judaic Studies Conn. Coll., 1990. Fellow Jewish Acad. Arts and Scis., Am. Acad. Arts & Scis., Timothy Dwight Coll., Yale U.; mem. Fgn. Press Assn. (hon. life), Amnesty Internat., PEN, Writers & Artists for Peace in Middle East, Writers Guild of Am. East, The Author's Guild, Royal Norwegian Soc. Scis. and Letters, Soc. des auteurs Paris, European Acad. of Arts, Sci. and Humanities, 1992; Phi Beta Kappa. Office: Boston U Univ Profs Program 745 Commonwealth Ave Boston MA 02215-1401

WIESEL, TORSTEN NILS, neurobiologist, educator; b. Upsala, Sweden, June 3, 1924; came to U.S., 1955; s. Fritz Samuel and Anna-Lisa Elisabet (Bentzer) W.; 1 dau., Sara Elisabet. MD, Karolinska Inst., Stockholm, 1954; D Medicine (hon.), Karolinska Inst, Stockholm, 1989; AM (hon.), Harvard U., 1967; ScD (hon.), NYU, 1987, U. Bergen, 1987. Instr. physiology Karolinska Inst., 1954-55; asst. dept. child psychiatry Karolinska Hosp., 1954-55; fellow in ophthalmology Johns Hopkins U., 1955-58, asst. prof. ophthalmic physiology, 1958-59; assoc. in neurophysiology and neuropharmacology Harvard U. Med. Sch., Boston, 1959-60; asst. prof. neurophysiology and neuropharmacology Harvard U. Med. Sch., 1960-64, asst. prof. neurophysiology, dept. psychiatry, 1964-67, prof. physiology, 1967-68, prof. neurobiology, 1968-74, Robert Winthrop prof. neurobiology, 1974-83, chmn. dept. neurobiology, 1973-82; Vincent and Brooke Astor prof. neurobiology, head lab. Rockefeller U., N.Y.C., 1983—, pres., 1992—; Ferrier lectr. Royal Soc. London, 1972; NIH lectr., 1975; Grass lectr. Soc. Neurosci., 1976; lectr. Coll. de France, 1977; Hitchcock prof. U. Calif.-Berkeley, 1980; Sharpey-Schafer lectr. Phys. Soc. London; George Cotzias lectr. Am. Acad. Neurology, 1983. Contbr. numerous articles to profl. jours. Recipient Jules Stein award Trustees for Prevention of Blindness, 1971, Lewis S. Rosenstiel prize Brandeis U., 1972, Friedenwald award Assn. Rsch. in Vision and Ophthalmology, 1975, Karl Spencer Lashley prize Am. Philos. Soc., 1977, Louisa Gross Horwitz prize Columbia U., 1978, Dickson prize U. Pitts., 1979, Nobel prize in physiology and medicine, 1981, W.H. Helmerich III award 1989. Mem. Am. Physiol. Soc., Am. Philos. Soc., AAAS, Am. Acad. Arts and Scis., Nat. Acad. Arts and Scis., Swedish Physiol. Soc., Soc. Neurosci. (pres. 1978-79), Royal Soc. (fgn. mem.), Physiol. Soc. (Eng.) (hon. mem.). Office: Rockefeller U Office Pres 1230 York Ave New York NY 10021-6307*

WIESEN, DONALD GUY, retired diversified manufacturing company executive; b. N.Y.C., July 4, 1928; s. Benjamin and Grace (Heath) W.; m. Patricia Ann Elfers, Apr. 29, 1950; children: Mara, Caitlin, Elizabeth, Anne, Megan. B.S., Columbia U., 1948, M.S., 1954. C.P.A., N.Y. Sr. tax specialist Price Waterhouse & Co., N.Y.C., 1950-58; with Chesebrough-Pond's Inc., Greenwich, Conn., 1958-87; gen. mgr. ops. Europe Chesebrough-Pond's Inc., 1965-70, treas., 1970-72, group v.p., chief fin. officer, 1972-77, group v.p., internat., 1977-82, sr. group v.p., 1982-84, vice chmn., chief fin. officer, 1984-87, also dir., ret., 1987; bd. dirs. Skandia Am. Corp., 1985-91. Trustee Greenwich Libr., 1974-80; bd. govs. St. Bernard Coll., Cullman, Ala., 1973-75; rep. Columbia U. Alumni, Geneva, 1968; bd. dirs. Inner-City Found. for Charity and Edn., Bridgeport, Conn., 1992-93. Capt. USMC, 1951-54. Mem. AICPA, Indian Harbor Yacht Club, Univ. Club (N.Y.). Roman Catholic.

WIESENBERG, JACQUELINE LEONARDI, medical lecturer; b. West Haven, Conn., May 4, 1928; d. Curzio and Filomena Olga (Turrinziani) Leonardi; m. Russel John Wiesenberg, Nov. 23; children: James Wynne, Deborann Donna. BA, SUNY, Buffalo, 1970, postgrad., 1970-73, 80—. Interviewer, examiner U.S. Dept. Labor, New Haven, 1948-52; sec. W.I. Clark Co., Hamden, Conn., 1952-55; acct. VA Hosp., West Haven, 1956-60; acct.-commissary U.S. Air Force Missle Site, Niagara Falls, N.Y., 1961-62; tchr. Buffalo City Schs., 1970-73, 79; acct. Erie County Social Svcs., Buffalo, 1971-73; lectr., 1973—. Contbr. articles to CAP, U.S. Air Force mag., 1954—. Capt., Nat. Found. March of Dimes, 1969—, com. mem. telethon, 1983-86; den mother Boy Scouts Am., 1961-68; chmn. Meals on Wheels, Town of Amherst, 1975-76; leader, travel chmn. Girl Scouts Am., 1968-77; mem. Nat. Congress Parents and Tchrs., 1957—; heart fund vol. Heart Assn., 1960-86; rep. Am. Diabetes Assn., 1994—, vol. Diabetes collection, 1994-95. Mem. AAUW, NAFE, Internat. Platform Assn., Nat. Parks and Conservation Assn., Am. Astrol. Assn., Nat. Arbor Day Found., Western N.Y. Conf. Aging, Nat. Geographic Soc., The Wilderness Soc., Nat. Trust for Hist. Preservation, The Nature Conservancy, Epsilon Delta Chi, Alpha Iota. Home: 14 Norman Pl Amherst NY 14226-4233

WIESENBERG, RUSSEL JOHN, statistician; b. Kaukauna, Wis., Apr. 9, 1924; s. Emil Martin and Josephine (Appelbaker) W.; m. Jacqueline Leonardi, Nov. 23; children: James Wynne, Deborann Donna. BS, U. Wis., 1951; postgrad. Cornell U., 1960-61, U. Mich., 1969, George Washington U., 1976. Analyst, Gen. Electric Co., West Lynn, Mass., 1951-56; specialist Internat. Gen. Electric Co., Rio de Janeiro, Brazil, 1956-59; statistician Gen. Motors Corp., Lockport, N.Y., 1959-65, sr. statistician, Harrison Radiator div., 1965-78, sr. reliability engr., 1978-82, sr. reliability statistician, 1982-87. Auditor, Community Chest Fund, 1952-55; umpire Little League Baseball, 1962-65; committeeman Buffalo Area council Boy Scouts Am., 1962—, Cub Scout committeeman, 1962-64, Webelos cubmaster, 1963-64; mem. Nat. Congress Parents and Tchrs., 1963—; heart fund Vol. Heart Assn., 1968; tournament dir. Am. Legion Baseball, 1975; vol. United Way campaign, 1983, nat. telethon March of Dimes, 1983-84. Served with AUS, 1943-46. Decorated Bronze Star. Mem. AAAS, Am. Statis. Assn., Nat. Register Sci. and Tech. Pers., U. Wis. Alumni Assn., Artus, Internat. Platform Assn., Phi Kappa Phi. Lutheran. com.). Contbr. articles to profl. jours. Home: 14 Norman Pl Buffalo NY 14226-4233

WIESENECK, ROBERT L., business executive; b. 1938. Graduate, Roosevelt U., 1958; MBA, U. Chgo., 1963. Pres., CEO SPS Transaction Svc. Inc., 1997—. Office: SPS Payment Systems Inc 2500 Lake Cook Rd Riverwoods IL 60015-3851

WIESENFELD, JOHN RICHARD, chemistry educator; b. N.Y.C., July 26, 1944; s. Walter and Trude (Rosenberg) W. Stokes fellow, Pembroke Coll., Cambridge, Eng., 1971-72; BS with honors, CCNY, 1965; PhD, Case Inst. Tech., Cleve., 1969; MA, U. Cambridge, Eng., 1970. Asst. prof. Cornell U., Ithaca, N.Y., 1972-77, assoc. prof., 1978-84, prof., 1984-95, chair dept. chemistry, 1985-88, dep. v.p. for rsch., 1988-90, v.p. for plan, 1990-94; v.p. academic programs and planning, 1994-95; dean of sci. Fla. Atlantic U., Boca Raton, 1995—; vis. scholar Stanford U. Calif., 1978-79, U. Wash., 1988; cons. E.I. DuPont, Wilmington, Del., 1975, Phys. Dynamics, La Jolla, Calif., 1980-82, U.S. Dept. Energy, Pitts., 1982, NIH, 1994; bd. dirs. Associated Univs., 1989-92. Contbr. more than 100 sci. articles to profl. jours. Sloan Found. research fellow, 1975; recipient Tchr.-Scholar award, Dreyfus Found., 1975. Fellow AAAS; mem. Am. Chem. Soc., Coun. Chem. Rsch. (governing bd. 1987-90). Home: 3011 Jasmine Ct Delray Beach FL 33483 Office: Fla Atlantic U PO Box 3091 Boca Raton FL 33431

WIESENFELD, KURT ARN, physicist, educator; b. Roslyn Heights, N.Y., Feb. 12, 1958; s. David and Elaine Kaye (Dattner) W.; m. Karla Mari Jennings, Aug. 17, 1985. BS in Physics, MIT, 1979; MA in Physics, U. Calif., Berkeley, 1982, PhD in Physics, 1985. Lectr., rschr. physics U. Calif., Santa Cruz, 1984-85; rschr. Brookhaven Nat. Lab., Upton, N.Y., 1985-87; asst. prof. Ga. Inst. Tech., Atlanta, 1987-92, assoc. prof., 1992-97, prof., 1997—. Contbr. over 80 articles to sci. jours. Office: Ga Inst Tech Sch Physics State St Atlanta GA 30332

WIESER, SIEGFRIED, planetarium executive director; b. Linz, Austria, Oct. 30, 1933; came to Can., 1955; s. Florian Wieser and Michaela Josepha (Kaufmann) Wieser-Burgstaller; m. Joan Xaven Quick, Sept. 8, 1962; children: Leonard Franz, Bernard Sidney. BS in Physics, U. Calgary, Alta., Can., 1966. Lead chorus singer, dancer Landes Theatre, Linz, 1949-53; project engr. EBG, Linz, 1952-54; with Griffith Farms Ltd., Eng., 1954-55; seismic computer operator Shell Can., Calgary, 1956-61; GTA systems analyst U. Calgary, 1961-66; planetarium dir. Centennial Planetarium, Calgary, 1966-84, exec. dir., 1984-91; exec. dir. emeritus Alberta Sci. Ctr., 1991—; cons. Electro Controls, Salt Lake City, 1978-79. Contbr. articles to profl. publs. Recipient Violet Taylor award U. Calgary, 1964; Queen Elizabeth scholar Province Alta., 1961; Paul Harris fellow Rotary Internat. Mem. Calgary Region Arts Found., Alberta Coll. of Art Alumni Assn. (pres. 1991-92). Anglican. Club: Magic Circle (Calgary). Avocations: swimming, hiking, astronomy, lecturing.

WIESLER, JAMES BALLARD, retired banker; b. San Diego, July 25, 1927; s. Harry J. and Della B. (Ballard) W.; m. Mary Jane Hall, Oct. 3, 1953; children: Tom, Ann, Larry. B.S., U. Colo., 1949; postgrad., Stonier Sch. Banking, Rutgers U., 1962, Advanced Mgmt. Program, Harvard U., 1973. With Bank of Am., NT & SA, 1949-87; v.p., mgr. main office San Jose, Calif., 1964-69, regional v.p. Cen. Coast adminstrn., 1969-74; sr. v.p., head No. European Area office Frankfurt, Fed. Republic of Germany, 1974-78; exec. v.p., head Asia div. Tokyo, 1978-81; exec. v.p., head N.Am. div. Los Angeles, 1981-82; vice chmn., head retail banking San Francisco, 1982-87; ret., 1987; bd. dirs. Visa USA, Visa Internat., Sci. Applications Internat. Corp.; bd. dirs., chmn. Bank Adminstrn. Inst., 1986-87. Pres. Santa Clara County United Fund, 1969, 70, San Jose C. of C., 1968; fin. chmn. Santa Clara County Reps., 1967-74; bd. dirs. San Diego Armed Svcs., YMCA, Sidney Kimmell Cancer Ctr.; trustee Sharp Hosp.; hon. consul-gen. for Japan, 1990-95. With USN, 1945-46. Mem. San Diego Zool. Soc., Bohemian Club, DeAnza Country Club, San Diego Country Club, San Diego Yacht Club. Presbyterian. Home: 605 San Fernando St San Diego CA 92106-3312 Office: Bank Am Nat Trust & Savs 450 B St San Diego CA 92101-8001

WIESNER, DAVID, illustrator, children's writer. Author, illustrator: Free Fall, 1988, Hurricane, 1990, Tuesday, 1991 (Caldecott medal 1992), June 29, 1999, 1992; illustrator: Kite Flier, 1986, The Sorcerer's Apprentice, 1989, The Rainbow People, 1989, Tongues of Jade, 1991, Man From the Sky, 1992, Night of the Gargoyles, 1994. Office: care Houghton Mifflin 222 Berkeley St Boston MA 02116-3748

WIESNER, JOHN JOSEPH, retail chain store executive; b. Kansas City, Mo., Mar. 31, 1938; s. Vincent A. and Jane Ann (Hagerty) W.; m. Georgiana Schild, Oct. 15, 1960; children: Susan, John V., Gretchen. BS in Bus. Adminstrn., Rockhurst Coll., 1960. Vice pres., contr. Fisher Foods, Cleve., 1970-77; asst. corp. contr. Richardson Vicks, N.Y.C., 1960-70; sr. exec. v.p. Pamida, Inc., Omaha, 1977-85, vice chmn., chief exec. officer, 1985-87; CEO C.R. Anthony Co., Oklahoma City, 1987—. Bd. dirs. Omaha Girls' Club, 1983—, Omaha Area Council on Alcohol and Drug Abuse, 1983—; bd. dirs. Fontenelle Forest, Omaha, chmn., 1983, 84, A Chance to Change Fedn.; mem. bd. regents Rockhurst Coll., Okla. City Golf & Country Club, Beacon Club, Oklahoma City, Kansas City, Mo. Named Bus. Assoc. of Yr., Am. Bus. Women's Assn., 1983. Mem. Nat. Assn. Accts. Republican. Roman Catholic.

WIESSLER, DAVID ALBERT, correspondent; b. Cambridge, Mass., July 20, 1942; s. Albert Francis and Vivian Mary (Thomas) W.; m. Mary Judith Burton, Dec. 28, 1968. AB, Princeton U., 1964; MA, U. Tex., 1968. Editor UPI, Dallas, N.Y.C., Washington, 1966-82; assoc. editor U.S. News & World Report, Washington, 1982-84; Washington Bur. chief UPI, Washington, 1984-90, sr. polit. editor, 1990-93; news editor Bloomberg News Svc., 1994-95; editor nat. news Reuters, Washington, 1995—. Recipient Best Feature Writer award Dallas Press Club, 1970. Mem. Washington Gridiron Club. Avocations: reading, travel, cooking.

WIEST, WILLIAM MARVIN, education educator, psychologist; b. Loveland, Colo., May 8, 1933; s. William Walter and Katherine Elizabeth (Buxman) W.; m. Thelma Lee Bartel, Aug. 18, 1955; children: William Albert, Suzanne Kay, Cynthia May. BA in Psychology summa cum laude, Tabor Coll., 1955; MA, U. Kans., 1957; PhD, U. Calif., Berkeley, 1962. Rsch. asst. psychol. ecology U. Kans., 1955-57; rsch. asst. measurement cooperative behavior in dyads U. Calif., Berkeley, 1958-59; from asst. to assoc. prof. Reed Coll., Portland, Oreg., 1961-74, prof., 1974-95, prof. emeritus, 1995—; adj. investigator Ctr. Health Rsch., Portland, 1985—; project coord. WHO, Geneva, 1976-84; fgn. travel leader Assiniboine Travel, Winnipeg, Man., Can., 1990-91, Willamette Internat. Travel, Portland, 1993-95; lectr. Fgn. Travel Club, Portland, 1990, 94; vis. scientist Oceanic Inst., Waimanalo, Hawaii, 1967-68; chmn. dept. psychology Reed Coll., Portland, 1973-75, 86; social sci. adv. com. Population Resource Ctr., N.Y.C., 1978—; vis. investigator Health Svcs. Rsch. Ctr., Portland, 1975-76, cons. 1976-80; com. protection human subjects Kaiser Permanente Med. Care Program, Portland, 1978-81; cons. WHO, 1980-81, U.S. Dept. Energy, 1980-83; mem. panel population study sect. HHS. Consulting editor Population and Environment, 1981—; jour. referee Health Psychology, Jour. Social Biology, Jour. Personality and Social Psychology, Memory and Cognition; contbr. articles to profl. jours. Sloan Found. Faculty Rsch. fellow, 1972-73, NSF fellow, 1975-76, USPSH fellow U. Calif., 1957-58, Woodrow Wilson Found. fellow U. Calif., 1960-61. Mem. AAAS, APHA, Am. Hist. Soc. Germans from Russia (conv. spkr. 1991, 97), Germans from Russia Heritage Soc., Am. Psychol. Assn., Population Assn. Am., Phi Beta Kappa, Sigma Xi. Home: 5009 SE 46th Ave Portland OR 97206-5048 Office: Reed Coll Psych Dept SE Woodstock Blvd Portland OR 97202

WIETHOLTER, WILLIAM JAMES, automotive parts manufacturing company executive; b. Cin., Jan. 16, 1942; s. William James and Elvi (Elo) W.; m. Jane Druffel, Dec. 17, 1966; children: Laura, Melissa, Michael, Catherine. BSIM, U. Cin., 1966; postgrad., Murray (Ky.) State U., 1975-77. Prodn./maintenance foreman Ford Motor Co., Cleve., 1964-67; sr. process engr. Modine Mfg., Bloomington, Ill., 1970-72; mfg. engring. mgr. Modine Mfg., Trenton, Mo., 1972-74; asst. plant mgr./supt. Modine Mfg., Paducah, Ky., 1974-77; plant mgr. Modine Mfg., Emporia, Kans., 1977-83, Clinton, Tenn., 1983-89; exec. v.p., gen. mgr. Zexel Tex. Inc., Grand Prairie, 1989-92, also bd. dirs., 1989-92; exec. v.p. mfg. Zexel USA Corp., Grand Prairie, 1992—, also bd. dirs. City commr. Emporia City Govt., 1981-83, mayor, 1983. Lt. USNR, 1967-70. Mem. Soc. Automotive Engrs. Office: Zexel USA Corp 1102 W North Carrier Pky Grand Prairie TX 75050-1122

WIGDOR, LAWRENCE ALLEN, chemical company executive; b. N.Y.C., Sept. 7, 1941; s. Irving and Gertrude (Kuhlman) W.; divorced; children: Paul, Evan. BChemE, NYU, 1962; MBA, CUNY, 1964, PhD, 1969. Group v.p. chems. Tenneco, Saddle Brook, N.J., 1976-78, exec. v.p. chems. & plastics, 1978-82; exec. v.p., COO Nuodex, Piscataway, N.J., 1982-85, pres., CEO, 1985-87; pres., CEO Huls Am., Piscataway, 1987-90; CEO Kronos Inc., East Houston, Tex., 1990—; exec. v.p. NL Industries, 1992—; chmn. bd. dirs., CEO Rheox, Inc., 1990—; chmn. bd. dirs. MEMC, St. Louis, 1989-90; bd. dirs. Nuodex Mexicana, Guadalajara, Mex., Huls Can., Toronto. Contbr. articles to profl. jours. 2d lt. U.S. Army. Mem. Chem. Mfrs. Assn. (bd. dirs. 1989-91). Republican. Avocation: pvt. investments.

WIGGERS, CHARLOTTE SUZANNE WARD, magazine editor; b. Cleve., Dec. 14, 1943; d. Raymond Paul and Irene Mary (Knapp) W.; m. John Houston Black, Feb. 1975 (div. 1980). AB, Smith Coll., 1966. Asst. editor The Hudson Rev., N.Y.C., 1966-76; assoc. editor The Print Collector's Newsletter, N.Y.C., 1977-79; copy editor Electronics mag., McGraw-Hill, N.Y.C., 1979-81; sr. copy editor Spectrum mag., N.Y.C., 1981-85; mng. editor Essence mag., N.Y.C., 1985—. Avocations: swimming, writing, photography, tennis. Home: 50 W 85th St Apt 5 New York NY 10024-4572 Office: Essence Magazine 1500 Broadway New York NY 10036-4015

WIGGIN, KENDALL FRENCH, state librarian; b. Manchester, N.H., Aug. 21, 1951; s. Ralph M. Jr. and Frances (Miltimore) W.; m. Elaine M. Elliott, June 2, 1973 (div. Jan. 1989); children: Sara, Douglas; m. Laura A. Larson, May 26, 1990; children: Lindsey, Tess. BA, U. N.H., 1974; MS in LS, Simmons Coll., 1975. Libr. Litchfield (N.H.) Pub. Libr., 1975; dir. Merrimack (N.H.) Pub. Libr., 1975-83; coord. tech. svcs. Manchester City Libr., 1983-90; state libr. N.H. State Libr., Concord, 1990—. Mem. ALA, New Eng. Libr. Assn., N.H. Libr. Assn., Chief Officers State Libr. Agys., Chief Officers State Libr. Agys. in N.E., N.H. Writers and Publishers Project. Republican. Presbyterian. Avocations: philately, gardening. Office: Cultural Affairs Dept 20 Park St Concord NH 03301-6316

WIGGINS, CHARLES, secondary education educator; b. Boston, July 8, 1938; s. John and Jeanne Lee (Sargeant) W.; children: Sam, Christy. AB, Colby Coll., 1962; AM, Columbia U., 1967. Cert. tchr., Conn. Tchr. social studies Wilton (Conn.) High Sch., 1967-70, Brien McMahon High Sch., Norwalk, Conn., 1970—. Contbr. articles to profl. jours. Co-chair, cofounder Edn. 2000; mem. Sec. of State's Citizenship Task Force, 1992-93. Cpl. U.S. Army, 1963-65. NDEA grantee, U. Bridgeport, 1968, Fulbright scholar U. Ghana, 1969; named Outstanding Educator, Cornell U., 1992. Mem. Am. Fedn. Tchrs. (steward 1986-93), Conn. Coun. Social Studies (bd. dirs. 1986-89, editor Yankee Forum 1985-91). Democrat. Avocations: carpentry, travel. Office: Brien McMahon High Sch Highland St Norwalk CT 06854

WIGGINS, CHARLES EDWARD, judge; b. El Monte, Calif., Dec. 3, 1927; s. Louis J. and Margaret E. (Fanning) W.; m. Yvonne L. Boots, Dec. 30, 1946 (dec. Sept. 1971); children: Steven L., Scott D.; m. Betty J. Koontz, July 12, 1972. B.S., U. So. Calif., 1953, LL.B., 1956; LL.B. (hon.) Ohio Wesleyan, 1975, Han Yang. U., Seoul, Korea, 1976. Bar: Calif. 1957, D.C. 1978. Lawyer, Wood & Wiggins, El Monte, Calif., 1956-66, Musick, Peeler & Garrett, Los Angeles, 1979-81, Pierson, Ball & Dowd, Washington, 1982-84, Pillsbury, Madison & Sutro, San Francisco, 1984; mem. 90-95th congresses from 25th and 39th Calif. Dists.; judge U.S. Ct. Appeals 9th Circuit, 1984—. Mayor City of El Monte, Calif., 1964-66; mem. Planning Commn. City of El Monte, 1956-60; mem. Commn. on Bicentennial of U.S. Constitution, 1985—, mem. standing com. on rules of practice and procedure, 1987—. Served to 1st lt. U.S. Army, 1945-48, 50-52, Korea. Mem. ABA, State Bar Calif., D.C. Bar Assn. Republican. Lodge: Lions.

WIGGINS, CHARLES HENRY, JR., lawyer; b. Balt., July 15, 1939; s. Charles Henry and Kathryn Wilson (Walker) W.; m. Wendy Jane Horn, June 20, 1964 (div. 1996); children: Charles Hunter, Rebecca Rae, Melinda Marie. BSEE, U. Ill., Urbana, 1962; JD with honors, U. Ill., 1965. Bar: Ill. 1965, U.S. Dist. (no. dist.) Ill. 1970, U.S. Tax Ct. 1974, U.S. Ct. Appeals (7th cir.) 1983. Assoc. Vedder, Price, Kaufman & Kammholz, Chgo., 1969-73, ptnr., 1974—. Mem. zoning bd. appeals Village of Indian Head Pk., Ill., 1984-91. Capt. U.S. Army, 1965-68. Mem. Chgo. Bar Assn., University Club (Chgo.), Edgewood Valley Country Club (LaGrange, Ill., bd. dirs. 1991—), SAR. Avocations: golf, tennis, bridge. Office: Vedder Price Kaufman & Kammholz 222 N La Salle St Fl 26 Chicago IL 60601-1104

WIGGINS, JAMES BRYAN, religion educator; b. Mexia, Tex., Aug. 24, 1935; m. Elizabeth R. Wiggins, May 28, 1995; children: Bryan, Karis. BA, Tex. Wesleyan U., 1957; BD, So. Meth. U., 1959; PhD, Drew U., 1963; postgrad., Tübingen U., Fed. Republic Germany, 1968-69. Ordained to ministry Meth. Ch., 1959. Instr. humanities Union Jr. Coll., Cranford, N.J., 1960-63; asst. prof. religion Syracuse (N.Y.) U., 1963-69, assoc. prof., 1969-75, prof., 1975—, dir. grad. studies, 1975-80, chair dept., 1980—; exec. dir. Am. Acad. Religion, 1983-91, dir., 1973-75, 83-91; cons. in field; People to People del. leader to former Soviet Union, 1992. Author: The Embattled Saint, 1966, Foundations of Christianity, 1970; editor: Religion as Story, 1975, Christianity: A Cultural Perspective, 1987, In Praise of Religious Diversity, 1996; contbr. articles to profl. jours. Trustee Scholars Press, Atlanta, 1983-91, chmn., 1986-91; chair, bd. dirs. Onondaga Pastoral Counseling Ctr., 1997—; bd. dirs. Inter-religious Coun. Ctrl. N.Y., 1997—. Rockefeller Found. fellow, 1962-63; Lilly Endowment rsch. grantee, 1992-93. Fellow Soc. for Arts (bd. dirs. 1976—), Religion and Culture; mem. AAUP, Am. Acad. Religion, Am. Soc. Ch. History. Democrat. Avocations: golf, tennis, music, reading, travel. Office: Syracuse U Dept Religion 501 Hall of Langs Syracuse NY 13244

WIGGINS, JAMES RUSSELL, newspaper editor; b. Luverne, Minn., Dec. 4, 1903; s. James and Edith (Binford) W.; m. Mabel E. Preston, Feb. 8, 1923 (widowed Oct. 1990); children: William James (dec.), Geraldine Wiggins Thomssen (dec.), Patricia Wiggins Schroth, John Russell. Grad. high sch., Luverne; LLD (hon.), Colby Coll., 1954, U. Maine, Bates Coll., 1968; DLitt (hon.), Anna Maria Coll., 1976, Clark U., 1977; LHD (hon.), Husson Coll., Bangor, Maine, 1979, U. New Eng., 1983; DSci (hon.), Maine Maritime Acad., 1987; LittD (hon.), Bowdoin Coll., 1988. Reporter Rock County Star, Luverne, 1922-25; editor, pub. Luverne Star, 1925-30; editorial writer Dispatch-Pioneer Press, St. Paul, 1930-33, Washington corr., 1933-38, mng. editor, 1938-45, editor, 1945-46; asst. to pub. N.Y. Times, 1946-47; mng. editor Washington Post, 1947-53, v.p., mng. editor, 1953-55; v.p., exec. editor Washington Post and Times Herald, 1955-60, editor, exec. v.p., 1960-68; U.S. amb. to UN, 1968-69; editor, pub. Ellsworth (Maine) Am., 1969-91, editor, 1969—. Author: Freedom or Secrecy, 1956. Served to maj. USAAF, 1943-45; air combat intelligence officer 1943-44, MTO. Mem. Am. Soc. Newspaper Editors (past pres.), Am. Antiquarian Soc. (pres. 1969-77), Sigma Delta Chi. Clubs: Nat. Press, Cosmos, Gridiron (past pres.) (Washington). Lodge: Masons. Home: Carlton Cove HCR 64 Box 506 Brooklin ME 04616-9709 Office: Ellsworth American 63 Main St Ellsworth ME 04605-1902

WIGGINS, JEROME MEYER, apparel textile industry financial executive; b. Portsmouth, Ohio, July 28, 1940; s. Jerome M. and Mary Vallee (Harold) W.; m. Mary Lou Wetta, Aug. 3, 1963; children: Laura, Kelly, Kristin, Patrick. BA, U. Notre Dame, 1962; postgrad., Ohio State U., 1964-66. CPA, Ohio. Acct. Ernst & Young, Columbus, Ohio, 1965-72; v.p. fin. Greater Ohio Corp., Columbus, 1972-75; gen. auditor VF Corp., Reading, Pa., 1975-80, contr., 1980-81, v.p. fin., 1981-89; chief fin. officer Dyersburg (Tenn.) Corp., 1989-95, pres. ops., 1995—. Mem. Am. Inst. CPA's. Republican. Roman Catholic. Avocations: golf, sailing, bridge. Office: Dyersburg Corp Tenn Indsl Fin Exec Phillips St Dyersburg TN 38024

WIGGINS, KIM DOUGLAS, artist, art dealer; b. Roswell, N.Mex., Apr. 8, 1959; s. Walton Wray Wiggins and Barbara Jo (Chesser) Ortega; m. Mary Allison Raney, Sept. 4, 1977 (div. May 1984); children: Rebekah, Mona; m. Cynthia Meredith, Sept. 29, 1985 (div. Oct. 1994); m. Maria C. Trujillo, June 17, 1995; children: Gianna Josiah, Elisha Douglas. Student, Ea. N.Mex. U., Roswell, 1977, 83-84, San Antonio Coll., 1978-79, Ind. Bapt. Coll., Dallas, 1982-83, Santa Fe Inst. Fine Art, 1989, Rhema C.B.S., Tulsa, 1997. Dir. Clarke-Wiggins Fine Art, Palm Springs, Calif., 1986-89; owner, mgr. Wiggins Fine Art, Santa Fe, 1989-93, Wiggins Studio, Roswell, 1991—; owner Print & Promise, Roswell, 1996—; cons. Mus. N.Mex., Santa Fe, 1992—, Cline Fine Art, Santa Fe, 1993—. One man shows at Altermann Morris Galleries, Houston, Dallas, 1992-97; exhibited in group shows Pa. Acad. Fine Art, Phila., 1992-96, M.H. DeYoung Mus., San Francisco, 1993-96; represented in permanent collections Mus. of N.Mex., Anschutz Collection, Denver; editor: K. Douglas Wiggins: Sense of Spirit, 1993. Mem. Internat. Platform Assn., Soc. Am. Impressionists, Coun. for Art of West, Gladney Ctr., Assurance Home. Republican. Avocations: printmaking, poetry, pottery, flying, scuba diving. Home: 6 El Arco Iris Roswell NM 88201 Studio: Altermann & Morris Galleries 225 Canyon Rd Santa Fe NM 87501

WIGGINS, MARY ANN WISE, small business owner, educator; b. Coushatta, La., Dec. 25, 1940; d. George Wilkinson and Maitland (Allums) Wise; m. Gerald D. Paul (div. Nov. 1977); children: John Barron, James Gordon, Brenda Michelle; m. Billy J. Wiggins, Oct. 3, 1981; children: Marshall Wade, Brian David, William Joshua, George Justin; stepchildren: Joseph James, Winona Gail. BA, Northwestern State U., Natchitoches, La., 1964, postgrad., 1994; postgrad., Weaterford Coll., 1967, North Tex. State U., 1968. Lic. ins. agt., real estate agt., La., pvt. pilot. Tchr. U.S. Army Schs., Nuremberg, Germany, 1964-66, Mineral Wells (Tex.) Ind. Sch. Dist., 1967-70; bookkeeper Wise Dept. Store, Coushatta, 1966-67; amb. of good will South Vietnam, 1971; owner, mgr. Mary Ann's Furniture & Hardware, Coushatta, 1977—; tchr. Springville Mid. Sch., Coushatta, 1994-96, Red River Parish Alternative Sch., Coushatta, 1996—. Chmn. Am. Cancer Soc., Conway, Ark., 1972, Red River Parish United Way, Coushatta, 1985; treas., bd. dirs. Hall Summit United Meth. Ch. Recipient German-Am. hospitality award Orgn. German-Am. Women, Nuremberg, 1965. Mem. NEA, La. Assn. Educators, Red River Assn. Educators (v.p. 1994—), U.S. C. of C., Coushatta-Red River C. of C. (charter), Pi Kappa Sigma, Sigma Kappa. Democrat. Methodist. Avocations: gardening/landscaping, swimming, horseback riding, computers, week-enders with family. Home: 2217 E Carroll St Coushatta LA 71019 Office: Mary Ann's Furniture & Hardware 1802 Ringgold Ave Coushatta LA 71019-9087

WIGGINS, NANCY BOWEN, real estate broker, market research consultant; b. Richmond, Va., Oct. 9, 1948; d. William Roy and Mary Virginia (Colson) Bowen; m. Samuel Spence Saunders, Aug. 16, 1969 (div. 1977); m. Edwin Lindsey Wiggins, Jr., Apr. 16, 1983; children: Neal Bowen, Mark Edwin. AA, St. Mary's Coll., Raleigh, N.C., 1968; postgrad., Trinity U., 1968-69; BA, U.S. Internat. U., San Diego, 1970; MA, U. Tex., Arlington, 1975; postgrad., Tulane U., 1976-77. Cert. comml. investment mem. Bank teller Bank of Am., San Diego, 1971-72; lectr. U. Tex., Arlington, 1974-76; instr. Johnson C. Smith U., Charlotte, N.C., 1977-78; human svcs. planner Centralina Coun. of Govt., Charlotte, 1978-80; mktg. rsch. analyst First Union Nat. Bank, Charlotte, 1980-81; mktg. rep. Burroughs Corp., Charlotte, 1981-83; ptnr., mktg. researcher George Selden & Assocs., Charlotte, 1983-84; pres., broker Bowen Wiggins Co., Charlotte, 1984-92; pres. WRB, Inc. (merger Bowen Wiggins Co. and W. Roy Bowen Co., Inc.), Charlotte, 1992-96; mgr., prin. Nancy Wiggins, LLC, Charlotte, 1996—; instr. U. N.C., Charlotte, 1984-85, 87-90, Winthrop U., Rock Hill, S.C., 1985-86, 91-92; bd. dirs. Roy Bowen, Inc., Frogmore, S.C., v.p., sec., 1990. Contbr. articles to profl. jours. Vice chmn. United Cerebral Palsy Coun., Charlotte, 1984; chmn. bd. dirs. Carriage House Condominium Assn., Charlotte, 1980-82; mem. Charlotte Mayor's Budget Adv. Com., 1980-81, Charlotte-Mecklenburg Planning Commn., 1994—, mem. planning com., 1994-95, zoning com., 1995-97, vice-chmn. zoning com., 1997; pres. Mecklenburg Dem. Women's Club, 1990; mem. state exec. com. N.C. Dem. Party, 1991-95; mem. Charlotte Women's Polit. Caucus, Mecklenburg County Solid Waste Adv. Bd., 1991-92, chmn. recycling com., 1991-94, 95-96; mem. Altar Guild of Christ Ch. Mem. Com. of 100 Women for Johnson C. Smith Univ., Charlotte Region Comml. Bd. Realtors, N.C. Assn. Appraisers (bd. dirs., pres. 1989-90), Internat. Coun. Shopping Ctrs., Menninger Soc. Topeka, Am. Planner Assn., Charlotte C. of C. (bd. advisors 1997), Tower Club of Charlotte, Multimillion Dollar Club, Tournament Players Club Piper Glen, Good Friends, Pi Sigma Alpha. Democrat. Episcopalian. Avocations: gardening, tennis, golf. Home: 6919 Seton House Ln Charlotte NC 28277 Office: Nancy Wiggins LLC 501 N Church St Ste 300 Charlotte NC 28202-2207

WIGGINS, NORMAN ADRIAN, university administrator, legal educator; b. Burlington, N.C., Feb. 6, 1924; s. Walter James and Margaret Ann (Chason) W.; m. Mildred Alice Harmon. AA, Campbell Coll., 1948; BA, Wake Forest Coll., 1950, LLB, 1952; LLM, Columbia U., 1956, JSD, 1964; Exec. Program, U. N.C., 1968-69; LLD, Gardner-Webb Coll., 1972. Deacon Wake Forest Baptist Ch., Winston-Salem, N.C., 1963-66, Buies Creek (N.C.) Bapt. Ch., 1973—; deacon, tchr. Sunday sch., 1952—, lay preacher, 1953—; pres. N.C. Found. of Ch.-Related Coll., 1969-70, Campbell U., Buies Creek, 1967—; prof. law Campbell U., 1976—. Author: Wills and Administration of Estates in North Carolina, 1964—, (with Gilbert T. Stephenson) Estates and Trusts, 1973; Editor: N.C. Will Manual, 1958—, Trust Functions and Services, 1978; Contbr. articles to legal jours. Chmn. Gov.'s Task Force Com. on Adjudication of the Com. on Law and Order, 1969-71; mem. com. on Drafting Interstate Succession Act for N.C., 1957-59; mem. Com. for Revision of the Laws Relating to the Adminstrn. of Descs.' Estates, 1959-67, chmn., 1964-67; trustee Sunday Sch. Bd., So. Bapt. Conv., 1975—, chmn. bd. trustees, 1978—, nominations com., 1988—; pres. Bapt. State Conv. N.C., 1983-85; bd. dirs. N.C. Citizens for Bus. and Industry, 1982—. Recipient Outstanding Civilian Svc. award Dept. Army, 1985; Campbell Law Sch. renamed in his honor the Norman Adrian Wiggins Sch. of Law, 1989; recognized for outstanding svc. to high edn. and legal edn. Newcomen Soc. U.S., 1993; Comdr.'s award for Pub. Svc., 1995, Internat. Freedom of Mobility award, 1995. Mem. ABA, Nat. Assn. Coll. and Univ. Attys. (pres. 1972-73, Disting. Svc. award 1991), Am. Assn. Presidents Ind. Colls. and Univs. (pres. 1981-83), N.C. Assn. Colls. and Univs. (exec. com. 1980—, pres. 1984-85), N.C. Assn. Ind. Colls. and Univs. (pres. 1970-72, exec. com. 1980-81), N.C. Bar Assn., Harnett County Bar Assn., Nat. Fellowship Baptist Men (pres. 1987-90), Jay Waugh Evang. Assn. (dir./pres. 1970-72), Dunn Area C. of C., Wake Forest Alumni Assn., Rotary (hon. mem. Dunn club), Phi Alpha Delta, Phi Kappa Phi, Omicron Delta Kappa. Office: Campbell U PO Box 127 Buies Creek NC 27506-0127

WIGGINS, ROGER C., internist, educator, researcher; b. Tetbury, Eng., May 26, 1945. BA, Cambridge U., Eng., 1968; BChir, Middlesex Hosp. Med. Sch., London, 1971, MB, MA, 1972. House physician dept. medicine The Middlesex Hosp., London, 1971-72; house surgeon Ipswich (Eng.) and East Suffolk Hosps., 1972; sr. house officer Hammersmith Hosp., The Middlesex Hosp., Brompton Hosp., London, 1972-74; rsch. registrar The Middlesex Hosp. Med. Sch., London, 1975-76; postdoctoral fellow Scripps Clinic and Rsch. Found., La Jolla, Calif., 1976-78, rsch. assoc., 1978-79, asst. mem. 1, 1979-81; asst. prof. U. Mich., Ann Arbor, 1981-84, assoc. prof., 1984-90, prof., 1990—, chief nephrology, 1988—, dir. O'Brien Renal Ctr., 1988—, dir. NIH Nephrology Tng. Program, 1988-96; lectr., speaker in field. Author chpts. to books; assoc. editor: Jour. Am. Soc. Nephrology, Clin. Sci.; contbr.

articles to profl. jours. First Broderip scholar, 1971, Harold Boldero scholar, 1971, James McIntosh scholar, 1971, The Berkeley fellow Gonville and Caius Coll., 1976; recipient Leopold Hudson prize, 1971, The William Henry Rean prize, 1971, Disting. Rsch. Jerome W. Conn award, 1984. Fellow Royal Coll. Physicians (U.K.); mem. Am. Assn. Pathologists, Am. Assn. Immunologists, Am. Soc. Nephrology, Fedn. Clin. Rsch., Am. Soc. Clin. Investigation, Ctrl. Soc. Am. Fedn. Clin. Rsch., Assn. Am. Physicians. Home: 3142 Parkridge Dr Ann Arbor MI 48103-1741 Office: U Mich Nephrology Div 3914 Taubman Ctr Ann Arbor MI 48109-0364*

WIGGINS, SAMUEL PAUL, education educator; b. Salisbury, N.C., Sept. 20, 1919; s. James Andrew and Mollie (Wilhelm) W.; m. Linda Jean Bessent, June 29, 1947; children: Stanley, David, Timothy, Mark. B.S., Ga. Tchrs. Coll., 1940; M.Ed., Duke U., 1942; Ph.D., Peabody Coll., 1952. Teaching prin. Alma, Ga., 1939-40; dir. lab. sch. Ga. Southwestern Coll., 1940-42; dir. student teaching Emory U., 1947-53; prof., adminstr. Peabody Coll., 1953-67; dean Coll. Edn., Cleve. State U., 1967-75, prof., 1975-85; prof. Norfolk State U., 1985-96, co-dir. project nat. bd. tchg. stds., 1995-96; chief advisor ICA (AID), Korea Tchr. Edn. Project, 1961-62; Fulbright lectr., Colombia, S.Am., 1966, Lisbon, Portugal, 1978; pres. Am. Assn. Colls. Tchr. Edn., 1974-75; mem. forum of leaders Nat. Ednl. Orgns. USOE, 1975-77. Author: Successful High School Teaching, 1958, Student Teacher in Action, 1957, Southern High Schools and Jobless Youth, 1961, The Desegregation Era in Higher Education, 1966, Higher Education in the South, 1966, Battlefields in Teacher Education, 1964, Educating Personnel for Urban Schools, 1972, Improving Education for the Youth of Portugal, 1980, Revolution in Teacher Education: A Review of Reform Reports, 1985; co-author: Equity and Excellence for Minorities in T.Ed. (A.T.E.), 1988,. Served with USNR, 1942-47, comdr. Res. ret. Home: 609 Abbey Dr Virginia Beach VA 23455-6504

WIGGINS, STEPHEN EDWARD, family practice physician, medical administrator; b. Phila., May 7, 1951; s. Ralph Cannon and Bernice J. (Maslovitz) W.; m. Rebecca del Carmen, Oct. 3, 1992; 1 child, Daniel Stephen. BA, Rutgers U., 1973; MD, Med. Coll. Va., 1977. Diplomate Am. Bd. Family Practice. Resident in family practice Riverside Hosp., Newport News, Va., 1977-80; staff emergency physician North Arundal Hosp., Glen Burnie, Md., 1980-81, So. Md. Hosp. Ctr., Clinton, 1982-84; med. dir. Convenient Health Care, Waldorf, Md., 1984—; ptnr. Old Line Med. Partnership, Waldorf, 1990-96, Convenient Health Care Mgmt., Waldorf, 1989-96; instr. family practice Georgetown U. Sch. Medicine, Washington, 1995-96. Vol. physician and citizen diplomat Gesundheit Inst., Russia, 1991; citizen diplomate U.S.-China Peoples Friendship Assn., China, 1988; vol. physician March of Dimes Walk-a-thon, Md., 1985-86. William Demarest scholar, Rutgers U., New Brunswick, N.J., 1969-73. Fellow Am. Acad. Family Physicians; mem. Med. and Chirurgical Faculty of the State of Md., Md. Acad. Family Physicians, Charles County Med. Soc. Avocation: scuba diving. Office: Convenient Health Care 640 Old Line Ctr Waldorf MD 20602-2553

WIGGS, EUGENE OVERBEY, ophthalmologist, educator; b. Louisville, Apr. 27, 1928; s. Eugene Overbey and Marie Helen (Martin) W.; children: Susan, Christopher, Karen, Mark. AB, Johns Hopkins U., 1950; MD, Duke U., 1955. Intern Denver Gen. Hosp., 1955-56; resident in ophthalmology Wilmer Inst. Johns Hopkins Hosp., 1956-59; ophthalmic plastic fellow Byron Smith, MD, N.Y.C., 1969; pvt. practice specializing in oculoplastic surgery Denver, 1961—; clin. prof. U. Colo. Med. Ctr.; lectr. ophthalmic plastic surgery various med. ctrs. Contbr. articles to med. jours. With USNR, 1959-61. Mem. AMA, Denver Med. Soc., Colo. Med. Soc., Am. Soc. Ophthalmic Plastic and Reconstructive Surgery, Am. Acad. Ophthalmology (svc. award 1982), Colo. Ophthalmology Soc. Republican. Roman Catholic. Office: 2005 Franklin St Denver CO 80205-5401

WIGHT, DARLENE, retired speech educator; b. Andover, Kans., Jan. 5, 1926; d. Everett John and Claudia (Jennings) Van Biber; m. Lester Delin, Jan. 21, 1950; children: Lester Delin II, Claudia Leigh. AA, Graceland Coll., 1945; BA, U. Kans., 1948, MA, 1952. Permanent profl. cert., Iowa; life tchr.'s cert., Mo. Instr. U. Kans., Lawrence, 1949-50; instr. overseas program U. Md., Munich, 1954; speech pathologist Independence (Mo.) Pub. Sch. Dist., 1958-61; assoc. prof. Graceland Coll., Lamoni, Iowa, 1961-87; cons. Quad-County Sch. Dist., Leon, Iowa, 1966-67, Mt. Ayr (Iowa) Cmty. Sch. Dist., 1967-70; cons. Head Start program SCIAP, Leon, 1972-75, MATURA, Bedford, Iowa, 1973-75. Co-author: Speech Communication Handbook, 1979. Mem. Common Cause, 1989, Friends of Art, Nelson-Atkins Mus. Art, Planned Parenthood, U.S. English, Inc., Habitat for Humanity, Nat. Mus. Women in Arts, Am. Craft Coun. Recipient Award of Merit U. Kans., 1982, Award of Distinction U. Kans., 1947-48. Mem. AAUW, Am. Speech, Lang. and Hearing Assn. (speech pathology clin. competency), Coun. Exceptional Children, Archaeol. Inst. Am. Democrat. Mem. Reorganized Latter Day Saints Ch. Avocations: weaving/fibers, traveling, gardening, cooking. Office: Graceland Coll Speech Dept Lamoni IA 50140

WIGHT, NANCY ELIZABETH, neonatologist; b. N.Y.C., Aug. 27, 1947; d. John Joseph and Gisela (Landers) Probst; m. Robert C.S. Wight, Oct. 1, 1988; 1 child, Robert C.S. II. Student, Cornell U., 1965-67; AB in Psychology, U. Calif., Berkeley, 1968; postgrad., George Washington U., 1971-72; MD, U. N.C., 1976. Diplomate Am. Bd. Pediatrics. Resident in pediatrics U. N.C., Chapel Hill, 1976-79; fellow in neonatal/perinatal medicine U. Calif., San Diego, 1979-81; clin. instr. Dept. of Pediatrics La. State U. Sch. of Medicine, Baton Rouge, 1982-86; neonatologist The Baton Rouge Neonatology Group, 1981-86; co-dir. neonatology, med. dir. respiratory therapy Woman's Hosp., Baton Rouge, 1981-85; med. dir. newborn svcs., neonatal respiratory therapy HCA West Side Hosp. Centennial Med. Ctr., Nashville, 1986-88; staff pediatrician, neonatologist Balboa Naval Hosp., San Diego, 1988-89; attending neonatologist Sharp Meml. Hosp., San Diego, 1990—, Children's Hosp.-San Diego, 1990—; asst. clin. prof. U. Calif. San Diego, 1991—; physician assoc. La Leche League. Contbr. articles to profl. jours. mem. exec. bd. Capital Area Plantation chpt. March of Dimes, Baton Rouge, 1981-86, chmn. health adv. com., 1982-86; mem. health com. Capital Area United Way, Baton Rouge, 1982-86; bd. mem. Baton Rouge Coun. for Child Protection, 1983-86, NICU Parents, Baton Rouge, 1981-86; mem. health adv. com. Nashville Area March of Dime, 1987-88. Recipeint Am. Med. Women's Assn. award. Mem. AMA, Am. Acad. Pediatrics, Calif. Med. Assn., So. Med. Assn., San Diego County Med. Assn., Calif. Perinatal Assn., So. Perinatal Assn., Nat. Perinatal Assn., La. Perinatal Assn. (past 1st v.p. and pres.), Internat. Lactation Cons. Assn. (cert.), Hastings Soc. Home: 1230 Triest Dr San Diego CA 92107 Office: Children's Assoc Med Group 8001 Frost St San Diego CA 92123-2746

WIGHTMAN, ALEC, lawyer; b. Cleve., Jan. 23, 1951; s. John and Betty Jane (Follis) W.; m. Kathleen A. Little, June 19, 1976; children: Nora, Emily. BA, Duke U., 1972; JD, Ohio State U., 1975. Bar: Ohio 1975, U.S. Tax Ct. 1982, U.S. Ct. Appeals (6th cir.) 1983. Assoc. Krupman, Fromson & Henson, Columbus, Ohio, 1975-77; ptnr. Krupman, Fromson, Bownas & Wightman, Columbus, 1978-82; assoc. Baker & Hostetler, Columbus, 1982-83, ptnr., 1984—. Mem. ABA, Ohio Bar Assn., Columbus Bar Assn., Ohio Oil and Gas Assn., Nat. Health Lawyers Assn. Avocation: tennis. Office: Baker & Hostetler 65 E State St Ste 2100 Columbus OH 43215-4213

WIGHTMAN, ARTHUR STRONG, physicist, educator; b. Rochester, N.Y., Mar. 30, 1922; s. Eugene Pinckney and Edith Victoria (Stephenson) W.; m. Anna-Greta Larsson, Apr. 28, 1945 (dec. Feb. 11, 1976); 1 dau., Robin Letitia; m. Ludmilla Popova, Jan. 14, 1977. B.A., Yale, 1942; Ph.D., Princeton, 1949; D.Sc., Swiss Fed. Inst. Tech., Zurich, 1968, Göttingen U., 1987. Instr. physics Yale, 1943-44; from instr. to asso. prof. physics Princeton, 1949-60, prof. math. physics, 1960-92; prof. emeritus, 1992—; Thomas D. Jones prof. math. physics Princeton, 1971—; vis. prof. Sorbonne, 1957, École Polytechnique, 1977-78. Served to lt. (j.g.) USNR, 1944-46. NRC postdoctoral fellow Inst. Teoretisk Fysik, Copenhagen, Denmark, 1951-52; NSF sr. postdoctoral fellow, 1956-57; recipient Dannie Heineman prize math. physics, 1969. Fellow Am. Acad. Arts and Scis., Royal Acad. Arts; mem. Nat. Acad. Scis., Am. Math. Soc., Am. Phys. Soc., AAAS. Office: Princeton U 350 Jadwin Hall Princeton NJ 08544

WIGHTMAN, GLENN CHARLES, environmental, health and safety administrator; b. Abington, Pa., Apr. 1, 1961; s. Glenn Clayton and Margaret Ann (Wilkinson) W.; m. Lauren Marie Saraceni, June 29, 1985; children: Margaret Elizabeth, Annette Suzanne. BSCE cum laude, Bucknell U., 1983; MBA, Lehigh U., 1991. Registered profl. engr., Pa. Student engr. Bechtel Nat., Inc., Middletown, Pa., 1982; occupl. engr. AT&T Corp., Allentown, Pa., 1984-87, Berkeley Heights, N.J., 1987-90; sr. engr. AT&T Corp., Basking Ridge, N.J., 1990-93; tech. mgr. AT&T Corp., Morristown, N.J., 1994-96; tech. mgr. Lucent Tech., Warren, N.J., 1996-97, mgr., 1997—; mem. Toxic Substances Control Act course faculty Govt. Insts., Inc., Rockville, Md., 1990-92. Contbr. articles to profl. jours. Recipient ednl. award Kodak, 1981. Mem. Am. Electronics Assn. (environ. and occupl. health com. 1990-92), Phi Eta Sigma, Tau Beta Pi, Beta Gamma Sigma. Democrat. Roman Catholic. Avocations: fitness, trombone, personal finance. Office: Lucent Tech 283 King George Rd Rm D3a33 Warren NJ 07059-5134

WIGHTMAN, LUDMILLA G. POPOVA, language educator, foreign educator, translator; b. Sofia, Bulgaria, Sept. 29, 1933; came to U.S., 1977; d. Genko Mateev and Liliana (Kusseva) Popov; m. Ivan Todorov Todorov, Aug. 13, 1957 (div. 1976); 1 child, Todor; m. Arthur Strong Wightman, Jan. 14, 1977. MS, U. Sofia, 1956. Cons. Nat. Libr., Sofia, 1956-58; rsch. assoc. Joint Inst. for Nuclear Rsch., Moscow, 1958-65; lectr. Russian Rutgers U., New Brunswick, N.J., 1969-70; editor Bulgarian Ency., Sofia, 1973-77; tchr. lang. Princeton (N.J.) Lang. Group, 1977—; libr. Firestone Libr., Princeton U., 1983-87. Translator: Introduction to Axiomatic Field Theory, 1975, New Eng. Rev., Bread Loaf Quar., 1987, Mr. Cogito, 1989, N.Y. Rev. Books, 1990, Poetry East, 1990-91, Literary Rev., 1992, Partisan Rev., 1996, Shifting Borders: East European Poetries of the Eighties, 1993. Avocations: bird watching, music, photography, travel. Home and Office: 16 Balsam Ln Princeton NJ 08540-5327

WIGHTMAN, THOMAS VALENTINE, rancher, researcher; b. Sacramento, Oct. 7, 1921; s. Thomas Valentine and Pearl Mae (Cutbirth) W.; m. Lan Do Wightman. Student, U. Calif., Berkeley, 1945-46; B of Animal Husbandry, U. Calif., Davis, 1949; student, Cal. Poly. Inst., 1949-50. Jr. aircraft mechanic SAD (War Dept.), Sacramento, Calif., 1940-42; rancher Wightman Ranch, Elk Grove, Calif., 1950-59; machinest Craig Ship-Bldg. Co., Long Beach, Calif., 1959-70; rancher Wightman Ranch, Austin, Nev., 1970-88; dir. Wightman Found., Sacramento, 1988—. Dir. med. rsch. Staff sgt. U.S. Army, 1942-45. Recipient scholarship U.S. Fed. Govt., 1945-50. Fellow NRA, VFW, U. Calif. Alumni Assn., U. Calif. Davis Alumni Assn., Bowles Hall Assn.; mem. Confederate Air Force, The Oxford Club. Republican. Avocations: antique automobiles and aircraft. Home and Office: Wightman Found 2130 51st St Apt 129 Sacramento CA 95817

WIGINGTON, RONALD LEE, retired chemical information services executive; b. Topeka, May 11, 1932; s. Oscar and Virginia C. (Ritchie) W.; m. Margaret E. Willey, Aug. 17, 1951; children: Linda, Carol, David, Brian. BS in Engring. Physics, U. Kans., 1953; MEE, U. Md., 1959; PhD in Elec. Engring., U. Kans., 1964; postgrad. in advanced mgmt. program, Harvard Bus. Sch., 1976-77. Tech. staff mem. Bell Telephone Labs., Murray Hill, N.J., 1953-54; div. chief Dept. Def., Washington, 1956-68; dir. rsch. and devel. Chem. Abstracts Svc., Am. Chem. Soc., Columbus, Ohio, 1968-84; dir. Washington ops. Am. Chem. Soc., 1984-86; chief exec. officer, dir. Chem. Abstracts Svc., Am. Chem. Soc., Columbus, 1986-91; dir. info. tech. Am. Chem. Soc., Columbus, 1991-94; chmn. bd. Online Computer Libr. Ctr., Dublin, Ohio, 1985-87, trustee, 1978-92. Contbr. articles to profl. jours. Pres., various positions PTA Prince George's County, Md., 1966-68; moderator, treas. Cmty. Assn. Upper Arlington (Ohio) Schs., 1970-74; mem. Upper Arlington Civic Orch., 1970-84, pres., 1973, 76; bd. dirs. Nat. Fedn. Abstracting and Info. Svcs., 1979-84, pres. 1982-83, hon. fellow 1995—; bd. dirs. Ohio Ctr. of Sci. and Industry, 1988-93; trustee Health Coalition of Ctrl. Ohio, Columbus, 1991—, treas., 1994—, vice-chmn., 1996—. With U.S. Army, 1954-56. Summerfield scholar U. Kans., 1949; recipient Nat. Capital award D.C. Council Engring. and Archtl. Socs., 1967, Meritorious Civilian Service award Dept. Defense, 1967. Mem. IEEE (sr.), Am. Chem. Soc., Internat. Coun. Sci. and Tech. Info. (exec. bd. 1986-94, treas. 1992-94), Material Property Data Network (bd. dirs. 1987-94), Sigma Xi. Avocations: gardening, music. Home: 2470 Wimbledon Rd Columbus OH 43220-4212

WIGLER, ANDREW JEFFREY, lawyer; b. Bklyn., Aug. 11, 1965; s. Jerome L. and Florence (Hoffstein) W.; m. Nancy D. Wigler, Feb. 22, 1992. BA, Albany State U., 1987; JD, Yeshiva U., N.Y.C., 1990. Bar: N.J. 1990, U.S. Dist. Ct. N.J. 1990, N.Y. 1991, U.S. Dist. Ct. (so. and ea. dists.) N.Y. 1991, U.S. Ct. Appeals (2nd cir.) 1991, D.C. 1993. Legis. intern Hon. Thomas J. Bartosiewicz, Albany, N.Y., 1986; legis. aide Hon. Anthony J. Genovesi, Albany, 1987; assoc. Reisman, Peirez, Reisman & Calica, Garden City, N.Y., 1993-94; assoc. Berger & Ackman, P.C., N.Y.C., 1990-93, ptnr., 1994-95; ptnr. Law Offices of Andrew J. Wigler, Esq., Great Neck, N.Y., 1995—; atty. in pvt. practice Advanced Mortgage Sys., L.L.C., Great Neck, N.Y., 1995—; bd. dirs. Advanced Mortgage Sys., LLC, N.Y.C. Committeeman Queens County Dem. Com., 1993, Kings County Dem. Com., 1990. Recipient First Place Brief award Phillip C. Jessup Moot Ct. Competition, N.Y., 1989, Best Brief award Cardozo Advocacy Competition, N.Y.C., 1988. Mem. ABA, N.Y. State Women's Bar Assn., Nassau County Bar Assn., N.Y. State Bar Assn., N.Y. County Lawyers Assn., Washington Bar Assn. Democrat.

WIGMORE, BARRIE ATHERTON, investment banker; b. Moose Jaw, Sask., Can., Apr. 11, 1941; came to U.S., 1970; s. Fred Henry and Pauline Elizabeth (Atherton) W.; m. Deedee Dawson, Aug. 24, 1964. B. Edn., U. Sask., Can., 1962, B.A., 1963; M.A., U. Oreg., 1964; B.A., Oxford U., Eng., 1966, M.A., 1971. Investment banker Goldman, Sachs & Co., N.Y.C., 1970—; bd. dirs. Potash Corp. Sask. Author: The Crash and Its Aftermath, A History of U.S. Securities Markets 1929-33, 1985, Securities Markets in the 1980s, 1997. Trustee Progressive Policy Inst., Am. Friends of Worcester Coll. (Oxford U.) Inc. Democrat. Avocations: politics, financial history. Home: 1 W 72nd St New York NY 10023 Office: Goldman Sachs & Co 85 Broad St New York NY 10004-2434

WIGMORE, JOHN GRANT, lawyer; b. L.A., Mar. 14, 1928; s. George Theodore and Mary (Grant) W.; m. Dina Burnaby, July 27, 1968 (dec. 1994); children: Alexander Trueblood, Adam Trueblood, John G. Jr., Mary. BS in Geology, Stanford U., 1949; JD, UCLA, 1958. Geologist Western Geophys., Calif., Colo., Mo., 1953-55; assoc. Lawler, Felix & Hall, L.A., 1958-62, ptnr., 1963-86; ptnr. Pillsbury, Madison & Sutro, L.A., 1986—; lectr. in field. Contbr. articles to profl. jours. Trustee, gov. L.A. County Mus. Natural History, 1970—; participant various local & state election campaigns, 1965-80. Officer USN, 1950-53. Fellow Am. Coll. Trial Lawyers, Am. Bar Found.; mem. ABA (chair litigation com. antitrust sect. 1970-74), Calif. State Bar (L.A. County bar del. 1965-75), L.A. County Bar Assn. (exec. com. trial sect. 1965-68), L.A. County Bus. Trial Lawyers (exec. com. 1984-87), Barristers (exec. com. 1960-65). Home: 114 Madison Ave PO Box 1328 Ketchum ID 83340 also: 870 Neptune Ave Encinitas CA 92024-2062 Office: Pillsbury Madison & Sutro Citicorp Plz 725 S Figueroa St Ste 1200 Los Angeles CA 90017-5443

WIGTON, PAUL NORTON, steel company consultant, former executive; b. Linesville, Pa., Aug. 13, 1932; s. Charles and Viola Grace (Dennis) W.; m. Janet Ohl, July 11, 1953; children: Bruce, Douglas. BS in Chemistry, Youngstown State U., 1957a; postgrad. exec. mgmt. program, MIT, 1974; hon. doctorate, Youngstown State U., 1980. Gen. supt. metal services Republic Steel Corp., Warren, Ohio, 1971-73, asst. to dist. mgr., 1973-75, dist. mgr., 1975-78; asst. v.p. ops. Republic Steel Corp., Cleve., 1978-80, v.p. steel ops., 1980-83, v.p., gen. mgr. flat rolled product group, 1983-84; pres. tubular products LTV Steel, 1984-91, ret., 1991; mem. Sr. Cons. Network Co., Inc., Beachwood, Ohio, 1991-92; prin. Paul N. Wigton & Assocs. Consultants, Sarasota, Fla., 1992—. Served to cpl. U.S. Army, 1953-54. Scholar Henry Roemer Found., 1957; scholar Am. Chem. Soc., 1957; named Industrialist of Yr. Mahoning Valley Econ. Devel. Corp., 1981, Mgr. of Yr., Mahoning Valley Econ. Devel. Corp., 1992. Mem. AIME, Am. Iron and Steel Inst., Assn. Iron and Steel Engrs. (nat. pres. 1988). Presbyterian. Clubs: Tournament Players (Prestancia-Sarasota, Fla.). Home: 3826 Torrey Pines Way Sarasota FL 34238-2839 Office: Paul N Wigton & Assocs Consultants 3826 Torrey Pines Way Sarasota FL 34238-2839

WIIG, ELISABETH HEMMERSAM, audiologist, educator; b. Esbjert, Denmark, May 22, 1935; came to U.S., 1957, naturalized, 1967; d. Svend Frederick and Ingeborg (Hemmersam) Nielsen; m. Karl Martin Wiig, June 10, 1958; children—Charlotte E., Erik D. B.A., Statsseminariet Emdrupborg, 1956; M.A., Western Res. U., 1960; Ph.D., Case Western Res. U., 1967; postgrad., U. Mich., 1967-68. Clin. audiologist Cleve. Hearing and Speech Center, 1959-60; instr. dept. phonetics Bergen (Norway) U., 1960-64; asst. prof., dir. aphasia rehab. program U. Mich., 1968-70; asst. prof. Boston U., 1970-73, asso. prof., chmn. dept., 1973-77, prof. dept. communication disorders, 1977-87, prof. emerita, 1987—; v.p. EDUCOM Assocs. Inc., 1992-93. Author: Language Disabilities in Children and Adolescents, 1976, Language Assessment and Intervention for the Learning Disabled, 1980, 84, CELF Screening Tests: Elementary and Secondary Levels, 1980, Clinical Evaluation of Language Fundamentals, rev. edit., 1987, Clinical Evaluation of Language Fundamentals 3, 1995, Test of Language Competence, 1985, expanded edit., 1989, Test of Word Knowledge, 1992, Clinical Evaluation of Language Fundamentals Preschool, 1992; editor: Human Communication Disorders: An Introduction, 1982, 86, 90, 94; contbr. articles to profl. jours. Recipient Metcalf Cup and Prize for excellence in teaching Boston U., 1967. Fellow Am. Speech and Hearing Assn. (cert. clin. competence in speech pathology and audiology); mem. Coun. for Learning Disabilities, Coun. for Exceptional Children, Internat. Assn. for Rsch. on Learning Disabilities, Am. Psychol. Soc. Address: 5211 Vicksburg Dr Arlington TX 76017-4941

WIIN-NIELSEN, AKSEL CHRISTOPHER, meteorologist educator; b. Juelsminde, Denmark, Dec. 17, 1924; emigrated to U.S., 1959; s. Aage Nielsen and Marie Christophersen; m. Bente Havsteen Zimsen, Dec. 5, 1953; children: Charlotte, Barbro Marianne, Karen Margrete. BS in Math, U. Copenhagen, Denmark, 1947, MS in Math, 1950; Fil. Lic. in Meteorology, U. Stockholm, Sweden, 1957, PhD in Meteorology, 1960; DSc (h.c.), U. Reading, 1981; DSc (honoris causa), U. Copenhagen, 1986. Staff meteorologist Danish Meteorol. Inst., 1952-55; research meteorologist Internat. Meteorol. Inst. U. Stockholm, 1955-58, asst. prof. Internat. Meteorol. Inst., 1957-58, exec. editor publ. Internat. Meteorol. Inst., Tellus, 1957-58; research meteorologist Air Weather Service, USAF; also staff mem. joint numerical weather prediction unit and lectr. George Washington U., 1959-61; research staff mem. Nat. Center Atmospheric Research, 1961-62, asst. dir., 1962-63; prof., chmn. dept. meteorology and oceanography U. Mich., 1963-71; prof. theoretical meteorology U. Bergen, Norway, 1971-72, U. Mich., 1972-74; dir. European Centre for Medium-Range Weather Forecasts, 1974-79; sec. gen. World Meteorol. Orgn., 1980-83; dir. Danish Meteorol. Inst., 1984-87; prof. U. Copenhagen, 1988-94; pres. Internat. Commn. for Dynamic Meteorology, 1971-79; chmn. working group on numerical experimentation, also mem. joint organizing com. Global Atmospheric Research Program, 1973-79; chmn. working group on earth scis., sci. adv. com. European Space Agy., 1977-79; sci. adv. com. Max Planck Inst. Meteorology, Hamburg, W. Ger.; v.p. Eumetsat Council, 1986-87; v.p. Council for European Ctr. for Medium-Range Weather Forecasts, 1985-86, pres., 1986-87; vis. scientist Nat. Ctr. Atmosphere Res., 1987; vis. prof. U. Mich., 1988; chmn. NATO-Panel on The Sci. of Global Environ. Changes, 1990-92. Recipient Ohridski medal Sofia (Bulgaria) U., 1980; Buys-Ballot medal Acad. Sci., Netherlands, 1981; Wihuri prize, Finland, 1983; Rossby prize Swedish Geophys. Soc., 1985, Friedman Rescue award, 1993. Fellow Am. Meteorol. Soc. (hon.); mem. Am. Geophys. Union, Swedish Acad. Sci., Royal Meteorol. Soc. (hon.), Finnish Acad. Arts and Scis., Euopean Geophys. Soc. (pres. 1988-90), Danish Acad. Tech. Scis. (v.p. 1989-92), Royal Danish Soc. Scis., N.Y. Acad. Scis., Tau Beta Pi. Home: Solbakken 6, 3230 Grasted Denmark

WIKANDER, LAWRENCE EINAR, librarian; b. Pitts., Dec. 16, 1915; s. Oscar Ragnar and Mary Edna (Gerdes) W.; m. Ethel Marie Whitlow, Nov. 23, 1940; children: Frederick Whitlow, Matthew Hays. B.A., Williams Coll., 1937; B.S. in Library Sci, Columbia U., 1939; M.A., U. Pa., 1949. Gen. asst. Carnegie Library, Pitts., 1939-40; supr. circulation Mt. Pleasant Br., D.C. Public Library, Washington, 1940-42; asst. librarian Temple U., Phila., 1946-50; librarian Forbes Library, Northampton, Mass., 1950-68; librarian Williams Coll., Williamstown, Mass., 1968-82, librarian emeritus, 1982—; curator Calvin Coolidge Meml. Room Forbes Library, Northampton, Mass., 1982-93. Author: Disposed to Learn, 1972, Completing a Century: History of the Northampton Social and Literary Club, 1962, Calvin Coolidge: A Chronological Summary, 1957; editor: The Hampshire History, 1962, The Northampton Book, 1954, A Guide to the Personal Files of Calvin Coolidge, 1986, (with Robert H. Ferrell) Grace Coolidge: An Autobiography, 1992. Pres. Northampton Community Chest, 1958-60; bd. dirs. Civil Liberties Union Mass., Hampshire, 1957-68; trustee Calvin Coolidge Meml. Found., 1969—; dir. South Mountain Concert Assn., 1975—; clk. Northampton Hist. Soc., 1955-68; dir. Hampshire Inter-Library Center, 1956-68. Served to capt. AUS, 1942-46; military intelligence in Africa, Italy, Austria. Mem. Am. Library Assn. (mem. council 1962-68), New Eng. Library Assn. (pres. 1967-68), Mass. Library Assn. (pres. 1960-61), Western Mass. Library Club (pres. 1953-55). Home: 21 Cluett Dr Williamstown MA 01267-2804

WIKARSKI, NANCY SUSAN, information technology consultant; b. Chgo., Jan. 26, 1954; d. Walter Alexander and Emily Regina (Wejnerowski) W.; m. Michael F. Maciekowich, Dec. 5, 1976 (div. Feb. 1985). BA, Loyola U., Chgo., 1976, MA, 1978; PhD, U. Chgo., 1990. Paralegal Winston & Strawn, Chgo., 1978-79; real estate analyst Continental Bank, Chgo., 1979-84, systems analyst, 1984-88, ops. officer, 1988-89, automation cons., 1989-92; systems mgr. PNC Mortgage Co. of Am., Vernon Hills, Ill., 1992-94; ind. cons. Lake Bluff, Ill., 1994—. Author: German Expressionist Film, 1990, The Fall of White City, 1996. Fellow U. Chgo., 1987-90. Mem. NAFE, Am. Mensa, Chgo. Computer Soc., Alpha Sigma Nu. Avocations: music, writing.

WIKSTROM, FRANCIS M., lawyer; b. Missoula, Mont., Aug. 20, 1949. BS, Weber State Univ., 1971; JD, Yale U., 1974. Bar: Utah 1974, U.S. Supreme Ct. 1980. Asst. U.S. atty. U.S. Dist. Ct. Utah, 1979-80, U.S. atty., 1981; mem., chmn. litigation dept. Parsons Behle & Latimer, Salt Lake City; mem. Utah State Bar Commn., Utah Judicial Conduct Commn.; mem. adv. com. on rules civil procedure Utah Supreme Ct. Fellow Am. Coll. Trial Lawyers; mem. ABA, Salt Lake County Bar Assn. (pres. 1993-94), Am. Inns Ct. II (master bench). Office: Parsons Behle & Latimer PO Box 45898 One Utah Ctr 201 S Main St Ste 1800 Salt Lake City UT 84111-2218

WILBANKS, JAN JOSEPH, philosopher; b. Lynchburg, Ohio, Dec. 17, 1928; s. James Odell and Bernice Elizabeth (Daugherty) W.; m. Alice Ramona Pacheco, Nov. 14, 1953; children—Elise, Anita, Jennifer. B.S., Cin. Coll. Pharmacy, 1951; Ph.D. in Philosophy, Ohio State U., 1964. Instr. Purdue U., 1961-64; mem. faculty Marietta (Ohio) Coll., 1964-89, prof. philosophy, 1973-89. Author: Hume's Theory of Imagination, 1968, also articles. With AUS, 1951-53. Home: 122 High St Marietta OH 45750-2636

WILBER, CHARLES GRADY, forensic science educator, consultant; b. Waukesha, Wis., June 18, 1916; s. Charles Bernard and Charlotte Agnes (Grady) W.; m. Ruth Mary Bodden, July 12, 1944 (dec. 1950); children: Maureen, Charles Bodden, Michael; m. Clare Marie O'Keefe, June 14, 1952; children: Thomas Grady (dec.), Kathleen, Aileen, John Joseph. BSc, Marquette U., 1938; MA, Johns Hopkins U., 1941, PhD, 1942. Asst. prof. physiology Fordham U., 1945-49; assoc. prof. physiology, dir. biol. labs. St. Louis U., 1949-52; leader Arctic expdns., 1943-44, 48, 50, 51; physiologist Chem. Corps, U.S. Army, 1952-61; assoc. physiology and pharmacology U. Pa., 1953-61, chief comparative physiology, 1956-61; prof. lectr. biol. scis. Loyola Coll., Balt., 1957-61; dir. Loyola Coll. (In-Service Inst. Sci. Tchrs.), 1958-61; prof. biol. scis., univ. rsch. coord., dean Grad. Sch. Kent State U., 1961-64; dir. marine laboratories U. Del., 1964-67; chmn., prof. dept. zoology Colo. State U., 1967-73, prof., 1967-87, emeritus prof. and chmn., 1987—, dir. forensic sci. lab., 1965—; dep. coroner Larimer County, Colo., 1968-78; pres. Manresa Co., 1978—; mem. Ctr. for Human Identification; expert witness fed. and state cts. on poisons, firearms, others; life mem. Marine Biol. Lab., Woods Hole, Mass., 1947—; mem. U.S. Army Panel Environ. Physiology, 1952-61; mem. study group Nat. Acad. Scis.-USAF, 1958-61; Wellcome vis. prof. basic med. scis. Ohio U. Med. Sch., 1983-84; vis. lectr. Am. Inst. Biol. Scis., 1957—; life mem. Corp. of Marine Biol. Lab., Woods Hole, Mass. Author: Biological Aspects of Water Pollution, 2d edit, 1971, Japanese edit., 1970, Forensic Biology for the Law Enforcement Officer, 1975, Contemporary Violence, 1975, Ballistic Science for the Law Enforcement Officer, 1977, Medicolegal Investigation of The President John

F. Kennedy Murder, 1978, Chemical Trauma from Pesticides, 1979, Forensic Toxicology, 1980, Beryllium, 1980, Agent Orange, 1980; Author: Turbidity, 1983, Selenium, 1983; contbr. articles to profl. jours.; exec. editor: Adaption to the Environment, vol. in series, 1962; editor: Am. Lecture Series in Environ. Studies; mem. editorial bd.: Am. Jour. Forensic Medicine and Pathology; contbr.: Harper Ency. Nat. Capt. USAAF, 1942-46; col. USAF, ret. Disting. scholar in criminal justice Albany State Coll., 1993. Fellow N.Y. Acad. Scis., Am. Acad. Forensic Sci.; mem. Am. Physiol. Soc., Cosmos Club (Washington), Phi Beta Kappa, Sigma Xi, Phi Sigma, Gamma Alpha. Republican. Roman Catholic. Home: 900 Edwards St Fort Collins CO 80524-3824 Office: Colo State U Dept Biology Fort Collins CO 80523 *The accident of history which has enabled me to study as I wished, work at what I enjoyed, and live as I chose is a mystery for which I must be eternally thankful.*

WILBER, DAVID JAMES, cardiologist; b. Ft. Atkinson, Wis., Apr. 1, 1951; s. Howard Spencer and Leona (Von Reuden) W.; m. Sandra Irene Reynertson, June 28, 1992. BS, U. Wis., 1973; MD, Northwestern U., 1977. Intern medicine Northwestern Meml. Hosps., 1977-80; fellow cardiology U. Mich., 1982-84; fellow electrophysiology Mass. Gen. Hosp., Boston, 1984-86; asst. prof. medicine Loyola U., Maywood, Ill., 1986-90, assoc. prof. medicine, 1990-94; prof. medicine U. Chgo., 1994—. Fellow Am. Coll. Cardiology, Am. Heart Assn. Office: Univ Chgo Hosps Sect Cardiology 5758 S Maryland Ave # C9024 Chicago IL 60637-1426

WILBER, ROBERT EDWIN, corporate executive; b. Boston, Dec. 15, 1932; s. Charles Edwin and Mary Charles (Gay) W.; m. Bonnie Marilyn Jones; children: Debra, Kathleen, Robert Jr., Thomas, Jeffrey, Mark, Matthew. BSBA in Acctg., Bowling Green State U., 1954. CPA, Mass., Tex. Sr. acct. Peat, Marwick, Mitchell and Co., Boston, 1954-58; gen. mgr. Door Controls Inc., Boston, 1958-59; asst. controller MKM Knitting Mills Inc., Manchester, N.H., 1959-63; internal audit supr. Raytheon Co., Lexington, Mass., 1963; asst. treas. Glens Falls (N.Y.) Ins. Co., 1963-66; controller Pnobscott Co., Boston, 1966-67; v.p. fin. and adminstrn. S.S. Pierce Co., Boston, 1967-73, Samson Ocean Systems Inc., Boston, 1973-79; v.p., chief acctg. officer Enserch Corp., Dallas, 1979-88; pres. Trade U.S.A., 1990—. Mem. Rep. Nat. Com. Mem. AICPAs, Nat. Assn. Trade Exchanges, Tex. Soc. CPAs, Mass. Soc. CPAs, , Fin. Execs. Inst., Inter City Assn., Pres.'s Club (Bowling Green, Ohio). Republican. Home: 5804 Goliad Ave Dallas TX 75206-6818 Office: 5740 Prospect Ave Dallas TX 75206-8808

WILBUR, ANDREW CLAYTON, radiologist; b. Phila., May 30, 1952; s. Richard Sloan and Betty Lou (Fannin) W. AB in Human Biology, Stanford U., 1974; MD, George Washington U., 1978. Diplomate Am. Bd. Radiology. Extern in diagnostic radiology Palo Alto (Calif.) Med. Found., 1978-79; resident in diagnostic radiology U. Ill. Hosp., Chgo., 1979-83, fellow in body imaging, 1983-84; asst. prof. radiology U. Ill. Coll. Medicine, Chgo., 1984-90, assoc. prof., 1990—, dir. body imaging dept. radiology, 1988—, dir. radiology residency program, 1989—. Contbr. articles to profl. jours. Mem. Radiol. Soc. N.Am., Am. Coll. Radiology, Am. Roentgen Ray Soc. Office: Univ of Illinois Hosp M/C 931 1740 W Taylor St Chicago IL 60612-7232

WILBUR, BARBARA MARIE, elementary education educator; b. Homer City, Pa., Dec. 1, 1945; d. Nicholas and Ann (Bender) Hrebik; m. Samuel Scime, Nov. 21, 1970 (div. Jan. 1974); m. Frederick Layton Wilbur, June 21, 1986 (dec. June 1989). BS in Elem. Edn., SUNY, Buffalo, 1967, EdM in Guidance Counseling, 1971; postgrad., Harvard U., 1969; grad., John Robert Powers Modeling Sch., Buffalo, 1974. Cert. permanent elem. sch. tchr., N.Y. Elem. tchr. Buffalo Pub. Schs., 1967-70, 94—, Diocese of Ft. Lauderdale, Fla., 1971-72, Diocese of Buffalo, 1973-94. Mem. State U. Buffalo Alumni Assn., State U. Coll. Buffalo Alumni Assn. (Outstanding Svc. award 1982), Buffalo State Coll. Alumni Assn. (bd. dirs. 1980-87, active various coms.). Republican. Roman Catholic. Avocations: modeling, volleyball, ice skating, tennis. Home: 301 Lowell Rd Tonawanda NY 14217-1236 Office: Buffalo Pub Schs Sch #18 118 Hampshire St Buffalo NY 14213-2014

WILBUR, BRAYTON, JR., distribution company executive; b. San Francisco, Oct. 2, 1935; s. Brayton and Matilda (Baker) W.; m. Judith Flood, June 29, 1963; children: Jennifer, Edward, Claire, Michael. B.A., Yale U., 1957; M.B.A., Stanford U., 1961. With Arthur Young & Co., San Francisco, 1962-63; v.p. Wilbur-Ellis Co., San Francisco, 1963-74, exec. v.p., 1974—, also dir.; dir. Chronicle Pub. Co., San Francisco, 1983-89; pres. Wilbur-Ellis Co., San Francisco, 1989—; bd. dir. Safeway Stores, 1977-86. Pres. San Francisco Symphony, 1980-87; v.p. Sponsors for Performing Arts Ctr., San Francisco, 1975—; trustee Fine Art Mus. of San Francisco, 1978-81, Asia Found., 1972—, chmn. 1990—. Served with USAR, 1958-63. Mem. Council on Fgn. Relations, Bohemian Club, Pacific Union Club, Cypress Point Club, Burlingame Country Club. Republican. Home: 821 Irwin Dr Burlingame CA 94010-6327 Office: Wilbur-Ellis Co 320 California St Fl 2 San Francisco CA 94104*

WILBUR, COLBURN SLOAN, foundation administrator, chief executive officer; b. Palo Alto, Calif., Jan. 20, 1935; s. Blake Colburn and Mary (Sloan) W.; m. Maria Grace Verburg, Sept. 1, 1961; children: Marguerite Louise, Anne Noelle. BA in Polit. Sci., Stanford U., 1956, MBA, 1960. Asst. cashier United Calif. Bank, San Francisco, 1960-65; v.p. Standata, San Francisco, 1965-68; adminstrv. mgr. Tab Products, San Francisco, 1968-69; exec. dir. Sierra Club Found., San Francisco, 1969-76, David and Lucile Packard Found., Los Altos, Calif., 1976—; bd. dirs., mem. adv. bd. Coun. Founds., Washington, Found. Ctr., N.Y.C. Former bd. dirs., mem. adv bd. Global Fund Women, Palo Alto, Calif.; past bd. dirs. Big Bros. San Francisco, Calif. Confederation Arts, Peninsula Grantmakers, Women's Fund Santa Clara; former bd. dirs., pres. Big Bros. Peninsula, North Fork Assn., Peninsula Conservation Ctr.; past bd. dirs., chmn. No. Calif. Grantmakers; bd. dirs., mem. adv. bd. Sierra Club Found., Stanford Theater Found., Palo Alto, U. San Francisco/Inst. Nonprofit Orgn. Mgmt. With U.S. Army, 1957-58. Office: David and Lucile Packard Found 300 2nd St Los Altos CA 94022-3632

WILBUR, DWIGHT LOCKE, physician; b. Harrow-on-the-Hill, Eng., Sept. 18, 1903; came to U.S., 1904; s. Ray Lyman and Marguerite May (Blake) W.; m. Ruth Esther Jordan, Oct. 20, 1928; children: Dwight L., Jordan R., Gregory F. AB, Stanford U., 1923; MD, U. Pa., 1926; MS in Medicine, U. Minn.-Mpls., 1933; DSc (hon.), Dartmouth Coll., 1973. Diplomate Am. Bd. Internal Medicine. Intern, U. Pa. Hosp., Phila., 1926-28; resident, Mayo Found., Rochester, Minn., 1929-31; staff Mayo Clinic, Rochester, 1931-37; clin. prof. medicine Stanford U., Calif., 1937-68; pvt. practice medicine, San Francisco, 1937-83; physician U.S. Naval Res., Oakland, Calif., 1942-46; clin. prof. medicine emeritus Stanford U. from 1968. Editor, Calif. Medicine, 1946-67. Author (with J.R. Gamble): Chemistry of Digestive Diseases, 1961, Current Concepts of Clinical Gastroenterology, 1965. Contbr. articles to profl. jours. Trustee Mayo Found., 1951-71, emeritus from 1971. Served to comdr., USNR, 1942-46. Recipient Julius Friedenwald medal, Am. Gastroenterol. Assn., 1961; Spl. Commendation for Outstanding Achievement, U. Minn., 1964; Outstanding Civilian Service medal, Dept. Army, 1966; First Disting. Internist award, Am. Soc. Internal Medicine, 1970. Mem. Calif. Med. Assn. (hon. past pres.), Inst. Medicine Nat. Acad. Scis. (charter), ACP (charter, Alfred Stengel Meml. award 1964, pres. 1958-59, fellow), AMA (pres. 1968-69), Am. Gastroenterologic Assn. (pres. 1954-55). Republican. Club: Commonwealth, Bohemian. Died March 9, 1997. Home: 140 Sea Cliff Ave San Francisco CA 94121-1125

WILBUR, E. PACKER, investment company executive; b. Bridgeport, Conn., Sept. 9, 1936; s. E. Packer and Elizabeth (Wells) W.; m. Laura Mary Ferrier, Sept. 17, 1965; children—Alison Mary, Andrew Packer, Gillian Elizabeth. B.A., Yale U., 1959; M.B.A., Harvard U., 1965. Cons. McKinsey & Co. Inc., N.Y.C., 1964-67; dir. corp. planning Am. Express Co., N.Y.C., 1967-69; v.p. Van Alstyne Noel & Co., N.Y.C., 1969-70; exec. v.p., dir., mem. exec. com. Newburger Loeb & Co. Inc., N.Y.C., 1970-73; pres. E.P. Wilbur & Co., Inc., Southport, Conn., 1973—, Southport Fin. Corp., 1986—; chmn. bd. Criterion Mgmt., Inc., Lafayette, Ind., Trend Mgmt., Inc., Tampa, Fla., Fairfield Advisors, Inc., Southport, EPW Securities, Inc., Southport; gen. ptnr. Grandland Realty Assos., Embankment Properties Ltd., London, Autumn Woods Assos., others; former allied mem. N.Y. Stock Exchange. Contbr. articles to fin. jours. Bd. dirs. Harvard U. Inst. for Social and Econ. Policy in the Middle East, Inst. Govt. Assested Housing, Washington, Mus. Art, Sci., Industry, Bridgeport, Wakeman Meml. Boys' Club, Southport, Greater Bridgeport Jr. Hockey League, Pequot Library, Southport, Bridgeport U., Northfield-Mt. Hermon Sch.; mem. dean's coun. John F. Kennedy Sch. of Govt. at Harvard U. Served AUS, 1959-60. Clubs: Pequot Yacht (Southport), Pequot Running (Southport) (chmn.); Country Club of Fairfield; Yale (N.Y.C.). Home: 648 Harbor Rd Southport CT 06490-1321 Office: 2507 Post Rd Southport CT 06490-1259

WILBUR, HENRY MILES, zoologist, educator; b. Bridgeport, Conn., Jan. 25, 1944; s. Robert Leonard and Martha (Miles) W.; m. Dorothy Spates, Jan. 27, 1967 (div. Dec. 1980); 1 child, Sarah; m. Rebecca Burchell, May 22, 1981; children: Helen, Lindsay. BS, Duke U., 1966; PhD, U. Mich., 1971. Asst. prof. Duke U., Durham, N.C., 1973-77, assoc. prof., 1977-81, prof., 1981-91, chmn., 1990-91; B.F.D. Runk prof. U. Va., Charlottesville, 1991—; dir. Mt. Lake Biol. Sta., Charlottesville, 1991—. Assoc. editor Ecol. Soc. Am., Soc. Study of Evolution, Soc. Am. Naturalists. Recipient Disting. Herpetologist Herpetologists League, 1990. Mem. Am. Soc. Icthyologists and Herpetologists, Am. Soc. Naturalists (treas., pres. 1996), Ecol. Soc. Am. (MacArthur award 1995), Soc. of Study of Evolution, Herpetologists League, Brit. Ecol. Soc. Office: U Va Dept Biology Gilmer Hall Charlottesville VA 22903-2477

WILBUR, LESLIE CLIFFORD, mechanical engineering educator; b. Johnston, R.I., May 12, 1924; s. Clifford Elwood and Isabel (Winsor) W.; m. Gertrude Monica Widmer, Sept. 9, 1950; children—Clifford Leslie, Kenneth Charles, Ted Winsor, Christopher Francis. B.S. in Mech. Engring, U. R.I., 1948; M.S., Stevens Inst. Tech., 1949. Registered profl. engr., Mass. Instr., then asst. prof. Duke, 1949-57; mem. faculty Worcester Poly. Inst., 1957—, prof. mech. engring., 1961—, dir. nuclear reactor facility, 1959-86, prof. emeritus, 1987—; Mem. N.E. adv. council Atomic Indsl. Forum, 1972—. Editor-in-chief: Handbook of Energy Systems. Served with AUS, 1943-46, ETO. Mem. Am. Nuclear Soc. (mem. at large exec. com. Northeastern sect. 1961-62, 66-67, chmn. Northeastern sect. 1968-69), ASME (vice chmn. Eastern N.C. sect. 1956-57), Am. Soc. Engring. Edn., AAAS, Sigma Xi, Tau Beta Pi, Phi Kappa Phi, Pi Tau Sigma. Baptist (deacon 1962-65). Home: PO Box 105 Sebasco Estates ME 04565-0105 also (summer): 94 Parkway N Brewer ME 04412-1235 Office: Worcester Poly Inst Dept Mech Engring Ed Worcester MA 01609

WILBUR, MARK, environmental executive. V.p. engring. Kemron Environ. Svcs., Inc., McLean, Va. Office: Kemron Environ Svcs Inc 7926 Jones Branch Dr Ste 1100 Mc Lean VA 22102-3303

WILBUR, RICHARD PURDY, writer, educator; b. N.Y.C., Mar. 1, 1921; s. Lawrence L. and Helen (Purdy) W.; m. Mary Charlotte Hayes Ward, June 20, 1942; children: Ellen Dickinson, Christopher Hayes, Nathan Lord, Aaron Hammond. AB, Amherst Coll., 1942, AM, 1952, DLitt (hon.), 1967; AM, Harvard U., 1947; LHD (hon.), Lawrence Coll., Washington U., Williams Coll., U. Rochester, SUNY, Potsdam, 1986, Skidmore Coll., 1987, U. Lowell, 1990; DLitt (hon.), Clark U.; DLitt, Am. Internat. Coll., Marquette U., Wesleyan U., Carnegie-Mellon U.; D.Litt. (hon.), Lake Forest Coll., 1982, Smith Coll., 1996; LittD (hon.), Sewanee U., 1996. Jr. fellow Harvard U., Cambridge, Mass., 1947-50, Asst. prof. English, 1950-54; assoc. prof. Wellesley Coll., 1955-57; prof. Wesleyan U., 1957-77; writer in residence Smith Coll., 1977-86. Author: The Beautiful Changes, 1947, Ceremony, 1950, A Bestiary, 1955, reprint, 1993, Things of This World, 1956, Poems 1943-56, 1957, Advice to a Prophet, 1961, Poems of Richard Wilbur, 1963, Walking to Sleep, 1969, The Mind-Reader, 1976, Seven Poems, 1981, The Whale, 1982, New and Collected Poems, 1988 (Pulitzer prize for poetry 1989); (children's books) Loudmouse, 1963, Opposites, 1973, More Opposites, 1991, A Game of Catch, 1994, Runaway Opposites, 1995; (criticism) Responses, 1976, (prose pieces) The Catbird's Song, 1997; co-author: (comic opera, with Lillian Hellman) Candide, 1957, (cantata, with William Schuman) On Freedom's Ground, 1986; translator: (Moliere) The Misanthrope, 1955, Tartuffe, 1963 (co-recipient Bollingen Translation prize 1963), The School for Wives, 1971, The Learned Ladies, 1978, Four Comedies, 1982, (Racine) Andromache, 1982, Phaedra, 1986, Molière's The School for Husbands, 1992, Imaginary Cuckold, 1993, Molière's Amphitryon, 1995; editor: Complete Poems of Poe, 1959, Poems of Shakespeare, 1966, Selected Poems of Witter Bynner, 1978. Decorated chevalier Ordre des Palmes Academiques; recipient Harriet Monroe prize Poetry mag., 1948, Oscar Blumenthal prize, 1950, Prix de Rome, Am. Acad. Arts and Letters, 1954, Edna St. Vincent Millay Meml. award, 1957, Nat. Book award, 1957, Pulitzer prize, 1957, Sarah Josepha Hale award, 1968, Bollingen prize, 1971, Brandeis U. Creative Arts award, 1971, Prix Henri Desfeuilles, 1971, Shelley Meml. award, 1973, Harriet Monroe Poetry award, 1978, St. Botolph's Club Found. award, 1983, Drama Desk award, 1983, Aiken-Taylor award, 1988, Bunn award, 1988, Washington Coll. Lit. award, 1988, St. Louis Lit. award, 1989, Grand Master award Birmingham-So. Coll., 1989, Gold Medal for Poetry, Am. Acad. Inst. Arts and Letters, 1991, Edward MacDowell medal, 1992, Nat. Arts Club Medal of Honor for Lit., 1994, PEN/Manheim Medal for Translation, 1994, Milton Ctr. prize, 1995, Acad. Am. Achievement award, 1995, Robert Frost medal Poetry Soc. of Am., 1996, T.S. Eliot award, 1996; Guggenheim fellow, 1952-53, 63, Ford fellow, 1960-61, Camargo Found. fellow, 1985; named U.S. Poet Laureate, Libr. Congress, 1987, Nat. Medal of the Arts, 1994. Fellow MLA (hon.); mem. AAAL (pres. 1974-76, chancellor 1976-78, 80-81), ASCAP, PEN (Transl. award 1983), Am. Acad. Arts and Scis., Acad. Am. Poets (chancellor emeritus), Dramatists Guild, Century Club. Home: 87 Dodwells Rd Cummington MA 01026-9705 also: 715R Windsor Ln Key West FL 33040-6430

WILBUR, RICHARD SLOAN, physician, foundation executive; b. Boston, Apr. 8, 1924; s. Blake Colburn and Mary Caldwell (Sloan) W.; m. Betty Lou Fannin, Jan. 20, 1951; children: Andrew, Peter, Thomas. BA, Stanford U., 1943, MD, 1946; JD, John Marshall Law Sch., 1990. Intern San Francisco County Hosp., 1946-47; resident Stanford Hosp., 1949-51, U. Pa. Hosp., 1951-52; postgrad. tng. U. Mich. Hosp., 1957, Karolinska Sjukhuset, Stockholm, 1960; mem. staff Palo Alto (Calif.) Med. Clinic, 1952-69; dep. exec. v.p. AMA, Chgo., 1969-71, 73-74; asst. sec. for health and environment Dept. Def., 1971-73; sr. v.p. Baxter Labs., Inc., Deerfield, Ill., 1974-76; exec. v.p. Council Med. Splty. Socs., 1976-91, sec. accreditation council for continuing med. edn., 1979-91; asso. prof. medicine Georgetown U. Med. Sch., 1971-77, Stanford Med. Sch., 1952-69; pres. Nat. Resident Matching Plan, 1991-92; chmn. bd. Calif. Med. Assn., 1968-69, Calif. Blue Shield, 1966-68, Am. Medico-Legal Found., 1987—; chmn. bd., CEO Inst. for Clin. Info., 1994—; CEO Medic Alert, 1992-94; pres. Am. Bd. Med. Mgmt., 1992; mem. Am. Bd. Electrodiagnostic Medicine, 1993—. Contbr. articles to med. jours. Vice chmn. Rep. Cen. Com. Santa Clara County, Calif., 1966-89; bd. govs. ARC; chmn. bd. dirs. Medic Alert Found.; bd. dirs. Nat. Adv. Cancer Coun., Nat. Health Coun., 1993-95; bd. visitors Drew U. Postgrad. Med. Sch.; chmn. Mid-Am. Blood Svcs. Bd., Lifesource Blood Bank, 1996. With USNR, 1942-49. Recipient Disting. Svc. medal Dept. Def., 1973, scroll of merit Nat. Med. Assn., 1971. Fellow ACP, Am. Coll. Legal Medicine (bd. dirs.), Am. Coll. Physician Execs. (bd. regents 1985-89, pres.-elect 1987, pres. 1988-89), Internat. Coll. Dentistry (hon.); mem. Inst. Medicine, Ill. Med. Assn., Lake County Med. Soc., Am. Gastroent. Assn., Pacific Interurban Clin. Club, Am. Soc. Internal Medicine, Santa Clara County Med. Soc. (hon.), Cedars Club (Soda Springs, Calif.), Union League Phila., Phi Beta Kappa, Alpha Omega Alpha. Home: 985 Hawthorne Pl Lake Forest IL 60045-2217 Office: 207 Westminster Rd Lake Forest IL 60045-1885

WILBURN, MARY NELSON, retired lawyer, writer; b. Balt., Feb. 18, 1932; d. David Alfred and Phoebe Blanche (Novotny) Nelson; m. Adolph Yarbrough Wilburn, Mar. 5, 1957; children: Adolph II, Jason David. AB cum laude, Howard U., 1952; MA, U. Wis., 1955, JD, 1975. Bar: Wis. 1975, U.S. Supreme Ct 1981. Commr. Nat. Coun. of Negro Women Commn. on Edn., 1986—; judge NAACP ACT-SO Competition, 1994—; vol. One Ch. One Addict, 1995—; mem. bd. edn. Cath. Archdiocese of Washington, 1995—; bd. mem. Office Employer Appeals, D.C., 1997—; bd. dirs. One Ch.-One Inmate, 1997—. Mem. Fedn. Internat. de Abogadas (bd. dirs. 1996—), Howard U. Alumni Assn., Links, Inc., Leadership Greater Washington (bd. dirs. 1992-94, v.p. 1995-96), Coun. Black Catholics, Alpha Kappa Alpha.

WILBURN, ROBERT CHARLES, institute executive; b. Latrobe, Pa., July 1, 1943; s. Robert Charles and Annabel Grace (McWherter) W.; m. Patricia Ellen Zuidema, May 18, 1968; children: Jason, Rae, Jesse, Benjamin. BS, U.S. Air Force Acad., 1965; MPA, Princeton U., 1967, PhD, 1970; LLD (hon.), U. Scranton, Pa., 1983, Hahneman U., 1984, Duquesne U., 1985. Econometrician Dept. of Def., Washington, 1967-69, policy analyst, 1970-72; economist The White House, Washington, 1969-70; v.p. Chase Manhattan Bank, N.Y.C., 1972-75; pres. Indiana U. of Pa., Indiana, 1975-79; sec. of budget Commonwealth of Pa., Harrisburg, 1979-83, sec. edn., 1983-84; pres. Carnegie Inst., Pitts., 1984-92, Colonial Williamsburg (Va.) Found., 1992—; bd. dirs. Harsco Corp., Wormleysburg, Pa., Crestar Corp., Richmond, Va. Trustee Carnegie Mellon U., 1985-92, Shadyside Hosp., Pitts., 1985-92; sec. Allegheny Conf. on Community Devel., Pitts. Capt. USAF, 1965-72. Named Man of Yr., Pitts. Vectors, 1992. Mem. ALA, Am. Mus. Assn. (bd. dirs. 1989-92), Urban Librs. Coun. Chgo. (pres. 1991-93), World Affairs Coun. (bd. dirs. 1988-92), Duquesne Club (bd. dirs. 1990-92), Hampton Roads Partnership, 1996—, Pitts. Athletic Assn. Republican. Roman Catholic. Office: Colonial Williamsburg Found PO Box 1776 Williamsburg VA 23187-1776

WILBY, WILLIAM LANGFITT, global mutual fund manager, economist; b. New Orleans, May 10, 1944; s. Langfitt Bowditch and Routh (Trowbridge) W.; m. Cynthia Warren Pike, Mar. 19, 1982; 1 child, Molly. BS in Engring., U.S. Mil. Acad., 1967; MA in Econs., U. Colo., 1978, PhD in Econs., 1980. Commd. lt. U.S. Army, 1967, advanced through grades to capt., 1969, served in Europe, Vietnam, Washington, resigned, 1974; internat. economist Fed. Res. Bank Chgo., 1980-81; v.p., economist No. Trust Bank, Chgo., 1981-86; mng. dir. AIG Global Investors, N.Y.C., 1986-90; dir. Global Equities Oppenheimer Funds, N.Y.C., 1990—; vis. prof. Am. Grad. Sch. Internat. Mgmt., Glendale, Ariz., 1978-79, Kellogg Grad. Sch. Bus. Northwestern U., Evanston, Ill., 1981-84. Mem. Assn. Investment Mgmt. and Rsch. Office: Oppenheimer Funds Two World Trade Ctr 34th Fl New York NY 10048-0203

WILCHER, LARRY K., lawyer; b. Lebanon, Ky., July 19, 1950; s. Dwain LaRue and Juanita (Tungate) W.; m. Mary Jo Hayden, Aug. 21, 1971; children: Emily Jane, Joseph Keith. BS in Pharmacy, St. Louis Coll. Pharmacy, 1973; JD, No. Ky. U., 1983; program of instrn. for lawyers, Harvard U., 1987, 91, 94. Dir. real estate SuperX Drugs Corp., Cin., 1975-84; dir. real estate, real estate counsel Dollar Gen. Corp., Scottsville, Ky., 1984-85, gen. counsel, 1985—, asst. sec., 1988—; bd. dirs. TransFin., Inc. Contbr. to book: Kentucky Business Organizations, 1989. Chmn. Warren County Young Reps., Bowling Green, Ky., 1977-79; sec., dir. Scottsville-Allen County Leasing Corp., 1992—; sec., dir. Scottsville-Allen County Indsl. Devel. Authority, Inc., 1991—; dir. Leadership Ky., 1994—. Named to Hon. Order Ky. Cols., 1968, One of Outstanding Young Men of Am., U.S. Jaycees, 1978; recipient Johnson & Johnson award St. Louis Coll. Pharmacy, 1973, Thurston B. Morton Leadership award Ky. Young Rep. Fedn., 1979. Mem. ABA, Nat. Assn. Corp. Dirs., Ky. Bar Assn. (recognition award 1987), Louisville Bar Assn., Def. Rsch. Inst., Am. Corp. Counsel Assn. Republican. Baptist. Office: Dollar Gen Corp 427 Beech St Scottsville KY 42164-1670

WILCHER, SHIRLEY J., lawyer; b. Erie, Pa., July 28, 1951; d. James S. Wilcher and Jeanne (Evans) Cheatham. AB cum laude, Mt. Holyoke Coll., 1973; MA, New Sch. Social Research, 1976; JD, Harvard U., 1979. Bar: N.Y. 1980. Assoc. Proskauer Rose Goetz and Mendelsohn, N.Y.C., 1979-80; staff atty. Nat. Women's Law Ctr., Washington, 1980-85; assoc. counsel Com. on Edn. and Labor U.S. Ho. Reps., Washington, 1985-90; dir. state rels., gen. counsel Nat. Assn. Ind. Colls. and Univs., Washington, 1990-94; dep. asst. sec. Office Fed. Contract Compliance Programs, U.S. Dept. Labor, Washington, 1994—. Editor Harvard U. Civil Rights/Civil Liberties Law Rev., 1978-79; contbr. articles to profl. jours. Nat. bd. dirs. Nat. Polit. Congress of Black Women, Washington, 1985-87; convenor Black Women's Roundtable on Voter Participation, Washington, 1984-85. Mem. ABA, Nat. Bar Assn., Nat. Conf. Black Lawyers (local bd. dirs. 1980-87, nat. bd. dirs. 1986-87). Democrat. Buddhist. Avocations: music, Oriental art. Office: US Dept Labor Fed Contract Compliance Programs FPB 200 Constitution Ave NW Washington DC 20210-1531

WILCHINS, SIDNEY A., gynecologist; b. Paterson, N.J., Feb. 2, 1940; s. Philip Aaron and Esther (Blake) W.; m. Carole Diane Brill, June 23, 1963, (div. Mar. 1985); children: Joan Helen, Edward Victor; m. Estelle Angel, Mar. 15, 1985; children: Jacqueline, Susan. BA in Biol. Scis., Rutgers U., 1961; MD, Georgetown U., 1965. Diplomate Am. Bd. Ob Gyn. Clin. instr. N.J. Med. Sch., Newark, N.J., 1971-73; clin. asst. prof. N.J. Med. Sch., Newark, 1973-78, clin. assoc. prof., 1978—; adj. rsch. prof. N.J. Inst. Tech., Newark, 1978—; assoc. dir. Pilgrim Med. Ctr., Montclair, N.J., 1982-93; med. dir. Ultrasound Diagnostic Sch., Union, N.J., 1989-91, N.J. Menopause Found., 1992—; gynecol. cons. Organon/Akzo, 1991—; med. dir. Gynchoices of Cen. Jersey, 1994—; pres. Soc. of Forensic Obstetricians & Gynecologists, 1994-96; bd. dirs. N.Y. Met. MSO Physicians Network, 1996—. Author, editor: Cryosurgery and Medicine, 1990; contbr. articles to profl. jours. Lt. USNR, 1965-69. Fellow ACOG, ACS, N.Y. Acad. Medicine; mem. N.Y. Acad. Scis., Forensic Soc. Ob-Gyn. (pres. 1994-95), Colonia Country Club. Achievements include patent pending on Intraperitoneal Hyperthermia Device, pregnancy conducto for labor software copyright; application of chaost level to analysis of labor physiology. Home: 154 Devon Rd Colonia NJ 07067-3205 Office: Union County Ob-Gyn 236 E Westfield Ave Roselle Park NJ 07204-2084

WILCOCK, DONALD FREDERICK, mechanical engineer; b. Bklyn., Sept. 24, 1913; s. Frederick and Jennie Marie (Young) W.; m. Marjorie Ellen Ferris, Sept. 3, 1938; 1 son, Donald Everett. B.S. in Civil Engring, Harvard U., 1934; D.Engring. Sci., U. Cin., 1939. Research chemist Sherwin Williams Co., Chgo., 1939-42; with Gen. Electric Co., 1942-65; mgr. tribology dept. Mech. Tech., Inc., Latham, N.Y., 1965-78; pres. Tribolock Inc., Schenectady, 1978—, Inst. for Innovation Through Tribology, 1980-82. Author: Bearing Design and Application, 1957. Fellow ASME (Nat. Hersey award), Am. Soc. Lubrication Engrs. Patentee. Home and Office: 40 Autumn Dr Apt 200 Slingerlands NY 12159-9346

WILCOX, ARTHUR MANIGAULT, newspaper editor; b. Phila., May 2, 1922; s. John Walter and Caroline (Manigault) W.; m. Katharine Moore McMurray, Nov. 25, 1944; children: Margaret Moore, Arthur Manigault, Priscilla McMurray, Robert Manigault. B.S., Ga. Inst. Tech., 1943. Reporter Charleston (S.C.) Eve. Post, 1946-52, city editor, 1952-57, editor, 1968-74; asst. editor Charleston News and Courier, 1957-68, editor, 1974-90; sec., cons. Evening Post Pub. Co., pubs. Post-Courier, 1990—. Curator S.C. Hist. Soc., 1957-60; trustee Hist. Charleston Found., 1985-94; trustee Charleston Mus., 1967-96, trustee emeritus, 1996, pres. bd., 1971-81; mem. bd. visitors Winthrop Coll., Rock Hill, S.C., 1984-87; chmn. Nat. Com. to Save Ft. Sumter Flags, 1983-89; vestryman Protestant Episcopal Ch., 1954-59, 62-66, 68-72, 79-82, 96—, sr. warden, 1981. Lt. (j.g.) USN, 1943-46; rear adm. USNR. Mem. Am. Soc. Newspaper Editors, New Eng. Soc., St. Cecilia Soc., Soc. Colonial Wars (registrar 1991—), Caroline Art Assn., U.S. Naval Inst., Audubon Soc., Nat. Trust, Huguenot Soc. S.C. (v.p. 1990-91, pres. 1991-96), Charleston Club, Carolina Yacht Club, Tennis Club, Army and Navy Club (Washington), Wild Dunes Club (Isle of Palms, S.C.), Rotary, Yeaman's Hall Club (Charleston, S.C.). Home: 26 St Augustine Dr Charleston SC 29407-6018 Office: 171 Church St Ste 300 Charleston SC 29401-3165

WILCOX, BENSON REID, cardiothoracic surgeon, educator; b. Charlotte, N.C., May 26, 1932; s. James Simpson and Louisa (Reid) W.; m. Lucinda Holderness, July 25, 1959; children: Adelaide, Alexandra, Melissa, Reid. BA, U. N.C., 1953, MD, 1957. Diplomate Am. Bd. Surgery, Am. Bd. Thoracic Surgery (chmn. 1991-93). Resident Barnes Hosp., St. Louis, 1958-59, N.C. Meml. Hosp., Chapel Hill, 1959-60, 62-64; clin. assoc. Nat. Heart Inst., Bethesda, Md., 1960-62; instr. U. N.C., Chapel Hill, 1963-65, asst. prof., 1965-68, assoc. prof., 1968-71, chief divsn. of cardiothoracic surgery, 1969—, prof., 1971—; cons. NIH Grant Com., Bethesda, 1986-89. Contbr. articles to profl. jours.; author (with others): Atlas of the Heart, 1988, Surgical Anatomy of the Heart, 1992. Pres. Atlantic Coast Conf., Greensboro, N.C., 1980-81; dir. Am. Bd. Thoracic Surgery, 1983-93, chmn., 1991-93. Markle scholar John and Mary Markle Found., 1967; recipient

Hadassah Myrtle Wreath award, 1979. Mem. Am. Assn. Thoracic Surgery, Am. Surg. Assn., Soc. Thoracic Surgeons (treas. 1980-86, pres. 1994-95), Soc. Univ. Surgeons, So. Surg. Assn., Thoracic Surgery Dirs. Assn. (pres. 1985-87), Womack Soc. (pres. 1991-93). Democrat. Presbyterian. Avocations: medical history, tennis, golf, hiking. Office: U NC Med Sch Div Cardiothoracic Surgery 108 Burnett-Womack CB-7065 Chapel Hill NC 27599-7065

WILCOX, BRUCE GORDON, publisher; b. Boston, Sept. 3, 1947; s. Edward Teed and Maud (Eckert) W.; m. Greta Green, Apr. 7, 1974; children: Sarah M., Thor E., Hilary A. BA, Harvard U., 1969; postgrad., Peace Corps, Senegal, 1969-70, NYU, 1972-75. Asst. sales mgr. U. Wash. Press, Seattle, 1971-72, editor, 1975-82; program officer Franklin Book Programs, N.Y.C. and Dacca, Bangladesh, 1972-75; dir. U. Mass. Press, Amherst, 1983—; cons. NEH, Washington, 1983, 85, NEA, Washington, 1991. Mem. editl. adv. bd. Jour. Scholarly Publ., 1992—. Bd. dirs. Mass. Rev., 1987—. Mem. Assn. Am. Univ. Presses (del. to USSR and Ea. Europe 1977, to China 1985, to Estonia and CSFR 1992, bd. dirs. 1990-96, pres. 1994-95). Home: 191 Lincoln Ave Amherst MA 01002-2009

WILCOX, CHARLES JULIAN, geneticist, educator; b. Harrisburg, Pa., Mar. 28, 1930; s. Charles John and Gertrude May (Hill) W.; m. Eileen Louise Armstrong, Aug. 27, 1955; children: Marsha Lou, Douglas Edward. BS, U. Vt., 1950; MS, Rutgers U., 1955, PhD, 1959. Registered profl. animal scientist. Dairy farm owner, operator Charlotte, Vt., 1955-56; prof. U. Fla., Gainesville, 1959-95; prof. emeritus, 1995—; cons. in internat. animal agrl. Gt. Britain, France, Sudan, Pakistan, Can., Mex., El Salavador, Ecuador, Brazil, Bolivia, Peru, Colombia, Venezuela, Dominican Republic, Saudi Arabia, Sweden, Norway, 1965—. Author: (with others) Animal Agriculture, 1973, 2d edit., 1980, Improvement of Milk Production in Tropics, 1990; editor: Large Dairy Herd Management, 1978, 93. 1st Lt. U.S. Army, 1951-53, Korea. Decorated Combat Infantryman badge; 3 Korean campaigns. Recipient Disting. Svc. award Fla. Purebred Dairy Assn., 1986, Jr. Faculty award Gamma Sigma Delta, 1968, Sr. Faculty award, 1984, Internat. award for Disting. Svc. to Agr., 1987, Sr. Rsch. Scientist award Sigma Xi, 1994. Mem. Am. Dairy Sci. Assn., Am. Soc. Animal Sci., Brazilian Soc. Genetics (editorial bd. 1979—), Am. Registry Profls. Animal Sci. (examining bd. 1987—), Fla. Holstein Assn. (pres. 1979), Fla. Jersey Cattle Club (bd. dirs.), Fla. Guernsey Cattle Club (pres. 1974-76), Fla. Jersey Cattle Club (bd. dirs.). Republican. Avocations: spectator sports (baseball, football, basketball, tennis). Office: Univ Fla Dairy and Poultry Sci Dept Gainesville FL 32611-0920

WILCOX, DAVID ERIC, educational consultant, electrical engineer; b. Cortland, N.Y., Sept. 4, 1939; s. James A. and Lucille (Fiske) C.; B.S. in Elec. Engring., U. Buffalo, 1961; postgrad. Syracuse U., 1965, Marist Coll.; M.S., U. Bridgeport, 1977; Ed.D. candidate Rutgers U.; m. Phyllipa Ann Wilcox, Jan. 23, 1977; children: Terri L., Cindy A., Jana L. Research engring. mgr. input/output devices Rome (N.Y.) Air Devel. Center, 1966-70; dir. sales Mercon Inc., Winsooki, Vt., 1970-73, dir., 1972—; pres. Wilcox Tng. Systems, Newburgh, N.Y., 1973—; prin. Exec. Effectiveness, Inc., N.Y.C.; instr. Dale Carnegie courses. Pres. N.Y. State Jaycees, 1972-73, chmn. bd., 1973-74; dir. U.S. Jaycees, 1970-71; bd. dirs., v.p. N.Y. State Spl. Olympics, 1972-73; bd. dirs., treas. Family Counseling Service, Inc.; mem. Orange County Pvt. Industry Coun.; mem. N.Y. State Excelsior Examiner, 1995. Served to lt. USAF, 1961-65. Registered profl. engr., N.Y. Mem. Soc. Info. Display, IEEE, N.Y., State Soc. Profl. Engrs., Internat. Transactional Analysis Assn., Internat. Platform Assn., Am. Soc. Quality Control. Methodist. Author: Information System Sciences, 1965; also articles. Patentee in field. Home: 511 River Rd Newburgh NY 12550-1304 Office: Rock Cut Rd Newburgh NY 12550 also: 30 W 60th St New York NY 10023-7902

WILCOX, HARRY HAMMOND, retired medical educator; b. Canton, Ohio, May 31, 1918; s. Harry Hammond and Hattie Estelle (Richner) W.; m. D. June Freed., June 21, 1941; children: Joyce L. Wilcox Graff, Margaret J. (Mrs. Grayson S. Smith), James Hammond. B.S., U. Mich., 1939, M.S., 1940, Ph.D., 1948. Asso. prof. biology Morningside Coll., Sioux City, Iowa, 1947-48; asso. in anatomy U. Pa., 1948-52; mem. faculty U. Tenn. Center for Health Scis., 1952-83, Goodman prof. anatomy, 1966-83, emeritus prof. anatomy, 1983—. Assoc. editor: Anat. Record, 1968-83. Served with AUS, 1945-46. Mem. AAAS, Am. Assn. Anatomists, Am. Soc. Zoologists, Sigma Xi. Home: 1031 Marcia Rd Memphis TN 38117-5513

WILCOX, HARRY WILBUR, JR., retired corporate executive; b. Phila., Feb. 13, 1925; s. Harry Wilbur and Justine Elizabeth (Doolittle) W.; m. Colleen Ann Cerra, Apr. 6, 1946; children: Justine, Harry Wilbur III. B.S., Yale U., 1949. With Gen. Electric Co., N.Y.C., 1949-50; mfg. supt. Sylvania Electric Products, 1951-67; v.p., gen. mgr. Granger Assocs. (electronics), Palo Alto, Calif., 1967-70; gen. mgr. ITT-Cannon Electric Co., Phoenix, 1970-72; pres. Hills McCanna Co., Carpentersville, Ill., 1972-75; pres. VSI, and group v.p. IU Internat. Corp., 1975-78; exec. v.p. ITT-Grinnell, 1978-85; pres. ITT Valve Div, Lancaster, Pa., 1985-88; dir. Meyer Industries, Nat. Temperature Control Centers, Paul N. Howard Co.; former chmn. VSI, VSI-UK. Mem. adv. com. Town of Sherborn, Mass. Served with U.S. Army, 1943-46. Decorated Bronze star. Mem. R.I. Country Club, Yale Club of Vero Beach, Grand Harbor Golf and Beach Club (Vero Beach), Bristol (R.I.) Yacht Club. Patentee in electroluminescence. Home: 31 Sea Breeze Ln Bristol RI 02809-1520 also: 1135 Harbor Links Cir Vero Beach FL 32967-7202

WILCOX, HARVEY JOHN, lawyer; b. Elyria, Ohio, Nov. 1, 1937; s. Hubbard Clyde and Sylvia (Wahter) W.; m. Leslie Louise Coleman, Apr. 11, 1970. BA cum laude, Amherst Coll., 1959; LLB, Yale U., 1962. Bar: Ohio 1962, Va. 1994. Mem. firm Wilcox & Wilcox, 1962-78; with office gen. counsel Dept. Navy, Washington, 1966-94; asst. to gen. counsel Dept. Navy, 1969-72, counsel Naval Air Systems Command, 1972-76, dep. gen. counsel, 1976-94, cons. atty., arbitrator, 1994—; guest lectr. U.S. Army Logistics Mgmt. Center; mem. Navy Contract Adjustment Bd., 1968-72. Designed Arlington County (Va.) flag, 1983. Bd. dirs. Navy Fed. Credit Union, 1974-77, sec.-treas., 1974-75, 2d v.p., 1975-77; mem. Def. Adv. Panel on Streamlining Acquisition Laws, 1991-92. Lt. USNR, 1963-66. Recipient Meritorious Exec. rank 1990, Disting Exec. rank, 1981, 89, Navy Disting. Civilian Svc. award, 1989, Defense Disting. Civilian Svc. award, 1994. Mem. Ohio Bar Assn., Va. State Bar, Charlottesville-Albemarle Bar Assn., Nat. Trust Hist. Preservation, Nature Conservancy. Home: PO Box 338 Turner Mountain Rd Ivy VA 22945-0338

WILCOX, JOHN CAVEN, lawyer, corporate consultant; b. N.Y.C., Nov. 12, 1942; s. Daniel A. and Jessie Alexandra (Caven) W.; m. Vanessa Guerrini-Maraldi, Sept. 30, 1983; children: Daniel D.G., William G.M., Julia G.M. BA magna cum laude, Harvard U., 1964, JD, 1968; MA, U. Calif., Berkeley, 1965; LLM, NYU, 1981. Bar: N.Y. 1973. Account exec. Georgeson & Co. Inc., N.Y.C., 1973-79, mng. dir., 1979-90, chmn. 1990—; trustee Family Dynamics, Inc., N.Y.C., 1979-96, Woodrow Wilson Nat. Fellowship Found., 1996. With U.S. Army, 1968-70, Vietnam. Woodrow Wilson fellow, 1965. Mem. ABA, NYSE (mem. shareholders comm. com. 1989—), N.Y. State Bar Assn., Am. Soc. Corp. Secs. (mem. securities industry com. 1987-95, securities law com. 1995—), Nat. Assn. Security Dealers (mem. issuer affairs com. 1990—), Downtown Assn., Harvard Club (N.Y.C.), Phi Beta Kappa. Democrat. Home: 580 W End Ave New York NY 10024-1723 Office: Georgeson & Co Inc Wall Street Plz New York NY 10005

WILCOX, JON P., justice; b. Berlin, Wis., Sept. 5, 1936; m. Jane Ann; children: Jeffrey, Jennifer. AB in Polit. Sci., Ripon Coll., 1958; JD, U. Wis., 1965. Pvt. practice Steele, Smyth, Klos and Flynn, LaCrosse, Wis., 1965-66, Hacker and Wilcox, Wautoma, Wis., 1966-69, Wilcox, Rudolph, Kubasta & Rathjen, Wautoma, 1969-79; elected judge Waushara County Cir. Ct., 1979-92; apptd. justice Wis. Supreme Ct., 1992—; commr. Family Ct., Waushara County, 1977-79; vice chmn., chmn. Wis. Sentencing Commn., 1984-92; chief judge 6th Jud. Dist., 1985-92; co-chair State-Fed. Jud. Coun., 1992, Jud. Coun. Wis., 1993; mem. Prison Overcrowding Task Force, 1988-90; mem. numerous coms. Wis. Judiciary; mem. faculty Wis. Jud. Coll., 1986—; chmn. Wis. Chief Judges Com., 1990-92; co-chair comm. on judiciary as co-equal br. of govt. Wis. State Bar; lectr. in field. Co-author: Wisconsin News Reporter's Legal Handbook: Wisconsin Courts and Court Procedures, 1987. Bd. visitors U. Wis. Law Sch, 1970-76. Lt. U.S. Army, 1959-61. Named Outstanding Jaycee Wautoma, 1974; recipient Disting. Alumni award Ripon Coll., 1993. Fellow Am. Bar Found.; mem. ABA (com. on continuing appellate edn.), Nat. Coun. Juvenile and Family Ct. Judges, Wis. Bar Assn. (bench bar com.), Wis. Law Found., Tri-County Bar Assn., Dane County Bar Assn., Trout Unltd., Ruffed Grouse Soc., Ducks Unltd., Rotary, Phi Alpha Delta. Office: Supreme Court State Capitol PO Box 1688 Madison WI 53701-1688

WILCOX, MARK DEAN, lawyer; b. Chgo., May 25, 1952; s. Fabian Joseph and Zeryle Lucille (Tase) W.; m. Catherine J. Wertjes, Mar. 12, 1983; children: Glenna Lynn, Joanna Tessie, Andrew Fabian Joseph. BBA, U. Notre Dame, 1973; JD, Northwestern U., 1976; CLU, Am. Coll., 1979, ChFC, 1992. Bar: Ill. 1976, U.S. Dist. Ct. (no. dist.) Ill. 1976, Trial Bar 1982, U.S. Ct. Appeals (7th cir.) 1987, U.S. Supreme Ct. 1989. Staff asst. Nat. Dist. Attys. Assn., Chgo., 1974-75; trial asst. Cook County States Atty., Chgo., 1975; intern U.S. Atty. No. Dist. Ill., Chgo., 1975-76; assoc. Lord, Bissell & Brook, Chgo., 1976-85, ptnr., 1986—. Bd. mgrs. YMCA Metropolitan Chgo., Internat. Spl. Olympics. Mem. ABA (tort and ins. practice sect.), Am. Soc. CLU and ChFC, Chgo. Bar Assn. (ins. law com.), Def. Rsch. Inst., Trial Lawyers Club Chgo., Notre Dame Nat. Monogram Club, Union League Club (Chgo.), Beta Gamma Sigma. Office: Lord Bissell & Brook 115 S La Salle St Chicago IL 60603-3801

WILCOX, MAUD, editor; b. N.Y.C., Feb. 14, 1923; d. Thor Fredrik and Gerda (Ysberg) Eckert; m. Edward T. Wilcox, Feb. 9, 1944; children: Thor (dec.), Bruce, Eric, Karen. A.B. summa cum laude, Smith Coll., 1944; A.M., Harvard U., 1945. Teaching fellow Harvard U., 1945-46, 48-51; instr. English Smith Coll., Northampton, Mass., 1947-48, Wellesley Coll., Mass., 1951-52; exec. editor Harvard U. Press, 1958-66, humanities editor, 1966-73, editor-in-chief, 1973-89, ret.; freelance editorial cons. Cambridge, 1989—; cons., panelist NEH, Washington, 1974-76, 82-84; cons. Radcliffe Pub. Course, 1991. Mem. MLA (com. scholarly edits. 1982-86), Assn. Am. Univ. Presses (chair com. admissions and standards 1976-77, v.p. 1978-79, chair program com. 1981-82), Phi Beta Kappa. Democrat. Episcopalian. Home and Office: 63 Francis Ave Cambridge MA 02138-1911

WILCOX, MICHAEL WING, lawyer; b. Buffalo, July 21, 1941; s. Paul Wing and Barbara Ann (Bauter) W.; m. Diane Rose Dell, June 18, 1966; children: Timothy, Katherine, Matthew. AB, UCLA, 1963; JD, Marquette U., 1966. Bar: Wis. 1966, U.S. Ct. Appeals (7th cir.) 1967. Law clk. to judge U.S. Ct. Appeals (7th cir.), Chgo., 1966-67; with firm Boardman, Suhr, Curry & Field, Madison, Wis., 1967-83; ptnr. Quarles & Brady, Madison, Wis., 1983-90, Stolper, Koritzinsky, Brewster & Neider, Madison, 1990-94, Stolper, Wilcox & Hughes, Madison, 1995—; lectr. in field. Author: (with others) Marital Property Law in Wisconsin, 1986. Bd. dirs. Meriter Found. Mem. ABA (chmn. marital property com. of real property probate and trust law sect. 1986-89), Wis. State Bar Assn. (chmn. taxation sect. 1983-84), Am. Coll. Trust and Estate Counsel, Rotary (bd. dirs. Madison West chpt.). Club: The Madison. Home: 6318 Keelson Dr Madison WI 53705-4367 Office: Stolper Wilcox & Hughes 6510 Grand Teton Plz Madison WI 53719-1029

WILCOX, NANCY DIANE, nurse, administrator; b. Griffin, Ga., Oct. 28, 1951; d. Robert Wayne Birdwell and Eula F. (Maddox) Tatum; m. David Reed Wilcox, May 29, 1970; children: David Jr., Melanie, Bradley, Amy. AS, Panola Coll., 1971; lic. vocat. nurse, Kilgore Coll., 1990, ASN, 1993; BSN magna cum laude, U. Tex., Tyler, 1994. RN, Tex. Hemodialysis nurse Good Shepherd Hosp., Longview, Tex., 1990-91, critical care and telemetry nurse, 1993-94; staff nurse Roy H. Laird Hosp., Kilgore, 1991-93; case mgr. TLC Home Health Agy., Longview, 1994-95; owner, operator LifeCare Home Nursing, Inc., Kilgore, Longview, 1995—. Mem. ANA, Tex. Nurses Assn., Home Care Nurses Assn., Phi Theta Kappa, Alpha Chi, Sigma Theta Tau. Avocation: collecting dolls. Home: 1705 Oakwood Dr Kilgore TX 75662-8803

WILCOX, RHODA DAVIS, elementary education educator; b. Boyero, Colo., Nov. 4, 1918; d. Harold Francis and Louise Wilhelmina (Wilfert) Davis; m. Kenneth Edward Wilcox, Nov. 1945 (div. 1952); 1 child, Michele Ann. BA in Elem. Edn., U. No. Colo., 1941; postgrad., Colo. Coll., 1955-65. Life cert. tchr., Colo. Elem. tchr. Fruita (Colo.) Pub. Sch., 1938-40, Boise, Idaho, 1940-42; sec. civil service USAF, Ogden, Utah, 1942-43, Colorado Springs, Colo., 1943-44; sec. civil service hdqtrs. command USAF, Panama Canal Zone; sec. Tech. Libr., Eglin Field, Fla., 1945-46; elem. tchr. Colorado Springs Sch. Dist. 11, 1952-82, mem. curriculum devel. com., 1968-69; lectr. civic, profl. and edn. groups, Colo.; judge for Excellence in Literacy Coldwell Bankers Sch. Dist. 11, Colo. Coun. Internat. Reading. Assn. Author: Man on the Iron Horse, 1959, Colorado Slim and His Spectacklers, 1964, (with Jean Pierpoint) Changing Colorado (Social Studies), 1968-69, The Founding Fathers and Their Friends in Denver Posse of the Westerners Brand Bank, 1971, The Bells of Manitou, 1973, (with Len Froisland) In the Footsteps of the Founder, 1993. Mem. hist. adv. bd. State Colo., Denver, 1976; mem. Garden of the Gods master plan rev. com. City of Colorado Springs, 1987—; mem. cemetery adv. bd. City of Colorado Springs, 1988-91; mem. adv. bd. centennial com., 1971; mem. steering com. Spirit of Palmer Festival, 1986; judge Nat. Hist. Day, U. Colo., Colorado Springs, and Colo. Coll., Colorado Springs; hon. trustee Palmer Found., 1986—; mem. Am. the Beautiful Centennial Celebrations, Inc., 1992-93; active Friends of the Garden of the Gods, Friends of Winfield Scott Stratton, Friends of the Libr. Named Tchr. of the Yr., Colorado Springs Sch. Dist. 11, 1968. Mem. AAUW (Woman of Yr. 1987), Colo. Ret. Educators Assn., Colorado Springs Ret. Educators Assn., Helen Hunt Jackson Commemorative Coun., Women's Ednl. Soc. Colo. Coll. Avocations: lecturing, conducting tours and writing tour scripts, volunteering in Pioneers Mus. Archives, Ecumenical Social Ministries, Garden of the Gods, Rock Ledge Ranch. Home: 1620 E Cache La Poudre St Colorado Springs CO 80909-4612

WILCOX, RONALD BRUCE, biochemistry educator, researcher; b. Seattle, Sept. 23, 1934; s. Howard Bruce and Edna Jane (McKeown) W.; m. Susan Lenore Folkenberg, May 15, 1937; children: Deanna Marie, Lisa Suzanne. B.S., Pacific Union Coll., 1957; Ph.D., U. Utah, 1962. Research fellow Harvard Med. Sch., Boston, 1962-65; asst. prof. Loma Linda U., Calif., 1965-70, assoc. prof., 1970-73, prof., 1973—, chmn. dept. biochemistry, 1973-83. Mem. gen. plan rev. com. City of Loma Linda, 1981-92; bd. dirs. East Valley United Way, 1990—. Fellow Danforth Found., St. Louis, 1957; fellow Bank Am. Giannini Found. San Francisco, 1965. Mem. Am. Thyroid Assn., Endocrine Soc. Democrat. Seventh-day Adventist. Home: 25516 Lomas Verdes St Loma Linda CA 92354-2417 Office: Loma Linda U Dept Biochemistry Loma Linda CA 92350

WILCOXSON, ROY DELL, plant pathology educator and researcher; b. Columbia, Utah, Jan. 12, 1926; m. Iva Wall, 1949; children: Bonnie, Paul, Karren, John. BS, Utah State U., 1953; MS, U. Minn., 1955, PhD in Plant Pathlogy, 1957. Asst. prof., 1957-66; prof. plant pathology U. Minn., St. Paul, 1966-91, prof. emeritus, 1991—; spl. staff mem. Rockefeller Found.; vis. prof. Indian Agrl. Rsch. Inst., New Delhi; dir. Morocco project U. Minn., 1983-87; adj. prof. Inst. Agronomy and Vet. Medicine, Hassan II, Rabat, Morocco, 1985—. Fellow Am. Phytopath Soc., Indian NAS, Indian Phytopath Soc., AAAS. Research in diseases of forage crops and cereal crops; cereal rust diseases. Office: 1669 County Road 8230 West Plains MO 65775-5766 Address: Dept Plant Path U Minn Saint Paul MN 55101

WILCZEK, FRANK ANTHONY, physics educator; b. Mineola, N.Y., May 15, 1951; s. Frank John and Mary Rose (Cona) W.; m. Elizabeth Jordan Devine, July 3, 1973; children: Amity, Mira. BS in Math., U. Chgo., 1970; MA in Math., Princeton U., 1971, PhD in Physics, 1973. Instr. Princeton (N.J.) U., 1973-74, asst. prof., 1974-76, assoc. prof., 1978-79, prof., 1980-81; prof. Inst. for Theoretical Physics, Santa Barbara, Calif., 1981-88, Inst. for Advanced Study, Princeton, 1989—; vis. fellow Inst. for Advanced Study, Princeton, 1977-78; vis. prof. Harvard U., 1987-88. Author: Longing for the Harmonies, 1988, Fractional Statistics and Anyon Superconductivity, 1990; contbr. articles to profl. jours. Recipient J.J. Sakurai prize Am. Phys. Soc., 1986, Dirac medal UNESCO, 1994; A.P. Sloan fellow, 1975-77, MacArthur fellow, 1982-87, Huttenback prof. U. Calif., Santa Barbara, 1984-88, Lorentz prof. Leiden U., 1998. Mem. NAS, Am. Acad. Arts & Scis. Avocations: chess, music, logic puzzles. Home: 112 Mercer St Princeton NJ 08540-6827 Office: Inst Advanced Study Dept Natural Scis Olden Ln Princeton NJ 08540-4920

WILCZEK, JOHN FRANKLIN, history educator; b. San Francisco, Jan. 9, 1929; s. Leonard Matthew and Teresa Edith (Silvey) W.; m. Kuniko Akabane, Nov. 14, 1966; 1 child, Mary Theresa Shepherd. BA in History with honors, U. Calif., Berkeley, 1952; MA, U. Calif., 1953; PhD, Pacific Western U., Encino, Calif., 1978. Cert. secondary tchr., Calif. Instr. history and polit. sci. City Coll. San Francisco, 1956-94, instr. history of Japan, 1995; tchr. Japan History part-time City Coll. of San Francisco, 1996—; instr. Kobe (Japan) Women's Coll., 1979-81; instr. Seido Lang. Inst., Kobe, 1979-81; sec.-treas. Tokyo TV Broadcasting Corp., San Francisco, 1975—. Author: The Teaching of Japanese History on the Community College Level, 1978. Sgt. U.S. Army, 1953-55. Mem. U. Calif. Alumni Assn. Republican. Roman Catholic. Avocations: art, numismatics, philately, classical music, photography. Home: 5 Windsor Dr Daly City CA 94015-3257 Office: City Coll of San Francisco 50 Phelan Ave San Francisco CA 94112-1821

WILD, DIRK JONATHAN, accountant; b. Metairie, La., Sept. 15, 1967; s. Karcher Charles Jr. and Betty Ann (Crowley) W.; m. Kathryn Leigh Gates, Aug. 10, 1991. BS in Acctg., La. Tech. U., 1989; M Profl. Acctg., U. Tex., 1990. CPA, La. Experienced mgr. Arthur Andersen, New Orleans, 1990—. Mem. AICPA. Office: Arthur Andersen & Co 201 Saint Charles Ave Ste 4500 New Orleans LA 70170-4500

WILD, HARRY E., engineering company executive; b. Province, R.I., Sept. 25, 1940; s. Harry Edward and Lula Elizabeth (Johnson) W.; m. Marjorie D. Dompe, Nov. 26, 1981; children: Elizabeth Ann, Eric Johnson. BCE, U. Fla., 1966, MS, 1967. Registered profl. engr. Fla., Ga., Maine. Draftsman, inspector, surveyor Briley Wild & Assocs., Ormond Beach, Fla., 1959-65; treatment plant operator U. Fla., Gainesville, 1965-66; design engr. Metcalf & Eddy, Boston, 1966-68, project engr., 1968-71; v.p. Briley, Wild & Assocs., Ormond Beach, 1971, pres., chief exec. officer, 1972—; peer reviewer in field. Contbr. articles to profl. jours. Served with U.S. Army. Recipient Harrison P. Eddy award, Water Pollution Control Fedn., 1972. Fellow Fla. Engring. Soc. (v.p. 1977-78, 81-83), Am. Cons. Engrs. Council; mem. ASCE, Am. Water Works Assn., Fla. Inst. Cons. Engrs. (officer 1974-80, pres. 1979-80, Ormond Beach C. of C. (bd. govs.). Presbyterian. Club: Halifax (Daytona Beach, Fla.). Home: 110 Knollwood Estate Dr Ormond Beach FL 32174-4223 Office: Briley Wild & Assocs Inc PO Box 1023 Ormond Beach FL 32175-1023

WILD, JAMES ROBERT, biochemistry and genetics educator; b. Sedalia, Mo., Nov. 24, 1945; s. Robert Lee and Frances Elleta (Wheeler) W.; m. Ann Lynn Brenner, Aug. 1, 1973; 1 child, Kalli Ann. BA in Zoology, U. Calif., Davis, Calif., 1967; PhD in Cell Biology, U. Calif., Riverside, 1971; post doctoral fellow, U. Calif., 1972. Rsch. microbiologist NMR Inst., Active Duty USN, Bethesda, Md., 1972-75; from asst. to assoc. prof. genetics and plant sci. Tex. A&M U., Coll. Sta., Tex., 1975-84; prof., chair genetics faculty Tex. A&M U., Coll. Sta., 1984-87, prof. biochemistry & genetics, 1984—, head biochemistry and biophysics dept., 1986-90; exec. assoc. dean Coll. Agriculture & Life Scs., Tex. A&M U., Coll. Sta., 1987-92; prof., head dept. biochemistry and biophysics, 1994—. Recipient Incentive in Excellence award Ctr. for Teaching Excellence, 1984-85, Outstanding Youth Educator, Tex. Conf., United Meth. Ch., 1984, So. Regional award for excellence in coll. and univ. teaching in food and agrl. scis. Higher Edn. program USDA, 1992. Methodist. Office: Tex A&M U Biochemistry Bldg Rm 339 College Station TX 77843-2128

WILD, JOHN JULIAN, surgeon, director medical research institute; b. Sydenham, Kent, Eng., Aug. 11, 1914; came to U.S., 1946; s. Ovid Frederick and Ellen Louise (Cuttance) W.; m. Nancy Wallace, Nov. 14, 1949 (div. 1966); children: John O., Douglas J.; m. Valerie Claudia Grosenick, Aug. 9, 1968; 1 child, Ellen Louise. BA, U. Cambridge, Eng., 1936, MA, 1940, MD, 1942, PhD, 1971. Intern, resident U. Coll. Hosp., London, 1938-42; intern U. College Hosp., London, 1938-42; staff surgeon Miller Gen., St. Charles and North Middlesex Hosps., London, 1942-44; venereologist Royal Army Med. Corps, 1944-45; rsch. fellow, instr. depts. surgery and elec. engring., prin. investigator U. Minn., Mpls., 1946-51; dir. rsch. Medico-Technol. Rsch. Dept. St. Barnabas Hosp., Mpls., 1953-60; dir. Medico-Technol. Rsch. Unit Minn. Found., St. Paul, 1960-63; pvt. practice Mpls., 1966—; dir. Medico-Technol. Rsch. Inst. Mpls., St. Louis Park, Minn., 1965—; lectr. in field of medical instruments, ultrasound. Contbr. articles to profl. jours. Recipient Japan prize in Medical Imaging, Sci. and Tech. Found. Japan, 1991. Fellow Am. Inst. Ultrasound in Medicine (Pioneer award 1978); mem. AMA, World Fedn. Ultrasound in Medicine and Biology, Minn. State Med. Assn., Hennepin County Med. Soc., N.Am. Alvis Owners Club; hon. mem. British Inst. of Radiology, Japan Soc. of Ultrasound in Medicine. Achievements include patents in field; origination of ultrasonic medical imaging instruments and diagnostic techniques; origination of the field of pulse-echo ultrasonic diagnostic medicine. Avocations: automobile restoration, antique collecting and restoration. Home and Office: Medico-Technol Rsch Inst 4262 Alabama Ave S Minneapolis MN 55416-3105

WILD, NELSON HOPKINS, lawyer; b. Milw., July 16, 1933; s. Henry Goetseels and Virginia Douglas (Weller) W.; m. Joan Ruth Miles, Apr. 12, 1969; children: Mark, Eric. A.B., Princeton U., 1955; LL.B., U. Wis., 1961. Bar: Wis. 1962, Calif. 1967; cert. specialist in probate, estate planning and trust law State Bar of Calif. Research assoc. Wis. Legis. Council, Madison, 1955-56; assoc. Whyte, Hirschboeck, Minahan, Harding & Harland, Milw., 1961-67, Thelen, Marin, Johnson & Bridges, San Francisco, 1967-70; sole practice law San Francisco, 1970—; mem. State Bar Calif. Client Trust Fund Commn., 1983, mem. exec. com. conf. dels., 1985-88. Contbr. articles to legal jours. Bd. dirs. Neighborhood Legal Assistance Found., San Francisco, 1974-85, chmn. bd., 1978-81. Served with USAF, 1956-58. Mem. ABA, Calif. Bar Assn., San Francisco Bar Assn., Am. Bar Found., Lawyers of San Francisco Club (gov. 1975, treas. 1981, v.p. 1982, pres.-elect 1983, pres. 1984), Calif. Tennis Club (bd. dirs. 1995—, pres. 1997). Office: 220 Montgomery St Ste 1006 San Francisco CA 94104-3419

WILD, RICHARD P., lawyer; b. N.Y.C., Aug. 13, 1947; s. Alfred P. and Harriet C. (Hoffman) W.; m. Deirdre L. Felbin, June 15, 1969; children: Nicholas B., Daniel M. AB, Columbia U., 1968; JD, Yale U., 1971. Bar: Pa. 1971, U.S. Dist. Ct. (ea. dist.) Pa. 1971, U.S. Tax Ct. 1973, U.S. Claims Ct. 1977. Assoc. Dechert Price & Rhoads, Phila., 1971-78, ptnr., 1978—; bd. dirs. Penn Fuel Gas, Inc. Mem. Phila. Bar Assn. (mem. tax sect.). Office: Dechert Price & Rhoads 4000 Bell Atlantic Tower 1717 Arch St Philadelphia PA 19103-2713

WILD, ROBERT LEE, physics educator; b. Sedalia, Mo., Oct. 9, 1921; s. Alwin Bernard and Nellie Marie (Nowlin) W.; m. Frances Elleta Wheeler, Oct. 7, 1943; children: James Robert, Janet Gayle, Margaret Nell. B.S., Central Mo. State U., 1943; M.A., U. Mo., 1948, Ph.D., 1950. Asst. prof. physics U. N.D., Grand Forks, 1950-52; prof. U. Calif., Riverside, 1953-88, prof. emeritus, 1988; Fulbright lectr. U. Philippines, 1981-82; mem. adv. com. Calif. Sci. Project, 1988—. Contbr. articles profl. jours. Served with AUS, 1943-45. NSF fellow, 1959-60; recipient Disting. Teaching award U. Calif., Riverside, 1973, Faculty of the Yr. award U. Calif.-Riverside Alumni, 1993. Pub. Svc. award Citizens U. Com., 1994. Mem. Am. Phys. Soc., Am. Assn. Physics Tchrs. (v.p. sect. 1983-84, pres. So. Calif. sect. 1985-86, pres., 1986-87, award 1966), Sigma Xi. Baptist. Home: 5709 Durango Rd Riverside CA 92506-3216 Office: U Calif Dept Physics Riverside CA 92521

WILD, ROBERT WARREN, lawyer; b. Syracuse, N.Y., Mar. 25, 1942; s. Robert Sumner and Evelyn I. (Yorman) W.; m. Elizabeth Trowbridge, Sept. 5, 1965; children: Robert Mason, Alexander Lewis, Elizabeth Anne. BS, MIT, 1964; JD, Cornell U., 1970. Bar: N.Y. 1971, D.C. 1973. Engr. Smithsonian Astrophysical Obs., Cambridge, Mass., 1965-67; atty., advisor U.S. Dept. Justice, Washington, 1970-72; law clk. to Hon. Justice William H. Rehnquist U.S. Supreme Ct., Washington, 1972-73; ptnr. Nixon, Hargrave, Devans & Doyle, Rochester, N.Y., 1973—. Trustee Rochester Police Benevolent Assn., 1994—. Mem. Monroe County Bar Assn. (trustee 1990-91, 92-94, treas. 1992-94, counsel 1994—). Office: Nixon Hargrave Devans & Doyle LLP Clinton Sq PO Box 1051 Rochester NY 14603

WILDE, CARLTON D., lawyer; b. Houston, Apr. 11, 1935; s. Henry Dayton and Louise (Key) W.; m. Martha Cloyes, July 26, 1958; children: Carlton D. Jr., Jennifer. Student, Coll. of William and Mary, 1953-55; B.A., U. Tex., 1957, J.D., 1959. Assoc. Bracewell & Patterson, Houston, 1959-62, ptnr., 1962-67, 85—, mng. ptnr., 1967-85. Trustee Presbyn. Sch., So. Tex. Coll. Law. Fellow Am. Bar Found., Tex. Bar Found., Houston Bar Found.; mem. ABA, State Bar Tex., River Oaks Country Club, Coronado Club (Houston), Biltmore Forest Country Club (Asheville, N.C.). Republican. Home: 3105 Reba Dr Houston TX 77019-6209 Office: Bracewell & Patterson 2900 S Tower Pennzoil Pl 711 Louisiana St Ste 2900 Houston TX 77002-2721

WILDE, DANIEL UNDERWOOD, computer engineering educator; b. Wilmington, Ohio, Dec. 27, 1937; s. Arthur John and Ruby Dale (Underwood) W. BSEE, U. Ill., 1960; MS, M.I.T., 1962, Ph.D., 1966. Research instr. medicine Boston U. Med. Sch., 1964-66; asst. prof. info. adminstrn. U. Conn., 1966-69, assoc. prof., 1970-75, prof., 1976-85; assoc. dir. New Eng. Rsch. Application Ctr., Storrs, Conn., 1966-72, dir., 1973-85; dir. NASA Indsl. Application Ctr., 1972-91; pres. NERAC, Inc., Tolland, Conn., 1985—; trustee Engring. Index, Inc.; cons. Am. Soc. Metals, 1973—. Author: Introduction to Computing: Problem Solving, Algorithms and Data Structures, 1973; contbr. articles to profl. jours. Served with USAF. Recipient NASA Public Service award, 1975. Mem. IEEE, Am. Soc. Info. Sci., Assn. Computing Machinery, Assn. Info. and Dissemination Centers (sec.-treas. 1976-79, pres. 1979-81). Office: Nerac Inc 1 Technology Dr Tolland CT 06084-3902

WILDE, DAVID, publisher, writer, biographer; b. Hereford, Nov. 12, 1944; s. Elizabeth Lillian (Price-Slawson) W. Diploma, Kneller Hall, London, 1965; pvt. mus. studies with Carmello Pace, Malta, 1964-68; student, Cardiff (Wales) Coll. Music, 1970-71; diploma in art, Open U., Leicester, Eng., 1980; student, Lancaster (Eng.) U., 1980-81, U. N.Mex., 1984. With BBC Radio, Eng., 1975-79; resident mem. wind ensemble Loughborough (Eng.) U., 1976-79; oil field worker Western Oceanic Inc. and Bawden Drilling, North Sea, Scotland, 1983-84; tutor U. N.Mex., Albuquerque, 1986-88, tchr. dept. continuing edn., 1989-90; musician/composer Civic Orch., Albuquerque, 1988-89; legal rschr. Wilde & Sprague, Albuquerque, 1988-90; pub., author Wilde Pub., Albuquerque, 1989—; clerical officer Severn-Trent Water, Eng., 1972-74, Social Security, Eng., 1983; rschr. Ctr. Southwest Rsch. U. N.Mex., 1994-97; spkr. in field. Author: The Spirit That Wants Me, 1989, In the South: The Five Year Diary of a Journey Across America, 1991, Route 66: The Five Year Diary of a Journey Across America, 1991, Wildeland: Prose, 1992, North Sea Saga, 1960s: Opera of Oil, 1993, Desert Meditations: A Fairy Tale of New Mexico, 1993, Black Innocence: The Immigrant, 1993, Poems, People, Places: Travels on My Own, 1994, Basic Horn Technique: Studies for the French Horn, 1994, The Life and Times of Cdr. E.C. Zeke Cortez, USNR, 1996, (with others) La Puerta: A Doorway Into the Academy, 1997; contbr. to National Library of Poetry, 1996; editor 6 books; actor Geronimo prodn. Turner Network TV, 1993; extra various prodns., 1969-84. Rschr. SRIC, Albuquerque, 1989-96; cons. N.Mex. Bd. Appraisers, Albuquerque, 1989-90. Roman Catholic. Avocations: travel, classical music, spirituality, history, mathematics. Office: 105 Stanford Dr SE Albuquerque NM 87106-3537 also: Wilde Pub PO Box 4581 Albuquerque NM 87196-4581

WILDE, EDWIN FREDERICK, mathematics educator; b. Lombard, Ill., Jan. 14, 1931; s. Edwin Frederick and Carrie Belle (Hammond) W.; m. Connie Mae Rawlings, Aug. 23, 1952; children—Brad Alan, Bruce Ramon, Elizabeth Lynn. B.S., Ill. State U., 1952, M.S., 1953; M.A., U. Ill., 1955, Ph.D., 1959; postgrad., U. Wis., part time, 1955-58, Stanford U., 1964-65. With Beloit (Wis.) Coll., 1955-76, prof. math., dean faculty, 1969-71, v.p. for planning, 1971-75; dean Roger Williams Coll., Bristol, R.I., 1976-80; provost, dean of faculty U. Tampa, Fla., 1980-86; vice chancellor U. S.C., Spartanburg, 1986-91, prof. math., 1991—; cons. AID insts., India, 1964, Insts. Internat. Edn., East Pakistan, 1969. NSF Sr. Sci. Faculty fellow, 1964-65. Mem. Math. Assn. Am. (bd. govs. 1968-69, 72-75). Home: 275 James Rd Gaffney SC 29341-4013 Office: Math Dept Univ SC Spartanburg SC 29303

WILDE, HAROLD RICHARD, college president; b. Wauwatosa, Wis., May 14, 1945; s. Harold Richard and Winifred (Wiley) W.; m. Benna Brecher, Feb. 4, 1970; children: Anna, Henry, Elizabeth Ty. BA, Amherst Coll., 1967; MA, PhD, Harvard U., Cambridge, Mass., 1973. Spl. asst. to gov. Office of Gov., State of Wis., Madison, 1972-75; ins. commr. Office of Commr. of Ins., State of Wis., Madison, 1975-79; spl. asst. to pres. U. Wis. System, Madison, 1979-81; v.p. for external affairs Beloit (Wis.) Coll., 1981-91; pres. North Ctrl. Coll., Naperville, Ill., 1991—. Bd. dirs. Ctr. for Pub. Representation, Inc., Madison, 1981-87, Beloit Community Found., 1988-91, Budget Funding Corp., 1993—. Mem. Phi Beta Kappa. Home: 329 S Brainard St Naperville IL 60540-5401 Office: North Ctrl Coll 30 N Brainard St Naperville IL 60540-4607

WILDE, JAMES DALE, archaeologist, educator; b. Las Vegas, N.Mex., May 9, 1950; s. Ralph M. and Joyce (Anderson) W.; m. Deborah Thompson, Oct. 6, 1973 (div. 1979); 1 child, Colin James Post; m. Deborah E. Newman, June 4, 1983; children: Matthew Catlow, Russell James. BA, U. N.Mex., 1972; MA, U. Oreg., 1978, PhD, 1985. Archaeologist Deerlodge Nat. Forest, U.S. Forest Svc., Butte, Mont., 1977, Earth Tech. Corp., Seattle, 1981-82, Geo-Recon Internat., Ltd., Seattle, 1982-84; asst. dir. office pub. archaeology Brigham Young U., Provo, Utah, 1984-88, dir., 1988-95, adj. prof. dept. anthropology, 1985-95; archaeologist Hdqrs. USAF Ctr. for Environ. Excellence, San Antonio, 1995—; mem. com. on archaeology Brigham Young U., 1986-90, mem. mus. adv. com., 1990-95; mem. subcom. on antiquities legis. Utah Legislature, Salt Lake City, 1988-90. Author: Utah Avocational Archaeologist Certification Program: Teaching Guide (vols. I-III), 1988, Utah Avocational Archaeologist Certification Program: Student Handbook (vols. I-III), 1988; contbr. articles to profl. publs., encys. and books. Mem. vestry St. Mary's Episc. Ch., Provo, 1992-95. Mem. Am. Anthropol. Assn., Soc. Am. Archaeology, Soc. Profl. Archaeologists, Utah Profl. Archaeol. Coun. (treas. 1986-88, pres. 1988-90), Sigma Xi. Democrat. Avocations: reading, golf, tennis, fishing, hiking. Home: 7923 Moon Walk San Antonio TX 78250 Office: HQ AFCEE/ECR 3207 North Rd Brooks AFB TX 78235-5363

WILDE, JAMES L., lawyer; b. Provo, Utah, May 27, 1940. BS, Brigham Young U., 1965; JD, Columbia U., 1968. Bar: Utah 1968. Mem. Ray, Quinney & Nebeker, Provo. Former LDS mission pres. Hungary-Budapest Mission, 1990-94. Mem. Utah State Bar, Am. Inn Ct. I (master bench), Blue Key, Pi Sigma Alpha. Office: Ray Quinney & Nebeker 210 First Security Bank Bldg 92 N University Ave Provo UT 84601-4420

WILDE, JOHN, artist, educator; b. Milw., Dec. 12, 1919; s. Emil F. and Mathilda (Lotz) W.; m. Helen Ashman, July 1943 (dec. Dec. 1966); children: Jonathan, Phoebe; m. Shirley Miller, 1969. B.S., U. Wis., 1942, M.S., 1948. Mem. faculty U. Wis., 1948—, prof. art, 1960—, chmn. dept. art and art edn., 1960-62, Alfred Sessler Distinguished prof. art, 1969-82, prof. emeritus, 1982—; elected mem. Nat. Acad. Design, 1994. Works exhibited Met. Mus. Art, Mus. Modern Art, Whitney Mus. Am. Art, Corcoran Mus. Art, Mpls. Art Mus., San Francisco Mus. Art, Whitney Mus. Am. Art, 1978-80, Nat. Portrait Gallery, Smithsonian Instn., 1980, Nat. Gallery, Washington, 1988; retrospective Elvehjem Mus. Art, U. Wis., 1984-85; 3-man retrospective, Milw. Art Mus., 1982, others; represented in permanent collections, Pa. Acad. Art, Detroit Inst. Fine Art, Worcester Art Mus., Wadsworth Atheneum, Whitney Mus. Am. Art, Carnegie Inst., Nat. Collection Art, Smithsonian Instn., Yale U. Art Gallery, Butler Inst. Am. Art, Art Inst. Chgo., Sheldon Meml. Art Gallery, U. Nebr., Zimmerli Mus. Art, Rutgers U., N. Brunswick, N.J., Mus. Contemporary Art, Chgo., others, also extensive exhbns. abroad. Recipient numerous awards for painting and drawing in regional and nat. exhbns. including, Childe Hassam purchase award Am. Acad. and Inst. Arts and Letters, 1981, 87.

WILDE, NORMAN TAYLOR, JR., investment banking company executive; b. Phila., Sept. 13, 1930; s. Norman Taylor and Elizabeth (Duthie) W.; m. Ruth Nancy Osterndorf, Sept. 26, 1959; children: Karen, Suzanne, Norman Taylor III. B.S., U. Pa., 1953. Vice pres. Janney, Montgomery, Scott, Inc., Phila., 1966-69; pres. Janney, Montgomery, Soctt, Inc., Phila., 1969—; trustee Penn Mut. Life Ins. Co.; chmn. Pa. Trust Co., 1995—, Abington Meml. Hosp., 1995—. Served to lt. USN, 1953-55. Mem. Nat. Assn. Security Dealers (chmn. 1983—), Securities Industries Assn. (gov. 1979-82), Pine Valley Golf Club, Phila. Cricket Club. Office: Janney Montgomery Scott Inc 1801 Market St Philadelphia PA 19103-1628

WILDE, PATRICIA, artistic director; b. Ottawa, Ont., Can., July 16, 1928; m. George Bardyguine; children: Anya, Youri. Dancer Am. Concert Ballet, Marquis de Cuevas Ballet Internat., N.Y.C., 1944-45, Ballet Russe de Monte Carlo, N.Y.C., 1945-49, Roland Petit's Ballet Paris, Met. Ballet Britain, London, 1949-50; prin. ballerina N.Y.C. Ballet, 1950-65; dir. Harkness Sch. Ballet, N.Y.C., 1965-67; ballet mistress, tchr. Am. Ballet Theatre, N.Y.C., 1969-77; dir. Am. Ballet Theatre Sch., N.Y.C., 1977-82; artistic dir. Pitts. Ballet Theatre, 1982—; tchr. Am. Ballet Theatre, 1969-77, Joffrey scholarship program, N.Y.C. Ballet, 1968-69; established Sch. of Grand Theatre of Geneva, 1968-69; adjudicator Regional Ballet in Am. S.E. and S.W., 1969-82; choreographer N.Y. Philharmonic; guest tchr. various ballet cos. and colls.; trustee Dance U.S.A.; panelist Nat. Choreographic Project. Recipient Leadership award in Arts and Letters YWCA, 1990, Pitts. Woman of Yr. in Arts award, 1993, Cultural award for outstanding contbns. to cultural climate of region Pitts. Ctr. for Arts, 1997. Office: Pitts Ballet Theatre 2900 Liberty Ave Pittsburgh PA 15201-1511

WILDE, WILLIAM KEY, lawyer; b. Houston, May 3, 1933; s. Henry Dayton and Louise (Key) W.; m. Ann Jeannine Austin, Aug. 3, 1957; children—William Key, Austin, Adrienne, Michael. A.B., Coll. William and Mary, Williamsburg, Va., 1955; J.D., U. Tex., Austin, 1958. Bar: Tex. 1958. Assoc. Bracewell & Patterson, Houston, 1958-61, ptnr., 1961—. Bd. dirs. Goodwill Industries Houston, 1972—; elder 1st Presbyn. Ch.; trustee Presbyn. Found. U.S.A., Ky., 1983-391, Schriener Coll., 1991—. Fellow ABA, Am. Bar Found., Am. Coll. Trial Lawyers; mem. Tex. Bar Assn. (bd. dirs. 1984-87), Houston Bar Assn. (pres. 1982-83), Houston Club (pres. 1981-82), Houston Country Club (bd. dirs., pres. 1989-90). Republican. Avocations: golf; tennis; skiing; scuba diving. Home: 6206 Woods Bridge Way Houston TX 77007-7041 Office: Bracewell & Patterson 2900 S Tower Pennzoil Place Houston TX 77002

WILDE, WILLIAM RICHARD, lawyer; b. Markesan, Wis., Mar. 1, 1953; s. Leslie Maurice and Elaine Margaret (Schweder) W.; m. Carolyn Margaret Zieman, July 17, 1981 (div. 1987); 1 child, Leah Marie; m. Barbara Joan Rohlf, Jan. 6, 1990. BA, U. Wis., Milw., 1975; JD, Marquette U., 1980. Bar: Wis. 1980, U.S. Dist. Ct. (ea. and we. dists.) Wis. 1980. Dist. atty. Green Lake County, Green Lake, Wis., 1980-83, corp.counsel, 1981; ptnr. Curtis, Wilde and Neal, Oshkosh, Wis., 1983—. Mem. Assn. Trial Lawyers Am., Wis. Bar Assn., Wis. Acad. Trial Lawyers (Amicus Curiae Brief com. 1987-92, bd. dirs., assoc. editor The Verdict, treas. 1993, sec. 1994, v.p. 1995, pres.-elect 1996, pres. 1997), Wis. Assn. Criminal Def. Lawyers (bd. dirs. 1987-91), Winnebbago County Bar Assn., Green Lake County Bar Assn., Lions. Home: PO Box 282 Markesan WI 53946-0282 Office: Curtis Wilde & Neal PO Box 3422 Oshkosh WI 54903-3422

WILDE, WILSON, insurance company executive; b. Hartford, Conn., Sept. 24, 1927; s. Philip Alden and Alice Augusta (Wilson) W.; m. Joanne Gerta Menzel, June 19, 1953; children—Stephen W., David W., Elisabeth L., Richard A. Student, Swarthmore Coll., 1945-46; BA, Williams Coll., 1949. Sales agt. Conn. Gen. Life Ins. Co., Hartford, 1949-53; with Hartford Steam Boiler Inspection & Ins. Co., 1953—, exec. v.p., 1970-71, pres., CEO, 1971—, chmn., CEO, 1993-94, chmn. exec. com., 1994—; bd. dirs. PXRE Corp. Corporator Inst. Living, Hartford; hon. bd. dirs. Hartford Stage Co., 1973—, Jr. Achievement, Old State House Assn., 1976—; trustee Loomis-Chaffee Sch., 1974—, chmn. bd., 1988—. Served with USNR, 1945-47, 51-53. Club: Hartford (pres. 1974). Office: Hartford Steam Boiler 1 State St PO Box 5024 Hartford CT 06102-5024

WILDEBUSH, JOSEPH FREDERICK, economist; b. Bklyn., July 18, 1910; s. Harry Frederick and Elizabeth (Stolzenberg) W.; AB, Columbia, 1931, postgrad Law Sch., 1932; LLB, Bklyn. Law Sch., 1934, JD, 1967; m. Martha Janssens, July 18, 1935; children: Diane Elaine (Mrs. Solon Finkelstein), Joan Marilyn (Mrs. Bobby Sanford Berry); m. Edith Sorensen, May 30, 1964. Admitted to N.Y. State bar, 1934, Fed. bar, 1935; practice law, N.Y.C., 1934-41; labor relations dir. Botany Mills, Passaic, N.J., 1945-48; exec. v.p. Silk and Rayon Printers and Dyers Assn. Am., Inc., Paterson, N.J., 1948-70; exec. v.p. Textile Printers and Dyers Labor Rels. Inst., Paterson, 1954-70; mem. panel labor arbitrators Fed. Mediation and Conciliation Svc., N.Y. State Mediation Bd., N.J. State Mediation Bd., N.J. Pub. Employment Relations Commn., Am. Arbitration Assn.; co-adj. faculty Rutgers U., 1948-90; lectr. Pres. Pascack Valley Hosp., Westwood, N.J., 1950-64, chmn. bd., 1964-67, chmn. emeritus, 1967-80; dir. Group Health Ins. N.Y., 1950-56. Served as maj. Engrs. Corps, U.S. Army, 1941-43. Mem. N.Y. County Lawyers Assn., Am. Acad. Polit. and Social Sci., Indsl. Rels. Rsch. Assn., Ret. Officers Assn., Nat. Geog. Soc. Lutheran. Contbr. articles profl. jours. Home and Office: 37 James Ter Pompton Lakes NJ 07442-1921

WILDENTHAL, BRYAN HOBSON, university administrator; b. San Marcos, Tex., Nov. 4, 1937; s. Bryan and Doris (Kellam) W.; m. Joyce Lockhart; children: Rebecca, Bryan, Lora; m. Adele Sutton; children: Kerry, Andrea. BA, Sul Ross State Coll., 1958; PhD, U. Kans., 1964. Rsch. assoc. Rice U., Houston, 1964-66; AEC postdoctoral fellow Oak Ridge (Tenn.) Nat. Lab., 1966-68; asst. prof. physics Tex. A&M U., College Station, 1968-69; assoc. prof. physics Mich. State U., East Lansing, 1969-72, prof. physics, 1972-83; head physics and atmospheric sci. Drexel U., Phila., 1983-87; dean arts and scis. U. N.Mex., Albuquerque, 1987-92; v.p. acad. affairs U. Tex., Dallas, 1992-94; provost, v.p. acad. affairs, 1994—; cons. Los Alamos (N.Mex.) Nat. Lab., 1987-92; sr. U.S. prof. Humboldt Found., Germany, 1973. Fellow J.S. Guggenheim Found., 1977. Mem. Phi Beta Kappa. Home: 3002 Cross Timbers Ln Garland TX 75044-2008 Office: U Tex Office Academic Affairs Richardson TX 75083

WILDENTHAL, C(LAUD) KERN, physician, educator; b. San Marcos, Tex., July 1, 1941; s. Bryan and Doris (Kellam) W.; m. Margaret Dehlinger, Oct. 15, 1964; children—Pamela, Catharine. B.A., Sul Ross Coll., 1960; M.D., U. Tex. Southwestern Med. Ctr., Dallas, 1964; Ph.D., U. Cambridge, Eng., 1970. Intern Bellevue Hosp., N.Y.C., 1964-65; resident in medicine, fellow cardiology Parkland Hosp., Dallas, 1965-67; research fellow Nat. Heart Inst., Bethesda, Md., 1967-68; vis. research fellow Strangeways Research Lab., Cambridge, 1968-70; asst. prof. to prof. internal medicine and physiology U. Tex. Southwestern Med. Ctr., Dallas, 1970-76, prof., dean grad. sch., 1976-80, prof., dean Southwestern Med. Sch., 1980-86, prof., pres., 1986—; hon. fellow Hughes Hall, U. Cambridge, 1994—. Author: Regulation of Cardiac Metabolism, 1976, Degradative Processes in Heart and Skeletal Muscle, 1980; contbr. articles to profl. jours. Bd. dirs. Dallas Symphony, Dallas Opera, Dallas Mus. Art, S.W. Mus. Sci. and Tech., Dallas Citizen's Coun., Am. Friends Cambridge U. Recipient rsch. career devel. award NIH, 1972; spl. rsch. fellow USPHS, 1968-70; Guggenheim fellow, 1975-76. Mem. AMA, Am. Soc. Clin. Investigation, Am. Coll. Cardiology, Royal Soc. Medicine Gt. Britain, Am. Physiol. Soc., Internat. Soc. Heart Rsch. (past pres. Am. sect.), Am. Fedn. Clin. Rsch., Assn. Am. Med Colls., Assn. Am. Physicians, Am. Heart Assn. (past chmn. sci. policy com.), Assn. Acad. Health Ctrs. (past chmn. sci. policy com.). Home: 4001 Hanover Ave Dallas TX 75225-7010 Office: U Tex Southwestern Med Ctr 5323 Harry Hines Blvd Dallas TX 75235-7208

WILDER, BILLY, motion picture director, writer, producer; b. Vienna, Austria, June 22, 1906; came to U.S., 1934; m. Audrey Young. Reporter Berlin. Began: film writing with People On Sunday, produced in, Berlin; followed by Emil and the Detectives; now in, Mus. Modern Art, went to, Paris; writer, dir.: Mauvaise Graine; placed under contract as writer, Paramount Studios; writer: (in collaboration) screenplays Bluebeard's Eighth Wife, 1938, Midnight, 1939, Ninotchka, 1939, Arise My Love, 1940, Hold Back the Dawn, 1941; dir., writer: (in collaboration) Five Graves to Cairo, 1943, Double Indemnity, 1944, The Lost Weekend (Acad. award Best Dir.), 1945 (co-award with Charles Brackett for screenplay), The Emperor Waltz, 1948, A Foreign Affair, 1948, Sunset Boulevard, 1950 (Acad. award co-award best story, screenplay); producer, dir., writer: (in collaboration) The Big Carnival (Ace in the Hole), 1951, Stalag 17, 1953, Sabrina, 1954, Love in the Afternoon, 1957, Some Like It Hot, 1959, The Apartment, 1960 (Acad. awards best direction, best picture, co-award best story and screenplay); co-producer, dir., writer: (in collaboration) The Seven Year Itch, 1959; dir., collaborator: The Spirit of St. Louis, 1957, Witness for the Prosecution, 1957, Buddy, Buddy, 1981; producer, dir., writer: One, Two, Three, 1961, Irma La Douce, 1963, Kiss Me, Stupid, 1964, The Fortune Cookie, 1966, The Private Life of Sherlock Holmes, 1970, Avanti, 1972, Fedora, 1979; dir., author: screenplay The Front Page, 1974. Head film sect. Psychol. Warfare div. U.S. Army, 1945. Recipient Poses Creative Art medal for film Brandeis U., 1983, Irving G. Thalberg award Motion Picture Acad., 1988, D.W. Griffith Dirs. award, 6 Acad. awards, 2 Laurel awards Screen Writers Guild. Address: Care Paul Kohner 9300 Wilshire Blve Ste 555 Beverly Hills CA 90212*

WILDER, CHARLES WILLOUGHBY, lawyer, consultant; b. Newton, Mass., Jan. 27, 1929; s. Philip Sawyer and Elisabeth (Clark) W.; m. Elinor Gardner Dean, Nov. 2, 1957; children: Michael, Stephen, Elisabeth. BA, Bowdoin Coll., 1950; LLB, Columbia U., 1957. Bar: N.Y. 1958. Assoc. White & Case, N.Y.C., 1957-58; law clk. to judge U.S. Ct. Appeals (2d cir.), N.Y.C., 1958-59; atty. Gen. Electric Co., 1959-67; from counsel to v.p., dep. gen. counsel, sec. Tex. Gulf Sulphur Co. (name changed to Texasgulf Inc. 1973), N.Y.C. and Stamford, Conn., 1967-90; v.p., dep. gen. counsel, sec. Elf Aquitaine, Inc., Stamford, 1983-90; now legal cons. Served to lt. (j.g.) USNR, 1951-54. Mem. ABA, N.Y. State Bar Assn., Assn. Bar City N.Y. Democrat. Office: Elf Aquitaine Inc 280 Park Ave 36th Fl New York NY 10017-1216

WILDER, DAVID RANDOLPH, materials engineer, consultant; b. Lorimor, Iowa, June 11, 1929; s. Rex Marshall and Ethel Marie (Busch) W.; m. Donna Jean Moore, June 17, 1951; children: Susan, Michael, Margaret, Bruce. BS, Iowa State U., 1951, MS, 1952, PhD, 1958. Registered profl. engr., Iowa. Engr. Ames Lab., 1951-81; faculty mem. dept. materials sci. and engring. Iowa State U., Ames, 1955—, prof. engring., chmn. dept., 1961-89, prof. engring., 1989-91, prof. emeritus, 1991—; cons. to various industries, fed. agys, 1955—. Contbr. numerous tech. paper to profl. lit.; patentee in field. Fellow Am. Ceramic Soc., Accreditation Bd. for Engring. and Tech.; mem. Nat. Inst. Ceramic Engrs., Am. Soc. for Engring. Edn., Keramos. Home: 1214 Ridgewood Ave Ames IA 50010-5208

WILDER, GENE, actor, director, writer; b. Milw., June 11, 1935; s. William J. and Jeanne (Baer) Silberman; m. Mary Joan Schutz, Oct. 27, 1967 (div. 1974); 1 child, Katharine Anastasia; m. Gilda Radner, 1984 (dec.); m. Karen Boyer, Sept. 8, 1991. BA, U. Iowa, 1955; postgrad., Bristol Old Vic Theatre Sch., 1955-56. Appeared in Broadway play: The Complaisant Lover, 1962 (Clarence Derwent award); appeared in motion pictures: Bonnie and Clyde, 1966, The Producers, 1967 (Acad. award nomination), Start the Revolution Without Me, 1968, Quackser Fortune Has a Cousin in the Bronx, 1969, Willy Wonka and the Chocolate Factory, 1970, Everything You Always Wanted to Know About Sex, 1971, Rhinoceros, 1972, Blazing Saddles, 1973, The Little Prince, 1974, Silver Streak, 1976, The Frisco Kid, 1979, Stir Crazy, 1980; Hanky Panky, 1982, See No Evil, Hear No Evil, 1989, Funny About Love, 1990, Another You, 1991; dir., writer, actor film: The Adventures of Sherlock Holmes' Smarter Brother, 1975, The World's Greatest Lover, 1977, Sunday Lovers, 1980, The Woman in Red, 1984, Haunted Honeymoon, 1986; actor, co-writer film: Young Frankenstein, 1974 (Acad. award nomination); TV appearances include: The Trouble With People, 1973, Marlo Thomas Spl., 1973, The Scarecrow, 1972, Thursday's Games, 1973, (series) Something Wilder, 1994—. Campaigned with Elaine May and Rene Taylor for Eugene McCarthy, Allard Lowenstein and Paul O'Dwyer, 1968. Served with U.S. Army, 1956-58. Office: William Morris Agency 151 S El Camino Dr Beverly Hills CA 90212-2704*

WILDER, JOHN SHELTON, state official, state legislator; b. Fayette City, Tenn., June 3, 1921; s. John Chamblee and Martha (Shelton) W.; m. Marcelle Morton, Dec. 31, 1941; children: John Shelton, David Morton. Student, U. Tenn.; LL.B., Memphis Law U., 1957. Bar: Tenn. 1957. Engaged in farming Longtown, Tenn., 1943—; supr. mgmt. Longtown Supply Co.; judge Fayette County Ct.; mem. Tenn. Senate, 1959—; lt. gov. Tenn., 1971—; past pres. Nat. Assn. Soil Conservation Dists., Tenn. Soil Conservation Assn., Tenn. Agrl. Council; exec. com. So. Legis. Conf., Conf. Lt. Govs.; dir. Oakland Deposit Bank, Tenn., Somerville Bank and Trust Co., Tenn. Served with U.S. Army, 1942-43. Mem. Tenn. Cotton Ginners Assn. (past pres.), Delta Theta Phi. Democrat. Methodist. Club: Shriners. Office: Legislative Plz Ste 1 Nashville TN 37243-0026*

WILDER, MICHAEL STEPHEN, insurance company executive; b. New Haven, Conn., Sept. 8, 1941. BA, Yale U., 1963; JD, Harvard U., 1966. Bar: Conn. 1966. Atty. Hartford (Conn.) Fire Ins. Co., 1967-69, asst. gen. counsel, 1969-71, assoc. gen. counsel, 1971-75, gen. coun., sec., 1975-87, sr. v.p., gen. counsel, sec., 1987-95; sr. v.p., gen. counsel The Hartford Fin. Svcs. Group, Inc., 1995—. Mem. ABA, Conn. Bar Assn. Office: Hartford Fin Svcs Group Inc Hartford Plz Hartford CT 06115

WILDER, PELHAM, JR., chemist, pharmacologist, educator, academic administrator; b. Americus, Ga., July 20, 1920; s. Pelham and Hattie (Wilder) W.; m. Alma Sterly Lebey, Mar. 20, 1945; children: Alma Ann, Pelham III, Sterly Lebey. A.B., Emory U., 1942, M.A., 1943; M.A., Harvard U., 1947, Ph.D., 1950. Teaching fellow Harvard U., 1943-44, 46-49; instr. chemistry Duke U., 1949-52, asst. prof., 1952-58, assoc. prof., 1958-62, prof., 1962-67, prof. chemistry and pharmacology, 1967-87, Univ. Disting. Svc. prof. chemistry and pharmacology, 1987-90, Univ. Disting. Svc. prof. emeritus, 1990—, univ. marshal, chief of protocol, 1977—; cons. NSF, Washington, 1960-68; Research Triangle Inst., Durham, 1965—, E.I. duPont deNemours & Co., 1966-69; Mem. advanced placement com. Coll. Entrance Exam. Bd., N.Y., 1967-75, chmn. chemistry com., 1969-75, cons., 1975—; mem. exec. com. Gov. N.C. Sci. Advisory Com., 1962-64. Author: (with W.C. Vosburgh) Laboratory Manual of Fundamentals of Analytical Chemistry, 1956, Laboratory Manual of Physical Chemistry of Aqueous Solutions, 1967; Contbr. articles to profl. jours. Bd. dirs. Durham Acad., chmn., 1970-72; chmn. Exptl. Study of Religion and Soc., Raleigh, N.C., 1966-69. Served with USNR, 1944-46. Recipient 1st annual Alumni Distinguished Undergrad. Teaching award Duke, 1971, Disting. Pub. Svc. award USN, 1989. Mem. Am. Chem. Soc. (chmn. N.C. sect. 1956, com. on profl. tng.), Assn. Naval ROTC Colls. and Univs. (pres. 1982-88), Chem. Soc. London, Phi Beta Kappa (chpt. pres. 1974-75), Sigma Xi, Omicron Delta Kappa. Democrat. Presbyn. (ruling elder; exec. com. Ednl. Instns. Synod of N.C. 1966-72). Lodge: Rotary Club: Univ. (Durham, N.C.). Home: 2514 Wrightwood Ave Durham NC 27705-5830 Office: Duke U Dept Chemistry PO Box 90357 Durham NC 27708-0357

WILDER, ROBERT GEORGE, advertising and public relations executive; b. Hornell, N.Y., Mar. 27, 1920; s. George Reuben and Laura (Nolan) W.; m. Annabel D. Heritage, Feb. 21, 1953; children: Loraine Wilder Powell, Gordon Heritage. B.A., Coll. Wooster, 1942. Propr. Robert G. Wilder & Co., Inc. (public relations), Phila., 1945-50; dir. public relations Lewis & Gilman (advt.-public relations), Phila., 1950-55; v.p. Lewis & Gilman (advt.-public relations), 1955-59, exec. v.p., 1959-64, pres., from 1964; chmn. Lewis, Gilman & Kynett ((merger with Foote, Cone & Belding)), 1983-90, chmn. emeritus, 1990—; bd. dirs. Rittenhouse Trust Co.; dir. emeritus Round Hill Devel. Co. Ltd., Montego Bay, Jamaica. Trustee emeritus Franklin Inst., Lankenau Hosp., Phila.; bd. dirs. Independence Hall Assn.; life trustee emeritus Coll. of Wooster, Ohio. Served to lt. comdr. USNR, 1942-46. Recipient award Charles M. Price Sch., 1971, Bus. and Industry award Opportunities Industrialization Ctr., 1971, Disting. Alumni award Coll. Wooster, 1971, Area Council Econ. Edn. Enterprise award, 1980, Gold Liberty Bell award TV, Radio & Advt. Club Phila., 1982, Vol. of Yr. award Leukemia Soc. Eastern Pa., 1983, Silver medal Phila. Club of Advt. Women, 1984, ann. achievers award Wheels, 1985, Good Scout award Phila. coun. Boy Scouts Am., 1986, Heart of Phila. award Am. Heart Assn., 1989, Great Am. award Poor Richard Club Phila., 1990; named to Bus./Profl. Advt. Assn. Hall of Fame, 1988; inducted into First Annual Hall of Fame of Broadcast Pioneers, Phila. chpt., 1992. Mem. Res. Officers Assn. (past pres. Pa.), Greater Phila. C. of C. (past chmn., bd. dirs., William Penn award 1991); Clubs: Union League (past pres.), Penn, Bachelors Barge (chmn.), Phila. Country, Merion Cricket, Sunday Breakfast. Home: Grays Ln House 100 Grays Ln Haverford PA 19041-1727 Office: Tierney & Ptnrs 200 S Broad St Philadelphia PA 19102-3803

WILDER, RONALD PARKER, economics educator; b. Freeport, Tex., Jan. 15, 1941; s. J. Barton and Lois (Parker) W.; m. Charlotte D. Pearson, Sept. 4, 1965; children: Erika, Rachel, David. BA, Rice U., 1963, MA, 1964; PhD, Vanderbilt U., 1969. Asst. prof. econs. U. S.C., Columbia, 1970-75, assoc. prof., 1975-80, prof., 1980—, chmn. dept. econs., 1987—. Co-author: Stock Life Insurance Profitability, 1986; mem. editorial bd. So. Econ. J., 1978-80; contbr. articles to profl. jours. Capt. U.S. Army, 1968-70. Fellow Ford Found., Vanderbilt U., 1964-65. Mem. Am. Econ. Assn., So. Econ. Assn., Omicron Delta Epsilon. United Methodist. Avocations: hiking, canoeing. Office: U of SC Dept of Econs Columbia SC 29208

WILDER, VALERIE, ballet company administrator; b. Pasadena, Calif., Aug. 5, 1947; d. Douglas Wilder and Helen Marie (Wilson) Morrill; m. Geoffrey Duer Perry, Nov. 24, 1973; children: Stuart Whittier, Sabina Woodman. Student, Butler U., Indpls., 1966-68, U. Toronto, 1969-75. Dancer Nat. Ballet Can., Toronto, 1970-78; ptnr. Perry & Wilder Inc., Toronto, 1976-83; artistic adminstr. Nat. Ballet Can., Toronto, 1983-86, assoc. artistic dir., 1986-87, co-artistic dir., 1987-89, assoc. dir., 1989-96, exec. dir., 1996—; adv. bd. Dancer Transition Ctr., Toronto, 1986—; dance adv. panel Can. Coun., 1984-89; dance adv. com. Ont. Arts. Coun., 1985-90. Bd. dirs. Toronto Arts Coun., 1990-94. Mem. Dance in Can. Assn., Can. Assn. Profl. Dance Orgns. (bd. dirs.). Avocations: competitive running, triathlon. Office: Nat Ballet of Can, 470 Queens Quay West, Toronto, ON Canada M5V 3K4

WILDEROTTER, JAMES ARTHUR, lawyer; b. Newark, July 25, 1944; s. Arthur Walter and Dorothy Theresa (King) W.; m. Cheryl Lynn Clifford; children: James, Kristin, Kathryn. BA, Georgetown U., 1966; JD, U. Ill., 1969. Bar: D.C. 1969, U.S. Supreme Ct. 1974. Assoc. Covington & Burling, Washington, 1969-71; spl. asst. to Under Sec. Commerce, Washington, 1971-73; exec. asst. to Sec. HUD, Washington, 1973-74; assoc. dept. atty. gen. U.S. Washington, 1974-75, assoc. counsel to Pres. U.S., 1975-76; gen. counsel U.S. Energy Research and Devel. Adminstrn., Washington, 1976-77; of counsel Morgan, Lewis & Bockius, Washington, 1977-78; ptnr. Jones, Day, Reavis & Pogue, Washington, 1978-91, 95—; v.p., gen. counsel Internat. Paper Co., Purchase, N.Y., 1991-94. Editor in chief: U. Ill. Law Rev., 1968-69. Gen. counsel rules com. Rep. Nat. Conv., 1980; sec. James S. Brady Presdl. Found., 1982-88; gen. counsel Nat. Sudden Infant Death Syndrome Found., 1986-90, sec. Sudden Infant Death Syndrome Alliance, 1990-93. With USN, 1962-68. Mem. ABA. Republican. Roman Catholic. Home: 518 Duke St Alexandria VA 22314-3738 Office: Jones Day Reavis and Pogue 1450 G St NW Washington DC 20005-2001

WILDES, LEON, lawyer, educator; b. Scranton, Pa., Mar. 4, 1933. BA magna cum laude, Yeshiva U., 1954; JD, NYU, 1957, LLM, 1959. Bar: N.Y. 1958, U.S. Dist. Ct. (so. dist.) N.Y. 1960, U.S. Supreme Ct. 1961. Ptnr. Wildes and Weinberg, N.Y.C., 1960—; adj. prof. law Benjamin N. Cardozo Sch. Law, N.Y.C., 1981—. Contbr. numerous articles to law revs. Mem. ABA, Assn. of Bar of City of N.Y. (com. immigration and nationality law 1975-78, 88-91, 95—), Am. Immigration Lawyers Assn. (nat. pres. 1970-71, bd. govs. 1971—, co-chair ethics com. 1993—, editor Immigration and Nationality Law Symposium 1983). Office: 515 Madison Ave New York NY 10022-5403

WILDHABER, MICHAEL RENE, accountant; b. Jefferson City, Mo., Aug. 4, 1952; s. Rainey A. and Velma W.; m. Paula M. Wildhaber, Sept. 28, 1974; 1 child, Wendy. AA, Florissant Valley Coll., 1972; BS, U. Mo., 1974. CPA, Mo.; cert. info. sys. auditor, cert. internal auditor, cert. tax preparer, assoc. ins. acctg. and fin., enrolled agt. Sr. auditor I.T.T. Fin., St. Louis, 1974-79; audit mgr. Navco, St. Louis, 1980-85; contr. Millers mutual, Alton, Ill., 1985-88; pres. R&M Tax and Acctg., St. Louis, 1988—. Tchr. Jr. Achievement, St. Louis, 1993-94; vol. Olympic Festival, St. Louis, 1994, 100 Neediest Cases, St. Louis, 1990-94, Old News Boy, St. Louis, 1992-94. Mem. AICPA, Mo. Soc. CPAs, Inst. Internal Auditors. Office: R&M Tax and Acctg 3805 S Kings Hwy Saint Louis MO 63109

WILDHACK, JOHN ROBERT, producer, broadcast executive; b. Buffalo, Oct. 23, 1958; s. Robert Henry and Beth Mae (Hankin) W. BA in TV/Radio, Syracuse U., 1980. Prodn. asst. Sta. ESPN-TV, Bristol, Conn., 1980-81; assoc. producer Sta. ESPN-TV, Bristol, 1981-82, sr. assoc. producer, 1982-84, producer, 1984-85, sr. producer, sr. v.p. programming, 1985—. Mem. Nat. Acad. Cable Programming. Republican. Roman Catholic. Avocations: golf, music. •

WILDHACK, WILLIAM AUGUST, JR., lawyer; b. Takoma Park, Md., Nov. 28, 1935; s. William August and Martha Elizabeth (Parks) W.; m. Martha Moore Allston, Aug. 1, 1959; children: William A. III, Elizabeth L. B.S., Miami U., Oxford, Ohio, 1957; J.D., George Washington U., 1963. Bar: Va. 1963, D.C. 1965, Md. 1983, U.S. Supreme Ct. 1967. Agt. IRS, No. Va., 1957-65; assoc. Morris, Pearce, Gardner & Beitel, Washington, 1965-69; sole practice Washington, 1969; v.p., corp. counsel B.F. Saul Co. and affiliates, Chevy Chase, Md., 1969-87, Chevy Chase Bank, F.S.B. and affiliates, 1987-90; atty. pvt. practice, Arlington, Va., 1990—; sec. B.F. Saul Real Estate Investment Trust, Chevy Chase, 1972-87. Mem. Arlington Tenant Landlord Commn., 1976-91. Mem. ABA, Md. Bar Assn., D.C. Bar, Va. Bar, Arlington County Bar Assn., Nat. Acad. Elder Law Attys., Am. Soc. Corp. Secs., Phi Alpha Delta. Presbyterian.

WILDIN, MAURICE WILBERT, mechanical engineering educator; b. Hutchinson, Kans., June 24, 1935; s. John Frederick and Mildred Minerva (Dawson) W.; m. Mary Ann Brovan Christiansen, Aug. 9, 1958; children: Molly, Mildred. AA, Hutchinson Jr. Coll., 1955; BSME, U. Kans., 1958; MSME, Purdue U., 1959, PhD, 1963. Grad. asst. and instr. mech. engring. Purdue U., West Lafayette, Ind., 1958-61; from asst. prof. to assoc. prof. mech. engring. U. N.Mex., Albuquerque, 1961—, prof., 1973, dept. chair, 1968-73; mem. tech. staff Sandia Nat. Labs., Albuquerque, 1984-85; cons. several domestic and fgn. firms on stratified thermal storage, 1985—. Contbr. articles to profl. jours. Fellow ASHRAE; mem. ASME, Am. Solar Energy Soc. Office: U NMex Dept Mech Engring Albuquerque NM 87131

WILDING, DIANE, marketing, financial and information systems executive; b. Chicago Heights, Ill., Nov. 7, 1942; d. Michael Edward and Katherine Surian; m. Manfred Georg Wilding, May 7, 1975 (div. 1980). BSBA in Acctg. magna cum laude, No. Ill. U., 1963; postgrad., U. Chgo., 1972-74; cert. in German lang., Goethe Inst., Rothenburg, Germany, 1984; cert. in internat. bus. German, Goethe Inst., Atlanta, 1994. Lic. cosmetologist. Systems engr. IBM, Chgo., 1963-68; data processing mgr. Am. Res. Corp., Chgo., 1969-72; system rsch. and devel. project mgr. Continental Bank, Chgo., 1972-75; fin. industry mktg. rep. IBM Can., Ltd., Toronto, Ont., 1976-79; regional telecommunications mktg. exec. Control Data Corp., Atlanta, 1980-84; gen. mgr. The Plant Plant, Atlanta, 1985-92; cons. SAP IBM Corp., Atlanta, 1993—; pioneer installer on-line Automatic Teller Machines, Pos Equipment. Author: The Canadian Payment System: An International Perspective, 1977. Mem. Chgo. Coun. on Fgn. Rels.; bd. dirs. Easter House Adoption Agy., Chgo., 1974-76. Mem. Internat. Brass Soc., Goethe Inst., Mensa. Clubs: Ponte Verde (Fla.); Royal Ont. Yacht, Libertyville Racquet. Avocations: horticulture, travel, dancing, gourmet cooking, foreign languages. Home: 2350 Cobb Pkwy #28-J Smyrna GA 30080

WILDING, JAMES ANTHONY, airport administrator; b. Washington, Dec. 22, 1937; s. Anthony Warwick and Dorothy (Lauten) W.; m. Marcella Anne Gibbons, Aug. 5, 1961; children: Matthew, William, Patricia, Marcella. B.S. in Civil Engring., Catholic U., 1959. With planning dept. Bur. Nat. Capital Airports, Washington, 1959-63, with civil engring. dept., 1963-72, acting dir., 1974; chief engring. staff Met. Washington Airports, 1972-75, dep. dir., 1975-79, dir., 1979-87; gen. mgr. Met. Washington Apts. Authority, Alexandria, Va., 1987—; chmn. Airports Coun. Internat. N.A., 1995. Recipient Sr. Exec. Service Performance award Dept. Transp., 1981, Meritorious Exec. award Pres. of U.S., 1982, Outstanding Achievement award Sec. Transp., 1985. Roman Catholic. Home: 1805 Crystal Ln Silver Spring MD 20906-2102 Office: Met Washington Airports Authority 44 Canal Center Plz Alexandria VA 22314-1592

WILDING, LAWRENCE PAUL, pedology educator, soil science consultant; b. Winner, S.D., Oct. 1, 1934; s. William Kasper and Ruth Inez (Root) W.; m. Gladys Dora Milne, Nov. 25, 1956; children: Linda Kay, Doris Bertha, Charles William, David Lawrence. BSc, S.D. State U., 1956, MSc, 1959; PhD, U. Ill., 1962. Asst. in agronomy S.D. State U., Brookings, 1956-59; rsch. fellow U. Ill., Urbana, 1959-62; prof. agronomy Ohio State U., Columbus, 1962-76; prof. pedology Tex. A&M U., College Station, 1976—; vis. prof. U. Guelph, Ont. Can., 1971-72; mem. NATO Advanced Rsch. Workshop on Expansive Soils, Cornell U., 1990-91. Author or/and editor 3 books; assoc. editor Catena Verlag, 1989, Geoderma, 1988-92; contbr. over 130 articles to profl. jours., chpts. to books. Sgt. S.D. N.G., 1956-59. Recipient Mem. award Sigma XI, 1988, Superior Svc. Group award sci. rsch. USDA, 1993; Campbell Soup fellow, 1959-62; grantee USDA, AID, 1986—. Fellow Am. Soc. Agronomy (cert.), Soil Sci. Soc. Am. (Soil Sci. Rsch. award 1987, opportunities in soil sci. com., chmn. subcommn. B 1989-92, chmn. divsn. S-5, bd. dirs. rep., mem. steering com. 1990-91, pres. elect 1992-93, pres. 1993-94, pst pres. 1994-95), Am. Inst. Chemists; mem. Soil Scientists Assn. Tex., Soil and Water Conservation Soc. Am., Tex. A&M Faculty Club, Gamma Sigma Delta. Democrat. Presbyterian. Avocations: golf, woodworking, travelling, sports, antiques. Office: Texas A&M U Dept Soil and Crop Scis College Station TX 77843

WILDMAN, C.J. (BUD), political organization official; b. Ottawa, Ont., Can., June 3, 1946; m. Anne Wildman; children: Rob, Jody, Cary, Tiana, Kendra (dec.). BA in History and Polit. Sci., Carleton U., 1967. Tchr. H.S. Sault Ste Marie Bd. Edn.; mem. Provincial Parliament for Algoma; min. natural resources New Dem. Party Govt., min. environ. and energy, min. responsible for native affairs; caucus chair Ont. New Dem. Party, edn. and tng. critic, interim head; salary negotiator Ont. Secondary Sch. Tchrs. Fedn.; critic to natural resources, agr. and food, small bus. and coops., no. devel. and mines, occupl. health and safety, native affairs, industry and trade devel., no. transp. and comm., econ. devel. and treasury and econs. Office: Rm 361 East Wing, Legis Bldg Queens Park, Toronto, ON Canada M4A 1A5

WILDMAN, GARY CECIL, chemist; b. Middlefield, Ohio, Nov. 25, 1942; s. Gerald Robert and Frances Jane (Swager) W.; m. Nancy Jackson, June 5, 1965; children: Debbie, Eric. A.B. in Chemistry, Thiel Coll., 1964; Ph.D. in Chemistry, Duke U., 1970. Research asst. B.F. Goodrich Research, Brecksville, Ohio, summer 1964; instr. Duke U., 1966-67; research chemist Hercules Research Center, Wilmington, Del., 1968-71; asso. prof. polymer sci. U. So. Miss., Hattiesburg, 1971-76; prof. U. So. Miss., 1976-83, chmn. dept., 1971-76, dean Coll. Sci. and Tech., 1976-83; v.p. research and devel. Schering Plough, Memphis, 1983—. Mem. Am. Chem. Soc., So. Soc. Coatings Tech., Soc. Plastics Engrs., Am. Crystallographic Assn., Phi Beta Kappa, Sigma Xi, Phi Lambda Upsilon, Sigma Pi Sigma, Omicron Delta Kappa. Republican. Methodist. Club: Rotary. Home: 8857 Aldershot Dr Memphis TN 38139-6522 Office: PO Box 377 Memphis TN 38151-0002

WILDMAN, MAX EDWARD, lawyer; b. Terre Haute, Ind., Dec. 4, 1919; s. Roscoe Ellsworth and Lena (Shaw) W.; m. Joyce Lenore Smith, Sept. 25, 1948; children: Leslie, William. B.S., Butler U., 1941; J.D., U. Mich., 1947; M.B.A., U. Chgo., 1952. Bar: Ill., Ind. Ptnr. Kirkland & Ellis, Chgo., 1947-67; mng. ptnr. Wildman, Harrold, Allen & Dixon, Chgo., 1967-89; dir. Colt Industries, N.Y., Nat. Blvd. Bank, Ill. Contbr. articles to profl. jours. Trustee Butler U., Indpls., Lake Forest Hosp., Ill., Lake Bluff Library Bd., Ill.; chmn. Lake Bluff Zoning Bd. Served to lt. col. USAF, 1943-46; PTO. Fellow Am. Coll. Trial Lawyers; mem. Soc. Trial Lawyers, Law Club, Legal Club, Trial Lawyers Club of Chgo. Presbyterian. Clubs: Anglers (Chgo.), Pere Marquette Rod and Gun (Baldwin, Mich.), Shoreacres (Lake Bluff), Univ. of Chgo. Office: Wildman Harrold Allen & Dixon 225 W Wacker Dr Chicago IL 60606-1224

WILDS, BONNIE, author, community volunteer; b. Phila., July 12, 1922; d. J.D. and Rose (Morris) Farber; m. Walter Warren Wilds, Jan. 18, 1946; children: Stephanie Wilds Shea, Eugenia Wilds Ardrey, Vanessa Wilds Cunningham Wassenar, Pamela Wilds Cole. BA, Sarah Lawrence Coll., 1942; MA, U. Pitts., 1957, PhD, 1973. Govt. intern Office of Coord. Inter-Am. Affairs Nat. Inst. Pub. Affairs, Washington, 1942-43; desk officer Dept. State, Washington, 1943-44, economist, 1944-46; resource coord. Inst. Internat. Edn., N.Y.C., 1975-76. Author: El Animal Profeta by Antonio Mira de Amescua, 1979. Mem. women's com. Carnegie Mus. Art, Pitts., 1958—; mem. social svc. bd. dirs. Shadyside Hosp., Pitts., 1958-61; mem. women's aux. bd. dirs. Magee Women's Hosp., Pitts., 1958-63, pres., 1961-63; bd. dirs., v.p. Bethany Lenox Hill Day Care Ctr., N.Y.C., 1974-92, Mary Walton Children's Ctr., N.Y.C., 1974-92; bd. dirs. Musicians Emergency Fund, 1980-84, pres., 1982-84, hon. dir., 1985—; mem. Hospitality Com. for UN Dels., 1984—, dir., 1992—, v.p., 1995-96. Recipient Pub. Svc. citation City of Pitts., 1959. Fellow Pierpont Morgan Libr., Frick Collection; mem. The New England Soc., Colony Club (N.Y.), Rolling Rock Club (Ligonier, Pa.). Republican. Episcopalian. Avocations: community service, travel, reading. Home: 20 E 68th St New York NY 10021-5844

WILE, JULIUS, former corporate executive, educator; b. N.Y.C., Apr. 17, 1915; s. Irwin and Harriet (Brussel) W.; m. Ruth Miller, June 26, 1941 (dec. Feb. 1992); children: Barbara Miller Wile Schwarz, Andrew Brussel. B.S. in Mech. Engring. and Aeronautics, NYU, 1936; DFA (hon.), Culinary Inst. Am., 1994. With Julius Wile Sons & Co. Inc., N.Y.C., 1936-41, 45-76, v.p., 1955-66, sr. v.p., 1967-76; prodn. engr. Brewster Aero. Corp., L.I City, N.Y., 1942-44, Greer Hydraulics Inc., Bklyn., 1944-45; trustee Culinary Inst. Am., Hyde Park, N.Y., 1970-79, 81-90, chmn. bd. trustees, 1981-83; vis. lectr. Sch. Hotel Adminstrn. Cornell U., Ithaca, N.Y., 1953-82; wines and spirits lectr.; v.p. New Eng. Distillers Inc., Teterboro, N.J., 1955-72. Contbr. Brit. Book of Yr, 1957-75; editor: Frank Schoonmaker's Encyclopedia of Wine, 7th edit., 1978. V.p. Spain-U.S. C. of C., N.Y.C., 1972; bd. dirs. Scarsdale Family Counseling Service, N.Y., 1973-79; chmn. ann. drive ARC, Scarsdale, 1976. Decorated Ordre de l'Economie Nationale France, Ordre National du Merite France, Membre d'Honneur Academie du Vin de Bordeaux. Mem. Commanderie de Bordeaux (gov. 1959—, dep. grand maitre 1978-88, grand chancelier 1988—), Soc. Wine Educators (bd. dirs. 1980—, treas. 1986-93), Wine and Food Soc. N.Y. (bd. dirs. 1971-73, 77-83), Nat. Assn. Beverage Importers (chmn. table wine com. 1954-60, 65-76). Republican. Jewish. Clubs: Explorers, Quaker Ridge Golf (Scarsdale). Home and Office: 27 Grand Park Ave Scarsdale NY 10583-7611 *Fifteen years of Prohibition led to public ignorance of fine wines and spirits. Education of myself, employees, the trade and the public has been an important part of my career. It was and still is both a duty and a pleasure to pass on what I have learned and enjoyed. My tenet is that 'there is no premium for good taste.'*

WILEMAN, GEORGE ROBERT, lawyer; b. Ironton, Ohio, June 1, 1938; s. George Merchant and Marguerite (McCormack) W.; children: John Chandler, Julie Jo. AB, Duke U., 1960; JD, Georgetown U., 1963. Bar: Ohio 1968, Tex. 1977, U.S. Supreme Ct. 1993. Pvt. practice Dallas, 1977—. Mem. Coll. State Bar of Tex. Republican. Avocations: boating, running. Home: 5200 Keller Springs #1136 Dallas TX 75248 Office: 5220 Spring Valley Rd Ste 520 Dallas TX 75240-2414

WILENSKY, GAIL ROGGIN, economist; b. Detroit, June 14, 1943; d. Albert Alan and Sophia (Blitz) Roggin; AB with honors, U. Mich., 1964, MA in Econs., 1965, PhD in Econs., 1968; hon. degree Hahnemann U., 1993; m. Robert Joel Wilensky, Aug. 4, 1963; children: Peter Benjamin, Sara Elizabeth. Economist, President's Commn. on Income Maintenance Programs, exec. dir. Md. Council of Econ. Advs., 1969-71; sr. researcher Urban Inst., Washington, 1971-73; assoc. research scientist, public policy and public health U. Mich., Ann Arbor 1973-75, vis. asst. prof. econs., 1973-75; sr. research mgr. Nat. Center for Health Services Research, Hyattsville, Md., 1975-83; assoc. profl. lectr. George Washington U., 1976-78; v.p. div. health affairs Project HOPE, Millwood, Va., 1983-90; adminstr. Health Care Fin. Adminstrn., Washington, 1990-92, dep. asst. to the pres. for policy devel., White House, 1992-93; sr. fellow Project Hope, Bethesda, Md., 1993—, chair phys. payment rev. com., 1995—. Vol. Am. Heart Assn., 1980-85; mem. health adv. com. Compt. Gen. U.S., 1987-90, 93—; bd. dirs. United Healthcare Corp., Adv.Tiss Sci., Coram, St. Jude Med., Syncor Internat., Capstone Pharmacy, Shared Med. Sys. Mem. vis. com. med. sch. U. Mich., 1993—; trustee United Mine Workers Am. Retirement Fund, 1993—. Flinn Found. disting. scholar, 1985; recipient Dean Conley award Am. Coll. Healthcare Execs, 1989. Mem. NAS (mem. inst. medicine 1989—), Am. Econ. Assn. (women's com. 1982-84), Fedn. Orgns. of Profl. Women (chmn. econ. task force 1981-83), Am. Statis. Assn., Nat. Tax Assn., Washington Women Economists, Assn. Health Svcs. Rsch. (dir. 1984-87), Found. Health Svcs. Rsch. (bd. dirs. 1987-90, commr. physician payment rev. com. 1989-90). Contbr. 90 articles in field to profl. jours. Mem. Cosmos Club (Washington). Home: 2807 Battery Pl NW Washington DC 20016-3439

WILENSKY, HAROLD L., political science and industrial relations educator; b. New Rochelle, N.Y., Mar. 3, 1923; s. Joseph and Mary Jane (Wainsten) W.; children: Stephen David, Michael Alan, Daniel Lewis. Student, Goddard Coll., 1940-42; AB, Antioch Coll., 1947; MA, U. Chgo., 1949, PhD, 1955. Asst. prof. sociology U. Chgo., 1951-53, asst. prof. indsl. relations, 1953-54; asst. prof. sociology U. Mich., Ann Arbor, 1954-57, assoc. prof., 1957-61, prof., 1961-62; prof. U. Calif., Berkeley, 1963-82, prof. polit. sci., 1982—, research sociologist Inst. Indsl. Relations, 1963—, project dir. Inst. Internat. Studies, 1970-90; project dir. Ctr. for German and European Studies, Berkeley, 1994—; mem. research career awards com. Nat. Inst. Mental Health, 1964-67; cons. in field. Author: Industrial Relations: A Guide to Reading and Research, 1954, Intellectuals in Labor Unions: Organizational Pressures on Professional Roles, 1956, Organizational Intelligence: Knowledge and Policy in Government and Industry, 1967, The Welfare State and Equality: Structural and Ideological Roots of Public Expenditures, 1975, The New Corporatism, Centralization, and the Welfare State, 1976, (with C.N. Lebeaux) Industrial Society and Social Welfare, 1965, (with others) Comparative Social Policy, 1985, (with L. Turner) Democratic Corporatism and Policy Linkages, 1987; editor: (with C. Arensberg and others) Research in Industrial Human Relations, 1957, (with P.F. Lazarsfeld and W. H. Sewell) The Uses of Sociology, 1967; contbr. articles to profl. jours. Recipient aux. award Social Sci. Rsch. Coun., 1962, Book award McKinsey Found., 1967; fellow Ctr. for Advanced Study in Behavioral Scis., 1956-57, 62-63, German Marshall Fund, 1978-79; Harry A. Millis rsch. awardee U. Chgo., 1950-51. Fellow AAAS; mem. AAUP, Internat. Sociol. Assn., Internat. Polit. Sci. Assn., Indsl. Relations Research Assn. (exec. com. 1965-68), Soc. for Study Social Problems (chmn. editorial com.), Am. Polit. Sci. Assn., Am. Sociol. Assn. (exec. council 1969-72, chmn. com. on info. tech. and privacy 1970-72), Council European Studies (steering com. 1980-83). Democrat. Jewish. Avocations: music, trumpet, skiing. Office: U Calif Dept Polit Sci 210 Barrows Hall Berkeley CA 94720-1951

WILENSKY, JULIUS M., publishing company executive; b. Stamford, Conn., Oct. 10, 1916; s. Joseph and Mary (Wainstein) W.; m. Dorothy T. Jobrack, July 2, 1939; children—Joseph L. (dec.), Nancy L. Jamie, Martha J. Hansen. Student, Rensselaer Poly. Inst., 1934-36. Methods engr. Yale & Towne Mfg. Co., Stamford, 1939-49; prodn. mgr. Yale & Towne Mfg. Co., 1953-57; dir. purchasing lock and hardware div. Eaton Yale & Towne, Rye, N.Y., 1957-67; mayor of Stamford, 1969-73; dir. materials, arms operations Winchester div. Olin Corp., New Haven, 1973-78; pres. Wescott Cove Pub. Co., 1978—; lectr. in field. Author guide books on cruising L.I. Sound, Cape Code, Windward Islands, Bay Islands of Honduras and Abacos; contbr. articles to boating mags. and newspapers; contbg. editor: Rudder, 1970-77; author cruising columns Ea. and So. edits. Sea mag., 1978-80, Rudder mag., 1981-83; editor cruising guides to Tahiti, French Soc. Islands, Maine (2 vols.), Turkey, Belize, Mexico's Caribbean Coast, I Don't Do Portholes, Lights and Legends, Beachcombing and Beachcrafting, Pacific Wanderer, Irma Quarterdeck Reports, Inside American Paradise, Beachcruising and Coastal Camping, Circumnavigation: Sail the Trade Winds (2 vols.), First Time Around, Chesapeake Bay Cruising Guide-Vol. I, Upper Bay, Florida Keys and Everglades Cruising Guide. Bd. dirs. Stamford Ctr. for Arts, 1981-90; treas. Lifeline, 1983-85; first v.p. Met. Regional Coun., 1973; mem. Tri-State Regional Planning Commn., 1971-73, Stamford Bd. Fin., 1965-69, Stamford Planning Bd., 1963-65; chmn. Coun. Rep. Clubs, Stamford, 1961-62. With USAAF, 1943-46. Named Republican of Yr. Stamford Reps., 1962. Mem. Am. Mgmt. Assn., Stamford Power Squadron, Stamford Good Govt. Assn. (dir., treas. 1949-57), Stamford Chamber Residences (pres. 1953-55). Home: 51 Barrett Ave Stamford CT 06905-3212 *To be productive in fields or enterprises which are useful to other people has been my aspiration, and it's a high one. It's important to set goals early in life, then follow a plan to obtain the education and experience required to achieve these goals. Courage, honesty, objectivity, determination, hard work, and consideration for others will enable one to become outstanding in any field.*

WILENSKY, SAUL, lawyer; b. Bklyn., Dec. 9, 1941; s. Morris and Pearl (Wagman) W.; m. Sandra J. Brunault, Nov. 11, 1979; 1 child, Margot. BA, Hunter Coll., 1963; LLB, St. John's U., Bklyn., 1966; LLM, NYU, 1976. Bar: N.Y. 1967, U.S. Dist. Ct. (ea. and so. dists.) N.Y. 1970, U.S. Supreme Ct. 1971, U.S. Ct. Appeals (2d cir.) 1973, U.S. Dist. Ct. (no. dist.) N.Y. 1974. Ptnr. Lester, Schwab, Katz & Dwyer, N.Y.C., 1966—. Office: Lester Schwab Katz & Dwyer 120 Broadway New York NY 10271-0002

WILES, ANDREW J., mathematician, educator; b. England, Apr. 11, 1953; married; children. BS in Math., Oxford U., England; PhD in Math., Cambridge U., England. Lecturer Inst. Advanced Studies, Princeton, N.J.; asst., assoc. prof. math. Harvard U., Cambridge, Mass.; prof. math. Princeton U., Princeton, N.J., 1982—. Recipient Wolf Prize in Mathematics, 1995. Achievements include solving (with Richard Taylor) Pierre de Fermat's last theory of 1637. Office: Princeton U Dept Math Princeton NJ 08544

WILES, CHARLES PRESTON, minister; b. Frederick, Md., Aug. 5, 1918; s. Charles Wesley and Nellie (Burgess) W.; m. Mary McCallum; children: Mary Margaret, Charles Preston, Wade Burgess. A.B., Washington Coll., 1939; postgrad., U. Va., 1940; M.A., Duke U., 1945, Ph.D. (Univ. fellow 1947-51, Kearns Honor fellow 1949-50), 1951; B.D., Va. Theol. Sem., 1947. Ordained to ministry Episc. Ch., 1947. Priest-in-charge St. Joseph's Ch., Durham, N.C., 1947-51; rector St. Mary's Episcopal Ch., Burlington, N.J., 1951-64; pres., trustee Burlington Coll., 1951-64, faculty cons., 1956-64; mem. faculty Phila. Div. Sch., 1959-62, lectr. ch. history, 1960-62; dean St. Matthew's Episcopal Cathedral, Dallas, 1964-87, dean emeritus, 1989; assoc. priest St. Luke's, Dallas, 1987—; dep. gen. Conv. from Diocese Dallas, 1967, 69, 70, 73, 76, 79; del. Provincial Synod from Diocese Dallas, 1966, 69, 72, 75, 78; mem. exec. council Diocese Dallas, 1967-77, 84-86, pres. mem. standing com., 1970-73, pres., 1971-73, mem. bd. missions, 1967-69, chmn. dept. coll. work, 1965-71, mem. bd. examing chaplains, 1965-71; mem. standing liturgical commn.; dean, warden Cathedral Center for Continuing Edn. and Pastoral Concern, 1971-87, Commn. Ministry, 1971-76; dean Dallas Deanery, 1965-69, 84-86, Bicentennial preacher, 1975; pres. convocation and clericus Diocese of N.J., 1961-64; examining chaplain, mem. bd. missions, mem. bd. christina edn., dean Burlington-Trenton convocation; instr., dean Drew Conf. for Adults in N.J., 1952-56; retreat conductor St. Martin's House, Bernardsville, N.J., St. John Bapt. Convent, Mendhan, N.J.; dean Diocesan Sch. Religion, N.J., 1962-63; parish life lab. and weekend conductor Nat. Dept. Christian Edn., 1962; co-founder, dean Princeton (N.J.) Conf., 1956-64; mem. Goals for Dallas Com.; co-chmn. N.Am. Cathedral Deans' Conf., 1980-81. Author: Sacrament and Sacrifice, 2d edit., 1973, Lancelot Andrews, Caroline Divine, 1951, Lift Up Your Hearts, 1956, A Manual of Prayers, 1975, The Holy Eucharist: Word and Sacrament, 1993, The Gate of Heaven, 1993, A Centennial Narrative History of the Episcopal Diocese of Dallas, 1995. Trustee Gen. Theol. Sem., 1968-80; bd. dirs. Evergreen Home for Aging, St. Philip's Community Center, Overseas Mission Soc. Named Priest of Yr., 1969. Mem. Navy League, Ch. Hist. Soc. (dir. 1960-68), Kiwanian Club (Disting. Svc. award 1951, Disting. Citizen award Brunswick, Md. 1986), Dallas Athletic club, Chaparral, Vesper (Phila.) Club, Burlington County Country Club. Home: 7023 Northwood Rd Dallas TX 75225-2439

WILES, DAVID MCKEEN, chemist; b. Springhill, N.S., Can., Dec. 28, 1932; s. Roy McKeen and Olwen Gertrude (Jones) W.; m. Valerie Joan Rowlands, June 8, 1957; children: Gordon Stuart, Sandra Lorraine. B.Sc. with honors, McMaster U., 1954, M.Sc., 1955; Ph.D. in Chemistry, McGill U., 1957. Research officer chemistry div. Nat. Research Council of Can., Ottawa, 1959-66; head textile chemistry sect. chemistry div. Nat. Research Council of Can., 1966-75, dir. chemistry div., 1975-90; pres. Plastichem Cons., Victoria, B.C., Can., 1990—; bd. dirs. MLB Industries, Malahat Sys. Corp.; chmn. Can. High Polymer Forum, 1967-69; v.p. N.Am. Chem. Congress, Mexico City, 1975. Contbr. articles to profl. jours.; mem. editl. adv. bd. numerous profl. jours. Can. Ramsay Meml. fellow, 1957-59. Fellow Chem. Inst. Can. (chmn. bd. dirs. 1972-74, pres. 1975-76, Dunlop Lectr.

award 1981), Royal Soc. Chem. London, Royal Soc. Can.; mem. Am. Chem. Soc. (Polymer Chem. div.). Patentee in field. Home and Office: 3965 Juan de Fuca Terr, Victoria, BC Canada V8N 5W9

WILES, WILLIAM DIXON, III, lawyer; b. Wellington, Tex., Apr. 1, 1949; s. William Dixon Wiles Sr. and Metha (Bacon) Chapman; m. Betsy Flowers, Mar. 21, 1971; children: Dixon, Robert. BA magna cum laude, U. Houston, 1971; JD, So. Meth. U., 1974. Bar: Tex. 1974, U.S. Dist. Ct. (no., so., ea. and we. dists.) Tex., U.S. Dist. Ct. Ark., U.S. Ct. Appeals (5th and 11th cirs.). Ptnr. Bailey & Williams, Dallas; now ptnr. Fowler, Wiles & Keith L.L.P., Dallas. Mem. ABA, Am. Bd. Trial Advs., Am. Soc. Law and Medicine, Nat. Health Lawyers Assn., Tex. Assn. Def. Counsel, Dallas Assn. Def. Counsel. Democrat. Episcopalian. Club: Lakewood Country (Dallas). Home: 5527 Swiss Ave Dallas TX 75214-4948 Office: Fowler Wiles & Keith LLP 1900 City Place Center LB19 2711 N Haskell Ave Dallas TX 75204

WILETS, LAWRENCE, physics educator; b. Oconomowoc, Wis., Jan. 4, 1927; s. Edward and Sophia (Finger) W.; m. Dulcy Elaine Margoles, Dec. 21, 1947; children—Ileen Sue, Edward E., James D.; m. Vivian C. Wolf, Feb. 8, 1976. BS, U. Wis., 1948; MA, Princeton, 1950, PhD, 1952. Research asso. Project Matterhorn, Princeton, N.J., 1951-53, U. Calif. Radiation Lab., Livermore, 1953; NSF postdoctoral fellow Inst. Theoretical Physics, Copenhagen, Denmark, 1953-55; staff mem. Los Alamos Sci. Lab., 1955-58; mem. Inst. Advanced Study, Princeton, 1957-58; mem. faculty U. Wash., Seattle, 1958—; prof. physics U. Wash., 1962-95; prof. emeritus U. Wash., Seattle, 1995—; cons. to pvt. and govt. labs.; vis. prof. Princeton, 1969, Calif. Inst. Tech., 1971. Author: Theories of Nuclear Fission, 1964, Nontopological Solitons, 1989; contbr. over 180 articles to profl. jours. Del. Dem. Nat. Conv., 1968. NSF sr. fellow Weizmann Inst. Sci., Rehovot, Israel, 1961-62; Nordita prof. and Guggenheim fellow Lund (Sweden) U., also Weizmann Inst., 1976—; Sir Thomas Lyle rsch. fellow U. Melbourne, Australia, 1989; recipient Alexander von Humboldt sr. U.S. scientist award, 1983. Fellow Am. Phys. Soc., AAAS; mem. Fedn. Am. Scientists, AAUP (pres. chpt. 1969-70, 73-75, pres. state conf. 1975-76), Phi Beta Kappa, Sigma Xi. Club: Explorers. Research on theory of nuclear structure and reactions, nuclear fission, atomic structure, atomic collisions, many body problems, subnuclear structure and elementary particles. Office: Univ Washington Dept Physics PO Box 351560 Seattle WA 98195-1560

WILEY, ALBERT LEE, JR., physician, engineer, educator; b. Forest City, N.C., June 9, 1936; s. Albert Lee and Mary Louise (Davis) W.; m. Janet Lee Pratt, June 18, 1960; children: Allison Lee, Susan Caroline, Mary Catherine, Heather Elizabeth. B in Nuclear Engring., N.C. State U., 1958, postgrad., 1958-59; MD, U. Rochester, N.Y., 1963; PhD, U. Wis., 1972. Diplomate Am. Bd. Nuclear Medicine, Am. Bd. Radiology, Am. Bd. Med. Physics. Nuclear engr. Lockheed Corp., Marietta, Ga., 1958; intern in surgery-medicine U. Va. Med. Sch., Charlottesville, 1963-64; resident in radiation therapy Sanford U., Palo Alto, Calif., 1964-65; resident and NCI postdoctoral fellow U. Wis. Hosp., Madison, 1965-68; med. dir. USN Radiol. Def. Lab., San Francisco, 1968-69; staff physician Balboa Hosp., USN, San Diego, 1969-70; asst. prof. radiotherapy M.D. Anderson Hosp. U. Tex., Houston, 1972-73; assoc. dir., clin. dir. radiation oncology U. Wis., Madison, prof. radiology, human oncology, med. physics, 1970-88; prof., chmn. radiation oncology, dir. cancer ctr. East Carolina U. Med. Sch., Greenville, N.C., 1988-93; cons. U.S. NRC, 1981-82, Nat. Cancer Inst., U.S. Dept. VA, 1990-93; advisor, cons. numerous univs., govt. agys. and biotech. corps.; mem. Wis. Radioactive Waste Bd., Wis. Gov.'s Coun. on Biotech., Gov.'s Com. on UN., com. on Nuclear Reactor Safeguards. Author more than 150 articles and abstracts on med. physics, environ. health, nuclear medicine, biology and cancer treatment; assoc. editor Jour. Med. Physics. Rep. candidate for U.S. Congress for 2d Wis. dist., 1982, 84; rep. primary candidate for gov., State of Wis., 1986; mem. Greenville Drug Task Force; bd. dirs. Greenville Salvation Army. Lt. comdr. USNR, ret. Oak Ridge Inst. Nuclear Studies fellow N.C. State U., 1958-59. Fellow Am. Coll. Radiology, Am. Coll. Preventive Medicine, Am. Coll. Nuclear Medicine, N.C. Inst. Polit. Leadership; mem. IEEE, AMA, AAUP, Am. Assn. Physicists in Medicine, Am. Soc. Therapeutic Radiation Oncologists, Am. Assn. Physics Tchrs., Am. Bd. Sci. in Nuclear Medicine (sec.-treas.), Am. Acad. Health Physics, Am. Cancer Soc. (N.C. bd. dirs.), C. of C., VFW, Vietnam Vets. Am., Am. Legion, Masons, Rotary, Sigma Xi, Tau Beta Pi. Avocations: fishing, skiing, scuba diving, hiking. Home: Box 588 797 Salter Path Rd Box 588 Indian Beach NC 28575

WILEY, BONNIE JEAN, journalism educator; b. Portland, Oreg.; d. Myron Eugene and Bonnie Jean (Galliher) W. BA, U. Wash., 1948; MS, Columbia U., 1957; PhD, So. Ill. U., 1965. Mng. editor Yakima (Wash.) Morning Herald; reporter, photographer Portland Oregonian; feature writer Seattle Times; war correspondent PTO AP; western feature editor AP, San Francisco; reporter Yakima Daily Republic; journalism tchr. U. Wash., Seattle, Cen. Wash. U., Ellensburg, U. Hawaii, Honolulu; mem. grad. faculty Bangkok U., Thailand, 1991; mem. faculty journalism program U. Hawaii, Honolulu, 1992—; Adminstr. Am. Samoa Coll., Pago Pago; news features advisor Xinhua News Agy., Beijing, Yunnan Normal U., Kumming, China, 1995. Mem. Women in Communications (Hawaii Headliner award 1985, Nat. Headliner award 1990), Theta Sigma Phi. Home: 1434 Punahou St Apt 1212 Honolulu HI 96822-4748

WILEY, CARL ROSS, timber company executive; b. Astoria, Oreg., Apr. 17, 1930; s. Hamilton Ross and Ada Ellen (Smith) W.; m. Dolores Eileen Brice, Dec. 19, 1953; children: Susan, Steven, Kenneth. BS in Indsl. Engring., Oreg. State U., 1958; grad. exec. tng. program, MIT, 1974. Quality control engr. Oreg. Metall. Corp., 1958-59; indsl. engr. Osborne Electronics Corp., Portland, Oreg., 1959-62; v.p. timber and mfg. Boise Cascade Corp., Idaho, 1962-80; exec. v.p. Roseburg (Oreg.) Lumber Co., 1980-85; chief exec. officer Puget Sound Plywood, Tacoma, 1986-93; pres., CEO Lane Plywood, Eugene, Oreg., 1993-96; retired, 1996. Bd. dirs. Boise YMCA, 1975-78. With AUS, 1951-53. Mem. Am. Plywood Assn. (trustee), Western Wood Products Assn. (bd. dirs., chmn. econ. svcs. 1974-80). Lutheran.

WILEY, DON CRAIG, biochemistry and biophysics educator; b. Akron, Ohio, Oct. 21, 1944; s. William Childs and Phyllis Rita (Norton) W.; m. Katrin Valgeirsdottir; children: William Valgeir, Lara; children from previous marriage: Kristen D., Craig S. BS in Physics and Chemistry, Tufts U., 1966; PhD in Biophysics, Harvard U., 1971; PhD (hon.), U. Leiden, The Netherlands, 1995; Doctorate (hon.), U. Leiden, Netherlands, 1995. Asst. prof. dept. biochemistry and molecular biology Harvard U., Cambridge, Mass., 1971-75, assoc. prof., 1975-79, prof. biochemistry and biophysics, 1979—, chmn. dept. molecular and cellular biology, 1992-95, investigator Howard Hughes Med. Inst., 1987—; mem. biophys. chemistry study sect. NIH, 1981-85; Shipley Symposium lectr. Harvard Med. Sch., 1985, Peter A. Leermakers Symposium lectr. Wesleyan U., 1986, K.F. Meyer lectr. U. Calif., San Francisco, 1986, John T. Edsall lectr. Harvard U., 1987, Washburn lectr. Boston Mus. Sci., 1987, Harvey lectr. N.Y. Acad. Sci., 1988, XVI Linus Pauling lectr. Stanford U., 1989; rsch. assoc. in medicine Children's Hosp., Boston, 1990—. Contbr. numerous articles to profl. jours. Recipient Ledlie prize Harvard U., 1982, Louisa Gross Horwitz prize Columbia U., 1990, William B. Coley award Cancer Rsch. Inst., 1992, V.D. Mattia award, 1992, Passano Found. Laureate award, 1993, Emil von Behring prize, 1993, Gairdner Found. Internat. award, 1994, Lasker award, 1995, Rose Payne Disting. Scientist award, 1996; European Molecular Biology fellow, 1976. Fellow NAS (lectr. 1988); mem. AAAS, Am. Acad. Arts and Scis., Am. Chem. Soc. (Nichol's Disting. Symposium lectr. N.E. sect. 1988), Am. Crystallographic Assn., Am. Soc. for Chemistry and Molecular Biology, Am. Soc. for Virology, Biophys. Soc. (Nat. lectr. 1989), Protein Soc., Am. Phil. Soc. Achievements include research on amino acid sequences of haemagglutinins of influenza viruses of the H3 subtype isolated from horses, studies of infuenza haemagglutinin mediated membrane fusion. Office: Harvard U Dept Molecular and Cellular Biology 7 Divinity Ave Cambridge MA 02138-2019 also: Children's Hosp Lab of Molecular Medicine 320 Longwood Ave Boston MA 02115-5746

WILEY, EDWIN PACKARD, lawyer; b. Chgo., Dec. 10, 1929; s. Edwin Garnet and Marjorie Chastina (Packard) W.; m. Barbara Jean Miller, May 21, 1949; children: Edwin Miller, Clayton Alexander, Stephen Packard. BA, U. Chgo., 1949, JD, 1952. Bar: Wis. 1952, Ill. 1952, U.S. Dist. Ct. (ea. dist.) Wis. 1953, U.S. Supreme Ct. 1978. Assoc. Foley & Lardner, Milw., 1952-60, ptnr., 1960—; bd. dirs. Genetic Testing Inst., Inc., Nat. Rivet and Mfg. Co., Shaler Co., Waukesha Cutting Tools, other corps. and founds. Co-author: Bank Holding Companies: A Practical Guide to Bank Acquisitions and Mergers, 1988, Wisconsin Uniform Commercial Code Handbook, 1971; author: Promotional Arrangements: Discrimination in Advertising and Promotional Allowances, 1976; editor in chief U. Chgo. Law Rev., 1952; contbr. articles to legal jours. Bd. dirs. Blood Ctr. of Southeastern Wis., pres., 1978-82; pres. Blood Ctr. Rsch. Found., Inc., 1983-87; v.p. Friends of Schlitz Audubon Ctr., Inc., 1975-87; active United Performing Arts Fund of Milw.; pres. Wis. Conservatory of Music, 1968-74; pres. First Unitarian Soc. Milw., 1961-63; v.p. Mid-Am. Ballet Co., 1971-73, Milw. Ballet Co., 1973-74; pres. Florentine Opera Co., 1983-86; bd. dirs. Milw. Symphony Orch., pres., 1993-95; bd. dirs. Milw. Pub. Mus., Inc., sec. 1992—; bd. dirs. Wis. History Found. Mem. ABA, State Bar of Wis., Milw. Bar Assn., Am. Law Inst., Order of Coif, Milw. Club, Univ. Club, Phi Beta Kappa (pres. Greater Milw. assn. 1962-63). Unitarian-Universalist. Home: 929 N Astor St Unit 2101 Milwaukee WI 53202-3488 Office: Foley & Lardner Firstar Ctr 777 E Wisconsin Ave Milwaukee WI 53202-5302

WILEY, GREGORY ROBERT, publisher; b. Mpls., Sept. 21, 1951; s. William Joseph and Terese (Kunz) W.; m. Sheila Francis, May 25, 1979; children: Kathleen, Mary Glennon. BA in Personnel Adminstrn., U. Kans., 1972-74. Dist. sales mgr. Reader's Digest, St. Louis, 1976-80, regional sales dir., Chgo., 1980-82; nat. sales mgr. retail div. Rand McNally & Co., Chgo., 1982-83, nat. sales mgr. premium incentive div., 1983-86, nat. sales mgr. bookstore and mass market sales, 1986-88; book publisher, The Sporting News, St. Louis, 1988-90, v.p. mktg. Marketmakers Internat., St. louis, 1990-93; v.p. mktg. Sofsource Inc., 1993—. Mem Nat. Premium Sales Execs., Promotional Mktg. Assn. Am. Roman Catholic. Avocations: pvt. pilot., historic restoration, golf. Home: 1867 Ironstone Rd Saint Louis MO 63131-3804 Office: Sofsource Inc 14615 Manchester Rd Ste 203 Saint Louis MO 63105

WILEY, JASON LARUE, JR., neurosurgeon; b. Canandaigua, N.Y., Dec. 2, 1917; s. Jason LaRue and Eva Althea (Moore) W.; m. Alma Williams, Jan. 4, 1944 (div. Feb. 1956); children: Robert W., Richard L.; m. Ann Valentine Gerrish, Apr. 14, 1956 (div. July 1979); children: Martha V., Pamela M., Catherine A. Student, Antioch Coll., 1934-37; MD, Harvard U., 1941. Diplomate Am. Bd. Surgery, Am. Bd. Neurol. Surgery. Intern Kings County Hosp., Bklyn., 1941-42; asst. resident surgery Ellis Hosp., Schenectady, N.Y., 1948-49; from asst. to assoc. resident surgery Rochester (N.Y.) Gen. Hosp., 1949-51; from asst. to assoc. to chief resident neurosurgery Yale U. and Hartford Hosp., New Haven and Hartford Conn., 1951-54; practice medicine specializing in neurosurgery Kansa City, Mo., 1954-56, Rochester, 1956—; chief neurosurgery Rochester Gen. Hosp., 1959-71, emeritus neurosurgeon, 1989—; clin. asst. prof. neurosurgery U. Rochester, 1961-88. Mem. Bd. for Profl. Med. Conduct, N.Y. State Dept. Health, Albany, N.Y., 1985—. Served to lt. comdr. USN, 1942-47, PTO. Mem. Med. Soc. County Monroe, Med. Soc. State N.Y., N.Y. State Neurosurg. Soc. (bd. dirs.), Congress Neurol. Surgeons, Am. Assn. Neurol. Surgeons, Canandaigua Yacht Club. Republican. Episcopalian. Avocations: sailing, skiing, fishing, genealogy. Office: 1445 Portland Ave Rochester NY 14621-3008

WILEY, MYRA, mental health nurse, educator; b. Lexington, Ala., Jan. 20, 1938; d. Joseph Aaron and Annie Lura (Putnam) Haraway; m. Robert Harold Wiley, Sept. 17, 1960; children: Sonya, Robert, Marie. BSN, U. Ala., Huntsville, 1989. RN, Ala.; cert. in chem. dependency. Nursing asst., night-weekend coord. Upjohn Health Care, Huntsville, 1983-87; nursing asst. North Ala. Rehab. Hosp., Huntsville, 1987-89; staff nurse Humana Hosp., Huntsville, 1989-91; staff nurse counselor Bradford-Parkside, Madison, Ala., 1991-95; relief charge nurse for behavioral health Columbia Med. Ctr. of Huntsville (formerly Crestwood Hosp.), Huntsville, Ala., 1995-96; with Bradford Health Svcs., Huntsville Bus. Inst., 1997—. Mem. ANA, Ala. State Nurses Assn., Madison County Nurses Assn., Nat. Consortium Chm. Dependency Nurses, Inc., Nurses Soc. on Addictions. Baptist. Avocations: reading, traveling, hiking, embroidery.

WILEY, RICHARD ARTHUR, lawyer; b. Bklyn., July 18, 1928; s. Arthur Ross and Anna Thorsen (Holder) W.; m. Carole Jean Smith, Aug. 13, 1955; children: Kendra Elizabeth, Stewart Alan, Garett Smith. AB, Bowdoin Coll., Brunswick, Maine, 1948; BCL, Oxford (Eng.) U., 1951; LLM, Harvard U., 1959; LLD, Bowdoin Coll., 1994. Bar: Mass. 1954, U.S. Ct. Mil. Appeals 1954, U.S. Dist. Ct. Mass. 1962, U.S. Supreme Ct. 1985. Atty. John Hancock Mut. Life Ins. Co., Boston, 1956-58; from atty. to mng. ptnr. Bingham, Dana & Gould, Boston, 1959-76; gen. counsel, asst. sec. Dept. Def., 1976-77; v.p., counsel First Nat. Bank Boston, 1977-78, exec. v.p., 1978-85; exec. v.p. Bank of Boston Corp., 1985; ptnr. Csaplar & Bok, Boston, 1986-90, mem. exec. com., 1987-90, chmn., 1989-90, of counsel, 1990; of counsel Gaston & Snow, Boston, 1990-91; dir. Powers and Hall P.C., Boston, 1991-94, of counsel, 1994-95; of counsel Hill & Barlow, Boston, 1995—; bd. dirs., chmn. Automated Assemblies Corp., Mass. Higher Edn. Assistance Corp.; bd. dirs. Nomadic Structures, Inc., Nypro, Inc., Carlo Gavazzi, Inc., Edn. Resources Inst., World Shelters, Inc.; lectr. Boston U. Law Sch., 1961-64; past vice chmn. New Eng. Conf. on Doing Bus. Abroad; trustee New Eng. Legal Found., chmn., 1980-83; adj. lectr. govt. and legal studies Bowdoin Coll., 1995—. Author: Cases and Materials on Law of International Trade and Investment, 1961; contbr. articles to profl. jours. Bd. overseers Bowdoin Coll., 1966-81, pres., 1977-80, trustee, 1981-93, trustee emeritus, 1993—; mem. Mass. Edn. Financing Authority, 1986-91, chmn., 1987-91; mem. Wellesley (Mass.) Town Meeting, 1971-75, mem. fin. adv. com., 1973-74; chmn. Mass. Bd. Regents of Higher Edn., 1991; bd. regents Task Force on Student Fin. Aid, 1987; mem. Mass. Higher Edn. Coord. Coun., 1991-95, vice chmn., 1991-93, chmn., 1993-95; chmn. lawyers divsn. United Way Mass. Bay, 1975; mem. devel. com., trustees of donations Episcopal Diocese Mass., 1971-75; trustee, exec. com. North Conway Inst., mem., 1980-92, chmn., 1988-92; bd. trustees Internat. Coun. Trust, Boston; trustee, mem. exec. com., chmn. Mass. Taxpayers Found., 1989-92; chmn. bd. trustees World Peace Found., Boston, 1983-95; corporator Schepens Eye Rsch. Inst., 1991-95; dep. chmn. planning Mass. rep. state com., 1971, vice chmn. fin. com., 1971-72. Officer USAF, 1953-56. Decorated Air Force Commendation medal; recipient Dep. Def. Disting. Pub. Svc. medal, 1977; Rhodes scholar, 1949. Mem. ABA (vice chmn. fgn. and internat. bus. law com. 1967-69), Boston Bar Assn. (exec. com., antitrust com. 1965-68), Council on Fgn. Relations, Boston Com. on Fgn. Relations (mem. exec. com., chmn. 1980-83), Phi Beta Kappa.

WILEY, RICHARD EMERSON, lawyer; b. Peoria, Ill., July 20, 1934; s. Joseph Henry and Jean W. (Farrell) W.; m. Elizabeth J. Edwards, Aug. 6, 1960; children: Douglas S., Pamela L. B.S. with distinction, Northwestern U., 1955, J.D., 1958; LL.M., Georgetown U., 1962. Bar: Ill. 1958, D.C. 1972. Pvt. practice Chgo., 1962-70; gen. counsel FCC, Washington, 1970-72, mem., 1972-74, chmn., 1974-77, chmn. FCC's adv. com. on advanced TV svc., 1987—; mng. ptnr. Wiley, Rein & Fielding, Washington, 1983—; prof. law John Marshall Law Sch., U. Chgo., 1963-70. Chmn. adv. bd. Inst. for Tele-Info., Columbia U., 1989—. Capt. AUS, 1959-62. Fellow Am. Bar Found.; mem. ABA (mem. ho. of dels. 1969-71, 77-84, chmn. young lawyers sect., 1977-84, chmn. Forum com. on communications 1969, chmn. bd. editors ABA Jour. 1984-89, chmn. com. on scope and correlation of work 1989, chmn. adminstrv. law and regulatory practice 1993-94), Fed. Bar Assn. (pres. 1977), Fed. Communications Bar Assn. (pres. 1987), Ill. Bar Assn., Chgo. Bar Assn., Adminstrv. Conf. U.S. (coun., sr. fellow), Phi Delta Phi, Phi Delta Kappa. Methodist. Home: 3818 N Woodrow St Arlington VA 22207-4345 Office: Wiley Rein & Fielding 1776 K St NW Ste 1100 Washington DC 20006-2304

WILEY, RICHARD GORDON, electrical engineer; b. Wind Ridge, Pa., Aug. 25, 1937; s. Asa Gordon and Mildred Louise (Fisher) W.; m. Jane Bradley Wilmes, Oct. 15, 1960; children: Richard Bradley, John Gordon, Laura Jane, Timothy Scott, Martha Anne, James Robert. BS, Carnegie-Mellon U., 1959, MS, 1960; PhD, Syracuse U., 1975. Rsch. engr. Syracuse (N.Y.) Rsch. Corp., 1960-67, staff cons. engr., 1975-86; asst. dir. applied rsch. Lab. Microwave Systems, Inc., Syracuse, 1967-75; v.p., chief scientist Rsch. Assocs. Syracuse, Inc., 1986—. Author: Electronic Intelligence: The Analysis of Radar Signals, 1982, 2d edit. 1993, Electronic Intelligence: The Interception of Radar Signals, 1985; co-author: Radar Vulnerability to Jamming, 1990; co-inventor pulse train analysis using personal computer, 1987. 1st lt. U.S. Army, 1961-63. Fellow IEEE; mem. Assn. Old Crows. Republican. Episcopalian. Office: Rsch Assocs Syracuse Inc 6280 Northern Blvd Ste 100 East Syracuse NY 13057

WILEY, THOMAS GLEN, retired investment company executive; b. Salt Lake City, Feb. 1, 1928; s. Thomas J. and Juanita (Dean) W.; children: Jana Lynn, Jill, Tina Elizabeth, Tova Suzanne. B.B.A. cum laude, U. Wash., 1951, postgrad., 1954. With Shell Chem. Co., 1954-61; fin. analyst Shell Chem. Co., N.Y.C., 1960-63; mgr. fin. analysis and pricing Lear Siegler, Los Angeles, 1963-72; v.p. finance, treas. Electronic Memories & Magnetics Corp., Los Angeles, 1963-72; exec. v.p. Hale Bros. Assocs., San Francisco, 1972-80; pres. Computer Election Systems, Berkeley, Calif., 1980-84, Texport, Inc., Anaheim, Calif., 1988-89; dir. Osmotics, Denver, 1994—. 1st lt. AUS, 1951-53. Home: 1765 Broadway St San Francisco CA 94109-2425

WILFORD, BONNIE BAIRD, health policy specialist; b. Chgo., Jan. 11, 1946; d. George Martin and Ruth Eleanor (Anderson) Baird; m. David Edward Wilford, Oct. 2, 1967; children: Heather Lynn, Edward Baird. BA, Knox Coll., 1967; postgrad., Roosevelt U., 1969-71. Staff assoc. Am. Hosp. Assn., Chgo., 1967-70; mgr. plan devel. Blue Cross & Blue Shield Assn., Chgo., 1970-79; dir. dept. substance abuse AMA, Chgo., 1979-91, dir. divsn. clin. sci., 1988-91; exec. office of the Pres. The White House, 1991-92; sr. rsch. scientist; dir. Pharm. Policy Project, George Washington U. Med. Ctr., Washington, 1992—. Author: Balancing the Response to Prescription Drug Abuse, 1990, Pharmaceutical Benefits for HIV/AIDS, 1996; editor Pharmaceutical Policy Rev., 1996—; contbr. articles to profl. jours. Recipient Outstanding Svc. award Fla. Task Force on Alcohol and Drug Abuse, 1986, Merit award State of Mo., 1985, Disting. Svc. award U.S. Dept. Health and Human Svcs., 1990. Mem. APHA, Internat. Narcotic Enforcement Officers Assn. (Award of Honor 1985), Assn. for Med. Edn. and Rsch. Substance Abuse, Informal Steering Com. Prescription Drug Abuse (bd. dirs.). Avocations: travel, gardening, needlework. Office: CHPR/George Washington U 2021 K St NW Ste 800 Washington DC 20006-1003

WILFORD, JOHN NOBLE, JR., news correspondent; b. Murray, Ky., Oct. 4, 1933; s. John Noble and Pauline (Hendricks) W.; m. Nancy Everett Watts, Dec. 25, 1966; 1 child, Nona. Student, Lambuth Coll., 1951-52; BS, U. Tenn., 1955; MA, Syracuse U., 1956; Internat. Reporting fellow, Columbia, 1961-62; DHL (hon.), R.I. Coll., 1987; DSc (hon.), Middlebury Coll., 1991. Reporter Comml. Appeal, Memphis, summers 1954-55; reporter Wall St. Jour., N.Y.C., 1956, 59-61; contbg. editor Time mag., N.Y.C., 1962-65; sci. reporter N.Y. Times, 1965-73, asst. nat. editor, 1973-75, dir. sci. news, 1975-79, sci. corr., 1979—; vis. journalist Duke U., 1984; McGraw lectr. Princeton U., 1985; Disting. prof. journalism, U. Tenn., Knoxville, 1989-90; mem. Am. Mus.-Mongolian Gobi Expdn., 1991, Dir.'s Visitor, Inst. for Advanced Study, 1995. Author: We Reach The Moon, 1969, The Mapmakers, 1981, The Riddle of the Dinosaur, 1985, Mars Beckons, 1990, The Mysterious History of Columbus, 1991; co-author: The New York Times Guide to the Return of Halley's Comet, 1985, (with William Stockton) Spaceliner, 1981; editor: Scientists at Work, 1979. With CIC AUS, 1957-59. Recipient Book award Aviation/Space Writers, 1970, Writing award Aviation/Space Writers, 1983, G.M. Loeb Achievement award U. Conn, 1972, Press award Nat. Sci. Club, 1974, AAAS-Westinghouse Sci. Writing award, 1983, Ralph Coats Roe medal ASME, 1995, Pulitzer prize nat. reporting, 1984, N.Y. Times Pulitzer Prize Winning Team, 1987. Mem. Nat. Assn. Sci. Writers, Authors Guild, Soc. Profl. Journalists, Am. Geog. Soc. (councilor 1994—), Century Assn., Sigma Chi, Phi Kappa Phi, Phi Beta Kappa. Home: 232 W 10th St New York NY 10014-2976 Office: 229 W 43rd St New York NY 10036-3913

WILGIS, HERBERT E., JR., corporate executive; b. Balt., Apr. 30, 1935; s. Herbert E. and Margaret S. (Shaw) W.; m. Jane VandeGrift; children—Jeffery, Herbert, Edward. A.B. in History, Princeton U., 1957. Foreign service officer U.S. Dept. State, numerous countries, 1958-86; counselor Am. embassy, Budapest, 1977-80; minister-counselor Am. embassy, Warsaw, Poland, 1981-83; consul gen. U.S. consulate gen., Barcelona, Spain, 1983-86; pres., chief exec. officer Penniman and Browne, Balt., 1986—. Served with U.S. Army, 1957. Recipient Superior and Meritorious Honor awards Dept. State, 1978, 86. Mem. Am. Fgn. Service Assn. Office: Penniman and Browne Inc 6252 Falls Rd Baltimore MD 21209-2126

WILHELM, DAVID C., political organization administrator; m. Degee Dodds; children: Luke, Logan. BA, Ohio U., 1977; MPP, Harvard U., 1990. Rsch. dir. pub. employee dept. AFL-CIO, 1981-83; campaign mgr. Senator Paul Simon, 1984, Senator Joseph Biden for Pres., Iowa, 1985-87, Richard M. Daley for Mayor, Chgo., 1989, 91, Gov. Bill Clinton for Pres., 1991-92; chmn. Nat. Dem. Com., 1993-94; rsch. dir. Pub. Employee Dept. AFL-CIO, Chgo., 1981-83; exec. dir. Citizens for Tax Justice, Chgo., 1985-87; pres. The Strategy Group, Chgo., 1988-91; sr. mng. dir. investment banking Kemper Everen Securities, Inc., Chgo., 1994—; dir. Fed. Home Loan Bank Chgo., Citizen Action of Ill.; bd. dirs. The Christian Century Mag., Democrats 2000, Parkways; mem. Chgo. Com. Chgo. Coun. Fgn. Rels. Recipient medal of Merit, Ohio U., 1994. Fellow Inst. Politics. Office: EVEREN Securities Inc. 77 W Wacker Dr Ste 3000 Chicago IL 60601

WILHELM, GAYLE BRIAN, lawyer; b. Springfield, Mass., Sept. 1, 1936; s. William E. and Margaret (Koerber) W.; m. Emogene Chase, Sept. 1, 1957; children: Gayle Barrett, Erica Chase Fotta, Laura Elizabeth. BA, Harvard U., 1957, LLB, 1964. Bar: Conn. 1964. Sr. ptnr. Cummings & Lockwood, Stamford, Conn., 1964—. Author: Connecticut Estates Practice, 6 vols., 1970—, The Executor's Handbook, 1985, The Connecicut Living Trust, 1993. 1st lt. USAF, 1957-61, Japan. Fellow Am. Coll. Trust and Estate Counsel. Avocations: tennis, bicycling, fishing. Office: Cummings & Lockwood 4 Stamford Plaza Stamford CT 06901-3202

WILHELM, JAMES HOYT, retired baseball player; b. Huntersville, NC, July 26, 1923. Pitcher New York Giants, 1952-57, St. Louis Cardinals, 1957-58, Cleve. Indians, 1958-59, Balt. Orioles, 1959-63, CHI A, 1963-69, Calif. Angels, 1969-70, Atlanta Braves, 1970-72. Sgt., U.S. Army. Recipient Purple Heart; selected to Nat. League All-Star Team, 1953-70; selected to Am. League All-Star Team, 1959, 61-62; named to Baseball Hall of Fame, 1985. Achievements include most games ever pitched (1070). Office: c/o Baseball Hall of Fame Mus PO Box 590 Cooperstown NY 13326-0590

WILHELM, KATE (KATY GERTRUDE), author; b. Toledo, June 8, 1928; d. Jesse Thomas and Ann (McDowell) Meredith; m. Joseph B. Wilhelm, May 24, 1947 (div. 1962); children: Douglas, Richard; m. Damon Knight, Feb. 23, 1963; 1 child, Jonathan. PhD in Humanities(hon.), Mich. State U., 1996. Writer, 1956—; co-dir. Milford Sci. Fiction Writers Conf., 1963-76; lectr. Clarion Fantasy Workshop Mich. State U., 1968-94. Author: (novels) More Bitter Than Death, 1962, (with Theodore L. Thomas) The Clone, 1965, The Nevermore Affair, 1966, The Killer Thing, 1967, Let the Fire Fall, 1969, (with Theodore L. Thomas) The Year of the Cloud, 1970, Abyss: Two Novellas, 1971, Margaret and I, 1971, City of Cain, 1971, The Clewiston Test, 1976, Where Late the Sweet Birds Sang, 1976, Fault Lines, 1976, Somerset Dreams and Other Fictions, 1978, Juniper Time, 1979, (with Damon Knight) Better Than One, 1980, A Sense of Shadow, 1981, Listen, Listen, 1981, Oh! Susannah, 1982, Welcome Chaos, 1983, Huysman's Pets, 1986, (with R. Wilhelm) The Hills Are Dancing, 1986, The Hamlet Trap, 1987, Crazy Time, 1988, Dark Door, 1988, Smart House, 1989, Children of the Wind: Five Novellas, 1989, Cambio Bay, 1990, Sweet, Sweet Poison, 1990, Death Qualified, 1991, And the Angels Sing, 1992, Seven Kinds of Death, 1992, Naming the Flowers, 1992, Justice for Some, 1993, The Best Defense, 1994, A Flush of Shadows, 1995, Malice Prepense, 1996, (multimedia space fantasy) Axoltl, U. Oreg. Art Mus., 1979, (radio play) The Hindenburg Effect, 1985; editor: Nebula Award Stories #9, 1974, Clarion SF, 1976; contbr. short stories to anthologies and periodicals. Mem. PEN, Nat. Writers Union, Mystery Writers Am., Sci. Fiction Writers Am., Authors Guild. Address: 1645 Horn Ln Eugene OR 97404-2957

WILHELM, MARILYN, private school administrator. Founder-dir. The Wilhelm Sch., Houston. Office: The Wilhelm Sch 3003 Richmond Ave Houston TX 77098-3107*

WILHELM, MORTON, surgery educator; b. Roanoke, Va., June 22, 1923; s. Walter LeRoy and Della Mae (Turner) W.; m. Jean Osborne, June 3, 1949; children: Melissa, Christina. BS, Va. Mil. Inst., 1944; MD, U. Va., 1947. Diplomate Am. Bd. Surgery. Intern, resident in surgery VA Mason Hosp., Seattle, 1947-51, 52-53; fellow, instr. surgery Med. Ctr. U. Va., Charlottesville, 53-54, 56-66, assoc. prof. surgery Med. Ctr., 1966-80, prof. surgery Med. Ctr., 1980-93, chief dept. surg. oncology Med. Ctr., 1990-93, Joseph Farrow prof. surg. oncology Med. Ctr., 1990-93. Pres. Va. div. Am. Cancer Soc., Meritorious Svc. award, Horsley award, Nat. Teresa Lasser award. Lt. U.S. Army, 1951-53. Fellow Am. Coll. Surgeons (vice chmn. commn. on cancer 1989-90, pres. Va. chpt.); mem. Am. Soc. Clin. Oncology, So. Surg. Assn., So. Soc. Clin. Surgeons, Soc. Surg. Oncology. Avocations: tennis, golf, woodworking. Office: U Va Med Ctr Box 334 Cancer Ctr Charlottesville VA 22908

WILHELM, ROBERT OSCAR, lawyer, civil engineer, developer; b. Balt., July 7, 1918; s. Clarence Oscar and Agnes Virginia (Grimm) W.; m. Grace Sanborn Luckie, Apr. 4, 1959. B.S. in Civil Engring., Ga. Tech. Inst., 1947, M.S.I.M., 1948; J.D., Stanford U., 1951. Bar: Calif. 1952, U.S. Supreme Ct. Mem. Wilhelm, Thompson, Wentholt and Gibbs, Redwood City, Calif., 1952—; gen. counsel Bay Counties Gen. Contractors; pvt. practice civil engring., Redwood City, 1952—; pres. Bay Counties Builders Escrow, Inc., 1972-88. With C.E., AUS, 1942-46. Mem. Bay Counties Civil Engrs. (pres. 1957), Peninsula Builders Exchange (pres. 1958-71, dir.), Calif. State Builders Exchange (treas. 1971), Del Mesa Carmel Cmty. Assn. (bd. dirs. 1997—). Clubs: Mason, Odd Fellows, Eagle, Elks. Author: The Manual of Procedures for the Construction Industry, 1971, Manual of Procedures and Form Book for Construction Industry, 9th edit., 1995; columnist Law and You in Daily Pacific Builder, 1955—; author: Construction Law for Contractors, Architects and Engineers. Home: 134 Del Mesa Carmel Carmel CA 93923-7950 Office: 600 Allerton St Redwood City CA 94063-1504

WILHELM, SISTER PHYLLIS, principal; b. Toledo, Aug. 3, 1941; d. Edward John and Ellen Catherine (Sorg) W. BA, St. Francis Coll., 1964; MEd in Instruction, U. Wis., Superior, 1994. Cert. tchr., Wis., elem. tchr. spl. edn., Ill.; joined Sisters of St. Francis of Mary Immaculate, 1959. Tchr. primary St. Rita of Casica Sch., Aurora, Ill., 1963-65, St. Joseph Sch., Manhattan, Ill., 1965-74; tchr. primary Holy Family-St. Francis Sch., Bayfield, Wis., 1974-77, prin., tchr., 1979—, peace edn. instr. K-6, 1989—; tchr. spl. edn. Guardian Angel Sch., Joliet, Ill., 1977-79. Mem. Superior Diocesan Prin. Assn. (treas. 1981-83, 96—, Educator of Yr. award 1991), Phi Delta Kappa. Avocations: crafts, gardening, cooking. Home: RR 1 Box 92 Bayfield WI 54814-9724

WILHELM, WALTER TINKHAM, information systems consultant; b. Miami, Fla., Nov. 29, 1938; s. Walter Scott and Gladys (Tinkham) W.; m. Margaret Beverly Bryson, June 12, 1959; children: Walter Manning, Stephanie Renee. BS, U. So. Calif., 1966, MBA, 1968. Systems specialist Gen. Dynamics, Ft. Worth, 1960-62; telemetry engr. Lockheed Space Systems, Vandenberg AFB, Calif., 1962-64, Hughes Aircraft Co., Culver City, Calif., 1964-68; mktg. and sales mgr. Hughes Aircraft Co., Carlsbad, Calif., 1968-72; asst. to pres. Ratner Corp., San Diego, 1972-74; Euroean mgr. Hughes Aircraft Co., Weybridge, Eng., 1974-80; v.p. sales and mktg. Microdynamics, Inc., Dallas, 1980-86; mng. dir. Microdynamics Europe, Munich, Germany, 1986-90; sr. v.p., dir. Microdynamics Inc., Dallas, 1990-94; prin. Wilhelm Leslie Assocs., 1995—. Contbr. articles to profl. jours. With USAF, 1956-60. Avocations: tennis, travel, reading, cooking. Office: Wilhelm-Leslie Assocs PO Box 745 Allen TX 75013-0013

WILHELM, WILLIAM JEAN, civil engineering educator; b. St. Louis, Oct. 5, 1935; s. Maurice Ferdinand and Eileen Winifred (McClintock) W.; m. Patricia Jane Zietz, Aug. 17, 1957; children—William, Robert, Andrew, Mary, David. BME, Auburn U., 1958, MS, 1963; PhD, N.C. State U., 1968. Registered profl. engr., Kans., W.Va. Structural engr. Palmer & Baker Engrs., Mobile, Ala., 1958-60; instr. engring. graphics Auburn U., 1960-64; asst. prof. civil engring. W.Va. U., Morgantown, 1967-72; assoc. prof. W.Va. U., 1972-76, prof., 1976-79, chmn., 1974-79; dean engring., prof. Wichita State U., 1979—, dir. Ctr. for Productivity Enhancement, 1984-86, exec. dir. Ctr. for Tech. Application, 1988-91; bd. dirs. Kans. Tech. Enterprise Corp., Orthopaedic Rsch. Inst. Via Christi Regional Med. Sys., Wichita Industries and Svcs. for the Blind, Inc. Contbr. articles to profl. jours. Served with C.E. U.S. Army, 1959, 62. Recipient Recognition award Wichita State U. Alumni Assn., 1993. Fellow ASCE, Am. Concrete Inst. (Joe W. Kelley award 1986, Henry L. Kennedy award 1994); mem. NSPE, Soc. Women Engrs. (sr.), Am. Soc. Engring. Edn., Kans. Engring. Soc. (pres. 1994-95, Outstanding Engr. of Yr. award 1989), Order of the Engr., Sigma Xi, Phi Kappa Phi, Tau Beta Pi, Pi Tau Sigma, Chi Epsilon (chpt. hon. W.Va. U. 1979). Roman Catholic. Home: 2500 Banbury Cir Wichita KS 67226-1046 Office: Wichita State U Coll Engring Wichita KS 67260-0044

WILHELMI, MARY CHARLOTTE, education educator, college official; b. Williamsburg, Iowa, Oct. 2, 1928; d. Charles E. and Loretto (Judge) Harris; m. Sylvester Lee Wilhelmi, May 26, 1951; children: Theresa Ann, Sylvia Marie, Thomas Lee, Kathryn Lyn, Nancy Louise. BS, Iowa State U., 1950; MA in Edn., Va. Poly. Inst. and State U., 1973, cert. advanced grad. studies, 1978. Edn. coord. Nova Ctr. U. Va., Falls Church, 1969-73; asst. adminstr. Consortium for Continuing Higher Edn. George Mason U., Fairfax, Va., 1973-78; adminstr., asst. prof. George Mason U., Fairfax, 1978-83; dir. coll. rels. and devel., assoc. prof. No. Va. C.C., Annandale, 1983—; bd. dirs. No. Va. C.C. Ednl. Found., Inc., Annandale, 1984—; v.p. mktg. Fairfax (Va.) Symphony, 1995—; chmn. Health Systems Agy. No. Va., Fairfax; mem. George Mason U. Inst. for Ednl. Transformation. Edtl. bd. Va. Forum, 1990-93; contbr. articles to profl. jours. Bd. dirs. Fairfax County chpt. ARC, 1981-86, Va. Inst. Polit. Leadership, 1996—, Fairfax Com. of 100, 1986-88, 90—, Hospice No. Va., 1983-88, No. Va. Mental Health Inst., Fairfax County, 1978-81, Fairfax Profl. Women's Network, 1981, Arts Coun. Fairfax County, 1989—; vice chmn. Va. Commonwealth U. Ctr. on Aging, Richmond, 1978—; mem. supt.'s adv. coun. Fairfax County Pub. Schs., 1974-86, No. Va. Press Club, 1978—; mktg. chair Internat. Childrens Festival, 1997; pres. Fairfax Ext. Leadership Coun., 1995; mem. Leadership Fairfax Class of 1992. Named Woman of Distinction, Soroptomists, Fairfax, 1988, Bus. Woman of Yr., Falls Church Bus. and Profl. Women's Group, 1993; fellow Va. Inst. Polit. Leadership, 1995. Mem. State Coun. Higher Edn. Va. (pub. affairs adv. com. 1985—), Greater Washington Bd. Trade, Fairfax County C. of C. (legis. affairs com. 1984—) Va. Women Lobbyists, 1991—, No. Va. Bus. Roundtable, Internat. Platform Assn., Phi Delta Kappa (10-Yr. Continuous Svc. award 1991), Kappa Delta Alumni No. Va., Psi Chi, Phi Kappa Phi. Roman Catholic. Avocations: piano, organ, reading, hiking. Home: 4902 Ravensworth Rd Annandale VA 22003-5552 Office: No Va CC 4001 Wakefield Chapel Rd Annandale VA 22003-3724

WILHELMSEN, HAROLD JOHN, accountant, operations controller; b. Kansas City, Mo., July 13, 1928; s. Karl John and Cora Irene (Reynolds) W.; m. Audrey Loraine Woodard, Oct. 14, 1950. BBA, U. Wis., 1950. CPA, Wis. With S.C. Johnson & Son Inc., Racine, Wis., 1953-90, dir. fin. South Pacific, 1970-72, mgr. overseas fin. svcs., 1972-76, contr. U.S. ops., 1976-78, v.p., contr. internat. ops., 1978-90, ret., 1990. Pres. Racine Symphony Orch. Assn., 1957-60; trustee Carthage Coll., Kenosha, Wis., 1984-91, dir., sec. Pinnacle Peak Country Club Estates, 1992-95; dir., pres. Pinnacle Peak Country Club; treas. Christ the Lord Luth. Ch. Served with U.S. Army, 1950-52. Republican. Lutheran. Clubs: Pinnacle Peak Country (Scottsdale, Ariz.); Am. Nat. (Sydney, Australia). Avocations: golf, squash, bridge, reading, music.

WILHELMY, ODIN, JR., insurance agent; b. New Kensington, Pa., Oct. 9, 1920; s. Odin and May (Hazeltine) W.; m. Betty M. Rollins, Nov. 23, 1945; children: Ann Leslie, Margaret Linn, Janet Lee. BA with honors, U. Cin., 1941; PhD, Cornell U., 1950. CLU, ChFC. Asst. prof. Cornell U., Ithaca, N.Y., 1949-52; div. chief Battelle Meml. Inst., Columbus, Ohio, 1952-70; sr. agt. Prin. Mut. Life Ins. Co., Columbus, 1970—. Scoutmaster Boy Scouts Am., Ithaca, N.Y., Columbus, Ohio, 1946-74. Sgt. U.S. Army, 1942-46, Aleutian Islands. Recipient Silver Beaver award Boy Scouts Am. Mem. Phi Beta Kappa, Phi Kappa Phi, Pi Kappa Alpha, Omicron Delta Kappa. Presbyterian. Avocations: church work, scouting, gardening. Home: 2942 N Star Rd Columbus OH 43221-2961

WILHOIT, CAROL DIANE, special education educator; b. Rockford, Ill., June 2, 1950; d. Iris May (Zeigler) Cleeton; m. Jerry Dean Wilhoit, Aug. 15, 1971; children: David, Heather, Hilary, Erin. BSE, N.E. Mo. State U., 1972; MS in Edn., 1991. Cert. spl. edn. tchr., Mo. Tchr. emotionally handicapped Clarence Cannon Elem., Elsberry, Mo., 1972-73; EMH tchr. Bowling Green (Mo.) Elem., 1973-77, Clopton High Sch., Clarksville, Mo., 1979-82; tchr. learning disabilities Eugene Field Elem., Hannibal, Mo., 1982—; active Accelerated Sch., chair curriculum cadre, intervention cadre, steering com., 1992-93, mem. parent involvement com., 1994; del. Northeast Dist. Tchrs. Assn. Assembly, 1994. Mem. state due process subcom., 1994; PL-94-142 adv. com., 1992—. Mem. Coun. Exceptional Children (pres. 1986-88, bd. dirs. Mo. chpt. 1986, 1988-91, organizer local chpt. 1988, awards chmn., chair profl. devel. subcom., chair registration com. 1991-92, chair membership com. Mark Twain chpt. 1991—, spring conf. session leader, del. to internat. coun. assembly 1992-93, spring conf. chair 1994, del. to internat. conf. 1995), Mo. State Tchrs. Assn. (del. to state assembly 1989-90, superintendent's com. 1989-91, dist. prof. devel. com. 1990—, mentor tchr. 1990-92, state spl. edn. monitoring com. 1991-92), Hannibal Cmty. Tchrs. Assn. (bldg. rep. exec. com. 1987—, v.p. 1988, pres. 1989), Learning Disabilities Assn. Avocations: reading, crafts, sewing. Office: Eugene Field Elem 1405 Pearl St Hannibal MO 63401-4151

WILHOIT, GENE, state agency administrator. Edn. dir. Ark. Dept. Edn., Little Rock. Office: Ark Dept Edn Capitol Mall Bldg 4 Little Rock AR 72201-1071*

WILHOIT, HENRY RUPERT, JR., federal judge; b. Grayson, Ky., Feb. 11, 1935; s. H. Rupert and Kathryn (Reynolds) W.; m. Jane Horton, Apr. 7, 1956; children: Mary Jane, H. Rupert, William. LLB, U. Ky., 1960. Ptnr. Wilhoit & Wilhoit, 1960-81; city atty. City of Grayson, Ky., 1962-66; county atty. Carter County, Ky., 1966-70; judge U.S. Dist. Ct. (ea. dist.) Ky., 1981—. Recipient Disting. Service award U. Ky. Alumni Assn., 1980. Mem. ABA, Ky. Bar Assn. Office: US Dist Ct 320 Fed Bldg 1405 Greenup Ave Ashland KY 41101-7542*

WILKE, CHET, real estate executive; b. Chgo., Dec. 10, 1942; m. Beverly J. Galuska, July 31, 1981; children: Lisa Michelle, Rebecca Ann, Christa Leann. BA in Comm., Columbia Coll., L.A., 1970. Cert. real estate specialist. Sta. mgr., dir. TV news, personality Armed Forces Radio & TV, 1965-69; acct. exec. Sta. KALI, L.A., 1969-72; sr. acct. exec. HR/Stone Radio Reps., L.A., 1972-75; gen. sales mgr. Sta. KYXY-FM, San Diego, 1975-77; pres., founder Wilke Enterprises Inc., San Diego and Houston, 1977-81; gen. sales mgr. Sta. KEYH, Houston, 1982; gen. sales mgr., acting mgr. Sta. KYST, Houston, 1982-85; mgr., mktg./creative dir. Advt. Concepts Inc., Houston, 1985-88; exec. v.p. First Hanover Real Estate/Mortgage, Houston and Sugar Land, Tex., 1988-89; pres., real estate broker Ameristar Group Corp., Plano, Tex., 1989—; CEO PRO, Profl. Realty Office Network, Inc., Plano, Tex., 1995—, PRO, AmeriStar Realty, Inc., 1996—, PRO Anderson Realty, Inc., Richardson, Tex., 1996—. With USAF, 1964-69. Mem. Nat. Assn. Realtors, Tex. Assn. Realtors, Greater Dallas Assn. Realtors, Collin County Assn. Realtors, Womens Coun. Realtors, Lions. Republican. Methodist. Home: 2312 Cardinal Dr Plano TX 75023-1470 Office: PRO Network 3033 W Parker Rd Ste 106 Plano TX 75023-8000

WILKE, CONSTANCE REGINA, elementary education educator; b. Camden, N.J., Mar. 20, 1944; d. Matthew Stanley Sr. and Regina Rita (Przeradzki) Wojtkowiak; m. Alvin Frank Wilke Jr., Apr. 20, 1968; children: Joseph Alvin, Suzanne Renee. BA in Elem. Edn., Glassboro State U., 1967, MA in Reading and Supervision, 1979. Cert. tchr. and reading speicalist, N.J. Tchr. 5th grade Bellmawr (N.J.) Bd. Edn., 1967-70; tchr. 2d grade Ethel M. Burke Sch., Bellmawr, N.J., 1970—. Author: Wojtkowiak Family History, 1992. Vol. Gloucester (N.J.) City Libr., 1972-75, Vet.'s Standdown, Meals on Wheels, Cathedral Soup Kitchen; sec. E.M. Burke Sch. PTA, Bellmawr, 1973-78, publicity person, 1980-85, pres., 1982-85, author and editor publicity book, 1980-81, 82-83, rec. sec., 1995-97; advisor Community Edn. Bd., Gloucester City, 1973-74; eucharistic minster St. Mary's Ch., Gloucester City, 1990—, mem. renew com., lector; dir. and founder of Internat. Day at E.M. Burke Sch., dir. and founder Vet.'s Day Program. Named Citizen of Yr., Polish-Am. Congress, 1983. Mem. NEA, N.J. Epilepsy Found., N.J. Edn. Assn., Bellmawr Edn. Assn. (faculty rep.), Asthma Assn. Roman Catholic. Avocations: needle crafts, reading, gardening, family historian. Office: E M Burke Sch 112 S Black Horse Pike Bellmawr NJ 08031-2309

WILKE, DUANE ANDREW, educator; b. Chgo., July 2, 1948; s. Joseph V. and Helena (Komulainen) W.; m. Sue Rowley, Oct. 9, 1970; children: Mya, Kira, Noah. BS, Ill. State U., Normal, 1970; MS in Edn., No. Ill. U., 1978. Cert. tchr., Ill. Tchr. Glencoe (Ill.) Pub. Schs., 1970-71; English tchr. middle sch. U.S. Peace Corps, Daegu, S. Korea, 1971-73; tchr. tng. coord U.S. Peace Corps, S. Korea, 1973-74; diagnostician, tchr. Singer Mental Health Ctr., Rockford, Ill., 1974-78; spl. edn. cons., diagnostician Rockford Pub. Schs., 1978-90; edn. instrn. specialist EduQuest/IBM, Rockford, 1992-93; tech. specialist Title 1 Rockford Pub. Schs., 1993—; adj. instr. No. Ill. U., De Kalb, 1980-90; evaluator North Cen. Evaluation Team, Ottawa, Ill., 1989; instr. coord. St. Xavier U., Internat. Renewal Inst., Chgo., Rockford, 1990-94; featured spkr. 1991 conv. Coun. for Exceptional Children. Co-author: (asessment instrument) Task Assessment for Prescriptive Teaching, 1979. V.p. bd. Kantorei Boys Choir, 1996; pres. bd. trustees Unitarian Ch., Rockford, 1991-93. Recipient ASCD Ill. Profl. Devel. award 1996; named Svc. Personnel of Yr., Those Who Excel, Rockford, Ill., 1987. Avocation: singing. Home: 1419 Post Ave Rockford IL 61103-6222

WILKE, LEROY, church administrator. Dir. dept. youth ministry Luth. Ch.-Mo. Synod, St. Louis, St. Louis. Office: 1333 S Kirkwood Rd Saint Louis MO 63122-7226

WILKEN, CLAUDIA, judge; b. Mpls., Aug. 17, 1949; d. Claudius W. and Dolores Ann (Grass) W. BA with honors, Stanford U., 1971; JD, U. Calif., Berkeley, 1975. Bar: Calif. 1975, U.S. Dist. Ct. (no. dist.) Calif. 1975, U.S. Ct. Appeals (9th cir.) 1976, U.S. Supreme Ct. 1981. Asst. fed. pub. defender U.S. Dist. Ct. (no. dist.) Calif., San Francisco, 1975-78, U.S. magistrate judge, 1983-93, dist. judge, 1993—; ptnr. Wilken & Leverett, Berkeley, Calif., 1978-84; adj. prof. U. Calif., Berkeley, 1978-84; prof. New Coll. Sch. Law, 1980-85; mem. jud. br. com. Jud. Conf. U.S.; past mem. edn. com. Fed. Jud. Ctr. Magistrate Judges, 9th Cir. Magistrate Judges; chair 9th cir. Magistrates Conf., 1987-88. Mem. ABA (mem. jud. adminstrn. divsn.), Alameda County Bar Assn. (judge's membership), Nat. Assn. Women Judges, Order of Coif, Phi Beta Kappa. Office: US Dist Ct No Dist 1301 Clay St # 2 Oakland CA 94612-5217

WILKENING, LAUREL LYNN, academic administrator, planetary scientist; b. Richland, Wash., Nov. 23, 1944; d. Marvin Hubert and Ruby Alma (Barks) W.; m. Godfrey Theodore Sill, May 18, 1974. BA, Reed Coll., Portland, Oreg., 1966; PhD, U. Calif., San Diego, 1970; DSc (hon.), U. Ariz., 1996. Asst. prof. to assoc. prof. U. Ariz., Tucson, 1973-80, dir. Lunar and Planetary Lab., head planetary scis., 1981-83, vice provost, prof. planetary scis., 1983-85, v.p. rsch., dean Grad. Coll., 1985-88; div. scientist NASA Hdqrs., Washington, 1980; prof. geol scis., adj. prof. astronomy, provost U. Washington, Seattle, 1988-93; prof. earth system sci., chancellor U. Calif., Irvine, 1993—; dir. Seagate Tech., Inc., 1993—, Rsch. Corp., 1991—; vice chmn. Nat. Commn. on Space, Washington, 1984-86, Adv. Com. on the Future of U.S. Space Program, 1990-91; chair Space Policy Adv. Bd., Nat. Space Coun., 1991-92; co-chmn. primitive bodies mission study team NASA/European Space Agy., 1984-85; chmn. com. rendezvous sci. working group NASA, 1983-85; mem. panel on internat. cooperation and competition in space Congl. Office Tech. Assessment, 1982-83; trustee NASULGC, 1994-97, UCAR, 1988-89, 97—, Reed Coll., 1992—. Author: (monograph) Particle Track Studies and the Origin of Gas-Rich Meteorites, 1971; editor: Comets, 1982. U. Calif. Regents fellow, 1966-67; NASA trainee, 1967-70. Fellow Meteoritical Soc. (councilor 1976-80), Am. Assn. Advanced Sci.; mem. Am. Astron. Soc. (chmn. div. planetary scis. 1984-85), Am. Geophys. Union, AAAS, Planetary Soc. (dir. 1994—), Phi Beta Kappa. Democrat. Avocations: gardening, camping, swimming. Office: U Calif Chancellors Office 501 Adminstrn Bldg Irvine CA 92697-1900

WILKENS, LEONARD RANDOLPH, JR. (LENNY WILKENS), professional basketball coach; b. Bklyn., Oct. 28, 1937; s. Leonard Randolph Sr. and Henrietta (Cross) W.; m. Marilyn J. Reed, July 28, 1962; children: Leesha Marie, Leonard Randolph III, Jamée McGregor. BS in Econs., Providence Coll., 1960, HHD (hon.), 1980. Counselor Jewish Employment Vocat. Services, 1962-63; salesman packaging div. Monsanto Co., 1966; profl. basketball player St. Louis Hawks, 1960-68; player-coach Seattle SuperSonics, 1969-72, head coach, 1977-85, gen. mgr., 1985-86; profl. basketball player Cleve. Cavaliers, 1972-74, player NBA All-Star Game, 1973, head coach, 1986-93; player-coach Portland (Oreg.) Trail Blazers, 1974-76; head coach Atlanta Hawks, 1993—; coach 4 NBA All-Star Teams including Ea. Conf. team All-Star game, Mpls., 1994, World Champion basketball team, 1979, IBM NBA Coach of the Year, 1994; winningest coach of all time, 1995, coach 1996 Olympic Basketball Team, asst. coach 1992 Olympic Basketball. Author: The Lenny Wilkens Story, 1974. Bd. regents Gonzaga U., Spokane; bd. dirs. Seattle Ctr., Big Bros. Seattle, Bellevue (Wash.) Boys Club, Seattle Opportunities Industrialization Ctr., Seattle U.; co-chmn. UN Internat. Yr. of Child program, 1979; organizer Lenny Wilkens Celebrity Golf Tournament for Spl. Olympics. 2d lt. U.S. Army, 1961-62. Recipient Whitney Young Jr. award N.Y. Urban League, 1979, Disting. Citizens award Boy Scouts Am., 1980; named MVP in NBA All-Star Game, 1971, Man of Yr., Boys High Alumni chpt. L.A., 1979, Sportsman of Yr., Seattle chpt. City of Hope, 1979, Congl. Black Caucus Coach of Yr., 1979, CBA Coach of Yr., 1979, Coach of Yr., Black Pubs. Assn., 1979, NBA Coach of Yr., 1994; named to NIT-NIKE Hall of Fame, 1988; named to 9 NBA All-Star Teams, elected to Naismith Memorial Basketball Hall of Fame, 1988. *

WILKENS, ROBERT ALLEN, utilities executive, electrical engineer; b. Esmond, S.D., Jan. 3, 1929; s. William J. and Hazel C. (Girch) W.; m. Barbara M. Davis, Apr. 15, 1952; children—Bradley Alan, Beth Ann, Bonnie Sue, William Frank. B.S.E.E., S.D. State U., 1951. Dispatcher, engr. G.O., Northwestern Pub. Service Co., Huron, 1953-55, div. engr., Huron 1955-58, div. elec. supt., 1958-59, div. mgr., 1959-66, asst. to pres., 1966-69, vice pres. ops., G.O., 1969-80, pres., chief operating officer, 1980-90, pres., chief exec. officer, 1990-94, chmn. bd. dirs. 1994-97, also dir.; v.p., past pres. N. Cen. Electric Assn., past dir. Midwest Gas Assn.; dir. Farmers & Mchts. Bank Huron; past adminstrv. chmn., treas. Mid-Continent Area Power Pool. Mem. Salvation Army Adv. Bd., 1962-87; S.D. State R.R. Bd., 1982-87; past pres. Huron United Way. Served to capt. USAF, 1951-53. Named Disting. Engr., S.D. State U., 1977. Mem. North Central Elec. Assn., Midwest Gas Assn., S.D. Engring. Soc., Huron C. of C. (pres. 1963). Republican. Methodist. Lodges: Kiwanis, Masons, Shriners. Office: Northwestern Pub Svc Co 33 3rd St SE Huron SD 57350-2015

WILKER, LAWRENCE J., performing arts association administrator; b. Boston; m. Elizabeth Cross. BA in Econs., U. Mass., MFA; PhD in Theater, U. Ill. Dir. properties Shubert Orgn.; v.p. Eugene O'Neill Theater Found.; pres. Playhouse Sq. Found., Cleve., John F. Kennedy Ctr. for the Performing Arts, Washington, 1991—. Mem. exec. com. Fed. City Coun.; consulting dir. Riggs Nat. Bank; trustee Nat. Found. Advancement of the Arts; founder Del. Ctr. for the Performing Arts. Recipient 125th Anniversary Alumni award U. Mass., 1988, Outstanding Alumnus award U. Ill., 1990; named Arts Adminstr. of Yr. Arts Mgmt. newsletter, 1991. Mem. League Hist. Am. Theatres (pres.), Assn. of Performing Arts Presenters (pres.), Assn. Performing Arts Ctrs. (chmn.). Office: The Kennedy Ctr John F Kennedy Ctr for Performing Arts Washington DC 20566-0001

WILKERSON, CHARLES EDWARD, architect; b. Essex County, Va., Apr. 1, 1921; s. John Pullen, Jr. and Eva Lee (Eubank) W.; m. Sallie Ray Bowers, Feb. 14, 1959; children: Judith Gardner, Ann Hunter, Edward Ray. B.Arch., Va. Poly. Inst. and State U., 1943. Registered architect, Va. Bookkeeping clk. Crawford Mfg. Co., Richmond, Va., 1937-39; draftsman Dixon & Norman Architects, Richmond, 1946-47, John S. Efford Architect, Richmond, 1947-49; draftsman Walford & Wright Architects, Richmond, 1949-54, ptnr., 1955-60; ptnr. Wright, Jones & Wilkerson, Richmond, 1961-88; sole practice Richmond, 1988-91. Pres., sec.-treas., bd. dirs. Va. Found. Architecture, 1964-86. Tech. sgt. C.E., U.S. Army, 1943-46, PTO. Fellow AIA (dir. Va. chpt., sec. Va. chpt. 1959-61, dir. James River chpt. 1979-82, William C. Noland award Va. Soc.). Baptist.

WILKERSON, MATHA ANN, oil company executive; b. Mill Creek, Okla., Sept. 1, 1937; d. Frank and Lottie Evelyn (Cordell) Stie; m. Ronald Gene Wilkerson, Dec. 22, 1956; 1 child, Mitchell Linn. BS in Edn., East Cen. U., 1966. Elem. sch. tchr. Moore (Okla.) Pub. Schs., 1966-74; office mgr. S. S. Sanbar, M.D., Oklahoma City, 1974-78; ops. mgr., acct. John A. Taylor Oil Co., Oklahoma City, 1978-84; office mgr., controller Lance Ruffel Oil & Gas Corp., Oklahoma City, 1984—. Mem. Coun. of Petroleum Accounts Soc. (com. mem. 1979—). Baptist. Avocations: handicrafts, reading. theatre, cooking. Office: Lance Ruffel Oil & Gas 100 Park Ave Ste 500 Oklahoma City OK 73102-8003

WILKERSON, RITA LYNN, special education educator, consultant; b. Crescent, Okla., Apr. 22. BA, Cen. State U., Edmond, Okla., 1963; MEd, Cen. State U., 1969; postgrad., U. Okla., 1975, Kans. State U. Elem. tchr. music Hillsdale (Okla.) Pub. Sch., 1963-64; jr. high sch. music and spl. edn. Okarche (Okla.) Pub. Sch., 1965-71; cons. Title III Project, Woodward, Okla., 1971-72; dir. Regional Edn. Svc. Ctr., Guymon, Okla., 1972-81; dir., psychologist Project W.O.R.K., Guymon, 1981-90; tchr. behavioral disorders Unified Sch. Dist. 480, Liberal, Kans., 1990—; sch. psychologist Hardesty (Okla.) Schs., 1994; cons. Optima (Okla.) Pub. Schs., 1990, Felt (Okla.) Pub. Schs., 1990, Texhoma (Okla.) Schs., 1994, Balko (Okla.) Pub. Schs., 1996; spl. edn. cons. Optima Pub. Schs., 1992—, Goodwell (Okla.) Pub. Schs., 1992—; diagnostician Tyrone, Okla. Pub. Schs., 1992-95; home svcs. provider Dept. Human Svcs., Guymon, 1990; active Kans. Dept. Social and Rehab. Svcs., 1993—; adj. tchr. Seward County C.C., 1994—. Grantee Cen. State U., 1968-69, Oklahoma City Dept. Edn., 1988-89. Mem. ASCD, NAFE, NEA (liberal Kans. chpt.), AAUW, Coun. Exceptional Children, Okla. Assn. Retarded Citizens, Okla. Assn. for Children with Learning Disabilities, Phi Delta Kappa. Republican. Avocation: crafts. Home: 616 N Crumley St Guymon OK 73942-4341 Office: Unified Sch Dist 480 7th And Western Liberal KS 67901

WILKERSON, THOMAS L., career military officer; b. Pocatello, Idaho, Feb. 11, 1946; m. Lynn Reid; children: Jennifer Lynn, Catherine Aileen. BS, U.S. Naval Acad., 1967. Commd. 2d lt. USMC, 1967, advanced through ranks to major gen.; dep. asst. chief of staff ops. II Marine Expeditionary Force USMC, Camp Lejeune, N.C., 1990-92, dep. comdr. gen. II Marine Expeditionary Force, 1992, asst. dep. chief of staff plans, policies & ops., 1992; cmdr. reserve USMC, New Orleans, 1992—. Office: HQ Marine Corps Divsn Pub Affairs Washington DC 20380

WILKERSON, WILLIAM HOLTON, banker; b. Greenville, N.C., Feb. 16, 1947; s. Edwin Cisco and Agnes Holton (Gaskins) W.; m. Ellen Logan Tomskey, Oct. 27, 1973; 1 child, William Holton Jr. AB in Econs., U. N.C., 1970. Asst. v.p. First Union Nat. Bank, Greensboro, N.C., 1972-77; v.p. Peoples Bank & Trust Co., Rocky Mount, N.C., 1977-79; sr. v.p. Hibernia Nat. Bank, New Orleans, 1979-86; exec. v.p. Peoples Bank and Trust Co., 1987-89, pres., 1989-90; group exec officer, vice chmn. bd. dirs. Centura Banks, Inc., 1990—; chmn., Centura Ins. Svcs., Inc., 1995-97, Centura Securities, Inc., 1995-97, Carolinas Gateway Partnership, Inc., 1995-96, Centura Leasing Co.; exec. v.p., bd. dirs. CLS Inc.; bd. dirs. 1st greensboro Home Equity, Inc. Mem. Robert Morris Assoc., Rocky Mount C. of C. (bd. dirs. 1989-96, vice chmn. 1992-94, chmn.-elect 1994, chmn. 1995), Benvenue Country Club, Kiwanis, Omicron Delta Epsilon, Chi Beta Phi, Phi Sigma Pi. Republican. Home: 336 Iron Horse Rd Rocky Mount NC 27804-2118

WILKES, BRENT AMES, management consultant; b. Melrose, Mass., Sept. 30, 1952; s. Gordon Borthwick and Frances (Ames) W.; 1 child, Erin. Bachelor, U. Mass., 1974; M of Pub. Affairs, U. Conn., 1977. Adminstrv. asst. Town of Tolland, Conn., 1975-76; mgmt. specialist Mass. Dept. Community Affairs, Boston, 1976-79; adminstrv.. asst. to mayor City of Gloucester, Mass., 1979-80; assoc. dir., dir. of field svcs. Mass. Mcpl. Assn., Boston, 1980-89; v.p., treas. Mass. Interlocal Ins. Assn., Boston, 1984-89; pres. MMA Consulting Group, Inc., Boston, 1989-94, MMA Mgmt. Svcs. Inc., Boston, 1995—; v.p., treas. Pub. Employer Risk Mgmt. Assn., Albany, N.Y., 1989-97, pres., 1997—; adj. prof. Suffolk U. Grad. Sch.

Mgmt., Boston, 1980-82; lectr. numerous regional and nat. trade assns. Author and editor: Managing Small Towns, 1986; contbr. articles to profl. jours. Mem. fin. com. Town of Acton, Mass., 1977-79; mem. town meeting Town of Reading, Mass., 1987-89; pres. Unitarian Universalist Ch. of Reading, 1990-93. Mem. Internat. City Mgmt. Assn. (cert. in mgmt.), Mass. Mcpl. Mgmt. Assn. Democrat. Unitarian Universalist. Avocations: golf, tennis, volleyball, reading. Office: MMA Mgmt Svcs Inc 60 Temple Pl Boston MA 02111-1306

WILKES, DAVID ROSS, therapist, social worker; b. Springfield, Ohio, Sept. 4, 1951; s. Carol Monroe and Margaret (Perdi) W.; m. Donna Marie Roach, Apr. 11, 1987; children: Andrew David, Lauren Rose. AAS in Community Mental Health Tech., Borough Manhattan C.C., 1980; BA in Psychology, Queens Coll., 1985; postgrad., Ctr. Modern Psychoanalytic Studies, 1986-89, Union Inst., 1990—. Admission interviewer, referral counselor Westside Social Setting/Manhattan Bowery Project, N.Y.C., 1978-79; with dept. psychiatry City Hosp. Elmhurst, 1980-83; behavioral counselor Assn. Children with Retarded Mental Devel., 1985-87; therapist, social worker West Lawrence Care Ctr., 1987-90; case mgr. Nassau Case Mgmt. Program Nassau County Dept. Mental Health, Hempstead, N.Y., 1990—. Recipient Note of Commendation from Commr. Nassau County Dept. Mental Health and Devel. Disabilities, 1992. Mem. Am. Counseling Assn., Am. Psychol. Assn., Nat. Psychology Adv. Assn., Nat. Assn. Advancement of Psychoanalysis (assoc.), Phi Theta Kappa. Avocation: history of jazz, jazz musician. Office: Babylon Cons Ctr 210 Deer Park Ave Babylon NY 11702-2832

WILKES, DELANO ANGUS, architect; b. Panama City, Fla., Jan. 25, 1935; s. Burnice Angus and Flora Mae (Scott) W.; m. Dona Jean Murren, June 25, 1960. B.Arch., U. Fla., 1958. Cert. Nat. Council Archtl.; registration bds. cert. personal trainer, older adult specialty cert. Am. Coun. on Exercise. Designer, Perkins & Will Partnership, Chgo., 1960-63; designer, job capt. Harry Weese, Ltd., Chgo., 1963-66; project architect Fitch Larocca Carrington, Chgo., 1967-69; architect Mittelbusher & Tourtelot, Chgo., 1970-71; assoc. Bank Bldg. Corp., Chgo., 1972-75; sr. assoc. Charles Edward Stade & Assocs., Park Ridge, Ill., 1975-77; sr. architect Consoer Morgan Architect, Chgo., 1977-83, mktg. coord., 1980-83; design cons. Chamlin & Assocs., Peru and Morris, Ill., 1969-82, dir. architecture, 1983-86, v.p. architecture, 1986—; archtl. cons. Sweet's div. McGraw Hill., Inc., Chgo., 1984-90; ptnr. Deri Wilkes Assocs., 1990—; trainer Fitness Barn, 1995-96, Q Sports Club, 1997. Mem. coordinating com. Dune Acres Plan Commn. (Ind.), 1983-91; bldg.commr. City of Dune Acres, 1984-89; chmn. Ind. party Dune Acres, 1987; elected trustee Dune Acres Town Bd. 1988-91, pres. Town Bd., 1988-89; mem. Dune Acres Civic Improvement Found., 1988-91 (leadership recognition for drive to restore Dune Acres Clubhouse); cons. Inst. of Crippled and Disabled, N.Y.C., 1978-83; guest lectr., field trip guide Coll. DuPage, Glen Ellyn, Ill., 1968-76; guest architect med. adv. com. to Pres.'s Com. for Handicapped, 1977, 78. Vice chmn. Westchester County Dem. Precinct, Porter County, Ind., 1986; chmn. selection com. Dem. Hdqrs., Porter County, 1986; mem. Dem. Cen. Com., Porter County, 1986; treas. Com. to elect Kovach to Council, Porter County, 1986; vice chmn. Duneland Dems., 1988-92; pres. Ocean House Condominium Assn., St. Augustine, Fla., 1993-94. Mem. Businessmen for Pub. Interest, Folsom Family Assn. Am. (pres. 1978-82, v.p. 1982—, nominating com. 1983, host ann. meeting, Chgo. 1981), AIA, Chgo AIA (chmn. design awards display com. 1978-79, producer New Mem. Show 1979, chmn. pub. relations com. 1980), Art Inst. Chgo., Chgo. Lyric Opera Guild, Chgo. Assn. Commerce and Industry (display dir. 1979 meeting), Am. Soc. Interior Design (coordinator Info. Fair 1979), N.C. Geneal. Soc., New Eng. Hist. Geneal. Soc., Putnam County Hist. Soc., Cook County Hist. Soc., Soc. Colonial Wars, Gargoyle. Democrat. Unitarian. Author: Colonel Ebenezer Folsom, 1778-1789, North Carolina Patriot and Tory Scourge, 1975; editor Folsom Bull., 1977-80; producer documentary film The Angry Minority, Menninger Found., 1978. Home: 23 Circle Dr Chesterton IN 46304-1002

WILKES, JAMES E., telecommunications industry executive; b. 1937. BA, Mich. State U., 1959, MBA, 1962. With Ameritech Corp. and/or related cos., 1962—; pres., chief exec. officer Mich. Bell Telephone, Detroit, 1993—. Office: Mich Bell Tel Co 444 Michigan Ave Detroit MI 48226-2517

WILKES, JOSEPH ALLEN, architect; b. N.Y.C., Aug. 14, 1919; s. Abraham P. and Rose W.; m. Margaret Wilcoxson, Dec. 7, 1946; children—Jeffrey, Roger. B.A., Dartmouth Coll., 1941; M.Arch., Columbia U., 1949. Registered architect, N.Y., Fla., Md., D.C., Va. Assoc. prof. architecture U. Fla., Gainesville, 1952-59; project dir. Bldg. Research Adv. Bd. Nat. Acad. Sci., Washington, 1959-62; assoc. architect Keyes, Lethbridge & Condon, Washington, 1962-66; ptnr. Wilkes & Faulkner, Washington, 1966-82, Wilkes Faulkner Jenkins & Bass, Washington, 1983-90; lectr. architecture U. Md., 1971-85. Editor: Ency. of Architecture, 5 vols., 1988-89: chmn. editorial rev. bd.: Architectural Graphic Standards, 7th edit., 1980; archtl. works include: bldgs. Nat. Zool. Park; (bldg. renovation) Fed. Res. Bd. Bldg., Washington. Pres. Nat. Ctr. for a Barrier Free Environment, Washington, 1978; mem. profl. adv. council Nat. Easter Seals Soc. for Crippled Children, 1977-80; mem. Pres. Com. for Employment of Handicapped, Washington, 1976-82. Served to capt. AC U.S. Army, 1942-45; ETO. Fellow AIA; mem. Alpha Rho Chi. Home: 1720 Winchester Rd Annapolis MD 21401-5851

WILKES, SHAR (JOAN CHARLENE WILKES), elementary education educator; b. Chgo., July 15, 1951; d. Marcus and Hattie (Ehrich) Wexman; 1 child, McKinnon. Student, U. Okla., 1973, U. Wyo., 1975—. Rsch. dirs., exhibit designer Nicolaysen Art Mus.-Children's Ctr., Casper, Wyo., 1984-85; tchr. Natrona County Sch. Dist. 1, Casper, Wyo., 1974-96, 97—; reading specialist Southridge Elem. Sch., 1995—; enrichment coord. Paradise Valley Elem. Sch., 1993-94; co-coord. Children's Health Fair/Body Works Healthfair, Ptnrs. in Edn., Paradise Valley Elem. Sch./Wyo. Med. Ctr. and Blue Envelope, 1994. Author: Fantastic Phonics Food Factory. Dem. candidate Wyo. State Legis., 1986, 88; edn. chair United Way, Casper, 1988; chairperson Very Spl. Arts Festival, 1988, March of Dimes, 1989; grants person Casper Symphony, 1990; NCSD coord. Bear Trap Meadow Blue Grass Festival, 1995, 96, 97. Mem. NEA, LWV, Coun. Exceptional Children, Nat. Coun. Edn. Assn., Internat. Reading Assn., Wyo. Edn. Assn., Natrona County Sch. Dist. # 1 (spelling bee coord.), Soroptimist (charter), Phi Delta Kappa (exec. bd. 1988-90), Delta Kappa Gamma. Home: 4353 Coffman Ct Casper WY 82604

WILKEY, MALCOLM RICHARD, retired ambassador, former federal judge; b. Murfreesboro, Tenn., Dec. 6, 1918; s. Malcolm Newton and Elizabeth (Gilbert) W.; m. Emma Secul Depolo, Dec. 21, 1959. AB, Harvard U., 1940, LLB, 1948; LLD (hon.), Rose-Hulman Inst. Tech., 1984. Bar: Tex. 1948, N.Y. 1963, U.S. Supreme Ct. 1952, D.C. 1970. U.S. atty. So. Dist. Tex., 1954-58; asst. atty. gen. U.S., 1958-61; ptnr. Butler Binion Rice & Cook, 1961-63; gen. counsel, sec. Kennecott Copper Corp., 1963-70; judge U.S. Ct. Appeals D.C. Circuit, 1970-85; U.S. amb. to Uruguay, 1985-90; official in charge fed. forces at Little Rock Sch. Crisis, Dept. Justice, 1958; mem. U.S.-Chile Arbitration Commn., 1991—; lectr. internat. constl. and adminstrv. law London Poly., 1979, 80; lectr. Tulane U. Law Summer Sch., Grenoble, France, 1981, 83, San Diego Law Summer Sch., Oxford, Eng., 1983, Brigham Young Law Sch., 1984, 93; vis. fellow Wolfson Coll., Cambridge U., 1985; chmn. Pres.'s Commn. on Revision Fed. Ethics Laws, 1989; spl. counsel to Atty. Gen. for inquiry into the House Banking Facility, 1992. Author: Is It Time For A Second Constitutional Convention, 1995. Del. Republican Nat. Conv., 1960. Served from 2d lt. to lt. col. AUS, 1941-45. Hon. fellow Wolfson Coll., Cambridge. Fellow Am. Bar Found.; mem. Am. Law Inst. (adv. com. restatement fgn. rels. law of U.S.), Jud. Conf. U.S. (com. on standards for admission to fed. cts. 1976-79), Phi Beta Kappa, Delta Sigma Rho, Phi Delta Phi (hon.). Address: Av El Bosque 379, Providencia, Santiago Chile

WILKIE, DONALD WALTER, biologist, aquarium museum director; b. Vancouver, B.C., Can., June 20, 1931; s. Otway James and Jessie Margaret (McLeod) W.; m. Patricia Ann Archer, May 18, 1980; children: Linda, Douglas, Susanne. B.A., U. B.C., 1960, M.Sc., 1966. Curator Vancouver Pub. Aquarium, 1961-63, Phila. Aquarama, 1963-65; exec. dir. aquarium-mus. Scripps Instn. Oceanography, La Jolla, Calif., 1965-93, exec. dir. emeritus, 1993—; cons. aquarium design, rschg. exhibit content; sci. writer and editor naturalist-marine edn. programs. Author books on aquaria and marine ednl. materials; contbr. numerous articles to profl. jours. Mem. Am. Soc. Ichthyologists and Herpetologists, San Diego Zool. Soc. (animal health and conservation com.). Home: 4548 Cather Ave San Diego CA 92122-2632 Office: U Calif San Diego Scripps Instn Oceanography Libr 9500 Gilman Dr La Jolla CA 92093-5003 *As a biologist and teacher my major goal has been to increase public interest in learning about our environment and promoting proper use of the earth's resources.*

WILKIE, EVERETT CLEVELAND, JR., librarian; b. Kinston, N.C., June 27, 1947; s. Everett Cleveland, Sr. and Nancy Frances (Stroup) W.; m. Barbara Lande Turman, Feb., 1986; 1 child, Lauren Llewellyn. Student, Campbell Coll., 1965-67; BA in English, Wake Forest U., 1969, MA in English, 1970; PhD in Comparative Lit., U. S.C., 1977, M Librarianship, 1978. Instr. dept. English McDowell Tech. Inst., Marion, N.C., 1970-71, Anderson (S.C.) Coll., 1971-72; adminstrv. asst. office dean freshmen U. S.C., Columbia, 1973-76, adminstrv. asst. office dean Coll. Humanities and Social Scis., 1976-78; rsch. assoc. dept. comparative lit. Brown U., Providence, 1978-80, bibliographer John Carter Brown Libr., 1981-84; reference libr. Lilly Libr. Ind. U., Bloomington, 1980-81; head libr., Crofut curator rare books and manuscripts, editor Bulletin Conn. Hist. Soc., Hartford, 1985—; mem. publ. adv. com. Conn. Jewish History; mem. state Hist. Records Adv. Bd., 1994, subcom. on membership, 1994; mem. RBMS Security & Seminars Com.; presenter papers in field. Contbr. 29 articles to profl. jours. McClean fellow Libr. Co. Phila., 1989, Mellon fellow, 1992; Travel to Collections grantee NEH, 1992. Mem. ALA, Bibliographical Soc. Am., Am. Printing History Assn., Soc. Am. Archivists, New England Printing History Assn., New England Archivists. Office: Conn Hist Soc 1 Elizabeth St Hartford CT 06105-2213

WILKIE, VALLEAU, JR., foundation executive; b. Summit, N.J., July 3, 1923; s. Valleau and Amelia Wilkie (Parry) W.; m. Donna Hartwell, Oct. 28, 1985; children: Janice, Robert. A.B., Yale U., 1948; M.A., Harvard U., 1954. Instr. history Phillips Acad., 1948-59; headmaster Gov. Dummer Acad., Byfield, Mass., 1959-72; mem. bd. trustees Gov. Dummer Acad., 1960-72, dir. devel., 1972-73; exec. v.p. Sid W. Richardson Found., Ft. Worth, 1973—; bd. dirs. Nat. Charities Info. Bureau;. Bd. dirs. S.W. Ednl. Devel. Lab., 1976-82, pres. 1981-82; mem. Council on Founds., Inc., 1980—, bd. dirs., 1981-87, chmn. bd., 1985-87; bd. dirs. Conf. of S.W. Founds., 1977-82, pres., 1981-82; bd. dirs. Found. Ctr., 1982-91, Nat. Charities Info. Bur., 1991—. Served to 1st lt. USAAF, 1942-45. Mem. Headmasters Assn., N.E. Assn. Schs. and Colls. (chmn. commn. on ind. secondary schs. 1967-70, pres. 1972-73), Delta Kappa Epsilon. Episcopalian. Office: Sid W Richardson Found 309 Main St Fort Worth TX 76102-4006

WILKIN, MILES CLIFFORD, theatrical group executive; b. Norfolk, Va., Aug. 9, 1948; s. Winton Reynold and Elizabeth (Lawrence) W.; m. Kathleen Burke, June 13, 1968 (div. Aug. 1984); children: Miles Clifford II, Stephen Joseph; m. Constance Beth Weinstein, Feb. 4, 1991. BSBA, U. Fla., 1971. Asst. to dean of students U. Fla., Gainesville, 1971-78; dir. Orlando (Fla.) Centroplex, 1978-79; gen. mgr. Saenger Theatre, New Orleans, La., 1979-82; pres., chief exec. officer Pace Theatrical Group, Inc., Houston, N.Y.C., Miami, 1982—. Assoc. producer (plays) Jerome Robbins Broadway, 1989, Gypsy, 1990; producer (plays) Long Day's Journey into Night, 1986, South Pacific, 1987, Into The Woods, 1988, Starlight Express, 1989, Grand Hotel, 1991, Magic of David Copperfield, 1991, Bye Bye Birdie, 1991, Fiddler on the Roof, 1991 (Tony award). Pres. Story Theatre Prodn., Ft. Lauderdale, Fla.; mem. Performing Arts Ctr. Trust., Miami. Mem. League Am. Theatres & Producers (gov., mem. exec. com.). Avocation: scuba diving. Office: Pace Theatrical Group Inc 1515 Broadway Ste 3804 New York NY 10036*

WILKIN, RICHARD EDWIN, clergyman, religious organization executive; b. nr. Paulding, Ohio, Nov. 3, 1930; s. Gaylord D. and Beulah E. (Tarlton) W.; m. Barbara A. Zehender, Aug. 10, 1952; children—Richard Edward, James Lee, Deborah Ann. Student, Giffin Jr. Coll., 1948-49; B.S., Findlay Coll., 1952, D.D., 1975; postgrad., Ind. U., 1959-60. Ordained to ministry Churches of God Gen. Conf., 1953; pastor Neptune Ch. of God, Celina, Ohio, 1952-59, Wharton (Ohio) Ch. of God, 1959-64, Anthony Wayne Ch. of God, Ft. Wayne, Ind., 1964-70; adminstr., chief exec. Chs. of God Gen. Conf., Findlay, Ohio, 1970-87; supr. mission work India, Bangladesh, Haiti, 1970-85; dir. field edn. and Inst. for. Biblical Studies, faculty mem. Winebrenner Theol. Sem., Findlay, 1987-92, adj. facult O.T., 1993—; interim sr. pastor Coll. 1st Ch. of God, Findlay, 1992-93; Dir. summer youth camps, sec., mem. exec. com. Ohio Conf., 1952-59, state clk., pres., 1959-64; chmn. Commn. on Edn., mem. exec. com. Ind. Conf., 1964-70; adv. com. Am. Bible Soc.; steering com. U.S. Ch. Leaders, 1979; pres. Ft. Wayne Ministerial Assn.; bd. dirs. Associated Chs. of Ft. Wayne and Allen County, 1966-70; tchr. Center Twp. Jr. High Sch., Celina, Mendon (Ohio) Union High Sch., Van Del High Sch., Van Wert, Ohio, 1954-59; interim pastor Shawnee First Ch. of God, Lima, Ohio, 1987-88, ch. cons., 1987—. Vice pres. bd. trustees Winebrenner Haven, mem. adv. com. in race relations regarding sch. reorgn. and busing, Ft. Wayne, 1967-69; trustee Winebrenner Theol. Sem., 1980-87, sec. bd. trustees; trustee U. Findlay, 1985—, chmn. of com. on trustees of bd. of trustees; sec. Bd. of Pensions of Ch. of God, Gen. Conf., 1986—. Recipient Outstanding Tchr. award, 1958; Disting. Alumnus award Findlay Coll., 1973, Outstanding Leadership award Ohio Conf. Chs. of God, 1986, Disting. Assoc. award U. Findlay, 1992; named Hon. Alumnus Winebrenner Theol. Sem., 1978. Mem. NEA, Ohio Edn. Assn., NAACP, Farm Bur. Home: 1806 Greendale Ave Findlay OH 45840-6918

WILKINS, (GEORGE) BARRATT, librarian; b. Atlanta, Nov. 6, 1943; s. George Barratt and Mabel Blanche (Brooks) W. B.A., Emory U., 1965; M.A., Ga. State U., 1968, U. Wis., 1969. Reference libr. S.C. State Libr., Columbia, 1969-71; instl. libr. cons. Mo. State Libr., Jefferson City, 1971-73; asst. state libr. State Libr. Fla., Tallahassee, 1973-77; state libr. State Libr. Fla., 1977—; dir. div. Libr. and Info. Svcs. State of Fla., Tallahassee, 1986—, acting asst. sec. state, 1987; abstractor Hist. Abstracts, 1967-71; dir. survey project Nat. Ctr. Edn. Statistics, 1976-77; del. The White House Conf. on Libr. and Info. Svcs., 1991; mem. planning com. Fla. Gov.'s Conf. on Libraries and Info. Svcs.; bd. dirs. Southeastern Libr. Network, Inc., 1979-82, treas., 1980-81, vice chmn., 1981-82; mem. adv. coun. U.S. Pub. Printer, 1983-86, Southeastern/Atlantic Regional Med. Libr. Svcs. 1986-89; mem. planning com., Fla. Automated Edn. Commn., 1989-94; bd. dirs. Fla. Distance Learning Network, Inc., First Am. Found., Inc.; cons. in field. Contbr. articles to profl. jours. Mem. adv. com. statewide jail project Mo. Assn. Social Welfare, 1971-73, bd. dirs. central div., 1971-73; mem. State Univ. System Interinstl. Library Com., 1977—; bd. dirs. Fla. Ctr. Libr. Automation, 1984—, Fla. Ctr. for the Book, 1984—, Fla. Coll. Ctr. for Libr. Automation, 1990—. Recipient Exceptional Achievement award Assn. Specialized and Coop. Libr. Agys., 1991, Outstanding Pub. Svc. award Gov. of Fla., 1991; U. Wis. fellow, 1969. Mem. ALA (coun. 1981-85, legis. com. 1982-86, com. on orgn. 1988-90, planning com., 1993-95, standards, 1996—), Assn. State Libr. Agys. (pres. 1976-77), Assn. Hosp. Instl. Librs. (bd. dirs. 1973-74), Am. Correctional Assn. (instn. libr. com.), Southeastern Libr. Assn. (pres. 1982-84), Chief Officers of State Libr. Agys. (bd. dirs. 1980-82, pres. 1990-92, chair legis. com. 1992-96), Beta Phi Mu, Phi Alpha Theta. Democrat. Episcopalian. Office: Dept State Divsn Libr Svcs RA Gray Bldg Tallahassee FL 32399-0250

WILKINS, BURLEIGH TAYLOR, philosophy educator; b. Bridgetown, Va., July 1, 1932; s. Burleigh and Helen Marie (Taylor) W.; children: Brita Taylor, Carla Cowgill, Burleigh William. BA summa cum laude, Duke U., 1952; MA, Harvard U., 1954, Princeton U., 1963; PhD, Princeton U., 1965. Instr. MIT, Cambridge, 1957-60, Princeton U., 1960-61, 63; asst. prof. Rice U., Houston, 1965-66, assoc. prof., 1966-67; assoc. prof. U. Calif., Santa Barbara, 1967-68, prof., 1968—. Author: Carl Becker, 1961, The Problem of Burke's Political Philosophy, 1967, Hegel's Philosophy of History, 1974, Has History Any Meaning?, 1978, Terrorism and Collective Responsibility, 1992. Mem. Phi Beta Kappa. Office: Univ of Calif Dept of Philosophy Santa Barbara CA 93106

WILKINS, CAROLINE HANKE, consumer agency administrator, political worker; b. Corpus Christi, Tex., May 12, 1937; d. Louis Allen and Jean Guckian Hanke; m. B. Hughel Wilkins, 1957; 1 child, Brian Hughel. Student, Tex. Coll. Arts and Industries, 1956-57, Tex. Tech. U., 1957-58; BA, U. Tex., 1961; MA magna cum laude, U. Ams., 1964. Instr. history Oreg. State U., 1967-68; adminstr. Consumer Svcs. divsn. State of Oreg., 1977-80, Wilkins Assoc., 1980—; mem. PFMC Salmon Adv. subpanel, 1982-86. Author: (with B. H. Wilkins) Implications of the U.S.-Mexican Water Treaty for Interregional Water Transfer, 1968. Dem. precinct committeewoman, Benton County, Oreg., 1964-90; publicity chmn. Benton County Gen. Election, 1964; chmn. Get-Out-the-Vote Com., Benton County, 1966; vice chmn.Benton County Dem. Ctrl. Com., 1966-70; vice chmn. 1st Congl. Dist., Oreg., 1966-68, chmn., 1969-74; mem. exec. com. Western States Dem. Conf., 1970-72; vice chmn. Dem. Nat. Com., 1972-77, mem. arrangements com., 1972, 76, mem. Dem. Charter Commn., 1973-74; mem. Dem. Nat. Com., 1972-77, 85-89, mem. size and composition com., 1987-89, rules com., 1988; mem. Oreg. Govt. Ethics Commn., 1974-76; del., mem. rules com. Dem. Nat. Conv., 1988; 1st v.p. Nat. Fedn. Dem. Women, 1983-85, pres., 1985-87, parliamentarian, 1993-95; mem. Kerr Libr. bd. Oreg. State U., 1989-95, pres., 1994-95; mem. Corvallis-Benton County Libr. Found., 1991—, sec., 1993, v.p., 1994, pres., 1995; bd. dirs. Oreg. chpt. U.S. Lighthouse Soc., pres., 1997—. Named Outstanding Mem., Nat. Fedn. Dem. Women, 1992. Mem. Nat. Assn. Consumer Agy. Adminstrs., Soc. Consumer Affairs Profls., Oreg. State U. Folk Club (pres. faculty wives 1989-90), Zonta Internat. (vice area bd. dirs. dist. 8 1992-94, area dir., bd. dist. 8 1994-96, by laws and resolutions chair, found. liaison 1997—). Office: 3311 NW Roosevelt Dr Corvallis OR 97330-1169

WILKINS, CHARLES L., chemistry educator; b. Los Angeles, Calif., Aug. 14, 1938; s. Richard and Lenore M. W.; m. Ingrid Fritsch, 1997; 1 child, Mark R. BS, Chapman Coll., 1961; PhD, U. Oreg., 1966. Prof. chemistry U. Nebr., Lincoln, 1967-81; prof. U. Calif., Riverside, 1981—. Office: Univ of Calif-Riverside Dept Of Chemistry Riverside CA 92521

WILKINS, DAVID GEORGE, fine arts educator; b. Battle Creek, Mich., Sept. 12, 1939; s. George Henry and Marjorie Ewing (Pierce) W.; m. Ann Thomas, June 25, 1966; children: Rebecca Louise, Katherine May. BA, Oberlin Coll., 1961; MA, U. Mich., 1963, PhD, 1969. Instr. U. N.H., Durham, 1963-64; prof. dept. history of art and arch. U. Pitts., 1967—, chair, 1989-92, dir. univ. art gallery, 1976-92; faculty mem. summer sessions Sarah Lawrence Coll.-U. Mich., Florence, Italy, 1975-81. uthor: (with Bernard Schultz and Katheryn M. Linduff) Art Past/Art Present, 2nd edit., 1994, (with Bonnie A. Bennett) Donatello, 1984, Maso di Banco, 1985, (with K.J. Arbitman) The Illustrated Bartsch, Vol. 53, Pre-Rembrandt Etchers, 1985, Paintings and Sculpture of the Duquesne Club, 1986 (with Mark M. Brown and Lu Donnelly) The History of the Duquesne Club, 1989; revising editor: Hartt History of Italian Renaissance Art, 4th edit., 1994; co-editor (with Rebecca L. Wilkins): The Search for a Patron in the Middle Ages and the Renaissance, 1996. Bd. dirs. Pitts. Ctr. for Arts, 1979-93—; bd. dirs. Mendelssohn Choir of Pitts., 1979-84; mem. Pa. Humanities Coun., 1984-88; mus. adv. panel Pa. Coun. on Arts, 1985-87. William E. Suida fellow Kress Found., Kunsthistorisches Inst., Florence, 1966-67; recipient Chancellor's Disting. Teaching award U. Pitts., 1987. Mem. Coll. Art Assn., Italian Art Soc., Renaissance Soc. Am. Democrat. Home: 1217 Shady Ave Pittsburgh PA 15232-2811 Office: U Pitts Dept History Art & Arch 104 Frick Fine Arts Pittsburgh PA 15260-7601

WILKINS, (JACQUES) DOMINIQUE, professional basketball player; b. Orléans, France, Jan. 12, 1960; came to U.S., 1964; s. John and Geraldine Wilkins; m. Nicole Berry, Sept. 26, 1992; children: Iyisha, Chloe. BBA, U. Ga., 1982. Basketball player Atlanta Hawks, 1982-94, Los Angeles Clippers, 1994, Boston Celtics, 1994-95, Panathinaikos-Athens, Athens, Greece, 1995-96, San Antonio Spurs, 1996—. Mem. NBA All-Star team, 1986-91, 93-94; NBA scoring leader, 1986; mem. All-NBA first team, 1986; mem. NBA All-Rookie team, 1983; Sporting News NCAA All-American, 1981, 82; mem. Dream Team II; slam dunk champion NBA, 1985, 90; mem. Panathinaikos-Athens european championship team, 1996. Holds single game record for most free throws without a miss-23, 1992; currently 6th all-time leading scorer in NBA history. Office: Kauffman Sports 29350 Pacific Coast Hwy Malibu CA 90265-3957

WILKINS, EARLE WAYNE, JR., surgery educator emeritus; b. Albany, N.Y., Aug. 17, 1919; s. Earle Wayne and Mildred Anna (Dana) W.; m. Suzanne Porter, Aug. 26, 1944; children: Clinton Porter, Wendy Dana Wilkins Hopkins, Wayne Lawrence. AB, Williams Coll., 1941; MD, Harvard U., 1944. Diplomate Am. Bd. Surgery, Am. Bd. Thoracic Surgery. Surg. resident Mass. Gen. Hosp., Boston, 1944-46, 48-51, mem. staff, 1952—, vis. surgeon, 1968—; mem. staff Harvard Med. Sch., Boston, 1953—, clin. prof. surgery, 1979-89, prof. emeritus, 1989—; Fulbright vis. prof. Allgemeines Krankenhaus, Vienna, Austria, 1964-65; vis. prof. Nat. Def. Med. Ctr., Taipei, Taiwan, 1989; surgeon Boston Bruins Hockey Club, 1969-85; physician tech. advisor div. of Emergency Med. Svcs., Washington, 1977-81, med. dir. Mass. Region IV, Boston, 1980-82; chmn. bd. Boston Med. Flight, 1985-87. Editor: Current Therapy in Cardiothoracic Surgery, 1989, Esophageal Cancer, 1988, Emergency Medicine: Scientific Foundations and Current Practice, 1989; contbr. numerous articles to profl. jours. Trustee Williams Coll., Williamstown, Mass., 1971-89, pres. Soc. of Alumni, 1967-69. Lt. (j.g.) USNR, 1946-48. Recipient Sports Illustrated Silver Anniversary award All-American Time Inc., N.Y.C., 1965, Commonwealth award Commonwealth Mass., 1986, Disting. Alumnus award Albany Acad., 1988, Rogerson Cup Williams Coll., 1991, Bicentenniel Medal Williams Coll., 1993. Fellow ACS, Am. Surg. Assn.; mem. AMA, Mass. Med. Soc., Boston Surg. Soc., Am. Assn. Thoracic Surgery (councillor 1984-88), Soc. Thoracic Surgeons, New Eng. Surg. Soc. (pres. 1980-81), Gen. Thoracic Surg. Club, Taconic Golf Club (pres. 1990-95). Republican. Avocations: golf, tennis, skiing, travel, stamps. Home: 240 South St Williamstown MA 01267-2822

WILKINS, FLOYD, JR., retired lawyer, consultant; b. Fowler, Calif., Sept. 8, 1925; s. Floyd and Kathryn (Springborg) W.; m. Holly Blee, June 18, 1949 (div. Jan. 1964); children: Douglas B., Janet H., Steven B., Kevin D.; m. Sybil Ann Perrault, Feb. 22, 1964. BS, U. Calif., Berkeley, 1946; LLB, Harvard U., 1952. Bar: N.Y. 1953, Calif. 1959. Assoc. Dwight, Royall, Harris, Koegel & Caskey, N.Y.C., 1952-58; v.p., trust officer San Diego Trust & Savs. Bank, 1958-63; assoc., then ptnr., prin. Seltzer Caplan Wilkins & McMahon, P.C. and predecessors, San Diego, 1963-91; lectr. U. So. Calif. Tax Inst., L.A., 1975, Title Ins. and Trust Co., L.A. and Santa Ana, Calif., 1973, 78, 83, Trust Svcs. of Am. Tax Forum, San Diego, U. Calif. Continuing Edn. of Bar, San Diego, 1977-91. Bd. dirs., pres. San Diego County Citizens Scholarship Found. Served with USNR, 1944-46. Mem. ABA, State Bar Calif., San Diego County Bar Assn. Republican. Avocations: travel, photography, wine, gardening. Home: 2005 Soledad Ave La Jolla CA 92037-3904

WILKINS, HERBERT PUTNAM, judge; b. Cambridge, Mass., Jan. 10, 1930; s. Raymond Sanger and Mary Louisa (Aldrich) W.; m. Angela Joy Middleton, June 21, 1952; children: Douglas H., Stephen M., Christopher P., Kate W. McManus. A.B., Harvard U., 1951, LL.B. magna cum laude, 1954; LL.D., Suffolk U., 1976; J.D., New Eng. Sch. Law, 1979. Bar: Mass. 1954. Assoc. firm Palmer & Dodge, Boston, 1954-59; ptnr. Palmer & Dodge, 1960-72; assoc. justice Mass. Supreme Jud. Ct., 1972-96, chief justice, 1996—. Editor: Harvard U. Law Rev, 1953-54. Bd. overseers Harvard U., 1977-83, pres. bd., 1981-83; trustee Milton Acad., 1971-76, Phillips Exeter Acad., 1972-78; mem. Concord (Mass.) Planning Bd., 1957-60; selectman Town of Concord, 1960-66, town counsel, 1969-72; town counsel Town of Acton, Mass., 1966-72. Mem. Am. Law Inst. (council), Am. Coll. Trial Lawyers (jud. fellow). Republican. Unitarian-Universalist. Office: Mass Supreme Jud Ct Pemberton Sq 1300 New Courthouse Boston MA 02108

WILKINS, J. ERNEST, JR., mathematician; b. Chgo., Nov. 27, 1923; s. J. Ernest and Lucille B. (Robinson) W.; m. Gloria Louise Stewart, June 22, 1947 (dec.); children: Sharon Wilkins Hill, J. Ernest III; m. Maxine G. Malone, June 2, 1984. BS, U. Chgo., 1940, MS, 1941, PhD, 1942; BME, NYU, 1957, MME, 1960. Mathematician Am. Optical Co., Buffalo, 1946-50; mgr. R&D United Nuclear Corp., White Plains, N.Y., 1950-60; assoc. dir. lab. Gen. Atomic Co., San Diego, 1960-70; Disting. prof. applied math. physics Howard U., Washington, 1970-77; vis. scientist Argonne (Ill.) Nat. Lab., 1976-77, fellow, 1984-85; v.p., dep. gen. mgr. EG & G Idaho, Idaho Falls, 1977-84; Disting. prof. Clark Atlanta U., 1990—; chmn. Army Sci. Bd. Dept. Army, 1978-81; mem. Adv. Com. on Reactor Safeguards, Washington, 1990-94, chmn., 1993-94. Contbr. articles to profl. jours. With AUS, 1946-

47. Recipient Outstanding Civilian Svc. medal U.S. Army, 1980. Mem. Am. Nuclear Soc. (pres. 1974-75, cons. 1987-90), Am. Math. Soc., Math. Assn. Am., Oak Ridge Assn. Univs. (coun. 1990—). Office: Clark Atlanta U Box J Atlanta GA 30314

WILKINS, JOHN WARREN, physics educator; b. Des Moines, Mar. 11, 1936; s. Carl Daniel and Ruth Elizabeth (Warren) W. B.S. in Engring, Northwestern U., 1959; M.S., U. Ill., 1960, Ph.D., 1963; D.Tech. (hon.), Chalmers Tekniska Hogskola, Göteborg, 1990. NSF postdoctoral fellow U. Cambridge, Eng., 1963-64; asst. prof. physics Cornell U., 1964-68, assoc. prof., 1968-74, prof., 1974-88; Ohio Eminent scholar, prof. physics Ohio State U., 1988—; vis. prof. H.C. Ørsted Inst., Copenhagen, 1968, Nordita, Copenhagen, 1972-73, 75-76, 79-81; cons. Los Alamos Nat. Lab., 1984—. Assoc. editor Physica Scripta, 1977-85, Phys. Rev. Letters, 1982-85, Rev. Modern Physics, 1983-95; mem. editorial bd. Phys. Rev. B, 1991-94; coord. Comments on Condensed Matter Physics, 1985-90. Fellow AAAS, Am. Phys. Soc. (publs. oversight com. 1995—, chmn. 1995-96, councillor divsn. condensed matter physics 1989-93, exec. com. divsn. biol. physics 1973-77); mem. European Phys. Soc. Office: Ohio State U Dept Physics 174 W 18th Ave Columbus OH 43210-1106

WILKINS, LUCIEN SANDERS, gastroenterologist; b. Sanford, N.C., Mar. 30, 1942; s. Alexander Betts and Olive Elizabeth (Pittman) W.; m. Freda Barry Hartness, July 16, 1966; children: Lucien Sanders Jr., Elise Perryman. BA, Duke U., 1963; MD, Med. Coll. Va., 1967. Diplomate Am. Bd. Internal Medicine. Intern Medical Coll. Va., Richmond, 1967-68, resident in internal medicine, 1970-72, gastreoenterology fellow, 1972-73; clin. gastroenterologist Wilmington (N.C.) Health Assoc., 1973—; vis. physician Hopital St. Croix, Leogane, Haiti, 1979-84; founder Divsn. Gastrointestinal Endoscopy Hopital St. Croix, Leogane, 1984, 1st Endoscopic Ambulatory Surgery Facility in State of N.C., 1990; chmn. dept. medicine New Hanover Regional Med. Ctr., Wilmington, N.C., 1990-92; asst. prof. clin. medicine U. N.C., Chapel Hill, 1974—; bd. dirs. Br. Banking and Trust, Wilmington, 1991—; physican adv. Nat. Found. Ileitis and Colitis, 1976-78. Author: Progeny, 1994. Bd. dirs. Cape Fear Coun. for the Arts, Wilmington, 1976-77, New Hanover Regional Med. Ctr. Found., Wilmington, 1993-95, exec. com., 1994-95, Com. of 100, Wilmington, 1992-95. Lt. comdr. M.C., USN, 1968-70. A. D. Williams rsch. fellow, 1965, Paul Harris fellow Rotary, 1986; winner GTP-L Al Holbert Meml. Race, Sebring, Fla., 1995. Mem. ACP, New Hanover-Pender County Med. Soc. (pres. 1980), Cape Fear Country Club, Surf Club, Hist. Stock Car Racing Group, Figure Eight Island Yacht Club (charter), Wrightsville Beach Ocean Racing Assn. (commodore). Presbyterian. Avocations: vintage automobile racing, tennis, sailing, skiing, outdoors. Home: 2215 Lynnwood Dr Wilmington NC 28403-8026 Office: Wilmington Health Assoc 1202 Medical Ctr Dr Wilmington NC 28401-7307 *Being a true physician means continually learning from your patients, about your patients, and on behalf of your patients.*

WILKINS, MICHAEL JON, judge; b. Murray, Utah, May 13, 1948; s. Jack L. and Mary June (Phillips) W.; m. Diane W. Wilkins, Nov. 9, 1967; children: Jennifer, Stephanie, Bradley J. BS, U. Utah, 1975, JD, 1976. Bar: Utah 1977, U.S. Dist. Ct. Utah 1977, U.S. Ct. Appeals (10th cir.) 1987, U.S. Supreme Ct. 1986. Mng. ptnr. Wilkins, Oritt & Headman, Salt Lake City, 1989-94; judge Utah Ct. Appeals, 1994—; mem. Gov.'s Adv. Com. on Corp., Salt Lake City, 1989-94; mem. Utah Supreme Ct. Complex Steering Com., 1993-94; mem. Judiciary Standing Com. on Info., Automation and Records, 1995—, chmn., 1995—; mem. Legis. Compensation Commn., 1994-95. Trustee Utah Law Related Edn. Project, Inc., Salt Lake City, 1991-95, chmn., 1992-94. 1st lt. U.S. Army, 1968-72. Mem. LDS Ch. Office: Utah Ct Appeals 230 S 500 E Ste 400 Salt Lake City UT 84102-2015

WILKINS, ORMSBY, music director, conductor, pianist; b. Sydney, Australia. Student, Sydney Conservatory Music, Melbourne (Australia) Conservatory Music. Joined Australian Ballet, 1973, condr., 1976-82, resident condr., 1982-83, guest condr. tour USSR and Eng., 1988, guest condr. tour Am., 1990; condr. Sadler's Wells Royal Ballet (now Birmingham Royal Ballet), 1984-90; music dir., prin. condr. Nat. Ballet Can., Toronto, Ont., Can., 1990—; condr. Royal Swedish Ballet, Royal Opera House Orch. at Covent Garden, Opera Ballet de Lyon, Philharmonic Orch. London, Royal Philharm. Orch. Lodon, Hong Kong Philharmonic Orch., Winnipeg Symphony Orch. Performances include Swan Lake, Sleeping Beauty, Coppelia, Raymonda, Petrouchka, Rite of Spring; debut at Rome Opera House, 1996, at La Scala, Milan, Italy, 1997. office: Nat Ballet Can, 470 Queens Quay West, Toronto, ON Canada M5V 3K4

WILKINS, PHILIP CHARLES, judge; b. Jan. 27, 1913; student Sacramento Jr. Coll.; LL.B., U. Calif., San Francisco, 1939; m. Sue Wilkins, Aug. 9, 1941. Bar: Calif. 1939. Mem. firm A.D. McDougall, Sacramento, 1940-42, Rowland & Craven, Sacramento, 1946-54; individual practice law, Sacramento, 1954-59; ptnr. firm Wilkins, Little & Mix, Sacramento, 1959-65, Wilkins & Mix, Sacramento, 1966-69; judge U.S. Dist. Ct., Eastern Dist. Calif., Sacramento, 1969—, now sr. judge. Served to lt. USNR, 1942-46. Office: US Dist Ct 4028 US Courthouse 650 Capitol Mall Sacramento CA 95814*

WILKINS, RITA DENISE, researcher, multimedia design consultant; b. Detroit, June 21, 1951; d. William H. and Alice L. (Hayes) Smith. Student, George Peabody Coll., 1969-70, Cleveland (Tenn.) State Community Coll., 1973-75. Mgmt. coord., legal coord. Arlen Realty and Devel. Corp., Chattanooga, Tenn., 1973-76; asst. v.p., office mgr. Newburger Andes & Co., Atlanta, 1976-78, asst. v.p., project mgr., 1978-79; project mgr. Robinson-Humphrey, Atlanta, 1979-80; dept. head Office Properties Group Merrill Lynch Realty Comml. Svcs., Atlanta, 1980-83; acquisition devel. mgmt. rep. Cardinal Industries, Inc., Atlanta, 1983-86; pres., sr. cons. CPC/Foresite, Charleston, S.C., 1986—; guest lectr. Ga. State U. Contbr. articles to profl. jours. Mem. Indsl. Devel. Rsch. Coun. Office: CPC/Foresite 240 Kimberly Ave Apt 4 Asheville NC 28804-3553

WILKINS, ROBERT HENRY, neurosurgeon, editor; b. Pitts., Aug. 18, 1934; s. George H. and Mary M. (Lemon) W.; m. Gloria A. Kohl, Dec. 28, 1957; children: Michael I., Jeffrey K., Elizabeth A. BS, U. Pitts., 1955, MD, 1959. Diplomate Am. Bd. Neurol. Surgery. Intern, resident gen. surgery Duke U. Med. Ctr., Durham, N.C., 1959-61, resident neurosurgery, 1963-68, asst. prof. neurosurgery, 1968-72, prof. neurosurgery, 1976—; chief divsn. neurosurgery, 1976-96; clin. assoc. surgery br. Nat. Cancer Inst., Bethesda, Md., 1961-63; chmn. dept. neurosurgery Scott and White Clinic, Temple, Tex., 1972-75; assoc. prof. neurosurgery U. Pitts., 1975-76; lectr. Cook County Grad. Sch. Medicine, Chgo., 1976—; attending neurosurgeon Durham VA Hosp., 1968-72, 78—; mem. Nat. Adv. Coun. Nat. Inst. Neurol. Disorders and Stroke, 1989-92. Co-editor: Neurosurgery, 2d edit., 3 vols., 1996, Neurosurgery Updates I and II, 1990, 91, Neurosurgery Operative Atlas, 1991—, Principles of Neurosurgery, 1994; editor Clin. Neurosurgery, 1972-75; assoc. editor Surg. Neurology, 1975-76; founding editor Neurosurgery, 1977-82; mem. editl. bd. Jour. Neurosurgery, 1987-96, chmn., 1996-97; neurosurgery editor Key Neurology and Neurosurgery, 1993-96, Yr. Book of Neurology and Neurosurgery, 1994-97. Recipient Travel award Copenhagen, Nat. Inst. Neurol. Diseases and Blindness, Royal Australasian Coll. Surgeons, Found. lectr. Adelaide 1986. Fellow ACS (gov. 1996); mem. Congress Neurol. Surgeons (pres. 1979-80), Am. Assn. Neurol. Surgeons (treas. 1989-92), So. Neurosurg. Soc. (sec. 1988-91, pres. 1992-93), Soc. Neurol. Surgeons (v.p. 1995-96), Am. Bd. Neurol. Surgery (dir. 1991-97, chmn. 1996-97), Phi Beta Kappa, Alpha Omega Alpha. Democrat. Episcopalian. Avocations: medical writing and editing. Office: Duke U Med Ctr PO Box 3807 Durham NC 27710-3807

WILKINS, ROBERT PEARCE, lawyer; b. Jesup, Ga., Sept. 10, 1933; s. Ransom Little and Sarah (Pearce) W.; m. Rose Truesdale, Jan. 7, 1956; children: Robert Pearce, Chisolm Wallace (dec.), Sarah Ruth Weiss, Rose Anne Brooks. B.A., U. S.C., 1953, J.D., 1954; LL.M., Georgetown U., 1957. Bar: S.C. 1954; cert. mediator and arbitrator, S.C. Atty. Office Gen. Counsel, Sec. Army, Washington, 1956; trust officer First Nat. Bank S.C., Columbia, 1957-60; practice law Columbia, 1960-64; ptnr. McLain, Sherrill & Wilkins, Columbia, 1964-68, McKay, Sherrill, Walker, Townsend & Wilkins, Columbia, 1969-75; sole practice law Columbia and Lexington, S.C., 1975-88; of counsel Nelson, Mullins, Riley & Scarborough, Lexington, 1988—; pres. Sandlapper Press, Inc., 1967-72, pub. Sandlapper Mag. S.C., 1968-72; editor Sandlapper Mag. S.C., 1968-69, 89—; editor, pub. S.C. History Illustrated, 1970; pres. R.P.W. Pub. Corp.; mem., chmn. S.C. Splty. Adv. Bd. Estate Planning and Probate, 1982-85; lectr. in law U. S.C., 1971-78. Author: Draftin Wills and Trust Agreements in South Carolina, 1971, Drafting Wills and Trust Agreements in Michigan, 1978, Wills and Trust System (Arkansas), 1978, Drafting Wills and Trust Agreements: A Systems Approach, 1995, 3d edit., 1995, software edit.; (with others) Word Processing for a Law Office, 1979, also articles; editor: The Lawyer's Microcomputer, 1982-85, The Lawyer's PC, 1983-97, What a Lawyer Needs to Know to Buy and Use a Computer, 1984, The Perfect Lawyer, 1990-97, The Lawyers' Word, 1991, Shepard's Elder Care/Law Newsletter, 1991-95, Hot docs Toolbox, 1996-97, Drafting Wills and Trust Agreements Newsletter, 1997—. Del., Spl. Liaison Tax Com. Southeastern Region, 1967-70; exec. com. Richland County Rep. Com., 1960-64; sec.-treas. Richland County Rep. Club, 1960; bd. dirs. Ctrl. Tb-RD Assn.; trustee Sch. Dist. 1, Lexington County, S.C., 1971-78, sec., 1972-75, chmn., 1975-78; mem. S.C. Commn. on Higher Edn., 1978-80, S.C. Commn. on Lawyer Competence, 1980-82; bd. dirs. Crime Stoppers of the Midlands, 1983-85, RPW Learning Ctr., 1987-94, Mt. Hope Cemetary, 1991—, also v.p., 1992—; v.p. 11th cir. Alumni Coun. U. S.C., 1993-95, mem. awards com., 1995—; mem. commn. Riverbanks Zoo, 1986—, sec., 1991-95, chmn., 1995-96, vice-chmn., 1996—. With AUS, 1954-55. Recipient Compleat Lawyer award Law Sch. U. S.C., 1997. Fellow Am. Bar Found., Am. Coll. Trust and Estate Counsel (publs. com. 1984-87, bd. regents 1986-87, mem. tech. com. 1989—), Am. Coll. Tax Counsel, Coll. Law Practice Mgmt. (charter, trustee), S.C. Bar (tax coordinating com. 1968-70, chmn. legal econs. com. 1973-75, ho. of dels. 1978-80, editor S.C. Lawyer 1989-91, mem. alternative dispute resolution sect. 1993—), S.C. Bar Found. (life, bd. dirs. 1984-88, v.p. 1986-87, pres. 1987-88); mem. ABA (ho. of dels. 1986-87, chmn. valuation subcom., estate and gift tax com., taxation sect. 1967-73, vice chmn. svc. and assistance to law student div. com. gen. practice sect. 1971-72, vice chmn. corp. counsel com. gen. practice sect. 1972-74, editor econs. of law practice sect. legal econs. 1974-78, sec. 1977-78, vice chmn. 1978-79, chmn. 1980-81, mem. standing com. assn. comm. 1981-84, real property, probate and trust law, mem. publs. com. 1985-89, editor Probate and Property, 1986-89), Richland County Bar Assn. (chmn. probate sect. 1973-74, unauthorized practice of law com. 1976), Lexington County Bar (chmn. mediation com. 1994—), Columbia Jaycees (sec.-treas. 1958-59), Columbia Estate Planning Coun. (pres. 1964-65), Am. Y-Flyer Yacht Racing Assn. (area v.p. 1971, internat. dir. 1972-73), Omicron Delta Kappa, Sigma Chi. Clubs: Columbia Sailing (dir. 1968-71), Columbia Tip Off (dir. 1968-73), Columbia (pres. 1971-72). Home: PO Box 729 Lexington SC 29071-0729 Office: 334 Old Chapin Rd Lexington SC 29072-8801

WILKINS, ROGER CARSON, retired insurance company executive; b. Houlton, Maine, June 9, 1906; s. George W. and Amanda (Carson) W.; m. Evelyn McFadden, Aug. 23, 1933; 1 child, Susan J. Student, Ricker Classical Inst., 1919-24; B.A., U. Maine, 1929; LL.D., U. Hartford, 1966, Ricker Coll., 1970, Trinity Coll., 1973. With Travelers Ins. Companies, Hartford, from 1929; beginning as mgr. mortgage loan dept. for Travelers Ins. Companies, Tex., 1930; successively asst. mgr. home office, mgr., sec. v.p. Travelers Ins. Companies, 1953-65, sr. v.p., 1965-69, pres., 1969-71, chmn. bd., from 1971; also chief exec. officer; chmn. bd. Travelers Corp., 1971-73, chmn. exec. com., from 1974; former dir. Allis-Chalmers Corp., United Tech., Conn. Bank and Trust Co., Conn. Natural Gas Co.; former trustee Wells Fargo Mortgage Investor. Bd. dirs. U.S. C. of C. Corporator Hartford Hosp.; pres. Hartford Inst. Living; trustee St. Joseph Coll. Clubs: Hartford, Hartford Golf; Gulf Stream Golf (Fla.); Ekwanok Country (Manchester, Vt.).

WILKINS, TRACY DALE, microbiologist, educator; b. Sparkman, Ark., July 25, 1943; s. James Edward and Lena Belle (Wilcox) W. BS, U. Ark., 1965; PhD, U. Tex., 1969. Postdoctoral U. Ky. Med. Sch., Lexington, 1969-71; asst. prof. Va. Poly. Inst. State U., Blacksburg, 1972-75, assoc. prof., 1972-75, prof., 1980-85, head dept. anaerobic microbiology, 1985-93; dir. Fralin Biotechnology Ctr. Va. Tech., Blacksburg, Va., 1993—; pres. TechLab., Inc., 1990—. Contbr. articles to profl. jours.; patentee in field. NIH grantee, 1975—, Nat. Cancer Inst. grantee, 1979—. Mem. Am. Soc. Microbiology, Soc. Intestinal Microecology and Disease (pres. 1989-91). Avocations: flying, hunting, fishing. Office: Va Tech Fralin Biotechnology Ctr W Campus Dr Blacksburg VA 24061-0346

WILKINS, WILLIAM WALTER, JR., federal judge; b. Anderson, S.C., Mar. 29, 1942; s. William Walter and Evelyn Louise (Horton) W.; m. Carolyn Louise Adams, Aug. 15, 1964; children: Lauren, Lyn, Walt. B.A., Davidson Coll., 1964; J.D., U. S.C., 1967. Bar: S.C., 1967, U.S. Dist. Ct. S.C. 1967, U.S. Ct. Appeals (4th cir.) 1969, U.S. Supreme Ct. 1970. Law clk. to judge U.S. Ct. Appeals 4th Cir., 1969; legal asst. to U.S. Senator Strom Thurmond, 1970; ptnr. Wilkins & Wilkins, Greenville, S.C., 1971-75; solicitor 13th Jud. Cir., 1974-81; judge U.S. Dist. Ct., Greenville, 1981-86, U.S. Ct. Appeals (4th cir.), 1986—; lectr. Greenville Tech. Coll.; chmn. U.S. Sentencing Commn., 1985-94. Editor-in-chief S.C. Law Rev., 1967; contbr. articles to legal jours. Served with U.S. Army, 1967-69. Named Outstanding Grad. of Yr. U. S.C. Sch. Law, 1967. Mem. S.C. Bar Assn., Wig and Robe. Republican. Baptist. Office: US Cir Ct 4th Ct PO Box 10857 Greenville SC 29603-0857

WILKINSON, ALAN HERBERT, nephrologist, medical educator; b. Johannesburg, So. Africa, July 11, 1948; came to U.S., 1985; s. Raymond C. and Nonie (Levick) W.; m. Angelika A. E. Adami, Dec. 22, 1973; one child: Rebecca Kate Adami. BS in Physiology, Biochem., Philosophy, U. Witwatersrand, So. Africa, 1969, BS with honors in Biochemistry, 1970, MB, BCh, 1975. Visiting assoc. Dept. Internal Medicine U. Iowa, Iowa City, 1987-88; assoc. prof. of medicine UCLA Sch. Med., L.A., 1988-95, prof. med., 1995—; dir. clin. nephrology UCLA Dept. Med., L.A., 1988-93, dir. kidney and pancreas transplantation, 1993—; bd. dirs. UCLA Ctr. Health Schs., 1994-97. Contbr. articles to profl. jours. Mem. Nat. Kidney Fdn. Steering Comm., U.S. Transplant Games, L.A., 1992. Recipient Exceptional Svc. award, Nat. Kidney Fdn, S.C., 1992. Fellow Nat. Kidney Rsch.; mem. Am. Soc. Transplant Physicians, Internat. Nephrology Soc., Am. Soc. Nephrology, Royal Coll. Physicians (Eng.). Avocations: Ornithology. Office: UCLA Dept of Med Box 951693 200 Medical Plz Los Angeles CA 90095-1693

WILKINSON, ALBERT MIMS, JR., lawyer; b. Nashville, June 29, 1925; s. Albert Mims and Mary Nelle (Derryberry) W.; m. Edythe Bush, Mar. 27, 1953 (div.); children: William Terry, Elizabeth Ann, David Bush; m. Dolores Jean Attard, Oct. 22, 1971 (div.); 1 child, Mary Dolores. Student, Emory U., 1942-43; JD, U. Ga., 1949. Bar: Ga. 1948. Pvt. practice law Atlanta, 1950-85; gen. counsel GEC-Marconi Avionics Inc., Atlanta, 1985—; hon. legal adviser to Brit. Consul Gen. at Atlanta. Author: The Winning of the Revolutionary War in the South, 1976, The Rights of Unsecured Creditors-The Law in Georgia, 1979. Mem. DeKalb County Bd. Elections, 1966-72; chmn. 4th Congl. Dist. Republican Exec. Com., 1968-70, Ga. State Rep. Exec. Com., 1968-74; 1st vice chmn. Ga. Rep. Party, 1972-74, asst. gen. counsel, 1974-75; vice chmn., trustee Atlanta Counseling Center, Inc., 1960-83. Served with USCGR, 1943-46. Decorated Order Brit. Empire. Fellow Comml. Law Found.; mem. BA, Ga. Bar Assn., Atlanta Bar Assn., Ga. Soc. (pres. 1962-63), SAR, Southeastern Mem.'s Assn. (pres. 1960-61), Comml. Law League Am., Ga. Soc. Colonial Wars, Old Guard of Gate City Guard (comdt. 1986), N.C. Soc. of Cincinnati, Sphinx Club, Gridiron Club, Commerce Club, Civitan, Masons, Blue Key, Omicron Delta Kappa. Baptist. Home and Office: 333 Sky Vly Dillard GA 30537-9507 *By precept and example my parents pointed out the upward way in life, on a foundation of religious faith. "To do justly, to love mercy, to walk humbly with thy God." Later a beloved teacher taught the lines from Ulysses as he prepared to set sail, "To strive, to seek, to find and never yield." Their inspiration has continued throughout my life.*

WILKINSON, BEN, chancellor, evangelist, ministry organizer, writer; b. Gloster, Miss., July 6, 1932; s. Thomas Lamar and Evie (Quackenbush) W.; m. Mary Pittman; children: Evangeline Patricia Wilkinson Light, William Dwight, Manford Leighton, Glen Calvin. BA in Pub. Speaking, U. So. Miss., 1954; MDiv, Columbia Theol. Sem., Decatur, Ga., 1957, postgrad., 1964-65; DD, Whitefield Theol. Sem., 1992. Pastor Trinity Presbyn. Ch., Huntsville, Ala., 1955-62; pastor Ga. Ave Presbyn. Ch., Atlanta, 1962-66, evangelist, 1966—, exec. dir., 1973-95; founder, dir. Synod of the City-PEF Planting Bibl. Chs. in the Inner City, 1993—; with Presbyn. Evangelistic fellowship, Decatur, Ga.; bd. dirs. Atlanta Sch. Bibl. Studies, Westminster Bibl. Missions, World Harvest Missions, Lords Day Alliance; founder, dean, pres. Atlanta Sch. Bibl. Studies, 1971-85, chancelor, prof., 1986—. Editor: Come...Follow, 1973-95. Recipient John Calvin Internat. award The Christian Observer, 1995; Ben Wilkinson Sch. of Missions at Atlanta Sch. Bibl. Studies named in his honor, 1997. Avocations: sports, writing, reading, family life. Home: 214 Inman Dr Decatur GA 30030-3833 Office: Presbyn Evangelistic Fellowship Synod of the City 214 Inman Dr Decatur GA 30030-3833

WILKINSON, DAVID TODD, physics educator; b. Hillsdale, Mich., May 13, 1935; s. Harold Arba and Thelma Ellen (Todd) W.; m. Sharon E. Harper, June 14, 1958 (div. June 1979); children: Wendy, Kenton; m. Eunice H. Dowell, Oct. 13, 1984. BS in Engring. Physics, U. Mich., 1957, MS in Nuclear Engring., 1959, PhD in Physics, 1962. Lectr. physics U. Mich., Ann Arbor, 1962-63; instr. Princeton U., N.J., 1963-65; asst. prof. Princeton U., 1965-68, assoc. prof., 1968-71; prof. Princeton U., N.J., 1971—, chmn. dept., 1987-90; cons. NASA, mem. COBE satellite team. Contbr. articles to profl. jours. Alfred P. Sloane fellow, 1965-67, John Simon Guggenheim fellow, 1977-78. Mem. NAS. Office: Princeton U Jadwin Hall PO Box 708 Dept Princeton NJ 08544

WILKINSON, DONALD MCLEAN, investment counsel; b. Richmond, Va., Jan. 27, 1938; s. Donald McLean and Nancy Carroll (Ridenour) W.; m. Lucinda Pina Moles, July 6, 1963; children: Donald McLean III, Duncan Austin, Charles Carroll, Margot Carolina. BA in English, Va. Mil. Inst., Lexington, 1961; postgrad., U. Madrid, 1962; MBA, U. Va., 1996. Mgr. Keystone Internat. Fund, Boston, 1968-69; portfolio mgr. Tsai Mgmt. & Rsch., N.Y.C., 1968-69; v.p. New Ct. Capital, N.Y.C., 1970-72; chmn., CEO Wilkinson O'Grady & Co., Inc., N.Y.C., 1972—; chmn., chief exec. officer Helvetia Capital Corp., N.Y.C., 1987-93; pres., CEO The Swiss Helvetia Fund, Inc., N.Y.C., 1987-93. Confederate naval historian. Trustee The VMI Found. Inc., Lexington, Va., Darden Grad. Bus. Sch. Found., Charlottesville, Va.; dir. The Battle Abbey Coun. of Va. Hist. Soc. 1st lt. U.S. Army, 1962-64. Mem. Internat. Fin. Analysts Fedn., Assn. Investment Mgmt. and Rsch., N.Y. Soc. Security Analysts, Racquet and Tennis Club, Holland Lodge. Episcopalian. Home: 200 E 71st St New York NY 10021-5137 Office: Wilkinson O'Grady and Co 520 Madison Ave Fl 25 New York NY 10022-4213

WILKINSON, DORIS, medical sociology educator; b. Lexington, Ky., June 13, 1936; d. Howard Thomas and Regina Wilkinson. BA, U. Ky., 1958; MA, Case Western Res. U., 1960, PhD, 1968; MPH, Johns Hopkins U., 1985. Asst. prof. U. Ky., Lexington, 1968-70; assoc. prof., then prof. Macalester Coll., St. Paul, 1970-77; exec. assoc. Am. Sociol. Assn., Washington, 1977-80; prof. med. sociology Howard U., Washington, 1980-84; vis. prof. U. Va., 1984-85; prof. sociology U. Ky., Lexington, 1985—; chmn. panel women in sci. program NSF, Washington, 1976; rev. panelist Nat. Inst. Drug Abuse, Washington, 1978-79; mem. bd. sci. counselors Nat. Cancer Inst., Bethesda, Md., 1980-84; vis. scholar Harvard U., Cambridge, Mass., 1989-90, vis. prof., summers 1992, 93, 94; Rapoport vis. prof. social theory Smith Coll., summer 1995. Author: Wookbook for Introductory Sociology, 1968; editor: Black Revolt: Strategies of Protest, 1969; co-editor: The Black Male in America, 1977, Alternative Health Maintenance and Healing Systems, 1987, Race, Gender and the Life Cycle, 1991; social history photographic exhbn. "The African American Presence in Medicine" Harvard Med. Libr., 1991, Pearson Mus.- So. Ill. U. Med. Sch., 1992, N.J. Coll. Medicine and Dentistry, 1993, Louisville Mus. History and Sci., 1994, U. Cin. Med. Sch. Libr., 1994, Albert Einstein Coll. of Medicine, 1995, Midway Coll., 1996; contbr. articles to profl. jours. Bd. overseers Case Western Res. U., Cleve., 1982-87; apptd. Ky. Commn. on Women, 1993-96. Recipient Pub. Humanities award U. Ky., 1990, Midway Coll. Women's History Month award, 1991, Gt. Tchr. award Nat. Alumni Assn. U. Ky., Disting. Scholar award Assn. Black Sociologists, 1993; inducted into Hall of Disting. Alumni, U. Ky., 1989; fellow Woodrow Wilson Found., 1959-61, Ford Found., 1989-90; grantee Social Sci. Rsch. Coun., 1975, Nat. Inst. Edn., 1978-80, Nat. Cancer Inst., 1986-88, Ky. Humanities Coun., 1988, Am. Coun. Learned Soc., 1989-90, NEH, 1991; Disting. Prof. in Coll. Arts and Scis., U. Ky., 1992-93. Mem. So. Sociol. Soc. (honors com. 1993-94), Am. Sociol. Assn. (exec. assoc., budget com. 1985-88, v.p. 1991-92, mem. coun. 1994—, Dubois-Johnson-Frazier award 1988), D.C. Sociol. Soc. (pres. 1982-83), Soc. for Study of Social Problems (v.p. 1984-85, pres. 1987-88), Ea. Sociol. Soc. (v.p. 1983-84, pres. 1992-93, I. Peter Gellman award 1987), Phi Beta Kappa (valedictorian), Alpha Kappa Delta. Unitarian.

WILKINSON, EDWARD ANDERSON, JR., retired naval officer, business executive; b. Selma, Ala., Sept. 21, 1933; s. Edward Anderson and Alice Margaret (Moorer) W.; m. Barbara Anne Parker, June 4, 1955 (dec. June 1991); children: Daryl Edward, Daniel Bryan, Edward Anderson III, David Park; m. Sondra Marie Moore, Oct. 2, 1994. B.S., U.S. Naval Acad., 1955; M.S. in Mech. Engring., 1964; grad., Nat. War Coll., 1972. Commd. ensign U.S. Navy, 1955, advanced through grades to rear adm., 1979; dir. Anti-Submarine Warfare Systems Program Office, Washington, 1978-79; dep. dir. Def. Mapping Agy., Washington, 1979-81; cmdr. Patrol Wings, U.S. Atlanta Fleet, Brunswick, Maine, 1981-83; dir. Def. Mapping Agy., Washington, 1983-85; ret., 1985; exec. v.p. Internat. Fed. Systems Intergraph Corp., Reston, Va. Decorated Legion of Merit, D.S.M. (Dept. Def.). Methodist. Home: 1555 Regatta Ln Reston VA 20194 Office: Intergraph Corp Reston VA

WILKINSON, EUGENE PARKS, nuclear engineer; b. Long Beach, Calif., Aug. 10, 1918; s. Dennis William and Daisy Amelia (Parks) W.; m. Janice Edith Thuli, Mar. 28, 1942; children: Dennis Eugene, Stephen James, Marian Lynn, Rodney David. AB in Chemistry, San Diego State U., 1938. Instr. chemistry San Diego State U., 1938-39; commd. ensign U.S. Navy, 1940, advanced through grades to vice adm., 1970; served various locations including 1st comdg. officer USS Nautilus (1st nuclear-powered submarine), 1953-57; 1st comdg. officer USS Long Beach, 1959-63, 1st nuclear-powered surface ship; ret., 1974; exec. v.p. Data Design Labs., Cucamonga, Calif., 1977-80; pres., chief exec. officer Inst. Nuclear Power Ops., Atlanta, 1980-84, pres. emeritus, 1984—; bd. dirs. Data Design Labs., Advanced Resource Devel. Environ. Inc.; chmn. bd. dirs. MDM Engring. Corp., Laguna Niguel, Calif. Decorated Legion of Merit, Silver Star, D.S.M. with three oak leaf clusters, others, Second Order Sacred Treasure Japan; recipient George Westinghouse Gold medal ASME, 1983, Oliver Townsend medal Atomic Indsl. Forum, 1984, Gold medal Uranium Inst., 1989. Mem. Am. Soc. Naval Engrs., Am. Nuclear Soc. (Henry DeWolf Smyth Nuclear Statesman medal 1994), Navy League, Submarine League, Nat. Acad. Engring. Avocations: tennis, bridge. Home: 1449 Crest Rd Del Mar CA 92014-2530

WILKINSON, GRANT ROBERT, pharmacology educator; b. Derby, U.K., Aug. 27, 1941; came to U.S., 1966; s. Arthur Henry and Gwendoline Mary (Fox) W.; m. Margaret Kay Fletcher, Aug. 8, 1964 (div. Apr. 1978); children: Grant Russell, Nicole Estelle; m. June Zoe Dass, July 12, 1978 (div. Jan. 1995); children: Tracey Allyson, Erika Lynne. BSc in Pharmacy, U. Manchester, 1963; PhD, U. London, 1966. Postdoctoral fellow U. Calif., San Francisco, 1966-68; asst. prof. U. Ky., Lexington, 1968-71; asst. prof. Vanderbilt U., Nashville, 1971-73, assoc. prof., 1973-78, prof. of pharmacology, 1978—; cons. NIH, Bethesda, Md., 1972—, NRC, NAS, Washington, 1986-87, 92-94, also pharm. industry: mem. editorial adv. bd. various jours. in field. Author: Drug Metabolism and Disposition: Considerations in Clinical Pharmacology, 1985; contbr. over 200 articles and revs. to profl. publs. Recipient NIH Merit award, 1991. Fellow AAAS (sect. chmn. 1986-87), Am. Assn. Pharm. Sci.; mem. Am. Soc. for Pharmacology and Exptl. Therapeutics, Am. Soc. Clin. Pharmacology and Therapeutics (Rawls-Palmer Progress in Medicine award 1996). Achievements include research on drug metabolism in humans, effects of disease-states, pharmacokinetics, clinical pharmacology. Office: Vanderbilt U Dept Pharmacology Nashville TN 37232-6600

WILKINSON, HAROLD ARTHUR, neurosurgeon; b. Wake Forest, N.C., June 17, 1935; s. Charles T. and Ursula (Bernstein) W.; m. Alice D. Speas, June 22, 1957; children: Arthur, Edward. BS, Wake Forest Coll., 1955; MD, Duke U., 1959, PhD, 1962. NIH postdoctoral rsch. fellow Duke U. Med.

Ctr., Durham, N.C., 1959-61, intern, 1961-62; resident in neurosurgery Mass. Gen. Hosp., Boston, 1962-66; mem. faculty Harvard U. Med. Ctr., Cambridge, Mass., 1966-78; mem. staff Boston City Hosp., 1966-71, Beth Israel Hosp., Boston, 1971-78; prof. neurosurgery, chmn. div. U. Mass. Med. Ctr., Worcester, 1979—, prof. anatomy cell biology program, 1985—, residency program dir., 1991—. Contbr. articles to profl. jours.; inventor intracranial pressure monitoring cup catheter. Med. Found. fellow, 1966-69. Mem. AMA, ACS, Am. Assn. Neurol. Surgery, Congress of Neurosurgery, New Eng. Neurol. Soc. Office: U Mass Med Ctr Div Neurosurgery 55 Lake Ave N Worcester MA 01655-0002

WILKINSON, HARRY EDWARD, management educator and consultant; b. Richmond Heights, Mo., June 30, 1930; s. Harry Edward and Virginia Flo (Shelton) W.; m. Sara Beth Kikendall, Aug. 30, 1958; children: Linda Beth, Cheryl Susan. BA in Physics, Princeton U., 1952; MBA, Washington U., St. Louis, 1957; D Bus. Adminstrn., Harvard U., 1960. Lic. psychologist, Mass. Staff engr. Southwestern Bell Tel. Co., St. Louis, 1954-57; traffic engr. New Eng. Tel. & Telegraph Co., Boston, 1957-60; sr. mgmt. cons. Harbridge House Inc., Boston, 1961-65; dean bus. adminstrn., dir. Mgmt. Inst., Northeastern U., Boston, 1965-67; pres., chmn. bd. Univ. Affiliates Inc., North Port, Fla., 1967—; vis. prof. mgmt. Rice U., Houston, 1990-94, dir. office of exec. devel., 1994—; cons. to various industries and govt., 1961—. Author: Influencing People in Organizations, 1993; contbr. articles to mgmt. jours. Lt. (j.g.) USN, 1952-54, Korea. Mem. APA, Acad. Mgmt., N.Am. Case Rsch. Assn., S.W. Case Rsch. Assn., Harvard Bus. Sch. Assn. Office: Jones Grad Sch Rice U 6100 Main St Houston TX 77005-1827

WILKINSON, HARRY J., retired technical company executive; b. Phila., Nov. 15, 1937; s. Frank and Annie Wilkinson; children: Tracey, Todd, Betsey. BS in Indsl. Engring., Temple U., 1965. Mktg. mgr. aerospace div. SPS Techs., Jenkintown, Pa., 1969-75; mng. dir. Unbrako, Ltd. div. SPS Techs., Coventry, Eng., 1975-79; pres. Unbrako, Ltd. div. SPS Techs., Jenkintown, 1979-82; pres. aerospace and indsl. products div., group v.p. domestic ops. SPS Techs., Newtown, Pa., 1984-86, pres., chief operating officer, 1986-97, also bd. dirs.; bd. dirs. Drexelbrook Engring., Horsham, Pa., Flexible Cirs., Inc., Warrington, Pa. Served to lt. U.S. Army, 1957-59. Office: SPS Technologies 301 Highland Ave Jenkintown PA 19046-2630

WILKINSON, JAMES ALLAN, lawyer, healthcare executive; b. Cumberland, Md., Feb. 10, 1945; s. John Robinson and Dorothy Jane (Kelley) W.; m. Elizabeth Susanne Quinlan, Apr. 14, 1973; 1 child, Kathryn Barrett. BS in Fgn. Service, Georgetown U., 1967; JD, Duquesne U., 1978. Bar: Pa., U.S. Dist. Ct. (we. dist.) Pa. Legis. analyst Office of Mgmt. and Budget, Washington, 1972-73; dep. exec. sec. Cost of Living Coun., Washington, 1973-74; sr. fin. analyst U.S. Steel Corp., Pitts., 1974-82; ptnr. Buchanan Ingersoll, Pitts., 1982-88; CFO, gen. counsel Meritcare, Sewickley, Pa., 1988—; sr. v.p. Culwell Health Inc., 1991—; adj. prof. U. Pitts. Sch. Law, 1988-91. Author: Financing and Refinancing Under Prospective Payment, 1985; contbr. articles to profl. jours. Chmn. Oversight Com. on Organ Transplantation, Pitts., 1986—; sec.-treas. bd. dirs. Pitts. Symphony Soc., 1986—, Western Pa. Com. of Prevention of Child Abuse, 1987-90, Comprehensive Safety Compliance, 1988-91, Buchanan Ingersoll Profl. corp., 1988-90, Parental Stress Ctr., 1990-94; sec. Ross Mountain Club, 1995—. Mem. ABA, Am. Acad. Hosp. Attys., Am. Soc. of Law and Medicine, Nat. Assn. of Bond Lawyers, Nat. Health Lawyers Assn., Healthcare Fin. Mgrs. Assn., Audubon Soc. Southwestern Pa. (treas. 1996—), Duquesne Club, Pitts. Athletic Assn. Republican. Episcopalian. Home: 1005 Elmhurst Rd Pittsburgh PA 15215-1819 Office: Meritcare Inc 400 Broad St Ste 203 Sewickley PA 15143-1500

WILKINSON, JAMES HARVIE, III, federal judge; b. N.Y.C., Sept. 29, 1944; s. James Harvie and Letitia (Nelson) W.; m. Lossie Grist Noell, June 30, 1973; children: James Nelson, Porter Noell. B.A., Yale U., 1963-67; J.D., U. Va., 1972. Bar: Va. 1972. Law clk. to U.S. Supreme Ct. Justice Lewis F. Powell, Jr., Washington, 1972-73; asst. prof. law U. Va., 1973-75, assoc. prof., 1975-78; editor Norfolk (Va.) Virginian-Pilot, 1978-81; prof. law U. Va., 1981-82, 83-84; dep. asst. atty. gen. Civil Rights div. Dept. Justice, 1982-83; judge U.S. Ct. Appeals (4th cir.), 1984—, chief judge, 1996—. Author: Harry Byrd and the Changing Face of Virginia Politics, 1968, Serving Justice: A Supreme Court Clerk's View, 1974, From Brown to Bakke: The Supreme Court and School Integration, 1979. Bd. visitors U. Va., 1970-73; Republican candidate for Congress from 3d Dist. Va., 1970. Served with U.S. Army, 1968-69. Mem. Va. State Bar, Va. Bar Assn., Am. Law Inst. Episcopalian. Home: 1713 Yorktown Dr Charlottesville VA 22901-3035 Office: US Ct Appeals 255 W Main St Ste 230 Charlottesville VA 22902-5058

WILKINSON, JAMES SPENCER, general physician; b. Wake Forest, N.C., Sept. 26, 1974; s. Robert Watson and Ella Houston (Holding) W.; m. Eva Elizabeth Hitchner, June 21, 1939; children Carol Lynn, James Spencer Jr. MD, U. Pa., 1938, MSc, 1949. Diplomate Am. Bd. Dermatology. Intern Jersey City Med. Ctr., 1939-40, Marine Hosp., Boston, 1940-41; fellow U. Pa. Grad. Sch., Phila., 1946-49; pvt. practice James Wilkinson MD, PA, Raleigh, N.C., 1949—. Capt. U.S. Air Force, 1942-46. Mem. AMA, Raleigh Acad. Medicine, Assn. Mil. Surgeons U.S., Wake County Med. Soc., N.C. Med. Soc., Air Force Assn. Avocations: sailing, hunting, fishing. Office: James S Wilkinson MD PA 903 W Peace St Raleigh NC 27605-1417

WILKINSON, JOHN HART, lawyer; b. Newton, Mass., Dec. 31, 1940; s. Roger Melvin and Margaret (Carter) W.; children: Heather, Carter. BA, Williams Coll., 1962; LLB, Fordham U., 1965. Bar: N.Y. 1965, U.S. Dist. Ct. (so. and ea. dists.) 1968, U.S. Ct. Appeals (2d cir.) 1981, U.S. Ct. Appeals (11th cir.) 1982, U.S. Ct. Appeals (3d cir.) 1984, U.S. Ct. Appeals (5th cir.) 1987. Assoc. Donovan, Leisure, Newton & Irvine, N.Y.C., 1965, 67-73, ptnr., 1973—, editor, contbg. author to firm's ADR Practice Book, 1990; law clk. to presiding justice U.S. Dist. Ct. N.Y. (so. dist.), 1967-68; frequent speaker on litigation. Contbr. numerous articles to profl. jours. Bd. dirs., pres. Childfind of Am., Inc., 1993-94; v.p. bd. dirs. Pelham (N.Y. Family Svc., 1982-85; vol. learning disabled children Chelsea Neighborhood, N.Y.C., 1965-67; bd. dirs. Catskill Ctr. for Conservation and Devel., 1993—. Recipient Am. Jurisprudence award Fordham U. Mem. ABA (alt. dispute resolution com. 1989—), N.Y. State Bar Assn. (alt. dispute resolution com. 1989-93), Fed. Bar Coun., Assn. Bar City N.Y. (profl. responsibility com. 1987-89, pub. assistance com. 1991-94). Avocation: woodworking, flyfishing, biking, camping. Office: Donovan Leisure Newton & Irvine 30 Rockefeller Plz New York NY 10112

WILKINSON, LOUISE CHERRY, psychology educator, dean; b. Phila., May 15, 1948; m. Alex Cherry Wilkinson; 1 child, Jennifer Cherry. B.A. magna cum laude with honors, Oberlin Coll., 1970; Ed.M., Ed.D., Harvard U., 1974. Prof., chmn. dept. ednl. psychology U. Wis., Madison, 1976-85; prof., exec. officer Grad. Sch. Ph.D. Program CUNY, N.Y.C., 1984-86; prof. II, dean Grad. Sch. Edn. Rutgers U., 1986—; mem. Nat. rev. bd. Nat. Inst. Edn., 1977, 85, 87; cons. Nat. Ctr. for Bilingual Rsch., 1982, 84, U.S. Dept. Edn., 1995-96; adv. bd. Nat. Reading Rsch. Ctr., 1992—. Co-author: Communicating for Learning, 1991; editor: Communicating in Classroom, 1982, Social Context of Instruction, 1984, Gender Influences in the Classroom; mem. editorial bds. and contbr. articles to profl. jours. Fellow Am. Psychol. Assn., Am. Psychol. Soc.; mem. Internat. Assn. for Study Child Lang., Am. Ednl. Rsch. Assn. (v.p. 1990-92, program chair 1997). Home: 3 Andrews Ln Princeton NJ 08540-7633 Office: Rutgers U Grad Sch Edn 10 Seminary Pl New Brunswick NJ 08901-1108

WILKINSON, MICHAEL KENNERLY, physicist; b. Palatka, Fla., Feb. 9, 1921; s. Robert Ridley and Henrietta Lucille (Kennerly) W.; m. Virginia Sleap, June 18, 1944; children: Robert Warren, William Michael, Lucille Elizabeth. B.S., The Citadel, 1942; Ph.D., M.I.T., 1950. Research asso. M.I.T., 1948-50; research scientist Oak Ridge Nat. Lab., 1950-64, assoc. dir. Solid State div., 1964-72, dir. Solid State div., 1972-86, sr. advisor Solid State div., 1986-91; cons., 1991—; vis. prof. physics Ga. Inst. Tech., 1961-62, adj. prof., 1962-91; mem. adv. com. div. materials research NSF.; mem. council on materials sci. Dept. Energy. Contbr. articles on solid state physics to profl. jours. Served with AUS, 1942-46. Fellow Am. Phys. Soc., AAAS; mem. Am. Crystallog. Assn., Tenn. Acad. Sci., Sigma Xi, Sigma Pi Sigma. Episcopalian. Home: 124 Morningside Dr Oak Ridge TN 37830-8320 Office: Oak Ridge Nat Lab Oak Ridge TN 37831

WILKINSON, RALPH RUSSELL, biochemistry educator, toxicologist; b. Portland, Oreg., Feb. 20, 1930; s. Tracy Chandler and Lavern (Russell) W.; m. Evelyn Marie Wickman, Aug. 5, 1956. BA, Reed Coll., 1953; PhD, U. Oreg., 1962; MBA, U. Mo., Kansas City, 1974. Rsch. chemist VA Hosp., Kansas City, Mo., 1973-74; sr. rsch. chemist Midwest Rsch. Inst., Kansas City, 1975-84; prof. Rockhurst Coll., Kansas City, 1985-86, Cleve. Chiropractic Coll., Kansas City, 1987—; cons. in biochemistry, toxicology, environ. impact, tech. assessment, Kansas City, 1984—. Author: (book) Neurotoxins and Neurobiological Function, 1987; contbr. articles to profl. jours. Mem. Southtown Coun., Kansas City, Mo., 1989—, Spina Bifida Assn. Am., Kansas City, 1989—. Recipient NSF fellowship, 1959-60. Mem. Am. Chem. Soc., Sigma Xi. Avocations: travel, history, biography, music, antiques. Home: 7911 Charlotte St Kansas City MO 64131-2175

WILKINSON, REBECCA ELAINE, human resources application specialist; b. Dallas, Nov. 11, 1960; d. John Cephas and Mary Magdeline (Rhea) Bishop; m. Billy Don Wilkinson, July 31, 1982; children: Eric Tyler, Kristen Rhea. BEd, U. Dallas, 1982, MBA, 1995. Adminstrv. asst. IBM, Irving, Tex., 1982-85; equal opportunity coord. IBM, Irving, 1985-90; human resources data analyst IBM, Roanoke, Tex., 1990-94; sr. human resources/payroll application specialist Westinghouse Security Systems, Irving, 1994—; team leader finance & adminstrv. sys. Westinghouse Security Sys., 1996-97; cons. Cambridge Technology Ptnrs., 1997—. Mem. NOW, Greenpeace, Sigma Iota Epsilon. Democrat. Episcopalian. Avocations: needlework, rollerblading, reading, golfing, bowling.

WILKINSON, ROBERT EUGENE, plant physiologist; b. Oilton, Okla., Oct. 24, 1926; s. Olney Samuel and Grace Elma (Curry) W.; m. Evelyn Dolores Smith, Jan. 31, 1951; children: Olney Thomas, Randall David. BS in Botany, U. Ill., Champaign, 1950; MS in Plant Physiology, U. Okla., 1952; PhD in Plant Physiology, U. Calif., Davis, 1956. Plant physiologist USDA, Clarkdale, Ark., 1957-62, Los Lunas, N.Mex., 1962-65; assoc. agronomist U. Ga. Agrl. Ext. Sta., 1965-74; agronomist U. Ga., 1974-94; ret., 1994; cons. U. Sao Paulo, Piricicaba, Brazil, 1978. Contbr. articles to profl. jours. With USNR, 1944-45; to lt. USAFR, 1950-58. Sr. Fulbright grantee, Turku, Finland, 1974-75, Teaching Rsch. Fulbright grantee, Nova Sad, Yugoslavia, 1975. Fellow Am. Inst. Chemistry; mem. Weeds Sci. Soc. Am., Am. Soc. Plant Physiologists, Kiwanis. Home: 655 Laura Dr Griffin GA 30224-5315

WILKINSON, RONALD STERNE, science administrator, environmentalist, historian; b. Chgo., Feb. 16, 1934; s. Maurice Sterne and Florence Marie (Colby) W.; m. Karen Ensinger, June 14, 1969 (div. 1976). BA, Mich. State U., 1960, PhD, 1969. Chemist Berry Bros., Detroit, 1955-57; mem. faculty Mich. State U., East Lansing, 1960-70; sci. specialist Libr. of Congress, Washington, 1970-90, sr. sci. specialist, 1990—; assoc. in bibliography Am. Mus. Nat. History, N.Y.C., 1976-82; trustee William T. Hornaday Conservation Trust, La Jolla, Calif., 1989—. Author: John Winthrop, Jr. and the Origins of American Chemistry, 1969, Benjamin Wilkes, The British Aurelian, 1982; editor-in-chief The Mich. Entomologist (later The Great Lakes Entomologist), 1966-71; contbr. more than 160 articles to sci. and history of sci. publs. Ryder scholar Mich. State U., U. London, 1960, Woodrow Wilson Found. fellow Harvard U., 1960-61, Fulbright scholar Univ. Coll., London, 1965-66. Fellow Linnean Soc. London, Geol. Soc. London, Royal Entomol. Soc. London; mem. Grolier Club (N.Y.C., asst. editor 1979-82). Democrat. Home: 228 9th St NE Washington DC 20002-6110 Office: Libr of Congress Washington DC 20540

WILKINSON, SIGNE, cartoonist; b. Phila.. BA in English, 1972. Reporter West Chester (Pa.) Daily Local News, Academy of Natural Scis., Phila.; freelance cartoonist Phila. and N.Y. publs.; cartoonist San Jose (Calif.) Mercury News, 1982-85, Phila. Daily News, 1985—. Contbr. Organic Gardening mag., Univ. Barge Club News. Recipient Pulitzer Prize for editorial cartooning, 1992. Mem. Assn. Am. Editl. Cartoonists (pres. 1994-95). Avocation: gardening. Office: Phila Daily News PO Box 8263 400 N Broad St Philadelphia PA 19101

WILKINSON, STANLEY RALPH, agronomist; b. West Amboy, N.Y., Mar. 28, 1931; s. Ralph Ward and Eva Goldie (Perkins) W.; m. Jean Saye; children: Rachael, Stanley R. Jr., Augusta J. BS, Cornell U., 1954; MS, Purdue U., 1956, PhD, 1961. Soil scientist U.S. Regional Pasture Rsch. Lab., University Park, Pa., 1960-64, So. Piedmont Conservation Rsch. Ctr., Watkinsville, Ga., 1965—. Past advance chmn. Boy Scouts Am. Served to capt. USAF, 1955-57. Recipient 3d prize Freedoms Found., 1956. Fellow Soil and Water Conservation Soc. Am., Am. Soc. Agronomy; mem. Am. Soc. Agronomy, Soil Sci. Soc. Am., Soil and Water Conservation Soc., Sigma Xi. Methodist. Contbr. 18 chpts. to books and 140 tech. articles to profl. jours.

WILKINSON, WARREN SCRIPPS, manufacturing company executive; b. Detroit, Feb. 2, 1920; s. Almadus DeGrasse and Harriet Gertrude (Whitcomb) W.; m. Joan Todd, June 14, 1941; m. Mireille De Bary, Dec. 17, 1966. Grad., Hotchkiss Sch., Lakeville, Conn., 1937; BS in Math, Harvard U., 1941; student, Calif. Inst. Tech., 1941-42. With U.S. Rubber Co., Detroit, 1942-43, Hanson Van Winkle-Munning Co., Matawan, N.J., 1946-64; pres. Hanson Van Winkle-Munning Co., 1961-64; v.p., gen. mgr. Hanson-Van Winkle-Munning div. M & Chems. Inc., 1964-66; chmn. RPI Designs, Marlette, Mich., 1966—. Pres. Detroit Hist. Commn., 1994; mem. overseer's com. on univ. resources Harvard U. John Harvard fellow, 1946. Home: 2 Woodland Pl Grosse Pointe MI 48230-1920

WILKINSON, WILLIAM DURFEE, museum director; b. Utica, N.Y., Sept. 2, 1924; s. Winfred Durfee and Edith (Lockwood) W.; m. Dorothy May Spencer, Apr. 2, 1966. B.S., Harvard U., 1949; postgrad., Munson Inst. Am. Maritime History, Mystic, Conn., 1961-62. Group ins. underwriter Home Life Ins. Co., N.Y.C., 1949-59; adminstr., marine curator Mus. City of New York, 1960-63; registrar Met. Mus. Art, N.Y.C., 1963-71; assoc. dir. Mariners Mus., Newport News, Va., 1971-73, dir., 1973-94, dir. emeritus, 1994—; ret., 1994. Mem. Sec. of Navy Adv. Com. on Naval History, 1986-88, 91-96, chmn. 1991-95; mem. Exec. Coun. Internat. Congress Maritime Mus., 1989-93; bd. dirs. Coun. Am. Maritime Mus., 1975-79, pres., 1978-79; bd. dirs. Mus. Computer Network, Inc., 1972-83, Assn. for Rescue at Sea, Inc., 1977—, Coast Guard Acad. Found., Inc., 1981-87, U.S. Life Saving Svc. Heritage Assn., 1995—. With C.E. AUS, 1943-45. Mem. Am. Assn. Mus., Nat. Trust Hist. Preservation (maritime preservation com. 1978-80), Explorers Club. Home and Office: 747 W Springfield Rd Springfield PA 19064-1337

WILKINSON, WILLIAM SHERWOOD, lawyer; b. Williston, N.D., Sept. 6, 1933; s. John Thomas and Evelyn (Landon) W.; m. Carol Ann Burns, Aug. 20, 1960; children—Leslie Ann, Richard Sherwood, Greta Dinnen. B.S. in Bus, U. Idaho, 1955; J.D., U. Denver, 1960. Bar: Colo. bar 1960, Mich. bar 1966. Practiced in Canon City, Colo., 1960-66; asst. dist. atty. 11th Jud. Dist., Colo., 1961-65; gen. counsel, sec. Mich. Farm Bur. Family Cos., Lansing, 1966-96; lectr. Pre-Parole Release Center, Colo. State Penitentiary, 1961-65; instr. adult edn., Canon City, 1965; counsel Canon City Recreation Dist., 1964-65. Mem. lay adv. bd. St. Thomas More Hosp., Canon City, 1963-66; Del., county, dist. and congl. convs. Republican party, 1964. Served to capt. USAF, 1955-58. Recipient Cmty. Disting. Svc. award Canon City Jr. C. of C., 1964. Mem. ABA, Colo. Bar Assn., Mich. Bar Assn., Am. Judicature Soc., Am. Corp. Counsel Assn., Nat. Coun. Farmer Coops. (legal, tax and acctg. com.), Phi Delta Phi, Tau Kappa Epsilon. Methodist (lay leader, mem. ch. ofcl. bd.). Home: 1707 Foxcroft Rd East Lansing MI 48823-2131

WILKNISS, PETER E., foundation administrator, researcher; b. Berlin, Germany, Sept. 28, 1934; U.S. citizen.; s. Fritz and Else (Stueber) W.; m. Edith P. Koester, May 25, 1963; children: Peter F., Sandra M. MS in Chemistry, Tech. U., Munich, Ger., 1958, PhD in Radio and Nuclear Chemistry, 1961. Rsch. chemist, radiological protection officer U.S. Naval Ordnance Sta., 1961-64, head nuclear chemistry branch, 1964-66; rsch. oceanographer U.S. Naval Rsch. Lab., 1966-70, head chemical oceanography branch, 1970-75; mgr. Nat. Ctr. Atmospheric Rsch. Program NSF, Washington, 1975-76, mgr. Internat. Phase of Ocean Drilling/Ocean Sediment Coring Program, 1976-80, mgr. Ocean Drilling Project Team, AAEO Directorate, 1980, dir. divsn. Ocean Drilling Programs, 1980-81, sr. sci. assoc. Office of Dir., 1981-82, dep. asst. dir. Sci, Tech., Internat. Affairs Directorate, 1982-84, dir. divsn. Polar Programs, 1984-93, sr. sci. assoc. Geoscis. Directorate, 1993-96; pres. Polar Kybernetes Internat. LLC, Fairbanks, Alaska, 1997—; liaison mem. NRC, NAS, Marine Bd., 1978-81, Polar Rsch. Bd., 1984-93; mem. atmospheric chemistry and radioactivity com. Am. Meteorological Soc., 1975-78; mem. interagy. com. atmospheric scis., 1975-76, space station adv. com., NASA, 1988-93. Contbr. 61 articles to sci., tech. jours., USN reports; over 100 formal presentations nat., internat. sci. confs., symposia, meetings; participant 16 nat., internat. workshops. Presdl. citation AIA, 1993; Wilkniss mountain Antarctic named in his honor Sec. Interior, U.S. Bd. Geographic Names, 1992. Mem. AAAS, Am. Geophysical Union, Antarctican Soc., Sigma Xi. Episcopalian. Avocations: soccer, swimming, skiing. Home: 8814 Stockton Pky Alexandria VA 22308-2360 Office: Polar Kybernetes Internat PO Box 82900 Fairbanks AK 99708

WILKS, DUFFY JEAN, counselor, educator; b. Spur, Tex., Feb. 15, 1936; d. Rube Lee Jay and Elizabeth Audeen (Simmons) Austin; children: Vicki Ratheal, Juli Ratheal, Randy Ratheal, Rodney Ratheal; m. W.B. Wilks, Oct. 22, 1986. BA in Psychology, Tex. Tech. U., 1981, MEd in Psychology, 1984, EdD in Ednl. Psychology, 1995. Cert. substance abuse counsleor; lic. profl. counselor, Tex.; lic. marriage and family therapist, Tex. Editor writer Floydada (Tex.) newspaper, 1972-80; probation officer Adult/Juvenile Probation, Lubbock, Tex., 1982-86; pvt. practice Horseshoe Bay, Tex., 1986—; prof. Western Tex. Coll., Snyder. Mem. ACA, Tex. Assn. Counseling and Devel. (editorial bd. jour. 1989-91, author revs., editor Disting. Svc. award 1991), Tex. Counseling Assn., Tex. C.C. Tchrs. Assn., Internat. Assn. for Addictions and Offender Counselors. Avocations: playing piano, writing, researching.

WILKS, LARRY DEAN, lawyer; b. Columbia, S.C., Jan. 8, 1955; s. Ray Dean and Jean (Garrett) W.; m. Jan Elizabeth McIllwain, May 2,1981; children: John Ray, Adam Garrett. BS, U. Tenn., 1977, JD, 1980. Bar: Tenn. 1981, U.S. Dist. Ct. (mid. dist.) Tenn. 1981, U.S. Supreme Ct. 1986, U.S. Ct. Appeals (6th cir.) 1993, U.S. Dist. Ct. (we. dist.) Tenn. 1996. Assoc. Mayo & Norris, Nashville, 1981-82; sole practice Springfield, Tenn., 1982-84; ptnr. Walton, Jones & Wilks, 1984, Jones & Wilks, 1984-89. Chmn. Dem. Orgn. Robertson County Tenn., 1986-93. Fellow Tenn. Bar Found.; mem. ABA, ATLA, Tenn. Bar Assn. (assoc. gen. counsel 1991-94, gen. counsel 1994—, bd. profl. responsibility 1993—, bd. govs. 1991—, young lawyers divsn. lifetime fellow), Tenn. Assn. Criminal Def. Lawyers, Tenn. Trial Lawyers Assn., Robertson County Bar Assn. (pres. 1993-96), Nat. Assn. Criminal Def. Laywers, Tenn. Young Lawyers Conf. (bd. dirs. 1987, editor quar. newsletter 1987-88, Mid. Tenn. v.p. 1988-89, v.p. 1989-90, pres.-elect 1990-91, pres. 1991-92). Methodist. Office: 509 W Court Sq Springfield TN 37172-2413

WILKS, R(ALPH) KENNETH, JR., state official; b. Springfield, Mo., Sept. 25, 1956; s. Ralph Kenneth and Virginia Lacy (Phillips) W.; m. Melinda Sue Maxwell, July 21, 1984. BA, Evangel Coll., 1978; MPA, U. Mo., Kansas City, 1980. Adminstrv. aide City of Leawood (Kans.), 1979-80; theater mgr. Crown Cinema Corp., Jefferson City, Mo., 1981-84; rsch. analyst II Mo. Dept. Social Svcs., Jefferson City, 1984-86, planner II, 1986-93; planner III Mo. Dept. Corrections, Jefferson City, 1993—; legis. intern U.S. Sen. Robert Dole, Washington, 1978; lectr. in field. Contbr. articles to profl. jours. Mem. Am. Soc. Pub. Adminstrn., Am. Corrections Assn., Mo. Inst. Pub. Adminstrn., Social Sci. Honor Soc. (life). Avocations: photography, biking, hiking, gardening, reading. Home: 4802 Rainbow Hills Rd Jefferson City MO 65109-0277

WILKS, WILLIAM LEE, retired educator, dean; b. Ft. Wayne, Ind., Nov. 12, 1931; s. Lee and Mildred (Roberts) W.; children: Sara P., Margaret E., Amy P., David E., Ariel J., Cordelia L. BA, Yale U., 1952; JD, U. Mich., 1955; LLM, George Washington U., 1973; LLD, Dickinson Sch. Law, 1988. Bar: Ind. 1955, Mich. 1955. With Hunt, Suedhoff & Wilks, Ft. Wayne, 1957-70; asst. prof. Dickinson Sch. Law, Carlisle, Pa., 1970-73, assoc. prof., 1973-74, prof., asst. dean, 1974-77, prof., dean, 1977-89; pres., dean South Tex. Coll. Law., Houston, 1989-95; cons. Juvenile Ct. Judges Commn., 1971-75; reporter Commonwealth Ct. of Pa., 1973-89; adv. Motor Vehicle Code Revision, 1973-74; lectr. Pa. Law Enforcement Acad., 1971-88, Pa. Bar Inst., 1970-88. Contbr. articles to legal jours. Bd. dirs. Cumberland-Perry Assn. Retarded Citizens, 1973-76, Legal Svcs., Inc., 1973-77; mem. bd. advisors Cumberland County Children's Svcs., 1975-78; pres. United Way Carlisle, 1986. With U.S. Army, 1955-57. Fellow Am. Bar Found.; mem. ABA, ATLA, Def. Rsch. Inst., Ind. Bar Assn., Pa. Bar Assn., Houston Bar Assn. Home: 10734 Old Coach Ln Houston TX 77024-3124 Office: S Tex Coll Law 1303 San Jacinto St Houston TX 77002-7013

WILKS-OWENS, DIXIE RAE, conference/meeting planner; b. Oakland, Calif., Nov. 1, 1943; d. James D. Wilks and Pauline Ruth (Peoples) Biddulph; m. August Edward Slagle (div. 1974); children: Tonya Davina Slagle, Victor Scott Slagle; m. Howard Laverne Owens, Dec. 15, 1984. AA, Ohlone Coll., 1973; attended, U. Calif., Davis, 1993-94; cert. mgmt. effectiveness, U. So. Calif. Unemployment ins. specialist, employment and tng. generalist. Employment supr. Calif. Employment Devel. Dept., Sacramento, 1969-86, employment specialist, 1986-88, legis. analyst, 1988-90, legis. re-employment ctr. mgr., 1990-91, mktg. mgr., 1991-94, mgr. workforce preparation conf., 1994-96; pres. Meeting Masters, Sacramento, 1996—; state mgr. Dept. Labor's Nationwide One-Stop Career Ctr. Conf., 1997. Bd. dirs., membership chair Sacramento Women's Campaign Fund, 1993—. Mem. Internat. Assn. Pers. in Employment Security (mem. internat. rels. com. 1991, Calif. chpt. pres. 1992-94, bd. dirs. conf. planning bd. 1993-94, legis. chair 1995—), Soc. Govt. Meeting Profls. Democrat. Unitarian Universalist. Avocation: conference planner. Office: Meeting Masters 1151 Oak Hall Way Sacramento CA 95822-3209 also: State Job Tng Coord Coun 800 Capitol Mall MIC67 Sacramento CA 95814

WILL, CLIFFORD MARTIN, physicist, educator; b. Hamilton, Ont., Can., Nov. 13, 1946; m. Leslie Saxe, June 26, 1970; children: Elizabeth, Rosalie. BS, McMaster U., Hamilton, 1968; PhD, Calif. Inst. Tech., 1971. Enrico Fermi fellow U. Chgo., 1972-74; asst. prof. physics Stanford U., Palo Alto, Calif., 1974-81; assoc. prof. physics Washington U., St. Louis, 1981-85, prof. physics, 1985—, chmn. dept. physics, 1991—; chmn. com. on time transfer in satellite systems Air Force Studies Bd., Washington, 1984-86. Assoc. editor Physical Rev. Letters, 1989-92; author: Theory and Experiment in Gravitational Physics, 1981, rev. edit., 1993, Was Einstein Right?, 1986, rev. edit., 1993. Alfred P. Sloan Found. fellow, 1975-79, J.S. Guggenheim Found. fellow, 1996-97, J.W. Fulbright fellow, 1996-97; recipient Sci. Writing award Am. Inst. Physics, 1987, Disting. Alumni award, McMaster U., 1996. Fellow Am. Phys. Soc. (exec. com. astrophysics div. 1988-90); mem. Am. Astron. Soc., Am. Assn. Physics Tchrs. (Richtmyer Meml. Lectr. 1987), Internat. Soc. Gen. Relativity and Gravitation. Office: Washington U Dept Physics Campus Box 1105 1 Brookings Dr Saint Louis MO 63130-4862

WILL, ERIC JOHN, state senator; b. Omaha, Nebr., Apr. 16, 1959; s. John Babcock and Patricia Elaine (Propst) W. BA in Polit. Sci., U. So. Calif., 1981; postgrad., Creighton U., 1993—. Legis. researcher Nebr. State Legis., Omaha, 1981-90, senator, 1991—; chmn. enrollment and rev. com., 1991-93, rules com., 1993—; vice chmn. gen. affairs com., 1991—; mem. revenue and urban affairs com., 1991—. Mem. Phi Beta Kappa. Democrat. Presbyterian. Avocations: softball, bowling, volleyball. Home: 6029 Pinkney St Omaha NE 68104-3411 Office: Nebr State Capitol District 8 Lincoln NE 68509

WILL, GEORGE FREDERICK, editor, political columnist, news commentator; b. Champaign, Ill., May 4, 1941; s. Frederick L. and Louise Will. BA, Trinity Coll., 1962, Oxford (Eng.) U., 1964; MA, Ph.D., Princeton U., 1967; LLD (hon.), U. San Diego, 1977; LittD (hon.), Dickinson Coll. and Georgetown U., 1978; hon. degree, U. Ill., 1988. Prof. polit. philosophy Mich. State U., 1967-68, U. Toronto, 1968-70; mem. staff of Sen. Gordon Allott U.S. Senate, Washington, Can., 1970-72; editor The Nat. Rev., Washington, 1973-76; contbg. editor Newsweek mag., 1976—; syndicated columnist Washington Post, 1974—; TV news analyst ABC-Capitol Cities, 1981—; bd. dirs. Ctr. for Strategic Internat. Studies, Washington, Balt. Orioles. Author: The Pursuit of Happiness and Other Sobering Thoughts, 1979, The Pursuit of Virtue and Other Tory Notions, 1982, Statecraft as Soulcraft: What Government Does, 1983, The Morning After:

American Successes and Excesses, 1986, The New Season: A Spectator's Guide to the 1988 Election, 1987, Men at Work, 1990, Suddenly: The American Idea at Home and Abroad 1988-89, 1990, Restoration: Congress, Term Limits and the Recovery of Deliberate Democracy, 1992, The Leveling Wind: Politics, the Culture and Other News, 1994; participant This Week With David Brinkley, ABC-TV, 1981—; commentator World News Tonight, 1984—. Recipient Pulitzer prize for Commentary, 1977; named Young Leader Am. Time mag., 1974. Avocation: baseball. Office: The Washington Post 1150 15th St NW Washington DC 20071-0001

WILL, JAMES FREDRICK, steel company executive; b. Pitts., Oct. 12, 1938; s. Fred F. and Mary Agnes (Ganter) W.; m. Mary Ellen Bowser, Dec. 19, 1964; children: Mary Beth, Kerry Ann. BSEE, Pa. State U., 1961; MBA, Duquesne U., 1972. Works mgr. Kaiser Steel Corp., Fontana, Calif., 1976-78, v.p. ops., 1978-80, v.p. planning, 1980-81, exec. v.p., 1981, pres., 1981-82; exec. v.p., pres. indsl. group Cyclops Corp., Pitts, 1982-86; pres., chief operating officer Cyclops Corp., Pitts., 1986-88, pres., chief exec. officer, 1989-92; pres., chief oper. officer Armco, Inc., Parsippany, NJ, 1992-93; pres., chief exec. officer Armco, Inc., Pitts., 1994-96; chmn., pres., CEO Armco, Inc., 1996—; vice-chmn. 1994, chmn. 1995, Specialty Steel Industry of N.Am. Office: Armco Inc 1 Oxford Center Pittsburgh PA 15219-1407

WILL, JANE ANNE, psychologist; b. Evansville, Ind., Feb. 6, 1945; d. Edwin Francis and Frances Elizabeth (Patry) W. BA in Edn., St. Benedict's Coll., Ferdinand, Ind., 1968; MA in Edn., MS in Clin. Psychology, U. Evansville, 1973, 1987; MA in Christian Spirituality, Creighton U., 1979; D Psychology, Fla. Tech., Melbourne, 1991. Lic. psychologist, Ind.; joined Sisters of St. Benedict, Inc., Roman Cath. Ch. Tchr. Ireland (Ind.) Jr. H.S., 1969-76, Meml. H.S., Evansville, Ind., 1976-77; dir. recruitment and tng. Sisters of St. Benedict, Inc., Ferdinand, Ind., 1978-84, cons. admissions bd., 1984—; tchr. Mater Dei H.S., Evansville, 1984-88; therapist Osceola Ctr., Kissimme, Fla., 1989-90, Charter Hosp., Kissimme, Fla., 1989-90; intern VA Med. Ctr., St. Louis, 1990-91; clin. psychologist St. Mary's Health Care Svcs., Evansville, 1991—; adj. prof. Brescia Coll., Owensboro, Ky., 1978-80, St. Mary's of the Woods Coll., Terre Haute, Ind., 1980-84. Author jour. Ind. Reading Quarterly, 1973. Bd. dirs. Nat. Formation Dirs., Washington, 1982-84; chairperson region VII Formation Conf., Mich. and Ind., 1982-84. Luise Whiting Bell scholar, 1986. Mem. APA, Ind. Psychol. Assn., Southwestern Ind. Psychol. Assn. (treas. 1992, sec. 1993, v.p. 1994, pres. 1995), Vanderburgh County Mental Health Assn. (bd. dirs. 1994—, v.p. 1996, pres. 1997). Roman Catholic. Avocations: hiking, crocheting, music, reading. Home: 725 Wedeking Ave Evansville IN 47711-3861

WILL, JOANNE MARIE, food and consumer services executive, communications consultant, writer; b. Mpls., Mar. 18, 1937; d. Lester John and Dorothea Amelia (Kuenzel) W. BS in Home Econs. and Journalism, Iowa State U., 1959. Food writer, editor food guide Chgo. Tribune, 1959-67; account supr., home econs. coordinator J. Walter Thompson Co., Chgo., 1967-73; assoc. food editor, then food editor Chgo. Tribune, 1973-81; dir. food and consumer services Hill and Knowlton, Inc., Chgo., 1981-87; dir., group mgr. food and consumer svcs. Selz/Seabolt Comms., Inc., Chgo. Mem. bd. govs. Iowa State U. Found., past mem. home econs. adv. bd.; past bd. dirs., officer Sr. Ctrs. Met. Chgo. Recipient Alumnae Recognition medal Iowa State U., 1994; named Outstanding Young Alumnus Iowa State U., 1968. Mem. Am. Assn. Family Consumer Scis. (Chgo. bus. sect.), Ill. Assn. Family and Consumer Scis., Chgo. Nutrition Assn. (pres.-elect 1993-94, pres. 1994-95), Dames d'Escoffier (bd. dirs. Chgo. chpt., past v.p.).

WILL, ROBERT ERWIN, economics educator; b. Dousman, Wis., Mar. 8, 1928; s. Erwin and Gena (Luedtke) W.; m. Barbara Anne Couture, Dec. 22, 1956; children: Jonathan (dec.), Leslie Anne, Jennifer. B.A. cum magna laude, Carleton Coll., 1950; M.A., Yale U., 1951, Ph.D., 1965. Mem. faculty Yale, 1951-54, U. Mass., 1954-57; mem. faculty econs. Carleton Coll., Northfield, Minn., 1957—; prof. Carleton Coll., 1968-73, W.A. Williams prof., 1973-82, Plank prof., 1982-92, chmn. dept. econs., dir. First Bank System execs. seminars, 1971-80, prof. emeritus, 1992—; vis. prof. U. Minn., 1965; vis. fellow Inst. Devel. Studies, U. Sussex, Eng., 1970-71, H.H. Humphrey Inst., 1981-82; John de Quedville Briggs lectr., St. Paul Acad., 1966-70; dir. Kings' Coll. seminar in econs. Cambridge (Eng.) U., 1990; pres. NBC Found., 1997—. Author: Poverty in Affluence: The Social, Political and Economic Dimensions of Poverty in the United States, 1965, Scalar Economies and Urban Service Requirements, 1965, also articles and research on manpower, tourism, and devel. Mem. Minn. Dept. Manpower Svcs. Adv. Coun., 1966-80, Wilton Pk., Brit. Fgn. Office Study Ctr., 1970—; dir., chief fin. officer Cmty. Electronics Corp., Mpls., 1968-91; dir. Minn. World Affairs Ctr., 1972-90, Minn. Internat. Ctr., 1979-86; pres. Minn. Trade Conf., 1996—; mem. policy com. United Shareowners Am., 1960-80; mem. Northfield Heritage Preservation Commn., 1982—, Northfield Sister Cities Commn., 1991-94, Mpls. Inst. Art, Walker Art Ctr., Northfield Arts Guild; bd. visitors Am. Grad. Sch. Internat. Mgmt., 1980-90; bd. dirs. Northfield United Way, 1983-86, Minn. UN Rally Bd., 1973-97, Lutheran Home Cannon Valley, Northfield Manor, Northfield Parkview, 1993—; chmn. Northfield Hist. Soc. Endowment, 1993—. Ford Found. Faculty fellow, 1962-63, NSF Faculty fellow, 1970-71; Interuniv. Ctr. for European Studies fellow, 1975-85; Mellon grantee, Mex., 1976, Spain, 1981; Devel. Fund grantee, France, 1985, World Tourism grantee, Eng., 1990. Mem. World Future Soc., Assn. for 3d World Studies, Soc. for Internat. Devel., Bus. and Econ. History Soc., Assn. Cultural Econs., Assn. Comparative Econ. Studies, Am. Friends Wilton Pk, Assn. for Pvt. Enterprise Edn., Nat. Assn. Bus. Economists, Assn. Evolutionary Econs., History Econ. Assn., Caribbean Studies Assn., N.Am. Econ. and Fin. Assn., Population Action Coun. (nat. com.), Minn. Econ. Ass., Chactonbury Ring Club (Sussex), Rotary (Rotary Found. Svc. award 1995), Phi Beta Kappa. Democrat. Episcopalian. Home: 708 3rd St E Northfield MN 55057-2311

WILL, TREVOR JONATHAN, lawyer; b. Ashland, Wis., Aug. 11, 1953; s. William Taylor and Geraldine Sue (Trevor) W.; m. Margaret Ann Johnson, Aug. 28, 1976; children: Tyler William, Alexandra Marie, Jennifer Catherine. BA summa cum laude, Augustana Coll., 1975; JD cum laude, Harvard U., 1978. Bar: Wis. 1978, U.S. Dist. Ct. (ea. dist.) Wis. 1978, U.S. DIst. Ct. (we. dist.) Wis. 1980, U.S. Ct. Appeals (7th cir.) 1983, U.S. Supreme Ct. 1984, U.S. Dist. Ct. (ea. dist.) Mich. 1985. Assoc. Foley & Lardner, Milw., 1978-87, ptnr., 1987—; adj. law prof. Marquette U. Law Sch., 1994—. Mem. ABA, State Bar Wis., Milw. Bar Assn., Def. Rsch. Inst. Home: 10011 N Waterleaf Dr Mequon WI 53092-6146 Office: Foley & Lardner 777 E Wisconsin Ave Milwaukee WI 53202-5302

WILLADSEN, MICHAEL CHRIS, marketing professional, sales executive; b. Cheboygan, Mich., Sept. 18, 1946; s. Chris Jens and Helen Margaret (Barr) W.; m. Kay Ann Brooks, Dec. 10, 1964, (div. Dec. 10, 1989); children: Michael Jr., Erik; m. Linda Sue Degroff, Apr. 4, 1992; children: Stephanie, Gretchen, Ross. Student, Delta Coll., 1964-66; A in Bus. Mgmt., Northwood Inst., 1968, BA in Bus. Mgmt., 1969. Mktg. rep. Detroit dist. Petemco, Inc., 1970-73, mktg. rep. Indpls. Dist., 1973-74; dist. mgr. Petemco Inc.-Ind. Ohio Mich., Ind., Ohio, Mich., 1974-76, Consolidated Stas. Marathon Oil, Oshkosh, Wis., 1976-79; sales mgr. Champaign (Ill.) Dist. Marathon Oil, 1981-82; supr. Credit Card Ctr. Marathon Oil, Findlay, Ohio, 1982-84; wholesale mktg. profl. Marathon Brand Mktg./Ohio, Mich., Ky., 1982-84; jobber sales Marathon Oil/Ohio, Pa., W.Va., Ohio, Pa., W. Va., 1984-92, Marathon Oil/Ill., Wisc., Chgo., Chgo., 1992—. Named to Nat. Assn. Intercollegiate Athletes Sml. Coll. All-State Football Team/Dist. 23, 1968. Mem. Cleve. Petroleum Club (v.p. 1988-91), Chgo. Oilmens. Republican. Presbyterian. Avocations: camping, softball, basketball, physical work out. Office: Marathon Oil Co P O Box 1635 Bolingbrook IL 60440

WILLANS, JEAN STONE, religious organization executive; b. Hillsboro, Ohio, Oct. 3, 1924; d. Homer and Ella (Keys) Hammond; student San Diego Jr. Coll.; D.D. (hon.) Ch. of the East, 1996; m. Richard James Willans, Mar. 28, 1966; 1 dau., Suzanne Jeanne. Asst. to v.p. Family Loan Co., Miami, Fla., 1946-49; civilian supr. USAF, Washington, 1953-55; founder, dir. Blessed Trinity Soc., editor Trinity mag., Los Angeles, 1960-66; co-founder, exec. v.p., dir. Soc. of Stephen, Altadena, Calif., 1967—, exec. dir., Hong Kong, 1975-81; lectr. in field. Republican. Episcopalian. Author: The Acts of the Green Apples, 1974, rev. edit 1995; co-editor: Charisma in Hong Kong, 1970; Spiritual Songs, 1970; The People Who Walked in Darkness, 1977; The People Who Walked in Darkness II, 1992. Recipient Achievement award Nat. Assn. Pentecostal Women, 1964; monument erected in her honor Kowloon Walled City Park, Hong Kong Govt., 1996. Office: Soc of Stephen PO Box 6225 Altadena CA 91003-6225 *I am interested in telling as many people as possible about the experience with the Holy Spirit which brings a language unknown to the speaker. I believe this experience is the source of the power of the early church and that anyone who appropriates it receives the power to change many things, not the least of these being himself.*

WILLANS, RICHARD JAMES, religious organization executive, human resources management consultant; b. Detroit, July 24, 1943; s. James Cyril and Georgie Agnes (Ray) W.; m. Jean Stone, Mar. 28, 1966; 1 child, Suzanne Jeanne. Student, Dartmouth Coll., 1960-63; BS in Orgnl. Behavior, U. San Francisco, 1984; DD (hon.), All. Coll. Seminarians, Santa Cruz, Calif., 1996. Assoc. editor Trinity Mag., Van Nuys, Calif., 1963-66; co-founder, pres., chmn. Soc. of Stephen, Altadena, Calif., 1967—; missionary pastor Soc. of Stephen, Hong Kong, 1968-81; tchr. Hong Kong Christian Coll., Caineway English Coll., Hong Kong, 1968-71; ops. mgr. RCM Svcs., Hong Kong, 1972-74; dir. exec. selection Peat, Marwick, Mitchell & Co., Hong Kong, 1974-81; pers. dir. Gen. Bank, L.A., 1982-83; dir. human resources Calif. Commerce Bank, L.A., 1984-88; mgr. human resources info. ctr. Union Bank of Calif., Monterey Pk., 1988-96; lectr. in field. Co-editor: (collection of personal stories) Charisma in Hong Kong, 1970, (song book) Spiritual Songs, 1970, (book series) The People Who Walked in Darkness, Vol. I, 1977, Vol. II, 1992, (book) The Acts of the Green Apples, 1995. Monument in his honor for drug addict rehab. work-Kowloon Walled City Pk., Hong Kong, 1996. Republican. Office: Soc of Stephen PO Box 6225 Altadena CA 91003-6225

WILLARD, GREGORY DALE, lawyer; b. Pittsfield, Ill., Feb. 8, 1954; s. Wesley Dale and Rosmary (Stark) W.; m. Ann Julia Grier, June 3, 1978; children: Michael, David, John. BA summa cum laude, Westminster Coll., Fulton, Mo., 1976; JD cum laude, U. Ill., 1979. Bar: Mo., U.S. Dist. Ct. (ea. dist.) Mo., U.S. Ct. Appeals (8th Cir.). Staff asst. to Pres. Exec. Office of the Pres. The White House, Washington, 1976-77; ptnr. Bryan Cave, St. Louis, 1979—; co-chmn. bankruptcy com. Met. Bar Assn., St. Louis, 1983-84. Bd. Dirs. St. Louis Children's Hosp., 1985-89, Found. for Spl. Edn., 1990—. Mem. Noonday Club. Office: Bryan Cave 211 N Broadway Saint Louis MO 63102-2733

WILLARD, LOUIS CHARLES, librarian; b. Tallahassee, Fla., Sept. 28, 1937; s. Bert and Rose (De Milly) W.; m. Nancy Booth, June 22, 1963. BA, U. Fla., 1959; BD, Yale, 1965, MA, 1967, PhD, 1970. Tchr. Tripoli (Lebanon) Boys' Sch., 1959-62; ordained to ministry Presbyn. Ch., 1965; acting librarian Princeton Theol. Sem., 1968-69, librarian, 1969-86; librarian, mem. faculty Harvard Div. Sch., 1986—. Mem. A.L.A., Theol. Library Assn., Soc. Bibl. Lit., Am. Acad. Religion, Phi Beta Kappa, Chi Phi. Home: 24 Concord Greene Unit 8 PO Box 1250 Concord MA 01742-1250 Office: Andover-Harvard Theol Libr Divinity Sch 45 Francis Ave Cambridge MA 02138-1911

WILLARD, NANCY MARGARET, writer, educator; b. Ann Arbor, Mich.; d. Hobart Hurd and Margaret (Sheppard) W.; m. Eric Lindbloom, Aug. 15, 1964; 1 child, James Anatole. B.A., U. Mich., 1958, Ph.D., 1963; M.A., Stanford U., 1960. Lectr. English Vassar Coll., Poughkeepsie, N.Y., 1965—. Author: (poems) In His Country: Poems, 1966; Skin of Grace, 1967; A New Herball: Poems, 1968, Testimony of the Invisible Man: William Carlos Williams, Francis Ponge, Rainer Maria Rilke, Pablo Neruda, 1970, Nineteen Masks for the Naked Poet: Poems, 1971, The Carpenter of the Sun: Poems, 1974, A Visit to William Blake's Inn: Poems for Innocent and Experienced Travelers, 1981 (Newbery Medal 1982), Household Tales of Moon and Water, 1983, Water Walker, 1989, The Ballad of Biddy Early, 1989; (short stories) The Lively Anatomy of God, 1968, Childhood of the Magician, 1973; (juveniles) Sailing to Cythera and Other Anatole Stories, 1974, All on a May Morning, 1975, The Snow Rabbit, 1975, Shoes Without Leather, 1976, T0e Well-Mannered Balloon, 1976, Night Story, 1986, Simple Pictures are Best, 1977, Stranger's Bread, 1977, The Highest Hit, 1978, Papa's Panda, 1979, The Island of the Grass King, 1979, The Marzipan Moon 1981, Uncle Terrible, 1982, (adult) Angel in the Parlor: Five Stories and Eight Essays, 1983, The Nightgown of the Sullen Moon, 1983, Night Story, 1986, The Voyage of the Ludgate Hill, 1987, The Mountains of Quilt, 1987, Firebrat, 1988; (novel) Things Invisible To See, 1984, Sister Water, 1993; (play) East of the Sun, West of the Moon, 1989, The High Rise Glorious Skittle Skat Roarious Sky Pie Angel Food Cake, 1991, A Nancy Willard Reader, 1991, Pish Posh said Hieronymus Bosch, 1991, Beauty and the Beast, 1992; illustrator: The Letter of John to James, Another Letter of John to James, 1982, The Octopus Who Wanted to Juggle (Robert Pack), 1990, (novel) Sister Water, 1993, (essays) Telling Time, 1993, (juvenile) A Starlit Somersault Downhill, 1993, (juvenile) The Sorcerer's Apprentice, 1993; author, illustrator: An Alphabet of Angels, 1994; (juvenile) Gutenberg's Gift, 1995, The Good Night Blessing Book, 1996; (poems, with Jane Yolen) Among Angels, 1995, Swimming Lessons, 1996, The Magic Cornfield, 1997. Recipient Hopwood award, 1958, Devins Meml. award, 1967, John Newbery award, 1981, Empire State award, 1996; Woodrow Wilson fellow, 1960; NEA grantee, 1987. Mem. The Lewis Carroll Soc., The George MacDonald Soc. Office: Vassar Coll Dept English Raymond Ave Poughkeepsie NY 12601

WILLARD, RALPH LAWRENCE, surgery educator, physician, former college president; b. Manchester, Iowa, Apr. 6, 1922; s. Hosea B. and Ruth A. (Hazelrigg) W.; m. Margaret Dyer Dennis, Sept. 26, 1969; children: Laurie, Jane, Ann, H. Thomas. Student, Cornell Coll., 1940-42, Coe Coll., 1945; D.O., Kirksville Coll. Osteo. Medicine, 1949; EdD (hon.), U. North Tex., 1985; ScD (hon.), W.Va. Sch. Osteo. Medicine, 1993. Intern Kirksville Osteo. Hosp., 1949-50, resident in surgery, 1954-57; chmn. dept. surgery Davenport Osteo. Hosp., 1957-68; dean, prof. surgery Kirksville Coll. Osteo. Medicine, 1969-73; asso. dean acad. affairs, prof. surgery Mich. State U. Coll. Osteo. Medicine, 1974-75; dean Tex. Coll. Osteopathic Medicine, 1975-76, pres., 1981-85, prof. surgery, 1985-87; v.p. med. affairs North Tex. State U., Denton, 1976-81; assoc. dean W.Va. Sch. Osteo. Medicine, Lewisburg, 1988-91; mem. Nat. Adv. Council Edn. for Health Professions, 1971-73, Iowa Gov.'s Council Hosps. and Health Related Facilities, 1965-68; chmn. council deans Am. Assn. Colls. Osteo. Medicine, 1970-73, pres., 1979-80. Served with USAAF, 1942-45; Served with USAF, 1952-53; col. USAFR, ret. Decorated D.F.C., Air medal with 4 oak leaf clusters, Meritorious Svc. medal, Legion of Merit; recipient Robert A. Kistner Educator award Am. Assn. Colls. Osteo. Medicine, 1989. Fellow Am. Coll. Physician Execs., Am. Coll. Osteo. Surgeons; mem. Am. Osteo. Assn. (Disting. Svc. cert. 1992), Tex. Osteo. Assn., W.Va. Soc. Osteo. Medicine, Am. Acad. Osteopathy, Acad. Osteo. Dirs. Med. Edn., Aerospace Med. Assn., Flying Physicians Assn., Quiet Birdmen, Davis-Monthan Officers Club, Masons, Shriners, Lewisburg Rotary (Paul Harris fellow), Internat. Comanche Soc., Order of Daedalians. Democrat. Episcopalian. Home: PO Box 749 Lewisburg WV 24901-0749 Office: WVa Sch Osteo Medicine 400 N Lee St Lewisburg WV 24901-1128 *The wise man has faith, the fool is he who betrays that faith.*

WILLARD, RICHARD KENNON, lawyer; b. Houston, Sept. 1, 1948; s. Fair McDaniel Willard and Elsbeth Rowe (Kennon) Willard Armistead; m. Leslie Harral Hopkins, July 10, 1976; children: Stephen Hopkins, Lauren Suzanne. B.A., Emory U., 1969; J.D., Harvard U., 1975. Bar: D.C. 1988, Tex. 1978, Ga. 1975. Law clk. U.S. Ct. Appeals, San Francisco, 1975-76, U.S. Supreme Ct., Washington, 1976-77; atty. Baker & Botts, Houston, 1977-81; counsel for intelligence policy U.S. Dept. Justice, Washington, 1981-82, dep. asst. atty. gen. civil div., 1982-83, asst. atty. gen., 1983-88; ptnr. Steptoe & Johnson, Washington, 1988—; adj. prof. Georgetown U. Law Ctr., 1991096. Note editor: Harvard U. Law Rev., 1974-75. Gen. counsel Republican Party of Tex., Austin, 1980-81. Served to 1st lt. U.S. Army, 1969-72. Mem. Met. Club. Episcopalian. Office: 1330 Connecticut Ave NW Washington DC 20036-1704

WILLARD, ROBERT EDGAR, lawyer; b. Bronxville, N.Y., Dec. 13, 1929; s. William Edgar and Ethel Marie (Van Ness) W.; m. Shirley Fay Cooper, May 29, 1954; children: Laura Marie, Linda Ann, John Judson. B.A. in Econs., Wash. State U., 1954; J.D., Harvard U., 1958. Bar: Calif. 1959. Law clk. to U.S. dist. judge, 1958-59; pvt. practice L.A., 1959-82; assoc. firm Flint & Mackay, 1959-61; pvt. practice, 1962-64; mem. firm Willard & Baltaxe, 1964-65, Baird, Holley, Baird & Galen, 1966-69, Baird, Holley, Galen & Willard, 1970-74, Holley, Galen & Willard, 1975-82, Galvin & Willard, Newport Beach, Calif., 1982-86; pvt. practice Newport Beach, 1987-89; mem. firm Davis, Punelli Keathley & Willard, Newport Beach, 1990—; Dir. various corps. Served with AUS, 1946-48, 50-51. Mem. ABA, Los Angeles County Bar Assn., State Bar Calif., Assn. Trial Lawyers Am., Am. Judicature Soc., Acacia Frat. Congregationalist. Club: Calcutta Saddle and Cycle. Home: 1840 Oriole Dr Costa Mesa CA 92626-4758 Office: 610 Newport Center Dr Ste 1000 Newport Beach CA 92660-6449

WILLAUER, WHITING RUSSELL, consultant; b. Boston, May 24, 1931; s. Whiting and Louise Knapp (Russell) W.; m. Julie Matheson Arnold, July 11, 1959 (div.); children—Whiting Russell, Jr., William Arnold. B.S., Princeton U., 1955, M.S., 1959; Ph.D., Georgetown U., 1964. Research assoc. joint research com. Dept. Def., 1951-52; ops. mgr. Civil Air Transport Airline Taiwan, 1952-53; scientist Analytic Services, Inc., 1958-61; asst. prof. astronomy Georgetown U., 1965-68; mgr. TRW Systems Group support to chief Naval ops., McLean, Va., 1968-73, TRW Antisubmarine projects, 1973-79, TRW Ship Acquisition project, 1979-85; advanced systems mgr. TRW Systems Integration Group, 1985-90, cost estimating mgr., 1990-95; sr. cons., 1995—; cons. Nat. Geog. Soc., 1961-65, U. Tex., 1962, NSF, 1963, Booz-Allen & Hamilton, 1966-67. Mng. editor: Jour. Astronautical Scis, 1969-71; Designer: Orrery (planetarium) on permanent exhibit, New Explorers Hall, Nat. Geog. Soc. Asst. chief steward Alpine Venue XIII Olympic Winter Games, Lake Placid, 1980; mem. U.S. Olympic Com., bd. dirs., 1987-94, sec. nat. governing bodies, 1989-92, mem. membership svcs. com., 1988-92, mem. athletic devel. com., 1992-96; chef de mission Winter Pan Am. Games, Las Lenas, Argentina, 1990; asst. chief de mission XVI Winter Olympics, Albertville, France, 1992; U.S. Olympic Com. liaison to VI Paralympic Winter Games, Lillehammer, Norway, 1994. Research fellow Georgetown U., 1961-65. Fellow AAAS (coun.); mem. Am. Astronautical Soc. (v.p. fin.), Blue Ridge Ski Coun. (pres. 1976-78), U.S. Ski Assn. (pres. 1982-87, Julius Blegan award 1988), U.S. Skiing (vice chmn. 1994-96), Internat. Ski Fedn. (chmn. U.S. del. 1983, 85, chmn. recreational skiing com. 1987—, eligibility com. 1988—), Ea. Ski Assn. (treas. 1980-82), Pan Am Sports Orgn. (winter games adv. com. 1988—), Sigma Xi, Chevy Chase Club (Md.), Nantucket Yacht Club (Mass.) (commodore 1981-83, bd. govs. 1957-59, 68—). Home: 4201 Cathedral Ave NW Apt 701W Washington DC 20016-4946

WILLCOTT, MARK ROBERT, III, chemist, educator, researcher; b. Muskogee, Okla., July 23, 1933; s. Mark Robert Willcott Jr. and Josephine Oliver; m. Earline Faye Hinkle, June 4, 1955; children: Julie, June Elinor, Mark Robert IV, Ashley. BA, Rice U., 1955; MS, Yale U., 1959, PhD, 1963. Asst. prof. chemistry Emory U., Atlanta, 1962-64; asst. prof. chemistry U. Houston, 1965-68, assoc. prof., 1968-73, prof., 1973-83; head biomed. Nuc. Magnetic Resonance lab. Baylor Coll. Medicine, Houston, 1982-83; pres., chmn. bd. Nuc. Magnegic Resonance Imaging, Inc., Houston, 1983-88; prof. chemistry and radiology Vanderbilt U., Nashville, 1989-94; prof., dir. of rsch. U. Tex. Med. Br., Galveston, 1994—; cons. Codman & Shurtleff, Inc., Randolph, Mass., 1991—. Advanced NMR Sys., Andover, Mass., 1994—, Cooper and Dunham, N.Y.C., 1994—, Kenyon and Kenyon, N.Y.C., 1997—; adj. prof. chemistry Rice U., Houston, 1995—; adj. prof. medicine Baylor Coll. Medicine, 1996—. Author patents for magnetic resonance imaging, 1988-94. Bd. dirs. Bay Oaks Cmty. Assn., Houston, 1996—. Lt. (j.g.) USN, 1955-58. John Simon Guggenheim fellow Guggenheim Found., 1972; recipient Alexander von Humboldt Sr. Scientist prize Humboldt Found., 1978. Mem. Am. Chem. Soc., Am. Assn. Physicists in Medicine, Internat. Soc. Magnetic Resonance. Democrat. Presbyterian. Avocations: mountaineering, photography, philately. Home: 1807 Orchard Country Ln Houston TX 77062-2338 Office: U Tex Med Br Dept Radiology Houston TX 77555-0793

WILLCOX, CHRISTOPHER PATRICK, magazine editor; b. Chgo., Nov. 2, 1946; s. James Christopher and Rita (Donovan) W.; m. Emily Turner, July 6, 1976; 1 child, Kathleen. BA, U. Notre Dame, 1968. Editl. writer Detroit News, 1980-82, dep. editl. page editor, 1982-84; program advisor Radio Free Europe/Radio Liberty, Munich, Germany, 1984-88; sr. editor Reader's Digest, Pleasantville, N.Y., 1988-90, sr. staff editor, 1990-91, exec. editor, 1991—, editor-in-chief; adj. prof. journalism Columbia U., N.Y.C., 1993-96. Mem. Am. Soc. Mag. Editors, Deadline Club. Office: Readers Digest Assn Readers Digest Rd Pleasantville NY 10570*

WILLE, KARIN L., lawyer; b. Northfield, Minn., Dec. 14, 1949; d. James Virginia Wille. BA summa cum laude, Macalester Coll., 1971; JD cum laude, U. Minn., 1974. Bar: Minn. 1974, U.S. Dist. Ct. Minn. 1974. Atty. Dresselhuis & Assocs., Mpls., 1974-75; assoc. Dorsey & Whitney, Mpls., 1975-76; atty. Dayton-Hudson Corp., Mpls., 1976-84; gen. counsel B. Dalton Booksellers, Edina, Minn., 1985-87; assoc. Briggs & Morgan, Mpls., 1987-88; shareholder Briggs and Briggs, 1988—; co-chair Upper Midwest Employment Law Inst., 1983-94. Mem. ABA, Minn. State Bar Assn. (labor and employment sect., corp. counsel sect., dir. 1989-91), Hennepin County Bar Assn. (labor and employment sect.), Minn. Women Lawyers, Phi Beta Kappa. Office: Briggs & Morgan 2400 IDS Ctr Minneapolis MN 55402

WILLE, LOIS JEAN, retired newspaper editor; b. Chgo., Sept. 19, 1931; d. Walter and Adele S. (Taege) Kroeber; m. Wayne M. Wille, June 6, 1954. B.S., Northwestern U., 1953, M.S., 1954; Litt.D. (hon.), Columbia Coll., Chgo., 1980, Northwestern U., 1990, Rosary Coll., 1990. Reporter Chgo. Daily News, 1958-74, nat. corr., 1975-76, assoc. editor charge editorial page, 1977; assoc. editor charge editorial and opinion pages Chgo. Sun-Times, 1978-83; assoc. editor editorial page Chgo. Tribune, 1984-87, editor editorial page, 1987-91, ret., 1991. Author: Forever Open, Clear and Free: the Historic Struggle for Chicago's Lakefront, 1972, At Home in the Loop: How Clout and Community Built Chicago's Dearborn Park, 1997. Recipient Pulitzer prize for public svc., 1963, Pulitzer prize for editorial writing, 1989, William Allen White Found. award for excellence in editorial writing, 1978, numerous awards Chgo. Newspaper Guild, numerous awards Chgo. Headline Club, numerous awards Nat. Assn. Edn. Writers, numerous awards Ill. AP, numerous awards Ill. UPI. Home: 120 Charmont Dr Radford VA 24141-4205

WILLE, WAYNE MARTIN, retired editor; b. Des Plaines, Ill., Nov. 17, 1930; s. Clarence Louis and Lois Naomi (Martin) W.; m. Lois Jean Kroeber, June 6, 1954. B.S.J., Northwestern U., 1952, M.S.J., 1953. Reporter Chgo. Sun Times, 1956-57; dir. press info. WBBM-TV and CBS-TV, Chgo., 1957-58; feature editor Sci. and Mechanics mag., 1958-60, mng. editor, 1960-62; news editor Nat. Safety Council, Chgo., 1962-64, asst. dir. pub. info., 1964-67; mng. editor World Book Year Book, Chgo., 1967-69; exec. editor World Book Yr. Book, 1969-83; mng. editor World Book Yr. Book and Sci. Yr. and Health & Med. Ann., 1983-91. Served with AUS, 1953-55. Mem. Chgo. Headline Club (pres. 1967-68), Soc. Profl. Journalists. Clubs: La Salle Street Rod and Gun.

WILLEMS, CONSTANCE CHARLES, lawyer; b. Zuilen, Utrecht, Netherlands, Oct. 31, 1942; came to U.S., 1967, naturalized, 1977; d. Anton Henri and Maria (Van der Meys) Charles; m. Cornelis Franciscus Willems, May 25, 1965; 1 son, Maurice. B.A. in Sociology magna cum laude, U. New Orleans, 1974; J.D. with honors, Tulane U., 1977. Bar: La. 1977, U.S. Dist. Ct. (ea. dist.) La. 1977, U.S. Ct. Appeals (5th cir.) 1977, U.S. Supreme Ct. 1983. Assoc. McGlinchey, Stafford, Mintz, Cellini, and Lang, New Orleans, 1977-81, ptnr., 1982—; instr. law office mgmt. Loyola U. Sch. Law, 1986-90; instr. European law Tulane U. Sch. Law, New Orleans, 1994, 96. Mem. Task Force on Municipalization; hon. consul for The Netherlands, 1989—; bd. dirs. United Way Agy. REls. Com., 1987-91, Coun. Internat. Visitors, 1992-94, Com. of 21, 1994—, New Orleans Opera Assn., 1995—; sec./treas. Consular Corps; bd. visitors Coll. Liberal Arts U. New Orleans, 1995—. Recipient Disting. Alumni award U. New Orleans, 1989. Mem. ABA, La. Assn. Women Attys. (pres. 1983-85, 86-87), La. State Bar Assn. (mem. ho. of dels. 1984-85, chair internat. law sect. 1994—). Office: McGlinchey Stafford Lang 643 Magazine St New Orleans LA 70130-3405

WILLENBECHER, JOHN, artist; b. Macungie, Pa., May 5, 1936; s. John George and Geneva (Bacon) W. B.A., Brown U., 1958; postgrad., N.Y. U., Inst. Fine Arts, 1958-61. sculptor-mem. N.Y.C. Art Commn., 1980-92; mem. commn. for plaza and pavillion, Mpls. Inst. Arts, 1991. Exhibited in one-man shows including Hamilton Gallery Contemporary Art, N.Y.C., 1977, 80, U. Mass. Art Gallery, Amherst, 1977, Wright State U. Art Gallery,

Dayton, Ohio, 1977, Jaffe-Friede Gallery, Dartmouth Coll., Hanover, N.H., 1977, Fine Arts Ctr. U. R.I., Kingston, 1978, Neuberger Mus., SUNY at Purchase, 1979, Allentown (Pa.) Art Mus., 1979, Mpls. Inst. Arts, 1993, U. N.Mex. Art Gallery, Albuquerque, 1996; exhibited in numerous group shoes including Albright-Knox Art Gallery, Buffalo, 1963, Whitney Mus. Am. Art, N.Y.C., 1964-68; represented in permanent collections including Solomon R. Guggenheim Mus., N.Y.C., Met. Mus., N.Y.C., Whitney Mus. Am. Art, Albright-Knox Art Gallery, Phila. Mus. Art, Centre d'Art et Culture Georges Pompidou, Paris, Hirshhorn Mus. and Sculpture Garden, Washington, Art Inst. Chgo. Nat. Endowment for Arts grantee, 1977, Esther and Adolph Gottlieb Found. grantee, 1994. Subject of profl. articles and catalogues.

WILLENBRINK, ROSE ANN, lawyer; b. Louisville, Ky., Apr. 20, 1950; d. J.L. Jr. and Mary Margaret (Williams) W. Student, U. Chgo., 1968-70; BA in Anthropology with highest honors, U. Louisville, 1973, JD, 1975. Bar: Ky. 1976, Ind. 1976, U.S. Dist. Ct. (we. dist.) Ky. 1976. Atty. Mapother & Mapother, Louisville, 1976-79; v.p., counsel Nat. City Bank, Louisville, 1980—. Mem. ABA, NAFE, Ky. Bar Assn., Louisville Bar Assn., Women Lawyers Assn., Conf. on Consumer Fin. Law, Corp. House Counsel Assn., Phi Kappa Phi. Home: 2356 Valley Vista Rd Louisville KY 40205-2002 Office: Nat City Bank 3700 Nat City Tower Louisville KY 40202

WILLENS, ALAN RUSH, management consultant; b. Detroit, Jan. 14, 1936; s. Gerald Lionel Willens and Gertrude Virginia Rush; m. Harriet Lois Sinclair (June 30, 1958 (div. 1985); children: Beth Willens Hollander, Scott Sinclair Willens, Lori Helen Willens. BBA, U. Mich., 1957, MBA, 1958. Project dir. United Rsch., Inc., Cambridge, Mass., 1958-61; sr. assoc. Systems Analysis and Rsch. Corp., Boston, 1961-64; sr. cons. Regional and Urban Planning Implementation, Inc., Cambridge, 1964-65; v.p. Charles River Assocs., Inc., Boston, 1965-87, exec. v.p., 1987-92, pres., 1992-95, exec. v.p., 1992-95, sr. advisor, 1996—. Chmn. com. Ellis Neighborhood Assn., Boston, 1985-88; trustee Dartmouth Sq. Condo. Assn., Boston, 1992-96, chmn., 1994. Mem. Profl. Svcs. Mgmt. Assn. (bd. dirs. 1977-80, treas. 1978-80, First Fellow 1979). Avocations: sailing, skiing, photography, personal computers, tennis. Home: 130 Appleton St Apt 1G Boston MA 02116-6045 Office: Charles River Assocs Inc John Hancock Tower 200 Clarendon St # T-33 Boston MA 02116-5021

WILLENSON, KIM JEREMY, publisher, journalist, author; b. Milw., Feb. 10, 1937; s. Lawrence Alvin and Miriam Hannah W.; m. Keiko Okubo, Dec. 1964 (div. Aug. 1977); m. Ayako Doi, Oct. 10, 1981. BS, U. Wis., 1960; MS, Columbia U., 1962. Reporter Wis. State Jour., Madison, 1959-61, Washington Post, 1962-63; corr. UPI, Tokyo, 1963-65, Asia div. news editor, 1965-66; chief S.E. Asia corr. UPI, Bangkok, Thailand, 1966-69; corr. UPI, Saigon, Republic of Vietnam, 1970-72; chief nat. security reporting team UPI, Washington, 1972-74, internat. mng. editor, 1987; assoc. editor fgn. and mil. affairs Newsweek, N.Y.C., 1974-78; corr. Newsweek, Washington, 1978-80, Tokyo bur. chief, 1980-83, nat. security corr., Washington, 1983-86; pub. The Daily Japan Digest, 1990—. Author: The Bad War, 1987. Served with U.S. Army, 1957-59. Recipient Best War Corr. award Overseas Press Club, N.Y., 1977, Best Mag. Fgn. Affairs Article award Overseas Press Club, N.Y., 1981. Mem. Nat. Press Club. Jewish. Avocation: sailing. Office: Japan Digest 5510 Columbia Pike Ste 207 Arlington VA 22204-3123

WILLERDING, MARGARET FRANCES, mathematician; b. St. Louis, Apr. 26, 1919; d. Herman J. and Mildred F. (Icenhower) W. A.B., Harris Tchrs. Coll., 1940; M.A., St. Louis U., 1943, Ph.D., 1947. Tchr. (Pub. Schs.), St. Louis, 1940-46; instr. math. Washington U., St. Louis, 1947-48; asst. prof. Harris Tchrs. Coll., St. Louis, 1948-56; mem. faculty San Diego State Coll., 1956—, asso. prof., 1959-65, prof. math., 1966-76, prof. emeritus, 1976—. Author: Intermediate Algebra, 1969, Elementary Mathematics, 1971, College Algebra, 1971, College Algebra and Trigonometry, 1971, Arithmetic, 1968, Probability: The Science of Chance, 1969, Mathematics Around the Clock, 1969, Mathematical Concepts, 1967, From Fingers to Computers, 1969, Probability Primer, 1968, Mathematics: The Alphabet of Science, 1972, 74, 77, A First Course in College Mathematics, 1973, 77, 80, Mathematics Worktext, 1973, 77, Business and Consumer Mathematics for College Students, 1976, The Numbers Game, 1977. Mem. Nat. Council Tchrs. Math., Assn. Tchrs. Sci. and Math., Am. Math. Soc., Math. Assn. Am., Greater San Diego Math. Council (dir. 1963-65), Sigma Xi, Pi Mu Epsilon. Home: 10241 Vivera Dr La Mesa CA 91941-4370 Office: Dept Math San Diego State Coll San Diego CA 92085

WILLES, MARK HINCKLEY, media industry executive; b. Salt Lake City, July 16, 1941; s. Joseph Simmons and Ruth (Hinckley) W.; m. Laura Fayone, June 7, 1961; children: Wendy Anne, Susan Kay, Keith Mark, Stephen Joseph, Matthew Bryant. AB, Columbia U., 1963, PhD, 1967. Mem. staff banking and currency com. Ho. of Reps., Washington, 1966-67; asst. prof. fin. U. Pa., Phila., 1967-69; economist Fed. Res. Bank, Phila., 1967, sr. economist, 1969-70, dir. research, 1970-71, v.p., dir. research, 1971, 1st v.p., 1971-77; pres. Fed. Res. Bank of Mpls., 1977-80; exec. v.p., chief fin. officer Gen. Mills, Inc., Mpls., 1980-85, pres., chief oper. officer, 1985-92, vice chmn., 1992-95; chmn., pres., CEO Times Mirror Co., L.A., 1995—. Office: Times Mirror Co Times Mirror Sq Los Angeles CA 90053 *My success is based on adherence to principles I learned in the home, which is the most basic and important organizational unit in the world. Three of those principles stand out in my mind: Be just, honest and moral—do things not only because they are required, but because they are right. Have mercy—care enough about others to be fair and kind. Be humble—you can get more done effectively with the help of others than you can do on your own.*

WILLETT, A. L. THOMPSON, public relations executive, consultant; b. Bardstown, Ky., Jan. 27, 1909; s. Aloysius Lambert and Mary Catherine (Thompson) W.; BA, Xavier U., Cin., 1931; m. Mary Virginia Sheehan, Jan. 14, 1942; children: Mary Tabitha (Mrs. Frank J. Fisher, Jr.), James (dec.), Martha Harriet (Mrs. Even Kulsveen), John David, Susan Virginia, Richard Francis, Alice Jane. Editor Loveland (Ohio) Herald, 1931-32; comptroller Ky. Hwy. Dept., 1932-33; asst. supt. Bernheim Distilling Co., Louisville, 1933-36; pres. Willett Distilling Co., Bardstown, Ky., 1936-82, also dir.; pres. Thompson Willett, pub. rels., Bardstown, 1982—; officer Willett Distributing , Inc., Wines Importer, 1982—; internat. rep. Pub. Translation of Lemarié Life of Bishop Flaget. Chmn. Bardstown-Nelson County Hist. Commn., 1938-53; Ky. advisor Nat. Trust for Historic Preservation, Washington, 1943-40. Bd. dirs. Xavier U., 1960-63; bd. dirs. Bellarmine Coll., 1964—; dir. Ida Lee Willis Meml. Found., Frankfort, Ky., 1982—. Recipient Disting. Cath. Alumnus award Archdiocese of Louisville, 1994. Mem. Ky. Distillers Assn. (pres. 1960), Newcomen Soc. N.Am., Distilled Spirits Coun. U.S. (dir. 1940-82). Club: Old Kentucky Home Country (Bardstown), Xavier U. 1931 Soc. Lodge: K.C. Contbr. articles to various publs. Home: Beechwold E Stephen Foster PO Box 91 Bardstown KY 40004 Office: PO Box 91 Bardstown KY 40004-0091

WILLETT, ANNA HART, composer; b. Bartlesville, Okla., June 18, 1931; d. Thomas Kellogg and Mary Kathryn (Feist) Willett Dalferes; m. Roger Garland Horn, Aug. 1956 (div. June 1962). B in Music Edn., Southwestern La. Inst., 1954; MA, La. State U., 1964, postgrad., 1976-87. Lifetime tchr. cert., La. Pub. sch. vocal music tchr. Iberville Parish, Plaquemine, La., 1954-55, Orleans Parish, New Orleans, 1966-71; elem. music pedagogy tchr. St. Mary's Dominican Coll., New Orleans, 1972. Composer: Dances for Solo Violin, 1981, Weaving Song, 1982, Entertainer's Song, 1983, Hercules Variations, 1986, En Ivrez, 1989. Scholar Loyola U. of the South, New Orleans, 1972-73. Mem. AAUW. Episcopalian. Avocations: gardening, bridge. Home: 2244 Ferndale Ave Baton Rouge LA 70808

WILLETT, ROSLYN LEONORE, public relations executive, food service consultant; b. N.Y.C., Oct. 18, 1924; d. Edward and Celia (Stickler) S.; m. Edward Willett (separated); 1 child, Jonathan Stanley. BA, Hunter Coll., N.Y.C., 1944; postgrad., Columbia U., 1944, CUNY, 1947-48, NYU, 1947-48, 52, New Sch., 1987-88. Dietitian YWCA, N.Y.C., 1944; tech. and patents libr. Stein Hall & Co., N.Y.C., 1944-46, food technologist tech. svcs. and devel. dept., 1946-48; editor McGraw-Hill, Inc., N.Y.C., 1949-50, Harcourt Brace Jovanovich, Inc., N.Y.C., 1950-54; pub. rels. writer Farley Manning Assocs., N.Y.C., 1954-58; cons. pub. rels. and food svc. Roslyn Willett Assocs., Inc., N.Y.C., 1959—; adj. prof. Hunter Coll., 1955-56, Polytech. Univ., N.Y., 1981-82, Columbia U. Sch. of Pub. Health, 1975-78; seminar presenter in field. Author: The Woman Executive in Woman in Sexist Society, 1971, short stories. chmn. Woman's Polit. Caucus, Inc., N.Y., N.J., Conn., 1971-73; v.p. Mid Hudson Arts and Sci. Ctr., Poughkeepsie, N.Y.; bd. dirs. Small Bus. Task Force, Assn. for Small Bus. and Professions, 1981-85, Regional Adv. Coun. Fed. SBA, 1976-78, Rhinebeck Chamber Music Soc., 1985-86, Will Inst. , New Paltz, 1980—; bd. dirs. Women Studies Abstracts, 1971-81. Mem. Pub. Rels. Soc. Am. (accredited), Food Svc. Cons. Soc. Internat., N.Y. Acad. Scis., Inst. Food Technologists, Paris Club. Avocations: writing, dance, art collecting, hiking, swimming. Home: Hunn's Lake Rd Stanfordville NY 12581 Office: 441 W End Ave New York NY 10024-5328

WILLETT, THOMAS EDWARD, lawyer; b. N.Y.C., Nov. 8, 1947; s. Oscar Edward and Alice (Fleming) W.; m. Marilyn Kenney, Dec. 28, 1969; children: Thomas Justin, Christopher Joseph. BS, USAF Acad., Colo., 1969; JD with distinction, Cornell U., 1972. Bar: N.Y. 1973, U.S. Ct. Claims 1973, U.S. Supreme Ct. 1977. Judge advocate USAF, Syracuse, N.Y., 1973-75, Kincheloe AFB, Mich., 1975-77; judge advocate USAF Hdqs., Washington, 1977-79; assoc. Harris, Beach & Wilcox, Rochester, N.Y., 1979-84, ptnr., 1985—. Pres. Monroe County Legal Assistance Corp., Rochester, 1983-89. Capt. USAF, 1969-79. Mem. ABA, N.Y. State Bar Assn., Monroe County Bar Assn., Order of Coif. Office: Harris Beach & Wilcox Granite Bldg 130 Main St E Rochester NY 14604-1620

WILLETTE, DONALD CORLISS, reverend; b. Lemmon, S.D., June 26, 1941; s. Corliss Noah Willette and Marion Alice (Egland) Allen. BA, St. Mary's Coll./Sem., 1963; MDiv, St. Thomas Sem., Denver, 1984. ordained Roman Catholic priest. Owner, operator Edel Haus Restaurant, Estes Park, Colo., 1975-77; owner, real estate broker Better Homes Gardens, Estes Park, 1977-84; assoc. pastor St. Thomas More, Englewood, Colo., 1984-87, St. Jude Ch., Lakewood, Colo., 1987-88; pastor St. Theresa Ch., Frederick, Colo., 1988-91, St. Louis Ch., Louisville, Colo., 1991—; founding bd. dirs. Mary's Dream Ltd., Frederick, 1989-92, Migrant Outreach Ministry, Longmont, Colo., 1991-95; tour leader Holy Land Pilgrimages, Jerusalem, 1984-94. With USAF, 1967-73, advanced through grades to col. USAFR, Colo. NG. Mem. Am. Legion (chaplain 1977—), K. of C. (chaplain 1984—), VFW, Elks (chaplain 1979-96, 96—). Avocations: salt water sailing, Holy Land pilgrimage leader. Office: St Louis Ch 902 Grant Ave Louisville CO 80027-1916

WILLEY, GORDON RANDOLPH, retired anthropologist, archaeologist, educator; b. Chariton, Iowa, Mar. 7, 1913; s. Frank and Agnes Caroline (Wilson) W.; m. Katharine W. Whaley, Sept. 17, 1938; children: Alexandra, Winston. AB, U. Ariz., 1935, AM, 1936, LittD (hon.), 1981; PhD, Columbia U., 1942; A.M. honoris causa, Harvard U., 1950; Litt.D. honoris causa, Cambridge U., 1977, U. N.Mex., 1984. Archaeol. asst. Nat. Pk. Svc., Macon, Ga., 1936-38; archaeologist La. State U., 1938-39; archaeol. field supr. Peru, 1941-42; instr. anthropology Columbia U., 1942-43; anthropologist Bur. Am. Ethnology, Smithsonian Instn., 1943-50; Bowditch prof. archaeology Harvard U., 1950-83; Bowditch prof. emeritus Havard U., 1984—; sr. prof. anthropology Harvard U., 1983-87, chmn. dept. anthropology, 1954-57; vis. prof. Am. archaeology Cambridge (Eng.) U., 1962-63; mem. expdns. to Peru, Panama, 1941-52, Brit. Honduras, 1953-56, Guatemala, 1958, 60, 62, 64, 65, 66, 67, 68, Nicaragua, 1959, 61, Honduras, 1973, 75-77. Author: Excavations in the Chancay Valley, Peru, 1943, Archaeology of the Florida Gulf Coast, 1949, Prehistoric Settlement Patterns in the Viru Valley, Peru, 1953, Introduction to American Archaeology, 2 vols, 1966-71, The Artifacts of Altar de Sacrificios, 1972, Excavations of Altarde Sacrificious, Guatemala: Summary and Conclusions, 1973, Das Alte Amerika, 1974, The Artifacts of Seibal, Guatemala, 1978, Essays in Maya Archaeology, 1987, Portraits in American Archaeology, 1988, New World Archaeology and Culture History, 1990, Excavations at Seibal: Summary and Conclusions, 1990; co-author: Early Ancon and Early Supe Cultures, 1954, The Monagrillo Culture of Panama, 1954, Method and Theory in American Archaeology, 1958, Prehistoric Maya Settlements in the Belize Valley, 1965, The Ruins of Altar de Sacrificios, Department of Peten, Guatemala: An Introduction, 1969, the Maya Collapse: An Appraisal, 1973, A History of American Archaeology, 1974, 3d edit., 1993, The Origins of Maya Civilization, 1977, Lowland Maya Settlement Patterns: A Summary View, 1981, the Copan Residential Zone, 1994; co-editor: Courses Toward Urban Life, 1962, Precolumbian Archaeology, 1980, A Consideration of the Early Classic Period in the Maya Lowlands, 1985; editor: Prehistoric Settlement Patterns of the New World, 1956, Archaeological Researches in Retrospect, 1974. Overseas fellow Churchill Coll., Cambridge U., 1968-69; decorated Order of Quetzal Guatemala; recipient Viking Fund medal, 1953; Gold medal Archaeol. Inst. Am., 1973; Alfred V. Kidder medal for achievement in Am. Archaeology, 1974; Huxley medal Royal Anthrop. Inst., London, 1979; Walker prize Boston Mus. Sci., 1981; Drexel medal for archaeology Univ. Mus., Phila., 1981, Golden Plate award Am. Acad. Achievement, 1987. Fellow Am. Anthrop. Assn. (pres. 1961), Am. Acad. Arts and Sci., London Soc. Antiquaries, Soc. Am. Archaeology (pres. 1968, Disting. Svc. award 1980); mem. Nat. Acad. Sci., Am. Philos. Soc., Royal Anthrop. Inst. Gt. Britain and Ireland, Cosmos Club (Washington), Tavern Club (Boston), Phi Beta Kappa, Brit. Acad. (corr.).

WILLEY, JAMES LEE, dentist; b. Colorado Springs, Colo., Oct. 26, 1953; s. Elwood James and Dorothy Jean (Norton) W.; m. Catherine Margaret Whitmer, Aug. 23, 1975; children: Andrew James and David Lee (twins). BA, So. Ill. U., 1975; BS in Dentistry, U. Ill., Chgo., 1977, DDS, 1979; MBA, No. Ill. U., 1986. Pvt. practice Elburn, Ill., 1979—; lectr. Dental Arts Labs., Peoria, Ill., 1981-90. Trustee Paul W. Clopper Meml. Found., 1989—, chmn. fund raising com., 1991—, treas., 1992—; mem. adminstrv. bd. Geneva United Meth. Ch., 1991-92; asst. scoutmaster Boy Scouts Am., Elburn, 1995—; spokesperson Prevent Abuse and Neglect Through Dental Awareness, 1995—; village trustee Village of Elburn, 1995-97, fin. com., 1995-97, police com., 1995-96, pub. works com., 1996-97, village pres., 1997—. Recipient Certificate of Merit, Swissedent Found., Glendale, Calif., 1983; benefactor Clopper Found., 1992. Fellow Am. Endodontic Soc.; mem. ADA (Outstanding Young Dentist Leader award 1992), Ill. State Dental Soc. (alt. del. 1990, spokesperson 1990—, del. 1991-92, dental edn. com. 1991-93, chmn. 1994—, vice-spkr. ho. of dels. 1992-93), Fox River Valley Dental Soc. (bd. dirs. 1988-93, sec. 1989, treas. 1990, v.p. 1991, pres. 1992), The Dental PAC of Ill. (bd. dirs. 1988-97, exec. com. 1989-97, 2d v.p. 1991-93, 1st v.p. 1993-95, pres. 1995-97). Avocations: fishing, photography. Home: 711 N 3rd St Elburn IL 60119-8968 Office: 135 S Main St # 7G Elburn IL 60119-9142

WILLEY, JOHN DOUGLAS, retired newspaper executive; b. Melrose, Mass., June 4, 1917; s. Arthur Peach and Lillian (Holden) W.; m. Marilynn Miller, July 3, 1943; children: Margery Lynn Willey Marshall (dec.), John Douglas, James Campbell, David Spencer, Peter Whitney. LLD (hon.), U. Toledo, 1972. Sec. Boston & Maine R.R., Boston, 1935-40, Jones & Lamson Machine Co., Springfield, Vt., 1940-41; reporter The Blade, Toledo, 1946-49, asst. to pub., 1949-51, city editor, 1952-54, asst. mng. editor, 1954-56, dir. pub. rels., 1956-58, treas., 1962-69, assoc. pub., 1965-81, pres., 1969-81, also bd. dirs.; pres. Clear Water, Inc., 1966-89; bd. dirs. Buckeye Cablevision, Inc., Monterey Peninsula Herald; v.p., dir. Lima Communications Corp., 1971-81, Red Bank Register, 1975-81; mem. Ohio adv. bd. Liberty Mut. Ins. Co., 1976-82. Mem. exec. com. of bd. trustees, treas. Toledo Area Med. Coll. and Edn. Found., 1960-75, hon. trustee, 1975—; mem. adv. bd. St. Vincent Hosp., 1961-75; trustee Maumee Valley Country Day Sch., 1974-77, Med. Coll. Ohio, 1982-91; treas. Amateur Athletic Union Task Force Com., 1976-82, Ohio chmn. U.S. Olympic Commn. 1979-80; mem. Inter-Univ. Coun., Ohio, 1988-91. Capt. A.C., U.S. Army, 1942-46. Recipient Disting. Citizen award Med. Coll. Ohio, 1994. Mem. Belmont Country Club, Med. Coll. Ohio Faculty Club, Sigma Delta Chi. Home: 3534 River Rd Toledo OH 43614-4326

WILLGING, PAUL RAYMOND, trade association executive; b. New Rochelle, N.Y., Feb. 14, 1942; s. Herbert Martin and Pauline Mary (Mast) W.; m. Monika Guenther, Aug. 25, 1967; children: Kirsten, Birgit. BA, U. St. Thomas, 1963; M in Internat. Affairs, Columbia U., 1966, PhD, 1973. Assoc. adminstr. Health Services Adminstrn., Parklawn, Md., 1973-75; dep. commr. Med. Services Adminstrn., Washington, 1975-80; dep. adminstr. Health Care Fin. Adminstrn., Balt., 1980-82; asst. v.p. Blue Cross/Blue Shield Greater N.Y., N.Y.C., 1982-83; exec. v.p. Am. Health Care Assn., Washington, 1983—. Contbr. articles to profl. jours. Bd. dirs. Nat. Health Coun., Washington, 1986—, Howard County Gen. Hosp., Columbia, 1987—. Fulbright scholar, 1964; fellow Woodrow Wilson Found., 1965, Ford Found., 1966. Avocations: skiing, jogging. Home: 10366 Crossbeam Ct Columbia MD 21044-3819 Office: Am Health Care Association 1201 L St NW Washington DC 20005-4024*

WILLHAM, RICHARD LEWIS, animal science educator; b. Hutchinson, Kans., May 4, 1932; s. Oliver S. and Susan E. (Hurt) W.; m. Esther B. Burkhart, June 1, 1954; children: Karen Nell, Oliver Lee. B.S., Okla. State U., 1954; M.S., Iowa State U., 1955, Ph.D., 1960. Asst. prof. Iowa State U., Ames, 1959-63, assoc. prof., 1966-71, prof. dept. animal sci., 1971-78, Disting. prof., 1978—; assoc. prof. Okla. State U., Stillwater, 1963-66; cons. in field; tchr. livestock history; guest curator exhbn. Art About Livestock, 1990. Author: A Heritage of Leadership - The First 100 Years of Animal Science at Iowa State University, 1996. Recipient Svc. award Beef Improvement Fedn., 1974, Edn. and Rsch. award Am. Polled Herefore Assn., 1979, Rsch. award Nat. Cattlemen's Assn., 1986, 91, Disting. Alumnus award Okla. State U., 1978, Regents Faculty Excellence award Iowa State U., 1993; named to Hall of Fame Am. Hereford Assn., 1982, Am. Angus Assn., 1988. Fellow Am. Soc. Animal Sci. (animal breeding and genetics award 1978, industry service award 1986). Home: 316 E 20th St Ames IA 50010-5563 Office: Iowa State U Dept Animal Sci Ames IA 50011

WILLHITE, CALVIN CAMPBELL, toxicologist; b. Salt Lake City, Apr. 27, 1952; s. Jed Butler and Carol (Campbell) W. BS, Utah State U., 1974, MS, 1977; PhD, Dartmouth Coll., 1980. Toxicologist USDA, Berkeley, Calif., 1980-85, State of Calif., Berkeley, 1985—; adj. assoc. prof. toxicol. Utah State U., 1984-94; mem. data safety rev. bd. Johns Hopkins Sch. Medicine, 1996—; mem. Calif./OSHA Gen. Industry Safety Order/Lead in Constrn. PEL Adv. Bd., 1994, 96. Mem. editl. bd. Toxicology and Applied Pharmacology, 1989—; editor N.Y. Acad. Scis., 1993, Toxicology, 1996—, Jour. Toxicological Environ. Health, 1996—; contbr. articles on birth defects to profl. jours. Nat. Inst. Child Health and Human Devel. grantee, 1985, 89, 92, March of Dimes Birth Defects Found. grantee, 1987-91, Hoffmann LaRoche grantee, 1992-94, Chem. Mfg. Assn., Nat. Ctr. Toxicol. Rsch., 1996. Mem. Soc. Toxicology (mem. program com. 1995—, Frank R. Blood award 1986), Teratology Soc. (chair pub. affairs), Am. Conf. Govt. Ind. Hygienists (vice-chair TLV com.), Internat. Occupl. Hygiene Assoc. Democrat. Mem. United Ch. of Christ. Home: 2863 Sanderling Dr Fremont CA 94555-1368 Office: State Calif 700 Heinz Ave Berkeley CA 94710-2721

WILLIAM, DAVID, director, actor; b. London, Eng., June 24, 1926; arrived in Can., 1986; s. Eric Hugh and Olwen (Roose) W. BA, U. Coll., Oxford, Eng., 1950. Artistic dir. Glasgow Citizen's Theatre, The Nottingham Playhouse, The New Shakespeare Co., London, The National Theatre of Israel, Stratford Festival, Can., 1989-93; instr. U.S., Can., Britain; founder, 1st artistic dir. Ludlow Festival. Theatre directing credits include: Bacchae, The Importance of Being Earnest, The Tempest, Entertaining Mr. Sloane, Love Letters, Treasure Island, Hamlet, Love for Love, The Shoemaker's Holiday, Murder in the Cathedral, Troilus and Cressida, The Winter's Tale, She Stoops to Conquer, Antigone, Separate Tables, Romeo and Juliet, Othello, King Lear, Volpone, Albert Herring, The Merry Wives of Windosr, Twelfth Night; directing world premiers of operas include: Therese, Royal Opera House Covent Garden, The Lighthouse, Edinburgh festival, Red Emma; other operas directed include Iphigenie en Tauride, The Fairy Queen, Lisbon, La Traviata, Scottish Opera, Il Re Pastore, Camden Festival, Albert Herring, Aldeburgh Festival, Cosl Fan Tutte, Opera St. Louis; appeared in Uncle Vanya as Serebryakov, As You Like It as Jaques, Twelfth Night as Malvolio, Hamlet as Rosencrantz to Richard Burton's (Hamlet); appeared in numerous TV prodns. most notably as Richard the Second in the BBC series An Age of Kings; compiled, directed and acted in My Shakespeare, Stratford Festival and CBC Radio. Home: 194 Langarth St E, London, ON Canada N6C 1Z5

WILLIAMS, AENEAS DEMETRIUS, professional football player; b. New Orleans, Jan. 29, 1968. Degree in acctg., So. Univ. La., 1990. Cornerback Ariz. Cardinals, 1991. Selected to Pro Bowl, 1994-96; tied for NFL lead in interceptions (9), 1994. Office: c/o Ariz Cardinals PO Box 888 Phoenix AZ 85001-0888*

WILLIAMS, ALAN DAVISON, publishing company executive; b. Duluth, Minn., Oct. 25, 1925; s. Curtis Gilbert and Marjorie Barton (Townsend) W.; m. Beverly Alexander, Apr. 1, 1951 (div. May 1988); children: Wistar W. Rawls, Anne Alexander, Marjorie Williams Noah; m. Rosina Rue, June 25, 1988; 1 child, Rosina Barton. Grad., Phillips Exeter Acad., 1944; B.A., Yale U., 1949. Advt. mgr. McGraw-Hill Book Co., 1949-53; publicity mgr., editor J.B. Lippincott Co., 1953-58; N.Y. editor Little, Brown & Co., 1959-65; mng. editor, editorial dir., v.p. Viking Press, Inc., N.Y.C., 1965-84; v.p. editorial Viking-Penguin Inc., 1975-84; exec. editor, v.p. G.P. Putnam Co., N.Y.C., 1985-87; pub., editor in chief Arbor House/William Morrow, N.Y.C., 1987-89; pub. Grove Weidenfeld Inc., N.Y.C., 1990-92; Mem. adv. council English dept. Princeton, 1972-86. Editor: Fifty Years-A Farrar, Straus and Giroux Reader, 1996. Bd. dirs. Friends of Princeton Art Mus., 1980-85; trustee Princeton U. Press, 1991-95. Served with USAAF, 1944-45. Woodrow Wilson vis. fellow; recipient Career Achievement award PEN/Roger Klein Found., 1997. Club: Century Assn. (N.Y.C.). Home: 560 Palisade Ave Jersey City NJ 07307-1125

WILLIAMS, ALUN GWYN, publishing company executive; b. Newtown, Powys, Wales, Oct. 31, 1953; s. Edgar Pugh and Pamela Beresford (Jones) W.; m. Deborah Elaine Smith, May 1, 1982; children: Megan Elizabeth, Gareth Huw. BA in Math., Worcester Coll., Oxford (Eng.) U., 1975, MA, 1980. Chartered acct. Audit mgr. Touche Ross, London, 1980-83; group fin. contr. October Pub., London, 1986-88; comml. dir. Reed Consumer Books, London, 1988-92; v.p. fin. Reed Reference Pub., New Providence, N.J., 1992-95, exec. v.p. fin. and ops., 1995—. Mem. Inst. Chartered Accts. Eng. and Wales (Strachan prize 1980). Office: Reed Reference Pub 121 Chanlon Rd New Providence NJ 07974-1541

WILLIAMS, ANDY, entertainer; b. Wall Lake, Iowa, Dec. 3, 1930; s. Jay Emerson and Florence (Finley) W.; m. Claudine Longet, Dec. 15, 1961 (div.); children: Noelle, Christian, Robert; m. Debbie Haas, May 3, 1991. pres. Barnaby Records, Barnaby Prodns., Barnaby Sports; owner Moon River Enterprises; host Andy Williams San Diego Golf Open, 1969-89. Worked with 3 brothers as Williams Brothers Quartet, on radio stations in Des Moines, Chgo., Cin. and Los Angeles, 1938-47, Williams Brothers, (teamed with Kay Thompson); worked for night clubs, U.S. and Europe, 1947-52; regular performer: Steve Allen Tonight TV show, 1953-55; star: Andy Williams TV Show, 1962-71; night club and concert entertainer, rec. artist for Columbia Records; recordings include Moon River, Love Story, theme from The Godfather, Can't Get Used to Losing You, Days of Wine and Roses, Born Free, Hawaiian Wedding Song, Butterfly. Named Number One Male Vocalist Top Artist on Campus Poll, 1968; recipient 17 gold albums, 3 Emmy awards, 6 Grammy awards. Office: Moon River Theatre 2500 W Highway 76 Branson MO 65616-2164*

WILLIAMS, ANN CLAIRE, federal judge; b. 1949; m. David J. Stewart. BS, Wayne State U., 1970; MA, U. Mich., 1972; JD, U. Notre Dame, 1975. Law clk. to hon. Robert A. Sprecher, 1975-76; asst. U.S. atty. U.S. Dist. Ct. (no. dist.) Ill., Chgo., 1976-85; faculty mem. Nat. Inst. for Trial Advocacy, 1979—; judge U.S. Dist. Ct. (no. dist.) Ill., Chgo., 1985—; chief Crime Drug Enforecement Task Froce North Ctrl. Region, 1983-85; chair ct. adminstrn. and case mgmt. com. Jud. Conf. U.S., 1993—. Trustee U. Chgo. Lab Sch.; sec. bd. trustees U. Notre Dame, Mus. Sci. and Industry. Mem. Fed. Bar Assn., Fed. Judges Assn. (treas.), Women's Bar Assn. of Ill. Office: US Dist Ct 219 S Dearborn St Ste 1988 Chicago IL 60604-1801*

WILLIAMS, ANNEMARIE HAUBER, secondary education educator; b. Schorndorf, Baden Württenburg, Germany, Mar. 6, 1946; came to U.S., 1951; d. William Carl and Hertha (Franze) Hauber; m. William C. Young, Nov. 23, 1972 (div.); 1 child, Niccole Anne Young; m. Evan J. Williams, Aug. 1, 1982. BA, U. S.C., 1968; postgrad., U. London Sch. Econs., 1969; MA, SUNY, New Paltz, 1974. Cert. social studies educator. Tchr. history Monticello (N.Y.) High Sch., 1968-70; tchr. history, coach male varsity and jr. varsity tennis, varsity basketball cheerleaders Yorktown (N.Y.) High Sch., 1970-71; tchr. history Hendrick Hudson High Sch., Montrose, N.Y., 1971—;

coach male varsity tennis Hendrick Hudson High Sch., Montrose, 1971-73; textbook rater in field. Mem. Dems. for Am., U. S.C., 1965-68. Recipient Outstanding Tchr. award U. Chgo., 1988, Study grant U. Hawaii, 1969. Mem. ASCD, N.Y. State Coun. for Social Studies, Nat. Coun. for Social Studies. Democrat. Lutheran. Avocations: tennis, gardening, reading, swimming, art collecting. Home: Box 365 7 Lord Rd Rock Hill NY 12775-5019

WILLIAMS, ANTHONY A., federal official; m. Diana Lynn Simmons; 1 child. BA in Polit. Sci. magna cum laude, Yale U., 1982; JD, M of Pub. Policy, Harvard U., 1987. Law clk. to Hon. David Nelson U.S. Dist. Ct., Boston, 1987-88; asst. dir. Boston Redevel. Authority, 1988-89; exec. dir. Cmty. Devel. Agy., St. Louis, 1989-91; dep. comptr. State of Conn., Boston, 1991-93; CFO Dept. Agrl., 1993—; exec. dir. Cmty. Devel. Agy., St. Louis, 1989-91; dept. contr. State of Conn., 1991-93; CFO Dept. Agr., Washington, 1993—; adj. prof. pub. affairs Columbia U., N.Y.C., 1992-93. Pres. pro tempore, chmn. cmty. devel. com. Conn. Bd. Alderman, 1980-83; dir. comm. Conn. Spkr. House and Assembly Dem., 1983. Kellogg Found. Nat. fellow, 1991. Office: Dept of Agrl Chief Fin Officer 441 4th St NW Ste 350N Washington DC 20001-2700*

WILLIAMS, ARTHUR BENJAMIN, JR., bishop; b. Providence, R.I., June 25, 1935; m. Lynette Rhodes, 1985. AB, Brown U., 1957; MDiv, Gen. Theol. Sem., 1964; MA, U. Mich., 1974; DD, Gen. Theol. Sem., 1986. Clarence Horner fellow Grace Ch., Providence, 1964-65; asst. St. Mark, Riverside, R.I., 1965-67; sub-dean St. John Cathedral, Providence, 1967-68; assoc. & interim rector Grace Ch., Detroit, 1968-70; asst. to bishop Diocese of Mich., 1970-77; archdeacon Ohio Cleve., 1977-85; suffragan bishop Episcopal Diocese of Ohio, Cleve., 1986—; v.p. House of Bishops, 1995—; chair Com. on Justice, Peace and Integrity of Creation, 1995—. Chair editl. com. Lift Every Voice and Sing II, 1993. Office: Diocese of Ohio 2230 Euclid Ave Cleveland OH 44115-2405

WILLIAMS, ARTHUR COZAD, broadcasting executive; b. Forty Fort, Pa., Feb. 12, 1926; s. John Bedford and Emily Irene (Poyck) W.; m. Ann Cale Bragan, Oct. 1, 1955; children: Emily Williams Van Hoorickx, Douglas, Craig. Student, Wilkes U., 1943-44; B.A. cum laude, U. So. Calif., 1949. With Kaiser Aluminum, 1949, Sta. KPMC, 1950-51; v.p., mgr. KFBK and KFBK-FM Radio Stas., Sacramento, 1951-80; with public relations dept. Sacramento Bee, McClatchy Newspapers, 1981-86; dir.-treas. Norkal Opportunities, Inc.; pres. Sacramento Bee Credit Union. Served with AUS, 1944-46. Mem. Sigma Delta Chi. Clubs: Rotary, Sutter, Valley Hi Country, Masons, Shriners. Home: 1209 Nevis Ct Sacramento CA 95822-2532 Office: 1125 Brownwyk Dr Sacramento CA 95822-1028

WILLIAMS, AUBREY WILLIS, anthropology educator; b. Madison, Wis., July 31, 1924; s. Aubrey Willis and Anita (Schreck) W.; m. Alice Rebecca Williams, Sept. 20, 1950 (div. June 1972); children: Jonathan Goree, Nancy Clark; m. Graceanne Adamo, Dec. 21, 1974 (div. June 1992); 1 child, Aubrey Philip Rhys. BA, U. N.C., 1955, MA, 1957; PhD, U. Ariz., 1964. Circulation mgr. So. Farmer Inc., Montgomery, Ala., 1950-53, pub. rep., 1953-55; research asst. dept. anthropology U. N.C., Chapel Hill, 1956; field camp dir. Am. Friends Service Com., San Salvador el Verde, Puebla, Mex., 1957-58; teaching asst. U. Ariz., Tucson, 1958-60; ethnologist Navajo Tribe, Window Rock, Ariz., 1961-62; asst. prof. U. Md., College Park, 1962-66, assoc. prof., dir. div. of anthropology, 1967-71, full prof., 1971—; research assoc. Smithsonian Instn., Washington, 1966-67; Fulbright prof., USSR, 1982, Fulbright-Hays prof., Mex., 1984, USIA prof. Tampere (Finland) U., 1990-91. Mem. Am. Anthrop. Assn., Soc. for Applied Anthropology. Democrat. Office: U Md Dept Anthropology College Park MD 20472

WILLIAMS, B. JOHN, JR., lawyer, former federal judge; b. Lancaster, Pa., Dec. 13, 1949; s. Bernard John and Sarah Elizabeth (Sykes) W.; m. Martha Caroline Roberts, Aug. 6, 1977; children: Robert, Sarah, Anne, Bernard. BA, George Washington U., 1971, JD, 1974. Bar: D.C., Pa., U.S. Ct. Appeals (fed. cir.). Law clk. to judge U.S. Tax Ct., Washington, 1974-76; assoc. Ballard, Spahr, Andrews & Ingersoll, Phila., 1976-81; spl. asst. to chief counsel IRS, Washington, 1981-83; dep. asst. atty. gen. Tax Div. Dept. Justice, Washington, 1983-84; ptnr. Morgan, Lewis & Bockius, Washington, 1984-85; judge U.S. Tax Ct., Washington, 1985-90; ptnr. Morgan, Lewis & Bockius, Washington, 1990—; mem. adv. com. U.S. Ct. Appeals, Fed. Cir. Fellow Am. Coll. Tax Counsel; mem. ABA, Am. Law Inst., Phi Beta Kappa, Omicron Delta Kappa. Republican. Office: Morgan Lewis & Bockius 1800 M St NW Washington DC 20036-5802

WILLIAMS, BARBARA ANNE, college president; b. Camden, N.J., Oct. 14, 1938; d. Frank and Laura Dorothy (Szweda) W. BA cum laude, Georgian Court Coll., 1963; MLS, Rutgers U., 1965; MA, Manhattan Coll., 1973; postgrad., NYU, 1976-81, 93—. Cert. English tchr., N.J.; joined Sisters of Mercy, 1957. Sec. Camden Cath. High Sch., 1956-57; registrar Georgian Ct. Coll., Lakewood, N.J., 1960-66, dir. libr. svcs., 1966-74, dean acad. affairs, 1974-80, pres., 1980—; bd. dirs. N.J. Natural Gas Co., 1986-91. Mem. editorial bd. N.J. Woman mag. Bd. dirs., mem. ednl. adv. coun. Diocese of Trenton, N.J., 1983-90; mem. adv. bd. Ocean County Ctr. for Arts, Lakewood, N.J., 1983-91; mem. Ocean County Pvt. Industry Coun., 1983-92; bd. dirs. Monmouth/Ocean Devel. Coun., 1981-84; mem. State of N.J. Student Assistance Bd., 1995—; mem. Ocean County School-to-Work Com., 1996—. Named Outstanding Woman N.J. Assn. Women Bus. Owners, 1983; recipient Humanitarian award Monmouth/Ocean Devel. Coun., 1985, Salute to Policymakers award Exec. Women N.J., 1986, Woman in Leadership award Monmouth Coun. Girl Scouts, 1987, Citizen of Yr. Alcoholism & Drug Abuse Coun. Ocean County, 1993, Brotherhood/Sisterhood award Monmouth/Ocean County chpts. NCCJ, 1994. Mem. Assn. of Mercy Colls. (pres. 1981-83), Mercy Higher Edn. Colloquium (mem. exec. com. 1980-87, sec. 1996—), Ocean County Bus. Assn. (trustee 1982-84), Nat. Assn. Inc. Colls. and Univs. (secretariat 1981-83, 87-91), NAIA (coun. of pres. 1997—). Home and Office: Georgian Ct Coll 900 Lakewood Ave Lakewood NJ 08701-2600

WILLIAMS, BEN FRANKLIN, JR., mayor, lawyer; b. El Paso, Tex., Aug. 12, 1929; s. Ben Franklin and Dorothy (Whitaker) W.; m. Daisy Federighi, June 2, 1951; children: Elizabeth Lee, Diane Marie, Katherine Ann, Benjamin Franklin III. BA, U. Ariz., 1951, JD, 1956. Bar: Ariz. 1956. With Bd. Immigration Appeals, Dept. Justice, 1957, ICC, 1959; pvt. practice Tucson, Ariz., 1956—; city atty. Douglas and Tombstone, 1962; atty. Mexican consul, 1960; mayor of Douglas, 1980-88; bd. dirs. Ariz. Pub. Service Co., Univ. Med. Ctr. Corp. Pres. Ariz. League Cities and Towns, pres. Douglas Sch. Bd., 1963, 69, 70; mem. bd. Ariz. Dept. Econ. Planning and Devel.; bd. dirs. Ariz.-Mex. Commn., Ariz. Acad. (Town Hall), Merabank & Ariz. Pub. Service Co.; ward committeeman Douglas Republican Com., 1962. Served to 1st lt. AUS, 1951-53. Mem. ABA, Internat. Bar Assn., Ariz. Bar Assn. (treas. 1963), Cochise County Bar Assn. (pres. 1959), Pima County Bar Assn., Am. Judicature Soc., U. Ariz. Law Coll. Assn. (dir.), Ariz. Hist. Soc. (dir.), Sigma Nu, Phi Delta Phi, Blue Key. Episcopalian. Lodge: Elks. Home: 6555 N St Andrews Dr Tucson AZ 85718-2615 Office: 3773 E Broadway Blvd Tucson AZ 85716-5409

WILLIAMS, BERNABE FIGUEROA, professional baseball player; b. San Juan, P.R., Sept. 13, 1968. Outfielder New York Yankees, 1991—. Named Am. League Championship Series MVP, 1996. Office: New York Yankees Yankee Stadium E 161 St and River Ave Bronx NY 10451*

WILLIAMS, BILL, academic administrator. Pres. Grand Canyon U. Office: Grand Canyon U 3300 W Camelback Rd Phoenix AZ 85017-3030

WILLIAMS, BOBBY See EVERHART, ROBERT PHILLIP

WILLIAMS, BROWN F, television media services company executive; b. Evanston, Ill., Dec. 22, 1940; s. Jack Kermit Williams and Virginia Helen (Benjamin) Likar; m. Linda Francee Ludt, Sept. 1961 (div. 1968); 1 child, Eden Carol Williams McCarthy; m. Martha Amidon Powers, 1970 (div. 1974); m. Sandra Ann Matkowski, Jan. 1984; 1 child, Bronwyn Emily. AB in Math. and Physics, U. Calif., Riverside, 1962, MA in Physics, 1964, PhD in Physics, 1966. Mgr. Electro-Optics Lab., Princeton, N.J., 1969-75; dir. RCA Labs., Princeton, 1976-82, v.p., 1982-87; pres. Williams Cons. Group, Princeton, 1988-90; pres. Princeton Video Image, 1990—. Fellow IEEE; mem. AAAS, Am. Phys. Soc., Sigma Xi. Avocations: skiing, ocean sailing, tennis. Office: 47 Hulfish St Princeton NJ 08542-3709

WILLIAMS, BRYAN, university dean, medical educator; b. Longview, Tex., July 28; s. Lewis Bryan and Margaret Louise (Smart) W.; m. Frances Montgomery, Mar. 31, 1950; children: Harrison, Amy, Philip, Nickolas, Margaret, Lincoln. MD, Southwestern Med. Sch., 1947. Diplomate Am. Bd. Internal Medicine. Pvt. practice Dallas, 1957-70; prof. internal medicine, assoc. dean student affairs Southwestern Med. Sch., 1970-90, prof. internal medicine emeritus, dean student affairs emeritus. Fellow ACP; mem. Inst. Medicine Nat. Acad. Scis. (charter). Home: 3419 Dartmouth Ave Dallas TX 75205-2806

WILLIAMS, CAMILLA, soprano, voice educator; b. Danville, Va.; d. Booker and Fannie (Cary) W.; m. Charles T. Beavers, Aug. 28, 1950. BS, Va. State Coll., 1941; postgrad., U. Pa., 1942; studies with, Mme. Marian Szekely-Freschl, 1943-44, 1952, Berkowitz and Cesare Sodero, 1944-46, Rose Dirman, 1948-52, Sergius Kagen, 1958-62; MusD (hon.), Va. State U., 1986, D. (hon.), 1985. Prof. voice Bronx Coll., N.Y.C., 1970, Bklyn. Coll., 1970-73, Queens Coll., N.Y.C., 1974, Ind. U., Bloomington, 1977—; 1st black prof. voice Cen. Conservatory Music, Beijing, People's Republic China, 1983. Created role of Madame Butterfly as 1st black contract singer, N.Y.C. Ctr., 1946, 1st Aida, 1948; 1st N.Y. performance of Mozart's Idomeneo with Little Orch. Soc., 1950; 1st Viennese performance Menotti's Saint of Bleecker Street, 1955; 1st N.Y. performance of Handel's Orlando, 1971; other roles include Nedda in Pagliacci, Mimi in La Boheme, Marguerite in Faust; major tours include Alaska, 1950, London, 1954, Am. Festival in Belgium, 1955, tour of 14 African countries for U.S. Dept. State, 1958-59, Israel, 1959, concert for Crown Prince of Japan as guest of Gen. Eisenhower, 1960, tour of Formosa, Australia, New Zealand, Korea, Japan, Philippines, Laos, South Vietnam, 1971, Poland, 1974; appearances with orchs. including Royal Philharm., Vienna Symphony, Berlin Philharm., Chgo. Symphony, Phila. Orch., BBC Orch., Stuttgart Orch., many others; contract with RCA Victor as exclusive Victor Red Seal rec. artist, 1944—. Recipient Marian Anderson award (1st winner), 1943, 44, Newspaper Guild award as First Lady of Am. Opera, 1947, Va. State Coll. 75th anniv. cert. of merit, 1957, NYU Presdl. Citation, 1959, Gold medal Emperor of Ethiopia and Key to City of Taiwan during Pres. Johnson's Cultural Exchange Program, 1962, Art, Culture and Civic Guild award, 1962, Negro Musician's Assn. plaque, 1963, Harlem Opera and World Fellowship Soc. award, 1963; named Disting. Virginian Gov. of Va., 1972; inducted Danville (Va.) Mus. Fine Arts and History Hall of Fame, 1974; Camilla Williams Park designated in her honor, Danville, 1974; honored by Ind. U. Sch. Music Black Music Students' Orgn., 1979; named to Hon. Order Ky. Cols., 1979; honored by Phila. Pro Arte Soc., 1982; Disting. award of Ctr. for Leadership and Devel., 1983; Taylor-Williams student residence hall at Va. State U. named in Billy Taylor's and her honor, 1985. Mem. NAACP (hon. life), Internat. Platform Assn., Alpha Kappa Alpha. Office: Ind U Sch Music Bloomington IN 47401 *Years of travel have given me the chance to meet people of every race, kind, and condition. I have been a witness to the brotherhood and sisterhood of mankind, for we are all children of God. The most important lesson of my life is the value of giving. When you give of yourself you receive the blessings of your talents.*

WILLIAMS, CARL CHANSON, oil company executive; b. Cin., Oct. 16, 1937; s. Charles J. and Alcie (Brazile) W.; m. Claire Bathé, May 26, 1985; 1 child, Michelle. A.S., U. Cin., 1965; B.S., SUNY-Brockport, 1974; M.B.A., U. Rochester, 1975. Mgr. fin. systems Xerox Corp., Rochester, N.Y., 1972-77; dir. info. mgmt. Am. Can Co., Greenwich, Conn., 1977-79, mng. dir. info. mgmt., 1979-80, mng. dir. ops. control, 1980-82; sr. v.p., dir. mgmt. info. systems DDB Needham Worldwide, N.Y.C., 1982-90; pres. The Intertechnology Group, Inc., N.Y.C., 1990-91; v.p. infosystems and tech. Macmillan Pub. Co., N.Y.C., 1991-93; gen. mgr. info. tech. Amoco Corp., Chgo., 1993-94, v.p. info. tech., 1994—; cons. Stamford (Conn.) Bd. Edn., 1981-82; lectr. U. Rochester, N.Y., 1975-77; adj. prof. Fordham U., 1991—. Exec. dir. Concerned Assn. Rochester, N.Y., 1971-75; bd. dirs. Stamford Cmty. Arts Coun., 1983-84; trustee Roosevelt U., 1995—. Mem. Soc. Info. Mgmr. (exec. coun. 1980-83, pres. 1985, pres. coun. 1986—), Exec. Leadership Coun. Office: Amoco Corp 200 E Randolph St Chicago IL 60601-6436

WILLIAMS, CARL E., SR., bishop. Presiding bishop Ch. of God in Christ, Internat., N.Y.C., 1978—. Office: Ch of God in Christ Internat 170 Adelphi St Brooklyn NY 11205-3302*

WILLIAMS, CARL HARWELL, utilities executive; b. Mansfield, Ga., Oct. 22, 1915; s. John Horace and Mary Ruby (Harwell) W.; m. Diane Barnes, June 25, 1967; children: Edward Vincent, Lesa Anne. Student, U. Fla., 1934-35; B.S., Ga. Sch. Tech., 1939; postgrad., Harvard Advanced Mgmt. Program, U. Hawaii, 1956. Registered profl. engr., Hawaii. Engr. Fla. Power & Light Co., Miami, 1939-41; with Hawaiian Electric Co., Inc., Honolulu, 1945-80; mgr. engring. Hawaiian Electric Co., Inc., 1955-62, v.p., 1962-71, exec. v.p., 1971-72, pres., 1972-80, dir., 1970-85, chmn. exec. com., 1980-85; chmn. bd., dir. Maui Electric Co. (subsidiary), 1972-80, Hawaii Electric Light Co. (subsidiary), 1972-80; dir. Bank of Hawaii., Hawaiian Electric Industries, Inc., Bancorp Hawaii, Inc. Bd. dirs. Aloha United Way, 1973-79; bd. dirs. Oahu Devel. Conf., 1972-81, chmn., 1979-80; bd. visitors Coll. Bus. Adminstrn., Hawaii, mem. adv. com. advanced mgmt. program, 1969-75, mem. adv. com. Hawaii geothermal project, 1973-78; mem. State Energy Policy Task Force, 1974-78, Hawaii Energy Conservation Council, 1978-80, Gov.'s Com. Alt. Energy Devel., 1978-80; bd. dirs. Am.-Samoa Power Authority, 1981-83. Served to lt. col., Signal Corps AUS, 1941-45. Decorated Legion of Merit. Fellow IEEE; mem. Hawaii C. of C., Engring. Assn. Hawaii, Nat. Soc. Profl. Engrs. (past dir.), Hawaii Soc. Profl. Engrs. (past dir., pres.), Pacific Coast Elec. Assn. (dir. 1972-81, pres. 1979-80), AIEE (past chmn. Hawaii sect.). Clubs: Pacific, Outrigger Canoe. Home: 2969 Kalakaua Ave Apt 501 Honolulu HI 96815-4620

WILLIAMS, CAROL JORGENSEN, social work educator; b. New Brunswick, N.J., Aug. 12, 1944; d. Einar Arthur and Mildred Estelle (Clayton) Jorgensen; m. Oneal Alexander Williams, July 4, 1980. BA, Douglass Coll., 1966; MS in Computer Sci., Stevens Inst. Tech., 1986; MSW, Rutgers U., 1971, PhD in Social Policy, 1981. Child welfare worker Bur. Children's Svcs., Jersey City, 1966-67, Outagamie County Dept. Social Svcs., Appleton, Wis., 1967-69; supr. WIN N.J. Divsn. Youth and Family Svcs., New Brunswick, 1969-70; coord. Outreach Plainfield (N.J.) Pub. Libr., 1972-76; rsch. project dir. County and Mcpl. Govt. Study Commn., N.J. State Legislature, 1976-79; prof. social work Kean Coll. N.J., Union, 1979—; assessment liaison social work program Kean Coll. of N.J., Union, 1987—, dir. MSW program, 1995—; chmn. faculty senate gen. edn. com., Kean Coll. N.J., 1990-94, chmn. faculty senate ad hoc com. for 5-yr. review of gen. edn. program, 1991-93, mem. retention and tenure com. Sch. of Liberal Arts, 1988-94, vice chmn., 1992-94; cons. N.J. div. Youth and Family Svcs., 1979-93, Assn. for Children N.J., 1985-88; cons., evaluator Thomas A. Edison Coll., 1977—, emm. acad. coun. and others. Mem. NOW, Coun. on Social Work Edn. (com. on info. tech.), Nat. Assn. Social Workers (chpt. com. on nominating and leadership identification 1990-92, co-chmn. 1991-92), Kean Coll. Fedn. Tchrs., Assn. Baccalaureate Program Dirs. (mem. com. on info. tech.). Democrat. Clubs: Good Sam (Agoura, Calif.); Outdoor World (Bushkill, Pa.). Home: 32 Halstead Rd New Brunswick NJ 08901-1619 Office: Kean Coll of NJ Social Work Program Morris Ave Union NJ 07083-7117

WILLIAMS, CAROLYN ELIZABETH, manufacturing executive; b. L.A., Jan. 24, 1943; d. George Kissam and Mary Eloise (Chamberlain) W.; m. Richard Terrill White, Apr. 9, 1972; children: Sarah Anne, William Daniel. BS, Ga. Inst. Tech., 1969; MM, Northwestern U., 1988. Saleswoman Ea. Airlines, Atlanta, Montreal (Can.) and Seattle, 1964-69; job analyst Allied Products Corp., Atlanta, 1969-70; mgr. Allied Products Corp., Frankfort, Mich., 1970-71; planning analyst, sr. planning analyst Allied Products Corp., Chgo., 1972-74, dir. planning, 1974-76, staff v.p. planning, 1976-79, v.p. planning and bus. research, 1979-86, v.p. corp. devel., chief planning officer, 1986-93; pres. White, Williams & Daniels, 1993—. Mem. adv. bd. Ga. Inst. Tech. Mem. Winnteka Yacht Club (dir. jr. sailing), Midwest Youth Sailing Assn. (bd. dirs., treas.).

WILLIAMS, CAROLYN WOODWORTH, retired elementary education educator, consultant; b. Binghamton, N.Y., Aug. 29, 1937; d. Charles Byron Woodworth and Dorothy Louise (Wheeler) Krum; m. James C. Williams, Mar. 29, 1958; children: Christopher, Lizette Macaluso, Matthew (dec.). BS in Elem. Edn., SUNY, Cortland, 1958; postgrad., SUNY, Geneseo, 1973-74, U. Vt., 1988; MS in Edn., SUNY, Brockport, 1989. Cert. tchr. K-6, N.Y. Elem. tchr. grade 6 Whitney Point (N.Y.) Ctrl. Sch., 1959-69; elem. tchr. grade 6 Palmyra (N.Y.)-Macedon Ctrl. Sch., 1969-71, elem. tchr. grade 4, 1971-79, 84-95, elem. tchr. grade 1, 1979-84, ret., 1995. Author, editor booklets. Active Women's Rep. Club, Binghamton, N.Y., 1959-67. Recipient Bring Local History Live into Classroom award Griffiss-McLouth Fund, 1993. Mem. ASCD, AAUW, N.Y. State United Tchrs., N.Y. State Hist. Soc., Wayne County Hist. Soc. (bicentennial history fair coord. 1989), Ea. Star (sister). Methodist. Avocations: children's welfare, literacy, women's issues, history, technology. Home: 3304 Fallbrook Park Canandaigua NY 14424

WILLIAMS, CHARLES D., bishop. Bishop of Alaska Ch. of God in Christ, Anchorage. Office: Ch of God in Christ 2212 Vanderbilt Cir Anchorage AK 99508-4563*

WILLIAMS, CHARLES DAVID, oil and steel company executive; b. Mineola, Tex., July 16, 1935; s. Floyd L. and Audie N. (Hall) W.; m. Shirley R. Dodd, Jan. 23, 1954; children: Jan, Charles David. BS in Petroleum Engring., Tex. A&M U., 1957, MS in Petroleum Engring., 1959; MBA in Fin., So. Meth. U., 1971. Asst. to exec. v.p. Atlantic Richfield Co., N.Y.C., 1971-72; dir. planning Atlantic Richfield Co., Dallas, 1972-76; mgr. investor relations Atlantic Richfield Co., L.A., 1976-79; v.p. investor affairs Tex. Oil and Gas Corp., Dallas, 1979-86; v.p. investor relations USX Corp., Pitts., 1986—. Mem. Soc. Petroleum Engrs., N.Y. Soc. Security Analysts, Petroleum Investor Relations Assn., Sigma Xi, Beta Gamma Sigma. Republican. Baptist. Avocations: golf, fishing. Office: USX Corp 600 Grant St Pittsburgh PA 15219-2702

WILLIAMS, C(HARLES) FRED, history professor; b. Allen, Okla., Dec. 24, 1943; s. Charley Howard and Willie Mae (Brooks) W.; m. Glenda Belcher, June 6, 1963 (dec. Oct. 1970); 1 child, Laura; m. Janet Hamm, Dec. 27, 1971; children: Brad, Libby. BE, East Cen. State U., Ada, Okla., 1965; MA, Wichita State U., 1966; PhD, U. Okla., 1970. Asst., then assoc. prof. History Univ. Ark., Little Rock, 1969-73, dept. chmn., 1973-80, assoc. dean Coll. Liberal Arts, 1980-83, assoc. vice chmn. Edn. Program, 1983-88; prof. history, dir. Ctr. Ark. Studies U. Ark., Little Rock, 1988-. Author: A History of Pharmacy in Arkansas, 1982, Arkansas: An Illustrated History, 1986; editor: A Documentary History of Arkansas, 1984, A Cartoon History of Arkansas. Bd. dirs. Old State House Assocs., Little Rock, 1981-85, Ark. Hist. Preservation Alliance, 1985-86; pres. Vol. in Pub. Schs., Little Rock, 1986—. Recipient Cert. of Merit State of Ark., 1976, Supt.'s Citation Little Rock Sch. Dists., 1984; named Humanist of Yr. Ark. Endowment for the Humanities, Little Rock, 1983. Mem. Orgn. Am. Historians, Agriculture History Soc., Western History Assn., Ark. Hist. Assn., Phi Delta Kappa (pres. 1987-88). Home: 8214 Reymere Dr Little Rock AR 72227-3942 Office: U Ark Dept Edn 2801 S University Ave Little Rock AR 72204-1000

WILLIAMS, C(HARLES) K(ENNETH), poet, literature and writing educator; b. Newark, N.J., Nov. 4, 1936; s. Paul Bernard and Dossie (Kasdin) W.; m. Sarah Dean Jones, June, 1966 (div. 1975); 1 child, Jessica Anne; m. Catherine Justine Mauger, Apr. 15, 1975; 1 child, Jed Mauger. BA, U. Pa., 1958. Vis. prof. lit. Beaver Coll., Jenkintown, Pa., 1975, Drexel U., Phila., 1976, U. Calif., Irvine, 1978, Boston U., 1979-80, Bklyn. Coll., 1982-83; Mellon vis. prof. lit. Franklin and Marshall Coll., Lancaster, Pa., 1977; prof. writing Columbia U., N.Y.C., 1981-85; prof. lit. George Mason U., Fairfax, Va., 1992-95; Halloway lectr. U. Calif., Berkeley, 1986, Princeton U., 1995—. Author: A Day for Anne Frank, 1968, Lies, 1969, I Am the Bitter Name, 1972, With Ignorance, 1977, The Lark, The Thrush, The Starling, 1983, Tar, 1983, Flesh and Blood, 1987, Poems, 1963-1983, 1988, The Bacchae of Euripides, 1990, Helen, 1991, A Dream of Mind: Poems, 1992, Selected Poems, 1994, The Vigil, 1997; contbr. editor Am. Poetry Rev., 1972—; translator: Women of Trachis (Sophocles), 1978. Sponsor People's Fund, Phila., 1967—. Recipient Nat. Book Critics Circle award in poetry, 1987, Morton Dauwen Zabel prize Am. Acad. of Arts and Letters, 1989, Harriet Monroe prize, 1993; fellow Guggenheim Found., 1975, Nat. Endowment for Arts, 1985, 93; Lila Wallace-Reader's Digest grantee, 1993—. Mem. PEN, Poetry Soc. Am. Avocations: piano, guitar, drawing. Home: 82 Rue d'Hauteville, 75010 Paris France

WILLIAMS, CHARLES LAVAL, JR., physician, international organization official; b. New Orleans, Jan. 19, 1916; s. Charles Laval and Lewise (McLaurine) W.; m. Ellen Clendenin Ustick, Dec. 14, 1946; children: Ellen Clendenin, Katherine McLaurine. Student, U. Va., 1933-35; M.D., Tulane U., 1940; M.P.H., U. Mich., 1945. Diplomate: Am. Bd. Preventive Medicine and Pub. Health. Intern U.S. Marine Hosp., New Orleans, 1941; with USPHS, 1941-67; assigned N.C. State Health Dept., 1941-44, USPHS States Relations div., 1944, U. Mich., 1944-45, Am. Acad. Pediatrics Nat. Study Child Health Services, 1945-47; chief planning unit, asst. chief div. commd. officers, 1947-51; with US/AID Div. Pub. Health, 1951-62; chief pub. health adviser AID Mission to Peru, 1959-62; assoc. dir. internat. relations Office Internat. Health, 1962-64; chief Office Internat. Research, NIH, Bethesda, Md., 1965-66; dep. dir., then dir. Office Internat. Health, Office Surgeon General, USPHS, Washington, 1966-67; dep. dir. Pan Am. Health Orgn., 1967-79; ret.; exec. v.p. Am. Assn. World Health, 1980-84; U.S. del./alt. or advisor to eight world health assemblies between 1955 and 1967, and to ten sessions of the Directing Coun. of the Pan Am. Health Orgn. between 1953 and 1966. Fellow Am. Pub. Health Assn.; mem. U.S.-Mexico Border Pub. Health Assn., Phi Kappa Phi, Delta Omega. Home: 5600 Wisconsin Ave 1009 Chevy Chase MD 20815-4411

WILLIAMS, CHARLES LINWOOD (BUCK WILLIAMS), professional basketball player; b. Rocky Mount, N.C., Mar. 8, 1960; s. Moses and Betty Williams. Student, U. Md. Basketball player New Jersey Nets, NBA, 1981-89; player Portland Trail Blazers, 1989-96, N.Y. Knicks, 1996—. Mem. U.S. Olympic Team, 1980, NBA All-Rookie Team, 1982; player NBA All-Star Games, 1982, 83, 86; named NBA Rookie of Yr., 1982; named to NBA All-Defensive Team, 1990, 91. Office: NY Knicks 2 Pennsylvania Plz New York NY 10121-0091*

WILLIAMS, CHARLES MARVIN, commercial banking educator; b. Romney, W. Va., Apr. 20, 1917; s. W. Marvin and Lula H. (Taylor) W.; m. Elizabeth Huffman, Oct. 19, 1946; children: Holland H., Andrea L. AB, Washington and Lee U., 1937; MBA, Harvard U., 1939, DCS, 1951; LLD, Washington and Lee U., 1966. Credit trainee Mfrs. Trust Co., N.Y.C., 1939-41; asst. prof. finance Harvard Grad. Sch. Bus. Adminstrn., 1947-51, assoc. prof., 1951-56, prof. bus. adminstrn., 1956-60, Edmund Cogswell Converse prof. banking and finance, 1960-66, George Gund prof. comml. banking, 1966-86, prof. emeritus, 1986—; pres. Charles M. Williams Assocs. Author: Cumulative Voting for Directors, 1951, (P. Hunt) Case Problems in Finance, 1949, (with P. Hunt and G. Donaldson) Basic Business Finance, 1958. Served to lt. comdr., Supply Corps USNR. Mem. Phi Beta Kappa, Kappa Alpha. Clubs: Harvard (N.Y.C.); Weston Golf. Home: 50 Cherry Brook Rd Weston MA 02193-1306 Office: Soldiers Field Boston MA 02163

WILLIAMS, CHARLES MURRAY, computer information systems educator, consultant; b. Ft. Bliss, Tex., Dec. 26, 1931; s. Robert Parvin and Barbara (Murray) W.; m. Stanley Bright, Dec. 31, 1956; children: Margaret Allen Williams Becker, Robert Parvin, Mary Linton Williams Bondurant. BS, Va. Mil. Inst., 1953; MS, Stanford U., 1964; PhD, U. Tex., 1967. Physicist USAF, Kirtland AFB, N.Mex., 1956-58; staff mem. Sandia Labs., Albuquerque, 1958-62; programmer analyst Control Data Corp., Palo Alto, Calif., 1962-63; mathematician Panoramic Rsch., Inc., Palo Alto, 1963-64; mem. tech. staff Thomas Bede Found., Los Altos, Calif., 1964-65; rsch. scientist assoc. U. Tex., Austin, 1965-67; asst. prof. Computer Sci. Pa. State U., State College, 1967-72, Va. Poly. Inst. and State U., Blacksburg, 1972-75; assoc. prof. Computer Info. Systems Ga. State U., Atlanta, 1975-83, prof. Computer Info. Systems, 1983—; cons. Visicon Inc., State Coll., 1970-72, Broomall (Pa.) Industries Inc., 1973-79, Bausch & Lomb Inc., Rochester, N.Y. 1981, Bell South Media Techs. Inc., Atlanta, 1987-90; mem. tech. staff Bell Labs., Whippany, N.J., 1979; textbook reviewer various publs. including

Harper & Row, Prentice Hall, Simon & Schuster, 1976—. Contbr. articles to profl. computer graphics and image processing publs. Bd. dirs. Ga. Striders, 1993—; numerous presentations Fitness and the Fountain of Youth Seminar, 27 municipalities in 6 states, 1992—. Grantee Xerox Corp., 1985, Ga. Rsch. Alliance Telemedicine Project, 1993; recipient Silver medals in 1500-meter and 3000 meter runs 60-64 age divsn. Athletic Congress (now U.S.A. Track & Field) Nat. Masters Indoor Track and Field Championships, 1992, Gold medals in 5000-meter and 10,000-meter runs, Bronze medal in 1500-meter run, 1992, Gold medals in 1500-meter and 3000-meter runs U.S.A. Track & Field Indoor Championships, 1993, Gold medals in 5000-meter and 10,000 meter runs, Bronze medal in 1500-meter run U.S. Track and Field Outdoor Championships, 1993, Bronze medal in 5000-meter run and 10,000-meter runs U.S.A. Track & Field Outdoor Championships, 1994, Gold medal in 3000-meter run U.S.A. Track & Field Indoor Championships, 1994; ranked 3d nationally in road racing Running Times, 1992; ranked 5th, (2nd honorable mention) 1993. Mem. Nat. Computer Graphics Assn. (hon., Ga. bd. dirs. 1979-85, bd. dirs. Ga. chpt. 1985-89, sec. 1988-89), Computer Graphics Pioneers, Nat. Platform Assn., Upsilon Pi Epsilon, Omicron Delta Kappa. Republican. Episcopalian. Avocation: competitive road running (recipient numerous gold and silver medals). Home: 316 Argonne Dr NW Atlanta GA 30305-2814 Office: Ga State U Dept of Computer Info Sys University Pla Atlanta GA 30303 *Throughout life, gain inspiration from the actions of your elders. Emulate them by focusing your energies so that your own actions may inspire the young. You are never too old to begin new ventures.*

WILLIAMS, CHARLES WESLEY, technical executive, researcher; b. Palestine, Ark.; s. Fredrick Charles and Fannie Rochet (Southall) W.; m. Nancy Sue Rhea, Sept. 5, 1959; children: Brent L., Brian E. B.S.E.E., U. Tenn.-Knoxville, 1959, M.S., 1963. Registered profl. engr., Ohio. Devel. engr. Mead Research Lab., Chillicothe, Ohio, 1959-60, Oak Ridge Nat. Lab., 1960-63; tech. mgr. EG & G Ortec, Oak Ridge, 1963-76, tech. dir. phys. and life sci., 1976-81; mgr. Assay Inst. EG & Ortec, Oak Ridge, 1981-85; pres. Autograffix Inc., Knoxville, Tenn., 1985—. Contbr. articles to tech. jours., chpt. to book. Fellow IEEE (v.p. Nuclear and Plasma Sci. Soc. 1979); mem. Tau Beta Pi, Eta Kappa Nu. Baptist.

WILLIAMS, CHARLOTTE EVELYN FORRESTER, civic worker; b. Kansas City, Mo., Aug. 7, 1905; d. John Dougal and Georgia (Lowerre) Forrester; student Kans. U., 1924-25; m. Walker Alonzo Williams, Sept. 25, 1926; children: Walker Forrester, John Haviland. Trustee, Detroit Grand Opera Assn., 1960-87, dir., 1955-60; chmn. Grinnell Opera Scholarship, 1958-66; founder, dir., chmn. adv. bd. Cranbrook Music Guild, Inc., 1952-59, life mem.; bd. dirs. Detroit Opera Theater, 1959-61, Severo Ballet, 1959-61; Detroit dist. chmn. Met. Opera Regional Auditions, 1958-66; Fla. Atlantic U. Found.; past pres. Friends of Caldwell Playhouse, Boca Raton. Mem. Debbie-Rand Meml. Svc. League (life), DAR, English-Speaking Union, Vol. League Fla. Atlantic U., PEO, Order Eastern Star. Home: 2679 S Ocean Blvd Apt 5C Boca Raton FL 33432-8353

WILLIAMS, CHESTER ARTHUR, JR., insurance educator; b. Blakely, Pa., Mar. 6, 1924; s. C. Arthur and Alice (Robinson) W.; m. Roberta Riegel, Sept. 1, 1951; children—Robert Arthur, Bruce Allan. A.B., Columbia U., 1947; A.M., 1949, Ph.D., 1952. Lectr. ins. U. Buffalo, N.Y., 1950-52; asst. prof. U. Minn., 1952-55, assoc. prof., 1955-58, Ford Found. faculty fellow, 1957-58, prof., 1958-80, acting dean, 1970-71, asso. dean, 1971-72, dean, 1972-78, Minn. Ins. Industry chair prof., 1980-92, prof. emeritus, 1992—; vis. prof. U. Pa., 1960-61, Keio U., Tokyo, 1984. Author: Price Discrimination in Property and Liability Insurance, 1959, Economic and Social Security, 1957, Risk Management and Insurance, 1964, Insurance Arrangements under Workmen's Compensation, 1969, Insurance Principles and Practices: Property and Liability, 1976, Principles of Risk Management and Insurance, 1978, Insurance and Risk Management, 1980, Ocean Marine Insurance, 1988, An International Comparison of Workers' Compensation, 1991; editor Jour. of Risk and Ins., 1981-86. Contbr. articles to profl. jours. Bd. dirs. State Capitol Credit Union, 1965-68, pres., 1967-68; bd. dirs. Consumers Union, 1972-75; bd. dirs. Minn. State Coun. on Econ. Edn., 1973-78, chmn., 1975-77; bd. dirs. St. Paul Cos., Inc., 1975-90. Served to 1st lt. USAF, 1943-46. Recipient Gold medal Internat Ins. Soc., 1993, Elizur Wright award Am. Risk and Ins. Assocs., 1993; laureate Ins. Hall of Fame. Mem. Am. Risk Ins. Assn. (dir. 1960-65, 81-86, pres. 1965), Am. Acad. Actuaries, Decision Sci. Inst., Am. Statis. Assn., Am. Finance Assn., AAUP, Phi Beta Kappa, Beta Gamma Sigma. Episcopalian. Home: 1984 Shryer Ave W Saint Paul MN 55113-5415

WILLIAMS, CLYDE E., JR., lawyer; b. Niagara Falls, N.Y., Dec. 17, 1919; s. Clyde E. and Martha (Barlow) W.; m. Ruth Van Aken, Oct. 16, 1948; children: Clyde E. III (dec.), Mark Van Aken, Sara. AB, Denison U., Granville, Ohio, 1942; LLB, Harvard U., 1945. Bar: Ohio 1945. Practice corp. and real estate law, 1945—; v.p. Spieth, Bell, McCurdy & newell Co., L.P.A., Cleve., 1964—; also bd. dirs. Spieth, Bell, McCurdy & Newell Co., Cleve.; gen. counsel Growth Cos., Inc., Phila., 1950-55; pres., dir. Williams Investment Co., Cleve., 1954—; sec., dir. Williams Internat. Corp., Walled Lake, Mich., 1954—; dir., gen. Counsel Techno-fund, Inc., Columbus, Ohio, 1960-67; dir. rAdio Seaway, Inc. (Sta. WCLV-FM), 1962—; mem. faculty Fenn Coll. and Cleve. Coll. divsn. Western Res. U., 1945-50. Trustee, mem. exec. com., v.p. Cleve. Soc. for Blind, 1979—, pres., 1985-87, mem. adv. council, 1987—. Mem. ABA, Ohio Bar Assn., Cleve. Bar Assn., Union Club, Skating Club. Office: Spieth Bell McCurdy et al 2000 Huntington Bldg 925 Euclid Ave Cleveland OH 44115

WILLIAMS, DARRYL MARLOWE, medical educator; b. Denver, Apr. 3, 1938; s. Archie Malvin and Dorothy Merle (Grapes) W.; m. Susan Arlene Moore, June 24, 1966; children: Carol Ruth, Peter Todd, Sarah Elizabeth. Student, U. Colo., 1956-58; BS, Colo. State U., 1993; MD, MS in Anatomy, Baylor U., 1964. Diplomate Am. Bd. Internal Medicine, Am. Bd. Hematology. Intern and resident Baylor Affiliated Hosps., Houston, 1964-66, 67-68; resident U. Utah, Salt Lake City, 1966-67, fellow in hematology, 1968-73, asst. prof., 1973-77; assoc. prof. La State U., Shreveport, 1977-81, prof., 1981-90, chief hematology sect., 1977-85, asst. dean/rsch., 1981-85, dean Sch. Medicine, 1985-90; prof. medicine, dean Sch. Medicine Tex. Tech U. Health Scis. Ctr., Lubbock, 1990-95; prof. medicine office border health and area health edn. Tex. Tech. Health Scis. Ctr., El Paso, 1995—, also bd. dirs., 1995—; dir. med. edn. Cmty. Partnership Tex. Tech. Health Sci. Ctr., El Paso, 1995—; mem. hemophilia adv. com. La. Legislature, Baton Rouge, 1977-83; vice chair La. Lung and Cancer Bd., New Orleans, 1984-90; pres. N.W. La. AIDS Task Force, Shreveport, 1987. Mem. editl. bd. Tex. Jour. Rural Health, 1990—. Mem. Am. Heart Assn., Lubbock chpt., Shreveport Biracial Commn., 1988, Lubbock Indigent Health Care Coalition Task Force, 1991-92, Health Professions Edn. Adv. Com., Lubbock Friends of Pub. Radio; vice chair health profls. edn. adv. com. Tex. Coord. Bd. Higher Edn., 1992-95; sec. Health Edn. and Tng. Consortium of Tex., 1990—; mem. Border Vision Fronteriza Steering Com., 1995—. Recipient award Nat. Ski Patrol System, Salt Lake City, 1975. Fellow ACP, Am. Coll. Nutrition; mem. AMA, Am. Soc. Hematology, Am. Inst. Nutrition, Am. Soc. Clin. Nutrition, Tex. Med. Assn. (physicians oncology edn. com.), Royal Soc. Medicine, Alpha Omega Alpha. Office: Tex Tech Health Sci Ctr Health Scis Ctr 4800 Alberta Ave El Paso TX 79905-2709

WILLIAMS, DAVE HARRELL, investment executive; b. Beaumont, Tex., Oct. 5, 1932; s. George Davis and Mary (Hardin) W.; m. Reba White, Mar. 15, 1975. B.S. in Chem. Engring, U. Tex., 1956; M.B.A. (Baker scholar, Teagle fellow), Harvard U., 1961. Chartered fin. analyst. Chem. engr. Exxon Corp., Baton Rouge, 1959; security analyst deVegh & Co., N.Y.C., 1961-64; dir. research Waddell & Reed, Kansas City, Mo., 1964-67; exec. v.p. Mitchell Hutchins, Inc., N.Y.C., 1967-77; chmn. bd. Alliance Capital Mgmt. Corp., N.Y.C., 1977—; bd. dirs. The Equitable Cos., Inc. Contbr.: articles to Fin. Analysts Jour. Trustee Am. Fedn. of Art, Fgn. Policy Assn, Metropolitan Mus. of Art. Served with USNR, 1956-59. Mem. Fin. Analysts Fedn. (past officer, dir.), N.Y. Soc. Security Analysts (past pres.), Bond Club N.Y., Econ. Club N.Y., Knickerbocker Club, Down Town Assn., Century Assn., Grolier Club. Presbyterian. Office: Alliance Capital Mgmt Corp 1345 Avenue Of The Americas New York NY 10105-0302

WILLIAMS, DAVID ARTHUR, marketing professional; b. Lima, Ohio, Jan. 22, 1953; s. Arthur Henry and Jane Elenor (Davisson) W. AA Bus., Coll. DuPage, 1973; BA Mktg., Columbia Coll., Chgo., 1976. Dir. mktg. Breckenridge (Colo.) Ski Corp., 1976-81; pres. Williams & Assocs., Denver, 1981-84; dir. real estate advt. Kohler (Wis.) Co., 1984-89; v.p. mktg. The Anvan Cos., Glencoe, Ill., 1989-96; v.p.mktg. Coldwell Banker/Kahn, Glencoe, Ill., 1996-97; v.p. account svcs. Waldman & Assocs., Chgo., 1997—. Office: Waldman & Assocs 57 W Grand Ave Chicago IL 60610

WILLIAMS, DAVID HOWARD, lawyer; b. Las Vegas, Nev., Sept. 21, 1945; s. Howard Cummins and Alice Emma (Taufenbach) W.; m. Kathleen Graham, Sept. 2, 1967; children: David Howard Jr., Jonathan Graham. BA in History cum laude, Denison U., 1967; MA in Polit. Sci., Columbia U., 1969; JD cum laude, Ohio State U., 1973. Bar: Ohio 1973, Ga. 1980. Assoc. Vorys, Sater, Seymour & Pease, Columbus, Ohio, 1973-79; from assoc. to ptnr. Powell, Goldstein, Frazer & Murphy, Atlanta; ptnr. Hunton & Williams, Atlanta; adj. prof. U. Ga. Sch. Law, 1995—; lectr. in field. Bd. dirs. Atlanta Ballet, 1991-92, Ga. Assn. for Primary Health Care; former trustee, co-pres. parents' assn. Trinity Sch., Atlanta; past trustee Northside Youth Orgn., Atlanta; former asst. gen. counsel Ga. Rep. Party; former mem. coun. legal advisors Rep. nat. Com. Mem. ABA, State Bar Ga., Atlanta Bar Assn., Atlanta C. of C. Office: Hunton & Williams NationsBank Plz 600 Peachtree St NE Atlanta GA 30308-2214

WILLIAMS, DAVID KEITH, technical trainer; b. Exeter, N.H., Mar. 4, 1965; s. Horace Robert and Arlene Emily (Locke) W. BS, U. N.H., 1987. Software engr. Micro-Integration, Newmarket, N.H., 1988-89, Alloy Computer Products, Marlboro, Mass., 1989-90; sr. software engr. Cabletron Systems, Inc., Rochester, N.H., 1990-95, tech. trainer, 1995—; cons. in computer software. Asst. scoutmaster Boy Scouts Am., Newton Junction, N.H., 1986-91; bd. dirs. Newton Junction Fireman's Assn., 1983-95. Mem. Amnesty Internat. Ptnrs. of Conscience. Baptist. Avocations: foreign languages, musical instruments, hiking, skiing, karate.

WILLIAMS, DAVID PERRY, manufacturing company executive; b. Detroit, Nov. 16, 1934; s. M.S. Perry and Virginia (Hayes) W.; m. Jill Schneider, July 27, 1972; children: Tracy, Perry, David, William, Nell. B.A., Mich. State U., 1956, M.B.A., 1964. V.p. sales Automotive div. Kelsey Hayes Co., Romulus, Mich., 1958-71; v.p., mgr. automotive product line ITT, N.Y.C., 1971-76; v.p., dir. Budd Co., Troy, Mich., 1976-79, sr. v.p. ops., dir., 1979-80, sr. v.p., chief ops. officer, 1980-86, pres., chief operating officer, dir., 1986—; dir. Standard Fed. Bank, Troy, Mich., 1990—, SPX Corp., Muskegon, Mich., 1992—, Budd Canada, Inc., Kitchener, Ont., 1981—, Thyssen Prodn. Systems, 1994. Served to 1st lt. USAF, 1956-58. Mem. Soc. Automotive Engrs., Engring. Soc. Detroit, Soc. Jfg. Engrs., Bloomfield Hills Country Club, Country of Detroit, Yondotega, PGA Nat. Club (Fla.), Tournament Players Club (Mich.), Question Club, Royal and Ancient Golf Club of St. Andrews (Scotland), Beta Gamma Sigma. Republican. Episcopalian. Home: 333 Lincoln Rd Grosse Pointe MI 48230-1604 Office: Budd Co PO Box 2601 3155 Big Beaver Rd Troy MI 48084

WILLIAMS, DAVID ROGERSON, JR., engineer, business executive; b. Tulsa, Oct. 20, 1921; s. David Rogerson and Martha Reynolds (Hill) W.; m. Pauline Bolton, May 28, 1944 (dec. Feb. 4, 1988); children: Pauline B. Williams Lampshire, David Rogerson III, Rachel K. Williams Zebrowski; m. Anne W. Kerr, Jan. 5, 1990. B.S., Yale U., 1943. Constrn. foreman, supt. Williams Bros. Corp., 1939-49; co-founder, v.p. Williams Bros. Co., 1949-56, exec. v.p., 1956-66, chmn. exec. com., 1966-70; chmn. bd. Resource Scis. Corp., Tulsa, 1970-83, Williams Techs. Inc., Carbon Resources, Inc.; chmn. Integrated Carbons Corp., Tulsa; co-founder, dir. Patagonia Corp., Tucson; dir. The Williams Cos., Tulsa. Trustee Hudson Inst., Indpls. Served to capt. USAAF, World War II. Fellow ASCE; mem. Am. Petroleum Inst., Alta. Assn. Profl. Engrs., Am. Gas Assn., Yale Engring. Assn., Ind. Natural Gas Assn., Royal Soc. Arts, Duke of Edinburgh's World Fellowship, Springdale Hall (Camden, S.C.), Racquet and Tennis Club, Yale Club N.Y., So. Hills (Tulsa) Club, River Club (N.Y.), Maidstone Club (East Hampton, N.Y.). Office: 320 S Boston Ave Ste 831 Tulsa OK 74103-3728

WILLIAMS, DAVID RUSSELL, music educator; b. Indpls., Oct. 21, 1932; s. H. Russell and Mary Dean (Whitmer) W.; m. Elsa Bühlmann, Jan. 30, 1960. AB, Columbia U., 1954, MA, 1956; PhD, U. Rochester, 1965. Dir. music Windham Coll., Putney, Vt., 1959-62; opera coach Eastman Sch. Music, Rochester, N.Y., 1962-65, assoc. prof. theory, adminstr. of MusM program, 1965-80; prof., chmn. dept. music U. Memphis (formerly Memphis State U.), 1980-87, prof. music, 1980—; bd. dirs. Memphis Youth Symphony, Memphis Symphony, 1984-90; mem. exec. bd. Opera Memphis, 1980-87, Salute to Memphis Music, 1980-87. Author: Bibliography of the History of Music Theory, 1971, Conversations with Howard Hanson, 1988, Music Theory from Zarlino to Schenker: A Bibliography and Guide, 1990; producer: Highwater Records album 8201 featuring John Stover, classical guitar, 1983; composer Suite for Oboe, Clarinet and Piano, 1968, Five States of Mind, 1970. Bd. dirs., sec. Rochester Philharm. Orch., 1976-78; v.p., bd. dirs. Rochester Chamber Orch., 1974-78; pres., bd. dirs. Opera Theatre of Rochester, 1973-74; bd. dirs., chmn. Am. Ritual Theatre, 1979-80; bd. sponsors Met. Opera Mid. South Region, Memphis, 1983—. Served as cpl. U.S. Army, 1957-59. Recipient Eastman Sch. Music Pub. award, 1970. Mem. NARAS (treas. Memphis chpt. 1984-86), Coll. Music Soc. (sec. 1973-83), Music Tchrs. Nat. Assn. Sci. (state chmn. 1971-74), Nat. Assn. Schs. of Music (chmn. region 8 1989-92), Tenn. Assn. Music Execs. in Colls. and Univs. (pres. 1986-87), Southeastern Composers League (composer mem.), Pi Kappa Lambda (pres. U. Memphis chpt. 1988-90), Phi Beta Kappa, Phi Mu Alpha (hon.), Sigma Alpha Iota (hon.). Clubs: Rochester, Univ., Summit. Avocations: language study, word puzzles. Home: 273 W Central Park St Apt 1 Memphis TN 38111-4570 Office: U Memphis Dept Music Memphis TN 38152 *Having had a family background that was superior in so many ways has helped me to sharpen my purpose in life, in that it has made me realize to what an extent affirmative action is necessary in order to provide a milieu in which truly equal opportunity can exist. Many doors of opportunity have been held open for me; those of disadvantaged access are often not aware that these doors exist. The more individuals I can lead to these portals, the more I will have achieved in my lifetime.*

WILLIAMS, DAVID SAMUEL, insurance company executive; b. Purcell, Okla., Oct. 16, 1926; s. David Skelton and Mattie Carolyn (Kimberlin) W.; m. Gloria Jean Trudgeon, Jan. 14, 1951; children: Mellanie K., David R., Gary B., Kimberly R. BA, U. Okla., 1950; LLB, LaSalle U., 1968. With U.S. Fidelity & Guaranty Cos., various locations, 1952-74; asst. mgr. U.S. Fidelity & Guaranty Cos., Albuquerque, 1963-66; mgr. U.S. Fidelity & Guaranty Cos., San Jose, Calif., 1966-74; v.p. Eldorado Ins. Co., Palo Alto, Calif., 1974-77, exec. v.p., chief operating officer, 1977-78; v.p. Eldorado Mgmt. Co., Palo Alto, Calif., 1973-78, chief operating officer, exec. v.p., 1978; mng. dir. Eldorado Service Corp., 1974-76, exec. v.p., 1976-78; ptnr. Williams Ranch Co., 1977—; owner David S. Williams and Assocs. L.C., 1988—; chmn. bd., pres. Homeland Gen. Corp., Homeland Ins. Co. and Homeland Indsl. Corp., San Jose, Calif., 1978-87; pres. Homeland Mgmt. Corp. (Cayman) Ltd., 1980-87, Homeland Internat. (Bermuda) Ltd., 1982-87; chmn. bd. On Line Ins. Systems, Inc., 1982-92; underwriting mem. Lloyds of London, 1979—; adv. bd. Pacific Valley Bank, 1975-87; tchr. Albuquerque U., 1957-58, N.Mex. U., 1958-59, bd. dirs. Fin. Guardian Group, Inc., Kansas City, Mo., Kestrel Aircraft Co. Mem. indsl. panel Stanford Research Inst., 1968; mgmt. cons. County Santa Clara Edn. Dept., 1968-73; mem. Calif. adv. com. Ins. Services Office; bd. dirs. ins. council City of Hope, Los Angeles; committeeman pioneer council Boy Scouts Am., 1968; pres. Immanuel Luth. Ch., Saratoga, Calif., 1989-90. Served to lt. col. AC U.S. Army, 1944-46, 50-52. Recipient Outstanding Fieldman's award for N.Mex., N.Mex. Insurors Assn., 1959. Mem. Internat. Bar Assn., Cen. Coast Fieldmen's Assn., Assn. Calif. Ins. Cos. (dir.), Sigma Alpha Epsilon. Lutheran. Clubs: San Jose Athletic, Rotary (pres. 1974, Paul Harris fellow 1976); Univ. San Jose, British-Am., Center., San Francisco Comml. Home: 4220 Ridgeline Cir Norman OK 73072-1731

WILLIAMS, DAVID VANDERGRIFT, organizational psychologist; b. Balt., Feb. 5, 1943; s. Laurence Leighton and Mary Duke (Warfield) W.; m. Diane M. Gayeski, Aug. 23, 1980; 1 child, Evan David Williams. BA, Gettysburg (Pa.) Coll., 1965; MA, Temple U., 1967; PhD, U. Pa., 1971. Asst. prof. psychology Ithaca (N.Y.) Coll., 1970-75, assoc. prof. psychology, 1975—; ptnr. OmniCom Assocs., Ithaca, 1979—; co-dir. Inst. Behavior-Econs., Ithaca, 1993—; cons. and speaker in field. Co-author: Interactive Media, 1985, (multimedia comms.), interactive multimedia software, 1979—; contbr. to books and articles to profl. jours. Bd. dirs. Ctr. for Religion, Ethics and Social Policy, Cornell U., 1975-77, Eco-Justice Task Force, Ithaca, 1975-78; trustee Montessori Sch. Ithaca, 1993—; Alternatives Fed. Credit Union, Ithaca, 1994-96. Rsch. fellow U.S. Office of Edn., 1967-70; recipient various grants. Mem. APA, Canadian Psychol. Assn., Environ. Design Rsch. Assn., Internat. Soc. Applied Psychology, Intergenerational Network, Nat. Soc. for Performance and Instrn., Am. Montessori Soc., Campbell Soc., Vandergrift Hist. Soc., Welsh Nat. Gymanfa Ganu Assn., Ithaca Yacht Club, Tau Kappa Epsilon, Psi Chi. Avocations: singing, sailing, sign language, geneology, travel. Office: OmniCom Assocs 407 Coddington Rd Ithaca NY 14850-6011

WILLIAMS, DAVID WELFORD, federal judge; b. Atlanta, Mar. 20, 1910; s. William W. and Maude (Lee) W.; m. Ouida Maie White, June 11, 1939; children: David Welford, Vaughn Charles. A.A., Los Angeles Jr. Coll., 1932; A.B., UCLA, 1934; LL.B., U. So. Calif., 1937. Bar: Calif. 1937. Practiced in Los Angeles, 1937-55; judge Mcpl. Ct., Los Angeles, 1956-62, Superior Ct., Los Angeles, 1962-69, U.S. Dist. Ct. (cen. dist.) Calif., Los Angeles, 1969—; now sr. judge U.S. Dist. Ct. (cen. dist.) Calif.; judge Los Angeles County Grand Jury, 1965. Recipient Russwurm award Nat. Assn. Newspapers, 1958; Profl. Achievement award UCLA Alumni Assn., 1966. Office: US Dist Ct 255 E Temple St Rm 7100 Los Angeles CA 90012-3334

WILLIAMS, DEBBIE KAYE, optometrist; b. Benham, Ky., Mar. 13, 1960; d. Charles Hughes and Bernice (Knotts) W.; m. Gregory Allen Collins, July 2, 1983 (div. July 1989); re-married, Dec. 28, 1990; 1 child, Arianna Courtney, 1994. AS, U. Louisville, 1980-82, BS, 1985; DO, Ill. Coll. Optometry, 1989. Pvt. practice Whitesburg, Ky., 1989—; cons. LKLP Head Start, Whitesburg, 1991—. Mem. Letcher County Bd. Health, 1993. Mem. Am. Optometric Assn., Ky. Optometric Assn., U. Louisville Alumni Assn., Ill. Coll. of Optometry Alumni Assn., Retinitis Pigmetosa Found. (Letcher county chpt. v.p. 1990-91), Beta Simga Kappa. Democrat. Baptist. Avocations: travel, walking, reading, painting. Home and Office: Dr DK Williams OD PSC 120 River Rd Whitesburg KY 41858-1178

WILLIAMS, DELWYN CHARLES, telephone company executive; b. Idaho Falls, Idaho, Apr. 27, 1936; s. Charles H. and Vonda (Wood) W.; m. Marlene Grace Nordland, Feb. 29, 1964; children—Stephen, Kirstin, Nicole. B.S. in Bus., U. Idaho, 1959. C.P.A., Calif. Accountant Peat, Marwick, Mitchell & Co. (C.P.A.s), San Francisco, 1960-65; treas. Dohrmann Instruments Co., Mountain View, Calif., 1965-68; with Continental Telephone Co. of Calif., Bakersfield, 1968-84; controller Continental Telephone Co. of Calif., 1969-70, v.p., treas., 1970-77, v.p., gen. mgr., 1977-79, pres., 1977-84, also dir.; pres. J.H. Evans, Inc., and subs., 1984-95, CEO, 1995—. Home: 10052 Oak Branch Cir Carmel CA 93923-8000 Office: 4918 Taylor Ct Turlock CA 95382-9579

WILLIAMS, DONALD CLYDE, lawyer; b. Oxnard, Calif., Oct. 12, 1939; s. Leslie Allen and Elizabeth Esther (Orton) W.; m. Miriam Arline, Oct. 5, 1966; children—Erin K., Nikki Dawn. B.A. in Gen. Bus, Fresno State Coll., 1963; J.D., Willamette U., 1967. Bar: Oreg. 1967. Practice in Grants Pass, 1967-70; ptnr. Myrick, Seagraves, Williams & Nealy, 1968-70, Carlsmith, Ball, Wichman, Murray & Ichiki, 1977—; asst. atty. gen. Am. Samoa, 1970-71, atty. gen., 1971-75; assoc. justice High Ct. Trust Ter. of Pacific Islands, 1975-77. Served with USCGR, 1958-59. Mem. ABA, Calif. Bar Assn., Oreg. Bar Assn., Am. Samoa Bar Assn., Guam Bar Assn., Hawaii Bar Assn., Commonwealth No. Mariana Islands Bar Assn., Fed. States of Micronesia Bar Assn., Guam C. of C. Office: Carlsmith Ball Wichman & Ichiki 555 S Flower St Fl 25 Los Angeles CA 90071-2300

WILLIAMS, DONALD JOHN, research physicist; b. Fitchburg, Mass., Dec. 25, 1933; s. Toivo John and Ina (Kokkinen) W.; m. Priscilla Mary Gagnon, July 4, 1953; children: Steven John, Craig Mitchell, Eino Stenroos. B.S., Yale U., 1955, M.S., 1958, Ph.D., 1962. Sr. staff physicist Applied Physics Lab., Johns Hopkins U., 1961-65; head particle physics br. Goddard Space Flight Center, NASA, 1965-70; dir. Space Environ. Lab., NOAA, Boulder, Colo., 1970-82; prin. investigator Energetic Particles expt. NASA Galileo Mission, 1977—; prin. staff physicist Johns Hopkins U. Applied Physics Lab., 1982-89, dir. Milton S. Eisenhower Rsch. Ctr., 1990-96; chief scientist rsch. ctr., 1996—; mem. nat. and internat. sci. planning coms.; chmn. NAS com. on solar-terrestrial rsch., 1989-93; mem. sci. adv. bd. USAF, 1993—. Author: (with L.R. Lyons) Quantitative Aspects of Magnetospheric Physics, 1983; assoc. editor: Jour. Geophys. Research, 1967-69, Revs. of Geophysics and Space Research, 1984-86; editor: (with G.D. Mead) Physics of the Magnetosphere, 1969, Physics of Solar-Planetary Environments, 1976; mem. editorial bd.: Space Sci. Revs., 1975-85; contbr. articles to profl. jours. Mem. USAF Sci. Adv. Bd., 1994—. Lt. USAF, 1955-57. Recipient Sci. Research award, 1974; Disting. Authorship award, 1976, 85. Fellow Am. Geophys. Soc.; mem. Am. Phys. Soc., Internat. Assn. Geomagnetism and Aeronomy (pres. 1991-95), Internat. Acad. Astronautics, Sigma Xi. Home: 14870 Triadelphia Rd Glenelg MD 21737

WILLIAMS, DONALD MAXEY, dancer, singer, actor; b. Chgo., June 23, 1959; s. Arlandus Maxey and Florida (Jelks) W. Student, pub. schs., Chgo. Prin. dancer Dancer Theatre of Harlem, N.Y.C., 1977—. Dancer in movie Cotton Club, 1983-84. Mem. Am. Guild Mus. Artists, Screen Actors Guild. Baptist. Club: The Sevens (co-founder). Avocations: basketball; bowling; table tennis. Office: Dance Theatre of Harlem 466 W 152nd St New York NY 10031-1814*

WILLIAMS, DONNA LEE H., state agency adminstrator; b. Wilmington, Del., Nov. 13, 1960; d. Ronald Lee and Loretta M. (Simonson) H.; m. John R. Williams, Oct. 8, 1988. AA, Wesley Coll., 1979; BA in Govt., Coll. William and Mary, 1981; JD, Widener U., 1984. Atty. Prickett, Jones, Elliott, Kristol & Shnee, Dover, Del., 1983-87, Bayard Handelman & Murdock, Dover, 1987-92; ins. commr. State Del., Dover, 1993—. mem. Del. Bd. Accts., Dover. Mem. Nat. Assn. Ins. Commrs., Del. Bar Assn., Kent County Bar Assn. (past pres.), Women Bus. Leaders, Women's Rep. Club Dover (pres. 1985-87). Methodist. Avocations: travel, sewing, English handsmocking, golf. Office: Del Dept Ins PO Box 7007 841 Silver Lake Blvd Dover DE 19903-1507

WILLIAMS, DOROTHY PUTNEY, middle school educator; b. Richmond, Va., Sept. 18, 1952; d. Meriwether Vaughan and Dorothy Louise (Martin) Putney; m. Gary Davis Williams, July 24, 1982; children: Gary Davis, Michael Dale, Mark Vaughan. BA, Averett Coll., 1974. Cert. tchr., Va. Tchr. New Kent County Pub. Schs., Quinton, Va., 1974-79, Salem Ch. (Va.) Elem. Sch., Chesterfield County Schs., 1979-90, Cloverhill Elem. Sch., Midlothian, Va., 1990-94; tchr. fgn. langs., English, social scis., history Swift Creek Middle Sch., Chesterfield County Schs., Midlothian, Va., 1994—; mem. Fgn. Lang. Curriculum Coun., Chesterfield, 1992; delegation leader Pres. Ambs. Team-World Travel, People to People; tchr. humanities, multicultural lit. Mary Baldwin Coll. Author: A Holistic Appraoch to Foreign Languages and Cultures in the Elementary School Classroom, 1992; author fgn. langs. global awareness program, 1990; author curriculum on ancient Egypt taught at Ctr. for Gifted Edn., Coll. William and Mary. Named Tchr. of Yr., 1990-91; recipient award for Tchr. Excellence, 1992. Mem. Nat. Coun. Tchrs. of English, Internat. Reading Assn., Va. State Reading Assn., Richmond Area Reading Coun., Alpha Delta Kappa, Phi Delta Kappa (educator of the year award 1993). Baptist. Avocations: writing children's literature, world travel, anthropology, archeology, foreign languages. Home: 5118 Rock Harbour Rd Midlothian VA 23112-6211 Office: Swift Creek Middle Sch 3700 Old Hundred Rd Midlothian VA 23112-4702

WILLIAMS, DOYLE Z., university dean, educator; b. Shreveport, La., Dec. 18, 1939; s. Nuell O. and Lurline (Isbell) W.; m. Maynette Derr, Aug. 20, 1967; children: Zane Derr, Elizabeth Marie. B.S., Northwestern State U., 1960; M.S. in Acctg., La. State U., 1962, Ph.D., 1965. CPA, Tex. Mgr. spl. edn. projects AICPA, N.Y.C., 1967-69; assoc. prof. Tex. Tech. U., Lubbock, 1969-71, prof. acctg., 1972-73, prof. area acctg., coord., 1973-78; prof. acctg. U. So. Calif., L.A., 1978-93, dean Sch. Acctg., 1979-87, interim dean Sch. Bus., 1986-88; dean U. Ark. Coll. Bus. Adminstrn., Fayetteville, 1993—; vis. prof. U. Hawaii, Honolulu, 1971-72. Author over 40 jour. articles and books. Chmn. Acctg. Edn. Change Commn., 1989-93. Named Mem. of Yr. N.Y. chpt. Nat. Assn. Accts., 1967, Outstanding Acctg. Educator Beta

Alpha Psi, 1982; recipient Disting. Faculty award Calif. CPA Found., 1983, Nat. Leadership award Acad. Bus. Adminstrs., 1995. Mem. AICPA (coun. 1983-91, v.p. 1987-88, bd. dirs. 1987-91, Outstanding Educator award 1990), Am. Acctg. Assn. (dir. edn. 1973-75, pres. 1984-85, Outstanding Educator award 1996), Fedn. Schs. Accountancy (pres. 1982, Faculty Merit award 1993), Adminstrs. Acctg. Programs (pres. 1977-78). Home: 2447 Boston Mountain Vw Fayetteville AR 72701-2802 Office: Coll Bus Adminstrn U Ark Fayetteville AR 72701

WILLIAMS, DREW DAVIS, surgeon; b. San Augustine, Tex., Jan. 18, 1935; s. Floyd Everett and Villamae (Morehead) W.; m. Marilyn Raus, June 27, 1958; children: Leslie, Cynthia, Matthew, Jennifer, Amelia. BS, Tex. A&M Coll., 1957; MD, U. Tex., 1960; grad., naval flight surgeon, U.S. Naval Sch. Aviation Medicine, Jan.-June, 1963. Diplomate Am. Bd. Surgery, Am. Bd. Quality Assurance and Utilization Rev. Physicians. Intern USPHS Hosp., Seattle, 1960-61; resident in gen. surgery U. Tex. Med. Br., Galveston, 1961-62, 64-68; resident pulmonary svc. M.D. Anderson Hosp., Houston, 3 months, 1968; pvt. practice gen. surgery Baytown, Tex., 1968—; active staff San Jacinto (Tex.) Meth. Hosp., 1968-95, chief of surgery, 1972, 73, pres. med. staff, 1976; mem. courtesy staff Bay Coast Hosp., Baytown, 1968-95; cons. staff Baytown Med. Ctr. Hosp., 1972-95; 1st chmn. dept. surgery in devel. of family practice residency program affiliated with Tex. Med. Sch., Houston, 1977; mem. Tex. State Bd. Med. Examiners, 1983-89, sec.-treas., 1984-88, pres., 1988-89; unit med. dir., clin. instr. dept. preventive medicine and cmty. health U. Tex. Med. Br., Galveston, 1995—. Contbr. articles to med. publs. Flight surgeon USN, 1962-64; lt. comdr. USNR, ret., 1967. Am. Cancer Soc. clin. fellow, 1966-67. Fellow ACS, AMA (Physicians Recognition award), Tex. Med. Assn.; mem. Tex. Med. Found. (fed. peer rev. group), Houston Surg. Soc. (pres. 1994), Southwestern Surg. Congress, Tex. Surg. Soc., Singleton Surg. Soc. (past pres.), Harris County Med. Soc. (chmn. coun. med. splty., mem. exec. bd. 1994), East Harris County Med. Soc. (pres. 1982), Baytown Surg. Soc., Sir William Osler Soc., Am. Cancer Soc. (pres. Baytown chpt. 1970-71), Sons of Republic Tex. (at large life), SAR (past pres. local chpt.), Soc. Descendents of Colonial Clergy, Magna Carta Barons (Somerset chpt.), Colonial Order of the Crown, Sovereign Colonial Soc.-Ams. of Royal Descent, Masons (32 degree), Shriners, KT, Gideons Internat., Phi Beta Pi. Democrat. Mem. Ch. of Christ. Avocations: gardening, hunting, fishing, genealogy, golf. Home and Office: 1217 Kilgore Rd Baytown TX 77520-3912

WILLIAMS, EARLE CARTER, retired professional services company executive; b. Selma, Ala., Oct. 15, 1929; s. Henry Earle and Nora Elizabeth (Carter) W.; m. June Esther Anson, Sept. 7, 1951; children: Gayle Marie, Carol Patrice, Sharon Elaine. B.E.E., Auburn U., 1951; postgrad., U. N.Mex., 1959-62; DSc (hon.), Auburn U., 1991. Registered profl. engr., N.Mex. Utilities design engr. Standard Oil Co. Ind., Whiting, 1954-56; mem. tech. staff Sandia Corp., Albuquerque, 1956-62; sr. engr. BDM Internat., Inc., El Paso, Tex., 1962-64, spl. projects dir., 1964-66, dir. ops., 1966-68; v.p., gen. mgr. BDM Internat., Inc., Vienna, Va., 1968-72; pres., CEO, BDM Internat., Inc., Vienna and McLean, Va., 1972-92, bd. dirs., 1972—; ret. as CEO, BDM Internat. Inc., Vienna and McLean, Va., 1992; bd. dirs. Parsons Corp., GTS Duratek, Inc., Gamma-A Techs., Inc.; mem. Naval Rsch. Adv. Com., 1984-90, chmn., 1986-90; dir. Am. Bus. Conf., 1985-88. Exec. com., steering com. El Paso C.C., 1968-69, trustee, 1969-70; commr. Fairfax County Econ. Devel. Authority, 1976-80, chmn., 1978-80; mem. Va. State Bd. for C.C., 1980-87; bd. dirs. Ctrl. Va. Ednl. TV Corp., 1978-87, Atlantic Coun. U.S., 1987-93; chmn. George Mason Inst. Indsl. Policy Bd., 1982-91; bd. dirs. Wolf Trap Found., 1984-92, vice chmn., 1985-87, chmn., 1988-90, emeritus dir., 1992—; trustee Va. Found. for Ind. Colls., 1984-87, 90-94, Flint Hill Sch., Oakton, Va., 1990-95, George Mason U. Found., 1987—, Auburn U. Found., 1991—; bd. dirs. Potomac KnowledgeWay Project, 1995—; mem. Va. Bus. Higher Edn. Coun., 1995—. With AUS, 1951-53. Recipient Engr. of Yr. award Va. Soc. Profl. Engrs., 1989, Superior Pub. Svc. award Dept. Navy, 1990; named to Ala. Engring. Hall of Fame, 1994. Mem. NSPE, Profl. Svcs. Coun. (bd. dirs. 1974-92, emeritus bd. dirs. 1992—, pres. 1976-79), Armed Force Comm. and Electronics Assn. (bd. dirs. 1978-82, 86-87, permanent dir. 1990, internat. v.p. 1979-82, 84-85, chmn. 1988-90, Disting. Svc. award 1987), Coun. on Fgn. Rels., Fairfax County C. of C. (bd. dirs. 1978-86), City Club (D.C.), Met. Club (D.C.), Tower Club (Vienna, Va.), Bay Colony Club (Naples, Fla.), Eta Kappa Nu. Presbyterian.

WILLIAMS, EDDIE NATHAN, research institution executive; b. Memphis, Aug. 18, 1932; s. Ed and Georgia Lee (Barr) W.; m. Jearline F. Reddick, July 18, 1981; children: Traci Lynne, Edward Lawrence, Terence Reddick. BS, U. Ill., 1954; postgrad., Atlanta U., 1957, Howard U., 1960; LLD (hon.), U. D.C., 1986; DHL, Bowie State Coll., 1980, Chgo. State U., 1994. Reporter Atlanta Daily World Newspaper, 1957-58; staff asst. U.S. Senate Com. on Fgn. Relations, Washington, 1959-60; fgn. service res. officer U.S. Dept. State, Washington, 1961-68; v.p. U. Chgo., 1968-72; pres. Joint Ctr. for Polit. and Econ. Studies, Washington, 1972—; vice chmn. Black Leadership Forum, 1996; bd. dirs. Harrah's Entertainment, Inc., The Riggs Nat. Bank Washington, Blue Cross Blue Shield Nat. Capital Area, LeMoyne-Owen Coll.; advisor Ctrs. for Disease Control, 1992—. Editorial columnist: Chgo. Sun Times, 1970-72; contbr. articles to profl. jours. Bd. dirs. Nat. Opinion Rsch. Ctr., 1992—; chmn. Pew Partnerships for Civic Change, 1993—. Am. Polit. Sci. Assn. fellow, 1958, MacArthur Found. fellow, 1988, Nat. Acad. Pub. Adminstrn. fellow, 1993; recipient Adam Clayton Powell Award Congl. Black Caucus, 1981, Washingtonian of Yr. award Washingtonian Mag., 1991, Nation Builder award Nat. Black Caucus of State Legislators, 1993, Outstanding Leadership award Korean Am. Alliance, 1994. Mem. Coun. Fgn. Rels., Kappa Tau Alpha, Omega Psi Phi, Sigma Pi Phi. Office: Joint Ctr Polit & Econ Studies 1090 Vermont Ave NW Ste 1100 Washington DC 20005-4905

WILLIAMS, EDGAR GENE, university administrator; b. Posey County, Ind., May 4, 1922; s. Noley Wesley and Anna Lena (Wilsey) W.; m. Joyce Ellen Grigsby, May 7, 1944; children: Cynthia Ellen Williams Mahigian, Thomas Gene. A.B., Evansville Coll., 1947; M.B.A., Ind. U., 1948, D.B.A., 1952. Instr. Ind. U., Bloomington, 1948-52; asst. prof. Ind. U., 1952-55, assoc. prof., 1955-58, prof. bus. adminstrn., 1958—, assoc. dean, 1965-69, v.p., 1974-88, now emeritus. Bd. dirs. Found. for Sch. of Bus., Ind. U., Bloomington, 1966—, Bloomington Community Found.. Served with U.S. Army, 1943-46. Mem. Beta Gamma Sigma. Democrat. Methodist. Clubs: Masons, Bloomington Country. Home: 1126 E 1st St Bloomington IN 47401-5076

WILLIAMS, EDSON POE, retired automotive company executive; b. Mpls., July 31, 1923; s. Homer A. and Florence C. Williams; m. Irene Mae Streed, June 16, 1950; children: Thomas, Louise, Steven, Linnea, Elisa. B.S.M.E. cum laude, U. Minn., 1950. Spl. purpose machinery operator, 1946-50; mfg. mgr., project engr. Crestliner div. Bigelow Sanford Inc., 1950-53, v.p., mgr. mfg. and engring., 1953-58, pres., 1958-63; with Ford Motor Co., 1963-87, mgr. customer svc. div., 1973; gen. mgr. Ford Motor Co. (Ford Mexico), 1973-75; pres. Ford Motor Co. (Ford Mid-East & Africa), 1975-79, Ford Motor Co. (Ford Asia-Pacific Inc.), 1979-87; v.p. Ford Motor Co., 1979-82, v.p.-gen. mgr. N.Am. truck ops., 1982-86, v.p. Ford Diversified Products ops., 1986-87. Served with USAAF, 1942-46. Mem. Naples Yacht and Sailing Club. Home: 688 21st Ave S Naples FL 34102-7610

WILLIAMS, EDWARD DAVID, consulting executive; b. Scranton, Pa., June 20, 1932; s. David Thomas and Mabel (Sims) W. m. Natalie Imnadze, Oct. 18, 1952; children: Denise, Claudia. BBA, Hofstra U., 1960; postgrad. in Bus. Adminstrn., Fairleigh Dickenson U., 1979. Cons. Cresap, McCormick and Paget, N.Y.C., 1964-65; sr. mgmt. cons. Union Carbide Corp., N.Y.C., 1965-67; asst. contr. data processing Western Union, N.Y.C., 1967-69; v.p. mgmt. info. systems ABC, Hackensack, N.J., 1970-86; v.p., chief info. officer Blue Cross Blue Shield of N.J., Newark, 1986-88; v.p. Chantico Pub. Co., Carrellton, Tex., 1989-90; pres. SMC-BIS Inc., Basking Ridge, N.J., 1990-93; pres., CEO Strategic Outsourcing Svcs. Inc., Mountain Lakes, N.J., 1993—; speaker in field. Mem. adv. bd. YMCA. With U.S. Army, 1948-52. Decorated Silver Star with oak leaf cluster, Bronze Star with V, Purple Heart with 2 oak leaf clusters. Mem. Soc. Mgmt. Info. Systems, N.J. C. of C., Profit Oriented Systems Planning Bd. (bd. dirs.), Masons. Republican. Office: Strategic Outsourcing Svcs 49 Old Bloomfield Ave Mountain Lakes NJ 07046-1449

WILLIAMS, EDWARD EARL, JR., entrepreneur, educator; b. Houston, Aug. 21, 1945; s. Edward Earl and Doris Jewel (Jones) W.; m. Susan M. Warren, June 28, 1983; children: Laura Michelle, David Brian. BS, U. Pa., 1966; PhD, U. Tex., 1968. Asst. prof. econs. Rutgers U., New Brunswick, N.J., 1968-70; assoc. prof. fin. McGill U., Montreal, Que., Can., 1970-73; v.p., economist Service Corp. Internat., Houston, 1973-77; prof. adminstrv. sci. Rice U., Houston, 1978-82, Henry Gardiner Symonds prof., 1982—, prof. stats., 1995—; chmn. bd. Edward E. Williams & Co., Houston, 1976-92; chmn. bd., pres. Tex. Capital Investment Co., 1979-95; chmn. bd. First Tex. Venture Capital Corp., 1983-92; mng. dir. First Tex. Venture Capital, LLC, 1992—; dir. Video Rental of Pa. Inc., Svc. Corp. Internat, EQUUS II, Inc.; adv. dir. Frost Nat. Bank. Benjamin Franklin scholar, Jesse Jones scholar, U. Pa., 1966, Tex. Savs. and Loan League fellow, NDEA fellow, U. Tex., 1968. Mem. Am. Statis. Assn., Coll. Innovation Mgmt. and Entrepreneurship, Fin. Mgmt. Assn., Raveneaux Country Club, Jewish Comm. North. Beta Gamma Sigma, Alpha Kappa Psi. Author: Prospects for the Savings and Loan Industry, 1968, An Integrated Analysis for Managerial Finance, 1970, Investment Analysis, 1974, Business Planning for the Entrepreneur, 1983, The Economics of Production and Productivity: A Modeling Approach, 1996; contbr. articles to profl. jours. Republican. Home: 7602 Wilton Park Dr Spring TX 77379-4672 Office: Rice U Jesse H Jones Grad Sch Adminstrn Houston TX 77251

WILLIAMS, EDWARD GILMAN, retired banker; b. Ware, Mass., Apr. 11, 1926; s. Carl Emmons and Susan Helen (Gilman) W.; m. Barbara Thompson Russell, June 19, 1959; children: Thomas Clarke, Susan Gilman. B.A., Trinity Coll., Conn., 1950. With Union Trust Co., New Haven, 1951-89; asst. trust officer Union & New Haven Trust Co., 1956-59, trust officer, 1959-64, v.p., 1964-65, v.p., sr. adminstrv. officer, 1965-69; sr. v.p. Union Trust Co., 1969-72, exec. v.p., 1972-89; v.p. Northeast Bancorp., Inc., 1972-89. Former treas. Leila Day Nurseries, Inc., New Haven; treas., pres. Ridge Rd. Sch. PTA, Hamden Hall Country Day Sch. Parents Assn.; bd. dirs. Vis. Nurse Assn., New Haven, 1963-86, pres., treas., 1970-75; trustee New Eng. Sch. Banking, 1971-74, 81-88, vice chmn., 1985-86, chmn. 1986-88; trustee Shubert Performing Arts Ctr., New Haven, 1985-90; bd. dirs. New Haven Colony Hist. Soc., 1987-89; trustee, deacon, chmn. music com. Ch. of Redeemer, New Haven; bd. dirs., treas. Edgerton Garden Ctr., 1992—; bd. dirs. Easter Seals Goodwill Rehab. Ctr., New Haven, 1993—. Mem. English-Speaking Union (treas. New Haven chpt. 1994—), New Haven Lawn Club (pres. 1979-82), Masons. Home: 900 Mix Ave Apt 17 Hamden CT 06514-5107 Office: 3074 Whitney Ave # 3-10 Hamden CT 06518-2391

WILLIAMS, EDWARD JOSEPH, banker; b. Chgo., May 5, 1942; s. Joseph and Lillian (Watkins) W.; children: Elaine, Paul; m. Ana J. Ortiz, Apr. 20, 1996. BBA, Roosevelt U., 1973. Owner Mut. Home Delivery, Chgo., 1961-63; exec. v.p. Harris Trust and Savs. Bank, Chgo., 1964—; mem. Consumer Adv. Council, Washington, 1986—. Trustee Adler Planetarium, Chgo., 1982, Roosevelt U., Chgo.; chmn. Provident Med. Ctr., Chgo., 1986; bd. dirs. Voices for Ill. Children, Chgo. Coun. on Urban Affairs; pres. Neighborhood Housing Svcs. Recipient Disting. Alumni award Clark Coll., Atlanta, 1985. Mem. Nat. Bankers Assn., Urban Bankers Forum (Pioneer award 1986), Econ. Club. Chgo. Clubs: Metropolitan, Plaza (Chgo.). Office: Harris Trust & Savs Bank 111 W Monroe St Chicago IL 60603

WILLIAMS, EDWARD VINSON, music history educator; b. Orlando, Fla., July 12, 1935. B.M., Fla. State U., 1957; M.M., Ind. U., 1962; M.A., Yale U., 1966, Ph.D., 1968. Prof. music history dept. music U. Kans., Lawrence, 1969-90, chmn. dept. music history, 1975-84; assoc. dean rsch. and grad. studies Coll. Arts and Architecture, prof. music Pa. State U., University Park, Pa., 1990—. Author: The Bells of Russia: History and Technology, 1985. Served with U.S. Army, 1957-60. Recipient Chancellor's award for Excellence in Teaching, U. Kans., 1975; Kennan Inst. fellow Wilson Ctr., Washington, 1985; fellow Nat. Humanities Ctr., Research Triangle Park, N.C., 1980-81. Mem. Am. Musicological Soc., Am. Assn. for Advancement Slavic Studies, Assn. Bell Art (Moscow). Home: 330 Toftrees Ave Apt 149 State College PA 16803-2043 Office: Pa State U Coll Arts and Architecture 115 Arts Bldg University Park PA 16802-2900

WILLIAMS, EDWIN NEEL, newspaper editor; b. Rives, Mo., Jan. 14, 1942; s. Carl Edwin and Vina Marie (Edmonston) W.; m. Marylyn Lentine, 1973; 1 child, Jonathan Lentine. BA in History, U. Miss., 1965. Reporter Clarksdale (Miss) Press-Register, 1965; reporter, editor Delta Dem.-Times, Greenville, Miss., 1967-72; Nieman fellow Harvard U., Cambridge, Mass., 1972-73; writer, researcher Ford Found., N.Y.C., 1973; editorial writer Charlotte (N.C.) Observer, 1973-76, editor of editorial pages, 1976-80, 87—. Chmn. KinderMourn, Charlotte, 1988, N.C. Harvest, 1993-94; bd. dirs. N.C. Ctr. for Pub. Policy Rsch., Raleigh, 1992-95. With U.S. Army, 1965-67. Baptist. Home: 916 Mount Vernon Ave Charlotte NC 28203-4845 Office: Charlotte Observer PO Box 30308 Charlotte NC 28230-0308

WILLIAMS, ELEANOR JOYCE, government air traffic control specialist; b. College Station, Tex., Dec. 21, 1936; d. Robert Ira and Viola (Ford) Toliver; m. Tollie Williams, Dec. 30, 1955 (div. July 1978); children: Rodrick, Viola Williams Smith, Darryl, Eric, Dana Williams Jones, Sheila Williams Watkins, Kenneth. Student Prairie View A&M Coll., 1955-56, Anchorage Community Coll., 1964-65, U. Alaska-Anchorage, 1976. Clk./stenographer FAA, Anchorage, 1965-66, adminstrv. clk., 1966-67, pers. staffing asst., 1967-68, air traffic control specialist, 1968-79, air traffic contr. supr., San Juan, P.R., 1979-80, Anchorage, 1983-85, airspace specialist, Atlanta, 1980-83 ; with FAA, Washington, 1985-87; area mgr. Kansas City Air Rt. Traffic Control Ctr., Olathe, Kans., 1987-89, asst. mgr. quality Assurance, 1989-91, supr. traffic mgmt., 1991, supr. system effectiveness section, 1991-93, asst. air traffic mgr., 1993-94, air traffic mgr. Cleve. Air Route Traffic Control Ctr., Oberlin, Ohio, 1994—, acting mgr. sys. mgmt. br., Des Plaines, Ill., 1995-96, mem. human resource reform team task force, Washington, 1996—, acting regional exec. mgr. Great Lakes Region, Des Plaines, Ill., 1996—. Sec. Fairview Neighborhood Coun., Anchorage, 1967-69; mem. Anchorage Bicentennial Commn., 1975-76; bd. dirs. Mt. Patmos Youth Dept., Decatur, Ga., 1981-82; mem. NAACP; del. to USSR Women in Mgmt., 1990; mem. citizens amb. program People to People Internat. Recipient Mary K. Goddard award Anchorage Fed. Exec. Assn. and Fed. Women's Program, 1985, Sec.'s award Dept. transp., 1985, Pres. VIP award, 1988, C. Alfred Anderson award, 1991, Disting. Svc. award Nat. Black Coalition of Fed. Aviation Employees, 1991, Paul K. Bohr award FAA, 1994, Nat. Performance Rev. Hammer award from V.P. Al Gore, 1996; A salute to Her Name in the Congl. Record 104th Congress, 1995. Mem. Nat. Assn Negro Bus. and Profl, Women (North to the Future club, charter pres. 1975-76), Blacks in Govt., Nat. Black Coalition of Fed. Aviation Employees (pres. cen. region chpt. 1987-92, Over Achievers award, 1987, Disting. Svc. award 1988, Sojourner Truth award Great Lakes region 1997), Profl. Women Contrs. Orgn., Air Traffic Contrs. Assn., Fed. Mgrs. Assn., Internat. Platform Assn., Women in Mgmt. (del. Soviet Union), Gamma Phi Delta. Democrat. Baptist. Avocations: singing; sewing. Home: 5421 NE River Rd # 708 Chicago IL 60656 Office: FAA 326 E Lorain St Oberlin OH 44074-1216

WILLIAMS, ELIZABETH EVENSON, writer; b. Sioux Falls, S.D., Sept. 25, 1940; d. A. Duane and Eleanor (Kelton) Evenson; m. Louis P. Williams Jr., Aug. 31, 1968; 1 child, Katherine. BS, S.D. State U., 1962; MA, U. Wis., 1964; postgrad., U. Minn., 1969-70; MA, S.D. State U., 1983, postgrad., 1997—. Dir. pubs. No. State Coll., Aberdeen, S.D., 1965-68; instr. journalism S.D. State U., Brookings, 1968-69, 85—; asst. editor Journalism Quar., Mpls., 1969-70; pub. info. specialist S.D. Com. on Humanities, Brookings, 1975-78; asst. and instr. speech dept. S.D. State U., Brookings, 1981-92; part-time dir. Women's Ctr., Brookings, 1988-90; reading series coord. S.D. Com. on Humanities, Brookings, 1986-91. Author: Emil Loriks: Builder of a New Economic Order, 1987, More Reflections of a Prairie Daughter, 1993; weekly columnist Brookings Daily Register, 1985-92, RFD News, 1992-95; contbr. articles to profl. jours. Vestry mem. St. Paul's Ch., Brookings, 1975-76, 84-86, 92-97, sr. warden, 1995-97; pres. LWV of S.D., 1985-89, treas., 1990-92. S.D. Humanities Com. grantee, 1984, 87, 90. Mem. Nat. Fedn. Press Women (1st place nat. writing contest 1977), Phi Kappa Phi, Pi Kappa Delta, Alpha Kappa Delta. Episcopalian. Avocations: golf, photography, travel. Home: 1103 3rd St Brookings SD 57006-2230 Office: SD State U Journalism Dept Brookings SD 57007

WILLIAMS, ELIZABETH YAHN, author, lecturer, lawyer; b. Columbus, Ohio, July 20, 1942; d. Wilbert Henry and Elizabeth Dulson (Brophy) Yahn. BA cum laude, Loyola Marymount U., 1964; secondary tchg. credential, UCLA, 1965; JD, Loyola U., 1971. Cert. tchr. h.s. and jr. coll. law, English and history. Writer West Covina, Calif., 1964—; designer West Covina, 1966-68; tchr. jr./sr. h.s. L.A. City Schs., Santa Monica, Calif., 1964-65, La Puente (Calif.) H.S. Dist., 1965-67; legal intern, lawyer Garvey, Ingram, Baker & Uhler, Covina, Calif., 1969-72; lawyer, corp. counsel Avco Fin. Svcs., Inc., Newport Beach, Calif., 1972-74; sole practitioner and arbitrator Santa Ana, Calif., 1974-80, Newport Beach, 1980-87; mem. faculty continuing edn. State Bar of Calif., 1979; adj. prof. Western State U. Sch. Law, Fullerton, Calif., 1980; mem. fed. cts. com. Calif. State Bar, San Francisco, 1977-80. Author: (1-act plays) Acting-Out Acts, 1990, Grading Graciela, 1992, Boundaries in the Dirt, 1993; author, lyricist: (1-act children's musical) Peter and the Worry Wrens, 1995; editor: The Music of Poetry, 1997; contbr. articles to profl. jours.; panelist TV show Action Now, 1971; interviewee TV show Women, 1987; scriptwriter, TV show Four/Four, 1994, (3-act adaptation) Saved in Sedona, 1995; scriptwriter, prodr., host TV show Guidelights to Success, 1996. Mem. alumni bd. Loyola-Marymount U., L.A., 1980-84; mem. adv. bd. Rancho Santiago Coll., Santa Ana, 1983-84; spkr. Commn. on Status on Women, Santa Ana, 1979. Recipient Editor's Choice award Nat. Libr. of Poetry, 1995-96, Telly award finalist, 1996; grantee Ford Found., 1964-65; French scholar Ohio State U., 1959, acad. scholar Loyola-Marymount U., 1960-64. Mem. Calif. Women Lawyers (co-founder, life, bd. dirs. 1975-76), Orange County Bar Assn. (faculty Orange County Coll. Trial Advocacy 1982, chmn. human and individual rights com. 1974-75, comml. law and bankruptcy com. 1978-79, corp. and bus. law sect. 1980-81), So. Calif. Book Writers and Illustrators, Magee Park Poets, Phi Theta Kappa (most disting. hon. life mem.). Avocation: directing and producing ensemble and liturgical dramas and musicals. Office: PO Box 146 San Luis Rey CA 92068-0146

WILLIAMS, EMMA CRAWFORD, business owner; b. Dillon, S.C., Aug. 16, 1945; d. Moses and Sallie Lee (McInnis) Crawford; m. Johnny Lee Williams, Nov. 25, 1967; 1 child, GiGi T. A in Bus. Adminstrn., Durham (N.C.) Bus. Coll., 1964; A in Acctg., Strayer Coll., Washington, 1969. From sec. to office mgr. Ferris & Co., Washington, 1965-68; exec. asst. mgr. Manpower Assistance Program, Washington, 1968-71; adminstrv. asst./office mgr. Appalachian Regional Com., Washington, 1971-81; adminstrv. sec. Home Owners Warranty Ins., Washington, 1981-82; office mgr. Hilton Internat. Hotels, Washington, 1986-89; pres., CEO, owner AHA Enterprises, Inc. (Added Hands Agy.), Ft. Washington, Md., 1989—; mem. Fairfax County Commerce Dept.; motivational spkr. D.C. Treatment Facility; guest spkr. Julia Jackson's Other Office on Bus. and Fins., Va., 1996. Block capt. Ft. Washington Citizen Assn., 1975—; active Laura House Assn., Tex., 1992—; vol. office asst. nat. presdl. campaign, Washington, 1976. Mem. Am. Woman's Econ. Devel., Nat. Notary Assn., Dillionite, Inc. Democrat. Avocations: reading journals and self-help publications, collecting antiques, polo, fundraising campaigns. Home: 9108 Overlook Trail Washington MD 20744 Office: AHA Enterprises Inc Added Hands Agy 1800 Diagonal Rd Ste 600 Alexandria VA 22314-2840

WILLIAMS, EMORY, former retail company executive, banker; b. Falco, Ala., Oct. 26, 1911; s. William Emory and Nelle (Turner) W.; m. Janet Hatcher Allcorn, May 15, 1943; children: Nelle (Mrs. Gilbert Brown), Janet (Mrs. Edwin Harrison), Bliss (Mrs. Howell Browne), Carol (Mrs. James Schroeder), Emory III. A.B., Emory U., 1932. With Sears, Roebuck & Co., 1933-75; pres. Sears, Roebuck (S.A.), Brazil, 1958-60, Homart Devel. Co., 1960-67; treas. parent co., 1962-64, v.p., treas., 1964-75; chmn. bd., chief exec. officer Sears Bank & Trust Co., 1975-81, also dir.; chmn. bd. dirs., pres. Chgo. Milw. Corp., 1981-85; ptnr. Williams Realdy Co.; chmn. Williams & Nichols Co., SureBlock Co., Am. Investors in China. Div. chmn. Chgo. Crusade of Mercy, 1962-64, gen. chmn., 1966, pres, 1976-78; chmn. Ill. Health Edn. Commn., 1968-70; pres. Adler Planetarium, 1972-75, Ravinia Festival Assn., 1972-78; ptrs. bd. dirs. Community Fund, 1970-73; trustee Emory U., Chgo. Community Trust, Northwestern Meml. Hosps., Episcopal Diocesan Found., Kellstadt Found.; chmn. Chgo. Chamber Musicians. Lt. col. C.E., U.S. Army, World War II, CBI. Mem. Piedmont Driving Club (Atlanta); Chgo. Club, Old Elm Club (Chgo.), Commercial Club; Indian Hill Club (Winnetka, Ill.), Loblolly Bay Yacht Club, Loblolly Pines Golf Club (Hobe Sound, Fla.), Seminole Golf Club (North Palm Beach). Home: 1630 Sheridan Rd Wilmette IL 60091 Also: 7760 SE Lake Shore Dr Hobe Sound FL 33455-3833

WILLIAMS, ERIK GEORGE, professional football player; b. Phila., Sept. 7, 1968. Student, Ctrl. State U. Offensive tackle Dallas Cowboys, 1991—; mem. Superbowl Championship team, 1993, 94. Named to Pro Bowl Team, 1993; named offensive tackle on The Sporting News NFL All-Pro Team, 1993; selected to Pro Bowl, 1996. Office: Dallas Cowboys 1 Cowboys Pky Irving TX 75063-4945*

WILLIAMS, ERNEST GOING, retired paper company executive; b. Macon, Miss., Sept. 24, 1915; s. Augustus Gaines and Mary (Sanford) W.; m. Cecil Louise Butler, Aug. 18, 1951; children: Ernest Sanford, Turner Butler, Elizabeth Cecil. BS in Commerce and Bus. Adminstrn., U. Ala., 1938, LLD, 1987. Asst. to treas. U. Ala., 1938-42, 45-48, treas., 1948-56; v.p. First Nat. Bank Tuscaloosa, Ala., 1956-58; dir. First Nat. Bank Tuscaloosa, 1956-84; v.p., dir. Gulf States Paper Corp., Tuscaloosa, 1958-77; chmn. bd., dir. Affiliated Paper Cos., Inc., Tuscaloosa, 1977-94; bd. dirs., past chmn. Southland Nat. Ins. Corp.; past pres. Associated Industries Ala. Trustee emeritus U. Ala., David Warner Found.; past pres. YMCA, United Way of Tuscaloosa County; past chmn. Tuscaloosa County chpt. ARC; past pres. DCH Found.; chmn. Williams Fund, Inc., Alyth Properties, Ltd. With USNR, 1942-45. Named Tuscaloosa Citizen of Year Civitan Club, 1974. Mem. Newcomen Soc. N.Am., Ala. Acad. of Honor, Univ. Club, River Club, Indian Hills Country Club, North River Yacht Club (vice commodore), Exch. Club (past pres.), Kappa Alpha, Omicron Delta Kappa, Beta Gamma Sigma. Presbyterian. Home: 156 The Highlands Tuscaloosa AL 35404-2900 Office: Affiliated Paper Co Inc 1806 6th St Tuscaloosa AL 35401-1721

WILLIAMS, ERNEST WILLIAM, JR., economist, educator; b. Scranton, Pa., Oct. 27, 1916; s. Ernest William and Kathryn (Winterstein) W.; m. Thelma Foxwell Klohr, Dec. 7, 1957 (dec. 1984). B.S., Columbia U., 1938, M.S., 1939, Ph.D., 1951. Economist Nat. Resources Planning Bd., 1940-42, WPB, 1942-44; chief transp. div. U.S. Strategic Bombing Survey, 1944-45; fiscal analyst U.S. Bur. Budget, 1945-46; lectr. transp. Grad. Sch. Bus. Columbia, 1947-52, assoc. prof., 1952-58, prof. transp., 1958-86, prof. emeritus, 1987—, vice dean, 1977-79; vis. prof. mgmt. U. Ariz., 1972, 74; cons. ODM, 1951-60; dir. transp. study Dept. Commerce, 1959-60; dir. ACF Industries, Inc., N.Y.C., 1960-84; mem. N.Y.-N.J. Met. Rapid Transit Commn., 1955-58; mem. task force Pres.'s Adv. Com. Transp. Policy and Orgn., 1954-55; mem. task force on regulatory agencies First Hoover Commn., 1948. Author: (with Marvin L. Fair) Economics of Transportation, rev. edit, 1959, The Regulation of Rail-Motor Rate Competition, 1958, Freight Transportation in the Soviet Union, 1962, The Future of American Transportation, 1971, Economics of Transportation and Logistics, 1974, rev. edit., 1981, (with G.K. Sletmo) Liner Conferences in the Container Age, 1981; contbr. articles to profl. publs. Trustee TAA Research Fund, 1962-65; bd. visitors U.S. Army Transp. Sch., 1963-66. Recipient Medal for Freedom. Mem. Am. Econ. Assn., Am. Soc. Transp. and Logistics. Home: 415 Janes Ln Stamford CT 06903-4818

WILLIAMS, ERVIN EUGENE, religious organization administrator; b. Corning, N.Y., Feb. 25, 1923; s. Douglas Lewis and Mina P. (Barnes) W.; m. Ruth Evelyn Snyder, June 12, 1945; children: Roger Eugene, Virginia Ruth. Student, Toccoa Falls (Ga.) Bible Coll., 1939, Cornell U., 1942; BA, Pa. State U., 1949; MA, Mich. State U., 1961, PhD in Communications, 1971. Ordained to ministry Ind. Bapt. Ch., 1950. Acad. dean Greensburg (Pa.) Bible Inst., 1949-51; min. Bapt. Ch., New Kensington, Pa., 1951-53; instr. Pa. State U., 1953-55; sr. min. East Lansing (Mich.) Trinity Ch., 1955-71; vis. prof. Trinity Evang. Div. Sch., Deerfield, Ill., 1968-71, prof. communication and practical theology, 1971-77, dir. D Ministry program, 1975-76; gen. dir. Am. Missionary Fellowship, Villanova, Pa., 1977-92; exec. min. Ch. of the Apostles, Atlanta, 1993-95; ch. and instl. cons. Smyrna, Ga., 1995-97; sr. pastor New Life Bible Ch., Abaco, The Bahamas, 1997—; chaplain Mich. State U., East Lansing, 1955-71; cons. Haggai Inst. for Advanced Leadership Tng., Atlanta, 1969—; lectr. Calvary Bapt. Coll., Kansas City, Mo., 1962, Haggai Inst. Third World Leaders, Singapore, 1970—; Staley lectr. Robert Wesleyan Coll., North Chili, N.Y., 1973, Judson Coll., Elgin, Ill., 1977-79; cons. to mission bds., 1967-76; assoc. dir. Camp of Woods, Speculator, N.Y., 1971-77. Author: 3 books; contbr. numerous articles to religious periodicals, also monographs. Trustee Dorothy H. Theis Meml. Found., Sierra Vista, Ariz., 1987—; trustee Gospel Vols., Speculator, N.Y., 1963-93; mem. bd. regents Owosso (Mich.) Coll., 1971-73. Pilot USAAF, 1942-45, prisoner of war, ETO, 1945. Mem. Nat. Sunday Sch. Assn., Christian Assn. Psychol. Studies, Mich. Acad. Arts and Scis., Aircraft Owners and Pilots Assn., Phi Beta Kappa, Pi Gamma Mu, Phi Kappa Phi, Alpha Kappa Delta. *It is much more difficult to conceal ignorance and prejudice than it is to acquire knowledge and fairness.*

WILLIAMS, FORMAN ARTHUR, engineering science educator, combustion theorist; b. New Brunswick, N.J., Jan. 12, 1934; s. Forman J. and Alice (Pooley) W.; m. Elsie Vivian Kara, June 15, 1955 (div. 1978); children: F. Gary, Glen A., Nancy L., Susan D., Michael S., Michelle K.; m. Elizabeth Acevedo, Aug. 19, 1978. BSE, Princeton U., 1955; PhD, Calif. Inst. Tech., 1958. Asst. prof. Harvard U., Cambridge, Mass., 1958-64; prof. U. Calif.-San Diego, 1964-81; Robert H. Goddard prof. Princeton U., N.J., 1981-88; prof. dept. applied mechs. and engring. scis. U. Calif., San Diego, 1988—; predsidential chair in Energy and Combustion Rsch U. Calif., San Diego, Ca., 1994—. Author: Combustion Theory, 1965, 2d edit., 1985; contbr. articles to profl. jours. Fellow NSF, 1962; fellow Guggenheim Found., 1970; recipient U.S. Sr. Scientist award Alexander von Humboldt Found., 1982, Silver medal Combustion Inst., 1978, Bernard Lewis Gold medal Combustion Inst., 1990, Pendray Aerospace Literature award Am. Inst. of Aeronautics and Astronautics, 1993. Fellow AIAA ; mem. Am. Phys. Soc., Combustion Inst., Soc. for Indsl. and Applied Math., Nat. Acad. Engring., Nat. Acad. Engring Mex. (fgn. corr. mem.), Sigma Xi. Home: 8002 La Jolla Shores Dr La Jolla CA 92037-3230 Office: U Calif San Diego Ctr Energy & Combustion Rsch 9500 Gilman Dr La Jolla CA 92093-5003

WILLIAMS, FRANK JAMES, JR., department store chain executive, lawyer; b. St. Louis, July 2, 1938; s. Frank James and Alberta Klaus Williams; children by previous marriage: Kimberly, Andrew, Renee; m. Sandra M. Garbe, Feb. 13, 1988. B.S.B.A., Washington U., St. Louis, 1960; J.D., Washington U., 1963; postgrad., U. Mo., 1960-61. Bar: Mo. 1963. Asst. gen. counsel May Dept. Stores, St. Louis, 1963-66, v.p.-labor relations, 1970-75, v.p.-labor relations and govt. affairs, 1975-80, v.p.-pub. affairs, 1980—; atty. Pet, Inc., St. Louis, 1966-67; lectr. various trade, profl. orgns. Treas. May Dept. Stores Polit. Action Com., St. Louis, 1981—. Mem. Mo. Bar Assn., Nat. Retail Mchts. Assn. (chmn. employee rels. com. 1977-78, silver plaque), Am. Retail Fedn. (chmn. employee rels. com. 1973-76), Nat. Retail Fedn. Roman Catholic. Club: Mo. Athletic (1st v.p. and treas. 1980-81) (St. Louis). Home: 2907 Bayberry Ridge Dr Saint Louis MO 63129-6422 Office: May Dept Stores 611 Olive St Saint Louis MO 63101-1721

WILLIAMS, FRANKLIN CADMUS, JR., bibliographer; b. Palestine, Tex., July 30, 1941; s. Franklin Cadmus and Cathryn Lucille (Pessoney) W. BA, Baylor U., 1963; MA, Stephen F. Austin State U., 1965; PhD, U. Wis., 1975. Cert. in secondary edn. English and History. Teaching fellow Stephen F. Austin State U., Nacogdoches, Tex., 1964-65, U. Wis., Madison, 1965-68; instr. English Austin Peay State U., Clarksville, Tenn., 1970-71; adj. asst. prof. East Tex. State U., Commerce, 1975; asst. prof. English Jarvis Christian Coll., Hawkins, Tex., 1976-78, 79-81; ind. scholar Palestine, Tex., 1981—; owner, bibliographer Goldsmith Archive, Palestine, 1981—; cons. Diocese of Galveston-Houston, 1977-84, Tex. State Hist. Assn., Austin, 1988; speaker, editor Jarvis Christian Coll., Hawkins, Tex., 1976-78, 79-81; nat. teaching fellow Office Edn., Washington, 1976-77; del. to Baylor U., U. Wis. System, Madison, 1981. Author: Lone Star Bishops: The Roman Catholic Hierarchy in Texas, 1997; contbr. articles to profl. jours. Mem. Modern Lang. Assn., Tex. State Hist. Assn., Tex. Cath. Hist. Soc., Baylor Alumni Assn. (life), Wis. Alumni Assn. (life), Sigma Tau Delta. Avocations: reading, record collecting, historical genealogy, tennis, swimming. Office: PO Box 96 Palestine TX 75802-0096

WILLIAMS, FREDERICK, statistics educator; b. Middlesbrough, Eng., Feb. 9, 1922; came to U.S., 1926; s. Frederick William and Violet (Taylor) W.; m. Frances Marian Sacks, July 7, 1945. B.S.E., U. Mich., 1947, M.B.A. with distinction, 1948; Ph.D., Northwestern U., 1958. Teaching asst. statistics U. Mich., 1947-48; instr. statistics Northwestern U., 1948-54; instr., then asst. prof. statistics U. Ill., 1954-58; asso. prof. statistics U. Mo., 1958-61, prof., 1961—, chmn. dept., 1966-71, 1973-76, acting chmn., 1980-81, tchr. exec. devel. program, 1959-65, dir. grad. studies statistics, 1971-72; prof. emeritus, 1992—; cons., lectr. in field. Co-author: An Introduction to Probability, 1965. Served with USNR, 1943-46. Mem. Am. Statis. Assn. (pres. Mid-Mo. chpt. 1982, 93-94, past pres. 1995, mem. nat. coun. 1982-83, 85-97), Ops. Rsch. Soc. Am., Beta Gamma Sigma, Phi Kappa Phi. Home: 2501 N Leisurely Way Columbia MO 65202-2204 Office: Dept Statistics Math Scis Bldg Rm 320A U Mo Columbia MO 65211-0001

WILLIAMS, GARY, collegiate basketball team coach. B.Bus., U. Md., 1968. Asst. coach U. Md., College Park, 1969; asst. coach Woodrow Wilson H.S., Camden, N.J., head coach; asst. coach Lafayette Coll., head soccer coach; asst. coach, head coach Boston Coll., 1978-79, 83-87, American U., Washington, 1979-83; head coach Ohio State U., Columbus, U. Md., College Park, 1989—. Named Dist. Coach of Yr., 1981. Office: University of Maryland PO Box 295 College Park MD 20741-0295*

WILLIAMS, GARY MURRAY, medical researcher, pathology educator; b. Regina, Sask., Can., May 7, 1940; s. Murray Austin and Selma Ruby (Domstad) W.; m. Julia Christine Lundberg; children: Walter, Jeffrey, Ingrid. BA, Washington and Jefferson Coll., 1963; MD, U. Pitts, 1967. Diplomate Am. Bd. Pathology, Am. Bd. Toxicology. Assoc. prof. pathology Temple U., Phila., 1971-75; mem. Fels Rsch. Inst., Phila., 1971-75; rsch. prof. N.Y. Med. Coll., Valhalla, 1975—; chief pathology and toxicology div. Am. Health Found., Valhalla, 1975—; mem. toxicology study sect. NIH, Bethesda, Md., 1985-87; mem. working groups Internat. Agy. Rsch. on Cancer, Lyon, France, 1976, 80, 82, 83, 85, 86, 87, 89, 91, 96, 97; bd. dirs. Naylor Dana Inst., 1997—. Editor: Sweeteners; Health Effects, 1988; co-editor: Cellular System for Toxicity Testing, 1983; founding editor: Cell Biology and Toxicology, 1984—, Antioxidants: Chemical, Physiological, Nutritional and Toxicological Aspects, 1993; mem. editl. bd. Nutrition and Cancer, 1981—, Archives of Toxicology, 1988—, European Jour. Cancer Prevention, 1991—, Drug and Chem. Toxicology, 1994—; contbr. more than 410 sci. papers to profl. publs. Lt. comdr. USPHS, 1969-71. Recipient Sheard-Sanford award Am. Soc. Clin. Pathologists U. Pitts., 1967. Mem. Am. Assn. Cancer Rsch., Soc. Toxicology (Arthur J. Lehman award 1982, Lectr. award 1996), Soc. Toxicol. Pathology, Phi Beta Kappa, Alpha Omega Alpha. Home: 8 Elm Rd Scarsdale NY 10583-1410 Office: Am Health Found 1 Dana Rd Valhalla NY 10595-1549

WILLIAMS, GEORGE CHRISTOPHER, biologist, ecology and evolution educator; b. Charlotte, N.C., May 12, 1926; s. George Felix and Margaret (Steuart) W.; m. Doris Lee Calhoun, Jan. 25, 1951; children: Jacques, Sibyl, Judith, Phoebe. AB, U. Calif., Berkeley, 1949; PhD, UCLA, 1955; ScD (hon.), Queen's U., Kingston, Ont., Can., 1995. Instr. and asst. prof. Mich. State U., East Lansing, 1955-60; assoc. prof. dept. ecology and evolution SUNY, Stony Brook, 1960-66, prof., 1966-90; adj. prof. Queens U., Kingston, Ont., Can., 1980—. Author: Adaptation and Natural Selection, 1966, Sex and Evolution, 1975, Natural Selection: Domains, Levels and Challenges, 1992; co-author: Evolution and Ethics, 1989, (with R.M. Nesse) Why We Get Sick: The New Science of Darwinian Medicine, 1995; editor Quar. Rev. Biology, SUNY, 1965—. With U.S. Army, 1944-46. Recipient Eminent Ecologist award Ecol. Soc. Am., 1989, Daniel Giraud Elliot medal Nat. Acad. Sci., 1992; fellow Ctr. Adv. Study Behavioral Sci., Stanford, 1981-82, Guggenheim Found., 1988-89. Fellow AAAS, Soc. Study Evolution (v.p. 1973, pres. 1989), Nat. Acad. Sci., Am. Soc. Ichthyologists and Herpetologists, Am. Soc. Naturalists (editor 1974-79), Icelandic Natural History Soc. Office: SUNY Quarterly Review of Biology Stony Brook NY 11794

WILLIAMS, GEORGE EARNEST, engineer, retired business executive; b. Bartow, Fla., Nov. 27, 1923; s. Earnest Roscoe and Ruby Barnett (Mathews) W.; m. Muriel Theodorsen, June 9, 1949. BS in Engring. with honors, USCG Acad., 1944; postgrad., Harvard U., 1945-46; SM in Mgmt., MIT, 1949. Registered profl. engr. 2 states. Project engr., bus. cons. Ebasco, N.Y.C.; design engr., prodn. supr. Minute Maid Corp., Orlando, Fla.; asst. contr., div. contr., group contr., corp. dir. fin. planning and analysis United Technologies Corp., Hartford, 1957-76, v.p., 1977-82; sr. v.p. Kensington Mgmt. Cons., 1982-84; sr. v.p. fin. Otis Elevator Co., N.Y.C., 1976-77; Mem. exec. com. Conn. Commn. Services and Expenditures, 1971. Contbr. articles to fin. jours., chpts. to books. Served with USCG, 1941-47. Mem. AIAA, Fin. Execs. Inst., Army and Navy Club (Washington), Naples Yacht Club, Port Royal Club. Originator pricing system purchase of Fla. oranges for concentrate mfg.; avocation: yachtsman. Home: 1325 7th St S Naples FL 34102-7316

WILLIAMS, GEORGE HOWARD, lawyer, association executive; b. Hempstead, N.Y., Feb. 12, 1918; s. George R. and Marcella (Hogan) W.; m. Mary Celeste Madden, Nov. 23, 1946; children—Mary Beth Williams Barritt, Stephen, Kevin, Jeanne Marie. A.B., Hofstra Coll., 1939, LL.D. (hon.), 1969; J.D., N.Y. U., 1946, LL.D. (hon.), 1969; postgrad., NYU, 1959. Bar: N.Y. 1946. Adminstrv. asst. to dean NYU Law Sch., N.Y.C., 1946-48, instr. law, 1948-50, asst. prof., 1950-52, assoc. prof., 1952-55, prof., 1956-62, v.p. univ. devel., 1962-66, exec. v.p. planning and devel., 1966-68; pres. Am. U., Washington, 1968-75; exec. v.p., dir. Am. Judicature Soc., Chgo., 1976-87. Author: (with A.T. Vanderbilt and L.L. Pelletier) Report on Liberal Adult Education, 1955; (with K. Sampson) Handbook for Judges, 1984. Bd. dirs. Nat. Ctr. Edn. Politics, 1948-58, trustee, 1958-65; trustee Hofstra U., 1961-64; chmn. bd. trustees Trinity Coll., Vt., 1978-86; bd. dirs. Ctr. for Conflict Resolution, 1988—, Univ. Support Svcs. Served to lt. col., inf. AUS, World War II. Decorated Legion of Merit, Silver Star. Mem. Am. Polit. Sci. Assn., ABA Assn. Bar City N.Y., Alpha Kappa Delta, Phi Delta Phi. Clubs: N.Y. U. (N.Y.C.); Nat. Lawyers (Washington). Home: 1322 Judson Ave Evanston IL 60201-4720 Office: Am Judicature Soc 25 E Washington St Ste 1600 Chicago IL 60602-1805

WILLIAMS, GEORGE HUNTSTON, church historian, educator; b. Huntsburg, Ohio, Apr. 7, 1914; s. David Rhys and Lucy Adams (Pease) W.; m. Marjorie Louise Derr, July 27, 1941; children: Portia, Jeremy, Jonathan, Roger. Student, U. Munich, 1934-35; AB, St. Lawrence U., 1936; BDiv, U. Chgo., 1939, LittD (hon.), 1965; postgrad., U. Strasbourg, 1939-40, U. Calif., 1943-45; ThD, Union Theol. Sem., 1946; DD (hon.), Meadville Theological Sch., 1954; DHL (hon.), Loyola U., 1980, St. Anselm Coll., 1984; DCnL (hon.), King's Coll. U., 1986; DD, U. Edinburgh, Scotland, 1987. Ordained to ministry Unitarian and Congl. Chs., 1940. Asst. minister Ch. of Christian Union, Rockford, Ill., 1940-41; mem. faculty Starr King Sch. for Ministry, Pacific Sch. Religion, Berkeley, Calif., 1941-47; asso. prof. ch. history Starr King Sch. for Ministry, Pacific Sch. Religion, 1946-47; lectr. ch. history, head dept. Harvard Div. Sch., 1947-53, asso. prof., acting dean, 1953-55, prof., 1955—, Winn prof. ecclesiastical history, 1956, Hollis prof. div., 1963-81, emeritus, 1981—; Fulbright lectr. U. Strasbourg, 1960-61; Gunning lectr. U. Edinburgh, Scotland, 1987. Author: The Church and the Democratic State and the Crisis in Religious Education, 1948, An Examination of the Thought of Frederic Henry Hedge, 1949, The Norman Anonymous of ca. 1100, 1951, Public Aid to Parochial Education, 1951, Christology and ChurchState Relations in the Fourth Century, 1951, Church History in the U.S 1900-1950, 1951, Church, State and Society in John Paul II, 1983; editor, contbr. Harvard Divinity School History, 1954, Ministry in the Patristic Period, 1956, Golden Priesthood and the Leaden State1, 1957, Anabaptist and Spiritual Writers, 1957, Anselm, 1960, The Radical Reformation, 1962 (enlarged Spanish edit. 1983, 2d English edit. 1992), Wilderness and Paradise, 1962, Camillo Renato, 1965, Georges Florovsky, 1965, Sacred Condominium in American Debate on Abortion, 1970, The Last Catholic Modernist, 1973, Two Social Strands Italian Anabaptism, 1973, The Stancarist Schism, 1980; co-editor: Writings of Thomas Hooker before 1633, 1976, Polish Brethren, 1601-85, 1980, Protestantism in The Ukraine, 1550-1701, 1978, The Mind of John Paul II, 1981; translator, editor Lubieniecki's History of the Polish Reformation, 1995, Divinings: Religion at Harvard, 1636-1992, 1993; mem. editorial bd. or co-editor: Harvard Theol. Rev. and Studies, Church History, Greek, Roman, and Byzantine Studies, Jour. Church and State, Studies in Romanticism, Mennonite Quar. Rev., Reflections, Bibliotheca Unitariorum. Decorated knight Order of St. Gregory the Great (John Paul II); Guggenheim fellow and IREX scholar U. Lublin, Poland, 1972-73; NEH 1980. Fellow Deputizatione di Storia Patria per le Venezie (hon.); mem. Am. Soc. Reformation Rsch. (pres. 1967), Patristic Soc., Am. Acad. Arts and Scis., Medieval Acad. Am., Am. Soc. Ch. History (pres. 1958), Cath. Hist. Assn., European Soc. Culture, Civil Liberties Union Mass. (adv. com.), Americans United for Life (pres. 1971-77), Mass. Hist. Soc., Phi Beta Kappa. Honored by jubilee vol. Continuity in Church History, 1979. Home: 58 Pinehurst Rd Belmont MA 02178-1504 Office: Widener Libr 747 Harvard U Cambridge MA 02138

WILLIAMS, GEORGE LEO, retired secondary education educator; b. N.Y.C., June 29, 1931; s. Leo Dominick and Cathryn Margaret (Schellderfer) W.; m. Adelia Gilda Musa, Feb. 26, 1958; children: Adelia, Marina, Gilda. BA, CUNY, 1953, MA, 1955; PhD, NYU, 1966. Tchr. Port Washington (N.Y.) Pub. Schs., 1953, chairperson integrated studies, 1960-65, coord. Amherst project, 1968-69, chairperson English dept., 1970-90; adminstrv. asst. secondary and higher edn. dept. NYU, N.Y.C., 1965-66; adj. prof. NYU, 1966-74, Adelphi U., Garden City, N.Y. 1967-69, Hofstra U., Hempstead, N.Y., 1967-74; chmn. profl. growth and devel. com. Port Washington Pub. Schs., 1973-90, chmn. bicentennial com. 1989-90, mem. policy bd. Port Washington Tchr. Ctr., 1987-90; mem. alumni bd. Queens Coll. History Dept., 1996—. Co-author: (play) The Triumph of the Constitution, 1988; author: Fascist Thought and Totalitarianism in Italy's Secondary Schools: Theory and Practice, 1922-1943, 1993, Port Washington in the Twentieth Century: Places and People, 1995, (play) Remembrances of the First Colonial Settlement, 1993; editor Port Arrow Community Newsletter, 1973-84, Cow Neck Peninsula Hist. Soc. Newsletter, 1974-77; contbg. editor L.I. Forum, 1985—; author, prodr. (video) Port Washington into the 21st Century, 1996. Chairperson landmarks com. Cow Neck Peninsula Hist. Soc., Port Washington, 1980—, trustee, 1974-77; commr. landmarks com. Village of Port Washington North, 1983—, chmn., 1991; chairperson Hist. Landmark Preservation Commn., North Hempstead, N.Y., 1984-97, 1701 Roslyn Grist Mill Com., 1997—; mem. Port Washington Continuing Edn. Adv. Coun., 1988-97; co-chair 1895 Roslyn Clock Tower Com., 1994-96. Recipient environ. award Residents for a More Beautiful Port Washington, 1994. Mem. ASCD, Nat. Coun. Tchrs. English, Soc. for Preservation L.I. Antiquities, Port Washington Tchrs. Assn. (v.p. 1963-64, bd. dirs. 1966-74, founder ret. tchrs. chpt. 1991, newsletter editor 1990-92), Am. Hist. Assn. (cert. recognition 1988), Friends for L.I.'s Heritage, Roslyn Landmark Soc., N.Y. Geneal./Biog. Soc., N.Y. State Hist. Assn., Fulbright Assn., Hofstra Univ. Club, Residents for a More Beautiful Port Washington (1994 Environ. award), Phi Beta Kappa, Phi Alpha Theta, Pi Sigma Alpha. Home: 84 Radcliff Ave Port Washington NY 11050-1600

WILLIAMS, G(EORGE) MELVILLE, surgeon, medical educator; b. Soochow, China, Nov. 16, 1930; came to U.S., 1940; s. Melville Owens and Annie Lee (Young) W.; m. Lee Logan, June 12, 1955 (div. 1985); children: Curtiss John, Steven Hoyt, Lucy Roxanna, Elizabeth; m. Elizabeth Hopkins, Feb. 14, 1986 (div.); m. Linda Parsons, Apr. 14, 1996. BA, Oberlin Coll., 1953; MD, Harvard U., 1957. Diplomate Am. Bd. Surgery. Spl. fellow NIH, Melbourne, Australia, 1963-64; instr. surgery Med. Coll. Va., Richmond, 1964-65, asst. prof. surgery, 1965-66, assoc. prof. surgery, 1966-67, prof. surgery, 1967-69; prof. surgery The Johns Hopkins U. Sch. Medicine, Balt., 1969—. Author: Atlas of Aortic Surgery, Editor: Transplant Rejection. United Network Organ Sharing (pres. 1984-85). Capt. U.S. Army, 1960-62. Grantee NIH, 1969, 82, Am. Heart Assn., 1991. Mem. Am. Surg Assn., The Halsted Soc. (pres. 1983), Am. Soc. Transplant Surgeons (pres. 1982-83), So. Assn. for Vascular Surgery (pres. 1991). Democrat. Methodist. Avocations: carpentry, fishing, boating. Office: Johns Hopkins Hosp 600 N Wolfe St Baltimore MD 21205-2110

WILLIAMS, GEORGE RAINEY, retired surgeon, educator; b. Atlanta, Oct. 25, 1926; s. George Rainey and Hildred (Russell) W.; m. Martha Vose, June 16, 1950; children: Bruce, Alden, Margaret, Rainey. Student, U. Tex., 1944-46; B.S., Northwestern U., 1948; M.B., 1950, M.D., 1950. Intern Johns Hopkins Hosp., 1950-51, William Stewart Halsted fellow surgery, 1951-52, asst. resident surgery, 1952-53, asst. resident surgeon, 1955-57, resident surgeon, 1957-58; practice medicine specializing in gen. and thoracic surgery Oklahoma City, 1958-96; asst. prof. surgery U. Okla. Health Scis. Center, Oklahoma City, 1958-61; assoc. prof. U. Okla. Health Scis. Center, 1961-63; prof. surgery U. Okla. Health Scis. Center Coll. of Medicine, 1963-96, chmn. dept. surgery, 1974—; interim dean U. Okla. Coll. Medicine, 1981-82, 85-86, 88-89; dir. Am. Bd. Surgery, 1975-81, vice chmn., 1979-81. Contbr. articles on gen. and thoracic surgery to profl. jours. Served lt., MC, 3d Inf. Div. AUS, 1953-55. Recipient Disting. Service citation U. Okla., 1982; named to Okla. Hall of Fame, 1986. Fellow ACS (sec. bd. govs. 1985-87, 1st v.p. 1989-90), Soc. Univ. Surgeons, Am. Assn. Thoracic Surgery, So. Surg. Assn., Am. Surg. Assn., Phi Beta Kappa, Delta Kappa Epsilon, Phi Beta Pi, Alpha Epsilon Delta, Alpha Omega Alpha, Pi Kappa Epsilon. Home: 6722 Country Club Dr Oklahoma City OK 73116-4706 Office: U Okla Dept Surgery PO Box 26307 Oklahoma City OK 73126-0307

WILLIAMS, GEORGE WALTON, English educator; b. Charleston, S.C., Oct. 10, 1922; s. Ellison Adger and Elizabeth Simonton (Dillingham) W.; m. Harriet Porcher Simons, Nov. 28, 1953; children: George Walton Jr., Ellison Adger II, Harriet Porcher Stoney. B.A., Yale U., 1947; M.A., U. Va., 1949, Ph.D., 1957. Asst. cashier Carolina Savs. Bank, Charleston, 1949-54; asst. prof. English, Duke U., 1957-63, asso. prof., 1963-67, prof., 1967, chmn. dept. English, 1982-86, prof. emeritus, 1993—; dir. summer inst. Commn. on English, Coll. Entrance Exam. Bd., 1962; pres. Durham Savoyards, Ltd., 1966-68, 81-82; sr. fellow Coop. Program in Humanities, Duke-U. N.C., 1969; Historiographer, Diocese of S.C., 1960-78; vis. prof. U.S. Mil. Acad., 1982-83. Author: St. Michael's, Charleston, 1751-1951, 1951, Image and Symbol in the Sacred Poetry of Richard Crashaw, 1963, The Craft of Printing and the Publication of Shakespeare's Plays, 1985; editor: Romeo and Juliet, 1964, Complete Poetry of Richard Crashaw, 1970, Jacob Eckhard's Choirmaster's Book, 1971, Shakespeare's Speech-Headings, 1997; contbg. editor Dramatic Works of Beaumont and Fletcher, 1966-96; assoc. editor Arden Shakespeare, 1996—. Served with inf. U.S. Army, 1943-45, ETO. Decorated Combat Inf. badge; recipient Outstanding Civilian Service medal Dept. Army, 1983; Guggenheim Found. fellow, 1977-78; Huntington Library fellow, 1981. Mem. MLA (com. on new variorum 1980-92, chmn. Shakespeare divsn. 1990), South Atlantic MLA (pres. 1980-81), Southeastern Renaissance Conf. (editor 1960-70, 91-95, pres. 1973), Bibliog. Soc., Royal Soc. Arts London, S.C. Hist. Soc., Carolina Yacht Club (Charleston), St. Cecilia Soc. (Charleston), Elizabethan Club Yale U., Phi Beta Kappa, Phi Kappa Phi. Home: 6 Sylvan Rd Durham NC 27701-2849 Office: Duke U Dept English Box 90015 Durham NC 27708

WILLIAMS, GLADYS TUCKER, elementary school principal; d. Lee William and Cora Lena (Barksdale) Tucker; m. John Thomas Williams, June 6, 1964; children: Jon Trevor, Jamia Tiffani. BS, D.C. Tchrs. Coll., 1971; MA, George Washington U., 1981. From speech/lang. pathologist to prin. Prince Georges County Schs., Upper Marlboro, Md., 1971—. Pres. Largo (Md.) H.S. Choir Parents Assn., 1992-93; 2d v.p. Melwood Elem. Sch. PTA, Upper Marlboro, 1987-89. Mem. Nat. Assn. Elem. Prins. & Adminstrs., Assn. Sch.-Based Adminstrs. & Supervisors, Md. State Tchrs. Assn., Prince Georges County Tchrs. Assn., Alpha Delta Kappa, Delta Kappa Gamma (v.p. 1994-95). Office: James McHenry Elem Sch 8909 Mchenry Ln Lanham Seabrook MD 20706-4198

WILLIAMS, GLEN MORGAN, federal judge; b. Jonesville, Va., Feb. 17, 1920; s. Hughy May and Hattie Mae W.; m. Jane Slemp, Nov. 17, 1962; children: Susan, Judy, Rebecca, Melinda. A.B. magna cum laude, Milligan Coll., 1940; J.D., U. Va., 1948. Bar: Va. 1947. Pvt. practice law Jonesville, 1948-76; judge U.S. Dist. Ct. (we. dist.) Va., 1976-88, sr. judge, 1988—; commonwealth's atty. Lee County, Va., 1948-51; mem. Va. Senate, 1953-55. Mem. editorial bd.: Va. Law Rev, 1946-47. Mem. Lee County Sch. Bd., 1972-76; trustee, elder First Christian Ch., Pennington Gap, Va. Lt. USN, 1942-46, MTO. Recipient Citation of Merit Va. Def. Lawyers Assn., Oustanding Alumnus award Milligan Coll., 1980, Svc. to Region award Emory & Henry Coll., 1996. Mem. ABA, Va. State Bar (citation of merit), Va. Bar Assn. (citation of merit), Fed. Bar Assn., Va. Trial Lawyers Assn. (Meritorious Svc. award 1986, Disting. Svc. award), Am. Legion, 40 and 8. Clubs: Lions, Masons, Shriners. Office: US Dist Ct Fed Bldg PO Box 339 Abingdon VA 24212

WILLIAMS, GLORIA LOUISE, gifted and talented education educator; b. Greenville, S.C., Sept. 29, 1949; d. Harding and Gladys Louise (Burgess) Hendricks; children: Lisa, Philip. BA, Spelman Coll., 1971; MusB, Mich. State U., 1973; MS in Edn., Ind. U., 1979. Cert. elem. tchr., Ind. Dir. christian edn. Second Christian Ch., Indpls., 1975-77; staff devel. intern Indpls. Pub. Schs., 1977-78; tchr. elem. and mid. sch. Lawrence Twp. Schs., Indpls., 1980—; head human rels. com. Lawrence Twp. Sch., 1982-83. Part-time dir. children's ministry Light of the World Christian Ch., Indpls., 1984-89. Recipient Gloria and James Williams Day award Light of the World Christian Ch., 1989. Mem. Jack and Jill of Am., NAACP, Alpha Kappa Alpha. Avocations: piano, reading, singing. Office: MSD Lawrence Twp Sch 7601 E 56th St Indianapolis IN 46226-1310

WILLIAMS, GORDON HAROLD, internist, medical educator, researcher; b. Denver, Colo., May 23, 1937; s. Freeman Royal and Vonda Larcine (Olsen) W.; m. Dorrell Deen Ward, June 11, 1963; children: Jeffrey Scott, Christopher Shawn, Jonathan Sylvan, TarrynSue, Megan Suzanne, Brenya Shannon. BA, Harvard U., 1959, MD, 1963. Diplomate Am. Bd. Internal Medicine, 1970, endocrinology, 1975. Intern U. Chicago Hosps., 1963-64; resident Peter Bent Brigham Hosp., Boston, Mass., 1966-67; fellow, endocrinology, 1967-70; sr. physician Brigham Women's Hosp., Boston, Mass., 1981—; asst. prof. medicine Harvard U., Boston, 1970-73, assoc. prof., 1973-80, prof., 1980—; chief endocrine and hypertension divsn. Brigham and Women's Hosp., Boston, 1973—, dir. Clin. Rsch. Ctr., 1973—. Lt. USN, 1964-66. Fellow ACP, Coun. High Blood Pressure Rsch.; mem. Endocrine Soc., Am. Soc. Clin. Investigation, Am. Physiol. Soc., Am. Assn. Physicians. Mem. LDS Ch. Office: Brigham and Womens Hosp Dept Endocrinology/Hypertension 221 Longwood Ave Boston MA 02115-5822

WILLIAMS, GREGORY HOWARD, lawyer, educator; b. Muncie, Ind., Nov. 12, 1943; s. James Anthony Williams; m. Sara Catherine Whitney, Aug. 29, 1969; children: Natalia Dora, Zachary Benjamin, Anthony Bladimir, Carlos Gregory. B.A., Ball State U., 1966; M.A., U. Md., 1969; Ph.D., George Washington U., 1982, M.Ph., 1977, J.D., 1971. Bar: Va. 1971, D.C. 1972. Dep. sheriff Delaware County, Muncie, Ind., 1963-66; tchr. Falls Ch. Public Sch., Va., 1966-70; legis. asst. U.S. Senate, Washington, 1971-73; dir. exptl. programs George Washington U., 1973-77; prof. law U. Iowa Coll. Law, Iowa City, 1977-93; assoc. v.p. Acad. Affairs U. Iowa, 1991-93; dean, prof. law Ohio State U., Columbus, 1993—. Author: Law and Politics of Police Discretion, 1984, Iowa Guide to Search and Seizure, 1986, Life on the Color Line: The True Story of a White Boy Who Discovered He Was Black, 1995. Mem. Iowa Adv. Commn. to U.S. Commn. on Civil Rights, Washington, 1978-86; chmn., mem. Iowa Law Enforcement Acad., Camp Dodge, 1979-85. Recipient Cert. of Appreciation Black Law Students Assn., 1984, GW Edn. Opportunity Program, 1977, Disting. Alumnus award George Washington U., Nat. Law Ctr., 1994, L.A. Times Book prize Current Interest Category, 1995, Disting. Alumnus award Ball State U., 1996. Mem. Assn. Am. Law Schs. (exec. com. 1997—). Office: Ohio State U Coll of Law 55 W 12th Ave Columbus OH 43210-1338

WILLIAMS, HAROLD, geology educator; b. St. John's, Nfld., Can., Mar. 14, 1934; s. Alexander and Catherine (Snow) W.; m. Emily Jean King, Sept. 19, 1957; children: Alexander, David, Steven. B.Sc., Meml. U., 1956, diploma in engring., 1956, M.Sc., 1958; Ph.D., U. Toronto, 1961. Research scientist Geol. Survey Can., Ottawa, Ont., 1961-68; prof. geology Meml. U., St. John's, 1968—, Alexander Murray prof., 1990—. Contbr. numerous articles and geol. maps to profl. jours. Killam scholar Can. Council, 1977-81, Miller medal Royal Soc. Can., 1987, Gov. Gen.'s medal Meml. U. Fellow Royal Soc. Can., Geol. Assn. Can. (Disting. fellow, Past Pres. medal 1976, Logan medal 1988), Geol. Soc. Am., Can. Soc. Petroleum Geologists

(Douglas medal 1981). Avocation: folk musician. Office: Meml Univ Dept Earth Sci, SJ Carew Bldg, Saint Johns, NF Canada A1B 3X5

WILLIAMS, HAROLD ANTHONY, retired newspaper editor; b. Milw., Apr. 22, 1916; s. Harold Ambrose and Helen Theresa (Schmitt) W.; m. Ruth Edna Smith, Oct. 17, 1942; children—Anne Meredith Williams Gibson, Mary Helen Williams Winter, Sara B. Williams Cherner, Julie C. Williams Stewart. A.B., U. Notre Dame, 1938. Editor Towson (Md.) Union News, 1938-40; mem. staff Balt. Sunpapers, 1940-81; fgn. corr. Balt. Sunpapers, Europe, 1949-50; asst. to exec. editor, then city desk editor Balt. Sunpapers, 1950-54, Sunday editor, 1954-79, asst. mng. editor, 1979-81; sr. instr. Towson (Md.) State U., 1982-89; chmn. Newspaper Comics Coun., 1970-72, mem. exec. com., 1972-81; chmn. curriculum com., lectr. Renaissance Inst., Coll. Notre Dame of Md., 1989-92; discussion leader Am. Press Inst.; lectr. Towson State U. Elderhostel, 1993—. Author: A History of the Western Maryland Railway, 1952, Baltimore Afire, 3d edit, 1990, Guide to Baltimore and Annapolis, 1957, History of the Hibernian Society of Baltimore, 1957, A History of Eudowood, 1964, Robert Garrett and Sons, 1965, Bodine, A Legend in His Time, 1971; The Baltimore Sun, 1837-1987. Chmn. Friends Coun., Albin O. Kuhn Libr. and Gallery, U. Md., Balt. County, 1990-94; mem. adv. coun. Friends of the Johns Hopkins U. Librs., 1990—, pres., 1993-95. With CIC, AUS, 1942-46. Named Marylander of Yr., Md. Colonial Soc., 1989. Mem. Am. Assn. Sunday and Feature Editors, Wine and Food Soc. Balt. (pres. 1979-81), Balt. Bibliophiles (pres. 1978-79, exec. com.), Md. Hist. Soc., 14 W Hamilton St. Club (Balt.), Johns Hopkins Club. Democrat. Roman Catholic. Home: 307 Cedarcroft Rd Baltimore MD 21212-2520

WILLIAMS, HAROLD MARVIN, foundation official, former government official, former university dean, former corporate executive; b. Phila., Jan. 5, 1928; s. Louis W. and Sophie (Fox) W.; m. Nancy Englander; children: Ralph A., Susan J., Derek M. AB, UCLA, 1946; JD, Harvard U., 1949; postgrad. U. So. Calif. Grad. Sch. Law, 1955-56; DHL (hon.), Johns Hopkins U., 1987, Occidental Coll., 1997. Bar: Calif. 1950; practiced in Los Angeles, 1950, 53-55; with Hunt Foods and Industries, Inc., Los Angeles, 1955-68, v.p. 1958-60, exec. v.p., 1960-68, pres., 1968; gen., mgr. Hunt-Wesson Foods, 1964-66, pres., 1966-68; chmn. finance com. Norton Simon, Inc., 1968-70, chmn. bd., 1969-70, dir., 1959-77; dir. Times-Mirror Corp., SunAmerica, Calif. Endowment, Pub. Policy Inst.; prof. mgmt., dean Grad. Sch. Mgmt., UCLA, 1970-77; pres., dir. Special Investments & Securities Inc., 1961-66; chmn. SEC, Washington, 1977-81; pres., chief exec. officer J. Paul Getty Trust, 1981—; regent U. Calif., 1983-94. Mem. Commn. for Econ. Devel. State of Calif., 1973-77; energy coordinator City of Los Angeles, 1973-74; public mem. Nat. Advt. Review Bd., 1971-75; co-chmn. Public Commn. on Los Angeles County Govt.; mem. Coun. on Fgn. Rels., Com. for Econ. Devel.; commn. to rev. Master Plan for Higher Edn., State of Calif., 1985-87; co-chair Calif. Citizens Commn. Higher Edn.; trustee Nat. Humanities Ctr., 1987-93; dir. Ethics Resource Ctr.; mem. Pres.' Com. on Arts and Humanities; mem. Commn. on the Acad. Presidency. Served as 1st lt. AUS, 1950- 53. Mem. State Bar Calif. Office: J Paul Getty Trust 1200 Getty Center Dr Ste 400 Los Angeles CA 90049-1657

WILLIAMS, HAROLD ROGER, economist, educator; b. Arcade, N.Y., Aug. 22, 1935; s. Harry Alfred and Gertrude Anna (Scharf) W.; m. Lucia Dorothy Preuschoff, Apr. 23, 1955; children: Theresa Lynn, Mark Roger. B.A., Harpur Coll., SUNY, Binghamton, 1961; M.A., Pa. State U., 1963; Ph.D., U. Nebr., 1966; postgrad., Harvard U., 1969-70. Instr., Pa. State U., 1962-63; Instr. U. Nebr., 1965-66; mem. faculty Kent (Ohio) State U., 1966—, prof. econs. and internat. bus., 1972—, chmn. dept., 1974-81, dir. Internat. Bus. Program, Grad. Sch. Mgmt., 1980-86, chmn. faculty senate, 1988-89; assoc. dean Grad. Sch. Mgmt., 1994-96; program dir. Kent State-Geneva Program, Geneva, Switzerland, 1996—; econ. cons. and adv. to numerous govt., bus. and internat. orgns. Author over 100 books and articles in field. Served with AUS, 1954-57. Grantee NSF. Mem. Am. Econ. Assn., Internat. Econs. Assn., Acad. Internat. Bus., Midwest Econ. Assn. (v.p. 1969-70), So. Econ. Assn., Phi Gamma Mu, Omicron Delta Epsilon, Beta Gamma Sigma, Phi Beta Delta. Home: 415 Suzanne Dr Kent OH 44240-1933 Office: Dept Econs Kent State U Kent OH 44242

WILLIAMS, HARRIET CLARKE, retired academic administrator, artist; b. Bklyn., Sept. 5, 1922; d. Herbert Edward and Emma Clarke (Gibbs) W. AA, Bklyn. Coll., 1958; student, Art Career Sch., N.Y.C., 1960; cert., Hunter Coll., 1965, CPU Inst. Data Processing, 1967; student, Chineses Cultural Ctr., N.Y.C., 1973; hon. certs., St. Labre Sch./St. Joseph's, Ind. Sch., Mont., 1990. Adminstr. Baruch Coll., N.Y.C., 1959-85; mktg. researcher 1st Presbyn. Arts and Crafts Shop, Jamaica, N.Y., 1986-96; tutor in art St. John's U., Jamaica, 1986-96; founder, curator Internat. Art Gallery, Queens, N.Y., 1991—. Exhibited in group shows at Union Carbide Art Exhibit, N.Y.C., 1975, Queens Day Exhbn., N.Y.C., 1980, 1st Presbyn. Arts and Crafts Shop, N.Y.C., 1986, others; contbr. articles to profl. publs. Vol. reading tchr. Mabel Dean Vocat. High Sch., N.Y.C., 1965-67; mem. polit. action com. dist. council 37, N.Y.C., 1973-77; mem. negotiating team adminstrv. contracts, N.Y.C., 1975-78; mem. Com. To Save CCNY, 1976-77, Statue Liberty Ellis Island Found., Woodrow Wilson Internat. Ctr. Scholars, Wilson Ctr. Assocs., Washington, St. Labre Indian Sch., Ashland, Mont. Appreciation award Dist. Coun. 37, 1979; recipient Plaque Appreciation Svcs., Baruch Coll., Key award St. Joseph's Indian Sch., 1990, Key award in Edn. and Art, 1990, others. Mem. NAFE, AAUW, Women in Mil. Svc., Assn. Am. Indian Affairs, Nat. Mus. of Am. Indian, Artist Equity Assn. N.Y., Lakota Devel. Coun., Am. Film Inst., Bklyn. Coll. Alumni, Nat. Geographic Soc., Nat. Mus. Woman in the Arts, Statue of Liberty Ellis Island Found., Inc., Alliance of Queens Artists, U.S. Naval Inst., El Museo Del Barrio, Am. Mus. Natural History, Internat. Ctr. for Scholars-Wilson Ctr. Assocs., Arrow Club-St. Labre Indian Sch., Mus. of Television and Radio, Women in Military Meml. Found., Nat. Mus. of Am. Indian, U.S. Holocaust Mus., Navy Meml. (adv. coun.). Roman Catholic. Avocations: aerobics, vol. work, world travel, music. Office: Baruch Coll 17 Lexington Ave New York NY 10010

WILLIAMS, HENRY STRATTON, radiologist, educator; b. N.Y.C., Aug. 26, 1929; m. Frances S. Williams; children: Mark I, Paul S., Bart H. BS, CCNY, 1950; MD, Howard U., 1955. Diplomate Nat. Bd. Med. Examiners. Intern Brooke Army Hosp., San Antonio, 1956; resident in radiology Letterman Army Hosp., San Francisco, 1957-60; pvt. practice radiology L.A., 1963—; assoc. clin. prof. radiology Charles R. Drew Med. Sch., L.A.; chmn. bd. Charles Drew U. Medicine and Sci. Found.; interim pres. Charles R. Drew U. of Medicine and Sci. Mem. ad hoc adv. com. Joint Commn. Accreditation Hosps. Served to maj. U.S. Army, 1960-63. Fellow Am. Coll. Radiology; mem. Calif. Physicians Service (bd. dirs. 1971-77), Calif. Med. Assn. (counselor, mem. appeals bd., del., chmn. urban health com.), Los Angeles County Med. Assn.

WILLIAMS, HENRY THOMAS, retired banker, real estate agent; b. Worton, Md., Mar. 27, 1932; s. Henry Thomas W. and Ivy Lorraine (Urie) Francis; m. Marion Dwyer, Aug. 1953 (div. 1954); m. Laura Lynne Davis, Sept. 13, 1958; children: Lisa C. Ross, Henry Thomas III, Davis F. Student, Washington Coll., 1951-52; grad., ABA Nat. Installment Credit Sch. at U. Chgo., 1968, Va.-Md. Sch. Bank Mgmt. at U. Va., 1972. Grad. Realtors Inst. Teller Chestertown Bank Md., 1960-61, note teller, 1961-63, asst. cashier, 1963-68, mgr. installment loans, 1968-73, v.p., sr. loan officer, sec., 1973-85; v.p., br. mgr. Chestertown Bank Md., Rock Hall, 1985-88; now assoc. broker-realtor The Hogans Agy., Inc., Chestertown; mem. Queen Anne's County Real Estate Bd. Past dir. United Way Kent County, Chestertown; past vestryman, past chmn. budget com. St. Paul's Ch., Chestertown. Mem. Bank Adminstrn. Inst. (past sec., past chmn. Ea. Shore Chpt.), Md. Bankers Assn. (past v.p., past chmn. group 5), Md. Young Bankers Com., Chester River Yacht and Country Club, Lions (bd. dirs., past sec., past v.p.). Democrat. Home: 21139 Green Ln Rock Hall MD 21661-1634 Office: The Hogans Agy Inc Rt 213 N 515 Washington Ave Chestertown MD 21620-1217

WILLIAMS, HENRY WARD, JR., lawyer; b. Rochester, N.Y., Jan. 12, 1930; s. Henry Ward and Margaret Elizabeth (Simpson) W.; children: Edith Williams Linares, Margaret Williams Warren, Sarah Williams Farrand, Ann Williams Treacy, Elizabeth DeLancey, Victoria Maureen. AB, Dartmouth Coll., 1952; LLB, U.Va., 1958. Bar: N.Y. 1959, U.S. Dist. Ct. (we. dist.) N.Y. 1959, U.S. Dist. Ct. (so. dist.) Mich. 1982, U.S. Ct. Appeals (2d cir.) 1963, U.S. Tax Ct. 1960, U.S. Supreme Ct. 1968, D.C. 1978. Ptnr. Harris, Beach & Wilcox, Rochester, 1958-78, Robinson, Williams, Angeloff & Frank, Rochester, 1978-80, Weidman, Williams, Jordon, Angeloff & Frank, Rochester, 1980-82, The Williams Law Firm, Rochester, 1982—. Mem. Va. Law Rev., 1957-58. Chmn. Geva, Genesee Finger/Lakes Regional Planning Coun., 1973-89; majority leader Monroe County Legislature, 1967-73; mem. alumni coun. Dartmouth Coll., 1995—; mem. Nat. Ski Patrol Sys. Lt. (j.g.) USN, 1952-55. Mem. ABA, N.Y. State Bar Assn., Monroe County Bar Assn. (trustee 1982-85), Rochester Yacht Club, Royal Can. Yacht Club, Lake Yacht Racing Assn. (pres. 1985-87, hon. pres. 1988-90), Royal Ocean Racing Club, Raven Soc., Order of Coif, Omicron Delta Kappa. Home: 69 B Main St Pittsford NY 14534-1903 Office: The Williams Law Firm 10 Grove St Pittsford NY 14534-1327

WILLIAMS, HERBERT J., bishop. Bishop of N. Cen. Mich. Ch. of God in Christ, Saginaw. Office: Ch of God in Christ 1600 Cedar St Saginaw MI 48601-2837*

WILLIAMS, HERMAN, JR., protective services offical. Fire chief Balt. Fire Dept., 1994—. Office: Balt Fire Dept Hdqrs 414 N Calvert St Baltimore MD 21202-3603*

WILLIAMS, HIBBARD EARL, medical educator, physician; b. Utica, N.Y., Sept. 28, 1932; s. Hibbard G. and Beatrice M. W.; m. Sharon Towne, Sept. 3, 1982; children: Robin, Hans. AB, Cornell U., 1954, MD, 1958. Diplomate Am. Bd. Internal Medicine. Intern Mass. Gen. Hosp., Boston, 1958-59, resident in medicine, 1959-60, 62-64, asst. physician, 1964-65; clin. assoc. Nat. Inst. Arthritis and Metabolic Diseases, NIH, Bethesda, MD, 1960-62; instr. medicine Harvard U., Boston, 1964-65; asst. prof. medicine U. Calif., San Francisco, 1965-68, assoc. prof., 1968-72, prof., 1972-78, chief divsn. med. genetics, 1968-70, vice chmn. dept. medicine, 1970-78; prof., chmn. dept. medicine Cornell U. Med. Coll., N.Y.C., 1978-80; physician-in-chief N.Y. Hosp.-Cornell Med. Ctr., N.Y.C., 1978-80; dean Sch. Medicine U. Calif., Davis, 1980-92, prof. internal medicine, 1980—; mem. program project com. NIH, Nat. Inst. Arthritis and Metabolic Diseases, 1971-73. Editor med. staff confs. Calif. Medicine, 1966-70; mem. editl. bd. Clin. Rsch., 1968-71, Am. Jour. Medicine, 1978-88; cons. editor Medicine, 1978-86; assoc. editor Metabolism, 1970-80; mem. adv. bd. physiology in medicine New Eng. Jour. Medicine, 1970-75; contbr. articles to med. jours. With USPHS, 1960-62. Recipient Career Devel. award USPHS, 1968; recipient award for excellence in teaching Kaiser Found., 1970, Disting. Faculty award U. Calif. Alumni-Faculty Assn., 1978; John and Mary R. Markle scholar in medicine, 1968. Fellow ACP; mem. AAAS, Am. Fedn. Clin. Rsch., Am. Soc. Clin. Investigation (sec.-treas. 1974-77), Assn. Am. Physicians, Assn. Am. Med. Colls. (adminstrv. bd., coun. deans 1989-92, exec. coun. 1990-92), Calif. Acad. Medicine (pres. 1984), San Francisco Diabetes Assn. (bd. dirs. 1971-72), Western Assn. Physicians (v.p. 1977-78), Western Soc. Clin. Rsch., Calif. Med. Assn. (chmn. coun. sci. affairs 1990-95, bd. dirs. 1990-95, chair bd. dirs. 1996—), Giannini Found. (sci. adv. bd. 1990—), St. Francis Yacht Club, Alpha Omega Alpha. Office: U Calif Sch Medicine TB150 Davis CA 95616

WILLIAMS, HIRAM DRAPER, artist, educator; b. Indpls., Feb. 11, 1917; s. Earl Boring and Inez Mary (Draper) W.; m. Avonell Baumunk, July 7, 1941; children—Curtis Earl, Kim Avonell. B.S., Pa. State U., 1950, M.Ed., 1951. Tchr. art U. So. Calif., 1953-54, UCLA, summer 1959, U. Tex., 1954-60; mem. faculty and pres's. coun. U. Fla., Gainesville, 1960—; Disting. Service prof. U. Fla., until 1982, prof. emeritus, 1982; Mem. chancellor's council U. Tex. System. Exhibited, Pa. Acad. Fine Arts anns., Whitney Mus. Am. Art bi-anns., Corcoran Gallery Bi-anns., U. Ill. bi-anns., Mus. Modern Art exhbns., also Nordness Gallery, N.Y.C.; represented in permanent exhbns., Mus. Modern Art, Wilmington Art Center, Whitney Mus. of Am. Art, N.Y.C., Sheldon Meml. Art Mus., Milw. Art Center, Guggenheim Mus., Smithsonian Inst., Harn Art Mus., U. Fla., Yale; also pvt. collections.; author: Notes for a Young Painter, 1963, rev., 1985; contbr. articles to mags. Served to capt. C.E. U.S. Army, World War II, ETO. Tex. Rsch. grantee, 1958; Guggenheim fellow, 1962-63; inducted into Fla. Artists Hall of Fame, 1994. Address: 2804 NW 30th Ter Gainesville FL 32605-2727 *My desire as a painter is to animate material with imagery that strikes conjunctions of art and life.*

WILLIAMS, HOWARD RUSSELL, lawyer, educator; b. Evansville, Ind., Sept. 26, 1915; s. Clyde Alfred and Grace (Preston) W.; m. Virginia Merle Thompson, Nov. 3, 1942; 1 son, Frederick S.T. AB, Washington U., St. Louis, 1937; LLB, Columbia U., 1940. Bar: N.Y. 1941. With firm Root, Clark, Buckner & Ballantine, N.Y.C., 1940-41; prof. law, asst. dean U. Tex. Law Sch., Austin, 1946-51; prof. law Columbia U. Law Sch., N.Y.C., 1951-63; Dwight prof. Columbia Law Sch., 1959-63; prof. law Stanford U., 1963-85, Stella W. and Ira S. Lillick prof., 1968-82, prof. emeritus, 1982, Robert E. Paradise prof. natural resources, 1983-85, prof. emeritus, 1985—; Oil and gas cons. President's Materials Policy Commn., 1951; mem. Calif. Law Revision Commn., 1971-79, vice chmn., 1976-77, chmn., 1978-79. Author or co-author: Cases on Property, 1954, Cases on Oil and Gas, 1956, 5th edit., 1987, Decedents' Estates and Trusts, 1968, Future Interests, 1970, Oil and Gas Law, 8 vols., 1959-64 (with ann. supplements/rev. 1964-95), abridged edit., 1973, Manual of Oil and Gas Terms, 1957, 9th edit., 1994. Bd. regents Berkeley Bapt. Divinity Sch., 1966-67; trustee Rocky Mountain Mineral Law Found., 1964-66, 68-85. With U.S. Army, 1941-46. Recipient Clyde O. Martz Tchg. award Rocky Mountain Mineral Law Found., 1994. Mem. Phi Beta Kappa. Democrat. Home: 360 Everett Ave Apt 4B Palo Alto CA 94301-1422 Office: Stanford U Sch Law Nathan Abbott Way Stanford CA 94305

WILLIAMS, HUGH ALEXANDER, JR., retired mechanical engineer, consultant; b. Spencer, N.C., Aug. 18, 1926; s. Hugh Alexander and Mattie Blanche (Megginson) W.; BS in Mech. Engring., N.C. State U., 1948, MS in Diesel Engring. (Norfolk So. R.R. fellow), 1950; postgrad. Benedictine U. Inst. Mgmt.; m. Ruth Ann Gray, Feb. 21, 1950; children: David Gray, Martha Blanche Williams Heidengren. Jr. engr.-field service engr. Baldwin-Lima Hamilton Corp., Hamilton, Ohio, 1950-52, project engr., 1953-55; project engr. Electro-Motive div. Gen. Motors Corp., La Grange, Ill., 1955-58, sr. project engr., 1958-63, supr. product devel. engine design sect., 1963-86, staff engr., advanced mech. tech., 1986-87. Trustee Downers Grove (Ill.) San. Dist., 1965-92, pres., 1974-91, v.p., 1991-92; pres. Ill. Assn. San. Dists., 1976-77, bd. dirs., 1977-89; mem. statewide policy adv. com. Ill. EPA, 1977-79; mem. DuPage County Intergovtl. Task Force Com., 1988-92; elder Presbyn. Ch. Served with USAAC, 1945. Registered profl. engr., Ill. Recipient Trustee Svc. award Ill. Assn. San. Dists., 1986, Citizens award Downers Grove Evening chpt. Kiwanis, 1991. Fellow ASME (chmn. honors and awards com. 1993-96, Diesel and Gas Engine Power Div. Speaker awards 1968, 84, Div. citation 1977, Internal Combustion Engine award 1987, exec. com. Internal Combustion Engine div. 1981-87, 88-92, chmn. 1985-86, sec. 1988-92); mem. Soc. Automotive Engrs. (life), ASME (chmn. Soichiro Honda medal com. 1987-92, chmn. internat. combustion engine award com., 1993—), Ill. Assn. Wastewater Agys. (Outstanding Mem. award 1990, hon. mem. 1992), Raleigh Host Lions Club (pres. 1996—), Masons (32 degree), Sigma Pi. Republican. Editor: So. Engr., 1947-48; contbr. articles to profl. jours. Patentee in field. Home: 2108 Weybridge Dr Raleigh NC 27615-5562

WILLIAMS, HULEN BROWN, former university dean; b. Lauratown, Ark., Oct. 8, 1920; s. Ernest Burdett and Ann Jeanette (Miller) W.; m. Virginia Anne Rice, June 20, 1942 (dec. June 1970); children: James Browning, Virginia Jean; m. Michaela Galasso, Mar. 20, 1971. BA, Hendrix Coll., 1941; MS, La. State U., 1943, PhD, 1948; postgrad., Cornell U., summer 1950, U. Calif., Berkeley, 1953. Instr. through asso. prof. La. State U., Baton Rouge, 1947-56; prof., head chemistry dept. La. State U., 1956-68, dean Coll. Chemistry and Physics, 1968-82; ret., 1982; Cons. to chem. and legal professions. Co-author books on chemistry; contbr. articles to profl. jours. Served to lt. (j.g.) USNR, 1944-46. Mem. Am. Chem. Soc., Sigma Xi, Sigma Pi Sigma, Phi Lambda Upslion, Phi Kappa Phi, Omicron Delta Kappa. Home: 470 Castle Kirk Dr Baton Rouge LA 70808-6011

WILLIAMS, IDA JONES, consumer and home economics educator, writer; b. Coatesville, Pa., Dec. 1, 1911; d. William Oscar and Ida Ella (Ruth) Jones; m. Charles Nathaniel Williams, Mar. 17, 1940 (dec. July 1971). BS, Hampton Inst., 1935; MA, U. Conn., 1965; cert. recognition, Famous Writers Sch., Westport, Conn., 1976, 78. Cert. high sch. tchr., English, sci., home econs., Va., Pa. Sci. and home econs. tchr. Richmond County H.S., Ivondale, Va., 1935-36; English and home econs. tchr. Northampton County H.S., Chesaepeake, Va., 1936-40; consumer and home econs. tchr. Northampton County H.S., Machipongo, Va., 1940-71, Northampton Jr. H.S., Machipongo, 1971-76. Author: Starting Anew After Seventy, 1980 (plaque 1980), News and Views of Northampton County High Principals and Alumni, 1981; co-author: The History fo Virginia State Federation of Colored Women's Clubs, Inc., 1996; editor: Fifty Year Book 1935-1985 - Hampton Institute Class, 1985, Favorite Recipes of Ruth Family & Friends, 1986. V.p. Ea. Lit. Coun., Melfa, Va., 1987-89; mem. Ea. Shore Coll. Found., Inc.,Melfa, 1988-94; mem. Gov.'s Adv. Bd. on Aging, Richmond, Va., 1992-94; instr. Ladies Community Bible Class, 1976-80 (Plaque 1980); sec., treas., v.p. Hospice Support of Ea. Shore, 1980-94; mem. Northampton/Accomack Adv. Counc., 1992-94; marshall 28th anniv. commencement Ea. Shore Cmty. Coll., 1996. Recipient Nat. Sojourner Truth Meritorious Svc. award Nat. Assn. Negro Bus. and Profl. Women's Clubs, Gavel Ea. Shore Ret. Tchrs. Assn., 1994, Jefferson award Am. Inst. Pub. Svc., Wavy-TV-Bell Atlantic and Mattress Discounters, 1991, Gov.'s award for vol. excellence, 1994, Contribution to Edn. award Ea. Shore Coll. Found., 1997; named Home Econs. Tchr. of Yr., Am. Home Econs. Assn. and Family Cir., 1975, Woman of Yr., Prog. Women of E.S., 1997. Mem. AARP (Citation award 1996, Mem. of Yr. 1997), Progressive Women of Ea. Shore (pres. 1985-93, Gold Necklace 1993, Woman of Yr. 1997), C. of C., Univ. Women (v.p. Portsmouth br. 1985-87), Ea. Shore Ret. Tchrs. (pres. 1977-84), Dist. L Ret. Tchrs. (pres. 1989-91), Va. State Fedn. Colored Women's Club (pres. 1990-94, editor history com. 1996—), Am. Assn. Ret. Persons (Va. state legis. com. 1995—). Mem. Ch. of Christ. Avocations: crafts, travel, writing, lecturing. Home and Office: PO Box 236 14213 Lankford Hwy Eastville VA 23347-0236

WILLIAMS, IRVING LAURENCE, physics educator; b. Newport, R.I., Dec. 3, 1935; s. Leroy Payton and Alberta Helen (Troy) W.; m. Carrie Mae Graves, Aug. 26, 1967; children: Cheryl Anita, Carla Chantrase. EdB, R.I. Coll., 1957; MA in Teaching, Brown U., 1962; PhD, NYU, 1975. Cert. teaching, R.I. Classroom tchr. Newport (R.I.) Sch. Dept., 1962-63; prof. physics Morgan State U., Balt., 1963-67; prof. physics Nassau Community Coll., Garden City, N.Y., 1967-97, asst. to pres., 1980-85, retired, 1997; adj. prof. Hofstra U., Hempstead, N.Y., 1980-87; dist. clk. Roosevelt (N.Y.) Sch. Bd., 1989-91. Co-author: (lab. workbook) Meterology Lab. Exercises, 1975, 76. Treas. Econ. Opportunity Commn., Nassau County, N.Y., 1984; trustee Grace Lutheran Ch., Malverne, N.Y., 1987, Roosevelt Bd. Edn., 1988; active Roosevelt Rep. Club, 1989; mem. sch. bd. Grace Lutheran Sch., Malverne, 1991. With U.S. Army, 1957-60. Recipient Chancellor's award SUNY, 1975, Citzen's award EOC Nassau County, Hempstead, 1987, Roosevelt Educator's award, Roosevelt Coun., 1989; NSF Weather Svc. grantee, Washington, 1989. Mem. AAUP, Nat. Sci. Tchrs. Assn., Am. Assn. Physics Tchrs., Soc. Coll. Sci. Tchrs., N.Y. Acad. Sci., Am. Assn. Higher Edn., N.Y. Assn. Two Yr. Colls. Republican. Avocation: piano. Home: 2 Leeward Ct Greensboro NC 27455-0812

WILLIAMS, J. BRYAN, lawyer; b. Detroit, July 23, 1947; s. Walter J. and Maureen June (Kay) W.; m. Jane Elizabeth Eisele, Aug. 24, 1974; children: Kyle Joseph, Ryan Patrick. AB, U. Notre Dame, 1969; JD, U. Mich., 1972. Bar: Mich. 1972, U.S. Dist. Ct. (ea. dist.) Mich. 1972. Exec. ptnr. Dickinson, Wright, Moon, Van Dusen & Freeman, Detroit, 1972—. Mem. ABA, Mich. Bar Assn., Detroit Bar Assn., Notre Dame Club of Detroit (pres. 1984), Oakland Hills Country Club, Nat. Club Assn. (bd. dirs., sec. 1995-97), Greater Detroit C. of C. (bd. dirs.), Detroit Inst. Arts (corp. rels. com.), Chamber Music Soc. of Detroit (bd. dirs.), Econ. Club Detroit (bd. dirs.), Detroit Legal News Co. (bd. dirs.). Roman Catholic. Home: 993 Suffield Ave Birmingham MI 48009-1242 Office: 500 Woodward Ave Ste 4000 Detroit MI 48226-3423

WILLIAMS, J. VERNON, lawyer; b. Honolulu, Apr. 26, 1921; s. Urban and W. Amelia (Olson) W.; m. Malvina H. Hitchcock, Oct. 4, 1947 (dec. May 1970); children—Carl H., Karin, Frances E., Scott S.; m. Mary McLellan, Sept. 6, 1980. Student, Phillips Andover Acad., 1937-39; B.A. cum laude, Amherst Coll., 1943; LL.B., Yale, 1948. Bar: Wash. 1948. Assoc. Riddell, Riddell & Hemphill, 1948-50; ptnr. Riddell, Williams, Bullitt & Walkinshaw (and predecessor firms), 1950-95; prin. Graham & James L.L.P./Riddell Williams, P.S., Seattle, 1996—; sec., dir. Airborne Freight Corp., 1968-79, gen. counsel, 1968-96. Chmn. March of Dimes, Seattle, 1954-55; Mem. Mayor's City Charter Rev. Com., 1968-69; chmn. Seattle Bd. Park Commrs., 1966-68; co-chmn. parks and open space com. Forward Thrust, 1966-69; dir. bd. and commrs. br. Nat. Recreation and Parks Assn., 1968-69; chmn. Gov.'s adv. com. Social and Health Services, 1972-75; Bd. dirs. Seattle Met. YMCA, 1965—, pres., 1976-79; trustee Lakeside Sch., 1971-79; mem. alumni council Phillps Andover Acad., 1970-73, Yale Law Sch., 1969-77; chancellor St. Mark's Cathedral, Seattle, 1964—. Served with USAAF, 1943-45. Mem. Univ. Club, Seattle Tennis Club, Birnam Wood Golf Club. Home: 1100 38th Ave E Seattle WA 98112-4434 Office: 4500 1001 4th Ave Plz Seattle WA 98154-1065

WILLIAMS, JACK MARVIN, research chemist; b. Delta, Colo., Sept. 26, 1938; s. John Davis and Ruth Emma (Gallup) W. B.S. with honors, Lewis and Clark Coll., 1960; M.S., Wash. State U., 1964, Ph.D., 1966. Postdoctoral fellow Argonne (Ill.), Nat. Lab., 1966-68, asst. chemist, 1968-70, assoc. chemist, 1970-72, chemist, 1972-77, sr. chemist, group leader, 1977—; vis. guest prof. U. Mo., Columbia, 1980, 81, 82, U. Copenhagen, 1980, 83, 85; chair Gordon Rsch. Conf. (Inorganic Chemistry), 1980. Bd. editors: Inorganic Chemistry, 1979-96, assoc. editor, 1982-93. Crown-Zellerbach scholar, 1959-60; NDEA fellow, 1960-63; recipient Disting. Performance at Argonne Nat. Labs. award U. Chgo., 1987, Centennial Disting. Alumni award Wash. State U., 1990. Mem. Am. Crystallographic Assn., Am. Chem. Soc. (treas. inorganic div. 1982-84), Am. Phys. Soc., AAAS. Office: Chemistry Div 9700 Cass Ave Lemont IL 60439-4803

WILLIAMS, JACKSON JAY, education consultant; b. Mitchell, Ind., Sept. 14, 1961; s. Jackie Eugene and Judith Ann (Chastain) W. Student, Drake U., 1979-80, 81-84, George Williams Coll., 1984-85; BS in Leisure and Environ. Resource Adm., Aurora U., 1986; MS in Experiential Edn., Mankato (Minn.) State U., 1990; postgrad., U. Ky., 1992—. Course instr., coord. George Williams Coll., Williams Bay, Wis., 1984-86; course dir. Inner Quest Inc., Leesburg, Va., 1986-88; instr. Voyager Outward Bound Sch., Ely, Minn., 1989; challenge course coord., Outdoor Edn. Inst. Tex. A&M U., Coll. Sta., 1990-91; substitute tchr. Mitchell (Ind.) H.S., 1994-95; grad. asst., dept. ednl. policy studies U. Ky., Lexington, 1995—; cons. Ednl. Consultants, Mitchell, 1990—; cons. Chgo. Area Girl Scout Coun., 1985. CPR instr. ARC, Ill., Iowa 1980-88. Ill. State Scholar, 1979; recipient Vigil Honor, Order of the Arrow, Boy Scouts Am., 1979. Mem. Assn. Experiential Edn., Assn. for Challenge Course Tech., Ohio Valley Philosophy of Edn. Soc., Nat. Eagle Scout Assn., Mitchell (Ind.) C. of C., Loyal Order of Moose. Avocations: ice hockey, reading. Home: 516 Marion St Mitchell IN 47446-1056 Office: Univ Kentucky Dept Ednl Policy Studies 134 Taylor Education Bldg Lexington KY 40506

WILLIAMS, JAMES ALEXANDER, lawyer; b. Pine Bluff, Ark., Oct. 30, 1929; s. Absalom Alexander and Kyle (Baggarly) W.; m. Janet L. Bray, Nov. 27, 1953; children: Laura Kay, Victoria Lynn, Diana Leigh. Student, U. Ark., 1948; B.A., So. Methodist U., 1951, J.D., 1952, M.L.A., 1971. Bar: Tex. 1952. Since practiced in Dallas; mem. firm Touchstone, Bernays & Johnston, 1955-57; partner firm Bailey and Williams, 1957—. Bd. dirs. Spl. Care Sch.; bd. mgmt. YMCA; chmn. adminstrv. bd. Univ. Park United Meth. Ch., 1973; bd. dirs. Dallas Opera. Lt. USNR, 1952-55. Mem. ABA, Dallas Bar Assn., State Bar Tex., Dallas, Tex. Assn. Def. Counsel, Internat. Assn. Def. Counsel, Fedn. Ins. and Corp. Counsel, Am. Bd. Trial Advocates, Acad. Hosp. Attys., Trial Attys. Am., So. Meth. U. Law Alumni Assn. (pres. 1970-72), Exch. Club (pres. 1967), Dallas Club, Northwood Club, Crescent Club, Giraud Club (San Antonio), Lambda Chi Alpha, Phi Alpha Delta. Democrat. Home: 4630 Northaven Rd Dallas TX 75229-4225 Office: 7502 Greenville Ave Ste 500 Dallas TX 75231-3812 *Honesty and fair dealing with one's fellow man are essential to real success.*

WILLIAMS, JAMES ARTHUR, retired army officer, information systems company executive; b. Paterson, N.J., Mar. 29, 1932; s. Charles M. and Elsie (Kretszchmar) W.; m. Barbara Widnall, June 26, 1959; children: Steven, Karen. BS, U.S. Mil. Acad.; MA in Latin Am. Studies, U. N.Mex. Commd. 2d lt. U.S. Army, 1954, advanced through grades to lt. gen.; asst. army attache U.S. Def. Attache Office, Caracas, Venezuela, 1966-72; exch. officer State-Def. Exch. Program Office of Sec. Def., Washington, 1972-74; comdr. 650th MI Group, Shape, 1974-76; dep. dir. estimates Def. Intelligence Agy., Washington, 1977-80; dep. chief staff for intelligence U.S. Army, Europe, 1980-81; dir. Def. Intelligence Agy., Washington, 1981-85; ret., 1985; v.p. PSC Corp., 1986; pres. Direct Info. Access Corp., Annandale, Va., 1987—. Decorated Legion of Merit, Bronze Star with oak leaf cluster, Air medals, D.S.M., Nat. Intelligence D.S.M., Army Commendation medal, French Legion of Honor; Dist. Mem. Mil. Intelligence Hall of Fame. Mem. Assn. U.S. Army, Nat. Mil. Intelligence Assn. (chmn. bd. 1987—). Methodist. Home: 8928 Maurice Ln Annandale VA 22003-3914 Office: Direct Info Access Corp PO Box 721 Annandale VA 22003-0721

WILLIAMS, JAMES BRYAN, banker; b. Sewanee, Tenn., Mar. 21, 1933; s. Eugene G. and Ellen (Bryan) W.; m. Betty G. Williams, July 11, 1980; children: Ellen, Elizabeth, Bryan. AB, Emory U., 1955. Chmn., CEO SunTrust Banks, Inc., Atlanta, 1991—; bd. dirs. The Coca-Cola Co., Atlanta, Genuine Parts Co., Atlanta, Rollins, Inc., Ga.-Pacific Corp., Atlanta, RPC, Inc., Atlanta, Sonat Inc., Birmingham, Ala. Trustee Emory U.; chmn. bd. trustees Robert W. Woodruff Health Scis. Ctr. Lt. USAF, 1955-57. Mem. Bankers Roundtable. Presbyterian. Clubs: Piedmont Driving (Atlanta), Capital City (Atlanta), Commerce (Atlanta), Peachtree Golf (Atlanta), Augusta Country. Office: SunTrust Banks Inc 25 Park Pl NE Atlanta GA 30303

WILLIAMS, JAMES CASE, metallurgist; b. Salina, Kans., Dec. 7, 1938; s. Luther Owen and Clarice (Case) W.; m. Joanne Rufener, Sept. 17, 1960; children: Teresa A., Patrick J. B.S. in Metall. Engring, U. Wash., 1962, M.S., 1964, Ph.D., 1968. Rsch. engr., lead engr. Boeing Co., Seattle, 1961-67; tech. staff N.Am. Rockwell Corp., Thousand Oaks, Calif., 1968-74; mgr. interdivisional tech. program N.Am. Aerospace group, 1974, program devel. mgr. structural materials, 1974-75; prof. metallurgy, co-dir. Ctr. for Joining of Materials, Carnegie-Mellon U., Pitts., 1975-81; pres. Mellon Inst., Pitts., 1981-83; dean Carnegie Inst. Tech., Carnegie-Mellon U., Pitts., 1983-88; gen. mgr. materials dept. GE Aircraft Engines, 1988—; Mem bd. NRC, com. on Engrin. and Tech. Systems, 1996—; chmn. Nat. Materials Adv. Bd., 1988-95, materials and structures com. NASA Aero. Adv. Com. 1992—; mem. Materials Sci. and Engring. Study, 1986-88; bd. govs. Inst. for Mechs. and Materials, U. Calif., San Diego, 1989-95; trustee Min. Math. Sci. & Engring., Cin., 1988—; mem. scientific adv. bd. USAF, 1996—. Co-editor: Scientific and Technological Aspects of Titanium and Titanium Alloys, 1976; contbr. numerous articles to tech. jours. Trustee Oreg. Grad. Inst. Sci. and Tech., 1988-94; cons. Cubmaster Boy Scouts Am., 1976-77. Recipient Ladd award Carnegie Inst. Tech.; Adams award Am. Welding Soc.; Boeing doctoral fellow. Fellow Am. Soc. Metals (Gold medal 1992); mem. NAE, ASM, AIME (Leadership award 1993), ARPA Materials Rsch. Coun., Alpha Sigma Mu. Republican. Episcopalian. Home: 3307 Brinton Trl Cincinnati OH 45241-4814 Office: GE Aircraft Engines Gen Mgr Material Dept MD H85 Cincinnati OH 45215

WILLIAMS, JAMES E., food products manufacturing company executive; married. With Golden State foods Corp., 1961—; chief exec. officer Golden State foods Corp., Pasadena, Calif., 1978—. Office: Golden State Foods Corp 18301 Von Karman Ave Ste 1100 Irvine CA 92612-1009*

WILLIAMS, JAMES EUGENE, management consultant; b. Macon, Ga., June 23, 1927; s. James Eugene and Margaret Elizabeth (Tinker) W.; m. Linda K. Magnuson, June 23, 1984; children: Paul David, Lisa Jane Williams Robertson, Philip Alan, Gail Ellen Williams Feeney, Amanda Allen Thompson, Jason Douglas Allen, Joel Winston Allen. BS in Aero. Engring., Iowa State Coll., 1950. Engr. Robins AFB, Ga., 1950-54, Hdqrs. USAF, Washington, 1954-61; dep. asst. sec. Office Asst. Sec. Air Force, Washington, 1961-85; dir. govt. bus. policy Northrop Corp., Washington, 1986-88; mgmt. cons. Tempe, Ariz., 1988—. Recipient Presdl. Meritorious Exec. award, 1981, Presdl. Disting. Exec. award, 1982. Home: 3223 S College Ave Tempe AZ 85282-3773

WILLIAMS, JAMES FRANCIS, JR., religious organization administrator; b. Coffeyville, Kans., June 20, 1938; s. James Francis and Sarah Kathryn (Tavenner) W.; m. Alice Carol Kinney, June 1, 1963; children: James F. III, Todd Alexander, Leslie. BA, So. Meth. U., 1960; ThM, Dallas Theol. Sem., 1964; HHD, U. Tex., 1988. Campus dir. Campus Crusade for Christ, Dallas, 1961-64; area dir. Campus Crusade for Christ, various North Tex. locations, 1964-68; regional dir. Campus Crusade for Christ, Southwestern U.S., 1968-71; nat. dir. tng. Campus Crusade for Christ, U.S., 1971-72; founder, pres. Probe Ministries, Internat., Dallas, 1973—; dir. music Campus Crusade for Christ, Arrowhead, Calif., 1967-71. soloist, chorus Dallas Opera, 1982-84. Named one of Outstanding Young Men in Am. Dallas Jaycees, 1965. Evangelical Christian. Office: Probe Ministries 1900 Firman Dr Ste 100 Richardson TX 75081-1869

WILLIAMS, JAMES FRANKLIN, II, university dean, librarian; b. Montgomery, Ala., Jan. 22, 1944; s. James Franklin and Anne (Wester) W.; m. Madeline McClellan, Jan. 1966 (div. May 1988); 1 child, Madeline Marie; m. Nancy Allen, Aug. 1989; 1 child, Audrey Grace. BA, Morehouse Coll., 1966; MLS, Atlanta U., 1967. Reference libr. Wayne State U. Sci. Libr., Detroit, 1968-69; document delivery libr. Wayne State U. Med. Libr., Detroit, 1969-70, head of reference, 1971-72, dir. med. libr. and regional med. libr. network, 1972-81, regional dir., 1975-82; assoc. dir. of librs. Wayne State U., 1981-88; dean librs. U. Colo., Boulder, 1988—; bd. regents Nat. Libr. Medicine, Bethesda, Md., 1978-81. Mem. editl. bd. ACRL Publications in Librarianship, College and Research Libraries; contbr. articles to profl. jours., chpts. to books; book editor and author. Subject of feature interview in centennial issue Am. Librs. jour., 1976. Mem. ALA (Visionary Leader award 1988), Coll. and Rsch. Librs. (editl. bd.), Assn. Rsch. Librs. (bd. dirs. 1994-96). Avocations: cycling, travel, fishing. Office: U Colo Office of Dean Librs Campus Box 184 Boulder CO 80309-0184

WILLIAMS, JAMES HENRY, JR., mechanical engineer, educator, consultant; b. Newport News, Va., Apr. 4, 1941; s. James H. Williams and Margaret L. (Holt) Mitchell; children: James Henry III, Sky Margaret Melodie. Mech. designer (Homer L. Ferguson scholar), Newport News Apprentice Sch., 1965; S.B., MIT, 1967, S.M., 1968; Ph.D., Trinity Coll., Cambridge U., 1970. Sr. design engr. Newport News Shipyard, 1960-70; asst. prof. mech. engring. M.I.T., 1970-74, assoc. prof., 1974-81, prof., 1981—, duPont prof., 1973, Edgerton prof., 1974-76; cons. engring. to numerous cos. Contbr. numerous articles on stress analysis, vibration, fracture mechanics, composite materials and nondestructive testing to profl. jours. Recipient Charles F. Bailey Bronze medal, 1961, Charles F. Bailey Silver medal, 1962, Charles F. Bailey Gold medal, 1963, Baker award M.I.T., 1973, Den Hartog Disting. Educator award, 1981; named prof. teaching excellence Sch. Engring., 1991; C.F. Hopewell faculty fellow, 1993—. Mem. ASME, Am. Soc. Nondestructive Testing, Nat. Tech. Assn. Subspecialties: Theoretical and applied mechanics; Composite materials. Office: MIT Room 3-360 77 Massachusetts Ave Rm 3-360 Cambridge MA 02139-4301

WILLIAMS, JAMES KENDRICK, bishop. Ed., St. Mary's Coll., St. Mary's, Ky., St. Maur's Sch. Theology, South Union, Ky. Ordained priest Roman Catholic Ch., 1963; ordained titular bishop Catula and aux. bishop of Covington, 1984; ordained first bishop of Lexington, Ky., installed 1988. Office: Bishop of Lexington PO Box 12350 1310 Leestown Rd Lexington KY 40582-2350*

WILLIAMS, JAMES LEE, financial industries executive; b. Tampa, Fla., Nov. 5, 1941; s. Donald Clark and Nell (Medlin) W.; m. Linda Taylor, Dec. 28, 1968; children: Donald Clark II, Taylor Lee. AA, St. Petersburg (Fla.) Jr. Coll., 1965; BS, Fla. State U., 1967. Mgmt. Ryder Truck Lines, Jacksonville, Fla., 1967-69; dist. mgr. underwriting div. U.S. Leasing Corp., Dallas, 1969-73; area v.p. Mfrs. Hanover Leasing Corp., Houston and London, 1973-79; v.p. corp. fin. Underwood Neuhause & Co. Inc., Houston, 1979-81; chmn., chief exec. officer 1st City Leasing Corp., Houston, 1981-85; mng. dir. capital markets 1st City Bancorp., Houston, 1985-89; mng. dir. fin. svcs. M.P.S.I. Systems Inc., Dallas, 1989-90; pres., chief exec. officer Strategic Decisions Holdings Corp., Dallas, 1990-92; sr. mng. dir. Williams and Assocs., 1992; pres. Global Svcs. Capital Corp., Houston, 1993-96; v.p. Ikon Hov. Adminstrv. Svc. Ctr., 1997—. Served with USN, 1959-62. Mem. Equipment Leasing Assn. (fed. govt. rels. com. 1984-88, 95—), Tex. Assn. Equipment Lessors (bd. dirs. 1985-89), Greater Houston Partnership. Republican. Presbyterian. Clubs: Houston Ctr. (bd. dirs. 1985-89), Lakeside Racquet (athletic com. 1986-89), Forum (Houston). Avocations: golf, jogging, swimming. Office: Global Svcs Capital Corp 2902 W 12th St Houston TX 77008-6114

WILLIAMS, JAMES ORRIN, university administrator, educator; b. New Orleans, Jan. 8, 1937; married, 1956; 3 children. BS, Auburn U., 1960, MEd, 1963, EdD, 1967; postgrad., Tchrs. Coll., Columbia U., summer 1964. Tchr. social sci., coach Columbus High Sch. Ga., 1960-61; tchr., coach Eufaula High Sch. Ala., 1961-63; prin. Troy Jr. High Sch., 1963-65; grad. asst. Sch. Edn. Auburn U., 1965-66, interim dir. field service, 1966-67; asst. prof. edn. adminstrn. U. Fla., 1967-68; asst. prof. Columbus Coll., 1968-69; assoc. prof., chmn. div. Auburn U., Montgomery, 1969-73, vice chancellor acad. affairs, 1973-80, chancellor, 1980—. Contbr. articles to profl. jours. Phi Delta Kappa grantee, 1967. Mem. Am. Assn. State Colls. and Univs., Am. Assn. Coll. Tchr. Edn., Assn. Tchr. Edn., So. Regional Council Edn. Adminstrn., Phi Delta Kappa (v.p. 1965), Phi Kappa Phi.

WILLIAMS, JANE CROUCH, mental health counselor, social worker; b. Knoxville, Tenn., Apr. 23, 1931; d. Brockway and Elsie Irene (Wayland) Crouch; m. James Bowers Bell, June 27, 1950 (div. Sept. 1971); children: Steven Easterly Bell, Sharon Irene Bell Mann Trotter, Joseph Brockway Bell, Robert Wayland Bell; m. Don Roy Williams, Mar. 28, 1989. Student, U. Cin., 1949-50, Ft. Sanders Hosp. Sch. Nursing, 1950; BS in Social Work, U. Tenn., 1985. Office nurse Knoxville Surg. Group, 1955-82; therapist Overlook Health Ctr., Sevierville, Tenn., 1985-89; therapist, counselor Seymour (Tenn.) Family Physicians, 1985-89; coord. mental health day treatment Ridgeview Psychiat., Campbell County, Tenn., 1989-94; mental health counselor Wynn-Habersham Health, Campbell County, 1995—; rschr. Mountain Heritage Rsch., La Follette, Tenn., 1993—; rsch. cons. for family historians, 1955—. Author: Descendants of William Goddard of Sullivan County, Tennessee, 1994. Christian counselor Presbyn. Ch., La Follette, 1993—; elder 1st Presbyn. Ch., La Follette, 1993—; mem. divsn. reconciliation and compassion East Tenn. Presbytery, Knoxville, 1995-97; life mem. East Tenn. Hist. Soc., Knoxville, 1955—, Meml. Found. Germanna Colonies of Va., Culpeper, Va., 1981—. Mem. NSW, Nat. Geneal. Soc., Phi Kappa Phi, Phi Beta Kappa. Republican. Avocations: genealogy, oil painting, spending time with grandchildren. Home: 1007 Ellison Rd La Follette TN 37766-3011 Office: Wynn Habersham Health Clin RR 3 La Follette TN 37766-9803

WILLIAMS, JEFFRY CEPHAS, business executive; b. Streator, Ill., Jan. 3, 1960; s. Kenneth Joseph Williams and Betty Patricia (Brooks) Brassfield; m. Linda Ann Danko, Oct. 1, 1993. B of Fin., Ill. State U., Normal, 1982, B of Econs., 1982. Corp. sec. Westgate, Inc., Streator, 1977—, Chris' Flower Shop, Inc., Streator, 1985—, Wilfield, Inc., Streator, 1986—. Sec. Streator Police Pension Bd., 1992—; co-chair KEEP Com., Streator, 1992; mem. budget com. United Way, Streator. Recipient Eagle Scout Boy Scouts Am. Mem. Masons. Avocations: outdoor activities, alternative-renewable energy interests, investments and stock market. Office: Westgate Inc 116 S 1st St PO Box 942 Streator IL 61364-0942

WILLIAMS, JESSIE WILLMON, lay religious worker, retired librarian; b. Boynton, Okla., Feb. 23, 1907; d. Thomas Woodard and Eliza Jane (Adams) Willmon; m. Austin Guest, Aug. 13, 1932 (div. 1945); m. Thomas Washington Williams, Dec. 12, 1946 (dec.). BA, East Tex. State U., 1930, MA, 1944. cert. English and Spanish tchr., Tex. Libr. Gladewater (Tex.) Pub. Libr., 1935-46; med. libr. VA Hosp., North Little Rock, Ark., 1946-58; base libr. Little Rock AFB, 1958-68; ret., 1968; lay worker 1st Bapt. Ch., Pecan Gap, Tex., 1988—. Mem. Delta Kappa Gamma, Phi Beta Kappa. Democrat. Mem. So. Bapt. Conv. Home: PO Box 43 Pecan Gap TX 75469-0043 *Proverbs 30: 8-9 summarizes the good life for me! "Remove far from me vanity and lies; give me neither poverty nor riches; feed me with food convenient for me; lest I be full and deny thee and say 'Who is the Lord?' or lest I be poor and steal, and take the name of my God in vain.*

WILLIAMS, JOCELYN JONES, reading educator; b. Greenville, N.C., Sept. 24, 1948; d. William Edward and Elinor Suejette (Albritton) Jones; m. Robert Alexander Simpkins Jr., Sept. 7, 1969 (div. May 1972); m. Oscar James Williams Jr., July 12, 1985 (div. Mar. 1989). BS, Bennett Coll., 1970; MEd, N.C. Cen. U., 1988; MS, N.C. Agrl. & Tech. State U., 1992. Kindergarten/1st grade tchr. Greenville City Schs., 1970-74; elem./reading tchr. Orange County Schs., Hillsborough, N.C., 1974—; mem. N.C. Reading Recovery Adv. Bd., 1994—, Reading Recovery Coun. N.Am., 1994—. Mem. NEA, ASCD, Internat. Reading Assn., Nat. Assn. Edn. Young Children, N.C. Assn. Educators, Phi Delta Kappa, Alpha Kappa Alpha, Progressive Sertoma Club. Democrat. Baptist. Avocations: reading, singing, sewing, cooking. Home: 47 Celtic Dr Durham NC 27703-2894

WILLIAMS, JOEL MANN, polymer material scientist; b. Suffolk, Va., Apr. 6, 1940; s. Joel Mann and Mildred (Barlow) W.; m. Mary Carol Gregory, Sept. 1, 1962; children: Catherine Reine, Michael Gregory. BS, Coll. William and Mary, 1962; PhD, Northwestern U., 1966. Asst. prof. chemistry U. Minn., Mpls., 1967-68; research chemist E.I. DuPont de Nemours, Waynesboro, Va., 1968-72; mem. staff Los Alamos (N.Mex.) Nat. Lab., 1972-93; contractor Ray Raskin Assocs., 1995—; cons., 1993—. Author: The Electronic Puzzle, 1994, The Delta State: Molecular Carpooling, 1995, Moles, Bits and Cubes, 1996; co-author: Advances in Physical Organic Chemistry, 1968, Analytical Chemistry of Liquid Fuel Sources, 1978, Coal Science and Chemistry, 1986. Fellow NIH, 1963-66, NSF, 1966-67. Mem. Sigma Xi. Republican. Roman Catholic. Clubs: Tennis (Los Alamos) (tres. 1984-86), Mountain Mixers Square Dance (treas. 1977-79), Barranca Mesa Pool Assn. (treas. 1975-76). Avocations: skiing, camping, tennis, gardening. Home: 51 Zuni St Los Alamos NM 87544-2647

WILLIAMS, JOHN ALAN, secondary education educator, coach; b. Watertown, N.Y., May 30, 1949; s. John F. and Doris (Fuess) W.; m. Ana Maria Delima Moniz, Feb. 22, 1977; children: Timothy John, Katherine Evelyn. BS in Oceanography, U.S. Naval Acad., 1971; MS in Sci. Edn., Syracuse U., 1978; postgrad., SUNY, Oswego, 1989-90. Sci. tchr., coach Liverpool (N.Y.) High Sch., 1977-80, sci. tchr., coach, dir. sci. and tech. fair, 1981—, advisor, coach Olympiad Team, 1987—; application engr. Hoffman Air & Filtration, Syracuse, N.Y., 1980-81. Coach wrestling team Liverpool High Sch., 1982—; coach local Pee Wee wrestling team, 1982—; bd. dirs. sci. fair com. Syracuse Discovery Ctr., 1986—. Lt. USN, 1971-76, Vietnam. Named Ctrl. N.Y. Sci. Tchr. of Yr. Syracuse Discovery Ctr., 1986-87, Onondaga High Sch. League-North Wrestling Coach of Yr., 1984-85, 88-89, 92-93. Mem. Nat. Earth Sci. Tchrs. Assn., United Liverpool Faculty Assn., N.Y. State Sci. Tchrs. Assn. (10 Yr. award 1990), Assn. Sci. Tech. Ctrs. (Honor Roll Tchrs. 1987), Syracuse Tech. Club (Outstanding Tchr. award 1990), NFL (Tchr. of Yr. 1990), Sigma Xi (Outstanding Sci. Tchr. award 1989). Home: 4320 Luna Crse Liverpool NY 13090-2050 Office: Liverpool High Sch 4338 Wetzel Rd Liverpool NY 13090-2011

WILLIAMS, JOHN ALFRED, educator, author; b. Jackson, Miss., 1925; m. Lorrain Isaac; 1 son, Adam; children by previous marriage: Gregory, Dennis. Grad., Syracuse U., Nat. Inst. Arts and Letters, 1962; LL.D., U. Mass., Dartmouth, 1978; Lit.D, Syracuse U., 1995. With Am. Com. on Africa, N.Y.C.; Disting. prof. English La Guardia Community Coll., 1973-74, 74-75; prof. English Rutgers U., 1979—, Paul Robeson prof. English, 1990—; Bard Ctr. fellow Bard Coll., 1994-95; lectr. CCNY; guest writer Sarah Lawrence Coll.; Regents lectr. U. Calif., Santa Barbara, 1972, U. Hawaii, 1974, Nat. Endowment for the Arts, 1977; vis. prof. Boston U., 1978-79, NYU, 1986-87. Started writing poetry during World War II, in Pacific; Author: The Angry Ones, 1960; novels Night Song, 1961, Sissie, 1963, The Man Who Cried I Am, 1967, Sons of Darkness, Sons of Light, 1969, Captain Blackman, 1972, Mothersill and the Foxes, 1975, The Junior Bachelor Society, 1976, (plays) Last Flight from Ambo Ber, 1981, The Berhama Account, 1985, Jacob's Ladder, 1987, also 8 vols. of non-fiction, vol. of poems; !Click Song, 1982 (Before Columbus Found. Am. Book award 1983); 7 anthologies. Recipient Centennial medal for outstanding achievement Syracuse U., 1970, Lindback award for Disting. Teaching Rutgers U., 1982. Home: 693 Forest Ave Teaneck NJ 07666-2042 *I've tried to adhere to the philosophies of W.E.B. DuBois. He never quit.*

WILLIAMS, JOHN ANDREW, physiology educator, consultant; b. Des Moines, Aug. 3, 1941; s. Harold Southall and Marjorie (Larsen) W.; m. Christa A. Smith, Dec. 26, 1965; children: Rachel Jo, Matthew Dallas. BA, Cen. Wash. State Coll., 1963; MD, U. Wash., Seattle, 1968, PhD, 1968. Staff fellow NIH, Bethesda, Md., 1969-71; research fellow U. Cambridge, Eng., 1971-72; from asst. to prof. physiology U. Calif., San Francisco, 1973-87; prof. physiology, chair dept. physiology, prof. internal medicine U. Mich., Ann Arbor, 1987—; mem. gen. medicine study sect. NIH, Bethesda, 1985-88, DDK-C study sect., 1991-95. Contbr. numerous articles to profl. jours.; editor Am. Jour. Physiology: Gastrointestinal Physiology, 1985-91; assoc. editor Jour. Clin. Investigation, 1997—. Trustee Friends Sch. in Detroit, 1992—. NIH grantee, 1973—. Mem. Am. Physiol. Soc. (Hoffman LaRoche prize 1985, mem. coun. 1996-99), Am. Soc. Cell Biology, Am. Soc. Clin. Investigation, Am. Gastroenterology Assn., Am. Pancreatic Assn. (pres. 1985-86). Democrat. Home: 1115 Woodlawn Ave Ann Arbor MI 48104-3956 Office: Dept Physiology Univ of Mich Med Sch Ann Arbor MI 48109

WILLIAMS, JOHN CHRISTOPHER RICHARD, bishop; b. Sale, Cheshire, Eng., May 22, 1936; arrived in Can., 1960; s. Frank Harold and Ceridwen Roberts (Hughes) W.; m. Rona Macrae Aitken, Mar. 18, 1964; children: Andrew David, Judith Ann. BA in Commerce, Manchester U., Eng., 1958; diploma in theology, Cranmer Hall, Durham, Eng., 1960; DD, Emmanuel St. Chad Coll., Saskatoon, Can., 1997. Ordained deacon Anglican Ch. of Can., 1960, priest, 1962. Missionary in charge Anglican Ch. Can., Sugluk, Que., Can., 1961-72, Cape Dorset, N.W.T., Can., 1972-75, Baker Lake, N.W.T., 1975-78; archdeacon of the Keewatim Anglican Ch. Can., 1975-87; rector Holy Trinity Anglican Ch. Can., Yellowknife, N.W.T., 1978-87; bishop suffagan Diocese of the Arctic, Can., 1987-90, diocesan bishop, 1990—; trustee Can. Churchman, Anglican Ch. Can., 1976-82, mem. nat. exec. com., 1976-79, 92-95. Coord., trans. into Eskimo Inukkitut New Testament, 1992. Avocations: reading, skiing, swimming.

WILLIAMS, JOHN CORNELIUS, lawyer; b. Lee Valley, Tenn., Jan. 24, 1903; s. Hugh and Kitty (Lawrence) W.; 1 son by former marriage, John Cornelius; m. Darthey I. Black, Aug. 12, 1954; 1 dau., Kitty. A.B., Wofford Coll., 1927; LL.B., U. S.C., 1931. Bar: S.C. bar 1931. Prin. Campobello High Sch., Spartanburg County, S.C., 1927-28; practiced in Spartanburg, 1931-61; U.S. atty. Western Dist. S.C., 1951-54, 61-68; partner law firm Williams and Williams, Spartanburg, 1968—; Mem. S.C. Legislature, 1931-32, 49-50. Served to col. U.S. Army, 1940-46. Mem. S.C. Bar Assn., Spartanburg County Bar Assn. (past pres.), 4th U.S. Jud. Conf., V.F.W. (past comdr. S.C.), Am. Legion, 40 and 8, Blue Key, Pi Kappa Delta, Phi Kappa Sigma, Phi Alpha Delta. Democrat. Baptist. Club: Masons (32 degree). Home: 318 S Park Dr Spartanburg SC 29302-3244

WILLIAMS, JOHN EDWARD, lawyer; b. Atlanta, May 21, 1946; s. Edward Carl and Mary E. (Griffin) W.; m. Kristin Forsberg, May 22, 1976; children: Alexandra, Courtney, Charles. BA, Yale U., 1968; JD, U. Va., 1974; LLM in Taxation, Georgetown U., 1977. Bar: Va. 1974, D.C. 1975, U.S. Dist. Ct. D.C. 1975, U.S. Tax Ct. 1975, U.S. Ct. Appeals (D.C. cir.) 1975, U.S. Supreme Ct. 1977. Law clk. to Judge Charles R. Richey U.S. Dist. Ct. (D.C. dist.), 1974-75; assoc. Patton, Boggs & Blow, Washington, 1975-78, Cadwalader, Wickersham & Taft, Washington, 1978-81; asst. to the commr. IRS, Washington, 1981-84; tax counsel Ropes & Gray, Washington, 1984-86; ptnr. David & Hagner, P.C., Washington, 1986-90, Winston & Strawn, Washington, 1990—; mem. Jud. Conf. of D.C. Circuit, 1978, 82, 85, 87, 92. With U.S. Army, 1968-74. Mem. ABA (tax sect., chmn. tech. subcom., adminstrv. practice com. 1986-88), Met., Yale N.Y.C., Chevy Chase Club. Home: 4526 36th St NW Washington DC 20008-4250 Office: Winston & Strawn 1400 L St NW Washington DC 20005-3509

WILLIAMS, JOHN FRANKLIN, real estate broker; b. Durham, N.C., Apr. 23, 1959; m. Stacey Williams. BSBA, Appalachian State U., 1981; MBA, So. Ill. U., 1984. Cert. real estate brokerage mgr., residential specialist, relocation profl., real estate appraiser. Computer analyst McDonnell Douglas, St. Louis, 1981-86; real estate broker Christian Bros. Realty, Bridgeton, Mo., 1986-92, Re/Max Properties West, Chesterfield, Mo., 1992—. Mem. St. Louis Assn. of Realtors (multimillion dollar club 1989-91), Mo. Assn. of Realtors (life mem. million dollar club 1989). Avocation: karate. Office: Re/Max Properties West 361 Chesterfield Ctr Chesterfield MO 63017-4801

WILLIAMS, JOHN HORTER, civil engineer, oil, gas, telecommunications and allied products distribution company executive; b. Havana, Cuba, Aug. 17, 1918; s. Charles P. and Alice Magruder (Dyer) W.; m. Emily Alice Ijams, June 6, 1942 (dec.); children—John H., Burch I., S. Miller; m. Joanne Harwell Simpson., Feb. 1, 1975. B.S., Yale U., 1940. Registered profl. engr., Okla., Minn. With The Williams Cos. Inc., Tulsa, 1940-42, 46-50, pres., dir., 1950-70, chmn., chief exec. officer, 1971-78, now hon. dir.; bd. dirs. Apco Argentina, Inc., Unit Corp., Willbros Group, Inc. Served with USNR, 1942-46. Decorated Order of Condor of Andes (Bolivia); named Okla. Hall of Fame, 1977; recipient Outstanding Okla. Oil Man awad Okla.-Kans. Oil and Gas Assn., 1982, Disting. Svc. award Nat. Petroleum Hall of Fame, 1985; inducted into Okla. Commerce and Industry Hall of Honor, 1986, Tulsa Hall of Fame, 1993. Mem. ASCE, Yale Engring. Assn. Office: The Williams Cos Inc 1 Williams Ctr Fl 49 Tulsa OK 74172-0150

WILLIAMS, JOHN JAMES, JR., architect; b. Denver, July 13, 1949; s. John James and Virginia Lee (Thompson) W.; m. Mary Serene Morck, July 29, 1972. BArch, U. Colo., 1974. Registered architect, Colo., Calif., Idaho, Va., Utah, Nev. Project architect Gensler Assoc. Architects, Denver, 1976, Heinzman Assoc. Architects, Boulder, Colo., 1977, EZTH Architects, Boulder, 1978-79; prin. Knudson/Williams PC, Boulder, 1980-82, Faber, Williams & Brown, Boulder, 1982-86, John Williams & Assocs., Denver, 1986—; panel chmn. U. Colo. World Affairs Conf.; vis. faculty U. Colo. Sch. Architecture and Planning, Coll. Environ. Design, 1986-91. Author (with others) State of Colorado architect licensing law, 1986. Commr. Downtown Boulder Mall Commn., 1985-88; bd. dirs. U. Colo. Fairway Club, 1986-88; mem. Gov's. Natural Hazard Mitigation Coun., State of Colo., 1990. Recipient Teaching Honorarium, U. Colo. Coll. Architecture and Planning, 1977, 78, 79, 80, 88, Excellence in Design and Planning award City of Boulder, 1981, 82, Citation for Excellenc, WOOD Inc., 1982, 93, Disting. Profl. Svc. award Coll. Environ. Design U. Colo., 1988. Mem. AIA (sec. 1988, bd. dirs. Colo. North chpt. 1985-86, chair Colo. govtl. affairs com., Design award 1993, pres. 1990, v.p. 1989, sec. 1987, sec. Colo. chpt. 1988, ednl. fund Fisher I traveling scholar 1988, state design conf. chair 1991, North chpt. Design award 1993), Architects and Planners of Boulder (v.p. 1982), Nat. Coun. Architect Registration Bd., Nat. Golf Found. (sponsor), Kappa Sigma (chpt. pres. 1970). Avocations: golf, polit. history, fitness and health. Home: 1031 Turnberry Cir Louisville CO 80027-9594 Office: John Williams and Assocs 821 17th St Ste 502 Denver CO 80202-3018

WILLIAMS, JOHN LEE, lawyer; b. Nashville, Dec. 23, 1942; s. Leslie Elwood and Gladys Mae (Ridings) W.; m. Norma Jean Givens, May 27, 1967; 1 child, Jacob Andrew. BA, Tenn. Technol. U., 1964; JD, U. Tenn., 1967. Bar: Tenn 1967. Ptnr. Porch, Peeler & Williams, Waverly, Tenn., 1967-78, Porch, Peeler, Williams Thomason, Waverly, 1978—; asst. dist. atty. 21st Jud. Cir. Ct. Tenn., 1972-74; judge Ct. Gen. Sessions of Humphreys County, Tenn., 1978-82; county atty. Humphreys County, 1968-72, 82-86, 94—; city atty. City of Waverly, 1978—, City of McEwen, Tenn., 1978—, City of Lobelville, Tenn., 1985-89; gen. counsel Meriwether Lewis Elec. Coop., Centerville, Tenn., 1980—; cmty. dir. NationsBank, Humphreys County, 1984-95. State legal counsel Tenn. Jaycees, 1970; treas., sec. Humphreys County Dem. Exec. Com., 1978—; chmn. Humphreys County Election Commn., 1968-72. Col. Tenn. Army N.G., 1990—. Mem. ABA, Am. Judicature Soc., Tenn. Bar Assn. (ho. of dels.), Humphreys County Bar Assn. (pres. 1978—), Masons (master 1985). Home: 102 S Court Sq Waverly TN 37185-2113

WILLIAMS, JOHN MICHAEL, physical therapist, sports medicine educator; b. Columbus, Ohio, Oct. 19, 1951; s. James Hutchison and Helen Lucille (Knight) W.; m. Karen Sue Eaglen, June 23, 1973; children: Michelle Rene, Elizabeth Ann. BS in Phys. Therapy, Ohio State U., 1975, MS in Allied Medicine, 1983. Lic. phys. therapist, Ohio. Asst. dir. phys. therapy Licking Meml. Hosp., Newark, Ohio, 1978-80; pvt. practice Westerville, Ohio, 1977-80; asst. dir. rehab. St. Anthony Hosp., Columbus, 1980-88; from chief phys. therpist to dir. phys. and sports medicine St. Ann's Sports Medicine, Westerville, 1988-95; mgr. Nova Care Rehab., 1995—; clin. instr. Ohio State U., Columbus, 1984—, faculty instr., 1997—; adj. faculty sports medicine Otterbein Coll., Westerville, 1989-96; cons. Licking County Arthritis Found., Newark, 1978-80; phys. therapy adv. bd. Ctrl. Ohio Tech. Coll., Newark, 1978—; bd. dirs. SAHCU Credit Union, Westerville; asst. prof. phys. and occupl. therapy programs U. Findlay, Ohio, 1996—. Author monograph. Med. team capt. Columbus Marathon, 1989—, U.S. Men's Olympic Marathon Trials, Columbus, 1992. Lt. col. USAR, 1969—. Decorated Army Commendation medal; recipient Mayor's award for vol. svc. City of Columbus, 1993. Mem. Am. Acad. Med. Adminstrs., Am. Phys. Therapy Assn. (rep. to state assembly 1987—), Rotary Internat. Episcopalian. Avocations: volleyball, golf, running. Home: 132 Ormsbee Ave Westerville OH 43081-1151

WILLIAMS, JOHN TAYLOR, lawyer; b. Cambridge, Mass., June 19, 1938; s. Paul Merchant Taylor and Audrey Arlene Dowling; m. Leonora Hall; children: Caleb, Jared, Nathaniel. AB, Harvard U., 1960; LLB, U. Pa., 1965. Bar: Mass. 1965, U.S. Dist. Ct. Mass., U.S. Ct. Appeals (1st cir.), U.S. Supreme Ct. Corp. loans officer State St. Bank & Trust Co., Boston, 1960-62; from assoc. to ptnr. Haussermann, Davison & Shattuck, Boston, 1965-83; ptnr. Palmer & Dodge, Boston, 1983—; bd. dirs. Blackwell Sci. Inc.; lectr. on 1st amendment, copyright, pub. and intellectual property law for Practicing Law Inst., Mass. CLE/New Eng. Law Inst., Nat. Assn. Archivists, Boston Patent Lawyers Assn., others; apptd. mem. U.S. Courthouse Arts Comm., U.S. Publ. Del. to China, 1993; mem. lit. panel Nat. Endowment for the Arts, 1990, 91, 94, mem. presentation and creation panel, 1996. Author: (screenplay) Rolf in the Woods, 1987, (screenplay) Toussaint L'Overture, 1989, (with E. Gabriel Perle) The Publishing Law Handbook, 2 vols. (revised annually); contbg. author: Legal Problems in Book Publishing, 1981, 84, 86; contbg. editor: Small Voices and Great Trumpets: Minorities and the Media, 1980. Bd. dirs. City of Cambridge Arts Coun., 1973-83, chmn., 1981-83; bd. dirs. Ploughshares Inc., 1988-89; trustee Arthur Fiedler Meml. Inc., 1983—, Boston Philharm. Orch., 1983-85, Petra Found., 1988—; trustee, gen. counsel Inst. Contemporary Art, 1970-92; mem. corp. Mass. Gen. Hosp., 1985—; mem. Patent and Tech Conflicts Coms., 1985-91; clk. John F. Kennedy Meml. Commn. Inc., 1986—; mem. adv. bd. Provincetown Fine Arts Work Ctr., 1992—. Mrm. ABA (sect. patent, trademark, copyright law, chmn. com. on authors 1978-81, communications and entertainment law forum coms.), Boston Bar Assn. (former chmn. com. on delivery of legal svcs. to indigent), Lawyers' Com. for Civil Rights under Law (chmn. steering com. 1988-91), Mass. Bar Assn. (bus. law and computer law sects.), Nat. Lawyers' Com. for Civil Rights (bd. dirs. 1989—), Tavern Club (Boston). Home: 9 Orchard St Cambridge MA 02140-1321 Office: Palmer & Dodge 1 Beacon St Boston MA 02108-3107

WILLIAMS, J(OHN) TILMAN, insurance executive, real estate broker, city official; b. Detroit, Feb. 26, 1925; s. Aubrey and Martha (Lou) W.; m. Sally Jane Robinson, Aug. 22, 1947; children: Leslie Ann, Martha Lou. B.S. in Agr. Mich. State U., 1951. Pres. Satellite Ins. Brokerage, Garden Grove, Calif., 1959—; pres. Satellite Real Estate, Satellite Mortgage & Loan Co. Mayor Garden Grove, 1976-78, re-elected, 1987, mem. coun., 1980-92, apptd. vice mayor, 1989—; mem. Ad Hoc Com. on Property Tax to Limit Govt. Spending with Spirit of 13 Initiative; elected to Orange County Dem. Cen. Com., 68th Assembly Dist., 1996; past pres. Garden Grove High Sch. Band Boosters. With USAAF, World War II, PTO. Mem. Bd. Realtors, Ind. Ins. Agts. Assn., Orange County Esperanto Assn. (pres. 1985—), Am. Legion, VFW. Democrat. Methodist. Clubs: Toastmasters (Anaheim, Calif.); Fifty-Plus Sr. Citizens of Garden Grove (pres. 1986—). Lodges: Lions, Elks. Home: 11241 Chapman Ave Garden Grove CA 92840-3301 Office: 12311 Harbor Blvd Garden Grove CA 92840-3809 *Service to one's fellowman and community is the greatest avocation and pleasure one can follow.*

WILLIAMS, JOHN TOWNER, composer, conductor; b. Flushing, N.Y., Feb. 8, 1932. Student, UCLA; pvt. studies with Mario Castelnuovo-Tedesco, Los Angeles; student, Juilliard Sch.; pvt. studies with, Madame Rosina Lhevinne, N.Y.C.; hon. degree, Berklee Coll. Music, Boston, Northeastern U., Boston, Tufts U., U. So. Calif., Boston U., New Eng. Conservatory Music, Providence Coll.; others. Condr. Boston Pops Orch., 1980—. Works include: composer (film scores) I Passed for White, 1960, Because They're Young, 1960, The Secret Ways, 1961, Bachelor Flat, 1962, Diamond Head, 1962, Gidget Goes to Rome, 1963, The Killers, 1964, John Goldfarb, Please Come Home, 1964, None But the Brave, 1965, How to Steal a Million, 1966, The Rare Breed, 1966, Not With My Wife, You Don't, 1966, The Plainsman, 1966, Penelope, 1966, A Guide for the Married Man, 1967, Valley of the Dolls, 1967 (Acad. award nominee), Fitzwilly, 1968, Sergeant Ryker, 1968, The Reivers, 1969 (Acad. award nominee), Daddy's Gone A-Hunting, 1969, Goodbye, Mr. Chips, 1969 (Acad. award nominee), The Story of A Woman, 1970, Fiddler on the Roof, 1971 (Acad. award for musical adaptation 1971), The Cowboys, 1972, The Poseidon Adventure, 1972 (Acad. award nominee), Images, 1972 (Acad. award nominee), Pete 'n' Tillie, 1972, The Paper Chase, 1973, The Long Goodbye, 1973, The Man Who Loved Cat Dancing, 1973, Cinderella Liberty, 1973 (Acad. award nominee), Tom Sawyer, 1973 (Acad. award nominee), Sugarland Express, 1974, Earthquake, 1974, The Towering Inferno, 1974 (Acad. award nominee), Conrack, 1974, Jaws, 1975 (Acad. award 1976, Grammy award, Golden Globe award), The Eiger Sanction, 1976, Family Plot, 1976, Midway, 1976, The Missouri Breaks, 1976, Raggedy Ann and Andy, 1977, Black Sunday, 1977, Star Wars, 1977 (Acad. award, 3 Grammy awards, Golden Globe award), Close Encounters of the Third Kind, 1977 (2 Grammy awards, Acad. award nominee), The Fury, 1978, Jaws II, 1978, Superman, 1978 (2 Grammy awards), Meteor, 1979, Quintet, 1979, Dracula, 1979, "1941", 1979, The Empire Strikes Back, 1980 (2 Grammy awards, Acad. award nominee), Raiders of the Lost Ark, 1981 (Grammy award, Acad. award nominee), Heartbeeps, 1981, E.T., 1982 (Acad. award for best original score, 3 Grammy awards, Golden Globe award), Monsignor, 1982, Yes, Giorgio, 1982 (Acad. award nominee), Superman III, 1983, Return of the Jedi, 1983 (Acad. award nominee), Indiana Jones and the Temple of Doom, 1984 (Acad. award nominee), The River, 1984 (Acad. award nominee), Space Camp, 1986, Emma's War, 1986, The Witches of Eastwick, 1987 (Acad. award nominee), Empire of the Sun, 1987 (Acad. award nominee), Jaws: The Revenge, 1987, Superman IV: The Quest for Peace, 1987, The Secret of My Success, 1987, The Accidental Tourist, 1988 (Acad. award nominee, Indiana Jones and the Last Crusade, 1989 (Acad. award nominee), Always, 1989, Born On The Fourth of July, 1989 (Acad. award nominee), Stanley and Iris, 1990, Presumed Innocent, 1990, Home Alone, 1990 (Acad. award nominee), Hook, 1991 (Acad. award nominee), JFK, 1991 (Acad. award nominee), Far and Away, 1992, Home Alone II, 1992, Jurassic Park, 1993, Schindler's List, 1993 (Acad. award for best original score 1993), Sabrina, 1995 (Acad. award nominee for best original score 1996, Nixon, 1995 (Acad. award nominee for best dramatic score 1996); composer music for songs including: (from Sabrina, lyrics by Alan and Marilyn Bergman) Moonlight, 1995 (Acad. award nominee for best original song 1996); composer: (TV programs) Heidi, 1969 (Emmy award), Jane Eyre, 1971 (Emmy award), others; composer numerous concert pieces and symphonies including Jubilee 350 Fanfare for the Boston Pops, 1980, theme to the 1984 Summer Olympic Games, Liberty Fanfare, 1987; recorded numerous albums with Boston Pops Orch. including Pops in Space, That's Entertainment (Pops on Broadway), Pops on the March, Pops Around the World (Digital Overtures), Aisle Seat, Pops Out of This World, Boston Pops on Stage, America, the Dream Goes On; collaborator: (with Jessye Norman) With A Song in My Heart, Swing, Swing, Unforgettable; guest condr. major orchs. including London Symphony Orch., Cleve. Orch., Phila. Orch., Toronto Orch., Montreal Orch. Served with USAF. Recipient several gold and platinum records Rec. Industry Assn. Am. Office: Gorfaine & Schwartz care of Michael Gorfaine 3301 Barham Blvd Ste 201 Los Angeles CA 90068-1477*

WILLIAMS, JOHN TROY, librarian, educator; b. Oak Park, Ill., Mar. 11, 1924; s. Michael Daniel and Donna Marie (Shaffer) W.; B.A., Central Mich. U., 1949; M.A. in Libr. Sci., U. Mich., 1951, M.A., 1954; Ph.D., Mich. State U., 1973. Reference libr. U. Mich., Ann Arbor, 1955-59; instr. Bowling Green (Ohio) State U., 1959-60; reference librarian Mich. State U., East Lansing, 1960-62; 1st asst. reference dept. Flint (Mich.) Pub. Library, 1962-65; head reference svcs., Purdue U., West Lafayette, Ind., 1965-72; head pub. svcs. No. Ill. U., Dekalb, 1972-75; asst. dean, asst. univ. libr. Wright State U., Dayton, Ohio, 1975-80; vis. scholar U. Mich., Ann Arbor, 1980—; cons. in field. Served with U.S. Army, 1943-46. Mich. State fellow, 1963-64; HEW fellow, 1971-72. Mem. Am. Libr. Assn., Spl. Libraries Assn., Am. Soc. for Info. Scis., Am. Sociol. Assn., AAUP, Coun. on Fgn. Rels. Contbr. articles to profl. jours. Home: PO Box 7531 Ann Arbor MI 48107-7531

WILLIAMS, JOHN WESLEY, fine arts educator; b. Memphis, Feb. 25, 1928; s. Wesley Alfred and Anna Belle (Curtis) W.; m. Mary Ellen Schmidt, Dec. 26, 1955; children: Maxwell, Katherine, Sarah, Cyril, Elena, Amelia. Student, Duke U., 1948-50; B.A., Yale U., 1952; M.A., U. Mich., 1953, Ph.D., 1960. Instr., assoc. prof. Swarthmore Coll., Pa., 1960-72; prof. fine arts U. Pitts., 1972—, Disting. Svc. prof., 1993—; dir. Internat. Center Medieval Art, N.Y.C., 1982-85. Author: Early Spanish Illum, 1977, Apocalypse in Spain, 1991, The Illustrated Beatus, 1994. Served with USMC, 1946-48. Guggenheim fellow, 1984-85, Inst. for Advanced Study member, 1991-92. Home: 749 S Linden Ave Pittsburgh PA 15208-2814 Office: Dept History History of Art & Architecture University of Pittsburgh Pittsburgh PA 15260

WILLIAMS, JOHN YOUNG, merchant banker; b. Cordele, Ga., Apr. 13, 1943; s. George Wilmer and Minnie Converse (Roberts) W.; m. Julian Perdue Boykin; m. Joyce, Isabel. BS in Indsl. Engring., Ga. Inst. Tech., 1965; MBA in Fin., Harvard U., 1969. CFA, Ga. Assoc. Kuhn, Loeb & Co., N.Y.C., 1969-71; asst. v.p. Stone & Webster Securities Corp., N.Y.C., 1971-74, Chem. Bank, N.Y.C., 1974-75; mng. dir. Dean Witter Reynolds, Inc., Atlanta, 1975-84; sr. v.p., ltd. ptnr. Bear Stearns & Co., Atlanta, 1984-85; mng. dir. Robinson Humphrey Co., Atlanta, 1985-87; mng. dir., co-founder Grubb & Williams, Ltd., Atlanta, 1987—, Equity South Ptnrs., 1995—; bd. dirs. Tech Data Corp., Clearwater, Fla., Law Cos. Group, Inc., Atlanta, Frisco Furniture Co., High Point, N.C., co-chmn. 1st lt. U.S. Army, 1965-67, Korea. Fellow Soc. Internat. Bus. Fellows (sec. 1988-89); mem. Assn. for Investment Mgmt. and Rsch. (CFA), Assn. for Corp. Growth (pres. 1983-84), Harvard Bus. Sch. Club (pres. 1982-83), Phi Delta Theta (alumni pres. 1980-81). Episcopalian. Avocation: military history. Home: 750 Arden Close NW Atlanta GA 30327-1275 Office: Equity South Advisors LLC 3399 Peachtree Rd NE Ste 1790 Atlanta GA 30326-1151

WILLIAMS, JOSEPH DALTON, pharmaceutical company executive; b. Washington, Pa., Aug. 15, 1926; s. Joseph Dalton and Jane (Day) W.; m. Mildred E. Bellaire, June 28, 1973; children: Terri, Daniel. BS in Pharmacy, U. Nebr., 1950; DSc (hon.), Union U., 1991, U. Nebr., 1989; LHD (hon.), Albany Coll. Pharmacy, Union U., 1980, Rutgers U., 1987, Long Island U., 1988; DSc (hon.), Phila. Coll. Pharmacy and Sci., 1988, Long Island U., 1988, Albany Coll. Pharmacy of Union U., 1991; D Human Svcs. (hon.), Caldwell Coll., 1989; LLD (hon.), Bethune-Cookman Coll., 1990, Coll. St. Elizabeth, 1990, Seton Hall U., 1990, U. Md., 1991, St. Augustine Coll., 1992. Pres. Parke-Davis Co., Detroit, 1973-76; pres. pharm. group Warner-Lambert Co., Morris Plains, N.J., 1976-77; pres. Internat. Group, 1977-79; pres., dir. Warner-Lambert Corp., 1979-80, pres., chief operating officer, 1980-84, chmn., CEO, 1985-91, chmn. exec. com., 1991—; bd. dirs. AT&T, J.C. Penney & Co., Exxon Corp., Rockefeller Fin. Svcs., Inc., Rockefeller and Co., Inc., Eckerd Corp. Bd. dirs. People to People Health Found., United Negro Coll. Fund; trustee emeritus Columbia U.; chmn. Commn. on Higher Edn. for State of N.J. With USNR, 1943-46. Mem. Am. Pharm. Assn., N.J. Pharm. Assn., Somerset Hills Country Club, Links Club, Pine Valley Golf Club, Baltusrol Golf Club, Mid Ocean Club, Robert Trent Jones Internat. Golf Club. Office: Warner-Lambert Co 182 Tabor Rd Morris Plains NJ 07950-2536

WILLIAMS, JOSEPH HILL, retired diversified industry executive; b. Tulsa, June 2, 1933; s. David Rogerson and Martha Reynolds (Hill) W.; children: Joseph Hill Jr., Peter B., James C.; m. Terese T. Ross, May 7, 1977; stepchildren: Margot Ross, Jennifer Ross. Diploma, St. Paul's Sch., 1952; B.A., Yale U., 1956, M.A. (hon.), 1977; postgrad., Sch. Pipeline Tech. U. Tex., 1960. Field employee div. domestic constrn. The Williams Cos., Inc., Tulsa, 1958-60; project coord. div. engring. The Williams Cos. Inc., Tulsa, 1960-61; project supt. Iran, 1961-62, asst. resident mgr., 1962-64; project mgr., 1964-65, resident mgr., 1965-67; exec. v.p. Tulsa, 1968—, pres., chief operating officer, 1971-78; chmn., chief exec. officer The Williams Cos., Inc., Tulsa, 1979-93; chmn. bd. The Williams Cos., Inc., 1994; now chmn. & CEO The Williams Co., Inc., Tulsa, O.K.; dir. The Williams Co., Inc., Tulsa, 1995—. Former fellow, trustee Yale Corp. Served with AUS, 1956-58. Mem. (hon.) Am. Petroleum Inst. (hon. bd. dirs.), Met. Tulsa C. of C. (past chmn.), Okla. State C. of C. and Industry (past. chmn.), Bus. Coun., Nature Conservancy (past chmn. bd. govs.). Episcopalian. Clubs: Springdale Hall (Camden, S.C.); Augusta (Ga.); Grandfather Golf and Country (Linville, N.C.); Old Baldy Club, (Saratoga, Wyo). Office: Williams Cos Inc 1 Williams Ctr PO Box 2400 Tulsa OK 74102-2400

WILLIAMS, JOSEPH THEODORE, oil and gas company executive; b. Oklahoma City, June 19, 1937; s. Roland Leslie and Mary Virginia (Maloy) W.; m. Marilyn Kay Hansen, Sept. 3, 1948; children: Joseph Kent, John Kevin, Katharine Ann, Jennifer Lyn. BS in Petroleum Engring., U. Tex., 1960. Engr. Chevron Corp., New Orleans and Brookhaven, Miss., 1960-65; engr. mgr. Arabian Am. Oil Co., Dhahran, Saudi Arabia, 1965-70, Chevron Corp., Denver and San Francisco, 1970-74; gen. mgr. ops. Chevron Petroleum (U.K.) Ltd., London, 1974-78; sr. v.p. Mitchell Energy and Devel. Corp., Houston, 1978-81; pres., chmn. Sovran Energy Corp., Houston, 1981-83; v.p. Lear Petroleum Corp., Dallas, 1983-85, pres., chief exec. officer, 1985-89, also chmn. bd. dirs.; pres., CEO DALEN Resources Corp. (formerly PG&E Resources Co.), Dallas, 1989-95; vice chmn., CEO Enserch Exploration, Inc., 1995-96; pvt. practice Dallas, 1996—. Mem. AIME, Soc. Petroleum Engrs., Tex. Ind. Producers and Royalty Owners Assn., Ind. Petroleum Assn. Am., Domestic Petroleum Coun., Dallas Petroleum Club, Northwood Club. Avocations: golf, tennis, bridge, music.

WILLIAMS, JULIE BELLE, psychiatric social worker; b. Algona, Iowa, July 29, 1950; d. George Howard and Leta Maribelle (Durschmidt) W. BA, U. Iowa, 1972, MSW, 1973. Lic. psychologist, ind. clin. social worker, marriage and family therapist, Minn.; lic. social worker, Iowa. Social worker Psychopathic Hosp., Iowa City, 1971-72; OEO counselor YOUR, Webster City, Iowa, 1972; social worker Child Devel. Clinic, Iowa City, 1973; therapist Mid-Eastern Iowa Community Mental Health Ctr., Iowa City, 1973; psychiat. social worker Mental Health Ctr. No. Iowa, Mason City, 1974-79, chief psychiat. social worker, 1979-80; asst. dir. Community Counseling Ctr., White Bear Lake, Minn., 1980-85, dir., 1985—; lectr., cons. in field. NIMH grantee, 1972-73. Mem. NASW (Acad. Cert. Social Workers, Qualified Clin. Social Workers, diplomate), NOW, Am. Orthopsychiat. Assn., Am. Assn. Sex Educators, Counselors and Therapists, Minn. Women Psychologists, Minn. Lic. Psychologists, Phi Beta Kappa. Democrat. Office: 1280 N Birch Lake Blvd White Bear Lake MN 55110-6708

WILLIAMS, JULIE FORD, mutual fund officer; b. Long Beach, Calif., Aug. 7, 1948; d. Julious Hunter and Bessie May (Wood) Ford; m. Walter Edward Williams, Oct. 20, 1984; 1 child, Andrew Ford. BA in Econs., Occidental Coll., 1970. Legal sec. Kadison, Pfaelzer, Woodard, Quinn & Rossi, L.A., 1970-71, 74-77; legal sec. Fried, Frank, Harris, Shriver & Jacobson, N.Y.C., 1971-72, Pallot, Poppell, Goodman & Shapo, Miami, Fla., 1973-74; adminstrv. asst. Capital Research-Mgmt., Los Angeles, 1978-82; corp. officer Cash Mgmt. Trust Am., 1982—, Bond Fund Am., 1982—, Tax-Exempt Bond Fund Am., 1982—, AMCAP Fund, 1984—, Am. Funds Income Series, 1985—, Am. Funds Tax-Exempt Series II, 1986—, Capital World Bond Fund, 1987—, Am. High-Income Trust, 1987—, Intermediate Bond Fund Am., 1987—, Tax-Exempt Money Fund Am., 1989—, U.S. Treasury Money Fund Am., 1991—, Fundamental Investors, 1992—, Ltd. Term Tax-Exempt Bond Fund Am., 1993—, Am. High-Income Mcpl. Bond Fund, 1994—; v.p. fund bus. mgmt. group Capital Rsch. Mgmt., 1986—. Pres.-elect Alumni Bd. Govs. Occidental Coll., 1996-97, pres., 1997-98. Democrat. Episcopalian. Avocations: scuba diving, RVing, theatre. Office: Capital Rsch and Mgmt Co 333 S Hope St Los Angeles CA 90071-1406

WILLIAMS, JUSTIN W., government official; b. N.Y.C., Jan. 4, 1942; s. Louis P. and Edith W. Williams. BA, Columbia U., 1963; LLB, U. Va., 1967. Bar: Va. 1967. Atty. Dept. Justice, 1967-68; asst. commonwealth atty. Arlington County, Va., 1968-70; asst. U.S. atty. Ea. Dist. Va., 1970-78, 1st asst. U.S. atty., 1978-79; U.S. atty. Alexandria, Va., 1979-81; asst. U.S. atty., 1981-86; U.S. atty. Ea. dist. Va., 1986; asst. U.S. atty., chief criminal divsn. Ea. dist. Va., Alexandria, Va., 1986—. Episcopalian. Office: US Atty's Office 2100 Jamieson Ave Alexandria VA 22314-5702

WILLIAMS, KAREN HASTIE, lawyer, think tank executive; b. Washington, Sept. 30, 1944; d. William Henry and Beryl (Lockhart) Hastie; m. Wesley S. Williams, Jr.; children: Amanda Pedersen, Wesley Hastie, Bailey Lockhart. Cert., U. Neuchatel, Switzerland, 1965; BA, Bates Coll., 1966; MA, Tufts U., 1967; JD, Cath. U. Am., 1973. Bar: D.C. 1973. Staff asst. internat. gov. relations dept. Mobil Oil Corp., N.Y.C., 1967-69; staff asst. com. Dist. Columbia U.S. Senate, 1970, chief counsel com. on the budget, 1977-80; law clk. to judge Spottswood Robinson III U.S. Ct. Appeals (D.C. Cir.), Washington, 1973-74; law clk. to assoc. justice Thurgood Marshall U.S. Supreme Ct., Washington, 1974-75; assoc. Fried, Frank, Harris, Shriver & Kampelman, Washington, 1975-77, 1975-77; adminstr. Office Mgmt. and Budget, Washington, 1980-81; of counsel Crowell & Moring, Washington, 1982, ptnr., 1982—; Bd. dirs. Crestar Fin. Services Corp., Fannie Mae, Washington Gas Light Co., Continental Airlines, SunAmerica, Inc. Chair, trustee Greater Washington Research Ctr., chair. Mem. ABA (pub. contract law sect., past chair), Nat. Bar Assn., Washington Bar Assn., Nat. Contract Mgmt. Assn., NAACP (bd. dirs. legal defense fund). Office: Crowell & Moring Ste 1200W 1001 Pennsylvania Ave NW Washington DC 20004-2505

WILLIAMS, KAREN JOHNSON, federal judge; b. Orangeburg, S.C., Aug. 4, 1951; d. James G. Johnson and Marcia (Reynolds) Johnson Dantzler; m. Charles H. Williams, Dec. 27, 1968; children: Marian, Ashley, Charlie, David. BA, Columbia Coll., 1972; postgrad., U. S.C., 1973, JD cum laude, 1980. Bar: S.C. 1980, U.S. Dist. Ct. S.C. 1980, U.S. Ct. Appeals (4th cir.) 1981. Tchr. Irmo (S.C.) Mid. Sch., 1972-74, O-W High Sch., Orangeburg, 1974-76; assoc. Charles H. Williams P.A., Orangeburg, 1980-92; circuit judge U.S. Ct. Appeals (4th cir.), 1992—; mem. exec. bd. grievance commn. S.C. Supreme Ct., Columbia, 1983-92. Mem. child devel. bd. First Bapt. Ch., Orangeburg; bd. dirs. Orangeburg County Mental Retardation Bd., 1986-94, Orangeburg-Calhoun Hosp. Found.; bd. visitors Columbia Coll., 1988-92; dir. Reg. Med. Ctr. Hosp. Found., 1988-92; mem. adv. bd. Orangeburg-Calhoun Tech. Coll., 1987-92. Mem. ABA, Am. Judicature Soc., Fed. Judges Assn., S.C. Bar Assn., Orangeburg County Bar Assn. (co-chair Law Day 1981), S.C. Trial Lawyers Assn., Bus. and profl. Women Assn., Rotary, Order of Wig and Robe, Order of Coif. Home: 2503 Five Chop Rd Orangeburg SC 29115 Office: 1021 Middleton St Orangeburg SC 29115-4783

WILLIAMS, KENNETH JAMES, retired county official; b. Eureka, Calif., Apr. 28, 1924; s. E. J. and Thelma (Hall) W.; student Humboldt State Coll., 1942-43; B.S., U. Oreg., 1949, M.Ed., 1952; m. Mary Patricia Warring, Sept. 3, 1949; children—James Clayton, Susan May, Christopher Kenneth. Engaged as mountain triangulation observer with U.S. Coast and Geodetic Survey, 1942; instr. bus. and geography Boise (Idaho) Jr. Coll., 1949-51; tchr. Prospect High Sch., 1952-54; prin. Oakland (Oreg.) High Sch., 1954-58; supt. prin. Coburg Public Schs., 1958-64; supt. Yoncalla (Oreg.) Public Schs., 1964-66, Amity (Oreg.) Public Schs., 1966-72; adminstr. Yamhill County, McMinnville, Oreg., 1974-85; cons., 1985—; county liaison officer Land and Water Conservation Fund, 1977-85. Dist. lay leader Oreg.-Idaho ann. conf. United Methodist Ch., 1968-80, bd. dirs. western dist. Ch. Extension Soc., 1976; mem. Mid-Willamette Manpower Council, 1974-85; bd. dirs. Lafayette Noble Homes, 1970-72; mem. adv. com. local budget law sect. State of Oreg. Served with AUS, 1943-46. Decorated Purple Heart. Mem. NEA, Oreg. Edn. Assn., Oreg. Assn. Secondary Prins., Nat. Assn. Secondary Prins., AAUP, Oreg., Am. Assn. Sch. Adminstrs., Assn. Supervision and Curriculum Devel., Nat. Sch. Pub. Relations Assn., Phi Delta Kappa. Mason (Shriner), Lion. Home: 21801 SE Webfoot Rd Dayton OR 97114-8832

WILLIAMS, KENNETH OGDEN, farmer; b. Clarksdale, Miss., Jan. 18, 1924; s. Peter Fairley and Robbie (Casey) W.; m. Frances Dyer Lott, June 14, 1969; 1 child, Frances. BS, Vanderbilt U., 1949. Ptnr. P.F. Williams and Sons, Clarksdale, 1949-88, Swan Lake Farms, Clarksdale, 1989—. Mem. Miss. Ho. of Reps., Jackson, 1960-84, Miss. Senate, 1988-94. Sgt. U.S. Army, 1942-46. Decorated Bronze Star. Republican. Baptist. Home: 1505 Holly St Clarksdale MS 38614-2912

WILLIAMS, KENNETH SCOTT, entertainment company executive; b. Tulsa, Okla., Dec. 31, 1955; s. David Vorhees Williams and Mary Louise (Newell) Rose; m. Jann Catherine Wolfe, May 20, 1989; children: Catherine Eloise, Michael Holbrook. BA, Harvard Coll., 1978; MS, Columbia U., 1985. Bank officer Chase Manhattan Bank, N.Y.C., 1978-82; asst. treas. Columbia Pictures Entertainment, N.Y.C., 1982-84, v.p., treas., 1984-89; sr. v.p. fin. and adminstrn. Columbia Pictures Entertainment, Burbank, Calif., 1990-91; sr. v.p. corp. ops. Sony Pictures Entertainment, Culver City, Calif., 1991-95; exec. v.p. Sony Pictures Entertainment, Culver City, 1995-96; pres. Digital Studio divsn. Sony Pictures Entertainment, 1996—. Mem. Blue Hill Troupe, N.Y.C., 1979—; bd. dirs. L.A. Conservancy; bd. govs. L.A. Music Ctr.; chmn. Entertainment Tech. Ctr., U. So. Calif.; bd. govs. L.A. Music Ctr.; chmn. entertainment tech. ctr. U. So. Calif.; trustee the Buckley Sch. Mem. N.Y. Soc. Securities Analysts, Fin. Execs. Inst., Harvard Club. So. Calif. (bd. dirs.), Beta Gamma Sigma. Home: 966 Stone Canyon Rd Los Angeles CA 90077-2914 Office: Sony Pictures Entertainment 10202 Washington Blvd Culver City CA 90232-3119

WILLIAMS, KENT HARLAN, coast guard officer; b. Forty Fort, Pa., Aug. 18, 1943; m. Geraldine M. Boyle, 1965; children: Deborah, Rebecca, Jessica. BS in Engring., USCG Acad., 1965; postgrad., Naval Postgrad. Sch., 1969-70, Naval War Coll., 1978-79, MIT, 1983-84. Commd. ensign USCG, 1965, advanced through grades to vice adm., 1994; resource dir., comptr. USCG, Washington, 1990-91, chief, office acquisition, 1991-93; dist. comdr. USCG, Boston, 1993-94, chief of staff, 1994-96. Decorated D.S.M., Legion of Merit with three oak leaf clusters, Bronze Star with combat V; Sloan medal MIT, 1983-84. Mem. Am. Soc. Mil. Comptr., Coast Guard Acad. Alumni Assn., MIT Club. Office: USCG 2100 2d St SW Washington DC 20593-0001

WILLIAMS, LARRY BILL, academic administrator; b. Cushing, Okla., June 9, 1945; s. Louis Albert and Morene Ruth (Cox) W.; m. Pam Bryan, May 1, 1993; children: Natalie Michelle, Nicole Diane, Louis Bradley, Sharla Dianne Bryan, Vanessa Joy Bryan. BS, Ctrl. State U., Edmond, Okla., 1967, MBA, 1972; PhD, U. Okla., 1985; grad. Inst. Ednl. Mgmt. program, Harvard U., 1996. Office mgr. Okla. State U., Stillwater, 1967-69; from asst. comptr. to dir. univ. pers. svcs. Ctrl. State U., 1969-80, from asst. v.p. adminstrn. to v.p. adminstrn., 1980-87; interim pres. Southeastern Okla. State U., Durant, 1987, pres., 1987-97; pres. Northeastern State U., Tahlequah, Okla., 1997—; managerial cons. various municipalities; mktg. cons. State of Okla.; arbitrator Met. Fraternal Order of Police; bd. dirs. Okla. Small Bus. Devel. Ctr., Okla. Acad. State Goals, chmn. S.E. region, 1995. Bd. dirs. Bryan County Econ. Devel. Corp., 1989—, Bryan County United Way, 1988-94; mem. adv. bd. Med. Ctr. Southeastern Okla., 1987-92; bd. dirs. Bryan County Ret. Sr. Vol. Program, 1990-92, Leadership Okla. Class IV, 1991, mem. adv. bd., 1991-95; mem. exec. bd. Boy Scouts Am., 1991; com. mem. Okla. Ctr. for Advancement Sci. and Tech. Long Range Planning Task Force, Most Eminent Scholars and Rsch. Equipment, 1990-91; mem. higher edn. alumni coun. Okla. State Regent for Higher Edn. Tuition Com., mem. budget com., mem. outreach com., mem. quality initiative com., mem. capital com., chmn. legis. affairs com., chmn. acad. affairs com.; mem. adv. coun. Ea. Okla. Schs., 1987—; trustee Southeastern Found., 1990—; past pres. Kickingbird Golf Course Mgmt., Edmond; bd. dirs. Edmond C. of C., 1984; mem. Okla. State Regents for Higher Edn. Coun. of Pres., 1987—, chair, 1994; Chocktaw Nation of Okla. JTPA Adv. Coun., 1987—; mem. Okla. Regional Pres.' Coun., 1987—, chair, 1994; vice chmn. Diamond Jubilee Commn., Edmond; mem. found. bd. trustees Ctrl. State U., Edmond; mem. adv. com. Durant Airport. With USNG, 1962-70. Named One of Outstanding Young Men of Am., Edmond Jaycees, 1971, 74, 79;

recipient Presdl. Leadership award Nat. U.S. Jaycee Pres., 1971, Presdl. Leadership, Achievement and Honor awards Nat. Jaycees, 1972, Nat. Presdl. award of Honor Nat. Coll. and Univ. Pers. Assn., 1973, Disting. Svc. award City of Edmond, 1974, Dwight F. Whelan Meml. award for Outstanding Leadership, Edmond, 1972, Disting. Former Student award U. Ctrl. Okla., 1996; named to Cushing Alumni Hall of Fame, 1988, recipient Nat. Order Omega (charter hon. mem), 1991. Mem. Okla. Assn. Coll. and Univ. Pers. Adminstrs. (founder, bd. dirs., chmn.), Nat. Coll. and Univ. Pers. Assn., Nat. Coll. and Univ. Bus. Officers Assn., Okla. Assn. Affirmative Action (co-founder, pres., bd. dirs.), Okla. City Pers. Assn. , Am. Assn. State Colls. and Univs., Okla. Assn. Coll. and Univ. Bus. Officers (bd. dirs., pres.), Acad. Cert. Adminstrv. Mgrs., Okla. Small Bus. Devel. Ctr. (bd. dirs. 1987—), Industry Edni. Coun. McCurtain County, Okla. Acad. for State Goals (bd. dirs. 1992—, vice chair S.E. region 1995), Okla. Advs. for Arts and Humanities (mem. steering com. 1995), Durant C. of C. (past pres., bd. dirs.), Okla. State C. of C. (bd. dirs. 1991—), Blue Key, Rotary. Democrat. Presbyterian. Lodge: Rotary (sec. Edmond club 1986-87). Avocation: golf. Office: Southeastern Okla State U Office of Pres Durant OK 74701

WILLIAMS, LARRY ROSS, surgeon; b. Murphysboro, Ill., July 20, 1952; s. Laurel Ross and Mary Elizabeth (Blankinship) W.; m. Sarah Elizabeth Hecht, June 17, 1978; children: Gretchen Elizabeth, Noelle Louisa. BS, So. Ill. U., 1974; MD, U. Ill., Chgo., 1978, MS, 1982. Resident in surgery U. Ill., Chgo., 1978-83, fellow in surgery, 1983-84; fellow in vascular surgery Northwestern U., Chgo., 1984-85; asst. prof. U. South Fla., Tampa, 1985-92, clin. asst. prof., 1992—; chief vascular surgery Bay Pines VA Hosp., St. Petersburg, Fla., 1985-89; pvt. practice St. Anthony's Hosp., St. Petersburg, 1985—, chief of surgery, 1993-95, pres.-elect med. staff, 1993-95, pres. med. staff, 1996—; bd. govs. Physician-Hosp. Orgn., 1994-97. Contbr. articles to profl. jours. Active First United Meth. Ch., St. Petersburg, 1985—, Vinoy Resort, St. Petersburg, 1992—, Polywogs, St. Petersburg, 1989—. Fellow ACS; mem. Internat. Soc. Cardiovascular Surgery, Soc. Non-Invasive Vascular Technology, Assn. for Acad. Surgery, Pinellas County Med. Soc. (bd. govs. 1994-97), Fla. Med. Assn. (splty. soc. rep. 1994-96), Am. Inst. Ultrasound in Medicine, Fla. Assn. Gen. Surgeons, Peripheral Vascular Surg. Assn., Warren Cole Surg. Soc., So. Assn. for Vascular Surgery, Fla. Vascular Soc. (sec. 1991-94, pres. 1994-95), Fla. Surg. Soc., Southeastern Surg. Congress, Acad. Med. Arts and Scis., Frederick A. Coller Surg. Soc., Soc. for Clin. Vascular Surgery, Fla. Assn. Cardiovascular and Pulmonary Rehab., Phi Eta Sigma, Phi Kappa Phi, Phi Beta Kappa. Avocations: family activities, golf, tennis. Office: 1111 7th Ave N Saint Petersburg FL 33705-1348

WILLIAMS, LAWRENCE FLOYD, conservation organization official; b. Eugene, Oreg., Mar. 26, 1937; s. Carroll Parven and Catherene (Dorris) W.; m. Patricia Ann Pride, Feb. 25, 1978. Student, Portland State U. Advt. staff asst. Omark Industries, Portland, Oreg., 1963-67; internat. advt. liaison Hyster Co., Portland, 1968; exec. dir. Oreg. Environ. Coun., Portland, 1969-78; policy analyst pub. land mgmt. White House Coun. on Environ. Quality, Washington, 1978-81; spl. cons. Sierra Club, Portland, 1969; Washington rep. Sierra Club, 1981-85; dir. internat. program Sierra Club, Washington, 1985—; Former mem. dist. adv. bd. Bur. Land Mgmt.; former mem. Adv. Com. on Forest Mgmt. Policy; former cons. Coun. on Econ. Priorities; former mem. acv. com. Bonneville Power Adminstrn.; mgr. N.W. Workshops for Conservation Found. on Implementation Clean Air Act, 1972, Clean Water Act, 1975, U.S. Energy Policy, 1976; former mem. Western Forst Environ.-Industry Policy Discussion Group. Author: (with Raymond Mikesell) International Banks and the Environment, from Growth to Sustainability: An Unfinished Agenda, 1992; mng. editor: Bankrolling Disasters, International Development Banks and the Global Environment, 1986. Past mem. bd. dirs. Inst. for Transp. and Devel. Policy, N.W. Environ. Def. Ctr.; past chmn. Nat. Coalition for Clean Water, Pacific N.W. chpt. Sierra Club; founder, past 1st chmn. Portland Sierra Club; past v.p. Fedn. Western Outdoor Clubs; past pres. Trails Club Oreg.; past assembly pres. Inst. Ecology; organizer, past chmn. Com. for Volcanic Cascades Study, People Against Nerve Gas; organizer Oreg. League Conservation Voters; mem. steering com. Biodiversity Action Network, 1993; mem. adv. bd. Global Forest Policy Project, 1994. With USAF, 1956-70. Recipient Richard L. Neuberger award Oreg. Environ. Coun., 1988. Democrat. Home: 4607 Van Ness St NW Washington DC 20016-5631 Office: Sierra Club 408 C St NE Washington DC 20002-5818

WILLIAMS, LEA EVERARD, history educator; b. Milw., July 25, 1924; s. William Everard and Paula Herndon (Pratt) W.; m. Daisy Shen, Sept. 15, 1949; children—Adrienne Paula Covington, William Herndon. B.A., Cornell U., 1950; M.A., Harvard U., 1952, Ph.D., 1956. With U.S. Fgn. Service, Chungking, China, 1944-45; Am. vice consul U.S. Fgn. Service, Shanghai, 1945-48; with Brown U., 1956—, prof. Asian history, 1969-76, prof. history, 1976-89, prof. history emeritus, 1989—; dir. East Asia Lang. and Area Ctr., 1969-84; vis. prof. history U. Singapore, 1961-63; vis. prof. Asian affairs Fletcher Sch., 1964-65; lectr. Fgn. Svcs. Inst., U.S. Dept. State, staff lectr. spl. expeditions, 1993—. Author: Overseas Chinese Nationalism, 1960, The Future of the Overseas Chinese in Southeast Asia, 1966, Southeast Asia: A History, 1976; editor, transl.: The Origins of the Modern Chinese Movement in Indonesia, 1969. Served with U.S. Army, 1943. Social Sci. Research fellow, 1957; Fulbright-Hays fellow, 1966-67; Am. Council Learned Socs. fellow, 1969; Nat. Sci. Council vis. scholar Taiwan, 1980; Gulbenkian Found. travel grantee, 1980, 82, 85, 89. Mem. The South Seas Soc., Assn. Asian Studies, Royal Asiatic Soc. (Malayan br.), Koninklijk Instiuut voor Taal, Land-en Volkenkunde, Hakluyt Soc., Providence Athenaeum, Phi Beta Kappa. Clubs: Bristol Yacht (R.I.); Catboat Assn., Am. Club (Singapore); Royal Singapore Yacht, U.S. Coast Guard Aux. Home: 73 Transit St Providence RI 02906-1022 Office: Brown U History Dept Providence RI 02912

WILLIAMS, LENA HARDING, English language educator; b. Portsmouth, Va., June 12, 1947; d. Arthur McKinley and Mildred (Smith) Harding; m. Leroy Stephen Williams, July 8, 1966; children: Michael LaMar, Darryl LaVon, Stephen LaSean. AB in English Edn. and Speech, Norfolk State U., 1969; postgrad., U. Va., 1972-73, Norfolk State U., 1987, Old Dominion U., 1973-88; MS in Ednl. Adminstrn., Old Dominion U., 1993. Cert. 7-12 English and speech tchr., mid. sch. and h.s. prin., collegiate profl., Va. English tchr. S.H. Clarke Sch. Portsmouth Schs., 1969-70, English tchr., W.E. Waters Sch., 1970-71, English tchr., Churchland Mid. Sch., 1971-74, English dept. chmn., 1974-86, 88—; fieldtester Va. Standards of Learning Lang. Arts; tchr./trainer Portsmouth Schs., 1986-88, lead mentor tchr., 1990—; presenter SAT prep. workshop, New-Tchr. Insvc., Writing Across the Curriculum, Reading to Learn, Technology in the Classroom. Active Hodges Manor Civic League, Portsmouth, 1985—, PTA; dir. Christian edn., summer camp youth adv., coord. vol. tutorial svc., mem. sr. choir, usher, coord. youth activities, mem. ch. coun., bd. dir. kindegarten, Edna Hyke Corbett Achievement award found.; coord. Multiple Sclerosis Read-a-Thon, Back to Sch. Seminar; community campaign vol. Mother's March, Am. Cancer Soc., Muscular Dystrophy, Am. Heart Assn.; co-sponsor Cavalier Manor Deep Doubles Tennis Tounament. Named State Tchr. of Yr., State Bd. Edn., Richmond, Va., 1992, Outstanding Young Educator, Portsmouth Jaycees, 1978; recipient 25 svc. and honor awards from local orgns. Fellow Hampton Rds Inst. for Advanced Study of Teaching; mem. ASCD, NEA, NAACP, Va. Edn. Assn., Nat. State Tchrs. of Yr. Assn., Va. State Secondary Reading Assn., Va. Congress English Teachers, Va. Assn. Tchrs. of English, Portsmouth Edn. Assn., Portsmouth Reading Coun.,Tidewater Assn. Tchrs. English, Hampton Roads Inst. for the Advanced Study of Teaching, Delta Sigma Theta. Democrat. Avocations: singing, speaking, reading, collecting dolls. Home: 801 Nottingham Rd Portsmouth VA 23701-2118 Office: Churchland Mid Sch 4051 River Shore Rd Portsmouth VA 23703-2001

WILLIAMS, LESLIE PEARCE, history educator; b. Harmon-on Hudson, N.Y., Sept. 8, 1927; s. George and Addie Adelia (Williams) Greenberg; m. Sylvia Irene Alessandrini, Sept. 3, 1949; children: David Rhys, Alison Ruth, Adam Jonathan, Sarah Lucille. BA, Cornell U., 1949, PhD, 1952. Instr. history Yale U., 1952-56; assoc. historian Nat. Found. for Infantile Paralysis, N.Y.C., 1956-57; asst. prof. U. Del., 1956-59; asst. prof. history Cornell U., 1960-62, assoc. prof., 1962-65, prof., 1965-71, John Stambaugh prof. history of sci., 1971-94, prof. emeritus, 1994—, chmn. dept. history, 1969-74, dir. program in history and philosophy sci. and tech., 1984-91. Author: Michael Faraday, A Biography, 1965, The Origins of Field Theory, 1967, Album of Science: The Nineteenth Century, 1978, (with Henry John Steffens) A History of Science in Western Civilization, 3 vols, 1978; editor: The Selected Correspondence of Michael Faraday, 2 vols, 1972, Relativity Theory: Its Origin and Impact on Modern Thought, 1968, (with B. Tierney and D. Kagan) Great Issues in Western Civilization, 2 vols., 1968; cons. editor Italian jour. Physis, Rivista della Storia della Scienza. With USNR, 1945-46. NSF fellow, 1959-60; 1st degree black belt Hayashi-ha Shito-ryu Karate. Mem. History of Sci. Soc., Internat. Acad. History of Sci., French Acad. Scis. (mem. com. Lavoisier), Phi Beta Kappa. Home and Office: 207 Iradell Rd Ithaca NY 14850-9207 Office: Cornell Univ Dept Sci and Tech Studies Ithaca NY 14853

WILLIAMS, LESTER FREDERICK, JR., general surgeon; b. Brockton, Mass., June 28, 1930; s. Lester Frederick Sr. and Frances (Sullivan) W.; m. Sara Jayne Conroy. AB, Brown U., 1952; MD, Boston U., 1956. Diplomate Am. Bd. Surgery. Intern Letterman U.S. Army Hosp., San Francisco, 1956-57; surg. resident Tripler U.S. Army Hosp., Honolulu, 1957-61; surgeon-in-chief U. Hosp., Boston, 1977-84; program dir. Boston U. Affiliated, 1972-84; chmn. div. surgery Boston U., 1972-84; chief of surgery VA Med. Ctr., Nashville, 1985-89; dir. gallstone ctr. Vanderbilt U. Med. Ctr., Nashville, prof. surgery, 1985—; chief of surgery St. Thomas Hosp., Nashville, 1989—; examination cons. Am. Bd. Surgery, 1987—. Editor: Fundamental Approach to Surgical Problems, 1961, Vascular Insufficency of the Bowels, 1970, Vascular Disorders of the Intestinal Tract, 1971, Core Textbook of Surgery, 1972, Self Assessment of Current Knowledge in General Surgery, 1974, Difficult Problems in General Surgery, 1988; contbr. numerous articles to profl. jours. Maj. USAF, 1956-65. USA Rsch. grants, 1965-72, NIH Rsch. grants, 1971-89. Fellow ACS; mem. AMA, Am. Assn. for the Surgery of Trauma, Am. Fedn. for Clin. Rsch., Am. Gastroenterol. Assn., Am. Lithotripsy Soc., Am. Motility Soc., Am. Surg. Assn., Am. Trauma Soc., Assn. for Acad. Minority Physicians, Inc., Assn. Program Dirs. in Surgery, Assn. of VA Surgeons, Boston Surg. Soc., Honolulu Surg. Soc., Collegium Internationale Chirurgiae Digestivae, Internat. Assn. for the Surgery of Trauma and Surg. Intensive Care, Internat. Hepato-Biliary-Pancreas Assn., Soc. Univ. Surgeons, So. Surgical Assn., Societe Internationale de Chirurgi, Soc. for Surgery of Alimentary Tract, New England Surgical Soc., Alpha Omega Alpha. Office: Vanderbilt U Med Ctr Garland and 21st Ave Nashville TN 37232-5729 also: Vanderbilt U Sch Medicine PO Box 380 4220 Harding Rd Nashville TN 37202

WILLIAMS, LINDA BERGENDAHL, information specialist; b. Glen Cove, N.Y., June 1, 1946; d. Eigil and Lilliam Gertrude (Bettine) Bergendahl; children from previous marriage: Heidi, Garth; m. Arthur G. Williams, 1993. BA, L.I. U., 1969; MA, SUNY, Stony Brook, 1984. Asst. curator Nat. Pk. Svc., Mastic, N.Y., 1980-84; office mgr. Coogan, Swanson and Lange, Burlington, Vt., 1985-87; rsch. officer U. Vt., Burlington, Vt., 1987-93; pres. Impact Info., Burlington, 1991—. Founder Brookhaven Hist. Dists., Patchogue, N.Y., 1978, Community Connection Program, Burlington, 1988, Holiday Basket Program, Burlington, 1988. Mem. Soc. Competitive Intelligence Profls., Womens Bus. Owners Network (bd. dirs.), Vt. Cons. Network, New Eng. Devel. Rsch. Assn. Avocations: sailing, skiing, gardening. Office: Impact Information PO Box 1044 Burlington VT 05402-1044

WILLIAMS, LISLE EDWARD, civil and structural engineer; b. Indiana, Pa., Feb. 10, 1945; s. Lisle Edward and Marguerite Lighte (Roadarmel) W.; m. Pamela Jayne Long, Aug. 12, 1972; children: April, Andrew, Amy. Assoc. Degree, Gateway Tech. Inst., Pitts., 1967; Cert., Carnegie-Mellon U., 1970, U. Pitts., 1974, Pa. State U., 1982. Registered profl. engr., Pa.; profl. land surveyor; fallout shelter analysis lic. Numerous managerial and tech. positions dist. 11-0 Pa. Dept. Transp., Pitts., 1964-90; program mgr. transp. HDR Engring., Inc., Pitts., 1991-92; asst. v.p. Parsons Brinckerhoff, Inc., Pitts., 1992-93; dep. dir. ops. Buchart-Horn, Inc., Pitts., 1993—; bd. dirs. TRB Com., Washington, Planning & Design Divsn. ARTBA, Washington; pres. Constrn. Legis. Coun., 1988. Author, editor, editl. bd. newsletter Cross-Sect., 1968-97, Pitts. Profl. Engr., 1974-97; contbr. numerous tech. articles to PE Reporter and Scanner mag. Elder, deacon, chmn. Plum Creek Presbyn. Ch., Pitts., 1972-97; instl. rep. Boy Scouts Am., Troop #77, Pitts., 1980-90; mem. Plum Parent Tchr. Soccer Assn., Plum Area Soccer League, Pitts., 1983-97; mem. Southwestern Pa. Regional Planning Orgn./Met. Planning Orgn. Citizens Adv. Panel, 1996-99, Mon-Fayette Expressway/So. Beltway Projects Alliance Group, 1996—, Pa. Hwy. Info. Assn., 1990—. Named Pitts. Outstanding Young Civil Engr. of Yr., ASCE, 1983; recipient Svc. to People award ASCE, 1988, citation Pa. Senate, 1991, Pa. House of Reps., 1991; Resolution in his honor, City of Pitts., 1995, Proclamation, County of Allegheny, 1995. Mem. Am. Soc. Hwy. Engrs. (life, nat. bd. dirs. 1964—, pres. 1983-84, testimonial 1987, Pres.'s award 1983, 84, Disting. Svc. award 1984), Pa. Soc. Profl. Engrs. (v.p., pres.-elect, pres., bd. dirs. 1970—, Young Engr. of Yr. award 1980, L.W. Hornfeck award 1984, President's Four Star award, 1986, Past Pres.'s plaque 1997), Pa. Engring. Found. (trustee 1991—), Internat. Bridge Conf. (gen. chmn. 1992-93, chmn. 1993); chmn. CEC/Pa. Trans. subcom. 1992—, Greater Pitts. C. of C., 1992-97, Western Pa. Conservancy, 1992-97. Democrat. Presbyterian. Home: 15 Plumcrest Dr Pittsburgh PA 15239-1503 Office: Buchart Horn Inc Conestoga Bldg 7 Wood St 2d Fl Pittsburgh PA 15222-1920

WILLIAMS, LOUIS CLAIR, JR., public relations executive; b. Huntington, Ind., Nov. 7, 1940; s. Louis Clair and Marian Eileen (Bowers) W.; children—Terri Lynn, L. Bradley, Lisa C.; m. Mary Clare Moster. B.A., Eastern Mich. U., 1963. Copywriter, Rochester (N.Y.) Gas and Electric Co., 1963-65, editor RG&E News, 1965-66; employee info. specialist Gen. Ry. Signal Co., Rochester, 1966-67, supr. employment and employee rels., 1967-69; supr. pub. rels. Heublein, Inc., Hartford, Conn., 1969-70; dir. corp. communications Jewel Cos., Inc., Chgo., 1970-71; account exec. Ruder & Finn of Mid-Am., Chgo., 1971-73, v.p., 1973-76, sr. v.p., 1976-78; cons. Towers, Perrin, Forster & Crosby, Los Angeles, 1978-79; exec. v.p., gen. mgr. Harshe-Rotman & Druck, Inc., Chgo., 1979, pres. midwest region, 1979-80; v.p. Hill & Knowlton, Inc., Chgo., 1980-81, sr. v.p., 1981-83; pres. Savlin Williams Assocs., Evanston, Ill., 1983-85, L.C. Williams & Assocs., Chgo., 1985—. Recipient Clarion award Women in Communications, 1978, award of Excellence, Internat. Coun. Indsl. Editors, 1969, Bronze Oscar-of-Ind., Fin. World, 1974. Mem. Internat. Assn. Bus. Communicators (pres. 1979-80), Chgo. Assn. Bus. Communicators (pres.), Publicity Club Chgo., Pub. Rels. Soc. Am.

WILLIAMS, LOUIS STANTON, glass and chemical manufacturing executive; b. Honolulu, Oct. 7, 1919; s. Urban and Amelia (Olson) W.; m. Dorothy Webster Reed, June 12, 1943; children: Eric Reed, Timothy Howell, Steven Neil, Deborah Reed Sawin. A.B., Amherst Coll., 1941, LL.D., 1981; M.B.A., Harvard U., 1943; D.H.L., Thiel Coll., 1985. With PPG Industries (formerly Pitts. Plate Glass Co.), 1946-84, various acctg. positions, 1946-56, became controller, 1956, v.p. finance, 1963-75, dir., 1975-90, exec. v.p., 1975-76, vice chmn., 1976-78, chmn., chief exec. officer, 1979-84; chmn. Fed. Home Loan Bank, Pitts., 1971-73; bd. dirs. Duplate Can., 1976-84, Rubbermaid Inc., 1977-90, Dravo Corp., 1978-91, Prudential Ins. Co. Am., 1981-89, Mellon Bank Corp, 1981-92, Texaco Inc., 1988-92. Trustee Family and Children's Service, Pitts., 1955-61; bd. dirs. YMCA, Pitts., 1959-93, pres., 1975-77, mem. YMCA nat. bd., 1973-88, chmn., 1983-85; trustee YMCA Retirement Fund, 1989-94; pres. exec. com. Allegheny Conf. on Community Devel., 1982-83, chmn., 1983-85; bd. dirs. Pa. Economy League, 1978-83, Community Chest Allegheny County, 1961-67, Pitts. Symphony Soc., 1978-90; chmn. United Way Campaign of Southwestern Pa., 1981; bd. dirs. United Way of Allegheny County, 1978—, pres., 1984-86; trustee St. Margaret's Meml. Hosp., Pitts., 1969-83, Carnegie-Mellon U., 1978-95, Carnegie Inst., 1977-95, Com. Econ. Devel., 1981-84, Tax Found., 1980-84, Pitts. Cultural Trust, 1984-93. Lt. USNR, 1943-46. Mem. Financial Execs. Inst. (pres. Pitts. 1965-66, nat. dir. 1968-73, nat. v.p. 1972-73), Bus. Roundtable (Policy Com. 1982-84), Duquesne Club, Fox Chapel Golf Club (Pitts.), Rolling Rock Club (Ligonier, Pa.), Iron City Fishing Club (Can.), John's Island Club, Bent Pine Golf Club (Fla.), Phi Beta Kappa. Presbyn. Home: 5 The Trillium Pittsburgh PA 15238-1928 Office: PPG Industries 1 Ppg Pl Pittsburgh PA 15272-0001

WILLIAMS, LOVIE JEAN, elementary education educator; b. Kinston, N.C., Aug. 28; d. Robert Lee and Effie Mae (Hardy) W. BS, Mill. Coll. Edn., N.Y.C., 1973; MA, Columbia U., 1979, postgrad. Cert. tchr., N.Y. Instr. math. Coll. of New Rochelle, Bronx, N.Y.; tchr., asst. prin., prin. Christ Crusader Acad., N.Y.C.; elem. tchr. math. and sci. N.Y.C. Bd. Edn., Bklyn. Recipient Excellence in Teaching award, Rookie Tchr. award N.Y.C. Bd. Edn. Mem. ASCD, Elem. Sch. Sci. Assn., Math. Edn. through Mid. Grades, Delta Sigma Theta. Office: John Peter Zenger Elem Sch 502 Morris Ave Bronx NY 10451-5549

WILLIAMS, LOWELL CRAIG, lawyer, employee relations executive; b. Tehachapi, Calif., Dec. 3, 1947; s. Lyndon Williams and Gertrude (White) Sievert; m. Marsha Mendelssohn; children: John S., Jeffrey A. Bescheinigungsgeschichte, Georg August U., Germany, 1968; BA, U. Calif., Santa Barbara, 1969; JD, Columbia U., 1972. Bar: N.Y. 1973, U.S. Ct. Appeals (2nd cir.) 1974, U.S. Supreme Ct. 1974. Assoc. Sullivan & Cromwell, N.Y.C., 1972-75; sr. v.p. Elf Aquitaine, Inc., N.Y.C., 1976-95; v.p. Compagnie des Machines Bull, N.Y.C., 1995—. Pres. emeritus Scarsdale Synagogue. Mem. Internat. Bar Assn., German Law Assn. (dir.). Home: 37 Paddington Rd Scarsdale NY 10583-2321 Office: Bull Info Sys 1211 Avenue Of The Americas New York NY 10036-8701

WILLIAMS, LUTHER STEWARD, science foundation administrator; b. Sawyerville, Ala., Aug. 19, 1940; s. Roosevelt and Mattie B. (Wallace) W.; m. Constance Marie Marion, Aug. 23, 1963; children: Mark Steward, Monique Marie. BA magna cum laude, Miles Coll., 1961; MS, Atlanta U., 1963; PhD, Purdue U., 1968, DSc (hon.), 1987; DSc (hon.), U. Louisville, 1992, Capitol Coll., 1996, Bowie State U., 1996. NSF lab. asst. Spelman Coll., 1961-62; NSF lab. asst. Atlanta U., 1962-63, instr. biology, faculty rsch. grantee, 1963-64, asst. prof. biology, 1969-70, prof. biology, 1984-87, pres., 1984-87; grad. tchg. asst. Purdue U., West Lafayette, Ind., 1964-65, grad. rsch. asst., 1965-66, asst. prof. biology, 1970-73, assoc. prof., 1973-79, prof., 1979-80, NIH Career Devel. awardee, 1971-75, asst. provost, 1976-80; dean Grad. Sch., prof. biology Washington U., St. Louis, 1980-83; v.p. acad. affairs, dean Grad. Sch. U. Colo., Boulder, 1983-84; Am. Cancer Soc. postdoctoral fellow SUNY-Stony Brook, 1968-69; assoc. prof. biology MIT, 1973-74; spl. asst. to dir. Nat. Inst. Gen. Med. Scis., NIH, Bethesda, Md., 1987-88; dep. dir. Nat. Inst. Gen. Med. Scis. NIH, Bethesda, 1988-89; sr. sci. advisor to dir. NSF, Washington, 1989-90, asst. dir. for edn. and human resources, 1990—; chmn. rev. com. MARC Program, Nat. Inst. Gen. Med. Scis., NIH, 1972-76; grant reviewer NIH, 1971-73, 76, NSF, 1973, 76-80, Med. Research Council of N.Z., 1976; mem. life scis. sreening com. recombinant DNA adv. com. HEW, 1979-81; mem. nat. adv. gen. med. sci. council NIH, 1980-85; mem. adv. com. Office Tech. Assessment, Washington, 1984-87; chmn. fellowship adv. com. NRC Ford Found., 1984-85; mem.-at-large Grad. Record Exam. Bd., 1981-85, chmn. minority grad. edn. com., 1983-85; mem. health, safety and environ. affairs. com. Nat. Labs., U. Calif., 1981-87; mem. adv. panel Office Tech. Assessment, U.S. Congress, 1985-86; mem. fed. task force on women, minorities and the handicapped in sci. and tech., 1987-91; mem. adv. panel to dir. sci. and tech. ctrs. devel. NSF, 1987-88; mem. nat. adv. com. White House Initiative on Historically Black Colls. and Univs. on Sci. and Tech., 1986-89; numerous other adv. bds. and coms. Contbr. sci. articles to profl. jours. Vice chmn. bd. advisors Atlanta Neighborhood Justice Ctr., 1984-87; bd. dirs. Met. Atlanta United Way, 1986-87, Butler St. YMCA, Atlanta, 1985-87; trustee Atlanta Zool. Assn., 1985-87, Miles Coll., 1984-87, Atlanta U., 1984-87, 90-96; mem. nominating com. Dana Found. NIH predoctoral fellow Purdue U., 1966-68. Fellow AAAS, Am. Acad. Microbiology; mem. Am. Soc. Microbiology, Am. Chem. Soc., Am. Soc. Biol. Chemists (mem. ednl. affairs com. 1979-82, com. on equal opportunities for minorities 1972-84), AAAS, N.Y. Acad. Scis. Home: 11608 Split Rail Ct Rockville MD 20852-4423 Office: NSF Education & Human Resources 4201 Wilson Blvd Arlington VA 22230-0001

WILLIAMS, MARGARET, federal official. BA, Trinity Coll.; MA in Comm., U. Pa. Asst. to Pres., chief of staff to First Lady The White House, Washington, 1993—. Office: Office of the First Lady The White House 1600 Pennsylvania Ave NW Washington DC 20500-0005*

WILLIAMS, MARGARET LU WERTHA HIETT, nurse; b. Midland, Tex., Aug. 30, 1938; d. Cotter Craven and Mollie Jo (Tarter) Hiett; m. James Troy Lary, Nov. 16, 1960 (div. Jan. 1963); 1 child, James Cotter; m. Tuck Williams, Aug. 11, 1985. BS, Tex. Woman's U., 1960; MA, Tchrs. Coll., N.Y.C., 1964, EdM, 1974, doctoral studies, 1981; postgrad., U. Tex., 1991-92, U. Wis.; cert. completion, U. Wis., Scotland. Cert. clin. nurse specialist, advanced practice nurse; cert. psychiat./mental health nurse, nursing continuing edn. and staff devel. Nurse Midland Meml. Hosp., 1960-63; instr. Odessa (Tex.) Coll., 1963-67; dir. ADNP Laredo (Tex.) Jr. Coll., 1967-70; asst. prof. Pan Am. U., Edinburgh, Tex., 1970-72; rsch. asst. Tchrs. Coll., 1973-74; nursing practitioner St. Luke's Hosp., N.Y.C., 1975-79; sgt. Burns Security, Midland, 1979-81; with Area Builders, Odessa, 1981-83; field supr. We Care Home Health Agy., Midland, 1983-87; clin. educator, supr. Glenwood, A Psychiat. Hosp., Midland, 1987-92; dir. nursing Charter Healthcare Systems, Corpus Christi, Tex., 1992-93; RN III Brown Sch., San Marcos, Tex., 1993—; owner MTW Nursing Consultation, Lockhart, Tex., 1996—, Margaret Hiett Williams RN, CNS, Lockhart, Tex., 1996—; co-owner, operator MTW Med. Legal Cons.; adj. prof. Pace U., 1974-75, S.W. Tex. State U., 1995. Mem. Gov. Richards' Exec. Leadership Coun., 1991-95, re-election steering com., 1994. Recipient Isabelle Hampton-Robb award Nat. League for Nursing, 1976, Achievement award Community Leaders of Am., 1989, Ladies 1st of Midland, 1974. Mem. NAFE, ANA, Tex. Nurses Assn. (pres. dist. 21 1962-65, dist. 32 1970-72), Am. Psychiat. Nurses Assn., Parkland Meml. Hosp. Nurses Alumnae Assn., Tex. Women's U. Alumnae Assn., Midland H.S. Alumni, Bus. and Profl. Women's Club, Mensa, Lockhart Breakfast Lions Club. Democrat. Avocations: songwriting, public speaking, singing, travel. Office: PO Box 324 Lockhart TX 78644-0324

WILLIAMS, MARIE CLONEY, rehabilitation nurse administrator, business owner; b. Abilene, Tex., Oct. 20, 1944; d. Morton Earl and Emily Marie (Stepanek) Phillips; m. Richard Morgan Cloney, Aug. 25, 1965 (div. Nov., 1989); children: Kellen Frances, Shannon Cooper.; m. Clifford John Williams, Jr., May 17, 1992. BSN, U. N.C., 1966, MPH, 1967. RN, Pa.; cert. nurse adminstr. Rsch. assoc. U. N.C. Sch. of Pub. Health, Chapel Hill, N.C., 1967-68; head nurse Comty. Dr. Nursing Ctr., Manhasset, N.Y., 1968; staff nurse Hackettstown (N.J.), 1973-74; dir. nursing Welkind Neurol. Hosp., Chester, N.J., 1974-78; dir. nursing svcs. Healthbank Rehab. Ctr., Columbia, Pa., 1978-81; adminstr. for nursing svcs. Pa. State U.-Elizabethtown (Pa.) Rehab., 1981-83; assoc. adminstr. nursing svcs. Rehab. Hosp. York, Pa., 1983-85; adminstr., CEO Rehab. Hosp. York, 1985-88; v.p. ops. Rehab. Systems Co., Camp Hill, Pa., 1988-93; owner, ptnr. Interactive Health Co., Mechanicsburg, Pa., 1993—; mem. profl. adv. com. VNA of York, Pa., 1985-88; asst. sec., bd. dirs. York County Health Corp., York, 1986-88; bd. dirs. Mt. View Regional Rehab. Hosp., Morgantown, W. Va., 1990-92; owner, mgr., cons. Marie Williams Assocs., Mechanicsburg, Pa., 1993—. Contbr. articles to profl. jours. Com. mem. Country and Town Bapt. Ch., Mechanicsburg, Pa., 1989—. Mem. Assn. Rehab. Nurses, Ctrl. Pa. Tech. Coun., Am. Electronics Assn., Nat. Disting. Svc. Registry: Med. Rehab., Sigma Theta Tau, Delta Omicron. Republican. Avocations: tennis, piano. Home: 26 Cumberland Estates Dr Mechanicsburg PA 17055-1719 Office: Interactive Health Co 2415-A Old Gettysburg Rd Camp Hill PA 17011

WILLIAMS, MARK H., marketing communications agency executive; b. Omaha, Apr. 30, 1959; s. Perry T. and Donna M. (Hodges) W. BA in Comm. and Bus., Loyola U., Chgo., 1981. Account mgmt. Bozell, Jacobs, Kenyon & Eckhardt, Omaha, 1981-88, v.p., 1988—; sr. v.p. account mgmt. and devel. Bozell Worldwide, Chgo., 1987—; speaker Creighton U., U. Nebr., Harvard U., Northwestern U., numerous confs. and seminars. Contbr. articles to profl. jours. Mem. Am. Advt. Fedn., and numerous trade assns. Home: 910 Lake Shore Dr Chicago IL 60611-1540 Office: Bozell Worldwide Inc 625 N Michigan Ave Chicago IL 60611

WILLIAMS, MARSHA KAY, data processing executive; b. Norman, Okla., Oct. 26, 1963; d. Charles Michael and Marilyn Louise (Bauman) Williams; m. Dale Lee Carabetta, Dec. 13, 1981. BS in Computer Mgmt. & Sci., Metro. State Coll., Denver, 1996. Data processing supr. Rose Mfg. Co., Englewood, Colo., 1981-84, Mile High Equip. Co., Denver, 1984-88; mgr. info. tech. Ohmeda Monitoring Sys., Louisville, Colo., 1988—. Mem. info. tech. adv. bd. Warren Tech. Sch., 1994—, chair 1996—. Mem. Bus. and Profl. Women's Assn. (Young Careerist 1991), Data Processing Mgmt. Assn. Home: 4700 Yates Ct Broomfield CO 80020 Office: Ohmeda Monitoring Systems 1315 W Century Dr Louisville CO 80027-9560

WILLIAMS, MARSHALL HENRY, JR., physician, educator; b. New Haven, July 15, 1924; s. Marshall Henry and Henrietta (English) W.; m. Mary Butler, Aug. 27, 1948; children: Stuart, Patricia, Marshall, Frances, Richard. Grad., Pomfret Sch., 1942; B.S., Yale, 1945, M.D., 1947. Diplomate Nat. Bd. Med. Examiners, Am. Bd. Internal Medicine. Intern Presbyn. Hosp., N.Y.C., 1947-48; asst. resident medicine Presbyn. Hosp., 1948-49; asst. resident medicine New Haven Hosp., 1949-50, asst. in medicine, 1950; trainee Nat. Heart Inst., 1950; practice medicine, specializing in internal medicine Bronx, N.Y.; chief respiratory sect., dept. cardiorespiratory diseases Army Med. Service Grad. Sch., Walter Reed Army Med. Center, 1953-55; dir. cardiorespiratory lab. Grasslands Hosp., Valhalla, N.Y., 1955-59; dir. chest svc. Bronx Mcpl. Hosp. Ctr., 1959-94; vis. asst. prof. physiology Albert Einstein Coll. Medicine, Bronx, 1955-59, assoc. prof. medicine and physiology, 1959-66, prof. medicine, 1966-95, prof. emeritus, 1995—; dir. pulmonary div. Montefiore Med. Ctr., Albert Einstein Coll. Medicine, 1981-94. Author: Clinical Applications of Cardiopulmonary Physiology, 1960, Essentials of Pulmonary Medicine, 1982, Consultation in Chest Medicine, 1985; contbr. articles to profl. jours. Served from 1st lt. to capt. U.S. Army, 1950-52. Mem. Am. Physiol. Soc., AAAS, Am. Heart Assn., Westchester Heart Assn (past pres.), Am. Thoracic Soc., Am. Fedn. Clin. Research, N.Y. Acad. Sci., N.Y. Trudeau Soc. (past pres.), Am. Soc. Clin. Investigation, Soc. Urban Physicians (past pres.), N.Y. Tb. and Health Assn. (past dir.), Alpha Omega Alpha. Home: 103 Fox Meadow Rd Scarsdale NY 10583-2301 Office: Albert Einstein Coll Medicine Bronx NY 10461

WILLIAMS, MARTHA ETHELYN, information science educator; b. Chgo., Sept. 21, 1934; d. Harold Milton and Alice Rosemond (Fox) W. B.A., Barat Coll., 1955; M.A., Loyola U., 1957. With IIT Rsch.Inst., Chgo., 1957-72, mgr. info. scis., 1962-72, mgr. computer search ctr., 1968-72; adj. assoc. prof. sci. info. Ill. Inst. Tech., Chgo., 1965-73, lectr. chemistry dept., 1968-70, rsch. prof. info. sci., coordinated sci. lab. Coll. engring.; also dir. info. retrieval research lab. U. Ill., Urbana, 1972—, prof. info. sci. grad. sch. of libr. info. sci., 1974—, affiliate, computer sci. dept., 1979—; chmn. large data base conf. Nat. Acad. Sci./NRC, 1974, mem. ad hoc panel on info. storage and retrieval, 1977, numerical data adv. bd., 1979-82, computer sci. and tech. bd., nat. rsch. network rev. com., 1987-88, chmn. utility sub-com., 1987-88; mem. task force on sci. info. activities NSF, 1977; U.S. rep. review com. for project on broad system of ordering, UNESCO, Hague, Netherlands, 1974; vice chmn. Gordon Rshc. Conf. on Sci. Info. Problems in Rsch., 1978, chmn., 1980; mem. panel on intellectual property rights in age of electronics and info. U.S. Congress, Office of Tech. Assessment; program chmn. Nat. Online Meeting, 1980—; cons. to numerous cos., govt. agys. and rsch. founds.; invited lectr. Commn. European Communities, Industrial R&D adv. com., Brussels, 1992. Editor in chief Computer-Readable Databases Directory and Data Sourcebook, 1976-89, founding editor, 1989-92; editor Ann. Rev. Info. Sci. and Tech., 1976—, Online Rev., 1979-92, Online and CDROM Rev., 1993—, procs. nat. online meeting, 1981—; contbg. editor column on databases to Bull. Am. Soc. Info. Sci., 1974-78; mem. editorial adv. bd. Database, 1978-88; mem. editorial bd. Info. Processing and Mgmt., 1982-89, The Reference Libr.; contbr. more than 200 articles to profl. jours. Trustee Engirng. Info., Inc., 1974-87, bd. dirs., 1976-91, chmn. bd. dirs., 1982-91, v.p., 1978-79, pres., 1980-81; regent Nat. Libr. Medicine, 1978-82, chmn. bd. regents, 1981; mem. task force on sci. info. activities NSF, 1977-78; mem. nat. adv. com. ACCESS ERIC, 1989-91. Recipient best paper of year award H. W. Wilson Co., 1975; NSF travel grantee Luxembourg, 1972; NSF travel grantee Honolulu, 1973; NSF travel grantee Tokyo, 1973; NSF travel grantee Mexico City, 1975; NSF travel grantee Scotland, 1976. Fellow AAAS (computers, info. and comm. mem.-at-large 1978-81, nominating com. 1983, 85), Inst. Info. Sci. (hon.); mem. NAS (joint com. with NRC on chem. info. 1971-73), Am. Chem. Soc., Am. Soc. Info. Sci. (councilor 1971-72, 87-89, chmn. networks com. 1973-74, spl. interest group of SDI 1974-75, pres.-elect 1986-87, pres. 1987-88, past pres., mem. planning com. 1988-89, publs. com. 1974—, chmn. 1989, mem. nominations com. 1989, chmn. budget and fin. com. 1987-89, award of merit 1984, Pioneer Info. Sci. award 1987, Watson Davis award 1995), Assn. for Computing Machinery (pub. bd. 1972-76), Assn. Sci. Info. Dissemination Ctrs. (v.p. 1971-73, pres. 1975-77), Internat. Fedn. for Documentation (U.S. nat. com.). Home: 2134 Sandra Ln Monticello IL 61856-8036 Office: U Ill 1308 W Main St Urbana IL 61801-2307

WILLIAMS, MARTHA SPRING, psychologist; b. Dallas, Oct. 5, 1951; d. Thomas Ayers and Emma Martha (Felmet) Spring; m. James Walter Williams, June 30, 1979; children: Dane Ayers, Jake Austin. BA, East Tex. State U., 1972, MEd, 1974, EdD, 1978. Cert. and lic. psychologist, Tex.; lic. profl. counselor, marriage and family therapist. Tchr. Dallas Ind. Sch.; grad. asst. to dean Coll. Edn. East Tex. State U., 1975-77; intern Terrell State Hosp. Outreach Clinic and Hunt County Clinic, Greenville, Tex., 1975-76, Univ. Counseling Ctr., East Tex. State U., 1976-77; learning dir. Man and His Environ. Program, 1978-85; pvt. practice psychology Dallas, 1981—; adolescent group therapist in-patient psychiat. facility, 1986-91; mem. staff Baylor/Richardson (Tex.) Med. Ctr., clin. dir. allied mental health profls., 1992-94; v.p. for provider rels. Advanced Behavioral Health Care Sys., Inc., 1995—; mem. staff Green Oaks, St. Paul, Seay Behavioral Hosps. Author: (with others) The Role Innovative Woman and Her Positive Impact on Family Functioning, 1981, Women and Intimacy, 1982, Permenstral Syndrome: A Family Affair, 1984, The Expanding Horizons of Traditional Private Pracitce: High Tech High/Touch, 1986, Adolescent Suicide: Consequences of an Anti-Child Society, 1986, Therapist as a Partner, 1987. Nat. del. Dem. Conv., San Francisco, 1984; Dem. county chair Kaufman County, 1993—; mem. state Dem. Exec. Com. 1993—. Mem. APA, Am. Assn. Marriage and Family Therapists, Am. Soc. Clin. Hypnosis. Lutheran. Avocations: snow skiing, travel, politics, tap dancing. Home: PO Box 1119 Terrell TX 75160-1119 Office: Ste 825 4835 Lyndon B Johnson Fwy Dallas TX 75244-6003 *In this increasingly complex, mobile, and hurried world, it is vital that people seek out and nurture healthy relationships to maintain a sense of connection which in times past flowed more naturally from extended family and communities.*

WILLIAMS, MARY ELEANOR NICOLE, writer; b. Atlanta, May 14, 1938; d. Edward King Merrell and Bernice I. (Pitts) Smith; m. Charlie Lloyd Williams, July 25, 1993 (dec. June 1997); children: Mary Palmer, Susan Gober, Traci Cox. Student, Fla. Jr. Coll., 1974. Lic. real estate broker, Fla. Editor, writer, former owner Southwestern Advt. and Pub., Carrollton, Ga., 1991-94; freelance writer children's stories, 1992—. Author, editor: West Georgia Area Guide, 1991-93. Mem. Carroll County C. of C. Avocations: writing, music, travel, walking, art. Home: 103 Ferndale Rd Carrollton GA 30117-4312

WILLIAMS, MARY ELIZABETH, elementary school educator; b. Gary, Ind., Nov. 14, 1943; d. Morris O. and Mary C. (Hall) Douglas; m. Timothy Williams Jr., July 30, 1966; children: Donna M., Brian T., Derrick A. BS, Purdue U., 1965; MS, Ind. U., Gary, 1973, reading endorsement, 1990, lic. adminstr., 1994. Tchr. Hammond (Ind.) Schs., 1965-66, Gary Cmty. Sch., 1966—. Author: Building Public Confidence Through Communication, 1983. Deaconess, Sunday sch. tchr. St. John Bapt. Ch., Gary, 1967—; founder, coord. Boys and Girls Club, 1994-97. Recipient Outstanding Svc. award Kappa Delta Pi, 1991, Svc. award Nobel Sch. PTA, 1993, Adult Vol. Literacy award Gary Pub. Libr., 1991, Women of Distinction award YWCA, 1995. Mem. Am. Fedn. Tchrs., Gary Reading Coun. (sec. 1993, v.p. 1994—, pres. 1995), Ind. State Reading Assn. (mem. family involvement in reading com. 1993-97), N.W. Ind. Alliance Black Sch. Educators, Alpha Kappa Alpha (sec. 1987-90), Afrocentric Curriculum Cadre, Phi Delta Kappa (v.p. Krinon Club 1991). Democrat. Avocations: reading, sewing, cooking, photography, gardening. Home: 8535 Lakewood Ave Gary IN 46403-2250

WILLIAMS, MARY IRENE, dean; b. Hugo, Okla., June 30, 1944; d. Primer and Hyler B. (Tarkington) Jackson; m. Lee A. Williams (div. June 1981); 1 child, Monica Ariane. BS in Bus. Edn., Langston U., 1967; MS in Bus., Emporia (Kans.) State U., 1973; EdS, U. Nev., Las Vegas, 1977; D of Bus. Adminstrn. in Internat. Bus., U.S. Internat. U., 1992. Instr. Spokane (Wash.) C.C., 1967-70; tchr. bus. Topeka Pub. Schs., 1970-73; prof. C.C. So. Nev., Las Vegas, 1973—, assoc. dean of bus., 1978-93, dean acad. support svcs., 1993-95; prof. bus. adminstrn. Langston U., Tulsa, 1993—; asst. to assoc. v.p., asst. coord. bus., prof. bus. admin. Rogers U., Tulsa, 1996—; asst. to assoc. v.p., asst. coord. bus., adj. prof. So. Nazarene U., 1996-97; adj. prof. Tulsa Jr. Coll., 1997. Named Educator of Yr. Nucleus Plaza Assn., 1985, New Visions, Inc., 1986. Mem. AAUW, Internat. Assn. Bus. Communicators, Nat. Bus. Edn. Assn. Avocations: exercising, studying languages, reading. Office: CC So Nev 3200 E Cheyenne Ave North Las Vegas NV 89030-4228

WILLIAMS, MARY LEE, elementary school educator; b. Hearne, Tex., Feb. 24, 1950; d. William Penn and Joanna (Wiley) Robinson; m. James Curtis Williams, July 22, 1972; children: Uhura Michelle, James Curtis II, Charles Istan. BS, Bishop Coll., Dallas, 1972; MS, Stephen F. Austin State U., 1979. Tchr. Rosemont Sch., Dallas, 1973-75; tchr. Blackshear Sch., Hearne, Tex., 1977-93, asst. prin., 1993-94, tchr., TAAS coord. alternative acad. edn., 1994—, summer sch. program adminstr./tchr., 1996. Mem. NAACP, NEA, Tex. tchrs. Assn., Robertson County Tchrs. Assn. (pres. 1988-92), Order Ea. Star (worthy matron), Chums Club (pres. 1994—), Phi Delta Kappa. Democrat. Baptist. Avocations: reading, gardening, fishing. Home: Box 715 700 W Gregg Calvert TX 77837-0715 Office: Blackshear Elementary School 1401 Blackshear Dr Hearne TX 77859-2483

WILLIAMS, MARY PEARL, judge, lawyer; b. Brownsville, Tex., Jan. 12, 1928; d. Marvin Redman and Theo Mae (Kethley) Hall; m. Jerre Stockton Williams, May 28, 1950; children—Jerre Stockton, Shelley Hall, Stephanie Kethley. B.A., U. Tex., 1948, J.D., 1949. Bar: Tex. 1949, U.S. Supreme Ct. 1955, U.S. Dist. Ct. (we. dist.) Tex., 1987. Asst. atty. gen. State of Tex. Austin, 1949-50, relief judge Municipal Ct., summer 1964; asst. instr. dept. govt. U. Tex., Austin, 1966-67; atty. Office of Emergency Preparedness, Exec. Office of Pres., Washington, 1968-70; labor arbitrator, mem. arbitration panel Am. Arbitration Assn., 1972-73; judge County Ct. at Law 2, Travis County, Tex., 1973-80, 53d Judicial Dist. Ct., 1981—; cons. Dept. HEW, 1966-67. Mem. adv. com. Juvenile Bd. of Travis County, 1964-67; trustee United Way, 1974-78. Named Outstanding Woman, Austin Am.-Statesman, 1974, Austin Citizen, 1978; named Woman of Yr., Austin Dist. Bus. and Profl. Women, 1977; elected to Austin H.S. Hall of Fame, 1996. Fellow ABA, Am. Bar Found.; mem. State Bar Tex., Coll. State Bar Tex., Travis County Bar Assn., Am. Law Inst., Am. Judicature Soc., Inst. Jud. Adminstrn., Jr. League Austin, Kappa Alpha Theta, Delta Kappa Gamma (hon.). Democrat. Methodist. Office: Travis County Courthouse PO Box 1748 Austin TX 78767-1748

WILLIAMS, MATT (MATTHEW DERRICK WILLIAMS), professional baseball player; b. Bishop, Calif., Nov. 28, 1965. Student, U. Nev., Las Vegas. With San Francisco Giants, 1987-96, Cleveland Indians, 1997—; player Nat. League All-Star Team, 1990, 94. Recipient Gold Glove award, 1991, 93, 94, Silver Slugger award, 1990, 93-94; named to Sporting News Nat. League All-Star team, 1990, 93-94, Coll. All-Am. team Sporting News, 1986; Nat. League RBI Leader, 1990. Office: Cleveland Indians 2401 Ontario St Cleveland OH 44115*

WILLIAMS, MATTIE PEARL, accounting educator; b. Shreveport, La., June 22, 1951; d. Robert Lee and Janie Ellen (Culpepper) Williams. BS, Grambling (La.) State U., 1973; MBA, U. Tampa, 1983; postgrad., La. State U., 1972, So. U., 1972. Fin. clk. for La. Arthritis Found. of La., Inc., New Orleans, 1974; marine ins. asst. Johnson & Higgins of La., Inc., New Orleans, 1975-76; employee rels. asst. Exxon U.S.A. Esso Ea., Houston, 1977—; mktg. asst. Gen. Dynamics Stromberg Carlson, 1978-81; acctg. instr. St Petersburg (Fla.) Jr. Coll., 1983—, instr.-in-chg., 1983-95, faculty governance rep., 1988-90. Founding mem. Tampa Orgn. Black Affairs, 1978-80. Mem. Nat. Black MBA Assn., Nat. Assn. Black Accts., Am. Assn. for Higher Edn., Fla. Assn. C.C. Democrat. Roman Catholic. Avocations: golf, tennis, health fitness. Home: 104 Gardenwood Dr College Park GA 30349

WILLIAMS, MAURICE JACOUTOT, development organization executive; b. New Brunswick, Can., Nov. 13, 1920; s. Alfred Jacoutot and Yvonne (Theberge) W.; m. Betty Jane Bath, Dec. 18, 1943; children: Jon, Peter, Stephen. Student, Northwestern U., 1940-42, U. Manchester, Eng., 1945; M.A., U. Chgo., 1949. Research fellow London Sch. Econs., summer 1948; Dir. U.S. student program U. Fribourg, Switzerland, 1946; prin. examiner Chgo. Civil Service Commn., 1949; economist Office Internat. Trade Policy, Dept. State, Washington, 1950-53; econ. officer Am. embassy, London, 1953-55; chief Econ. Def. Coordination, 1955-58; asst. dir. U.S. Operations Mission to Iran, ICA, 1958-60, dep. dir., 1961-63; dep. dir. USAID/Pakistan, 1963-65, dir., 1965-67; chief program div. Near East-South Asia, 1961; asst. adminstr. Nr. East-South Asia AID/W, 1967-70; dep. adminstr. AID, 1970-74; chmn. Devel. Assistance Com. OECD, Paris, 1974-78; exec. dir. UN World Food Council, 1978-86; sec.-gen., pres. emeritus Soc. Internat. Devel., 1986—; Presdl. coordinator Fgn. Disaster Relief, Bangladesh, Peru, Philippines, Managua, Sahel, 1971-74; chief U.S. del. U.S.-N. Vietnam Joint Econ. Commn., 1974—. Recipient Nat. Civil Service award, 1971, AID Distinguished Honor award, 1974, Rockefeller Pub. Service award, 1974. Club: Cosmos. Address: Overseas Devel Council 1875 Connecticut Ave NW Washington DC 20009-5728 *The principles guiding me have been those of middle-America at mid-century, namely that integrity and concentrated efforts yield their own reward. Implicit are beliefs in democratic values, equity in opportunities for social and economic progress, and the need to build up institutions for their realization. The challenge of our time has been to extend these goals worldwide. They are best pursued in cooperative endeavors through the United Nations. A decent standard of food, health and personal security is possible for all people and nations. Endeavors to these ends have been personally rewarding.*

WILLIAMS, MAX LEA, JR., engineer, educator; b. Aspinwall, Pa., Feb. 22, 1922; s. Max Lea and Marguerite (Scott) W.; m. Melba Cameron, July 26, 1967; children: Gregory S., Christine C. Williams Mann, Richard L. BS in Mech. Engring, Carnegie Inst. Tech., 1942; MS, Calif. Inst. Tech., Aero. Engr. and PhD in Aeronautics, 1950. Registered profl. engr. Calif., La., Pa., Utah. Mem. faculty, successively lectr., asst. prof., assoc. prof., prof. aeronautics Calif. Inst. Tech., 1948-66; dean, prof. engring. U. Utah, 1965-73, disting. prof. engring., 1973; dean, prof. engring. U. Pitts., 1973-85, disting. service prof. engring., 1985-90, disting. svc. prof. engring. emeritus, 1990—, dean emeritus, 1985—; rsch. scholar von Humbolt Found., 1992-94; vis. prof. aero. U. Tex., Austin, 1995—; mem. exec. com. Internat. Congress Fracture, founding editor Internat. Jour. Fracture, 1965-96, editor emeritus, 1997—; Gen. Lew Allen disting. vis. prof. aero. Air Force Inst. Tech., 1985-87; mem. sci. adv. bd. USAF, 1985-89, ad hoc mem., 1989-94; sci. advisor Acquisition Logistic Ctr. USAF, 1987-88; sci. dir. NATO Adv. Study Inst., Italy, 1967; mem. biomaterials advisory commn. Nat. Inst. Dental Research, 1967-70; mem. chem. rocket advisory com. NASA, 1968-73; mem. engring. advisory com. NSF, 1969-72; mem. nat. materials adv. bd. NRC, chmn. Council on Materials Structures and Design, 1975-77; assoc. mem. Def. Sci. Bd., 1975-76, 82-85; chmn. structural mechanics com. Interagy. Task Force OSTP, coop. automotive res. program, 1979-80; cons., lectr. in field; cons. Dept. Def., 1970-93, Dept. State, 1973-81; dir. MPC Corp., Pitts., 1974-87; bd. dirs. U.S. World Energy Conf., Washington, 1977-83; pres. Utah Engring. Devel. Found., 1969-79; founding chmn. BCR Nat. Lab., U. Pitts., 1983-85; adviser Regional Indsl. Devel. Corp., Pitts., 1973-83, Ams. for Energy Independence, Washington, 1976-82; mem. nat. engr. adv. bd. Mercer U., 1988-94. Cons. editor Ency. Solid State, 1969-79; contbr. numerous articles to profl. jours. Served to capt. USAAF, 1943-46. Recipient Adhesion Rsch. award ASTM, 1975, Solid Rocket Tech. Achievement award AIAA, 1988, Merit Civilian Svc. citation USAF, 1989; NSF sr. postdoctoral fellow Imperial Coll., London, 1971-72; von Humboldt Found. rsch. scholar, 1992-94; named Disting. Alumnus Calif. Inst. Tech., 1995. Fellow Soc. Exptl. Mechanics, AIAA (assoc.), AAAS; mem. Utah Acad. Scis., N.Y. Acad. Scis., Am. Soc. Engring. Edn., Am. Chem. Soc., Internat. Congress on Fracture (exec. com. 1965, hon. fellow 1989), Soc. Rheology, Cosmos Club (Washington), Univ. Club (Pitts.), Sigma Xi (nat. lectr. 1972), Theta Tau, Tau Beta Pi. Home: 29514 235th Ave SE Kent WA 98042-7078

WILLIAMS, MELVIN JOHN, sociologist, educator; b. Stovall, N.C., Feb. 13, 1915; s. John Presley and Mary Jenera (Wilkerson) W.; m. Frances Clark, Oct. 15, 1936; children—Kay Frances (Mrs. Bradley Yount), Dorothy Virginia (dec.), Melvin John, Deborah Susan (Mrs. Monte F. Little), Steven Clark, Eric Stanton. A.B., Duke, 1936, B.D., 1939, Ph.D., 1941. From instr. to asst. prof. sociology Albion (Mich.) Coll., 1941-44; prof. sociology, head dept. Wesleyan Coll., Macon, Ga., 1944-47; asso. prof. sociology Fla. State U., Tallahassee, 1947-52; prof. sociology, head dept. Stetson U., De Land, Fla., 1952-60; prof. sociology, chmn. social work Stetson U., 1960-63; prof. sociology. East Carolina U., Greenville, 1963—; chmn. dept. sociology East Carolina U., 1963-71; vis. prof. summers Mich. State Normal Coll., 1943, Whittier Coll., 1957, U. N.C., 1970; With Duke Found., summer 1936. Author: with others Contemporary Social Theory, 1940, Catholic Social Thought, Its Approach to Contemporary Problems, 1950, Social Norms of Adolescents, A Study in Social Guidance, 1959, Moral and Spiritual Values in Education, 1955; Contbr. articles to profl. publs. Co-dir. Addison project Kresge Found., 1942-44; dir. YWCA Community Survey, Macon, Ga., 1944; dir., family counselor Children's Center, Macon, 1946-47; dir. Adolescent Research project Wesleyan Coll., 1944-46, East Carolina U., 1963; research and sociol. cons., 1946—; dir. NSF Inst. in Sociology, 1967. Fellow Am. Sociol. Assn.; mem. AAAS, AAUP, Am. Acad. Polit. and Social Sci., So. Sociol. Soc. (sec. treas. 1953-55, 1st v.p. 1955-56), Groves Conf., Nat. Council Family Relations, S.A.R., Omicron Delta Kappa, Alpha Kappa Delta, Pi Gamma Mu. Methodist. Club: Lion (pres. DeLand, Fla. 1960). Home: 103 Poplar Dr Greenville NC 27834-6435

WILLIAMS, MICHAEL ALAN, psychologist; b. Cin., May 20, 1948; s. Chester and Gentry Mae (Canada) W.; m. Linda Ann Presswood, Aug. 8, 1970; children: Michael Alan II, Derrick Alexander. BA, U. Cin., 1970, MA, 1971, EdD, 1980. Instr. U. Cin., 1972-75; sch. psychologist Dayton Bd. Edn., Ohio, 1975-78; assoc. prof. Wright State U., Dayton, 1978—, coord. spl. edn. program, 1992—; clin. psychologist Profl. Psychol. Services, Dayton, 1981—; psychol. services coordinator Montgomery County Children's Services, Dayton, 1983-88; psychol. cons. Diversion Alternative for Youth, Dayton, 1990—; program mgr. Head Start Supplementary Tng. Program, Cin., 1973-74; cons. Ohio Luth. Synod, Dayton, 1981-83, Blacks in Govt., Dayton, 1982-85, Montgomery County, Stillwater Health Ctr., Dayton, 1982-86. Co-editor (book): Teaching in a Multicultural Pluralistic Society, 1982, 2d edit., 1987. Treas. Dayton Free Clinic and Counseling Ctr., Dayton, 1983; bd. dirs. Planned Parenthood Assn., Dayton, 1983, Miami Valley Literacy Coun., Dayton, 1990-97, Dayton Mediation Ctr., 1995—, S. Cmty., Inc., 1996. Named Outstanding Young Man Am., Jaycees, 1984, Top Ten African-Am. Males, Dayton chpt. Urban League, 1995; McCall Scholarship, 1966-70. Mem. Am. Psychol. Assn., Nat. Assn. Black Psychologists, Nat. Assn. Sch. Psychologists, Dayton Assn. Black Psychologists (v.p. 1986-88, pres. 1988-89), Mental Health Assn. (bd. dirs. 1985), Assn. Tchr. Educators. Avocations: bible student, music, handiwork, writing. Home: 4830 Old Hickory Pl Dayton OH 45426-2149 Office: Wright State U 373 Millett Hall Dayton OH 45435

WILLIAMS, MICHAEL ANTHONY, lawyer; b. Mandan, N.D., Sept. 14, 1932; s. Melvin Douglas and Lucille Ann (Gavin) W.; m. Marjorie Ann Harrer, Aug. 25, 1962 (div. 1989); children: Ann Margaret, Douglas Raymond, David Michael; m. Dorothy Ruth Hand, 1989. B.A., Coll. of St. Thomas, 1954; LL.B., Harvard U., 1959. Bar: Colo. 1959, N.D. 1959, U.S. Dist. Ct. Colo. 1959, U.S. Ct. Appeals (10th cir.) 1959, U.S. Supreme Ct. 1967. Assoc. Sherman & Howard and predecessor Dawson, Nagel, Sherman & Howard, Denver, 1959-65, ptnr., 1965-91; pres. Williams, Youle & Koenigs, P.C., Denver, 1991—. Served as 1st lt. USAF, 1955-57. Mem. Am. Coll. Trial Lawyers, Am. Bd. Trial Advs., Colo. Bar Found., Am. Law Inst., ABA, Colo. Bar Assn., Denver Bar Assn., Arapahoe County Bar Assn. Office: Williams Youle & Koenigs PC 1200 17th St Ste 1420 Denver CO 80202-5835

WILLIAMS, MICHAEL JAMES, health care services consultant; b. Royal Oak, Mich., Sept. 23, 1951; s. Robert Burgett and Elizabeth (McGuire) W.; m. Juliana Caitlin. BA in Police Adminstrn., Wayne State U., 1974, BS in Psychology, 1974; MPA, Calif. State U., Fullerton, 1978. Asst. mgr. Suburban Ambulance Co., Royal Oak, 1970-74; dir. Emergency Med. Services Imperial County, El Centro, Calif., 1974-76, Orange County, Santa Ana, Calif., 1976-80; pres. EMS Systems Design, Irvine, Calif., 1980-89, The Abaris Group, Tustin, 1989—; instr., trainer ACLS, Am. Heart Assn., 1978-80, CPr, 1989—; spl. cons. Hosp. Coun. So. Calif., Calif. Assn. Hosps. and Health Systems; EMS med. coord. trauma emergencies Pyramid Films, Santa Monica, Calif., 1989 (Am. Film Inst. Blue Ribbon award). Contbr. numerous articles to profl. jours. Recipient Recognition award Orange County Emergency Care Commn., 1980, Appreciation award UCI Med. Ctr., Orange, Calif., 1980, Orange County Fire Chiefs Assn., 1980. Mem. Healthcare Fin. Mgmt. Assn., Am. Trauma Soc., Am. Heart Assn. (bd. dirs. Orange County chpt., 1976-82), No. Calif. Healthcare Execs., Orange County Trauma Soc. (bd. dirs. 1981-89, program achievement award, 1987), Internat. Assn. Fire Chiefs (EMS sect.), EMS Adminstrs. Assn. Calif. (founding). Democrat. Avocations: jogging, racquetball, fishing. Office: 700 Ygnacio Valley Rd Ste 250 Walnut Creek CA 94596-3859

WILLIAMS, MILLER, poet, translator; b. Hoxie, Ark., Apr. 8, 1930; s. Ernest Burdette and Ann Jeanette (Miller) W.; m. Lucille Day, Dec. 29, 1951 (div.); m. Rebecca Jordan Hall, Apr. 11, 1969; children: Lucinda, Robert, Karyn. BS, Ark. State Coll., 1951; MS, U. Ark., 1952; postgrad., La. State U., 1951, U. Miss., 1957; HHD (hon.), Lander Coll., 1983; DHL, Hendrix Coll., 1995. Instr. in English La. State U., 1962-63, asst. prof., 1964-66; vis. prof. U. Chile, Santiago, 1963-64; assoc. prof. Loyola U., New Orleans, 1966-70; Fulbright prof. Nat. U. Mex., Mexico City, 1970; co-dir. grad. program in creative writing U. Ark., 1970-84, assoc. prof., 1971-73, prof. English and fgn. langs., dir. program in transl., 1973-87, univ. prof., 1987—, dir. poetry-in-the prisons programs div. continuing edn., 1974-79, chmn. program in comparative lit., 1978-80; dir. U. Ark. Press, 1980-97, Bank of Elkins, Ark. 1988—; fellow Am. Acad. in Rome, 1976—, mem. adv. coun. Sch. Classical Studies, 1985-91; first U.S. del. Pan Am. Conf. Univ. Artists and Writers, Concepcion, Chile, 1964; invited del. Internat. Assembly Univ. Press Dirs., Guadalajara, Mex., 1991; mem. poetry staff Bread Loaf Writers Conf., 1967-72; founder, exec. dir. Ark. Poetry Cir., 1975; participant Assn. Am. Univ. Presses Soviet Mission, 1989. Author: (poems) A Circle of Stone, 1964, Recital, 1965, So Long At the Fair, 1968, The Only World There Is, 1971; (criticism) The Achievement of John Ciardi, 1968, The Poetry of John Crowe Ransom, 1971; (with John Ciardi) (criticism) How Does a Poem Mean?, 1974; (poems) Halfway From Hoxie: New & Selected Poems, 1973, Why God Permits Evil, 1977, Distractions, 1981, The Boys on Their Bony Mules, 1983; translator: (poems) Poems & Antipoems (Nicanor Parra), 1967, Emergency Poems (Nicanor Parra), 1972, Sonnets of Giuseppe Belli, 1981; editor: (poems) 19 Poetas de Hoy en Los Estados Unidos, 1966, (with John William Corrington) Southern Writing in the Sixties: Poetry, 1967, Southern Writing in the Sixties: Fiction, 1966, Chile: An Anthology of New Writing, 1968, Contemporary Poetry in America, 1972, (with James A. McPherson) Railroad: Trains and Train People in American Culture, 1976, A Roman Collection: An Anthology of Writing about Rome and Italy, 1980, Ozark, Ozark: A Hillside Reader, 1981, (criticism) Patterns of Poetry, 1986, (poetry) Imperfect Love, 1986, Living on the Surface: New and Selected Poems, 1989, Adjusting to the Light, 1992, Points of Departure, 1995, The Ways We Touch, 1997; poetry editor La. State U. Press, 1966-68; contbr. articles to profl. publs. Mem. ACLU. Recipient Henry Bellaman Poetry award, 1957, award in poetry Arts Fund, 1973, Prix de Rome, Am. Acad. Arts and Letters, 1976, Nat. Poets prize, 1990, Charity Randall citation Internat. Poetry Forum, 1993, John William Corrington award for excellence in lit., Centenary Coll., Shreveport, La., 1994, Acad. Lit. award AAAL, 1995, Presdl. Inaugural Poet award, 1997; named Bread Loaf fellow in poetry, 1963. Mem. MLA, PEN, AAUP, South Ctrl. MLA, Am. Lit. Translators Assn. (v.p. 1978-79, pres. 1979-81), Authors' Guild, Soc. Benemerito dell'Assn. Centro Romanesco Trilussa (Rome). Home: 1111 Valley View Dr Fayetteville AR 72701-1603 Office: U Ark Press 201 Ozark Ave Fayetteville AR 72701-4041

WILLIAMS, MORGAN LLOYD, retired investment banker; b. N.Y.C., Mar. 30, 1935; s. John Lloyd and Adelaide Veronica (Patchell) W.; m. Margaret Patricia Rooney, May 13, 1961; children: Morgan Lloyd Jr., John Graham, Christine Joyce. BS in Econs., Wharton Sch., U. Pa., 1957; MBA, Columbia U., 1961. V.p., stockholder Kidder, Peabody & Co., N.Y.C., 1970-90, mng. dir., 1985-87. Trustee Inc. Village of Plandome, N.Y., 1982-86, mayor, 1986-87. Lt. USN, 1957-59. Mem. Nassau Country Club (Glen Cove, N.Y.). Republican. Roman Catholic. Home: 2040 Broadway St Apt 403 San Francisco CA 94115-1587

WILLIAMS, NATHANIEL, JR., elementary education educator; b. Jacksonville, Fla., June 7, 1940; s. Nathaniel Sr. and Alice Elizabeth (Dusom) W.;

m. Carol Ann Odom, Sept. 6, 1969; children: Monica C., Nathaniel Joshua. BS in Chemistry and Math., Bethune-Cookman Coll., Daytona Beach, Fla., 1965; M in Teaching Elem., U. Pitts., 1973. Chemist Pitts. Plate Glass Coating and Resin, Springdale, Pa., 1966-67; ins. agt. Can. Life Assurance Co., Pitts., 1967-70; tutorial tchr. Model Cities Program, Pitts., 1968-69; employment adminstr. South Oakland Citizen Coun., Pitts., 1969-70; substitute tchr. Bd. Edn., Pitts., 1970-72; elem. tchr. Penn Hills (Pa.) Sch. Dist., 1973—; dir. edn. Pitts. Challenge, Wilkinsburg, Pa., 1974-79; bd. dirs. East End Family Ctr., Pitts., 1982-84; elem. evaluator Pa. Dept. Edn., Harrisburg, 1992—. Editor newsletter Ethnic Minority News, 1989—; coord. sci. program Invent Am., 1993. Ch. trustee, deacon Lincoln Ave. Ch. of God, Pitts., 1980-90, 94, mem. scholarship com., 1990-94. Recipient 1st place Mural award WQED/MacDonald, Pitts., 1992, plaque Ethnic Minority Caucus, Gettysburg, Pa., 1993. Mem. NEA, Pa. State Edn. Assn. (Western region com. chair 1988-94, bd. dirs. 1989-91), Penn Hills Edn. Assn. (com. chair 1983-94). Democrat. Avocations: reading, science projects, plays. Home: 218 Hawkins Ave Braddock PA 15104-2117 Office: Dibble Elem Sch 1079 Jefferson Rd Pittsburgh PA 15235-4723

WILLIAMS, NEIL, JR., lawyer; b. Charlotte, N.C., Mar. 22, 1936; s. Lyman Neil and Thelma (Peterson) W.; m. Sue Sigmon, Aug. 23, 1958; children: Fred R., Susan S. AB, Duke U., 1958, JD, 1961. Bar: Ga. 1962, U.S. Dist. Ct. (no. dist.) Ga. 1977, U.S. Ct. Appeals (11th cir.) 1977. Assoc. Alston & Bird (and predecessor firm), Atlanta, 1961-65, ptnr., 1966—, mng. ptnr., 1984-96; bd. dirs. Nat. Data Corp., Atlanta, Printpack, Inc., Atlanta, Atty's Liability Assurance Soc., Inc., Chgo. Chmn. bd. trustees Duke U., 1983-88, trustee, 1980-93; chmn. bd. trustees Vasser Woolley Found., Atlanta, 1975—, Leadership Atlanta, 1976-80; trustee Brevard Music Ctr., 1977-86, 91—, Presbyn. Ch. USA Found., Jeffersonville, Ind., 1983-90, Research Triangle Inst., 1983-88; bd. dirs. Atlanta Symphony Orch., 1970-76, 84-93, 95—, pres. 1988-90; Woodruff Arts Ctr., 1987—; bd. counsellors The Carter Ctr., Atlanta, 1987-96; Cen. Atlanta Progress, 1984-96; bd. dirs. Am. Symphony Orch. League, Washington, 1990—, chmn., 1995—. Recipient Disting. Alumni award Duke U., 1991, Rhyne award, 1996. Mem. ABA, Am. Bar Found., State Bar Ga., Am. Law Inst., Atlanta C. of C. (bd. dirs., 1994—, vice chmn. 1994—), Phi Beta Kappa, Omicron Delta Kappa. Clubs: Piedmont Driving, Commerce (Atlanta); University (N.Y.C.). Home: 3 Nacoochee Pl NW Atlanta GA 30305-4164 Office: Alston & Bird 1 Atlantic Ctr 1201 W Peachtree St NW Atlanta GA 30309-3400

WILLIAMS, NEVILLE, international development organization executive; b. Muncie, Ind., Mar. 28, 1943; s. Donald Charles and Rose Eileen (Boughton) W. Student, U. Colo., 1964-66, U. Neuchatel, Switzerland, 1967. Freelance corr. Vietnam, 1968-69; freelance journalist Montreal, Que., Can., 1970-71, London, 1971-73; writer, producer Sta. WNBC-TV News, N.Y.C., 1973-74; freelance writer Telluride, Colo., 1975-79; media liaison Office of Solar Energy U.S. Dept. Energy, Washington, 1979-80; dir. of mktg. Telluride Ski Resort, Inc., 1981-83; owner, operator Hist. Sheridan Opera Ho., Telluride, 1983-85; nat. media dir. Greenpeace U.S.A., Washington, 1987-89; founder, pres., chmn. Solar Electric Light Fund, Washington, 1990—; also, bd. dirs.; bd. dirs. Solar Electric Light Co. Inc.; pres. Williams & Assocs., Telluride and Washington, 1983-90. Author: The New Exiles, 1971, (monograph) Great Telluride Strike, 1977; contbr. articles to N.Y. Times mag., Penthouse, Outside, New Times, The Nation, The New Republic, Nature, others. Apptd. mem. Adv. Com. for Commerce and Devel., State of Colo., 1980-85; apptd. mem. Gov.'s Motion Picture & TV Commn., 1981-85. Fellow Am. Solar Energy Soc., Internat. Solar Energy Soc. Avocations: mountaineering, hiking, history, metaphysics. Office: Solar Electric Light Fund 1734 20th St NW Washington DC 20009-1105

WILLIAMS, NORMAN DALE, geneticist, researcher; b. Roca, Nebr., Nov. 4, 1924; s. John Alva and L. Carrie (Crawford) W.; m. Elaine Elizabeth Kuster, Aug. 7, 1947; children: David N., Curtis A. BS, U. Nebr., 1951, MS, 1954, PhD, 1956. Assoc. trainee Argonne Nat. Lab., Lemont, Ill., 1954-56, rsch. assoc., 1956; rsch. geneticist USDA Agrl. Rsch. Svc., Fargo, N.D., 1956-72, rsch. leader, 1972—; adj. prof. N.D. State U., Fargo, 1961—. Contbr. articles to profl. jours. With U.S. Army, 1945-47. Fellow AAAS, Am. Soc. Agronomy, Crop Sci. Soc. Am.; mem. Am. Genetics Assn., Genetics Soc. Am., Coun. for Agrl. Sci. and Tech., Masons, Sigma Xi (pres., pres.-elect N.D. chpt. 1976-78). Presbyterian. Avocations: golf, fishing, bowling, woodworking, gardening. Home: 809 South Dr Fargo ND 58103-4933 Office: USDA Agrl Rsch Svcs State University Sta PO Box 5677 Fargo ND 58105-5677

WILLIAMS, NORRIS HAGAN, JR., biologist, educator, curator; b. Birmingham, Ala., Mar. 31, 1943; s. Norris Hagan Sr. and Ernestyne Edna (Brown) W.; m. Nancy Jane Fraser, June 26, 1970; children: Matthew Ian, Luke Fraser. BS, U. Ala., 1964, MS, 1967; PhD, U. Miami, 1971. Asst. prof. Fla. State U., Tallahassee, 1973-78, assoc. prof., 1978-81; assoc. curator U. Fla., Gainesville, 1981-83, curator, 1983—, dept. chmn., 1985-94. Co-author: Orchid Genera of Costa Rica, 1986, Identification Manual for Wetland Plant Species of Florida, 1987; author: (chpt.) Orchid Biology II, 1982, Handbook of Experimental Pollination Biology, 1983; contbr. article to Biol. Bull., 1983. Mem. Assn. for Tropical Biology, Bot. Soc. Am., Soc. for Study Evolution, Linnean Soc. of London. Democrat. Office: U Fla Fla Mus Natural History Gainesville FL 32611

WILLIAMS, OMER S. J., lawyer; b. Rushville, Ind., June 20, 1940; s. John Thomas and Dorothy June (Jackson) W.; m. Gail Duff Shute, July 17, 1965; children: James Jackson, John Wesley. BA, Yale U., 1962, LLB, 1965. Assoc. Thacher Proffitt & Wood, N.Y.C., 1965-71, ptnr., 1971—, chmn. exec. com., mng. ptnr., 1992—. Dir. Greater N.Y. Coun. Boy Scouts Am., coun. commr.; dir. Downtown Lower Manhattan Assn. Mem. ABA (coms. new devels. bus. financing, banking law), N.Y. State Bar Assn., Assn. of the Bar of the City of N.Y. (coms. savings instns., banking law), The Downtown Assn. Club. Mem. Christian Ch. Avocations: tennis, genealogy, civil war history. Home: 206 N Franklin Tpke Ho Ho Kus NJ 07423-1425 Office: Thacher Proffitt & Wood 2 World Trade Ctr New York NY 10048-0203

WILLIAMS, PAMELA R., secondary school administrator; b. Tacoma, Feb. 9, 1950; d. Richard Bartle and Elaine Staab; m. Raymond L. Williams, 1972. BA in Edn. with distinction, Wash. State U., 1972; MA in Adminstrn., Washington U., St. Louis, 1983. Cert. tchr., Mo., Colo., adminstr., Colo. Tchr. Countryside Elem., DeSoto, Kans., 1972-77, U. Chgo. Lab Sch., 1977-78, Francis Parker Sch., Chgo., 1978-80; mid. sch. tchr., coord. English, Mary Inst., St. Louis, 1980-88; elem. bilingual tchr. Boulder (Colo.) Valley Schs., 1988-91, asst. prin., 1991-96, prin., 1996—. Mem. ASCD, NEA, Am. Assn. Sch. Adminstrs. (women's caucus), Nat. Assn. Secondary Sch. Prins., CORO Women in Leadership Alumnae Assn., Phi Delta Kappa. Office: Base Line MS 700 20th St Boulder CO 80302-7702

WILLIAMS, PAT, former congressman; b. Helena, Mont., Oct. 30, 1937; m. Carol Griffith, 1965; children: Griff, Erin, Whitney. Student, U. Mont., 1956-57, William Jewell U.; BA, U. Denver, 1961; postgrad., Western Mont. Coll.; LLD (hon.), Carroll Coll., Montana Coll. of Mineral Sci. and Tech. Mem. Mont. Ho. of Reps., 1967, 69; exec. dir. Hubert Humphrey Presdl. campaign, Mont., 1968; exec. asst. to U.S. Rep. John Melcher, 1969-71; mem. Gov.'s Employment and Tng. Council, 1972-78, Mont. Legis. Reapportionment Commn., 1973; co-chmn. Jimmy Carter Presdl. campaign, Mont., 1976; mem. 96th-102nd Congresses from 1st Mont. dist., 1979-96; sr. fellow Ctr. Rocky Mountain W. U. Mont., Missoula, 1996—; ranking mem. postsecondary edn. subcom. Coordinator Mont. Family Edn. Program, 1971-78. Served with U.S. Army, 1960-61; Served with Army N.G., 1962-69. Mem. Mont. Fedn. Tchrs. Democrat. Lodge: Elks. Home: 907 Beckwith Missoula MT 59801 Office: U Montana Ctr Rocky Mountain West Missoula MT 59801*

WILLIAMS, PAT, professional basketball team executive; b. Phila., May 3, 1940; m. Jill Marie Paige; children: Jimmy, Bobby Karyn. Asst. gen. mgr. Miami Marlines, 1964; gen. mgr. Spartanburg Phillies, West Carolina League, Spartanburg, S.C., 1965-67, pres., 1967-68; bus. mgr. Phila. 76ers, 1968-69; gen. mgr. Chgo. Bulls, 1969-73, Atlanta Hawks, 1973-74; gen. mgr., v.p. Phila. 76ers, 1974; gen. mgr., COO Orlando Magic, sr. exec. v.p. Mem. Fellowship of Christian Athletes. Office: Orlando Magic 1 Magic Pl Orlando FL 32801-1116*

WILLIAMS, PATRICK MOODY, composer; b. Bonne Terre, Mo., Apr. 23, 1939; s. Wilson Moody and Jean (Murphy) W.; m. Catherine Greer, Apr. 7, 1962; children: Elizabeth, Greer, Patrick. B.A., Duke U., 1961; hon. doctorate, U. Colo., 1983. vis. prof. U. Utah, 1970-71, U. Colo., 1975-77. Composer, N.Y.C., 1961-68, Los Angeles, 1968—; composer 60 film scores, music for TV series; artist 11 record albums; works include An American Concerto, 1977, (for jazz quartet and symphony orch.) Rhapsody (for concert band, jazz ensemble), 1975, (for solo cello and orch.) The Silent Spring, 1974, (for narrator and orch.) Gulliver, 1985 (for symphony orch. and narrator) Romances, (jazz soloist, orch.) 1986, Theme For Earth Day, 1990, An Overture To A Time, 1990. Served with U.S. Army. Acad. award nominee, 1980, nominee for Grammy 10 times, winner, 1974, 86, Pulitzer prize music nominee, 1977, nominee for Emmy 19 times, winner, 1979, 81, 93, nominee for Cable ACE award 2 times, winner 1994. Mem. Acad. Motion Picture Arts and Scis., Acad. TV Arts and Scis., Acad. Recording Arts and Scis., Broadcast Music, Inc. Democrat. *I am a convinced believer in the apprenticeship system of learning. There were a few people in my life that taught me many things, and I will be forever grateful that I had the opportunity to know them and learn from them. What they knew about music was invaluable to me, and what they were as people was even better.*

WILLIAMS, PAUL, retired federal agency administrator; b. Jacksonville, Ill., Aug. 6, 1929; s. Russell and Bernice (Wheeler) W.; m. Ora B. Mosby; 1 child, Reva Williams. BA, Ill. Coll., 1956, LHD, 1980. Dir. fin. City of Chgo., 1956-63; assoc. dir. fin. United Planning Orgn., Washington, 1964-65; internat. adminstrv. officer U.S. Dept. State, Washington, 1965-68; dir. of office mgmt. U.S. HUD, Washington, 1968-93, gen. deputy dept. fair housing and equal opportunity, 1993-94, dep. ops. and mgmt., 1994-97, ret., 1997. Author: Questionnaire on Execution of Urban Renewal Programs, 1959. Pres. Bel Pre Civic Assn., Wheaton, Md., 1978, bd. dirs., 1971, 79; pres. Bel Pre PTA, Wheaton, 1973. Sgt. U.S. Army, 1948-52. Recipient letter of recognition for 36 yrs. fed. svc. U.S. Pres., letter of recognition for 36 yrs. govt. svc. Senators of Md., citation for 36 yrs. dedicated govt. svc. Gov. of Md., cert. of recognition Nat. Assn. Black and Minority C. of C., 1987. Methodist. Avocations: racquetball, jogging. Home: 14009 Blazer Ln Silver Spring MD 20906-2321 Office: Dept Housing and Urban Devel 451 7th St SW Rm 5100 Washington DC 20410-0001

WILLIAMS, PAULETTE W., state agency administrator; b. Moulton, Ala., Oct. 21, 1944; d. Paul Price and Sallie Davis (Bass) Wiley; m. Robert Thomas Williams, Oct. 11, 1968; 1 child, Shannon Thomas. Student, Florence State Coll., 1963-64. Planning and ops. officer civil def Decatur (Ill.)/Morgan Co., 1964-74, planning and ops. officer emergency mgmt., 1975-77; planning and ops. officer, dep. dir. emergency mgmt. Mobile (Ala.) Co., 1977-89; emergency mgmt. area coord. I State of Ala., Clanton, 1989-95; dir. Ala. Emergency Mgmt. Agy., Clanton, 1994-95; observer nuc. power plant Dept. Def., Romania, 1994; mem. gov. cabinet State of Ala., Clanton, 1994-95. Mem. cmty. advisor coun. Occidental Chem. Co., Muscle Shoals, Ala., 1993—; mem. state disaster svcs. com. ARC, Ala., 1993—. Recipient Spl. Recognition award Ala. Police Acad., 1986, Appreciation cert. Mobile (Ala.) Police Acad., 1986, Outstanding Svc. and Dedication cert. and flag, 1988, Hon. Adm. cert. Mayor of Decatur, 1988, Outstanding Svc. and Contbns. Appreciation cert. Nat. Coordinating Coun. on Emergency Mgmt., 1988, Appreciation plaque Greater Mobile Indsl. Assn., 1989, Appreciation for Profl. Assistance plaque Kerr McGee Chem. Corp., 1989, Appreciation cert. State of Ala., 1989, Meritorious Svc. cert. City of Mobile, 1989, Appreciation for Help and Support plaque City of Mobile Police Dept. Hazardous Materials Unit, 1989, Outstanding Dedication and Svc. plaque Mobile County Local Emergency Planning Com., 1989, Appreciation cert. FEMA-Floods of 1990, 1990, Pub. Svc. award U.S. Dept. Commerce, NOAA, 1994. Mem. Ala. Emergency Mgmt. Coun. (pres., Sec.-treas. plaque 1986, Appreciation cert. 1986, Legis. Chmn. plaque 1987), Nat. Emergency Mgmt. Assn. (mem. recovery com.). Episcopal. Home: 2224 Marietta Ave Muscle Shoals AL 35661-2620 Office: Alabama Emergency Mgmt PO Drawer 2160 Clanton AL 35045

WILLIAMS, PHYLLIS CUTFORTH, retired realtor; b. Moreland, Idaho, June 6, 1917; d. William Claude and Kathleen Jessie (Jenkins) Cutforth; m. Joseph Marsden Williams, Jan. 21, 1938 (dec. 1986); children: Joseph Marlis, Bonnie L. Williams Thompson, Nancy K. Williams Stewart, Marjorie Williams Karren, Douglas Claude, Thomas Marsden, Wendy K. Williams Clark, Shannon I. Williams Ostler. Grad., Ricks Coll., 1935. Tchr. Grace (Idaho) Elem. Sch., 1935-38; realtor Williams Realty, Idaho Falls, Idaho, 1972-77; mem. Idaho Senate, Boise, 1977; owner, mgr. river property. Compiler: Idaho Legisladies Cookbook, Cookin' Together, 1981. With MicroFilm Ctr., LDS Ch. Mission, Salt Lake City, 1989-90; block chmn. March of Dimes Soc.; active Idaho State Legisladies Club, 1966-84, v.p., 1982-84. Republican. Avocations: genealogy, cooking, music, politics, photography, travel. Home: 1950 Carmel Dr Idaho Falls ID 83402-3020

WILLIAMS, PRESTON NOAH, theology educator; b. Alcolu, S.C., May 23, 1926; s. Anderson James and Bertha Bell (McRae) W.; m. Constance Marie Willard, June 4, 1956; children—Mark Gordon, David Bruce. A.B., Washington and Jefferson Coll., 1947, M.A., 1948; B.D., Johnson C. Smith U., 1950; S.T.M., Yale, 1954; Ph.D., Harvard, 1967. Ordained to ministry Presbyn. Ch., 1950. Martin Luther King. Jr. prof. social ethics Boston U. Sch. Theology, 1970-71; Houghton prof. theology and contemporary change Harvard U. Div. Sch., Cambridge, Mass., 1971—; acting dean Harvard U. Div. Sch., 1974-75; acting dir. W.E.B. DuBois Inst., 1975-77. Editor-at-large: Christian Century, 1972—; contbr. articles to profl. jours. Mem. Am. Acad. Religion (pres. 1975—), Am. Soc. Christian Ethics (dir., pres. 1974-75), Phi Beta Kappa. Home: 36 Fairmont St Belmont MA 02178-2919 Office: 45 Francis Ave Cambridge MA 02138-1911

WILLIAMS, QUENTIN CHRISTOPHER, geophysicist, educator; b. Wilmington, Del., Jan. 1, 1964; s. Ferd Elton and Anne Katherine (Lindberg) W.; m. Elise Barbara Knittle, Dec. 19, 1987; children: Byron Frederick, Alanna Katherine. AB, Princeton U., 1983; PhD, U. Calif., Berkeley, 1988. Rsch. geophysicist Inst. of Tectonics, U. Calif., Santa Cruz, 1988-91; asst. prof. dept. earth sci. U. Calif., Santa Cruz, 1991-95, assoc. prof. dept. earth sci., 1995—. Contbr. articles to profl. jours. Presdl. Faculty fellow, 1993—. Mem. Am. Geophys. Union, Am. Phys. Soc. Office: U Calif Santa Cruz Dept Earth Sciences Santa Cruz CA 95064

WILLIAMS, QUINN PATRICK, lawyer; b. Evergreen Park, Ill., May 6, 1949; s. William Albert and Jeanne Marie (Quinlan) W.; children: Michael Ryan, Mark Reed, Kelly Elizabeth. BBA, U. Wis., 1972; JD, U. Ariz., 1974. Bar: Ariz. 1975, N.Y. 1984, U.S. Dist. Ct. Ariz. 1976. Vice pres., sec., gen. counsel Combined Comm. Corp., Phoenix, 1975-80; v.p., sec., gen. counsel Swensen's Ice Cream Co., Phoenix, 1980-83; sr. v.p. legal and adminstrn. Swensen's Inc., Phoenix, 1983-86; of counsel Winston & Strawn, Phoenix, 1985-87, ptnr., 1987-89, ptnr Snell & Wilmer, Phoenix, 1989—. Chmn. Ariz. Tech. Incubator, 1993-94; chair Ariz. Venture Capital Conf. 1993, 94; co-chair Gov. Small Bus. Advocate Exec. Coun., 1993—; bd. dirs. Greater Phoenix Econ. Coun., 1996; vice chair Gov. Regulatory Coun., 1995. Served with USAR, 1967-73. Mem. ABA, Maricopa County Bar Assn., N.Y. Bar Assn., State Bar Ariz., Internat. Franchise Assn., Paradise Valley Country Club, Scottsdale Charos. Republican. Roman Catholic. Home: 8131 N 75th St Scottsdale AZ 85258-2781 Office: Snell & Wilmer One Arizona Ctr Phoenix AZ 85004

WILLIAMS, RALPH CHESTER, JR., physician, educator; b. Washington, Feb. 17, 1928; s. Ralph Chester and Annie (Perry) W.; m. Mary Elizabeth Adams, June 23, 1951; children—Cathy, Frederick, John (dec.), Michael, Ann. AB with distinction, Cornell U., 1950, MD, 1954; MD (hon.), U. Lund, Sweden, 1991. Diplomate: Am. Bd. Internal Medicine. Intern Mass. Gen. Hosp., Boston, 1954-55; asst. resident internal medicine Mass. Gen. Hosp., 1955-56; resident internal medicine N.Y. Hosp., 1956-57; chief resident Mass. Gen. Hosp., Boston, 1959-60; guest investigator Rockefeller Inst., N.Y.C., 1961-63; practice medicine specializing in internal medicine (subspecialty rheumatology), 1963—; asso. prof. U. Minn. at Mpls., 1963-68, prof., 1968-69; prof., chmn. dept. medicine U. N.Mex., Albuquerque, 1969-88; Schott prof. rheumatology and medicine U. Fla., Gainesville, 1988—; Diplomate Am. Bd. Internal Medicine. Asso. editor: Jour. Lab. and Clin. Medicine, 1966-69; editorial bd.: Arthritis and Rheumatism, 1968—; Contbr. numerous articles to profl. jours. Served to capt. USAF, 1957-59. Master Am. Coll. Rheumatology; fellow ACP; mem. Am. Assn. Immunology, Assn. Am. Physicians, Am. Fedn. Clin. Rsch., Am. Soc. Clin. Investigation, Ctrl. Soc. Clin. Rsch., Western Soc. Clin. Rsch., Phi Beta Kappa, Alpha Omega Alpha. Research in immunologic processes and connective tissue diseases. Home: 2516 NW 20th St Gainesville FL 32605-2981

WILLIAMS, RALPH WATSON, JR., retired securities company executive; b. Atlanta, July 2, 1933; s. Ralph Watson and Minnie Covington (Hicks) W.; m. Nancy Jo Morgan, Mar. 19, 1955 (dec. Dec. 1989); children: Ralph Watson III, Nancy Jane, John Martin Hicks; m. Almonese Brown Clifton, Nov. 24, 1990. Student, Davidson Coll., 1951; B.B.A., U. Ga., 1955. Trainee banking Trust Co. Ga., Atlanta, 1955; mcpl. sales staff Courts & Co., Atlanta, 1955-57; v.p., salesman securities First Southeastern Corp., Atlanta, 1957-60; br. mgr. Francis I. duPont & Co., 1960-69; spl. partner duPont Glore Forgan Inc., N.Y.C., 1969-70; gen. partner Glore Forgan Inc., 1970, exec. v.p., 1971—, sr. v.p., 1972—; also dir.; sr. v.p., dir., mem. exec. com. duPont-Walston Inc., 1973-74; sr. v.p. E.F. Hutton & Co. Inc., 1974-81; exec. v.p., dir. E.F. Hutton & Co., Inc., 1981-88; exec. v.p. Shearson Lehman Hutton Inc., Atlanta, 1988-89; ret., 1989. Mem. Nat. Assn. Security Dealers (chmn. dist. com. 7), Benedicts Atlanta, Phi Delta Theta. Methodist. Clubs: Commerce (Atlanta), Capital City (Atlanta), Piedmont Driving (Atlanta). Home: 3504 Dumbarton Rd NW Atlanta GA 30327-2614

WILLIAMS, REDFORD BROWN, medical educator; b. Raleigh, N.C., Dec. 14, 1940; s. Redford Brown Sr. and Annie Virginia (Betts) W.; m. Virginia Carter Parrott, August 9, 1940; children: Jennifer Betts, Lloyd Carter. AB, Harvard U., 1963; MD, Yale U., 1967. Diplomate Am. Bd. Internal Medicine. Intern, then resident Yale-New Haven Med. Ctr., 1967-70; sr. surgeon USPHS, Bethesda, Md., 1970-72; asst. prof. Duke U. Med. Ctr., Durham, N.C., 1972, prof. psychiatry, 1977—, prof. psychology, 1990—, dir. behavioral medicine rsch. ctr., 1985—; cons. NIH rev. coms., Bethesda, 1977—. Author: The Trusting Heart, 1989, Anger Kills, 1993, The Caring Family, 1997; contbr. articles to profl. jours. Dir. N.C. Heart Assn., Chapel Hill, 1980-83. Recipient Rsch. Scientist award NIMH, 1974—; NIH grantee, 1986—. Fellow Soc. Behavioral Medicine (pres. 1984-85, Upjohn Disting. Scientist award 1992), Acad. Behavioral Medicine Rsch. (pres. 1995—); mem. Am. Psychosomatic Soc. (bd. dirs. 1978-81, pres. 1992). Unitarian Universalist. Avocation: tennis. Office: Duke U Med Ctr Box 3926 Durham NC 27710

WILLIAMS, RHYS, minister; b. San Francisco, Feb. 27, 1929; s. Albert Rhys and Lucita (Squier) W.; m. Eleanor Hoyle Barnhart, Sept. 22, 1956; children: Rhys Hoyle, Eleanor Pierce. AB, St. Lawrence U., 1951, BD, MDiv, 1953, DD, 1966; postgrad., Union Sem., summer 1956; LLD (hon.), Emerson Coll., 1962. Ordained to ministry Unitarian Ch., 1954. Min. Unitarian Ch., Charleston, S.C., 1953-60, 1st and 2d Ch., Boston, 1960—; mem. faculty, field edn. supr. Harvard U., 1969—; Russell lectr. Tufts U., 1965, Minns lectr., 1986. Pres. Edward Everett Hale House, 1987—, Soc. of Cincinnati, State of N.H., 1986-89; v.p. Franklin Inst., 1960—, sec., 1990-96; v.p. Benevolent Frat. Unitarian Universalist Chs., 1982-93; pres. Unitarian Universalist Urban Ministries, 1991—; sec. bd. trustees Emerson Coll., 1961-94, trustee, 1994—; chaplain Gen. Soc. Cin., Washington, 1977—, New Eng. coun. Navy League, 1980—, Founders and Patriots of Mass., SR; chmn. Festival Fund, Inc., Am.-Soviet Cultural Exch., 1989-91; trustee Opera Co. Boston, 1970—; trustee Meadville Lombard Theol. Sch., Chgo., 1971-77, mem. ministerial fellowship com., 1961-69, chmn., 1968-69; fin. chmn. Ch. Larger Fellowship, 1968-86; bd. dirs. Peter Faneuil Housing Corp., 1992—, AIDS Housing, 1995, clk. 1996—; trustee Franklin Square House, 1993—; acting chmn. Franklin Found., 1997. Mem. Unitarian Universalist Mins. Assn. (pres. 1968-70), Unitarian Hist. Soc. (pres. 1960-75), Evang. Missionary Soc. (pres. 1965-80, v.p. 1980—), Soc. for Propagation Gospel Among Indians and Others in N.Am. (v.p. 1975—), Unitarian Svc. Pension Soc. (pres. 1973—), Soc. Ministerial Relief (pres. 1973—, mem. com. for ch. staff fin.), Mass. Hist. Soc., Colonial Soc. Mass., Union Club (Boston), Union Boat Club (Boston), Beta Theta Pi (pres. New Eng. 1964-66). Office: 1st and 2d Church in Boston 66 Marlborough St Boston MA 02116-2007

WILLIAMS, RICHARD CHARLES, computer programmer, consultant; b. Boston, Dec. 25, 1955; s. Richard Clayton and Nancy Karolyn (Kerr) W. BA, SUNY, New Paltz, 1991. Cert. in software engring. Programmer/cons. Shared Ednl. Computing, Poughkeepsie, N.Y., 1976-78; systems programmer, comms. mgr. Cornell U. Med. Sch., N.Y.C., 1978-79; staff programmer IBM Corp. Hdqrs., White Plains, N.Y., 1979-84; systems programmer IBM Data Systems Div., Poughkeepsie, 1984-86; adv. programmer IBM Network Systems, White Plains, 1986-89; open systems cons. IBM Large Systems, Kingston, N.Y., 1989-95; sr. R/3 basis architect, cert. SAP cons. IBM-SAP Competency Ctr., Phila., 1996-97, sr. architect, 1997—; cons. IBM Hudson Valley Fed. Credit Union, Poughkeepsie, 1986—, C-Net, Broomfield, Colo., 1988-89, Toastmasters Bd. Dirs., Santa Ana, Calif., 1987, Landmark Edn., N.Y.C., 1989—. Author: Lasting Legacy, 1987; co-author: Migrating to TSO from VSPC, 1986; inventor, patentee. Bd. dirs. Hudson Valley FCU, 1995—, 2d vice chair, 1996-97, 1st vice-chair, 1997—; bd. dirs. SUNY Alumni Bd. Named one of Outstanding Young Men of Am., 1985, Vol. of Yr., NACUSAC, 1995. Mem. IEEE, ACM, SUNY Alumni Assn. (bd. dirs. 1994-97—), Poughkeepsie Toastmasters nternat. (chpt. pres. 1982, dist. gov. 1985, Toastmaster of Yr. 1984), Open Online Transactional Programming Users Group (mem. planning bd.). Democrat. Methodist. Avocations: skiing, community organizing, travel. Home: 2 Jansen Rd New Paltz NY 12561-3810 Office: IBM-SAP Competency Ctr 100 Stevens Dr Philadelphia PA 19113-1521 also: SAP, Neurottstrasse 16, D-69190 Walldorf Germany

WILLIAMS, RICHARD CLARENCE, retired librarian; b. Guide Rock, Nebr., Apr. 9, 1923; s. Lyall Wesley and Elsie Marie (Guy) W. Student, Southwestern U., Georgetown, Tex., 1944-45; student, U. Tex., Austin, 1945-46; BA, U. Idaho, Moscow, 1948; BA in Librarianship, U. Wash., Seattle, 1949; MLS, U. Mich., Ann Arbor, 1952. Sec. Schaefer-Hitchcock Co., Sandpoint, Idaho, 1941-42; asst. librarian Willamette U. Library, Salem, Oreg., 1949-51; cataloger U. Mich. Library, Ann Arbor, 1951-59; serials cataloger N.Y.C. Pub. Library, 1959-66, asst. dir. for cataloging, 1967-88, Astor fellow for library research, 1988-89; mem. subcom. on cataloging standards Research Libraries Group, Palo Alto, Calif., 1978-88. Contbr. poetry to coll. publs., 1944-48; bibliographer for Mexicon, 1986—. Bd. dirs. Eugene James Dance Co., N.Y.C., 1978—. Served with USN, 1943-46. Mem. ALA, Soc. Am. Archaeology, Am. Anthrop. Assn., Archeol. Inst. Am., John Bartram Assn., Bot. Soc. Am., Coun. on Bot. and Hort. Librs., Pre-Columbian Art Rsch. Inst., Soc. for Econ. Botany, Phi Beta Kappa (U. Idaho chpt.). Avocations: New World archeology, Black studies, botany.

WILLIAMS, RICHARD DONALD, retired wholesale food company executive; b. Audubon, Iowa, Feb. 19, 1926; s. Walter Edward and Olga M. (Christensen) W.; m. Carol Francis, June 17, 1950; children: Gayle, Todd, Scott. B.A., Ohio Wesleyan U., 1948; M.B.A., Northwestern U., 1949. Dir. indsl. and pub. rels. Gardner div. Diamond Nat. Corp., Middletown, Ohio, 1949-61; with Fleming Cos., Inc., 1961-89; v.p. pers. Fleming Cos., Inc., Oklahoma City, 1972-76; sr. v.p. human resources Fleming Cos., Inc., 1976-80, exec. v.p. human resources, 1980-89, ret., 1989. Pres. Jr. Achievement, Topeka, Kans., 1972; v.p. Last Frontier council Boy Scouts Am., Oklahoma City, 1980; campaign chmn. United Way Greater Oklahoma City, 1980, pres., 1985-87; bd. dirs. Community Council Central Okla., Oklahoma City chpt. ARC, Support Ctr. Okla., Better Bus. Bur., Okla. City Beautiful. Served with USN, 1944-46. Mem. Am. Soc. Personnel Adminstrn., Soc. Advancement Mgmt., Am. Mgmt. Assn., Phi Gamma Delta. Clubs: Quail Creek Country (Oklahoma City), Petroleum (Oklahoma City); Baille 'd Oklahoma (hon.), La Chaine des Rotisseurs. Home: 2940 Brush Creek Rd Oklahoma City OK 73120-1858

WILLIAMS, RICHARD FRANCIS, insurance executive; b. Oak Park, Ill., Sept. 9, 1941; s. Harvey B. and Marie (Gallery) W.; m. Barbara Ann Zdon, Aug. 8, 1964; children: Ann Marie, Richard Lewis. Student, DePaul U., 1964. Various positions CNA Ins., Chgo., 1964-80; 2asst. v.p. Zurich Ins. Co., Chgo., 1980-84; pres., CEO, Empire Fire & Marine, Omaha, 1984-93, Fidelity & Deposit Co. Md., Balt., 1993—. Republican. Roman Catholic. Home: 15404 Duncan Hill Rd Sparks MD 21152-9765 Office: Fidelity & Deposit Co Md 300 Saint Paul St Baltimore MD 21202-2103

WILLIAMS, RICHARD LEROY, federal judge; b. Morrisville, Va., Apr. 6, 1923; s. Wilcie Edward and Minnie Mae (Brinkley) W.; m. Eugenia Kellogg, Sept. 11, 1948; children: Nancy Williams Davies, R. Gregory, Walter L., Gwendolyn Mason. LLB, U. Va., 1951. Bar: Va. 1951. Ptnr. McGuire, Woods & Battle and predecessor firms, 1951-72; judge Cir. Ct. City of Richmond, 1972-76; ptnr. McGuire, Woods & Battle, 1976-80; dist. judge U.S. Dist. Ct., Richmond, Va., 1980—, sr. judge, 1992—. Served to 2d lt., USAAF, 1940-45. Fellow Am. Coll. Trial Lawyers; mem. Va. State Bar, Va. Bar Assn., Richmond Bar Assn. Office: US Dist Ct/Lewis F Powell 1000 E Main St Ste 228 Richmond VA 23219-3514*

WILLIAMS, RICHARD LUCAS, III, electronics company executive, lawyer; b. Evanston, Ill., Oct. 30, 1940; s. Richard Lucas Jr. and Ellen Gene (Munster) W.; m. Karen Louise Carmody, Nov. 11, 1967. AB, Princeton U., 1962; LLB, U. Va., 1965. Bar: Ill. 1965, D.C. 1968, U.S. Supreme Ct. 1968. Assoc. Winston & Strawn, Chgo., 1968-74; ptnr. Winston & Strawn, 1974-79; sr. v.p., gen. counsel Gould Inc., Rolling Meadows, Ill., 1979-81; sr. v.p., adminstrn., gen. counsel Gould Inc., 1981-90, also bd. dir., 1985-88; ptnr. Smith Williams and Lodge, Chgo., 1990-95, Vedder, Price, Kaufman & Kammholz, Chgo., 1995—; bd. dirs. GNB Batteries, Inc., 1984-86, ULINE Inc., Lake Bluff, Ill. Bd. dirs. Internat. Tennis Hall of Fame, Newport, R.I., 1993-97; v.p. Chgo. Dist. Tennis Assn., 1968-70; vice chmn. Am. Cancer Soc., Chgo., 1984; bd. dirs., pres. Lake Shore Found. for Animals, Chgo., 1990-94. With JAGC USNR, 1965-68. Mem. ABA, Ill. Bar Assn., Chgo. Bar Assn., Execs. Club Chgo. (co-chmn. Western Europe internat. com. 1990-97), Law Club (Chgo.), Meadow Club (Rolling Meadows, gov. 1979—, chmn. 1985-90). Home: 1200 N Lake Shore Dr Chicago IL 60610-2370 Office: Vedder Price 222 N La Salle St Ste 2500 Chicago IL 60601-1002

WILLIAMS, RICHARD THOMAS, lawyer; b. Evergreen Park, Ill., Jan. 14, 1945; s. Raymond Theodore and Elizabeth Dorothy (Williams) W. AB with honors, Stanford U., 1967, MBA, JD, 1972. Bar: Calif. 1972, U.S. Supreme Ct. 1977. Assoc., then ptnr. Kadison Pfaelzer Woodard Quinn & Rossi, L.A., 1972-87; ptnr. Whitman & Ransom, 1987-93, Whitman Breed Abbott & Morgan, L.A., 1993—. Contbg. editor Oil and Gas Analyst, 1978-84. Mem. ABA, L.A. County Bar Assn. Office: Whitman Breed Abbott & Morgan 633 W 5th St Los Angeles CA 90071-2005

WILLIAMS, RICHMOND DEAN, library appraiser, consultant; b. Reading, Mass., Dec. 10, 1925; s. Theodore Ryder and Anabel Lee (Hutchison) W.; m. Eleanor Davidson Washbourne, Sept. 26, 1953; children—Richmond Lyttleton, Eleanor Davidson, Anne Ryder. AB cum laude, Williams Coll., 1950; MA, U. Pa., 1952, PhD, 1959. Instr., asst. dean Williams Coll., Williamstown, Mass., 1954-56; dir. Wyo. Hist. and Geol. Soc., Wilkes-Barre, Pa., 1956-60; asst. dir. Am. Assn. State and Local History, Madison, Wis., 1960-61; dir. libraries Eleutherian Mills-Hagley Found., Wilmington, Del., 1962-87; instr. Acad. Lifelong Learning U. Del., 1996—; cons. archivist M.S. Hershey Found., Pa., 1981—, Md. Dept. Housing and Community Devel., 1993-94; bd. dirs. Scholarly Resources Inc. Co-author: A Look at Ourselves, 1962; author: They Also Served, 1965; compiler: Directory of Historical Records in Delaware, 1995, Writing Haiku, 1997. Sec., U. Del. Library Assocs., Wilmington, 1972-86; mem. adv. bd. Del. Hist. Records, Dover, 1982—; mem. Del. Humanities Forum, Wilmington, 1984-91; trustee Conservation Ctr. Phila., 1984-86. Served to lt. AUS, 1943-47. Pennfield fellow U. Pa., 1953. Mem. Econ. History Assn (sec.-treas. 1975-88), Mid-Atlantic Regional Archives Com., Am. Assn. State and Local History (pres. 1974-76), Am. Antiquarian Soc., Phi Beta Kappa. Avocations: golf; sailing; book collecting. Home and Office: 202 Brecks Ln Wilmington DE 19807-3011

WILLIAMS, ROBERT BENJAMIN, convention center executive; b. Newton, Miss., Jan. 19, 1935; s. Lee W. and Bessie L. (Dowdell) W.; m. Cornelia I. Holiday, June 4, 1963 (div. Jan. 15, 1991); children: Robert Jr., Vincent, Andrea, Lisa, John. BA in Polit. Sci., U. Dayton, 1958; MA in Polit. Sci., Villanova (Pa.) U., 1964; grad., Nat. War Coll., 1979. Commd. 2d lt. U.S. Army, 1958, advanced through grades to col.; prof. mil. sci. Ga. Inst. Tech., 1970-72; chief pers. svc. divsn. U.S. Army, 1973-75, comdr. inf. battalion, 1975-76, strategic policy planner Joint Chiefs of Staff, 1976-78; dep. chief Joint Chiefs of Staff Nuclear Negotiation Divsn., Washington, 1979-82; sr. mil. adviser U.S. delegation to START U.S. Army, Geneva, 1982-83; ret. U.S. Army, 1983; v.p. for student affairs Morehouse Coll., Atlanta, 1983-84; exec. dir. human resources com. of cabinet Commonwealth of Pa., Harrisburg, 1984-87; v.p. of adminstrn. Pa. Convention Ctr. Authority, Phila., 1987—. Vice chmn. Urban Edn. Found., Phila., 1989-94; bd. dirs. Mercy Douglas Human Svcs. Camp, Phila., 1990—; chmn. Housing and Devel. Corp., Phila., 1993—, Trevors Campaign for the Homeless, 1988-93. Republican. Baptist. Office: Pa Conv Ctr Authority 1101 Arch St Philadelphia PA 19107-2208

WILLIAMS, ROBERT BRICKLEY, lawyer; b. Moon Run, Pa., July 3, 1944; s. David Emanuel and Margaret E. (Brickley) W.; m. Teresa Maria Kutzavitch, Aug. 26, 1967; children: R. Benjamin, Lizabeth A., Matthew M. BA, Swarthmore Coll., 1966; JD, Georgetown U., 1969. Bar: Pa. 1969, U.S. Tax Ct. 1974, U.S. Claims Ct. 1978; accredited estate planner. Sr. ptnr. Eckert Seamans Cherin & Mellott, Pitts., 1969-95, Williams, Coulson, Johnson, Lloyd, Parker & Tedesco, LLC, Pitts., 1995—. Trustee Union Cemetery Assn., 1974-97; chmn. Allegheny Tax Soc., Pitts., 1976, Pa. State Tax Conf., 1978, Family Firm Inst., Pitts., 1993, United Way Endowment, Pitts., 1995-97; pres. Union Ch., Gayly, Pa., 1988-92; dir. Estate Planning Coun., Pitts., 1989, Pitts. (Pa.) Presbyn. Found., 1995-97, YMCA Pitts., Cancer Support Network, Neighborhood Elder Care. Fellow Am. Coll. Trusts and Estates Counsel; mem. ABA, Pa. Bar Assn., Allegheny County Bar Assn., Pitts. Rotary (found. chair 1990-96, citation of merit 1993), Pitts. Tax Club. Republican. Avocations: family, travel, charitable and church activities. Office: Williams Coulson Johnson Lloyd Parker & Tedesco LLC 1550 Two Chatham Ctr Pittsburgh PA 15219

WILLIAMS, ROBERT C., company executive. From chmn. to emeritus chmn. James River Corp. Address: PO Box 2218 Richmond VA 23218*

WILLIAMS, ROBERT CHADWELL, history educator; b. Boston, Oct. 14, 1938; s. Charles Reagan and Dorothy (Chadwell) W.; m. Ann Bennett Kingman, Aug. 27, 1960; children: Peter, Margaret, Katharine. B.A., Wesleyan U., 1960; A.M., Harvard U., 1962, Ph.D., 1966. Asst. prof. history Williams Coll., Williamstown, Mass., 1965-70; prof. history Washington U., St. Louis, 1970-86; dean of faculty Davidson Coll., N.C., 1986—; pres. Central Slavic Conf., 1971-72; v.p. History Assocs. Inc., Gaithersburg, Md., 1980—; sr. research assoc. St. Antony's Coll., Oxford, 1985. Author: Culture in Exile, 1972, Artists in Revolution, 1976, Russian Art and American Money, 1980 (Pulitzer nominee), The Other Bolsheviks, 1986, Klaus Fuchs, Atom Spy, 1987, Russia Imagined, 1997; co-author: Crisis Contained, 1982; mem. editorial bd.: Slavic Rev., 1979-82. Fellow Kennan Inst., 1976-77; fellow Am. Council Learned Socs., 1973-74, W. Wilson Found., 1960-61. Mem. Am. Assn. for Advancement of Slavic Studies, Phi Beta Kappa, Sigma Xi. Presbyterian. Office: Davidson Coll Office VP Acad Affairs Davidson NC 28036

WILLIAMS, ROBERT DANA, lawyer; b. Hyannis, Mass., Feb. 21, 1939; s. Harold Warren and Winifred Josephine (Shores) W.; m. Gaye Carol Gorringe, May 30, 1964 (div. 1974); children: Sarah Ann, Amy Alden; m. Barbara Ellen Bruce, Aug. 7, 1976; children: Dana Ariana Brix, Nathaniel Shepard. AB magna cum laude, Harvard U., 1961, LLB, 1964. Bar: Mass. 1965. Rsch. asst. Am. Law Inst., Cambridge, Mass., 1964-65; assoc. Warner & Stackpole, Boston, 1965-71; ptnr. Warner & Stackpole, 1971-85; of counsel Hinckley, Allen, Tobin & Silverstein, Boston, 1985-87; ptnr. Hinckley, Allen, Snyder & Comen, Boston, 1987-90, Wayne, Lazares & Chappell, Boston, 1990-95, Masterman, Culbert & Tully, Boston, 1995—; firm rep. New Eng. Entrepreneurship Coun., Inc. Boston, 1986-89. Bd. govs., exec. com. Concord (Mass.) Mus., 1980-86, capital campaign steering com., 1990-92; bd. dirs. Found. of Mass. Eye and Ear Infirmary, Boston, 1980-91; trustee, sec. Guidance Camps, Inc., 1968-86; trustee Mass. Eye and Ear Infirmary, 1971—, bd. mgrs., 1980-91, chmn. nominating com., 1984-91; dir., sec. Napoleonic Soc. of Am., Clearwater, Fla., 1985-95; bd. dirs. Psychomotor Inst., Inc., Cambridge, Mass., 1979-95. Mem. Orgn. Am. Historians, Am. Soc. Legal History (com. on documentary preservation 1980-88), Phi Beta Kappa. Congregationalist. Avocations: history, antiquarian books. Home: 41 Monument St Concord MA 01742-1841 Office: Masterman Culbert & Tully One Lewis Wharf Boston MA 02110-3985

WILLIAMS, ROBERT EUGENE, astronomer; b. Dunsmuir, Calif., Oct. 14, 1940; s. Francis Henry and Lois Evangeline (Youde) W.; m. Elaine Carolyn Eckwall, Dec. 29, 1961; 1 child, Scott Francis. AB, U. Calif., Berkeley, 1962; PhD, U. Wis., 1965. Rsch. asst. U. Calif., Berkeley, 1960-62; Wis. Alumni Rsch. Found. fellow U. Wis., 1962-65; from asst. prof. to assoc. prof. U. Ariz., Tucson, 1965-78, prof., 1978-83; vis. rsch. assoc. European So. Obs., Garching, 1983-84; NRC sr. rsch. fellow NASA-Ames Rsch. Ctr., 1984-85; dir. Cerro Tololo Inter-Am. Obs., La Serena, Chile, 1985-93, Space Telescope Sci. Inst., 1993—; mem. NRC Spl. Studies Bd., 1995—; mem. exec. com. Aspen (Colo.) Ctr. for Physics, 1983-88, trustee/treas., 1982-88; adj. prof. The Johns Hopkins U., 1993—; sr. Fulbright prof. Univ. Coll. London, 1972-73; mem. NSF Minority Grad. Fellowship Panel, 1982-85, CTID Users Com., 1978-81, Kitt Peak Nat. Observatory Telescope Allocation Com., 1978-80, Cerro Tololo Inter-Am. Observatory Telescope Allocation Com., 1976-78; chmn. U.S. Nat. Fulbright Com., Astronomy, 1974-78. Author 100 profl. papers. Recipient Alexander von Humboldt award German Govt., 1991, Dorothy Klumpke Roberts prize, 1962; Fulbright prof. U. London, 1971-72; Heinz Pagels Meml. lectr., 1995, Stanford Bunyan lectr., 1995, Princeton U. Evain lectr., 1997. Mem. Internat. Astron. Union (U.S. nat. commn. 1990-92), Am. Astron. Soc. (com. on astronomy and pub. policy 1994-96, edn. adv. bd. 1981-83), Astron. Soc. of the Pacific. Avocations: running, biking. Office: Space Telescope Science Institute 3700 San Martin Dr Baltimore MD 21218-2410

WILLIAMS, ROBERT HENRY, oil company executive; b. El Paso, Jan. 12, 1946; s. William Frederick and Mary (Page) W.; m. Joanne Marie Mudd, Oct. 22, 1967; children: Lara, Michael, Suzanne, Jennifer. BS in Physics, U. Tex., El Paso, 1968; PhD in Physics, U. Tex., Austin, 1973; MS in Physics, Va. Poly. Inst., 1971. Dir. Gulf Oil R&D, Houston, 1978-81; tech. mgr. Gulf Oil Internat., Houston, 1981-83; exploration mgr. Gulf Oil Co., Houston, 1983-85; mgr. geophys. rsch. Tenneco Oil Co., Houston, 1985-87, mgr., chief geophysicist, 1987-88; founder, mng. dir. Dover Energy, Houston, 1988—; exec. v.p. Tatham Offshore Inc, Houston, 1989-95, also bd. dirs.; chmn., CEO Dover Tech. Inc., Houston, 1989—; cons. Tenneco Inc., Houston, 1989—; DeepTech Internat., 1992-95; Ukraine Acad. Sci., 1993; bd. dirs., exec. v.p. DeepTech Inc., 1991-95; founder, pres. Westway tech. Assocs., 1986—; co-founder, chmn. CEO Castaway Graphite Rods, Inc., 1990—; owner, CEO Team Tex. Inc., 1993—; Bulldog Lures, Inc., 1994—; founder, CEO Houston Books Inc., 1994—; founder, CEO, chmn. Dover Energy Exploration, 1995—; pres. Westway Interests, 1995—; mng. dir. Swep, LLC; CEO, bd. dirs. Dover (Belize), 1996—; bd. dirs. Tatham Offshore, Swep, Inc. Contbr. articles to profl. jours. Mem. coun. Boy Scouts Am., Houston, 1989—; patron Mus. Fine Arts, Houston, 1990-97, Houston Zool. Soc., 1990-97; leader Girl Scouts U.S., Houston, 1989—, life mem. Mem. Soc. Exploration Geophysics, Am. Assn. Petroleum Geologists, Am. Geophys. Union. Republican. Avocations: scuba diving, book collecting, fishing. Office: Dover Tech 11767 Katy Fwy Ste 1000 Houston TX 77079-1730

WILLIAMS, ROBERT JENE, lawyer, rail car company executive; b. Darby, Pa., Oct. 30, 1931; s. Joslyn Justus and Dolores Marie (Dugan) W.; m. Shirley Geraldine Fiedler, Aug. 8, 1953; children: Robin Jeanne, Sara Ann. B.S., Ursinus Coll., 1953; J.D., U. Pa., 1956. Bar: N.J. 1957, Pa. 1959, Ill. 1973. Asso. firm Bleakly, Stockwell & Zink, Camden, N.J., 1956-58; atty., asst. gen. atty. Reading Co., Phila., 1958-69; gen. counsel, sec. Trailer Train Co., Phila., 1969-71, Trailer Train Co. (now TTX Co.), Chgo., 1971-94; v.p. Trailer Train Co., 1975-94; ret., 1994. Mem. Ill. Bar Assn. Home: 1349 Woodland Dr Deerfield IL 60015-2017

WILLIAMS, ROBERT JOSEPH, museum director, educator; b. Bennington, Vt., June 21, 1944; s. Joseph and Ruthe Allison (Moody) W. BS in Edn., U. Vt., 1970; MA in Interdisciplinary Social Sci., San Francisco State U., 1981. Tchr. adult edn. Mt. Anthony Union High Sch., Bennington, Vt., 1972-74; columnist Bennington Banner, 1972-77; tchr. San Francisco State U., 1976-79; founder, dir. NORRAD Drug Rehab. Ctr., San Francisco, 1986-88; museum curator Shaftsbury (Vt.) Historical Soc., 1989—; founder, dir. Bennington Tutorial Ctr., 1971-74. Author: Toward Humanness in Education, 1981, Chalice of Leaves: Selected Essays and Poems, 1988, Modern Salvation: Guidelines from Cosmology, 1994; author: (with others) Intimacy, 1985. Recipient Edmunds Essay medal Vt. Historical Soc., Montpelier, 1961, award of the League of Vt. Writers, 1972, Golden Poet award World of Poetry, Sacramento, Calif., 1990. Democrat. Avocation: cosmology. Home: 102 Putnam St Bennington VT 05201-2348 Office: Shaftsbury Hist Soc PO Box 401 Shaftsbury VT 05262-0401 *I sought the truth, and sought to live by it.*

WILLIAMS, ROBERT LEON, psychiatrist, neurologist, educator; b. Buffalo, July 22, 1922; s. Leon R. and L. Paulyne (Ingraham) W.; m. Shirley Glynn Miller, Feb. 5, 1949; Karen, Kevin. B.A., Alfred U., 1944; M.D., Albany Med. Coll., Union U., 1946. Chief neurology and psychiatry Lackland AFB Hosp., USAF, San Antonio, 1952-55; cons. neurology and psychiatry to USAF Surgeon Gen., 1955-58; faculty Coll. Medicine, U. Fla., Gainesville, 1958-72, prof., chmn. dept. psychiatry, 1964-72; prof. psychiatry Baylor Coll. Medicine, Houston, 1972-92, chmn. dept., 1972-90, prof. neurology, 1976-92, acting chmn. dept., 1976-77, prof. emeritus psychiatry and neurology, 1992—; mem. faculty various univs., part time 1949-58 including Albany Med. Coll. at Union U., Columbia Coll. Physicians and Surgeons, Boston U., U. Tex., Georgetown U. Author: (with W.B. Webb) Sleep Therapy: A. Bibliography and Commentary, 1966, (with others) EEG of Human Sleep: Clinical Applications, 1974; editor: (with Ismet Karacan and Carolyn J. Hursch) Psychopharmacology of Sleep, 1976, Sleep Disorders: Diagnosis and Treatment, 1978, 2d edit., 1988; (with others) Phenomenology and Treatment of Anxiety, 1979, of Alcoholism, 1980, of Psychophysiological Disorders, 1982, of Psychosexual Disorders, 1983, of Psychiatric Emergencies, 1984. Served from 1st lt. to lt. col. USAF, 1949-58; col. Res., ret. Recipient Cert. Profl. Achievement USAF Surgeon Gen., 1967. Mem. Am. Psychiat. Assn., Am. Electroencephalographic Soc., Am. Coll. Psychiatrists (pres. 1982-83), Am. Acad. Neurology, AMA, Group for Advancement of Psychiatry, Benjamin Rush Soc. (pres. 1986-88), Accreditation Coun. for grad. Med. Edn. (residency rev. com. for psychiatry 1985-93), Alpha Omega Alpha. Research and publs. on basic psychophysiology of human sleep.

WILLIAMS, ROBERT LUTHER, city planning consultant; b. Porterville, Calif., June 24, 1923; s. Luther Esco and Mary (Lyon) W.; children: Jeffrey Robert, Derrick Paul, Gail Diane. Student, Utah State Coll., 1944; A.B., U. Calif.-Berkeley, 1949, M.C.P., 1951. Asst. planning dir. Stockton, Calif., 1951-54; planning dir. Alameda, Calif., 1954-57, Alameda County, 1957-63; exec. dir. Am. Inst. Planners, Washington, 1963-69; v.p. Hill Devel. Corp., Middletown, Conn., 1969-71; dir. land mgmt. dept. Gulf Oil Corp., Reston, Va., 1971-74; pres. Coleman-Williams, Inc., Greenbrae, Calif., 1975-78, Robert Williams Assocs., Inc., San Rafael, Calif., 1978-87; mem. community affairs panel KQED-TV, San Francisco, 1991-94; lectr. U. Calif. at Berkeley extension, 1956-59; tech. adviser regional planning Assn. Bay Area Govts., Calif., 1961-63; vis. prof. U. R.I., 1969-71; pres. G.I.F.T. Inst., Inc., 1991-94. Bd. dirs. Planning Found. Am., 1965-70, Communities Found., Inc., 1973-77. Served to 1st lt. AUS, 1943-46, 52, ETO. Named Young Man of Year Alameda, 1956. Mem. Am. Inst. Cert. Planners (pres. Calif. chpt. 1960), Am. Planning Assn., World Future Soc., Lambda Alpha, Lambda Chi Alpha. Presbyterian. Home: RR #2 Box 379 Pitcher Pond Rd Lincolnville ME 04849

WILLIAMS, ROBERT LYLE, corporate executive, consultant; b. Nowata, Okla., June 22, 1942; s. Clifford Lyle and Eula Mae (Barnes) W.; m. Lorene Linnet Dillahunty, June 12, 1965; 1 child, Eleanor Lynn. B.S., Okla. State U., 1964; M.B.A., Baylor U., 1965. Acctg. supr. Southwestern Bell Telephone Co., Houston, 1965-66; fin. exec. Ford Motor Co., Dearborn, Mich., 1969-80; treas. Ford Brazil, Sao Paulo, 1976-79, Agrico Chem. Co., Tulsa, 1980-82; v.p., chief fin. officer Texas City Refining, Inc., Tex., 1983-88; sr. v.p. Furnishings 2000, Inc., San Diego, 1988-89; pvt. cons. Houston, 1990—; chmn. Galveston County Taxpayers Research Council, 1987-88. Served to lt. USN, 1966-69. Republican. Presbyterian. Avocation: travel. Office: 2500 E T C Jester Blvd Ste 200 Houston TX 77008-1375

WILLIAMS, ROBERT MARTIN, economist, consultant; b. N.Y.C., May 4, 1913; s. Joseph Tuttle and Mary Adeline (Johnson) W.; m. Vera Jean Bobsene, July 31, 1956; 1 son, Kenneth Martin. B.A., Pomona Coll., 1934; M.A., UCLA, 1942; Ph.D., Harvard U., 1950. Teaching fellow physics Dartmouth Coll., 1935-36; mgmt. trainee Western Electric Co., Inc., Los Angeles, 1936-40; lectr. UCLA, 1947-51, asst. prof., 1951-56, assoc. prof., 1956-63, prof. bus. econs. and statis. Grad. Sch. Mgmt., 1963-83, prof. emeritus, 1983—, vice chmn. dept. mgmt., 1961-67, dir. bus. forecasting project, 1952-81, consulting, 1981—; dir. Imperial Corp. Am., 1975-86, emeritus dir., 1986—; dir. Am. Savs. and Loan Assn. Kans., 1982-86, Silver State Savs. and Loan Assn. Colo., 1982-86; mem. exec. com., dir. Imperial Savs. and Loan Assn. Calif., 1978-82; econ. cons. Fed. Res. Bank Kansas City, Lockheed Aircraft Corp., others, also state and fed. agys. Editor, contbr. The UCLA Business Forecast for the Nation and California, 1961-88; contbr. numerous articles on bus. forecasting and regional econ. devel. Served to lt. comdr. USNR, 1942-46. Resources for Future, Inc. Research grantee, 1962; NSF grantee, 1965. Mem. Am. Econ. Assn., Am. Statis. Assn., Nat. Assn. Bus. Economists, World Future Soc., Centre for Internat. Rsch. on Econ. Tendency Surveys, Ostomy Assn. L.A. (exec. v.p. 1989—). Home: 750 Enchanted Way Pacific Palisades CA 90272-2818 Office: UCLA John E Anderson Grad Sch Mgmt Bus Forecasting Project Los Angeles CA 90095

WILLIAMS, ROBERT ROY, trade association administrator; b. Lima, Ohio, Aug. 31, 1909; s. Forrest Clyde and Minnie May (McKee) W.; m. Alyce Hogarth, Aug. 14, 1937 (dec. Mar. 1996); children: Cheryl Elizabeth Williams Lucks, Robert Roy Williams, Jr. Student, Miami U., Oxford, Ohio, 1929-33; LHD (hon.), Urbana U., 1996. Exec. v.p. Ohio State Restaurant Assn., Columbus, 1938-53, Nat. Food Svc. Assn., Columbus, 1953—; lectr. trade assn. mgmt., Ohio State U., Columbus, 1947-53. Benefactor Cuyahoga Falls Schs. Found. Mem. Am. Soc. Assn. Execs. (Distinguished Svc. award, 1986), Nat. Rep. Assn. (pres. 1992—), Nat. Rep. Found. (life), Am. Legion (life), Navy League U.S. (life), Sigma Chi (Constantine award, 1994), Rotary Club (Paul Harris fellow, 1986), Masons. Methodist. Developer continental cadre sys. for Nat. Rep. Found., creator term food service. Avocations: world travel, photography, genealogical research. Home: 3010 Sunset Dr Columbus OH 43202-1954 Office: Nat Food Svc Assn PO Box 1932 Columbus OH 43216-1932

WILLIAMS, ROBERT WALTER, physics educator; b. Palo Alto, Calif., June 3, 1920; s. Philip S. and Louise (Brown) W.; m. Erica Lehman, Sept. 23, 1969; children: Paul, David, Eric. AB, Stanford U., 1941; MA, Princeton U., 1943; PhD, MIT, 1948. Assoc. physicist Los Alamos Lab., 1943-46; rsch. assoc. MIT, 1946-48, asst. prof., 1948-52, assoc. prof., 1952-59; prof. physics U. Wash., Seattle, 1959-90, prof. emeritus, 1990—; cons. Boeing Co., Seattle, 1961-64; vis. scientist CERN (European Orgn. Nuclear Rsch.) Lab., Geneva, 1967, 74, 81, 88—; trustee Univs. Rsch. Assn., 1978-84. Contbr. articles to profl. jours. Fellow Am. Phys. Soc., Am. Acad. Arts and Scis. Research on properties of fundamental particles. Home: 3413 E Laurelhurst Dr NE Seattle WA 98105-5357 Office: Univ Wash Dept Physics Box 351560 Seattle WA 98195-1560

WILLIAMS, ROBERTA GAY, pediatric cardiologist, educator; b. Rocky Mount, N.C., Oct. 23, 1941. BS, Duke U., 1963; MD, U. N.C., 1968. Diplomate Am. Bd. Pediats. (mem. com. ofcl. examiners 1985—, bd. dirs. and rep. sub-bd. chmn. com. 1992—, mem. exec. com. 1993—), Am. Bd. Pediat. Cardiology (chmn. 1991-92, cons. 1993). Med.-pediat. intern N.C. Meml. Hosp., Chapel Hill, 1968-69; pediat. resident Columbia Presbyn. Med. Ctr., N.Y., 1969-70; fellow in cardiology Children's Hosp. Med. Ctr., Boston, 1970-73, from asst. in cardiology to assoc. in cardiology, 1973-75, sr. assoc. in cardiology, 1976-82; from instr. pediats. to asst. prof. pediats. Harvard Med. Sch.-Children's Hosp., Boston, 1973-82; assoc. prof. pediats. UCLA Med. Ctr., 1982-86, chief divsn. pediat. cardiology, 1982-95, prof. pediats., 1986-95; chair pediatrics U. N.C. Sch. Medicine, Chapel Hill, 1995—; attending physician Cardiac Med. Svcs., Children's Hosp. Med. Ctr., Boston, 1974, cardiology cons. Cardiothoracic Surgery Svc., 1974, med. dir. Cardiovasc. Surgery ICU, 1974-79, dir. Cardiac Graphic Lab. and Cost Ctr., 1977-82, mem. com. neonatal ICU, 1978-79, v.p. med. staff, 1980-81; guest lectr., invited spkr., seminar leader in field. Mem. editl. bd.: Pediat. Cardiology, 1979, Circulation, 1983-91, Am. Jour. Cardiology, 1984-91, Jour. Applied Cardiology, 1985, Clin. Cardiology, 1988, Internat. Jour. Cardiology, 1992-95, Archives of Pediats. and Adolescent Medicine, 1994—; editl. cons. Jour. of Am. Coll. of Cardiology, 1992-94. Mem. exec. coun. cardiovasc. disease in the young Am. Heart Assn., 1979-85, mem. subcom. congenital cardiac defects, 1980-82, subcom. nominating com., 1982-83; mem. Am. Heart Assn.-Greater L.A. affiliate, 1983—, exec. com. and rsch. com., 1984—, judge young investigator competition, 1984, mem. program com., 1986-90, v.p. med.-exec. com., 1991-92, pres.-elect, 1992-93, and numerous other coms. Fellow Am. Coll. Cardiology (allied health profls. com. 1984-87, mem. physician workforce adv. com. 1988-94, mem. manpower adv. com. 1988—, mem. extramural continuing edn. com. Heart House 1990—, co-chmn. Bethesda conf. 1993, gov. So. Calif. chpt. 1994—, pres. Calif. chpt. 1994—), Am. Acad. Pediats. (sec. exec. com. sect. on cardiology 1985-87, mem. com. on fetus and newborn 1985-88, mem. exec. com. sect. on cardiology 1985—, chmn. program com. 1988-89, mem. subcom. Am. Heart Assn. task force on assessment of diagnosis and therapeutic cardiovascular procedures 1989, chairperson sec. cardiology 1989, mem. credentials com. 1991—, mem. coun. on sects. mgmt. com. 1995—); mem. Soc. for Pediat. Rsch., Am. Pediat. Soc., Am. Soc. Echocardiography (mem. exec. com. 1975-78, com. on guidelines for technician tng. 1975-78, bd. dirs. 1976-80, treas. exec. coun. com. 1981-83). Avocations: photography, hiking. Office: U NC Dept Pediatrics CB 7220 509 Burnett-Womack Chapel Hill NC 27599

WILLIAMS, ROBIN, actor, comedian; b. Chgo., July 21, 1951; s. Mr. and Mrs. Robert W.; m. Valerie Velardi, June 4, 1978 (div.); 1 child, Zachary; m. Marsha Garces, Apr. 30, 1989; children: Zelda, Cody. Attended, Claremont Men's Coll., Marin Coll., Juilliard Sch., N.Y.C. Started as stand-up comedian in San Francisco clubs, including Holy City Zoo, The Boardinghouse; later became regular at Comedy Store, Los Angeles; appeared in TV series Laugh-In, The Richard Pryor Show, America 2-Night, Happy Days, Homicide: Life on the Streets, 1993 (Emmy nomination, Guest Actor - Drama Series, 1994); star of TV series Mork and Mindy, 1978-82 (People's Choice award), (cable) Robin Williams: An Evening at the Met, 1986 (Grammy award), host of HBO's Shakespeare: The Animated Tales, 1993 (CableAce Award, Best Entertainment Host); film appearances include: Popeye, 1980, The World According to Garp, 1982, The Survivors, 1983, Moscow on the Hudson, 1984, Club Paradise, 1986, Good Morning Vietnam, 1987 (Golden Globe award 1988, Acad. Award nominee for best actor), The Adventures of Baron Munchausen, 1989, Dead Poets Society, 1989 (Best Actor nomination Golden Globe award, 1994, nominated best actor Acad. award), Cadillac Man, 1990, The Fisher King, 1991 (Golden Globe award, Acad. award nominee for best actor 1991), Dead Again, 1991, Hook, 1991, Aladdin (voice) (Spl. Achievement award Hollywood Fgn. Press, Nat. Bd. Rev. 1992), 1992, Toys, 1992, Mrs. Doubtfire, 1993 (Best Picture, Best Actor in a Musical or Comedy, Golden Globe, 1994, Best Picture, Best Actor, People's Choice award), Nine Months, 1995, Jumanji, 1995, The Bird Cage, 1996, Jack, 1996, The Secret Agent, 1996, Hamlet, 1996; theatre: Waiting for Godot, 1988; recorded albums: Reality, What a Concept, 1979 (Grammy award), Throbbing Python of Love, A Night at the Met (Grammy award); host Comic Relief, 1986; appeared in TV variety programs, ABC Presents a Royal Gala, 1988 (Emmy award, 1988), Carol, Carl, Whoopi & Robin, 1987 (Emmy award). Recipient Golden Apple award Hollywood Women's Press Club; Golden Globe award; ACE award; Am. Comedy award, 1987, 88; Grammy award for best comedy rec., 1987. Office: PO Box 480909 Los Angeles CA 90048-9509

WILLIAMS, ROGER LAWRENCE, historian, educator; b. Boulder, Colo., June 22, 1923; s. Raymond Ustick and Mabel (Woolf) W. BA, Colo. Coll., 1947; MA, U. Mich., 1948, PhD, 1951. Asst. prof. Minn. State Coll., Mankato, 1950-52, MIT, Cambridge, 1952-55; vis. prof. Mich. State U., East Lansing, 1955-56; assoc. prof. Antioch Coll., Yellow Springs, Ohio, 1956-65; prof. U. Calif., Santa Barbara, 1965-71; prof. U. Wyo., Laramie, 1971-78, Disting. prof., 1978-88. Author: French Revolution of 1870-71, 1969, The Mortal Napoleon III, 1971, The Horror of Life, 1980, Aven Nelson of Wyoming, 1984, Gérard and Jaume: Two Neglected Figures in the History of the Jussiaean Classification, 1988, Napoleon III and the Stoffel Affair, 1993, The Letters of Dominique Chaix, Botanist-Curé, 1997; co-author: How

Modernity Came to a Provençal Town, 1988, Handbook of Rocky Mountain Plants, 1992; mem. editorial bd. Antioch Rev., 1958-64. Vol. Rocky Mountain Nat. Park, Estes Park, Colo., 1986-87. Mem. French Hist. Studies (life), History Sci. Soc. (life), Nat. Coun. for History Edn., N.Y. Bot. Soc., Denver Bot. Soc. Home: 1701 S 17th St Laramie WY 82070-5406

WILLIAMS, ROGER STEWART, physician; b. San Diego, Feb. 15, 1941; s. Manley Samuel and Ethelyn Mae W.; children: Roger S., Karen E., David G., Sarah E. MD cum laude, Emory U., 1966. Diplomate Am. Bd. Psychiatry and Neurology. Intern, Grady Hosp., Atlanta, 1966-67. Med. resident Emory U., Atlanta, 1966-68; resident neurology Mass. Gen. Hosp., Boston, 1970-73, assoc. neurologist, 1973-87; assoc. prof. neurology Harvard Med. Sch., Boston, 1977-87; neurologist Billings (Mont.) Clinic, 1987—; adj. prof. Mont. State U., Bozeman. Contbr. articles to profl. jours. Served to lt. comdr. USN, 1968-70. Kennedy fellow Kennedy Found., Washington, 1973-75; NIMH grantee, Bethesda, Md., 1979-87. Mem. Am. Acad. Neurology, Mont. Med. Assn., AMA, Alpha Omega Alpha.

WILLIAMS, ROGER WRIGHT, public health educator; b. Great Falls, Mont., Jan. 24, 1918; s. Elmer Howard and Mary (Stuart-Davidson) W.; m. Marjorie Madeline Jones, May 9, 1943; children: Barbara, Stuart Roger. B.S., U. Ill., 1939, M.S., 1941; postgrad., Cornell U., U. N.C. Sch. Pub. Health; Ph.D., Columbia Sch. Pub. Health, 1947; cert. applied parasitology and entomology, U. London, 1957. Mem. faculty Columbia Sch. Pub. Health, N.Y.C., 1944-83, prof. med. entomology, 1966-82, prof. emeritus, 1983, acting head div. tropical medicine, 1970; cons. USPHS, Alaska, 1949, Newton, Ga., 1952, Therapeutic Research Found. of Phila. Inc., 1949, Jackson Hole Preserve Inc., Govt. V.I., U.S. Nat. Park Service, 1959-61, Rockefeller Found., Trinidad, W.I. and Brazil, 1963; filariasis research project WHO, Rangoon, Burma, 1966-70; mem. arbovirus field staff Rockefeller Found., Nigeria, 1964-65; mem. Corp. Bermuda Biol. Sta. for Rsch., 1955-80. Contbr. articles on arthropods of med. importance and diseases they transmit to profl. jours. and books. Mem. Tenafly (N.J.) Cmty. Orch., 1960-63; mem. Tenafly Town-Wide Com., 1970; mem. Boys Activities Com., 1968-72, trustee, 1969-72, pres., 1970-72; chmn. dads' com. troop 140 Boy Scouts Am., Tenafly, 1968-69, merit badge councilor, 1965-83, 88-92; mem. Ocean County Coun., 1991-92; dist. coord. Manchester Township, N.J., 1989-91; trustee Tenafly Nature Ctr., 1967-71, v.p., 1968-71; adv. bd. Am. Christian Coll., 1971-78; deacon Tenafly Presbyn. Ch., 1968-74, elder, 1974-79, 81-82; deacon Lakehurst Presbyn. Ch., 1984-87, elder, 1988-93, chmn. Vesper com., mem. chapel com. and exec. com. Crestwood Manor, 1993—; vol. Meals on Wheels program, 1989-92. Officer USNR, 1943-46. Recipient commendation Boy Scouts Am., 1990; Rockefeller traveling fellow, 1947; Childs Frick fellow Bermuda, 1955, 57; NSF sr. postdoctoral fellow U. London (Eng.) Sch. Hygiene and Tropical Medicine, 1956-57; La. State U. Sch. Medicine fellow in tropical medicine Central Am., 1957. Fellow AAAS; mem. Internat. Coll. Tropical Medicine, Internat. Filariasis Assn., Am. Wash. Entomol. Socs., Am. Mosquito Control Assn., Am. Soc. Parasitologists, Am. Royal Socs. Tropical Medicine and Hygiene, Elisha Mitchel Sci. Soc., N.Y. Soc. Tropical Medicine (pres. 1969-70), Tenafly Swim Club (trustee 1972-74, v.p. 1973, pres. 1974), Travel Club of Leisure Village West (bd. dirs. 1983-89, v.p. 1988), Nature Club (pres. 1989), Kiwanis (pres. elect Leisure Village West chpt. 1985-86, pres. 1986-87, Disting. past pres. 1987-88), Mens Club Crestwood Manor, 1993—, Phi Sigma. Achievements include discovery of a Filariasis model for laboratory research on human filariasis; the first filariid parasite to be demonstrated to be transmitted by a mite; co-discoverer West African Arbovirus, Dugbe virus. Home: 50 Lacey Rd Ste B103 Whiting NJ 08759-2954 *Success is living in peace and contentment with one's self. I have attempted to achieve this by leading what I consider to be a Christian Life and helping others to do the same, by giving some of my time to help improve the world around us for others, and by giving a little more effort to a task than the minimum necessary to just get it done.*

WILLIAMS, RONALD BOAL, JR., financial consulting company executive, software designer, consultant; b. Lake Forest, Ill., Dec. 23, 1938; s. Ronald Boal Sr. and Dorothy (Herreman) W.; m. Sue Ellen White, Dec. 23, 1961; children: Elizabeth Daugherty, Anna O'Dwyer, Abigail. BA, U. Wis., 1961; MBA, Northwestern U., Evanston, Ill., 1969. Cert. mgmt. cons. Fin. analyst The Richardson Co., Melrose Park, Ill., 1965-68; from exec. coord. to dir. corp. planning Beatrice Foods Co., Chgo., 1968-82; exec. v.p. Systema Corp., Chgo., 1980-82; pres. RW Assocs., Hinsdale, Ill., 1982-84; exec. v.p. Fin. Tng. Resources, Lombard, Ill., 1983—. Author: Positive Outlook Calendar, 1996, 97; contbr. articles to profl. jours. Mem. Dist. 58 Sch. Bd., 1976-79; adv. bd. Clear Air Engring., 1996—. Lt. USN, 1961-65. Avocations: marathon running. Home: 4825 Seeley Ave Downers Grove IL 60515-3411 Office: Fin Tng Resources 905 Parkview Blvd Lombard IL 60148-3267

WILLIAMS, RONALD DEAN, minister, religious organization executive; b. Decatur, Ill., Oct. 23, 1940; s. Henry Lawrence and Ella Loudica Williams; m. Carole Jeanette Lane, June 16, 1962; children: Scott Allan, Mark Lawrence, Derek James. BTh, LIFE Bible Coll., L.A., 1965; DD, Internat. Ch. Foursquare Gospel, L.A., 1992. Ordained to ministry Internat. Ch. Foursquare Gospel, 1966. Pastor Foursquare Gospel Ch., Surrey, B.C., Can., 1965-69; missionary Foursquare Gospel Ch., Hong Kong, 1969-85; prof. LIFE Bible Coll., 1985-95; mng. editor Foursquare World ADVANCE, 1993—; comm. officer Internat. Ch. of Foursquare Gospel, 1988—; bd. dirs. Foursquare Gospel Ch.; pres. exec. bd. Internat. Pentecostal Press Assn., Oklahoma City, 1990—; comm. officer Pentecostal/Charismatic Chs. North Am., Memphis, 1994—; coord. E. Coun. Foursquare Miss., 1979-82. Editor: The Vine and The Branches, 1992; mng. editor Foursquare World ADVANCE mag., 1985. With USAF, 1958-61. Avocations: writing, golf, reading, music. Office: Internat Ch Foursquare Gospel 1910 W Sunset Blvd Ste 200 Los Angeles CA 90026-3247

WILLIAMS, RONALD L., pharmaceutical association executive; b. Akron, Ohio, July 30, 1935; s. Reuben and Thelma W. BS in Pharmacy, Ohio No. U., 1957. Pharmacist, pharmacy owner Akron, 1957-66; exec. sec. Student Am. Pharm. Assn., Washington, 1968-71, 77-81; asst. exec. sec. Am. Pharm. Assn. Acad. Pharm. Practice, Washington, 1971-72; exec. sec. Am. Pharm. Assn. Acad. Pharm. Practice, 1972-83, Am. Pharm. Assn. Acad. Pharm. Sci., 1978-83; dir. liaison and state relations Am. Pharm. Assn., 1983-85, dir. profl. affairs, 1985-86, dir. communications, 1986-90, exec. dir. planning, exec. officer ops., 1990-95, dir. comm., strategic planning, 1995—, coord. pharm. recovery program, 1984-95; nat. high blood pressure coord. com., 1977-86, Interdisciplinary Task Force on Provider Roles, 1979-80, U.S. Drug Enforcement Adminstrn./Pharmacy Working Com., 1974-86; co-chmn. Nat. Conf. on High Blood Pressure Control, 1979-80; ann. meeting planning com. Nat. Coun. on Patient Info. and Edn., 1985-86; mem. Medic Alert Nat. Pharmacy Task Group, 1985-92, Poison Prevention Week Coun., 1988-94; mem. informal steering com. Com. on Prescription Drug Abuse, 1982-86; leader pharmacists sect. U. Utah Sch. Alcohol and Other Drug Dependencies, 1984-95; adv. bd. Ohio No. U. Coll. Pharmacy, 1987-94, Campbell U. Coll. Pharmacy, 1993—; planning com. Nat. Conf. on Impaired Health Profl., 1986-88. Editor: Pharmacy Practice, 1971-86, Pharmacy Student, 1977-82, Acad. Reporter, 1978-83. Named Distiguished Person of Yr., Pharmacist Planning Svc., Inc., 1996; recipient Ewart A. Swinyard award U. Utah Sch. on Alcoholism and Other Drug Dependencies, 1996. Mem. AMA (affiliate), Am. Pharm. Assn., Washington Pharm. Assn., Am. Soc. Assn. Execs., Soc. for Profl. Well-Being, Cuyahoga Falls Schs., Found., Am. Legion, Kappa Psi. Democrat. Methodist. Office: Am Pharm Assn 2215 Constitution Ave NW Washington DC 20037-2907

WILLIAMS, RONALD LEE, pharmacologist; b. Koleen, Ind., June 26, 1936; s. Marion Raymond and Doris May (Lynch) W.; m. Sondra Sue Cobb, June 7, 1957; children: Robin Lee, Christopher P., David R., Jonathan V. BS, Butler U., 1959, MS, 1961; PhD, Tulane U., 1964. Registered pharmacist, Colo. From instr. to assoc. prof. pharmacology La. State U., New Orleans, 1964-84, assoc. prof. medicine, 1978-84, ret., 1984; asst. dir. Dept. of Corrections Hosp. Pharmacy, Canon City, Colo., 1986-93; with Canon Pharmacy, Canon City, Colo., 1994-95; with pharmacy svc. VA Med. Ctr., Ft. Lyon, Colo., 1996—; expert adv. panel renal drugs U.S. Pharmacopeia Drug Info., 1981-85; cons. in field. Editorial bd. jour. Pharmacology, 1979; reviewer jour. Pharmaceutical Sci., 1976; contbr. articles to profl. jours. La. Heart Assn. grantee, 1964, 66. Mem. Am. Soc. Pharmacology, N.Y. Acad. Sci., Fedn. Am. Soc. Exptl. Biology, So. Colo. Soc. Hosp. Pharm. Assn., Sigma Xi, Rho Chi. Republican. Baptist. Avocations: hiking, camping, back-packing, hunting.

WILLIAMS, RONALD OSCAR, systems engineer; b. Denver, May 10, 1940; s. Oscar H. and Evelyn (Johnson) W. BS in Applied Math., U. Colo. Coll. Engring., 1964, postgrad. U. Colo., U. Denver, George Washington U. Computer programmer Apollo Systems dept., missile and space divsn. Gen. Electric Co., Kennedy Space Ctr., Fla., 1965-67, Manned Spacecraft Ctr., Houston, 1967-68; computer programmer U. Colo., Boulder, 1968-73; computer programmer analyst def. systems divsn. System Devel. Corp. for NORAD, Colorado Springs, 1974-75; engr. def. systems and command-and-info. systems Martin Marietta Aerospace, Denver, 1976-80; systems engr. space and comm. group, def. info. systems divsn. Hughes Aircraft Co., Aurora, Colo., 1980-89; rsch. analyst, 1990—. Vol. fireman Clear Lake City (Tex.) Fire Dept., 1968; officer Boulder Emergency Squad, 1969-76, rescue squadman, 1969-76, liaison to cadets, 1971, pers. officer, 1971-76, exec. bd., 1971-76, award of merit, 1971, 72, emergency med. technician 1973—; spl. police officer Boulder Police Dept., 1970-75; spl. dep. sheriff Boulder County Sheriff's Dept., 1970-71; nat. adv. bd. Am. Security Coun., 1979-91, Coalition of Peace through Strength, 1979-91. Served with USMCR, 1958-66. Decorated Organized Res. medal; recipient Cost Improvement Program award Hughes Aircraft Co., 1982, Systems Improvement award, 1982, Top Cost Improvement Program award, 1983. Mem. AAAS, AIAA (sr.), Math. Assn. Am., Am. Math. Soc., Soc. Indsl. and Applied Math., Math. Study Unit of the Am. Topical Assn., Armed Forces Comm. and Electronics Assn., Assn. Old Crows, Am. Def. Preparedness Assn., Marine Corps Assn., Air Force Assn., U.S. Naval Inst., Nat. Geog. Soc., Smithsonian Instn., Soc. Amateur Radio Astronomers, Met. Opera Guild, Colo. Hist. Soc., Hist. Denver, Inc., Historic Boulder, Inc., Hawaiian Hist. Soc., Denver Botanic Gardens, Denver Mus. Natural History, Denver Zool. Found., Inc., Mensa. Lutheran.

WILLIAMS, ROSS EDWARD, physicist; b. Carlinville, Ill., June 28, 1922; s. Cyrus Hillis and Mildred Denby (Ross) W.; m. Carolyn Chenoweth Williams, July 5, 1958 (div. June 12, 1986); children: Robert H. (dec.), Katherine J., Ross E. Jr.; m. Madeleine D. Peters, Sept. 14, 1996. BS in Physics and Math., Bowdoin Coll., Brunswick, Maine, 1940-43; MS in Physics, Columbia U., 1947; PhD in Physics, 1955. Instr. in Physics Bowdoin Coll., Brunswick, Maine, 1942-43; project engr. Spl. Devices Ctr. ONR, Sands Point, L.I., 1946; sr. rsch. engr. Sperry Products, Inc., Danbury, Conn., 1947-49; cons., govt. and indsl. pvt. practice, 1953-60; sr. rsch. assoc. Hudson Labs Columbia U., Dobbs Ferry, N.Y., 1960-65; assoc. dir., 1965-68; prof. Engring. and Applied Sci. Columbia U., N.Y.C., 1968-74; pres., CEO Ocean and Atmospheric Scis., Inc., Dobbs Ferry, N.Y., 1974—; cons. Nat. Acad. Scis., Washington, 1967—, Naval Rsch. Lab., Washington, 1968-78; dir. Ocean and Atmospheric Sci. Inc., Dobbs Ferry, N.Y., 1968—, Optimum Applied Systems, Inc., Dobbs Ferry, N.Y., 1974—, Valleywood Realty, Inc., Yonkers, N.Y., 1991—, Esthetic Challenges, Inc., Exeter, N.H., 1993—. Lay leader, 1976-79, trustee, 1985-94, Asbury United Meth. Ch., Tuckahoe, N.Y., 1976-79. Lt. USNR, 1943-46. Fellow Acoustical Soc. Am., 1994. Mem. Am. Phys. Soc., Phi Beta Kappa, Sigma Xi. Avocations: hiking, ice skating. Home: 24 Laurel Hill Rd Hollis NH 03149 Office: Ocean & Atmospheric Science Inc 145 Palisade St Dobbs Ferry NY 10522-1617

WILLIAMS, ROY, university athletic coach. Head coach U. Kansas Jayhawks, 1988—. Named Nat. Rookie Coach of Yr., Basketball Times, 1989, Coach of Yr., Basketball Writers Assn., 1990, Big 8 Coach of Yr., AP and UPI, 1990, Big 8 Coach of Yr., AP, 1992, Nat. Coach of Yr., 1992. 1991 NCAA Tournament runner-up. Office: Univ Kansas Allen Fieldhouse Lawrence KS 66045*

WILLIAMS, RUTH ELIZABETH (BETTY WILLIAMS), retired secondary school educator; b. Newport News, Va., July 31, 1938; d. Lloyd Haynes and Erma Ruth (Goodrich) W. BA, Mary Washington Coll., 1960; cert. d'etudes, Converse Coll., 1961, U. Oreg., 1962. Cert. tchr., Va. French tchr. York High Sch., York County Pub. Schs., Yorktown, Va., 1960-65; French resource tchr. Newport News Pub. Schs., 1966-74, tchr. French and photography, 1974-81, tchr. French, Spanish, German and Latin, 1981-91, ret., 1991; pres. Cresset Publs., Williamsburg, Va., 1977—; lectr. Sch. Edn., Coll. Williamand Mary, Williamsburg, 1962-65; French tchr., coord. fgn. langs. York County Pub. Schs., 1962-65; workshop leader dept. pub. instrn. State of Del., Dover, 1965; cons. Health de Rochemont Co., Boston, 1962-71. Driver Meals on Wheels, Williamsburg, 1989-90; contbr. Va. Spl. Olympics, Richmond, 1987—; charter mem. Capitol Soc. Colonial Williamsburg Found., Inc., 1994; mem. Colonial Williamsburg Assembly, Colonial Williamsburg Found., Inc.; mem. Altar Guild, Bruton Parish Ch., Williamsburg, 1960—. Grantee Nat. Def. Edn. Act, 1961, 1962. Mem. AAAU, Fgn. Lang. Assn. Va., AARP (ret. tchrs. divsn.), Heritage Soc., Mary Washington Coll. Alumni Assn., Va. Hist. Soc., Am. Assn. Tchrs. French, Mortar Bd., Women in the Arts, Alpha Phi Sigma, Phi Sigma Iota. Episcopalian. Avocations: photography, coin and stamp collecting, geology, walking, sailing. Home and Office: 471 Catesby Ln Williamsburg VA 23185-4732

WILLIAMS, RUTH L., rehabilitation counselor, consultant; b. Dubois, Pa., July 28, 1945. Student, Massasoit C.C., Brockton, Mass., 1985, Empire State Coll.-SUNY, Saratoga Springs, 1992—. Nurses aid instr. Goddard Hosp., Brockton, 1963-72; counselor, cons. North Attleboro (Mass.) Rehab. Assoc., 1992-95; founder, dir. advocacy L.I.F.E. Orgn., Brockton, 1981-86; v.p. Abilities Unltd., Brockton, 1984-86; info. and referral vols. Stavros CIL, Amherst, Mass., 1990. Cmty. access monitor Mass. Office Disability, Boston, 1982—; mem. commn. disabilities, Brockton, 1984-96, North Attleborough, 1992—; arts and crafts dir. Sr. Citizen Ctr., East Bridgewater, Mass., 1990-91. Recipient Ednl. Scholarship grant Deaf Blind Multi-Disabled Unit Mass. Commn. for the Blind, 1992—. Mem. AAUW, Independence Assoc. Roman Catholic. Avocations: writing poetry, reading, playing cards. Home: 111 Raymond Hall Dr North Attleboro MA 02760-6401

WILLIAMS, RUTH LEE, clinical social worker; b. Dallas, June 24, 1944; d. Carl Woodley and Nancy Ruth (Gardner) W. BA, So. Meth. U., 1966; M Sci.in Social Work, U. Tex., Austin, 1969. Milieu coordinator Starr Commonwealth, Albion, Mich., 1969-73; clin. social worker Katherine Hamilton Mental Health Care, Terre Haute, Ind., 1973-74; clin. social worker, supr. Pikes Peak Mental Health Ctr., Colorado Springs, Colo., 1974-78; pvt. practice social work Colorado Springs, 1978—; pres. Hearthstone Inn, Inc., Colorado Springs, 1978—; practitioner Jin Shin Jyutsu, Colorado Springs, 1978—; pres., v.p. bd. dirs. Premier Care (formerly Colorado Springs Mental Health Care Providers Inc.), 1986-87, chmn. quality assurance com., 1987-89, v.p. bd. dirs., 1992-93; bd. dirs. Beth Haven, Inc. Author, editor: From the Kitchen of The Hearthstone Inn, 1981, 2d rev. edit., 1986, 3d rev. edit., 1992. Mem. Am. Bd. Examiners in Clin. Social Work (charter mem., cert.), Colo. Soc. Clin. Social Work (editor 1976), Nat. Assn. Soc. Workers (diplomate), Nat. Bd. Social Work Examiners (cert.), Nat. Assn. Ind. Innkeepers, So. Meth. U. Alumni Assn. (life). Avocations: gardening, hiking, sailing. Home: 11555 Howells Rd Colorado Springs CO 80908-3735 Office: 536 E Uintah St Colorado Springs CO 80903-2515

WILLIAMS, S. LINN, lawyer; b. St. Louis, July 1, 1946; s. Sidney Duane and Elizabeth Gertrude (Relfe) W.; m. Noriko Kurosawa, Sept. 13, 1975. B.A., Princeton U., 1968, J.D., Harvard U., 1971, postgrad. Cambridge U., 1972-74. Bar: Mass. 1971, D.C. 1972, Pa. 1987. Law clk. to Hon. I.L. Goldberg, U.S. Ct. Appeals 5th Cir., Dallas, 1971-72; assoc. Blakemore & Mitsuki, Tokyo, 1974; assoc., then ptnr. Leva, Hawes, Symington, Martin & Oppenheimer, Washington, 1975-81; v.p., gen. counsel Overseas Pvt. Investment Corp., Washington, 1981-84; v.p., gen. counsel Sears World Trade, Inc., 1984-85; ptnr. Gibson Dunn and Crutcher, Washington and Tokyo, 1985-89, 92-93, Jones Day Reavis & Pogue, Washington, 1993-94; sr. v.p., gen. counsel Edison Mission Energy, Irvine, Calif., 1995—; Japanese fgn. legal cons. Tokyo Dainibengoshikai, 1987-89; dep. U.S. trade rep., amb., Washington, 1989-91; mem. bd. dirs. Japan-Am. Soc. So. Calif.; sr. fellow Ctr. Strategic and Internat. Studies, Washington. Fulbright scholar, 1972, NEH fellow, 1972, McConnell fellow, 1967, Ford Found. fellow, 1972. Mem. United Oxford & Cambridge Club (London), Met. Club (Washington). Author: Developing an Export Trading Business, 1989; contbr. chpts. in book, also numerous articles on trade and investments. Office: Edison Mission Energy Co 18101 Von Karman Ave Irvine CA 92612-1010

WILLIAMS, SALLY BROADRICK, infection control nurse and consultant; b. Dalton, Ga., Dec. 25, 1943; d. Columbus N. and Anne M. (McHan) Broadrick; m. Joe P. Williams, Aug. 30, 1969; children: Michael J., Andrew B. Diploma in Nursing, Grady Meml. Hosp., Atlanta, 1969; BS in Health Arts, Coll. of St. Francis, Joliet, Ill., 1981. Cert. in infection control. Emergency dept. nurse Hamilton Med. Ctr., Dalton, 1963-69; patient care coord. Wesley Woods Health Ctr., Atlanta, 1969-70; critical care nurse DeKalb Gen. Hosp., Decatur, Ga., 1970-71, emergency dept. nurse, 1971-73, infection control and employee health nurse, 1973-75; infection control dir. DeKalb Med. Ctr., Decatur, 1973-94; infection control/employee health dir. R.T. Jones Hosp., Canton, 1994—; tng. cons. CDC, Atlanta, 1984-89; bloodborne pathogen cons. Merck, 1992, 93. Author: Infection Control for Emergency Medical Technicians, 1990, Infection Control for Pre-Hospital Care Givers, 1989, Infection Control for Pre-Hospital Care Givers and Emergency Departments, 1994. Trustee APIC Rsch. Found.; observer/reporter Cherokee LWV, Cherokee County, Ga., 1993-94; vol. Am. Cancer Soc.; fin. chairperson Cherokee County Relay for Life; mem. adv. com. Boy Scouts Am. Med. Explorer Post #23, Canton, Ga. Mem. NAFE, Ga. Infection Control Network (pres. 1981-84, 90, 95, dist. 3 liaison 1981-84, 90, dist. 1 liaison 1995-97, Infection Control Practitioner of Yr. award 1984, 89, Outstanding Contbr. award 1985, 87, 91), Assn. Practitioners in Infection Control (pres. 1978, Outstanding Practitioner award 1990), Assn. for Profls. in Infection Control and Epidemiology (nominating chmn. 1993, pres.-elect 1995, pres. Greater Atlanta chpt. 1996), Internat. Assn. for AIDS Educators, Southeastern Assn. Microbiologists. Democrat. Methodist. Avocations: reading, travel. Home: 1454 White Columns Blvd Canton GA 30115 Office: RT Jones Hosp 201 Hospital Rd Canton GA 30114-2408

WILLIAMS, SANDRA CASTALDO, elementary school educator; b. Rahway, N.J., Sept. 19, 1941; d. Neil and Loretta Margaret (Gleason) Castaldo; m. Arthur Williams III, 1962; children: Arthur IV, Melinda S., Thomas N. Student, Syracuse U., 1959-61; AB, Kean Coll., 1969, MA magna cum laude, 1978. Cert. tchr. K-8, early childhood, N.J. Preschool tchr. St. Andrew's Nursery & Kindergarten, New Providence, N.J., 1973-82; kindergarten tchr. Walnut Ave. Sch. Cranford (N.J.) Sch. Dist., 1978-79; adjunct prof. Farleigh Dickinson Coll., Rutherford, Teaneck, N.J., 1983-86; tchr. 4th grade The Peck Sch., Morristown, N.J., 1986-89; dir. Summit Child Care Ctr., 1990-91; tchr. 1st grade Oak Knoll Sch. of Holy Child Jesus, Summit, N.J., 1992—, tchr. Confraternity of Christian Doctrine, 1995—; bd. dirs. Summit Child Care Ctr., 1970-71, cons., 1991; cert. instr. Jacki Soresen Aerobic Dancing, Inc., Summit, 1990, Westfield, 1992-95. Co-chair United Way, Summit, 1991; Eucharistic min. St. Teresa's Ch., Summit, 1994—. Mem. ASCD, Internat. Reading Assn., Phi Kappa Phi, Alpha Sigma Lambda, Kappa Kappa Gamma. Republican. Roman Catholic. Avocations: needle work, gardening, church, physical fitness. Home: 8 Sunset Dr Summit NJ 07901-2323 Office: Oak Knoll Sch Holy Child Jesus 44 Blackburn Rd Summit NJ 07901-2408

WILLIAMS, SANDRA KELLER, postal service executive; b. Bethesda, Md., Oct. 3, 1944; d. Park Dudley and Julia Mildred (Hunter) Keller; m. Tommy Allen Williams, Dec. 24, 1970; children: Chris Allen, Wakenna, Barbara. BA, U. Colo., 1966; MBA, U. Mo., Kansas City, 1971; MS, Ga. Inst. Tech., 1973. Mathematician Colo. State U., Ft. Collins, 1966; sr. scientist Booz-Allen Applied Rsch., Kansas City, Mo., 1967-68; computer sci. instr. Mo. Western Coll., St. Joseph, 1968-71; systems planning analyst Decatur (Ga.) Fed. Savs. and Loan Assn., 1972-73; planning analyst Fed. Res. Bank, Atlanta, 1974-75; indsl. engr. so. region hdqrs. U.S. Postal Svc., Memphis, 1975-79; nat. mgr. quality control U.S. Postal Svc., Washington, 1979-86; dir. city ops. so. Md. div. U.S. Postal Svc., Capital Heights, 1986-87, dir., oper. supt. so. Md. div., 1987-88; postmaster U.S. Postal Svc., Reading, Pa., 1988—; cons. Personal Bus., St. Joseph, 1968-69; grad. teaching asst. Ga. Inst. Tech., Atlanta, 1971-73; adj. faculty Dekalb C.C., Clarkston, Ga., 1973-75, Memphis State U., 1976-78; owner Custom Florals, 1995—. Chmn. Combined Fed. Campaign, Reading, 1988-96, U.S. Postal Svc.-Berks County Savs. Bond Program, 1988-95, United Way's Govt. divsn., 1989-90; bd. dirs. YWCA, Reading and Berks County, treas., 1990, pres., 1991. Mem. Nat. League Postmasters (legis. officer 1988-91), Berks County Women's Network (bd. dirs. 1994-95, treas. 1995). Republican. Avocations: interior design, gardening, investment portfolio management. Home: 1514 Hill Rd Reading PA 19602-1410

WILLIAMS, SANKEY VAUGHAN, health services researcher, internist; b. San Antonio, Apr. 15, 1944; s. James Sankey and Helen (Long) W.; m. Constance Hess, June 27, 1972; children: Elizabeth Helen, Jennifer Lee. AB, Princeton U., 1966; MD, Harvard U., 1970. Diplomate Am. Bd. Internal Medicine. Intern Hosp. of U. Pa., 1970-71, jr. resident, 1971-72, chief med. resident, 1974-75; assoc. dir. clin. rsch. Ctr. for Study of Aging, U. Pa., 1982-86; assoc. dir. for med. affairs Leonard Davis Inst. for Health Econs., U. Pa., 1978-90; dir. clin. scholars program U. Pa., Phila., 1988-96; prof. health care systems Wharton Sch., U. Pa., Phila., 1989—; prof. medicine U. Pa., Phila., 1989—, chief div. gen. internal medicine, 1992—, Sol Katz prof. medicine, 1992—; commr. Prospective Payment Assessment Commn., U.S. Congress, Washington, 1988-91; chairman health svcs. rsch. devel. grants study sect. Agy. for Health Care Policy and Rsch., 1991-94; counselor for med. affiars to the pres. U. Pa., 1990-92. Co-editor: The Physician's Practice, 1980; author 25 revs, chpt. or editorials; contbr. 48 articles to various sci. jours. Lt. comdr. USPHS, 1972-74. Recipient Career Devel. award Henry S. Kaiser Family Found., 1981-86. Mem. ACP (master, chmn. clin. privileges com. 1989-93, Am. Fedn. Clin. Rsch. (program chmn. health svcs. rsch. 1985), Soc. for Med. Decision Making (pres. 1985-86), Soc. for Gen. Internal Medicine (coun. 1979-84, editor Jour. Gen. Internal Medicine 1995-2000). Office: Hosp Univ of Pa Divsn Gen Internal Medicine Silverstein 3 Philadelphia PA 19104

WILLIAMS, SPENCER MORTIMER, federal judge; b. Reading, Mass., Feb. 24, 1922; s. Theodore Ryder and Anabel (Hutchison) W.; m. Kathryn Bramlage, Aug. 20, 1943; children: Carol Marcia (Mrs. James B. Garvey), Peter, Spencer, Clark, Janice, Diane (Mrs. Sean Quinn). AB, UCLA, 1943; postgrad., Hastings Coll. Law, 1946; JD, U. Calif., Berkeley, 1948. Bar: Calif. 1949, U.S. Supreme Ct. 1952. Assoc. Beresford & Adams, San Jose, Calif., 1949, Rankin, O'Neal, Center, Luckhardt, Bonney, Marlais & Lund, San Jose, Evans, Jackson & Kennedy, Sacramento; county counsel Santa Clara County, 1955-67; adminstr. Calif. Health and Welfare Agy., Sacramento, 1967-69; judge U.S. Dist. Ct. (no. dist.) Calif., San Francisco, from 1971, now sr. judge; County exec. pro tem, Santa Clara County; adminstr. Calif. Youth and Adult Corrections Agy., Sacramento; sec. Calif. Human Relations Agy., Sacramento, 1967-70. Chmn. San Jose Christmas Seals Drive, 1953, San Jose Muscular Dystrophy Drive, 1953, 54; team capt. fund raising drive San Jose YMCA, 1960; co-chmn. indsl. sect. fund raising drive Alexian Bros. Hosp., San Jose, 1964; team capt. fund raising drive San Jose Hosp.; mem. com. on youth and govt. YMCA, 1967-68; Candidate for Calif. Assembly, 1954, Calif. Atty. Gen., 1966, 70; bd. dirs. San Jose Better Bus. Bur., 1955-66, Boys City Boys' Club, San Jose, 1965-67; pres. trustees Santa Clara County Law Library, 1955-66. Served with USNR, 1943-46; to lt. comdr. JAG Corps USNR, 1950-52, PTO. Named San Jose Man of Year, 1954. Mem. ABA, Calif. Bar Assn. (vice chmn. com. on publicly employed attys. 1962-63), Santa Clara County Bar Assn., Sacramento Bar Assn., Internat. Assn. Trial Judges (pres. 1995-96), Calif. Dist. Attys. Assn. (pres. 1963-64), Nat. Assn. County Civil Attys. (pres. 1963-64), 9th Cir. Dist. Judges Assn. (pres. 1981-83), Fed. Judges Assn. (pres. 1982-87), Kiwanis, Theta Delta Chi. Office: US Dist Ct 280 S 1st St San Jose CA 95113-3002

WILLIAMS, STANLEY, ballet dancer and teacher; b. Chappel, Eng., 1925. guest tchr. Sch. Am. Ballet, N.Y.C. Ballet Co., 1960-62; mem. faculty Sch. Am. Ballet, N.Y.C., 1964—, now co-chmn. faculty; guest instr. Royal Danish Ballet, 1966-80; sr. faculty chair The Brown Found., Inc., 1987. Staged: Bournonville Divertissement for, N.Y.C. Ballet (Dance Mag. award 1981); studied at school, Royal Danish Ballet, also in, Paris; accepted into the company, 1943, became solo dancer, 1949, tchr., 1950—, guest artist, Iceland, 1947, Brussels and Stockholm, 1948, ballet master, leading dancer with, George Kirsta's Ballet Comique in Eng., 1953-54; repertoire in Denmark includes leading roles in Coppelia, others. Knighted by King of

Denmark; recipient Mae L. Wien award, 1992. Address: Sch Am Ballet 70 Lincoln Center Plz New York NY 10023-6548

WILLIAMS, STEPHEN, anthropologist, educator; b. Mpls., Aug. 28, 1926; s. Clyde Garfield and Lois (Simmons) W.; m. Eunice Ford, Jan. 6, 1962; children: Stephen John, Timothy. BA, Yale U., 1949, PhD, 1954; MA, U. Mich., 1950; MA (hon.), Harvard, 1962. Asst. anthropology dept. Peabody Mus., Yale U., 1950-52; mem. faculty Harvard U., Cambridge, Mass., 1958—, prof. anthropology, 1967-72, Peabody prof., 1972-93, prof. emeritus, 1993—, chmn. dept., 1967-69; rsch. fellow Peabody Mus., Harvard U., Cambridge, Mass., 1954-57, mem. staff, 1954—, dir. mus., 1967-77; curator N.Am. Archaeology, 1962-93, hon. curator 1993—; dir. rsch. of Peabody Mus.'s Lower Miss. Survey, 1958-93. Author books and articles on N.Am. archaeology and "Fantastic" archaeology. Home: 1017 Foothills Trl Santa Fe NM 87505-4537 Office: PO Box 22354 Santa Fe NM 87502-2354

WILLIAMS, STEPHEN FAIN, federal judge; b. N.Y.C., N.Y., Sept. 23, 1936; s. Charles Dickerman and Virginia (Fain) W.; m. Faith Morrow, June 11, 1966; children: Susan, Geoffrey Fain, Sarah Margot Nu, Timothy Dwight, Nicholas Morrow. B.A., Yale U., 1958; J.D., Harvard U., 1961. Bar: N.Y. 1962, Colo. 1977. Assoc. Debevoise, Plimpton, Lyons & Gates, N.Y.C., 1962-66; asst. U.S. atty. So. Dist. N.Y., 1966-69; asst. prof. law U. Colo., Boulder, 1969-77; prof. U. Colo., 1977-86; judge U.S. Ct. Appeals (D.C. cir.), Washington, 1986—; vis. prof. UCLA, 1975-76; vis. prof., fellow in law and econs. U. Chgo., 1979-80; vis. William L. Hutchison prof. energy law So. Meth. U., 1983-84; cons. Adminstrv. Conf. U.S., 1974-76, FTC, 1983-85; mem. Boulder Area Growth Study Commn., 1972-73. Contbr. articles to law revs., mags. Served with U.S. Army, 1961-62. Mem. Am. Law Inst. Office: US Courthouse 3rd Constitution Ave NW Washington DC 20001

WILLIAMS, SUE DARDEN, library director; b. Miami, Fla., Aug. 13, 1943; d. Archie Yelverton and Bobbie (Jones) Eagles; m. Richard Williams, Sept. 30, 1989. B.A., Barton Coll., Wilson, N.C., 1965; M.L.S., U. Tex., Austin, 1970. Cert. librarian, N.C., Va. Instr. Chowan Coll., Murfreesboro, N.C., 1966-68; libr.'s asst. Albemarle Regional Libr., Winston, N.C., 1968-69; br. libr. Multnomah County Pub. Libr., Portland, Oreg., 1971-72; asst. dir. Stanly County Pub. Libr., Albemarle, N.C., 1973-76; dir. Stanly County Pub. Libr., 1976-80; asst. dir. Norfolk (Va.) Pub. Libr., 1980-83; dir., 1983-94, Rockingham County Pub. Libr., Eden, N.C., 1996—. Mem. ALA (orientation com. 1990-92, chair 1991), Libr. Adminstrv. and Mgmt. Assn. (pub. rels. sec. 1985-87), Southeastern Libr. Assn. (staff devel. com. 1986-88, Rothrock award com. 1984-86, sec. pub. libr. sect. 1982-84), Va. Libr. Assn. (SELA rep. 1993-96, coun. 1984, 88-91, 93-96, ad hoc conf. guidelines com. 1985-86, chmn. conf. program 1984, awards and recognition com. 1983), Pub. Libr. Assn. (bd. dirs.-at-large Met. area 1986-89), Va. State Libr. (coop edn. com. 88-89). Home: 817A Carter St Eden NC 27288-5923 Office: Rockingham County Pub Libr 527 Boone Rd Eden NC 27288-4905

WILLIAMS, SYLVESTER EMANUAL, III, elementary school educator, consultant; b. Chgo., Feb. 4, 1937; s. Sylvester Emanual and Carita (Brown) W.; children: Sylvia, Sylvester, Sydnee, Steven. BS, No. Ill. U., 1958; MA, Chgo. State U., 1968; PhD, U. S.C., 1992. Cert. tchr., S.C., N.C., Ill. From asst. to supt. Washington D.C. Pub. Schs., 1968-69; tchr. Chgo. Pub. Schs., 1958-68; program officer Dept. Edn., Washington, 1971-86; prof. Lander U., Greenwood, S.C., 1986-89, U. S.C., Akin, 1990-91; tchr., coach Charlotte (N.C.) Mecklenburg Pub. Schs., 1992—; bd. dirs. John de Home Sch., McCormick, S.C., 1986—. Mem. Phi Delta Kappa. Republican. Baptist. Avocation: motion picture prodn. Home: 205 Briggs Ave Greenwood SC 29649-1603

WILLIAMS, TED (THEODORE SAMUEL WILLIAMS), former baseball player, former manager, consultant; b. San Diego, Aug. 30, 1918; s. Samuel Steward and May W.; m. Doris Soule; 3 children. Played with Boston Red Sox, 1939-42, 46-60; now cons. and spring tng. instr.; mgr. Washington Senators, 1969-71, Tex. Rangers, 1972; sports cons. Sears, Roebuck & Co. Author: (with John Underwood) My Turn at Bat: The Story of My Life, 1968, The Science of Hitting, 1972. Served to 2d lt. USMCR, 1942-45. Named to Am. League All-Star Team, 1940-42, 46-51, 54-60; named Sporting News Player of Year, 1941, 42, 47, 49, 57, Am. League Most Valuable Player, 1946, 49, Am. League Mgr. of Year, 1969; inducted to Baseball Hall of Fame, 1966. Address: c/o Baseball Hall of Fame PO Box 590 Cooperstown NY 13326*

WILLIAMS, TED VAUGHNELL, physical education educator; b. Bronx, N.Y., Apr. 1, 1952; s. Joseph Alexander and Annie (Canady) W. BS, Springfield Coll., 1977. Cert. tchr., N.Y. Substitute tchr. Valhalla (N.Y.) High Sch., 1977; tchr. aide for handicapped children, tchr. spl. edn. Rye Lake Campus, Valhalla, 1978; supr. recreation activities Springfield (Mass.) Girl's Club Family Ctr., 1979; assoc. dir. boy's and men's phys. edn. dept. Trenton YMCA, 1979—; house supr. Cardinal McCloskey's Group Home, Tappan, N.Y., 1980-81; phys. edn. tchr. Our Lady of Refuge Sch., Bronx, N.Y., 1982-83; tchr. phys. edn. various Cath. elem. schs. Yonkers, N.Y., 1983—; with ops. dept. Hudson Valley Nat. Bank, 1990-92. Active Walk Am. for Healthier Babies, March of Dimes, 1990-93. Recipient Ed Steitz award Basketball Hall of Fame, 1975, Capitol award Nat. Leadership Coun., 1991. Mem. ASCD, AAHPERD, Am. Assn. Leisure and Recreation, Hudson Valley Leisure Svcs. Assn. Democrat. Baptist. Home: 49 Bradford Ave White Plains NY 10603-2143 Office: Saint Denis Sch 73 Lawrence Ave Yonkers NY 10707-1417

WILLIAMS, TEMPLE WEATHERLY, JR., internist, educator; b. Wichita Falls, Tex., Apr. 19, 1934; s. Temple Weatherly and Dorothy (Coleman) W.; married; children: Holly Clare, Temple Weatherly III; m. Joan Loos, Apr. 6, 1991. Student, Midwestern U., 1951-53; B.S., So. Meth. U., 1955; M.D., Baylor U., 1959. Intern, resident in internal medicine Duke U. Hosp., Durham, N.C., 1959-60, 62-63; fellow in infectious disease Baylor U., 1960-62; clin. assoc. infectious disease NIH, Bethesda, Md.; prof. medicine and microbiology/immunology Baylor Coll. Medicine, Houston, 1974—. Contbr. 100 articles on infectious diseases to profl. jours., chpts. to books. Served with USPHS, 1963-65. Fellow ACP, Infectious Disease Soc. Am.; mem. AMA. Republican. Methodist. Office: 6565 Fannin MS 910 Houston TX 77030

WILLIAMS, THELMA JEAN, social worker; b. Blytheville, Ark., Nov. 2, 1934; d. Willie Louis and Louise (Witherspoon) Morgan; m. Raymond Augustus Williams, Sr., July 22, 1955 (div. Jan. 1961); children: Ronald Duane, Derrick Lamont, Raymond Augustus Jr. BA, U. Mo., St. Louis, 1971; MPA, U. Mo., Kansas City, 1994. Caseworker Mo. Divsn. Welfare, St. Louis, 1959-69, casework supr., 1969-73; quality assurance specialist Dept. Health, Edn. and Welfare, Kansas City, Mo., 1973-74, program integrity specialist, 1974-82; supervisory quality control specialist Dept. Health Human Svcs., Kansas City, Mo., 1982-88, sr. quality control specialist, 1988-90, children and families program specialist, 1990—. Tutor Deramus Br. YMCA, Kansas City, 1994; mem. U. Mo. Coordinating Bd. on Diversity, 1995-96; mem. U. Mo. Minority Affairs Com., 1995-96; project leader Focus Kansas City, 1996; del. Citizen Ambassador Program, 1994-96. Recipient Pres.'s 1000 Points of Light award, 1991, Sec. Health and Human Svcs.' Disting. Vol. Svcs. award, 1991, Cert. of Appreciation Interagency Coun. on Homeless, 1992, Spl. Act of Svc., Dept. Health and Human Svcs. Dept., Family Support Administrn., 1989 (all Washington). Mem. ASPA, AAUW, People to People Internat. Methodist. Avocations: travel, reading, professional studies, classical music, continuing education. Home: 803 W 48th St Kansas City MO 64112-1855 Office: Dept Health Human Svcs Children & Families Admins 601 E 12th St Ste 276 Kansas City MO 64106-2808

WILLIAMS, THEODORE EARLE, industrial distribution company executive; b. Cleve., May 9, 1920; s. Stanley S. and Blanche (Albaum) W.; m. Rita Cohen, Aug. 28, 1952; children: Lezlie, Richard Atlas, Shelley, William Atlas, Wayne, Marsha, Patti Blake, Jeff Blake. Student, Wayne U., 1937-38; BS in Engring, U. Mich., 1942, postgrad. in bus. adminstrn, 1942. Pres. Wayne Products Co., Detroit, 1942-43, L.A., 1947-49; pres. Williams Metal Products Co., Inglewood, Calif., 1950-69; chmn. bd., pres., chief exec. officer Bell Industries, L.A., 1970—; instr. U. Mich., 1942. Patentee in field. Served to 1st lt. AUS, 1943-46. Recipient Humanitarian award City of L.A., 1977. Democrat. Home: 435 N Layton Way Los Angeles CA 90049-2022 Office: Bell Industries Inc 11812 San Vicente Blvd Los Angeles CA 90049-5022 *It seems to me that many of our current problems in this world originate from the drift away from concern for other people to the emphasis on self. We are reluctant to get involved, and as this spaceship gets smaller, we become more interdependent all the time. If we don't learn to live together, I'm afraid we may all perish together.*

WILLIAMS, THEODORE JOSEPH, engineering educator; b. Black Lick, Pa., Sept. 2, 1923; s. Theodore Finley and Mary Ellen (Shields) W.; m. Isabel Annette McAnulty, July 18, 1946; children: Theodore Joseph, Mary Margaret, Charles Augustus, Elizabeth Ann. B.S.Ch.E., Pa. State U., 1949, M.S.Ch.E., 1950, Ph.D., 1955; M.S. in Elec. Engring., Ohio State U., 1956. Research fellow Pa. State U., University Park, 1947-51; asst. prof. Air Force Inst. Tech., 1953-56; technologist Monsanto Co., 1956-57, sr. engring. supr., 1957-65; prof. engring. Purdue U., Lafayette, Ind., 1965-94, prof. emeritus, 1995—, dir. control and info. systems lab., 1965-66; dir. Purdue Lab. Applied Indsl. Control, 1966-94, dir. emeritus, 1995—; cons., 1964—; vis. prof. Washington U., St. Louis, 1962-65. Author: Systems Engineering for the Process Industries, 1961, Automatic Control of Chemical and Petroleum Processes, 1961, Progress in Direct Digital Control, 1969, Interfaces with the Process Control Computer, 1971, Modeling and Control of Kraft Production Systems, 1975, Modelling, Estimation and Control of the Soaking Pit, 1983, The Use of Digital Computers in Process Control, 1983, Analysis and Design of Hierarchical Control Systems - With Special Reference to Steel Plant Operations, 1985, A Reference Model for Computer Integrated Manufacturing (CIM) - A Description from the Viewpoint of Industrial Automation, 1989, The Purdue Enterprise Reference Architecture, 1992; editor: Computer Applications in Shipping and Shipbuilding, 6 vols., 1973-79, Proceedings Advanced Control Confs., 19 vols., 1974-93. Served to 1st lt. USAAF, 1942-45; to capt. USAF, 1951-56. Decorated Air medal with 2 oak leaf clusters. Fellow AAAS, AIChE, Instrument Soc. Am. (hon. mem., pres. 1968-69, Albert F. Sperry gold medal 1990, Lifetime Achievement award 1995), Am. Inst. Chemists, Inst. Measurement and Control (London, sr. Harold Hartley silver medal 1975), Indsl. Computing Soc.; mem. IEEE (sr.), Soc. for Computer Simulation (hon.), Am. Chem. Soc., Am. Automatic Control Coun. (pres. 1965-67), Am. Fedn. Info. Processing Socs. (pres. 1976-78), Sigma Xi, Tau Beta Pi, Phi Kappa Phi, Phi Lambda Upsilon. Home: 208 Chippewa St West Lafayette IN 47906-2123 Office: Purdue U Potter Rsch Ctr Inst Interdisciplinary Enging Studies West Lafayette IN 47907-1293

WILLIAMS, THEODORE JOSEPH, JR., lawyer; b. Pitts., July 23, 1947; s. Theodore Joseph and Isabel (McAnulty) W.; m. Sherri Lynne Foust, July 4, 1970; children: Kelley Shields, Jonathan Stewart, Jordan Fuller. BA, Purdue U., 1969; JD, U. Tulsa, 1974. Bar: Ill. 1975, U.S. Ct. Appeals (7th cir.) 1975, U.S. Dist. Ct. (no., so. and cen. dists.) Ill. 1975, Mo. 1978, U.S. Ct. Appeals (8th cir.) 1978, U.S. Dist. Ct. (ea. and we. dists.) Mo. 1978, U.S. Supreme Ct. 1978, D.C. 1981, U.S. Ct. Appeals (D.C. cir.) 1988, U.S. Ct. Appeals (10th cir.), U.S. Dist. Ct. D.C 1988, U.S. Ct. Mil. Appeals 1991, Colo. 1996, U.S. Ct. Appeals (10th cir.) 1996, Colo. 1996. Asst. city prosecutor City of Tulsa, 1974; trial atty., law dept. Chgo. and North Western R.R., Chgo., 1975-78; assoc. Thompson and Mitchell, St. Louis, 1978-81; assoc. Shepherd, Sandberg & Phoenix, P.C., St. Louis, 1981-84, ptnr., 1984-88; ptnr., chmn. transp. law dept. Armstrong, Teasdale, Schlafly & Davis, St. Louis, 1988—. Assoc. editor Law. Jour., U. Tulsa, 1974. Treas. sch. bd. Mary Queen of Peace Sch., Webster Groves, Mo., 1986, v.p., 1987. Major U.S. Army Res., 1991—. Mem. ABA (vice chmn. rail and motor carrier law com., torts and ins. practice law sect. 1989-90, chair-elect 1990-91, chair 1991-92), Ill. Bar Assn., Mo. Bar Assn., Def. Rsch. Inst. (chair, railroad law commn. 1996—), Nat. Assn. R.R. Coun., We. Conf. Ry. Coun., Assn. ICC Practitioners, Maritime Law Assn., Internat. Assn. Def. Coun., Transp. Lawyers Assn., Assn. Transp. Practitioners. Republican. Roman Catholic. Office: Armstrong Teasdale Schlafly & Davis One Metropolitan Sq Saint Louis MO 63102

WILLIAMS, THOMAS ALLISON, lawyer; b. Port Chester, N.Y., Dec. 19, 1936; s. Howard Hunter and Mary Katharine (Covell) W.; m. Anne Lamson Bell, Sept. 7, 1961; children: Thomas Allison, Laura L., James C., David D. BA in Econs., Yale U., 1959, LLB, 1962. Bar: N.Y. 1963. Assoc. Milbank, Tweed, Hadley & McCloy, N.Y.C., 1962-70, ptnr., 1971-94, pres., dir., The Depository Trust Co., N.Y.C., 1994—. Trustee Rye Free Reading Room (N.Y.), 1965-85, pres., 1978-85; trustee Rye Presbyn. Ch., 1972-75; trustee, chmn. planning com. United Hosp., Port Chester, N.Y., 1978-86, chmn. bd., 1986-96; trustee Westchester Libr. System, Westchester, N.Y., 1968-73, pres., 1972-73. Mem. ABA, N.Y. State Bar Assn., Assn. of Bar of City of N.Y., Am. Yacht Club (commodore), N.Y. Yacht Club, Apawamis Club. Republican. Presbyterian. Office: The Depository Trust Co 55 Water St New York NY 10041

WILLIAMS, THOMAS ARTHUR, biomedical computing consultant, psychiatrist; b. Racine, Wis., May 11, 1936; s. Robert Klinkert and Marion Anne (Wisneski) W.; m. Rexanne Louise Smith, Aug. 8, 1988; children: Jennifer, Thomas, Ted, Susan, Hailey, Renata. BA, Harvard Coll., 1958; MD, Columbia U., 1963; postgrad., NIH, 1967-68. Diplomate Nat. Bd. Med. Examiners, Am. Bd. Psychiatry and Neurology. Intern in surgery Presbyn. Hosp., N.Y.C., 1963-64; resident in psychiatry N.Y. State Psychiat. Inst., N.Y.C., 1964-67; chief depression sect. NIMH, Bethesda, Rockville, Md., 1967-71; asst. prof. U. Pitts., 1969-70; assoc. prof. U. Utah, Salt Lake City, 1971-77; prof., chmn. dept. psychiatry Eastern Va. Med. Sch., Norfolk, Va., 1977-78; clin. dir. Sheppard & Enoch Pratt Hosp., Towson, Md., 1978-80; prof. U. South Fla., Tampa, 1980-83; practitioner psychiat. medicine, med. dir. St. Augustine (Fla.) Psychiat. Ctr., 1983-89, 89-90; prin. Williams & Assocs., Tampa, 1990—. Chief editor: Psychobiology of Depression, 1972, Mental Health in the 21st Century, 1979; contbr. numerous articles to profl. jours. and chpts. to books. Mem. Gov.'s Adv. Com. on Mental Health, Salt Lake City, 1971-77, Gov.'s Adv. Com. on Penal Code, Richmond, Va., 1978, Dist. Mental Health Bd., Tampa, 1980-83; mem. U.S. Govt. Mission on Psychiatry to USSR, 1974; sponsor, coach Forest Hills Little League Baseball, Tampa, 1980-83. Sr. surgeon USPHS, 1958-67. Recipient Predoctoral fellowship NIMH, 1960-61, Alumni Rsch. award N.Y. State Psychiat. Inst., 1964, Rush Bronze Medal award Am. Psychiat. Assn., 1973, Rsch. grants VA, 1971-77. Mem. AMA, Fla. Med. Assn., Hillsborough County Med. Assn., Columbia U. Alumni Club (dir. 1995—), Harvard Club of the West Coast of Fla. Avocations: personal computing, classical music, opera, profl. basketball. Home: 831 S Delaware Ave Tampa FL 33606 Office: Williams & Assocs 831 S Delaware Ave Tampa FL 33606-2914

WILLIAMS, THOMAS FFRANCON, chemist, educator; b. Colwyn Bay, Wales, Jan. 30, 1928; came to U.S., 1961; s. David and Margaret (Williams) W.; m. Astra Silvia Birins, Jan. 31, 1959; children: Ifor Rainis, Gwyn David. B.Sc., Univ. Coll., London, Eng., 1949; Ph.D., U. London, 1960. Sci. officer U.K. Atomic Energy Authority, Harwell, Eng., 1949-55; sr. sci. officer U.K. Atomic Energy Authority, 1955-61, prin. sci. officer, 1961; research scientist Ill. Inst. Tech. Research Inst., Chgo., 1961; asst. prof. chemistry U. Tenn., Knoxville, 1961-63; assoc. prof. U. Tenn., 1963-67, prof., 1967—, Alumni Distinguished Service prof., 1974—; tchg. and rsch. assoc. Northwestern U., Evanston, Ill., 1957-58; NSF vis. scientist Kyoto (Japan) U., 1965-66; coord. U.S.-Japan Sci. Sem., Hakone, Japan, 1969; chmn. Gordon Rsch. Conf. on Radiation Chemistry, New Hampton, N.H., 1971, Gordon Rsch. Conf. Radical Ions, Wolfeboro, N.H., 1984; John Simon Guggenheim Meml. Found. fellow, Swedish Rsch. Coun. Lab., Studsvik, Nykoping, 1972-73; vis. scientist Royal Inst. Tech., Stockholm, Sweden, 1972-73; chmn. 10th Southeastern Magnetic Resonance Conf., 1978; mem. chemistry div. rev. com. Argonne (Ill.) Nat. Lab., 1988, 91, 95; cons. Pacific N.W. Nat. Lab., 1996-97. Contbg. author: Fundamental Processes in Radiation Chemistry, 1968, Radiation Chemistry of Macromolecules, 1972; mem. editorial bd. Radiation Rsch., 1993-97; contbr. numerous articles on chem. effects of high energy radiation to profl. jours. AEC, ERDA, Dept. Energy grantee, 1962—. Mem. Am. Chem. Soc. (program chmn. sect. 1968-69, exec. com. 1986-88), Brit. Chem. Soc., Radiation Rsch. Soc., Phi Beta Kappa (hon.), Sigma Xi (pres. U. Tenn. chpt. 1993-94). Home: 3117 Montlake Dr Knoxville TN 37920-2836 Office: U Tenn Dept Of Chemistry Knoxville TN 37996

WILLIAMS, THOMAS FRANKLIN, physician, educator; b. Belmont, N.C., Nov. 26, 1921; s. T.F. and Mary L. (Deaton) W.; m. Catharine Carter Catlett, Dec. 15, 1951; children: Mary Wright, Thomas Nelson. BS, U. N.C., 1942; MA, Columbia U., 1943; MD, Harvard U., 1950; DSc (hon.), Med. Coll. Ohio, 1987, U. N.C., 1992. Diplomate Am. Bd. Internal Medicine. Intern Johns Hopkins, Balt., 1950-51; asst. resident physician Johns Hopkins, 1951-53; resident physician Boston VA Hosp., 1953-54; research fellow U. N.C., Chapel Hill, 1954-56; instr. dept. medicine and preventive medicine U. N.C., 1956-57, asst. prof., 1957-61, assoc. prof., 1961-68, prof., 1968; attending physician Strong Meml. Hosp., Rochester, N.Y., 1968—; cons. physician Genesee Hosp., Rochester, N.Y., 1973—, St. Mary's Hosp., Rochester, N.Y., 1974-83, Highland Hosp., Rochester, N.Y., 1973; prof. medicine, preventive medicine and community health U. Rochester, 1968-92, also prof. radiation biology and biophysics, 1968-91, on leave, 1983-91, prof. emeritus, 1992—; mem. adv. bd. U. Rochester (Sch. Medicine and Dentistry), 1968-83; clin. prof. medicine U. Va., 1983-89; lectr. medicine Johns Hopkins U., 1983-89; clin. prof. depts family medicine and medicine Georgetown U., 1983-89; dir. Nat. Inst. on Aging NIH, 1983-91; asst. surgeon gen. USPHS, 1983-91, ret., 1991; attending physician Monroe Community Hosp., Rochester, 1991—, vice chmn. Cmty. Coalition for Long Term Care, 1991—; disting. physician VA Med. Ctr., Canandigua, N.Y., 1995—; med. dir. Monroe Cmty. Hosp., Rochester, 1968-83; mem. rev. coms. Nat. Ctr. for Health Svcs. Rsch.; mem. adv. bd. St. Ann's Home; mem. gov. bd. NRC, 1981-83; sci. dir. Am Fedn. Aging Rsch., 1992—; bd. dirs. Kirkhaven, Nat. Coun. on Aging. Contbr. articles on endocrine disorders, diabetes, health care delivery in chronic illness and aging to profl. publs. Served with USNR, 1943-46. USPHS fellow, 1966-67; Markle scholar, 1957-61. Fellow Am. Pub. Health Assn., ACP; mem. AAAS, Inst. Medicine, NAS (coun. 1980-83, governing bd. 1981-83), Assn. Am. Physicians, N.Y. State Med. Soc., Monroe County Med. Soc., Am. Diabetes Assn. (bd. dir. 1974-80), Am. Fedn. Clin. Rsch., Soc. Exptl. Biology and Medicine, Am. Geriatrics Soc., Am. Gerontol. Soc., Rochester Regional Diabetes Assn. (pres. 1977-79), N.C. Coun. for Human Rels. (chmn. 1963-66), Am. Clin. Climatol. Assn. Episcopalian. Home: 287 Dartmouth St Rochester NY 14607-3202 Office: Monroe Community Hosp Office Med Dir Rochester NY 14620

WILLIAMS, THOMAS LLOYD, psychiatrist; b. Mt. Carmel, Pa., May 8, 1925; s. Thomas Lloyd and Anna (Roberts) W.; m. Lucille H. Held, June 23, 1993; children: Scott, Michael. BS, U. Pitts., 1949, MD, 1952. Diplomate Am. Bd. Neurology and Psychiatry. Intern Allegheny Gen. Hosp., Pitts., 1952-53; family practice Gilbert, Pa., 1953-59; resident Mental Health Hosp. affiliated with U. Iowa, Cherokee, 1959-62, mem. staff, 1962-63; pvt. practice Bethlehem, Pa., 1963—; chief of psychiatry St. Lukes Hosp., Bethlehem, Pa., 1976-88, mem. staff emeritus, 1988—. 1st lt. navigator, U.S. Army Air Corps, 1943-45, ETO. Decorated 7 Battle Stars, Air medal with 3 clusters, Disting. Flying Cross. Fellow Am. Psychiat. Assn. (life). Republican. Avocations: hunting, fishing, carving.

WILLIAMS, THOMAS RAYMOND, lawyer; b. Meridian, Miss., Aug. 26, 1940. BS, U. Ala., 1962, LLB, 1964. Bar: Ala. 1964, Tex. 1979, U.S. Supreme Ct. 1980, D.C. 1983. Ptnr. McDermott, Will & Emery, Washington. Mem. D.C. Bar Assn., Ala. State Bar Assn., State Bar Tex. Office: McDermott Will & Emery 1850 K St NW Washington DC 20006-2213

WILLIAMS, THOMAS RHYS, anthropologist, educator; b. Martins Ferry, Ohio, June 13, 1928; s. Harold K. and Dorothy (Lehew) W.; m. Margaret Martin, July 12, 1952; children: Rhys M., Ian T., Tom R. B.A., Miami U., Oxford, Ohio, 1951; M.A., U. Ariz., 1956; Ph.D., Syracuse U., 1956. Asst. prof., asso. prof. anthropology Calif. State U., Sacramento, 1956-65; vis. asso. prof. anthropology U. Calif. Berkeley, 1962; vis. prof. anthropology Stanford U., 1976; prof. anthropology Ohio State U., Columbus, 1965-78; chmn. dept Ohio State U., 1967-71, mem. grad. council, 1969-72, mem. univ. athletic council, 1968-74, chmn. univ. athletic council, 1973-74, exec. com. Coll. Social and Behavior Scis., 1967-71; dean Grad. Sch. George Mason U., Fairfax, Va., 1978-81, prof. anthropology, 1981—; dir. Ctr. for Rsch. and Advanced Studies George Mason U., 1978-81, fed. liaison officer, 1978-81, chmn. faculty adv. bd. grad. degree program in conflict resolution, 1980-86. Author: The Dusun: A North Borneo Society, 1965, Field Methods in the Study of Culture, 1967, A Borneo Childhood: Enculturation in Dusun Society, 1969, Introduction to Socialization: Human Culture Transmitted, 1972, Socialization, 1983; editor, contbg. author: Psychological Anthropology, 1975, Socialization and Communication in Primary Groups, 1975, Cultural Anthropology, 1990; contbr. articles to profl. jours. Mem. United Democrats for Humphrey, 1968, Citizens for Humphrey, 1968. Served with USN, 1946-48. Research grantee NSF, 1958, 62, Am. Council Learned Socs.-Social Sci. Research Council, 1959, 63; Ford Found. S.E. Asia, 1974, 76; recipient Disting. Faculty award Calif. State U., Sacramento, 1961, George Mason U., 1983; Disting. Teaching awards Ohio State U., 1968, 76. Fellow Am. Anthrop. Assn., Royal Anthrop. Inst. Gt. Britain; assoc. mem. Current Anthropology; mem. AAAS, Sigma Xi. Office: George Mason U Robinson Hall B-315 4400 University Dr Fairfax VA 22030-4422

WILLIAMS, TONDA, entrepreneur, consultant; b. N.Y.C., Nov. 21, 1949; d. William and Juanita (Rainey) W.; 1 child, Tywana. Student, Collegiate Inst., N.Y.C., 1975-78, C.W. Post Coll., 1981-83; BA in Bus. Mgmt., Am. Nat. U., Phoenix, 1983; grad., L.I. Bus. Inst., 1996. Notary pub. N.Y. Asst. controller Acad. Ednl. Devel., N.Y.C., 1971-81; mgr. office Chapman-Apex Constrn. Co., Bayshore, N.Y., 1982-84; specialist computer RGM Liquid Waste Removal, Deerpark, N.Y., 1985-87; contr. LaMar Lighting Co., Freeport, N.Y., 1987—; owner, pres. Omni-Star, Bklyn., 1981—; pres. Omni-Data Tech., Bayshore, N.Y., 1996—. Author: Tonda's Songs in Poetry, 1978, The Magic of Life, 1991; co-author: Computer Management of Liquid Waste Industry, 1986. Recipient Golden Poet award World of Poetry, 1992. Mem. Am. Mus. Natural History, Am. Soc. Notary Pubs. Avocations: bowling, chess, singing. Home: 74 Cedar Dr Bay Shore NY 11706-2419

WILLIAMS, UNA JOYCE, psychiatric social worker; b. Youngstown, Ohio, June 24, 1934; d. Samuel Wilfred and Frances Josephine (Woods) Ellis; children: Wendy Louise, Christopher Ellis, Sharon Elizabeth. BA, U. Ala., 1957; MSW, Adelphi U., 1963. Diplomate CSW, Am. Bd. Examiners in Clin. Social Work, Internat. Acad. Behavioral Medicine, Counseling, Psychotherapy. Dir. Huntington Program for Sr. Citizens; psychiat. social worker-supr. N.Y. State Dept. Mental Hygiene, Suffolk Psychiat. Hosp., Central Islip; info.-referral counselor Mental Health Assn. Nassau County, Hempstead, N.Y.; therapist Madonna Heights Family Clinic, Dix Hills, N.Y.; med. and psychiat. social worker Northport (N.Y.) VA Med. Ctr., psychiat. social worker acute psychiat. treatment svs.; med. social worker dialysis svcs. Northport (N.Y.) Va. Med. Ctr.; cons. on programs for aging Luth. Social Svcs. Mt. N.Y., 1959, sr. citizens cons. Port Jefferson-L.I. Bd. Edn., 1963. Chmn. Huntington Twp. Com. Human Rels., 1970; sec. bd. trustees Unitarian Universalist Fellowship Huntington, 1984. Named Mem. of Yr. Germany Philetelic Soc. Mem. NASW (cert., diplomte), Am. Assn. Family Counselors and Mediators, Germany Philetelic Soc. (pres. chpt. 30, 1990). Avocations: oil painting, stamp collecting, music (voice & piano), family geneology. Home: 316 Lenox Rd Huntington Station NY 11746-2640

WILLIAMS, VANESSA, recording artist, actress; b. Millwood, N.Y., Mar. 18, 1963; m. Ramon Hervey II, 1988; children: Melanie, Jillian, Devin. Recording artist, 1988—. Stage appearances include: (Broadway) Kiss of the Spider Woman, 1994-95; film appearances include Pick-up Artist, 1987, Under the Gun, 1989, Another You, 1991, Harley Davidson and the Marlboro Man, 1991, Eraser, 1996, Hoodlum, 1997, Soul Food, 1997; (TV films) Full Exposure: The Sex Tapes Scandal, 1989, Perry Mason: The Case of the Silenced Singer, 1990, Stompin' at the Savoy, 1992, Jacksons: An American Dream, 1992, Bye Bye Birdie, 1995, (TV mini series) Nothing Lasts Forever, 1995, The Odyssey, 1997; (TV guest appearance) The Fresh Prince of Bel-Air, 1990; albums: The Right Stuff, 1988, The Comfort Zone, 1991, The Sweetest Days, 1994; # 1 hit single Save the Best for Last. Recipient 8 Grammy award nominations; named one of 50 Most Beautiful People, People Mag. First Black to be named Miss America, 1983 (resigned title 1983). Office: Mercury Records care Dawn Bridges 825 8th Ave New York NY 10019-7416*

WILLIAMS, VIDA VERONICA, guidance counselor; b. Charleston, S.C., May 4, 1956; d. Timothy and Dotlee (Pendarvis) W. BA, Fisk U., 1978; MS in Edn., Queens Coll., 1986, postgrad., 1994-95. Cert. sch. counselor, spl. edn. tchr., N.Y. Job counselor Trident Work Experience, Charleston, 1980; spl. edn. tchr. Jr. High Sch. 158, Bayside, N.Y., 1983-86, Pub. Sch. 214,

Bklyn., 1986-90; guidance counselor I.S. 171, 364, Pub. Sch. 214, Bklyn., 1990-95, I.S. 302, Bklyn., 1995—; co-dir. I.S. 302 Gospel Chorus, 1994-95; counselor Dist. 19 Bereavement, Bklyn., 1991-95; bd. dirs. Alpha Kappa Alpha Day Care Ctr., St. Albans, N.Y., 1992-94. Vol. Voter Registration, Jamaica, 1992, Increase the Peace Corps, N.Y.C., 1992, Feeding of 5,000, Jamaica, 1993, Victim Svcs., Bklyn., 1994-95; chair activities Harlem Dowling Foster Care, Jamaica, N.Y., 1995; active Allen A.M.E. Ch. Gospel Choir, 1994-95, Voices of Victory, 1994-95. Named one of Outstanding Young Women Am., 1980. Mem. Alpha Kappa Alpha. Avocations: reading, singing, sewing, arts and crafts. Home: 159-19 137th Ave Jamaica NY 11434 Office: IS 302 350 Linwood St Brooklyn NY 11208-2116

WILLIAMS, W. CLYDE, religious organization administrator. Exec. sec. Christian Meth. Episcopal Ch., Atlanta, 1987—. Office: Christian Meth Episcopal Ch 2805 Shoreland Dr SW Atlanta GA 30331-6714 Office: 201 Ashby St NW Ste 212 Atlanta GA 30314-3422

WILLIAMS, W. VAIL, psychologist; b. Denver, Apr. 13, 1940; s. Warren J. and Edna M. (Follen) W.; m. Sandra M. Eisenrich (div. 1972); 1 child, Jason; m. Linda Lou Fain, Dec. 27, 1975; children: Ken, Dan, Davis, Jeremiah. BS, Bradley U., 1963, MA, 1964; PhD, U. Okla., 1968. Lic. psychologist, S.D., Colo., Calif. Owner Social Systems Devel., 1970-78; sr. psychologist Ft. Logan Mental Health Ctr., Denver, 1968-74; sr. rsch. assoc. Mental Rsch. Inst., Palo Alto, Calif., 1974-78; assoc. prof. Med. Sch. U. S. D., Sioux Falls, 1978—; chmn. curriuclum and evaluation com. Sch. Medicine U. S.D., Sioux Falls, 1989-92; bd. dirs. Univ. Physicians, U. S.D. Sch. Medicine; cons. Charter Hosp., Sioux Falls, 1989-94; clin. dir. Psychiatry Assocs., 1989—. Contbr. to books and articles to profl. jours. Bd. dirs. S.D. Jr. Football Assn., Sioux Falls, 1988-92, Citizens Against Rape and Violence, Sioux Falls, 1988-89, Post 15 Baseball Program, 1995—. Fellow Am. Orthopsychiat. Assn.; mem. APA, AAAS, S.D. Psychol. Assn. (pres. Div. 1 1993-94), Woodlake Athletic Club. Avocation: computers. Office: Psychiatry Assoc 4009 W 49th St Ste 308 Sioux Falls SD 57106-5221

WILLIAMS, WADE HAMPTON, III, motion picture producer, director, distributor; b. Kansas City, Mo., Sept. 18, 1942; s. Wade H. and Mary (Hawkins) W. Pres. Film Works Studio, Kansas City, Mo., 1980—; owner, exhibitor Englewood Theatre, Independence, Mo., Rio Theatre, Overland Park, Kans. Author: (screenplay) Detour, 1992; producer: Helter Skelter, 1972, Invaders from Mars, 1986, Midnight Movie Massacre, 1986; producer, director: Detour, 1992; contbr. articles to profl. jours. Recipient Hugo award Rome Film Festival, 1981, Golden Palm award Ft. Lauderdale Film Festival, 1990. Republican. Home: 13001 Wornall Rd Kansas City MO 64145-1211 Office: Wade Williams Prodns 13001 Wornall Rd Kansas City MO 64145-1211

WILLIAMS, WALTER BAKER, mortgage banker; b. Seattle, May 12, 1921; s. William Walter and Anna Leland (Baker) W.; m. Marie Davis Wilson, July 6, 1945; children: Kathryn Williams-Mullins, Marcia Frances Williams Swanson, Bruce Wilson, Wendy Susan. BA, U. Wash., 1943; JD, Harvard U., 1948. With Bogle & Gates, Seattle, 1948-63, ptnr., 1960-63; pres. Continental Inc., Seattle, 1963-91, chmn., 1991—; bd. dirs. United Graphics Inc., Seattle, 1973-86, Fed. Nat. Mortgage Assn., 1976-77; chmn. Continental Savings Bank, 1991—. Rep. Wash. State Ho. of Reps., Olympia, 1961-63; sen. Wash. State Senate, Olympia, 1963-71; chmn. Econ. Devel. Council of Puget Sound, Seattle, 1981-82; pres. Japan-Am. Soc. of Seattle, 1971-72; chmn. Woodland Park Zoo Commn., Seattle, 1984-85. Served to capt. USMC, 1942-46, PTO. Recipient Brotherhood Citation, NCCJ, Seattle, 1980, First Citizen award Seattle-King County Asn. Realtors, 1997. Mem. Mortgage Bankers Assn. Am. (pres. 1973-74), Wash. Mortgage Bankers Assn. (pres. 1971), Fed. Home Loan Mortgage Corp. (adv. com.), Wash. Savs. League (bd. dirs., chmn. 1991-92), Rotary (pres. local club 1984-85), Rainier Club Seattle (pres. 1987-88). Republican. Congregationalist. Office: Continental Inc 601 Union St Ste 2000 Seattle WA 98101-2326

WILLIAMS, WALTER DAVID, aerospace executive, consultant; b. Chgo., July 22, 1931; s. Walter William and Theresa Barbara (Gilman) W.; m. Joan Haven Armstrong, Oct. 22, 1960; children: Latham Lloyd, Clayton Chapell, William Haven. BS, Ohio U., 1951; MBA, Harvard U., 1955; MS, MIT, 1972. Supr. fin. policy and systems Hughes Aircraft Co., Culver City, Calif., 1955-57; staff mem. Rand Corp. and SDC, Santa Monica, Calif., 1957-60; mgr. adminstrn. and fin. Microwave Div. TRW Inc., Canoga Park, Calif., 1960-63; exec. asst. Space Labs. Northrop Corp., Hawthorne, Calif., 1963-66; fin. mgr. comml. group Aircraft Div. Northrop Corp., Hawthorne, Calif., 1966-72; dir. internat. plans Northrop Corp., L.A., 1972-74, dir. internat. mkt. devel., 1974-77, exec. dir. internat., 1977-93; pres. Williams Internat. Assocs., L.A., 1994—; export advisor U.S. Sec. Commerce, Washington, 1986—. Author (study/lect. series) Internat. Def. Mktg., 1982. Dir. KCET Men's Coun., L.A., 1970; pres. Westwood Rep. Club, L.A., 1970; assoc. mem. Rep. State Ctrl. Com., Calif., 1968; div. chmn. Rep. Ctrl. Com., L.A. County, 1968. Served to capt. U.S. Army, 1951-53. Recipient fellowship Alfred P. Sloan Found., 1971-72. Mem. AIAA, Soc. Sloan Fellows, MIT Club, Harvard Bus. Sch. Assn., Newcomen Soc., Chaine des Rotisseurs, L.A. Country Club, Harvard Club, Soc. Bacchus Am., Delta Sigma Pi, Pi Kappa Alpha. Avocations: golf, tennis, paddle tennis. Office: Williams Internat Assocs PO Box 491178 Los Angeles CA 90049-9178

WILLIAMS, WALTER JACKSON, JR., electrical engineer, consultant; b. Elkhart, Ind., Jan. 17, 1925; s. Walter Jackson and Mary (Delcamp) W.; m. Helen L. Evans, July 20, 1944 (dec. Aug. 1980); children: David, Eileen, Valerie; m. Evelyn M. Bowyer, May 26, 1984 (dec. Oct. 1990); m. Margaret M. McLaughlin, Aug. 26, 1995. BSEE, Purdue U., 1948, MS, 1950; PhD, 1954. From grad. asst. to instr. Purdue U., Layfayette, Ind., 1948-54; jr. engr. Argonne (Ill.) Nat. Lab., Ill., 1950, Naval Ordnance Plant, Indpls., 1951; engr. Internat. Tel. & Tel. Co., Ft. Wayne, Ind., 1954-60, cons., 1961-63, sr. tech. advisor Aerospace Optical divsn., 1975-80, tech. dir., 1980-87, ret., 1987, cons., 1987—; chmn. dept. elec. engring. Ind. Inst. Tech., Ft. Wayne, 1961-65, dean engring., 1963-67, v.p., acad. dean, 1967-75, interim pres., 1970-72; cons. in field, 1960—. Patentee in field. Bd. dirs. Assoc. Chs., Ft. Wayne, 1965-67. With AUS, 1943-46. Mem. IEEE (mem. com. on accreditation activities com. 1984-89), NSPE, Am. Soc. Engring. Edn., Accreditation Bd. for Engring. and Tech. (mem. engring. accreditation commn. 1990-95), Ind. Soc. Profl. Engrs. (bd. dirs. Ft. Wayne chpt. 1968-70), Ft. Wayne Engrs. Club (pres. 1967-68, bd. dirs. 1969-71), Sigma Xi, Tau Beta Pi, Eta Kappa Nu. Home: 8707 Stellhorn Rd Fort Wayne IN 46815-4410

WILLIAMS, WALTER JOSEPH, lawyer; b. Detroit, Oct. 5, 1918; s. Joseph Louis and Emma Geraldine (Hewitt) W.; m. Maureen June Kay, Jan. 15, 1944; 1 child, John Bryan. Student, Bowling Green State U., 1935-36; B.S.B.A., Ohio State U., 1940; J.D., LL.B., U. Detroit, 1942. Bar: Mich. bar 1942. Title atty. Abstract & Title Guaranty Co., 1946-47; corp. atty. Ford Motor Co., 1947-51, Studebaker-Packard Corp., 1951-56; asst. sec., house counsel Am. Motors Corp., Am. Motors Sales Corp., Am. Motors Pan-Am. Corp., Evart Products Co., Ltd., 1956-65, corp. sec. house counsel, 1965-72; asst. corp. sec., dir. Am. Motors (Can.) Ltd.; dir. Evart Products Co., 1959-72; dir., corporate sec., house counsel Jeep Corp., Jeep Sales Corp., Jeep Internat. Corp., 1968-72; partner Gilman and Williams, Southfield, Mich., 1972-74; atty. Detroit Edison Co., 1974-75; asst. sec., sr. staff atty. Burroughs Corp. (and subsidiaries), 1975-84; pvt. practice, pres. Walter J. Williams P.C., Bloomfield Hills, Mich., 1984—. Charter commr., city of Dearborn Heights, Mich., 1960-63; dir. Detroit Met. Indsl. Devel. Corp., 1962-72, also asst. sec. Served to capt. U.S. Army, 1942-46. Mem. ABA, Detroit Bar Assn. (chmn. corp. gen. counsel com. 1965-68), Fed. Bar Assn., State Bar Mich., Ohio State U. Alumni Assn. (pres. Detroit 1961-63), U. Detroit Law Alumni, Delta Theta Phi. Club: Oakland Hills Country. Home and Office: 3644 Darcy Dr Bloomfield Hills MI 48301-2125

WILLIAMS, WALTER WAYLON, lawyer, pecan grower; b. Gause, Tex., Nov. 12, 1933; s. Jesse Nathaniel and Lola Fay (Matthews) W.; m. Velmalene Von Gonten, Mar. 6, 1953; children—Diana Lee, Virginia Marie. B.B.A. with honors, U. Tex., 1959, J.D. with honors, 1960. Bar: Tex. bar 1960. Since practiced in Houston; mem. firm Fulbright, Crooker, Freeman, Bates & Jaworski, 1960-63, Bates & Brock, 1964-66, Brock, Williams & Boyd, 1966-79, Williams & Boyd, 1979-88; pres. Nat. Pecan Growers Coun., 1976-78, Tex. Pecan Growers Assn., 1976-78. Served with AUS, 1953-55. Named Outstanding Soldier of Second Army, 1955. Mem. ABA, Houston Bar Assn., State Bar Tex., Tex. Trial Lawyers Assn. (dir. 1972-76), Houston Trial Lawyers Assn. (dir. 1969), Assn. Trial Lawyers Am., Chancellors, Beta Gamma Sigma, Phi Delta Phi. Home: RR 3 Box 101 Yoakum TX 77995-9711

WILLIAMS, WAYNE DE ARMOND, lawyer; b. Denver, Sept. 24, 1914; s. Wayne Cullen and Lena Belle (Day) W.; m. Virginia Brinton Deal, Sept. 9, 1937; children: Marcia Lee, Daniel Deal; m. Thelma Ralston, Apr. 8, 1995. A.B., U. Denver, 1936; J.D., Columbia U., 1938. Bar: Colo. 1938. Pvt. practice Denver, 1938-43, 46-58; ptnr. firm Williams & Erickson (and predecessors), Denver, 1958-77; gen. counsel Denver Water Dept., 1977-91; asst. city atty. Denver, 1939-43, spl. asst. city atty., 1946-49; chmn. Denver County Ct. Nominating Commn., 1968-69; mem. Denver Dist. Ct. Nominating Commn., 1969-75; lectr. in field U. Denver, 1947-60. Contbr. articles to legal jours. Chmn. Denver Mcpl. Airport Adv. Commn., 1963-65; chancellor Rocky Mountain Meth. Ann. Conf., 1978-86; former mem. governing bd. Colo. chpt. English Speaking Union, Colo. Tuberculosis Assn., Colo. Soc. for Prevention Blindness; mem. adv. bd. Anchor Ctr. for Blind Children. Capt. JAGD U.S. Army, 1943-46. Mem. ABA (Ross Essay prize 1944), Colo. Bar Assn. (gov. 1974-77), Denver Bar Assn. (pres. 1974-75), Sigma Alpha Epsilon, Phi Delta Phi, Omicron Delta Kappa. Democrat. Methodist. Clubs: Lions, Masons. Home: 625 S Alton Way Apt 3A Denver CO 80231-1752

WILLIAMS, WILLIAM ARNOLD, agronomy educator; b. Johnson City, N.Y., Aug. 2, 1922; s. William Truesdall and Nellie Viola (Tompkins) W.; m. Madeline Patricia Moore, Nov. 27, 1943; children—David, Kathleen, Andrew. B.S., Cornell U., 1947, M.S., 1948, Ph.D., 1951. Prof. emeritus U. Calif., Davis, 1993—. Editor agr. sect. McGraw-Hill Ency. Sci. & Tech.; contbr. articles to profl. jours. Mem. Nat. Alliance for Mentally Ill. Served to lt. U.S. Army, 1943-46. Grantee NSF, 1965-82, Kellogg Found., 1963-67; Fulbright scholar, Australia, 1960, Rockefeller Found. scholar, Costa Rica, 1966. Fellow AAAS, Am. Soc. Agronomy, Crop Sci. Soc. Am.; mem. Soil Sci. Soc. Am., Soc. Range Mgmt., Am. Statis. Assn., Assn. for Tropical Biology, Fedn. Am. Scientists, Am. Math Soc. Democrat. Home: 718 Oeste Dr Davis CA 95616-3531 Office: Univ California Dept Agronomy And Rang Davis CA 95616

WILLIAMS, WILLIAM COREY, theology educator, consultant; b. Wilkes-Barre, Pa., July 12, 1937; s. Edward Douglas and Elizabeth Irene (Schooley) W.; m. Alma Simmenroth Williams, June 27, 1959; 1 child, Linda. Diploma in Ministerial Studies, NE Bible Inst., 1962; BA in Bibl. Studies, Cen. Bible Coll., 1963, MA in Religion, 1964; MA in Hebrew and Near Ea. Studies, NYU, 1966, PhD in Hebrew Lang. and Lit., 1975; postgrad., Hebrew U., 1977-78, Inst. Holyland Studies, 1986. Ref. libr. Hebraic section Libr. of Congress, Washington, 1967-69; prof. Old Testament So. Calif. Coll., Costa Mesa, 1969—; adj. prof. Old Testament Melodyland Sch. Theology, Anaheim, Calif., 1975-77; vis. prof. Old Testament Fuller Theol. Sem., Pasadena, Calif., 1978-81, 84, Asian Theol. Ctr. for Evangelism and Missions, Singapore and Sabah, E. Malaysia, 1985, Continental Bible Coll., Saint Pieters-Leeuw, Belgium, 1985, Mattersey Bible Coll., Eng., 1985, Inst. Holy Land Studies, Jerusalem, 1986, Regent U., 1994; transl. cons. and reviser New Am. Std. Bible, 1969-94; transl. cons. The New Internat. Version, 1975-76, New Century Version, 1991, The New Living Translation, 1992-95, New Internat. Version, Reader's Version, 1993-94; transl. cons. and editor Internat. Children's Version, 1985-86. Author: (books, tapes) Hebrew I: A Study Guide, 1986, Hebrew II: A Study Guide, 1986; contbr. articles to International Standard Bible Encyclopedia, New International Dictionary of Old Testment Theology and Evangelical Dictionary of Biblical Theology; contbr. articles to profl. jours.; contbr. notes to Spirit Filled Life Study Bible. Nat. Def. Fgn. Lang. fellow NYU, 1964-67; Alumni scholar N.E. Bible Inst., 1960-61; NEH fellow, summer 1992. Mem. Soc. Bibl. Lit., Evang. Theol. Soc. (exec. office 1974-77), Am. Acad. Religion, Nat. Assn. Profs. of Hebrew, Inst. Bibl. Rsch., The Lockman Found. (hon. mem. bd. dirs. 1992-94, mem. editorial bd. 1974-94). Home: 1817 Peninsula Pl Costa Mesa CA 92627-4591 Office: So Calif Coll 55 Fair Dr Costa Mesa CA 92626-6520

WILLIAMS, WILLIAM HARRISON, retired librarian; b. Seattle, Apr. 18, 1924; s. William E. and Letah M. (Hollenback) W.; m. Mary Helen Sims, Apr. 19, 1945; children: Linda Lee, Dee Ann. B.S., Brigham Young U., 1969, M.L.S., 1970. Dir. Provo Pub. Library, Utah, 1969-70; Wyo. State Librarian, 1970-78; dir. Wyo. state Archives and Hist. dept., 1971-78; exec. sec. Wyo. Hist. Soc., 1971-78; sr. research analyst Wyo. Taxpayers Assn., 1978-84. Served to lt. col. USAAF, 1943-64. Decorated USAF commendation with oak leaf cluster. Mem. Beta Phi Mu, Phi Alpha Theta. Home: 21607 N 123rd Dr Sun City West AZ 85375-1950

WILLIAMS, WILLIAM HENRY, II, publisher; b. Birmingham, Ala., Oct. 21, 1931; s. Calvin Thomas and Lillian Elizabeth (Levey) W.; m. Lewis Mozelle Hensley, Feb. 28, 1959; 1 child, William Henry III. Student, Baylor U., 1952-55. Printer Waco (Tex.) Tribune-Herald, 1950-59; internat. rep. Internat. Typog. Union, Colorado Springs, Colo., 1960-68; editor, gen. mgr. Colorado Springs Free Press, 1969-70; dir. labor relations The Morning Telegraph, N.Y.C., 1970-72; gen. mgr. Daily Racing Form, Hightstown, N.J., 1972-89, nat. gen. mgr. for U.S. and Can., 1990-91, pub., 1991-92; ret., 1992; pub. Kerrville (Tex.) Mountain Sun, 1993-96; mem. adv. council journalsim dept. Baylor U., Waco, 1970-72. Chmn. CentraState Med. Ctr., Freehold, N.J., 1982-83, CentraState Health Affiliates, Freehold, 1987-94; vice chmn. Ctr. for Aging, Inc., Freehold, 1985-90; dep. mayor Freehold Twp. Com., 1987, mayor, 1989-90, 93, committeeman, 1985-94; chmn. Freehold Mayor's Task Force on Substance Abuse, 1987-91; mem. Upper Guadalupe River Authority, 1995—, Kerr Econ. Devel. Found.; mem. devel. bd. Alamo Area Workforce, 1997—. Named an Hon. Trustee Freehold Area Hosp., 1985—. Mem. Am. Newspaper Pubs. Assn., Newspaper Pers. Rels. Assn., Tex. Press Assn. (bd. dirs. 1995-96), NCCJ (Brotherhood award 1986), Exch. Club (Hightstown; carter pres.), Masons (32 deg.), Shriners, Optimists (charter mem. Freehold chpt.), Lions Club (host). Republican. Lutheran. Club: Exchange (Hightstown) (charter pres.). Lodges: Masons (32 degree), Shriners, Optimists (charter mem. Freehold chpt.). Avocations: music, golf, football, skiing. Home and Office: 172 Saint Andrews Loop Kerrville TX 78028-6441

WILLIAMS, WILLIAM JOHN, JR., lawyer; b. New Rochelle, N.Y., Feb. 6, 1937; s. William John and Jane (Gormley) W.; m. Barbara Reuter. BA, Holy Cross Coll., Worcester, Mass., 1958; LLB, NYU, 1961. Bar: N.Y. 1961. Practiced in N.Y.C., 1962—; ptnr. firm Sullivan & Cromwell, 1969—. Trustee NYU Law Sch. Found., 1977—, Holy Cross Coll., 1988-96. Fellow Am. Bar Found.; mem. ABA, Am. Law Inst., N.Y. State Bar Assn., Assn. of Bar of City of N.Y., U.S. Golf Assn. (mem. exec. com. 1978-87, sec. 1980-81, v.p. 1982-85, pres. 1986-87). Democrat. Roman Catholic.

WILLIAMS, WILLIAM JOSEPH, physician, educator; b. Bridgeton, N.J., Dec. 8, 1926; s. Edward Carlaw and Mary Hood (English) W.; m. Margaret Myrick Lyman, Aug. 12, 1950 (dec. Aug., 1985) ; children: Susan Lyman, William Prescott, Sarah Robb; m. Karen A. Hughes, Feb. 18, 1989. Student, Bucknell U., 1943-45; MD, U. Pa., 1949. Diplomate: Am. Bd. Internal Medicine. (hematology com. 1976-80). Intern U. Pa., 1949-50, Am. Cancer Soc. research fellow in Biochemistry, 1950-52, resident medicine, 1954-55, assoc. to asst. prof. medicine, 1955-58, assoc. prof. to prof. medicine, chief hematology, 1961-69; sr. instr. microbiology Case Western Res. U., 1952; asst. prof. medicine Washington U., St. Louis, 1959-60; research fellow Oxford U., Eng., 1960-61; mem. hematology tng. com. Nat. Inst. Arthritis and Metabolic Disease, 1964-68, research career program com., 1968-72; chmn. dept. medicine SUNY Health Sci. Ctr., Syracuse, N.Y., 1969-92, prof. medicine, 1969—; interim dean Coll. Medicine SUNY Health Sci. Ctr., Syracuse, 1991-92; vis. scientist Walter and Eliza Hall Inst., Melbourne, Australia, 1980; vis. prof. Monash U., Melbourne, 1980; mem. thrombosis adv. com. Nat. Heart and Lung Inst., 1969-73, chmn., 1971-73; adv. coun. Nat. Arthritis, Metabolism and Digestive Diseases, 1975-79; mem. residency rev. com. internal medicine Accreditation Coun. Grad. Med. Edn., 1983-89, mem. bd. appeals panel for internal medicine, 1989—; mem. N.Y. State Coun. Grad. Med. Edn., 1987-89. Editor-in-chief: Hematology, 1972, 4th edit., 1989, Williams Hematology Companion Handbook, 1996; contbr. articles to med. lit. Trustee Everson Mus. Art, 1975-81, 83-89. With USNR, 1944-46, 52-54. Recipient Research Career Devel. award Nat. Heart Inst., 1963-68; Daland fellow Am. Philos. Soc., 1955-57; Markle scholar, 1957-62. Mem. AMA, ACP (gov. Upstate N.Y. 1976-81), Am. Soc. Biol. Chemists, Am. Soc. Clin. Investigation, Assn. Am. Physicians, Am. Clin. and Climatol. Assn., Am. Heart Assn. (council on thrombosis exec. com. 1977-81), Internat. Soc. Thrombosis and Haemostasis, Assn. Profs. Medicine, Am. Soc. Hematology, Interurban Clin. Club (sec. 1964-70), Internat. Hematology Soc., Alpha Omega Alpha. Mem. Soc. Friends. Home: 5160 Peck Hill Rd Jamesville NY 13078-9724 Office: 750 E Adams St Syracuse NY 13210-2306

WILLIAMS, WILLIAM MAGAVERN, headmaster; b. Niles, Mich., Dec. 22, 1931; s. Errol Edwin and Mary Elizabeth (Magavern) W.; m. Linda Carol Grush, June 15, 1958; children: Diana, William Jr., Sarah. BA, Williams Coll., 1953, LHD (hon.), 1984; postgrad. in Philosophy, Columbia U., 1954-58, MA in Ednl. Psychology, 1966. Tchr. elem. English, history, phys. edn. McTernan Sch., Waterbury, Conn., 1953-54; head guidance, boarding, and humanities depts., instr. English, coach varsity wrestling Riverdale Country Sch., Bronx, N.Y., 1955-66; headmaster Doane Acad., Burlington, N.J., 1966-70, Poly. Prep. Country Day Sch., Bklyn., 1970—. Trustee Bklyn Inst. Arts and Scis., 1972-79, Bklyn. Ctrl. YMCA, 1974-78, Profl. Children's Sch., 1976-79, Bklyn. Children's Mus., 1979-82, Plymouth Ch. Pilgrims, 1979-86, N.Y. State Assn. Ind. Schs., 1980-86. Mem. Headmasters' Assn., Country Day Sch. Headmasters' Assn., Cum Laude Soc. (regent dist. III 1971-87, dep. pres. gen. 1981-87, pres. gen. 1987-96), Guild Ind. Schs. N.Y. (pres. 1986-88). Avocations: skiing, chess, travel, Civil War history. Home: 195 Amity St Brooklyn NY 11201-6203 Office: Poly Prep Country Day Sch 92d St and 7th Ave Brooklyn NY 11228

WILLIAMS, WILLIAM RALSTON, retired bank and trust company executive; b. Hattiesburg, Miss., Jan. 20, 1910; s. William Ralston and Beulah (Smith) W.; m. Mary E. Marsh, May 8, 1936; chiildren—Mary J. (Mrs. Charles W. Cargill, Jr.), Julie D. Sher. Student, Central State Coll., Edmond, Okla., 1929-32, Okla. State U., 1933. Dist. mgr. Oklahoma City area Internat. Harvester Co., 1935-43; owner Stipes-Williams Co., Altus, Okla., 1943-55, Williams Investment and Ins. Co., Altus, 1955-69; sr. v.p. Fidelity Nat. Bank & Trust Co., Oklahoma City, 1968-83; ret., 1983; Regent A. and M. Colls. Okla., 1952-69, chmn., 1957-64; v.p. Am. Assn. Gov. Bds. Colls. and Univs. Am., 1958. Mem. Altus City Council, 1948-52. Served to lt. USNR, 1944-46. Mem. Oklahoma City C. of C., Am. Legion, Beta Theta Pi. Democrat. Episcopalian. Clubs: Kiwanis (pres. Altus 1947, lt. gov. 1952), Masons (33 deg., K.T., Jester), Elks; Quail Creek Country (Oklahoma City). Home: 3012 Thorn Ridge Rd Oklahoma City OK 73120-1924

WILLIAMS, WILLIAM STANLEY COSSOM, physics educator and researcher; b. Margate, Kent, England, Aug. 4, 1929; s. Stanley Charles and Winifred Florence (Cossom) W.; m. Renée Emilienne Maria Duval-Destin, Sept. 5, 1956; children: Claire, Matthieu. BSc, U. Coll. London, 1950, PhD, 1953. Univ. lectr. U. Glasgow, 1955-61; sr. rsch. officer dept. nuclear physics U. Oxford, 1961-90, re-designated lectr. physics, 1990-96; fellow and tutor St. Edmund Hall, Oxford, 1963-96, emeritus fellow, 1996—. Author: Introduction to Elementary Particle Physics, 1961, 2d edit. 1971, Nuclear and Particle Physics, 1991; contbr. articles to profl. jours. Mem. Inst. Physics London, Am. Phys. Soc. Office: Nuclear and Astrophys Lab Dept Physics, 1 Keble Rd, Oxford OX1 3RH, England

WILLIAMS, WILLIAM THOMAS, artist, educator; b. Cross Creek, N.C., July 17, 1942; s. William Thomas and Hazel (Davis) W.; m. Patricia Ayn Deweese; children—Nila Winona, Aaron Thomas. B.F.A., Pratt Inst., 1966; M.F.A., Yale U., 1968. Mem. faculty Sch. Visual Arts, Pratt Inst., 1969-70; mem. faculty dept. art Bklyn. Coll., City U., N.Y., 1970—; prof. art Bklyn. Coll., City U., 1977—. Home: 654 Broadway New York NY 10012-2327

WILLIAMS, WILLIE, protective services official; b. 1943; m. Evelina; children: Lisa, Willie Jr., Eric. AS, Phila. Coll. Textiles and Sci., 1982; postgrad., St. Joseph U., 1991. Police officer City of Phila., 1964-72, police detective, 1972-74, police sgt., 1974-76, police lt. juvenile aid div., 1976-83, police capt. 22nd and 23rd dists., 1984-86, police inspector, head tng. bur., civil affairs div., North police div., 1986-88, dep. commr. adminstrn., 1988, police commr., 1988-92; chief of police L.A. Police Dept., 1992—; lecture, instr. Temple U., Univ. Pa., Univ. Del. Former scoutmaster Boy Scouts Am.; mem. Pa. Juvenile Officers' Assn., Southeastern Pa. Chiefs of Police, West Angeles Ch. of God in Christ; past bd. dirs. Rebuild L.A. Mem. Nat. Orgn. Black Law Enforcement Execs. (past nat. pres.), Internat. Assn. Chiefs of Police, Alpha Sigma Lambda. Office: Office of Police Chief 150 N Los Angeles St Los Angeles CA 90012-3309*

WILLIAMS, WILLIE, JR., physicist, educator; b. Independence, La., Mar. 24, 1947; s. Willie Sr. and Lee Anner (Booker) W.; 1 child, Willie Williams III. B.S., So. U., 1970; M.S., Iowa State U., 1972, Ph.D., 1974. Mem. faculty Lincoln U., Lincoln University, Pa., 1974—, assoc. prof. physics, 1979-84; prof. physics Lincoln U., Lincoln University, 1984—, chmn. dept., 1976—, chmn. sci. and math. div., 1978-80, 83—, founder, dir. Lincoln Advance Sci. and Engring. Reinforcement (LASER) Program, 1980-96, dir. pre-engring., 1976-96, dir., prin. investigator Early Alert-Young Scholars Program, 1992-96; bd. dirs. women tech. program Lincoln U. Urban Ctr., Phila.; vis. prof. Ctr. for Teaching Innovation, Drexel U., 1975; liaison officer Nat. Assn. for Equal Opportunity in Higher Edn., Dept. Def. Program., 1987—; mem. steering com. NSF Comprehensive Ctr. for Minorities, Phila.; bd. dirs. Prime Inc., Phila. Contbr. articles to profl. jours. Chmn. Cheyney Lincoln Temple Cluster, 1974-78; pres. The Men Fedn., So. U., 1968-69. Recipient Lindback award for Outstanding Teaching, 1976, Outstanding Scientist award White House Initiative, 1988; named one of Outstanding Young Men of Am., 1979; fellow NASA, 1979, Mobil Oil Corp., 1977, Nat. Bur. Standards, 1979, Dept. Def., 1980-81, Navy fellow, 1982. Mem. AAAS, AAUP, Am. Assn. Physics, N.Y. Acad. Scis., Math. Assn. Am., Am. Phys. Soc., Nat. Soc. Black Physicists, Nat. Geog. Soc., Iowa State Alumna Assn., Sigma Xi, Sigma Pi Sigma. Baptist. Home: 448 W Baltimore Pk West Grove PA 19390 Office: Lincoln U Dept Physics Lincoln University PA 19352 *Throughout my life I have always striven to achieve the very best and have held on to the belief that wherever possible improve upon today, so that everyone might have a better tomorrow! I have been guided by the the principle of being selective in my endeavors, having specific objectives, followed by detailed analysis, concise actions and intense work with continous review.*

WILLIAMS, WILLIE JOHN, II, marketing consultant; b. Mobile, Ala., Mar. 3, 1960; s. Willie John and Augustine (Dacus) W. BS in Mktg. and Mgmt., Ala. State U., 1984. Account exec. Thomas May & Assocs., Montgomery, Ala., 1984-85, v.p. mktg., 1986-88; dir. mktg. Imex Comm., Atlanta, 1985-86; v.p. mktg. Tempo Advt. & Mktg., Mobile, 1988-91; mktg. cons., Mobile, 1991-97; v.p. mktg. Thomas May & Assocs., Montgomery, Ala., 1994-97; v.p. advt. WIQR-AM, WYVC-FM, WCOX-AM, Montgomery; mem. bd. Ala. Dept. Human Resources, Montgomery, 1991—, sec. bd., 1992-95. Founder Baldwin County Reverend M.L. King Celebration Com., 1989; v.p. Young Rep. Club Baldwin County, 1993-94, sec., 1991, pres., 1994-96, 97—; mem. Baldwin County Rep. Exec. Com., 1991—; mem. State of Ala Voter Registration Adv. Bd. Recipient award of merit City of Daphne, Ala., 1990, 91; named to Mobile PressRegister Top 60 young leaders for the next century. Mem. Masons, Alpha Phi Omega (v.p., pres.). Baptist. Avocations: golf, chess, basketball, reading, travel. Home: PO Box 434 Point Clear AL 36564-0434 Office: 11370 Confederate Rest Rd Point Clear AL 36564

WILLIAMS, WINTON HUGH, civil engineer; b. Tampa, Fla., Feb. 14, 1920; s. Herbert DeMain and Alice (Grant) W.; m. Elizabeth Walser Seelye, Dec. 18, 1949; children: Jan, Dick, Bill, Ann. Grad. Adj Gens. Sch., Gainesville, Fla., 1943; student U. Tampa, 1948; grad. Transp. Sch., Ft. Eustis, Va., 1949; BCE, U. Fla., 1959; grad. Command and Gen. Staff Coll., Ft. Levenworth, Kans., 1964, Engrs. Sch., Ft. Belvoir, 1965, Indsl. Coll. Armed Forces, Washington, 1966, Logistics Mgmt. Center, Ft. Lee, Va., 1972. Registered profl. engr., Fla., N.C. Constrn. engr. air fields C.E., U.S. Army, McCoy AFB, Fla., 1959-61, Homestead AFB, Miami, Fla., 1961-62; civil engr. C.E., Jacksonville (Fla.) Dist. Office, 1962-64, chief master planning and layout sect., mil. br., engring. div., 1964-70; chief master planning and real estate div. Hdqrs. U.S. Army So. Command, Ft. Amador, C.Z., 1970-75, spl. asst. planning and mil. constrn. programming Marine Corps Air Bases Eastern Area, Marine Corps Air Sta., Cherry Point, N.C., 1975-82;

cons. engr., Morehead City, N.C., 1982—. Mem. Morehead City Planning Bd., 1982-94; mem. Carteret County N.C. Health Bd., 1990—, chmn. 1995-97; active Boy Scouts, C.Z.; mem. nat. council U. Tampa. Served with AUS, World War II, ETO, Korean War; col. Res. Decorated Breast Order of Yun Hi (Republic of China); presdl. citation, Meritorious Service medal (Republic of Korea); eagle scout with gold palm. Fellow ASCE (life); mem. NSPE (life), Res. Officers Assn. (life, v.p. C.Am. and S.Am.), Profl. Engrs. N.C., Am. Soc. Photogrammetry, Prestressed Concrete Inst. (profl.), Soc. Am. Mil. Engrs. (life, engr.), Nat. Eagle Scout Assn., Nat. Rifle Assn. Am., Am. Legion (life), Order Arrow, Theta Chi. Presbyterian. Home and Office: 4322 Coral Point Dr Morehead City NC 28557-2745

WILLIAMS, YVONNE G., corporate trainer; b. Waycross, Ga., Jan. 27, 1953; d. Alfred Hayward and Elizabeth Thomas; 1 child, Benjamin Nkrumah Williams. BA in Bus. Mgmt., Eckerd Coll., 1993; MA in Adult Edn., U. South Fla., 1995, postgrad. Mktg. rep. Xerox, Tampa, Fla., 1987-90, account exec., 1990-92, document mgmt. tng. rep., 1992-96; edn. specialist Xerox, Tampa, 1996—; adv. bd. PIMEG, St. Petersburg, Fla., 1995—. Active First Bapt. Instnl. Ch., St. Petersburg. Mem. NAACP, ASTD, Nat. Coun. Negro Women, Tamp Educators Sertoma Club, South Ctrl. Rotary, Phi Kappa Phi. Office: Xerox Corp 4200 W Cypress St Tampa FL 33607-4156

WILLIAMS-ASHMAN, HOWARD GUY, biochemistry educator; b. London, Eng., Sept. 3, 1925; came to U.S., 1950, naturalized, 1962; s. Edward Harold and Violet Rosamund (Sturge) Williams-A.; m. Elisabeth Bächli, Jan. 25, 1959; children—Anne Clare, Christian, Charlotte, Geraldine. B.A., U. Cambridge, 1946; Ph.D., U. London, 1949. From asst. prof. to prof. biochemistry U. Chgo., 1953-64; prof. pharmacology and exptl. therapeutics, also prof. reproductive biology Johns Hopkins Sch. Medicine, 1964-69; prof. biochemistry Ben May Inst., U. Chgo., 1969—, Maurice Goldblatt prof., 1973-91, prof. emeritus, 1991. Contbr. numerous articles in field to publs. Recipient Research Career award USPHS, 1962-64. Fellow Am. Acad. Arts and Scis. (Amory prize 1975); mem. Am. Soc. Biochemistry and Molecular Biology. Home: 5421 S Cornell Ave Chicago IL 60615-5646 Office: U Chgo Ben May Inst Chicago IL 60637

WILLIAMS-BRIDGERS, JACQUELYN, federal government official; b. Washington, Feb. 27, 1956; m. Daniel Bridgers; 2 children. BA, Syracuse U., 1977, MA in Pub. Administration, 1978; DHL (hon.), Southeastern U., 1996. With U.S. General Acctg. Office, 1978-95; assoc. dir. for housing and cmty. devel. issues U.S. Dept HUD, 1983-84; now inspector general U.S. State Dept., Washington, 1996—. Recipient Arthur S. Flemming award, GAO Meritorious Svc. award, 1992. Office: Office Inspector Gen Dept State 2201 C St NW Rm 6817 Washington DC 20520-0001*

WILLIAMS JONES, ELIZABETH, financial planner, business consultant; b. San Francisco, Jan. 16, 1948; d. John and Myrtle Mary (Thierry) W.; children: Brian, Jonathan; m. Archie W. Jones Jr. Cert. in bus., U. Calif., 1979. Cert. computers loan processing. Manpower coord., fed. programs U.S. Govt., San Francisco; patient svc. rep. Health Care Svc., Oakland, Calif.; ins. and real estate cons.; pres. Investments Unlimited, Oakland, EWJ & Assocs. Mktg. Firm; leisure svcs. commr. City of Pitts.; CEO Ultimate Vacations Inc. Mem. NAACP. Recipient Pub. Speaking award; European Investment fellow. Mem. AAUW, NAFE, Nat. Real Estate Owners Assn., Nat. Notary Assn., Order Ea. Star, Heroines Jericho, Daus. Isis, Toastmistress Club.

WILLIAMS-MONEGAIN, LOUISE JOEL, science educator, administrator, retired; b. Chgo., June 13, 1941; d. Sylvester Emanuel Jr. and Carita Bell (Brown) Williams; m. Martin Monegain, Aug. 19, 1961; children: Michael Martin, Martin Marion II. BS, Shaw U., 1975; JD, Antioch Sch. of Law, Washington, 1979; cert. adminstrn., Roosevelt U., 1988; PhD, U. Ill., 1994. Tchr. Chgo. Archdiocese, 1968-73; assoc. dir. pub. affairs Warren Regional Planning Commn., Soul City, N.C., 1973-74; comm. specialist Coun. of the Great City Schs., Washington, 1974-76; lawyer Equal Employment Opportunity Commn., Washington, 1979-80; tchr. Olive Harvey City Coll., Chgo., 1981-83; mgr. Joy Travel Agt., Chgo., 1981-83; owner, pres. MJS Your Travel Agt., Chgo., 1983-86; sci. tchr. Chgo. Pub. Schs., 1986-91; program leader, evaluator Argonne (Ill.) Nat. Lab., 1991-97; ret., 1997; pres. Monegain & Assocs.; program leader, evaluation rep. Nat. Cancer Program, Accra and Jumasi, Ghana, West Africa, 1995. Vol. Art Inst., Chgo., 1994; green team adv. bd. Lincoln Park Zool. Soc., Chgo., 1992—. Scholarship State of Ill., 1987. Mem. ASCD, Am. Edn. Rsch. Assn., Nat. Sci. Tchrs. Assn., Assn. for Coll. and Univ. Women, Phi Delta Kappa. Avocations: attending opera, dance performances, plays, galleries, swimming, traveling.

WILLIAMSON, ALAN BACHER, English literature educator, poet, writer; b. Chgo., Jan. 24, 1944; s. George and Jehanne (Bacher) W.; m. Anne Winters, Oct. 12, 1968 (div. Feb. 1988); 1 child, Elizabeth Kilner. BA, Haverford Coll., 1964; MA, Harvard U., 1965, PhD, 1969. Asst. prof. U. Va., Charlottesville, 1969-75; Briggs-Copeland lectr. Harvard U., Cambridge, Mass., 1977-80; Fannie Hurst lectr. Brandeis U., Waltham, Mass., 1980-82; prof. English, U. Calif., Davis, 1982—; poetry panelist Nat. Endowment for Arts, 1989. Author: (criticism) Pity the Monsters, 1974, Introspection and Contemporary Poetry, 1984, Eloquence and Mere Life, 1994, (poetry) Presence, 1983, The Muse of Distance, 1988, Love and the Soul, 1995. Poetry fellow Nat. Endowment for Arts, 1973; Guggenheim fellow, 1991. Mem. MLA (exec. com. div. on poetry 1987-91). Democrat. Zen Buddhist. Office: U Calif Dept English Davis CA 95616

WILLIAMSON, BRIAN DAVID, information systems executive, consultant; b. Danbury, Conn., May 14, 1973; s. Robert Garth and Celeste Marie (D'Alessio) W. AA in Specialized Bus., Art Inst. Phila., 1993; BS in Gen. Studies, Teikyo Post U., 1994; postgrad. in Tech. Mgmt., Polytech. U., 1997—. Asst. mgr. The New Milford (Conn.) Music Ctr., 1991-93; prodn. asst. Med. Broadcasting Co., Conshohocken, Pa., 1993; owner Custom Designs, Inc., Danbury, Conn., 1991-96; info. systems and telecomms. analyst Datahr Rehab. Inst., Brookfield, Conn., 1996—; video technician Danbury Corp., Bethel, Conn., 1992—. Author, writer (film script) The Senior, 1994. Republican. Roman Catholic. Avocations: tennis, computer graphics, movies, music. Home: 34 Lindencrest Dr Danbury CT 06811-4232 Office: Datahr Rehab Inst 135 Old State Rd # 5189 Brookfield CT 06804-2535

WILLIAMSON, CLARENCE KELLY, microbiologist, educator; b. McKeesport, Pa., Jan. 19, 1924; s. James Frederick and Loretta (McDermott) W.; m. Dorothy Birgit Ohlsson, Aug. 18, 1951; children: Lisa Ann, Erik James. B.S., U. Pitts., 1949, M.S., 1951, Ph.D., 1955. Bacteriologist E.S. Magee Hosp., Pitts., 1951; instr. bacteriology U. Pitts., 1951-55, Pa. State U., summer 1953; mem. faculty Miami U., Oxford, Ohio, 1955—, chmn. dept. microbiology, 1962-72, prof., 1963-85, dean Coll. Arts and Sci., 1971-82, prof. emeritus, 1985—, exec. v.p. acad. affairs, provost, 1982-85, provost, exec. v.p. acad. affairs emeritus, 1985—; cons. Warren-Teed Products Co., Columbus, Ohio, 1953-62; cons. editor microbiology World Pub. Co., Cleve., 1965-68. Sec.-treas. McCullough-Hyde Meml. Hosp., 1968-70, trustee, bd. dirs., 1967-77, vice chmn., 1970-71, 72-74, chmn., 1974-76; trustee Hospice of the Miami Valley, 1984-92, United Campus Ministry, 1992-96; mem. commn. on arts and scis. Nat. Assn. State Univs. and Land-Grant Colls., 1974-80; bd. govs. Am. Inst. Biol. Scis., 1977-83; bd. dirs. Coun. Colls. of Arts and Scis., 1975-79, pres., 1977-78; trustee S.W. Ohio and No. Ky. chpt. Nat. Multiple Sclerosis Soc., 1981-89; trustee Lakeside Assn., Chautauqua, Lakeside, Ohio, 1990—. With USNR, 1943-46. Recipient Benjamin Harrison medallion, 1982. Fellow Am. Acad. Microbiology, Ohio Acad. Sci. (v.p. med. sci. sect. 1970-71); mem. Am. Soc. Microbiology, Sigma Xi, Beta Gamma Sigma, Phi Kappa Phi, Omicron Delta Kappa, Rho Chi, Phi Sigma (nat. v.p. 1975-77, pres. 1977-83). Club: Torch (pres. Butler County 1969-70). Lodge: Rotary (pres. Oxford 1967-68). Spl. research poststreptococcal glomerulonephritis, classification of viridans streptococci, dissociation of Pseudomonas aeruginosa. Home: 104 Mckee Ave Oxford OH 45056-9056

WILLIAMSON, DONALD E., state official; b. Louisville, Miss., June 17, 1955; m. Anita Hudspeth; 1 child, Jonathan Stuart. Student, East Miss. Jr. Coll., 1972-73, Miss. State U., 1973-75; MD cum laude, U. Miss., 1979. Diplomate Am. Bd. Internal Medicine. Intern, resident internal medicine U. Va. Hosp., Charlottesville, 1979-82; with East Miss. State Hosp., Meridian, 1979; state tb control oficer Miss. State Dept. Health, 1982-86; dir. divsn. disease control Ala. Dept. Pub. Health, 1986-88, dir. bur. preventive health svcs., 1988-92, state health officer, 1992—; faculty mem. Injury Control Rsch. Ctr. U. Ala., Birmingham; clin. assoc. prof. dept. internal medicine U. South Ala.; presenter in field. Contbr. articles to profl. jours. Chmn. Ala. Pub. Health Care Authority, Ala. Radiation Adv. Bd. Health; mem. Ala. Commn. Aging, State Bldg. Commn., Statewide Health Coordinating Coun., Ala. Youth Svcs. Bd., Gov.'s Task Force Health Care, 1993, Ala. Child Abuse & Neglect Prevention Bd., Ala. Resource Devel. Com., Ala. Anatomical Bd., Planning and Adv. Coun. Devel. Disabilities, Ala. Bd. Med. Scholarship Awards, Pesticides Adv. Com., Gov.'s Interagy. Coordinating Coun., Ala. Juvenile Justice Coordinating Coun., Emergency Med. Svcs. Adv. Coun., 1986-92, Legis. Adv. Com. AIDS, 1988-90, Atty. Gen.'s Task Force Med.Waste, 1989, Water Resources Adv. Coun., exec. coun. Ala. Children's Svcs. Facilitation Team, 1993—; mem. med. adv. com. ARC. Recipient Mosby Book award, 1979, D.G. Gill award, 1997; Pub. Health Leadership Inst. scholar, 1996. Mem. APHA, Assn. State and Territorial Health Ofcls. (pres.-elect), Med. Assn. State Ala., Ala. Pub. Health Assn. (bd. dirs. 1991—, chmn. disease control and epidemiology sect. 1991-92), Phi Theta Kappa, Phi Kappa Phi, Alpha Omega Alpha. Home: 813 Lichfield Ct Montgomery AL 36117 Office: Ala Dept Pub Health 434 Monroe St Montgomery AL 36104-3725

WILLIAMSON, DONALD RAY, retired career Army officer; b. Amarillo, Tex., Oct. 13, 1943; s. Floy Edwin and Dorothy Lorene (Orr) W.; m. Beverly Ann Howard, Aug. 31, 1963; children: Rebecca Ann, Catherine Paige. BS in Econs., W. Tex. State U., 1966; MA in Bus., Cen. Mich. U., 1977; degree, Dept. Def. Program Mgrs., 1982, U.S. Army Command and Gen. Staff Coll., 1980. Commd. 2d lt. U.S. Army, 1966, advanced through grades to lt. col., 1982, retired, 1986; comdg. officer combat support co. U.S. Army, Ft. Hood, Tex., 1973-74; comdg. officer 2d aviation co. U.S. Army, Ft. Hood, 1974-75; dep. insp. gen. U.S. Army, Ft. Leavenworth, Kans., 1975-78; comdg. officer 213th aviation co. U.S. Army, Rep. of Korea, 1978-79; asst. program mgr. advanced scout helicopter program U.S. Army, 1981-86; owner Witan Group, Chesterfield, Mo., 1986-88; pres. Sys. Test Evaluation Inc., St. Louis, Mo., 1988—. Contbr. articles to profl. jours. Decorated Bronze Star, 37 Air medals with "V" device, D.F.C. with oak leaf cluster, Legion of Merit. Mem. Army Aviation Assn. Am., Assn. U.S. Army, Lansing Jaycees (past pres.), Mensa. Avocations: flying, reading, tennis. Home: 50 Orange Hills Dr Chesterfield MO 63017-3248 Office: 4433 Woodson Rd Saint Louis MO 63134-3713

WILLIAMSON, DONNA MARIA, pastoral counselor; b. Oswego, N.Y., Feb. 26, 1944; d. Donald Carl and Helen Mary (Saber) Townsley; m. Patrick H. Williamson, July 7, 1962; children: Kevin Patrick, Michael Brian, Timothy Daniel. Grad. pub. schs., Fulton, N.Y. Cert. in clin. pastoral edn., pastoral care, Onondaga Pastoral Counseling Ctr.; weight loss counselor. Chaplain Loretto Geriatric Ctr., Syracuse, 1981-82; hosp. chaplain St. Rose of Lima Parish, Syracuse, 1982-84, pastoral counselor, 1984—; weight loss counselor Nutri-System, Syracuse, 1988-91. Founding mem. Fulton Community Nursery Sch., 1967, Commn. on Women in Ch. and Society, Syracuse, 1984; mem. Alethea, Ctr. on Death and Dying, Inc., Syracuse, 1978, Syracuse Area Domestic Violence Coalition's Religious Task Force, 1994—. Mem. Charles F. Menninger Soc. Roman Catholic. Avocations: flower arranging, vocalist. Office: St Rose of Lima Parish 409 S Main St N Syracuse NY 13212-2811

WILLIAMSON, DOUGLAS FRANKLIN, JR., lawyer; b. Anniston, Ala., Mar. 23, 1930; s. Douglas Franklin and Elizabeth Louise (Connor) W.; m. Barbara Tuerk, Dec. 28, 1957; children: Mary Leyden, Douglas Franklin III, Bruce Reynolds. AB summa cum laude, Amherst Coll., 1952; LLB, Yale U., 1955. Bar: N.Y. 1958, Fla. 1976. Assoc. Breed, Abbott & Morgan, N.Y.C., 1957-63, ptnr., 1963-72; ptnr. Williamson & Hess and predecessor firm, N.Y.C., 1972-79; of counsel Winthrop, Stimson, Putnam & Roberts, N.Y.C., 1979-81, ptnr., 1982-95, sr. counsel, 1996—. Bd. dirs. World Wildlife Fund, Washington, 1979-88, treas., 1986-88, mem. nat. coun., 1988—; bd. dirs. Conservation Found., Washington, 1985-88, treas., 1986-88; bd. dirs. Lower Hudson chpt. Nature Conservancy, Mt. Kisco, N.Y., 1976-87, 93—, sec., 1976-87, hon. dir., 1987—, chmn., 1993-94; bd. dirs. Oblong Land Conservancy, Pawling, N.Y., 1990—, chmn. 1996—; bd. dirs. Quaker Hill Civic Assn., Pawling, 1974—, past pres.; chmn. Pawling Assessment Rev. Bd., 1976—. With U.S. Army, 1955-57. Fellow Am. Coll. Trust and Estate Counsel, N.Y. State Bar Found.; mem. N.Y. State Bar Assn., Assn. of Bar of City of N.Y. (mem. com. on trusts, estates and surrogate cts. 1973-78, chmn. 1975-78), Everglades Club, Quaker Hill Country Club (pres. 1980-81), Old Guard Soc. of Palm Beach Golfers, English Speaking Union, Phi Beta Kappa, Phi Beta Kappa Assocs. (sec. 1975-77, v.p. 1977-79). Office: Winthrop Stimson Putnam & Roberts One Battery Park Plz New York NY 10004

WILLIAMSON, EDWIN DARGAN, lawyer, former federal official; b. Florence, S.C., Sept. 23, 1939; s. Benjamin F. and Sara (Dargan) W.; m. Kathe Gates, July 12, 1969; children: Samuel Gates, Edwin Dargan Jr., Sara Elizabeth. BA cum laude, U. of the South, 1961, DCL (hon.), 1992; JD, NYU, 1964. Bar: N.Y. 1965, D.C. 1988. Assoc. Sullivan & Cromwell, N.Y.C., 1964-70, ptnr., 1971-76; ptnr. Sullivan & Cromwell, London, 1976-79, N.Y.C., 1979-88, Washington, 1988-90, 93—; legal adviser U.S. Dept. State, Washington, 1990-93, Permanent Ct. of Arbitration, 1991—; bd. dirs. Triton Energy Corp., 1994—. Regent U. of the South, Sewanee, Tenn., 1981-87, chmn., 1985-87, coun. frn. rels., 1995—; bd. dirs. Nat. Dance Inst., N.Y.C., 1984-88, Episcopal Ch. Found., N.Y.C., 1986-94; vestryman St. James Episcopal Ch., N.Y.C., 1984-88. Mem. ABA U.S. Coun. Internat. Bus. and Industy Adv. Coun. to OECD (vice chmn. coms. on multinat. enterprise and investments 1993—, chmn. BIAC expert group on Multinat. mgmt. investment 1996—), Internat. Rep. Inst. (rule of law adv. bd. 1993—), Raquet and Tennis Club (N.Y.C.), Met. Club. Republican.

WILLIAMSON, ERNEST LAVONE, petroleum company executive; b. Perryton, Tex., Sept. 10, 1924; s. Ernest and Mabel Robert (Donnell) W.; m. Gertrude Florence Watkins, Dec. 2, 1950; children: Richard Dean, Judith Watkins, Mary Nan, David Ernest. BSEE, U. Okla., 1950; student, Hill's Bus. Coll., 1943. Sales and svc. rep. Hughes Tool Co., 1950-52; with land dept. Phillips Petroleum Co., 1952-54; with La. Land & Exploration Co., New Orleans, 1954—, exec. v.p., 1967-74, pres., 1974-84, COO, 1982-83, CEO, 1984-88, chmn., 1985-88, also dir.; bd. dirs. Hibernia Nat. Bank, New Orleans, Halliburton Co., Cen. La. Electric Co. Mem. adv. bd. Salvation Army, 1971—; bd. visitors U. Okla.; bd. dirs. New Orleans Jr. Achievement. With U.S. Army, 1943-46. Mem. Am. Assn. Petroleum Landmen, Ind. Petroleum Assn. Am., Mid-Continent Oil and Gas Assn. (chmn. 1980-81), Am. Petroleum Inst., Petroleum Club, Tchefuncta Country Club. Presbyterian. Office: La Land & Exploration Co 909 Poydras St PO Box 60350 New Orleans LA 70160

WILLIAMSON, FLETCHER PHILLIPS, real estate executive; b. Cambridge, Md., Dec. 16, 1923; s. William Fletcher and Florence M. (Phillips) W.; student U. Md., 1941, 42; m. Betty June (Stoker), Apr. 6, 1943; 1 son, Jeffrey Phillips; m. 2d, Helen M. Stumberg, Aug. 28, 1972. Test engr. Engring. Lab., Glen Martin Co., 1942-43; salesman Corkran Ice Cream Co., Cambridge, 1946-50; real estate broker, 1950—; chmn. bd. Williamson Real Estate, Dorchester Corp., 1963-72; bd. dirs. WCEM, Inc., 1966-75; vice chmn. bd., dir. Nat. Bank of Cambridge, 1979—; dir. Cam-Storage Inc., Dorchester Indsl. Devel. Corp., Delmarva Bank Data Processing Ctr.; co-receiver White & Nelson, Inc. Bd. dirs. Delmarva council Boy Scouts Am.; past pres. Cambridge Hosp., United Fund of Dorchester County; bd. dirs. Del. Mus. Natural History, Dorchester County Pub. Library; bd. dirs., v.p. Game Conservation Internat.; v.p. Del. Mus. Natural History. Served as ordnance tech. intelligence engr. AUS, 1943-46; ETO. Mem. Md. Real Estate Assn. (gov. 1956-66), Outdoor Writers Assn., Nat. Rifle Assn., Nat. Def. Preparedness Assn., Cambridge Dorchester C. of C. (dir. 1955—), Power Squadron (comdr. 1954-56), Dorchester County Bd. Realtors (pres.), Scandinavian Atlantic Salmon Group, Explorers Club, Soc. of S. Pole. Methodist. Clubs: Rolling Rock, Shikar Safari, Anglers, Chesapeake Bay Yacht, Camp Fire, Md., Georgetown. Lodges: Masons, Shriners.

WILLIAMSON, FREDERICK BEASLEY, III, rubber company executive; b. Balt., June 21, 1918; s. Frederick Beasley and Virginia Ogden (Ranson) W.; m. Katherine Stryker, Apr. 19, 1941; children—Katherine L., Frederick Beasley IV, Marsha R. Student, Princeton, 1937-40. With Goodall Rubber Co., Trenton, N.J., 1940-41, 46-88, pres., chmn. bd., 1957-85, dir., 1950-89; bd. dirs. N.J. Nat. Bank. Bd. dirs. Mercer Med. Center, Trenton, N.J, 1965-89, New Jobs, 1962-91 ; campaign chmn. Delaware Valley United Way, 1964. Served to capt., 5th Armored Div. U.S. Army, 1942-46. Mem. Rubber Mfrs. Assn. (dir. 1958-86), Nat. Assn. Mfrs. (bd. dirs. 1981-82), N.J. Mfrs. Ins. Co. (bd. dirs. 1965-90, dir. emeritus 1990—, chmn. 1977-79), N.J. Bus. Industry Assn. (dir. emeritus 1990—). Clubs: Princeton (N.Y.C.); Trenton Country; Hartwood (Port Jervis, N.Y.); Pine Valley Golf. Home: 1265 Eagle Rd New Hope PA 18938-9221

WILLIAMSON, JACK (JOHN STEWART), writer; b. Bisbee, Ariz., Apr. 29, 1908; s. Asa Lee and Lucy Betty (Hunt) W.; m. Blanche Slaten Harp, Aug. 15, 1947 (dec. Jan. 1985); stepchildren: Keign Harp (dec.), Adele Harp Lovorn. BA, MA, Eastern N.Mex. U., 1957, LHD (hon.), 1981; PhD, U. Colo., 1964. Prof. English Eastern N.Mex. U., Portales, 1960-77. Author numerous sci. fiction books including The Legion of Space, 1947, Darker Than You Think, 1948, The Humanoids, 1949, The Green Girl, 1950, The Cometeers, 1950, One Against the Legion, 1950, Seetee Scock, 1950, Seetee Ship, 1950, Dragon's Island, 1951, The Legion of Time, 1952, (with Frederik Phhl) Star Bridge, 1955, Dome Around America, 1955, The Trial of Terra, 1962, Golden Blood, 1964, The Reign of Wizardry, 1965, Bright New Universe, 1967, Trapped in Space, 1968, The Pandora Effect, 1969, People Machines, 1971, The Moon Children, 1972, H.G. Wells: Critic of Progress, 1973, Teaching SF, 1975, The Early Williamson, 1975, The Power of Blackness, 1976, The Best of Jack Williamson, 1978, Brother to Demons, Brother To Gods, 1979, Teaching Science Fiction: Education for Tomorrow, 1980, The Alien Intelligence, 1980, The Humanoid Touch, 1980, Manseed, 1982, The Queen of a Legion, 1983, Wonder's Child: My Life in Science Fiction, 1984 (Hugo award 1985), Lifeburst, 1984, Firechild, 1986, Mazeway, 1990: (with Fredrick Pohl) Undersea Quest, 1954, Undersea Fleet, 1955, Undersea City, 1956, The Reefs of Sapce, 1964, Starchild, 1965, Rogue Star, 1969, The Farthest Star, 1975, Wall Around a Star, 1983, Land's End, 1988, Mazeway, 1990. (with Frederik Phol) The Singers Of Time, 1991, Beachhead, 1992, Demon Moon, 1994, The Black Sun, 1996; (with Miles J. Breuer) The Birth of an New Republic, 1981. Served as staff sgt. USAAF, 1942-45. Mem. Sci. Fiction Writers Am. (pres. 1978-80, Grand Master Nebula award 1976), Sci. Fiction Research Assn. (Pilgrim award 1968), World Sci. Fiction, Planetary Soc. Avocations: travel, astronomy, photography. Home: PO Box 761 Portales NM 88130-0761 Office: Ea NMex U Golden Libr Portales NM 88130

WILLIAMSON, JOEL RUDOLPH, humanities educator; b. Anderson County, S.C., Oct. 27, 1929; s. James Henry and Carrie Mae (Swaney) W.; m. Marie Ahern, Nov. 17, 1953 (div. May 1983); children: Joele, William, Alethea; m. Anna Woodson, Oct. 18, 1986. AB, U. S.C., 1949, MA, 1951; PhD, U. Calif., 1964. Instr. dept. history U. N.C., Chapel Hill, 1960-64, asst. prof., 1964-66, assoc. prof., 1966-69, prof., 1969-85, Lineberger prof. in humanities, 1985—; resident fellow Rockefeller Ctr., Bellagio, Italy, 1988; Eudora Welty prof. in so. studies Millsaps Coll., 1984; disting. vis. prof. Rhodes Coll., 1984; vis. prof. dept. history, assoc. Lowell House Harvard U., 1981-82. Author: After Slavery: The Negro in South Carolina During Reconstruction, 1861-1877, 1965, The Origins of Segregation, 1968, New People: Miscegenation and Mulattoes in the United States, 1980, The Crucible of Race, 1984 (Francis Parkman prize Soc. Am. Historians, Ralph Waldo Emerson award Phi Beta Kappa, Mayflower Cup, Frank L. and Harriet C. Owsley award 1985, Robert Francis Kennedy Book award, Pulitzer prize in History nomination 1985), A Rage for Order, 1986, William Faulkner and Southern History, 1993 (Pulitzer prize in History nomination 1994, Mayflower Cup), also articles. Lt. USN, 1951-55. Fellow Guggenheim Found., 1970-71, NEH, 1987-88, Ctr. for Advanced Study in Behavioral Scis., Stanford, Calif., 1977-78, summer 1979, 80, 81, So. fellow, 1961-62, Charles Warren Ctr., 1981-82. Mem. Soc. Am. Historians. Avocation: travel. Home: 211 Hillsborough St Chapel Hill NC 27514 Office: U NC Dept History 567 Hamilton Chapel Hill NC 27599-3195

WILLIAMSON, JOHN HENRY, III, school administrator; b. San Mateo, Calif., Feb. 20, 1960; s. Ronald Clay and Kathryn (Kennedy) W.; m. Trisha Glenell Hair, Aug. 11, 1990; 1 child, Matthew. BA, St. Mary's Coll. of Calif., 1982; MA, Monterey Inst. Internat. Studies, 1984. Cert. tchr. Calif. Tchr. Ojai (Calif.) Valley Sch., 1985-92; acad. dean Ojai Valley Sch., 1987-89, asst. headmaster, 1989-90, dean of faculty, 1990-92, dir. summer sch. and camp, 1988-92, assoc. dir. admissions, 1992-96, dir. of admission, 1997—. Mem. Western Boarding Schs. Assn. (steering com. 1992-95). Avocations: reading, running, camping. Home: 381 Baker Ave Ventura CA 93004-1558

WILLIAMSON, JOHN PRITCHARD, utility executive; b. Cleve., Feb. 22, 1922; s. John and Jane (Pritchard) W.; m. Helen Morgan, Aug. 3, 1945; children: John Morgan, James Russell, Wayne Arthur. BBA, Kent State U., 1945; postgrad., U. Toledo, 1953-56, U. Mich., 1956. CPA, Ohio. Sr. acct. Arthur Andersen & Co., Detroit and Cleve., 1945-51; dir. methods and procs. Toledo Edison Co., 1951-59, asst. treas., 1959-60, sec., 1960-62, sec.-treas., 1962-65, v.p. finance, 1965-68, sr. v.p., 1968-72, pres., chief exec. officer, 1972-79, chmn., chief exec. officer, 1979-86; chmn. Centerior Energy Corp., 1985-86; chmn. emeritus Toledo Edison Co., Centerior Energy Corp., 1986—; dir. emeritus, chmn. 1st Nat. Bank of Toledo, 1974-75; chmn. N.Am. Electric Reliability Coun., 1984-87; chmn. Nat. Electric Security Com., 1987-88. Pres. Ohio Electric Utility Inst., 1972; chmn. East Cen. Area Power Coordination Pool, 1971-72, mem. exec. com. Edison Electric Inst., 1981-85; trustee Assn. Edison Illuminating Cos., 1982-84; pres. Toledo C. of C., 1970; chmn. Ohio C. of C., 1979-81, life dir.; pres. Toledo Symphony Orch., 1985-86; hon. trustee Toledo Mus. Art, Toledo Hosp.; trustee U. Toledo Found., 1980-87, Kent State U. Found., Rio Verde Cmty. Assn.; vice chmn. Greater Toledo Corp., 1984-86; trustee, treas. Rio Verde Cmty. Ch., 1989-92; elder Presbyn. Ch.; pres. Toledo Cmty. Chest, 1972; chmn. Greater Toledo Area United Way, 1971. Named Toledo Outstanding Citizen, 1976; recipient Kent State U. medallion, 1992;Williamson Alumni Ctr. named in his honor, 1991. Mem. Fin. Analysts Soc. Toledo (pres. 1968-69), Systems and Procs. Assn. (internat. treas. 1960), Inst. Pub. Utilities (chmn. exec. com. 1969-70), Toledo Boys Club (Echo award 1974), Kent State U. Alumni Assn. (pres. 1971-72, Outstanding Alumnus 1974), Belmont Country Club, Rio Verde Country Club, Inverness Club (gov. 1967-76), Rio Verde Saddle Club (past pres.), Kiwanis (past pres. Toledo, Disting. Svc. award 1977), Blue Key, Delta Sigma Pi, Beta Alpha Psi, Delta Upsilon. Republican. Home: 10661 Cardiff Rd Perrysburg OH 43551-3404 also: 18524 E Poco Vista Rio Verde AZ 85263-7125

WILLIAMSON, KENNETH LEE, chemistry educator; b. Tarentum, Pa., Apr. 13, 1934; s. James D. and Mary June (Becker) W.; m. Mary Louise Hoerner, Sept. 15, 1956; children—Christopher Lee, Tania Louise, Kevin Keith. B.A. cum laude (Nat. scholar), Harvard, 1956; Ph.D. (Allied Chem. and Dye Co. fellow), U. Wis., 1960. Mem. faculty Mt. Holyoke Coll., 1961—, prof. chemistry, 1969—, Mary E. Woolley prof. chemistry, 1984—; mem. Grad. faculty U. Mass., 1965—; vis. prof. Cornell U., 1966, Dartmouth Coll., 1986-87, Harvard U., 1989-90, U. Trondheim, Norway, 1991, U. Louis Pasteur, Stasbourg, France, 1991, Basel U., Switzerland, 1992, U. Canterbury, New Zealand and U. Auckland, New Zealand, 1994; vis. prof. MIT, 1996, 97. Author papers and books in field; patentee in field. Mem. South Hadley Hist. Commn., 1983—. NIH postdoctoral fellow Stanford, 1960-61; NSF sci. faculty fellow U. Liverpool, Eng.; also fellow of univ., 1968-69; Guggenheim fellow, 1975-76, Oxford (Eng.) U. fellow of univ., 1976, 1983; research assoc., Calif. Inst. Tech., 1975, 82. Mem. Am. Chem. Soc., AAAS, Sigma Xi. Home: 43 Woodbridge St South Hadley MA 01075-1138

WILLIAMSON, LAIRD, stage director, actor; b. Chgo., Dec. 13, 1937; s. Walter B. and Florence M. (Hemwell) W. B.S. in Speech, Northwestern U., 1960; M.F.A. in Drama, U. Tex., 1965. Dir. Am. Conservatory Theatre, San Francisco, 1974—; stage dir. A Christmas Carol, 1976-81, The Matchmaker (tour of Soviet Union), 1976, A Month in the Country, 1978, The Visit, 1979, Pantagleize, 1980, Sunday in the Park, 1986, End of the World, 1988, Imaginary Invalid, 1990, Machinal, 1997; dir. Oreg. Shakespearean Festival, Ashland, 1972-74, Western Opera Theatre, San Francisco, 1976-77, Theater

Fest, Santa Maria, Calif., 1971-84, Denver Theater Ctr., 1981, Bklyn. Acad. Music, 1981, Denver Ctr. Theatre Co., 1985-97, Seattle Repertory Theatre, 1990, Old Globe Theatre, San Diego, 1977, 92, 94; artistic dir. Theater Fest, Solvang, Calif., 1981-83, Intiman Theatre, 1986, 88, Seattle Repertory Theatre, 1990, Berkeley Shakespeare Festival, 1990, Guthrie Theatre, 1991, 93, The Shakespeare Theatre, Washington, 1995, 96; actor in Othello, 1973, Twelfth Night, 1974, Cyrano, 1974, Enrico IV, 1977, Judas, 1978, Hamlet, 1979, The Bacchae, 1981. Mem. Soc. Stage Dirs. Actors Equity Assn., Screen Actors Guild.

WILLIAMSON, MARILYN LAMMERT, English educator, university adminstrator; b. Chgo., Sept. 6, 1927; d. Raymond Ferdinand and Edith Louise (Eisenbies) Lammert; m. Robert M. Williamson, Oct. 28, 1950 (div. Apr. 1973); 1 child, Timothy L.; m. James H. McKay, Aug. 15, 1974. BA, Vassar Coll., 1949; MA, U. Wis., 1950; PhD, Duke U., 1956. Instr. Duke U., Durham, N.C., 1955-56, 58-59; lectr. N.C. State U., Raleigh, 1957-58, 61-62; asst. prof. Oakland U., Rochester, Mich., 1965-68, assoc. prof., 1968-72; prof. English Wayne State U., Detroit, 1972-90, Disting. prof. English, 1990—, chmn. dept. English, 1972-74, 81-83, assoc. dean Coll. Liberal Arts, 1974-79; dir. women's studies Wayne State U., 1976-87; dep. provost Wayne State U., Detroit, 1987-91, sr. v.p. for acad. affairs, provost, 1991-95; pres. Assn. Depts. English, 1976-77. Author: Infinite Variety, 1974, Patriarchy of Shakespeare's Comedies, 1986, British Women Writers 1650-1750, 1990; editor: Renaissance Studies, 1972, Female Poets of Great Britain, 1981; contbr. articles to profl. jours. Pres. LWV, Rochester, 1963-65. Recipient Detroit Disting. Svc. award, 1986, Faculty Recognition award Bd. Govs., Wayne State U., 1991; Bunting Inst. fellow, 1969-70, AAUW fellow, 1982-83, J.N. Keal fellow, 1985-86. Mem. MLA (exec. coun. 1977-80, mem. editorial bd. 1992-94), Renaissance Soc. Am., Coll. English Assn., Mich. Acad. (pres. 1978-79), Shakespeare Assn. Am., Mich. Coun. Humanities (chair 1991-93), Fed. State Humanities Coun. (bd. dirs. 1994—). Democrat. Home: 2275 Oakway Dr West Bloomfield MI 48324-1855 Office: Wayne State Univ Dept of English Detroit MI 48202

WILLIAMSON, MYRNA HENNRICH, retired army officer, lecturer, consultant; b. Gregory, S.D., Jan. 27, 1937; d. Walter Ferdinand and Alma Lillian (Rajewich) H. BS with highest honors, S.D. State U., 1960; MA, U. Okla., 1973; grad., U.S. Army Command and Gen. Staff Coll., 1977, Nat. War Coll., 1980. Commd. 2d lt. U.S. Army, 1960, advanced through grades to brig. gen., 1985; bn. comdr. Mil. Police Sch. U.S. Army, Fort McClellan, Ala., 1977-79; chief plans policy and service div. Jl 8th Army U.S. Army, Korea, 1980-81; chief mgmt. support Office Dep. Chief Staff for Research, Devel. and Acquisition U.S. Army, Washington, 1981-82; brigade comdr. U.S. Army, Fort Benjamin Harrison, Ind., 1983-84; comdg. gen. 3d ROTC Region U.S. Army, Fort Riley, Kans., 1984-87; dep. dir. mil. personnel mgmt. U.S. Army, Washington, 1987-89, ret., 1989; U.S. del. com. on women in NATO Forces, 1986-89. Pres., bd. dirs. S.D. State U. Found., 1988—; bd. dirs. Women in Mil. Svc. to Am. Found.. Recipient Disting. Alumnus award S.D. State U., 1984. Mem. Internat. Platform Assn., Assn. U.S. Army (trustee), United Svcs. Automobile Assn. (bd. dirs.), The Internat. Alliance, Phi Kappa Phi.

WILLIAMSON, NORMA BETH, adult education educator; b. Hamilton, Tex., Nov. 2, 1939; d. Joseph Lawrence and Gladys (Wilkins) Drake; m. Stuart Williamson, Mar. 14, 1981. BA, Baylor U., 1962; MA, Tex. A&I U., 1969; postgrad., Tex. Tech. U., 1976-80, CIDOC, Cuernavaca, Mex., 1973, 75. Instr. English, Tex. Southmost Coll., Brownsville; coll. prep. tchr. Tex. Dept. Corrections, 1995—; lectr. Spanish Sam Houston State U. Music chmn. Huntsville Unitarian Universalist Ch.; pres. S.W. Dist. Unitarian Universalist Assn., 1982-86. Mem. AAUW (pres. Huntsville br. 1995-96), Delta Kappa Gamma, Alpha Mu (pres. 1980-81), Upsilon (pres. 1994-96). Home: RR 1 Box 349 Bedias TX 77831-9625

WILLIAMSON, OLIVER EATON, economics and law educator; b. Superior, Wis., Sept. 27, 1932; s. Scott Gilbert and Lucille S. (Dunn) W.; m. Dolores Jean Celeni, Sept. 28, 1957; children: Scott, Tamara, Karen, Oliver, Dean. SB, MIT, 1955; MBA, Stanford U., 1960; PhD, Carnegie-Mellon U., 1963; PhD (hon.), Norwegian Sch. Econs. and Bus. Adminstrn., 1986; PhD in Econ. Sci. (hon.), Hochschule St. Gallen, Switzerland, 1987, Groningen U., 1989, Turku Sch. Econs. & Bus. Admin, 1995. Project. engr. U.S. Govt., 1955-58; asst. prof. econs. U. Calif., Berkeley, 1963-65; assoc. prof. U. Pa., Phila., 1965-68, prof., 1968-83, Charles and William L. Day prof. econs. and social sci., 1977-83; Gordon B. Tweedy prof. econs. law and orgn. Yale U., 1983-88; Transam. prof. of bus., econs. and law U. Calif., Berkeley, 1988-94, Edgar F. Kaiser prof. bus. adminstrn., prof. econs. and law, 1994—; spl. econ. asst. to asst. atty. gen. for antitrust Dept. Justice, 1966-67; dir. Ctr. for Study Orgnl. Innovation, U. Pa., 1976-83; Edgar F. Kaiser prof. bus., econs. and law U. Calif., Berkeley, 1988—; cons. in field. Author: The Economics of Discretionary Behavior, 1964, Corporate Control and Business Behavior, 1970, Markets and Hierarchies, 1975, The Economic Institutions of Capitalism, 1985, Economic Organization, 1986, Antitrust Economics, 1987, The Mechanisms of Governance, 1996; assoc. editor Bell. Jour. Econs., 1973-74, editor, 1975-82; co-editor Jour. Law, Econs. and Orgn., 1983—. Fellow Ctr. for Advanced Study in Behavioral Scis., 1977-78; Guggenheim fellow, 1977-78; Am. Acad. Arts and Scis. fellow, 1983; recipient Alexander Henderson award Carnegie-Mellon U., 1962, Alexander von Humboldt Rsch. prize, 1987, Irwin award Acad. of Mgmt., 1988. Fellow Econometric Soc., Am. Acad. Polit. and Social Scis., Am. Acad. Political and Social Sci.; mem. Nat. Acad. Scis., Am. Econ. Assn. Office: U Calif Dept Econs Berkeley CA 94720

WILLIAMSON, PETER DAVID, lawyer; b. Houston, Oct. 13, 1944; s. Sam and Sophie Ann (Kaplan) W.; m. Patricia Golemon; children: Heather, Amber, Asia, Ginger. B.A., U. Ill., 1966; J.D., U. Tex., 1969. Bar: Tex. 1969, U.S. Supreme Ct. 1974, U.S. Ct. Appeals (4th, 9th, 5th, 8th, 10th, 11th and D.C. cirs.); lic. comml. pilot. Pvt. practice Houston, 1971—; founder IMMLAW, The Nat. Consortium of Immigration Law Firms. Mem. Am. Immigration Lawyers Assn. (pres. 1994-95). Home: 2417 Branard St Houston TX 77098-2213 Office: 1111 Fannin St Ste 1360 Houston TX 77002-6923 *I do not believe in the existence of national boundaries. The philosophy of my practice of the law is to help my clients achieve the ability to pass freely through such artificial political barriers.*

WILLIAMSON, PHILIP, apparel executive. CEO Williamson-Dickie Mfg. Co., Ft. Worth. Office: Williamson-Dickie Mfg Co PO Box 1779 Fort Worth TX 76101*

WILLIAMSON, RICHARD CARDINAL, physicist; b. Minocqua, Wis., Sept. 10, 1939; s. Lyman Olaf and Edna (Cardinal) W.; m. Christine Bauer, Sept. 2, 1961; children—Kari, Meagan, Heidi, Ryan. B.S. in Physics, MIT, 1961, Ph.D. in Physics, 1966. Staff physicist NASA Electronics Research Ctr., Cambridge, Mass., 1965-70; staff mem. and assoc. group leader MIT Lincoln Lab., Lexington, Mass., 1970-80, group leader applied physics, electrooptic device rsch., 1980-95, sr. staff electro-optical devices and materials group, 1995—. Contbr. articles to jours., chpts. to books; patentee in field. Fellow IEEE (Centennial award 1984, Sonics and Ultrasonics Achievement award 1985); mem. IEEE, Am. Phys. Soc., Optical Soc. Am., Sigma Xi. Methodist. Home: 21 Pendleton Rd Sudbury MA 01776-1612 Office: MIT Lincoln Lab 244 Wood St Rm C-317 Lexington MA 02173-6426

WILLIAMSON, RICHARD HALL, association executive; b. Canton, N.C., July 29, 1940; s. James Eustace and Gwendolyn (Nevada) H.; m. Julia Draper Brown, Nov. 7, 1965 (div. Jan. 1981); children: Shawn Nicol, Kevin Carson. BS in Physics, N.C. State U., 1962, MS in Nuclear Engring., 1970, PhD in Econs., 1972. Instr. N.C. State U., Raleigh, 1968-72; chief, energy systems analysis AEC, Washington, 1972-75; asst. dir., energy analysis U.S. Energy R & D Adminstrn., Washington, 1975-77; dir., program analysis U.S. Dept. Energy, Washington, 1977-80, dir., policy devel., 1980-84, dep. asst. sec. for internat. affairs, 1984-94; dep. exec. dir. U.S. Energy Assn., Washington, 1995—. Author: A Group Strategy for Energy Research, Development and Demonstration, 1980; contbr. articles to jours. in field. Football ofcl. Atlantic Coast Conf., Greensboro, N.C., 1980—, Rose Bowl, Pasadena, Calif., 1995. 1st lt. U.S. Army, 1962-64; col. USAR, 1964-93. NSF fellow, 1964-65; AEC fellow, 1965-68; recipient Outstanding alumnus award IFC, N.C. State U., 1971, Presdl. Rank award U.S. Dept. Energy, 1990. Mem. Sigma Alpha Mu (nat. pres. 1984-86), Tau Beta Pi, Phi Kappa Phi, Omicron Delta Kappa, Sigma Pi Sigma, Pi Mu Epsilon. Republican. Methodist. Avocations: stamp collecting, tennis, golf, skiing. Home: Apr 1107-S 3705 S George Mason Dr Falls Church VA 22041-3720 Office: US Energy Assn 1620 I St NW Ste 1000 Washington DC 20006-4005

WILLIAMSON, RICHARD SALISBURY, lawyer; b. Evanston, Ill., May 9, 1949; s. Donald G. and Marion (Salisbury) W.; m. Jane Thatcher, Aug. 25, 1973; children: Elizabeth Jean, Craig Salisbury, Richard Middleton. A.B. with honors, Princeton U., 1971; J.D., U. Va., 1974. Bar: Ill. bar 1974, D.C. bar 1975. Legis. counsel, adminstrv. asst. to Congressman Philip M. Crane of Ill., 1974-76; assoc. firm Winston & Strawn, Washington, 1977-80; ptnr. Winston & Strawn, 1980; asst. to Pres. for intergovtl. affairs, Washington, also assoc. dir. President's Task Force on Regulatory Relief, 1981-83; U.S. ambassador Vienna, Austria, 1983-85; sr. v.p., corp. and internat. relations Beatrice Cos., Inc., Chgo., 1985-86; ptnr. Mayer, Brown & Platt, Chgo., 1986-88, 89—; asst. sec. of state internat. orgn. affairs Dept. of State, Washington, 1988-89; rep. UN Orgns., Vienna, 1983-85; dep. ref. with rank of ambassador IAEA. Editor: Trade & Economic Growth, 1993, United States Foreign Policy and the United Nations System, 1996; coeditor: (with Paul Laxalt) A Changing America: Conservatives View the 80's From the United States Senate, 1980, Reagan's Federalism: His Efforts to Decentralize Government, 1990, The United Nations: A Place of Promise and of Mischief, 1991. Republican. Office: Mayer Brown & Platt 190 S La Salle St Chicago IL 60603-3410

WILLIAMSON, ROBERT CHARLES, marketing executive; b. West Chester, Pa., Jan. 3, 1925; s. Herman Gideon and Grace (Faddis) W.; m. Frances Yvonne Ishmael, Apr. 10, 1945 (div. July 1969); children: Robert C. Jr., Edward H., Richard F., Kathryn G.; m. Mary Elizabeth Bogle, Oct. 1, 1983. BS, Naval Sci. Sch., Monterey, Calif., 1959; postgrad. in Internat. Rels., Naval War Coll., Newport, R.I., 1960. Commd. ensign, designated naval aviator USN, 1944, advanced through grades to comdr., 1963, ret., 1966; gen. mgr. Springfield (Va.) Assocs., 1966-69; v.p. CCC Corp., Rosslyn, Va., 1969-70; pres. WILCO Assocs., Mt. Vernon, Va., 1970-73; dir. mktg. Documail Systems, Lenexa, Kans., 1973-80; N.Am. mktg. mgr. Leigh Instruments, Waterloo, Ont., Can., 1981-83; v.p. Tabs Assocs., Abingdon, Md., 1983-87; pres. WILLMAR Assocs. Internat., Brandon, Fla., 1987—. Mem. Nat. Assn. Presort Mailers (exec. dir. 1984—), Ret. Officers' Assn., Assn. Former Intelligence Officers, Assn. Naval Aviation. Club: Army and Navy. Home and Office: 3906 Butternut Ct Brandon FL 33511-7961

WILLIAMSON, ROBERT ELMORE, agricultural engineering educator; b. York County, S.C., Nov. 8, 1937; s. Charles Edward Jr. and Margaret Gladys (Elmore) W.; m. Eva Evelyn Simpson, June 27, 1964; children: Margaret Edye, Robert Elmore Jr. BS, Clemson U., 1959, MS, 1964; PhD, Miss. State U., 1972. Registered profl. engr., Ga. Rsch. assoc. Miss. State U., Starkville, 1966-71; asst. prof. agrl. engring. U. Ga., Tifton, 1971-78; assoc. prof. Clemson (S.C.) U., 1978-81, prof. agrl. engring., 1981—. Co-inventor bulb, root and leafy vegetable harvester, improved harvesting machinery, multi-purpose horticultural tractor; contbr., co-contbr. over 54 articles to scholarly jours.; contbr., co-contbr. over 24 articles to sci. jours. Asst. scoutmaster Clemson area Boy Scouts Am., 1972-78, 80—. 1st lt. USAF, 1959-62. Mem. Am. Soc. AGrl. Engrs., Phi Kappa Phi, Gamma Sigma Delta, Alpha Zeta, Sigma Xi. Presbyterian. Avocations: hunting, camping, backpacking, woodworking, tennis. Home: 303 Princess Grace Ave Clemson SC 29631-1215 Office: Agrl Engring McAdams Hall Clemson U Clemson SC 29631

WILLIAMSON, ROBERT WEBSTER, brokerage house executive; b. Springfield, Ill., Dec. 10, 1942; s. Robert W. and Catherine (Jackson) W.; m. M. Eleanor Brushwood, June 23, 1984; children: R. Todd, Elizabeth, Thomas. BS, Northwestern U., 1965, JD, 1968; AMP, Harvard U., 1995. Bar: Ill. 1968. V.p. internat. Continental Ill. Nat. Bank, Chgo., 1967-73; mgr. corp. fin. Continental Ill. Ltd., London, 1973-77; sr. v.p. Merrill Lynch and Co., London, Hong Kong, N.Y.C., 1977—; bd. dirs. Rykoff Sexton. Mem. Chgo. Bar Assn., Hong Kong Jockey Club. Office: Merrill Lynch & Co Inc World Fin Ctr New York NY 10281

WILLIAMSON, RONALD THOMAS, lawyer; b. Paterson, N.J., Nov. 12, 1948; s. Thomas Sim and Jessie Carnegie (Sandilands) W.; m. Nancy Anne Hough, June 13, 1982; children: Kate Elizabeth, Brad Francis Thomas. BA, Rutgers U., 1970; JD cum laude, Widener U., 1975. Bar: Pa. 1976, U.S. Dist. Ct. (ea. dist.) Pa. 1976, U.S. Supreme Ct. 1979, U.S. Ct. Appeals (3d cir.) 1980. Assoc. Modell, Pincus, Hahn and Reich, Phila., 1976-77; asst. dist. atty., chief of appeals County of Montgomery, Norristown, Pa., 1977-85; sr. dep. atty. gen. organized crime sect. Pa. Atty. Gen., Harrisburg, 1985—, atty.-in-charge ea. regional office, 1985—; instr. search and seizure Southeastern Tng. Ctr., Pa. State Police, Worcester, 1979-85; legal instr. Montgomery County C.C., Whitpain, Pa., 1984. Contbr. to profl. publs. Bd. dirs. Denbigh Group Foster Home, Bridgeport, Pa., 1979-83, pres., 1984; mem. Cen. Montgomery Optimist Club, Norristown, 1980-81. Mem. Pa. Bar Assn., Montgomery County Bar Assn. Republican. Presbyterian. Avocations: tennis, squash, sailing, triathlon, reading. Office: Pa Office Atty Gen 2490 Boulevard Of Generals Norristown PA 19403-5234

WILLIAMSON, SAMUEL RUTHVEN, JR., historian, university administrator; b. Bogalusa, La., Nov. 10, 1935; s. Samuel Ruthven and Frances Mitchell (Page) W.; m. Joan Chaffe Andress, Dec. 30, 1961; children: George Samuel, Treeby Andress, Thaddeus Miller. BA, Tulane U., 1958; AM, Harvard U., 1960, PhD, 1966, grad. advanced mgmt. program, 1986; hon. degrees, Furman U. Va. Theol. Sem. Asst. prof. U.S. Mil. Acad., 1963-66; instr. history Harvard U., 1966-68, asst. prof., 1968-72, Allston Burr sr. tutor, 1968-72, asst. to dean of Harvard Coll., 1969-70; rsch. assoc. Inst. Politics, faculty assoc. Ctr. for Internat. Affairs, 1971-72; mem. faculty J.F. Kennedy Sch. Govt., 1971-72; assoc. prof. history U. N.C., Chapel Hill, 1972-74; prof. U. N.C., 1974-88, dean Coll. Arts and Scis., 1977-85, provost univ., 1984-88; pres., vice chancellor The U. of the South, Sewanee, Tenn., 1988—; cons. Historian's Office, Office of Sec. Def., 1974-76; vis. fellow Churchill Coll., 1976-77; mem. vis. com. Harvard Coll., 1986-92; dir. Research Triangle Inst., 1984-88; trustee N.C. Sch. Sci. and Math., 1985-88, Day Found., 1990-93; mem. bd. visitors Air U., 1994—. Author: The Politics of Grand Strategy: Britain and France Prepare for War, 1904-1914, 1969, 2d edit., 1990; co-author: The Origins of U.S. Nuclear Strategy, 1945-53, 1993; editor: The Origins of a Tragedy: July 1914, 1981; co-editor: Essays on World War I: Origins and Prisoners of War, 1983, Austria-Hungary and the Origins of the First World War, 1991; Am. editor: War and Soc. Newsletter, 1973-88. Mem. cen. com. Morehead Found., 1978-93; vice chmn. bd. visitors Air U., 1996—. Capt. U.S. Army, 1963-66. Fulbright scholar U. Edinburgh, 1958-59; Woodrow Wilson fellow, 1958-63; Danforth fellow, 1958-63; Nat. Endowment Humanities fellow, 1976-77; Ford Found. grantee, 1976; fellow Nat. Humanities Ctr., 1983; recipient George Louis Beer prize for best book on internat. history Am. Hist. Assn., 1970. Mem. Am. Hist. Assn., Internat. Inst. Strategic Studies, Nat. Assn. Ind. Colls. and Univs. (chairperson bd. dirs. 1994-95). Democrat. Episcopalian. Home: PO Box 837 Sewanee TN 37375-0837 Office: U of the South Office of Pres Sewanee TN 37375-4013

WILLIAMSON, THOMAS GARNETT, nuclear engineering and engineering physics educator; b. Quincy, Mass., Jan. 27, 1934; s. Robert Burwell and Elizabeth B. (McNeer) W.; m. Kaye Darlan Love, Aug. 16, 1961; children: Allen, Sarah, David. BS, Va. Mil. Inst., 1955; MS, Rensselaer Poly. Inst., 1957; PhD, U. Va., 1960. Asst. prof. nuclear engring. and engring. physics dept. U. Va., Charlottesville, 1960-62, assoc. prof., 1962-69, prof., 1969-90, prof. emeritus, 1990—, chmn. dept., 1977-90; sr. scientist Westinghouse Savannah River Labs., Aiken, S.C., 1990—; with Gen. Atomic (Calif.), 1965, Combustion Engring., Windsor, Conn., 1970-71, Los Alamos Sci. Lab., 1969, Nat. Bur. Standards, Gaithersburg, Md., 1984-85; cons. Philippine Atomic Energy Commn., 1963, Va. Power Co., 1975-90, Babcock & Wilcox, Lynchburg, Va., 1975-90. Vestryman Ch. of Our Savior, Charlottesville, St. Thaddeus, Aiken, S.C. Fellow Am. Nuclear Soc.; mem. AAAS, Am. Soc. Engring. Edn., Sigma Xi, Tau Beta Pi. Episcopalian. Home: 217 Colleton Ave Aiken SC 29801 Office: Westinghouse Bldg 730 B Savannah River Co Aiken SC 29808*

WILLIAMSON, THOMAS SAMUEL, JR., lawyer; b. Plainfield, N.J., July 14, 1946; s. Thomas Samuel and Winifred (Hall) W.; married; 2 children. BA, Harvard U., 1968; postgrad., Oxford U., Eng., 1968-69; JD, U. Calif., Berkeley, 1974. Bar: D.C. 1975, Calif. 1975, U.S. Dist. Ct. D.C. 1977. Dir. tng. div. Alem Pub. Relations, Addis Ababa, Ethiopia, 1970-71; assoc. Covington & Burling, Washington, 1974-78, 81-82, ptnr., 1982-93; dep. inspector gen. U.S. Dept. Energy, Washington, 1978-81; solicitor U.S. Dept. Labor, Washington; ptnr. Covington & Burling, Washington; mem. exec. com. Washington Lawyers for Civil Rights Under Law, 1983-93, co-chair, 1990-92. Mem. vis. com. to dept. of athletics Harvard U., 1985-87. Rhodes scholar, 1968. Mem. ABA, Nat. Bar Assn., Coun. on Fgn. Rels., Washington Coun. Lawyers (bd. dirs. 1975-90). Avocations: camping, cycling. Home: 1745 Poplar Ln NW Washington DC 20012-1117 Office: Covington and Burling PO Box 7566 1201 Pennsylvania Ave NW Washington DC 20044

WILLIAMSON, WILLIAM PAUL, JR., journalist; b. Des Moines, Mar. 30, 1929; s. William Paul and Florence Alice (Dawson) W.; m. Vania Torres Nogueira, Nov. 27, 1959; children—Mary Liz (Mrs. Omar Fernandez), Jon Thadeus, Margaret Ann(Mrs. Cesar Rocha). Student, Mex. City Coll., 1952, U. Havanna, 1955; BA, U. No. Iowa, 1953; M.A., U. Iowa, 1954. Editor Brazilian Bus., Rio de Janeiro, 1958-60; mng. ptnr. Editora Mory Ltd., Rio de Janeiro, 1960-79; editor Brazil Herald, Rio de Janeiro, 1960-80; exec. dir. Inter Am. Press Assn., Miami, Fla., 1981-94, hon. life mem., mem. adv. coun., 1994—; dir. Inter Am. Press Assn., 1966-80, chmn. awards com., 1975-80; solo navigator 1st passage Madeira Island, Portugal-Madeira Island, Brazil, 1994-95. Editor for Brazil, Fodor's South America, 1970-79; contbr. articles to various newspapers and mags. Pres. Am. Soc., Rio de Janeiro, 1968; bd. dirs. Instituto Brasil-Estados Unidos, Rio de Janeiro, 1977-80, Am. C. of C. for Brazil, Rio de Janeiro, 1964-68. Served with USMC, 1946-48. Decorated Order of Rio Branco (Brazil); recipient Citizen of Rio de Janeiro award State Legislature, 1975; Hon. Carioca award O Globo Newspaper, Rio de Janeiro, 1972; Ralph Greenbuerg award Am. Soc. Rio de Janeiro, 1977; Outstanding Svc. to Freedom of Expression and Newspapers awards Internat. Fedn. of Newspaper Pubs. and Internat. Assn. of Broadcasting, 1994; Benemeritous Citizen award Mcpl. Legislature, Itaquai, Brazil, 1995. Mem. Am. Soc. Assn. Execs., South Fla. Soc. Assn. Execs. (pres. 1987), Soc. Profl. Journalists, Overseas Press Club Am., Rio Yacht Club, Ilha da Madeira Yacht Club, Kappa Tau Alpha. Home: 2600 Castilla Is Fort Lauderdale FL 33301-1594 Office: Inter Am Press Assn 2911 NW 39th St Miami FL 33142-5148

WILLIE, CHARLES VERT, sociology educator; b. Dallas, Oct. 8, 1927; s. Louis James and Carrie (Sykes) W.; m. Mary Susannah Conklin, Mar. 31, 1962; children: Sarah Susannah, Martin Charles, James Theodore. BA, Morehouse Coll., 1948, DHL (hon.), 1983; MA, Atlanta U., 1949; PhD, Syracuse U., 1957, DHL (hon.), 1992; DD (hon.), Gen. Sem., 1974; DHL (hon.), Berkeley Div. Sch., Yale U., 1972, R.I. Coll., 1983, Johnson C. Smith U., Charlotte N.C., 1991; MA (hon.), Harvard U., 1974; DL (hon.), Framingham (Mass.) State Coll., 1992; DHL (hon.), Franklin Pierce Coll., Rindge, N.H., 1996; D of Engring. Tech. (hon.), Wentworth Inst. Tech., 1996. Instr. to asst. prof. sociology Syracuse (N.Y.) U., 1952-63, assoc. prof., 1964-67, prof., 1968-74, chmn. dept. sociology, 1967-71, v.p., 1972-74; prof. edn. and urban studies Grad. Sch. Edn. Harvard U., 1974—; instr. dept. preventive medicine SUNY Upstate Med. Center, Syracuse, 1955-60; research dir. Washington Action for Youth delinquency prevention project, Pres.' Com. on Juvenile Delinquency and Youth Crime, Washington, 1962-64; vis. lectr. Lab. Community Psychiatry, Harvard U. Med. Sch., Boston, Mass., 1966-67; vis. lectr. ch. and soc. Episcopal Div. Sch., Cambridge, Mass., 1966-67; commr. Pres.'s Commn. on Mental Health, 1977-78; mem. tech. adv. bd. Maurice Falk Med. Fund, 1968—; bd. dirs. Social Sci. Rsch. Coun., 1969-75; master Boston Sch. Desegregation case, Fed. Dist. Ct., 1975. Author: Church Action in the World, 1969, Black Students at White Colleges, 1972, Race Mixing in the Public Schools, 1973, Oreo, 1975, A New Look at Black Families, 1976, 2d edit., 1981, 3d edit., 1988, 4th edit., 1991, The Sociology of Urban Education, 1978, The Caste and Class Controversy on Race and Poverty, 1979, 2d edit., 1989, The Ivory and Ebony Towers, 1981, Race, Ethnicity and Socioeconomic Status, 1983, School Desegregation Plans That Work, 1984, Black and White Families, 1985, Five Black Scholars, 1986, (with Michael Grady) Metropolitan School Desegregation, 1986, Effective Education, 1987, (with Michael Grady and Richard Hope) African-Americans and the Doctoral Experience, 1991, Theories of Human Social Action, 1994, Controlled Choice, 1996; editor: The Family Life of Black People, 1970, (with B. Brown and B. Kramer) Racism and Mental Health, 1973, Black/Brown/White Relations, 1977, (with R. Edmonds) Black Colleges in America, 1978, (with S. Greenblatt) Community Politics and Educational Change, 1981, (with Inabeth Miller) Social Goals and Educational Reforms, 1988, (with A. Garibaldi and W. Reed), The Education of African-Americans, 1991, (with P. Rieker, B. Kramer and B. Brown) Mental Health, Racism and Sexism, 1995. Hon. trustee Episcopal Div. Sch., Cambridge, Mass.; mem. United Negro Coll. Fund, 1983-90; mem. nat. exec. coun. Episcopal ch., 1967-74, v.p. gen. conv., 1970-74; host Inner City Beat nat. pub. affairs weekly television program, monitor channel, 1991-92; mem. Maxwell Sch. Adv. bd. of Syracuse U., 1992—. Recipient faculty svc. award Nat. Univ. Ext. Assn., 1969, 50th Anniversary Disting. Alumnus award Syracuse U. Maxwell Sch., 1974; Lee-Founders award Soc. for Study Social Problems, 1983, Family Scholar award, 1986; Disting. Career Contbn. award com. on role and status minorities in ednl. R & D, Am. Ednl. Rsch. Assn., 1990, Benjamin E. Mays Svc. award Morehouse Coll., 1994, Father John LaFarge, S.J. award Fairfield U., 1995, Disting. Career award Assn. Black Sociologists, 1996, Outstanding Book award for mental health, racism and sexism Myers Ctr. for Study of Human Rights in N.Am., 1996. Mem. Am. Ednl. Rsch. Assn., Am. Sociol. Assn. (coun. 1980-83, 95-98, v.p. 1996-97, DuBois-Johnson-Frazier award 1994), Phi Beta Kappa, Alpha Phi Alpha. Episcopalian. Home: 41 Hillcrest Rd Concord MA 01742-4615 Office: Harvard U Grad Sch Edn 457 Gutman Libr 6 Appian Way Cambridge MA 02138-3704

WILLIFORD, DONALD BRATTON, accounting company executive; b. York, S.C., Sept. 20, 1936; s. Thomas Leslie and Florence Odessa (Brown) W.; m. Linda Craven, June 12, 1959; 1 child, Linda Sharon. BSBA, U.S.C., 1958. CPA, N.C. Jr. acct. J. P. Stevens, Charlotte, N.C., 1959; staff acct. Haskins & Sells, CPAs, Charlotte, 1959-62; with audit and tax div. Belk Stores Svcs., Inc., Charlotte, 1962-69; corp. sec. Ruddick Corp., Charlotte, 1969—. Mem. AICPA, N.C. Assn. CPA, Am. Soc. Corp. Secs., Risk and Ins. Mgmt. Soc., Employee Stock Ownership Plans Assn. (chair 1991-93), River Hills Country Club. Avocation: golf. Office: Ruddick Corp 2000 Two 1st Union Ctr Charlotte NC 28282

WILLIG, KARL VICTOR, computer firm executive; b. Idaho Falls, Idaho, June 4, 1944; s. Louis Victor and Ethel (McCarty) W.; m. Julianne Erickson, June 10, 1972; 1 son, Ray. BA magna cum laude, Coll. of Idaho, 1968; MBA (Dean Donald Kirk David fellow), Harvard U., 1970. Pres. Ariz. Beef, Inc., Phoenix, 1971-73; group v.p. Ariz.-Colo. Land & Cattle Co., Phoenix, 1973-76; v.p. Rufenacht, Bromagen & Hertz, Inc., Chgo., 1976-77; pres. Sambo's Restaurants, Inc., Santa Barbara, Calif., 1977-79; ptnr. Santa Barbara Capital, 1979-85; pres. EURUSA Equities Corp., 1985-86; pres., chief exec. officer InfoGenesis, 1986—; trustee Am. Bapt. Sem. of West, 1977-85; mem. Chog. Merc. Exch., 1976-77, mem. audit com., 1976-77. Named one of Outstanding Young Men of Am., 1972; recipient Assn. of U.S. Army award, 1964.

WILLIG, ROBERT DANIEL, economics educator; b. Bklyn., Jan. 16, 1947; s. Jack David and Meg W.; m. Virginia Mason, July 8, 1973; children: Jared Mason, Robert Mason, Alexandra Mason. BA, Harvard U., 1967; MS in Ops. Rsch., Stanford U., 1968, PhD in Econs, 1973. Lectr. Stanford U., Palo Alto, Calif., 1971-73; mem. tech. staff Bell Labs., Holmdel, N.J., 1973-77; supr. dept. econs. rsch. Bell Labs., 1977-78; prof. econs. and pub. affairs Princeton U., 1978—; mem. Aspen Inst. Task Force on Future of Postal Svc., 1978-80; dep. asst. atty. gen. U.S. Dept. Justice, Washington, 1989-91; cons. in field; rsch. fellow U. Warwick, Eng., 1977; mem. organizing com. Telecom Policy Rsch. Conf., 1977-78; mem. rsch. adv. bd. Am. Enterprise Inst., 1980-88; mem. N.J. Gov.'s Task Force on Market-Based Pricing of Electricity, 1987; bd. dirs. Consultants in Industry Econs., Inc., 1983—; mem. Def. Sci. Bd. Task Force on Antitrust for the Def. Industry, 1993-94, Transp. Rsch. Bd. Task Force, 1995-96; advisor Inter-Am. Devel. Bank, 1997—. Author: Welfare Analysis of Policies Affecting Prices and Products, 1973, Contestable Markets and the Theory of Industry Structure, 1982; editor: Handbook of Industrial Organization, 1986; contbr. articles to profl.

jours. mem. editorial bd.: M.I.T. Press Series on Govt. Regulation, 1978—, Am. Econ. Rev., 1980-83, Jour. Indsl. Econs., 1985-89, Utility Policy, 1989—. Mem. adv. bd. B'nai B'rith Hillel Found., Princeton U., 1978—. NSF grantee, 1979-85. Fellow Econometric Soc. (program com. 1978-81); mem. Am. Econ. Assn. (nominating com. 1980-81). Office: Princeton Univ Economics Dept Princeton NJ 08540

WILLINGHAM, CLARK SUTTLES, lawyer; b. Houston, Nov. 29, 1944; s. Paul Suttles and Elsie Dell (Clark) W.; m. Jane Joyce Hitch, Aug. 16, 1969; children: Meredith Moores, James Barrett. BBA, Tex. Tech U., 1967; JD, So. Meth. U., 1971, LLM, 1984. Bar: Tex. 1971. Ptnr. Kasmir, Willingham & Krage, Dallas, 1972-86, Finley, Kumble et al, Dallas, 1986-87, Hill, Held & Metzger and predecessor, Dallas, 1988—; mem. Tex. Bd. Vet. Med. Examiners, 1991-95, pres., 1994. Contbr. articles to profl. jours. Mem. exec. com. Dallas Summer Musicals, 1979-93, pres., 1994-95. Mem. ABA (chmn. agrl. com. tax sect. 1984-86), State Bar Tex. (chmn. agrl. tax com. 1985-87), Am. Law Inst., Nat. Cattlemen's Beef Assn. (bd. dirs., pres.-elect 1997), U.S. Meat Export Fedn. (exec. com. 1991-93), Beef Industry Coun. (exec. com. 1990-91, promotion chmn. 1992-94), Tex. Cattle Feeders Assn. (bd. dirs., pres. 1988), Dallas Bar Assn., Dallas Country Club. Republican. Episcopalian. Home: 3824 Shenandoah St Dallas TX 75205-1702 Office: Hill Held & Metzger 1 Turtle Creek Village Dallas TX 75219

WILLINGHAM, EDWARD BACON, JR., ecumenical minister, administrator; b. St. Louis, July 27, 1934; s. Edward and Harriet (Sharon) W.; m. Angeline Walton Pettit, June 14, 1957; children: Katie, Carol. BS in Physics, U. Richmond, 1956; postgrad., U. Rochester, 1958-59; MDiv., Colgate Rochester Div. Sch., 1960. Ordained to ministry Am. Bapt. Ch., 1960. Min. Christian edn. Delaware Ave. Bapt. Ch., Buffalo, N.Y., 1960-62; dir. radio and TV Met. Detroit Coun. Chs., 1962-75; exec. dir. Christian Communication Coun. Met. Detroit Chs., 1976—; bus. mgr. N.Am. Broadcast sect. WACC, 1972—, chmn., 1970-71; broadcast cons. Mich. Coun. Chs., 1965-75; guest cons. religious broadcasting Germany, 1968; mem. coord. com. Mich. Ecumenical Forum, 1986, 90-92, chmn., 1991-92. Bd. mgrs. Broadcasting and Film Commn., Nat. Coun. Chs., 1965-73; mem. Muslim-Christian-Jewish Leadership Forum, 1987—; bd. deacons 1st Bapt. Ch. Birmingham, chmn., 1994. Recipient Gabriel award Cath. Broadcasting Assn., 1972, 1st Ann. Ecumenical award Am. Bapt. Chs. of Mich., 1992, Race Rels. award Booker T. Washington Bus. Assn. of Detroit, 1983. Mem. Assn. Regional Religious Communicators (pres. 1969-71), World Assn. Christian Comm. (ctrl. com. 1973-78), Phi Gamma Delta, Sigma Pi Sigma. Office: 1300 Mutual Bldg Detroit MI 48226

WILLINGHAM, JEANNE MAGGART, dance educator, ballet company executive; b. Fresno, Calif., May 8, 1923; d. Harold F. and Gladys (Ellis) Maggart. student Tex. Woman's U., 1942; student profl. dancing schs., worldwide. dance tchr. Beaux Arts Dance Studio, Pampa, Tex., 1948—; artistic dir. Pampa Civic Ballet, 1972—. Mem. Tex. Arts and Humanities, Tex. Arts Alliance, Pampa C. of C. (fine arts com.), Pampa Fine Arts Assn. Office: Pampa Civic Ballet Beaux Arts Dance Studio 315 N Nelson St Pampa TX 79065-6013

WILLINGHAM, MARY MAXINE, fashion retailer; b. Childress, Tex., Sept. 12, 1928; d. Charles Bryan and Mary (Bohannon) McCollum; m. Welborn Kiefer Willingham, Aug. 14, 1950; children: Sharon, Douglas, Sheila. BA, Tex. Tech U., 1949. Interviewer Univ. Placement Svc., Tex. Tech U., Lubbock, 1964-69; owner, mgr., buyer Maxine's Accent, Lubbock, 1969—; speaker in field. Leader Campfire Girls, Lubbock, 1964-65; sec. Community Theatre, Lubbock, 1962-64. Named Outstanding Mcht., Fashion Retailor mag., 1971, Outstanding Retailer; recipient Golden Sun award Dallas Market, May 1985. Mem. Lubbock Symphony Guild, Ranch and Heritage Ctr. Club: Faculty Women's. Office: 16 Briercroft Shopping Ctr Lubbock TX 79412-3022

WILLINGHAM, WARREN WILLCOX, psychologist, testing service executive; b. Rome, Ga., Mar. 1, 1930; s. Calder Baynard and Eleanor (Willcox) W.; m. Anna Michal, Mar. 17, 1954; children: Sherry, Judith, Daniel. Student, Ga. Inst. Tech., 1952; PhD, U. Tenn., 1955. Rsch. assoc. World Book Co., N.Y.C., 1959-60; dir. evaluation studies Ga. Inst. Tech., Atlanta, 1960-64; dir. rsch. Coll. Bd., N.Y.C., 1964-68; dir. access rsch. office Coll. Bd., Palo Alto, Calif., 1968-72; asst. v.p., disting. rsch. scientist Ednl. Testing Svc., Princeton, N.J., 1972—; vis. prof. U. Minn., 1988; mem. adv. bd. on ednl. requirements on Sec. Navy, 1968; cons. to numerous schs., colls. U.S. Office Edn. Author: Free Access Higher Education, 1970, Source Book for Higher Education, 1973, College Placement and Exemption, 1974, Assessing Experimental Learning, 1977, Selective Admissions in Higher Education, 1977, Personal Qualities and College Admissions, 1982, Success in College, 1985, Testing Handicapped People, 1988, Predicting College Grades, 1990; Gender and Fair Assessment, 1997; editor: Measurement in Education, 1969-72; mem. editl. bd. Jour. Ednl. Measurement, 1971-75, Alternate Higher Edn., 1976-80, Am. Ednl. Rsch. Jour., 1968-71; contbr. articles, tech. reports to profl. jours. Served to lt. USNR, 1955-59. Recipient Ann. award So. Soc. Philosophy and Psychology, 1958. Fellow Am. Psychol. Assn., AAAS; mem. Nat. Council on Measurement in Edn. (dir.), Am. Ednl. Research Assn., Am. Psychol. Soc., CAEL (hon. life mem.), Sigma Xi. Office: Edn Testing Svc Princeton NJ 08540

WILLIS, ARNOLD JAY, urologic surgeon, educator; b. Phila., Feb. 12, 1949; s. Alexander and Rosaline May (Dortort) W.; m. Lilian Marie Mortensen, Aug. 29, 1981; children: Adam Mark, Simon Matt, Andreas Morton. BA, Franklin & Marshall U., 1970; MD, Thomas Jefferson Med. Ctr., 1974. Intern George Washington U. Hosp., Washington, 1974-75, resident in surgery, 1975-77, resident in urology, 1977-80; instr. in urology George Washington U. Med. Ctr., Washington, 1980-82, asst. clin. prof., 1982-88, assoc. clin. prof., 1988—; mem. Del Marva Found. Med. care, Washingotn, 1985-90; mem. profl. adv. bd. Nat. Kidney Found., Washington, 1988-92; cons. Caremark Internat., Washington, 1990-93, Managed Care Options, Bethesda, Md., 1993-95. Mem. editl. bd. Health Educator, 1995-96; contbr. articles to sci. jours.; inventor ultrasound guide. Clin. Oncology Tng. grantee NIH, 1974; named Tchr. of Yr., Georgetown Family Practice Residency, 1991. Fellow Internat. Coll. Surgeons (v.p. U.S. sect. 1986—, Washington regent); mem. Am. Urologic Assn., Am. Assn. Clin. Urologists, Washington Urol. Assn. (Resident's prize 1980). Jewish. Avocations: tennis, squash, skiing, fishing, sailing. Home: 2011 Whiteoaks Dr Alexandria VA 22306 Office: 650 Pennsylvania Ave SE Ste 450 Washington DC 20003-4339

WILLIS, ARTHUR CLIFTON, writer, educator; b. Macon County, Ala., Aug. 1, 1923; s. Arthur II and Frances E. Willis; divorced; 1 child, Arthur C. IV. BS, Cheyney U., 1964; MA, Temple U., 1966; PhD, Howard U., 1972. Cert. secondary edn. tchr., Pa. Tchr. Phila. Sch. Dist., Phila., 1964-74; clk. State Treas. Office, Columbus, Ohio, 1954-62; prof. Cheyney (Pa.) U., 1974-86; writer Phila., 1986—; cons. Model Cities, Phila., 1967-68, Native Am. Schs., N.D., 1977; mem. curriculum devel. team Phila. Sch. Dist., 1977-81. Author: Cecil's City: A History of Blacks in Philadelphia, 1638-1971, 1990, Cheyney: Mother of Higher Education of African Americans, 1995. Mem. African Heritage Studies Assn., African Studies Assn. Avocations: jogging, reading history, swimming, fishing, attending live theater. Home: Box 9321 W Market St Philadelphia PA 19139

WILLIS, BEN, writer, artist; b. Racine, Wis., Dec. 4, 1930; s. Ben Sherlock Willis and Beryl Hester (Smith) Young; div. 1971. Attended, Phila. Coll. Art, 1953-54, Pa. Acad. Fine Arts, 1954-55, Academie Julian, Paris, 1955-57. Author: The Tao of Art, 1987; collaborator: The Art of Oriental Embroidery, 1980; exhibited in group shows Salmagundi Club, N.Y.C., 1971-75, Am. Watercolor Soc., Nat. Acad. Design, N.Y.C., 1978, Cicchinelli Galleries, N.Y.C., 1980, Nat. Arts Club, N.Y.C., 1980, Salmagundi Club, 1980, Manasquan Group Artists, 1981, Pastel Soc., N.Y.C., 1982, Allied Artists Am., N.Y.C., 1982, Am. Artists Profl. League, N.Y.C., 1984; represented in numerous pvt. collections. Seaman 1st class, USN, 1948-52, Korea. Recipient 1st prize N.Y.C. Ctr., 1960, Manasquan Outdoor Art Show, 1981, Best in Show award Manasquan Group Artists, 1981, others. Fellow Alumni Fellowship Pa. Acad. Fine Art, Author's Guild. Episcopalian. Avocations: languages, music, reading, judo. Home: 249 Morris Ave Elizabeth NJ 07208-3610

WILLIS, BEVERLY ANN, architect; b. Tulsa, Feb. 17, 1928; d. Ralph William and Margaret Amanda (Porter) W. BFA, U. Hawaii, 1954; PhD in Fine Arts (hon.), Mt. Holyoke Coll., 1983. Registered architect, Calif. Prin. Willis Atelier, Honolulu, 1954-66, Willis & Assocs., Inc., San Francisco, 1966-80, Beverly Willis Architects, N.Y.C., 1990—; dir., Architecture Rsch. Inst., Inc., N.Y.C. 1993—. Prin. works include Union St. Stores (merit award San Francisco AIA, award of distinction State of Calif.), Nob Hill Cts. (merit award AIA), 1970, Margaret Hayward Park (grand and merit awards Pacific Coast Bldg. Con., Honor award Design Internat.), 1983, San Francisco Ballet Bldg., 1984, Manhattan Village Acad. Loft H.S., N.Y.C., 1995; contbr. articles to profl. jours., chpts. to books. Trustee Nat. Bldg. Mus., Washington, 1976—; bldng. rsch. adv. bd. Nat. Acad. Sci., 1971-79, chair Fed. Construction Coun., 1976-79. Recipient Phoebe Hearst Gold Medal award, 1969. Fellow AIA; mem. Achievement Rewards for Coll. Scientists, Internat. Women's Forum, Villa Taverna Club, Lambda Alpha Internat. (pres. San Francisco chpt. 1981-82). Club: Villa Taverna (San Francisco). Avocations: poetry, sketching, walking. Office: 119 E 35th St New York NY 10016-3805

WILLIS, BRUCE WALTER, actor, singer; b. Fed. Republic of Germany, Mar. 19, 1955; came to U.S., 1957; s. David and Marlene Willis; m. Demi Moore; children: Rumer Glenn, Scout Larve, Tallulah Belle. Student, Montclair State Coll.; studied with Stella Adler. mem. First Amendment Comedy Theatre. Actor: (off-Broadway prodns.) Heaven and Earth, 1977, Fool for Love, 1984, The Bullpen, The Bayside Boys, The Ballad of Railroad William, (TV film) Trackdown, (feature films) Prince of the City, 1981, The Verdict, 1982, Blind Date, 1987, Sunset, 1988, Die Hard, 1988, In Country, 1989 (Golden Globe nomination 1990), Look Who's Talking (voice), 1989, Die Hard 2: Die Harder, 1990, Bonfire of the Vanities, 1990, Mortal Thoughts, 1991, Hudson Hawk, 1991, Billy Bathgate, 1991, The Last Boy Scout, 1991, Death Becomes Her, 1992, Striking Distance, 1993, Color of Night, 1994, North, 1994, Pulp Fiction, 1994, Nobody's Fool, 1994, Color of Night, 1994, Die Hard With a Vengeance, 1995, 12 Monkeys, 1995, Four Rooms, 1995, Last Man Standing, 1996; guest star (TV series) Miami Vice, The Twilight Zone; regular (TV series) Moonlighting, 1985-89 (People's Choice award 1986, Emmy award 1987, Golden Globe award 1987), musician (TV spl.) The Return of Bruno, 1986; rec. artist (album) The Return of Bruno, 1987, If It Don't Kill You, It Just Makes You Stronger, 1989; appeared in numerous commls. Named Internat. Broadcasting Man of Yr. Hollywood Radio and TV Soc.

WILLIS, C. PAUL, minister; b. Harkers Island, N.C., Dec. 14, 1932; s. Cleveland Paul and Bertha Gray (Lewis) W.; m. Mary Jane Roberts, June 1, 1951; children: Deborah, Tamalie, Dennis. BA, Campbell U., 1966; Clin. Pastoral Edn. degree, Bowman Gray Sch. Medicine, Winston Salem, N.C., 1969; MDiv, Southeastern Bapt. Sem., Wake Forest, N.C., 1970; DMin, Oral Roberts U., 1989. Pastor Northside Bapt. Ch., Greensboro, N.C., 1970-73; pres. Christian Word Ministries, Greensboro, 1973-82; sr. pastor Cathedral of His Glory, Greensboro, 1982—; pres. Ministerio de Su Gloria, Antigua, Guatemala, 1990—. Author: Bells and Pomegranates, 1991, Born to Triumph, 1992, Christ of the Apocalypse, 1993; (booklets) Abiding Power, 1976, Visions of the Victory, 1976, Signs That Make You Wonder, 1993, When the Spirit Comes, Whoosh, 1994. Mem. Charismatic Bible Ministries. Republican. Office: Cathedral of His Glory 4501 Lake Jeanette Rd Greensboro NC 27455-2807 *A life of hope and joy is built on the possibility of a miracle. I have staked everything on my belief in the miracle of the resurrection of Jesus Christ. The miracle of His resurrection gives hope for a present miracle. It is upon this truth that Christianity stands or falls!.*

WILLIS, CLAYTON, broadcaster, author, corporation executive, former government official, educator, arts consultant, photojournalist, lecturer, author; b. Washington, Aug. 11, 1933; s. William H. and Elizabeth Carl (Kerferstein) W. Student, The Sorbonne, Paris, 1953-54; BA, George Washington U., 1957; student, U. Oslo, 1953; grad., N.Y. Inst. Fin., 1966, Assn. Commodities Exch. Firms Inc., 1966. Spl. assignment Am. Embassy, London, 1957; writer NBC Network radio show Tex and Jinx, 1958; spl. corr. NBC News, La Paz, Bolivia, 1959; spl. Washington corr. Fin. News TV Network (now CNBC), N.Y.C., 1988; contbr., anchor, TV prodr., corr. Saudi Arabian TV, Newsweek mag., Philips News Svc. The Hope (Ark.) Star; contbr., corr. Christian Sci. Monitor, L.A. Times-Mirror Syndicate, The Palm Beach (Fla.) Post, The Greenwich (Conn.) Time, The Bar Harbor (Maine) Times, Info-Explo Mining Jour., Rouyn-Noranda, Que., Can., Fin. News TV Network, New York, The Mainichi, Tokyo, The China Post, Taipei, Taiwan, Chattanooga Times, The Nashville Tennesseean, the Daily Nation of Kenya, The Khartoum Echo, Sudan, The Washington Daily News, Washington Post, Cape Argus of Capetown, South Africa, Bangkok Post, Irish Times, Dublin; reporter, movie, art critic Albuquerque Tribune, 1959-61; asst. editor Newsweek Mag., N.Y.C., 1961-62; TV broadcaster-writer UPI Newsfilm, N.Y.C., 1962; White House corr., chief bur., anchor World Radio News, Houston; White House, Washington corr. WAVA Radio Sta., Washington, 1963-65; editorial writer, corr. Hearst Newspapers, N.Y.C., 1965; press officer UN, N.Y.C., 1965-66; spl. assignment Am. Embassy, Reykjavik, Iceland, 1967; editorial writer, critic, reporter N.Y. Amsterdam News, N.Y.C., 1967-68; cons. govt., law, and ethics programs Ford Found., N.Y.C., 1968-69; dir. pub. affairs U.S. EEOC, Washington, 1969-70; cons. OEO, Washington, 1970, Pres.'s Nat. Coun. on Indian Opportunity, Washington, 1970-71, Community Rels. Svc., U.S. Dept. Justice, Washington, 1970-73, Cabinet Com. on Opportunities for Spanish-Speaking People, 1971-72, Fed. Energy Adminstrn., Washington, 1973-74; dir. pub. affairs Office Petroleum Allocation U.S. Dept. Interior, 1973-74; dir. Congl. rels., dir. pub. affairs Pres.'s Nat. Commn. on Fire Prevention and Control, 1971-73; pub., editor, owner Four Corners Chieftain, Ignacio and Durango, Colo., 1972-73; lectr. Sch. of Bus., U. D.C., Washington, 1973-74; owner, White House corr., photojournalist Willis News Svc., Washington, 1974—; pub. affairs dir. Inaugural Vets. Com., 1976-77; White House corr., photojournalist Washington Life mag., 1993—; anchor Channel 33, Arlington, Va., 1991—; adviser to Fernando E.C. de Baca, spl. asst. to the Pres., White House, 1974-76; lectr. nat., internat. affairs, Haiti, art, communications, strategic and precious metals, diamond, nickel, copper, and cobalt mining, energy; corr.-broadcaster Sta. KTEN-TV, Ada, Okla., 1985; mem. staff presdl. transition office U.S. Pres. Bush, 1988-89, 90; anchor, pres. 30 minutes with Clayton Willis, 2000 Today With Clayton Willis; pres., anchor, exec. producer TV show 30 Minutes with Clayton Willis, PBS, 1990; dir. and curator L. Clayton Willis Art Collection, Washington; anchor, corr. Channel 33 Arlington, Va., 1991—; pres., White House corr., congressional corr., photojournalist, Evening News Broadcasting Co., Collector Watch TV Show Ltd. with Clayton Willis, Alexandria, 1991—, 30 Mins. with Clayton Willis, and Willis News Service; prodr., anchor documentary programs Saudi Arabian TV, 1992—; exec. prodr., anchor Glimpses of the World documentaries, 1993; White House corr., photojournalist Hope (Ark.) Star, 1994—; dir., curator L. Clayton Willis Art Collection, Washington. Coauthor: Capital Fare, 1977, When Americans Vote, Anything Can Happen, 1997. Lott-Willis Pictorial Digest of U.S. Presidential Elections and Inaugurations, 1997; contbr. articles to Daily Mail, London, London Sunday Express, Umtali Post, Zimbabwe, Gwelo (Zimbabwe) Times, To the Point news mag., Johannesburg, The Citizen, Johannesburg, Hartford Courant, Sacramento Union, Chattanooga Times, UPI Radio Networks, Washington Post, The Hope (Ark.) Star, Phillpis News Svc., also other mags. and newspapers. Broadcaster with Bush/Quayle Nat. Campaign Hdqrs., Washington, 1988; adviser Presdl. Transition Office of Pres. George Bush, 1988-89; loaned Haitian paintings for spl. exhbn. to Haitian Embassy, Washington, 1991, Milw. Art Mus., 1992. Recipient Outstanding Svc. award Harlem Prep. Sch., Johannes Gutenberg medal (Mainz, Germany), 1984, Letters of Cert. Appreciation Pres. of U.S., 1989. Mem. Overseas Press Club Am. Covered Vietnam, Congo, Mid. East, Rhodesian and South African wars; visited 150 countries; specialist gold, diamond, energy, silver, platinum, nickel, copper and cobalt mining and strategic minerals; covered Clarence Thomas and Robert Gates U.S. Senate confirmation hearings, 1991. Home and Office: Evening News Broadcasting Co PO Box 25615 Washington DC 20007

WILLIS, CLIFFORD LEON, geologist; b. Chanute, Kans., Feb. 20, 1913; s. Arthur Edward and Flossie Duckworth (Fouts) W.; m. Serreta Margaret Thiel, Aug. 21, 1947 (dec.); 1 child, David Gerard. BS in Mining Engring., U. Kans., 1939; PhD, U. Wash., 1950. Geophysicist The Carter Oil Co. (Exxon), Tulsa, 1939-42; instr. U. Wash., Seattle, 1946-50, asst. prof., 1950-54; cons. geologist Harza Engring. Co., Chgo., 1952-54, 80-82, chief geologist, 1954-57, assoc. and chief geologist, 1957-67, v.p., chief geologist, 1967-80; pvt. practice cons. geologist Tucson, Ariz., 1982—; cons. on major dam projects in Iran, Iraq, Pakistan, Greece, Turkey, Ethiopia, Argentina, Venezuela, Colombia, Honduras, El Salvador, Iceland, U.S. Lt. USCG, 1942-46. Recipient Haworth Disting. Alumnus award U. Kans., 1963. Fellow Geol. Soc. Am., Geol. Soc. London; mem. Am. Assn. Petroleum Geologists, Soc. Mining, Metallurgy and Exploration Inc., Assn. Engring. Geologists, Sigma Xi, Tau Beta Pi, Sigma Tau, Theta Tau. Republican. Roman Catholic. Avocations: travel, reading. Home: 4795 E Quail Creek Dr Tucson AZ 85718-2630

WILLIS, CONNIE (CONSTANCE E. WILLIS), author; b. 1945. Tchr. elem. and jr. H.S. Branford, Conn., 1967-69. Author: (short stories/novels) Letter from the Clearys (Nebula award 1982, Hugo award 1983), Lincoln's Dreams, 1987, Doomsday Book (Nebula award 1992, Hugo award 1993), Impossible Things, 1993, Uncharted Territory, 1994, Even the Queen (Nebula award 1992, Hugo award 1993), (novelette) Fire Watch (Nebula award 1982, Hugo award 1983), At the Rialto (Nebula award 1990), The Last of the Winnebagos (Nebula award 1988, Hugo award 1989), Death on the Nile (Hugo award 1994), (novel) Uncharted Territory, 1994, Remake, 1995, Bellwether, 1996; (with Cynthia Felice) Water Witch, 1982, Light Raid, 1989, Promised Land, 1997. Address: 1716 13th Ave Greeley CO 80631-5418

WILLIS, CRAIG DEAN, academic administrator; b. Cambridge, Ohio, Mar. 21, 1935; s. John Russell and Glenna (Stevens) W.; m. Marilyn Elaine Foster, June 9, 1956; Mark Craig, Bruce Dean, Todd Laine, Garth John. B.A., Ohio Wesleyan U, 1957; M.A., Ohio State U., 1960, Ph.D., 1969. Registrar Ohio Wesleyan U., 1964-69; dir. admissions Wright State U., 1970-72, dean, 1971-77; v.p. acad. affairs Concord Coll., 1977-82; pres. Lock Haven U. Pa., 1982—; chmn. Internat. Affairs com. Am. Assn. State Colls. and Univs.; A.C.E. pres.'s commn. on internat. edn.; vice chmn. Clinton region Mellon Bank Ctr., 1987, chmn., 1988, also bd. dirs.; bd. dirs. Lock Haven U., Lock Haven Hosp.; chmn. Lock Haven Hosp. Health Fund; cons. Ellis Assocs., Princeton, W.Va., 1980-82. Chmn. bd. Kirkmont Preschool, Beavercreek, Ohio, 1974-77, Beavercreek Library, 1976-77, Regional Edn. Service Agy., Beckley, W.Va., 1978-82; mem. N.E.-Midwest leadership Coun., 1989—. Recipient Disting. Alumnus award dept. edn. Ohio Wesleyan U., 1991; scholar Sohio Oil, 1953, Govt. of France, Paris, 1964, Shell Oil Co, 1967. Mem. Commn. State Coll. and Univ. Pres., Assn. State Colls. annd Univs., Clinton County C. of C. (pres.), Rotary (v.p., pres. elect, Citizen of Yr. award Lock Haven 1989), Ohio Wesleyan U. Alumni Assn. (Disting. Sesquicentennial Alumnus of the Edn. 1992), Phi Kappa Phi, Kappa Kappa Psi, Phi Delta Kappa, Kappa Delta Pi. Presbyterian. Office: Lock Haven U North Fairview St Lock Haven PA 17745

WILLIS, DAVID EDWIN, retired geophysicist; b. Cleve., Mar. 13, 1926; s. Russell E. and Eleanor Marie (Himebaugh) W.; m. Martha Louise Mumma, Jan. 3, 1948; children: Karen, Mark, Marta, Seth. B.S., Case Western Res. U., 1950; M.S. (U. Mich. Engring. Research Inst. fellow), U. Mich., 1957, Ph.D., 1968. Party chief, asst. supr. Keystone Exploration Co., Houston, 1950-55; research geophysicist, geophysics lab. head U. Mich., Ann Arbor, 1955-70; asso. prof. U. Mich., 1968-70; prof. dept. geol. scis. U. Wis., Milw., 1970-82; chmn. dept. U. Wis., 1972-76; v.p. Geo-Aid Corp., 1975-80; sr. geophysicist UNOCAL, L.A., 1982-92; geophysical cons. Richmond, Tex., 1992-96. Contbr. articles to profl. jours. Served with USNR, 1944-46. NSF grantee, 1964-79; Air Force Office Sci. Research grantee, 1958-76; AEC grantee, 1971-74; ERDA grantee, 1974-77. Fellow Geol. Soc. Am.; mem. Seismol. Soc. Am., Soc. Exploration Geophysicists, Am. Assn. Petroleum Geologists, L.A. Basin Geol. Soc., Phi Beta Kappa, Sigma Xi, Phi Kappa Phi. Home: 1311 Woodfair Dr Richmond TX 77469-6650

WILLIS, DAVID LEE, radiation biology educator; b. Pasadena, Calif., Mar. 15, 1927; s. Olan Garnet and Ida May (Lott) W.; m. Earline L. Fleischman, Dec. 26, 1950; children: David Lee, Paul J., Daniel N. B.Th., Biola Sem., Los Angeles, 1949; B.A., Biola U., 1951; B.S., Wheaton (Ill.) Coll., 1952; M.A., Calif. State U., Long Beach, 1954; Ph.D., Oreg. State U., 1963. Tchr. sci. various high schs., Calif., 1952-57; instr. biology Fullerton (Calif.) Coll., 1957-61; mem. faculty Oreg. State U., Corvallis, 1962—, prof. radiation biology, 1971-87, prof. emeritus, 1987—, chmn. dept. gen. sci., 1969-85; mem. Hanford Health Effects Panel, 1986; cons. in radioecology. Co-author: Radiotracer Methodology in Biological Science, 1965, Life in the Laboratory, 1965, Radiotracer Methodology in the Biological, Environmental and Physical Sciences, 1975. Mem. Am. Sci. Affiliation (pres. 1975), Health Physics Soc., Radiation Research Soc. Republican. Baptist. Home: 3135 NW McKinley Dr Corvallis OR 97330-1139 Office: Oreg State Univ Radiation Ctr Corvallis OR 97331-5901

WILLIS, DOUGLAS ALAN, lawyer; b. Taylorville, Ill., Feb. 22, 1963; s. Roy Willis and Sharon (Peel) Boaden. BA, Ill. Coll., 1985; JD, DePaul Coll. of Law, 1988. Bar: Ill. 1988, U.S. Dist. Ct. (no. dist.) Ill. 1988, U.S. Ct. Appeals (7th cir.) 1992. Intern BBC, Dallas, 1984, Ill. Dept. Registration/Edn., Springfield, 1983, Ill. State Senate Staff, Springfield, 1982, 84; rsch. asst. M.C. Bassiouni, Chgo., 1986-87; summer clk. Hon. Richard Mills, U.S. Dist. Judge, Springfield, 1987; asst. corp. sec. Profl. Svc. Industries, Inc., Lombard, Ill., 1991—, assoc. corp. counsel, 1989—. Intern U.S. House Minority Leader Robert Michel, Jacksonville, Ill., 1983. Named to Order of the Barrister, 1988, DePaul Exec. Moot Ct. Bd., 1988. Mem. Ill. State Bar Assn., Delta Theta Phi. Republican. Methodist. Home: 1510 Lakeview Dr Apt 145 Darien IL 60561-4932 Office: Profl Svc Industries Inc 510 E 22nd St Lombard IL 60148-6110

WILLIS, DOYLE HENRY, state legislator, lawyer; b. Kaufman, Tex., Aug. 18, 1908; s. Alvin and Eliza Jane (Phillips) W.; m. Evelyn McDavid, 1942; children: Doyle Jr., Dan, Dina, Dale. BS, BA, U. Tex., 1934; LLB, Georgetown U., 1938. Bar: D.C. 1937, Tex. 1938, U.S. Supreme Ct. 1942. Mem. coun. City of Fort Worth, 1963-64; mem. Tex. Ho. of Reps., Austin, 1946-52, 1969—, Tex. State Senate, Austin, 1952-62. Maj. USAF, 1941-46, PTO. Decorated Bronze Star, 4 battle stars, USAF. Mem. KP (life), Masons (life), Shriners (life), Ind. Order Odd Fellows., Lions Club. Democrat. Methodist. Avocations: golf, fishing, reading. Home: 3316 Browning Ct E Fort Worth TX 76111-5021 Office: Sinclair Bldg Fort Worth TX 76102

WILLIS, EVERETT IRVING, lawyer; b. Canadian, Tex., Oct. 28, 1908; s. Newton Percy and Lena (Powers) W.; m. Margaret Virginia Wilson, Dec. 25, 1935; children: Everett Irving, Robert Frampton. Student, Austin Coll., Sherman, Tex., 1924-26; AB, U. Mo., 1928; LLB magna cum laude, Harvard U., 1932. Bar: N.Y. 1933. With firm Dewey Ballantine (and predecessors), N.Y.C., 1932—, ptnr., 1944—. Mem. Bd. of Edn., Rye, N.Y., 1946-52, pres., 1951-52. Recipient drug industry Man of Year award, 1964. Mem. ABA (coun. pub. utilities sect. 1966-69), N.Y. State Bar Assn., Assn. Bar City N.Y., N.Y. County Lawyers Assn., Univ. Club (N.Y.C.), City Midday Club (N.Y.c.), Apawamis Club (Rye, N.Y.), Phi Beta Kappa, Sigma Nu, Alpha Pi Zeta. Republican, Presbyterian. Home: 59 Hillandale Rd Rye Brook NY 10573-1704 Office: 1301 Avenue Of The Americas New York NY 10019-6022

WILLIS, FRANK EDWARD, retired air force officer; b. Clinton, Ill., June 19, 1939; s. William Edward and Bernardine (Saveley) W.; m. Clarice Marie Hull, June 7, 1961; children: Michael, Steven, William. BS in Engring., USAF Acad., Colorado Springs, Colo., 1961; MA in Bus. Mgmt., U. Nebr., 1973. Commd. 2d lt. USAF, 1961, advanced through grades to maj. gen., 1989; dep. comdr. 314th Tactical Airlift Group, Little Rock AFB, 1978-79, comdr., 1979-80; vice comdr. 374th Tactical Airlift Wing, Clark Air Base, The Philippines, 1980-81, comdr., 1981-83; comdr. 317th Tactical Airlift Wing, Pope AFB, N.C., 1983-84; vice comdr. Air Force Manpower and Pers. Ctr., Randolph AFB, Tex., 1984-85; comdt. Air Command and Staff Coll., Maxwell AFB, Ala., 1985-88; vice comdr. 22d Air Force, Travis AFB, Calif., 1988-89; dir. and dep. chief of staff for requirements Air Mobility and Mil. Airlift Command, Scott AFB, Ill., 1989-93; ret., 1993; co-owner retail hobby shop Tinker Town, Inc., St. Louis, 1994—. Decorated D.S.M. (2), Legion of Merit (2), Air medal (7), Meritorious Svc. medal (2). Presbyterian. Avocations: electronics, computers, model railroading. Home: 1901 Mistflower Glen Ct Chesterfield MO 63005-4713

WILLIS, FRANK ROY, history educator; b. Prescot, Lancashire, Eng., July 25, 1930; s. Harry and Gladys Reid (Birchall) W.; children from previous marriage, Jane, Clare, Geoffrey. BA, Cambridge (Eng.) U., 1952, cert. in edn., 1955, diploma in devel. econs., 1974; PhD, Stanford U., 1959. Instr. Stanford (Calif.) U., 1959-60; from instr. to assoc. prof. history U. Wash., Seattle, 1960-64; assoc. prof. then prof. U. Calif., Davis, 1964—. Author: The French in Germany, 1962, France, Germany and the New Europe, 1945-1967, 1968, Europe in the Global Age, 1968, Italy Chooses Europe, 1971, Western Civilization: An Urban Perspective, 1973, World Civilizations, 1982, The French Paradox, 1982, Western Civilization: A Brief Introduction, 1987. Fellow Rockefeller Found., Paris, 1962-63, Guggenheim Found., 1966-67, Social Scis. Research Council, Cambridge, 1973-74. Avocation: travel. Office: Univ of Calif Davis Dept Of History Davis CA 95616

WILLIS, GUYE HENRY, JR., soil chemist; b. L.A., July 1, 1937; s. Guye Henry and Esther Mae (Bloomer) W.; m. Phyllis Joy Payne, Dec. 27, 1960; children: Michael Guye, Mark Charles. BS, Okla. State U., 1961; MS, Auburn U., 1963, PhD, 1965. Soil chemist USDA Agrl. Rsch. Svc., Baton Rouge, 1965—. Contbr. articles to profl. jours. Mem. Am. Soc. Agronomy, Am. Chem. Soc., Am. Soc. Agrl. Engrs. Achievements include discovery that less than 5% of applied pesticides are lost in surface runoff; volatile loss to atmosphere is pathway of greatest loss of surface applied pesticides; rainfall amount more important than rainfall intensity in washing pesticides from plant foliar surfaces. Office: USDA Agrl Rsch Svc 4115 Gourrier Ave Baton Rouge LA 70808-4443

WILLIS, HAROLD WENDT, SR., real estate developer; b. Marion, Ala., Oct. 7, 1927; s. Robert James and Della (Wendt) W.; student Loma Linda U., 1950, various courses San Bernardino Valley Coll.; m. Patsy Gay Bacon, Aug. 2, 1947 (div. Jan. 1975); children: Harold Wendt II, Timothy Gay, April Ann, Brian Tad, Suzanne Gail; m. Vernette Jacobson Osborne, Mar. 30, 1980 (div. 1984); m. Ofelia Alvarez, Sept. 23, 1984; children: Ryan Robert, Samantha Ofelia. Ptnr., Victoria Guernsey, San Bernardino, Calif., 1950-63, co-pres., 1963-74, pres., 1974—; owner Quik-Save, 9th & Waterman shopping ctr., 1966—, Ninth and Waterman Shopping Ctr., San Bernardino, 1969—; pres. Energy Delivery Systems, Food and Fuel, Inc. San Bernardino City water commr., 1965—, pres. bd. water commrs., 1994—. Bd. councillors Loma Linda (Calif.) U., 1968-85, pres., 1971-74; mem. So. Calif. Strider's Relay Team (set indoor Am. record in 4x800 1992, set distance medley relay U.S. and World record for 60 yr. old 1992). Served as officer U.S. Mcht. Marine, 1945-46. Mem. Calif. Dairy Industries Assn. (pres. 1963, 64), Liga Internat. (2d v.p. 1978, pres. 1982, 83). Seventh-day Adventist (deacon 1950-67). Lic. pvt. pilot; rated multi engr. in 601 P aerostar. Office: PO Box 5607 San Bernardino CA 92412-5607

WILLIS, ISAAC, dermatologist, educator; b. Albany, Ga., July 13, 1940; s. R.L. and Susie M. (Miller) W.; m. Alliene Horne, June 12, 1965; children: Isaac Horne, Alliric Isaac. BS, Morehouse Coll., 1961, DSc (hon.), 1989; MD, Howard U., 1965. Diplomate Am. Bd. Dermatology. Intern Phila. Gen. Hosp., 1965-66; fellow Howard U., Washington, 1966-67; resident, fellow U. Pa., Phila., 1967-69, assoc. in dermatology, 1969-70; instr. dept. dermatology U. Calif., San Francisco, 1970-72; asst. prof. Johns Hopkins U. and Johns Hopkins Hosp., Balt., 1972-73, Emory U., Atlanta, 1973-77, assoc. prof., 1977-82; prof. Morehouse Sch. Medicine, Atlanta, 1982—, chief dermatology, 1991—; dep. commdr. of 3297th USA Hosp. (1000B), 1990—; attending staff Phila. Gen. Hosp., 1969-70, Moffit Hosp., U. Calif., 1970-72, Johns Hopkins Hosp., Balt. City Hosp., Good Samaritan Hosp., 1972-74, Crawford W. Long Meml. Hosp., Atlanta, 1974—, West Paces Ferry Hosp., 1974—, others; mem. grants rev. panel EPA, 1986—; mem. gen. medicine group IA study sect. NIH, 1985—, mem. nat. adv. bd. Arthritis and Musculoskeletal and Skin Diseases, 1991—; chmn. instl. rev. bd., mem. pharmacy and therapeutic com.; mem. nat. adv. coun. U. Pa. Sch. Medicine, 1995—, charter mem. nat. alumni coun., 1995—; bd. mem. Comml. Bank Gwinnett; West Paces Med. Ctr.; mem. gov.'s commn. on effectiveness and economy in govt. State of Ga. Human Resources Task Force, 1991—; charter mem. Nat. Alumni Adv. Coun. U. Pa. Med. Ctr., 1995—; mem. com. adv. bd. sch. pub. health Emory U., 1994—; cons. in field. Bd. dirs. Heritage Bank, Comml. Bank of Ga., chmn. audit rev. com., 1988-96; chmn. State of Ga. Dermatology Found., 1995; bd. dirs. Lupus Specialists, Inc., 1996—, InterVu, Inc., 1995—. Served to col. USAR, 1983-95. EPA grantee, 1985—. Author: Textbook of Dermatology, 1971—; Contbr. articles to profl. jours. Chmn. bd. med. dirs. Lupus Erythematrosus Found., Atlanta, 1975-83; bd. dirs. Jacquelyn McClure Lupus Erythematrosus Clinic, 1982—; bd. med. dirs. Skin Cancer Found., 1980—; trustee Friendship Bapt. Ch., Atlanta, 1980-82; mem. Ga. State Bd. of Workers' Compensation Med. Subcom., 1997—. Nat. Cancer Inst. grantee, 1974-77, 78—; EPA grantee, 1980—. Fellow Am. Acad. Dermatolgy, Am. Dermtol. Assn.; mem. AAAS, Soc. Investigative Dermatology, Am. Fedn. Clin. Research, Am. Soc. Photobiology, Am. Med. Assn., Nat. Med. Assn., Internat. Soc. Tropical Dermatology, Pan Am. Med. Assn., Phi Beta Kappa, Omicron Delta Kappa. Clubs: Frontiers Internat., Sportsman Internat. Subspecialties: dermatology; cancer research (medicine). Home: 1141 Regency Rd NW Atlanta GA 30327-2719 Office: NW Med Ctr 3280 Howell Mill Rd NW Ste 342 Atlanta GA 30327-4109

WILLIS, JOHN ALVIN, editor; b. Morristown, Tenn., Oct. 16, 1916; s. John Bradford and George Ann (Myers) W.; m. Claire Olivier, Sept. 25, 1960 (div.); m. Marina Sarda, Jan. 26, 1978 (div.). BA cum laude, Milligan Coll., 1938; MA, U. Tenn., 1941; postgrad., Ind U., Harvard U. Asst. editor Theatre World, N.Y.C., 1945-65, editor, 1965—; asst. editor Screen World, N.Y.C., 1948-65, editor, 1965—; tchr. pub. high schs., N.Y.C., 1950-76; editor Dance World, 1966-80; asst. editor Opera World, 1952-54, Great Stars of Am. Stage, 1952, Pictorial History of Silent Screen, 1953, Pictorial History of Opera in America, 1959, Pictorial History of the American Theatre, 1950, 60, 70, 80, 85; mem. Tony Theatre Awards Com. Nat. bd. dirs. U. Tenn. Theatre; mem. com. to select recipients for Mus. Theatre Hall of Fame, NYU. Lt. USNR, 1943-45. Recipient Lucille Lortel Lifetime Achievement award, 1993, Drama Desk Lifetime Achievement award, 1994; high sch. auditorium renamed John Willis Performing Arts Ctr. in his honor, Morristown, 1993. Mem. Actors Equity Assn., Nat. Bd. Rev. Motion Pictures (past bd. dirs.). Home and Office: 190 Riverside Dr New York NY 10024-1008

WILLIS, JOHN T., state official; b. Nov. 1, 1946; m. Kathy S. Mangan; children: Karen M., James T. BA in Econs. cum laude, Bucknell U., 1968; JD, Harvard Law Sch., 1971. Clk. Army Ct. of Mil. Rev., 1971-74; legal assistance officer Aberdeen Proving Grounds, 1974-75; pvt. practice atty. Westminster, Balt. City, Md., 1975-90; chief of staff County Exec. of Prince George's County, 1990-94; apptd. sec. of state State of Md., 1995—; adj. prof. Western Md. Coll., 1979—; chmn. Gov.'s Commn. on Md. Mil. Monuments; adv. bd. U. Balt.'s Schaefer Ctr. for Pub. Policy. Author: Presidential Elections in Maryland, 1984; contbg. author: Western Maryland: A Profile, 1980, Justice and the Military, 1972; contbr. articles to profl. jours.; editor: The Advocate, 1973-74. Vice-chmn. Md. Dem. Party, 1987-89, mem. various coms. and del. to Dem. Nat. Convs., 1976-96; chair Dem. Secs. of State, 1995—. Judge advocate gen. corps U.S. Army, 1968-75. Mem. Md. Bar Assn., Carroll County Bar Assn., Md. Hist. Soc., Carroll County Arts Coun. (past pres.). Office: Office of Sec of State State House Annapolis MD 21401*

WILLIS, JUDY ANN, lawyer; b. Hartford, Conn., July 7, 1949; d. Durward Joseph and Angeline Raphael (Riccardo) W. BA, Cen. Conn. State U., 1971; postgrad., U. Conn. Law Sch., 1976-77; JD, Boston Coll., 1979. Bar: Mass. 1979, U.S. Dist. Ct. Mass. 1980, Calif. 1990. Sr. atty. H.P. Hood Inc., Chelsea, Mass., 1979-83; v.p. law Parker Bros., Beverly, Mass., 1983-89; sr. v.p. bus. affairs Mattel, Inc., El Segundo, Calif., 1989—. Bd. dirs. Children Affected by AIDS Found. Office: Mattel Inc 333 Continental Blvd El Segundo CA 90245-5032

WILLIS, KEVIN ALVIN, professional basketball player; b. L.A., Sept. 6, 1962. Student, Jackson C.C., Mich., Mich. State U. Basketball player Atlanta Hawks, 1984-94; with MiamiHeat, 1994-95, Golden State Warriors, 1995-96, Houston Rockets, 1996—. Named NBA All-Star, 1992. Office: Houston Rockets Two Greenway Plz Ste 400 Houston TX 77046*

WILLIS, PAUL ALLEN, librarian; b. Floyd County, Ind., Oct. 1, 1941; s. Clarence Charles and Dorothy Jane (Harritt) W.; m. Barbara Marcum, June 15, 1963; children: Mark, Sally. AB, U. Ky., 1963, JD, 1969; MLS, U. Md., 1966. Cataloger Libr. of Congress, Washington, 1963; head descriptive cataloging br. Sci. and Tech. Info. Facility NASA, College Park, Md., 1963-66; law libr., prof. law U. Ky., Lexington, 1966-73; dir. librs. U. Ky., 1973—, acting dean Coll. Libr. Sci., 1975-76, 88; exec. sec. Ky. Jud. Retirement and Removal Commn., 1977-81; mem. adv. com. Ctr. for Jud. Conduct Orgns., Am. Judicature Soc., Chgo., 1979-81; bd. dirs. Southea. Libr. Network, Atlanta, 1980-83, 96—; mem. exec. com. Ky. Hist. Soc., 1984-88; mem. Ky. Adv. Coun. on Librs., 1985—, adv. com. Online Computer Libr. Ctr., 1986-90; cons. S.E. Consortium for Internat. Devel., U. Sriwijaya, Palembang, Sumatera, Indonesia, 1987-88. Sr. fellow UCLA, summer 1982. Mem. Assn. Southea. Rsch. Librs. (chair 1986-88). Home: 2055 Bridgeport Dr Lexington KY 40502-2615 Office: U Ky Libr Office of Dir Lexington KY 40506

WILLIS, RALPH HOUSTON, mathematics educator; b. McMinnville, Tenn., Dec. 26, 1942; s. Carl Houston and Carrie Lee (Hill) W.; m. Gayle Catherine Celestin, June 29, 1973 (div. Apr. 1985); m. Velma Inez Church, Aug. 10, 1985; stepchild, Bobbie Lynn White. BS in Math., Mid. Tenn. State U., 1964, MA in Math., 1966. Cert. secondary edn. Instr. math. dept. Western Carolina U., Cullowhee, N.C., 1968-73, asst. prof. math. dept., 1973-83, assoc. prof. math. dept., 1983—. Editor: (newsletters) Abelian Grapevine-Secondary Math, 1970-88, The Child of Mathematics-Elementary-Middle Grade Math., 1972-78; mem. editl. bd. The Centroid, 1995—; contbr. articles to profl. jours. Dir., coord. Western Carolina U. High Sch. Math. Contest, Cullowhee, 1970—; solicitor-coord. Math. Contest Scholarship Program, Cullowhee, 1971-82; initiator-coord. Math. Dept.'s Vis. Speaker Program, Western Carolina U., Cullowhee, 1974-77; faculty sponsor N.C. Coun. Tchrs. Math. Student Affiliate, Cullowhee, 1988—. 1st lt. U.S. Army, 1966-68. Recipient Paul A. Reid Disting. Svc. award Western Carolina U., 1991, hon. mention N.C. Gov.'s Award for Excellence, 1991, Innovator award N.C. Coun. Tchrs. in Math., 1994. Mem. Nat. Coun. Tchrs. Math. (Innovator award 1994), N.C. Coun. Tchrs. Math. (historian 1993—, Innovator award 1994. editl. bd. Centroid 1995—), Phi Kappa Phi, Kappa Mu Epsilon. Avocations: genealogy, gardening, military history, model building, carpentry. Office: Western Carolina U Math Dept Stillwell Bldg Cullowhee NC 28723

WILLIS, ROBERT ADDISON, dentist; b. Wichita, Kans., Apr. 27, 1949; s. Everett Clayton and Mary Ann (Rohlin) W.; m. Janet Sue Jones, Jan. 21, 1968 (div. Dec. 1986); children: Gregory, Jeffrey; m. Sherryl Ann Galloway, Apr. 26, 1991; children: Wes Misak, Wendy Misak. Student, Okaloosa Walton Jr. Coll., Niceville, Fla., 1970-71, Wichita State U., 1972-74; DDS, U. Mo., 1978. Dentist Wellington, Kans., 1978—; cons. Sumner County Regional Hosp., 1980—, Lakeside Lodge Nursing Home, Wellington, 1980—. Bd. dirs. Kans. Babe Ruth Leagues, Inc., dist. commr., 1990—; bd. of elders Calvary Luth. Ch., 1989-94. With USAF, 1968-71. Mem. ADA, Acad. Gen. Dentistry, So. Dist. Dental Soc. (pres. 1980), Kans. Dental Assn. (coun. on peer rev. 1988-89), Wellington Dental Soc. (treas. 1981—), Optimist CLub, Wellington Area C. of C. (com. on indsl. devel. 1992), Am. Legion, Xi Psi Psi. Republican. Avocations: golf, photography, jogging, collecting music records, woodworking. Home: 620 Circle Dr Wellington KS 67152-3206 Office: 204 E Lincoln Ave Wellington KS 67152-3061

WILLIS, RONI MAY LEWIS, library administrator; b. Springfield, Mass., Dec. 27, 1954; d. Ralph Mansfield and Ruth Harriet (Williamson) Lewis; m. Arnold Thomas Willis, Aug. 7, 1976; 1 child, Dana Rene. BS in Edn., Winthrop Coll., 1976, MEd, 1979; M of Librarianship, U. S.C., 1982. Cert. pub. libr., Ga. Media specialist Chesterfield County S.C. Schs., Pogeland, 1976-79, Lancaster County S.C. Schs., 1979-81; young adult and audiovisual libr. West Ga. Reg. Libr., Carrollton, 1983-84; asst. dir. West Ga. Reg. Libr., 1984—; chair-elect, chair North Ga. Associated Librs., 1988-90. Mem. Carroll County Cmty. Theatre; treas. Carroll County Heart unit Am. Heart Assn., 1994—, sec., 1992-94. Mem. ALA, Ga. Libr. Assn. (chair pub. rels. com. 1988-90), Pub. Libr. Assn., Carroll County C. of C., Pilot Club of Carrollton (pres. 1986-87). Republican. Baptist. Avocations: puppetry, storytelling, dramatic arts, cross stitch, gardening. Office: West Ga Reg Libr Carrollton GA 30117

WILLIS, SELENE LOWE, electrical engineer, software consultant; b. Birmingham, Ala., Mar. 4, 1958; d. Lewis Russell and Bernice (Wilson) Lowe; m. André Maurice Willis, June 12, 1987. BSEE, Tuskegee (Ala.) U., 1980; postgrad. in Computer Programing, UCLA, 1993-94; student, U. So. Calif., 1996. Component engr. Hughes Aircraft Corp., El Segundo, Calif., 1980-82; reliability and lead engr. Aero Jet Electro Systems Corp., Azusa, Calif., 1982-84; sr. component engr. Rockwell Internat. Corp., Anaheim, Calif., 1984, Gen. Data Comm. Corp., Danbury, Conn., 1984-85; design engr. Lockheed Missile & Space Co., Sunnyvale, Calif., 1985-86; property mgr. Penmar Mgmt. Co., L.A., 1987-88; aircraft mechanic McDonnell Douglas Corp., Long Beach, 1989-93; Unix system adminstrn. Santa Cruz Ops., 1994; mem. tech. staff Space Applications Corp., El Segundo, Calif., 1995-96; bus. ops. mgr., cons. New Start, Santa Monica, Calif., 1995; software developer Nat. Advancement Corp., 1996; entrepreneur Datatronics, 1996—; exec. v.p., owner L.A. Network Engr. Jet Propulsion Lab., L.A., 1996—; software engr. Jet Propulsion Lab, Pasadena, Calif., 1996, network engr., application engr., 1996—; cons., software designer Kern & Wooley, attys., Westwood, Calif., 1995; software developer Nat. Advancement Corp., Santa Ana, Calif., 1995—. Vol. Mercy Hosp. and Children's Hosp., Birmingham, 1972-74; mrm. L.A. Gospel Messengers, 1982-84, West Angeles Ch. of God and Christ, L.A., 1990; cons., mgr. bus. ops. New Start/ Santa Monica (Calif.) Bay Area Drug Abuse Coun., 1995. Scholar Bell Labs., 1976-80, UCLA, 1994. Mem. IEEE, ASME, Aerospace and Aircraft Engrs., So. Calif. Profl. Engring. Assn., Tuskegee U. Alumni Assn., UCLA Alumni Assn. (scholarship and adv. com.), Eta Kappa Nu. Mem. Christian Ch. Avocations: piano, computers, softball, real estate.

WILLIS, THORNTON WILSON, painter; b. Pensacola, Fla., May 25, 1936; s. Willard Wilson and Edna Mae (Hall) W.; m. Peggy Jean Whisenhant, June, 1960; 1 son, David Shaw.; m. Vered Lieb, 1983; 1 dau., Rachel Elizabeth. B.S., U. So. Miss., 1962; M.A., U. Ala., 1966. vis. artist-in-residence La. State U., New Orleans, 1971-72. Represented in U.S. by André Zarre Gallery, N.Y.C., in Europe by Galerie Nordenhake, Stockholm.; assoc. editor: Re-View, 1978—; one-man exhbns. include: Henri Gallery, Washington, 1968, Paley and Lowe, N.Y.C., 1970, New Orleans Mus. Art, 1972, 55 Mercer St. Gallery, 1979, Galerie Nordenhake, Sweden, 1980, Oscarsson Hood Gallery, N.Y.C., 1980-84, Gloria Luria Gallery, Miami, 1985, Pensacola Mus. retrospective, 1988, Galerie Nordenhake retrospective, Stockholm, 1988, 89, Twining Gallery retrospective, 1990, André Zarre Gallery, N.Y.C., 1993; group exhbns. include: Phila. Civic Center, 1970, Whitney Mus., 1971, Contemporary Art Mus., Houston, 1980, 81, Sidney Janis Gallery, N.Y.C., 1980, 81, Johnson Mus., Ithaca, N.Y., 1981, Mus. Modern Art, N.Y.C., 1981, 84, 85-86, Galerie Arnesen, Copenhagen, 1981, ARS '83, Helsinki, André Emmerich Gallery, N.Y.C., 1992, Anita Shapolsky Gallery, N.Y.C., 1993; represented in permanent collections, Whitney Mus., N.Y.C., Mus. Modern Art, N.Y.C., New Orleans Mus. Art, Denver Mus. Fine Art, Rochester Meml. Gallery, Albright-Knox Mus., Phillips Collection, Washington, Herbert F. Johnson Mus., Cornell U., Chase Manhattan Collection, William Paley Collection, CBS, Power Collection, Sidney, Australia, Solomon R. Guggenheim Mus., N.Y.C., various collections, museums Europe, Scandanavia. With USMC, 1954-57. Recipient award Adolph & Esther Gottlieb Found., 1991; John Simon Guggenheim fellow, 1978-79; Nat. Endowment Arts grantee, 1980-81. Mem. U.S. Golf Assn. Avocation: golf. Home: 85 Mercer St New York NY 10012-4438 Office: 87 Mercer St New York NY 10012-4402

WILLIS, WESLEY ROBERT, college administrator; b. Rahway, N.J., Mar. 16, 1941; s. Meachen William and Mildred (Sisco) W.; m. Elaine Stanislaw, May 22, 1965; children: Mark, Kevin, Nathan. BS, Phila. Coll. Bible, 1963; ThM, Dallas Theol. Sem., 1967; EdD, Ind. U., 1978. Prof., dept. chmn. Washington Bible Coll., 1967-70; minister edn. Forcey Meml. Ch., Washington, 1967-71; prof., acad. v.p. Ft. Wayne (Ind.) Bible Coll., 1971-78; exec. v.p. Scripture Press Ministries, Wheaton, Ill., 1978-80; sr. v.p. Scripture Press Publs., Inc., Wheaton, 1980-90; v.p. acad. affairs Phila. Coll. Bible, Langhorne, Pa., 1990-97; pres. Northwestern Coll., St. Paul, 1997—; bd. dirs. Scripture Press Publs., Ltd., Whitby, Ont., Can.; bd. dirs., chmn. bd. Christian Svc. Brigade, Wheaton, 1972-88. Author: 200 Years and Still Counting, 1981, Make Your Teaching Count, 1984, Developing the Teacher in You, 1990, also 6 others; ocntbr. over 150 articles to religious publs. Sunday sch. tchr., elder Coll. Ch., Wheaton; bd. regents Dallas Theol. Sem., 1987—. Recipient Disting. Edn. Alumnus award Phila. Coll. Bible, 1988, Gold Medallion award Evang. Pubs. Assn., 1990. Mem. Nat. Assn. Profs. Christian Edn., Nat. Assn. Dirs. Christian Edn., Evang. Theol. Soc. Office: Northwestern Coll 3003 Snelling Ave N Saint Paul MN 55113-1501

WILLIS, WILLIAM DARRELL, JR., neurophysiologist, educator; b. Dallas, July 19, 1934; s. William Darrell and Dorcas (Chamberlain) W.; m. Jean Colette Schini, May 28, 1960; 1 child, Thomas Darrell. BS, BA, Tex. A&M U., 1956; MD, U. Tex. Southwestern Med. Sch., 1960; PhD, Australian Nat. U., 1963. Postdoctoral research fellow Nat. Inst. Neurol. Diseases and Blindness, Australian Nat. U., 1960-62, Istituto di Fisiologia, U. Pisa, Italy, 1962-63; from asst. prof. to prof. anatomy, chmn. dept. U. Tex. Southwestern Med. Sch., Dallas, 1963-70; chief lab. comparative neurobiology Marine Biomed. Inst., prof. anatomy and physiology U. Tex. Med. Br., Galveston, 1970—, dir. Marine Biomed. Inst., 1978—, chmn. dept. anatomy and neurosci., 1986—, Ashbel Smith prof., 1986-95, Cecil and Ida Green prof., 1995—; mem. neurology B study sect. NIH, 1968-72, chmn., 1970-72, mem. neurol. disorders Program Project rev. com., 1972-76, Nat. Adv. Neurol. and Communicative Disorders and Stroke Coun., 1987-90; tng. grant com. Nat. Inst. of Neurol. Disorders and Stroke, 1994—. Mem. editl. bd. Neurosci., Exptl. Neurology, 1970-90, Archives Italienne Biologie, Neurosci. Letters, 1976-92; chief editor Jour. Neurophysiology, 1978-83, Pain, 1986-89; assoc. editor Jour. Neurosci., 1986-89, editor-in-chief, 1993-94; sect. editor Exptl. Brain Rsch., 1990-92, 95—. Mem. AAAS, Am. Assn. Anatomists (exec. com. 1980-86), Am. Pain Soc. (pres. 1982-83), Internat. Assn. Study Pain (coun. 1984-90), Am. Physiol. Soc., Soc. Exptl. Biol. Medicine, Soc. Neurosci. (pres. 1984-85), Internat. Brain Rsch. Orgn., Cajal Club, Sigma Xi, Alpha Omega Alpha. Home: 2925 Beluche Dr Galveston TX 77551-1511 Office: U Tex Med Br Marine Biomed Inst 301 University Blvd Galveston TX 77555-5302

WILLIS, WILLIAM ERVIN, lawyer; b. Huntington, W.Va., Oct. 11, 1926; s. Asa Hannon and Mae (Davis) W.; m. Joyce Litteral, Sept. 1, 1949; children: Kathryn Cunningham, Anne Dresser, William. Student, Ind. U., 1944, NYU, 1945; AB, Marshall U., 1948; JD, Harvard, 1951; LHD (hon.), Marshall U., 1997. Bar: N.Y. 1952. Pvt. practice N.Y.C., 1951—; ptnr. Sullivan & Cromwell, 1960-94, sr. counsel, 1994—; lectr. Practising Law Inst., 1963—; trustee Fed. Bar Council, 1968-72; mem. 2d Circuit Commn. on Reduction Burdens and Costs Civil Litigation, 1977-82. Co-author Doing Business in America; contbr. Edn. Civil Practice Law Rev. Forms and Guidance for Lawyers, also articles to legal jours. Mem. panel arbitrators Pub. Resources; trustee Tenafly (N.J.) Nature Ctr., 1994—; dir. Soc. Yeager Scholars, Marshall U., Huntington, 1995—. With AUS, 1944-46. Fellow Am. Coll. Trial Lawyers, Am. Bar Found.; mem. ABA (standing com. on fed. judiciary 1987-95, chair 1992-93, 94-95), N.Y. Bar Assn. (chmn. antitrust sect. 1976-77, exec. com. 1976-83), Assn. Bar City of N.Y. (chmn. profl. discipline com. 1983-86), Fed. Bar Coun. (trustee 1969-72), Am. Judicature Soc., Am. Arbitration Assn. (panel arbitrators), N.Y. Law Inst., N.Y. County Lawyers, Ins. Judicial Adminstrn., India House, World Trade Ctr. Home: 190 Tekening Dr Tenafly NJ 07670-1219 Also: Otterhole Rd West Milford NJ 07480 Office: Sullivan & Cromwell 125 Broad St New York NY 10004-2400

WILLIS, WILLIAM HARRIS, internist, cardiologist; b. St. Augustine, Fla., June 26, 1943; m. Jan Willis; children: Brandon, Patrick. BA in Biology, So. Coll., 1961-65; MD, Loma Linda U., 1969. MD, Fla., Calif., Ala., Tex.; Diplomate Am. Bd. Internal Medicine, Am. Bd. Cardiovascular Diseases, Nat. Bd. Med. Examiners. Intern U. Ala. Hosp. and Clinics, Birmingham, 1969-70, resident, 1970-72; fellowship U. Ala. Med. Ctr., Birmingham, 1972-74, chief fellow of cardiology, 1973-74, instr. in medicine, 1973-74; staff cardiologist USAF Med. Ctr., San Antonio, 1974-76; asst. clin. prof. medicine U. Tex., San Antonio, 1975-76; asst. prof. medicine Loma Linda (Calif.) U. Sch. of Medicine, 1976-78, co-dir. Cardiovascular Labs., 1976-80, assoc. prof. medicine, 1978-84; dir. Cardiology Fellowship Program Loma Linda U. Med. Ctr., 1978-88, dir. Cardiovascular Labs., 1980-89; prof. medicine Loma Linda (Calif.) U. Sch. Medicine, 1984-89; asst. chief cardiology Loma Linda U. Med. Ctr., 1986; med. dir. Loma Linda (Calif.) Internat. Heart Inst., 1988; co-dir. cardiac catheterization lab. Fla. Hosp., Orlando, 1990-96, dir. CCU, 1992-96. Mem. editorial bd. Catheterization and Cardiovascular Diagnosis, 1987-95; reviewer Am. Coll. Cardiology, 1988—. Fellow ACP, Am. Coll. Cardiology, Soc. Cardiac Angiography and Interventions (chmn. program com. 1980-88); mem. Soc. Cardiog Angiography and Intervention (bd. dirs. 1989-92). Avocations: golf, fishing, skiing, scuba diving. Office: Fla Heart Group PA 1613 N Mills Ave Orlando FL 32803-1849

WILLIS, WILLIAM HENRY, marketing executive; b. Canton, Ohio, Mar. 15, 1951; s. William Lincoln and Gwendolyn Ann (Wasem) W.; m. Rebecca Ann Klinker, June 16, 1973; children: Kristen Ann, Patrick Michael, Susan Kathleen. BSBA, Ohio State U., 1973; M of Mgmt., Northwestern U., 1974. Assoc. product mgr. H.J. Heinz Co., Pitts., 1974-76; product mgr. Pillsbury Co., Mpls., 1976-77, mktg. mgr., 1977-79, group mktg. mgr., 1979-81; dir. bus. planning Pepsico, Inc., Purchase, N.Y., 1981-82, dir. mktg., 1982-85; exec. v.p. mktg. Ogden Svcs. Corp., N.Y.C., 1985-87, exec. v.p. indsl. svcs., 1987-93; pres. spl. mkts. divn. Reader's Digest Inc., Pleasantville, N.Y., 1994-95; pres. Pacific region Reader's Digest Inc., Pleasantville, 1995—. Exec. fundraiser Minn. Orch. Guaranty Fund, Mpls., 1979; United Way chmn. Pillsbury Co., Mpls., 1980. Named Advertiser of Yr. Aviation mag., 1986. Republican. Roman Catholic. Avocations: real estate management, renovating old homes. Office: Reader's Digest Inc Reader's Digest Rd Pleasantville NY 10570

WILLISCROFT, BEVERLY RUTH, lawyer; b. Conrad, Mont., Feb. 24, 1945; d. Paul A. and Gladys L. (Buck) W.; m. Kent J. Barcus, Oct. 1984. BA in Music, So. Calif. Coll., 1967; JD, John F. Kennedy U., 1977. Bar: Calif., 1977. Elem. tchr., Sunnyvale, Calif., 1968-72; legal sec., legal asst. various law firms, Bay Area, 1972-77; assoc. Neil D. Reid, Inc., San Francisco, 1977-79; sole practice, Concord, Calif., 1979—; exam. grader Calif. Bar, 1979—; real estate broker, 1980-88; tchr. real estate King Coll., Concord, 1979-80; lectr. in field; judge pro-tem Mcpl. Ct., 1981-93. Bd dirs. Contra Costa Musical Theatre, Inc., 1978-82, v.p. adminstrn., 1980-81, v.p. prodn., 1981-82; mem. community devel. adv. com. City of Concord, 1981-83, vice chmn., 1982-83, mem. status of women com., 1980-81, mem. redevel. adv. com., 1984-86, planning commnr. 1986-92, chmn., 1990; mem. exec. bd. Mt. Diablo coun. Boy Scouts Am., 1981-85; bd. dirs. Pregnancy Ctrs. Contra Costa County, 1991—, chmn., 1993—. Recipient award of merit Bus. and Profl. Women, Bay Valley Dist., 1981. Mem. Concord C. of C. (bd. dir., chmn. govt. affairs com. 1981-83, v.p. 1985-87, pres. 1988-89, Bus. Person of Yr. 1986), Calif. State Bar (chmn. adoptions subcom. north, 1994), Contra Costa County Bar Assn., Todos Santos Bus. and Profl. Women (co-founder, pres. 1983-84, pub. rels. chmn. 1982-83, Woman of Achievement 1980, 81), Soroptimists (fin. sec. 1980-81). Office: 3018 Willow Pass Rd Ste 205 Concord CA 94519-2570

WILLKE, THOMAS ALOYS, university official, statistics educator; b. Rome City, Ind., Apr. 22, 1932; s. Gerard Thomas and Marie Margaret (Wuennemann) W.; m. Geraldine Ann Page, Dec. 28, 1954; children: Richard, Susan, Donald, Jeanne, Mary, Kathleen. AB, Xavier U., 1954; MS, Ohio State U., 1956, PhD, 1960. Sr. engr. N.Am. Aviation, Columbus, Ohio, 1959-60; instr. math. Ohio State U., Columbus, 1960-61, assoc. prof., 1966-70, assoc. prof. statistics, 1970-72, prof., 1972—, dir. stats. lab., 1971-73, vice provost Arts and Scis., 1973-86, acting dean Univ. Coll., 1983-85, dean undergrad. studies Arts and Scis., 1987; prof. math. scis. Otterbein coll., Westerville, Ohio, 1987-97, chmn. dept. math. scis., 1988-96; rsch. mathematician U.S. Nat. Bur. Standards, Washington, 1961-66; asst. prof. math. U. Md., College Park, 1963-66. Contbr. articles on statis. non parametric methods and robustness to profl. jours. Mem. Am. Statis. Assn., Math. Assn. Am. Roman Catholic. Home: 4375 Mumford Dr Columbus OH 43220-4438 Office: Otterbein Coll Dept Of Math Scis Westerville OH 43081

WILLKIE, WENDELL LEWIS, II, lawyer; b. Indpls., Oct. 29, 1951; s. Philip Herman Willkie and Rosalie (Heffelfinger) Hall; m. Carlotta Fendig, June 27, 1987; children: Alexandra Elizabeth, Diana Fendig, Caroline Heffelfinger. AB, Harvard U., 1973; BA, Oxford (Eng.) U., 1975, MA, 1983; JD, U. Chgo., 1978. Bar: N.Y. 1979. Assoc. Simpson Thacher and Bartlett, N.Y.C., 1978-82; gen. counsel NEH, Washington, 1982-84; assoc. counsel to Pres. The White House, Washington, 1984-85; chief of staff, counselor to Sec. U.S. Dept. Edn., Washington, 1985, gen. counsel, 1985-88; counsel Office of the Pres.-elect, Washington, 1988-89; gen. counsel Dept. of Commerce, Washington, 1989-93; v.p. Westvaco Corp., N.Y.C., 1995-96, sr. v.p., gen. counsel, 1996—; vis. fellow Am. Enterprise Inst., Washington, 1993-94. Co-author, editor: (with J.R. Lilley) Beyond MFN: Trade with China and American Interests, 1994. Harvard U. scholar, 1969-73, Rhodes scholar, 1973-75. Republican. Episcopalian. Home: 155 Christie Hill Rd Darien CT 06820-3017 Office: Westvaco Corp 299 Park Ave New York NY 10171

WILLMAN, JOHN NORMAN, management consultant; b. St. Joseph, Mo., Jan. 19, 1915; s. John N. and Frances (Potter) W.; m. Victoria King, May 9, 1941; 1 dau., Victoria. Student, St. Benedict's Coll., 1936; B.A., St. Louis U., 1979. With Am. Hosp. Supply Corp., 1940-59, v.p., 1954-59; with Brunswick Corp., St. Louis, 1959-68; v.p. Brunswick Corp., 1961-68, pres. Health and Sci. div., 1961-68; v.p. Sherwood Med. Industries, Inc., St. Louis, 1961-67; pres. Sherwood Med. Industries, Inc., 1967-72, vice chmn. bd., 1972-73, also dir.; pres., chief exec. officer, dir. IPCO Corp., White Plains, N.Y., 1973-78; mgmt. cons., 1978—. Mem. Old Warson Country Club (St. Louis), St. Louis Club, Noonday Club (St. Louis), Univ. Club (St. Louis). Home: 530 N Spoede Rd Saint Louis MO 63141-7754

WILLMAN, VALLEE LOUIS, physician, surgery educator; b. Greenville, Ill., May 4, 1925; s. Philip L. and Marie A. (Dall) W.; m. Melba L. Carr, Feb. 2, 1952; children: Philip, Elizabeth, Susan, Stephen, Mark, Timothy, Jane, Vallee, Sarah. Student, U. Ill., 1942-43, 45-47; MD, St. Louis U., 1951. Diplomate Am. Bd. Surgery (sr. examiner 1976—), Am. Bd. Thoracic Surgery. Intern Phila. Gen. Hosp., 1951-52; intern, resident St. Louis U. Group Hosps., 1952-56; Ellen McBride fellow in surgery St. Louis U., 1956-57, sr. instr. surgery, 1957-58, asst. prof. surgery, 1958-61, assoc. prof., 1961-63, prof., 1963—, C. Rollins Hanlon prof. surgery, chmn. dept., 1969—, vice chmn. dept., 1967-69; attending physician St. Louis U. Hosp., 1969—; chief of surgery, 1969—; mem. staff Cardinal Glennon Children's Hosp., 1969—; cons. St. Louis VA Hosp., 1969—. Mem. editorial bd. Jour. Thoracic and Cardiovascular Surgery, 1976-86, Archives of Surgery, 1977-87, Jour. Cardiovascular Surgery, 1982-87, N.Am. editor, 1987—; contbr. over 250 articles to profl. jours. With USN, 1943-45. Recipient Merit award St. Louis Med. Soc., 1973, Health Care Leadership award Hosp. Assn. Met. St. Louis, 1988. Fellow Am. Surg. Assn., Am. Assn. Thoracic Surgery, Cen. Surg. Assn. (pres., mem. ad hoc com. on coronary artery surgery 1971-72); mem. ACS (Disting. Svc. award 1987), Soc. for Vascular Surgery, Internat. Soc. for Cardiovascular Surgery (pres. N.Am. chpt. 1985-87), Phi Beta Kappa, Phi Eta Sigma, Alpha Omega Alpha. Roman Catholic. Office: St Louis U Hosp 3635 Vista Ave Saint Louis MO 63110-2539

WILLMARTH, WILLIAM WALTER, aerospace engineering educator; b. Highland Park, Ill., Mar. 25, 1924; s. Sinclair Anson and Dorothy (Cox) W.; m. Nancy Robinson, Nov. 20, 1959; children—Robert, Deborah, Elizabeth, Kathleen. B.S. in Mech. Engring, Purdue U., 1949; M.S. in Aero. Engring, Calif. Inst. Tech., 1950, Ph.D., 1954. Research fellow, then sr. research fellow Calif. Inst. Tech., 1954-58; mem. faculty U. Mich., Ann Arbor, 1958—; prof. aerospace engring. U. Mich., 1961-90, prof. emeritus aerospace engring., 1990—; cons. to industry, 1952—. Author papers, reports. Served with AUS, 1943-46. Vis. fellow Joint Inst. Lab. Astrophysics, Boulder, Colo., 1963-64; fellow Max Planck Inst. für Stromungsforschung, Göttingen, Fed. Republic Germany, summer 1975. Fellow AIAA, Am. Phys. Soc. (Fluid Dynamics prize 1989); mem. AAUP, Sigma Xi, Tau Beta Pi, Tau Sigma. Home: 765 Country Club Rd Ann Arbor MI 48105-1034

WILLMORE, ROBERT LOUIS, lawyer; b. Ramstein AFB, Fed. Republic Germany, July 16, 1955; s. Wendell James and Theresia (Galler) W. BS in Econs., MIT, 1977; JD, Yale U., 1980. Bar: D.C. 1981, U.S. Ct. Appeals (D.C. cir.) 1985. Legis. asst. Senator Carl T. Curtis, Washington, 1977-78; law clk. to presiding judge U.S. Dist. Ct. (no. dist.) Tex., Dallas, 1980-81; assoc. Shaw, Pittman, Potts & Trowbridge, Washington, 1981-82; asst. gen. counsel Office of Mgmt. and Budget, Exec. Office of the Pres., Washington, 1982-85; dep. asst. atty. gen. civil div. U.S. Dept. Justice, Washington, 1985-88; of counsel Arent, Fox, Kintner, Plotkin & Kahn, Washington, 1988-93; ptnr. Crowell & Moring LLP, Washington, 1993—; exec. sec. Cabinet Council Tort Policy Working Group, Washington, 1985-88; chmn. task force on liability ins. availability, Washington, 1985-88. Editor Yale Law Jour., 1979-80. Mem. ABA, D.C. Bar Assn. Republican. Roman Catholic. Home: 6879 St Albans Rd Mc Lean VA 22101-2810 Office: Crowell & Moring 1001 Pennsylvania Ave NW Washington DC 20004-2505

WILLNER, ALAN ELI, electrical engineer, educator; b. Bklyn., Nov. 16, 1962; s. Gerald and Sondra (Bernstein) W.; m. Michelle Frida Green, June 25, 1991. BA, Yeshiva U., 1982; MS, Columbia U., 1984, PhD, 1988. Summer tech. staff David Sarnoff Rsch. Ctr., Princeton, N.J., 1983, 84; grad. rsch. asst. dept. elec. engring. Columbia U., N.Y.C., 1984-88; postdoctoral mem. tech. staff AT&T Bell Labs., Holmdel, N.J., 1988-90; mem. tech. staff Bell Communications Rsch., Red Bank, N.J., 1990-91; assoc. prof. U. So. Calif., L.A., 1992—, assoc. dir. Ctr. Photonic Tech., 1994—; head del. Harvard Model UN Yeshiva U., 1982; instr. Columbia U., 1987; rev. panel mem. NSF, Washington, 1992, 93, 94; invited optical comm. workshop NSF, Washington, 1994, chair panel on optical info. and comm., 1994. Author 1 book; contbr. articles to IEEE Photonics Tech. Letters, Jour Lightwave Tech., Jour. Optical Engring., Jour. Electrochem. Soc., Electronics Letters, Applied Physics Letters, Applied Optics; assoc. editor Jour. Lighwave Tech., guest editor. Mem. faculty adv. bd. U. So. Calif. Hillel Orgn., 1992. Grantee NSF, Advanced Rsch. Projects Agy., Packard Found., Powell Found., Ballistic Missile Def. Orgn.; fellow Semiconductor Rsch. Corp., 1986, NATO/NSF, 1985, Sci. and Engring. fellow David and Lucile Packard Found., 1993, presdl. faculty fellow NSF, 1994, Sr. Scholar fellow Fulbright Found., 1997; recipient Armstrong Found. prize Columbia U., 1984, young investigator award NSF, 1992. Fellow Optical Soc. Am. (vice chair optical comm. group, symposium organizer ann. mtg. 1992, 95, panel organizer ann. mtg., 1993, 95, program com. for conf. on optical fiber commn. 1996, 97); mem. IEEE (sr. mem.), IEEE Lasers and Electro-Optics Soc. (v.p. tech. affairs, mem. optical comm. tech. com., bd. govs., chmn. optical commn. tech. com., chmn. optical comm. subcom. ann. mtg. 1994, mem. optical networks tech. com.), Soc. Photo-Instrumentation Eng ring. (program chair telecomm. engring. photonics west 1995, chmn. conf. on emerging technologies for all-optical networks, photonics west, 1995, program com. for conf. on Optical Fiber Comm., 1996, conf. program com. components for WDM), Sigma Xi. Achievements include patents for localized photochemical etching of multilayered semiconductor body, optical star coupler utilizing fiber amplifier technology, and one-to-many simultaneous optical WDM 2-dim. plane interconnections. Home: 1200 S Shenandoah St Apt 201 Los Angeles CA 90035-2265 Office: U So Calif Dept Elec Engring EEB 538 Los Angeles CA 90089-2565

WILLNER, ANN RUTH, political scientist, educator; b. N.Y.C., Sept. 2, 1924; d. Norbert and Bella (Richman) W. BA cum laude, Hunter Coll., 1945; MA, Yale U., 1946; PhD, U. Chgo., 1961. Lectr. U. Chgo., 1946-47, research assoc. Ctr. for Econ. Devel. and Cultural Change, 1954-56, 61-62; advisor on orgn. and tng. Indonesian Ministry for Fgn. Affairs, Jakarta, 1952-53; expert for small scale indsl. planning Indonesian Nat. Planning Bur., Jakarta, 1953-54; fgn. affairs analyst Congl. Reference Service, Library of Congress, 1960; asst. prof. polit. sci. Harpur Coll., Binghamton, N.Y., 1962-63; postdoctoral fellow polit. sci. and Southeast Asian studies Yale U., New Haven, 1963-64; research assoc. Ctr. Internat. Studies, Princeton U., 1964-69; assoc. prof. polit. sci. U. Kans., Lawrence, 1969-70, prof., 1970—; vis. prof. polit. sci. CUNY, 1975; cons. govt. agys. and pvt. industry. Polit. sci. editor: Ency. of the Social Scis., 1961; mem. editorial bd. Econ. Devel. and Cultural Change, 1954-57, Jour. Comparative Adminstrn., 1969-74, Comparative Politics, 1977—; author: The Neotraditional Accomodation to Political Independence, 1966, Charismatic Political Leadership: A Theory, 1968, The Spellbinders, 1984; also monographs, articles, chpts. to books. Grantee Rockefeller Found., 1965, Social Sci. Research and Am. Council Learned Socs., 1966. Mem. Am. Polit. Sci. Assn. (gov. council 1979-81). Home: 2112 Terrace Rd Lawrence KS 66049-2733

WILLNER, DOROTHY, anthropologist, educator; b. N.Y.C., Aug. 26, 1927; d. Norbert and Bella (Richman) W. Ph.B., U. Chgo., 1947, M.A., 1953, Ph.D., 1961; postgrad., Ecole Pratique des Hautes Études, U. Paris, France, 1953-54. Anthropologist Jewish Agy., Israel, 1955-58; tech. asst., adminstrn. expert in community devel. UN, Mexico, 1958; asst. prof. dept. sociology and anthropology U. Iowa, Iowa City, 1959-60; research assoc. U. Chgo., 1961-62; asst. prof. dept. sociology and anthropology U. N.C., Chapel Hill, 1962-63, Hunter Coll., N.Y.C., 1964-65; assoc. prof. dept. anthropology U. Kans., Lawrence, 1967-70; prof. U. Kans., 1970-90; professorial lectr. Johns Hopkins U. Sch. Advanced Internat. Studies, 1992. Author: Community Leadership, 1960, Nation-Building and Community in Israel, 1969. Contbr. numerous articles to profl. publs. Fellow Am. Anthrop. Assn., Soc. Applied Anthropology, Royal Anthrop. Inst.; mem. Cen. States Anthrop. Soc. (past pres.), Assn. Polit. and Legal Anthropology (past pres.). Home: 5480 Wisconsin Ave Bethesda MD 20815-3530

WILLNER, JAY R., consulting company executive; b. Aurora, Ill., Sept. 22, 1924; s. Charles R. and Ida (Winer) W.; m. Suzanne Wehmann, July 17, 1958; 1 child, Adam. Student, UCLA, 1946-48; BS, MIT, 1950; MBA, Rutgers U., 1959. Researcher Andrew Brown Co., Los Angeles, 1950-52; tech. salesman Glidden Co., Los Angeles, 1952-54; market researcher Roger Williams Inc., N.Y.C., 1954-59; sr. market analyst Calif. Chem. Co., San Francisco, 1959-63; mgr. planning chem. coatings div. Mobil Chem. Co., N.Y.C., 1963-68; pres. WEH Corp., San Francisco, 1968—; lectr. U. Calif., Berkeley, 1962—; adj. faculty U. San Francisco, 1977—; U.S. corr. German mag. Farbe & Lack. Contbg. editor Jour. Protective Coatings and Linings; editor The WEH Report. Supporter San Francisco Mus. of Modern Art. 2d lt. A.C., AUS, 1943-46. Mem. Am. Chem. Soc., Steel Structures Painting Coun., Mechs. Libr., SFMOMA (supporter), San Francisco Comml. Club, Chemists Club (N.Y.C.), MIT Club No. Calif. Home: 700 Presidio Ave San Francisco CA 94115 Office: WEH Corp PO Box 470038 San Francisco CA 94147-0038

WILLNOW, RONALD DALE, editor; b. Adrian, Mich., Mar. 12, 1933; s. Wilbur A. and Irene L. (Sword) W.; m. Onnalee Thompson, Aug. 24, 1957; childrn: Lindle, Randall, Evan. AB, Adrian Coll., 1954; MA, U. Mich., 1959. Reporter St. Louis Post-Dispatch, 1959-66, asst. city editor, 1966-71, city editor, 1971-76, news editor, 1976-81, asst. mng. editor, 1981-90, dep. mng. editor, 1990—. With U.S. Army, 1954-56. Mem. Mid-Am. Press Inst. (bd. dirs. 1978—, past pres.), Mo. Associated Press Editors Assn. (pres. 1995—), St. Louis Journalism Found. (chmn. 1973-79), Press Club St. Louis (pres. 1983-86). Unitarian. Home: 7432 Cornell Ave Saint Louis MO 63130-2914 Office: St Louis Post-Dispatch 900 N Tucker Blvd Saint Louis MO 63101-1069

WILLOCKS, ROBERT MAX, retired librarian; b. Maryville, Tenn., Oct. 1, 1924; s. Willis Lemuel and Hannah (Emert) W.; m. Neysa Nerene Ferguson, May 23, 1947; children—Margret Sharon, Samuel David, Mark Timothy, Robert Daniel, Kent Max. B.A., Maryville Coll., 1949; B.D., Golden Gate Bapt. Theol. Sem., 1951, Th.M., 1962; M.A. in Library Sci, Peabody Coll., 1962. Ordained to ministry Bapt. Ch., 1950; pastor in Calif., 1950-56; missionary to Korea So. Bapt. Fgn. Mission Bd., Taejon, 1956- 65; assoc. dir. library Heidelberg Coll., Tiffin, Ohio, 1965-67; dir. library Columbia (S.C.) Coll., 1967-70; asst. dir. libraries Syracuse (N.Y.) U., 1970-76; assoc. dir. libraries U. Fla., Gainesville, 1976-83, acting dir. libraries, 1983-84, dep. dir. libraries, 1984-89, ret., 1989; pastor Northwood Bapt. Ch., Gainesville, 1981-92; libr. Bapt. Theol. Sem., Lusaka, Zambia, 1994-97; ret., 1995; cons. Choong Chung Nam Province Library Assn., Korea, 1962-65; dir. Korea Bapt. Press, 1959-61; prof. ch. history Korea Bapt. Sem., 1957-65, acting pres., 1958-59, librarian, 1959-65; Vice chmn. Korea Bapt. Mission, 1962-64; del. Fla. Gov.'s Conf. on Libraries, 1978. Editor: Korean translations Thus it is Written, 1963, The Progress of Worldwide Missions, 1965. Chmn. trustees Wallace Meml. Bapt. Hosp., Pusan, Korea, 1964-65; pres. bd. dirs. Phoenix Homeowners Assn., 1980-88. With USNR, 1943-46. Mem. ALA (chmn. telefacsimile com. 1976-78, tech. com. 1980-84, chmn. standards com. 1985-88), Fla. Libr. Assn., Southeastern Library Assn., AAUP, Peabody Coll. Alumni Assn. (pres. S.C. 1968-69). Home: 1930 NW 12th Rd Gainesville FL 32605-5338

WILLON, MYCHAEL COLE, school system administrator; b. Cambridge, Md., Apr. 1, 1955; s. Wallace Edwin and Iris Mary (Slacum). BS, U. Md., 1973-77, MEd, 1984; PhD, LaSalle U., 1992. Notary pub., Kans. Tchr. Charles Co. Bd. of Edn., Pomfret, Md., 1977-78; tchr. Howard Co. Bd. of Edn., Columbia, Md., 1978-85, gifted and talented resource tchr., 1985-86; asst. prin. Frederick County Bd. Edn., Md., 1986-88, gifted and talented coord., 1987; prin. McCollom Elem. Sch., Wichita, Kans., 1988-89, coord. spl. projects in curriculum, 1989-90, coord. elem. social studies, 1990-91, dir. elem. programs, 1991-93, asst. to supt., 1993-95; dir. Horace Mann/Irving/Park Complex, 1995—. Recipient MATE Cooperating Teacher of the Year. Md. Assoc. of Teacher Education, 1984, Excellence in Teaching award Howard County C. of C., Columbia, Md. 1984. Mem. Wichita Reading Assn., Am. Numismatic Soc., U. Md. Alumni Assn., Assn. Tchr. Educators. Republican. Avocations: traveling, running. Home: 1249 N Saint Francis Wichita KS 67214-2838 Office: Unified Sch Dist # 259 HIP Complex 1243 N Market St Wichita KS 67214-2834

WILLOUGHBY, JOHN WALLACE, former college dean, provost; b. Brumanna, Lebanon, July 30, 1932; s. James Wallace and Ida Cecilia (Frost) W.; m. Joanne Arnoldt DeWitt, Sept. 2, 1959; children—James Wallace, David Frost. B.A., Yale U., 1952; B.A., M.A., Oxford U., Eng., 1954; Ph.D., U. Rochester, 1959. Instr. English U. N.Mex., Albuquerque, 1959-60; instr. U. Chgo., 1960-63; from asst. prof. to prof., dean faculty Southampton Coll. Long Island, N.Y., 1963-73; v.p. for acad. affairs S.W. Minn. State Coll., Marshall, 1973-74, St. Francis Coll., Loretto, Pa., 1974-83; provost, dean of faculty, dir. continuing edn. Southwestern Coll., Winfield, Kans., 1983-92; distributor Success Motivation Inst., 1988—. Editor: English: Selected Readings, 1963; assoc. editor Brownings Correspondence Wedgestone Press, 1993—; dcontbr. articles to profl. jours. Treas. Cambria-Somerset Coun. for Health Edn., Johnstown, Pa., 1976-83; v.p. for scouting Penns Woods Coun. Boy Scouts Am., 1978-82; mem. com. on preparation fro ministry South Kans. Presbytery, 1989-95; pres. Winfield (Kans.) Lions Club, 1996-97. Rhodes scholar, Oxford, 1952-54. Mem. Am. Assn. Rhodes Scholars. Democrat. Presbyterian. Avocations: bicycling; camping; philately; gardening; singing. Home: 518 E 15th Ave Winfield KS 67156-4403

WILLOUGHBY, RODNEY ERWIN, retired oil company executive; b. Dallas, July 24, 1925; s. Charles V. and Juanita (Jones) W.; m. Marie J. Johnston, Feb. 27, 1954; five children. B.B.A., Tulane U., 1945; M.B.A., Harvard U., 1947. Mem. dean's staff Harvard Bus. Sch., 1947-48; with ECA, Paris, France, 1948-49; petroleum attache Am. embassy, London, Eng., 1949-52; concession mgr. Gulf Oil Corp., N.Y.C., 1952-55; mem. fgn. staff Standard Oil Co. Calif., San Francisco, 1955-65; pres. Refineria Conchan Chevron, Peru, 1965-69, Chevron Oil Co. Latin Am., 1969-71; v.p., treas. Chevron Corp. (formerly Standard Oil Co.), Calif., San Francisco, 1971-84; v.p. fgn. Chevron Corp. (formerly Standard Oil Co.), 1984-89. Trustee U. San Francisco, Fine Arts Mus. San Francisco. Served to lt. (j.g.) USNR, 1943-46. Clubs: Pacific Union, Burlingame Country. Office: 55 New Place Rd Hillsborough CA 94010-6446

WILLOUGHBY, STEPHEN SCHUYLER, mathematics educator; b. Madison, Wis., Sept. 27, 1932; s. Alfred and Elizabeth Frances (Cassell) W.; m. Helen Sali Shapiro, Aug. 29, 1954; children: Wendy Valentine (Mrs. Peter Gallen), Todd Alan. AB (scholar), Harvard U., 1953, AM in Teaching, 1955; EdD (Clifford Brewster Upton fellow), Columbia U., 1961. Tchr. Newton (Mass.) Pub. Schs., 1954-57, Greenwich (Conn.) Pub. Schs., 1957-59; instr. U. Wis., Madison, 1960-61, asst. prof. math. edn. and math., 1961-65; prof. math. edn. and math. NYU, 1965-87, dir. math. edn. dept., 1967-83, chmn. math., sci. and stats. edn. dept., 1970-80, 86-87, chmn. Univ. Faculty Council, 1981-82; prof. math. U. Ariz., Tucson, 1987—; mem. nat. bd. advisor Sq. One TV, 1983-94, U.S. Commn. on Math. Instrn., 1984-95, chmn., 1991-95; math. adv. com. Nat. Tchr. Exam. Successor (Praxis), 1989-94; edn. panel New Am. Schs. Devel. Corp., 1991—; U.S. Nat. rep. Internat. Commn. on Math. Instrn., 1991-95. Author: Contemporary Teaching of Secondary School Mathematics, 1967, Probability and Statistics, 1968, Teaching Mathematics: What Is Basic, 1981, Mathematics Education for a Changing World, 1990, Real Math, 1981, 85, 87, 91—; contbr. articles to profl. jours. and encys., chpts. to yearbooks and anthologies. Recipient Leadership in Math. Edn. Lifetime Achievement medal, 1995. Mem. Nat. Coun. Tchrs. Math. (dir. 1968-71, pres. 1982-84), Coun. Sci. Soc. Pres. (exec. bd. 1984, 85, 86, 87, chmn. 1988). Home: 5435 E Gleneagles Dr Tucson AZ 85718-1805 Office: U Ariz Dept Math Tucson AZ 85721

WILLOUGHBY, WILLIAM, II, retired nuclear engineer; b. Birmingham, Ala., Jan. 14, 1933; s. William and Marion Louise (Hart) W.; m. Doris Jean Lindsey, Oct. 16, 1954; 1 child, William III. BSChemE, MIT, 1954; MS in Nuclear Engring., U. Calif., Berkeley, 1960. Registered profl. engr., S.C. Physicist U. Calif. Lawrence Livermore (Calif.) Lab., 1957-61; tech. support supr. Carolina Va. Nuclear Power Assocs., Parr, S.C., 1962-67; mgr. nuclear engr. S.C. Elec. & Gas, Columbia, 1967-76; sr. project mgr., consulting engr. Stone & Webster Engring., N.Y.C., 1976-93; ret., 1993; mem. S.C. Nuclear Adv. Coun., Columbia, 1974-76; instr. Bridgeport Engring. Inst., Fairfield, Conn., 1994, Midlands Tech. Coll., Columbia, S.C., 1994-97. Contbr. articles to profl. jours. Commodore Columbia Sailing Club, 1974. 1st lt. U.S. Army, 1955-57. Mem. AAAS, Am. Nuclear Soc., Sigma Xi, Tau Beta Pi. Episcopalian. Home: 506 Killington Ct Columbia SC 29212

WILLOUGHBY, WILLIAM FRANKLIN, II, physician, researcher; b. Washington, Feb. 4, 1936; s. William Westel and Patricia (DeZychlinska) W.; m. Mary Scott Fishburne, 1963 (div. 1974); children: Westel Woodbury, William Franklin III, Laura Fishburne, Mary Scott; m. Judith Eleanor Barbaras, Oct. 25, 1975; 1 child, Robert Alexander Willoughby. AB, Johns Hopkins U., 1957, MD, 1965, PhD in Microbiology, 1965; grad. with distinction, USAF War Coll., 1985. Diplomate Am. Bd. Pathology. Intern then resident in pathology Johns Hopkins Hosp., 1965-67; asst. prof. depts. pathology and microbiology Case Western Res. U., Cleve.; dir. Virginia Mason Rsch. Ctr., Seattle, 1972-75; assoc. prof. dept. pathology Sch. Medicine, Johns Hopkins U., Balt., 1975-87; prof., chmn. dept. pathology Sch. Medicine, U. S.C., Columbia, 1987-92; dir. labs. Cook County Hosp., Chgo., 1992—, interim med. dir., 1994-96; cons. NIH, Bethesda, Md., 1979—, mem. pathology A study sect., 1982-86; cons. NRC, Washington, 1981-84; mem. Res. Component Med. Coun., Dept. Def., Pentagon, 1991-93; dep. surgeon gen. for res. affairs USAF, Bolling AFB, D.C., 1993-95; asst. surg. gen. USAF, Desert Storm/Desert Shield, 1990-91. Mem. editorial bd. Am. Rev. Respiratory Disease, 1978-84; contbr. articles to profl. jours., reviewer numerous sci. manuscripts. Vestryman Trinity Episcopal Ch., Long Green, Md., 1984-87; bd. dirs. Ctrl. S.C. chpt. ARC, Columbia, 1989-92; bd. fellow Norwich U., 1992-95. Maj. USAFR, 1975-95, advanced through grades to maj. gen., 1992-95. Decorated D.S.M., Legion of Merit, Meritorious Svc. medal; recipient Edwin E. Osgood prize Va. Mason Rsch. Ctr., 1973; Arthritis Found. fellow Scripps Clinic and Rsch. Found., 1967-69; Poncine scholar Poncine Found., 1972-74; NIH rsch. grantee, 1976-91. Fellow Coll. Am. Pathologists; mem. AAAS, Am. Soc. Investigative Pathology, Am. Assn. Immunologists, Am. Soc. Cell Biologists, Chgo. Coun. Fgn. Rels., Internat. Acad. Pathology, Assn. Pathology Chmns., Aerospace Med. Assn., Soc. USAF Flight Surgeons (bd. govs. 1993—), Soc. Cons. to Armed Forces, Am. Thoracic Soc., Assn. Mil. Surgeons U.S., Army Navy Club (Washington), Midtown Tennis Club (Chgo.). Avocations: aviation, music, tennis. Home: 1416A S Federal St Chicago IL 60605-2710 Office: Cook County Hosp Hektoen Inst 627 S Wood St Chicago IL 60612-3810

WILLRICH, MASON, utilities executive, consultant; b. L.A., 1933; m. Patricia Rowe, June 11, 1960 (dec. July 1996); children: Christopher, Stephen, Michael, Katharine. BA magna cum laude, Yale U., 1954; JD, U. Calif., Berkeley, 1960. Atty. Pillsbury Madison and Sutro, San Francisco, 1960-62; asst. gen. coun. U.S. Arms Control and Disarmament Agy., 1962-65; assoc. prof. law U. Va., 1965-68, prof. law, 1968-75, John Stennis prof. law, 1975-79; dir. internat. rels. Rockefeller Found., N.Y.C., 1976-79; v.p. Pacific Gas & Electric, San Francisco, 1979-84, sr. v.p., 1984-88, exec. v.p., 1988-89; CEO, pres. PG&E Enterprises, San Francisco, 1989-94; exec. Pacific Gas and Electric Co., San Francisco, 1979-94; chmn. EnergyWorks, 1995—; prin. Nth Power Technologies, Inc., 1996—; cons., 1994—. Author: Non-Proliferation Treaty, 1969, Global Politics of Nuclear Energy, 1971, (with T.B. Taylor) Nuclear Theft, 1974, Administration of Energy Shortages, 1976 (with R.K. Lester) Radioactive Waste Management and Regulation, 1977. Trustee, past chmn. World Affairs Coun. No. Calif.; pres. Midland Sch.; dir. Resources for the Future, Atlantic Coun. Guggenheim Meml. fellow, 1973. Mem. Phi Beta Kappa, Order of Coif. Office: PO Box 50907 Palo Alto CA 94303-0673

WILLS, CHARLES FRANCIS, former church executive, retired career officer; b. Avalon, N.J., July 26, 1914; s. Charles H. and Anna Margaret (Diemand) W.; m. Charlotte Emily Robson, Aug. 22, 1936; children: C. Frederic, Emily, Sally and Larry (twins). B.S., Wheaton (Ill.) Coll., 1935; B.D., Eastern Bapt. Theol. Sem., 1938, Th.M., 1941; grad., Air War Coll., 1961. Commd. 1st lt. U.S. Army, 1941; advanced through grades to col. U.S. Air Force, 1963; chaplain AUS, 1941-49, U.S. Air Force, 1949-67; ret., 1967; exec. dir. chaplaincy services Am. Bapt. Chs., Valley Forge, Pa., 1969-75; exec. dir. profl. services Am. Bapt. Chs., 1975-78; assoc. sec. Bapt. World Alliance, Washington, 1978-80; treas. Bapt. World Alliance, 1980-81; mem. Commn. on Doctrine and Interchurch Cooperation, 1980-90. Decorated Legion of Merit, Bronze Star, Purple Heart. Mem. Mil. Chaplains Assn., Mil. Order of Purple Heart.

WILLS, DAVID WOOD, minister, educator; b. Portland, Ind., Jan. 25, 1942; s. Theodore Oscar Mitchell and Elizabeth Lochore (Wood) W.; m. Carolyn Reynolds Montgomery, Aug. 22, 1964; children: John Brookings, Theodore Worcester, Thomas Churchill. BA, Yale U., 1962; BD, Princeton Theol. Sem., 1966; PhD, Harvard U., 1975. Ordained to ministry Presbyn. Ch., 1970. Asst. prof. Sch. of Religion, U. So. Calif., 1970-72; asst. prof. dept. of religion Amherst Coll., Mass., 1972-78, assoc. prof., 1978-83, prof., 1983-90, prof. religion and Black studies, 1990-94, Winthrop H. Smith '16 prof. Am. history and Am. studies, dept. religion and Black studies, 1994—, also dir. Luce Program in Comparative Religious Ethics 1978-88. Editor (with Richard Newman) Black Apostles at Home and Abroad, 1982, (with Albert Raboteau) Afro-American Religion: A Documentary History Project, 1987—. Kent fellow Danforth Found., 1966-70, 75, Ford Found. fellow, 1972, Inst. for Ecumenical and Cultural Rsch. fellow, 1972, Nat. Humanities Ctr. fellow, 1980-81, 94, NEH fellow for Coll. Tchrs., 1988-89, W. E. B. DuBois Inst. for Afro-Am. Rsch. fellow, 1989-91. Mem. Am. Acad. Religion (chair Afro-Am. religious history group 1975-78), Am. Hist. Assn., Am. Soc. Ch. History, Am. Studies Assn., Orgn. Am. Historians, So. Hist. Assn., Phi Beta Kappa. Home: 100 Woodside Ave Amherst MA 01002-2526 Office: Amherst Coll Dept Religion Amherst MA 01002

WILLS, GARRY, journalist, educator; b. Atlanta, May 22, 1934; s. John and Mayno (Collins) W.; m. Natalie Cavallo, May 30, 1959; children: John, Garry, Lydia. BA, St. Louis U., 1957; MA, Xavier U., Cin., 1958, Yale U., 1959; PhD, Yale U., 1961; LittD (hon.), Coll. Holy Cross, 1982, Columbia Coll., 1982, Beloit Coll., 1988, Xavier U., 1993, St. Xavier U., 1993, Union Coll., 1993, Macalester Coll., 1995, Bates Coll., 1995; St. Ambrose, 1997. Fellow Center Hellenic Studies, 1961-62; assoc. prof. classics Johns Hopkins U., 1962-67, adj. prof., 1968-80; Henry R. Luce prof. Am. culture and public policy Northwestern U., 1980-88, adj. prof., 1988—; newspaper columnist Universal Press Syndicate, 1970—; mem. adv. com. Internat. Ctr. Jefferson Studies; mem. Historians' adv. bd., Mt. Vernon. Author: Chesterton, 1961, Politics and Catholic Freedom, 1964, Roman Culture, 1966, Jack Ruby, 1967, Second Civil War, 1968, Nixon Agonistes, 1970, Bare Ruined Choirs, 1972, Inventing America, 1978, At Button's, 1979, Confessions of a Conservative, 1979, Explaining America, 1980, The Kennedy Imprisonment, 1982, Lead Time, 1983, Cincinnatus, 1984, Reagan's America, 1987, Under God, 1990, Lincoln at Gettysburg, 1992 (Pulitzer Prize for gen. non-fiction 1993), Certain Trumpets: The Call of Leaders, 1994, Witches and Jesuits: Shakespeare's Macbeth, 1994, John Wayne's America, 1997. Recipient Pulitzer prize, 1993, Merle Curti award Orgn. Am. Historians, Nat. Book Critics Circle award (2), Wilbur Cross medal Yale U., Peabody award. Mem. AAAL, Am. Acad. Arts and Scis., Am. Antiquarian Soc., Mass. Hist. Soc. Roman Catholic. Office: Northwestern U Dept History Evanston IL 60201

WILLS, IRENE YOUNG, accountant; b. Wellington, Tex., Aug. 9, 1950; d. William Tiffin and Edith Irene (Lindsey) Young; m. James Randolph Ward, Aug. 22, 1970 (div. 1987); m. Donald Eugene Wills, June 17, 1988; children: James Tiffin Ward, Lindsey DeAnne Ward. BA, Tex. Christian U., 1972; MBA, Angelo State U., 1992. Cert. cash mgr. Sr. acct. Grogan & Dane, CPAs, San Angelo, Tex., 1985-91, GTE, San Angelo, 1991-93; cash mgr. USAA Buying Svc., San Antonio, 1993-96; treasury mgr. H.E. Butt Grocery Co., San Antonio, Tex., 1997—; mem. supervisory com. 1st Cmty. Fed., San Angelo, 1988-89, bd. dirs., 1989-91, chmn. bd. dirs., 1991. Pres. Shannon Med. Aux., San Angelo, 1982; bd. dirs. Tom Green County Child Welfare Bd., San Angelo, 1980-83, San Angelo Cultural Affairs Coun., 1983-89; chmn. Regional Child Welfare Coun., San Angelo, 1983. Mem. San Antonio Treasury Mgmt. Assn. (bd. dirs. 1997), Treasury Mgmt. Assn. (cert. cash mgr.), Inst. Mgmt. Accts., Jr. League San Angelo. Home: 7517 Fair Oaks Pkwy Fair Oaks Ranch TX 78015 Office: HE Butt Grocery Co 646 S Main Ave San Antonio TX 78204-1210

WILLS, J. ROBERT, academic administrator, drama educator, writer; b. Akron, Ohio, May 5, 1940; s. J. Robert and Helen Elizabeth (Lapham) W.; m. Barbara T. Salisbury, Aug. 4, 1984. B.A., Coll. of Wooster, 1962; M.A., U. Ill., 1963; Ph.D., Case-Western Res. U., 1971; cert. in arts adminstrn, Harvard U., 1976. Instr. to asst. prof., dir. theatre Wittenberg U., Springfield, Ohio, 1963-72; assoc. prof., dir. grad. studies, chmn. dept. theatre U. Ky., Lexington, 1972-77; prof. theatre, dean U. Ky. (Coll. Fine Arts), 1977-81; prof. drama, dean Coll. Fine Arts, U. Tex., Austin, 1981-89, Effie Marie Cain Regents chair in Fine Arts, 1986-89; provost, prof. theatre Pacific Luth. U., Tacoma, Wash., 1989-94; prof. theatre, dean coll. fine arts Ariz. State U., Tempe, 1994—; cons. colls., univs., arts orgns., govt. agencies. Author: The Director in a Changing Theatre, 1976, Directing in the Theatre: A Casebook, 1980, rev. edit., 1994; dir. 92 plays; contbr. articles to profl. jours. Bd. dirs. various art orgns., Ky., Tex., Wash., Ariz. Recipient grants public and pvt. agencies. Mem. Nat. Assn. State Univs. and Land-Grant Colls.(chmn. commn. on arts 1981-83), Coun. Fine Arts Deans (exec. com. 1984-89, sec./treas. 1986-89), Univ. and Coll. Theatre Assn. (pres. 1981-82), Assn. for Communication Adminstrn. (pres. 1986-87), Ky. Theatre Assn. (pres. 1976). Office: Ariz State U Coll Fine Arts Tempe AZ 85287-2101

WILLS, JOHN ELLIOT, JR., history educator, writer; b. Urbana, Ill., Aug. 8, 1936; s. John Elliot and George Anne (Hicks) W.; m. Carolin Connell, July 19, 1958; children: Catherine, Christopher John, Jeffrey David, Joanne, Lucinda. BA in Philosophy, U. Ill., 1956; MA in East Asian Studies, Harvard U., 1960, PhD in History and Far Ea. Langs., 1967. History instr. Stanford (Calif.) U., 1964-65; history instr. U. So. Calif., L.A., 1965-67, asst. prof., 1967-72, assoc. prof., 1972-84, prof., 1984—, acting chair East Asian Langs. and Cultures, 1987-89; dir. East Asian Studies Ctr. USC-UCLA Joint East Asian Studies Ctr., L.A., 1990-94; rsch. abroad in The Netherlands, Taiwan, China, Japan, Macao, Philippines, Indonesia, India, Italy, Spain, Portugal, Eng. Author: Pepper, Guns, and Parleys: The Dutch East India Company and China, 1662-1681, 1974, Embassies and Illusions: Dutch and Portuguese Envoys to K'ang-hsi, 1666-1687, 1984, Mountain of Fame: Portraits in Chinese History, 1994; co-editor: (with Jonathan D. Spence) From Ming to Ch'ing: Conquest, Region, and Continuity in Seventeeth-Century China, 1979; contbr. articles to profl. jours. Grantee Nat. Acad. Scis., 1985, Am. Coun. Learned Soc., 1979-80; Younger Humanist fellow NEH, 1972-73. Mem. Assn. for Asian Studies, Am. Hist. Assn., Phi Beta Kappa, Phi Kappa Phi (Recognition award 1986, 95). Avocation: travel. Office: U So Calif Dept History Los Angeles CA 90089-0034

WILLS, MICHAEL RALPH, medical educator; b. Bath, Somerset, Eng., May 4, 1931; came to U.S., 1977; s. Ralph Herbert and Una Read (Hearse) W.; m. Margaret Christine Lewis, Sept. 12, 1955; children: Matthew, Catherine, Sarah, Benjamin, Thomas. M.B., Ch.B., U. Bristol, Eng., 1954, M.D., 1964, Ph.D., 1978. Intern Bristol Royal Infirmary, 1954-55, fellow, resident, 1957-64; sr. lectr. Royal Free Hosp. and Med. Sch., London, 1964-70, reader, 1970-74, prof., 1974-77; dir. clin. labs. U. Va., Charlottesville, 1977—. Author books, films; contbr. articles to profl. jours. Lt. comdr. Royal Naval Res., Eng. NIH rsch. fellow, 1967-68. Fellow ACP, Royal Coll. Physicians, Royal Coll. Pathologists. Roman Catholic. Avocations: reading, wood carving, gardening, military modelling. Home: 236 Rookwood Dr Charlottesville VA 22903-4644 Office: U Va Dept Pathology Charlottesville VA 22908

WILLS, OLIVE BOLINE, elementary education educator; b. Augusta, Ga., May 10, 1928; d. Francis Ensey and Gazena (Visscher) Boline; m. James Wingfield Wills, Apr. 16, 1952; children: Anne Visscher, Deana Boline Wills Burgess, Ensey James. Student, U. Chgo., 1948; AB in Social Sci. and Edn., Ga. State Coll. for Women, 1949; student, Emory U., 1950. Cert. tchr., Ga. Teen-age program dir. YWCA, Charleston, S.C., 1949-50; dir. voluntary religious activities Ga. State Coll. for Women, Milledgeville, 1950-52; social studies tchr. Washington (Ga.) High Sch., 1952-53, Wilkes Acad., Washington, 1970-91; 5th grade language arts tchr. John Milledge Acad., Milledgeville, 1991-92; curator, callaway restoration City of Washington, 1992—. Program chmn. PTA, Washington, 1965-66, fund raising chmn., 1966-67, dist. chmn., 1968-69; baton twirling tchr. Ga. Music Educators Assn., Washington, 1975-88; chmn. Wilkes County ARC, Washington, 1982—; pres. Ga. State Coll. For Women Alumni Assn., Milledgeville, 1965-67, Starlight Garden Club, Washington, 1963; sec. Friends the Libr., Washington, 1990-91, Womens Club, Washington, 1964-65, 96-97; Sunday sch. tchr. First Bapt. Ch., Washington, 1952—, choir mem., 1965—. Recipient Clara Barton award ARC, Washington, 1989, Cert. Appreciation, 1965, 79, 89, 91; named one of Outstanding Secondary Tchrs. Am. Wilkes Acad., Washington, 1974, U.S. History Tchr. of Yr., DAR, Washington, 1983. Avocations: swimming, embroidery, reading, grandchildren. Home: 509 E Robert Toombs Ave Washington GA 30673-2045

WILLS, ROBERT HAMILTON, retired newspaper executive; b. Colfax, Ill., June 21, 1926; s. Robert Orson and Ressie Mae (Hamilton) W.; m. Sherilyn Lou Niersteimer, Jan. 16, 1949; children: Robert L., Michael H., Kendall J. B.S., M.S., Northwestern U., 1950. Reporter Duluth (Minn.) Herald & News-Tribune, 1950-51; reporter Milw. Jour., 1951-59, asst. city editor, 1959-62; city editor Milw. Sentinel, 1962-75, editor, 1975-91; exec. v.p. Jour./Sentinel, Inc., Milw., 1991-92, pres., 1992-93; vice-chmn., 1993; also bd. dirs. Jour./Sentinel, Inc., Milw.; pub. Milw. Jour.; sr. v.p., bd. dirs. Jour. Communications; pres. Wis. Freedom of Info. Council, 1979-86, charter mem., 1997; Pulitzer Prize juror, 1982, 83, 90. Mem. media-law rels. com. State Bar Wis.; vice chmn. privacy coun. Wis. Pub. Svc. Commn., 1996-97; chmn. Wis. Privacy Coun., 1994-95. Recipient Leadership award Women's Ct. and Civic Conf. Greater Milw., 1987, Freedom of Info. award, 1988. Mem. Wis. Newspaper Assn. (pres. 1985-86, Disting. Svc. award 1992), Wis. AP (pres. 1975-76, Dion Henderson award Svc. 1993), Am. Soc. Newspaper Editors, Internat. Press Inst., Milw. Press Club (Media Hall Fame 1993), Soc. Profl. Journalists (prs. Milw. chpt. 1979-80, nat. pres. 1986-87), Sigma Delta Chi Found. (bd. dirs. 1993-96, Wis. Newsman of Yr. Milw. chpt. 1973). Home: 2030 Allen Blvd Apt 3 Middleton WI 53562-3469

WILLS, WALTER JOE, agricultural marketing educator; b. Beecher City, Ill., Oct. 8, 1915; s. Joe J. and Lillian L. (Buzzard) W.; m. Mary E. Triffet, May 22, 1942 (dec. 1981); m. Martha Jane Smith Peck, June 12, 1982. Student, Blackburn Coll., Carlinville, Ill., 1934; B.S. in Agr, U. Ill., 1936, M.S. in Agrl. Econs, 1937, Ph.D., 1952. Credit examiner Prodn. Credit Corp., St. Louis, 1937-47; asst. prof. U. Ill., 1947-52; dir. farm relations Am. Trucking Assn., 1953-54; extension marketing specialist Wash. State Coll., 1954-56; prof. agrl. marketing So. Ill. U., Carbondale, 1956-83, chmn. agrl. industries dept., 1957-72, cons., 1983—; Fulbright lectr. Ege U., Izmir, Turkey, 1969-70. Author: Introduction to Grain Marketing, 1972, Introduction to Agribusiness Management, 1973, (with Michael E. Newman) Agribusiness Management and Entrepreneurship, 3d edit., 1993, Introduction to Agricultural Sales, 1982. Served to capt., ordnance dept. U.S. Army, 1941-46. Recipient Outstanding Coop. Educator award Am. Inst. Cooperation, 1978; Great Tchr. award So. Ill. U., 1984, Disting. Svc. award, 1992. Mem. Goldern Key, Phi Kappa Phi, Gamma Sigma Delta, Alpha Zeta. Club: Rotarian. Home: 904 S Valley Rd Carbondale IL 62901-2421

WILLS, WILLIAM RIDLEY, II, former insurance company executive, historian; b. Nashville, June 19, 1934; s. Jesse Ely and Ellen (Buckner) W.; m. Irene Weaver Jackson, July 21, 1962; children: William Ridley III, Morgan Jackson, Thomas Weaver. BA, Vanderbilt U., 1956. Agt., staff mgr. Nat. Life & Accident Ins. Co., Nashville, 1958-62, supr., 1962-64, asst. sec., 1964-67, asst. v.p., 1967-70, 2d v.p., 1970-75, v.p., 1975-81, sr. v.p., 1981-83; sr. v.p. Am. General Services Co., 1982-83; dir. Nat. Life & Accident Ins. Co., Nashville, 1976-83; pres. Tenn. Hist. Soc., 1985-87; bd. dirs. Nat. Trust for Hist. Preservation, 1988-91. Author: History of Belle Meade: Mansion, Plantation and Stud, 1991, Old Enough to Die, 1996, Touring Tennessee: A Post Card Panorama, 1898-1955, 1996. Nat. chmn. Living Endowment Drive Vanderbilt U., 1974; pres. Cumberland Mus. and Sci. Ctr., Nashville, 1977; gen. chmn. campaign United Way, Nashville and Middle Tenn., 1978; pres. YMCA of Met. Nashville, 1984; trustee Ladies Hermitage Assn., 1981-90; mem. Tenn. Hist. Commn.; chmn. bd. Montgomery Bell Acad., 1988-97; bd. dirs. Vanderbilt U., 1988—. Lt. USN, 1956-58. Recipient awards YMCA, 1977, 1983, United Way De Tocqueville award, 1989, Tenn. History Book award Tenn. Lib. Assn. and Tenn. Hist. Comm., 1991, Disting. Alumnus award Montgomery Bell Acad., 1996. Fellow Life Office Mgmt. Assn.; mem. Assn. Preservation Tenn. Antiques (pres. Nashville chpt. 1987-89), Belle Meade Country Club, Coffee House Club, Round Table Literary Club. Presbyterian.

WILLSE, JAMES PATRICK, newspaper editor; b. N.Y.C., Mar. 17, 1944; s. Sherman Stokes and Katherine (Mackey) W.; m. Sharon Margaret Stack, Sept. 15, 1973; 1 child, Elizabeth Ruth. BA, Hamilton Coll., 1967; MS, Columbia U., 1968. Nat. editor AP, N.Y.C., 1969-74; news editor AP, San Francisco, 1975-78; city editor San Francisco Examiner, 1978-82, mng. editor, 1982-84; mng. editor N.Y. Daily News, 1984-89, editor, pub., 1989-95; editor Star Ledger, Newark, 1995—. Fellow Stanford U., 1975. Mem. Am. Soc. Newspaper Editors, AP Mng. Editors. Office: Star Ledger 1 Star Ledger Plz Newark NJ 07102-1200*

WILLSON, C. GRANT, chemistry educator, engineering educator; b. Vallejo, Calif., Mar. 30, 1939; s. Carlton P. and Margaret Ann (Cosner) W.; m. Deborah Jeanne Merritt, Dec. 13, 1975; children: William, Andrew. BS in Chemistry, U. Calif., Berkeley, 1962, PhD in Organic Chemistry, 1973; MS in Organic Chemistry, San Diego State U., 1969. With propellent rsch. Aeroject Gen. Corp., Sacramento, 1962-64; tchr., coach Fairfax High Sch., L.A., 1964-67; prof. Calif. State U., Long Beach, 1973-74, U. Calif., San Diego, 1974-78; mgr. polymer sci. and tech. IBM Almaden Rsch. Ctr., San Jose, Calif., 1978-93; prof. chemistry, chem. engrng. U. Tex., Austin, 1993—. Contbr. articles to profl. jours.; patentee in field. Mem. NAE, AAAS, Soc. Photographic and Instrumentation Engrs., Am. Phys. Soc., Am. Chem. Soc. (Arthur K. Doolittle award 1986, award Chemistry of Materials 1991, Carouthers award 1992, Coop. Rsch. award in Polymer Sci. 1993), St. Francis Yacht Club, Sigma Xi. Avocations: sailing, skiing. Office: U Tex Dept Chem Engrng CPE3 474 Austin TX 78712

WILLSON, JAMES DOUGLAS, aerospace executive; b. Edinburgh, Scotland, May 24, 1915; came to U.S., 1921; s. George William and Margaret (Douglas) W.; m. Genevieve Best, Nov. 11, 1939; children: James Douglas, Stephen J., Wendy. B.S. with honors, Ohio State U., 1937, M.B.A., 1938. C.P.A., N.Y. Sr. auditor Arthur Andersen & Co. (C.P.A.'s), N.Y.C., 1938-42; controller Stinson div. Consol. Vultee Aircraft Corp., 1946-48, Plaskon div. Libbey-Owens-Ford Glass Co., 1948-53; treas. Affiliated Gas Equipment Co., Cleve., 1953; v.p. finance, treas. Norris-Thermador Corp., Los Angeles, 1957-59; controller, mgr. finance Tidewater Oil Co., Los Angeles, 1959-60; v.p. finance Tidewater Oil Co., 1960-66, Northrop Corp., Los Angeles, 1966-70; sr. v.p. finance, treas. Northrop Corp., 1970-80, also dir. Author: Controllership, 1952, 63, 81, 90, 95, Business Budgeting and Control, 1956, 57, Internal Auditing Manual, 1983, 89, Budgeting and Profit Planning, 1983, 89, 92, Financial Information Systems, 1986. Served to lt. comdr. USNR, 1942-46. Mem. Nat. Assn. Accts. (Lybrand Gold medal 1960), Am. Inst. C.P.A.s, Controllers Inst. Am. Home: 1715 Chevy Chase Dr Beverly Hills CA 90210-2709

WILLSON, JOHN MICHAEL, mining company executive; b. Sheffield, England, Feb. 21, 1940; s. Jack Desmond and Cicely Rosamond (Long Price) W.; m. Susan Mary Partridge, Aug. 26, 1942; children: Marcus J., Carolyn A. BSc in Mining Engrng. with honors, Imperial Coll., London, 1962, MSc in Mining Engrng., 1985. With Cominco Ltd., 1966-74; v.p. No. Group Cominco Ltd., Vancouver, B.C., Can., 1981-84; pres. Garaventa (Canada) Ltd., Vancouver, 1974-81; pres., CEO Western Can. Steel Ltd., Vancouver, 1985-88, Pegasus Gold Inc., Spokane, Wash., 1989-92, Placer Dome, Inc., Vancouver, B.C., Can., 1993—; chmn. bd. dirs. Placer Pacific Ltd., Sydney, Australia, Placer Dome U.S., San Francisco, Placer Dome Can. Ltd., Placer Dome Latin Am.; bd. dirs. Can. Occidental Petroleum Ltd. Pres. N.W.T. Chamber Mines, Yellowknife, Can., 1982-84; chmn. bd. dirs. Western States Pub. Lands Coalition, Pueblo, Colo., 1990-91; bd. dirs. World Gold Coun. Mem. AIME, Can. Inst. Mining and Metallurgy, Inst. Mining and Metallurgy (London), Assn. Profl. Engrs. B.C., Assn. Profl. Engrs. and Geologists N.W.T., N.W. Mining Assn. (bd. dirs. Corp. Leadership award 1991), World Gold Coun. (bd. dirs.). Avocations: cycling, tennis, squash, sailing, skiing. Home: 4722 Drummond Dr, Vancouver, BC Canada V6T 1B4 Office: Placer Dome Inc, 1055 W Dunsmuir St Ste 1600, Vancouver, BC Canada V7X 1P1

WILLSON, MARY F., ecology researcher, educator; b. Madison, Wis., July 28, 1938; d. Gordon L. and Sarah (Loomans) W.; m. R.A. von Neumann, May 29, 1972 (dec.). B.A. with honors, Grinnell Coll., 1960; Ph.D., U. Wash., 1964. Asst. prof. U. Ill., Urbana, 1965-71, assoc. prof., 1971-76, prof. ecology, 1976-90; rsch. ecologist Forestry Scis. Lab., Juneau, Alaska, 1989—; prin. rsch. scientist, affiliate prof. biology Inst. Arctic Biology U. Alaska, Fairbanks; faculty assoc. divsn. biol. scis. U. Mont., Missoula. Author: Plant Reproductive Ecology, 1983, Vertebrate Natural History, 1984; co-author: Mate Choice in Plants, 1983. Fellow AAAS, Am. Ornithologists Union; mem. Soc. for Study Evolution, Am. Soc. Naturalists (hon. mem.), Ecol. Soc. Am., Brit. Ecol. Soc. Office: Forestry Scis Lab 2770 Sherwood Ln Juneau AK 99801-8545

WILLSON, PRENTISS, JR., lawyer; b. Durham, N.C., Sept. 20, 1943; s. Prentiss and Lucille (Giles) W. AB, Occidental Coll., 1965; JD, Harvard U., 1968. Bar: Calif. 1969, U.S. Dist. Ct. (no. dist.) Calif. 1971, U.S. Ct. Appeals (9th cir.) 1971, U.S. Tax Ct. 1971, U.S. Supreme Ct. 1975. Instr. law Miles Coll., Birmingham, Ala., 1968-70; ptnr. Morrison & Foerster, San Francisco, 1970—; prof. Golden Gate U., 1971-84; lectr. Stanford U. Sch. Law, 1985-88. Contbr. articles to legal publs. Mem. ABA, Calif. Bar Assn. Democrat. Office: Morrison & Foerster 425 Market St San Francisco CA 94105

WILLSON, ROBERT (WILLIAM), glass sculpture and watercolor artist; b. Mertzon, Tex., May 28, 1912; s. James Thomas and Birdie Alice (Blanks) W.; m. Virginia Lambert, Aug. 12, 1941 (div. 1977); 1 child, Mark Joseph; m. Margaret Pace, May 30, 1981. BA, U. Tex., 1934; MFA, U. Bellas Artes, Mex., 1941. Pub. sch. tchr. various small Tex. towns, 1936-40; chmn. art dept. Tex. Wesleyan Coll., Ft. Worth, 1940-48; owner Nob Hill Tourist Resort, Winslow, Ark., 1948-52; prof. art U. Miami, 1952-77, ret., 1977; represented by Sol Del Rio Gallery, San Antonio, Galleria d'Arte Moderna Ravagnan, Venice, Italy, Lyons-Matrix Gallery, Austin, Tex., Sandra Ainsley Gallery, Toronto, Stein Gallery, Portland, Maine, Painted Horse Gallery, Aspen, Colo., Parchman-Stremmel Gallery, San Antonio; tchr. U. Mex., 1935; dir. Nob Hill Art Gallery, Ark. Ozarks, 1948-52; dir. Tex. Wesleyan Coll. Art Gallery, 1940-48; cons.-dir. Peoria Art Mus., Ill., 1969. One-man shows include U. Tex., Austin, 1980, McNay Art Mus., San Antonio, 1982, Art Inst. of the Permian Basin, Odessa, Tex. 1985, 96, Tulane U., New Orleans, 1986, San Antonio Mus. Art, 1986, San Angelo (Tex.) Mus. of Art, 1989, Lyons-Matrix Gallery, Austin, 1989, 92, 95, Mus. of Modern Art, Venice, Italy, 1984, Galleria d'Arte Sant'Apollonia, 1989, Galleria d'Arte Moderna, San Marco, Vencie, 1984-89, Martin Mus. of Art, Baylor U., Waco, Tex., 1991-92, N.Mex. Mus. of Fine Art, Santa Fe, 1993, Bee County Coll., Beeville, Tex., 1996; exhibited in group shows at Internat. Glass Art 982 Show, Venice, Italy, 1994; juried shows include San Francisco Mus. Art, 1971, Mus. Modern Art, Mexico City, Adria Gallery, N.Y.C., Harmon Gallery, Naples, Fla., Lowe Art Mus., Fucina degli Angeli Internat. Glass Sculpture Exhbns., Venice, 1966-88, La Biennale di Venizia, 1972; selected to 1st Biennial of Glass, Correr Mus., Venezia Aperto Vetro, 1996; permanent collections include Museo Correr, Venice, Victoria and Albert Mus., London, Nat. Italian Glass Mus., Murano, Italy, Auckland Nat. Art Mus., New Zealand, U. Tex., Austin, Corning Mus. Glass, N.Y., Witte Art Mus., San Antonio, San Antonio Mus. Art, Phila. Mus. Art, Little Rock Ctr., Ark., Ft. Lauderdale (Fla.) Art Mus., Peoria Art Mus., Lowe Art Mus., Miami, Fla., Columbus (Ga.) Art Mus., Duke U. Art Mus., N.C., Oxford (Eng.)-Wilson-Willson Glass Collection, New Orleans Mus. Art, New Mex. Mus. Fine Art, Santa Fe, others; contbr. articles to profl. jours. Capt. USMCR, 1942-45. Tex. Regents scholarship U. Tex., 1930-34, Farmer Internat. fellowship to Mex., 1935; Nat. study grant Corning Mus. of Glass, 1956, rsch. grant U. Miami, 1964, 66, Feldman Found., 1976, Internat. rsch. grant U.S. Office of Edn., 1966-68, Coll. grants Shell Co. Found., 1971, 73. Mem. AAUP, Coun. of Ozark Artists and Craftsmen (founder), Fla. Craftsmen, Coll. Art Assn., Am. Assn. Mus., Fla. Sculptors, Tex. Sculptors, Tex. Watercolor Soc., others. Avocations: collecting ancient glass, Indian poetry. Home: 207 Terrell Rd San Antonio TX 78209-5915

WILLUMSON, GLENN GARDNER, curator, art historian; b. Glendale, Calif., June 22, 1949; s. Donald Herbert and Aileen Ann (Gardner) W.; m. Margaret Julia Moore, June 20, 1970; children: Erik Ryan, Ashley Aileen. BA, St. Mary's Coll., 1971; MA, U. Calif., Davis, 1984; PhD in Art History, U. Calif., Santa Barbara, 1988. Asst. curator Nelson Art Gallery, Davis, Calif., 1982-83; with collection devel. Getty Ctr. for History of Art and Humanities, Santa Monica, Calif., 1988-92; curator Palmer Mus. of Art, University Park, Pa., 1992—; fellow Nat. Writing Project, 1987; vis. prof. U. Calif., Irvine, 1990; adj. prof. art history Pa. State U., University Park, 1994—. Author: W. Eugene Smith and the Photo-Essay, 1992 (grantee J. Paul Getty Trust 1991), Collecting With a Passion, 1993; mem. editl. bd. History of Photography mag., London, 1991-94, Cambridge Univ. Press., N.Y.C., 1993—. Univ. Tchr.'s fellow NEH, 1997—. Mem. Am. Studies Assn. (Annette K. Baxter prize 1987), Coll. Art Assn., Soc. Photog. Edn. (mem. governing bd. Mid-Atlantic region), Assn. Historians Am. Art. Office: Palmer Mus Art Curtin Rd University Park PA 16802

WILMERDING, JOHN, art history educator, museum curator; b. Boston, Apr. 28, 1938; s. John Currie and Lila Vanderbilt (Webb) W. A.B., Harvard U., 1960, A.M., 1961, Ph.D., 1965. Asst. prof. art Dartmouth Coll., 1965-68, asso. prof., 1968-73, Leon E. Williams prof., 1973-77, chmn. dept. art, 1968-72, chmn. humanities div., 1971-72; sr. curator Am. art Nat. Gallery of Art, 1977-83, dep. dir., 1983-88; Sarofim prof. Am. art Princeton (N.J.) U., 1988—, chmn. dept. art and archeology, 1992—; vis. lectr. history of art Yale U., 1972; vis. prof. fine arts Harvard U., 1976; vis. prof. art U. Md., 1979; vis. prof. art history U. Del., 1982; hon. curator painting Peabody Mus., Salem, Mass.; vis. curator Met. Mus., 1988—. Author: Fitz Hugh Lane, American Marine Painter, 1964, A History of American Marine Painting, 1968, Pittura Americana dell' Ottocento, 1969, Robert Salmon, Painter of Ship and Shore, 1971, Fitz Hugh Lane, 1971, Winslow Homer, 1972, Audubon, Homer, Whistler and 19th Century America, 1972, The Genius of American Painting, 1973, American Art, 1976, American Light, The Luminist Movement, 1980, American Masterpieces from the National Gallery of Art, 1980, An American Perspective, 1981, Important Information Inside, 1982, Andrew Wyeth, The Helga Pictures, 1987, American Marine Paintings, 2d edit., 1987, Paintings by Fitz Hugh Lane, 1988; American Views: Essays on American Art, 1991, The Artist's Mount Desert: American Painters on the Maine Coast, 1994. Trustee Shelburne Mus., Vt., Guggenheim Mus., N.Y.C., N.E. Harbor Libr., Maine, Wendell Gilley Mus., S.W. Harbor, Maine, Wyeth Endowment for Am. Art, Wilmington, Del. Guggenheim fellow, 1973-74. Fellow Phila. Atheneum (hon.); Mem. Coll. Art Assn., Am. Studies Assn. Office: Princeton U Dept Art and Archaeology 105 McCormick Hall Princeton NJ 08544-1018

WILMERS, ROBERT GEORGE, banker; b. N.Y.C., Apr. 20, 1934; s. Charles K. and Cecilia (Eitingon) W.; children: Robert George, Christopher C. B.A., Harvard U., 1956; postgrad., Harvard Bus. Sch., 1958-59. Dep. fin. adminstr. City of N.Y., 1966-70; v.p. Morgan Guaranty Trust Co., N.Y.C. and Belgium, 1970-80; chmn., pres., chief exec. officer, dir. First Empire State Corp., Buffalo, 1982—; chmn. bd., chief exec. officer, dir. Mfrs. & Traders Trust Co., Buffalo, 1983—; bd. dirs. Fed. Res. Bank N.Y., The Bus. Coun. N.Y. State, A/Knox Art Gallery, ENY Savs. Bank, Greater Buffalo Partnership; mem. gov. coun. N.Y. State Bankers Assn. Bd. dirs. Buffalo Found., 1986. Decorated officer de l'Ordre de la Couronne (Belgium). Mem. Coun. Fgn. Rels. Home: 800 W Ferry St Buffalo NY 14222-1660 also: 1 W 64th St New York NY 10023-6731 Office: Mfrs & Traders Trust Co 1 M&T Plz Buffalo NY 14211-1638

WILMETH, DON BURTON, theater arts educator, theater historian, administrator, editor; b. Houston, Dec. 15, 1939; s. Perry Davis and Pauline Wilmeth; m. Judy Eslie Hansgen, June 10, 1963; 1 child, Michael Tyler. BA, Abilene Christian U., 1961; MA, U. Ark., 1962; PhD, U. Ill., 1964; MA Ad Eundem (hon.), Brown U., 1970. Teaching asst. U. Ark., Fayetteville, 1961-62, U. Ill., Urbana, 1962-64; asst. prof., head drama dept. Eastern N.Mex. U., Portales, 1964-67; from asst. to prof. theatre arts, dept. chmn. Brown U., Providence, 1967—; curator H. Adrian Smith Collection of Conjuring Books and Magicana, 1988—; cons. Internat. Exchange of Scholars (Fulbright), Washington, 1982-84, Am. memory Libr. Congress, 1992-95, Am. Theatre series Sta, WNET-TV, N.Y.C.; bd. dirs. Inst. Am. Theatre Studies, Bloomington, Ind., 1981-84; juror George Freedley Theatre Book Award com., 1971-93, 94-97, Barnard Hewitt Book Award com., 1985-89; mem. Theatre Hall of Fame Com. Hist. Figures, 1993—; O.R. and Eva Mitchell Vis. Disting. prof. Trinity U., San Antonio, 1995. Dir. numerous theatrical prodns. including (Brown U. prodns.) Carousel (Rodgers and Hammerstein), 1968, The Devils, 1969, The Night of the Iguana (Tennesee Williams), 1970, Much Ado About Nothing (Shakespeare), 1971, Too True to be Good, 1972, Dial "M" for Murder, 1972, The Beggar's Opera (John Gay), 1973, Company (Stephen Sondheim), 1974, Look Homeward, Angel, 1975, Secret Service, 1976, Romeo and Juliet (Shakespeare), 1977, The Hostage (Brendan Behan), 1978, The Seagull (Chekhov), 1979, The Importance of Being Earnest (Oscar Wilde), 1980, The Playboy of the Western World (J.M. Synge), 1982, The Rivals (Sheridan), 1983, Our Town (Thornton Wilder), 1985, Philadelphia Story, 1987, Mrs. Warren's Profession (Shaw), 1989, The Duchess of Malfi (John Webster), 1992, The Illusion, 1994, also numerous prodns. at other venues; acting roles include Twelfth Night (Colo. Shakespeare Festival 1960), The Tempest (Champlain Shakespeare Festival 1962), The Passion of Dracula, 1979, The Runner Stumbles, 1984, Follies, 1991; author: The American Stage to World War I, 1978, American and English Popular Entertainment, 1980, George Frederick Cooke, 1980 (Hewitt award 1981), The Language of American Popular Entertainment, 1981, Variety Entertainment and Outdoor Amusements, 1982; co-author: Theatre in the United States: A Documentary History, Vol. 1, 1750-1915, 1996; co-editor: Plays by Augustin Daly, 1984, Plays by William Hooker Gillette, 1983, Mud Show, American Tent Circus Life, 1988, Cambridge Guide to America Theatre, 1993, sole edit., 1996; editor (book series) Cambridge Studies Am. Theatre and Drama, 1992—; co-editor Cambridge History of Am. Theatre (3 vols., 1997—); contbg. editor: Cambridge Guide to World Theatre, 1988, 95; contbr. articles to profl. jours., chpts. to books and reviewer of books; adv. editor of 6 jours; contbr. articles to World Book Encyclopedia, Dictionary of Am. Biography, Encyclopedia of New York City, and other reference material. Corp. mem. Providence Pub. Library, 1983—; bd. mgrs. The Players of Providence, 1968-80; mem. adv. bd. East Lynne Theatre Co., Secaucus, N.J., 1981—, Langston Hughes Cultural Arts Ctr., Providence, 1982-92, Actors Theatre of Louisville, 1987—; grants panelist R.I. State Council on the Arts, Providence, 1981—; cons. Libr. of Congress, 1992—. John Simon Guggenheim fellow, 1982. Fellow Am. Theatre Assn. (chmn. publs. 1975-77); mem. Theatre Library Assn. (v.p. 1981-84), Internat. Fed. Theatre Research (exec. bd. 1995-97), Theatre Hist. Soc., Am. Soc. Theatre Research (exec. com. 1976-78, 80-83, 85-88, 94—, pres. 1991-94, sec. 1995—), Soc. for Advancement of Edn.-N.Y.C. (bd. trustees 1977-91), Coll. Fellows of Am. Theatre (bd. dirs. 1995-96, dean 1996-97), Nat. Theatre Conf. Avocations: reading, collecting theatre books and memorabilia, bookbinding. Home: 525 Hope St Providence RI 02906-1630 Office: Brown U Dept Theatre Speech and Dance PO Box 1897 Providence RI 02912-1897

WILMORE, DOUGLAS WAYNE, physician, surgeon; b. Newton, Kans., July 22, 1938; s. Waldo Wayne and Hilda Gard (Adrian) W.; m. Judith Kay Shabert; 1 child, Carol Kristann. BA, Washburn U., 1960; MD, Kans. U., 1964; MS (hon.), Harvard U., 1979; PhD (hon.), Washburn U., 1995. Diplomate Am. Bd. Surgery. Intern Hosp. U. Pa., Phila., 1964-65, resident, fellow, 1965-71; chief clin. rsch. and staff surgeon U.S. Army Inst. Surg.

Rsch., Ft. Sam Houston, 1971-79; staff surgeon Brigham and Women's Hosp., Boston, 1979—. Editor: Scientific American Surgery, 1988. Lt. Col. U.S. Army, 1971-74. Achievements include development of safe modern techniques for providing parenteral nutrition to critically-ill patients.

WILMOT, IRVIN GORSAGE, former hospital administrator, educator, consultant; b. Nanking, China, June 30, 1922; s. Frank Alonzo and Ethel (Ranney) W.; m. Dorothy Agnes Mohlfeld, Feb. 6, 1943; children: Marcia Beth, David Michael. BS, Northwestern U., 1955; MBA, U. Chgo., 1957. With Internat. Register Co., Chgo., 1946-47; buyer U. Chgo., 1947-49; adminstrv. asst., then asst. supt. U. Chgo. Clinics, 1949-61; adminstr. NYU Med. Center-Univ. Hosp., 1961-68, exec. v.p., 1968-81; exec. v.p. Blue Cross-Blue Shield Greater N.Y., 1981-83, dir., 1977-81; exec. v.p., chief operating officer Montefiore Hosp. and Med. Ctr., N.Y.C., 1984-85; healthcare cons., 1985—; instr. then asst. prof. U. Chgo., 1957-61; asso. prof. NYU, 1961-68; prof., 1968—; assoc. dir. U. Chgo. Grad. Program Hosp. Adminstrn., 1959-61; mem. hosp. rev. and planning council State of N.Y., 1979-87. Bd. dirs. N.Y. Blood Center, 1978-81. With USN, 1940-46. Fellow Am. Coll. Hosp. Adminstrs. (chmn. central. com. insts. 1959-65, regent N.Y. State and P.R. 1974—); mem. Assn. U. Programs Hosp. Adminstrs. (exec. sec. 1959-61), Am. Hosp. Assn. (mem. council research and planning 1965-68, council on mgmt. 1979-80, council on fin. 1981-84, trustee 1979-81), Assn. Am. Med. Colls. (chmn. council teaching hosps. 1970-71), Greater N.Y. Hosp. Assn. (bd. govs., pres. 1973-74), Hosp. Assn. N.Y. State (trustee, chmn. 1976-77). Home: 34 Helen Ave Rye NY 10580-2447 Office: PO Box 672 Rye NY 10580-0672

WILMOT, LOUISE C., retired naval commander, charitable organization executive; b. Wayne, N.J., Dec. 31, 1942; d. W.J. Currie and Dorothy Murphy; m. James E. Wilmot. BA in History, Coll. St. Elizabeth, Convent Sta., N.J., 1964; student, Naval War Coll., Newport, R.I., 1977; M in Legis. Affairs, George Washington U., 1978. Commd. ensign USN, 1964; advanced through grades to rear adm., 1991; comm. watch officer, registered publs. custodian, women's barracks officer Naval Air Sta., Pensacola, Fla.; with NATO staff Allied Forces, So. Europe, 1966-68; officer recruiter Recruiting Area Seven, Dallas; Naval Senate liaison officer Office Legis. Affairs, Washington; head women's equal opportunity br. Bur. Naval Pers., 1974-76; exec. officer Navy Recruiting Dist., Montgomery, Ala., 1977-79; command of Navy Recruiting Dist., Omaha, 1979-82; dep. dir accession policy Asst. Sec. Def. for Manpower, Installations, and Logistics, Washington, 1982-85; comdr. Navy Recruiting Area Five, Gt. Lakes, Ill., 1985-87; exec. asst., Naval aide Asst. Sec. Navy for Manpower and Reserve Affairs, Washington, 1987-89; comdr. Naval Tng. Ctr., Orlando, Fla., 1989-91; vice chief Naval Edn. and Tng., Pensacola, 1991-93; comdr. Naval Base, Phila., 1993-94; ret. U.S. Navy, 1994; dep. exec. dir. Cath. Relief Svcs., Balt., 1994—. Decorated DSM, Def. Superior Svc. medal, Legion of Merit with 3 gold stars. Office: Cath Relief Svcs 209 W Fayette St Baltimore MD 21201-3403

WILMOT, THOMAS RAY, medical entomologist, educator; b. Great Falls, Mont., Sept. 9, 1953; s. Donald D. and Jeanne M. W.; m. Gail A. Ballard, June 26, 1976; children: Lacey A., Eric T. BS in Entomology, Mont. State U., 1975; MS in Entomology, Oreg. State U., 1978; MPH, UCLA, 1984, PhD in Epidemiology, 1986. Inspector Cacade County Pesticide Program, Great Falls, Mont., 1970-75; mgr. Yakima County Mosquito Control, Wash., 1978-80; entomologist Midland County Mosquito Control, Sanford, Mich., 1984—; adj. instr. Saginaw Valley State U., University Center, Mich., 1988—; vector control cons., Midland, Mich., 1988—. Contbr. articles to profl. jours. Mem. Local Emergency Plan Com., Midland, Mich., 1990-96; spkr. Dow Corning Spkrs. Bur., Midland, 1992-96. Pub. Health traineeship USPHS, 1980-84; recipient Achievement award Nat. Assn. Counties, 1994. Mem. Am. Mosquito Control Assn. (mem. editl. bd. 1989-92), Entomol. Soc. Am. (bd. cert. entomologist), Soc. for Vector Ecology (regional dir. 1990-96), Mich. Mosquito Control Assn. (pres. 1989, disting. svc. award 1994), Phi Kappa Phi. Avocation: coaching youth athletics. Office: Midland County Mosquito Control 2180 N Meridian Rd Sanford MI 48657-9501

WILMOTH, WILLIAM DAVID, prosecutor; b. Elkins, W.Va., July 11, 1950; s. Stark Amasa and Goldie (Johnson) W.; m. Rebecca Weaver, Aug. 21, 1971; children: Charles, Anne, Samuel, Peter. BS in Fin. cum laude, W.Va. U., 1972, JD, 1975. Bar: W.Va. 1975, U.S. Dist. Ct. (so. dist.) W.Va. 1975, U.S. Dist. Ct. (no. dist.) W.Va. 1976, U.S. Ct. Appeals (4th cir.) 1977, U.S. Supreme Ct. 1981, Pa. 1986. Law clk. to presiding judge U.S. Dist. Ct. (no. dist.) W.Va., Elkins, 1975-76; assoc. Bachmann, Hess, Bachmann & Garden, Wheeling, W.Va., 1976-77; asst. U.S. atty. U.S. Dept. Justice, Wheeling, 1977-80; ptnr. Schrader, Byrd, Byrum & Companion, Wheeling, 1980-93; U.S. atty. U.S. Dist. Ct. (no. dist.) W.Va., Wheeling, W.Va., 1993—. Past pres., bd. dirs. nat. trial coun. Boy Scouts Am., Wheeling; bd. dirs. Wheeling Nat. Heritage Area Corp., Wheeling YMCA, OVations Youth Orch., State Coll. Sys. W.Va., past chmn. Mem. ABA, Am. Bankruptcy Inst., Def. Research Inst., Def. Trial Lawyers W.Va., Rotary Club Wheeling (past pres.). Democrat. Lodge: Rotary. Home: 4 Highland Park Wheeling WV 26003-5473 Office: US Atty Office PO Box 591 Wheeling WV 26003-0076

WILMOT-WEIDMAN, KIMBERLY JO, journalist; b. Milw., Dec. 30, 1970; d. Timothy Fredrick and Mary Jo (Handel) W.; m. Jade Matthew, June 18, 1994. BA, U. Wis., Milw., 1993; MA, Cardinal Stritch Coll., 1995, Towson State U., 1996. Reporter Cmty. Newspapers, Milw., 1992-95; editor ARI/AP, Milw., 1993-95; asst. editor Metro Parent Mag., Milw., 1995; reporter Patuxent Publ., Balt., 1995—; adj. prof. Towson State U., 1996—; freelance writer Chgo. Tribune. Co-author: New Faces, 1994. Tutor Milw. Literacy Coalition, 1992-95. Mem. Alpha Epsilon Lambda. Office: Patuxent Pub 409 Washington Ave Towson MD 21204-4920

WILMOUTH, ROBERT K., commodities executive; b. Worcester, Mass., Nov. 9, 1928; s. Alfred F. and Aileen E. (Kearney) W.; m. Ellen M. Boyle, Sept. 10, 1955; children: Robert J., John J., James P., Thomas G., Anne Marie. BA, Holy Cross Coll., 1949; MA, U. Notre Dame, 1950, LLD, 1984. Exec. v.p., dir. 1st Nat. Bank Chgo., 1972-75; pres., chief adminstrv. officer Crocker Nat. Bank, San Francisco, 1975-77; pres., chief exec. officer Chgo. Bd. Trade, 1977-82; chmn. LaSalle Nat. Bank, 1982—; pres., chief exec. officer Nat. Futures Assn. Trustee U. Notre Dame, investment com.; mem. adv. coun. Kellogg Grad. Sch. Mgmt., Northwestern U. Mem. Chgo. Club, Barrington Hill Country Club, Econ. Club. Home: 429 Caesar Dr Barrington IL 60010-4029 Office: Nat Futures Assn 200 W Madison St Ste 1600 Chicago IL 60606-3415

WILNER, JUDITH, journalist; b. Framingham, Mass., Mar. 30, 1943; d. John C. and Marjorie E. (Devonshire) Earley; m. David Alan Wilner, Aug. 27, 1964 (div. Aug. 1968); 1 child, Erica Susan; m. Fred Karp, July 28, 1991; 1 child, Shai Shalom Karp. BA in Letters, U. Okla., 1964. Wire editor, copy editor The Norman (Okla.) Transcript, 1967-72; news editor Loveland (Colo.) Reporter-Herald, 1972-73; editor of editl. page The Albuquerque Tribune, 1974-76, city editor, 1974-76; copy editor The Denver Post, 1976-77, copy desk chief, 1977-80, mgr. editl. sys., 1980-84; dep. tech. editor N.Y. Times, 1984-86, tech. editor, 1986—; women's editor The Norman Transcript, 1964-66. Mem. Newspaper Assn. of Am. (tech. com., chmn. wire svc. guidelines com. 1992—).

WILNER, MORTON HARRISON, retired lawyer; b. Balt., May 28, 1908; s. Joseph A. and Ida (Berkow) W.; m. Zelda Dunkelman, Nov. 3, 1940; children: James D., Thomas B., Lawrence J., Theodora. B.S. in Econs, U. Pa., 1930; J.D., Georgetown U., 1934. Bar: D.C. 1933. Gen. counsel emeritus Armed Forces Benefit Assn.; vice chmn. AFBA Indsl. Bank; bd. dirs. Armed Forces Benefit Svcs., Inc.; mem. emeritus Giant Food, Inc. Past pres. Jewish Community Center of Greater Washington.; Emeritus life trustee U. Pa.; past pres. Nat. Child Research Center; bd. govs. St. Albans Sch., 1968-72. Served to maj. USAAF; dep. dir. aircraft div. WPB 1942-45. Decorated Legion of Merit; recipient Ourisman Meml. award for civic achievement, 1970; Ben Franklin award U. Pa., 1973; alumni award of merit, 1975; Friar of Yr. award U. Pa., 1976; Wharton Sch. Club Joseph Wharton award, 1980. Mem. Fed. Bar Assn., ABA (ho. dels. 1971-73), D.C. Bar Assn., Internat. Bar Assn., Fed. Communications Bar Assn. (pres. 1969-70). Clubs: Army and Navy, Woodmont Country. Home: 2701 Chesapeake St NW Washington DC 20008-1042 Office: AFBA 909 N Washington St Alexandria VA 22314-1555

WILNER, PAUL ANDREW, journalist; b. N.Y.C., Feb. 12, 1950; s. Norman and Sylvia (Rubenstein) W.; m. Alyson Paula Bromberg, June 3, 1980; children: Anne Charlotte, Daniel Joseph. Student, U. Calif., Berkeley, 1968; BA, CUNY, 1976. Copy clk. N.Y. Times, 1976-80; reporter L.A. Herald Examiner, 1980-85; mng. editor Hollywood Reporter, L.A., 1985-87; asst. mng. editor features San Francisco Examiner, 1987—; sr. instr. U. So. Calif., L.A., 1983-85. Author: (poetry) Serious Business, The Paris Rev., 1977. Office: SF Examiner Mag 110 5th St San Francisco CA 94103-2918

WILNER, THOMAS BERNARD, lawyer; b. Toronto, Ont., Can., July 7, 1944; came to U.S., 1944; s. Morton H. and Zelda (Dunkelman) W.; m. Jane Ten Broeck; children: Amanda, Adam, David. BA, Yale U., 1966; LLB, U. Pa., 1969. Clk. U.S. Ct. Appeals, Phila., 1969-70; assoc. Debevoise Plimpton, N.Y.C., 1970-72; counsel Amtrak, Washington, 1972-73; ptnr. Arnold & Porter, Washington, 1973-89, Shearman & Sterling, Washington and Tokyo, 1989—.

WILPON, FRED, real estate developer, baseball team executive; b. Bklyn., Nov. 22, 1936; s. Nathan and Frances (Altman) W.; m. Judith Anne Kessler, Sept. 27, 1958; children: Jeffrey Scott, Robin Lynn, Bruce Nathan. B.A., U. Mich., 1958. Vice pres. Hanover Equities Corp., N.Y.C., 1959-69, Peter Sharp & Co., N.Y.C., 1969-71; chmn. bd. Sterling Equities, Inc., Manhasset, N.Y., 1971—; pres. N.Y. Mets Profl. Baseball Team, 1980—, now also chief exec. officer. Mem. Vol. Urban Cons. Group, Mayor N.Y.C. Housing Task Force; trustee Jewish Inst. Geriatric Care, New Hyde Park, N.Y., 1976—, Green Vale Sch., Glen Head, N.Y., 1977—. Served with USAF, 1959. Mem. Young Pres. Orgn. Club: KP. Office: NY Mets Shea Stadium Roosevelt Ave & 126th St Flushing NY 11368*

WILSDON, THOMAS ARTHUR, product development engineer, administrator; b. Waterbury, Conn., Aug. 18, 1942; s. Arthur and Ruth (Wellington) W.; m. Yvonne Jeanne Pettit, June 19, 1964 (div. Apr. 1986); children: Thomas Charles, Beth Jeanne; m. Sharon Diann Culbertson, Feb. 14, 1988; children: Vandee Hyder, Jacklynn Hyder. BSEE, U. Conn., 1964; MBA, SUNY, Buffalo, 1978. Product design engr. Westinghouse Gen. Control Divsn., Buffalo, 1964-78; mgr. product devel. Westinghouse Control Divsn., Asheville, N.C., 1978-87; mgr. Advantage engrng. Westinghouse Elec. Components Divsn., Asheville, 1987-94; mgr. logic control products devel. engrng. Eaton/Cutler Hammer, Milw., 1994—. Mem. IEEE, NSPE, Am. Mgmt. Assn. Methodist. Achievements include development of low voltage AC and DC motor starters, Ampgard 7200V motor starter components, solid state controlled Advantage motor starters, PLC, DCI, sensor development, pushbuttons, limit switch, electronic product engineering. Home: PO Box 250 Pewaukee WI 53072-0250 Office: Eaton/Cutler Hammer 4201 N 27th St Milwaukee WI 53216-1807

WILSEY, PHILIP ARTHUR, computer science educator; b. Kewanee, Ill., Sept. 24, 1958; s. George A. and Mary Lee (Smith) W.; m. Marilyn L. Hargis, Jan. 2, 1982; children: Patrick A., Zackary E., Alexis L. BS in Math., Ill. State U., 1981; MS in Computer Sci., U. Southwestern La., 1985, PhD in Computer Sci., 1987. Computer programmer Union Ins. Group, Bloomington, Ill., 1980-81, Bob White Computing & Software, Bloomington, 1981-82; rsch. asst. Univ Southwestern La., Lafayette, La., 1983-87; asst. prof. U. Cin., 1987—; cons. MTL, Dayton, 1992—; mem. editorial bd. VLSI Design, 1993-95. Assoc. editor: Potentiais Mag., 1992—; contbr. articles to profl. jours. Mem. AAAS, IEEE, Assn. Computing Machinery. Home: 4654 Leadwell Ln Cincinnati OH 45242-7936 Office: Computer Architecture Design Lab Dept ECECS PO Box 210030 Cincinnati OH 45221-0030

WILSKE, KENNETH RAY, internist, rheumatologist, researcher; b. American Falls, Idaho, Jan. 4, 1935; s. Emil and Emelia (Levi) W.; m. Edna Janean Walsh, June 23, 1958; children: Lisa Janean, Ashley Renee, Kendell Colleen. BA in Biology, Coll. Idaho, 1955; MD with honors, U. Wash., Seattle, 1959. Diplomate Am. Bd. Internal Medicine, Am. Bd. Rheumatology. Intern in medicine Columbia Presbyn. Hosp., N.Y.C., 1959-60, asst. resident in medicine, 1960-61; asst. resident in medicine U. Wash., Seattle, 1961-62, postdoctoral rsch. fellow in arthritis, 1962-64; with Virginia Mason Clinic, Seattle, 1968—, chmn. continuing med. edn. com., 1968-78, head section allergy, immunology and rheumatic diseases, 1969—, dep. chief of medicine, staff physician, 1976—, mem. clin. pharmacology com., 1983—, co-chmn. ad hoc com. on establishment Ctr. for Asian & Internat. Memdine, 1984—; pres. bd. trustees and chmn. exec. com. Virgina Mason Rsch. Ctr., 1978-82, mem. long range planning com., other coms., 1979—; mem. pub. rels. and devel. com. Virgina Mason Med. Found., 1978—, bd. dirs., 1979—, v.p., 1984-86; clin. assoc. prof. medicine U. Wash., 1970; cons. arthritis Pub. Health Svc. Hosp., Seattle, VA Hosp., Seattle; cons. staff physician Univ. Hosp., Seattle; staff physician Harborview Hosp., St. Francis Xavier Hosp., Drs. Hosp., all Seattle; clin. prof. medicine U. Wash.; mem. nat. teaching faculty Merck, Sharp & Dohme, 1984-86; mem. arthritis adv. com. FDA, 1979; speaker, presenter, vis. lectr. numerous profl. orgns., symposia, confs. and hosps. U.S.A., Can., Buenos Aries, Prague, Czechoslovakia, Eng., Indonesia, Japan. Author: (with L.A. Healy, B.H. Hansen) Beyond the Copper Bracelet, 1972, (with Healey), Systemic Manifestation of Temporal Arteritis, 1978; contbr. numerous articles, revs. to profl. jours. Recipient Physicians Recognition award AMA, 1969. Fellow ACP, Am. Coll. Rheumatologists; mem. N.W. Soc. Clin. Rsch. (pres. 1972), N.W. Rheumatism Soc. (pres. 1970), N.W. Med. Assn., N. Pacific Soc. Internal Medicine (prgram com. 1977-79), Am. Rheumatism Assn. (program com., chmn. local arrangements Western sect. 1983, mem. nat. exec. com. 1974-76), Am. Group Practice Assn. (continuing med. edn. com. 1971-76), Am. Soc. Clin. Rheumatology, Am. Soc. Rheumatology, Wash. State Med. Assn. (various coms. 1974-78, liaison sub-com. Bd. Med. Axaminers 1978, Aesculapius award 1967), Seattle Acad. Internal Medicine, King County Med. Soc. (trustee 1979-81, jud. coun. 1984), Arthritis Found. (bd. dirs. and exec. com. 1974-76, bd. dirs. Western Wash. chpt. 1965—, mem. med. and sci. com. 1965—, Disting. Svc. award 1966), Pacific Interurban Clin. Club, U. Wash. Med. Alumni Assn. (sec./treas. 1977, exec. com. 1977-79, pres. 1978). Home: 6529 NE Windermere Rd Seattle WA 98105-2057 Office: Virginia Mason Clinic 1000 9th Ave Seattle WA 98104-1227

WILSNACK, ROGER E., retired medical association administrator. Dir. Becton Dickinson Rsch. Ctr., Research Triangle Park, N.C.; ret., 1997. Office: Becton Dickinson & Co Becton Dickinson Rsch Ctr PO Box 12016 Research Triangle Park NC 27709-2016

WILSON, AARON MARTIN, religious studies educator, college executive; b. Bazette, Tex., Sept. 30, 1926; s. John Albert and Myrtle (Hulsey) W.; m. Marthel Shoults, Jan. 31, 1947; children: Gloria Dallis, John Bert. BA, So. Bible Coll., 1963, DD (hon.), 1980; MA, Pitts. State U., 1972; PhD, Valley Christian U., 1980. Pastor various chs., 1947-58, Pentecostal Ch. of God, Houston, 1958-64, Pentacostal Ch. of God, Modesto, Calif., 1985-88; nat. dir. Christian edn. Pentecostal Ch. of God, Joplin, Mo., 1964-79, 88-93; pres. Evang. Christian Ch., Fresno, Calif., 1979-85; v.p. devel. Messenger Coll., Joplin, 1993-95; editor The Pentecostal Messenger, Joplin, 1995—; treas. Evang. Curriculum Commn., 1988-93; prof. So. Bible Coll., Houston, 1962-64. Author: Basic Bible Truth, 1988, Studies on Stewardship, 1989, My Church Can Grow, 1996. Republican. Home: 4701 Connecticut Ave Joplin MO 64804-5147 Office: Messenger Publ House PO Box 850 Joplin MO 64802-0850

WILSON, ADDISON GRAVES (JOE WILSON), lawyer, state senator; b. Charleston, S.C., July 31, 1947; s. Hugh deVeaux and Wray Smart (Graves) W.; m. Roxanne Dusenbury McCrory, Dec. 30, 1977; children—Michael Alan, Addison Graves, Julian Dusenbury, Hunter Taylor. B.A., Washington and Lee U., 1969; J.D., U. S.C.-Columbia, 1972. Bar: S.C. 1972. Staff mem. Sen. Strom Thurmond, Washington, 1967, Congressman Floyd Spence, Columbia, S.C., 1970-72; ptnr. Kirkland, Wilson, Moore, Allen, Taylor & O'Day and predecessor, West Columbia, S.C., 1972—; dep. gen. counsel U.S. Energy Sec. Jim Edwards, Washington, 1981-82; bd. dirs. NationsBank, Lexington, S.C.; senator State of S.C., Columbia, 1984—; presdl. appointee to Intergovtl. Adv. Coun. on Edn., 1990-91; mem. Internat. Observation Del. for 1990 Bulgarian parliamentary election. Campaign mgr. Congressman Floyd Spence, Columbia, 1974, 78, 80, 82; dist. campaign mgr. Gov. Carroll Campbell, 1986; vice chmn. S.C. Republican Party, 1972-74 . Served to lt. col. USNG, 1975—. Presbyterian. Lodges: Rotary, Masons, Shriners. Home: 2825 Wilton Rd Springdale SC 29170 Office: Kirkland Wilson Moore Allen Taylor & O'Day 1700 Sunset Blvd West Columbia SC 29169-5940 also: PO Box 5709 West Columbia SC 29171-5709

WILSON, ALLAN BYRON, graphics company executive; b. Jackson, Miss., Aug. 19, 1948; s. Allen Bernice Wilson and Mary Pickering (Levereault) W.; m. Ines Ghinato, May 19, 1975; 1 child, Lucas Ghinato. B.S., Rice U., 1970, M.S. in Elec. Engring., 1971. Systems adminstr. Max Planck Institut für Kohlenforschung, Mülheim Ruhr, Fed. Republic Germany, 1971; systems programmer Digital Equipment Corp., Maynard, Mass., 1972-74, mktg. specialist, 1974-75, mktg. mgr., 1976-79; internat. ops. dir. Intergraph Corp., Huntsville, Ala., 1980-82, v.p. corp. and internat. ops., 1982-83, exec. v.p., 1983—. Contbr. articles to profl. jours. Mem. Assn. for Computing Machinery, IEEE. Home: PO Box 6607 Huntsville AL 35824-0607 Office: Intergraph Corp Huntsville AL 35894-0001

WILSON, ALMA, state supreme court justice; b. Pauls Valley, Okla.; d. William R. and Anna L. (Schuppert) Bell; m. William A. Wilson, May 30, 1948 (dec. Mar. 1994); 1 child, Lee Anne. AB, U. Okla., 1939, JD, 1941, LLD (hon.), 1992. Bar: Okla. 1941. Sole practice Muskogee, Okla., 1941-43; sole practice Oklahoma City, 1943-47, Pauls Valley, 1948-69; judge Pauls Valley Mcpl. Ct., 1967-68; apptd. spl. judge Garvin & McLain Counties, Norman, Okla., 1969-75; dist. judge Cleveland County, Norman, Okla., 1975-79; justice Okla. Supreme Ct., Oklahoma City, 1982—, now chief justice, 1995-96. Mem. alumni bd. dirs. U. Okla.; mem. Assistance League; trustee Univ.Okla. Meml. Union. Recipient Guy Brown award, 1974, Woman of Yr. award Norman Bus. and Profl. Women, 1975, Okla. Women's Hall of Fame award, 1983, Okla Hall of Fame, 1996, Pauls Valley Hall of Fame, 1997, Pioneer Woman award, 1985, Disting. Svc. Citation U. Okla., 1985. Mem. AAUW, Garvin County Bar Assn. (past pres.), Okla. Bar Assn. (co-chmn. law and citizenship edn. com.), Okla. Trial Lawyers Assn. (Appellate Judge of Yr. 1986, 89), Altrusa, Am. Legion Aux. Office: Okla Supreme Ct State Capitol Rm 204 Oklahoma City OK 73105

WILSON, ALMON CHAPMAN, surgeon, physician, retired naval officer; b. Hudson Falls, N.Y., July 13, 1924; s. Almon Chapman and Edith May (Truesdale) W.; m. Sofia M. Bogdons, Jan. 24, 1945; 1 child, Geoffrey Peter. B.A., Union Coll., Schenectady, 1946; M.D., Albany Med. Coll., 1952; M.S., George Washington U., 1969; student, Naval War Coll., Newport, R.I., 1968-69. Diplomate: Am. Bd. Surgery. Served as enlisted man and officer U.S. Navy, 1943-46, lt. j.g., M.C., 1952, advanced through grades to rear adm., 1976; intern U.S. Naval Hosp., Bremerton, Wash., 1952-53; resident VA Hosp., Salt Lake City, 1954-58; chief of surgery Sta. Hosp. Naval Sta., Subic Bay, Philippines, 1959-61; staff surgeon Naval Hosp., San Diego, 1961-64; asst. chief surgery Naval Hosp., Chelsea, Mass., 1964-65; comdg. officer 3d Med. Bn., 3d Marine Div. Fleet Marine Force, Pacific, Vietnam, 1965-66; chief surgery Naval Hosp., Yososuka, Japan, 1966-68; assigned Naval War Coll., 1968-69; fleet med. officer, comdr. in chief U.S. Naval Forces, Europe; sr. med. officer Naval Activities London, 1969-71; dep. dir. planning div. Bur. Medicine and Surgery Navy Dept., Washington, 1971-72; dir. planning div. Navy Dept., 1972-74; with additional duty as med. adv. to dep. chief naval ops. (logistics) and personal physician to chmn. Joint Chiefs of Staff, 1972-74; comdg. officer Naval Hosp., Great Lakes, Ill., 1974-76; asst. chief for material resources Bur. Medicine and Surgery Navy Dept., Washington, 1976-79; comdg. officer (Navy Health Scis. Edn. and Tng. Command), 1979-80; the med. officer U.S. Marine Corps., 1980-81, project mgr. Fleet Hosp. Programs, 1981-82; dir. Resources Div., 1982-83; dep. dir. naval medicine, dep. surgeon gen. Dept. Navy, 1983-84; ret., 1984; mem. grad. med. edn. adv. com. Dept. Def. Decorated Legion of Merit with gold V (2 stars), Meritorious Service medal, Joint Service Commendation medal. Fellow ACS (gov.); mem. Assn. Mil. Surgeons U.S.

WILSON, ALPHUS DAN, plant pathologist, researcher; b. Ft. Worth, Tex., Sept. 27, 1958; s. Alphus James and Essie Morris (Nugent) W.; m. Lisa Beth Forse, July 11, 1992; 1 child, Jon Colter. BS in Bioenviron. Sci., Tex. A&M U., 1981, MS in Plant Pathology, 1983; PhD in Plant Pathology, Wash. State U., 1988. Grad. rsch. asst. Tex. A&M U., College Station, 1981-83, Wash. State U., Pullman, 1984-88; postdoctoral plant pathologist USDA-Agrl. Rsch. Svc., Pullman, 1989-90, rsch. plant pathologist, 1990-91; rsch. plant pathologist USDA-Forest Svc., Stoneville, Miss., 1991-95, prin. rsch. pathologist, 1996—; tech. cons. Tex. Oak Wilt Suppression Adv. Bd., Austin, 1992—, Tex. Forest Svc. Strategic Plan Team, Austin, 1994—. Author: (chpt.) Systematics, Ecology, and Evolution of Endophytic fungi in Grasses and Woody Plants, 1996; contbr. articles to profl. jours. Project judge Delta Regional Sci. Fair, Greenville, Miss., 1992; sci. demonstrator Delta Schs. Sci. Awareness Day, Stoneville, 1993. Recipient fellowship Chevron Chem. Corp., 1981-83, Rsch. fellowship Wash. State U., 1984-88. Mem. AAAS, N.Y. Acad. Scis., Am. Phytopathological Soc., Mycol. Soc. Am., Soc. Am. Foresters, Alpha Zeta. Republican. Methodist. Achievements include discovery of genetic system controlling mating incompatibility in the Indian paint fungus, E. tinctorium; discovery of endosymbiotic Acremonium endophytes in wild Hordeum cereal grass species; development of Giemsa protocol for permanent nuclear staining of fungi; discovery of genetic system controlling sexual incompatibility in the chickpea blight fungus, D. rabiei. Avocations: fly fishing, backpacking, exploring wilderness areas, snow skiing, photography, hunting. Home: 2202 Highway 1 N Greenville MS 38703-9471 Office: USDA Forest Svc So Hardwoods Lab PO Box 227 Stoneville MS 38776

WILSON, ANNE GAWTHROP, artist, educator; b. Detroit, Apr. 16, 1949; d. Gerald Shepard and Nancy Craighead (Gawthrop) Wilson; m. Michael Andreas Nagelbach. Student, U. Mich. Sch. of Art, 1967-69; BFA, Cranbrook Acad. Art, Bloomfield Hills, Mich., 1972; MFA, Calif. Coll. Arts and Crafts, 1976. Chair textile dept. The De Young Mus. Art Sch., San Francisco, 1973-78; prof. fiber dept. Sch. of the Art Inst., Chgo., 1979—; adj. instr. Calif. Coll. Arts and Crafts, Oakland, Calif., 1975-78; panelist Nat. Endowment for Arts, Washington, 1986, Western States Arts Fedn./ Nat. Endowment for Arts Regional Fellowships for Visual Artists, Santa Fe, 1995; co-curator Artemisia Gallery, Chgo., 1988; juror Fiber Nat. '90, Adams Art Gallery, Dunkirk, N.Y., 1990; co-moderator Women's Caucus for Art, Chgo., 1992; panelist, workshop instr. Internat. Symposium '92, Toyama, Japan, 1992; panelist The Textile Mus., Washington, 1994; bd. trustees Haystack Sch., Deer Isle, Maine, 1990-95; artists adv. bd. Kohler Arts Ctr., Sheboygan, Wis., 1994—; lectr. Kansas City Art Inst., 1996, Australian Nat. U. Canberra Sch. Art, 1996, Textile Conservation Ctr./ Courtauld Inst. Art, London, 1995, others. One person shows include Chgo. Pub. Libr. Cultural Ctr., Randolph Gallery, 1988, Roy Boyd Gallery, Chgo., 1994, Halsey Gallery, Sch. of Arts, Coll. Charleston, S.C., 1992, Madison (Wis.) Art Ctr., 1993-94, Ill. Wesleyan U., Bloomington, Ill., 1995; exhibited in group shows Netherlands Textile Mus., 1989, Musee Cantonal des Beaux-Arts, Palais de Rumine, Lausanne, Switzerland, 1989, Gallery and Mus., Newhouse Ctr. for Contemporary Art, Snug Harbor Cultural Ctr., S.I., N.Y., 1991, Calif. Coll. Arts and Crafts, Oakland, Calif., 1992, John Michael Kohler Arts Ctr., Sheboygan, Wis., 1992-93, Art Inst. of Chgo., 1993, Textile Mus., Washington, 1994, Gallery 2, Chgo., 1994, Hyde Park Art Ctr., Chgo., 1994, Cranbrook Acad. Art Mus., Bloomfield Hills, 1994-95, Ariz. State U. Art Mus., Tempe, 1997, REVOLUTION, Detroit, 1997, Mus. Contemporary Art, Chgo., 1996-97, City Gallery at Chastain, Atlanta, 1995; represented in permanent collections Calif. Poly. State U., San Luis Obispo, Calif., Robert L. Kidd Assocs., Inc., Birmingham, Mich., Sandoz Crop Protection Corp., Chgo., M. H. De Young Meml. Mus., San Francisco, Art Inst. Chgo., Cranbrook Acad. Art Mus., Bloomfield Hills; contbr. articles and revs. to profl. jours. Recipient Louis Comfort Tiffany Found. award, 1989; Nat. Endowment for Arts curatorial fellow in decorative arts and mus. edn. Fine Arts Mus. San Francisco, 1978; Nat. Endowment for Arts Visual Artists Fellowship grantee, 1982, 88, Chgo. Artists Abroad grantee, 1988, 89, Ill. Arts Coun. Individual Artist grantee, 1983, 84, 87, 93, Chgo. Artists Internat. Program grantee, 1996. Office: Sch of the Art Inst Fiber Dept 37 S Wabash Ave Chicago IL 60603-3017

WILSON, ARCHIE FREDRIC, medical educator; b. L.A., May 7, 1931; s. Louis H. and Ruth (Kert) W.; m. Tamar Braverman, Feb. 11, 1937; children: Lee A., Daniel B. BA, UCLA, 1953, PhD, 1967; MD, U. Calif., San Francisco, 1957. Intern L.A. County Gen. Hosp., 1957-58; resident U. Calif., San Francisco, 1958-61; fellow in chest disease dept. medicine UCLA, 1966-67, asst. prof., 1967-70; asst. prof. U. Calif., Irvine, 1970-73, assoc. prof., 1973-79, prof., 1979—. Editor: Pulmonary Function Test: Interpretation, 1986; contbr. articles to profl. jours. Bd. mem. Am. Lung Assn., Orange County, 1970-90, Am. Heart Assn., Calif., 1990—. Capt. USMC, 1961-63. Mem. Am. Fedn. Clin. Rsch., Western Soc. Clin. Investigation. Office: Univ Calif 101 The City Dr S Orange CA 92868-3201

WILSON, ARTHUR JESS, psychologist; b. Yonkers, N.Y., Oct. 25, 1910; s. Samuel Louis and Anna (Gilbert) W.; BS, NYU, 1935, MA, 1949, PhD, 1961; LLB, St. Lawrence U., 1940; JD, Bklyn. Law Sch., 1967; m. Lillian Moss, Sept. 16, 1941; children—Warren David, Anton Francis. Tchr., Yonkers Pub. Schs., 1935-40; dir. adult edn. Yonkers, 1940-42; supr. vocat. rehab. N.Y. State Dept. Edn., 1942-44; personnel exec. Abraham & Straus, Bklyn., 1946-47; rehab. field sec. N.Y. Tb and Health Assn., 1947-48; dir. rehab. Westchester County Med. Center, Valhalla, N.Y., 1948-67; dir. Manhattan Narcotic Rehab. Center, N.Y. State Drug Abuse Control Commn., 1967-68; clin. psychologist VA Hosp., Montrose, N.Y., 1968-73; pvt. practice clin. psychology, Yonkers, 1973—; cons. N.Y. State Dept. Edn., HEW; spl. lectr. Sch. Pub. Health and Adminstrv. Medicine, Columbia U. and Grad. Sch., N.Y. U.; instr. Westchester Community Coll., Valhalla, N.Y.; selected participant Clin. Study Tour of China, 1980. With USN, 1944-46. Recipient Founders Day award NYU, 1961. Mem. APA, Internat. Mark Twain Soc. (hon.), N.Y. Acad. Scis., N.Y. State Psychol. Assn., Internat. Platform Assn. (selected mem.), Kappa Delta Pi, Phi Delta Kappa, Epsilon Pi Tau. Author: The Emotional Life of the Ill and Injured, 1950; A Guide to the Genius of Cardozo, 1939; The Wilson Teaching Inventory, 1941; also articles. Honored as Westchester Author, Westchester County Hist. Soc., 1957. Home and Office: 4121 NW 88th Ave Apt 204 Coral Springs FL 33065-1820 also: 487 Park Ave Yonkers NY 10703-2121

WILSON, AUGUST, playwright; b. Pitts., 1945; s. David Bedford (stepfather) and Daisy Wilson; 1 child, Sakina Ansari. Founder Black Horizons Theatre Co., Pitts., 1968; script writer Sci. Mus. of Minn., 1979. Author: (playwright) The Homecoming, 1979, The Coldest Day of the Year, 1979, Fullerton Street, 1980, Black Bart and the Sacred Hills, 1981, Jitney, 1982, Ma Rainey's Black Bottom, 1984 (N.Y. Drama Critics Circle award for best play 1985, Tony award nomination for best play 1985, Whiting Writers' award 1986), Fences, 1985 (Am. Theatre Critics Outstanding Play award 1986, Drama Desk award for outstanding new play 1986, N.Y. Drama Critics' Circle award for best play 1986, Pulitzer Prize for drama 1987, Tony award for best play 1987, Outer Critics' Circle award for best play 1987), Joe Turner's Come and Gone, 1986 (N.Y. Drama Critics Circle award for best play 1988, Tony award nomination for best play 1988), The Piano Lesson, 1987 (Drama Desk award for outstanding new play 1990, N.Y. Drama Critics' Circle award for best play 1990, Pulitzer Prize for drama 1990, Tony award nomination for best play 1990, Am. Theatre Critics Outstanding Play award 1990), Two Trains Running, 1990 (Am. Theatre Critics Assn. award 1992, N.Y. Drama Critics Circle award for best play 1992, Tony award nomination for best play 1992), Seven Guitars, 1995 (N.Y. Drama Critics Cir. award 1996, Tony nomination Best Play 1996). Recipient John Gassner Best Am. Playwright award Outer Critics Circle, 1987; named Artist of Yr., Chgo. Tribune, 1987, Literary Lion award N.Y. Pub. Libr., 1988. Mem. AAAL. Office: care John Breglio Paul Weiss Rifkind Wharton & Garrison 1285 Avenue Of The Americas New York NY 10019-6028

WILSON, BARBARA LOUISE, communications executive; b. Bremerton, Wash., Aug. 3, 1952; d. Algernon Frances and Dorothy Virginia (Martin) W.; m. Ashby A. Riley III, Feb. 7, 1979 (div. Dec. 1983). BA in Fin. and Econs., U. Puget Sound, 1974; MBA, U. Wash., Seattle, 1985. With Pacific N.W. Bell, Seattle and Portland, Oreg., 1974-86, divsn. mgr. pub. comm., 1983-85, asst. v.p., exec. dir. number svcs. mktg., 1985-86; v.p. implementation planning US West, Inc., Englewood, Colo., 1986-87; pres. US West Info. Systems, Englewood, 1987-89; v.p. govt. and edn. svcs. US West Comm., Englewood, 1989; v.p. human resources U.S. West Comm., Denver, 1989-92; v.p., chief exec. officer Idaho state U.S. West Communications, Boise, 1992—, regional v.p., Idaho v.p., 1993—; bd. dirs. U.S. West New Vector Group, Bellevue, Wash., 1988-90, U.S. Bank Idaho, Idaho Bus. Coun.; audit com. chair U.S. Bank; chair nat. adv. com. Tel. Pioneers Am., N.Y.C., 1989; chair adv. bd. Coll. Bus. and Boise State U., 1994-96, mem. adv. bd., 1996—. Bd. dirs., mem. exec. com. Wash. Coun. for Edn., Seattle, 1985-86; team capt. major gifts com. Boys and Girls Club, Seattle, 1986; chairperson co. campaign United Way, Seattle, 1985; bd. dirs. Denver Arts Ctr. Found., 1989-91; bd. advisors U. Wash. Exec. MBA Program, 1991-93; mem. adv. bd. Boise State U. Sch. Bus.; mem. bd. Boise State U. Found. Mem. adv. bd. Boise State U. Sch. Bus.; bd. mem. Mountain States Med. Rsch. Inst.; bd. dirs. Bouse State U. Found., U.S. Bank, Bishop Kelly Found., St. Luke's Regional Med. Ctr.; mem. Gov.'s Econ. Stimulus Com. Mem. Idaho Bus. Coun. (bd. dirs., chair-elect), Idaho Assn. Commerce and Industry (vice chmn. bd. dirs. 1992—), Boise C. of C. (bd. dirs. 1992—), Arid Club Boise. Roman Catholic. Avocations: golf, snow skiing, travel, boating. Office: US West Communications 999 Main St Fl 11 Boise ID 83702-9001

WILSON, BARBARA MITCHELL, nurse; b. Daytona Beach, Fla., July 11, 1962; d. Joe Hamilton and Mary Joyce (Clark) Mitchell; m. Timothy Steve Wilson, Sept. 24, 1983; children: Michael Timothy, Elizabeth Alene. Diploma, Piedmont Hosp. Sch. Nursing, 1983. RN, CNOR, CRNFA. Nursing asst. Gwinnett Hosp. Sys., Lawrenceville, Ga., 1978-80; staf nurse Piedmont Hosp., Atlanta, 1983-84; staf nurse Gwinnett Hosp. Sys., 1984—, nurse neurosurgery resource, 1984-93, nurse trauma resource, oper. rm., 1991-95, educator oper. rm. nursing, 1994-95; RN, 1st asst. pvt. practice, Atlanta, 1994—; cons. in field. Mem. AORN, ANA, RN First Asst Splty. Assembly (edn. com. 1994-95, governing coun. 1995-98, sec. 1995-96, election coord. 1996-98), RN First Assts. Ga. (sec./treas. 1995-97), Ga. Nurses Assn. Baptist. Avocations: family, camping, horses. Home: 415 Clark Lake Estates Grayson GA 30017

WILSON, BARBARA T., physical education educator; b. Pisgah, Ala., June 5, 1944; d. Jesse Leroy and Lillie Belle (Long) Tinker; m. Jimmy Dale Wilson, June 30, 1963; childern: Eric Dale, Christopher, Chadwick, Jeremy Lance. BS in Heatlh Phys. Edn., Biology, Jacksonville State U., 1967; MS in Health Phys. Edn., U. Ala., 1969, EdS Heatlh Edn., 1980. Cert. tchr. Tchr. Calhoun County Bd. Edn., Anniston, Ala., 1967-74, Jacksonville (Ala.) State U., 1974—. Author: Aqua Robics, 1991; co-author: Curriculum Voices, 1986; editor Jacksonville State U. H.P.E.R. Alumni newsletter, 1993-95. Mem. AAHPERD, NEA, Coll. Assn. Health, Phys. Edn., Recreation and Dance (sec., treas. 1986-87, 84-85, pres. elect 1994-95, pres. 1995—), Ala. Assn. Health, Phys. Edn., Recreation and Dance, Ala. Edn. Assn., Delta Kappa Gamma (pres. Beta Phi chpt. 1996—, dist. II dir.). Avocations: jogging, ceramics, gardening, cooking, traveling. Office: Jacksonville State U Pete Mathews Coliseum Jacksonville AL 36265

WILSON, BARRY WILLIAM, biology educator; b. Bklyn., Aug. 20, 1931; s. Albert Abraham Wilson and Ethel (Lubart) Bedsow; m. Joyce Ann Sisson, June 7, 1957; 1 child, Sean. BA, U. Chgo., 1950; BS, MS, Ill. Inst. Tech., 1957; PhD, UCLA, 1962. Asst. prof. biology U. Calif., Davis, 1962-1972, prof. avian sci. and environ. toxicology, 1972—, chmn. dept. Avian scis., 1991-96; mem. drug task force Muscular Dystrophy Assn., N.Y.C., 1980—; councilor NeuroToxicology subsect. Soc. Toxicology, Washington, 1985-86; pres. Calif. br. Tissue Culture Assn., Washington, 1978; mem. editorial bd. NeuroToxicology, Little Rock, 1986-91; ad hoc mem. NIH Toxicology Study Sect., Washington, 1985; mem. EPA sci. adv. panel Cholinesterase, 1989—; chair EPA Cholinesterase Methodologies Workshop, 1991. Editor: Birds: Readings From Science American, 1980; assoc. editor Bulletin Environ. Contamination and Toxicology, 1990—; contbr. numerous articles to profl. jours. Mem. Am. Physiol. Soc., Am. Soc. Cell Biology, Am. Ornithologists Union, Soc. Neurosci., Soc. Toxicology, Soc. Environ. Toxicology and Chemistry, Tissue Culture Assn., Soc. Devel. Biology, Am. Chem. Soc., Soc. for In Vitro Biology. Avocations: bird watching, photography, music. Office: U Calif Dept Avian Scis Davis CA 95616

WILSON, BEN, elementary school principal. Prin. Ingleside Sch., Athens, Tenn. Recipient Elem. Sch. Recognition award U.S. Dept. Edn., 1989-90. Office: Ingleside Sch 600 Guille St Athens TN 37303*

WILSON, BENJAMIN FRANKLIN, JR., education educator; b. Shreveport, La., Aug. 13, 1933; s. Benjamin Franklin Wilson and Charlotte (Cornman) Dudley; m. Verna Chorine Walker, May 21, 1953; children: Carolyn Coleith, Cynthia Denise, Ben Edward. BS, U. Houston, 1956, MEd, 1964; PhD, Nat. Christian U., 1974; DEd, Baylor U., 1977. Cert. tchr., adminstr., counselor, vocat. counselor, Tex.; lic. profl. counselor, Tex. Tchr., counselor Houston Ind. Sch. Dist., 1957-65; dir. guidance and counseling Gary Job Corps, San Marcos, Tex., 1965-73; disability examiner Tex. Vocat. Rehab. Commn., Austin, 1973-74; asst. prof. edn. Southwest Tex. State U., San Marcos, 1974-79; counselor Hays Consolidated Ind. Sch. Dist., Buda, Tex., 1979-81; asst. supt., elem. prin., jr. h.s. prin. Pearsall (Tex.) Ind. Sch. Dist., 1981-89; prof. edn. Sul Ross State U, Rio Grande Coll., Rio Grande College Uvalde, Tex., 1989—; edn. cons. Contbr. articles to profl. jours. V.p. Save America's Vital Environment; mem. Prairie Lea (Tex.) Ind. Sch. Dist. Sch. Bd., 1967-74. 2d lt. USMCR, 1956. Mem. ACA, Am. Assn. Sch. Adminstrs., AF&AM Prairie Lea Lodge #114, Gonzales Commandery # 30, OES Wimberley Chpt. # 1130, Phi Delta Kappa (treas. 1976). Avocations: travel, writing poetry, fishing, hunting, crafts. Home: HCR 34 Box 1016 Uvalde TX 78801 Office: Sul Ross State U Rio Grande Coll 400 Sul Ross Dr Uvalde TX 78801-6907

WILSON, BENJAMIN FRANKLIN, JR., steamship agency executive; b. Balt., Dec. 29, 1945; s. Benjamin Franklin and Priscilla Lee (Harris) W.; m. Brenda Gay Zonn, June 8, 1968; children: Jeanine Carol, Shawn David. Degree in bus. mgmt., Johns Hopkins U., 1972. Asst. mgr. ops. Lavino Shipping Svcs., Balt., 1969-82, ops. mgr., 1982-89, pt. mgr., 1989-92; v.p. East Coast Inchcape Shipping Svcs., Balt., 1992—; mem. agts. com. Steamship Trade Assn., Balt., 1970-89. Chmn. bd. deacons Weems Creek Bapt. Ch., Annapolis, Md., 1991-94; treas. Annapolis H.S. Band, 1988-92. Recipient award for 2,000 hours of vol. svc. Bd. Edn. Anne Arundel County, 1992. Mem. Balt. Maritime Assn., Propeller Club (mng. bd. dirs. 1989-92). Republican. Baptist. Avocations: computers, fishing, sports memorabilia. Home: 1839 Brett Ct Annapolis MD 21401

WILSON, BETTY MAY, resort company executive; b. Moberly, Mo., Mar. 13, 1947; d. Arthur Bunyon and Martha Elizabeth (Denham) Stephens; m. Ralph Felix Martin, Aug. 22, 1970 (div. May 1982); m. Gerald Robert Wilson Sr., Mar. 3, 1984; stepchildren: Gerald Robert Jr., Heather Lynn, Jeffrey Michael. BS in Acctg. and Bus. Adminstrn., Colo. State U., 1969. CPA, Mo. Tax mgr. Arthur Andersen and Co., St. Louis, 1969-75; v.p., asst. sec., dir. taxes ITT Fin. Corp., St. Louis, 1975-95; v.p. taxes Caesars World, Inc., Las Vegas, Nev., 1995—; sr. v.p., bd. dirs. Lyndon Ins. Co., St. Louis, 1977-95, ITT Lyndon Life Ins. Co., ITT Lyndon Property Ins. Co., St. Louis, 1977-95. Mem. AICPA, Nev. Soc. CPAs, Am. Fin. Svcs. Assn. (chmn. tax com. 1987-88), Tax Execs. Inst. (chmn. corp. tax mgmt. com. 1993-95, regional v.p. 1995-96, exec. com. 1995-96, treas., 1997-98, bd. dirs. St. Louis chpt., past sec., past pres.), Mo. Girls Racing Assn. (pres. 1977-82). Baptist. Avocations: country western dancing, Harley Davidson motorcycles. Office: Caesars World Inc 3800 Howard Hughes Pkwy Las Vegas NV 89109-0925

WILSON, BLENDA JACQUELINE, academic administrator; b. Woodbridge, N.J., Jan. 28, 1941; d. Horace and Margaret (Brogsdale) Wilson; m. Louis Fair Jr. AB, Cedar Crest Coll., 1962; AM, Seton Hall U., 1965; PhD, Boston Coll., 1979; DHL (hon.), Cedar Crest Coll., 1987, Loretto Heights Coll., 1988, Colo. Tech. Coll., 1988, U. Detroit, 1989; LLD (hon.), Rutgers U., 1989, Ea. Mich. U., 1990, Cambridge Coll., 1991, Schoolcraft Coll., 1992. Tchr. Woodbridge Twp. Pub. Schs., 1962-66; exec. dir. Middlesex County Econ. Opportunity Corp., New Brunswick, N.J., 1966-69; exec. asst. to pres. Rutgers U., New Brunswick, N.J., 1969-72; sr. assoc. dean Grad. Sch. Edn. Harvard U., Cambridge, Mass., 1972-82; v.p. effective sector mgmt. Ind. Sector, Washington, 1982-84; exec. dir. Colo. Commn. Higher Edn., Denver, 1984-88; chancellor and prof. pub. adminstrn. & edn. U. Mich., Dearborn, 1988-92; pres. Calif. State U., Northridge, 1992—; Am. del. U.S./U.K. Dialogue About Quality Judgments in Higher Edn.; adv. bd. Mich. Consolidated Gas Co., Stanford Inst. Higher Edn. Rsch., U. So. Col. Dist. 60 Nat. Alliance, Nat. Ctr. for Rsch. to Improve Postsecondary Teaching and Learning, 1988-90; bd. dirs. Alpha Capital Mgmt.; mem. higher edn. colloquium Am. Coun. Edn., vis. com. Divsn. Continuing Edn. in Faculty of Arts & Scis., Harvard Coll., Pew Forum on K-12 Edn. Reform in U.S. Dir. U. Detroit Jesuit High Sch., Northridge Hosp. Med. Ctr., Arab Cmty. Ctr. for Econ. and Social Svcs., Union Bank, J. Paul Getty Trust, James Irvine Found., Internat. Found. Edn. and Self-Help, Achievement Coun., L.A.; dir., vice chair Met. Affairs Corp.; exec. bd. Detroit area coun. Boy Scouts Am.; bd. dirs. Commonwealth Fund, Henry Ford Hosp.-Fairlane Ctr., Henry Ford Health System, Met. Ctr. for High Tech., United Way Southeastern Mich.; mem. Nat. Coalition 100 Black Women, Detroit, Race Rels. Coun. Met. Detroit, Women & Founds., Greater Detroit Interfaith Round Table NCCJ, Adv. Bd. Valley Cultural Ctr., Woodland Hills; trustee assoc. Boston Coll.; trustee emeritus Cambridge Coll.; trustee emeritus, bd. dirs. Found. Ctr.; trustee Henry Ford Mus. & Greenfield Village, Sammy Davis Jr. Nat. Liver Inst. Mem. AAUW, Assn. Governing Bds. (adv. coun. of pres.'s), Edn. Commn. of the States (student minority task force), Am. Assn. Higher Edn. (chair-elect), Am. Assn. State Colls. & Univs. (com. on policies & purposes, acad. leadership fellows selection com.), Assn. Black Profls. and Adminstrs., Assn. Black Women in Higher Edn., Women Execs. State Govt., Internat. Women's Forum, Mich. Women's Forum, Women's Econ. Club Detroit, Econ. Club, Rotary. Office: Calif State Univ Office of President 18111 Nordhoff St Northridge CA 91330-0001

WILSON, BRANDON LAINE, writer, advertising and public relations consultant, explorer; b. Sewickley, Pa., Oct. 2, 1953; s. Edgar C. and Mary Beth (Tuttle) W.; m. Cheryl Ann Keefe, June 23, 1989. BA, U. N.C., 1973; Cert. Am. Acad. Dramatic Arts, 1974. actor stage mgr., lighting, Red Barn Theatre, Little Patriot Theatre, Pittsburgh, 1969-70, actor, Carolina Playmakers, Chapel Hill, 1971-73, Asst. acct. exec. Hill & Knowlton Pub. Rels., Pitts., 1973; dir. video Seattle Repertory Theatre/2d Stage Theatre, 1975-76; asst. dir., videographer pub. broadcasting Network, Chapel Hill, 1976-77, wrote 7 long-format videos for Sheraton Hotels Hawaii, Japan, wrote and produce numerous TV comml.; dir. advt. and TV Prodn. N.Am. Films, Eugene, Oreg., 1977-79; gen. mgr. Boulder Community Coops., 1980-81; pub. info. officer, asst. to mayor City of Barrow, Alaska, 1981-82; dir. advt. and promotion Anchorage Conv. and Visitors Bur., Anchorage, 1983-85; mgr. mktg. communications GTE, Honolulu, 1986-87; v.p., sr. copywriter, producer Peck, Sims, Mueller Advt. (NW Ayer affiliate), Honolulu, 1987-89; pres., creative dir. Wilson & Assoc., Inc., Hawaii, 1987—, pres. Brandon Wilson Lit. Svcs., 1991—. Author: Dead Men Don't Leave Tips - A Couple's Trans-African Odyssey, 1991, Yak Butter Blues, 1994; prin. works (TV) include The General Assembly Today, 1976-77, (films) Sasquatch, Mystery of the Sacred Shroud, Buffalo Rider; (Theatre) L'Histoire du Soldat Benito Cereno made for TV, One Flew over the Cuckoo's Nest, Street Car Named Desire, Suddenly Last Summer, Rose Tattoo, Typist and the Tiger, Star Sprangled Girl, Everything in the Garden, Period of Adjustment, Any Wednesday, The Great Soc.; contbr. articles to nat. mags. and newspapers. Named Eagle Scout Boy Scouts Am., one of Exceptionally Able Youth, 1970, Literary award U. Pitts., 1970, one of Outstanding Young Men in Am., 1986, Men of Achievement award U.K., 1987, 93, Dict. of Internat. Biography, U.K., 1993; recipient Order of the Arrow, two Ike Pono Gold awards Internat. TV Assn., 6 creative advt. awards. Mem. (accreditation) PRSA, Soc. of Friends, Mensa, Internat. Campaign for Tibet, Amnesty Internat. Journeyed length of Africa overland (Ceuta to Cape Town), 1990; half of first western couple to hike Himalayas from Lhasa, Tibet to Kathmandu, Nepal, 1992; climbed Mt. Nyragongo, Zaire, Mt. Kilimanjaro, Tanzania, Mt. Olympus, Greece, Mt. Everest Base Camp, Tibet, Mt Miyajima, Japan, Crough Patrick, Ireland, Te Rua Manga, Rarotonga, Mt. Zeus, Greece; rafted down the Zambezi River; tracked mountain gorillas in Zaire; journeyed overland across C.Am.; explored Eastern Europe, 1989; hiked Alps and Tyrennes, 1996.

WILSON, BRIAN DOUGLAS, recording artist, composer, record producer; b. Inglewood, Calif., June 20, 1942; s. Murry Gage and Audree Neva (Korthof) W.; m. Marilyn Sandra Rovell, Dec. 7, 1964; children: Carnie, Wendy. Student, El Camino Coll. Mem. musical group, The Beach Boys, 1961—; also composer; albums include Surfin Safari, 1962, Surfin' USA, 1963, Surfer Girl, 1963, Little Deuce Coupe, 1963, All Summer Long, 1964, Christmas Album, 1964, Beach Boys Party, 1965, Pet Sounds, 1966, All Summer Long, 1994, The Beach Boys Today, 1994, Smiley Smile, 1994, Stack-O-Tracks, 1994, Surger Girl, 1994, 20/20, 1994, Wild Honey, 1994, Endless Summer, 1995, The Greatest Hits, 1995, Stars and Stripes Vol. 1, 1996, Pet Sounds, 1996; solo album: Brian Wilson, 1988, Sire, 1988, Sweet Insanity, 1991; author: (autobiography) Wouldn't It Be Nice, 1991. Named to Rock and Roll Hall of Fame, 1988. also: William Morris Agy 151 S El Camino Dr Beverly Hills CA 90212-2704 also: Capitol Records 1750 Vine St Los Angeles CA 90028*

WILSON, BRUCE BRIGHTON, transportation executive; b. Boston, Feb. 6, 1936; s. Robert Lee and Jane (Schlotterer) W.; m. Elizabeth Ann MacFarland, Dec. 31, 1958; children: Mabeth, Mary, Bruce Robert, Caroline Daly. AB, Princeton U., 1958; LLB, U. Pa., 1961. Bar: Pa. 1962. Assoc. Montgomery, McCracken, Walker & Rhoads, Phila., 1962-69; atty. U.S. Dept. Justice, Washington, 1969-79; dep. asst. atty. gen. antitrust div. U.S. Dept. Justice, 1971-76; spl. counsel Consol. Rail Corp., Phila., 1979-81, gen. counsel litigation and antitrust, 1981-82, v.p., gen. counsel, 1982-84, v.p. law, 1984-87, sr. v.p. law, 1987-97, sr. v.p. merger, 1997—; bd. dirs. Phila. Indsl. Devel. Corp.; mem. mgmt. com. Concord Resources Group, 1989-91. Mem. corp. adv. bd. Phila. Mus. Art. Fellow Salzburg Seminar in Am. Studies (Austria), 1965; fellow Felz Inst. State and Local Govt., 1967. Mem. ABA, Phila. Bar Assn. Clubs: Corinthian Yacht, Pyramid. Home: 224 Chamounix Rd Wayne PA 19087-3606 Office: Consol Rail Corp PO Box 41417 2001 Market St 17th Flr Philadelphia PA 19101-1417

WILSON, BRUCE KEITH, men's health nurse; b. Alton, Ill., Aug. 18, 1946; s. Lewis Philip and Ruth Caroline Wilson; m. Karen Loughrey, Aug. 14, 1977; children: Sarah Ann, Andrew James. BSN, U. Tex., San Antonio, 1975, MSN, 1977; PhD, North Tex. State U., Denton, 1987. Cert. in nursing informatics Am. Nurses Credentialing Ctr. Coord. Pan Am. U., Edinburg, Tex., 1982-83; house supr. HCA Rio Grande Regional Hosp., McAllen, Tex., 1986-87; program dir. Tex. Southmost Coll., Brownsville, 1983-86; mem. faculty U. Tex.-Pan Am., Edinburg, 1986—. Author: Logical Nursing Math., 1987. With U.S. Army, 1966-68. Mem. ANA, Nat. League for Nursing, Am. Assembly for Men in Nursing, Tex. League for Nursing (bd. dirs. 1993-97). Avocations: photography, computer. Home: 1702 Ivy Ln Edinburg TX 78539-5367 Office: U Tex-Pan Am Dept Nursing Edinburg TX 78539

WILSON, C. DANIEL, JR., library director; b. Middletown, Conn., Nov. 8, 1941; s. Clyde D. and Dorothy M. (Neal) W.; m. M. April Jackson, Apr. 1986; children: Christine, Cindy, Clyde, Ben. BA, Elmhurst Coll., 1967; MA, Rosary Coll., 1968; MPA, U. New Orleans, 1995. Trainee Chgo. Pub. Libr., 1967-68; instr. U. Ill., 1968-70; asst. dir. Perrot Meml. Libr., Greenwich, Conn., 1970-76; dir. Wilton Pub. Libr., Wilton, Conn., 1976-79; assoc. dir. Birmingham Pub. Libr., Birmingham, Ala., 1979-83; dir. Davenport Pub. Libr., Davenport, Iowa, 1983-85, New Orleans Pub. Libr., 1985—. With USMC, 1962-65. Mem. Am. Libr. Assn., La. Libr. Assn., Am. Soc. Pub. Adminstrs., Pi Gamma Mu, Rotary. Episcopalian. Office: New Orleans Pub Libr Simon Heinsheim & Fisk Libe 219 Loyola Ave New Orleans LA 70112-2007

WILSON, C. NICK, health educator, consultant, researcher, lecturer; b. Balt., Feb. 18, 1942; s. Anna May (Gallion) W.; m. Nancy Ann King, Sept. 17, 1966 (div. Apr. 1976); children: Eve Anna Nicole, Tara Stacia; m. Linda Persons, Feb. 25, 1984; children: Melissa Anne, Kristin Marie. BS, U. Hartford, 1966; MHA, George Washington U., 1972; PhD, U. Miss., 1983. Dir. ops. Health Am., Louisville, 1976-79, So. Health Svcs., Marks, Miss., 1979-81; rsch. and teaching asst. U. Miss., Oxford, 1981-83; asst. prof. U. Tex., Galveston, 1983-85, U. Okla., Oklahoma City, 1987-91; pres. Shriners Burn Hosp., Galveston, 1985-87; assoc. prof. health, cons., sr. lectr. U. North Fla., Jacksonville, 1991—; cons., Jacksonville, 1991—. Author: Health Care Management, 1983; contbr. chpts. to books and over 150 articles to profl. jours. Bd. dirs., treas. First Coast Healthcare Execs. Group, Jacksonville, 1991—. Lt. USAF, 1966-69. Fellow Am. Coll. Healthcare Execs. (various offices, faculty advisor student chpt. Jacksonville 1991—), Royal Soc. Health; mem. APHA (various offices), Am. Hosp. Assn. (various offices). Republican. Episcopalian. Avocations: golf, tennis, hunting, fishing, sailing. Office: U North Fla Coll Health 4567 Saint Johns Bluff Rd S Jacksonville FL 32224-2646

WILSON, CARL ARTHUR, real estate broker; b. Manhasset, N.Y., Sept. 29, 1947; s. Archie and Florence (Hefner) W.; divorced; children: Melissa Starr, Clay Alan. Student UCLA, 1966-68, 70-71. Tournament bridge dir. North Hollywood (Calif.) Bridge Club, 1967-68, 70-71; computer operator IBM, L.A., 1967-68, 70-71; bus. devel. mgr. Walker & Lee Real Estate, Anaheim, Calif., 1972-76; v.p. sales and mktg. The Estes Co., Phoenix, 1976-82, Continental Homes Inc., 1982-84; pres. Roadrunner Homes Corp., Phoenix, 1984-86, Lexington Homes, Inc., 1986, Barrington Homes, 1986-90; gen. mgr. Starr Homes, 1991—, pres., 1996—; pres. Offsite Utilities, Inc., 1992—; adv. dir. Liberty Bank. Mem. Glendale (Ariz.) Citizens Bond Coun., 1986-87, Ariz. Housing Study Commn., 1988-89, Valley Leadership, 1988—; pres.'s coun. Am. Grad. Sch. Internat. Mgmt., 1985-89; vice-chmn. Glendale Planning and Zoning Commn., 1986-87, chmn., 1987-91; mem. bd. trustees Valley of Sun United Way, 1987-92, chmn. com. Community Problem Solving and Fund Distbn., 1988-89; mem. City of Glendale RTC Task Force, 1990, Maricopa County Citizens Jud. Reform Com., 1990-92, Maricopa County Citizens Jud. Adv. Coun., 1990-91; co-founder, bd. dirs. Leaderhsip West, Inc., 1993-94; mem. Maricopa County Trial Ct. Appointment Commn., 1993—. Mem. Nat. Assn. Homebuilders (bd. dirs. 1985-93, nat. rep. Ariz. 1990-92), Cen. Ariz. Homebuilders Assn. (adv. com. 1979-82, treas. 1986, sec. 1987, v.p. 1987-89, chmn. 1989-90, bd. dirs. 1985—, life dir. 1994—); mem. bd. adjustments City of Glendale, 1976-81, chmn., 1980-81, mem. bond coun., 1981-82; mem. real estate edn. adv. coun. State Bd. Community Coll., 1981-82; precinct committeeman, dep. registrar, 1980-81. With U.S. Army, 1968-70. Mem. Glendale C. of C. (dir. 1980-83, 89-91), Sales and Mktg. Coun. (chmn. edn. com. 1980, chmn. coun. 1981-82, Mame grand award 1981). Home: PO Box 39985 Phoenix AZ 85069-0985 Office: Starr Homes Inc Offsite Utilities Inc PO Box 39985 Phoenix AZ 85069-0985

WILSON, CAROLYN ROSS, school administrator; b. Lake Charles, La., June 25, 1941; d. Charles Wesley and Lucille Gertrude (Payne) Ross; m. James David Wilson, Apr. 10, 1971; 1 child, Charlise. BS in Music Edn. cum laude, Xavier U., 1962; MMus in Music Edn., Cath. U., Washington, 1968; postgrad., U. D.C., 1985-86, George Washington U., 1987-88, Harvard U., 1989. Tchr. Xavier U. Jr. Sch. Music, New Orleans, 1960-61, Orleans Parish Schs., New Orleans, 1962-63; tchr. D.C. Pub. Schs., Washington, 1964-87, curriculum writer, summer 1984, 85, adminstrv. intern Ea. High Sch., 1987-88, asst. prin. Cardozo High Sch., 1988-89, asst. prin. Duke Ellington Sch. of Arts, 1989-93; prin. Duke Ellington Sch. Arts, Washington, 1993—; curriculum writer music dept. D.C. Pub. Schs., Washington, 1984-85, dir. All City High Sch. Chorus, 1973. Composer: A Dedication to Federal City Alumnae Chapter of Delta, Sigma Theta Sorority, Inc., 1973. Lector Immaculate Conception Ch., Washington, 1986—; named D.C. Tchr. of Yr., 1987. Recipient Cert. of Merit-Outstanding Tchr. and Prin. award D.C. Govt., 1994; U.S. Dept. Edn. Effective Schs. grantee, Washington, 1992. Mem. ASCD, Instn. for Devel. Ednl. Activities (6th yr. fellow, session chair 1988, seminar leader 1991, 92, 93, 94), Delta Sigma Theta (Federal City Alumnae chpt.). Roman Catholic. Avocations: reading, travel, bowling, musical arranging, playing the piano. Office: Duke Ellington Sch Arts 35th And R St NW Washington DC 20912

WILSON, CHARLES (CHARLIE WILSON), former congressman; b. Trinity, Tex., June 1, 1933. Student, Sam Houston State U., Huntsville, Tex., 1951-52; B.S., U.S. Naval Acad., 1956. Commd. ensign U.S. Navy, 1956, advanced through grades to lt.; ret., 1960; mem. Tex. Ho. of Reps., 1960-66, Tex. Senate, 1966-72, 93nd-104th Congresses from 2nd Tex. dist., Washington, D.C., 1973-96; ranking minority mem. appropriations subcom. on fgn. ops., export financing & related programs; partner Hooper, Hooper, Owen & Gould, 1996—; mgr. lumber yard, 1962-72. Democrat. Office: Hooper, Hooper, Owen & Gould 801 Pennsylvania Ave NW Ste 730 Washington DC 20004*

WILSON, CHARLES B., neurosurgeon, educator; b. Neosho, Mo., Aug. 31, 1929; married; 3 children. BS, Tulane U., 1951, MD, 1954. Resident pathologist Tulane U., 1955-56, instr. neurosurgery, 1960-61; resident Ochsner Clinic, 1956-60; instr. La. State U., 1961-63; from asst. prof. to prof. U. Ky., 1963-68; prof. neurosurgery U. Calif., San Francisco, 1968—. Mem. Am. Assn. Neurol. Surgery, Soc. Neurol. Surgery. Achievements include research in brain and pituitary tumors. Office: U Calif Sch Medicine Box 0350 San Francisco CA 94143

WILSON, CHARLES BANKS, artist; b. Springdale, Ark., Aug. 6, 1918; s. Charles Bertram and Bertha Juanita (Banks) W.; m. Edna Frances McKibben, Oct. 10, 1941; children—Geoffrey Banks, Carrie Vee. Student, Art Inst. Chgo., 1936-41. Mag. and book illustrator, 1943-60; head art dept. N.E. Okla. A. & M. Coll., Miami, Okla., 1947-61; painter, printmaker. Executed mural, Okla. State Capitol, 1975; represented in permanent collections, Met. Mus., N.Y.C., Library of Congress, Washington, U.S. Capitol Bldg., D.C. Corcoran Gallery, Smithsonian Inst., Will Rogers Meml. Mus., Philbrook Art Center, Tulsa, Nat. Cowboy Hall of Fame, Oklahoma City.; Illustrator numerous books. Bd. dirs. Thomas Gilcrease Mus. History and Art, Tulsa, 1957-61; chmn. Pub. Libr. Bd., Miami, Okla., 1954-59. Named to Okla. Hall of Fame; recipient Western Heritage award Cowboy Hall of Fame, D.S.C., U. Okla.; subject of books The Lithographs of Charles Banks Wilson, 1989, Search for the Purebloods, 1989, An Oklahoma Portrait, 1989. Mem. Internat. Inst. Arts and Letters (Geneva). Office: 1611 Mission Blvd Fayetteville AR 72703-3043

WILSON, CHARLES GLEN, zoo administrator; b. Clinton, Okla., Aug. 24, 1948; s. Claude Lee and Alva Dean (Gaskins) W.; m. Susan Elizabeth Mosher, Nov. 21, 1975; children: Erica Dean, Grant Mosher. BS, Okla. State U., 1972, MS, 1980. Dir. Memphis Zool. Gardens and Aquarium, 1976—. Contbr. articles to profl. jours. Served with U.S. Army, 1968-70. Recipient Ark. Traveler award, 1977. Profl. fellow Am. Zool. Parks and Aquariums. Office: Memphis Zoo & Aquarium 2000 Galloway Ave Memphis TN 38112-5033

WILSON, CHARLES HAVEN, lawyer; b. Waltham, Mass., July 27, 1936; s. Charles Haven Sr. and Kathryn (Sullivan) W.; children: Kathryn Wilson Self, Charles H. Jr. AB in Govt. magna cum laude, Tufts U., 1958; MS in Journalism, Columbia U., 1959; JD, U. Calif., Berkeley, 1967. Bar: D.C. 1968, U.S. Supreme Ct. 1972. Sr. law clk. to Chief Justice Earl Warren, 1967-68; from assoc. to counsel Williams & Connolly, Washington, 1968-90; sr. lawyer ACLU of Nat. Capital Area, Washington, 1992—; adj. prof. constitutional law Georgetown U. Law Ctr., 1971, 72. With U.S. Army, 1959-62. Mem. ABA (litigation sect. coun. 1976-79, dir publs. 1975-90, founding editor jour. Litigation 1974, bd. editors ABA Jour. 1985-91), Order of Coif. Democrat. Roman Catholic. Avocation: reading. Office: ACLU of Nat Capital Area S 119 1400 20th St NW Washington DC 20036

WILSON, CHARLES REGINALD, real estate executive; b. Bear Lake, Pa., Nov. 7, 1904; s. Earl Ayling and Edith (Finch) W.; m. Josephine Harrison, Sept. 8, 1927; children—Charles Reginald, Jacquelyn Ann. Student, U. Pitts., 1927. Asst. dean men U. Pitts., 1927-29; bus. promotion mgr. Hotel Schenley, Pitts., 1929-35; sales mgr. William Penn Hotel, Pitts., 1935-39; v.p., gen. mgr. William Penn Hotel, 1952; mgr. Roosevelt Hotel, Pitts., 1939-52; sr. v.p. Union Nat. Bank of Pitts. (formerly Commonwealth Bank & Trust Company), 1952-71, Realty Growth Corp., Pitts., 1972—; pres. Commonwealth Real Estate Co., 1957-64. Pres. Panther Found., U. Pitts.; exec. com. Pitts. Conv. and Visitors Bur. Mem. Pitts. Athletic Assn., Soc. Indsl. Realtors, Delta Tau Delta, Omicron Delta Kappa. Clubs: Mason, Pittsburgh Field, Duquesne. Home: 4601 5th Ave Pittsburgh PA 15213-3666 Office: Roosevelt Bldg Sixth St and Penn Ave Pittsburgh PA 15222

WILSON, CHARLES VINCENT, human resources executive; b. Rockledge, Fla., May 7, 1949; s. Phillip J. and Etta R. (Talley) W.; m. Priscilla A. Johnson, Mar. 22, 1976; children: Stephanie Brooke, Rachel Marie. BSBA, Pa. State U., 1971. Dir. human resources Kendall Co., Boston, 1971-84; zone E.R. mgr. Frito-Lay, Dallas, 1984-86, group human resources mgr.-sales, 1986-87, group human resources mgr.-hdqrs., 1987-89; dir. mgmt. planning & devel. Pearle, Inc., Dallas, 1989; v.p. cultural diversity & pers. devel. Grand Met. Food Sector, Mpls., 1989-91, v.p., dir. human resources tech., 1991-94; v.p. for human resources U. Md. Med. Sys., Balt., 1994-96; sr. v.p. human resources Clarian Health Ptnrs., Inc., Indpls., 1996—; mem. tech. adv. coun. Olympus Corp., Inc., 1993-94; chmn. Univ. Med. System/Frederick Douglas H.S. Partnership Steering Com., 1996; mem. Univ. Hosp. Consortium Human Resources Officers Coun., 1994-96. Bd. dirs. Big Brothers/Big Sisters of Ctrl. Md., 1994-96. Recipient Black Achiever award Chgo. YMCA, 1975; Nat. Merit scholar, 1967. Mem. Nat. Black Human Resources Soc., Soc. for Human Resource Mgmt. Democrat. Baptist. Avocations: fitness workouts, golf, reading, travel, music. Office: Clarian Health Ptnrs Inc PO Box 1367 I-65 & 21st St PO Box 1367 Indianapolis IN 46206

WILSON, CHARLES ZACHARY, JR., newspaper publisher; b. Greenwood, Miss., Apr. 21, 1929; s. Charles Zachary and Ora Lee (Means) W.; m. Doris J. Wilson, Aug. 18, 1951 (dec. Nov. 1974); children: Charles III, Joyce Lynne, Joanne Catherine, Gary Thomas, Jonathan Keith; m. Kelly Freeman, Apr. 21, 1986; children: Amanda Fox, Walter Bremond. BS in Econs., U. Ill., 1952, PhD in Econs. and Stats., 1956. Asst. to v.p. Commonwealth Edison Co., Chgo., 1956-59; asst. prof. econs. De Paul U., Chgo., 1959-61; assoc. prof. bus. SUNY, Binghamton, 1961-67, prof. econs. and bus., 1967-68; prof. mgmt. and edn. UCLA, 1968-84, vice chancellor acad. programs, 1985-87; CEO, pub., pres. Cen. News-Wave Publs., L.A., 1987—; pres. Czand Assocs., Pacific Palisades, Calif., 1994—; mem. adv. council Fed. Res. Bank, San Francisco, 1986-88, 2001 com. Office of Mayor of Los Angeles, 1986-89. Author: Organizational Decision-Making, 1967; contbr. articles on bus. to jours. Bd. dirs. Los Angeles County Mus. Art, 1972-84; com. on Los Angeles City Revenue, 1975-76, United Nations Assn. panel for advancement of U. and Japan Relations, N.Y.C. 1972-74; chmn. Mayor's task force on Africa, 1979-82. Fellow John Hay Whitney, U. Ill., 1955-56, Ford Found., 1960-61, 81-82, 84, Am. Council of Edn., UCLA, 1967-68, Aspen Inst. for Human Studies; named one of Young Men of Yr., Jaycees, 1965. Mem. AAAS, Am. Econ. Assn., Nat. Newspaper Pub. Assn., Am. Mgmt. Assn., Alpha Phi Alpha (pres., pledgemaster 1952-54), Phi Kappa Phi, Order of Artus (pres.). Avocations: tennis, jogging, collecting old bus. texts. Home: 1053 Tellem Dr Pacific Palisades CA 90272-2243 Office: Cen Newspaper Publs 2621 W 54th St Los Angeles CA 90043-2614

WILSON, CLARENCE SYLVESTER, JR., lawyer, educator; b. Bklyn., Oct. 22, 1945; s. Clarence Sylvester and Thelma Louise (Richards) W.; m. Helena Chapellin Iribarren, Jan. 26, 1972. BA, Williams Coll., 1967; JD, Northwestern U., 1974. Bar: Ill., 1975; U.S. Supreme Ct., 1985. Fgn. Svc. Res. officer U.S. Dept. of State, 1969-74; vice consul 3d sec. Am. Embassy, Caracas, Venezuela, 1969-71; adj. prof. law Kent Coll. of Law, Ill. Inst. Tech., Chgo., 1981-94; lecturer, Columbia Coll., Chgo., 1995—; mem. vis. com. music dept. U. Chgo., 1991—; mem. bd. govs. Sch. of Art Inst. of Chgo., 1994—; vice chmn. Jazz Mus. of Chgo., 1994-97. Trustee Chgo. Symphony Orch., 1987-96, Art Inst. Chgo., 1990—; mem. adv. bd. Chgo. Dept. Cultural Affairs, 1988—; bd. dirs. Arts Midwest, Mpls., 1985-89, Harold Washington Found., Chgo., 1989-91; mem. MERIT Music Program, 1991-96, Ill. Arts Coun., 1984-89; project mgr. Dept. Justice Task Force. The Pres.'s Pvt. Sector Survey on Cost Control in the Fed. Govt. (Grace Commn.), 1982-84. Mem. Lawyers for the Creative Arts (pres. 1987-88). Republican. Episcopalian. Avocations: music, art collecting. Home: 5555 S Everett Ave Chicago IL 60637-1968 Office: 25 E Washington St Ste 1500 Chicago IL 60602-1804

WILSON, CLAUDE RAYMOND, JR., lawyer; b. Dallas, Feb. 22, 1933; s. Claude Raymond and Lottie (Watts) W.; m. Emilynn; children: Deidra Wilson Frazier, Melissa Woodland Utley, Michelle Woodard Dunn. BBA, So. Meth. U., 1954, JD, 1956. Bar: Tex. 1956; CPA, Calif., Tex. Asso. firm Cervin & Melton, Dallas, 1956-58; atty. Tex. & Pacific R.R. Co., Dallas, 1958-60; atty. office regional counsel IRS, San Francisco, 1960-63; sr. trial atty. office chief counsel IRS, Washington, 1963-65; ptnr. Wilson & White, Dallas, 1965—; chmn., Dallas dist. dir. IRS Adv. Commn., 1990-91. Mem. ABA, AICPA (coun. 1989-93), State Bar Tex., Dallas Bar Assn. (pres. sect. taxation 1969-70), Tex. Soc. CPAs (pres. 1989-90, pres. Dallas chpt. 1983-84), Greater Dallas C. of C. (chmn. appropriations and tax com. 1990-91), Crescent Club, Montaigne Club, Masons, Shriners, Jesters, Delta Sigma Phi, Delta Theta Phi. Republican. Episcopalian. Office: 3500 Bank One Ctr 1717 Main St Dallas TX 75201-4605

WILSON, COLIN HENRY, writer; b. Leicester, Eng., June 26, 1931; s. Arthur and Anetta W.; m. Joy Stewart; children: Sally, Damon, Rowan; 1 child from previous marriage, Roderick. writer in residence Hollins (Va.) Coll., 1966-67; vis. prof. U. Wash., Seattle, 1967, Rutgers U., New Brunswick, N.J., 1974. Author (numerous books including novels): The Glass Cage, 1967, The Occult, 1971, The Black Room, 1971, The Space Vampires, 1975, Mysteries, 1978; 6 critical studies in the Outsider series; non-fiction: Access to Inner Worlds, 1982, A Criminal History of Mankind, 1983, (with Donald Seaman) Modern Encyclopedia of Murder, 1983, The Essential Colin Wilson, 1984, The Personality Surgeon, 1986, (with Damon Wilson) Encyclopedia of Unsolved Mysteries, 1987, Spiderworld, 1987, The Misfits, 1988, Beyond The Occult, 1988, Written in Blood, 1989, (with Donald Seaman) The Serial Killers, 1990; (play) Mozart's Journey to Prague, 1991, Spiderworld: The Magician, 1992, The Strange Life of P.D. Ouspensky, 1993, Unsolved Mysteries Past and Present (with Damon Wilson), 1993, From Atlantis To The Sphinx, 1996, Atlas of Holy Places and Sacred Sites, 1996. Club: Savage.

WILSON, DANIEL DONALD, engineering executive; b. Pitts., Oct. 28, 1958; s. Howard Raymond and Eleanor Hinsdale (Clark) W.; m. Jean Basia Sitko, Oct. 26, 1991. BS in Math., U. Vt., 1979; MS in Ops. Rsch., Stanford U., 1988. Systems analyst Raytheon System Design Lab., Bedford, Mass., 1979-83; software engr. Raytheon Svc. Co., Huntsville, Ala., 1983-85; sr. engr. Raytheon System Design Lab., Bedford, 1986-88; mgr. analytical models Raytheon System Design Lab., Tewksbury, Mass., 1988—. Mem. AIAA (treas. 1990-92, sec. 1992-93, N.E. coun. 1993-95), Ops. Rsch. Soc. Am., Am. Assn. Cost Estimators, Soc. Cost Estimation and Analysis. Home: 21 Symmes Rd Winchester MA 01890-3014 Office: Raytheon Sys Design Lab PO Box 1201 m/s T3TG6 Tewksbury MA 01876-0901

WILSON, DARRYL CEDRIC, lawyer, law educator, consultant; b. Chgo., Nov. 5, 1961. BFA, BBA, So. Meth. U., 1982; JD, U. Fla., 1984; LLM, John Marshall Law Sch., 1989. Bar: Ill. 1986, U.S. Ct. Appeal (7th cir.) 1986, Fla. 1995, U.S. Supreme Ct. 1995. Law clk. Ctr. for Govtl. Responsibility, Gainesville, Fla., 1984-85; Reginald Heber Smith law fellow Cook County Legal Assistance, Harvey, Ill., 1985-86, staff atty. property specialist, 1986-87; pro bono coord. Cook County Legal Assistance, Oak Park, Ill., 1987; corp. atty. intellectual property divsn. Soft Sheen Products Corp., Chgo., 1987; real estate atty. UAW, Ford Legal Svcs., Lansing, Ill., 1988-89; of counsel Steck & Spataro, Chgo., 1989-93; pvt. practice Wilson and Assocs., Chgo., 1989—; prof. law Detroit Coll. Law, 1992-94; mng. ptnr., gen. counsel Freico Diversified Svcs., 1988—; prof. law Stetson U. Sch. Law, 1994—; cons. Pvt. Minority Small Bus. Assocs., Chgo., 1992, Detroit, 1992. Contbr. articles to profl. and acad. jours. Mem. ABA, Am. Intellectual Property Lawyers Assn., Black Entertainment and Sports Lawyers Assn., Internat. Trademark Assn., Ill. Bar Assn., Fla. Bar Assn., Sports Lawyers Assn., Lawyers for Creative Arts. Avocations: music, sports, history. Office: Stetson U Coll Law Saint Petersburg FL 33711 also: Wilson & Assoc Box 27023 Saint Petersburg FL 33711

WILSON, DAVID EUGENE, magistrate judge; b. Columbia, S.C., Jan. 12, 1940; s. David W. and Emma (Moseley) W.; m. Nancy Ireland, Sept. 5, 1964; children: Amy R., Cara S. BA, U. S.C., 1963, JD, 1966; MA, Boston U., 1971. Bar: Vt. 1972, D.C. 1973, Wash. 1980, U.S. Dist. Ct. Vt. 1972, U.S. Dist. Ct. (we. dist.) Wash. 1976. Asst. atty. gen. State of Vt., Montpelier, 1972-73; asst. U.S. atty. U.S. Dist. Ct. D.C., Washington, 1973-76; asst. U.S. atty. U.S. Dist. Ct. (we. dist.) Wash., Seattle, 1976-89, U.S. atty., 1989, asst. U.S. atty., chief criminal div., 1989-92; U.S. magistrate judge Seattle, 1992—; mem. faculty Atty. Gen.'s Advocacy Inst., Washington, 1979—, Nat. Inst. Trial Advocacy, Seattle, 1987—. Capt. U.S. Army, 1966-71, col. USAR. Recipient Disting. Community Svc. award B'nai Brith, 1987. Fellow Am. Coll. Trial Lawyers; mem. Fed. Bar Assn., Wash. State Bar, Seattle-King County Bar. Avocations: hunting, fishing, skiing, books. Office: 304 US Courthouse Seattle WA 98104

WILSON, DAVID GORDON, mechanical engineering educator; b. Sutton Coldfield, Warwick., Eng., Feb. 11, 1928; s. William and Florence Ida (Boulton) W.; m. Anne Ware Sears, July 18, 1963 (div. May 1988); children: John M.B., Erica Sears; m. Ellen Cecilia Warner, Dec. 20, 1988; 1 child, Susan Speck. Postgrad., MIT, Harvard U., 1955-57; BS with honors, U. Birmingham, UK, 1948; PhD, U. Nottingham, UK, 1953. Brush fellow, rsch. asst. Nottingham U., 1950-53; ship's 7th engr. officer Donaldson Line, Glasgow, UK, 1953; engr. Brush Elec. Engring. Co., Ltd., UK, 1953-55; sr. gas-turbine designer Ruston & Hornsby, Lincoln, UK, 1957-58; sr. lectr., mech. engring. U. Ibadan, Zaria, Nigeria, 1958-60; v.p., tech. dir. No. Rsch. and Engring. Corp., Cambridge, Mass., also U.K., 1960-66; assoc. prof. mech. engring. MIT, Cambridge, 1966-71, prof., 1971-94; prof. emeritus, 1994—; vis. engr., Boeing Airplane Co., 1956-57; vis. fellow MIT and Harvard U., 1955-56; cons., lectr. in field. Author: The Design of Gas-Turbine Engines, 1991, The Design of High-Efficiency Turbomachinery and Gas Turbines, 1984; co-author: (with Frank Rowland Whitt) Bicycling Science, 1974, 2d edit., 1982, (with Richard Wilson et al) The Health Effects of Fossil-Fuel Burning, 1981, (with Douglas Stephen Beck) Gas-Turbine Regenerators, 1996; co-editor: (with Allan V. Abbott) Human-Powered Vehicles, 1995; editor: Solid-Waste-Management Handbook, 1977, The Treatment and Management of Urban Solid Waste, 1972. Recipient T. Bernard Hall prize Inst. Mech. Engrs., 1954, Lord Weir 1st prize Inst. Mech. Engrs., 1955, Indsl. Rsch. IR-100 award, 1974, Reclamation Industries Internat. prize, 1974; Power-Jets-Sch. scholar, 1954; Commonwealth Fund fellow MIT and Harvard U., 1955-57. Avocations: human power, biking, hiking, tennis, music. Office: MIT/Mech Engring Rm 3-455 Cambridge MA 02139

WILSON, DAVID JAMES, chemistry researcher, educator; b. Ames, Ia., June 25, 1930; s. James Calmar and Alice Winona (Olmsted) W.; m. Martha Carolyn Meyers, Sept. 6, 1952; children: John Wesley, Charles Steven, William David, Andrew Lyman, Joyce Ballin. BS in Chemistry, Stanford U., 1952; postgrad., 1952-53, 55-57; PhD, Calif. Inst. Tech., 1958. Mem. faculty U. Rochester, N.Y., 1957-69, assoc. prof., 1963-67, prof. phys. chemistry, 1967-69; prof. Vanderbilt U., Nashville, 1969-95, prof. chemistry and environ. engring., 1977-95, prof. emeritus, 1995—, Alexander Heard disting. service prof., 1983-84; sr. rsch. assoc. Eckenfelder, Inc., Nashville, 1988-95, sr. rsch. fellow, 1995—; vis. sr. lectr. chemistry U. Ife, Nigeria, 1964-65; vis. prof. U. Málaga, Spain, 1993-94; mem. Rochester Com. for Sci. Info., 1960-69, v.p., 1966-69; chmn. Nashville Com. for Sci. Info., 1971-74. Pres. Tenn. Environ. Coun., 1985-87. With AUS, 1953-55. Recipient award Monroe County Conservation Coun., 1967, Tenn. Conservation League, 1971; Alfred P. Sloan Found. fellow, 1964-66. Mem. AAAS, Am. Chem. Soc., Tenn. Acad. Sci., Sigma Xi, Phi Beta Kappa. Home: 3600 Wilbur Pl Nashville TN 37204-3829

WILSON, DAVID LEE, clinical psychologist; b. Mooresville, N.C., July 5, 1941; s. William John Mack and Joyce Evelyn (Evans) W.; m. Barbara Ann Klepfer, Apr. 22, 1960 (div. Jan. 1982); children: Cheryl, Lisa, David; m. Cheryl Andersen, May 22, 1983 (div. Jan. 1992). Student, Auburn U., 1959-60; AB in Psychology, Davidson Coll., 1963; PhD in Clin. Psychology, U. N.C., 1967. Tchg. fellow U. N.C., Chapel Hill, 1964; psychology intern Letterman Hosp., San Francisco, 1966-67, supr., 1967-70; sr. psychologist Kaiser Hosp., Hayward, Calif., 1970-72; pvt. practice psychology San Francisco, 1970-72; mem. staff Far No. Regional Ctr., Redding, Calif., 1970-74; dir. Redding Psychotherapy Group, 1974—, Vietnam Vets. Readjustment Program, Shasta and Tehama, 1984—; cons. in field. Author: (play) The Moon Cannot Be Stolen, 1985; contbr. articles to profl. jours. Chmn. Shasta Dam P.U.D. Com., Shasta County, 1981-82, Shasta County Headstart Bd., 1982-85, Criminal Justice Adv. Bd. Shasta County, 1982-87, Youth and Family Counseling Ctr., Shasta County, 1986-89. Capt. U.S. Army, 1965-70. Recipient Danforth award Danforth Found., 1959; Woodrow Wilson Found. fellow, 1963; Smith Fund grantee, 1966; Dana scholar, 1960-63. Fellow Am. Bd. Med. Psychotherapy; mem. APA, Calif. State Psychol. Assn. (chpt. rep. 1990-95, bd. dirs. 1990-95, chair membership com. 1993-95, exec. com. 1993-95, chair publs. com. 1994-95, chair divsn. VI 1996, chair divsn. I 1997, Silver PSI award 1995), Shasta Cascade Psychol. Assn. (pres. 1990-91, mem. bd. dirs. 1990—, Outstanding Psychologist 1993), Am. Assn. Advancement of Behavior Therapy, Eye Movement Desensitization and Reprocessing Network (Outstanding Rsch. award 1994), Eye Movement Desensitization and Reprocessing Internat. Assn. (bd. dirs. 1995—, chair 1996—). Democrat. Avocations: fly fishing, backpacking, camping, white water rafting. Office: Redding Psychotherapy Group 616 Azalea Ave Redding CA 96002-0217

WILSON, DEBRA, oil, gas industry executive. Mgr. devel., adminstr. United Aviation Fuels Corp., Arlington Heights, Ill., 1995—, mgr. elect. purchasing. Office: United Aviation Fuels Corp 1200 E Algonquin Rd Arlington Heights IL 60005-4712

WILSON, DELANO DEE, consultant; b. Great Falls, Mont., Apr. 15, 1934; s. William McKinley and Alvina Henrietta (Beck) W.; m. Marilyn Ann Harant, Nov. 14, 1959; children: Robin David, Leslie Ann Wilson, Christian William. BSEE, Mont. State U., 1959. Analytical engr. GE, Schenectady, N.Y., 1960-69, sr. engr., 1964-69, mgr. alternating current studies, 1969-72; mgr. engring. projects GE, Phila., 1972-74; prin. engr. Power Techs., Inc., Schenectady, 1974-82; v.p., prin. engr. Power Techs., Inc.-Tech. Assessment Group, Schenectady, 1980-85; pres., CEO Power Techs. Inc., Schenectady, 1986-95, chmn. bd. dirs., 1989-95; expert eyewitness, cons. Internat. Conf. on High Voltage Systems, Paris, 1974-90. U.S. rep., 1986-92. Author, co-author 6 books; contbr. numerous tech. papers to profl. jours.; patentee in field. Bd. dirs. Ellis Hosp., Schenectady, 1987—; trustee Capital Dist. YMCA, 1989—. With U.S. Army, 1954-56. Fellow IEEE (mem. transp. and dist. com., exec. bd. Power Engring. Soc. 1988-94, Disting. Svc. award 1988). Avocations: skiing, fishing, amateur auto rebuilding. Office: Power Techs Inc 1482 Erie Blvd PO Box 1058 Schenectady NY 12301

WILSON, DON WHITMAN, archivist, historian; b. Clay Center, Kans., Dec. 17, 1942; s. Donald J. Wilson and Lois M. (Sutton) Walker; m. Patricia Ann Sherrod, July 9, 1983; children—Todd, Jeffrey, Michael, Denise. AB, Washburn U., Topeka, 1964; MA, U. Cin., 1965, PhD, 1972, LittD (hon.), 1988. Archivist Kans. State Hist. Soc., Topeka, 1967-69; instr. history Washburn U., 1967-69; historian, dept. dir. Dwight D. Eisenhower Library, Abilene, Kans., 1969-78; assoc. dir. State Hist. Soc. Wis., Madison, 1978-81; dir. Gerald R. Ford Library and Mus., Ann Arbor, Mich., 1981-87; lectr. history U. Mich., 1982-87; Archivist of the U.S. Washington, 1987-93; rsch. prof. Tex. A&M U., College Station, 1993—, exec. dir. George Bush libr. ctr., 1993—. Author: Governor Charles Robinson of Kansas, 1975; editor: D-Day: The Normandy Invasion, 1971. Mem. Abilene Library Bd., 1973-76; mem. Abilene City Commn., 1976-78; pres. Dickinson County Hist. Soc., Abilene, 1976-77. NDEA fellow, 1964-67; recipient Pub. Service award Gen. Services Adminstrn., 1973. Mem. Am. Hist. Assn. (mem. Beveridge Book Prize com. 1979-82), Am. Assn. State and Local History, Kans. Hist. Soc. (bd. dirs. 1987—), Am. Antiquarian Soc. Republican. Baptist. Home: 209 Chimney Hill Cir College Station TX 77840-1829 Office: Tex A&M U PO Box 1145 George Bush Libr Ctr College Station TX 77843-1145*

WILSON, DONALD EDWARD, physician, educator; b. Worcester, Mass., Aug. 28, 1936; s. Rivers Rivo and Licine (Bradshaw) W.; m. Patricia C. Littell, Aug. 27, 1977; children: Jeffrey D.E., Sean D., Monique, Sheila L. A.B., Harvard U., 1958; M.D., Tufts U., 1962. Diplomate Am. Bd. Internal Medicine. Intern St. Elizabeth Hosp., Boston, 1962-63; resident in medicine, research fellow in gastroenterology VA Hosp. and Lemuel Shattuck Hosp., Boston, 1963-66; assoc. chief gastroenterology Bklyn. Hosp., 1968-71; instr. medicine SUNY Downstate Med. Center, Bklyn., 1968-71; asst. prof. medicine U. Ill., Chgo., 1971-73; asso. prof. U. Ill., 1973-75, prof., 1975-80, acting head dept. medicine, 1976-77; dir. div. gastroenterology U. Ill. Hosp., Chgo., 1971-80; chief of gastroenterology U. Ill. Hosp., 1973-80, physician-in-chief, 1976-77; prof., chmn. dept. medicine SUNY Downstate Med. Center, Bklyn., 1980-91; physician-in-chief State U. and Kings County Hosp., 1980-91; dean, prof. medicine U. Md.Sch. Medicine, Balt., 1991—; vis. prof. medicine U. London, Kings Coll. Med. Sch., 1977-78; mem. gastrointestinal drugs adv. bd. FDA, 1985-87, chmn., 1986-87; mem. Part II test com. Nat. Bd. Med. Examiners, 1985-88; mem. nat. digestive adv. bd. NIH, 1985-87, chmn., 1986-87; mem. gen. clin. rsch. ctrs. com. NIH, 1987—; mem. nat. adv. com. Agy. for Health Care Policy and Rsch., Dept. HHS, 1991—, chmn., 1992—; mem. residency rev. com. for internal medicine Acque, 1993—; mem. nat. com. fgn. med. edn. and accreditation U.S. Dept. Edn., 1994—. Contbr. articles to med. jours. Bd. vis. Harvard Sch. of Pub. Health, 1992-94. Served to capt. M.C., USAF, 1966-68. Recipient Rsch. award HEW, 1971, 74, Rsch. award John A. Hartford Found., Inc., 1972-79, Rsch. award Distilled Spirits Coun. U.S., 1972-74, Rsch. award VA, 1974. Master ACP; mem. NAS, AAAS, Am. Gastroent. Assn., Am. Fedn. Clin. Rsch., Am. Assn. Study Liver Disease, Accreditation Coun. Grad. Med. Edn. (rev. com. internal medicine), Central Soc. Clin. Rsch., Central Rsch. Club, Chgo. Soc. Gastroenterology (pres. 1978-79), Digestive Disease Found., Midwest Gut Club, Soc. Exptl. Biology and Medicine, N.Y. Acad. Scis., N.Y. Acad. Medicine, N.Y. Soc. Gastroenterology, Chgo. Soc. Gastrointestinal Endoscopy (pres. 1979-80), Assn. Am. Physicians, Assn. for Acad. Minority Physicians (sec./treas. 1986—), Nat. Med. Assn., Am. Clin. and Climatological Assn., 1994—, Assn. Profs. Medicine (sec.-treas. 1990-91), Inst. of Medicine, Med. Club Bklyn., Sigma Pi Phi (grand boule). Club: Harvard (Chgo., N.Y.C.), 14 West Hamilton St. Club (Balt.), The Ctr. Club, (Balt.). Office: U Md Sch Medicine 655 W Baltimore St Baltimore MD 21201-1509*

WILSON, DONALD GREY, management consultant; b. Bridgeport, Conn., Sept. 20, 1917; s. William Gray and Jeannetta McAvoy (Kerr) W.; m. Elizabeth Jean Lanning, Apr. 24, 1943 (div. Mar. 1971); children: Kirk Lanning, Craig Gardner, William Grey. B.S. in Elec. Engring, Rensselaer Poly. Inst., 1938; S.M., Harvard U., 1939, M.E.S., 1947, Ph.D., 1948. Mgr. automatic fire alarm div. Sealand Corp., Bridgeport, Conn., 1939-40; instr. elec. engring. Rensselaer Poly. Inst., 1940-42; staff mem. Radiation Lab. Mass. Inst. Tech., 1942-45; prof. elec. engring. U. Kan., Lawrence, 1947-55; chmn. dept. U. Kan., 1948-55; dir. Phila. Brass & Bronze, 1962-64, Mallory-Xerox Corp., 1964-65; cons. U.S. Naval Ordance Test Sta., China Lake, Calif., 1953-54; assoc. dir. rsch. dept. Stromberg-Carlson Co., San Diego, 1955-59, gen. mgr., 1959, asst. v.p., 1959-60; v.p. rsch. P.R. Mallory & Co., Indpls., 1960, v.p. rsch. and engring., 1961-71, v.p. rsch., engring. and environ. affairs, 1971-75; alt. dir. Mallory Metal. Products, Eng., 1967; pres. Contemporary Custom Cabinets, San Diego, 1975-76; v.p. Continental Resources and Minerals Corp., Dayton, Ohio, 1978-79; sr. v.p. Tanzi Mergers/Acquisitions, San Diego, 1983-86; mgmt. cons., 1976—; sr. lectr. U. Rochester, 1956-57; lectr. dept. elec. engring. San Diego State U., 1981-92, asst. dean coll. engring., 1987, prof. emeritus, 1992—; mng. dir., exec. bd. nat. Bur. Prof. Cons., 1988-94, sr. counsel, 1994—. Contbr. articles to profl. jours. Bd. dirs. Speech and Hearing Clinic, Indpls., 1960-66; Bd. dirs. Washington Twp. Sch. Dist., 1964-68, pres., 1966-67. Recipient Outstanding Acad. Advisor award San Diego State U., 1992. Fellow AAAS; mem. IEEE (sr.), Affiliation Profl. Cons. Orgns. (chmn. bd. govs. 1991-93), Internat. IEEE Outstanding Br. Counselor award 1992), Intertel, Sigma Xi, Sigma Phi Epsilon, Tau Beta Pi, Eta Kappa Nu. Home: 3110 Levante St Carlsbad CA 92009-8332

WILSON, DONALD HURST, III, computer training services executive; b. Balt., Mar. 1, 1946; s. Donald H. Jr. and Winifred Arnold (Leist) W.; m. Beverly Lee Wright, Oct. 3, 1975; children: Beverly Callaway, Sarah Elizabeth. AB, Yale U., 1968; MBA, Harvard U., 1976, JD, 1976. Bar: Mass. 1977. Cons. Boston Cons. Group, 1976-78; dir. mktg. I/C divsn. Black & Decker, Hampstead, Md., 1978-83; pres. MWI Tng. Svcs., Inc., Hunt Valley, Md., 1983-96; v.p. worldwide classroom line of bus. Global Knowledge Network, Inc., Hunt Valley, Md., 1996—. Mem. vestry St. John's Episcopal Ch., 1993-96, lay eucharistic min., 1995—; dir. The Bishop Claggett Ctr., 1995-97. Mem. Info. Tech. Tng. Assn. (bd. dirs. 1993-95), Assn. Microcomputer Distbrs. (bd. dirs. 1988-90), Archaeol. Soc. Md. (trustee 1994—). Republican. Avocations: Bible study, archaeology, hunting, farming, horseback riding. Home: Oak Meadow Farm 3919 Butler Rd Reisterstown MD 21136-4804 Office: Global Knowledge Network Inc 140 Lakefront Dr Hunt Valley MD 21030-2238

WILSON, DONALD MALCOLM, publishing executive; b. Glen Ridge, N.J., June 27, 1925; s. Robert and Adelaide (Streubel) W.; m. Susan M. Neuberger, Apr. 6, 1957; children: Dwight Malcolm, Katherine Loudon, Penelope. Grad., Deerfield (Mass.) Acad., 1943; B.A., Yale U., 1948. Reporter Life mag., 1949-53, chief Far Ea. corr., 1953-56, chief Washington corr., 1956-60, asso. pub., 1968-69; gen. mgr. Time- Life Internat., 1965-68; v.p. corporate and pub. affairs Time, Inc., 1969-81, corp. v.p. pub. affairs, 1981-89; pu. Business News N.J., New Brunswick, 1989—; dep. dir. USIA, 1961-65; mem. adv. council Edward R. Murrow Ctr., Tufts U., The Nat. Council of La Raza, 1985-89; mem. Pub. Broadcasting Authority of N.J., 1969-73, 76-79. Trustee Vassar Coll., 1971-79, The Brearley Sch., 1977-86;

bd. dirs. Solomon R. Guggenheim Mus., The Schumann Fund for N.J., Ctr. for Analysis of Pub. Issues. Decorated Air medal. Mem. Council on Fgn. Relations. Clubs: Federal City (Washington); Century Assn. (N.Y.C.). Home: 4574 Province Line Rd Princeton NJ 08540-2212 Office: Business News NJ 391 George St New Brunswick NJ 08901-2017

WILSON, DONNA MAE, foreign language educator, administrator; b. Columbus, Ohio, Feb. 25, 1947; d. Everett John and Hazel Margaret (Bruck) Palmer; m. Steven L. Wilson, Nov. 16, 1968. BA, Ohio State U., 1973, MA, 1976; postgrad studies, U. Wash., Seattle Pacific U., 1980-93; cert., U. Salamanca, Spain, 1985. Tchg. assoc. Ohio State U., Columbus, 1974-76; lectr. U. Wash., Seattle, 1977-78; grants officer Seattle U., 1978-82; adj. prof. Shoreline Coll., Seattle, 1982-84; coord. fgn. langs., prof. Spanish Bellevue (Wash.) Coll., 1984-87; prof. Spanish Highline Coll., Des Moines, Wash., 1987—, chair fgn. lang. dept., 1990-94; chair arts and humanities Highline Coll., Des Moines, 1994—; bd. dirs. Wash. C.C.s, Olympia, 1991—; spkr. at lang. orgns., confs. regional and nat., 1985—. Editor: (book) Fronteras: En Contacto, 1992-93; (jours.) Modern Lang. Jour., 1991, 92, 94, 96, 97, Hispania, 1993, 95; text editor D. C. Heath and Co., Harcourt, Brace and Jovanovich, Houghton Mifflin, Prentice Hall; contbr. articles to profl. jours., chpt. to book. Recipient cert. of excellence Phi Theta Kappa, 1990, Pathfinder award Phi Beta Kappa, 1995; fellowshp grant Coun. Internat. Edn. Exchange, Santiago, Chile, 1992. Mem. Am. Assn. Tchrs. of Spanish (v.p. Wash.), Am. Coun. Tchrs. of Fgn. Langs. (cert. oral proficiency), Assn. Dept of Fgn. Langs. (exec. bd. 1994—), Pacific N.W. Coun. Fgn. Langs., 1986—, Nat. Assn. Fgn. Lang. Suprs., Sigma Delta Mu. (nat. exec. sec. 1992—). Avocations: travel, rsch. on 2d lang., outdoors. Home: 8720 229th Pl SW Edmonds WA 98026-8438 Office: Highline Coll 240th & Pacific Hwy S Des Moines WA 98198

WILSON, DOROTHY CLARKE, author; b. Gardiner, Maine, May 9, 1904; d. Lewis Herbert and Flora Eva (Cross) Clarke; m. Elwin L. Wilson, Aug. 31, 1925; adopted children: Joan S., Harold Elwin (dec.). A.B., Bates Coll., 1925, Litt.D., 1947; L.H.D., U. Maine, 1984. Author of: about seventy religious plays, vol. religious plays Twelve Months of Drama for the Average Church, 1934; novels The Brother, 1944, The Herdsman, 1946, Prince of Egypt, 1949 (winner Westminster $7500 award for best religious novel), House of Earth, 1952, Fly With Me to India, 1954, Jezebel, 1955, The Gifts, 1957, Dr. Ida: A Biography Dr. Ida S. Scudder of India, 1959, The Journey, 1962, Take My Hands: Biography Dr. Mary Verghese, 1963, The Three Gifts, 1963, Ten Fingers for God: Biography Dr. Paul Brand, 1965, Handicap Race: The Story of Roger Arnett, 1967, Palace of Healing, The Story of Dr. Clara Swain, 1968, Lone Woman: Biography of Dr. Elizabeth Blackwell, 1970, The Big-Little World of Doc Pritham, 1971, Hilary, The Brave World of Hilary Pole, 1973, Bright Eyes, the Story of Susette La Flesche-an Omaha Indian, 1974, Stranger and Traveler, The Story of Dorothea Dix, American Reformer, 1975, Climb Every Mountain, 1976, Granny Brand, Her Story, 1976, Twelve Who Cared: My Adventures with Christian Courage, 1977, Apostle of Sight, Story of Dr. Victor Rambo, 1980, Lincoln's Mothers: A Story of Nancy and Sally Lincoln, 1981, Lady Washington, 1984, Queen Dolley: A Story of Dolley Madison, 1987, Alice and Edith: The Wives of Theodore Roosevelt, 1989, Union in Diversity: The Story of Our Marriage, 1993, Leaves in the Wind: A Lifetime in Verse, 1994; lectr. on India, Middle East. Trustee Bates Coll. Recipient Woman of Distinction award Alpha Delta Kappa, 1971, New Eng. United Meth. award, 1975, Distinguished Achievement award U. Maine, 1977, achievement citation award AAUW, 1988, MaryAnn Hartman award U. Maine, 1989, Deborah Morton award Westbrook Coll., 1989. Mem. Phi Beta Kappa. Home: 117 Bennoch Rd Orono ME 04473-1121

WILSON, DWIGHT LISTON, former military officer, investment advisor; b. Hereford, Tex., Oct. 30, 1931; s. Liston Oscar and Pauline (Smart) W.; m. Barbara Ann Alderman, Sept. 4, 1955; children: Terri Ann, Ron Alan, Diana Kay. B.A. in Govt., Okla. U., 1953; M.A. in Public Adminstrn., Shippensburg (Pa.) U., 1973. Commd. 2d lt. U.S. Army, 1953, advanced through grades to maj. gen., 1980; service in Vietnam, W.Ger.; dir. force mgmt. (Hdqrs. Dept. Army), Washington, 1979-80; ret., 1980; fin. cons., resident mgr. Merrill Lynch, Pierce, Fenner and Smith, Punta Gorda, Fla., 1981-95. Decorated D.S.M., Legion of Merit, Bronze Star, Meritorious Service medal, Army Commendation medal (3), Air medal (10). Mem. Assn. U.S. Army. Methodist.

WILSON, EARLE LAWRENCE, church administrator; b. Rensselaer, N.Y., Dec. 8, 1934; s. Lawrence Wilbur Wilson and Wilhelaminia Knapp; m. Sylvia M. Beck; children: Deborah, Stephen, Colleen. B in Theology, United Wesleyan Coll., 1956, BS, 1961; M of Divinity, Evang. Sch. of Theology, 1965; M of Theology, Princeton Theol. Sem., 1967; D of Divinity, Houghton Coll., 1974. Sr. pastor Wesleyan Church, Gloversville, N.Y., 1956-61; gen. supt. Wesleyan Church, Indpls., 1984—; sr. pastor First Wesleyan Church, Bethlehem, Pa., 1961-72; pres. United Wesleyan Coll., Allentown, Pa., 1972-84. Author: When You Get Where You're Going, 1966, Within a Hair's Breadth, 1989. Mem. chaplain Rotary. Republican. Home: 11697 Pompano Dr Indianapolis IN 46236-8819 Office: Wesleyan Ch PO Box 50434 Indianapolis IN 46250-0434*

WILSON, EDWARD CONVERSE, JR., oil and natural gas production company executive; b. Cambridge, Mass., Jan. 1, 1928; s. Edward Converse and Jean (McLean) W.; m. Patricia Ann Cairns, Sept. 10, 1953; children—Amy Cairns, Sarah Converse. A.B., Harvard U., 1949. Brokerage trainee Estabrook & Co., Boston, 1951; Midwest Stock Exchange clk. Paul H. Davis & Co., Chgo., 1951-52; mem. Chgo. Bd. Trade, 1952-78, dir., 1966-67, chmn., 1970-71; partner Nolan & Wilson Co. (specialists on Midwest Stock Exchange), 1965-72; sr. partner Wilson Prodn. Co., Ft. Smith, Ark., 1972-74; dir. Rutledge Assos., Wakefield, Mass., 1965-74, Paul H. Robinson Inc., Chgo., 1972-81. Mem. devel. com. Chgo. chpt. Nat. Multiple Sclerosis Soc., 1970; mem. vis. com. on univ. resources Harvard, 1971-74, 76-81; Bd. dirs. Franklin Blvd. Community Hosp., 1970-74. Served with USAAF, 1946-47. Mem. Racquet Club (Chgo.). Home: 11114 Wickwood Dr Houston TX 77024-7523 Office: 1770 Saint James Pl Houston TX 77056-3405

WILSON, EDWARD COX, minister; b. Danville, Va., Sept. 30, 1938; s. James Thomas and Sallie Estelle (Cox) W.; m. Nancy Alva Hudson, Aug. 9, 1960; children: Michael Edward, Suzanne Adams. AB magna cum laude, Elon Coll., 1960; MDiv, Union Sem., 1965. Ordained to ministry Presbyn. Ch. (U.S.A.), 1965. Pastor Meadowbrook Presbyn. Ch., Greenville, N.C., 1965-67, Indian Trail (N.C.) Presbyn. Ch., 1971-86, Locust (N.C.) Presbyn. Ch., 1987-92; assoc. pastor Selwyn Ave Presbyn. Ch., Charlotte, N.C., 1968-71; pastor Williams Meml. Presbyn. Ch., Charlotte, 1992-97; interim min., 1997—; commr. Gen. Assembly, Presbyn. Ch. (U.S.A.), 1973, 79, 86; mem. com. on ministry, nomination com., mem. coun. Presbytery, also moderator, 1976-77. Author: Broken--But Not Beyond Repair, 1992, Play Ball! Reflections on Coaching Young Folk, 1994; contbr. articles, sermons and prayers to religious jours. Union Theol. Sem. fellow, 1965. Mem. Alban Inst. Democrat. Home: 8618 Appaloosa Way Ln Charlotte NC 28216-8732 *In my life I am discovering that love is the primary law and the basic creed.*

WILSON, EDWARD NATHAN, mathematician, educator; b. Warsaw, N.Y., Dec. 2, 1941; s. Hugh Monroe and Margaret Jane (Northrup) W.; m. Mary Katherine Schooling, Aug. 19, 1976; children: Nathan Edward, Emily Katherine. BA, Cornell U., 1963; MS, Stanford U., 1965; PhD, Washington U., St. Louis, 1971. Instr. Ft. Valley (Ga.) State Coll., 1965-67, Washington U., St. Louis, 1968-69, U. Calif., Irvine, 1970-71, Brandeis U., Waltham, Mass., 1971-73; asst. prof. Washington U., St. Louis, 1973-77, assoc. prof., 1977-87, dean grad. sch., 1983-93, dean univ. coll., 1986-88, prof., 1987—, chair dept. math., 1995—; mem. Grad. Record Exams. Bd., Princeton, N.J., 1986-90; sec.-treas. Assn. Grad. Schs. Contbr. articles to profl. jours. Mem. Brentwood Sch. Bd., Mo., 1984. Woodrow Wilson fellow, 1963; NSF fellow, 1963-65; NDEA fellow, 1967-70. Mem. Am. Math. Soc., Math. Assn. of Am. Democrat. Office: Washington U Campus Box 1146 1 Brookings Dr Saint Louis MO 63130-4862

WILSON, EDWARD OSBORNE, biologist, educator, author; b. Birmingham, Ala., June 10, 1929; s. Edward Osborne and Inez (Freeman) W.; m. Irene Kelley, Oct. 30, 1955; 1 dau., Catherine Irene; BS, U. Ala., 1949, MS, 1950, LHD (hon.), 1980; PhD, Harvard U., 1955; DPhil, Uppsala (Sweden) U.; DS (hon.), Duke U., 1978, Grinnell Coll., 1978, U. West Fla., 1979, Lawrence U., 1979, Fitchburg State Coll., 1989, Macalester Coll., U. Mass., 1990, Oxford U., 1993, Ripon Coll., 1994, U. Conn., 1995, Ohio U., 1996, Bates Coll., 1996, Coll. Wooster, 1997; U. Guelph, 1997, U. Portland, 1997; DPhil, Uppsala U., 1987; LHD (hon.), Hofstra U., 1986; Pa. State U., Bradford Coll., 1997; D.h.c., U. Madrid Complutense, 1995; LLD, Simon Fraser U.; U. Portland, 1997. Jr. fellow Soc. Fellows, Harvard U., 1953-56, mem. faculty, 1956—, Baird prof. sci., 1976-94, Pellegrino U. prof., 1994—, curator entomology, 1971—; fellow Guggenheim Found., 1978, mem. selection com., 1982-89; bd. dirs. World Wildlife Fund, 1983-94, Orgn. Tropical Studies, 1984-91, N.Y. Bot. Gardens, 1991-95, Am. Mus. Natural History, 1992—, Am. Acad. Liberal Edn., 1993—, Nature Conservancy, 1994—, Conservation Internat., 1997—. Author: The Insect Societies, 1971, Sociobiology: The New Synthesis, 1975, On Human Nature, 1978 (Pulitzer prize for non-fiction 1979), (with C.J. Lumsden) Promethean Fire, 1983, Biophilia, 1984, (with Bert Holldobler) The Ants, 1990 (Pulitzer prize for non-fiction 1991), Success and Dominance in Ecosystems, 1990, The Diversity of Life, 1992 (Nat. Wildlife Assn. award Sir Peter Kent Conservation prize), (with Bert Holldobler) Journey to the Ants, 1994 (Phi Beta Kappa prize sci. 1995), Naturalist, 1994 (L.A. Times Book prize sci. 1995), In Search of Nature, 1996. Recipient Cleve.-AAAS rsch. prize, 1967, Nat. Medal Sci., 1976, Leidy medal Acad. Natural Sci., Phila., 1979, Disting. Svc. award Am. Inst. Biol. Scis., 1976, Mercer award Ecol. Soc. Am., 1971, Founders Meml. award and L.O. Howard award Entomol. Soc. Am., 1972, 85, Archie Carr medal U. Fla., 1978, Disting. Svc. award Am. Humanist Soc., 1982, Tyler ecology prize, 1984, Silver medal Nat. Zool. Park, German Ecol. Inst. prize, 1987, Weaver award scholarly letters Ingersoll Found., 1989, Crafoord prize Royal Swedish Acad. Scis., 1990, Prix d'Inst. de la Vie, Paris, 1990, Revelle medal, 1990, Gold medal Worldwide Fund for Nature, 1990, Achievement award Nat. Wildlife Fedn., 1992, Shaw medal Mo. Bot. Garden, 1993, Internat. prize Biology Govt. of Japan, 1993, Eminent Ecologist award, 1994, Audubon medal Audubon Soc., 1995, AAAS Pub. Understanding Sci. award, 1995, John Hay award Orion Audubon Soc., 1995, Schubert prize, Germany, 1996, Washburn award Mus. Sci., 1996, Hutchinson Medal Garden Club Am., 1997, others. Fellow Am. Acad. Arts and Scis., Am. Phil. Soc., Deutsche Akad. Naturforsch; mem. NAS, Am. Genetics Assn. (hon. life), Brit. Ecol. Soc. (hon. life), Entomol. Soc. Am. (hon. life), Zool. Soc. London (hon. life), Am. Humanist Soc. (hon. life), Acad. Humanism (hon. life), Netherlands Entomol. Soc. (hon. life), Royal Soc. London, Finnish Acad. Sci. and Letters, Russian Acad. Nat. Sci., Royal Soc. Sci. Uppsala (Sweden), others. Home: 9 Foster Rd Lexington MA 02173-5505 Office: Harvard U Mus Comparative Zoology Cambridge MA 02138

WILSON, EMERY ALLEN, university dean, obstetrician-gynecologist, educator; b. Frankfort, Ky., Apr. 8, 1942; s. Emery Lee and Mary Catheryne (Cooper) W.; m. Clara Bullock, June 18, 1966; children: Emily, Bryan. BA, Emory U., 1964; MD, U. Ky., 1968. Diplomate Am. Bd. Ob-Gyn (examiner 1979-89), Am. Bd. Reproductive Endocrinology. Intern, resident U. Ky., 1968-72; instr. Harvard U. Med. Sch., Boston, 1974-76; asst. prof. ob-gyn U. Ky. Coll. Medicine, Lexington, 1976-79, assoc. prof., 1979-81, prof., 1981—, dean, 1987—, dir. Ctr. for Reproductive Medicine, 1983-87; vice chancellor for clin. profession svcs. U. Ky., 1987—; cons. Nat. Inst. Occupational Safety and Health, Cin., 1980-82; dir. Florence Crittendon House, Lexington, 1986-89. Editor: Nutrition in Pregnancy, 1980, Endometriosis, 1987, Professional Management and Practice Management, 1989; author over 100 articles, book chpts., abstracts; reviewer several profl. jours. Maj. USAF, 1972-74. Recipient Acad. Tng. award Ortho Pharms., 1972. Fellow Am. Coll. Obstetricians and Gynecologists; mem. Am. Fertility Soc., Soc. Gynecologic Investigation, Alpha Omega Alpha, Omicron Delta Kappa. Mem. Disciples of Christ Ch. Home: 967 Edgewater Dr Lexington KY 40502-3011 Office: U Ky Coll Medicine 800 Rose St Lexington KY 40536-0001*

WILSON, ESTHER ELINORE, technical college educator; b. Uehling, Nebr., Nov. 4, 1921; d. Lorenz John and Dorothea Emma Rosena (Schmidt) Paulsen; m. Billy LeRoy Wilson, Nov. 14, 1919; 1 child, Frances Ann Wilson Dellar. BS, Morningside Coll., 1950; postgrad., U. Nebr., 1947-80, U. S.D., 1954-83; MS, U. Minn., 1963. Cert. postsecondary tchr., Iowa. Tchr. Irvington (Nebr.) Pub. Schs., 1942-44, Immanuel Luth. Schs., Wichita, Kans., 1944-45, Winnebago (Nebr.) Pub. Schs., 1946-50, Nat. Bus. Coll., Sioux City, Iowa, 1950-51; tchr., asst. prin. Liberty Consol. Sch., Merrill, Iowa, 1951-55; mktg. tchr. coord. South Sioux City (Nebr.) Community Schs., 1955-86; adj. faculty prof. adult basic edn. Western Iowa Tech. Coll., Sioux City, 1989-94; mgr. rental properties Sioux City, 1950—; real estate assoc. State Nat., Dakota City, Nebr., 1988-92, Century 21 Marketplace, Sioux City, 1987-88; advt. sales mgr. Auto Hotline, South Sioux City, 1986-87. Author: I Said I Would, 1995; contbg. author: Siouxland Anthology, 1995, Capturing Our Heritage, 1996. Vol. tchr. N.E. Nebr. C.C., South Sioux City, 1987-90; supt. St. Paul's Luth. Sunday Sch., Sioux City, 1972-76; treas. Hope Luth. Ch., 1989-95; SBA counselor SCORE, 1995—; co-pres. Friends of Libr., South Sioux City, 1986-88; fundraiser South Sioux City Pub. Libr., 1984-85; pres. Am. Cancer Soc., Dakota County, Nebr., 1979-88; state pres. Nebr. Bus. Edn. Assn., 1979, Distributive Edn. Tchrs. Assn., 1980. Recipient Outstanding Svc. to State Orgns., Nebr. Vocat. Edn. Assn., 1976, Woman of the Yr. Am. Bus. Women Assn., 1972. Mem. Nebr. State Edn. Assn. (sec., treas., v.p., pres., Dedicated Svc. award 1986), NEA, South Sioux City Chamberettes (sec., v.p., pres. 1972-89), Am. Federated Women's Club (sec., v.p., pres.). Avocations: reading, political and economic studies, gardening, evangelism. Home and Office: 435 Dixon Path South Sioux City NE 68776

WILSON, EUGENE ROLLAND, foundation executive; b. Findlay, Ohio, Jan. 14, 1938; s. Clair and Ethel Bernice (Cryer) W.; m. Mary Ann Dalton; children: Jeff, Andy. B.A., Bowling Green State U., 1960; M.S., Syracuse U., 1961. Dir. devel., asst. to pres. Bowling Green (Ohio) State U., 1966-70; mgr. radio-TV advt. Columbia Gas of Ohio, Inc., Columbus, 1964-66; assoc. dir. devel. Calif. Inst. Tech., Pasadena, 1971-77, v.p. for inst. relations, 1979-80; assoc. dir. ARCO Found., Los Angeles, 1977-79, exec. dir., 1980-83, pres., 1984-94; pres. youth devel. Ewing Marion Kauffman Found., Kansas City, Mo., 1995—; chmn. contbns. coun. Conf. Bd.; mem. corp. grant makers com. Coun. of Founds. Nat. bd. of visitors Ctr. on Philanthropy; founding trustee Arcadia (Calif.) Edn. Found.; elder trustee Presbyn. Ch. Named Outstanding Young Man Bowling Green Jaycees, 1967; recipient hon. service award Hugo Reid Sch. PTA, 1977, Corp. Social Responsibility award Mex.-Am. Legal Def. and Edn. Fund, 1989, Nat. Leadership award in edn. Inst. for Ednl. Leadership, 1992. Mem. Bowling Green State U. Alumni Assn. (pres. 1965), Gnome and Athenaeum Clubs of Caltech, Omicron Delta Kappa. Home: 14117 W 56th Ct Shawnee KS 66216-4696 Office: 4900 Oak St Kansas City MO 64112-2702 *Our values and judgments are shaped by our roots. The special relationships developed in small-town rural America, and the many opportunities to enjoy a variety of leadership experiences, prove invaluable later in life to cope with the broader, more vexing problems of pluralistic society. Later sophistication—tempered by the humility of those early roots—then becomes more meaningful.*

WILSON, EWEN MACLELLAN, economist; b. Nairobi, Kenya, July 29, 1944; came to U.S., 1969; s. Walter Maclellan and Barbara (Gange) Maclellan W.; m. Kay Stephens, May 31, 1969; children: Libby, Cindy, Riara. BS, U. London, 1965; MS, W.Va. U., 1970; PhD, N.C. State U., 1973. With conservation and extension dept. Ministry of Agrl., Banket, Rhodesia, 1965-68; research fellow U. Rhodesia, Salisbury, 1973-74; asst. prof. Va. Tech. Inst., Blacksburg, 1975-77; dir. econs. and stats. Am. Meat Inst., Arlington, Va., 1977-83, v.p., 1983-85; apptd. dep. asst. sec. U.S. Dept. Agrl., Washington, 1985-87, asst. sec., 1987-89; pres. Wilson Agribus. Analysis, 1989-90; exec. dir. Commodity Futures Trading Commn., Washington, 1990-94; chief agriculture and fin. statistics div. Bur. of Census, Washington, 1994—; bd. dirs. Nat. Cooperative Bank, 1988-90, Commodity Credit Corp, 1987-89. Mem. Am. Agrl. Econs. Assn. Republican. Episcopalian. Office: Bur of Census 437 Iverson AGFS Washington DC 20233

WILSON, FRANCES EDNA, protective services official; b. Keokuk, Iowa, Aug. 4, 1955; d. David Eugene and Anna Bell (Hootman) W. BA, St. Ambrose Coll., 1982; MA, Western Ill., 1990; cert. massage therapist, Shocks Ctr. for Edn., Moline, Ill., 1993. Lic. massage therapist, Iowa. Trainer, defensive tactics Davenport (Iowa) Police, 1990—, police corporal, 1985-94; police sgt. Iowa Assn. Women Police, Davenport, 1994—, apptd. recs. bur. comdr., 1996—, pres., 1989-92; cons., def. tactics Scott C.C., Bettendorf, Iowa, 1993—; owner Wilson Enterprises Ltd., Davenport, 1995—; spkr. workshops; guest spkr. Genesis Employee Assistance Program, 1996. Bd. dirs. Scott County Family YMCA, Davenport, 1990-95, instr., 1989—, The Family Connection, Ltd.; instr. Davenport Cmty. Adult Edn., 1991-94; mem. Iowa SAFE KIDS Coalition, 1992—; mem. First Presbyn. Ch., Davenport, 1986—, bd. deacons, 1995; vol. asst. Davenport Police Dept.'s Sgts. Planning Com. on Tng., 1991, K-9 Unit, 1990-94. Recipient Law Enforcement award Davenport Optimist Club, 1997. Mem. Am. Soc. Law Enforcement Trainers, Law Enforcement Alliance Am., Am. Women Self Def. Assn., Nat. Ctr. for Women and Policing, Iowa Assn. Women Police (pres. 1989-92, Officer of Yr. 1995), Iowa State Police Assn., Internat. Platform Assn., Internat. Assn. Women Police. Avocations: photography, reading, education, massage therapy, enjoying life. Office: Davenport Police Dept 420 N Harrison St Davenport IA 52801-1304

WILSON, F(RANCIS) PAUL, novelist, screenwriter; b. Jersey City, May 17, 1946; s. Frank P. and Mary (Sullivan) W.; m. Mary Murphy, Aug. 23, 1969. BS, Georgetown U., 1968. With Cedar Bridge Med. Group, Bricktown, N.Y., 1974—. Author: Healer, 1976, 2d edit., 1992, Wheels Within Wheels, 1978, 2d edit., 1992, An Enemy of the State, 1980, 2d edit., 1992, The Keep, 1981 (N.Y. Times bestseller list), 2d edit., 1982, The Tomb, 1984 (N.Y. Times bestseller list, Porgie award West Coast Rev. Books 1984), The Touch, 1986, Black Wind, 1988, Soft and Others, 1989, Dydeetown World, 1989, The Tery, 1990, Reborn, 1990, Reprisal, 1991, Sibs, 1991, Nightworld, 1991, The Select, 1994, Implant, 1995, Deep as the Marrow, 1996; co-author: (with Matthew J. Costello) Mirage, 1996, (TV teleplay) Glim-Glim, 1989, (with Matthew J. Costello) FTL NewsFeed, 1992-96; editor: Freak Show, 1992, Diagnosis: Terminal, 1996; also numerous short stories. Office: care Albert Zuckerman Writers House 21 W 26th St New York NY 10010-1003

WILSON, FRANK HENRY, electrical engineer; b. Dinuba, Calif., Dec. 4, 1935; s. Frank Henry and Lurene (Copley) W.; m. Carol B. Greening, Mar. 28, 1964; children: Frank, Scott E. BS, Oreg. State U., 1957. Electronic engr. Varian Assoc., Palo Alto, Calif., 1960-61, Stanford U. Med. Sch., Palo Alto, 1961-68, U. Calif. Med. Sch., Davis, 1968-77, Litronix, Cupertino, Calif., 1978-81, Quantel, Santa Clara, Calif., 1981-87, Heraeus Lasersonics, Milpitas, Calif., 1987-91, Continuum Electro-Optics, Santa Clara, Calif., 1992-96. 1st lt. Signal Corps U.S. Army, 1958-60. Mem. IEEE. Home: 3826 Nathan Way Palo Alto CA 94303-4519

WILSON, FRANK LYNDALL, surgeon; b. Oct. 29, 1926; children: Frank L. III, Patricia W. Major; m. Kristina F. Wilson, June 29, 1984. BS, Emory U., 1948, MD, 1952. Diplomate Am. Bd. Surgery, 1960. Surg. intern Univ. Hosps. Cleve., 1952-53; asst. surg. resident Grady Meml. Hosp., Atlanta, 1953, 55-58, chief surg. resident, 1958-59, now mem. surg. staff; pvt. practice surgery, Atlanta, 1959—; chmn. dept. surgery Piedmont Hosp., Atlanta, 1984-91 , also trustee, mem. surg. staff; clin. asst. prof. surgery Emory U. Sch. Medicine; mem. staff Crawford W. Long Meml. Hosp. Trustee Lovett Sch., 1971-79, Piedmont Hosp., 1984-91; chmn. med. div. United Way Atlanta, 1978. Served with USN, 1944-46, 53-55. Fellow ACS (pres. Ga. chpt. 1976-77); mem. Med. Assn. Atlanta (dir. 1977-82, pres. 1980, chmn. med. adv. com. selective service, peer rev. com.), Atlanta Med. Heritage Inc. (pres. 1980-83), Med. Assn. Ga. (vice councilor 1966-68, del.), Ga. Surg. Soc. (pres. 1990-91), So. Med. Assn., AMA, Atlanta Clin. Soc. Rocky Mountain Traumatological Soc. Presbyterian. Club: Piedmont Driving, Highlands Country (N.C.). Office: 95 Collier Rd NW Ste 6015 Atlanta GA 30309-1721

WILSON, FRANKLIN D., sociology educator; b. Birmingham, Ala., Sept. 3, 1942; s. Ernest and Ollie Lee (Carter) W.; children—Rachel, Chareese. B.A., Miles Coll., 1964; postgrad., Atlanta U., 1964-65; M.A., Wash. State U., 1971, Ph.D., 1973. Instr. Grambling U., La., 1965-66; prof. sociology U. Wis.-Madison, 1973—; cons. Madison Pub. Schs. 1976—; cons. planning dept. City of Madison, Wis., 1984—. Author: Residential Consumption, Economic Opportunities and Race, 1979. Served with U.S. Army, 1966-69; Vietnam. Decorated Purple Heart, Silver Star, Vietnam medal of Valor. Mem. Am. Statis. Assn., Population Assn. Am., Am. Sociol. Assn. Unitarian. Avocation: swimming. Office: U Wis Ctr for Demography and Ecology Social Sci Bldg Madison WI 53713

WILSON, FRED M., II, ophthalmologist, educator; b. Indpls., Dec. 10, 1940; s. Fred Madison and Elizabeth (Fredrick) W.; m. Karen Joy Lyman, Sept. 10, 1959 (div. June 1962); 1 child, Teresa Wilson Kulick; m. Claytonia Leigh Pemberton, Aug. 28, 1964; children: Yvonne Wilson Hacker, Jennifer, Benjamin James. AB in Med. Scis., Ind. U., 1962, MD, 1965. Cert. Am. Bd. Ophthalmology. Intern Sacred Heart Hosp., Spokane, Wash., 1965-66; resident in ophthalmology Ind. U., Indpls., 1968-71, fellow in ophthalmology, 1971-72; fellow in ophthalmology F.I. Proctor Found., San Francisco, 1972-73; from asst. prof. to assoc. prof. ophthalmology Ind. U., Indpls., 1972-76, prof. ophthalmology, 1981—; med. dir. Ind. Lions Eye Bank, Inc., Indpls., 1973—; cons. surgeon Ind. U., Indpls., 1973—. Author or editor numerous sci. articles, book chpts. and books on ophthalmology. Lt. comdr. USNR, 1966-68, PTO. Mem. Am. Acad. Ophthalmology (assoc. sec. 1988-93, Sr. Teaching award 1989), Assn. Proctor Fellows, Soc. Heed Fellows, Am. Ophthalmol. Soc., Am. Bd. Ophthalmology (bd. dirs. 1993—), Ill. Soc. Ophthalmology (hon.), Mont. Acad. Ophthalmology (hon.), Pacific-Coast Ophthalmol. Soc. (hon.). Republican. Avocations: photography, guitar, history, language, natural history. Home: 12262 Crestwood Dr Carmel IN 46033-4323 Office: Ind U Sch Medicine Dept Ophthalmolgy 702 Rotary Cir Indianapolis IN 46202-5133

WILSON, FREDERIC SANDFORD, pharmaceutical company executive; b. Schenectady, NY, Mar. 28, 1944; s. Robert Omer and Isabel May (Sandford) W.; children: Amy Kathleen, Adrienne Ann; m. Judith Ann Goettsche, Feb. 7, 1973; children: Marla Ann, Brian Bennett, Jessica Lea, Jennifer Lynn. BS, Syracuse U., 1968. Acct. exec. Mastropaul Design Inc., Syracuse, N.Y., 1969-70; copy editor Norwich Eaton Pharms., Norwich, N.Y., 1970-72; sales rep. Norwich Eaton Pharms., Gary, Ind., 1972-73; asst. product mgr. Norwich Eaton Pharms., Norwich, 1974-75, mktg. svcs. mgr., 1975-76, product mgr., 1977-81, bus. devel. mgr., 1981-83, sr. product mgr., 1983-85, mgr. med. foods, 1986-89; assoc. mktg. mgr. P&G Pharms., Norwich, 1989-92; dir. profl. rels. P & G Pharms., Cin., 1993-96; mgr. mktg. svcs. P&G, Cin., 1997—; cons. Sandoz Nutrition Corp., Mpls., 1992. Inventor Jejunostomy Kit, 1981, Vivonex T.E.N. med. food, 1983, Tolerex med. food, 1987. Bd. dirs. Syracuse U. Minority Access Program, 1989-91, Nat. Osteo. Found.; mem. Alliance for Continuing Med. Edn. Mem. Pharms. Assn. for Continuing Med. Edn. (chmn.), Am. Dietetic Assn. (corp. leadership coun.). Office: Procter & Gamble 2 Procter And Gamble Plz # Tn3 Cincinnati OH 45202-3314

WILSON, FREDERICK ALLEN, medical educator, medical center administrator, gastroenterologist; b. Winchester, Mass., Aug. 22, 1937; s. Warren Archibald and Alice Jane (Springall) W.; m. Lynne Stewart Cantley, Feb. 24, 1962; children: Douglas, Victoria. A.B., Colgate U., 1959; M.D., Albany Med. Coll., 1963. Intern Hartford Hosp., Conn., 1963-64, resident in medicine, 1964-66; fellow in gastroenterology Albany Med. Coll., N.Y., 1966-67; USPHS postdoctoral fellow in gastroenterology U. Tex. Southwestern Med. Sch., Dallas, 1969-72; asst. prof. medicine Vanderbilt U. Sch. Medicine, Nashville, 1972-76, assoc. prof., 1976-82, mem. adv. com. clin. research ctr., 1978-81; prof. medicine, chief div. gastroenterology Milton S. Hershey Med. Ctr., Pa. State U., Hershey, 1982-90; prof. medicine, dir. div. gastroenterology Med. U. S.C., Charleston, 1990-94; mem. ACP Med. Knowledge Self-Assessment Program VI, 1980-81; mem. gastroenterology and clin. nutrition rev. group Nat. Inst. ARthritis, Diabetes, Digestive and Kidney Disease, NIH, Bethesda, Md., 1985-89; pre=reviewer Am. Coun. Grad. Med. Edn., 1994-95. Contbr. numerous articles, abstracts, chpts. to profl. pubs.; reviewer for sci. jours. Served to maj. M.C., U.S. Army, 1967-69. Recipient Clin. Investigator award VA Med. Ctr., Nashville, 1972-75; recipient Investigator award Howard Hughes Med. Inst., Vanderbilt U., 1975-78; NIH Fogarty Internat. Ctr. sr. internat. fellow Max Planck Inst. for Biophysics, Frankfurt, W.Ger., 1979-80. Mem. Am. Fedn. Clin. Research, Central Soc. Clin. Research, Am. Gastroenterology Assn., Am. Assn. Study Liver Diseases, Am. Soc. Clin. Investigation, N.Y. Acad. Scis., So. Car. Med. Assn., Eastern Gut Club, Pa. Soc. Gastroenterology. Office: Med U SC Div Gastroenterology 171 Ashley Ave Charleston SC 29425-0001

WILSON, GARY DEAN, lawyer; b. Wichita, Kans., June 7, 1943; s. Glenn E. and Roe Zella (Mills) W.; m. Diane Kay Williams, Dec. 29, 1965; children: Mark R., Matthew C., Christopher G. BA, Stanford U., 1965, LLB, 1968. Bar: D.C. 1970, U.S. Dist. Ct. D.C. 1970, U.S. Ct. Appeals (D.C. cir.) 1972, U.S. Ct. Appeals (7th cir.) 1979, U.S. Ct. Appeals (2d cir.) 1983. Law clk. U.S. Ct. Appeals, 2d cir., N.Y.C., 1968-69, U.S. Supreme Ct., Washington, 1969-70; assoc. Wilmer, Cutler & Pickering, Washington, 1970-75, ptnr., 1976—; acting prof. law Stanford (Calif.) Law Sch., 1981-82. Bd. visitors Stanford Law Sch., 1990-92. Democrat. Home: 4636 30th St NW Washington DC 20008-2127 Office: Wilmer Cutler & Pickering 2445 M St NW Washington DC 20037-1435

WILSON, GARY LEE, airline company executive; b. Alliance, Ohio, Jan. 16, 1940; s. Elvin John and Fern Helen (Donaldson) W.; children: Derek, Christopher. BA, Duke U., 1962; MBA, U. Pa., 1963. V.p. fin., dir. Trans-Philippines Investment Co., Manila, 1964-70; exec. v.p., dir. Checchi & Co., Washington, 1971-73; exec. v.p. Marriott Corp., Washington, 1973-85; exec. v.p., chief exec. officer, dir. The Walt Disney Co., Burbank, Calif., 1985-89, dir., 1990; chmn. bd. Northwest Airlines, Inc., St. Paul, Minn., 1990—.

WILSON, GENEVA JUNE, gerontology nurse, consultant; b. Albany, Tex., July 30, 1931; d. Alford Addison and Francis Aliene (Smith) Alexander; children: Carla, Jeff, Susan, Laura. AA with honors, Ranger (Tex.) Jr. Coll., 1951; BSN, Tex. Christian U., 1957; diploma with honors, LNHA Wayland Bapt. U., Plainview, Tex., 1989. Cert. CPR; lic. nursing home adminstr. Dir. nursing svc. Univ. Hosp., Lubbock, Tex.; assoc. dir. nursing edn., instr. Sch. Nursing Meth. Hosp., Lubbock; discharge planner Lubbock Gen. Hosp.; nursing cons. ARA Living Ctrs., Houston; quality assurance profl. Beverly Enterprises (now Complete Care Svcs.), Austin, Tex.; adminstr. Lubbock Health Care & Rehab. Ctr./Beverly Enterprises; owner Big Country Home Health Agy., Abilene, Tex. Mem. Am. Bus. Women's Assn., Harris Coll. Nursing-Tex. Christian U. Alumni Assn.

WILSON, GEORGE PETER, international organization executive; b. Perth, Scotland, July 6, 1935; came to U.S., 1985; s. Alan Johnson and Doris L. (Allan) W.; m. Sandra Graham, Feb. 6, 1960 (div. 1984); 1 child, Iain; m. Robbyn Dee LaCroix, Nov. 17, 1984; 1 stepchild, Orion. Diploma in Hotel Mgmt., Scottish Coll. Commerce, Glasgow, 1954. Chartered acct., 1965, cert. internal auditor, 1985. Hotel mgr., auditor Can. Nat. Rys., Ottawa and Montreal, 1956-65; fin. officer Treasury Bd. Can., asst. sec. to Cabinet, dir. Pub. Service Commn., counsellor external affairs Govt. of Can., Ottawa, Geneva, 1965-78; dir. gen. audit UN, N.Y.C., 1978-80; dep. auditor gen. of Can. Govt. of Can., Ottawa, 1980-85; pres. Inst. Internal Auditors, Orlando, Fla., 1985-92; dir. audit FAO UN, Rome, 1992—. Contbr. articles to profl. jours. Mem. Can. Inst. Chartered Accts. (com. mem.), Inst. Internal Auditors (com. mem.), Can. Comprehensive Audit Found. (gov. 1985-88), Internat. Consortium on Govt. Fin. Mgmt. (bd. dirs. 1983-92), Inst. for Fin. Crime Prevention. Home: Via Giulia 98 # 9, 00186 Rome Italy Office: FAO HQ, Viale delle Terme di, Caracalla, 00100 Rome Italy

WILSON, GEORGE WHARTON, newspaper editor; b. Phila., Feb. 22, 1923; s. Joshua Wharton and Eva (Frear) W.; m. Neva Jean Gossett, Nov. 18, 1950; children: Guy Richard, Lee Robert. B.A., Western Md. Coll., 1947; postgrad., U. Pa., 1948. Reporter, city editor News-Chronicle, Shippensburg, Pa., 1945-46; asst. news dir. Sta. WILM-Radio, Wilmington, Del., 1947-48; sports editor Evening Chronicle, Uhrichsville, Ohio, 1948-49, editor, 1949-50; editor Daily Record, Morristown, N.J., 1950-54; chief editorial writer Standard-Times, New Bedford, Mass., 1954-59; editorial writer Phila. Inquirer, 1959-64, chief editorial writer, 1964-87. Author: Yesterday's Philadelphia, 1975, Stephen Girard: America's First Tycoon, 1995. Served with USAAF, 1942-45. Recipient George Washington honor medal Freedoms Found., 1961, 67, 72; Phila. Press Assn. award editorial writing, 1967, 68; award for editorial writing Pa. Press Assn., 1972, 79; award for editorial writing U.S. Indsl. Council, 1975, 77; Disting. Service award Sigma Delta Chi, 1977; Disting. Journalism award Citizens Com. on Public Edn. in Phila., 1978; Public Service award Phila. Convention and Visitors Bur., 1980; award for column writing N.J. Soc. Profl. Journalists, 1981; Elm award Fishtown Civic Assn., 1982. Mem. Am. Acad. Polit. and Social Sci., Franklin Inst., Acad. Natural Sci., Hist. Soc. Pa., Soc. Profl. Journalists, Phila. Mus. Art, Phila. Maritime Mus., Phila. Writers Orgn., Phila. Zool. Soc., Pa. Soc., Friends of Independence Nat. Hist. Park, Huguenot Hist. Soc., Pa. Acad. Fine Arts, Pen and Pencil Club (Phila.), Elks, Am. Legion. Republican. Congregationalist. Club: Pen and Pencil (Phila.). Home: PO Box 617 Albrightsville PA 18210-0617

WILSON, GEORGE WILTON, economics educator; b. Winnipeg, Man., Can., Feb. 15, 1928; came to U.S., 1952, naturalized, 1970; s. Walter and Ida (Wilton) W.; m. I. Marie McKinney, Sept. 6, 1952 (dec. July 1986); children: Ronald Leslie, Douglas Scott, Suzanne Rita; m. Joan Murdock, May 16, 1988. B.Commerce, Carleton U., Ottawa, Can., 1947-50; M.A., U. Ky., 1951; Ph.D., Cornell U., 1955. Economist Bd. Transp. Commrs., Ottawa, 1951-52; teaching fellow Cornell U., 1952-55; asst. prof. econs. Middlebury (Vt.) Coll., 1955-57; prof. transp. Ind. U., Bloomington, 1957-66; prof. bus. econs., chmn. dept. Ind. U., 1966-70, dean Coll. Arts and Scis., 1970-73, disting. prof. bus. econs., 1978-92, disting. prof. emeritus bus. econs., prof. emeritus econs., 1992; Collaborator study South Asia 20th Century Fund, 1962-65, dir. research Can.'s needs and resources, 1964-65; dir. case studies role transp. in econ. devel. Brookings Instn., 1964, study transport and econ. devel. of Indochina, 1974; mem. Presdl. Task Force Transp., 1964, 68; dir. Transp. Res. Ctr., Ind. U., 1990-92. Author: Essays on Some Unsettled Questions in the Economics of Transportation, 1962, Economic Analysis of Intercity Freight Transportation, 1980, Inflation: Causes, Consequences and Cures, 1982, U.S. Intercity Passenger Transportation Policy, 1930-91, An Interpretive Essay, 1992; co-author: Mathematical Models and Methods in Marketing, 1961, Canada: An Appraisal of Its Needs and Resources, 1965, The Impact of Highway Investment on Development, 1966, Growth and Change at Indiana U, 1966, Transportation on the Prairies, 1968, Asian Drama, 1968, Essays in Economic Analysis and Policy, 1970, Southeast Asian Regional Transport Survey, 1972, Regional Study of the Impact of the Energy Situation on Transport Development, 1983; Editor: Classics of Economic Theory, 1964, Technological Development and Economic Growth, 1971. Recipient A. Davidson Dunton Alumni award Carleton U., Salzberg Hon. Medallion Syracuse U., 1992. Mem. Am. Econ. Assn. (Disting. Mem. award 1986), Transp. Rsch. Forum (pres. 1969, Transp. Rsch. award 1990), Gamma Sigma. Address: RD 3 Box 1132 Butternut Ridge Rd Middlebury VT 05753-8744

WILSON, GERALD EINAR, mechanical and industrial engineer, business executive; b. Newhill, Alta., Can., Mar. 20, 1922; s. Robert E. and Cecelia (Stephenson) W.; m. Helen M. Martens, June 9, 1945. B.A.Sc., U. Toronto, 1950. Registered profl. engr., 8 provinces. Asst. brewmaster John Labatt Ltd., London, Ont., Can., 1950-62; v.p. prodn. Labatt Ont. Breweries, 1962-64; v.p. engring. John Labatt Ltd., 1964-69, v.p. engring. services, 1969-85, v.p., 1986-87, retired; pres. Carpools Environ. Protection Services Ltd., 1977—. Patentee solar quilt, continuous separator, others. Bd. dirs. Ont.a Environ. Assessment Bd., 1977-83; chmn. Boys and Girls Club Found., London; bd. dirs. Boys and Girls Clubs, Can., Heritage London Found. Served to 1st lt. RCAF, 1942-45. Decorated D.F.C., others. Mem. Assn. Profl. Engrs., Engring. Inst. Can., Master Brewers Assn., Internat. C. of C. Conservative. Anglican. Clubs: London Hunt (London); Union (Victoria, B.C.). Lodge: Royal Can. Legion (pres. 1981-82). Home: Sir Adam Beck Suite, 240 Sydenham St, London, ON Canada N6A 1W5

WILSON, GERALDINE O'CONNOR, psychologist; b. Hartford, Conn., Oct. 18, 1933; d. Dennis Paul and Florence Marguerite (Sheehan) O'Connor; m. Richard Thomas Wilson, Apr. 12, 1958; children: Susan, Deirdre P., Moira, Megan. BA, Marymount Coll., 1955; MS, So. Conn. State U., 1971, dipl. advanced studies, 1976. Social worker Southbury (Conn.) Tng. Sch., 1956-58; sch. psychologist Waterbury (Conn.) Bd. Edn., 1970-71, Brookfield (Conn.) Bd. Edn., 1971-95; pvt. practice Southbury, 1995—. Mem. Nat. Assn. Sch. Psychologists (cert.), Conn. Assn. Sch. Psychologists (cert., regional dir. 1972-74, treas. 1975-80, newspaper editor 1975-77, practioner of year 1995). Democrat. Roman Catholic. Avocations: reading, music, gardening, travel. Home and Office: 51 Stillson Rd Southbury CT 06488-1116

WILSON, GLEN PARTEN, professional society administrator; b. Waco, Tex., Dec. 10, 1922; s. Glen P. and Hazel (Parnell) W. BS in Aero. Engring., U. Tex., Austin, 1943, MA in Psychology, 1948, PhD in Psychology, 1952. Engr. Lockheed Aircraft Co., Burbank, Calif., 1943-44; teaching fellow, rsch. asst., instr. U. Tex., Austin, 1946-52; rsch. psychologist USAF, Lackland AFB, Tex., 1952-53; gen. mgr. Tex. Ednl. Devices Co., Austin, 1953-54; asst. to Senator Lyndon B. Johnson Washington, 1955-57; staff Senate Preparedness Investigating Subcom. and Senate Spl. Com. on Space and Astronautics, Washington, 1957-59; chief clk., profl. staff mem. Senate Com. on Aero. and Space Scis., Washington, 1959-77; cons. Washington, 1977-79; spl. asst. for student activities NASA, Washington, 1979-80, acting dir. acad. affairs div., 1980-82; pres. Marie D. and Glen P. Wilson Found., Washington, 1982-87; exec. dir. Nat. Space Soc., Washington, 1984-88, exec. dir. emeritus, 1988—; lectr. on aero. and space programs, Senate orgn., sci. policy, tech. assessment, student activities, space activism. Participant as staff passage of Nat. Aeros. and Space Act, 1958, Communications Satellite Act, 1962, NASA Authorization Acts, 1958-77; editor Policy Planning for Aeronautical Rsch. and Devel., Senate Document 90, 89th Congress, 1966; developer NASA shuttle student involvement program, 1980, space edn. orgn., 1984—. With USN, 1944-46. Recipient Exceptional Svc. medal NASA, 1981; Nat. Space Soc. Hdqrs. renamed The Glen P. Wilson Internat. Space Ctr., 1988. Mem. AIAA (spl. presdl. citation 1976), AAAS, Nat. Space Soc., Internat. Acad. of Astronautics, Sigma Xi, Nat. Space Club, Cosmos Club. Home: 433 New Jersey Ave SE Washington DC 20003-4034 Office: 600 Pennsylvania Ave SE Ste 201 Washington DC 20003-4344

WILSON, GLENN, economist, educator; b. East St. Louis, Ill., Feb. 4, 1929; s. Herschel and Regina (Hayes) W.; m. Helen Janice O'Dell, Jan. 28, 1951; children—David, Thomas, Ann. B.A., U. Okla., 1951; M.A., 1952. Adminstr., Welfare and Retirement Fund United Mine Workers, Pitts., Knoxville, Tenn., 1952-58; dir. med. care research Nationwide Ins. Co., Columbus, 1958-62; exec. dir. Community Health Found., Cleve., 1962-68; exec. v.p. Kaiser Community Health Found., Cleve., 1968-69; assoc. dean U. N.C. Med. Sch., Chapel Hill, 1970-88, prof. dept. social medicine, 1977—, chmn. dept., 1977-89; cons. Sault Ste. Marie and Dist. Group Health Assn.; health adv. Mayor Stokes, Cleve., 1967-69. Contbr. articles to profl. jours. Home: 214 Glandon Dr Chapel Hill NC 27514-3816 Office: U NC Med Sc Dept Social Medicine Chapel Hill NC 27514

WILSON, GRAHAM MCGREGOR, energy company executive; b. Kilwinning, Scotland, Aug. 2, 1944; s. Peter and Jessie (Scott) W.; m. Josee Perrault; children: Stefanie, Richard, Patrick. BS, McGill U., Montreal, Que., Can., 1967; MBA, U. Western Ont., London, Can., 1969. Investment analyst Greenshields Inc., 1969-72; asst. treas. Genstar, 1972-74; various fin. positions, v.p. fin. MacMillan Bloedel Ltd., Vancouver, B.C., Can., 1974-83; v.p. fin. and adminstrn. Petro-Can. Inc., Calgary, Alta., 1983-88; exec. v.p., CFO Westcoast Energy Inc., Vancouver, 1988—; bd. dirs. Foothills Pipe Lines Ltd., Calgary, Pacific No. Gas Ltd., Vancouver, Pacific Coast Energy Corp., Vancouver, Westcoast Power Inc., Vancouver, Westcoast Gas Svcs., Calgary, Centra Gas Inc., Toronto, Ont., Centra Gas Alta., Inc., Leduc Centra Gas B.C. Inc., Victoria, Itron Inc., Spokane, Wash., Union Gas Ltd., Chatham, Ont., Union Energy Inc., Chatham, Westcoast Energy Internat. Inc., Lake Superior Power Inc., Sta. KCTS-VT, Seattle, Westcoast Capital Corp., Engage Energy. Avocations: squash, golf. Office: Westcoast Energy Inc, Park Pl 666 Burrard St Ste 3400, Vancouver, BC Canada V6C 3M8

WILSON, H. DAVID, dean; b. West Frankfort, Ill., Sept. 13, 1939; m. Jeannette Wilson; children: Jennifer, Jacqueline, Mary Jeanne. AB in Zoology, Wabash Coll., 1961; MD, St. Louis Sch. Medicine, 1966. Diplomate Nat. Bd. Med. Examiners, Am. Bd. Pediatrics. Intern pediatrics Cardinal Glennon Meml. Hosp. for Children, St. Louis U., 1966-67; resident dept. pediatrics U. Ky. Med. Ctr., Lexington, 1967-68, chief resident, 1968-69; NIH rsch. fellow U. Tex. Health Scis. Ctr., Dallas, 1971-73; fellowship Am. Coun. on Edn., 1988-89; dir. admissions Coll. of Medicine, U. Ky., 1986-88; assoc. dean for acad. affairs, prof. Coll. Medicine, U. Ky., 1989-95; dean, prof. U. N.D. Sch. of Medicine, Grand Forks, 1995—; Author: (TV series) For Kids Sake, 1987-88; dir. pediatric infectious diseases U. Ky. Med. Ctr., Lexington, 1973-95, dir. cystic fibrosis care and tchg. ctr., 1975-80, med. dir., clin. virology lab., 1982-95; staff United Hosp., Grand Forks, 1995—; elected univ. senate U. Ky., 1993-96, bd. trustees Gluck Equine Rsch. Found., 1991-95, rules and elections univ. senate standing com., 1991-92, steering com. for U.K. self-study, 1990-95, co-chmn. steering com., 1990-95, chmn. review and search com. for chmn. dept. obstetrics and gynecology, 1990, chmn. curriculum com. Coll. of Medicine, 1989-95; elected acad. coun. of med. ctr. U. Ky. Med. Ctr., 1989-92; lectr. in field. Contbr. numerous articles to profl. jours. Fellow Pediatric Infectious Dieseases Soc.; mem. AMA, Am. Soc. of Microbiology, Am. Thoracic Soc., Am. Acad. Pediatrics, Pan Am. Group for Rapid Viral Diagnosis. Home: 10 Shadyridge Estates Grand Forks ND 58201 Office: U ND Sch of Medicine Rm 1925 501 N Columbia Rd Box 9037 Grand Forks ND 58202-9037*

WILSON, H(AROLD) FRED(ERICK), chemist, research scientist; b. Columbiana, Ohio, Aug. 15, 1922; s. Lloyd Ralph and Erma Rebecca (Frederick) W.; m. Alice Marjorie Steer, Aug. 20, 1949; children: Janice, Deborah, James, Kathleen. B.A., Oberlin Coll., 1947; Ph.D., U. Rochester, 1950. With Rohm & Haas Co., Phila., 1950-83; beginning as rsch. scientist, successively lab. head, rsch. supr., asst. dir., assoc. dir., dir. rsch. Rohm & Haas Co., 1950-74, v.p., 1974-83, chief sci. officer, from 1981; now with Wilson Assocs., Cape May, N.J.; mem. U.S. nat. com. IUPAC, 1977-84, vice chmn., 1980-82, chmn., 1982-84, fin. com., 1979-89, chmn., 1981-89; chmn. I.R.I. Research Corp., 1980-82, dir., 1979-82. Served to 1st lt. USAAF, 1942-46. Decorated Air Medal. Mem. Am. Chem. Soc., AAAS, Soc. Chem. Industry, Dirs. Indsl. Research. Patentee in field. Home: 214 Gilmore Ave Merchantville NJ 08109-2531 Office: Wilson Assocs 24 Congress St Cape May NJ 08204-5308

WILSON, HARRY B., retired public relations company executive; b. St. Louis, May 17, 1917; s. H. Burgoyne and Margaret (Drew) W.; m. Helen Cain, July 27, 1940 (dec. Oct. 1983); children: Margaret Wilson Pennington, Harry B., Andrew B., Daniel B., Josephine Wilson Havlak, Julie Wilson Sakellariadis, Ellen Wilson Shumway; m. Mary Virginia Peisch, Apr. 7, 1984. Ph.B., St. Louis U., 1938. Mng. editor Sedalia (Mo.) Capital, 1939-40; reporter Kansas City Star; also state capital bur. chief St. Louis Globe-Democrat, 1940-42, polit. writer, columnist, 1946-52; corr. Business Week mag., 1948-52; with Fleishman-Hillard Inc., St. Louis, 1953; sr. ptnr. Fleishman-Hillard Inc., 1964-70, pres., 1970-74, chmn. bd., 1974-88, sr. ptnr., 1989-92. Bd. dirs. St. Louis Family Support Network, Friends of the New Cathedral. With USNR, 1942-46. Home: # 901 625 S Skimkar Blvd Saint Louis MO 63105-2301

WILSON, HENRY ARTHUR, JR., management consultant; b. Detroit, June 12, 1939; s. Henry Arthur and Ruth (Scott) W.; m. Mildred Rendell, June 17, 1961; 1 child, Suzanne. B.S., Mich. Luth. Coll., 1968; M.A., U. Detroit, 1976. Police officer Grosse Pointe Park Police Dept., Mich., 1960-68; v.p. Uniflight, Inc., St. Clare Shore, Mich., 1968-73; coordinator Criminal Justice Inst., Detroit, 1973-76; ptnr. Grant Thornton (formerly Alexander Grant & Co.), Detroit, 1976-92; grand sec., CEO Grand Lodge F & A.M., Mich.; CEO Mich. Masonic Home; pres., CEO, Mich. Masonic Home Charitably Found. Author: Masonic Etiquette and Protocol, 1985; usher St. Columba Episcopal Ch., Detroit, 1976—. Served with USAF, 1957-60. Mem. Certified Data Processing Auditors Assn., Masons (grand master Mich. 1984-85). Republican. Avocation: boating. Office: 1022 Nottingham Rd Grosse Pointe MI 48230-1332

WILSON, HERSCHEL MANUEL (PETE WILSON), retired journalism educator; b. Candler, N.C., July 17, 1930; s. Shuford Arnold and Ida Camilla (Landreth) W.; m. Ruby Jean Herring, Aug. 10, 1952. AB in Journalism, San Diego State U., 1956; MS in Journalism, Ohio U., Athens, 1959; postgrad., U. So. Calif., 1966-70. Reporter, copy editor, picture editor The San Diego Union, 1955-58; reporter, wire editor Long Beach (Calif.) Ind., 1959-65; prof. journalism Calif. State U., Northridge, 1965-71; fgn. desk copy editor L.A. Times, 1966-71; prof. and former chmn. journalism Humboldt State U., Arcata, Calif., 1971-91; ret., 1991; cons. KVIQ-TV News Dept., Eureka, Calif., 1985-87. Contbr. articles to profl. jours. Publicity dir. Simi Valley (Calif.) Fair Housing Coun., 1967; bd. dirs., publicity dir. NAACP, Eureka, Calif., 1978-80. Journalist with USN, 1948-52, Korea. Named Nat. Outstanding Advisor, Theta Sigma Phi, 1970. Mem. Soc. Profl. Journalists. (named Disting. Campus Advisor 1982), San Fernando Valley Press Club (v.p. 1969-70), Beau Pre Men's Golf Club (McKinleyville, Calif., pub. rels. dir., treas. 1978). Democrat. Methodist. Avocations: golf, walking, gardening, reading. Home: 115 Bent Creek Ranch Rd Asheville NC 28806-9521

WILSON, HUGH STEVEN, lawyer; b. Paducah, Ky., Nov. 27, 1947; s. Hugh Gipson and Rebekah (Dunn) W.; m. Clare Maloney, Apr. 28, 1973; children: Morgan Elizabeth, Zachary Hunter, Samuel Gipson. BS, Ind. U., 1968; JD, U. Chgo., 1971; LLM, Harvard U., 1972. Bar: Calif. 1972, U.S. Dist. Ct. (cen. dist.) Calif. 1972, U.S. Dist. Ct. (so. dist.) Calif. 1973, U.S. Ct. Appeals (9th cir.) 1975, U.S. Dist. Ct. (no. dist.) Calif. 1977, U.S. Dist. Ct. (ea. dist.) 1980. Assoc. Latham & Watkins, Los Angeles, 1972-78, ptnr., 1978—. Recipient Jerome N. Frank prize U. Chgo. Law Sch., 1971. Mem. ABA, Los Angeles County Bar Assn., Order of Coif, Calif. Club. Republican. Avocations: lit., zoology.

WILSON, I. DODD, dean; b. St. Peter, Minn., July 10, 1936. AB summa cum laude, Dartmouth Coll., 1958; MD, Harvard U., 1961. Diplomate Am. Bd. Internal Medicine. Intern dept. medicine U. Minn. Hosps., Mpls., 1961-62; med. fellow Dept. of Medicine, 1962-63, 65-66; instr. dept. of medicine U. Minn. Med. Sch., Mpls., 1967-68, asst. prof., 1968-71, assoc. prof., 1971-76, dir. sect. of gastroenterology, 1972-83, vice chmn. dept. of medicine, 1983-86, prof. medicine, 1976-86; dean, prof. medicine U. Ark. Coll. of Medicine, Little Rock, 1986—; exec. vice chancellor U. Ark. Med. Scis., 1994—; mem. Univ. Hosp. Consortium Rsch. Task Force, 1994; adv. bd. UALR Donaghey Project, 1994—; mem. State Crime Lab. Bd., 1992—, chmn. 1991-92; bd. dirs. First Comml. Nat. Bank, Ark. Children's Hosp. Rsch. Inst., Inc.; mem. Ark. Rice Depot Bd., 1988-94; mem. State Med. Examiner's Commn., 1986-90; med. bd. Univ. Hosp., 1986—; mem. chancellor's cabinet U. Ark. for Med. Scis., 1986—; chmn. U. Minn. Clin. Assocs., ad hoc com. for fin matters, 1986; vice chmn. U. Minn. Clin. Assocs., 1986, clin. assoc. exec. com., 1985; mem. univ. com. Univ. Press, 1985-86; clin. assoc. planning and mktg. com. U. Minn., 1985; mem. Hosp. Quality Assurance Steering com., 1984-96, chmn. hosp. utilization mgmt. com., 1985; mem. Univ. Bookstore com., 1985; mem. Univ. Senate, 1985-86; chmn. dept. medicine search com. for Dir. of Gen. Internal Medicine, 1985; chmn. med. sch. search com. head of dept. dermatology U. Minn., 1984, chmn. dept. medicine search com. for dir. pulmonary sect. 1984, mem. hosp. bd. govs. com. on planning and devel., 1983-86, med.=surg. hosp. facilities com., 1982-83, mem. steering com. of self-study task force U. of Minn. Med. Sch., 1982-83, many more coms. Contbr. numerous articles to profl. jours. Lt. USNR, 1963-65. Fellow ACP; mem. AMA, Am. Fedn. for Clin. Rsch., Am. Gastroenterol. Assn., Ctrl. Soc. for Clin. Rsch., Am. Assn. for the Study of Liver Disease, Ark. Med. Soc. (editl. bd. 1988-93, ex-officio mem., coun. 1987—), Pulaski County Med. Soc., Assn. of Am. Med. Colls. (coun. of deans, chair 1995-96, mgmt. edn. program planning com. 1993—, adv. panel on strategic positioning for health care reform 1992—, exec. coun. 1992—, adminstrv. bd. 1992—, DEANS-VA coordinating com. 1990-94, ad hoc com. on nursing svcs. and the tchg. hosp. 1989, adv. com. on medicare regulations for payment of physicians in tchg. hosps. 1989), So. Med. Phi Beta Kappa, Alpha Omega Alpha. Office: Univ Ark for Med Scis Mail Slot #550 4301 W Markham St Little Rock AR 72205-7101*

WILSON, IAN EDWIN, cultural organization administrator, archivist; b. Montreal, Que., Can., Apr. 2, 1943; s. Andrew and Marion (Mundy) W.; m. Ruth Dyck, Mar. 24, 1979. BA, Queen's U., Kingston, Ont., 1968, MA History, 1974. Archivist Queen's U., Kingston, Ont., Can., 1966-76; provincial archivist Sask. (Can.) Archives, 1976-86; archivist of Ont. Ont. Govt., Toronto, 1986—; dir. gen. info. resource mgmt. divsn. Ministry Culture, Tourism and Recreation, Toronto, 1990-93; sec. Kingston Hist. Soc., 1967-72, v.p., 1972-76; chair cons. group Social Sci. and Humanities Rsch. Coun. Can., Ottawa, 1979-80; adj. prof. Faculty Info. Studies U. Toronto, 1993—; spkr. in field. Author: (with J. Douglas Stewart) Heritage Kingston, 1973; editor: Kingston City Hall, 1975; producer: (with J. William Brennan) Regina Before Yesterday, 1978; contbr. articles to profl. jours. Chmn. congregation Mennonite Ch., Regina, 1981-84; mem. Sask. award merit selection com., 1985-86; chair Sask. Heritage adv. bd., 1978-83, mem., 1983-86; Ont. dir. Forum for Young Canadians, 1995—. Recipient Queen Elizabeth II silver jubilee medal, 1977, W.G. Leland cert. commendation Soc. Am. Archivists, 1981, W. Kaye Lamb prize Assn. Can. Archivists, 1983; Woodrow Wilson hon. fellow, 1967. Mem. Assn. Can. Archivists (various coms., editl. bd. 1986-88), Ont. Hist. Soc. (exec. coun. 1970-73, v.p. 1973-75, pres. 1975-76), Can. Hist. Assn. (past chmn., vice chmn., pres. archives sect. 1972-74), Champlain Soc. (bd. dirs., v.p. 1989-95, pres. 1995—). Home: 30 Holly St #604, Toronto, ON Canada M4S 3C2 Office: Archives of Ontario, 77 Grenville St, Toronto, ON Canada M7A 2R9

WILSON, IAN HOLROYDE, management consultant, futurist; b. Harrow, England, June 16, 1925; came to U.S., 1954; s. William Brash and Dorothy (Holroyde) W.; m. Page Tuttle Hedden, Mar. 17, 1951 (div. Dec. 1983); children: Rebecca, Dorothy, Ellen, Holly, Alexandra; m. Adrianne Marcus, July 12, 1992. MA, Oxford U., 1948. Orgn. cons. Imperial Chem. Industries, London, 1948-54; various staff exec. positions in strategic planning, mgmt. devel. Gen. Electric Co., Fairfield, Conn., 1954-80; sr. cons. to maj. U.S. and internat. cos. SRI Internat., Menlo Park, Calif., 1980-93; prin. Wolf Enterprises, San Rafael, Calif., 1993—; exec. in residence Va. Commonwealth U., Richmond, 1976. Author: Planning for Major Change, 1976, The Power of Strategic Vision, 1991, Rewriting the Corporate Social Charter, 1992, Managing Strategically in the 1990s, 1993, Executive Leadership, 1995; mem. editl. bd. Planning Rev., 1973-81; Am. editor Long Range Planning Jour., London, 1981-89; sr. editor Strategy and Leadership, 1993—. Mem. adv. bd. Technol. Forecasting and Social Change, 1989—; chmn. Citizen's Long Range Ednl. Goals Com., Westport, Conn., 1967-70; mem. strategic process com. United Way of Am., Alexandria, Va., 1985-94. Capt. Brit. Army, 1943-45, ETO. Mem. AAAS, Strategic Leadership Forum, World Future Soc. Unitarian. Avocations: camping, writing, photography. Home and Office: 79 Twin Oaks Ave San Rafael CA 94901-1915

WILSON, IAN ROBERT, food company executive; b. Pietermaritzburg, South Africa, Sept. 22, 1929; s. Brian J. and Edna C. W.; m. Susan Diana Lasch, Jan. 14, 1970; children: Timothy Robert, Christopher James, Diana Louise, Jason Luke. B.Commerce, U. Natal, South Africa, 1952; postgrad., Harvard U. Bus. Sch., 1968. With Coca-Cola Export Corp., Johannesburg, South Africa, 1956-74; mgr. Coca-Cola Export Corp., 1969-72, v.p., regional mgr., 1972-73, area mgr., 1973; pres., chief exec. officer Coca-Cola Ltd., Toronto, Ont., Can., 1974-76; chmn. bd., dir. Coca-Cola Ltd., 1976-81; exec. v.p. Coca-Cola Co., Atlanta, 1976-79; vice chmn. Coca-Cola Co., 1979-81, pres. Pacific group; dir. Coca-Cola Export Corp., Atlanta, 1976-81; pres., chief exec. officer, dir. Castle & Cooke, Inc., San Francisco, 1983-84, Wyndham Foods, Inc., 1985-89; chmn. bd., chief exec. officer Windmill Corp., San Francisco, 1989-94; mng. ptnr. Dartford Partnership and Induna Ptnrs., San Francisco, 1993—; also bd. dirs. Dartford Partnership and Induna Ptnrs.; bd. dirs. Novell Inc., Golden State Foods, Inc., Egoli Ptnrs., New Age Beverages Ltd., U.S./Asean Coun., East-West Ctr.; chmn. bd. dirs. Windy Hill Pet Foods, Van de Kamp Inc. and MBW Foods Inc. Mem. Church of Eng. Clubs: Durban Country and Johannesburg Country, Inanda Hunt and Polo, Atlantic Salmon, San Francisco Golf, Pacific Union, Burlingame Country. Home: 945 Green St San Francisco CA 94133-3639 Office: Dartford Partnership 801 Montgomery St Ste 400 San Francisco CA 94133-5164

WILSON, JACK, aeronautical engineer; b. Sheffield, Yorkshire, Eng., Jan. 5, 1933; came to U.S., 1956; s. George and Nellie (Place) W.; m. Marjorie Reynolds, June 3, 1961 (div. Jan. 1991); children: Tanya Ruth, Cara; m. Carol Blixen, Jan. 3, 1997. BS in Engring., Imperial Coll., London, 1954; MS in Aero. Engring., Cornell U., 1958, PhD in Aero. Engring., 1962. Sr. scientific officer Royal Aircraft Establishment, Farnborough, Eng., 1962-63; prin. rsch. sci. Avco-Everett Rsch. Lab., Everett, Mass., 1963-72; vis. prof. Inst. de Mecanique des Fluides, Marseille, France, 1972-73; sr. scientist U. Rochester (N.Y.), 1973-80; sr. rsch. assoc. Sohio/BP Am., Cleve., 1980-90; sr. engring. specialist Sverdrup Tech. Inc., Cleve., 1990-93, NYMA, Brook Park, 1994—. Author: (chpt.) "Gas Lasers" of Applied Optics in Engineering VI, 1980, "Laser Sources" of Techniques in Chemistry XVII, 1982; contbr. articles to profl. jours. Co-recipient S.A.E. Manley Meml.

award, 1995. Mem. AIAA (sr., mem. tech. com. 1991-92). Achievements include first to demonstrate gas-dynamic laser; patent in application of high speed flow to gas laser media; patent in devel. of antimony dopant sources; measurement of air ionization rate at very high speeds. Office: NYMA 2001 Aerospace Pky Brook Park OH 44142-1002

WILSON, JACK FREDRICK, retired federal government official; b. Salt Lake City, Apr. 2, 1920; s. John Lorimer and Mayme J. (James) W.; m. Gwendolyn Gwynn, Nov. 20, 1947; children—Wendy, Elaine, Barbara Ann, Laurel, John F. Jr., James C. B.S., Brigham Young U., 1942; postgrad., Mont. State U., 1962, Pa. State U., 1965. Range conservationist Bur. Land Mgmt., Rawlins, Wyo., 1949-57; dist. mgr. Bur. Land Mgmt., Burley, Idaho, 1957-67; dist. and land office mgr. Bur. Land Mgmt., Riverside, Calif., 1967-72; dir. Boise Interagy. Fire Ctr., Idaho, 1972-81; dir. Office Aircraft Services U.S. Dept. Interior, Boise, 1981-87; dir. Boise Interagy. Fire Ctr., 1987-92; ret., 1992. Contbr. articles to profl. jours. Dir. county disaster com. ARC, 1982-88. Maj. USAF, 1942-47. Recipient Meritorious award U.S. Dept. Interior, 1976, Disting. Service award, 1981, EEO Performance award, 1985; Outstanding Contbn. to Fire Mgmt. award U.S. Dept. Agr. Forest Service, 1976. Mem. Soc. Am. Foresters (chmn. fire com. 1980-82), Am. Soc. Range Mgmt. (sec. pres. 1967), So. Calif. Assn. Foresters and Fire Wardens, Lions (sec. 1954-57), Rotary. Mem. Ch. of Jesus Christ of Latter-day Saints. Avocations: long range weather forecasting, genealogy, reading, golf. Home: 1820 Sunrise Rim Rd Boise ID 83705-5138

WILSON, JACK MARTIN, dean, scientific association executive, physics educator; b. Camp Atterbury, Ind., June 29, 1945; s. Jack Maurer and Ruth L. (Leiseder) W.,. m. Judi Chang, Aug. 18, 1990; children: John, Jessica, Erika, Gretchen. A.B., Thiel Coll., Greenville, Pa., 1967; M.A., Kent State U., 1970, Ph.D., 1972. Assoc. prof. physics Sam Houston State U., Huntsville, Tex., 1972-80; chmn. dept. physics Sam Houston State U., Huntsville, 1980-81, chmn. div. chemistry and physics, 1981-82; prof. physics U. Md., College Park, 1984-90; dir. Anderson Ctr. for Innovation in Undergrad. Edn. Rensselaer Poly. Inst., Troy, N.Y., 1990-95, dean undergrad. and continuing edn., 1995—; mem. U.S. com. Internat. Union Pure and Applied Physics, Washington, 1984-90, IBM consulting scholar, 1992-95; dir. U.S. team in Internat. Physics Olympia, 1985-90. Editor: Teacher Institutes and Workshops, 1984, The Education of the Physicist, 1985; also articles in field. Recipient Computers in Physics award Dept. Edn., Washington, 1985; Physics Teaching Resource Agents award NSF, 1985; Developing Student Confidence award Exxon Edn. Found., 1983; grantee various fed. agys. and pvt. founds. Mem. AAAS, Am. Assn. Physics Tchrs. (exec. officer 1982-90), Am. Phys. Soc. (edn. com. 1982—), Am. Inst. Physics (governing bd. 1984-91), Am. Soc. for Engring. Edn. (Theodore Hesburgh award 1995, Boeing Outstanding Engring. Educator award 1995), Sigma Xi (del., rsch. award 1972). Office: Rensselaer Poly Inst Undergrad & Continuing Edn 212 Pittsburgh Bldg Troy NY 12180

WILSON, JAMES HARGROVE, JR., lawyer; b. Oliver, Ga., Nov. 26, 1920; s. James Hargrove and Louise (Sealy) W.; m. Frances Audra Schaffer, Dec. 24, 1942 (dec. Nov. 1990); children: Susan Frances, James Hargrove. A.B. with honors, Emory U., 1940; LL.B. summa cum laude, Harvard U., 1947. Bar: Ga. 1947, D.C. 1951. Assoc. firm Sutherland, Tuttle & Brennan (now Sutherland, Asbill & Brennan), Atlanta and Washington, 1947-53, ptnr., 1953—; lectr. Emory U., 1959, chmn. bd. visitors, 1967-68; trustee The Northwestern Mut. Life Ins. Co., Milw., 1972-91; mem. advisory group Commr. of Internal Revenue, 1963-64. Pres.: Harvard Law Review, 1946-47. Chmn. bd. trustees Met. Atlanta Crime Commn., 1970-71; mem. Harvard U. Overseers Com. to Visit Law Sch., 1959-65; trustee Emory U., 1983-90, trustee emeritus, 1990—. Served to lt. comdr. USNR, 1942-46. Fellow Am. Bar Found., Am. Coll. Tax Counsel; mem. ABA, State Bar Ga., D.C. Bar, Atlanta Bar Assn., Am. Law Inst. (coun. 1974—), Lawyers Club Atlanta (pres. 1960-61), Am. Judicature Soc., Harvard Law Sch. Assn. (coun. 1981-85), Emory U. Alumni Assn. (pres. 1966-67), Capital City Club, Piedmont Driving Club, Commerce Club, Peachtree Club, Phi Beta Kappa, Omicron Delta Kappa, Kappa Alpha. Methodist. Home: 3171 Marne Dr NW Atlanta GA 30305-1931 Office: Sutherland Asbill & Brennan 999 Peachtree St NE Ste 2300 Atlanta GA 30309-3964

WILSON, JAMES LAWRENCE, chemical company executive; b. Rosedale, Miss., Mar. 2, 1936; s. James Lawrence and Mary Margaret (Klingman) W.; m. Barbara Louise Burroughs, Aug. 30, 1958; children: Lawrence Burroughs, Alexander Elliott. B.Mech. Engring., Vanderbilt U., 1958; M.B.A., Harvard, 1963. Vice pres. Nyala Properties, Inc., Phila., 1963-65; staff assoc. Rohm & Haas Co., Phila., 1965-67; exec. asst. to pres. Rohm & Haas Co., 1971-72, treas., 1972-74; regional dir. Rohm & Haas Co., Europe, 1974-77; group v.p. Rohm & Haas Co., 1977-86, vice-chmn., 1986-88, chmn., CEO, 1988—; treas. Warren-Teed Pharms., Inc., Columbus, Ohio, 1967-68, v.p., 1969; pres. Consol. Biomed. Labs., Inc., Dublin, Ohio, 1970-71; bd. dirs. Rohm and Haas Co., Vanguard Group Investment Cos., Cummins Engine Co., Inc. Co-author: Creative Collective Bargaining, 1964. Trustee Vanderbilt U., 1987—, Culver Ednl. Found., 1988—; chmn. Phila. High Sch. Acads., 1989—. Mem. Chem. Mfrs. Assn. (bd. dirs. 1988—, chmn. 1996). Office: Rohm & Haas Co 100 Independence Mall W Philadelphia PA 19106

WILSON, JAMES LEE, retired geology educator, consultant; b. Waxahachie, Tex., Dec. 1, 1920; s. James Burney and Hallie Christine (Hawkins) W.; m. Della I. Moore, May 8, 1944; children: James Lee Jr., Burney Grant, Dale Ross (dec.). Student, Rice U., 1938-40; BA, U. Tex., 1942, MA, 1944; PhD, Yale U., 1949. Geologist Carter Oil Co., Tulsa, 1943-44; asst. and assoc. prof. U. Tex., Austin, 1949-52; rsch. geologist Shell Devel. Co., Houston, 1952-66; prof. Rice U., Houston, 1966-79, U. Mich., Ann Arbor, 1979-86; geol. cons. New Braunfels, Tex., 1986—; cons. Erico Corp., London, 1985-88, Masera Corp., Tulsa, 1988—, Coyote Geol. Svcs., Boulder, Col., 1990—; adj. prof. Rice U., 1986—. Author: Carbonate Facies in Geologic History, 1975; contbr. articles to tech. jours. With C.E., U.S. Army, 1944-46, Italy. Grantee NSF. Fellow Geol. Soc. Am.; mem. Am. Assn. Petroleum Geologists (hon., Disting. Educator award), Internat. Sedimentological Soc., Soc. Econ. Paleontology and Minerology (pres. 1972-73, field trip guide books 1989), Paleontological Soc., West Tex. Geol. Soc., South Tex. Geol. Soc., Can. Soc. Petroleum Geologists. Avocations: piano, languages. Home and Office: 1316 Patio Dr New Braunfels TX 78130-8505

WILSON, JAMES MILLER, IV, cardiovascular surgeon, educator; b. Atlanta, Mar. 11, 1946; s. James Miller Wilson III and Sara Sharp; children: James Miller V, Robert Paul, Michael Simpson, Sara Ann. Student, Emory U.; MD, Duke U., 1971. Diplomate Am. Bd. Surgery, Am. Bd. Thoracic Surgery. Intern N.Y. Hosp., 1971-72; resident N.Y. Hosp.-Cornell Med. Ctr., 1972-73, U. Calif., San Francisco, 1975-80; attending staff Christ Hosp., Cin., 1980—, Bethesda Hosp., Cin., 1980—, Jewish Hosp., Cin., 1980—, Univ. Hosp., Cin., 1982—, Deaconess Hosp, Cin., 1982—; chmn. dept. cardiovasc. surgery Deaconess Hosp., Cin., 1985—; attending staff VA Med Ctr., Cin., 1983—, Children's Hosp., Cin., 1984—, Good Samaritan Hosp., Cin., 1994—; assoc. prof. clin. surgery U. Cin. Coll. Med., 1985—; open heart surgery adv. com., Ohio, 1995—: lectr. in field. Contbr. articles to profl. jours. Lt. Comdr. submarine svc. USN, 1973-75. Fellow ACS, Am. Coll. Cardiology; mem. AMA, U.S. Naval Submarine League, Am. Assn. Thoracic Surgery, Assn. Acad. Surgery, Soc. Thoracic Surgeons, Am. Heart Assn. (mem. cardiovasc. coun.), Ohio State Med. Assn., Cin. Acad. Medicine, Howard C. Nafziger Soc. Avocations: music, diving, hiking, skiing, horses. Office: 311 Straight St Cincinnati OH 45219-1018

WILSON, JAMES NEWMAN, retired laboratory executive; b. San Diego, Aug. 28, 1927; s. Jack Alexander and Irene (Newman) W.; m. Alice Ann Gorte, Sept. 19, 1954 (div. July 1979); children: Patricia Ann Brugman, Martin James; m. Sibyl Winslow-Bloom, Dec. 14, 1993. BS, U. Calif., Berkeley, 1951; SM, MIT, 1952. With Calif. Inst. Tech. Jet Propulsion Lab., Pasadena, 1952-89; asst. spacecraft system mgr. Mariner Venus Mercury 1973 Project, 1969-74; project mgr. Calif. Inst. Tech. Jet Propulsion Lab., Pasadena, 1985-89. Author: An Arm and a Leg or Two, 1989. Ednl. officer U.S. Power Squadron, Pasadena, 1982-84. With U.S. Army, 1945-46. Recipient Exceptional Svc. medal NASA, 1974, Presidential award Gerald R. Ford, 1974. Mem. Los Angeles Yacht Club. Avocations: classical guitarist, yachtsman. Home: 3200 Alta Laguna Blvd Laguna Beach CA 92651-2060

WILSON, JAMES QUINN, government, management educator; married; 2 children. Henry Lee Shattuck prof. govt. Harvard U., 1961-86; now James Collins prof. mgmt., UCLA; bd. dirs. Am. Enterprise Inst., New Eng. Electric Sys., Rand Corp., State Farm Ins, Protection One. Author: Negro Politics, 1960, Political Organizations, 1961, Varieties of Police Behavior, 1968, The Amateur Democrat, 1973, The Investigators, 1978, Thinking About Crime, 1983; (with R.J. Herrnstein) Crime and Human Nature, 1985, (with Roberta Wilson) Watching Fishes, 1985; Bureaucracy: What Government Agencies Do and Why They Do It., 1989, American Government: Institutions and Policies, 1991, The Moral Sense, 1993, On Character, 1994, Moral Judgment, 1997. Former chmn. Nat. Adv. Coun. for Drug Abuse Prevention, Police Found.; former mem. com. on rsch. on law enforcement and the adminstrn. of justice NRC, Pres.'s Fgn. Intelligence Adv. Bd.; former mem. U.S. Atty. Gen.'s Task Force on Violent Crime; former mem. Commn. on Presdl. Scholars, Sloan Commn. on Cable Comms.; former dir. Joint Ctr. for Urban Studies MIT and Harvard. Fellow Am. Acad. Arts and Scis.; mem. Am. Philos. Soc., Am. Polit. Sci. Assn. (pres., James Madison award). Office: UCLA Grad Sch Mgmt 405 Hilgard Ave Los Angeles CA 90095-9000

WILSON, JAMES RAY, international business educator; b. Hamilton, Ohio, Mar. 7, 1930; s. Ray Crawford and Ruth Lee (Walthers) W.; B.A. (U.S. Navy Coll. Tng. Program scholar), Miami U., Oxford, Ohio, 1952, postgrad., 1967-68; M.A., Ohio State U., 1956; Ph.D., U. Minn., 1984; m. Carolyn Dempsey, Feb. 1, 1952; children—Robin E., Victoria, Mark, Jamie. Grad. asst. Ohio State U., 1955-56; grain mcht. Cargill Inc., Balt., 1956-58; pres. Granexport Corp., Manila, Philippines, 1959-66; mng. dir. Tradax Graanhandel B.V., Amsterdam, 1966-67; instr. in geography Miami U., 1967-68; pres. Cargill Agricola S.A., Sao Paulo, Brazil, 1968-78; dir. indsl. div. Tradax Geneve S.A., Geneva, 1978-80; corp. v.p. Cargill Inc., Mpls., 1980-83; pres. Cargill Southeast Asia, Ltd., Singapore, 1984-88; internat. bus. prof. Miami U., Oxford, Ohio, 1988-92, prof. mgmt. dept., 1994-97; chmn. Cargill Tech. Svcs., Ltd., Thame, Eng., 1992-94. Served with USN, 1952-55. Fellow Royal Geog. Soc.; mem. Assn. Am. Geographers. Congregationalist. Home: 6533 Buckley Rd Oxford OH 45056-9727

WILSON, JAMES ROBERT, lawyer; b. Meade, Kans., Dec. 3, 1927; s. Robert J. and Bess O. (Osborne) W.; m. Marguerite Jean Reiter, Nov. 27, 1960; 1 son, John Ramsey. B.A., Kans. U., 1950, LL.B., 1953. Bar: Kans. 1953, Nebr. 1961, Colo. 1981. Pvt. practice Meade, Kans., 1953-57, Lakewood, Colo., 1989-93; county atty. Meade County, 1954-57; city atty. Meade, 1954-57; asst. gen. counsel Kans. Corp. Commn., 1957-59, gen. counsel, 1959-61, mem., 1961; atty. KN Energy, Inc., 1961-75, personnel dir., 1964-67, v.p., treas., 1968-75, exec. v.p., 1975-78, pres., chief operating officer, 1978-82, pres., chief exec. officer, 1982-85, chmn., pres., chief exec. officer, 1985-88, chmn., 1988-89; bd. dirs. Alliance Ins. Cos. With USNR, 1945-46. Mem. Phi Kappa Sigma. Home: 1725 Foothills Dr S Golden CO 80401-9167

WILSON, JAMES WILLIAM, lawyer; b. Spartanburg, S.C., June 19, 1928; s. James William and Ruth (Greenwaldt) W.; m. Elizabeth Clair Pickett, May 23, 1952; children: Susan Alexandra Wilson Albright, James William. Student, Tulane U., 1945-46; BA, U. Tex., Austin, 1950, LLB, 1951. Bar: Tex. 1951. Practiced in Austin, 1951-79; ptnr. McGinnis, Lochridge & Kilgore (and predecessors), 1960-76; of counsel Stubbeman, McRae, Sealy, Laughlin & Browder, 1976-79; sr. v.p. and gen. counsel Brown & Root, Inc., Houston, 1980-93, also dir.; of counsel Sewell & Riggs, Houston, 1993-95; asst. atty. gen., 1957-58; legis. asst. to senate majority leader Lyndon B. Johnson, 1959-60; adj. prof. U. Tex. Law Sch., 1962-63, 95-97. Lt. (j.g.) USNR, 1952-55. Fellow Tex. Bar Found., Houston Bar Found.; mem. ABA, Tex. Bar Assn., Am. Law Inst., Order of Coif, Phi Beta Kappa. Home: 3412 Timberwood Cir Austin TX 78703-1013

WILSON, JANE, artist; b. Seymour, Iowa, Apr. 29, 1924; d. Wayne and Cleone (Marquis) W.; m. John Gruen, Mar. 28, 1948; 1 child, Julia. BA, U. Iowa, 1945, MA, 1947. Mem. fine arts faculty Parsons Sch. Design, 1973-83, 89-90; vis. artist U. Iowa, 1974; adj. assoc. prof. painting and drawing Columbia U., 1975-85, assoc. prof., 1985-86, prof., 1986-88, acting chair, 1986-88; Andrew Mellon vis. prof. painting Cooper Union, 1977-78. One-woman shows include Hansa Gallery, N.Y.C., 1953, 55, 57, Stuttman Gallery, N.Y.C., 1958-59, Tibor de Nagy Gallery, N.Y.C., annually, 1960-66, Graham Gallery, N.Y.C., 1968, 69, 71, 73, 75, Fischbach Gallery, N.Y.C., 1978-81, 84, 88, 90, 91, 93, 95, 97, Munson-Williams-Proctor Inst., Utica, N.Y., 1980, Cornell U., Ithaca, N.Y., 1982, Compass Rose Gallery, Chgo, 1988, Am. U., Washington, 1989, U. Richmond, Va., 1990, Earl McGrath Gallery, L.A., 1990-91, 93, Dartmouth Coll., Hanover, N.H., 1991, Arnot Mus., Elmira, N.Y., 1993-94, Parrish Mus., Southampton, N.Y., 1996, Glenn Horowitz Gallery, East Hampton, N.Y., 1996; represented in permanent collections Met. Mus., Mus. Modern Art, Whitney Mus., Wadsworth Athenaeum, Heron Art Mus., NYU Rockefeller Inst., Vassar Coll., Pa. Acad. Fine Arts, Hirschorn Mus., Washington, Nelson-Atkins Mus., Kansas City, Mo., San Francisco Mus. Modern Art. Recipient Purchase prize Childe Hassam Fund, 1971, 73, Ranger Fund Purchase prize 1977; Ingram-Merrill grantee, 1963, Louis Comfort Tiffany grantee, 1967, Eloise Spaeth award The Guild Hall, East Hampton, N.Y., 1988. Mem. Am. Acad. Arts and Letters (treas. 1992-95, Award in Art 1981), Nat. Acad. Design (pres. 1992-94), Phi Beta Kappa.

WILSON, JANIE MENCHACA, nursing educator, researcher; b. Lytle, Tex., Mar. 15, 1936; m. Patrick W. Wilson; 1 child, Kathryn Lynn Kohlleppel. BSN, Incarnate Word Coll., San Antonio, 1958; MSN, U. Tex., San Antonio, 1973; PhD in Nursing, U. Tex., Austin, 1978. RN. Oper. rm. nurse Santa Rosa Hosp., San Antonio, 1958-59; instr. Brackenridge Hosp. Sch. Nursing, Austin, 1963-66; staff nurse Med. Coll. Ga., Augusta, 1967-68; instr. dept. nursing San Antonio Coll., 1968-72, prof. dept. nursing edn., 1976—; counselor Project GAIN Tex. Nurses Assn., Austin, 1973-76; rsch. assoc. Ctr. for Health Care Rsch. and Evaluation, U. Tex. System, Austin, 1974-75; cons. Nurse Aide Competency Evaluation Program, San Antonio, 1989—; mem. manuscript rev. panel Nursing Rsch., N.Y.C., 1989-91. Contbr. chpts. to books, articles to profl. jours. Bd. dirs. Ctr. for Health Policy Devel., San Antonio, 1988-92; mem. Nat. Adv. Coun. on Nurse Edn. and Practice, 1995—. 1st lt. USAF, 1960-63. Mem. AAUP, ANA (coun. nurse rschrs., coun. cultural diversity, fellow program for ethnic minorities 1975-77), Am. Acad. Nursing, Nat. League Nursing, Nat. Assn. Hispanic Nurses, Sigma Theta Tau. Roman Catholic. Avocations: music, reading, fishing, dancing, sewing. Home: 4126 Longvale Dr San Antonio TX 78217-3525 Office: San Antonio Coll 1300 San Pedro Ave San Antonio TX 78212-4201

WILSON, JEAN DONALD, endocrinologist, educator; b. Wellington, Tex., Aug. 26, 1932; s. J.D. and Maggie E. (Hill) W. BA in Chemistry, U. Tex., 1951, MD, 1955. Diplomate: Am. Bd. Internal Medicine. Intern, then resident in internal medicine Parkland Meml. Hosp., Dallas, 1955-58; clin. assoc. Nat. Heart Inst., Bethesda, Md., 1958-60; instr. internal medicine U. Tex. Southwestern Med. Sch., Dallas, 1960-61; prof. U. Tex. Southwestern Med. Sch., 1968—. Editor: Jour. Clin. Investigation, 1972-77. Served as sr. asst. surgeon USPHS, 1958-60. Recipient Amory prize Am. Acad. Arts and Scis., 1977, Fuller prize Am. Urol. Assn., 1983, Lita Annenberg Hazen award, 1986, Dale medal Soc. for Endocrinology, 1991, Pincus medal Worchester Found., 1992. Fellow Royal Coll. Physicians; mem. NAS, Am. Acad. Arts and Scis., Inst. Medicine, Am. Fedn. Med. Rsch., Am. Soc. Clin. Investigation, Assn. Am. Physicians, Soc. Exptl. Biology and Medicine, Am. Soc. Biochemistry and Molecular Biology, Endocrine Soc. (Oppenheimer award 1972, Koch award 1993). Office: U Tex Southwestern Med Ctr Dept Internal Medicine 5323 Harry Hines Blvd Dallas TX 75235-7208

WILSON, JIM, Canadian provincial official; b. Alliston, Ont., Can., 1963. Grad., U. Toronto. Constituency asst. to former chair Mgmt. Bd. of Cabinet, Mem. Parliament; spl. asst. to local MP; mem. Ont. Legislature, 1990—; min. of health Province of Ont., 1995—. Active Ont. Progressive Conservative Small Bus. Task Force, Ont. Progressive Conservative Task Force on Rural Econ. Devel., Ont. Progressive Conservative Health Adv. Coun. Conservative. Office: Hepburn Block, 80 Grosvenor St 10th Flr, Toronto, ON Canada M7A 2C4

WILSON, JOHN, artist; b. Boston, Apr. 14, 1922; s. Reginald and Violet (Caesar) W.; m. Julia Kowitch, June 25, 1950; children—Rebecca, Roy, Erica. Diploma with highest honors, Boston Mus. Sch. (Paige fellow for European study), 1944; B.S. in Edn, Tufts U., 1947; student, Fernand Leger's Sch., Paris, France, 1948-49; student (John Hay Whitney fellow), Esmeralda Sch. of Art, Mex. Instr. Boston Mus. Sch., 1949-50, Bd. Edn., N.Y.C., 1959-64; prof. Boston U., 1964-86, prof. emeritus, 1986—. Exhibited at, Atlanta U., Smith Coll., Carnegie Inst. Annual Art Show, Library of Congress Print Nationals, Mus. Modern Art, at N.Y.C. Met. Mus. Art, N.Y.C., Rose Art Mus., Brandeis U., Detroit Inst. Arts, Mus. Fine Arts, Boston; represented in permanent collections, Boston Pub. Library, Smith Coll., Mus. Modern Art, Atlanta U., Carnegie Inst., Bezalel Mus., Jerusalem, Rose Art Mus., Brandeis U., Howard U., Tufts U., Dept. Fine Arts, French govt., Mus. Nat. Ctr. Afro-Am. Artists, Boston; winner competitions for monument, Statue of Martin Luther King, Jr., Buffalo, 1983, U.S. Capitol, Washington, 1986, monument, Roxbury Community Coll., Boston, 1985. Illustrator: children's books Spring Comes to the Ocean (Jean Craighead George), 1965, Becky (Julia Wilson), 1970, Striped Ice Cream (Joan Lexau), 1968, Malcolm X (Arnold Adoff), 1970. Bd. dirs. Elma Lewis Sch. Fine Arts, Boston, 1970-75. Sculpture fellow Mass. Arts and Humanities Found., 1976. Home: 44 Harris St Brookline MA 02146-4933

WILSON, JOHN DONALD, banker, economist; b. McKeesport, Pa., Feb. 8, 1913; s. John Johnston and Katherine A. (Hollerman) W.; m. Myriam Rohr, Mar. 10, 1942 (div. Feb. 18, 1950); 1 dau., Nina Marie; m. Danesi Matthews Hilton, Nov. 3, 1951; children: John Douglas, David Matthews, Mary Danesi. B.A. magna cum laude, U. Colo., 1935; M.A. in Econs. (Braker teaching fellow), Tufts Coll., 1937; M.A. in Econs., Harvard U., 1940. Instr. econs. Harvard U., 1937-40; editor Survey of Current Bus., U.S. Dept. Commerce, 1940-42; economist Editor and Publisher McGraw-Hill Pub. Co., 1946-50; established McGraw-Hill Am. Letter; mem. research and devel. staff N.Y. Life Ins. Co., 1950-51; v.p. charge ops. Inst. Internat. Edn., 1951-53; with Chase Manhattan Bank, 1953-81, successively bus. cons., v.p. and dir. econ. research, group exec. econ. research, pub. relations and market research, 1961-63, sr. v.p., dir. bank's corp. plans, 1963-69, sr. v.p., dir. econ. group, 1969-72, sr. v.p., chief economist, dir. econs., 1972-81, econ. cons., 1981-84; cons. U.S. Govt. Intelligence Svcs., 1984-92; dir. Chase Econometric Assos., 1971-81, chmn., 1971-75. Author: The Chase—The Chase Manhattan Bank, N.A., 1945-1985, 1986. Bd. dirs. United Neighborhood Houses, N.Y.C., 1955-68; treas., organizing trustee Found. Libr. Ctr., 1956-63; dir. Associated Alumni U. Colo., 1959-63; trustee Inst. Internat. Edn., N.Y.C., 1964-85. Lt. (j.g.) USNR, 1943-46, OSS. Mem. Council Fgn. Relations, Internat. C. of C. (exec. com. U.S. council internat. bus. 1969—, sr. trustee), Am. Econ. Assn., Am. Statis. Assn., Phi Beta Kappa, Sigma Chi. Presbyn. Club: Harvard (N.Y.C.), Field (Bronxville, N.Y.). Home: 6 Sunset Ave Bronxville NY 10708

WILSON, JOHN DOUGLAS, economics educator; b. Bronxville, N.Y., Sept. 30, 1952; s. John Donald and Danesi (Hilton) W.; m. Patricia Furlong, July 19, 1986; 1 child, Elizabeth Danesi. AB magna cum laude, Brown U., 1975; PhD, MIT, 1979. Asst. prof. Columbia U., N.Y.C., 1979-84; assoc. prof. Ind. U., Bloomington, 1985-90, prof., 1990—, chair econs. dept., 1992-96; vis. asst. prof. U. Wis., Madison, 1984-85. Co-editor: Income Taxation and International Personal Mobility. 1989; mem. editorial bd. Jour. Urban Econs., 1991—; assoc. editor Econs. & Politics, 1990—; co-editor Jour. Internat. Econs., 1992-95; mem. bd. editors Am. Econ. Rev., 1989-94; contbr. articles to profl. jours. NSF Rsch. grantee, 1993-94. Mem. Phi Beta Kappa. Presbyterian. Avocation: running. Office: Ind U Econs Dept Wylie Hall Bloomington IN 47405

WILSON, JOHN ERIC, biochemistry educator; b. Champaign, Ill., Dec. 13, 1919; s. William Courtney and Marie Winette (Lytle) W.; m. Marion Ruth Heaton, June 7, 1947; children: Kenneth Heaton, Douglas Courtney, Richard Mosher. SB, U. Chgo., 1941; MS, U. Ill., 1944; PhD, Cornell U., 1948. Rsch. asst. Pyroxylin Products, Inc., Chgo., summers 1941-42, Gen. Foods Corp., Hoboken, N.J., summer, 1943; asst. in chemistry U. Ill., 1941-44; asst. in biochemistry Cornell U. Med. Coll., N.Y.C., 1944-48, rsch. assoc., 1948-50; asst. prof. biochemistry U. N.C., Chapel Hill, 1950-60, assoc. prof., 1960-65, prof., 1965-90, prof. emeritus, 1990—, dir. grad. studies, dept. biochemistry, 1965-71, acting dir. neurobiology program, 1968-69, assoc. dir., 1969-72, dir., 1972-73; Kenan prof. U. Utrecht, The Netherlands, 1978. Mem. editl. bd. Jour. Neurochemistry, 1987-94; contbr. numerous articles on biochemistry and neurochemistry to profl. publs. Scoutmaster Occoneechee coun. Boy Scouts Am., 1959-66; mem. Chapel Hill Twp. Adv. Coun., 1978-85, Orange County (N.C.) Planning Bd., 1979-85. Fellow AAAS; mem. Am. Chem. Soc., Am. Soc. for Biochemistry and Molecular Biology, Am. Soc. Neurochemistry, N.C. Acad. Sci., Internat. Soc. for Neurochemistry, Internat. Brain Rsch. Orgn., Soc. Neurosci. (coun. 1969-70, chmn. fin. com. 1973-78, organizer and mem. exec. com. N.C. chpt. 1974-75), Harvey Soc., Sigma Xi, Phi Lambda Upsilon, Alpha Chi Sigma, Beta Theta Pi. Home: 214 Spring Ln Chapel Hill NC 27514-3540 Office: U NC Sch Medicine Dept Biochemistry Chapel Hill NC 27599-7260

WILSON, JOHN FRANCIS, religion educator, educational institution administrator; b. Springfield, Mo., Nov. 4, 1937; s. Frederick Marion and Jesse Ferrel (Latimer) W.; m. L. Claudette Faulk, June 9, 1961; children: Laura, Amy, Emily. BA, Harding U., Searcy, Ark., 1959; MA, Harding U., Memphis, 1961; PhD, U. Iowa, 1967. Dir. Christian Student Ctr., Springfield, 1959-73; prof. religious studies S.W. Mo. State U., Springfield, 1961-83; prof. of religion, dean Seaver Coll. Arts, Letters and Scis. Pepperdine U., Malibu, Calif., 1983—. Author: Religion: A Preface, 1982, 2d edit., 1989; co-author: Discovering the Bible, 1986, Excavations at Capernaum, 1989; contbr. articles, revs. to profl. publs. Mem. Archaeol. Inst. Am., Am. Schs. of Oriental Rsch., Soc. Bib. Lit., Am. Numismatic Soc., Am. Coun. Acad. Deans. Mem. Ch. of Christ. Office: Pepperdine U Seaver Coll 24255 Pacific Coast Hwy Malibu CA 90263-0001

WILSON, JOHN LEWIS, university official; b. Columbus, Ohio, Mar. 18, 1943; s. John Robert and Betty Marie (Barker) W.; m. Linda Patricia Kiernan, Apr. 23, 1966; 1 child, Heidi Annette. BA in Internat. Rels., Am. U., 1963, MA in Econs., 1973, PhD, 1977. Staff asst. Congressman Paul N. McCloskey, Washington, 1968-72; sr. assoc. Govt. Affairs Inst., Washington, 1973-77; pres. Experience Devel., Inc., Tucson, 1978-85; from asst. to assoc. dean faculty sci. U. Ariz., Tucson, 1985-93, acting asst. to sr. v.p. adminstrn. and fin., 1988-89, dir. decision and planning support, 1994—; instr. U. Phoenix, Tucson, 1980-83. Author: (with others) Managing Planned Agricultural Development, 1976. 1st lt. U.S. Army, Vietnam, 1964-68. Decorated Bronze Star with oak leaf cluster and V device. Mem. Am. Econ. Assn., Am. Soc. Quality Control, Assn. for Instnl. Rsch., Tucson Met. C. of C. Democrat. Avocations: walking, computers, reading, bicycle racing. Home: 8030 E Garland Rd Tucson AZ 85750-2830 Office: U Ariz Administration 116 Tucson AZ 85721

WILSON, JOHN OLIVER, economist, educator, banker; b. St. James, Mo., May 22, 1938; s. John Riffie and Jacquetta Ruth (Linck) W.; B.A. in Math., Northwestern U., 1960; Ph.D. in Econs., U. Mich., 1967; m. Beclee Newcomer, Jan. 28, 1961; children—Beth Anne, Benjamin Duncan. Asst. prof. Yale U., 1967-70; asst. dir. Office Econ. Opportunity, Washington, 1969-71; asst. sec. HEW, 1972; dir. North Star Research Inst., Mpls., 1972-74; exec. v.p., chief economist Bank of Am., San Francisco 1975—, chief economist, 1982—; prof. Grad. Sch. Pub. Policy and Haas Sch. Bus. U. Calif., Berkeley, 1979-92. bd. dirs. Nat. Bur. Econ. Rsch., Cambridge, Mass. Bd. visitors Joint Center for Urban Studies, Harvard U.-M.I.T., 1978-87; trustee Grad. Theol. Union, Berkeley, Calif. Served with U.S. Navy, 1960-63. Ford Found. fellow, 1966-67. Mem. Am. Econ. Assn., Western Econ. Assn., Nat. Assn. Bus. Economists. Republican. Presbyterian. Author: After Affluence, Economics to Meet Human Needs 1980, Middle Class Crisis: The American and Japanese Experience, 1983, The Power Economy, Building An Economy That Works, 1985; contbr. articles to profl. jours. Office: Bank of America Ctr 555 California St San Francisco CA 94104

WILSON, JOHN ROSS, retired law educator; b. Memphis, Aug. 8, 1920; s. Charles Monroe and Lida Scott (Christenberry) W.; m. Anne Woodruff Talley, Feb. 7, 1944; children—Margaret Anne, Andrew Ross. B.B.A., So. Meth. U., 1943, LL.B., 1948; student, U. Tex., Austin, 1939-41. Bar: Tex. bar 1948. Mem. faculty Baylor U. Law Sch., Waco, Tex., 1948-86; assoc.

prof. law Baylor U. Law Sch., 1951-55, prof., 1955-86, prof. emeritus, 1986; cons. on bankruptcy and judicial remedies. Author: Cases and Materials on Judicial Remedies, 1966; contbr. articles to profl. jours. Served to lt. USNR, 1943-46. Mem. Am. Judicature Soc., Tex. Bar Assn., Am. Bar Assn., Waco-McLennan County Bar Assn., Tex. Trial Lawyers Assn., Delta Theta Phi, Sigma Alpha Epsilon. Republican. Methodist. Office: Baylor Univ Law Sch Waco TX 76703

WILSON, JOSEPH CHARLES, IV, ambassador; b. Bridgeport, Conn., Nov. 6, 1949; s. Joseph Charles III and Phyllis (Finnell) W.; m. Susan Dale Otchis, Apr. 27, 1973 (div. 1986); children: Sabrina Cecile, Joseph Charles; m. Jacqueline Marylene Giorgi, July 1, 1986. BA in History, U. Calif., Santa Barbara, 1972. Fgn. svc. officer Dept. of State, Washington, 1976—; congl. fellow Am. Polit. Sci. Assn., Washington, 1985-86; dep. chief of mission Am. Embassy, Bujumbura, Burundi, 1982-85, Brazzaville, Congo, 1986-88, Baghdad, Iraq, 1988-91; amb. Dept. of State Am. Embassy, Libreville, Gabon, Sao Tome and Principe, 1992-95; polit. adv. to Commdr. in Chief U.S. Armed Forces Europe, 1995—. Recipient Disting. Alumni award U. Calif. Santa Barbara, 1991, Comdr. in Order of Equatorial Star govt. Gabon award, 1995; named hon. adm. County Commr., El Paso, Tex., 1991. Mem. Am. Polit. Sci. Assn., Am. Fgn. Svc. Assn. (William R. Rivkin award 1987), U. Calif. Santa Barbara Alumni Assn., San Onofre Surfing Club. Avocations: golf, bicycling, weight lifting. Home and Office: HQ USEUCom Unit 30400 Box 1458 APO AE 09128-1458

WILSON, JOSEPH MORRIS, III, lawyer; b. Milw., July 26, 1945; s. Joseph Morris Jr. and Phyllis Elizabeth (Cresson) W.; children: Elizabeth J., Eric M.; m. Dixie Lee Brock, Mar. 23, 1984. BA, Calif. State U., Chico, 1967; MA, U. Washington, 1968; JD summa cum laude, Ohio State U., 1976. Bar: Alaska 1976, U.S. Dist. Ct. Alaska 1976, U.S. Ct. Appeals (9th cir.) 1986. Recruiter and vol. U.S. Peace Corps, People's Republic of Benin, 1969-73; legal intern U.S. Ho. of Reps., Washington, 1975; ptnr. Guess & Rudd P.C., Anchorage, 1976-88, chmn. comml. dept., 1981-82, ptnr. compensation com., 1982-84; mgr. Alaska taxes, sr. tax atty. BP Exploration Inc., Alaska, 1990—; bus. law instr. U. Alaska, Anchorage, 1977-78. Mem. ABA, Alaska Bar Assn. (taxation sect.), Anchorage Bar Assn. Democrat. Club: UAA Basketball Boosters, World Affairs Coun. Avocations: music, sports, travel. Home: 1779 Morningtide Ct Anchorage AK 99501-5722 Office: MB6-4 PO Box 196193 Anchorage AK 99519-6193

WILSON, JUDY, small business owner. From order desk clk. to sales rep. Pacific Fasteners; sales rep. Wire & Cable; outside sales rep. Standard Wire & Cable Co., L.A.; owner Wilco Wire & Cable. Office: Wilco Wire & Cable Co 1035 Mission Ct Fremont CA 94539-8203

WILSON, KAREN LEE, museum director; b. Somerville, N.J., Apr. 2, 1949; d. Jon Milton and Laura Virginia (Van Dyke) W.; m. Paul Ernest Walker, 1980; 1 child, Jeremy Nathaniel. AB, Harvard U., 1971; MA, NYU, 1973, PhD, 1985. Rsch. assoc., dir. excavation at Mendes, Egypt Inst. Fine Arts, NYU, 1979-81; coord. exhbn. The Jewish Mus., N.Y.C., 1981-82, adminstrv. cataloguer, 1982-83, coord. curatorial affairs, 1984-86; curator Oriental Inst. Mus. U. Chgo., 1988-96, mus. dir., 1996—. Author, editor: Mendes, 1982; contbr. articles to profl. jours. Mem. Am. Oriental Soc., Am. Rsch. Ctr. in Egypt. Office: Oriental Institute Museum 1155 E 58th St Chicago IL 60637-1540

WILSON, KAREN WILKERSON, paralegal; b. Reidsville, N.C., June 28, 1957; d. William Henry and Jean Gloria (Tiller) W.; divorced. Student, N.C. State U., 1975-77, Western Carolina U., Cullowhee, N.C., 1978-80; diploma, Profl. Ctr. Paralegal Studies, Columbia, S.C., 1988. Paralegal Ken H. Lester, Esquire, Columbia, 1989—; spkr. Alumni Profl. Ctr. Paralegal Studies, Columbia, 1988-95. Mem. ATLA, S.C. Trial Lawyers Assn. (paralegal rep. 1993—). Democrat. Methodist. Office: Lester & Jones 1716 Main St Columbia SC 29201-2820

WILSON, KATHY, principal; b. East Providence, R.I., Aug. 10, 1951; d. Marion A. and Rita (Castergine) Higdon; m. Paul O. Wilson, Dec. 21, 1974; children: Casey Rose, Fletcher Todd. BS in Edn., U. Mo., 1973, MA in Edn., 1976. Cert. in tchg., Mo. Social sci. rsch. analyst Dept. Labor, Washington, 1977-80; nat. pres. Nat. Women's Polit. Caucus, Washington, 1981-85; substitute tchr. Alexandria (Va.) City Pub. Schs., 1989-91; tchr. Resurrection Children's Ctr., Alexandria, Va., 1991-93; dir. Abracadabra Child Care & Devel. Ctr., Alexandria, Va., 1993—; model tchr. The Danny Chitwood Early Learning Ctr., Alexandria, Va., 1993, The Danny Chitwood Early Learning Inst. Family Child Care, Alexandria, 1992-93; jr. gt. books tchr. Maury & Lykes Crouch Elem. Schs., 1986-89. Contbr. articles to newspapers. Youth Soccer Coach Alexandria Soccer Assn., 1989-90; recording sec. PTA, gift wrap chmn.; chmn. All Night Grad. Party, T.C. William H.S., 1995—; mem. adv. bd. Nat. Womens Polit. Caucus; founder, bd. dirs. Nat. Rep. Coalition for Choice, Washington, 1989-91. Received award for one of Washington's Most Influential Washington Mag., 1985; named one of Am.'s 100 Most Important Women Ladies Home Jour. editl. bd., 1983. Mem. Nat. Assn. for the Edn. of Young Children, Alexandria Child Care Dirs. Assn. (co-chmn. 1995—). Republican. Baptist. Avocations: reading, writing, soccer, politics, friends. Home: 1402 Orchard St Alexandria VA 22302 Office: Abracadabra Child Care & Devel Ctr 700 Commonwealth Ave Alexandria VA 22301-2308

WILSON, KATHY KAY, foundation executive; b. Monticello, Ind., Jan. 25, 1961; d. Kenneth L. and Janet I. (Linback) Kruger; m. Kenneth Culp III, June 18, 1983 (div. Jan. 1986); m. Douglas M. Wilson, July 20, 1991. AS, Ball State U., 1981; BS, Ind. Wesleyan U., 1989. Legal sec. Nesbitt Law Firm, Rensselaer, Ind., 1981-84; asst. to dir. Office of Patents and Copyrights Purdue Rsch. Found., West Lafayette, Ind., 1984-86; legal sec. Barnes & Thornburg, Indpls., 1986-87; rsch. and info. specialist Ind. U. Found., Indpls., 1987-91; dir. prospect rsch. Ind. U. Found., Bloomington, 1991—; cons. Prospect Rsch., Indpls., 1991—; mem. faculty Fund Raising Sch., 1988-90. Mem. adv. coun. Bloomington Hosp., 1992—. Mem. NAFE, Am. Prospect Rsch. Assn. (v.p. bd. dirs. 1991, pres. 1992, Ind. chpt. pres. 1988-90), Phi Gamma Nu, Delta Delta Delta. Home: 1225 Pickwick Pt Bloomington IN 47401-6118 Office: Ind U Found PO Box 500 Bloomington IN 47402-0500

WILSON, KEITH DUDLEY, media and music educator; b. Windermere, July 13, 1936; s. Charles Alexander and Fanny (Shaw) W.; 1 child, Nicholas. BA with honors, Kings Coll., Cambridge, 1957, MA, 1960. Lectr. Brit. Coun./Zagreb Univ., Croatia, 1957-58; assoc. prof., dir. TV Brit. Coun. Tehran U., Iran, 1958-64; reader Brit. Coun. Osmania U., Hyderabad, India, 1964-66; head of liberal edn. Salford Coll. of Tech., U.K., 1967-72, head of humanities, 1972-85; head of performing arts and media U. Coll. Salford, 1985-90; dir. ctr. for media performance and comm. U. Salford, 1990-96, founding dir. internat. media ctr., 1993—; dean faculty of media, music and performance Salford U., 1996—; tutor, counsellor Open U., 1972-90; dir. Aspects Prodn. Assocs., TVUK, Adelphi Prodns., Salford, 1988—; chair PRS John Lennon awards, London, 1990-93; co-chair NYNEX Cable TV, Manchester, 1993-95; vis. acad. The Brit. Coun., Korea, 1992; founder over 20 higher edn. courses in music, media and recording. Contbr. articles to profl. jours. and nat. papers; concert tours to Brazil, Belgium, Holland, Iceland, Norway, Denmark, Greece, Ecuador, Russia and Hungary; residencies at Edinburgh Internat. Festival, broadcasts and recordings, 1986-97. Mem. U. Salford Centenary Com., 1994-96, City of Salford LS Lowry Centenary, 1988, City of Salford Millenium Lowry Centre for performing and visual arts and Nat. Indsl. Ctr. for Virtual Reality, 1994—; founder Salford U. Brass Band, Wind Band, Big Band, Soundworks, Jazz Ensembles, Groove Machine, Aspects Theatre; mem. City Pride Initiative, Manchester, 1993—, Fellowship Great Britain Sasakawa Found., Japan, 1991. Fellow Royal Soc. of Arts; mem. Royal TV Soc., British Film Inst., British Acad. of Film and TV., Prodrs. Assn. Cinema and TV, Producers Assn. Cinema and Television. Avocations: nordic culture, wines of the world, fellwalking. Office: Internat Media Centre, Adelphi House The Crescent Salford, Manchester M3 6EN, England

WILSON, KENNETH GEDDES, physics research administrator, educator; b. Waltham, Mass., June 8, 1936; s. E. Bright and Emily Fisher (Buckingham) W.; m. Alison Brown, 1982. A.B., Harvard U., 1956, DSc hon., 1981; Ph.D., Calif. Tech. Inst., 1961; Ph.D. (hon.), U. Chgo., 1976. From asst. prof. to prof. physics Cornell U., Ithaca, N.Y., 1963-88, James A. Weeks prof. in phys. sci., 1974-87; Hazel C. Youngberg Trustees Disting prof. The Ohio State U., Columbus, 1988—. Co-author: Redesigning Education, 1974. Recipient Nobel prize in physics, 1982, Dannie Heinemann prize, 1973, Boltzmann medal, 1975, Wolf prize, 1980, A.C. Eringen medal, 1984, Franklin medal, 1982, Aneesur Rahman prize, 1993. Mem. NAS, Am. Philos. Soc., Am. Phys. Soc., Am. Acad. Arts and Scis.

WILSON, KENNETH JAY, writer; b. Oklahoma City, Aug. 25, 1944; s. Kenneth J. and Betty Wallace (Bleakmore) W. B.A. magna cum laude, Yale U., 1966, M.Phil., 1969; postgrad. Queen's Coll., Oxford U., Eng., 1969-70; Ph.D., Yale U., 1973. From instr. to assoc. prof. English U. Rochester, N.Y., 1970-83; assoc. Clare Hall, Cambridge U., Eng., 1977; vis. assoc. prof. English Coll. William and Mary, Williamsburg, Va., 1983; editor in chief Peter Lang Pub., N.Y.C., 1983-87; dir. of rights and permissions Princeton U. Press, 1987-88; commissioning editor polit. sci. and psychology Routledge, N.Y.C., 1988-90; adminstrv. dir. HIV Clin. Rsch. Ctr. Mt. Zion Med. Ctr./U. Calif., San Francisco, 1994-95; cons. USIA, 1985. Editor: Letters of Sir Thomas Elyot, 1976, English Works of Thomas More, 1978; author: Incomplete Fictions, 1985, Pope John Paul II, 1992; contbr. essays, book revs. and short fiction to mags. and profl. jours. Woodrow Wilson fellow, 1966, 83; sr. fellow Folger Shakespeare Library, Washington, 1976; Am. Philos. Soc. grantee, 1976; Am. Council Learned Soc. fellow, 1977. Mem. Mory's Club, Elizabethan Club (New Haven), Yale Club (N.Y.C.), Palm-Aire Country Club, Phi Beta Kappa. Democrat. Roman Catholic. Home and Office: 5570 Country Club Way Sarasota FL 34243-3759

WILSON, LANFORD, playwright; b. Lebanon, Mo., Apr. 13, 1937; s. Ralph E(ugene) and Violetta (Tate) W. Student, San Diego State Coll., 1955-56; PhD in Humanities, U. Mo., 1985, Grinnell Coll., 1994; PhD in Literature, Southampton Coll., 1995. Playwright, 1962—; resident playwright, dir., co-founder Circle Repertory Co., N.Y.C., 1969-95. Author: (plays) So Long at the Fair, 1963, Home Free, 1964, No Trespassing, 1964, The Sandcastle, 1964, The Madness of Lady Bright, 1964, Ludlow Fair, 1965, Balm in Gilead, 1965, This is the Rill Speaking, 1965, Days Ahead, 1965, Sex in Between Two People, 1965, The Gingham Dog, 1966, The Rimers of Eldritch, 1966, Wandering, 1966, Days Ahead, 1967, Lemon Sky, 1969, Serenading Louie, 1970, The Great Nebula in Orion, 1970, The Hot L Baltimore, 1972, The Family Continues, 1972, The Mound Builders, 1975, Fifth of July, 1978, Brontasaurus, 1978, Talley's Folly, 1979, A Tale Told, 1981, Angels Fall, 1983, A Betrothal, 1984, Talley & Son, 1985, Burn This, 1987, A Poster of the Cosmos, 1987, The Moonshot Tape, 1990, Redwood Curtain, 1991, Trinity, 1993, I'm Not the Ocean, 1995, Sympathetic Magic, 1995, Virgil is Still the Frogboy, 1996; translator Three Sisters, 1984; author: (books) Balm in Gilead and Other Plays, 1966, The Rimers of Eldritch and Other Plays, 1968, The Gingham Dog, 1969, Lemon Sky, 1970, The Hot L Baltimore, 1973, The Mound Builders, 1976, Fifth of July, 1979, Talley's Folly, 1980, Angels Fall, 1983, Serenading Louie, 1985, Talley & Son, 1986, Burn This, 1988, Redwood Curtain, 1992, 21 Short Plays, 1994, By the Sea, 1996, Collected Plays, Vol. I, 1997. ABC Yale fellow, 1969; Rockefeller grantee, 1967, 73, Guggenheim grantee, 1970, NEA grantee, 1990; recipient Vernon Rice award, 1966-67, Inst. Arts and Letters award, 1970, Obie award, 1972, 75, 84, 97, Outer Critics Circle award, 1973, Drama Critics Circle award, 1973, 80, Pulitzer prize, 1980, Brandeis award, 1981, John Steinbeck award, 1990, Edward Albee Last Frontier award, 1994, Am. Acad. of Achievement award, 1995. Mem. Dramatists Guild Council.

WILSON, LAUREN ROSS, academic administrator; b. Yates Center, Kans., May 4, 1936; s. Roscoe C. and Margaret D. W.; m. Janie Haskin, Jan. 25, 1959; children—Lance Kevin, Keela Lynn. B.S., Baker U., Baldwin, Kans., 1958; Ph.D., U. Kans., 1963. Mem. faculty Ohio Wesleyan U., Delaware, 1963-87; prof. chemistry Ohio Wesleyan U., 1971-87, Homer Lucas U. prof., dean acad. affairs, 1978-86, acting provost, 1985-86, asst. to pres., 1986, 87; vice chancellor for acad. affairs U. N.C., Asheville, 1987-95, prof. chemistry, 1987-95, interim chancellor, 1993-94; pres., prof. chemistry Marietta Coll., 1995—; vis. prof. Ohio State U., 1968, 74; vis. research assoc. Oak Ridge Nat. Lab., 1972-73. Recipient Outstanding Tchr. award Ohio Wesleyan U., 1968. Mem. AAAS, AAUP, Am. Chem. Soc., Am. Assn. Higher Edn., Coun. Undergrad. Rsch., Sigma Xi. Office: Marietta Coll 215 5th St Marietta OH 45750-4033

WILSON, LAWRENCE FRANK (LARRY WILSON), professional football team executive; b. Rigby, Idaho, Mar. 24, 1938; m. Nancy Drew, Apr. 15, 1980. Student, U. Utah, 1956-60. Defensive back St. Louis Cardinals, NFL, 1960-72, dir. profl. scouting, 1973-76, dir. profl. pers., 1977-88; v.p., former gen. mgr. Ariz. Cardinals, NFL, 1988—. Mem. All-NFL Team, 1963, 66, 67, 68, 69; player Pro Bowl, 1962-63, 65-70; inducted Pro Football Hall of Fame, 1978; led in interceptions NFL, 1966. Office: Ariz Cardinals PO Box 888 Phoenix AZ 85001-0888*

WILSON, LELAND EARL, petroleum engineering consultant; b. Ft. Recovery, Ohio, Oct. 28, 1925; s. John Huffman and Matilda Caroline (Sunderhaus) W.; m. Marian Ruthetta Trygstad, Nov. 27, 1948; children: Kathleen Ann, Linda Kay, Mary Lee, John Russell. BS in Petroleum Engring., Tulsa U., 1950. Registered profl. engr., Alaska, Tex. Drilling engr. Atlantic Refining Co., Tex., Ark., and La., 1950-56; drilling supr. Atlantic Refining Co., La., Tex., 1956-65; drilling supt. Atlantic Richfield, Anchorage, 1965-67, prodn. and drilling supt., 1967-72; ops. mgr. ARCO Oil Prodn. Co., London, 1972-75; resident mgr. ARCO Greenland, Copenhagen, 1975-78; pres. ARCO Indonesia, Inc., Jakarta, 1978-82; v.p. ARCO China, Hong Kong, 1982-85; petroleum cons. Lindale, Tex., 1985—; bd. dirs. Houma Oil Treaters, Inc., DPM Non-Destructive Testing, Odessa, Tex. Author family history Dear John, 1989; contbr. articles to profl. jours.; inventor in field. Aviation cadet AAF, 1943-45. Mem. NSPE, Tex. Soc. Profl. Engrs., Tyler Petroleum Club, Soc. Petroleum Engrs., Petroleum Club (pres. Anchorage 1971-72), Indonesian Petroleum Assn. (pres. 1981-82). Republican. Roman Catholic. Avocations: geneaology, golf, travel. Home: PO Box 893 428 Lonestar Ln Lindale TX 75771 Office: PO Box 893 2715 S Main Lindale TX 75771

WILSON, LEONARD GILCHRIST, history of medicine educator; b. Orillia, Ont., Can., June 11, 1928; s. George Edward and Mary Agnes (MacPhee) W.; m. Adelia Katherine Hans, June 7, 1969; 1 child, George Edward Hans. B.A., U. Toronto, Can., 1949; M.Sc., U. London, 1955; Ph.D., U. Wis., Madison, 1958. Lectr. Mount Allison U., Sackville, N.B., Can., 1950-53; vis. instr. U. Calif., Berkeley, 1958-59; asst. prof. Cornell U., Ithaca, N.Y., 1959-60; asst. prof. Yale U., New Haven, 1960-65, assoc. prof., 1965-67; prof., head dept. history of medicine U. Minn., Mpls., 1967—. Author: Charles Lyell: The Years to 1841: The Revolution in Geology, 1972, Medical Revolution in Minnesota, 1989; editor: Benjamin Silliman and His Circle, 1979, Sir Charles Lyell's Scientific Journals on the Species Question, 1971; editor Jour. History Medicine and Allied Scis., 1973-82; co-editor: Readings in History of Physiology, 1966; mem. bd. mgrs. Jour. Hist. Medicine, 1962—. Fellow AAAS; mem. Am. Assn. History of Medicine, Am. Hist. Assn., History of Sci. Soc., Minn. Acad. Medicine (pres. 1984-85, sec.-treas. 1989—), Brit. Soc. for the History of Sci., Soc. for the History of natural History. Home: 797 Goodrich Ave Saint Paul MN 55105-3344 Office: U Minn Dept History of Medicine 420 Delaware St SE Minneapolis MN 55455-0374

WILSON, LEROY, retired glass manufacturing company executive; b. Indpls., July 15, 1928; s. Paul Allison and Lula (Berry) W.; m. Claudie Leenaert, Aug. 9, 1968; children: Paul Neil, Daniel Stuart, Benjamin, Antoine, Virginie. B.S. in Mech. Engring, Purdue U., 1950. With Corning Glass Works, N.Y., 1950-87; v.p. gen. mgr. electronic products div. Corning Glass Works, 1975-80; pres. Corning Europe Inc., Neuilly, France, 1980-87. Mem. dean's adv. council Krannert Sch., Purdue U. Served with AUS, 1954-56. Named Disting. Engring. Alumnus, Purdue U., 1981. Fellow Inst. Dirs.; mem. Royal Automobile Club (London). Ch. of Eng. Home: Egypt House, Rushlake Green, Heathfield East Sussex TN21 9QT, England

WILSON, LESLIE, biochemist, cell biologist, biology educator; b. Boston, June 29, 1941; s. Samuel Paul Wilson and Lee (Melnicker) Kamerling; m. Carla Helena Van Wingerden, Sept. 9, 1989; children from previous marriage: Sebastian A. Michael, Naomi Beth. BS, Mass. Coll. Pharmacy and Allied Health Scis., 1963; PhD, Tufts U., 1967; postdoctoral study, U. Calif. at Berkeley, 1967-69. Asst. prof. dept. pharmacology Stanford U. Sch. Medicine, 1969-74; assoc. prof. dept. biol. scis. U. Calif., Santa Barbara, 1975-78, prof. biochemistry, 1979—, chmn. dept. biol. scis., 1987-91, head divsn. molecular, cellular, devel. biol., 1992-93; sci. adv. panel mem. cell and devel. biology Am. Cancer Soc., Atlanta, 1984-88; cons. Eli Lilly & Co., Indpls., 1980—; scientific adv. bd. Myco Genetics, Inc., 1997—. Editor: (book series) Methods in Cell Biology, 1987—; assoc. editor Biochemistry; contbr. numerous rsch. papers to profl. publs. Bd. dirs. Cancer Found. Santa Barbara. Rsch. grantee NIH, 1970—, Am. Cancer Soc., 1986—. Mem. AAAS, Am. Soc. Cell Biology (chmn. sci. program 1977), Am. Soc. Biol. Chemistry and Molecular Biology, Am. Soc. Pharmacology and Exptl. Therapeutics, Am. chem. Soc. Democrat. Office: Univ Calif Dept Molecular Cellular and Devel Biology Santa Barbara CA 93106

WILSON, LINDA, librarian; b. Rochester, Minn., Nov. 17, 1945; d. Eunice Gloria Irene Wilson. BA, U. Minn., Morris, 1967; MA, U. Minn., 1968. Libr. rsch. svcs. U. Calif., Riverside, 1968-69, head dept. phys. scis. catalog, 1969-71; city libr. Belle Glade (Fla). Mcpl. Libr., 1972-74; instr. part-time Palm Beach Jr. Coll., Belle Glade, 1973; head adult-young adult ext. Kern County Libr. Sys., Bakersfield, Calif., 1974-80; dir. dist. libr. Lake Agassiz Regional Libr. System, Crookston, Minn., 1980-85; supervising libr. San Diego County Libr., 1985-87; county libr. Merced (Calif.) County Libr., 1987-93; learning network mgr. Merced Coll., 1994-95; libr. dir. Monterey Park (Calif.) Bruggemeyer Meml. Libr., 1995—. Active Leadership Merced, 1987-88; mem. East Site Based Coordinating Coun., Merced, 1990-92, Merced Gen. Plan Citizens Adv. Com., 1992-95, Sister City Com., Merced, 1992-95, East L.A. Bus. and Profl. Women, 1996—, Monterey Pk. Rotary, 1996—. Recipient Libr. award Eagles Aux., 1984, Woman of Achievement award Commn. on the Status of Women, 1990, Libr. award Calif. Libr. Trustees and Commrs., 1990, Woman of Yr. award Merced Bus. and Profl. Women, 1987. Mem. ALA (sec. pub. libr. sys. sect. 1988-89), Calif. Libr. Assn. (sec. govt. rels. com. 1991-92, continuing edn. com. 1993-96), Minn. Libr. Assn. (pres. pub. libr. divsn. 1985), Merced County Mgmt. Coun. (pres. 1989), Merced Bus. and Profl. Women (pres. 1988-89). Democrat. Lutheran. Avocations: travel, walking, reading, swimming, stamp collecting. Home: 1000 E Newmark Ave Apt 22 Monterey Park CA 91755-3129

WILSON, LINDA SMITH, academic administrator; b. Washington, Nov. 10, 1936; d. Fred M. and Virginia D. (Thompson) Smith; m. Paul A. Wilson, Jan. 22, 1970; 1 dau. by previous marriage: Helen K. Whatley, a stepdau., Beth A. Wilson. B.A., Newcomb Coll., Tulane U., 1957; Ph.D., U. Wis., 1962; HLD (hon.), Tulane U., 1993; DLitt. (hon.), U. Md., 1993. Postdoctoral rsch. assoc. U. Md., College Park, 1962-64, rsch. asst. prof., 1964-67; vis. asst. prof. U. Mo.-St. Louis, 1967-68; asst. to vice chancellor for rsch., asst. vice chancellor for rsch., assoc. vice chancellor for rsch. Washington U., St. Louis, 1968-75; assoc. vice chancellor for rsch. U. Ill., Urbana, 1975-85; assoc. dean Grad. Coll., U. Ill., Urbana, 1978-85; v.p. for rsch. U. Mich., Ann Arbor, 1985-89; pres. Radcliffe Coll., Cambridge, Mass., 1989—; chmn. adv. com. office sci. and engring. pers. NRC, 1990-96; mem. dir.'s adv. coun. NSF, Washington, 1980-89, adv. com. edn. and human resources, 1990-95; mem. Nat. Commn. on Rsch., Washington, 1978-80; mem. com. on govt.-univ. relationships NAS, 1981-83, mem. govt.-univ.-industry rsch. roundtable, 1984-89; mem. rsch. resources adv. coun. NIH, Bethesda, Md., 1978-82, energy rsch. adv. bd. DOE, 1987-90; mem. sci., tech. and states task force Carnegie Commn. on Sci., Tech. and Govt., 1991-92; trustee Com. on Econ. Devel., 1995—, overseer Mus. of Sci., Boston, 1992—. Author book chpts.; contbr. articles to profl. jours. Bd. govs. YMCA, Champaign-Urbana, Ill., 1980-83; mem. adv. bd. Nat. Coalition for Sci. and Tech., Washington, 1983-87; trustee Mass. Gen. Hosp., 1992—; dir. Citizen's Fin. Group, 1996—. Recipient Centennial award Newcomb Coll., 1986; named One of 100 Emerging Leaders Am. Coun. Edn. and Change, 1978. Fellow AAAS (bd. dirs. 1984-88); mem. NAS (coord. coun. for edn. 1991-93), Am. Chem. Soc. (bd. coun. com. on chemistry and pub. affairs 1978-80), Soc. Rsch. Adminstrs. (Disting. Contbn. to Rsch. Adminstrn. award 1984), Nat. Coun. Univ. Rsch. Adminstrs., Assn. for Biomed. Rsch. (bd. dirs. 1983-86), Inst. Medicine (mem. coun. 1986-89), Am. Coun. Edn. (commn. on women in higher edn. 1991-93, chair 1993), Phi Beta Kappa, Sigma Xi, Alpha Lambda Delta, Phi Delta Kappa, Phi Kappa Phi. Home: 76 Brattle St Cambridge MA 02138-3452 Office: Radcliffe Coll Office of Pres Fay House 10 Garden St Cambridge MA 02138

WILSON, LLOYD LEE, organization administrator; b. Elkton, Md., Sept. 14, 1947; s. Clifton Laws and Betty Raye (Bare) W.; m. Susan Sieg Wilson, 1992; children: Asa, Ryan, Morgan, Daniel. BS in Mgmt., MIT, 1969, MS in Mgmt., 1977. Bus. mgr. med. clinics Mass. Gen. Hosp., Boston, 1970-73; ptnr. Willow Co., mgmt. cons., Cambridge, Mass., 1974-77; dir. community relations Wilson Neuropsychiat. Hosp., Charlottesville, Va., 1977-78; exec. dir. Jefferson Area United Transp. Inc., Charlottesville, Va., 1978-80, Va. Mountain Housing Inc., Blacksburg, 1980-82; gen. sec. Friends Gen. Conf. Religious Soc. Friends, Phila., 1982-85; dir. rsch. and devel. Va. Mountain Housing, Inc., Christiansburg, 1985-88, dir. multifamily housing, 1989-91, regional dir., 1991-92; pres. Friendly Mgmt. Svcs. Corp., Norfolk, Va., 1992-95, Not-for-Profit Mgmt., Inc., Norfolk, Va., 1995—; pres., dir. Va. Housing Coalition, Inc., 1981-82; treas., bd. dirs. Fiddle Hill Farm, Inc., Barboursville, Va., 1982-89; bd. mgrs. Bible Assn. Friends in Am., Phila., 1983-85; mem. com. rec. ministers Balt. Yearly Meeting Friends, Sandy Spring, Md., 1984-86; asst. sec.-treas. Friends Meeting House Fund, Inc., Phila., 1984-85; asst. presiding clk. Communications Commn. of Friends United Meeting, Richmond, Ind., 1987-88; recorded minister of the gospel, Soc. of Friends, 1989— (presiding clk. Va. Beach monthly meeting 1990-92); dir. coordinating cabinet Va. Coun. Chs., 1988; presiding clk. N.C. Yearly Meeting of Friends, 1991-92. Author: Essays on the Quaker Vision of Gospel Order, 1993; contbr. articles to profl. jours. Treas., bd. dirs. Norfolk (Va.) Quaker House, Inc., 1995—; bd. dirs. New Dominion Housing, Inc., Norfolk, 1992-94; vice chmn. Montgomery County Cmty. Svc. Commn., Christianburg, Va., 1980-82; mem. ednl. coun. MIT, 19777-89; bd. dirs. Am. Friends Svc. Com., Inc., Phila., 1980-83; bd. dirs. Interfaith Housing Corp. Cambridge, Inc., 1975-77, treas., 1976-77, also numerous others. Home: 536 Carnaby Ct Virginia Beach VA 23454-3473 Office: Not for Profit Mgmt Inc PO Box 7891 Norfolk VA 23509-0891

WILSON, LOIS M., minister; b. Winnipeg, Man., Can., Apr. 8, 1927; d. Edwin Gardiner Dunn and Ada Minnie (Davis) Freeman; m. Roy F. Wilson, June 9, 1950; children: Ruth, Jean, Neil, Bruce. BA, United Coll., Winnipeg, 1947, BDiv, 1969; Diploma in TV prodn., Ryerson Tech. Inst., 1974; DDiv (hon.), Victoria U., Toronto, 1978, United Theol. Coll., Montreal, 1978, Wycliff Coll., 1983, Queens U., Kingston, 1984, U. Winnipeg, 1986, Mt. Allison U., 1988; LLD (hon.), Trent U., Peterborough, 1984, Dalhousie U., 1989, Dalhousie U., 1989, Ripon Coll., Wis., 1992; DCL (hon.), Acadia U., 1984; DHuml (hon.), Mt. St. Vincent, Halifax, 1984. Ordained to ministry United Church of Can., 1965. Minister Thunder Bay, 1965-69, Hamilton, 1969-78, Kingston, 1978-80; moderator United Church of Can., Kingston, 1980-82; McGeachy sr. scholar United Church of Can., 1989-91; pres. Can. Council of Chs., Toronto, Ont., 1976-79; co-dir. Ecumenical Forum Can., Toronto, Ont., 1983-89; pres. World Council of Chs., Geneva, 1983-91; chancellor Lakehead U., Thurder Bay, Ont., 1990—; chmn. contemporary theology Lafayette-Orinda (Calif.) Presbyn. Ch., 1995; mem. adv. coun. internt. devel. studies U. Toronto, 1987-93; spokesperson Project Ploughshares, 1st and 2d UN Conf. on Disarmament, N.Y.C., 1978-82; lectr. Vancouver Sch. Theology, 1980, Queens Theol. Coll., 1982-83, 92, Chancellor's lectr., 1992; officer Human Rights Commn., Ont., 1973; mem. bd. regents Victoria U., 1990—; chief Can. Fact finding Mission to Sri Lanka, 1992; team mem. Ctrl. Am. Monitoring Group to El Salvador and Guatemala, 1993. Author: Like a Mighty River, 1980, Turning the World Upside Down, 1989, Miriam, Mary and Me, 1992, Telling Her Story, 1992, Stories Seldom Told, 1997; mem. adv. bd. Can. Woman Studies Jour., York U., 1993—; contbr. articles to profl. publs. Pres. Social Planning Coun., Thunder Bay, 1967-68, Can. Com. for Scientists and Scholars, Toronto, 1982; bd. dirs. Elizabeth Fry Soc., Hamilton, 1976-79, Amnesty Internat., 1978-90, Can. Inst. for Internat. Peace and Security, 1984-88, Energy Probe, 1981-86, Internat. Ctr. Human Rights and Dem. Devel., 1997—; active Refugee Status Adv. Com., 1985-89; bd. dirs. Can. Univ. Svc. Overseas, 1983-85, Inernat. Ctr. Human Rights & Dem. Devel.; chmn. Urban Rural Mission, Can., 1990—; mem. Environ. Assessment Panel Govt. Can., Nuclear Fuel Waste Mgmt. and Disposal Concept, 1989—; trustee Nelson Mandela Fund, 1990-92. Decorated Order of Can., 1984, Order of Ont., 1991; recipient Queens Jubilee medal, Commemorative medal for 125th Anniversary of Confederation of Can., 1992, World Federalist Peace award, 1985, Pearson Peace medal UN Assn. of Can., 1985; named hon. pres. Student Christian Movement of Can., Toronto, 1976. Mem. CAW (pub. rev. bd. 1986—), Can. Assn. Adult Edn. (bd. dirs. 1986-90), Friends Can. Broadcasting (bd. dirs. 1986—, v.p.), Civil Liberties Assn. (v.p. 1986—), UNIFEM (nat. v.p. 1993-95, mem. CCIC team to monitor El Salvador election 1994), World Federalists (pres. Can. chpt. 1996—), Parliament of World's Religions (del. 1993), Christian-Jewish Dialogue Jerusalem (keynote speaker 1994). Home and Office: 40 Glen Rd Apt 310, Toronto, ON Canada M4W 2V1

WILSON, LORRAINE M., medical and surgical nurse, nursing educator; b. Mich., Nov. 18, 1931; d. Bert and Frances Fern (White) McCarty; m. Harold A. Wilson, June 9, 1953; children: David Scott, Ann Elizabeth. Diploma in Nursing, Bronson Meth. Sch. Nursing, Kalamazoo, Mich., 1953; BS in Chemistry, Siena Heights Coll., 1969; MSN, U. Mich., 1972; PhD, Wayne State U., Detroit, 1985. RN, Mich. Staff nurse U. Mich. Med. Ctr., Ann Arbor, 1953-54, Herrick Meml. Hosp., Tecumseh, Mich., 1954-69; asst. prof. nursing U. Mich., Ann Arbor, 1972-78, Wayne State U., Detroit, 1978-79; assoc. prof. nursing Sch. of Nursing Oakland U., Rochester, Mich., 1986-89; prof. nursing Ea. Mich. U., Ypsilanti, Mich., 1989—; researcher in field; bd. advs. Profl. Fitness Systems, Warren, Mich., 1986—; cons. wellness and exercise program General Motors CPC Hdqs., Warren, 1986; cons. and faculty liaison nurse extern program in critical care Ea. Mich. U. Catherine McAuley Health Ctr., 1989—. Author: (with S. Price and L. Wilson) Pathophysiology, 5th edit., 1997; contbr. articles to profl. jours. Vol. Community Health Screening Drives, Tecumseh, 1960-70, leader Girl Scouts U.S., Tecumseh, 1960; sunday sch. tchr. Gloria Dei Luth. Ch., Tecumseh, 1960; mem. PTA. Grantee Mich. Heart Assn., 1984, 88, R.C. Mahon Found., 1988. Mem. ANA (various offices and com. chairs), Midwest Nursing Rsch. Soc. (v.p., sec.-treas., bd. dirs.), Mich. Nurses Assn. (del.), Nat. League Nursing, Nat. Orgn. Women, Sigma Theta Tau. Lutheran. Avocations: traveling, theatre, jogging. Home: 1010 Red Mill Dr Tecumseh MI 49286-1145 Office: Ea Mich U 53 W Michigan Ave Ypsilanti MI 48197-5436

WILSON, LUCY JEAN, librarian; b. Cin., Dec. 27, 1938; d. Gregory Girard and Harriet Elsa (Wiggers) Wright; m. Paul Robert Wilson, Aug. 25, 1962 (div. 1968); 1 child, Ellen Field; m. William Carl Schutzius, Dec. 12, 1976; stepchildren: Christopher Matthew, Catharine Alexander, John Benedict, Margaret Elizabeth. BA in French, Middlebury (Vt.) Coll., 1960; MS in Libr. Sci., U. Ill., 1963. Tech. libr. Chanute AFB, Rantoul, Ill., 1963-65; libr. Coll. Prep. Sch., Cin., 1969-74; pub. svcs. libr. Raymond Walters Coll., Cin., 1974-79, dir. libr., 1979-92, sr. libr., 1988—; dir. libr. and instructional media program Raymond Walters Coll., U. Cin., 1979-92, dir. media profl. cert. program, 1989-93; access svcs. libr. U Cin. Coll. Engring., 1992—; bd. dirs. Ohio-Ky. Cooperating Librs., Union List of Serials, 1984-87; sec. instrn. and tng. coun. Ohionet, 1981-82. Mem. ALA, AAUP, Am. Soc. Info. Sci. (sec. 1980-81), Midwest Federating of Libr. Assn. (registration com. 1983), Acad. Libr. Assn. Ohio (nominating com. 1985), Greater Cin. Libr. Consortium (bd. dirs. 1979-92), Am. Soc. for Profl. Sci., Spl. Librs. Assn., Libr. Guild U. Cin. Home: 3444 Stettinius Ave Cincinnati OH 45208-1204 Office: U Cin Engring Coll Libr 880 Baldwin Hall U Cin Cincinnati OH 45221-0018

WILSON, LUCY LYNN WILLMARTH, postal service administrator; b. Russellville, Ala., May 18, 1953; d. Richard Bert and Alice Josephine (Gantt) Willmarth; m. Donald Wayne Wilson, Dec. 21, 1974; children: Beau Evan and Heath Edward (twins). BS in Home Econs., U. Ala., 1975; BS Ed. Sec. Biology/Psychology, Athens (Ala.) State Coll., 1996. Dietetic technician Athens (Ala.) Limestone Hosp., 1975-76, Med. Ctr. Hosp., Huntsville, Ala., 1976-78; kitchen supr. Lurleen B. Wallace Ctr., Decatur, Ala., 1979; food svc. dir. Limestone Nursing Hosp., Athens, 1980; city carrier U.S. Postal Svc., Huntsville, 1986; city carrier U.S. Postal Svc., Athens, 1986-88, distbn. clk., 1988—; officer in charge U.S. Postal Svc., Lester, Ala., 1992-93. Mem. Cowart Elem. Sch. PTA, Athens, 1985-91; clinic vol. Cowart Elem. Sch., 1985; team mother Dixie Youth Baseball, Athens, 1991; mem. Athens H.S. Athletic Boosters Club, 1994—. Recipient Good Citizenship award Civitan Club, Russellville, 1971. Mem. MADD (Ala. chpt.), Nat. Assn. Postmasters of U.S. (assoc.), Ala. Sci. Tchrs. Assn., U. Ala. Nat. Alumni Assn, Athens State Coll. Alumni Assn., Nature Conservancy, The Studebaker Drivers Club. Avocations: genealogy, reading, music, photography, travel, college studies. Home: 209 Cascade Dr Athens AL 35611-2215 Office: US Postal Svc 1110 W Market St Athens AL 35611-2466

WILSON, LYNTON RONALD, telecommunications company executive; b. Port Colborne, Ont., Can., Apr. 3, 1940; s. Ronald Alfred and Blanche Evelyn (Matthews) W.; m. Brenda Jean Black, Dec. 23, 1968; children: Edward Ronald, Margot Jean, Jennifer Lyn. BA, McMaster U., 1962, LLD, 1995; MA, Cornell U., 1967; D honoris causa, U. Montreal, 1995. Dep. minister Ministry Industry and Tourism, Ont., 1978-81; pres., CEO Redpath Industries, Ltd., Toronto, 1981-88; mng. dir. N.Am. Tate & Lyle, PLC, 1986-89; chmn. bd. Redpath Industries, Ltd., 1988-89; vice chmn. Bank of N.S., Toronto, 1989-90; pres., chief operating officer BCE, Inc., Montreal, 1990-92; pres., CEO BCE Inc., Montreal, 1992-93, chmn., pres. CEO, 1993-96, chmn., CEO, 1996—; chmn. Bell Can.; bd. dirs. Tate & Lyle plc, London, Stelco Inc., BCE, Inc., Bell Can., No. Telecom, Teleglobe Inc., C.W. Howe Inst., Bell Can. Internat., BCE Mobile Comm., Inc., Chrysler Can. Ltd., Chrysler Corp., Bell-No. Rsch. Ltd., Can. Inst. for Advanced Rsch.; mem. internat. coun. J.P. Morgan and Co., N.Y.C. Bd. govs. Olympic Trust Can.; mem. policy com. Bus. Coun. on Nat. Issues; mem. The Trilateral Commn.; trustee Montreal Mus. of Fine Arts Found. Mem. The Mount Royal Club of Montreal, York Club, Toronto Club, Toronto Golf Club, Rideau Club, Univ. Club of Montreal, Royal Montreal Golf Club, Mount Bruno Country Club. Home: 1321 Sherbrooke St W Apt A-110, Montreal, PQ Canada H3G 1J4 Office: BCE Inc / Ste 3700, 1000 Rue de la Gauchetière O, Montreal, PQ Canada H3B 4Y7

WILSON, M. ROY, medical educator; b. Yokohama, Japan, Nov. 28, 1953. BS, Allegheny Coll., 1976; MD, Harvard Med. Sch., 1980; MS in Epidemiology, UCLA, 1990. Diplomate Nat. Bd. Medicine, Am. Bd. Ophthalmology. Intern Harlem Hosp. Ctr., N.Y.C., 1980-81; resident in ophthalmology Mass. Eye & Ear Infirmary/Harvard Med. Sch., Boston, 1981-84, glaucoma, 1984-85; clin. fellow in ophthalmology Harvard Med. Sch., 1980-85, clin. asst. ophthalmology, 1985-86; clin. instr. dept. surgery, Divsn. Ophthalmology Howard U. Sch. Medicine, Washington, 1985-86; asst. prof. ophthalmology UCLA, 1986-91; asst. prof., chief Divsn. Ophthalmology Charles R. Drew U. of Medicine and Sci., L.A., 1986-90, assoc. prof., chief Divsn. Ophthalmology, 1991-94, acad. dean, 1993-95, dean, 1995—, prof., 1994—; prof. UCLA, 1994—; asst. in ophthalmology Mass. Eye and Ear Infirmary, 1985-86; cons. ophthalmologist, Victoria Hosp., Castries, St. Lucia, 1985-86; hosp. appointment, UCLA; chief physician Martin Luther King, Jr. Hosp., L.A., 1986—; project dir. Internat. Eye Found., Ministry of Health, 1985-86; biology lab instr., Allegheny coll., 1975; instr. in biochemistry Harvard U. Summer Sch., 1977-78; instr. Harvard Med. Sch., 1980-85, others; cons. and presenter in field; participant coms. in field. Mem. AMA, Assn. Rsch. in Vision and Ophthalmology, Chandler-Grant Glaucoma Soc., Nat. Med. Assn., Am. Acad. Ophthalmology, Soc. Eye Surgeons Internat. Eye Found., Mass. Eye and Ear Infirmary Alumni Assn., So. Calif. Glaucoma Soc., West Coast Glaucoma Study Club, Assn. Univ. Profs. in Ophthalmology, L.A. Eye Soc., Calif. Med. Assn., Am. Glaucoma Soc., Soc. Epidemiol. Rsch., Am. Pub. Health Assn. Office: 1621 E 120th St Los Angeles CA 90059-3025

WILSON, MARC FRASER, art museum administrator and curator; b. Akron, Ohio, Sept. 12, 1941; s. Fraser Eugene and Pauline Christine (Hoff) W.; m. Elizabeth Marie Fulder, Aug. 2, 1975. BA, Yale U., 1963, MA, 1967. Departmental asst. Cleve. Mus. Art, 1964; translator, project cons. Nat. Palace Mus., Taipei, Taiwan, 1968-71; assoc. curator of Chinese art Nelson Gallery-Atkins Mus., Kansas City, Mo., 1971-73, curator of Oriental art, 1973—, interim dir., 1982, dir. and curator Oriental art, 1982—; mem., rapporteur Indo-US Subcom. on Edn. and Culture, Washington, 1976-79; mem. adv. com. Asia Soc. Galleries, N.Y.C., 1984—, China Inst. in Am., 1985—. Mem. adv. com. Muni-Art Commn. on Urban Sculpture, Kansas City, 1984-87; com. mem. Kansas City-Xi'an, China, Sister City program, 1986—; mem. humanities coun. Johnson County Cmty. Coll., 1976-79; commr. Japan-U.S. Friendship Commn., Washington, 1986-88; panelist Japan-U.S. Cultural and Edn. Cooperation, Washington, 1986-88; mem. mayor's task force on race relations, 1996—; mem. indemnity adv. panel, 1995—; v.p. Brush Creek Ptnrs. 1995—. Recipient The William Yates Medallion Civic Svc. award William Jewell Coll., 1995. Mem. Assn. Art Mus. Dirs. (treas., trustee 1988-90, chmn. works of art com. 1986-90), Mo. China Coun., Fed. Coun. Arts and Humanities (chmn. arts and artifacts indemnity adv. panel 1986-89, 1995-96). Office: Nelson-Atkins Mus Art 4525 Oak St Kansas City MO 64111-1818

WILSON, MARGARET BUSH, lawyer, civil rights leader; b. St. Louis, Jan. 30, 1919; married; 1 child, Robert Edmund. B.A. cum laude, Talladega Coll., 1940; LL.B., Lincoln U., 1943. Ptnr. Wilson & Wilson, St. Louis, 1947-65; now with firm Wilson & Assocs.; asst. dir. St. Louis Lawyers for Housing, 1969-72; asst. atty. gen. Mo., 1961-62; atty. Rural Electrification Adminstrn., Dept. Agr., St. Louis, 1943-45; instr. civil procedure St. Louis U. Sch. Law, 1971; chmn. St. Louis Land Reutilization Authority, 1975-76; mem. Mo. Coun. Criminal Justice, 1972—; chmn. Intergroup Corp., 1985-87; bd. dirs. Mut. of N.Y. Mem. gen. adv. com. ACDA, 1978-81; trustee emeritus Washington U., St. Louis; chmn. bd. trustees Talladega Coll., Ala., 1988-92; nat. bd. dirs. ARC, 1975-81, United Way, 1978-84, Police Found., 1976-93; treas. NAACP Nat. Housing Corp., 1971-84, chmn. nat. bd., 1975-84; dep. dir./acting dir. St. Louis Model City Agy., 1968-69; adminstr. Mo. Commn. Svc. and Continuing Edn., 1967-68. Recipient Bishop's award Episcopal Diocese Mo., 1962; Juliette Derricotte fellow, 1939-40, Disting. Lawyer award Bar Assn. Metro St. Louis, 1997. Mem. ABA (chmn. youth edn. for citizenship 1991-94), Nat. Bar Assn., Mo. Bar Assn., Mound City Bar Assn., St. Louis Bar Assn., Alpha Kappa Alpha. Office: Wilson & Assocs 4054 Lindell Blvd Saint Louis MO 63108-3202

WILSON, MARGARET DAULER, philosophy educator; b. Pitts., Jan. 29, 1939; d. Lee Van Voorhis and Margaret (Hodge) D.; m. Emmett Wilson, Jr., June 12, 1962. A.B., Vassar Coll., 1960; A.M., Harvard U., 1963, Ph.D., 1965; postgrad., Oxford U., 1963-64. Asst. prof. philosophy Columbia U., 1965-67; asst. prof. Rockefeller U., 1967-70; asso. prof. philosophy Princeton (N.J.) U., 1970-75, prof., 1975—, acting chmn. dept. philosophy, 1987-88; dir. Summer Inst. Early Modern Philosophy, Bristol, R.I., 1974; vis. asst. prof. Barnard Coll., part-time 1969-70. Author: Descartes, 1978; editor: The Essential Descartes, 1969. Mem. Planning Bd. Franklin Twp., N.J., 1988-92, Environ. Commn., 1988-95. Recipient Centennial medal Harvard Grad. Sch. Arts and Scis., 1989, Behrman prize for distinction in humanities Princeton U., 1994; Japan Soc. for Promotion of Sci. fellow, 1990, Guggenheim fellow, 1977-79, Am. Coun. Learned Socs. fellow, 1982-83; visitor Inst. Advanced Study, spring 1973. Fellow Am. Acad. Arts and Scis.; mem. Am. Philos. Assn. (v.p. ea. divsn. 1993-94, pres. ea. divsn. 1994-95), Leibniz Soc. N.Am. (pres. 1986-90), Internat. Berkeley Soc. Home: 943 Canal Rd Princeton NJ 08540-8509 Office: Princeton U Dept Philosophy 1879 Hall Princeton NJ 08544

WILSON, MARGARET EILEEN, retired physical education educator; b. Kansas City, Mo., Aug. 4, 1925; d. Edward Leslie and Bertha Mae (Coe) W. BS in Edn., U. Ark., 1944, MS, 1949; PhD, U. Iowa, 1960. Cert. secondary tchr., Ark. Recreation dir. Pine Bluff (Ark.) Arsenal, 1944-45; instr. Ctrl. High Sch., Muskogee, Okla., 1945-48; grad. asst. U. Ark., Fayetteville, 1948-49; instr. Fayetteville High Sch., 1949-52; from instr. to asst. prof. Ark. Poly. Coll., Russellville, 1952-57, assoc. prof., 1959-65; grad. asst. U. Iowa, Iowa City, 1957-59; prof. Tex. Tech. U., Lubbock, 1965-90, dept. chair health, phys. edn. and recreation for women, 1967-76, prof. emerita, 1990—; mem. Tex. Tech. Faculty Senate, 1978-90, pres., 1978-79, 85-86. Active Lubbock County Dem. Ctrl. Com., 1993, 94, 96. Recipient AMOCO Found. Disting. Tchg. award, 1978, Disting. Faculty award in Tex. Tech. Moms and Dads Assn., 1987. Mem. AAHPERD (life), Tex. Assn. for Health, Phys. Edn., Recreation and Dance (Honor award 1979, David K. Bruce award 1992), Tex. Tech. Faculty Legal Action Assn. (pres. 1990-96), Lubbock Ret. Tchrs. Assn. (cmty. svc. chair 1994-96, co-treas. 1996—), Double T Connection (chair membership 1991-94), Delta Gamma (house corp. treas. 1982-91, Cable award 1978), Delta Kappa Gamma (chpt. pres. 1972-74, Chpt. Achievement award 1976, state corr. sec. 1979-81, state conv. chair 1979-80, state nominations com. 1985-87, state pers. com. 1987-89, State Achievement award 1987, state necrology com. 1993-95, state fin. com. 1995-96). Presbyterian. Avocations: gardening, needlepoint, reading. Home: 5411 46th St Lubbock TX 79414-1513 Office: Tex Tech U Womens Gymnasium Lubbock TX 79409

WILSON, MARY ELIZABETH, physician, educator; b. Indpls., Nov. 19, 1942; d. Ralph Richard and Catheryn Rebecca (Kurtz) Lausch; m. Harvey Vernon Fineberg, May 16, 1975. AB, Ind. U., 1963; MD, U. Wis., 1971. Diplomate Am. Bd. Internal Medicine, Am. Bd. Infectious Diseases. Tchr. of French and English Marquette Sch., Madison, Wis., 1963-66; intern in medicine Beth Israel Hosp., Boston, 1971-72, resident in medicine, 1972-73, fellow in infectious diseases, 1973-75; physician Albert Schweitzer Hosp., Deschapelles, Haiti, 1974-75, Harvard Health Svcs., Cambridge, Mass., 1974-75; asst. physician Cambridge Hosp., 1975-78; hosp. epidemiologist Mt. Auburn Hosp., Cambridge, 1975-79, chief of infectious diseases, 1978—, dir. Travel Resource Ctr., 1996—; adv. com. immunization practices Ctrs. for Disease Control, Atlanta, 1988-92; acad. adv. com. Nat. Inst. Pub. Health, Mex., 1989-91; cons. Ford Found., 1988; instr. in medicine Harvard Med. Sch., Boston, 1975-93, asst. clin. prof., 1994—, assoc. Ctr. Health & Global Environ., 1996—; asst. prof. depts. epidemiology and population and internat. health Harvard Sch. Pub. Health, 1994—; lectr. Sultan Qaboos U., Oman, 1991; chair Woods Hole Workshop, Emerging Infectious Diseases, 1993. Author: A World Guide to Infections: Diseases, Distribution, Diagnosis, 1991; co-editor: (with Richard Levins and Andrew Spielman) Disease in Evolution: Global Changes and Emergence of Infectious Diseases, 1994; mem. editl. bd. Current Issues in Pub. Health; sect. editor, travel medicine & tropical diseases, editl. bd. Infectious Diseases in Clinical Practice. Mem. Cambridge Task Force on AIDS, 1987-90, Earthwatch, Watertown, Mass., Cultural Survival, Inc., Cambridge; bd. dirs. Horizon Communications, West Cornwall, Conn., 1990. Recipient Lewis E. and Edith Phillips award U. Wis. Med. Sch., 1969, Cora M. and Edward Van Liere award, 1971, Mosby Scholarship Book award, 1971; scholar in residence Bellagio (Italy) Study Ctr., Rockefeller Found., 1996. Fellow ACP, Infectious Diseases Soc. Am., Royal Soc. Tropical Medicine and Hygiene; mem. Am. Soc. Microbiology, N.Y. Acad. Scis., Am. Soc. Tropical Medicine and Hygiene, Mass. Infectious Diseases Soc., Peabody Soc., Internat. Soc. Travel Medicine, Wilderness Med. Soc., Soc. for Vector Ecology, Internat. Union Against Tuberculosis and Lung Disease, Soc. for Epidemiol. Rsch., Sigma Sigma, Phi Sigma Iota, Alpha Omega Alpha. Avocations: playing the flute, hiking, reading, travel. Office: Mt Auburn Hosp 330 Mount Auburn St Cambridge MA 02138-5502

WILSON, MARY LOUISE, publishing executive; b. Chgo., June 29, 1940; d. John Baptiste and Marion Margaret (Coveney) Sweig; m. John Paul Wilson, June 7, 1969; 1 son, Devin Sweig. Student, U. Toronto, 1960-61; B.A., Smith Coll., 1962; M.A., Emerson Coll., 1965; Ph.D., Northwestern U., 1968. Assoc. prof. speech pathology California (Pa.) State Coll., 1968-69; prof. communication scis. and disorders U. Vt., Burlington, 1969-94, prof. emerita, 1994—, dir. program in communication sci. and disorders, 1971-77, acting chmn., 1977-80; dir. E. M. Luse Center for Communication Disorders, 1971-81; disting. vis. scholar Worcester State Coll., Mass., 1984; pres. Laureate Learning Systems, Inc., 1982—; mem. Vt. State Adv. Com. on Spl. Edn., 1974; project dir. Bur. Edn. of Handicapped, 1971-83. Author: Wilson Initial Syntax Program, 1972, Wilson Expanded Syntax Program, 1976, Syntax Remediation: A Generative Grammar Approach to Language Development, 1977, Prescriptive Analysis of Language Disorders, 1979, Expressive Syntax Assessment, 1979, Sequential Software for Language Development Intervention, 1991, 2d edit.; co-author: First Words, 1982, 3d edit., 1989, Speak Up, 1983, First Categories, 1983, Microcomputer Language Assessment and Development System, 1984, 2d edit., 1988, First Verbs, 1985, 2d edit., 1989, Fast Access Scan Talker, 1985, First Words II, 1986, 2d edit., 1989, Twenty Categories, 1986, 2d edit., 1989, Talking Series, 1987, Creature Antics, 1987, Creature Chorus, 1987, Creature Capers, 1988, Words and Concepts, 1989, Concentrate! On Words and Concepts, 1989, Early Emergins Rules, 1990, Creature Features, 1992, Exploring Vocabulary, 1994, Simple Sentence Structure, 1994, Swim, Swam, Swum: Mastering Irregular Verbs, 1995. Mem. Am. Speech and Hearing Assn., Am. Assn. Mental Retardation (pres. region X), Coun. Exceptional Children, Vt. Speech and Hearing Assn. Home: RR 2 Box 355 Hinesburg VT 05461-9409 Office: Laureate Learning Systems Inc 110 E Spring St Winooski VT 05404-1837

WILSON, MATTHEW FREDERICK, newspaper editor; b. San Francisco, May 10, 1956; s. Kenneth E. and Verna Lee (Hunter) W. BA in Philosophy, U. Calif., Berkeley, 1978. Copy person San Francisco Chronicle, summers 1975, 76, 77, copy editor, 1978-82, editorial systems coord., 1982-84; budget analyst San Francisco Newspaper Agy., 1984085; asst. news editor San Francisco Chronicle, 1985-87, asst. to exec. editor, 1987-88, mng. editor, 1988-95, exec. editor, 1995—. Mem. Am. Soc. Newspaper Editors, AP Mng. Editors, Calif. Soc. Newspaper Editors. Office: San Francisco Chronicle 901 Mission St San Francisco CA 94103-2905*

WILSON, MELVIN EDMOND, civil engineer; b. Bremerton, Wash., Aug. 3, 1935; s. Edmond Curt and Madeline Rose (Deal) W.; m. Deanna May Stevens, Nov. 22, 1957 (div. Mar. 1971); children: Kathleen, Debra Wilson Frank. BSCE, U. Wash., 1957, MSCE, 1958. Registered profl. engr., Wash. Asst. civil engr. City of Seattle, 1958-60, assoc. civil engr., 1960-64, sr. civil engr., 1964-66, supervising civil engr., 1966-75, sr. civil engr., 1975-77, mgr. X, 1977-88; owner Wilson Cons. Svcs., Seattle, 1988-89; transp. sys. dir. City of Renton, Wash., 1989-96, ret., 1996; owner Mel Wilson Photographer, Seattle, 1975-84. Contbr. reports to profl. jours. Rep. Renton transp. work group King County (Wash.) Growth Mgmt. Policy Com.; rep. Renton tech. adv. com. South County Area Transp. Bd., King County, 1992-96, developer svc. policy (adopted by Puget Sound Govtl. Conf.) to encourage travel by transit. successfuly led effort to make Renton first suburban city to receive direct transit svc. under Met. King County Plan, 1994. Mem. ASCE, Am. Pub. Works Assn., Inst. Transp. Engrs., Tau Beta Pi, Sigma Xi. Avocations: pphotography, weight lifting, hiking.

WILSON, MICHAEL E., lawyer; b. Rantoul, Ill., Oct. 28, 1951. BA cum laude, Washington U., 1973, JD, 1977. Bar: Mo. 1977. Principal Greensfelder, Hemker & Gale, P.C., St. Louis; instr. legal writing Washington U. Sch. Law, 1979-82; mem. nat. panel constrn. industry arbitrators and co-chmn. St. Louis Constrn. Adv. Com., 1987-91. Mem. ABA, The Mo. Bar (contbr. jour.), Bar Assn. Metro. St. Louis (contbr. jour.), Order Coif. Office: Greensfelder Hemker & Gale PC 2000 Equitable Bldg 10 S Broadway Saint Louis MO 63102-1712

WILSON, MILNER BRADLEY, III, retired banker; b. Spartanburg, S.C., Nov. 17, 1933; s. Milner Bradley and Margaret (Nash) W.; m. Nancy Brock, Aug. 18, 1956; children—Margaret, Julia, Bradley. A.B., Duke U., 1955; LL.B., U.S.C., 1961; A.M.P., Harvard U., 1973. CLU. With Citizens & So. Nat. Bank S.C., Charleston, 1961-84, gen. trust officer, 1971-72, exec. v.p., 1972-84; v.p. Barnett Banks Trust Co. N.A., Hallandale, Fla., 1984-86; regional v.p. Barnett Banks Trust Co. N.A., Tampa, Fla., 1986-87; sr. v.p. Barnett Banks Trust Co. N.A., Jacksonville, Fla., 1987-89; v.p. No. Trust Bank of Fla., Miami, 1989-95. Served with USMC, 1955-58. Mem. ABA. Home: 1603 Hunters Rd Huntersville NC 28078

WILSON, MINTER LOWTHER, JR., retired officers association executive; b. Morgantown, W.Va., Aug. 19, 1925; s. Minter Lowther and Mary Mildred (Friend) W.; m. Helen Hope Sauerwein, June 18, 1946; children—Mary Florence, Barbara Ann, Karen Lee, Stephen David. B.S. in Mil. Sci. and Engring., U.S. Mil. Acad., 1946; M.S. in Journalism, U. Wis., Madison, 1963; diploma, NATO Def. Coll., Rome, 1969, U.S. Army War Coll., 1971. Commd. officer U.S. Army, 1946, advanced through grades to col., comdg. officer 1st Brigade, 1st Armored Div., 1968-69; chief of pub. info. Supreme Hdqrs. Allied Powers, Europe, 1969-72; editor Ret. Officer Mag., Alexandria, Va., 1972-88; dir. communications Ret. Officers Assn., Alexandria, 1972-88. Contbr. articles to profl. jours. Chmn. bd. deacons Ch. of the Covenant, Arlington, 1974-77, elder, 1977-80, 88-93, clk. of session, 1991-94, chmn. bd. trustees, 1982-86; mem. troop com. Boy Scouts Am., 1972-78. Decorated Commendation medal, Legion of Merit (2); recipient George Washington Honor medal Freedoms Found., 1975, 76, 77, George Washington Honor medal encased Freedoms Found., 1979, Honor cert. Freedoms Found., 1973, 74, 78. Mem. West Point Soc. of D.C. (life, bd. govs. 1978-81), Army Distaff Found. (bd. dirs. 1980-83), Assn. U.S. Army, Ret. Officers Assn. (life). Presbyterian. Club: Army Navy Country. Avocations: photography; golf; skiing; tennis; racquetball. Home: 3116 N Thomas St Arlington VA 22207-4120

WILSON, MIRIAM GEISENDORFER, retired physician, educator; b. Yakima, Wash., Dec. 3, 1922; d. Emil and Frances Geisendorfer; m. Howard G. Wilson, June 21, 1947; children—Claire, Paula, Geoffrey, Nicola, Marla. B.S., U. Wash., Seattle, 1944, M.S., 1945; M.D., U. Calif., San Francisco, 1950. Mem. faculty U. So. Calif. Sch. Medicine, L.A., 1965—, prof. pediatrics, 1969—. Office: U So Calif Med Ctr 1129 N State St Rm 1g24 Los Angeles CA 90033-1069

WILSON, MIRIAM JANET WILLIAMS, publishing executive; b. London, Ont., Can., July 13, 1939; d. Ralph George and Lillian Conn Williams; m. Carson Winnette, Nov. 20, 1960 (div. 1971); children: Barrie Carson Winnette, Rebecca Lynn Winnette; m. Charles Lindsay Wilson, Dec. 14, 1973; 1 child, Charles William Wilson; stepchildren: Kenneth M., Carol Ann, Catherine S., Nancy L., Patrick L. Diploma in nursing, Glendale (Calif.) Sanitarium & Hosp., 1960. RN, Calif., Va., Ohio, Md., W.Va. Head nurse emergency and med. fls. Glendale Sanitarium and Hosp., 1960-65; psychometrist Harding Hosp., Worthington, Ohio, 1969-73; biofeedback specialist in assn. Dr. Randolph P. Johnston, Winchester, Va., 1980-84; dir. Stress Ctr. for Children and Adults, Shepherdstown, W.Va., 1985-87; pres. Rocky River Pubs., Shepherdstown, 1987—; lectr. ednl., profl. and civic groups, 1984—. Author: Help For Children, 6 edits., 1987-95, Stress Stoppers, 2 edits., 1987-89; contbr. articles to profl. pubs. Active Shepherdstown Women's Club, 1986-95. Mem. NAFE, Internat. Platform Assn., Am. Booksellers Assn., N.Y. Acad. Scis. Avocations: gardening, music, reading. Office: Rocky River Pubs PO Box 1679 Shepherdstown WV 25443-1679

WILSON, MITCHELL B., fraternal organization administrator; b. Berea, Ky., Jan. 27, 1956; s. William Paul and Shirley Ann (Rose) W.; m. Joan Gentry, May 25, 1985; 1 child, Theodore Mitchell. BA, U. Ky., Lexington, 1980. Chpt. cons. Kappa Sigma Frat., Charlottesville, Va., 1980-82, exec. asst., 1982-83, dir. chpt. ops., 1983-85, dir. pub. rels., 1985-87, exec. dir., 1987—. Editor: The Caducens Mag., 1987—. Mem. Am. Soc. Assoc. Execs., Frat. Execs. Assn. Home: 506 Nottingham Rd Charlottesville VA 22901-1239 Office: Kappa Sigma PO Box 5066 Charlottesville VA 22905-5066*

WILSON, MYRON ROBERT, JR., retired psychiatrist; b. Helena, Mont., Sept. 21, 1932; s. Myron Robert Sr. and Constance Ernestine (Bultman) W. BA, Stanford U., 1954, MD, 1957. Diplomate Am. Bd. Psychiatry and Neurology. Dir. adolescent psychiatry Mayo Clinc, Rochester, Minn., 1965-71; pres. and psychiatrist in chief Wilson Ctr., Faribault, Minn., 1971-86; ret., 1986; chmn. Wilson Ctr., 1986-90; ret., 1990; assoc. clin. prof. psychiatry UCLA, 1985—. Contbr. articles to profl. jours. Chmn., chief exec. officer C.B. Wilson Found., L.A., 1986—; mem. bd. dirs. Pasadena Symphony Orchestra Assn., Calif., 1987. Served to lt. comdr., 1958-60. Fellow Mayo Grad. Sch. Medicine, Rochester, 1960-65. Fellow Am. Psychiat. Assn., Am. Soc. for Adolescent Psychiatry, Internat. Soc. for Adolescent Psychiatry (founder, treas. 1985-88, sec. 1985-88, treas. 1988-92); mem. Soc. Sigma Xi (Mayo Found. chpt.). Episcopalian. Office: Wilson Found 8033 W Sunset Blvd # 4019 West Hollywood CA 90046-2427

WILSON, NANCY, singer; b. Chillicothe, Ohio, Feb. 20, 1937; d. Olden and Lillian (Ryan) W.; m. Kenneth C. Dennis (div. 1969); 1 child, Kenneth C.; m. Wiley Burton, 1974; children: Samantha, Sheryl. Ed., Columbus (Ohio) schs. Began career as singer with local groups, then joined Rusty Bryant band, 1956, toured Midwest and Can., until 1958, singing independently, 1959—, rec. artist Capitol Records, EMI Records, Japan, Nippon Columbia, Japan, Interface, Japan, Columbia Records, USA, Epic/Sony Japan; recs. include I'll Be a Song, Just To Keep You Satisfied, Forbidden Lover, Nancy Now, Lady With A Song, With My Lover Beside Me, 1991; internat. concert tours, U.S., Japan, Europe, Indonesia, Australia; rec. artist; TV appearances include Police Story, Hawaii Five-O, It's A

Living; hostess: TV series Nancy Wilson Show, Sta. KNBC, L.A., 1974-75, Red Hot & Cool (syndicated), 1990—; appeared in film: The Big Score. Recipient Grammy award for Best R&B Vocal Nat. Acad. Rec. Arts and Scis., Best Female Vocalist award Playboy and Down Beat Jazz Polls, Image award NAACP, 1986, award Nat. Med. Assn., Equitable (17th Black Achievement) award, Urban Network Lifetime Achievement award, 1990, Whitney Young awd., Los Angeles Urban League, Essence awd., Essence Magazine, 1992; Star on Hollywood Walk of Fame, 1990. *

WILSON, NANCY JEANNE, laboratory director, medical technologist; b. Neptune, N.J., Apr. 17, 1951; d. Harry E. Sr. and Kathryn E. (O'Shea) W. BS, Monmouth Coll., 1975; MPA, Fairleigh Dickinson U., 1988. Clin. intern med. tech., staff med. technologist Riverview Med. Ctr., 1975; staff med. technologist Rush Clin. Labs., Red Bank, N.J., 1975; staff med. technologist Kimball Med. Ctr., Lakewood, N.J., 1975-76, clin. lab. supr., 1976-86; infection control practice Jersey Shore Med. Ctr., Neptune, N.J., 1990; dir. lab. and diagnostic svcs. Carrier Found., Belle Meade, N.J., 1991—. Mem. Am. Soc. Clin. Pathologists (diplomate lab. mgmt.), Am. Assn. Clin. Chemistry, Am. Soc. Microbiology, Clin. Lab. Mgmt. Assn., Am. Soc. Clinics Lab. Sci., Pi Alpha Alpha. Avocations: golf, walking, relaxing. Home: 42 Monument St Freehold NJ 07728-1721 Office: Carrier Found Rt 601 PO Box 147 Belle Mead NJ 08502

WILSON, NANCY LINDA, church officer; b. Mineola, N.Y., July 13, 1950. Grad., Allegheny Coll.; student, Boston U.; MDiv, SS, Cyril and Methodius Sem. Ordained to ministry Universal Fellowship of Met. Cmty. Chs. Dist. coord. N.E. dist. Universal Fellowship of Met. Cmty. Chs.; clk. bd. of elders Fellowship hdqrs. Universal Fellowship of Met. Cmty. Chs., L.A., 1979-86, sr. pastor Met. Comty. Ch., 1986—; vice-moderator UFMCC, L.A., 1993—; bd. trustees Samaritan Inst. Religious Studies; founder, chief ecumenical officer Ecumenical Witness and Ministry; vice chair Progressive Religious Alliance. Author: Our Tribe: Queer Folks, God, Jesus and the Bible, 1995; co-author: Amazing Grace; prodr.: (brochure) Our Story Too. Rockefeller scholar. Office: Met Cmty Ch PO Box 46609 Los Angeles CA 90046

WILSON, NORMAN GLENN, church administrator, writer; b. Rensselaer, N.Y., Nov. 3, 1936; s. Lawrence Wilbur and Wilhelmena Augusta (Knapp) W.; m. Nancy Ann Deyo, Nov. 17, 1956; children: Beth, Lawrence, Jonathon. BRE in Religious Edn., United Wesleyan Coll., 1958, DD (hon.), 1986; MA in Biblical Studies, Winona Lake Sch. Theology, 1968. Pastor The Wesleyan Ch., 1958-76, Gloversville, N.Y., 1963-66, North Lakeport, Mich., 1966-70, Owosso, Mich., 1970-76; dir. comm. The Wesleyan Ch., Indpls., 1992—; program prodr., speaker The Wesleyan Hour, Indpls., 1975—; mem. gen. bd. adminstrn. The Wesleyan Ch., Indpls., 1992—; disting. lectr. Staley Found., 1986. Author: How to Have a Happy Home, 1976, Christianity in Shoe Leather, 1978, The Constitution of the Kingdom, 1989, People Just Like Us, 1994, Follow the Leader, A Daily Spiritual Journey, 1996; editor The Wesleyan Advocate, 1992—. Mem. Nat. Religious Broadcasters (bd. dirs. 1984—, Merit award 1984). Avocations: oil painting, antique cars. Home: 304 Scarborough Way Noblesville IN 46060-3881

WILSON, NORMAN LOUIS, psychiatrist, educator; b. Buffalo, Oct. 4, 1937; s. Norman Louis and Martha W.; m. Ly Thi Phien, Aug. 22, 1988; 1 child, Daniel. BS in Biophysics summa cum laude, Yale U., 1959; MD, Harvard Med. Sch., Boston, 1963. Diplomate Am. Bd. Psychiatry and Neurology, Am. Coll. Forensic Examiners, Am. Bd. Forensic Medicine, Am. Acad. Experts in Traumatic Stress, Nat. Registry Group Therapists; cert. Hypnosis and cons. in hypnosis, Am. Soc. Clin. Hypnosis. Med. intern Rush-Presbyn.-St. Luke's Med. Ctr., Chgo., 1963-64; resident in psychiatry, tchg. fellow Mass. Mental Health Ctr.-Harvard U., Boston, 1964-66, Peter Bent Brigham Hosp.-Harvard U., 1966-67; pvt. practice, Washington, 1969—; condr. workshops on use of hypnosis in treatment of multiple personality disorder, mood disorders, psychopharmacology, forensic evaluations and testimony; asst. clin. prof. dept. psychiatry and behavioral sci. George Washington U. Sch. Medicine, Washington, 1973—; founding mem., mem. faculty Washington Psychotherapy Tng. Inst., 1989—; staff psychiatrist Cmty. Psychiat. Clinic, Bethesda, Md., 1969-71, D.C. Forensic Psychiat. Adminstrn., 1974-89; psychiatrist NIH Employee Health Svc., 1971-74, John Howard Pavilion, St. Elizabeth's Hosp., Washington, 1987-89; cons. Clin. Ctr., NIH, 1974-80, Mental Health Assocs., Adelphi, Md., 1983-92, Luth. Social Svcs., Washington, 1990-93, occupl. med. svc. NIH, 1989-93; chmn. dept. psychiatry Washington Hosp. Ctr., 1987-92, admitting privileges; admitting privileges George Washington U. Hosp., Psychiat. Inst. Washington, Dominion Hosp.; mem. mktg. com. Nat. Capital Reciprocal Ins. Co. Capt. M.C., USAF, 1967-69. Fellow Am. Psychiat. Assn.; mem. Am. Group Therapy Assn., Am. Coll. Forensic Examiners, Am. Acad. Psychiat. and Law, Internat. Soc. for Study Dissociation, Washington Psychiat. Soc. (former mem. coms. on liaison with non-psychiatry mental health works, forensic psychiatry, pub. rels.), Med. Soc. D.C. (past mem. alcohol com. and mental health com.), Amnesty Internat., Physicians for Social Responsibility, Am. Coalition for Abuse Awareness, Phi Beta Kappa. Avocations: scuba diving, backpacking, canoe tripping, movies, classical and folk music. Office: 4025 Connecticut Ave NW Washington DC 20008-1148 *I quote Spinoza: "Learn as if you will live forever, live as if you will die tomorrow." Work to achieve balance in your life.*

WILSON, OWEN MEREDITH, JR., lawyer; b. Oakland, Calif., Dec. 22, 1939; s. O. Meredith and Marian Wilson; m. Sandra A. Wilson (div.); children: Ann, Melissa, Jennifer; m. Teddi Anne Wilson; children: Amanda, Lisa. Student, U. Utah, 1957-59; AB, Harvard U., 1961; LLB, U. Minn., 1965. Bar: Oreg. 1965, Wash. 1985. Ptnr. Lane Powell Spears Lubersky, Portland, Oreg., 1965—; mem. mediation panel U.S. Dist. Ct., 1986—. Mem. bd. visitors Law Sch. U. Minn., 1990-96. Mem. ABA, Oreg. State Bar Assn., Wash. State Bar, Multnomah Bar Assn. Office: 520 SW Yamhill St Ste 800 Portland OR 97204-1331

WILSON, PAMELA AIRD, physician; b. Milw., May 13, 1947; d. Rushen Arnold and Marianna (Dickie) W.; m. Paul Quin, June 20, 1981. BS in Zoology, U. Md., 1969; MS in Physiology, U. Wis., 1971; MD, U. Md., Balt., 1976. Diplomate Am. Bd. Internal Medicine. Asst. prof. U. Wis., Madison, 1983-90, assoc. prof., 1990—. Bd. dirs. Wis. chpt. Am. Lung Assn.; exec. com. Wis. Thoracic Soc.; past pres. Gov.'s Coun. on Phys. Disabilities, 1990—. Office: 600 Highland Ave # H6 380 Madison WI 53792-0001

WILSON, PATRICIA POTTER, library science and reading educator, educational and library consultant; b. Jennings, La., May 3, 1946; d. Ralph Harold and Wilda Ruth (Smith) Potter; m. Wendell Merlin Wilson, Aug. 24, 1968. BS, La. State U., 1967; MS, U. Houston-Clear Lake, 1979; EdD, U. Houston, 1985. Cert. tchr., learning resources specialist (librarian), Tex. Tchr., England AFB (La.) Elem. Sch., 1967-68, Edward White Elem. Sch., Clear Creek Ind. Schs., Seabrook, Tex., 1972-77; librarian C.D. Landolt Elem. Sch., Friendswood, Tex., 1979-81; instr./lectr. children's lit. U. Houston 1983-86; with U. Houston/Clear Lake, 1984-87, asst. prof. libr. sci. and reading, 1988-94, assoc. prof. learning resources and reading edn., 1994—, faculty devel com. chair, 1997— mem. faculty senate, 1992-93; cons. Hermann Hosp., Baywood Hosp., 1986-87, Bedford Meadows Hosp., 1989-90, Wetcher Clinic, 1989; v.p., sec. Potter Farms, Inc., 1994—. Trustee, Freeman Meml. Library, Houston, 1982-87, v.p., 1985-86, pres., 1986-87; trustee Evelyn Meador Libr., 1993-94; adv. bd. Evelyn Meador Libr., 1994—; mem. adv. bd. Bay Area Soc. Prevention Cruelty Animals, 1994—; mem. Armand Bayou Nature Ctr., Houston, 1980—, bd. dirs. 1989-94; bd. dirs. Sta. KUHT-TV, 1984-87; mem. Bay Area Houston Symphony League; mem. Bay Area Assistance League, 1997—. Editor A Rev. Sampler, 1985-86, 89-90; dir. Learning Resources Book Rev. Ctr., 1989-90. Author: HAPPENINGS: Developing Successful Programs for School Libraries, 1987, The Professional Collection for Elementary Educators, 1996; contbg. editor Tex. Library Jour., 1988-94; contbr. articles to profl. jours. Recipient Rsch. award Tex. State Reading Assn., 1993, Pres. award Tex. Coun. Tchrs. of English, Disting. Teaching award Enron Corp., 1996; grantee Tex. Libr. Assn., 1993. Mem. ALA, Am. Assn. Sch. Librarians, Internat. Reading Assn., Nat. Coun. Tchrs. English, (Books for You review com. 1985-88, Your Reading review com., 1993-96), Tex. Coun. Tchrs. English, Antarctican Soc., Assist. League, Bay area, 1996—. Mem: Bay Oaks Country Club, Phi Delta Kappa, Phi Kappa Phi. Methodist. Home: 629 Bay Vista Dr Seabrook TX 77586-3001 Office: U Houston Clear Lake 2700 Bay Area Blvd Houston TX 77058-1002

WILSON, PAUL EDWIN, lawyer, educator; b. Quenemo, Kans., Nov. 2, 1913; s. Dale Edwin and Clara (Jacobs) W.; m. Harriet Eileen Stephens, June 16, 1941; children: Elizabeth, Mary Paulette, Eileen, David. BA, U. Kans., 1937, MA, 1938; LLB, Washburn U., 1940. Bar: Kans. 1940, U.S. Supreme Ct. 1952, U.S. Ct. Appeals 1950. Pvt. practice law Ashland, Kans., 1941-42, Lyndon, Kans., 1946-50; atty. County of Osage, Kans., 1947-50; gen. counsel dept. social welfare State of Kans., 1950-51, asst. atty. gen., 1951-53, 1st asst. atty. gen., 1953-57; assoc. prof. law U. of Kans., 1957-62, prof., 1962-68, Kane prof., 1968-81, prof. emeritus, 1981—; assoc. dir. Inst. Judicial Adminstrn., 1964-65; vis. prof. The Menninger Found., 1972; cons. in field. Author: (with Reams) Segregation and the Fourteenth Amendment in the States, 1975, Pattern Rules of Court and Code Provisions, 1975, Judicial Education in the United States, 1965, A Time to Lose, 1995; editor: American Criminal Law Quar. 1963-70; contbr. articles in field to profl. jours. Mem. Lawrence (Kans.) Planning Commn., 1962-65; chmn. Bd. Zoning Appeals, Lawrence, 1966-67; mem. Kans. Hist. Sites Bd. Rev., 1973-77; trustee Ft. Burgwin (N.Mex.) Rsch. Ctr., 1976-79, Task Force for Hist. Preservation, Lawrence, Kans. (Disting. Svc. citation 1991), 1987-89. With U.S. Army, 1942-46. Recipient Justice award Kans. Supreme Ct., 1992; cited for Disting. Svc. to Bar and Pub., Kans. Bar Assn., 1987, Gov. Kans., Ho. Reps., Kans.; Disting. Svc. award S.W.Kans. Bar Assn., 1995. Mem. Am. Bar Assn., Kans. Bar Assn. (chmn. com. criminal law 1960-68), Am. Law Inst., Am. Bar Found., Selden Soc., Nat. Trust Historic Preservation (bd. advisors 1972-78), Kans. State Hist. Soc. (v.p. 1987-89, pres. elect 1990, pres. 1990-91f, Phi Alpha Delta. Republican. Methodist. Office: U Kans 301 Green Hall Lawrence KS 66045 *Few things in my life have happened according to a preconceived plan. My admonition to the young is "Don't plan, just live." Perhaps I should add "also let live," by which I mean a concern for humanity, contemporary and prospective.*

WILSON, PAUL HOLLIDAY, JR., lawyer; b. Schenectady, N.Y., Sept. 4, 1942; s. Paul H. and Sarah Elizabeth (MacLean) W.; m. Elaine Hawley Griffin, May 30, 1964; children: Hollace, Paul, Kirsten, Katherine. AB, Brown U., 1964; LLB, MBA, Columbia U., 1967. Bar: N.Y. 1967, U.S. Dist. Ct. (so. dist.) 1968. Law clk. U.S. Dist. Ct. (so. dist.) N.Y., N.Y.C., 1967-68; assoc. Debevoise & Plimpton, N.Y.C., 1968-75, ptnr., 1976—, fin. ptnr., 1980-88, 91-93, dep. presiding ptnr., 1993—. Vice-chmn., trustee St. Michael's Montessori Sch., N.Y.C., 1977-79, chmn. bd. trustees, 1979-81. Mem. ABA, Assn. Bar City N.Y. (mem. commn. on securities regulations 1985-88). Club: Vineyard Haven Yacht (Mass.) (vice-commodore 1985, commodore 1986-87). Avocations: sailing, reading, music. Office: Debevoise & Plimpton 875 3rd Ave New York NY 10022-6225

WILSON, PAUL W., JR., lawyer, entrepreneur; b. Salt Lake City, July 18, 1948; s. Paul W. and Helen June (Jackson) W.; m. Ann Stevens, Jan. 29, 1971; children: Paul III, Laura, Jenny, Jane, Lisa, Mary. BA cum laude high honors with distinction, Brigham Young U., 1972; JD, U. Minn., 1975. Bar: Minn. 1975. Pres. LW Enterprises, Mpls., 1972-89; chief exec. officer Sights on Svc., Inc., Mpls., 1989—; bd. dirs. Am. Harvest, Chaska, Minn. Commr. Viking coun. Boy Scouts Am., Mpls., 1988-90, bd. dirs.; coach Plymouth, Minn., 1981—; bd. dirs. Brigham Young U. Alumni Bd., Provo, 1987-91, NHCP, 1987-95, pres. 1991-93. Recipient Silver Beaver Boy Scouts Am., 1988, Award of Merit Boy Scouts Am., 1984; Hinckley scholar, 1971-72, Univ. scholar, 1972. Mem. Minn. Bar Assn., Am. Mgmt. Assn. Mem. Ch. of Jesus Christ of Latter Day Saints. Avocations: reading, water skiing, basketball, scouting, youth activities.

WILSON, PETE, governor; b. Lake Forest, Ill., Aug. 23, 1933; s. James Boone and Margaret (Callaghan) W.; m. Betty Robertson (div.); m. Gayle Edlund, May 29, 1983. B.A. in English Lit., Yale U., 1955; J.D., U. Calif., Berkeley, 1962; LL.D., Grove City Coll., 1983, U. Calif., San Diego, 1983, U. San Diego, 1984. Bar: Calif. 1962. Mem. Calif. Legislature, Sacramento, 1966-71; mayor City of San Diego, 1971-83; U.S. Senator from Calif., 1983-91; gov. State of Calif., 1991—. Trustee Conservation Found.; mem. exec. bd. San Diego County council Boy Scouts Am.; hon. trustee So. Calif. Council Soviet Jews; adv. mem. Urban Land Inst., 1985-86; founding dir. Retinitis Pigmentosa Internat.; hon. dir. Alzheimer's Family Ctr., Inc., 1985; hon. bd. dirs. Shakespeare-San Francisco, 1985. Recipient Golden Bulldog award, 1984, 85, 86, Guardian of Small Bus. award, 1984, Cuauhtemoc plaque for disting. svc. to farm workers in Calif., 1991, Julius award for outstanding pub. leadership U. So. Calif., 1992, award of appreciation Nat. Head Start, 1992; named Legislator of Yr., League Calif. Cities, 1985, Man of Yr. N.G. Assn. Calif., 1986, Man of Yr. citation U. Calif. Boalt Hall, 1986; ROTC scholar Yale U., 1951-55. Mem. Nat. Mil. Family Assn. (adv. bd.), Phi Delta Phi, Zeta Psi. Republican. Episcopalian. Office: State Capitol Office Of Governor Sacramento CA 95814*

WILSON, PETER MASON, computer programmer; b. N.Y.C., Mar. 14, 1934; s. Kenneth Mason and Priscilla (Nickerson) W.; m. Lois S., July 13, 1957; children: Katherine Rose, Kenneth Mason II. BS, Ga. Tech., 1960; MS, Fla. State U., 1965, PhD, 1975. Asst. prof. Fla. A&M U., Tallahassee, 1966-77; sys. analyst U. Fla., Tallahassee, 1977-79; instrnl. designer Control Data Corp., Rockville, Md., 1979-85, Booze, Allen & Hamilton, Rockville, 1985-88, Pace Enterprises, Falls Church, Md., 1989-91; sr. tech. trainer Arbitron, Laurel, Md., 1991-94; project mgr., instrnl. designer Bell Atlantic, Balt., 1994—; chair computer usage in pub. schs. Fairfax (Va.) Bd. of Edn., 1985-88; cons. evaluation spl. edn. Howard County Bd. of Edn., Ellicott City, Md., 1991-93. Active vestry Holy Comforter, Vienna, Va., 1985-89, demographics com. St. John's Ch., Ellicott City, 1992-93. Nat. Urban League fellow, 1969, Atomic Energy Commn. fellow, 1972; recipient Howard County Bd. of Edn. commendation, 1993. Mem. AERA (session chair), SALT (presenter), Math. Assn. Am. (presenter), Theta Chi. Episcopalian. Home: 7810 Rockburn Dr Ellicott City MD 21043 Office: Bell Atlantic 1 E Pratt St Baltimore MD 21202-1038

WILSON, PETER MICHAEL, insurance company executive; b. Greenwich, Conn., Sept. 21, 1948; s. James T. Jr. and Alice Theresa (Trefrey) W.; m. Karen Mary Burgett Johnson, Dec. 31, 1969 (div. Feb. 1978); 1 child, Kimberley Ann. BBA in Mgmt., U. Wis., Whitewater, 1980, MBA in Fin., 1985. Acctg. asst. United Svcs. Life Ins. Co., Washington, 1970-71; asst. treas. Gen. Life Ins. Corp., Milw., 1971-82; v.p. fin. analysis Monogram Reins. Corp., Providence, 1982-85; pres., treas. Mystic Ins. Intermediaries, Inc., Hartland, Wis., 1985—. Fin. chmn. Vietnam Moving Wall Event Com., Merton, Wis., 1992. Sgt. USMC, 1966-70, Vietnam. Fellow Life Mgmt. Inst.; mem. Ins. Acctg. and Systems Assn. Democrat. Roman Catholic. Avocations: golf, computers, reading, videomaking. Home: W298N7011 Ridgeview Ln Hartland WI 53029-9127 Office: Mystic Ins Intermediaries W298n7011 Ridgeview Ln Hartland WI 53029-9127

WILSON, PHILIP DUNCAN, JR., orthopedic surgeon; b. Boston, Feb. 14, 1920; s. Philip Duncan and Germaine Wilson; m. Katherine Stern. Grad., Harvard U.; MD, Columbia U., 1944. Diplomate Am. Bd. Orthopaedic Surgery. Surg. intern, then resident Mass. Gen. Hosp., Boston, 1944-46; resident in orthopaedic surgery Hosp. for Spl. Surgery, N.Y.C., 1948-50, attending surgeon, 1951-72, surgeon in chief, 1972-89, surgeon in chief emeritus, trustee, 1989—; resident orthopaedic surgery San Francisco Med. Ctr., U. Calif., 1950-51; attending orthopaedic surgeon N.Y. Hosp., 1951—; prof. surgery Med. Ctr., Cornell U., N.Y.C., 1951—; cons. dept. surgery VA Hosp., Bronx, N.Y., 1972-89, North Shore U. Hosp., Manhasset, N.Y., 1975—, Meml. Hosp., N.Y.C., 1978—, Jamaica Hosp., Queens, N.Y., 1989—; civilian cons. Cho Ray Hosp.-Cholon, South Vietnam, 1962; mem. adv. panel on total hip replacements FDA, Washington, 1969, adv. panel on prophylactic antibiotic in surgery, 1977; chmn. consensus devel. panel on total hip replacements NIH, Bethesda, Md., 1982; mem., sec. Adv. Coun. on Orthopaedic Resident Edn., 1981-93. Bd. dirs. M.E. Muller Found., 1989—. Capt. U.S. Army, 1946-48. Fellow ACS; mem. AMA, Am. Acad. Orthopaedic Surgeons (pres. 1972-73), U.S. Hip Soc. (pres. 1980-81), Orthopaedic Rsch. Soc., Assn. Hip and Knee Surgery, Am. Orthopaedis Assn., Internat. Hip. Soc., Internat. Soc. Orthopaedic Surgery and Traumatology, N.Y. Acad. Medicine (chmn. orthopaedic sect. 1962-63, chmn. biochem. sect. 1969-70), Orthopaedic Rsch. and Edn. Found. (trustee 1981-83), N.Y. State Soc. Orthopaedic Surgeons, N.Y. Clin. Soc. Office: Hosp Spl Surgery 535 E 70th St New York NY 10021-4892

WILSON, R. DALE, marketing educator, consultant; b. Ironton, Ohio, July 16, 1949; s. Robert J. and Treva L. (Shively) W.; m. Emily J. Ray, June 19, 1971; 1 child, Travis Ray. BBA cum laude, Ohio U., 1971; MBA, U. Toledo, 1972; PhD, U. Iowa, 1977. Asst. prof. mktg. Pa. State U., University Park, 1976-80; v.p., dir. mktg. scis. Batten, Barton, Durstine & Osborn, Inc., N.Y.C., 1980-83; vis. prof. Cornell U., Ithaca, N.Y., 1983-84; assoc. prof. Mich. State U., East Lansing, 1984-87, prof., 1987—; cons. in field. Contbr. articles to profl. jours. Youth baseball and basketball coach, East Lansing, 1989—. Faculty research grantee Pa. State U., Mich. State U. Mem. Am. Acad. Advt., Am. Mktg. Assn., Inst. Ops. Rsch. and Mgmt. Scis. (assoc. editor Interfaces, cert. recognition 1983), Assn. Consumer Rsch., Product Devel. and Mgmt. Assn., Beta Gamma Sigma. Home: 859 Audubon Rd East Lansing MI 48823-3003 Office: Mich State U Eli Broad Grad Sch Mgmt Dept Mktg/Supply Chain Mgmt N322 N Business Complex East Lansing MI 48824-1122

WILSON, RALPH EDWIN, lawyer, justice; b. Osceola, Ark., Sept. 28, 1921; s. Emmett A. and Lillie (Simmons) W.; m. Mary Ann Murray, Apr. 23, 1949; children: Ralph Edwin, Teresa Ann, Don Alan. Student, U.S. Naval Acad., 1943; A.B., Union U., 1946; J.D., Vanderbilt U., 1949. Bar: Tenn. 1948, Ark. 1948. Practice in Osceola, 1949—, city atty. Osceola, 1949; dep. pros. atty. 2d Jud. Dist. Ark., 1950-53; spl. asst. to atty. gen. Ark., 1956-60, spl. assoc. justice Supreme Ct. Ark., 1984; pres. Liberal State Bank, Gt. Eastern Assurance Co., North Little Rock; sec. Farmers Agri Export, Inc.; dir. Allied Cos., Inc., Does-More Products Corp., Allied Real Estate Investment Trust, Osceola Land Devel. Co.; Mem. adv. council Nat. Pub. Works Week, 1964. Alderman Osceola City Council, 1958-61. Served as lt. U.S. Mcht. Marines USNR, 1943-45. Recipient Ark. House and Senate Concurrent Resolutions Commendation, 1971. Mem. Ark. Bar Assn. (past mem. exec. com.), Osceola Bar Assn. (pres.), Am. Trial Lawyers Assn., U.S. Bar (Supreme Ct.), Am. Legion, Phi Alpha Delta, Alpha Tau Omega, Tau Kappa Alpha. Democrat. Methodist. Club: Kiwanian (internat. v.p. 1970-71, trustee 1966-70, life fellow internat. found.). Home: 903 W Hale Ave Osceola AR 72370-2428 Office: 109 N Maple St Osceola AR 72370-2537 *I believe it is man's highest achievement to reach far and find truth. The adversary system in law is this searching and finding truth. The drama of the courtroom involves all that is precious—life, liberty, property, dominion over children. These interacting forces play against each other, but if all facts are before the court, truth invariably prevails.*

WILSON, RAMON B., educator, administrator; b. Ogden, Utah, Sept. 22, 1922; s. Benjamin Andrew and Hannah Josephine (Browning) W.; m. Ruth G. Worlton, July 27, 1945; children: Lynn, William Scott, Bruce Ramon, JoAnne, Kathleen. B.S., Utah State U., 1947; M.S., Purdue U., 1948, Ph.D., 1950; postgrad., U. Calif., Berkeley, 1972, Georgetown U., 1976. Extension economist Utah State U., Logan, 1950-53; mktg. economist Calif. Dept. Agr., Sacramento, 1953-55; asst. prof. Purdue U., West Lafayette, Ind., 1955-57; assoc. prof. Purdue U., 1957-63, prof. agrl. econs., 1963-78, prof. emeritus, 1978—, market service dir., 1960-68; asst. dir. Ind. Coop. Extension Service, 1963-74, assoc. dir. agrl. expt. sta., asst. to dean agr., 1968-74; from asst. to assoc. dir. Benson Agrl. Food Inst. Brigham Young U., Provo, Utah, 1979-82; asst. to sec. U.S. Dept. Agr., Washington, 1974-76; cons., lectr. in field. Served with U.S. Army, 1943-46. Home: 435 E 2200 N Provo UT 84604-1725

WILSON, RAYMOND CLARK, former hospital executive; b. Birmingham, Ala., July 8, 1915; s. Raymond Clyde and Lida (Gay) W.; m. Sara Elizabeth Paris, Feb. 17, 1940; children: Margery Jo, Richard Clark, Sara Elizabeth, Raymond Paul. Student, Oglethorpe U., 1933-34, U. Ga., 1934-37, Tulane U., 1948; D.Bus. Adminstrn. (hon.), William Carey Coll. Office mgr. firm C.R. Justi (contractor), Atlanta, 1933-42; paymaster J.A. Jones Constrn. Co., Brunswick, Ga., 1942-45; asst. supt. So. Bapt. Hosp., New Orleans, 1946-53; adminstr. So. Bapt. Hosp., 1953-68, exec. dir., 1969-77; pres. Affiliated Bapt. Hosps., Inc., 1977-80, Health Care Cons. & Mgmt. Services, Inc., 1977-80; ret., 1980; exec. dir. Bapt. Meml. Hosp., Jacksonville, Fla., 1973-77; dir., chmn. La. Health and Indemnity Co.; dir. New Orleans Area Health Planning Council, 1969-74. Bd. dirs. Bapt. Hosp. Found., 1970-78; bd. trustees Crosby Meml. Hosp., 1992-94, chmn., 1993-94. With USAAF, 1945-46. Paul Harris fellow Rotary Found. Fellow Am. Coll. Healthcare Execs. (bd. regents 1972-75); mem. Hosp. Svc. Assn. (bd. dirs., treas. 1953-74), Am. Hosp. Assn. (ho. dels. 1972-75), La. Hosp. Assn. (pres. 1956), New Orleans Hosp. Coun. (pres. 1954-55), Southeastern Hosp. Conf. (pres. 1963), Bapt. Hosp. Assn. (pres. 1964-65). Baptist (trustee, deacon). Home: 200 W Sunnybrook Rd Carriere MS 39426-7831

WILSON, REBECCA LYNN, lawyer; b. Glen Ellyn, Ill., July 22, 1965; d. Wayne Robert Wilson and Rosemary Phylis (Stoecklin) Maglio. BA, U. Wis., 1987; JD, William Mitchell Coll., 1990; cert. mediation, Lakewood (Minn.) C.C., 1994. Bar: Minn. 1990, U.S. Dist. Ct. Minn. 1992. Law clk., assoc. Jack S. Jaycox Law Offices, Bloomington, Minn., 1988-93; assoc. Steffens, Wilkerson & Lang, Edina, Minn., 1993, Wilkerson, Lang & Hegna, Bloomington, 1993-95, Wilkerson, Hegna & Walsten, Bloomington, 1996—. Mem. ABA, Minn. State Bar Assn., Hennepin County Bar Assn. Office: Wilkerson Hegna & Walsten Ste 1100 3800 W 80th St Bloomington MN 55431-4426

WILSON, RICHARD ALEXANDER, career officer; b. San Francisco, Apr. 5, 1941; s. William Alexander and Myrlin Francis (Ralph) W.; m. Elizabeth Ray Esleeck, Feb. 24, 1962; children: Richard Scott, David Alexander. BS in Naval Sci., U.S. Naval Academy, 1963; MS in Systems Acquisition, Navy Postgrad. Sch., 1975; grad., USN Test Pilot Sch. Commd. ensign USN, advanced through grades to rear adm.; commdg. officer Fighter Squadron 154, Miramar, Calif., 1976-78; comdr. Carrier Airwing 14, Miramar, 1981-82; chief of staff Comfitaewing PAC, Miramar, 1982-84; commdg. officer USS Camden, Bremerton, Wash., 1984-86; with OPNAV Staff, Pentagon, Washington, 1986-87; commdg. officer USS Midway, Yokosuka, Japan, 1987-89; with Joint Staff, Pentagon, Washington, 1989-91; comdr. Carrier Group 7, San Diego, 1991-92; dep. chief staff ops. and plans CINCPACFLT, Pearl Harbor, Hawaii, 1993-95; dep. dir.-space electronic warfare OPNAV, Washington D.C., 1995—. Named Outstanding Young Man of Am., Jaycees, 1970. Mem. Naval Inst. Procs. (life), Assn. Naval Aviation (life), Naval Aviation Mus. Found. (life), U.S. Naval Acad. Alumni Assn. (life), Order Daedalians.

WILSON, RICHARD ALLAN, landscape architect; b. Chgo., Feb. 5, 1927; s. Edgar Allan and Lois Helena (Hearn) W.; m. Lisabet Julie Horchler, May 31, 1958; children: Gary Allan, Carl Bruce. BS, U. Calif., Berkeley, 1952. Engring. draftsman Freeland Evanson & Christenson, San Diego, 1952-53; designer, estimator Blue Pacific Nursery & Landscape Co., San Diego, 1955-59; prin. Richard A. Wilson, FASLA and Assocs., San Diego, 1959—; sec. Calif. Coun. Landscape Architects, 1982-85; expert witness for law firms, 1983—. Designer Phil Swing Meml. Fountain, 1967. Mem. landscape com. Clairemont Town Coun., San Diego, 1955. With U.S. Army, 1944-46, Korea. Recipient First Pl. award for landscape So. Calif. Expdn., Del Mar, 1963. Fellow Am. Soc. Landscape Architects (del. coun. 1982-85), Am. Inst. Landscape Architects (treas. 1970, 2d v.p. 1971). Republican. Home and Office: 2570 Tokalon Ct San Diego CA 92110-2232

WILSON, RICHARD CHRISTIAN, engineering firm executive; b. Bethlehem, Pa., July 17, 1921; s. Christian and Laura Barrows (Langham) W.; m. Jean M. Avis, July 16, 1949; children—Richard A., Christy. B.S., Carnegie-Mellon U., 1943; M.S., Lehigh U., 1947; Ph.D., U. Mich., 1961. Mfg. engr. Westinghouse Electric Corp., East Pittsburgh, 1943; instr. mech. engring. Carnegie-Mellon U., Pitts., 1943-44; vacuum test engr. Kellex Corp., N.Y.C., 1944; area supr. Carbide & Carbon Chem. Co., Oak Ridge, 1945-46; apparatus engr. Westinghouse Electric Corp., Jackson, Mich., 1947-55; instr. indsl. and operation engring. U. Mich., 1955-61, asst. prof., 1961-63, assoc. prof., 1963-66, prof., 1966-85, chmn. dept., 1973-77, assoc. dean Coll. Engring., 1968-72; pres. Techware, Inc., 1985-86, ret., 1986; dir. Cascade Data Corp., 1969-72. Contbr. articles to profl. jours. Bd. dirs. Ecumenical Assn. Internat. Understanding, 1970-87, pres., 1975-76, 86-87. Mem. IEEE, Inst. Mgmt. Sci., Am. Inst. Indsl. Engrs., Ops. Research Soc. Am., Sigma Xi, Beta Theta Pi, Phi Kappa Phi. Club: Rotary. Home: 805 Mt Pleasant Ave Ann Arbor MI 48103-4776 Office: U Mich Dept Indsl Engring Ann Arbor MI 48109

WILSON, RICHARD EDWARD, composer, pianist, music educator; b. Cleve., May 15, 1941; s. James F. and Edith Ann (Zingler) W.; m. Adene Stevenson Green, May 15, 1971; children: Katherine Blanca, James Graham. A.B. magna cum laude, Harvard U., 1963; M.A., Rutgers U., 1966. Asst. prof. music Vassar Coll., Poughkeepsie, N.Y., 1966-70, assoc. prof. music, 1970-76, prof. music, 1976—, chmn. dept. music, 1979-82, 85-88; Mary Conover Mellon Chair Vassar Coll., Poughkeepsie, 1988—. Composer: Music for Violin and Violoncello, 1969, Eclogue for Piano Solo, 1974 (Burge prize 1979), Figuration 1980, String Quartet No. 3, 1982, two symphonies, 1984, 87; Opera: Aethelred the Unready, 1994. Recipient 23 ann. awards for profl. distinction ASCAP, 1970—, Walter Henrichsen award Am. Acad. Inst. Arts and Letters, 1986, Cleve. Arts prize, 1988, Exec.'s award Dutchess County, 1989, Stoeger prize Chamber Music Soc. Lincoln Ctr., 1994; named Guggenheim fellow, 1992, composer-in-residence Am. Symphony Orch., 1992—. Mem. Am. Music Ctr., Am. Soc. Composers, ASCAP, Phi Beta Kappa. Club: Harvard (N.Y.C.). Home: 8 Vassar Lake Dr Poughkeepsie NY 12601-3021 Office: Vassar Coll Dept Music Box 18 Poughkeepsie NY 12604

WILSON, RICHARD FERROL, plant physiologist, educator; b. Macomb, Ill., July 6, 1947; s. Elmer Ferrol and Velma Lucille (Swartzbaugh) W.; m. Pamela Ann Magerl, Aug. 28, 1971. BS, Western Ill. U., 1970; MS, U. Ill., 1973, PhD, 1975. Plant physiologist USDA Agrl. Rsch. Svc., Raleigh, N.C., 1975—; prof. crop sci. N.C. State U., Raleigh, 1975—. Recipient Arthur S. Fleming award Downtown Jaycees, D.C., 1986, Alumni Achievement award Western Ill. U., 1989, Merit award Gamma Sigma Delta, 1989, Disting. Svc. award USDA, 1989, Utilization Rsch. award Am. Soybean Assn., 1990, Soybean Team Rsch. award Am. Soybean Assn., 1991; named Disting. Scientist of Yr., USDA Agrl. Rsch. Svc., 1987. Fellow Am. Soc. Agronomy, Crop Sci. Soc. Am.; mem. Am. Oil Chemists Soc., Am. Soc. Crop Sci., N.Y. Acad. Sci., Am. Soc. Plant Physiologists, Kiwanis, Sigma Xi, Alpha Zeta (chancellor 1969-70, Outstanding Alumni award 1991). Republican. Methodist. Avocations: bicycling, bowling, golf. Home: 110 Chattel Close Cary NC 27511-9745 Office: USDA Agrl Rsch Svc PO Box 7620 Raleigh NC 27695

WILSON, RICHARD HAROLD, government official; b. Waterloo, Iowa, July 15, 1930; s. Clarence Hough and Mary (Dillon) W.; m. Elaine Elizabeth Aniol., June 14, 1957; children: Elizabeth Aniol Wilson Adams, Andrew Edward. B.A., U. Ill., 1952; M.P.A., U. Kans., 1958. Lic. real estate broker, Tex.; cert. econs. devel. specialist Nat. Devel. Coun. Adminstrv. asst. to city mgr. San Antonio, 1956-58; budget analyst Kansas City, Mo., 1959; research asso. Internat. Union Local Authorities, The Hague, 1959-60; city mgr. Nevada, Mo., 1960-65; asst. to city mgr. Ft. Worth, 1965-67; asst. city mgr. Albuquerque, 1967-68, city mgr., 1968-72; dir. housing and urban rehab. Dallas, 1972-82; sr. v.p. Metroplex R&D Cons., Dallas, 1982-83; regional dir. comty. planning and devel. HUD Region V, Chgo., 1983-94; CPD program advisor HUD, Chgo., 1994—; lectr. real estate U. Tex.-Arlington; instr. govt. Dallas County Community Coll. Dist.; exec. v.p. Designs for Worship, Inc., Dallas, 1982-83. Bd. dirs. Neighborhood Housing Svcs. Am., Inc., 1974-82; chmn. Housing Tax Force of North Cen. Tex. Coun. Govts., 1974-80, chmn. human resources com., 1981-82; active Boy Scouts Am.; docent Prairie Ave. House Mus., 1995—; bd. dirs. Marina Towers Condominium Assn., 1991-96. Fulbright fellow Leiden (The Netherlands) U., 1959-60, Kennedy Sch., Harvard U., 1981, Fed. Exec. Inst., 1995, NEH, U. Calif., Santa Barbara, 1978, Urban Execs. Exch. Program, Internat. City-County Mgmt. Assn., 1979-80. Mem. Nat. Assn. Housing and Redevel. Ofcls. (v.p. Tex. chpt. 1975-80, mem. S.W. regional coun. 1975-82), Internat. City-Coun. Mgmt. Assn. (fellow 1979-80), Am. Soc. Pub. Adminstrn. (pres. N.Mex. 1968-69, v.p. North Tex. 1976-77, pres. North Tex. 1977-78, mem. nat. coun. 1979-82, Greater Chgo. chpt. coun. 1987-93, 95-96), Naval Res. Assn., Chgo. Arch. Found. (docent 1990—), Fed. Exec. Inst. Alumni Assn., Phi Gamma Delta, Pi Sigma Alpha, Alpha Phi Omega. Episcopalian. Club: Rotary (Chicago). Home: 300 N State St Apt 2833 Chicago IL 60610-4816 Office: HUD 77 W Jackson Blvd 24th Floor Chicago IL 60604-3507

WILSON, RICK KEITH, political science educator; b. New Underwood, S.D., Sept. 19, 1953; s. Richard K. and Darlene J. (Klosterman) W.; m. Patricia M. Dupras. BA, Creighton U., 1975, MA in History, 1977; PhD in Polit. Sci., Ind. U., 1982. Vis. lectr. Washington U., St. Louis, 1982-83; asst. prof. Rice U., Houston, 1983-88, assoc. prof., 1990-95, chmn. polit. sci. dept., 1991-94, prof., 1995—; vis. prof. Calif. Inst. Tech., Pasadena, 1989, Ind. U., Bloomington, 1989-90; program dir. polit. sci. NSF, 1996—. Author: (book) Congressional Dynamics, 1994; contbr. articles to Legislative Studies Quarterly, 1989—. Pres. Willow Meadows Civic Assn., Houston, 1991-93. Grantee NSF, Bloomington, Ind., 1981-83, Houston, Tex., 1988-90. Mem. Am. Polit. Sci. Assn., Econ. Sci. Assn., Midwest Polit. Sci. Assn. Democrat. Avocations: biking, baseball, computer programming. Home: 4327 McDermed Houston TX 77035 Office: Rice Univ Dept Polit Sci PO Box 1892 Houston TX 77251

WILSON, RITA P., insurance company executive. Sr. v.p. corp. rels. Allstate Ins. Co., Northbrook, Ill. Office: Allstate Ins Co 2775 Sanders Rd Ste F8 Northbrook IL 60062-6110

WILSON, ROBERT ALBERT, communications consultant; b. Jamestown, N.Y., Dec. 20, 1936; s. Albert C. and Minnie M. (Leroy) W.; m. Marcia K. Milton, Aug. 22, 1959; children: Jonathan, Kathryn. BA magna cum laude, Colgate U., 1959; diploma, Sch. Advanced Internat Studies, Bologna, Italy, 1960; MA, Johns Hopkins, 1961. News editor/announcer Sta. WJOC, Jamestown, 1953-57; staff reporter Post-Jour., Jamestown, 1958-61; intelligence research specialist U.S. Info. Agy., Washington, 1963-66, sr. editor, 1966-72; sr. assoc. pub. affairs Pfizer, Inc., N.Y.C., 1972-78, assoc. dir. pub. affairs, 1978-81, v.p. pub. affairs, 1981-96; pres. Pfizer Found., Inc., N.Y.C., 1981-95; dir. Nat. Health Coun., 1987-94; chmn. pub. affairs sect. Pharm. Rsch. and Mfrs. Am., 1982-83. Exec. com. Religion in Am. Life, N.Y.C., 1988—; pres. bd. dirs. Conn. Grand Opera & Orch., 1994—. Mem. Pub. Rels. Soc. Am., Riverside Yacht Club, Phi Beta Kappa. Avocations: sailing, skiing. Office: Conn Grand Opera and Orch 4 Landmark Sq Stamford CT 06901-2502

WILSON, ROBERT ALLEN, religion educator; b. Geff, Ill., Oct. 7, 1936; s. Perry Arthur and Eva Mae (Dye) W.; m. Patsy Ann Jarrett, June 1, 1957; children: Elizabeth Ann, Angela Dawn, Christine Joy. AB, Lincoln (Ill.) Christian Coll., 1958, Hanover Coll., 1961; MRE, So. Bapt. Seminary, 1965, EdD, 1972. Ordained to ministry Ch. of Christ, 1958. Minister Fowler (Ind.) Christian Ch., 1955-59, Zoah Christian Ch., Scottsburg, Ind., 1959-64; minister of edn. and youth Shively Christian Ch., Louisville, 1964-69; prof. Christian edn. and family life Lincoln (Ill.) Christian Seminary, 1969—; pres. Christian Marriage and Family Enrichment Services, Lincoln, 1980—. Contbr. articles to profl. jours. Mem. Nat. Assn. Profs. Christian Edn. (editor newsletter 1975-79, pres. 1979-80), Religious Edn. Assn. Lodge: Rotary (bd. dirs. Lincoln chpt. 1988—, pres. 1993-94). Home: 330 Campus View Dr Lincoln IL 62656-2106 Office: Lincoln Christian Coll & Seminary 100 Campus View Dr # 178 Lincoln IL 62656-2111

WILSON, ROBERT BURTON, veterinary and medical educator; b. Salt Lake City, June 29, 1936; s. Stanley Burton and Jessie Adelia (Hassell) W.; m. Janet Diane McMurdie, June 1, 1962; children: Robert Burton Jr., Janet Diane. BS, Utah State U., 1958; DVM with highest honors, Wash. State U., 1961; PhD, U. Toronto, Ont., Can., 1967. Lic. veterinarian, Mass., Wash., Utah. Intern Angell Meml. Animal Hosp., Boston, 1962-63; asst. prof. Brigham Young U., Provo, Utah, 1963-64; asst. scientist Hosp. for Sick Children, Toronto, 1964-69; assoc. prof. MIT, Cambridge, 1969-73; prof. vet. medicine U. Mo., Columbia, 1973-76; prof., chmn. vet. micro. and pathology Wash. State U., Pullman, 1976-83, dean coll. vet. medicine, 1983-88; vet. cons. Forsyth Dental Inst., Boston, 1972-73; mem., chmn. adv. com. NIH, Bethesda, Md., 1976-80, 89-93. Contbr. over 100 articles to profl. jours. Recipient Mary Mitchell award Mass. Soc. Prevention Cruelty to Animals, 1964, Tchr. of Yr. award MIT, 1971, Tchr. of Yr. award W.A.M.I. Med. Program, 1992, 94, 95. Fellow Am. Heart Assn. (coun. of arteriosclerosis); mem. Am. Vet. Med. Assn., Am. Inst. Nutrition. Mem. LDS Ch. Avocations: genealogy, history, golf, fishing. Home: 505 SE Crestview St Pullman WA 99163-2212 Office: Wash State U Coll Vet Medicine Bustad Hall Pullman WA 99164-7040

WILSON, ROBERT FOSTER, lawyer; b. Windsor, Colo., Apr. 6, 1926; s. Foster W. and Anne Lucille (Svedman) W.; m. Mary Elizabeth Clark, Mar. 4, 1951 (div. Feb. 1972); children: Robert F., Katharine A.; m. Sally Anne Nemec, June 8, 1982. BA in Econs., U. Iowa, 1950, JD, 1951. Bar: Iowa 1951, U.S. Dist. Ct. (no. and so. dists.) Iowa 1956, U.S. Ct. Appeals (8th cir.) 1967. Atty., FTC, Chgo., 1951-55; pvt. practice, Cedar Rapids, Iowa, 1955—; pres. Lawyer Forms, Inc.; dir. Lawyers Forms, Inc. Democratic state rep. Iowa Legislature, Linn County, 1959-60; mem. Iowa Reapportionment Com., 1968; pres. Linn County Day Care, Cedar Repids, 1968-70; del. to U.S. and Japan Bilateral Session on Legal and Econ. Rels. Conf., Tokyo, 1988, Moscow Conf. on Law and Bilateral Rels., Moscow, 1990; U.S. del. to Moscow conf. on legal and econ. rels., 1990. Sgt. U.S. Army, 1944-46. Mem. ATLA, Am. Arbitration Assn. (mem. panel arbitrators), Am. Legion (judge advocate 1970-75, 1987-93), Iowa Trial Lawyers Assn., Iowa Bar Assn., Linn County Bar Assn., Delta Theta Phi. Club: Cedar View Country. Lodges: Elks, Eagles. Home: 100 1st Ave NE Cedar Rapids IA 52401-1109 Office: 810 Dows Rd Cedar Rapids IA 52403-7010

WILSON, ROBERT GODFREY, radiologist; b. Montgomery, Ala., Mar. 18, 1937; s. Robert Woodridge and Lucille (Godfrey) W.; B.A., Huntingdon Coll., 1957; M.D., Med. Coll. Ala., 1961; m. Dorothy June Waters, Aug. 31, 1957; children—Amy Lucille, Robert Darwin, Robert Woodridge II, Lucy Elizabeth. Intern, Letterman Gen. Hosp., San Francisco, 1961-62; resident in radiology U. Okla. Med. Center, Oklahoma City, 1965-68, clin. instr. in radiology, 1968—; practice medicine specializing in diagnostic and therapeutic radiology, nuclear medicine, Shawnee, Okla., 1968—; mem. med. staff Shawnee Med. Center, Mission Hill Meml. Hosp., Shawnee, 1968—. Served to capt. M.C., USAF, 1960-65. Diplomate Nat. Bd. Med. Examiners, Am. Bd. Radiology, Am. Bd. Nuclear Medicine. Mem. AMA, Okla., Pottawatomie County med. socs., Okla., Greater Oklahoma City radiol. socs., Am. Coll. Radiology, Soc. Nuclear Medicine, Radiol. Soc. N.Am. Methodist. Home: 26 Sequoyah Blvd Shawnee OK 74801-5570 Office: 1110 N Harrison St Shawnee OK 74801-5202

WILSON, ROBERT GORDON, investment banker; b. Mt. Vernon, N.Y., Dec. 16, 1933; s. Gerald and Ella Baxter (Close) W.; m. Valerie Ann Wilson, Apr. 25, 1966 (div. 1986); children: Jennifer Lynn, Kimberly Ann; m. Anne Marie Henriquez, Sept. 27, 1986; 1 child, Anthony H. Crotti. BA, Haverford Coll., 1955; MBA, Columbia U., 1957. Gen. ptnr. Goldman Sachs & Co., N.Y.C., 1967-80, ltd. ptnr., 1981-89; pres. Goldman Sachs Internat., London, 1977-80; chmn., pres. Ecologic Waste Svcs., Inc., Miami, Fla., 1990-94; vice chmn. Carter Kaplan & Co., Richmond, Va., 1993-94; chmn., pres. Ziani Internat. Capital, Inc., Miami, 1995—; bd. dirs. Phoenix Home Life Mut. Ins. Co., Hartford, Conn., RealShare Internat., Inc., N.Y.C.; CEO Credit Source USA, Inc., Charlottesville, Va., 1997—. Former chmn. bd. trustees YMCA Greater N.Y., N.Y.C., 1985. Republican. Avocations: golf, wines, travel. Home: Apt 1127 151 Crandon Blvd Key Biscayne FL 33149-1573 Office: Ziani Internat Capital Inc 151 Crandon Blvd Apt 1127 Key Biscayne FL 33149-1566

WILSON, ROBERT GOULD, management consultant; b. Springfield, Mass., July 29, 1929; s. George Winthrop Wilson and Clara Margret (Smyth) Turnbull; m. Jane Seaman, Sept. 14, 1952; children: Roberta Wilson DiBlasi, Richard Jan. BA in Eng., Bates Coll., 1951. Various positions Gen. Electric Co., Bridgeport, Conn., 1953-64; v.p. planning Warnco, Inc., Bridgeport, 1964-76; pres. Hathaway Can., Prescott, Ont., 1976-79; sr. mgmt. cons. Arthur D. Little, Cambridge, Mass., 1979-84; pres. Northeast Cons., Boston, 1984—, now chmn. Co-author: Business Strategy, 1983. Trustee Bates Coll., Lewiston, Maine, 1984-89. Office: NE Cons Resources Inc One Liberty Sq11th Fl Boston MA 02109

WILSON, ROBERT JAMES MONTGOMERY, investment company executive; b. Millbrook, N.Y., Feb. 8, 1920; s. Albert James Montgomery and Charlotte (Kaye) W.; m. Yvette Laneres, May 10, 1952; children—Robert James Montgomery, Olivia Laneres Wilson Welbourn, Geoffrey Laneres. Grad., Choate Sch., 1938; A.B., Yale U., 1942. Securities analyst buying dept. Union Securities Corp., N.Y.C., 1946-49; securities analyst Union Service Corp., N.Y.C., 1949-59; v.p. Union Service Corp., 1959-63; pres., dir. Surveyor Fund, Inc. (formerly Gen. Public Service Corp.), N.Y.C., 1963-71; with Rockefeller Family and Assos., 1972-75; pres. Adams Express Co., N.Y.C., 1975-86, also bd. dirs., 1975—; pres. Petroleum & Resources Corp. (formerly Petroleum Corp. Am.), N.Y.C., 1975-86, also bd. dirs., 1975—; mem. adv. investment com. Md. State Retirement Systems, 1979-82; bd. dirs. Assn. Publicly Traded Investment Cos., 1968-71, chmn., 1969-71. Mem. 1940 Fahnestock Expdn. of Am. Mus. Natural History to South Seas. Served to capt. AUS, World War II. Mem. Md. Club, Sea Oaks Beach and Tennis Club.

WILSON, ROBERT M., theatre artist; b. Waco, Tex., Oct. 4, 1941; s. D.M. and Loree Velma (Hamilton) W. Student, U. Tex., 1962; BFA, Pratt Inst., 1966, DFA (hon.), 1991. Artistic dir. Byrd Hoffman Found., N.Y.C., 1969—; lectr. Internat. Sch., Paris, 1971, Atelje Festival, Belgrade, Yugoslavia, Internat. Theater Inst. of UNESCO, Durdan, France, 1971, Skowhegan Art Sch., Maine, 1977, Harvard U., 1982; condr. seminars U. Calif.-Berkeley, 1970, George Sch., New Hope, Pa., 1970, U. Iowa, 1970, Newark State Coll., 1971; condr. workshops Royaumont, France, 1972, Boulder, Colo., 1973, Ohio State U., 1973, Centre de Development du Potential Humain, Paris, 1973, 74, NEA, Seattle, 1982, UCLA, 1985. Theatrical and operatic performances U.S. and Europe include: Deafman Glance, 1970 (Best Fgn. Play award Le Syndicat de la Critique Dramatique et Musicale, Paris 1970, Drama Desk award for best direction 1971), The Life and Times of Joseph Stalin (Obie Spl. Citation award for direction 1974), A Mad Man A Mad Giant A Mad Dog A Mad Urge A Mad Face, 1974, The Life and Times of Dave Clark, 1974, A Letter for Queen Victoria, 1974 (Maharam Found. award for scenic design 1975, nominee Tony award for best score and libretto 1975, Best Lyric Theatre award Le Syndicat de la Critique Dramatique et Musicale Paris, 1977), The $ Value of Man, 1974, Dialog, 1974, Einstein on the Beach, 1976, 84 (Best Play award Theatre of Nations, Belgrade, Yugoslavia, 1977, Lumen award, 1977), I Was Sitting on my Patio This Guy Appeared I Thought I Was Hallucinating, 1977, Dialog/Network, 1978, Death, Destruction and Detroit, 1979 (German Critics award 1979, German Press award 1979), Edison, 1979, Dialog/Curious George, 1980, The Man in the Raincoat, 1981, Prologue to Fourth Act of Deafman Glance, 1982, Medea, 1984, Great Day in the Morning, 1982, The Golden Windows, 1982, 85 (Der Rosenstrauss award 1982), The Civil Wars, 1983-85 (Pulitzer prize nominee for drama 1986), Hamletmachine, 1986 (Obie award for direction Village Voice 1986), Alceste, 1986, Salome, 1987, Parzival, 1987, Quartett, 1987, Death, Destruction and Detroit II, 1987, The Martyrdom of St. Sebastian, 1988, Cosmopolitan Greetings, 1988, The Forest, 1988, DeMaterie, 1989, Doktor Faustus, 1989 (Best Prodn. award Italian Theatre Critics, 1989), Swan Song, 1989, Orlando, 1989, The Black Rider, 1990, (German Theater Critics award for Best Prodn. of Yr.), King Lear, 1990, When We Dead Awaken, 1991, Parsifal, 1991, The Magic Flute, 1991, Lohengrin, 1992, Dr. Faustus Lights the Lights, 1992, Alice, 1993, Alice in Bed, 1993, Madame Butterfly, 1993, The Black Rider, 1993, Orlando, 1993, Der Mond im Gras, 1994, Hanjo/Hagoromo, 1994, T.S.E., 1994, The Meek Girl, 1994, The Death of Moliere, 1994, Hamlet: A Monologue, Bluebeard's Castle and Erwartung, Persephone, Snow on the Mesa, 1995, Four Saints in Three Acts, Time Rocker, Oedipus Rex, G.A. Story, 1996, Prometeo, 1997; author (plays): Two Conversations with Edwin Denby, 1973, A Letter for Queen Victoria, 1974, I Was Sitting on my Patio This Guy Appeared I Thought I Was Hallucinating, 1977, Death, Destruction and Detroit, 1979, The Golden Windows, 1981, The Civil Wars, 1983, Death, Destruction and Detroit II, 1987; contbg. author: (anthology) New American Plays Vol. III, 1970; films include: Overture for a Deafman, Murder; video works include: Spaceman, 1976, 84, Video 50, 1978, Deafman Glance, 1981, Stations, 1982, La Femme a la Cafeterie, 1989 (Grand Prize Biennale Festival of Cinema Art, Barcelona), The Death of King Lear, 1989, Mr. Bojangles' Memory, 1991, La Mort de Moliere, 1993; exhibited drawings and sculpture one-man shows: Iolas Gallery, N.Y.C., Palazzi Gallery, Milan, Galerie Fred Lanzenberg, Brussels, Paula Cooper Gallery, N.Y.C., Musée Galliera, Paris, 1972, 74, Multiples/Goodman Gallery, 1977, 79, Neuberger Mus., Purchase, N.Y., 1980, Contemporary Art Ctr., Cin., 1980, Castelli Feigen Corcoran, N.Y.C., Portia Harcus Gallery, Cambridge, Mass., Alpha Gallery, Cambridge, Richard Kunlenschmidt Gallery, Los Angeles, Hewlet Gallery, Pitts., Lehman Coll. Arts Gallery, Bronx, Walker Art Ctr., Mpls., 1984, Rhona Hoffman Gallery, 1986, Galerie der Stadt Stuttgart, 1987, Galerie Herald Behm, Hamburg, 1988, AnneMarie Verna Galerie, Zurich, 1989, Galerie Ha Galerie Yvon Lambert, 1989, Feigen Gallery, Chgo., 1990, Mus. Fine Arts, Boston, 1991, Centre Georges Pompidou, Paris, 1991, Galerie Fred Jahn, Munich, 1991, Hiram Butler Gallery, Houston, 1992, Laura Carpenter Gallery, Sante Fe, 1992, IVAM, Valencia, 1992, Produzenentengalerie, Hamburg, 1992, Deichtorhallen, Hamburg, 1993, Mus. Boymans-van Beuningen, Rotterdam, 1993, Akira Ikeda Gallery, N.Y.C., 1994, Galeria Luis Serpa, Lisbon, 1995, Thaddeus Ropac Gallery, Salzburg and Paris, Clink Street Vaults, London, Galeries Lafayette, Paris, Art Cologne, Cologne, 1996; exhibited numerous other maj. galleries, U.S. and abroad, including: Willard Gallery, N.Y.C., 1971, Marian Goodman Gallery, 1982, Pavillion des Arts, Paris, 1983, Otis-Parsons, Los Angeles, 1984, Inst. Contemporary Art, Boston, 1985, Galeria Gamarra y Garrigues, Madrid, 1992, Kamakura Gallery, Tokyo, 1992, Galerie van Rijsbergen, Rotterdam, 1993; works represented in permanent collections: Mus. Modern Art, N.Y.C., Boston Mus. Fine Arts, Australian Nat. Gallery, Canberra, Kunst Mus., Bern, Lannan Mus., L.A., Mus. Modern Art, Paris, Mus. Art, R.I. Sch. Design, Providence, The French Govt., Paris, Mus. Contemporary Art, Los Angeles, Boymans Mus., Rotterdam, Stedelijk Mus., Amsterdam, Menil Mus., Houston, Tex., Centre Georges Pompidou, Paris, Art Inst., Chgo., Huntington Art Mus. U. Tex., Austin, Met. Mus. Art, N.Y.C., Phila. Mus. Art. Recipient Chgo. Art Inst. Skowhegan medal for drawing Skowhegan Sch. Painting, 1987, Inst. Honor award AIA, 1988, Mondello award, Palermo, 1988, Brandeis Univ. Poses Creative Arts award, 1991, Golden Lion award in sculpture, Venice Bienniale, 1993, Tex. Artist of the Yr., 1995, Premio Europa per il Teatro, Dorothy and Lillian Gish prize, 1996, B-Z Kulturpries, 1997; named Most Outstanding Theater Designer of the Seventies, U.S. Inst. Theater Tech., Washington, 1977; Rockefeller grantee, 1970, 77-80; Guggenheim fellow, 1971, 80. Mem. Nat. Inst. Music Theatre (trustee), Am. Repertory Theatre (hon. bd. dirs.), The Dramatists Guild, Soc. des Auteurs et Compositeurs Dramatiques, Soc. Stage Dirs. and Choreographers, PEN Am. Ctr., I.C.A. Boston (bd. overseers). Office: RW Work Ltd 131 Varick St Rm 908 New York NY 10013-1410

WILSON, ROBERT M., financial executive; b. St. Louis, Aug. 10, 1952; s. William H. and Mary E. (Sacksteder) W.; m. Joli S. Schneeberger, Oct. 7, 1978; 1 child, William Wilcox. BS, Miami U., Oxford, Ohio, 1974; JD, Cleve. State U., 1977. Bar: Ohio; CPA, Ohio. Ptnr. Touche Ross & Co., Dayton, Ohio, 1972-88; exec. v.p. Roberds, Inc., Dayton, 1988—. Chmn. Dayton Ballet Assn., 1979-91; trustee Carillon Park, Dayton, 1988-94, City-Wide Devl. Corp., 1991—; assoc. bd. Dayton Art Inst., 1989-95. Mem. ABA (com. chmn. 1990-92), Ohio Soc. CPAs (pres. 1985-86). Republican. Roman Catholic. Office: Roberds Inc 1100 E Central Ave Dayton OH 45449-1812

WILSON, ROBERT NATHAN, health care company executive; b. Covington, Ky., Aug. 7, 1940; s. Robert Thomas and Ruth (Pearce) W.; m. Anne Wright, Mar. 29, 1969; children: Julie Anne, Jonathan Robert. BA in Bus., Georgetown (Ky.) Coll., 1962; grad. exec. program Grad. Sch. Bus. Adminstrn., Columbia U., 1975; LLD (hon.), Phila. Coll. Pharmacy and Sci., 1991. Sales rep. Ortho Pharm. Corp., Raritan, N.J., 1964; various exec. and mgr. positions, 1964-77; pres. Johnson & Johnson Dental Products Co., East Windsor, N.J., 1977-79; co. group chmn. Johnson & Johnson, New Brunswick, N.J., 1981-83, mem. exec. com., 1983—, apptd. vice chmn. exec. com., 1994—, vice chmn., bd. dirs., 1989—; pres. Ortho Pharm. Corp., Raritan, N.J., 1979-83; chmn. Ortho Pharm. Ltd. Can., 1979-83; bd. dirs. U.S. Trust Corp. 1991—, James Black Found., London, Amerada Hess Corp. Trustee Mus. Am. Folk Art, N.Y.C., 1981-95; chmn., bd. dirs. Healthcare Inst. N.J., 1996—; bd. dirs. World Wildlife Fund, 1995—, Georgetown Coll. Found., World Bus. Coun. for Sustainable Devel., Pharm. Rsch. and Mfrs. Am. Found., 1994—; mem. Trilateral Commn. Recipient Alumni Achievement award Georgetown Coll., 1987. Mem. Pharm. Rsch. and Mfrs. Am. (bd. dirs. 1984—, exec. com. 1988—, policy analysis and planning com. 1989—). Presbyterian. Office: Johnson & Johnson 1 Johnson And Johnson Plz New Brunswick NJ 08933-0001

WILSON, ROBERT NEAL, sociologist, educator; b. Syracuse, N.Y., Nov. 15, 1924; s. Robert Marchant and May Eloise (Neal) W.; m. Arleene Eleanor Smith, Aug. 21, 1948 (div. 1973); children—Lynda Lee, Deborah Eloise; m. Joan Wallace, Aug. 1, 1973. B.A., Union Coll., 1948; Ph.D., Harvard U., 1952. Research assoc. Cornell U., Ithaca, N.Y., 1951-53; staff Social Sci. Research Council, Washington, 1953-56; lectr. Harvard U., Cambridge, Mass., 1957-60; assoc. prof. Yale U., New Haven, 1960-63; prof. sociology U. N.C., Chapel Hill., 1963—; trustee Easter Seal Research Found., Chgo., 1966-72; cons. NIMH, Washington, 1968-72, Nat. Inst. Child Health and Human Devel., Washington, 1970-77; reviewer NEH, Washington, 1977—. Author: Man Made Plain, 1958, Sociology of Health, 1970, The Writer as Social Seer, 1979, Experiencing Creativity, 1986; author, editor: The Arts in Soc., 1964. Served to sgt. U.S. Army, 1943-46, ETO. Ctr. for Advanced Study Behavioral Scis. fellow, 1956-57; Fulbright scholar, 1975. Fellow Am. Sociol. Assn., Am. Pub. Health Assn., So. Sociol. Soc. Democrat. Episcopalian. Avocation: poetry. Home: 103 Springvalley Rd Carrboro NC 27510-1246 Office: Univ NC Chapel Hill NC 27514

WILSON, ROBERT RATHBUN, retired physicist; b. Frontier, Wyo., Mar. 4, 1914; s. Platt Elvin and Edith (Rathbun) W.; m. Jane Inez Scheyer., Aug. 20, 1940; children—Daniel, Jonathan, and Rand. AB, U. of Calif., 1936; PhD, 1940; DSc (hon.), Notre Dame U., U. Bonn, Harvard U., 1986, Wesleyan U., 1987. Instr. Princeton U., 1940-42, asst. prof., 1942-45; head rsch. divsn. Los Alamos Lab., 1944-45, 1944-45; assoc. prof. physics Harvard, 1946-47; prof. physics and dir. Lab Nuclear Studies Cornell U., 1947-67; prof. physics U. Chgo., 1967-78, Peter B. Ritzma prof., 1978-80; dir. Fermi Nat. Accelerator Lab., Batavia, Ill., 1967-78; Michael Pupin prof. Columbia U., 1980-83; now ret. Contbr. articles to Physics Rev. Recipient Elliott Cresson medal Franklin Inst., 1964, Nat. medal sci., 1973, Enrico Fermi award, 1984, The Wright prize, 1986, del Regato medal, 1989, Gemant award, 1995. Fellow NAS, Am. Phys. Soc. (pres. 1985), Am. Acad. Arts and Scis., Fedn. Am. Scientists (chmn. 1946, 63), Am. Philos. Soc., Sigma Xi. Address: 916 Stewart Ave Ithaca NY 14850-2123

WILSON, ROBERT SPENCER, magazine editor; b. Bolling Field, D.C., Feb. 21, 1951; s. Joseph Griswold and Helen (Hodnett) W.; m. Martha Elaine Ritchie, Oct. 19, 1974; children: Matthew Spencer, Cole Ritchie, Robert Samuel. BA, Washington and Lee U., 1973; MA, U. Va., 1977. Lectr. U. Va., Charlottesville, 1977-80; asst. editor Washington Post, 1977-83; book editor, book columnist USA Today, Washington, 1983-94; lit. editor Civilization mag., Washington, 1994-95; editor Preservation mag., Manassas, Va., 1996—. Home and Office: 9301 Grant Ave Manassas VA 20110-5040

WILSON, ROBERT WILLIAM, defense systems company executive; b. Green Island, N.Y., July 26, 1935; s. William James and Margaret Ann (Ayotte) W.; m. Dolores Ann Kirchert; children: Kirk, Kathy Doherty, Karen McBride. BS in Chemistry, St. Michael's Coll., Winooski, Vt., 1956; MS in Physics, Boston U., 1964; MS in Mgmt., MIT, 1972. Program mgr., v.p. Avco Systems div., Wilmington, Mass., 1960-82; dir. TAC E/O systems Honeywell Corp., Lexington, Mass., 1982-85; v.p., asst. gen. mgr. Avco Everett (Mass.) Rsch. Lab., 1984-87, Textron Def. Systems, Wilmington, 1987-94; mng. ptnr. Tech. Applications Ptnrs., Tarpon Springs, Fla., 1994—. With USAF, 1956-60. Recipient Firepower award Am. Def. Preparedness, 1986. Mem. AIAA, Nat. Security Indsl. Assn., Air Force Assn. Roman Catholic. Avocation: piloting. Home: 1111 Mainsail Dr Tarpon Springs FL 34689-8318

WILSON, ROBERT WOODROW, radio astronomer; b. Houston, Tex., Jan. 10, 1936; s. Ralph Woodrow and Fannie May (Willis) W.; m. Elizabeth Rhoads Sawin, Sept. 4, 1958; children—Philip Garrett, Suzanne Katherine, Randal Woodrow. B.A. with honors in Physics, Rice U., 1957; Ph.D., Calif. Inst. Tech., 1962. Research fellow Calif. Inst. Tech., Pasadena, 1962-63; mem. tech. staff AT&T Bell Labs., Holmdel, N.J., 1963-76; head wireless tech. rsch. dept. AT&T Bell Labs., 1976-94; sr. sci. Harvard-Smithsonian Ctr. for Astrophysics, Cambridge, Mass., 1994—. Discoverer 3 deg. k microwave background radiation, 1965; discoverer CO and other molecules in interstellar space using their millimeter wavelength radiation. Recipient Henry Draper medal Royal Astron. Soc., London, 1977, Herschel medal Nat. Acad. Scis., 1977; named Fairchild Disting. scholar Caltech., 1987;

Nobel prize in physics, 1978; NSF fellow, 1958-61, Cole fellow, 1957-58. Mem. Am. Astron. Soc., Internat. Astron. Union, Am. Phys. Soc., Internat. Sci. Radio Union, Nat. Acad. Scis., Phi Beta Kappa, Sigma Xi. Home: 9 Valley Point Dr Holmdel NJ 07733-1320 Office: Harvard-Smithsonian Ctr Astrophysics 60 Garden St # 42 Cambridge MA 02138-1516

WILSON, ROBIN SCOTT, university president, writer; b. Columbus, Ohio, Sept. 19, 1928; s. John Harold and Helen Louise (Walker) W.; m. Patricia Ann Van Kirk, Jan. 20, 1951; children: Kelpie, Leslie, Kari, Andrew. B.A., Ohio State U., 1950; M.A., U. Ill., 1951, Ph.D., 1959. Fgn. intelligence officer CIA, Washington, 1959-67; prof. English Clarion State Coll., (Pa.), 1967-70; assoc. dir. Com. Instnl. Cooperation, Evanston, Ill., 1970-77; assoc. provost instrn. Ohio State U., Columbus, 1977-80; univ. pres. Calif. State U., Chico, 1980-93, pres. emeritus, 1993—. Author: Those Who Can, 1973, Death By Degrees, 1995, Paragons, 1996; short stories, criticism, articles on edn. Lt. USN, 1953-57. Mem. AAAS, Phi Kappa Phi.

WILSON, ROBLEY CONANT, JR., English educator, editor, author; b. Brunswick, Maine, June 15, 1930; s. Robley Conant and Dorothy May (Stimpson) W.; m. Charlotte A. Lehon, Aug. 20, 1955 (div. 1991); children: Stephen, Philip; m. Susan Hubbard, June 17, 1995. B.A., Bowdoin Coll., 1957, D.Litt (hon.), 1987; M.F.A., U. Iowa, 1968. Reporter Raymondville Chronicle, Tex., 1950-1951; asst. publicity dir. N.Y. State Fair Syracuse, 1956; instr. Valparaiso U., Ind., 1958-63; asst. prof. English U. No. Iowa, Cedar Falls, 1963-69, assoc. prof., 1969-75, prof., 1975—, editor N.Am. Rev., 1969—. Author: The Pleasures of Manhood, 1977, Living Alone, 1978, Dancing for Men, 1983 (Drue Heinz Lit. prize 1982), Kingdoms of the Ordinary, 1987 (Agnes Lynch Starrett award 1986), Terrible Kisses, 1989, A Pleasure Tree, 1990 (soc. Midland Authors Poetry award 1990), The Victim's Daughter, 1991, A Walk Through the Human Heart, 1996. Bd. dirs. Associated Writing Programs, Norfolk, Va., 1983-86; pres. Iowa Woman Endeavors, Inc., 1986-90. With USAF, 1951-55. Guggenheim fellow, 1983-84, Nicholl Screenwriting fellow, 1996. Mem. Am. Soc. Mag. Editors, Authors' Guild. Home: 415 London Rd Winter Park FL 32792-4837 Office: Univ Northern Iowa North Am Review Cedar Falls IA 50614

WILSON, ROGER BYRON, lieutenant governor, school administrator; b. Columbia, Mo., Oct. 10, 1948; m. Patricia O' Brien; children: Erin, Drew. BA, Ctrl. Methodist Coll.; MA in Edn., U. Mo.; grad., Harvard U., 1990. Asst. prin. Russell Blvd. Elem. Sch., Columbia, Mo.; real estate broker; collector Boone County, Mo., 1976-79; mem. Mo. State Senate from Dist. 19, 1979-92; lt. gov. State of Mo., 1993—; chmn. senate appropriations com., apportionment com., chmn. tourism commn.; mem. Mo. bus. and edn. partnership commn., transportation devel. commn., gov.'s adv. coun. phys. fitness. Bd. dirs. United Way, Columbia; mem. Mo. Assn. Cmty. Arts Agys., Boone County Hist. Soc.; mem. com. Mo. Parents as Tchrs. Recipient Everett award Mo. State Tchr.'s Assn., Outstanding Legislator of Yr. award, 1991, Boss of Yr. award Am. Businesswomen's Assn., Disting. Legislator award Nat. Conf. of State Legislatures, Horace Mann award Mo. Nat. Edn. Assn., Pub. Ofcl. of Yr. award Mo. Assn. Homes for Aging, M.U. Alumni award, 1991, Kirkpatrick award Northwest Mo. Press Assn., 1997. Mem. Columbia C. of C., Cosmopolitan Internat. Office: State Capitol Building Bldg 121 Jefferson City MO 65101-1556

WILSON, ROGER GOODWIN, lawyer; b. Evanston, Ill., Sept. 3, 1950; s. G. Turner Jr. and Lois (Shay) W.; m. Giovinella Gonthier, Mar. 7, 1975. AB, Dartmouth Coll., 1972; JD, Harvard U., 1975. Bar: Ill. 1975, U.S. Dist. Ct. (no. dist.) Ill. 1976, U.S. Ct. Appeals (7th cir.) 1977, U.S. Dist. Ct. (no. dist.) Ind. 1985. Assoc. Kirkland & Ellis, Chgo., 1975-81, ptnr., 1981-86; sr. v.p., gen. counsel, corp. sec. Blue Cross/Blue Shield, 1986—; speaker Nat. Healthcare Inst., U. Mich., 1987-93, Am. Law Inst.-ABA Conf. on Mng. and Resolving Domestic and Internat. Bus. Disputes, N.Y.C., 1988, Washington, 1990; cert. health cons. program Purdue U., 1993-94, Inst. for Bus. Strategy Devel., Northwestern U., 1993-94, The Health Care Antitrust Forum, Chgo., 1995, Nat. Health Lawyers Assn Managed Care Law Inst., 1995, Nat. Health Lawyers Assn. Conf. on Tax Issues in Healthcare Orgns., 1996. Advisor Constl. Rights Found., Chgo., 1982-87; mem. So. Poverty Law Ctr., Montgomery, Ala., 1981—. Mem. ABA, Nat. Health Lawyers Assn. (spkr. 1984), Chgo. Coun. Lawyers (bd. govs. 1988-92), Coun. Chief Legal Officers (conf. bd. 1995—), Dartmouth Lawyers Assn., Sinfonietta (bd. dirs. 1987—), Univ. Club, Mid-Am. Club, Phi Beta Kappa. Avocations: French lang. and culture. Home: 2800 N Lake Shore Dr Apt 1917 Chicago IL 60657-6246 Office: Blue Cross/Blue Shield 676 N Saint Clair St Chicago IL 60611

WILSON, RONALD JAMES, geologist; b. San Antonio, Dec. 24, 1948; s. James Robert and Robbie Lee (Bell) W.; m. Beverly Ann Engelhorn, June 23, 1970 (div. May 1980); children: Jennifer, Jason; m. June Guynette Nolin, Aug. 5, 1983; 1 child, Heather. BA, Rice U., 1971. Sr. logging engr. Schlumberger, Houston, 1971-75; sr. petrophysicist Delta Drilling Co., Tyler, Tex., 1975-78; sr. log analyst Dresser Industries, Houston, 1978-81; mgr., geology and petrophysics Intercomp, Houston, 1981-83; cons. geologist C G & A, Ft. Worth, 1983-90; exec. v.p. Alpha Bio Internat., Ltd., Dallas, 1990-91; pres. Integrated Energy Solutions, Ft. Worth, 1991-94, Lahd Energy, Inc., Granbury, Tex., 1994—; bd. dirs. Tex. Energy Resources Internat., Ft. Worth, Tex., 1996. Author: Practical Log Analysis, 1981, Quick-Look Techniques, 1981; contbr. articles to jour. Prodn. Log Analyst, Log Analyst. Mem. nat. edn. bd. Luth. Ch. Am., Denver, 1975; deacon Richland Hills Ch. of Christ, Ft. Worth, 1991; edn. com. Action United Meth. Ch., Acton, Tex., 1994-95; pres. bd. trustees The White Lake Sch., 1995—. Mem. Am. Assn. Petroleum Geologists (cert.), Soc. Profl. Well Log Analysts (pres. 1987-88), Soc. Petroleum Engrs. (bd. edn. 1976—), Divsn. Environ. Geoscientists (charter). Republican. Avocations: reading, crafts, wood-working, golfing. Home: 301 Willow Ridge Rd Fort Worth TX 76103 Office: Lahd Energy Inc 307 W 7th St Ste 1717 Fort Worth TX 76102-5114

WILSON, RONALD LAWRENCE, professional hockey coach; b. Windsor, Ont., Can., May 28, 1955. BA in Econs., Providence Coll. Profl. hockey player Toronto Maple Leafs, 1975-85, Minn. North Stars, 1986-88; asst. coach Milw., Vancouver Canucks, 1989-90, Vancouver Canucks, 1990-93; interim coach Milw. Admirals, 1990; head coach Anaheim (Calif.) Mighty Ducks, 1993—, Team USA, 1996. Named to NCAA All-Am. East 1st team, 1974-76; Team USA World Cup Champaions, 1996. Office: Mighty Ducks PO Box 61077 2695 E Katella Ave Anaheim CA 92803-6177

WILSON, ROOSEVELT LEDELL, secondary education educator; b. Baton Rouge, La., Aug. 8, 1941; m. Barbara Batiste; 1 child, Janile. BS, So. U., 1964, MEd, 1970; MS, U. Okla., 1973; PhD, U. Iowa, 1975. Cert. tchr. math. and sci., La. Tchr. East Baton Rouge Parish Sch. Bd., 1964-75, 81—; teaching asst. U. Iowa, Iowa City, 1974; asst. prof. Jackson (Miss.) State U., 1976-81; tchr. earth and physical sci., dean of students Baton Rouge Prep. Acad., 1994—; club sponsors, dept. chairperson McKinley Mid. Magnet, Baton Rouge, 1981—; dir. workshops E. Baton Rouge Parish Schs., 1983, 85; coord. after-sch. tutorial program Jordan United Meth. Ch., Baton Rouge, 1992—; participant adminstrv. internship program E. Baton Rouge Parish, 1993-94. Contbr. articles to profl. jours. Mem. male chorus Jordan United Meth. Ch., Baton Rouge. Fellow Nat. Fellowship Fund; grantee NSF. Mem. NEA, Nat. Sci. Tchrs. Assn., La. Assn. Educators, Phi Delta Kappa. Methodist. Avocations: golf, tennis, fishing. Home: 21253 Old Scenic Hwy Zachary LA 70791 Office: Baton Rouge Prep Acad 5959 Cadillac St Baton Rouge LA 70811-5802

WILSON, RUBY LEILA, nurse, educator; b. Punxsutawney, Pa., May 29, 1931; d. Clark H. and Alda E. (Armstrong) W. BS in Nursing Edn., U. Pitts., 1954; MSN, Case Western Res. U., 1959; EdD, Duke U., 1969. Staff nurse, asst. head nurse Allegheny Gen. Hosp., Pitts., 1951-52; night clin. instr., adminstrv. suppr. Allegheny Gen. Hosp., 1951-55; staff nurse, asst. head nurse Fort Miley VA Hosp., San Francisco, 1957-58; instr. nursing Duke U. Sch. Nursing, Durham, N.C., 1955-57; asst. prof. med. surg. nursing Duke U. Sch. Nursing, 1959-66, assoc. in medicine, 1963-66, prof. nursing, 1971—, dean sch. nursing., 1971-84, asst. to chancellor for health affairs, 1984—; asst. prof. dept. community and family medicine Duke U. Sch. Medicine, 1971—; cons., vis. prof. Rockefeller Found., Thailand, 1968-71; vis. prof. Case Western Res. U., 1982-84; mem. Gov.'s Commn. on Health Care Reform in N.C., 1994. Contbr. articles to profl. jours. Active N.C. Med. Care Commn., Gov.'s Commn. on N.C. Health Care Reform, 1994—. Fellow Am. Acad. Nursing, Inst. Medicine; mem. ANA, Am. Assn. Colls. Nursing, Am. Assn. Higher Edn., Nat. League Nursing, Assn. for Acad. Health Ctrs. (mem. inst. planning com.), Women's Forum N.C. (bd. dirs. 1984-88, 95—), N.C. Found. for Nursing (pres. 1990-94). Office: Duke U Med Ctr PO Box 3243 Durham NC 27715-3243

WILSON, SAMUEL GRAYSON, federal judge; b. 1949. BS, U. Richmond, 1971; JD cum laude, Wake Forest U., 1974. Asst. commonwealth atty. City of Roanoke, Va., 1974-76; asst. U.S. atty. Western Dist. Va., 1976; U.S. magistrate U.S. Dist. Ct. for Western Dist. Va., 1976-81; mem. Woods, Rogers & Hazlegrove, Roanoke, 1981-90; dist. judge U.S. Dist. Ct. for Western Dist. Va., Roanoke, Va., 1990—. Mem. staff Wake Forest Law Rev., 1973-74. Mem. law bd. visitors Wake Forest U. Mem. Va. State Bar, Fed. Bar Assn., Va. Bar Assn., Roanoke Bar Assn., Supreme Ct. Hist. Soc. Methodist. Office: Ricard H. Poff Fed Bldg PO Box 2421 210 Franklin Rd SW Roanoke VA 24010-2421*

WILSON, SAMUEL MAYHEW, surgeon; b. Phila., June 26, 1950; s. Samuel Mack and Lois Elisabeth (Graf) W.; m. Dorothy Hay Barrus, June 9, 1990; children: Elisabeth Hay, Mary Jaudon. BA, Swarthmore Coll., 1972; MS, Drexel U., 1975; MD, Temple U., 1979. Diplomate Am. Bd. Surgery. Resident in surgery Temple U. Hosp., Phila., 1979-84; fellow in vascular surgery Presbyn.-U. Pa. Med. Ctr., Phila., 1984-86; attending surgeon Evang. Cmty. Hosp., Lewisburg, Pa., 1986-88, Albert Einstein Med. Ctr., Phila., 1988-95; attending surgeon Elkins Park (Pa.) Hosp., 1988-95, Frankford Hosp., Phila., 1988-95, JFK Meml. Hosp., Phila., 1988-95; staff surgeon Kent Gen. Hosp., Dover, 1996—; asst. clin. instr. surgery U. Pa. Med. Sch., Phila., 1984-85, assoc. clin. instr., 1985-86; clin. instr. surgery Temple U. Sch. Medicine, Phila., 1988-95. Contbr. articles to profl. jours. Active Christ Episcopal Ch., Dover, 1996—. Corp. USMCR, 1972-78. Fellow ACS; mem. AMA (Physician Recognition award), Med. Soc. Del., Kent County Med. Soc., Delaware Valley Vascular Soc., Eastern Vascular Soc. Avocations: sailing, skiing, hiking, photography, reading. Home: 2 Drake Ct Wyoming DE 19934 Office: 807 S Bradford St Dover DE 19904-4137

WILSON, SAMUEL V., academic adminstrator. Pres. Hampden-Sydney (Va.) Coll. Office: Hampden-Sydney Coll Office of Pres PO Box 128 Hampden Sydney VA 23943-0128

WILSON, SHERYL A., pharmacist; b. Nashville, Apr. 6, 1957; d. Robert Lewis and Norma Anne (Cox) W. BS in Biology, David Lipscomb U., 1979; BS in Pharmacy, Auburn U., 1985. Lic. pharmacist, Tenn. Student extern/intern East Alabama Med. Ctr., Opelika, Ala., 1982-86; staff pharmacist Metro Nashville Gen. Hosp., 1987-95, PharmaThera, Inc., Nashville, 1995—. Flutist Nashville Community Concert Band, 1973—; preschool tchr. Donelson Ch. of Christ, 1988—. Mem. Am. Pharm. Assn., Am. Soc. Health Sys. Pharmacists, Am. Soc. Parenteral and Enteral Nutrition, Tenn. Soc. Hosp. Pharmacists, Nashville Area Pharmacists Assn. Democrat. Avocations: art, music, reading, cooking, sewing. Home: 1439 Mcgavock Pike Nashville TN 37216-3231 Office: PharmaThera Inc 1410 Donelson Pike Ste B-3 Nashville TN 37217-2933

WILSON, SLOAN, author, lecturer; b. Norwalk, Conn., May 8, 1920; s. Albert F. and Ruth (Danenhower) W.; m. Elise Pickhardt, Feb. 4, 1941 (div.); children—Lisa, Rebecca, David Sloan; m. Betty Stephens; 1 dau., Jessica. Grad., Fla. Adirondack Sch., 1938; AB, Harvard, 1942; LHD (hon.), Rollins Coll., 1982. Writer, contbr. New Yorker and other mags.; with Providence Jour., 1946-47, Time, Inc., 1947-49, Nat. Citizens Commn. for Pub. Schs., 1949-53; dir. information services, asst. prof. English Buffalo U., 1953-55; asst. dir. White House Conf. on Edn., 1955-56; Disting. writer-in-residence Rollins Coll., Winter Park, Fla., 1981-82; dir. Winter Park Artists Workshop, 1983-85; cons. Philip Crosby Assocs., Winter Park, 1984-87; lectr. Va. Commwealth U., 1990. Author: Voyage to Somewhere, 1946, The Man in the Gray Flannel Suit, 1955, A Summer Place, 1958, A Sense of Values, 1960, Georgie Winthrop, 1962, Janus Island, 1966, Away From It All, 1969, All The Best People, 1970, What Shall We Wear to This Party, 1976, Small Town, 1978, Ice Brothers, 1979, The Greatest Crime, 1980, Pacific Interlude, 1982, The Man in the Gray Flannel Suit II, 1983. Served to lt. USCGR, World War II. *Although some of my books have been widely read, I of course am not as successful as a writer as I would like to be. Almost all writers, after all, must, if they are honest, suspect that their triumphs are temporary. This is no cause for lament, for the same happens to almost everybody in all walks of life. I am lucky to have a wife who makes my private life a joy and three daughters and a son who with my ten grandchildren give me a kind of immortality. Much like the characters in most of my books, I find my family the only part of my life which does not disappoint. My children and my wife always give me excellent reviews which never yellow in a scrapbook. I sometimes lecture on the topic of "Success." Nowadays that word seems to me to be much more complex than it did when I was young. As I grow old I love life more and more.*

WILSON, STANLEY P., retired lawyer; b. Hamlin, Tex., Sept. 1, 1922; s. Milton Young and Ethel M. (Patterson) W.; m. Claudie Park, Sept. 23, 1944; children: Stanley P., Russell Park, Marianne. BS, U. North Tex., Denton, 1943; LLB, U. Tex., Austin, 1948. Bar: Tex. 1948. Ptnr. McMahon, Smart, Wilson, Surovik & Suttle, Abilene, Tex., 1948-81; sr. v.p., gen. counsel Central and S.W. Corp., Dallas, 1981-86; exec. v.p., gen. counsel Central and S.W. Corp., 1986-88, ret., 1988. Lt. (j.g.) USN, 1943-46, PTO. Mem. ABA, State Bar Tex., Am. Coll. Trial Lawyers, Internat. Assn. Def. Counsel, Abilene Bar Assn., Abilene Country Club, Preston Trail Club. Methodist. Home: 1921 Elmwood Dr Abilene TX 79605-4802 Office: Ste 800 First Nat Bank Bldg Abilene TX 79601

WILSON, STEPHEN RIP, public policy consultant; b. Twin Falls, ID, Apr. 26, 1948; s. Jerome P. and Epsy Jane (Griggs) W.; m. Judith Ann Newcomb, June 2, 1972 (dec. Nov. 16, 1977); children: Paul, Sloan; m. Judith E. Allen, Apr. 11, 1992. BA, Columbia U., 1970. Editor Sta. KABC TV, Los Angeles, 1970-72; owner, mgr. Oro Verde Farms, Hagerman, ID, 1972-77; new dir. Sta. KAET TV, Phoenix, 1978-83; adminstrv. aide U.S. Senator Dennis DeConcini, Phoenix, 1983-89; chief exec. officer Flatt & Assocs., Mesa, Ariz., 1989-90; exec. asst. to Gov. Rose Mofford State of Ariz., Phoenix, 1990-91; pres. SRW Cos., Phoenix, Ariz., 1991—; commr. Gov.'s Coun. Phys. Fitness, Phoenix, 1988-90; bd. dirs. Crime Victim Found., Phoenix, 1984; mem. Jefferson Forum. Mem. Nucleus Club, Com. on Fgn. Relations. Democrat. Avocations: scuba diving, skiing, tennis, fly fishing, golf, writing. Home: 2017 E Marshall Ave Phoenix AZ 85016-3110

WILSON, STEPHEN VICTOR, federal judge; b. N.Y.C., Mar. 26, 1942; s. Harry and Rae (Ross) W. B.A. in Econs., Lehigh U., 1963; J.D., Bklyn. Law Sch., 1967; LL.M., George Washington U., 1973. Bars: N.Y. 1967, D.C. 1971, Calif. 1972, U.S. Ct. Appeals (9th cir.) U.S. Dist. Ct. (so., cen. and no. dists.) Calif. Trial atty. Tax div. U.S. Dept. Justice, 1968-71; asst. U.S. atty., L.A., 1971-77, chief spl. prosecutions, 1973-77; ptnr. Hochman, Salkin & Deroy, Beverly Hills, Calif., from 1977; judge U.S. Dist. Ct. (cen. dist.) Calif., L.A., 1985—; adj. prof. law Loyola U. Law Sch., 1976-79; U.S. Dept. State rep. to govt. W.Ger. on 20th anniversary of Marshall Plan, 1967; del. jud. conf. U.S. Ct. Appeals (9th cir.), 1982-86. Recipient Spl. Commendation award U.S. Dept. Justice, 1977. Mem. ABA, L.A. County Bar Assn., Beverly Hills Bar Assn. (chmn. criminal law com.), Fed. Bar Assn. Jewish. Contbr. articles to profl. jours. Home: 9100 Wilshire Blvd Beverly Hills CA 90212-3415 Office: US Dist Ct 312 N Spring St Los Angeles CA 90012-4701*

WILSON, STEVEN J., metal products executive; b. 1943. BSME, Northwestern U., Evanston, Ill., 1966; MBA, U. Chgo., 1973. With Vapor Corp., Niles, Ill., 1966-69; with Electro Products Co., Niles, 1969-71, Signode Corp., Lincolnshire, Ill., 1971-89; v.p. opers. Duo-Fast Corp., Franklin Park, Ill., 1991—, v.p. engring. and tool mfg. Office: Duo-Fast Corp 3702 River Rd Franklin Park IL 60131-2121

WILSON, TERRENCE RAYMOND, manufacturing executive; b. St. Louis, July 1, 1943; s. Raymond Lemuel and Eula Ellen (Sutton) W.; m. Judy Marie Coleman, May 23, 1964; children: John Scott, Dustin Marint. Student, Drury Coll., 1961-62, St. Louis Jr. Coll., 1962-64, Mo. U., 1965-67. Program control planning adminstr. McDonnell Aircraft, St. Louis, 1962-65, 67; mgmt. control mgr. Vitro Labs., Silver Spring, Md., 1966; mgr. customer svc. Teledyne Wis. Motor, Milw., 1968-69, dir. ops., 1970-71, dir. mktg., 1972-73; gen. mgr. Teledyne Still-Man, Cookeville, Tenn., 1973-74; pres. multiplant div. Teledyne Still-Man, Cookeville, 1975-78; group exec. Teledyne, Inc., 1979-84; pres. Teledyne Indsl. Engines, 1984-87; pres., chief exec. officer Morgan Corp., Morgantown, Pa., 1987-92; pres. Magnatech Internat. L.P., Sinking Spring, Pa., 1992—; mng. dir. Spirka Maschinenbay GmbH, Alfeld, Germany, 1996-97. Bd. dirs. Tenn. Tech. U. Coll. Bus. Found.; mem. exec. bd. Hawk Mountain Coun. Boy Scouts Am.; bd. trustees Kutztown U. Found., mem. pres. adv. com. Mem. Beta Gamma Sigma. Roman Catholic. Home: 411 Green Ln Reading PA 19601-1009 Office: Magnatech Internat LP 796 Fritztown Rd Sinking Spg PA 19608-1522

WILSON, THEODORE HENRY, retired electronics company executive, aerospace engineer; b. Eufaula, Okla., Apr. 23, 1940; s. Theodore V. and Maggie E. (Buie) W.; m. Barbara Ann Tassara, May 16, 1958 (div. 1982); children: Debbie Marie, Nita Leigh, Wilson Axten, Pamela Ann, Brenda Louise, Theodore Henry II, Thomas John; m. Colleen Fagan, Jan. 1, 1983 (div. 1987); m. Karen L. Lerohl, Sept. 26, 1987 (div. 1997); m. Sandra Rivadeneira, Mar. 27, 1997. BSME, U. Calif., Berkeley, 1962; MSME, U. So. Calif., 1964, MBA, 1970, MSBA, 1971. Sr. rsch. engr. N.Am. Aviation Co. div. Rockwell Internat., Downey, Calif., 1962-65; propulsion analyst, supr. div. applied tech. TRW, Redondo Beach, Calif., 1965-67, mem. devel. staff systems group, 1967-71; sr. fin. analyst worldwide automotive dept. TRW, Cleve., 1971-72; contr. systems and energy group TRW, Redondo Beach, 1972-79; dir. fin. control equipment group TRW, Cleve., 1979-82, v.p. fin. control indsl. and energy group, 1982-85; mem. space and def. group TRW, Redondo Beach, 1985-93, ret., 1993; lectr., mem. com. acctg. curriculum UCLA Extension, 1974-79. Mem. Fin. Execs. Inst. (com. govt. bus.), Machinery and Allied Products Inst. (govt. contracts coun.), Nat. Contract Mgmt. Assn. (bd. advisors), Aerospace Industries Assn. (procurement and fin. coun.), UCLA Chancellors Assocs., Tau Beta Pi, Beta Gamma Sigma, Pi Tau Sigma. Republican. Avocations: golf, bridge. Home: 3617 Via La Selva Palos Verdes Peninsula CA 90274-1115

WILSON, THOMAS ARTHUR, economics educator; b. Vancouver, B.C., Canada, Aug. 5, 1935; s. Victor and Edith Christina (Grange) W.; m. Julia Ann Dillon, Feb. 8, 1958; children: Christine Diana, Arthur Dillon. B.A., U. B.C., 1957; Ph.D., Harvard U., 1961. Instr. Harvard U., 1961-62, asst. prof., 1962-67; assoc. prof. U. Toronto, 1967-68, prof., 1968—, dir. Inst. for Policy Analysis, 1969-75, dir. econs., 1979-82, chmn. econs. dept., 1982-85, dir. policy and econ. analysis program, 1987—, area coord. bus. econs. Faculty of Mgmt., 1989—; cons. various govtl. depts. Author: Advertising and Market Power, 1974, Canadian Competition Policy, 1979, Fiscal Policy in Canada, 1993, The Future of Telecommunications Policy in Canada, 1995. Fellow Royal Soc. Can.; mem. Am. Econs. Assn., Canadian Econ. Assn. (pres. 1984-85). Office: 140 St George St, Toronto, ON Canada M5S 1A1

WILSON, THOMAS LEON, physicist; b. Alpine, Tex., May 21, 1942; s. Homer Marvin and Ogarita Maude (Bailey) W.; m. Joyce Ann Krevosky, May 7, 1978; children: Kenneth Edward Byron, Bailey Elizabeth Victoria. BA, Rice U., 1964, BS, 1965, MA, 1974, PhD, 1976. With NASA, Houston, 1965—, astronaut instr., 1965-74, high-energy theoretical physicist, 1969—. Author of two books on cosmic dust and astrophysics; contbr. articles in field to profl. jours. including Phys. Rev. Recipient Hugo Gernsback award IEEE, 1964; NASA fellow, 1969-76. Mem. AAAS, Am. Phys. Soc., N.Y. Acad. Scis., Am. Assn. Physicists in Medicine. Research on grand unified field theory, relativistic quantum field theory, quantum chromodynamics, quantum probability theory, supergravity, quantum cosmology, astrophysics, deep inelastic scattering, neutrino astronomy, neutrino tomography, discoverer classical uncertainty principle; subspecialty: relativity and gravitation. Patentee in field; contributor to design of NASA's proposed lunar base; originator olive branch as symbol of man's 1st landing on moon (on Susan B. Anthony and Eisenhower dollars); and manual Saturn takeover for Apollo moon program. Home: 206 Woodcombe Dr Houston TX 77062-2538 Office: NASA Johnson Space Ctr Houston TX 77058

WILSON, THOMAS S., professional basketball team administrator. CEO Detroit Pistons, pres. Office: Detroit Pistons 2 Championship Dr Pontiac MI 48342-1938*

WILSON, THOMAS WILLIAM, lawyer; b. Bklyn., Sept. 14, 1935; s. Matthew and Alice (McCrory) W.; m. Eileen Marie McGann, June 4, 1960; children—Jeanne Alice, Thomas William, David Matthew, A.B., Columbia U., 1957, LL.B., 1960. Bar: N.Y. 1962, U.S. Dist. Ct. (so. and ea. dists.) N.Y. 1962, D.C. 1972. Assoc. Mendes and Mount, N.Y.C., 1961-65, Haller & Small, N.Y.C., 1965-66; gen. counsel Prudential of Gt. Brit., N.Y.C., 1966-68; mng. ptnr. Wilson, Elser, Moskowitz, Edelman & Dicker, N.Y.C., 1968—. Contbr. articles to profl. jours. Served with U.S. Army, 1960-65. Mem. ABA, N.Y. State Bar Assn., Def. Research Inst. (editorial bd. profl. liability reporter). Office: Wilson Elser Moskowitz Edelman & Dicker 150 E 42nd St New York NY 10017-5612

WILSON, THOMAS WOODROW, III, research scientist, consultant; b. Greensboro, N.C., Mar. 29, 1956; s. Thomas Woodrow Jr. and Ruth Hanes (Friddle) W.; m. Rhonda Gayle Beeson, May 16, 1980. BS in Textile Chemistry with honors, N.C. State U., 1978, MS in Textile Chemistry, 1981, PhD in Fiber and Polymer Sci., 1986. Registered patent agent. Polymer scientist Rsch. Triangle Inst., Research Triangle Park, N.C., 1989-91; rsch. scientist Family Health Internat., Research Triangle Park, 1991-93, sr. rsch. scientist, 1993-94, assoc. dir., 1994-95; mgr. intellectual property and regulatory affairs Mayer Labs., Oakland, Calif., 1996-97; materials engr. Tetra Plastics, Portland, Oreg., 1997—; cons. IPAS, Carrboro, N.C., 1991-94. Patentee med. devices; contbr. numerous articles to profl. jours. Grantee USDA, NASA, NIH/Nat. Inst. Dental Rsch., 1986. Mem. AAAS, Am. Chem. Soc. (polymeric materials sci. and engring. divsn., polymer divsn., rubber divsn., N.C. polymer group, divsn. chemistry and law), ASTM, Sigma Xi. Avocations: leatherworking, woodworking, writing fiction. Office: Tetra Plastics 15705 SW 72nd Ave Portland OR 97224-7937

WILSON, TISH, children's services administrator; b. San Diego, Feb. 27, 1950; d. Kelley Frank and Evelyn Jewel (Parr) Scott; m. David Alexander Stephenson, Apr. 17, 1983; children: Wes, Dwight. BS, San Diego State U., 1973, MS, Utah State U., 1976. Tchr. Neighborhood Assoc./Head Start, San Diego, 1970-72, San Diego Unified Schs., 1972-73; instr. Utah State U., Logan, 1973-78; edn. coord. Ute Indian Tribe, Ft. Duchesne, Utah, 1975-78; edn. specialist Community Devel. Inst., Kansas City, Mo., 1978-79; exec. dir. Community Devel. Inst., Albuquerque, 1979-88; divsn. head early childhood multicultural edn. program Santa Fe C.C., 1988-95; dirs. opers. devel. children's svcs. Presbyn. Med. Svcs., Santa Fe, 1995—; bd. dirs. Community Devel. Inst., Albuquerque, Work Systems by Design, Kansas City, Twisted Pine Nursery, Inc., Santa Fe; validator Acad. of Early Childhood Programs, Washington, 1984—; rep. Cun. for Early Childhood Profl. Recognition, Washington, 1978—. Mem. City of Santa Fe Children & Youth Commn., 1990-92; task force mem. State of N.M., House Meml., Santa Fe, 1989-95, Senate Joint Meml., 1996—. Recipient Gov.'s Outstanding N.Mex. Women award, 1995. Mem. Nat. Assn. for the Edn. of Young Children, N.Mex. Head Start Assn. Democrat. Avocations: hiking, swimming, camping. Office: Presbyn Med Svcs PO Box 2267 1422 Paseo De Peralta Santa Fe NM 87504

WILSON, TOM, cartoonist, greeting card company executive; b. Grant Town, W.Va., Aug. 1, 1931; s. Charles Albert and Hazel Marie W.; m. Carol; children: Tom, Ava. Grad., Art Inst. Pitts., 1955. Advt. layout man Uniontown Newspapers Inc., Uniontown, PA, 1950-53; designer Am. Greetings Corp., Cleveland, OH, 1955-56; creative dir. Am. Greetings Corp., 1957-78, v.p. creative devel., 1978-81; pres. Those Characters from Cleve., 1981—; former mem. faculty Cooper Sch. Art. Cartoonist: Ziggy, 1971—, syndicated in newspapers across U.S. by Universal Press Syndicate, Kansas City; collections include: Life is Just a Bunch of Ziggys, 1973, It's a Ziggy World, 1974, Ziggy Coloring Book, 1974, Never Get Too Personally Involved with Your Own Life, 1975, Promises to Myself: Ziggy's Thirty-Day Ledger of I Owe Me's, 1975, Plants are Some of My Favorite People, 1976, Ziggys of the World Unite!, 1976, Pets Are Friends You Like Who Like You Right Back, 1977, The Ziggy Treasury, 1977, This Book is for the Birds, 1978, Encore! Encore!, 1979, Ziggy's Love Notes, 1979, Ziggy's Thinking of

You Notebook, 1979, Ziggy's Fleeting Thoughts Notebook, 1979, A Ziggy Christmas, 1980, Ziggy's Door Openers, 1980, Ziggy Faces Life, 1981, One Thing You Can Say About Living Alone...There's Never Any Question About Who Didn't Jiggle the Handle on the John, 1981, Short People Arise, 1981, A Word to the Wide is Sufficient, 1981, Ziggy's Sunday Funnies, 1981, Ziggy & Friends, 1982, Ziggy Faces Life...Again!, 1982, Ziggy's For You With Love, 1982, Ziggy's Gift, 1982, Ziggy's Big Little Book, 1983, Ziggy and Friends, 1983, Ziggy's Funday Sunnies, 1983, Alphabet Soup Isn't Supposed to Make Sense, 1984, Ziggy Weighs In, 1984, Ziggy's Ship Comes In, 1984, Ug! The Original Hunk, 1985, Ziggy In the Rough, 1985, Ziggy's Ins and Outs, 1985, Ziggy's Ups and Downs, 1985, Ziggy In the Fast Lane, 1987, Ziggy's Follies, 1988, Ziggy's Star Performances, 1989, Ziggy's School of Hard Knocks, 1989, Ziggy On the Outside Looking In, 1990, (also illustrator) Ziggy's Christmas Book Levels 1, 2, 1991, (also illustrator) Ziggy's Play Today Guitar Method, 1991, Look Out World...Here I Come! Ziggy's Own Down-to-Earth Humor: A Look At the Environment and Ourselves, 1991, Ziggy...A Rumor in His Own Time, 1992, The Ziggy Cookbook: Great Food From Mom's Diner, 1993, A Day in the Life of Ziggy, 1993, One-Eight Hundred-Ziggy, 1994, My Life As a Cartoon: A Ziggy Collection, 1995, Ziggy's Place. Served with U.S. Army, 1953-55. Recipient Purchase award Butler Mus. Nat. Painting Competition, Emmy award for best animated spl., 1982. Developer Soft Touch line of greeting cards. Home: 22905 Ruple Pky Cleveland OH 44142-1100 Office: Universal Press Syndicate 4520 Main St Kansas City MO 64111-1816 *My objective and chief motivation has always been to bring something about that wasn't there before.**

WILSON, VICTORIA JANE SIMPSON, farmer, former nurse; b. Floresville, Tex., Nov. 30, 1952; d. Joseph Eugene and Eva Gertrude (Ferguson) Simpson; m. Richard Royce Wilson, May 15, 1976; children: Sarah Beth, Nathan Lawrence. BSN, U. Cen. Ark., 1977; MS in Nursing, Northwestern State U., 1981. Charge nurse surg. St. Vincent Infirmary, Little Rock; staff nurse ICU La. State U. Med. Ctr., Shreveport, La.; patient edn. coord. White River Med. Ctr., Batesville, Ark.; co-owner, chief exec. officer Health Plus, Stuttgart, Ark.; co-owner, mgr. Wilson & Son Fish Farm. Mem. Catfish Farmers Am. (bd. dirs.), Catfish Farmers Ark., Sigma Theta Tau. Home and Office: 51 Wilson Ln Humphrey AR 72073-0310

WILSON, W. STEPHEN, mathematics educator, researcher; b. Iowa City, Iowa, Nov. 11, 1946; s. Charles William and Frances Preshia (Stephenson) W.; m. Norma Jean Kriger, June 9, 1990; 1 child, Saul Kriger. SB in Math., MIT, 1968, SM in Math., 1969, PhD in Math., 1972. Instr., then asst. prof. Princeton (N.J.) U., 1972-78; assoc. prof. math. Johns Hopkins U., Balt., 1977-80, prof., 1980—, chair dept., 1993-96; mem., Inst. Advanced Study, Princeton, 1974-75, 77-78. Contbr. articles on algebraic topology to math. jours. Alfred P. Sloan Found. fellow, 1977-79. Mem. Am. Math. Soc. Office: Johns Hopkins U Dept Math 34th and Charles Sts Baltimore MD 21218

WILSON, WALLACE, art educator, artist; b. Dallas, June 10, 1947; s. William Wallace and Zoe (Naylor) W.; m. Mary Claire Straw, Apr. 3, 1982; 1 child, Erin Rebecca. Student, Tex. Tech. U., 1965-67; B.A., U. Tex., 1970; MFA, Sch. of Art Inst. Chgo., 1975. Asst. prof. U. Ky., Lexington, 1970-75, U. Del., Newark, 1975-79; assoc. prof. U. Fla., Gainesville, 1979-90, prof., 1990-94; prof., chmn. art dept. U. South Fla., Tampa, 1994—; vis. prof. U. Gothenburg, Sweden, 1984, 86, London Study Ctr. Fla. State U., 1988. One-man shows O.K. Harris Gallery, N.Y.C., 1977, 87, Photopia, Mancini Gallery, Phila., 1977, Balt. Mus. Art, 1977, Images Gallery, New Orleans, 1979, U. Ala., Birmingham, 1983, Francesca Anderson Gallery, Boston, 1986, Marcuse Pfeifer Gallery, N.Y.C., 1987, 89, Tartt Gallery, Washington, 1987, 90, 92, The Photographers Gallery, London, 1989, Robert Klein Gallery, Boston, 1991, Southeast Mus. Photography. Fla., 1993; group exhbns. include U. Nebr., Lincoln, 1972, Galerie Zabriskie, Paris, 1978, Boston Visual Arts Union, 1981, Santa Barbara Mus. Art, Calif., 1982, Robert Freidus Gallery, N.Y.C., 1983, N.Mex. State U. Gallery, Las Cruces, 1987, Spl. Photographers Co., London, 1989, Douglas Drake Gallery, N.Y.C., 1992, Art Network, Atlanta, 1993, The Art Inst. Chgo., 1994; represented in permanent collections Mus. Modern Art, N.Y.C., Art. Inst. Chgo., Oakland Mus., Calif., New Orleans Mus. Art, Balt. Mus. Art, City Mus. Munich, Houston Mus. Fine Arts, The Bklyn. Mus. Recognized in various publs. including Village Voice, N.Y.C., 1977, 87, 89, Le Figaro, Paris, 1978, Art Voices, Palm Beach, Fla., 1981, Art Papers, Atlanta, 1982, Miami Herald, 1989, 90, The Sunday Times, 1989, Photo Metro, San Francisco, 93, Washington Post, 1987, 92; recipient U. Del. Faculty research award, 1978, 20x24 Camera award Polaroid, 1985; fellow Swedish Found., Stockholm, 1986; U. Fla. Faculty research grantee, 1980, 88, 93; Individual Artist fellow State of Fla. Div. Cultural Affairs, 1982, 88. Mem. Soc. for Photog. Edn. (vice chmn. S.E. region 1982-85). Office: U South Fla Art Dept Tampa FL 33620-7350

WILSON, WARNER RUSHING, psychology educator; b. Jackson, Miss., July 27, 1935; s. William Enouch and Ruby (Goyne) W. A.B., U. Chgo., 1956; M.A., U. Ark., 1958; Ph.D., Northwestern U., 1960. Teaching asst. Northwestern U., 1957-60; research psychologist E.I. duPont de Nemours & Co., Wilmington, Del., 1960; asst. prof. U. Hawaii, 1960-65; asso. prof. U. Ala., 1965-73; prof. Wright State U., Dayton, Ohio, 1973-93; pvt. practice Las Vegas, Nev., 1993—; Cons. Bryce State Hosp., Tuscaloosa, Ala., 1966, Ednl. Testing Service, 1968, Tuscaloosa VA Hosp., 1968-74, H.R.B. Singer Co., 1972; Trainee Downey (Ill.) VA Hosp., summer 1959. Contbr. articles to profl. jours. spl. summer fellow in evaluation research Northwestern U., 1973-74, NSF grantee, 1976-78, Johnson Assocs. Postdoctoral Clin. fellow, 1981-82; Research grantee DuPont Co., 1961-62; Research grantee NIMH, 1965, 68-70; Research grantee NSF, 1966-68; Named Outstanding Psychology student U. Ark., 1956-57. Mem. Soc. Exptl. Social Psychology. Home: 2117 Flower Ave N Las Vegas NV 89109 Office: 3376 S Eastern Ave Las Vegas NV 89109-3367

WILSON, WARREN SAMUEL, clergyman, bishop; b. New Orleans, May 15, 1927; s. Charlie Price and Warnie (Heart) W.; m. Lillie Pearl Harvey, Mar. 31, 1949; 1 child, Barbara LaJoyce. BA, So. U., Baton Rouge, 1950; DDiv, Moody Coll., Chgo., 1952; DDiv (hon.), Trinity Hall Coll. and Sem., Springfield, Ill., 1975. Ordained to ministry Ch. of God in Christ, 1952, crowned bishop, apptd. state bishop, Calif., 1970. Min. St. Bernard St. Church of God in Christ, New Orleans, until 1960, Fresno (Calif.) Temple Ch. of God in Christ, 1960—. Served with USN, 1942-46, PTO. Mem. NAACP (life). Avocations: bass fishing, boating. Office: Fresno Temple Ch of God in Christ 1435 S Modoc St Fresno CA 93706-3032*

WILSON, WENDY MELGARD, primary and elementary school educator; b. Fargo, N.D., Jan. 13, 1952; d. Howard A. Melgard and Grace B. (Alphson) Watkins; m. Henry Milton Wilson II, July 31, 1982; children: Andrew J., Aaron C. BA/BS in Edn., U. N.D., 1972-77; postgrad., Drake U., 1984-86, Simpson Coll., 1992-94. Secondary spl. edn. tchr. Ctrl. Decatur Community Schs., Leon, Iowa, 1978-80; work experience instr. Green Valley AEA, Creston, Iowa, 1980-82; elem. spl. edn. tchr. Stuart (Iowa) Menlo Community Schs., 1983-86; elem. spl. edn. tchr. Greenfield (Iowa) Community Schs., 1986-93, kindergarten tchr., 1993—; pres., bd. dirs. Little Lambs Presch., Greenfield, 1991-92; sec., v.p. bd. Sunshine Daycare Ctr., Greenfield, 1987-90; co-chairperson S.W. Iowa Very Spl. Art Festival, Creston, 1981; innkeeper, co-owner Wilson Home Bed & Breakfast, 1986-95; team mem. New Iowa Schs. Devel. Corp., 1996—. com. mem. Greenfield Tourism Com., 1988-94; mem. Greenfield Mother's Club, 1987—, sec., 1991; mem. Adair County Meml. Hosp. Aux., 1987—; mem. Greenfield Elem. PTA. Mem. NEA, PEO, ISEA, Greenfield Edn. Assn. (pres., v.p., com. ch. 1989—), Nat. Assn. for Educating Young Children, Iowa Bed and Breakfast Innkeepers Assn. (sec. 1990-92), Greenfield C. of C., Winterset C. of C., Greenfield Bus. Women, Iowa Aviation Preservation Soc. Home: PO Box 93 Greenfield IA 50849-9757

WILSON, WILLIAM ALEXANDER, manufacturing engineer; b. Cleve., Sept. 8, 1959; s. Raymond and Lydia (Lima) W. Student, Cuyahoga C.C.; BME, Cleve. State U., 1986. Mfg. engr. Physics Internat., Wadsworth, Ohio, 1986-88; sr. mfg. engr. Lucas Aerospace, Broadview Heights, Ohio, 1988-89; mfg. engr. Siemens Energy and Automation, Inc., Norwood, Ohio, 1989—. Mem. SME (5 Yr. award 1992). Avocation: competitive swimming. Office: Siemens Energy & Automation 4620 Forest Ave Norwood OH 45212-3306 also: Lemforder Corp 1100 Aviation Blvd Hebron KY 41048-9332

WILSON, WILLIAM BERRY, lawyer; b. Cape Girardeau, Mo., June 17, 1947; s. Charles F. and Anita (Bartlum) W.; m. Suzanne T. Wilson; children: Matthew James, Sarah Talbot. BA summa cum laude, Westminster Coll., 1969; JD, U. Mich., 1972. Bar: Fla. 1972, U.S. Dist. Ct. (mid. dist.) Fla. 1972, U.S. Ct. Appeals (11th cir.) 1972, U.S. Supreme Ct. 1976; bd. cert. Civil Trial Lawyer, 1983—. Ptnr. Maguire, Voorhis & Wells P.A., Orlando, Fla., 1977—; mng. dir. Maguire, Voorhis & Wells P.A., Orlando, 1982-84, pres., 1984-97, chmn., 1997—; mem. exec. com. and trust com., bd. dirs. SunTrust N.A., Bank Ctrl. Fla. Bd. dirs. Econ. Devel. Authority, Orlando, 1992—, chmn. 1994-95, subcom. chmn. Project 2000, Orlando, 1985-87; bd. dirs. Fla. Symphony, Orlando, 1985-93, Fla. TaxWatch, Inc., 1992—, Rotary, Univ. Club, Country Club of Orlando, Citrus Club, 1994—, U. Ctrl. Fla. Found., 1996—; trustee Orlando Mus. Art, 1993—; bd. overseers Crummer Sch. Bus. Rollins Coll., 1994—; chmn. Fla. Residential Property & Casualty Joint Underwriting Assn., 1995—. Mem. ABA, Fla. Bar Assn. (mem. exec. coun. trial lawyers sect. 1987—, chmn. code and rules of evidence com. 1986-88, chmn. 1996-97), Orange County Bar Assn. (chmn. fed. and state practice sect. 1982-84, chmn. jud. rels. com. 1989-90), Am. Bd. Trial Advocacy, Def. Rsch. Inst., Fla. Def. Lawyers Assn. Republican. Presbyterian. Avocations: tennis, scuba diving. Office: Maguire Voorhis & Wells PA 2 S Orange Ave # 633 Orlando FL 32801-2606

WILSON, WILLIAM C.M., gastroenterologist; b. Pitts., June 8, 1953; s. George Lincoln and Nancy Adair (Lytle) W.; m. Marlis Howland, June 25, 1977; children: Sarah, Stephen, Corrie. BS in Biology, Va. Tech, 1975; MD, Hahnemann U., 1979. Intern, residency R.I. Hosp., Providence, 1978-82; staff internist USAF Med. Ctr., Wright-Patterson AFB, Ohio, 1982-86; fellowship Hahnemann U., Phila., 1986-88; with Digestive Care, Dayton, Ohio, 1988—; chmn. planning com. Dayton Gastroenterology Symposium, 1990—; com. patient edn. Miami Valley Hosp., Dayton, 1990-94, quality assurance Miami Valley Hosp., 1992—; vice chmn. dept. medicine Miami Valley Hosp., 1994-96; chmn. dept. medicine, Miami Valley Hosp., 1996—. Bd. Fairhaven Ch., Dayton, 1990-94, Dayton Christian Schs. Inc., 1995—; physician Dayton Christian Schs. Inc., 1993—; Pastor USAF, 1979-86. Mem. AMA, ACP, Am. Gastroenterological Assn., Am. Coll. Gastroenterology, Am. Soc. Gastrointestinal Endoscopy, Montgomery County Med. Assn., Alpha Omega Alpha. Avocations: tennis, computer, wood working, bicycling, photography. Office: 75 Sylvania Dr Dayton OH 45440

WILSON, WILLIAM GLENN, JR., graphic designer; b. McKeesport, Pa., Mar. 16, 1955; s. William Glenn Sr. and Anna Elizabeth (Johnson) W.; m. Marie Estelle Spillias, July 13, 1983 (div. June 1986); m. Beth Lynn Lewis, July 9, 1988. Student, Art. Inst., 1977-78. Pressman, mgr. Prince Printing, Clairton, Pa., 1968-76; pressman, layout artist Multiscope, Inc., Pitts., 1976-77, mgr., 1977-79; editor, pub., dir. Questar Mag., Pitts., 1978-81; artist, designer Dick Z Assocs., Pitts., 1979-81; designer, pub., adminstr. Imagine, Inc., Pitts., 1982-83; graphic designer St. (Fla.) Petersburg Times, 1983-90; owner Wilson-Lewis-Wilson Design, Palm Harbor, Fla., 1990—; comm. cons. ABR Info. Svcs., 1993—. Assoc. prodr. 7th Ann. Sci. Fiction Film Awards, Hollywood, Calif., 1980; prodr. corp. video Mus. African-Am. Art, Tampa, Fla., 1991; editor, ghostwriter Grande Illusions, 1983; editor, pub. comic book mag. The Collector, 1966-74, sci. fiction mag. Questar, 1978-81; fie. corres. Starlog Mag. Contbr. Popular Culture Collection Hillman Libr., U. Pitts., 1990; cons. Mus. African-Am. Art, Tampa, 1991—; designer, cons., contbr. Tampa Bay History Ctr., 1993—. Recipient Hon. Mention Printing Industry Assn. Western Pa., 1979, 80, Lifetime Achievement award Acad. Sci. Fiction, 1980, Mag. Cover of Yr., Mktg. Bestsellers, N.Y.C., 1980, Pub. Svc. award Distilled Spirits Coun., 1981, Nat. Agri-Mktg. Assn. award as designer of award winning curriculum materials for Am. Egg Bd., 1993, Graphic Arts Excellence award for outstanding achievement in design, Consolidated Papers, Inc., 1996. Avocations: swimming, racquetball, tennis, film, photography.

WILSON, WILLIAM JULIUS, sociologist, educator; b. Derry Twp., Pa., Dec. 20, 1935; s. Esco and Pauline (Bracy) W.; m. Mildred Marie Hood, Aug. 31, 1957; children—Colleen, Lisa; m. Beverly Ann Huebner, Aug. 30, 1970; children—Carter, Paula. BA, Wilberforce U., 1958; MA, Bowling Green State U., 1961; PhD, Wash. State U., 1966; LHD (hon.), U. Mass., 1982, L.I. U., 1982, Columbia Coll., Santa Clara U., Loyola Coll., 1988, De Paul U., 1989; LLD (hon.), Marquette U., Mt. Holyoke Coll., 1989; LHD (hon.), New Sch. for Social Rsch., 1991, Bard Coll., 1992, John Jay Sch. Criminal Justice, 1992, U. Pa., 1993, So. Ill. U., 1993, Northwestern U., 1993, Bowling Green State U., 1994, SUNY, Binghamton, 1994, Princeton U., 1994, Columbia U., Rutgers U., Haverford Coll., Johns Hopkins U. Asst. prof. U. Mass., Amherst, 1965-69; assoc. prof. U. Mass., 1969-71; vis. asso. prof. U. Chgo., 1971-72, assoc. prof. dept. sociology, 1972-75, prof., 1975—, chmn. dept. sociology, 1978—, Lucy Flower prof. urban sociology, 1980-84, Lucy Flower disting. service prof., 1984—; Lucy Flower Univ. prof., 1990-96; Malcolm Wiener Prof. of social policy Harvard U., 1996—; mem. bd. univ. publs. U. Chgo. Press, 1975-79; bd. dirs. Ctr. for Nat. Policy, 1988—, Ctr. for Advanced Study of Behavioral Scis., 1988—, Twentieth Century Fund, 1992—, Jerome Levy Inst., 1992—, Manpower Demonstration Rsch. Corp., 1993—; mem. domestic strategy group Aspen Inst., 1992—; bd. dirs. Pub./Private Ventures, Phila. Author: Power, Racism and Privilege, 1973, Through Different Eyes, 1973, The Declining Significance of Race, 1978, The Truly Disadvantaged, 1987, The Ghetto Underclass, 1993, Sociology and the Public Agenda, 1993, When Work Disppears, 1996. Bd. dirs. Social Sci. Rsch. Coun., 1979-84, Chgo. Urban League, 1983—, Spencer Found., George M. Pullman Found., Russell Sage Found., 1989—, Ctr. for the Advanced Study of the Behaviorial Scis., 1989—, Nat. Humanities Ctr., 1990; mem. Environment, Devel., and Public Policy, 1980—; nat. bd. dirs. A. Philip Randolph Inst., Inst. Rsch. on Poverty, 1983—; trustee Spelman Coll., 1989—; mem. Pres. Commn. on White House Fellowships, 1994—; mem. Pres. Com. Nat. Medal Sci., 1994—; trustee Wilberforce U. With U.S. Army, 1958-60. Recipient Disting. Tchr. of Year award U. Mass., Amherst, 1970, Regents Disting. Alumnus award Wash. State U., 1988, Burton Gordon Feldman award Brandeis U., 1991, Frank E. Seidman Disting. award in polit. econ., 1994; MacArthur Prize fellow, 1987. Fellow AAAS, Am. Acad. Arts and Scis.; mem. NAS, Am. Philos. Soc., Am. Sociol. Assn. (pres. 1989-90, Sydney M. Spivack award 1977, DuBois, Johnson, Frazier award 1990), Soc. for Study Social Problems (C. Wright Mills award 1988), Sociol. Rsch. Assn. (pres. 1987-88), Consortium Of Social Sci. Assn. (pres. 1993-94), Internat. Sociol. Assn., Chgo. Urban League (Beautiful People award 1979). Democrat. Home: 75 Cambridge Pkwy Unit E406 Cambridge MA 02142 Office: John F Kennedy Sch Govt Harvard Univ 79 John F Kennedy St Cambridge MA 02138-5801

WILSON, WILLIAM PRESTON, psychiatrist, emeritus educator; b. Fayetteville, N.C., Nov. 6, 1922; s. Preston Puckett and Rosa Mae (VanHook) W.; m. Dorothy Elizabeth Taylor, Aug. 21, 1950; children: William Preston, Benjamin V., Karen E., Tammy E., Robert E. B.S., Duke U., 1943, M.D., 1947. Diplomate: Am. Bd. Psychiatry and Neurology (examiner). Intern Gorgas Hosp., Ancon, C.Z.; then resident psychiatry Duke U. Med. Center, later resident neurology, 1949-54; asst. prof. psychiatry Duke U. Med. Sch., 1955-58; asso. prof. psychiatry, dir. psychiat. research U. Tex. Med. Br., Galveston, 1958-60; asso. prof. psychiatry Duke U. Med. Center, 1961-64, head div. clin. neurophysiology, 1961-83, prof. psychiatry, head div. biol. psychiatry, 1964-84, emeritus prof. psychiatry, 1985—; dir. Inst. Christian Growth, Burlington, N.C., 1985—; chief neurophysiol. labs. VA Hosp., Durham, N.C., 1961-76; sec. Am. Bd. Qualification in Electroencephalography, 1971-77; mem. N.C. Gov.'s Task force on Diagnosis and Treatment; mem. med. adv. com. N.C. Found. Mental Health Rsch.; bd. dirs. nat. div. Contact Teleminstry USA, also mem. internat. commn. healing; cons. numerous area hosps.; Finch lectr. Fuller Theol. Sem., Pasadena, Calif., 1974; vis. prof. psychiatry Marshall U. Sch. Medicine, Huntington, W.Va., 1985-89. Co-author: The Grace to Grow; editor: Applications of Electroencephalography in Psychiatry; co-editor: EEG and Evoked Potentials in Psychiatry and Behavioral Neurology; Contbr. med. jours. Mem. ofcl. bd. Asbury United Methodist Ch., Durham; mem. program and curriculum com. United Meth. Ch., 1973-81; trustee Meth. Retirement Home, Durham, N.C.; pres. United Meth. Renewal Services, Inc., 1978-82. Served with AUS, 1943-46. Recipient Ephraim McDowell award Christian Med. Found., 1982, Pioneer in Christian Psychiatry award Congress on Christian Counseling, 1988; named Educator of Yr., Christian Med. and Dental Soc., 1996; EEG Montreal Neurol. Inst. fellow, 1954-55, postdoctoral fellow NIMH. Mem. Am. Psychiatric Assn., So. Psychiatric Assn. (pres. 1977-78), AMA, So. Med. Assn. (chmn. sect. neurology and psychiatry 1970), Med. Soc. N.C., Durham-Orange County Med. Soc. (chmn. student recruitment com. 1965), Soc. Biol. Psychiatry, Am. EEG Soc. (councillor), So. EEG Soc. (pres. 1964), Assn. Research Nervous and Mental Diseases, Am. Epilepsy Soc., AAAS, Am. Acad. Neurology, Sigma Xi, Alpha Omega Alpha. Republican. Club: U.S. Power Squadron (comdr. Durham 1971). Home: 1209 Virginia Ave Durham NC 27705-3263 Office: PO Box 2347 Burlington NC 27216-2347

WILSON, WILLIAM R., JR., judge; b. 1939. Student, U. Ark., 1957-58; BA, Hendrix Coll., 1962; JD, Vanderbilt U., 1965. Atty. Autrey & Goodson, Texarkana, Ark., 1965-66, Wright, Lindsey & Jennings, Little Rock, 1969-72, Wilson & Hodge, Little Rock, 1972-74; prin. William R. Wilson Jr., P.A., Little Rock, 1974-80, Wilson & Engstrom, Little Rock, 1980-83, Wilson, Engstrom & Vowell, Little Rock, 1984, Wilson, Engstrom, Corum & Dudley, Little Rock, 1984-93; judge U.S. Dist. Ct. (ea. dist.) Ark., Little Rock, 1993—; chair Ark. Supreme Ct. Com. on Model Criminal Jury Instrns., 1978—; active Ark. Supreme Ct. Com. on Civil Practice, 1982—. Lt. USN, 1966-69. Named Disting. Alumnus, Hendrix Coll., 1993, Outstanding Lawyer, Pulaski County Bar Assn., 1993. Mem. ABA, ATLA, Am. Bd. Trial Advocates (Nat. Civil Justice award 1992), Am. Coll. Trial Lawyers, Internat. Acad. Trial Lawyers, Internat. Soc. Barristers, Ark. Bar Assn. (Outstanding Lawyer 1991), S.W. Ark. Bar Assn., Ark. Trial Lawyers Assn. (pres. 1982, Outstanding Trial Lawyer 1988-89). Office: US Dist Ct Ark 600 W Capitol Ave Rm 153 Little Rock AR 72201-3329*

WILSON, WILLIAM STANLEY, oceanographer; b. Alexander City, Ala., June 5, 1938; s. Norman W. and Helen C. (Hackemack) W.; m. Anne M. Stout; children: Lauren, Jonathan (dec.). BS, William & Mary Coll., 1959, MA, 1965; PhD, Johns Hopkins U., 1972. Marine biol. collector Va. Inst. Marine Sci., Gloucester Point, 1959-62, computer systems analyst, 1964-65; computer systems analyst Chesapeake Bay Inst., Balt., 1965-66; phys. oceanography program mgr. Office of Naval Rsch., Washington, 1972-78; chief oceanic processes program NASA, Washington, 1979-89, program scientist earth observing system, 1989-92; asst. adminstr. for ocean svcs. and coastal zone mgmt. NOAA, Washington, 1992-95, deputy chief scientist, 1995—. Recipient Antarctica Svc. medal NSF, 1961, Superior Civilian Svc. award USN, 1979, Exceptional Sci. Achievement medal NASA, 1981, Disting. Achievement award MIS and Compass Publs., 1989, award Remote Sensing Soc., 1992, medal French Space Agy., 1994, Portuguese Naval Cross, 1997/. Mem. Am. Meteorol. Soc., Am. Geophys. Union (Ocean Scis. award 1984), Oceanography Soc. (com. chmn. 1989-92), The Coastal Soc., Sigma Xi, Omicron Delta Kappa. Avocations: bicycling, scuba diving, gardening. Home: 219 Tunbridge Rd Baltimore MD 21212-3423 Office: HCHB Rm 5224 14th & Constituion NW Washington DC 20230

WILSON-WEBB, NANCY LOU, adult educational administrator; b. Maypearl, Tex., Jan. 20, 1932; d. Madison Grady and Mary Nancy Pearson (Haney) Wilson; m. John Crawford Webb, July 29, 1972. BS magna cum laude, Abilene (Tex.) Christian U., 1953; MEd with high honors, Tex. Christian U., 1985. Cert. tchr., adult edn. dir., sch. adminstr., Tex. Tchr. elem. grades Ft. Worth Ind. Sch. Dist., 1953-67, adult edn. tchr., 1970-73; dir. adult edn. consortium for 38 sch. dists. Tex. Edn. Agy., 1973—; pres. Nat. Commn. on Adult Basic Edn., 1994-95; pres. Tex. Adult Edn. Adminstrn., 1994; apptd. mem. Tex. State Literacy Coun., 1987—, Tex. State Sch. Bd. Commn., 1994-95; exec. bd. Tex. Coun. Co-op Dirs., 1989—; apptd. to Gov. Ann Richard's Task Force for Edn. Cons. to textbooks: On Your Mark?, 1994, others. Pres. Jr. Womans Club, Ft. Worth, 1969, Fine Arts Guild, Tex. Christian U., Ft. Worth, 1970-72, Ft. Worth Womens Civic Club Coun., 1970; active Exec. Libr. Bd., Ft. Worth, 1990—; apptd. bd. dirs. Literacy Plus in North Tex., 1988, Greater Ft. Worth Literacy Coun.; commr. Ed-16 Task Forces Tex. Edn. Agy., 1985-94; literacy bd. dirs. Friends of Libr., 1967—, Opera Guild Bd. Ft. Worth, 1965—, Johnson County (Tex.) Corrs. Bd.; bd. dirs. Salvation Army, 1991-95. Recipient Bevy award Jr. Womans Club, 1968, Proclamation Commrs. Ct. Outstanding 43 Yr. Literacy Svc. to Tarrant County, 1994, Tarrant County Woman of Yr. award, Fort Worth Star Telegram, 1995, Outstanding Leadership award Ft. Worth ISD Sch. Bd., 1995; named one of Most Outstanding Educators in U.S. Nat. Assn. Adult Edn., 1983, Most Outstanding Woman Edn., City of Ft. Worth, 1991, others; nominated to Tex. Hall of Fame for Women, 1991; scholar Germany, 1983. Mem. NEA, DAR (v.p. Mitshan Keith chpt. 1997-98, Nat. Most Outstanding Literacy award 1992, Leadership Literacy award 1985-87, 89, 94), AAUW, Am. Assn. Adult and Cont. Edn. (v.p. 1987-89, chair 1993 internat. conv. 1992), Tex. Assn. Adult and Cont. Edn. (pres. 1985-86, Most Outstanding Adult Adminstr. in Tex. 1984), Tex. Coun. Adult Edn. Dirs. (pres.), Coun. World Affairs (bd. dirs. 1980-92), Am. Bus. Women's Assn., Ft. Worth C. of C., Lecture Found., Internat. Reading Assn. (Literacy Challenge award 1991), Ft. Worth Adminstrv. Assn., Zonta, Ft. Worth Garden Club, Woman's Club, Ft. Worth Petroleum Club, Carousel Dance Assn., Optimist Club (Ft. Worth), Met. Dinner Dance Club, Ridglea County Club, Crescent Club, Alpha Delta Kappa (Nat. Literacy award 1992), Phi Delta Kappa. Mem. Church of Christ. Home: 3716 Fox Hollow St Fort Worth TX 76109-2616 Office: 100 N University Dr Fort Worth TX 76107-1360

WILSTED, JOY, elementary education educator, reading specialist, parenting consultant; b. St. Marys, Pa., Aug. 12, 1935; d. Wayne and Carrie (Neiger) Furman; m. Richard William Wilsted, Feb. 14, 1982; 2 children. BA, Fla. Atlantic U., 1970; MS in Edn., Old Dominion U., Norfolk, Va., 1975. Cert. reading specialist, elem. tchr., Mo.; cert. permanent tchr., N.Y. Tchr. creative dramatics Hillsboro Country Day Sch., Pompano Beach, Fla., 1966-68; tchr. PTA Kindergarten, Boca Raton, Fla., 1968-69; tchr. creative dramatics Wee-Wisdom Montessori Sch., Delray Beach, Fla., 1969-70; elem. tchr. Birmingham (Mich.) Pub. Schs., 1970-72; classroom and reading resource tchr. Chesapeake (Va.) Pub. Schs., 1972-79; reading coord. Harrisonville (Mo.) Pub. Schs., 1979-81; Chpt. I reading tchr., reading improvement tchr. North Kansas City Pub. Schs., Kansas City, Mo., 1981-96; instr. continuing edn. U. Mo., Kansas City, 1980-87, Ottawa U., Overland Park, Kans., 1990—; cons. Young Authors' Conf., Oakland U., Rochester, Mich., 1971; coord. fine arts Alpha Phi Alpha Tutorial Project, Chesapeake, 1973-75; presenter Chpt. I Summer Inst., Tech. Asistance Ctr., Mo., 1984; cons. on parenting Reading Success Unltd., Gallatin, Mo., 1987—; mem. adv. bd. Parents & Children Together, Ind. U. Family Literacy Ctr., Bloomington, 1990-93; keynote speaker ann conf. Nat. Coalition of Chapter I Parents. Author: Dramatics for Self-Expression, 1967, Now Johnny CAN Learn to Read, 1987, Reading Songs and Poems of Joy, 1987, Character-Building Poems for Young People. Mem. Internat. Reading Assn. (mem. coun., pres. local coun. 1986-88, state chmn. parents and reading com. 1988-89, mem. nat. parents and reading com. 1989-92, keynote spkr. IRA Conf. Inst. 1990, local coun., Literacy award 1989). Office: Reading SUCCESS Unltd PO Box 215 Gallatin MO 64640-0215

WILT, JEFFREY LYNN, pulmonary and critical care physician; b. Fairmont, W.Va., Nov. 15, 1963; s. Paul Lynn and Linda (Amos) W. BA, U. Mich., 1986, MD, 1988. Diplomate Am. Bd. Internat. Medicine, subspecialty pulmonary diseases and critical care medicine, Am. Bd. Med. Examiners; cert. ACLS. Resident in internal medicine Blodgett/St. Mary's Hosp., Grand Rapids, Mich., 1988-91, chief med. resident in internal medicine, 1990-91; asst. dir. internal medicine residency St. Mary's Hosp., Grand Rapids, 1992; fellow sect. pulmonary and critical care W.Va. U., Morgantown, 1992-95; asst. dir. MICU Blodgett Meml. Med. Ctr. Mem. ACP (Nat. Clin. Vignette winner 1991), AMA, Am. Thoracic Soc., Am. Coll Chest Physicians (Young Investigators award 1993), Soc. Crit. Care Medicine. Republican. Avocations: bicycling, karate, magic, reading, swimming. Home: 3410 Winterberry Ct SE Grand Rapids MI 49546-7251 Office: 1900 Wealthy St SE Ste 150 Grand Rapids MI 49506-2969

WILTROUT, ANN ELIZABETH, foreign language educator; b. Elkhart, Ind., Aug. 3, 1939; d. F. LeRoy and Margaret Elizabeth (Williams) W. BA, Hanover Coll., 1961; MA, Ind. U., 1964, PhD, 1968. Vis. asst. prof. Ind. U., Bloomington, 1968-69; asst. prof. Miss. State U., Mississippi State, 1969-71, assoc. prof., 1971-87, prof., 1987—; NEH fellow in residence Duke U., 1977-78. Author: A Patron and a Playwright in Renaissance Spain, 1987; contbr. articles to profl. publs. Recipient Disting. Svc. cert. Inst. Internat. Edn., 1986. Mem. AAUP, MLA (del. to assembly 1975-78), Assn. Internat. Hispanistas, Cervantes Soc. Am., Am. Assn. Tchrs. of Spanish and Portuguese, Assn. Hispanic Classical Theater, Soc. Scholars in Arts and Scis.,

Phi Kappa Phi, Sigma Delta Pi. Avocations: Shakespeare, travel, reading, roses. Office: Miss State U Dept Fgn Langs Drawer FL Mississippi State MS 39762

WILTSE, JAMES CLARK, civil engineer; b. Dearborn, Mich., Apr. 14, 1927; s. Cecil C. and Mary G. (Brashear) W.; m. Marlyn R. Glatus, Feb. 14, 1953; children: Richard, Mary, Michael. BSCE, U. Mich., 1953. Registered profl. engr., Mass. Civil engr. U.S. Army C.E., Detroit, 1954-67; project engr. USAF Civil Engring., London, 1968-72; civil engr. USN Facilities Engring. Command, Norfolk, Va., 1973-75; chief engr. USN Resident Office, Keflavik, Iceland, 1976-81; staff civil engr. USAF Electronic Systems Div., Kaiserslautern, Germany, 1982-91; spl. asst. ROICC Norfolk, Lantnavfac Eng Com, Norfolk, Va., 1992-93; quality assurance engr. HQ Lantnavfac, 1993-94; ret., 1994. Sgt. U.S. Army, 1946-47, Japan. Fellow ASCE (life); mem. Soc. Am. Mil. Engrs. Home: 8555 Lawson Ave Norfolk VA 23503-5220

WIMBERLY, EVELYN LOUISE RUSSELL, nursing coordinator; b. Tallulah, La., Feb. 7, 1941; d. Luther Franklin and Marion Gertrude (Martin) Russell; m. William Lary Wimberly, Mar. 29, 1963; children: Collin, Holly, Allison. BSN, Northwestern State U., 1963; MSN, Northwestern State U. La., 1994. Head nurse Hanna Hosp., Coushatta, La.; dir. nurses Sr. Citizen Ctrs., Coushatta; evening supr. Riverside Med. Ctr., Bossier City, La.; house supr. La. State U. Hosp., Shreveport, coord. nursing quality improvement and policy and procedure. Mem. ANA, La. Nurses Assn., Sigma Theta Tau (Beta Chi chpt.). Home: PO Box 145 Hall Summit LA 71034-0145

WIMBERLY, MARK VINCENT, utility executive; b. Port St. Joe, Fla., Aug. 28, 1957; s. George Herbert Jr. and Dorothy Mae (Minus) W.; m. Mary Susan Hendrix, Sept. 13, 1980; children: Ashleigh Kristen, John Raymond, Allison Kathleen. BS in Indsl. Rels. Mgmt., Auburn U., 1980. EEO rep. Ala. Power Co., Birmingham, 1980-81, staff asst., 1980-81; supr. compliance Ala. Power Co., Wilsonville, 1981-83; asst. to sr. v.p. Ala. Power Co., Birmingham, 1995-96; coord. coop. program Miss. Power Co., Gulfport, 1985-90; mgr. fed. affairs Miss. Power Co., Washington, 1990-92; mgr. bus. devel. So. Energy, Melbourne, Australia, 1992-94; dist. mgr. Gulf Power Co., Panama City, Fla., 1996—; bd. dirs., mem. exec. com. Australian Infrastructure Devel. Com., Sydney, 1993-94. Pres. Ocean Springs (Fla.) Kiwanis Club,, 1988, 89; bd. dirs. United Way of N.W. Fla., Panama, 1997, ARC, Panama City, 1997; mem. adv. bd. Fla. State U. Panama City Found., 1996-97. Mem. Rotary. Methodist. Office: Gulf Power Co 1230 E 15th St Panama City FL 32405-6132

WIMBROW, PETER AYERS, III, lawyer; b. Salisbury, Md., Apr. 11, 1947; s. Peter Ayers Jr. and Margaret (Johnson) W. BS, East Tenn. State U., 1970; JD, Washington and Lee U., 1973. Bar: Md. 1973, U.S. Dist. Ct. Md. 1974, U.S. Ct. Appeals (4th cir.) 1979, U.S. Supreme Ct. 1979, U.S. Tax Ct. 1981, U.S. Ct. Appeals (D.C. cir.) 1981, U.S. Ct. Appeals (3d cir.) 1985. Sole practice, Ocean City, Md., 1974—. Photographer, cast mem.: (film) Clear and Present Danger. Mem. City Solicitor Feasibility Study Com., Ocean City; contbg. editor Coconut Times. Mem. WWII com. Berlin Heritage Found. Mem. ABA, ATLA, Md. Bar Assn. (bd. govs., program com., membership com., centennial com.), Worcester County Bar Assn. (sec., treas., v.p., pres., chmn. com. on athletic endeavors), Md. Trial Lawyers Assn., Md. Criminal Def. Attys. Assn., Appellate Jud. Nominating Commn., Nat. Criminal Def. Attys. Assn. Republican. Home: Seatime Condominium 136 St 502-n Ocean City MD 21842 Office: PO Box 56 4100 Coastal Hwy Ocean City MD 21842

WIMMER, MAUREEN KATHRYN, chemical engineer; b. Quakertown, Pa., Oct. 25, 1969; d. Ronald Homer and Jane (Astheimer) W. BSChemE, Lehigh U., 1992. Engring. intern Gen. Chem., Claymont, Del., 1991; process control engr. Johnson Matthey CSD, Wayne, Pa., 1992-94, washcoat engr., 1994-97; process engr. Ashland Chem. Co., Easton, Pa., 1997—. Mem. AIChE. Republican. Lutheran. Avocations: music, movies. Home: 2212B Catasauqua Rd Bethlehem PA 18018 Office: 400 Island Park Rd Easton PA 18042-6814

WIMMER, NANCY T., lawyer; b. Newark, Jan. 13, 1951; d. Harold and Gilda (Schwartz) Tainow; m. Howard A. Wimmer, Sept. 1, 1974; 2 children. BS magna cum laude, Temple U., 1973; JD, Temple U. Sch. Law, 1994. Bar: Pa. 1995. Staff atty. Cmty. Health Law Project, Camden, N.J., 1993-96; legal cons. elder law project Temple U., Phila., 1994; mng. atty., dir. Cancer Patient Legal Advocacy Network, Pa., 1994—. Mem. Pa. Bar Assn., Phila. Bar Assn., Northeast Reg. Ca. Inst. (adv. bd.), Linda Creed Br. Ca. Found. (adv. bd.), Nat. Br. Ca. Coalition.

WIMPEE, MARY ELIZABETH, elementary school educator; b. Karnes City, Tex., Nov. 23, 1952; d. Bernarr Floyd and Mary Jane (Putnam) Plummer; m. William Eugene Wimpee, June 7, 1975; 1 child, Matthew David. BS in Elem. Edn., Baylor U., 1974. Cert. elem. tchr., Tex. Resource tchr. 1st and 2nd grades Kenedy (Tex.) Ind. Sch. Dist., 1975-76; kindergarten tutor Stride Learning Ctr., F.E. Warren AFB, Wyo., 1976-78, infant stimulation therapy asst., 1978-80; kindergarten tchr. Stockdale (Tex.) Ind. Sch. Dist., 1980-81; kindergarten tchr. Edgewood Ind. Sch. Dist., San Antonio, 1981-83, 1st grade tchr., 1983-85, 2nd grade tchr., reading lang., gifted and talented tchr., 1989-93, instrnl. specialist, gifted and talented tchr., 1993-94; 3rd grade tchr. Winston Elem. Sch., San Antonio, 1994—; 2nd grade tchr. Winston Elem. Sch., 1996-97; 3rd grade tutor Wake County, Cary, N.C., 1985-86, 3rd grade tchr., 1986-89. Co-author: Curriculum Writing for Kindergarten and Second Grade Gifted and Talented, 1991. Mem. Edgewood Classrm. Tchrs. Assn. (rep. 1990—). Baptist. Avocations: Longaberger basket collecting, cross stitching, reading, collecting cook books, collecting cat meow houses. Home: 9658 Chelmsford San Antonio TX 78239-2308 Office: Winston Elem 2500 S General Mcmullen Dr San Antonio TX 78226-1657

WIMPRESS, GORDON DUNCAN, JR., corporate consultant, foundation executive; b. Riverside, Calif., Apr. 10, 1922; s. Gordon Duncan and Maude A. (Waldo) W.; m. Jean Margaret Skerry, Nov. 30, 1946; children—Wendy Jo, Victoria Jean, Gordon Duncan III. B.A., U. Oreg., Eugene, 1946, M.A., 1951; Ph.D., U. Denver, 1958; LL.D., Monmouth Coll., Ill., 1970; L.H.D., Tusculum Coll., Greenville, Tenn., 1971. Lic. comml. pilot. Dir. pub. relations, instr. journalism Whittier (Calif.) Coll., 1946-51; asst. to pres. Colo. Sch. Mines, Golden, 1951-59; pres. Monticello Coll., Alton, Ill., 1959-64, Monmouth Coll., Ill., 1964-70, Trinity U., San Antonio, 1970-77; vice chmn. S.W. Found. for Biomed. Rsch., San Antonio, 1977-82, pres., 1982-92, also bd. govs.; pres. Duncan Wimpress & Assocs., Inc., San Antonio, 1992—; commr. Burlington No. R.R. scholarship selection com.; chmn. Valero Energy Corp. scholarship commn.; bd. dirs. Southwest Rsch. Inst. Author: American Journalism Comes of Age, 1950. Bd. dirs. Am. Inst. Character Edn., ARC, Am. Heart Assn., Cancer Therapy and Rsch. Found.; trustee San Antonio Med. Found., Eisenhower Med. Ctr., Rancho Mirage, Calif.; mem. San Antonio Fiesta Commn.; ruling elder United Presbyn. Ch., U.S.A.; mem. adv. bd. Alamo Area chpt. Am. Diabetes Assn. 1st lt. AUS, 1942-45, ETO. Decorated Bronze Star. Mem. Aircraft Owners and Pilots Assn., Am. Acad. Polit. and Social Sci., Am. Assn. Higher Edn., MENSA, Nat. Pilots Assn., Pilots Internat. Assn., Inc., Quiet Birdmen, Greater San Antonio C. of C. (bd. dirs.), North San Antonio C. of C. (bd. dirs.), Assn. Former Intelligence Officers, Confederate Air Force, Pi Gamma Mu, Sigma Delta Chi, Sigma Delta Pi, Sigma Phi Epsilon (trustee found.), Sigma Upsilon, Newcomen Soc. N.Am. Clubs: Argyle, St. Anthony, San Antonio Country, the Dominion (bd. govs.), City , Plaza, San Antonio Golf Assn. Lodge: Rotary (dist. gov. 1983-84, San Antonio). Avocations: golf, skiing, flying. Office: PO Box 780818 San Antonio TX 78278-0818

WIN, KHIN SWE, anesthesiologist; b. Rangoon, Burma, Sept. 27, 1934; came to U.S., 1962; d. U Mg and Daw Aye (Kyin) Maung; m. M. Shein Win, May 28, 1959; children: Tha Shein, Thwe Shein, Maw Shein, Thet Shein, Htoo Shein. Intermediate of Sci. Degree, U. Rangoon, 1954, MB, BS, 1962. Intern Waltham (Mass.) Hosp., 1962-63; resident anesthesiology Boston City Hosp., 1963-65; fellow pediatric anesthesiology New Eng. Med. Ctr. Hosps., Boston, 1965-66; fellow anesthesiology Martin Luther King Jr. Gen. Hosp., L.A., 1978-79; pvt. practice anesthesiology Apple Valley, Calif., 1984—; asst. prof. anesthesiology Martin Luther King Jr./Charles R. Drew Med. Ctr., L.A., 1979-84. Republican. Buddhist. Avocations: gardening, meditation. Home: 13850 Pamlico Rd Apple Valley CA 92307-5400 Office: St Mary Desert Valley Hosp Dept Anesthesiology 18300 Us Highway 18 Apple Valley CA 92307-2206

WINAWER, SIDNEY JEROME, physician, clinical investigator, educator; b. N.Y.C.; s. Nathan and Sally Winawer; children: Daniel, Jonathan, Joanna. BA, NYU, 1952; MD, SUNY, N.Y.C., 1956. Asst. in medicine Harvard Med. Sch., Boston, 1962-66; asst. physician Harvard Med. Svc. Boston City Hosp., 1964-66; with Meml. Sloan-Kettering Cancer Ctr., N.Y.C., 1978—, head lab for gastroent. cancer rsch., 1988—, chief gastroent. and nutrition svc., 1988—, mem. with tenure of title, 1988—, Paul Sherlock chair, 1991—; prof. medicine Cornell U. Coll. Medicine, N.Y.C., 1980—; head Ctr. for Prevention Colon Cancer WHO, Geneva, 1985; liason rep. Nat. Cancer Adv. Bd., Washington, 1984-89; mem. adv. com. on cancer prevention Am. Cancer Soc., 1988-90; mem. sci. adv. bd. ICRF; cons. various rev. coms., Nat. Cancer Inst., Washington. Editor: Prevention Colorectal Cancer, 1980, Basic and Clinical Perspectives of Colorectal Polyps and Cancer, 1988, Lar Bowel Cancers: Policy, Prevention, Research and Treatment, 1991, Management of Gastrointestinal Disease, 1992, Gastrointestinal Cancer, 1992, Cancer of the Colon, Rectum and Anus, 1994, Cancer Free, 1995; contbr. chpts. to books, articles to profl. jours. Capt. USAF, 1959-61. Nat. Cancer Inst. grantee 1974, 77, 80 (2), 85, 88 , 90. Fellow ACP, Am. Coll. Gastroenterology (pres. 1979-80, Disting. Sci. Achievement award 1982, Baker Presdl. lectr. 1992, Master 1993); mem. Am. Soc. Gastrointestinal Endoscopy (bd. dirs. 1974-78, disting. lectr. 1985, Schindler award 1994), Am. Gastroent. Assn. (nat. chmn. cancer sect. 1989-91), Am. Soc. Clin. Oncology, Am. Assn. Cancer Rsch., N.Y. Soc. Gastrointestinal Endoscopy (founder, pres. 1978-79, ann. lectr. 1985). Jewish. Avocations: opera, biking, cross-country skiing, sailing, dancing. Office: Meml Sloan-Kettering Cancer Ctr 1275 York Ave New York NY 10021-6007

WINBERRY, JOSEPH PAUL, JR., optometrist; b. Passaic, N.J., Apr. 25, 1957; s. Joseph Paul Sr. and Doris Evelyn (Tiernan) W.; m. Paula Ann Winberry, Oct. 14, 1989. BS, Dickinson Coll., 1979; OD, Ill. Coll. Optometry, 1987. Assoc. optometrist Eye Care Assocs., Harrisburg, Pa., 1987-88; optometrist Sears Optical, York, Pa., 1989-91, Camp Hill (Pa.) Eye Care, Camp Hill, Pa., 1991—; bd. dirs. Tri-County Assn. for Blind, Harrisburg, 1992—. Author The Keystoner newsletter, 1992; contbr. articles to profl. jours. Pres. Dickinson Club Chgo., 1993-87; mem. Big Bros. Chgo., 1985-87; chairperson Alumni Admission Program, Dickinson Coll., 1987—, chmn. 15th class reunion, 1994. Recipient Harold Kohn award Am. Optometric Found., 1987; named one of Outstanding Young Men Am., 1984. Fellow Am. Acad. Optometry; mem. Am. Aptometric Assn., Ctrl. Pa. Optometry Soc. (pres., v.p., sec., treas. 1989—, Optometrist of Yr. 1991), Pa. Optometric Assn. (trustee 1996, sec.-treas. 1997), Astron. Soc. Harrisburg, KC, Lions (Camp Hill v.p. 1991-97), Beta Theta Pi (scholarship 1976). Democrat. Methodist. Avocations: golf, astronomy, sailing, hiking, travel. Home: 134 Lancaster Blvd Mechanicsburg PA 17055 Office: Camp Hill Eye Care 3028 Market St Ste 3 Camp Hill PA 17011-4592

WINBURY, MARTIN MAURICE, pharmaceutical executive, educator; b. N.Y.C., Aug. 4, 1918; s. Ervin and Helen (Stein) W.; m. Blanche Mary Simons, July 11, 1942; children: Nancy Ellen, Gail Elizabeth. BS, L.I. U., 1940; MS, U. Md., 1942; PhD, NYU, 1951. Rsch. fellow U. Md., College Park, 1940-42, U.S. Bur. of Mines, College Park, 1942-44; scientist Merck Inst. Therapy Rsch., Rahway, N.J., 1944-47; pharmacologist G. D. Searle, Skokie, Ill., 1947-55; dir. pharmacology Schering Corp., Bloomfield, N.J., 1955-61, Warner Lambert, Morris Plains, N.J., 1961-80; dir. sci. devel. Warner Lambert, Ann Arbor, Mich., 1980-86, ret., 1986; pres. InterPharm, Ann Arbor, 1986—; mem. faculty U. Mich. Med. Sch., Ann Arbor, 1986—. Contbr. articles to profl. jours. Fellow AAAS, Am Coll. Cardiology, N.Y. Acad. Scis.; mem. Am. Soc. Pharmacology and Exptl. Therapy, Am. Heart Assn., Gordon Rsch. Conf. (chmn.). Achievements include findings in mechanism of nitroglycerin action-redistribution of coronary blood flow. Home: 3600 Windemere Dr Ann Arbor MI 48105-2844 Office: InterPharm PO Box 8335 Ann Arbor MI 48107-8335

WINBY, MARY BERNADETTE, marketing executive; b. N.Y.C., Sept. 16, 1958; d. John Joseph and Theresa Eunice (Schoeffler) Vasile; m. Allan Gerard Winby, July 21, 1990. BSBA, St. John's U., Jamaica, N.Y., 1980. V.p. mktg. IBM Mid-Hudson Employees Fed. Credit Union, Kingston, N.Y., 1989-92; officer, dir. mktg. Mid-Hudson Savings Bank, FSB, 1992-94; pres., owner The Mktg. Analysts, Patterson, N.Y., 1994—; pres., owner Freelance Advt. Co., Poughkeepsie, N.Y., 1982-88; cons., tchr. in field. Office: The Mktg Analysts Hampshire Ctr Rte 311 Patterson NY 12563

WINCENC, CAROL, concertizing flutist, educator; b. Buffalo, June 29, 1949; d. Joseph and Margaret (Miller) Wincenc; m. Douglas Webster; 1 child, Nicola Wincenc-Webster. Grad., Santa Cecilia Acad., Rome, 1967, Chigiana Acad., Siena, Italy, 1968; MusB, Manhattan Sch. Music, N.Y.C., 1971; MusM, Juilliard Sch. Music, N.Y.C., 1972. Concertizing flutist recs. with Deutsche, Gramaphon, Nonesuch, New World, Music Masters, and Decca records; soloist with major symphony orchs.; artist faculty Juilliard Sch., 1988—. Bd. dirs., v.p. Chamber Music Am., N.Y.C., 1990-91, 91—. Recipient Naumburg award, 1978. Mem. Nat. Flute Assn. (life, bd. dirs.). Home: 875 W End Ave Apt 14E New York NY 10025-4954 Office: The Juilliard Sch Lincoln Ctr New York NY 10023

WINCER, SIMON, film director. Films include Harlequin, 1980, The Day After Halloween, 1981, Phar Lap, 1984, D.A.R.Y.L., 1985, The Lighthorsemen, 1987, Quigley Down Under, 1990, Harley Davidson and the Marlboro Man, 1991, Free Willy, 1993, Operation Dumbo Drop, 1995, The Phantom, 1996; exec. prodr.: The Man From Snowy River, 1982, One Night Stand, 1983; TV dir.: The Girl Who Spelled Freedom, 1986, The Last Frontier, 1986, Bluegrass, Lonesome Dove, 1989 (Outstanding Direction Emmy award 1989); cons. The Adventures of the Black Stallion, 1990. Office: c/o Creative Artists Agency 9830 Wilshire Blvd Beverly Hills CA 90212-1804

WINCE-SMITH, DEBORAH L., federal agency administrator; m. Michael B. Smith; 2 children. Grad. magna cum laude, Vassar Coll., 1972; Master's, Cambridge (Eng.) U., 1974. Former program mgr. internat. programs NSF; asst. dir. internat. affairs and global competitiveness Office of Sci. and Tech. Policy The White House, 1984-89; asst. sec. tech. policy Dept. Commerce, Washington, 1989-93; sr. fellow Coun. on Competitiveness, Washington, 1993—; sr. fellow Congl. Econ. Leadership Inst., Washington, 1993—. Office: Coun on Competitiveness 1401 H St NW Ste 650 Washington DC 20005-2110*

WINCH, TERENCE PATRICK, publications director, writer; b. N.Y.C., Nov. 1, 1945; s. Patrick and Bridie (Flynn) W.; m. Susan Francis Campbell, Nov. 8, 1981; 1 child, Michael Campbell. BA summa cum laude, Iona Coll., 1967; MA, Fordham U., 1968, postgrad. Book critic Book World The Washington Post, 1975-81; editor-in-chief Revue Mag. Olsson's Books and Records, 1983-84; editor, resident assoc. program Smithsonian Instn., Washington, 1985-86, acting chief of publs., sr. editor Nat. Mus. Am. Art, 1986-92, head of publs. Nat. Mus. Am. Indian, 1992—. Author: (book of poems) Irish Musicians/American Friends, 1986 (Am. Book award 1986), The Great Indoors, 1995 (Columbia Book award 1996), (collection of short stories) Contenders, 1989; musician, composer: (album with group Celtic Thunder) The Light of Other Days, 1988 (INDIE award 1989); editor: (books) American Art at the 19th-Century Paris Salons, 1990, Homecoming: The Art and Life of William H. Johnson, 1991, Between Home and Heaven: Contemporary American Landscape Photography, 1992, Native American Dance, 1992, All Roads Are Good: Native Voices on Life and Culture, 1994; contbr. to periodicals including Washington Post, New Republic, Paris Rev., Am. Poetry Rev. Bklyn. Rev. Creative writing fellow NEA, 1992, Yaddo fellow, 1975, NDEA doctoral fellow Fordham U.; writing grantee D.C. Commn. on Arts and Humanities, 1992, Md. State Arts Commn., 1997; artist-in-residence Corcoran Sch. of Art, 1975-76; scholar Iona Coll. Mem. Nat. Acad. Rec. Arts and Scis. Democrat. Office: Smithsonian Instn Nat Mus Am Indian # 7103 470 Lenfant Plz SW Ste 7103 Washington DC 20024-2124

WINCHELL, GEORGE WILLIAM, curriculum and technology educator; b. Coldwater, Mich., Nov. 12, 1948; s. Elwood F. and Ethel L. (DeBray) W.; m. Marcia A. Hersh, June 7, 1969 (dec.); 1 child, Paul Michael. BA, Mich. State U., 1969; diploma, Leningrad (USSR) State U., 1967; MA, Mich. State U., 1973; EdS, Cen. Mich. U., 1982. Cert. elem., secondary, Russian, lang. arts and social sci. tchr.; cert. adminstr., supt., elem. prin. Elem. tchr. Silverton (Colo.) Pub. Schs.; tech. edn. cons. Stanton, Mich.; off-campus instr. Cen. Mich. U., Mt. Pleasant; profl. devel. coord., facilitator strategic planning, dir. instrn. Ctrl. Montcalm Pub. Sch., Stanton; dir. tech. edn. Cen. Montcalm Pub. Sch., Stanton; continuing edn. instr. Grand Valley State U., Allendale. Mem. ASCD, Internat. Soc. Tech. Edn., Mich. Assn. Computer Users in Learning, Nat. Staff Devel. Coun. Office: Ctrl Montcalm Pub Sch PO Box 9 Stanton MI 48888-0009

WINCHELL, MARGARET WEBSTER ST. CLAIR, realtor; b. Clinton, Tenn., Jan. 26, 1923; d. Robert Love and Mayme Jane (Warwick) Webster; student Denison U., 1940, Miami U., Oxford (Ohio), 1947, 48; m. Charles M. Winchell, June 7, 1941; children—David Alan (dec.), Margaret Winchell Boyle; m. 2d, Robert George Sterrett, July 15, 1977 (dec. 1982). Saleswoman Fred K.A. Schmidt & Shirmer real estate, Cin., 1960-66, Cline Realtors, Cin., 1966-70; owner, broker Winchell's Showplace Realtors, Cin., 1972—; ins. agt. United Liberty Life Ins. Co., 1966—, dist. mgr., 1967-70, 77-82, regional mgr., 1982—; stockbroker Waddell & Reed, Columbus, Ohio, 1972—, Security Counselors; ins. broker, 1984, gen. agent; dir. Fin. Consultants, 1984, 85, 86, 87, owner; instr. evening coll. Treas., v.p. Parents without Partners, 1969, sec., 1968; pres. PTA; dir. Children's Bible Fellowship Ohio, 1953-76; dir. Child Evangelism Cin.; nat. speaker Child Evangelism Fellowship and Nat. Sunday Sch. Convs., 1955-57; pres. Christian Solos, 1974, Hamilton Fairfield Singles; chaplain Bethesda N. Hosp.; leader singles groups Hyde Park Community United Meth. Ch.; vol leader, sr. dance leader Sycamore Sr. Ctr., 1990-97; annuity and ins. specialist for Fin. Consultants, 1982—. Mem. Nat. Assn. Real Estate Bds. West Shell Realtors (v.p.), Womens Council Real Estate Bd. (treas.). Clubs: Alfonta, Travel go go, Guys and Gals Singles (founder, 1st pres.), Hamilton Singles (pres.). Home and Office: 8221 Margaret Ln Cincinnati OH 45242-5309

WINCHESTER, KENNETH JAMES, publisher; b. N.Y.C., Aug. 21, 1952; s. James and Josephine Winchester; m. Fiona Gilsenan, Feb. 14, 1993; children: Maeve, James, Patricia. BA in History, Coll. of Wooster, Ohio, 1974; MS in Forestry, U. Toronto, 1976. Staff writer Outdoor Can. Mag., Toronto, 1976-77; assoc. editor Reader's Digest Can., Montreal, 1978-83; founder, pub. St. Remy Press, Montreal and N.Y.C., 1983-94; editorial dir. Sunset Pub., Menlo Park, Calif., 1994-96; pub. new media Time Inc., San Francisco, 1996—. Pub. website Virtual Garden, 1996; editor: Western Garden Book, 1995; pub. series Art of Woodworking, 1993—, Explore Am., 1995—. Recipient Interactive Summit award I.I.C.S., 1995, i Magic award Select Media, 1996, Best of the Web, PC World, 1996. Office: Time Inc New Media 221 Main St # 460 San Francisco CA 94105

WINCOR, MICHAEL Z., psychopharmacology educator, clinician, researcher; b. Chgo., Feb. 9, 1946; s. Emanuel and Rose (Kershner) W.; m. Emily E.M. Smythe; children: Meghan Heather, Katherine Rose. SB in Zoology, U. Chgo., 1966; PharmD, U. So. Calif., 1978. Rsch. project specialist U. Chgo. Sleep Lab., 1968-75; psychiat. pharmacist Brotman Med. Ctr., Culver City, Calif., 1979-83; asst. prof. U. So. Calif., L.A., 1983-97, assoc. prof., 1997—; cons. Fed. Bur. Prisons Drug Abuse Program, Terminal Island, Calif., 1978-81, Nat. Inst. Drug Abuse, Bethesda, Md., 1981, The Upjohn Co., Kalamazoo, 1982-87, 91-92, Area XXIV Profl. Stds. Rev. Orgn., L.A., 1983, Brotman Med. Ctr., Culver City, Calif., 1983-88, SmithKline Beecham Pharms., Phila., 1990-93, Tokyo Coll. of Pharmacy, 1991, G. D. Searle & Co., Chgo., 1992—. Contbr. more than 40 articles to profl. jours., chpts. to books, papers presented at nat. and internat. meetings and reviewer. Mem. adv. coun. Franklin Avenue Sch., 1986-89; trustee Sequoyah Sch., 1992-93; mem. tech. com. Ivanhoe Sch., 1993-96. Recipient Cert. Appreciation, Mayor of L.A., 1981, Bristol Labs Award, 1978, DuPont Pharma Innovative Pharmacy Practice award, 1995, Pharmacy Coun. Mental Health award, 1996; Faculty scholar U. So. Calif. Sch. Pharmacy, 1978. Mem. Am. Coll. Clin. Pharmacy (chmn. constn. and bylaws com. 1983-84, mem. credentials com. 1991-93, 95-97, ednl. affairs com. 1994), Am. Assn. Colls. Pharmacy (focus group on liberalization profl. curriculum 1990-92, mem. pharmacy practice planning commn. 1996-97), Am. Soc. Health-Sys. Pharmacists (chmn. edn. and tng. adv. working group 1985-88, chmn. com. on academia 1996-97), Am. Pharm. Assn. (del. ann. meeting ho. of dels. 1989), Sleep Rsch. Soc., Am. Sleep Disorders Assn., Calif. Pharmacists Assn. (trustee 1997—), U. So. Calif. Sch. Pharmacy Alumni Assn. (bd. dirs. 1979—), Rho Chi. Avocation: photography. Office: U So Calif 1985 Zonal Ave Los Angeles CA 90033-1058

WIND, HERBERT WARREN, writer; b. Brockton, Mass., Aug. 11, 1916; s. Max E. and Dora O. Wind. BA, Yale U., 1937; MA, Cambridge U., Eng., 1939. Staff writer New Yorker mag., N.Y.C., 1947-54, 62-90, Sporting Scene; editor, writer Sports Illustrated mag., N.Y.C., 1954-60; cons., writer, assoc. producer TV series Shell's Wonderful World of Golf, 1961-62; tchr. seminar on lit. of sports, Yale U., 1973. Author: The Story of American Golf, 1948, revised 1956, 75, (with Ben Hogan) The Modern Fundamentals of Golf, 1957, (with Jack Nicklaus) The Greatest Game of All, 1969, Game, Set, and Match, collection of tennis articles, 1979, Following Through, collection of golf articles, 1985; editor The Classics of Golf reprint series, 1983—. With USAAF, 1942-46, PTO. Mem. Oxford and Cambridge Golfing Soc., Yale Golf Assn., Royal and Ancient Golf Club of St. Andrews. Home: 32 Jericho Rd Weston MA 02193-1210

WINDELS, PAUL, JR., lawyer; b. Bklyn., Nov. 13, 1921; s. Paul and Louise E. (Gross) W.; m. Patricia Ripley, Sept. 10, 1955; children: Paul III, Mary H., James H.R., Patrick D. AB, Princeton U., 1943; LLB, Harvard U., 1948. Bar: N.Y. 1949. Spl. asst. counsel N.Y. State Crime Commn., 1951; asst. U.S. atty. Ea. Dist. N.Y., 1953-56; N.Y. regional adminstr. SEC, 1956-61, also spl. asst. U.S. atty. for prosecution securities frauds, 1956-58; lectr. law Am. Inst. Banking, 1950-57; mem. Windels, Marx, Davies & Ives and predecessor firms, 1961-88, of counsel, 1988—. Author: Our Securities Markets-Some SEC Problems and Techniques, 1962. Trustee, chmn. Bklyn. Law Sch., Lycée Francais N.Y.; trustee Princeton U. Rowing Assn., Knox Sch., Lexington Sch. for the Deaf, Gerta Charitable trust; past pres. Fed. Bar Coun.; mem. adv. bd. NYU Inst. French Studies, SUNY Marine Scis. Rsch. Sta.; bd. dirs. Horticulture Soc. N.Y. Capt. F.A., AUS, 1943-46, ETO; maj. USAR. Recipient Flemming award for fed. svc.; decorated chevalier Order French Acad. Palms; officer Nat. Order Merit France. Fellow Am. Bar Found.; mem. ABA, N.Y. State Bar Assn., Assn. of Bar of City of N.Y. Republican. Presbyterian. Office: Windels Marx Davies & Ives 156 W 56th St New York NY 10019-3800

WINDER, ALVIN ELIOT, public health educator, clinical psychologist; b. N.Y.C., Feb. 17, 1923; s. Martin Winder and Frances (Erdrick) Isaacson; m. Barbara Ina Dietz, July 19, 1949; children: Mark, Joshua, Sarah, Susan. BA, CUNY, 1947; MS, U. Ill., 1948; PhD, U. Chgo., 1952; MPH, U. Calif., Berkeley, 1980. Lic. clin. psychologist, Mass. Chief psychologist VA Hosp., Downey, Ill., 1953-56; rsch. asst., asst. prof. Clark U., Worcester, Mass., 1956-58; chief psychologist VA Clinic, Springfield, Mass., 1958-61; assoc. prof. psychology Springfield Coll., 1961-63; chmn. psychology dept. Westfield (Mass.) State Coll., 1963-65; assoc. prof. counseling edn. Sch. Edn., U. Mass., Amherst, 1965-69, prof., dir. grad. program div. nursing, 1969-78, prof. Sch. Pub. Health, 1978-93; dir. planning, cons. Springfield (Mass.) Pub. Health Dept., 1993-95; adj. prof. Sch. Pub. Health, Boston U., 1995—; assoc. to exec. sec. Asian Pacific Assn. for Control of Tobacco, 1988—. Author: Introduction to Health Education, 1984, Solid Waste Education Recycling Directory, 1989; editor: Adolescence Contemporary Studies, 1974; guest editor Jour. Applied Behavior, 1970; co-editor: Internat. Quar. of Cmty. Health Edn., 1992—. Sr. selectman Town of Leverett, Mass., 1988-90; Lilly Found. mentor U. Mass., 1989. Grantee U.S. Childrens Bur., 1966, 67, Dexter Found., 1969, NIMH, 1974, Nat. Cancer Inst., 1986-91. Mem. APHA, APA. Avocations: dressage, handball, tennis. Home and Office: 84 Booth Rd Dedham MA 02026-5702

WINDER, CLARENCE LELAND, psychologist, educator; b. Osborne County, Kans., June 16, 1921; s. Clarence McKinley and Edna (Ikenberry) W.; m. Elizabeth Jane Jacobs, Aug. 14, 1943; children: David William, Christina Louise. Student, Santa Barbara State Coll., 1941; AB with honors, U. Calif. at Los Angeles, 1943; MA, Stanford U., 1946, PhD, 1949. From instr. to assoc. prof. Stanford U., 1949-61; dir. Psychol. Clinic, 1953-61;

prof., dir. Psychol. Clinic, Mich. State U., 1961-62, prof. psychology, 1961-91, prof. emeritus, 1991—, chmn. dept., 1963-67; dean Coll. Social Sci. Mich. State U., 1967-74, assoc. provost, 1974-77, provost, 1977-86, provost emeritus, 1991—; prof., dir. Psychol. Svcs. Ctr., U. So. Calif., 1962-63; spl. rsch. psychol. aspects schizophrenia, parent-child rels., personality devel., and higher edn. adminstrn. 1st lt. USAAF, 1943-45. Decorated Air medal with 7 clusters, D.F.C. Fellow APA, AAAS; mem. Sigma Xi. Home: 1776 Hitching Post Rd East Lansing MI 48823-2144

WINDER, DAVID KENT, federal judge; b. Salt Lake City, June 8, 1932; s. Edwin Kent and Alma Eliza (Cannon) W.; m. Pamela Martin, June 24, 1955; children: Ann, Kay, James. BA, U. Utah, 1955; LLB, Stanford U., 1958. Bar: Utah 1958, Calif. 1958. Assoc. firm Clyde, Mecham & Pratt Salt Lake City, 1958-66; law clk. to chief justice Utah Supreme Ct., 1958-59; dep. county atty. Salt Lake County, 1959-63; chief dep. dist. atty., 1965-66; asst. U.S. atty. Salt Lake City, 1963-65; partner firm Strong & Hanni, Salt Lake City, 1966-77; judge State of Utah Dist. Ct., Salt Lake City, 1977-79; U.S. Dist. judge Utah, 1979-93, chief U.S. Dist. judge, 1993-97; examiner Utah Bar Examiners, 1975-79, chmn., 1977-79. Served with USAF, 1951-52. Mem. Am. Bd. Trial Advocates, Utah State Bar (Judge of Yr. award 1978), Salt Lake County Bar Assn., Calif. State Bar. Democrat. Office: US Dist Ct 235 US Courthouse 350 S Main St Salt Lake City UT 84101-2106

WINDER, RICHARD EARNEST, legal foundation administrator, writer, consultant; b. Vernal, Utah, Sept. 23, 1950; s. William Wallace and Winnifred (Jenkins) W.; m. Janice Fay Walker, Apr. 19, 1975; children: Scott Christian, Eric John, Brian Geoffrey, Laura Jeanne, Amy Elizabeth. BA magna cum laude, Brigham Young U., 1974, JD cum laude, 1978; MBA with honors, U. Michigan, Flint, 1988. Bar: Utah 1978, U.S. Dist. Ct. Utah 1978, Mich. 1979, U.S. Dist. Ct. (ea. and we. dists.) Mich. 1979. Tchg. asst., grad. instr. Brigham Young U., Provo, Utah, 1976-78; law clk. Willingham & Coté, E. Lansing, Mich., 1978-79, atty., 1979-87; exec. v.p. Mgmt. Leasing, Inc., Battle Creek, Mich., 1987-88, Mgmt. Options, Inc., Lansing, Mich., 1988-91; fin. mgr. Mich. State Bar Found., Lansing, Mich., 1991-94, dep. dir., fin. mgr., 1994—; panelist 9th Nat. Legis. Conf. Small Bus., San Antonio, 1987; adj. prof. Davenport Coll. Bus., Lansing, 1990-92, mgmt. adv. com., 1993-96; mem. founding steering com. Capital Quality Initiative, Lansing, 1992-96; liaison State Bar Mich. Long Range Planning Process, 1996—; co-founder, rsch. prin. Quality Dynamics Rsch. Inst., Haslett, Mich., 1994—. Author: (with others) Value Sharing: Value Building, 1990, Corporate Orienteering, 1995; contbr., bd. editors: Summary of Utah Real Property Law, 1978. Vol. leader Boy Scouts Am., Chief Okemos Coun., Lansing, 1978—. Mem. ABA, Am. Soc. Quality Control (chmn. Lansing-Jackson sect. 1994-95, spkr. and writer 1992—), Mich. Bar Assn., Utah Bar Assn., Lansing Regional C. of C. (small bus. coun., MBA task force Bus. and Edn. com. 1988-92, recipient Chmn.'s award 1992), Beta Gamma Sigma. Republican. Mem. LDS Ch. Avocations: writing, speaking, computer technology, research, teaching. Office: Michigan State Bar Found 306 Townsend St Lansing MI 48933-2012

WINDER, ROBERT OWEN, retired mathematician, computer engineer executive; b. Boston, Oct. 9, 1934; s. Claude V. and Harriet O. W.; m. Kathleen C. Winder; children by previous marriage: Katherine, Amy. A.B., U. Chgo., 1954; B.S., U. Mich., 1956; M.S., Princeton U., 1958, Ph.D., 1962. With RCA, 1957-78; group head RCA, Princeton and Somerville, N.J., 1969-75; dir. microprocessors RCA, 1975-77, dir. systems, 1977-78; mgr. workstation devel. Exxon Enterprises, Inc., Princeton, 1978-85; v.p. Syntex Computer Systems Inc., Bordentown, N.J., 1985-88; mgr. product engring., Princeton Operation Intel Corp., 1988-93; mgr. engring. ops. Video Products Div., Intel, Chandler, Ariz., 1993-95; ret., 1995. Contbr. articles to profl. jours.; patentee in field. NSF fellow, 1956-57; Recipient David Sarnoff award RCA, 1975. Fellow IEEE.

WINDHAGER, ERICH ERNST, physiologist, educator; b. Vienna, Austria, Nov. 4, 1928; came to U.S., 1954; s. Maximilian and Bertha (Feitzinger) W.; m. Helga A. Rapant, June 18, 1956; children: Evelyn Ann, Karen Alice. MD, U. Vienna, 1954. Research fellow in biophysics Harvard Med. Sch., Boston, 1956-58; instr. in physiology Cornell U. Med. Coll., N.Y.C., 1958-61; vis. scientist U. Copenhagen, 1961-63; asst. to prof. physiology Cornell U. Med. Coll., N.Y.C., 1963—, Maxwell M. Upson prof. physiology and biophysics, 1978—, chmn. dept. physiology, 1973—. Recipient Homer W. Smith award N.Y. Heart Assn., 1978. Office: Cornell U Med Coll Dept Physiology 1300 York Ave New York NY 10021-4805

WINDHAM, CUYLER LARUE, police official; b. Lamar, S.C., Nov. 29, 1936; s. Raymond Baxter and Zeloise (Parnell) W.; m. Mary Frances Dowling, Aug. 24, 1955; children: Cuyler LaRue Jr., David Baxter. Student, Ben Franklin U., 1956. With fingerprint divsn. FBI, Washington, 1955-57; night security clk. Charlotte (N.C.) divsn. FBI, 1957-62; condr. investigations resident agy. FBI, Fayetteville, N.C., 1962-67; spl. agt. N.C. State Bur. Investigation, Fayetteville & Kannapolis, 1967-72; supr. inter-agy. narcotics squad N.C. State Bur. Investigation, Fayetteville, 1968-72; asst. supr. Fayetteville divsn. N.C. State Bur. Investigation, 1972-73, asst. dir., 1974-85; sr. asst. dir. N.C. State Bur. Investigation, Fayetteville, 1985-94; ret., 1994; maj., chief of detectives Cumberland County Sheriff's Office, Fayetteville, 1994-95; chief dep. Cumberland County Sheriff's Office, Fayetteville, N.C., 1995—; speaker on law enforcement, violent crimes and narcotics problems, N.C. and southeastern U.S.; chmn. drug subcom. Law Enforcement Coord. Com., Ea. Dist. N.C.; mem. law enforcement adv. com. Seventh Congrl. Dist. N.C., 1997. Pres. Christian Peace Officers Assn., Cumberland County chpt., Fayetteville, 1991-92; deacon Southview Bapt. Ch., Hope Mills, N.C. Named Outstanding Young Law Enforcement Officer Cumberland County, Cape Fear Jaycees, 1970-71; recipient 1st place award for outstanding young law enforcement officer N.C., N.C. Jaycees, 1971. Mem. Law Enforcement Officers Assn. (com. mem. statewide violent crimes task force, violent crimes com.), Law Enforcement Officers Alumni Assn. (pres. nat. tng. inst. drug enforcement adminstrn. 1977), Gamecock Club. Democrat. Baptist. Home: 112 Bledsoe St Hope Mills NC 28348-9701

WINDHAUSER, JOHN WILLIAM, journalism educator; b. Rochester, N.Y., Jan. 30, 1943; s. Milton Edward and Mary Ellen (McDonald) W.; m. Marlene Marie Most. BS, Tri-State U., 1966; MA, Ball State U., 1967; PhD, Ohio U., 1975. Editor, reporter, advt. and pub. relations positions, 1964-77; asst. prof. journalism Colo. State U., Ft. Collins, 1971-77, Bradley U., Peoria, Ill., 1977-78; assoc. prof., dir. research ctr. U. Miss., Oxford, 1978-82; prof. La. State U., Baton Rouge, 1982—; cons. in field; research judge Soc. Profl. Journalists; editorial bd. Journalism Quarterly, Coll. Media Rev., Newspaper Research Jour. Author: The Editorial Process, 1978, 2d edit., 1985; co-editor, co-author: The Media in the 1984 and 1988 Presidential Campaigns, 1991; contbr. numerous articles to profl. jours.; editor Profl. Jour., Coll. Press Rev., 1972-81. Recipient Life Membership award Nat. Council Coll. Publs. Advisers, 1981, Presdl. award Nat. Council Coll. Publs. Advisers, 1973-81. Mem. Assn. for Edn. in Journalism, Speech Communication Assn., The So. Speech Assn. Office: Sch Journalism La State U Baton Rouge LA 70803

WINDHORST, JOHN WILLIAM, JR., lawyer; b. Mpls., July 6, 1940; s. John William and Ardus Ruth (Bottge) W.; m. Diana Margarita Aranda, Feb. 15, 1975; 1 child, Diana Elizabeth. AB, Harvard U., 1962; LLB, U. Minn., 1965. Bar: Minn. 1965, U.S. Tax Ct., U.S. Ct. Appeals (8th cir.) 1965, U.S. Dist. Ct. Minn. 1967, U.S. Supreme Ct. 1975. Law clk. to Hon. H.A. Blackmun U.S. Cir. Ct., Rochester, Minn., 1965-66; assoc. Dorsey & Whitney, Mpls., 1966-70; with office of Revisor of Statutes State of Minn., 1967, 69; ptnr. Dorsey & Whitney, 1971-96, of counsel, 1997—. Bd. dirs. St. Paul Chamber Orch., 1980-86, Harry A. Blackmun Scholarship Found., 1996—. Mem. ABA (com. on state and local taxes), Minn. State Bar Assn., Hennepin County Bar Assn., Mpls. Athletic Club, Skylight Club, Harvard Club of Minn. (pres. 1977-78). Home: 4907 Lakeview Dr Minneapolis MN 55424-1525

WINDMAN, ARNOLD LEWIS, retired mechanical engineer; b. N.Y.C., Oct. 17, 1926; s. Raphael and Anna (Wexler) W.; m. Patricia Foley, Dec. 13, 1967; children—Richard, Marjorie, Kevin, Colleen, Sean, JoAnn, Brian, William. B.M.E., Coll. City N.Y., 1947. Bar: registered profl. engr., N.Y., 13 other states. Project engr. F.E. Sutton, N.Y.C., 1947-50; with Syska & Hennessy, Inc., N.Y.C., 1950-90, pres., 1976-86, vice chmn., 1986-90, also bd. dirs.; pres. Am. Cons. Engrs. Coun., 1985-86; chmn. N.Y. State Bd. Engring. and Land Surveying, 1982-84; bd. dirs., v.p. Sea Pines Plantation. Bd. dirs. Phelps Meml. Hosp., Tarrytown, N.Y., 1974-82; planning commn. Hilton Head Island. Mem. Am. Soc. Heating, Refrigerating and Air Conditioning Engrs., chpt. pres. (1965), N.Y. Assn. Cons. Engrs. (pres. 1981-82, dir. 1977), ASME, Tau Beta Pi, Pi Tau Sigma. Democrat. Jewish. Home: 1919 S Beach Club Vl Hilton Head Island SC 29928-4068 *Professional integrity, enthusiasm, and a continuing effort to train younger people for advancement are three key ingredients of a successful career.*

WINDMULLER, JOHN PHILIP, industrial relations educator, consultant; b. Dortmund, Germany, Dec. 4, 1923; came to U.S., 1942; s. Solomon and Bertha (Kahn) W.; m. Ruth Heilbrun, Aug. 15, 1947; children: Betsey, Thomas. B.A., U. Ill., 1948; Ph.D., Cornell U., Ithaca, N.Y., 1951; postgrad., Grad. Inst. Internat. Studies, U. Geneva, 1957-58. Elections examiner NLRB, St. Louis, 1949; asst. prof. indsl. and labor relations Cornell U., 1951-54, assoc. prof., 1954-61, prof., 1961-83, dir. internat. activities N.Y. State Sch. Indsl. and Labor Relations, 1961-64, assoc. dean sch., 1975-77, Martin P. Catherwood prof. indsl. and labor relations, 1983-87; prof. emeritus, 1987—; vis. prof. Free U., Amsterdam, Netherlands, 1964-65; sr. staff mem. ILO, Geneva, 1971-72, ILO Dir. Gen.'s rep. in Netherlands, 1984; vis. lectr. Dept. State, Germany, Austria, Netherlands, 1957-58, U. Istanbul, Turkey, 1958, Dept. State, Germany, 1964-65. Author: American Labor and the International Labor Movement, 1954, Labor Relations in the Netherlands, 1970, Collective Bargaining in Industrialized Market Economies: A Reappraisal, 1987, The International Trade Secretariats, 1991, rev., 1995; co-author: Convergence and Diversity in International and Comparative Industrial Relations, 1995; editor: Industrial Democracy in International Perspective, 1977; co-editor: Employers Associations and Industrial Relations, 1984; mem. editl. bd. Indsl. and Labor Relations Rev., 1953—; bd. editors Cornell U. Press, 1981-84, Labour (Rome), 1987-94. Recipient Silver medal Gov. Netherlands Minister Social Affairs, 1970; Fulbright sr. research fellow U.S. Commn. on Internat. Exchange, Netherlands, 1964-65; Ford Found. internat. relations fellow, 1957-58. Mem. Indsl. Relations Research Assn., Conseil Scientifique Institut de Travail, U. Bordeaux, Phi Beta Kappa, Phi Kappa Phi. Office: Cornell U NY State Indsl & Labor Rels Ithaca NY 14853-3901

WINDOM, HERBERT LYNN, oceanographer, environmental scientist; b. Macon, Ga., Apr. 23, 1941; m. Patricia Woodruff, 1963; children: Kevin, Elizabeth. BS, Fla. State U., 1963; MS, U. Calif., San Diego, 1965, PhD in Earth Sci., 1968. Prof. oceanography Skidaway Inst. Oceanography and Ga. Inst. Technology, Savannah, Ga., 1968-93, acting dir., 1994—. Mem. Am. Soc. Limnol. and Oceanography, Internat. Coun. ExplorSea, Am. Geophys. Union, Oceanography Soc. Office: Skidaway Inst of Oceanography 10 Ocean Science Cir Savannah GA 31411-1011

WINDSOR, JAMES THOMAS, JR., printing company executive, newspaper publisher; b. Blakely, Ga., July 30, 1924; s. James Thomas and Mary Alice (Blitch) W. Student, Emory Jr. Coll., Valdosta, Ga., 1941-42, Cardiff (Wales) U., 1945-46; BA, Emory U., 1947. Insp./scientist U.S. Argl. Rsch. Adminstrn., San Augustine, Tex., 1948; pres. J.T. Windsor & Co., McRae, Ga., 1949-65; v.p. McRae Industries, Inc., 1963-64; pers. dir. Sunbeam Corp., McRae, 1965-71; editor, pub. The Laurens County News, 1973-74; editor, publisher The Soperton (Ga.) News, 1971—, The Wheeler County Eagle, Alamo, Ga., 1975—, The Montgomery Monitor, Mt. Vernon, Ga., 1987—; pres. The Mulberry Bush, Inc., Soperton, 1985-89, Suburban Printing Corp., Higgston, Ga., 1972—. Editor: Blueprint for Progress, 1963 (Washington Model award), also cookbooks and hist. books; area newspaper columnist, 1971—. Mayor City of McRae, 1962-70; adminstr. Telfair County, McRae, 1965; pres. Telfair Redevel. Corp., 1963-64; former coun. bd. dirs. Boy Scouts Am., Macon, Ga.; bd. dirs. Million Pines Festival, Soperton, 1973-87, Ga. Mcpl. Assn., Atlanta, 1963-66; dir. Eastman (Ga.) Planning and Devel. Commn., 1965-70; supt. sch. McRae Meth. Ch., 1951-71; active Eagle Scouts Am. With AUS, 1943-46, ETO. Recipient 20 yrs. perfect attendance award McRae Meth. Ch. Sch. Mem. Ga. Press Assn. (numerous awards 1972—), Nat. Newspaper Assn., Montgomery County C. of C., Soperton-Treutlen C. of C., Telfair County C. of C. (pres.), Wheeler county C. of C., Jaycees (editor jour. 1959, 1st place Jour. in Nation award, Rebel Corps col. 1991—, One of 5 Ga. Outstanding Young Men award 1961), VFW, Am. Legion (post comdr. 1957-58), Treutlen County Sportsman Club, McRae Rotary Club (pres.), Toastmasters, Lions (pres. Soperton 1975-76, 15 yrs. perfect attendance award). Avocations: photography, reading, walking, writing, graphic arts. Home: 308 3rd St # 537 Soperton GA 30457 Office: Suburban Printing Corp RR 1 Ailey GA 30410-9801

WINDSOR, LAURENCE CHARLES, JR., publishing executive; b. Bronxville, N.Y., July 4, 1935; s. Laurence Charles and Margaret (Phalen) W.; m. Ruth Ester Lindstrom, 1977. Disting. grad., St. John's Mil. Acad., 1953; student, Grinnell Coll., 1953-55, U.S. Mil. Acad., 1957-58. V.p., dir. promotion Conover-Mast, 1960-67; assoc. promotion dir. Life mag., N.Y.C., 1967-70; merchandising dir. Life mag., 1970—; v.p., dir. advt. and pub. relations Sterling Communications subsidiary Time-Life; exec. v.p. Calderhead, Jackson, Inc., 1974-78; sr. v.p., dir. promotion Young and Rubicam Army Group, N.Y.C., 1978—; pub. relations cons. Penobscot Charitable Trust, 1966.; spl. asst. to postmaster gen. U.S., 1972-74. Appeared in motion picture The D.I., 1957. Mem. pub. edn. com. N.Y. Gov.'s Conf. on Alcohol Problems; mem. coun. Episcopal Ch. Found., pres.'s coun. Phoenix House; mem. adv. bd. Army ROTC. With USMC, 1955-61. Decorated Commemorative War Cross Royal Yugoslav Army; recipient citation of merit Wis. Res. Officers Assn., Am. Spirit Honor medal Citizen's Com. for Army, Navy, and Air Force, Inc., 1956. Mem. U.S. Sales Promotion Exec. Assn. (dir., named Promotion Exec. of Yr. 1969), Marine Corps Combat Corr. Assn. (sec.), West Point Soc. N.Y. (gov. 1967—), Publicity Club N.Y., Publicity Club Chgo., Nat. Acad. TV Arts and Scis., Internat. Radio and TV Soc., Am. Inst. Plant Engrs., Order Vet. Corps Arty. (lt. col., aide-de-camp, comdg. gen., coun. of adminstrn., Disting. Expert pistol award, 1st Provincial Regtl. medal, Order Centennial Legion), 7th Regt. Rifle Club, Marine Corps Pub. Affairs Unit, U.S. Darting Assn., Nat. Sci. Tchrs. Assn., Assn. U.S. Army (v.p. N.Y. chpt.), Am. Def. Preparedness Assn., Kosciuszko Assn., Marine Corps League, Employer Support of the Guard and Res. (N.Y. State Exec. Com.), Army-Navy Union, NRA, Conn. AAU of U.S., Nat. Jogging Assn., New Eng. Soc., Ends of Earth Assn. (chaplain), English Speaking Union, Sovereign Mil. Order of the Temple of Jerusalem, Time-Life Alumni Soc., Nat. Com. for Responsible Patriotism, St. Georges Soc., Nat. Eagle Scout Assn., Old Boys Assn., Nat. Fedn. Breeders of Giant Flemish Rabbits, Soc. Colonial Wars, Soc. Colonial Clergy, Order Descs. Colonial Govs., Order Colonial Acorn, SAR, Soc. Descs. Founders of Hartford, Order of St. Vincent, Soc. of 1812, Order Crown of Charlemagne in U.S.A., Order Lafayette, Sons and Daus. of Pilgrims, The Pilgrims, Sons of Colonial New England, N.Y. Geneal. and Biog. Soc., Met. Squash Racquets Assn., Church Club N.Y., Union League (v.p., bd. govs., chmn. pub. and mil. affairs), Manhattan Club, Bedford Bicycle Polo Club, Bombay Bicycle Club, Squadron A Club, Soldiers, Sailors and Airmens Club (bd. advisors), Road Runners Club, Alpha Phi Omega. Republican. Episcopalian (vestryman, lay reader). Office: Union League Club Box 7 38 E 37th St New York NY 10016-3095

WINDSOR, MARGARET EDEN, writer; b. Flemington, Mo., Aug. 10, 1917; d. John Denny and Rhoda Belle (Morgan) Head; m. Eugene B. Windsor, Jan. 10, 1987. Ret. med. technologist, 1982. Author: Murder in St. James, 1990, The Outhouse, 1996; editor: From Pandora's Box, 1993. Cpl. USAF, 1944-45. Mem. Columbia Chpt. Mo. Writers Guild (v.p. 1989-90). Democrat. Roman Catholic. Avocations: music, theatre, reading, television. Home: 2404 Iris Dr Columbia MO 65202-1265

WINDSOR, PATRICIA (KATONAH SUMMERTREE), author, educator, lecturer; b. N.Y.C., Sept. 21, 1938; d. Bernhard Edward and Antoinette (Gaus) Seelinger; m. Laurence Charles Windsor, Jr., Apr. 3, 1959 (div. 1978); children: Patience Wells, Laurence Edward; m. Stephen E. Altman, Sept. 21, 1986 (div. 1989). Student, Bennington Coll., 1956-58, Westchester Community Coll.; AA, NYU. V.p. Windsor-Morehead Assocs. N.Y.C., 1960-63; info. mgr. Family Planning Assn., London, 1974-76; faculty mem. Inst. Children's Lit., Redding Ridge, Conn., 1976-94; editor-in-chief AT&T, Washington, 1978-80; instr. U. Md. Writers Inst., Open Univ., Washington, 1980-82; creative developer, faculty mem. Long Ridge Writer's Group, Danbury, Conn., 1988—; dir. Summertree Studios, Savannah, Ga., 1992—; dir. Wordspring Lit. Cons., 1989—; dir. Devel. Writing Workshops, Katonah, N.Y., 1976-78; judge Internat. Assn. Bus. Communicators, Washington, 1979, 89; lectr. L.I. U., Jersey City State Coll., Skidmore Coll., others, 1987—; instr. Coastal Ga. Ctr. for Continuing Edn., 1996—, Armstrong Atlantic U. Continuing Edn., 1997—. Author: The Summer Before, 1973 (ALA Best Book award 1973, transl. 1980 Austrian State prize 1980, also Brit., Norwegian, German edits.), Something's Waiting for You, Baker D, 1974 (starred selection Libr. Jour., Brit., Japanese edits.), Home Is Where Your Feet Are Standing, 1975, Diving for Roses, 1976 (N.Y. Times Outstanding Book for Young Adults award, starred selection Libr. Jour.), Mad Martin, 1976, Killing Time, 1980, Demon Tree, 1983 (pen name Colin Daniel), The Sandman's Eyes, 1985 (Edgar Allan Poe Best Juvenile Mystery award Mystery Writers Am.), How a Weirdo and a Ghost Can Change Your Life, 1986, The Hero, 1988 (highest rating Voice of Youth Advocate), Just Like the Movies, 1990, The Christmas Killer, 1991 (Edgar nominee, Brit., Danish, French edits.), Two Weirdos and a Ghost, 1991, A Weird and Moogly Christmas, 1991, The Blooding, 1996, The House of Death, 1996; columnist The Blood Rev., 1990-92, Savannah Parent, 1990-92; columnist Coastal Senior, 1997—; also short stories in anthologies and mags.; actress: The Haunting of Hill House, City Lights Theatre Co., 1991. Mem. City Lights Theatre Co., Savannah, Ga., 1991. Mem. Children's Book Guild, Authors Guild, Poetry Soc. Ga., Savannah Storytellers. Avocations: skiing, painting, modern dance. Office: Writers House 21 W 26th St New York NY 10010-1003 Address: c/o Scholastic Books 555 Broadway New York NY 10012-3999

WINDSOR, WILLIAM EARL, consulting engineer, sales representative; b. Evansville, Ind., Jan. 24, 1927; s. Charles H. and Lora E. (Archey) W.; divorced; children: Kim, William, Robert. Student, Purdue U., 1946-50. Field engr. Philco Corp., Phila., 1950-53, Europe, Africa, Arabia; studio ops. engr. Sta. WFBM, Indpls., 1953-55; field engr. RCA Svc. Co., Cherry Hill, N.J., 1955-56; audio facilities engr. ABC, N.Y.C., 1956-62; rsch. engr. Fine Recording, Inc., N.Y.C., 1962-66; chief engr. A & R Recording, Inc., N.Y.C., 1966-68; chief engr., corp. sec. DB Audio Corp., N.Y.C., 1968-70; pres. Studio Cons., Inc., N.Y.C., 1970-72; sr. v.p., v.p., gen. mgr. Quad Eight Electronics-Quad Eight/Westrex, San Fernando, Calif., 1972-85; sr. mktg. exec. Mitsubishi Pro Audio Group, San Fernando, Calif., 1985-89; pres., CEO Quad Eight Electronics, Inc., Valencia, Calif., 1989-90; ind. cons., Valencia, 1991—. Inventor monitor mixer for multitrack audio consoles, 1967, update function for audio console automation, 1973; designer of new architecture for film scoring and film re-recording sound mixing consoles, 1974 (Acad. award 1974). Served with USNR, 1945-50. Fellow Audio Engring. Soc. (chmn. N.Y. sect. 1970); mem. Soc. Motion Picture & TV Engrs. Avocations: photography, foreign travel, art collecting. Home and Office: 23112 Yvette Ln Valencia CA 91355-3060

WINE, DONALD ARTHUR, lawyer; b. Oelwein, Iowa, Oct. 8, 1922; s. George A. and Gladys E. (Lisle) W.; m. Mary L. Schneider, Dec. 27, 1947; children: Mark, Marcia, James. B.A., Drake U., 1946; JD, State U. Iowa, 1949. Bar: Iowa 1949, D.C. 1968. Pvt. practice in Newport and Wine, 1949-61; U.S. atty. So. Dist. Iowa, 1961-65; of counsel Davis, Brown, Koehn, Shors & Roberts. Bd. dirs. Des Moines YMCA, 1963-75; bd. dirs. Salvation Army, 1969—, chmn., 1971; bd. dirs. Davenport YMCA, 1961; bd. dirs. Internat. Assn. Y's Men, 1957-59, area v.p., 1961; bd. dirs. Polk County Assn. Retarded Persons, 1991-95; mem. internat. com. YMCA's U.S. and Can., 1961-75; v.p. Iowa Council Chs.; pres. Des Moines Area Religious Coun. Found., 1992—; chmn. bd. trustees First Bapt. Ch., 1975; trustee U. Osteo. Medicine and Health Scis., 1980-95; Organizer Young Dems., Iowa, 1946; co-chmn. Scott County Citizens for Kennedy, 1960. Served to capt., navigator USAAF, 1943-45. Decorated D.F.C. Mem. ABA (chmn. com. jud. adminstrn. jr. bar sect. 1958), Iowa Bar Assn. (pres. jr. bar sect. 1957), Polk County Bar Assn. (sec. 1973-74), Des Moines C. of C. (chmn. city-state tax com. 1978-79, chmn. legis. com. 1979-84, bd. dirs. 1981), Des Moines Club, Masons, Kiwanis (pres. Downtown club 1969), Order of Coif, Sigma Alpha Epsilon. Office: 2500 Financial Ctr 666 Walnut St Des Moines IA 50309-3904

WINE, L. MARK, lawyer; b. Norfolk, Va., Apr. 16, 1945; s. Melvin Leon and Mildred Sylvia (Weiss) W.; m. Blanche Weintraub, June 8, 1969; children—Kim, Lara, Dana. B.A. with high honors, U. Va., 1967; J.D., U. Chgo., 1970. Bar: D.C. 1970, U.S. Supreme Ct. 1977. Assoc., Kirkland, Ellis & Rowe, Washington, 1970-72; trial atty. land and natural resources div. Dept. of Justice, Washington, 1972-78; ptnr. Kirkland & Ellis, Washington, 1978—. Mem. ABA. Office: Kirkland & Ellis 655 15th St NW Ste 1200 Washington DC 20005-5701

WINE, MARK PHILIP, lawyer; b. Iowa City, Jan. 6, 1949; s. Donald Arthur and Mary Lepha (Schneider) W.; children: Nicholas, Meredith Kathryn; m. Kathryn Bouquet Arneson, May 31, 1986. AB, Princeton U., 1971; JD, U. Iowa, 1974. Bar: Iowa 1974, Minn. 1976, U.S. Dist. Ct. Minn. 1976, U.S. Ct. Appeals (8th cir.) 1976, U.S. Supreme Ct. 1984, U.S. Ct. Appeals (4th cir.) 1985, U.S. Ct. Appeals (7th and Fed. cirs.) 1992. Law clk. to judge U.S. Ct. Appeals (8th cir.), St. Louis, 1974-76; ptnr. Oppenheimer Wolff & Donnelly, Mpls., 1976—. Mem. ABA, Minn. Bar Assn., Internat. Assn. Def. Counsel, Princeton Club N.W. Democrat. Congregationalist. Avocations: cooking, reading, biking, golf. Home: 2014 Stradella Rd Los Angeles CA 90077 Office: Oppenheimer Poms Smith 2029 Century Park E Fl 38 Los Angeles CA 90067-2901

WINE, SHERWIN THEODORE, rabbi; b. Detroit, Jan. 25, 1928; s. William Harry and Tillie (Israel) W. B.A., U. Mich., 1950, A.M., 1952; B.H.L., Hebrew Union Coll., Cin., M.H.L., 1956, rabbi, 1956. Rabbi Temple Beth El, Detroit, 1956-60, Windsor, Ont., Can., 1960-64; Rabbi Birmingham (Mich.) Temple, 1964—; cons. editor Humanistic Judaism, 1966—. Author: A Philosophy of Humanistic Judaism, 1965, Meditation Services for Humanistic Judaism, 1977, Humanistic Judaism-What Is It?, 1977, Humanist Haggadah, 1980, High Holidays for Humanists, 1980, Judaism Beyond God, 1985, Celebration, 1988, Staying Sane in a Crazy World, 1996. Founder Ctr. for New Thinking, Birmingham, 1977—; founder Soc. Humanistic Judaism, 1969; pres. N.Am. Com. for Humanism, 1982-93. Chaplain U.S. Army, 1956-58. Mem. Conf. Liberal Religion (chmn. 1985-96), Leadership Conf. Secular and Humanistic Jews (chmn. 1983-93), Internat. Inst. Secular Humanistic Judaism (co-chmn. 1986—), Internat. Assn. Humanist Educators, Counselors and Leaders (pres. 1988-93), Internat. Fedn. Secular Humanistic Jews (co-chmn. 1993—). Home: 362 Southfield Rd Birmingham MI 48009-3739 Office: 28611 W 12 Mile Rd Farmington MI 48334-4225

WINE-BANKS, JILL SUSAN, lawyer; b. Chgo., May 5, 1943; d. Bert S. and Sylvia Dawn (Simon) Wine; m. Ian David Volner, Aug. 21, 1965; m. Michael A. Banks, Jan. 12, 1980. BS, U. Ill.-Champaign-Urbana, 1964; JD, Columbia U., 1968; LLD (hon.), Hood Coll., 1975. Bar: N.Y. 1969, U.S. Ct. Appeals (4th cir.) 1969, U.S. Ct. Appeals (6th and 9th cirs.) 1973, U.S. Supreme Ct. 1974, D.C. 1976, Ill. 1980. Asst. press. and pub. rels. dir. Assembly of Captive European Nations, N.Y.C., 1965-66; trial atty. criminal div. organized crime and racketeering sect. and labor racketeering sect. U.S. Dept. Justice, 1969-73; asst. spl. prosecutor Watergate Spl. Prosecutor's Office, 1973-75; lectr. law seminar on trial practice Columbia U. Sch. Law, N.Y.C., 1975-77; assoc. Fried, Frank, Harris, Shriver & Kampelman, Washington, 1975-77; gen. counsel Dept. Army, Pentagon, Washington, 1977-79; ptnr. Jenner & Block, Chgo., 1980-84; solicitor gen. State of Ill. Office of Atty. Gen., 1984-86, dep. atty. gen., 1986-87; exec. v.p., chief oper. officer ABA, Chgo., 1987-90; pvt. practice law, 1990-92; bd. dirs. Cenvill Devel. Corp., 1991-92; v.p. Motorola Internat. Network Ventures Inc. and dir. transaction and govt. rels. group, Network Ventures Divsn., Motorola, 1992-97, chmn. bd., St Peters Telecom and Omni capital Inc.; dir. bus. devel. Motorola Cellular Infrastructure Group, 1997—; mem. EEC disting. vis. program European Parliament, 1987; bd. dirs. Cenvill Devel. Corp., 1991-92; chmn. bd. dirs. St. Petersburg Telecom, Russia, 1994—, Omni Capital Ptnrs., Inc., 1994—; mem. bd. assocs. program for the study of cultural values & ethics U. Ill. Recipient Spl. Achievement award U.S. Dept. Justice, 1972, Meritorious award, 1973, Cert. Outstanding Svc., 1975; decoration for Disting. Civilian Svc., Dept. Army, 1979; named Disting. Visitor to European Econ. Community. Mem. Internat. Women's Forum, The Chgo. Network, Econ. Club. Address: 3-4A 1441 W Shure Dr Arlington Heights IL 60004

WINEBERG, HOWARD, research director; b. N.Y.C., Aug. 30, 1955; s. Moe and Ruth (Blinder) W. BA, Bowling Green (Ohio) State U., 1977, MA, 1980; PhD, Johns Hopkins U., 1985. Demographer Indian Nations Coun. of Govts., Tulsa, 1985; asst. dir. Population Rsch. Ctr., prof. urban studies and planning Portland (Oreg.) State U., 1986—; co-founder Oreg. Demographic Group, Portland, 1990; Oreg. rep. to Fed.-State Coop. Program for Population Estimates, 1986—; mem. steering com. Fed.-State Coop. Program for Population Estimates, 1994—. Author: Do All Trails Lead to Oregon? Population Estimates for Oregon 1980-90, 91, 92, 93, 94, 95, 96; contbr. articles to profl. jours. Johns Hopkins U. fellow, 1980-82; Children's Svcs. Commn., grantee, 1989. Mem. Internat. Soc. for Philos. Enquiry, Population Assn. Am., Population Reference Bur., Soc. for Study of Social Biology, So. Demographic Assn., Oreg. Acad. Sci., Internat. Platform Assn. Avocations: racquetball, music. Office: Portland State U Population Rsch Ctr 1604 SW 10th Ave Portland OR 97201-3202

WINEGAR, ALBERT LEE, computer systems company executive; b. Beloit, Wis., Apr. 23, 1931; s. Albert Richard and Theo Rayneta (Hubbell) W.; m. Phyllis M. Everill, June 21, 1953; children: Bradford, Steven, Kristine, Kathleen. B.B.A., U. Wis., 1954; Stanford Sloan Exec. fellow, Stanford U., 1970. With IBM Corp., 1956-79, div. dir. mgmt. services, 1977-79; v.p. corp. planning, then group v.p. field ops. Olivetti Corp., Tarrytown, N.Y., 1979-80; pres. Olivetti Corp., 1980-81; v.p. field ops. NBI Inc., Boulder, Colo., 1981-84; pres., chief exec. officer Sensory, Inc., Santa Clara, Calif., 1984-85; pres., chief exec. officer VICOM Systems, Inc., Fremont, Calif., 1985-91, ret., 1991; bd. dirs. JRL Systems, Inc., ASI. V.p. bd. trustees Valley Hosp., Ridgewood, N.J., 1978-81; pres. N.J. Bus. Arts Found., 1977-78, Estates of Barton Creek Homeowners Assn., 1992-94. Capt. AUS, 1954-56. Mem. Computer and Bus. Equipment Mfrs. Assn. (dir. 1980-81), Barton Creek Country Club, Beta Theta Pi. Republican. Home: 8401 Hickory Creek Dr Austin TX 78735-1530

WINEGARDNER, ROSE MARY, special education educator; b. Granite City, Ill., Feb. 4, 1933; d. Arthur Udell and Margaret Helen (Brown) Barco; m. Carl Norman Winegardner, July 23, 1954; children: Laura Helen, Thelma Rose Winegardner Gordon, Jacob Harrison (dec.). BS in Edn., Mo. U., Columbia, 1954; MA in Ednl. Adminstrn., Wyo. U., 1977; edn. specialist, Nebr. U., 1988. Cert. tchr., Nebr., Iowa, Mo. Tchr. Elem. Sch. Grandview & Belton, Mo., 1957-64; tchr. mid. sch. Schleswig (Iowa) Community Schs., 1978-82; spl. edn. resource tchr. Ednl. Svc. Unit #4, Auburn, Nebr., 1982-94, Kans. U. Inst. Rsch. Learning trainer strategy implementation model, 1989—; spl. edn. resource tchr. Dawson-Verdon Consol. Schs., 1990—. Grantee Nebr. Dept. Edn., 1990-93. Mem. Internat. Reading Assn., Coun. for Exceptional Children (v.p. S.E. Nebr. chpt. 1990-92, pres. 1992-94, 94-96), DAR, Phi Delta Kappa, Zeta Tau Alpha. Lutheran. Home: 2100 23rd St Auburn NE 68305-2400

WINEKE, WILLIAM ROBERT, reporter, clergyman; b. Madison, Wis., Apr. 4, 1942; s. Edward Ervin and Jennie Mae (Lanigan) W.; m. Susan L. Detering, Dec. 9, 1964 (div. June 1975); children: Gregory, Andrew; m. Jacqueline Cone, Mar. 18, 1990. BS, U. Wis., 1965; BDiv, Chgo. Theol. Sem., 1969. Reporter Wis. State Jour., Madison, 1963-65; writer United Ch. of Christ, N.Y.C., 1966-68; pub. rels. dir. Chgo. (Ill.) Theol. Sem., Chgo., 1968-69; reporter Wis. State Jour., Madison, 1969—; chaplain Wis. Rescue Mission, Madison, 1977—; bd. rev. Wis. Health Policy Network, Madison, 1994—. Fellow Religions Pub. Rels. Soc., 1974; recipient Disting. Svc. award State Med. Soc. Wis., 1992, Disting. Svc. award LWV, Madison, 1994. Democrat. Home: 1024 Ridgewood Dr Stoughton WI 53589-4125 Office: Wis State Jour 1901 Fish Hatchery Rd Madison WI 53713-1248

WINELL, MARVIN, orthopaedic surgeon; b. N.Y.C., June 2, 1934; s. Irving David and Frances W.; children: Kenneth, Jonathan, Andrew; m. Dale Francine Lehmann, Nov. 2, 1968; children: Jennifer, Rachel, Douglas. BA, Columbia Coll., 1955; MD, SUNY, N.Y.C., 1961. Intern Kings County Hosp., N.Y.C., 1961-62, resident in surgery, 1962-63; rsch. fellow Columbia U. Orthop. Rsch. Lab., N.Y.C., 1963-64; orthop. surgery resident Columbia Presbyn. Med. Ctr., N.Y.C., 1964-67; orthop. surgeon Orthop. Tri-County Assoc., Plainfield, N.J., 1969—; asst. clin. prof. orthop. surgery Rutgers U., New Brunswick, N.J., 1975-80; chief orthop. surgery Muhlenberg Hosp., Plainfield, N.J., 1980-85; asst. clin. prof. orthop. surgery Columbia U., N.Y.C., 1988—. Maj. U.S. Army, 1967-69. Fellow Am. Acad. Orthop. Surgeons; mem. Am. Trauma Soc., Ea. Orthop. Soc. (founding mem.), N.J. Orthop. Soc. Office: Orthop Tri-County Assoc 1038 Edgewood Ave Plainfield NJ 07060-2612

WINER, WARD OTIS, mechanical engineer, educator; b. Grand Rapids, Mich., June 27, 1936; s. Mervin Augustus and Ina Katherine (Wood) W.; m. Mary Jo Wielinga, June 15, 1957; children: Mathew Owen, James Edward, Paul Andrew, Mary Margaret. Asso., Grand Rapids Jr. Coll., 1956; B.S., U. Mich., 1958, M.S., 1959, Ph.D., 1961; Ph.D. (Cavendish Lab. fellow), Cambridge (Eng.) U., 1961-63. Asst. prof. dept. mech. engring. U. Mich., Ann Arbor, 1963-66, assoc. prof., 1966-69; assoc. prof. mech. engring. Ga. Inst. Tech., 1969-71, prof., 1971-84, Regents' prof., 1984—, dir. George W. Woodruff Sch. Mech. Engring., 1988—, mem. exec. bd., 1983-88, chmn., 1984-86; chmn. Gordon Research Conf. on Friction, Lubrication and Wear, 1980; mem. NRC, 1980-88; chmn. Com. on Recommendations for U.S. Army Basic Sci. Research, 1985-87; mem. div. mech., structural, materials engring. adv. bd. NSF Engring. Directorate, 1984-89. Co-editor: Wear Control Handbook, 1980; tech. editor: Jour. Lubrication Tech., 1980-84, Jour. of Tribology, 1984-87; contbr. articles to profl. jours. Democratic precinct chmn., 1967-68; Mem. exec. bd. Horace H. Rackham Sch. Grad. Studies, U. Mich., 1968. Recipient Disting. Faculty Svc. award Coll. Engring. U. Mich., 1967, Cert. Recognition, NASA, 1977, Clarence E. Earle Meml. award Nat. Grease Lubricating Inst., 1979, Disting. Prof. award Ga. Inst. Tech., 1987. Fellow AAAS, ASME (bd. comms. 1987-81, v.p. rsch. 1989-93, Melville medal 1975, Centennial medallion 1980, Mayor D. Hersey award 1986, Charles Russ Richards Meml. award 1988), Soc. Tribologists and Lubrication Engrs. (bd. dirs. 1983-86, Nat. award 1997), Brit. Tribology Trust (gold medal 1987); mem. Am. Soc. Engring. Educators (Benjamin Garver Lamme award 1995, Donald Marlowe award 1996), NAE, Metro Atlanta Engring. Soc. (Engr. of Yr. 1989), Am. Acad. Mechanics, Soc. Rheology, Soc. Engring. Sci. (dir. 1980-84), AAUP (pres. Ga. Tech. chpt. 1972-74, v.p. state conf. 1973-75), Sigma Xi (chpt. pres. 1982-83, Sustained Rsch. in Engring. award 1975), Tau Beta Pi, Pi Tau Sigma, Phi Kappa Phi. Home: 1025 Mountain Creek Trl NW Atlanta GA 30328-3535

WINER, WARREN JAMES, insurance executive; b. Wichita, Kans., June 16, 1946; s. Henry Charles and Isabel (Ginsburg) W.; m. Mary Jean Kovacs, June 23, 1968 (div. Feb. 1973); m. Jo Lynn Sondag, May 3, 1975; children: Adam, Lauren. BS in Math., Stanford U., 1968. With Gen. Am. Life Ins. Co., St. Louis, 1968-73, dir. retirement plans, 1973-76, 2d v.p., 1976-80; v.p., sr. actuary Powers, Carpenter & Hall, St. Louis, 1980-84, sr. v.p., dir. pension div., 1984-85, pres., chief operating officer, 1985-86, lobbyist, commentator, 1985—, pres., chief exec. officer, 1986—; pres. W F Corroon, 1988-93; prin. William M. Mercer, 1993—, mng. dir., 1994-95; exec. v.p. Gen. Am. Life Ins. Co., St. Louis, 1995—; mem. Actuarial Exam. Com., Chgo., 1973-74. Contbr. articles to profl. jours. Bd. dirs. Lucky Lane Nursery Sch. Assn., St. Louis, 1978-93, pilot divsn. United Way, 1986-87; co-pres. Conway Sch. Parent Assn., 1986-87; bd. dirs. Paraquad, 1991—, chmn., 1994—; bd. dirs. ATD, 1992—. Fellow Soc. Actuaries; mem. Am. Acad. Actuaries, Enrollment of Actuaries (joint bd.), Am. Life Ins. Assn. (small case task force 1979-80), Life Office Mgmt. Assn. (ICPAC com. 1975-80), St. Louis Actuaries Club. Jewish. Clubs: St. Louis, Clayton (St. Louis). Avocations: bridge, wine tasting, swimming, weight tng. Office: Gen Am Life Ins Co 13045 Tesson Ferry Rd Saint Louis MO 63128-3407

WINETT, SAMUEL JOSEPH, manufacturing company executive; b. Chgo., June 15, 1934; s. Maurice and Ruby (Caplan) W.; m. Susan Carol Finkel, Apr. 24, 1957; children: Bradley, William, James. BS in Acctg., U. Ill., 1956; MBA, U. Chgo., 1970. CPA, Ill. Staff auditor Arthur Young & Co., Chgo., 1958-63; with Outboard Marine Corp., Waukegan, Ill., 1963-91, asst. controller, 1974-78, controller ops., 1978-86, v.p. fin., 1986-91; cons. QED Ptnrs., Chgo., 1993—. Served as 1st lt. U.S. Army, 1956-58. Mem. AICPA, Ill. CPA Soc., Fin. Execs. Inst., Assn. for Corp. Growth. Home: 3128 Mapleleaf Dr Glenview IL 60025-1123

WINFIELD, DAVID MARK, former professional baseball player, commentator; b. St. Paul, Oct. 3, 1951. Student, U. Minn.; LL.D.(hon.), Syracuse U., 1987. Player San Diego Padres (Nat. League), 1973-80, N.Y. Yankees (Am. League), 1980-90, Calif. Angels (Am. League), 1990-91; with Toronto Blue Jays (Am. League), 1991-92, Minnesota Twins (Am. League), 1992-94, Cleve. Indians, 1995; commentator Fox Broadcasting Co., Beverly Hills, Calif., 1996—; mem. Nat. League All-Star team, 1977-80, Am. League All-Star team, 1981-88; led Nat. League in total bases, 1979; played in World Series, 1981. Author (with Tom Parker) autobiography Winfield: A Player's Life, 1988. Recipient Golden glove, 1979-80, 82-85, 87, Silver Slugger award, 1981-85, 92; named top Sporting News All-Star Team, 1979, 82-84, 92; named Sporting News Am. League Comeback Player of Yr., 1990. Office: Fox Broadcasting Co PO Box 900 Beverly Hills CA 90213*

WINFIELD, JOHN BUCKNER, rheumatologist, educator; b. Kentfield, Calif., Mar. 19, 1942; s. R. Buckner and Margaret G. (Katterfelt) W.; m. Patricia Nichols (div. 1968); 1 child, Ann Gibson; m. Teresa Lee McGrath, 1969; children: John Buckner III, Virginia Lee. BA, Williams Coll., 1964; MD, Cornell U., 1968. Diplomate Am. Bd. Internal Medicine. Intern in medicine N.Y. Hosp., N.Y.C., 1968-69; staff assoc. LI/Nat. Inst. Allergy and Infectious Diseases NIH, Bethesda, Md., 1969-71; resident in medicine, fellow in rheumatology U. Va. Sch. Medicine, Charlottesville, 1971-73; fellow in immunology Rockefeller U., N.Y.C., 1973-75; asst. prof. medicine U. Va. Sch. Medicine, Charlottesville, 1975-76, assoc. prof. medicine, 1976-78; assoc. prof. medicine U. N.C., Chapel Hill, 1978-81, prof. medicine, 1981—, chief div. rheumatology and immunology, 1978—; dir. Thurston Arthritis Rsch. Ctr. U. N.C. Sch. Medicine, Chapel Hill, 1982—; Smith prof. medicine U. N.C. Sch. Med., Chapel Hill, 1987—; adv. coun. Nat. Inst. Arthritis and Musculoskeletal and Skin Diseases, NIH, 1988-92; chmn. edn. com. Am. Rheumatism Assn., Atlanta, 1980-84; immunol. scis. study sect. NIH, 1979-83, Arthritis Musculoskeletal and Skin study sect., 1992—; vice-chair fellowship com. Arthritis Found., 1982; med. coun. Lupus Found. Am., 1987—. Author more than 100 med. and sci. articles in peer reviewer rheumatology and immunology jours.; mem. editl. bd. Arthritis and Rheumatism, Bull. Rheumatic Diseases, Rheumatology Internat., Clin. Exptl. Rheumatology, Am. Jour. Medicine. Sr. asst. surgeon with USPHS, NIH, Bethesda, Md., 1968-71. Recipient Borden prize Cornell U. Med. Coll., 1964, numerous rsch. grants NIH and Arthritis Found., 1975—, Sr. Investigator award Arthritis Found., 1976-79, Kenan award U. N.C., 1985, NIH merit award, 1992. Fellow ACP; mem. Am. Assn. Immunologists, Am. Coll. Rheumatology, Am. Fedn. Clin. Rsch., Am. Soc. Clin. Investigation, Assn. Am. Physicians, Am. Clin. Climatol. Assn., Chapel Hill Country Club. Republican. Episcopalian. Avocations: golf, off-road motorcycling, scuba diving instructor. Home: 801 Kings Mill Rd Chapel Hill NC 27514-4920 Office: U NC Sch Medicine Thurston Arthritis Rsch Ctr CB 7280 Rm 3310 Chapel Hill NC 27599

WINFIELD, MICHAEL D., engineering company executive; b. 1939. BS in Chem. Engring., Ohio State U.; MBA, U. Chgo. Chem. engr. UOP, Des Plaines, Ill., 1962-74, mgr. refinery projects, 1974-76, asst. dir. tech. svcs., 1976-81, dir. bus. devel., 1981-83, v.p. tech. svcs., 1983-84, v.p. process svcs., 1984-92, pres., CEO, 1992—. Office: UOP 25 E Algonquin Rd Des Plaines IL 60016-6101*

WINFIELD, PAUL EDWARD, actor; b. L.A., May 22, 1941. Student, U. Portland, 1957-59, Stanford U., 1959, L.A. City Coll., 1959-63, UCLA, 1962-64. artist-in-residence Stanford U., 1964-65, U. Hawaii, 1965, U. Calif., Santa Barbara, 1970-71. Films include Gordons War, 1973, Huckleberry Finn, 1974, Conrack, 1974, Guess Who's Minding the Mint, 1969, Sounder, 1972 (Acad. Award nomination 1973), Hustle, 1975, Twilights Last Gleaming, 1976, A Hero Ain't Nothing But A Sandwich, 1978, Carbon Copy, 1981, White Dog, 1981, Star Trek II, 1982, Mike's Murder, 1982, On the Run, 1982, The Terminator, 1985, Blue City, 1986, Death Before Dishonor, 1987, The Serpent and the Rainbow, 1988, Presumed Innocent, 1990, Cliff Hanger, 1993, Dennis the Menace (The Movie), 1993, Kingdom of The Blind, 1994, The Mike Tyson Story, 1994, Fluke, 1994, Original Gangsters, 1995, Mars Attacks, 1995; TV appearances include Green Eyes, 1976, All Deliberate Speed, 1976, King, 1978 (Emmy nomination), Backstairs at the White House, 1979, The Blue and the Gray, 1982, Star Trek: Next Generation, 1992; guest star: TV appearances include Roots II (Emmy nomination), Angel City, 1980, Sisters, 1981, Sophisticated Gents, 1981, Go Tell It on the Mountain, 1983, Queen (miniseries), 1993, Scarlett (miniseries), 1994, Picket Fences, 1994 (Guest Actor in a Drama Emmy award), Touched By An Angel, 1995, Secrets of the Rose Garden, 1995; theatrical appearances include Checkmates, 1988, nat. tour A Few Good Men, 1992, Othello, Guthrie Theatre, 1993. Office: 5750 Wilshire Blvd Ste 590 Los Angeles CA 90036-3697

WINFREE, ARTHUR TAYLOR, biologist, educator; b. St. Petersburg, Fla., May 15, 1942; s. Charles Van and Dorothy Rose (Scheb) W.; m. Ji-Yun Yang, June 18, 1983; children: Rachael, Erik from previous marriage. B.Engring. in Physics, Cornell U., 1965; Ph.D. in Biology, Princeton U., 1970. Lic. pvt. pilot. Asst. prof. theoretical biology U. Chgo., 1969-72; assoc. prof. biology Purdue U., West Lafayette, Ind., 1972-79; prof. Purdue U., 1979-86; prof. ecology and evolutionary biology U. Ariz., Tucson, 1986-88, Regents' prof., 1989—; pres., dir. research Inst. Natural Philosophy, Inc., 1979-88. Author: The Geometry of Biological Time, 1980, When Time Breaks Down, 1986, The Timing of Biological Clocks, 1987. Recipient Career Devel. award NIH, 1973-78, The Einthoven award Einthoven Found. and Netherlands Royal Acad. Scis., 1989; NSF grantee, 1966—; MacArthur fellow, 1984-89, John Simon Guggenheim Meml. fellow, 1982. Home: 1210 E Placita De Graciela Tucson AZ 85718-2834 Office: U Ariz Dept Biology 326 BSW Tucson AZ 85721

WINFREY, CAREY WELLS, journalist, magazine editor; b. N.Y.C., Aug. 1, 1941; s. William Colin and Mary (Robinson) W.; m. Laurie Beardsley Platt, July 30, 1972 (div. 1980); m. Jane Elizabeth Keeney, Feb. 13, 1982; children: Graham William, Wells Millar. AB, Columbia U., N.Y.C., 1963, MS in Journalism, 1967. With Pub. Broadcasting Lab., NET; assoc. editor Time Inc., N.Y.C., 1968-71; exec. producer Ednl. Broadcast Corp., N.Y.C., 1971-77; reporter, fgn. corr. for Africa N.Y. Times, N.Y.C., 1977-80; mag. editor CBS Mags., N.Y.C., 1981-90, dir. video devel., 1981-83, editor Cuisine mag., 1983-84, v.p., editorial dir., 1985-87; v.p. Diamandis Comm., Inc. (formerly mag. divsn. CBS), N.Y.C., 1987-90, editor-in-chief Memories mag., 1987-90; editor-in-chief Am. Health mag. Reader's Digest Publs., N.Y.C., 9190-96; dir. Delacorte Ctr. for Mag. Journalism, N.Y.C., 1996—; cons. Ford Found., N.Y.C., 1976. Author: Starts and Finishes, 1975; exec. producer: (TV programs) Behind the Lines, 1971-75 (Emmy award 1973-74, NYU Don Hollenback award 1974), Assignment America, 1975, WNET Reports, 1976-77; columnist: "Eye on Books" for Book of the Month Club News, 1980, Parenting mag., 1986-89; producer Mixed Bag, twice-weekly video arts mag. for CBS Cable; contbr. articles to numerous publs. including The N.Y. Times Mag., Harpers, N.Y. Mag. Served to capt. USMC, 1963-66. Pulitzer Travelling fellow, 1967; recipient Meyer Berger award for Disting. Reporting Columbia U., 1978. Home: 340 Riverside Dr New York NY 10025-3423 Office: Columbia U Grad Sch Journalism New York NY 10027

WINFREY, JOHN CRAWFORD, economist, educator; b. Somerville, Tenn., July 2, 1935; s. Arthur Peter and Frances (Crawford) W.; m. Barbara Ann Strickland, July 20, 1957; 1 child, Mae Millicent. A.B., Davidson Coll., 1957; Ph.D., Duke U., 1965. Asst. dir. data processing Hanes Hosiery, Winston Salem, N.C., 1959-62; research asst. in econs. Duke U., Durham, N.C., 1963-64; asst. prof. econs. Washington and Lee U., Lexington, Va., 1965-68, assoc. prof., 1969-73, prof., 1974—; vis. prof. Vanderbilt U., Nashville, 1966, Tufts U., Boston, 1975, UCLA, 1978, U. Ill., 1982, U. Va., 1986, Duke U., 1989, 95, U. Calif., Berkeley, 1993, U. Utrecht, The Netherlands, 1995. Co-author: The Motion Commotion, 1972; author: Public Finance, Public Choice and the Public Sector, 1973. Bd. dirs. Lexington Tennis Clinic, Va., 1968-72, Rockridge Area Conservation Council, 1982-84; pres. Rockbridge Arts Guild, 1986-88. Recipient Comunity Svc. Lexington Jaycees, 1971; NEH fellow, 1975, 78, 82, 86, 89, 93; vis. fellow U. Coll. Oxford U., Eng., 1979, 95. Fellow Soc. for Values in Higher Edn.; mem. Am. Econ. Assn., So. Econ. Assn., History of Econs. Soc., Eastern Econ. Assn. Democrat. Presbyterian. Club: High Wheelers (Lexington). Home: 628 Stonewall St Lexington VA 24450-1933 Office: Washington and Lee U Dept Econs Lexington VA 24450

WINFREY, MARION LEE, television critic; b. Knoxville, Tenn., July 7, 1932; s. Charles Houston and Norma Elsa (Wesenberg) W.; m. Mary Anne Hight, Sept. 5, 1958 (div. 1977); 1 son, David Dylan; m. Kiki Olson, Aug. 24, 1978 (div. 1982). B.S., U. Tenn., 1966; M.F.A., U. Iowa, 1968. Reporter Nashville Tennessean, 1957-58, Knoxville News-Sentinel, 1958-60, Miami bur. UPI, 1960-62, Miami Herald, 1962-63, Washington bur. Knight Newspapers, 1963-66, Detroit Free Press, 1968-71; reporter Phila. Inquirer, 1972-74, TV critic, 1974—; instr. journalism U. Iowa, 1966-68; Bernard Kilgore journalism counselor DePauw U., 1971. Author: Kent State Report, The President's Commission on Campus Unrest, 1970; included in Best Sports Stories (edited by Marsh and Ehre), 1963. Served with U.S. Army, 1954-56. Nieman fellow Harvard U., 1971-72. Mem. TV Critics Assn. (founding pres. 1978-79), Sigma Delta Chi, Phi Gamma Delta. Baptist. Clubs: Harvard (Phila.); Pen and Pencil; Nat. Press (Washington). Home: 1700 Benjamin Franklin Pky Philadelphia PA 19103-1210 Office: 400 N Broad St Philadelphia PA 19130-4015

WINFREY, OPRAH, television talk show host, actress, producer; b. Kosciusko, Miss., Jan. 29, 1954; d. Vernon Winfrey and Vernita Lee. BA in Speech and Drama, Tenn. State U. News reporter Sta. WVOL Radio, Nashville, 1971-72; reporter, news anchorperson Sta. WTVF-TV, Nashville, 1973-76; news anchorperson Sta. WJZ-TV, Balt., 1976-77, host morning talk show People Are Talking, 1977-83; host talk show A.M. Chgo. Sta. WLS-TV, 1984; host The Oprah Winfrey Show, Chgo., 1985—; nationally syndicated, 1986—; host series of celebrity interview spls. Oprah: Behind the Scenes, 1992—; owner, prodr., chmn., CEO Harpo Prodns., 1986—. Appeared in films The Color Purple, 1985 (nominated Acad. award and Golden Globe award), Native Son, 1986, Throw Momma From the Train, 1988, Listen Up: The Lives of Quincy Jones, 1990; prodr., actress ABC-TV miniseries The Women of Brewster Place, 1989, also series Brewster Place, 1990, movie There Are No Children Here, 1993; exec. prodr. (ABC Movie of the Week) Overexposed, 1992; host, supervising prodr. celebrity interview series Oprah: Behind the Scenes, 1992, ABC Aftersch. Spls., 1991-93; host, exec. prodr. Michael Jackson Talks...to Oprah-90 Prime-Time Minutes with the King of Pop, 1993. Recipient Woman of Achievement award NOW, 1986, Emmy award for Best Daytime Talk Show Host, 1987, 91, 92, 94, 95, America's Hope award, 1990, Industry Achievement award Broadcast Promotion Mktg. Execs./Broadcast Design Assn., 1991, Image awards NAACP, 1989, 90, 91, 92, Entertainer of the Yr. award NAACP, 1989, CEBA awards, 1989, 90, 91, George Foster Peabody's Individual Achievement award, Gold Medal award IRTS; named Broadcaster of Yr. Internat. Radio and TV Soc., 1988; recognized as one of America's 25 Most Influential People, Time mag. Office: Harpo Prodns 110 N Carpenter St Chicago IL 60607-2101*

WING, ADRIEN KATHERINE, law educator; b. Oceanside, Calif., Aug. 7, 1956; d. John Ellison and Katherine (Pruitt) Wing; children: Che-Cabral, Nolan Felipe. A.B. magna cum laude, Princeton U., 1978; M.A., UCLA, 1979; J.D., Stanford Law Sch., 1982. Bar: N.Y. 1983, U.S. Dist. Ct. (so. and ea. dists.) N.Y. 1983, U.S. Ct. Appeals (5th and 9th cirs.). Assoc. Curtis, Mallet-Prevost, Colt & Mosle, N.Y.C., 1982-86, Rabinowitz, Boudin, Standard, Krinsky & Lieberman, 1986-87; assoc. prof. law U. Iowa, Iowa City, 1987-93, prof. law, 1993—; mem. alumni council Princeton U., 1983-85, trustee Class of '78 Alumni Found., 1984-87, v.p. Princeton Class of 1978 Alumni, 1993—; mem. bd. visitors Stanford Law Sch., 1993-96. Mem. bd. editors Am. Jour. Comp. Law, 1993—. Mem. ABA (exec. com. young lawyers sect. 1985-87), Nat. Conf. Black Lawyers (UN rep., chmn. internat. affairs sect. 1982-95), Internat. Assn. Dem. Lawyers (UN rep. 1984-87), Am. Soc. Internat. Law (exec. council 1986-89, group chair S. Africa 1996—, nom. com. 1991, 93), Black Alumni of Princeton U. (bd. dirs. 1982-87), Transafrica Scholars Forum Coun. (bd. dirs 1993—), Iowa City Foreign Rels. Coun. (bd. dirs. 1989-94), Iowa Peace Inst. (bd. dirs. 1993-95), Council on Fgn. Rels., Internat. Third World Legal Studies Assn. (bd. dirs. 1996—). Democrat. Avocations: photography, jogging, writing, poetry. Office: U Iowa Sch Law Boyd Law Bldg Iowa City IA 52242

WING, ELIZABETH SCHWARZ, museum curator, educator; b. Cambridge, Mass., Mar. 5, 1932; d. Henry F. and Maria Lisa Schwarz; m. James E. Wing, Apr. 18, 1957; children: Mary Elizabeth Wing-Berman, Stephen R. BA, Mt. Holyoke Coll., 1955; MS, U. Fla., 1957, PhD, 1962. Interim asst. curator Fla. Mus. Natural History, U. Fla., Gainesville, 1961-69, asst. curator, 1969-73, assoc. curator, 1973-78, curator, 1978—; U. Fla., Fla. Mus. Natural History, Gainesville, 1990-92; U.S. rep. Internat. Congress Archaeozoology, 1981—. Author: (with A.B. Brown) Paleonutrition, 1979; editor (with J.C. Wheeler) Economic Prehistory of the Central Andes, 1988; contbr. articles to profl. jours. Recipient Fryxell award Soc. Am. Archaeology, 1996; NSF grantee, 1961-64, 68-73, 79-80, 84-85, 89-91, 95-96. Mem. Soc. Ethnobiology (pres. 1989-91, trustee 1991—). Office: U Fla Fla Mus Natural History PO Box 117800 Museum Rd Gainesville FL 32611-7800

WING, JAMES DAVID, lawyer; b. Milw., May 4, 1943; s. William H. and Elaine E. (Koehler) W.; m. Marilyn Lee Walsh, Aug. 21, 1965 (div. June 1980); children: Benjamin, Tracy, Nathaniel, John; m. Eunide Valcin, Nov. 28, 1980. BA, Beloit (Wis.) Coll., 1965; MA, U. Chgo., 1966, JD, 1969. Bar: Wis. 1969, Fla. 1975, U.S. Ct. Appeals (7th cir.) 1973, U.S. Dist. Ct. (mid. dist.) Fla. 1975, U.S. Ct. Appeals (5th cir.) 1978, U.S. Dist. Ct. (so. dist.) Fla. 1981, U.S. Ct. Appeals (11th cir.) 1981, U.S. Supreme Ct. 1979. Assoc. Whyte, Hirschboeck, Minahan, Harding & Harland, Milw., 1969-75, Carlton, Fields, Ward, Emmanuel, Smith & Cutler, Tampa, Fla., 1975-85, Myers, Kenin, Levinson & Richards/Shea & Gould, Miami, Fla., 1985-88, Fine, Jacobson, Schwartz, Nash & Block, Miami, 1988-94, Holland & Knight, Miami, 1994—. Mem. Phi Beta Kappa, Phi Eta Sigma, Omicron Delta Kappa. Avocation: Germanistics, tennis.

WING, JOHN RUSSELL, lawyer; b. Mt. Vernon, N.Y., Jan. 20, 1937; s. John R. and Elinore (Smith) W.; m. Mary Zeller, Aug. 24, 1963 (div. June 1975); children: Ethan Lincoln, Catherine Dorothy; m. Audrey Strauss, Aug. 12, 1979; children: Carlin Elinore, Matthew Lawrence. BA, Yale U., 1960; JD, U. Chgo., 1963. Bar: N.Y. 1964. Assoc. Sherman & Sterling, N.Y.C., 1963-66; asst. U.S. atty. So. Dist. N.Y., N.Y.C., 1966-78; chief fraud unit U.S. Dist. Atty. So. Dist. N.Y., 1971-78; ptnr. Weil, Gotshal & Manges, N.Y.C., 1978—. Contbr. articles to profl. jours. Fellow Am. Coll. Trial Lawyers; mem. ABA (white collar crime com. criminal justice sect. 1978—, environ. task force com. 1983-85), Assn. Bar of City of N.Y. (criminal advocacy com. 1985-88), Fed. Bar Coun. (2d cir. cts. com. 1982-84), N.Y. Coun. Def. Lawyers (bd. dirs. 1986-90). Republican. Episcopalian. Avocation: sailing. Home: 52 Livingston St Brooklyn NY 11201-4813 Office: Weil Gotshal & Manges 767 5th Ave New York NY 10153-0001

WING, LILLY KELLY RAYNOR, health services administrator; b. Florence, S.C., Oct. 1, 1953; d. Harold and Adlyne (Gaddy) Kelly; m. Terry Michael Wing, Apr. 29, 1989; children: Kelly Ann, Stuart James. ADN, Florence Darlington Tech, Florence, S.C., 1985; BS in Nursing, Med. U. S.C., 1987; MSN, U. S.C., 1992. RN, S.C.; lic. nat. long term care adminstr.; N.C.; lic. long term care adminstr. Staff nurse McLeod Regional Med. Ctr., Florence, S.C., 1985-88; neuro rehab. nurse mgr. HealthSouth Rehab. Ctr., Florence, 1988; dir. nursing HealthSouth Rehab Ctr., Columbia, S.C., 1988-89; program dir. orthopedic, rehab. Bruce Hosp. System, Florence, S.C., 1989-91; adminstr., mem. adv. bd. Inpatient Rehab. Svcs. of Carolinas Hosp. Svcs., Florence, S.C., 1992-95; exec. dir. Transitional Health Svcs. of Cary, N.C., 1995-96; corp. sub. mgr. WelCare Internat., Atlanta, 1995—; adj. prof. Limestone Coll., Gaffney, S.C., 1993; mem. S.C. TB Task Force, 1994, TB stds. in long term care subcom., 1994, edn. with state TB plan subcom., 1994. Mem. N.C. Peer Rev. Team for N.C. Health Care Facilities Assn., ANA (cert. nursing adminstr., past pres. local chpt. 1991-93, sec., bd. dirs. 1994), AACN, S.C. Nurses Assn., Assn. Rehab. Nurses, Pee Dee Nurses Assn., S.C. Assn. Rehab. Faculties (sec., bd. dirs. 1992—), S.C. Health Care Assn., S.C. Hosp. Assn. (long term care coun. 1994).

WINGARD, RAYMOND RANDOLPH, transportation products executive; b. Goshen, Ala., Nov. 6, 1930; s. Raymond T. and Mary (Sanders) W.; student So. Meth. U., 1948-49, Birmingham-So. Coll., 1949-50, Harvard, 1973; m. Gainnell Harris, June 2, 1951; children: Renee, Kay, Beckie, Robin, Randy. With Koppers Co., Inc., 1951-62, area mgr., Montgomery, Ala.,

1963-64, mgr. R.R. sales and planning Western region, Chgo., 1964-71, divsn. mgr., asst. v.p. R.R. sales and planning, 1971-74, asst. v.p., mktg. mgr., Pitts., 1974-75, v.p., mgr. human resources, 1975-80, v.p., mgr. mktg. dept., 1981-85, v.p., mgr. adminstrv. svcs. and corp. planning, 1985-88; agy. mgr. Ala. Farm Bur. Svc. Analusia, 1962-63, exec. dir. Railway Tie Assn., 1988-96; chmn. Telemed Techs., Internat., 1996—, Cardiac Telecom Corp., 1996—. Chmn. R-1 Sch. Dist. Adv. Coun., Independence, Mo., 1960; pres. Independence Suburban Cmty. Improvement League, 1959-60; mem. dist. 58 Bd. Edn., 1969-71; trustee Pitts. Coun. Internat. Visitors, 1978-84, pres., 1982-83; pres. Minority Engring. Edn. Effect, Inc., 1977-80; bd. dirs. Allegheny coun. Boy Scouts Am., Blue Cross of Pa., vice-chmn., 1986-89; bd. dirs. Diversified Benefits Svc., Inc., 1990-95, Children's Make-A-Wish Found., 1995-96, Christian Svc. Ctr., 1996—, Baldwin Anti-Violence Ctr., 1996—, pres.-elect, 1997. With AUS, 1950-51. Mem. Am. Wood Preservers Assn., Japan Mgmt. Assn., Railway Tie Assn., Western Ry. Club, Duquesne Club, Harvard Club Mobile. Methodist. Home: 15300 State Hwy 180 Gulf Shores AL 36542-8242 Office: PO Box 1039 140 Cove Ave Gulf Shores AL 36547

WINGATE, BETTYE FAYE, librarian, educator; b. Hillsboro, Tex., Oct. 31, 1950; d. Warren Randolph and Faye (Gilmore) W. BA summa cum laude, Baylor U., 1971, MA, 1975; MLS, Tex. Womans U., 1985. Cert. prov. sec., learning resources endorsement. English tchr. Mexia (Tex.) H.S.; reading tchr. Connally Ind. Sch. Dist., Waco, Tex.; reading tchr., libr. Grapevine-Colleyville Ind. Sch. Dist., Grapevine, Tex.; libr. Crockett Jr. H.S., Irving, Tex.; mem. librs. coms., Campus Action Planning Com., 1989-93, Irving Ind. Sch. Dist. Site Based Decision-Making Com., 1992-94, mem. staff devel. coun., 1994-96, chairperson media fair com., 1996-97; speaker, presenter in field. Founding sponsor Challenger Ctr. Recipient Tex. Media awards, 1988, 89, 94. Mem. ALA, NEA, Am. Assn. Sch. Librs., Tex. State Tchrs. Assn. (assn. rep.), Tex. Libr. Assn. (chmn. state media awards com. 1989-91), Tex. Assn. Edn. Tech., Tex. Computer Edn. and Tech., Assn. Ednl. Comm. and Tech., Planetary Soc., Nat. Space Soc., Nat. Parks & Conservation Assn., Baylor Alumni Assn. (life), Beta Phi Mu, Delta Kappa Gamma (scholar 1985).

WINGATE, C. KEITH, law educator; b. Darlington, S.C., May 12, 1953; s. Clarence L. and Lilly W.; m. Gloria Farley; stepchildren: Brenda, Marvin, Terry and Oliver Champion. BA in Polit. Sci., U. Ill., 1974, JD cum laude, 1978. Bar: Calif., 1978. Assoc. litigation dept. Morrison & Foerster, San Francisco, 1978-80; from asst. to assoc. prof. law U. Calif.-Hastings, San Francisco, 1980-86, prof., 1986—; dir. Coun. Legal Edn. Opportunity Region I Inst., 1989; vis. prof. law Stanford (Calif) Law Sch., fall 1990, 94; chair Minority Law Tchrs.' Conf. Com., 1990; mem. acad. assistance work group, law sch. admissions coun., 1991; mem. bd. trustees Law Sch. Admission Coun., 1997-98. Author: (with David I. Levine and William R. Slomanson) Cases and Materials on California Civil Procedure, 1991, (with William R. Slomanson) California Civil Procedure in a Nutshell, 1992, (with Donald L. Doernberg) Federal Courts, Federalism and Separation of Powers, 1994. Bd. dirs. Community Housing Devel. Corp., North Richmond. Recipient 10 Outstanding Persons award U. Ill. Black Alumni Assn., 1980; Harno fellow U. Ill., Coll. of Law, 1976. Mem. Assn. Am. Law Schs. (chair sect. minority groups 1990, exec. com. mem. sect. civil proceedure 1991), Charles Housting Bar Assn., Phi Sigma Alpha. Office: U Calif Hastings Coll Law 200 Mcallister St San Francisco CA 94102-4707

WINGATE, HENRY TAYLOR, JR., foundation administrator, fundraiser; b. Opelika, Ala., Mar. 2, 1929; s. Henry T. and Dorothy Inez (Mathews) W.; m. Mary Frances Grimes, Sept. 17, 1949; children: Frances, Kenneth, Mathew. BS in Agrl. Sci., Auburn U., 1950. Field rep. agrl. chems. div. Swift Co., Birmingham, Ala., 1953-57; regional dir. Muscular Dystrophy Assn. Am., Birmingham, 1958-64; dir. state crusade Am. Cancer Soc., Atlanta, 1964-65; regional fund raising rep. Nat. Assn. Retarded Citizens, Atlanta, 1965-69; regional dir. Nat. Multiple Sclerosis Soc., Atlanta, 1969-77; asst. dir. field services Epilepsy Found. Am., Washington, 1977-78; group v.p. fin. devel. Nat. Arthritis Found., Atlanta, 1978-89. Vol. counselor Svc. Corp. Retired Execs., 1991—. 1st lt. U.S. Army, 1951-53. Named to Gov.'s com. on employment of handicapped Gov. of Ga., 1977, Col. Aide de Camp, Gov. of Tenn., 1982, 86. Mem. Nat. Soc. Fund Raising Execs. (bd. dirs. 1971-72, cert.), Arthritis Found. Staff Assn., Nat. Vol. Health Agys. (chmn. 1981-82), Combined Health Appeals Am. (bd. dirs. 1985-88). Republican. Baptist. Avocations: photography, fishing. Home: 4860 Mountain West Ct Stone Mountain GA 30087-1038

WINGATE, HENRY TRAVILLION, federal judge; b. Jackson, Miss., Jan. 6, 1947; s. J.T. and Eloise (Anderson) W.; m. Turner Arnita Ward, Aug. 10, 1974. BA, Grinnell Coll., 1969; JD, Yale U., 1973; LLD (hon.), Grinnell Coll., 1986. Bar: Miss. 1973, U.S. Dist. Ct. (so. dist.) Miss. 1973, U.S. Ct. Appeals (5th cir.) 1973, U.S. Mil. Ct. 1973. Law clk. New Haven (Conn.) Legal Assistance, 1971-72, Community Legal Aid, Jackson, 1972-73; spl. asst. atty. gen. State of Miss., Jackson, 1976-80; asst. dist. atty. (7th cir.), Jackson, 1980-84; asst. U.S. atty. U.S. Dist. Ct. (so. dist.), Jackson, 1984-85; judge U.S. Dist. Ct. (so. dist.) Miss., Jackson, 1985—; lectr. Miss. Prosecutors Coll., 1980-84, Law Enforcement Tng. Acad., Pearl, Miss., 1980-84, Miss. Jud. Coll., 1980-84, Nat. Coll. Dist. Attys., 1984-85; adj. prof. law Golden Gate U., Norfolk, Va, 1975-76, Tidewater Community Coll., 1976, Miss. Coll. Sch. Law, 1978-84. Former mem. adv. bd. Jackson Parks and Recreation Dept.; former mem. bd. dirs. SCAN Am. of Miss., Inc., Jackson Arts Alliance, Drug Rsch. and Edn. Assn. in Miss., Inc., United Way Jackson; mem. exec. com. Yale U. Law sch., 1989—; chmn. bd. dirs. YMCA, 1978-80. Racquetball State Singles Champion Jr. Vets. Div., 1981, State Singles Champion Srs. Div., 1982, Outstanding Legal Service award NAACP (Jackson br. and Miss. br.), 1982, Civil Liberties award Elks, 1983, Community Service award Women for Progress Orgn., 1984. Mem. ABA (co-chmn. sect. litigation liaison with judiciary 1989-91), Miss. Bar Assn., Hinds County Bar Assn., Fed. Bar Assn., Yale Club Miss. Avocations: reading, theater, racquetball, jogging, bowling. Home: 6018 Huntview Dr Jackson MS 39206-2130 Office: James O Eastland Courthouse 245 E Capitol St Ste 109 Jackson MS 39201-2411*

WINGATE, ROBERT LEE, JR., internist; b. Columbia, S.C., May 28, 1936; s. Robert Lee and Helen (Owen) W.; m. Ritanne Cooper, Apr. 19, 1962 (div. 1965); 1 child, Elizabeth Butterfield-Wingate; m. Jeannette DeLatte, Mar. 27, 1968 (div. 1980); children: Laura Owen, Charlotte Cramer. BS, U. S.C., 1957; MD, Med. Coll. S.C., 1961. Intern Cin. Gen. Hosp., 1961-62, jr. resident internal medicine, 1964-65; asst. resident in internal medicine Med. Coll. of Va., Richmond, 1965-66; resident in internal medicine Charity Hosp. of La., New Orleans, 1966-67, resident in neurology, 1967-68; pvt. practice Columbia, 1968-78; PruCare physician Memphis, 1983-85; med. dir. M. Lowennstein and Celanese Corps., Rock Hill, S.C., 1978-80; med. dir. nursing home care unit Dorn VA Hosp., Columbia, 1980-82; med. cons. disability determination div. Vocat. Rehab. S.C., Columbia, 1982-83; cons. Student Health Ctr. U. S.C., Columbia, 1985-86; cons. Urgent Care Ctrs. S.C., 1986-87; pvt. practice Pelion, S.C., 1987-92; staff internist, cons. internal medicine Western Mental Health Inst., Western Institute, Tenn., 1992—; med. dir. Forest Hills Nursing Ctr., Columbia, 1968-78; med. cons. S.C. Commn. for Blind, Columbia, 1970-78, Mid-Carolina Coun. on Alcoholism, Columbia, 1970-74; instr. internal medicine U. S.C. Sch. Medicine, 1980-82; cons. internal medicine and urgent care Pelion Cmty. Care Ctr., 1989-92; instr. Sch. Nursing, Med. Coll. S.C., Winthrop divsn., 1978-80; lectr. in field. Contbr. articles to newspapers. Ofcl. physician Peanut Party S.C., 1990-92. Lt. comdr. M.C., USNR, 1958-66. Grantee Burroughs-Wellcome Co., 1958, Med. Coll. S.C., 1960, Congress of U.S., 1987. Mem. ACP, AMA (physician's recognition award 1969, 74, 79, 85, 86, 94-96, 96-99), Am. Soc. Internal Medicine, Am. Occupational Med. Assn., So. Med. Assn., S.C. Med. Assn., Lexington County Med. Assn., Soc. of 1824, Ruritan, Phi Rho Sigma. Avocations: chess, hunting, fishing, movie making, collecting stamps and coins. Office: Western Mental Health Inst Bolivar TN 38074

WINGATE, THOMAS MARIE JOSEPH, assistant headmaster; b. Guildford, Surrey, England, May 23, 1959; came to the U.S., 1993; s. Peter Henry and Therese M. (Vachon) W.; m. Maria Elena Espinosa de los Reyes Bolanos, July 10, 1982; children: Elenita, Juliet, Thomas Philip. BA in English, History, Theory Art, U. Kent, Canterbury, Kent, U.K., 1981; postgrad. cert. in edn. in English, U. Leeds, U.K., 1982; MEd, Ga. State U., 1996. English tchr. St. George's Coll., Weybridge, Surrey, 1985-86; English tchr. Brit. Internat. Sch., Mexico City, 1986-89, head English, 1989-91, head intermediate sch., 1991-93; lang. arts tchr. Wesleyan Sch., Atlanta, 1993-94, prin., 1994-96, asst. headmaster, 1996—. Author: The Chapel on the Heath, 1985. Vol. Saint Vincent de Paul Soc., Atlanta, 1994. Grantee Ga. State U., Atlanta, 1993-94, Wesleyan Sch. Governing Bd., Atlanta, 1994. Mem. ASCD, Kappa Delta Pi. Roman Catholic. Avocations: photography, mountain climbing, cricket, coin collecting. Office: Wesleyan Sch 5405 Spalding Dr Norcross GA 30092-2614

WINGENBACH, GREGORY CHARLES, priest, religious-ecumenical agency director; b. Washington, Feb. 1, 1938; s. Charles Edward and Pearl Adeline (Stanton) W.; m. MaryAnn Pearce, Sept. 16, 1961; children: Mary-Adele, Karl Eduard, John Clair, Evgenia Kisa Maria. Student, Georgetown U., 1958-62; BA, Goddard Coll., 1972; postgrad., U. Thessalonike, Greece, 1973-74; MDiv, Louisville Presbyn. Theol. Sem., 1976, D of Ministry in Pastoral and Ecumenical Theology, 1982. Ordained to ministry Greek Orthodox Archdiocese North and South Am. as deacon, 1971, assoc. priest, 1973. Editl. asst., mem. staff Washington Star and N.Y. Herald-Tribune, 1957-62; rsch. and legis. asst. U.S. Senator Clair Engle, Calif., 1962-63; cmty. rels. programs mgr. U.S. Exec. OEO, Washington, 1965-69; regional program devel. officer AEC-Oak Ridge (Tenn.) Associated Univs., 1970-73; assoc. St. George's Ch., Knoxville, Tenn., 1971-73; chaplain St. John Chrysostomos Ch. and Vlatadon Monastery, Thessalonike, 1973-74; named steward/oikonomos, preacher Met. Archdiocese of Thessalonike, 1974; pastor Assumption of Virgin Mary Ch., Louisville, 1974-79, Holy Trinity Ch., Nashville, 1979-82, St. Spyridon's Ch., Monessen, Pa., 1983-86; nat. dir. family life/pastoral ministries Greek Orthodox Archdiocese North and South Am., N.Y.C. and Brookline (Mass.), 1986-90; exec. dir. Kentuckiana Interfaith Community, Louisville, 1990—; Orthodox del. Louisville Area Interch. Coun. and Ecumedia Com., 1974-79; pres., exec. adminstr. LAIOS-Kentuckiana Interfaith Coun., 1977-79; diocesan rep. Archdiocese Nat. Presbyters Coun., 1982-85; archdiocese del. Nat. Coun. Chs., Orthodox/Luth. Dialogues Consultation, 1986—, Orthodox Nat. Missions Bd., 1981-90; named protopresbyter Greek Orthodox Archdiocese, 1980, Pitts. Diocese, 1983, Detroit Diocese, 1995; ecumenical officer Greek Orthodox Diocese Pitts., 1983-86. Author: The Peace Corps, 1961, Guide to the Peace Corps, 1965, Broken...Yet Never Sundered: The Ecumenical Tradition, 1987; editorial researcher: Richard Nixon, 1959, Duel at the Brink, 1960, The Floating Revolution, 1962. Mem. Fellowship St. Alban and St. Sergius, Orthodox Theol. Soc. Am. (exec. bd.), N.Am. Acad. Ecumenists (exec. bd.). Office: Kentuckiana Interfaith Community 1115 S 4th St Louisville KY 40203-3101

WINGER, DEBRA, actress; b. Cleve., 1955; d. Robert and Ruth W.; m. Timothy Hutton, March 16, 1986 (div.); 1 child, Emanuel Noah. Student, Calif. State U., Northridge. Made 1st profl. appearance in Wonder Woman TV series, 1976-77; appeared TV film Spl. Olympics, 1977; appeared in films Thank God It's Friday, 1978, French Postcards, 1979, Urban Cowboy, 1980, Cannery Row, 1982, An Officer and a Gentleman, 1982, Terms of Endearment, 1983, Mike's Murder, 1984, Legal Eagles, 1986, Black Widow, 1987, Made in Heaven, 1987, Betrayed, 1988, Everybody Wins, 1990, The Sheltering Sky, 1990, Leap of Faith, 1992, Wilder Napalm, 1993, Shadowlands, 1993 (Academy award nominee, Best Actress, 1993), A Dangerous Woman, 1993, Forget Paris, 1995. Office: care Creative Artists Agency 9830 Wilshire Blvd Beverly Hills CA 90212-1804*

WINGER, RALPH O., lawyer; b. Keokuk, Iowa, July 8, 1919; s. Ralph O. and Mary Ellen (Lee) W.; m. Irene L. Sutton, Apr. 5, 1941; children: Ralph O. (dec.), Allen, Louise, Robert. BA, State U. Iowa, 1940; LLB, Harvard U., 1947. Bar: N.Y. 1948. Assoc. Cahill Gordon & Reindel and predecessor firms, N.Y.C., 1947-60, ptnr., 1960-91, sr. counsel, 1992—. Lt. USNR, 1942-46, PTO. Mem. ABA, N.Y. State Bar Assn. (chmn. tax sect. 1973-74, ho. of dels. 1974-75), Bay Terrace Country Club (N.Y.). Republican. Home: 20908 28th Rd Flushing NY 11360-2413 Office: Cahill Gordon & Reindel 80 Pine St New York NY 10005-1702

WINGER, ROGER ELSON, church administrator; b. Fisherville, Ont., Can., Dec. 25, 1933; s. Elson Clare and Bertha Caroline (Schweyer) W.; m. Della Bertha Lebien, June 7, 1958; children: Jeffrey, Karen Mohr, David, Thomas, Susan. AA, Concordia Jr. Coll., Ft. Wayne, Ind., 1953; BA, Concordia Sem., St. Louis, 1955, theol. diploma, 1958; DD (hon.), Concordia Luth. Sem., Edmonton, Alta., Can., 1991. Ordained to ministry, Luth. Ch., 1958. Pastor Holy Trinity Luth. Ch., London, 1958-64, Good Shepherd Luth. Ch., Coventry, Eng., 1964-69, Luth. Mission, Liverpool, Eng., 1969-72, Faith Luth. Ch., Dunnville, Ont., 1972-78, St. Matthew Luth. Ch., Smithville, Ont., 1972-78, St. Paul's Luth. Ch., Kitchener, Ont., 1978-91; pres. ea. dist. Luth. Ch.-Can., Kitchener, 1991—; v.p. Ont. dist. Luth. Ch.-Can., 1982-88; sec. Luth. Ch.-Can., Winnipeg, Man., 1988-91; mem. bd. regents Concordia Luth. Sem., Edmonton, Alta., 1984-88, Concordia Luth. Sem., St. Catharines Ont., 1991—. Avocations: photography, golf, woodworking. Home: 76 Deerwood Crescent, Kitchener, ON Canada N2N 1R3 Office: Luth Ch Can East Dist, 275 Lawrence Ave, Kitchener, ON Canada N2M 1Y3

WINGERT, HANNELORE CHRISTIANE, real estate sales executive, chemical company executive; b. Karlsbad, Czechoslavakia; came to U.S., 1962, naturalized, 1967; d. Andreas and Gisela Maria (Ciharz) Zwickel; m. Rudolf Wingert, Feb. 9, 1963; children: Angela Helene, Christopher Rudolf. I.B.A., Stadt. Berufsschule, Fed. Republic Germany, 1961; postgrad. in mgmt., Bergen Community Coll., 1983. Lic. real estate, N.J. Clk. various cos., N.J., 1963, bilingual sec., 1963-78; exec. sec., adminstrv. asst. Lurgi Corp., Hasbrouck Heights, N.J., 1978-81; sr. exec. sec. Degussa Corp., Teterboro, N.J., 1981-83, asst. product mgr. silica, 1983-85, asst. product mgr. H202, 1985-87, sales promotion coord., 1987; sales assoc. Schlott Realtors, Kinnelon, N.J., 1987-90; Caldwell Banker, 1990—; million dollar club, 1988, multi-million dollar club, 1990, N.J. million dollar club, 1992. Author real estate newsletter, 1992—, community newsletter, 1977-79. Mem. Bd. Realtors Morris and Passaic (N.J.) Counties; chmn. master planning com. High Crest Lake, West Milford, N.J., 1974-75; advisor Jr. Woman's Club Kinnelon-Butler (N.J.), 1973-74; techr. computer classes Bd. Realtors, Passaic County, 1989-92. Mem. N.J. Fed. of Woman's Clubs (past pres.), High Crest Lake Woman's Club (pres. 1972-73) (West Milford, N.J.). Republican. Roman Catholic. Home: 204 High Crest Dr West Milford NJ 07480-3710 Office: Caldwell Banker Realtors Kinnelon 1450 State Rt 23 Butler NJ 07405-1624

WINGLE, JAMES MATHEW, bishop; b. Pembroke, Ont., Can., Sept. 23, 1946; s. James Mathew and Elizabeth Anne (Coyne) W. BA, U. Windsor, 1966-69, MA, 1971-75; STL, Alfonsiano Acad., 1979-82. Ordained priest Roman Cath. Ch., 1977. Probation officer Ministry Correctional Svcs., Ont., 1970-75; priest (parish ministry) Diocese of Pembroke, Mattawa, Ont., 1977-79; asst. prof. St. Augustine's Sem., Toronto, Ont., 1987-93, pres., rector, 1987-93; consecrated bishop, 1993; bishop Diocese of Yarmouth, N.S., 1993—; sec. Toronto Sch. of Theology, 1985-87, bd. dirs. 1987-93; bd. dirs. Villa St. Joseph, Yarmouth, 1993—. Cons. and bd. dirs. Big Sisters Assn., Windsor, Ont., 1972-75. Avocations: cycling, skiing, music (organ), poetry, gardening. Office: Diocese of Yarmouth, PO Box 278, Yarmouth, NS Canada B5A 4B2

WINHAM, GEORGE KEETH, retired mental health nurse; b. Plain Dealing, La., Nov. 25, 1934; s. Henderson and Lula Mae (Kelly) W.; m. Patricia Annie Weise, Nov. 7, 1959; children: Adrian Keeth, George Kevin, Karla Ann. ADN, La. State U., 1974; BS in Health Care, Carolina Christian U., 1986. Cert. chem. dependency nurse specialist; RN, La. Staff nurse preceptor ward 10 VAMC, Shreveport, La., 1992-96, staff nurse ward 10, 1976-88, 96; ret. Overton Brooks VA Med. Ctr., Shreveport, 1996; guest speaker in field. With USAFR, 1982-95. Mem. Drug and Alcohol Nurses Assn., Am. Soc. Pain Mgmt. Nurses, Nat. Fedn. Federal Employees (local treas. 1956, nurse of yr. 1989), Air Force Sgts. Assn., Nat. Consortium Chem. Dependency Nurses, Consol. Assn. Nurses in Substance Abuse, Masons. Baptist. Avocations: repairing antique furnitures, framing pictures. Home: 106 Lancashire Dr Bossier City LA 71111-2023

WINHAM, GILBERT RATHBONE, political science educator; b. Flushing, N.Y., May 11, 1938; s. Alfred Rathbone and Margery Rankin (Post) W.; m. Linda Joyce Tanner, June 11, 1960; children: Nina Gail, Russell Post, Karla Joyce. A.B., Bowdoin Coll., 1959; diploma in internat. law, U. Manchester, Eng., 1964; Ph.D., U. N.C., 1967. Asst. prof., then assoc. prof. polit. sci. McMaster U., Hamilton, Ont., Can., 1967-75; assoc. prof., then prof. polit. sci. Dalhousie U., Halifax, N.S., Can., 1975-92; Eric Dennis Meml. prof. govt. and polit. Sci. Dalhousie U., Halifax, N.S., 1992—, dir. Centre Fgn. Policy Studies, 1975-82, chmn. dept., 1985-88; Claude T. Bissell prof. Can.-Am. studies U. Toronto, Ont., 1990-91; cons. GATT/WTO, numerous govt. agys. in Can. and U.S.; guest scholar Brookings Instn., 1972; vis. scholar Ctr. Internat. Affairs Harvard U., 1979-80; external faculty Internat. Peace Acad., N.Y.C., 1981-85; vis. prof. Colegio de Mex., 1991, 93; chmn. N.S. Adjustment Adv. Coun., 1988-90; mem. internat. trade adv. com. Govt. Can., 1988-94, dispute settlement panels for Can.-U.S. Free Trade Agreement, NAFTA and World Trade Orgn., 1989—; rsch. coord. Royal Commn. on Econ. Union and Devel. Prospects for Can., 1983-85. Author: International Trade and the Tokyo Round Negotiation, 1986, Trading with Canada: The Canada-U.S. Free Trade Agreement, 1988, The Evolution of International Trade Agreements, 1992; co-editor: The Hallifax 6-7 Summit: Issues on the Table, 1995; mem. editorial bd. Internat. Jour., 1983-88, Negotiation Jour., 1983-88, Can. Fgn. Policy, 1992—; contbr. articles to profl. jours. Served to lt. USNR, 1959-62. Can. Coun. leave fellow, 1973-74, 82-83, Rockefeller fellow in internat. rels., 1979-80, Killam rsch. fellow, 1988-90. Fellow Royal Soc. of Canada; Mem. Can. Polit. Sci. Assn. (dir. 1974-76), Am. Polit. Sci. Assn., Can. Civil Liberties Assn., Can. Inst. Internat. Affairs (chmn. Halifax br. 1978-82), Bedford Basin Yacht Club. Home: 120 Shore Dr, Bedford, NS Canada B4A 2E1 Office: Dalhousie U, Dept Polit Sci, Halifax, NS Canada B3H 4H6

WINIK, JAY B., writer, political scientist, consultant; b. New Haven, Feb. 8, 1957; s. Herbert Edward Winik and Marilyn Joan (Fishman) Abrams; m. Lyric Wallwork, Nov. 17, 1991. BA in Psychology cum laude, Yale U., 1980, PhD in Polit. Sci., 1993; MS in Internat. Rels. with distinction, London Sch. Econs., 1981. Arms control cons. Rand Corp., Santa Monica, Calif., 1983; chief speechwriter Ambassador Benjamin Netanyahu, N.Y.C., 1984; sr. profl. staff mem. House Com. on Armed Svcs., Washington, 1985-88; vis. fellow Ctr. for Strategic and Internat. Studies, Washington, 1988; dep. exec. dir. Def. Sec.'s Commn. on Base Realignment and Closure, Washington, 1988; legis. asst. for def. and fgn. policy Office of Sen. Charls S. Robb & Senate Com. on Fgn. Rels., Washington, 1989-91; sr. fellow Sch. Pub. Affairs U. Md., College Park, 1991—; advisor to Sec. Defense, 1993; prin. advisor for def. and fgn. policy, 1986 policy commn. Dem. Nat. Com.; assoc. staff mem. select com to investigate covert arms transactions with Iran, 1987. Author: On the Brink, 1996; editl. contbr. Wall Street Jour., N.Y. Times, Washington Post, others pubs., 1981—. Grantee U.S. Inst. Peace, 1987; fellow Bradley Found. Fellow Ctr. for Strategic and Internat. Studies (adj.); mem. Coun. on Fgn. Rels. (term mem.). Jewish. Avocation: tennis. Home: 4628 Hunt Ave Chevy Chase MD 20815-5425 Office: U Md CISSM Sch Pub Affairs College Park MD 20740

WINK, DOREEN MUSTO, interior designer; b. Rochester, N.Y., Oct. 18; d. Nunzio Edward and Ann (Iaculli) Musto; m. Douglas L. Wink; 1 stepdaughter, Melissa Lynn; 1 child, Douglas III. AAS in Psychology cum laude, Monroe C.C., 1973; BSW cum laude, SUNY, Brockport, 1975. Social worker, dir. mental health Cobbs Hill Nursing Home, Rochester, N.Y., 1975-78; social worker Rochester, N.Y., 1980-89; interior designer for retail stores Washington, 1989-91; CEO Three-D-Wink Inc., Washington, 1991—; panel mem. bd. on gardens Better Homes & Gardens. Mem. Peerless Rockville (Md.) Hist. Soc.; judge, mem. 4-H Orgn., 1985—; vol. to staff White House, Washington, 1994—; head art dept. Young Reps. Club, Rochester, 1964-69; organizer, pres. Rockshire New Comers Club, Rockville, Md.; active nat., local politics; chmn. Rockshire Arch. Com. Mem. NOW, Nat. Trust for Hist. Preservation, White House Hist. Soc., Decorative Arts Trust (cons.), Nat. Mus. of Women in the Arts (charter), Tex. State Soc. (inaugural ball com. 1985-94), Nat. Italian Am. Found., Smithsonian Instn., Md. Design, Space Planning and Props Soc. (founder, dir.), Pres. Woodrow Wilson Hist. Soc., Pres. James Monroe Hist. Soc., Rockville Garden Club of Rockshire. Avocations: painting, biking, crochet, walking, reading.

WINKEL, RAYMOND NORMAN, avionics manufacturing executive, retired naval officer; b. Flint, Mich., Dec. 8, 1928; s. Norman Martin and Evelyn Matilda (Hylen) W.; m. Ellen Stefula, Dec. 29, 1955; children: Raymond Norman, Ann, Maryellen. B.S., U.S. Naval Postgrad. Sch., Monterey, Calif., 1964; M.S., Villanova (Pa.) U., 1967; grad., Advanced Mgmt. Program, Harvard U., 1973. Enlisted in U.S. Navy, 1948, commd. ensign, designated naval aviator, 1951, advanced through grades to rear adm., 1979; service in Far East; comdg. officer Naval Electronics Systems Test and Evaluation Facility St. Inigoes, Md., 1969-71; dir. avionics U.S. Navy, 1973-76; project mgr. Navy/Marine Corps heavy lift helicopter, 1976-78; gen. mgr. Navy/industry team to develop new ship/aircraft weapon system for anti-submarine warfare LAMPS Mark III, 1978-81; ret. U.S. Navy, 1981; v.p. Washington ops. Telephonics Corp., Huntington, N.Y., 1981-82; v.p. programs and contracts Astronautics Corp. Am., Milw., 1982-94; aerospace industry cons. Heathsville, Va., 1994-95; sr. dir. DCH Tech., Inc., Sherman Oaks, Calif., 1995—. Decorated Legion of Merit, Meritorious Service medal, Air medal, Navy Achievement medal. Mem. Am. Helicopter Soc., Armed Forces Comms. and Electronics Assn., Navy Helicopter Assn., Exptl. Aircraft Assn., U.S. Naval Inst., Assn. Naval Aviation, Ret. Officers Assn., Kiwanis, Rappahannock River Yacht Club, U.S. Power Squadron. Republican. Roman Catholic. Home and Office: Island Point Rd RR 2 Box 123 Heathsville VA 22473

WINKELMAN, JAMES WARREN, hospital administrator, pathology educator; b. Bklyn., Oct. 29, 1935; s. Charles Winkelman and Augusta Spiselman; m. Sidra Levi, Sept. 1, 1957 (div. Sept. 1972); children: Elizabeth, Claudia, Recha; m. Rina Lavie, Sept. 20, 1977; 1 child, Zev. AB, U. Chgo., 1955; MD, Johns Hopkins U., 1959; MA (hon.), Harvard U., 1990. Diplomate Am. Bd. Pathology. Intern in medicine Johns Hopkins Hosp., 1959-60; resident in pathology NYU Hosp., Bellevue Hosp., 1962-65; asst. prof. pathology NYU, 1965-67; assoc. clin. prof. UCLA, 1969-80; asst. dir. Bio-Sci. Labs., Van Nuys, Calif., 1967-70, v.p., 1970-72, pres., 1972-77, bd. dirs., 1970-77; exec. v.p. Nat. Health Labs., La Jolla, Calif., 1977-80; prof. pathology SUNY Health Sci. Ctr., Syracuse, 1980-86, Harvard U. Med. Sch., Boston, 1986—; v.p., dir. clin. labs. Brigham and Women's Hosp., Boston, 1986—; cons. to numerous govt. agys. and industry; vis. prof. Soroka Med. Ctr., Beersheva, Israel, 1982. Author: Clinical Chemistry, 1974; also over 100 articles; patentee in field lab. sci. Capt. USPHS, 1960-62. Mem. Coll. Am. Pathologists, Assn. Clin. Lab. Scientists, Am. Soc. Clin. Pathology, Clin. Lab. Mgmt. Assn., Alpha Omega Alpha. Republican. Jewish. Avocations: tennis, golf, travel, classical music. Office: Brigham and Women's Hosp 75 Francis St Boston MA 02115-6110

WINKLER, AGNIESZKA M., advertising agency executive; b. Rome, Italy, Feb. 22, 1946; came to U.S., 1953, naturalized, 1959; d. Wojciech A. and Halina Z. (Owsiany) W.; children from previous marriage: children: Renata G. Ritcheson, Dana C Sworakowski.; m. Arthur K. Lund. BA, Coll. Holy Name, 1967; MA, San Jose State U., 1971; MBA, U. Santa Clara, 1981. Teaching asst., San Jose State U., 1968-70; cons. to ea. European bus., Palo Alto, Calif., 1970-72; pres./founder Commart Communications, Palo Alto, 1973-84; pres./founder, chmn. bd. Winkler McManus, Santa Clara, Calif., 1984—; bd. dirs. Reno Air, Lifeguard, Lifeguard Life Ins. Trustee Santa Clara U., 1991—; trustee O'Connor Found., 1987-93, mem. exec. com., 1988—, mem. Capital Campaign steering com., 1989; mem. nat. adv. bd. Comprehensive Health Enhancement Support System, 1991—; mem. mgmt. west com. A.A.A.A. Agy., 1991—, vice chair no. Calif. coun., 1996—; project dir. Poland Free Enterprise Plan, 1989-92; mem. adv. bd. Normandy France Bus. Devel., 1989-92; mem. bd. regents Holy Names Coll., 1987—; bd. dirs. San Jose Mus. Art, 1987; mem. San Jose Symphony, Gold Baton, 1986; mem. nat. adv. com. CHESS, 1991—; dir. Bay Area Coun., 1994—. Recipient CLIO award in Advt., Addy award and numerous others; named to 100 Best Women in Advt., Ad Age, 1988, Best Woman in Advt., AdWeek and McCall's Mag., 1993, one of 100 Best and Brightest Women in Mktg. & Advt., NAWBO, 1996. Mem. Family Svc. Assn. (trustee 1980-82), Am. Assn. Advt. Agys. (agy. mgmt. west com. 1991), Bus. Profl. Advt. Assn., Polish Am. Congress, San Jose Advt. Club, San Francisco Ad Club, Beta Gamma Sigma (hon.), Pi Gamma Mu, Pi Delta Phi (Lester-Tinneman award 1966, Bill Raskob Found. grantee 1965). Office: Winkler Advt 301 Howard St 21st Fl San Francisco CA 94105

WINKLER, ALLAN MICHAEL, history educator; b. Cin., Jan. 7, 1945; s. Henry Ralph and Clare (Sapadin) W.; div.; children: Jennifer, David; m. Sara Penhale, May 2, 1992. BA, Harvard U., 1966; MA, Columbia U., 1967; PhD, Yale U., 1974. Vol. Peace Corps, The Philippines, 1967-69; instr., asst. prof. history Yale U., New Haven, 1973-78; asst. prof., assoc. prof. U. Oreg., Eugene, 1979-86; prof. history Miami U., Oxford, Ohio, 1986—, chmn. dept., 1986-95; prof. Helsinki (Finland) U., 1978-79, U. Amsterdam, The Netherlands, 1984-85, U. Nairobi, Kenya, 1995-96. Author: The Politics of Propaganda, 1978, Modern America, 1985, Home Front, U.S.A., 1986, The American People, 1986, The Recent Past, 1989, Life Under a Cloud, 1993, America: Pathways to the Present, 1994, Cassie's War, 1994. Fulbright grantee, 1978-79, 84-85, 95-96, NEH grantee, 1981-82. Mem. Am. Hist. Assn., Orgn. Am. Historians, Am. Studies Assn., Harvard Club (Cin.). Avocations: running, bicycling, squash, tennis, golf. Home: 925 Cedar Dr Oxford OH 45056-3443 Office: Miami U Dept History Oxford OH 45056

WINKLER, CHARLES HOWARD, lawyer, investment management company executive; b. N.Y.C., Aug. 4, 1954; s. Joseph Conrad and Geraldine Miriam (Borok) W.; m. Joni S. Taylor, Aug. 28, 1993. BBA with highest distinction, Emory U., 1976; JD, Northwestern U., 1979. Bar: Ill. 1979, U.S. Dist. Ct (no. dist.) Ill. 1979. Assoc. Levenfeld & Kanter, Chgo., 1979-80; assoc. Kanter & Eisenberg, Chgo., 1980-84, ptnr., 1985-86; ptnr. Neal Gerber & Eisenberg, Chgo., 1986-96; sr. mng. dir., COO Citadel Investment Group, LLC, Chgo., 1996—; sr. mng. dir. Taft Securities LLC, Chgo., 1996—, Titan Securities LLC, Chgo., 1996—, Aragon Investments Ltd., Chgo., 1996—. Author: (with others) Basic Tax Shelters, 1982, Limited Liability Companies: The Entity of Choice, 1995; mng. editor Northwestern Jour. Internat. Law and Bus., 1979. Mem. ABA (mem. sect. on taxation), Beta Gamma Sigma. Home: 50 E Bellevue Pl Chicago IL 60611-1129 Office: Citadel Investment Group LLC 225 W Washington St Fl 9 Chicago IL 60606-3418

WINKLER, DOLORES EUGENIA, retired hospital administrator; b. Milw., Aug. 10, 1929; d. Charles Peter and Eugenia Anne (Zamka) Kowalski; m. Donald James Winkler, Aug. 18, 1951; 1 child, David John. Grad., Milw. Bus. Inst., 1949. Acct. Curative Rehab. Ctr., Milw., 1949-60; staff acct. West Allis (Wis.) Meml. Hosp., 1968-70, chief acct., 1970-78, reimbursement analyst, 1978-85, dir. budgets and reimbursement, 1985-95; ret., 1995; mem. adv. coun./fin. com. Tau Home Health Care Agy., Milw., 1981-83. Mem. Healthcare Fin. Mgmt. Assn. (pres. 1989-90, Follmer Bronze award 1980, Reeves Silver award 1986, Muncie Gold award 1989, medal of honor 1993), Inst. Mgmt. Accts. (pres. 1983-84, nat. dir. 1986-88, pres. Mid Am. Regional Coun. 1988-89, award of excellence 1989), Beta Chi Rho (pres. 1948). Avocations: travel, photography, golf. Home: 12805 W Honey Ln New Berlin WI 53151-2652

WINKLER, GUNTHER, biotechnology executive, drug development expert; b. Laa Thaya, Noe, Austria, Aug. 20, 1957; came to U.S., 1986; s. Kurt and Irmgard (Lahner) W.; m. Maria Toifl, Sept. 11, 1979; children: Claudia, Marc. MS in Biochemistry, U. Vienna, Austria, 1983, PhD in Biochemistry, 1986. Rsch. assoc. Inst. Virology U. Vienna, 1982-86; postdoctoral fellow U. Medicine and Dentistry of N.J., Piscataway, 1986-88; rsch. scientist Biogen, Inc., Cambridge, Mass., 1988-91, dir. med. ops., 1991—; program exec. Biogen, Inc., Cambridge, 1995—; contbr. to sci. confs.; expert presentations and articles on drug devel. strategies and mgmt. of clin. studies, chair clin. confs. Contbr. articles to profl. jours. Recipient Outstanding Achievement award Austrian Soc. Microbiology, 1986. Mem. Am. Mgmt. Assn., Drug Info. Assn., Assocs. Clin. Pharmacology. Achievement include research in virology dealing with structure function relationship of proteins, HIV, flaviviruses; industrial research in CD4, CD4-toxins, complement proteins; 3 patent applications; international clinical development of Hirulog and Beta-Interferon from phase I to phase III in cardiovascular indications, infectious diseases, and multiple sclerosis; preparations for FDA and internat. market approvals; registration of AVONEX, postmarketing studies; pre-clinical and clinical development of anti-inflammatory drugs. Home: 8 Churchill Rd Winchester MA 01890-1008 Office: Biogen Inc 14 Cambridge Ctr Cambridge MA 02142-1401

WINKLER, HENRY FRANKLIN, actor; b. N.Y.C., Oct. 30, 1945; s. Harry Irving and Ilse Anna Maria (Hadra) W.; m. Stacey Weitzman, May 5, 1978; 1 dau., Zoe Emily. Student, Emerson Coll., 1963-67, D.H.L., 1978; student, Yale Sch. Drama, 1967-70. With Yale Repertory Theatre, 1970-71; founder New Haven Free Theatre, 1968, Off The Wall N.Y., improvisation co., 1972; tchr. drama UCLA Adult Extension. Off-Broadway shows, 1972-73, Cin. Playhouse, 1973; films include The Lords of Flatbush, 1972, Crazy Joe, 1974, Heroes, 1977, The One and Only, 1977, Night Shift, 1983, Wes Craven's Scream, 1996; starred in TV series Happy Days, 1973-84, Monty, 1994, Mr. Sunshine; appeared in TV movie An American Christmas Carol, 1979 (ABC), Absolute Strangers, 1991 (CBS), The Only Way Out, 1994 (ABC), Truman Capote's One Christmas, 1994 (NBC), A Child is Missing, 1995 (CBS), Dad's Week Off, 1996 (Showtime); prodr. Sightings; exec. producer TV program Who Are the Debolts and Where Did They Get Nineteen Kids, TV series for ABC Ryan's Four, 1983, TV movie Scandal Sheet, 1984, MacGyver, 1985, producer, host home video Strong Kids, Safe Kids, 1985, PBS animated spl. Happy Ever After, 1985, Two Daddies to Love Me, 1988; producer ABC After Sch. Spl. Losing a Sister, 1988; pres. Fair Dinkum Prodns., Hollywood, Calif., 1979—, Winkler-Daniels Prodns., Hollywood, 1987-91; producer TV program Run, Don't Walk for own co. JZM Prodns., 1981; dir. TV movie A Smokey Mountain Christmas, 1986, feature film Memories of Me, 1988, Cop and a Half, 1992. Named Best Actor in Comedy Series, Photoplay mag. 1976-77, recipient Golden Globe award 1976, 77, 78; named King of Baccus, Mardi Gras, New Orleans 1977, Emmy nominee 1975, 76, 77; recipient Golden Plate award Am. Acad. Achievement 1980, Daytime Emmy nomination best dir. All The Kids Do It, produced for JZM Prodns., 1985; Sorrisi e Canzoni Telegatto award (Italian TV award) 1980; nat. spokesperson United Friends of the Children, 1982—. Recipient Humanitarian award Women in Film, 1988; named hon. youth chmn. Epilepsy Found.; chmn. Toys for Tots, 1977. Mem. AFTRA, Screen Actors Guild, Actors Equity. Office: care Richard Grant & Assoc 8484 Wilshire Blvd Ste 500 Beverly Hills CA 90211-3214

WINKLER, HENRY RALPH, retired academic administrator, historian; b. Waterbury, Conn., Oct. 27, 1916; s. Jacob and Ethel (Rieger) W.; m. Clare Sapadin, Aug. 18, 1940; children—Allan Michael, Karen Jean; m. Beatrice Ross, Jan. 28, 1973. A.B., U. Cin., 1938, M.A., 1940; Ph.D., U. Chgo., 1947; hon. degrees, Lehigh U., 1974, Rutgers U., 1977, No. Ky. U., 1978, St. Thomas Inst., 1979, Hebrew Union Coll., 1980, Xavier U., 1981, U. Akron, 1984, U. Cin., 1987, Thomas More Coll., 1989. Instr. U. Cin., 1939-40; asst. prof. Roosevelt Coll., 1946-47; mem. faculty Rutgers U., 1947-77, prof. history, 1958-77, chmn. dept., 1960-64; dean faculty Liberal Arts, 1967, vice provost, 1968-70, acting provost, 1970, v.p. for acad. affairs, 1970-72, sr. v.p. for acad. affairs, 1972-76, exec. v.p., 1976-77; exec. v.p. U. Cin., 1977, pres., 1977-84, pres. emeritus, 1984—, Univ. prof. history, 1977-86, prof. emeritus, 1986—; mng. editor Am. Hist. Rev., 1964-68; vis. prof. Bryn Mawr Coll., 1959-60, Harvard, summer 1964, Columbia, summer 1967; faculty John Hay Fellows Inst. Humanities, 1960-65; bd. overseers Hebrew Union Coll., 1984—. Author: The League of Nations Movement in Great Britain, 1914-19, 1952, Great Britain in the Twentieth Century, 1960, 2d edit., 1966; editor: (with K.M. Setton) Great Problems in European Civilization, 1954, 2d edit., 1966, Twentieth-Century Britain, 1977, Paths Not Taken: British Labour and International Policy in the Nineteen Twenties, 1994; mem. editorial bd. Historian, 1958-64, Liberal Edn., 1986—; mem. adv. bd. Partisan Rev., 1972-79; contbr. articles to jours., revs. Nat. chmn. European history advanced placement com. Coll. Entrance Exam. Bd., 1960-64; mem. Nat. Commn. on Humanities in Schs., 1967-68, Am. specialist Eastern Asia, 1968; exec. com. Conf. on Brit. Studies, 1968-75; chmn. bd. Nat. Humanities Faculty, 1970-73; chmn. adv. com. on history Coll. Entrance Exam. Bd., 1977-80; mem. council on acad. affairs, mem. bd. trustees, chmn., 1982-84; pres. Highland Park (N.J.) Bd. Edn., 1962-63; mem. exec. com. Nat. Assn. State Univs. and Land-Grant Colls., 1978-81, mem. Cin. Lit. Club, 1978—, pres., 1993—; bd. dirs. Am. Council on Edn., 1979-81; trustee Seasongood Good Govt. Found., 1979—, pres., 1991-93; trustee Thomas More Coll., 1986-93; mem. Ohio Indsl. Tech. and Enterprise Bd., 1983-89; bd. dirs. Nat. Civic League, 1986—, Planning Accreditation Bd., 1988—; mem. adv coun. Clin. Valley State Coll., Ohio Humanities Coun., 1994— With USNR, 1943-46. Recipient Lifetime Achievement award N.Am. Conf. on Brit. Studies, 1995, Bishop William Hughes award for disting. svc. to Cath. higher edn., 1997. Mem. Am. Hist. Assn., Phi Beta Kappa, Tau Kappa Alpha, Phi Alpha Theta. Clubs: Comml., Bankers, Cin., Lit. Office: U Cin 571 Langsam Library Cincinnati OH 45221

WINKLER, HOWARD LESLIE, investment banker, business and financial consultant; b. N.Y.C., Aug. 16, 1950; s. Martin and Magda (Stark) W.; m. Robin Lynn Richards, Sept. 12, 1976; 1 child, David Menachem. AA in Mktg., Los Angeles City Coll., 1973, AA in Bus. Data Processing, 1977, AA in Bus. Mgmt., 1981. Sr. cons. Fin. Cons. Inc., Los Angeles, 1972-81; asst. v.p. Merrill Lynch, Inc., Los Angeles, 1981-83; v.p. Drexel, Burnham, Lambert, Inc., Beverly Hills, Calif., 1983-84; pres. Howard Winkler Investments, Beverly Hills, Calif., 1984-90, Landmark Fin. Group, L.A., 1990-96; ptnr. N.W.B. Assocs., L.A., 1988-91; chmn. bd. United Cmty. and Housing Devel. Corp., L.A., 1986-96; bd. mem./sec. United Housing & Cmty. Svcs. Corp., 1996—; chmn. bd. United Housing and Cmty. Svcs. Corp., 1986-96; bd. dirs. Earth Products Internat., Inc., Kansas City, Kans., 1992, Fed. Home Loan Bank of San Francisco, 1991-93. Nat. polit. editor B'nai B'rith Messenger, 1986-95. Mem. Calif. Rep. Cent. Com., 1985-93; mem. L.A. County Rep. Cent. Com., 1985-92, chmn. 45th Assembly Dist., 1985-90; mem. Rep. Senatorial Inner Circle, 1986—, Rep. Presdl. Task Force, 1985— (Legion of Merit award 1992); mem. Rep. Eagles, 1988-92; Nat. Rep. Senatorial Com., 1986—, Golden Circle Calif., 1986-92, GOP Platform Planning Com. at Large del., 1992, 96; del. to GOP nat conv., Houston, 1992, San Diego, 1996; Calif. chmn. Jack Kemp for Pres., 1988, mem. nat. steering com. Bush-Quayle '88, 1987, nat. exec. com. Bush-Quayle '92, 1991; mil. adminstrv. supr. CID US Army, 1969-72, SE Asia; legis. and civic action Agudath Israel Calif., 1985—; mem. L.A. County Narcotics and Dangerous Drugs Commn., 1988—, L.A. County Drug Ct. Planning Com., 1996—; trustee, sec.-treas. Minority Health Professions Edn. Found., 1989-94; program chmn. Calif. Lincoln Clubs Polit. Action Com., 1987-88; state co-chmn. Pete Wilson for Gov. Campaign, 1989, John Seymour for Lt. Gov. Campaign, 1989-90; chpt. pres. Calif. Congress of Reps., 1989-93; chmn. Claude Parrish for Bd. of Equalization, 1989-90; founder, dir. Community Rsch. & Info. Ctr., 1986—; mem. fin. com. John Seymour for Senate '92, 1991. Decorated Legion of Merit; recipient Cmty. Svc. award Agudath Israel Calif., 1986, Pres.'s Cmty. Leadership award, 1986, Disting. Cmty. Svc. U.S. Senator Pete Wilson, 1986, Calif. Gov.'s Leadership award, 1986, Cmty. Svc. award U.S. Congresswoman Bobbi Fiedler, 1986, Resolution of Commendation Calif. State Assembly, 1986, Outstanding Cmty. Svc. Commendation Los Angeles County Bd. Suprs., 1986, 90, Outstanding Citizenship award City of Los Angeles, 1986, 90, 94, Cmty. Leadership award Iranian-Jewish Community L.A., 1990, 95, Resolution of Commendation, State of Calif., 1992, Cmty. Svc. Commendation, 1993, Rep. Senatorial Medal of Freedom award, Sentorial Inner Circle, 1994, Commendation L.A. County Bd. Suprs., 1994. Mem. Calif. Young Reps., Calif. Rep. Assembly, VFW, Jewish War Veterans. Jewish. Avocations: philanthropy, family time. Office: PO Box 480454 Los Angeles CA 90048-1454

WINKLER, IRA SAMUEL, information security consultant, educator, author; b. Bklyn., Dec. 31, 1962; s. Seymour and Sheila (Kaplan) W.; m. Molly Ann Wray, Sept. 3, 1989; children: Matthew Ray, Jason Benjamin. BA, Syracuse U., 1984; MS, Bowie State U., 1989; PhD, U. Md., Balt., 1997. Computer sys. analyst Nat. Security Agy., Ft. Meade, Md., 1984-90; computer scientist Computer Scis. Corp., Hanover, Md., 1990-92; sr. software engr. BTG, Inc., Vienna, Va., 1992-93; faculty assoc. Johns Hopkins U., Balt., 1994—; project mgr. Sci. Applications Internat. Corp., Annapolis, Md., 1993-96; dir. technology Nat. Computer Security Assn., Carlisle, Pa., 1996—; pres. Argo Prodns., Las Vegas, Nev., 1997—; U.S. adv. group Internat. Stds. Orgsn. Com. on Ergonomics, 1993—; mem. ANSI 200 Com. for Human Computer Interaction, 1993—; adj. faculty Anne Arundel C.C., Arnold, Md., 1990-92; adj. asst. prof. U. Md., College Park, 1992—; presenter in field. Author: Corporate Espionage, 1997; co-author: Through the Eyes of the Enemy, 1997; co-author: People Before Technology, 1991, The Official Internetworld Internet Security Handbook, 1995, The Internet and Internetworking Security Handbook, 1997; editl. asst. Sigchi Bull., 1994—; reviewer MIS Quar., 1992—; contbg. editor: Internetwork, 1996—; contbr. articles to profl. jours. Mem. Assn. for Computing Machinery, Info. Sys. Security Assn., Nat. Computer Security Assn. (cons. 1995—), Soc. for Competitive Intelligence Profls., Armed Forces Comm. and Electronics Assn. (scholarship com. 1990), Chesapeake Bay Country Wanderers (club rep. 1995-96), Mensa, Intertel, Phi Kappa Phi. Avocations: volksmarching, karate. Home: 35 Sunset Dr Severna Park MD 21146 Office: Nat Computer Security Assn 1200 Walnut Bottom Rd Carlisle PA 17013-7635

WINKLER, IRWIN, motion picture producer; b. N.Y.C., May 28, 1934; s. Sol and Anna Winkler. BA, NYU, 1955. Mailroom messenger William Morris Agy., N.Y.C., 1955-62; motion picture producer, owner Winkler Films, Culver City, Calif., 1982—; pres., Chartoff-Winkler Prodns., 1966—. Producer: Rocky, 1976 (10 Acad. award nominations, winner 3 including Best Picture, Los Angeles Film Critics award for best picture), They Shoot Horses Don't They, 1969 (9 Acad. award nominations), Nickelodeon, 1976, The Gambler, 1974, Up the Sandbox, 1972, The New Centurions, 1972, Point Blank, 1967, Double Trouble, 1967, Leo the Last, 1970 (Best Dir. award Cannes Film Festival, Belgrade Film Festival), The Strawberry Statement, 1970 (Jury prize Cannes Film Festival), The Split, 1968, Breakout, 1975, Believe in Me, 1971, The Gang That Couldn't Shoot Straight, 1971, The Mechanic, 1972, Busting, 1974, S.P.Y.S, 1974, Peeper, 1975, New York, New York, 1977, Valentino, 1977, Uncle Joe Shannon, 1978, Comes a Horseman, 1978, Rocky II, 1979, Raging Bull, 1980 (8 Acad. award nominations, winner 2, Los Angeles Film Critics award for best picture), Rocky III, 1981, True Confessions, 1981, Author, Author, 1982, The Right Stuff, 1983 (8 Acad. award nominations), Rocky IV, 1984, Revolution, 1985, 'Round Midnight, 1986 (2 Acad. award nomiations, Acad. award Best Original Score), Betrayed, 1988 (Chgo. Film Festival Lifetime Irwin Achievement award 1987), Goodfellas, 1990 (6 Acad. award nominationThe Net, 1995, The Juror, 1996; dir, writer: The Net, 1995, Guilty by Suspicion,1991.s, winner 1, Brit. Acad. award Best Picture, N.Y. Film Critics Best Picture, L.A. Film Critics Best Picture), Rocky V, 1990, Music Box, 1990 (Golden Bear award for best film Berlin Film Festival); writer/dir.: Guilty by Suspicion, 1991 (U.S. selection Cannes Film Festival); producer/dir.: Night and the City, 1992 (N.Y. Film Festival, London Film Festival), The Net, 1995; retrospectives Brit. Film Inst., 1989, Chgo. Film Festival, 1989, Mus. Modern Art, N.Y.C., 1990, L.A. County Mus. Art, 1992. Served with U.S. Army, 1951-53. Named Commander d'Artes et de Lettres, French Govt. Minister of Culture, 1985. Mem. Am. Film Inst. (bd. govs.), Prodrs. Guild Am. (bd. dirs.). Office: Winkler Films 211 S Beverly Dr Ste 200 Beverly Hills CA 90212-3828

WINKLER, JOANN MARY, secondary school educator; b. Savanna, Ill., Dec. 17, 1955; d. Donald Edgar and Genevieve Eleanor (Withhart) Winkler; m. Russell Arthur Ehlers, May 25, 1990; 1 child, Genevieve Rose Winkler Ehlers. BS in Art Edn., No. Ill. U., 1979; MA in Art Edn., N.E. Mo. State U., 1984. Tchr. art, chmn. dept. art Clinton (Iowa) H.S., 1979—; Coll. for Kids instr. Area Edn. Agy. #9, Clinton, summers, 1986—, Davenport, summers, 1987—; instr. St. Ambrose U., Clinton, 1990, Mt. St. Clare Coll., Clinton, 1993—. Costume designer Utah Mus. Theatre, "Two by Two," 1987; exhibited in group shows at Clinton Art Assn., 1990-93. Judge Art in the Park, Clinton, 1988, 93; co. mgr. Utah Mus. Theager, Ogden, 1987; founding bd. dirs. Art's Alive, Clinton, 1985-86; bd. dirs. Gateway Contemporary Ballet, Clinton, 1987-89; founding com. mem. Louis Sullivan's Van Allen Bldg. Jr. Mus., Clinton, 1991-93. Recipient Gold Key Group award Clinton Sch. Bd., 1990, Gold Key Individual award, 1989; R.I. Sch. Design scholar, 1989, Alliance for Ind. Colls. of Art scholar, summers 1988. Mem. NEA, Ill. Art Edn. Assn., Chgo. Art Inst., Clinton Art Assn., Art Educators of Iowa, Nat. Art Edn. Assn., PEO. Avocations: swimming, travel, theater. Home: 722 Melrose Ct Clinton IA 52732-5508 Office: Clinton High Sch 817 8th Ave S Clinton IA 52732-5616

WINKLER, JOSEPH CONRAD, former recreational products manufacturing executive; b. Newark, May 20, 1916; s. Charles and Mollie (Abrams) W.; m. Geraldine M. Borok, Sept. 20, 1953; children: Charles H., David J. B.S., NYU, 1941. Gen. mgr. Indsl. Washing Machine Corp., New Brunswick, N.J., 1941-48; controller Mojud Corp., N.Y.C., 1948-52; controller, asst. treas. Barbizon Corp., N.Y.C., 1952-57; controller Ideal Toy Corp., N.Y.C., 1957-58; dir. fin. and adminstrn. Ideal Toy Corp., 1960-62, v.p. fin., 1962-68, sr. v.p. fin., 1968-78, exec. v.p., chief operating officer, dir., 1978-81, pres., dir., 1981-83; exec. in residence, mem. bus. adv. coun. Sch. Bus. Adminstrn., Montclair (N.J.) State U., 1983-90; controller McGregor-Doniger, Inc., N.Y.C., 1958-59; dir. Ideal of Australia Ltd., Melbourne, 1963-82, Ideal of Canada Ltd., Toronto, 1963-82, Ideal of Japan Ltd., Tokyo and Kiowa, 1963-80, Ideal Toy Co. Ltd., High Wycombe and Wokingham, Eng., 1966-82, Arxon Spiel & Freizeit GmbH, Rotgau, Germany, 1968-82, Perfekta Ltd. and Hollis Industries Ltd., Hong Kong, 1970-74, Ideal Loisirs S.A., Paris, 1972-82. Mem. editorial rev. bd. Issues in Internat. Bus., 1985—. Committeeman, troop treas. Boy Scouts Am., Tenafly, N.J., 1965-71; bd. dirs. N.Y. League Hard of Hearing, 1982-88; active Nat. Roster Sci. and Splized. Pers., War Manpower Commn., 1941-46. Served with Office Statis. Control USAAF, 1945. Mem. Fin. Execs. Inst. Home: 3546 S Ocean Blvd Apt 605 Palm Beach FL 33480-5720

WINKLER, LEE B., business consultant; b. Buffalo, Dec. 31, 1925; s. Jack W. and Caroline (Marienthal) W.; children: James, Cristina Ehrlich, Richard Ehrlich Jr.; m. Maria Mal Verde. B.S. cum laude, NYU, 1945, M.S. cum laude, 1947. Mgr. LBW, Inc. (formerly Winkler Assocs. Ltd.), N.Y.C., 1948-58; pres. Winkler Assocs. Ltd., Beverly Hills, Calif., and N.Y.C., 1958—; exec. dir. Global Bus. Mgmt. Inc., Beverly Hills, 1967—; v.p. Bayly Martin & Fay Inc., N.Y.C., 1965-68, John C. Paige & Co., N.Y.C., 1968-71; cons. Albert G. Ruben Co., Beverly Hills, 1971—. Served with AUS, 1943-45. Decorated chevalier comdr. Order Holy Cross Jerusalem, also spl. exec. asst., charge d'affaires, 1970; chevalier comdr. Sovereign Order Cyprus, 1970. Mem. Nat. Acad. TV Arts and Scis., Nat. Acad. Recording Arts and Scis., Beverly Hills C. of C., Phi Beta Kappa, Beta Gamma Sigma, Mu Gamma Tau, Psi Chi Omega. Office: 15250 Ventura Blvd Sherman Oaks CA 91403-3201 *In the final analysis, the bottom line, if you will—the only thing that truly matters in life are those friends and family that hold you dear to them. Success, and its attendant monies, rise and fall like the tides, and even vanish at times, but earned love is as constant as the earth's rotation is independent of the tides.*

WINKLER, PAUL FRANK, JR., astrophysicist, educator; b. Nashville, Nov. 10, 1942; s. Paul Frank and Estelle (Pye) W.; m. Geraldine Huck, Aug. 20, 1966 (div. 1979); children: Katharine Estelle, Johanna Pye; m. Janet Pippit Beers, June 25, 1983; stepchildren: Sarah Creighton Beers, Nathan Pippitt Beers. B.S., Calif. Inst. Tech., 1964; A.M., Harvard U., 1965, Ph.D., 1970. From instr. to prof. physics Middlebury Coll., Vt., 1969—, chmn. dept., 1980-88, William R. Kenan Jr. prof. physics, 1984-87, chmn. nat. scis. div., 1988-93, asst. to pres. for sci. planning, 1993-96; vis. scientist MIT, Cambridge, 1973-74, 78-80; sr. vis. fellow Inst. Astronomy U. Cambridge, 1985-86; vis. resident astronomer Cerro Tololo InterAm. Observatory, La Serena, Chile, 1990-91, 96-97; vis. fellow Joint Inst. for Laboratory Astrophysics, U. Colo., Boulder, 1991. Contbr. articles to profl. jours. NSF fellow, 1965-69, Alfred P. Sloan Found. fellow, 1976-80. Mem. Am. Phys. Soc., Am. Astron. Soc., Internat. Astron. Union, Coun. on Undergraduate Rsch. Office: Middlebury Coll Dept Physics Middlebury VT 05753

WINKLER, SHELDON, dentist, educator; b. N.Y.C., Jan. 25, 1932; s. Ben and Lillian (Barsh) W.; m. Sandra M. Cohen, Aug. 13, 1961; children: Mitchell, Lori. BA, Washington Sq. Coll., 1953; DDS, NYU, 1956. Asst. prof. denture prosthesis NYU Coll. Dentistry, N.Y.C., 1958-61, 66-68, rsch. asst. prof., 1962-63; dir. materials rsch. Consol. Metal Products Industries Inc., Albany, N.Y., 1963-65, cons. materials rsch., 1966-68; asst. prof. removable prosthodontics sch. dentistry SUNY, Buffalo, 1968-70; assoc. prof. SUNY, 1970-79; prof., chmn. dept. prosthodontics Temple U. Sch. Dentistry, Phila., 1979-86, 94-96, asst. dean for advanced studies, continuing edn./rsch., 1987-89, acting asst. dean, 1993-95; asst. dir., vis. dentist, dental dept. NYU Med. Center, Goldwater Meml. Hosp., N.Y.C., 1966-68; attending in prosthodontics E.J. Meyer Meml. Hosp., Buffalo, 1975-79; postgrad. instr. First Dist. Dental Soc. N.Y., N.Y.C., 1963—; cons. Coe Labs., Chgo., 1967-87, Harkness Center, Buffalo, Rosa Coplon Home and Infirmary, Buffalo, 1970-79, Erie C.C., Buffalo, 1979—, Lever Bros. Co., N.Y.C., 1981—, VA Hosp., Phila., 1989—; lectr. dept. dental hygiene N.Y.C. Cmty. Coll., 1967-68. Author: (with A. Davidoff and M.H.M. Lee) Dentistry for the Special Patient: The Aged, Chronically Ill and Handicapped, 1972, Essentials of Complete Denture Prosthodontics, 1979, 2d edit., 1988; editor: Resins in Dentistry, 1975, Complete Dentures, 1977, Removable Prosthodontics, 1984; editor Jour. Implant Dentistry, 1990—; contbr. articles to profl. lit.; co-designer McGowan-Winkler complete denture trays. Served as capt. AUS, 1956-58, 61-62. Recipient Outstanding Layman award Vocat. Tech. Alumni and Student Assn., SUNY, Buffalo, 1974, Internat. Edn. award Internat. Congress Oral Implantologists, 1992, journalism award Internat. Coll. Dentists, 1993, Academic Devotion award Chulalongkorn U., Bangkok, 1995. Fellow Am. Coll. Dentists, Greater N.Y. Acad. Prosthodontics; mem. ADA, Internat. Assn. Dental Rsch., Am. Assn. Dental Schs., Am. Acad. Implant Prosthodontics, Sci. Rsch. Soc. Am., Acad. Plastics Rsch., Am. Prosthodontic Soc., Am. Soc. Geriatric Dentistry, Internat. Congress of Oral Implantologists, Sigma Xi, Sigma Epsilon Delta, Omicron Kappa Upsilon. Home: 1224 Liberty Bell Dr Cherry Hill NJ 08003-2759 Office: Sch Dentistry Temple U Philadelphia PA 19140

WINKS, ROBIN WILLIAM, history educator; b. West Lafayette, Ind., Dec. 5, 1930; s. Evert McKinley and Jewell (Sampson) W.; m. Avril Flockton, Sept. 27, 1952; children: Honor Leigh, Eliot Myles. BA magna cum laude, U. Colo., 1952, MA, 1953; PhD with distinction, Johns Hopkins U., 1957; MA (hon.), Yale U., 1967; DLitt (hon.), U. Nebr., 1976, U. Colo., 1987; MA (hon.), Oxford U., 1992; DPhil, Westminster Coll., 1995. From instr. to Randolph W. Townsend prof. history Yale U., New Haven, 1957—, dir. office of spl. projects and founds., 1974-76, master Berkeley Coll., 1977-90; Eastman prof. Oxford U., 1992-93, chair studies in environment, 1993-96, chair dept. history, 1996—. Author: Canada and the U.S., 1960, The Cold War, 1964, Historiography of the British Empire-Commonwealth, 1966, History of Malaysia, 1967, Age of Imperialism, 1969, Pastmasters, 1969; The Historian as Detective, 1969, A Forty-Year Minuet, 1970, The Blacks in Canada, 1971, Slavery, 1972, An American's Guide to Britain, 1977, Other Voices, Other Views, 1978, Relevance of Canadian History, 1979, Western Civilization, 1979, Detective Fiction, 1980, Modus Operandi, 1982, History of Civilization, 1984, Cloak and Gown, 1987, Asia in Western Fiction, 1990, Frederick Billings, 1991, The Imperial Revolution, 1994, Laurance S. Rockefeller, Catalyst for Conservation, 1997. Cultural attache U.S. Embassy, London, 1969-71; chair Nat. Park System Adv. Bd., Washington, 1981-83, bicentennial com. for Internat. Confs. of Americanists Dept. State, 1974-77. Smith-Mundt prof. U. Malaya, 1962; Inst. Commonwealth Studies at U. London fellow, 1966-67; Guggenheim fellow, 1976-77; grantee Social Sci. Rsch. Coun., 1959, 75; Resident scholar Sch. Am. Rsch., 1985, 91, 94. Fellow Royal Hist. Soc., Explorers Club; mem. Am. Hist. Assn., Can. Hist. Assn., Royal Commonwealth Soc. (life), Yale Club (N.Y.C.), Athenaeum, Spl. Forces Club. Office: Yale U Dept History PO Box 1504 A New Haven CT 06506-1504

WINN, ALBERT CURRY, clergyman; b. Ocala, Fla., Aug. 16, 1921; s. James Anderson and Elizabeth (Curry) W.; m. Grace Neely Walker, Aug. 29, 1944; children: Grace Walker (Mrs. Stewart E. Ellis), James Anderson, Albert Bruce Curry, Randolph Axson. A.B., Davidson Coll., 1942, LL.D., 1968; B.D., Union Theol. Sem., Va., 1945, Th.D., 1956; Th.M., Princeton Theol. Sem., 1949; LL.D., Stillman Coll., 1975. Ordained to ministry Presbyn. Ch., 1945; asst. prof. Davidson Coll., 1946-47; pastor Potomac Rural Parish, Va., 1948-53; prof. Bible Stillman Coll., 1953-60; prof. theology Louisville Presbyn. Theol. Sem., 1960-73, pres., 1966-73; pastor 2d Presbyn. Ch., Richmond, Va., 1974-81, N. Decatur Presbyn. Ch., Decatur, Ga., 1981-86; Moderator Presbyn. Synod Ala., 1958, Presbyn. Synod Ky., 1969, Gen. Assembly, Presbyn. Ch. in U.S., 1979; vis. prof. Union Theol. Sem. in Va., 1987, Columbia Theol. Sem., 1987, Louisville Presbyn. Theol. Sem., 1988; interim pastor Cen. Presbyn. Ch., Atlanta, 1989-90, St. Andrews Presbyn. Ch., Tucker, Ga., 1993-94. Author: Layman's Bible Commentary on Acts, 1960, The Worry and Wonder of Being Human, 1966, Where Do I Go From Here, 1972, Proclamation Two: Epiphany, 1980, A Sense of Mission, 1981, Christ the Peacemaker, 1982, Plain Talk about the Apostles' Creed, 1985, The Christian Primer, 1990, Ain't Gonna Study War No More, 1993. Chmn. trustees Stillman Coll., 1965-70. Served as chaplain USNR, 1945-46. Mem. Phi Beta Kappa, Beta Theta Pi, Omicron Delta Kappa. Office: 3812 Forrestgate Dr Winston Salem NC 27103

WINN, C(OLMAN) BYRON, mechanical engineering educator; b. Canton, Mo., Nov. 21, 1933; s. Colman Kersey and Kiula Elmeda (Ingold) W.; m.

Donna Sue Taylor, Aug. 25, 1957; children: Byron, Derek, Julie. BS in Aeronautics, U. Ill., 1958; MS in Aeronautics, Stanford U., 1960, PhD, 1967. Engr. Lockheed Missiles & Space Co., Palo Alto, Calif., 1958-60, sr. engr., 1962-64; rsch. scientist Martin-Marietta, Denver, 1960-62; lectr. Santa Clara (Calif.) U., 1963-65; assoc. prof. Colo. State U., Ft. Collins, 1966-74, prof. mech. engring., 1974—, prof., head dept., 1982-95, assoc. dean, 1995—; cons. Space Rsch. Corp., North Troy, Vt., 1969-73; pres. Solar Environ. Engring. Co., 1973-85. Author: Controls in Solar Energy Systems, 1982, Controls in Solar Energy Systems, 1993; assoc. editor Jour. Solar Energy Engring., 1982-89, Passive Solar Jour., 1987, Advances in Solar Energy, 1996—. Loaned exec. United Way, Ft. Collins, 1992. With U.S. Army, 1953-55. Named Disting. Alumnus U. Ill., 1984, J.E. Cermak Adv. award, 1986, EPPEC award Platte River Power Authority, 1992, ABELL Svc. award, 1997. Fellow ASME; mem. AIAA (Energy Systems award 1991), Internat. Solar Energy Soc. (bd. dirs. 1980-89), Am. Solar Energy Soc. (bd. dirs. 1979-86, solar action com. 1991-93), Tau Beta Pi. Achievements include development of controllers for solar energy systems; design and development of the reconfigurable passive evaluation analysis and test facility; founding of the Energy Analysis and Diagnostic Center, The Waste Minimization Assessment Center, The Industrial Assessment Center and Manufacturing Excellence Center at Colo. State U. Office: Colo State U Dept Mech Engring Fort Collins CO 80523

WINN, H. RICHARD, surgeon; b. Chester, Pa., 1947. MD, U. Pa., 1968; BA, Princeton U., 1964. Diplomate Am Bd. Neurological Surgeons. Intern U. Hosp., Cleve., 1968-69, resident surgery, 1969-70; resident neurolog. surgery U. Hosp. Va., Charlottesville, 1970-74; neurol. surgeon U. Wash. Hosp., Seattle, 1983—; prof., chmn. neurol. surgery U. Wash., Seattle, 1983—; dir. Am. Bd. Neurol. Surgery. Founding editor Neurosurgical Clinics of North Amercia; mem. editl. bd. Jour. Neurosurgery, Am. Jour. Physiology, Am. Jour. Surgery. Fellow AAAS, Soc. Brit. Neurol. Surgeons (hon.); mem. AMA, Coll. Neurol. Surgery, Am. Assn. Neurol. Surgeons. Office: U Wash Dept Neurosurg 325 9th Ave # 359766 Seattle WA 98104-2420

WINN, JAMES JULIUS, JR., lawyer; b. Colon, Panama, Nov. 7, 1941; came to U.S., 1941; s. James Julius and Molly (Brown) W.; m. Elizabeth Kokernot Lacy, Aug. 15, 1970; children: Mary Ann, Elizabeth Lacy, James Julius VI. AB, Princeton U., 1964; JD cum laude, Washington and Lee U., 1970. Bar: Md. 1970, U.S. Dist. Ct. Md. 1971, U.S. Dist. Ct. D.C. 1982. Assoc. Piper & Marbury L.L.P., Balt., 1970-78, ptnr., 1978—. Assoc. editor, contbr. author Washington & Lee U. Law Rev., 1968-70. Counselor St. John's Ch., Western Run Parish, Glyndon, Md., 1974—; mem. com. on canons and other bus., investment com. Episc. Diocese Md., 1986—; dir. Ctr. for Ethics and Corp. Policy, 1988-95, chmn., 1991-95; dir. Ctr. Stage, 1986—; dir. Oldfields Sch., 1991-96; v.p., dir. Ruxton Country Sch., 1988-91. Mem. ABA (chmn. subcom. on publs. of com. on law and acctg. of sect. of bus. law), Md. State Bar Assn. (com. on corp. law of sect. of bus. law). Office: Piper & Marbury LLP 36 S Charles St Baltimore MD 21201-3020

WINN, KENNETH HUGH, archivist, historian; b. Seattle, June 27, 1953; s. John Hugh and Elaine (Spoor) W.; m. Karen Anderson, June 13, 1981; children: Alice Anderson, David Dysart. BA, Colo. State U., 1975, MA, 1977; AM, Washington U., 1979, PhD, 1985. Resident historian Mo. Hist. Soc., St. Louis, 1987-90, jour. editor, 1987-91, dir. publications, 1989-91; state archivist Sec. State, Jefferson City, Mo., 1991—; vis. asst. prof. Washington U., St. Louis, 1984-87, adj. asst. prof., 1987-90, adj. prof., 1991—; cons. St. Louis Art Mus., 1989-90; dep. coord. Mo. Hist. Records adv. bd., 1991—; adv. bd. Mo. Ctr. for Book, 1993-97; bd. dirs. Mo. Conf. History, 1991-95, pres., 1994-95; vice chair Mo. Bd. Geog. Place Names, 1995—. Author: Exiles in a Land of Liberty, 1989; co-author Differing Visions, 1994. Charlotte W. Newcombe fellow Woodrow Wilson Found., 1981-82; grantee Richard S. Brownlee Fund, 1992-93, 93-94, 95-97. Mem. Nat. Assn. Govt. Archives and Records Adminstrs. (pubs. com. 1996—), Am. Hist. Assn., Orgn. Am. Historians, Coun. State Hist. Records Coords. (chair steering com. 1997—), Soc. Historians Early Am. Republic. Home: 814 Primrose Ln Jefferson City MO 65109-1888 Office: Mo State Archives 600 W Main St Jefferson City MO 65101-1532

WINN, ROBERT CHEEVER, rehabilitation services professional; b. N.Y.C., Apr. 11, 1939; s. Richard Wilkens and Ella Jane (Mackenzie) W.; m. Margery Ellen Irwin (div. Sept. 1983); children: Elizabeth Jane, Margaret Ruth, Nancy Louise; m. Susan Elizabeth Gengler, June 4, 1988. BA, U. Bridgeport, 1962; MA, Ball State U., 1975. Advanced through grades to maj. USAF, 1963-83; customer support rep. Boeing Mil. Airplanes, Wichita, Kans., 1983-89; counselor Wichita Counseling Ctr., 1988; vocat. rehab. counselor Kans. Rehab. Svcs., Wellington, 1989—. Mem. Sumner County ADA Accsssibility Adv. Bd., 1994—; deacon Hillside Christian Ch., 1991-94, elder, 1995—. Named one of Outstanding Young Men of Am., 1974. Mem. Nat. Rehab. Assn., Kans. Rehab. Assn., Kans. Head Injury Assn., Lions (pres. 1994-95, zone chmn. 1991-92, 94-95), VFW (jr. vice comdr. Derby, Kans. chpt. 1989, adj. 1988), Kans. Rehab. Couselors Assn. (sec., treas. 1994-96). Republican. Home: 924 Bristol Ter Wichita KS 67207-4306 Office: Kans Rehab Svcs 1116 W 8th St Wellington KS 67152-3423

WINN, STEVEN JAY, critic; b. Phila., Apr. 25, 1951; s. Willis Jay and Lois (Gengelbach) W.; m. Katharine Weber, Sept. 15, 1979 (div. Dec. 1985); m. Sally Ann Noble, July 22, 1989; 1 child, Phoebe Ann. BA, U. Pa., 1973; MA, U. Wash., 1975. Staff writer, editor Seattle Weekly, 1975-79; staff critic San Francisco Chronicle, 1980—. Co-author: Ted Bundy: The Killer Next Door, 1980; contbr. articles to various publs. Wallace Stegner fellow Stanford U., 1979-80. Office: San Francisco Chronicle 901 Mission St San Francisco CA 94103-2905

WINNEKER, CRAIG ANTHONY, journalist; b. Chgo., Dec. 19, 1966; s. Allan Seymour and Betty Sue (Stone) W.; m. Karen Elizabeth Hoehn, Apr. 21, 1990. BA, Tex. Christian U., 1987. Rschr. Capitol Jour./PBS, Washington, 1986; asst. prodr. The McLaughlin Group/PBS, Washington, 1987-89; staff writer Roll Call Newspaper, Washington, 1989-91, assoc. editor, 1991-93, sr. editor, 1993-95, mng. editor, 1995—; guest lectr. Close Up Found., Washington, 1991—; treas. exec. com. of corr. Periodical Press Gallery, U.S. Congress, Washington, 1994-96, chmn., 1997—. Recipient Disting. Alumni award The Washington Ctr. for Internships and Acad. Seminars, 1995. Office: Roll Call Newspaper 900 2nd St NE Washington DC 20002-3557

WINNER, KARIN, newspaper editor. Editor San Diego Union-Tribune. Office: Copley Press Inc 350 Camino De La Reina San Diego CA 92108-3003

WINNER, MICHAEL ROBERT, film director, writer, producer; b. London, Oct. 30, 1935; s. George Joseph and Helen (Zloty) W. Degree in law and econs. with honors, Cambridge (Eng.) U., 1956. Writer Fleet St. (newspapers), London, 1956-58; columnist London Sunday Times, 1990—, London News of the World, 1995—. Engaged in film prodn., 1956—; dir. films Play it Cool, 1962, West 11, 1963, The Mechanic, 1972, Death Wish II, 1981; dir., writer The Cool Mikado, 1962, You Must be Joking, 1965, The Wicked Lady, 1982; producer, dir. The System, 1963, I'll Never Forget What's 'isname, 1967, The Games, 1969, Lawman, 1970, The Nightcomers, 1971, Chato's Land, 1971, Scorpio, 1972, The Stone Killer, 1973, Death Wish, 1974, Won Ton Ton The Dog Who Saved Hollywood, 1975, Firepower, 1978, Scream for Help, 1983, Death Wish III, 1985; producer, writer, dir. films The Jokers, 1966, Hannibal Brooks, 1968, The Sentinel, 1976, The Big Sleep, 1977, Appointment With Death, 1987, A Chorus of Disapproval, 1988, Bullseye!, 1989, Dirty Weekend, 1992, Parting Shots, 1997; producer plays Nights at the Comedy, Comedy Theatre, London, 1960, The Silence of St. Just, Gardner Centre, Brighton, 1971, The Tempest, Wyndhams Theatre, London, 1974, A Day in Hollywood, A Night in the Ukraine, Mayfair Theatre, London, 1978, (TV series London Weekend TV) Michael Winner's True Crimes, 1990, 91, 92, 93, 94. Founder, chmn. Police Meml. Trust, 1984. Mem. Dirs. Guild Gt. Britain (coun., trustee, chief censorship officer 1983). Office: Scimitar Films Ltd, 6-8 Sackville St, London W1X 1DD, England

WINNER, THOMAS GUSTAV, foreign literature educator; b. Prague, Czechoslovakia, May 4, 1917; came to U.S., 1939, naturalized, 1950; s. Julius and Franziska (Grünhutová) Wiener; m. Irene Portis, Sept. 25, 1942; children: Ellen, Lucy Franziska. Student, Charles U., Prague, 1936-38, U. Lille, France, 1936; B.A., Harvard U., 1942, M.A., 1943; Ph.D., Columbia U., 1950; M.A. (hon.), Brown U., 1966; PhD (hon.), Masaryk U., 1995. With OWI, 1943-46; vis. fellow Johns Hopkins, 1947-48; from instr. Russian to asso. prof. Duke, 1948-58; asso. prof., then prof. Slavic langs. and lits. U. Mich., 1958-65; prof. Slavic langs. and comparative lit. Brown U., 1965-82, chmn. dept. Slavic langs., 1968-72, prof. emeritus, 1982—; dir. Center for Research in Semiotics, 1977-83; dir. Program in Semiotic Studies Boston U., 1984—; Fulbright lectr. Sorbonne, Paris, 1956-57, Ruhr Univ., Bochum, Fed. Republic Germany, 1989; exchange prof. U. Warsaw, 1972-73, U. Zagreb, spring 1973; mem. seminar theory lit. Columbia, 1968—. Author: Oral Art and Literature of the Kazakhs of Russian Central Asia, 1958, Chekhov and his Prose, 1965; editor: Brown U. Slavic Reprints; editor Am. Jour. Semiotics, 1980-85; spl. interests Russian lit., Czech lit., semiotics and poetics. Ford Found. sr. fellow, 1951-52, NEH sr. fellow, 1972, 92-93; Rockefeller grantee, 1977, IREX grantee, 1972, 78, 79, 90, 92, Fulbright-Hayes, 1973; recipient Josef Dobrovsky medal Acad. Scis. Czech Republic, 1997. Mem. MLA, Am. Com. Slavists, Internat. Assn. for Semiotic Studies, Semiotics Soc. Am. (pres. 1977-78), Czech. Semiotic Soc. (hon.), Am. Soc. Tchrs. Slavic and East European Langs., Czechoslovak Soc. for Arts and Scis. (v.p. 1982-85), Comparative Lit. Assn., Internat. Assn. Slavists, Am. Assn. Advancement of Slavic Studies, Karel Teige Soc. (Czech Republic), F.X. Salda Soc. (Czech Republic). Address: 986 Memorial Dr Apt 404 Cambridge MA 02138-5739

WINNIE, ALON PALM, anesthesiologist, educator; b. Milw., May 16, 1932; s. Russell Griffith and Evelyn Dorothy (Olson) W.; m. June Patton Bethune, July 16, 1960 (div.); children: Alon Palm Jr., Russell, Debra. B.A., Princeton U., 1954; M.D., Northwestern U., 1958. Diplomate Am. Bd. Anesthesiology. Mem. teaching staff Cook County Hosp., Chgo., 1963-72; assoc. dir. anesthesia Cook County Hosp., 1968-72; prof. anesthesiology, head dept. U. Ill. Coll. Medicine, 1972-89; dir. Pain Control Ctr., U. Ill. Hosp., Chgo., 1989-92; chmn. dept. anesthesiology & pain mgmt. Cook County Hosp., Chgo., 1992—. Author: Plexus Anesthesia (Book of Yr. award Anesthesia Found. 1983). Served as 1st lt. M.C. USAF. Recipient Humanitarian award Mil. Soc. Anesthesiologists, 1980, Gillespie award Faculty of Anesthetists of Royal Australasian Coll. Surgery, 1986, Nils Lofgren award Astra Pharmm. Products inc., 1987, Duncan Ferguson Meml. award Brigham & Women's Hosp., 1988, 92, Dhunes Meml. Lectureship U. Goteborg (Sweden), 1990, Corrino Meml. Lectureship Harvard Med. Sch., 1993, Caribbean Lectureship, 1996. Fellow Am. Coll. Anesthesiologists, Australian and New Zealand Coll. Anesthetists, Royal Coll. Anesthetists; mem. AMA, Am. Soc. Regional Anesthesia (pres. 1976-80, Gaston Labat award 1982), Am. Soc. Anesthesiologists, Ill. Soc. Anesthesiologists (pres. 1971-72, Disting. Svc. award 1974, McQuiston award 1983), Ill. Soc. Anesthesiologists, Chgo. Soc. Anesthesiologists (pres. 1968-74). Republican. Episcopalian. Office: 1835 W Harrison St Chicago IL 60612-3701

WINNIE, GLENNA BARBARA, pediatric pulmonologist; b. Lansing, Mich., Oct. 14; d. Robert John and Irene (Fetchik) W.; m. Jeffrey Alan Cooper, Mar. 17, 1990; children: Robert Jefferson Cooper, David Jamison Cooper. BS, Mich. State U., 1973; MD, Vanderbilt U., 1977. Diplomate Am. Bd. Pediatrics, Am. Bd. Pediatric Pumonology. Resident in pediatrics Case Western Res. U./Babies and Childrens Hosp., Cleve., 1977-79, fellow in pediatric pulmonology, 1979-82; asst. prof. pediatrics Albany (N.Y.) Med. Coll., 1982-90, assoc. prof. pediatrcis, 1990-95, head pediatric pulmonology sect., 1982-95; assoc. prof. pediat. U. Pitts., 1995—; dir. Albany Pediat. Pulmonary and Cystic Fibrosis Ctr., 1982-95; adminstrv. dir. pulmonary divsn. Children's Hosp. of Pitts., 1995—, co-dir. Cystic Fibrosis Ctr., 1995—. Contbr. articles to profl. jours. Bd. dirs. Albany Ronald McDonald Ho., 1986-88. Rsch. grantee Nat. Cystic Fibrosis Found., 1984-88, 88-90, NIH, 1987-93. Mem. Am. Acad. Pediatrics (exec. com. chest sect. 1996—), Am. Thoracic Soc. (rsch. fellowship review com. 1989-92), Capital Dist. Pediatric Soc. (treas. 1985-90, pres. 1990-91), Soc. Pediat. Rsch. Episcopalian. Achievements include description of role of Epstein Barr virus in pulmonary exacerbations in cystic fibrosis. Office: Childrens Hosp of Pitts 3705 5th Ave Pittsburgh PA 15213-2524

WINNING, JOHN PATRICK, lawyer; b. Murphysboro, Ill., Oct. 29, 1952; s. William T. Jr. and Lillian (Albers) W.; m. Jessica Anne Yoder, June 17, 1978; children: Erika Anne, Brian Patrick, Derek Matthew. AB with distinction, Mo. Bapt. Coll., 1974; JD, St. Louis U., 1979. Bar: Mo. 1979, U.S. Dist. Ct. (ea. dist.) Mo. 1979, U.S. Ct. Appeals (8th cir.) 1979, U.S. Dist. Ct. (so. dist.) Tex. 1985, U.S. Ct. Appeals (5th cir.) 1987, U.S. Dist. Ct. (we. dist.) Tex. 1988, Tex. 1989. Assoc. Chused, Strauss, Chorlins, Goldfarb, Bini & Kohn, St. Louis, 1979-81; assoc. counsel Mfrs. Hanover Fin. Services, Phila., 1981-83; corp. counsel Cessna Fin. Corp., Wichita, Kans., 1983-85; atty. Southwestern Bell Publs., Inc., St. Louis, 1985-90; pvt. practice St. Louis, 1990—; pres. Butler Hill Investments, Inc., St. Louis, 1990-91; prin. Success Mgmt. Group, 1991-96; ptnr. DPPC Mgmt. Group, St. Louis, 1996—; sec., bd. dirs. Winning Equipment Co.; asst. prof. bus. adminstn. Mo. Bapt. Coll., 1986-91. Treas. Concerned Citizens of Chesterfield, 1989-91; deacon, mem. fin. com. 1st Bapt. Ch., Ellisville, Mo., 1992-93, vice chmn. fin. com., 1993-94, chmn. fin. com., 1994-95, vice chmn. deacons, 1993-95, dir. Sunday sch., 1993-94; bd. trustees, chmn. athletic com., chmn. by-laws com. Mo. Bapt. Coll., 1992—, sec. presidl. search com., 1994, mem. exec. com., bd. trustees, 1994—; mgr. St. Louis Flames Youth Baseball, 1992-95; mgr. St. Louis Thunder Youth Baseball, 1995—; coach St. Clare Bulls Basketball Team, 1994—; asst. scoutmaster troop 313 Boy Scouts Am., 1997—. Named one of Outstanding Young Men of Am., 1987, Outstanding Alumnus Mo. Bapt. Coll., 1987-88, Athletic Hall of Fame, Mo. Bapt. Coll., 1989. Mem. Nat. Lawyers Assn., Eagle Scouts Assn., Met. St. Louis Bar Assn., Christian Legal Soc., Acad. Family Mediators, Assn. Family and Conciliation Cts., Mo. Bapt. Coll. Alumni Assn. (pres. 1980-81, 88-90), St. Louis Assn., Christian Attys., West County C. of C., Chesterfield C. of C. Republican. Southern Baptist. Avocations: coaching baseball and basketball, reading. Home: 13261 Romany Way Ct Saint Louis MO 63131-1610 Office: Ste 107 12855 Flushing Meadow Dr Saint Louis MO 63131

WINNINGHAM, MARE, actress; b. Phoenix, May 16, 1959. Appeared in (TV movies and miniseries): The Thorn Birds, 1983, Special Olympics/A Special Kind of Love, 1978, Amber Waves, 1980 (Emmy award 1980), The Women's Room, 1980, Off the Minnesota Strip, 1980, A Few Days in Weasel Creek, 1981, Freedom, 1981, Missing Children: A Mother's Story, 1982, Helen Keller: The Miracle Continues, 1984, Single Bars, Single Women, 1984, Love is Never Silent, 1985 (Emmy award nomination 1986), Who Is Julia?, 1986, A Winner Never Quits, 1986, Eye on the Sparrow, 1991, God Bless the Child, 1988, Love and Lies, Crossing to Freedom, Fatal Exposure, 1991, She Stood Alone, Those Secrets, Intruders, 1992, Better Off Dead, 1994, Betrayed by Love, Letter to My Killer; appeared in (films): One Trick Pony, 1980, Threshold, 1983, St. Elmo's Fire, 1985, Nobody's Fool, 1986, Shy People, 1987, Made in Heaven, 1987, Miracle Mile, 1988, Turner and Hooch, 1989, Hard Promises, 1992, Teresa's Tattoo, Wyatt Earp, 1994, Georgia, 1995 (Acad. award nomination best supporting actress 1995); sang title song in (film) Freedom, 1981; singer (solo album) What Might Be, 1992, Red and Brown, 1996. Office: care William Morris Agy 151 S El Camino Dr Beverly Hills CA 90212-2704

WINNOWSKI, THADDEUS RICHARD (TED WINNOWSKI), bank executive; b. Albany, N.Y., Feb. 20, 1942; s. Thaddeus Walter and Harriet Frances (Witko) W.; m. Sheila Margaret Neary, June 15, 1968; children: Dona, Paul. BS in Econs., Siena Coll., 1963. Adminstrv. v.p. Key Bank N.A., Albany, 1978-80; pres. Key Bank L.I., Sayville, N.Y., 1980-85; pres., CEO Key Bank of Oreg., Woodburn, 1985-86, chmn., CEO, Portland, 1986-95, chmn., 1995—, exec. v.p., group exec. N.W. region Key Corp, Seattle, 1995—, chmn. CEO, 1996—. Bd. dirs. Blue Cross/Blue Shield reg. Benchmark, 1996—; bd. regents U. Portland, Oreg. 1st lt. U.S. Army, 1964-66. Mem. Oreg. SBA (mem. adv. coun.), Oreg. Bankers Assn., Seattle C. of C. (bd. dirs. 1996—), Portland Met. C. of C. (hon. bd. dirs.). Roman Catholic. Home: 4220 E Lynn St Unit One Seattle WA 98112-2768

WINOGRAD, BERNARD, financial adviser; b. Detroit, Dec. 31, 1950; s. Daniel and Lillian (Walder) W.; m. Carol Leslie Snodgrass, Mar. 8, 1974; children: Simon James Bartholomew, Christina Lynn. B.A., U. Chgo., 1970. Pub. affairs mgr. Bendix Corp., Southfield, Mich., 1975; exec. asst. to W.M. Blumenthal, 1975-77, dir. corp. communications, 1977-79, treas., 1979-83; exec. v.p. Taubman Investments, 1983-84; pres. Taubman Investment Co., 1984-96; exec. v.p., CFO Taubman Ctrs., Inc., 1996; exec. asst. to W. Michael Blumenthal, U.S. Sec. Treasury, Washington, 1977; pres., chief exec. Prudential Real Estate Investors. Mem. Urban Land Inst. (NAREIT exec. com.). Home: 189 Oak Ridge Ave Summit NJ 07901 Office: Prudential Real Estate Investors 8 Campus Dr Parsippany NJ 07054-4401

WINOGRAD, NICHOLAS, chemist; b. New London, Conn., Dec. 27, 1945; s. Arthur Selig Winograd and Winifred (Schaefer) Winograd Mayes; m. Barbara J. Garrison. BS, Rensselaer Poly. Inst., 1967; PhD, Case Western Reserve U., 1970. Asst. prof. chemistry Purdue U., West Lafayette, Ind., 1970-75, assoc. prof. chemistry, 1975-79; prof. chemistry Pa. State U., University Park, 1979-85, Evan Pugh prof. chemistry, 1985—; cons. Shell Devel. Co., Houston, 1975—; mem. chemistry adv. bd. NSF, Washington, 1987-90, analytical chemistry adv. bd., 1986-89. Contbr. articles to profl. jours. A.P. Sloan Found. fellow, 1974; Guggenheim Found. fellow, 1977; recipient Founder's prize Tex. Instruments Found., 1984, Faculty Scholar's Pa. State U., 1985, Bennedetti Pichler award Am. Microchem. Soc., 1991, Outstanding Alumnus award Case Western Res. U., 1991. Fellow AAAS (Sect. award); mem. Am. Chem. Soc. Home: RR 1 Box 49F Spring Mills PA 16875 Office: Pa State U Dept of Chemistry 152 Davey Lab University Park PA 16802-6300

WINOGRAD, SHMUEL, mathematician; b. Tel Aviv, Jan. 4, 1936; came to U.S., 1956, naturalized, 1965; s. Pinchas Mordechai and Rachel Winograd; m. Elaine Ruth Tates, Jan 5, 1958; children: Daniel H., Sharon A. BSEE, MIT, MSEE; PhD in Math., NYU, 1968. Mem. research staff IBM, Yorktown Heights, N.Y., 1961-70, dir. math. sci. dept., 1970-74, 81-94; IBM fellow, 1972—; permanent vis. prof. Technion, Israel. Author: (with J.D. Cowan) Reliable Computations in the Presence of Noise; research on complexity of computations and algorithms for signal processing. Fellow IEEE (W. Wallace McDowell award 1974), Assn. Computing Machinery, N.Y. Acad. Scis.; mem. NAS, Am. Math. Soc., Math. Assn. Am., Am. Philos. Soc., Soc. Indsl. and Applied Math., Am. Acad. Arts & Scis. Home: 235 Glendale Rd Scarsdale NY 10583-1533 Office: IBM Research PO Box 218 Yorktown Heights NY 10598-0218

WINOKUR, ROBERT S., federal agency administrator. BS, Rensselaer Polytech Inst.; MS, Am. U. Tech. dir. Office of Oceanographer USN, Washington, 1985-93; asst. adminstr. Satellite and Info. Svcs. Nat. Oceanic and Atmospheric Adminstrn., Washington, 1993—. Vice chmn. Interagy. Task Force on Observations and Data Mgmt. Recipient Presdl. Disting. Exec., Meritorious Rank award. Fellow Acoustical Soc. Am.; mem. Marine Tech. Soc. (v.p. tech. affairs), Internat. Global Climate Observing Sys. (vice chmn. joint sci. and tech. com.). Office: Dept Commerce-Nat Enviromental Satellite Data & Info Srv #2069 Federal Bldg 4 Washington DC 20233

WINSHIP, FREDERICK MOERY, journalist; b. Franklin, Ohio, Sept. 24, 1924; s. Wilbur William and Edna B. (Moery) W.; m. Joanne Tree Thompson, Aug. 29, 1967. A.B., DePauw U., 1945; M.S., Columbia, 1946. Corr. UPI, 1946—; assigned UN, 1947-49; editorial staff N.Y.C., 1950-60, cultural affairs editor, 1960-72, sr. editor, 1972-75, asst. mng. editor, 1975-80; sr. editor arts/theater N.Y.C., 1980-97; Broadway critic, 1985-97. Contbr. articles mags. Pres. Letters Abroad, Inc., 1962-83; chmn. Easter Seal Soc., N.Y.C., 1964-73, Oratorio Soc. N.Y., 1965-75, N.Y. Conf. Patriotic Socs., 1967-72; Bd. dirs. Odell House-Rochambeau Hdgrs., 1965-75, N.Y. State Easter Seal Soc., 1969-72, Mus. of City of N.Y., 1974—, Am. Philharm. Orch., 1981-82, Friends of the Am. Theater Wing, 1990—. Recipient Am. Legion Journalism award, 1955; Whitelaw Reid Journalism fellow India, 1958; Creative Club Journalism award, 1962. Mem. S.A.R. (sec. N.Y. chpt. 1963-68), St. Nicholas, Founders and Patriots, Mayflower Descs., Soc. Colonial Wars (bd. dirs.), S.R., Soc. Cincinnati, Sigma Delta Chi. Republican. Episcopalian. Home: 417 Park Ave New York NY 10022-4401 Office: UPI 2 Penn Plz New York NY 10121

WINSHIP, WADLEIGH CHICHESTER, holding company executive; b. San Francisco, Oct. 3, 1940; s. Henry Dillon and Anne Eliza (Chichester) W.; m. Lynne McPherson, Dec. 28, 1970; children: Wadleigh Chichester, Kelly McPherson. BA, U. Ga., 1964. Trainee Ga. Hwy. Express, Inc., Atlanta, 1964-68, v.p., dir., mem. exec. com., 1968-78; v.p., dir., mem. exec. com. Transus, Inc., Atlanta, 1978-84, pres., chief exec. officer, mem. exec. com., 1984-88, chmn. bd. SurfAir div., 1970—; pres., chief exec. officer Winship Group Inc., Atlanta, 1988—; past chmn. Regional and Dist. Carriers Conf.; bd. govs. Regular Common Carriers Conf., 1970-88. Chmn. transp. com. Atlanta chpt. ARC, 1968; life bd. dirs., past mem. exec. com. Alliance Theatre Co., Atlanta; bd. dirs., past chmn. Goodwill Industries Atlanta; bd. dirs., past chmn. Ga. Soc. to Prevent Blindness; past bd. dirs. Pace Acad., Darlington Sch. Mem. Am. Trucking Assn. (v.p. exec. com. 1982-88), Ga. Bus. and Industry Assn. (bd. dirs. 1972-78), World Pres. Orgn., Peachtree Golf Club, The Nine O'Clocks, Piedmont Driving Club, Highlands Country Club, Chi Phi. Libertarian. Episcopalian. Home: 3296 Rilman Rd NW Atlanta GA 30327-1551 Office: Winship Group Inc 4751 Best Rd Ste 190 Atlanta GA 30337-5609

WINSKILL, ROBERT WALLACE, manufacturing executive; b. Tacoma, Oct. 30, 1925; s. Edward Francis William and Margaret Eyre (Myers) W. BA, Coll. Puget Sound, Tacoma, 1947. Field rep. Ray Burner Co., San Francisco, 1954-57, nat. sales mgr., 1960-69; v.p. sales Western Boiler Co., L.A., 1957-60; gen. sales mgr. Ray Burner Co., San Francisco, 1973-82; v.p., chief exec. officer Orr & Sembower, Inc., Middletown, Pa., 1969-73; pres. Combustion Systems Assocs., Inc., Mill Valley, Calif., 1982—; bd. dirs. Sino-Am. Boiler Engring. Co., Shanghai, China, S. T. Johnson Co., Oakland, Calif. Contbr. articles to profl. jours.; columnist Marin Scope, Mill Valley Harold, 1991—. With U.S. Army, 1943-44. Mem. ASME, Olympic Club (San Francisco), Rotary. Avocation: vineyard. Office: Combustion Systems Assocs Inc PO Box 749 Mill Valley CA 94942-0749

WINSLET, KATE, actress; b. Reading, Eng., Oct. 5, 1975. Appeared in plays including Peter Pan, What the Butler Saw (Manchester Evening News award for Best Supporting Actress), A Game of Soldiers, Titanic, 1997, (musical) Adrian Mole; appeared in TV shows including Anglo-Saxon Attitudes, Shrinks, Dark Season, Casualty, Get Back; appeared in films including Heavenly Creatures, 1994 (Best Fgn. Actress award New Zealand Film and TV Awards), Sense and Sensibility, 1995 (SAG award, Brit. Acad. of Film and TV award for Best Supporting Actress, Golden Globe nominee, Am. Acad. of Motion Picture Arts and Scis. nominee), A Kid in King Arthur's Court, 1995, Jude, 1996, Hamlet, 1996; appeared in various TV commls. Office: The William Morris Agy 151 S El Camino Dr Beverly Hills CA 90212-2704*

WINSLETT, STONER, artistic director; 1 child, Alexander. Student, Am. Ballet Theatre Sch., N.C. Sch. of the Arts; grad. summa cum laude, Smith Coll., 1980. Artistic dir. Richmond Ballet; trustee Dance/USA. Mem. Phi Beta Kappa. Office: Richmond Ballet 614 N Lombardy St Richmond VA 23220

WINSLOW, DAVID ALLEN, chaplain, naval officer; b. Dexter, Iowa, July 12, 1944; s. Franklin E. and Inez Maude (McPherson) W.; m. Frances Lavinia Edwards, June 6, 1970; children: Frances, David. BA, Bethany Nazarene Coll., 1968; MDiv, Drew U., 1971, STM, 1973. Ordained to ministry United Meth. Ch., 1969; cert. FEMA instr. Clergyman, 1969—; assoc. minister All Sts. Episcopal. Ch., Millington, N.J., 1969-70; asst. minister Marble Collegiate Ch., N.Y.C., 1970-71; min. No. N.J. Conf., 1971-75; joined chaplain corps USN, 1974, advanced through grades to lt. comdr., 1980, ret., 1995; exec. dir. Marina Ministries, 1995—. Author: The Utmost for the Highest, 1993, Epiphany: God Still Speaks, 1994, Be Thou My Vision, 1994, Evening Prayers At Sea, 1995, Wiseman Still Adore Him, 1995, God's Power At Work, 1996; (with Walsh) A Year of Promise: Meditations, 1995, editor: The Road to Bethlehem: Advent, 1993, Preparation for Resurrection: Lent, 1994, God's Promise: Advent, 1994, The Way of the Cross: Lent, 1995; contbr. articles to profl. jours. Bd. dirs. disaster svcs. and family svcs. ARC, Santa Ana, Calif., 1988-91, Child Abuse Prevention Ctr., Orange, Calif., 1990-91; bd. dirs. Santa Clara County Coun. Chs., 1993-94, del., 1995—; bd. dirs. The Salvation Army Adult Rehab. Ctr. Adv. Coun., San Jose, Calif; bd. dirs. disaster svcs. ARC, Santa Clara Valley chpt., San

Jose, 1995—. Mem. ACA, USN League (hon.), Sunrise Exch. Club (chaplain 1989-91), Dick Richards Breakfast Club (chaplain 1988-91), Masons (charter), Shriners, Scottish Rite. Avocations: golf, skiing, sailing. Home: 20405 Via Volante Cupertino CA 95014-6318

WINSLOW, JAMES DAVID, international trade analyst; b. Cleve., Sept. 9, 1965; s. Erik Kenelm and Elda Lydia (Colavincenzo) W.; m. Allison Sue Katzen, Dec. 5, 1992; children: Dillon James, Zoë Rose. BA in Psychology, George Washington U., 1987, MBA in Fin. & Investment, 1991. Rsch. analyst Proserv, Inc., Washington, 1986; legal asst. Spriggs & Hollingsworth, Washington, 1987-89; rsch. analyst Sumitomo Corp., Washington, 1989-90, bus. devel. analyst, 1990-94; sr. analyst, 1994-95; mgr. bus. devel. Sumitomo Corp., Washington, 1996—; guest lectr. George Washington U., Washington. Mem. Am. Mgmt. Assn., Asia Soc., Japan-Am. Soc., Sigma Alpha Epsilon. Roman Catholic. Avocations: golf, skiing, reading, photography. Home: 20401 Lindos Ct Gaithersburg MD 20879-4367 Office: Sumitomo Corp of Am 800 Connecticut Ave NW Washington DC 20006-2709

WINSLOW, JOHN FRANKLIN, lawyer; b. Houston, Nov. 15, 1933; s. Franklin Jarnigan and Jane (Shipley) W. BA, U. Tex., 1957, LLB, 1960. Bar: Tex. 1959, D.C. 1961. Atty., Hispanic law div. Library Congress, Washington, 1965-68; counsel, com. on the judiciary Ho. of Reps., Washington, 1968-71; atty., editor Matthew Bender & Co., Washington, 1973-79; atty. FERC, Washington, 1979-84; sole practice Washington, 1984—; researcher Hispanic Law Research, Washington, 1979—. Author: Conglomerates Unlimited: The Failure of Regulation, 1974, The Acquisitors, 1997; editor: Fed. Power Service, 1974-79; contbr. articles to Washington Monthly, Nation, 1975—. Mem. Tex. Bar Assn., D.C. Bar Assn.

WINSLOW, PAUL DAVID, architect; b. Phoenix, June 12, 1941; s. Fred D. and Thelma E. (Ward) W.; m. Carole Lynn Walker, June 13, 1964; 1 child, Kirk David. B.Arch., Ariz. State U., 1964. Lic. architect, Ariz., Calif., Nev. Ptnr. The Orcutt/Winslow Partnership, Phoenix, 1972—; speaker solar energy workshops, Phoenix, 1986-89; adj. prof. Ariz. State Univ., 1991; mem. faculty Advanced Mgmt. Inst., San Francisco. Mem. profl. adv. council Ariz. State U. Coll. Architecture, Tempe, 1970—, bd. dirs. Architecture Found., 1972-76; mem. adv. com. City of Phoenix Bldg. Safety Bd., 1981; mem. adv. bd. Herberger Ctr. Ariz. State U. Coll. Archictecture, Herberger Ctr. Design Excellence. Bd. dirs. Ctrl. Ariz. Project Assn., Phoenix, 1971-74, Ariz. Ctr. for Law in the Pub. Interest, Phoenix, 1979-86, Phoenix Cmty. Alliance; chmn. Encanto Village Planning Com., Phoenix, 1981-86; chmn. Indian Sch. Citizens adv. com. Ind. Sch. Land Use Planning Team; lectr. on planning Ariz. State Univ. planning dept., 1989, city of Presott, Phoenix and Tempe, 1988-89; active Coun. Ednl. Facilities Planners Internat. Fellow AIA (bd. dirs. Central Ariz. chpt. also sec., treas. and pres.); mem. Ariz. Soc. Architects (bd. dirs. 1970-71, 78-82), Bldg. Owners and Mgrs. Assn. Greater Phoenix (pres. 1989-90, 90-91), Boar Valley Forward Assn.. (exec. com. 1994—). Methodist. Club: Arizona (Phoenix). Home: 816 E Circle Rd Phoenix AZ 85020-4144 Office: The Orcutt.Winslow Partnership 1130 N 2nd St Phoenix AZ 85004-1806

WINSLOW, WALTER WILLIAM, psychiatrist; b. Lacombe, Alta., Can., Nov. 23, 1925; came to U.S., 1959, naturalized, 1964; s. Floyd Raymond and Lily Evangeline (Palmer) W.; m. Barbara Ann Spiker; children: Colleen Denise, Dwight Walter, Barbara Jean, Wendi Jae. BS, La Sierra Coll., 1949; MD, Loma Linda U., 1952. Diplomate: Am. Bd. Psychiatry and Neurology. Intern Vancouver Gen. Hosp., 1952; psychiat. resident Provincial Mental Hosp., Essondale, B.C., 1957-59, Harding Hosp., Worthington, Ohio, 1959-60; instr. dept. psychiatry and indsl. medicine U. Cin., 1960-66, dept. preventive medicine, 1964-66; asst. prof. psychiatry U. N.Mex., Albuquerque, 1966-68, assoc. prof. psychiatry, 1969-74, prof., chmn. dept. psychiatry, 1974-91, dir. mental health programs, 1976-91; med. dir. Charter Hosp. of Albuquerque, 1991-95, Charter-Heights BHS, Albuquerque, 1995—; assoc. prof. psychiatry Georgetown U., Washington, 1968-69; dir. bernalillo County Mental Health/Mental Retardation Ctr., 1970-78, 81-91. Contbr. articles to profl. jours. Recipient N.Mex. Gov.'s Commendation for 10 yrs. service in mental health, 1979. Fellow Am. Psychiat. Assn. (life, area VII rep. 1981-85, Assembly Speaker's award 1984), Am. Coll. of Psychiatrists, Am. Assn. Community Psychiatrists (hon.); mem. AMA, Am. Assn. Psychiatry and the Law, N.Mex. Psychiat. Assn. (pres. 1974-75). Republican. Office: 101 Hospital Loop NE Ste 215 Albuquerque NM 87109-2128

WINSOR, KATHLEEN, writer; b. Olivia, Minn., Oct. 13, 1919; d. Harold Lee and Myrtle Belle (Crowder) W.; m. Robert John Herwig, 1936 (div. 1946); m. Paul A. Porter, June 26, 1956 (dec. Nov. 1975). AB, U. Calif., 1938. Author: Forever Amber, 1944, Star Money, 1950, The Lovers, 1952, America, With Love, 1957, Wanderers Eastward, Wanderers West, 1965, Calais, 1979, Jacintha, 1984, Robert and Arabella, 1986. Mem. Authors Guild. Democrat. Presbyterian. Office: care Roslyn Targ Lit Agy Inc 105 W 13th St Apt 15E New York NY 10011-7848

WINSTEAD, CLINT, financial publisher; b. Stanford, Ky., Jan. 31, 1956; m. Catherine R. Venturini; 1 child, Alexander Clay. BA, Columbia U., 1983, MBA, 1986. Dir. publs. Loan Pricing Corp., N.Y.C., 1986-87; v.p., editor-in-chief Investment Dealers' Digest Inc., N.Y.C., 1987-96; v.p., gen. mgr. IDD Enterprises, N.Y.C., 1996—. Home: 593 S Maple Ave Glen Rock NJ 07452-1853 Office: IDD Enterprises LP 2 World Trade Ctr Fl 18 New York NY 10048-1898

WINSTEAD, DANIEL KEITH, psychiatrist; b. Cin., Dec. 30, 1944; s. Daniel Sebastian and Betty Jane (Kirsch) W.; m. Jennifer Reiner, June 15, 1968; children: Laura Suzanne, Nathaniel Scott. BA, U. Cin., 1966; MD, Vanderbilt U., 1970. Diplomate Am. Bd. Psychiatry and Neurology. Resident U. Cin., 1970-72, fellow, 1972-73; chief VA Med. Ctr. psychiat. svc. Tulane U., New Orleans, 1976-79, dir., consultation/liaison psychiat. tng., 1979-83, dir. psychiatric edn. and residency tng., 1983-87, assoc. prof., 1979-84, prof., 1984—, chmn. dept. psychiatry and neurology, 1987—; chief psychiat. svc. VA Med. Ctr., New Orleans, 1976-80; assoc. chief staff for edn. VA Med Ctr., New Orleans, 1979-87; staff psychiatrist VA Med. Ctr., New Orleans, 1987—; med. dir. Jefferson Parish Substance Abuse Clinic, 1980-81; cons. E.R. Squibb and Sons, 1985-86; vis. physician psychiatry Charity Hosp., New Orleans, 1979-90. Contbr. articles to profl. jours. Maj. U.S. Army, 1973-76. Mem. AMA, Am. Coll. Psychiatrists, Am. Acad. Psychiatry and Law, Am. Psychiat. Assn., La. State Med. Soc., So. Assn. for Rsch. in Psychiatry, Acad. Psychosomatic Medicine, Am. Assn. Chairmen Depts. Psychiatry, Am. Assn. Dirs. Psychiat. Residency Tng., Assn. Acad. Psychiatry, La. Psychiat. Assn. (pres. 1991-92), Soc. Biol. Psychiatry, New Orleans Area Psychiat. Assn., New Orleans Neurol. Soc., Orleans Parish Med. Soc. Republican. Presbyterian. Avocations: oenology, travel. Home: 5348 Bellaire Dr New Orleans LA 70124-1033 Office: Tulane Med Sch 1430 Tulane Ave New Orleans LA 70112-2699

WINSTEAD, GEORGE ALVIS, law librarian, biochemist, educator, consultant; b. Owensboro, Ky., Jan. 14, 1916; s. Robert Lee and Mary Oma (Dempsey) W.; m. Elisabeth Donelson Weaver, July 18, 1943. BS, We. Ky. U., 1938; MA, George Peabody Coll., 1940, MLS, 1957, MEd, 1958. Head chemistry and biology dept. Belmont Coll., Nashville, 1952-56; head chemistry dept. George Peabody Coll., Vanderbilt U., Nashville, 1956-58; assoc. law librarian Vanderbilt U., Nashville, 1958-76; dir. Tenn. State Supreme Ct. Law Libraries, Nashville, 1976—; law cons. Tenn. Youth Legis., Nashville, 1976—; cons. civic clubs, local colls., 1976—, Tenn. State Govt. Depts. Archives, Nashville, 1976—. Author: Tenn. State Law Library Progress Reports, 1975, Supreme Court Library Personnel Guide, 1981, Designing Future Law Libraries' Growth and Expansion, 1982, Problem Identification and Solutions in Law Libraries, Tenn. Supreme Courts, 1985. Mem. Col. Tenn. Gov.'s staff, Nashville, 1978. With USAAF, 1943-46. Named to Gov.'s Staff of Ky. Cols., Lexington, 1988. Fellow Am. Inst. Chemists, SAR. Baptist. Avocations: camping, hiking, traveling, crafts, antique cars. Home: 3819 Gallatin Rd Nashville TN 37216-2609 Office: Tenn Supreme Ct Libr Nashville TN 37219

WINSTEAD, JOY, journalist, consultant; b. Washington, May 31, 1934; d. Purnell Judson and Mellie Richardson (Winstead) W.; m. David Boyd Propert, Jul. 28, 1956 (div. June 1980); children: Kathleen Joy, David Bruce; m. Fred L. Frechette, Mar. 15, 1997. BA in pol. sci., U. Richmond, 1955. Reporter Richmond (Va.) Times-Dispatch, 1955-56; staff writer, pub. rels. U. Pa., Phila., 1956-58; dir. publicity Children's Hosp., Washington, 1958-59; staff writer Richmond News Leader, 1972-77; features editor Columbia (S.C.) Record, 1977-81; asst. editor lifestyles Richmond Times-Dispatch, 1981-83, fashion editor, 1983-92; coord. pub. rels. Sci. Mus. Va., Richmond, 1992-93; dir. communications Medical Soc. Va., Richmond, 1993-96; guest lectr. U. Richmond, Va. Commonwealth U., U. S.C.; book reviewer Richmond Times-Dispatch. Contbg. author: Richmond Reader; contbg. editor: A Gem of a Coll. History of Westhampton Coll.; author (introduction): University of Richmond, A Portrait. Co-chmn. alumni weekend U. Richmond, 1968, chmn. alumnae fund, 1989, chmn. lectr. series, 1992-94, mem. 75th Anniversary Com. Recipient 1st pl. award for spl. articles Nat. Fedn. Press Women, 1975, Va. Press Women, 1975, 95, Va. Press Assn., 1978. Mem. Soc. Profl. Journalists (bd. dirs. 1975), Va. Press Women (hospitality chmn. 1993), Soc. Profl. Journalists Found. (bd. dirs. 1987-91), Va. Assn. Med. Soc. Execs. (assoc.), Am. Assn. Med. Soc. Execs., Richmond Pub. Rels. Assn., Fashion Editors and Reporters Assn. (bd. dirs. 1985-91, nominating com. chmn. 1991). Presbyterian. Avocations: theater, music, travel. Home: 122 Holly Rd Williamsburg VA 23185

WINSTEAD, NASH NICKS, university administrator, phytopathologist; b. Durham County,, N.C., June 12, 1925; s. Nash L. and Lizzy (Featherston) W.; m. Geraldine Larkin Kelly, Sept. 17, 1949; 1 dau., Karen Jewell. B.S., N.C. State U., 1948, M.S., 1951; Ph.D., U. Wis., 1953. Asst. prof. plant pathology Raleigh, 1953-58; assoc. prof. N.C. State U., Raleigh, 1958-61; prof. N.C. State U., 1961-90, prof. emeritus, 1991—, dir. inst. biol. scis., 1965-67, asst. dir. agrl. exptl. sta., 1965-67, asst. provost, 1967-73, assoc. provost, 1973-74, provost and vice chancellor, 1974-90, acting chancellor, 1981-82; Phillip Found. intern acad. adminstrn. Ind. U., 1965-66; bd. trustees N.C. Sch. Sci. and Math., 1985-90. Contbr. articles profl. jours. Mem. N.C. Council on Higher Edn. for Adults, 1967-75; inst. rep. So. Assn. for Colls. and Schs., 1967-74; mem. Cooperating Raleigh Colls., 1968-90, pres., 1971-73, 83-85; chmn. interaction between protoplasm and toxicants com. So. Regional Edn. Bd., 1964-65; Bd. dirs. N.C. State U. YMCA, 1963-65; trustee Meth. Home for Children, 1980-88, pres., 1983-84, N.C. Wesleyan Coll., 1987-97. Served with USAAF, 1943-46. Recipient Sigma Xi research award, 1960. Fellow AAAS; Mem. Am. Phytopath. Soc. (chmn. disease, pathogen physiology com.), Am. Inst. Biol. Scis., N.C. Assn. Colls. and Univs. (exec. com. 1974-80, pres. 1978-79), Nat. Assn. State Univs. and Land Grant Colls. (edn. telecommunications com. 1980-85, equal opportunity com. 1985-88), Acad. Deans for So. States, N.C. Assn. of Acad. Officers (exec. com. 1986-89, v.p., pres. 1987-88), Sigma Xi, Phi Kappa Phi, Omicron Delta Kappa. Club: Torch Internat. (sec.). Home: 1109 Glendale Dr Raleigh NC 27612-4709 Office: NC State U Box 7111 Raleigh NC 27695-7101

WINSTEN, SAUL NATHAN, lawyer; b. Providence, Feb. 23, 1953; s. Harold H. and Anita E. Winsten; m. Patricia J. Miller, Aug. 7, 1977; children: David A., J. Benjamin, Jennifer M. BA with honors, Beloit Coll., 1976; JD, Drake U., 1980. Ptnr. Michael, Best & Friedrich, Milw., 1988—. Contbr. articles to profl. jours. Mem. devel. com. Milw. Sch. Engring.; apptd. co-chair Govs. Adv. Coun. on Internat. Trade, 1996. Mem. ABA (chmn. com. young lawyers divsn. 1989-90, governing coun., mem. antitrust, bus. and internat. law sects.), Wis. Bar Assn., Internat. Bar Assn., Japan-Am. Soc. Wis. (pres. 1993-94, co-founder 1990, sec. 1990-92), Nat. Assn. Japan-Am. Socs. (bd. dirs. 1991—, mem. exec. com. 1993—), Am. Soc. Assn. Execs. (legal sect.), Wis. Found. Ind. Colls. (bd. dirs., strategic planning com.), Order of Barristers. Office: Michael Best & Friedrich 100 E Wisconsin Ave Milwaukee WI 53202-4107

WINSTON, GEORGE, pianist, guitarist, harmonica player; b. Hart, Mich., 1949. Ind. musician, 1967—; founder Dancing Cat Productions, Santa Cruz, CA, 1983—. Seven solo piano albums, including Ballads and Blues, 1972, Autumn, 1980, Winter Into Spring, 1982, December, 1982, Summer, 1991, Forest, 1995, Linus & Lucy: The Music of Vince Guaraldi, 1996; audiobook soundtracks: (with Meryl Streep) The Velveteen Rabbit, 1985, (Peanuts) Birth of the Constitution, 1988, (with Liv Ullmann) Sadako and the Thousand Paper Cranes, 1995; prodr. albums of the masters of traditional Hawaiian slack key (finger style) guitar. Office: care Dancing Cat Productions PO Box 639 Santa Cruz CA 95061-0639

WINSTON, HAROLD RONALD, lawyer; b. Atlantic, Iowa, Feb. 7, 1932; s. Louis D. and Leta B. (Carter) W.; m. Carol J. Sundeen, June 11, 1955; children: Leslie Winston Yannetti, Lisa, Laura L. BA, U. Iowa, 1954, JD, 1958. Bar: Iowa 1958, U.S. District Ct. (no. and so. dists.) Iowa 1962, U.S. Tax Ct. 1962, U.S. Ct. Appeals (8th cir.) 1970, U.S. Supreme Ct. 1969. Trust Officer United Home Bank & Trust Co., Mason City, Iowa, 1958-59; mem. Breese & Cornwell, 1960-62, Breese, Cornwell, Winston & Reuber, 1963-73, Winston, Schroeder & Reuber, 1974-79, Winston, Reuber, Swanson & Byrne, P.C., Mason City, 1980-92, Winston, Reuber & Byrne, 1992-96, Winston & Byrne P.C., 1996—. Police judge, Mason City, 1961-73. Contbr. articles to profl. jours. Past pres. Family YMCA, Mason City, Cerro Gordo County Estate Planning Coun.; active local charitable orgns. Capt. USAF, 1955-57. Fellow Am. Coll. Trust and Estate Counsel, Am. Bar Found. (life), Iowa Bar Found. (life); mem. ABA, Iowa Bar Assn. (gov., lectr. ann. meeting 1977-79), 2d Jud. Dist. Bar Assn. (lectr. meeting 1981-82), Cerro Gordo County Bar Assn. (past pres.), Am. Judicature Soc., Assn. Trial Lawyers Am., Euchre and Cycle Club, Mason City Country Club, Kiwanis, Masons. Republican. Presbyterian (elder). Office: Winston & Byrne 119 2nd St NW Mason City IA 50401-3105

WINSTON, JUDITH ANN, lawyer; b. Atlantic City, Nov. 23, 1943; d. Edward Carlton and Margaret Ann (Goodman) Marianno; B.A. magna cum laude, Howard U., Washington, 1966; J.D., Georgetown U., 1977; m. Michael Russell Winston, Aug. 10, 1963; children: Lisa Marie, Cynthia Eileen. Bar: D.C. 1977, U.S. Supreme Ct. Dir. EEO Project, Coun. Gt. City Schs., Washington, 1971-74; legal asst. Lawyers Com. for Civil Rights Under Law, Washington, 1975-77; spl. asst. to dir. Office for Civil Rights, HEW, Washington, 1977-79; exec. asst., legal counsel to chair U.S. EEO Commn., Washington, 1979-80; asst. gen. counsel U.S. Dept. Edn., 1980-86; dep. dir. Lawyers Com. for Civil Rights Under Law, 1986-88; dep. dir. pub. policy Women's Legal Def. Fund, Washington, 1988-90, chair employment discrimination com., 1979-88; ednl. cons., 1974-77; asst. prof. law Washington Coll. Law of Am. U., 1990-93. assoc. prof. law, 1993-95; gen. counsel U.S. Dept. Edn., Washington, 1993—. Pres. bd. dirs. Higher Achievement Program. Named Woman Lawyer of Yr., Women's Bar Assn., 1997. Fellow ABA Found.; mem. ACLU (pres. Nat. Capital Area, bd. dirs.), Fed. Bar Assn. (chair gen. counsels sect. 1993—), D.C. Bar Assn., Washington Coun. Lawyers, Washington Bar Assn., Nat. Bar Assn., Lawyers' Com. for Civil Rights Under Law (treas., bd. dirs.), Links Inc., Alpha Kappa Alpha, Phi Beta Kappa, Delta Theta Phi. Democrat. Episcopalian. Author: Desegregating Schools in the Great Cities: Philadelphia, 1970, Chronicle of a Decade 1961-1970, 1970, Desegregating Urban Schools: Educational Equality/Quality, 1970; contbr. articles to profl. jours. Home: 1371 Kalmia Rd NW Washington DC 20012-1444 Office: Dept Edn 600 Independence Ave SW Washington DC 20202-0004

WINSTON, KRISHNA RICARDA, foreign language professional; b. Greenfield, Mass., June 7, 1944; d. Richard and Clara (Brussel) W.; 1 child, Danielle Billingsley. BA, Smith Coll., 1965; MPhil, Yale U., 1969, PhD, 1974. Instr. Wesleyan U., Middletown, Conn., 1970-74, asst. prof., 1974-77; assoc. prof. Wesleyan U., Middletown, 1977-84, prof., 1984—, acting dean, 1993-94; coord. Mellon Minority Undergrad. Program, 1993—. Author: O v. Horváth: Close Readings of Six Plays, 1975; translator: O. Schlemmer, Letters and Diaries, 1972, S. Lenz, The Heritage, 1981, G. Grass, Two States, One Nation, 1990, C. Hein, The Distant Lover, 1989, G. Mann, Reminiscences and Reflections, 1990, J. W. V. Goethe, Wilhelm Meister's Journeyman Years, 1989, C. v. Krockow, The Hour of the Women, 1991, E. Heller, With the Next Man Everything Will be Different, 1992, R. W. Fassbinder, The Anarchy of the Imagination, 1992, G. Reuth, Goebbels, 1994, E. Lappin, editor, Jewish Voices, German Words, 1994, P. Handke, Essay on the Jukebox, 1994. Vol. Planned Parenthood, Middletown, 1972-77; mem. Recycling Task Force, Middletown, 1986-87; chmn. Resource Recycling Adv. Coun., Middletown, 1989—. Recipient Schlegel-Tieck prize for translation, 1994; German Acad. Exch. Svc. fellow. Mem. MLA, NEMLA, Soc. for Exile Studies, Am. Lit. Translators' Assn., Am. Assn. Tchrs. German, PEN, Phi Beta Kappa (pres. Wesleyan chpt. 1987-90). Home: 655 Bow Ln Middletown CT 06457-4808 Office: Wesleyan Univ German Studies Dept Middletown CT 06459

WINSTON, MICHAEL RUSSELL, foundation executive, historian; b. N.Y.C., May 26, 1941; s. Charles Russell and Jocelyn Anita Prem Das Winston; m. Judith Ann Marianno, Aug. 10, 1963; children: Lisa Marie, Cynthia Eileen. BA magna cum laude, Howard U., 1962; MA, U. Calif.-Berkeley, 1964, PhD, 1974. Instr. dept. history Howard U., Washington, 1964-66, asst. dean Coll. Liberal Arts, 1968-69, asst. prof. dept. history, 1970-73, v.p. acad. affairs, 1983-90, prof. emeritus, 1990—; assoc. dir. Inst. Svcs. to Edn., Washington, 1966; fellow Haus. Hof-und Staatsarchiv, Vienna, Austria, 1969; dir. Moorland Spingarn Rsch. Ctr., 1973-83; v.p., bd. dirs. Alfred Harcourt Found., Silver Spring, Md., 1992-93, pres., 1993—; cons. Smithsonian Instn., 1979—, nat. Inst. Edn., 1978-85, NSF, 1985—. Author: (with R.W. Logan) The Negro in the United States, 1970, The Howard University Department of History, 1913-73, 1973; editor: (with R.W. Logan) Dictionary of American Negro Biography, 1982, (with G.R. McNeil) Historical Judgements Reconsidered, 1988; mem. editorial bd. Washington History, 1993—. Trustee spl. contbn. fund NAACP, 1980-82; trustee D.C. Pub. Defender Svc., 1985-88; bd. trustees Woodrow Wilson Nat. Fellowship Found., 1997—; mem. exec. bd. Nat. Capital Area coun. Boy Scouts Am., 1988-90; bd. mgrs. Hist. Soc. Washington; bd. dirs. Harcourt Brace Jovanovich, 1980-91, D.C. Pub. Libr. Found., 1994—, pres., 1995—, Nat. Coun. for History Standards; mem. Commn. on Coll. and Univ. Nonprofl. Studies, ABA; mem. Nat. Ctr. for History in the Schs., UCLA/NEH; mem. nat. adv. com. and coun. of scholars Libr. of Congress, nat. adv. bd. Protect Historic Am. Moten fellow U. Edinburgh, 1962, Wilson fellow U. Calif., 1962, Ford fellow, 1969-70, Woodrow Wilson Internat. Ctr. Scholars fellow, 1979-80. Mem. Am. Hist. Assn., Orgn. Am. Historians, Am. Antiquarian Soc., Hist. Soc. Washington, Atlantic Coun. of U.S., Coun. on Fgn. Rels., Nat. Coun. for History Standards, Epsilon Boule, Sigma Pi Phi, Phi Beta Kappa. Democrat. Episcopalian. Club: Cosmos (Washington), The Century Assn. (N.Y.). Home: 1371 Kalmia Rd NW Washington DC 20012-1444 Office: Alfred Harcourt Found 8401 Colesville Rd Silver Spring MD 20910-3312

WINSTON, MORTON MANUEL, equipment executive; b. N.Y.C., Dec. 9, 1930; s. Myron Hugh and Minna (Schneller) W.; m. Katherine Tupper Winn, Feb. 3, 1979; 1 child, Kate Winston; children by previous marriages: Gregory Winston, Livia Winston; stepchildren—Wesley Hudson, Laura Hudson. A.B., U. Vt., 1951; M.A., U. Conn., 1953; LL.B. magna cum laude, Harvard U., 1958. Bar: D.C. 1961. Law clk. to Justice Frankfurter, Supreme Ct. U.S., 1959-60; asso. firm Cleary, Gottlieb, Steen & Hamilton, N.Y.C., Washington, 1960-67; v.p. Tosco Corp., N.Y.C., 1964-67; exec. v.p. Tosco Corp., 1967-71, pres., 1971-83, chief exec. officer, 1976-83, chmn., 1983-84, dir., 1984-86; pres., chmn. Stamet, Inc., Gardena, Calif., 1987—; chmn. Norad Corp., 1986—; dir. Stamet, Inc. and Norad Corp, 1986—; bd. dir. Baker Hughes Corp. trustee George C. Marshall Research Found., Lexington, Va., Mus. Contemporary Art, L.A.; chmn. Station KLON-FM, Long Beach, Calif.; trustee Calif. State Summer Sch. for the Arts Found. Served to lt. (j.g.) USCGR, 1953-55. Office: Stamet Inc 17244 S Main St Gardena CA 90248-3101

WINSTON, ROLAND, physicist, educator; b. Moscow, USSR, Feb. 12, 1936; s. Joseph and Claudia (Goretskaya) W.; m. Patricia Louise LeGette, June 10, 1957; children—Joseph, John, Gregory. A.B., Shimer Coll., 1953; B.S., U. Chgo., 1956, M.S., 1957, Ph.D., 1963. Asst. prof. physics U. Pa., 1963-64; mem. faculty U. Chgo., 1964—, prof. physics, 1975—, chmn. physics dept., 1989-95. Recipient Kraus medal Franklin Inst., 1996. Fellow AAAS, Am. Phys. Soc., Am. Optical Soc.; mem. Internat. Solar Energy Soc. (Abbot award 1987). Achievements include patent for ideal light collector for solar concentrators. Home: 5217 S University Ave Apt C Chicago IL 60615-4439 Office: Physics Dept U Chgo 5640 S Ellis Ave Chicago IL 60637-1433

WINSTON, STANLEY S., advertising executive. Vice chmn., chief creative officer Ogilvy & Mather Direct, 1973—. Recipient Andi Emerson award for outstanding svc. to direct mktg. creative cmty., 1992, Silver Apple award Direct Mktg. Club N.Y., 1993. Mem. Direct Mktg. Assn. (chmn. Echo com., John Caples com.), Direct Mktg. Creative Guild. Office: Ogilvy & Mather Direct 309 W 49th St New York NY 10019-7316

WINT, DENNIS MICHAEL, museum director; b. Macon, Ga., Mar. 17, 1943; s. Paul Kenneth and Mary (McClure) W.; m. Patricia McLaughlin, Dec. 27, 1970; 1 child, Laurel Julia. B.S., U. Mich., 1965; tchr.'s cert., Lake Erie Coll., 1970; Ph.D., Case Western Res. U., 1977. Dir. environ. edn. Wiloughby Eastlake City Schs., 1968-70; dir. Ctr. Devel. Environment Curiculum, 1970-75; cons. Ohio Dept. Edn., 1975-77; dir. mus. and edn. Acad. Natural Scis., Phila., 1977-79; v.p., dir. natural history mus. Acad. Natural Scis., 1979-82; dir. Cranbrook Inst. Sci., Bloomfield Hills, Mich., 1982-86; pres. St. Louis Sci. Ctr., 1986-95; pres., CEO The Franklin Inst., Phila., 1995—; adj. asst. prof. Temple U.; past chmn. edn. and human resources adv. com. NSF, 1991-92; past pres. St. Louis Area Mus. Collaborative, 1991-92, mem. exec. com. Grantee in field. Mem. Am. Assn. Mus., Assn. Sci.-Tech. Ctrs. (mem. nominating com., v.p. 1993-95, pres. 1995—), Greater Phila. Cultural Alliance. Home: 8205 Ardmore Ave Wyndmoor PA 19038

WINTER, ALAN, retired publishing company executive; b. Rogate, Sussex, Eng., Oct. 14, 1937; came to U.S., 1982; s. George Adolph and Muriel (Burton) W.; m. Anne Claire, Sept. 22, 1962; children: Mark, Paul. B.S., U. Wales, 1959, Ph.D., 1963; M.A., U. Cambridge, Eng., 1972. Instr. Harvard U., Cambridge, Mass., 1964-65; lectr. U. York, Eng., 1965-68; editor Cambridge U. Press, 1968-82; dir. Cambridge U. Press, N.Y.C., 1982-93. Contbr. numerous articles to sci. jours. Chmn. Govs. of Newnham Croft Sch., Cambridge, Eng., 1975-81. Clubs: Athenaeum (London).

WINTER, ARCH REESE, architect; b. Mobile, Ala., Sept. 13, 1913; s. Augustus Reese and Winona (Battson). BArch, Auburn U., 1935; MArch, Cath. U. Am., 1937; postgrad., Cranbrook Acad. Art, Bloomfield Hills, Mich., 1939-41. Cons. Nat. Resources Planning Bd., Washington, 1941-43; practice architecture city planning firm as Arch R. Winter, Mobile, 1945-84. City plans include Natchez and Gulfport, Miss., Shreveport and Monroe, La., Old Louisville, Ky., restoration area archtl. includes YWCA Youth Center and Residence, Isle Dauphine Country Club, Dauphin Island (Gulf States region AIA Honor award, 1957). Cons. Mobile Planning Commn. Recipient medal of merit Tenn. Soc. Architects, 1971, Thomas Jefferson medal selection com U. Va. Sch. Architecture, 1976-79, cert. of commendation Mobile Historic Devel. Commn., 1981; named Ala. Disting. Arch. Ala. Archtl. Found., 1996. Fellow AIA (pres. Ala. chpt. 1955, nat. AIA engrs. joint coun. 1957-59, urban design com. 1959-64, chmn., del to commn. d'Urbanisme, 1962, design com. 1972-78, bd. dirs. 1968-71, chmn. Honor award, 1969, chmn. environ. commn. 1970-71, Citation for Excellence in Community Architecture 1965); mem. Am. Planning Assn. (Disting Svc. Plaque Ala. chpt. 1984). Address: 9 Bienville Ave Mobile AL 36606-1463

WINTER, CHESTER CALDWELL, physician, surgery educator; b. Cazenovia, N.Y., June 2, 1922; s. Chester Caldwell and Cora Evelyn (Martin) W.; m. Mary Antonia Merullo, Oct. 22, 1983; children by previous marriage: Paul, Ann, Jane. B.A., U. Iowa, 1943, M.D., 1946. Diplomate: Am. Bd. Urology. Intern Meth. Hosp., Indpls., 1946-47; med. resident St. Luke's Hosp., Cedar Rapids, Iowa, 1947; resident gen. surgery VA Hosp., Los Angeles, 1952-53; resident urology VA Hosp.-U. Calif. at Los Angeles Med. Center, 1953-57; physician Mentone, Calif., 1950-51; clin. asst. surgery UCLA, 1954-57, instr. surgery and urology, 1957-58, asst. prof. surgery and urology, 1958-59, asst. prof. Step II, 1959-60; prof. surgery and urology Ohio State U., 1960-88, prof. emeritus surgery and urology, 1988—, Louis Levy prof. urology, 1980-88; dir. urology Ohio State U. Hosp., Columbus, 1960-78; cons. urology VA, Air Force hosps., Dayton. Author: Radioisotope Renography, 1963, Correctable Renal Hypertension, 1964, Nursing Care of Patients with Urologic Diseases, 4th edit, 1977, Practical Urology, 1969, Vesicoureteral Reflux, 1969; Editorial cons.: Exerpta Medica: Nuclear Medicine, Jour. AMA; editorial bd.: Andrology, Jour. Urology; Contbr. articles to med. jours. Served to capt. M.C. U.S. Army, 1943-46, 48-49. Fellow Am. Acad. Pediatricians, Am. Coll. Surgeons; mem. Am. Assn. Genitourinary Surgeons, Am. Urol. Assn., Soc. Univ. Surgeons, Soc. Pediatric Urology, Soc. Univ. Urologists, Internat. Soc. Urology, Urol. Investigators Forum, Ohio State Med. Assn., Columbus Surg. Soc., Central Ohio Urology Soc., Columbus Acad. Medicine, Ohio State U. Med. Soc., York Country Club (Worthington, Ohio), Kiwanis. Home: 6425 Evening St Worthington OH 43085-3054

WINTER, DAVID FERDINAND, electrical engineering educator, consultant; b. St. Louis, Nov. 9, 1920; s. Ferdinand Conrad and Annie (Schaffer) W.; m. Bettie Jeanne Turner; children: Suzanne, Sharie Winter Chappeau. BSEE, Washington U., St.Louis, 1942; MSEE, MIT, 1948. Registered profl. engr., Mo. Staff mem. radiation lab. MIT, Cambridge, 1942-45, rsch. assoc. electronics lab., 1945-48; prof. elec. engring. Washington U., 1948-55, affiliate prof. elec. engring., 1955-67; v.p. engring. and rsch. Moloney Elec. Co., St. Louis, 1955-74; v.p. rsch. and engring. Blackburn div. IT&T, St. Louis, 1974-82, dir. advanced tech. devel., 1982-86; pvt. practice cons. St. Louis, 1986—; tech. expert on effects of stray voltage on dairy cattle for Wis. Pub. Svc. Commn.; cons. Naval Ordanance Lab. of Ind., Indpls., 1950-53, other industries, St. Louis, 1979—. Contbr. articles to profl. jours.; holder 28 patents. Elder, pastor Maplewood Bible Chapel, St. Louis. Fellow IEEE (life), Inst. Radio Engrs.; mem. NSPE, Am. Soc. Agrl. Engrs., Mo. Soc. Profl. Engrs., Sigma Xi, Tau Beta Pi, Eta Kappa Nu. Avocations: cabinet maker, photography, music instruments. Home and Office: 629 Meadowridge Ln Saint Louis MO 63122-3021

WINTER, DAVID LOUIS, systems engineer, human factors scientist, retired; b. Pitts., July 30, 1930; s. Louis A. and Gladys M. (Quinn) W.; m. Nancy L. Tear, July 1, 1952; children: Leeson, Blaise, Gregory, Lauren. BA, U. Pitts., 1952; MA, Columbia U., 1960; cert. computer sci., Northeastern U., 1971. Assoc. rsch. scientist Am. Insts. Rsch., Washington, 1961-66; sr. rsch. scientist Am. Insts. Rsch., Bedford, Mass., 1966-71, prin. rsch. scientist, 1976-94, retired, 1995; sr. systems analyst RCA Corp.-Sarnoff Labs., Princeton, N.J., 1971-73; mgr. systems engring. Codon Corp., Bedford, 1973-76; computer systems cons. Mass. Dept. Mental Health, 1971-73. Pres. Mayo Peninsula Civic Assn., Edgewater, Md., 1964-65; v.p. Bedford Human Rels. Coun., 1992-94. Capt. USAF, 1952-64. Mem. Am. Acad. Polit. Sci., Human Factors Soc., Soc. Ednl. Tech. Democrat. Roman Catholic. Achievements include design and human factors test for 8 USAF electronic, intelligence and backscatter radar systems; design of 4 computer-assisted training systems for USAF E3 AWACS radar, computer displays, communications and navigation subsystems; cons. engr. for design and test of E6 Joint Stars battlefield surveillance system. Office: MicroVentures Ltd 27 Gould Rd Bedford MA 01730-1250

WINTER, DONALD FRANCIS, lawyer; b. Hackensack, N.J., June 11, 1941; s. Frank Joseph and Ina Beulah (Swanson) W.; m. Katherine C. Blodgett, Nov. 30, 1963 (div. 1974); children: Andrew Blodgett, Matthew Francis, Anthony Reed. AB, Harvard U., 1963, JD, 1966. Bar: Mass. 1966, U.S. Dist. Ct.Mass. 1966. Assoc. Palmer & Dodge, Boston, 1966-73, ptnr., 1973—; bd. dirs. Ellis Meml. Assn. Chmn. Back Bay Archtl. Commn., 1969-82; trustee Boston Ballet Co., 1969—, Provincetown Art Assn. and Mus., 1991—, Provincetown Fine Arts Work Ctr., 1992—; mem. Park Pla. Civic Adv. Com., 1980—. Mem. ABA, Mass. Bar Assn., Boston Bar Assn., Nat. Assn. Bond Lawyers, Somerset Club, Harvard Club. Lutheran. Home: 19 Commercial St Provincetown MA 02657 Office: Palmer & Dodge 1 Beacon St Boston MA 02108-3107

WINTER, DOUGLAS E., lawyer, writer; b. St. Louis, Oct. 30, 1950; s. William E. and Dorothy E. (Schuster) W.; m. Lynne G. Turner, July 9, 1977; step-children: John, Stephen. BS, U. Ill., 1971, MS, 1972; JD, Harvard U., 1975; postgrad., Judge Advocate Gen.'s Sch., 1977. Bar: Mo. 1975, Ill. 1976, D.C. 1976. Clk. to Hon. William H. Webster U.S. Ct. Appeals (8th cir.), St. Louis, 1975-76; assoc. Covington & Burling, Washington, 1976-84; ptnr. Bryan Cave LLP, Washington, 1985—; vis. prof. U. Iowa, Iowa City, 1980-81. Author: Stephen King, 1982, Shadowings: The Reader's Guide to Horror Fiction, 1983, Stephen King: The Art of Darkness, 1984, Faces of Fear, 1985, Black Wine, 1986, Splatter: A Cautionary Tale, 1987, Prime Evil, 1988, Darkness Absolute, 1991, Black Sun, 1994, American Zombie, 1997, Millennium, 1997, Revelations, 1997; contbr. articles and short stories to popular mags. and newspapers. Capt. U.S. Army, 1973-77. Recipient world fantasy award World Fantasy Conv., 1986, award Internat. Horror Critics Guild, 1995, 96. Mem. Nat. Book Critics Circle, Horror Writers Assn. (chmn. grievance com. 1989—). Office: Bryan Cave LLP 700 13th St NW Washington DC 20005-3960

WINTER, FOSTER, III, environmental engineer; b. Detroit, Oct. 6, 1957; s. Foster II and Sandra Rae (Schmelzer) W.; m. Karen Lee Rosenberg, Aug. 25, 1990. BSChemE, U. So. Calif., L.A., 1985, MS in Environ. Engr., 1988. Registered profl. engr., Calif., civil engr., chem. engr. Mem. tech. staff Rocketdyne Div./Rockwell Internat., Canoga Park, Calif., 1985-87; project engr. Tetra Tech., Inc., Pasadena, Calif., 1987-88, L.A. County Sanitation Dist., Whittier, Calif., 1988—. Mem. Water Pollution Control Fedn., Am. Inst. Chem. Engrs., ASCE. Office: LA County Sanitation Dists PO Box 4998 Whittier CA 90607-4998

WINTER, FREDERICK ELLIOT, fine arts educator; b. Barbados, W.I., June 19, 1922; s. Edward Elliot and Constance Mabel (Gill) W.; m. Joan Elizabeth Hay, June 9, 1951; children: Elizabeth, Penelope, Mary, Michael. B.A., McGill U., 1945; Ph.D., U. Toronto, 1957. Instr. U. Toronto, 1947-49, 50-51, lectr., 1951-57, asst. prof., 1957-61, asso. prof., 1961-68, prof., 1968-90, prof. emeritus, 1990—, chmn. dept. fine art, 1971-77, grad. coord. history of art, 1978-81, spl. lectr. history of art, 1990—; chmn. U. Toronto Assn. Teaching Staff, 1968-69; mem. mng. com. Am. Sch. Classical Studies, Athens, Greece, 1968-90, chair pers. com., 1975-77; mem. programme com. Can. Archaeol. Inst. at Athens, 1990-94; dir. Can. Acad. Inst., Athens, 1994—. Author: (with G.S. Vickers, P.H. Brieger) Art and Man, Vol. I, 1963, Greek Fortifications, 1971; contbr. articles Jour. Classical Assn. Can., Am. Jour. of Archaeology, Echos du Moude Classique/Classical Views. Recipient Gold medal in classics McGill U., 1945; Flavelle fellow U. Toronto, 1947-48; White fellow Am. Sch., Athens, 1949-50; spl. research fellow, 1977-78, 87-88; sr. assoc. fellow, 1982, 83-84, 86, 91; Am. Philos. Soc. grantee, 1957; grantee Soc. Scis. Humanities Rsch. Coun. Can., 1962, 68, 71, 75, 77-78, 82, 83-84, 86, 87-88, 91; grantee U. Toronto Humanities and Social Scis. Rsch. Com., 1993. Mem. Classical Assn. Can., Archeol. Inst. Am. (editorial adv. bd. Am. Jour. Archaeology 1981-85). Home: 164 Highgate Ave, Willowdale, ON Canada M2N 5G8 Office: Dept Fine Art, U Toronto, Toronto, ON Canada

WINTER, HARLAND STEVEN, pediatric gastroenterologist; b. San Francisco, Sept. 25, 1948; s. Milton and Madeline (Price) W.; m. Susan Weinstein, Oct. 9, 1983. BA, U. Calif., Berkeley, 1970; MD, UCLA, 1974. Intern UCLA, 1974-75, jr. asst. resident pediatrics, 1975-76, sr. asst. resident, 1976-77; clin. fellow gastroenterology Children's Hosp., Boston, 1977-80; rsch. fellow pediatrics Harvard U. Med. Sch., Boston, 1977-79, instr. pediatrics, 1979-82, asst. prof. pediatrics, 1983-91, assoc. prof. pediatrics, 1991—; chief pediatric gastroenterology Boston City Hosp., 1992—; trustee Crohn's & Colitis Found., N.Y.C., 1991-93, regional med. adv. chmn., 1990-93. Editor: (books) Infant Nutrition, the First Three Years, 1984, Managing Your Child's Crohn's Disease or Ulcerative Colitis, 1996. Named New Investigator, NIH, 1981-84, Prin. Investigator, 1984-87, 87-93, Co-PI, 1994-99. Mem. N.Am. Soc. for Pediat. Gastroenterology and Nutrition (pres.-elect 1996-98).

WINTER, HARVEY JOHN, government official; b. New Albion, N.Y., Apr. 6, 1915; s. George J. and Irene (Harvey) W.; m. Virginia M. Shaw, Sept. 2, 1939; 1 child, Jeffrey S. B.A. magna cum laude, U. Buffalo, 1938, M.A., 1939; teaching fellow, George Washington U., 1939-40. Historian U.S. Nat. Park Service, 1940-42; archivist U.S. Nat. Archives, 1942-43; with U.S. Office Alien Property Custodian, 1943-51, chief reports and stats. sect., 1948- 51; with State Dept., 1951—, chief internat. bus. practices div., 1959-61, asst. chief, 1961-70, chief bus. practices div., 1970-71, dir. office bus. protection, 1971-73, dir. office bus. practices, 1973-90, dir. office intellectual property and competition, 1991-92; U.S. del. European Productivity Agy. cartel meetings, Paris, 1958-60; mem. U.S. del. diplomatic confs. Internat. Design Agreement, The Hague, 1960, 17th session GATT, Geneva, Switzerland, 1960; U.S. alt. rep. 5th session Intergovtl. Copyright Com., London, 1960, 6th session, Madrid, 1961, 7th session, New Delhi, 1963; U.S. alt. rep. Interunion Coordinating Com., Geneva, 1963-69; U.S. observer African Seminar on Indsl. Property, Brazzaville, Congo, 1963; U.S. alt. observer Latin Am. Indsl. Property Seminar, Bogota, Colombia, 1964, Asian Indsl. Property Seminar, Colombo, Ceylon, 1966, Com. of Experts on Inventors' Certificates, Geneva, 1965, Com. of Experts on Adminstrv. Agreement, Geneva, 1965, Intellectual Property Diplomatic Conf., Stockholm, 1967, Diplomatic Conf. on Agreement for Classification of Indsl. Designs, Locarno, Switzerland, 1968, Diplomatic Conf. on Patent Cooperation Treaty, Washington, 1970, Diplomatic Conf. on Agreement for Internat. Patent Classification, Strasbourg, France, 1971, Diplomatic Conf. on Universal Copyright Conv., Paris, 1971; U.S. alt. rep. Diplomatic Conf. on Phonogram Conv., Geneva, 1971, Diplomatic Conf. on Indsl. Property, Vienna, 1973; U.S. rep. Com. Experts on Type Face Agreement, Geneva, 1972, Com. Experts on Communications Satellites Problems, Nairobi, Kenya, 1973; U.S. del. Diplomatic Conf. on Communications Satellites Conv., Brussels, 1974, Diplomatic Conf. on Treaty for Deposit Microorganisms, Budapest, Hungary, 1977, Diplomatic Conf. on Plant Protection Conv., Geneva, 1978, World Intellectual Property Orgn. Governing Bodies, Geneva, 1979-82; alt. del. World Intellectual Property Orgn. Governing Bodies, 1983-91; alt. U.S. del. Diplomatic Conf. on Revision of Paris Conv., Geneva, 1980, 82, 83, 84 Nairobi, 1981; U.S. del. UNESCO Experts on Rental of Videograms, Paris, 1984, Com. Govtl. Experts on Audiovisual Works and Phonograms, Paris, 1986, Com. Govtl. Experts on Internat. Register of Audiovisual Works, Geneva, 1988, Diplomatic Conf. on Treaty for Internat. Registration of Audiovisual Works, Geneva, 1989, Com. Experts on Disputes Steelement Treaty on Intellectual Property, 1990; chmn. Internat. Patent Classification Assembly, 1992. Recipient Superior Honor award Dept. State, 1971, 75, 89, 92, 50-Yr. Svc. award, 1990, Jefferson meda. N.J. Patent Law Assn., 1982; honoree Copyright Soc. U.S.A., 1989. Mem. Phi Beta Kappa. Episcopalian (vestry). Home: 1019 22nd St S Arlington VA 22202-2137 Office: Dept of State Washington DC 20520

WINTER, JOHN DAWSON, III, blues guitarist, singer; b. Beaumont, Tex., Feb. 23, 1944; s. John Dawson II and Edwina (Holland) W. Grad. high sch. Organizer, performer numerous rock and blues bands, rec. artist, CBS Records, Inc., 1969—, TV and concert appearances through, U.S. and Europe, 1969—; albums include Johnny Winter, 1969, Second Winter, 1969, Johnny Winter-And, 1970, Live, 1971 (Gold Record award 1974), Still Alive and Well, 1973, Saints and Sinners, 1974, John Dawson Winter III, 1974, Nothin' But the Blues, 1977, White Hot and Blue, 1978, The Johnny Winter Story, 1980, Raisin' Cain, Serious Business, 1985, 3rd Degree, 1986, The Winter of '88, 1988, Winter Scene, 1990, Let Me In, 1991, Scorchin' Blues, 1992, A Rock n' Roll Collection, 1994; producer recs. by Muddy Waters: albums include Still Hard (Artist of Yr., Rolling Stone mag. 1969). Mem. Broadcast Music Inc., Musicians Union. Office: care Aligator Records PO Box 60234 Chicago IL 60660

WINTER, LARRY EUGENE, accountant; b. Williamsport, Pa., Jan. 17, 1950; s. Robert Schrader and Betty Irene (Foresman) W.; m. Constance Dianne Snyder, June 2, 1973; children: John, Matthew, Noël, James. A in Bus. Adminstrn., Palm Beach Jr. Coll., 1969; BSBA, U. Fla., 1971; cert. bus., U. Pa., 1977. Cert. valuation analyst, cert. fraud examiner, CPA, Fla., Ga.; accredited fin. planning specialist. Audit supr. Touche Ross & Co., Atlanta, 1971-74; chief fin. officer Hawthorne Industries, Dalton, Ga., 1974-79; pvt. practice acctg. Dalton, 1979-89; mng. ptnr. Winter & Harris, CPAs, Dalton, 1990—; mem. White House Conf. Small Bus., Atlanta, 1979; instr. West Ga. Coll., Carollton, 1985, Ea. European Bus. Coll., Budapest, Hungary, 1995; acct. in residence Ga. Coll., Milledgeville, Ga., 1989; cons. Christian Businessman, Chattanooga, 1986—. Author: The American Free Enterprise System and the Ethics that Make it Work, 1991. Trustee Dalton Jr. Coll. Found.; chair Whitfield County/Dalton Day Care Ctrs., 1987-92; elder Fellowship Bible Ch., 1985—; mem. adv. coun. Ga. State Bd. Workers Compensation, 1991—; mem. fee arbitration panel State Bar Ga., 1987—. Mem. AICCPA, Nat. Assn. Cert. Valuation Analysts, Ga. Soc. CPAs (pres. 1983-84), Fla. Inst. CPAs (recipient), Ga. Sheriff's Assn. (Disting. Humanitarian award), Dalton-Whitfield C. of C. (Leadership 1990-91, treas. 1992-94), Assn. Cert. Fraud Examiners, Walden Club, Kiwanis (life, pres. 1978-79, lt. gov. 1981-84). Avocations: cooking, credit and fin. counseling. Office: PO Box 2644 Dalton GA 30722-2644

WINTER, MIRIAM THERESE (GLORIA FRANCES WINTER), nun, religious education educator; b. Passaic, N.J., June 14, 1938; d. Mathias William and Irene Theresa (Marton) W. BMus, Cath. U. Am., 1964; M in Religious Edn., McMaster Divinity Coll., Hamilton, Ont., Can., 1976; PhD in Liturgical Studies, Princeton Theol. Sem., 1983; LHD (hon.), Albertus Magnus Coll., 1991, St. Joseph Coll., 1993. Joined Med. Mission Sisters, Roman Cath. Ch., 1955. Dir. liturgy and liturgical music Med. Mission Sisters, Phila., 1960-76, pub. rels. dir., coord., 1963-72; assoc. prof. liturgy, worship and spirituality Hartford (Conn.) Sem., 1980-85, prof., 1985—, prof. liturgy, worship, spirituality, and feminist studies, 1994—; mem. faculty St. Therese's Inst., Phila., 1964-68, acad. dir., 1968-72, Immaculate Conception Sem. Summer Program, Mo., 1969, Cath. U. Summer Grad. Program, Washington, 1970, Hope Ecumenical Inst., Jerusalem, summer 1974, 75, 76, McMaster Divinity Coll. Grad. Program, 1976, Continuing Edn. Program, 1976, N.Y. Archdiocesan Sch. Liturgical Music, summer 1980, 82, Vancouver Sch. Theology, summer 1982, USN Chaplains through Auburn Theol. Sem., 1990; mem. adj. faculty Union Inst., Cin., 1992-94; with emergency relief work Internat. Rescue Com., Cambodia, 1979-80, Malteser-Hilfsdienst Auslandsdienst, Germany, 1984, Med. Mission Sisters, Ethiopia, 1985; lectr., instr., performer, worship leader, song leader for various groups by invitation, nat. and internat., 1967—. Author: Preparing the Way of the Lord, 1978, God-With-Us: Resources for Prayer and Praise, 1979, An Anthology of Scripture Songs, 1982, Why Sing? Toward a Theology of Catholic Church Music, 1984, WomanPrayer, WomanSong: Resources for Ritual, 1987, WomanWord: A Feminist Lectionary and Psalter, 1990, WomanWisdom: A Feminist Lectionary and Psalter, Women of the Hebrew Scriptures, Part I, 1992 (First Place award for books on liturgy Cath. Press Assn. 1992), WomanWitness: A Feminist Lectionary and Psalter, Women of the Hebrew Scriptures, Part II, 1992 (First Place award for books on liturgy Cath. Press Assn. 1993), The Gospel According to Mary: A New Testament for Women, 1993; co-author: Defecting in Place: Women Claiming Responsibility for Their Own Spiritual Lives, 1994, (Second place award for books on gender studies Cath. Press Assn. 1995;), The Chronicles of Noah and Her Sisters: Genesis and Exodus According to Women, 1995 (2d place award for books on gender studies Cath. Press Assn. 1996); Songlines: Hymns, Songs, Rounds, and Refrains, 1996; author numerous songs included in albums EarthSong, WomanSong, Remember Me, Sandstone, Songs of Promise, RSVP: Let Us Pray, Gold, Incense and Myrrh, In Love, Seasons (Christian Oscar award Nat. Evang. Film Found. 1971), Knock, Knock, Praise the Lord in Many Voices (live recording of Mass of A Pilgrim People premiered at Carnegie Hall, 1967), I Know the Secret, Joy is Like the Rain (Gold album in USA and Australia); contbr. articles to profl. jours. Bd. dirs. Capitol Region Conf. Chs., 1984-91, v.p., 1986-88, pres. bd. dirs., 1988-90, past pres., 1990-91, Archdiocesan Office Urban Affairs, 1986-95; mem. Christian Conf. ann. event WINFEST, 1986, 87; mem. small christian communities design team Archdiocese of Hartford, 1987-91; mem. major events design team RENEW, 1986; subcommn. chair Archdiocesan Office of Synod, 1991; mem. New Eng. team Ministry of Money, 1984-90, 93; mem. The New Century Hymnal editl. com. United Ch. of Christ, 1993-95; active Ho. of Bread, Pediats. AIDS Unit Yale-New Haven Hosp., Covenant to Care, Voices of Joy Gospel Choir women imprisioned at Niantic. Grantee Lilly Endowment, 1989-90, 91-93; recipient Ho. of Reps. citation Commonwealth of Pa., 1968, Women in Leadership Edn. award YWCA Conn., 1989, Convenant to Care award for ministry to children, 1993; named to McMaster U. Alumni Gallery, 1982, Celebration of 120 Women in Leadership, 1987, Bayley-Ellard H.S. Hall of Fame, 1993. Mem. ASCAP (Popular Awards list 1968—), AAUW (Excellence in Equity award Conn. chpt. 1995), Nat. Assn. Pastoral Musicians, N.Am. Acad. of Liturgy, Societas Liturgica. Avocations: photography, calligraphy. Office: Hartford Sem 77 Sherman St Hartford CT 06105-2260

WINTER, PAUL THEODORE, musician; b. Altoona, Pa., Aug. 31, 1939; s. Paul Theodore and Beaulah (Harnish) W.; m. Cherry Liley, 1991. B.A., Northwestern U., 1961. Leader: Paul Winter Sextet, 1961-65, Winter Consort, 1967—; performed concerts in 26 countries and throughout U.S., 1st jazz group to perform at White House, 1962, recorded numerous albums; founder Living Music Records, Inc., 1980. Founder Living Music Found., 1976. Fellow Lindisfarne Assn., 1977; recipient Global 500 award UN, 7 Grammy nominations, Best New Age Album Grammy Award, 1994 for Spanish Angel, 1995 for Prayer for the Wild Things. Address: Living Music Records Inc PO Box 72 Litchfield CT 06759-0072

WINTER, PETER MICHAEL, physician, anesthesiologist, educator; b. Sverdlovsk, Russia, Aug. 5, 1934; came to U.S., 1938, naturalized, 1944; s. George and Anne Winter; m. Michelle Yakopec, Dec. 28, 1991; children: Karin Anne, Christopher George, Lia Lynn, Tori Anne. BA, Cornell U., 1958; MD, U. Rochester, 1962. Intern U. Utah, Salt Lake City, 1962-63; resident in anesthesiology, pharmacology and respiratory physiology Mass. Gen. Hosp., Boston, 1963-65; USPHS fellow Harvard U. Med. Sch., 1964-66; Buswell fellow dept. physiology, asst. prof. SUNY, Buffalo, 1966-69; assoc. prof. dept. anesthesiology Sch. Medicine, U. Wash., Seattle, 1969-74; prof. Sch. Medicine, U. Wash., 1974-79; prof., chmn. dept. anesthesiology and critical care medicine U. Pitts. Sch. Medicine, 1979-96, Peter and Eva Safar prof. anesthesiology/critical care med.; anesthesiologist in chief Univ. Health Ctr. Hosps., Pitts., 1979-96. Editorial cons. Anesthesiology CCMJ; contbr. chpts. to books, papers and abstracts on anesthesia, environ. phys. pharmacology and med. edn. to publs. Served with U.S. Army, 1953-56. Recipient NIH career devel. award, 1971. Mem. AMA, Am. Coll. Chest Physicians, Am. Soc. Anesthesiologists, Royal Soc. Medicine, N.Y. Acad. Scis., Soc. Critical Care Medicine, Undersea Med. Soc., Internat. Anesthesia Research Soc., Assn. Univ. Anesthetists, Morton Soc. (founding mem.). Club: Am. Alpine. Office: 3471 5th Ave Ste 910 Pittsburgh PA 15213-3221

WINTER, RALPH KARL, JR., federal judge; b. Waterbury, Conn., July 30, 1935; married. B.A., Yale U., 1957, J.D., 1960. Bar: Conn. 1973. Research assoc., lectr. Yale U., 1962-64, asst. prof. to assoc. prof. law, 1964-68, prof. law, 1968-82; spl. cons. subcom. on separation of powers U.S. Senate Com. on Judiciary, 1968-72; sr. fellow Brookings Inst., 1968-70; adj. scholar Am. Enterprise Inst., 1972-82; judge U.S. Ct. Appeals (2d cir.), New Haven, 1982—; vis. prof. law U. Chgo., 1966; mem. adv. com. civil rules Jud. Conf. U.S., 1987-92, chair adv. com. rules evidence, 1993. Contbr. articles to profl. jours. Office: Second Circuit 141 Church St New Haven CT 06510-2030

WINTER, RICHARD LAWRENCE, financial and health care consulting company executive; b. St. Louis, Dec. 17, 1945; s. Melvin Lawrence and Kathleen Jane (O'Leary) W.; children from previous marriage: Leigh Ellen, Jessica Marie, George Bradford; m. Kathryn Ann Geppert, Dec. 4, 1993. B.S. in Math., St. Louis U., 1967, M.S. in Math. (fellow), 1969; M.B.A., U. Mo., St. Louis, 1976. Rsch. analyst Mo. Pacific R.R., St. Louis, 1971-73; dir. fin. relations Linclay Corp., St. Louis, 1973-74; asst. v.p. 1st Nat. Bank in St. Louis (name now Centerre Bank, N.A.) subs. Boatmen's Nat. Bank, 1974-79; v.p. fin. UDE Corp., St. Louis, 1979-81; pres. Health Care Investments, Ltd., St. Louis, 1981—, Larus Corp., St. Louis, 1981—, Garden View Care Ctr., Inc., O'Fallon, Mo., 1987—; mem. exec. bd. Duchesne Bank, St. Peters, Mo., 1989—; lectr. math. U. Mo.-St. Louis, 1972-74, St. Louis U., 1982-90. Active various fund raising activities including St. Louis Symphony, Jr. Achievement, United Way St. Louis, Arts and Edn. Fund, St. Louis, 1974-79. Served with U.S. Army, 1969-71. Mem. Nat. Health Lawyers Assn., Pi Mu Epsilon. Roman Catholic. Club: Mo. Athletic (St. Louis). Home: 1321 Green Tree Ln Saint Louis MO 63122-4744 Office: 12412 Powerscourt Dr Saint Louis MO 63131-3635

WINTER, ROGER PAUL, government official; b. Hartford, Conn., July 13, 1942; s. Raymond Gustav and Marion Nellie (Stafford) W.; m. Delorise Allen, Aug. 22, 1966; children: Jonathan, Raymond Todd, Nicole. B.A. in Psychology, Wheaton Coll., 1964; LLD (hon.), Holy Family Coll., 1993. Asst. sec. Md. Dept. Human Resources, Balt., 1970-79, Md. Dept. Budget and Fiscal Planning, Annapolis, 1979-80; dir. Office of Refugee Resettlement, HHS, Washington, 1980-81, U.S. Com. for Refugees, Washington, 1981—; exec. dir. Immigration and Refugee Svcs. Am., Washington, 1994—; cons. on refugee affairs Women's Refugee Project, Washington, 1981-84; adv. bd. Refugee Policy Group, 1981-86; mem. bd. Refugee Voices, 1988-96; mem. exec. com. Coun. Washington Reps. on UN, 1989-91. Recipient Disting. Service Cambodian Assn. Am., 1982, Disting. Service award Indochina Resource Action Ctr., 1988. Mem. Nat. Ry. Hist. Soc.-Balt., Sudan Relief and Rehab. Assn. (bd. dirs., sec. 1991-93). Lodge: Eagles. Home: 6328 Departed Sunset Columbia MD 21044-6009 Office: US Com for Refugees 1717 Massachusetts Ave NW Washington DC 20036-2001

WINTER, RUTH GROSMAN (MRS. ARTHUR WINTER), journalist; b. Newark, May 29, 1930; d. Robert Delmas and Rose (Rich) Grosman; m. Arthur Winter, June 16, 1955; children: Robin, Craig, Grant. B.A., Upsala Coll., 1951; MS, Pace U., 1989. With Houston Press, 1955-56; gen. assignment Newark Star Ledger, 1951-55, sci. editor, 1956-69; columnist L.A. Times Syndicate, 1973-78, Register and Tribune, syndicate, 1981-85; contbr. to consumer mags.; instr. St. Peters Coll., Jersey City.; vis. lectr. mag. writing Rutgers U. Author: Poisons in Your Food, rev. edits., 1971, 91, How to Reduce Your Medical Bills, 1970, A Consumer's Dictionary of Food Additives, 1972, 3d rev. edit. 1994, Vitamin E, The Miracle Worker, 1972, So You Have Sinus Trouble, 1973, Ageless Aging, 1973, So You Have a Pain in the Neck, 1974, A Consumer's Dictionary of Cosmetic Ingredients, 1974, 4th rev. edit., 1994, Don't Panic, 1975, The Fragile Bond: Marriage in the 70's, 1976, Triumph Over Tension, 1976 (N.J. Press Women's Book award), Scent Talks Among Animals, 1977, Cancer Causing Agents: A Preventive Guide, 1979, The Great Self-Improvement Sourcebook, 1980, The Scientific Case Against Smoking, 1980, People's Guide to Allergies and Allergens, 1984, A Consumer's Guide to Medicines in Food, 1995; co-author: The Lean Line One Month Lighter Program, 1985, Thin Kids Program, 1985, Build Your Brain Power, 1986, Eat Right: Be Bright, 1988, A Consumer's Dictionary of Medicines: Prescription, Over-the-Counter and Hebral, 1994, 97, Super Soy,: The Miracle Bean, 1996. Recipient award of merit ADA, 1966, Cecil award Arthritis Found., 1967, Am. Soc. Anesthesiologists award, 1969, Arthritis Found. award, 1978; named Alumnus of Year Upsala Coll., 1971, Woman of Year N.J. Daily Newspaper Women, 1971, Woman of Achievement Millburn Short Hills Profl. and Bus. Women's Assn., 1991. Mem. Soc. Mag. Writers, Authors League, Nat. Assn. Sci. Writers, Am. Med. Writers Assn. (Eric Martin Meml. award), N.J. Daily Newspaper Women (awards news series 1958, 70, named Woman of Achievement 1971, 83), Am. Soc. Journalists and Authors (pres. 1977-78, spl. service award 1983), N.J. Press Women (pres. 1982-84). Home and Office: 44 Holly Dr Short Hills NJ 07078-1318

WINTER, THOMAS SWANSON, editor, newspaper executive; b. Teaneck, N.J., Dec. 28, 1937; s. Frank J. and Beulah (Swanson) W.; m. Dawne Cina, Mar. 28, 1978; children—Victoria Ruth, Abigail Swanson. A.B., Harvard U., 1959, M.B.A., 1961. Asst. editor Human Events newspaper Human Events, Inc., Washington, 1961-64, editor, 1964—, co-owner, pres., 1966—; pres. Fund for Objective News Reporting. Treas. Conservative Victory Fund, Washington, 1975—; 1st vice chmn. Am. Conservative Union, 1972—. Lutheran. Clubs: Nat. Press, Capitol Hill. Home: 16 4th St SE Washington DC 20003-3804 Office: Human Events 422 1st St SE Washington DC 20003-1803

WINTER, WILBURN JACKSON, JR., financial executive; b. Savannah, Ga., June 23, 1944. BSBA, U. N.C., 1966. Asst. v.p. Nations Bank, Charlotte, N.C., 1969-74; v.p. 1st Nat. Bank Chgo., Atlanta, 1974-86; prin. Acorn Fin. Svcs., Inc., Atlanta, 1986-88; v.p. Greyhound Fin. Corp., Atlanta, 1988-89; mng. dir. LBO Capital Corp., Atlanta, 1989-90; sr. v.p., CFO, Rosser Internat., Inc., Atlanta, 1990-95; bus. cons. Atlanta, 1995—. Lt. USN, 1966-69; capt. USNR, 1969-96. Mem. Assn. for Corp. Growth, Atlanta Venture Forum, S.R. Home: No 8 3050 Margaret Mitchell Dr Atlanta GA 30327

WINTER, WILLIAM EARL, mayor, retired beverage company executive; b. Granite City, Ill., Sept. 21, 1920; s. William M. and Ada M. (Compton) W.; m. Dorothy E. Schuster, Feb. 20, 1944 (dec. 1976); children: William C., Douglas E.; m. Mildred E. Stiebel, Mar. 18, 1977. AB, U. Ill., 1942. With Seven-Up Co., St. Louis, 1946-81; v.p., dir. mktg. Seven-Up Co., 1969-71, exec. v.p., 1971-74, pres., chief operating officer, 1974-76, pres., chief exec. officer, 1976-79, chmn. bd., 1979-81, also former dir., cons.; chmn. emeritus, 1996—; cons. Cadbury Beverages/Seven-Up, chmn. emeritus, 1996. Bd. dirs. Combined Health Appeals Am., YMCA Greater St. Louis, U. Ill. Found., Deaconess Hosp. Found.; mem. exec. bd. St. Louis Area coun. Boy Scouts

Am. Capt. U.S. Army, 1942-46. Named to Promotion Mktg. Hall of Fame, 1979, Beverage World Hall of Fame, 1986. Mem. Am. Mktg. Assn., Sales and Mktg. Execs. St. Louis, Promotion Mktg. Assn. Am. (chmn. bd. 1971-72), Phi Beta Kappa, Phi Eta Sigma, Omicron Delta Gamma. Home: 12310 Boothbay Ct Saint Louis MO 63141-8119 Office: Dr Pepper/Seven Up Cos Inc 8900 Page Ave Saint Louis MO 63114-6108

WINTER, WILLIAM FORREST, former governor, lawyer; b. Grenada, Miss., Feb. 21, 1923; s. William Aylmer and Inez (Parker) W.; m. Elise Varner, Oct. 10, 1950; children: Anne, Elise, Eleanor. BA, U. Miss., 1943, LLB, 1949; LLD, William Carey Coll., 1980, Millsaps Coll., 1983, Troy State U., 1988, Davidson Coll., 1996. Bar: Miss. 1949. Practice in Grenada, 1949-58; practice in Jackson, Miss., 1968—; ptnr. Watkins, Pyle, Ludlam, Winter and Stennis, 1968-80; sr. ptnr. Watkins, Ludlam & Stennis, 1985—; mem. Miss. Ho. of Reps., 1948-56; state tax collector, 1956-64, state treas., 1964-68; lt. gov. State of Miss., 1972-76; gov., 1980-84; Eudora Welty prof. So. studies Millsaps Coll., 1989, Jamie Whitten prof. law U. Miss., 1989; chmn. So. Growth Policies Bd., 1981, So. Regional Edn. Bd., 1982, Adv. Commn. on Intergovtl. Rels., 1993—; chmn. MDC, Inc. Pres. bd. trustees Miss. Dept. Archives and History; chmn. Kettering Found., 1990-93, Appalachian Regional Commn., 1983, Commn. on Future of South, 1986, Nat. Civic League, 1987-88, Nat. Commn. on State and Local Pub. Svc., Stennis Ctr. for Pub. Svc., Found. for the Mid South. With AUS, 1943-46, 51. Harvard U. Inst. Politics fellow, 1985. Mem. Am., Miss., Hinds County bar assns., U. Miss. Alumni Assn. (pres. 1979), Phi Delta Phi, Omicron Delta Kappa, Phi Delta Theta. Democrat. Presbyterian. Club: Univ. (Jackson). Office: 633 N State St Jackson MS 39202-3300

WINTER, WINTON ALLEN, JR., lawyer, state senator; b. Ft. Knox, Ky., Apr. 19, 1953; s. Winton A. and Nancy (Morsbach) W.; m. Mary Boyd, July 28, 1978; children: Katie, Molly, Elizabeth. BA, U. Kans., 1975, JD, 1978. Bar: Kans. 1978. Ptnr. law firm Stevens, Brand, Golden, Winter & Skepnek, Lawrence, Kans., 1978—; pres. Corp. for Change; mem. Kans. Senate, 1982-92. Bd. dirs. Lawrence United Fund, Boys Club of Lawrence. Mem. ABA, Kans. Bar Assn., Douglas County Bar Assn. Kans. U. Law Soc. Republican. Roman Catholic. Club: Rotary. Note and comment editor Kans. Law Rev., 1977-78. Office: PO Box 189 502 Mercantile Bank Tower Lawrence KS 66044-0189

WINTERER, PHILIP STEELE, lawyer; b. San Francisco, July 8, 1931; s. Steele Leland and Esther (Hardy) W.; m. Patricia Dowling, June 15, 1955; children: Edward J., Amey C. BA, Amherst Coll., 1953; LLB, Harvard U., 1956. Bar: N.Y. 1957, Republic of Korea 1958. Assoc., then ptnr. Debevoise & Plimpton, N.Y.C., 1956-93, ret. ptnr., 1993, of counsel, 1994-96; dir. Am. Savs. Bank, 1972-92. Contbr. articles to profl. publs. Trustee Amherst Coll., Adelphi U.; chmn. emeritus Sch. of Am. Ballet; mem. Com. on the Folger Shakespeare Libr.; past pres. Am. Italy Soc.; chmn. exec. com. Phipps Houses; chn. Austen Riggs Ctr.; bd. dirs. N.Y. State Bd. Nature Conservancy; bd. dirs. Phi Beta Kappa Assocs. Recipient Amherst Coll. medal for Eminent Svc., 1980. Mem. Coun. on Fgn. Rels., Am. Law Inst., Citizens Housing and Planning Coun. N.Y., N.Y. Sci. Policy Assn., N.Y. Acad. Scis., Tax Forum, Am. Coll. Tax Counsel. Home: 1165 Fifth Ave New York NY 10029-6931 also: East Hill Rd Keene NY 12942 Office: Debevoise & Plimpton 875 3rd Ave New York NY 10022-6225

WINTERER, VICTORIA THOMPSON, hospitality executive; b. Chgo., May 4, 1943; d. Henry Lawrence and Charlotte (Mather) Thompson; m. William George Winterer, Sept. 2, 1967; children: William G. Jr., Andrew H., Britton T., Mark L. Cert., Emma Willard Sch., Troy, N.Y., 1961; BA, Vassar Coll., 1965. Picture rschr. Time, Inc., N.Y.C., 1965-72; pres. bd. trustees Conn. River Mus., Essex, 1983-86; dir. Rockfall Found., Middletown, Conn., 1986-92; chairwoman Campaign for Emma Willard, Troy, 1992—; v.p., trustee Emma Willard Sch., 1986—; owner, exec. Griswold Inn, Inc., Essex, 1972-96. Bd. dirs. Conn. River Valley and Shoreline Visitors' Coun., Middletown, 1994-96; sec. Essex Twp. Bd. Trade, Essex, 1990-96; mem. Essex Rep. Town Com., 1976-84. Recipient Disting. Alumnae award for Svc. to Emma Willard Sch., 1996; named Disting. Citizen of Yr., Middlesex County C. of C., 1996. Home: 93 River Rd Essex CT 06426-1307 also: Snail's Pace PO Box 640 Bokeelia FL 33922

WINTERER-SCHULZ, BARBARA JEAN, art designer, author; b. Manchester, N.H., Apr. 1, 1938; d. John Edward and Elizabeth Virginia Grace; m. Allen George Winterer, Mar. 30, 1959 (div. 1977); children: Audrey Lyn Winterer, Amy Jo Winterer DeNoble; m. James Robert Schulz, May 28, 1983. AA, Mesa (Ariz.) C.C., 1980; BS summa cum laude, U. Md., Heidelberg, Germany, 1996. Art designer Morningstar Art Design Studio, Cortez, Colo., 1988—. Contbr. articles to newspapers and jours. Ofcl. U.S. reporter at World Eskimo Indian Olympics, Faribanks, Alaska, 1994; asst. dir. Ariz. Myasthenia Gravis Found., 1977-80. Recipient Humanitarian award Phila. Inst. Human Potential, 1972, Chancellor of Germany award for acad. achievement, 1986. Mem. Am. Landscape Contractors Assn., Alpha Sigma Lambda, Phi Theta Kappa. Avocations: gardening, gourmet cooking. Office: Morningstar Art Design Studio 201 W Downey Ave Cortez CO 81321-2727

WINTERGERST, ANN CHARLOTTE, language educator; b. Memmingen, Bavaria, Germany, Mar. 11, 1950; came to U.S., 1958; d. Martin and Charlotte Frieda (Denk) W. BA summa cum laude, St. John's U., 1972; MA, Columbia U., 1974, EdM, 1981, EdD, 1989. Teaching fellow U. Pa., Phila., 1972-73; lang. arts tchr. Our Lady Miraculous Medal Sch., Ridgewood, N.Y., 1973-81; assoc. tchr. Columbia U., N.Y.C., 1978-82; asst. prof. St. John's U., Queens, N.Y., 1981-86, 92-93, dir. ESL, 1986-91, assoc. prof., 1993—; cons. Ednl. Testing Svc., Oakland, Calif., 1989—, Bd. Regents N.Y. State, Albany, 1992-95, St. Martin's Press, N.Y.C., 1993-95, United Nations, N.Y.C., 1994-95, 96-97. Author: Second-Language Classroom Interaction, 1994; editor: Focus on Self-Study, 1995; contbr. articles to profl. jours. Mem. Dem. Nat. Com., Washington, 1990—. Mem. N.Y. State TESOL (officer, 1st v.p. 1994-95, pres. 1995-96, immediate past pres. 1996-97), N.Y. State Coun. Langs. (officer, pres. 1988-90), Internat. TESOL (higher edn. chair 1993-94, officer). Democrat. Roman Catholic. Avocations: soprano in Diocesan choir, German folkdancer, traveling, bowling, skiing. Home: 70-15 71st Pl Glendale NY 11385 Office: St Johns Univ Dept Fgn Langs Jamaica NY 11439

WINTERHALTER, DOLORES AUGUST (DEE WINTERHALTER), art educator; b. Pitts., Mar. 22, 1928; d. Joseph Peter and Helen August; m. Paul Joseph Winterhalter, June 21, 1947 (dec.); children: Noreen, Audrey, Mark; m. Marvin Bernard Hoeing, Mar. 26, 1988 (div. Dec. 1994). Student, Yokohama, Japan, 1963-64, Paris, 1968-70. Cert. tchr. Japanese Flower Arranging, Kamakuri Wood Carving. Tchr. YWCA, Greenwich, Conn., 1978-84, Friends of the Arts and Scis., Sarasota, Fla., 1992—; lectr. Sarasota Art Assn., 1984—; tchr., workshop presenter, Bangkok, 1971; mem. staff Hilton Leech Art Studio and Gallery, Sarasota; events chmn. State of Fla. Watercolor Exhbn., Sarasota, 1995; cultural exch. tchr. univs., fine arts acads., China; mem., tchr. Venice Art Ctr., Sarasota, 1996-97, Hilton Leech Tchr., Sarasota, 1996. Exhbns. Xiam, China, 1994; numerous works in watercolor, ink, oriental brushwork; paintings in numerous corp. collections. Pres., Am. Women's Club, Genoa, Italy, 1962; participant to help raise money for scholarships Collectors and Creators Tour of Fine ARts Soc. of Sarasota, 1994. Recipient numerous awards Old Greenwich (Conn.) Art Assn., 1971-84, Sarasota, 1985, Collectors and Creators Tour award Fine Arts Soc. Sarasota, 1994; named Artist of Yr., Fine Arts Soc. Sarasota, 1994. Mem. Nat. League Am. Pen Women (pres. Sarasota br. 1994—), Suncoast Fla. Watercolor Soc. (life), Fla. Watercolor Soc., Long Boat Key Art Assn., Sarasota Art Assn., Sumi-e Soc. Am., Nat. League Am. PEN Women (pres. 1994-96). Democrat. Roman Catholic. Avocations: wood carving, travel, bridge, creative design in crochet and fashion. Home and Office: 4027 Westbourne Cir Sarasota FL 34238-3249

WINTERMANS, JOSEPH JACK GERARD FRANCIS, financial services executive; b. Eindhoven, North Brabant, The Netherlands, Oct. 4, 1946; arrived in Can., 1973; s. Joseph J.F.G. and Catherine (Van Dijk) W.; m. Eileen Simon, Oct. 30, 1972. LLB, Leyden, The Netherlands, 1967, LLM, 1972; MBA, Queens, Kingston, Ont., Can., 1972. V.p. Bristol Myers Can., Toronto, Ont., 1981-82; sr. v.p. Am. Express Can., Markham, Ont., 1982-87; pres. Can. Tire Acceptance Ltd., Welland, Ont., 1988—; sr. v.p. diversified bus. Can. Tire Corp., 1995—. Hon. fellow Ryerson Poly. Univ., Toronto, 1993. Mem. Am. Mktg. Assn. (pres. Toronto chpt. 1981-82). Office: Can Tire Acceptance Ltd, 555 Prince Charles Dr, Welland, ON Canada L3C 6B5

WINTER-NEIGHBORS, GWEN CAROLE, special education educator, art educator; b. Greenville, S.C., July 14, 1938; d. James Edward and Evelyn (Lee) Walters; m. David M. Winter Jr., Aug., 1963 (dec. Feb. 1982); children: Robin Carole Winter, Charles G. McCuen, Dustin Winter TeBrugge; m. Thomas Frederick Neighbors, Mar. 24, 1989. BA in Edn. & Art, Furman U., 1960, MA in Psychology, 1967; cert. in guidance/pers., Clemson U., 1981; EdD in Youth & Mid. Childhood Edn., Nova Southeastern U., 1988; postgrad., U. S.C., Spartanburg, 1981-89; cert. clear specialist instruction, Calif. State U., Northridge, 1991; art edn. cert., Calif. State U., L.A., 1990—; postgrad., Glendale U., 1996—. Cert. tchr. art, elem. edn., psychology, secondary guidance, S.C. Tchr. 7th grade Greenville Jr. H.S., 1960-63; art tchr. Wade Hampton H.S., Greenville, 1963-67; prin. adult edn. Woodmont H.S., Piedmont, S.C., 1983-85, Mauldin H.S., Greenville and Mauldin, S.C., 1981; tchr. ednl. psychology edn. dept. Allen U., Columbia, S.C., 1969; activity therapist edn. dept. S.C. Dept. of Corrections, Columbia, 1973-76; art specialist gifted edn. Westcliffe Elem. Sch., Greenville, 1976-89; tchr. self-contained spl. day class Elysian Heights Elem. Sch., Echo Park and L.A., Calif., 1989-91; art tchr. medh. drawing Sch. Dist. Greenville County Blue Ridge Mid. Sch., Greer, S.C., 1991-95; participant nat. conf. U.S. Dept. Edn./So. Bell, Columbia, 1989; com. mem. nat. exec. com. Nova Southeastern U., 1988-89. Illustrator: Mozart Book, 1988; author: (drama) Let's Sing a Song About America, 1988 (1st pl. Nat. Music award 1990). Life mem. Rep. Presdl. Task Force, 1970—; mem. voter registration com. Lexington County Rep. Party, 1970-80; grand jury participant 13th Jud. Ct. Sys., Greenville, 1987-88, guardian ad litem, 1988-89. Tchr. Incentive grantee Sch. Dist. Greenville County, 1986-88, Project Earth grantee Bell South, 1988-89, 94-95, Edn. Improvement Act/Nat. Dissimination Network grantee S.C. State Dept. Edn., 1987-88, Targett 2,000 Arts in Curricular grantee S.C. Dept. Edn., 1994-95, Alliance grantee Bus. Cmty. Greenville, 1992-95, Greer Art Rsch. grantee, 1993-94, S.C. Govs. Sch. Study grantee, 1994, Edn. Improvement Act Competitive Tchr. grantee S.C. Dept. Edn., 1994-95, Alliance Grand grant, 1995-96; recipient Am. Jurisprudence Bancroft-Whitney award Glendale U. Sch. Law. Mem. NEA, ABA (student orgn.), Nat. Art Edn. Assn., Nat. Mus. Women in Arts, S.C. Arts Alliance, S.C. Art Edn. Assn., Phi Delta Kappa (com. mem. 1976-90), Upstate IBM-PC Users Group. Baptist/Lutheran. Avocations: computers, art, writing, music composition, law. Home: 26 Charterhouse Ave Piedmont SC 29673-9139 Office: Neighbors Enterprises 3075 Foothill Blvd Unit 138 La Crescenta CA 91214-2742

WINTERNITZ, FELIX THOMAS, editor, educator; b. Wichita Falls, Tex., Sept. 15, 1958; s. Walter Hines and Josephine (Thomas) W.; m. Connie Yeager, May 28, 1988; children; Kathryn Ann, Abigail Grace. Attended, Temple U., 1978-81. Police reporter Wilmington (Del.) News-Jour., 1981-83; Sunday editor Savannah (Ga.) News-Press, 1983-85; asst. features editor Rochester (N.Y.) Times-Union, 1985-86; dep. features editor Cin. Enquirer, 1986-89; editorial dir. Cin. mag., 1989-96; spl. projects editor Cin. City Beat, 1996—; adj. prof. journalism U. Cin., 1991—; fellow Poynter Inst. Media Studies, St. Petersburg, Fla., 1991, Knight Ctr. for Specialized Journalism, U. Md., College Park, 1993; prof. journalism No. Ky. U., 1995—. Contbr. articles to profl. jours. Mem. Cin. Soc. Profl. Journalists (pres. 1995—). Office: 23 E 7th St Ste 617 Cincinnati OH 45202-2456

WINTEROWD, WALTER ROSS, English educator; b. Salt Lake City, Jan. 24, 1930; s. Harold Ross and Henrietta Ethel (Fike) W.; m. Norma Graham, Aug. 2, 1952; children: Geoffrey Ross, Anthony Gordon. B.S., Utah State U., 1952; Ph.D., U. Utah, 1962. Asst. prof. U. Mont., Missoula, 1962-66; assoc. prof. U. So. Calif., Los Angeles, 1966-71, prof. English, 1971-79; McElderry prof. English U. So. Calif., 1979—. Author: Rhetoric: A Synthesis, 1967, Contemporary Rhetoric, 1975, The Contemporary Writer, 1975, Composition/Rhetoric: A Synthesis, 1986, The Culture and Politics of Literacy, 1989, The Rhetoric of the "Other" Literature, 1990, (with Geoffrey Winterowd) The Critical Reader, Thinker, and Writer, 1992. Served with U.S. Army, 1953-55. Mem. Nat. Council Tchrs. English, AAUP. Democrat. Home: 17551 San Roque Ln Huntington Beach CA 92647-6641 Office: Dept English U So Calif Los Angeles CA 90089-0354

WINTERROWD, WILLIAM J., bishop. Bishop Diocese of Colo., Denver, 1991—. Office: Diocese of Colo 1300 Washington St Denver CO 80203-2008*

WINTERS, BARBARA JO, musician; b. Salt Lake City; d. Louis McClain and Gwendolyn (Bradley) W. AB cum laude, UCLA, 1960, postgrad., 1961; postgrad., Yale, 1960. Mem. oboe sect. L.A. Philharm., 1961-94, prin. oboist, 1972-94; ret.; clinician oboe, English horn, Oboe d'amore. Recs. movie, TV sound tracks. Avocation: painting in oils and mixed media. Home: 3529 Coldwater Canyon Ave Studio City CA 91604-4060 Office: 135 N Grand Ave Los Angeles CA 90012-3013

WINTERS, BRIAN JOSEPH, professional sports team executive; b. Rockaway, N.Y., Mar. 1, 1952. Profl. player L.A. Lakers, Milw. Bucks; head coach Vancouver Grizzlies, 1995—. Office: Vancouver Grizzlies, 800 Griffiths Way, Vancouver, BC Canada VGB 6G1

WINTERS, HAROLD FRANKLIN, physicist; b. Renton, Wash., May 19, 1932; s. Walter Wade and Ruth Elizabeth (Meyer) W.; m. Marjorie Ann Neiswender, June 9, 1956; children: Kathie Moe, David Winters, John Winters, Janice Assadi, Judy Ahlquist. Attended, Biola Coll., 1950-51; BS, Whitworth Coll., 1958; PhD, Washington State U., 1963. Rsch. staff mem. IBM Almaden Rsch. Ctr., San Jose, Calif., 1963-93; emeritus IBM Almaden Rsch. Ctr., San Jose, 1993—; vis. prof. Odense U., Denmark, 1979-80; past N.Am. rep. Subcom. on Plasma Chemistry, Internat. Union Pure and Applied Chemistry; past trustee Am. Vacuum Soc.; past lectr. numerous major nat. and internat. confs. throughout the world. Past mem. editl. bd. Plasma Materials Interactions, Jour. Nuc. Inst. and Methods; contbr. numerous articles to sci. jours. Corp. U.S. Army, 1952-54. Recipient (with John Coburn) Thinkers award Tegal Corp., 1983, Disting. Alumni Achievement award Wash. State U., 1992, John A. Thornton Meml. award and lectr. Am. Vacuum Soc., 1993, honored by plasma sci. divsn. of Am. Vacuum Soc. with naming of John Coburn and Harold Winters Student Award, 1994. Mem. AAAS, Am. Vacuum Soc., Am. Sci. Affiliation. Achievements include patents for plasma processing, ion sources and ion pumps; scientific contributions in the fields of plasma science, surface science, thin films, ion bombardment of solids, dissociation of gases by electron impact. Home: 632 Lanfair Dr San Jose CA 95136-1947 *My conversion to evangelical Christianity in high school led to a change in my attitude, lifesyle, behavior, and study habits. I changed from a poor student with a bad attitude to an excellent student with a great love for science. These changes led to a successful and enjoyable scientific career. I find no contradiction or conflict between science and my Christian faith; on the contrary science has increased my respect for God.*

WINTERS, J. OTIS, oil industry consultant; b. Tulsa, Nov. 6, 1932; s. John McAfee, Jr. and Marian Dunn (McClintock) W.; m. Ann Allene Varnadow, Oct. 18, 1958; children: John, Richard, David, Paul. MS in Petroleum Engring., Stanford U., 1955; MBA, Harvard U., 1962. Registered profl. engr., Okla. V.p. Warren Am. Oil Co., Tulsa, 1962-65; pres. Ednl. Devel. Corp., Tulsa, 1965-73; exec. v.p., dir. Williams Cos., Tulsa, 1973-77, First Nat. Bank of Tulsa, 1978-79; pres. Avanti Energy Corp., Tulsa, 1980-87, Zephyr Corp., Tulsa, 1980-90; chmn. Pate Winters & Stone Inc., 1990—; bd. dirs. Walden Residential Properties, Inc., NGC Corp., Hat Brands, Inc., Liberty Bancorp Inc., Amx Corp. Chmn. bd. First United Meth. Ch., 1977-79; pres. Downtown Tulsa Unltd., 1977; former vice chmn. bd. Oral Roberts U.; bd. dirs. Jr. Achievement; commr. Tulsa Urban Renewal Authority; 1st v.p. Ark. Basin Devel. Assn. Served as 1st lt., C.E. U.S. Army, 1955-57. Recipient various pub. service awards. Mem. Tulsa C. of C. (bd. dirs.), So. Hills Country Club (Tulsa), Pine Valley Golf Club, Augusta Nat. Golf Club, Cypress Point Club, Royal and Ancient Club, St. Andrews. Home: 4616 Christopher Pl Dallas TX 75204-1611 Office: Pate Winters & Stone Inc 5956 Sherry Ln Ste 2001 Dallas TX 75225-8301

WINTERS, J. SAM, lawyer, federal government official; b. Amarillo, Tex., July 7, 1922; m. Dorothy Jean Rushing, Dec. 21, 1947; 1 child, Leila Winters Mischer. BA, U. Tex., 1944, JD, 1948. Bar: Tex. 1948. Briefing atty. Supreme Ct. Tex., Austin, 1948-49; chief Charter div. Sec. of State, State of Tex., Austin, 1949-50; ptnr. Bagby & Winters, Austin, 1950-57; shareholder Clark, Thomas, & Winters, Austin, 1957—; bd. govs. U.S. Postal Svc., Washington, 1991-95, chmn. bd. govs., 1994-95, vice chair, 1996-97; mem. stds. com. Nat. Flood Inst. Program, Washington, 1990-93, dir., 1990-94. Bd. dirs. Tex. Assn. Taxpayers; mem. devel. bd. U. Tex., Austin, 1988—, mem. Pres.'s Assocs., 1981—; mem. chancellor's coun. U. Tex. Sys., 1983—; mem. symposium planning com. Lyndon B. Johnson Sch. Pub. Affairs, Austin, 1987—. Mem. ABA (past chair, sect. pub. utility comm. and transp. law, chair sect. pub. utility, comms. and transp. law 1995-96), State Bar Tex., Travis County Bar Assn., Tex. Bar Found., Internat. Assn. Def. Counsel, Tex. Assn. Def. Counsel, Fedn. Ins. and Corp. Counsel, Tex. Rsch. League (past chair), Tex. Coun. Econ. Edn., Tex. Hist. Soc., Panhandle Plains Hist. Soc., SAR. Democrat. Episcopalian. Office: Clark Thomas & Winters PO Box 1148 Austin TX 78767-1148

WINTERS, JONATHAN, actor; b. Dayton, Ohio, Nov. 11, 1925; s. Jonathan H. and Alice Kilgore (Rodgers) W.; m. Eileen Ann Schauder, Sept. 11, 1948; children: Jonathan IV, Lucinda Kelley. Student, Kenyon Coll., 1946; B.F.A., Dayton Art Inst., 1950. With radio sta. WING, Dayton, 1949; disc jockey sta. WBNS-TV, Columbus, Ohio, 1950-53. Appeared on: Garry Moore Show, 1954-63, Steve Allen Show, 1954-61, Omnibus, 1954, NBC Comedy Hour, 1956, Jonathan Winters Show, 1956-57, Jack Paar Show, 1963-64, Andy Williams Show, 1966-67, Dean Martin Show, 1966-67, Jonathan Winters Show, CBS-TV, 1968-69, Wacky World of Jonathan Winters, 1972-73; numerous appearances NBC Monitor show, 1963—, Hollywood Squares, 1975—; TV series include Mork & Mindy, 1982-83, Davis Rules, (Emmy award for best supporting actor) 1991-92, 5 spls. Showtime Cable TV; night club appearances, 1953-60; motion picture appearances: It's a Mad, Mad, Mad World, 1963, The Loved One, 1964, The Russians Are Coming, The Russians Are Coming, 1966, Penelope, 1967, The Midnight Oil, 1967, 8 On the Lam, 1967, Oh Dad, Poor Dad, 1968, Viva Max, 1969, The Fish That Saved Pittsburgh, 1979, The Longshot, 1986, Say Yes, 1986, Moon Over Parador, 1988, The Flintstones, 1994, The Shadow, 1994; rec. artist, Columbia Records.; author: Mouse Breath, Conformity and Other Social Ills, 1965, Winter's Tales, 1987, Hang-Ups, 1990; voice numerous cartoon characters. Served with USMCR, 1943-46, PTO. Named to Comedy Hall of Fame U.S., 1993, Comedy Hall of Fame Can., 1994; recipient Grammy for Comedy Album of Yr., 1996.

WINTERS, NOLA FRANCES, food company executive; b. Achilles, Kans., Aug. 27, 1925; d. Edward Earl and Mary Ruby (Mikesell) Ginther; divorced. Student, U. Kans., 1943-45; BA, U. Colo., 1972. Exec. sec. Holly Sugar Corp., Colorado Springs, Colo., 1953-66, asst. sec., 1966-84, dir. corp. rels., asst. sec., 1981-84, dir. corp. and pub. rels., asst. sec., 1984-90; asst. sec. HSC Export Corp., Colorado Springs, 1980-90, Imperial Holly Corp., Colorado Springs, 1988-90. Mem. Phi Beta Kappa. Republican. Methodist.

WINTERS, RALPH E., film editor. Films include Gaslight, Little Women, King Solomon's Mines, Quo Vadis (Acad. award nomination), Kiss Me Kate, Executive Suite, Seven Brides for Seven Brothers (Acad. award nomination), High Society, Jailhouse Rock, Ben-hur (Acad. award), Butterfield 8, Soldier in the Rain, The Pink Panther, The Great Race (Acad. award nomination), Fitzwilly, How to Succeed in Business without Really Trying, The Party, The Thomas Crown Affair, The Hawaiians, Kotch (Acad. award nomination), The Front Page, Mr. Majestyk, King Kong, 10, S.O.B., Victor Victoria, Curse of the Pink Panther, Big Trouble, Let's Get Harry, Moving, Tagget. Office: The Mirisch Agy 10100 Santa Monica Blvd Ste 700 Los Angeles CA 90067-4011*

WINTERS, RICHARD ALLEN, mineral economist; b. Butte, Mont., Feb. 19, 1963; s. Allen S. and Doris Ellen (Taylor) W.; m. Malinna J. Winters, June 30, 1994. BS in Fin., Econs., U. Mont., 1986; MS in Mineral Econs., Colo. Sch. Mines, 1990, postgrad., 1991—. Office engr. Morrison Knudsen Engrs., Richland, Wash., 1986-88; project acct. Morrison Knudsen Engrs., Richland, 1987-88; ops. analyst Echo Bay Mines, Denver, 1989; instr. Colo. Sch. Mines, Golden, Colo., 1991-92; cons. Coors Brewing Co., Golden, 1991-92; sr. rsch. engr. Phelps Dodge Mining Co., Morenci, Ariz., 1992-94; gold analyst Robertson, Stephens and Co., San Francisco, 1994-95; v.p. corp. devel. Golden Star Resources Ltd., Denver, 1995—. Pres. Mineral Econ. Grad. Student Assn., 1989-90. Mem. Soc. Mining, Metallurgy and Exploration, Assn. Environ. Resource Economists, Mineral, Econs. and Mgmt. Soc. Avocations: outdoors, jewelry craft. Home: 1250 Galapago St #605 Denver CO 80204-3588 Office: Golden Star Resources Ltd Robertson Stephens & Co Denver CO 80203

WINTERS, ROBERT W., medical educator, pediatrician; b. Evansville, Ind., May 23, 1926; s. Frank and Clara (Flentke) W.; m. Madoris Seiler, Sept. 5, 1948 (div. Feb. 1972); children: Henry N., R. George; m. Agnete Thomsen, Feb. 11, 1976; children: Charlotte, Anne. AB magna cum laude, Indiana U., 1948; MD cum laude, Yale U., 1952. Diplomate Am. Bd. Pediatrics. Intern, resident, and fellow U. N.C., Chapel Hill, 1954-58; asst. prof. U. Pa., Phila., 1959-61; prof. Columbia U., N.Y.C., 1962-81; CEO HNS-Healthdyne, Parsippany, N.J., 1985-89; chmn. Nat. Alliance Infusion Therapy, Washington, 1990-92; pres. Winters Assocs., Inc., Mendham, N.J., 1989—. Contbr. to profl. jour.; author 5 books. 2nd lt. cav. U.S. Army, 1944-46. Recipient Mead Johnson award Am. Acad. Pediatrics, 1966, Borden award, 1972. Office: PO Box 188 Mendham NJ 07945-0188

WINTERS, SAM, federal agency administrator, lawyer. BA, JD, U. Tex. Ptnr. Clark, Thomas & Winters, Austin, Tex.; bd. govs. U.S. Postal Svc., Washington, 1991—, chmn. bd. govs., 1994-96. Chmn. Tex. Rsch. League, 1990, 91; past mem. Nat. Hwy. Safety Adv. Com.; mem. devel. bd. U. Tex., Austin. With USN, World War II. Mem. ABA (chmn.-elect sect. utilities, comm. and transp.), Am. Law Inst. (life), State Bar Tex. Office: US Post Office 475 L'Enfant Plz SW Washington DC 20260*

WINTERSHEIMER, DONALD CARL, state supreme court justice; b. Covington, Ky., Apr. 21, 1932; s. Carl E. and Marie A. (Kohl) W.; m. Alice T. Rabe, June 24, 1961; children: Mark D., Lisa Ann, Craig P., Amy T., Blaise Q. BA, Thomas More Coll., 1953; MA, Xavier U., 1956; JD, U. Cin., 1959. Bar: Ky. 1960, Ohio 1960. Pvt. practice Covington, Ky., 1960-76; city solicitor City of Covington, 1962-76; judge Ky. Ct. Appeals, Frankfort, 1976-83; justice Ky. Supreme Ct., Frankfort, 1983—, chmn. criminal rules com., 1988-94, chmn. continuing jud. edn. com., 1983—, chmn. rules com., 1994—; del. Foster Parent Rev. Bd., 1985—; mem. adv. bd. Sta. WNKU-FM, 1984-94, Am. Soc. Writers on Legal Subjects. Trustee Sta. WNKU-FM. Recipient Cmty. Svc. award Thomas More Coll., 1968; recipient Disting. Alumnus award Thomas More Coll., 1982; named Disting. Jurist Chase Coll. Law, 1983, Outstanding Jurist Phi Alpha Delta Law Frat., 1990. Mem. ABA, Am. Judicature Soc., Ky. Bar Assn., Ohio Bar Assn., Cin. Bar Assn., Inst. Jud. Adminstrn. Democrat. Roman Catholic. Home: 224 Adams Ave Covington KY 41014-1712 Office: Ky Supreme Ct Capitol Building Rm 201 Frankfort KY 40601

WINTERSTEIN, JAMES FREDRICK, academic administrator; b. Copperas Cove, Tex., Apr. 8, 1943; s. Arno Fredrick Herman and Ada Amanda Johanna (Wagnr) W.; m. Diane Marie Bochmann, July 13, 1963; children: Russell, Lisa, Steven, Amy. Student, U. N.M., 1962; D of Chiropractic cum laude, Nat. Coll. Chiropractic, 1968; cert., Harvard Inst. for Ednl. Mgmt., 1988. Diplomate Am. Chiropractic Bd. Radiology; lic. chiropractic, Ill., Fla., S.D., Md. Night supr. x-ray dept. DuPage Meml. Hosp., Elmhurst, Ill., 1964-66; x-ray technologist Lombard (Ill.) Chiropractic Clinic, 1966-68, asst. dir., 1968-71; chmn. dept. diagnostic imaging Nat. Coll. Chiropractic, Lombard, Ill., 1971-73, chief of staff, 1985-86, pres., 1986—; pvt. practice West Chicago, Ill., 1968-73, Fla., 1973-85; faculty Nat.-Lincoln Sch. Postgrad. Edn., 1967—; chmn. x-ray test com. Nat. Bd. Chiropractic Examiners, 1971-73; govs. adv. panel on coal worker's pneumoconiosis and chiropractic State of Pa., 1979; v.p. Am. Chiropractic Coll. Radiology, 1981-83; mem. adv. coun. on radiation protection Dept. Health and Rehabilitative Svcs. State of Fla., 1984-85; cons. to bd. examiners State of S.C., 1983-84, State of Fla., 1980-85; cons. to peer review bd. State of Fla., 1980-84; trustee Chiropractic Centennial Found., 1989-90; speaker in field. Pub. Outreach, monthly Nat. Coll. Chiropractic; author numerous monographs on chiropractic edn. and practice; inventor composite shielding and mounting means for x-ray machines; contbr. articles to profl. jours. Chmn., bd. dirs. Trinity Luth. Ch., West Chgo., 1970-72, Luth. High Sch., Pinellas County, Fla., 1979-82, St. John Luth. Ch., Lombard, 1988; chmn. bd. edn. First Luth. Sch., 1975-79; chmn. First Luth. Congregation, Clearwater, Fla., 1979-82; chmn. bldg. planning com. Grace Luth. Ch. and Sch., St. Petersburg, Fla., 1984-85; bldg. planning com. ch. expansion, new elem. sch., First Luth. Sch., 1975-79; stewardship adv. coun. Fla./Ga. dist. Luth. Ch. Mo. Synod, 1983-85; trustee West Suburban Regional Acad. Consortium, 1993—. With U.S. Army, 1961-64. Recipient Cert. Meritorious Svc. Am. Chiropractic Registry of Radiologic Technologists, Cert. Recognition for Inspiration, Guidance, and Support Delta Tau Alpha, 1989, Cert. Appreciation Chiropractic Assn. South Africa, 1988. Mem. Am. Chiropractic Assn., Am. Chiropractic Coll. Radiology (pres. 1983-85, exec. com. 1985-86), Am. Chiropractic Coun. on Diagnostic Imaging, Am. Chiropractic Coun. on Diagnosis and Internal Disorders, Am. Chiropractic Coun. on Nutrition, Nat. Coll. Alumni Assn., Am. Pub. Health Assn., Assn. Chiropractic Colls. (sec.-treas. 1986-91), Coun. Chiropractic Edn. (sec.-treas. 1988-90, v.p. 1990-92, pres. 1992-94, immediate past pres. 1994), Fla. Chiropractic Assn. (chmn. radiol. health com. 1977-. Republican. Lutheran. Avocations: racketball, reading, automobile rehabilitation, Harley-Davidson motorcycles, fishing. Home: 276 E Edward St Lombard IL 60148-3905

WINTHROP, JOHN, investment company executive; b. Boston, June 22, 1936; s. Nathaniel Thayer and Serita Bartlett (Harwood) W.; m. Elizabeth Goltra; children: John, H. Grenville, Bayard, Edward Field Winthrop. BA, Harvard U., 1958; MBA, Columbia U., 1962. With Wood, Struthers & Winthrop, N.Y.C., 1964-79; former chmn. Mgmt. Co. (subs. DJL); pres. de Vegh Fund, 1973-79, dir., 1973—; founder, pres. John Winthrop & Co., S.C.; dir. Nat. Utilities & Industries, N.J., Ivanhoe Plantation, Inc., S.C., Pioneer Funds, Boston; bd. dirs. Am. Farmland Trust, Washington. Former bd. govs. Investment Co. Inst., Washington. With USNR, 1958-60. Mem. N.Y. Soc. Security Analysts, Mass. Hist. Soc., Harvard Alumni Assn. (bd. dirs.), Pilgrims. Republican. Clubs: Harvard (past bd. mgrs. N.Y.C. club), Knickerbocker (N.Y.C.). Home: 9 Ladson St Charleston SC 29401-2703 Office: One North Adger's Wharf Charleston SC 29401-2571

WINTHROP, JOHN, business executive; b. Salt Lake City, Apr. 20, 1947; m. Marilyn MacDonald, May 17, 1975; children: Grant Gordon, Clayton Hanford. AB cum laude, Yale U., 1969; JD magna cum laude, U. Tex., 1972. Bar: Calif. 1972. Law clk. 9th cir. U.S. Ct. Appeals, L.A., 1972-73; conseil juridique Coudert Freres, Paris, 1973-75; v.p. gen. counsel MacDonald Group, Ltd., L.A., 1976-82; pres., CEO MacDonald Mgmt. Corp. and MacDonald Group Ltd., L.A., 1982-86; pres., chief exec. officer MacDonald Corp. (gen. contractors), L.A., 1982-86; chmn., CEO Comstock Mgmt. Co., L.A., 1986—; pres., CEO Winthrop Investment Properties, Los Angeles, 1986—; CEO Veritas Imports, L.A., 1995—; bd. dirs. Plus Prods., Tiger's Milk Prods., Irvine, Calif., 1977-80. Bd. dirs., sec. L.A. Sheriff's Dept. Found.; bd. dirs. L.A. Opera. Mem. Calif. Bus. Properties Assn. (mem. bd. advisors 1981-87), Internat. Coun. Shopping Ctrs., Nat. Eagle Scout Assn. (life), French-Am. C. of C. (bd. dirs. 1982-87), Urban Land Inst., Nat. Realty Bd., Regency Club, Yale Club N.Y., Calif. Club, The Beach Club, Elizabethan Club. Republican. Office: Comstock Mgmt Co Penthouse 9460 Wilshire Blvd Beverly Hills CA 90212

WINTHROP, LAWRENCE FREDRICK, lawyer; b. L.A., Apr. 18, 1952; s. Murray and Vauneta (Cardwell) W.; BA with honors, Whittier Coll., 1974; JD magna cum laude, Calif. Western Sch., 1977. Bar: Ariz. 1977, Calif. 1977, U.S. Dist. Ct. Ariz. 1977, U.S. Dist. Ct. (so. dist.) Calif. 1981, U.S. Ct. Appeals (9th cir.) 1981, U.S. Dist. Ct. (cen. dist.) Calif. 1983, U.S. Supreme Ct. 1983. Assoc. Snell and Wilmer, Phoenix, 1977-83, ptnr., 1984-93, Doyle, Winthrop, & Oberbillig, P.C., Phoenix, 1993—. judge pro tem Maricopa County Superior Ct., 1987—, Ariz. Ct. Appeals, 1992—; lectr. Ariz. personal injury law and practice and state and local tax law Tax Exec. Inst., Nat. Bus. Inst., Profl. Edn. Systems, Inc., Ariz. Trial Lawyers Assn., Maricopa County Bar Assn.; bd. dirs. Valley of the Sun Sch., 1989—, chmn., 1994-96; mem. Vol. Lawyers Program, Phoenix, 1980—. Fellow Ariz. Bar Found., Maricopa Bar Found.; mem. ABA, Calif. Bar Assn., Ariz. Bar Assn. (mem. com. on exam, 1995—), Ariz. Tax Rsch. Assn. (bd. dirs. 1989-93), Maricopa County Bar Assn., Ariz. Assn. Def. Counsel (bd. dirs., pres. 1988-89, chmn. med.-malpractice com. 1993-95), Aspen Valley Club, LaMancha Racquet Club. Republican. Methodist. Avocations: music, golf, tennis. Editor-in-chief Calif. Western Law Rev., 1976-77. Home: 6031 N 2nd St Phoenix AZ 85012-1210 Office: Doyle Winthrop & Oberbillig PC PO Box 10417 Ste 1550 2800 N Central Ave Phoenix AZ 85016-4666

WINTLE, ROSEMARIE, bio-medical electronic engineer; b. Brigham City, Utah, Sept. 13, 1951; d. DeVere and Kathleen (Layton) W. Student, Weber State U., 1972-76, Brigham Young U., 1978-79, U. Utah, 1980-87, ITT Electronic Tech. Inst., 1986-88, Utah State U., 1991-92. Engr. Morton Internat., Brigham City, Utah; computer technician Salt Lake City; engr. Nuclear Med., Mesa, Ariz., 1976-77, U. Utah Hosp. Lab., Salt Lake City, 1980-87; electronic engr. Varian Assocs., Inc., Salt Lake City, 1987-88; electronic bio-med. experiment and rsch. engr. Clin. Rsch. Assocs., Provo, Utah, 1988-89. Contbr. articles to profl. jours. Designer, builder Honeyville (Utah) town playground equipment; designer, mgr. Honeyville town water system. Recipient grant Brigham City. Mem. IEEE (pres.), NSPE, Inst. for Sci. Info., Am. Statis. Assn., Sci. Am. Libr., Computer Club, Amnesty Internat., Libr. of Science, Newbridge Book Club. Mem. LDS Ch.

WINTON, HOWARD PHILLIP, optometrist; b. Springfield, Mo., June 23, 1925; s. George Lecoumpt and Emma Pearl (Schoonover) W.; m. Frances Jeanne Zellweger, June 29, 1946; children: Susan, James, Stephen, Gary, Carolyn. Student, Northern Ill. Coll. of Optometry, Midwest Sch. of Optics; LHD, Ill. Coll. of Optometry, 1965. Pvt. practice optometry Melbourne, Fla.; nat. cons. to Surgeon Gen. USAF, 1979. Pres. Melbourne C. of C.; pres., chmn. bd. dirs. Brevard Econ. Devel. Coun., Brevard County, 1970-79. With USN, 1943-46, PTO. Named Optometrist of the Yr., Fla. Optometric Assn., 1972. Fellow Am. Acad. Optometry; mem. Fla. Optometric Assn. (pres. 1965), Am. Optometric Assn. (pres. 1975-76, mem. coun.), So. Coun. Optometrics (pres. 1968), Brevard Optometric Assn. (founder, pres. 1973), Rotary Internat. (founder Interact Club 1962, pres. Melbourne 1962).

WINTON, JEFFREY BLAKE, arbitrator; b. Chgo., Feb. 16, 1945; s. Stanley A. and Phyllis R. (Levin) W.; B.S., U. Ill., 1966, M.S. in Labor Relations, 1968; m. Deborah Stein, 1994. With Midwest Stock Exchange, Chgo., 1968-70; dir. mediation services Office of State Sch. Supt., 1970-73; pres., chief exec. officer, chmn. Radionic Industries, Inc. (formerly Radionic Transformers Corp.), Chgo., 1973—; pres. Jeffrey B. Winton & Assocs., Chgo., 1972—. Lectr. labor relations and mgmt. Northwestern U., 1974-78. Asst. to Senator Adlai E. Stevenson, III, 1966, 70, 74; arbitrator, mediator Fact-Finder: Federal Mediation and Conciliation Service, Am. Arbitration Assn., Iowa Public Employment Relations Bd., Wis. Employment Relations Commn., Ind. Edn. Relations Bd., Nat. Mediation Bd., Ill. Pub. Employment Relations Bd., Ill. Tchr. Hearing Panel, Ill. Edn. Employment Relations Bd.; pres. Radionic High-Tech, Inc., 1982—. Recipient Gold Key to City of Champaign, Ill., 1968. Mem. Nat. Acad. Arbitrators, Am. Arbitration Assn. (labor panel), Fed. Mediation and Conciliation Service (labor panel), Indsl. Relations Research Assn., Nat. Mediation Bd., Soc. Profls. in Dispute Resolution (v.p.), Chgo. Assn. Commerce. Contbr. articles to profl. publs. Office: 6625 W Diversey Ave Chicago IL 60707-2218

WINTOUR, ANNA, editor; b. Eng., Nov. 3, 1949; came to U.S., 1976; d. Charles and Elinor W.; m. David Shaffer, Sept. 1984; children: Charles, Kate. Student, Queens Coll., 1963-67. Deputy fashion editor Harper's and Queen Mag., London, 1970-76; fashion editor Harper's Bazaar, New York, 1976-77; fashion and beauty editor Viva Mag., New York, 1977-78; contbg. editor fashion and style Savvy Mag., New York, 1980-81; sr. editor N.Y. Mag., 1981-83; creative dir. U.S. Vogue, N.Y., 1983-86; editor-in-chief British Vogue, London, 1986-87, House and Garden, N.Y., 1987-88, Vogue, N.Y., 1988—. Office: Vogue Mag Conde Nast Bldg 350 Madison Ave New York NY 10017-3704*

WINTRODE, RALPH CHARLES, lawyer; b. Hollywood, Calif., Dec. 21, 1942; s. Ralph Osborne and Maureen (Kavanagh) W.; m. Leslie Ann O'Rourke, July 2, 1966 (div. Feb. 1994); children: R. Christopher, Patrick L., Ryan B. BS in Acctg., U. So. Calif., 1966, JD, 1967. Bar: Calif. 1967, N.Y. 1984, Japan 1989, Washington 1990. From assoc. to ptnr. Gibson, Dunn & Crutcher, Tokyo, L.A., Newport Beach and Irvine, Calif., 1967—. Sec. Music Ctr. Los Angeles County, 1986-88; bd. dirs. Coro Found., L.A. County, 1986-87. Mem. Newport Harbor Club, Am. Club Tokyo. Avocations: sailboat racing, car racing, flying. Office: Gibson Dunn & Crutcher 4 Park Plz Irvine CA 92614-8560 also: Gibson Dunn & Crutcher 333 S Grand Ave Los Angeles CA 90071-1504

WINTROL, JOHN PATRICK, lawyer; b. Wichita, Kans., Feb. 13, 1941; s. Clarence Joseph and Margaret (Gill) W.; m. Janet Lee Mitchell; children: John Howard, Joanna Lee. BA cum laude, Rockhurst Coll., 1963; JD, Georgetown U., 1969. Bar. D.C. 1969, U.S. Ct. Appeals (4th, 5th, 11th and D.C. cirs.) 1981, U.S. Dist. Ct. Md. 1984. Law clk. to Hon. Howard Corcoran U.S. Dist. Ct., Washington, 1969-71; assoc. Howrey & Simon, Washington, 1971-77; mng. ptnr. Perito, Duerk & Pinco, Washington, 1978-85; ptnr. Finley Kumble, Washington, 1985-87, Laxalt, Washington, Perito & Dubuc, Washington, 1988-91, McDermott, Will & Emery, Washington, 1991—; mem. jud. conf. U.S. Ct. Appeals (D.C. cir.). Vol. Peace Corps, Turkey, 1963-66. Mem. ABA. Roman Catholic. Office: McDermott Will & Emery 1850 K St NW Washington DC 20006-2213

WINTROUB, BRUCE URICH, dermatologist, educator, researcher; b. Milw., Nov. 8, 1943; s. Ernest Bernard and Janet (Zien) W.; m. Marya Kraus, Jan. 20, 1973; children: Annie, Ben, Molly. BA, Amherst Coll., 1965; MD, Washington U., St. Louis, 1969. Diplomate Am. Bd. Internal Medicine, Am. Bd. Dermatology. Intern in medicine Peter Bent Brigham Hosp., Boston, 1969-70, jr. asst. resident in medicine, 1970-71, jr. assoc. in medicine, 1976-80, asst. then attending physician, 1976-81; resident in dermatology Harvard Med. Sch., Boston, 1974-76, instr., 1976-78, asst. prof., 1978-82; assoc. prof. dermatology Sch. Medicine, U. Calif., San Francisco, 1982-85, attending physician med. ctr., 1982—, prof., mem. exec. com. dept. dermatology, 1985-95; chmn. exec. com. dept. dermatology U. Calif., San Francisco, 1985-95; mem. dean's adv. com., governing bd. continuing med. edn., other coms. Sch. Medicine, U. Calif., San Francisco, 1986—; exec. vice dean Sch. Medicine U. Calif., San Francisco, 1995-97; chief med. officer U. Calif., Stanford, 1997—; assoc.dean Sch. Medicine, U. Calif., Mount Zion, 1990—; dir. Dermatology Assocs., San Francisco, 1982-85; cons. in dermatology Mass. Gen. Hosp., Boston, 1976-82, Beth Israel Hosp. and Children's Hosp. Med. Ctr., Boston, 1978-82, Parker Hill Med. Ctr., Boston, 1980-82; attending physician Robert B. Brigham Hosp. div. Brigham and Women's Hosp., Boston, 1980-81, assoc., 1980-82; chief dermatology svc. Brockton (Mass.) VA Med. Ctr., 1980-82; asst. chief dermatology VA Med. Ctr., San Francisco, 1982-85, mem. space com., 1984-85, dean's adv. com., 1985—, chmn. budget com., 1987—; clin. investigator Nat. Inst. Allergy, Metabolism and Digestive Disease, NIH, 1978; assoc. dean Sch. Medicine Stanford U., 1997—. Author: (with others) Biochemistry of the Acute Allergic Reactions, Fifth International Symposium, 1988; contbr. numerous articles, abstracts to profl. jours. NIH clin. fellow and grantee, 1967-69. Fellow Am. Acad. Dermatology (com. evaluations 1985—, coun. govt. liaison 1987—, congress on tech. plannning commn. 1988—, assoc. editor Dialogues in Dermatology jour. 1982-85, Stellwagon prize 1976); mem. Soc. Investigative Dermatology (chmn. pub. rels. com. 1987-88), Assn. Profs. Dermatology (chmn. program com. 1987—, bd. dirs.), Pacific Dermatol. Assn. (chmn. program com. 1987—), San Francisco Dermatol. Soc., Am. Fedn. Clin. Rsch. (chmn. dermatology program 1988-89), Am. Assn. Immunology, Dystrophic Epidermolysis Bullosa Rsch. Am. (bd. dirs. 1981), Internat. Soc. Dermatology, Internat. Soc. Cutaneous Pharmacology (founding mem.), Am. Soc. Clin. Investigation, Skin Pharmacology Soc., Calif. Med. Soc., San Francisco Med. Soc., Clin. Immunology Soc., Dermatology Found., (bd. dirs., exec. com.), AAAS, Am. Assn. Physicians, Calif. Acad. Medicine, Am. Dermatol. Assn., Sigma Xi, Alpha Omega Alpha. Avocation: golf. Office: Deans Office Sch Medicine U Calif San Francisco 513 Parnassus Ave Rm S224 San Francisco CA 94122-2722

WINWOOD, STEPHEN LAWRENCE, musician, composer; b. Birmingham, Eng., May 12, 1948; s. Lawrence Samuel and Lillian Mary (Saunders) W.; m. Eugenia Crafton, Jan. 17, 1987; children: Mary Clare, Elizabeth Dawn, Stephen Calhoun, Lillian Eugenia. Rec. artist Spencer Davis Group, 1964-67, Blind Faith, 1970, Traffic, 1967-74; solo artist N.Y.C. and in England, 1974—; dir. F.S. Ltd. Albums include: Arc of a Diver, 1980, Talking Back to the Night, 1982, Back in the High Life, 1986, Roll With It, 1988 (Grammy 1989), Chronicles, Refugees of the Heart, 1991, Traffic: Far From Home, 1994, Junction 7, 1997. Recipient 14 Gold Record awards, 4 Platinum Record awards, 2 Grammy awards.

WINZENRIED, JESSE DAVID, retired petroleum executive; b. Byron, Wyo., June 13, 1922; s. Fritz and Margaret Smith W.; m. Marion Suzan Jacobson, Mar. 15, 1945 (dec. 1984); children: Suzan Winzenried Carlston, Jay Albert, Keith Frederic; m. Lela Madsen, Mar. 12, 1988. BS, U. Wyo., 1945; MS, U. Denver, 1946; PhD, NYU, 1955. Dir. rsch. Tax Found., N.Y.C., 1947-56; sr. v.p. Husky Oil Ltd., Cody, Wyo., 1956-65, Calgary, Alta., Can., 1965-67; v.p. firm Booz, Allen & Hamilton, Cleve., 1968-69; v.p. Coastal States Gas Corp., Houston, 1969-74; group v.p., dir. Crown Ctrl. Petroleum Corp., Balt., 1974-81; vice chmn., dir. Securities Investor Protection Corp., Washington, 1988-95; lectr. mgmt. NYU, 1955-56. Contbr. articles to profl. jours. With U.S. Air Corps, 1942-43. Republican. Mem. LDS Ch.

WINZER, P.J., lawyer; b. Shreveport, La., June 7, 1947; d. C.W. Winzer and Pearlene Hall Winzer Tobin. BA in Polit. Sci., So. U., Baton Rouge, 1968; JD, UCLA, 1971. Bar: Bar: Calif. 1972, U.S. Supreme Ct. 1986. Staff atty. Office of Gen. Counsel, U.S. HEW, Washington, 1971-80; asst. spl. counsel U.S. Office of Spl. Counsel Merit Systems Protection Bd., Dallas, 1980-82; regional dir. U.S. Merit Systems Protection Bd., Falls Church, Va., 1982—. Mem. Calif. Bar Assn., Fed. Cir. Bar Assn., Delta Sigma Theta. Office: US Merit System Protection 5203 Leesburg Pike Ste 1109 Falls Church VA 22041-3401

WIOT, JEROME FRANCIS, radiologist; b. Cin., Aug. 24, 1927; s. Daniel and Elvera (Weisgerber) W.; m. Andrea Kockritz, July 29, 1972; children—J. Geoffrey, Jason. M.D., U. Cin., 1953. Diplomate: Am. Bd. Radiology (trustee, pres.). Intern Cin. Gen. Hosp., 1953-54, resident, 1954-55, 58-59; gen. practice medicine Wyoming, Ohio, 1955-57; mem. faculty U. Cin., 1959-67, 68—, prof., chmn. radiology, 1973-93, acting sr. v.p., provost for med. affairs, 1985-86; practice medicine specializing in radiology Tampa, Fla., 1967-68. Contbr. articles to med. jours. Bd. dirs. Ruth Lyons Fund, U. Cin. Found., 1997—. Served with USN, 1945-46. Fellow Am. Coll. Radiology (pres. 1983-84, chmn. commn. on diagnostic radiology); mem. Radiol. Soc. N.Am., Am. Roentgen Ray Soc. (pres. 1986-87), Am. Bd. Radiology (pres. 1982-84), Ohio Med. Assn., Cin. Acad. Medicine, Radiol. Soc. Greater Cin., Ohio Radiol. Soc., Am. Thoracic Soc., Ohio Thoracic Soc., Fleischner Soc., Soc. Gastrointestinal Radiologists. Office: U Cin Med Ctr 234 Goodman St Cincinnati OH 45267

WIPKE, W. TODD, chemistry educator; b. St. Charles, Mo., Dec. 16, 1940; BS, U. Mo., Columbia, 1962; PhD, U. Calif., Berkeley, 1965. Research chemist Esso Research and Engring. Co., Baton Rouge, 1962; postdoctoral research fellow Harvard U., 1967-69; asst. prof. Princeton U., 1969-75; assoc. prof. chemistry, U. Calif., Santa Cruz, 1975-81, prof. chemistry, 1981—; founder, cons. Molecular Design Ltd., San Leandro, Calif., 1978-91, Ciba-Geigy, Basle, Switzerland, 1978-82, BASF, Ludwigshafen, Fed. Republic Germany, 1974-78, Squibb, Princeton, N.J., 1976-81; adv. EPA, 1984—, chmn. of the bd. InfoPoint, Inc. Editor: Computer Representation and Manipulation of Chemical Information, 1973, Computer-Assisted Organic Synthesis, 1977 ; editor in chief: (jour.) Tetrahedron Computer Methodology, 1987-92; editor Tetrahedron and Tetrahedron Letters, 1987-92; contbr. articles to profl. jours. Served to capt. U.S. Army, 1966-67. Recipient Eastman Kodak Research award, 1964, Texaco Outstanding Research award, 1962; Alexander von Humboldt Sr. Scientist award, 1987; Merck Career Devel. grantee, 1970; NIH, fellow, 1964-65. Mem. NAS, Am. Chem. Soc. (assoc., Computers in Chemistry award 1987, Herman Skolnik award 1991), Assn. Computing Machinery, Chem. Soc., Am. Assn. Artificial Intelligence (charter), Chemical Structure Assn. (charter), Internat. Soc. Study Xenobiotics. Office: U Calif Dept Chemistry Santa Cruz CA 95064

WIPPEL, JOHN FRANCIS, philosophy educator; b. Pomeroy, Ohio, Aug. 21, 1933; s. Joseph Edward and Mary Josephine (Andrews) W. BA in Philosophy, Cath. U. Am., 1955, MA in Philosophy, 1956, STL in Theology, 1960; PhD in Philosophy, Louvain, Belgium, 1965; Maitre agrégé in Philosophy, Louvain, 1981. Ordained priest Roman Cath. Ch., 1960. Instr. philosophy Cath. U., Washington, 1960-61, 63-65, asst. prof. philosophy, 1965-67, assoc. prof. philosophy, 1967-72, ord. prof. philosophy, 1972—, acad. v.p., 1989-96, provost, 1996—; vis. assoc. prof. U. Calif., San Diego, 1969. Assoc. editor Yale Libr. of Medieval Philosophy; author: Metaphysical Thought of Godfrey of Fontaines, 1981 (Mercier prize 1981), Metaphysical Themes in Thomas Aquinas, 1984, Boethius of Dacia, 1987, Mediaeval Reactions to the Encounter between Faith and Reason, 1995; co-author: Medieval Philosophy, 1969, Les questions disputées et les questions quoblibétiques dans les facultés de théologie, de droit et de médécine, 1985; editor: Studies in Medieval Philosophy, 1987; contbr. numerous articles to profl. jours., chpts. to books. Basselin scholar, 1953-56, Penfield fellow, 1961-63; NEH fellow, 1970-71, 84-85. Mem. Medieval Acad. Am., Metaphys. Soc. Am., Am. Cath. Philos. Assn. (pres. 1986-87), Soc. Medieval and Renaissance Philosophy (pres. 1982-84), Société international pour l'étude de la philosophie médiévale. Office: Cath Univ of Am 620 Michigan Ave NE Washington DC 20064-0001

WIRE, WILLIAM SHIDAKER, II, retired apparel and footwear manufacturing company executive; b. Cin., Jan. 5, 1932; s. William Shidaker and Gladys (Buckmaster) W.; m. Alice Dumas Jones, Aug. 31, 1957; children: Alice Wire Freeman, Deborah Wire Suber. Student, U. of South, 1950; AB, U. Ala., 1954, JD, 1956; LLM, NYU, 1957. Bar: Ala. 1956. Atty. Hamilton, Denniston, Butler & Riddick, Mobile, 1959-60; with Talladega Ins. Agy., Ala., 1961-62; with Genesco, Inc., Nashville, 1962-94, former chmn. and CEO; bd. dirs. Genesco Inc., 1st Am. Corp., 1st Am. Nat. Bank Nashville, Dollar Gen. Corp. Mem. Belle Meade Country Club (Nashville), University Club (N.Y.), Shoal Creek (Ala.) Club, Golf Club Tenn., Kappa Alpha. Presbyterian. Home: 6119 Stonehaven Dr Nashville TN 37215-5613

WIREMAN, BILLY OVERTON, college president; b. Jackson, Ky., Oct. 7, 1932; s. William and Emily (Bach) W.; m. Katie Marie Coomer, Mar. 3, 1955; children: J. Gary, Emily Kay Crigler. B.A., Georgetown Coll. (Ky.), 1954, LHD, 1987; M.A., U. Ky., 1957; Ed.D., Peabody Coll., Vanderbilt U., 1960; L.H.D., U. Tampa, 1970, Eckerd Coll., 1977, Georgetown Coll., 1987. Mem. faculty Eckerd Coll., St. Petersburg, Fla., 1960-63, v.p. devel., 1963-68, pres., 1968-77; pres. Queens Coll., Charlotte, N.C., 1978—; guest lectr. People's U. Beijing (China), 1982, also Hong Kong, Taiwan, Philippines; pub. interviews with polit. leaders in Phillipines and South Korea, 1988, 89; rsch. work in USSR, 1989; spkr. fundraising panel, evaluator, accrediting agy. So. Assn. Colls. and Schs., 1989; past v.p. Ormond Beach Pier, Inc., Fla. Co-author: Getting It All Together: The New American Imperative, 1973, Dangerous Grace, 1992, The Peninsula Plot, 1995; contbr. over 150 articles to profl. publs. Chmn. edn. divsn. St. Petersburg United Fund, 1966-67; del. White House Conf. children and Youth, 1970, White House Conf. You, 1971; trustee, chmn. devel. cabinet United Bd. Christian Higher Edn. in Asia, 1974-83; chmn., trustee Bd. for Need-Based Med. Student Loans, State of N.C., 1982; past bd. dirs. Coll. Fund Pinellas County; mem. internat. adv. bd. Han Nam U., Korea, 1987-92, OALS Coll. Bd.; rep. Charlotte C. of C. in China; chair Charlotte-Mecklenburg Cmty. Rels. Com., 1989-95, bd. dirs. Friendship Trays, Charlotte World Affairs Coun.; vice chair Multiple Sclerosis Dinner of Champions Hope Award event, 1988; chmn. Charlotte-Mecklenburg Cmty. Rels. Com. Bd., co-chair Common Ground; mem. steering com. Wildacres Inititiative; bd. dirs. Johnson C. Smith U.; bd. visitors Charlotte Country Day Sch.; mem. Billy Graham Crusade Com., 1996; chmn. selection com. Wilderacres Leadership Initiative. Recipient Liberty Bell award St. Petersburg Bar Assn., 1971, Univ. Medal of Honor Han Nam U., South Korea, 1988, Dinner of Champions Hope award Multiple Sclerosis Soc., Charlotte, 1989. Mem. AAUP, Am. acad. Polit. and Socil Sci., Am. Mgmt. Assn. (dir.), Club of Rome, Am. Coun. Edn. (Internat. Commn.), Young Pres. Orgn., Univ. Club of N.Y.C., N.C. Soc. of N.Y., Charlotte Squires, Tower Club, City Club of Charlotte, Goodfellows, N.C. Trade Assn. (bd. dirs.), British Am. Bus. Assn. (bd. dirs.), Friday Fellows. Office: Queens Coll 1900 Selwyn Ave Charlotte NC 28274-0001

WIRKEN, JAMES CHARLES, lawyer; b. Lansing, Mich., July 3, 1944; s. Frank and Mary (Brosnahan) W.; m. Mary Morse, June 12, 1971; children: Christopher, Erika, Kurt, Gretchen, Jeffrey, Matthew. BA in English, Rockhurst Coll., 1967; JD, St. Louis U., 1970. Bar: Mo. 1970, U.S. Dist. Ct. (we. dist.) Mo. 1970. Asst. prosecuter Jackson County, Kansas City, Mo., 1970-72; assoc. Morris, Larson, King, Stamper & Bold, Kansas City, Mo., 1972-75; dir. Spradley, Wirken, Reismeyer & King, Kansas City, Mo., 1976-88, Wirken & King, Kansas City, Mo., 1988-93; pres. The Wirken Group, Kansas City, Mo., 1993—; adj. prof. law U. Mo., Kansas City, 1984—. Author: Managing a Practice and Avoiding Malpractice, 1983; co-author Missouri Civil Procedure Form Book, 1984; mem. editorial bd. Mo. Law Weekly, 1989—, Lender Liability News, 1990—. Mem. ABA, Nat. Conf. Bar Pres. (coun. 1993—), Met. Bar Caucus (pres. 1992-93), Am. Trial Lawyers Assn., Mo. Bar Assn. (bd. govs. 1976-78, chmn. econs. and methods practice com. 1982-84, quality and methods of practice com. 1989-91, vice chmn. young lawyers sect. 1976-78), Mo. Assn. Trial Attys. (bd. govs. 1983-85), Kansas City Met. Bar Assn. (pres. young lawyers sect. 1975, chair legal assistance com. 1977-78, chair tort law com. 1982, pres. 1990), L.P. Gas Group (founder, chair 1991—). Home: 47 W 53rd Kansas City MO 64112 Office: The Wirken Group PC 4717 Grand Ave Ste 620 Kansas City MO 64112-2206

WIRKLER, NORMAN EDWARD, architectural, engineering, construction management firm executive; b. Garnavillo, Iowa, Apr. 1, 1937; s. Herbert J. and Irene (Kregel) W.; m. Margaret Anne Gift, Oct. 16, 1959; children: Chris Edward, Scott Norman, Elizabeth Anne. BArch, Iowa State U., 1959. Designer The Durrant Group Inc., Dubuque, Iowa, 1959-64, assoc., 1964-67, prin., 1967-82; pres. The Durrant Group Inc., Denver, 1982—; co-owner Wirkler Property Mgmt. Snowmass Co., 1993; pres. Foresite Capital Facilities Corp., Denver County, 1993—; commr., mem. exec. com. Commn. on Accreditation on Corrections, 1985-91; archtl. cons. to Am. Correctional Assn. Standards Program; mem. Am. Correctional Assn. Standards Com., 1992-98; v.p. Garnavillo (Iowa) Bank Corp. Co-author: Design Guide for Secure Adult Correctional Facilities, 1983;. Bd. dirs. United Way, Dubuque, 1984. Fellow AIA (pres. Iowa chpt. 1977; mem. nat. com. on arch. for justice 1974—, chmn. 1979; chmn. AIA Ins. Trust 1985-87, mem. Colo. chpt. 1987—); mem. ASTM (detention component standards com. 1982-84), Dubuque C. of C. (legis. com. 1978-83, chmn. 1979; v.p. 1984, exec. com. 1982-85), Iowa State U. Devel. Coun. Club. Republican. Avocations: flying, skiing, jogging, golf, hunting. Office: The Durrant Group Inc Ste 240 3773 Cherry Creek North Dr Denver CO 80209-3812

WIRSCHING, CHARLES PHILIPP, JR., brokerage house executive, investor; b. Chgo., Oct. 26, 1935; s. Charles Philipp and Mamie Ethel (York) W.; m. Beverly Ann Bryan, May 28, 1966. BA, U. N.C., 1957. Sales rep. Adams-Millis Corp., Chgo., 1963-67; ptnr. Schwartz-Wirsching, Chgo., 1968-70; sec., dir. Edwin H. Mann, Inc., Chgo., 1971-74; stockbroker Paine Webber, Inc., Chgo., 1975-85, account v.p., 1986-95; ret., 1995; ind. cons. Paine Webber, Inc., Chgo., 1996—. Mem. adv. coun. John Nuveen & Co., Inc., 1993-95; trustee Wirsching Charitable Trust, 1987—. Republican. Episcopalian. Avocation: foreign travel. Home and Office: 434 Clinton Pl River Forest IL 60305-2249

WIRSIG, WOODROW, magazine editor, trade organization executive, business executive; b. Spokane, Wash., June 28, 1916; s. Otto Alan and Beulah Juliet (Marohn) W.; m. Jane Barbara Dealy, Dec. 11, 1942; children: Alan Robert, Guy Rodney, Paul Harold. Student, Kearney (Nebr.) State Tchrs. Coll., Los Angeles City Coll., UCLA, 1933-39; B.A., Occidental Coll., 1941; M.S., Columbia Grad. Sch. Journalism, 1942. Dir. Occidental Coll. News Bur., 1939-41; radio newswriter WQXR, N.Y.C., 1941-42; news writer, propaganda analyst CBS, 1942-43; rewrite man Los Angeles Times, 1943-44; asst. editor This Week mag., 1944-45; staff writer Look mag., 1946, asst. mng. editor, 1946-49, exec. editor, 1950-52; mng. editor Quick mag., 1949-50; asso. editor Newsweek mag., Ladies' Home Jour., 1952; editor Woman's Home Companion, 1952-56; editorial cons. Ednl. Testing Service, Princeton, 1957-67; TV cons. NBC-TV, ABC-TV; creator Nat. Daytime Radio Programs, 1957-60; radio documentary Companion; pres. communications firm Wirsig, Gordon and O'Connor, Inc., 1956-58; editor Printers' Ink mag., N.Y.C., 1958-65, Salesweek mag., 1959-60; editorial dir. Overseas Press Club ann. mag. Dateline, 1961, 62; creator, editorial dir. Calif. Life mag.; pres. Better Bus. Bur. Met. N.Y., Inc., 1966-77; also pres. Edn. Research Found.; pres. Bus. Advocacy Center, Inc., 1977—; creator Corp. Social Accountability Audit and Customer Services/Consumer Affairs Audit.; Cons. to Office Sec. HEW, 1965-66. Author: I Love You, Too., 1990; editor, contbr.: Your Diabetes (Dr. Herbert Pollack), 1951; editor: Advertising: Today-Yesterday-Tomorrow; New Products Marketing; cons. editor: Principles of Advertising; contbr. nat. mags.; lectr.; syndicated columnist: other newspapers L.A. Times, 1964-65. Recipient gold medal Benjamin Franklin Mag. Awards, 1956. Mem. Soc. Consumer Affairs Profls. (pres. 1983), Newcomen Soc., Archons, Players Club, Overseas Press Club, Nat. Press Club, N.Y. Advt. Club, N.Y.C. Club, Springdale Country Club, Evergreen Country Club (v.p.), Nassau Club, Century Assn., Families for Alzheimers Rights Assn. (pres. 1994—), Univ. Club, Sigma Delta Chi, Phi Gamma Delta, Gamma Delta Upsilon. Democrat. Presbyterian. Home and Office: Sandhill Cove 1459 SW Shoreline Dr Palm City FL 34990-4533

WIRSZUP, IZAAK, mathematician, educator; b. Wilno, Poland, Jan. 5, 1915; came to U.S., 1949, naturalized, 1955; s. Samuel and Pera (Golomb) W.; m. Pola Ofman, July 19, 1940 (dec. 1943); 1 son Vladimir (dec. 1943); m. Pera Poswianska, Apr. 23, 1949; 1 dau., Marina (Mrs. Arnold M. Tatar). Magister of Philosophy in Math, U. Wilno, 1939; Ph.D. in Math, U. Chgo., 1955. Lectr. math. Tech. Inst. Wilno, 1939-41; dir. Bur. d'Études et de Statistiques Spéciales, Société Centrale d'Achat-Société Anonyme des Monoprix, Paris, 1946-49; mem. faculty U. Chgo., 1949—, prof. math., 1965-85, prof. math. emeritus, 1985—, prin. investigator U. Chgo. Sch. Math. Project (sponsored by Amoco Found., also dir. resource devel. component), 1983—, dir. Internat. Math. Edn. Resource Ctr., 1988—; dir. NSF Survey Applied Soviet Rsch. in Math. Edn., 1985-91; cons. Ford Found., Colombia, Peru, 1965-66, Sch. Math Study Group, 1960, 61, 66-68; participant, writer tchr. tng. material African Math. Program, Entebbe, Uganda, summer 1964, Mombasa, Kenya, summers 1965-66; assoc. dir. Survey Recent Ea. European Math. Lit., 1956-68, dir., 1968-84; dir. NSF program application computers to mgmt., 1976-83; cons. NSF-AID Sci. Edn. Program, India, 1969; mem. U.S. Commn. on Math. Instn., 1969-73. Contbr. articles to profl. jours.; Editor Math. books, transls., adaptions from Russian.; Adviser math.: Ency. Brit., 1971—. Recipient Lewellyn John and Harriet Manchester Quantrell award U. Chgo., 1958, Univ. Alumni Svc. medal, U. Chgo., 1994; resident master Woodward Ct., U. Chgo., 1971-85; endowed Wirszup Lecture Series, U. Chgo., 1986. Mem. N.Y. Acad. Scis., Am. Math. Soc., Math. Assn. Am., AAAS, Nat. Council Tchrs. Math. (chmn. com. internat. math. edn. 1967-69, Lifetime Achievement medal for Leadership, Tchg., and Svc. in Math. Edn. 1996). Home: 5750 S Kenwood Ave Chicago IL 60637-1744 Office: U Chgo Dept Math 5734 S University Ave Chicago IL 60637-1514

WIRT, FREDERICK MARSHALL, political scientist; b. Radford, Va., July 27, 1924; s. Harry Johnson, Sr. and Goldie (Turpin) W.; m. Elizabeth Cook, Sept. 6, 1947; children: Leslie Lee, Sandra Sue, Wendy Ann. B.A., DePauw U., 1948; M.A., Ohio State U., 1949, Ph.D., 1956. Instr. to prof. polit. sci. Denison U., Granville, Ohio, 1952-66; vis. prof., lectr. U. Calif., Berkeley, 1966-68, 69-72; dir. policy scis. grad. program U. Md. Balt. County, 1972-75; prof. polit. sci. U. Ill., Urbana, 1975—; dir. Inst. for Desegregation Problems, U. Calif.-Berkeley, 1970-72; cons. Motion Picture Assn. Am., Rand Corp., Nat. Inst. Edn., SUNY Sch. Edn. Albany; vis. prof. U. Rochester, Nova U., U. Melbourne; acad. visitor London Sch. Econs. Author: Politics of Southern Equality, 1970 (honorable mention for best book 1972), Power in the City, 1974; (with others) The Polity of the School, 1975, Political Science and School Politics, 1977, Education, Recession, and the World Village, 1986, (with others) Culture and Education Policy in the American States, 1992, I Ain' What I Was: Civil Rights in the New South, 1996, We Ain't What We Was, 1997, The Political Dynamics of American Education, 1997. Mem. Granville City Charter Commn., 1964. Grantee Am. Philos. Soc., Denison Rsch. Assn., U. Ill. Rsch. Bd., NEH, Ford Found., Ctr. Advanced Studies; fellow U. Ill., Dept. Edn., Spencer Found.; recipient Lifetime Achievement awards Am. Ednl. Rsch. Assn., 1995, Am. Polit. Sci. Assn., 1994. Mem. Am. Polit. Sci. Assn. (nat. council, Career Achievement award 1993, 91), Midwestern Polit. Sci. Assn., Am. Ednl. Rsch. Assn., Policy Studies Orgn. Home: 2007B Eagle Ridge Ct Urbana IL 61801-8617 Office: U Ill Dept of Polit Sci Urbana IL 61801

WIRT, MICHAEL JAMES, library director; b. Sault Ste. Marie, Mich., May 21, 1947; s. Arthur James and Blanche Marian (Carruth) W.; m. Barbara Ann Hallesy, Aug. 12, 1972; 1 child, Brendan. BA, Mich. State U., 1969; MLS, U. Mich., 1971; postgrad. U. Wash., 1990. Cert. librarian, Wash. Acting librarian Univ. Mich., Ctr. for Research on Econ. Devel., Ann Arbor, 1971-72; instnl. services librarian Spokane County Library Dist., Wash., 1972-76, asst. dir., 1976-79, acting dir., 1979, dir., 1980—. Mem. Adv. com. Partnership for Rural Improvement, Spokane, 1982-85, Wash. State Libr. Planning and Devel. Com., 1984-85, Ea. Wash. U. Young Writers Project Adv. Bd., 1988-89; mem. issues selection com. Citizens League of Greater Spokane, 1991-93, City of Spokane Indian Trail Specific Plan Task Force, 1992-95; mem. comm. com. United Way Spokane County, 1994, campaign chair local govt. divsn., 1996. Mem. Wash. Libr. Assn. (2d v.p. 1984-86, Merit award 1984, dir. 1989-91, legis. planning com., 1991—, pub. rels. com. 1993—, coord. comm. 1996—), Wash. Libr. Network (rep. Computer Svc. Coun. 1983-86, v.p., treas. State Users Group 1986-87), Am. Libr. Assn. (Pub. Libr. Affiliates Network 1990-93, PLA Bus. Coun. 1990-94, chmn. 1991-94), Spokane Valley C. of C. (local govt. affairs com. 1987—, co-chair 1996—), Spokane Area C. of C. (local govt. com. 1990-94, human svcs. com. 1990-92, chmn. 1991-92, govt. reorgn. task force 1995), Spokane Civic Theatre (bd. dirs. 1996—), Momentum (local govt. strategy com. 1992-94). Office: Spokane Ct Libr Dist 4322 N Argonne Rd Spokane WA 99212-1853

WIRTH, DAVID EUGENE, software designer, consultant; b. Norfolk, Va., Oct. 20, 1951; s. Eugene Ross and Darlene (Worley) W. BA, Luther Coll., 1975. Systems analyst ASI Computer Systems, Waterloo, Iowa, 1974-87, v.p. ops., 1987—. Avocations: basketball, softball, fishing, hunting. Office: ASI Computer Systems Inc PO Box 1527 Waterloo IA 50704-1527

WIRTH, DYANN FERGUS, public health educator, microbiologist; b. Racine, Wis., Jan. 31, 1951; d. Russell and Phyllis Rose (Muratone) Fergus; m. Peter Wirth, Aug. 25, 1973. BA with highest honors, U. Wis., 1972; PhD, MIT, 1978; AM (hon.), Harvard U., 1990. Instr. Marine Biol. Lab., Woods Hole, Mass., 1980-84; asst. prof. Harvard Sch. of Pub. Health, Boston, 1981-86, assoc. prof., 1986-90, prof., 1990—; editor-in-chief Academic Press Exptl. Parasitology, Boston, 1987—; NIH study sect. mem. tropical medicine and parasitology NIH, Bethesda, 1987-91; chmn. steering com. on chemotherapy of Malaria WHO, Geneva, 1986-91, 91—; mem. sci. adv. bd. Edna McConnell Clark Found.; chair sci. adv. com. Burroughs Wellcome Fund Career Awards, 1994—. Contbr. numerous articles to profl. jours. Fellowship Fulbright Found., 1972-73, Predoctoral fellowship NIH, 1973-78, Helen Hay Whitney fellowship, 1978-81; recipient Burroughs-Wellcome award in Molecular Parasitology, 1982, 85-90. Mem. AAAS, Am. Soc. Microbiology, Am. Soc. Tropical Medicine and Hygiene (Bailey K. Ashford award 1995), Am. Soc. Virology, Phi Beta Kappa. Office: Harvard Sch of Pub Health 665 Huntington Ave Boston MA 02115-6021

WIRTH, FREMONT PHILIP, neurosurgeon, educator; b. Nashville, July 23, 1940; s. Fremont P. and Willa (Dean) W.; m. Penelope Simpson, July 25, 1964; children: Fremont Philip II, Andrew Simpson, Carolyn Howe. BA with honors in History, Williams Coll., 1962; MD, Vanderbilt U., 1966. Diplomate Am. Bd. Neurol. Surgery (guest examiner 1989, bd. dirs. 1992—), Nat. Bd. Med. Examiners; cert. advanced trauma life support ACS. Surg. intern Johns Hopkins Hosp., Balt., 1966-67, resident and fellow in surgery, 1967-68; asst. resident in neurosurgery Barnes Hosp., Washington U., St. Louis, 1970-72, fellow in neurosurgery, 1972-74; pvt. practice, Savannah, Ga., 1974—; asst. clin. prof. neurosurgery Med. Coll. Ga., Augusta, 1991—, vis. prof., 1978, 79, 86, 87; mem. staff, neurosurg. ICU, St. Joseph's Hosp., 1974—, dir. 1978—; mem. staff Meml. Med. Ctr., 1974—, dir. rehab., 1983; mem. staff Candler Gen. Hosp., 1974—; med. dir. Head and Spinal Cord Injury Prevention Project for Ga., 1984—; presenter in field, 1970—; vis. prof. U. Md., Balt., 1981, Tufts New Eng. Med. Ctr., Boston, 1982. Series editor (with R.A. Ratcheson) Concepts in Neurosurgery, 1986-93; editor: (with Ratcheson) Neurosurgical Critical Care, Concepts in Neurological Surgery, Vol. 1, 1987, Ruptured Cerebral Aneurysms, Concepts in Neurological Surgery, Vol. 6, 1994; contbr. articles and book revs. to med. jours., chpts. to books. Elder Skidaway Island Presbyn. Ch., 1981-83; mem. pack 57 com. Cub Scouts Am., Savannah, 1979-84; mem. troop 57 com. Boy Scouts Am., Savannah, 1980-85, mem. fin. com. Coastal Empire coun., 1987-90, mem. adv. bd., 1990—; chmn. physicians' solicitation United Way Coastal Empire, 1987; bd. dirs. Think First Found., 1990-95. With USPHS, 1968-70. Fellow ACS (bd. govs. 1984-90, sr. mem. trauma com. 1991-93); mem. AMA (physician's recognition award 1973-76, 77-79, 80-82, 83-85, 88-91, 91-94, 95—), Congress Neurol. Surgeons (profl. conduct com. 1989-93, Disting. Svc. award 1989), Neurol. Soc. Am., Am. Assn. Neurologic Surgeons (nominating com. 1994-96), Brain Surgery Soc., Ga. Med. Soc., Med. Assn. Ga. (editl. bd. 1987-93), pres. 1995, Ga. Neurosurg. Soc. (exec. com. 1981-88, pres. 1988-89, Semmes lectr. 1997), So. Neurosurg. Soc. (exec. com. 1982-91, pres. 1988-89), Am. Heart Assn. (fellow stroke coun.). Avocations: golf, fly fishing, hunting. Office: Neurol Inst Savannah 4 E Jackson Blvd Savannah GA 31405-5810

WIRTH, PETER, lawyer; b. Halgehausen, Germany, July 17, 1950; came to U.S., 1956; BA, U. Wis., 1972; JD, Harvard U., 1975. Bar: Mass. 1975. Assoc. Palmer & Dodge, Boston, 1975-81, ptnr., 1982-96, of counsel, 1996—; exec. v.p., chief legal officer Genzyme Corp., 1996—; lectr. grad. tax program Boston U., 1982-85. Mem. ABA, Mass. Bar Assn., Phi Beta Kappa. Office: Genzyme Corporation One Kendall Square Cambridge MA 02139

WIRTH, TIMOTHY ENDICOTT, federal official, former senator; b. Santa Fe, Sept. 22, 1939; s. Cecil and Virginia Maude (Davis) W.; m. Wren Winslow, Nov. 26, 1965; children: Christopher, Kelsey. B.A., Harvard U., 1961, M.Ed., 1964; Ph.D., Stanford U., 1973; hon. degree, U. Colo., Denver U., Colo. Coll., Washington Coll., Clark U. White House fellow, spl. asst. to sec. HEW, Washington, 1967; asst. to chmn. Nat. Urban Coalition, Washington, 1968; dep. asst. sec. for edn. HEW, Washington, 1969; v.p. Great Western United Corp., Denver, 1970; mgr. Rocky Mountain office Arthur D. Little, Inc. (cons. firm), Denver, 1971-73; mem. 94th-99th Congresses from 2d Colo. Dist., 1975-87, mem. energy and commerce com., sci. and tech. com., budget com., chmn. subcom. telecommunications, fin. and consumer protection; U.S. senator from Colo., 1987-93, mem. armed services com., energy and natural resources com., budget com., banking com., housing and urban affairs com.; counselor U.S. Dept. State, Washington, 1993-94, Under Sec. of State for global affairs, 1994—. Mem. bd. overseers Harvard U.; chair vis. com. Harvard Grad. Sch. Edn. Recipient Disting. Service award HEW, 1969; Ford Found. fellow, 1964-66. Mem. White House Fellows Assn. (pres. 1968-69), Denver Council Fgn. Relations (exec. com. 1974-75). Office: Dept of State Under Sec State Global Affr 2201 C St NW Washington DC 20520-0001

WIRTHLIN, JOSEPH B., church official; b. Salt Lake City, June 11, 1917; s. Joseph L. and Madeline (Bitner) W.; m. Elisa Young Rogers, May 26, 1941; 8 children. Degree in Bus. Adminstrn., U. Utah. Ordained apostle LDS Ch., 1986. Served a mission to Germany, Austria and Switzerland LDS Ch., 1930s, served in stake and ward aux. positions, counselor, bishop to mem. stake presidency, until 1971, 1st counselor Sunday Sch. Gen. Presidency, 1971-75, asst. to coun. of 12 apostles, 1975-76, gen. authority area supr. Europe area, 1975-78, mem. 1st Quorum of Seventy, 1976-86, exec. adminstr. to S.E. area U.S. and Caribbean Islands, 1978-82, mng. dir. Melchizedek Priesthood Com., Relief Soc. and Mil. Rels. Com., 1978-84; exec. adminstr. LDS Ch., Brazil, 1982-84; pres. Europe area of ch. LDS Ch., 1984-86, mem. presidency of 1st Quorum of Seventy, exec. dir. curriculum dept., editor ch. mags., 1986, apostle, 1986—, mem. missionary exec. coun., mem. gen. welfare svcs. com., ch. bd. edn. and bd. trustees, 1986—. Office: LDS Ch Joseph Smith Meml Bldg 47 E North Temple Salt Lake City UT 84150-1001*

WIRTHLIN, MILTON ROBERT, JR., periodontist; b. Little Rock, July 13, 1932; s. Milton Robert and Margaret Frances (Clark) W.; m. Joan Krieger, Aug. 1, 1954; children: Michael, Steven, Laurie, David, Aina. DDS, U. Calif., San Francisco, 1956, MS, 1968. Commd. ensign USN, 1955, advanced through grades to capt., 1976, retired, 1985; assoc. prof. U. Pacific, San Francisco, 1985-86; assoc. clin. prof. U. Calif., San Francisco, 1986-96, clin. prof., 1996—, dir. postgrad. periodontology, 1996—. Contbr. articles to profl. jours. Asst. scoutmaster Boy Scouts Am., San Bruno, Calif., 1968, com. chmn. Explorer Post, San Francisco, 1981-83; bd. dirs. ARC, Chgo., 1976-81, chiir social svc. com., San Francisco, 1981-83. Decorated Meritorious Svc. medal with 2 gold stars; recipient Gabbs prize U. Calif., 1956. Fellow Internat. Coll. Dentists; mem. Am. Dental Assn., Am. Acad. Perdioontology, Western Soc. Periodontology, Med-Dental Study Guild San Francisco (pres. 1993), Internat. Assn. Dental Rsch., Omicron Kappa Upsilon. Avocations: HO scale model railroading, fly tying, trout fishing, genealogy. Office: U Calif Med Ctr Sch Dentistry San Francisco CA 94143-0762

WIRTHS, THEODORE WILLIAM, public policy consultant; b. Ansonia, Conn., June 23, 1924; s. Theodore Eugene and Elizabeth (McLean) W.; m. Claudine Turner Gibson, Dec. 28, 1945; children: William M., David G. B.A., Yale, 1947; M.A., U. Ky., 1949; postgrad., U. N.C., 1948-51. Teaching fellow U. N.C., 1949-50, field dir. urban studies, 1951-53; with AEC, 1953-66; chief reports and emergency planning Savannah River Ops., Aiken, S.C., 1960-62; real estate officer Washington, 1962-64; planning officer, 1964-65, Congl. fellow, 1965-66; congl. liaison officer NSF, Washington, 1966-70, dep. for govt. liaison, 1970-73, dir. Office of Govt. and Pub. Programs, 1973-76, dir. Office Small Bus. R&D, 1976-83; cons. in sci. and pub. policy, 1983—. Author: (with Chapin, Gould and Denton) In the Shadow of a Defense Plant, 1954. Chmn. Aiken Zoning Bd. Adjustment, 1956-62; vol. Hospice of Frederick County, 1986— (Hospice Vol. of Yr. 1994, 95, Hall of Fame, 1996). With AUS, 1943-45, ETO. Recipient Meritorious Service award NSF, 1970, Disting. Service award NSF, 1983. Mem. AAAS. Episcopalian. Home: 6608 Jefferson Blvd PO Box 335 Braddock Heights MD 21714

WIRTSCHAFTER, JONATHAN DINE, neuro-ophthalmology educator, scientist; b. Cleve., Apr. 4, 1935; s. Zolton Tilson and Reitza (Dine) W.; m. Carol Lavenstein, Sept. 13, 1959; children: Jacob Daniel, Benjamin Zolton, Joshua Joel, Sara Louise, David Dine, Brooke Ann. Student, UCLA, 1953; BA, Reed Coll., 1956; MD, Harvard U., 1960; MS in Physiology, Linfield Coll., 1963. Diplomate Am. Bd. Ophthalmology (assoc. examiner 1975—), Am. Bd. Neurology. Intern Phila. Gen. Hosp., 1960-61; resident in neurology Good Samaritan Hosp., Portland, Oreg., 1961-63; resident in ophthalmology Johns Hopkins Hosp., Balt., 1963-66; fellow in neurology Columbia-Presbyn. Hosp., N.Y.C., 1966-67; asst. prof. ophthalmology, neurology and neurosurgery U. Ky., Lexington, 1967-70, assoc. prof., 1970-74, prof., chmn. dept., 1974-77, dir. div. ophthalmology, 1967-74; prof. ophthalmology, neurology, neurosurgery U. Minn. Med. Sch., Mpls., 1977—, Frank E. Burch endowed chair in ophthalmology, 1990—; vis. prof. Hadassah-Hebrew U. Med. Ctr., Jerusalem, 1973-74; Earl G. Padfield, Jr., M.D. Meml. lectr. U. Kans., 1986; vis. prof., lectr. numerous other univs.; cons. VA Hosps., Lexington, 1967-77, Mpls., 1977—; spl. cons. Nat. Eye Inst., 1981. Co-author: Ophthalmic Anatomy: A Manual with Some Clinical Applications, 1970, rev. edit., 1981, A Decision-Oriented Manual of Retinoscopy, 1976, Computed Tomography: An Atlas for Ophthalmologists, 1982, Magnetic Resonance Imaging and Computed Tomography: Clinical Neuro-orbital Anatomy, 1992; contbr. numerous articles to profl. jours.; patentee in field. Bd. mem. Temple Israel, Lexington, 1970-73, McPhail Suzuki Music Assn., 1979-81, Mpls. Talmud Torah, 1979-85; founder, bd. mem. Jewish Community Assn. of Lexington, 1969-77; alumni interviewer Reed Coll., 1968—. Grantee Nat. Eye Inst., 1968-71, 78-81, 89—, Fight for Sight, 1974, Benign Essential Belpharospasm Found., 1988. Fellow ACS, N.Am. Neuro-Ophthalmology Soc. (pres., 1996-97), Am. Acad. Ophthalmology (Sr. honor award 1994); mem. AAAS, AMA (Hon. Mention award-sci. exhibit 1970), Am. Acad. Neurology, Am. Ophthal. Soc., Assn. for Rsch. in Vision and Ophthalmology, Soc. for Neurosci., Internat. Soc. Neuro-Ophthalmology, Am. Israeli Ophthal. Soc. (bd. mem. 1984—), Boylston Med. Soc. Harvard Med. Sch., Alpha Omega Alpha. Democrat. Office: Fairview U Hosp 520 Delaware St SE Minneapolis MN 55455-0501

WIRTZ, ARTHUR MICHAEL, JR., professional hockey team executive; m. Sunny Wirtz; children: Laura, Arthur III, Jimmy. BS, U. Pa. From v.p. to exec. v.p. Chgo. Black Hawks, 1958—. Office: Consol Enterprises 680 N Lake Shore Dr Fl 19 Chicago IL 60611-3495 also: Chgo Black Hawks 1901 W Madison St Chicago IL 60612-2459*

WIRTZ, WILLEM KINDLER, garden and lighting designer, public relations consultant; b. N.Y.C., Jan. 8, 1912; s. Carel Augustus Marie and Wilhelmina Johanetta (Kindler) W. Ed., Ethical Culture Sch., N.Y.C., also Inst. Musical Art, N.Y.C. Dir. exhibits svc. Pa. Art Program, 1937-42, pub. rels. dir., 1937-42; ptnr. Campbell-Wirtz Assos., Phila., 1942-51; pres. Willem Wirtz Assos., Phila., 1952—; founder, 1961, since pres. Willem Wirtz Garden Assos., Inc., and Willem Wirtz Assocs., mfrs. of Ribbonlite; design assoc. Am. Soc. Interior Decorators; dir. Am. Jour. Nursing Co.; also chmn. Pa. bull. award com., 1964; guest lectr. Charles Morris Price Sch., Phila.; pres. Phila. chpt. Am. Pub. Relations Assn., 1954-56, nat. sec., 1955-57, Eastern v.p., 1960. Inventor (with Isaiah Roossine): Ribbonlite. Mem. Nat. Assn. Pub. Rels. Counsel (dir.), Pub. Rels. Soc. Am. (v.p. 1961, assembly del. 1961-63), Pa. Hort. Soc., Phila. Art Alliance, Zool. Soc. Palm Beaches (sec. 1971), Netherlands-Am. Soc., Poinciana Club (Palm Beach, Fla.). Office: 228 Phipps Plz Palm Beach FL 33480-4241

WIRTZ, WILLIAM WADSWORTH, real estate and sports executive; b. Chgo., Oct. 5, 1929; s. Arthur Michael and Virginia (Wadsworth) W.; m. Joan Roney, Dec. 15, 1950 (dec. May 1983); children: William R., Gail W., Karen K., Peter R., Alison M.; m. Alice Pirie Hargrave, Dec. 1, 1987. A.B., Brown U., 1950. Pres. Chgo. Blackhawk Hockey Team, Inc., 1966—, Chgo. Stadium Corp., 1966—, Consol. Enterprises, Inc., Chgo., 1966—, Forman Realty Corp., Chgo., 1965—, 333 Bldg. Corp., Chgo., 1966—, Wirtz Corp., Chgo., 1964—; chmn. bd. govs. Nat. Hockey League. Inducted into NHL Hall of Fame, 1976; recipient Lester Patrick trophy, 1978. Clubs: Saddle and Cycle (Chgo.), Racquet (Chgo.), Mid-America (Chgo.); Fin and Feather (Elgin, Ill.); Sunset Ridge Country (Northbrook, Ill.). Office: Wirtz 680 N Lake Shore Dr Fl 19 Chicago IL 60611-3495 also: Chgo Stadium 1800 W Madison St Chicago IL 60612-2620 also: Nat Hockey Leage, 1155 Metcalfe St Ste 960, Montreal, PQ Canada H3B 2W2*

WIRTZ, WILLIAM WILLARD, lawyer; b. DeKalb, Ill., Mar. 14, 1912; s. William Wilbur and Alfa Belle (White) W.; m. Mary Jane Quisenberry, Sept. 8, 1936; children—Richard, Philip. Ed., No. Ill. State Teachers Coll., DeKalb, Ill., 1928-30, U. Calif. at Berkeley, 1930-31; A.B., Beloit Coll., 1933; LL.B., Harvard, 1937. Instr. Kewanee (Ill.) High Sch., 1933-34, U. Iowa, 1937-39; asst. prof. Sch. Law, Northwestern U., 1939-42; asst. gen. counsel Bd. Econ. Warfare, 1942-43; with War Labor Bd., 1943-45, gen. counsel and pub. mem., 1945; chmn. Nat. Wage Stblzn. Bd., 1946; prof. law Northwestern U., 1946-54; engaged law practice, 1955-61; sec. of labor Dept. Labor, 1962-69; prof. law U. San Diego;. Mem. Ill. Liquor Control Commn., 1950-56. Mem. Am., D.C., Ill. bar assns., Phi Beta Kappa, Beta Theta Pi, Delta Sigma Rho. Office: 1211 Connecticut Ave NW Washington DC 20036

WIRZ, GEORGE O., bishop; b. Monroe, Wis., Jan. 17, 1929. Student, St. Francis Sem., Milw., Marquette U., Milw., Cath. U. Ordained priest Roman Cath. Ch., 1952. Appointed titular bishop of Municipa Roman Cath. Ch., Madison, Wis., 1978—; aux. bishop Roman Cath. Ch., Madison, 1978—. Office: St Patrick Church 404 E Main St Madison WI 53703-2816 also: Box 11 15 E Wilson St Madison WI 53701*

WIRZ, PASCAL FRANCOIS, trust company executive; b. Paris, Dec. 26, 1943; came to U.S., 1971; s. Boris and Armande (Martini) W.;m. Sharon T. Oller, Aug. 16, 1968; children: Matthieu, Benoit, Colette, Severin. BA in Econs., U. Paris, 1966; MBA in Bus., Hautes Etudes Commerciales, Paris, 1965; MBA in Fin., Lehigh U., 1968. Audit traine Peat Marwick & Mitchell, N.Y.C., 1968-69; tchr. auditing CESA (HEC), Jouy en Josas, France, 1969-71; security analyst European-Am. Econ. Corp., N.Y.C., 1971-82; sr. v.p. Fiduciary Trust Internat., N.Y.C., 1982—. Trustee Corlette Glorney Found. Served with French Air Force, 1969-70. Mem. India House, Paris-Am. Club. Home: 186 Christopher St Montclair NJ 07042-4206 Office: Fiduciary Trust Internat 2 World Trade Ctr New York NY 10048-0203

WISBAUM, WAYNE DAVID, lawyer; b. Niagara Falls, N.Y., May 29, 1935; s. Franklin C. and Elizabeth (Boff) W.; m. Janet Katz, July 3, 1960; children—Karen, Wendy, Deborah. B.A., Cornell U., 1956; LL.B., Harvard U., 1959. Bar: N.Y. 1960. Assoc. Kavinoky & Cook, Buffalo, 1960-66; sr. ptnr. Kavinoky & Cook, 1966—; mem. adv. com. Ticor Title Co.; bd. dirs., pres., chmn. bd. Kleinhans Music Hall Mgmt. Inc. Pres. Buffalo Coun. on World Affairs, 1968-70: mem. Young Leadership Cabinet Nat. United Jewish Appeal, 1967-73; mem. com. on leadership devel. Nat. Coun. Jewish Fedn. and Welfare Funds, 1967—; mem. Mayor's Com. on Youth Opportunity; bd. dirs. Anti-Defamation League; mem. Coun. Internat. Studies, SUNY, Buffalo; chmn. Buffalo chpt. Am. Jewish Com.; treas. Buffalo Fedn. Jewish Philanthropies; bd. govs. United Jewish Fedn., Buffalo; chmn. bd. dirs. Buffalo Philharm. Orch. Soc.; bd. dirs., mem. exec. com. Burchfield Art Ctr.; bd. dirs., pres. Jewish Family Service of Erie County. Served to capt. U.S. Army, 1964. Recipient United Jewish Fedn. Buffalo Leadership award, 1967, Community Relations award Am. Jewish Com., 1985, Abram Pugash award Jewish Family Service, 1985; named Harvard Alumnus of Yr., 1990. Mem. ABA, N.Y. State Bar Assn. (chmn. com. lawyers title guaranty funds), Erie County Bar Assn., Am. Law Inst., Harvard Law Sch. Assn. Western N.Y. (sec.), Zool. Soc. Buffalo (dir., mem. exec. com.), Harvard Club (pres. Buffalo chpt., mem. N.Y.C. chpt.), Buffalo Club, Cornell Club (N.Y.C. chpt.), Zeta Beta Tau. Home: 180 Greenaway Rd Buffalo NY 14226-4166 Office: Kavinoky & Cook 120 Delaware Ave Buffalo NY 14202-2704

WISCH, DAVID JOHN, structural engineer; b. Jefferson City, Mo., Dec. 6, 1953; s. Theodore A. and Josephine (Lauf) W.; m. Leslie Babin, Oct. 24, 1981; 1 child, Christine. BSCE, U. Mo., Rolla, 1975, MSCE, 1977. Registered profl. engr., La., Calif. Civil engr. Texaco-Ctrl. Offshore Engring., New Orleans, 1977-81, advanced civil engr., 1981-86, sr. project engr., 1986-92; specialist Texaco-Ctrl. Offshore Engring., Bellaire, Tex., 1992-96; sr. specialist Texaco-Ctrl. Offshore Engring., 1997—, fellow, 1997—; chmn. fixed systems subcom. Am. Petroleum Inst., Dallas, Washington, 1991-93, mem. adv. bd. offshore standardization com., 1991-94, chmn., 1993-94, mem. exec. com. on standardization, 1994—, chmn. offshore and subsea com., 1994—, head U.S. Delegation Internat. Orgn. Stds. Tech. Com. 1967/Subcom 7, 1993—, mem. Tech. Com. 67/Subcom. 7/AG1, 1993—, convener Tech. Com. 67/Subcom 7/WG3-Fixed Steel Structures, 1993—; mem. structure subcom. Oil Soc. Internat. Exploration and Prodn. Forum, London, 1993-93; mem. spl. com. on offshore facilities Am. Bur. Shipping, 1996—. Author numerous papers/presentations, 1984—. Mem. Am. Bur. Shipping (spl. com. on offshore structures), ASCE (program. subcom. for Offshore Tech. Conf. 1993—), Sigma Xi, Phi Kappa Phi, Tau Beta Pi, Chi Epsilon (chpt. pres. 1975-76). Office: Texaco Offshore Engring Dept 4800 Fournace Pl Bellaire TX 77401-2324

WISDOM, JOHN MINOR, federal judge; b. New Orleans, May 17, 1905; s. Mortimer Norton and Adelaide (Labatt) W.; m. Bonnie Stewart Mathews, Oct. 24, 1931; children: John Minor (dec.), Kathleen Mathews, Penelope Stewart Wisdom Tose. AB, Washington and Lee U., 1925; LLB, Tulane U., 1929, LLD (hon.), 1976; LLD (hon.), Oberlin Coll., 1963, San Diego U., 1979, Haverford Coll., 1982, Middlebury Coll., 1987, Harvard U., 1987, So. Meth. U., 1994. Bar: La. 1929. Mem. Wisdom, Stone, Pigman & Benjamin, New Orleans, 1929-57; judge U.S. Ct. Appeals (5th cir.), 1957—, now sr. judge; mem. Multi-Dist. Litigation Panel, 1968-78, chmn., 1975-78; mem. Spl. Ct. Regional Reorgn. of R.R.s, 1975-86, presiding judge, 1986—; adj. prof. law Tulane U., 1938-57; faculty IJA Appellate Judges Seminar, 1961-70; vis. coms. law schs. U. Chgo., Harvard U., U. Miami, U. San Diego. Mem. Pres.'s Com. on Govt. Contracts, 1953-57; past pres. New Orleans Council Social Agys.; Republican nat. committeeman for La., 1952-57; trustee Washington and Lee U., 1953—. Served from capt. to lt. col. USAAF, 1942-46. Decorated Legion of Merit, Army Commendation medal; recipient 1st Disting. Jurist award La. Bar Found., 1986, St. Thomas More Medallion, Loyola U. of L.A., 1987, Devitt Disting. Svc. to Justice award, 1989, Tulane Disting. Alumnus award, 1989, Alfred E. Clay award Children's Bur., 1992, Strength in Aging award (with Mrs. Wisdom) LSU Geriatric Ctr., 1992, LPB Living Legends award, 1993, Trumpet award Turner Broadcasting, 1994. Mem. ABA (chmn. appellate judges conf. 1966-67, 1st recipient John Minor Wisdom pub. svc. and profl. award sect. litigation 1990, Am. Inns of Ct. Lewis F. Powell Jr. award 1991, Fellows award young lawyers div. 1991, Pres.'s medal of Freedom 1993, medal 1996), Am. Acad. Arts and Scis., La. Bar Assn., New Orleans Bar Assn., La. Bar Found., Am. Law Inst. (coun. mem. 1961), La. Law Inst., Am. Judicature Soc., Order of Coif, Delta Kappa Epsilon, Phi Alpha Delta (Tom C. Clark Equal Justice under Law award 1982), Omicron Delta Kappa. Episcopalian. Clubs: Boston (New Orleans), Louisiana (New Orleans); Metropolitan (Washington). Office: John Minor Wisdom 200 John Minor Wisdom Bldg 600 Camp St New Orleans LA 70130-3425

WISE, CHARLES CONRAD, JR., educator, past government official, author; b. Washington, Apr. 1, 1913; s. Charles Conrad and Lorena May (Sweeney) W.; m. Ruth Miles Baxter, Nov. 19, 1938; children: Gregory Baxter, Charles Conrad III, Jenifer; m. Norma Lee Clasbey, Apr. 28, 1984. A.B., George Washington U., 1938, J.D., 1936; M. Fiscal Adminstrn., Columbus U., 1943. Bar: D.C. 1935. Clk. U.S. Dept. Agr., 1933-36; adminstrv. asst. Bur. Accounts, Treasury Dept., 1936-39; atty. R.R. Retirement Bd., 1939-41; claims atty. Q.M.C., C.E., U.S. War Dept., 1941-43; asst. counsel Office Gen. Counsel, U.S. Navy Dept., 1946-47; gen. counsel War Contracts Price Adjustment Bd., 1948-51, mem., 1950-51; legislative counsel R.F.C., 1951-53; exec. sec. Subversive Activities Control Bd., 1953-61; dept. counsel indsl. plant security Dept. Def., 1962-71, chief dept. counsel, 1971-73; instr. thanatology, religion and philosophy Blue Ridge C.C., 1973-89; assoc. English dept. George Washington U., 1960, Am. U., 1961. Author: Windows on the Passion, 1967, Windows on the Master, 1968, Ruth and Naomi, 1971, Mind Is It: Meditation, Prayer, Healing and the Psychic, 1978, Picture Windows on the Christ, 1979, The Magian Gospel, 1979, Thus Saith the Lord: The Autobiography of God, 1984, The Holy Families, 1990; various articles for mags. Served as lt. USNR, 1944-46. Mem. Fed. Bar Assn., Delta Theta Phi, Phi Beta Kappa. Home: PO Box 117 Penn Laird VA 22846-0117

WISE, DAVID, author, journalist; b. N.Y.C., May 10, 1930; s. Raymond L. and Karena (Post) W.; m. Joan Sylvester, Dec. 16, 1962; children: Christopher James, Jonathan William. BA, Columbia Coll., 1951. Reporter N.Y. Herald Tribune, 1951-66, N.Y. city hall bur. chief, 1953-57; bur. chief N.Y. Herald Tribune, Albany, N.Y., 1956-57; mem. Washington bur. N.Y. Herald Tribune, 1958-66, chief Washington bur., 1963-66; fellow Woodrow Wilson Internat. Center for Scholars, 1970-71; lectr. in polit. sci. U. Calif. at Santa Barbara, 1977-79. Author: The Politics of Lying: Government Deception, Secrecy, and Power, 1973, The American Police State: The Government Against the People, 1976, Spectrum, 1981, The Children's Game, 1983, The Samarkand Dimension, 1987, The Spy Who Got Away, 1988, Molehunt: The Secret Search for Traitors that Shattered the CIA, 1992, Nightmover: How Aldrich Ames Sold the CIA to the KGB for $4.6 Million, 1995; co-author: (with Thomas B. Ross) The U-2 Affair, 1962, The Invisible Government, 1964, The Espionage Establishment, 1967 (with Milton C. Cummings, Jr.), Democracy Under Pressure: An Introduction to the American Political System, 1971, 8th edit., 1997; contbg. author: The Kennedy Circle, 1961, None of Your Business, 1974, The CIA File, 1976; contbr. articles to nat. mags. Recipient Page One award Newspaper Guild N.Y., 1969, George Polk Meml. award, 1974. Mem. Washington Ind. Writers, Am. Polit. Sci. Assn. Clubs: Fed. City (Washington), Gridiron (Washington). Office: c/o Sterling Lord Literistic Inc 65 Bleecker St New York NY 10012-2420

WISE, EDMUND JOSEPH, physician assistant, industrial hygienist; b. Pitts., June 18, 1947; s. Edmund Joseph and Marian Elizabeth (Burdelski) W. BA in Biology, Washington and Jefferson Coll., 1969; B of Health Scis., Duke U., 1974; MPH, U. Tenn., 1990. Clin. care tech. II Duke U. Med. Ctr., Durham, N.C., 1971-72; physician asst. Oak Ridge (Tenn.) Nat. Lab., 1974—; mem. toxic substance control act task team Lockheed Martin Energy Sys., Oak Ridge, 1995—; mem. hazardous waste com. Oak Ridge Nat. Lab., 1993—, ergonomics com., 1994—, hearing conservation com., 1984—. Author: History Medical Activities 1/12 Infantry, 1970; co-author: AAPA Guidelines Continuing Medical Education, 1977, ORNL Hazwoper Program Manual, 1993; co-author: (chpt.) Tennessee Academy Constitution and Bylaws, 1976. Mem. malpractice review bd. Tenn. Dept. Pub. Health, Nashville, 1981—. Capt. U.S. Army, 1969-75, Vietnam. Decorated Bronze Star, Combat Med. badge; recipient Gold cert. of Appreciation, Am. Heart Assn., 1983. Fellow Am. Acad. Physician Assts. (house del. 1979, 86, profl. and continuing med. edn. com. 1975-80), Tenn. Acad. Physician Assts. (co-founder, v.p. 1975, pres. 1977); mem. Tenn. Heart Assn. (cert. BCLS, affiliate faculty 1978—), East Tenn. Region Heart Assn. (CPR-Emergency Cardiac Care com. 1980—), Duke U. Alumni Assn., Nat. 4th Infantry Divsn. Assn., Washington and Jefferson Alumni Assn. Republican. Roman Catholic. Avocations: model railroading, stamp collecting, gardening, tennis, exercise. Home: 1238 Venido Dr Knoxville TN 37932-2598 Office: Oak Ridge Nat Lab Health Divsn PO Box 2008 MS6220 Oak Ridge TN 37831-6220

WISE, GEORGE EDWARD, lawyer; b. Chgo., Feb. 26, 1924; s. George E. and Helen L. (Gray) W.; m. Patricia E. Finn, Aug. 3, 1945; children: Erich, Peter, Abbe, Raoul, John. J.D., U. Chgo. Bar: Calif. 1949, U.S. Dist. Ct. (no. dist.) Calif. 1948, U.S. Ct. Appeals (9th cir.) 1948, U.S. Dist. Ct. (cen. dist.) 1950, U.S. Supreme CT. 1955. Law clk. Calif. Supreme Ct., 1948-49; sr. ptnr. Wise, Wiezorek, Timmons & Wise, Long Beach, 1949—. With USNR, 1943-45. Fellow Am. Coll. Trial Lawyers; mem. ABA, Los Angeles County Bar Assn., Long Beach Bar Assn. (pres. 1970, Atty. of Yr. 1990), Calif. State Bar. Home: 5401 E El Cedral St Long Beach CA 90815-4112 Office: Wise Wiezorek Timmons & Wise 3700 Santa Fe Ave Ste 300 Long Beach CA 90810-2171

WISE, JOHN AUGUSTUS, lawyer; b. Detroit, Mar. 30, 1938; s. John Augustus and Mary Blanche (Parent) W.; m. Helga M. Bessin, Nov. 27, 1965; children: Monique Elizabeth, John Eric. Student, U. Vienna, 1957-58; AB cum laude, Coll. Holy Cross, 1959; JD, U. Mich., 1962; postgrad., U. Munich, 1962-63. Bar: Mich. 1963, D.C. 1966. Assoc. Dykema, Gossett, Detroit, 1962-64; asst. to pres. Internat. Econ. Policy Assn., Washington, 1964-66; assoc. Parsons, Tennent, Hammond, Hardig & Ziegelman, Detroit, 1967-70; pres. Wise & Marsac P.C., 1970—; dir. Peltzer & Ehlers Am. Corp., 1975-80, Colombian Am. Friends Inc., 1974-89. Mem. Detroit Com. on Fgn. Rels.; bd. dirs. Hyde Park Coop., 1974-77; trustee Friends Sch., Detroit, 1977-81, Brighton Health Svcs. Corp., 1991-94; chmn. bd. trustees Brighton Hosp., 1995—. Ford Found. grantee U. Munich, 1962-63. Mem. ABA, Mich. Bar Assn., Detroit Bar Assn., Internat. Bar Assn., Detroit Athletic Club, Detroit Club, Detroit Econ. Club. Roman Catholic. Home: 1221 Yorkshire Rd Grosse Pointe MI 48230-1105 Office: BUHL Bldg Buhl Building Fl 11 Detroit MI 48226-3604

WISE, JOHN JAMES, oil company executive; b. Cambridge, Mass., Feb. 28, 1932; s. Daniel and Alice E. (Donlon) W.; m. Rosemary S. Bishop, Mar. 4, 1967; children: Susannah, Jean. BS, Tufts U., 1953; PhD, MIT, 1966. Rsch. scientist Mobil R & D Corp., Paulsboro, N.J., 1953-76, mgr. process R & D, 1976-77, sect. mgr., 1976-77; v.p. planning Mobil R & D Corp., N.Y.C., 1977-81; mgr. exploration and producing rsch. Mobil R & D Corp., Dallas, 1981-82; v.p. planning Mobil R & D Corp., N.Y.C., 1982-84; mgr. process and products R & D Mobil R & D Corp., Paulsboro, N.J., 1984-87, v.p. rsch., 1987—. Patentee in field (25); contbr. articles to profl. jours. Mem. NAE, Am. Inst. Chem. Engrs., Indsl. Rsch. Inst. (Achievement award 1995), World Petroleum Congress, Sigma Xi. Office: Mobil R & D Corp PO Box 0480 Paulsboro NJ 08066-0480

WISE, KELLY, private school educator, photographer, critic; b. New Castle, Ind., Dec. 1, 1932; s. John Kenneth W. and Geraldine (Kelly) Edwards Wise; m. Sybil Anahid Zulalian, Aug. 15, 1959; children: Jocelyn Anne, Adam Kelly, Lydia Louise. B.S., Purdue U., 1955; M.A., Columbia U., 1959. Instr. English Mt. Hermon Sch., Gill, Mass., 1960-66; instr. English Phillips Acad., Andover, Mass., 1966—, chmn. dept., 1978-82, acting dean faculty, 1982-83, dean faculty, 1985-90; founder, dir. Inst. for Recruitment of Tchrs., Andover, Mass., 1989—; photography critic The Boston Globe, 1982-93; art commentator Nat. Pub. Radio, 1987-89; photography and English cons. Nat. Humanities Faculty, Concord, Mass., 1970-83; mem. Pub. Art Adv. Bd. of Mass. Coun.; cons. editor Addison House Pubs., Danbury, N.J., 1974-79. Author: (with Kalkstein and Regan) English Competence Handbook, 1972; editor: The Photographers' Choice, 1975, Lotte Jacobi, 1978, Portrait: Theory, 1981, Photo Facts and Opinions, 1981; author, photographer: Still Points, 1977, A Church, A People, 1979; editor photographer: City Limits, 1987; assoc. editor: Views, Jour. Photography, 1980-81; works included in anthologies, one-man shows, Portland Museum Art, Maine, 1974, Silver Image Gallery, Columbus, Ohio, 1975, Canon Photo Gallery, Amsterdam, Holland, 1977, Focus Gallery, San Francisco, 1977, Art Mus., U. Mass., Amherst, 1978, Neikrug Gallery, N.Y.C., 1979, Sheldon Gallery, U. Nebr., Lincoln, 1980, Yuen Lui Gallery, Seattle, 1980, Rose Art Mus., Brandeis U., Waltham, Mass., 1981, Blixt Gallery, Ann Arbor, Mich., 1981, Snite Art Gallery, U. Notre Dame, 1981, Jeb Gallery, Providence, 1981, Currier Gallery Art, Manchester, N.H., 1985, Addison Gallery Am. Art, Andover, Mass., 1985, Art Ctr., DePauw U., 1986, Art Gallery, Conn. Coll., 1986, Yuen Lui Gallery, Seattle, 1986, Kresge Art Mus., Mich. State U., 1987, Brockton Art Mus., 1987; group shows include Inst. Contemporary Art, Boston, 1972, Mus. Fine Arts, Boston, 1974, Fogg Art Mus., Cambridge, 1976, Sidney Janis Gallery, N.Y.C., 1977, The Photographer's Gallery, London, 1979, II Diaframma, Milan, Italy, 1979, Iisalmen Kamera, Helsinki, Finland, 1984, Archive Gallery, N.Y., 1987, Mass. Coll. Art, 1988, Martin Schweig Gallery, St. Louis, 1988, Satellite Gallery, Cultural Affairs Dept., Los Angeles; works included in book Flesh and Blood: Photographers' Images of Their Own Families. Served with USN, 1955-57, PTO. Recipient Disting. Alumnus award Purdue U., 1996. Office: Phillips Academy Andover MA 01810-4161

WISE, MARVIN JAY, lawyer; b. San Antonio, Apr. 6, 1926; s. Philip and Anna Edith (Corman) W.; m. Gloria Marian Johnston, Sept. 19, 1954; children: Philip Johnston, Jennifer Lea, Amelia Ann. B.A. magna cum laude, U. Tex., 1945; LL.B. cum laude, Harvard U., 1949; diploma comparative legal studies, U. Cambridge, Eng., 1950. Bar: Tex. 1949. Assoc. Thompson & Knight, Dallas, 1950-57; ptnr. Wise and Stuhl, Dallas, 1957-88; of counsel Novakov, Davidson & Flynn, Dallas, 1988—. Bd. dirs. Dallas Assn. Mental Health, Isthmus Inst., Dallas Home Jewish Aged, Dallas Civic Ballet Soc., Walden Prep. Sch. Served with AUS, 1945-46. Fulbright scholar, 1949-50. Fellow Tex. Bar Found.; mem. ABA, Tex. Bar Assn., Dallas Bar Assn. (chmn. probate, trusts and estates sect. 1981-82), Am. Coll. Trust and Estate Counsel, UN Assn. (dir. Dallas chpt.), Phi Beta Kappa, Alpha Phi Omega, Phi Eta Sigma, Pi Sigma Alpha. Jewish. Club: Crescent. Home: 3444 University Blvd Dallas TX 75205-1834 Office: 2000 St Paul Pl 750 N Saint Paul St Dallas TX 75201-7105

WISE, PATRICIA, lyric coloratura; b. Wichita, Kans.; d. Melvin R. and Genevieve F. (Dotson) W.; 1 child, Jennifer. B. Music Edn., U. Kans., Lawrence, 1966. Prof. voice Ind. U. Sch. Music, Bloomington, 1995—. Debut as Susanna in Marriage of Figaro, Kansas City, 1966; prin. roles include Lucia, Gilda, Micaela, Juliette, Zerbinetta, Pamina, Musetta, Lulu, Violetta, Nedda, numerous others; appeared with leading Am. opera cos. including, Chgo., Santa Fe, N.Y.C., San Francisco, Houston, San Diego, Miami, Balt., Phila., Pitts.; European appearances, 1971-76, London Royal Opera, Glyndebourne Festival, Vienna Volksoper, Geneva Opera; guest artist with Vienna, Hamburg, Munich, Cologne, Frankfurt, and Berlin State Operas; guest appearances in Madrid, Barcelona, Rome, La Scala Milan, Nice, Paris Chatelet, Zurich, Dresden, Salzburg Festival, Theatro Colon, Buenos Aires; appeared with orchs. including, Chgo. Symphony Orch., Los Angeles Symphony Orch., N.Y. Handel Soc., Israel Philharm. Orch., Vienna Philharm. Orch., N.Y. Philharm., Cleve. Orch., Berlin Symphonic Orch., BBC Orch., Nat. Orch. France; Angel Recordings; internat. TV, film appearances. Recipient Morton Baum award N.Y.C. Ctr., 1971, Dealey Meml. award Dallas Symphony, 1966, Naftzger young Artist award Wichita Symphony, 1966, Midland Young Artist award Midland (Tex.) Symphony Orch., 1966; M.B. Rockefeller Fund grantee, 1967-70; Sullivan Found. grantee, 1967-68; named Kammersänger Vienna Staatsoper, 1989.

WISE, PAUL SCHUYLER, insurance company executive; b. Pratt, Kans., July 16, 1920; s. George Warren and Bess Grace (Cossairt) W.; m. Frances H. Christie, Oct. 26, 1975; children by previous marriage: Schuyler, David, Betsy. Student, U. Kans., 1938-40; BA, Washburn U., 1942, JD, 1947; student, U. Mich., 1945-46. Bar: Kans. Atty. Kans. Ins. Dept., 1947, asst. commr. ins., 1948-51, commr. workmen's compensation, 1951-52; atty.-ins. legislation Alliance of Am. Insurers, Chgo., 1952-56, mgr. legis. bur., 1956-61, asst. mgr., 1961-62, gen. mgr., 1962-68, pres., chief exec. officer, 1968-84, chmn. bd., 1984-85; dir. Ins. Inst. for Hwy. Safety, Coll. of Ins.; bd. overseers Inst. for Civil Justice; lectr. in field; bd. dirs. United Funds, Kansas City, Mo., Potash Corp. of Sask., Can. Contbr. articles to profl. jours. Co-founder, bd. dirs. Hospice of North Shore; bd. dirs. Sr. Net. Lt. USN. Recipient Man of Yr. award Fedn. Ins. Counsel, 1982; inducted into Hall of Fame, Kans. Ins. Ednl. Found., 1983. Home: 8648 Silver Saddle Dr PO Box 5248 Carefree AZ 85377-5248

WISE, RITA J., writer, poet; b. Indpls., June 8, 1954; d. Arlessie T. Byrd; children: Chajuana Marita, Russell Aaron. BGS, Purdue U., Indpls., 1995. Cert. beauty/image cons. Office mgr. State Atty. Gen.'s Office, Indpls., 1973-81; adminstrv. sec. student affairs Ind. U., Indpls., 1980-90; part-time bus. instr. Ind. U.-Purdue U., Indpls., 1993-95; loaned assoc. United Way Ctrl. Ind., Indpls., 1995; adminstrv. sec. materials engrng. dept. Kelly Svcs./Allison Gas Turbine, 1996—. Author: (poetry) Relief, 1995, Windows of the World, 1991, What Shall I Tell My Children, 1994, A Mothers' Pay Message, 1989. Telefundraiser local charities, 1996-97. Recipient scholarship and Diamond Homer award Soc. Famous Poets, Anaheim, Calif., 1996. Mem. Ind. U.-Purdue U. Sch. of Bus. Alumni. Avocations: writing poetry, aerobics, dancing. Home: 3319 Manor Ct Indianapolis IN 46218-2310 Office: Wise Pub Co PO Box 18066 Indianapolis IN 46204

WISE, ROBERT, film producer, director; b. Winchester, Ind., Sept. 10, 1914. Student, Franklin Coll., D.F.A. (hon.), 1968. Staff cutting dept. R.K.O., 1933, became sound cutter, asst. editor, film editor, 1939-43, dir., 1943-49; with 20th Century-Fox, 1949-52, M.G.M., 1954-57; free-lance, 1958—, ptnr. ind. film co., 1970—; Past mem. Nat. Council of Arts. Ind. producer/dir. various studios; motion pictures include The Curse of the Cat People, 1944, Mademoiselle Fifi, 1944, The Body Snatcher, 1945, A Game of Death, 1945, Criminal Court, 1946, Born to Kill, 1947, Mystery in Mexico, 1948, Blood on the Moon, 1948, The Set-Up, 1949, Two Flags West, 1950, Three Secrets, 1950, The House on Telegraph Hill, 1951, The Day the Earth Stood Still, 1951, The Captive City, 1952, Something For the Birds, 1952, The Desert Rats, 1953, Destination Gobi, 1953, So Big, 1953, Executive Suite, 1954, Helen of Troy, 1955, Tribute to a Bad Man, 1956, Somebody Up There Likes Me, 1957, This Could Be the Night, 1957, Until They Sail, 1957, Run Silent, Run Deep, 1958, I Want to Live, 1958, Odds Against Tomorrow, 1959, West Side Story (Acad. awards best dir. with Jerome Robbins, and best picture), 1961, Two For the Seasaw, 1962, The Haunting, 1963, The Sound of Music, 1965 (Acad. award best dir., best picture), The Sand Pebbles, 1966, Star!, 1968, The Andromeda Strain, 1971, Two People, 1973, The Hindenburg, 1975, Audrey Rose, 1977, Star Trek-The Motion Picture, 1979, Rooftops, 1989. Recipient Nat. Medal of Arts award, 1992. Mem. Dirs. Guild (pres. 1971-74), Acad. Motion Picture Arts and Scis. (pres. 1985-87). Office: Robert Wise Prodns 315 S Beverly Dr Ste 214 Beverly Hills CA 90212-4310

WISE, ROBERT EDWARD, radiologist; b. Pitts., May 21, 1918; s. Joseph Frank and Victoria Rose (Conley) W.; m. Yvonne Burkhard, Mar. 27, 1943; children: Lynne Dailey, Robert Edward, John Burkhard. B.S., U. Pitts., 1941; M.D., U. Md., 1943. Intern U.S. Naval Hosp., Phila., 1943-44; fellow in radiology Cleve. Clin. Found., 1947-49; radiologist Cleve. Clinic, 1949-52; practice medicine specializing in radiology Pitts., 1952-53; radiologist Lahey Clinic Found., Boston, 1953—, CEO, chmn. bd. govs., 1975-91; chmn. bd. Lahey Clinic Found., 1986—; instr. radiology U. Pitts., 1952-53; clin. prof. radiology Sch. Medicine, Boston U.; dir. Bay State Skills Corp., Boston; adj. staff rsch. and edn. Cleveland Clinic, Ft. Lauderdale, Fla., 1996—. Author: Intravenous Cholangiography, 1962, Accessory Digestive Organs, 1973, Radiology, Gallbladder and Bile Ducts. Trustee Eleanor Naylor Dana Charitable Trust, Lahey Clinic Hosp., Boston Ballet Co., Lahey Clinic Found.; bd. dirs. Boston Pub. Libr. Found.; corporator New Eng. Deaconess Hosp., Boston Opera Assn., Lahey-Hitchcock Clinic; chmn. Robert E. Wise M.D. Rsch. and Edn. Inst. of Lahey Clinic Found.; bd. govs. Hist. Soc., Palm Beach County, 1997—. Mem. Am. Coll. Radiology (pres. 1975), Radiol. Soc. N.Am. (pres. 1974), New Eng. Roentgen Ray Soc. (pres. 1963), AMA, Mass. Med. Soc. Mass. Radiol. Soc. (pres. 1973), Eastern Radiol. Soc. (pres. 1965), N. Suburban C. of C. (dir.). Roman Catholic. Clubs: Algonquin (Boston) (dir); Brae Burn Country (West Newton, Mass.); Webhannet Golf (Kennebunk Beach, Maine), Kennebunk River (Kennebunkport), Atlantis Golf (Atlantis, Fla.), La Coquille (Manalapan, Fla.), Beach (Palm Beach). Home: 1545 Lands End Rd Manalapan FL 33462 Office: Lahey Clinic Found 31 Mall Rd Burlington MA 01803-4138

WISE, ROBERT ELLSWORTH, JR. (BOB ELLSWORTH), congressman; b. Washington, D.C., Jan. 6, 1948; m. Sandra Casber, 1984. BA, Duke U., 1970; JD, Tulane U., 1975. Bar: W.Va., 1975. Sole practice Charleston, W.Va., 1975-80; atty., legis. council for judiciary com. W.Va. Ho. of Dels., 1977-78; mem. W.Va. Senate, 1980-82, 97th-105th Congresses from 2nd W.Va. dist., Washington, 1982—; whip at large, 1986—, mem. govt. reform and oversight com., transp. and infrastructure com. Dir. West Virginians for Fair and Equitable Assessment of Taxes, Inc. Mem. ABA, W.Va. State Bar Assn. Democrat. Avocations: physical fitness, bluegrass music. Office: US Ho of Reps 2367 Rayburn Bldg Washington DC 20515-4802*

WISE, ROBERT LESTER, utilities executive; b. Curwensville, Pa., Oct. 4, 1943; s. Robert Lester Wise and Kathryn Elizabeth (Riddle) Husak; m. Sandra Lee Leonard, June 12, 1965; 1 child: Robert L. III. BSME, Lafayette Coll., 1965. Registered profl. engr., Pa. Cadet engr., jr. engr. Pa. Electric Co., Johnstown, 1965-68, stat. supr. prodn., sta. supt. ops., 1968-71, sta. supt., mgr. generating stas., 1971-79, asst. v.p. ops., v.p. ops., 1979-82, v.p. generation engrng. and support, 1982-83, v.p. ops., 1984-86, pres., bd. dirs., 1986-94; pres. fossil generation GPU Svc. Corp., Johnstown, Pa., 1994-96; pres. GPU Generation Inc., Johnstown, 1996—, also bd. dirs.; bd. dirs. GPU Svc. Inc., GPU Nuclear Inc., GPU Internat., Inc., Parsippany, N.J., U.S. Nat. Bank, USBANCORP, Inc., USBANCORP Trust Co., Greater Johnstown/Cambria county C. of C., Utilities Mutual Ins. Co., Johnstown Area Regional Industries; mem. Pa. Bus. Roundtable, 1990; mem. Edison Electric Inst. Policy com. on environ. affairs, 1995, Assn. of Edison Illuminating Cos. Power Generation Com., St. Francis Coll. Bus. Dept. adv. coun. Bd. dirs. Johnstown Symphony Orch., 1988; mem. adv. coun. of exec. bd. Penn's Woods coun. Boy Scouts Am., 1980—; mem. exec. com. Greater Johnstown Com., 1987, Pa. Electric Assn., Harrisburg, 1987, Cambria-Somerset Labor Mgmt. Com., 1987; mem. exec. adv. com. Johnstown Bus. Coun. on Health Care, 1987; trustee United Way Greater Johnstown, 1991, So. Alleghenies Mus. Art. Mem. Sunnehanna Country Club. Republican. Avocations: sailing, racquet sports, golf. Office: GPU Generation Inc 1001 Broad St Johnstown PA 15906-2437

WISE, SANDRA CASBER, lawyer. BA, Macalester Coll., 1969; JD, U. Minn., 1972. Bar: Minn. 1972, D.C., 1986, W.Va., 1987. Legis asst. to Rep. Martha Keys, Washington, 1977-78; asst. to asst. to the pres. for women's issues Sara Weddington, The White Ho., Washington, 1979; staff sub-com. on pub. assistance Ho. Com. on Ways and Means, Washington, 1980, staff sub-com. on health, 1981-85; atty. White, Fine and Verville, 1986; staff dir. sub-com. on social security Ho. Com. on Ways and Means, Washington, 1987-94, minority counsel subcom. on social security, 1995—. Office: House Com on Ways & Means 1106 Longworth Bldg Ofc Bldg Washington DC 20515-0004

WISE, WARREN ROBERTS, lawyer; b. Beaver City, Nebr., Oct. 8, 1929; s. Harold Edward and Doris Lorene (Roberts) W.; m. Marcia Hench, Oct. 14, 1961; children: Debra, David, Susan. BS, U. Nebr., 1950, LLB, 1953; LLM, Georgetown U., 1960. Atty. U.S. Dept. Justice Lands Div., Washington, 1955-61, U.S. Dept. Justice Tax Div., Washington, 1961-63; assoc. counsel Mass. Mut. Life Ins. Co., Springfield, 1963-67, asst. gen. counsel, 1967-72, 2d v.p., assoc. gen. counsel, 1972-74, v.p., assoc. gen. counsel, 1974-85, sr. v.p., assoc. gen. counsel, 1985-88, exec. v.p., gen. counsel, 1988-93; ret., 1993. Author: Business Insurance Agreements, 1970, 80, 91; editor; Massachusetts Life Insurance Law, 1980. Chmn. bd. East Coast Conf., Evang. Covenant Ch., 1987-89, chmn. pension bd., 1984-86, exec. bd., 1995—; bd. dirs. Mass. Family Inst., 1994—, vol. policy analyst, 1994—. Mem. ABA (chmn. life ins. law com. torts and ins. sect. 1992-93), Assn. Life Inst. Counsel (bd. dirs. 1987-92, pres. 1992-93), Longmeadow Country Club, Laurel Oak Country Club. Republican. Avocation: golf. Home: 7831 Allen Robertson Pl Sarasota FL 34240

WISE, WILLIAM ALLAN, oil company executive, lawyer; b. Davenport, Iowa, July 10, 1945; s. A. Walter and Mary Virginia (Kuhl) W.; m. Marie Figge, Sept. 27, 1969; children—Vivian Marie, Genevieve Marie, Mary Elizabeth. B.A., Vanderbilt U.; J.D., U. Colo. Bar: Colo. 1970. Prin. counsel El Paso Natural Gas, Tex., 1970-80, sr. v.p. mktg., 1985-87, exec. v.p. mktg., 1987-89; pres., chief oper. officer El Paso Natural Gas, 1989-90, pres., chief exec. officer, 1990-93, chmn, pres. & CEO, 1994-96; asst. gen. counsel in Houston The El Paso Co., 1980-82, v.p., gen. counsel, 1983, sr. v.p., gen. counsel and sec., 1983-85; chmn., pres. & CEO El Paso Natural Gas Co. dba El Paso Energy Corp., 1996—; also bd. dirs. El Paso Energy Corp.; bd. dirs. Tex. Commerce Bank, El Paso, Tex. Commerce Bancshres, Inc., Houston, Interstate Natural Gas Assn. Am., Washington: mem. N.Y. Merc. Exch., Tri-Regional Com. Contbr. articles to profl. jours. Bd. dirs. Battle Mountain Gold Co., U. Colo. Found., Boulder, Gas Industry Stds., Natural Gas Coun., Tex. Gov.'s Bus. Coun.; mem. bus. adv. coun. and devel. bd. U. Tex., El Paso; bd. visitors M.D. Anderson Cancer Ctr. Mem. Nat. Petroleum Coun. (bd. dirs.), Colo. Bar Assn., El Paso Country Club, George Town Club (Washington), River Oaks Country Club (Houston), Old Baldy Club (Saratoga, Wyo.). Republican. Roman Catholic. Avocations: golf, running. Home: 5605 Westside Dr El Paso TX 79932-2921 Office: El Paso Energy Corp. 100 N Stanton One Paul Kayser Cen El Paso TX 79901

WISE, WILLIAM JERRARD, lawyer; b. Chgo., May 27, 1934; s. Gerald Paul and Harriet Muriel (Rosenblum) W.; m. Peggy Spero, Sept. 3, 1959; children: Deborah, Stephen, Betsy, Lynne. B.B.A., U. Mich., 1955, M.B.A., 1958, J.D. with distinction, 1958. Bar: Ill. 1959. Spl. atty. Office Regional Counsel, IRS, Milw., 1959-63; with firm McDermott, Will & Emery, Chgo., 1963-70, Coles & Wise, Ltd., 1971-81, Wise & Stracks, Ltd., 1982—; Lectr., contbr. Ill. Inst. Continuing Legal Edn.; arbitrator Cir. Ct. Cook County Ill., 1990—. Mem. Village of Winnetka (Ill.) Caucus, 1974-75; Bd. dirs. Blind Service Assn., Chgo., 1964-74; dir., treas. Suzuki Orff Sch. for Young Musicians, Chgo., 1981-91. Served with AUS, 1958-59. Mem. Chgo. Bar Assn. Home: 1401 Tower Rd Winnetka IL 60093-1628 Office: Wise & Stracks Ltd 20 N Clark St Ste 1000 Chicago IL 60602-4111 *I believe that one succeeds best in our society if one gives as little thought as possible to one's personal well being.*

WISEHART, MARY RUTH, academic administrator; b. Myrtle, Mo., Nov. 2, 1932; d. William Henry and Ora (Harbison) W. BA, Free Will Baptist Bible Coll., 1955; BA, George Peabody Coll. Tchrs., 1959, MA, 1960, PhD, 1976. Tchr. Free Will Bapt. Bible Coll., Nashville, 1956-60, chmn. English dept., 1961-85; exec. sec.-treas. Free Will Bapt. Women Nat. Active for Christ, 1985—. Author: Sparks Into Flame, 1985; contbr. poetry to jours. Mem. Nat. Coun. Tchrs. English, Christian Mgmt. Assn., Religious Conf. Mgmt. Assn., Scribbler's Club. Avocations: photography, music, drama. Office: Women Nat Active for Christ Free Will Bapt PO Box 5002 Antioch TN 37011-5002

WISEMAN, ALAN M(ITCHELL), lawyer; b. Long Branch, N.J., July 6, 1944; s. Lincoln B. and Gertrude (Gorcey) W.; m. Paula Wiseman, July 8, 1965; children—Steven, David, Julie. B.A., Johns Hopkins U., 1965; J.D., Georgetown U., 1968. Bar: Md. 1968, Ill. 1970, D.C. 1973. Law clk. to Hon. William J. McWilliams Md. Ct. Appeals, 1968-69; assoc. Schiff Hardin & Waite, Chgo., 1970-74; ptnr. Howrey & Simon, Washington, 1976—. Editor Georgetown Law Jour., 1967-68. Mem. U.S. C. of C. (council on antitrust policy). Office: 1299 Pennsylvania Ave NW Washington DC 20004-2400

WISEMAN, DENNIS GENE, university dean; b. Anderson, Ind., Sept. 25, 1947; s. Harold Leslie and Lillian Loetta (Woods) W.; m. Susan Jean Reidenbach, June 10, 1971; children: Matthew Benjamin, Andrew Joseph. BA, U. Indpls., 1969; MA, U. Ill., 1970, PhD, 1974; postgrad., Ind. U., 1970-71. Tchr. Indpls. Pub. Schs., 1970-71; rsch. asst. U. Ill., Urbana, 1971-74, clinician, supr., 1972-74, coord. Office for Profl. Svc., 1973-74; dir., tchr. Champaign (Ill.) pub. schs., 1972-73; asst. prof. U. S.C. Coastal Carolina Coll., Conway, 1974-77, assoc. prof., 1977-84, prof., 1984—, dean Sch. Edn., 1982—; dean Sch. Edn. and Grad. Studies, Coastal Carolina U.,

1993—; field disseminator Social Sci. Edn. Consortium, Boulder, Colo., 1979-81; reviewer Ethnic Heritage Studies Program, U.S. Office Edn., Washington, 1980-81; cons. S.C. State Dept. Edn., Columbia, 1986—; dir. Oxford program U. S.C. Coastal Carolina Coll., summer, 1990; evaluator So. Assn. Colls. and Schs., Atlanta, 1991; folio reviewer for Nat. Coun. for Social Studies, Nat. Coun. for Accreditation of Tchr. Edn., 1994—. Co-author: Effective Teaching, 1st edit., 1984, 2d edit. 1991, Wondering about Thinking, 1988, The Middle Level Teachers' Handbook: Becoming a Reflective Practitioner, 1997; contbr. articles to jours. in field. Mem. Horry County Human Rels. Coun., Conway, 1990-93; mem. curriculum frameworks rev. panel S.C. Dept. Edn., 1993—. Named Tchr. of Yr., U. S.C. Coastal Carolina Coll., 1980; S.C. Com. for the Humanities grantee, 1984, S.C. Com. on Higher Edn. grantee, 1985, 86; Japan Study Program scholar U.S. Office Edn., 1980. Mem. S.C. Assn. Colls. for Tchr. Edn. (pres. elect 1989, pres. 1989-91), Coun. Edn. Deans (pres. 1986-90, pres. 1996—), Nat. Coun. for the Social Studies, Am. Assn. Colls. for Tchr. Edn. (instl. rep. 1980—), Assn. Tchr. Educators, Phi Delta Kappa (pres. Coastal Carolina chpt. 1984-85). Methodist. Avocations: reading, travel, tennis, writing. Office: Coastal Carolina U Dean Sch Edn & Grad Studies PO Box 261954 Conway SC 29528-6054

WISEMAN, DOUGLAS CARL, education educator; b. Nashua, N.H., Feb. 28, 1935; s. Howard W. and Ruth D. (Aiken) W.; m. Donna Wiseman; children: Mark, Cynthia, Lori, Alan, Kathleen, Steve. BEd, Plymouth (N.H.) State Coll., 1961; MS, Ind. U., 1962, PED, 1970. Cert. tchr. health, math., phys. edn., sci. Tchr. high sch. Nashua (N.H.) Pub. Schs., 1960-61, tchr. jr. high, 1962-63; teaching asst. Ind. U., Bloomington, 1961-62; tchr. high sch. Portage (Mich.) High Sch., 1963-64; instr., asst. prof. Plymouth (N.H.) State Coll., 1964-69; asst. prof. Northeastern U., Boston, 1969-71; dir. athletics, chmn. dept. Plymouth State Coll., 1971-80, prof., chair dept. edn., 1980—, assoc. dean, 1993-96, prof., 1996—; cons. Am./Nat. Red Cross, Laconia, N.H., 1971—, State Dept. Edn., Concord, 1980—. Author, contbg. editor: Adapted Physical Education, 1982, Practical Research, 1989, Physical Education for Exceptional Students, 1994; contbr. articles to profl. jours. Cert. police officer Ashland, N.H., 1992—; chair sch. bd. Plymouth Regional Sch. Dist., 1989-91. AAHPERD Ea. Dist. scholar, 1990-91. Republican. Avocations: reading, scuba. Office: Plymouth State Coll Rounds # 035 Plymouth NH 03264

WISEMAN, FREDERICK, filmmaker; b. Boston, Jan. 1, 1930; s. Jacob Leo and Gertrude Leah (Kotzen) W.; m. Zipporah Batshaw, May 29, 1955; children: David B., Eric T. BA, Williams Coll., 1951; LLB, Yale U., 1954; LHD (hon.), U. Cin., 1973, Williams Coll., 1976, John Jay Coll. Crim. Justice, 1994; DFA (hon.), Lake Forest Coll., 1991, Princeton U., 1994. Bar: Mass. 1955. Lectr. law Boston U. Law Sch., 1958-61; research assoc. Brandeis U., Waltham, Mass., 1962-66; treas. Orgn. for Social and Tech. Innovation, 1966-70; filmmaker Zipporah Films, Cambridge, Mass., 1970—; vis. lectr. numerous schs. Filmmaker: Titicut Follies, 1967, High School, 1968, Law and Order, 1969 (Emmy award Best News Documentary 1969), Hospital, 1970 (Emmy award Best Dir. and Best News Documentary 1970, Columbia Dupont award for excellence in broadcast journalism 1970), Basic Training, 1971, Essene, 1972, Juvenile Court, 1973 (Columbia Dupont award for excellence in broadcast journalism 1975), Primate, 1974, Welfare, 1975, Meat, 1976, Canal Zone, 1977, Sinai Field Mission, 1978, Manoeuvre, 1979, Model, 1980, Seraphita's Diary, 1982, The Store, 1983, Racetrack, 1985, Deaf, 1986, Blind, 1986, Multi-Handicapped, 1986, Adjustment and Work, 1986, Missile, 1987, Near Death, 1989, Central Park, 1989, Aspen, 1991, Zoo, 1993, High School II, 1994, Ballet, 1995, La Comedie Française, 1996; dir. theatre Tonight We Improvise, 1986-87, Life and Fate, 1988, Hate, 1991, Am. Repertory Theatre, Welfare: The Opera, Am. Music Theater Festival, 1992. Served with U.S. Army, 1955-56. Fellow Russell Sage Found., 1961-62. NATAS fellow, 1991; Guggenheim Found. fellow, 1980-81; MacArthur fellow, 1982-87; recipient The Peabody award, Personal award, 1991. Fellow Am. Acad. Arts and Scis. Office: 1 Richdale Ave # 4 Cambridge MA 02140-2627

WISEMAN, GLORIA DIANA, medical educator, physician; b. N.Y.C.. BS, CCNY, 1977; MD, Columbia U., 1981. Diplomate Nat. Bd. Medical Examiners. Intern and resident in pediatrics NYU Med. Ctr., 1981-84, teaching asst., 1983-84; neonatal-perinatal medicine fellow Babies' Hosp. Columbia U., 1984-86, asst. pediatrician Babies' Hosp., 1984-86, staff assoc., 1984-86; instr. U. Medicine and Dentistry of N.J.-N.J. Med. Sch., 1986-87, asst. prof. clin. pediatrics, 1987-88; neonatology/pediatric attending physician U. Hosp. N.J., 1986-88; rsch. fellow in allergy and immunology Albert Einstein Coll. Medicine, Bronx, N.Y., 1988-91; fellow in allergy and immunology Weiler Hosp. of Albert Einstein Coll. Medicine, Bronx, 1988-91; dir. neonatal-perinatal medicine Englewood (N.J.) Hosp., 1991-96, Holy Name Hosp., N.J., 1996—; asst. attending physician divsn. newborn medicine Mount Sinai-Babies' and Children's Hosp. of N.Y., N.Y.C., 1991—; attending physician divsn. perinatal medicine Columbia-Presbyn. Med. Ctr., N.Y.C., 1996—; asst. prof. pediatrics Columbia U., N.Y.C., 1996—; divsn. bd. of inquiry faculty of medicine Columbina U., 1978-80; com. of admissions U.M.D.N.J.-N.J. Med. Sch., 1986-88; crit. care com. intensive care nursery U. Hosp. N.J., 1986-88; perinatal morbidity rate mortality com. Englewood Hosp., 1991-96, co-chmn. perinatal policy com., 1991-96, pharmacy and therapeutics com., 1992-96, future devel. com., 1992-96, ob-gyn. quality improvement com., 1995-96, chmn. neonatal intensive care quality assurance com., 1993-96, mem. pediatric quality assurance com., 1996—, mem. breastfeeding task force, 1996—; co-chmn. neonatal clin. stds. com., 1994-96, level of care design com., 1995-96, pediatric/neonatal quality assurance com., 1996—, chmn. neonatal policy and procedure com., 1997—; asst. prof. pediatrics Columbia U., 1996—. Contbr. articles to profl. jours. Recipient Internat. Cultural Diploma of Honor Order Internat. Ambassadors, Internat. Order of Merit Women's Inner Circle of Achievement. Fellow Am. Acad. Pediatrics; mem. AMA (Physician's Recognition awards (2), Am. Acad. Allergy and Immunology, Clin. Immunology Soc., Joint Coun. Allergy and Immunology, N.Y. Perinatal Soc., Babies' Hosp. Alumni Assn., NYU Pediatric Alumni Assn., P&S Columbia U. Alumni Assn., Alumni Orgn. City Coll., Phi Beta Kappa (Gamma chpt.). Office: Holy Name Hosp 718 Teaneck Rd Teaneck NJ 07666-4245

WISEMAN, JAMES RICHARD, classicist, archaeologist, educator; b. North Little Rock, Ark., Aug. 29, 1934; s. James Morgan and Bertie Lou (Sullivan) W.; m. Margaret Lucille Mayhue, Aug. 20, 1954; children: James Alexander, Stephen Michael. BA, U. Mo., Columbia, 1957; MA, U. Chgo., 1960, PhD, 1966; postgrad., Am. Sch. Classical Studies, Athens, Greece, 1959-60. Instr. U. Tex., Austin, 1960-64; asst. prof. classics U. Tex., 1964-66, asso. prof., 1966-70, prof., 1970-73; dir. archaeol. excavations at Ancient Corinth, Greece, 1965-72; chmn. archaeol. studies program, 1969-73; prof. classics Boston U., 1973—, prof. art history, 1975—, prof. archaeology, 1980—, chmn. dept. classical studies, 1974-82, chmn. dept. archaeology, 1982-96, dir. archaeol. studies program, 1975-76, 79-82, dir. Ctr. Archeol. Studies, 1980—; dir. summer program Greece, 1976-77, 81, 91-94; vis. assoc. prof. classics U. Colo., Boulder, 1970; Am. prin. investigator, co-dir. Am.-Yugoslav Archaeol. Excavations at Stobi, Yugoslavia, 1970-81; project supr. Boston U. Archaeol. Excavations in Temple, N.H., 1975-76; vis. rsch. prof. Am. Sch. Classical Studies, Athens, 1978-79; cons. archaeology; chmn. exec. com. Ctr. Remote Sensing; dir. Boston U. Nikopolis Project in N.W. Greece; vis. fellow Clare Hall and McDonald Inst. for Archaeol. Rsch., Cambridge, 1997. Author: Stobi, A Guide to the Excavations, 1973, The Land of the Ancient Corinthians, 1978, (with Thomas Sever) Remote Sensing and Archaeology: Potential for the Future, 1985; contbr. numerous articles on ancient history, epigraphy, classical studies, archaeology to profl. jours.; editor, contbg. author: Studies in the Antiquities of Stobi I, 1973, II, 1975, III, 1981; founding editor: Jour. Field Archaeology, 1974—; contbg. editor Archaeology Mag., 1995—. Trustee Am. Ctr. Oriental Rsch., Am. Schs. Oriental Rsch., 1985-89. Served with USN, 1952-55. Recipient Bromberg award U. Tex., 1964, Bronze Plaque award City of Titov Veles, SR Makedonija, Yugoslavia; disting. alumnus award Coll. Arts and Sci. U. Mo. Columbia, 1989; Am. Council Learned Socs. fellow, 1967-68, 78-79, 90-91; Guggenheim fellow, 1971-72; U. Tex. Research Inst. grantee, summers 1961, 66, 67, and 1967-68, 71-72; NEH grantee, 1968, 69, 76-80; Ford Found. grantee, 1968-72; Smithsonian Instn. grantee, 1970-75, 79-81; Dumbarton Oaks fellow, 1983-84; NGS grantee, 1984, 92; NASA grantee, 1984, 91; W.M. Keck Found. grantee, 1985, 86, 88, 92; J.M. Kaplan Fund grantee, 1997; NEH fellow, 1990; Mellon fellow Inst. Advanced Study, Princeton U., 1990-91. Fellow Soc. Antiquaries of London, Explorers Club; mem. Archaeol. Inst. Am. (nat. pres. 1985-88, exec. com. 1973-77, 81-92, trustee 1993—, pres. Ctrl. Tex. Soc. 1962-64, pres. Boston Soc. 1979-81, Gold Seal award 1989, Chase Eliot Norton lectr.), Am. Philol. Assn., Am. Sch. Classical Studies at Athens (exec. com. 1973-76), Am. Acad. at Rome, Assn. Ancient Historians, Assn. Field Archaeology (exec. com. 1970-85), Am. Inst. Nautical Archaeology, Internat. Assn. Archaeology, Ctr. Materials Rsch. in Archaeology and Ethnology (exec. com. 1975-78, 79-83), Soc. Am. Archaeology, Soc. Hist. Archaeology, Am. Coun. Learned Soc. (del. 1985-89), German Archeol. Inst. (corr.). Democrat. Office: Boston U Dept Archaeology 675 Commonwealth Ave Boston MA 02215-1406

WISEMAN, JAY DONALD, photographer, mechanical designer and contractor; b. Salt Lake City, Dec. 23, 1952; s. Donald Thomas and Reva (Stewart) W.; m. Barbara Helen Taylor, June 25, 1977; children: Jill Reva, Steve Jay. Ed. Utah State U., Logan, U. Utah. Cert. profl. photographer. Pvt. practice photography; owner, pres. JB&W Corp. Recipient Grand prize Utah State Fair, 1986, Kodak Crystal for Photographic Excellence, 1986, 87, Master of Photography degree, 1989, Best of Show award, 1991-92; Profl. Photographer Mag. cover photo, 1988; numerous photos inducted for permanent collection Internat. Photographic Hall of Fame, 1989; photo named one of World's Greatest, Kodak, 1987-88; 2 photos named among World's Best, Walt Disney World and Profl. Photographers Assn., 1988, 2 prints tied for Best of Show award RMPPA Regional contest, 1991; recipient Gold Medallion award Best in Show (world wide). Mem. Profl. Photographers Assn. Am. (one of top 10 scores internat. photo contest), Rocky Mountain Profl. Photographers (Best of Show, highest score ever 1987, Master Photographer of Yr. 1991, Ct. of Honour 1981-91), Intermountain Profl. Photographers Assn. (Master's Trophy Best of Show 1982, 86, 88, Photographer of Yr. award 1986, Ct. of Honour 1981-91), Photographers Soc. Am (Best of Show award Utah chpt. 1986). Latter Day Saints. Represented in Salt Lake City Internat. Airport permanent photo exhibit, various traveling loan collections, U.S. and Europe, 1988, loan collection Epcot Ctr., 1988-91; photographs published numerous profl. jours.

WISEMAN, LAURENCE DONALD, foundation executive; b. Washington, Feb. 24, 1947; s. Leon Robert and Marion (Zuckerman) W.; m. Robin Lynn Jeweler, May 29, 1978; children: Justin J., David B. AB with highest distinction, Dartmouth Coll., 1969; M in Pub. Affairs, Princeton U., 1971. Exec. producer Sta. WQED-TV (pub. broadcasting), Pitts., 1971-75; prin. Moses, Epstein and Wiseman, Washington, 1975-78; v.p. Yankelovich, Skelly and White, N.Y.C., 1978-81; v.p. Am. Forest Council, Washington, 1981-84, pres., 1984—; pres. Am. Forest Coun., 1984-92, Am. Forest Found., 1993—. Author: Coalition Building, 1977. Bd. dirs. Cystic Fibrosis Found., N.Y.C., 1979-80, Urban Philharmonic, Washington, 1980-83, Sasha Bruce House, Washington, 1980-82; adv. com. Soc. for Profl. Journalists, Washington, 1984; hon. trustee Nat. Arbor Day Found., Nebraska City, Nebr., 1984—; chairperson Nat. Coun. on Pvt. Forests, 1997—. Mem. Am. Forestry Assn., Soc. Am. Foresters, Pub. Rels. Soc. Am. Home: 10621 Democracy Ln Potomac MD 20854-4016 Office: Am Forest Found 1111 19th St NW Washington DC 20036-3603

WISEMAN, RANDOLPH CARSON, lawyer; b. Staunton, Va., Jan. 25, 1946; s. Malcolm Bell Wiseman and Alberta Elizabeth (Forbus) Marshall; m. Patty Joanne Gray, June 28, 1969; 1 child, Michael Randolph. BS, East Tenn. State U., Johnson City, 1968; JD, Capital U., Columbus, Ohio, 1974. Bar: Ohio 1974, U.S. Dist. Ct. (so. dist.) Ohio 1974, U.S. Supreme Ct. 1977. Assoc. Tyack, Scott & Colley, Columbus, 1974-77; ptnr. Tyack, Scott, Grossman & Wiseman, Columbus, 1977-79, Tyack, Scott & Wiseman, Columbus, 1979-81, Bricker & Eckler, Columbus, 1981—. Contbr.: Evidence in America: The Federal Rules in the States, 1987; contbr. law articles to profl. jours. Bd. trustees Nat. Multiple Sclerosis Soc., Columbus, 1987—, chmn. 1991-93, Big Bros. Assn., Columbus, 1976-78. Mem. ABA, Internat. Assn. Def. Counsel, Ohio State Bar Assn., Columbus Bar Assn., Franklin County Trial Lawyers Assn. (pres.). Republican. Avocations: running, reading, auto racing. Office: Brickler & Eckler 100 S 3rd St Columbus OH 43215-4236

WISEMAN, THOMAS ANDERTON, JR., federal judge; b. Tullahoma, Tenn., Nov. 3, 1930; s. Thomas Anderton and Vera Seleta (Poe) W.; m. Emily Barbara Matlack, Mar. 30, 1957; children: Thomas Anderton III, Mary Alice, Sarah Emily. B.A., Vanderbilt U., 1952, LL.B., 1954; LLM, U. Va., 1990. Bar: Tenn. Pvt. practice Tullahoma, 1956-63; ptnr. Haynes, Wiseman & Hull, Tullahoma and Winchester, Tenn., 1963-71; treas. State of Tenn., 1971-74; ptnr. Chambers & Wiseman, 1974-78; judge U.S. Dist. Ct. (mid. dist.) Tenn., Nashville, 1978—, chief judge, 1984-91, sr. judge, 1995—; mem. Tenn. Ho. of Reps., 1964-68; adj. prof. law Vanderbilt U. Sch. Law. Asso. editor: Vanderbilt Law Rev, 1953-54. Democratic candidate for gov., Tenn., 1974; Chmn. Tenn. Heart Fund, 1973, Middle Tenn. Heart Fund, 1972. Served with U.S. Army, 1954-56. Fellow Tenn. Bar Found.; mem. Masons (33 deg.), Shriners, Amateur Chefs Soc. Presbyterian. Office: US Dist Ct 736 US Courthouse 801 Broadway Nashville TN 37203

WISER, JAMES LOUIS, political science educator; b. Detroit, Mar. 4, 1945; s. Louis Bernard and Nita Pauline (Neff) W.; m. Bethany Marie Goodall, Dec. 27, 1967; children: Steven Louis, Michael James. B.A., U. Notre Dame, 1967; M.A., Duke U., 1968, Ph.D., 1971. Asst. prof. Loyola U., Chgo., 1971-74, assoc. prof., 1974-81, prof., 1981—, chmn. dept. polit. sci., 1980-84, dean Coll. Arts and Scis., 1987-89, sr. v.p., dean of faculties, 1989—. Author: Political Philosophy: A History of the Search for Order, 1983; Political Theory: A Thematic Inquiry, 1986. Bd. dirs. Am. Cancer Soc., Chgo., 1982-84. Recipient dissertation award Woodrow Wilson Found., 1970; Fulbright-Hayes grantee, 1969; NEH grantee, 1979. Mem. Am. Polit. Sci. Assn., Conf. for Study of Polit. Thought (chmn. 1975-77), Internat. Seminar for Philosophy and Polit. Theory. Democrat. Roman Catholic. Home: 6725 N Wildwood Ave Chicago IL 60646-1306 Office: Loyola U 820 N Michigan Ave Chicago IL 60611-2103

WISH, JAY BARRY, nephrologist, specialist; b. Hartford, Mar. 30, 1950; s. Martin and Evelyn Lillian (Lassman) W.; m. Linda Kristina Hansen, June 29, 1971; (div. 1980); children: Allen Jeremy, Robin Lindsey; m. Diane Elizabeth Perkins, June 5, 1983; children: Jeffrey Bryan, David Phillip. BA, Wesleyan U., 1970; MD, Tufts U., 1974. Diplomate Am. Bd. Internal Medicine, Am. Bd. Nephrology. Resident in medicine New England Med. Ctr., Boston, 1974-79; instr. in medicine Tufts U., Boston, 1978-79; lectr. in health sci. Northeastern U., Boston, 1978-79; asst. prof. of medicine Case Western Res. U., Cleve., 1979-85, assoc. prof. of medicine, 1985-96, prof. medicine, 1996—; dir. hemodialysis U. Hosps. of Cleve., 1980—, dir. continuing edn., 1987-95; chmn. Med. Adv. Bd. Kidney Found. of Ohio, Cleve., 1985-88. Author: Renal Disease and Hypertension, 1982, Disorders of Potassium, 1984, Metabolic Diseases, 1986, Rheumatic Diseases of the Kidney, 1993, Acid-Base and Electrolyte Disorders in the Critically Ill Patient, 1993, Assuring Quality of Care in Dialysis Patients, 1994; contbr. articles to med. jours. Chmn. med. rev. bd. End-Stage Renal Disease Network #22, Pitts., 1982-87, End-Stage Renal Disease Network #9, Indpls., 1992—; mem. exec. com. Forum of End-Stage Renal Disease Networks, 1992—, v.p., 1996—; bd. dirs. Renal Phys. Assn., 1993—, sec. 1996-97, treas., 1997—; mem. Nat. Kidney Found. Fellow Am. Coll. of Physicians; mem. Cleve. Restoration Soc., Am. Soc. of Nephrology, Internat. Soc. of Nephrology, Alpha Omega Alpha. Democrat. Jewish. Avocation: performing arts. Office: U Hosps Cleve 11100 Euclid Ave Cleveland OH 44106-1736

WISHARD, DELLA MAE, state legislator; b. Bison, S.D., Oct. 21, 1934; d. Ervin E. and Alma J. (Albertson) Preszler; m. Glenn L. Wishard, Oct. 18, 1953; children: Glenda Lee, Pamela A., Glen Ervin. Grad. high sch., Bison. Mem. S.D. Ho. of Reps., Pierre, 1984-96; pub., editor Bison (S.D.) Courier, 1996—. Columnist County Farm Bur., 1970-96. Committeewoman state Rep. Cen. Com., Perkins County, S.D., 1980-84. Mem. Am. Legis. Exch. Coun. (state coord. 1985-91, state chmn. 1991—), Fed. Rep. Women (chmn. Perkins County chpt. 1978-84), S.D. Farm Bur. (state officer 1982). Lutheran. Avocations: writing, gardening. Home: HC 1 Box 139 Prairie City SD 57649-9714 Office: Bison Courier Box 429 Bison SD 57260

WISHARD, GORDON DAVIS, lawyer; b. Indpls., Jan. 7, 1945; s. William Niles Jr. and Caroline (Davis) W.; m. Anne Emison; children: Claire Clark, Gordon Davis Jr. BA, Williams Coll., 1966; JD, Ind. U., 1969. Bar: Ind. 1969, U.S. Dist. Ct. (so. dist.) Ind. 1969, U.S. Ct. Appeals (7th cir.) 1976, U.S. Supreme Ct. 1980, U.S. Tax Ct. 1983. Ptnr. Ice Miller Donadio & Ryan, Indpls. Mem. Am. Coll. Trust and Estate Coun. (Ind. chmn. 1990-95). Avocations: hunting, fishing. Office: Ice Miller Donadio & Ryan 1 American Sq Indianapolis IN 46282-0001

WISHART, ALFRED WILBUR, JR., foundation administrator; b. Pitts., Dec. 21, 1931; s. Alfred W. and Corrinne C. (Bell) W.; m. Barbara J. Scott, June 30, 1956; children: Scott S., Kathryn A., Craig C. BA, Coll. Wooster, 1953; MDiv, Union Theol. Seminary, 1956; DHL (hon.), Waynesburg U., 1976; DD (hon.), Washington and Jefferson Coll., 1983. Asst. min. Shadyside Presbyn. Ch., Pitts., 1956-60; sr. min. Arlington Ave. Presbyn. Ch., East Orange, N.J., 1961-70; exec. dir. Howard Heinz Endowment, Pitts., 1970-92, Vira I. Heinz Endowment, Pitts., 1985-92; sec. H.J. II Charitable and Family Trust, Pitts., 1970-89; exec. sec. Pitcairn-Crabbe Found., Pitts., 1970—; pres., CEO Pitts. Edn. Found., Pitts., 1970—. Mem. Duquesne Club (bd. dirs. 1983-86), Fox Chapel Golf Club, Rolling Rock Club. Republican. Avocations: tennis, golf, squash, shooting, fishing. Home: 408 Buckingham Rd Pittsburgh PA 15215-1555 also: Pitts Found One PPG Pl 30th Fl Pittsburgh PA 15222-5401*

WISHART, LEONARD PLUMER, III, army officer; b. Newark, Sept. 24, 1934; s. Leonard Plumer and Mabel Dorothea (Womsley) W.; m. Sandra Frances De Vito, Apr. 12, 1958; children: Leonard Plumer IV, Scott Brian. Student, Va. Mil. Inst., 1952-53; BS in Engring., U.S. Mil. Acad., 1957; MS in Nuclear Physics, U. Va., 1966. Commd. 2d lt. U.S. Army, 1957, advanced through grades to lt. gen., 1988; served in Germany and Vietnam; tactical officer U.S. Mil. Acad., West Point, N.Y., 1971-73; sr. mil. asst. to Sec. of Army, 1975-76; comdr. 1st Brigade, 24th Inf. Div., Ft. Stewart, Ga., 1977-78; chief of staff 24th Inf. Div., 1979, VII Corps in Germany, 1979-81; asst. div. comdr. 1st Armored Div., 1981-83; dep. comdr. CACDA, Ft. Leavenworth, Kans., 1983-86; comdr. 1st Inf. Div., Ft. Riley, Kans., 1986-88, Combined Arms Command, Ft. Leavenworth, Kans., 1988-91; dep. comdr. TRADOC, Ft. Leavenworth, Kans., 1988-91, ret., 1991; assoc. Burdeshaw Assocs. Ltd., Bethesda, Md., 1991-92; apptd. 1st dir. non-legis. and fin. svcs. U.S. Ho. of Reps., Washington, 1992-94, resigned, 1994; assoc. Burdeshow Assocs., Ltd., Bethesda, Md., 1994—; program mgr. INNOLOG, McLean, Va., 1996—. Active in cmty. activities. Decorated Disting. Service Medal (2), Legion of Merit (2), D.F.C., Bronze Star medal (2), Army Commendation medal, Air medals. Mem. Assn. U.S. Army, Assn. Grads. U.S. Mil. Acad., Alumni Assn. U. Va., VFW, Soc. of the First Divsn. Methodist. Office: Burdeshaw Assocs Ltd 4701 Sangamore Rd Bethesda MD 20816-2508

WISHART, RONALD SINCLAIR, retired chemical company executive; b. Bklyn., Mar. 1, 1925; s. Ronald Sinclair and Elizabeth Lathrop (Phillips) W.; m. Betty B. Burnup, Sept. 14, 1951 (dec. Dec. 1973); children: Michael Sinclair, James Ronald; m. Eleanor Dorothy Parrish Dooley, Jan. 11, 1975; stepchildren: Donna Dooley Willix, Arthur D. Dooley. BChemE, Rensselaer Poly. Inst., 1948. Engr., chemist Linde air div. Union Carbide Corp., Tonawanda, N.Y., 1948-51; sales rep. Chgo., Cleve., 1951-56; region mgr. Chgo., 1956-57; product mgr., mktg. mgr. Silicones div. N.Y.C., 1957-64, gen. mgr., pres., 1964-66, pres. devel. and coating materials divs., 1966-71, corp. dir. energy and transp. policy, 1972-82, v.p. fed. govt. regulations, 1983-85; v.p. pub. affairs Danbury, Conn., 1985-90; chief of staff to chmn. of corp. Union Carbide, N.Y.C., 1984-85; mem. adv. coun. Gas Rsch. Inst., Energy Modeling Ctr., Stanford U., 1979-83, Environ. and Energy Policy Ctr., John F. Kennedy Sch. Pub. Policy, Harvard U., 1980-87; energy com. Aspen Inst., 1976-88; chmn., exec. dir. Electricity Consumers Resource Coun., Washington, 1976-79. Author: The Marketing Factor, 1966; contbr. chpts. to books and articles to profl. jours.; patentee silicone formulas. Vol. Am. Field Svc., Burma, 1944-45; pres., trustee, elder White Plains (N.Y.) Presbyn. Ch., 1987-90; elder Palm City Presbyn. Ch., 1996—; treas., bd. dirs. St. Christopher's Jenni Clarkson Home, 1968-91; mem. exec. bd. Westchester Putnam coun. Boy Scouts Am., White Plains, 1985-91; v.p. Carbide Retiree Corps.; dir. Hospice Martin and St. Lucie, Inc., 1994—; pres. Lancewood Assn., 1997. Mem. NAM (mem. energy com.), Am. Mgmt. Assn. (v.p. 1966-69), Chem. Mfrs. Assn. (chmn. energy com. 1974-78), Nat. Petroleum Refiners Assn. (v.p. 1972-76, chmn. issues com. 1985-89), Internat. Fedn. Ind. Energy Users (chmn. 1978), Am. Chem. Soc., Soc. Chem. Industry, U.S. C. of C. (mem. energy com.), Met. Club Washington, Harbor Ridge Yacht and Country Club. Republican. Presbyterian. Avocations: golf, skiing, reading. Home: 1329 NW Lancewood Ter Palm City FL 34990-8050

WISHNER, HOWARD E., public relations executive; b. Miami Beach, Fla., May 31, 1952. AS in Polit. Sci., Miami Dade Jr. Coll., 1969; BA in Polit. Sci./Journalism, U. S.C., 1971, MBA in Bus./Journalism, 1972. Mktg. dir. Ringling Bros. & Barnum & Bailey Circus, 1973-75; acct. exec. Ruder & Finn, N.Y.C., 1975-77; sr. acct. exec. The Softness Group, N.Y.C., 1978-80; pres. Wishner Comm., N.Y.C., 1981-94; exec. v.p., gen. mgr. Aaron D. Cushman and Assocs., N.Y.C., 1994-95; mng. ptnr. KCSA Pub. Rels., N.Y.C., 1995—. Mem. Am. Auto Racing Writers Assn., Broadcasters Assn. Office: KCSA Pub Rels 820 2nd Ave New York NY 10017-4504

WISHNER, MAYNARD IRA, finance company executive, lawyer; b. Chgo., Sept. 17, 1923; s. Hyman L. and Frances (Fisher) W.; m. Elaine Loewenberg, July 4, 1954; children: Ellen (Mrs. Tom Kenemore), Jane, Miriam. B.A., U. Chgo., 1944, J.D., 1947. Bar: Ill. 1947. Exec. dir. Chgo. Commn. on Human Relations, 1947-52; chief ordinance enforcement div. Law Dept., City of Chgo., 1952-55; mem. law firm Cole, Wishner, Epstein & Manilow, Chgo., 1955-63; with Walter E. Heller & Co., Chgo., 1963-86, pres., 1974-86; of counsel Rosenthal and Schanfield, Chgo., 1986-95; dir. Walter E. Heller Internat. Corp., Am. Nat. Bank & Trust Co., and br. cos., Chgo. Pres. Jewish Fedn. Met. Chgo., 1987-89; chair adv. coun. Nat. Jewish Community Rels., 1992-94, pres. Coun. Jewish Fedn., 1993-96; chmn. nat. exec. coun. Am. Jewish Com., 1973-76, chmn. bd. govs., 1977-80, nat. pres. 1980-83, hon. pres., recipient Human Rights medallion, 1975; bd. dirs. Nat. Found. for Jewish Culture; chmn. Ill. Humanities Coun.; commr. Nat. Hillel Found.; mem. vis. com. U. Chgo. Sch. Social Svc. Adminstrn.; chair Ill. Humanities Coun., 1991-93. Served with AUS, 1943. Home: 1410 Sheridan Rd Wilmette IL 60091-1840 Office: Rosenthal & Schanfield 55 E Monroe St Chicago IL 60603-5701

WISHNER, STEVEN R., retail executive; b. N.Y.C., Mar. 21, 1950; s. Jerome and Florence (Wanger) W.; m. Lauri Ruth Berkson, June 5, 1977; children: Andrew R., Sara M. BA, Colgate U., 1972; MBA, Cornell U., 1976. 2nd v.p. Chase Manhattan Bank, N.Y.C., 1976-78; functional v.p. Chase Manhattan Bank, 1978; dir. fin. svcs. Gen. Instrument Corp., Clifton, N.J., 1978-79; asst. to treas. Gen. Instrument Corp., 1979-81; dir. fin. svcs. Viacom Internat. Inc., N.Y.C., 1981-82; asst. treas. Viacom Internat. Inc., 1982-86; v.p., treas. Zayre Corp., Framingham, Mass., 1987-89; v.p. fin., treas. The TJX Cos., Inc., Framingham, 1987—; mem. ea. adv. bd. Protection Mut. Ins. Co., 1987-91. Vice chmn. fin. com. Town of Sudbury, Mass. Mem. Fin. Execs. Inst., Nat. Assn. Corp. Treas., Nat. Investor Rels. Inst., Cornell U. Alumni Assn. (co-chmn. admissions com., alumni exec. coun. 1987-90), Masons. Home: 92 Fox Run Rd Sudbury MA 01776-2768 Office: The TJX Companies Inc 770 Cochituate Rd Framingham MA 01701-4672

WISHNICK, MARCIA MARGOLIS, pediatrician, geneticist, educator; b. N.Y.C., Oct. 10, 1938; d. Hyman and Tillie (Stoller) Margolis; m. Stanley Wishnick, June 12, 1960; 1 child, Elizabeth Anne. BA, Barnard Coll., 1960; PhD, NYU, 1970, MD, 1974. Diplomate Am. Bd. Pediatrics, Nat. Bd. Med. Examiners. Rsch. technician Lederle Labs./Am. Cyanamid, Pearl River, N.Y., 1960-66; postdoctoral fellow N.Y. Pub. Health Lab., N.Y.C., 1970-71; resident in pediatrics NYU-Bellevue Med. Ctr., N.Y.C., 1974-77, asst. prof. pediatrics, 1977-82; clin. assoc. prof. pediatrics Bellevue Med. Ctr. NYU Med. Ctr., N.Y.C., 1982-87; clin. prof. pediatrics NYU-Bellevue Med. Ctr., N.Y.C., 1987—; pvt. practice, N.Y.C., 1977—. Contbr. articles to profl. jours. Fellow Am. Acad. Pediatrics; mem. AMA, N.Y. Pediatric Soc., N.Y. Med. Soc., N.Y. Women's Med. Assn. Office: 157 E 81st St New York NY 10028-1844

WISLER, CHARLES CLIFTON, JR., retired cotton oil company executive; b. Oklahoma City, June 6, 1926; s. Charles Clifton and Lucille Sunshine (McCormick) W.; m. Frances Joan Higgins, Sept. 21, 1946; children: Karen Lynn Collins-Eiland, Gary Clifton, David Charles. Student, Oklahoma City

U., 1945-47. Bookkeeper Magnolia Petroleum Co., Oklahoma City, 1947-51; cotton buyer C.S. Higgins Co., Lubbock, Tex., 1951-52; office mgr. Sharp & Glover, Harlingen, Tex., 1952; with Toyo Cotton Co., Dallas, 1952-81, pres., 1972-81; pres. Chickasha Cotton Oil Co., Ft. Worth, 1981-86, chmn., 1986-88; advisor to bd. dirs. Nat. Cotton Coun., 1985-91. Bd. dirs. Nat. Kidney Found., Dallas, 1976-83, Granbury Opera House Assn., 1992-94; mem. Agr. Policy Adv. Com. for Trade Negotiations, Washington, 1975-77. With USAAF, 1944-45. Mem. Tex. Cotton Assn. (dir. 1971-75, 79-80, pres. 1974), Am. Cotton Shippers Assn. (dir. 1972, 74-75, 77). Republican. Methodist. Home: 6115 Belvidere Cir Granbury TX 76049 *I have always believed in living a disciplined life and the practice of Christian principles in business.*

WISLER, DARLA LEE, pastor; b. Balt., May 14, 1940; d. Hugh Charles Douglas and Angela Rita (Poffel) Mayer; m. Norman Marvin Wisler, Dec. 26, 1960; children: David Paul, Diane Lynn. A in Biblical Studies, Christian Internat. U., 1982, BTh, 1984, MDiv, 1990, D in Ministry, 1993. Asst. pastor Anderson (S.C.) Christian Assembly, 1978-80; founder, sr. pastor Living Water Ch., Anderson, 1981—; mid-week devotion min. Anderson Health Care Ctr., 1980—, pres. adv. bd., 1988—; dean Living Water Bible Coll., Anderson, 1982—; prin. Living Water Christian Sch., Anderson, 1983-88; regular co-host Dove Broadcasting TV-16, Greenville, S.C., 1984—; coord. Christian Internat. Network of Chs. Mid-East Region, 1994-96. Author: Basic Christian Teaching Made Plain and Clear, 1994, Advanced Christian Teaching Made Plain and Clear, 1995. Pres. clergy staff exec. com. Anderson Area Med. Ctr., 1993-94; sec. Anderson County Sheriff's Dept. Chaplaincy, Anderson, 1996; chaplain Anderson County Sheriff's Dept., 1996—. Republican. Avocations: walking, reading, crocheting, cooking. Office: Living Water Ch PO Box 1823 Anderson SC 29622

WISLER, WILLARD EUGENE, health care management executive; b. Cliffside Park, N.J., May 31, 1933; s. Willard Walter and Doris Alice (McGlone) W.; m. Carol M. Askey, Aug. 19, 1966; children: Diana Marie, Jennifer Lee. BBA, U. Fla., 1955; MBA, The George Washington U., 1963. Asst. adminstr. Halifax Dist. Hosp., Daytona Beach, Fla., 1963-64; CFO Waterman Meml. Hosp., Eustis, Fla., 1964-67, COO, 1967-72; COO Suburban Hosp., Louisville, 1972-73; exec. dir. Gen. Hosp. of Fort Walton Beach, Fla., 1973-77; pres. Winter Pk. (Fla.) Meml. Hosp., 1977-91, Park Health Corp., Winter Pk., 1985-91, The Tampa Bay Hosp. Assn., St. Petersburg, Fla., 1991—; bd. dirs. Village on the Green, Longwood, Fla., 1983-88; mem. ho. of dels. Am. Hsp. Assn., Chgo., 1985-88; regent State of Fla. Am. Coll. Healthcare Execs., Chgo., 1988-93. Adv. council mem. Hamilton Holt Sch., Rollins Coll., Winter Pk., 1986-89, Orlando Bus. Jour., 1989, Pioneer Savings Bank, Winter Pk., 1986-88. Sgt. U.S. Army, 1955-59. Fellow Am. Coll. Healthcare Execs., Citrus Club, Winter Park Racquet, Interlachen Country. Democrat. Home: 3414 W Mullen Ave Tampa FL 33609-4632 Office: The Tampa Bay Hosp Assn 9455 Koger Blvd N Ste 118 Saint Petersburg FL 33702-2431

WISMER, PATRICIA ANN, secondary education educator; b. York, Pa., Mar. 23, 1936; d. John Bernhardt and Frances Elizabeth Loreen Marie (Fry) Feiser; m. Lawrence Howard Wismer, Aug. 4, 1961. BA in English, Mt. Holyoke Coll., 1958; MA in Speech/Drama, U. Wis., 1960; postgrad., U. Oreg., 1962, Calif. State U., Chico, 1963-64, U. So. Calif., 1973-74. Tchr., co-dir. drama program William Penn Sr. High Sch., York, 1960-61; instr. English, dir. drama York Jr. Coll., 1961-62; assoc. church editor San Francisco Examiner, 1962-63; reporter, publicist News Bur. Calif. State U., Chico, 1963-64; chmn. English Dept. Chico Sr. H.S., 1966-96; mentor tchr. Chico Sr. High Sch., Chico Unified Sch. Dist., 1983-93; judge writing awards Nat. Coun. Tchr. English, 1970—; cons. No. Calif. Writing Project, 1977—; curriculum cons., freelance writer and photographer, 1996—. Mem. Educators for Social Responsibility, Calif. Assn. for Gifted, Upper Calif. Coun. Tchrs. English (bd. dirs. 1966-85, pres. 1970-71), Calif. Assn. Tchrs. English, Nat. Coun. Tchrs. English, NEA, Calif. Tchrs. Assn., Chico Unified Tchrs. Assn. Democrat. Lutheran. Avocations: photography, play prodn., video prodn. Home: 623 Arcadian Ave Chico CA 95926-4504 Office: PO Box 1250 Cannon Beach OR 97110-1250

WISNE, LAWRENCE A., metal products executive; b. 1947; s. Anthony E. W. With Prog Tool & Indsl. Co., Southfield, Mich., v.p., 1977-79, pres., 1979—. Office: Prog Tool & Inds Co 21000 Telegraph Rd Southfield MI 48034-4280*

WISNER, FRANK GEORGE, ambassador; b. N.Y.C., July 2, 1938; s. Frank Gardiner W. and Mary Knowles (Fritchey) W.; m. Genevieve de Virel, July, 1969 (dec. 1974); 1 dau., Sabrina; m. Christine de Ganay, June, 1976; 1 son, David; stepchildren: Caroline Sarkozy, Olivier Sarkozy. BA, Princeton U., 1961. With Fgn. Svc. Dept. Dept. State, Algiers, Morocco, 1962-64; from staff aide to sr. advisor Vietnamese province Tuyen Duc Agy. Internat. Devel., Vietnam, 1964-68; officer-in-charge Tunisian affairs Dept. State, Washington, 1968-71; chief econ.-comml. sect. Am. Embassy, Tunis, Tunisia, 1971-73; chief polit. sect. Am. Embassy, Dacca, Bangladesh, 1973-74; dir. plans and mgmt. Bur. Pub. Affairs, Washington, 1974-75; spl. asst. to dir., then dep. dir. Pres.' Interagy. Task Force Refugee Resettlement, Washington, 1975; spl. asst. to undersec. polit. affairs, 1975-76; dir. office So. African affairs Dept. State, Washington, 1976-77, dep. exec. sec., 1977-79; U.S. amb. to Zambia Lusaka, 1977-82; dep. asst. sec. African affairs Dept. State, Washington, 1982-86; U.S. amb. to Egypt Cairo, 1986-91; U.S. amb. to Philippines Manila, 1991-92; under sec. of state for internat. security affairs Washington, 1992-93; under sec. of def. for policy Dept. Def., Washington, 1993-94; U.S. amb. to India, 1994—. Recipient meritorious honor award Dept. State, 1973, superior honor award, 1992; recipient Mil. Medal of Honor Govt. Vietnam, 1968, Social Welfare medal of honor, 1968. Mem. Council on Fgn. Relations, Metropolitan Club (Washington), Ivy Club (Princeton, N.J.), Knickerbocker Club (N.Y.). Episcopalian. Office: Am Embassy New Delhi State Dept Washington DC 20521-9000

WISNER, ROSCOE WILLIAM, JR., retired human resources executive; b. Beatrice, Nebr., Mar. 17, 1926; s. Roscoe William Sr. and Genevieve M. (McVey) W.; m. Louise Jackson, Mar. 15, 1952; children: Jacqueline Louise, Valerie Joyce. BA, Lincoln U., Oxford, Pa., 1950; MEd, Temple U., 1963. Accredited profl. in human resource mgmt. Sr. personnel examiner Phila. Personnel Dept., 1954-64; supr. testing and rsch. Port Authority of N.Y. and N.J., N.Y.C., 1964-76, coord. spl. programs for people with disabilities, 1976-91; ret.; instr., adj. faculty LaGuardia C.C. Author: Performance Test Procedures and Problems, 1964; contbr. articles to profl. jours. Adv. coun. Industry-Labor Coun., Albertson, N.Y., 1976-91, Kessler's Rehab. Inst., East and West Orange, N.J., 1979-91, Rusk Rehab. Inst., N.Y.C., 1980-91, Mayor's Office People with Disabilities, N.Y.C., 1980-96, Internat. Ctr. for Disabled, N.Y.C., 1980-91, N.Y.C. Bd. Edn. Spl. Edn. Project Future, 1986-91; exec. dir. Cmty. Action Program, Westbury, 1965; mem. Watchful Eye Civic Assn., Roosvelt, N.Y., 1983—; life mem. NAACP. Sgt. U.S. Army, 1944-46. Recipient Exec. Dir. Unit citation Port Authority N.Y. and N.J., 1984, Disting. Svc. award, 1990, Profl. Achievement award Ea. Region/Pub. Pers. Assn. Conf., 1969. Mem. APA (assoc.), ASPA, NAACP (life), Internat. Pers. Mgmt. Assn., Soc. Human Resource Mgmt. (life), Masons, Alpha Phi Alpha (life). Home: 266 E Greenwich Ave Roosevelt NY 11575-1205

WISNESKI, MARY JO ELIZABETH, reading specialist, educator; b. Saginaw, Mich., Dec. 18, 1938; d. Walter Frank and Hedwig Josephine (Borowicz) W. BS, Cen. Mich. U., 1961; MS, So. Ill. U., 1969; EdD, U. No. Colo., 1979; postdoctoral, U. Calif., Berkeley, 1980-81. Cert. elem. educator, elem. adminstr., reading specialist, Calif.; reading recovery tchr. Elem. educator various schs., 1960-75; instr. U. No. Colo., Greeley, 1976-78, 79; reading specialist Vacaville (Calif.) Unified Sch. Dist., 1980—; lectr. San Francisco State U., 1983-86; prof. Chapman Coll., Travis AFB, Calif., 1986-90; med. transcriptionist, office mgr. collections, 1991-94; cons. in field. Author: Clifford Books Teacher Manual, 1991, Reading Recovery Position Paper, 1995. Vol. ARC, Travis Air Mus., Travis AFB; bd. dirs. Polish Arts and Culture Found., San Francisco, 1988-91, Vistula Dancers; mem. Reading Del. to Vietnam, People-to-People Internat. Amb. Program, 1995. Recipient Tchr. in Space Certificate NASA, 1986, Outstanding Tchr. Commendation Dept. of Defense, 1973. Mem. AAUW, ACSA, Nat. Women's Polit. Caucus, Nat. Reading Conf., Internat. Reading Assn., CTA, Reading Recovery Coun., Western Coll. Reading Assn., Calif. Profs. Reading (v.p., treas.), Calif. Edn. Assn., Solano County Reading Assn. (pres., v.p., sec.), Lowiczanie Folk Dance Ensemble (pres. pro tem, treas.), Polish Am. Congress, Phi Delta Kappa, Phi Kappa Phi, Kappa Delta Pi, Pi Lambda Theta. Avocations: modeling, travel, skiing, gardening, nature. Home: 314 Creekview Ct Vacaville CA 95688-5318

WISNESKI, SHARON M., critical care nurse, educator; b. Phila., June 22, 1952; d. Charles Edward and Hilda Marie (Riley) Ashley. AS, Wesley Coll., Dover, Del., 1979, BS, 1985; MSN, Widener U., Chester, Pa., 1991, cert. in nursing edn., 1993, postgrad., 1994—. ACLS. Charge nurse, med.-surg. ICU Milford (Del.) Meml. Hosp.; clin. instr. Wesley Coll., Del. Tech. and Community Coll., Dover; critical care per-diem nurse Med. Ctr. Del., Newark; instr. nursing Del. State U., Dover, 1991-95, asst. prof., 1995—; part-time staff nurse med. ICU Med. Ctr. of Del., Newark; apptd. rev. bd. Del. Medicaid Drug Utilization Rev. Bd., 1993—; mem. Del. Bd. Nursing Practice Adv. Com., 1994—. Contbr. chpt. to book. Mem. ANA (rev. panelist ANA continuing edn. ind. study 1995—), AACCN (southeastern Pa. chpt.), AAUW, Assn. Black Nursing Faculty, Del. Nurses Assn. (chmn. nursing practice com. 1992, Del. Nurse of Yr. 1993), Inst. Constituent Mems. in Nursing Practice, Sigma Theta Tau, Chi Eta Phi. Home: 336 Pine Valley Rd Dover DE 19904-7113

WISNICKI, JEFFREY LEONARD, plastic surgeon; b. N.Y.C., May 15, 1957; s. Joseph and Lorraine (Justman) W. BS summa cum laude, Rensselaer Poly. Inst., 1976; MD cum laude with honors, Union U., 1980. Diplomate Am. Bd. Plastic Surgery. Intern in surgery Stanford (Calif.) U. Med. Ctr., 1980-81, resident in gen., plastic and reconstructive surgery, 1981-84, chief resident in plastic and reconstructive surgery, 1985-86; fellow in plastic and reconstructive surgery Dartmouth-Hitchcock Med. Ctr., Hanover, N.H., 1984; active staff Good Samaritan Hosp., West Palm Beach, Fla., 1986—, Wellington Regional Hosp., West Palm Beach, 1986—; chief divsn. plastic surgery John F. Kennedy Meml. Hosp., West Palm Beach, 1990-93; chmn. dept. surgery Palms West Hosp., West Palm Beach, 1991-93, chief med. staff, 1994—; chief divsn. of plastic surgery Good Samaritan and St. Mary's Hosp., West Palm Beach, 1997—; clin. instr. surgery U. Calif., San Francisco, 1985; bd. dirs. Interplast, 1985-86, clin. faculty, 1986—; presenter in field. Contbr. chpts. to books and articles to profl. jours. Fellow ACS; mem. Am. Soc. Plastic & Reconstructive Surgeons, Alpha Omega Alpha. Office: 2047 Palm Beach Lakes Blvd West Palm Beach FL 33409-6501

WISNIEWSKI, HENRYK MIROSLAW, pathology and neuropathology educator, research facility administrator, research scientist; b. Luszkowko, Poland, Feb. 27, 1931; came to U.S., 1966; s. Alexander and Ewa (Korthals) W.; m. Krystyna Wylon, Feb. 14, 1954; children: Alexander (dec.), Thomas. MD, Med. Sch., Gdansk, Poland, 1955, DSc (hon.), 1991; PhD in Exptl. Neuropathology, Med. Sch., Warsaw, Poland, 1960; DSc (hon.), Coll. of S.I., 1992, Med. Sch., Poznan, Poland, 1996. From asst. to assoc. prof., head. lab. exptl. neuropathology, assoc. dir. Inst. Neuropathology Polish Acad. Sci., Warsaw, 1958-66; rsch. assoc., from asst. prof. to prof. Albert Einstein Coll. Medicine, N.Y.C., 1966-75; dir. MRC Demyelinating Diseases Unit, Newcastle upon Tyne, Eng., 1974-76; prof. neuropathology SUNY Health Sci. Ctr., Bklyn., 1976—; dir. N.Y. State Inst. Basic Rsch. in Devel. Disabilities, S.I., 1976—; vis. neuropathologist U. Toronto, Ont., Can., 1961-62; vis. scientist Lab. of Neuropathology Nat. Inst. Neurol. and Communicative Diseases and Stroke, NIH, 1962-63; docent Med. Sch., Warsaw, 1965; past mem. Neuology B study sect. NIH; past mem. mental retardation rsch. com. Nat. Inst. Child Health and Human Devel. Mem. editl. bd. Acta Neuropathologica, Jour. Neuropathology and Exptl. Neurology, Devel. Neurosci., Internat. Jour. Geriatric Psychiatry, Alzheimer Disease and Assoc. Disorders Internat. Jour., Brain Dysfunction, Dementia, Jour. Neural Transmission-Dementia Sect., Amyloid: Internat. Jour. Exp. and Clin. Investigation; mem. editl. adv. bd. Neurobiology of Aging; contbr. over 645 articles to profl. jours. and symposia procs. Decorated Officer's Cross (Poland); recipient N.Y.C. chpt. award Assn. for Help of Retarded Children, 1984, Welfare League award letchworth Village chpt. Assn. for Help of Retarded Children, 1985, Staten Island Chpt. award Benevolent Soc. for Retarded Children, 1986, Alfred Jurzkowski Found. award in neurobiology, 1996; named Career Scientist, Health Rsch. Coun. of City of N.Y., Neuropathologist of 20th Century, XI Internat. Congress Neuropathologists, 1990. Fellow AAAS; mem. Am. Assn. Neuropathologists (pres. 1984, Weil award 1969, Moore award 1972), British Soc. Neuropathology, Can. Assn. Neuropathologists, Am. Assn. Retarded Citizens, Assn. Rsch. in Nervous and Mental Disease, Am. Assn. Mental Deficiency, Internat. Soc. Devel. Neuroscis., Soc. Exptl. Neuropathology, World Fedn. Neurology, Sigma Xi. Roman Catholic. Achievements include research of developmental disabilities, aging, Alzheimer disease, Down syndrome, amyloidosis, neuronal fibrous protein pathology; demyelinating diseases. Office: NY State Inst Basic Rsch Devel Disabilities 1050 Forest Hill Rd Staten Island NY 10314-6330

WISNIEWSKI, JOHN WILLIAM, mining engineer, bank engineering executive; b. Portage, Pa., Jan. 22, 1932; s. John and Agnes (Ease) W.; m. Joan Smith, Aug. 24, 1957; children: John Andrew, Jean Marie, Maria. BS in Mining Engring., U. Pitts., 1954, postgrad., 1967-68. Mining engr. Bethlehem Mines Corp., Johnstown, Pa., 1956-61, Fairmont, W.Va., 1961-62; mining and gen. engr. IRS, Pitts., 1962-69; mining engr., then coordinating engr. IRS, Washington, 1969-72, supervisory gen. engr., chief rsch., planning and studies sect., 1972-76; mining engr., then dep. chief engr. Export-Import Bank U.S., Washington, 1976-82, chief engr., 1982, v.p. engring., 1982-94; v.p. engring. and environ. div., 1994-95, ret., 1995. With U.S. Army, 1954-56; Korea. AIME scholar U. Pitts., 1950. Home: 9308 Ironhorse Ln Gaithersburg MD 20879-2161

WISNIEWSKI, ROBERT JUDE, publishing company sales and marketing executive; b. Milw., Dec. 9, 1950; s. Boleslaw T. and Dolores F. (Bzdawka) W.; m. Rebecca M. Meyhoff, Apr. 16, 1977. BA, U. Wis., Milw., 1973. Dist. mgr. Trade Press Pub. Co., Milw., 1973-85, nat. sales mgr., 1985-88, dir. sales and mktg., 1988—, pres. pub., 1988. Bd. dirs. Gt. Lakes Hemophilia Found., Milw., 1987—. Mem. Sales and Mktg. Execs. (bd. dirs. Milw. 1988—). Office: Trade Press Pub Corp 2100 W Florist Ave Milwaukee WI 53209-3721

WISNIEWSKI, STEPHEN ADAM, professional football player; b. Rutland, Vt., Apr. 7, 1967. Student, Pa. State U. Offensive guard L.A. Raiders, 1989—. Named All-Pro Team Guard by Sporting News, 1990-93, Coll. All-Am. Team, 1987, 88. Played in Pro Bowl, 1990-91, 93. Office: L A Raiders 1220 Harbor Bay Pkwy Alameda CA 94502-6501*

WISNIEWSKI, THOMAS JOSEPH, music educator; b. Chgo., Sept. 17, 1926; s. George Wisniewski and Rose (Jelewski) W.; children: Dieter, Lisa Ann, Ericka. B.Mus., Am. Conservatory of Music, Chgo., 1948; M.Mus., No. Ill. U., 1964. Instr. string instrument Sch. Dist. 89, Maywood, Ill., 1950-55; orch. dir. Sch. Dist. 44, Lombard, Ill., 1955-67; dir. orchs. Glenbard East High Sch., Lombard, 1959-67; prof. music U. Ill., Urbana, 1967-94, emeritus prof., 1994—, chair music edn. div., 1988-92; music cons. Webster Internat. Illustrated Dictionary, 1993. Prodr. films Playing the String Bass, 1967, Playing the Cello, 1968; developer (with Rodney Mueller) computer software program Visualized Vibrato, 1995. Author: Learning Unlimited String Program, Vol. 1, 1975, Vol. 2, 1976; editor Orch. Publs., 1990; music editor Webster International Illustrated Dictionary, 1994. Mem. Am. String Tchrs. Assn. Assn. (Disting. Svc. award Ill. unit 1991, Disting. Svc. award Tenn. unit 1993), Ill. Music Educators Assn. (Pres.'s award 1996), Music Educators Nat. Conf., Ill. String Tchrs. Assn. (editor 1967, 87, pres. 1970), Nat. Jazz Educators Assn. (nat. orch. chmn. 1976), Pi Kappa Lambda, Phi Mu Alpha. Office: U Ill 1114 W Nevada St Urbana IL 61801

WISOTSKY, SERGE SIDOROVICH, SR., engineering executive; b. Chelsea, Mass., Oct. 19, 1919; s. Sidor Radionovich and Anna Epatiovna (Fariba) W.; m. Marion Ellen Ramsdell, Aug. 10, 1952; children: Serge S. Jr. (dec.), Tanya Lloyd, Stephan, John and Alexander (twins), Phillip. Student, Boston Trade Sch., 1933-37, Lowell Inst. Sch., 1937-43; BS in Physics, MIT, 1950; MS in Physics, Brown U., 1952. Registered profl. mech. engr., Mass., Okla.; lic. electrician, Mass. Elec. motor mech./armature winder United Motors Corp., Boston, 1937-40; machinist apprentice, mfg. methods, steam turbine test GE River Works, Lynn, Mass., 1940-44; engr. R & D Ultrasonics Corp., Cambridge, Mass., 1952-53; instrument engr. Control Engring. Corp., Canton and Norwood, Mass., 1953-57; staff engr. MIT/Draper Lab., Cambridge, Mass., 1957-59; hydroacoustic transducer sect. head Raytheon/Submarine Signal Divsn., Portsmouth, R.I., 1959-70; MSR engr. Raytheon Equipment Divsn. North Dighton, Mass. and Kwajalein Atoll, 1958; v.p. engring. ORB Inc., Sharon, Mass. and Tulsa, 1970—; chief engr. Indsl. Vehicles, Internat., (geophys. prospecting vehicles using VIBROSEIS, worldwide), Tulsa, 1974-84; cons. Amoco Prodn. Rsch. Ctr. (geophys. prospecting sound sources), Tulsa, 1985-86, 93. Contbr. articles to profl. jours. including Jour. Underwater Acoustics, Jour. Geophys. Rsch., Jour. Inst. Navigation, ONR, Jour. Acoustical Soc. Am., Offshore Tech. Conf., Soc. Exptl. Geophys., Sea Tech.; appeared on Dave Garroway's morning TV show, 1953. Brass band clarinetist Stoughton VFW, 1937-42, Bklyn. Armed Guard Ctr., 1945, Brockton Cosmopolitan, 1951-65, Aleppo Shrine, 1965—, Lawrence Colonial, 1989—, Canton/Am. Legion, 1992—. With USNR, 1944-46. Mem. ASME, Acoustical Soc. Am., Am. Soc. Materials, Soc. Exploration Geophysicists (life), Masons. Russian Orthodox, Congregationalist and Baptist. Achievements include patents for Electro/Syn Pressure Gauge, Electro-HydroSonic Transducer, 6 Water Hammer Piledrivers, and WastePile, also numerous foreign patents. Home and Office: PO Box 422 89 Bullard St Sharon MA 02067-1007

WISS, MARCIA A., lawyer; b. Columbus, Ohio, May 15, 1947; d. John William and Margaret Ann (Cook) W.; m. Donald Gordon MacDonald, Nov. 18, 1921; children: Christopher C. Wiss, Joan Merle. BS in Fgn. Svc., Georgetown U., 1969, JD, 1972. Bar: D.C. 1972. Econ. analyst World Bank, Washington, 1969; atty. U.S. Dept. Justice, Washington, 1972-73; atty. office gen. counsel Overseas Pvt. Investment Corp., Washington, 1973-78; assoc. Stroock & Stroock & Lavan, Washington, 1978-79; gen counsel-designate Inst. for Sci. and Tech. Cooperation, Washington, 1979; affiliate Curtis, Mallet-Prevost, Colt & Mosle, Washington, 1979-80; ptnr. Anderson & Pendleton, Chartered Attys., Washington, 1980-87, Kaplan Russin & Vecchi, Washington, 1987-92, Whitman & Ransom, 1992-93, Whitman, Breed, Abbott & Morgan, Washington, 1993—; gen. counsel Washington chpt., Soc. Internat. Devel., 1980—; gen. counsel, Assn. for Women in Devel., 1982—; bd. advisers, Procedural Aspects of Internat. Law Inst., 1985—. editor Georgetown Law Ctr. Jour. Law and Policy in Internat. Bus., 1971-72. Chairperson Holy Trinity Parish Coun., Washington, 1976; mem. bd. advisers Trees for Life, Wichita, Kans., 1984—. Mem. Am. Fedn. Govt. Employees (chmn. 1975-76), D.C. Bar (steering com. divsn. 12, 1985-88, co-chmn. fin. and banking com. 1985), Am. Soc. Internat. Law (v.p. 1991-94, coun. 1987-90), Washington Fgn. Law Soc. (pres. 1983-84). Roman Catholic. Office: Wilmer Cutler & Pickering 2445 M St NW Washington DC 20037-1435

WISSBRUN, KURT FALKE, chemist, consultant; b. Brackwede, Westphalia, Germany, Mar. 19, 1930; came to the U.S., 1939; s. Hermann and Bertha (Falke) W. BS, U. Pa., 1952; PhD, Yale U., 1956. Rsch. chemist Hoechst-Celanese (formerly Celanese Corp.), Summit, N.J., 1957-60; group leader Hoechst-Celanese, Summit, N.J., 1960-62; rsch. assoc. Hoerst-Celanese (formerly Celanese Corp.), Summit, N.J., 1966-70, sr. rsch. assoc., 1970-90; polymer cons. Summit, 1990—. Author: Melt Rheology and Plastics Processing, 1989, (with others) Blow Molding Handbook, 1988; contbr. articles to profl. jours.; patentee, inventor in field. Mem. Am. Chem. Soc., Soc. Rheology (pres. 1995-97, Bingham medal 1992), British Soc. Rheology, Sigma Xi. Jewish. Avocations: golf, opera, travel. Home: 1 Euclid Ave Apt 4E Summit NJ 07901-2164

WISSNER, GARY CHARLES, motion picture art director, production designer; b. N.Y.C., Feb. 9, 1964; s. Sidney and Penina (Gologor) W.; m. Tambre Hemstreet, Nov. 13, 1993. BFA, NYU, 1986. Scenic artist Cape Code Melody Tent, Hyannas, Mass., 1983; prodn. technician Imero Fiorentino Assocs., N.Y.C., 1984-86; asst. scenic designer Radio City Music Hall, N.Y.C., 1986; art dir. MTV Networks, N.Y.C., 1987-88; asst. art dir. Country Music Awards, L.A., 1987; asst. art dir. TV show Young and the Restless, L.A., 1987; asst. art dir. Patty Hearst Atlantic Entertainment, L.A., 1987. Art dir.: (commls.) Chrysler, Laser Tag, Michelob, (theme parks/indsls.) Tomorrowland, 1990, Korean World Expo, 1991, AT&T Futurecom, 1993, (TV) Road to Daytona (MTV segment), 1987, Superbowl in San Diego (MTV spl.), 1988, Family of Spies (CBS mini-series), 1989, In Living Color, 1991, (feature films) Teenage Mutant Ninja Turtles, 1989, Another 48 Hours, 1990, Hoffa, 1992, Wyatt Earp, 1993, Junior, 1994, Seven, 1995; prodn. designer: (comml.) Balance Health Foods, 1993, (television) Millenium, 1996, (feature film) Stephen King's Graveyard Shift, 1990, Last Man Standing, 1995, Steel, 1996, Frosty, 1997, I Know What You Did, 1997; asst. art dir. feature films Warlock, 1988, The Abyss, 1988. Mem. Acad. Motion Picture Arts and Scis. (voting mem.), Soc. Motion Picture Art Dirs. (voting mem.), United Scenic Artists (voting mem.). Avocations: computers, sculpture, sports, fitness. Office: care Art Directors Guild 11365 Ventura Blvd Ste 315 Studio City CA 91604-3148

WIST, ABUND OTTOKAR, biomedical engineer, radiation physicist, educator; b. Vienna, Austria, May 23, 1926; s. Engelbert Johannes and Augusta Barbara (Ungewitter) W.; m. Suzanne Gregson Smiley, Nov. 30, 1963; children: John Joseph, Abund Charles. BS in Engring., Tech U. Graz, 1947; MEd, U. Vienna, 1950, PhD in Theoretical Physics, 1951. Research and devel. engr. Hornyphon AG, Vienna, 1952-54, Siemens & Halske AG, Munich, Germany, 1954-58; dir. research and devel. Brinkman Instruments Co., Westbury, N.Y., 1958-64; sr. scientist Fisher Sci. Inc., Pitts., 1964-69; mem. faculty U. Pitts., 1970-73; asst. prof. computer sci. Va. Commonwealth U., 1973-76, asst. prof. biophysics, 1976-82, asst. prof. physiology and biophysics, 1982-84, asst. prof. radiology, 1984-92, adj. prof. radiology, 1992-95; radiation safety specialist Bur. Radiol. Health, Va. Dept. Health, Richmond; pres. CEO, Inn Tech Inc., Richmond Va., 1995—; founder, gen. chmn. Symposium Computer Applications in Med. Care, Washington, 1977-79, chmn. Biomedical Optics Conf., Clin. Application of Modern Imaging Tech. I and II, L.A., 1993, 94; session chmn., lectr. European Radiology Conf., Vienna, 1993, Advanced Laser Dentistry Conf., St. Petersburg, Russia, 1994; session chmn., lectr. Biomedical Optics Europe Conf., Lille, France, 1994; invited speaker, session chmn., co-chmn. poster session Internat. Conf. Light and Biol. Systems, Wroclaw, Poland, 1995; lectr. and session chmn. BIOS Europe 95 Conf., Barcelona, Spain, 1995; lectr. 5th European Congresson Dental and Maxillofacial Radiology, Cologne, Germany, 1995; pres. Inntech, Inc., 1985—. Author: Electronic Design of Microprocessor Based Instrumentation and Control Systems, 1986; contbr. numerous articles and chpts. to profl. jours. and books; patentee in electronic and lab. instrumentation (10). NASA/Am. Soc. Engring. Edn. faculty fellow, summer 1975; U.S. biomed. engring. del. People's Republic China, 1987, 93, Russia, 1993; lectr. in field; bd. regents Liberty U., Lynchburg, Va., 1991—. Mem. AAAS, IEEE (sr., sec. cen. Va., vice chmn. Richmond sect.), ASTM, SPIE (editor proceedings, 1993, 94), N.Y. Acad. Scis., Am. Coll. Radiology (assoc.), Richmond Computer Club (founder, pres. 1977-79), Biomed. Engring. Soc., Am. Assn. Physics in Medicine, Sigma Xi. Roman Catholic. Home: 9304 Farmington Dr Richmond VA 23229-5336 Office: Med Coll Va/VCA 1101 E Marshall St Richmond VA 23298-5008

WISTISEN, MARTIN J., agricultural business executive; b. Bancroft, Idaho, May 30, 1938; s. Raoul and Cora (Johnson) W.; m. Katherine Callister, Dec. 28, 1960; children: Kevin, Diane, Kaeleen, Janette, Richard, Michelle, R. Brent, N. Greg. BS, Brigham Young U., 1962; MBA, Northwestern U., 1964; PhD, Columbia U., 1976. Fin. analyst Esso Internat., Inc., N.Y.C., 1964-65; dir. fin. analysis, mgr. econ. analysis TWA, N.Y.C., 1967-70; dir. bus. and econs., prof. bus. mgmt. and bus. econs., dir. MBA program, asst. dean Grad. Sch. Mgmt. Brigham Young U., Provo, Utah, 1971-80; v.p. sales and mktg. U & I, Inc., Kennewick, Wash., 1980-82; exec. v.p., chief oper. officer UI Group, Kennewick, 1982-86; pres., chief exec. officer AgriNorthwest, Kennewick, 1986—. Pres. Blue Mountain Coun. Boy Scouts Am., Kennewick, 1987-89, 96—; bd. dirs. Wash. State Potato Commn., Moses Lake, 1990-93; mem. strategy commn. Wash. State Energy Adv. Bd., 1991-92. Mem. Assn. Wash. Bus. (bd. dirs. 1987—), Tri City Cmty. Hosp. Physician Orgn. (pres. 1995—), Beta Gamma Sigma, Phi Kappa Phi. Republican. Mem. LDS Ch. Office: AgriNorthwest 2810 W Clearwater Ave Kennewick WA 99336-2963

WISWALL, FRANK LAWRENCE, JR., lawyer, educator; b. Albany, N.Y., Sept. 21, 1939; s. Frank Lawrence and Clara Elizabeth (Chapman) W.; m. Elizabeth Curtiss Nelson, Aug. 9, 1975; children by previous marriage: Anne W. Kowalski, Frank Lawrence III. BA, Colby Coll., 1962; JD, Cornell U.,

1965; PhD in Law, Cambridge U., 1967. Bar: Maine 1965, N.Y. 1968, U.S. Supreme Ct. 1968, D.C. 1975; lic. master near coastal steam and motor vessels, 1960—. Assoc. Burlingham, Underwood, Barron, Wright & White, N.Y.C., 1967-73; maritime legal adviser Rep. of Liberia, 1968-88; mem. legal com. Internat. Maritime Orgn., London, 1972-74, vice chmn. 1974-79, chmn., 1980-84; tutorial supr. internat. law Clare Coll., Cambridge, Eng., 1966-67; vis. lectr. Cornell Law Sch., 1969-76, 82; lectr. U. Va. Law Sch. and Ctr. for Oceans Law and Policy, 1978-82; prof. law Cornell U., 1984; Johnsen prof. maritime law Tulane U., 1985; adj. prof. law World Maritime U., Malmo, Sweden, 1986—; prof. Internat. Maritime Law Inst., Malta, 1991—, mem. governing bd., 1992—; prof. admiralty law Maine Maritime Acad., 1993-94; del. Internat. Conf. Marine Pollution, London, 1973; del., chmn. drafting com. Internat. Conf. Carriage of Passengers and Luggage by Sea, Athens, 1974; del. Internat. Conf. on Safety of Life at Sea, London, 1974, 3d UN Conf. on Law of Sea, Caracas, Venezuela, 1974, 3d UN Conf. on Law of Sea (all subsequent sessions); del., chmn. com. final clauses Internat. Conf. on Limitation of Liability for Maritime Claims, London, 1976; del. UN Conf. Carriage of Goods by Sea, Hamburg, 1978, XIII Diplomatic Conf. on Maritime Law, Brussels, 1979; chmn. com. of the whole Internat. Conf. Carriage of Hazardous Substances by Sea, 1984; del. internat. conf. on Maritime Terrorism, Rome, 1988; counsel various marine casualty bds. of investigation, 1970—, harbormaster, Port of Castine, 1960-62. Author: The Development of Admiralty Jurisdiction and Practice Since 1800, 1970; editor-in-chief Benedict on Admiralty, Vols. 6, 6A-6C (treaties and convs.), 1992—; contbr. articles to profl. jours. Ofcl. prin. Diocese of Mid-Atlantic States, Anglican Cath. Ch., 1988—, chancellor Missionary Diocese of N.E., 1993—; spkr. assembly laity Anglican Cath. Ch., 1995—. Recipient Yorke prize U. Cambridge, 1968-69. Fellow Royal Hist. Soc.; mem. Nat. Lawyers Assn., Titulaire of the Comité Maritime Internat. (exec. councillor 1989—), Maritime Law Assn. U.S. (chmn. com. on intergovtl. orgns. 1983-87, chmn. com. on CMI 1987-95), Ecclesiastical Law Soc., Selden Soc., Am. Soc. Legal History, U.K. Assn. Average Adjusters, U.S. Assn. Average Adjusters, Maine Bar Assn., Assn. Bar City N.Y., U.S. Navy League (pres. Penobscot coun. 1997), United Oxford and Cambridge U. Club (London), Century Assn., Alpha Delta Phi, Phi Delta Phi. Office: PO Box 201 Castine ME 04421-0201

WIT, DANIEL, international consultant; b. N.Y.C., June 8, 1923; s. Benjamin and Stella (Bloom) W.; m. Phyllis J. Citron, June 15, 1947; children: Pamela S., Frederick W. AB, Union Coll., N.Y., 1943; postgrad., Yale U. Italian program, Paris, 1943-44, Inst. d'Etudes Politiques, Paris, 1945-46; AM, Princeton U., 1948, PhD, 1950. Mem. dept. polit. sci. Ohio State U., 1948-50, U. Cin., 1950-54, U. Mich., 1954-56, Ind. U., 1956-58; mem. dept. polit. sci. George Washington U., 1959-61; head dept. polit. sci. No. Ill. U., Dekalb, 1961-69; dir. internat. programs No. Ill. U., 1969-77, dean internat. and spl. programs, 1977-92, acting v.p., provost, 1986-87; internat. mgmt. cons., 1992—; co-dir. Ctr. S.E. Asian Studies and Tng., 1962-69; Fulbright prof. pub. adminstrn., master's degree dir. Inst. social Studies, The Hague, The Netherlands, 1966-67; vis. prof. pub. adminstrn., adv. Ind. U.-ICA program, Thailand, 1956-58; dir. internat. studies Govtl. Affairs Inst., Washington, 1959-61; project dir. Thai Labor Law and Practice, 1960, Brazailan Labor-A Mgmt. Survey, 1960, Indonesian Labor-A Mgmt. Survey, 1961; cons. tng. program Peace Corps S.E. Asia, Thai Dept. Interior; prof. fgn. affairs Nat. War Coll., 1963-64. Author: Comparative Political Institutions, 1953, A Comparative Survey of Local Government and Administration, 1958, Local Government in Thailand, 1958, Manpower Problems in Southeast Asia, 1960, Labor Conditions in Thailand, 1960, Labor Law and Practice in Thailand, 1964, Thailand: Another Vietnam?, 1968; co-author: Our American Government and Political System, 1972, 77, 82; contbr. articles to profl. jours. Inst. Am. Univs. fellow, France, 1981. Mem. Am. Polit. Sci. Assn. (nat. coun. 1967-69), Phi Beta Kappa. Home: 222 Fairmont Dr De Kalb IL 60115-2332

WIT, DAVID EDMUND, software and test preparation company executive; b. N.Y.C., Feb. 25, 1962; s. Harold Maurice W. and Joan Leta (Rosenthal) Sovern; m. Kathleen Mary Bentley, Sept. 9, 1989. BA summa cum laude, Hamilton Coll., 1985. Rsch. assoc. E.M. Warburg Pincus and Co., N.Y.C., 1985-86; CEO Logicat Inc., N.Y.C., 1986—; bd. dirs. Calif. Energy Co., Omaha, 1987—. Mem. N.Y. Software Industry Assn., Phi Beta Kappa. Avocation: running. Home: 3 Stratford Rd Larchmont NY 10538-1341 Office: Logicat Inc 201 E 16th St New York NY 10003-3706

WIT, HAROLD MAURICE, investment banker, lawyer, investor; b. Boston, Sept. 6, 1928; s. Maurice and Martha (Bassist) W.; m. Judith Haworth, Apr. 1989; children from previous marriage: David Edmund, Hannah Edna. A.B. magna cum laude, Harvard, 1949; J.D. (editor law jour.), Yale, 1954. Bar: N.Y. 1954. Assoc. Cravath, Swaine & Moore, N.Y.C., 1954-58; asst. sec. One William St. Fund, Inc., N.Y.C., 1958-59; v.p., sec. One William St. Fund, Inc., 1959-60; assoc. Allen & Co., 1960-70; assoc Allen & Co., Inc., 1965—, v.p., 1965-70, exec. v.p., 1970—, mng. dir., mem. exec. com.; dir., mem. exec. com., chmn. audit com., Toys-R-Us, Inc.; dir. Allen Investments, Inc. Trustee The Nature Conservancy, South Folk-Shelter Island chpt.; co-founder Group for South Fork; mem. Panel on Future of Govt. in N.Y., 1979-80; mem. vis. coms. Harvard U. Div. Sch.; mem. nat. adv. bd. Project on Being with Dying Upaya Found. With Mass. N.G., 1947-50; lt. (j.g.) USNR, 1951-53, Korea. Mem. VFW, Am. Legion, Korean War Vets. Assn., University Club (N.Y.C.), Harvard Club (N.Y.C.), Phi Beta Kappa, Phi Delta Phi. Home: 150 E 69th St New York NY 10021-5704 also: 57 Cross Hwy PO Box 348 East Hampton NY 11937 Office: Allen & Co Inc 711 5th Ave New York NY 10022-3111

WITCHER, DANIEL DOUGHERTY, retired pharmaceutical company executive; b. Atlanta, May 17, 1924; s. Julius Gordon and Myrtice Eleanor (Daniel) W.; divorced; children: Beth S., Daniel Dougherty Jr., J. Wright, Benjamin G.; m. Betty Lou Middaugh, Oct. 30, 1982. Student, Mercer U., 1946-47, Am. Grad. Sch. Internat. Mgmt., 1949-50. Regional dir. Sterling Drug Co., Rio de Janeiro and Sao Paulo, Brazil, 1951-56; gen. mgr. Mead Johnson & Co., Sao Paulo, 1956-60; area mgr. Upjohn Internat., Inc., Sao Paulo, 1960-64; v.p. Upjohn Internat., Inc., Kalamazoo, 1964-70, group v.p., 1970-73; pres., gen. mgr. Upjohn Internat., 1973-86; v.p. Upjohn Co., 1973-86, sr. v.p., 1986-89, asst. to pres., 1988-89; chmn. Upjohn Healthcare Svcs., 1982-87; ret., 1989; bd. dirs. Upjohn Co.; trustee Am. Grad. Sch. Internat. Mgmt., 1981—. With USNR, 1943-46. Mem. Pharm. Mfrs. Assn. (chmn. internat. sect. 1981-82, 85-86), Am. Grad. Sch. Internat. Mgmt. Alumni Assn. (pres. 1989-91). Republican. Episcopalian. Avocations: tennis, golf.

WITCHER, GARY ROYAL, minister, educator; b. Clinton, Okla., July 4, 1950; s. Alton Gale and Frances Loraine (Royal) W.; m. Victoria Amy Waddington, June 6, 1970; children: Jessica, Toni, Monica. BA in Art, Southwestern Okla. State U., 1973, BA in Art Edn., 1975, MEd in Art, 1978. Minister, 1979. Tchr. Window Rock Sch. Dist., Ft. Defiance, Ariz., 1973-76, Western Heights (Okla.) Sch. Dist., Oklahoma City, 1976-77, Mustang (Okla.) Sch. Dist., 1977-79; minister Ch. of Christ, Cervignano, Italy, 1979-86, Watertown, S.D., 1986—; instr. Harmony Hill Coll., Watertown, 1987—; part-time tchr. Watertown Sch. Dist., 1987—; bd. dirs. East River Bible Camp, 1988—. Recipient 1st Place Slide Program Competition prize Am. Fedn. Mineralogical Socs., 1993, 95. Mem. Coteau des Plains Gem and Mineral Soc. (pres. 1991-92, 95). Republican. Avocations: photography, car restoration, collecting rocks, coins and stamps. Home: PO Box 1622 1105 4th St NE Watertown SD 57201 Office: Ch of Christ 1103 4th St NE Watertown SD 57201-1202

WITCHER, ROBERT CAMPBELL, bishop; b. New Orleans, Oct. 5, 1926; s. Charles Swanson and Lily Sebastian (Campbell) W.; m. Elisabeth Alice Cole, June 4, 1957; 2 children. BA, Tulane U., 1949; MDiv, Seabury-Western Theol. Sem., 1952, DD, 1974; MA, La. State U., 1960, PhD, 1968; DCL (hon.), Nashotah House, 1989. Ordained priest Episc. Ch., 1953; consecrated bishop, 1975. Priest-in-charge St. Andrew Ch., Linton, La. and St. Patrick Ch., Zachary, La., 1953-56; priest-in-charge St. Augustine Ch., Baton Rouge, La., 1953-54; rector St. Augustine Ch., 1954-61; canon pastor Christ Ch. Cathedral, New Orleans, 1961-62; rector St. James Ch., Baton Rouge, 1962-75; coadjutor bishop L.I., 1975-77; bishop, 1977-91; prof. ch. history Mercer Sch. Theology, 1975-91; interim bishop of Armed Forces, 1989-90; bishop in residence Baton Rouge, New Orleans, 1991-92; pres. Mercer Scholarship Fund; trustee Ch. Pension Fund, 1991-92; pres. bd. trustees estate belonging to Diocese of L.I., 1975-91; pres. Anglican Soc. N.Am., 1980-83; chmn. pastoral com. House of Bishops, 1980-90, Com. to Revise Title III, 1980-90; chmn. Com. on Developing Guidelines for Theol. Edn.; cons. Episc. Health Fund L.I.; historiographer Diocese of La. Author: The Episcopal Church in Louisiana, 1801-1861. Trustee U. of South, 1963-69, Seabury-Western Theol. Sem., 1963-82, Gen. Theol. Sem., 1979-88, Ch. Pension Fund, 1985-91, Bch. Reins. Corp.; pres. Episc. Health Svcs.; bd. dirs. Nat. Coun. Alcoholism, L.I. Coun. Alcoholism, Alcohol and Drug Abuse Coun., Baton Rouge, St. Mary's Hosp. for Children, Baton Rouge Green, La. Urban Forestry Coun., United Way; bd. dirs., trustee St. James Place; active NCCJ (Baton Rouge chpt.). Capt. USNR, ret. Mem. N.Y. State Coun. Chs., L.I. Coun. Chs. (com. social justice), Am. Legion, Mil. Order of World Wars, Naval Res. Assn., Res. Officers Assn. Address: 1934 Steele Blvd Baton Rouge LA 70808-1673

WITCOFF, SHELDON WILLIAM, lawyer; b. Washington, July 10, 1925; s. Joseph and Zina (Ceppos) W.; m. Margot Gail Hoffner, Sept. 6, 1953; children: Lauren Jill, David Lawrence, Lisa Ann, Julie Beth. B.S. in Elec. Engring, U. Md., 1949; J.D., George Washington U., 1953. Bar: D.C. 1953, N.Y. 1955, Ill. 1956. Patent examiner Patent Office, Dept. Commerce, 1949-53; patent lawyer Bell Telephone Labs., Murray Hill, N.J., 1953-55; ptnr. Bair, Freeman & Molinare, Chgo., 1955-69, Allegretti, Newitt, Witcoff & McAndrews, Chgo., 1970-88, Allegretti & Witcoff, LTD, Chgo., 1988-95, Banner & Witcoff Ltd., Chgo., 1995—; v.p. Art Splty. Co., Chgo., 1967—; v.p. Caspian Fur Trading Co., N.Y.C.; dir. Child Abuse Unit for Studies, Edn. and Svcs., Chgo. Fire and police commr., Skokie, Ill., 1960-63. Served with USNR, 1943-46. Mem. Am. Bar Assn., Bar Assn. 7th Circuit, Intellectual Property Assn. of Chgo., Order of Coif, Tau Epsilon Phi, Phi Delta Phi., B'nai B'rith. Home: 235 Maple Hill Rd Glencoe IL 60022-1257 Office: 10 S Wacker Dr Chicago IL 60606-7407

WITCOVER, JULES JOSEPH, newspaper columnist, author; b. Union City, N.J., July 16, 1927; s. Samuel and Sarah (Carpenter) W.; m. Marian Laverty, June 14, 1952 (div. Oct. 1990); children: Paul, Amy, Julie, Peter; m. Marion Elizabeth Rodgers, June 21, 1997. AB, Columbia Coll., 1949, MS in Journalism, 1951. Reporter Hackensack (N.J.) Star-Telegram, 1949-50, Providence Jour., 1951-52, Newark Star-Ledger, 1953, Washington br. Newhouse Newspapers, 1954-69, L.A. Times, Washington, 1970-72, Washington Post, 1973-76; columnist Washington Star and Tribune Media Svcs., 1977-81, Balt. Sun, Washington, 1981—. Author: 85 Days: The Last Campaign of Robert Kennedy, 1969, The Resurrection of Richard Nixon, 1970, White Knight: The Rise of Spiro Agnew, 1972, (with Richard M. Cohen) A Heartbeat Away: The Investigation and Resignation of Vice President Spiro T. Agnew, 1974, Marathon: The Pursuit of the Presidency, 1972-76, 1977, (novel) The Main Chance, 1978, (with Jack W. Germond) Blue Smoke and Mirrors: How Reagan Won and Why Carter Lost the Election of 1980, 1981, (with Germond) Wake Us When It's Over: Presidential Politics of 1984, 1985, (with Germond) Whose Broad Stripes and Bright Stars?: The Trivial Pursuit of the Presidency 1988, 1989, Sabotage at Black Tom: Imperial Germany's Secret War in America, 1914-1917, 1989, Crapshoot: Rolling the Dice on the Vice Presidency, 1992, (with Germond) Mad as Hell: Revolt at the Ballot Box 1992, 1993, The Year the Dream Died: Revisiting 1968 in America, 1997. With USN, 1945-46. Recipient Washington Corr. award Sigma Delta Chi, 1963, Alumni award Columbia Grad. Sch. Journalism, 1972; Reid Found. fellow, Europe, 1958. Roman Catholic. Home: 3042 Q St NW Washington DC 20007-3080 Office: Washington Bur Balt Sun 1627 K St NW Washington DC 20006-1702

WITEK, JAMES EUGENE, public relations executive; b. LaPorte, Ind., Sept. 14, 1932; s. Stanley and Victoria (Peret) W.; m. Mary Carolyn Hood, June 18, 1955; children: James Jay, Janet Marie, Jeffrey Patrick, Jean Theresa. A.B., Ind. U., 1954; M.A., U. Mo., 1970. Joined U.S. Army, 1954, commd. 2d lt., 1954, advanced through grades to lt. col., 1968; editor, pub. Infantry Mag., Fort Benning, Ga., 1968-70; advisor to Vietnamese Mil. Region IV Ranger Comdr., 1970-71; plans officer CINCPAC, Hawaii, 1971-75; exec. editor Soldiers, Washington, 1975-77; editor in chief Soldiers, 1977-79; dir. public affairs Nat. Com. for Employer Support Guard and Res., Arlington, Va., 1979-82, ret., 1982; dep. dir. pub. relations Am. Legion, Washington, 1982-86; mgr. pub. rels. Dowty Aerospace, Sterling, Va., 1986—. Decorated Legion of Merit, Bronze Star, Air Medal, Purple Heart, Vietnamese Cross of Gallantry with Silver Star. Mem. Assn. U.S. Army, Am. Legion, Ret. Officers Assn., Phi Beta Kappa, Tau Kappa Alpha, Pi Kappa Phi. Roman Catholic. Home: 3240 Atlanta St Fairfax VA 22030-2128 Office: Dowty Aerospace PO Box 5000 Sterling VA 20167-1050

WITH, GERDA BECKER, artist; b. Hamburg, Germany, Mar. 4, 1910; came to U.S., 1939; d. Ludwig and Martha (De Bruycker) Becker; m. Karl E. With, July 17, 1939 (dec. Dec. 1980); children: Christopher B., Nela W. Dwyer. M in Decorative Arts, Charlottenburg, Berlin, 1938. One woman shows include Otis Art Inst., Mus. St. Barbara, also pvt. galleries throughout Europe and U.S., 1958—; illustrator: (book) The Man Who Stole the Word "Beautiful", 1991, others. Avocations: reading, traveling, friends and family. Home: 3045 Kelton Ave Los Angeles CA 90034-3021

WITHERELL, MICHAEL S., physics educator; b. Toledo, Sept. 22, 1949; s. Thomas W. and Marie (Savage) W.; m. Elizabeth Hall. BS, U. Mich., 1968; MS, U. Wis., 1970, PhD, 1973. Instr. Princeton (N.J.) U., 1973-75, asst. prof., 1975-81; asst. prof. U. Calif., Santa Barbara, 1981-83, assoc. prof., 1983-86, prof., 1986—; chmn. physics adv. com. Fermi Nat. Accelerator Lab., Batavia, Ill., 1987-89; mem. high energy physics adv. panel U.S. Dept. Energy, Washington, 1990-93; chmn. sci. policy com. Stanford Linear Accelerator Ctr., 1995—. Guggenheim fellow John S. Guggenheim Found., 1988; recipient W. K. H. Panofsky prize Am. Phys. Soc., 1990. Fellow AAAS. Office: U Calif Dept Physics Santa Barbara CA 93106

WITHERINGTON, JENNIFER LEE, sales and marketing executive; b. Albuquerque, Sept. 8, 1960; d. Terrence Lee and Pamela Ann (Hoerter) W. BA in Polit. Sci., James Madison U., 1982. Asst. press sec. U.S. Senate, Washington, 1983-85; nat. sales mgr. Madison Hotels, Washington, 1986-88; dir. sales Madison Air Charter Svcs., Washington, 1987-88; nat. sales mgr. Ritz-Carlton Hotels, Palm Springs, Calif., 1988-90; dir. sales and mktg. Cappa and Graham, Inc., San Francisco, 1990-95; gen. mgr. USA Hosts, San Francisco, 1995—; spkr. in field. Contbr. articles to profl. jours. Vol. San Francisco Emergency Rescue Team, Yerba Buena Ctr. for Arts. Mem. Am. Soc. Assn. Execs., Soc. Incentive Travel Execs., Hospitality Sales and Mktg. Assn. Internat. (pres. San Francisco chpt. 1994—), Meeting Profls. Internat. Republican. Roman Catholic. Avocations: golf, gourmet food. Home: 1565 Green St Apt 304 San Francisco CA 94123-5129 Office: USA Hosts 177 Post St Ste 550 San Francisco CA 94108-4700

WITHEROW, JIMMIE DAVID, secondary school educator; b. Dalton, Ga., Nov. 13, 1961; s. Jimmie W. and Jimmie Lou (Nixon) W. BA in English, Emory U., 1983; MEd in Secondary Edn., Ga. State U., 1989. Cert. English tchr., Ga. Tchr. SE Whitfield High Sch., Whitfield County Bd. Edn., Dalton, 1983-92, Murray County High Sch., Chatsworth, Ga., 1992—. Contbr. article to profl. jour. Mem. NEA, Nat. Coun. Tchrs. English, Ga. Edn. Assn., Ga. Coun. Tchrs. English, Kappa Delta Pi. Home: PO Box 891 Chatsworth GA 30705-0891

WITHERS, HUBERT RODNEY, radiotherapist, radiobiologist, educator; b. Queensland, Australia, Sept. 21, 1932; came to the U.S., 1966; s. Hubert and Gertrude Ethel (Tremayne) W.; m. Janet Macfie, Oct. 9, 1959; 1 child, Genevieve. MBBS, U. Queensland, Brisbane, Australia, 1956; PhD, U. London, 1965, DSc, 1982. Bd. cert. Ednl. Coun. for Fgn. Med. Grads. Intern Royal Brisbane (Australia) and Associated Hosps., 1957; resident in radiotherapy and pathology Queensland Radium Inst. and Royal Brisbane (Australia) Hosp., 1958-63; Univ. Queensland Gaggin fellow Gray Lab., Mt. Vernon Hosp., Northwood, Middlesex, Eng., 1963-65, Royal Brisbane (Australia) Hosp., 1966; radiotherapist Prince of Wales Hosp., Randwick, Sydney, Australia, 1966; vis. rsch. scientist Lab. Physiology, Nat. Cancer Inst., Bethesda, Md., 1966-68; assoc. prof. radiotherapy sect. exptl. radiotherapy U. Tex. Sys. Cancer Ctr. M.D. Anderson Hosp. & Tumor Inst., Houston, 1968-71; prof. radiotherapy, chief sect. sect. exptl. radiotherapy U. Tex. Sys. Cancer Ctr. M.D. Anderson Hsop. & Tumor Inst., Houston, 1971-80; prof. dir. exptl. radiation oncology dept. radiation oncology UCLA, 1980-89, prof., vice-chair dir. exptl. radiation oncology dept. radiation oncology, 1991-94, Am. Cancer Soc. Clin. Rsch. prof. dept. radiation oncology, 1992—, interim dir. Jonsson Comprehensive Cancer Ctr., 1994-95, chmn. radiation oncology, 1994—; assoc. grad. faculty U. Tex., Grad. Sch. Biomed. Scis, Houston, 1969-73, mem. grad. faculty, 1973-80; prof. dept. radiotherapy Med. Sch., U. Tex. Health Sci. Ctr., Houston, U. Tex. Med. Sch., Houston, 1975-80; prof., dir. Inst. Oncology, The Prince of Wales Hosp., U. NSW, Sydney, Australia, 1989-91; mem. com. mortality mil. pers. present-at-atmosphere tests of nuclear weapons Inst. Medicine, 1993-94; mem. radiation effects rsch. bd. NRC, 1993—; mem. com. neutron dose reporting Internat. Commn. Radiation Units and Measurements, 1982—, mem. report com. clin. dosimetry for neutrons, 1993—; mem. task force non-stochastic effects radiation Internat. Com. Radiation Protection, 1980-84, mem. com. 1, 1993—; mem. radiobiology com. Radiation Therapy Oncology Group, 1979—, mem. dose-time com., 1980-89, mem. gastroenterology com., 1982-89; mem. edn. bd. Royal Australian Coll. Radiology, 1989-91; mem. cancer rsch. coord. com. U. Calif., 1991-97, mem. standing curriculum com. UCLA biomed. physics grad. program, 1993—; cons. exptl. radiotherapy U. Tex. System Cancer Ctr., 1980—. Mem. Am. editl. bd.: Internat. Jour. Radiat. Oncol. Biol. Phys., 1982-89, 91—, internat. editl. bd., 1989-91; cons. editor: The European Jour. Cancer, 1990-95; editl. bd. dirs.: Endocurietherapy/Hyperthermia Oncology, 1991—, Radiation Oncology Investigations, 1992—; assoc. editor: Cancer Rsch., 1993-94, editl. bd. 1995-97. Mem. Kettering selection com. Gen. Motors Cancer Rsch. Found., 1988-89, chmn., 1989, awards assembly, 1990-94. Recipient Medicine prize Polish Acad. Sci., 1989, Second H.S. Kaplan Disting. Scientist award Internat. Assn. for Radiation Rsch., 1991, Gray medal Internat. Commn. Radiation Units, 1995U.S. Dept. Energy Fermi award 1997, Am. Radium Soc. Janeway medal, 1994, A,/ Soc. Therapeutic Radiology, Oncolody Gold medal, 1991, Radiation Rsch. Soc. Failla award, 1988); named Gilbert H. Fletcher lectr. U. Tex. Sys. Cancer Ctr., 1989, Clifford Ash lectr. Ont. Cancer Inst., Princess Margaret Hosp., 1987, Erskine lectr. Radiol. Soc. N.Am., 1988, Ruvelson lectr. U. Minn., 1988, Milford Schultz lectr. Mass. Gen. Hosp., 1989, Del Regato Found. lectr. Hahnemann U., 1990, Bruce Cain Meml. lectr. New Zealand Soc. Oncology, 1990, others. Fellow Royal Australasian Coll. Radiologists (bd. cert.), Am. Coll. Radiology (bd. cert. therapeutic radiology, adv. com. patterns of care study 1988—, radiation oncology advisory group 1993-97, others), Am. Radium Soc. (mem. and credential c om. 1986-89, 93-94, treas. 1993-94, pres.-elect 1995-96, pres. 1996-97, others), Am. Soc. Therapeutic Radiology and Oncology (awards com. 1993, publs. com. 1993-97, vice chair Publs. Commn., 1996-98, keynote address 1990, , others); mem. Nat. Cancer Inst. (various ad-hoc rev. coms. 1970—, radiation sudy sect. 1971-75, cons. U.S.-Japan Coop. Study high LET Radiotherapy 1975-77, cancer rsch. emphasis grant rev. com. 1976, clin. cancer ctr. rev. com. 1976-79, toxicology working group 1977-78, reviewer outstanding investigator grants 1984-93, bd. sci. counselors, 1986-88), Nat. Cancer Inst. Can. (adv. com. rsch. 1992-95), Pacific N.W. Radiol. Soc. (hon.), Tex. Radiol. Soc. (hon.), So. Calif. Radiation Oncology Soc. (sec., treas., 1992-94, pres. 1996-97), European Soc. Therapeutic Radiology an d Oncology (hon.), Polish Oncology Soc. (hon.) Austrian Radiation Oncology Soc. (hon.), Phila. Roentgen Ray Soc. (hon.), Radiation Rsch. Soc. (pres. 1982-83, honors and awards com. 1984-88, ad hoc com. funds utilization 1987-89, adv. com. Radiation Rsch. Jour., 1988—). Office: UCLA Med Ctr 10833 Le Conte Ave Los Angeles CA 90095-3075

WITHERS, RAMSEY MUIR, government consultant, former government official; b. Toronto, Ont., Can., July 28, 1930; s. William Muir and Alice Smith Hope (Hannah) W.; m. Jean Alison Saunders, May 8, 1954; children—James Scott, Leslie Susan, Deidre Ann. BSc, Royal Mil. Coll. Can., Kingston, Ont., 1952, DEng (hon.), 1994; BSc in Elec. Engring., Queen's U., Kingston, 1954; D Mil. Sci. honoris causa, Royal Roads Mil. Coll., Victoria, B.C., 1992. Registered profl. engr., Ont. Commd. officer Can. Army, 1948, advanced through grades to gen., 1980; sta. in Can., Republic of Korea, Fed. Republic of Germany and U.K., 1952-76; comdr. Can. Forces Europe, Fed. Republic of Germany, 1976-77; vice chief def. staff Can. Forces, 1977-80, chief def. staff, 1980-83, ret., 1983; dep. minister transport Dept. of Transp., Ottawa, Ont., 1983-88; pres., chief oper. officer Govt. Cons. Internat., Ottawa, 1988-93; dir. Can. Inst. Strategic Studies, 1990-96, ATS Aerospace Inc., 1993-97; chmn. Industry Govt. Rels. Group Inc. (IGRG Inc.), Ottawa, 1993—. V.p., sec. nat. coun. Boy Scouts Can., 1977-84, internat. commr., 1985-90, hon. v.p., 1990—; chmn. Can. War Mus. Com., 1988-95; trustee Can. Mus. Civilization, 1990-95; elected mem. Queen's U. Coun., Kingston, 1997—. Decorated comdr. Order of Mil. Merit, comdr. Order of St. John, Can. Forces Decoration with two bars; Georgian Coll. fellow, 1987; recipient Outstanding Achievement Pub. Svc. award, 1986, Silver Wolf award Boy Scouts Can., 1990, Alumni Achievement award Queen's U., Kingston, 1995. Mem. Assn. Profl. Engrs. Ont., Rideau Club. Avocations: boating; cycling. Home: 150 Waverly St Apt 2C, Ottawa, ON Canada K2P OV4

WITHERS, W. RUSSELL, JR., broadcast executive; b. Cape Girardeau, Mo., Dec. 10, 1936; s. Waldo Russell Sr. and Dorothy Ruth (Harrelson) W.; 1 child, Dana Ruth. BA, S.E. Mo. State U., 1958. Disc jockey Sta. KGMO Radio, Cape Girardeau, 1955-58; account exec. Sta. WGGH Radio, Marion, Ill., 1961-62; v.p. LIN Broadcasting Corp., Nashville, 1962-69; exec. v.p., dir. Laser Link Corp., Woodbury, N.Y., 1970-72; owner Withers Broadcasting of Hawaii, 1975-79, Withers Broadcasting of Minn., 1974-79, Withers Broadcasting Cos., Iowa, 1981—, Mood Music Ill., Mt. Vernon, 1973—, Mood Music, Inc., Cape Girardeau, 1972—, Royal Hawaiian Radio Co., Inc., others; owner various radio and TV stas., including KREX-TV, Grand Junction, Colo., KREY-TV, Montrose, Colo., KREG-TV, Glenwood Springs, Colo., KREZ-TV, Durango, Colo., KAVU-TV, Victoria, Tex., Page Ins. and Real Estate, Mt. Vernon, Ill.; chmn. bd., CEO Withers Beverage Corp., Mobile Ala., 1973-79; chmn. adv. bd. Mut. Network; bd. dirs. Theatrevision, Inc., Turneffe Island Lodge, Ltd., Belize, Sta. WDTV, Clarksburg, W.Va., WMIX-AM-TV, Mt. Vernon, KGMO-KAPE, Cape Girardeau, KOKX AM-FM, Keokuk, Iowa, KTRC, Santa Fe, KNAL, Victoria, KMPL and KBXB, Sikeston, Mo., KVSF, Santa Fe, KBOM-FM, Santa Fe; pres. Ill. Pub. Airports assn.; co-chmn. TARPAC. Bd. dirs., chmn. bd. Mt. Vernon Tourism and Conv. Bur.; chmn. Mt. Vernon Airport Authority; bd. regents Lincoln Acad. With U.S. Army, 1957-58. Mem. Mt. Vernon C. of C. (bd. dirs.), Nat. Assn. Broadcasters, Ill. Broadcasters Assn., Stadium Club, Mo. Athletic Club, Elks, Moose, AmVets, Masons, Shriners, Sigma Chi. Christian Scientist. Home: 1 Sleepy Hollow Ln Mount Vernon IL 62864-2852 Office: PO Box 1508 Mount Vernon IL 62864-1508

WITHERSPOON, CAROLYN BRACK, lawyer; b. Little Rock, Mar. 29, 1950; d. Gordon Paisley and Mildred Louise (Lemon) Brack; m. Joseph Roger Armbrust, July 25, 1970 (div. 1976); 1 child, Catherine Paisley; m. John Leslie Witherspoon, June 15, 1979. Student, U. Ark., 1968-70, So. Meth. U., 1970; BA, U. Ark., 1974, JD with honors, 1978. Bar: Ark. 1978, U.S. Dist. Ct. (ea. and we. dists) Ark. 1978, U.S. Ct. Appeals (8th cir.) 1979, U.S. Supreme Ct. 1981. Asst. atty. City of Little Rock, 1978, chief dep. atty., acting city atty., 1984-85; assoc. House, Wallace & Jewell, Little Rock, 1985-87, ptnr., 1987-90; dir. McGlinchey Stafford Lang, Little Rock, 1990-97, Cross, Dunter, Witherspoon & Galchus, 1997—; mem. com. Fed. Ct. Practice, 1988-91, Ark. Supreme Ct. Civil Practice Com., 1989—; chair adv. com. Civil Justice Reform Act, 1993-95. Contbr. articles to profl. jours. Commr. Ark. Real Estate Commn., 1978-81; past chmn. Little Rock Housing Authority Bd. of Comm., past pres., bd. dirs. Advs. for Battered Women; past bd. dirs., pub. rels. chmn. LWV; past pres. Ark. Women's History Inst. Recipient Am. Jurisprudence labor law award, 1977. Fellow Am. Bar Found.; mem. ABA (EEO com.), Am. Law Inst., Nat. Conf. Bar Pres. (exec. coun. 1996—), Transp. Lawyers Assn., Ark. Bar Assn. (pres. 1995-96, Golden Gavel award 1989, 93, Ark. Inst. for Continuing Legal Edn. award 1991), Ark. Assn. Women Lawyers (pres. 1982-83), Pulaski County Bar Assn. (pres. 1989-90), Nat. Inst. Mcpl. Law Officers (state chmn. 1985-87, v.p. 1987-89), William R. Overton Inn of Ct. (pres. 1992-93). Avocations: hunting, fishing, reading, traveling. Office: McGlinchey Stafford Lang 500 E Markham St # 200 Little Rock AR 72201-1756

WITHERSPOON, JAMES DONALD, biology educator; b. Springfield, Mo., Dec. 19, 1933; s. Harry H. and Lucy Catherine (Applegate) W.; m. Rebecca Jane Hutto, Jan. 24, 1958; children: Sarah Jane, John Edward. BS, Purdue U., 1955, MS, 1960, PhD, 1963. From instr. to asst. prof. biology Western Md. Coll., Westminster, 1960-68; assoc. prof. Southwestern at Memphis Coll., 1968-76; free-lance writer Phoenix, 1976-82; adj. prof. Grand Canyon Coll., Phoenix, 1982-84, prof., 1984—, chmn. dept. scis., 1985-92, acting chmn. dept. math. and computer scis., 1988-89; coord. allied health Grand Canyon U. (formerly Grand Canyon Coll.), Phoenix, 1992-94, assoc.

dean Coll. Sci. and Applied Health, 1994—; cons. Doubleday & Co., Garden City, N.Y., 1960-62, Narco Bio-Sys., Houston, 1972-76; assoc. coord. med. edn. S.W. Kirksville Coll. Osteo. Medicine, 1990-94; leader Am. tchr.: Eszterhazy Karoly Tchrs. Tng. Coll., Hungary, summers 1991-93, Vilnius Pedagogical Univ., Lithuania, summer 1995-97. Author: The Functions of Life, 1970, Human Physiology, 1984, From Field to Lab, 1993; co-author: The Living Laboratory, 1960; co-author numerous tapes and computer programs, 1973-87. Grantee Grass Found., 1962-72, Ariz. Commn. for Postsecondary Edn., 1985-87. Mem. AAAS, Am. Inst. Biol. Scis., Ariz. Alliance for Sci., Maths. and Tech. Edn. (bd. dirs. 1986-88), Sigma Xi. Republican. Presbyterian. Achievements include rsch. on relation of hypoxia to body temperature, innovative methods for biological education. Home: 17122 E Grande Blvd Fountain Hills AZ 85268-3224 Office: Grand Canyon U 3300 W Camelback Rd Phoenix AZ 85017-3030

WITHERSPOON, JOHN KNOX, JR., investment banking executive; b. Chattanooga, May 3, 1928; s. John Knox and Helen (Newell) W.; m. Norma Cofer, Sept. 28, 1957; children: Laura, Alice, Mark, Eric, Cary, Clay. BA, Princeton U., 1950. CLU. Pension analyst Provident Life and Accident Ins. Co., Chattanooga, 1953-57, asst. mgr. pension div., 1957-60, agy. sec., 1960-64, asst. v.p., 1964-69, v.p., 1969-84, sr. v.p., 1984-90; mng. dir. Crownpoint Fin. Group, Chattanooga, 1990-92; v.p. Porter, White & Co., Inc., Chattanooga, 1993—. Chmn. Hamilton County Bd. Edn., Chattanooga, 1984-85; pres. Met. Council Community Services, Chattanooga, 1977; v.p. Family and Children's Services, Chattanooga, 1978-80. Served as cpl. U.S. Army, Korea. Mem. Am. Soc. CLUs, Assn. for Corp. Growth, Phi Beta Kappa. Republican. Presbyterian. Lodge: Kiwanis. Office: Porter White & Co 651 E 4th St Ste 100 Chattanooga TN 37403-1912

WITHERSPOON, WILLIAM, investment economist; b. St. Louis, Nov. 21, 1909; s. William Conner and Mary Louise (Houston) W.; student Washington U. Evening Sch., 1928-47; m. Margaret Telford Johanson, June 25, 1938; children: James Tomlin, Jane Telford, Elizabeth Witherspoon Vodra. Rsch. dept. A. G. Edwards & Sons, 1928-31; pres. Witherspoon Investment Co., 1931-34; head rsch. dept. Newhard Cook & Co., 1934-43; chief price analysis St. Louis Ordnance Dist., 1943-45; head rsch. dept. Newhard Cook & Co., 1945-53; owner Witherspoon Investment Counsel, 1953-64; ltd. ptnr. Newhard Cook & Co., economist, investment analyst, 1965-68; v.p. rsch. Stifel, Nicolaus & Co., 1968-81; lectr. on investments Washington U., 1948-67. Mem. Clayton Bd. of Edn., 1955-68, treas., 1956-68, pres., 1966-67; mem. Clayton Park and Recreation Commn., 1959-60; trustee Ednl. TV, KETC, 1963-64; mem. investment com. Gen. Assembly Mission Bd. Presbyn. Ch. (USA), Atlanta, 1976-79, mem. permanent com. ordination exams, 1979-85; cons. to investment com. Ctr. Theol. Inquiry, Princeton, N.J., 1995—. Served as civilian Ordnance Dept., AUS, 1943-45. Chartered fin. analyst. Mem. St. Louis Soc. Fin. Analysts (pres. 1949-50). Club: Mo. Athletic (St. Louis). Home: 6401 Ellenwood Ave Saint Louis MO 63105-2228 *Many of the current social and ethical problems of today might be partially resolved if theology would be influenced by the 4th dimension of spacetime plus the 5th dimension of the mind, the 6th dimension of the spirit and the 7th dimension of God the Father.*

WITHERSPOON, W(ILLIAM) TOM, engineering consultant; b. Dallas, Feb. 1, 1949; s. Vernon H. and Mary Witherspoon; m. Sandra Stein, July 10, 1970; children: Mary Jac, Stephen. BSCE, So. Meth. U., 1971; MS in Mgmt. and Adminstrv. Sci., U. Tex., Dallas, 1979. Registered profl. engr., Tex. Field engr. Robert E. McKee Constrn., 1972-73; supt. Batson Cook County, 1973-77; project mgr. Rucker Constrn. Co., 1977-81; v.p. Wynn Oil Co., 1981-85; pres. Sandco Petroleum Corp., 1985; pres. S & W Found. Contractors, Richardson, Tex., 1986—, pres., soil dr., 1992—; speaker in field. Contbr. articles to profl. jours.; patentee in field. Deacon Ch. of Christ. Recipient Gold medal Masters Pan Am. Championship; named 5-time Tex. State Weightlifting Champion. Mem. ASCE, Am. Soc. Petroleum Engrs., Am. Soc. Petroleum Geologists, Tex. Found. Repair Soc. (pres., exec. dir. 1997), Found. Repair Assn. Tex., North Tex. Weightlifting Assn. (pres.), Internat. Assn. Found. Drillers (bd. dirs.). Office: 1030 E Belt Line Rd Richardson TX 75081-3703

WITHROW, LUCILLE MONNOT, nursing home administrator; b. Alliance, Ohio, July 28, 1923; d. Charles Edward Monnot and Freda Aldine (Guy) Monnot Cameron; m. Alvin Robert Withrow, June 6, 1945 (dec. 1984); children: Cindi Withrow Johnson, Nancy Withrow Townley, Sharon Withrow Hodgkins, Wendel Alvin. AA in Health Adminstrn., Eastfield Coll., 1976. Lic. nursing home adminstr., Tex.; cert. nursing home ombudsman. Held various clerical positions Dallas, 1950-72; office mgr., asst. adminstr. Christian Care Ctr. Nursing Home, Mesquite, Tex., 1972-76; head adminstr. Christian Care Ctr. Nursing Home and Retirement Complex, Mesquite, 1976-91; nursing home ombudsman Tex. Dept. Aging and Tex. Dept. Health, Dallas, 1991-93; legal asst. Law Offices of Wendel A. Withrow, Carrollton, Tex., 1993—; mem. con. on geriatric curriculum devel. Eastfield Coll., Mesquite, 1979, 87; mem. ombudsman adv. com. Sr. Citizens Greater Dallas; nursing home cons.; notary pub., 1995—. Vol. Dallas Arboretum and Bot. Soc., Dallas Summer Musicals Guild; mem. Ombudsman adv. com. Sr. Citizens of Greater Dallas, Health Svcs. Speakers Bur.; charter mem. Stage Show Prodns. Recipient Volunteerism awards Tex. Atty. Gen., 1987, Tex. Gov., 1992. Mem. Tex. Assn. Homes for Aging, Am. Assn. Homes for Aging, Health Svcs. Speakers Bur., White Rock Kiwanis. Republican. Mem. Ch. of Christ. Avocations: reading, travel, theater. Home: 11344 Lippitt Ave Dallas TX 75218-1922 Office: Law Office of W A Withrow 1120 Metrocrest Dr Ste 200 Carrollton TX 75006-5787

WITHROW, MARY ELLEN, treasurer of United States; b. Marion, Ohio, Oct. 2, 1930; d. Clyde Welsh and Mildred (Stump) Hinamon; m. Norman David Withrow, Sept. 4, 1948; children: Linda Rizzo, Leslie Legge, Norma, Rebecca Gooding. Mem. Elgin Local Bd. Edn., Marion, Ohio, 1969-73, pres., 1972; safety programs dir. ARC, Marion, 1968-72; dep. registrar State of Ohio, Marion, 1972-75; dep. county auditor Marion County, Ohio, 1975-77, county treas., 1977-83; treas. State of Ohio, Columbus, 1983-94; treas. of the U.S. Dept. Treasury, Washington, 1994—; chmn. Ohio Bd. Deposits, 1983—, Anthony Commn. on Pub. Fin. Mem. exec. com. Ohio Dem. Com., mem. exec. com. women's caucus; mem. Dem. Nat. Com.; mem. Met. Women's Ctr.; pres. Marion County Dem. Club, 1976; participant Harvard U. Strategic Leadership Conf., 1990.; mem. Dem. Leadership Coun. Recipient Donald L. Scantlebury Meml. award, 1991, Women of Achievement award YWCA of Met. Columbus, 1993, Outstanding Govt. Svc. award Am. Numis. Assn., 1995; inducted Ohio Women's Hall of Fame, 1986; named Outstanding Elected Dem. Woman Holding Pub. Office, Nat. Fedn. Dem. Women, 1987, Advocate of Yr., SBA, 1988, Most Valuable State Pub. Ofcl., City and State newspaper, 1990; Women Execs. in State Govt. fellow Harvard U., 1987. Mem. LWV (dem. leadership coun.), State Assn. County Treas. (legis. com. 1979-83, treas. 1982), Nat. Assn. State Treas. (pres. 1992, Jesse Unruh award 1993, chair long range planning com., mem. exec. com.), Nat. Assn. State Auditors Comtps. and Treas. (pres. 1990, strategic planning com., intergov. rels. com., chair state and mcpl. bonds com.), Coun. State Govts. (exec. com., internat. affairs com., orgnl. planning and coord. com., strategic planning task force), Women Execs. in State Govt. (chair fund devel. com.), Altrusa Bus. and Profl. Women's Club (hon.), Delta Kappa Gamma (hon.), Delta Sigma Pi (hon.). Club: Bus. and Profl. Women's. Office: Dept Treasury 1500 Pennsylvania Ave NW Washington DC 20005-1007

WITHROW, WILLIAM N., JR., lawyer; b. Toccoa, Ga., June 26, 1954. BA magna cum laude, U. Ga., 1975, JD magna cum laude, 1978. Bar: Ga. 1978. Law clk. to Hon. James C. Hill U.S. Ct. Appeals, 5th Cir., 1978-79; ptnr. Troutman Sanders, Atlanta. Mem. ABA, State Bar Ga., Atlanta Bar Assn. Office: Troutman Sanders 5200 NationsBank Pla 600 Peachtree St NE Atlanta GA 30308-2214

WITHUHN, WILLIAM LAWRENCE, museum curator, railroad economics and management consultant; b. Portland, Oreg., Aug. 12, 1941; s. Vernon Lawrence and Ruth Eleanor (Ferguson) W.; m. Gail Joy Hartman, Nov. 22, 1964; children: James, Thomas, Harold. BA, U. Calif.-Berkeley, 1963; MBA with distinction, Cornell U., 1977, MA, 1980. Commd. regular 2d lt. USAF, 1963, advanced through grades to capt., 1967; indsl. engr., asst. dir. manpower and orgn. USAF, Travis AFB, Calif., 1964-65; global, polar, tactical, and instr. navigator worldwide USAF, 1965-72; spl. ops. navigator USAF, Vietnam; select lead navigator Mil. Airlift Command USAF, 1970-72; ret., 1972; intern, then staff asst. U.S. Ho. of Reps., 1973-74; v.p. Va. & Md. R.R. Co., Cape Charles, Va., 1977-81, Md. & Del. R.R., Federalsburg, Md., 1977-81; sr. v.p. Ont. Midland R.R., Ont. Cent. R.R., Sodus, N.Y., 1979-83; v.p. Rail Mgmt. Svcs., Inc., Syracuse, N.Y., 1979-83, RSA Leasing Co., Syracuse, 1980-83; exec. v.p. Am. Coal Enterprises, Inc., Akron, Ohio, 1980-82; v.p., gen. mgr. Allegheny So. Ry., Martinsburg, Pa., 1982-83; acting dir. R.R. Mus. of Pa., 1982-83; curator transp. Nat. Mus. Am. History Smithsonian Inst., Washington, 1983—, dep. chmn. dept. sci. and tech., 1984-91, spl. asst. to dir., 1990-94; bd. dirs., chmn. The Waring Group Inc., Transp. Cons., Salisbury, Md., 1983-89; cons. Nat. Pk. Svc., Pa. Hist. Soc. & Mus. Commn., Expo 2000, Germany, Fed. Railroad Admnstrn., Nat. Transp. Safety Bd. Author: Spirit of Steam, 1995; editor, co-author: Rails Across America, 1993; contbr. articles to profl. jours. Decorated D.F.C. with cluster, Bronze Star, Air medal with 12 clusters, Antarctic Svc. medal; De Karman fellow, 1979-80, Smithsonian fellow, 1980-81; recipient Golden Apple award Nat. Ednl. Film Festival, 1996. Mem. Am. Inst. Indsl. Engrs., Soc. for History of Tech., Ry. and Locomotive Hist. Soc. (dir., v.p.), Internat. Assn. Ry. Operating Officers, Cornell Club Washington, Theta Chi. Office: Nat Mus Am History Smithsonian Inst Rm 5010 Washington DC 20560

WITIAK, DONALD THEODORE, medicinal chemistry educator; b. Milw., Nov. 16, 1935; s. Theodore and Elvi (Dahlbacka) W.; m. Deanne Beth Knapton, Dec. 16, 1958; children—Mark Donald, Elizabeth Jane. B.S. in Pharmacy, U. Wis.-Madison, 1958, postgrad., 1959-60, Ph.D. in Medicinal Chemistry, 1961; postgrad., U. Kans., 1960-61. Asst. prof. U. Iowa, Iowa City, 1961-66, assoc. prof., 1966-67; assoc. prof. Ohio State U., Columbus, 1967-71, prof. medicinal chemistry, 1971-93, chmn. div. medicinal chemistry, 1973-82, dir. basic rsch. univ. Comprehensive Cancer Ctr., 1987-93, prof. emeritus, 1993—; prof. med. chemistry U. Wis., Madison, 1993—, Dean Sch. Pharmacy, 1993-95; mem. study sect. NIH, 1980-83; U.S. rep. to provisional sect. com. Internat. Union Pure and Applied Chemistry, 1986-88; mem. Can. Govt. internat. multidisciplinary peer-rev. com. for networks of Ctr. Excellence; mem. drug. devel., hematology and pathology study sect. Am. Cancer Soc., 1995—. Editor: Calcium Regulation, 1982, Antilipidemic Drugs Medicinal, Chemical and Biochemical Aspects, vol. 17, 1991; assoc. editor Current Medicinal Chemistry, 1995; mem. editl. bd. Jour. Medicinal Chemistry, 1971-75, European Jour. Med. Chemistry, 1986—, Pharmacochemistry Libr., 1987—; assoc. editor Current Medicinal Chemistry, 1994—; contbr. numerous articles to profl. jours., chpts. to books; holder 15 patents in field. Mem. Columbus Biotech. Adv. Com., 1985, Columbus Tech. Roundtable, 1983. Served with USNR, 1955-63. Recipient Kimberly prof. rsch. award, 1985, Apha Found./Acad. Pharm. Scis. Rsch. Achievement award, 1985, Taito O. Soine Meml. award U. Minn., 1988, Thirty-First Annual Bergg award Sch. Pharmacy Rho Chi Soc., W. Va. U., 1994; grantee NIH 1971—, EPA, 1984—. Fellow Am. Pharm. Assn., Acad. Pharm. Scis., Am. Assn. Pharm. Scis.; mem. Am. Chem. Soc. (com. nomenclature 1984-85, chmn. com. to rev. Jour. Medicinal Chemistry 1983, councilor div. med. chem. 1990-92), Am. Cancer Soc. (supported rsch. com. Ohio div. 1988, bd. dirs. 1991-93). Home: 3046 Bosshard Dr Madison WI 53711-5860 Office: U Wis 425 N Charter St Madison WI 53706-1508

WITKE, DAVID RODNEY, newspaper editor; b. Council Bluffs, Iowa, Mar. 24, 1937; s. Arnold and Rosamond Louise (Storer) W.; m. Priscilla Bill Smith, Oct. 8, 1960; 1 son, Carl. B.S. in Journalism, Northwestern U., 1959. Reporter, editor The Courier, Champaign-Urbana, Ill., 1962-66; copy editor The Register, Des Moines, 1966-70, city editor, 1970-73, asst. mng. editor adminstrn., 1973-74, asst. mng. editor electronics, 1974-75, mng. editor, 1975-83, dir. ops., 1983-85, dep. editor, ombudsman, 1985-87, exec. sports editor, 1987—; rep. Iowa Freedom of Info. Coun., Des Moines, 1973—, pres., 1986-88; vis. lectr. Drake U., 1986—, Iowa State U., 1990—; juror Pulitzer Prize, 1989-91. Served to lt. (j.g.) USN, 1959-62, PTO. Mem. Assoc. Press Mng. Editors Assn., Mid-Am. Newspaper Assn., AP Sports Editors Assn., The Prairie Club, Sigma Delta Chi. Unitarian. Home: 2521 48th Pl Des Moines IA 50310-2506 Office: Des Moines Register and Tribune Co 715 Locust St Des Moines IA 50309-3703

WITKIN, ERIC DOUGLAS, lawyer; b. Trenton, N.J., May 14, 1948; s. Nathan and Norma Shirley (Stein) W.; m. Regina Ann Bilotta, June 8, 1980; children: Daniel Robert, Sarah Ann. AB magna cum laude, Columbia U., 1969; JD, Harvard U., 1972. Bar: N.Y. 1973, D.C. 1989, U.S. Dist. Ct. (so. and ea. dists.) N.Y. 1974, U.S. Ct. Appeals (2d and D.C. cirs.) 1974, U.S. Supreme Ct. 1977, U.S. Dist. Ct. D.C. 1989. Assoc. Poletti, Freidin, Prashker & Gartner, N.Y.C., 1972-80, ptnr., 1980-85; sr. atty. labor Kaye, Scholer, Fierman, Hays & Handler, N.Y.C., 1985-88; of counsel Akin, Gump, Strauss, Hauer & Feld, Washington, 1988-90; counsel Benetar, Bernstein, Schair & Stein, N.Y.C., 1990—. treas., founder Property Owners Against Unfair Taxation, N.Y.C., 1983-90; trustee Temple Emanu-El of Westchester, 1996—. Lawrence Chamberlain scholar Columbia U., N.Y.C., 1968; recipient Alumni medal Alumni Fedn. Columbia U., 1982. Mem. ABA (labor and employment law sect.), N.Y. State Bar Assn. (labor and employment law sect., com. on equal employment opportunity law), Assn. of Bar of City of N.Y. (spl. com. on sex and law, com. on labor and employment law), Westchester County Bar Assn., Columbia Coll. Alumni Assn. (pres. 1988-90, bd. dirs. 1974—, Robert Lincoln Carey prize, Alumni prize 1969, Lions award 1990), Alumni Fedn. Columbia U. (alumni trustee nominating com. 1990-97, pres. 1997—), Am. Soc. Pers. Adminstrn. (contbr. monthly newsletter 1986-88), Soc. Human Resource Mgmt., Soc. Columbia Grads. (bd. dirs. 1994—), Phi Beta Kappa. Club: Harvard (N.Y.C.). Avocations: piano, sailing. Home: 103 Wendover Rd Rye NY 10580-1939 Office: Benetar Bernstein Schair & Stein 330 Madison Ave New York NY 10017-5001

WITKIN, EVELYN MAISEL, geneticist; b. N.Y.C., Mar. 9, 1921; d. Joseph and Mary (Levin) Maisel; m. Herman A. Witkin, July 9, 1943 (dec. July 1979); children—Joseph, Andrew. AB, NYU, 1941; MA, Columbia U., 1943, PhD, 1947; DSc honoris causa, N.Y. Med. Coll., 1978, Rutgers U., 1995. Mem. staff genetics dept. Carnegie Inst., Washington, 1950-55; mem. faculty State U. N.Y. Downstate Med. Center, Bklyn., 1955-71; prof. medicine State U. N.Y. Downstate Med. Center, 1968-71; prof. biol. scis. Douglass Coll., Rutgers U., 1971-79, Barbara McClintock prof. genetics, 1979-83; Barbara McClintock prof. genetics Waksman Inst. Microbiology, 1983-91; Barbara McClintock prof. emerita Waksman Inst. Microbiology, Rutgers U., 1991—. Author articles; mem. editorial bds. profl. jours. Postdoctoral fellow Am. Cancer Soc., 1947-49; fellow Carnegie Instn., 1957; Selman A. Waksman lectr., 1960; Phi Beta Kappa vis. scholar, 1980-81; grantee NIH, 1956-89; recipient Prix Charles Leopold Mayer French Acad. Scis., 1977, Lindback award, 1979. Fellow AAAS, Am. Acad. Microbiology; mem. NAS, Am. Acad. Arts and Scis., Environ. Mutagen Soc., Am. Genetics Soc., Am. Soc. Microbiology. Home: 1 Firestone Ct Princeton NJ 08540-5220 Office: Rutgers U Waksman Inst Microbiology Piscataway NJ 08854

WITKIN, ISAAC, sculptor; b. Johannesburg, South Africa, May 10, 1936; children: Tamar, Nadine. Student, St. Martin's Sch. Art, London, 1957-60. Asst. to Henry Moore, 1961-63; tchr. St. Martin's Sch. Art, London, 1963-65; artist in residence Bennington (Vt.) Coll., 1965-79; tchr. Parson's Sch. Design, N.Y.C., 1975-78; vis. prof. Middlebury Coll., Vt., 1981; mem. Yale U. Adv. Com. to the Art Sch., 1987-90; mem. Bennington Coll. Art Collection Com., 1987-91; bd. mem. Internat. Sculpture Ctr., 1990—. One-person shows include Hamilton Gallery Contemporary Art, N.Y.C., 1981, Mattingly Baker Gallery, Dallas, 1982, McIntosh/Drysdale Gallery, Washington, 1982, 1986, Hirschl & Adler Modern, N.Y.C., 1985, 1988, Jan Turner Gallery, L.A., Patricia Hamilton, N.Y.C., Locks Gallery, Phila., 1991, 93, Walker Hill Art Ctr., Seoul, Korea, 1992, others; exhibited in group shows at Hamilton Gallery, N.Y.C., 1981, Freeman Gallery, Albright Coll., 1982, Fuller Goldeen Gallery, San Francisco, 1982, The Berkshire Mus., Pittsfield, Mass., 1982, Washington Square Plaza, Washington, 1983, Wave Hill, Bronx, N.Y., 1983, Pratt Inst. Gallery, N.Y.C., 1984, Sonoma State U., Calif., 1984, N.J. State Mus., Trenton, 1984, Number One Penn Plaza, N.Y.C., 1984, Williams Coll. Mus. Art, Williamstown, Mass., 1984, N.J. Ctr. for the Visual Arts, Summit, 1987, Zone Arts Ctr., Springfield, Mass., 1988, James A. Michener Fine Arts Ctr., Doylestown, Pa., 1989, Robeson Ctr. Gallery, Rutgers U., Trenton, 1989, Locks Gallery, Phila., 1990-91, Robert Morrison Gallery, N.Y.C., 1993, Marc de Montebello Gallery, N.Y.C., 19995, Atlantic Found., Hamilton, N.J., 1995, Hunterdon Art Ctr., Clinton, N.J., 1995, others; represented in permanent collections Alcoa Co., Pitts., Am. Rep. Ins. Co., Des Moines, Arts Coun. Gt. Brit., London, Atlantic Found., Princeton, Carnegie Inst., Pitts., Chase Manhattan Bank, N.Y.C., CIGNA Corp., Phila., Columbus (Ohio) Mus. Fine Art, Denver (Colo.) Mus. Art, Fine Arts Mus., U. Sydney, Australia, MIT, Boston, Nat. Mus. Am. Art, Washington, numerous others. Recipient First prize Paris Biennale, 1965, Guggenheim fellowship, 1981; grantee N.J. State Coun. on the Arts, 1985, Adolph and Esther Gottlieb Found., 1994. Studio: 137 Scrapetown Rd Pemberton NJ 08068-1909*

WITKIN, JOEL-PETER, photographer; b. Bklyn., Sept. 13, 1939; s. Max and Mary (Pellegrino) W.; m. Cynthia Jean Bency, June 30, 1978; one child, Kersen Ahanu. B.F.A., Cooper Union, 1974; M.F.A., U. N.Mex., 1986; student (fellow), Columbia U., 1973-74. Artist in residence Zerybthia Rome, Italy, summer 1996; represented by Pace/McGill, N.Y.C., Fraenkel Gallery, San Francisco, Baudion Lebon Gallery, Paris; lectr. Am. Acad. Rome. Exhibited in Projects Studio One, N.Y.C., 1980, Galerie Texbraun, Paris, 1982, Kansas Ctiy Art Inst., 1983, Stedelijk Mus., Amsterdam, 1983, Fraenkel Gallery, 1983-84, 87, 91, 93, 95, 97, Pace Wilden-Stein MacGill Gallery, N.Y.C., 1983, 84, 87, 89, 91, 93, 95, 97, San Francisco Mus. Modern Art, 1985, Bklyn. Mus., 1986, Galerie Baudoin Lebon, Paris, 1987, 89, 91, 95, Centro de Arte Reina Sofia Mus., Madrid, 1988, Palais de Tokyo, Paris, 1989, Fahey/Klein Gallery, L.A., 1987, 89, 91, 97, Mus. Modern Art, Haifa, Israel, 1991, Photo Picture Space Gallery, Osaka, Japan, 1993, Guggenheim Mus., N.Y.C., 1995, Interkamera, Prague, 1995, Il Castello de Rivoli Mus., Turin, 1995, Encontros de Fotografia, Colombia, Portugal, 1996, Rencontres de la Photographie, Arles, France, 1996, Taipei Photo Gallery, Taiwan; group shows: Mus. Moder Art, N.Y.C., 1959, San Francisco Mus. Moder Art, 1981, Whitney Biennial, 1985, Palais de Tokyo, Paris, 1986, La Phorographie Contemporaine en France, 1996, Foto Masson, Goteberg, Sweden, 1997; represented in permanent collections, Mus. Modern Art, N.Y.C., San Francisco Mus. Modern Art, 1980, Nat. Gallery Art, Washington, Victoria and Albert Mus., London, George Eastman House, N.Y., The Getty Collection, Moder Museet, Stockholm, Sweden, Whitney Mus., N.Y.C., The Guggenheim Mus., N.Y.C., Tokyo Met. Mus. Photography; subject of monographs: Joel-Peter Witkin, 1985, 88-89, 91, 93, 95-96; editor: Masterpieces of Medical Photography, 1987, Harms Way, 1994; artist residency, Rome, 1996. Served with U.S. Army, 1961-64. Decorated Chevalier Des Arts et de Letters (France), 1990, The Augustus Saint Gaudens medal The Cooper Union, 1996; recipient Disting. Alumni award The Cooper Union, 1986, Internat. Ctr. Photography award, 1988; Ford Found. grantee, 1977, 78, Nat. Endowment in Photography grantee, 1980, 81, 86, 92. Address: 1707 Five Points Rd SW Albuquerque NM 87105-3017 *My need is to understand existence. That need becomes art when it reaches into the extreme limit of the possible.*

WITKIN, MILDRED HOPE FISHER, psychotherapist, educator; b. N.Y.C.; d. Samuel and Sadie (Goldschmidt) Fisher; children: Georgia Hope, Roy Thomas, Laurie Phillips, Kimberly, Nicole, Scott, Joshua, Jennifer; m. Jorge Radovic, Aug. 26, 1983. AB, Hunter Coll., MA, Columbia U., 1968; PhD, NYU, 1973. Diplomate Am. Bd. Sexology, Am. Bd. Sexuality; cert. supr. Head counselor Camp White Lake, Camp Emanuel, Long Beach, N.J.; tchr. econs., polit. sci. Hunter Coll. High Sch.; dir., group leader follow-up program Jewish Vacation Assn., N.Y.C.; investigator N.Y.C. Housing Authority; psychol. counselor Montclair State Coll., Upper Montclair, N.J., 1967-68; mem., lectr. Creative Problem-Solving Inst., U. Buffalo, 1968; psychol. counselor Fairleigh Dickinson U., Teaneck, N.J., 1968, dir. Counseling Center, 1969-74; pvt. practice psychotherapy, N.Y.C., also Westport, Conn.; sr. faculty supr., family therapist and psychotherapist Payne Whitney Psychiat. Clinic, N.Y. Hosp., 1973—; clin. asst. prof. dept. psychiatry Cornell U. Med. Coll., 1974—; assoc. dir. sex therapy and edn. program Cornell-N.Y. Hosp. Med. Ctr., 1974—; sr. cons. Kaplan Inst. for Evaluation and Treatment of Sexual Disorders, 1981—; supr. master's and doctoral candidates, NYU, 1975-82; pvt. practice psychotherapy and sex therapy, N.Y.C., also Westport, Conn.; cons. counselor edn. tng. programs N.Y.C. Bd. Edn., 1971-75; cons. Health Info. Systems, 1972-79; vis. prof. numerous colls. and univs.; chmn. sci. com. 1st Internat. Symposium on Female Sexuality, Buenos Aires, 1984. Exhibited in group shows at Scarsdale (N.Y.) Art Show, 1959, Edn. legislation chmn. PTA, Yonkers, 1955; publicity chmn. United Jewish Appeal, Scarsdale, 1959-65; Scarsdale chmn. mothers com. Boy Scouts Am., 1961-64; mem. Morrow Assn. on Correction N.J., 1969-91; bd. dirs. Girl Scouts of Am. Recipient Bronze medal for svcs. Hunter Coll.; United Jewish Appeal plaque, 1962; Founders Day award N.Y. U., 1973, citation N.Y. Hosp./Cornell U. Med. Ctr., 1990. Fellow Internat. Coun. Sex Edn. and Parenthood of Am. U., Am. Acad. Clin. Sexologists; mem. AAUW, APA, ACA, Assn. Counseling Supervision, Am. Coll. Personnel Assn., Internat. Assn. Marriage and Family Counselors, Am. Coll. Sexuality (cert.), Women's Med. Assn. N.Y.C., N.Y. Acad. Sci., Am. Coll. Pers. Assn. (nat. mem. commn. II 1973-76), Nat. Assn. Women Deans and Counselors, Am. Assn. Sex Educators, Counselors and Therapists (regional bd., nat. accreditation bd., cert. internat. supr.), Soc. for Sci. Study Sex Therapy and Rsch., Eastern Assn. Sex Therapists, Am. Assn. Marriage and Family Counselors, N.J. Assn. Marriage and Family Counselors, Ackerman Family Inst., Am. Personnel and Guidance Assn., Am., N.Y., N.J. psychol. assns., Creative Edn. Found., Am. Assn. Higher Edn., Assn. Counselor Supervision and Edn., Profl. Women's Caucus, LWV, Am. Assn. counseling and Devel., Am. Women's Med. Assn., Nat. Coun. on Women in Medicine, Argentine Soc. Human Sexuality (hon.), Am. Assn. Sexology (diplomate), Conn. Assn. Marriage and Family Therapy, Pi Lambda Theta, Kappa Delta Pi, Alpha Chi Alpha. Author: 45-And Single Again, 1985, Single Again, 1994; contbr. articles to profl. jours. and textbooks; lectr. internat. and nat. workshops, radio and TV. Home: 9 Sturges Commons Westport CT 06880-2832 Office: 35 Park Ave New York NY 10016-3838

WITKOP, BERNHARD, chemist; b. Freiburg, Baden, Germany, May 9, 1917; came to U.S., 1947, naturalized, 1953; s. Philipp W. and Hedwig M. (Hirschhorn) W.; m. Marlene Prinz, Aug. 8, 1945; children: Cornelia Johanna, Phyllis, Thomas. Diploma, U. Munich, 1938, PhD, 1940, Golden Dr. Diploma, 1990; ScD, Privat-Dozent, 1947. Matthew T. Mellon research fellow Harvard U., 1947-48, mem. faculty, 1948-50; spl. USPHS fellow Nat. Heart Inst., NIH, 1950-52; vis. scientist Nat. Inst. Arthritis and Metabolic Diseases, 1953, chemist, 1954-55, chief sect. metabolites, 1956-87, chief lab. chemistry, 1957-87, scholar, 1987-92, hon. scholar emeritus, 1993; vis. prof. U. Kyoto, Japan, 1961, U. Freiburg, Fed. Repubic Germany, 1962; adj. prof. U. Md. Med. Sch., Balt.; Nobel symposium lectr. Stockholm-Karlskoga, 1981; mem. bd. Internat. Sci. Exchange, 1974; mem. exec. com. NRC, 1975; mem. Com. Internat. Exchange, 1977, Paul Ehrlich Award Com., Frankfurt, 1980-97. Editor: Fedn. European Biochem. Soc. Letters, 1979-90. Recipient Superior Service award USPHS, 1967; Paul Karrer gold medal U. Zurich, 1971; Kun-ni-to (medal of sci. and culture 2d class) Emperor of Japan, 1975; Alexander von Humboldt award for sr. U.S. scientists, 1978. Mem. NAS, Am. Chem. Soc. (Hillebrand award 1958), Am. Acad. Arts and Sci., Acad. Leopoldina (fgn.), Pharm. Soc. Japan (hon.), Chem. Soc. Japan (hon.), Japanese Biochem. Soc. (hon.). Office: NIH-Dept Health Edn & Welfare Bldg 8-B1A-11A Bethesda MD 20892 *A career between two worlds and two wars, spanning 50 years of research aims changing from structural to dynamic aspects, may be considered epigonal in the sense that my teacher H. Wieland (Nobel Prize 1928) always considered biochemistry as a neglected area of organic chemistry. In a small way I tried to follow his example and interests, such as oxidation mechanisms, natural products and highly active toxins.*

WITKOWSKY, GIZELLA, dancer; b. Toronto, Ont., Can.. Student, Nat. Ballet Sch. With Nat. Ballet Can., 1975—, 2nd soloist, 1977, 1st soloist, 1978, prin. dancer, 1985—; dancer David Allan's Italian Tour, 1985. Performances include Swan Queen/Black Queen in Swan Lake, Snow Queen/Sugar Plum Fairy in Nutcracker, Queen of the Wilis in Giselle, Swanild in Coppélia, Hanna in Merry Widow, Tatiana in Onegin, others; lead roles in Sphinx, Alice, Voluntaries, Rite of Spring; other roles include Serenade, Four Temperaments, Les Sylphides, Paquita, La Bayadere Act II, Offenbach in the Underworld, Elite Syncopations; created roles Pastorale, Compenents, L'Ile Inconnue, Oiseaux Exotiques, Concerto for the Elements, Lostin Twilights; guest performances include inaugural Huntsville Festival of Arts, 1993, Hungarian Nat. Ballet, Budapest, 1992, Bermuda Festival, 1991, 93, Annual Nijinsky Gala, Hamburg, 1991, Stars and Soloists of Can. Ballet, Italy, 1985. Home: 77 Langley Ave, Toronto, ON Canada M4K 1B4*

WITMAN, FRANK MCCONNELL, clergyman, educator; b. Altoona, Pa., Dec. 1, 1931; s. Edwin Henry and Mary Frances (Grose) W.; m. Elsie Ellen McLaughlin, Mar. 28, 1953; children: Mark Allan, Paul David. BA, Calif. State U., L.A., 1956; ThM, Sch. Theology at Claremont, Calif., 1959, D Ministry, 1977; cert. supervising pastor, Fuller Theol. Sem., 1983. Ordained elder United Meth. Ch., 1961; cert. L.A. Police Dept. Acad., Advanced Police Chaplain Sch. Assoc. pastor Trinity United Meth. Ch., Pomona, Calif., 1959-62; sr. pastor Rialto (Calif.) United Meth. Ch., 1962-69, United Meth. Ch., Simi Valley, Calif., 1969—; bd. dirs. United Meth. Fed. Credit Union, Montclair, Calif., chmn. bd., 1976—; mem. adj. faculty Sch. Theology at Claremont, 1992—, trustee, 1966-69; mem. CKW Partnership, adminstrn. and fin. cons., Vista, Calif., 1988—. Co-author: Christian Response in a Hungry World, 1978, Church Administration and Finance, 1995. Chaplain Simi Valley Police Dept., 1978—; guest chaplain U.S. Ho. of Reps., Washington, 1990. Sgt. U.S. Army, 1953-55. Named Young Man of Yr., Rialto Jr. C. of C., 1965, Citizen of Yr., Rialto C. of C., 1969; recipient Disting. Ministry award Sch. Theology at Claremont, 1993, Walter Teagle fellow, 1976-77. Mem. Sch. Theology at Claremont Alumni Assn. (pres. 1965-69), Rotary (bd. dirs. Rialto 1964-65, Simi Valley 1973-74, Paul Harris fellow 1985). Republican. Avocations: camping, leading youth and adult camps, travel. Home: 1892 Suntree Ln Simi Valley CA 93063-4193 Office: United Meth Ch 2394 Erringer Rd Simi Valley CA 93065-2222

WITMER, DIANE F., communication educator; b. Pasadena, Calif., Jan. 20, 1945; d. Stanley Lamar and Mary Evelyn Witmer; m. Robert D. Joyce (div. 1987); 1 child, David William Penkoff. AA, Golden West Coll., Huntington Beach, Calif., 1977; BS in BA, U. LaVerne (Calif.), 1980; MS in Sys. Mgmt., U. So. Calif., L.A., 1989; MA in Communication Arts, U. So. Calif., 1993, PhD in Orgnl. Comm., 1994. Dir. pub. rels. Weight Watchers, Santa Ana, Calif., 1980-84; dir. comm. March of Dimes, Costa Mesa, Calif., 1986-90; prin. Penkoff Comm. Resources, L.A., 1990-92; instr. Calif. State U., Fullerton, 1990-94; asst. lectr. comm. arts and scis. U. So. Calif., University Park, 1991-94; asst. prof. Purdue U., West Lafayette, Ind., 1994—. Editor, The Paper Weight, 1981-84. Chmn. award com. March of Dimes, Costa Mesa, nat. vol., 1980—, also chair speakers bur. Sagemore divsn., mem. exec. com. Mem. Pub. Rels. Soc. Am. (accredited mem.), U. So. Calif. Alumni Assn., Indpls. Symphony Chorus. Avocations: singing.

WITMER, G. ROBERT, retired state supreme court justice; b. Webster, N.Y., Dec. 26, 1904; s. George H. and Lillian (Woodhull) W.; m. Marian P. Costello, June 27, 1936; children: George Robert, John R., Thomas W., Sylvia Witmer Bissell. A.B., U. Rochester, N.Y., 1926; LL.B., Harvard U., 1929. Bar: N.Y. 1929. Pvt. practice Rochester, 1929-45; ptnr. Easton & Witmer, 1931-45; surrogate Monroe County, 1946-53; justice N.Y. State Supreme Ct., 1954-81, assoc. justice appellate div. 1st dept., 1963-67, appellate div. 4th dept., 1968-81; jud. adminstrv. officer, appellate div. N.Y. State Supreme Ct. (4th dept.), 1981-94; adminstrv. judge N.Y. State Supreme Ct. (7th Jud. Dist.), 1962-68; ret., 1994; town atty., Webster, 1934-35; served on N.Y. State Ct. Appeals, 1974. Co-author: N.Y. Pattern Jury Instructions-Civil, Vol. 1, 1965, rev. edit., 1974, Vol. 11, 1968; co-chmn. pub. com. Practitioner's Handbook for Appeals Appellate Divs. N.Y., 1979, Practitioner's Handbook for Appeals to the Court of Appeals of New York, 1981. Supr. Town of Webster and County of Monroe, 1936-45; chmn. Webster Republican Com., 1933-45, mem. exec. com. of Monroe County Republican Com., 1933-45. Mem. Am., N.Y. State, Monroe County Bar Assns., Am. Law Inst., Webster Grange, Univ. Club (Rochester), Masons, Theta Chi. Home: 45 Corning Park Webster NY 14580-3503

WITMER, GEORGE ROBERT, JR., lawyer; b. Rochester, N.Y., Mar. 23, 1937; s. George Robert and Marian Pauline (Costello) W.; m. Nancy Rosetta Wenner, Dec. 28, 1968; children: Wendy Lynn, Heidi Dawn, George Robert, III, Frank David. A.B., U. Rochester, 1959; LL.B., Harvard U., 1962. Bar: N.Y. 1962, U.S. Dist. Ct. (we. dist.) N.Y. 1963, U.S. Supreme Ct. 1967, U.S Dist. Ct. (no. dist.) N.Y. 1977. Assoc. Nixon, Hargrave, Devans & Doyle, Rochester, 1962-70; ptnr. Nixon, Hargrave, Devans & Doyle, 1970—; instr. in bus. law U. Rochester, 1965-66; mem. com. to advise and cons. Jud. Conf. State N.Y. on Civil Practice Law and Rules, 1970-77. Mem. N.Y. State Rep. Com., 1976-93; trustee Eastman Dental Ctr. Rochester, 1977—, pres. bd. trustees, 1989-90; trustee U. Rochester, 1979—, chmn. exec. com., 1992—. Fellow N.Y. Bar Found. (dir. 1991-96), ABA Found.; mem. ABA, Monroe County (N.Y.) Bar Assn., N.Y. State Bar Assn. (ho. of dels. 1978—, v.p. 1984-88, sec. 1989-90, pres.-elect 1993-94, pres. 1994-95, exec. com. environ. law sect. 1981-96, environ. law sect. Disting. Svc. award), Am. Law Inst., Rochester Rotary Club (dir. local club 1977-79), Masons (master 1971), Phi Beta Kappa. Republican. Lutheran. Home: 892 Lake Rd Webster NY 14580-9008 Office: Nixon Hargrave Devans & Doyle PO Box 1051 Clinton Sq Rochester NY 14604-1729

WITMER, JOHN ALBERT, librarian; b. Lancaster, Pa., Nov. 29, 1920; s. Albert Franklin and Mary Esther (Conrad) W.; m. Doris May Ferry, June 10, 1943; children: Marilyn May Witmer Custis, John Richard, Deborah Witmer Jones. AB, Wheaton Coll., 1942, AM, 1946; ThM, Dallas Theol. Sem., 1946, ThD, 1953; MS in L.S., E. Tex. State U., 1969; cert. Archival Adminstrn., U. Tex., Arlington, 1988. Grad. fellow Wheaton Coll., 1942-44; mng. editor Child Evangelism mag., Dallas, 1944-46; instr. Child Evangelism Inst., Dallas and Chgo., 1945-47; instr. systematic theology Dallas Theol. Sem., 1947-54, asst. prof., 1954-86, assoc. prof., 1986-87, assoc. prof. emeritus, 1987—; librarian Mosher Library, 1964-86, archivist, 1987—; cert. instr. Dale Carnegie Course, 1956-92, instr. emeritus, 1992—. Contbr. articles to profl. jours., essays; editor: The Christian Librarian, 1972-74. Treas. Evang. Communications Research Found., 1970-73; bd. dirs. Dallas Bible Coll., 1972-83, chmn., 1974-77, sec., 1979-82; bd. dirs. Evang. Projects, 1975-92. Mem. Assn. Christian Librs., Evang. Philos. Soc., Evan. Theol. Soc., Soc. Am. Archivists, Soc. Southwest Archivists, Grace Evang. Soc. Home: 6630 Westlake Ave Dallas TX 75214-3441

WITMER, JOHN HARPER, JR., lawyer; b. Phila., May 5, 1940; s. John Harper and Jane Carolyn (Lentz) Witmer; m. Arlene Marie Rosipal, June 9, 1962; 1 dau., Tara Leah. BA, Pa. State U., 1962; JD, George Washington U., 1969. Bar: Md. 1969, D.C. 1970, Ill. 1979. Mgmt. analyst Nat. Security Agy., Ft. Meade, Md., 1963-66; mem. Sidley & Austin, Washington, 1969-78; sr. v.p., gen. counsel DEKALB Energy Co., 1978-95, DEKALB Genetics Corp., 1978—. Mem. ABA, Ill. State Bar Assn., Md. State Bar Assn., D.C. Bar Assn. Home: 2575 Greenwood Acres Dr De Kalb IL 60115-4916 Office: DEKALB Genetics Corp 3100 Sycamore Rd De Kalb IL 60115-9621

WITMEYER, JOHN JACOB, III, lawyer; b. New Orleans, Dec. 18, 1946; s. John J. and Thais Audrey (Dolese) W. B.S., Tulane U., 1968; J.D. with distinction, Duke U., 1971. Bar: N.Y. Assoc. Mudge Rose Guthrie & Alexander, N.Y.C., 1971-76; ptnr. Ford Marrin Esposito & Witmeyer (now Ford, Marrin, Esposito, Witmeyer & Gleser, L.L.P.), N.Y.C., 1976—. Col. USAR. Office: Ford Marrin Esposito Witmeyer & Gleser LLP Wall St Plz New York NY 10005-1875

WITOVER, STEPHEN BARRY, pediatrician; b. Bklyn., Jan. 7, 1941; s. Nat and Frances (Posner) W.; m. Joyce Bonnie Weiss; children: Julie Lyn, Gary Lee. AB, Adelphi U., 1961; MD, Chgo. Med. Sch., 1965. Intern, resident, chief resident Montefiore Hosp. and Med. Ctr., Bronx, N.Y.; intern to chief resident pediatrics, 1965-68; pres. Merrimack Valley Pediat. Assocs., Billerica, Mass., 1972—; med. dir. Teen Health Svcs. Saints Meml. Hosp., Lowell, Mass., 1974—; chief of pediatrics Teen Health Svcs. St. Johns Hosp., 1982—. Maj. U.S. Army, 1968-70. Office: Merrimack Pediatric Assocs 221 Boston Rd North Billerica MA 01862-2321 also: Merrimack Valley Pediatric Assn 1501 Main St Tewksbury MA 01876-4725

WITSCHEY, WALTER ROBERT THURMOND, science museum administrator, archaeologist, computer systems consultant; b. Charleston, W.Va., June 19, 1941; s. Robert E. and Sarah Elizabeth (Thurmond) W.; m. Joan DuRelle Vincent, July 19, 1980; children: Anne Elizabeth, Schon Roberts Parris, Sarah C. Brauner, Walter Robert Thurmond II, Benjamin Hart Vincent. BA in Physics, Princeton U., 1963; MBA in Ops. Rsch., U. Va., 1965; MA in Anthropology-Maya Archaeology, Tulane U., 1989, PhD in Anthropology-Maya Archaeology, 1993. Systems engr. IBM Corp., Richmond, Va., 1965-67, mktg. rep., 1967-69; v.p. The Computer Co., Richmond, Va., 1969-70, pres., CEO, 1970-84; cons., pub., proprietorship Gatewood Co., Richmond, Va., 1978—; dir., CEO Sci. Mus. Va., Richmond, Va., 1992—; bd. dirs. Highland Data Svcs., 1982-85; vis. instr. computer systems U. Va., 1985-86; instr. word processing, Delgado Community Coll., 1989; lectr. microcomputer applications, Our Lady Of Holy Cross Coll., 1989-92; lectr. dept. Anthropology, Tulane U., 1987-92, asst. to the dir., 1987-88, lectr., curriculum cons., 1988-92, adj. instr. A.B. Freeman Sch., 1991; adj. faculty dept. Sociology, Anthropology and Mathematical Scis., Va. Commonwealth U., 1992—. Contbr. articles to profl. jours. Dir. Assn. Sci.-Tech. Ctrs., 1995—, Sci. Mus. Va. Found., Richmond, 1981-90, La. Sci. Ctr., New Orleans, 1985-90; pres., dir. Richmond-on-the-James, 1984-85; sec., dir. Richmond Cmty. H.S. Policy Bd.; cons. Federated Arts Coun., Richmond. Tinker Found. archaeol. rsch. grantee (3), Middle Am. Rsch. Inst. archaeol. grantee, Mesoam. Ecology Inst. archaeol. rsch. grantee (3), Middle Am. Rsch. Inst. archaeol. rsch. grantee (3), pvt. archaeol. rsch. grantee. Mem. AAAS, Am. Assn. Mus., Assn. Sci.-Tech. Ctrs. (dir.), Soc. Am. Archaeology, Va. Acad. Sci., Va. Assn. Mus. (mem. coun.), Va. Space Grant Consortium, Assn. Computing Machinery, Sigma Xi. Presbyterian. Avocation: field archaeology. Office: Sci Mus Va 2500 W Broad St Richmond VA 23220-2057

WITT, CATHERINE LEWIS, neonatal nurse practitioner, writer; b. Burlington, Iowa, Nov. 21, 1957; d. Rodney Darrell and Neola Ann (Wharton) Lewis; m. John Robert Witt, Mar. 31, 1984; children: Jeffrey Lewis, Jennifer Diane. BSN, U. No. Colo., 1980; MSN, U. Colo., 1987. Cert. neonatal nurse practitioner. Staff nurse St. Joseph's Hosp., Denver, 1980-85; neonatal nurse practitioner Denver Children's Hosp., 1986-88; coord. neonatal nurse practitioner and neonatal transport Presbyn.-St. Luke's Med. Ctr., Denver, 1988—. Column editor Neonatal Network; contbr. chpts. to books. Troop leader Girl Scouts U.S. Mem. Nat. Assn. Neonatal Nurses (co-chair program com. 1992-94, bd. dirs., dir.-at-large 1997—), Nat. Cert. Corp. (test. com. 1994-96). Democrat. Episcopalian. Avocations: reading, sewing, church tape ministry, children's church education. Home: 17586 E Dickinson Pl Aurora CO 80013 Office: Presbyn-St Luke's Med Ctr 1719 E 19th Ave Denver CO 80218-1235

WITT, DAVID L., curator, writer; b. Kansas City, Mo., Nov. 3, 1951; s. Lloyd Vernon and Dean W. B.S. in Polit. Sci., Kans. State U., 1974. Naturalist Naish Nature Ctr., Edwardsville, Kans., summers 1967-70; asst. curator Seton Mus., Cimarron, N.Mex., summers 1972-74; curatorial asst. Riley County Hist. Mus., Manhattan, Kans., 1973-74; mus. asst. Millicent Rogers Mus., Taos, N.Mex., 1976-77; curator The Gaspard House Mus., Taos, N.Mex., 1978-79, The Harwood Found., Taos; 1979—. Author: The Taos Artists, 1984, Taos Moderns: Art of the New, 1992 (Southwest Book award Border Regional Libr. Assn. 1993); co-author: Spirit Ascendant: The Art and Life of Patrociño Barela, 1996; contbr. articles to profl. jours. Organizer first N.Mex. Art History Conf., 1986; founder Southwest Art History Coun., 1990. Mem. PEN, N.Mex. Assn. Mus. (pres. 1986-88). Democrat. Home: PO Box 317 Taos NM 87571-0317 Office: 4081 Ndcbu Taos NM 87571-6004

WITT, ELIZABETH NOWLIN (BETH WITT), special education educator, speech-language pathologist; b. Columbus, Miss., Apr. 11, 1941; d. Mervyn Davis and Elizabeth (Moody) Smith; m. Lawrence V. Witt Jr., Feb. 10, 1963; children: Lawrence V. III, Ben, John, Catherine, Elizabeth. BS in Journalism and English, Miss. U. for Women, Columbus, 1963; MA in Spl. Edn., La. Tech. U., Ruston, 1979; postgrad., La. State U., 1990—. Cert. in English, learning disabilities, mental retardation, presch. handicapped severe/profound, also prin., ednl. cons., ednl. diagnostician, La.; lic. speech-lang. pathologist. Tchr. spl. edn. Caddo-Bossier Assn. for Retarded Citizens, Shreveport, La., 1976-79; tchr presch. handicapped Bossier Parish Schs., Bossier City, La., 1979-83; ednl. diagnostician Caddo Parish Schs., Shreveport, 1983-96; ednl. cons. Ruston (La.) State Sch., summer 1981; instr. La. Tech. U., 1990-95; mem. author adv. bd. Comm. Skill Builders, Tucson, 1986-88; ex officio mem. Region VII Infant Coun., Shreveport, 1990-92; bd. dirs. Childcare of N.W. La., Shreveport, 1986-90, Head Start, Shreveport, 1984-85, pt. asst. prof. Speech-Language Pathology La. Tech. U., 1996—, Ruston, pt. Speech Pathologist at C-BARC early intervention program in Shreveport, La., 1996—. Mem. editorial adv. bd. JCCD, DCCD; author lang. activity kits and programs. Vol. edn. cons. Lighthouse Presch. Program, Vols. of Am., Shreveport, 1986—; elder First Presbyn. Ch., Bossier City, 1989-91. Mem. Am. Speech and Hearing Assn., Coun. for Exceptional Children (editor newsletter La. Fedn. 1988-90, pres. La. div. early childhood 1989-90, pres. La. div. mental retardation 1986-87, editl. rev. bd., jour. DSSD-CEC 1990-95). Avocations: reading, anthropology, archaeology, country decorating, travel. Office: C-BARC Goldman Sch 351 Jordan St Shreveport LA 71101-4846

WITT, HUGH ERNEST, technology consultant; b. Winchester, Ky., Nov. 18, 1921; s. Hugh E. and Louella (Milliken) W.; m. Janie Bryan (dec. Oct. 1990); m. Evelyn Chapman, Apr. 22, 1993. Student, Transylvania U., 1941-43; BS, U. Ky., 1945; MS, MIT, 1957. Asst. to dep. asst. sec. Dept. of Air Force, Washington, 1954-61, dep. asst. sec., 1961-70; dep. asst. sec. Dept. of Navy, Washington, 1970-73; prin. dep. asst. sec. of Def., Washington, 1973-74; fed. procurement policy adminstr. Office Mgmt. and Budget, Washington, 1974-77; dir., govt. liaison United Techs. Corp., Washington, 1977-81, v.p., govt. liaison, 1981-87, cons. to United Techs. Corp., 1987—. Pres. Old Town Civic Assn., Alexandria, Va., 1961-63; bd. dirs. Alexandria Hist. Found.; mem. Alexandria Bd. Archtl. Rev., 1964-77; trustee Alexandria Hosp. Found., 1992-94. Alfred P. Sloan fellow MIT, Cambridge, Mass., 1956-57. Fellow Nat. Contract Mgmt. Assn.; mem. Aerospace Industries Assn., Nat. Security Indsl. Assn., MIT Alumni Assn., Soc. Sloan Fellows, Kappa Alpha.

WITT, JAMES LEE, federal agency administrator; b. Dardanelle, Ark., 1944; m. Lea; children: Jimmy, Michael. Founder Witt Constrn. Co.; county judge Yell County, Ark.; state dir. Office Emergency Svcs., Ark.; dir. Fed. Emergency Mgmt. Agy., Washington, 1993—. Chmn. bd. Child Devel., Inc., charter; Gov.'s rep. state disasters, Presdl. disasters. Recognized for outstanding efforts Nat. Assn. Counties. Office: Federal Emergency Mgmt Agency Office of Dir 500 C St SW Washington DC 20024-2523

WITT, RAY, automotive manufacturing executive. CEO CMI Internat., Southfield, Mich. Office: 30333 Southfield Rd Southfield MI 48076-1352*

WITT, RAYMOND BUCKNER, JR., lawyer; b. Lenoir City, Tenn., Apr. 20, 1915; s. Raymond Buckner and Gertrude (Jackson) W.; m. Florence Elder Bagley, Sept. 14, 1943; children—Florence Elder, Mary Alice, George Evans. A.B., U. Chattanooga, 1937; LL.B., U. N.C., 1939. Bar: Tenn. 1939. Since practiced in Chattanooga; with Witt, Gaither, Whitaker and predecessor firms, 1945—, partner, 1946—; dir., gen. counsel Dixie Yarns, Inc., 1947-92. Pres. Met. Council Community Services, 1966-68; mem. Chattanooga Bd. Edn., 1953-65, vice chmn., 1963-65; chmn. Chattanooga Bicentennial Religious Com., 1976; chmn. bd. Chattanooga-Hamilton County Bicentennial Library, 1976-78; trustee Westend Found.; mem. U. Chatanooga Found. Inc., 1969—, trustee, sec., gen. counsel , chmn. 1988-90; pres. Chattanooga YMCA, 1986-87; chmn. United Way Fund campaign, 1987; chmn. bd. trustees 1st Centenary United Methodist, 1989, chmn. adminstrv. bd., 1993, 94. Served to lt. comdr. USNR, 1942-45, PTO. Recipient Distinguished Service award Chattanooga Kiwanis, 1963, Tenn. Sch. Bds. Assn., 1963. Mem. ABA, Tenn. Bar Assn. Methodist (chmn. commn. on Christian edn. 1953-55, ch. sch. supt. 1955-60). Home: 1615 Minnekahda Rd Chattanooga TN 37405-2411 Office: American Natl Bank Bldg Chattanooga TN 37402-4402

WITT, ROBERT WAYNE, English educator; b. Scottsville, Ky., Mar. 26, 1937; s. Aubrey G. Witt and Nina Loyce (Cook) Jackson. BA, Georgetown Coll., 1959; MA, U. Miss., 1961, PhD, 1970. Instr. U. Miss., Oxford, 1965-70; asst. prof. Ea. Ky. U., Richmond, 1970-75, assoc. prof., 1975-80, prof., 1980—. Author: Mirrow-within, 1975, Shakespeare's Sonnets, 1979, Rocking Chair, 1987, Combining Modes, 1992, Hour in Paradise, 1993, Toxic, 1995. Mem. MLA, South Atlantic Modern Lang., Dramatists Guild, Automatic Musical Instruments Collectors. Avocations: playing piano, collecting antique automatic musical instruments. Home: PO Box 419 Richmond KY 40476-0419

WITT, TOM, economics researcher, educator; b. Borger, Tex., Apr. 22, 1944; s. Eugene Thomason and Helen C. (Hathaway) W.; m. Grethe A. Myles, Mar. 4, 1976. BA, Okla. State U., 1966; MA, Washington U., St. Louis, 1968, PhD, 1974. Asst. prof. Dept. Econs., W.V. U., Morgantown, 1970-75, assoc. prof., 1975-80; acting asst. dean Grad. Sch., W.V. U., Morgantown, 1977-78; exec. dir. Bureau of Bus. Rsch., W.V. U., Morgantown, 1985—; dir. Ctr. Econs. Rsch., W.Va. U., Morgantown, 1985—; acting assoc. dean Coll. Bus. and Econs., W.V. U., Morgantown, 1985-86; assoc. dean rsch. and outreach Coll. Bus. and Econs. W.Va. U., Morgantown, 1994—; cons. Nat. Regulatory Rsch. Inst., Columbia, Ohio, 1980-81; cons., expert witness W.Va. Human Rights Commn., Charleston, 1984; expert witness W.Va. Atty. Gen., 1987-88, Ashland Oil, 1992-93. Author: (monograph) Guidelines for Attracting Private Capital to Corps of Engineers Projects, 1977; The Cost of Doing Business in West Virginia, 1988; (book) Power from the Appalachians, 1989; co-editor: (book) West Virginia in the Nineties: Policies for Econ. Progress; contbr. articles to profl. jours. Pres. Cheat Canyon Park Homeowners, Morgantwon, 1979-87, Monongalia Arts Ctr., 1980-81; bd. dirs., treas. Friends of W.Va. Pub. Radio, Charleston, 1985-93, chmn., 1989-91; sec.-treas. Cheat Neck Pub. Svc. Dist., 1989-95, Main Street Morgantown, 1994—; mem. Monongalia County Econ. Devel. Authority, 1994—; assoc. dean. rsch. and outreach Coll. of Bus. and Econ. W.Va. U., 1995—. Mem. Am. Econ. Assn., Am. Stats. Assn., Regional Sci. Assn., So. Econ. Assn., Rotary. Home: 3202 Deerfield Ct Morgantown WV 26505-8612 Office: Bureau of Bus Rsch WV U PO Box 6025 Morgantown WV 26506-6052

WITT, WALTER FRANCIS, JR., lawyer; b. Richmond, Va., Feb. 18, 1933; s. Walter Francis and Evelyn Virginia (Riggleman) W.; m. Rosemary Winter, Sept. 5, 1964; children: Leslie Anne Millman, Walter Francis III. BS, U. Richmond, 1954, JD, 1966. Bar: Va. 1966, D.C. 1974. Assoc. Hunton and Williams, Richmond, 1966-74, ptnr., 1974—. Contbr. articles to profl. jours. 1st lt. U.S. Army, 1955-57. Mem. ABA (chmn. real property com. sect. gen. practice 1995—, dep. chair urban, state and local govt. com. 1995—, sect. gen. practice), Va. Bar Assn., Richmond Bar Assn., D.C. Bar Assn., Phi Beta Kappa, Phi Delta Phi. Home: 8901 Tresco Rd Richmond VA 23229-7725 Office: Hunton & Williams Riverfront Plaza East Twr 951 E Byrd St Richmond VA 23219-4040

WITTBRODT, EDWIN STANLEY, consultant, former bank executive, former air force officer; b. Flint, Mich., Aug. 13, 1918; s. Stanley Frank and Marie (Ross) W.; m. Joan Helen Miller, Apr. 22, 1950; children: Stephanie Rita, Candace Lee, Edwin Stanley. Student, Gen. Motors Inst. Tech., 1936-38, Grad. Sch. Dept. Agr., 1950-51, Indsl. Coll. Armed Forces, 1961-62, George Washington U., 1962, U. So. Calif., 1963-64. Joined U.S. Army, 1941, commd. 2d lt., 1942; advanced through grades to brig. gen. USAF, 1968; various assignments U.S., 1941-49; budget officer Hdqrs. USAF, 1949-53, 56-61; dir. budget and acctg. Hdqrs. N.E. Air Command, Nfld., 1953-56; comptroller space systems div. Los Angeles, 1962-64; comptroller aero., systems div. Wright-Patterson AFB, 1964-66; asst. comptroller USAF, 1966-67; dir. acctg. and fin. Hdqrs. USAF, 1967-68; asst. comptroller air force for acctg. and fin., comdr. Air Force Acctg. and Fin. Ctr., Denver, 1968-71; v.p. systems Cen. Bank Denver, 1971-81, v.p. info. resources mgmt., 1981-84; dir. Computer Congenerics Corp. Colo., Hasa Corp. Co-chmn. Combined Fed. Campaign, Denver, 1968-87; Hon. dir. USO, Denver, 1968-71, mem. council, 1971-87 . Decorated D.S.M., Legion of Merit, Soldier's Medal, Commendation medal with oak leaf cluster; recipient Gen. Jimmy Doolittle Disting. Fellow award, Flint No. Alumni Assn. Disting. Fellow award, 1990, Treas. Dept. Pioneer in Elec. Commerce award, 1995. Mem. Am. Soc. Mil. Comptrollers (past pres. Washington chpt., nat. v.p. 1968-70, pres. Denver chpt. 1971-72), Assn. Govt. Accountants, Assn. Mil. Banks (dir. 1974-84), Am. Inst. Banking, Denver C. of C. (chmn. mil. affairs com. 1979-82), Aurora C. of C. (mil. affairs coun. 1987—), Air Force Assn. (v.p. N. Colo. 1971-72, pres. Silver and Gold chpt. 1972-73, state treas. 1976-83, pres. Mile High chpt. 1987-88). Club: Columbine Country. Home: 10 Niblick Ln Columbine Valley CO 80123 *I have adopted two attitudes that I believe assisted me in all of my undertakings: (1)—that of being what I call a "responsible non-conformist" and (2)—"no problems—just opportunities.".*

WITTBRODT, FREDERICK JOSEPH, JR., automotive designer; b. Detroit, Feb. 6, 1955; s. Frederick Joseph Sr. and Hilda Lottie (Neubert) W.; m. Deborah Carrie Kay, Apr. 11, 1992; stepchildren: Angela Defer, Michael Defer II; children from previous marriage: Robin Lynn, Daniel Joseph. G-rad., Philpot Sch. Automotive Body Drafting, Royal Oak, Mich., 1977, Entech. Engring., Troy, Mich., 1984. Designer Modern Engring Co.-Design, Troy, Mich., 1977-78, Detroit Indsl. engring., Troy, Mich., 1978-80, Engring Tech., Ltd., Troy, Mich., 1980-86, Pioneer Engring., Dearborn, Mich., 1986, APD, Dearborn, Mich., 1988-89, Mega-Tech. Engring., Warren, Mich., 1989-90, Uni-Tech, Madison Heights, Mich., 1990-91, Harman at Harvard, Southfield, Mich., 1991; sr. automotive designer Lincoln Tech. at Schlegel, Madison Heights, 1991-92; sr. designer, surface devel. specialist Resource Techs. at Harvard Industries, Farmington Hills, Mich., 1992-95; sr. designer, surface devel. specialist Resource Tech. at Britax-Rainford, Inc., Marysville, Mich., 1995—; owner Wittbrodt Design Co., Chesterfield, Mich. Mem. NRA, Internat. Platform Soc. Avocations: furniture design, landscape design, coin collecting. Home: 8030 Harbour Dr Fair Haven MI 48023

WITTCOFF, HAROLD AARON, chemist; b. Marion, Ind., July 3, 1918; s. Morris and Bessie (Pruss) W.; m. Dorothy Brochin, 1946; 2 sons. A.B. magna cum laude, DePauw U., 1940; Ph.D., Northwestern U., 1943; grad., Advanced Mgmt. Program, Harvard U., 1964. With Gen. Mills, Inc., Mpls., 1943-79; head chem. research dept. Gen. Mills, Inc., 1952-56, Dir. chem. research, 1956-67, v.p., dir. chem. research and devel., 1967-69, v.p., dir. corp. research, 1969-79; dir. research and devel. Koor Chems., Beer Sheva, Israel, 1979-82; dir. process evaluation and research planning Chem Systems, Tarrytown, N.Y., 1982-85; sci. adviser Chem. Systems Internat., Tarrytown, N.Y., 1985—; adj. prof. chemistry U. Minn., 1973-82. Author: The Phosphatides, 1951, Industrial Organic Chemistry: A Perspective 2 vols. 1980; Pharmaceutical Chemicals in Perspective, 1989, Industrial Organic Chemicals, 1996. Recipient Minn. award Am. Chem. Soc., 1976. Mem. Phi Beta Kappa, Sigma Xi, Phi Eta Sigma. Patentee in field. Home: Box 307 Scarborough Manor Scarborough NY 10510

WITTE, MARLYS HEARST, internist, educator; b. N.Y.C., 1934. MD, NYU Sch. Medicine, 1960. Intern N.C. Meml. Hosp., Chapel Hill, 1960-61; resident Bellevue Hosp. Ctr., N.Y.C., 1961-63; fellow NYU Hosp., Washington U., St. Louis, 1964-66; prof. surgery U. Ariz., 1965-69, 69—; attending internist Ariz. Health Sci. Ctr., Tucson, 1965-69, 69—. Rsch. fellow Am. Heart Assn., 1995-96. Mem. AAAS, Am. Hosp. Assn., Alpha Omega Alpha. Office: U Ariz Coll Medicine PO Box 245063 1501 N Campbell Ave Tucson AZ 85724-5063

WITTE, MERLIN MICHAEL, oil company executive; b. Los Angeles, Mar. 28, 1926; s. Anthony A. and Julia (Macke) W.; m. Donna Patricia Hurth, Jan. 22, 1949; children: James Anthony, Daniel Michael, Catherine Ann, Michael Leon, Robert Joseph, Joseph William, Anne Marie, William Benson, Janet Mary. B.A., Loyola U., Los Angeles, 1949. With IRS, U.S. Treasury Dept., 1949-51; investment, tax mgr. McCulloch Motors Corp., also Robert P. McCulloch, 1951-55; pres., gen. mgr., dir. McCulloch Oil Corp., Los Angeles, 1956-80; pres., dir. Merlin Assocs., Inc., Los Angeles, 1980—, M.M. Witte & Assocs., Inc., Los Angeles, 1980—; mgr., chief exec. United Oil Producers, Los Angeles, 1984-86; bd. dirs. Kent Fin. Svcs., Inc., Search Exploration, Inc.; bd. dirs., chmn. McCulloch Energy, Inc., 1991-95; co-chmn. The Am. Drilling Co., L.L.C., 1995—; pres., CEO South Coast Oil Corp., 1996—. Mem. bd. regents Loyola Marymount U., L.A., 1991—. Served with USAAF, 1944-45. Mem. Ind. Oil and Gas Producers Assn., Ind. Petroleum Assn., Western, West Cen. Tex. oil and gas assns., Town Hall, Bel-Air Country Club (pres. 1990-91), PGA West Golf Club.

WITTE, RAYMOND HENRY, psychologist, educator; b. Dayton, Ky., Mar. 22, 1957; s. Raymond Henry and Irma Mae (Henry) W.; m. Susan Evans Weih; children: sarah, Ashleigh. BA, Ky. U., 1979, MS, 1982, PhD, 1991. Nat. cert. sch. psychologist; std. sch. psychology, Ky.; lic. sch. psychologist. Prof. Midway (Ky.) Coll., 1981-87; rsch. asst., neuropsychologist Albert Chandler Med. Ctr., Univ. Ky., Lexington, 1985-87; sch. psychologist Jessamine County Sch. System, Nicholasville, Ky., 1988-93; preschool co-dir. Jessamine County Sch. System, Nicholasville, 1992-93; asst. prof. Miami U., Oxford, Ohio, 1993—. Contbr. articles to profl. jours. Recipient Univ. scholarship U. Ky., Lexington, 1978. Mem. APA, Nat.

Assn. Sch. Psychologists, Ohio Sch. Psychol. Assn. Avocations: horses, hiking.

WITTEBORT, ROBERT JOHN, JR., lawyer; b. Chgo., Dec. 29, 1947; s. Robert John and Marguerite (Shaughnessy) W.; m. Nancy Joan Hertel, July 2, 1988. BA, Yale U., 1969; JD, Notre Dame U., 1974. Bar: Ill. 1974, U.S. Dist. Ct. (no. dist.) Ill. 1974, U.S. Ct. Appeals (7th cir.) 1975, U.S. Tax Ct. 1977, U.S. Ct. Mil. Appeals 1982. Assoc. Hopkins & Sutter, Chgo., 1974-77; gen. counsel, asst. dir. Ill. Housing Devel. Authority, Chgo., 1977-82; ptnr. Chapman and Cutler, Chgo., 1982-90; sr. ptnr. Law Offices Robert J. Wittebort, Jr., 1990—; co-founder, exec. v.p., gen. counsel Chgo. Bldg. Svcs., Inc., 1990—. Contbg. editor: Business Law, 4th edit., 1977; contbg. author: Notre Dame Lawyer, 1974; author: The Chicago Club 1960-1994, 1995. Bd. dirs. Music of the Baroque, Met. Housing Devel. Corp., Chgo.; trustee Chgo. Acad. Scis. Comdr. USNR, 1969—. Mem. Nat. Assn. Bond Lawyers, Naval Order U.S. (vice comdr.-gen.), Ill. Commandery Naval Order U.S. (comdr. 1987-88), Chgo. Club, Saddle & Cycle Club, Lambda Alpha. Republican.

WITTEN, DAVID MELVIN, radiology educator; b. Trenton, Mo., Aug. 16, 1926; s. Buford Isom and Mary Louise (Melvin) W.; m. Netta Lee Watkins, Dec. 23, 1950; children—David Melvin, II, Michael Lee. Student, Trenton Jr. Coll., 1943-44, 46-47; A.B., Washington U., St. Louis, 1950, M.D., 1954; M.S. in Radiology, Mayo Grad. Sch. Medicine, U. Minn., 1960. Diplomate: Am. Bd. Radiology. Intern Virginia Mason Hosp., Seattle, 1954-55; practice medicine specializing in family medicine Trenton, Mo., 1955-57; fellow in radiology Mayo Clinic/Mayo Found., Rochester, Minn., 1957-60; cons. in diagnostic roentgenology Mayo Clinic, 1960-70; instr. Mayo Grad. Sch. Medicine, Rochester, 1960-66; asst. prof. radiology Mayo Grad. Sch. Medicine, 1966-70; pvt. practice medicine specializing in radiology Aberdeen, Wash., 1970-71; clin. assoc. prof. U. Wash., 1970-71; prof. diagnostic radiology, chmn. dept. diagnostic radiology U. Ala., Birmingham, 1971-82; diagnostic radiologist in chief Univ. Hosp., Birmingham, 1971-82; prof., chmn. dept. radiology U. Mo., Columbia, 1982-87, prof. emeritus, 1987—; pres. U. Ala. Health Services Found., 1973-75. Author: Atlas of Tumor Radiology-The Breast, 1969, Clinical Urography, 1977; contbr. articles on radiology of breast cancer, urologic and gastrointestinal disease to profl. jours.; mem. editorial bd. Am. Jour. Roentgenology, 1976-87, Applied Radiology, 1978-87, Urologic Radiology, 1979-87, Radiographics, 1983-87. Served with USNR, 1944-46. Fellow Am. Coll. Radiology; mem. Radiol. Soc. N.Am., Am. Roentgen Ray Soc., AAAS, Soc. Genitourinary Radiology (pres. 1981-82), Assn. Univ. Radiologists, AMA, Mo. Radiol. Soc. (pres. 1988-89), Mo. State Med. Assn., Can. Assn. Radiologists (hon.), Audubon Soc. (editor The Bluebird (Mo.) chpt. 1990-95). Home: 601 Covered Bridge Rd Columbia MO 65203-9562 Office: Univ Mo Health Scis Ctr 1 Hospital Dr Columbia MO 65201-5276

WITTEN, LOUIS, physics educator; b. Balt., Apr. 13, 1921; s. Abraham and Bessie (Perman) W.; m. Lorraine Wollach, Mar. 27, 1949 (dec. 1987); children: Edward, Celia, Matthew, Jesse; m. Francis L. White, Jan. 2, 1992. B.E., Johns Hopkins U., 1941, Ph.D., 1951; B.S., NYU, 1944. Research assoc. Princeton U., N.J., 1951-53; research assoc. U. Md., College Park, 1953-54; staff scientist Lincoln Lab., MIT, 1954-55; assoc. dir. Martin Marietta Research Lab., Balt., 1955-68; prof. physics U. Cin., 1968—; trustee Gravity Research Found. Editor: Gravitation: An Introduction to Current Research, 1962, Relativity: Procs. of Relative Conf. in Midwest of 1969, Symposium on Asymptotic Structure of Space-Time, 1976; patentee in field; contbr. numerous articles to sci. jours. Served to 1st lt. USAF, 1942-46. Fulbright lectr. Weismann Inst. Scis., Rehovot, Israel, 1963-64. Fellow Am. Phys. Soc.; mem. Am. Math. Soc., Internat. Astron. Union, AAAS. Office: Univ Cincinnati Dept Physics Cincinnati OH 45221-0011

WITTEN, THOMAS JEFFERSON, JR., mathematics educator; b. Welch, W.Va., Feb. 10, 1942; s. Thomas Jefferson and Gladys Marium (McMeans) W.; m. Barbara Phyllis Honaker, Feb. 20, 1965; children: Thomas Jefferson III, Rebecca A. Dye, Timothy A., Stephanie L. Dye. BS in Edn., Concord Coll., Athens, W.Va., 1965; MA in Edn., W.Va. U., Morgantown, 1971. Cert. tchr., Va., W.Va. Tchr. math. McDowell County Schs., Gary (W.Va.) High Sch., 1965-71, asst. prin., 1971-73; asst. prin. inst. Tazewell County Schs., Richlands (Va.) High Sch., 1973-87; secondary supr. Jackson County Schs., Ripley, W.Va., 1987-88; asst. prof. math., tech. prep. coord. Southwest Va. Community Coll., Richlands, 1988—; math. cons. S.W. Va. C.C. Computer Math. Grant Project, Richlands, 1988-90; coord. S.W. Va. Tech Prep Consortium, 1992—; co-dir. Eisenhower Math Grant, 1996-97. Mem. sch. bd. Tazewell (Va.) County Schs., 1990-91, 95—, chair 1996; faculty senate pres. South Va. C.C., 1992-94. Recipient K-8 Tchr. Improvement grant, 1992-93. Mem. Va. C.C. Assn., Mountain Math Alliance (chmn. 1909—), PTA (life, pres. 1979-81), Richlands Rotary (pres. 1989-91), Masons (jr. deacon 1966-68), Shriners. Democrat. Methodist. Avocations: painting, cross-stitch, reading, computers, old cars, writing. Home: 737 Terry Dr Richlands VA 24641-2616 Office: SW Va C C Box SVCC Richlands VA 24641

WITTENBERG, KATE, editor; b. N.Y.C., Apr. 20, 1958; d. Stanley Jackson and Carmen Rita (Puglisi) W.; m. Bradbury Taylor, Aug. 9, 1989; children: Emma Taylor, Daniel Taylor. BA in English and History with honors, Wesleyan U., Middletown, Conn., 1980; postgrad., Columbia U., 1983-84. Asst. to copy chief The Viking Press, N.Y.C., 1980-82; asst. history editor Oxford Univ. Press, N.Y.C., 1982-84; acquisitions editor Columbia Univ. Press, N.Y.C., 1984-90, editor-in-chief and pub. for social scis., 1990—; lectr. in field. Contbr. articles to profl. jours. Mem. digital libr. task force Columbia U. Librs. Andrew W. Mellon Fund grantee, 1996. Mem. AAUP (chair libr. rels. com. 1997—), Assn. Am. Pubs. (mem. electronic info. com. profl. and scholarly divsn.). Office: Columbia University Press 562 W 113th St New York NY 10025-8004

WITTENBRINK, JEFFREY SCOTT, lawyer; b. Cairo, Ill., May 24, 1960; s. Howard Samuel and Cherie Ellen (Martin) W.; m. Tamara Inez Parker, Aug. 5, 1989; children: Charlotte Jane, Jeffrey Scott Jr. BA, La. State U., 1984, JD, 1987. Bar: La. 1988, U.S. Dist. Ct. (ea. and mid. dists.) La. 1988, U.S. Dist. Ct. (we. dist.) La. 1989, U.S. Ct. Appeals (5th cir.) 1989. Law clk. to Judge William H. Brown, 19th Jud. Dist. Ct., Baton Rouge, 1987-88; assoc. Roy, Kiesel, Aaron & Tucker, Baton Rouge, 1988-91, Winston G. DeCuir & Assocs., Baton Rouge, 1991-93; pvt. practice Wittenbrink Law Firm, Baton Rouge, 1993—; arbitrator Baton Rouge City Ct., 1993—; instr. CPCU's, Baton Rouge, 1991, Office Emergency Planning State of La., 1993. Contbr. articles to Around the Bar legal newsletter, 1987—. Coach debate team Cath. H.S., Baton Rouge, 1987-91, mock trial team Baton Rouge H.S., 1989-93; treas., trustee, bd. dirs. Ingleside United Meth. Ch., Baton Rouge, 1991—; mem., lectr. La. Vol. Lawyers for Arts, Baton Rouge, 1988—; bd. dirs. La. Crafts Coun., Baton Rouge, 1990—. Mem. ABA, ATLA, La. Bar Assn., Baton Rouge Bar Assn. (mem. newsletter com. 1987—, vol. indigent panel 1992, chair CLE 1992, chmn. membership com. 1993, Pres.'s award 1993), Dean Henry George McMahon Am. Inn of Ct. (barrister, reporter 1993-95), Kiwanis (bd. dirs. 1994—), Baton Rouge Youth (chmn., property com. 1995). Avocations: photography, fencing, writing. Office: Wittenbrink Law Firm 533 Europe St Baton Rouge LA 70802-6408

WITTENSTEIN, MICHAEL DAVID, marketing professional; b. Orlando, Fla., Dec. 29, 1958; s. Sheldon and Patsy Ruth (Printz) W.; m. Louis Ilene Green, Apr. 3, 1990; 1 child, Isaac David. BA with high honors, U. Fla., 1980; M in Internat. Mgmt., Am. Grad. Sch. Internat. Mgmt., Glendale, Ariz., 1985. Market analyst Cushman & Wakefield, Atlanta, 1986-87; info. sys. cons. Wittenstein & Assocs., Atlanta, 1987-90; co-pres., dir. mktg. strategies GALILEO Inc., Atlanta, Ga., 1991-94; CEO SupportWare, software pubs., 1991-92; cons. Apple Computer, Inc., The Nutrasweet Co., Xerox; speaker on implication of photo CD in digital imaging; internat. speaker including Comdex, Am. Mktg. Assn., Gergia Tech, Brazilian Mktg. Assn., Image World, Interactive TV Assn., Bus. OnLine, Internat. Assn. Bus. Communicators, Media/Options, others. Author: Managing Change: A Guide to Automation, (software) Business Presentation on PC, 1989, Help Service for PC, 1990, What Can Multimedia Do for Your Company?, Principles of Knowledge Navigation; developer: (interactive products) Talking Business Card, Laptop Sales System; contbr. articles to profl. jours.; prodr. 100 interactive multimedia projects and websites including AT&T, CNN, Coca-Cola, Delta Airlines, IBM, MCI Telecom., Turner Broadcasting, Goodwill Games, others; inventor of various electronic advertising delivery and measurement programs. Cons. ARC, The Ga. Shakespeare Festival, Atlanta, 1990—, Jewish Family Svcs., Atlanta, 1988—, Chabad of Cobb. Mem. Internat. Interactive Comm. Assn., Bus. and Tech. Alliance, Southeastern Software Assn., Am. Mktg. Assn., Sales & Mktg. Execs. Tech. Execs. Roundtable, Phi Beta Kappa, Omicron Delta Kappa. Avocations: racquetball, hiking, travel. Office: GALILEO Inc 6055 Barfield Rd NE Ste 200 Atlanta GA 30328-4400

WITTER, RICHARD LAWRENCE, veterinarian, educator; b. Bangor, Maine, Sept. 10, 1936; s. John Franklin and Verna Harriet (Church) W.; m. Joan Elizabeth Denny, June 30, 1962; children—Jane Katherine, Steven Franklin. B.S., Mich. State U., 1958, D.V.M., 1960; M.S., Cornell U., 1962, Ph.D., 1964. Rsch. veterinarian Agrl. Rsch. Svc., U.S. Dept. Agr., East Lansing, Mich., 1964-75, dir. Avian Disease and Oncology Lab., 1975—; clin. prof. pathology Mich. State U., East Lansing, 1965—. Contbr. articles to profl. jours. Recipient Disting. Alumni award Coll. Vet. Medicine, Mich. State U., 1985, Disting. Service award USDA, 1985. Mem. AVMA, Am. Assn. Avian Pathologists (P.P. Levine award 1967, 81, 88, 92, Upjohn Achievement award 1992), Poultry Sci. Assn. (CPC Internat. award 1976), Mich. Vet. Med. Assn., World Vet. Poultry Assn. (B. Rispens rsch. award 1983). Lodge: Kiwanis. Avocations: piano, hunting, fishing, gardening. Home: 1799 Elk Ln Okemos MI 48864 Office: Avian Disease and Oncology Lab 3606 E Mt Hope Rd East Lansing MI 48823-5338

WITTHUHN, BURTON ORRIN, university official; b. Allentown, Pa., Aug. 22, 1934; s. Ray Arthur and Mae Marcella (Kline) W.; m. Patricia King, June 24, 1961; children: Jonathan, Andrew. BS, Kutztown (Pa.) U., 1956; MEd, Pa. State U., 1962, PhD, 1968. Tchr. Allentown (Pa.) Pub. Schs., 1956-63; teaching asst., assoc. Pa. State U., University Park, 1963-66, research asst., 1965-66; asst. prof. Ohio State U., Columbus, 1967-70; prof., chmn. dept. geography Edinboro (Pa.) State Coll., 1970-79, assoc. v.p. acad. affairs, 1980-83; provost, v.p. acad. affairs Edinboro Univ. of Pa., 1984-88; provost, v.p. acad. affairs Western Ill. U., Macomb, 1988-93, acting pres., 1993, provost, v.p. acad. affairs, 1994—; is. rsch. prof. Nat. Taiwan Normal U., 1978; cons. Project Africa/Carnegie-Mellon U., Pitts., 1967-70, 92, 87, 95; mem. mid. states periodic rev. team, Phila., 1986; mem. mid. states evaluation team in conjunction with Am. Optometric Assn. , 1987; mem. evaluation team Pa. Dept. Edn., 1988; mem. accreditation team Am. Optometric, 1990, 91, 92; evaluator North Cen. Assn., 1994, 97; vice chmn. Quad Cities Grad. Ctr., 1991—; mem. nat. screening com. for Africa, Inst. of Internat. Edn., 1994, 95, 96. Author: Discovery in Geography, 1976; mem. editl. bd. Pa. Geographer, Chronicle of CQI; contbr. chpts. to books in field. Mem. Edinboro Planning & Zoning Commn., 1973-77. Recipient Disting. Alumnus award Kutztown U., 1990; Fulbright Hays fellow, Ethiopia, Kenya, Uganda, 1965. Mem. Nat. Coun. Geog. Edn. (exec. bd. 1977-80, mem. award com. for region IV 1981), Pa. Coun. Geog. Edn. (exec. sec. 1976-79, pres. 1975-76, Outstanding Prof. award 1978). Democrat. Episcopalian. Lodge: Rotary (pres. Edinboro club 1972-73). Avocations: reading, golf, photography, model constrn. Home: 1106 Bayberry Ln Macomb IL 61455-3518 Office: Western Ill U Sherman Hall 1 Circle Dr Macomb IL 61455

WITTICH, BRENDA JUNE, religious organization executive, minister; b. Muncie, Ind., Dec. 19, 1946; d. Plano Brentie and Norma June (Huggins) Gossett; m. Chester Edward Wittich, Dec. 24, 1980; 1 child, September Leigh Noonan. Lic., Morris Pratt Inst. Assn., 1979, postgrad., 1983-86. Ordained minister Nat. Spiritualist Assn. of Churches, 1986. Pastor Fifth Spiritualist Ch., St. Louis, 1988—. Co-author, editor: National Spiritualist Association Churches Public Relations Handbook, 1992; co-author booklet: Spiritualism - Pathway of Light, 1992; contbr. articles to Nat. Spiritualist Mag. Mem. St. Louis Pub. Sch. Clergy Leaders Forum, 1991-92, Tchrs. for Nat. Spiritualist Assn. of Chs. Ednl. Ctr.-Psychology and Parlimentary Procedures. Mem. Nat. Hemlock Soc., Nat. Spiritualist Assn. of Chs. (trustee 1990-92, supt. pub. rels. 1990-94, v.p. bd. trustees 1992-94, pres. bd. trustees 1994), Inst. Noetic Scis. Avocations: travel, reading. Home: 3903 Connecticut St Saint Louis MO 63116-3905 Office: Nat Spiritualist Assn Chs 13 Cottage Row PO Box 217 Lily Dale NY 14752 *Idealism is not dead, it lies dormant within all people. It is the responsibility of those of us who possess it to assist awakening it in others. We must dream our lofty dreams and see them fulfilled.*

WITTICH, JOHN JACOB, retired college president, corporation consultant; b. Huntley, Ill., Nov. 13, 1921; s. John and Eva (Karl) W.; m. Leah Elliott, Apr. 2, 1944; children: Karen Ann Zvonar, Jane Ellen Tock, John Elliott. B.A., DePauw U., 1943, LL.D. (hon.), 1971; M.A., U. N.Mex., 1949; Ph.D., Stanford U., 1952; L.H.D. (hon.), Ill. Coll., 1979; D.P.S. (hon.), MacMurray Coll., 1980. Tchr. Albuquerque High Sch., 1948-49; teaching asst. Stanford, 1949-51; asst. prof. psychology Coll. of Pacific, Stockton, Calif., 1951-52; dean of admissions, dir. scholarships, assoc. prof. DePauw U., Greencastle, Ind., 1952-61; exec. dir. Coll. Center of Finger Lakes, Corning, N.Y., 1961-63, Coll. Student Personnel Inst., Claremont, Calif., 1963-68; dir. grad. studies in student pers. Claremont Grad. Sch., 1963-68; pres. MacMurray Coll., Jacksonville, Ill., 1968-80; program dir. Fla. Assn. Colls. and Univs., 1980-84; dir. higher edn. program Stetson U., 1981-88; v.p. Capital Formation Counselors, Inc., Belleaire Bluffs, Fla., 1983—. Contbr. articles to popular and profl. jours. Mem. exec. com. Divsn. Higher Edn., Ctrl. Ill. Conf. of United Meth. Ch., 1968-80; mem. exec. com. Fedn. Independent Ill. Colls. and Univs. and Assoc. Colls. Ill.; mem. non-pub. adv. com. Ill. Bd. Higher Edn., 1972-78; mem. Nat. Merit Scholarship Selection Com., 1956, 61; cons. Calif. Gov.'s Conf. on Edn., 1965, on Youth, 1966; trustee Fla. Endowment for Humanities, 1982-85; presdl. counsellor Stetson U., 1987—; bd. dirs. DeLand House Next Door, 1990-94; adv. com. West Volusia County Hosps., 1992—. With USMC, 1943-46, PTO. Recipient Alumni citation DePauw U., 1994; Rockefeller fellow Aspen Inst. for Humanistic Studies, 1979. Mem. APA, Am. Coll. Pers. Assn. (commn. chmn.), Nat. Assn. Coll. Admissions Counselors (exec. bd. 1955-58), Cen. States Coll. Assn. (exec. com. 1969-77, sec.-treas. 1970-77), 4th Marine Divsn. Assn., Sigma Chi.

WITTING, CHRIS *See* **WITTING, CHRISTIAN JAMES, JR.**

WITTING, CHRISTIAN JAMES, JR. (CHRIS WITTING), broadcast executive; b. Plainfield, N.J., Jan. 20, 1953; s. Chris James and Grace Munson Meyers; m. Gale M. Witting, 1978 (div. 1993); children: John N., Karen A. BA in Econs., Williams Coll., 1975. Prodr., pub. affairs dir. WIND-AM, Chgo., 1975-77; exec. prodr. WBZ-AM, Boston, 1978-80; v.p. ops. WOWO-AM, Ft. Wayne, Ind., 1980-83; dir. news and programming KDKA-AM, Pitts., 1983-86, WBBM-AM (CBS), Chgo., 1986-89; v.p., gen. mgr. WCAU-AM (CBS), Phila., 1989-90, WCBS-AM (CBS), N.Y.C., 1990-92; pres. Harmony House, Inc., Chgo., 1993—; ops. mgr. WMAQ-AM (CBS), Chgo., 1994-96; pres. Creative Broadcast Cons., Chgo., 1991—; pres., CEO Success Jour. Corp. Author audio program Countdown to Success, 1993; host, creator syndicated radio program The Success Jour., 1993—, Tracking Business Leaders. Recipient Gold medal Internat. Radio-TV Festival, 1986. Mem. Broadcast Pioneers (life). Office: Success Journal Corp 1310 Waukegan Rd Ste 301 Glenview IL 60025

WITTLER, SHIRLEY JOYCE, former state official, state commissioner; b. Ravenna, Nebr., Oct. 10, 1927; d. Earl William and Minnie Ethel (Frink) Wade; m. LeRoy F. Wittler, Dec. 31, 1946; children: Julie Diane, Barbara Liane. Student, U. Nebr., 1944-47. Real estate saleswoman Harrington Assocs., Lincoln, Nebr., 1965-69; real estate broker Tom Searl Realty, Inc., Cheyenne, Wyo., 1970-76; dep. state treas. Wyo., 1976-78; state treas., 1979-83; chmn. state tax commn. and bd. equalization State of Wyo., 1985-90; ret., 1990. Pres. LWV, Lincoln, 1965-69; bd. dirs. LWV Wyo., 1970-72; fin. chmn. Republican Central Com. Laramie County, Wyo., 1974-76; chmn. Laramie County Pres. Ford Com., 1976; Rep. precinct committeewoman, 1972-77; mem. Laramie County Library Bd., 1976, Community Devel. Adv. Bd., 1974-77. Mem. Cheyenne Bd. Realtors (pres. 1976, Cheyenne Realtor of Yr. 1974), Women's Civic League (treas. 1974, legis. chmn. 1975-76). Lutheran. Home: 5022 Hoy Rd Cheyenne WY 82009-4850

WITTLICH, GARY EUGENE, music theory educator; b. Belleville, Ill., Dec. 3, 1934; s. Marvin Oscar W. and Erma Carrie (Garlich) Jackson Wittlich; m. Barbara L. Casey, Jan. 4, 1958 (div. Feb. 1969); children: M. Kent, Kristi L.; m. Mildred Elizabeth Read, Mar. 17, 1971. B.M.Ed., So. Ill. U., 1957, M.Mus., 1959; Ph.D., U. Iowa, 1969. Asst. prof. music Upper Iowa U., Fayette, 1959-63; prof. music, grad. studies in music theory Ind. U., Bloomington, 1975-94, asst. v.p., office of v.p. for info. tech., 1995—, dir. of computing Sch. of Music, 1989-95; Meadows disting. vis. prof. music So. Meth. U., Dallas, 1982-83; vis. prof. U. Mich., Ann Arbor, 1974; dir. Ctr. for Profl. Devel. in Music Tech., CMS/ATMI, 1995—; cons. U. Del. Music Videodisc Series, NEH, 1982-85; mem. vis. performing arts com. U. Del., 1996-98; mem. music test com. Ednl. Testing Svc., Princeton, N.J., 1983-85, chmn., 1986-90. Author: (with C. Lee Humphries) Ear Training: An Approach Through Music Literature, 1974, (with others) Aspects of Twentieth-Century Music, 1975, (with J. Schaffer and L. Babb) Microcomputers and Music, 1986, (with D. Martin) Tonal Harmony for the Keyboard, 1988. Served with U.S. Army, 1957, 61-62. NSF grantee Ind. U., 1970; fellow Inst. for Acad. Tech., 1992. Mem. Assn. for Tech. in Music Instrn. (founding), Coll. Music Soc. (bd. mem. for theory 1987-89), Soc. Music Theory (exec. bd. 1982-85, pres. 1988-91). Home: 3101 David Dr Bloomington IN 47401-4472 Office: Sch Music Ind U Bloomington IN 47405

WITTLINGER, TIMOTHY DAVID, lawyer; b. Dayton, Ohio, Oct. 12, 1940; s. Charles Frederick and Dorothy Elizabeth (Golden) W.; m. Diane Cleo Dominy, May 20, 1967; children: Kristine Elizabeth, David Matthew. BS in Math., Purdue U., 1962; JD with distinction, U. Mich., 1965. Bar: Mich. 1966, U.S. Dist. Ct. (ea. dist.) Mich. 1966, U.S. Ct. Appeals (6th cir.) 1968, U.S. Supreme Ct. 1971. Assoc. Hill Lewis (formerly Hill, Lewis, Adams, Goodrich & Tait), Detroit, 1965-72, ptnr., 1973—, head litigation dept., 1976—; mem. profl. assistance com. U.S. Dist. Ct. (ea. dist.) Mich., 1981-82. Mem. house of deps. Episc. Ch., N.Y.C., 1979—; vice chmn. Robert Whitaker Sch. Theology, 1983-87; sec. bd. trustees Episc. Ch., Diocese of Mich., Detroit, 1983—, sec. conv. Episc. Diocese Mich., 1990—, mem., sec. Episcopal nat. econ. justice implementation com., 1988—, mem. Episc. nat. exec. coun., 1991—; active Nat. Episc. Jubilee Minstry Com., Nat. Episc. Coalition for Social Witness and Justice, Fifth Province Episc. Ecclesiastical Ct. Appeal; bd. dirs. Episc. Student Found., U. Mich., 1990-93; chair Grubb Inst. Behavioral Studies Ltd., Washington, 1986—. Mem. ABA, State Bar Mich., Nat. Bd. Trial Advocacy (cert.), Engring. Soc. Detroit. Home: 736 N Glenhurst Dr Birmingham MI 48009-1143 Office: Hill Lewis 255 S Woodward Ave Birmingham MI 48009-6182

WITTMANN, OTTO, art museum executive; b. Kansas City, Mo., Sept. 1, 1911; s. Otto and Beatrice Knox (Billingsley) W.; m. Margaret Carlisle Hill, June 9, 1945; children: William Hill, John Carlisle. Student, Country Day Sch., Kansas City; AB, Harvard U., 1933; postgrad., 1937-38, postgrad. Carnegie scholar, summer 1937; LLD, U. Toledo; DFA, Hillsdale Coll., Bowling Green State U., U. Mich., Kenyon Coll., Skidmore Coll. Curator prints Nelson Gallery Art, Kansas City, 1933-37; instr. history of art Emerson Sch., Boston, 1937-38; curator Hyde Collection, Glens Falls, N.Y., 1938-41; instr. history of art Skidmore Coll., Saratoga Springs, N.Y., 1938-41; asst. dir. Portland (Oreg.) Mus. Art, 1941; assoc. dir. Toledo Mus. Art, 1946-59, trustee, 1958—, dir., 1959-76, dir. emeritus, 1977—; v.p., cons., art advisor, 1977—; trustee, cons. Los Angeles County Mus. Art, 1977-78; vice chmn., trustee, cons. J. Paul Getty Trust, 1977—; organizer exhbns. art activities Am. museums USIA, 1953-55; editl. cons. Gazette des Beaux Arts; vice chmn. Nat. Collection Fine Arts Commn.; bd. dirs. Toledo Trust Co.; cons. Clark Art Inst., 1990—. Editl. chmn. Toledo Mus. Catalogue of European Paintings and Guide to Collections; writer numerous museum catalogues, profl. articles. Founding mem. Nat. Coun. Arts; mem. mus. panel NEH; chmn. adv. panel Nat. Found. Arts and Humanities; mem. art adv. panel IRS; mem. nat. arts accessions com. U.S. embassies; mem. U.S.-ICOM Nat. Com.; former sec. gen. com. pour Musées du Verre, ICOM; founding mem. Ohio Arts Coun.; sponsor Nat. Trust Sch., Attingham, Shropshire, Eng. Maj. AUS, USAAF, OSS, 1941-46. Decorated officer Legion of Honor, France, officer Order Orange Nassau, Netherlands, comdr. Arts and Letters France; comdr. Order of Merit Italy). Fellow Museums Assn. (Eng.); mem. Intermus. Conservation Assn. (pres. 1955-56, trustee), Harvard Soc. Contemporary Art (co-dir. 1931-33), Assn. Art Mus. Dirs. (pres. 1961-62, 71-72), Am. Assn. Museums (former v.p., Disting. Service to Mus. award 1987), Coll. Art Assn., Archeol. Inst. Am., Internat. Inst. for Conservation of Hist. and Artistic Works, Soc. Archtl. Historians, Verien der Freunde Antiker Kunst, Am. Soc. French Legion Honneur, Alliance Francaise de Toledo (trustee), Phi Kappa Phi. Episcopalian (vestryman). Clubs: Traveller's (London); Century Assn. (N.Y.C.); Toledo, Harvard (pres. 1956-57), Rotary (pres. 1963-64). Home: 300 Hot Springs Rd Apt 163 Montecito CA 93108-2065 Office: J Paul Getty Trust 1200 Getty Center Dr Ste 400 Los Angeles CA 90049-1657

WITTMER, JAMES FREDERICK, preventive medicine physician, educator; b. Carlinville, Ill., Dec. 30, 1932; s. Franklin Benjamin and Eva Caroline (Zihlman) W.; m. Juanita Lou Wilkey, June 29, 1962; children: Ellen, Carol, Nancy. MD, Washington U., St. Louis, 1957; MPH, Harvard U., 1961. Diplomate Am. Bd. Preventive Medicine. Intern U. Va. Hosp., Charlottesville, 1857-58; commd. capt. USAF, 1958, advanced through grades to col., 1971; ret., 1979; dean allied health U. Tex. Health Sci. Ctr., San Antonio, 1979-80; asst. med. dir. Conoco Oil Co., Ponca City, Okla., 1980-81; assoc. med. dir. Mobil Oil Corp., N.Y.C., 1981-83; dir. health, environ. and safety ITT, N.Y.C., 1983-95; corp. v.p., 1990-95; clin. prof. medicine Cornell U. Med. Coll., N.Y.C., 1984—; lectr. environ. medicine NYU, N.Y.C., 1984—; adj. prof. U. Tex. Sch. Pub. Health, Houston, 1987-96, prof. occupl. health, 1996—; nat. coord. com. on clin. preventive svcs. USPHS, 1994—. Mem. med. and ins. com. Pres.'s Com. on Employment People with Disabilities, Washington, 1986-94, chmn., 1986-90. Fellow ACP, Am. Coll. Occupational and Environ. Medicine (bd. dirs. 1990-97, sec. 1992-94), Am. Coll. Preventive Medicine, Aerospace Med. Assn., N.Y. Acad. Medicine; mem. AMA, Tex. Occupational Med. Assn. Home and Office: 159 Sabine Rd Boerne TX 78006-6217

WITTNER, LOREN ANTONOW, lawyer, former public relations executive; b. N.Y.C., May 2, 1938; s. Henry Warren and Miriam Margo (Antonow) W.; m. Judith Ginsberg, June 21, 1959 (div. Sept. 1972); children: Jennifer Leslie, Elizabeth Anne; m. Dianna Marks, Apr. 2, 1975. AB, Columbia U., 1958; JD, Harvard U., 1961. Bar: N.Y. 1961, Ill. 1966. Assoc. O'Dwyer & Bernstien, N.Y.C., 1961-62, Emil & Kobrin, N.Y.C., 1962-66; assoc. Antonow & Fink, Chgo., 1966-70, ptnr., 1970-77; rep. of Sec. U.S. Dept. Commerce, Chgo. and Washington, 1977-81; exec. v.p. Daniel J. Edelman, Inc., Chgo., 1981-90; ptnr. Winston & Strawn, Chgo., 1990-94; dir. client svcs. Lewis and Roca, Phoenix, 1994—; chmn. Midwest region Fed. Regional Council, 1978-79. Served with USAR, 1961-65. Mem. ABA. Avocation: classical music.

WITTREICH, WARREN JAMES, psychologist, consultant; b. Weehawken, N.J., Aug. 18, 1929; s. Andrew Otto and Muriel Viola (Wilson) W.; m. Mary Shirley Wells, Sept. 10, 1951 (div. Sept. 1959); children: Michael, Peter; m. Lois Vivian Llewellyn, Sept. 8, 1959 (div. July 1996); children: Benjamin, Debra, Susie (dec.), Andrea; m. Eileen Burke, Aug. 20, 1996. AB in Psychology summa cum laude, Princeton U., 1951, MA in Psychology, 1953, PhD in Psychology, 1954; PhD in Clin. Psychology, Cath. U., Washington, 1958. Lic. psychologist, Pa. Guest scientist Naval Med. Rsch. Inst., Bethesda, Md., 1953-54; postdoctoral trainee VA, East Orange, N.J., 1954-55; clin. psychologist Lancaster and Phila., Pa., 1955—; exec. v.p. Nat. Analysts, Inc., Phila., 1959-64; pres. Daniel Yankelovich of Pa., Phila., 1964-67; pres., CEO Crossroads Career Planning Corp., Phila., 1967-85; adj. prof., rsch. cons. U. Pa., Phila., 1968-73; CEO Focus Group Assocs. Ltd., Bethlehem, Pa., 1995—; advisor to Sec. of Transp., U.S. Dept. Transp., Washington, 1968-72; expert witness FTC, Washington, 1957, U.S. Congress, Washington, 1959, N.Y. State Supreme Ct., N.Y.C., 1963. Exhibited in 4 one-man shows; 2 commd. paintings; contbr. articles to profl. jours. Worker Robert F. Kennedy Campaign Com., Washington, 1967; mem. Citizens Adv. Com. on Transp. Quality, U.S. Dept. Transp., Washington, 1968-74. Recipient fellowship NSF, 1952-53. Fellow Pa. Psychol. Assn.; mem. APA, Phi Beta Kappa, Sigma Xi. Episcopalian. Avocation: oil painting. Home: 1158 W Main St Ste F1-1 Lansdale PA 19446

WITTROCK, MERLIN CARL, educational psychologist; b. Twin Falls, Idaho, Jan. 3, 1931; s. Herman C. and Mary Ellen (Baumann) W.; m. Nancy McNulty, Apr. 3, 1953; children: Steven, Catherine, Rebecca. BS in Biology, U. Mo., Columbia, 1953, MS in Ednl. Psychology, 1956; PhD in Ednl. Psychology, U. Ill., Urbana, 1960. Prof. grad. sch. edn. UCLA,

1960—, founder Ctr. Study Evaluation, chmn. div. ednl. psychology, chmn. faculty, exec. com.; univ. com. on outstanding teaching; co-founder Urban Tchr. Edn. Program, 1996; fellow Ctr. for Advanced Study in Behavioral Scis., 1967-68; vis. prof. U. Wis., U. Ill., Ind. U., Monash U., Australia; bd. dirs. Far West Labs., San Francisco; chmn. com. on evaluation and assessment L.A. Unified Sch. Dist.; mem. nat. adv. panel for math. scis. NRC of NAS, 1988-89; chmn. nat. bd. Nat. Ctr. for Rsch. in Math. Scis. Edn., chmn. charges com. UCLA; adv. bd. Kauffman Found., Kansas City, Mo., 1995—; bd. dirs. Western Edn. Lab. for Edn. Rsch. Author, editor: The Evaluation of Instruction, 1970, Changing Education, 1973, Learning and Instruction, 1977, The Human Brain, 1977, Danish transl., 1980, Spanish transl., 1982, The Brain and Psychology, 1980, Instructional Psychology: Education and Cognitive Processes of the Brain, Neuropsychological and Cognitive Processes of Reading, 1981, Handbook of Research on Teaching, 3d edit., 1986, The Future of Educational Psychology, 1989, Research in Learning and Teaching, 1990, Testing and Cognition, 1991, Generative Science Teaching, 1994, Metacognitiion 1995. Capt. USAF, 1953-55. Recipient Thorndike award for outstanding psychol. rsch., 1987, Disting. Tchr. of Univ. award UCLA, 1990; Ford Found. grantee. Fellow AAAS, APA (pres. divsn. ednl. psychology 1984-85, assn. coun. 1988-91, award for Outstanding Svc. to Ednl. Psychology 1991, 93, Disting. Svc. award for svc. to sci. adv. coun.), Am. Psychol. Soc., (charter fellow), Am. Ednl. Rsch. Assn. (chmn. ann. conv., chmn. publs. 1980-83, assn. coun. 1986-89, bd. dirs. 1987-89, chmn. com. on ednl. TV 1989—, Outstanding Contbns. award 1986, Outstanding Svc. award 1989); mem. Phi Delta Kappa. Office: UCLA 3022 Moore Hall Los Angeles CA 90095

WITTRUP, RICHARD DERALD, health care executive; b. Marne, Iowa, Oct. 2, 1926; s. Otis Kermit and Ruby Beatrice (Olsen) W.; m. Marilyn Eleanor Sorensen, June 7, 1949; children: Kenton Lawrence, Alan Scott, Eleanor Elizabeth. BA in Econs., U. Mo., 1951; MBA, U. Chgo., 1955. Adminstrv. asst. U. Chgo. Hosp., 1952-57; adminstr. U. Ky. Hosp., Lexington, 1957-68; asst. exec. v.p. Brigham Women's Hosp., Boston, 1968-69, exec. v.p., 1970-78; adminstr. Herman Smith Assocs. Internat., Jeddah, Saudia Arabia, 1978-80, mng. dir., 1981-88, v.p. profl. affairs, 1980-88; asst. to pres. and CEO Henry Ford Health System, Detroit, 1988-93, corp. v.p., 1993—. Sgt. U.S. Army, 1945-47, Italy. Fellow ACHE; mem. Am. Hosp. Assn., Healthcare Execs. Study Soc. Baptist. Office: Henry Ford Health System 1 Ford Pl Detroit MI 48202-3450

WITTRY, DAVID BERYLE, physicist, educator; b. Mason City, Iowa, Feb. 7, 1929; s. Herman Joseph and Edna Pearl (Filbey) W.; m. Mildred Elizabeth DuBois, July 1, 1955; children—James David, Robert Andrew, Kristopher Lee, Diane Marie, Linda Beryle. B.S., U. Wis., 1951; M.S., Calif. Inst. Tech., 1953, Ph.D., 1957. Research fellow Calif. Inst. Tech., Pasadena, 1957-59; asst. prof. U. So. Calif., Los Angeles, 1959-61; assoc. prof. dept. elec. engring. U. So. Calif., 1961-69, prof. dept. materials sci. and elec. engring., 1969—; cons. Hughes Semiconductors, 1958-59, Applied Research Labs., Inc., 1958-83, Exptl. Sta., E.I. du Pont de Nemours & Co., 1962-71, Gen. Telephone and Electronics Research Labs., 1966-72, Autonetics div. N. Am. Aviation, 1961-63, Electronics Research div. Rockwell Internat., 1976-81, Atlantic Richfield Co. Corp. Tech. Lab., 1981-87, Jet Propulsion Lab., 1985-88, Hitachi Instruments, 1989-90; vis. scientist Japan Soc. Promotion of Sci., U. Osaka Prefecture, 1974. Editor 3 proceedings of cons. Contbr. articles to profl. jours. Patentee in field. Recipient first award essays on gravity, Gravity Research Found., 1949, Disting. Scientist award phys. scis. Microscopy Soc. Am., 1995, Disting. Svc. citation U. Wis. Coll. Engring., 1996; Guggenheim fellow, 1967-68; Knapp scholar U. Wis., 1949-51. Mem. IEEE, Electron Microscopy Soc. Am. (dir. phys. scis. 1979-81, pres. 1983), Microbeam Analysis Soc. (sec. organizing com. 1966, exec. council 1970-72, pres. 1988, Presdl. award 1980, Birks award 1987, 89, hon. mem.), Am. Phys. Soc., Sigma Xi. Methodist. Office: U So Calif Dept Materials Sci Los Angeles CA 90089-0241

WITTSTEIN, EDWIN FRANK, stage and film production designer; b. Mt. Vernon, N.Y., Apr. 7, 1929; s. Nathan Harry and Miriam (Goldman) W. Student, Parsons Sch. Design, 1946-50; BS, NYU, 1950; postgrad., Cooper Union, 1950-52. Stage designer Dramatic Workshop prodn. The Inspector General, 1947; set designer Gertrude Stein's Yes Is for a Very Young Man; set and costume designer Ounga Opera, Phila., 1950, (opera) The Celebrated Jumping Frog of Calaveras County, Venice, Italy, 1953, The Transposed Heads, 1958, The Fantasticks, 1960 (still running); designer Broadway prodn. Kean, 1961; set and costume designer The Gondoliers, N.Y.C. Opera, 1963, The Knack (directed by Mike Nichols), 1964, The Marriage of Figaro, N.Y.C. Opera, 1965, The Amen Corner, 1965, Happy Birthday Wanda June, Enter Laughing, 1965, The Room, A Slight Ache, 1965, The Yearling, 1965, Serjeant Musgrave's Dance, 1966 (Obie award 1966), You Know I Can't Hear You When the Water's Running, 1967, set designer Merchant of Venice, Shakespeare Festival Conn., 1967, As You Like It, Richard II, Shakespeare Festival Conn., 1968, The Man in the Glass Booth, 1968, The Basement, The Tea Party, Celebration, 1969, (for Cin. Playhouse) The Miser, Volpone, The Good Woman of Setzuan, Angel Street, He Who Gets Slapped, 1968-70, The Country Wife, Shakespeare Theatre, Conn., 1973, Ulysses in Nightown, 1974 (Tony award nomination 1974, Maharam award 1974), The Torchbearers, 1978, The Aspern Papers, 1978, Love's Labors Lost, 1983, Berkshire Theatre Festival, 1988, Tusitala, 1988, Tete a Tete, 1989, The Hasty Heart, 1990, Trains, 1991, (sets, costumes 30th anniversary tour) The Fantasticks, 1990, Sarah, Plain and Tall, 1991 (Emmy nomination 1991), Colette Collage, 1991, March of the Falsettos, 1991, Falsettoland, 1991, (prodn. designer Hallmark Hall of Fame TV) An American Story, 1992, (prodn. designer Hallmark Hall of Fame TV) Skylark, 1993, (prodn. designer Hallmark Hall of Fame TV) A Place for Annie, 1993, (set designer off-Broadway) I Do! I Do!, 1996; designer TV shows Armstrong Circle Theatre, The Tonight Show with Steve Allen, NBC operas Cosi Fan Tutte, La Traviata, La Boheme, Boris Godounov, Cavalleria Rusticana, Blithe Spirit, The Diary of Anne Frank, Camino Real, The Royal Family, The Prince of Homburg; prodn. designer TV series The Adams Chronicles (Emmy nomination 1975); designer TV films A Memory of Two Mondays, 1971, For Ladies Only, 1982, Legs, 1982, Samson and Delilah, 1983, Heartsounds, 1984; designer TV spl. Echoes in the Darkness, 1987; designer films Bananas, 1971, Play It Again Sam, 1971, The Seven-Ups, 1972; art dir. films Smile, 1975, Fame, 1979; prodn. designer film Endless Love, 1981; set and costume designer (ballet) Coppelia, 1992. Home: 339 E 87th St New York NY 10128-4801

WITUCKI, JANET MARIE, nursing educator, geriatric researcher; b. Stevens Point, Wis., Nov. 27, 1946; d. Joseph John and Victoria Rose Tylka; m. Elmer Andrew Witucki, Aug. 19, 1967; 1 child, William James. Diploma, St. Joseph's Sch. Nursing, 1967; BSN, Ball State U., 1991, MSN, 1994; postgrad., U. Tenn., 1996—. Staff nurse Meml. Hosp., Wausau, Wis., 1967-69; charge nurse, insvc. dir. Colonial Manor, Wausau, 1969-73, The Willows, Alexandria, Ind., 1979-81; allied health instr. North Ctrl. Tech. Inst., Wausau, 1973-79; staff nurse Cmty. Hosp., Anderson, Ind., 1981-85; instr., allied health coord. Ivy Tech. State Coll., Muncie, Ind., 1985-93; dir. practical nursing program Ivy Tech. State Coll., Muncie, 1993-94; mem. nursing faculty Ball State U., Muncie, 1994-96; bd. dirs. Day Star Alzheimer Adult Day Care Ctr., Muncie, 1993-96; mem. empathy rsch. team U. Tenn., Knoxville; presenter in field. Contbr. articles to profl. jours. Mem. So. Nursing Rsch. Soc., Tenn. Nurses Assn., Ball State U. Nursing Alumni (bd. dirs. 1994-96), Sigma Theta Tau. Avocations: reading, travel. Home: 609 Park Rd Apt 4 Sevierville TN 37862

WITWER, SAMUEL WEILER, JR., lawyer; b. Chgo., Aug. 5, 1941; s. Samuel Weiler and Ethyl Loraine (Wilkins) W.; m. Susan P. Stewart, Sept. 18, 1971; children: Samuel Stewart, Michael Douglas. AB with honors, Dickinson Coll., 1963; JD, U. Mich., 1966. Bar: Ill. 1967, U.S. Dist. Ct. (no. dist.) Ill. 1967, U.S. Ct. Appeals (7th cir.) 1972, U.S. Supreme Ct. 1973, U.S. Ct. Appeals (6th cir.) 1985, U.S. Dist. Ct. (ea. dist.) Mich., 1987. Assoc. Witwer, Moran, Burlage & Atkinson, Chgo., 1967-74; ptnr. Witwer, Poltrock & Giampietro, 1974—; mem. Fed. Trial Bar Admissions Com. No. Dist. Ill., 1982—. Governing mem. Chgo. Zool. Soc., 1986-90; trustee United Meth. Homes and Services, Chgo., 1974—, Dickinson Coll., Carlisle, Pa., 1976—; mem. Cook County Home Rule Commn., Chgo., 1974-75; chmn. Agy. Appeals Com. Chgo., 1975-78; atty. Glenview Park Dist., 1982—; spl. asst. atty. gen. Auditor Gen. Ill., 1984-92. Mem. ABA, Meth. Bar Assn. (pres. 1972-73), Chgo. Bar Assn., Ill. Bar Assn., Law Club of Chgo., Sigma Chi, Phi Delta Phi. Republican. Methodist. Club: Union League. Home: 1330 Overlook Dr Glenview IL 60025-5166 Office: Witwer Poltrock & Giampietro 125 S Wacker Dr Chicago IL 60606-4402

WITZ, GISELA, chemist, educator; b. Breslau, Federal Republic of Germany, Mar. 16, 1939; came to U.S., 1955; d. Gerhardt Witz and Hildegard (Sufeida) Minzak. BA, NYU, 1962, MS, 1965, PhD, 1969. Assoc. rsch. scientist NYU Med. Ctr., N.Y.C., 1970-73, rsch. scientist, 1973-77, asst. prof., 1977-80; asst. prof. Univ. of Medicine and Dentistry of N.J.-Rutgers Med. Sch., Piscataway, N.J., 1980-86; assoc. prof. U. Medicine and Dentistry N.J.-Robert Wood Johnson Med. Sch., Piscataway, 1986-93, prof., 1993—; dep. dir. Joint Grad. Program in Toxicology, Rutgers U./Univ. Medicine and Dentistry of N.J.-Robert Wood Johnson Med. Sch., 1988, assoc. dir. 1992—; cons. Nat. Rsch. Coun., Washington, 1982-83, 85-86. Contbr. articles to profl. jours. Recipient Dupont Teaching award, NYU, 1966, Univ. Scholar, Founders Day award, N.Y. U., 1969, Student Appreciation award Rutgers Assn. Toxicology Grad. Students, 1996. Mem. Am. Assn. Cancer Research, Am. Chem. Soc., Soc. Toxicology, N.Y. Acad. Sci., Sigma Xi. Avocation: gardening. Office: U Medicine and Dentistry NJ Robert Wood Johnson Med Sch Piscataway NJ 08854

WITZGALL, CHRISTOPH JOHANN, mathematician; b. Hindelang, Bavaria, Germany, Feb. 25, 1929; came to U.S., 1959; s. Otto and Hanna (Schulte-Liese) W.; m. Elizabeth Bingham, Oct. 10, 1964; children: John Chandler, Hanna Elizabeth, George Matheus. PhD in Maths., Universitat Munich, 1958. Rsch. assoc. Princeton (N.J.) U., 1959-61, U. Mainz, Germany, 1961; postdoctoral RAND Corp., Santa Monica, Calif., 1961, Argonne Nat. Lab., Joliet, Ill., 1962; mathematician Nat. Bur. of Stds., Washington, 1962-66, Boeing Scientific Rsch. Labs., Seattle, 1966-73, Nat. Inst. Stds. and Tech., Gaithersburg, Md., 1973—; acting chief ops. rsch. div. Nat. Inst. Standards and Tech., Gaithersburg, Md., 1979-82; vis. prof. U. Tex., Austin, 1971, Universitat Wurzburg, Germany, 1972, U. Md., College Park, 1977, Johns Hopkin's U., Balt., 1985. Co-author: Convexity and Optimization in Finite Dimensions, 1970. Mem. AAAS, Informs, Soc. for Indsl. and Applied Maths., Am. Math. Soc. Office: Nat Inst Stds and Tech Gaithersburg MD 20899

WITZIG, WARREN FRANK, nuclear engineer, educator; b. Detroit, Mar. 26, 1921; s. Arthur Judson and Mary (Bender) W.; m. Bernadette Sullivan, Mar. 31, 1942; children: Eric, Leah, Marc, Lisa Witzig Davidson. B.E.E., Rensselaer Poly. Inst., 1942; M.S., U. Pitts., 1944, Ph.D., 1952. Registered profl. engr., Pa., Washington. Research engr. Westinghouse Research, Pitts., 1942-48; mgr. reactor physics, engr. Bettis Atomic, Pitts., 1948-60; co-founder, sr. v.p., dir. NUS Corp., Washington, 1960-67; head dept. nuclear engring. Pa. State U., 1967-87, emeritus, 1987—; cons. nuclear engr. utilities industry; chmn. Pa. Gov.'s Com. on Atomic Energy Devel., 1970-80; mem. Saxton safety com., 1970-72; mem. waste com. Atomic Indsl. Forum, 1971-73; mem. adv. com. Dept. Energy, 1980-82; mem. ops. rev. com. Tex. Utility; mem. nuclear safety and compliance com., bd. dirs. GPU, 1983-92; mem. nuclear oversight com. PSE&G, 1983-91; mem. accrediting bd. Inst. Nuclear Power Ops., 1992-96; mem. safety rev. bd. TVA, 1986-91; chmn. Westinghouse Nuclear Safety and Environ. Commn., 1988-93; chmn. safety audit bd. Centichem., 1989; mem. safeguards com. Pa. State U., 1993—. Designer S5W submarine reactor, 1956-60. Mem. bd. mgmt. YMCA, 1955-64. Fellow AAAS, Am. Nuclear Soc. (mem. exec. com. edn. div., past chmn. nat. com. on public info., chmn. nuclear engring. dept. head com. 1980); mem. Am. Phys. Soc., IEEE (past chmn. nuclear eng. and plasma div.), Sigma Xi, Eta Kappa Nu, Pi Kappa Alpha, Sigma Pi Sigma (Power Engring. Educator spl. citation). Presbyterian (elder). Achievements include design of S5W submarine reactor; criticality engineer on Nautilus maiden voyage; developed continuing and long distance education in nuclear engineering. Home: 1330 E Park Hills Ave State College PA 16803-3244 Office: Pa State U 231 Sackett Bldg University Park PA 16802-1408

WITZKE, DAVID JOHN, plastic surgeon, educator; b. Rochester, Minn., Jan. 7, 1951; s. Walton E. and Adeline (Altermatt) W.; m. Barbara-Jo Weko, July 20, 1978; children: Sterling, Mercedes, Beckett, Peyton. BA in Math. summa cum laude, U. Minn., 1973; MD, Mayo Med. Sch., 1977. Diplomate Am. Bd. Surgery, Am. Bd. Plastic Surgery, Nat. Bd. Med. Examiners. Intern gen. surgery Mayo Clinic, 1977-78, resident gen. surgery, 1978-82, resident plastic surgery, 1982-84; rsch. asst. U. Minn., Mpls., 1969-73, Mayo Grad. Sch. Medicine, Rochester, 1973-77; pvt. practice, Sioux Falls, S.D., 1984—; dir. burn unit McKennan Hosp., Sioux Falls, 1986—; clin. instr. surgery U. S.D. Med. Sch., Sioux Falls, 1986—; presenter in field. Contbg. author: Methods in Cell Biology, 1978, Hypertrophic Cardiomyopathy, 1982; contbr. articles to med. jours. Recipient Donald C. Balfour Alumni award, 1978. Fellow ACS; mem. AMA, Am. Soc. Plastic and Reconstructive Surgeons, Am. Soc. Maxillofacial Surgeons, Am. Burn Assn., Am. Cleft Palate Assn., Am. Assn. for Hand Surgery, Am. Soc. for Reconstructive Microsurgery, Internat. Soc. Craniomaxillofacial Surgery, Internat. Congress Plastic and Reconstructive Surgery, Midwestern Assn. Plastic Surgery, Acad. Plastic Surgeons Minn., S.D. Med. Assn., Mayo Clinic Priestley Surg. Soc., Mayo Alumni Assn., Phi Beta Kappa. Avocations: statistical equity analysis, scuba diving. Office: Plastic Surgery Assocs SD 911 E 20th St Ste 602 Sioux Falls SD 57105-1048

WIWCHAR, MICHAEL, bishop; b. Komarno, Manitoba, Canada, May 9, 1932. ordained priest June 28, 1959. Pastor St. John the Baptist Church, Newark, NJ, 1990-93; bishop Diocese of St. Nicholas of Chicago for the Ukrainians, 1993—. Office: Chancery Office 2245 W Rice St Chicago IL 60622-4858

WIXOM, WILLIAM DAVID, art historian, museum administrator, educator; b. Phila., July 17, 1929; s. Clinton Wood and Beatrice Rachel (Hunt) W.; BA, Haverford (Pa.) Coll., 1951; MA, Inst. Fine Arts NYU, 1963; m. Nancy Coe, Aug. 8, 1959; 3 children. Asst. curator to curator medieval and renaissance decorative arts Cleve. Mus. Art, 1958-78, chief curator early western art, 1979; chmn. dept. medieval art and The Cloisters, Met. Mus. Art, N.Y.C., 1979—; adj. assoc. prof. history of art Case Western Res. U., Cleve., 1967-78, adj. prof., 1978; adj. prof. N.Y.U., 1981-82; mem. adv. council for Snite Mus. Art Notre Dame U., 1974-95. Bd. dirs. Internat. Ctr. Medieval Art, N.Y.C., 1971-82, pres., 1971-74. Belgium-Am. Ednl. Found. fellow, 1962; Nat. Endowment Arts grantee, 1973; fellow Pierpont Morgan Library, 1979—; J. Paul Getty Mus. Guest Scholar, 1996. Fellow Soc. of Antiquaries of London; mem. Coll. Art Assn. (dir. 1979-83), Medieval Acad. Am., Internat. Center Medieval Art. Quaker. Author: Treasures from Medieval France, 1967; Renaissance Bronzes from Ohio Collections, 1975; contbg. author The Royal Abbey of Saint Denis in the Time of Abbot Suger, 1981, The Treasury of San Marco, 1985; Gothic and Renaissance Art in Nuremberg, 1986, Festschrift Gerhard Bott, 1987, Hommage à Hubert Landais, 1987, The Cloisters, Studies in Honor of the Fiftieth Anniversary, 1992, Festschrift Gerhard Schmidt, 1994, Enamels of Limoges 1100-1350, 1996, Studies in Honor of Kurt Weitzmann, 1995, The Glory of Byzantium, Art and Culture of the Middle Byzantine Era, AD-843-1261, 1997; contbr. articles to profl. jours. Office: Cloisters Fort Tryon Park New York NY 10040

WIZARD, BRIAN, publisher, author; b. Newburyport, Mass., June 24, 1949; s. Russell and Ruth (Hidden) Willard. BA, Sonoma (Calif.) State U., 1976; D of Metaphysics, Universal Life Ch., 1997. Ordained to ministry Universal Life Ch., 1997. Pvt. practice as jeweler, sculptor and craftsman Calif., 1974-79; Wallowa, Oreg., 1991—; prin. The Starquill Pub., Port Douglas, Queensland, Australia, 1981-86; owner Starquill Internat., Wallowa, Oreg. Author: (novels) Permission to Kill, 1985, Shindara, 1987, Heaven on Earth, 1990, Coming of Age, 1990, Permission to Live, 1992, Pollution IV, 1993, Back in the World, 1995, (short stories) Tropical Pair, 1986, Metempsychosis, 1988 (In Search of) The Silver Lining, 1994, The Moon Whistling By on a Cloud, 1994, (The Princess of the) Wildflowers, 1995, Mushroom Magic, 1996; contbr. to Smithsonian Inst.'s The Vietnam War Generation; contbr. to SpaceArc; prodr. (video documentaries) Thunderhawks, 1987, Swift Action Newsteam, Tope Creek Lookout, 1995; songwriter, prodr. (cassette) Brian Wizard Sings for His Supper, 1989 (cert. of achievement Billboard 1993); songwriter, singer, prodr. (music videos) (I Don't Want) Permission to Kill, 1989, Busker's Theme Song, Living in North Queensland, Circus Act, Hitch Hiking Man, Self-Portrait, The Love We Share Will Never End, 1994, Never Met a Girl Like You, Folk-Rock Opera: A Cover Story: After That Ugly Saloon Incident. Renovator hist. landmark The Tope Creek Lookout (Skyship); sponsor Adopt A Hwy., 1995; min. Universal Life Ch. With U.S. Army, 1967-70. Decorated Air medals (26), Aviator Flight Wings; recipient Cert. of Appreciation, Pres. Richard M. Nixon. Mem. Vietnam Helicopter Crewmember Assn., 145th Combat Aviation Bn. Assn., Vietnam Combat Vets. Assn., Vietnam Vets. Am., Vietnam Vets. Australia Assn. Office: PO Box 42 Wallowa OR 97885-0042 *Vietnam combat veteran Brian Wizard upgraded his combat experience to creative insight. He turns his inner visions into expressive art with the same gusto developed as a crew member of the historical assault helicopter Pollution IV. His art work is wide ranging and top quality. He can write a good story, compose a catchy tune, produce amazing videos, and make outrageous sculptures and jewelry. Brian Wizard is a turn-of-the-millennium artist/author who has locked and loaded his mind with clear and concise thoughts.*

WLEUGEL, JOHN PETER, manufacturing company executive; b. Hoyanger, Sogn, Norway, July 1, 1929; s. Johan and Helga (Faye) W.; m. Leonor Abaroa, Dec. 1959; children—Jan Andrew, Cecilia Maria. B.A., U. Copenhagen, 1953; M.B.A., U. Toronto, 1957. With Belgium Machine Tool Assn., 1953-54; with Massey-Ferguson Ltd., Toronto, 1954-71, treas., 1968-71, also dir. several subs.; sr. v.p. Bata Ltd., Toronto, also bd. dirs.; dir., officer several subsidiaries (Bata Shoe Org.), Don Mills, Ont., Can., 1972-89; exec.-in-residence Schulich Sch. Bus., York U., North York, Can., 1990—; bd. dirs. Advanced Material Resources Ltd., The Can. Coun. for the Ams. Mem. Financial Execs. Inst., Univ. Club (Toronto). Home: 5 Campbell Crescent, North York, ON Canada M2P 1P1 Office: York U, Schulich Sch Bus, 4700 Keele St, North York, ON Canada M3J 1P3

WOBBLETON, JUDY KAREN, artist, educator; b. Williamston, N.C., Aug. 31, 1947; d. Lloyd Thomas and Lillian Edith (Hudson) Letchworth; m. Albert Virgil Wobbleton Jr., Apr. 7, 1968; children: Olivia Elizabeth, Virgil Alan. Clk. Beaufort County Hosp., Washington, N.C., 1965-68; ins. supr. Mercy Hosp., Sacramento, 1968-72; adminstrv. asst. hosp. svcs. Fairbanks (Alaska) Meml. Hosp., 1972-75; basketry artist Williamston, 1983—; instr. basketry N.C. Basketmakers, 1984-97, co-founder, 1984; instr. Wayne C.C., Goldsboro, N.C., 1986-91. Contbg. artist: The Basket Book, 1988, Basketmaker's Baskets, 1990, Craft Works in The Home, 1990. Troop leader Girl Scouts U.S., Goldsboro, 1983-88, svc. unit mgr., 1987-91; active Roanoke Arts & Crafts Guild, 1991-96, v.p., 1991-97. Recipient 2d Pl. award Wilson Arts Coun., 1987, 3d Pl. award Martin County Arts Coun., 1992. Mem. N.C. Basketmakers Assn. (hon., co-founder 1984, bd. dirs. 1984-94, membership chmn. 1984-87, pres. 1990-94, conv. rev. com. 1994-96), Goldweavers Basketry Guild (hon.). Avocations: reading, cooking, painting. Home and Office: Baskets By Judy 1325 Oakview Rd Williamston NC 27892

WOBUS, REINHARD ARTHUR, geologist, educator; b. Norfolk, Va., Jan. 11, 1941; s. Reinhard Schaffer and Oral (Phares) W.; m. Sheridan Whitcher, Mar. 18, 1967; children: Erik Reinhard, Cameron Wright. BA, Washington U., St. Louis, 1962; MA, Harvard U., 1963; PhD, Stanford U., 1966. Asst. prof. geology Williams Coll., Williamstown, Mass., 1966-72, assoc. prof., 1972-78, prof., 1978-85, Edna McConnell Clark prof. geology, 1985—, dept. chmn., 1988-96; geologist U.S. Geol. Survey, Denver, 1967-86; vis. prof. Colo. Coll., Colorado Springs, 1976, 82-83, Colo. State U., Ft. Collins, summers 1977-84; staff geologist Colo. Outdoor Edn. Ct., Florissant, 1983; co-founder Keck Twelve-Coll. Geol. Consortium, mem. gov. bd., 1986—. Contbr. maps and articles on Precambrian geology of So. Rocky Mountains to profl. jours. Danforth fellow, 1962, Woodrow Wilson felow, 1962, NSF fellow, 1962-66. Fellow Geol. Soc. Am.; mem. Am. Geophys. Union, Nat. Assn. Geology Tchrs., Coun. on Undergrad. Rsch., Colo. Sci. Soc., Mineral Soc. Am., Phi Beta Kappa, Sigma Xi. Current work: Petrology and geochronology of Precambrian igneous and metamorphic rocks and mid-Tertiary volcanic rocks, so. Rocky Mountains. Subspecialties: Petrology, Geology. Home: 20 Grandview Dr Williamstown MA 01267-2528 Office: Williams Coll Dept Geoscis Williamstown MA 01267

WODARCZYK, FRANCIS JOHN, chemist; b. Chgo., Dec. 11, 1944; s. Sigmund Frank and Josephine Aurelia (Boblak) W. BS, Ill. Inst. Tech., 1966; AM, Harvard U., 1967, PhD, 1971. Postdoctoral U. Calif., Berkeley, 1971-73; rsch. chemist Cambridge Rsch. Labs., Hanscom AFB, Mass., 1973-77; program mgr. Office of Sci. Rsch., Bolling AFB, D.C., 1977-78; mem. tech. staff Rockwell Internat. Sci. Ctr., Thousand Oaks, Calif., 1978-85; program mgr. Office of Sci. Rsch., Bolling AFB, 1985-90; program dir. NSF, Washington, 1990—. Recipient scholarship, George M. Pullman Found., 1962, Ill. Inst. Tech., 1962-66, Ill. State scholarship, 1962-66, NSF fellowship, 1966-71, 71-72. Mem. AAAS, Am. Chem. Soc., Sigma Xi, Alpha Chi Sigma (chpt. v.p. 1965-66, chpt. award 1964). Achievements include development of radio frequency-microwave double resonance spectroscopy; first demonstration cw optically pumped molecular laser; laser-excited electronic to vibrational energy transfer studies. Office: NSF 4201 Wilson Blvd Arlington VA 22230-0001

WODLINGER, MARK LOUIS, broadcast executive; b. Jacksonville, Fla., July 13, 1922; s. Mark H. and Beatrice Mae (Boney) W.; m. Marilyn Stone-Birk; children: Kevin, Michael, Stephen, Mark. BS, U. Fla., 1943. Salesman Sta. WQUA, Moline, Ill., 1948; mgr. Sta. WOC-AM-FM-TV, Davenport, Iowa, 1949-58; v.p. Sta. WMBD-TV, Peoria, Ill., 1959-61; v.p., gen. mgr. Sta. WZZM-TV, Grand Rapids, Mich., 1962-63, Sta. KMBC-TV, Kansas City, Mo., 1963-69; pres. Intermedia, Kansas City, 1969-73; builder, owner comml. radio stas. Swaziland, Africa; operator Radio Malawi, Blantyre, and Marknews TV and Radio News Bur., Nairobe, Kenya, 1971-74; owner, pres. Sta. KBEQ, Kansas City, 1973-77; owner Sta. WCJX-FM, Miami, 1985-86, Sta. WIXI-FM, Naples and Ft. Myers, Fla., 1986-95, Sta. KKLO-AM, Leavenworth, Kans., 1982-92, Sta. KCWV, Kansas City, Mo., 1982-90, TV-5, Hit Video USA, Satellite Music Network, Houston, 1985-88; owner SMR-2-way radio/telephone, Naples, Fla., 1993—, San Francisco, 1993—; chmn. bd. dirs. Wodlinger Broadcasting Co., Naples, 1978—; ptnr. Wireless Cable, Naples, 1990—; owner, ptnr. KABELTEL KFT (Hungary), Budapest, Sopron, Nagykanizsa, Szombathely, 1991-96; owner, comml. FM Radio Ikva, Sopron, 1993—, comml. FM Love Radio 97.8, Tallinn, Paide, Rakvere, Tartu, Sindi, Viliandi and Marjamaa, Estonia, 1993—, comml. FM Radio Kecskemet, Hungary, 1995—, FM Radio Zalaegerszeg, 1995—, comml. FM Reflex Radio 99.2 MHz, Szekesfehervar, Hungary, 1996—; ptnr., chmn. bd. dirs. wireless cable TV Ukrainian-Am. Broadcasting, Kiev, Ukraine, 1990—, comml. TV Channel 7, 1990—, comml. FM Radio 69.89, Kiev, 1992—; owner, ptnr. comml. FM Radiocentras, Vilnius, Lithuania, 1992-96; owner, ptnr. comml. FM Radio 99.70 MHz, 1996—; ptnr. joint mktg. AT&T Paradyne, Largo, Fla., 1992-94, Bellcore, Morristown, N.J., 1995—; owner, ptnr., chmn. bd. dirs. real estate devel., Croatia, 1991—; owner outdoor advt. billboards, Tallinn, Estonia, 1993-95; owner, ptnr. real estate devel., Hungary, 1991—. Bd. dirs. Kansas City Philharm., Kansas City Civic Coun., Naples YMCA; mem. Conservancy, Naples Civic Assn. Served to lt. USN, 1941-45. Mem. Nat. Assn. Broadcasters, Mo. Assn. Broadcasters, Broadcast Pioneers. Republican. Episcopalian. Clubs: Kansas City, Univ., Vanguard, Carriage, Port Royal, Naples Yacht, Houston Yacht, White Lake Yacht (Whitehall, Mich.). Lodge: Rotary. Home: 800 Galleon Dr Naples FL 34102 Office: 3355 Tamiami Trl N Naples FL 34103

WOELFEL, JAMES WARREN, philosophy educator; b. Galveston, Tex., Aug. 16, 1937; s. Warren Charles and Mary Frances (Washinka) W.; m. Sarah Chappell Trulove, Nov. 24, 1982; children by previous marriages: Skye Caitlin, Allegra Eve, Sarah Judith; stepchildren: Ann Marie and Paul Trulove. BA, U. Okla., 1959; MDiv, Episcopal Div. Sch., Cambridge, Mass., 1962; MA, Yale U., 1964; PhD, U. St. Andrews, Scotland, 1967. Asst. prof. philosophy and religion U. Kans., Lawrence, 1966-70, asst. prof. philosophy, 1970-71; assoc. prof. philosophy and religion, 1971-75, prof. philosophy and religious studies, 1975-88, prof. philosophy, 1988—, acting chmn. dept. religious studies, 1983-84, dir. Western civilization program, 1985—; manuscript reader for various presses, jours. Author: Bonhoeffer's Theology, 1970, Borderland Christianity, 1973, Camus: A Theological Perspective, 1975 (republished as Albert Camus on the Sacred and the Secular, 1987), Augustinian Humanism, 1979, The Agnostic Spirit as a Common Motif in Liberal Theology and Liberal Scepticism, 1990; editor (with Sarah Chappell Trulove) and contbr.; Patterns in Western Civilization, 1991; contbr. numerous articles, essays, revs. to profl. publs. Danforth grad. fellow Episcopal Div. Sch., Cambridge, Mass., 1959-62, U. St. Andrews, 1962-63, 65-66, Yale U., New Haven, 1963-65; Fulbright scholar U. St. Andrews, 1962-63; grantee NEH, Exxon Found., Mellon Found., Menninger Found.,

Inst. for Ecumenical and Cultural Research. Mem. Am. Acad. Religion, Highlands Inst. for Am. Religious Thought, Phi Beta Kappa. Democrat. Avocations: piano; walking. Home: 808 Alabama St Lawrence KS 66044-3942 Office: U Kans Western Civilization Program 2106 Wescoe Hall Lawrence KS 66045-2178

WOELFEL, JOSEPH DONALD, communications educator; b. Buffalo, June 3, 1940; s. Richard Joseph and Elizabeth Lillian (Graeber) W.; children: Charles, Joseph, Johanna, Evan, Alaina, Alec. BS in Sociology, Canisius Coll., 1962; MA in Sociology, U. Wis., 1963, PhD in Sociology, 1968. Asst. prof. sociology U. Ill., Urbana, 1968-72; assoc. prof. communications Mich. State U., East Lansing, 1972-78; prof. communications SUNY, Albany, N.Y., 1978-89; prof., chair communications SUNY, Buffalo, N.Y., 1989—; pres. The Galileo Co., Amherst, N.Y., 1978—; dir. rsch. Terra Rsch. Computing Co., Birmingham, Mich., 1990—; cons. Agy. Internat. Devel., Albany Rsch. Svcs., Almeth Rsch., Am. Mktg. Assn., Arbitron, ASG, Blue Cross/Blue Shield Mich., others; bd. dirs. Multimedia Moguls, Lancaster, N.Y. Author: Communication and Science, 1992, 94, What's Wrong With This Picture?, 1995, Variational Principles of Communication, 1995, (with others) The Measurement of Communication Process: Galileo Theory and Method, 1980; editor Systemsletter, 1983-85; editor-in-chief RAH Press, 1995—; assoc. editor Human Communication Rsch., 1976, 79, Communication Quar., 1977-83, Informatologia Jugoslavia, 1985—; cons. editor Am. Sociol. Rev., Am. Jour. Sociology, Rural Sociology, Jour. Cross Cultural Rsch., Human Orgn., Human Communication Rsch., Communication Rsch.; contbr. chpts. in books and articles to profl. publs. Bd. dirs. WBFO, Buffalo, 1991-92. Sr. fellow East-West Communication Inst., Honolulu, 1977-83, Faculty fellow Rockefeller Inst. Govt., 1985—; Richard W.D. Nicholas Agrl. Sci. scholar U. Melbourne, 1986; recipient Pres.'s award for Excellence in Rsch., SUNY, 1983, Fulbright award Conf. Dubrovnik, 1983. Mem. AAAS, N.Am. Classification Soc., N.Y. Acad. Scis., Internat. Soc. Network Analysis, Neural Network Soc., Psychometric Soc., Soc. Scientific Study of Communication. Office: U Buffalo Dept Communication 332 MFAC-Fillmore Buffalo NY 14261

WOELFFER, EMERSON SEVILLE, artist; b. Chgo., July 27, 1914; s. George K. and Marguerite (Seville) W.; m. Diane Anderson, Dec. 7, 1945. Student, Art Inst. Chgo., 1935-38; B.F.A., Inst. Design, Chgo., 1949; PhD (hon.), New Sch. for Social Rsch., 1991, Otis Parsons Sch. Design, L.A., 1993, Otis Parson's Art Inst., 1993, New Sch. Social Rsch., Otis Sch. head painting dept. Otis Art Inst., Los Angeles, 1974—; artist in residence. One-man shows include Paul Kantor Gallery, Beverly Hills, Calif., 1953, 60, Poindexter Gallery, N.Y.C., 1958, 61, Primus-Stuart Gallery, L.A., 1961, Santa Barbara (Calif.) Mus. Art, 1964, Quay Gallery, San Francisco, 1967, Honolulu Acad. Arts, 1970, Jodi Scully Gallery, L.A., 1972, 73, Newport Harbour Art Mus., Newport Beach, Calif., 1974, Phillips Collection, Washington, 1975, Gruenebaum Gallery, N.Y.C., 1978, New Orleans Mus. Art, 1987, Wenger Gallery, L.A., Manny Silverman Gallery, L.A., 1991, 93, Parsons Sch. Design, L.A., 1992, Otis Art Inst., James Corcoran Gallery, 1993, Hyundai Art Gallery, Seoul, Korea, 1995; traveling exhbn. at Modern Art Mus., New Delhi, India, 1988, collages of 1987-89 Manny Silverman Gallery, L.A.; two-person show Harcourt Gallery, San Francisco, 1990; exhibited in group shows at UCLA, 1987-88; represented in permanent collections British Mus., Art Inst. Chgo., Whitney Mus. Am. Art, Mus. Modern Art, N.Y.C., L.A. County Mus. Art, Washington Gallery Modern Art, Wight Galleries of UCLA, San Francisco Mus. Art, Bauhaus Archives, Berlin, Smithsonian Archives Am. Art, Washington, Santa Fe Mus. Art, Seattle Art Mus., Biblioteque Nationale, Paris, Acad. Arts and Sci., N.Y., Israel mus., also numerous others. Grantee Guggenheim Found., 1968-69, NEA, 1974, Pollock Krasner, 1986, Greenburger Found., 1988; prints given Israel Mus., Vienna, 1996. Home: 475 Dustin Dr Los Angeles CA 90065-5023

WOELFLEIN, KEVIN GERARD, banker; b. Haverhill, Mass., Feb. 9, 1933; s. John Henry and Helen Margaret (Hoar) W.; m. Ann Buckley, Sept. 9, 1957; children: Karl G., Luise A., Andrew B., Peter H. B.S., MIT, 1954; M.B.A., U. Pa., 1958, postgrad., 1959-65. Venture analyst Atlas Chem. Industries, Wilmington, Del., 1959-66; economist Fed. Res. Bank Phila., 1966-67; asst. v.p. 1st Nat. Bank Chgo., 1967-70, v.p., 1970-72; v.p., gen. mgr. (Tokyo br.), 1972-75; pres., chief exec. officer, dir. UBAF Arab Am. Bank, N.Y.C., 1975-81; pres., chief operating officer, dir. Am. Security Bank, Washington, 1981-83; pres., dir. Mass. Co., Inc., Boston, 1983-86; pres. U.S. Capital Investments Co., Alexandria, Va., 1983—; chmn. bd. Conn. Bancorp, Inc., also bd. dirs.; chmn. bd. Norwalk (Conn.) Bank, 1990-92, also bd. dirs.; mem. The Spectrum Group, Alexandria, 1995—; trustee Meridian Internat. Ctr., Washington, 1982-87, counselor, 1987—. Bd. dirs. Small Bus. High Tech. Inst., 1982-85; mem. exec. com. MIT Enterprise Forum, Washington, 1982-85; mem. MIT Corp. vis. com. Ctr. for Internat. Studies; mem. adv. council U.S.-Japan Study Ctr., Johns Hopkins U. Sch. Advanced Internat. Studies, 1982-85; trustee Convent of Sacred Heart, Greenwich, Conn., 1977-81; mem. U.S.-Saudi Arabian Joint Commn. on Econ. Cooperation, 1982-84. Served to lt. U.S. Army, 1954-56. Recipient Corp. Leadership award MIT, 1980; Knight of Malta, Fed. Assn., 1984. Mem. Riverside Yacht Club, Columbia Country Club. Office: The Spectrum Group 11 Canal Center Plz Ste 110 Alexandria VA 22314-1595

WOERNER, FREDERICK FRANK, international relations educator; b. Phila., Aug. 12, 1933; s. Frederick Frank and Mary Ann (McCabe) W.; m. Gennie Ehrhorn, Jan. 21, 1956; children: Frederick Frank III, Charles Anthony, Robert John, Michael Scott. BS, U.S. Mil. Acad., West Point, N.Y., 1955; MA, U. Ariz., 1965. Advanced through grades to gen. U.S. Army, 1955-89, ret., 1989; prof. Boston U., 1990—; chmn. Am. Battle Monuments Commn., Washington, 1994—; v.p. U.S. Strategic Inst., Boston, 1992—. Mem. Assn. Grads. of Mil. Acad., Assn. U.S. Army, Coun. Fgn. Rels., Inter-Am. dialogue. Lutheran. Avocations: reading, jogging, fishing. Home: 4 Arbor Cir Natick MA 01760 Office: Dept Internat Rels Boston U 152 Bay State Rd Boston MA 02215-1501

WOERNER, ROBERT LESTER, landscape architect; b. Rochester, N.Y., Jan. 31, 1925; s. William John and Loretta Bertha (Hettel) W.; m. Mary Jane Warn, May 12, 1952; children: Jane Marie, Anne Louise. B.S., SUNY Coll. Forestry, Syracuse, 1949. Cert. landscape architect, Wash., Idaho. Draftsman N.A., Rotunno Landscape Architects, Syracuse, 1947-49; landscape architect Park Dist., Plan Commn., Yakima, Wash., 1949-50; asst. supt. parks Spokane Park Dept., Spokane, Wash., 1950-56; dir. Denver Bot. Gardens, 1956-58; pvt. practice landscape architect Spokane, 1959—; chmn. bd. registration Landscape Architects State of Wash., 1976-78; pres. Council Landscape Archtl. Registration Bds., 1978-79. Mem. Zoning Bd. Adjustment, Spokane, 1983; mem. Urban Design Com., 1983; mem. Capitol Campus Design Adv. Com., 1982-94. Cpl. U.S. Army, 1943-45, ETO. Recipient Indsl. Landscaping Award Am. Assn. Nurserymen, Lincoln Bldg., Spokane, 1966; recipient Cert. of Merit Wash. Water Power, 1967, State Indsl. Landscaping award Wash State Nurserymen's Assn., Wash. Water Power, 1968. Fellow Am. Soc. Landscape Architects (pres. 1979-80, Disting. Svc. award 1976). Republican. Roman Catholic. Lodge: Kiwanis.

WOESSNER, FREDERICK T., composer, pianist; b. Teaneck, N.J., July 23, 1935; s. Fred and Bertha W.; m. Lise, Feb. 14, 1960 (div. 1973); children: Betty, Allison. Student, Peabody Conservatory of Music, Balt., 1960-61; MBA, NYU, 1968; MA, Calif. State U., Los Angeles, 1975; pvt. study with, David Diamond, Charles Haubiel, Albert Harris. Owner Al-Fre-Bett Music, Los Angeles, 1980—. Composer (for orch.) Nursery Song, Variations on an Irish Air, Reflections for Strings, Fanfare for Winds, String Quartet, Concerto for piano improvisations and orch., Secret Gospels (Cantata), Sonic studies for Piano I Elegy for Trumpet and Winds, (music for films) Sky Bandits, Gunbus, Pale Horse, Pale Rider, The Curb Your Appetite Diet, Centerfold, (title music for TV) Actors Forum, (for stage) From Berlin to Broadway, Oh Atlantis, Kurt, Lil Nell, Another Town, Victorian Atmospheres; composer and pianist, album-film/video, Vincent Moreaux, His Finest Hour In My Forest Cathedral, Songs from the Sea; rec. artist Sonic Arts and Repertoire Records. Pres. bd. dirs. Inst. for Recording and Multimedia Arts; mem. bd. govs.Music and the Arts Found. of Am., Inc.; dir. West Coast Musical Theatre Lab. Mem. ASCAP, Nat. Acad. Recording Arts and Scis., Dramatists Guild, Soc. Composers and Lyricists, Am. Fedn. Musicians, Am. Soc. Music Arrangers and Composers (treas. 1978—), Composers and Arrangers Found. Am. (sec.). Democrat. Office: Al-Fre-Bett Music PO Box 45 Los Angeles CA 90078-0045

WOESTENDIEK, (WILLIAM) JOHN, JR., columnist; b. Winston-Salem, N.C., Sept. 5, 1953; s. William John Sr. and Josephine (Pugh) W.; m. Jennifer Ann Swartz, Sept. 1, 1979; 1 child, Joseph Yoon Tae. BJ, U. N.C., 1975. Reporter Ariz. Daily Star, Tucson, 1975-78; reporter, asst. city editor, city editor Lexington (Ky.) Herald-Leader, 1978-81; reporter Phila. Inquirer, 1981-90; nat. corr. West Coast bur. Phila. Inquirer, Newport Beach, Calif., 1990-93; reporter Phila. Inquirer, 1994-96, columnist, 1996—. Recipient Paul Tobenkin Meml. award Columbia U., 1984, Nat. Headliners award Press Club Atlantic City, 1987, Pulitzer Prize for Investigative Reporting Columbia U., 1987, Ernie Pyle award, 1994, Best Feature Story award Ky. Press. Assn., 1978, Best Investigative Story award Ky. Press Assn., 1979, Nat. Arc of Excellence Nat. Assn. Retarded Citizens, 1984, Best News Reporting First Place award AP Mng. Editors Pa., 1985, Sigma Delta Chi award for Feature Writing, 1994; John S. Knight fellow Stanford U., 1988-89. Office: The Phila Inquirer PO Box 8263 Philadelphia PA 19101-8263

WOETZEL, DAMIAN ABDO, ballet dancer, educator; b. Newton, Mass., May 17, 1967; s. Robert Kurt and Sheila Marilyn (Barry) W. Grad. high sch., Holllywood, Calif., 1983. Prin. dancer L.A. Ballet, 1983-85; mem. corps de ballet N.Y.C. Ballet, 1985-88, soloist, then prin. dancer, 1989—; Dir. ballet program New York State Summer School for the Arts, Saratoga Springs, N.Y., 1994—; dancer, choreographer New York City Opera, 1994-95. Performed in Jerome Robbins' Four Seasons Dance at a Gathering: Goldberg Variations, Glass Pieces, Interplay, Other Dances; Balanchine's La Sonnambula, Stars and Stripes, Mozariana, Ballo della Regina, Tarantella, The Nutcracker, La Source,Coppelia, Donizetti Variations, Raymonda Variations, Martin's the Sleeping Beauty, Jeu de Cartes, Musical Offering, Paulenc Sonata, Les Petits Riens, The Waltz Project; also Tschaikovsky's Pas de Deux; danced in N.Y.C. Ballet's Balanchine Celebration, 1993, danced in film George Balanchine's The Nutcracker, 1993; choreographed Ebony Concerto, 1994, Glazounov Pas de Deux, 1994; danced in Alexander Borodin's opera Prince Igor, 1994. Recipient 1st prize Commemorative award Nat. Ballet Achievement Fund, Phila., 1984. Avocations: carpentry, gardening, guitar playing, surfing. Office: NYC Ballet Inc NY State Theater Lincoln Ctr Plz New York NY 10023*

WOFFORD, HARRIS LLEWELLYN, former senator, national service executive; b. N.Y.C., Apr. 9, 1926; s. Harris Llewellyn and Estelle (Gardner) W.; m. Emmy Lou Clare Lindgren, Aug. 14, 1948 (dec. Jan. 1996); children: Susanne, Daniel, David. BA, U. Chgo., 1948; study fellow, India, 1949, Israel, 1950; LLB, Yale U., 1954; LL.B., Howard U., 1954. Bar: D.C. 1954, U.S. Supreme Ct. 1958, Pa. 1978. Asst. to Chester Bowles, 1953-54; law assoc. Covington & Burling, Washington, 1954-58; legal asst. to Rev. Theodore Hesburgh, Commn. on Civil Rights, 1958-59; assoc. prof. Notre Dame Law Sch., 1959-60, on leave, 1961-66; asst. to Sen. Kennedy, 1960; spl. asst. to Pres. Kennedy, 1961-62; spl. rep. for Africa, dir. Ethiopian program U.S. Peace Corps, 1962-64; assoc. dir. Peace Corps, Washington, 1964-66; pres. Coll. at Old Westbury, SUNY, 1966-70, Bryn Mawr (Pa.) Coll., 1970-78; counsel firm Schnader, Harrison, Segal and Lewis, Phila., 1979-86; chmn. Pa. Dem. State Com., 1986; sec. labor and industry Commonwealth of Pa., 1987-91; U.S. senator from Pa., 1991-95; CEO Corp. Nat. Svc., Washington, 1995—; vis. lectr. Howard Law Sch., 1956. Author: It's Up to Us, 1946, (with Clare Wofford) India Afire, 1951, Of Kennedys and Kings, 1980; editor: Embers of the World, 1970; co-editor: Report of the U.S. Commission on Civil Rights, 1959. Mem. Coun. Fgn. Rels., 1968—; co-chmn. Com. for Study of Nat. Svc., 1977-80; mem. U.S. Adv. Com. on Nat. Growth Policy Processes, 1975-76; trustee The Am. Coll. , Bryn Mawr, 1975-83; mem. coun. U.S.-South Africa Leader Exch. Program, 1971-87; bd. dirs. Internat. League for Human Rights, 1979-87, pres., 1980-81; bd. dirs. Pub. Interest Law Ctr. Phila., 1978-87; trustee Martin Luther King Ctr. for Nonviolent Social Change, 1983-87; governing coun. Wilderness Soc., 1983-87. With USAF, 1944-45. Mem. ABA. Roman Catholic. Office: Corporation for Nat Svc 1201 New York Ave NW Washington DC 20525-0001

WOGAMAN, JOHN PHILIP, minister, educator; b. Toledo, Mar. 18, 1932; s. Donald Ford and Ella Louise (Kilbury) W.; m. Carolyn Jane Gattis, Aug. 4, 1956; children—Stephen Neil, Donald George, Paul Joseph, Jean Ann. B.A., U. Pacific, 1954; S.T.B., Boston U., 1957, Ph.D., 1960. Ordained to ministry United Methodist Ch., 1957. Pastor First Meth. Ch., Marlborough, Mass., 1956-58; staff asst., div. world missions United Meth. Ch., 1960-61; asst. prof., then assoc. prof. U. Pacific, 1961-66; prof. Christian social ethics Wesley Theol. Sem., Washington, 1966—, dean, 1972-83; sr. pastor Foundry United Meth. Ch., Washington; mem. com. religious and civil liberties Nat. Council Chs., 1966-68, mem. com. internat. affairs, 1967-69; chairperson United Meth. Infant Formula Task Force, 1980-84, Muskie Com., 1982-91, World Meth. Council, 1986—, United Meth. Gen. Conf., 1988, 92, 96; v.p. Interfaith Alliance, 1996—. Author: Methodism's Challenge in Race Relations, 1960; Protestant Faith and Religious Liberty, 1967; Guaranteed Annual Income: The Moral Issues, 1968; A Christian Method of Moral Judgement, 1976; Christians and the Great Economic Debate, 1977; Faith and Fragmentation, 1985; Economics and Ethics, 1986; Christian Perspectives on Politics, 1988, Christian Moral Judgment, 1989, Making Moral Decisions, 1990, Christian Ethics, 1993, To Serve the Present Age, 1995. Editor: The Population Crisis and Moral Responsibility, 1973, Readings in Christian Ethics, 1996. Pres. Stockton (Calif.) Fair Housing Com., 1963-64, Suburban Md. Fiar Housing, 1970; mem. Calif. Democratic Central Com., 1964-66. Lilly fellow, 1959-60; recipient Research award Assn. Theol. Schs., 1975. Mem. Am. Soc. Christian Ethics (pres. 1976-77), Am. Theol. Soc. Home: 4620 45th St NW Washington DC 20016-4479 Office: 1500 16th St NW Washington DC 20036

WOGAN, GERALD NORMAN, toxicology educator; b. Altoona, Pa., Jan. 11, 1930; s. Thomas B. and Florence E. (Corl) W.; m. Henrietta E. Hoenicke, Aug. 24, 1957; children: Christine F., Eugene E. BS, Juniata Coll., 1951; MS, U. Ill., 1953, PhD, 1957. Asst. prof. physiology Rutgers U., New Brunswick, N.J., 1957-61; asst. prof. toxicology MIT, Cambridge, 1962-65, assoc. prof., 1965-69, prof. toxicology, 1969—, head dept. applied biol. scis., 1979-88, prof. chemistry, 1989—, dir. divsn. toxicology, 1988—; cons. to nat. and internat. govt. agys., industries. NIH grantee, 1963—. Mem. editl. bd. Cancer Rsch., 1971-79, Applied Microbiology, 1971-79, Chem.-Biol. Interactions, 1975-78, Toxicology, Environ. Health, 1974-84, Jour. Nat. Cancer Inst., 1988—; contbr. articles and revs. to profl. jours. Recipient Disting. Alumni award U. Ill. Fellow Am. Acad. Microbiology; mem. AAAS, NAS, Inst. Medicine, Am. Assn. Cancer Rsch., Am. Soc. Pharmacology and Exptl. Therapeutics, Am. Soc. Microbiology, Soc. Toxicology, Am. Inst. Nutrition, Sigma Xi. Office: MIT Divsn of Toxicology 77 Massachusetts Ave Rm 415 Cambridge MA 02139-4301

WOGAN, ROBERT, broadcasting company executive; b. N.Y.C., Oct. 13, 1925; s. Robert and Johanna (Hilderbrandt) W.; m. Phyllis Jayn Volz, Nov. 21, 1965 (div. 1991); children—Robert, Stephen. Grad. pub. schs. Page NBC, 1943, asst. mgr. guest relations, 1945-46, night announcer, sec., 1946, asst. supr. announcing, 1946-47; asst. supr. announcing NBC (prodn. div.), 1947-48, night adminstrv. asst., 1948-50, supr. network program operations, 1950-55, Eastern radio program and prodn. mgr., 1955-63, exec. producer "Monitor" program, 1963-65, v.p. radio network programs, 1965-73; exec. producer spl. programs NBC Radio Network, 1973-75, regional mgr. affiliate relations, 1975-81, regional dir. affiliate relations, 1981-89; regional mgr. Westwood One Cos., 1989—, Mut. Broadcasting System, 1989—, NBC Radio Network, 1989—, Talknet Programs, 1989—; exec. producer conv. entertainment, coordinator NBC/Mus. of Broadcasting to preserve history radio data. Exec. producer X Minus One radio program, 1974-75. Mem. Nat. council Boy Scouts Am., 1970—; chmn. Radio com. United Hosp. Fund, 1972. Served with AUS, 1944-45. Recipient Radio-TV All-Am. of Year award for Experiment in Drama, 1963, Gabriel award for pub. service programming, 1967, Freedoms Found. award, 1972, Peabody awards for "Monitor", 1972, for "Project I Experiment", 1973. Mem. Broadcast Pioneers, Internat. Radio and TV Soc. Home: 360 W 22nd St New York NY 10011-2600 Office: 30 Rockefeller Plz New York NY 10112 also: 1700 Broadway New York NY 10019-5905 also: 1775 S Jefferson Davis Hwy Arlington VA 22202

WOGEN, WARREN RONALD, mathematics educator; b. Forest City, Iowa, Feb. 19, 1943; s. Milford N. and Olive A. (Sime) W.; m. Sherry D., Aug. 23, 1969; children—Shannon, Lori. A.B., Luther Coll., 1965; M.A. in Math., Ind.U., 1967, Ph.D. in Math., 1969. Prof. math. U. N.C., Chapel Hill, 1969—. Contbr. articles to profl. jours. Mem. Am. Math. Soc. Office: U NC Math Dept. Chapel Hill NC 27599-3250

WOGLOM, ERIC COOKE, lawyer; b. Bklyn., Mar. 14, 1943; s. Joseph F. and Rita Mary (Cooke) W.; m. Joshan Robin Levitsky, May 11, 1968; children—Peter Douglas, Brian Stewart. B.A., Yale U., 1964; LL.B., U. Pa. 1967. Bar: N.Y. 1968, U.S. Patent and Trademark Office 1970, U.S. Ct. Appeals (9th cir.) 1972, U.S. Ct. Appeals (2d cir.) 1973, U.S. Dist. Ct. (so. and ea. dist.) N.Y. 1974, U.S. Supreme Ct. 1974, U.S. Ct. Appeals (7th cir.) 1980, U.S. Ct. Appeals (Fed. cir.) 1982. With Fish & Neave, N.Y.C., 1967—, sr. ptnr., 1976—; mem. intellectual property adv. com. U.S. Dist. Ct. Del. Served with U.S. Army, 1967. Mem. ABA, Am. Intellectual Property Law Assn., Assn. Bar City N.Y. (past chair com. on patents), N.Y. Law Inst., N.Y. Intellectual Property Law Assn. (past chair com. on econ. matters effecting the profession), N.Y. State Bar Assn. Republican. Roman Catholic. Clubs: Yale of N.Y.C., Shelter Island Yacht. Home: 430 North St Harrison NY 10528-1118 Office: Fish & Neave 1251 Avenue Of The Americas New York NY 10020-1104

WOGSLAND, JAMES WILLARD, retired heavy machinery manufacturing executive; b. Devils Lake, N.D., Apr. 17, 1931; s. Melvin LeRoy and Mable Bertina (Paulson) W.; m. Marlene Claudia Clark, June 1957; children: Karen Lynn, Steven James. BA in Econs., U. Minn., 1957. Various positions fin. dept. Caterpillar Tractor Co., Peoria, Ill., 1957-64, treas., 1976-81; mgr. fin. Caterpillar Overseas S.A., Geneva, 1965-70, sec.-treas., 1970-76; dir.-pres. Caterpillar Brasil S.A., São Paulo, 1981-87; exec. v.p. Caterpillar, Inc., Peoria, 198-90, also bd. dirs., vice-chmn., 1990-95; bd. dirs. Cipsco, Inc., Springfield, Ill. Mem. adv. bd. St. Francis Hosp., Peoria, 1987-95; bd. dirs. Peoria Area Cmty. Found., 1986-92; trustee Eureka Coll., 1987-95. Sgt. USAF, 1951-55. Mem. Hayden Lake Golf and Country Club. Republican. Presbyterian. Home: 9675 Easy St Hayden Lake ID 83835-9526

WOHL, ARMAND JEFFREY, cardiologist; b. Phila., Dec. 11, 1946; s. Herman Lewis and Selma (Paul) W.; m. Marylouise Katherine Giangrossi, Sept. 4, 1977; children: Michael Adam, Todd David. Student, Temple U., 1967; MD, Hahnemann U., 1971. Intern Bexar County Hosp., San Antonio, 1971-72; resident in internal medicine Parkland Hosp., Dallas, 1972-74; fellow in cardiology U. Tex. Southwestern Med. Ctr., Dallas, 1974-76; chief of cardiology USAF Hosp. Elmendorf, Anchorage, 1976-78; chief cardiologist Riverside (Calif.) Med. Clin., 1978-79; cardiologist Grossmont Cardiology Med. Group, La Mesa, Calif., 1980-84; pvt. practice, La Mesa, 1985—; chief of cardiology Grossmont Hosp., La Mesa, 1988-90; asst. clin. prof. Sch. Medicine. U. Calif., San Diego, 1990—. Contbr. articles to profl. jours. Bd. dirs. Grossmont Healthcare Dist., 1995—, San Diego County chpt. Am. Heart Assn., 1981-87. Maj. USAF, 1976-78. Fellow Am. Coll. Cardiology (councilor Calif. chpt. 1991—), Am. Coll. Physicians, Coun. on Clin. Cardiology. Avocations: tennis, travel. Office: 5565 Grossmont Center Dr La Mesa CA 91942-3020 *Personal philosophy: Work hard, respect others, enjoy life.*

WOHL, DAVID, humanities educator, college dean-theatre director; b. Washington, Nov. 28, 1950; s. Joseph Gene and Carol (Weiss) W.; children: Isaac, Gabriele. BA, Clark U., 1972; MA, U. Conn., 1975; PhD, Kent State U., 1988. Staff asst. Am. Theatre Assn., Washington, 1975-76; prof. W.Va. State Coll., Institute, 1976-79, chmn. dept. comm., 1979-88, dean divsn. arts and humanities, 1988—; artistic dir. Charleston (W.Va.) Stage Co., 1991—; gen. mgr. Porthouse Theatre Festival, Cuyahoga Falls, Ohio, 1984-85; cons. U. South Ala., Mobile, 1988; bd. dirs., treas., pres. Southeastern Theatre Conf., 1993—; co-dir. W.Va. Gt. Tchrs. Seminar. Stage dir. Kanawha Players, 1978—, Nutmeg Summer Playhouse, 1975-76, W.Va. Theatre Festival, Charleston Playhouse; prodr.: (films) Chillers, 1985, Strangest Dreams, 1990, Paradise Park, 1992 (Gold medal Houston Internat. Film Festival 1992, 1st place award Chgo. Film Festival 1992); contbr. articles to theatre jours. Bd. dirs. Kanawha Arts Alliance, Charleston, 1979-81, Kanawha Players, 1982-85; pres. W.Va. Theatre Conf., 1987-89; v.p. Arts Advocacy W.Va., 1994—. NEH Fellow, 1977, 80; Dept. Edn. teaching fellow, 1976-77. Mem. Am. Soc. for Theatre Rsch., Assn. for Theatre in Higher Edn., Speech Comm. Assn. Home: 1411 Summit Ln Charleston WV 25302-2639 Office: W Va State Coll PO Box 28 Institute WV 25112-0028

WOHL, RONALD H., management consultant, writing and editorial expert; b. Washington, Sept. 3, 1942; s. Bernard Carl and Martha (Aberbach) W.; m. Myrna Zelda Chevelier, June 27, 1965; children: Jennifer Lynn, Amy Beth. Student, Fla. State U., 1960-62; BA in Anthropology, George Washington U., 1965; postgrad., George Washington U. Law Sch., 1965-67, Am. U., Washington, 1969-74. Cert. mgmt. cons. Asst. to regional credit mgr. Sears, Roebuck & Co., Bethesda, Md., 1966-67; supr. payroll & ins. Montgomery Coll., Rockville, Md., 1967-71; supr. program info. & analysis Nat. Rural Elec. Coop. Assn., Washington, 1971-74; employee benefits comms. cons. Wyatt Co., Washington, 1974-77; pres. R.H. Wohl & Assocs./In Plain English, Gaithersburg, Md., 1977—; columnist Gazette Newspapers, Gaithersburg, 1987, Montgomery Jour., Rockville, 1989-90; bd. dirs. Braille Tech., LLC, 1995; prin. Future Solutions. Mem. editl. bd., author Employers Guide to Managed Health Care, 1994—, Civic Action Handbook, 1994—. Precinct chair Montgomery County Dems., 1978—; Dem. candidate for Md. Ho. of Dels., Annapolis, 1986; chmn. Commn. on Humanities, Montgomery County Md., 1987—; dir. North Potomac (Md.) Citizens Assn., 1988-95; citizen mem. Comty. Policing Steering Com., Montgomery County, Md., 1992—; tchr. Am. Jewish history and comparative religion; bd. dirs. Temple Beth Ami Congregation, Temple Beth Ami Brotherhood, Rockville, 1981-95, pres. 1990-92. Mem. Am. Assn. Home Based Bus. (nat. bd. dirs.), Inst. for Mgmt. Cons. (v.p. mem. Washington D.C. chpt. 1994-95). Home: 14501 Antigone Dr North Potomac MD 20878-2484 Office: R H Wohl & Assocs/ In Plain English PO Box 3300 Gaithersburg MD 20885-3300

WOHLEBER, LYNNE FARR, archivist, librarian; b. Pitts., Mar. 16, 1939; d. Donald Elmer and Helen Rose (Lula) F.; m. David Louis Wohleber, Oct. 14, 1972 (div. Sept. 1989); 1 child, Jeffrey David. AB, Allegheny, 1961; MLS, U. Pitts., 1991. Comms. sec. Aluminum Co. of Am., Pitts., 1968-73; shop mgr. The Thread Shed, Pitts., 1986-90; libr. Coun. Am. Embroiderer's Libr., Carnegie, Pa., 1985-93; archivist Episcopal Diocese of Pitts., 1989—; libr. Bower Hill Cmty. Ch., 1996—; cons. Calvary Epixcopal Ch. Archives, Pitts., 1992-93, Bapt. Home Libr., Mt. Lebanon, 1994, First United Meth. Ch. Archives, Pitss., 1995; bldg. archives workshop instr., 1995. Coord. presch. program Am. Lung Assn., Pitts., 1977-87; capt., ward chair Am. Cancer Soc., Pitts., 1978-84; mem., newsletter editor Mendelssohn Choir of Pitts., 1973-87; cub scout den leader Boy Scouts Am., Mt. Lebanon, Pa., 1983-84; bd. deacons, Bower Hill Cmty. Ch., 1996—. Bd. deacon Bower Hill Cmty. Ch., 1996—; coord. presch. program Am. Lung Assn., Pitts., 1977-87; capt., ward chair Am. Cancer Soc., Pitts., 1978-84; mem. newsletter editor Mendelssohn Choir of Pitts., 1973-87; cub scout den leader Boy Scouts Am., Mt. Lebanon, Pa., 1983-84. Mem. Soc. Am. Archivists, Mid-Atlantic Regional Archives Conf. (co-chair spl. events 1992, pubs. com. 1996—), Nat. Episcopal Historians and Archivists (Pitts. coord. for 1997 Episcopal Tri-History Conf., bd. dirs. 1996-97), Pitts. Curators Coalition, Women's Episcopal History Project, Beta Phi Mu. Republican. Presbyterian and Episcopalian. Home: 110 Skylark Cir Pittsburgh PA 15234 Office: Episcopal Diocese of Pitts 325 Oliver Ave Pittsburgh PA 15222-2403

WOHLERT, EARL ROSS, health care analyst; b. Phila., Oct. 19, 1963; s. Anton Emil and Dona Lee (Zimmerman) WW.; m. Karen Lynn Bauer, Mar. 12, 1994; children: Ryan Chandler, Maia Katharine. BA, Hawaii Loa Coll., Kaneohe, 1986; MBA, U. New Haven, 1992. Acct. Yale U. Sch. Medicine, New Haven, 1987-88, fin. analyst, 1988-90, assoc. adminstr. fin., 1990-93, assoc. adminstr. fin. svcs., 1993-95; health care analyst M.D. Health Plan, North Haven, Conn., 1995-96, dir. healthcare analysis, 1996—; mktg. and mgmt. cons. Lt. USNR, 1992. Avocations: sailing, tennis, golf, traveling. Home: 11 Crofut Rd Orange CT 06477-2509 Office: MD Health Plan 6 Devine St North Haven CT 06473-2183

WOHLFORD, JAMES GREGORY, pharmacist; b. Virginia, Minn., Nov. 4, 1956; s. James Hoover and Jeanne Katherine (Imgrund) W. AA, Indian River C.C., Ft. Pierce, Fla., 1977; BS in Pharmacy, U. Fla., 1981; MBA, Fla. Inst. Tech., 1987; PhD in Pharmacy, Southeastern U. Health Sci., 1994. Registered pharmacist, Fla., Ala. Rsch. asst. U. Fla., Gainesville, 1979-81; pharmacist Lawnwood Med. Ctr., Ft. Pierce, 1981—. Mem. Fla. Soc. Hosp. Pharmacists, Am. Soc. Hosp. Pharmacists. Roman Catholic. Avocations: snow skiing, scuba diving, water skiing. Home: 4250 N A 1 A Apt 904 Fort Pierce FL 34949-8340 Office: Lawnwood Regional Med Ctr PO Box 188 Fort Pierce FL 34954-0188

WOHLGELERNTER, BETH, organization executive; b. N.Y.C., Jan. 30, 1956; d. Maurice Nathaniel and Esther Rachel (Feinerman) W. BA, Barnard Coll., 1977. Exec. aide to pres. Barnard Coll., N.Y.C., 1977-80; spl. asst. to pres. The Commonwealth Fund, N.Y.C., 1980-81; asst. to chief exec. officer/pres. Mary McFadden, Inc., N.Y.C., 1981-84; exec. adminstr. The Donna Karan Co., N.Y.C., 1984-90; nat. exec. dir. Hadassah, The Women's Zionist Orgn. Am., Inc., N.Y.C., 1990—; comm. adv. coun. AT&T, 1992—. Bd. dirs., v.p. N.Am. Conf. on Ethiopian Jewry, N.Y.C., 1981-85, bd. advisors, 1985—; bd. govs. Lincoln Sq. Synagogue, N.Y.C., 1988-94, bd. trustees, 1994—; bd. trustees United Israel Appeal, 1991—. Office: Hadassah The Women's Zionist Orgn Am Inc 50 W 58th St New York NY 10019-2505

WOHLGENANT, RICHARD GLEN, lawyer; b. Porterville, Calif., Dec. 2, 1930; s. Carl Ferdinand and Sara Alice (Moore) W.; m. Teresa Joan Bristow, Dec. 27, 1959; children: Mark Thomas, Tracy Patrice, Timothy James. B.A., U. Mont., Missoula, 1952; LL.B., Harvard U., Cambridge, Mass., 1957. Bar: Colo. 1957, U.S. Dist. Ct. Colo. 1957. Assoc. Holme Roberts & Owen LLC, Denver, 1957-62; ptnr./mem. Holme Roberts & Owen, Denver, 1962—. Bd. dirs. Adopt-A-Sch., Denver, 1976-80, St. Joseph Found., Denver, 1990-93, Denver Com. Coun. Fgn. Rels., Japanese-Am. Soc. Colo., Rocky Mountain chpt. U.S. Mex. C. of C. Mem. ABA, Colo. Bar Assn., Denver Bar Assn., Am. Coll. Real Estate Lawyers, Univ. Club, Law Club, City Club. Republican. Roman Catholic. Home: 300 Ivy St Denver CO 80220-5855 Office: Holme Roberts & Owen LLP 1700 Lincoln St Denver CO 80203-4500

WOHLLEBEN, RUDOLF, microwave and antenna researcher; b. Bad Kreuznach, Germany, June 4, 1936; s. Georg Konrad and Kathrin (Lellbach) W.; m. Walburg Groehler, Aug. 27, 1967 (div. Nov. 1982); children: Niclas-Jakob, Philipp-Andreas; m. Rosemarie Rudloff, Dec. 21, 1982; stepchildren: Viola Ehrenheim, Mathias Ehrenheim. BSEE, U. Karlsruhe, Germany, 1958; MSEE, diploma in elec. engring., Tech. U. Munich, 1960; Dr.Ing., Tech. Hochschule, Aachen, Germany, 1969. R & D engr. Forschungsinst. HF-Physik, Rolandseck, Rhein, Germany, 1961-64; rsch. and teaching asst. Inst. Tech. Electronics RWTH, Aachen, 1964-70; group leader antennas and electronics divsn. Max-Planck Inst. for Radioastronomie, Bonn, Germany, 1971—; lectr. antennas, radar radioastronomy U. Kaiserslautern, Germany, 1980—; cons. H. Schilling GmbH, Weiskirchen, Germany, 1969-71, Nuffield Obs., Manchester, Eng., 1975, ESA-ESTEC, Noordwijk, The Netherlands, A.N.T., Backnang, Elekluft, Bonn, Space Rsch. Inst., Moscow, R. Hirschmann-Antennen, Esslingen, Phys. Inst. of U. of Cologne, Dept. of Atomic Energy Comm. Sys. Group, Electr. Corp. India. Author, editor: Corps Alemannia/Karlsruhe in 250 Semstern, 1988; co-author: Antennas for Elliptical Polarization and its Measuring Techniques, 1968, Farfield Pattern Simulation of Linear Array Antennas on the Analog Computer, 1970, Interferometry in Radioastronomy and Radar Techniques, 1991, Interferometrie in Radioastronomie u. Radartechnik, 1973, Fruehe Spaetlese, 1997; contbr. 62 articles to sci. jours.; discoverer: (with Dirk Fiebig) beam squint of a radially displaced fed paraboloid reflector antenna, 1990. Recipient Th. Heuss medal, German Liberal Party, 1990. Mem. Informationstechnische Gesellschaft, US Planetary Soc., Corps Alemannia, Weinheimer Verband Alter Corpsstudenten (federal chmn. 1995-97). Mem. Free Democrat Party. Avocations: 16-millimeter film amateur, piano, soccer, poems, genealogy. Office: Max-Planck Inst Radioastronomie, Auf dem Huegel 69, D-53121 Bonn Germany

WOHLSCHLAG, DONALD EUGENE, zoologist, marine ecologist, educator emeritus; b. Bucyrus, Ohio, Nov. 6, 1918; s. Herman Albert and Agnes Mae (Canode) W.; m. Elsie Marjorie Baker, June 5, 1943; children: William Eugene, Nancy Sue, Sarah Ann. BS, Heidelberg Coll., 1940; PhD, Ind. U., 1949. Research assoc. in zoology U. Wis., 1948-49; asst. prof. biol. scis. Stanford U., 1949-56, asso. prof., 1956-64, prof., 1964-65; prof. zoology and marine scis. U. Tex., Aransas, 1965-86; prof. emeritus zoology and marine scis. U. Tex., Port Aransas, 1986—; dir. Marine Sci. Inst., 1965-70; mem. U.S. Marine Subcom. for Internat. Biol. Program, 1966-71; mem. com. on ecol. research interocean-canal Nat. Acad. Scis., 1969-70; mem. Tundra Biome Panel, NSF, 1971-74; mem. water ecosystems com. Inst. Ecology, 1974-76. Contbr. numerous articles on arctic, antarctic and Gulf Coast fish ecol. research to profl. publs.; editor: Contbns. in Marine Sci, 1974-88. Served to 1st lt. USAAF, 1942-46. Recipient Antarctic medal NSF, 1965; NSF grantee, 1955-70; NOAA grantee, 1976-79; Office Naval Research grantee, 1952-54; Tex. Dept. Water Resources grantee, 1975-79. Fellow AAAS, Am. Inst. Fisheries Research Biologists, Arctic Inst. N. Am., Explorers Club; mem. Am. Fisheries Soc., Am. Soc. Limnology and Oceanography, Am. Soc. Zoologists, Am. Soc. Ichthyology and Herpetology, Ecol. Soc. Am. (pres. Western sect. 1965), Estuarine Research Fedn. (dir. 1976-78), Gulf Estuarine Research Soc. (pres. 1976-78), Sigma Xi. Home: 625 E Ave C Port Aransas TX 78373 Office: U Tex Port Aransas Marine Lab Port Aransas TX 78373 *Maintain the habitat; preserve the species, humans included.*

WOHLTMANN, HULDA JUSTINE, pediatric endocrinologist, diabetologist; b. Charleston, S.C., Apr. 10, 1923; d. John Diedrich and Emma Lucia (Mohrmann) W. B.S., Coll. Charleston, 1944; M.D., Med. U. S.C., 1949. Diplomate Am. Bd. Pediatrics. Intern Louisville Gen. Hosp., 1949-50; resident in pediatrics St. Louis Children's Hosp., 1950-53; mem. faculty Washington U. Sch. Medicine, St. Louis, 1953-65, instr., 1953-58, asst. prof., 1958-65, postdoctoral fellow biochemistry, 1961-63; assoc. prof. pediatrics, head pediatric endocrinology Med. U. S.C., Charleston, 1965-70, prof., 1970-90, prof. emeritus, 1990—. Bd. dirs. Franke Home, Charleston, 1975—, treas., 1989-91; mem. adv. bd. for ethics ctr. Newberry (S.C.) Coll., 1989—; trustee Luth. Theol. So. Sem., 1991—. Mem. Am. Pediatric Soc., Ambulatory Pediatric Assn., Endocrine Soc., Am. Diabetes Assn., Am. Acad. Pediatrics, Am. Fedn. Clin. Rsch., Midwest Soc. Pediatric Rsch., So. Soc. Pediatric Rsch., S.C. Diabetes Assn. (bd. dirs. 1970-86, pres. 1970-73, 84-85, v.p., 1982-83, Profl Svc. award 1977), Lawson Wilkins Endocrine Soc., Sugar Club. Lutheran. Contbr. articles to sci. jours. Home: # 3 46th Ave Isle of Palms SC 29451-2607

WOIT, ERIK PETER, corporate executive, lawyer; b. Riga, Latvia, Mar. 10, 1931; s. Walter E. and Sigrid (Radzins) W.; m. Bonnie Jean Ford, June 16, 1953; children: Peter Gordon, Steven Ford. A.B., Allegheny Coll., 1953; J.D., Harvard U., 1956. Bar: N.Y. 1959, U.S. Supreme Ct., 1971. Asso. firm Mudge, Stern, Baldwin & Todd, N.Y.C., 1956-57, 60-62; asst. sec., internat. counsel Richardson-Merrell, Inc., 1962-71; sec., gen. counsel Amerace Corp., N.Y.C., 1971-73, v.p., group exec., 1973-74, pres. ESNA div., 1974-77, sr. v.p. adminstrn., chief adminstrv. and chief fin. officer, 1977-83; sr. v.p. Orient Express Hotels, Inc., N.Y.C., 1983—, also bd. dirs.; chmn. Sea Containers Am. Inc., 1984—; sr. v.p. Sea Containers Ltd., 1987—; participant Dept. Def. Joint Civilian Orientation Conf., 1994. Served to capt. USMCR, 1957-60. Recipient Maj. Gen. John H. Russell leadership award USMC Command and Staff Coll. Found., 1996. Mem. ABA, Assn. Bar City N.Y., Sigma Alpha Epsilon. Clubs: Harvard, Sky (N.Y.C.), 21 Club Inc. (N.Y.C.) (pres. 1995—). Home: 559 West Rd New Canaan CT 06840-2512 Office: 1155 Avenue Of The Americas New York NY 10036-2711

WOIWODE, LARRY (ALFRED WOIWODE), writer, poet; b. 1941. Writer in residence U. Wis., 1973-74; vis. prof. SUNY, Binghamton, 1983-85, prof., dir. creative writing program, 1985-88. Author: What I'm Goint to Do, I Think, 1969 (with others) Poetry North, 1970, Beyond the Bedroom Wall, 1975, (verse) Even Tide, 1977, Poppa John, 1981, Born Brothers, 1988, The Neumiller Stories, 1989. Recipient Award of Merit Am. Acad. of Arts and Letters, 1995. Office: c/o Michael di Capua Books Farrar Straus & Giroux 19 Union Sq W New York NY 10003-3304*

WOJCICKI, ANDREW ADALBERT, chemist, educator; b. Warsaw, Poland, May 5, 1935; s. Franciszek Wojcicki and Janina (Kozlowa) Hoskins; m. Marba L. Hart, Dec. 21, 1968; children: Katherine, Christina. BS, Brown U., 1956; PhD, Northwestern U., 1960; postdoctoral fellow, U. Nottingham, Eng., 1960-61. Asst. prof. chemistry Ohio State U., Columbus, 1961-66, assoc. prof., 1966-69, prof., 1969—, acting chmn., 1981-82; assoc. chmn. Ohio State U., 1982-83, 84-86; vis. prof. Case Western Res. U., 1967, U. Bologna, Italy, 1988; vis. researcher U. Coll. London, 1969; sr. U.S. scientist Alexander von Humboldt Found., Mulheim/Ruhr, Germany, 1975-76; vis. scholar U. Calif.-Berkeley, 1984; assoc. dean Coll. of Math. and Phys. Scis., Ohio State U., 1996—. Contbr. articles to profl. and scholarly jours. Guggenheim fellow U. Cambridge (Eng.), 1976; recipient Disting. Teaching award Ohio State U., 1968, Humboldt Sr. award Humboldt Found., 1975, 76. Mem. Am. Chem. Soc. (Columbus sect. award 1992), Royal Chem. Soc., Sigma Xi, Phi Lambda Upsilon. Home: 825 Greenridge Rd Columbus OH 43235-3411 Office: Ohio State U 120 W 18th Ave Columbus OH 43210-1106

WOJCICKI, STANLEY GEORGE, physicist, educator; b. Warsaw, Poland, Mar. 30, 1937; came to U.S., 1950; s. Franciszek and Janina (Kozlow) W.; m. Esther Denise Hochman, Nov. 17, 1961; children: Susan Diane, Janet Maia, Anne Elizabeth. A.B., Harvard U., 1957; Ph.D., U. Calif., Berkeley, 1962. Physicist Lawrence Radiation Lab., Berkeley, 1961-66; asst. prof. physics Stanford U., 1966-68, assoc. prof., 1968-74, prof., 1974—, chmn. dept., 1982-85, dep. dir. Superconducting Supercollider Central Design Group, 1984-89; chmn. Stanford Linear Accelerator Center Exptl. Program Adv. Com., 1979-81; chmn. High Energy Physics Adv. Panel, 1990-96. Assoc. editor Phys. Rev. Letters for Exptl. High Energy Physics, 1978-80. Recipient Alexander von Humboldt Sr. Am. Scientist award, 1981; NSF fellow, 1964-65; Sloan Found. fellow, 1968-72; Guggenheim fellow, 1973-74. Fellow Am. Phys. Soc. Office: Stanford U Physics Dept Stanford CA 94305

WOJCIK, ANTHONY STEPHEN, computer science educator; b. Chgo., Sept. 18, 1945; s. Casimir Anthony and Elizabeth Anne (Hudak) W.; m. Paula Jean Valaitis, Aug. 16, 1969; children: Laura Anne, Jeffrey Anthony. BS in Math., U. Ill., 1967, MS in Math., 1968, PhD in Computer Sci., 1971. Asst. prof. dept. computer sci. Ill. Inst. Tech., Chgo., 1971-76, assoc. prof. dept. computer sci., 1976-81, chmn. dept. computer sci., 1978-84, prof. dept. elec. and computer engring., 1984-86, prof. dept. computer sci., 1981-86; mem. tech. staff Bell Labs., Naperville, Ill., 1974; scientist in residence Argonne (Ill.) Nat. Lab., 1981, resident assoc., 1982-85, 86—, vis. scientist, 1985-86; prof. computer sci. Mich. State U., East Lansing, 1986—, chmn. dept. computer sci., 1986-95. Named Outstanding Young Man of Am., 1981-82. Mem. IEEE (chmn. midwestern area com. 1975-78), Assn. Computing Machinery. Roman Catholic. Office: Mich State U Dept Computer Sci East Lansing MI 48824

WOJCIK, CASS, decorative supply company executive, former city official; b. Rochester, N.Y., Dec. 3, 1920; s. Emil M. and Casimira C. (Krawiecz) W.; student Lawrence Inst. Tech., 1941-43, Yale U., 1943-44, U.S. Sch. for European Personnel, Czechoslovakia, 1945; m. Lilliam Leocadia Lendzion, Sept. 25, 1948; 1 child, Robert Cass. Owner, Nat. Florists Supply Co., Detroit, 1948-88, Nat. Decorative, Detroit, 1950-89; co-owner Creation Ctr., Detroit, 1955-60; cons.-contractor hort.-bot. design auto show displays, TV prodrs., designers and decorators. Mem. Regional Planning and Evaluation Coun., 1969-75; city-wide mem. Detroit Bd. Edn., 1970-75; commr. Detroit Public Schs. Employees Retirement Commn., until 1975; mem. Area Occupl. Ednl. Commn., Ednl. Task Force; chmn., grand marshal Ann. Gen. Pulaski Day Parade, Detroit, 1970, 71; mem. Friends of Belle Isle; mem. Nat. Arboretum Adv. Coun., U.S. Dept. Agr., 1982-83; mem. pastoral coun. Archidiocese of Detroit, 1983-86, 88-92; v.p. rsch. Barna Coll., Ft. Lauderdale, Fla., 1989-94; vice chmn. 13th Congl. Dist. Rep. Party Mich., 1987-91; elected to 1988 electoral coll. With U.S. Army, 1944-46. Decorated Bronze Star; recipient citation Polish-Am. Congress, 1971, Art in Park 3d prize City of Oakland Park, Fla. Mem. S.E. Mich. Coun. Govts., Mich., Nat. sch. bd. assns., Big Cities Sch. Bd. Com., Nat. Coun. Great Cities Schs., Mcpl. Fin. Officers Assn. U.S., Nat. Coun. Tchr. Retirement, Ctrl. Citizens Com. Detroit, Internat. Platform Assn., Mich. Heritage Coun., Nat. Geog. Soc., Polish Century Club. Home: 1729 SW 14th Ct Fort Lauderdale FL 33312-4109

WOJCIK, MARTIN HENRY, foundation development official; b. Chgo., May 10, 1948; s. Henry Martin and Mary Lorraine (Naughton) W. B.S., Ill. Inst. Tech., 1970; M. in Humanities, Bonn U., W. Ger., 1975. Price adminstr. R.R. Donnelley & Sons., Chgo., 1970-72; dir. devel. Citizens for a Better Environment, Milw., 1976-79; pres. Citizens for a Better Environment, Chgo., 1979-85, bd. dirs., 1979-85, 89—; chmn. bd. dirs. Citizens for a Better Environment, 1990-91; dir. found. relations Northwestern U., Evanston, Ill., 1987-89; dir. corp. and found. rels. Mayo Found., Rochester, Minn., 1989—; mem. policy adv. com. Ill. EPA, Springfield, 1980-82. Bd. dirs. Rochester Civic Theatre, 1991—, pres. bd. dirs. 1994-95; mem. adv. panel Minn. State Arts Bd., 1995, 97. Mem. Ill. Inst. Tech. Alumni Assn. Roman Catholic. Home: 535 19th St NW Rochester MN 55901-4901 Office: Mayo Found Med Edn and Rsch Rochester MN 55905

WOJEWODSKI, STAN, JR., artistic director, dean. MFA, Cath. U. of Am. Artistic dir. Ctr. Stage, Balt., 1977-91, Yale Repertory Theatre, 1991—; dean Yale Sch. of Drama, 1991—; tchr. Hammerstein Ctr. for Theater Studies, Columbia U.; advisor Theater Cornell; bd. dirs. Theatre Comms. Group; mem. theater panel Nat. Endowment for Arts. Dir.: Hamlet, The Baltimore Waltz, On the Verge, Edward the Second (Yale Repertory Theatre), The Countess Cathleen (Abbey Theatre, Dublin, Ireland), On the Verge, Volpone (Guthrie Theater), Don Quixote de la Jolla, The Heliotrope Bouquet by Scott Joplin and Louis Chauvin (La Jolla Playhouse), Much Ado About Nothing (Settle Repertory Theatre); staged David Mamet's Oleanna; dir. Williamstown Theatre Festival, Old Globe Theatre, San Diego, Hudson Guild Theatre, N.Y., Berkshire Theatre Festival. Office: Yale Repertory Theatre Box 208244 Yale Sta 222 York St New Haven CT 06520-8244*

WOJNILOWER, ALBERT MARTIN, economist; b. Vienna, Austria, Feb. 3, 1930; came to U.S., 1939; s. Theodore and Lissy (Koppel) W.; m. Sue Freudenfels, Apr. 6, 1952; children: Daniel, Michael, Joel, Samuel. A.B., Columbia U., 1951, A.M., 1951, Ph.D., 1960. Economist Fed. Res. Bank of N.Y., N.Y.C., 1951-62; assoc. economist First Nat. City Bank of N.Y.C., N.Y.C., 1962-63; chief economist The First Boston Corp., N.Y.C., 1964-86, sr. advisor, 1986—; cons. Rep. Nat. Bank of N.Y., N.Y.C., 1980—; adj. prof. fin. NYU Grad. Sch. Bus. Adminstrn., N.Y.C., 1961-66. Author: The Quality of Business Loans, 1960; co-author: Financial Institutions and Markets, 1970, 2d edit., 1981. Recipient A.A. Green prize Columbia Coll., 1951. Mem. Am. Fin. Assn. (bd. dirs. 1979-81), Am. Econ. Assn., Phi Beta Kappa. Democrat. Jewish. Office: The Clipper Group Corp 11 Madison Ave New York NY 10010-3629

WOJTYLA, KAROL JOZEF See JOHN PAUL, HIS HOLINESS POPE, II

WOLAHAN, CARYLE GOLDSACK, nursing educator; b. Somerville, N.J., July 27, 1942; d. Wilbur Wood and Jane (Hadley) Goldsack; m. Thomas Warren Hussey, June 26, 1965 (dec. Oct. 1970); 1 child, Timothy Stephen; m. William Kevin Wolahan, Sept. 30, 1983;. BS, Wagner Coll., 1964; MEd, Columbia U., 1973, EdD, 1979. Sch. nurse, tchr. Malverne (N.Y.) Pub. Schs., 1966-67, Dover-Wingdale Pub. Schs., Dover Plains, N.Y., 1967-68; head nurse Harlem Valley State Hosp., Wingdale, N.Y., 1968-69; asst. prof., acting dir. div. nursing Trenton (N.J.) State Coll., 1973-77; assoc. prof., acting dir. Felician Coll., Lodi, N.J., 1979-80, dir. div. nursing, 1982-87; dir. nursing program Stern Coll., Yeshiva U., N.Y.C., 1980-82; assoc. dean Coll. Nursing SUNY Health Sci. Ctr., Bklyn., 1987-91, acting dean Coll. Nursing, 1991-92; dean sch. nursing Adelphi U., 1992—. Contbr. articles to profl. jours., chpts. to books; editor Topics in Clin. Nursing, 1983. Recipient NEAA award; Named Woman of Achievement Alpha Omicron Pi. Mem. ANA (del. 1978-87), AAUP, N.J. State Nurses Assn. (coun. on edn. 1976-82, chmn. com. on ednl. preparation 1984-88), N.Y. State Nurses Assn. (chair pub. rels. com. 1990-92, spkrs. bur., recruitment com. Dist. 14, 1990, chair coun. on edn.), Nat. League for Nursing (accreditation com. 1985-90, site visitor 1984—), Am. Acad. Nursing, Nursing Edn. Alumni Assn. Tchrs. Coll. (pres. 1990-94), Lake Hopatcong Yacht Club, Sigma Theta Tau. Episcopalian. Avocations: boating, reading, theater, hand crafts. Home: 341 Maxim Dr Hopatcong NJ 07843-1744

WOLANER, ROBIN PEGGY, internet and magazine publisher; b. Queens, N.Y., May 6, 1954; d. David H. and Harriet (Radlow) W.; m. Steven J. Castleman, 1992; 1 child, Terry David. BS in Indsl. and Labor Rels., Cornell U., 1975. Sr. editor Viva Mag., N.Y.C., 1975-76; editor Impact Mag., N.Y.C., 1976-77; circulation mgr. Runner's World Mag., Mountain View, Calif., 1977-79; cons. Ladd Assocs., San Francisco, 1979-80; gen. mgr. Mother Jones Mag., San Francisco, 1980-81, pub., 1981-85; founder, pub. Parenting Mag., San Francisco, 1985-91, pres., 1991-92; v.p. Time Pub. Ventures, 1990-96; pres., CEO Sunset Pub. Corp., 1992-95; chmn. Online Ptnrs. LLC, 1997—. Bd. dirs. Med. Self Care Inc., 1996—, Ifusion Com. LLC, 1996—. Jewish. Office: 2240 Hyde St San Francisco CA 94109-1509

WOLANIN, BARBARA ANN BOESE, art curator, art historian; b. Dayton, Ohio, Dec. 12, 1943; d. William Carl and Elisabeth Cassell (Barnard) Boese; m. Thomas R. Wolanin, 1966 (div. 1980); children: Peter Michael, Andrew. AB, Oberlin Coll., 1966, AM, 1969; MAT, Harvard U., 1967; PhD, U. Wis., 1981. Art tchr. Lorain (Ohio) Pub. Schs., 1968-69, Newton (Mass.) Pub. Schs., 1969-71; teaching asst. U. Wis., Madison, 1972-74; asst. prof. art history Trinity Coll., Washington, 1978-83, James Madison U., Harrisonburg, Va., 1983-85; curator U.S. Capitol, Architect of the Capitol, Washington, 1985—; guest curator Pa. Acad. of Fine Arts, Phila, 1980-83. Author exhbn. catalog Arthur B. Carles, 1983, Constantino Brumidi, 1997; contbr. articles to profl. jours. Woodrow Wilson fellow, 1967, Kress fellow U. Wis., 1974, Smithsonian fellow, 1976; recipient Faculty Devel. award James Madison U., 1985. Mem. Women's Caucus for Art, Am. Assn. Mus., Coll. Art Assn., Am. Inst. for Conservation, Phi Beta Kappa (pres. Trinity Coll. 1982-83). Home: 4347 Brandywine St NW Washington DC 20016-4542 Office: US Capitol Office Capitol Architect Washington DC 20515

WOLANIN, JOHN CHARLES, realtor; b. Spangler, Pa., Jan. 8, 1957; s. George M. and Ellen (Chigas) W.; m. Andrea Katrina Donato, Oct. 21, 1978; children: Tricia Ann, John Paul. AA, Cuyahoga C.C., 1979; BA, Hiram Coll., 1981. Lic. broker, Ohio. Mail clk. Republic Steel, Cleve., 1975-79; payroll acct. LTV Steel, Cleve., 1979-89; regional credit mgr. Republic Engineered Steel, Massillon, Ohio, 1989-90; realtor Bob Princelon Realty, Massillon, Ohio, 1991-93, Re/Max Ptnrs. "The Massillon Man", Canton, Ohio, 1993—; prof. devel. com. Stark County Bd. Realtors, Canton, 1994-95; mktg. exec. Wolanin Enterprises, Cleve., 1979-89. Coach basketball Boys and Girls Club, Massillon, 1991—; parish coun. mem. St. Marys Ch., Massillon, 1991—. Mem. KC. Republican. Roman Catholic. Avocations: sports, coaching, hunting, cycling, computers. Home: 314 Sheffield Ave NE Massillon OH 44646-4577 Office: Re/Max Ptnrs 4535 Dressler Rd NW Canton OH 44718-4500

WOLANIN, THOMAS RICHARD, educator, researcher; b. Detroit, Dec. 1, 1942; s. Chester Richard and Helen Theresa (Luszki) W.; children: Peter, Andrew. BA magna cum laude, Oberlin Coll., 1965; MA, Harvard U., 1970, PhD, 1972. Staff dir. subcom. on labor-mgmt. rels. House Edn. and Labor Com., 1975-77, dep. staff dir. subcom. on select edn., 1977-78; exec. asst. to pres. NYU, 1981-82; analyst Senate Budget Com., 1982-83; staff dir. subcom. on investigations House P.O. and Civil Svc. Com., 1983-85, 87-91; staff dir. subcom. on postsecondary edn. House Edn. and Labor Com., 1978-81, 85-87;, 91-93; dep. ast. sec. legis. and congl. affairs U.S. Dept. Edn., Washington, 1993-96; sr. assoc. The Inst. for Higher Edn. Policy, Washington, 1996—; instr. govt. Oberlin Coll., 1967-69; asst. prof. polit. sci. U. Wis., Madison, 1971-78; adj. prof. edn. policy and polit. sci. George Washington U., Washington, 1997—. Author: Presidential Advisory Commissions: Truman to Nixon, 1975; co-author: Congress and the Colleges: Higher Education in National Politics, 1976; contbr. articles to profl. jours. Woodrow Wilson fellow, 1965-66, Harvard Grad. prize fellow, 1965-67, 69-71; guest scholar The Brookings Instn., 1970, Congl. fellow, 1971-72, Ford Found. travel and student grantee, 1972-73, 73-74, Spencer fellow Nat. Acad. Edn., 1975-81, acad. specialist grantee USIA, 1990. Mem. Am. Polit. Sci. Assn., Polish Am. Arts Assn. Washington, Polish Am. Congress, Congl. Fellowship Alumni Assn., Phi Beta Kappa. Democrat. Roman Catholic. Avocations: military history, Polish history, literature. Office: George Washington U Grad Sch Edn/Human Devel Washington DC 20052

WOLAS, HERBERT, lawyer; b. Bronx, N.Y., June 27, 1933; s. Irving and Mary (Kessner) W.; m. Annette Rudolph, Aug. 20, 1957; children: Cherise, Collette, Claudine. AA, UCLA, 1953, BA, 1954, JD, 1960. Bar: Calif. 1961. Since practiced in L.A. Served with F.A. AUS, 1955-56. Office: 1875 Century Park E Ste 2000 Los Angeles CA 90067-2521

WOLBRINK, DONALD HENRY, landscape architect, city planner; b. Ganges, Mich., May 13, 1911; s. Isaac M. and Ruby (Payne) W.; m. Florence Theresa Stack, Dec. 24, 1938; 1 child, Gretchen. B.A., U. Mich., 1932, M. Landscape Design, 1933. Landscape architect Nat. Park Service, Washington, 1934-41; landscape architect C.E., Omaha, 1941-44; assoc. Bartholomew Assocs., Honolulu, 1946-58, ptnr., 1958-64; pres. Donald Wolbrink, Honolulu, 1964-87, ret., 1989; dir. emeritus First Fed. Savs. and Loan, Honolulu; chmn. bd. Hawaii Architects and Engrs., Honolulu, 1979-84 (project dir. Melbourne strategy plan 1972-73); dir. Interplan, Melbourne, Australia, 1972-80. Co-author Hawaii State Law (land use law), 1961, sociophysical planning process, 1980; dir. (book) Tourism Standards, 1972. Bd. dirs. Oahu Devel. Conf., Honolulu, 1975-86 (project dir. 9 prin. Micronesian Islands 1961-75), C. of C., Honolulu, 1971-73, Downtown Improvement Assn., Honolulu, 1973-79; pres. Foresight, Inc., Honolulu, 1972-85. Served to lt. USN, 1944-46. Recipient Victorian Archtl. award Royal Australian Inst., 1977, Disting. Service award Engring. Assn. Hawaii, 1983, Spl. Achievement award Am. Plan Assn., 1990. Fellow ASCE, Am. Soc. Landscape Architects (trustee 1960-66, 77-78, merit award Hawaii chpt. 1983); mem. Am. Inst. Cert. Planners, Nat. Hist. Planning Pioneer Am., Inst. Consulting Planners. Avocation: photography. Home: 900 W Alpine Way Shelton WA 98584

WOLBRINK, JAMES FRANCIS, real estate investor; b. Charles City, Iowa, Sept. 8, 1942; s. Richard William and Anna (Bult) W.; m. Karen Ann Dunkerly, June 18, 1966. BS in Indsl. Engring., Iowa State U., 1966, postgrad., 1968-72. Cert. assn. exec. Tech. writer/editor Lawrence Radiation Lab., Livermore, Calif., 1966-67; editor, head engring. publs. Engring. Research Inst., Iowa State U., Ames, 1967-70; mng. dir., edn. and publs. Am. Inst. Indsl. Engrs., Norcross, Ga., 1971-83; commodities broker Clayton Brokerage, 1983-85; now pres. Wolbrink Properties, 1983—. Named Outstanding Young Alumnus Iowa State U., 1977. Mem. Sandy Springs Optimist Club (pres. 1989-90), Optimist Internat. (gov. Ga. dist. 1994-95), Delta Chi. Home and Office: 4520 Northside Dr NW Atlanta GA 30327-4548

WOLCHKO, MATTHEW JOHN, architect; b. Passaic, N.J., Jan. 10, 1961; s. John Stephen and Irene Wolchko; m. Marie Elena Theresa Malady, Feb. 15, 1992; 1 child, Katherine. BS in Architecture, Pa. State U., 1983; MArch, Ariz. State U., 1985. Registered architect, N.J.; lic. profl. planner, N.J.; cert. Nat. Coun. Archtl. Registration Bds.; notary pub., N.J. Draftsman Walter Kawecki, Montclair, N.J., 1984; rsch. asst. Coll. Architecture Ariz. State U., 1984-85; profl. intern Swanke, Hayden, Connell, N.Y.C., 1986; draftsman The Aybar Partnership, Ridgefield, N.J., 1985-89, ptnr., 1990—; presenter in field various confs. and workshops. Contbg. author: The Computability of Design, 1987. Mem. Three Saints Russian Orthodox Ch.; mem. Garfield (N.J.) Planning Bd., 1986-90, chmn., 1988-90; mcpl. rep. N.J. State Devel. and Redevel. Master Plan; mcpl. contact N.J. State Green Acres Program-Passaic River/Dundee Dam Hist. Park; mem. Garfield Zoning Bd. of Adjustment, 1994—; active Nat. Ry. Hist. Soc., Anthracite R.R. Hist. Soc. Mem. Architects League of No. N.J. (trustee 1996). Home: 105 Bergen St Garfield NJ 07026-2111 Office: Aybar Partnership 605 Broad Ave Ridgefield NJ 07657-1604

WOLCK, WOLFGANG HANS-JOACHIM, linguist, educator; b. Koenigsberg, Germany, Sept. 19, 1932; came to U.S., 1963; s. Walter Erich and

Margarete (Brettschneider) W.; m. Carolyn Ann Burch, June 18, 1966. Student, Birkbeck Coll., London, 1956; Staatsexamen, Christian Albrecht U., Kiel, Germany, 1960; Ph.D., J.W. Goethe U., Frankfurt, Germany, 1963. Instr. German and Latin Liverpool (Eng.) Inst., 1957-58; instr. Albert Ludwig U., Freiburg, Germany, 1964-65; asst. prof. Ind. U., Bloomington, 1966-69; assoc. prof. linguistics SUNY-Buffalo, 1970-74, prof., 1975—, chmn. dept., 1977-87, 89-91, dir. Latin Am. Studies program, 1972-76; research fellow Instituto de Estudios Peruanos, Lima, Peru, 1976-77; advisor Ministry of Edn., Lima, 1972, 82-83; rsch. prof. Belgian Nat. Sc. Found., 1991—; cons. Fischer-Price Toys, Inc., East Aurora, N.Y., 1980—; hon. prof. San Marcos Nat. U., Lima, 1972; mem. Fulbright Nat. Screening Com., 1993-96, E.C. Scientific Com. Linguistic Minorities, 1993-96. Author: Phonematische Analyse der Sprache von Buchan, 1965, Pequeño Breviario Quechua, 1987; co-author: Interkulturelle Mehrsprachigkeit, 1991; editor: The Social Dimension of Dialectology, 1976, The Fifth LACUS Forum, 1979, International Handbook on Contact Linguistics, 1996. Founding mem. Peru Earthquake Relief Com., Washington, 1972; field rep. United Way Campaign, Buffalo, 1977-81. Recipient Bronze medal Mazaryk U., Brno, Czech Republic, 1971; Fulbright grantee, 1963-64. Mem. Am. Dialect Soc., Linguistic Soc. Am., Societas Linguistica Europea, Linguistic Assn. Can. and U.S., Am. Assn. Applied Linguistics, Ctr. for Cognitive Sci., Centre for Multilingual Rsch., Sociedad Boliviana de Linguistica (hon.), Ellicottville Ski Club (dir. 1988-94). Home: 611 Skinnersville Rd Buffalo NY 14228-2505 Office: SUNY 685 Baldy Hall Buffalo NY 14260-1030

WOLCOTT, HUGH DIXON, obstetrics and gynecology educator; b. N.Y.C., Jan. 12, 1946; s. Charles Edmund and Joan Degrau (Loveland) W.; m. Jane Jarrell Smith; children: Allison, James. BS, U.S. Naval Acad., 1967; MSE, Princeton U., 1969; MD, Northwestern U., Chgo., 1979. Diplomate Am. Bd. Ob-Gyn, Am. Bd. Med. Examiners. Commd. ensign USN, 1967, advanced through grades to capt., 1990; aviator, Fighter Squadron 14 Naval Air Station, Oceana, Va., 1971-74; test pilot Naval Air Test Ctr., Patuxent River, Md., 1974-76; staff physician Naval Hosp., Portsmouth, Va., 1984, Jacksonville, Fla., 1984-86; dir. colposcopy and laser clins. Naval Hosp., Portsmouth, Va., 1986-89; dir. ob-gyn. residency program Naval Hosp., Portsmouth, 1989-91, acting chmn. dept. ob-gyn., 1990-91; ret., 1991; asst. prof. Med. Coll. Hampton Roads, Norfolk, Va., 1991—; head dept. ob-gyn. Sentara Hosps., Norfolk, 1996—. Contbr. articles profl. jours. Awarded 1st prize scientific paper by resident physician Am. Coll. Obstetricans and Gynecologists; recipient Guggenheim fellowship Princeton U., 1967-68; Trident scholar U.S. Naval Acad., 1966-67. Fellow Am. Coll. Ob.-Gyns. (chmn. Navy sect. armed forces dist. 1989-91), Assn. Profs. Ob.-Gyns. (assoc.); mem. Am. Assn. Gynecol. Laparoscopists. Episcopalian. Home: 835 Botetourt Gardens Norfolk VA 23507 Office: Woman Care Ctrs 811 Med Tower 400 Gresham Dr Norfolk VA 23507-1901

WOLCOTT, JOHN WINTHROP, III, corporate executive; b. Balt., Dec. 3, 1924; s. John Winthrop, Jr. and Dorothy C. (Fraser) W.; m. Elizabeth Thelin Hooper, Apr. 24, 1948 (div. 1985); children: John Winthrop IV, Elizabeth T., Katherine C.; m. Karen E. Jones, Oct. 1, 1985; 1 child, Oliver Lund. B.Indsl. Engring., Gen. Motors Inst., 1951. Registered profl. engr., Ohio. With Gen. Motors Corp., 1946-53, Weatherhead Co., Cleve., 1957-60; v.p. H.K. Porter Co., Inc., Pitts., 1960-64; pres., dir., CEO Ametek, Inc., N.Y.C., 1964-66; v.p. Am. Machine & Foundry Co., 1966-77, group exec. process equipment group, 1967-70; exec. v.p. ops., dir. AMF, Inc., 1970-77; pres., chief exec. officer, dir. Transway Internat. Corp., N.Y.C., 1978-86, chmn. bd., 1982-86. Served with USCGR, 1943-46. Mem. Soc. Colonial Wars, Md. Club (Balt.), Brook Club (N.Y.C.). Episcopalian. Home: 210 Carrsbrook Dr Charlottesville VA 22901-1004

WOLCOTT, OLIVER DWIGHT, international trading company executive; b. Marshfield, Oreg., Oct. 17, 1918; s. Dwight Oliver and Agnes Beatrice (Kunkel) W.; m. Valborg K. Rasmussen, Mar. 22, 1942; 1 child, John Oliver. BS, U. Calif., 1940; MBA, Stanford U., 1942. With Chemurgic Corp., 1943-50, pres., 1947-50; with subs. W.R. Grace & Co., 1950-60, v.p., 1958-60; with Balfour Guthrie & Co., San Francisco, 1961-77; from v.p. to pres. Balfour Guthrie & Co., 1964-77; dir. Barclays Bank Calif., 1974-88, chmn., 1979-85; dir. Wilson & Geo., Meyer & Co., 1981-92, Bd. Trade San Francisco, 1969-77. Mem. Pacific-Union Club. Address: 3773 Terra Granada Dr Walnut Creek CA 94595-3534

WOLCOTT, ROBERT WILSON, JR., consulting company executive; b. Phila., Nov. 20, 1926; s. Robert Wilson and Alice (Huston) W.; m. Margaret Hoopes, June 24, 1949; children: Allyn M., Anne H. BSCE, Princeton U., 1948. V.p., gen. mgr. Internat. Mill Service div. IU Internat. Corp., Phila., 1963-65, pres., 1965-70; group v.p. IU Internat. Corp., Phila., 1970-82, exec. v.p., 1982-88; cons. Phila., 1988—. Bd. dirs. The Church Farm. Sch., Exton, Pa., 1981—, Zool. Soc. Phila., 1983—. Mem. Am. Iron & Steel Inst., AIME. Clubs: Merion Cricket (Haverford, Pa.); Gulph Mills Golf (King of Prussia, Pa.); Phila. Home: 236 Atlee Rd Wayne PA 19087-3836 Office: 125 Strafford Ave Ste 130 Wayne PA 19087-3318

WOLCOTT, SAMUEL H., III, investment banker; b. Boston, June 1, 1935; s. Samuel H. and Mary (Weld) W.; m. Nora Bradley, Dec. 28, 1960; 1 child, Natalie. A.B., Harvard U., 1957. Ptnr. J. Barth & Co., San Francisco, 1961-70; exec. v.p. Dean Witter Reynolds, N.Y.C., 1970-87, E.F. Hutton, 1987-88, Dean Witter Reynolds, N.Y.C., 1988—. Office: Dean Witter Reynolds 2 World Trade Ctr Fl 65 New York NY 10048-0203

WOLCZYK, JOSEPH MICHAEL, lawyer; b. Auburn, N.Y., June 16, 1955; s. Constantine J. and Mary E. (Burke) W.; 1 child, Sarah Marie. AA, Auburn (N.Y.) C.C., 1975; BA, SUNY, Buffalo, 1977; MA, U. Notre Dame, 1978; JD, Valparaiso U., 1982; AAS, Cayuga (N.Y.) C.C., 1987. Bar: N.Y. 1984, U.S. Dist. Ct. (no. dist.) N.Y. 1985, D.C. 1986, U.S. Ct. Appeals (fed. cir.) 1989, Maine 1990. Pvt. practice Auburn, 1984—; atty., engr. Integrated Concepts, Inc., Rochester, N.Y., 1989-90; v.p. legal ops. White Earth Environ., Auburn, 1988-90; owner Commonwealth Funding of Auburn, 1986-87. Author: Small Town Solo, 5 The Compleat Lawyer 4. Mem. exec. bd. Boy Scouts Am. #366, Auburn, 1991-95; incorporator, bd. dirs. Tomatofest of Ctrl. N.Y., Auburn, 1988; vice chmn. Auburn Zoning Bd. Appeals, 1986-88; bd. dirs. Legal Svcs. of Ctrl. N.Y., 1995—. Named one of Outstanding Young Men of Am., 1988. Mem. ABA (sec. law student divsn. 1981, Silver Key 1981O, D.C. Bar, Maine Bar Assn., Irish Lawyers Assn. N.Y., Cayuga Mus. of History (treas. 1991-94, pres. 1994-96), Rotary Club Auburn (pres. 1988-90, Group Study Exch. team to Japan 1985, 96, Group Study Exch. dist. chmn. 1993-97, chmn. dist. 7150 found. com. 1996—, chmn. 1996—). Avocations: sailing, bicycling, hiking, skiing. Office: 164 State St Auburn NY 13021-1845

WOLD, DAVID C., bishop. Bishop of Southwestern Wash. Evang. Luth. Ch. in Am., Tacoma. Office: Synod of Southwestern Washington 420 121st St S Tacoma WA 98444-5218*

WOLD, FINN, biochemist, educator; b. Stavanger, Norway, Feb. 3, 1928; came to U.S., 1950, naturalized, 1957; s. Sverre and Herdis (Rasmussen) W.; m. Bernadine Moe, June 13, 1953; children—Eric Robert, Marc Sverre. Student, U. Oslo, 1946-50; M.S., Okla. State U., 1953; Ph.D., U. Calif. at Berkeley, 1956. Research asso. U. Calif. at Berkeley, 1956-57; asst. prof. biochemistry U. Ill., Urbana, 1957-62; asso. prof. U. Ill., 1962-66; prof. biochemistry U. Minn. Med. Sch., Mpls., 1966-74; prof. biochemistry U. Minn., St. Paul, 1974-81, head dept., 1974-79; Robert A. Welch prof. chemistry U. Tex. Med. Sch., Houston, 1981—; vis. prof. Nat. Taiwan U., 1971, Rice U., 1974, Amademia Sinica, Taiwan, 1990, U. Tromso, Norway, 1991-94; cons. in field. Author, contbg. author books; mem. editl. bd. Jour. Biol. Chemistry, 1974-79, 81-86, Biochemistry, 1974-83, Protein Sci., 1995—; contbr. articles to profl. jours. Fulbright fellow, 1950; John Simon Guggenheim fellow, 1960-61; recipient Lalor Found. Research award, 1958, NIH research career devel. award, 1961-66. Mem. AAAS, Am. Soc. Biochemistry and Molecular Biology (councilor 1978-81, sec. 1992-95), Am. Chem. Soc. (councilor 1980-83, chmn. divsn. biol. chemistry 1985-86), Protein Soc. (pres. 1989-91), Biochem. Soc. (London). Office: U Tex Med Sch PO Box 20708 Houston TX 77225-0708

WOLD, JOHN SCHILLER, geologist, former congressman; b. East Orange, N.J., Aug. 31, 1916; s. Peter Irving and Mary (Helff) W.; m. Jane Adele Pearson, Sept. 28, 1946; children: Peter Irving, Priscilla Adele, John Pearson. AB, St. Andrews U., Scotland and Union Coll., Schenectady, 1938; MS, Cornell U., 1939; LLD (hon.), U. Wyo., 1991. Dir. Fedn. Rocky Mountain States, 1966-68; v.p. Rocky Mountain Oil and Gas Assn., 1967, 68; mem. Wyo. Ho. of Reps., 1957-59; Wyo. Republican candidate for U.S. Senate, 1964, 70; mem. 91st Congress at large from, Wyo.; chmn., CEO Wold Trona Co., Inc.; pres., chmn. Wold Oil & Gas Co.; ret. Wold Nuclear Co., Wold Mineral Exploration Co., Casper, Wyo.; founding pres. Wyo. Heritage Soc.; founder Central Wyo. Ski Corp.; chmn. Wyo. Natural Gas Pipeline Authority, 1987-91; chmn. bd. Nuclear Exploration and Devel. Corp., Mineral Engring. Co. Contbr. articles to profl. jours. Chmn. Wyo. Rep. Com., 1960-64, Western State Rep. Chmns. Assn., 1963-64; mem. exec. com. Rep. Nat. Com., 1962-64; chmn. Wyo. Rep. State Fin. Com.; Active Little League Baseball, Boy Scouts Am., United Fund, YMCA, Boys Clubs Am.; former pres. bd. trustees Casper Coll.; trustee Union Coll. Served to lt. USNR, World War II. Named Wyo. Man of Yr. AP-UPI, 1968; Wyo. Mineral Man of Yr., 1979, Wyo. Heritage award, 1992; named Benefactor of Yr., Nat. Coun. for Resource Devel., 1993. Mem. Wyo. Geol. Assn. (hon. life, pres. 1956), Am. Assn. Petroleum Geologists, Ind. Petroleum Assn. Am., AAAS, Wyo. Mining Assn., Sigma Xi, Alpha Delta Phi. Episcopalian (past vestryman, warden). Home: 1231 W 30th St Casper WY 82604-4738 Office: Mineral Resource Ctr 139 W 2nd St Casper WY 82601-2473

WOLD, ROBERT LEE, architect, engineer; b. Oak Park, Ill., Oct. 20, 1931; s. Leaman A. and Helen Wold; m. Susan J. Olmstead, Dec. 18, 1854; children: Kyle, Eric, Karla. MArch with high honors, U. Ill., 1954. Registered architect, Ill., Mich., Fla., Pa., S.C., Mass. Designer DeLeuw Cather Co., Chgo., 1949-53; architect Perkins & Will, Chgo., 1954-55, Donker Assocs., Grand Rapids, Mich., 1957-59, Wold, Bowers, De Shane & Covert, Grand Rapids, 1960-76; prin. Robert Lee Wold & Assocs., Grand Rapids, 1976-96. Prin. works include Walker City Ctr., Kent Community Hosp. (AIA Design award 1972), Grand Valley State U. Campus Ctr. (AIA Design award 1975), First of Am. Bank Bldg. (AIA Design award 1983), Grand Valley State Downtown Campus (AIA Design award 1989). 1st lt. Corps of Engrs., U.S. Army, 1955-56. Recipient Gold medal Mich. Soc. Architects, 1982. Fellow AIA; mem. Rotary. Home: 3 Newhall Hilton Head Island SC 29928 Office: Tower Pinkster Titus Wold Inc 678 Front Ave NW Grand Rapids MI 49504-5323

WOLD, WILLIAM SYDNEY, molecular biology educator; b. Pine Falls, Manitoba, Can., Feb. 12, 1944; came to U.S., 1973; s. Roy and Nellie (Yurchison) W.; m. Susan Ann Lees, Dec. 30, 1967; m. Loralee Jane, William Guy, Jessica Ann, Jonathan Evered. BSc, U. Manitoba, 1965, MSc, 1968, PhD, 1973. Postdoctoral fellow St. Louis U., 1973-75, instr., 1975-76, from asst. prof. to prof. molecular virology, 1976-92, prof., chmn. dept. molecular microbiology and immunology, 1992—; reviewer's res. NIH, Washington, 1990—; cons. Genetic Therapy, Inc., 1994. Contbr. articles to Cell Jour., Jour. Biol. Chemistry, Jour. Immunology, Jour. Virology, Virology, others; assoc. editor jour. Virology, 1990—; mem. editl. bd. Jour. Virology, 1997—. NIH grantee, 1980—. Mem. AAAS, Am. Soc. Microbiology, Am. Soc. Virology, Internat. Soc. Antiviral Rsch. Achievements include discovery and characterization of human adenovirus proteins that counteract host immunosurveillance and that modulate virus-cell interactions by stimulating growth factor signal transduction. Office: St Louis U Molecular Microbiology & Immunology 1402 S Grand Blvd Saint Louis MO 63104-1004

WOLDEGABRIEL, GIDAY, research geologist; b. Mai Misham/Adwa, Tigray, Ethiopia, Sept. 3, 1955; came to U.S., 1982; s. Giday WoldeGabriel and Mislal Mesfin; m. Almaz Berhane Tesfamichael, Jan. 15, 1994. BS in Geology with honors, Addis Ababa (Ethiopia) U., 1978, MS in Geology, 1980; PhD in Geology, Case Western Res. U., 1987. Lectr. geology Addis Ababa U., 1980-82; dir.'s postdoctoral fellow Los Alamos (N.Mex.) Nat. Lab., 1987-90, contractor/collaborator, 1990-92, mem. tech. staff, 1992—. Author several publs. on volcanology, geochemistry and tectonics. Mem. Am. Geophysical Union. Avocations: running, camping, skiing, body building, swimming. Home: 45 Paige Cir Los Alamos NM 87544-3638 Office: Los Alamos Nat Lab EEES-1/MS D462 Los Alamos NM 87545

WOLDMAN, SHERMAN, pediatrician; b. Buffalo, Apr. 1, 1932; s. Joseph Harry and Sadie (Weinstein) W. m. Fern Marlene Weinstein, Dec. 28, 1952; children Deborah Janine Case, Scott Alan, Sabina Heide Muller. BS in Pharmacy Magna Cum Laude, U. Buffalo, 1953, MD with High Hons., 1957. Diplomate Am. Bd. Pediatrics. Intern Millard Fillmore Hosp., Buffalo, 1957-58; resident in pediatrics Children's Hosp., Buffalo, 1958-60; pvt. practice in pediatrics Buffalo, 1961-66, Cheektowaga, N.Y., 1962—; adj. clin. asst. pediatrics, SUNY Sch. Medicine, Buffalo, 1962, clin. assoc.m 1970, clin. asst. prof., 1973, preceptor Sch. Nursing, 1976-82; attending pediatrician Booth Meml. Hosp., Buffalo, 1969-72; sch. physician Williamsville (N.Y.) Ctrl. Schs., 1962-94, chmn. of physicians, 1970-94; courtesy staff St. Joseph Intercomty. Hosp., Cheektowaga, 1963-80, Kenmore (N.Y.) Mercy Hosp., 1963-70, 1974-82, Sisters of Charity Hosp., Buffalo, 1991—, Erie County Med. Ctr., Buffalo, 1979-83, Buffalo Gen. Hosp., 1987-95; provisional staff Mercy Hosp., Buffalo, 1982-83, courtesy staff 1983—. Vol. Leukemia Soc. Am., 1975—, bd. trustees Western N.Y. chpt. 1975—, pres. 1977-79, v.p. 1979-81, mem. profl. edn. com. 1975—, mem. nat. bd. trustees 1978-87, vice chmn. patient aid com., 1980-87; mem. task force on sch. health Erie County (N.Y.) Health Dept; trustee Temple Beth David Ner-Israel, Buffalo, 1964-5. Recipient PREP Fellowship award Am. Acad. Pediatrics, 1979-85; (with Mrs. Fern Woldman) Recognition cert. Cheektowaga C. of C., 1982, Myron L. Woldman Vol. of Yr. award, Leukemia Soc. Am., Western N.Y. chpt. 1987, Disting. Physician award MIllard Fillmore Health System, 1995. Fellow Am. Acad. Pediatrics; mem. Med. Soc. State of N.Y., Buffalo Pediatric Soc. (pres. 1969-70), Gibson Anatomical Soc. (hon.), Med. Soc. County of Erie, N.Y. (chmn. pub. health com. 1978-79), Maimonides Med. Soc. (pres. Buffalo 1982-83), Alpha Omega Alpha, Rho Chi (pres. U. Buffalo chpt. 1952-53), Phi Lambda Kappa (pres. student chpt. 1955-56, alumni 1965, v.p. alumni 1980-81). Avocations: gardening, computers. Office: 4427 Union Rd Cheektowaga NY 14225-2305

WOLDT, GERALD D. (JAY WOLDT), nurse anesthetist; b. Chippewa Falls, Wis., May 30, 1943; s. D.C. and Blanche A. (Patrie) W.; children: Michael B., Eve A. Diploma in Nursing, St. Mary's Sch. Nursing, Wausau, Wis., 1965; diploma, Tripler Army Sch. Anesthesia, Honolulu, 1970; BSN, Med. Coll. Ga., 1977; MSN, Oreg. Health Sci. U., 1980. Cert. RN Anesthetist. Staff nurse operating rm. Fitzsimons Hosp., Denver, 1966-67; commd. U.S. Army, 1966, advanced through grades to lt. col., 1981; staff anesthetist 93d Evac Hosp., Vietnam, 1970-71, 27th Surg. Hosp., Vietnam, 1971; clin. instr., staff anesthetist Madigan Army Hosp., Tacoma, Wash., 1971-72; staff anesthetist Munson Army Hosp., Leavenworth, Kans., 1972-76; chief anesthetist Dwight D. Eisenhower Hosp., Augusta, Ga., 1976-78, 2d Gen. Hosp., Landstuhl, Germany, 1980-83; nurse anesthesia cons. 7th MEDCOM, Germany, 1980-83; chief anesthetist, clin. instr. DeWitt Army Hosp., Ft. Belvoir, Va., 1983-87; staff anesthetist Potomac Hosp., Woodbridge, Va., 1986-91; dir. nurse anesthesia Mary Washington Hosp., Fredericksburg, Va., 1991-95; dir. nurse anesthesia Fredericksburg (Va.) Ambulatory Surgery Ctr., 1996—; co-facilitator death and dying seminars, 1980-83; lectr. in field. Mem. Am. Assn. Nurse Anesthetists, Sigma Theta Tau. Roman Catholic. Avocations: reading, racquetball, tennis, walking, painting. Home: One Charleston Ct Stafford VA 22554

WOLENSKY, JOAN, occupational therapist, interfaith minister; b. Wilkes Barre, Pa., Mar. 4, 1954; d. Paul and Anna (Havrilla) W.; children: Maurisa Ann Fela, Jennifer Andrea Fela. BS, Coll. Misericordia, Dallas, Pa., 1985; DDiv (hon.), New Theol. Sem., N.Y.C., 1992. Cert. interfaith minister; cert. minister Order of Melchizedek, 1992; Reiki master, USUI and Karuna Sys.; cert. nat. and internat. spiritual response therapy counselor/tchr.; cert. master tchr. magnified healing. Founder, adminstr. N.E. Pa. Interfaith Ministries/Celestial Pathways Ctr., Harveys Lake, Pa., 1988; founder, dir., adminstr. Occupational Therapy Cons. Svcs., Harveys Lake, 1989; dean, mem. adv. bd. Sage Inst., Shokan, N.Y.; mem. adv. bd. and quality assurance bd. At Home Health Care, Wilkes-Barre; mem., spkr. Am. Congress Rehab. Medicine, 1995. Contbr. articles to profl. jours. Recipient City of Richmond award City of Richmond Nursing Home, 1989; Mary K. Minglin scholar Am. Occupational Therapy Assn., 1984. Mem. Assn. for Interfaith Mins., Holistic Consortium of N.E. Pa., Inst. for Higher Healing/Wellness, Spiritual Response Assn., Universal Holistic Healers Assn. Avocations: martial arts, yoga, qingong, angels, guitar. Home: Po Box 197 Harveys Lake PA 18618

WOLENSKY, MICHAEL K., lawyer; b. Chattanooga, Aug. 16, 1946; s. Gabriel Albert and Irene (Northcutt) W.; m. Sandra Joy Silverman, Aug. 10, 1969; 1 child, David G. BME, Ga. Inst. Tech., 1967; JD, Am. U., 1971. Bar: Va. 1971, Fla. 1972, D.C. 1972, Ga. 1981, U.S. Supreme Ct. 1974. Patent examiner U.S. Patent Office, Washington, 1968-71; trial atty. SEC, Miami, Fla., 1971-75; chief enforcement atty. SEC, San Francisco, 1975-77; asst. gen. counsel SEC, Washington, 1977-82; regional adminstr. SEC, Atlanta, 1982-87; of counsel Kilpatrick & Cody, Atlanta, 1987-90; ptnr., chmn. litigation dept. Kutak Rock, Atlanta, 1990—; arbitrator Nat. Assn. Securities Dealers, N.Y.C., 1987—, Am. Arbitration Assn., Atlanta, 1988—, Nat. Futures Assn., 1996—. Contbr. articles to profl. publs. Mem. ABA, Atlanta Bar Assn. Avocations: tennis, coaching youth sports. Office: Kutak Rock 225 Peachtree St NE Ste 2100 Atlanta GA 30303-1731

WOLF, ALFRED, rabbi; b. Eberbach, Germany, Oct. 7, 1915; came to U.S., 1935, naturalized, 1941; s. Hermann and Regina (Levy) W.; m. Miriam Jean Office, June 16, 1940; children: David B., Judith C. (dec.), Dan L. BA, U. Cin., 1937; MHL, Hebrew Union Coll., 1941; DD, 1966; PhD, U. So. Calif., 1961; DHL, U. Judaism, 1987, Loyola Marymount U., 1990. Ordained rabbi, 1941. Rabbi Temple Emanuel, Dothan, Ala., 1941-46; S.E. regional dir. Union Am. Hebrew Congregations, 1944-46; Western regional dir. Union Am. Hebrew Congregations, Los Angeles, 1946-49; rabbi Wilshire Blvd. Temple Los Angeles, 1949-85, rabbi emeritus, 1985—; dir. Skirball Inst. on Am. Values of Am. Jewish Com., 1985-95; founding dir., 1996—; lectr. U. So. Calif., 1955-69, Hebrew Union Coll., Jewish Inst. Religion, Calif., 1963-65, 74; lectr. religion Seven Seas div. Chapman Coll., 1967; adj. prof. theology Loyola U. Los Angeles, 1967-74; lectr. sociology Calif. State U., Los Angeles, 1977; co-chair First Nationwide Conf. for Cath. Jewish and Protestant seminiaries, Chgo., 1993. Author: (with Joseph Gaer) Our Jewish Heritage, 1957, (with Monsignor Royale M. Vadakin) Journey Of Discovery - A Resource Manual for Catholic-Jewish Dialogue, 1989; editor Teaching About World Religions: A Teacher's Supplement, 1991. Mem. camp commn. adminstrv. com. Camp Hess Kramer, 1951—; mem. L.A. Com. on Human Rels., 1956-72, mem. exec. bd., 1960—, chmn., 1964-66, hon. mem., 1972—; pres. Anytown U.S.A., 1964-66; mem. United Way Planning Coun. Bd., chmn., 1974-78; mem. youth adv. com. NCCJ, 1968-72, exec. bd., 1972-93; founding pres. Interreligious Coun. So. Calif., 1970-72; chmn. clergy adv. com. L.A. Sch. Dist., 1971-81; chmn. Nat. Workshop on Christian-Jewish Rels., 1978; bd. govs. Hebrew Union Coll., bd. alumni overseers, 1972—; mem. L.A. 2000 Com., 1986-89, The 2000 Partnership, 1989-95, Berlin Sister City Com., L.A., 1987-89; bd. dirs. Jewish Fedn. Coun., 1978-85, bd. govs., 1985—; bd. dirs. Jewish Family Svc. L.A., sec., 1978-80. Recipient Samuel Kaminker award as Jewish educator of year Western Assn. Temple Educators, 1965, John Anson Ford Human Relations award County Commn. on Human Relations, 1972, 90, Harry Hollzer Meml. award Los Angeles Jewish Fedn. Council, 1978, Volpert Community Service award, 1986, Community Service award United Way of Los Angeles, 1980, Leadership award Los Angeles Bd. Edn., 1981, Service to Edn. award Associated Adminstrs. Los Angeles, 1983, Pub. Service award Jewish Chautauqua Soc., 1986, N.Am. Interfaith Leadership award Nat. Workshop for Christian-Jewish Rels., 1990. Mem. Bd. Rabbis So. Calif. (pres.), Am. Jewish Com. (exec. com. Los Angeles chpt., Max Bay Meml. award 1986), Central Conf. Am. Rabbis (exec. bd., mem. commn. on Jewish edn. 1970-72, treas. 1975-79, chmn. interreligious activities com. 1975-79, hon. mem. 1991—), Pacific Assn. Reform Rabbis (pres.), So. Calif. Assn. Liberal Rabbis (pres.), Synagogue Council Am. (mem. com. interreligious affairs), Alumni Assn. Hebrew Union Coll.-Jewish Inst. Religion, Town Hall, Los Angeles World Affairs Council, U. So. Calif. Alumni Assn. Home: 3389 Ley Dr Los Angeles CA 90027-1315 Office: Skirball Inst on Am Values 635 S Harvard Blvd Ste 214 Los Angeles CA 90005-2586

WOLF, ALFRED PETER, research chemist, educator; b. N.Y.C., Feb. 13, 1923; s. Josef and Margarete (Kunst) W.; m. Elizabeth H. Gross, June 15, 1946; 1 child, Roger O. B.A., Columbia U., 1944, M.A., 1948, Ph.D., 1952; Ph.D. (hon.), U. Uppsala, (Sweden), 1983, U. Rome, 1989. Chemist Brookhaven Nat. Lab., Upton, N.Y., 1951, chemist with tenure, 1957-64, sr. chemist, 1964—, chmn. chemistry dept., 1982-87; adj. prof. chemistry Columbia U., N.Y.C., 1953-83; vis. lectr. U. Calif., Berkeley, 1964; cons. Philip Morris, Inc., Richmond, Va., 1966-91, NIH, Bethesda, Md.; cons., advisor IAEA, Vienna, Austria; advisor Italian NRC, Rome, 1959—, Atomic Rsch. Inst., Julich, Germany, 1981-90; rsch. prof. psychiatry NYU, 1988—. Author: Synthesis of 11C, 18F and 13N Labelled Radiotracers for Biomedical Application, 1982; contbr. numerous articles to profl. jours.; patentee in field; editor: Jour. Labelled Compounds and Radiopharms., Radiochimica Acta. Served with AUS, 1943-46. Recipient JARI award Pergamon Jours., 1986, The Javits Neurosci. Investigator award, 1986, Georg V. Hevesy Meml. medal Georg V. Hevesy Found. Nuclear Medicine, 1986, disting. sci. award Inst. Clin. PET, 1996. Mem. NAS, Am. Chem. Soc. (Nuclear Applications in Chemistry award 1971, Esselen award 1988), Chem. Soc. (U.K.), Soc. Nuclear Medicine (1982 Paul Aebersold award, pres. radiopharm. council 1980, George Hevesy award 1991), German. Chem. Soc. Home: PO Box 1043 Setauket NY 11733-0803 Office: Brookhaven Nat Lab Dept Chemistry Upton NY 11973

WOLF, ARTHUR HENRY, museum administrator; b. New Rockford, N.D., June 18, 1953; s. Louis Irwin and Vivian Joyce (Grinde) W.; m. Holly M. Chaffee, Oct. 18, 1984. BA in Anthropology, U. Nebr., 1975; MA, U. Ariz., 1977. Lab. asst., acting curator anthropology U. Nebr. State Mus., Lincoln, 1973-75; rsch. asst. Ariz. State Mus., Tucson, 1975-77; curator of collections Sch. Am. Rsch., Santa Fe, N.Mex., 1977-79; dir. Millcent Rogers Mus., Taos, N.Mex., 1979-87, Nev. State Mus. and Hist. Soc., Las Vegas, 1988-92, Mus. of Rockies, Bozeman, Mont., 1992-96; pres. High Desert Mus., Bend, Oreg., 1996—; speaker in field; cons. Pueblos of Zuni, Picuris, San Ildefonso and Taos. Contbr. articles and revs. to profl. jours. Trustee Kokopelli Archeol. Rsch. Fund, Bozeman, 1992-96; active Mont. Ambs. Recipient Young Alumnus award U. Nebr. Lincoln, 1990. Mem. Am. Assn. Mus. (bd. dirs. 1994—, vis. com. roster 1989—, vice chair 1996-97), Rotary, Assn. Sci. Mus. Dirs. Avocations: travel, reading, music. Home: 110 NW Wau St Bend OR 97701 Office: Mus of Rockies Montana State U Bozeman MT 59717 also: High Desert Mus 59800 S Hwy 97 Bend OR 97702

WOLF, BARRY, genetics, pediatric educator; b. Chgo., June 19, 1947; s. Bert D. and Toby E. (Urkoff) W.; m. Gail Harriet Ross, Oct. 2, 1971; children: Michael Loren, Bryan Phillip. BS, U. Ill., 1969; MD, U. Ill. Coll. Medicine, 1974; PhD, U. Ill., 1974. Diplomate Am. Bd. Pediatrics, Med. and Biochem. Genetics. Intern, resident in pediatrics Childrens Meml. Hosp., Northwestern U., Chgo., 1974-76; fellow Yale U. Sch. Medicine, New Haven, Conn., 1976-78; prof. human genetics Med. Coll. Va., Richmond, 1978—, vice chair for rsch. dept. pediatrics, 1996—. Author over 140 jour. articles and book chpts. dealing with inherited disorders of metabolism and biochem. genetics, specifically disorders of biotin metabolism. Recipient E. Mead Johnson award for pediatric rsch. Am. Acad. Pediatrics, 1988, Borden award in nutrition Am. Inst. Nutrition, 1987, Outstanding Scientist of Va. award Va. Sci. Mus., 1986, Ounce of Prevention award Action for Prevention of Va., 1985. Mem. Am. Soc. Clin. Investigation, Soc. Pediatric Rsch., Soc. for Inherited Metabolic Diseases (bd. dirs.), Am. Soc. Clin. Nutrition, Am. Inst. Nutrition, Soc. for the Study of Inborn Errors of Metabolism, Am. Soc. Human Genetics. Avocations: oriental cloisonne. Office: Med Coll Va Dept Human Genetics PO Box 980033 Richmond VA 23298

WOLF, CHARLES, JR., economist, educator; b. N.Y.C., Aug. 1, 1924; s. Charles and Rosalie W.; m. Theresa van de Wint, Mar. 1, 1947; children: Charles Theodore, Timothy van de Wint. B.S., Harvard U., 1943, M.P.A., 1948, Ph.D. in Econs., 1949. Economist, fgn. service officer U.S. Dept. State, 1945-47, 49-53; mem. faculty Cornell U., 1953-54, U. Calif., Berkeley, 1954-55; sr. economist The Rand Corp., Santa Monica, Calif., 1955-67, head econs. dept., 1967-81; dean The Rand Grad. Sch., 1970—, sr. economist, 1981—, corp. fellow in internat. econs., 1996—; sr. fellow Hoover Inst., 1988—; bd. dirs. Fundamental Investors Fund, Capital Income Builder Fund, Am. Capital Fund, Capital World Growth Fund; mem. adv. com. UCLA Clin. Scholars Program; lectr. econs. UCLA, 1960-72; mem. adv. bd. grad. sch. pub. policy Carnegie-Mellon U., 1992—. Author: The Costs and Benefits of the Soviet Empire, 1986, Markets or Governments: Choosing

Between Imperfect Alternatives, 1988, 93, (with others) The Impoverished Superpower: Perestroika and the Soviet Military Burden, 1990, Linking Economic Policy and Foreign Policy, 1991, Defense Conversion and Economic Reform in Russia and Ukraine, 1994, Long-Term Economic and Military Hands: The United States and Asia, 1994-2015, 1995, The Economic Pivot in a Political Context, 1997; contbr. articles to profl. jours. Mem. Assn. for Public Policy Analysis and Mgmt. (pres. 1980-81), Am. Econs. Assn., Econometric Soc., Coun. on Fgn. Rels., Internat. Inst. Strategic Studies London. Clubs: Cosmos (Washington); Riviera Tennis (Los Angeles); Harvard (N.Y.). Office: RAND Grad Sch Policy Studies 1700 Main St Santa Monica CA 90401-3208

WOLF, CHARLES BENNO, lawyer; b. Chgo., Apr. 16, 1950; s. Ludwig and Hilde (Mandelbaum) W.; m. Sarah Lloyd, Sept. 1, 1973; children: Walter Ludwig, Peter Barton. AB, Brown U., 1972; JD, U. Chgo., 1975. Bar: Ill. 1975, U.S. Dist. Ct. (no. dist.) Ill. 1975, U.S. Ct. Appeals (4th, 5th, 6th, 7th, 8th, 9th, 10th, and 11th cirs.) 1985, U.S. Supreme Ct. 1985. Ptnr. Vedder, Price, Kaufman & Kammholz, Chgo., 1975—. Co-author: ERISA Claims and Litigation, 10th edit., 1995; contbr. articles to profl. jours. Mem. ABA, Chgo. Bar Assn., Internat. Found. Employee Benefit Plans. Office: Vedder Price Kaufman & Kammholz 222 N La Salle St Ste 2600 Chicago IL 60601-1002

WOLF, CHARLOTTE ELIZABETH, sociologist; b. Boulder, Colo., Sept. 14, 1926; d. Marion Guy and Ethel Eugenia (Thomas) Rosetta; m. René A. Wolf, Sept. 3, 1952; children: Christopher Robin, Michele Renee. B.A., U. Colo., 1949, M.A., 1959; Ph.D., U. Minn., 1968. Lectr. sociology U. Md., Tokyo, 1959-62, Turkey, 1965-67; instr. St. Mary Coll., Leavenworth, Kans., 1962-63; teaching asst. U. Minn., 1963-65; asst. prof. Colo. State U., 1968-69, Colo Woman's Coll., 1969-74; assoc. prof. sociology Ohio Wesleyan U., Delaware, 1974-80, prof., 1980, chmn. dept. sociology and anthropology, 1974-83; prof., chairperson dept. sociology and social work Memphis State U., 1983-92, prof. emeritus, 1992—. Author: Garrison Community: A Study of an Overseas American Military Colony, 1969, Southern Town/Two Communities, 1993; adv. editor Sociological Inquiry, 1988—, mem. bd. editors, 1990— ; contbr. chpts. to books and social sci. encys., articles to profl. jours.; mem. editorial bd. dirs. Sociological Spectrum, 1989-92. Recipient Ohio Wesleyan Outstanding Rsch. award, 1982, Faculty Devel. Leave Memphis State U., 1987-88; Mellon rsch. grantee, 1977, Shell Oil Co. grantee, 1978; Memphis State Ctr. for Humanities fellow, 1990. Mem. ACLU (bd. dirs. Memphis chpt. 1988—), AAUP (chpt. pres.), Am. Sociol. Assn. (chmn. com. status women 1974-76, nominations com. 1982-84), Soc. Study Social Problems (chair budget, audit and fin. com. 1975-79, treas. 1979-81), Western Social Sci. Assn. (exec. coun. 1974-77), Pacific Sociol. Assn., So. Sociol. Soc. (nominating com. 1987—, membership com. 1986-87), Mid South Sociol. Assn. (chair local arrangements 1986-87, awards com.), Sociologists Women in Soc. (chair nominations com. 1971-73, chair nominations com. South 1987-88), Soc. for Study Symbolic Interaction (C.H. Cooley award com. 1985-86, publs. com. 1989-92, chair George Herbert Mead publs. com. 1989-92, award com. 1988-89, mem. George Herbert Mead award com. 1994-95), North Ctrl. Sociol. Assn. (v.p. 1983-84), NOW (pres. Denver 1970-71, nat. bd. dirs. 1971-73, Woman of Yr. Denver chpt., chair nat. rsch. com. 1971-74), Memphis Bus. and Profl. Women's Network (exec. bd. 1991-93). Democrat. Home: APDO 604, Ajijic 45920 Jalisco Mexico

WOLF, CYNTHIA TRIBELHORN, librarian, library educator; b. Denver, Dec. 12, 1945; d. John Baltazar and Margaret (Kern) Tribelhorn; m. H.Y. Rassam, Mar. 21, 1969 (div. Jan. 1988); children: Najma C., Yousuf J.; adopted children: Leonard Joseph Lucero, Lakota E. Rassam-Lucero. BA, Colo. State U., 1970; MLS, U. Denver, 1985. Cert. permanent profl. librarian, N.Mex. Elem. tchr. Sacred Heart Sch., Farmington, N.Mex., 1973-78; asst. prof. library sci. edn. U. N.Mex., Albuquerque, 1985-90, dir. libr. sci. edn. divsn., 1989-90; pres. Info. Acquisitions, Albuquerque, 1990—; libr. dir. Southwestern Coll., Santa Fe, 1992-94; mem. youth resources Rio Grande Valley Libr. Sys., Albuquerque, 1994—; fine arts resource person for gifted edn. Farmington Pub. Schs., 1979-83; speaker Unofficial Mentorships & Market Research, 1992—. Mem. Farmington Planning and Zoning Commn., 1980-81; bd. dirs. Farmington Mus. Assn., 1983-84; pres. Farmington Symphony League, 1978. Mem. ALA, N.Mex. Library Assn., LWV (bd. dirs. Farmington, 1972-74, 75, pres.). Avocations: mixed media graphics design, market research, creative approaches to personal journals. Office: Rio Grande Valley Libr Sys Albuquerque NM 87000

WOLF, DALE EDWARD, state official; b. Kearney, Nebr., Sept. 6, 1924. BSc, U. Nebr., 1945; PhD in Agronomy and Weed Control, Rutgers U., 1949. With Dept. Agr., 1946; assoc. prof. agronomy Rutgers U., 1949; with E.I. duPont de Nemours & Co., Inc., from 1950, dir. agrichem. mktg., then gen. mgr. biochem. dept., 1972-79; v.p. biochems., also chmn. bd. subs. Endo Labs., Inc., Wilmington, Del., from 1979; group v.p. Agrl. Products, Wilmington, Del., from 1983; dir. Del. Devel. Office, Dover, 1987-89; lt. gov. of Del. Dover, 1989-93; gov. State of Del., Dover, 1993; sr. internat. cons. Mezzullo & McCandlish Law Firm, 1993—; chmn. Daynel Internat. LLC, Wilmington, Del., 1996—. Co-author: Principles of Weed Control, 1951. Bd. dirs. Del. chpt. ARC, 1975; gen. campaign chmn. United Way Del., 1978, also bd. dirs.; gen. campaign chmn. Girls Club Del., 1987; chmn. Del. Found. for Literacy, 1993—. 1st lt. AUS, 1943-46. Decorated Bronze Star, Purple Heart. Mem. Nat. Agrl. Chem. Assn. (chmn. 1981-83), Pharm. Mfrs. Assn. (dir.), Masons, Sigma Xi, Alpha Zeta.

WOLF, DAVID, lawyer; b. Boston, July 11, 1927; s. Ezekiel and Ray (Cohen) W.; m. Maxine Laura Bunnin, June 29, 1963; children—Eric E., Douglas R., James A. BA, U. Mass., 1949; LLB, Harvard U., 1952; postgrad., Northeastern U., 1952-55. Bar: Mass. 1952, U.S. Patent Office 1952, U.S. Ct. Customs and Patent Appeals 1955, U.S. Supreme Ct. 1958, U.S. Ct. Appeals (fed. cir.) 1983. Ptnr. Wolf, Greenfield & Sacks, P.C., Boston, 1952—; Watercolor artist; exhibited various local shows; holder of 13 U.S. letters patents in various arts. Watercolor artist; exhibited various local shows; holder of 12 U.S. letters patents in various arts. Bd. dirs. Newton Country Players, 1964-67, Killington East Homeowners Assn., pres. 1992—; mem. Com. for Accuracy in Mid. East Reporting in Am., 1989—, bd. dirs., gen. counsel, 1993—; mem. Am. Jewish Congress, 1990-92. Recipient various awards for art. Mem. Am. Patent Law Assn. (lectr. trademark trial adv. programs 1986-89), Lic. Execs. Soc., U.S. Trademark Assn., Harvard Law Sch. Alumni Assn., Boston Patent Law Assn. (pres. 1976), New Eng.-Israel C. of C. (v.p., bd. dirs. 1984-96), Hadassah Men's Assn., B'nai B'rith, Free Sons Israel, Alpha Epsilon Pi. Office: Wolf Greenfield & Sacks PC Fed Res Plz 600 Atlantic Ave Boston MA 02210-2211

WOLF, DON ALLEN, hardware wholesale executive; b. Allen County, Ind., June 18, 1929; s. Ellis Adolphus and Bessie Ruth (Fortman) W.; m. Virginia Ann Lunz, Oct. 8, 1949; children—Rebecca, Donna, Richard, Lisa. Student exec. course, Ind. U., 1969. With Hardware Wholesalers Inc., Fort Wayne, Ind., 1947—; purchasing mgr. Hardware Wholesalers Inc., 1957—, v.p., gen. mgr., 1967-80, pres., 1980-92; ret., 1992; bd. dirs. Ft. Wayne Nat. Bank, Clarcor. Pres., bd. dirs. Big Brothers, Fort Wayne, 1973-74; nat. pres. Big Brothers Soc. Am., 1977-80. Mem. Nat. Wholesale Hardware Assn. (dir. 1977—, pres. 1984-85, named Hardware Wholesaler of Year 1973, 85), Ind. State C. of C. (dir.). Republican. Lutheran. Office: Hardware Wholesalers Inc PO Box 868 Fort Wayne IN 46801-0868 also: 6502 Nelson Rd Fort Wayne IN 46803-1920

WOLF, DONALD JOSEPH, industrial engineer; b. Waynesboro, Pa., Feb. 28, 1925; s. Joseph Herman and Olive Mae (Kepner) W.; m. Betty Irene Stull, May 26, 1950; children: Darrell Joseph, Robert Lee, David Wayne. BS in Wood Tech., N.C. State U., 1953; MS in Indsl. Engring., LaSalle U., 1995, PhD, 1996. Registered profl. engr. Foreman, indsl. engr. York County Chair Co., Red Lion, Pa., 1953-57; supt. indsl. engr. Hoke Furniture Co., Thurmont, Md., 1957-60; plant mgr., indsl. engr. Statton Furniture Co., Hagerstown, Md., 1960-70; internat. cons. Ross Assocs., Inc., Asheville, N.C., 1970-78; pres., prin. cons. Wood Arts, Inc., Frederick, Md., 1978—; staff cons. Samuel Lawrence Furniture Co., Phoenix, 1990—, Princeton (W.Va.) New River Furniture Industries. Active Citizen Amb. program People to People Internat; forestry bd. V.CH. Frederick County, Md.; cubmaster, scoutmaster Boy Scouts Am., Red Lion and Thurmont, 1957-60; v.p. Jr. C. of C., Red Lion, 1958-59; v.p. St. John's Luth. Ch., Thurmont, 1986-88, lay asst. min., 1988-93. Sgt. U.S. Army C.E., 1943-47, ETO. Mem. NSPE (life), Md. Soc. Profl. Engrs. (life), Calif. Soc. Profl. Engrs., Inst. Indsl. Engrs. (life, sr.), Order of the Engr., Md. Hist. Soc., Frederick County (Md.) Hist. Soc., Adams County (Pa.) Hist. Soc., York County (Pa.) Hist. Soc., Buckinghamshire (Eng.) Hist. Soc., Kitochtinny Hist. Soc., Libr. of Congress (assoc.), Nat. Trust, Smithsonian Assocs., N.C. State Alumni Assn., Soc. of War of 1812, Elks, Am. Legion (life), VFW (life), SAR (past pres., v.p., newsletter editor, historian, Gold medal, Cert. of Disting. Svc., War Svc. medal), Soc. of Wood Sci. and Tech., Forest Products Rsch. Soc. (divsn. chmn.), Nat. Congress of Patriotic Orgns. (founding fellow), Ho. of Gordon, Clan MacLean Internat. (life), Clan McLaine of Lochbuie, Xi Sigma Pi. Republican. Avocation: genealogy. Home and Office: Wood Arts Inc 6905 Balsam Ct Frederick MD 21703-7146

WOLF, DUANE CARL, microbiologist; b. Forsyth, Mo., Apr. 7, 1946; s. Deward Carl and Mary Catherine (Collins) W. BS, U. Mo., 1968; PhD, U. Calif., Riverside, 1973. Asst. prof. dept. agronomy U. Md., College Park, 1973-78; assoc. prof. dept. agronomy U. Ark., Fayetteville, 1979-81; prof. dept. agronomy U. Ark., 1981—; presenter in field at nat. meetings. Contbr. articles to profl. jours.; author, co-author rsch. reports at regional meetings; co-author 5 book chpts. Fellow Am. Soc. Agronomy (chair environ. quality sect. 1988), Soil Sci. Soc. Am. (chair microbiol. biochem. sect. 1994); mem. AAAS, Am. Soc. Microbiology, Vietnam Vets. Am., Sigma Xi, Gamma Sigma Delta. Office: U Ark Dept Agronomy Fayetteville AR 72701

WOLF, EDWARD DEAN, electrical engineering educator; b. Quinter, Kans., May 30, 1935; s. Ezra Lawrence and Zora Blanche (Jamison) W.; m. Marlene Kay Simpson, Aug. 12, 1955; children: Julie Christine, LeAnn Cynthia, Shelly Diane. Student, Kans. State U., 1953; BS magna cum laude, McPherson Coll., 1957; PhD, Iowa State U., 1961; postgrad., Princeton U., 1961-62, U. Calif.-Berkeley, 1968. Mem. tech. staff Rockwell Internat. Sci. Ctr., Thousand Oaks, Calif., 1963-65; mem. tech. staff, sr. mem. tech. staff Hughes Research Labs., Malibu, Calif., 1965-67, 67-72, sect. head, 1972-78, sr. scientist, 1974-78; dir. Nat. Nanofabrication Facility, Cornell U., Ithaca, N.Y., 1978-88, prof. elec. engring., 1978-90, prof. emeritus, 1991—; dir. Office Technology Access and Bus. Assistance Cornell U., Ithaca, N.Y., 1995-96; co-owner, pres. Biolistics, Inc., 1986-89; cons. Dept. Def., 1978, 81-82, various indsl. cos., 1978—; mem. univ. adv. com. Semiconductor Rsch. Corp., Research Triangle, N.C., 1982-84, ad hoc com. NAS, 1977-79, steerinc com. European Microcircuits Engring. Conf., 1976-78; guest prof. Tech. U., Vienna, 1987; vis. fellow Trinity Coll, Cambridge (Eng.) U., 1986-87; fgn. fellow Erwin Schrodinger Soc., Vienna, 1987; bd. dirs. Phyton, Inc., Cornell Rsch. Found. Editorial bd.: IEEE Spectrum, 1983-85; contbr. numerous articles on microminiaturization to profl. jours.; patentee in field. Named outstanding young man of Am., 1966. Fellow Am. Inst. Chemists, IEEE; mem. Bohmische Phys. Soc. (sci. me.), Am. Phys. Soc., Am. Vacuum Soc., Electron Microscopy Soc. Am., Sigma Xi, Phi Lambda Upsilon. Republican. Home: 1691 Taughannock Blvd Trumansburg NY 14886-9120

WOLF, EDWARD LINCOLN, physics educator; b. Cocoa, Fla., Nov. 22, 1936; s. Norman Lincoln and Harriet (Burgess) W.; m. Carol Joyce Euwema, June 15, 1958; children: Douglas Wakefield, David Lincoln. BA, Swarthmore Coll., 1958; PhD, Cornell U., 1964. Postdoctoral fellow U. Ill. Dept. Physics, Urbana, 1964-66; research assoc. Eastman Kodak Co., Rochester, N.Y., 1967-75; prof. physics Iowa State U., Ames, 1975-85; head dept. physics, prof. Polytechnic U., Bklyn., 1986—, prof. physics, 1986—; sr. vis. fellow Cavendish Lab. U. Cambridge, U.K., 1973-74; vis. prof. U. Pa., Phila., 1982; program dir. condensed matter physics NSF, 1996-97. Author: Principles of Electron Tunneling Spectroscopy, 1985; editor: Materials and Mechanisms of Superconductivity, 1985. Fellow Am. Phys. Soc.; mem. Phi Beta Kappa, Sigma Xi. Presbyterian. Avocations: jogging, cycling, music. Office: Polytechnic U Dept Physics Six Metrotech Ctr Brooklyn NY 11201-2990

WOLF, EMIL, physics educator; b. Prague, July 30, 1922; naturalized U.S. citizen, 1967; BSc, U. Bristol, Eng., 1945, PhD, 1948; DSc, U. Edinburgh, Scotland, 1955; D. honoris causa, U. Groningen, 1989, U. Edinburgh, 1990, Palacky U., Czechoslovakia, 1992, U. Bristol, 1997, Laval U., Que., Can., 1997. Rsch. asst. observatory Cambridge U., Eng., 1948-51; rsch. asst. lectr. math. and physics U. Edinburgh, 1951-54; rsch. fellow theoretical physics U. Manchester, Eng., 1954-59; vis. rsch. scientist Courant Inst. NYU, 1957; assoc. prof. optics U. Rochester, N.Y., 1959-61; prof. physics U. Rochester, 1961—, prof. optics, 1978—, Wilson prof. optical physics, 1987—; Guggenheim fellow, vis. prof. U. Calif. at Berkeley, 1966-67; vis. prof. U. Toronto, 1974-75. Author: (with M. Born) Principles of Optics, 1959, (with L. Mandel) Optical Coherence and Quantum Optics, 1995; editor: Progress in Optics, Vol. I-XXXVI, 1961-96, (with L. Mandel) Selected Papers on Coherence and Fluctuations of Light, 2 vols., 1970, various confs.; contbr. articles to profl. jours. Recipient Marconi medal Italian Nat. Rsch. Coun., 1987, Gold medal Czechoslovak Acad. Scis., 1991, medal Union of Czechoslovak Mathematicians and Physicists, 1991, Gold medal Palacky U., Olomouc, Czechoslovakia, 1991. Fellow Optical Soc. Am. (Frederic Ives medal 1977, Max Born award 1987, dir.-at-large 1972-74, v.p. 1976, pres. 1978, hon. mem.), Am. Phys. Soc., Brit. Inst. Physics, Am. Inst. Physics (governing bd. 1977-78), Franklin Inst. (Albert A. Michelson medal 1980), Optical Soc. India (hon.), Optical Soc. Australia (hon.). Office: U Rochester Dept Physics and Astronomy Rochester NY 14627

WOLF, ERIC ROBERT, anthropologist, educator; b. Vienna, Austria, Feb. 1, 1923; came to U.S., 1940, naturalized, 1943; s. Arthur George and Maria (Ossinovski) W.; m. Kathleen Bakeman, Sept. 24, 1943; children: John David, Daniel Jacob; m. Sydel Finfer Silverman, Mar. 18, 1972. B.A., Queens Coll., 1946; Ph.D. (Viking Fund fellow), Columbia U., 1951; DL (hon.), U. Mich., 1992; D.h.c., U. Vienna, 1993, U. Amsterdam, 1997. Asst. prof. U. Ill., 1952-55, U. Va., 1955-58; vis. asst. prof. Yale U., 1958-59; assoc. prof. U. Chgo., 1959-61; prof. U. Mich., Ann Arbor, 1965-71, chmn. dept. anthropology, 1970-71; disting. prof. Herbert H. Lehman Coll. and Grad. Ctr., CUNY, 1971-92, disting. prof. emeritus, 1992—; field work, P.R., 1948-49, Mexico, 1951-52, Italy, 1960-61. Author: Sons of the Shaking Earth, 1958, Peasants, 1968, Peasant Wars of the Twentieth Century, 1969, Europe and the People Without History, 1982. Served with AUS, 1943-45. Decorated Silver Star; recipient Career award NIH, 1964-69, J.S. Staley prize Sch. for Am. Rsch., Santa Fe 1988, Kevin Lynch award MIT, 1989; Guggenheim fellow, 1960-61; sr. fellow NEH, 1973-74; MacArthur Found. fellow, 1990. Fellow NAS, Am. Acad. Arts and Scis, Nat. Acad. Scis.; mem. Am. Anthrop. Assn. Home: 4 Blueberry Hl Irvington NY 10533-1402

WOLF, FRANK R., congressman, lawyer; b. Philadelphia, Pa., Jan. 30, 1939; m. Carolyn Stover; children: Frank, Virginia, Anne, Brenda, Rebecca. B.A., Pa. State U., 1961; LL.B., Georgetown U., 1965. Bar: Va., D.C. Legis. asst. former Congressman Edward G. Biester, Jr., 1968-71; asst. to Sec. of Interior Rogers B. Morton, 1971-74; dep. asst. sec. for Congl. and Legis. Affairs, Dept. Interior, 1974-75; mem. 97th-105th Congresses from 10th Va. dist., Washington, 1981—; mem. appropriations com., chmn. transp. subcom., mem. TPS and fgn. affairs subcom. Served with USAR. Republican. Presbyterian. Office: US Ho of Reps 241 Cannon Bldg Ofc Bldg Washington DC 20515-4610*

WOLF, G. VAN VELSOR, JR., lawyer; b. Balt., Feb. 19, 1944; s. G. Van Velsor and Alice Roberts (Kimberly) W.; m. Ann Holmes Kavanagh, May 19, 1984; children: George Van Velsor III, Timothy Kavanagh (dec.), Christopher Kavanagh, Elisabeth Huxley. BA, Yale U., 1966; JD, Vanderbilt U., 1973. Bar: N.Y. 1974, Ariz. 1982, U.S. Dist. Ct. (so. dist.) N.Y. 1974, U.S. Dist. Ct. Ariz. 1982, U.S. Ct. Appeals (2d cir.) 1974, U.S. Ct. Appeals (9th cir.) 1982. Agrl. advisor U.S. Peace Corps, Tanzania and Kenya, 1966-70; assoc. Milbank, Tweed, Hadley & McCloy, N.Y.C., 1973-75; vis. lectr. law Airlangga U., Surabaya, Indonesia, 1975-76, U. Ariz. 1990, Vanderbilt U., 1991, U. Md., 1994, Ariz. State U., 1995; editor in chief Environ. Law Reporter, Washington, 1976-81; cons. Nat. Trust for Historic Preservation, Washington, 1981; assoc. Lewis & Roca, Phoenix, 1981-84, ptnr., 1984-91; ptnr. Snell & Wilmer, Phoenix, 1991—. Bd. dirs. Ariz. div. Am. Cancer Soc., 1985-96, sec. 1990-92, vice chmn. 1992-94, chmn., 1994-96; bd. dirs. S.W. divsn. Am. Cancer Soc., 1996—, chmn., 1996—. Editor: Toxic Substances Control, 1980; contbr. articles to profl. jours. Bd. dirs. Phoenix Little Theater, 1983-90, chmn., 1986-88. Mem. ABA (vice chmn. SONREEL commn. state and regional environ. coop.), Assn. Bar City N.Y., Ariz. State Bar Assn. (coun. environ. & nat. res. law sect. 1988-93, chmn. 1991-92), Maricopa County Bar Assn., Ariz. Acad., Union Club (N.Y.C.), Univ. Club (Phoenix), Phoenix Country Club. Office: Snell & Wilmer 1 Arizona Ctr Phoenix AZ 85004-0001

WOLF, GARY HERBERT, architect; b. Lansing, Mich., July 15, 1950; s. Herbert C. and Margaret Wolf; m. Bonnie L. Grad, June 21, 1980; children: Alexander, Theodore. BA, Cornell U., 1972; M Archtl. History, U. Va., 1974; MArch, Princeton U., 1978. Assoc. Graham Gund Archs., Inc., Cambridge, Mass., 1983-87; prin. Adams & Wolf Archs., Inc., Belmont, Mass., 1987-91, Gary Wolf Archs., Inc., Boston, 1991—; dir. design Heliotrope, Providence, R.I., 1993-96; mem. other archtl. firms, preservation orgns. and other instns. including constrn. mgmt. dept. Harvard U., Michael Graves Arch., Nat. Register Historic Places, 1974-83; vis. critic Harvard U. Grad. Sch. Design, Cambridge, Mass.; thesis advisor Boston Archtl. Ctr.; guest juror R.I. Sch. Design, Providence, Mass. Inst. Tech., Cambridge. Prin. archtl. works include Tree-House Porch, Brookline, Mass., 1987-88, 66 Leonard St., Belmont, Mass., 1988, Autumn Leaves House, Weston, Mass., 1988-94, Synectics Bldg. Restoration, Cambridge, Mass., 1987-88, 90-91, Mus. of Our Nat. Heritage Renovations, New Galleries and Meeting Hall, Lexington, Mass., 1993-96, Brookline Music Sch., 1991-94; designer Zephr Hammock, Glass Curtain Lamp, other objects; contbr. articles to profl. jours. Recipient Thomas Jefferson Meml. Found. Scholarship U. Va., 1972-74, Merit award Internat. Conceptual Furniture Competition, Progressive Archiecture Mag., 1980, 1st pl. Great Am. Facades Design Competition, 1990, Builder's Choice Design awards, 1991, 92, 93, Good Design Disting. Product award Chgo. Athenaeum: Mus. Architecture and Design, 1994, Gold Indsl. Design Excellence award Bus. Week/Indsl. Design Soc. Am., 1994, Best Products award Time Mag., 1994, Renovations of the Yr. award, 1996. Mem. AIA, Am. Assn. Mus., Nat. Trust Historic Preservation, Boston Soc. Archs. (past chair membership com.). Office: Gary Wolf Archs 145 Hanover St Boston MA 02108-2402

WOLF, GARY WICKERT, lawyer; b. Slinger, Wis., Apr. 19, 1938; s. Leonard A. and Cleo C. (Wickert) W.; m. Jacqueline Weltzin, Dec. 17, 1960; children: Gary, Jonathan. B.A.A., U. Minn., 1960, J.D. cum laude, 1963. Bar: N.Y. 1964, U.S. Ct. Appeals (2d cir.) 1969, U.S. Dist. Ct. (so. dist.) N.Y. 1969, U.S. Supreme Ct. 1971. Assoc. Cahill, Gordon & Reindel, N.Y.C., 1963-70, ptnr., 1970—; dir. Southwestern Pub. Svc. Co., 1986—, N.J. Resources Corp., 1995—. Mem. N.Y. State Bar Assn. (com. on securities regulation), Anglers Club (N.Y.C.), Downtown Assn. (N.Y.C.), Mashomack Fish and Game Club (Pine Plains, N.Y.). Home: Pleasantville Rd New Vernon NJ 07976 Office: Cahill Gordon & Reindel 80 Pine St New York NY 10005-1702

WOLF, HANS ABRAHAM, retired pharmaceutical company executive; b. Frankfurt, Fed. Republic Germany, June 27, 1928; came to U.S., 1936, naturalized, 1944; s. Franz Benjamin and Ilse (Nathan) W.; m. Elizabeth J. Bassett, Aug. 2, 1958; children: Heidi Elizabeth, Rebecca Anne, Deborah Wolf Streeter, Andrew Robert. AB magna cum laude, Harvard U., 1949, MBA, 1955; PhB, Oxford U., 1951. Math instr. Tutoring Sch., 1946-47; statis. research Nat. Bur. Econ. Research, N.Y.C., 1948-49; researcher Georgetown U., 1951-52; confidential aide Office Dir. Mut. Security, Washington, 1952; analyst Ford Motor div. Ford Motor Co., Dearborn, Mich., summer 1954; foreman prodn. M&C Nuclear Inc., Attleboro, Mass., 1955-57; asst. supt. prodn. Metals & Controls Corp., Attleboro, 1957-59, mgr. product dept., 1959-62, controller, 1962-67; asst. v.p., controller materials and services group Tex. Instruments Inc., Dallas, 1967-69, treas., v.p., 1969-75; v.p. fin., chief fin. officer Syntex Corp., Palo Alto, Calif., 1975-78, exec. v.p., 1978-86, vice chmn., chief adminstrv. officer, 1986-92, vice chmn., 1992-93, also bd. dirs., 1986-93; bd. dirs. Clean Sites, Inc., Alexandria, Va., Tab Products Co., Palo Alto, Calif., chmn., 1995—; bd. dirs. Network Equipment Techs., Redwood City, Calif., chmn., 1996—; bd. dirs. Satellite Dialysis Ctrs., Inc., Redwood City, Hyal Pharms., Mississauga, Ont. Author: Motivation Research—A New Aid to Understanding Your Markets, 1955. Mem. Norton (Mass.) Sch. Bd., 1959-62, chmn., 1961-62; pres., bd. dirs. Urban League Greater Dallas, 1971-74; bd. dirs. Dallas Health Planning Coun., mem. community adv. com., 1973-75; bd. dirs., pres. Children's Health Coun. of the Mid Peninsula; cubmaster Boy Scouts Am., 1976-78; elder United Ch. Christ, 1970-73, vice chmn. gen. bd., 1970-71, moderator, 1978-80; trustee Pacific Sch. Religion, 1986-94, chmn., 1990-94; trustee World Affairs Coun. San Francisco, 1986-92, 94-97; dir. Tech Mus. San Jose. With USAF, 1952-53. Mem. Am. Mgmt. Assn. (planning council fin. div. 1970-76), Phi Beta Kappa.

WOLF, HAROLD ARTHUR, finance educator; b. Lind, Wash., Feb. 10, 1923; s. Edward and Olga (Limert) W.; March 23, 1961; children: Mark, Suellen. B.A., U. Oreg., 1951; M.A., U. Mich., 1952, Ph.D., 1958. Instr. Lehigh U., 1955-56; economist Prudential Life Ins. Co., Newark, 1957-58; asst. prof. fin., money, banking U. Colo., 1958-60, assoc. prof., 1961-64, prof., 1965-68; prof. fin. U. Tex., Austin, 1969—; pvt. practice consulting for fin. instns., 1960—. Author: Personal Finance, 1978, 8th edit., 1989, Managing Your Money, 1977, Personal Financial Planning, 8th edit., 1989, alternate edit., 1991, 2nd alternate edit., 1992. Served with U.S. Navy, 1941-47. Mem. Am. Economic Assn., Am. Fin. Assn., So. Fin. Assn. Home: 7004 Edgefield Dr Austin TX 78731-2926 Office: Dept Finance University of Texas Austin TX 78712

WOLF, HAROLD HERBERT, pharmacy educator; b. Quincy, Mass., Dec. 19, 1934; s. John I. and Bertha F. (Sussman) W.; m. Joan Z. Silverman, Aug. 11, 1957; children: Gary Jerome, David Neal. B.S., Mass. Coll. Pharmacy, 1956; Ph.D., U. Utah, 1961; LLD (hon.), U. Md., 1994. Asst. prof. pharmacology Coll. Pharmacy Ohio State U., 1961-64, assoc. prof., 1964-69, prof., 1969-76, Kimberly prof., 1975-76, chmn. div. pharmacology, 1973-76; dean Coll. of Pharmacy, U. Utah, Salt Lake City, 1976-89, prof. pharmacology, 1989—, dir. Anticonvulsant Drug Devel. Program, 1989—; vis. prof. U. Sains Malaysia, 1973-74; mem. Nat. Joint Commn. on Prescription Drug Use, 1976-80; mem. NIH rev. com. Biomed. Rsch. Devel. Grant Program, 1978-79; external examiner U. Malaya, 1978, 92, 96, U. Sains Malaysia, 1980. Contbr. articles in field of central nervous system pharmacology and field of pharm. edn. Recipient Alumni Achievement award Mass. Coll. Pharmacy, 1978, Disting. Faculty award U. Utah, 1989, Rosenblatt prize, 1989, Disting. Alumnus award Coll. Pharmacy, U. Utah, 1991. Fellow AAAS, Acad. Pharm. Scis.; mem. Am. Soc. Pharmacology and Exptl. Therapeutics, Am. Pharm. Assn. (task force on edn. 1982-84), Am. Assn. Colls. of Pharmacy (pres. 1977, Disting. Pharmacy Educator award 1988, scholar in residence 1989, chmn. commn. on implementing change in pharmacy edn. 1989-92, 95-96), Am. Soc. Hosp. Pharmacists (commn. on goals 1982-84), Am. Coun. on Pharm. Edn. (bd. dirs. 1985-88), Soc. Neurosci. Jewish. Home: 4467 Adonis Dr Salt Lake City UT 84124-4720 Office: Univ Utah Coll Pharmacy Salt Lake City UT 84112

WOLF, IRVING, clinical psychologist; b. New Haven, Aug. 7, 1924; s. Samuel and Annie W.; m. Elizabeth Pennington Haughey, Aug. 1, 1949; children: Susan, Richard, Robert, William. A.B., Boston U., 1949, A.M., 1951, Ph.D., 1954. Diplomate Am. Bd. Profl. Psychology. Clin. psychologist VA Hosp., Brockton, Mass., 1954-57; clin. psychologist Mass. Gen. Hosp., Boston and research assoc. Harvard Med. Sch., 1957-59; prof. psychology, chmn. doctoral program clin. psychology, dir. fed. relations Boston U., 1959-75; vis. Fulbright prof. U. Philippines, Manila, 1965-66; dir. Nat. Ctr. Alcohol Edn., Washington, 1974; div. dir., sr. exec. Nat. Inst. Alcohol Abuse and Alcoholism, HEW, 1976-80; prof. psychology, sr. exec. Fed. Exec. Inst., Charlottesville, Va., 1981-85; pvt. practice, 1986-88; clin. dir. Devereux Found., Rutland, Mass., 1989-92; clin. assoc. Am. Geriatric Svcs., Rockland, Mass., 1992-95, Advanced Health Systems, 1996—. Author articles in field. Served with AUS, 1943-46. Named Disting. Alumnus Boston U. Coll. Liberal Arts, 1974. Fellow Am. Psychol. Assn.; mem. Eastern Psychol. Assn., Sr. Exec. Assn., Fed. Exec. Inst. Alumni Assn., Phi Beta Kappa. Home: 20 Pickwick Way Wayland MA 01778-3800

WOLF, JAMES ANTHONY, insurance company executive; b. Washington, May 10, 1945; s. Arthur William and Marie Antoinette (Dalton) Wolf; m. Sheila Marie Regan, June 27, 1968; children: Jayne Ann, Elizabeth. BS in Fin. cum laude, Boston Coll., 1967. Mktg. rep. IBM, Newark, N.J., 1967-68, Boston, 1970-78; mktg. mgr. IBM, N.Y.C., 1978-81; 2nd v.p. Tchrs. Ins. & Annuity Assn., N.Y.C., 1981-82, v.p., 1982-85, sr. v.p., 1985—. Served to sgt. U.S. Army, 1968-70, Vietnam. Mem. Am. Mgmt. Assn. Republican.

Roman Catholic. Home: 233 Ridge Common Fairfield CT 06430-7010 Office: Tchrs Ins & Annuity Assn Am 730 3rd Ave New York NY 10017-3206

WOLF, JEFFREY STEPHEN, physician; b. Hartford, Conn., July 30, 1946; s. Abraham and Norma Wolf; m. Nina Loving Lockridge; children: Sarah Loving, Lawren Hiley. BS, McGill U., 1968; MD, Med. Coll. Va., 1972, MS, 1973. Diplomate Am. Bd. Colon and Rectal Surgery, . Intern, in surgery Mt. Sinai Hosp., N.Y.C., 1972-73, resident, 1973-75; resident N.Y. Med. Coll.-Met. Hosp., N.Y.C., 1975-77; chief resident surgery Met. Hosp., 1977-78; fellow colon-rectal surgery Greater Balt. Med. Center, 1978-79; colon-rectal surgeon, Portsmouth, Va., 1979—. Fellow ACS, Am. Soc. Colon and Rectal Surgery; mem. AMA, Portsmouth Acad. Medicine, Med. Soc. Va., Am. Soc. Colon and Rectal Surgeons, So. Med. Assn., Chesapeake Colon-Rectal Soc.. Office: 3235 Academy Ave Ste 200 Portsmouth VA 23703-3200

WOLF, JOHN HOWELL, retired publisher; b. Narberth, Pa., Mar. 19, 1918; s. W. Dale and Ruth Coryell (Howell) W.; m. Jane Belmeur, May 18, 1946 (div. Dec. 16, 1969); children: John B., Wendy J.; m. Emily West Asbury, Dec. 21, 1969. Student, DePauw U., Greencastle, Ind., 1935-39, Xavier U., Cin., 1940-41. Pub. Cin. Suburban Newspapers, Inc., 1946-73; pres., pub. Cin. Suburban Newspapers, Inc./Clermont Newspapers, Inc., 1973-82; chmn. Nat. Better Newspaper Contests, Washington, 1957-58; adv. bd. U.S. Suburban Press, Inc., Chgo., 1970-75. Dir. Suburban Press Found., Chgo., 1972; del. 5th UNESCO Conf., 1956; chmn. Police Media Adv. Com., Cin., 1968; chmn. small media com. United Appeal, Cin., 1965; mem. com. of mgmt. YMCA, Norwood, Ohio, 1947—; pres. Y Men's Club, Norwood, 1952, Carlisle (Ky.) Nicholas County Indsl. Authority, 1984-89, chmn., 1988-89. Maj. U.S. Army, 1942-46. Recipient Silver medal Advertisers Club, Cin., 1973. Mem. Soc. Profl. Journalists, Suburban Newspapers of Am. (pres. 1973, pres. suburban newspapers sect. 1968), Nat. Newspaper Assn. (dir. 1978-83, exec. com. 1980-83, fin. com. 1980-83, Outstanding Dir. 1980), Accredited Home Newspapers of Am. (dir. 1972), Norwood Club (pres. 1950), Masons. Presbyterian. Avocations: reading, travel. Home: 244 Azalea Ct Carlisle KY 40311-9053

WOLF, JOHN STEVEN, construction executive, land developer; b. Portsmouth, Ohio, Sept. 4, 1947; s. John Andrew and Betty Lee Wolf, m. Pamela Gahm, Mar. 11, 1995; A.S. in Civil Engring. Tech., Ohio Coll. Applied Sci., 1967; B.S. in Civil Engring., Ohio U., 1975. Project engr. Columbus & So. Ohio Electric Co., 1974-75; staff project engr. Goodyear Atomic Corp., Piketon, Ohio, 1975-78; constrn. mgr., project engr. Am. Electric Power Service Corp., Lancaster, Ohio, 1978-83; project mgr. F. and P. Mgrs., Inc., Columbus, Ohio, 1983-85, Target Constrn. Co., Columbus, 1985-91; area mgr. Sherman R. Smoot Co., Indpls., 1991-93; dir. constrn. Pizzuti Devel., Inc., Columbus, 1993—; panel mem., speaker, seminars and classes in mgmt. and constrn. related areas. Served with U.S. Army, 1968-69; Vietnam. Decorated Army Commendation medal (2); registered profl. engr., Ohio, Ind. Nat. Soc. Profl. Engrs., Ohio Soc. Profl. Engrs, Ind. Soc. Profl. Engrs. Methodist. Club: Masons, Scottish Rite, Shriners. Home: 510 Wickham Way Gahanna OH 43230-2233 Office: 250 E Broad St Ste 1900 Columbus OH 43215-3708

WOLF, JOSEPH ALBERT, mathematician, educator; b. Chgo., Oct. 18, 1936; s. Albert M. and Goldie (Wykoff) W. BS, U. Chgo., 1956, MS, 1957, PhD, 1959. Mem. Inst. for Advanced Study, Princeton, 1960-62, 65-66; asst. prof. U. Calif., Berkeley, 1962-64, assoc. prof., 1964-66, prof., 1966—, Miller research prof., 1972-73, 83-84; prof. honorario Universidad Nacional de Cordoba, Argentina, 1989; vis. prof. Rutgers U., 1969-70, Hebrew U., Jerusalem, 1974-76, Tel Aviv U., 1974-76, Harvard U., 1979-80, 86. Author: Spaces of Constant Curvature, 1967, 72, 74, 77, 84, Unitary Representations on Partially Holomorphic Cohomology Spaces, 1974, Unitary Representations of Maximal Parabolic Subgroups of the Classical Groups, 1976, Classification and Fourier Inversion for Parabolic Subgroups with Square Integrable Nilradical, 1979; co-editor, author: Harmonic Analysis and Representations of Semisimple Lie Groups, 1980, The Penrose Transform and Analytic Cohomology in Representation Theory, 1993; editor Geometriae Dedicata, Math Reports, Jour. of Math. Systems, Estimation and Control, Letters in Math. Physics, Jour. of Group Theory in Physics; contbr. articles to profl. jours. Alfred P. Sloan rsch. fellow, 1965-67, NSF fellow, 1959-62; recipient Médaille de l'Université de Liège, 1977, Humboldt prize, 1995. Mem. Am., Swiss math. socs. Office: U Calif Dept Math Berkeley CA 94720-3840

WOLF, JULIUS, medical educator; b. Boston, Aug. 15, 1918; s. Herman and Rose (Kurgan) W.; m. Irene H. Bechtloff, May 4, 1945; children—Maritja Ann, Miriam Jeanne, Brenda Joyce. S.B., Boston U., 1940, M.D., 1943. Intern L.I. Coll. Hosp., 1943-44, resident, 1944-45; resident Bronx VA Hosp., 1947-48, sect. chief medicine, chief gastroenterology sec., chief med. service, 1948-72, chief staff, 1970-90; assoc. dean Mt. Sinai Med. Ctr., N.Y.C., 1974-90; assoc. prof. medicine Columbia Coll. Phys. and Surg., 1961-67; prof. medicine Mt. Sinai Sch. Medicine, 1968—. Chmn. VA Lung Cancer Group, 1962-75. Served to capt. AUS, 1943-45. Fellow ACP. Home: 315 Covert Ave New Hyde Park NY 11040-5436

WOLF, KARL EVERETT, aerospace and communications corporation executive; b. Hartford, Conn., Aug. 19, 1921; s. Carl Fred and Anna (Voss) W.; m. Lola Sue Stoner, Aug. 1, 1948; children: Paula R., Gloria J., Glenn K. B.S., U.S. Mil. Acad., 1943; J.D., U. Pa., 1953; S.J.D., George Washington U., 1963. Bar: D.C. 1953, Conn. 1953, U.S. Supreme Ct. 1960, Calif. 1971, Mich. 1975. Commd. 2d lt. U.S. Army, 1943, advanced through grades to lt. col., 1959, ret., 1963; assoc. counsel Philco. Corp., Phila., 1963-73; v.p., gen. counsel Ford Aerospace Corp., Detroit, 1973-88; ret., 1988; mem. adv. bd. Bur. Nat. Affairs, Fed. Contract Reports, Washington, 1963-73. Author: State Taxation of Government Contractors, 1964. Decorated Silver Star, Bronze Star; Croix de Guerre (Belgium). Mem. ABA, Fed. Bar Assn., Calif. Bar Assn. Home: 535 Dunnegan Dr Laguna Beach CA 92651-1432

WOLF, MARK LAWRENCE, federal judge; b. Boston, Nov. 23, 1946; s. Jason Harold and Beatrice (Meltzer) W.; m. Lynne Lichterman, Apr. 4, 1971; children: Jonathan, Matthew. BA cum laude, Yale U., 1968; JD cum laude, Harvard U., 1971; hon. degree, Boston Latin Sch., 1990. Bar: Mass. 1971, D.C. 1972, U.S. Supreme Ct. 1976. Assoc. Surrey, Karasik & Morse, Washington, 1971-74; spl. asst. to dep. atty. gen. U.S. Dept. Justice, Washington, 1974-75, spl. asst. to atty. gen., 1975-76; dep. U.S. atty. U.S. Dept. Justice, Boston, 1981-85; from assoc. to ptnr. Sullivan & Worcester, Boston, 1977-81; judge U.S. Dist. Ct. Mass., Boston, 1985—; lectr. Harvard U. Law Sch., Cambridge, Mass., 1990—; adj. prof. Boston Coll. Law Sch., 1992. Bd. dirs. Albert Schweitzer Fellowship, Boston, 1974—, pres., 1989—; chmn. John William Ward Fellowship, Boston, 1986—. Recipient cert. appreciation U.S. Pres., 1975, Disting. Service award U.S. Atty. Gen., 1985. Mem. Boston Bar Assn. (council 1982-85), Am. Law Inst. Office: US Dist Ct 90 Devonshire St Boston MA 02109-4501*

WOLF, MARTIN EUGENE, lawyer; b. Balt., Sept. 9, 1958; s. Eugene Bernard and Mary Anna (O'Neil) W.; m. Nancy Ann Reinsfelder, May 9, 1980; children: Matthew Adam, Allison Maria, Emily Elizabeth. BA, Johns Hopkins U., 1980; JD, U. Md., 1991. Bar: Md. 1991, U.S. Dist. Ct. Md. 1992, U.S. Ct. Appeals (4th cir.) 1992, U.S. Ct. Appeals (2d cir.) 1993. Mgmt. trainee Giant Foods, Inc., Landover, Md., 1980-82, dept. mgr., 1982-83, ops. analyst, 1983-86, fin. coord., 1986-89; law clk. Piper & Marbury, L.L.P., Balt., 1989-91, assoc., 1991-96; prin. Law Office of Martin E. Wolf, Abingdon, Md., 1996—; dir. Giant Food Fed. Credit Union, Landover, 1984-89; pres. Stalagmite Properties, Ltd., Abingdon, Md., 1995—; teaching asst. U. Md. Sch. Law, Balt., 1992-94; adj. prof. U. Md. Law Sch., Balt., 1996—. Mem. ABA, Md. State Bar Assn., Harford County Bar Assn., Harford County Bar Found. (Vol. Svc. award 1992, 94). Republican. Roman Catholic. Avocations: Lacrosse, hockey. Home: 11 Mitchell Dr Abingdon MD 21009

WOLF, MILTON ALBERT, economist, former ambassador, investor; b. Cleve., May 29, 1924; s. Sam and Sylvia (Davis) W.; m. Roslyn C. Zehman, June 23, 1948; children: Leslie Eric, Caryn Sue, Nancy Gail, Sherri Hope. BA in Chemistry and Biology, Ohio State U., 1948; BS in Civil Engring. summa cum laude, Case Inst. Tech., 1954; MA in Econs., Case Western Res. U., 1973, PhD in Econs., 1993, LHD (hon.), 1980; LLD (hon.), Cleve. State U., 1980. Pres. Zehman-Wolf Constrn. Co., Cleve., 1948-76; U.S. ambassador to Austria, 1977-80; disting. professorial lectr. in econs. Case Western Res. U., 1981-87; chmn. Milton A. Wolf Investors, 1980—; bd. dirs. Am. Greetings Corp., Town and Country Trust; U.S. del. UN conf. on Sci. and Tech. for Devel., 1979; U.S. del. dedication of UN Internat. Ctr., Vienna, 1979; host Salt II Summit, Vienna, 1979; trustee Cleve. Clinic; chmn. Fulbright Commn. for Austria, 1977-80. Trustee Ohio State U., 1986-96, chair, 1995-96; trustee Case Western Res. U., Cleve. Orch.; vice chmn. Coun. Am. Ambs.; chmn. Am. Austrian Found.; chmn. Am. Jewish Joint Distbn. Com.; mem. econ. adv. task force Carter Presdl. Campaign, 1976; mem. Carter Inauguration Com.; nat. fin. chmn. John Glenn Presdl. Campaign, 1983-84; dir. transition Gov. Celeste, State of Ohio, 1982-83; nat. trustee United Israel Appeal, United Jewish Appeal, Coun. Jewish Fedns.; trustee United Way Svcs.; life trustee Park Synagogue, Cleve.; past pres., life trustee Jewish Cmty. Fedn., Cleve. With USAAF 1943-48. Recipient Gt. Golden medal of honor with sash Republic of Austria, 1980, Gt. Golden medal of State Province of Salzburg, Republic of Austria, 1979, Eisenman award Jewish Cmty. Fedn. Cleve., 1990, Internat. Humanitarian award Raoul Wallenberg Com., 1995. Mem. Am. Econ. Assn., Cleve. Engring. Soc., Cleve. Builders Assn., Coun. Fgn. Rels., Fgn. Policy Assn., Acad. Polit. Sci., Cleve. Com. World Affairs, UN Assn.- U.S. (bd. govs.), Tau Beta Pi. Jewish. Home: 19200 S Park Blvd Shaker Heights OH 44122-1857 Office: 25700 Science Park Dr Beachwood OH 44122-7312

WOLF, PETER MICHAEL, investment management and land planning consultant, educator, author; b. New Orleans, Dec. 6, 1935; s. Morris and Ruth (New) W.; m. Alessandra Cantey, July 3, 1967; children—Phelan Godchaux, Alexis Ambler. B.A., Yale U., 1957; M.A., Tulane U., 1963; Ph.D., NYU, 1968. Ptnr. Wolf and Co., New Orleans, 1958-62; assoc. Wilbur Smith & Assocs., N.Y.C., 1968-70; faculty mem. NYU, 1966-67, Pratt Inst., N.Y.C., 1968-70; adj. prof. Cooper Union, N.Y.C., 1971-87; chmn. bd. fellows and mem. faculty Inst. Architecture and Urban Studies, N.Y.C., 1972-82; prin. Peter Wolf Assocs., N.Y.C., 1970—; organizer of exhbns. Mus. Modern Art, N.Y.C., 1969; writer exhbns. Whitney Mus. Art, N.Y.C., 1970; contbr. exhbns. Mus. Modern Art, N.Y.C., 1973, Albany Inst Art, 1975. Author: Land in America: Its Value, Use and Control, 1981; On Streets, 1979; The Future of the City: New Directions in Urban Planning, 1974; The Evolving City, Urban Design Proposals by Ulrich Franzen and Paul Rudolph, 1974. Trustee Guild Hall, East Hampton, N.Y., 1981-86, Van Allen Inst., 1995—, Godchaux Res. Plantation Fund (pres. 1994—). NEA Fellow, 1979; Graham Found. Fellow, 1967-68, 93-94; Fulbright Fellow, 1965-66; Ford Found. grantee, 1971-74. Recipient Charles B. Shattuck award Nat. Research and Edn. Trust Fund, 1983. Mem. Am. Inst. Cert. Planners. Avocation: tennis. Home: 325 W End Ave New York NY 10023-8135 Office: 7 W 36th St New York NY 10018-7911

WOLF, R. PETER, fundraising executive, harpsichordist; b. Washington, Dec. 5, 1942; s. Harry Edward and Virginia Anne (Simmons) W.; m. Rachel Irene Harrington Doggett, Sept. 2, 1994; m. Beniko Tsubaki, Apr. 15, 1977 (div. Oct. 1987). AB magna cum laude, Harvard U., 1965; MPhil, Yale U., 1969, PhD, 1977. Musician-in-residence N.C. State U., Raleigh, 1971-72; instr., asst. prof. SUNY, Stony Brook, 1972-78; asst. prof. Rutgers U., New Brunswick, N.J., 1980-85; editor, prodn. mgr. Broude Bros., Ltd., N.Y.C., 1985-89; dir. of devel. Hoboken (N.J.) Chamber Orchestra, 1989-90; devel. dir. Planned Parenthood/Essex County, Newark, N.J., 1991-93; dir. grants and spl. projects Nat. Coun. of Negro Women, Washington, 1994-96; devel. dir. Tudor Place Found., Washington, 1996-97, Family and Child Svcs. Washington, 1997—; cons. Partnership in Philanthropy, Newark, 1993-94; concert adv. com. The Meadows Found., Franklin Twp., N.J., 1987-93; dir. Sanctuary Concert Series, Highland Park, N.J., 1990-94; harpsichordist numerous ensembles, 1971—; vis. asst. prof. U. Utah, Salt Lake City, 1978-80. Editor 14 musical edits., 1984—; contbr. articles to profl. jours. Recipient solo recitalist's grant Nat. Endowment for the Arts, 1983, grant-in-aid Am. Coun. Learned Socs., 1982; fellow Summer Humanities Inst. NEH, 1984, Fulbright Hays, Amsterdam, 1965-66. Mem. Nat. Soc. Fund-Raising Execs. (cert.), Am. Fedn. Musicians, Soc. Jean-Philippe Rameau, Am. Musicol. Soc. Democrat. Avocations: philately, computers. Home: 7001 Barkwater Ct Bethesda MD 20817-4402

WOLF, ROBERT B., lawyer; b. Phila., Aug. 18, 1914; s. Morris and Pauline (Binswanger) W.; children—Edwin David, Virginia. B.A., Haverford Coll., 1936; LL.B., Harvard, 1939. Bar: Pa. 1939. Ptnr. Wolf, Block, Schorr & Solis-Cohen, 1940-43, 46-56, 57-85, of counsel, 1985—; gen. counsel FHA, Washington, 1956-57; instr. humanities Haverford Coll., 1948-49, 71-72. Chmn. mayor's coordinated housing improvement program, Phila., 1951, Phila. Youth Svcs. Coordinating Com., 1978-84; past chmn. Pa. Com. Crime and Delinquency; mem. juvenile adv. com. Pa. Commn. on Crime and Delinquency, 1976-86; ct. master Phila. Youth Study Ctr., 1989-91; trustee Benjamin Franklin Found., Berlin, Germany, 1955-56. 1st lt. inf. AUS, 1943-45; office Asst. Sec. War, 1945-46. Mem. Am., Pa., Phila. bar assns., Phi Beta Kappa. Home: 2101 Harts Ln Conshohocken PA 19428-2416 Office: Wolf Block Schorr & Solis-Cohen Packard Bldg Philadelphia PA 19102

WOLF, ROBERT IRWIN, psychoanalyst, art and art therapy educator; b. N.Y.C., Mar. 30, 1947; s. Arthur and Bernice (Rosenwasser) W.; children: Joshua Corey, Rebecca Melissa. B Indsl. Design, Pratt Inst., 1968, M Profl. Studies, 1973. Cert. Am. Bds. for Cert. and Accreditation in Psychoanalysis. Clin. dir. Henry Street Settlement Sch., N.Y.C., 1973-80; prof. art and art therapy Coll. of New Rochelle (N.Y.) Grad. Sch., 1980—; pvt. practice psychoanalysis, art therapy and supervision, N.Y.C., 1974—; dir. Inst. for Expressive Analysis, N.Y.C., 1993-96; vis. prof. art Pratt Inst., Bklyn., 1976—; keynote speaker Delaware Valley Art Therapy Assn., 1979; guest lectr. Ill. Art Therapy Assn., 1980. Contbr. articles to profl. jours., chpt. to book; exhibited sculptures in numerous galleries throughout U.S. Recipient 1st place sculpture award Ariel Gallery, N.Y.C., 1989. Mem. Nat. Psychol. Assn. for Psychoanalysis (sr.), Nat. Assn. for Advancement Psychoanalysis (cert.), Coun. Psychoanalytic Psychotherapists, Am. Art Therapy Assn. (registered, contbg. editor Art Therapy 1985—, workshop presenter 1970—), N.Y. Art Therapy Assn. (pres. 1975-76), Westchester Art Therapy Assn. (assoc.). Avocations: downhill skiing, jogging, snorkeling. Office: Coll New Rochelle Grad Art Programs New Rochelle NY 10801 also: 27 W 96th St New York NY 10025-6515

WOLF, ROSALIE JOYCE, financial executive; b. Southampton, N.Y., May 8, 1941; d. Saul and Anne W.; m. Milton Stern, May 15, 1979; 1 dau., Dina G. Pruzansky. A.B., Wellesley Coll., 1961; M.A. in Math, Northwestern U., 1962. With Mobil Oil Corp., N.Y.C., 1962-77; asst. treas. internat. Mobil Oil Corp., to 1977; v.p. venture capital group Donaldson, Lufkin, Jenrette, N.Y.C., 1977-79; asst. corp. contr. Internat. Paper Co., N.Y.C., 1979—, treas., 1981-86; prin., chief fin. officer Aldrich, Eastman & Waltch Inc., Boston, 1986-89; mng. dir. pvt. equity Merchant Banking Group, Bankers Trust Co., N.Y.C., 1989-93; treas., chief investment officer The Rockefeller Found., N.Y.C., 1994—; dir., mem. compensation com. Narragansett Capital Corp., 1983-86; trustee TIAA. Durant scholar Wellesley Coll., 1961. Mem. Fin. Women's Assn. N.Y., Women's Forum, Phi Beta Kappa.

WOLF, SARA HEVIA, art librarian; b. Havana, Cuba, Jan. 15, 1936; came to U.S., 1961; d. Policarpo and Manuela (Ruiz) Hevia; m. Luis A. Wolf, Sept. 23, 1960; 1 child, Sara Caroline. B in Bus., Havana Bus. U., 1956. Libr. asst. N.C. State U., Raleigh, 1963-65; cataloguer Ctrl. Piedmont C.C., Charlotte, N.C., 1970-71; libr. Mint Mus. Art, Charlotte, N.C., 1972—. Bd. dirs. YMCA, Charlotte, 1985-87; co-chair All Nations Festival, Inc., Charlotte, 1977-78; pres. Cath. Hispanic Ctr., Charlotte, 1981-82, editor Spanish Newsletter, 1972-75, chair Internat. Cultural Festival, 1973-76; steering com. Latin-Am. Week, Charlotte, 1993. Mem. Art Librs. Soc., N.Am. (mem. George Wittenborn Meml. Book Awards com. 1992, chair nominating com. S.E. chpt. 1987, chair Mary Ellen Lo Presti Publ. Awards com. S.E. chpt. 1989, v.p., pres.-elect S.E. chpt. 1990, pres. S.E. chpt. 1991), Metrolina Libr. Assn. (exec. bd. 1988), L.Am. Women's Assn. (pres. 1994-96), L.Am. Coalition. Office: Mint Mus of Art 2730 Randolph Rd Charlotte NC 28207-2012

WOLF, SHARON ANN, psychotherapist; b. Dallas, May 13, 1951; d. Frank Allan and Ursula (Mohnblatt) W.; 1 child, Allan. BA in Psychology, New Eng. Coll., 1973; MA in Counseling Psychology, Antioch Grad. Sch., 1976; PhD in Clin. Psychology, Union Grad. Sch., 1989. Cert. Mental Health Counselor, 1997. Behavioral spl. ednl. planner Philbrook Children's Learning Ctr., Concord, N.H., 1972; asst. to spl. edn. cons. N.H. Hosp., Concord, 1972-73; spl. edn. planner Rochester (N.H.) Child Devel. Ctr., 1973; counseling practicum Morrill Sch., Concord, N.H., 1973; counseling practicum Contoocook Valley Mental Health Ctr., Henniker, N.H., 1973-74, counseling psychology intern, 1974-76; lab. instr. New Eng. Coll., Henniker, 1973; ednl. and guidance counselor asst. Hillsboro (N.H.)-Deering Sch. Dist., 1973-74; pediatric psychology intern parent-infant devel. program Ctrl. N.H. C.M.H. Ctr., Concord, 1986-87; assoc. psychologist Easter Seal Rehab. Ctr., Manchester, N.H., 1976-80, Ctrl. N.H. Community Mental Health Svcs., Concord, 1980-88; intern forensic psychology Concord Dist. Ct., 1987-88; pvt. practice Northfield, N.H., 1988—; psychol. cons. children and youth program Twin Rivers Counseling Ctr., Franklin, N.H. 1980-83, therapist, 1984-86; therapist Ctrl. N.H. Comm. Mental Health Ctr., 1980-83, Parent-Infant Devel. Program, Concord, N.H., 1983-88. Fellow Am. Orthopsychiat. Assn.; mem. Am. Assn. Suicidology, Am. Assn. Counseling and Devel., New England Coun. on Crime and Delinquency, N.H. Assn. of the Deaf, N.H. Registry of Interpreters for the Deaf. Avocations: rug hooking, music, spending time with son. Office: PO Box 253 Tilton NH 03276-0253

WOLF, STEWART GEORGE, JR., physician, medical educator; b. Balt., Jan. 12, 1914; s. Stewart George and Angeline (Griffing) W.; m. Virginia Danforth, Aug. 1, 1942; children: Stewart George III, Angeline Griffing, Thomas Danforth. Student, Phillips Acad., 1927-31, Yale U., 1931-33; A.B., Johns Hopkins U., 1934, M.D., 1938; M.D. (hon.), U. Göteborg, Sweden, 1968. Intern N.Y. Hosp., 1938-39, resident medicine, 1939-42, NRC fellow, 1941-42; rsch. fellow Bellevue Hosp., 1939-42, clin. assoc. vis. neuropsychiatrist, 1946-52; rsch. head injury and motion sickness Harvard neurol. unit Boston City Hosp., 1942-43; asst., then assoc. prof. medicine Cornell U., 1946-52; prof., head dept. medicine U. Okla., 1952-67, Regents prof. medicine, psychiatry and behavioral scis., 1967—, prof. physiology, 1967-69; dir. Marine Biomed. Inst., U. Tex. Med. Br., Galveston, 1969-78; dir. emeritus Marine Biomed. Inst., U. Tex. Med. Br., 1978—, prof. medicine univ., also prof. internal medicine and physiology med. br., 1970-77; prof. medicine Temple U., Phila., 1977—; v.p. med. affairs St. Luke's Hosp., Bethlehem, Pa., 1977-82; dir. Totts Gap Inst., Bangor, Pa., 1958—; supr. clin. activities Okla. Med. Rsch. Found., 1953-55, head psychosomatic and neuromuscular sect., 1952-67, head neuroscis. sect., 1967-69; adv. com. Space Medicine and Behavioral Scis., NASA, 1960-61; cons. internal medicine VA Hosp., Oklahoma City, 1952-69; cons. (European Office), Paris, Office Internat. Rsch., NIH, 1963-64; mem. edn. and supply panel Nat. Adv. Commn. on Health Manpower, 1966-67; mem. Nat. Adv. Heart Coun., 1961-65, U.S. Phamacopeia Scope Panel on Gastroenterology, Regent Nat. Libr. Medicine, 1965-69; chmn., 1968-69; mem. Nat. Adv. Environ. Health Scis. Coun., 1966-70; exec. v.p. Frontiers Sci. Found., 1967-69; mem. sci. adv. bd. Muscular Dystrophy Assns. Am., Inc., 1974-91, chmn., 1980-89; mem. gastrointestinal drug adv. com. FDA, 1974-77; bd. Internat. Cardiology Fedn.; mem. bd. visitors dept. biology Boston U., 1978-88; mem. vis. com. Ctr. for Social Rsch., Lehigh U., 1980-90; chmn. adv. com. Wood Inst. on History of Medicine, Coll. Physicians, Phila., 1980-90, mem. program com. Coll. Physicians, 1990-91; dir. Inst. for Advanced Studies in Immunology and Aging, 1988—. Author: Human Gastric Function, 1943, The Stomach, 1965, Social Environment and Health, 1981, others; adv. editor Internat. Dictionary Biology and Medicine, 1978—; editor in chief Integrative Physiol & Behavioral Sci.: The Official Jour. of Pavlovian Soc., 1990—. Pres. Okla. City Symphony Soc., 1956-61; mem. Okla. Sch. of Sci. and Math. Found., 1961—. Recipient Disting. Svc. Citation U. Okla., 1968, Dean's award for disting. med. svc., 1992; Horsley Gantt medal Pavlovian Soc., 1987, Hans Selye award Am. Inst. Stress, 1988, Rsch. award Carolinska Inst., Stockholm, 1994, Wilém Laufberger medal Acad. Scis. of Czech Republic, Citation for sci. and humanitarian achievement The J.E. Purkyně Bohemian Med. Assn. Fellow Am. Psychiat. Assn. (disting., trustee 1992—, Hofheimer prize for rsch. 1952); mem. AMA (coun. mental health 1960-64), Am. Soc. Clin. Investigation, Am. Clin. and Climatol. Assn. (pres. 1975-76), Assn. Am. Physicians, Am. Psychosomatic Soc. (pres. 1961-62), Am. Gastroent. Assn. (rsch. award 1943, pres. 1969-70), Am. Heart Assn. (chmn. com. profl. edn., com. internat. program, awards), Romanian Acad. Med. Sci. (hon.), Coll. Physicians Phila., Collegium Internat. Activitas Nervosae Superioris (exec. com. 1992—, pres. 1994), Philos. Soc. Tex., Sigma Xi, Alpha Omega Alpha, Omicron Delta Kappa. Club: Cosmos (Washington). Home: 1430 Totts Gap Rd Bangor PA 18013-9716 Office: Totts Med Rsch Labs Bangor PA 18013

WOLF, WAYNE HENDRIX, electrical engineering educator; b. Washington, Aug. 12, 1958; s. Jesse David and Carolyn Josephine (Cunningham) W.; m. Nancy Jane Porter, Aug. 12, 1989. BS with distinction, Stanford U., 1980, MS, 1981, PhD, 1984. Lectr. Stanford (Calif.) U., 1984; staff mem. AT&T Bell Labs., Murray Hill, N.J., 1984-89; asst. prof. elec. engring. Princeton (N.J.) U., 1989-95, assoc. prof., 1995—; program chair First Internat. Workshop Hardware-Software Co-Design, 1991, gen. chair, 1993; program chair Internat. Conf. on Computer Design, 1995. Author: Modern VLSI Design, 1994; co-editor: High-Level VLSI Synthesis, 1991; contbg. author: Physical Design Automation of VLSI Systems, 1989. Mem. IEEE, Assn. Computing Machinery, Phi Beta Kappa, Tau Beta Pi. Avocations: bicycling, photography, films, flying. Office: Princeton U Dept Elec Engring Princeton NJ 08544

WOLF, WERNER PAUL, physicist, educator; b. Vienna, Austria, Apr. 22, 1930; came to U.S., 1963, naturalized, 1977; s. Paul and Wilhelmina Wolf; m. Elizabeth Eliot, Sept. 23, 1954; children: Peter Paul, Mary-Anne Githa. BA, Oxford (Eng.) U., 1951, DPhil, 1954, MA, 1954; MA (hon.), Yale U., 1965. Rsch. fellow Harvard U., 1956-57; Fulbright travelling fellow, 1956-57; Imperial Chem. Industries rsch. fellow Oxford U., 1957-59, univ. demonstrator, lectr., 1959-62; lectr. New Coll., 1957-62; faculty Yale U., 1963—, prof. physics and applied sci., 1965-76, dir. grad. studies dept. engring. and applied sci., 1973-76, Becton prof., 1976-84, chmn. dept. engring. and applied sci., 1976-81, chmn. council engring., 1981-84, Raymond J. Wean prof. engring. and applied sci., prof. physics, 1984—, dir. undergrad. studies dept. applied physics, 1987-94, dir. grad. studies coun. engring., 1989, chmn. dept. applied physics, 1990—, chair commn. on econ. status of faculty, 1990-92; dir. ednl. affairs, 1994—; cons. Dupont Exptl. Sta., Wilmington, Del., 1957, Hughes Aircraft, Culver City, Calif., 1957, GE Rsch. Lab., Schenectady, N.Y., 1960, Mullard Rsch. Labs., Salfords, England, 1961, IBM, Yorktown Heights, N.Y., 1962-66, Brookhaven Nat. Lab., 1966-80, GE R & D Ctr., Schenectady, 1966-93, U. Bridgeport, 1995—, Nat. U. Singapore, 1994-96; vis. prof. Technische Hochschule, Munich, Germany, 1969; Sci. Research Council sr. vis. fellow Oxford U., 1980, 84; vis. fellow Corpus Christi Coll., 1984, 87; mem. program com. Conf. Magnetism and Magnetic Materials, 1963, 65, 86, chmn., 1968, mem. adv. com., 1964-65, 70-76, 85-88, chmn., 1972, steering com., 1970-71, conf. gen. chmn., 1971; mem. organizing, program coms. Internat. Congress on Magnetism, 1967, internat. program com., 1978-79, planning com., 1979-85; vis. physicist Brookhaven Nat. Lab., 1966, 68, vis. sr. physicist, 1970, research collaborator, 1972, 74, 75, 77, 80; mem. vis. com. dept. phys./sci. U. Del., 1980, 84, 86; mem. NATO Advanced Study Inst. Program Com., 1983, 85, internat. adv. bd. Yamada Conf. XXV on Magnetic Phase Transitions, 1990; mem. bd. visitors Fairfield U., 1996—. Editor: CASE Reports, 1988-90; contbr. papers on magnetic materials and low temperature physics. Alexander von Humboldt Found. sr. U.S. scientist awardee, 1983; vis. guest fellow Royal Soc. London, 1987. Fellow IEEE, Am. Phys. Soc. (edn. com. 1977-80, program dir. Indsl. Grad. Intern Program 1978-79, chmn. fellowship com., Div. Condensed Matter Physics 1981-83); mem. Conn. Acad. Sci. and Engring., Yale Sci. and Engring. Assn. (Meritorious Svc. award 1985). Home: 37 Apple Tree Ln Woodbridge CT 06525-1258 Office: Yale U Dept Applied Physics PO Box 208284 New Haven CT 06520-8284

WOLF, WILLIAM MARTIN, computer company executive, consultant; b. Watertown, N.Y., Aug. 29, 1928; s. John and Rose (Emrich) W.; m. Eileen Marie Jolly, Aug. 19, 1952 (div. 1974); children: Rose, Sylvia, William. BS, St. Lawrence U., 1950; MS, U. N.H., 1951; postgrad., U. Pa., 1951-52, MIT, 1952-55. Programmer digital computer lab. MIT, Cambridge, Mass., 1952-54; pres. Wolf R & D Corp., Boston, 1954-69, Wolf Computer Corp., Boston, 1969-76, Planning Systems Internat., Boston, 1976-81, Micro Computer Software Inc., Cambridge, 1981-88, Tech. Acquisition Corp., Boston, 1989-91, Planning Internat., Inc., Boston, 1989-94, Wolfsort Corp., Boston, 1989—; chmn. Wolf & McManus, Brookline, Mass., 1995—; dir., exec. dir. Tech. Capital Network MIT, 1992-94; co-founder, pres. Assn. Ind. Software Cos., Washington, 1965-67, Design Sci. Inst., Phila., 1969-73, Nat. Coun. Profl. Svc. Firms, Washington, 1970-75; seminar leader MIT Sloan Sch., Cambridge, 1970; co-founder, bd. dirs. Harbor Nat. Bank, Boston. Author computer program; inventor management system, orbit calculator, sorting method. Co-founder X-10 Orgn., Boston, 1962; trustee Addison Gilbert Hosp., Gloucester, Mass., 1963; v.p. Young Pres. Orgn., Boston, 1970; overseer Mus. Sci., Boston, 1989—; mem. Computer Mus. Named Outstanding Young Man in Boston, Jaycees, 1962; recipient Speaker's award Data Processing Mgmt. Assn., 1966. Mem. World Bus. Coun., MIT Club (Alumni award 1991), Boston Computer Soc., Forty-Niners.

WOLFART, H.C., linguistics scholar, author, editor; b. Lindau im Bodensee, Germany, 1943. Grad. (BA equivalent), Albert-Ludwigs-U., Freiburg im Breisgau, Fed. Republic Germany, 1964; MA, Cornell U., 1967, Yale U., 1966; M.Phil., Yale U., 1967, PhD, 1969. Lectr. U. Alta., Edmonton, Can., 1967-68; asst. prof. U. Man., Winnipeg, Can., 1969-72; assoc. prof. U. Manitoba, Winnipeg, Can., 1972-77, prof., head anthropology dept., 1977-78, prof., coord. linguistics program, 1978-87, prof., head linguistics dept., 1987-93, Univ. Disting. prof., head linguistics dept., 1993-96, Univ. Disting. prof., Killam rsch. fellow, 1996—. Author: Plains Cree: A Grammatical Study, 1973, (with F. Pardo) Computer Assisted Linguistic Analysis, 1973, (with J.F. Carroll) Meet Cree: A Guide to the Cree Language, 2d edit., 1981, (with D.H. Pentland) Bibliography of Algonquian Linguistics, 1982; editor: Essays in Algonquian Bibliography in Honour of V.M. Dechene, 1984; editor and translator: (told by L. Beardy) pisiskiwak kâ-pîkiskwêcik/Talking Animals, 1988, (told by Nêhiyaw/Glecia Bear, co-edited and co-translated with F. Ahenakew wanisinwak iskwêsisak/Two Little Girsl Lost in the Bush, 1991; editor: Linguistic Studies Presented to John L. Finlay, 1991, (told by Nêhiyaw/Glecia Bear and others, co-edited and co-translated with F. Ahenakew) kôhkominawak otâcimowiniwâwa / Our Grandmothers' Lives as Told in their Own Words, 1992, (co-edited and co-translated with F. Ahenakew) kinêhiyâwiwininaw nêhiyawêwin / The Cree Language is Our Identity: The LaRonge Lectures of Sarah Whitecalf, 1993; mem. editl. bd. Actes du Congrès des Algonquinistes, 1982-94, Revue canadienne de linguistique, 1983-86; assoc. editor (supplements) Algonquian and Iroquoian Linguistics, 1985-96; gen. editor Sociètè d'Edition de textes algonquiens, 1985—. Recipient Rh Inst. award in the humanities, 1980; fellow Studienstiftung des deutschen Volkes, 1966-67, Can. Coun./Social Scis. and Humanities Rsch. Coun., 1975-76, 82-83, 86-96. Fellow Philol. Soc., Algonquian Text Soc., Royal Soc. of Can.; mem. Assn. canadienne de linguistique, Societas Linguistica Europaea, Linguistic Assn. Gt. Britain, Linguistic Soc. Am., Soc. for the Study of Indigenous Langs. of Ams., Soc. for Mesopotamian Studies, Rupert's Land Rsch. Ctr., British Assn. Can. Studies, Oxford Bibliog. Soc., Friends of the Bodleian, Henry Sweet Soc. Office: Linguistics Dept, U Manitoba, Winnipeg, MB Canada R3T 2N2

WOLFBEIN, SEYMOUR LOUIS, economist, educator; b. Bklyn., Nov. 8, 1915; s. Samuel and Fanny (Katz) W.; m. Mae Lachterman, Mar. 1, 1941; children: Susan Lois, Deeva Irene. BA, Bklyn. Coll., 1936; MA, Columbia U., 1937, PhD, 1941. Rsch. assoc. U.S. Senate Com. on Unemployment and Relief, 1938; economist, divsn. rsch. WPA, 1939-42; economist Bur. Labor Statistics, Dept. Labor, 1942-45, chief occpl. outlook divsn., 1946-49, chief div. manpower and productivity, 1949-50, chief div. manpower and employment, 1950-59, dep. asst. sec. labor, 1959-67; dir. Office Manpower, Automation and Tng., 1962-67, spl. asst. to sec. labor for econ. affairs, 1965-67; dean Sch. Bus. Adminstrn., Temple U., Phila., 1967-78; Joseph A. Boettner prof. bus. adminstrn. Sch. Bus. Adminstrn., Temple U., 1978-85; dean Temple U. in Japan, 1983-85; pres. T/W/O, 1986—; prof. econs. Am. U., Washington; dir. Lincoln Bank of Phila. Author: Decline of a Cotton Textile City, 1942, The World of Work, 1951, Employment and Unemployment in the U.S.--A Study of American Labor Force, 1964, Employment, Unemployment and Public Policy, 1965, Education and Training for Full Emplyment, 1967, Occupational Information: A Career Guidance View, 1968, Emerging Sectors of Collective Bargaining, 1970, Work in American Society, 1971, Manpower Policy: Perspectives and Prospects, 1973, Labor Market Information for Youth, 1975, Men in the Pre-Retirement Years, 1977, Establishment Reporting in the U.S., 1978, The New Labor Force, 1988, America's Service Economy, 1988, The Older Worker, 1988, Working and Not Working in the U.S.A., 1989, The Temporary Help Supply Industry, 1989, In the Year 2000: A New Look, 1990, Our Industrial Future, 1990, Our Occupational Future, 1990, To the Year 2000-- and Beyond: The World of Work, 1992, The Job Outlook in the U.S.A., 1994, Women at Work: A New Look, 1995, Education and Training for Work, 1996, Part Time Work in the U.S.A., 1996, The Philadelphia Story, 1996, An Election Lesson in Education, 1996, Employment in the U.S.A., 1997, Making a Living in the U.S.A., 1997; contbr. numerous articles to profl. and tech. jours. Mem. commn. on human resources Nat. Acad. Scis.; mem. adv. com. NSF; bd. mgrs. Springarden Coll.; mem. election com. Independence Blue Cross, Phila.; v.p. World Trade Coun.; mem. Mayor's Adv. Coun. on Employment, Phila.; bd. dirs. Jewish Employment and Vocat. Svc.. Served with U.S. Army, 1944-45. Recipient alumni award of honor Bklyn. Coll., 1954; Distinguished Service award Dept. Labor, 1955, 61. Fellow Am. Statis. Assn., AAAS; mem. Md. Civic Assn. (pres. Bannockburn 1957-59), Washington Statis. Soc. (pres.), Data Mgmt. Processing Assn. (hon. life), Am. Statis. Assn. (chmn. social statistics sect. 1956-57), Nat. Vocational Guidance Assn. (Eminent Career award 1970, chmn. occupational research com.), D.C. Guidance and Personnel Assn. (trustee). Home: E 706 Parktowne 2200 Benjamin Franklin Pky Philadelphia PA 19130 *Every year that goes by underscores the major common denominator to successful career development in America: the need to be responsive to social and economic change.*

WOLFBERG, MELVIN DONALD, optometrist, educational administrator, consultant; b. Altoona, Pa., June 24, 1926; s. Max Alex and Claire (Schiffman) Wolfberg; m. Audrey Iris Koch, Apr. 26, 1952; children: Debra Lynn, Michael Alex, Daniel Ben; m. Linda Diane Machesic, Dec. 4, 1979. OD, Pa. Coll. Optometry, Phila., 1951; D of Ocular Sci. (hon.), New England Coll. Optometry, 1989, Ill. Coll. Optometry, 1990. Lic. optometrist, Pa. Pvt. practice and ptnr. optometric practice Selinsgrove, Pa., 1951-79; pres. Pa. Coll. Optometry, Phila., 1979-89, chmn. bd., 1976-79; v.p. profl. rels. Bausch and Lomb, Rochester, N.Y., 1991-95; pres. In Vision Inst., Boston, 1991-95; ptnr./dir. Sylvan Learning Ctr., Vero Beach, Fla., 1996—; cons. to sec. HEW, Washington, 1970-77; dir. Better Vision Inst., N.Y.C., 1960-80. Mem. Selinsgrove City Coun., 1961-62; pres. Selinsgrove Community Chest, 1957; chmn. Optometrists Rep. Nat. Com., 1972, 76; chmn. Nat. Inter-Profl. Health Coun., Washington, 1972-77; dir. Univ. City Sci. Ctr., Phila., 1980-87; adv. com. Coun. Higher Edn., Commonwealth Pa., 1980-89. Served with U.S. Army, 1944-46, ETO. Decorated Purple Heart, Bronze Star, Silver Star; named Man of Yr. Central Pa. Optometric Soc., 1964, Alumnus of Yr. Pa. Coll. Optometry, 1970; recipient Carel C. Koch Meml. medal, 1989. Fellow Am. Acad. Optometry (pres. 1985-86); mem. Pa. Assn. Colls. and Univs. (exec. com. 1982-89, sec.-treas. 1985-88, vice chmn. 1988-89), Pa. Optometric Assn. (pres. 1959-61, Optometrist of Yr.), Am. Optometric Assn. (pres. 1969-70, Disting. Svc. award 1994), Pa. Coll. Optometry Alumni Assn. (pres. 1957), Beta Sigma Kappa.

WOLFE, AL, marketing and advertising consultant; b. Wyo., May 3, 1932; s. Clyde A. and Margaret V. (Joyce) W.; m. F. Carilouise, 1957 (div. 1994); children: Kirk, Kelley, Alison. B.A. in Psychology, U. Wyo., 1958. Product mgr., merchandising mgr. Gen. Mills, Mpls., 1958-62; asst. mktg. dir., v.p., account supr. Compton Advt., Chgo. and N.Y.C., 1963-66; v.p., account supr., exec. v.p., gen. mgr. Wells Rich Greene, N.Y.C., 1967-76; exec. v.p., dir. N.W. Ayer ABH Internat., N.Y.C., 1976-81; mng. dir., pres., bd. dirs. DDB Needham Worldwide, Chgo., 1981-87, pres. U.S. Div., 1987-88; pres. Al Wolfe Assocs., Inc., Mktg. and Advt. Cons., Sedona, Ariz., 1989—; bd. dirs. Clorox Co., Oakland, Calif., Dolphin Software, Inc., Lake Oswego, Oreg. Bd. dirs. U. Wyo. Found., pres., 1993-94; past pres. bd. dirs. U. Wyo. Art Mus.; chmn. Sedona Med. Ctr. Found.; bd. dirs. Sedona Acad.; bd. dirs. Sedona Cultural Park. Recipient Disting. Alumnus award U. Wyo. 1981. Mem. Econ. Club (Chgo.), Sedona 30 Club. Home: 405 Manzanita Dr Sedona AZ 86336-4002 Office: Al Wolfe Assocs Inc PO Box 2367 Sedona AZ 86339-2367

WOLFE, ALBERT BLAKESLEE, lawyer; b. Parkersburg, W.Va., Apr. 6, 1909; s. William Henry and Katharine (White) W.; m. Beatrice Ewan, Oct. 23, 1942 (dec. Nov. 1986); children: Katharine Ward, Diana Ewan Wolfe Larkin. Grad., Hill Sch., 1927; A.B., Princeton U., 1931; LL.B., Harvard U., 1934. Bar: Mass., W.Va. 1934. Assoc. Rackemann, Sawyer & Brewster, Boston, 1934-40; partner Rackemann, Sawyer & Brewster, 1940-74, of counsel, 1974—; pres. Parkersburg Property Mgmt. Co., 1956-78. Chmn. Cambridge Hist. Commn., 1963-73; mem. Mass. Hist. Commn., 1963-73; pres. Keystone Fund (charitable fund), W.Va., 1951-89; trustee Marietta Coll., 1961-74, life assoc., 1974—; trustee Nat. Trust for Historic Preservation, 1970-79; dir. Longfellow's Wayside Inn, 1972-89. Served to lt. comdr. USNR, 1942-45. Fellow Am. Bar Found. (life), Mass. Bar Found. (life); mem. ABA (chmn. real property, probate and trust law sect. 1968-69), Mass. Bar Assn., W.Va. Bar Assn., Am. Law Inst. (adviser model land devel. code 1963-76), Mass. Hist. Soc., Soc. Colonial Wars, Colonial Soc. Mass., Harvard Club Boston, Abstract Club Boston (pres. 1963-73), Harvard Faculty Club. Home: 311 Rivermead Rd Peterborough NH 03458-1762 also: High Wells Old Harrisville Rd Dublin OH 03444 *Conservation of resources—natural, cultural, and human, can, since space explorations have held a mirror to earth, be seen as the greatest challenge humankind has ever faced. We need more than ever before to understand all facets of human history, and to transcend allegiances to territory, home, country, ideology, religious sect, and even family, and to see all earth as home, and each and every man and woman, no matter how different from us, as a fellow sharer of the human experience. Building bridges of mutual understanding becomes ever more important.*

WOLFE, ALBERT J., state agency researcher; b. Long Branch, N.J., June 30, 1955; s. Albert J. and Gretchen (Gehlhaus) W. BA, Duquesne U., 1977; MA, U. Akron, 1985; MPA, Rutgers U., 1994. Chief Bur. of Mcpl. Inf. N.J. State League of Municipalities, Trenton, 1983-96; project specialist. divsn. local govt. svcs. N.J. Dept. Cmty. Affairs, Trenton, 1996—. Author: A History of Municipal Government in New Jersey Since 1798, 1990, The Faulkner Act: New Jersey's Optional Municipal Charter Law, 2d edit., 1993, There's Trouble in River City: The Dynamics of Local Regulation of New Technologies, 1988, Police Compensation in New Jersey: Who Says Crime Doesn't Pay?, 1992, New Jersey's Five Traditional Forms of Municipal Government, 1996. Office: NJ Dept Cmty Affairs Divsn Local Govt Svcs 101 S Broad St # 803 Trenton NJ 08608-2401

WOLFE, CAMERON WITHGOT, JR., lawyer; b. Oakland, Calif., July 7, 1939; s. Cameron W. and Jean (Brown) W.; m. Frances Evelyn Bishopric, Sept. 2, 1964; children: Brent Everett, Julie Frances, Karen Jean. AB, U. Calif.-Berkeley, 1961, JD, 1964. Bar: Calif. 1965, U.S. Dist. Ct. (no. dist.) Calif. 1965, U.S. Ct. Appeals (9th cir.) 1965, U.S. Tax Ct. 1966, U.S. Ct. Claims 1977, U.S. Ct. Appeals (3d cir.) 1980, U.S. Ct. Appeals (fed. cir.) 1983, U.S. Supreme Ct. 1986 . Assoc., then ptnr. Orrick, Herrington & Sutcliffe, San Francisco, 1964—; bd. dirs. Crowley Maritime Corp.; mem. steering com. Western Pension Conf. Pres. League to Save Lake Tahoe, 1979, 80; chmn. League to Save Lake Tahoe Charitable Trust, 1966-91, Piedmont Ednl. Fund Campaign, 1982-83; pres. Piedmont Ednl. Found., 1986-90; bd. dirs. Yosemite Fund., 1993—. Served with U.S. Army, 1957, with USAR, 1957-65. Mem. ABA (mem. taxation com.), Calif. State Bar, San Francisco Bar Assn., Order of Coif, Phi Beta Kappa. Clubs: Pacific Union (San Francisco); Claremont Country (Oakland, Calif.). Home: 59 Lakeview Ave Piedmont CA 94611-3514 Office: Orrick Herrington & Sutcliffe 400 Sansome St San Francisco CA 94111-3304

WOLFE, CHARLES MORGAN, electrical engineering educator; b. Morgantown, W.Va., Dec. 21, 1935; s. Slidell Brown and Mae Louise (Maness) W.; children—David Morgan, Diana Michele. B.S.E.E., W.Va. U., Morgantown, 1961, M.S.E.E., 1962; Ph.D., U. Ill., 1965. Research assoc. U. Ill., Urbana, 1965; mem. staff MIT Lincoln Lab., Lexington, Mass., 1965-75; prof. elec. engring Washington U., St. Louis, 1975—, Samuel C. Sachs prof., 1982-90, dir. semicondr. research lab., 1979-90; cons. MIT Lincoln Lab., 1975-76, Fairchild Semicondr., Palo Alto, Calif., 1975-76, Air Force Avionics Lab., Dayton, Ohio, 1976-79, U. Ill., 1983-85. Author: Physical Properties of Semiconductors, 1989; editor: Gallium Arsenide and Related Compounds, 1979; contbr. articles to profl. jours., chpts. to books. Served as sgt. USMC, 1955-58. Fellow IEEE (field awards com. 1984-87, Jack A. Morton award 1990); mem. NAE, AAAS, Electrochem. Soc. (Electronics divsn. award 1978). Office: Washington U Campus Box 1127 Saint Louis MO 63130-1127

WOLFE, DAVID LOUIS, lawyer; b. Kankakee, Ill., July 24, 1951; s. August Christian and Irma Marie (Nordmeyer) W.; m. Gail Lauret Fritz, Aug. 25, 1972; children: Laura Beth, Brian David, Kaitlin Ann. BS, U. Ill., 1973; JD, U. Mich., 1976. Bar: Ill. 1976, U.S. Dist. Ct. (no. dist.) Ill. 1976. Assoc., Gardner, Carton & Douglas, Chgo., 1976-82, ptnr., 1983—; lectr. estate planning Aid Assn. for Lutherans SMART Program, Chgo., 1980-84; lectr. Ill. Inst. Continuing Legal Edn., Chgo. Bar Assn., Lake Shore Nat. Bank, Ill. State Bar Assn. Contbr. articles to legal publs. Recipient Recognition award Ill. Inst. Continuing Legal Edn., 1981-84. Mem. ABA (sects. on taxation, corp. banking and bus. law 1981—, lectr.), NFL Players Assn. (cert. contract advisor 1983—), NCAA (cert. contract advisor), Chgo. Assn. Commerce and Industry (employee benefit subcom. 1983—), Ill. State Bar Assn. (employee benefits sect. council, 1986-95, recognition award 1983), Phi Kappa Phi, Beta Alpha Psi, Beta Gamma Sigma, Sigma Iota Lambda, Phi Eta Sigma. Office: Gardner Carton & Douglas 321 N Clark St Ste 3300 Chicago IL 60610

WOLFE, DEBORAH CANNON PARTRIDGE, government education consultant; b. Cranford, N.J.; d. David Wadsworth and Gertrude (Moody) Cannon; 1 son, Roy Partridge. BS, N.J. State Coll.; MA, EdD, Tchrs. Coll., Columbia U.; postgrad., Vassar Coll., U. Pa., Union Theol. Sem., Jewish Sem. Am.; hon. doctorates, Seton Hall U., 1963, Coll. New Rochelle, 1963, Morris Brown U., 1964, Glassboro/Rowan Coll., 1965, Bloomfield Coll., 1988, Monmouth Coll., 1988, William Paterson Coll., 1988; LLD (hon.), Kean Coll., 1981; LHD (hon.), Stockton State Coll., 1982; LLD (hon.), Jersey City State Coll., 1987, Centenary Coll., William Paterson Coll., 1989, Tuskegee U., 1989, Glassboro State Coll., 1985, Tuskegee U., 1989, St. Peter's Coll., 1989, Rider Coll., 1989, Georgian Court Coll., 1990; DSc (hon.), Stevens Inst. Tech., 1991; LLD (hon.), Rutgers U., 1992, Thomas Edison Coll., 1992; DSc, U. Med. and Dentistry N.J., 1989. Former prin., tchr. pub. schs. Cranford, also Tuskegee, Ala.; faculty Tuskegee Inst., Grambling Coll., NYU, Fordham U., U. Mich., Tex. Coll., Columbia U.; supervision and adminstrn. curriculum devel., social studies U. Ill., summers; prof. edn., affirmative action officer Queens Coll.; prof. edn. and children's lit. Wayne State U.; edn. chief U.S. Ho. of Reps. Com. on Edn. and Labor, 1962—; Fulbright prof. Am. lit. NYU; U.S. rep. 1st World Conf. on Women in Politics; chair non-govtl. reps. to UN (NGO/DPI exec. com.), 1983—; editl. cons. Macmillan Pub. Co.; cons. Ency. Brit.; adv. bd. Ednl. Testing Svc.; mem. State Bd. Edn., 1964-94; chairperson N.J. Bd. Higher Edn., 1967-94; mem. nat. adv. panel on vocat. edn. HEW; mem. citizen's adv. com. to Bd. Edn., Cranford; mem. Citizen's Adv. Com. on Youth Fitness, Pres.'s Adv. Com. on Youth Fitness, White House Conf. Edn., 1955, White House Conf. Aging, 1960, White House Conf. Civil Rights, 1966, White House Conf. on Children, 1970, Adv. Coun. for Innovations in Edn.; v.p. Nat. Alliance for Safer Cities; cons. Vista Corps, OEO; vis. scholar Princeton Theol. Sem., 1989—; active Human Rels. Coun., N.J., 1994—; vis. prof. U. Ill., U. N.C., Wayne State U.; theologian-in-residence Duke U.; mem. trustee bd. Sci. Svc.; mem. N.J. Commn. on Holocaust Edn., 1996. Contbr. articles to ednl. publs. Bd. dirs. Cranford Welfare Assn., Cmty. Ctr., 1st Bapt. Ch., Cranford Cmty. Ctr. Migratory Laborers, Hurlock, Md.; trustee Sci. Svc., Seton Hall U., bd. regents; mem. Pub. Broadcasting Authority, N.J. Commn. on Holocaust Edn., 1996—, Tuskegee U. Alumni, 1995, N.J. Conv. of Progressive Baptists, 1995; sec. Kappa Delta Pi Ednl. Found.; mem. adv. com. Elizabeth and Arthur Schlesinger Libr., Radcliffe Coll., trustee Edn. Devel. Ctr., 1965—; assoc. min. 1st Bapt. Ch.; chair Human Rels. Commn., 1995; v.p. N.J. Conv. Progressive Bapt., 1996—; mem. exec. com. Nat. Coun. Agrl. Rsch., Ext. and Teaching, 1997—; mem. N.J. Holocaust Commn., 1996—. Recipient Woman of Yr. award Delta Beta Zeta, Woman of Yr. award Morgan State Coll., Medal of Honor, DAR, 1990, Disting. Svc. medal Nat. Top Ladies of Distinction, 1991, Disting. Svc. award Nat. Assn. State Bds. Edn., 1992, 94, Disting. Svc. to Edn. award N.J. Commn. on Status of Women, 1993, Svc. to Children award N.J. Assn. Sch. Psychologists, 1993, Disting. Medal award U. Medicine and Dentistry N.J., Union Coll., citation N.J. State Coun. on Vacat. Edn., 1994, citation N.J. State Bd. Edn., 1994, Svc. award for 50 Yrs., Cranford Bd. Edn., 1995, Women Who Count award Zonta Internat., 1996, Minister's Appreciation award Progressive Nat. Baptist Convention, 1996, Edn. award Tuskegge U. Alumni, 1996, Women Whom Make a Difference award Zonta Internat., 1995; named to NABSE Hall of Fame. Mem. NEA (life), ASCD (rev. coun.), AAAS (chmn. tchr. edn. com.), LWV, NCCJ, AAUW (nat. edn. chmn.), AAUP, NAACP (Medal of Honor 1994), Coun. Nat. Orgns. Children and Youth, Am. Coun. Human Rights (v.p.), Nat. Panhellenic Coun. (dir.), Nat. Assn. Negro Bus. and Profl. Women (chmn. spkrs. bur., Nat. Achievement award 1958), Nat. Assn. Black Educators (pres.), N.Y. Tchrs. Assn., Am. Tchrs. Assn., Fellowship So. Churchmen, Internat. Reading Assn., Comparative Edn. Soc., Am. Acad. Polit. and Social Sci., Internat. Assn. Childhood Edn., Nat. Soc. Study Edn., Am. Coun. Edn. (commn. fed. rels.), Nat. Alliance Black Educators (pres.), Internat. Platform Assn., Ch. Women United (UN rep., mem. exec. com.), UN Assn.-U.S.A. (exec. com.), N.J. Fedn. Colored Women's Clubs, N.J. Holocaust Commn., 1996, CARAT of NASUCLGC (exec. bd. 1996), N.J. Commn. Holocaust Edn., Alliance of Black Clegywomen (pres.). Home: 326 E Nantucket Ln Jamesburg NJ 08831-1704 Office: NJ State Bd Edn 20 W State St Trenton NJ 08608-1206 *I feel I am extremely fortunate to have been born into a family where love of God and love of knowledge have been major concerns. The knowledge we have sought has not been 'knowledge for knowledge's sake' but 'knowledge to improve society and the world'. I have always felt that 'God power' linked with 'Brain power' was the greatest force in the world and I knew that in order to achieve such strength one must work diligently and constantly. Because knowledge changes so rapidly this quest for wisdom must be eternal. Hence I hope I'm still learning and growing for education must be involved from 'the womb to the tomb'.*

WOLFE, ELIZABETH ANNE, elementary education educator; b. Washington, July 26, 1954; d. William Arthur and Eleanore Elizabeth (Smith) Walsh; m. Christopher James Wolfe, Feb. 10, 1979; children: Daniel James Wolfe, Jeffrey Taylor Wolfe. AA, St. Petersburg Jr. Coll., Clearwater, Fla., 1975; BA, U. Md., 1977. Cert. elem., early childhood tchr., Fla. Kindergarten tchr. High Point Elem. Sch., Clearwater, 1978-83; 1st grade tchr. Curlew Creek Elem. Sch., Palm Harbor, Fla., 1983-87; 3rd grade tchr. math., social sci., sci. Curlew Creek Elem. Sch., Palm Harbor, 1987-89, 1st grade tchr., 1989-90, 5th grade lang. tchr., 1990-92, 4th grade lang. tchr., 1992-94, 5th grade self-contained tchr., 1994—. Cub Scout den leader Boy Scouts Am., Clearwater, 1991; coach Odyssey of the Mind, Curlew Creek Elem. Sch., 1991—. Recipient sci. fiction reading, writing grant Fla. Coun. Elem. Edn., 1992, sci. communication grant Dept. Instrnl. Tech., 1992, newspapers in edn. grant Teach for Excellence Edn. Found., 1990, mini-economy grant Teach for Excellence Edn. Found., 1988; winner Odyssey of the Mind State Championship, 1997. Mem. PTA, Pinellas Coun. Social Studies (elem. rep. 1990-92), Pinellas Classroom Tchrs. Assn., Pinellas Reading Coun. Avocations: Tae Kwon Do, roller blading, stepclass, computering. Home: 2732 Northridge Dr E Clearwater FL 34621-2318 Office: Curlew Creek Elem Sch 3030 Curlew Rd Palm Harbor FL 34684-5033

WOLFE, ELLEN DARLENE, school librarian, elementary school educator; b. Mattoon, Ill., Dec. 16, 1952; d. Floyd Dale and Irma Jane (Hensley) Robinson; m. Walter Ray Wolfe, Mar. 12, 1994; children: Gregory David, William Scott, Joseph Dean, Brian Matthew, Joshua Paul. BS, Ind. State U., 1987. Cert. elem. educator, Ill. Reading tchr. Marshall (Ill.) Community Dist. 2, 1987-91; law libr. Robinson (Ill.) Correctional Ctr., 1991-94; libr. Palestine (Ill.) Cmty. Unit Sch. Dist. # 3, 1994—; libr. City of Marshall, 1986—; dir. summer camp Clark County Handicapped Assn., Marshall, 1988—; law libr. Robinson Correctional Ctr., 1991. Coord. Jr. youth group St. Mary's Cath. Ch. Mem. Correctional Edn. Assn., Home Ext. Club, Kappa Delta Pi, Phi Delta Kappa. Roman Catholic. Home: 18993 E River Rd Palestine IL 62451-9705 Office: Robinson Correctional Ctr PO Box 1000 Robinson IL 62454-0919

WOLFE, ETHYLE RENEE (MRS. COLEMAN HAMILTON BENEDICT), college administrator; b. Burlington, Vt., Mar. 14, 1919; d. Max M. and Rose (Saiger) W.; m. Coleman Hamilton Benedict, Dec. 4, 1954. B.A., U. Vt., 1940, M.A., 1942; postgrad., Bryn Mawr Coll., 1942-43; Ph.D., N.Y. U., 1950; LHD (hon.), CUNY, 1989; LittD (hon.), Iona Coll., 1989. Teaching fellow U. Vt., 1940-42; research fellow Latin Bryn Mawr (Pa.) Coll., 1942-43; instr. classics Bklyn. Coll., 1947-49, instr. classical langs., 1949-54, asst. prof., 1954-59, assoc. prof., 1960-68, prof., 1968—, acting chmn. dept. classics and comparative lit., 1962-63, chmn. dept., 1967-72; dean Bklyn. Coll. (Sch. Humanities), 1971-78; exec. officer Humanities Inst. Bklyn. Coll., 1980-89, provost and v.p. for acad. affairs, 1982-88, provost emeritus, 1989—; mem. exec. com., chmn. com. on undergrad. affairs, com. on univ.-wide programs CUNY faculty senate; mem. study group AAAS, 1987-89; dir. Fund for Improvement of Postsecondary Edn.-funded Ctr. for Core Studies, 1987-88; co-chair senate report, Chancellor's Coll. Prep. Initiative, 1991; mem. exec. com for publ.: The Liberal art of science: Agenda for Action:, dir. Nat. Core Visitors Programs, 1985-89. Asso. editor: Classical World, 1965-71; co-editor: The American Classical Review, 1971-76; contbr. articles to jours. in field. Ethyle R. Wolfe Inst. for the Humanities Bklyn. Coll. named in honor, 1989; mem. Columbia U. Seminar in Classical Civilization. Recipient Kirby Flower Smith award, 1939, Goethe prize U. Vt., 1940, Alumni Achievement award U. Vt., 1985, Charles Frankel prize NEH, 1990; named to Hall of Honor U. Vt., 1991; named Disting. U. Faculty Sen. Emeritus, CUNY, 1992; NEH grantee, 1971, 1982-84, Andrew W. Mellon Found. grantee, 1984-88. Mem. Am. Philol. Assn., Archeol. Inst. Am., Vergilian Soc. Am., Classical Assn. Atlantic States (exec. com.), Am. Soc. Papyrologists, N.Y. Classical Club (past pres.), Phi Beta Kappa (past pres. Rho chpt., pres. 1988-90). Home: 360 W 22nd StApt 15 E New York NY 10011-2600 Office: Bklyn Coll care Insts of The Humanities Bedford Ave # H Brooklyn NY 11222

WOLFE, EVA AGNES, retired educator; b. Stockport, Iowa, Jan. 13, 1910; d. Marion J. and Hattie Florence (Webber) Munson; m. Donald Earl Wolfe, 1937; 1 child, Sharon Dawn. BA, Iowa Wesleyan U., 1951; student, U. Minn., 1928-89, State U. Iowa, 1928, 29, 30. Tchr. rural schs. Van Buren County, Stockport, 1929-30; grade sch. tchr. Van Buren County, Keosauqua, Iowa, 1930-37, Pleasant Lawn Consol. Sch., Mt. Pleasant, Iowa, 1946-50; tchr. home econs., English Danville (Iowa) Consol. High Sch., 1951-60; tchr. home econs. West Burlington (Iowa) Pub. Schs., 1961-74; ret., 1974. Mem. Am. Assn. Ret. Persons. Mem. DAR, AAUW, Henry County Ret. Tchrs. (pres. 1976-78), Daus of Nile, Order of Eastern Star, White Shrine, Alpha Xi Delta. Democrat. Methodist. Avocations: music, reading, sewing, dancing, exercise. Office: c/o Harold Munson 3199 Wheat Blvd Lockridge IA 52635-8054

WOLFE, GEORGE C., theater director, producer, playwright; b. Lexington, Ky., 1954. BA, Pomona Coll.; MFA, NYU. Prodr. N.Y. Shakespeare Festival, N.Y.C., 1993—; bd. dirs. Young Playwrights Festival, N.Y.C. Works include: (writer, lyricist) Paradise!, 1985; (writer, dir.) The Colored Museum, 1986 (Elizabeth Hull-Kate Warriner award Dramatists Guild 1986), Jelly's Last Jam, 1992 (Joe A. Callaway award Stage Dirs. and Choreographers Found. 1993, Drama Desk award); (librettist) Queenie Pie, 1987; (scene contbr.) Urban Blight, 1988; curator Festival of New Voices, 1990, 92; (adaptor, dir.) Spunk, 1990 (Obie award for best dir. 1990); (dir. plays) Caucasian Chalk Circle, 1990, Angels in America, 1992, (Tony award for best dir. in a play 1993), Twilight: Los Angeles, 1992, Perestroika, 1993 (Tony award nominee for best dir. 1994), Blade to the Heat, 1994, The Tempest, 1995; actor: A Delicate Balance, 1996 (Best Leading Actor Tony 1996). Grantee Rockefeller Found., Nat. Endowment for Arts, Nat. Inst. Musical Theatre; recipient Hull-Warriner award, Audleco awards (2), The George Oppenheimer/Newsday award, CBS-FDG New Play award, NYU Disting. Alumni award, HBO/USA Playwrights award, Person of Yr. award Nat. Theatre Conf., Spl. Achievement award Audleco, Spirit of the City award, LAMBDA award; named A Living Landmark, N.Y. Landmarks Conservancy. Mem. Dramatists Guild (mem. exec. bd.). Office: NY Shakespeare Festival Joseph Papp Pub Theater 425 Lafayette St New York NY 10003-7021*

WOLFE, GEORGE CROPPER, retired private school educator, artist, author; b. New Orleans, Sept. 6, 1933; s. Howard Edward and Amaryllis (Brannen) W.; m. Catherine Vasterling, June 2, 1955; children: David, Michael, Philip. BA in Fine Art, La. State U., 1956; MEd, U. New Orleans,

1972, MS in Urban Planning, 1975; postgrad., Tex. Tech U., Junction, 1986-93. Cert. tchr. art, social studies, La. Elem. tchr. Live Oak Manor Sch., Waggaman, La., 1962-65; tchr. art Isidore Newman Sch., New Orleans, 1965-96; adj. prof. art Northwestern State U., Natchitoches, La., 1997—; co-owner design studio Wolf Patrol Prodns.; adj. prof. art Northwestern State U., 1997—. Author: 3-D Wizardry (also video), Papier Maché Plaster and Foam, 1995; sculpture projects include New Alexandria (La.) Mus. Art; contbr. articles to profl. jours. Served with USCG, 1956-58. Recipient Telly award for How-to video 3D Wizardry, 1966. Mem. Nat. Art Edn. Assn. (La. Art Educator of Yr. 1990), La. Art Edn. Assn. (pres. 1978-79), Kappa Delta Pi, Phi Delta Kappa (v.p., Rsch. award 1996). Home: 342 Jefferson St Natchitoches LA 71457

WOLFE, GREGORY BAKER, international relations educator; b. Los Angeles, Jan. 27, 1922; s. Harry Norton and Laura May (Baker) W.; m. Mary Ann Nelson, June 15, 1946; children: Gregory Nelson, Laura Ann, Melissa Helene. A.B., Reed Coll., 1943; M.A., Fletcher Sch. Law and Diplomacy, 1947, Ph.D., 1961; Dr. honoris causa, U. Autonoma de Guadalajara, Mex., 1984; D.H.L., Southeast Coll. Osteo. Medicine, Miami, Fla., 1985. With internat. div. Arthur D. Little, Inc., Cambridge, Mass., 1951-57; dir. Greater Boston Econ. Study Com., 1957-61; dir. Latin Am. program Com. Econ. Devel., 1961-64; dir. intelligence and rsch. for Am. republics State Dept., 1964-68; pres. Portland State U., 1968-74; dean Sch. Internat. Svc. Am. U., Washington, 1975-79; pres. Fla. Internat. U., Miami, 1979-86; prof. internat. rels. Fla. Internat. U., 1979—; vis. scholar Cambridge U., Eng., 1986-87; sr. cons. Orion Comml. Realty Inc., 1991—; fed. negotiator Joint Transp. Com. Washington 1962-66. Contbr. articles to profl. jours. Chmn. bd. trustees Internat. Fine Arts Coll., 1993—; bd. dirs. Chopin Found. U.S., Inc., 1988-96, Concert Assn. Fla., Inc., 1988—, Am. Coll. Madrid, 1994—; founding chmn. Brickell Ave. Lit. Soc., 1988-96. Recipient Fla. Internat. Ctr. award, 1980, Leonard Abess award, 1984, Orden del Merito Civil, King of Spain, 1986, Fulbright lectr., Ecuador, 1989.

WOLFE, HAROLD JOEL, lawyer, business executive; b. Toronto, Ont., Can., July 21, 1940; s. Max and Beatrice Irene (Albert) W.; m. Carole S. Wolfe, Aug. 17, 1967; 3 children. B.Commerce, U. Toronto, 1963, LL.B., 1966. Mem. firm Goodman & Carr (Barristers), Toronto, 1968-69; with Oshawa Group Ltd., Toronto, 1970—; corp. v.p. real estate Oshawa Group Ltd., 1971—, also dir. Mem. Law Soc. Upper Can. Office: Oshawa Group Ltd, 302 East Mall, Toronto, ON Canada M9B 6B8

WOLFE, HARRIET MUNRETT, lawyer; b. Mt. Vernon, N.Y., Aug. 18, 1953; d. Lester John Francis Jr. and Olga Harriet (Miller) Munrett; m. Charles Briant Wolfe, Sept. 10, 1983. BA, U. Conn., 1975; postgrad., Oxford U. (Eng.), 1976; JD, Pepperdine U., 1978. Bar: Conn. 1979. Assoc. legal counsel, asst. sec. Citytrust, Bridgeport, Conn., 1979-90; v.p., sr. counsel, asst. sec. legal dept. Shawmut Bank Conn., N.A., Hartford, 1990-96; sole practice law, 1996-97; sr. v.p., counsel, sec. Webster Fin. Corp., Waterbury, Conn., 1997—; mem. govt. rels. com. Electronic Funds Transfer Assn., Washington, 1983—. Mem. Conn. Bar Assn. (mem. legis. com. banking law sect.), ABA, Conn. Bankers Assn. (trust legis. com.), Guilford Flotilla Coast Guard Aux., U.S. Sailing Assn., Phi Alpha Delta Internat. (Frank E. Gray award 1978, Shepherd chpt. Outstanding Student award 1977-78). Home: 621 Northwood Dr Guilford CT 06437-1124 Office: Shawmut Bank Conn NA Webster Fin Corp Webster Plaza Waterbury CT 06702

WOLFE, JAMES RONALD, lawyer; b. Pitts., Dec. 10, 1932; s. James Thaddeus and Helen Matilda (Corey) W.; m. Anne Lisbeth Dahle Eriksen, May 28, 1960; children: Ronald, Christopher, Geoffrey. B.A. summa cum laude, Duquesne U., 1954; LL.B. cum laude, NYU, 1959. Bar: N.Y. 1959. Assoc. Simpson Thacher & Bartlett, N.Y.C., 1959-69, ptnr., 1969-95, counsel, 1996—. Co-editor: West's McKinney's Forms, Uniform Commercial Code, 1965. Served to 1st lt. U.S. Army, 1955-57. Mem. ABA, N.Y. State Bar Assn., Assn. of Bar of City of N.Y., Am. Judicature Soc., N.Y. Law Inst. Republican. Roman Catholic. Home: 641 King St Chappaqua NY 10514-3807 Office: Simpson Thacher & Bartlett 425 Lexington Ave New York NY 10017-3903

WOLFE, JEAN ELIZABETH, medical illustrator, artist; b. Newark, Oct. 3, 1925; d. Arthur Howard and Ethel (Harper) Wolfe; BS, Russell Sage Coll., 1947; student Pratt Inst., 1949-50; MA in Medicine, U. Rochester Sch. Medicine and Dentistry, 1955; postgrad. (W.B. Saunders fellow), U. Pa., 1955-56, U. Pa., 1980, 95; MFA in Painting, U. Pa., 1973, MA (hon.), 1973. Cert. Med. Illustrator. Exhibitor, Pratt Inst. Galleries, Bklyn., 1958, N.Y. Med. Coll., 1958, Assn. Med. Illustrators, 1961-86, 90, AMA, N.Y.C., 1965, Phila., 1965, A.C.S., Atlantic City, 1965, Rsch. Study Club L.A., 1966, Phila. Art Alliance, 1967, 73, U. Pa. Alumni Ophthal. Assn., 1967-68, N.J. Med. Soc., 1968, Cayuga Mus. History and Art, 1968, Pensacola Art Ctr., 1969, FAA Aero. Center, Oklahoma City, 1970, Scheie Eye Inst., 1972-75, Assn. Med. Illustrators Traveling Salon, 1978, Moore Coll. Art, 1985, Mus. of Am. Illustration Soc. of Illustrators, 1986, Mutter Mus., Phila. Coll. of Physicians, 1990-92, Axis Gallery, 1992; represented in permanent collections Archives of Med. Visual Resources, Francis A. Countway Med. Libr., Harvard Univ., Mutter Mus., Phila. Coll. Physicians; collection of work donated by Scheie Eye Inst., memoirs and papers housed in The Arthur and Elizabeth Schlesinger Libr. on the History of Women in Am., Radcliffe Coll.; contbg. illustrator Adler's Textbook Ophthalmology, 8th edit., 1969; illustrations in med. books, jours., pharm. house pubs.; instr. Pembroke Coll. Brown U., 1947-49; dept. head Kimberley Sch., Upper Montclair, N.J., 1950-52; freelance med. illustration Studio N.Y. Med. Coll., 1956-60; instr. Pratt Inst., 1958-59; med. artist in ophthalmology, 1960-61, asst. instr. in med. illustration in ophthalmology, 1961-62, instr. in med. illustration in ophthalmology, 1962-65; assoc. in med. illustration U. Pa. Sch. Medicine, 1965-72, tenured sole artist in the hist. of the sch. of medicine, rsch. asst. prof. med. art in ophthalmology, 1972-85, rsch. asst. prof. emeritus, 1985—; independent studio (fine art) painting and med. illustration, 1985—; guest lectr. Johns Hopkins Med. Sch., 1973, NIH; guest artist USAF, Air Force Acad. and NORAD, 1971. Recipient Merit certificate AMA; Appreciation certificate ACS; 1st prize Pensacola Art Ctr., Am. Heart Assn., 1969, Gold medal Graphic Arts Soc. of Del. Valley, 1973. Fellow Assn. Med. Illustrators (emeritus); mem. Assn. Med. Illustrators (Ralph Sweet, Tom Jones awards, gov. 1970—, chmn. nominating com. 1972-73, vice chmn. bd. govs. 1973-74, chmn. bd. 1974-75, selection com., Lifetime Achievement award 1989—, adv. coun. Vesalius Trust 1990—), Soc. Illustrators (cert. merit 1986), Coll. Art Assn., Women's Caucus for Art, Faculty Club of U. Pa. Address: 55 Frazer Rd Beech 222 Malvern PA 19355-1981 also: Scheie Eye Inst 51 N 39th St Philadelphia PA 19104

WOLFE, JOHN THOMAS, JR., university president; b. Jackson, Miss., Feb. 22, 1942; s. John Thomas Sr. and Jeanette (Wallace) W.; children: Wyatt Bardouille, John Thomas Dantzler, David Andrew Dantzler. BEd, Chgo. Tchrs. Coll., 1964; MS, Purdue U., 1972, PhD, 1976. Tchr. English Englewood High Sch., Chgo., 1965-67; linguistics prof. Cuttington Coll., Liberia, West Africa, 1967-69; pres. Wolfe & Assocs., 1970-93; asst. mgr. residence hall Purdue U., West Lafayette, Ind., 1971-75, employee relations mgr., 1975-77; asst. prof. English Fayetteville (N.C.) State U., 1977-82, assoc. prof., 1982-85, coordinator area English and dramatic arts, 1978-83, head div. humaities and fine arts, 1979-84; acad. dean. Ft. Bragg U. Ctr., 1983-85; provost, v.p. for acad. affairs Bowie (Md.) State Coll., 1985-90; pres. Ky. State U., Frankfort, 1990-91; exec. dir. Nat. Rainbow Coalition, 1992-93; pres. Savannah (Ga.) State Coll., 1993—; lectr. Krannert Sch. Mgmt., 1976; mem. N.C. Humanities Commn., 1981-85. Contbr. articles in field. Active N.C. Humanities Com., Greensboro, 1979-83, Arts Coun. Fayetteville, Cumberland, N.C., 1979-85, Minority Bus. Resource Inst. Bd., Landover, Md., 1986—; bd. dirs. Entrepreneurial Devel. Program, Landover, 1986—, Savannah Econ. Devel. Auth., 1994, Savannah Area C. of C., 1994, Savannah Regional Small Bus. Capital Fund, 1994; del. White House Conf. on Librs., 1991; Ga. state rep. Am. Assn. State Colls. and Univs., 1993—. NEH grantee, 1979; Am. Council on Edn. fellow, 1982-83; recipient award Fayetteville Human Relations Commn., 1981. Mem. Nat. Coun. Tchrs. English (pres. Black Caucus 1981-88), Conf. Coll. Composition and Communication (chmn. resolutions com. 1982—), Am. Coun. Edn. (commn. leadership devel. 1995), Kappa Delta Pi, Omega Psi Phi, Alpha Kappa Mu (hon.). Roman Catholic. Avocations: poetry, reading, golfing, long distance motoring. Home: 247 Lyman Hall Rd Savannah GA 31410-1048 Office: Savannah State Coll Office of the Pres PO Box 20449 Savannah GA 31404*

WOLFE, JONATHAN A., food wholesaler, retailer. Pres., COO Oshawa Group Ltd., Toronto, Ont., Can. Office: The Oshawa Group Ltd, 302 E Mall, Toronto, ON Canada M9B 6B8

WOLFE, KENNETH L., food products manufacturing company executive; b. 1939; married. B.A., Yale U., 1961; M.B.A., U. Pa., 1967. With Bankers Trust Corp., 1961-62; chmn., CEO Hershey Foods Corp., 1994—; with Hershey Foods Corp., Pa., 1968—, asst. treas., 1968-69, budget dir., 1969-74, dir. ops. and fin. analysis, 1974-76, treas., 1986-80, v.p. fin. adminstrn. Hershey Chocolate Co., 1980-81, v.p., chief fin. officer, 1981-84, sr. v.p., chief fin. officer, 1984-85, pres., chief operating officer, 1985-93, chmn., CEO, 1994—, also dir. Office: Hershey Foods Corp 100 Crystal A Dr Hershey PA 17033-9529

WOLFE, LESLIE R., think-tank executive. Exec. dir. Ctr. for Women Policy Studies, Washington, D.C.; pres. Ctr. for Women Policy Studies. Office: Ctr Women Policy Studies 1211 Connecticut Ave NW Ste 312 Washington DC 20036-2709*

WOLFE, LILYAN, special education clinical educator; b. N.Y.C., Mar. 17, 1937; d. Alexander and Molly (Springer) Aven; m. Richard Wolfe, June 8, 1957; children: Brian, Stacey. BBA, CUNY, 1957; postgrad., Hunter Coll., 1962-65; MA, NYU, 1982, postgrad., 1983-85. Cert. tchr., N.J., N.Y.; cert. tchr. of handicapped, N.J. Tchr. PS 101 Manhattan, N.Y.C., 1962-65, Hazlet Twp. (N.J.) Schs., 1976-81; tchr. at risk mother-toddler program U. Medicine and Dentistry N.J., Newark, 1982-85, tchr. therapeutic nursery, 1982-84, head tchr., 1984—. Recipient cert. appreciation, Essex County Child Care Coalition, Newark, 1992. Mem. Nat. Assn. Edn. Young Children, NYU Alumni Assn., Kappa Delta Pi. Avocations: piano, gourmet cooking, travel, reading. Home: 120 Warren Aberdeen NJ 07747-1844 Office: U Medicine and Dentistry NJ Cmty Mental Health Ctr 215 S Orange Ave Newark NJ 07103-2700

WOLFE, MARGARET RIPLEY, historian, educator, consultant; b. Kingsport, Tenn., Feb. 3, 1947; d. Clarence Estill and Gertrude Blessing Ripley; m. David Earley Wolfe, Dec. 17, 1966; 1 child, Stephanie Ripley. BS magna cum laude, East Tenn. State U., 1967, MA, 1969; PhD, U. Ky., 1974. Instr. history East Tenn. State U., 1969-73, asst. prof., 1973-77, assoc. prof., 1977-80, prof., 1980—. Author: Lucius Polk Brown and Progressive Food and Drug Control, Tennessee and New York City, 1908-1920, 1978, An Industrial History of Hawkins County, Tennessee, 1983, Kingsport, Tennessee: A Planned American City, 1987, Daughters of Canaan: A Saga of Southern Women, 1995; contbg. author to books, also introductions to books; contbr. articles to profl. jours. Mem. Tenn. Com. for Humanities, 1983-85, exec. coun. mem., 1984-85; mem. Women's Symphony Com., Kingsport, 1990-95; exec. com. Tenn. Commemorative Woman's Suffrage Commn., 1994-95; mem. state rev. bd. Tenn. Hist. Commn., 1995—. Haggin fellow U. Ky., 1972-73; recipient Disting. Faculty award East Tenn. State U., 1977; East Tenn. State U. Found. rsch. award, 1979, Alumni cert. merit, 1984. Mem. AAUP, ACLU (exec. com. Tenn. 1991-92), NOW, Tenn. State Employees Assn., Am. Studies Assn. (John Hope Franklin Prize com. 1992), Am. Hist. Assn., Orgn. Am. Historians, So. Assn. Women Historians (pres. 1983-84, exec. com. 1984-86), So. Hist. Assn. (com. on the status of women 1987, program com. 1988, interim chair of program com. 1988, mem. com. 1993, 94, 95, nominating com. 1994, chair nominating com. 1995, chmn. mem. com. 1997), Smithsonian Assocs., Tenn. Hist. Soc. (editorial bd., 1995—), Coordinating Com. for Women in History, East Tenn. Hist. Soc. (mem. editorial bd. Jour. East Tenn. History), Phi Kappa Phi. Office: ETSU/UT at Kingsport Kingsport TN 37660 also: East Tenn State U Dept History Johnson City TN 37614

WOLFE, MARTHA, elementary education educator; b. Centralia, Ill., Apr. 16, 1944; d. Elmer A. and Dorothy L. (Stonecipher) Krietemeyer; children: Kimberly S., Debora L. BS, So. Ill. U., 1967, MS, 1973, adminstrv. cert., 1987. Cert. elem. tchr., K-12 adminstrn., Ill. Tchr. Title I reading, dir. Cobden (Ill.) Unit Sch. Dist.; presenter in field. Recipient Master Tchr. award Gov. of Ill., 1984. Mem. NEA, Internat. Reading Assn., So. Ill. Reading Assn. (pres., v.p., bd. dirs.), Delta Kappa Gamma (Lambda State scholar 1986). Home: 301 South St Anna IL 62906-1528

WOLFE, MARY JOAN, physician; b. Johnstown, Pa., May 26, 1949; d. Dermot F. and Jean M. (Litzinger) W.; m. Thomas R. Roberts, June 9, 1979; children: Douglas Roberts-Wolfe, Rebecca Roberts-Wolfe. AB in Chemistry, Cornell U., 1971; MD, M.S. Hershey (Pa.) Med. Ctr., 1976. Diplomate Am. Bd. Internal Medicine, Am. Bd. Emergency Medicine. Intern Rochester (N.Y.) Gen. Hosp., 1976-77; resident in internal medicine Westchester County Med. Ctr., Valhalla, N.Y., 1977-79, attending physician emergency dept., 1979-83; practice medicine specializing in internal medicine Ossining, N.Y., 1986—; attending physician emergency room No. Westchester Hosp., Mt. Kisco, N.Y., 1986-89; ind. distributor Biomagnetic Devices, Nikken. Mem. ethics com. Phelps Meml. Hosp., 1994-97, mem. bylaws com., 1989-96, chmn., 1996—. Mem. N.Y. Soc. Internal Medicine, Am. Soc. Internal Medicine. Avocations: gardening, camping, swimming, computers. Home: 6 Cecilia Ln Pleasantville NY 10570-1502 Office: 14 Church St Ossining NY 10562-4821

WOLFE, MAURICE RAYMOND, retired museum director, educator; b. Paris (Neuilly), France, Oct. 13, 1924; s. Guy Ellsworth and Genevieve (Plion) W.; m. Warwick Ellen Griffin, Nov. 4, 1955; 1 child, Shavaun. BA, U. Calif. in Sociology, Berkeley, 1948; MA in Sociology, U. Calif., Berkeley, 1952; postgrad. study, U. Paris Sorbonne, 1951; Cert. of Completion Sch. of Edn., U. Calif., Berkeley, 1954, postgrad., 1955. Rsch. asst. dept. of edn. U. Calif., Berkeley, 1949; tchr. of English and history Castlemont H.S., Oakland, Calif., 1954; lectr. in anthropology, philosophy, sociology and edn. U. Md. Overseas, 1956-59; lectr., instr. in philosopy and sociology U. Md., Munich, 1960-62; faculty mem. Merritt Coll., Oakland, Calif., 1962-88; chmn. dept. behavioral scis. Merritt Coll., Oakland, 1967-87; dir. and founder Merritt Coll. Anthropology Mus., Oakland, 1973-88; rsch. assoc. U. Calif. Lowie Mus. of Anthropology, 1985-89; lectr. Personnel Mgmt. for Execs., U.S. Govt. Sponsored, Berkeley, Calif. 1966-67, San Francisco State U. Dept Anthropology, 1967-68, Calif. State U., Hayward, Dept. Sociology, 1970-71; adj. instr. Monterey Peninsula Coll., Dept. Anthropology, 1990, 91, Hartnell Coll., Salinas, Calif., Chapman U., 1992-95, Golden Gate U., 1995-97. Editor: (jour.) Socioloqus, 1952. Recipient French Govt fellowship, Sorbonne, Paris, 1956; named to list of Great Teachers of Calif., Calif. Assn. Comty. Colls., Santa Barbara, 1984. Home: 33751 E Carmel Valley Rd Carmel Valley CA 93924-9303

WOLFE, MINDY RENÉ, early childhood education educator; b. Norton, Kans., Dec. 10, 1963; d. Roger L. and Celia Dee (Boxberger) W. Student, Colby C.C., 1982-83; BSBA, Ft. Hays State U., 1986, BS in Elem. Edn., 1988. Cert. tchr., Kans.; endorsement in early childhood spl. edn. Associated Colls. Cen. Kans. Tutor Ind. Teaching Svc., Norton, 1989-90; substitute tchr. Unified Sch. Dist. 211, Norton, 1989-90, Unified Sch. Dist. 295, Jennings, Kans., 1989-90, Kiddie Kampus Pre-sch., Norton, 1990; lead tchr. Jolly Junction Child Care Ctr., Lindsborg, Kans., 1990-92; policy adviser, toddler program dir. Children's Ctr., Lindsborg, 1992-93; dir. Newcomer Day Care Ctr., Marquette, Kans., 1993; asst. dir. Children's Ctr., Lindsborg, 1993-94; coord. early childhood spl. needs N.W. Kans. Ednl. Svc. Ctr., Oakley, 1994-95, head start tchr., 1995—. Fundraiser Community Fund, Lindsborg, 1992. Mem. AAUW, Student Kans.-NEA, Kans.-NEA, Nat. Assn. Edn. Young Children, Coun. for Exceptional Children, Kans. Head Start Assn. (staff rep.). Methodist. Avocations: crafts, fashion sewing, stationary bicycle, piano, church choir. Home: 417 Center Ave Oakley KS 67748-1717 Office: NW Kans Ednl Svc Ctr 703 W 2nd St Oakley KS 67748-1258

WOLFE, RALPH STONER, microbiology educator; b. Windsor, Md., July 18, 1921; s. Marshall Richard and Jennie Naomi (Weybright) W.; m. Gretka Margaret Young, Sept. 9, 1950; children: Daniel Binns, Jon Marshall, Sylvia Suzanne. Mem. faculty U. Ill., Urbana, 1953—, prof. microbiology, 1961—; cons. USPHS, Nat. Inst. Gen. Med. Scis. Contbr. microbial physiology rsch. papers to profl. jours. Guggenheim fellow, 1961, 75, USPHS spl. postdoctoral fellow, 1967; recipient Pasteur award Ill. Soc. for Microbiology, 1974, Selman A Waksman Award in Microbiology Nat. Acad. of Sciences, 1995. Mem. NAS (Selman Waksman award in microbiology 1995), Am. Acad. Arts and Scis., Am. Soc. Microbiology (Carski Disting. Teaching award 1971, Abbott Lifetime Achievement award 1996, hon. mem.), Am. Soc. Biol. Chemists. Office: U Ill Dept Microbiology B103 Chem & Life Scis Bldg 601 S Goodwin Ave Urbana IL 61801-3709

WOLFE, RICHARD RATCLIFFE, lawyer; b. Palmyra, Mo., Nov. 29, 1933; s. Francis Dunnan and Marie Ann (Ratcliffe) W.; m. Marilyn Jean McPheron, May 22, 1965; children: Richard Jr., Marie, John, Anne. BS in Engring., Okla. State U., 1955; JD, U. Mich., 1957. Patent atty. Cherry Burrell Corp., Chgo., 1958; designer rocket engring. NASA; tech. asst. U.S. Senate Com. on Aero. and Space Scis., Washington, 1961-64; adminstrv. asst. dir. revenue State of Ill., Springfield, 1964-67, adminstrv. asst. sec. of state, 1967-69; atty. Taylor, Miller, Magner, Sprowl & Hutchings, Chgo., 1969-81, Quinn, Jacobs, Barry & Miller, Chgo., 1981-86, Murchie, Calcutt & Boynton, Traverse City, Mich., 1986—. Author senate report on manned spaced flight program NASA. Dem. nominee 20th dist. U.S. Congress, Ill., 1966. With U.S. Army, 1958-60. Mem. Grand Traverse Yacht Club. Roman Catholic. Avocation: sailing. Office: 539 S Garfield Ave Traverse City MI 49686-3423

WOLFE, ROBERT RICHARD, bioresource engineer, educator; b. Chippewa Falls, Wis., Nov. 9, 1937; s. Lewis Samuel and Bernice (Quale) W.; m. Carol Abrams, June 23, 1974; children: Laura Allene, Richard Kevin. B.S., U. Wis., 1960, M.S., 1961; Ph.D., Purdue U., 1964. Research engr. A.O. Smith Corp., Milw., 1961; research asst. Purdue U., Lafayette, Ind., 1963; asst. prof. U. Wis., Madison, 1964-70; asso. prof. Rutgers U., New Brunswick, N.J., 1970-77; prof. Rutgers U., 1977—. Contbr. numerous articles to profl. jours. NSF grad. fellow, 1962. Mem. Am. Soc. Engring. Edn., Assn. Environ. Engring. Profs., ASME Machine Vision Soc., IEEE Computer Soc., Am. Soc. Agrl. Engrs. (Jour. Article award 1973, 77, 84, 86), Water Environ. Fedn., Inst. Food Technologists, Instruments Soc. Am., AAUP, Sigma Xi, Tau Beta Pi, Phi Kappa Phi, Alpha Epsilon, Alpha Zeta, Delta Theta Sigma. Home: 31 Wagner Rd Stockton NJ 08559-1413 Office: Rutgers U Dept Bioresource Engri New Brunswick NJ 08903

WOLFE, SHEILA A., journalist; b. Chgo.; d. Leonard M. and Rena (Karn) W. B.A., Drake U. Reporter Chgo. Tribune, 1956-73, asst. city editor, 1973-75, day city editor, 1975-79, city editor, 1979-81, met. coordinator, 1981-83, adminstrv. asst. to mng. editor, 1983—; pres. City News Bur. Chgo. 1986-88, 94-96. Recipient Beck award for outstanding profl. performance Chgo. Tribune, 1979; recipient Disting. Service award Drake U., 1982. Mem. Phi Beta Kappa. Home: 71 E Division St Chicago IL 60610-2367 Office: 435 N Michigan Ave Chicago IL 60611

WOLFE, STANLEY, composer, educator; b. N.Y.C., Feb. 7, 1924; s. Bert S. and Dorothy (Sanders) W.; m. Marguerite Wiberg, Aug. 10, 1960; children: Jeffrey, Madeleine. Student, Stetson U., 1946-47, Henry St. Music Sch., 1947-48; B.S. in Composition, Juilliard Sch. Music, 1952, M.S. in Composition, 1955. Faculty Juilliard Sch., N.Y.C., 1955—; dir. extension div. Juilliard Sch., 1956-89; adj. prof. music Lincoln Ctr. campus Fordham U., 1969-73; lectr. N.Y. Philharmonic Pre-Concert Series, 1985—. Prin. compositions include King's Heart; dance score, 1956, Canticle for Strings, 1957, Lincoln Square Overture, 1958, Symphony Number 3, 1959, String Quartet, 1961, Symphony Number 4, 1965, Symphony Number 5 (Lincoln Center Commn.), 1970, Symphony Number 6, 1981; Violin Concerto, 1987. Served with AUS, 1943-46. Recipient award Am. Acad. and Inst. Arts and Letters, 1990; Guggenheim fellow in composition, 1957; Nat. Endowment for Arts grantee, 1969, 70, 77. Mem. ASCAP, Am. Music Center, Am. Symphony Orch. League (Alice Ditson award 1961), U.S. Chess Fedn. Home: 32 Ferndale Dr Hastings On Hudson NY 10706

WOLFE, THAD ALLISON, air force officer; b. Coulee Dam, Wash., Oct. 26, 1942; s. Clyde Allison and Leona (Ruffner) W.; m. Jill Ann Strathern, June 4, 1964; children: Thori, Christian, Molly. BS in Mil. Sci., USAF Acad., 1964; MSEE, U. Wyo., 1969; grad., Squadron Officer Sch., 1972, Air Command and Staff Coll., 1978, Nat. War Coll., 1985; grad. sr. exec. program in nat. and internat. security, Harvard U., 1992. Commd. 2nd lt. USAF, 1964, advanced through grades to lt. gen., 1993; ops. flight comdr. 6950th Security Wing, RAF Sta. Chicksands, Eng., 1965-66; signals intelligence ops. officer 6994th Security Squadron, Pleiku, South Vietnam, 1966-67; devel. engr. Def. Intelligence Agy., Va., 1969-70; instr. pilot, flight comdr., asst. sect. comdr. Vance AFB, Okla., 1970-74; aircrew tng. Castle AFB, Calif., 1974-75; crew comdr., ops. officer 325th Bombardment Squadron, Fairchild AFB, Wash., 1975-77; readiness analyst, chief of pers. and adminstrn., exec. officer to dir., directorate ops. and readiness Hdqs. USAF, Washington, 1978-81; comdr. 9th Bombardment Squadron, Carswell AFB, Tex., 1981; dep. comdr. for standardization and evaluation 1st Combat Evaluation Group, Barksdale AFB, La., 1982; command ctr. sr. contr. Hdqs. Strategic Air Command, Offutt AFB, Nebr., 1982-84; vice comdr., then comdr. 509th Bombardment Wing, Pease AFB, N.H., 1985-88; spl. asst. to comdr. for officer profl. devel. Hdqs. Strategic Air Command, Offutt AFB, Nebr., 1988, dep. dir. nat. strategic target list, joint strategic target planning staff, 1988-90; comdr. Strategic Warfare Ctr., Ellsworth AFB, S.D., 1990-92; asst. dep. dir. for ops. Nat. Security Agy., Ft. George G. Meade, Md., 1992-93; vice comdr. Air Combat Command, Langley AFB, Va., 1993-95; chmn., CEO Internat. Youth Inst., 1996—; chmn. profl. mil. edn. bd. dirs. Air Combat Command, Langley AFB, Va., 1993-95, chief environ. leadership coun., 1993-95; bd. dirs. Air U., Maxwell AFB, Ala., 1995, Inst. Environ. and Natural Resources, Rsch. and Policy, U. Wyo., Laramie, 1995—, Western Rsch. Inst., Laramie, 1995—. Chmn. membership Boy Scouts Am., Rapid City, S.D., 1991. Decorated D.D.S.M., D.S.S.M., Legion of Merit, Bronze Star, Meriorious Svc. medal with three oak leaf clusters, Air medal, Air Force Commendation medal, Vietnam Svc. medal with svc. star, Republic of Vietnam Campaign medal. Mem. USAF Acad. Assn. of Grads., U. Wyo. Alumni Assn., Air Force Assn., Daedalians. Avocations: reading, sports, antiques, gardening. Office: Internat. Youth Inst Inc 901 N Pitt St Ste 250 Alexandria VA 22314-1536

WOLFE, THOMAS KENNERLY, JR., writer, journalist; b. Richmond, Va., Mar. 2, 1931; s. Thomas Kennerly and Helen (Hughes) W.; m. Sheila Berger; children: Alexandra, Thomas. AB, Washington and Lee U., 1951, DLitt (hon.), 1974; PhD in Am. Studies, Yale U., 1957; DFA (hon.), Mpls. Coll. Art, 1971, Sch. of Visual Arts, 1987; LHD (hon.), Va. Commonwealth U., 1983, Southampton Coll. (N.Y.), 1984, Randolph-Macon Coll., 1988, Manhattanville Coll., 1988, Longwood Coll., 1989; DLitt (hon.), St. Andrews Presbyn. Coll., 1990, Johns Hopkins U., 1990, U. Richmond, 1993. Reporter Springfield (Mass.) Union, 1956-59; reporter, Latin Am. corr. Washington Post, 1959-62; city reporter N.Y. Herald Tribune, 1962-66; mag. writer N.Y. World Jour. Tribune, 1966-67; contbg. editor New York mag., 1968-76, Esquire Mag., N.Y.C., from 1977; writer N.Y. Sunday Mag., 1962-66; contbg. artist Harper's Mag., N.Y.C., 1978-81. One-man show of drawings include Maynard Walker Gallery, N.Y.C., 1965, Tunnel Gallery, N.Y.C., 1974; author: The Kandy-Kolored Tangerine-Flake Streamline Baby, 1965, The Electric Kool-Aid Acid Test, 1968, The Pump House Gang, 1968, Radical Chic and Mau-mauing the Flak Catchers, 1970, The Painted Word, 1975, Mauve Gloves and Madmen, Clutter and Vine, 1976, The Right Stuff, 1979 (Am. Book award 1980), In Our Time, 1980, From Bauhaus to Our House, 1981, The Purple Decades: A Reader, 1982, The Bonfire of the Vanities, 1987; editor, contbr. The New Journalism, 1973; contbr. articles to Esquire Mag., others. Recipient Front Page awards for humor and fgn. news reporting Washington Newspaper Guild, 1961, Soc. Mag. Writers award for excellence, 1970, Frank Luther Mott Rsch. award, 1973, Harold D. Vursell Meml. award Am. Acad. and Inst. Arts and Letters, 1980, Columbia Journalism award, 1980, Nat. Sculpture Soc. citation for art history, 1980, John Dos Passos award, 1984, Gari Melchers medal, 1986, Benjamin Pierce Cheney medal Ea. Wash. U., 1986, Washington Irving medal St. Nicholas Soc., 1986, Theodore Roosevelt medal Theodore Roosevelt Assn., 1990, Wilbur Cross medal Yale Grad. Sch. Alumni Assn., 1990, St. Louis Literary award, 1990, Quinnipiac Coll. Pres. award, 1993; named Va. Laureate for Lit., 1977. Office: Farrar Straus & Giroux Inc 19 Union Sq W New York NY 10003-3304*

WOLFE, TOWNSEND DURANT, III, art museum director, curator; b. Hartsville, S.C., Aug. 15, 1935; m. Jane Rightor Lee; 1 child, Zibilla Lee; children (by previous marriage): Juliette Elizabeth, Mary Bryan, Townsend Durant. BFA, Atlanta Art Inst., 1958; MFA, Cranbrook Acad. Art, 1959;

postgrad, Harvard Inst. Arts Adminstrn., 1970; DFA (hon.), Memphis Coll. Art, 1996. Instr. Atlanta Art Assn., 1956-59, Memphis Acad. Art, 1959-64, Scarsdale Studio Workshop and Seamen Inst., N.Y.C., 1964-65; dir. Ford Found. Fund for Advancement of Edn. Wooster Community Art Ctr., Danbury, Conn., 1965-68; lectr. art U. Ark., Little Rock, 1969—; dir., chief curator The Ark. Arts Ctr., Little Rock, 1968—; sec. Ark. Arts Ctr. Found., 1973—; pres. Ark. Consortium Arts, 1976-80; pres. Ark. Arts in Edn. Adv. Coun., 1977-79; bd. dirs. Mid-Am. Arts Alliance, 1982-89; mem. adv. bd. Ark. Artists Registry, 1986—, Ark. Repertory Theatre, 1976-84; reviewer Inst. Mus. Svcs., 1984-87, examiner mus. assessment program, 1985-87; overview panel Nat. Endowment for Arts, 1986-88, rev. panel utilization of mus. resources, 1986, grant rev. panel conservation and collection maintenance, 1987; curator 20th Century Am. Sculpture Exhbn., First Ladies' Garden, The White House, 1995, Powerful Expressions: Recent American Drawings Nat. Acad. Design, N.Y., 1996. One-man shows include Madison Gallery, N.Y.C., 1961, U. Miss., 1963, Soutwestern U., Memphis, 1964, Ark. State U., Jonesboro, 1964, 70; group shows include Ball State Tchrs. Coll., Muncie, Ind., 1959, 63,65, 67, Ann. New Eng. Exhbn., 1966-67, Wadsworth Atheneum, Hartford, Conn., 1967, Audubon Artists, N.Y.C., 1968; represented in permanent collections Ark. State U., Union Planters Nat. Bank, Memphis, Mint Mus. Art, Charlotte, N.C., East Tenn. State U., others; author: Trustee Handbook, 1978, Appraiser Handbook, 1979, Selections from the Permanent Collection of the Arkansas Arts Center Foundation catalogue, 1983, Twentieth Century American Drawings from the Arkansas Arts Center Foundation Collection, 1984, American Drawings, 1986, National Drawings Invitational, 1986, 87, 88, 91, 92, 93, 94, 96, National Objects Invitational, 1987, 88, 89, 91, National Crafts Invitational, 1987, Picasso: The Classical Years 1917-1925, 1987, Carroll Cloar Arkansas Collections, 1987, Revelations Drawing/America catalogue, 1988, The Face, 1988, 90, American Abstract Drawings, 1989, The Figure, 1990, Will Barnet Drawings: 1930-90, 1991, Silverpoint Etc., 1992, Edward Faiers Retrospective, 1994, exhbn. catalogue Memphis Coll. Art, Paul Zwietnig-Rotterdam, 1995, Hans Burkhardt Drawings: 1932-1989, 1996, Large Drawings and Objects, 1996, various catalog essays. Presdl. appt. Nat. Mus. Svcs. Bd., 1995, Elizabeth Found. for the Arts, 1995, Nat. Coun. on the Arts, 1995. Recipient 20 awards for painting, 1958-68, Winthrop Rockefeller Meml. award, 1973, James R. Short award Southeastern Mus. Conf., 1981, Individual Achievement award Ark. Mus. Assn., 1984, Ark. Art Edn. Advocacy award, 1985, Promethean award for excellence in the arts March of Dimes, 1986, Chevalier dans l'ordre des Arts et Lettres, 1988, Diamond award Ark. chpt. Pub. Rels. Soc. Am., 1996, Dr. Martin Luther King Jr. Cmty. Svc. award, 1996, Disting. Svc. award outside the profession Nat. Art Edn. Assn., 1997. Mem. Assn. Art Mus. Dirs., Assn. Am. Museums (membership com. 1982-88, accreditation com., sr. examiner 1972—). Democrat. Episcopalian. Office: The Ark Arts Ctr MacArthur Park 9th and Commerce Little Rock AR 72202

WOLFE, VERDA NELL, pension consultant, financial planner; b. Sulphur Springs, Tex., Jan. 31, 1927; d. Marvin Alvin and Winnie Davis (Bass) Hamiter; m. James Braddy Wolfe, May 3, 1947; children: James Gordon, William Gregory, Charles Gary. Student, Baylor U., 1948-52, Tex. Tech U., 1974-76. CLU, CFP; cert. pension cons. Estate analyst Estate Fin. Planning Svc., Lubbock, Tex., 1973-76, Planning Cons., Lubbock, 1977-81; pres. DDRW Fin. Svcs., Lubbock, 1982-85, Pension Concepts and Administration, Lubbock, 1986—. Mem. Am. Soc. CLU and ChFC (chpt. pres. 1988-89), Inst. Cert. Fin. Planners, Am. Soc. Pension Actuaries and Cons. Avocations: music, oil painting, gardening. Home: 2125 57th St Lubbock TX 79412-2625 Office: Pension Concepts & Adminstn 2811A 74th St Lubbock TX 79423-1437

WOLFE, WILLIAM JEROME, librarian, English language educator; b. Chgo., Feb. 24, 1927; s. Fred Wiley and Helen Dorothea (Lovaas) W.; m. ViviAnn Lundin O'Connell, June 25, 1960 (div. 1962); 1 child, Lund. *Son Lund, Navy veteran and graduate of the University of Arizona, is a computer programmer. Father Fred Wolfe, World War II U.S. Army veteran, worked in the Railway Mail Service 1920-61 and practiced law in Chicago 1927-61. Grandparents Ludvig Lovaas (cabinetmaker) and Anna Anderson emigrated from Norway in 1888. Grandfather Alfred Wolfe, graduate of Tri-State Normal College, taught school in Kosciusko County, Indiana, 1897-1930. Great-grandfather James Wiley, from Ohio, served in the Union Army at the Battle of Shiloh. Great-great-great-grandfather Garret Wolfe served in the Pennsylvania militia during the American Revolution.* AB, U. Chgo., 1948; BA, Roosevelt U., Chgo., 1953; MEd, Chgo. State U., 1963; AA with high honors, Pima C.C., 1992; BA in Art magna cum laude, U. Ariz., 1994. Tchr. English John Marshall High Sch., Chgo., 1956-60; libr. Safford Jr. High Sch., Tucson, Ariz., 1961-71, Santa Rita High Sch., Tucson, 1971-75, Tucson High Sch., 1975-87; tutor Eastside Ctr., Tucson Adult Lit. Vols., 1988—, supr., 1993—. Co-founder Tucson Classic Guitar Soc., 1969-72; docent U. Ariz. Mus. Art, Tucson, 1989—; mem. adv. bd. U. Ariz. Sch. Music, 1995—; singer U. Ariz. Collegium Musicum, 1981-96, Sons of Orpheus Men's Chorus, Lane Justus Chorale. With U.S. Army, 1945-46, ETO. Mem. Sons of Norway, U. Ariz. Pres. Club, U. Ariz. Hon. Fellows Soc., Nat. Assn. Scholars, Assn. Lit. Scholars and Critics, Amnesty Internat., Human Life Found., Norsemen's Fedn., Phi Kappa Phi. Republican. Mem. Ch. of Christ Scientist. Avocations: poetry writing, drawing, singing, piano, calligraphy. Home: 8460 E Rosewood Tucson AZ 85710 *Through every turn of events, an always reliable and inspiring way to make a pleasing composition out of life consists in joyous thankfulness to the Creator for the love of family, wise counsel of teachers, and kind encouragement of friends.*

WOLFEN, WERNER F., lawyer; b. Berlin, May 15, 1930; came to U.S., 1939; s. Martin and Ruth Eva (Hamburger) W.; m. Mary Glasier, July 1, 1956; children: Richard, James, Lawrence (dec.). BS, U. Calif., Berkeley, 1950, JD, 1953. Bar: Calif. 1953. Assoc. Irell & Manella, L.A., 1953-57, ptnr., 1957—; co-chmn. exec. com. Irell & Manella, 1983-97; bd. dirs. Broadion Corp. Trustee UCLA Found.; pres. L.A. Goal, 1994—. Mem. ABA. Democrat. Jewish. Office: Irell & Manella 1800 Avenue Of The Stars Los Angeles CA 90067-4212

WOLFENDEN, RICHARD VANCE, biochemistry educator; b. Oxford, Eng., May 17, 1935; s. John Hulton and Josephine (Vance) W.; m. Anita Gaunitz, May 25, 1965; children: Peter, John. BA, Princeton U., 1956, Exeter Coll., Oxford U., Eng., 1958; MA, Exeter Coll., Oxford U., Eng., 1958; PhD, Rockefeller Inst., 1964. Asst. prof. chemistry Princeton U., N.J., 1964-70; assoc. prof. biochemistry U. N.C., Chapel Hill, 1970-73, prof. biochemistry, 1973-83, alumni disting. prof., 1983—; vis. fellow Exeter Coll., Oxford, 1969; vis. prof. U. Montpellier, France, 1976; mem. molecular biology panel NSF, Washington, 1973-76; mem. bio-organic and natural products study sect. NIH, Washington, 1981-86; cons. Schering Plough Corp., 1997—. Mem. editorial bd. Bioorganic Chemistry, 1983—, Biomed. Chem. Letters, 1993—. Fellow AAAS; mem. Am. Chem. Soc., Am. Soc. Biol. Chemists. Democrat. Home: 1307 Mason Farm Rd Chapel Hill NC 27514-4609 Office: U North Carolina Dept Biochemistry Chapel Hill NC 27514

WOLFENSON, AZI U., electrical, mechanical and industrial engineer, consultant; b. Rumania, Aug. 1, 1933; came to Peru, 1937; s. Samuel G. and Polea S. (Ulanowski) W.; m. Rebeca Sterental, Jan. 10, 1983; 1 child, Michael Ben; children by previous marriage: Ida, Jeannette, Ruth, Moises, Alex. Mech., Elec. Engr., Universidad Nacional de Ingenieria, Peru, 1955; MSc in Indsl. Engring., U. Mich., 1966; Indsl. Engr., U. Nacional de Ingenieria, Peru, 1967; PhD in Engring. Mgmt., Pacific Western U., 1983, PhD in Engring. Energy, Century U., 1985, D in Philosophy of Engring. (hon.) World U. Roundtable, Ariz., 1987. Power engr. Peruvian Trading Co., 1956-57; gen. mgr. AMSA Ingenieros S.A., 1957-60; prof. Universidad Nacional de Ingenieria, Peru, 1956-72, dean mech. and elec. engring., 1964-66, dean indsl. engring., 1967-72; dir. SWSA Automotive Parts, Peru, 1954-77; project mgr. Nat. Fin. Corp., Cofide, 1971-73; Peruvian dir. Corporacion Andina de Fomento, CAF, 1971-73; rep. in Peru, CAF, 1973-74; pres. DESPRO cons. firm, 1973-76; exec. pres. Electroperu, 1976-80; cons. engr., 1964—; dir. Tech. Transference Studies, 1971-72. Mem. Superior Coun. Electricity, 1964-66; metal mech. expert for andean group, 1970-71; Nat. Coun. Fgn. Investment and Tech. Transfer, 1972-73; councilman at the Concejo Provincial De Lima, 1969-75; mem. Consultive Coun. Ministry Economy and Fin., 1973-74; pres. Peruvian Jewish Community, 1966-70, Peruvian Hebrew Sch., 1976-78; promoter, co-founder, gen. mgr. La Republica Newspaper, Peru, 1981; pres. PROA project promotion AG, Switzerland, 1982—; chmn. Inst. for the Devel. of the Americas, Inc., Fla., 1993—; co-founder La Republica, 1981, El Popular, 1983, El Nacional, 1985, Todo Sport, 1993, El Chino, 1994, pres. bd. dirs., newspapers; chmn. Inst. Devel. Ams., Inc., Fla., 1993—; chmn. editl. bd. Sport Peru, 1994—; v.p. bd. dirs. Island Way Cmty. Assn., 1995-97; mem. exec. bd. dirs. Miami State Israel Bonds, 1997. Recipient awards Order Merit for Disting. Svcs., Peru, 1980, Disting. by City Coun. of Huancayo, 1980, Trujillo, 1978, Huaral, 1979, Piura, 1980, Disting. Contbn. award City of Lima, 1970, 71, Disting. Contbn. to Elec. Devel. in Peru, 1979, el Sol Radiante City Hall of Magdalena, Peru, 1995, others; disting. by the American Nuclear Soc. for contbn. to the advancement of nuclear sci. and tech., 1995—; named 1979 Exec., Gente mag., recognition Israel Govt., 1967, Disting. Comision Integracion Electrica Regional, CIER, medal, 1984, Disting. El Sol Radiante award City Hall of Magdalena, Peru, 1995. Fellow Inst. Prodn. Engrs., Brit. Inst. Mgmt.; mem. Colegio Ingenieros Peru, Instituto Peruano de Ingenieros Mecanicos (pres. 1965-66, v.p. 1967, dir. 1969, 70, 76), Asociacion Electrotechnica del Peru, ASME, AIIE (sr.), MTM Assn., Am. Soc. Engring. Edn., Am. Inst. Mgmt. Sci., AAAS, Assn. Mgmt. Sci. (dir. 1968), Asociacion Peruana Avance Ciencia, Inst. Adminstrv. Mgmt., British Inst. Mgmt., Am. Nuclear Soc. (vice chmn. 1988, 90, chmn. Swiss sect. 1991-93, Significant Contbn. to Advancement of Nuc. Sci. award 1995), Alumni Assn. of the Mich., Pacific Western and Century U., United Writers Assn., Swiss Soc. Writers, Swiss Sect. PEN Club Internat., others. Author: Work Communications, 1966, Programmed Learning, 1966, Production Planning and Control, 1968, Transfer of Technology, 1971, National Electrical Development, 1977, Energy and Development, 1979, El Gran Desafio, 1981, Hacia una politica economica alternativa, 1982, The Power of Communications: The Media, 1987. Contbr. articles to newspapers and jours. Clubs: Club der 200, FCL, Hebraica. Home: 3781 NE 208th Ter Miami FL 33180-3835

WOLFERT, RUTH, Gestalt therapist; b. N.Y.C., Nov. 10, 1933; d. Ira and Helen (Herschdorfer) W. BS summa cum laude, Columbia U., 1967, post-grad., 1966-68. Pvt. practice N.Y.C., 1972—; dir. Action Groups, N.Y.C., 1974-76, The Chrysalis Inst., N.Y.C., 1997—, Chrysalis, N.Y.C., 1996—; mem. faculty, mem. coordinating bd. Women's Interart Ctr., N.Y.C., 1971-75, also bd. dirs.; presenter Stockton (N.J.) State Coll., 1974-75; mem. faculty Inst. for Experiential Learning and Devel., 1988-92, Woodstock U., 1989-91, Gestalt Inst., Atlanta, 1989—; presenter in field. Author: The Broken Doll: A Survivor's Journey Into Life, 1997; contbg. author: (booklet) A Consumer's Guide to Non-Sexist Therapy, 1978. Mem. Assn. Humanist Psychology (bd. dirs. ea. regional network 1981-87, pres. 1985-87), N.Y. Isnt. Gestalt Therapy (trainer 1979—, chair workshops program 1979-83, co-chair conf. 1983-85, brochure com. 1987-95, interim exec. com. 1988-90, conf. com. 1989-91, v.p. 1993-95), Assn. Transpersonal Psychology (co-chair N.Y. discussion group 1991-92), Assn. Advancement Gestalt Therapy (bd. dirs. 1993—, co-chair Women's Issues in Gestalt Therapy interest group 1993—, conf. com. 1993-95). Office: 200 E 32nd St New York NY 10016-6306

WOLFF, ALAN WILLIAM, lawyer; b. Malden, Mass., June 12, 1942; s. Louis K. and Etta (Bernstein) W.; m. Helene N. Novick, Mar. 3, 1965; children: Anna, Jeremy, Ewan. AB, Harvard U., 1963; LLB, Columbia U., 1966. Bar: Mass. 1967, N.Y. 1966, U.S. Supreme Ct. 1971, D.C. 1972, U.S. Ct. Appeals (fed. cir.) 1982, Ct. Internat. Trade 1993. Atty., office of gen. counsel U.S. Treasury Dept., Washington, 1968-73; dep. gen. counsel Spl. Trade Rep. (now U.S. Trade Rep.), Washington, 1973-74, gen. counsel, 1974-76, dep. spl. trade rep. (with rank of ambassador), 1977-79; ptnr. Verner, Liipfert et al, Washington, 1979-85; ptnr. Dewey, Ballantine, Bushby, Palmer & Wood (now Dewey Ballantine), Washington, 1985—, mng. ptnr., 1992—; mem. Nat. Rsch. Coun. Bd. on Sci., Tech. and Econ. Policy, 1997—; mem. Pres.'s Adv. Com. for Trade Negotiations, 1980-82, U.S. Trade Rep.'s Svcs. Policy Adv. Com., 1980-86 (all located in Washington, D.C.); mem. adv. bd. Inst. for Internat. Econ., 1981—, Econ. Strategy Inst., 1990—; nat. adv. bd. Ctr. for Nat. Policy, 1988—; trustee Monterey Inst. Internat. Studies, 1992—; mem. Coun. Fgn. Rels., 1979—. Co-author: The Microelectronics Race, 1987, Steel and the State, 1988, Conflict Among Nations: Trade Policy for the 1990s, 1992; contbr. articles to profl. jours. Mem. ABA, Am. Soc. Internat. Law. Democrat. Unitarian. Office: Dewey Ballantine 1775 Pennsylvania Ave NW Washington DC 20006-4605 also: 1301 Avenue Of The Americas New York NY 10019-6022

WOLFF, BRIAN RICHARD, metal manufacturing company executive; b. L.A., Dec. 11, 1955; s. Arthur Richard and Dorothy Virginia (Johnson) W.; divorced; children: Ashley Rachael, Taryn Nicole. BSBA, Calif. State U., Chico, 1980; postgrad., U. Phoenix, 1990—. Registered counseling practitioner, Calif., 1996, guidance practitioner, Calif., 1996; ordained min. Progressive Universal Life Ch., 1996. Sales rep. Federated Metals Corp./ASARCO, Long Beach, Calif., 1980-82, dist. sales mgr., 1983-84; sales mgr. Copper Alloys Corp., Beverly Hills, Calif., 1982-83; dir. mktg. Federated-Fry Metals/Cookson, Long Beach, Industry and Paramount, Calif., 1984-87; regional sales mgr. Colonial Metals Co., L.A., 1987-91; nat. sales mgr. Calif. Metal X/Metal Briquetting Co., L.A., 1991-93; sales engr. Ervin Industries, Inc., Ann Arbor, Mich., 1993-95; sales mgr. Southbay Bronze, San Jose, Calif., 1996—; tech. sales mgr. GSP Metals & Chems. Co., 1987-91; cons. sales Calif. Metal Exch., L.A., 1987-91, Atlas Pacific Inc., Bloomington, Calif., 1993—; sales mgr. Southbay Bronze, San Jose, Calif., 1996—; dealer Mason Shoe Co., 1996—. Mem. citizens adv. com. on bus. Calif. Legis., 1983; ordained min. Universal Life, 1996. Mem. Non Ferrous Founders Soc., Am. Foundrymen Soc., Calif. Cast Metals Assn., Steel Structures Painting Coun., Am. Electroplaters Soc., Soc. Die Cast Engrs., NRA. Republican. Presbyterian. Avocations: scuba diving, tennis, freshwater fishing, trap shooting, hunting.

WOLFF, CHRISTOPH JOHANNES, music historian, educator; b. Solingen, Germany, May 24, 1940; came to U.S., 1970; s. Hans Walter and Annemarie (Halstenbach) W.; m. Barbara Mahrenholz, Aug. 28, 1964; children: Katharina, Dorothea, Stephanie. Ed., U. Berlin, 1960-63, U. Freiburg, Germany, 1963-65; Dr. Phil., U. Erlangen, Germany, 1966. Lectr. U. Erlangen, 1966-69; asst. prof. U. Toronto, Ont., Can., 1968-70; assoc. prof. musicology Columbia U., 1970-73, prof., 1973-76; prof. musicology Harvard U., 1976—, William Powell Mason prof., 1985—, dept. chmn., 1980-88, 90-91; vis. prof. Princeton U., 1973, 75; hon. prof. U. Freiburg, Germany, 1990—; acting dir. Harvard U. Libr., 1991-92; dean Grad Sch. Arts and Scis., 1992—. Author: Der Stile Antico in der Musik J.S. Bachs, 1968, The String Quartets of Haydn, Mozart, and Beethoven, 1980, Bach Compendium, 7 vols., 1986-89, Bach: Essays on His Life and Music, 1991, Mozart's Requiem, 1994; contbr. numerous articles to profl. jours.; editor: Bach-Jahrbuch, 1974—; critical edits. of music by, Scheidt, Buxtehude, Bach, Mozart, and Hindemith. Recipient Dent medal Royal Mus. Assn., London, 1978. Fellow Am. Acad. Arts and Scis.; Mem. Internat. Musicol. Soc., Am. Musicol. Soc., Gesellschaft fuer Musikforschung. Home: 182 Washington St Belmont MA 02178-3560 Office: Harvard U University Hall 18 Cambridge MA 02138-5723

WOLFF, CHRISTOPHER See KENDALL, CHRISTOPHER

WOLFF, CYNTHIA GRIFFIN, humanities educator, author; b. St. Louis, Aug. 20, 1936; d. James Thomas and Eunice (Heyn) Griffin; m. Robert Paul Wolff, June 9, 1962 (div. 1986); children—Patrick Gideon, Tobias Barrington; m. Nicholas J. White, May 21, 1988. B.A., Radcliffe Coll., 1958; Ph.D., Harvard U., 1965. Asst. prof. English Manhattanville Coll., Purchase, N.Y., 1968-70; asst. prof. English U. Mass., Amherst, 1971-74, assoc. prof., 1974-76, prof., 1976-80; prof. humanities MIT, Cambridge, 1980-85, Class of 1922 prof. lit. and writing, 1985—; mem. exec. com. for Am. lit. MLA, 1979-81; mem. selection bd. Literary Classics Am., 1981—; mem. exec. bd. for fgn. grants Am. Council Learned Socs., 1981-84. Author: (literary criticism) Samuel Richardson, 1972, (literary biography) A Feast of Words: The Triumph of Edith Wharton, 1977, 2d edit., 1995, Emily Dickinson, 1986; bd. editors Am. Quar., 1979-84. AAUW grantee, 1964-65; NEH grantee, 1975-76, 1983-84, 97-98; Am. Council Learned Socs. grantee, 1984-85. Mem. Am. Studies Assn. Home: 416 Commonwealth Ave Apt 619 Boston MA 02215-2812 Office: MIT Dept Humanities 14N-226 Cambridge MA 02139

WOLFF, DEBORAH H(OROWITZ), lawyer; b. Phila., Apr. 6, 1940; d. Samuel and Anne (Manstein) Horowitz; m. Morris H. Wolff, May 15, 1966 (div.); children: Michelle Lynn, Lesley Anne; m. Walter Allan Levy, June 7, 1987. BS, U. Pa., 1962, MS, 1966; postgrad., Sophia U., Tokyo, 1968; JD, Villanova U., 1979; LLM, 1988. Tchr. Overbrook High Sch., Phila., 1962-68; homebound tchr. Lower Merior Twp., Montgomery County, 1968-71; asst. dean U. Pa., Phila., 1975-76; law clk. Stassen, Kostos and Mason, Phila., 1977-78; assoc. Spencer, Sherr, Moses and Zuckerman, Norristown, Pa., 1980-81; ptnr. Wolff Assocs., 1981—; lectr. law and estate planning, Phila., 1980—; Recipient 3d Ann. Community Svc. award Phila. Mayor's Com. for Women, 1984; named Pa. Heroine of Month, Ladies Home Jour., July 1984. Founder Take a Brother Program; bd. dirs. Germantown Jewish Ctr.; high sch. sponsor World Affairs Club, Phila., 1962-68; mem. exec. com., sec. bd. Crime Prevention Assn., Phila., 1965—; bd. dirs. U. Pa. Alumnae Bd., Phila., 1965—, pres. bd. dirs., 1993—, v.p. organized classes, bd. crime prevention; chmn. urban conf. Boys Club Am., 1987; active Hahnaman Brain Tumor Rsch. Bd.; v.p., bd. dirs. Crime Prevention. Home and Office: 422 W Mermaid Ln Philadelphia PA 19118-4204

WOLFF, DEE IVONA, artist; b. Springfield, Minn., June 25, 1948; d. Herbert Edmond and Ivona Francis (Steffel) Ricke; m. Leonard Joe Wolff, Aug. 24, 1968. BA, U. Houston, 1971; cert. of art, Glassell Sch., Mus. Fine Arts, Houston, 1976; student, C.G. Jung Ctr., Houston, 1973-85, Oomoto Sch. Traditional Art, Japan, 1984. Fellow MacDowell Colony, Peterborough, N.H., 1987. One-man shows include Galveston (Tex.) Art Ctr., 1977, 90, Covo de Iongh Gallery, Houston, 1977, Watson de Nagy Gallery, Houston, 1978, Watson Gallery, Houston, 1981, 85, Tex. A&M U. Gallery, College Station, 1986, Marvin Seline Gallery, Austin, 1986, 88, Stephen F. Austin U. Gallery, Nacogdoches, Tex., 1987, Diverseworks Art-space, Houston, 1989, 90, Mus. S.E. Tex., Beaumont, 1990, C.G. Jung Ctr., 1990, D'Art, Dallas, 1990; numerous group exhbns. including Art League Houston, 1976, 96, U. Ill., 1977, Moody Gallery, Houston, 1978, Newport Harbor Art Mus., Calif., 1978, Bklyn. Mus., 1979, Witte Meml. Mus., San Antonio, 1979, So. Meth. U., Dallas, 1980, San Antonio Art Inst. Gallery, 1981, Stavanger Kunstforening, Norway, 1982, Waco (Tex.) Art Ctr., 1982, Salzburger Kunstverein, Austria, 1983-84, Houston Art League, 1983, 87, 96, Dallas Pub. Libr., 1983, Mus. Fine Arts, Houston, 1985, Midtown Arts Ctr., Houston, 1985, Galveston Art Ctr., 1986, 92, 93, 96, Aspen (Colo.) Art Mus., 1987, Judy Youens Gallery, Houston, 1987, 91, Mpls. Coll. Art & Design, 1988, Nat. Mus. Women in the Arts, Washington, 1988, Art Mus. SE Tex., Beaumont, 1989, 96, Longview (Tex.) Mus. and Art Ctr., 1989, Lynn Goode Gallery, Houston, 1990, 91, 96, Art Mus. South Tex., Corpus Christi, 1991, 96, Fine Arts Ctr., Lubbock, 1991, 96, Dallas Mus. Fine Arts, 1991, Tex. Fine Arts Assn., 1991, Karen Lanning Gallery, Houston, 1992, Women & Their Work Gallery, Austin, 1992, 96, Hooks-Epstein Gallery, Houston, 1993, 94, U. Tex. Med. Sch., 1993, Diverseworks Artspace, Houston, 1993, C.G. Jung Ctr., Houston, 1995, Houston Lawndale Art Ctr., 1996, Yekaterinburg, St. Petersburg, Russia, Tomsk, Rostovondon, Nizhnily-Novgorod, Russia, 1996, Slover McCutcheon Gallery, Houston, Concordia U., Austin, 1997, Nat. Art League, Douglaston, N.Y., 1997, Dallas Visual Art Ctr., Dallas, 1997; represented in permanent collections Aamoco Corp., Denver, Internat. Materials Mgmt. Engrs., Houston, Wilson Industries, Houston, Marriott Hotels, Jacksonville, Fla., Park Hotel, Charlotte, N.C., Oomoto, Kameoka City, Kyoto, Japan, Enron Corp., Houston, Mus. SE Tex., Art Mus. South Tex., Corpus Christi, Mus. Fine Arts, Houston; commd. St. Philip Presbyn. Ch., Houston, 23 stained glass windows St. Theresea of Lisieux, Sugarland, Tex., Corpus Christi Pub. Libr.; visual design stage sets Kabbalah; subject radio and TV interviews. Bd. dirs. Diverseworks Artspace, Houston, 1989-91, mem. artists adv. bd., 1990-91. Interdisciplinary Arts grantee Nat. Endowment Arts, 1988, Visual Arts Fellowship grantee, 1989; N.Y. State Coun. on Arts grantee, 1989; recipient Spirit of Am. Woman award Houston Performing Arts Soc. and J.C. Penney, 1989. Avocations: reading, yoga, gardening, walking, conversation. Studio: 421 Arlington St Houston TX 77007-2617

WOLFF, DERISH MICHAEL, economist, company executive; b. Boston, May 14, 1935; s. Nathan and Ruth Mae (Derish) W.; m. Maureen Robinson; children: Jeffrey Scott, Hayley Beth Kissel. BA, U. Pa., 1957; MBA, Harvard U., 1959. Fin. analyst Sigmund Werner, Inc., Belleville, N.J., 1959-61; devel. economist Louis Berger, Inc., East Orange, N.J., 1961-65, chief economist, 1965-67, v.p., 1968-74, exec. v.p., 1975-82, pres., CEO, 1982—; dir. Louis Berger Internat., Inc., Bronkonsult, CHELBI, Ammann & Whitney, Va. Maintenance Svcs., Inc.; guest lectr. Fgn. Svc. Inst., Newark Inst. Tech., U. Nev., MIT, Harvard U., Rutgers U., U. Denver; mem. Bretton Woods Com., 1987—. Mem. editl. bd. Modern Engring. Tech, 1978-80, Nat. Devel.-Modern Govt., 1972-79, Constrn. Bus. Review, 1991—. Mem. adv. com. to bd. trustees, mem. bldg. scis. challenge com. N.J. Inst. Tech.; class chmn. U. Pa. Ann. Giving, 1975-82, class pres., 1982-92; mem. U.S. Presdl. Trade Del. to Japan, 1986; mem. indsl. sector adv. com. Dept. of Commerce, 1988-92; mem. adv. com. U.S. Trade and Devel. Program, 1989-92. Mem. Am. Cons. Engrs. Coun. (chair internat. engring. com. 1983-85, vice chair 1986-93), Internat. Engring. and Constrn. Industries Coun. (del. 1986, 87, chmn. 1988-90, Bldg. Futures Coun. 1990—, vice chair 1994—), Ctr. for Strategic and Internat. Studies (steering group/GATT negotiations 1989), Phi Beta Kappa. Jewish. Clubs: Harvard, Penn. Office: Louis Berger Group 100 Halsted St East Orange NJ 07018-2612

WOLFF, EDWARD, physician; b. N.Y.C., Apr. 15, 1941; s. Julius and Molly W.; m. Marilyn Alice Pels; children: Shanna, Loryn, Kimberly. BS, Muhlenberg Coll., 1958; MD, Georgetown U., 1966. Intern U. Ala. Hosp., Brimingham, 1966-67; resident N.Y. Med. Coll., N.Y.C., 1967-71; physician pvt. practice, Great Neck, N.Y., 1976—; sr. asst. attending North Shore U. Hosp., Manhasset, N.Y.; attending physician St. Francis Hosp. Heart Ctr., Roslyn, N.Y. Contbr. articles to profl. jours. Fellow Am. Coll. Physicians; mem. AMA, N.Y. State Med. Soc., NAssau County Med. Soc. Office: 75 S Middle Neck Rd Great Neck NY 11021-3445

WOLFF, EDWARD A., electronics engineer; b. Chgo., Oct. 31, 1929; s. Samuel S. and Lillian P. W.; m. Anna Lee Tishk, June 19, 1951; children: David Steven, Elliot Marvin, Susan Toby. B.S.E.E., U. Ill., 1951; M.S., 1953; Ph.D., U. Md., 1961. Electronic scientist Naval Research Lab., Washington, 1951-54; project engr. Md. Electronic Mfg. Corp., Litton Industries, College Park, Md., 1956-59, Electromagnetic Research Corp., College Park, Md., 1959-61; engring. mgr. Aero Geo Astro-Keltec Industries/Aiken Industries, Alexandria, Va., 1961-67; v.p. Geotronics, Inc., Falls Church, Va., 1967-71; supervisory electronics engr. NASA Goddard Space Flight Ctr., Greenbelt, Md., 1971—; system mgr. Network TDRS System, 1981-89, MRJ, Inc., Oakton, Va., 1989—; instr. Tex. A&M U., 1962. Author: Spacecraft Technology, 1962, Antenna Analysis, 1966, 2d edit., 1988, Geoscience Instrumentation, 1974, Urban Alternatives, 1975, Microwave Engineering and Systems Applications, 1988. Mem. Md. Gov.'s Sci. Resources Adv. Bd., 1963-67; pres. U.S. Environment and Resources Council, 1972-75; treas. World Evironment and Resources Council, 1975-81. Served with U.S. Army, 1954-56. Fellow IEEE (dir. 1971-72), Washington Acad. Scis.; mem. AIAA, Nat. Soc. Profl. Engrs., Eta Kappa Nu, Sigma Tau, Phi Eta Sigma. Home: 1021 Cresthaven Dr Silver Spring MD 20903-1602 Office: MRJ Inc 10560 Arrowhead Dr Fairfax VA 22030-7305 *Everything I have done has been with the help of others. In return, as I have acquired management responsibilities, a primary objective has been to help others achieve their goals.*

WOLFF, EDWIN RAY, construction engineer; b. Continental, Ohio, Mar. 24, 1933; s. Ray Simeon and Datha Ruth (Donaldson) W.; m. Elizabeth I. Sutterlin, Feb. 16, 1963; children: Sandra Jean, Donald Scott. BSME, U. Toledo, 1969. Registered profl. engr., Ohio. Mem. design staff City of Ft. Lauderdale, Fla., 1965-67; mem. design/spl. orders staff Devilbliss Co., Toledo, 1967-69; engineer, mem. R & D staff Toledo Scale, 1969-70; design/constrn. engr. Lucas County Engr., Toledo, 1970—; cons. G.A.F., Inc., Oregon, Ohio, 1980—. Vol. Spl. Olympics, Lucas County, 1989—; trustee, bd. elders Fairgreen Ch., Toledo, 1975—; trustee Beneficial Union Pittsburg, 1986—; bd. dirs. Lucas County ARC. With Combat Engrs. Corps, 1956-58. Mem. Phi Kappa Chi, Pi Kappa Alpha. Democrat. Presbyterian. Home: 4312 Grantley Rd Toledo OH 43613-3738

WOLFF, ELEANOR BLUNK, actress; b. Bklyn., July 10, 1931; d. Sol and Bessie (Schultz) Blunk; m. William Howard Wolff, June 19, 1955; children: Ellen Jill, Rebecca Louise. BA in Edn., Speech and Theatre, Bklyn. Coll., 1972, MS in Spl. Edn., 1975; postgrad., Adelphi U., 1980-81. Cert. tchr.,

N.Y. Fashion model Garment Ctr., N.Y.C., 1949-50; sec. to v.p. out-of-town/export sales Liebmann Breweries Inc., Bklyn., 1950-58; tchr. N.Y.C. Bd. Edn., Bklyn., 1971-76; sec. to dir. environ. programs, pub. affairs officers, speakers bur. project leader Power Authority State of N.Y., N.Y.C., 1976-85; tchr. Hewlett-Woodmere (N.Y.) Sch. Dist., 1986-89; instr. adult edn. County of Nassau, N.Y., 1986-97; actress/model, N.Y.C., 1992—. V.p. program devel. for youth ctr. Wavecrest Gardens Community Assn., Far Rockaway, N.Y., 1959-63; teen leader Far Rockaway Jewish Ctr. Youth Coun., 1965-68; pres. Parents Assn. P.S. 215Q, Far Rockaway, 1966-67; tutor N.Y. C. Bd. Edn. Sch. Vol. Program, Far Rockaway, 1969-71; chair civic affairs Dem. Club, Far Rockaway, 1961-63; committeewoman Dem. Ctrl. Com., Queens County, N.Y., 1963-64; v.p. membership, mem. constn. com. Nassau County Dem. Women's Caucus, 1988, 89; awards com. Bklyn Coll.; mem. comm. adv. com. Hewlett-Woodmere Sch. Dist. 14, 1996-97. Named Mother of Yr. Congregation Shaaray Tefila, Far Rockaway, 1968; recipient Merit award Wavecrest Gardens Community Assn., 1960, Theater Arts Trophy for disting. svc. Bklyn. Coll. Alumni, 1992. Mem. AFTRA, SAG, Nassau Assn. Cmty./ Continuing Edn., Alumni Assn. Bklyn. Coll. (life). Avocations: painting, piano. Office: 1344 Broadway Hewlett NY 11557-1353

WOLFF, ELROY HARRIS, lawyer; b. N.Y.C., May 20, 1935; s. Samuel and Rose Marian (Katz) W.; children: Ethan, Anna Louise. A.B., Columbia U., 1957, LL.B., 1963. Bar: N.Y. 1963, D.C. 1969. Assoc. Kaye, Scholer, Fierman, Hays & Handler, N.Y.C., 1963-65; atty.-adviser to commr. FTC, Washington, 1965-67; sr. trial atty. Dept. Transp., 1967-69; assoc. Leibman, Williams, Bennett, Baird & Minow, Washington, 1969-70, ptnr., 1970-72; ptnr. Sidley & Austin, Washington, 1972—; mem. adv. com. on practice and procedure FTC, 1969-71; chmn. adv. com. on procedural reform CAB, 1975. Served to 1st lt. USAF, 1957-60. Mem. ABA (chmn. spring meeting program 1992-94, coun. 1995—), Union Internationale des advocats (chmn. competition law com. 1994—), Fed. City Club. Office: Sidley & Austin 1722 I St NW Washington DC 20006-3705

WOLFF, FRANK PIERCE, JR., lawyer; b. St. Louis, Feb. 27, 1946; s. Frank P. and Beatrice (Stein) W.; m. Susan Scallet, May 11, 1984; children: Elizabeth McLane, Victoria Hancox. BA, Middlebury Coll., 1968; JD, U. Va., 1971. Bar: Mo. 1971, U.S. Ct. Appeals (5th cir.) 1974, U.S. Ct. Appeals (8th cir.) 1975, U.S. Supreme Ct. 1975. Ptnr. Lewis, Rice & Fingersh, St. Louis, 1971-90; ptnr., sect. leader, bus. and transactional counseling sect. Bryan Cave LLP, St. Louis, 1990—; bd. dirs. Wood Ceilings, Inc. Bd. dirs. Leadership St. Louis, 1985-88, Washington U. Child Guidance Clinic, St. Louis, 1976-79, Jewish Family and Children's Svc., St. Louis, 1981-83, John Burroughs Sch., 1995—; gen. counsel Mo. Bot. Garden, St. Louis, 1981—, Mo. History Mus. Subdist., St. Louis, 1987—; spl. counsel Saint Louis Symphony Soc., 1989—; trustee St. Louis Children's Hosp., 1995—, chairperson mission vision and values com., 1996-97; mem. quality com. BJC Health Systems, Inc.; co-chmn. Parks Task Force, 2004 Inc. . Capt. USAR, 1968-76. Mem. ABA, Mo. Bar Assn., Bar Assn. Met. St. Louis (chmn. corp. sect. 1984-85), Noonday Club, Westwood County Club (chmn. fin. com. 1989-91, treas. 1989-91, v.p. 1991-93, pres. 1993-95, exec. com. 1989-95). Home: 21 Westwood Country Clb Saint Louis MO 63131-2411 Office: Bryan Cave One Metropolitan Sq Saint Louis MO 63102-2750

WOLFF, GEOFFREY ANSELL, novelist, critic, educator; b. L.A., Nov. 5, 1937; s. Arthur Saunders III and Rosemary (Loftus) W.; m. Priscilla Bradley Porter, Aug. 21, 1965; children: Nicholas Hinckley, Justin Porter. Grad., Choate Sch., 1955; student, Eastbourne (Eng.) Coll., 1955-56; BA summa cum laude, Princeton U., 1961; postgrad., Churchill Coll., Cambridge U., Eng., 1963-64. Lectr. in comparative lit. Robert Coll., Istanbul, Turkey, 1961-63; lectr. in Am. civilization Istanbul U., 1962-63; lectr. aesthetics Md. Inst. Coll. Art, 1965-69; vis. lectr. creative arts Princeton (N.J.) U., 1970-71, Ferris prof., 1980, 92; writer-in-residence Brandeis U., Waltham, Mass., 1982-95; prof. English and creative writing U. Calif., Irvine, 1995—; lectr. English lit. Middlebury (Vt.) Coll., 1976, 78; vis. lectr. Columbia U., N.Y.C., 1979, Brown U., Providence, 1981, 88, Boston U., 1981; mem. policy panel in lit. NEA; book critic Esquire mag., 1979-81; founder Golden Horn lit. mag., 1972; vis. prof. Williams Coll., 1994. Author: Bad Debts, 1969, The Sightseer, 1974, Black Sun, 1976, Inklings, 1978, The Duke of Deception, 1979, Providence, 1986; editor: Best American Essays, 1989, The Final Club, 1990, A Day at the Beach, 1992, The Age of Consent, 1995; book editor Washington Post, 1964-69, Newsweek mag., 1969-71, New Times mag., 1974-79; contbr. to mags. Recipient Award in Lit., Am. Acad. of Arts and Letters, 1994, R.I. Gov.'s Arts award, 1992; Woodrow Wilson fellow, 1961-62, 63-64, Fulbright fellow, 1963-64, Guggenheim fellow, 1972-73, 77-78, NEH sr. fellow, 1974-75, NEA fellow, 1979-80, 86-87, Am. Coun. Learned Socs. fellow, 1983-84, Lila Wallace Writing fellow, 1992. Mem. PEN, Princeton Club (N.Y.C.), Colonial CLub (Princeton), Dunes Club. Home: 202 S Orange Dr Los Angeles CA 90036 Office: U Calif-Irvine Program in Writing Dept of English Irvine CA 92717-2650

WOLFF, GRACE SUSAN, pediatrician; b. Rome, N.Y.. MD, Med. Coll. Wis., 1965. Diplomate Am. Bd. Pediatrics, Pediatric Cardiology. Intern St. Vincents Hosp., N.Y.C., 1965-66; resident Columbia-Presbyn Med. Ctr., N.Y.C., 1967-69; fellow in pediatrics and cardiology Childrens Hosp., Boston, 1969-71; pediatrician, pediatric cardiologist U. Miami (Fla.) -Jackson Meml. Hosp.; prof. U. Miami. Mem. Am. Assn. Pediatricians, Am. Coll. Cardiology, Am. Heart Assn. Office: U Miami-Jackson Meml Hosp PO Box 016960-R76 Miami FL 33101

WOLFF, HERBERT ERIC, banker, former army officer; b. Cologne, Germany, May 24, 1925; s. Hugo and Juanna Anna (Van Dam) W.; m. Alice (Billy) Rafael, Nov. 13, 1946 (dec. July, 1987); children: Karen (dec. Jan., 1992), Herbert E., Allen R. BA, Rutgers U., 1953; BS, U. Md., 1957; MA, George Washington U., 1962; grad., U.S. Army War Coll., 1962, Harvard U., 1979. Commd. 2nd lt. U.S. Army, 1945, advanced through grades to maj. gen.; served in Fed. Republic of Germany, Greece, Iran, Republic of Korea, Australia, New Guinea, The Phillipines, Japan and Socialist Republic of Vietnam; dep. dir. ops. NSA-CSS, Ft. Meade, Md., 1973-75; dep. corps. comdr. V. Corps U.S. Army, Frankfurt, Germany, 1975-77; comdr. gen. U.S. Army Western Command U.S. Army, Hawaii, 1977-81; with First Hawaiian Bank, Honolulu, 1981—, sr. v.p., corp. sec.; hon. consul gen. (Dató) U.S. Pacific region Govt. of Malaysia, Honolulu, 1985—. Author: The Man on Horseback, 1962, The Tenth Principle of War, 1964, Public Support, 1964, The Military Instructor, 1968. Mem. exec. bd. Aloha coun. Boy Socuts Am.; bd. dirs. USO, ASYMCA, Girl Scouts of U.S., Hawaii; v.p. Hawaiii Com. Fgn. Rels.; past pres. Pacific Asian Affairs Coun.; pres. Hawaii Army Mus. Soc. Decorated Bronze Star with V and 3 oak leaf clusters U.S. Army, Air medal (24) U.S. Army, Joint Services commendation medal U.S. Army, Army Commendation medal U.S. Army, Purple Heart, Gallantry Cross with 2 palms, Gallantry Cross with palm and silver star Nat. Order 5th class S. Vietnam, Order Nat. Security Merit Choen-Su S. Korea, D.S.M. with oak leaf clusters (2), U.S. Army, Silver Star with oak leaf cluster U.S. Army, Legion of Merit with 3 oak leaf clusters U.S. Army, D.F.C. U.S. Army, Combat Infantry Badge with two stars; named Citizen of Yr. Fed. Exec. Bd., 1987. Mem. Am. Soc. Corps. Secs., Assn. U.S. Army (trustee), 1st Inf. Divsn. Assn., 1st Cav. Divsn. Assn., U.S. Army Mus. Soc. (trustee), Plaza Club (bd. dirs.), Honolulu Country Club, Waialae Country Club, Rotary, Phi Kappa Phi. Office: First Hawaiian Bank PO Box 3200 Honolulu HI 96847-0001 *History is a gift we borrow and hope to pass on. Forget the past and be doomed to repeat it. Remember the past and accept the challenge to convince others.*

WOLFF, JESSE DAVID, lawyer; b. Mpls., Aug. 26, 1913; s. Maurice I. and Annalee (Weiskopf) W.; m. Elizabeth Hess, Nov. 22, 1939; children: Nancy Nicholas, Paula, Daniel Jesse. B.A. summa cum laude, Dartmouth Coll., 1935; J.D., Harvard U., 1938. Bar: N.Y. 1938. Practiced in N.Y.C., 1938—; assoc., then ptnr., to counsel Weil, Gotshal & Manges, 1938-88, 88—, sr. mng. ptnr., 1966-86; past dir., dep. chmn. Sotheby Parke Bernet Group (Eng.); past mem. adv. bd. Sotheby's Inc. Trustee, exec. com. Greatery N.Y. ARC; past mem. exec. com. Salvation Army, N.Y.C. Served with AUS, 1942-45. Mem. ABA, Judge Adv. Gen. Assn. Office: Weil Gotshal & Manges 767 5th Ave New York NY 10153-0001

WOLFF, KURT JAKOB, lawyer; b. Mannheim, Fed. Republic of Germany, Mar. 7, 1936; s. Ernest and Florence (Marx) W.; m. Sanda Lynn Dobrick, Dec. 28, 1958; children: Tracy Ellin, Brett Harris. AB, NYU, 1955; JD, U. Mich., 1958. Bar: N.Y. 1958, U.S. Supreme Ct. 1974, Hawaii 1985, Calif. 1988. Sole practice, N.Y.C., 1958—; assoc. Hays, Sklar & Herzberg, 1958-60; sr. assoc. Nathan, Mannheimer, Asche, Winer and Friedman, 1960-65; sr. assoc. Otterbourg, Steindler, Houston & Rosen, 1965-68, sr. ptnr., 1968-70, dir., treas. 1970—, chmn. bd., 1978-82, chief exec. officer, 1982— ; spl. master N.Y. Supreme Ct., 1977-85; vol. master U.S. Dist. Ct. (so. dist.) N.Y., 1978-82. Lectr., U. Mich. Law Sch.; mem. com. of visitors U. Mich. Law Sch., 1993—; spl. mediator Dept. Disciplinary Com. Appellate Divsn. First Judical Dept., 1991—. Mem. N.Y. State Bar Assn. (lectr.), Am. Arbitration Assn. (arbitrator), N.Y.C. Bar Assn. (arbitration com. 1979-83, state cts. of superior jurisdiction com. 1983-86, mem. com. on legal edn. and admission to the bar, 1991-94), ABA (chmn. ins. com. econs. sect. 1980-82, editor arbitration newsletter, arbitration com. sect. of litigation), Hawaii State Bar Assn., Calif. State Bar Assn., Gen. Arbitration Council Textile Industry N.Y.C., Fed. Bar Council. Contbr. articles to legal jours. Home: 9 Sunset Dr N Chappaqua NY 10514-1633 also: 48-641 Torrito Ct Palm Desert CA 92260 Office: 230 Park Ave New York NY 10169

WOLFF, LARRY F., dental educator, researcher; b. Mankato, Minn., May 25, 1948; m. Charles Harold and Madelyn Catherine (Burns) W.; m. Elizabeth Spencer Thompson, Aug. 7, 1976; children: Adam, Ryan, Sara. BA in Biology, Mankato State U., 1970, M in Biology and Chemistry, 1971; PhD in Microbiology, Northwestern U., 1974; DDS, U. Minn., 1978; M in Periodontology, NYU, 1980; cert. in dentistry, Aarhus (Denmark) Dental Coll., 1979. Rsch. fellow Northwestern U., Chgo., 1972-74; asst. prof. dentistry U. Minn., Mpls., 1980-85, assoc. prof., 1985-96, assoc. prof. periodontology, 1985-94; prof., 1996—. Contbr. articles to profl. jours. Grantee Nat. Inst. Dental Rsch. NIH, 1982—, numerous corps., 1988—. Mem. Am. Acad. Periodontology, Am. Dental Assn., Internat. Assn. Dental Rsch., Internat. Assn. Periodontists, Minn. Dental Assn., Minn. Assn. Dental Rsch. Office: U Minn Sch Dentistry 515 Delaware St SE Minneapolis MN 55455-0348

WOLFF, MANFRED ERNST, medicinal chemist, pharmaceutical company executive; b. Berlin, Feb. 14, 1930; came to U.S., 1933; s. Adolph Abraham and Kate (Fraenkel) W.; m. Helen S. Scandalis, Aug. 1, 1953 (div. 1971); children: Stephen Andrew, David James, Edward Allen; m. Susan E. Hurbert, Jan. 19, 1973 (div. 1975); m. A. Gloria Johnson, Dec. 25, 1982. BS, U. Calif. at Berkeley, 1951, MS, 1953, PhD, 1955. Rsch. fellow U. Va., 1955-57; sr. medicinal chemist Smith, Kline & French Labs., Phila., 1957-60; mem. faculty U. Calif., San Francisco, 1960-82, prof. medicinal chemistry, 1965-82, chmn. dept. pharm. chemistry, 1970-82; dir. discovery rsch. Allergan Labs, Irvine, Calif., 1982-84; v.p. discovery rsch. Allergan Pharms., Irvine, 1984-89; v.p. R & D Immunopharmaceutics Inc., San Diego, 1989-91, sr. v.p. R & D, 1991-95; pres. Intellepharm., Inc., Laguna Beach, Calif., 1997—; adj. prof. medicinal chemistry U. So. Calif., 1982—; elected mem. U.S. Pharm. Conv. Com. of Revision, 1990—. Editor: Burger's Medicinal Chemistry and Drug Discovery, Vol. 1-5, 5th edit., 1995-97; asst. editor Jour. Medicinal Chemistry, 1968-71; mem. editl. bd. Medicinal Chemistry Rsch., 1991-95; contbr. articles to profl. jours.; patentee in field. Fellow AAAS, Am Assn. Pharm. Scientists; mem. Am. Chem. Soc., Licensing Execs. Soc. Achievements include discovery of Alphagan and Zorac medicines for glaucoma and psoriasis.

WOLFF, PAUL MARTIN, lawyer; b. Kansas City, Mo., July 22, 1941; s. Joseph L. and Eleanor B. Wolff; m. Rhea S. Schwartz, Oct. 9, 1976. BA, U. Wis., 1963; LLB, Harvard U., 1966. Bar: D.C. 1968, U.S. Ct. Appeals (D.C. and 2d cir.) 1968, U.S. Supreme Ct. 1975, U.S. Ct. Appeals (10th and fed. cirs.) 1981, U.S. Ct. Appeals (8th cir.) 1982, U.S. Tax Ct. 1982, U.S. Ct. Claims 1984. Law clk. to Judge James R. Durfee U.S. Ct. Claims, Washington, 1966-67; assoc. Williams & Connolly, Washington, 1967-75, ptnr., 1976—; adj. prof. Catholic U. Law Sch., 1970-73. Co-author: Forensic Sciences; contbr. articles to legal jours. Bd. dirs. Stuart Stiller Found., Washington, Washington Coun. for Civil Rights Under Law, 1980-90, Renwick Alliance, Washington, 1987-93, Am. Jewish Com., Washington, 1988-92, Washington Legal Clinic for Homeless, 1988—, Opportunities for Older Ams. Found., 1988-92, Washington Performing Arts Soc., 1990—; dir. D.C. Sports Commn., Com. Pub. Edn.; trustee Fed. City Coun., Am. U. Mem. City Tavern Club, Econ. Club Washington (dir.), Phi Beta Kappa. Democrat. Avocations: photography, gardening, fly fishing. Home: 4770 Reservoir Rd NW Washington DC 20007-1905 also: Oak Ridge Warrenton VA 20186 Office: Williams & Connolly 725 12th St NW Washington DC 20005-3901

WOLFF, PETER ADALBERT, physicist, educator; b. Oakland, Calif., Nov. 15, 1923; s. Adalbert and Ruth Margaret W.; m. Catherine C. Carroll, Sept. 11, 1948; children: Catherine Mia, Peter Whitney. AB in Physics, U. Calif., Berkeley, 1945, PhD in Physics, 1951. Rsch. scientist Lawrence Radiation Lab., 1951-52; staff scientist Bell Telephone Lab., Murray Hill, N.J., 1952-63; dept. head, dir. electronic rsch. lab. Bell Telephone Lab., 1964-70; prof. physics U. Calif., San Diego, 1963-64; prof. physics, head solid state and atomic physics div., assoc. dir. Material Sci. Ctr. MIT, Cambridge, 1970-76, prof. physics, 1976-89, prof. emeritus, 1994—; dir. rsch. lab. of electronics MIT, 1976-81; dir. Francis Bitter Nat. Magnet Lab., 1981-87; dir. Draper Lab. Contbr. articles to profl. jours. Served with C.E. U.S. Army, 1945-46. Fellow Nippon Electric Co. Rsch. Inst., Princeton, 1989-94. Mem. Am. Phys. Soc., Am. Acad. Arts and Scis.

WOLFF, RICHARD JOSEPH, public relations executive, consultant, historian; b. Hackensack, N.J., Oct. 13, 1952; s. Richard Hamilton and Irene Marie (Ciruzzi) W. AB, Georgetown U., 1974; MA, Columbia U., 1976, PhD, 1979. Asst. dean, prof. St. John's U., Queens, N.Y., 1980-85; ptnr. pub. rels. Kekst & Co., Inc., N.Y.C., 1985-97; eec. v.p., gen. mgr., bd. dirs. Golin/Harris Comms., N.Y.C., 1997—; mem. Columbia U. Seminar on Modern Italy, N.Y.C., 1983—; founding mem. St. John's U. Seminar on Vatican Studies, Queens, 1994—. Author: Between Pope and Duce, 1990, Dorothy Day, 1994; contbr. articles to profl. jours.; editor Catholics, the State and the European Radical Right, 1987. Chmn., commr. North Hudson Sewerage Authority, Hudson County, N.J., 1988—; mem. adv. com. Congressman Robert Menendez, Jersey City, N.J., 1994—. Recipient Howard Marraro prize Am. Cath. Hist. Assn., 1982, Internat. fellow Columbia U., 1977. Mem. Phi Beta Kappa. Roman Catholic. Avocations: golf, reading, travel, politics. Office: Golin/Harris Comms Chrysler Bldg 405 Lexington Ave New York NY 10017

WOLFF, ROBERT PAUL, philosophy educator; b. N.Y.C., Dec. 27, 1933; s. Walter Harold and Charlotte (Ornstein) W.; m. Cynthia Griffin, June 9, 1962 (div. 1986); children: Patrick Gideon, Tobias Barrington; m. Susan Gould, Aug. 25, 1987. AB, Harvard U., 1953, MA in Philosophy, 1954, PhD, 1957. Instr. Harvard U., 1958-61; asst. prof. philosophy U. Chgo., 1961-63; vis. lectr. Wellesley Coll., 1963-64; assoc. prof. philosophy Columbia, 1964-69, prof., 1969-71; prof. philosophy U. Mass., Amherst, 1971-92, prof. Afro-Am. studies and philosophy, 1992—; grad. program dir. doctoral program in Afro-Am. Author: Kant's Theory of Mental Activity, 1963, A Critique of Pure Tolerance, 1965, Political Man and Social Man, 1966, Kant: A Collection of Critical Essays, 1967, Poverty of Liberalism, 1968, The Ideal of the University, 1969, In Defense of Anarchism, 1970, Philosophy: A Modern Encounter, 1971, The Autonomy of Reason, 1973, About Philosophy, 1975, 7th edit., 1998. Exec. dir. Harvard-Radcliffe Alumni/ae Against Apartheid, 1988-90; pres., exec. dir. Univ. Scholarships for South African Students, 1990—; co-dir. inst. advanced study in humanities U. Mass., 1992—, grad. program dir. Doctoral Program in Afro-Am. Studies, 1996—. Home: 107 Buffam Rd Amherst MA 01002-9723

WOLFF, SANFORD IRVING, lawyer; b. Chgo., Apr. 13, 1915; s. Herbert Barron and Libby (Levey) W.; m. Ann Barry, Mar. 21, 1970; children—Paul, David, Laura. BA, Knox Coll., 1936; grad., John Marshall Law Sch., U. Chgo., 1940. Bar: Ill. 1940, N.Y. 1973. Pvt. practice Chgo. and N.Y.C., 1945—; chief exec. AFTRA, AFL-CIO, N.Y.C., 1968-85; of counsel Becker, London & Kossow, N.Y.C., 1985—; chief exec. and counsel Am. Guild of Musical Artist, AFL-CIO, 1988-93. Trustee Harris Sch., Chgo. Served with AUS, 1940-45. Decorated Combat Inf. badge, Purple Heart, Bronze Star with cluster, Silver Star. Mem. ABA, Chgo. Bar Assn. Office: Becker London 1841 Broadway New York NY 10023-7603

WOLFF, SHELDON, radiobiologist, educator; b. Peabody, Mass., Sept. 22, 1928; s. Henry Herman and Goldie (Lipchitz) W.; m. Frances Faye Farbstein, Oct. 23, 1954; children: Victor Charles, Roger Kenneth, Jessica Raye. B.S. magna cum laude, Tufts U., 1950; M.A., Harvard U., 1951, Ph.D., 1953. Teaching fellow Harvard U., 1951-52; sr. research staff biology div. Oak Ridge Nat. Lab., 1953-66; prof. cytogenetics and radiology U. Calif., San Francisco, 1966-94; prof. emeritus, 1994—; dir. Lab. Radiobiology and Environ. Health U. Calif., San Francisco, 1983-95; vice chmn., chief rsch. Radiation Effects Rsch. Found., Hiroshima, Japan, 1996—; vis. prof. radiation biology U. Tenn., 1962, lectr., 1953-65; cons. several fed. sci. agys.; mem. health and environ. rsch. adv. com. U.S. Dept. Energy, 1986—, chmn., 1987-95; co-chmn. Joint NIH/Dept. Energy Subcom. on Human Genome, 1989-94. Editor: Chromosoma, 1983-97 ; assoc. editor: Cancer Research, 1983-97; Editorial bd.: Radiation Research, 1968-72, Photochemistry and Photobiology, 1962-72, Radiation Botany, 1964-86, Mutation Research, 1964-97, Caryologia, 1967-96, Radiation Effects, 1969-81, Genetics, 1972-85; Contbr. articles to sci. jours. Recipient E.O. Lawrence meml. award U.S. AEC, 1973. Mem. Genetics Soc. Am., Radiation Rsch. Soc. (counselor for biology 1968-72, Failla lectr. 1992, medal 1992), Am. Soc. Cell Biology, Environmental Mutagen Soc. (coun. 1972-75, pres. 1980-81, award 1982), Internat. Assn. Environ. Mutagen Socs. (treas. 1978-85), Sigma Xi. Democrat. Home: 41 Eugene St Mill Valley CA 94941-1717 Office: U Calif Lab Radiobiology San Francisco CA 94143

WOLFF, SIDNEY CARNE, astronomer, observatory administrator; b. Sioux City, Iowa, June 6, 1941; d. George Albert and Ethel (Smith) Carne; m. Richard J. Wolff, Aug. 29, 1962. BA, Carleton Coll., 1962, DSc (hon.), 1985; PhD, U. Calif., Berkeley, 1966. Postgrad. research fellow Lick Obs, Santa Cruz, Calif., 1969; asst. astronomer U. Hawaii, Honolulu, 1967-71, assoc. astronomer, 1971-76; astronomer, assoc. dir. Inst. Astronomy, Honolulu, 1976-83, acting dir., 1983-84; dir. Kitt Peak Nat. Obs., Tucson, 1984-87, Nat. Optical Astronomy Observatories, 1987—; dir. Gemini Project Gemini 8-Meter Telescopes Project, 1992-94. Author: The A-Type Stars--Problems and Perspectives, 1983, (with others) Exploration of the Universe, 1987, Realm of the Universe, 1988, Frontiers of Astronomy, 1990, Voyages Through the Universe, 1996; contrbr. articles to profl. jours. Trustee Carleton Coll., 1989—. Rsch. fellow Lick Obs. Santa Cruz, Calif., 1967; recipient Nat. Meritorious Svc. award NSF, 1994. Fellow Royal Astronical Soc.; mem. Astron. Soc. Pacific (pres. 1984-86, bd. dirs. 1979-85), Am. Astron. Soc. (coun. 1983-86, pres.-elect 1991, pres. 1992-94). Office: Nat Optical Astronomy Obs PO Box 26732 950 N Cherry Ave Tucson AZ 85719-4933

WOLFF, STEVEN ALEXANDER, arts and entertainment consultant; b. N.Y.C., July 18, 1957; s. Joel Charles and Joan (Mittlemark) W.; m. Gail English Loflin, June 12, 1988; children: Jessica Sadye, Ian Charles. BA in Econs., SUNY, Brockport, 1978; MFA in Theatre Adminstrn., Yale U., 1981. Cert. mgmt. cons. Cons. Artec Cons., N.Y.C., 1981-83; mgr. Theatre Projects Cons., N.Y.C., 1983-88; sr. v.p., prin. Hill Arts & Entertainment/ AMS/ArtSoft Mgmt. Svcs., Guilford, Conn., 1988-91; pres., founder AMS Planning & Rsch. Corp., Fairfield, Conn., 1991—, Audience Insight LLC, Fairfield, 1996—; lectr. in field. Major projects include Aronoff Ctr. for Arts, Cin., Calif. Ctr. for Arts, Escondido, Metro-Dade Arts Ctr., Miami; contbr. articles to profl. jours. Recipient Cert. of Honor, ARC (nat. chpt.), 1978. Mem. Internat. Soc. Performing Arts, Internat. Downtown Assn., Assn. Performing Arts Presenters, Young Entrepreneurs Orgn. Avocation: competitive offshore sailing. Office: AMS Planning & Rsch Corp 2150 Post Rd Fairfield CT 06430-5669

WOLFF, TOBIAS (JONATHAN ANSELL WOLFF), author; b. Birmingham, Ala., June 19, 1945; s. Arthur Saunders and Rosemary (Loftus) W.; m. Catherine Dolores Spohn, 1975; children: Michael, Patrick, Mary Elizabeth. BA, Oxford Univ., 1972, MA, 1975; MA, Stanford Univ., 1978. Mem. faculty Stanford (Calif.) U., Goddard Coll., Plainfield, Vt., Ariz. State U., Tempe, Syracuse (N.Y.) U., Stanford (Calif.) U.; reporter Washington Post. Author: In the Garden of the North American Martyrs, 1981 (St. Lawrence award for fiction 1982), The Barracks Thief, 1984 (PEN/Faulkner award for fiction 1985), Back in the World, 1985, This Boy's Life: A Memoir, 1989 (L.A. Times Book prize 1989), In Pharaoh's Army: Memories of the Lost War, 1994 (Esquire-Volvo-Winterstone's award, Eng. 1994); editor: Matters of Life and Death: New American Stories, 1983, The Stories of Anton Chekhov, 1987, Best American Short Stories, 1994, The Vintage Book of Contemporary American Stories, 1994, The Night in Question, 1996. Recipient Wallace Stegner fellowship in creative writing, 1975-76; Nat. Endowment for the Arts fellowship in creative writing, 1978, 85; Mary Roberts Rinehart award, 1979; Ariz. Coun. on Arts and Humanities fellowship in creative writing, 1980, Guggenheim fellowship, 1982; Rea award, 1989; Whiting Writer's award, 1989, Lila-Wallace-Reader's Digest award, 1993, Lyndhurst Found. award, 1994. Office: Stanford U Dept English Stanford CA 94305-2087

WOLFF, VIRGINIA EUWER, writer, secondary education educator; b. Portland, Oreg., Aug. 25, 1937; d. Eugene Courtney and Florence Evelyn (Craven) Euwer; m. Art Wolff, July 19, 1959 (div. July 1976); children: Anthony Richard, Juliet Dianne. AB, Smith Coll., 1959; postgrad., Goddard Coll., Warren Wilson Coll., L.I. U., Portland State U., Lewis & Clark Coll. Cert. tchr., Oreg. Tchr. The Miquon Sch., Phila., 1968-72, The Fiedel Sch., Glen Cove, N.Y., 1972-75, Hood River Valley (Oreg.) H.S., 1976-86, Mt. Hood Acad., Govt. Camp, Oreg., 1986—; 2d violinist Quartet con brio, Portland, 1989—, Parnassius Quartet, Portland, 1996. Author: Probably Still Nick Swansen, 1988, The Mozart Season, 1991, Make Lemonade, 1993. Violinist Mid-Columbia Sinfonietta, Hood River, 1976—, Oreg. Sinfonietta, Portland, 1988—. Recipient Young Adult Book award Internat. Reading Assn., 1989, PEN U.S.A. Ctr. West, 1989, Best Young Adult Book of Yr. award Mich. Libr. Assn., 1993, Child Study Children's Book award Bank Street Coll., 1994, Oreg. Book award Oreg. Lit. Arts, 1994. Mem. Soc. Children's Book Writers/Illustrators (Golden Kite 1994), Chamber Music Soc. Oreg. Avocations: chamber music, swimming, hiking, playing violin, gardening. Office: Curtis Brown Ltd care Marilyn E Marlow 10 Astor Pl New York NY 10003-6935

WOLFF, WILLIAM F., III, investment banker; b. N.Y.C., Apr. 12, 1945; s. William F. Jr. and Nancy (Wimpfheimer) W.; m. Phyllis Fox, June 1, 1969; children: Kenneth, Jonathan, Gillian. BA, U. Mich., 1967; JD, Columbia U., 1970, MBA, 1971. Bar: N.Y. 1970. V.p. Salomon Bros., Inc., N.Y.C., 1971-78; prin. Morgan Stanley & Co., N.Y.C., 1978-83; mng. dir. Lehman Brothers, N.Y.C., 1983—. Trustee St. David's Sch., N.Y.C., 1985—, Nat. Glaucoma Trust, 1992-96. Mem. Univ Club (N.Y.), Ocean Beach Club (Elberon, N.J.) (trustee 1985-89). Office: Lehman Bros Three World Fin Ctr New York NY 10285

WOLFGANG, GARY L., orthopaedic surgeon; b. Danville, Pa., May 27, 1940; s. Fred A. and Martha J. W.; children: Lynn, Kristi, Beth. BS, Lebanon Valley Coll., 1963; MD, Jefferson Med. Coll., 1967. Surgeon, chmn. surg. divsn. Geisinger Med. Ctr., Danville, Pa., 1967—. Lt. cmdr. USN, 1967-69. Mem. AAM. Presbyn.

WOLFGANG, LENORA D., foreign language educator; b. Phila, Sept. 25, 1934; d. Paul K. Poden and Mildred (Ross) Poden Wood; m. Marvin Eugene Wolfgang, June 1, 1957; children: Karen Wolfgang Swanson, Nina Victoria. BA, U. Pa., 1956, MA, 1965, PhD, 1973. Prof. French Lehigh U., Bethlehem, Pa., 1980—; tchr. at U. Pa., Rutgers U., Camden, Temple U., Friends' Select Sch., Phila., Ravenhill Acad., Phila., Swarthmore (Pa.) Sch. Author: Bliocadran: A Prologue to the Perceval of Chrétien de Troyes, 1976, Le Lai de L'Oiselet, 1990; contbr. 14 articles, 12 reviews to profl. jours. Fulbright scholar, 1956; Woodrow Wilson fellow, 1956, fellow NEH, 1984-85, 95-96. Mem. Modern Lang. Assn. Am., Medieval Acad. Am., Internat. Arthurian Soc., Internat. Courtly Literature Soc., Société Rencesvals, Cosmopolitan Club Phila., Phi Beta Kappa. Home: 4106 Locust St Philadelphia PA 19104 Office: Lehigh U Dept Modern Langs 9 W Packer Ave Bethlehem PA 18015-3082

WOLFGANG, MARVIN EUGENE, sociologist, criminologist, educator; b. Millersburg, Pa., Nov. 14, 1924; s. Charles T. and Pauline (Sweigard) W.; m. Lenora D. Poden, June 1, 1957; children: Karen Eleanor, Nina Victoria. B.A., Dickinson Coll., Carlisle, Pa., 1948; M.A., U. Pa., 1950, Ph.D.,

1955. Instr., asst. prof. Lebanon Valley Coll., 1948-52; instr. to prof. sociology U. Pa., Phila., 1952—; chmn. dept. U. Pa., 1968-72, prof. sociology and law, 1972—; also dir. Sellin Ctr. for Studies in Criminology and Criminal Law; vis. prof., fellow Churchill Coll., U. Cambridge, Eng., 1968-69; cons. Rand Corp.; Chmn. rev. com. on crime and delinquency NIMH, 1971-73; rsch. dir. Nat. Commn. on Causes and Prevention of Violence, 1968-69; commr. Nat. Commn. on Obscenity and Pornography, 1968-70. Author: Patterns in Criminal Homicide, 1958, Crime and Race, 1964, (with T. Sellin) The Measurement of Delinquency, 1964, (with F. Ferracuti) The Subculture of Violence, 1967, Crime and Culture, 1968, (with L. Radzinowicz) Crime and Justice, 3 vols, 1971, rev. edit., 1977, (with T. Sellin, R. Figlio) Delinquency in a Birth Cohort, 1972, (with R. Figlio, T. Thornberry) Criminology Index, 2 vols, 1975, Evaluating Criminology, 1978, (with N. Weiner) Criminal Violence, (with R. Figlio et al) National Survey of Crime Severity, 1986, (with T. Thornberry and R. Figlio) From Boy to Man: From Delinquency to Crime, 1987, (with N. Weiner) Violent Crime, Violent Criminals, Pathways to Criminal Violence, 1988, (with P. Tracy and R. Figlio) Delinquency Careers in Two Birth Cohorts, 1990, (with D. Nevares and P. Tracy) Delinquency in Puerto Rico: The 1970 Birth Cohort Study, 1991. Chmn., bd. dirs. Thomas Skelton Harrison Found.; chmn. Eisenhower Found. With AUS, 1943-45, ETO. Recipient Fulbright rsch. award, 1957-58, Hans von Hentig award World Soc. Victimology, 1988; Guggenheim fellow, 1957-58, 68-69. Mem. Am. Philos. Soc., Am. Acad. Arts and Scis., Internat. Soc. Criminology, Am. Soc. Criminology (past pres., rsch. award 1960, Edwin Sutherland award 1989), Am. Acad. Polit. and Social Sci. (pres.), Pa. Prison Soc. (bd. dirs., past pres.), Phi Beta Kappa. Home: 4106 Locust St Philadelphia PA 19104-3509 Office: Am Acad Polit & Social Sci 3937 Chestnut St Philadelphia PA 19104-3110

WOLFINGER, RAYMOND EDWIN, political science educator; b. San Francisco, June 29, 1931; s. Raymond Edwin and Hilda (Holm) W.; m. Barbara Kaye, Aug. 8, 1960; 1 son, Nicholas Holm. A.B., U. Calif.-Berkeley, 1951; M.A., U. Ill., 1955; Ph.D., Yale U., 1961. Asst. prof. polit. sci. Stanford (Calif.) U., Calif., 1961-66; assoc. prof. Stanford U., Calif., 1966-70, prof., 1970-71; prof. U. Calif.-Berkeley, 1971—, Heller prof. polit. sci., 1995—; dir. U. Calif. Data Archive and Tech. Assistance, 1980-92; chmn. bd. overseers Nat. Election Studies, Ann Arbor, Mich., 1982-86. Author: The Politics of Progress, 1974, (with others) Dynamics of American Politics, 1976, 80, (with Steven J. Rosenstone) Who Votes, 1980, (with others) The Myth of the Independent Voter, 1992; mem. editorial bd. Brit. Jour. Polit. Sci., 1980-84, Am. Polit. Sci. Rev., 1985-88. Bd. dirs. S.W. Voter Rsch. Inst. Inc., San Antonio, 1988-96, Consortium of Social Sci. Assns., 1987-93, pres. 1988-90. 1st lt. U.S. Army, 1951-53. Fellow Ctr. for Advanced Study in Behavioral Scis., 1960-61; Guggenheim fellow, 1965; Ford Found. faculty research fellow, 1970-71. Fellow Am. Acad. Arts and Scis.; mem. Am. Polit. Sci. Assn. (sec. 1981-82), AAUP (council 1981-84), Western Polit. Sci. Assn. (v.p. 1988-89, pres. 1989-90). Democrat. Office: U Calif Dept Polit Sci Berkeley CA 94720

WOLF-KLEIN, GISELE PATRICIA, geriatrician; b. Geneva, June 11, 1951; came to U.S., 1976; d. Francis and Patricia (Johnston) Wolf; m. Allen Klein. MD, Geneva U., 1975. Diplomate Am. Bd. Internal Medicine. Intern., resident L.I. Jewish Med. Ctr., 1976-78; fellow in geriatric medicine L.I. Jewish Med. Ctr., New Hyde Park, N.Y., 1978-80, chief geriatric medicine, 1991—; assoc. prof. medicine Albert Einstein Coll. of Medicine, N.Y. Author: Keys to Alzheimers Disease, 1992; contbr. numerous articles to profl. jours. Recipient 1 of Best Drs. in USA award Woodward-White, 1992-93. Fellow ACP, Am. Geriatric Soc.; mem. Gerontol. Soc. Am., Met. Area Geriatric Soc. (bd. dirs. 1991—), Sigma Xi. Avocations: skiing, mountain climbing, sculpture. Office: Parker Jewish Geriatric Inst 27111 76th Ave New Hyde Park NY 11040-1436

WOLFLE, DAEL LEE, public affairs educator; b. Puyallup, Wash., Mar. 5, 1906; s. David H. and Elizabeth (Pauly) W.; m. Helen Morrill, Dec. 28, 1929 (dec. July 1988); children: Janet Helen (Mrs. Wilhelm G. Christophersen), Lee Morrill, John Morrill. B.S., U. Wash., 1927, M.S., 1928; postgrad., U. Chgo., summers 1929, 30; Ph.D., Ohio State U., 1931, D.Sc., 1957; D.Sc., Drexel U., 1956, Western Mich. U., 1960. Instr. psychology Ohio State U., 1929-32; prof. psychology U. Miss., 1932-36; examiner in biol. scis. U. Chgo., 1936-39, asst. prof. psychology, 1938-43, assoc. prof., 1943-45; on leave for war work with Signal Corps, 1941-43; with OSRD, 1944-45; exec. sec. Am. Psychol. Assn., 1946-50; dir. commn. on human resources and advanced tng. Assoc. Research Councils, 1950-54; exec. officer AAAS, 1954-70; editor Sci., 1955, pub., 1955-70; prof. pub. affairs U. Wash., Seattle, 1970-76; prof. emeritus U. Wash., 1976—; mem. sci. adv. bd. USAF, 1953-57; mem. def. sci. bd. Dept. Def., 1957-61; mem. adv. council on mental health NIMH, 1960-64; mem. nat. adv. health council USPHS, 1965-66; mem. commn. on human resources NRC, 1974-78; mem. adv. bd. Geophys. Inst., Fairbanks, Alaska., 1970-93, chmn. adv. bd., 1972-81. Author: Factor Analysis to 1940, 1941, Science and Public Policy 1959, The Uses of Talent, 1971, The Home of Science, 1972, Renewing a Scientific Society, 1989; editor: America's Resources of Specialized Talent, 1954. Trustee Russell Sage Found., 1961-78, Pacific Sci. Cent. Found., 1962-80, Biol. Scis. Curriculum Study, 1980-85; chmn. bd. J. McK. Cattell Fund, 1962-82. Named Alumnus Summa Laude Dignatus, U. Wash., 1979. Mem. AAAS, (pres. Pacific divsn. 1991-92, exec. com. 1990—), AAUP, APA, Am. Acad. Arts and Scis. (exec. com. western sect. 1985-92), Sigma Xi. Home: 4545 Sand Point Way NE Apt 805 Seattle WA 98105-3926 Office: U Wash Box 353055 Grad Sch Pub Affairs Seattle WA 98195-3055

WOLFMAN, ALAN, medical educator, researcher; b. Bronx, N.Y., Mar. 12, 1956; married. Postdoctoral fellow dept. biophysics U. Rochester Med. Ctr., 1988-90; asst. staff dept. cell biology Cleve. Clinic Found., 1990—; adj. prof. dept. biology Cleve. State U., 1994—. Contbr. articles to profl. jours.; periodic reviewer for Molecular Cellular Biology, Jour. Biol. Chemistry, Biochemistry, BBA; ad hoc reviewer for program project Nat. Inst. Diabetes and Digestive and Kidney Diseases, 1995; invited reviewer for DRTC Pilot Project Ind. U., 1995—; presenter in field. Recipient NIH Postdoctoral fellowship award, 1985-88, Established Investigatorship award Am. Heart Assn., 1996—; NIH First grant, 1988-93, Cell Biology Tng. grant, 1979. Office: Cleve Clinic Found Rsch Inst Dept Cell Biology NC10 9500 Euclid Ave Cleveland OH 44195-0001

WOLFMAN, BERNARD, lawyer, educator; b. Phila., July 8, 1924; s. Nathan and Elizabeth (Coff) W.; m. Zelda Bernstein, Dec. 25, 1948 (dec. Oct. 1973); children: Jonathan L., Brian S., Dina A.; m. Toni A. Grotta, June 12, 1977. AB, U. Pa., 1946, JD, 1948; LLD (hon.), Jewish Theol. Sem., 1971, Capital U., 1990. Bar: Pa. 1949, Mass. 1976. Mem. law firm Wolf, Block, Schorr & Solis-Cohen, Phila., 1948-63; prof. law U. Pa. Law Sch., 1963-76, dean, 1970-75, Kenneth W. Gemmill prof. tax law and tax policy, 1973-76, chmn. Faculty Senate, 1969-70; Fessenden prof. law Harvard U., 1976—; vis. prof. Stanford U. Law Sch., summer 1982, NYU Law Sch., 1987-88; Irvine lectr. Cornell U. Law Sch., 1980; Halle lectr. Case Western Res. U. Law Sch., 1983, Sugarman lectr., 1989; Cleve. State U. Sch. Law, 1983; Altheimer lectr. U. Ark. Sch. Law, Little Rock, 1994; mem. editl. bds. law divsn. Aspen Law & Bus. (formerly Little Brown & Co.), Jour. Corp. Taxation; gen. counsel AAUP, 1966-68, mem. coun., 1979-82; cons. to ind. counsel Lawrence E. Walsh (Iran-Contra prosecution), 1987-89; mem. adv. group to commr. internal revenue, 1966-67; cons. tax policy U.S. Treasury Dept., 1963-68, 77-80; chmn. Task Force Univ. Governance, U. Pa., 1968-70; mem. steering com. IRS project Adminstrv. Conf. U.S., 1974-80; vice chmn. bd. advs. NYU-IRS Continuing Profl. Edn. Project, 1981-85; mem. legal activities policy bd. Tax Analysts, 1974—; mem. exec. com. Fed. Tax Inst. New Eng., 1976—. Author: Federal Income Taxation of Corporate Enterprise, 1971, 3d edit., 1990; (with J. Holden and D. Schenk) Ethical Problems in Federal Tax Practice, 1981 3d edit. 1995, (with J. Holden and K. Harris) Standards of Tax Practice, 1991, 4th edit. 1997; sr. author: Dissent Without Opinion: The Behavior of Justice William O. Douglas in Federal Tax Cases, 1975; contbr. articles to profl. jours. Adv. com. Commn. Philanthropy and Pub. Needs, 1973-75; mem. Phila. regional council Pa. Gov.'s Justice Commn., 1973-75; trustee Found. Center, N.Y.C., 1970-76, Fedn. Jewish Agys. Greater Phila., 1968-74; bd. dirs. Phila. Lawyers Com. Civil Rights Under Law, 1970-74, Phila. Defender Assn., 1955-69; mem. Nat. Lawyers Adv. Council of Earl Warren Legal Tng. Program. Served with AUS, 1943-45. Fellow Am. Bar Found., Am. Coll. Tax Counsel (regent 1st cir.); mem. ABA (past chmn. com. on taxation, coun. sect. individual rights and responsibilities 1978-82, coun. sect. taxation 1982-85), Am. Law Inst. (cons. fed. income tax project 1974—), ACLU (nat. dir. 1973-75), Order of Coif (exec. com. 1982-91, v.p. 1986-89, pres. 1989-91), Phi Beta Kappa. Home: 229 Brattle St Cambridge MA 02138-4623 Office: Law Sch Harvard U Cambridge MA 02138

WOLFMAN, BRUNETTA REID, education educator; b. Clarksdale, Miss., Sept. 4, 1931; d. Willie Orlando and Belle Victoria (Allen) Reid Griffin; m. Burton Wolfman, Oct. 4, 1952; children: Andrea, Jeffrey. BA, U. Calif., Berkeley, 1957, MA, 1968, PhD, 1971; DHL (hon.), Boston U., 1983; DP (hon.), Northeastern U., 1983; DL (hon.), Regis Coll., 1984, Stonehill Coll., 1985; DHL, Suffolk U., 1985; DET (hon.), Wentworth Inst., 1987; AA (hon.), Roxbury Community Coll., 1988. Asst. dean faculty Dartmouth Coll., Hanover, N.H., 1972-74; asst. v.p. acad. affairs U. Mass., Boston, 1974-76; acad. dean Wheelock Coll., Boston, 1976-78; cons. Arthur D. Little, Cambridge, Mass., 1978; dir. policy planning Dept. Edn., Boston, 1978-82; pres. Roxbury C.C., Boston, 1983-88, ACE sr. assoc., 1988-94, NAWE sr. assoc., 1994—; assoc. v.p. acad. affairs George Washington U., Washington, 1989-92, prof. edn., 1992-96, prof. edn. emeritus, 1996—; pres. bd. dirs. Literacy Vols. of Capitol Region; mem. comm. com. bd., pub. rels. com. LVA, Inc.; bd. dirs. Am. Coun. Edn., Harvard Cmty. Health Plan. Author: Roles, 1983; contbr. articles to profl. jours. Bd. overseers Wellesley (Mass.) Coll., 1981; bd. dirs. Boston-Fenway Program, 1977, Freedom House, Boston, 1983, Boston Pvt. Industry Coun., 1983, NCCJ, Boston, 1983, co-chmn.; bd. overseers Boston Symphony Orch.; trustee Mus. Fine Arts, Boston; councilor Coun. on Edn. for Pub. Health. Recipient Freedom award NAACP No. Calif., 1971, Amelia Earhart award Women's Edn. and Indsl. Union, Boston, 1983; Sr. scholar Nat. Assn. Women in Edn. Mem. Am. Sociol. Assn., Assn. Black Women in Higher Edn., D.C. Sociol. Soc., Greater Boston C. of C. (edn. com. 1982), Cosmos Club (Washington), Pi Lambda Theta, Alpha Kappa Alpha (Humanitarian award 1984), Phi Delta Kappa. Home: 657 Commercial St Provincetown MA 02657-1759

WOLFMAN, EARL FRANK, JR., surgeon, educator; b. Buffalo, Sept. 14, 1926; s. Earl Frank and Alfreda (Peterson) W.; m. Lois Jeannette Walker, Dec. 28, 1946; children—Nancy Jeannette, David Earl, Carol Anne. BS cum laude, Harvard U., 1946; MD cum laude, U. Mich., 1950. Diplomate Am. Bd. Surgery. Intern U. Mich., Ann Arbor, 1950-51, asst. resident in surgery, 1951-52, resident in surgery, 1954-55, from jr. clin. instr. surgery to assoc. prof., 1955-66, asst. to dean, 1960-61, asst. dean, 1961-64; practice medicine specializing in surgery, 1957—, Sacramento, 1966—; prof. surgery Sch. Medicine, U. Calif., Davis, 1966—, chmn. dept. surgery, 1966-78, assoc. dean, 1966-76, mem. staff, chief surg. svcs. Med. Ctr., 1966-78. Contbr. articles to profl. jours. Served to lt. M.C. USNR, 1952-54. Fellow ACS; mem. AMA (del. 1987—), Ctrl. Surg. Soc., Western Surg. Soc., Sacramento Surg. Soc., Pacific Coast Surg. Soc., Calif. Acad. Medicine, Frederick A. Coller Surg. Soc., Pan Am. Med. Assn., Soc. Surgery Alimentary Tract, Am. Assn. Endocrine Surgeons, Sacramento Med. Soc., Yolo Med. Soc., Calif. Med. Assn. (trustee 1991—), Am. Soc. Gen. Surgeons, Comstock Club. Methodist. Home: 44770 N El Macero Dr PO Box 3086 El Macero CA 95618 Office: U Calif-Davis Sch Medicine Dept Surgery 4301 X St Sacramento CA 95817-2214

WOLFMAN, IRA JOEL, editor, writer; b. Oct. 7, 1950; s. Aaron and Beatrice Ruth (Perlo) W.; m. Julia Diamant, June 24, 1979 (dec. 1982); m. Ronda Small, Dec. 20, 1991. B.A. cum laude, SUNY, Albany, 1971. News editor Washington Park Spirit, Albany, N.Y., 1971-73; sr. editor Smash mag., N.Y.C., 1975-76, Circus mag., N.Y.C., 1976-79; assoc. editor 3-2-1 Contact mag., N.Y.C., 1979-80; editor Sesame St Parents' Newsletter, N.Y.C., 1980-83; editor in chief Enter mag., N.Y.C., 1983-85, Sesame St. mag., Parents Guide, 1990-94; v.p., editor-in-chief Adult Consumer mags. Children's Television Workshop, N.Y.C., 1994—; newsletter editor Found. for Grandparenting, Mt. Kisco, N.Y., 1984-87; editor Am. Writer, 1988-89; freelance writer and editor, contbr. to Travel & Leisure, Architectural Record, Metropolis, N.Y. Daily News, Ms., Spy, 1985—. Author: Do People Grow on Family Trees? Genealogy for Kids and Other Beginners, 1991, My World and Globe, 1991. N.Y. State Legis. Corrs. scholar, 1970. Jewish.

WOLFORD, NANCY LOU, medical and surgical nurse; b. Cumberland, Md., Feb. 22, 1956; d. Charles Leo and Shirley Lou (Weicht) Westfall; m. Harry Edward Wolford, Aug. 20, 1977; 1 child, James. AA in Nursing, Allegany C.C., 1977. RN, Md.; cert. in med.-surg. nursing. Staff nurse in emergency dept. Frostburg (Md.) Community Hosp., 1978-88; staff nurse med. surg. unit Frostburg Hosp., Inc., 1988-95; staff nurse oncology/med.-surg. unit Meml. Hosp. and Med. Ctr., Cumberland, Md., 1995—; ind. beauty cons. Mary Kay Cosmetics, Inc., 1993—. Recipient Congl. scholarship Md. State Sen., 1974-77. Mem. AAUW, Nat. League Nurses, Order of Ea. Star. Republican. Methodist. Avocations: art, music. Home: 412 Park St Frostburg MD 21532-1511 Office: Meml Hosp and Med Ctr Memorial Ave Cumberland MD 21502

WOLFRAM, STEPHEN, physicist, computer company executive; b. London, Aug. 29, 1959; came to U.S., 1978; Degree, Eton Coll., 1976, Oxford U., 1978; PhD in Theoretical Physics, Calif. Inst. Tech., 1979. With Calif. Inst. Tech., Pasadena, 1979-82, Inst. for Advanced Study, Princeton, N.J., 1983-86; prof. physics, math, computer sci. U. Ill., Champaign, 1986—; pres., CEO Wolfram Rsch. Inc., Champaign, 1987—. Author: Theory and Applications of Cellular Automata, 1986, Mathematica, 1988, Cellular Automata and Complexity, 1994; editor jour. Complex Systems, 1987—. Fellow MacArthur Found., 1981. Office: Wolfram Rsch Inc 100 Trade Centre Dr Champaign IL 61820-7237

WOLFRAM, THOMAS, physicist; b. St. Louis, July 27, 1936; s. Ferdinand I. and Audrey H. (Calvert) W.; m. Eleanor Elaine Burger, May 22, 1965; children: Michael, Gregory, Melanie, Susan, Steven. BA, U. Calif., Riverside, 1959, PhD in Physics, 1963; MA in Physics, UCLA, 1960. Dir. divsn. physics and chemistry; Engr. Atomics Internat., Canoga Park, Calif., 1960-63; mem. tech. staff N.Am. Aviation Corp. Sci. Ctr., Thousand Oaks, Calif., 1963-68; group leader in solid state physics Rockwell Internat. Sci. Ctr., Thousand Oaks, 1968-72, dir. div. physics and chemistry, 1972-74; prof. physics, chmn. dept. physics and astronomy U. Mo., Columbia, 1974-83; dir. phys. tech. divsn. AMOCO Corp., 1983-87; v.p., gen. mgr. AMOCO Laser Co., 1987-95; bus. cons., 1995—; cons. in field. Editor: Inelastic Electron Tunneling Spectroscopy, 1978; contbr. rsch. articles to numerous publs. in field. Recipient Disting. Prof. award Argonne Univs. Assn., 1977. Fellow Am. Phys. Soc. Office: Tungsten Novela 2004 Somerset Ln Wheaton IL 60187-8128 *Crisis is the catalyst for constructive change.*

WOLFSCHMIDT, WILLI See FLINT, WILLIS WOLFSCHMIDT

WOLFSON, AARON HOWARD, radiation oncologist, educator; b. Nashville, May 13, 1955; s. Sorrell Louis and Jacqueline Adele (Falis) W.; m. Adrienne Sue Mates, Dec. 16, 1979; children: Alexis Ellyn, Andrew Lane. BA, U. Fla., 1978, MD, 1982. Diplomate Am. Bd. Radiology. Intern internal medicine Jackson Meml. Hosp., Miami, Fla., 1982-83; staff physician Pub. Health Svc., Miami, 1983-85; pvt. practice Palm Beach Gardens, Fla., 1985-86; resident in radiation oncology Med. Coll. Va., Richmond, 1986-89; instr. radiation oncology U. Miami Sch. Medicine, 1989-91, asst. prof., 1991-97, assoc. prof., 1997—. Contbr. articles to profl. jours. Bd. dirs. Children's Home Soc., Ft. Lauderdale, Fla., 1993—, Temple Beth Israel, Sunrise, Fla., 1994—; mem. spkrs. bur. U. Miami, 1993—; vol. spkr. Broward County Schs., 1990—; exec. v.p. Temple Beth Israel, 1996—. Sylvester Cancer Ctr. grantee, 1992. Mem. Gynecologic Oncology Group, Radiation Therapy Oncology Group, Am. Soc. Therapeutic Radiology and Oncology. Jewish. Achievements include research on malignant tumors of the female genital tract. Avocations: bridge, tennis, reading science fiction. Office: Univ of Miami 1475 NW 12th Ave # D-31 Miami FL 33136-1002

WOLFSON, HAROLD, public relations consultant; b. Pawtucket, R.I., Oct. 3, 1926; s. Samuel and Dora (Kasindorf) W.; m. Marian A. Granrud, Oct. 9, 1953; children: Nancy C. Jenne, Peter G. BA, Yale U., 1949. Feature writer N.Y. Jour.-Am., N.Y.C., 1949-55; v.p. Ruder & Finn Inc., N.Y.C., 1955-63; pres. Rubenstein, Wolfson & Co., N.Y.C., 1963-89; ret., 1989; cons., 1989—. Served with USN, 1944-46. Mem. Pub. Relations Soc. Am. (chmn. pub. relations com. N.Y. chpt. 1984-86). Home and Office: 20 Iselin Ter Larchmont NY 10538-2631

WOLFSON, IRWIN M., insurance company executive; b. Bronx, N.Y., May 29, 1937; s. Herman M. and Kate (Greenstein) W.; m. Pauline S. Frechtel, Dec. 25, 1962; children: Fran M., Lisa G. BS in Econs., NYU, 1960. Owner/CEO Wolfson Agency, Yonkers, N.Y., 1973—; instr., owner Successful Adult Fin. Seminars, Yonkers, 1990—. Mem. operating bd. Child Abuse Prevention Ctr., White Plains, N.Y., 1990—. Sgt. U.S. Army, 1960-66. Recipient Achievement award Congressman Elliot Engel, 1992, proclamation From T. Zaleski (Mayor) City of Yonkers, 1992, letter of Recognition from M. Cuomo (Governor) N.Y. 1992; Irwin M. Wolfson Day proclaimed by A. O'Rourk (County Exec.) N.Y. 1992. Mem. Yonkers Nat. Exch. Club (pres. 1990-91, N.Y. dist. dir. 1991-95, N.Y. dist. pres. 1996-97). Home: 11-4 Jackson Ave Scarsdale NY 10583-3104 Office: Wolfson Agency 475 Tuckahoe Rd Yonkers NY 10710-5716

WOLFSON, LARRY M., lawyer; b. Springfield, Ill., June 12, 1947; m. Cynthia Sherwood, 1972; children: Sharon Eve, Rachel Beth, Anna Faye. BSBA, Northwestern U., 1969; JD cum laude, U. Mich., 1974. Bar: Ill. 1974. Ptnr. Jenner & Block, Chgo. Mem. ABA, Ill. State Bar (lectr. Comml. Banking and Bankruptcy Law Edn. Series 1990), Chgo. Bar Assn., Chgo. Coun. Lawyers, Am. Bankruptcy Inst. Office: Jenner & Block 1 E Ibm Plz Chicago IL 60611-3586

WOLFSON, MARK ALAN, investor, business educator; b. Chgo., Sept. 25, 1952; s. Jack and Maribelle (Simen) W.; m. Sheila Rae Aronesti, Aug. 3, 1975; children: Laura Rachel, Charles Michael. BS in Acctg. and Fin., U. Ill., 1973, M Acctg. Sci., 1974; PhD in Acctg., U. Tex., 1977. Asst. prof. Stanford (Calif.) U., 1977-81, assoc. prof., 1981-85, prof. acctg., 1985-87, Joseph McDonald prof., 1987-92, assoc. dean, 1990-93; Dean Witter prof., 1992-96; Ford Found. vis. assoc. prof. U. Chgo., 1981-82; Thomas Henry Carroll vis. prof. Harvard U., Boston, 1988-89; cons. Fin. Acctg. Stds. Bd., Norwalk, Conn., 1985, 89-92; rsch. assoc. Nat. Bur. Econ. Rsch., Cambridge, Mass., 1988—; mem. steering com. Ctr. Econ. Policy Rsch., Stanford, 1990—; mem. task force Fed. Home Loan Bank Bd., 1989; v.p. Keystone Inc., 1995—; prin. Arbor Investors, 1995—; bd. dirs. Investment Tech. Group, Jefferies Group, L.A., Oreck Corp., Regina Home Care Corp.; bd. advisors FEP Capital; gen. ptnr. P & PK Family Ltd. Partnership. Mem. numerous editl. bds. of finance, econs., and acctg. jours.; contbr. numerous articles to profl. jours. Recipient Pomerance prize Chgo. Bd. Options Exch., 1981, Disting. Tchg. award Stanford U., 1990, Notable Contbn. to Lit. award AICPA-Am. Acctg. Assn., 1990, 92, Wildman award, 1991; named Disting. Accountancy Alumnus, U. Ill., 1989. Jewish. Office: Arbor Investors 2460 Sand Hill Rd Ste 300 Menlo Park CA 94025-6918

WOLFSON, MICHAEL GEORGE, lawyer; b. Chgo., Sept. 1, 1938; s. A. Lincoln M. Weingarten and Brina (Nelson) W.; m. Rita Sue Parsont, Sept. 11, 1966; children: Bethany Lynne, Sara Wynne, Deborah Kay. Student, MIT, 1956-58; BA, U. Chgo., 1961, JD, 1964, postdoctoral, 1964-65. Bar: Ill. 1964, N.Y. 1969. Assoc. Cravath, Swaine & Moore, N.Y.C., 1965-71, Brown, Wood, Fuller, Caldwell & Ivey, N.Y.C., 1971-73; ptnr. Brown & Wood LLP and predecessor firms, N.Y.C., 1974—. Woodrow Wilson fellow, 1961; Ford Found. fellow in internat. trade and devel., 1965. Fellow Am. Bar Found.; mem. ABA. Avocations: reading, photography, fly fishing, bicycling. Office: Brown & Wood LLP 1 World Trade Ctr New York NY 10048-0202

WOLFSON, NICHOLAS, law educator; b. N.Y.C., Feb. 29, 1932; s. Martin and Rose Wolfson; m. Judith Wolfson, Sept. 8, 1955; children: Amy, Adam. AB with highest honors, Columbia U., 1953; JD cum laude, Harvard U., 1956. Bar: N.Y. 1956, Mass. 1966. Atty. SEC, Washington, 1958-60; pvt. practice N.Y.C. and Boston, 1960-66; br. chief, spl. counsel, asst. dir. SEC, 1967-72; prof. U. Conn., 1972—, Ellen Ash Peters prof., 1990-92, George & Helen England prof., 1995—; vis. scholar Hoover Instn. on War, Revolution and Peace, Stanford (Calif.) U., fall 1985; lectr. in field. Author: The Modern Corporation: Free Markets vs. Regulation, 1984, Corporate First Amendments Rights and the SEC, 1990, Twentieth Century Fund Report: Conflicts of Interest: Investment Banking, 1976, Hate Speech, Sex Speech, Free Speech, 1997; co-author: Regulation of Brokers, Dealers and Securities Markets, 1979; contbr. articles to profl. jours. Past chair Fedn. Cmty. Rels. Coun.; pasr mem. exec. com. Nat. Jewish Cmty. Rels. Adv. Coun. Mem. ABA (chair legal edn. com. sect. bus. law 1984-88), Assn. Am. Law Schs. (chair bus. assns. sect. 1978). Office: U Conn Sch of Law 65 Elizabeth St Hartford CT 06105-2213

WOLGIN, DAVID LEWIS, psychology educator; b. Elizabeth, N.J., Oct. 17, 1945. BA, Rutgers U., 1967; MA, Vanderbilt U., 1968; PhD, Rutgers U., 1973. Postdoctoral fellow Inst. for Neurological Sci., U. Pa., Phila., 1973-74; rsch. assoc. U. Ill., Urbana, 1974-75; asst. prof. Fla. Atlantic U., Boca Raton, 1975-79, assoc. prof., 1979-85, prof., 1985—, dir. Inst. for the Study of Alcohol and Drug Dependence, 1986—, chmn. dept. psychology, 1996—. Author: (with others) Hunger: Basic Mechanisms and Clinical Implications, 1976, The Expression of Knowledge, 1982, Psychoactive Drugs: Tolerance and Sensitization, 1989; contbr. articles to profl. jours. Pres. Synagogue Inverrary-Chabad, Lauderhill, Fla., 1981-92; dir. Boca Raton Synagogue, 1995—, v.p. 1996-97. Rsch. grantee Nat. Inst. on Drug Abuse, 1990—. Mem. Soc. for Neurosci., N.Y. Acad. Sci., Soc. for Stimulus Properties Drugs, Soc. for the Study Ingestive Behavior, European Behavioural Pharmacology Soc., Ea. Psychol. Assn., Internat. Behavioral Neurosci. Soc. (charter). Office: Fla Atlantic U Dept Psychology Boca Raton FL 33431

WOLICKI, ELIGIUS ANTHONY, nuclear physicist, consultant; b. Buffalo, May 10, 1927; s. Karol Thaddeus and Katarzyna (Garbus) W.; m. Wilma Pitsenbarger, Aug. 28, 1954; children: Karol, Ann, Stasia, Stefanie. BS magna cum laude, Canisius Coll., 1946; PhD in Nuclear Physics, U. Notre Dame, 1950. Postdoctoral rsch. assoc. in nuclear physics, dept. physics State U. Iowa, Iowa City, 1950-52; rsch. physicist Van de Graaff Br. Naval Rsch. Lab., Washington, 1952-55, head charged particles reactions sect. Van de Graaff Br., 1955-66, assoc. div. supt. nuclear sci. and tech. div., 1966-84; program area reviewer for hardness assurance Dept. Def. Nuclear Agy., Washington, 1976-84, program area reviewer for single event upsets, 1981-84; chmn. Air Force NASA Hardness Assurance Com., 1979-90; pres. Wolicki Assocs. Inc., Alexandria, Va., 1984-94. Contbr. articles to jours., chpts. to books; patentee in field. Recipient Centennial award U. Notre Dame, 1965, Meritorious Civilian Svc. award Naval Rsch. Lab., 1971. Fellow IEEE (best paper award conf. on nuclear and space radiation effects 1987), Am. Phys. Soc. Roman Catholic. Achievements include early research on ion beam analysis of surfaces; ion implantation; radiation effects in electronic devices, SDI neutral particle beams; early work on single event upsets of microcircuits by cosmic rays in space. Avocations: travel, tennis, theater, music composition. Home and Office: 1310 Gatewood Dr Alexandria VA 22307-2032

WOLIN, ALFRED M., federal judge; b. Orange, N.J., Sept. 17, 1932; s. George and Juliet (Rosenstock) W.; m. Jane Zapiekov, Mar. 27, 1960; children: Roger, Marc. BA, U. Mich., 1954; LLB, JD, Rutgers U., 1959. Pvt. practice Elizabeth, N.J., 1960-80; judge Union County Dist. Ct., Elizabeth, N.J., 1980-85, Union County Superior Ct., Elizabeth, N.J., 1985-87, U.S. Dist. Ct., Newark, N.J., 1987—; atty. Roselle Bd. Adjustment, 1965-74; legis. aide to Senator Matthew J. Rinaldo, N.J. Senate, 1970-72; spl. asst. prosecutor Union County, 1970; congl. field rep. 12th congl. dist., 1972-79; mcpl. prosecutor Town of Westfield, N.J., 1973-74. Chief staff atty. Union County Legal Aid Soc., 1964-74; mem. Union County Ethics Com., sec., 1970-78, exec. com. Statewide Speedy Trial Com., Conf. Presiding Criminal Judges, Criminal Practice Com.; active Temple Emanuel, Jewish Fedn. Cen. N.J. SPC 2 U.S. Army, 1954-56, Germany. Mem. ABA, Am. Judicature Soc., N.J. Bar Assn. (judicial selection, discipline of the bar, lawyer referral coms.), Union County Bar Assn. (sec. 1970-74, pres. elect 1975, pres. 1976, judicial appointments com.), Fed. Judges Assn. Jewish. Office: US Dist Ct US Courthouse 50 Walnut St PO Box 999 Newark NJ 07101-0999 *Notable cases include: (as judge) presided over trademark rights suit involving Procter & Gamble vs. Revlon, 1990, which alleged that Revlon's creation of Ivory Coast shampoo infringed on name of Procter & Gamble's Ivory soap. The suit was settled for an undisclosed amount.**

WOLIN, JEFFREY ALAN, artist. AB, Kenyon Coll., 1972; MFA, Rochester Inst. Tech., 1977. Represented by Catherine Edelman Gallery,

Chgo.; photographer City of Kalamazoo (Mich.) Police Dept., 1973-74; asst. prof. photography Ind. U., Bloomington, 1980-86, assoc. prof. photography, 1986-92, prof., 1993—; head photographics svcs. George Eastman House, Rochester, 1976-80; adj. instr. photography U. Rochester, 1978-80. Exhbns. include Ryerson Photog. Are Ctr., Toronto, Can., 1978, Northlight Gallery, Tempe, Ariz., 1980, 88, Israel Mus., Jerusalem, 1980, George Eastman House, Rochester, 1981, 82, Seattle Arts Mus., 1986, Chgo. Cultural Ctr., 1986, 87, J.B. Speed Art Mus., Louisville, 1987, Silver Image Gallery, Columbus, Ohio, 1987, Marianne Deson Gallery, Chgo., 1988, Burden Gallery, N.Y., 1988, Nexus Contemporary Art Ctr., Atlanta, 1988, 89, Images Gallery, Cin., 1989, Catherine Edelman Gallery, Chgo., 1989, 91, 92, 93, 94, San Francisco Camerawork, 1990, U. Oreg. Mus. Art, Eugene, 1990, 92, Mus. Contemporary Photography, Chgo., 1991, 92, Blue Sky Gallery, Oreg. Ctr. for Photog. Arts, Portland, 1992, Mus. Fine Arts, Houston, 1992, L.A. County Art Mus., 1992, Opsis Gallery, N.Y.C., 1992, Mus. Modern Art, N.Y.C., 1992, Ctr. Creative Photography, Tucson, 1993, Robert Klein Gallery, Boston, 1994, Nelson-Atkins Mus. Art, Kansas City, 1994, Contemporary Art Ctr., New Orleans, 1995, Mpls. Mus. Am. Art, St. Paul, 1995, Art Inst. Chgo., 1996, Internat. Ctr. Photography, 1997, others; permanent collections include Seattle Arts Mus., San Francisco Mus. Modern Art, Mus. Modern Art, N.Y., Mus. Contemporary Photography, Chgo., Mus. Fine Arts, Houston, L.A. County Art Mus., Kalamazoo (Mich.) Inst. Art, Internat. Mus. Photography at George Eastman House, Met. Mus. Art, N.Y.C., Art Inst. Chgo., Ctr. Creative Photography, Tucson, Can. Ctr. for Architecture, Montreal, others. Visual Artist fellow NEA, 1988, 92, Master Artist fellow Ind. Arts Commn., 1991, John Simon Guggenheim fellow, 1991, ArtsLink fellow to Czechoslovakia, 1994, U.S./France fellow Cité Internationale des Arts-Paris, 1994. Subject of books and articles. Home: 2504 Poplar Ct Bloomington IN 47405

WOLIN, MICHAEL STUART, physiology educator; b. Bklyn., Sept. 11, 1953; s. Emanuel and Anita (Klein) W.; m. Theresa Marie Burke, Oct. 25, 1987; children: Joshua Mark, Seth Adam, Sarah Rachel. BA in Chemistry, SUNY, Binghamton, 1975; MS, Yale U., 1977, MPhil, 1978, PhD, 1981. NIH Nat. Rsch. Svc. fellow Tulane U. Sch. Medicine, New Orleans, 1981-82, instr. pharmacology, 1982-83; asst. prof. physiology N.Y. Med. Coll., Valhalla, 1983-89, assoc. prof., 1989-95; prof., 1995—; prin. investigator NIH, 1984—. Assoc. editor Am. Jour. Physiology, 1993—; mem. editl. bd. Microcirculation Jour., 1994—, Free Radical Biology and Medicine, 1997—, Nitric Oxide Biology and Chemistry, 1997—. Recipient Merit award NIH, 1996—; Biomed. rsch. scholar C.H. Revson Found., 1983-85. Mem. AAAS, Am. Thoracic Soc. (sci. program com. 1990-95), Am. Heart Assn. (vice chmn. 1995-96, chmn. 1996—, cardiopulmonary coun. 1984—, sci. program com. 1986-93, established investigator award recipient 1989-94, cardiovascular rsch. study com. 1992-95, co-chmn. Lung & Devel. Rsch. study com. 1995-96, mem. rsch. com. 1995—, com. on scientific sessions program 1996-99, scientific program com. chmn. cardiopulmonary and crititical care coun. 1996-99, exec. com. mem., 1992-94, 96—, Albert Hyman award La. chpt. 1983), Am. Physiol. Soc., Nitric Oxide Soc., Oxygen Soc. Microcirculatory Soc. (chmn. devel. com. 1994-95). Jewish. Achievements include elucidation of novel mechanisms of regulating vascular tone, tissue respiration and guanylate cyclase by reactive oxygen and nitrogen species. Home: 40 Goodwin Ave White Plains NY 10607-1014 Office: NY Med Coll Dept Physiology Valhalla NY 10595

WOLIN, NEAL STEVEN, lawyer; b. Chgo., Dec. 9, 1961; s. Harry S. and Doris (Wacker) W. BA summa cum laude, Yale U., 1983; MSc, U. Oxford, Eng., 1985; JD, Yale U., 1988. Bar: Ill. 1989, D.C. 1989. Adj. asst. prof. of law Bklyn. Law Sch., 1989; law clk. U.S. Judge Eugene H. Nickerson, Bklyn., 1988-89; assoc. Wilmer, Cutler & Pickering, Washington, 1989-90; spl. asst. to dirs. ctrl. intelligence Webster Gates & Woolsey, 1990-93; dep. legal adviser Nat. Sec. Coun. The White House, 1993-94; exec. asst. to the nat. sec. adviser The White House, 1994-95; dept. gen. counsel U.S. Dept. Treasury, 1995—. Coker Teaching fellow Yale Law Sch., 1987-88, Henry fellow, Henry Trust, U. Oxford, 1983-84. Mem. Coun. on Fgn. Rels., Phi Beta Kappa. Home: 4601 Connecticut Ave NW # 318 Washington DC 20008-5700

WOLINS, JOSEPH, artist; b. Atlantic City, Mar. 26, 1915; s. Morris and Rebecca (Katerinska) W.; m. Selma Lazaar, Dec. 7, 1957; children: Richard Lazaar, David Lazaar, John Wolins, Sarah Wolins. Student, Nat. Acad. Design, 1931-35. Painter with Fed. art projects, 1934-41; tchr. South Shore Art Sch., Rockville Center, N.Y., 1950-55, 92d St. YMHA, N.Y.C., 1960, Bklyn. Mus. Art Sch., 1961-62, Long Beach (N.Y.) High Sch., 1962-68; pvt. classes, 1961—. One-man shows include Contemporary Arts Gallery, N.Y.C., Bodley Gallery, N.Y.C., Silvermine Guild, Norwalk, Conn., Slater Mus., Norwich, Conn., Agra Gallery, Washington; exhibited in group shows at Everson Mus., Syracuse, N.Y., World's Fair, N.Y.C., 1939, J.B. Neumann Gallery, N.Y.C., Toledo Mus., Corcoran Art Gallery, U. Ill. Mus., Pa. Acad. Fine Art, Whitney Mus., Sao Paolo Mus. Modern Art, Norfolk (Va.) Mus., Smithsonian Instn., Butler Art Inst., Youngstown, Ohio, Met. Mus. Art, N.Y.C.; represented in permanent collections Met. Mus. Art, Norfolk Mus., Albert Gallery at St. Joseph's (Mo.) U., Ball State Mus. Art, Muncia, Ind., Fiske U. Art Gallery, Mobile, Mus. in Ein Horod, Israel, Butler Art Inst., Nat. Mus. Am. Art, Washington, Slater Mem. Mus., Norwich, Conn., Wichita (Kans.) Art Mus., Everson Mus. of Art, Syracuse, New Brit. Mus. Art, Conn., Boca Raton Art Mus., Fla., also pvt. collections. Grantee Mark Rothko Found., 1971; recipient Painting award Audubon Artists, 1976, Painting award Nat. Inst. Arts and Letters, 1976, Painting award Am. Soc. Contemporary Artists, 1976. Mem. Audubon Artists, Am. Soc. Contemporary Artists. Address: 463 West St New York NY 10014-2010

WOLINSKY, EMANUEL, physician, educator; b. N.Y.C., Sept. 23, 1917; s. Jacob and Bertha (Siegel) W.; m. Marjorie Claster, Nov. 15, 1946; children: Douglas, Peter. B.A., Cornell U., 1938, M.D., 1941. Diplomate Am. Bd. Med. Microbiology. Intern, resident medicine N.Y. Hosp., 1943-45; bacteriologist Trudeau Lab., Saranac Lake, N.Y., 1947-56; mem. faculty Case Western Res. U. Sch. Medicine, 1956—, prof. medicine, 1968-88, prof. pathology, 1981-88, prof. emeritus, 1988—; dir. microbiology Cleve. Met. Gen. Hosp., 1959-91, acting dir. dept. pathology, 1980-86, chief div. infectious diseases, 1961-83. Co-editor Textbook of Pulmonary Diseases, 5th edit., 1993; Asso. editor: Am. Rev. Respiratory Diseases, 1973-79; Contbr. articles to profl. jours., textbooks. Mem. Tb panel U.S.-Japan Co-op. Med. Sci. Program, 1969-75. Recipient Crystal Cross award Ohio Thoracic Soc., 1995, Louis Weinstein award Clin. Infectious Diseases, 1995. Mem. Am. Soc. Microbiology, Am. Thoracic Soc. (Trudeau medal 1986), Infectious Diseases Soc. Am., Phi Beta Kappa, Alpha Omega Alpha. Home: 24761 S Woodland Rd Cleveland OH 44122-3327 Office: Met Health Med Ctr 2500 Metrohealth Dr Cleveland OH 44109-1900

WOLINSKY, IRA, nutritionist; b. N.Y.C., Mar. 30, 1938; s. Abraham and Rachel (Stupsky) W.; m. Mary Ann C. Leonard, Jan. 9, 1965; children: Daniella, David. BS, CCNY, 1960; MS, Kans. U., 1965, PhD, 1968. Lectr. Hebrew U., Jerusalem, 1968-74; assoc. prof. Pa. State U., University Park, 1974-79; prof. U. Houston, 1979—. Editor of books and series on nutrition sci., sports nutrition, nutrition methods; contbr. articles to profl. jours. Office: U Houston Dept Human Devel Houston TX 77204-6861

WOLINSKY, LEO C., newspaper editor. BA in Journalism, U. So. Calif., 1972. Journalist, 1972—; staff writer L.A. Times, 1977-86, dep. chief Sacramento bur., 1987-89, city editor, 1990, Calif. polit. editor, 1991, metro editor, asst. mng. editor, 1994—. Office: Los Angeles Times Times Mirror Sq Los Angeles CA 90053

WOLINTZ, ARTHUR HARRY, physician, neuro-ophthalmologist; b. Bklyn., May 30, 1937; s. Louis and Celia (Ragofsky) W.; m. Carol Sue Bergstein, Nov. 28, 1963; children: Robyn Joy, Ellen Sharon. Student, NYU, 1955-58; MD summa cum laude, SUNY, Bklyn., 1962; postgrad., Columbia U., 1967-68. Diplomate Am. Bd. Psychiatry and Neurology, Am. Bd. Ophthalmology; licensee Nat. Bd. Med. Examiners, U. State of N.Y. Intern Maimonides Hosp., Bklyn., 1962-63, jr. resident in medicine, 1963-64; resident Nat. Inst. Neurol. Diseases and Blindness, Bethesda, Md., 1964-66; chief resident Mt. Sinai Hosp., N.Y.C., 1966-67; clin. asst. prof. neurology Downstate Med. Ctr. SUNY, Bklyn., 1968-69, resident in ophthalmology, 1969-71, from asst. prof. to prof., 1971—, prof. clin. ophthalmology and clin. neurology, 1977—, interim chief ophthalmology, 1983, acting regional chmn. dept. ophthalmology, 1984, prof. ophthalmology, 1987—, chmn. dept. ophthalmology, 1987-96; chair emeritus dept. ophthalmology SUNY-HSCB, 1996—; asst. neurologist Presbyn. Hosp., N.Y.C., 1967-68; instr. neuropathology Coll. Physicians and Surgeons Columbia U., N.Y.C., 1967-68; instr. neurology Mt. Sinai Sch. Medicine, N.Y.C., 1967-68; assoc. dir. neurology Maimonides Med. Ctr., Bklyn., 1968-69; asst. neurologist Coney Island Hosp., Bklyn., 1968-69; vis. neurologist Kings County Hosp. Ctr., Bklyn, 1968-69; chief div. ophthalmology and neuro-ophthalmology Kingsbrook Jewish Med. Ctr., Bklyn., 1971, sec. med. and dental staff 1976-77, v.p. 1978-79, pres. 1980-81, dir. ophthalmology 1981; attending physician State Univ. Hosp., Bklyn., 1971, Kings County Hosp. Ctr., Bklyn., 1971; cons. Luth. Med. Ctr., Beth Israel Med. Ctr., Brookdale Hosp. Med. Ctr., Bklyn., L.I. Coll. Hosp., Bklyn., Maimonides Med. Ctr., Cath. Med. Ctr. Bklyn. and Queens, Bklyn. VA Hosp. Author: Essentials of Clinical Neuro-Ophthalmology, 1976; contbr. chpts. to sci. textbooks and handbooks, articles to profl. jours. Treas. Flatbush Jewish Ctr., Bklyn. With USPHS 1964-66. Recipient J. Eugene Chalfin Meml. Lectr. award Alumni Assn. State Univ.-Kings County, 1981, Tchr. of Yr. award dept. ophthalmology Interfaith Med. Ctr., 1988; named Disting. Teaching Prof. SUNY, 1995. Fellow ACP, ACS, Am. Acad. Ophthalmology and Otolaryngology, Am. Acad. Neurology; mem. AMA, Med. Soc. County Kings, Med. Soc. State N.Y., Bklyn. Ophthal. Soc., N.Y. Acad. Medicine, AAAS, Am. Acad. Neurology, Alumni Assn. SUNY (Master Tchr. award 1987, pres.-elect 1989, pres. 1990-91), Oddfellows, Alpha Omega Alpha. Avocations: Torah reader, cantor. Home and Office: 100 Ocean Pky Brooklyn NY 11218-1755

WOLITARSKY, JAMES WILLIAM, securities industry executive; b. Tarrytown, N.Y., Feb. 19, 1946; s. Edward and Beulah (Kemmet) W.; m. Jean T. Nalle; children: James Jr., Matthew; stepchildren: Timothy, Joan. BA, Franklin & Marshall Coll., 1968; MBA, NYU, 1973. Auditor Hertz, Herson & Co., N.Y.C., 1970-73; comml. loan officer The Phila. Nat. Bank, 1973-76; chief fin. officer Almo Electronics Corp., Phila., 1976-80; dir. budget and control Paine Webber Inc., N.Y.C., 1981-82, dir. mktg. adminstrn., 1982-83, dir. mut. funds and asset mgmt., 1983-84; sr. v.p., dir. product mgmt. Phila. Nat. Bank, 1984-86; exec. v.p., chief fin. officer The Moseley Holding Corp., N.Y.C., 1986-87; pres., chief exec. officer Moseley Securities Corp., N.Y.C., 1987-88; exec. v.p. Gruntal Fin. Corp., N.Y.C., 1988-91; chief fin. officer, bd. dirs. Janney Montgomery Scott Inc., Phila., 1991—; bd. dirs. Phila. Depository Transfer Corp., Addison Capital Shares, Inc., treas.; treas. Addison Capital Mgmt. Corp. Bd. dirs. Cliveden of Nat. Hist. Trust, Inc. Sgt. U.S. Army, 1968-70. Decorated Bronze Star, Vietnam Cross of Gallantry. Mem. Securities Industry Assn. Episcopalian. Club: Phila. Racquet, Phila. Country. Avocations: fishing, skiing, tennis, golf. Home: 240 Church Rd Devon PA 19333 Office: Janney Montgomery Scott Inc 1801 Market St Philadelphia PA 19103-1628

WOLITZER, STEVEN BARRY, investment banker; b. Bklyn., Mar. 14, 1953; s. Philip and Regina (Wurm) W.; m. Joyce Sue Lindower, Dec. 7, 1985; children: David Joel, Scott Richard, Rachel. BS, NYU, 1973; MBA, Harvard U., 1977. CPA, N.Y. Mng. dir. Lehman Bros. Inc., N.Y.C., 1977—. Home: 250 E 87th St Apt 21B New York NY 10128-3120 Office: Lehman Bros Inc 3 World Fin Ctr New York NY 10285

WOLK, BRUCE ALAN, law educator; b. Bklyn., Mar. 2, 1946; s. Morton and Gertrude W.; m. Lois Gloria Krepliak, June 22, 1968; children: Adam, Daniel. BS, Antioch Coll., 1968; MS, Stanford U., 1972; JD, Harvard U., 1975. Bar: D.C. 1975. Assoc. Hogan & Hartson, Washington, 1975-78; prof. U. Calif. Sch. Law, Davis, 1978—, acting dean, 1990-91, dean, 1993—. Danforth Found. fellow, 1970-74, NSF fellow, 1970-72, Fulbright sr. research fellow, 1985-86. Mem. ABA, Am. Law Inst. Office: U Calif Sch Law King Hall Univ of Cal-Davis Davis CA 95616-5201

WOLK, MARTIN, electronic engineer, physicist; b. Long Branch, N.J., Jan. 13, 1930; s. Michael and Tillie (Barron) W.; 1 child, Brett Martin. BS, George Washington U., 1957, MS, 1968; PhD, U. N.Mex., 1973. Physicist Naval Ordnance Lab., White Oak, Md., 1957-59, Nat. Oceanic and Atmospheric Adminstrn., Suitland, Md., 1959-66; solid state physicist Night Vision Lab., Fort Belvoir, Va., 1967-69; rsch. asst. U. N.Mex., Albuquerque, 1969-73; electronics engr. Washington Navy Yard, 1976-83, TRW, Inc., Redondo Beach, Calif., 1983-84; physicist Metrology Engring. Ctr., Pomona, Calif., 1984-85; electronics engr. Naval Aviation Depot North Island, San Diego, 1985—; cons. Marine Corps Logistics Base, Barstow, Calif., 1985—, Naval Weapons Station, Fallbrook, Calif., 1987-89, Naval Weapons Support Ctr., Crane, Ind., 1989—. Contbr. articles to Jour. Quantitative Spectroscopy and Radiative Transfer, Monthly Weather Rev., Proceedings of SPIE, Procs. of EUROPTO. Cpl. U.S. Army, 1946-49, Japan. Mem. IEEE, Soc. Photo-Optical Instrumentation Engring., European Optical Soc., Sigma Pi Sigma, Sigma Tau. Achievements include development of first Tiros meterological satellites; research on electron-beam for micro-circuit device fabrication; development and implementation of electro-optical calibration systems for the TOW missile system optical and night vision sights for the Marine Corps. Home: 740 Eastshore Ter Chula Vista CA 91913-2421

WOLKEN, JEROME JAY, biophysicist, educator; b. Pitts., Mar. 28, 1917; s. Abraham I. and Dina (Lando) W.; m. Dorothy O. Mallinger, June 19, 1945 (dec. 1954); children: Ann A., Jonathan; m. Tobey J. Holestein, Jan. 26, 1956; children: H. Johanna, Erik Andrew. Student, Pa. State U., 1935-36, Duquesne U., 1937-39; BS, U. Pitts., 1946, MS, 1948, PhD, 1949. Rsch. fellow Mellon Inst., 1943-47, Princeton U., 1950-51, Rockefeller Inst., 1951-52; asst. prof. U. Pitts. Sch. Medicine, 1953-57, asso. prof., 1957-61, prof. biophysics physiology, 1962-66; head dept. bioscis. Carnegie Inst. Tech., Pitts., 1964-67; prof. biophysics and bioscis. Carnegie-Mellon U., 1964—, head biophys. rsch. lab., 1964-76; head biophys. rsch. lab. Eye and Ear Hosp., Pitts., 1953-64; rsch. assoc. Carnegie Mus.; guest prof. Pa. State U., 1963, U. Paris, 1967-68, U. Miami (Fla.) Inst. Theoretical Studies, 1966, Univ. Coll., London, 1971, Pasteur Inst., Paris, 1972, AEC, Saclay, France; rsch. fellow Princeton U., 1978; U.S. rsch. fellow Tohoku U., Sendai, Japan, 1988. Author 9 books; editor 2 books; contbr. 120 articles to profl. jours. With USNR, 1941-43. Recipient Career award USPHS, 1962-65. Fellow N.Y. Acad. Scis., AAAS, Optical Soc. Am. (pres. Pitts. sect. 1964-65), Am. Inst. Chemists, Explorers Club; mem. Am. Chem. Soc., Chemists Club N.Y., Am. Inst. Biol. Sci., Biophys. Soc., Soc. Gen. Physiologists, Am. Soc. Cell Biology, Am. Photobiol. Sci., Sigma Xi, Phi Sigma. Achievements include 2 patents for Light Concentrating Lens System. Home: 5817 Elmer St Pittsburgh PA 15232-1915 Office: Carnegie Mellon U Mellon Coll of Sci 4400 5th Ave Pittsburgh PA 15213-2617

WOLKOFF, EUGENE ARNOLD, lawyer; b. N.Y.C., June 9, 1932; s. Oscar and Jean (Zablow) W.; m. Judith Gail Edwards, Oct. 15, 1967; children—Mandy, Elana, Alexa, Justine. A.B., Bklyn. Coll., 1953; LL.B., St. John's U., 1961. Bar: N.Y. 1962, N.Mex. 1994. Practiced in N.Y.C and Santa Fe; mem. firm Callahan & Wolkoff, N.Y.C., 1965—; bd. dirs. Babylon Enterprises, Inc., Hist. Newspaper Archives, Inc., Data Image Processing Corp.; mem. nat. panel arbitrators Am. Arbitration Assn. Served to lt. col. USAFR, 1953-75. Mem. N.Y. State Bar Assn., N.Mex. Bar Assn., Pi Beta Gamma. Office: 17 Battery Pl New York NY 10004 also: 330 Garfield St Santa Fe NM 87501-2640

WOLL, HARRY J., electrical engineer; b. Farmington, Minn., Aug. 25, 1920; s. Henry L. and Clara M. (Fredrickson) W.; m. Mary V. Cowan, Feb. 15, 1947; children: Daniel, Alice. B.S.E.E., N.D. State U., 1940; postgrad., Ill. Inst. Tech., 1940-41; Ph.D., U. Pa., 1953. With RCA Corp., 1941-85; chief engr. aerospace systems div. RCA Corp., Burlington, Mass., 1963-69; div. v.p. govt. engring. RCA Corp., Moorestown, N.J., 1969-75; div. v.p., gen. mgr. RCA Automated Systems, Burlington, 1975-81; staff v.p., chief engr. RCA Electronic Products and Labs., Princeton, N.J., 1981-85. Chmn. bd. trustees Moore Sch. Elec. Engring., U. Pa., 1976-90; trustee U. Pa., 1989-91. Recipient 50th Anniversary gold medal Moore Sch. Elec. Engring., U. Pa., 1973. Fellow AAAS, IEEE (past chmn. Phila. sect., past chmn. fellow com.), Aerospace Industries Tech. Council (past chmn.); mem. Sigma Phi Delta, Phi Kappa Phi. Roman Catholic. Patentee in field. Home: PO Box 679 Concord MA 01742-0679

WOLLE, CHARLES ROBERT, federal judge; b. Sioux City, Iowa, Oct. 16, 1935; s. William Carl and Vivian (Down) W.; m. Kerstin Birgitta Wennerstrom, June 26, 1961; children: Karl Johan Knut, Erik Vernon, Thomas Dag, Aaron Charles. AB, Harvard U., 1959; JD, Iowa Law Sch., 1961. Bar: Iowa 1961. Assoc. Shull, Marshall & Marks, Sioux City, 1961-67, ptnr., 1968-80; judge Dist. Ct. Iowa, Sioux City, 1981-83; justice Iowa Supreme Ct., Sioux City and Des Moines, 1983-87; judge U.S. Dist. Ct. (so. dist.) Iowa, Des Moines, 1987-92, chief judge, 1992—; faculty Nat. Jud. Coll., Reno, 1983—. Editor Iowa Law Rev., 1960-61. Vice pres. bd. dirs. Sioux City Symphony, 1972-77; sec., bd. dirs. Morningside Coll., Sioux City, 1977-81. Fellow Am. Coll. Trial Lawyers; mem. ABA, Iowa Bar Assn., Sioux City C. of C. (bd. dirs. 1977-78). Avocations: sports, art, music, literature. Home: 1601 Pleasant View Dr Des Moines IA 50315-2129 Office: US Chief Dist Judge 103 US Courthouse 123 E Walnut St Des Moines IA 50309-2035

WOLLE, WILLIAM DOWN, foreign service officer; b. Sioux City, Iowa, Mar. 11, 1928; s. William Carl and Vivian Lucille (Down) W.; m. Zanie L. Donahue, Feb. 7, 1992; children from previous marriage: Laila Jean, William Nicholas. B.A., Morningside Coll., 1949; M.Internat. Affairs, Columbia U., 1951. Joined U.S. Fgn. Service, 1951; consular officer Baghdad, Iraq, 1951-52; econ. officer, 1952-53; consular officer Manchester, Eng., 1954-56; trainee Arab lang. and area Beirut, Lebanon, 1957-58; fgn. service officer gen. Aden, So. Yemen, 1958-59; econ. officer Jidda, Saudi Arabia, 1959-62; internat. economist Washington, 1962-64; internat. relations officer, 1964-65; officer in charge Arab-Israeli affairs, 1965-67; detailed Nat. War Coll., 1967-68; counselor polit. affairs Kuwait City, Kuwait, 1968-70; econ. officer, dir. AID, Amman, Jordan, 1970-73; econ. officer Nairobi, 1973-74; ambassador to Oman, Muscat, 1974-78; dir. Middle Eastern/South Asian Research Office, Dept. State, 1978-79; ambassador to United Arab Emirates, 1979-81; adviser internat. affairs Indsl. Coll. Armed Forces, 1982-84; chief sr. officer assignments, Washington, 1984-86. Served with AUS, 1946-47. Recipient Superior Service award Dept. State, 1974, Outstanding Civilian Service award Dept. Def., 1984. Home: 17284 Wexford Loop Dumfries VA 22026

WOLLENBERG, J. ROGER, lawyer; b. N.Y.C., May 1, 1919; s. Harry Lincoln and Gertrude (Arnstein) W.; m. Patricia S. Albright, Jan. 2, 1948; children: Christopher, Meredith, Pamela, Peter, Edward. B.A., U. Calif. at Berkeley, 1939, LL.B., 1942. Bar: Calif. 1946, D.C. 1954. Law clk. U.S. Supreme Ct. Justice William O. Douglas, 1946; with Dept. Justice, 1947-52; asst. gen. counsel FCC, 1952-54; pvt. practice, 1954—; ptnr. Wilmer, Cutler & Pickering, Washington, 1962-91, sr. counsel, 1992—. Mem. Falls Church (Va.) Sch. Bd., 1960-71, chmn., 1962-70; mem. city council City of Falls Church, 1982-88 ; chmn. adv. com. on procedures, U.S. Ct. Appeals, D.C. Cir., 1988-90. Served to lt. USNR, 1942-46. Mem. FCC Bar Assn. (pres. 1965-66), Am. Bar Assn. (ho. of dels. 1967-71). Home: 508 Lincoln Ave Falls Church VA 22046-2621 Office: Wilmer Cutler & Pickering 2445 M St NW Washington DC 20037-1435

WOLLENBERG, RICHARD PETER, paper manufacturing company executive; b. Juneau, Alaska, Aug. 1, 1915; s. Harry L. and Gertrude (Arnstein) W.; m. Leone Bonney, Dec. 22, 1940; children: Kenneth Roger, David Arthur, Keith Kermit, Richard Harry, Carol Lynne. BSME, U. Calif., Berkeley, 1936; MBA, Harvard U., 1938; grad., Army Indsl. Coll., 1941; D in Pub. Affairs (hon.), U. Puget Sound, 1977. Prodn. control Bethlehem Ship, Quincy, Mass., 1938-39; with Longview (Wash.) Fibre Co., 1939—, safety engr., asst. chief engr., chief engr., mgr. container operations, 1951-57, v.p., 1953-57, v.p. ops., 1957-60, exec. v.p., 1960-69, pres., 1969-78, pres., chief exec. officer, 1978-85, pres., chief exec. officer, chmn. bd., 1985—, also bd. dirs.; mem. Wash. State Council for Postsecondary Edn., 1969-79, chmn., 1970-73; mem. western adv. bd. Allendale Ins. Bassoonist SW Washington Symphony. Trustee Reed Coll., Portland, 1962—, chmn. bd. 1982-90. Served to lt. col. USAAF, 1941-45. Recipient Alumni Achievement award Harvard U., 1994. Mem. NAM (bd. dirs. 1981-86), Pacific Coast Assn. Pulp and Paper Mfrs. (pres. 1981-92), Inst. Paper Sci. and Tech. (trustee), Wash. State Roundtable, Crabbe Huson (bd. dirs.). Home: 1632 Kessler Blvd Longview WA 98632-3633 Office: Longview Fibre Co PO Box 606 Longview WA 98632-7391*

WOLLER, JAMES ALAN, lawyer; b. Adrian, Mich., Dec. 27, 1946; s. Robert Arthur and Florence Emma (Jacob) W.; m. Jill Ann Samis, Aug. 18, 1968 (div. Aug. 1978); 1 child, Emily Erin; m. Elizabeth Julia Frey, May 22, 1982. BA, U. Mich., 1969; JD, Columbia U., 1974. Bar: N.J. 1974, U.S. Dist. Ct. N.J. 1974, U.S. Tax Ct. 1976. Assoc. McCarter & English, Newark, 1974-79; v.p. Pfaltz & Woller, P.A., Summit, N.J., 1979-86, pres., 1987—. Editor Columbia U. Human Rights Law Rev., 1973-74. Mem. ABA, N.J. Bar Assn., Union County Bar Assn., Summit Bar Assn. (pres. 1987-88), Downtown Club (trustee 1997—), Raritan Yacht Club (fin. sec. Perth Amboy, N.J. 1988-89, treas. 1989-92, vice commodore 1993-94, commodore 1994-95), Columbia Law Sch. Assn. N.J. (trustee 1992—). Republican. Methodist. Avocation: sailing. Home: 207 Springfield Ave Summit NJ 07901-3907 Office: Pfaltz & Woller PA 382 Springfield Ave Summit NJ 07901-2707

WOLLERSHEIM, JANET PUCCINELLI, psychology educator; b. Anaconda, Mont., July 24, 1936; d. Nello J. and Inez Marie (Ungaretti) Puccinelli; m. David E. Wollersheim, Aug. 1, 1959 (div. June 1972); children: Danette Marie, Tod Neil; m. Daniel J. Smith, July 17, 1976. AB, Gonzaga U., 1958; MA, St. Louis U., 1960; PhD, U. Ill., 1968. Lic. psychologist, Mont. Asst. prof. psychology, asst. dir. testing and counseling ctr. U. Mo., 1968-71; prof. psychology U. Mont., Missoula, 1971—, dir. chin. psychology, 1980-87; chair Mont. Bd. Psychologists, 1977-78; cons. Mont. State Prison, 1971-85, Trapper Creek Job Corps, 1973—; pvt. practice, Missoula, 1971—. Author numerous rsch. articles. Bd. dirs. Crisis Ctr., Missoula, 1972-73; mem. profl. adv. bd. Head Start, Missoula, 1972-79. Recipient Disting. scholar award U. Montana, 1991. Fellow Am. Psychol. Assn. (bd. dirs. div. clin. psychology 1990-92); mem. Rocky Mountain Psychol. Assn. (pres. 1983-84), Nat. Council Univ. Dirs. Clin. Psychology (bd. dirs., 1982-88). Roman Catholic. Catholic. Home: 105 Greenwood Ln Missoula MT 59803-2401 Office: 900 N Orange St Ste 201 Missoula MT 59802-2998

WOLLERT, GERALD DALE, retired food company executive, investor; b. LaPorte, Ind., Jan. 21, 1935; s. Delmar Everette and Esther Mae W.; m. Carol Jean Burchby, Jan. 26, 1957; children—Karen Lynn, Edwin Del. B.S., Purdue U., 1957. With Gen. Foods Corp., 1959-89; dir. consumer affairs Gen. Foods Corp., White Plains, N.Y., 1973-74; mng. dir. Cottee Foods div. Gen. Foods Corp., Sydney, Australia, 1974-76; gen. mgr. Mexico div. Gen. Foods Corp., Mexico City, 1978-79; pres. Asia/Pacific ops. Gen. Foods Corp., Honolulu, corp. v.p. worldwide coffee and internat. div., 1979-89; ret., 1989; dir. Gen. Foods cos., Japan, Peoples Republic China, Korea, India, Taiwan, Singapore, Philippines. Webelos leader Boy Scouts Am., Mexico City, 1978-79; co. gen. chmn. United Fund campaign, Battle Creek, Mich., 1964-65, White Plains, N.Y., 1972-73. Served with U.S. Army, 1958. Mem. Asian-U.S. Bus. Coun., Oahu Country Club (Hawaii), Venice Golf and Country Club (Fla.), Beacon Hills and Beechwood (Ind.) Club.

WOLLMAN, HARRY, health care and executive search consultant; b. Bklyn., Sept. 26, 1932; s. Jacob and Florence Roslyn (Hoffman) W.; m. Anne Carolyn Hamel, Feb. 16, 1957; children: Julie Ellen, Emily Jane, Diana Leigh. AB summa cum laude, Harvard Coll., 1954, MD, 1958. Diplomate Am. Bd. Anesthesiology. Intern U. Chgo. Clinics, 1958-59; resident U. Pa., 1959-63, assoc. in anesthesia, 1963-65, mem. faculty, 1965-87, prof. anesthesia, 1970-87, prof. pharmacology, 1971-87, Robert Dunning Dripps prof., chmn. dept. anesthesia, 1972-87; prin. investigator Anesthesia Rsch. Ctr., 1972-78; program dir. Anesthesia Rsch. Tng. Grant, 1972-87; sr. v.p., chief acad. officer, dean Sch. Medicine Hahnemann U., Phila., 1987-92, prof. anesthesiology, 1987-92, prof. pharmacology, 1987-92, univ. prof., 1992-96; prin. Alexander, Wollman and Stark, Health Care Cons. Exec. Search, Woodstock, Vt., 1996—; Mem. anesthesia drug panel, drug efficacy study, com. on anesthesia Nat. Acad. Scis.-NRC, 1970-71, com. on adverse reactions to anesthesia drugs, 1971-72; mem. pharm. and toxicology tng. grants com. NIH, 1966-68, anesthesia tng. grants com., 1971-73, surgery, anesthesia and trauma study sect., 1974-78; chmn. com. on studies involving human beings U. Pa., 1972-76, chmn. clin. practice exec. com., 1976-80. Assoc. editor for revs.: Anesthesiology, 1970-75; Contbr. and editor books. Hon. John Harvard scholar Harvard Coll., 1950-53, Harvard Coll. scholar, 1953-54, Detur award, 1951; NIH rsch. traineeship fellow, 1959-63, Pharm. Mfg. Assn. fellow, 1960-61. Mem. AMA, Pa. Soc. Anesthesiologists (pres. 1972-73), Am. Physiol. Soc., Assn. U. Anesthetists (exec. coun. 1971-74, chmn.

scientific adv. bd. 1975-77), Soc. Acad. Anesthesia Chairmen (chmn. com. fin. resources 1973-77, pres. 1977-78), Am. Soc. Anesthesiologists, Am. Dental Soc., Anesthesiology (adv. bd. 1985-90), Assn. Am. Med. Coll., Phi Beta Kappa, Sigma Xi. Home: 13 Hathorn's Hill Woodstock VT 05091 Office: Alexander Wollmann and Stark 13 Hathorn Hl Woodstock VT 05091-1238

WOLLMAN, LEO, physician; b. N.Y.C., Mar. 14, 1914; s. Joseph and Sara (Samrick) W.; m. Eleanor Rakow, Aug. 16, 1936 (dec. 1953); children: Arthur Lee, Bryant Lee; m. Charlotte Kornberg Seidman, Oct. 6, 1954 (div. 1969); m. Ellen Hershenson, Mar. 25, 1985. BS, Columbia U., 1934; MS, NYU, 1938; MD, Royal Coll. Edinburgh, 1942; PhD (hon.), Rochdale, 1972; DSc (hon.), U. Mich., 1973. Diplomate Am. Bd. Hypnosis in Ob-Gyn, Nat. Bd. Acupuncture Medicine, Am. Acad. Pain Mgmt., Am. Bd. Psychiatry and Neurology, Am. Bd. Sexology. Intern Cumberland Hosp., Bklyn., 1942-43; resident Leith Gen. Hosp., 1942; practice medicine specializing in ob-gyn Bklyn., 1944-72; in psychiatry, 1972—; mem. staff Maimonides, Coney Island hosps., Bklyn. Hosp. Ctr., Bklyn., Park East, Mt. Sinai hosps., N.Y.C.; med. dir. acupuncture dept. Lexington Health Facility, N.Y.C. Author: Write Yourself Slim, 1976, Eating Your Way to a Better Sex Life, 1983, numerous articles in profl. jours.; editor-in-chief: Jour. Am. Soc. Psychosomatic Dentistry and Medicine, 1968-83; editor newsletter: Soc. Sci. Study Sex; editor: News Bull. of Inst. for Comprehensive Medicine; assoc. editor: Jour. Sex Research; internat. editor: Latin Am. Jour. Clin. Hypnosis; films I Am Not This Body, 1970, StrangeHer, 1971, Let Me Die a Woman, 1978. Pres. Jewish Com. Coun. Greater Coney Island, 1989—. Recipient Jules Weinstein Ann. Pioneer in Modern Hypnosis award, 1964. Fellow Am. Geriatrics Soc., N.Y. Acad. Scis. (life), Acad. Psychosomatic Medicine (sec. 1965), Soc. Clin. and Exptl. Hypnosis (life), Am. Soc. Clin. Hypnosis (life), Soc. Sci. Study Sex (pres. Eastern region 1979-81), Am. Soc. Psychical Research (life), Am. Med. Writers Assn. (life), Internat. Soc. Comprehensive Medicine, Am. Acad. Psychiatry and Neurology, Am. Coll. Sexology; mem. Nat. Geog. Soc. (life), AAAS (council 1971-73), Am. Assn. Social Psychiatry, Am. Soc. Abdominal Surgeons, Internat. Soc. Nonverbal Psychotherapy, N.Y. State Soc. Med. Research, Royal Medico-Psychol. Assn. (Eng.), N.Y. Soc. for Gen. Semantics, Nat. Assn. on Standard Med. Vocabulary (sec. 1964—), Am. Assn. History Medicine, Am. Assn. Study Headache, Am. Acad. Dental Medicine, Am. Assn. Marriage Counselors, Soc. Med. Jurisprudence, Bklyn. Psychol. Assn., Canadian Soc. for Study Fertility, Am. Fertility Soc. (life), Internat. Fertility Assn., Internat. Soc. for Clin. and Exptl. Hypnosis (life), Am. Soc. Psychosomatic Dentistry and Medicine (pres. 1969-72, exec. dir. 1973-83), Assn. Advancement Psychotherapy, Pan-Am. Med. Assn., Andalusian Soc. Sophrology and Psychosomatic Medicine, Brit. Med. Assn., Bklyn. Acad. Medicine, Internat. Soc. Psychoneuroendocrinology, L.I. Hist. Soc.; also hon. mem. numerous fgn. orgns. Address: 3813 Poplar Ave Brooklyn NY 11224-1301 *I have learned that to be busily occupied doing the work I like is to be happy. Doing what you like to do usually results in a job well done. To take pride in one's work is a virtue.*

WOLLMAN, NATHANIEL, economist, educator; b. Phila., May 15, 1915; s. Leon and Rose (Schimmel) W.; m. Lenora Levin, Dec. 25, 1939 (dec. Dec. 1994); children: Stephen, Eric. A.B., Pa. State U., 1936; Ph.D., Princeton U., 1940; LL.D., Colo. Coll., 1972. Instr., asst. prof. Colo. Coll., 1939-48; asso. prof., prof. econs. U. N.Mex., 1948-81, prof. emeritus, 1981—, chmn. dept. econs., 1960-69; dean Coll. Arts and Scis., 1969-81; economist Resources for the Future, 1959-60, 64-65; Chmn. Internat. Environ. Programs Com., 1976-79. Author: (with others) Water Supply and Demand, 1960, Value of Water in Alternative Uses, 1962, Water Resources of Chile, 1968, (with Gilbert Bonem) The Outlook for Water: Quality, Quantity and National Growth, 1971, (with others) Man, Materials and Environment, 1973. Served with USNR, World War II. Mem. Am. Econs. Assn. Home: 7010 Phoenix Ave NE Apt 713 Albuquerque NM 87110-3562

WOLLMAN, ROGER LELAND, judge; b. Frankfort, S.D., May 29, 1934; s. Edwin and Katherine Wollman; m. Diane Marie Schroeder, June 21, 1959; children: Steven James, John Mark, Thomas Roger. BA, Tabor Coll., Hillsboro, Kans., 1957; JD magna cum laude, U. S.D., 1962; LLM, Harvard U., 1964. Bar: S.D. 1964. Sole practice, Aberdeen, 1964-71; justice S.D. Supreme Ct., 1971-85, chief justice, 1978-82; judge U.S. Ct. Appeals (8th cir.), 1985—; states atty. Brown County, Aberdeen, 1967-71. Served with AUS, 1957-59. Office: US Ct Appeals 311 Fed Bldg and US Courthouse 400 S Phillips Ave Sioux Falls SD 57104-6824*

WOLLNER, THOMAS EDWARD, manufacturing company executive; b. Rochester, Minn., Dec. 30, 1936; s. Clarence E. and Grace W. (Day) W.; m. Marlene A. Hanson, July 12, 1958; children: Mark R., Jill M. BA, St. John's U., Collegeville, Minn., 1958; PhD, Wash. State U., 1964. Sr. research chemist tape research 3M Co., St. Paul, 1964-66, research supr., mgr. comml. tape div. lab., 1966-73, mgr. Cen. Research Labs., 1973-77, dir. Chem. Research Lab., 1977-81, dir. Indsl. and Consumer Sector Research Lab., 1981-84, exec. dir. research and devel. indsl. and consumer sector, 1984-86, v.p. research and devel. indsl. and consumer sector, 1986-87, staff v.p. Corp. Research Labs., 1987—. Served to lt. U.S. Army, 1960. Mem. Am. Chem. Soc., Indsl. Research Inst. (alt. rep.). Office: 3M Co 3M Center Bldg 01 Saint Paul MN 55144-0001

WOLLUM, ARTHUR GEORGE, II, microbiologist, researcher, educator; b. Chgo., July 26, 1937; s. Arthur George and Hertha (Christensen) W.; m. Karen Hanson, June 18, 1960; children: Steven Arthur, Mark Hanson. BS, U. Minn., 1959; MS, Oreg. State U., 1963, PhD, 1965. Rsch. assoc. Oreg. State U., Corvallis, 1965-67; asst. prof. microbiology N.Mex. State U., Las Cruces, 1967-71; assoc. prof. N.C. State U., Raleigh, 1971-76, prof., 1976—, head ecology program, 1984-89; vis. prof. Ohio State U., Columbus, 1978-79. Author more than 100 articles and book chpts. on biol. nitrogen fixation, microbial ecology, bioremediation. Fellow Soil Sci. Soc. Am., Am. Soc. Agronomy (divsn. chair, assoc. editor, coms.); mem. Am. Soc. Microbiology, Soc. Am. Forest (assoc. editor Forest Sci.), Soil Sci. Soc. Am. (tech. editor jour.), Sigma Xi, Gamma Sigma Delta. Achievements include advances in the understanding of stress ecology of Bradyrhizobium japonicum and its genetic diversity in soil environments,significant contrubutions to enhancing the teaching of soil microbiology. Office: NC State U Dept Soil Sci Box 7619 Raleigh NC 27695-7619

WOLMAN, J. MARTIN, retired newspaper publisher; b. Elizabeth, N.J., Mar. 8, 1919; s. Joseph D. and Dora (Baum) W.; m. Anne Paley, Sept. 12, 1943; children: Natalie, Jonathan, Ruth Ellen, Lewis Joel. Student, U. Wis., 1937-42. With Wis. State Jour., Madison, 1936-84; pub. Wis. State Jour., 1968-84; pres., gen. mgr. Madison Newspaper, Inc., 1969-84, ret., 1984, dir., 1969—; dir. Lee Enterprises, Inc., 1971-74; treas. Lee Endowment Trusts, 1988—; sec.-treas. Madison Improvement Corp., 1958-62. Treas. Wis. State Jour. Empty Stocking Club, 1948, Children and Youth Services Inc., 1962—; mem. Mayor Madison Adv. Com., 1965; bd. dirs. United Givers Fund, 1960-64, trustee, 1980—; ex-officio Roy L. Matson Scholarship Fund, 1961, Central Madison Com., Madison Art Assn.; trustee Edgewood Coll., Madison, U. Wis. Hosp. and Clinic; chmn. Madison Area Arts Coalition, 1984-85; bd. dirs. Univ. Health Sci. Center, 1975; chmn. U.S. Savs. Bond Met. Wis., 1983; coordinator Barneveld Disaster Fund, Wis., 1985-86; mem. U. Wis. Found., 1968-95; bd. dirs., trustee Wisc. Clin. Cancer Ctr., 1986—; Dir. Wisc. Newspaper Found., 1986-88; v.p., treas. Lee Endowment Found., 1989—. Served with AUS, 1942-46. Named Advt. Man of Year Madison Advt. Club, 1969, Madison Man of Achievement, 1976, Man of Yr. Salvation Army, 1993; recipient Disting. Service award Wis. Newspaper Assn., 1982, Community Service award Inland Daily Press Assn., 1983, Ralph D. Casey Minn. award for Disting. Service in Journalism, 1987, First Ringling Bros. Silver Smile award, 1993, Outstanding Svc. for Youth award Wis. State Jour., 1995. Mem. Madison C. of C. (dir. 1966-70, 74-84), Inland Daily Press Assn. (dir. 1961-65), Wis. Daily Newspaper League (pres. 1961-65), Wis. Newspaper Assn. (dir. 1977-84). Clubs: B'nai B'rith, Madison. Office: 1901 Fish Hatchery Rd Madison WI 53713-1248

WOLMAN, M. GORDON, geography educator; b. Balt., Aug. 16, 1924; s. Abel and Anna (Gordon) W.; m. Elaine Mielke, June 20, 1951; children: Elsa Anne, Abel Gordon, Abby Lucille, Fredericka Jeannette. Student, Haverford Coll.; AB in Geology, Johns Hopkins U., 1949; MA in Geology, Harvard U., 1951, PhD, 1953. Geologist U.S. Geol. Survey, 1951-58, part-time, 1958—; assoc. prof. geography Johns Hopkins U., Balt., 1958-62; prof. Johns Hopkins, 1962—; chmn. dept. geography and environ. engring., 1958-90, Interim provost, 1987, 90; adv. com. geography U.S. Office Naval Rsch., Oak Ridge Nat. Lab; exec. com. divsn. earth sci. NRC, internat. environ. programs com., environ. studies bd., com. water, com. mineral resources and environ., chmn. nat. commn. water quality policy NAS; chmn. NRC Com. Adv. U.S. Geol. Survey, NAS Commn. Geoscis., Environment and Resources; environ. adv. com. Savannah River Tech. Ctr.; cons. in field. Author: Fluvial Processes in Geomorphology, 1964; Editorial bd.: Science mag. Pres. bd. trustees Park Sch., Balt.; pres. bd. dirs. Sinai Hosp., Balt., Resources for Future, 1980-87; adv. com. Inst. Nuclear Power Ops., 1982-85; active Balt. City Charter Revision Commn., Cmty. Action Com., Balt. With USNR, 1943-46. Recipient Meritorious Contbn. award Assn. Am. Geographers, 1972, Disting. Career award Geomorphology, 1993, D.L. Linton award Brit. Geomorphological Rsch. Group, 1994, Rachel Carson award Chesapeake Appreciation Inc. Fellow Am. Acad. Arts and Scis.; mem. ASCE, NAS, Am. Geophys. Union (chmn. subcom. sedimentation, pres. hydrol. sect.), Geol. Soc. Am. (v.p. 1983, pres. 1984), Am. Geog. Soc. (councillor 1965-70, Cullum Geog. medal 1989), Washington Geol. Soc., Agrl. Hist. Soc., Md. Acad. Scis. (exec. com. 1970-75), Phi Beta Kappa, Sigma Xi. Home: 2104 W Rogers Ave Baltimore MD 21209-4553 Office: Johns Hopkins U Dept Geography/Environ Engr Baltimore MD 21218

WOLMAN, MARTIN, lawyer; b. Albany, N.Y., Feb. 2, 1937; s. Benjamin S. and Sonya (Kogan) W.; children: Koren M. Wolman-Tardy, Barton T., William B., Brandon S. AB, Brown U., 1958; LLB, U. Calif., Berkeley, 1964. Bar: Calif., 1964, Conn., 1965. Atty. Conn. Bank & Trust Co., Hartford, 1964-67; assoc. Day, Berry & Howard, Hartford, 1967-72, ptnr., 1972—; mem. Conn. Law Revision Commn. Trustee Russell-Sage Coll., Troy, N.Y., 1990-96, Wadsworth Atheneum, 1994; trustee Kingswood-Oxford Sch., West Hartford, Conn., 1980-93, chmn., 1986-89; bd. dirs. Hartford Hosp., 1991, Inst. of Living, 1994; mem. bd. govs. Hill-Stead Mus., Farmington, Conn., 1990-94. Lt. (j.g.) USN, 1958-61. Fellow Am. Coll. Trust and Estate Counsel (chmn. Conn. chpt. 1981-86); mem. Conn. Bar Assn. (chmn. exec. com. probate sect. 1979-82). Office: Day Berry & Howard City Place Hartford CT 06103

WOLMER, BRUCE RICHARD, magazine editor; b. N.Y.C., Mar. 9, 1948; s. Simon and Elaine (Richelson) Katz; m. Colleen Babington, Nov. 20, 1995. BA, Wesleyan U., Middletown, Conn., 1968; Licence es Lettres, U. Paris (Sorbonne), 1971; MPhil, Johns Hopkins U., 1976; postgrad., Ecole du Louvre, Paris, 1969-71. Rschr. dept. prints Met. Mus. Art, N.Y.C., 1972-73; editor Mus. Modern Art, N.Y.C., 1976-80; assoc. editor ARTnews Mag., N.Y.C., 1980-82, exec. editor, 1982-84; editor-in-chief Art and Antiques Mag., N.Y.C., 1984-85; pvt. art dealer London, Paris, 1986-90; exec. editor Art & Auction Mag., N.Y.C., 1990-94, editor-in-chief, 1994—; Author book, art revs. to N.Y. Observer, Sunday Times (London), ARTS, Artforum, others. Mem. Reform Club (London). Jewish. Home: 300 W 12th St New York NY 10014-1939 Office: Art & Auction Magazine 440 Park Ave S New York NY 10016-8012

WOLNER, RENA MERYL, publisher; b. Boston, Feb. 22, 1945; d. Samuel and Gertrude (Leaman) Tannenbaum. B.S., U. Bridgeport, 1967. Spl. asst. to pres. Bantam Books, N.Y.C., 1968-78; v.p. Berkley Books, N.Y.C., 1978-84, pres., 1985; pres., pub. Avon Books, N.Y.C., 1985-88; cons. Putnams Pub. Group., N.Y.C., 1989-94. Bd. dirs. Am. Book Awards, 1981-83. Mem. MS Soc. (bd. dirs. So. N.Y. chpt. 1889—).

WOLOSHCHUK, CANDACE DIXON, secondary school educator, artist, consultant; b. Joliet, Ill., Jan. 11, 1947; d. Harold Russell and Beatrice Diane (Johnson) Dixon; m. Christopher Ralph Jose, Mar. 1, 1969 (div. Sept. 1982); children: Amy Russell, Jennifer Seavey; m. Thomas Woloshchuk, Dec. 23, 1988; stepchildren: Michael, Debbie, Paul, John. BA in Art, Salem Coll., 1969; postgrad., Merrimac Coll., 1969; MA in Art Edn., U. Hartford, 1977; Cert. Dir. Fine Arts, Fitchburg State Coll., 1994. Cert. tchr., Mass., Conn. Art dir. Fred D. Wish Sch., Hartford, Conn., 1969-71; art tchr. Timothy Edwards Jr. H.S., South Windsor, Conn., 1971-72; art coord. Hebron (Conn.) Elem. Sch., Gilead Hill Sch., 1974-78; art tchr. Longmeadow (Mass.) Pub. Schs., 1978-82, Agawan (Mass.) Pub. Schs., 1982-85; visual arts coord. Wilbraham (Mass.) Mid. Sch., 1985—; coord. medieval festival Wilbraham Mid. Sch., 1986-87, coord. Oriental festival, 1987-88; pres., owner Scholarships Unltd., Monson, Mass., 1992-94; mem. tchr.-trainer program U. Hartford, 1974-78; enrichment, art tchr. Elms Coll., 1988-93; v.p. Pioneer Valley Decorative Painters, 1996-97. One-women show Garrett Gallery, 1981; group shows include Spencer Arts Ctr., 1993, Craft Adventure Expo '93, 1993 (2nd and 3rd pl. awards), Craft Expo '92, 1992 (2nd pl. award), Wilbraham Pub. Libr., 1992, 93, 94. Chairwomen, mem. Wilbraham Arts Lottery Coun., 1987-88; program chairwoman Pioneer Valley Decorative Painters of Mass., 1996—. Recipient Outstanding Visual and Performing Arts Edn. award, Mass. Alliance for Arts Edn., 1988, gold award Am. Sch. Food Svc. Assn., 1987. Mem. ASCD, NAFE, Nat. Art Edn. Assn., Mass. Art Edn. Assn., Mass. Tchrs. Assn., Wilbraham Tchrs. Assn., Am. Craft Coun. Republican. Avocations: sailing, needlepoint, painting, basketweaving. Office: Wilbraham Mid Sch 466 Stony Hill Rd Wilbraham MA 01095-1574

WOLOTKIEWICZ, MARIAN M., program director; b. Camden, N.J., Apr. 22, 1954; d. Edward J. and Rita J. Wolotkiewicz; m. Paul J. Sagan, Mar. 31, 1984 (div. Aug. 1, 1994). AB in Polit. Sci., Mount Holyoke Coll., 1976; JD, Suffolk U., 1979. Manuscript editor Little, Brown & Co., Boston, 1979-84; freelance editor, 1984-88; freelance writer Camp Dresser & McKee Inc., 1985-87; dir. pub. info. Regis Coll., Weston, Mass., 1988-90; assoc. dir. planned giving Clark U., Worcester, Mass., 1990-93; dir. gift planning & policy Mus. Fine Arts, Boston, 1993-94; pvt. practice cons. Boston, 1994-96; project mgr. Global Bus. Process Integration The Gillette Co., Boston, 1997—; various writing, editing and communications activities for Mass. Bar Assn., 1978-83, Womens Bar Assn., 1979-83; freelance editor for publishers including Little, Brown & Co., Artech Ho., Ballinger, Butterworth, 1984-88. Chmn. adv. com. Stow (Mass.) Cable TV, 1983-94; active fundraising Mass. Assn. Womens Lawyers charity auction, 1984, Mt. Holyoke Coll., 1986-96; pres. bd investors Mt. Holyoke Coll., 1997, Boston Alumnae Club, 1997; notary pub. State of Mass. Mem. Phi Delta Phi.

WOLOTSKY, HYMAN, retired college dean; b. N.Y.C., Nov. 27, 1918; s. Max and Bessie (Davis) W.; m. Ruth Schaffel, Mar. 31, 1946; children: Eugene, Paul. BA, CCNY, 1947; MA, Columbia U., 1948, doctoral studies, 1975-80. Cert. social worker. Program dir. Jewish Community Ctr., Portland, Maine, 1949-51; asst. exec. dir. Montgomery County Jewish Community, Chevy Chase, Md., 1951-53; exec. dir. Jewish Community Ctr. of Revere, Mass., 1953-59, YM-YWHA of Brockton, Mass., 1959-61, Mid-Westchester YM & YWHA, Eastchester, N.Y., 1961-65; exec. dir. early childhood ctr. Bank St. Coll. of Edn., N.Y.C., 1965-70, assoc. to provost, 1970-81, assoc. dean, 1981-84; cons. Assn. Mgmt. Svcs., New Rochelle, N.Y., 1984—; field instr. U. Md., College Pk., 1951-53, Boston U. Sch. Social Work, 1954-56, NYU Sch. Social Work, 1965-66, Hunter Coll. Sch. of Social Work, N.Y.C., 1967-70. Co-author: Career Development in Head Start, 1970, Brace Program of Systematic Observation, 1976; producer of videotapes including Experiencias Pre-escolares en Venezuela, 1978; contbr. articles to profl. jours. Trustee Fleetwood Synagogue, Mount Vernon, N.Y., 1963—, Clinton Child Care Assn., N.Y.C., 1970-80, Eastchester Youth Bd., 1961-64. Corp. U.S. Army, 1941-46. Mem. AAUP, Faculty Club Columbia U., Fleetwood Synagogue (pres. 1971-74). Democrat. Jewish. Avocations: travel, film/theatre, literature, museums. Office: Assn Mgmt Svcs 1270 North Ave New Rochelle NY 10804-2629

WOLPER, ALLAN L., journalist, educator; b. N.Y.C.; s. Sydelle Wolper; m. Joanna Birnbaum; children: Jill, Richard, Kim. BS, NYU, 1965. Reporter Providence Jour., 1965-67; polit. writer AP, N.Y.C., 1967-69, N.Y. Post, N.Y.C., 1970-63; writer, producer WABC Eyewitness News, N.Y.C., 1974-75; editor, columnist Soho Weekly News, N.Y.C., 1974-82; host, writer, producer of Right to Know Suburban Cablevision and N.J. Network, Sta. WNYC-TV, N.Y.C., Newark and Avenel, N.J., 1982-89; host, producer series on media Right to Know Right to Know syndicated pub. radio series on the media, Newark, 1989—; assoc. prof. journalism Rutgers U., 1978-92; prof. journalism Rutgers U., Newark, 1992—, prof., 1995—. Host, producer, writer documentary The Marielitos, 1984, Hillside: Desegregation, 1985, Impact, 1988, TV spl. The First Amendment, 1989 (Brechner award 1995); columnist Sports Media, Washington Journalism Rev., 1980-82, media N.J. Reporter, Princeton, 1982-85; contbg. writer Campus Journalism Editor and Pub. Mag., 1987—; contbr. articles to profl. jours. With U.S. Army, 1961-63. Recipient best pub. affairs program award Internat. TV and Video Festival, 1985, Nat. Cable TV Assn., 1986, award for cable excellence, 1986, 3 Aces award Nat. Cable TV, 1985, 86, Lowell Mellett award Pa. State U., 1985, Alfred I. DuPont award Columbia U., 1985, award in broadcast journalism (1st cable prodr. to win) N.J. Press Assn., 1987, N.J. Bell Enterprise award for best radio documentary, 1992, Best Radio Commentary and Media Nat. Headliner award 1993, Brechner award for writing on First Amendment & Freedom of Information, 1996. Mem. AAUP, Soc. Profl. Journalists (chmn. freedom of info. com. Dedline Club N.Y.C. br. 1980, Outstanding Broadcast Journalism award 1984, 87, Disting. Svc. award 1st Place Bicentennial Broadcast Competition 1989, spl. award N.J. Chpt., spl. award N.J. chpt. media criticism 1991, 1st Place Pub. Svc. award Mag. N.J. chpt. 1994, radio documentary 1992, investigative report 1992, winner Joseph Brechner 1st Amendment award 1995). NY Office: 327 Central Park W New York NY 10025-7631 Office: Rutgers U Journalism Dept Hill Hall Newark NJ 07102

WOLPER, DAVID LLOYD, motion picture and television executive; b. N.Y.C., Jan. 11, 1928; s. Irving S. and Anna (Fass) W.; m. Margaret Dawn Richard, May 11, 1958 (div.); children: Mark, Michael, Leslie; m. Gloria Diane Hill, July 11, 1974. Student, Drake U., 1946, U. So. Calif., 1948. V.p., treas. Flamingo Films, TV sales co., 1948-50, v.p. West Coast Ops., 1954-58; chmn., pres. Wolper Prodns., L.A., 1958—; cons., exec. producer Warner Bros., Inc., 1976—. TV prodns. include Race for Space, Making of the President 1960, 64, Biography series, Story of... series, The Yanks are Coming, Berlin: Kaiser to Khrushchev, December 7: Day of Infamy, The American Woman in the 20th Century, Hollywood and The Stars, March of Time Specials, The Rise and Fall of the Third Reich, The Legend of Marilyn Monroe, Four Days in November, Krebiozen and Cancer, National Geographic, Undersea World of Jacques Cousteau, China: Roots of Madness, The Journey of Robert F. Kennedy, Say Goodbye, George Plimpton, Appointment With Destiny, American Heritage, Smithsonian, They've Killed President Lincoln, Sandburg's Lincoln, Primal Man, The First Woman President, Chico and the Man, Get Christie Love, Welcome Back, Kotter!, Collison Course, Roots, Victory at Entebbe, Roots: The Next Generations, Moviola, The Thorn Birds, North and South Books I, II, III, Napoleon and Josephine, Alex Haley's Queen, Men Of The Dragon, Unwed Father, The Morning After; feature films include The Hellstrom Chronicle, Devil's Brigade, The Bridge at Remagen, If It's Tuesday, This Must Be Belgium, Willy Wonka and The Chocolate Factory, Visions of Eight, This is Elvis, Murder in the First, Surviving Picasso, L.A. Confidential; live spl. events include Opening and Closing Ceremonies 1984 Olympic Games, Liberty Weekend July 3-6, 1986. Trustee L.A. County Mus. Art, Am. Film Inst., L.A. Thoracic and Cardiovascular Found., Boys and Girls Clubs Am., U.S. Golf Assn. Found.; bd. dirs. Amateur Athletic Assn. L.A., L.A. Heart Inst., Acad. TV Arts and Scis. Found., So. Calif. Com. for Olympic Games, U. Soc. Calif. Cinema/TV Dept.; bd. govs. Cedars Sinai Med. Ctr.; com. mem. U.S. Olympic Team Benefit; mem. adv. com. Nat. Ctr. Jewish Film. Recipient award for documentaries San Francisco Internat. Film Festival, 1960, 7 Golden Globe awards, 5 George Foster Peabody awards, Disting. Service award U.S. Jr. C. of C.; 40 Emmy awards, 145 Emmy nominations Acad. TV Arts and Scis.; Monte Carlo Internat. Film Festival award, 1964, Cannes Film Festival Grand Prix for TV Programs, 1964; Oscar award, 11 Oscar nominations, Jean Hersholt Humanitarian award Acad. Motion Picture and TV Scis., medal of Chevalier The French Nat. Legion of Honor, 1990; named to TV Hall of Fame, 1988. Mem. Nat. Acad. TV Arts and Scis., Acad. Motion Picture Arts and Scis., Producers Guild Am., Caucus for Producers, Writers and Dirs. Office: care Warner Bros Inc 4000 Warner Blvd Burbank CA 91522-0001

WOLPER, MARSHALL, insurance and financial consultant; b. Chgo., Nov. 19, 1922; s. Harry B. and Bessie (Steiner) W.; m. Thelma R. Freedman, April 15, 1957 (div. Oct. 1968); m. Jacqueline N. Miller, Sept. 19, 1969 (div. Jan. 1976); m. Lucee I. G. Lee, Mar. 20, 1985; stepchildren—Robert Insinga, Cyndi Wolper. BA in Polit. Sci. and Econs., U. Ill., 1942. Chartered fin. cons. With Kent Products, Chgo., 1946; pres. Marshall Industries, Chgo., 1947-52; with Equitable Life Assurance Soc., 1953-89, nat. honor agt., 1966, nat. sales cons., 1967—; sr. ptnr. Wolper & Katz, 1958—; ptnr. Wolper and Katz Thoroughbred Racing Stable, 1977-86; instr. life underwriting and pensions U. Miami, 1959—; pres. Marshall Wolper Co., 1953—; chmn. bd. M.W. Computer Systems, Inc., 1971-80; pres. Marshall Wolper Pension Sers. Inc., 1978-80, Wolper Ross & Co., 1980-87; lectr. life ins., employee benefit plans, pensions, estate planning to various univs. and spl. meetings; pres. Greater Miami Tax Inst., 1963, Estate Planning Coun. Greater Miami, 1969-70; faculty Practicing Law Inst., 1967—; mem. adv. com., lectr. Inst. on Estate Planning. Author: Medical Entities Taxed as Corporations, 1961, Tax and Business Aspects of Professional Corporations and Associations, 1968; contbr. articles to profl. jours. Bd. dirs. Dade County chpt. ARC, Profl. Selling Inst. Served to 1st lt. AUS, Parachute Infantry, World War II, ETO. Decorated Bronze Star, Purple Heart; recipient Paragon award Equitable Life Assurance Soc., 1972; C.L.U. Mem. Am. Soc. CLUs (pres. Miami chpt. 1963, inst. faculty 1963-65, dir. 1966-67, regional v.p. 1968), The Am. Coll. (joint com. on continuing edn. 1965—), Nat. Assn. Life Underwriters (lectr. 1963, 66, 81), Million Dollar Round Table (life mem., speaker 1962-81, exec. com. 1974-78, pres. 1977), Assn. Advanced Life Underwriting (lectr. 1966, pres. 1972), Am. Soc. Pension Actuaries (dir.), Nat. Assn. Pension Consultants and Adminstrs. (treas.). Office: The Marshall Wolper Co 1546 NE Quayside Ter Miami FL 33138-2208

WOLPERT, EDWARD ALAN, psychiatrist; b. Chgo., Apr. 22, 1930; s. Sol and Dorothy (Greenwald) W.; m. Gloria Adele Yanoff, Mar. 23, 1958; children: Seth Isaac, Andrew Oxman, Edward Greenwald. B.A., U. Chgo., 1950, M.A., 1954, Ph.D., 1959, M.D., 1960. Diplomate: Am. Bd. Neurology and Psychiatry. Intern medicine U. Ill. Research Hosp., 1960-61; resident psychiatry Michael Reese Hosp., 1961-64; dir. clin. services Psychosomatic and Psychiat. Inst., 1966-79, dir. of hosp., 1979-93; clin. assoc. prof. psychiatry U. Chgo. Sch. Medicine, 1972-76, clin. prof. psychiatry, 1976-90; clin. prof. psychiatry U. Ill. Sch. Medicine, 1990-93; prof. psychiatry Rush Med. Coll., 1993—; sr. rsch. scholar Rush Inst. Mental Well-Being, 1993—; cons. Senila Shandman Orthogenic Sch., 1973-96; chmn. Ill. Dept. Mental Health and Devel. Disabilities Rev. Bd. Contbr. articles to profl. jours. Fellow Am. Psychiat. Assn.; mem. AMA, Ill., Chgo. med. socs., Ill. Psychiat. Soc. (pres. 1982-83), AAAS, Am. Psychoanalytic Assn. (certified in psychoanalysis), Assn. for Psychophysiol. Study of Sleep, Am. Psychol. Assn., N.Y. Acad. Scis., George S. Klein Meml. Psychoanalytic Research Forum, Am. Soc. for Clin. Pharmacology and Therapeutics, Chgo. Psychoanalytic Soc., Inst. Medicine Chgo., Wis. Acad. Arts, Letters and Scis. Home: 680 N Lake Shore Dr Ste 1004 Chicago IL 60611-4451 Office: Rush Inst Mental Well Being 1725 W Harrison St Chicago IL 60612-3828

WOLRAICH, MARK LEE, pediatrician. BA, SUNY, Binghamton, 1966; MD, SUNY, Syracuse, 1970. Diplomate Am. Bd. Pediatrics. Pediatric intern SUNY, Syracuse, 1970-71; pediatric resident U. Okla. Health Scis. Ctr., Oklahoma City, 1973-74; pediatric fellowship U. Oreg. Health Scis. Ctr., 1974-76; asst. prof. U. Iowa, 1976-81, assoc. prof., 1981-86, prof., 1986-90; prof. Vanderbilt U., 1990—, dir. divsn. child devel., dir. child devel. ctr., 1990—, dir. ctr. for chronic illnesses and disabilities in children, 1990—; assoc. dir. J.F. Kennedy Ctr. for Rsch. on Edn. and Human Devel., 1990-93; med. supr. U. Iowa Divsn. of Developmental Disabilities, 1980-90; vis. prof. Great Ormond St. Hosp. for Sick Children, London, 1983, U. Cape Town, Rondebosch Cape, South Africa, 1986, Columbus Children's Hosp., Ohio State U., Dept. Pediatrics, 1988; mem. Iowa State Foster Care Rev. Bd. Coeditor Advances in Developmental and Behavioral Pediatrics, 1981-92; cons. editor Am. Jour. on Mental Deficiency; editl. adv. bd. A Guide to Parent Counseling; cons. reviewer Developmental Medicine and Child Neurology, Pediatrics, Nutrition and Behavior, Jour. Pediatrics, Jou. of Social and Personal Relationships, Applied Rsch. in Mental Retardation, Jour. of Clin. Psychology, Jour. Developmental and Behavioral Pediatrics, Clin. Pediatrics, others; contbr. numerous articles to profl. publs.*. Recipient Disting. and Dedicated Svc. award Spina Bifida Assn. of Iowa, 1979, Lou Holloway award for rsch. Health Scis. Edn.; grantee NIMH, 1987-90, 92—, Nat. Inst. on Disability and Rehab. Rsch., 1987-89, 87-88, NIH, 1988-91, 91-94, Iowa Dept. of Human Svcs., 1986-88, 88-89, U. Iowa, 1979, 80-87, United Cerebral Palsy Rsch. and Endl. Found., Inc., 1978-87, 94, Iowa March of Dimes, 1980, Sugar Assn., Inc., 1983, Internat. Life Scis. Inst., 1988-91, W.T. Grant Found., 1989. Fellow Am. Acad. Pediatrics (com., grant 1992—), Am. Acad. Cerebral Palsy and Developmental Medicine; mem. Soc. for Behavioral Pediatrics (pres. 1994-95, program dir. 1990-93), Soc. Developmental Pediatrics, Soc. Pediatric Psychology Assn. (assoc.), Soc. for Pediatric Rsch. (sr.), Am. Acad. Physician and Patient (charter). Office: Vanderbilt U Child Devel Ctr 2100 Pierce Ave Nashville TN 37212-3162*

WOLSIFFER, PATRICIA RAE, insurance company executive; b. Indpls., Aug. 15, 1933; d. Charles L. and Dorothy M. (Smith) Bohlsen; m. Edward C. Wolsiffer, Oct. 5, 1956; children: John M., Anderson, Sherry L. Anderson Cooney, Edward J. Wolsiffer. Student, Ind. Central U., 1974-75. Various secretarial positions, 1964-71; with Blue Cross/Blue Shield Ind. (Associated Ins. Cos., Inc.), Indpls., 1971-88, supr. personnel, 1973-76, exec. asst. to pres., 1976-79, corp. sec., 1979-85, exec. asst. to chmn. bd., chief exec. officer, 1985-88, ret. Vol. Hancock Meml. Hosp. Guild, bd. dirs. Republican. Presbyterian. Clubs: Order Eastern Star, Daus. of Nile, Ladies Oriental Shrine. Home: 5550 E 100 N Greenfield IN 46140-9445 Office: 120 Monument Cir Indianapolis IN 46204-4906

WOLSON, CRAIG ALAN, lawyer; b. Toledo, Feb. 20, 1949; s. Max A. and Elaine B. (Cohn) W.; m. Janis Nan Braun, July 30, 1972 (div. Mar. 1986); m. Ellen Carol Schulgasser, Oct. 26, 1986; children: Lindsey, Michael and Geoffrey (triplets). BA, U. Mich., 1971, JD, 1974. Bar: N.Y. 1975, U.S. Dist. Ct. (so. and ea. dists.) N.Y. 1975, U.S. Ct. Appeals (2d cir.) 1975, U.S. Supreme Ct. 1978. Assoc. Shearman & Sterling, N.Y.C., 1974-81; v.p., asst. gen. counsel Thomson McKinnon Securities Inc., N.Y.C., 1981-85; v.p., sec., gen. counsel J.D. Mattus Co., Inc., Greenwich, Conn., 1985-88; also bd. dirs. J.D. Mattus Co., Inc. and affiliated cos., Greenwich; v.p., asst. gen. counsel Chem. Bank, N.Y.C., 1988-95; of counsel Williams and Harris, N.Y.C., 1995-96; ptnr. Williams & Harris LLP, N.Y.C., 1996—; dep. clk. Lucas County Courthouse, Toledo, 1968-69, 71-72. Articles and administrv. editor U. Mich. Law Rev., 1973-74. Mem. ABA, N.Y. State Bar Assn., Assn. of Bar of City of N.Y. (securities regulation com. 1994—), Corp. Bar. Assn. of Westchester and Fairfield, Phi Beta Kappa, Phi Eta Sigma, Pi Sigma Alpha. Avocations: reading, playing piano, fine dining, theater. Home: 41 Bonnie Brook Rd Westport CT 06880-1507 Office: Williams & Harris LLP 27th Fl One Battery Park Plz New York NY 10004

WOLTER, JOHN AMADEUS, librarian, government official; b. St. Paul, July 25, 1925; s. Amadeus Frank and Marjorie (Wears) W.; m. Joan Patricia Venard, July 6, 1956; children: Mark, Thomas, Matthew, David. Student, Coll. St. Thomas, 1950; BA, U. Minn., 1956, MA, 1965, PhD, 1975; post-grad., Georgetown U., 1957. Officer, seaman Isthmian Lines Inc., N.Y.C., 1943-50, 57-60; marine transp. officer Mil. Sea Transp. Ser., Washington, 1956-57; instr., map libr. U. Minn., 1961-64, asst. to dir. univ. librs., 1964-65, research fellow, 1965-66; asst. prof. Wis. State U., River Falls, 1966-68; asst. chief geography and map. div. Libr. of Congress, Washington, 1968-78, chief, 1978-91, acting dir. pub. svc. and collections MGMT I, 1989-90; cons. in geography, 1991-93; mem. U.S. Bd. Geog. Names, 1969-83, vice chmn., 1980-81, chmn., 1981-83. Editor: Progress of Discovery: Johann Georg Kohl, 1993, Images of the World: The Atlas Through History, 1996; rev. editor cartography divsn. Surveying and Mapping, 1971-72; mem. editl. bd. Cartographica, 1971-80, Am. Cartographer, 1974-79, Terrae Incognitae, 1973-75, ACSM Bull., 1974-80, Surveying and Mapping, 1972-80; editl. advisor The Portolan, 1986—; contbg. editor Imago Mundi, 1979-91; contbr. articles to profl. jours. Served with U.S. Army, 1950-52. Libr. of Congress Disting. Svc. award, 1992, Smithsonian Inst. Cert. of award, 1986. Mem. Internat. Geog. Union (U.S. nat. com. 1972-80, 84-88), Internat. Cartographic Assn. (U.S. mem. commn. on history of cartography 1972-76, corr. 1976-92, Assn. Am. Geographers (editorial bd. Annals 1988-92), Spl. Librs. Assn. (sec.-treas. geog.and map div. 1965), Soc. History Discoveries (sec.-treas. 1972-75, coun. 1976-78, v.p. 1983-85, pres. 1985-87), Can. Nautical Rsch. Soc., Am. Congress Surveying and Mapping (chmn. publs. com. 1978-80, Presdl. citation 1985), N.Am. Soc. Oceanic History, N.Mex. Geog. Soc. (bd. dirs., governing bd.), Washington Map Soc., Soc. Nautical Rsch., Ariz. Hist. Soc., U.S. Naval Hist. Found., Hakluyt Soc., Explorers Club, Theta Delta Chi. Home: 5430 Ring Dove Ln Columbia MD 21044-1716

WOLTERINK, LESTER FLOYD, biophysicist, educator; b. Marion, N.Y., July 28, 1915; s. John and Ruth Lavina (Voorhorst) W.; m. Lillian Ruth Nichols, June 30, 1938; children—Charles Paul, Timothy John. A.B., Hope Coll., 1936; M.A., U. Minn., 1940, Ph.D., 1943. Faculty Mich. State U., East Lansing, 1941—; prof. physiology Mich. State U., 1952-84, prof. emeritus, 1984—; asso. scientist AEC, Argonne Nat. Lab., 1948; cons., then biosatellite project scientist Ames Research Center, NASA, 1963-66; Mem. various coms. AEC Conf. on Isotopes in Plant and Animal Research, 1952-59; mem. NASA Manned Space Sta. Commn., 1966; cons. NSF, 1967-70; mem. panel on nitrogen oxides Nat. Acad. Sci./NRC, 1973-75. Contbr. articles to profl. publs., reports to govt. agys. Mem. Mich. Nucleonic Soc. (pres. 1961), Soc. Exptl. Biology and Medicine (sec. Mich. sect. 1961-63), Am. Astronautic Soc. (chmn. San Francisco sect. 1966), AAUP, Am. Inst. Biol. Scis., Am. Physiol. Soc., N.Y. Acad. Scis., IEEE, Biomed. Engring. Soc., Biophys. Soc., Sigma Xi (jr. scientist Mich. State U. 1954). Club: Torch (pres. 1983, sec. 1985-86). Home: 2277 Kewanee Way Okemos MI 48864-2514 Office: Mich State U Dept Physiology East Lansing MI 48824

WOLTERS, CURT CORNELIS FREDERIK, foreign service officer; b. Nymegen, The Netherlands, Mar. 13, 1938; came to U.S., 1957; s. Frederik and Cornelia Johanna (Jansen) W.; m. Sara J. Daughters, June 10, 1962 (div. 1980); children: Gwyneth, Chad; m. Charlotte Cooper, Sept. 22, 1980 (div. 1988); children: Lottena, Cicely; m. Sylvana K. Perry, Apr. 1989; 1 child, Roger. Student, Wash. State U., 1958-61, U. Bonn, Fed. Republic Germany, 1962-63; BA, U. Oreg., 1964, MA, 1966; MBA, U. Washington, 1976; PhD, Pacific Western U., 1989. Asst. sec. Rep. Botswana Govt., Gaborone, 1966-68; program advisor The Ford Found., N.Y.C., 1968-74; sr. rsch. analyst Seattle C. of C., 1974-76; sr. assoc. Inst. Pub. Adminstrn. N.Y., N.Y.C., 1976-78; freelance economist Africa, 1978-79; econ. program officer, diplomat (AID) Dept. State, Washington, 1979—; cons. Inst. for Puget Sound Needs, Seattle, 1975-76, Pacific Cons., Washington, 1976. Contbr. numerous articles to profl. jours.; author project evaluations. Mem. civic action com. Congress of Racial Equality, Eugene, Oreg., 1965-66; vol. campaign Dixie Lee Ray Gubernatorial Campaign, Seattle, 1976; treas., chmn. fin. com. Internat. Sch. Islamabad, 1989-92. Carnegie Found. fellow, 1964-65, Africa-Asia pub. svc. fellow Maxwell Sch., 1966-68, fellow German Govt., U. Bonn, 1962-63; recipient Air Def. Command Outstanding Achievement award USAF, 1960; Cmty. Svc. award U.S. Embassy, Islamabad, 1992-93, 93-94. Mem. Am. Econ. Assn., Air Force Assn., Wilson Ctr. (assoc. of Smithsonian Instn.), Am. Fgn. Svc. Assn., Holland Am. Club (treas. Greater Seattle area 1975-76), Am. Legion. Office: USAID/Zambia Lusaka Dept of State Washington DC 20521-2310

WOLTERS, OLIVER WILLIAM, history educator; b. Reading, Eng., June 8, 1915; came to U.S., 1964; s. Albert William and Gertrude (Lewis) W.; m. Euteen Khoo, Apr. 25, 1955; children: Pamela Gwyneth, Nigel Christopher. B.A., Lincoln Coll., Oxford U., 1937; Ph.D., Sch. Oriental and African Studies, London, 1961. With Malayan Civil Service, 1938-57; lectr. Sch. Oriental and African Studies, London, 1957-63; prof. S.E. Asian history Cornell U., Ithaca, N.Y., 1964-74, Goldwin Smith prof. S.E. Asian history, 1974-85; ret., 1985. Author: Early Indonesian Commerce, 1967, The Fall of Srivijaya, 1970, History, Culture, and Region in Southeast Asian Perspectives, 1982, Two Essays on Dai-Viet in the Fourteenth Century, 1988; editor: (with others) Southeast Asian History, 1976; sr. editor: The Vietnam Forum, 1985-93. Trustee Breezewood Found., Md., 1964-84. Decorated Officer Order Brit. Empire, 1952; Guggenheim fellow, 1972-73; Bellagio fellow Rockefeller Found., 1982; recipient Disting. Scholarship award Assn. for Asian Studies, 1990. Episcopalian.

WOLTERS, RAYMOND, historian, educator; b. Kansas City, Mo., July 25, 1938; s. Raymond M. and Margaret G. (Reilly) W.; m. Mary McCullough, June 23, 1962; children—Jeffrey, Kevin, Thomas. B.A., Stanford U., 1960; M.A., U. Calif.-Berkeley, 1962, Ph.D., 1967. Instr. dept. history U. Del., Newark, 1965-67, asst. prof., 1967-70, assoc. prof., 1970-75; prof. U. Del., 1975-96, Thomas Muncy Keith prof., 1996—. Mem. editl. adv. bd. Acad. Am. Ency.; author: Negroes and the Great Depression, 1970, The New Negro on Campus, 1975, The Burden of Brown, 1984, Right Turn, 1996. Fellow NEH, 1971-72, Am. Coun. Learned Socs., 1978-79, Earhart Found., 1989-90; recipient Silver Gavel award ABA. Mem. Am. Hist. Assn., Orgn. Am. Historians, So. Hist. Assn. Home: 20 Bridlebrook Ln Newark DE 19711-2061 Office: U Del History Dept Newark DE 19716

WOLTING, ROBERT ROY, city official; b. Faulkton, S.D., Dec. 29, 1928; s. George and Minnie (Meeter) W.; m. Nancy Catherine O'Brien, Nov. 26, 1953; children: Robert Roy, Linda Marie. Acct. Wolting Implement and Motor Co., Wessington Springs, S.D., 1954-60; city auditor City of Wessington Springs, 1960-64, City of Brookings, S.D., 1964-68; dir. fin. City of Fairbanks, Alaska, 1968-77, city mgr., 1977-79, 90-93, dir. fin., treas., 1984-90; city mgr., 1990-93; elected mem. City Coun., 1994—; city adminstr., clk. City of Union Springs, Ala., 1980-84. Mem. S.D. Retirement Bd., 1966-68. Sgt. USAF, 1950-54. Mem. Alaska Mcpl. Mgrs. Assn., Mcpl. Fin. Officers Assn. (pres. S.D. chpt. 1965-67, sec. Fairbanks chpt. 1976-78, bd. dirs. 1985-90). Democrat. Methodist. Avocation: photography. Home: 227 Iditarod Ave Fairbanks AK 99701-3232 Office: City of Fairbanks 800 Cushman St Fairbanks AK 99701-4615

WOLTZ, HOWARD OSLER, JR., steel and wire products company executive; b. Mt. Airy, N.C., Apr. 2, 1925; s. Howard Osler and Louise (Elliott) W.; m. Joan Elizabeth Moore, Dec. 29, 1949; children: Louise, Joan Woltz Robins, Howard O. III, Edwin Moore. LLB, U. Va., 1948. Bar: N.C., 1948. Ptnr. law firm Mt. Airy, 1948-54; pres., founder Dixie Concrete Products, Inc., Mt. Airy, 1953-69; founder Dixie Exposaic, Inc., Mt. Airy, 1963; pres., chmn. bd. Insteel Industries (formerly Eposaic Industries, Inc.), Mt. Airy, 1969-89, chmn., CEO, 1989-91. Mem. N.C. Ho. of Reps., 1951-53; chmn. Mt. Airy-Surry County Airport Authority, 1987-93; former pres. Greater Mt. Airy United Fund. Mem. Nat. Concrete Masonry Assn. (pres. 1965), N.C. Concrete Masonry Assn. (pres. 1959), Wire Reinforcement Inst. (chmn. 1982), Am. Wire Producers Assn. (bd. dirs. 1987-91), N.C. State Bar Assn., Mt. Airy C. of C. (Citizen of Yr. 1991). Rotary (past pres. Mt. Airy). Republican. Home: 819 Greenhill Rd Mount Airy NC 27030-9240 Office: Insteel Industries Inc 1373 Boggs Dr Mount Airy NC 27030-2145

WOLTZ, KENNETH ALLEN, consulting executive; b. Phila., Mar. 2, 1943; s. Herman and Florence (Varell) M.; m. Barbara Hand, June 18, 1966; children: Karyn, Diane, Kenneth. BS, U.S. Mil. Acad., 1966; MBA, Xavier U., 1971. Cert. mgmt. cons. Various mgmt. positions GE, Evansdale, Ohio and Bethesda, Md., 1968-73; mgr. systems Xerox Corp., Rochester, N.Y., 1973-75; dir. info. svcs. McGraw Edison, Des Plaines, Ill., 1975-77; mng. dir., mgmt. cons. Peat, Marwick, Mitchell, Chgo., 1977-80; mgmt. cons., CEO, Woltz & Assoc., Inc., Barrington, Ill., 1980—; mgmt. cons. Speaker at various Univs. With U.S. Army, 1966-68. Mem. Soc. Mgmt. Info. Systems, Inst. Mgmt. Cons., West Point Soc. (treas. 1975), Assn. Corp. Growth, Assn. Mgmt. Consulting Firms, Ind. Computer Cons. Assn., Forest Grove Club. Home: 19 Bow Ln Barrington Hills IL 60010-9802 Office: Woltz & Assocs Inc 526 Market Loop Dr West Dundee IL 60118-2184

WOLVERTON, ROBERT EARL, classics educator; b. Indpls., Aug. 4, 1925; s. Robert N. and Vivian (Lefflar) W.; m. Margaret Jester, Sept. 13, 1952; children: Robert Earl, Laurie Ann, Edwin J., Gary A. AB, Hanover Coll., 1948; MA, U. Mich., 1949; PhD, U. N.C., 1954; LittD, Coll. Mt. St. Joseph on the Ohio, 1977; postdoctoral, Oxford (Eng.) U., 1986. Asst. prof. classics U. Ga., 1954-59; asst. prof. classics, history Tufts U., 1959-62; asst. prof., assoc. prof. classics and humanities, dir. honors program Fla. State U., 1962-67; assoc. prof. classics, assoc. dean U. Ill. Grad. Coll., 1967-69; dean Grad. Sch. and Research; prof. classics Miami U., Oxford, Ohio, 1969-72; pres., prof. classics Coll. Mt. St. Joseph on Ohio, Cin., 1972-77; prof. Miss. State U., Starkville, 1977—, v.p. acad. affairs, 1977-86, prof. classics, 1986—, interim head dept. fgn. langs., 1991-92, head dept., 1992-96; vis. lectr. U. Perugia, Italy, 1985; fellow Acad. Adminstrn. Internship Program, 1965-66; field reader U.S. Office Edn.; cons., reviewer North Cen. Assn. Colls. and Schs., So. Assn. Colls. and Schs.; mem. exec. com. Coun. Grad. Schs. U.S., 1970-73; chmn. Midwest Assn. Grad. Schs., 1971; mem. Regents Adv. Com. Grad. Edn., Ohio, 1969-72, chmn., 1971-72; mem. Medford (Mass.) Edn. Coun., 1961-62. Author: Classical Elements in English Words, 1965, An Outline of Classical Mythology, 1966; contbg. translator: A Life of George Washington in Latin Prose (Francis Glass), 1976; editor: (with others) Graduate Programs and Admissions Manual, 1971, 72; contbr. (with others) articles to profl. jours. and encys. Trustee, v.p. Greater Cin. Consortium Colls. and Univs., St. Francis Hosp., Ohio; mem. Cin. coun. on econ. edn.; bd. dirs. Starkville Arts Alliance, pres., 1989-96, Starkville-Miss. State U. Symphony Assn., 1985—, pres., 1987-90, Miss. Opera Assn.; mem. Miss. Com. Humanities, 1982-86, Miss. Arts Commn., 1986-87; pres. coun. of laity St. Mary's of Oxford, 1969-70; mem. Starkville Cmty. Theatre, 1978-79, pres., 1982-82, 82-83; pres. parish coun. St. Joseph Ch., 1979, 89-90; pres. diocesan pastoral coun. Diocese of Jackson, Miss., 1983-84, 86-87. Recipient Outstanding Undergraduate Teaching award Miss. State U., 1990; John Grisham Master Tchr. award, 1994. Mem. Am. Classical League (pres. 1972-76), Am. Philol. Assn. Classical Assn. Middle West and South, Vergilian Soc., Am. Assn. Higher Edn., Assn. Ind. Colls. and Univs. Ohio (sec. 1973-75, vice chmn. 1975-77), Nat. Coun. Chief Acad. Officers (exec. com. 1981-84, chmn. 1983-94), Coun. Basic Edn., Nat. Faculty Humanities Arts and Scis., Acad. Polit. Sci., Ohio Program in Humanities, Golden Key Honor Soc., Cardinal Key Honor Soc., Sigma Chi, Omicron Delta Kappa, Eta Sigma Phi, Phi Kappa Phi (nat. editl. advisor 1984-89), Phi Delta Kappa, Phi Eta Sigma. Home: 102 Colonial Circle Starkville MS 39759-4201

WOLYNES, PETER GUY, chemistry researcher, educator; b. Chgo., Apr. 21, 1953; s. Peter and Evelyn Eleanor (Etter) W.; m. Jane Lee Fox, Nov. 26, 1976 (div. 1980); m. Kathleen Cull Bucher, Dec. 22, 1984; children: Margrethe Cull, Eve Cordelia. AB with highest distinction, Ind. U., 1971; AM, Harvard U., 1972, PhD in Chem. Physics, 1976; DSc (hon.), Ind. U., 1988. Rsch. assoc. MIT, Cambridge, 1975-76; asst. prof., assoc. prof. Harvard U., Cambridge, 1976-80; vis. scientist Max Planck Inst. für Biophysikalische Chemie, Gottingen, Fed. Republic Germany, 1977; assoc. prof. chemistry U. Ill., Urbana, 1980-83, prof., 1983—, prof. physics, 1985—; prof. physics and biophysics U. Ill., 1989—; permanent mem. Ctr. for Advanced Study U. Ill., Urbana, 1989—; William H. and Janet LyCan prof. chemistry Ctr. for Advanced Study U. Ill., Urbana, 1993-96, Robert Eiszner prof., 1996—; vis. prof. Inst. for Molecular Sci., Okazaki, Japan, 1982, 87; vis. scientist Inst. for Theoretical Physics, Santa Barbara, Calif., 1987, Ecole normale Supérieure, Paris, 1992, Merski lectr. U. Nebr., 1986, Denkewalter lectr., Loyola U., 1986; Hinshelwood lectr. Oxford U., 1997, Harkins lectr., U. Chgo., 1997. Contbr. numerous articles to profl. jours. Sloan fellow, 1981-83, J.S. Guggenheim fellow, 1986-87; Beckman assoc. Ctr. for Advanced Study, Urbana, 1984-85; Fogarty scholar NIH, 1994—. Fellow Am. Phys. Soc., Am. Acad. Arts and Scis.; mem. NAS, AAAS, Am. Chem. Soc. (Pure Chemistry award 1986), N.Y. Acad. Scis., Biophys. Soc., Phi Beta Kappa, Sigma Xi, Phi Lambda Upsilon (Fresenius award 1988), Sigma Pi Sigma, Alpha Chi Sigma. Home: 311 W Oregon St Urbana IL 61801-4125 Office: U Ill Sch of Chem Scis 505 S Mathews Ave Urbana IL 61801-3617

WOLYNIC, EDWARD THOMAS, specialty chemicals technology executive; b. Bklyn., May 29, 1948; s. Edward Joseph and Fortunata Wolynic; m. Loraine Cynthia Ciardullo. BS ChemE, Poly. Inst. N.Y., 1969; MS ChemE, Princeton U., 1972, PhD ChemE, 1974. Staff engr. Union Carbide Corp., Bound Brook, N.J., 1974-75; supr. Union Carbide Corp., Tarrytown, N.Y., 1975-77, mgr. mfg. tech., 1977-82, assoc. dir. tech., 1982-85, dir. tech., 1985-88; v.p. rsch. UOP, Tarrytown, 1988-90; v.p. devel. UOP, Des Plaines, Ill., 1990-92; dir. process R&D Internat. Specialty Products Corp., Wayne, N.J., 1993, v.p. R&D, 1993-95; dir. strategic tech. group Engelhard Corp., Iselin, N.J., 1995—. Contbr. tech. articles to profl. jours.; patentee in field. Mem. AIChe, Indsl. Rsch. Inst., Com. Devel. Assn., N.Am. Catalyst Soc. Avocations: fishing, tennis, skiing. Office: Engelhard Corp 101 Wood Ave S Iselin NJ 08830-2703

WOLYNIES, EVELYN See GRADO-WOLYNIES, EVELYN

WOMACH, EMILY HITCH, retired banker and marketing and public relations executive; b. Laurel, Del., Jan. 27, 1927; d. Elon G. and Jennie (Neal) Hitch; m. William S. Womach, Mar. 13, 1943 (Oct. 1982); 1 son, William Richard. Student, Salisbury (Md.) Bus. Inst., 1948; grad. Sch. Fin. Pub. Rels., Northwestern U., 1957; grad. Sch. Fin. Pub. Relations, Am. Inst. Banking, 1958, Stonier Grad. Sch. Banking, Rutgers U., 1968. With Sussex Trust Co., Laurel, 1945-68; sec., asst., cashier Sussex Trust Co., 1956-62, asst. v.p., sec., 1962-67, v.p., sec., 1967-68; adminstrv. asst. to gov. Del., 1968-69; sales rep. Robinson Real Estate, 1969-71; treas. State of Del., 1971-73; also dir. div. treasury dept. finance; v.p., mem. sr. mgmt. Farmers Bank State Del., Wilmington, 1973-76; chmn. bd., pres., chief exec. officer Women's Nat. Bank, Washington, 1976-83; chmn. bd., pres. Internat. Fin. Adv. Svcs., 1983-88; dir. mktg., pub. rels. Asbury Meth. Village, Gaithersburg, Md., 1986-92; pres. First WNB Corp., bank holding co., 1981-83; bd. dirs. Penjerdel Corp.; lectr. in field, 1958—; econ. commentator Spectrum on Economy, WCAV Radio, 1975-76; fin. cons. Past mem. nat. adv. coun. Small Bus. Adminstrn.; mem. Del. Bank Adv. Bd., 1963-71; participant Internat. Workshop Women Leaders in Banking and Fin., Amsterdam and San Remo, Italy. Chmn. budget com., auditor Laurel LWV, 1959-71; bd. dirs. Music at Noon, D.C. Performing Arts Soc., 1978-82; mem. edn. com., also fund drive com. Delmarva Poultry Industry, 1963-66; sec.-treas. Overall Econ. Devel. Program Com., 1967-71; mem. Del. State Small Bus. Adv. Council, 1965-71, Laurel Planning Commn., 1965-68, D.C. Employment Security Bd., 1978-80; v.p. Del. div. Am. Cancer Soc., 1964-68, mem. Del. exec. com. and bd., 1957-71; mem. Sussex County unit bd., 1957-71; bd. dirs. Nat. Capital Area region NCCJ, 1978-81; chmn. Del. Heart Fund, 1972; bd. dirs., treas. Community Fund. Greater Washington, 1978-81; mem. adv. coun. The Women's Inst./Am. U., 1978-83; trustee Wesley Coll., 1973-83. Recipient Outstanding Woman Who Works award Downtown Assn. Memphis, 1964, Merit award Del. Fed. Bus. and Profl. Women's Club, 1966; named Outstanding Citizen of Laurel, Outstanding Person of Yr. in Mktg. Washington Fin. Coun., 1981. Mem. Nat. Assn. Bank Women (v.p. Middle Atlantic div. 1960-61, nat. v.p. 1962-63, nat. pres. 1963-64), Am. Inst. Banking (pres. Sussex chpt. 1958-59), Am. Bankers Assn. (exec. com. savs. div. 1966-67, communication com. mktg. div. 1974-75, mem. adminstrv. com. govtl. rels. coun. 1975-76, 80-83), Del. Bankers Assn. (chmn. pub. rels. com. 1959-63, vice chmn. legis. com.), D.C. Bankers Assn. (adminstrv. coun. 1980-83), Friends of Women's World Banking/USA (pres. 1980-83), Am. Newspaper Women's Club (asso.), Del. C. of C. (dir. 1974-76, Josiah Marvel cup award 1967), Bus. and Profl. Women's Club (pres. Laurel 1951), Am. Acad. Polit. and Social Sci., Internat. Women's Forum, Rehoboth Art League, Nat. Audubon Soc. (bd. dirs. 1985-87), Delta Kappa Gamma (hon.). Democrat. Methodist.

WOMACK, EDGAR ALLEN, JR., technology executive; b. Humboldt, Tenn., Oct. 29, 1942; s. Edgar Allen Sr. and Lucy Opal (George) W.; m. Linda Jane Cochran, Dec. 28, 1963; children: Constance Elaine, Cynthia Lynn. BS, MIT, 1963, MS, 1965, PhD, 1969. With U.S. Atomic Energy Commn., Washington, 1968-73; with Babcock and Wilcox Co., Lynchburg, Va., 1975-85, v.p. sales and mktg., 1983-85; v.p. R&D Babcock and Wilcox Co., Alliance, Ohio, 1985-93; sr. v.p., chief tech. officer McDermott Internat., New Orleans, 1993—, sr. v.p., group exec. Indsl. Group, 1995—; bd. dirs. Ceramatec Corp., Indsl. Rsch. Inst., Washington, 1989-96, pres., 1994-95; bd. dirs. Universal Fabricators, Talleres Navales del Golfo. Patentee in field. Served to lt. USNR, 1968-70. Hon. Woodrow Wilson Found. fellow. Mem. ASME (ind. adv. bd. 1988—, chmn. 1997), Am. Mgmt. Assn. (rsch. and devel. coun. 1988-94), Indsl. Research Inst., AAAS, Soc. Sigma Xi. Presbyterian. Avocations: photography, diving, golf. Home: 7412 Jade St New Orleans LA 70124-3539 Office: McDermott Internat Inc PO Box 61961 New Orleans LA 70161-1961

WOMACK, JOSEPH DONALD, SR., manufacturing and telecommunications company executive, consultant; b. Ft. Worth, Aug. 15, 1926; s. Walter William and Hortense (McDonald) W.; m. Teresa Rose Parrette, June 1951; 1 son, Joseph Donald; m. Lewis Brennan O'Brien, Nov. 29, 1959; 1 son, Courtney Cralle; m. Marie Annette Thomas, Jan. 12, 1974. Student, U. Tex., 1943, Sophia U., Tokyo, 1951-53, Am. U., 1954-55. Fgn. service officer, Seoul, Tokyo, 1951-57, Beirut, 1961-64; exec. IBM World Trade, 1964; pres. Fed. Mktg. Services, Washington, 1965-69, AVMedia, Inc., Alexandria, Va., 1969-77; pres., chief exec. officer Solactor Corp., Alexandria, 1977—, Bakstop Info. Svcs., 1990—, Disabled Ams. Work Net Inc., Alexandria, 1994—, Disabled Ams. Empowerment Fund Inc., 1994—; chmn. Internat. Fund for Advanced Solar Energy, 1983—; cons. OEO, 1964, Army Chief Staff, 1969. Served with U.S. Maritime Service and U.S. Mcht. Marines, 1944-48; PTO. Mem. Internat. Solar Energy Soc. Office: Solactor Corp PO Box 6026 Alexandria VA 22306-0026

WOMACK, THOMAS HOUSTON, manufacturing company executive; b. Gallatin, Tenn., June 22, 1940; s. Thomas Houston and Jessie (Eckel) W.; Linda Walker Womack, July 20, 1963 (div. Dec. 1989); children: Britton Ryan, Kelley Elizabeth; m. Pamela Ann Reed, Apr. 20, 1991. BSME, Tenn. Tech. U., Cookeville, 1963. Project engr. U.S. Gypsum Co., Jacksonville, Fla., 1963-65; project mgr. Maxwell House Div. Gen. Foods Corp., Jacksonville, 1965-68; mfg. mgr. Maxwell House Div. Gen. Foods Corp., Hoboken, N.J., 1968-71, div. ops. planning mgr., 1971-73; industry sales mgr. J.R. Schneider Co., Tiburon, Calif., 1973-79; pres., CEO Womack Internat., Inc., Novato, Calif., 1979—; pres. Ceramic Microlight Technologies, LLC, Novato, Calif., 1995—; pres., CEO WestAmerica Engring. and Mfg. Co., 1997—. Holder 5 U.S. patents. Mem. Soc. Tribologists and Lubrication Engrs., Am. Filtration Soc., Soc. Mfg. Engrs., Am. Soc. Chem. Engrs. Avocations: skiing, vintage exotic sports cars. Office: Womack Internat Inc 105 Digital Dr Novato CA 94949-5734

WOMBLE, WILLIAM FLETCHER, lawyer; b. Winston-Salem, N.C., Oct. 29, 1916; s. Bunyan Snipes and Edith (Willingham) W.; m. Jane Payne Gilbert, Oct. 11, 1941; children: William Fletcher, Jr., Jane Womble Haver, Russell G., Ann Womble Strader. AB, Duke U., 1937, JD, 1939. Bar: N.C. 1939. Assoc. Womble Carlyle Sandridge & Rice P.L.L.C. and predecessors, Winston-Salem, 1939-47; ptnr. Womble Carlyle Sandridge & Rice P.L.L.C. and predecessors, 1947—. Campaign chmn. Forsyth County Community Chest, 1948; mem. N.C. Gen. Statutes Commn., 1953-55; mem. N.C. Bd. Higher Edn., 1955-57, 60-63; mem. N.C. Adv. Budget Commn., 1957-58; mem. N.C. Ho. of Reps., 1953-58, chmn. com. higher edn., 1957, vice chmn. fin. com., 1957; life trustee, past chmn. High Point U.; past trustee Winston-Salem State U., 1953-55; past trustee, past pres. Children's Home; bd. dirs. Triad United Methodist Home, 1976-87, 89—, treas., 1975-79, pres., 1979-85; mem. People-to-People Citizen Ambassador Program, 1981, 86; chmn. adminstrv. bd. Centenary United Meth. Ch., 1961-63, chmn. bd. trustees, 1983-85. Served to maj. USAAF, 1941-46. Named Trustee of Yr., Gen. Bd. Global Mins. of United Meth. Ch., Health and Welfare Mins. Dept., 1989. Fellow Am. Bar Found. (life, state chmn. 1984-89, Fifty Yr. award 1995); mem. ABA (ho. of dels. 1978-87, bd. govs. 1982-85, ethics com. 1985-91, chmn. jud. code subcom. 1988-91, exec. coun. Nat. Conf. Bar Pres. 1985-88, resource devel. coun. 1986-92, chair affiliate outreach com. 1994-97, coun. mem. sr. lawyers divsn. 1995-97), N.C. Bar Assn. (pres. 1966-67, chmn. endowment founders campaign 1986-87, chair sr. lawyers divsn. 1994-95, The Judge John J. Parker award 1984), N.C. State Bar (trustee Interest on Lawyers Trust Accounts 1983-91, vice chmn. 1989-91), Forsyth County Bar Assn.(pres. 1962), Am. Judicature Soc., U.S. Supreme Ct. Hist. Soc., N.C. Supreme Ct. Hist. Soc., Winston-Salem C. of C. (pres. 1960-61), Soc. of Cin., Old Town Club, Twin City Club, Piedmont Club, Rotary (local pres. 1964). Democrat. Methodist. Home: 1244 Arbor Rd # 441 Winston-Salem NC 27104 Office: Womble Carlyle Sandridge & Rice PO Box 84 1600 BBT Fin Ctr Winston Salem NC 27102-0084

WOMELDORFF, PORTER JOHN, utility executive; b. Milw., Feb. 26, 1933; s. Virgil Leslie and Leorra (Porter) W.; BSEE, U. Ill., 1954; m. Marilyn Sapp, Jan. 7, 1966; children: John Porter, Michael Wayne. With Ill. Power Co., Decatur, 1954-95, beginning as elec. engr., successively results supr., instrumentation engr., supr. system planning, mgr. planning, 1954-79, v.p., 1979-93, global climate program exec., 1993-95, ret. 1995; pres. Womeldorff Assocs. Ltd., 1995—; mem. Ill. Coal Devel. Bd., 1982-95, chair. Chair adv. bd. U. Ill. Coll. Engring., 1986-89; former hair sci. com. Global Climate Coalition; lay mem. Central Ill. Ann. Conf., United Methodist Ch., 1968—, lay leader, 1976-79, lay mem. North Central Jurisdictional Conf., 1972—, lay mem. Gen. Conf., 1976—; lay mem. Gen. Bd. Pubs., 1992—. Served to lt. C.E., AUS, 1955-57. Decorated Army Commendation Medal. Mem. Instrument Soc. Am. (v.p. 1971-73, Power Div. Achievement award 1983), IEEE, ASME, U. Ill. Elec. Engring. Alumni Assn. (pres., dir., Outstanding Alumni award 1994), Phi Kappa Phi, Tau Beta Pi, Sigma Tau, Eta

Kappa Nu, Alpha Kappa Lambda. Home and Office: 735 Country Manor Dr Decatur IL 62521-2524

WOMER, CHARLES BERRY, retired hospital executive, management consultant; b. Cleve., Mar. 30, 1926; s. Porter Blake and Margaret (Berry) W.; m. Elizabeth Benson, Oct. 7, 1950; children: Richard B., Carol E., John C. M.S. in Hosp. Adminstrn., Columbia U., 1953; B.S. in Mech. Engring., Case Inst. Tech., 1949. Asst. dir. Univ. Hosps., Cleve., 1957-61; assoc. dir. Univ. Hosps., 1961-65, pres., 1976-82; mgmt. cons., 1982-90, ret., 1990; adminstr. Yale-New Haven Hosp., 1965-67, dir., 1968-76, pres., 1976; lectr. Yale U., 1965-78, 87-91; adj. asst. prof. Case Western Res. U., 1976-83; mem. Conn. Commn. on Hosps. and Health Care, 1973-76; bd. dirs. New Haven Savings Bank, 1969-76. Bd. govs. U. New Haven, 1972-76. Served with AUS, 1944-46. Fellow Am. Coll. Healthcare Execs. (life); mem. Am. Hosp. Assn. (chmn. coun. on mgmt. and planning 1977-79), Conn. Hosp. Assn. (trustee 1970-74, pres. 1972-73, Disting. Svc. award 1976), Assn. Am. Med. Colls. (exec. coun. 1974-77, 78-80, treas. 1975-76, chmn. 1979-80, adminstrv. bd. coun. tchg. hosps. 1972-77, chmn. 1975-76). Home: 184 Rimmon Rd Woodbridge CT 06525-1920

WOMMACK, W(ILLIAM) W(ALTON), retired manufacturing company executive; b. Winston-Salem, N.C., Dec. 12, 1922; s. Sidney LaMar and Ada (Culler) W.; m. Jean Emery, Sept. 14, 1951; children: Judith J., Kent W., Lynne E., Mary E. B.Chem. Engring, N.C. State Coll., 1943; M.B.A., Harvard U., 1948. Engr. thru div. controller Libbey-Owens-Ford, Toledo, 1948; treas., controller Ottawa River Paper Co., Toledo, 1955-58; asst. gen. mgr. Mead. Corp., Cin., 1958-64; v.p. bd. Mead. Corp., Dayton, Ohio, 1964-66; group v.p. bd. Mead. Corp., Dayton, 1966-69, exec. v.p., 1969-71, vice chmn. bd., 1971-81, also dir., 1968-81. Lt. USNR, 1943-46.

WONDER, STEVIE (STEVLAND MORRIS), singer, musician, composer; b. Saginaw, Mich., May 13, 1950; m. Syreeta Wright, 1971 (div. 1972); children: Aisha, Keita, Mumtaz. Student pub. schs. in Detroit until age 12; then transferred to, Mich. Sch. for Blind. Solo singer, Whitestone Bapt. Ch., Detroit, 1959, rec. artist, Motown Records, Detroit, 1963-70; founder, pres. music pub. co., Black Bull Music, Inc., 1970—, Wondirection Records, Inc., 1982—; recs. include Fingertips, 1963, Uptight/Purple Raindrops, 1965, Someday At Christmas/The Miracles of Christmas, 1966, I'm Wondering/Everytime I See You I Go Wild, 1966, I Was Made To Love Her/Hold Me, 1967, Shoo-Be-Doo-Be-Doo-Da-Day/Why Don't You Lead Me To Love, 1968, You Met Your Match/My Girl, 1968, For Once In My Life, I Don't Know Why, My Cherie Amour, Yester-Me, Yester-You, Yesterday, Never Had a Dream Come True, Signed, Sealed, Delivered I'm Yours, Heaven Help Us All, I Wish (Grammy award 1977), Don't You Worry 'Bout a Thing, You Haven't Done Nothin', Boogie on Reggae Woman, (Grammy award 1975), Isn't She Lovely, Sir Duke, Another Star, As, You Are the Sunshine of My Life, (Grammy award 1974), Superstition, (Grammy award 1974), Higher Ground, Living For the City, (Grammy award 1975); albums include Little Stevie Wonder: The Twelve-Year Old Genius, 1963, Tribute to Uncle Ray, 1963, Jazz Soul of Little Steve, 1963, At The Beach, 1965, For Once in My Life, 1969, My Cherie Amour, 1970, Talk of The Town, 1970, Portrait, 1976, Uptight, 1966, Down To Earth, 1966, I Was Made To Love Her, 1967, Someday At Christmas, 1967, Stevie Wonder's Greatest Hits, 1968, Music of My Mind, 1972, Innervisions, 1973 (Grammy award 1974), Fulfillingness' First Finale (Grammy award 1975), Songs In the Key of Life, 1976 (Grammy award 1977), Stevie Wonder Live, Where I'm Coming From, 1972, Talking Book, 1972, Journey Through the Secret Life of Plants, 1979, Hotter than July, 1980, Woman in Red (Acad. award, Golden Globe award for single I Just Called to Say I Love You), 1984, In Square Circle (best soul/R&B album of yr., Down Beat mag. Readers' poll) 1986, Characters, 1987, Jungle Fever, 1991, Inner Peace, 1995, Motown Legends, 1995; (with others) Natural Wonders, 1995, Conversation Peace, 1996; numerous others; appeared in films: Bikini Beach, 1964, Muscle Beach Party, 1964; frequent TV appearances include Mike Douglas Show, guest host Saturday Night Live; named (Musician of Year, Down Beat mag. Rock/Blues Poll 1973-75, 77-78, Best Selling Male Soul Artist of Year, Nat. Assn. Rec. Merchandisers 1974), recipient numerous Grammy awards, also numerous awards for best singer/songwriter; Rock Music award 1977, Am. Music award 1978, Am. Video award for best rhythm and blues video for Ebony and Ivory 1982, Inducted Songwriters Hall of Fame 1982. Named to: Rock and Roll Hall of Fame, 1989; recipient Nelson Mandela Courage award, 1991. Office: 4616 W Magnolia Blvd Burbank CA 91505-2731 also: Motown Records 825 8th Ave New York NY 10019*

WONDERS, WILLIAM CLARE, geography educator; b. Toronto, Apr. 22, 1924; s. George Clarence and Ann Mary (Bell) W.; m. Lillian Paradise Johnson, June 2, 1951; children—Karen Elizabeth, Jennifer Anne, Glen William. B.A. with honors, Victoria Coll., U. Toronto, 1946; M.A., Syracuse U., 1948; Ph.D., U. Toronto, 1951; Fil. Dr. h.c., Uppsala U., 1981. Teaching asst. dept. geography Syracuse U., 1946-48; lectr. dept. geography U. Toronto, 1948-53; asst. prof. geography dept. polit. economy U. Alta., 1953-55, assoc. prof. geography, 1955-57, prof., head dept. geography, 1957-67, prof. dept. geography, 1967-87, Univ. prof., 1983—, prof. emeritus, 1987—; vis. prof. geography U. B.C., 1954, U. Okla., 1965-66, St. Mary's U., 1977, U. Victoria, 1989, J.F. Kennedy Inst., Free U. Berlin, 1990; guest prof. Inst. Geography, Uppsala (Sweden) U., 1962-63; rsch. fellow in Geography U. Aberdeen, Scotland, 1970-71, 78; vis. fellow in Can. Studies, U. Edinburgh, Scotland, 1987. Author: Looking at Maps, 1960, The Sawdust Fusiliers, 1991, Norden and Canada-A Geographer's Perspective, 1992, Alaska Highway Explorer, 1994; (with T. Drinkwater et al) Atlas of Alberta, 1969, (with J.C. Muller et al) Junior Atlas of Alberta, 1979; contbr., editor: Canada's Changing North, 1971, The North, 1972, The Arctic Circle, 1976, Knowing the North, 1988; contbr. articles to jours. and encys., chpts. to books. Mem. Nat. Adv. Com. on Geog. Rsch., 1965-69; chmn. Boreal Inst. No. Studies, 1960-62; mem. Can. Permanent Com. on Geog. Names, 1981-94, Alta. Hist. Sites Bd., 1978-83, vice chmn., 1982-83; mem. policy bd. Can. Plains Rsch. Centre, U. Regina (Sask.), 1975-86; mem. adv. bd. Royal Tyrrell Mus. Paleontology, 1984-89; bd. dirs. The Muttart Found., 1986-93, 95—, v.p., 1991-93, mem., 1991—. NSF sr. fgn. scientist fellow, 1965-66; Canada Council leave fellow, 1969-70, 77-78; Nuffield Found. fellow, 1970-71. Fellow Arctic Inst. N.Am., Royal Soc. Can., Royal Can. Geog. Soc.; mem. Can. Assn. Geographers (past pres.), Royal Scottish Geog. Soc., Can. Assn. Scottish Studies (councillor 1974-77), Scottish Soc. No. Studies, Champlain Soc. (councillor 1981-86), Sigma Xi, Gamma Theta Upsilon.

WONG, ANDREW, telecommunications company executive; b. Belmont, Mass., Feb. 17, 1953; s. Bing Yue and Sun Yan (Quan) W.; m. Kathleen Elaine Burchedean, June 22, 1984; 1 child, Brian Andrew. BA, BS, U. Pa., 1975; MA, MBA, Stanford U., 1979. Assoc. analyst Fed. Res. Bank of N.Y., N.Y.C., 1975-77; investment analyst Overseas Pvt. Investment Corp., Washington, 1979-82; sr. fin. analyst MCI Comm. Corp., Washington, 1982-83; mgr. corp. devel. Contel ASC, Rockville, Md., 1983-88; mgr. investment staff Potomac Capital Investment Corp., Washington, 1988-91; sr. cons. Riggs Mcht. Banking Group, Washington, 1991-92; dir. bus. devel. COMSAT Corp., Clarksburg, Md., 1992-95; v.p. mktg. GE Spacenet, McLean, Va., 1996—; bd. dirs. Exotech Corp., Marine Mgmt. Sys., Inc., Stamford, Conn., Teleport Internat., Inc., Arlington, Va.,; mem. adv. bd. Lawrence Livermore Nat. Labs., Livermore, Calif. Contbr. articles to profl. jours. Pub. Svc. fellow HEW, Stanford U., 1978. Mem. Washington Soc. Investment Analysts, Ctr. for Strategic and Internat. Studies, Washington Area Money Mgrs. Assn., Am. Mgmt. Assn., Westmoreland Citizens Assn. Presbyterian. Avocations: skiing, golf, running, foreign travel. Office: GE Spacenet 1750 Old Meadow Rd Mc Lean VA 22102-4304

WONG, ANTONIO HAM, family physician; b. San Pedro Sula, Honduras, Oct. 7, 1960; came to U.S., 1973; s. Hui Chung and Maria (Wong) H.; m. Heidi Wong, Apr. 7, 1990; children: Lawrence, Catherine, Kristen, Keith. BS, U. Miami, Fla., 1984, MD, 1990. Chief resident dept. family medicine Jackson Meml. Hosp., Miami, 1992-93; med. dir. PCA-Century Med. Ctr., Miami, 1993-95; CEO, founder Caduceus Med. Inst., Pembroke Pines, Fla., 1995—. Mem. AMA, Am. Acad. Family Physicians, Am. Soc. Bariatric Physicians, Fla. Med. Assn., Dade County Med. Assn. Avocations: reading, gourmet cooking, swimming, painting, photography. Home: 6523 Champlain Ter Davie FL 33331

WONG, CHING-PING, chemist, materials scientist, engineer, educator; b. Canton, China, Mar. 29, 1947; came to U.S., 1966; s. Kwok-Keung and Yun-Kwan (Lo) W.; m. Lorraine Homnack, May 27, 1978; children: Michelle, David. BS in Chemistry, Purdue U., 1969; PhD in Organic/Inorganic Chemistry, Pa. State U., 1975. Postdoctoral scholar Stanford (Calif.) U., 1975-77; mem. rsch. staff AT&T Bell Labs., Princeton, N.J., 1977-82, sr. mem. tech. staff, 1982-87, disting. mem. tech. staff, 1987-92; AT&T Bell Labs. fellow, 1992-96; prof. Sch. of Materials Sci. and Engring., Ga. Inst. Tech., Atlanta, 1996—; assembly, reliability and thermal mgmt. rsch. dir. NSF Packaging Rsch. Ctr.; program chmn. 39th Electronic Components Conf., 1989; gen. chmn. 41st Electronic Components and Tech. Conf., 1991; bd. govs. IEEE-Components, Hybrids and Mfg. Tech. Soc., 1987-89, tech. v.p., 1990-91, pres., 1992-93. Author, editor: Polymers for Electronic and Photonic Applications, 1993; contbr. articles to profl. jours. Recipient Outstanding Papers and Contbns. award IEEE-Components, Hybrids and Mfg. Tech. Soc., 1990, 91, 94, 96. Fellow IEEE (Outstanding Sustained Tech. Contbns. award 1995). Achievements include over 38 U.S. and numerous internat. patents for integrated device passivation and encepsulation area; pioneer in application of gel polymers for device reliability without hermeticity, a new application on electronic device packaging. Home: 3422 Glen Devon Ln Berkeley Lake CA 30136 Office: Ga Inst Tech Sch Materials Sci & Engring 778 Atlantic Dr Atlanta GA 30332-0245

WONG, DANIEL ON-CHEONG, geotechnical and environmental engineer; b. Macao, China, July 23, 1959; came to U.S., 1980; s. Yuen Fai and Kwan Heng (Luk) W.; m. Mei Ching Tsui Wong, Jan. 2, 1988; children: Matthew Anthony, Nathan Christopher. BS, U. Houston, 1983, MS, 1985, PhD, 1988. Registered profl. engr., Tex. Project engr. McBride-Ratcliff (A Badger Co.), Houston, 1989-93; chmn. bd. dirs., prin. Tolunay-Wong Engrs., Inc., Houston, 1993—; pres. R & D Constructors, Inc., Houston, 1997—; chmn. ASCE Tex. sect. Geotechnical com., 1994-95; friend of A2K03, Transp. Rsch. Bd., Washington, 1992. Contbr. articles to profl. jours. Deacon Houston Chinese Ch., 1989—; chmn. Chinese Student Christian Fellowship, U. Houston, 1985, 87. Recipient scholarships U. Houston, 1981-83, Young Engr. of the Year award Tex. Soc. Profl. Engrs. (Sam Houston chpt.), 1993. Mem. NSPE, ASCE (John Hawley award 1989, tech. paper award 1989, 94), Asian Am. Engrs./Architects (pres. 1997), Sigma Xi (assoc.). Avocations: reading, music, football, tennis. Office: Tolunay-Wong Engrs Inc 1706 W Sam Houston Pky N Houston TX 77043-2723

WONG, DAVID T., biochemist; b. Hong Kong, Nov. 6, 1935; s. Chi-Keung and Pui-King W.; m. Christina Lee, Dec. 28, 1963; children: Conrad, Melvin, Vincent. Student, Nat. Taiwan U., 1955-56; BS, Seattle Pacific U., 1961; MS, Oreg. State U., 1964; PhD, U. Oreg., 1966. Postdoctoral fellow U. Pa., Phila., 1966-68; sr. biochemist Lilly Rsch. Labs., Indpls., 1968-72, rsch. biochemist, 1973-77, sr. rsch. scientist, 1978-89; rsch. advisor, 1990—; adj. prof. biochemistry and molecular biology Ind. U. Sch. Medicine, 1986-96, adj. prof. neurobiology, 1991—. Mem. editl. bd. Chinese Jour. Physiology, 1996—; contbr. numerous articles to sci. jours.; patentee in field. Alumnus of Growing Vision Seattle Pacific U., 1989. Recipient Scientist of Yr., Pres. award Chinese Neuroscience Soc., 1991, Discoverers award Pharm. Mfr. Assn., 1993, Lifetime Rsch. award The Mental Health Assn. of Ind., 1996, World of Difference award Ind. Health Industry Forum, 1996, Pharm. Discoverer's award for Prozac, Nat. Alliance Rsch. on Schizophrenia. and Depression, 1996. Mem. Am. Coll. Neuropsychopharmaeology, Am. Soc. Pharmacology and Exptl. Therapeutics, Internat. Soc. Neurochemistry, Am. Soc. Neurochemistry, Soc. Neurosci. (pres. Indpls. chpt. 1987, 88), Soc. Chinese Bioscientists in Am., Indpls. Assn. Chinese Ams. (pres. 1987), Sigma Xi. Rsch. on biochemistry and pharmacology of neurotransmission; discovery and development of antidepressant drug, Prozac (Fluoxetine) and drug candidates including Tomoxetine, a selective inhibitor of norepinephrine uptake; duloxetine, an inhibitor for uptake of serotonin and norepinephrine; studies of potentially useful substances which enhance transmission of norepinephrine, dopamine (Permax (pergolide), an agent for treatment of Parkinson's disease), serotonin, acetylcholine and GABA-neurons; studies of natural products led to the discovery of carboxylic ionophores: Narasin and A204, which increase transport of cations across biomembranes. Office: Lilly Rsch Labs Eli Lilly and Co Lilly Corp Ctr Indianapolis IN 46285

WONG, DAVID YUE, academic administrator, physics educator; b. Swatow, China, Apr. 16, 1934; came to U.S., 1953; s. Fan and Wen (Tsang) W.; m. Katherine Young, Sept. 3, 1960 (div. Mar. 1988); children: Amy, Eric; m. Elizabeth Lewis, Mar. 26, 1988. BA, Hardin Simmons U., 1954; PhD, U. Md., 1957. Theoretical physicist Lawrence Radiation Lab., U. Calif., Berkeley, 1958-59; asst. prof. physics U. Calif., San Diego, 1960-63, assoc. prof., 1963-67, prof., 1967—, chair dept. physics, 1977-80, provost Warren Coll., 1985-94. Alfred P. Sloan fellow, 1966-68. Mem. Am. Inst. Physics.

WONG, HENRY LI-NAN, bank executive, economist; b. Rangoon, Burma, Nov. 3, 1940; s. Chew King and Jenny (Yu) W.; came to U.S., 1946. m. Laurie Yap, Apr. 11, 1968; children: Rachael S.Y., Remle S.W. BS, Waynesburg Coll., 1965; MS, U. Hawaii, 1968, PhD, 1969. Economist, Econ. Research Service U.S. Dept. Agr., Washington, 1969-70; economist Hawaii Dept. Budget and Fin., Honolulu, 1970-73; dir. Hawaii film office Hawaii Dept. Planning and Econ. Devel., Honolulu, 1973-84; exec. v.p. and chief adminstr., office of chmn. CB Bancshares Inc., Honolulu, 1984—; vice chmn., dir. Hawaii Strategic Devel. Corp., Honolulu, 1991-95; mem. coun. of revenue State of Hawaii, 1995—; v.p., bd. dirs. Friends of East West Ctr., Honolulu, 1983-84. NDEA fellow, 1965-69. Mem. Assn. Film Commrs. (pres. 1980), Am. Econ. Assn., Am. Agrl. Econs. Assn., Hawaii Internat. Film Festival, Chinese C. of C., Hawaii Soc. Corp. Planners, Lanakila Rehab. Ctr. (trustee), Alpha Kappa Psi, Theta Chi. Democrat. Presbyterian. Lodges: Elks, Masons (trustee), Shriners. Office: City Bank City Fin Tower 201 Merchant St Honolulu HI 96813-2928

WONG, JAMES BOK, economist, engineer, technologist; b. Canton, China, Dec. 9, 1922; came to U.S., 1938, naturalized, 1962; s. Gen Ham and Chen (Yee) W.; m. Wai Ping Lim, Aug. 3, 1946; children: John, Jane Doris, Julia Ann. BS in Agr., U. Md., 1949, BS in Chem. Engring., 1950; MS, U. Ill., 1951, PhD, 1954. Rsch. asst. U. Ill., Champaign-Urbana, 1950-53; chem. engr. Standard Oil of Ind., Whiting, 1953-55; process design engr., rsch. engr. Shell Devel. Co., Emeryville, Calif., 1955-61; sr. planning engr., prin. planning engr. Chem. Plastics Group, Dart Industries, Inc. (formerly Rexall Drug & Chem. Co.), L.A., 1961-66, supr. planning and econs., 1966-67, mgr. long range planning and econs., 1967, chief economist, 1967-72, dir. econs. and ops. analysis, 1972-78, dir. internat. techs., 1978-81; pres. James B. Wong Assocs., L.A., 1981—; chmn. bd. dirs. United Pacific Bank, 1988—; tech. cons. various corps. Contbr. articles to profl. jours. Bd. dirs., pres. Chinese Am. Citizens Alliance Found.; mem. Asian Am. Edn. Commn., 1971-81. Served with USAAF, 1943-46. Recipient Los Angeles Outstanding Vol. Service award, 1977. Mem. Am. Inst. Chem. Engrs., Am. Chem. Soc., VFW (vice comdr. 1959), Commodores (named to exec. order 1982), Sigma Xi, Tau Beta Pi, Phi Kappa Phi, Pi Mu Epsilon, Phi Lambda Upsilon, Phi Eta Sigma. Home: 2460 Venus Dr Los Angeles CA 90046-1646 *Personal philosophy: A man's reputation is his most prized possession.*

WONG, JOE, physical chemist; b. Hong Kong, Aug. 8, 1942; arrived in U.S., 1966; s. Po-lim and Mildred (Tam) W.; m. Mei-Ngan, Dec. 20, 1969; children: Glenn, Christina, Theresa. BSc, U. Tasmania, Australia, 1965; BSc with honors, U. Tesmania, Australia, 1966, DSc, 1986; PhD, Purdue U., 1970. Rsch. chemist Electrolytic Zinc of Australia, Tasmania, 1966; lectr. in phys. chemistry Royal Hobart Coll., Tasmania, 1966; rsch. chemist GE R&D Ctr., Schenectady, N.Y., 1970-86; sr. rsch. chemist Lawrence Livermore (Calif.) Nat. Lab., 1986—; adj. prof. chemistry SUNY, Albany, 1981-86; cons. prof. Stanford Synchrotron Rad. Lab., 1993—. Author: Glass: Structure by Spectroscopy, 1976; contbr. articles to profl. jours.; 7 patents in field. Sr. fellowship Sci. and Tech. Agy., 1991; recipient Humboldt Rsch. award Humboldt Found., 1991, RD-100 awards, 1990, 91. Fellow Am. Inst. Chemists; mem. AAAS, Am. Chem. Soc., Am. Phys. Soc., Materials Rsch. Soc., Sigma Xi. Home: 871 El Cerro Blvd Danville CA 94526-2704 Office: Lawrence Livermore Nat Lab PO Box 808 L-356 Livermore CA 94551

WONG, KUANG CHUNG, anesthesiologist; b. Chung King, People's Republic China, Nov. 12, 1936; m. Janny Wu; children: Jade, Shale, Amber, Kaston. BS in Chemistry, Iowa State U., 1959; MS in Pharmacology, State U. Iowa, 1962; PhD in Pharmacology, U. Nebr., Omaha, 1966, MD, 1968. Diplomate Am. Bd. Anesthesiology (assoc. examiner 1979—). Instr. then asst. prof. pharmacology U. Nebr., Omaha, 1965-69; intern Bishop Clarkson Hosp., Omaha, 1968; intern U. Nebr. Coll. Medicine, Omaha, 1968, resident in anesthesia, 1968-69; resident, then fellow U. Wash. Sch. Medicine, Seattle, 1969-70; mem. assoc. grad. faculty U. Nebr., Omaha, 1968-69; asst. to assoc. prof. anesthesiology and pharmacology U. Washington, Seattle, 1970-74; assoc. prof. anesthesiology and pharmacology U. Utah, Salt Lake City, 1974-76, chmn. dept., assoc. prof. anesthesiology and pharmacology, 1976-77, chmn. dept., prof. anesthesiology and pharmacology, 1977—; vis. prof. numerous univs. throughout world, also various hosps.; mem. adv. com. anesthetic and life support drugs FDA, 1982-83; attending anesthesiologist U. Wash. Med. Ctr. and affiliated hosps., Seattle, 1970-74; staff anesthesiologist U. Utah Med. Ctr., Salt Lake City, 1974—; mem. surgery, anesthesia and trauma study sects. NIH, 1982-86. Mem. editorial bd. Anesthesia and Analgesia, 1980-89. Served with U.S. Army, 1955-57. Recipient Dr. Ernest Tibbets Manning Meml. Scholarship, 1965-66, U. Nebr. Upper Regents' Scholarship, 1966-67; grantee NIH, 1969-72, 80-85, Wash. State Heart Assn., 1972-74, Utah Heart Assn., 1975-76, 78-80, U. Utah, 1975-76, 76-77, Knoll Pharm. Co., 1976-79; Riker Labs., Inc., 1976-78, Smith Kline and French, 1979-89. Mem. AMA, Am. Heart Assn., Am. Soc. Anesthesiologists (ad hoc com. self-evaluation 1979), Am. Soc. Clin. Pharmacology and Chemotherapy, Am. Soc. Pharmacology and Exptl. Therapeutics, Assn. Cardiac Anesthesiologists, Assn. Univ. Anesthesiologists, Internat. Anesthesia Rsch. Soc. (trustee 1989—), Salt Lake County Med. Soc., Utah Heart Assn., Utah Med. Soc., Utah Soc. Anesthesiologists, Soc. Acad. Anesthesia Chairmen, Sigma Xi, Alpha Omega Alpha. Office: Univ of Utah Sch of Medicine Dept of Anesthesiology Salt Lake City UT 84132

WONG, MA-LI, psychiatrist; b. Hong Kong; came to U.S., 1985; d. Kowk Keung and Yin Shang (Lau) W.; m. Julio Licinio, Nov. 15, 1985. MD, U. Sao Paulo, Brazil, 1982. Resident in medicine, then neurology U. Sao Paulo Med. Ctr., 1983-85; rsch. assoc. Albert Einstein Coll. Medicine, Bronx, N.Y., 1985-86; resident in psychiatry Albert Einstein Coll. Medicine, 1986-89; rsch. fellow Clin. Neuroendocrinology br. NIMH, Bethesda, Md., 1989-90; chief resident in psychiatry Yale U. Sch. Medicine, New Haven, 1990-91, instr. in psychiatry, 1991-93; vis. scientist clin. neuroendocrinology br. NIMH, Bethesda, Md., 1993—. Contbr. to profl. jours. Mem. N.Y. Acad. Scis., Am. Psychiat. Assn., Am. Fedn. Clin. Rsch., Soc. Neuroscience, Assn. Women Psychiatrists, Endocrine Soc. Avocations: poetry, photography. Office: 8135 N Brook Ln # 907 Bethesda MD 20814

WONG, MICHAEL HENRY, anesthesiologist; b. L.A., Feb. 10, 1965; s. Henry and Beulah (Chan) W.; m. Evelyn Wing Han Mark, Dec. 30, 1989; children: Bryce Michael, Kira Krishne. BS in Biol. Sci., U. So. Calif., 1987; DO, Coll. Osteo. Medicine Pacific, Pomona, Calif., 1991. Intern San Bernardino County Med. Ctr., San Bernardino, Calif., 1991; resident in anesthesiology Loma Linda (Calif.) U. Med. Ctr., 1991-95; dir. anesthesiology South Coast Surgery Ctr., Santa Ana, Calif., 1995—; pres., med. dir. Anesthetix Inc., Huntington Beach, Calif., 1995—, So. Calif. Pain Control Ctr., Inc., Garden Grove, Calif., 1995—. Recipient Alumni Meml. award Coll. Osteo. Medicine of Pacific, 1989. Mem. AMA, Am. Soc. Anesthesiologists, World Tae Kwon Do Fedn. (Dan instr.), Sigma Sigma Phi. Avocations: martial arts, skiing. Office: So Calif Pain Control Ctr 7077 Orangewood Ave Ste 150 Garden Grove CA 92841-1444

WONG, NANCY L., dermatologist; b. Chung King, China, Aug. 23, 1943; came to U.S., 1947; d. YinPao Harry and Alice Wang; m. Robert Lipshutz; children: Seth, Alison, David. BS magna cum laude, Pa. State U., 1963; MS in Physics, Columbia U., 1965; MD, Jefferson Med. Coll., Phila., 1971. Diplomate Am. Bd. Dermatology. Intern Wilmington Med. Ctr., 1972; resident Jackson Meml. Hosp., Miami, Mount Sinai Med. Ctr., Miami, 1977; pvt. practice Palo Alto, Calif., 1987—. Woodrow Wilson fellow 1963-64, NSF fellow, 1963-64, AEC fellow, 1963-64. Fellow Am. Acad. Dermatology. Avocations: tennis, music, writing, painting. Office: 1101 Welch Rd Ste C6 Palo Alto CA 94304-1904

WONG, PATRICK SECK LAI, chemical engineer; b. Canton, China, Aug. 8, 1936; came to U.S., 1957; m. Helen Wai Lun Wong, June 26, 1969; children: Julian, Francis, Alex. BSChemE, U. Mich., 1960, MS, MIT, 1962; PhD, Imperial Coll., London, 1967. Rsch. chemist W.R. Grace, Clifton, N.J., 1962-64; rsch. assoc. MIT, Cambridge, Mass., 1967-73; head transport process Alza Corp., Palo Alto, Calif., 1973-79, prin. scientist, 1981-85, dir. product rsch., 1985-87, sr. dir. rsch., 1987-91, exec. dir. R & D, 1991-94, v.p. rsch., 1994—; v.p. R & D Collins Indls. Co., Hong Kong, 1979-81, Bio-Electro System, Palo Alto, 1988-91. Contbr. articles to Jour. Polymer Sci. (London), AIChemE Jour., Ency. Pharm. Tech. Recipient Founder's award ALZA, 1996. Mem. Am. Chem. Soc., Am. Assn. Pharm. Scientists, Controlled Release Soc., Tau Beta Pi, Sigma Xi. Achievements include over 110 patents for Controlled Drug Delivery, Procardia XL. Office: Alza Corp 950 Page Mill Rd Palo Alto CA 94304-1012

WONG, PHILLIP ALLEN, osteopathic physician; b. Oakland, Calif., Dec. 8, 1956; s. Timothy Him and Lillian (Lee) W.; m. Lisa Perreautt, Apr. 30, 1983; children: Ashley, Heather. BS in Microbiology and Chemistry, No. Ariz. U., 1979; DO, Kirksville Coll. Osteo. Med., 1983. Intern Kirksville Osteo. Health Ctr., 1983-84; staff family physician USAF, Kirtland AFB, N.Mex., 1984-87; CEO, pvt. practice Albuquerque, 1987—. Capt. USAF, 1984-87. Mem. Am. Acad. Osteopathy (bd. cert. in osteo. manipulative medicine), Am. Osteo. Assn., Am. Coll. Osteo. Family Physicians (bd. cert. family practice), N.Mex. Osteo. Med. Assn. (bd. mem.), Ariz. Acad. Osteopathy (bd. mem.), Cranial Acad. (bd. cert. in cranial in the osteo. field). Office: 10211 Montgomery Blvd NE Ste A Albuquerque NM 87111-3604

WONG, PO KEE, research company executive, educator; b. Canton City, Kwangtung, China, May 5, 1934; came to U.S., 1959; s. Kum Fun Wong and Wai Chi Chun Wah, Aug. 1965; children, Adam, Anita. BS, Taiwan Provincial Cheng Kung U., Tainan, 1956; MS, U. Utah, 1961; PhD Mech. Engring., Calif. Inst. Tech., 1966; PhD in Aeronaut. and Astronaut. Engring., Stanford, 1970. Lic. mech. profl. engr., Taiwan; cert. tchr., Mass. Sr. scientist Lockheed Missile & Space Co., Palo Alto, Calif., 1966-68; lectr. U. Santa Clara, Calif., 1970-71; researcher NASA Ames Rsch. Ctr., Moffet Field, Calif., 1970-71; engr. G.E. Breeder Reactor Dept., Sunnyvale, Calif., 1972-73; specialist engr. Nuclear Svcs. Co., Campbell, Calif., 1973; engr. Stone & Webster Engring. Co., Boston, 1974-76; pres., chief exec. officer Systems Rsch. Co., Somerville, Mass., 1976—; tchr. Boston Public Schs., 1979—. Author, presenter tech. papers; patentee in field. Mem. ASME, AAAS, AIAA, The Math. Assn. of Am., Internat. Platform Assn., Internat. Assn. Structural Mechanics in Reactor Tech., N.Y. Acad. Scis. Achievements include patents in field. Avocations: tennis, table tennis, Chinese chess, Western chess, go-game. Home: 50 Bradley St Somerville MA 02145-2930 Office: Charlestown High Sch 240 Medford St Charlestown MA 02129-1930

WONG, RUTH ANN, nursing administrator; b. Chgo., July 24, 1946; d. Valentine Wally and Sally Sylvia (Poremski) Fronczak; m. James W. Wong, Apr. 20, 1974. Diploma in nursing, St. Mary of Nazareth Sch., 1967; pediatric nurse clinician cert., U. Va., 1973; BA, Occidental Coll., 1977; MPH, UCLA, 1979, perioperative nursing cert., 1990; pub. health nurse cert., Calif. State U., Long Beach, 1982. Cert. PNP. Commd. 2d lt. USAF, 1968, advanced through grades to col., 1994; charge nurse, staff nurse USAF, Barksdale AFB, La., 1968-70, Tachikawa AFB, Japan, 1970-72; charge nurse, staff nurse Kirtland AFB, N.Mex., 1972-74; chief flight nurse 146 Aeromedical Evacuation Squadron, Van Nuys, Calif., 1977-92; chief Air N.G. nursing svcs. Air N.G. Readiness Ctr., Andrews AFB, Md., 1992—; clin. instr. Calif. State U., L.A., 1974-77; field placement supr. grad. program Calif. State U., Northridge, 1981-87; PNP, Children's Hosp., L.A., 1974-77, Headstart Found., East Los Angeles, 1977-80; dir. nursing and health svcs. ARC, Pasadena, Calif., 1980-90, mem. adv. com. nurse asst. tng. program, Washington, 1989-91, enll. nurse cons., L.A., 1990-92, cons. nurse asst. tng., 1989; perioperative nurse UCLA, 1990-91. Decorated Air Force Commendation medal with one oakleaf cluster, Meritorious Svc. medal, Army Commendation medal. Roman Catholic. Avocations: reading, travel, interior decorating, snow skiing, gardening. Home: 7495 Digby Grn Alexandria VA 22315-5246 Office: Air NG 3500 Fetchet Ave Andrews AFB MD 20762

WONG, SUN YET, engineering consultant; b. Honolulu, Dec. 6, 1932; s. Chip Tong and Shiu Inn (Chang) W.; m. Janet Siu Hung Lau; children: Cathleen, Bryan, Jonathan. BS in Civil Engring. with honors, U. Hawaii, 1954; MS in Civil Engring., Yale U., 1955. Engr. N.Am. Aviation, Downey, Calif., 1955-58; mem. tech. staff Ramo Woolridge Space Tech. Labs., Redondo Beach, Calif., 1958-64; exec. v.p., treas., tech. dir. Mechanics Rsch. Inc., El Segundo, Calif., 1964-77; treas. System Devel. Corp., Santa Monica, Calif., 1977-79; chmn. bd., pres., treas. Applied Rsch. Inc., El Segundo, 1979-81; ind. cons. Rolling Hills Estates, Calif., 1981—; cons. Acurex, Mountain View, Calif., 1983, Ampex, Redwood City, Calif., 1991, Applied Tech., Mountain View, 1983-85, Astron, Mountain View, 1983-85, E Systems, Garland, Tex., 1986-93, Electromech. Systems Inc., Anaheim, Calif., 1984, Hughes, El Segundo, 1992, 94, 96—, Intercon, Cerritos, Calif., 1982-84, J.H. Wiggins Co., Redondo Beach, 1982-84, Kodak Datatape, Pasadena, Calif., 1989, Lion Engring., Rancho Palos Verdes, Calif., 1994—, Measurement Analysis Corp., Torrance, Calif., 1984-96, MRJ, Fairfax, Va., 1984, Odectics, Anaheim, 1990, Swales & Assocs., Beltsville, Md., 1992-93, Statis. Scis., Inc., Beverly Hills, Calif., 1986, Tompkins and Assocs., Torrance, 1984—, TRW, Redondo Beach, 1984; dir. Lion Engring. Avocation: metal machining. Home and Office: 7 Club View Ln Rolling Hills Estates CA 90274

WONG, VICTOR KENNETH, physics educator, academic administrator; b. San Francisco, Nov. 1, 1938; m. Nancy Wong; children: Cassandra, Pamela, Lianna. BS in Engring. Physics, U. Calif., Berkeley, 1960, PhD in Physics, 1966. Postdoctoral fellow Ohio State U., Columbus, 1966-68; lectr., asst. prof. U. Mich., Ann Arbor, 1968-76, adj. prof. physics, 1992-95; assoc. prof. physics U. Mich., Dearborn, 1976-82, prof. physics, 1982-86, chmn. dept. natural sci., 1980-83, dean Coll. Arts, Sci. and Letters, 1983-86; provost, vice chancellor acad. affairs U. Mich., Flint, 1986-95, prof. physics, 1986—; adj. rsch. scientist U. Mich., 1995—, dir. info. technology for rsch., 1995—. Assoc. editor: Math. Revs., 1980; contbr. articles to profl. jours. Mem. AAAS, Am. Phys. Soc., Am. Assn. Higher Edn. (1st chmn. Asian caucus 1986-88), Nat. U. Continuing Edn. Assn. (mem. minority com. 1989), North Ctrl. Assn. Colls. and Schs. (cons. evaluator com. 1989—), Am. Coun. Edn. (mem. commn. on minorities in higher edn. 1993-96), Assn. Computing Machinery, Phi Beta Kappa, Tau Beta Pi. Office: Univ Mich Info Tech Divsn 1071 Beal Ave Ann Arbor MI 48109-2134

WONG, WALLACE, medical supplies company executive, real estate investor; b. Honolulu, July 13, 1941; s. Jack Yung Hung and Theresa (Goo) W.; m. Amy Ju, June 17, 1963; children: Chris, Bradley, Jeffery. Student, UCLA, 1960-63. Chmn., pres. South Bay Coll., Hawthorne, Calif., 1965-86; chmn. Santa Barbara (Calif.) Bus. Coll., 1975—; gen. ptnr. W B Co., Redondo Beach, Calif., 1982—; CEO Cal Am. Med. Supplies, Rancho Santa Margarita, Calif., 1986-96, Cal Am. Exports, Inc., Rancho Santa Margarita, 1986-96, Pacific Am. Group, Rancho Santa Margarita, 1991-96; chmn., CEO Alpine, Inc., Rancho Santa Margarita, Calif., 1993-96; pres. Bayside Properties, Rancho Santa Margarita, 1993—; bd. dirs. Metrobank, L.A. FFF Enterprises; chmn. bd. 1st Ind. Fin. Group., Rancho Santa Margarita, 1994—; chmn. Affinity Fin. Corp., 1996—. Acting sec. of state State of Calif., Sacramento, 1982; founding mem. Opera Pacific, Orange County, Calif., 1985; mem. Hist. and Cultural Found., Orange County, 1986; v.p. Orange County Chinese Cultural Club, Orange County, 1985. Named for Spirit of Enterprise Resolution, Hist. & Cultural Found., Orange County, 1987; recipient resolution City of Hawthorne, 1973. Mem. Westren Accred Schs. & Colls. (v.p. 1978-79), Magic Castle (life), Singapore Club. Avocations: traveling, skiing. Office: Bayside Properties 23042 Arroyo Vis Rcho Station Marg CA 92688-2604

WONG, WARREN JAMES, mathematics educator; b. Masterton, N.Z., Oct. 16, 1934; came to U.S. 1964; s. Ken and Jessie (Ng) W.; m. Nellie Gee, May 12, 1962; children: Carole Frances, Andrea. BSc, U. Otago, Dunedin, N.Z., 1955, MSc, 1956; PhD, Harvard U., 1959. Lectr. U. Otago, Dunedin, 1960-64, sr. lectr., 1964; assoc. prof. math. U. Notre Dame, Ind., 1964-68, prof., 1968—. Proceedings editorial bd. Am. Math. Soc., Providence, R.I., 1988-90; contbr. articles to profl. jours. Vestryman St. Michael and All Angels Episcopal Ch., South Bend, 1988-90. Mem. Am. Math. Soc., Math. Assn. Am., Australian Math. Soc. Episcopalian. Office: Dept Math Univ Notre Dame Notre Dame IN 46556-5683

WONG, WILLIE, former mayor, automotive executive; b. Mesa, Ariz., Oct. 12, 1948; m. Cobina Wong; children: Kevin, Jeremy. Grad., Ariz. State U. Vice mayor City of Mesa (Ariz.), 1988-90; councilmem., 1990-91; mayor City of Mesa (Ariz.), 1992-96; mgr. Wilky's Performance Ctr., Mesa, 1992—; pres. Wilky's Performance Ctr., Mesa, Ariz.; prev. employment with AT&T. Treas. Regional Pub. Transp. Authority; chmn. Williams Redevel. Ptnrship., Maricopa Assn. Govts. Regional Devel. Policy Com.; vice-chmn. Williams Gateway Airport Authority, Mesa Sister Cities; exec. com. League of Ariz. Cities and Towns; bd. dirs. YMCA (past pres.), Child Crisis Ctr., Southwest Pub. Recycling Assn. Named Outstanding Young Man Mesa Leadership, Tng., & Devel. Assn., 1989. Mem. MAG Regional Coun., Econ. Devel. Adv. Bd., Rotary Club-Mesa West. Avocations: baseball, fishing, travel, reading. Home: 1343 E McLellan Mesa AZ 85203 also: Wilky's Performance Ctr 402 E Main Mesa AZ 85203*

WONG, WING KEUNG, trading, electronics company executive, physician; b. Hong Kong, Jan. 5, 1933; s. Lai Cho Wong and Sut Mui Chung; m. Ban Cho, May 28, 1957; children: Hoi Ling, Hoi Yin. MB, BS, Beijing Med. Coll., 1955. Lic. Med. Coun. Hong Kong. Physician 1st Hosp. of Beijing Med. Coll., 1955-69; with Hosp., Ganshu, China, 1970-73; pvt. practice Hong Kong, 1979-84; dir. Cheung Tai Hong Ltd., Hong Kong, 1974-86; chmn. bd. dirs. Computime Ltd., Hong Kong, 1979-93; dir. Computime Internat. Ltd., Brit. V.I., 1993-95; dep. chmn. Cheung Tai Hong Holdings Ltd., Bermuda, 1994-95; exec. dir. Cheung Tai Hong Ltd., Hong Kong, 1987-96. Mem. Hong Kong Med. Assn., Dynasty Club. Avocations: travel, music, diving, photography. Office: Cheung Tai Hong Ltd, 31/F Singga Comml Ctr, 144-151 Connaught Rd W Hong Kong Hong Kong

WONG-LIANG, EIRENE MING, psychologist; b. Nassau, Bahamas, Nov. 20, 1961; came to U.S., 1969; d. Menyu and Lim Ming (Chow) Wong; m. Danqing Liang. BA, Trinity U., San Antonio, 1984; PhD, Calif. Sch. Profl. Psychology, 1992. Crisis counselor United Way Crisis Hotline, San Antonio, 1983; lab. asst. Trinity U., 1983; counselor Bayer County Women's Ctr., San Antonio, 1984, Turning Point Juvenile Diversion Project, Garden Grove, Calif., 1985-86; psychol. trainee Wolters Elem. Sch., Fresno, 1987, San Luis Obispo (Calif.) Youth Day Treatment, 1987-88, Calif. Sch. Profl. Psychology Svc. Ctr., Fresno, 1988-89; staff psychologist 314th Med. Ctr., Little Rock, Ark., 1989-93; pvt. practice, clin. psychologist Houston, 1993—; psychologist USAFR, 1993-97. Mem. APA, Am. Soc. Clin. Hypnosis, Nat. Register Health Svc. Providers in Psychology, Tex. Psychol. Assn., Houston Psychol. Assn., Houston Assn. Clin. Hypnosis (charter, treas. 1996-97, pres. 1997—), Internat. Soc. Clin. Hypnosis. Office: 10101 Southwest Fwy Ste 445 Houston TX 77074-1114

WONG-STAAL, FLOSSIE, geneticist, medical educator. BA, UCLA, 1968, PhD, 1972. Tchg. asst. UCLA, 1969-70, rsch. asst., 1970-72; postdoctoral fellow U. Calif., San Diego, 1972-73; Fogarty fellow Nat. Cancer Inst., Bethesda, Md., 1973-75; vis. assoc. Nat. Cancer Inst., Bethesda, 1975-76, cancer expert, 1976-78, sr. investigator, 1978-81, chief molecular genetics of hematopoietic cells sect., 1982-89; Florence Seeley Riford chair in AIDS rsch., prof. medicine U. Calif. San Diego, La Jolla, 1990—; vis. prof. Inst. Gen. Pathology, First U. Rome, Italy, 1985. Mem. editl. bd. Gene Analysis Techniques, 1984—, Cancer Letters, 1984-94, Leukemia, 1987—, Cancer Rsch., 1987, AIDS Rsch. and Human Retroviruses (sect. editor), 1987—, DNA and Cell Biology (sect. editor), 1987—, Microbial Pathogenesis, 1987-90, AIDS: An Internat. Jour., 1987—, Internat. Jour. Acquired Immunodeficiency Syndrome, 1988—, Oncogene, 1988—, Jour. Virology, 1990—; contbr. articles to profl. jours. Recipient Outstanding Sci. award Chinese Med. and Health Assn., 1987, The Excellence 2000 award U.S. Pan Asian Am. C. of C. and the Orgn. of Chinese Am. Women, 1991. Mem. Am. Soc. for Virology (charter), Phi Beta Kappa. Office: Univ California Ctr for AIDS Rsch San Diego CA 92110

WONHAM, WALTER MURRAY, electrical engineer, educator; b. Montreal, Que., Can., Nov. 1, 1934; m. Vera Anne Hale; children: Marjorie Jane, Cynthia Margaret. B of Engring., McGill U., Montreal, 1956; PhD, U. Cambridge, Eng., 1961. Asst. prof. elec. engring. Purdue U., Lafayette, Ind., 1961-62; rsch. scientist Research Inst. for Advanced Studies, Balt., 1962-64; assoc. prof. Brown U., Providence, 1964-69; rsch. assoc. NASA, Cambridge, Mass., 1967-69, cons., 1969; prof. elec. engring. U. Toronto, Ont., Can., 1970—, J. Roy Cockburn Prof., U. Toronto, 1991—, Cockburn chair, 1991, univ. prof., 1996. Author: Linear Multivariable Control: A Geometric Approach, 1974, 3d edit., 1985 (Russian transl. 1980, Chinese transl. 1984); assoc. editor Soc. for Indsl. and Applied Math., Jour. on Control and Optimization, 1965-79, Systems Control Letter, 1981-85. Athlone fellow, Gt. Britain, 1956-58; spl. scholar Nat. Rsch. Coun. Can., 1958-60; sr. postdoctoral resident rsch. assoc. NAS U.S.A., 1967-69. Recipient Brouwer medal Netherlands Math Soc., 1990. Fellow Royal Soc. Can., IEEE (Control Systems Sci. and Engring. award 1987). Office: U Toronto Dept Elec Engring. 35 St George St, Toronto, ON Canada M5S 1A4

WONNACOTT, (GORDON) PAUL, economics educator; b. London, Ont., Can., Mar. 16, 1933; s. Gordon Elliott and Muriel Johnston Wonnacott; m. Donna Elizabeth Cochrane, July 2, 1960; children: David, Ann, Alan, Bruce. BA, U. Western Ont., 1955; MA, Princeton U., 1957, PhD, 1959. Instr., asst. prof. econs. Columbia U., N.Y.C., 1958-62; assoc. prof. then prof. econs. U. Md., College Pk., 1962-91; mem. Pres.'s Coun. Econ. Advisers, 1991-93; Alan Holmes vis. prof. econs. Middlebury Coll., 1994—; mem. rsch. staff Royal Commn. Banking and Fin., Toronto, 1962; sr. staff economist Coun. Econ. Advisers, Washington, 1968-70; assoc. dir. divsn. internat. fin. Fed. Res. Bd., Washington, 1974-75; vis. scholar Office Internat. Monetary Rsch., U.S. Treasury, 1980; econ. adviser to Under Sec. of State, 1990-91. Author: The Canadian Dollar, 1960, 2d rev. edit., 1965, (with R.J. Wonnacott) Free Trade between the United States and Canada: The Potential Economic Effects, 1967, (with H.G. Johnson and H. Shibata) Harmonization of National Economic Policies under Free Trade, 1968, Macroeconomics, 1974, 3d rev. edit., 1984, (with R.J. Wonnacott) Economics, 1979, 4th rev. edit. 1990, Spanish edit., 1981, 3d rev. edit., 1987, (with Y. and C. Crusius) Portuguese edit., 1982, 2d rev. edit., 1985, (with A. Blomquist) Can. edit., 1983, 4th rev. edit., 1994, The United States and Canada: The Quest for Free Trade, 1987; contbr. numerous articles to profl. jours. Fellow Brooking Inst., 1957-58, Ford Found., 1963-64; vis. fellow Inst. Internat. Econs., 1986, 93-94. Mem. Am. Econ. Assn. Avocations: skiing, tennis. Home: 8 Murdoch Ct Middlebury VT 05753 Office: Middlebury College Dept Econs Middlebury VT 05753

WONNACOTT, RONALD JOHNSTON, economics educator; b. London, Ont., Can., Sept. 11, 1930; s. Gordon and and Muriel (Johnston) W.; m. Eloise Howlett, Sept. 11, 1954; children: Douglas, Robert, Cathy Anne. B.A., U. Western Ont., 1955; A.M., Harvard U., 1957, Ph.D., 1959. Mem. faculty U. Western Ont., London, 1958—, prof. econs., 1964—, chmn. dept., 1969-72; vis. assoc. prof. U. Minn., Mpls., 1961-62; cons. Resources for the Future, Econ. Council Can., Can.-Am. Com., Nat. Planning Assn., C.D. Howe Inst. Author: Canadian-American Dependence: An Interindustry Analysis of Production and Prices, 1961, Canada's Trade Options, 1975, Selected New Developments in International Trade Theory, 1984, The Economics of Overlapping Free Trade Areas and the Mexican Challenge, 1991, (with G.L. Reuber) The Cost of Capital in Canada, 1961, (with Paul Wonnacott) Free Trade Between the U.S. and Canada, 1967, Economics, 1979, 4th edit., 1990, (with Thomas H. Wonnacott) Introductory Statistics, 1969, 5th edit., 1990, Econometrics, 1970, 2d edit., 1979, Regression, 1981. Fellow Royal Soc. Can.; mem. Am. Econ. Assn., Can. Econ. Assn. (pres. 1981), London Hunt Club, Sunningdale Golf Club (Eng.), Hon. Co. Edinburgh Golfers, Craigleith Ski Club. Home: 171 Wychwood Park, London, ON Canada N6G 1S1

WONSER, MICHAEL DEAN, retired public affairs director,; b. Long Beach, Calif., Mar. 12, 1940; s. Franklin Henry and Dorothy Mae (Harris) W.; children: Therice Michele, Sherice Michele, Christopher Franklin; m. Mary L. Van Epps, Dec. 22, 1990. BS, U. Oreg., 1963, MFA, 1965; postgrad., U. Colo., 1976. Instr. Cen. Oreg. Coll., Bend, 1966-68; prof. Adams State Coll., Alamosa, Colo., 1969-91, dir. pub. affairs, 1982-90; pres. Colo. Faculty Com. Trustees, 1980-82. Mem. Chamber Edn. Com., Monte Vista, Colo., 1982-88; pres. Luth. Ch. Alamosa, 1980-85; bd. dirs. Creede Repertory Theatre, 1989-91; mem. Commerce Comm. and Resources Comm., 1995, Cmty. Improvement Commn., Sisters, Oreg., 1996-97. Mem. Higher Edn. Assn. of Rockies (pres. Colo. chpt. 1985-88), C. of C. Ambassador (treas. 1982), Alamosa, C. of C. Tourism Bd., Alamosa (chmn. 1987-89), Sisters C. of C. (pres. 1996-97, bd. dirs.), Rotary. Republican. Avocations: golf, skiing. Home: 24 NW Shasta Pl Bend OR 97701-9186

WOO, PETER WING KEE, organic chemist; b. Canton, China, June 22, 1934; came to U.S., 1950; s. Yu Chang and Lim Tsing (Poon) W.; m. Katherine Liang, Aug. 27, 1966; children: Karen H.W., Lena H.A., Nelson H.Y. BS with great distinction, Stanford U., 1955; PhD, U. Ill., 1958. From assoc. rsch. chemist to sr. rsch. chemist Parke Davis & Co., Detroit, 1958-71; from rsch. scientist to sr. rsch. assoc. Parke Davis Pharm. Rsch. (divsn. Warner-Lambert Co.), Ann Arbor, Mich., 1971—. Co-inventor antileukemia drug; patentee in field; reviewer in field; contbr. articles to profl. jours. Mem. AAAS, Am. Chem. Soc. (excellence in indsl. chem. rsch. award 1983, Huron Valley sect.), Internat. Isotope Soc., Sigma Xi, Phi Beta Kappa. Avocations: tennis, table tennis, swimming, soccer, piano. Office: Parke-Davis Pharm Rsch 2800 Plymouth Rd Ann Arbor MI 48105-2430

WOO, S. B. (SHIEN-BIAU WOO), former lieutenant governor, physics educator; b. Shanghai, China, Aug. 13, 1937; came to U.S., 1955; s. C.K. and Kuo-Ying (Chang) W.; m. Katy K.N. Wu, July 20, 1963; children: Chih-I, Chih-Lan. B.S. in Physics and Math. summa cum laude, Georgetown Coll., Ky., 1956; M.S. in Physics, Washington U., St. Louis, 1962, Ph.D. in Physics, 1964. Prof. physics U. Del., Newark, 1966—; lt. gov. State of Del., Dover, 1985-89; pres. Del. State Senate; chmn. Bd. Pardons; cons. E.I. DuPont Co., Wilmington, Del., 1968, Del. State Coll., Dover, 1980-81. Contbr. articles to profl. jours. Chmn. bd., chief exec. officer Chinese Am. Community Ctr., Hockessin, Del., 1982-83; sec. Asian-Am. caucus Democratic Nat. Conv., 1983—; pres., co-chmn. Gov.'s Internat. Trade Council, 1985—; chmn. Gov.'s task force on High Tech., 1985—. Recipient Highest Achievement award Asian Am. High Tech. Conv., 1985; Army Rsch. grantee, 1972-87, NSF grantee, 1978-81; Inst. fellow Kennedy Sch., Harvard U. Mem. Am. Phys. Soc., AAAS, AAUP (exec. com. nat. council 1974-77), Orgn. Chinese Ams. (bd. dirs. 1977-79, nat. pres. 1990—), Sigma Xi. Home: 5 Farm House Rd Newark DE 19711-7458

WOO, SAVIO LAU-YUEN, bioengineering educator; b. Shanghai, China, June 3, 1942; s. Kwok CHong and Fung Sing (Yu) W.; m. Patricia Tak-kit Cheong, Sept. 6, 1969; children: Kirstin Wei-Chi, Jonathan I-Huei. BSME, Chico State U., 1965; MS, U. Wash., 1966, PhD, 1971. Research assoc. U. Wash., Seattle, 1965-70; asst. research prof. U. Calif.-San Diego, La Jolla, 1970-74, assoc. research prof., 1974-75, assoc. prof., 1975-80, prof. surgery and bioengring., 1980-90; vice chmn. for rsch. and dir. MSRC, 1990—; prof. ortho surgery U. Pitts., 1990—, prof. mech. engring., 1990—, Albert B. Ferguson Jr. prof. orthopaedic surgery, 1993—, prof. civil and environ. engring., 1994—, prof. rehab. sci. and tech., 1994—; prin. investigator VA Med. Ctr., San Diego, 1972-90, Pitts., 1990—; cons. bioengr. Children's Hosp., San Diego, 1973-80; cons. med. implant cos., 1978-85; vis. prof. biomechanics Kobe (Japan) U., 1981-82; dir., CEO M&D Coutts Inst. for Joint Reconstrn. and Rsch., 1984-90; mem. sci. adv. com. Whitaker Found., 1986-95, Steadman-Hawkins Sports Medicine Found., 1990—, OsteoArthritis Scis. Inc., 1992-95. Assoc. editor Jour. Biochem. Engring., 1979-87, Jour. Biomechanics, 1978—, Jour. Orthopedic Rsch., 1983-92, Materials Sci. Reports, 1990, Proc. Inst. Mech. Engrs. (Part H), 1990-94; mem. editl. adv. bd. Jour. Orthopedic Rsch., 1993—; internat. adv. bd. Jour. ESSKA, Knee Surgery, Sports Traumatology, Arthroscopy, 1993—; editl. bd. am. Jour. Sports Medicine, 1995—; mem. internat. adv. bd. Jour. Ortho. Sci. Recipient Elizabeth Winston Lanier Kappa Delta award, 1983, 86, awards for excellence in basic sci. rsch. Orthopaedic Rsch. Soc. and Am. Acad. Orthopaedic Surgeons, 1983, 86, 90, 94, O'Donoghue award Am. Orthopaedic Soc. Sports Medicine, 1990, Wartenweiler Meml. Lectureship, 1987, Citation award Am. Coll. Sports Medicine, 1988, Rsch. Career Devel. award NIH, 1977-82, Muybridge medal Internat. Soc. Internat. Biomechanics, 1995; Japan Soc. Promotion of Sci. fellow, 1981. Fellow ASME (sec., chmn. biomechanics com., chmn. honors com. bioengring. divsn., mem. exec. com. 1983-88, sec. 1985-86, chmn. 1986-87, H.R. Lissner award 1991), Am. Inst. Med. and Biol. Engring. (founding fellow, chmn. coll. fellows 1992-94, bd. dirs. 1992-94); mem. NAE, Inst. Medicine NAS, We. Orthopaedic Assn. (hon.), Biomed. Engring. Soc. (bd. dirs. 1984-86), Am. Acad. Orthopedic Surgeons, Orthopaedic Rsch. Soc. (exec. com. 1983-88, chmn. program com. 1983-84, pres. 1985-86), Am. Soc. Biomechanics (pres. 1985-86, sec. 1977-80, exec. com. 1984-87, Giovanni Borelli award 1993), Internat. Soc. Fractures Repair (bd. dirs. 1986-94, v.p. 1987-90, pres. 1990-92), Can. Orthopedic Rsch. Soc. (hon.), European Orthopedic Rsch. Soc., U.S. Nat. Commn. Biomechanics (chmn. 1994—, exec. com. 1988—). Home: 47 Pleasant View Ln Pittsburgh PA 15238-1859 Office: U Pitts Dept Ortho Surg Liliane Kaufmann Bldg 3471 5th Ave Ste 1010 Pittsburgh PA 15213-3221*

WOOD, ALLEN JOHN, electrical engineer, consultant; b. Milw., Oct. 1, 1925; s. Alfred John and Kathleen Francis (Welch) W.; m. Barbara Ann Cook, Oct. 29, 1949; children: John Scott, Susan Beth Wood Richmond. BEE, Marquette U., 1949; MS in Elec. Engring., Ill. Inst. Tech., 1951; PhD, Rensselaer Poly. Inst., 1959. Registered profl. engr., N.Y. Engr. Allis Chalmers Mfg. Co., West Allis, Wis., 1949-50; engr. GE, Lynn, Mass., 1951-52; engr. GE, Schenectady, N.Y., 1952-59, sr. engr., 1960-69; mem. tech. staff Hughes Aircraft Co., Culver City, Calif., 1959-60; cons., prin., dir. Power Techs., Inc., Schenectady, N.Y., 1969-91, treas., chief fin. officer, 1989-91; also bd. dirs. Power Techs., Inc., 1969-91; ind. cons., 1991—; adj. prof. Rensselaer Poly. Inst., Troy, 1966—; cons. in field, 1992—. Author: Power System Reliability Calculations, 1973, Power Generation Operation and Control, 1984, 2d edit. 1996; contbr. numerous articles to profl. jours. With U.S. Army, 1942-46, ETO, PTO. Fellow IEEE (life); mem. AAAS, Am. Nuclear Soc. Republican. Mem. Reformed Ch. in Am. Avocations: amateur radio, photography.

WOOD, ALLISON LORRAINE, lawyer; b. N.Y.C., May 30, 1962; d. Walter C. and Joan T. Wood. BA, Pace U., 1984; JD, DePaul U., 1987; postgrad., Northwestern U. Bar: Ill. 1987, U.S. Dist. Ct. (no. dist.) Ill. 1989, Fed. Trial Bar 1990. Judicial extern U.S. Bankruptcy Ct., Chgo., 1987; pub. defender, Office of Pub. Defender Cook County, Ill., 1987-89; counsel The Peoples Gas Light and Coke Co., Chgo., 1989-93; assoc Albert, Bates, Whitehead & McGaugh, Chgo., 1993—; adj. prof. DePaul U. Coll. Law, 1992—. Tutor, lectr. Minority Legal Edn. Resources, Inc., Chgo.; bd. dirs., sec. Ctrs. for New Horizons; panelist Atty. Registration and Disciplinary Commn. Supreme Ct. Ill.; mem. Target Hope-Mentor; spkr. We Care Role Model. Mem. ABA, Ill. State Bar Assn., Chgo. Bar Assn., Cook County Bar Assn. (bd. dirs., treas.), DePaul U. Coll. of Law Alumni Bd. Office: Albert Bates Whitehead & McGaugh 1 S Wacker Dr Ste 1990 Chicago IL 60606-4616

WOOD, ANDRÉE ROBITAILLE, archaeologist, researcher; b. Chgo., Feb. 10, 1929; d. Andrew George and Alice Marie (Fortier) Robitaille; m. Richard Lawrence Wood, Jan. 14, 1956; children: Mary Wood Molo, Matthew William Wood, Melissa Irene Wood, Elizabeth Wood Wesel, John Andrew Wood. BA, No. Ill. Univ., DeKalb, 1977, MA, 1982. Freelance archaeologist, 1981-84; rsch. asst. Prehistoric Project Oriental Inst., Univ. Chgo., Ill., 1984—; rsch., discovery, removal and analysis of ancient blood residues on lithic material Çayönü-Ergani, Turkey. Avocations: poetry, boating, tennis.

WOOD, ARTHUR MACDOUGALL, retired retail executive; b. Chgo., Jan. 27, 1913; s. R. Arthur and Emily (Smith) W.; m. Pauline Palmer, Nov. 17, 1945; children: Pauline, Arthur MacDougall Jr. AB, Princeton U., 1934, LLD (hon.), 1976; LLB, Harvard U., 1937; LHD (hon.), DePaul U., 1977; D in Humanics (hon., Springfield Coll., 1978; HHD (hon.), Beloit Coll., 1981. Bar: Ill. 1937. Atty. Bell, Boyd & Marshall, Chgo., 1937-40; atty. Sears, Roebuck & Co., 1946-52, sec., 1952-59, v.p., 1956-68, dir., 1959-83, comptroller, 1960-62, v.p. charge Pacific Coast ter., 1962-67, v.p. midwestern ter., 1967, pres., 1968-72, chmn., chief exec. officer, 1973-77. Gen. chmn. United Crusade, Los Angeles County, 1966; co-founder Chgo. United, 1975; gov. United Way Am., 1977; trustee Art Inst. Chgo., 1949—, also chmn., 1978-80; life trustee Rush-Presbyn.-St. Luke's Med. Ctr., Chgo.; former trustee Calif. Inst. Tech., U. Chgo.; mem. Chgo. Hort. Soc., trustee, 1992-93; active Pres. Nixon's Labor-Mgmt. Com., 1975, Pres. Coun. Minority Bus. Enterprises, 1970-74. With F.A. AUS; lt. col. USAAF, 1941-45. Decorated Legion of Merit. Mem. Bus. Coun. Office: PO Box 06619 9800 Sears Tower Chicago IL 60606-0619

WOOD, BARBARA ANN, financial executive; b. Davisburg, Mich., June 15, 1945; d. John Eakers and Florence Fay (Adams) Carter; m. Bruce Michael Wood, Nov. 21, 1964; children: Christine Ann Wood-Wall, Michael Nolan. Student, Oakland C.C., Rochester, Mich., 1970. Owner, pres. Keys Tax Svc., Auburn Hills, Mich., 1980-90; divsn. mgr. Advantage Capital Corp., Houston, 1984—, CEO, mem. coun., 1993—; bd. dirs. Chief Pontiac Fed. Credit Union; mem. prodr.'s adv. coun. Advantage Capital Corp. Mem. Internat. Assn. Fin. Planning, Am. Bus. Womens Assn. Republican. Avocations: bicycling, reading, walking, traveling. Office: Comprehensive Investment Sv Ste 102 1899 Orchard Lake Rd Sylvan Lake MI 48320-1775

WOOD, BARBARA BUTLER, secondary language arts and television production educator; b. L.A., Oct. 19, 1946; d. E. Reynolds and Frances (Swain) Butler; m. John M. Wood, Aug. 12, 1978; 1 child, Mark Douglas. BS in Edn., No. Ariz. U., 1968; MS in Cinema Edn., U. So. Calif., 1974. Lic. English tchr., Calif., secondary sch. English tchr., Ariz. Tchr. Whittier (Calif.) Union High Sch. Dist., 1968-73; mem. mgmt. staff Ramada Inns, Inc., Phoenix, 1975-79; tchr. Glendale (Ariz.) Union High Sch. Dist., 1985—; mem. part-time faculty English Glendale C.C., 1990-94; designer CD-ROM curriculum, English course developer Ednl. Mgmt. Group, Scottsdale, Ariz., 1996—; mem. adv. bd. on at-risk edn. Glendale Union High Sch. Dist., 1989-90, editor Viewpoint newsletter, 1991-92; cons. Ariz. Bus. Leaders for Edn., Phoenix, 1989-92. Active Jr. League Phoenix, 1983-87, Phoenix Zoo Aux., 1980-91. NEH fellow, Newark, N.J., 1990. Mem. ASCD, Nat. Coun. Tchrs. English. Office: Moon Valley High Sch 3625 W Cactus Rd Phoenix AZ 85029-3122 also: Ednl Mgmt Group 6710 E Camelback Rd Scottsdale AZ 85251

WOOD, BARBARA LOUISE CHAMPION, state legislator, retired; b. Swampscott, Mass., Jan. 10, 1924; d. John Duncan and Eva Louise (Moore) Champion; m. Newall Arthur Wood, June 12, 1948; children: Gary Duncan, Craig Newall, Brian Scott, Dennis Michael, Joan Wood Unger. Diploma in Nursing, Mary Hitchcock Meml. Hosp. Sch. Nursing, Hanover, N.H., 1945; student, Simmons Coll., 1947-48. RN. Rep., mem. ho. edn. com. Vt. Gen. Assembly, Montpelier, 1981-94, vice chmn. edn. com., 1983-87; ret., 1994; trustee Vt. State Colls., Waterbury, 1986-90, Gifford Meml. Hosp., Randolph, Vt., 1986-95; commr., Vt. rep. Edn. Commn. of the States, Denver, 1981-86. Sch. dir. Bethel Sch. Bd., Vt., 1963-85; mem.-at-large Vt. Sch. Bds. Assn., Montpelier, 1982-85. Served to 2d lt. U.S. Army, 1945-46. Mem. Am. Legion, Vis. Nurse Alliance Vt.-N.H. (bd. dirs. 1991—). Republican. Congregationalist. Clubs: Bethel Woman's (pres. 1976-78); Vt. Fedn. Women's Clubs (dist. pres. 1978-80). Home: Woodland Rd Bethel VT 05032 Office: Vt House of Reps State House Montpelier VT 05602

WOOD, C(HARLES) NORMAN, air force officer; b. Dallas, Mar. 7, 1938; s. Charles Camp Wood and Mary Louise (Wheatley) Ferguson; m. Jerre Louise Jones, June 10, 1961 (div. Sept. 1967); 1 child, Wende Louise; m. Elizabeth Burwell Dillard, June 27, 1969; 1 child, Elizabeth Burwell. BBA, U. Tex., 1960; MPA, Auburn U., 1974. Commd. 2d lt. USAF, 1960, advanced through grades to lt. gen., 1990; electronic warfare officer Strategic Air Command, Kans. and Okinawa, 1962-69; intelligence staff officer Hdqrs. Strategic Air Command, Offutt AFB, Nebr., 1969-72; chief def. analysis br. Hdqrs. Mil. Assistance Command, Saigon, Republic of Vietnam, 1972-73; air staff officer Hdqrs. USAF, Washington, 1974-76; exec. officer Office of Air Force History, Washington, 1976-77; student Nat. War Coll., Washington, 1978-79; dep. comdr. for ops. 544th Strategic Intelligence Wing, Offutt AFB, 1979, wing comdr., 1980; asst. dep. chief of staff intelligence Strategic Air Command, Offutt AFB, 1981-82; exec. dir. Pres.'s Fgn. Intelligence Adv. Bd. The White House, Washington, 1982-83; dep. dir. Nat. Strategic Target List, Joint Strategic Planning Staff, Offutt AFB, 1984; dep. asst. chief of staff intelligence USAF, Washington, 1985; dir. intelligence J-2 Hdqrs. U.S.

European Command, Fed. Republic Germany, 1986-87; asst. chief of staff intelligence Air Force Hdqrs., Washington, 1988-90; dir. Intelligence Community Staff, Washington, 1990-92; sr. v.p., gen. mgr. BDM Fed., 1992-96; pres., CEO Armed Forces Comms. and Electronics Assn., Fairfax, Va., 1996—. Decorated D.S.M., Legion of Merit, Def. Superior Svc. medal. Mem. Nat. Mil. Intelligence Assn., Security Affairs Support Assn., Armed Forces Communications and Electronics Assn., Air Force Assn. Republican. Mem. Christian Sci. Ch. Home: 5440 Mt Corcoran Pl Burke VA 22015-2147 Office: Armed Forces Comms and Electronics Assn 4400 Fair Lakes Ct Fairfax VA 22033-3801

WOOD, CHARLES TUTTLE, history educator; b. St. Paul, Oct. 29, 1933; s. Harold Eaton and Margaret (Frisbie) W.; m. Susan Danielson, July 9, 1955; children: Lucy Eaton, Timothy Walker, Martha Augusta, Mary Frisbie. A.B., Harvard, 1955, A.M., 1957, Ph.D., 1962. Investment analyst, trader Harold E. Wood & Co., St. Paul, 1955-56; teaching fellow gen. edn. Harvard, 1959-61, instr. history, 1961-64; mem. faculty Dartmouth, 1964—, prof. history, 1971—, Daniel Webster prof. history, 1980—, Daniel Webster prof. history and comparative lit., 1991—, chmn. dept. history, 1976-79, chmn. dept. comparative lit., 1977; vis. Keeney prof. of history Brown U., 1992-93; vis. prof. U. Coll. London, 1996. Author: The French Apanages and the Capetian Monarchy, 1223-1328, 1966, Philip the Fair and Boniface VIII, 2d edit., 1971, reprint, 1976, Felipe el Hermoso y Bonifacio VIII: Mexico: UTEHA, 1968, The age of Chivalry: Manners and Morals 1000-1450, 1970, The Quest for Eternity, reprint edit., 1983, Joan of Arc and Richard III, 1988, The Trial of Charles I, 1989, Fresh Verdicts on Joan of Arc, 1996; also articles. Chmn. Dresden Bd. Sch. Dirs., 1972-74. Guggenheim fellow, 1986-87; recipient Disting. Service award N.H. Sch. Bds. Assn., 1975; Am. Council Learned Socs. fellow, 1980-81; Am. Bar Found. fellow, 1981-82. Fellow Medieval Acad. Am. (treas. 1989—, fin. com. 1979—, council 1985-87); mem. Am. Hist. Assn. (chmn. nominating com. 1977, Adams prize com. 1976-78), Conf. Brit. Studies, Soc. for French Hist. Studies, N.H. Sch. Bds. Assn. (2d v.p. 1974-75), New Eng. Medieval Conf. (pres. 1978-79), Am. Soc. Legal History, Phi Beta Kappa. Club: St. Botolph (Boston). Home: 7 N Balch St Hanover NH 03755-1502

WOOD, CHRISTOPHER L. J., real estate consulting firm executive; b. London, Jan. 20, 1947; came to U.S., 1983; s. Sidney John and Lillian Ballantine (Pollock) W.; m. Pamela Wood, Dec. 14, 1978; 1 child, Alexander Wood. BSC, London U., 1969. Ptnr., dir. Debenham, Tewson & Chinnocks, London, U.S., 1972-96; COO America's Best, 1996—. Fellow Royal Instn. Chartered Surveyors; mem. Am. Soc. Real Estate Counselors, St. George's Soc. N.Y., Thames Rowing Club, Union League Club (Phila.). Office: America's Best 350 Hollow Tree Ridge Rd Darien CT 06820-3218

WOOD, CRAIG BRECKENRIDGE, paleobiologist, natural science educator; b. Washington, Jan. 27, 1943; s. William Ernest Wood and Christina Mae (DeBrito) Phillips; m. Sung He Lee, May 21, 1982; children: William, Violet, Virginia. AB in Geology, U. N.C., 1966; MS in Geology, U. Wyo., 1967; MA in Geology, Harvard U., 1980, PhD in Geology, 1992. Tchg. fellow geology, anthropology, biology depts. Harvard U., Cambridge, Mass., 1968-70, 73-74; rsch. assoc. geology dept. Princeton (N.J.) U., 1970-71; geologist Herbert & Assocs. Ltd., Virginia Beach, Va., 1972-73; lectr. biology and geology Asian divsn. U. Md., Yokota AFB, Japan, 1981-82; instr. natural sci. Providence Coll., 1974-79, asst. prof. natural sci., spl. lectr. geology, 1979-92, assoc. prof. natural sci., 1992—, dir. natural sci. program, 1993-95; Harvard U. exch. scholar dept. paleontology U. Calif., Berkeley, 1988-89; rsch. assoc. in mammalogy Mus. Comparative Zoology, Harvard U., 1994—; expdn. mem. Rift Valley Rsch. Mission in Ethiopia, Addis Ababa, 1976, Blue Nile region, Ethiopia, 1993, 96, 97. Co-discoverer of "Bodo Man", 1976, first Ethiopian highland mezozoic vertebrates, 1993, first Ethiopian dinosaurs, 1996. Mem. AAAS, Soc. Vertebrate Paleontology, Soc. for Study of Mammalian Evolution, Harvard Club R.I., R.I. Carolina Club (treas.), Humanities Forum of R.I., Sigma Xi, Phi Mu Alpha Sinfonia. Office: Providence Coll Biology Dept Providence RI 02918

WOOD, DANIEL BRIAN, educational consultant; b. Roseburg, Oreg., Mar. 5, 1960; s. Jack Livingston and E. June (Gamble) W. BS, U. Oreg., 1982, MS, 1985, PhD, 1989. Cert. folklore and ethnic studies. Fare policy analyst Lane Transit Dist., Eugene, Oreg., 1984-85; asst. to dean for internships Univ. Oreg., Eugene, 1987-88; rsch. analyst Oreg. System Higher Edn., Eugene, 1988; pvt. practice, ednl. rsch. Eugene, 1988—; co-designer, coauthor statewide exam. and analysis of transfer student performance in Oreg. higher edn.; manuscript reviewer for refereed jours.; vis. asst. prof., rsch. assoc. U. Miss., 1992-93; active Statewide Task Force on Transfer Followup, 1987-88. Reviewer Internat. Jour. Intercultural Rels., 1995—; contbr. articles to profl. jours. Mem. Am. Soc. Pub. Adminstrn., Oreg. Sect. Pub. Adminstrn. Edn., Pi Lambda Theta (pres.), Phi Delta Kappa. Home and Office: 122 E Howard Ave Eugene OR 97404-2617

WOOD, DAVID BRUCE, naturopathic physician; b. Fayetteville, N.C., Jan. 21, 1954; s. Marvin James and Rachel Elenor (Thom) W.; m. Wendy Ann McKiernan, Aug. 1974 (div. Aug. 1976); m. Cheryl Lynn Garbarino, Aug. 17, 1980. BS in Microbiology, U. Wash., 1977; D in Naturopathic Medicine, Bastyr U., Seattle, 1983. Pres., co-founder Trinity Family Health Clinic, Inc., P.S., Edmonds, Wash., 1984—; Spkr. local and nat. TV programs. Singer Sound of Praise Choir, Overlake Christian Ch., Kirkland, Wash., 1987-92; narrator Easter Pagent, 1989; mem. Cedar Park Assembly of God, Bothel, Wash. Mem. Am. Assn. Nutritional Cons., Nat. Health Fedn., Am. Assn. Naturopathic Physicians, Wash. Assn. Naturopathic Physicians (trustee, exec. bd. 1989-92). Avocations: singing, snow skiing, snorkeling, bicycling, travel. Home: 13721 Cascadian Way Everett WA 98208-7345 Office: Trinity Family Health Clinic Inc PS 7614 195th St SW Edmonds WA 98026-6260

WOOD, DAVID KENNEDY CORNELL, choreographer, educator; b. Fresno, Calif., Feb. 24, 1925; s. Earl Warner and Elsie Bliss (Kennedy) W.; m. Marni Pope Thomas, Dec. 28, 1958; children—Marina, Raegan, Ellis. B.A., U. Calif., 1945; student, Neighborhood Playhouse, N.Y.C., 1947-48, also other theatre and dance schs. Choreographer Broadway musicals, TV, N.Y.C. Opera Ballet, Met. Opera Ballet, 1950-58; soloist, Hanya Holm Co., 1948-50, soloist, rehearsal dir., Martha Graham Co., 1953-68, prof. dance, U. Calif., 1968—, artistic dir., Bay Area Repertory Dance Co., guest soloist, Belles Artes of Mexico, 1958-59, Sweden Ballet Akademien, 1960-61 (choreographic award Nat. Endowment for Arts 1973-74, 77-78); choreographer: Pre-Amble, 1971, Post Script, 1974, Cassandra, 1974, Changelings, 1970, The Immigrant, 1974, In the Glade, 1977, Jeux, 1978, Prometheus, 1980; Dusty Pools and Puddles, 1983, Rim of Heaven, 1984, Duad, 1985, Nova's prodn. Electrical Super Conductivity, 1986, Quiet Interludes, 1987, Graffitti, 1987, Persephone, 1988, American Decades, 1989, Dojoji, 1993. Served with USNR, 1943-46. Mem. Am. Guild Musican Artists, Actors Equity, AFTRA, Calif. Dance Educators Assn., Am. Assn. Dance Cos. Home: 3090 Buena Vista Way Berkeley CA 94708-2020 *The enjoyment of the act of doing, the willingness to accept the discipline of the moment and an awareness of one's individual growth all contribute to a total sense of achievement as well as a pleasure in it.*

WOOD, DAVID L., entomologist, educator; b. Jan. 8, 1931. BS, SUNY, Syracuse, 1952; PhD, U. Calif., Berkeley, 1960. Lic. forester, Calif. Prof. entomology, emeritis dept. Environ. Sci. Policy, Mgmt. U. Calif., Berkeley, 1960—; lectr., reviewer, cons. in field. Contbr. articles to profl. jours. Recipient Silver medal Swedish Coun. for Forestry and Agril. Rsch., 1983. Fellow Entomological Soc. Can. (Founder's award Lectr. Entomological Soc. Am. 1986, Founder's award Western Forest Insect Work Conf. 1992); mem. AAAS, AIBS, Entomol. Soc. Am., Entomol. Soc. Can., Internat. Soc. Chem. Ecology, Soc. Am. Foresters, Sigma Xi. Home: 26 Hardie Dr Moraga CA 94556-1134 Office: U Calif Divsn Insect Biology Berkeley CA 94720

WOOD, DIANE PAMELA, judge; b. Plainfield, N.J., July 4, 1950; d. Kenneth Reed and Lucille (Padmore) Wood; m. Dennis James Hutchinson, Sept. 2, 1978; children: Kathryn, David, Jane. BA, U. Tex.-Austin, 1971, JD, 1975. Bar: Tex. 1975, D.C. 1978. Law clk. U.S. Ct. Appeals (5th cir.), 1975-76, U.S. Supreme Ct., 1976-77; atty.-advisor U.S. Dept. State, Washington, 1977-78; assoc. law firm Covington & Burling, Washington, 1978-80; asst. prof. law Georgetown U. Law Ctr., Washington, 1980-81, U. Chgo., 1981-88, prof. law, 1988-95, assoc. dean, 1989-92, Harold J. and Marion F. Green prof. internat. legal studies, 1990-95, sr. lectr. in law, 1995—; spl. cons. antitrust divsn. internat. guide U.S. Dept. Justice, 1986-87, dep. asst. atty. gen. antitrust divsn., 1993-95; cir. judge U.S. Ct. Appeals (7th cir.), 1995—. Contbr. articles to profl. jours. Bd. dirs. Hyde-Park-Kenwood Cmty. Health Ctr., 1983-85. Mem. ABA (sec. antitrust and internat. law, chmn. internat. law sect. BIT com., co-chmn. internat. antitrust com., ILP coun. 1989-91, internat. legal scholar officer 1991-93, chmn., antitrust sec. subcom. on internat. unfair trade, vice-chair, sec. internat. antitrust com. 1991, standing com. on law and nat. security 1991-93), Am. Soc. Internat. Law, Am. Law Inst., Internat. Acad. Comparative Law. Democrat.

WOOD, DIRK GREGORY, surgeon, physician, forensic consultant; b. Springfield, Ohio, Sept. 19, 1953; s. Carlos Paul and Evelyn Cecelia (Bird) W.; m. Lashanda R. Daniels, Dec. 10, 1996. BA magna cum laude, Urbana (Ohio) U., 1973; postgrad., Ohio State U., 1973-75; MD, UAG Facultad de Medicina, Guadalajara, Mexico, 1980; JD, Capital Law Sch., Columbus, Ohio, 1991. Diplomate Am. Bd. Ob-Gyn, Am. Bd. Forensic Medicine. Intern Bronx (N.Y.) Lebanon Hosp., 1981-82; resident William Beaumont Hosp., Royal Oak, Mich., 1982-86; physician, surgeon Her Care, Inc., Springfield, 1986—; CEO Just What the Doctor Ordered, Springfield, 1992—. Coroner Clark County, Ohio, 1991-97. Fellow ACS, Am. Coll. Ob-gyn., Internat. Coll. Surgeons, Am. Coll. Legal Medicine, Royal Soc. Medicine (London), Phi Delta Epsilon (past chpt. pres.), Phi Alpha Delta. Republican. Avocations: scuba diving, bibliophilia, travel. Home: 202 Tuttle Rd Springfield OH 45503-5236 Office: Her Care Inc 2029 E High St Springfield OH 45505-1315

WOOD, DONALD CRAIG, retired marketing professional; b. Wilmington, Del., June 24, 1937; s. Thomas Henry and Madelyn (Brehm) W.; m. Elizabeth Haring, Apr. 28, 1962; children: Craig Standish, Allison Jean. BA, U. Del., 1959; MBA, Northwestern U., 1967. Sales engr. NVF Corp., Broadview, Ill., 1960-62, Synthane Corp., Morton Grove, Ill., 1962-68; account exec., mgr. sales Donnelley Mktg. subs. Dun and Bradstreet Corp., Oakbrook, Ill., 1968-69; from dir. to v.p. market devel. to v.p. mktg. Donnelley Mktg. subs. Dun and Bradstreet Corp., Stamford, Conn., 1977-1980; from v.p., gen. mgr. to pres. Info. Services Div. Donnelley Mktg. subs. Dun and Bradstreet Corp., Stamford, 1980-86, sr. v.p., 1987-90; v.p., gen. mgr. info. svcs. Triad Systems Corp., Livermore, Calif., 1990-96. Served to 1st lt. U.S. Army, 1959-60. Home: 45 Wood Duck Rd Hilton Head Island SC 29928

WOOD, DONALD EURIAH, lawyer; b. Guymon, Okla., May 27, 1935; s. Theodore and Lula Elizabeth (Rider) W.; m. Lynda Sharon Harris, Sept. 30, 1960; children—Donald Craig, Tana Dawn, Kristen Lynn. B.A., Panhandle A. and M. Coll., 1958; LL.B., Okla. U., 1964, J.D., 1970. Bar: Okla. bar 1964. Asst. county atty. Texas County, 1964; county atty., 1965-67; dist. atty. Okla. 1st Jud. Dist., Guymon, 1967—; Mem. adv. com. Okla. Commn. Criminal and Traffic Enforcement Systems, 1972; mem. Gov.'s Commn. Community Affairs and Planning, 1972-75; mem. faculty Panhandle State Coll., 1974-92; mem. Okla. Dist. Atty. Tng. Council, 1976—; mem. Okla. Bur. Narcotics and Dangerous Drugs Commn., 1992—. Served with inf. AUS, 1958-60. Named Okla. Prosecutor of Yr., Assn. Okla. Narcotic Enforcers, 1994-95. Mem. Okla. Bar Assn. (legal ethics com. 1971—), Texas County Bar Assn. (pres. 1966, 1970-71), Nat. Dist. Attys. Assn., Okla. Dist. Attys. Assn. (pres. 1972, exec. com. 1971—), Phi Alpha Delta. Presbyn. Clubs: Elk, Rotarian. Home: 605 Hillcrest Dr Guymon OK 73942-3345 Office: 319 N Main St Guymon OK 73942-4843

WOOD, DONALD FRANK, transportation educator, consultant; b. Waukesha, Wis., Feb. 22, 1935; s. Frank Blaine and Uilah (Mathson) W.; m. Doreen Johnson, July 5, 1968; children: Frank, Tamara. BA, U. Wis., 1957, MA, 1958; PhD, Harvard U., 1970. Transp. planner State of Wis., Madison, 1960-70; prof. San Francisco State U., 1970—. Author: El Camino, 1982, (with others) Motorized Fire Apparatus of the West, 1991, Contemporary Transportation, 1996, Contemporary Logistics, 1996, American Volunteer Fire Trucks, 1993, Commercial Trucks, 1993, International Logistics, 1994, Wreckers & Tow Trucks, 1995, Logging Trucks, 1996, Big City Fire Trucks, 1997; contbr. Ency. Britannica. 2d lt. U.S. Army, 1958. Mem. Coun. of Logistics Mgmt. (chpt. pres. 1975-76), Transp. Rsch. Forum (chpt. pres. 1974), Am. Truck Hist. Soc. Presbyterian. Home: 321 Riviera Cir Larkspur CA 94939-1508 Office: San Francisco State U Coll Bus San Francisco CA 94132

WOOD, EARL HOWARD, physiologist, educator; b. Mankato, Minn., Jan. 1, 1912; s. William Clark and Inez (Goff) W.; m. Ada C. Peterson, Dec. 20, 1936; children: Phoebe, Mark Goff, Guy Harland, Earl Andrew. B.A., Macalester Coll., 1934, D.Sc., 1950; B.S., U. Minn., 1939, M.S., M.B., Ph.D., 1941, M.D., 1942. Teaching fellow physiology U. Minn., 1936-39, instr., 1940; NRC fellow med. scis., dept. pharmacology U. Pa., 1941; instr. pharmacology Harvard Med. Sch., 1942; research asst. acceleration lab. Mayo Aero Med. Unit, 1943; asst. prof. physiology Mayo Found., U. Minn. Grad. Sch., 1944, prof. physiology and medicine, 1950—; staff mem. sect. physiology Mayo Clinic, 1947—; chmn. biophys. scis. unit Mayo Med. Sch.; career investigator Am. Heart Assn., 1961—; Sci. cons. air surgeon USAF Aero Med. Ctr., Heidelberg, Germany, 1946; vis. prof. U. Bern, 1965-66; vis. scientist dept. physiology Univ. Coll., London, 1972-73; rsch. cons. Canadian Air Force, DCIEM, Toronto, 1993-94. Contbr. articles to profl. jours., chpts. to books. Recipient Presdl. certificate of merit, Disting. Lectr. award Am. Coll. Chest Physicians, 1974, Sr. U.S. Scientist Humboldt award Kiel, Fed. Republic Germany, 1985, Phillips Meml. award ACP, 1983, Lucian award for research in cardiovascular diseases McGill U., 1985, Stewart Meml. lectr. Royal Aero. Soc., 1987, Outstanding Achievement award U. Minn., 1991. Fellow Aerospace Med. Assn. (Disting. Research award 1983); mem. Am. Physiol. Soc. (past chmn. circulation group, pres. 1980-81, Daggs award 1995), Am. Soc. Pharmacology and Exptl. Therapeutics, Am., Central socs. clin. investigation, Soc. Exptl. Biology and Medicine, Am. Heart Assn. (Research Achievement award 1973, past chmn. basic sci. sect.), AAAS, Nat. Acad. Medicine Mex., Nat. Acad. Arts and Scis. (Netherlands), Federated Am. Socs. Exptl. Biology (pres. 1981—), German Soc. for Heart and Circulation Rsch., Carl-Ludwig Ehrenmünze, Phi Beta Kappa, Sigma Xi, Alpha Omega Alpha (Outstanding Achievement award 1991). Research, numerous publs. on devel. instrumental techniques and procedures for study heart and circulation in health and disease; applications of these procedures to detection and quantitation of various types of acquired and congenital heart disease, study of effects and compensatory reaction of heart and circulation to various types of circulatory stress. Home: 211 2nd St NW Apt 1918 Rochester MN 55901-3101

WOOD, ELWOOD STEVEN, III, chemical company executive; b. Norfolk, Va., Mar. 8, 1934; s. Elwood Steven Jr. and Margaret (Schlegel) W.; m. Jean Elizabeth Abbott, Dec. 21, 1961; children: Michael Scott, Tracy Lee. S.B., MIT, 1956, S.M., 1957; M.B.A., U. Pa., 1962. With W.R. Grace & Co., 1961-95; asst. plant mgr. Organic Chems. div. W.R. Grace & Co., Owensboro, Ky., 1964-66; plant mgr. Polyfibron div. W.R. Grace & Co., Adams, Mass., 1966-67; v.p. W.R. Grace & Co., Lexington, Mass., 1967-77; exec. v.p. Constrn. Products div. W.R. Grace & Co., Cambridge, Mass., 1977-82; pres. Polyfibron div., v.p. parent co. W.R. Grace & Co., Lexington, Mass., 1982-95, worldwide GM printing products, 1993-95; ret., 1995. Served to 1st lt. U.S. Army, 1958.

WOOD, EMILY CHURCHILL, gifted and talented education educator; b. Summit, N.J., Apr. 11, 1925; d. Arthur Burdett and Ruth Vail (Pierson) Churchill; m. Philip Warren Wood, June 22, 1946; children: Martha, Arthur, Warren, Benjamin. BA, Smith Coll., 1946; MA in Teaching, Manhattanville Coll., 1971; postgrad., U. Tulsa, 1974-79, Langston U., 1990-92. Cert. tchr. social studies, learning disabilities, elem. edn., econs., Am. history, world history. Tchr. Miss Fines Sch., Princeton, N.J., 1946-47, Hallen Ctr. for Edn., Portchester, N.Y., 1973-74, Town and Country Sch., Tulsa, Okla., 1974-79, Tulsa Pub. Schs., 1979—, Tulsa Jr. Coll., 1990-92, 94; adv. bd. Great Expectations Educators, Tulsa, 1985—; leader colloquia bill of rights Arts and Humanities Coun., Tulsa, 1989; mem. literacy task force Tulsa 2000 Edn. Com., 1990-92; chmn. internat. student exch. Eisenhower Internat. Sch., Tulsa, 1992—. Author: (with others) Visual Arts in China, 1988, Applauding Our Constitution, 1989, The Bill of Rights: Who Guarantees What, 1993; contbr. articles to profl. jours. Dir. Smith Coll. Alumnae, Northampton, Mass., 1956-59; leader, founder Am. Field Svc., Tulsa, 1982-84; pres., v.p. Booker T. Washington H.S. PTA, Tulsa, 1985; campaign mgr. auditors race Dem. Party, Tulsa, 1988, 92, 94; bd. dirs., nominations chair Sister Cities Internat., Tulsa, 1992—. Named Tulsa Tchr. of Yr. Tulsa Classroom Tchrs. Assn., 1988, Nat. Elem. Tchr. of Yr., Nat. Bar Aux., 1992; recipient Elem. Medal of Excellence, Okla. Found. for Excellence, 1990, Valley Forge Tchrs. medal Freedoms Found., 1992, Paragon award Tulsa Commn. on Status of Women, 1996. Mem. Nat. Coun. Social Studies (religion program com. 1984—), DAR, Okla. Edn. Assn., Okla. Coun. Social Studies (pres. 1995, tchr. of yr. 1984), Okla. Bar Assn. (law related com. 1988—, tchr. of yr. 1990), Okla. Coun. Econ. Edn. (state and nat. awards 1981, 89, 92), Kent Place Alumnae Assn. (disting. alumna award 1992). Avocations: reading, swimming, traveling, bicycling. Home: 3622 S Yorktown Pl Tulsa OK 74105-3452

WOOD, EMMA S., nurse practitioner; b. Lancaster County, Pa., June 20, 1945; d. Moses H. and Elizabeth M. (Shirk) Zimmerman; m. George Wood, Feb. 4, 1977 (dec. July 1989); 1 child, George William Jr. ADN, Edison C.C., 1979; BSN, U. South Fla., 1987, MSN, 1989. RN, Fla.; cert. psychiat. and mental health nurse, cert. profl. in health care quality, clin. specialist in psychiat. mental health. Agy. adminstr., home health nurse VNA of Desoto County, Arcadia, Fla., 1979-81; utilization rev. coord. G. Pierce Wood Meml. Hosp., 1981-85, RN specialist, 1985-89, sr. nurse supr., mgr., 1989-95, nurse educator, 1995-97; advanced RN practitioner ARNP, 1997—. Mem. ANA, Fla. Nurses Assn., Nat. Assn. for Health Care Quality, Fla. Assn. for Health Care Quality, Am. Psychiat. Nurses Assn., NLN, Sigma Theta Tau. Home: 2808 Caribbean Dr Punta Gorda FL 33982-4302

WOOD, ERIC FRANKLIN, earth and environmental sciences educator; b. Vancouver, B.C., Can., Oct. 22, 1947; s. Lorne George and Olga Eugena (Hryvnak) W.; m. Katharine Holding Schwed; children: Eric Alexander, Emily Holding. BASc with hons., U. B.C., 1970; SM, MIT, 1972, MSCE, 1973, ScD, 1974. Rsch. asst. MIT, Cambridge, 1970-73; rsch. scholar Internat. Inst. for Applied Systems Analysis, Vienna, Austria, 1974-76; prof. civil engring. Princeton (N.J.) U., 1976—; EOS sci. steering com. NASA, 1984-87, sci. adv. working group, 1992, land surface processes adv. com., 1985-90, Landsat sci. working group, 1992-93; mem. Continental Internat. Project sci. steering com. World Climate Rsch. Program, 1993-95; mem. policy adv. panel Continental Water-Energy Climate Project, NOAA, Office of Global Programs, 1996-97. Co-author: An Introduction to Groundwater Contamination from Hazardous Wastes, 1984; assoc. editor: Water Resources Research, 1977-82, Applied Math. and Computation, 1983—, Jour. of Forecasting, 1984—, Rev. in Geophysics, 1988-93; editor (books) Recent Developments in Real-Time Forecasting/Control of Water Resources Systems, 1980, Scale Effects in Hyrology, 1986, Land Surface-Atmospheric Interactions for Climate Models: Observations, Modeling and Analysis, 1990; contbr. numerous articles to profl. jours. Recipient Rheinstein award Princton U., 1980. Fellow Am. Geophys. Union (mem. editl. bd. Water Resources Monographs, 1980-85, exec. mem. hydrology sect. 1984-85, 88-92, 94-95, union fellows com. 1994-98, union meeting com. 1988-90, chmn. remot sensing com., 1988-92, Horton rsch. com. 1992-95, Robert E. Horton award 1988), Am. Meteorol. Soc. (hydrology com. 1987-90, chair 1997—); mem. Inst. for Ops. Rsch. and the Mgmt. Scis., NAS (com. on flood levee policy), NSF (mem. com. of flood hazard mitigation 1979-80, panel on engring. and global climate change 1991), Brit. Hydrol. Soc. Avocations: squash, sailing, skiing. Office: Princeton U Dept of Civil Engring Princeton NJ 08544

WOOD, FERGUS JAMES, geophysicist, consultant; b. London, Ont., Can., May 13, 1917; came to U.S., 1924, naturalized, 1932; s. Louis Aubrey and Dora Isabel (Elson) W.; student U. Oreg., 1934-36; AB, U. Calif., Berkeley, 1938, postgrad., 1938-39; postgrad. U. Chgo., 1939-40, U. Mich., 1940-42, Calif. Inst. Tech., 1946; m. Doris M. Hack, Sept. 14, 1946; children: Kathryn Celeste Wood Madden, Bonnie Patricia Wood Ward. Teaching asst. U. Mich., 1940-42; instr. in physics and astronomy Pasadena City Coll., 1946-48, John Muir Coll., 1948-49; asst. prof. physics U. Md., 1949-50; assoc. physicist Johns Hopkins U. Applied Physics Lab., 1950-55; sci. editor Ency. Americana, N.Y.C., 1955-60; aero. and space rsch. scientist, sci. asst. to dir. Office Space Flight Programs, Hdqrs., NASA, Washington, 1960-61; program dir. fgn. sci. info. NSF, Washington, 1961-62; phys. scientist, chief sci. and tech. info. staff U.S. Coast and Geodetic Survey, Rockville, Md., 1962-66, phys. scientist Office of Dir., 1967-73, rsch. assoc. Office of Dir., 1973-77, Nat. Ocean Svc.; cons. tidal dynamics, Bonita, Calif., 1978—; mem. Am. Geophys. Union, ICSU-UNESCO Internat. Geol. Correlation Project 274, Working Group #1-Crescendo Events in Coastal Environments, Past and Future (The Millennium Project), 1988—. Capt. USAAF, 1942-46. Recipient Spl. Achievement award Dept. Commerce, NOAA, 1970, 74, 76, 77. Mem. Sigma Pi Sigma, Pi Mu Epsilon, Delta Phi Alpha. Democrat. Presbyterian. Author: The Strategic Role of Perigean Spring Tides in Nautical History and North American Coastal Flooding, 1635-1976, 1978; Tidal Dynamics: Coastal Flooding, and Cycles of Gravitational Force, 1986, Synergetic Gravitational Forces in Tides and the Solar System, 2 vols., 1997; contbr. numerous articles to encys., reference sources, profl. jours.; writer, tech. dir. documentary film: Pathfinders from the Stars, 1967; editor-in-chief: The Prince William Sound, Alaska, Earthquake of 1964 and Aftershocks, vols. 1-2A and sci. coordinator vols. 2B, 2C and 3, 1966-69. Home: 3103 Casa Bonita Dr Bonita CA 91902-1735

WOOD, FRANK PREUIT, educator, former air force officer; b. Greenville, Tex., Feb. 28, 1916; s. William L. and Ethel (Preuit) W.; m. Harriet Louise Brawner, Oct. 25, 1941; 1 son, Frank M. B.S. in Elec. Engring, U. Tex., 1939; grad., USAF pilot tng. schs., 1941. Commd. 2d lt. USAAF, 1941; advanced through grades to brig. gen. USAF, 1964; dep. chief staff personnel Air Tng. Command, Randolph AFB, Tex., 1962-66; comdr. Air Force Mil. Tng. Ctr. Lackland AFB, San Antonio, 1966-67; chief Mil. Assistance Adv. Group, Italy, 1967-69; dep. chief staff for personnel Tactical Air Command, Langley AFB, Va., 1969-70; ret., 1970; apptd. asso. dir. Bur. Engring. Research, U. Tex. Coll. Engring., Austin, 1970; dir. Bur. Engring. Research, U. Tex. Coll. Engring., 1971-78. Chmn. bd. equalization City of Austin, 1979—; elder Ctrl. Christian Ch., Austin, 1975-81, chmn. ofcl. bd., 1977; elder Ctrl. Christian Ch., San Antonio, 1985-89, 91-94, 95-98. Decorated Legion of Merit with 4 oak leaf clusters; named Disting. Grad., U. Tex. Coll. Engring., 1968. Club: Headliners (Austin). Home: 7400 Crestway Dr Apt 1003 San Antonio TX 78239-3094

WOOD, GEORGE H., investment executive; b. Kansas City, Mo., Sept. 7, 1946; s. George H. and Helen Lee (Hansen) W. BSBA, U. Mo., 1968, MBA, 1972. Securities analyst Kansas City Life Ins. Co., 1972-75, asst. dir. securities, 1975-76; sr. trust officer Commerce Bank of Kansas City, N.A., 1976-79, v.p., fixed income and portfolio group mgr., 1979-80, v.p., mgr. investment dept., 1980-82, sr. v.p., 1982-88, chief investment officer, 1988-90; mng. dir. Merus Capital Mgmt., 1990-94; v.p. Pacific Investment Mgmt. Co., 1994-97; sr. v.p. 1997—. Past bd. dirs., pres. Young Audiences, Inc. With AUS, 1969-71. Chartered fin. analyst . Mem. Inst. Chartered Fin. Analysts (past chmn. curriculum com.), Assn. Investment Mgmt. and Rsch., Fin. Analysts Fedn., San Francisco Soc. Fin. Analysts (bd. dirs.), U. Mo. Alumni Assn., Phi Delta Theta. Home: 2616 Temple Hills Dr Laguna Beach CA 92651-2036 Office: Pacific Investment Mgmt Co 840 Newport Center Dr Newport Beach CA 92660-6310

WOOD, GERALD DAVID, religious organization administrator; b. Narrows, Va., Oct. 16, 1947; s. Curtis Edmond and Myrtle Isabella (Jernigan) W.; m. Sandra Fay Harris, Aug. 24, 1968; children: Angela Dawn, Anthony David, Jonathan David, Beth Lynette. Student, Kjesaters, Vingaker, Sweden, 1966-67, Washington and Lee U., 1967-68, U. Va., 1968-69, Emmanuel Coll., 1973-81, Oxford U., 1994—; BREd, Maranatha Inst Christian Mins., 1994. Ordained to ministry Internat. Pentecostal Holiness Ch., 1968. Pastor Charlottesville (Va.) Pentecostal Holiness Ch., 1968-72, St. Paul Pentecostal Holiness Ch., Max Meadows, Va., 1972-82; sec.-treas. Va. Conf. Sunday Sch. Bd., Dublin, 1974-80; treas. Va. Conf. Christian Edn. Bd., 1980-86; pastor New Covenant Pentecostal Holiness Ch., Princeton, W.Va., 1982-86; dir. Christian edn. Appalachian Conf. Pentecostal Holiness Ch., Dublin, 1986-94; mem. Appalachian Conf. Bd., 1994; sr. pastor 1st Pentecostal Holiness Ch., Greenville, N.C., 1994—; mem. gen. Christian edn. bd. Internat. Pentecostal Holiness Ch., 1987-91, 93, mem. gen. bd. publs., 1993—; dir. radio ministry Wythe County Ministerial Assn., Wytheville, Va., 1978-80; pres. W.Va. Camp Meeting Assn., Princeton, 1982-84; bd. dirs. Church

Ministries United, Greenville, N.C., 1994—. Bd. dirs. Mountaineer Food Bank, Gassaway, W.Va., 1986; bd. dirs. Marantha Inst., Dublin, 1986-94, treas., 1989-92, registrar, 1992-94; pres. Dublin Elem. Sch. PTA, 1988-90, Pulaski County Advs. for Talented and Gifted, 1989-92, sec. New River Dist. PTA, 1990-92; chmn. bd. dirs., Ch. Ministries United, Greenville, N.C., 1996—. Mem. Coun. for Exceptional Children, Internat. Platform Assn., Am. Inst. Profl. Bookkeepers, Pentecostal Fellowship N.Am. (v.p. Princeton chpt. 1982-83). Republican. Avocation: amateur radio. Office: 1st Pentecostal Holiness Ch Brinkley Rd and Plaza Dr Greenville NC 27858 *My father taught me: "Always be honest with God, with others and with yourself. Love others the way God loves you. Serve God with everything you are." I have chosen to live in this way.*

WOOD, GLADYS BLANCHE, retired secondary education educator, journalist; b. Sanborn, N.D., Aug. 12, 1921; d. Charles Kershaw and Mina Blanche (Kee) Crowther; m. Newell Edwin Wood, June 13, 1943 (dec. 1990); children: Terry N., Lani, Brian R., Kevin C.; m. F.L. Stutzman, Nov. 30, 1991. BA in Journalism, U. Minn., 1943; MA in Mass Comm., San Jose State U., 1972. Cert. secondary tchr., Calif. Reporter St. Paul Pioneer-Dispatch, 1943-45; editor J.C. Penney Co., N.Y.C., 1945-46; tchr. English and journalism Willow Glen H.S., San Jose, Calif., 1968-87; freelance writer, photographer, 1947—; cons. in field. Named Secondary Journalism Tchr. of Yr. Calif. Newspaper Pubs. Assn., 1977. Mem. AAUW, Soc. Profl. Journalists, Journalism Edn. Assn., Calif. Tchrs. English, Calif. Ret. Tchrs. Assn., Women in Comm., Santa Clara County Med. Assn. Aux., Friends of Libr., Delta Kappa Gamma, Alpha Omicron Pi. Republican. Methodist. Avocations: music, journalism, photography, travel. Home: 14161 Douglass Ln Saratoga CA 95070-5535

WOOD, GORDON STEWART, historian, educator; b. Concord, Mass., Nov. 27, 1933; s. Herbert G. and Marion (Friberg) W.; m. Louise Goss, Apr. 30, 1956; children: Christopher, Elizabeth, Amy. AB, Tufts U., 1955; AM, Harvard, 1959; PhD, Harvard U., 1964. Fellow Inst. Early Am. History and Culture, Williamsburg, Va., 1964-66; asst. prof. Harvard U., Cambridge, Mass., 1966-67; assoc. prof. U. Mich., Ann Arbor, 1967-69; prof. history, Univ. prof. Brown U., Providence, 1969—; Pitt. prof. Cambridge U., 1982-83; bd. trustees Tufts U.; Bancroft lectr. U.S. Naval Acad., 1986; Anson G. Phelps lectr. NYU, 1986; Charles Edmundson lectr. Baylor U., 1987; Samuel Paley lectr. Hebrew U., Jerusalem, 1987; presdl. lecture series on presidency, 1991. Author: The Creation of the American Republic, 1776-1787, 1969, The Rising Glory of America, 1760-1820, 1971; co-author: The Great Republic, 1977, The Radicalism of the American Revolution, 1992 (Pulitzer Prize for history 1993). Mem. coun. Inst. Early Am. History and Culture, 1980-83; bd. trustees Colonial Williamsburg. With USAF, 1955-58. Recipient Bancroft prize Columbia U., 1970, Disting. Visitor award Australian-Am. Ednl. Found., 1976, Douglass Adair prize, 1984; Emerson prize Phi Beta Kappa, 1992; Sunderland fellow U. Mich. Law Sch., 1990; All Souls Coll. fellow, 1991; Woodrow Wilson Ctr. guest-scholar, 1993-94. Mem. Am. Hist. Assn. (John Dunning prize), Orgn. Am. Historians, Soc. Am. Historians, Nat. Hist. Soc. (chmn. bd. advisors), Soc. Historians of the Early Am. Republic (pres.), Am. Acad. Arts and Scis., Am. Philos. Soc. Home: 77 Keene St Providence RI 02906-1507 Office: Brown University Dept of History Box N Providence RI 02912-9040

WOOD, HARLINGTON, JR., federal judge; b. Springfield, Ill., Apr. 17, 1920; s. Harlington and Marie (Green) W. A.B., U. Ill., 1942, J.D., 1948. Bar: Ill. 1948. Practiced in Springfield, 1948-69; U.S. atty. So. Dist. Ill., 1958-61; mem. firm Wood & Wood, 1961-69; assoc. dep. atty. gen. for U.S. attys. U.S. dept. Justice, 1969-70; assoc. dep. atty. gen. Justice Dept., Washington, 1970-72; asst. atty. gen. civil div. Justice Dept., 1972-73; U.S. dist. judge So. Dist. Ill., Springfield, 1973-76; judge U.S. Ct. Appeals (7th cir.), 1976—; adj. prof. Sch. Law, U. Ill., Champaign, 1993; disting. vis. prof. St. Louis U. Law Sch., 1996. Chmn. Adminstrv. Office Oversight Com., 1988-90; mem. Long Range Planning Com., 1991-96. Office: US Ct Appeals PO Box 299 600 E Monroe St Springfield IL 62701-0299

WOOD, HENRY AUSTIN, architect; b. Waltham, Mass., June 18, 1929; s. Henry Austin Jr. and Dagmar (Lundholm) W.; m. Joan Klawans, Oct. 22, 1962 (div. 1983); children: Paul F., Joshua W., Daniel L.; m. Diane Sargent, May 24, 1987. BA, Harvard U., 1951, MArch, 1960. Registered arch., Mass., N.Y., R.I., N.J., Mo., Pa., Conn., Ohio, U.K. Jr. architect Samuel Glaser Assoc., Boston, 1960-62; architect Campbell, Aldrich & Nulty, Boston, 1962-65; project mgr. Kallmann & McKinnell, Boston, 1965-67, assoc., 1967-70, ptnr., 1970-73; prin. Kallmann, McKinnell & Wood Architects, Inc., Boston, 1973—. Fellow AIA. Office: Kallmann McKinnell & Wood 939 Boylston St Boston MA 02115-3104

WOOD, HOWARD GRAHAM, banker; b. Balt., July 27, 1910; s. Howard and Etta (Graham) W.; m. Florence Tottle, Apr. 2, 1977; children by previous marriage—Robert Graham, Virginia B. Delauney. BA, Johns Hopkins, 1932; LLB, U. Md., 1936. Bar: Md. bar 1936. With First Nat. Bank Md., 1932-85. Author: (with Robert H. Burgess) Steamboats Out of Baltimore, 1969. Mem. Commn. on Revision Balt. City Charter, 1965. Served to maj. Intelligence Div. AUS, 1942-46. Mem. Phi Beta Kappa, Phi Gamma Delta. Clubs: Elkridge, Johns Hopkins (Balt.). Home: 919 Bellemore Rd Baltimore MD 21210-1206 Office: First Md Bldg Baltimore MD 21202

WOOD, JACALYN KAY, education educator, educational consultant; b. Columbus, Ohio, May 25, 1949; d. Carleston John and Grace Anna (Schumacher) W. BA, Georgetown Coll., 1971; MS, Ohio State U., 1976; PhD, Miami U., 1981. Elem. tchr. Bethel-Tate Schs., Ohio, 1971-73, Columbus Christian Sch., 1973-74, Franklin (Ohio) Schs., 1974-79; teaching fellow Miami U., Oxford, Ohio, 1979-81; cons. intermediate grades Erie County Schs., Sandusky, Ohio, 1981-89, presenter, tchr. insvc. tng. Mem. coun. Sta. WVIZ-TV, 1981-88; assoc. prof. Ashland U., Elyria, Ohio, 1989, dir. elem. edn., 1989—; mem. Lorain County 20/20, mem. strategic planning bd., 1992—; mem. Leadership Lorain County, 1994—; mem. exec. com. Perkins Community Schs., 1981-85; mem. community adv. bd. Sandusky Vols. Am., 1985-89, Sandusky Sec. Bank, 1987-88, vol. Firelands Community Hosp., 1986-87; active Leadership Lorain County, 1994—. Mem. AAUW, ASCD, Am. Businesswomen's Assn. (local pres. 1985), Internat. Reading Assn., Assn. Childhood Edn. (internat. publications com. 1996), Ohio Sch. Suprs. Assn. (regional pres. 1986, state pres. 1986-87), Phi Delta Kappa (local sec. 1985, 86, v.p. 1991-93, pres. 1993—), Phi Kappa Phi, Kappa Delta Pi (local adv. 1991-93). Baptist. Home: 35873 Westminster Ave N Ridgeville OH 44039-1380 Office: Ashland U at LCCC 1005 Abbe Rd N Elyria OH 44035-1613

WOOD, JACK CALVIN, health care consultant, lawyer; b. Greenwood, Ind., Jan. 9, 1933; s. Earl Leon and Gertrude Ruby (Stott) W. A.B., DePauw U., Greencastle, Ind., 1954; J.D., Harvard U., 1961. Bar: Ill. 1961, Tex. 1965, D.C. 1978, Colo. 1983. Assoc. firm Hopkins-Sutter, Chgo., 1961-65; gen. counsel Sisters of Charity Health Care System, Houston, 1965-73; sr. partner firm Wood, Lucksinger & Epstein, Houston, 1973-87, of counsel, 1987-91; of counsel Vinson & Elkins, 1991—; editor-in-chief Topics In Health Care Financing, 1974-94; clin. prof. law St. Louis U. Med. Sch., 1976—; adj. prof. health care adminstrn. Tex. Women's U., 1977—; Pres. St. Joseph Hosp. Found., Houston, 1966-68; chmn. governing com. Am. Bar Assn. Health Law Forum, 1981-84. Author: Financial Management, 1973, Medicare Reimbursement, 1974, Private Third Party Reimbursement, 1975. Served to lt. comdr. USNR, 1954-65. Mem. Am. Soc. Hosp. Attys. (pres. 1974-75), Nat. Health Lawyers Assn. (bd. dirs. 1981-85), Am. Soc. Law and Medicine (bd. dirs. 1981-85). Home: Aldama # 1, San Miguel de Allede Mexico Office: 907 Zaragoza St Laredo TX 78040-5927

WOOD, JACKIE DALE, physiologist, educator, researcher; b. Picher, Okla., Feb. 16, 1937; s. Aubrey T. Wood and Wilma J. (Coleman) Wood Patterson. BS, Kans. State U., 1964, MS, 1966; PhD, U. Ill., 1969. Asst. prof. physiology Williams Coll., Williamstown, Mass., 1969-71; asst. prof. U. Kans. Med. Ctr., Kansas City, 1971-74, assoc. prof., 1974-78, prof., 1978-79; prof., chmn. dept. physiology Sch. Medicine, U. Nev., Reno, 1979-85; chmn. dept. physiology coll. medicine Ohio State U., Columbus, 1985—; cons. NIH, Bethesda, Md., 1982—. Recipient Research Career Devel. award NIH, 1974, Chancellor's award for teaching excellence U. Kans., 1975; named Hon. Citizen City of Atzugi Japan, 1987; Alexander von Humboldt fellow, W.Ger., 1976. Mem. Am. Physiol. Soc. (assoc. editor 1984-96, rsch. award 1986), Soc. Neurosci., Am. Gastroent. Assn., AAAS, Assn. Chairmen Depts. Physiology. Office: Ohio State U Dept Physiology 300 Hamilton Hall 1645 Neil Ave Columbus OH 43210-1218

WOOD, JAMES, supermarket executive; b. Newcastle-upon-Tyne, Eng., Jan. 19, 1930; came to U.S., 1974; s. Edward and Catherine Wilhelmina (Parker) W.; m. Colleen Margaret Taylor, Aug. 14, 1954; children: Julie, Sarah. Grad., Loughborough Coll., Leicestershire, England; hon. LHD, St. Peter's Coll., N.J. Chief food chain Newport Coop. Soc., S. Wales, U.K., 1959-62, Grays Food Coop. Soc., Eng., 1962-66; dir., joint dep. mng. dir. charge retailing Cavenham, Ttd., Hayes, Eng., 1966-80; pres. Grand Union Co., Elmwood Park, N.J., 1973-79; chief exec. officer, dir. Grand Union Co., from 1973, chmn. bd., 1979-80; chmn. bd., CEO Gt. Atlantic & Pacific Tea Co., Inc., 1980—; bd. dirs. Asarco, Inc., Irma Fabrikerne A/S, Denmark, Schering-Plough Corp. Active World USO, UNICEF, United Jersey Bank. With Brit. Army, 1948-50. Mem. Food Mktg. Inst. (bd. dirs.). Roman Catholic. Office: Gt Atlantic & Pacific Tea Co 2 Paragon Dr Montvale NJ 07645-1718

WOOD, JAMES, broker; b. Mt. Kisco, N.Y., May 2, 1927; s. L. Hollingsworth and Martha (Speakman) W.; m. Frances Randall, May 2, 1953; children: Emily Morris, Stephen H. Grad., Deerfield (Mass.) Acad., 1945; B.A., Haverford (Pa.) Coll., 1950. Mfrs. rep. distbn. fertilizers, 1950-54; with Bank of N.Y., 1954-82, asst. v.p., 1960-61, v.p., 1961-82; broker Prescott Ball & Turben, 1982-93, v.p., 1986-93; broker, v.p. Smith Barney, Mt. Kisco, 1993—. Trustee emeritus Bryn Mawr Coll., Jewish Found. for Edn. Women; bd. mgrs. Haverford Coll.; trustee, former chmn. bd. trustees Am. Bible Soc.; v.p., bd. dirs. Howard Meml. Fund. With USNR, 1945-46. Home: Braewold 153 Wood Rd Mount Kisco NY 10549 Office: Smith Barney 100 S Bedford Rd Mount Kisco NY 10549-3425

WOOD, JAMES ALBERT, foreign language educator; b. Enterprise, Oreg., Nov. 9, 1949; s. Ralph Albert and Charlotte Lavona (Johnson) Wood; m. Maritza Wood, Apr. 14, 1977; 1 child, Jamie Maritza. BS in Health and Phys. Edn., David Lipscomb U., Nashville, 1975; BA in Spanish, So. Oreg. Univ., 1979; MA in Health and Phys. Edn., So. Oreg. State Coll., 1979; EdD, Tex. A&M U., Kingsville, 1986; postgrad., U. Tenn., 1981-82. Cert. health and phys. edn. tchr., K-12, Spanish-ESL tchr., mid-mgmt. supr., supt., elem., bilingual all level ESL, Tex. Tchr. Spanish and ESL Galena Park Ind. Sch. Dist., Houston, 1986-88; tchr. ESL and reading Rice Consol. Ind. Sch. Dist., Altair, Tex., 1988-89; ESL tchr. K-5 Royalwood Elem.Sch., Sheldon Ind. Sch. Dist., Houston, 1989-90; vol. Peace Corps, El Salvador, 1976-77; sr. program devel. specialist bilingual programs U. Okla., Norman, 1990-92; assoc. prof. bilingual edn. Sul Ross State U. Rio Grande Coll., Uvalde, Tex., 1992—; adj. prof. Tex. So. U., Houston, U. Houston, Clear Lake, Tex., 1988-90. Contbr. articles to profl. jours. Sgt. U.S. Army, 1970-73. Dean's grantee Tex. A&M U.-Kingsville. Mem. ASCD, TESOL, Nat. Assn. Bilingual Edn., Tex. Assn. Bilingual Edn., Tex. Tchr. Educators Assn., Non-Commd. Officers Assn. (life), Am. Legion, VFW (life). Home: PO Box 1415 Uvalde TX 78802-1415

WOOD, JAMES ALLEN, lawyer; b. McMinnville, Tenn., Jan. 14, 1906; s. Ira and Emma (Calhoun) W.; m. Eva Beth Sellers, Dec. 28, 1941; 1 son, Eben Calhoun. A.B., U. Tenn., 1929; LL.B., U. Tex., 1934. Bar: Tex. 1934. Tchr. Bolton High Sch., Alexandria, La., 1929-32; since practiced in Corpus Christi; of counsel Wood, Burney, Cohn & Viles and predecessor firms, 1971—; state dist. judge, Corpus Christi, 1941-43; mem. rules adv. com. Supreme Ct. Tex., 1949-86. Author 7 vols. poetry; contbr. articles to profl. jours.; Life on a Warren County Farm (Tenn.) 1906-1923, Early Bench and Bar of Corpus Christi. Bd. dirs. Nueces River Authority, 1972-89, pres., 1981-84, life time hon. dir., 1989—. Lt. USNR, 1943-45. Fellow Am. Coll. Trial Lawyers; mem. ABA, Tex. Bar Assn., Nueces County Bar Assn. (pres. 1941). Home: 458 Dolphin Pl Corpus Christi TX 78411-1514

WOOD, JAMES E., JR., religion educator, author; b. Portsmouth, Va., July 29, 1922; s. James E. and Elsie Elizabeth (Bryant) W.; m. Alma Leacy McKenzie, Aug. 12, 1943; 1 son, James Edward III. BA, Carson-Newman Coll., 1943; BD, So. Bapt. Theol. Sem., 1947, ThM, 1948; MA, Columbia U., 1949; postgrad., U. Tenn., 1943-44; cert. in Chinese, Yale U., 1949-50; Japanese diploma, Naganuma Sch. Japanese Studies, Tokyo, 1950-51; LLD, Seinan Gakuin U., Japan, 1983; LLD (hon.), Capitol U., 1996; PhD, So. Baptist Theol. Sem., 1957. Ordained to ministry So. Bapt. Ch., 1942. Pastor So. Bapt. chs., Tenn. and Ky., 1942-48; Bapt. missionary to Japan, 1950-55; prof. religion and lit. Seinan Gakuin U., Japan, 1951-55; assoc. prof. history of religions Baylor U., Waco, Tex., 1955-58, prof. hist. religions, dir. J. M. Dawson Inst., 1958-73, 80-95, dir. honors program, 1959-64; chmn. interdeptl. grad. degree program in ch.-state studies Baylor U., 1962-73, 80-95, chmn. faculty-student Far Eastern exchange program, 1970-72, Simon and Ethel Bunn Disting. prof. ch.-state studies, 1980—; exec. dir. Bapt. Joint Com. on Public Affairs, Washington, 1972-80; mem. ctrl. panel Bapt. World Alliance Commn. on Religious Liberty and Human Rights, 1965-75, Commn. on Freedom, Justice and Peace, 1976-80; chmn. Bapt. Com. on Bicentennial, 1973-76; mem. So. Bapt. Inter-Agy. Coun., 1972-80, vice chmn., 1975-76, sec. 1976-77; vis. prof. So. Bapt. Theol. Sem., 1974, N.Am. Bapt. Theol. Sem., Sioux Falls, S.D., 1974, 79, Okla. Bapt. U., Shawnee, 1977, Naval Coll. of Chaplains, Providence, 1988—, others; vis. lectr. Ashland (Ohio) Theol. Sem., 1971; Vernon Richardson lectr. U. Bapt. Ch., Balt., 1975, Ea. Bapt. Theol. Sem., Phila., 1975; lectr. First World Congress on Religious Liberty, Amsterdam, 1977, 2d Congress, Rome, 1984, U. Faculty of Law, Warsaw, Poland, 1984, Brigham Young U., 1986, 95, U. Tirana, Albania, 1992, U. Malta, 1994, Austin Coll., 1995, numerous others; chair Internat. Consultation on Relig. Rights and Ethnic Identity, Budapest, 1992; co-chair Internat. Conf. Religious Freedom, Moscow, 1993; mem. internat. adv. bd. World Report on Freedom Conscious Human Rights Ctr., U. Sussex, U.K.; co-chair consultation on Freedom of Conscience and Belief, Moscow, 1993; chair Internat. Consultation Religious Liberty and Social Peace, Malta, 1994; Carver-Barnes lectr. Southeastern Bapt. Theol. Sem., 1981; Asian Found. lectr. Seinan Gakuin U., Japan, 1983; ecumenical consultation on edn. Nat. Coun. Chs., 1974; numerous other com. coun. positions. Author: A History of American Literature: An Anthology, 1952, (co-author) Church and State in Scripture, History and Constitutional Law, 1958, The Problem of Nationalism, 1969, Nationhood and the Kingdom, 1977, Secular Humanism and the Public Schools, 1986, Reflections on Church and State, 1995; (edited by Derek H. Davis) The Separation of Church and State Defended: Selected Writings of James E. Wood, Jr., 1995, Church-State Relations in the Modern World, 1996, and numerous others; editor: Markham Press Fund, Baylor U. Press, 1970-72; founding editor: Jour. Ch. and State, 1959-73, 80-93, mem. editl. coun., 1973-80; mem. editl. bd. Religion and Public Edn., Religious Freedom Reporter; editor; contbr. numerous profl. pubs. including Religion and Politics, Church and State, others; area editor, contbr. Ency. So. Bapts., 1982; contbr. Changing Trends in Education, 1992, Law, Religion and Human Rights in GLobal Perspective, 1995, Dialogue of Democracy: An American Politics Reader, 1996; contbr. over 300 articles to profl. jours. Speaker in field. Sponsor Ams. for Public Schs., 1963-68; bd. dirs. Waco (Tex.) Planned Parenthood, 1966-72, pres., 1971-72; sponsor Christians Concerned for Israel, 1968—, Tex. Conf. Chs. Consultation on Religion and Public Edn., 1971, Nat. Christian Leadership Conf. for Israel, 1978—; pres. Waco area ACLU, bd. dirs. Tex. unit, 1968-72; pres. Nat. Council Religion and Public Edn., 1979-83, exec. com., 1975—, bd. dirs., 1972—; chmn. exec. com. Council Washington Reps. on UN, 1977-80, mem. council exec. com., 1973-80; exec. com. Nat. Coalition on Public Edn. and Religious Liberty, 1973—; mem. religious liberty com. Nat. Council Chs. U.S.A., 1972—, also mem. com. internat. concerns on human rights; Am. rep. Chs. Montreux Colloquium on Helsinki Final Act, 1977; v.p. Waco Conf. Christians and Jews, 1983-86, Internat. Acad. for Freedom of Religion and Belief, 1985-90, pres., 1990—; mem. internat. adv. bd. World Report on Freedom of Conscience, Human Rights Ctr., U. Sussex, Eng.; trustee Internat. Devel. Conf., 1974-80; nat. coun. Am.-Israel Friendship League, 1977—; founder, chmn. Waco Human Rights Week, 1981—; mem. ch. rels. com., U.S. Holocaust Meml. Coun., 1990—. Recipient Disting. Alumnus award Carson-Newman Coll., 1974, Religious Liberty award Alliance for Preservation of Religious Liberty, 1980, Henrietta Szold award Tex. region Hadassah, 1981, Human Rights award Waco Conf. Christians and Jews, 1986, Cir. of Achievement award Baylor U. Mortar Bd., 1991, Religious Freedom Lifetime award Ams. United Ctrl. Tex., 1993, W.R. White Meritorious Svc. award, 1996; hon. Tex. col., 1969. Mem. Am. Soc. Ch. History, Am. Acad. Religion, Am. Soc. Internat. Law, Am. Soc. Sci. Study of Religion, N. Am. Soc. Ecumenists, NCCJ (ad. com. on ch. state and taxation 1979-85), Supreme Court Hist. Soc., Soc. for Scholarly Publishing, ACLU, Phi Eta Sigma, Pi Kappa Delta, Alpha Psi Omega. Democrat. Home: 3306 Lake Heights Dr Waco TX 76708-1543 Office: Baylor U PO Box 97308 Waco TX 76798-7308

WOOD, JAMES MICHAEL, lawyer; b. Oakland, Calif., Mar. 22, 1948; s. Donald James and Helen Winifred (Reiman) W.; div.; children: Nathan, Sarah, Ruth. BA, St. Mary's Coll., 1970; JD, U. San Francisco, 1973. Bar: Calif. 1973, U.S. Dist. Ct. (no., cen. and so. dists.) Calif. 1973. Rsch. atty. Alameda County Superior Ct., Oakland, 1973-76; ptnr. Crosby, Heafey, Roach & May, Oakland, 1976—; presenter at profl. confs. Contbr. articles to profl. jours. Chair alumni-faculty devel. fund St. Mary's Coll. Alumni Bd. Dirs., 1990-94. Mem. ABA (litigation sect., health law litigation com., litigation products liability com.), Assn. Trial Lawyers Am. (assoc.), State Bar Calif., Calif. Trial Lawyers Assn. (assoc.), No. Calif. Assn. Def. Counsel, Alameda County Bar Assn., Def. Rsch. and Trial Lawyers Assn., Am. Acad. Hosp. Attys., Am. Soc. Pharmacy Law, Nat. Health Lawyers Assn., Drug Info. Assn. Office: Crosby Heafey Roach & May 1999 Harrison St Oakland CA 94612-3520

WOOD, JAMES NOWELL, museum director and executive; b. Boston, Mar. 20, 1941; s. Charles H. and Helen N. (Nowell) W.; m. Emese Forizs, Dec. 30, 1966; children: Lenke Hancock, Rebecca Nowell. Diploma, Universita per Stranieri, Perugia, Italy, 1962; B.A., Williams Coll., Williamstown, Mass., 1963; M.A. (Ford Mus. Tng. fellow), NYU, 1966. Asst. to dir. Met. Mus., N.Y.C., 1967-68, asst. curator dept. 20th century art, 1968-70; curator Albright-Knox Art Gallery, Buffalo, 1970-73, assoc. dir., 1973-75; dir. St. Louis Art Mus., 1975-80, Art Inst. Chgo., 1980—; vis. com. visual arts U. Chgo., 1980-94; head com. Nat. Endowment Arts. Mem. Intermuseum Conservation Assn. (past pres.), Assn. Art Mus. Dirs. Office: Art Inst Chgo 111 S Michigan Ave Chicago IL 60603-6110

WOOD, JANE, dancer. Attended, Washington Sch. Ballet, Acad. Washington Ballet; studied with Patricia Neary, Geneva Ballet. Dancer Geneva Ballet, until 1978; dancer Ballet West, Salt Lake City, 1978-87, soloist, 1987-89, prin. artist, 1989—. Dance performances include Romeo & Juliet, Sleeping Beauty, Swan Lake, Giselle. Office: Ballet West 50 W 200 S Salt Lake City UT 84101-1642*

WOOD, JEANNE CLARKE, charitable organization executive; b. Pitts., Dec. 21, 1916; d. Joseph Calvitt and Helen Caroline (Mattson) Clarke; m. Herman Eugene Wood, Jr., May 6, 1936 (dec.); children: Helen Hamilton (Mrs. John Harry Mortenson), Herman Eugene III. Student, Collegiate Sch. for Girls, Richmond, Va., 1932-33. Asst. to Dr. and Mrs. J. Calvitt Clarke, Christian Children's Fund, Inc., Richmond, 1938-64; founder Children, Inc., Richmond, 1964; pres., internat. dir. Children, Inc., 1964—. Author: (with Helen C. Clarke) In Appreciation: A Story in Pictures of the World-Wide Family of Christian Children's Fund, Inc, 1958, Children's Christmastime Around the World, 1962, Children's Games Around the World, 1962, Children-Hope of the World-Their Needs, 1965, Children-Hope of the World-Their Friends, 1966; Editor: CI News, 1964. Recipient citation Eastern Council Navajo Tribe, 1970, citations Mayor of Pusan (Korea), 1971, citations Mayor of Seoul, 1971, citations Gov. of Kanagawa Prefecture (Japan), 1972, commendation Pres. of U.S., 1972, citation Stephen Philibosian Found., 1975, citation Santa Ana (El Salvador) Dept. Edn., 1975, citation Nat. Sch. for Blind, Dominican Republic, 1982, citation Navajo Tribal Council of Navajo Nation, Window Rock, Ariz., 1982. Office: Children Inc PO Box 5381 1000 Westover Rd Richmond VA 23220-6624 *While there are many things about which we can make no choice in this volatile world where change is constant and sometimes disastrous, it has seemed to me that one can make the choice between accepting things positively or negatively. I have chosen to accept them positively.*

WOOD, JEANNINE KAY, state official; b. Dalton, Nebr., Apr. 22, 1944; d. Grover L. and Elsie M. (Winkelman) Sanders; m. Charles S. Wood, Dec. 7, 1968; children: Craig C., Wendi L. Wood Armstrong. Exec. sec. Idaho Hosp. Assn., Boise, 1966-71; com. sec. Idaho State Senate, Boise, 1976-81, jour. clk., 1981-85, asst. to sec. of senate, 1985-91, sec. of senate, 1991—; pvt. practice typing svc. Boise, 1979-86. Mem. Am. Soc. Legis. Clks. and Secs. Methodist. Home: 3505 S Linder Meridian ID 83642 Office: Idaho State Capitol PO Box 83720 Boise ID 83720-0081

WOOD, JOETTA KAY, special education educator; b. Kirksville, Mo., Sept. 30, 1951; d. Vernon John Wood and Hazel Ellen (Lake) Ammon. BS in Elem. Edn., N.W. Mo. State U., 1973; MS in Spl. Edn., S.W. Mo. State U., 1993. Cert. tchr., Mo. Kindergarten Livingston County Sch., Wheeling, Mo., 1973-75; 1st grade tchr. Mercer (Mo.) Sch., 1975-77, Maysville (Mo.) Sch., 1978-80; learning disabilities tchr. Lakeland Sch., Lowery City, Mo., 1980-81, Tri-County Sch., Jamesport, Mo., 1981-84, Plato (Mo.) Sch., 1981-84; adj. faculty Columbia Coll., 1995. Mem. Coun. for Exceptional Children, Mo. State Tchrs. Assn. Home: PO Box 8 Plato MO 65552-0008

WOOD, JOHN ARMSTEAD, planetary scientist, geological sciences educator; b. Roanoke, Va., July 28, 1932; s. John Armstead and Lillian Cary (Hall) W.; m. Elisabeth Mathilde Heuser, June 12, 1958 (div.); children: Crispin S., Georgia K.; m. Julie Marie Nason, Sept. 9, 1989. B.S. in Geology, Va. Polytech. Inst., 1954; Ph.D. in Geology, Mass. Inst. Tech., 1958; post-doctoral study, U. Cambridge, Eng., 1959-60. Staff scientist Smithsonian Astrophys. Obs., Cambridge, Mass., 1959, 61-62, 65—; research asso. Enrico Fermi Inst. U. Chgo., 1962-65; prof. dept. geol. scis. Harvard, 1976-95; asso. dir. Harvard-Smithsonian Center for Astrophysics, 1981-86; Vice chmn. Lunar Sample Analysis Planning Team, 1971-72. Author: Meteorites and the Origin of Planets, 1968, The Solar System, 1979. Recipient NASA medal for exceptional sci. achievement, 1973, J.L. Smith medal NAS, 1976, G.K. Gilbert award Geol. Soc. Am., 1992. Fellow AAAS, Am. Geophys. Union, Meteoritical Soc. (pres. 1971-72, Leonard medal 1980); mem. NAS, Am. Acad. Arts and Scis., Cosmos Club. Asteroid no. 4736 named in his honor Johnwood. Home: 1716 Cambridge St # 15 Cambridge MA 02138-4343 Office: 60 Garden St Cambridge MA 02138-1516

WOOD, JOHN MARTIN, lawyer; b. Detroit, Mich., Mar. 29, 1944; s. John Francis and Margaret Kathleen (Lynch) W.; m. Judith Anne Messer; children—Timothy Peter, Meagan Anne. B.A., Boston Coll., 1966; J.D., Cath. U. Am., 1969. Bar: D.C. 1970, U.S. Dist. D.C. 1970, U.S. Ct. Appeals (D.C. cir., 3d cir., 4th cir.), U.S. Supreme Ct. 1973. Trial atty. tax div. Dept. Justice, Washington, 1969-73; assoc. Reed Smith Shaw & McClay, Washington, 1973-80, ptnr., 1980—, mng. ptnr., 1989-95, dir. legal personnel, 1995—. Dir. adv. bd. The Salvation Army, Va., Metro Washington; dir. The Franklin Sq. Assn., Leadership Washington, 1993—. Mem. D.C. Bar, Phi Alpha Delta, Delta Sigma Pi. Club: Barristers (Washington), River Bend Golf & C.C. Home: 9490 Oak Falls Ct Great Falls VA 22066-4143 Office: Reed Smith Shaw & McClay 1301 K St NW Washington DC 20005-3317

WOOD, JOSEPH GEORGE, neurobiologist, educator; b. Victoria, Tex., Dec. 8, 1928; s. Harold Robert and Frances Josephine (Marcak) W.; 1 dau., Marian. B.S., U. Houston, 1954, M.S., 1958; Ph.D., U. Tex., Galveston, 1962. Teaching asst. biology U. Houston, 1956-58; instr. anatomy U. Tex. Dental Br., Houston, 1961, Yale U., 1962-63; asst. prof. U. Ark. Med. Sch., Little Rock, 1963-66; assoc. prof. U. Tex., San Antonio, 1966-70; asst. dean acad. devel. U. Tex., 1967-69; prof. and chmn. dept. neurobiology and anatomy U. Tex., Houston, 1970-84; prof. neurobiology and anatomy U. Tex., 1984-88; prof., chmn. dept. anat. sci. U. Okla. Coll. Medicine, 1988-93; dir. Okla. Ctr. Neurosci., 1990-95; ret., 1995; guest prof. dept. pathobiology, cell biol. & Neuroanat U. Minn. Served with AUS, 1954-56. Recipient Basic Sci. Teaching award U. Tex. Houston, 1972, 75, 86, Disting. Alumnus award U. Tex. Med. Br., 1976. Mem. Am. Assn. Anatomists (exec. com. 1974-78), Soc. Neurosci. (exec. com. Houston chpt. 1971-77, pres. 1973-77), Assn. Am. Med. Colls., Cajal Club, Histochem. Soc., Assn. Anatomy Chmn., Tex. Soc. Electron Microscopy (pres. 1970-71, exec. council 1971-79), Sigma Xi (research award 1962), Phi Kappa Phi, Alpha Omega Alpha. Home and Office: 8638 Old Oak Dr Irving TX 75063

WOOD, JOSHUA WARREN, III, lawyer, foundation executive; b. Portsmouth, Va., Aug. 31, 1941; s. Joshua Warren and Mary Evelyn (Carter) W.; m. Marcia Neal Ramsey, Feb. 29, 1964; children: Lauren Elaine, Joshua Warren IV. A.B., Princeton U., 1963; J.D., U. Va., 1971. Bar: Va. 1971, N.J. 1976, U.S. Supreme Ct. 1977, N.Y. 1982. Comml. banking asst. Bankers Trust Co., N.Y.C., 1967-68; assoc. McGuire, Woods & Battle, Richmond, Va., 1971-75; v.p., gen. counsel, sec. The Robert Wood Johnson Found., Princeton, N.J., 1975—; spl. counsel Smith, Lambert, Hicks & Miller, Princeton, 1985-87, Drinker, Biddle & Reath, Princeton, N.J. and Phila., 1987-89; of counsel Lankenau & Bickford, N.Y.C., 1989-92. Mem. editorial bd. Va. Law Rev., 1969-71. Capt. arty. U.S. Army, 1963-67. Decorated Army Commendation medal. Mem. ABA, Princeton Bar Assn., N.Y. Bar Assn., Va. Bar Assn., N.J. Bar Assn., Nat. Health Lawyers Assn., Am. Arbitration Assn. (bd. dirs., mem. panel of arbitrators, task force Mass torts & alternative dispute resolution), Order of Coif, Princeton Club. Office: College Rd PO Box 2316 Princeton NJ 08543-2316

WOOD, KATHLEEN MARIE, physical therapist; b. Scranton, Pa., Nov. 18, 1968; d. Michael Joseph and Faye Ann (Hocker) Kostelnik; m. Robert Nevin Wood, Sept. 16, 1995. BS in Phys. Therapy, Beaver Coll., 1990. Phys. therapist Mercy Hosp., Scranton, 1990—; home health phys. therapist Mercy Hosp., Scranton, 1994—, quality assurance, 1994—. Mem. Altrusa Club Scranton (sec. 1993). Roman Catholic. Avocations: singing, shopping, aerobics, traveling. Home: 105 2nd St Dalton PA 18414 Office: Mercy Hosp 746 Jefferson Ave Scranton PA 18510-1624

WOOD, KENNETH ARTHUR, retired newspaper editor, writer; b. Hastings, Sussex, Eng., Feb. 25, 1926; came to U.S., 1965; s. Arthur Charles and Ellen Mary (Cox) W.; m. Hilda Muriel Harloe, Sept. 13, 1952. Educated in Eng. Editor Stamp Collector newspaper Van Dahl Publs., Albany, Oreg., 1968-80, editor emeritus, 1980—. Author (ency.) This Is Philately, 1982, (atlas) Where in the World, 1983, Basic Philately, 1984, Post Dates, 1985, Modern World, 1987; author several hundred articles and columns published in the U.K. and U.S.A., 1960—. Served with Brit. Army WW II. Recipient Disting. Philatelist award Northwest Fedn. Stamp Clubs, 1974, Phoenix award Ariz. State Philatelic Hall of Fame, 1979, Disting. Philatelist award Am. Topical Assn., 1979. Fellow Royal Philatelic Soc. (London); mem. Am. Philatelic Soc. (Luff award 1987, Hall of Fame Writers Unit, 1984). Avocations: philately, aviation history, modern history, gardening. Office: 2430 Tudor Way SE Albany OR 97321-5661

WOOD, KIMBA M., judge; b. Port Townsend, Wash., Jan. 2, 1944. BA cum laude, Conn. Coll., 1965; MSc, London Sch. Econs., 1966; JD, Harvard U., 1969. Bar: U.S. Dist. Ct. D.C. 1969, U.S. Ct. Appeals D.C. 1969, N.Y. 1972, U.S. Dist. Ct. (ea. and so. dists.) N.Y. 1974, U.S. Ct. Appeals (2d cir.) 1975, U.S. Supreme Ct. 1980, U.S. Dist. Ct. (we. dist.) N.Y. 1981. Assoc. Steptoe & Johnson, Washington, 1969-70; with Office Spl. Counsel, OEO Legal Svcs., Washington, 1970-71; assoc., then ptnr. LeBoeuf, Lamb, Leiby & MacRae, N.Y.C., 1971-88; judge, U.S. Dist. Ct. (so. dist.) N.Y., N.Y.C., 1988—. Mem. ABA (chmn. civil practice, procedure com. 1982-85, mem. coun. 1985-88, jud. rep. 1989-91), N.Y. State Bar Assn. (chmn. antitrust sect. 1983-84), Fed. Bar Coun. (trustee from 1978, v.p., 1984-85), Am. Law Inst. Office: US Dist Ct US Courthouse 500 Pearl St New York NY 10007-1316

WOOD, LARRY (MARY LAIRD), journalist, author, university educator, public relations executive, environmental consultant; b. Sandpoint, Idaho; d. Edward Hayes and Alice (McNeel) Small; children: Mary, Marcia, Barry. BA summa cum laude, U. Wash., 1939, MA summa cum laude, with highest honors, 1940; postgrad., Stanford U., 1941-42, U. Calif., Berkeley, 1946-47; cert. in photography, U. Calif., Berkeley, 1971; postgrad. journalism, U. Wis., 1971-72, U. Minn., 1971-72, U. Ga., 1972-73; postgrad. in art, architecture and marine biology, U. Calif., Santa Cruz, 1974-76, Stanford Hopkins Marine Sta., Santa Cruz, 1977-80. Lifetime secondary and jr. coll. teaching cert., Wash., Calif. Feature writer and columnist Oakland Tribune and San Francisco Chronicle, Calif., 1939—; archtl. and environ. feature and travel writer and columnist San Jose (Calif.) Mercury News (Knight Ridder), 1972-90; teaching fellow Stanford U., 1940-43; dir. pub. rels. 2-counties, 53-parks East Bay Regional Park Dist., No. Calif., 1948-68; pres. Larry Wood Pub. Rels., 1946—; pub. rels. dir. Calif. Children's Home Soc., 1947-58; prof. (tenure) pub. rels., mag. writing, journalism, investigative reporting San Diego State U., 1974, 75; disting. vis. prof. journalism San Jose State U., 1976; assoc. prof. journalism Calif. State U., Hayward, 1978; prof. sci. and environ. journalism U. Calif. Berkeley Ext. grad. divsn., 1979—; press del. nat. convs. Am. Geophys. Union Internat. Conf., 1986—, AAAS, 1989—, Nat. Park Svc. VIP Press Tour, Yellowstone after the fire, 1989—, Nat. Assn. Sci. Writers, 1989—, George Washington U./Am. Assn. Neurol. Surgeons Sci. Writers Conf., 1990, Am. Inst. Biol. Scis. Conf., 1990, Nat. Conf. Sci. Writers, Am. Heart Assn., 1995, Internat. Cardiologists Symposium for Med./Sci. Writers, 1995, Annenberg Program Electronic Media Symposium, Washington, 1995; EPA del. to USSR and Ea. Europe; expert witness on edn., pub. rels., journalism and copyright; cons. sci. writers interne project Stanford U., 1989—; spl. media guest Sigma Xi, 1990—; mem. numerous spl. press corps; selected White House Spl. Media, 1993—; selected mem. Duke U. 14th Ann. Sci. Reporters Conf., 1995; internat. press guest Can. Consulate Gen. Dateline Can., 1995—, French Govt. Tourist Office, 1996—, Ministerio delle Risorse Agricole Alimentari e Forestali and Assocs. Conf., 1995; appeared in TV documentary Larry Wood Covers Visit of Queen Elizabeth II. Contbr. over 5,000 articles on various topics for newspapers, nat. mags., nat. and internat. newspaper syndicates including L.A. Times-Mirror Syndicate, Washington Post, Phila. Inquirer, Chgo. Tribune, Miami Herald, Oakland Tribune, Seattle Times, San Francisco Chronicle, Parade, San Jose Mercury News (Nat. Headliner award), Christian Sci. Monitor, L.A. Times/Christian Monitor Worldwide News Syndicate, Washington Post, Phila. Inquirer, Hawaiian Airlines In Paradise and other in-flight mags., MonitoRadio, Sports Illus., Life, Mechanix Illus., Popular Mechanics, Parents (contbg. editor), House Beautiful, Am. Home (awards 1988, 89), Archl. Digest, Better Homes and Gardens, Sunset, Architectural Digest, National Geographic World, Travel & Leisure, Chevron USA/Odyssey (Calif. Pub.'s award 1984), Xerox Edn. Publs., Europe's Linguapress, PSA Mag., Off Duty, Oceans, Sea Frontiers, AAA Westways, AAA Motorland, Travelin', others. Significant works include home and garden columnist and editor, 5-part series Pacific Coast Ports, 5-part series Railroads of the West, series Immigration, Youth Gangs, Endangered Species, Calif. Lighthouse Chain, Lighthouses of the World, Pacific Coast Wetlands, Elkhorn Slough Nat. Estuarine Res., Ebey's Landing Nat. Hist. Island Res., Calif. Water Wars, BLM's Adopt a Horse Program, Mt. St. Helen's Eruption, Oreg's Covered Bridges, Loma Prieta Earthquake, Oakland Firestorm, Missing Children, Calif. Prison Reform, Columbia Alaska's Receding Glacier, Calif. Underwater Parks, and many others; author: Wonderful U.S.A.: A State-by-State Guide to Its Natural Resources, 1989; co-author over 21 books including: McGraw-Hill English for Social Living, 1944, Fawcett Boating Books, 1956-66, Fodor's San Francisco, Fodor's California, 1982-89, Charles Merrill Focus on Life Science, Focus on Physical Science, Focus on Earth Science, 1983, 87, Earth Science, 1987; contbr. Earth Science 1987; 8 works selected for use by Europe's Woltors-Nordoff-Longman English Language Texts, U.K., Netherlands, 1988; author: (with others) anthology West Winds, 1989; reviewer Charles Merrill texts, 1983-84; book reviewer Profl. Communicator, 1987—; selected writings in permanent collections Oakland Pub. Libr., U. Wash. Main Libr.; environ. works included in Dept. Edn. State of Md. textbook; contbr., author Journalism Quar.; author script PBS/AAA America series, 1992; contbg. editor: Parents. Nat. chmn. travel writing contest for U.S. univ. journalism students Assn. for Edn. in Journalism/Soc. Am. Travel Writers, 1979-83; judge writing contest for Nat. Assn. Real Estate Editors, 1982—; press del. 1st Internat. Symposium Volcanism and Aviation Safety, 1991, Coun. for Advancement of Sci. Writing, 1977—, Rockefeller Media Seminar Feeding the World-Protecting the Earth, 1992, Global Conf. on Mercury as Pollutant, 1992, Earth Summit Global Forum, Rio de Janeiro, 1992; invited Nat. Park Svc. Nat. Conf. Sci. Writers, 1985, Postmaster Gen.'s 1992 Stamps, 1991, Internat. Geophys. Union Conf., 1982—, The Conf. Bd., 1995, Corp. Comm. Conf., Calif. Inst. Tech.'s Media and Sci. Seminar, 1995—, EPA and Dept. Energy Tech. Conf., 1992, Am. Soc. Photogrammetry and Remote Sensing Internat. Conv. Mapping Global change, 1992, N.Y. Mus. Modern Art Matisse Retrospective Press Rev., 1992, celebration 150th anniversary Oreg. Trail, 1993, Coun. Advancement Sci. Writing, 1993-96, Sigma Xi Nat. Conf., 1988-96, Nat. Sci. Writers Confs., 1996, PRSA Travel and Tourism Conf., 1993—, Internat. Conf. Environment, 1994, 95, Quality Life Europe, Prague, 1994, Calif. Sesquicentennial, 1996, 14th Ann. Sci. Writers Conf., 1996, Picasso Retrospective, 1996, many others; mem. Gov.'s Conf. Tourism N.C., 1993, 94, 95, Calif., 1976—, Fla., 1987—; press guest 14 U.S. states and 12 fgn. countries' Depts. Tourism, 1986—. Recipient numerous awards, honors, citations, speaking engagements, including induction into Broadway Hall of Fame, U. Wash., 1984, Broadway Disting. Alumnus award, 1995; citations for environ. writing Nat. Park Svc., U.S. Forest Svc., Bur. Land Mgmt., Oakland Mus. Assn., Oakland C. of C., Chevron USA, USN plaque and citation, best mag. articles citation Calif. Pubs. Assn., 1984; co-recipient award for best Sunday newspaper mag. Nat. Headliners, citation for archtl. features Oakland Mus., 1983; honoree for achievements in journalism Nat. Mortar Bd., 1988, 89; selected as one of 10 V.I.P. press for Yellowstone Nat. Park field trip on "Let Burn" rsch., 1989; named one of Calif.'s top 40 contemporary authors for writings on Calif. underwater parks, 1989, nat. honoree Social Issues Resources Series, 1987; invited V.I.P. press, spl. press guest numerous events worldwide. Mem. Am. Bd. Forensic Examiners, Calif. Acad. Scis., San Francisco Press Club, Nat. Press Club, Pub. Rels. Soc. Am. (charter mem. travel, tourism, environment and edn. divs.), Nat. Sch. Pub. Rels. Assn., Environ. Cons. N.Am., Am. Assn. Edn. in Journalism and Comm. (exec. bd. nat. mag. div. 1978, panel chmn. 1979, 80, author Journalism Quar. jour.), Women in Comm. (nat. bd. officer 1975-77, book reviewer Prof. Communicator), Soc. Profl. Journalists (nat. bd. for hist. sites 1980—), Nat. Press Photographers Assn. (hon. life, cons. Bay Area interne project 1989—, honoree 1995), Investigative Reporters and Editors (charter), Bay Area Advt. and Mktg. Assn., Nat. Assn. Sci. Writers, Calif. Writers Club (state bd., Berkeley bd. 1989—, honoree ann. conv. Asilomar, Calif. 1990), Am. Assn. Med. Writers, Internat. Assn. Bus. Communicators, Soc. Environ. Journalists (charter), Am. Film Inst., Am. Heritage Found. (citation 1986, 87, 88), Soc. Am. Travel Writers, Internat. Oceanographic Found., Oceanic Soc., Calif. Acad. Environ. News Writers, Seattle Advt. and Sales Club (former officer), Nature Conservancy, Smithsonian Audubon Soc., Nat. Wildlife Fedn., Nat. Parks and Conservation Assn., Calif. State Parks Found., Calif. Environ. Leadership Roundtable, Fine Arts Mus., San Francisco, Seattle Jr. Advt. Club (charter), U. Wash. Comm. Alumni (Sch. Comm. alumni, life, charter mem. ocean scis. alumni, Disting. Alumni 1987), U. Calif., Berkeley Alumni (life, v.p., scholarship chmn. 1975-81), Stanford Alumni (life), Mortar Board Alumnae Assn. (life, honoree 1988, 89), Am. Mgmt. Assn., Nat. Soc. Environ. Journalists (charter), Calif. Environ. Leadership Roundtable, Phi Beta Kappa (v.p., bd. dirs. Calif. Alumni Assn., statewide chmn. scholarship awards 1975-81), Purple and Gold Soc. (planning com., charter, 1995—), Pi Lambda Theta, Theta Sigma Phi. Home: Piedmont Pines 6161 Castle Dr Oakland CA 94611-2737 *A creed I follow is Ralph Waldo Emerson's statement: "Nothing great was ever achieved without enthusiasm."*

WOOD, LAWRENCE CRANE, medical association administrator, educator; b. Phila., May 7, 1935; s. Francis Clark and Mary Louise (Woods) W.; m. Emma Mathis Hollingsworth, Aug. 29, 1959 (div. 1975); children: Lawrence C. Jr., Clinton Tyler; m. Shirley Ann Jacobsen, July 1, 1977; 1 child, Marianna Redd. AB, Princeton U., 1957; MD, U. Pa., 1961. Assoc. physician Mass. Gen. Hosp., Boston; instr. in medicine Harvard U. Med. Sch., Boston; pres., med. dir. Thyroid Found. Am., Boston, 1985—. Author: Your Thyroid: A Home Reference, 1982, 3rd edit., 1996. Pres. Thyroid Found. Internat., 1995—. Capt. USMC, 1965-68. Mem. ACP, Am. Thyroid Assn., Am. Assn. Clin. Endocrinologists, Mass. Med. Soc., Endocrine Soc. Avocations: fishing, sailing, banjo, guitar. Office: Mass Gen Hosp ACC 635 Parkman St Boston MA 02114

WOOD, LINCOLN JACKSON, aerospace engineer; b. Lyons, N.Y., Sept. 30, 1947; s. William Hulbert and Sarah Brock (Strumsky) W. BS with distinction, Cornell U., 1968; MS in Aeronautics and Astronautics, Stanford U., 1969, PhD, 1972. Staff engr. Hughes Aircraft Co., El Segundo, Calif., 1974-77; mem. tech. staff Jet Propulsion Lab. Calif. Inst. Tech., Pasadena, 1977-81, tech. group supr. Jet Propulsion Lab., 1981-89, tech. mgr., 1989-91, dep. tech. section mgr., 1991—; Bechtel instr. engring. Calif. Inst. Tech., Pasadena, 1972-74, lectr. in systems engring., 1975-76, vis. asst. prof., 1976-78, vis. assoc. prof., 1978-84; cons. in field. Contbr. articles on space navigation and optimal control theory to profl. jours. Bd. dirs. Boys Republic, Chino, Calif., 1991. Assoc. fellow AIAA (tech. com. on astrodynamics 1985-86, chmn. 1986-88, assoc. editor Jour. Guidance, Control and Dynamics 1983-89); sr. mem. Am. Astro. Soc. (space flight mechanics com. 1980—, chmn. 1993-95, assoc. editor Jour. of Astro. Scis. 1980-83, gen. chmn. AAS/AIAA Space Flight Mechanics Meeting, 1993), IEEE (sr. mem.), AAAS, Los Solteros (pres. 1991), Sigma Xi. Office: Jet Propulsion Lab 4800 Oak Grove Drive Mail Stop 301-125L Pasadena CA 91109

WOOD, MARCUS ANDREW, lawyer; b. Mobile, Ala., Jan. 18, 1947; s. George Franklin and Helen Eugenia (Fletcher) W.; m. Sandra Lee Pellonari, July 25, 1971; children: Edward Alan, Melinda Janel. BA cum laude, Vanderbilt U., 1969; JD, Yale U., 1974. Bar: Oreg. 1974, U.S. Dist. Ct. Oreg. 1974, U.S. Ct. Appeals (9th cir.) 1982. Assoc., then ptnr. Rives, Bonihadi & Smith, Portland, Oreg., 1974-78; ptnr. Stoel Rives LLP and predecessor firms, Portland, 1974—. Pres., bd. dirs. Indochinese Refugee Ctr., Portland, 1980, Pacific Ballet Theatre, Portland, 1986-87; bd. dirs. Outside In, Portland, 1989—. Lt. USNR, 1969-71. Mem. ABA, Phi Beta Kappa. Home: 9300 NW Finzer Ct Portland OR 97229 Office: Stoel Rives 900 SW 5th Ave Ste 2300 Portland OR 97204-1232

WOOD, MARGARET GRAY, dermatologist, educator; b. Jamaica, N.Y., May 23, 1918; d. C.W. Bromley and B. Eleanor (Niblack) Gray; m. Alfred Conard Wood, Mar. 24, 1950; children: M. Diana Wood, Deirdre Wood-Harper, Moira Dorothy Wood. BA, U. ALa., Tuscaloosa, 1941; MD, Woman's Med. Coll. Pa., 1948; D in Med. Scis. (hon.), Med. Coll. Pa., 1990, emeritus prof. medicine, 1993. Diplomate Am. Bd. Dermatology, Am. Bd. Dermatopathology. Intern Phila. Gen. Hosp., 1948-50; resident U. Pa. Hosp., 1950-53; instr. dept. dermatology U. Pa. Sch. Medicine, Phila., 1952-53, assoc., 1953-67, asst. prof., 1967-71, assoc. prof., 1971-75, clin. prof., 1975-80, prof. and chmn. dept. dermatology, 1980-82, prof., 1988-92, prof. emeritus, 1989—; assoc. prof. grad. Sch. Medicine U. Pa., Phila., 1957-71, cons. Sch. Dental Medicine, Sch. Vet. Medicine U. Pa., Phila.; asst. prof. Med. Coll. Pa., Phila., 1957-93, prof. emeritus, 1993—, vice chmn. bd. dirs. 1984—; vice chmn. bd. dirs. Med. Coll. Hosps., Phila., 1991—, Hahnemann U. Hosp., 1993—; mem. exec. com. Am. Med. Women's Hosp. Svc. Com., Washington, 1970—; dir. Alleghany Health Systems, Pitts., 1987-91, Alleghany Health Edn. and Rsch. Found., 1991-94; bd. dirs. St. Christophers Hosp. for Children, Alleghany U. Pitts., Alleghany Hosp. Systems. Author (with others) 4 books; contbr. numerous articles to med. jours. Recipient Rose Hershfeld award Women's Dermatology Soc., 1989. Mem. AMA, Internat. Dermatology Assn., Internat. Dermatopathology Assn., Phila. Dermatology Soc. (pres. 1978-79), Alpha Omega Alpha. Republican. Episcopalian. Avocations: gardening, medical research.

WOOD, MARIAN STARR, publishing company executive; b. N.Y.C., Mar. 30, 1938; d. Edward James and Betty (Starr) Markow; m. Anthony Stuart Wood, Mar. 21, 1963. B.A., Barnard Coll., 1959; postgrad., Columbia U., 1959-64. Teaching asst., lectr. Columbia U., N.Y.C., 1960-64; editor Praeger Pubs., N.Y.C., 1965-71; sr. editor Henry Holt & Co., N.Y.C., 1972-81, exec. editor, 1981-96; assoc. pub. Marian Wood Books, 1996—.

WOOD, MARION DOUGLAS, state legislator, lawyer; b. Detroit, Aug. 15, 1942; s. Marion Douglas and Kathryn Louise (Johnson) W.; m. Crystal Anne McAllister, Jan. 20, 1962; children: Gregory D., Jeffrey D. BS in Edn., Ark. State U., 1964; JD, U. Ark., 1974. Bar: Ark. 1974, U.S. Dist. Ct. Ark. 1974, U.S. Ct. Appeals (8th cir.) 1982. Trust officer Comml. Nat. Bank, Little Rock, 1972-74; pvt. practice law North Little Rock, 1974-89, Sherwood, Ark., 1989—; mem. Ark. Gen. Assembly, Little Rock, 1977-96. Maj. U.S. Army, 1964-70. Mem. Sherwood C. of C. (pres. 1993), Am. Legion, Vietnam Helicopter Pilots Assn., Rotary. Democrat. Methodist. Avocations: fishing, flying, woodworking. Office: Wood Law Firm PO Box 7078 Sherwood AR 72124-7078

WOOD, MAURICE, medical educator; b. Pelton, Eng., June 28, 1922; came to U.S., 1971; s. Joseph and Eugenie (Lumley) W.; m. Erica Joan Noble, May 1, 1948; children: Roger Lumley, Ashley Michael, Frances Jane. M.B., B.S., U. Durham, Eng., 1945; M.R.C.G.P., Royal Coll. Gen. Practice, London, 1966; F.R.C.G.P., Royal Coll. Gen. Practice, 1975. Diplomate: Am. Bd. Family Practice. Sr. ptnr. med. practice South Shields County, Durham, 1950-71; gen. practice teaching group U. Newcastle, Newcastle-on-Tyne, Eng., 1969-71; gen. clin. asst. dept. psychology-medicine South Shields Gen. Hosp., 1966-71; assoc. prof., dir. research family practice Med. Coll. Va.-Va. Commonwealth U., Richmond, 1971-73, prof., dir. research in family practice, 1973-87, prof. emeritus, 1987—; cons. advisor WHO, Geneva, 1979-90, chmn. working party to develop a classification for primary care, 1979-90; founding mem. exec. dir. N.Am. Primary Care Rsch. Group, Richmond, 1983-92, past pres., pres. emeritus, 1993—; chmn. com. on cmty. oriented primary care Insts. of Medicine, 1982-84. Assoc. editor: Jour. Family Practice, 1976-83. Recipient award for meritorious svc. Va. Acad. Family Physicians, 1976; Maurice Wood award for career achievement in primary care rsch. founded in his honor, 1995. Fellow Royal Coll. Gen. Practitioners, Am. Acad. Family Physicians; mem. Inst. Medicine-Nat. Acad. Sci., Soc. Tchrs. Family Medicine (Curtis Hames Career Research award 1984), Inst. of Medicine, NAS, Ambulatory Sentinel Practice Network, Internat. Primary Care Network (treas., bd. mem.), N.Am. Primary Care Rsch. Group (treas., bd. dirs., exec. dir., 1982-92). Episcopalian. Lodge: Rotary. Home: Wintergreen Rt 1 Box 672 Roseland VA 22967 Office: MCV-VCU Dept Family Practice PO Box 251 Richmond VA 23298-0251

WOOD, NANCY ELIZABETH, psychologist, educator; d. Donald Sterret and Orne Louise (Erwin) W. B.S., Ohio U., 1943, M.A., 1947; Ph.D., Northwestern U., Evanston, Ill., 1952. Prof. Case-Western Res. U., Cleve., 1952-60; specialist, expert Dept. HEW, Washington, 1960-62; chief of research Pub. Health, Washington, 1962-64; prof. U. So. Calif., Los Angeles, 1965—; learning disabilities cons., 1960-70; assoc. dir. Cleve. Hearing and Speech Ctr., 1952-60; dir. licensing program Brit. Nat. Trust, London. Author: Language Disorders, 1964, Language Development, 1970, Verbal Learning, 1975 (monograph) Auditory Disorders, 1978, Levity, 1980, Stoneskipping, 1989, Bird Cage, 1994. Pres. faculty senate U. So. Calif., 1987-88. Recipient Outstanding Faculty award Trojan Fourth Estate, 1982, Pres.' Svc. award U. So. Calif., 1992. Fellow Am. Speech and Hearing Assn. (elected, legis. council 1965-68), Am. Psychol. Assn. (cert.), AAAS; mem. Internat. Assn. of Scientists. Republican. Methodist. Office: U So Calif University Park Los Angeles CA 90089

WOOD, NATHANIEL FAY, editor, writer, public relations consultant; b. Worcester, Mass., June 23, 1919; s. Henry Fletcher and Edith (Fay) W.; m. Eleanor Norton, Dec. 19, 1945; children: Gary Nathaniel, Janet Ann. BS in Journalism, Bus. Adminstrn., Syracuse U., 1946. Editor, writer various publs., various cities, 1946-51; mng. editor Butane-Propane News, L.A., 1951-52; editor Western Metalworking Mag., L.A., 1952-62; western editorial mgr. Penton Pub. Co. Cleve., L.A., 1962-70; editor Orange County Illustrated, Orange County Bus., Newport Beach, Calif., 1970-71; western editor Hitchcock Pub., L.A., 1972-75; co-owner, mgr. Norton-Wood Pub. Rels. Svcs., Pasadena, Calif., 1975—; editorial dir. Security World, SDM and SCA Mags., Culver City, Calif., 1975-80; mgr. trade show Cahners Pub. and Expo Group, L.A., 1979-82; sr. editor Alarm Installer Dealer Mag., L.A., 1982-89; editor CNC West Mag., Westminster and Pasadena, Calif., 1982—. Freelance indsl. writer miscellaneous bus. pubs. Organizer Willkie Presdl. Campaign, Syracuse, N.Y., 1940; advisor various GOP campaigns, L.A., Washington, 1940-96; charter mem. Rep. Nat. Com., 1995, delegate-at-large GOP conv., 1996, mem. Pres.' Club, 1996, 97, convention guest, 1996; nat. adv. bd. Am. Security Coun.; donor L.A. Civic Light Opera and Ctr. Theatre Group; mem., donor L.A. Mus. Art, 1989—; founding mem. Western Heritage Mus., L.A., 1989—; active Met. Opera Guild, Colonial Williamsburg Found., Mus. Natural History L.A. 2nd lt. U.S. Army, 1943-45, PTO. Decorated Purple Heart; recipient Silver, Bronze and Gold medals for Editorial Excellence Gov. of Calif., 1959, 60, 62. Mem. Am. Legion, Am. Film Inst., Scabbard and Blade, L.A. World Affairs Coun., Smithsonian Instn., The Nat. Air and Space Soc., Soc. Profl. Journalists, Alpha Epsilon Rho, Tau Theta Upsilon. Avocations: swimming, boating, travel, photography, gardening. Home and Office: 1430 Tropical Ave Pasadena CA 91107-1623

WOOD, NEIL RODERICK, real estate development company executive; b. Winnipeg, Man., Can., Aug. 22, 1931; s. Reginald and Pearl (Beake) W.; m. Jean Mitchell Hume, Aug. 10, 1957; children: Barbara, David, John, Brian. B.Com., U. Man., 1952; M.B.A., Harvard U., 1955. Asst. mgr. Ont. real estate investment office Gt. West Life Assurance Co., 1955-59; with Cadillac Fairview Corp. Ltd. (and predecessor), Willowdale, Ont., 1959-61, 63-81; exec. v.p. Cadillac Fairview Corp. Ltd. (and predecessor), 1968-71, pres., 1971-81, vice chmn., 1980-81; pres. N.R. Wood Devel. Co. Ltd., 1982—; exec. v.p., dir. Campeau Corp., 1985-86; bd. dirs. Gentra Inc.; bd. govs. Roy Thompson Hall; past pres., trustee Internat. Coun. of Shopping Ctrs. Mem. Toronto Club, Rosedale Golf Club, Craigleith Ski Club, Beaumaris Club, Lost Tree Club, Loxahatchee Golf Club, Beacon Hall Club. Home and Office: RR # 3, Newmarket, ON Canada L3Y 4W1

WOOD, PAUL F., national health agency executive; b. Lockport, N.Y., Dec. 7, 1935; s. Dwight Edward and Frances (Fletcher) W.; m. Kathleen Frances Stretton, May 27, 1958; children: Paul S., Richard F. BA, Western Res. Univ., 1964; MA, Kent State U., 1970; PhD, Case Western Res. U., 1975. Assoc. exec. dir. United Way of Stark County, Canton, Ohio, 1967-70; owner Paul Wood Co., N. Canton, Ohio, 1970-86; dir. devel. The Salvation Army, N.Y.C., 1986-90; pres. Nat. Coun. on Alcoholism and Drug Dependence, Inc., N.Y.C., 1990—. Bd. dirs. Fairfield (Conn.) Chorale, 1991-94, Stepping Stones Found., 1996—, Bedford Hills, N.Y.; fin. com. Westport United Meth. Ch., 1993-96. Avocations: sailing, computer programming. Office: Nat Coun On Alcoholism & Drug Dependence 12 W 21st St New York NY 10010-6902

WOOD, QUENTIN EUGENE, oil company executive; b. Mechanicsburg, Pa., Mar. 5, 1923; s. Lloyd Paul and Greta (Myers) W.; m. Louise Lowe, Apr. 14, 1958. B.S., Pa. State U., 1948. Petroleum engr. Quaker State Oil Refining Corp., Parkersburg, W.Va., 1948-52; chief engr. Quaker State Oil Refining Corp., Bradford, Pa., 1952-55; mgr. prodn. Quaker State Oil Refining Corp., 1955-68; v.p. prodn. Quaker State Oil Refining Corp., Oil City, Pa., 1968-70; exec. v.p. Quaker State Oil Refining Corp., Oil City, 1970-73, pres., chief ops. officer, 1973-75; pres., chief exec. officer Quaker State Oil Refining Corp., 1975-82, chmn., chief executive officer, 1982-88, chmn. bd., 1988-90, dir., 1990-93; bd. dirs. Pa. Mfrs. Ins. Co.; chmn. industry tech. adv. com. U.S. Bur. Mines, 1960-70, Penn Grade Tech. Adv. Com., 1955-69, Pa. Oil and Gas Conservation Commn., 1961-71. Trustee Pa. State U., 1976-94, pres., 1979-87. 1st lt. USAAF, 1943-46. Mem. Am. Inst. Metall. Engrs., Pa. Grade Crude Oil Assn. (dir.), Pa. Oil Producers Assn. (past pres., dir. Bradford dist.), Am. Petroleum Inst. (dir.), Nat. Petroleum Refiners Assn. (dir.). Home: 1402 Spinnakers Reach Dr Ponte Vedra Beach FL 32082-4414 Office: Quaker State Corp Oil Creek Station Box G Oil City PA 16301

WOOD, R. STEWART, bishop; b. Detroit, June 25, 1934; s. Raymond and Marjorie Wood; m. Kristin Lie Miller, June 25, 1955; children: Lisa, Raymond, Michael. AB, Dartmouth Coll., 1956; MDiv, Va. Theol. Seminary, 1969; MA in Counseling and Sociology, Ball State U., 1973; postgrad., Va. Seminary. Ordained to diaconate and priesthood Episc. Ch., 1959. Vicar Episc. Ch., Seymour and Bean Blossom, Ind.; assoc. rector Grace Ch., Muncie, Ind., rector, 1966-70; exec. dir. Episc. Community Svcs., Indpls., 1970-76; rector All Saint's Episc. Ch., Christ Ch., Glendale, Ind., 1976-84, St. John's Ch., Memphis, 1984-88; elected Bishop Coadjutor Diocese Mich., Detroit, 1988-89, diocesan bishop, 1990—; dir. summer camps, conf. ctr.; dep. Gen. Conv. 1970, 73, 76, 82; exec. coun. Coalition for Ordination of Women, bd. dirs. Avocations: camping, golf, tennis, photography, motorcycling. Office: 4800 Woodward Ave Detroit MI 48201-1310

WOOD, RAYMUND FRANCIS, retired librarian; b. London, Nov. 9, 1911; came to U.S., 1924; s. George S. and Ida A. (Lawes) W.; m. Margaret Ann Peed, Feb. 26, 1943; children: Paul George, Gregory Leo, David Joseph. AB, St. Mary's U., Balt., 1931; MA, Gonzaga U., 1939; PhD, UCLA, 1949; MS in Libr. Sci., U. So. Calif., L.A., 1950. Instr. English U. Santa Clara (Calif.), 1939-41; rehab. officer VA, L.A., 1946-48; reference libr. Fresno (Calif.) State Coll., 1950-66; prof. libr. sci. UCLA, L.A., 1966-77, prof. emeritus, 1977—, from asst. dean to assoc. dean Grad. Sch. Libr. & Info. Sci., 1970-77. Author: California's Agua Fria, 1952, Life and Death of

Peter Lebec, 1954, The Saints of the California Landscape, 1987; co-author: Librarian and Laureate: Ina Coolbrith of California, 1973, many others. Vol. driver ARC, Van Nuys, Calif., 1977—; pres. Friends of the Encino/Tarzana Br. Libr., Tarzana, Calif., 1977-80, Jedediah Smith Soc., Stockton, Calif., 1987-90, knight comdr. Order of St. Gregory, 1994. With U.S. Army, 1942-46, ETO. Travel grantee Am. Book Found., 1964, Del Amo Found., 1974. Mem. ALA (book reviewer 1974—), Calif. Libr. Assn. (many offices), Mariposa County Hist. Assn. (life), Oral History Assn. (life), Fresno County Hist. Soc. (editor 1959-66), Westerners L.A. Corral (editor of Brand Book 1982). Democrat. Byzantine Catholic. Avocations: lecturing, writing, reading, traveling. Home: 18052 Rosita St Encino CA 91316-4217

WOOD, RICHARD COURTNEY, library director, educator; b. Spartanburg, S.C., Aug. 8, 1943; s. Herman Alva and Mildred Eloise (Porter) W.; m. Amy Louise Black, Aug. 16, 1974. BA, U. Tex., 1966; MLS, U. S.C., 1977. Head cataloging Wofford Coll. Libr., Spartanburg, 1969-78; hosp. libr. John Peter Smith Hosp., Ft. Worth, 1978-80; reference libr. Tex. Coll. Osteo. Medicine, Ft. Worth, 1980-82, assoc. dir. libr., 1982-91; dir. librs., assoc. prof. Sch. Medicine, chair HCOM dept. Tex. Tech U. Health Scis. Ctr., Lubbock, 1991—; cons. Tarrant County Med. Libr. Assn., Fort Worth, 1978-82, 84, Med. Plaza Hosp., Fort Worth, 1979-82, Grand Prairie (Tex.) Community Hosp., 1980-81, Cook-Fort Worth Children's Hosp., 1988—. Patron Kimball Art Mus. Fort Worth, 1987—; spokesman Neighborhood Assn., Fort Worth, 1989; vis. exec. United Way, Fort Worth, 1990. Mem. Dallas-Tarrant County Consortium (chmn. 1980-81), Metroplex Consortium Health Scis. (chmn. 1980-81), South Cen. Regional Group, Med. Libr. Assn. (chmn. osteo. librs. sect. 1986-87), South Cen. Acad. Med. Librs. (bd. dirs. 1991—, now chair), Nat. Network Librs. Medicine (bd. dirs. South Cen. region 1991-93), Deutsche Gesellschaft für Heereskunde, LIS Users Group (exec. bd.), Sigma Tau Delta. Republican. Presbyterian. Avocations: languages, travel, history, gardening, music. Home: 1805 Bangor Ave Lubbock TX 79416-5518 Office: Libr of Health Scis Tex Tech U Scis Ctr Lubbock TX 79430

WOOD, RICHARD D., JR., retail executive; b. 1938. BS in Commerce, U. Va., 1961; LLB, U. Pa., 1964. With Montgomery McCracken Walker & Rhoads, 1964-68; v.p., counsel Wawa Inc., Media, Pa., 1968-74, exec. v.p., 1974-79, pres., CEO, 1979—. With USMC, 1964-68. Office: Wawa Inc Red Roof 260 W Baltimore Pike Media PA 19063-5620*

WOOD, RICHARD ROBINSON, real estate executive; b. Salem, Mass., Nov. 8, 1922; s. Reginald and Irene Margaret (Robinson) W.; m. Pamela Vander Wiele, Mar. 8, 1951 (div. Apr. 1969); children: Christopher Robinson, Bryant Cornelius, Marcella Wood Mackenzie; m. Jane Philbin, Sept. 19, 1970. AB, Harvard Coll., 1944; postgrad., Mass. Inst. Tech., 1947-48. V.p. Hunneman & Co., Boston, 1959-72; trustee, sec. Mass. Real Estate Investment Trust, Boston, 1967-69; trustee Suffolk Franklin Savings Bank, 1967-74; pres., chmn. Continental Real Estate Equity, Boston, 1972-74; exec. v.p. ITEL Real Estate Corp., San Francisco, 1974-75; v.p. Baird & Warner, Chgo., 1976-80; pres., chmn. Renwood Properties, Inc., Peabody, Mass., 1981—; v.p., dir. Common Goal Capitol Group, Balt., 1986—; gen. ptnr. Common Goal Mortgage Fund, Balt., 1986—; v.p., bd. dirs. St. Katherines Care Ctrs., 1990—; pres., chmn. ILCO Properties, Chgo., 1981-87; mem. Coun. for Rural Housing and Devel., 1988—; trustee 19 Chauncy St. Trust, 1995—, Inst. for Responsible Housing Preservation, 1994—. Mem. Mayor's Citizen Adv. Bd., Boston, 1965-67; pres. Boston Rep. city Com., 1965-67; committeeman, treas. Mass. Rep. State Com., Boston, 1964-72; mem. Coun. for Rural Housing and Devel., 1988—. With Med. Corps U.S. Army, 1943-44. Mem. Nat. Leased Housing Assn., Harvard Club Boston, Longwood Cricket Club, Harvard Club of N.Y. Avocations: tennis, skiing. Home: 19 Chauncy St Cambridge MA 02138-2549 Office: Renwood Properties Inc 100 Corp Pl Ste 403 Peabody MA 01960

WOOD, ROBERT COLDWELL, political scientist; b. St. Louis, Sept. 16, 1923; s. Thomas Frank and Mary (Bradshaw) W.; m. Margaret Byers, Mar. 22, 1952; children—Frances, Margaret, Frank Randolph. AB, Princeton U., 1946; MA, Harvard U., 1947, MPA, 1948, PhD, 1950; LLD or DHL (hon.), St. Bonaventure Coll., U. Pitts., 1965, Bklyn. Poly. Inst., 1966, Princeton U., 1969, Rhode Island Coll., U. Mass., 1970, Worcester Poly. Inst., 1971, U. Maine, 1972, Hokkaido U., Japan, 1975, North Adams Coll., 1977, Boston U., 1978, Stonehill Coll., 1979. Assoc. dir. Fla. Legis. Reference Bur., Tallahassee, 1949-51; mgmt. orgn. expert U.S. Bur. Budget, Washington, 1951-54; lectr. govt. Harvard U., 1953-54, asst. prof., 1954-57; asst. prof. polit. sci. MIT, 1957-59, assoc. prof., 1959-62, prof., 1962-66, head dept., 1965-66, 69-70; undersec. HUD, Washington, 1966-68; sec. HUD, 1969; chmn. Mass. Bay Transp. Authority, Boston, 1969-70; dir. Harvard U.-MIT Joint Center for Urban Studies, Cambridge, 1969-70; pres. U. Mass., 1970-77; supt. Boston Public Schs., 1978-80; prof. U. Mass., Boston, 1981-83; Henry Luce prof. Dem. Instns. and the Social Order Wesleyan U., Middletown, Conn., 1983-93, John E. Andrus prof. govt., 1993; prof. emeritus U. Mass., Boston, 1994—; sr. fellow McCormack Inst. Pub. Affairs, U. Mass., Boston. Author: Suburbia, Its People and Their Politics, 1958, Metropolis Against Itself, 1959, 1400 Governments, The Political Economy of the New York Region, 1960, The Necessary Majority, Middle America and Urban Crisis, 1972, Whatever Possessed the President? Academic Experts and Presidential Policy, 1960-88, 1993; (with others) Schoolmen and Politics, 1962, Government and Politics of the U.S, 1965; author, editor: Remedial Law: When Courts Become Administrators, 1990. Trustee Coll. Bd., 1979-83, Kettering Found., 1971-76; mem. Commn. on Acad. Health Ctrs. and Economy New Eng.; bd. dirs. Lincoln Inst. Land Policy, 1976-80; chmn. Inst. for Resource Mgmt., 1982-84, 20th Century Task Force Fed. Ednl. Policy, 1983, Conn. Gov.'s Coalition on Adult Literacy, 1986-89; mem. Gov.'s Commn. on Quality and Integrated Edn., 1989-90. Served with inf. AUS, World War II, ETO. Decorated Bronze Star; recipient Hubert H. Humphrey award, 1985. Fellow Am. Acad. Arts and Scis., Am. Polit. Sci. Assn. (Career Achievmenet award 1989), Cosmos Club Washington, Phi Beta Kappa.

WOOD, ROBERT EMERSON, pediatrics educator; b. Jacksonville, Fla., Nov. 15, 1942; s. Waldo E. and Verda V. (von Hagen) W. BS in Chemistry magna cum laude, Stetson U., 1963; PhD in Physiology, Vanderbilt U., 1968, MD, 1970. Bd. cert. pediatrics; bd. cert. pediatric pulmonology. Intern in pediatrics Duke U. Med. Ctr., Durham, 1970-71, resident in pediatrics, 1971-72; fellow pediatric pulmonology Case Western Res. U., Cleve., 1974-76, asst. prof. pediatrics, 1976-82, assoc. prof. pediatrics, 1982-83; assoc. prof. pediatrics, chief divsn. pediatric pulmonary medicine Dept. Pediatrics, U. N.C., Chapel Hill, 1983-88, prof. pediatrics, chief divsn. pediatric pulmonary medicine, 1988-94; dir. pediat. ICU, 1984-86, dir. Ctr. Pediat. Bronchology, 1994—, now Stihh Prof. of pediatrics. Mem. editorial bd.: Pediatric Pulmonology, 1992—, Jour. Bronchology, 1993—; contbr. chpts. to books and articles to profl. jours. Lt. comdr. USPHS, 1972-74. Named Grad. fellow Danforth Found., 1963-68, Med. Scientist fellow Life Ins. Med. Rsch. Found., 1965-70, Clin. Rsch. fellow Cystic Fibrosis Found., 1974-76. Mem. Am. Bronchesophagological Assn., Am. Assn. for Bronchology, Soc. for Pediatric Rsch., Am. Thoracic Soc., N.C. Pediatric Soc. Office: U NC CB # 7220 Pediat Pulmonary Medicine Chapel Hill NC 27599-7220

WOOD, ROBERTA SUSAN, foreign service officer; b. Clarksdale, Miss., Oct. 4, 1948; d. Robert Larkin and Dorothy Eloise (Shelton) Wood. BA with distinction, Rhodes Coll., Memphis, 1970; postgrad. Nat. U. Cuyo, Mendoza, Argentina, 1970-71; MPA, Harvard U., 1980. Joined U.S. Fgn. Svc., 1972; svc. in Manila, Philippines, Naples and Turin, Italy, and Port-au-Prince, Haiti; mgmt. analyst Dept. State, Washington, 1980-84; U.S. consul gen., Jakarta, Indonesia, 1984-87, NATO Def. Coll., Rome, 1987-88; U.S. consul gen. Marseilles, France, 1988-91, Montreal, Que., Can., 1991-94; min., dep. chief of mission Am. Embassy, Quito, Ecuador, 1994-95; with U.S. Commn. Immigration Reform, Washington, 1995-96; consul gen. Am. Emassy, Moscow, 1997—. Fulbright scholar, 1970-71. Office: Am Embassy Moscow Psc 77 APO AE 09721-9998

WOOD, ROGER, publishing executive. Pres. Star Mag., Tarrytown, N.Y. Office: Star Mag 660 White Plains Rd Tarrytown NY 10591*

WOOD, RONALD, musician; b. London, June 1, 1947. Owner Woody's on the Beach (nightclub), Miami, 1987—. Guitarist and bassist with Jeff Beck Group, 1966-69, Faces, 1969-75, Rolling Stones, 1975—, New Barbarians, 1979; solo albums include Gimme Some Neck, 1979; albums (with Rolling Stones) Black and Blue, 1976, Love You Live, 1977, Some Girls, 1978, Sucking in the Seventies, 1981, Emotional Rescue, 1979, Tattoo You, 1981, Still Life, 1982, Undercover, 1983, Between the Sheets, 1985, Dirty Work, 1986, Rewind, 1986, Steel Wheels, 1988, Flashpoint, 1991, Voodoo Lounge, 1994 (Grammy award Best Rock Album); (with Faces) Long Player, A Nod's As Good As A Wink..., To a Blind Horse, Ooh-La-La; (with Small Faces) First Step, Ogden's Nut Gone Flake, There Are But Four Small Faces, 1991, All or Nothing, 1992; (solo) I've Got My Own Album To Do, Now Look; films include Let's Spend the Night Together, 1982, Digital Dreams, 1983. Office: Virgin Records 1790 Broadway Fl 6 New York NY 10019-1412*

WOOD, RUTH DIEHM, artist, design consultant; b. Cleve., July 31, 1916; d. Ellis Raymond and Frances Helen (Peshek) Diehm; m. Kenneth Anderson Wood, Sept. 14, 1937. Student, Spencerian Bus. Coll., 1935-36, John Huntington Inst., 1936, Cleve. Inst. Art, 1934-37, 45. Legal sec. Klein, Diehm & Farber, Attys., Cleve., 1936-37; freelance graphic designer Bailey Meter Co., Wickliffe, Ohio, 1967; interior design cons., lectr. One-woman shows include Artist & Craftsmen Assn., Cleve., 1949, Art Colony, Cleve., 1953, Women's City Club, Cleve., 1955, Cleve. Inst. Art Alumni, 1954, Malvina Freedson Gallery, Lakewood, Ohio, 1965, Intown Club, Cleve., 1953, Studio Inn, Painesville, Ohio, 1955, Little Gallery, Chesterland, Ohio, 1961, Hospitality Inn, Willoughby, Ohio, 1965, Coll. Club Cleve., 1965, Lakeland Community Coll., Mentor, Ohio, 1979, Holden Arboretum, Mentor, 1981, Fairmount Fine Arts Ctr., Russell, Ohio, 1992; represented in 12 nat. juried shows, 28 regional and local mus., many pvt. collections. Recipient 1st prize Oil Still Life, Cleve. Mus. Art, 1945, Grumbacher Merit award Lakeland Fla. Internat., 1952, Artistic Achievement award Gates Mills, 1973, numerous other awards; certs. of award in Nyumon and Shoden, Ikenobo Sch. Floral Art, Kyoto, Japan. Mem. Cleve. Inst. Art Alumni, Artists and Craftsmen, Geauga Artists, Women in the Arts. Republican. Mem. Seventh-Day Adventist. Avocations: travel, ikenobo floral art. Home and Studio: Kenwood Designers 11950 Sperry Rd Chesterland OH 44026-2225

WOOD, SAMUEL EUGENE, college administrator, psychology educator; b. Brotherton, Tenn., Aug. 16, 1934; s. Samuel Ernest and Daisy J. (Jernigan) W.; m. Helen J. Walker, June 2, 1956; children: Liane Wood Kelly, Susan Wood Benson, Alan Richard; m. Ellen Rosenthal Green, Sept. 8, 1977; stepchildren: Bart M. Green, Julie Alice Green. BS in English and Music, Tenn. Tech. U., 1961; M in Edn. Adminstrn., U. Fla., 1967, D in Edn., 1969. Asst. prof. edn. W.Va. U., 1968-70; asst. prof. edn. U. Mo., St. Louis, 1970-75, mem. doctoral faculty, 1973-75; dir. rsch. Ednl. Devel. Ctr., Belleville, Ill., 1976-81; prof. psychology Meramec Coll., St. Louis, 1981-94; pres. Higher Edn. Ctr., St. Louis, 1985—; prof. psychology Lindenwood Coll., 1995—; exec. dir. Edn. Opportunity Ctrs., St. Louis, 1985—, Project Talent Search, St. Louis, 1991—; bd. commrs. Pub. TV Com., St. Louis, 1985—; planning com. St. Louis Schs., 1985-90; adminstr. German-Am. student exch. program Internat. Bus. Students, 1985—; sponsor Higher Edn. Ctr. Internat. Edn. Coun., 1985—; co-founder, pres. Higher Edn. Cen. Cable TV Channel, Sta. HEC-TV, St. Louis, 1986; v.p. St. Louis County Cable TV Commn., 1991—. Musician, composer with USN Band, 1956-59; composer A Nautical Musical Comedy, A Child's Garden of Verses in Song, 1979; numerous poems set to music; co-author: (with Ellen Green Wood) (textbook) The World of Psychology, 1993, 2d edit., 1996, Can. edit., 1996; contbr. articles to ednl. and sci. jours. Served with USN, 1955-59. US Office Edn. grantee 1976-81, 85—. Mem. Internat. Edn. Consortium (bd. dirs. 1985-91), Phi Kappa Phi. Democrat. Baptist. Avocations: writing, reading, music composition and performance. Home: 5 Sona Ln Saint Louis MO 63141-7742 Office: Higher Edn Ctr 5 Sona Ln Saint Louis MO 63141-7742

WOOD, SHARON, mountaineer; b. Halifax, N.S., Can., May 18, 1957; d. Stan and Peggy Wood. LLD (hon.), U. Calgary, 1987. Climbed peaks Mt. McKinley (Alaska), Mt. Logan (Can.), Mt. Aconcagua (Argentina), Mt. Makalu (Himalayas), Mt. Everest (Himalayas, 1st N.Am. woman to climb); Can. Light Everest Expedition, 1986; lectr. in field. Recipient Tenzing Norgay Trophy, 1987. Address: 120 McNeil, Canmore, AB Canada T1W 2R8

WOOD, STEPHEN WRAY, educator, legislator, minister, singer, songwriter; b. Winston Salem, N.C., Oct. 6, 1948; s. D.W. and Annie Lee (Harris) W.; m. Starr Smith, June 18, 1978; children: Allyson, Joshua. BTh., John Wesley Coll., 1970; BA, Asbury Coll., 1973; MA, U. N.C., 1979; DMin, Luther Rice Sem., Fla., 1980; MDiv, Houston Grad. Sch. Theology, 1990. Ordained to ministry Soc. of Friends, 1980. Asst. dean, asst. prof. John Wesley Coll., High Point, N.C., 1975-81; min. Soc. of Friends, 1980—; adj. prof. Luther Rice Sem.; assoc. prof. Houston Grad. Sch. Theology; pres. Triad Christian Counseling, Greensboro, 1979. Contbr. articles to hist., ednl. and religious jours., Dictionary of N.C. Biography, Oxford Internat. Roundtable, 1997—; composer, singer religious music. Trustee John Wesley Coll., High Point, 1981—; bd. dirs. Friends Ctr.-Guilford Coll., Greensboro, 1982-89; vice chmn. Guilford County Rep. Party, N.C., 1981-85; mem. N.C. State Ho. Reps., 1985-86, 89-90, 91-92, 93-94, 95-96, 97—, spkr. pro tem, 1997—; chaplain High Point Jaycees. With U.S. Army, 1970-71; capt. N.C. State Militia. Mem. BMI (affiliate songwriter 1978—). Avocations: golf, book collecting, reading. Office: PO Box 5172 High Point NC 27262-5172 *I often reflect upon the maternal advice proffered me as a child, "Steve, if at first you don't succeed, try, try again." We may be down but not out. There is no such thing as the good old days because the future is just as bright as the promises of God. We conquer by continuing.*

WOOD, STUART KEE, retired engineering manager; b. Dallas, Mar. 8, 1925; s. William Henry and Harriet (Kee) Wood; m. Loris V. Poock, May 17, 1951 (dec. June 1990); children: Linda S. Kuehl, Thomas N., Richard D.; m. Lois H. Morton, Nov. 25, 1994. BS in Aero. Engring., Tex. A&M U., 1949. Aircraft sheet metal worker USAF SAC, Kelly Field, San Antonio, Tex., 1942-45; structural design engr. B-52, 367-80, KC-135, 707 Airplanes Boeing, Seattle and Renton, Wash., 1949-55; thrust reverser design engr. 707 and 747 Airplanes Boeing, Renton, 1955-66; supr. thrust reverser group 747 Airplane Boeing, Everett, Wash., 1966-69; supr. rsch. basic engine noise 727 airplane FAA, NASA, 1969-74; supr. jetfoil propulsion Jetfoil Hydrofoil Boeing, Renton, 1974-75; supr. rsch. basic engine performance loss JT9D Pratt & Whitney, 1975-79; supr. propulsion systems 757 Airplane Boeing, Renton, 1979-90; supr., propulsion systems thrust reverser 737, 747, 757, 767 Boeing, Kent, Wash., 1990-94, ret., 1994. Patentee in field. Recipient Ed Wells award AIAA, N.W. chpt., Bellevue, Wash., 1992. Republican. Presbyterian. Avocations: photography, computers, travel. Home: 3831 46th Ave SW Seattle WA 98116-3723

WOOD, THOMAS E., lawyer; b. L.A., Apr. 20, 1939; s. Louis Earl and Youda (Hays) W.; m. Sally Ann, June 22, 1963; children: Julia E. and Melissa H. BA, Amherst Coll., 1961; LLB, U. Pa., 1966. Bar: Pa. 1966. Assoc. Drinker Biddle & Reath, Phila., 1966-72, ptnr., 1972—. Chmn. Easttown Zoning Hearing Bd., Easttown Twp., Pa., 1976—. Mem. Phila. Club. Office: Drinker Biddle & Reath 1000 Westlakes Dr Ste 300 Berwyn PA 19312-2409

WOOD, VIVIAN POATES, mezzo soprano, educator, author; b. Washington, Aug. 19, 1923; d. Harold Poates and Mildred Georgette (Patterson) W.; studies with Walter Anderson, Antioch Coll., 1953-55, Denise Restout, Saint-Leu-La-Fôret, France and Lakeville, Conn., 1960-62, 64-70, Paul A. Pisk, 1968-71, Paul Ulanowsky, N.Y.C., 1958-68, Elemer Nagy, 1965-68, Vyautas Marijosius, 1967-68; MusB Hartt Coll. Music, 1968; postgrad. (fellow) Yale U., 1968; MusM (fellow), Washington U., St. Louis, 1971, PhD (fellow), 1973. Debut in recital series Internat. Jeunesse Musicals Arts Festival, 1953, solo fellowship Boston Symphony Orch., Berkshire Music Ctr., Tanglewood, 1964, St. Louis Symphony Orch., 1969, Washington Orch., 1949, Bach Cantata Series Berkshire Chamber Orch., 1964, Yale Symphony Orch., 1968; appearances in U.S. and European recitals, oratorios, operas, radio and TV, 1953-68; appeared as soloist in Internat. Harpsichord Festival, Westminster Choir Coll., Princeton, N.J., 1973; appeared as soloist in meml. concert, Landowska Ctr., Lakeville, 1969; prof. voice U. So. Miss., Hattiesburg, 1971—, asst. dean Coll. Fine Arts, 1974-76, acting dean, 1976-77; guest prof. Hochschule für Musik, Munich, 1978-79; prof. Italian Internat. Studies Program, Rome, 1986; Miss. coord. Alliance for Arts Edn., Kennedy Ctr. Performing Arts, 1974—; mem. Miss. Gov.'s Adv. Panel for Gifted and Talented Children, 1974—; mem. 1st Miss. Gov.'s Conf. on the Arts, 1974—; bd. dirs. Miss. Opera Assn. Author: Polenc's Songs: An Analysis of Style, 1971. Recipient Young Am. Artists Concert award N.Y.C., 1955; Wanda Landowska fellow, 1968-72. Mem. Miss. Music Tchrs. Assn., Nat. Assn. Tchrs. of Singing, Music Tchrs. Nat. Assn., Am. Musicology Soc., Golden Key, Mu Phi Epsilon, Delta Kappa Gamma, Tau Beta Kappa (hon.), Pi Kappa Lambda. Democrat. Episcopalian. Avocation: sailing. Office: U So Miss Sch Music South Pt # 8264 Hattiesburg MS 39406-9539

WOOD, WAYNE W., state legislator; b. Janesville, Wis., Jan. 21, 1930. Grad. high sch., Stoughton, Wis. Formerly builder, contractor, factory worker; mem. Janesville City Coun., 1972-76, pres., 1974-75; mem. Wis. Ho. of Reps., Madison, 1976—; mem. criminal justice and corrections com., rules com., ways and means com., 1985—, vice chmn., 1989-95, mem. state affairs com., 1987—. Mem. State VTAE Bd., 1975-76; mem. Coun. of State Govts. Legis. Oversight Task Force, 1983, Janesville Housing Authority, 1971-77; former mem. Children's Svc. Soc. Adv. Bd., Rock County Sr. 4-H Coun., Sinnissippi Coun. Boy Scouts Am. Mem. UAW. Home: 2429 Rockport Rd Janesville WI 53545-4445

WOOD, WELLINGTON GIBSON, III, biochemistry educator; b. Balt., Dec. 29, 1945; s. Wellington Gibson Jr. and Elsie Bernice (Johnson) W.; m. Beverly Jean Beaver, Feb. 8, 1969; children: Wellington Gibson IV, Katherine Brittingham. BA, Tex. Tech U., 1971, PhD, 1976. Postdoctoral fellow Syracuse (N.Y.) U., 1976-77; staff scientist Bangor (Maine) Mental Health Inst., 1978-80; evaluation coord. VA Med. Ctr., St. Louis, 1980-89; assoc. dir. for edn. and evaluation VA Med. Ctr., Mpls., 1989—; asst. prof. St. Louis U. Sch. Medicine, 1982-87, assoc. prof., 1987-89; assoc. prof. dept. pharmacology U. Minn. Sch. Medicine, Mpls., 1990-96, prof. dept. pharmacology, 1996—; mem. sci. editorial bd. Alcoholism and Drug Rsch. Comm. Ctr., Austin, Tex., 1990-96; mem. biochemistry, physiology and medicine study sect. NIH-Nat. Inst. Alcohol Abuse and Alcoholism, 1992-96, bd. sci. counselors, 1997—. Assoc. editor Exptl. Aging Rsch., 1977-82; contbr. numerous articles to profl. jours. Nat. Inst. on Alcohol Abuse and Alcoholism postdoctoral fellow, 1976-77; grantee Nat. Inst. on Alcohol Abuse and Alcoholism, 1987—, Nat. Inst. on Aging, 1993—, Dept. Vets. Affairs, 1981—. Mem. Am. Aging Assn. (bd. dirs. 1984-87), Rsch. Soc. on Alcoholism (chmn. membership com. 1988-91), Internat. Soc. for Biomed. Rsch. on Alcoholism, Am. Soc. for Neurochemistry, Internat. Soc. for Neurochemistry. Achievements include development of a new approach to understanding how cholesterol is regulated in brain neuronal membranes; cholesterol was asymmetrically distributed in the two leaflets of the membrane; this uneven distribution of cholesterol may involve the interaction of apolipoprotein E and the low density lipoprotein receptor; cholesterol asymmetry in neuronal membranes of mice deficient in apolipoprotein E and the low density lipoprotein receptor was altered; cholesterol asymmetry was changed in neuronal membranes of alcoholic animals and in membranes of aged animals; maintaining normal membrane cholesterol asymmetry is necessary for protein function and membrane structure and changes in cholesterol asymmetry may contribute to neuronal dysfunction induced by chronic alcohol consumption or advancing age. Home: 16091 Huron Path Lakeville MN 55044-8874 Office: VA Med Ctr GRECC 11G Minneapolis MN 55417

WOOD, WENDY DEBORAH, filmmaker; b. N.Y.C., Oct. 4, 1940; d. John Meyer and Marion Emily (Peters) W.; m. William Dismore Chapple, Dec. 7, 1963; 1 child, Samuel Eliot. BA cum laude, Vassar Coll., 1962; MA, Stanford U., 1964. Teaching asst. Stanford U., 1962-64; photographer, film editor Bristol (Eng.) U., 1964-66, asst. dir. Internat. Conf. Film Schs., 1966; rsch. asst. biology dept. U. Conn., Storrs, 1970-72; sr. media specialist Aetna Life & Casualty Co., Hartford, Conn., 1972-89; media writer, prodr., dir. U. Conn. Ctr. for Media and Tech., Storrs., 1989—; pres. Chapple Films, Inc., 1972—. Films include: Yankee Craftsman, 1972; Alcoholism, Industry's Costly Hangover, 1974; Draggerman's Haul, 1975; Flight Without Wings, 1977; Auto Insurance Affordability (2 awards), 1981; Where Rivers Run to the Sea (award), 1981; Our Town is Burning Down (6 awards), 1982; Wellness at the Worksite, 1984 (4 awards); Welcome to the Aetna Institute, 1985 (4 awards); Aenhance, 1989 (3 awards). Mem. peer rev. com. Conn. Commn. Higher Edn, 1992-96. Recipient CINE Golden Eagle award Council on Internat. Non-theatrical Events, 1972, 76, 84, 1st Place award Indsl. Photography, 1974, cert. Outstanding Creativity U.S. TV Commls. Festival, 1974, EFLA award Am. Film Festival, 1974, 76, Dir's. Choice award Sinking Creek Film Festival, 1975, award Columbus Film Festival, 1975, award Excellence Life Ins. Advtrs. Assn., 1975, Silver Screen award U.S. Indsl. Film Festival, 1976, 81, 1st place award Conn. Film Festival, 1977, 1st prize Nat. Outdoor Travel Film Festival, 1978, 1st pl. Houston Film Festival, 1982, CINE Golden Eagle, 1982, 84, award Am. Film Festival, 1982, N.Y. Film Festival, 1982, 83, Silver CINDY award Assn. Visual Communicators, 1985, others. Bd. dirs. Windham Regional Arts Council, 1987, 88, 89; mem. jury N.Y. Internat. Video and Film Festival. Mem. Info. Film Producers Am. (nat. dir., pres. chpt. 1981-82, Cindy award 1971, 72, 81, 82, 85, 87), Internat. Quorum Motion Picture Producers, Audio Visual Communicators (pres. Conn. chpt. 1985, treas. 1988). Democrat. Quaker. Home: 604 Phoenixville Rd Chaplin CT 06235-2211 Office: U Conn Media Ctr # U-1 Storrs CT 06269

WOOD, WILLIAM BARRY, III, biologist, educator; b. Balt., Feb. 19, 1938; s. William Barry, Jr. and Mary Lee (Hutchins) W.; m. Marie-Elisabeth Renate Hartisch, June 30, 1961; children: Oliver Hartisch, Christopher Barry. A.B., Harvard U., 1959; Ph.D., Stanford U., 1963. Asst. prof. biology Calif. Inst. Tech., Pasadena, 1965-68; assoc. prof. Calif. Inst. Tech., 1968-69, prof. biology, 1970-77; prof. molecular, cellular and developmental biology U. Colo., Boulder, 1977—; chmn. dept. U. Colo., 1978-83; mem. panel for developmental biology NSF, 1970-72; physiol. chemistry study sect. NIH, 1974-78; mem. com. on sci. and public policy Nat. Acad. Scis., 1979-80; mem. NIH Cellular and Molecular Basis of Disease Rev. Com., 1984-88. Author: (with J. H. Wilson, R.M. Benbow, L.E. Hood) Biochemistry: A Problems Approach, 2d edit., 1981, (with L.E. Hood and J.H. Wilson) Molecular Biology of Eucaryotic Cells, 1975, (with L.E. Hood and I.L. Weissman) Immunology, 1978, (with L.E. Hood, I.L. Weissman and J.H. Wilson) Immunology, 2d edit., 1984, (with L.E. Hood and I.L. Weissman) Concepts in Immunology, 1978; editl. rev. bd. Science, 1984-92; mem. editl. bd. Cell, 1984-87, Developmental Biology, 1995—; contbr. articles to profl. jours. Recipient U.S. Steel Molecular Biology award, 1969; NIH Rsch. grantee, 1965—, Merit awardee, 1986-96; Guggenheim fellow, 1975-76. Fellow AAAS; mem. Nat. Acad. Scis., Am. Acad. Arts and Scis., Am. Soc. for Cell Biology, Genetics Soc. Am. Soc. for Developmental Biology, Soc. Nematology. Office: Dept MCD Biology Box 347 U Colorado Boulder CO 80309

WOOD, WILLIAM JEROME, lawyer; b. Indpls., Feb. 14, 1928; s. Joseph Gilmore and Anne Cecilia (Morris) W.; m. Joann Janet Jones, Jan. 23, 1954; children: Steven, Matthew, Kathleen, Michael, Joseph, James, Julie, David. Student, Butler U., 1945-46; AB with honors, Ind. U., 1950, JD with distinction, 1952. Bar: Ind. bar 1952. Mem. firm Wood, Tuohy, Gleason, Mercer & Herrin (and predecessor), Indpls., 1952—; bd. dirs. Grain Dealers Mut. Ins. Co., Indpls., Am. Income Life Ins. Co., Waco, Tex.; gen. counsel Ind. Cath. Conf.; city atty., Indpls., 1959-60; instr. Ind. U. Sch. Law, 1960-62. Author: Indiana Pastors' Legal Handbook, 2nd edit., 1992, Realtors' Indiana Legal Handbook, 2d edit., 1991. Mem. Ind. Corp. Survey Commn., 1963—, chmn., 1977-86; mem. Ind. Corp. Law Study Commn., 1985-87; mem. Ind. Non Profit Corp. Law Study Commn., 1989-91; past bd. dirs. Alcoholic Rehab. Center, Indpls., Indpls. Lawyers' Commn., Community Svc. Coun. Indpls. Served with AUS, 1946-48. Recipient Brotherhood award Ind. region NCCJ, 1973. Mem. Ind. Bar Assn. (award 1968, sec. 1977-78), Indpls. Bar Assn. (pres. 1972-73, coun. bd. mgrs. 1992-93), Indpls. Bar Found., St. Thomas More Legal Soc. (pres. 1970), Indpl. Lit. Club (pres. 1973-74), Am. Legion. Democrat. Roman Catholic. Home: 3619 E 75th Pl Indianapolis IN 46240-3674 Office: 3400 Bank One Ctr Tower Indianapolis IN 46204-5134

WOOD, WILLIAM MCBRAYER, lawyer; b. Greenville, S.C., Jan. 27, 1942; s. Oliver Gillan and Grace (McBrayer) W.; m. Nancy Cooper, 1973 (dec. 1993); children: Walter, Lewis; m. Jeanette Dobson Haney, June 25, 1994. BS in Acctg., U. S.C., 1964, JD cum laude, 1972; LLM in Estate

Planning (scholar), U. Miami, 1980. Bar: S.C. 1972, Fla. 1979, D.C. 1973, U.S. Tax Ct. 1972, U.S. Ct. Claims 1972, U.S. Supreme Ct. 1977. Intern ct. of claims sect., tax div. U.S. Dept. Justice, 1971; law clk. to chief judge U.S. Ct. Claims, Washington, 1972-74; ptnr. firm Edwards Wood, Duggan & Reese, Greer and Greenville, 1974-78; asst. prof. law Cumberland Law Sch., Samford U., Birmingham, Ala., 1978-79; faculty Nat. Inst. Trial Advocacy: N.E. Regional Inst., 1979, 83-90, 95—, Fla. Regional Inst., 1989; teaching team 5th intensive trial techniques course Hofstra U., 1983; assoc. then capital ptnr. firm Shutts & Bowen, Miami, 1980-85; sole practice, Miami, 1985—, also Rock Hill, S.C., 1994—. Contbg. editor: The Lawyers PC; Fla. editor: Drafting Wills and Trust Agreements; substantive com. editor ABA: The Tax Lawyer, 1983—. Pres. Piedmont Heritage Fund., Inc. 1975-78; del. State Rep. Conv., 1985, 1987, 90; exec. committeeman Dade County Republicans, 1988-94, co-gen. counsel, 1990-91; apptd. Dade County Indsl. Devel. Authority, 1990-94; mem. vestry Episc. Ch., 1993-94. With USAF, 1965-69, Vietnam. Decorated Air Force Commendation medal; recipient Am. Jurisprudence award in real propery and tax I, 1971; winner Grand prize So. Living Mag. travel photo contest, 1969. Mem. ABA (taxation sect., teaching law com., 1994—), Greer C. of C. (pres. 1977, Outstanding leadership award 1976), Greater Greenville C. of C. (dir. 1977), Order Wig and Robe, Estate Planning Council South Fla., Omicron Delta Kappa. Club: Bankers (bd. govs. 1989—). Lodge: Masons, Rotary. Office: 5345 Wilgrove Mint Hill Rd Charlotte NC 28227-3467

WOOD, WILLIAM RANSOM, retired university president, city official, corporate executive; b. nr. Jacksonville, Ill., Feb. 3, 1907; s. William James and Elizabeth (Ransom) W.; m. Margaret Osborne, 1930 (dec. 1942); 1 son, William Osborne (dec. 1978); m. Dorothy Jane Irving, Mar. 18, 1944; children: Mark Irving, Karen Jane Parrish. A.B., Ill. Coll., 1927, LL.D., 1960; M.A., U. Iowa, 1936, Ph.D., 1939; LLD, U. Alaska, 1989. Tchr., coach pubs. schs. Mich., Iowa, Ill., 1928-46; asst. Supt. Evanston Twp. Schs., Ill., 1948-50; specialist jr. colls. and lower divs. U.S. Office Edn., 1950-53, program planning officer, 1953; dean statewide devel. higher edn. U. Nev., 1954-55, acting chmn. dept. English, 1955-56, acad. v.p., 1955-60, acting pres., 1958-60; pres. U. Alaska, 1960-73; mayor Fairbanks, Alaska, 1978-80; pres. Pacific Alaska Assocs., Ltd.; exec. v.p. Fairbanks Indsl. Devel. Corp., Festival Fairbanks '84; mem. staff study needs and resources higher edn. FAO, Libya, 1955; mem. study group off-duty ednl. program armed forces in Europe, U.S. Dept. Def., 1955; del. Am. Assembly Rgn. Rels., 1957-58; chmn. Nev. com. Fulbright scholarships, 1957-58; mem. chancellor's panel SUNY; mem. sci. group traveling to Antarctica, New Zealand, Australia; presenter sesquicentennial address Sigma Pi Literary Soc. of Ill. Coll., 1993. Editor: Looking Ahead, 1953, From Here On, 1954, All Around the Land, 1954, Youth and The World, 1955, To Be an American, 1957; author, editor: On Your Own, 1953; co-editor: Short Stories as You Like Them, 1940, Youth Thinks It Through, 1941, Just for Sport, 1943, Fact and Opinion, 1945, Short Stories, 1951, Study of Financing of Higher Education in Asia, 1968; author (verse): Not From Stone, 1983, Legacy of Dreams, 1993. Chmn. Alaska Am. Cancer Soc.; v.p. Alaska council Boy Scouts Am.; mem. bd. Rampart Dam adv. com.; mem. Gen. Med. Scis. Nat. Adv. Council, Alaska Higher Edn. Facilities Commn., 1967, Alaska Small Bus. Adv. Council, 1968, Satellite Communications Task Force; spl. asst. to mayor for trade and devel., Fairbanks North Star borough, 1984—; chmn. Greater Fairbanks Community Hosp. Found.; mem. White House Fellows Selection Panel, Nat. Adv. Council on Edn. Professions Devel.; chmn. Alaska Heart Assn.; mem. Alaskan Command Civilian Adv. Bd., 1962—; bd. dirs. U. Alaska Found., exec. dir. Fest. Fairbanks '84, 1981—. Served to lt. USNR, 1943-46; capt. USNR, ret. 1968. Recipient Outstanding Alaskan award, 1984, Alaskan of Yr. award, 1985, Centennial award Alexis de Tocqueville Soc., 1987, Disting. Citizen award Alaska coun. Boy Scouts Am., 1992; named to Ill. Coll. Athletic Hall of Fame, 1993, laureate Alaska Bus. Hall of Fame, 1996. Fellow Arctic Inst. N. Am.; mem. Am. Geog. Soc., Assn. Higher Edn. (exec. com.), Nat. Univ. Extension Assn., N.W. Assn. Secondary and Higher Schs., Western Assn. Colls., Navy League, AAAS, Assn. Applied Solar Energy (adv. council 1959), Am. Assn. Land-grant Colls. and State Univs., Internat. Assn. Univ. Presidents (exec. com.). Methodist. Clubs: Explorers, Fairbanks Petroleum, Washington Athletic. Lodge: Rotary (gov. dist. 503 1985-86). Home: 665 10th Ave Apt 305 Fairbanks AK 99701-4664

WOOD, WILLIS BOWNE, JR., utility holding company executive; b. Kansas City, Mo., Sept. 15, 1934; s. Willis Bowne Sr. and Mina (Henderson) W.; m. Dixie Gravel, Aug. 31, 1955; children: Bradley, William, Josh. BS in Petroleum Engring., U. Tulsa, 1957; grad. advanced mgmt. program, Harvard U., 1983; JD (hon.), Pepperdine U., 1996. With So. Calif. Gas Co., L.A., 1960-74, from v.p. to sr. v.p., 1975-80, exec. v.p., 1983-84; pres., CEO Pacific Lighting Gas Supply Co., L.A., 1981-83; from sr. v.p. to chmn., pres., CEO Pacific Enterprises, L.A., 1984-93, chmn., CEO, 1993—; bd. dirs. Gt. Western Fin. Corp., Gt. Western Bank, L.A.; dir. Automobile Club So. Calif.; trustee U. So. Calif.; bd. visitors Rand Grad. Sch. Trustee, vice-chmn. Harvey Mudd Coll., Claremont, Calif., 1984—; trustee, past chmn. Calif. Med. Ctr. Found., L.A., 1983—, past chmn.; trustee, past pres. S.W. Mus., L.A., 1983—; bd. dirs. L.A. World Affairs Coun.; dir., past chmn. bus. coun. for Sustainable Energy Future, 1994—; dir. Pacific Coun. for Internat. Affairs. Recipient Disting. Alumni U. Tulsa, 1995. Mem. Soc. Petroleum Energy Engrs., Am. Gas Assn., Pacific Coast Gas Assn. (past bd. dirs.), Pacific Energy Assn., Calif. Bus. Roundtable, Calif. State C. of C. (bd. dirs.), Nat. Assn. of Mfrs. (bd. dirs.), Hacienda Golf CLub, Ctr. Club, Calif. Club. Republican. Office: Pacific Enterprises 633 E 5th St Ste 5400 Los Angeles CA 90013-2109

WOODALL, DAVID MONROE, research engineer, dean; b. Perryville, Ark., Aug. 2, 1945; m. Linda Carol Page, June 6, 1966; 1 child, Zachary Page. B.A., Hendrix Coll., 1967; M.S., Columbia U., 1968; Ph.D., Cornell U., 1974. Registered profl. engr., Idaho, N.Mex. Nuclear engr. Westinghouse Corp., Pitts., 1968-70; asst. prof. U. Rochester, N.Y., 1974-77; asst. prof. U. N.Mex., Albuquerque, 1977-79, assoc. prof., 1979-83, prof., 1984-86, chair dept., 1980-83; group physics mgr. Idaho Nat. Engring. Lab., Idaho Falls, 1986-92; assoc. dean, dir. rsch. U. Idaho, 1992—; cons. to govt. Contbr. articles to sci. jours. Grantee NSF, DOE, AFOSR, Office Naval Research, others. Mem. IEEE, Am. Phys. Soc., Am. Nuclear Soc. (chpt. chair 1982-83), Am. Soc. for Engring. Edn. (divsn. chair 1983, 85). Office: Univ Idaho Engring Expt Station Coll Engring Moscow ID 83844-1011

WOODALL, GILBERT EARL, JR., medical administrator; b. Oak Ridge, Tenn., Dec. 21, 1954; m. Sarah Lee Blackburn, Sept., 1989; children: John Sage, Anna Alleen. BA, U. Tenn., 1976; MD, U. Tenn., Memphis, 1977; MS in Pub. Health, Western Ky. U., 1986. Med. dir. GM-Corvette Plant, Bowling Green, Ky., 1982-92, Alliant-Health at Work, Louisville, 1993-94, Jackson Madison-County Gen. Hosp.-Occupl. Medicine, Jackson, Tenn., 1995—. Mem. Mayor's Commn. on Employment and Disability Issues, Bowling Green, 1991, Meharry Med. Sch. Occupational Medicine Residency Adv. Bd., Nashville, 1987-88. Lt. comdr. USNR, 1978-82. Fellow Am. Coll. Occupational and Environ. Medicine (bd. dirs. 1987-90), Am. Coll. Preventive Medicine; mem. Tenn. Med. Assn. Avocation: computer science. Office: JMCGH-Occupational Medicine 708 W Forest Ave Jackson TN 38301-3901

WOODALL, JACK DAVID, manufacturing company executive; b. Ferndale, Mich., Aug. 1, 1936; s. William John and Florence Gladys (Feyen) W.; m. Janice Tracy Lanier, July 6, 1958; children: David Lanier, Kevin Langford, Elizabeth Tracy, Matthew Thomas. BS in Bus., Stetson U., 1958; MS in Internat. Affairs, George Washington U., 1969. Commd. 2d lt. U.S. Army, 1958, advanced through grades to lt. gen., 1989; comdr. 1st Brigade, 2d Inf. Div., Camp Casey, Republic of Korea, 1978-79; chief officer distbn. Mil. Pers. Ctr., Alexandria, Va., 1979-81, dir. plans and ops., 1981-82; chief plans and policy Allied Forces So. Europe, Naples, Italy, 1982-84; asst. div. comdr. 4th Inf. Div., Colorado Springs, Colo., 1984-86; comdg. gen. Berlin Brigade, 1986-87; dep. comdg. gen. V Corps, Frankfurt, Fed. Republic Germany, 1987-88; comdg. gen. 2d Inf. Div., Camp Casey, Korea, 1988-89, U.S. Army Japan, IX Corps, Camp Zama, 1989-92; pres. Innovative Tech., Brooksville, Fla., 1992—. V.p. West Pacific Girl Scouts Japan, Republic of Korea, The Philippines, 1989-92, Far East coun. Boy Scouts Am., 1990-92; v.p. Econ. Devel. Commn. Hernando County. Recipient Disting. Alumni award Stetson Alumni Assn., 1985, numerous mil. awards. Mem. Assn. U.S. Army (chpt. pres. 1986-88), Greater Hernando County C. of C. (dir.), Barnett Banks of the Sun Coast (dir.). Avocation: jogging.

WOODALL, JIM S., hospital administrator; b. Lumberton, N.C., Dec. 10, 1950; s. Julian Snelling and Margaret Jean (Daniel) W.; m. Angela Faye Lanier, Nov. 6, 1982; children: Angela Renee, Jimmie Daniel. BS in Biology, N.C. State U., 1972; MPH in Health Adminstrn., U. N.C., 1976; postgrad. studies Planning and Policy, Duke U., 1984; postgrad. studies Prins. of Leadership, Covey Leadership Ctr., 1994. Pesticide epidemiologist N.C. State Bd. of Health, Raleigh, 1972-77; mental health program analyst N.C. Dept. Human Resources, Raleigh, 1977-78, asst. dir. budget and analysis, 1978-81, dir. budget and analysis, 1981-86; dir. Caswell Ctr., Kinston, N.C., 1986—; chmn. Kinston Airport Commn., 1995-97. Mem. mental health adv. bd. Lenoir C.C., Kinston, 1988-94; program coord., instr. Leadership N.C., Greensboro, 1995-97; bd. dirs. Lenoir-Greene Partnership for Children, Kinston, 1997. Mem. Kinston Rotary Club (pres. 1992-93, Paul Harris fellow 1993), Lenoir County C. of C. (pres. 1996). Democrat. Baptist. Avocations: hunting, camping, flying. Office: Caswell Ctr 2415 W Vernon Ave Kinston NC 28504-3337

WOODALL, LEE, professional football player; b. Carlisle, Pa., Oct. 31, 1969. Student, U. Pa. Linebacker San Francisco 49'ers, 1994—. Selected to Pro Bowl, 1994. Achievements include member of San Francisco 49'ers Super Bowl XXIX Champions, 1994. Office: San Francisco 49'ers 4949 Centennial Blvd Santa Clara CA 95054-1229*

WOODALL, SAMUEL ROY, JR., trade association executive; b. July 8, 1936; s. Samuel Roy W.; m. Jane Marvin Brock, Aug. 5, 1958; children—Samuel Roy III, Lawrence B., Claiborne A., George G. B.A., U. Ky., 1958, LL.B., 1962; postgrad. (Woodrow Wilson fellow), Yale U., 1959. Bar: Ky. bar 1962. Atty. Ky. Dept. Ins., 1962-64, gen. counsel, 1965-66; commr. ins. Commonwealth Ky., 1966-68; assoc. firm Wyatt, Grafton and Sloss, Louisville, 1968-69; ptnr. Wyatt, Grafton and Sloss, 1969-72; pres. Western Pioneer Life Ins. Co. (and predecessors), Louisville, 1972-76; asst. to pres. Am. Life & Accident Ins. Co., Louisville, 1976-80; pres. Nat. Assn. Life Cos., Washington, 1980-93; v.p. and chief counsel state rels. Am. Coun. Life Ins., Washington, 1993—; guest instr. ins. law U. Louisville, 1968-69. Note editor: U. Ky. Law Rev, 1961-62. Pres. Citizen's Met. Planning Council, Louisville, 1970-71; chmn. City of Louisville Riverfront Commn., 1970-75, Ky. Heritage Commn., 1964-77; bd. dirs. Bingham Child Guidance Clinic, Louisville, 1969-76, Youth Performing Arts Council, 1979-80. Recipient Sullivan medallion U. Ky., 1958; named 1 of Ky.'s 3 Outstanding Young Men Ky. Jr. C. of C., 1968. Mem. ABA, Ky. Bar Assn., D.C. Bar Assn., Fedn. Ins. Counsel, Phi Beta Kappa, Phi Alpha Delta (pres. chpt. 1961-62). Home: 2851 29th St NW Washington DC 20008-4111 Office: Am Coun Life Ins 1001 Pennsylvania Ave NW Washington DC 20004-2505

WOODALL, WILLIAM LEON, retired insurance executive; b. Kirby, Ark., July 29, 1923; s. Ocie Doan and Hazel Cornelia (Paslay) W.; m. Patricia Ann Reese, Sept. 30, 1950; children: Michael Reese, David William, Stacy Ann. BS, Miami U., Oxford, Ohio, 1947. CPCU. Home office underwriter Ohio Casualty Group Ins. Cos., Hamilton, 1947-52, underwriter Mpls. br. office, 1952-53, field rep., Des Moines, 1953-54, underwriter Detroit br. office, 1962-64, mgr. Indpls. br. office, 1964-68, company v.p., Hamilton, 1968-77, sr. v.p., 1977-84, exec. v.p., sec., 1984-88, pres., chief oper. officer, 1988-91, also bd. dirs.; ptnr. Cady Ins. Agy., Burlington, Iowa, 1954-62. Republican. Methodist. Lodge: Elks. Home: 910 Macewen Dr Osprey FL 34229-9293

WOODARD, ALVA ABE, business consultant; b. Roy, N.Mex., June 28, 1928; s. Joseph Benjamin and Emma Lurania (Watkins) W.; m. Esther Josepha Kaufmann, Apr. 5, 1947 (div. Sept. 1991); children: Nannette, Gregory, Loreen, Arne, Mark, Kevin, Steven, Curtis, Marlee, Julie, Michelle; m. Margaret Adele Evenson, Oct. 1, 1994. Student, Kinman Bus. U., 1948-49, Whitworth Coll., 1956, Wash. State U., 1953-54. Sec.-treas., dir. Green Top Dairy Farms, Inc., Clarkston, Wash., 1948-52; v.p., treas., sec., dir. ASC Industries, Inc. (subs. Gifford-Hill and Co.), Spokane, Wash., 1953-75; dir. Guenther Irrigation, Inc., Pasco, Wash., 1966-71; mng. dir. Irrigation Rental, Inc., Pasco, 1968-75, Rain Chief Irrigation Co., Grand Island, Nebr., 1968-75; sec., dir. Keeling Supply Co., Little Rock, 1969-72; pres., dir. Renters, Inc., Salt Lake City, 1971-75, Woodard Western Corp., Spokane, 1976-86, Woodard Industries, Inc., Auburn, Wash., 1987-90; cons. Woodard Assocs., Spokane, Wash., 1985—; pres., dir. TFI Industries, Inc., Post Falls, Idaho, 1989-90; v.p., sec., treas., dir. Trans-Force, Inc., Post Falls, 1989-90, TFI Computer Scis., Inc., Post Falls, 1989-90. Newman Lake (Wash.) Rep. precinct committeeman, 1964-80; Spokane County del. Wash. Rep. Conv., 1968-80. Mem. Adminstrv. Mgmt. Soc. (bd. dirs. 1966-68), Optimists. Avocations: fishing, theater, golf, reading, dancing. Home and Office: 921 E 39th Ave Spokane WA 99203-3034

WOODARD, CAROL JANE, educational consultant; b. Buffalo, Jan. 19, 1929; d. Harold August and Violet Maybelle (Landsittel) Young; m. Ralph Arthur Woodard, Aug. 19, 1950; children: Camaron Jane, Carsen Jane, Cooper Ralph. BA, Hartwick Coll., 1950; MA, Syracuse U., 1952; PhD, SUNY, Buffalo, 1972; LHD (hon.), Hartwick Coll., 1991; postgrad., Bank St. Coll., Harvard U. Cert. tchr., N.Y. State. Tchr. Orchard Park, N.Y., 1950-51, Danville, Ind., 1951-52, Akron, N.Y., 1952-54; dir. Garden Nursery Sch., Williamsville, N.Y., 1955-65; tchr. Amherst (N.Y.) Coop. Nursery Sch., 1967-69; asst. prof. early childhood edn. SUNY, Buffalo, 1969-72; lab. demonstration tchr. and student teaching supr. SUNY, 1969-76, assoc. prof., 1972-79, prof., 1979-88, prof. emeritus, 1988—; co-dir. Consultants in Early Childhood, 1988—; cons. Lutheran Ch. Am., Villa Maria Coll., Buffalo Pub. Schs., Buffalo Mus. Sci., Headstart Tng. Programs, Erie Community Coll., N.Y. State Dept. Edn., numerous workshops.; cons. sch. systems, indsl. firms, pubs., civic orgns. in child devel.; vis. prof. The Netherlands and East China Univ., Shanghai, People's Republic of China; sci. trainer The Wright Group, 1995. Author 7 books for young children, 2 textbooks in field; co-author: Physical Science in Early Childhood, 1987; co-author nat. curriculum for ch. sch. for 3-yr.-olds; author: (booklet) You Can Help Your Baby Learn; author/coord. TAKE CARE child protection project, 1987; contbr. chpts. to books, articles to profl. jours. Trustee Hartwick Coll., Oneonta, N.Y., 1978-87; cons. EPIC Birth to Three Program, 1992; design cons. indoor playground Noah's Ark Jewish Ctr., Buffalo, 1992; Sites Project coord. Buffalo Pub. Schs., 1994—; student tchg. supr. SUNY, Fredonia, 1994—. Mem. Nat. Assn. Edn. Young Children, Early Childhood Edn. Council Western N.Y., Assn. Childhood Edn. Internat., Phi Delta Kappa, Pi Lambda Theta. Home: 1776 Sweet Rd East Aurora NY 14052-3028

WOODARD, CLARA VERONICA, nursing home official; b. Bayonne, N.J.; d. William George and Lula (Langston) Yelverton; m. John Henry Woodard; children: John Michael, Stephen Jay. Grad., Bayonne Hosp. Sch. Nursing, 1951, Manhattan Sch. Radiology, 1953, NYU-Bellevue Med. Ctr., 1955, Valencia Community Coll., Orlando, Fla. RN, N.J., Fla. Head nurse Bayonne Hosp., 1949-50; office nurse Dr. D.G. Morris, Bayonne, 1951-52; pvt. duty nurse Christ Hosp and Bayonne Hosp., 1954-58; tchr. kindergarten, Nuremburg, Fed. Republic Germany, 1972-73; ICU-CCU nurse Holy Spirit Hosp., Camp Hill, Pa., 1973-74; head nurse Orlando Gen. Hosp., 1974-76, house supr., 1976-78; dir. nurses Winter Park (Fla.) Care Ctr., 1980-83; Medicare coord. Pinar Terrace Manor, Orlando, 1987-92, clin. instr., 1992—, house supr., nurse mgr. Alzheimer unit, 1993—; instr. Valencia Coll., Orlando, Fla. Named Employee of Yr. and Employee of Month, Orlando Gen. Hosp., 1980, Employee of Month, Winter Park Care Ctr., 1983. Mem. NAFE, Nat. League Negro Women. Democrat. Roman Catholic. Avocations: poetry, short stories, public speaking, theology. Home: 2931 De Brocy Way Winter Park FL 32792-4505 Office: Pinar Terrace Manor 7950 Lake Underhill Rd Orlando FL 32822-8229

WOODARD, HAROLD RAYMOND, lawyer; b. Orient, Iowa, Mar. 13, 1911; s. Abram Sylvanus and Grace Lenora (Brown) W.; m. Clara F. Jarrell, Apr. 30, 1986; stepchildren: Walter J., Turner J., Laurel C. BS, Harvard U., 1933, LLB, 1936. Bar: Ind. 1936. Pvt. practice with firm and predecessor Woodard, Emhardt, Naughton, Moriarty & McNett, Indpls., 1936—; lawyer, 1936-46; ptnr. Woodard, Emhardt, Naughton, Moriarty & McNett, Indpls., 1950—; adj. prof. patent law Sch. Law Ind. U., Indpls., 1957-88. Lt. sr. grade USNR, 1942-46. Named Sagamore of the Wabash, Gov. of Ind., 1991. Fellow Am. Coll. Trial Lawyers; mem. ABA, Ind. 7th Cir. Bar Assn. (past pres.), Am. Patent Law Assn., Young Lawyers Assn. Indpls. (past pres.), Ind. U. Sch. Law-Indpls. Alumni Assn. (1st hon. mem.), Columbia Club (past pres.), Woodstock Club (past pres.), Univ. Club (past pres.), 100 Club (past pres.). Methodist. Office: Woodard Emhardt Naughton Moriarty & McNett 3700 Bank One Tower Indianapolis IN 46204-5137

WOODARD, JOHN ROGER, urologist; b. Hawkinsville, Ga., Dec. 18, 1932; s. John Alton and Mary Louise (Williams) W.; m. Inga Lou Harper, Sept. 3, 1955; children: John Roger, Susan, Stephen, Honor. Student, Emory U., Atlanta, 1950-53; M.D., Med. Coll. Ga., Augusta, 1957. Diplomate: Am. Bd. Urology. Intern in surgery Med. Coll. Va., 1957-58, resident in surgery, 1958-59; resident in urology N.Y. Hosp.-Cornell Med. Center, 1959-63; postgrad. fellow in pediatric urology Great Ormand St. Hosp. for Sick Children, London, 1963-64; instr. surgery, surgeon to outpatients N.Y. Hosp.-Cornell Med. Center, 1964; asso. in surgery Emory U., 1964-68; asso. prof. surgery U. Ala. Med. Center, 1968-69; prof. urol. surgery, dir. pediatric urology Emory U., 1969—; chief urology Henrietta Egleston Hosp. for Children., 1970—; numerous vis. professorships. Contbr. articles to sci. jours., chpts. to med. textbooks. Fellow ACS (bd. govs. 1986-92), Am. Acad. Pediatrics (chmn. urology sect. 1987-88); mem. AMA, Med. Assn. Atlanta (bd. dirs. 1986-89), Med. Assn. Ga., Soc. Pediatric Urology, Am. Urol. Assn., Am. Assn. Gen. Urol. Surgeons, Soc. Pediatric Urol. Surgeons, Nat. Urol. Forum, Cherokee Town and Country Club. Home: 10 Prescott Walk Atlanta GA 30307 Office: 1901 Century Blvd NE Ste 14 Atlanta GA 30345-3300

WOODARD, LARRY L., college official; b. Lebanon, Oreg., Apr. 16, 1936; s. Hugh Frank and Ima Ellen (Bilyeu) W.; m. Bette Jeanette Brown, Aug. 10, 1956; children: Perry, Craig, Stacy. BS in Forestry, Oreg. State U., 1957. Forester Bur. of Land Mgmt., Oreg., 1957-69, Washington, 1969-72; dist. mgr. Bur. of Land Mgmt., Coeur d'Alene, Idaho, 1972-76; assoc. state dir. Bur. of Land Mgmt., Boise, Idaho, 1976-78, Santa Fe, 1978-82, Boise, 1982-86; state dir. Bur. of Land Mgmt., Santa Fe, 1987-93; dir. devel. Boise Bible Coll., 1993—. Author: A to Z, The Biography of Arthur Zimmerman, 1988, Before the First Wave, 1994. Bd. dirs. Boise Bible Coll., 1977-87; trustee N.Mex. Nature Conservancy, 1987-90. Recipient Disting. Svc. award U.S. Dept. Interior, 1986, Sec.'s Stewardship award U.S. Dept. Interior, 1989, Pres.'s Meritorious Exec. award, 1991. Republican. Avocations: teaching history, writing, hunting, gardening. Home: PO Box 365 Meridian ID 83680-0365 Office: Boise Bible Coll 8695 Marigold St Boise ID 83714-1220

WOODARD, NINA ELIZABETH, banker; b. L.A., Apr. 3, 1947; d. Alexander Rhodes and Harriette Jane (Power) Mathews; divorced; children: Regina M., James D. Grad. Pacific Coast Banking Sch., 1987; BS in mgmt., Calif. Coast U., 1993; postgrad., Ctr. for Creative Leadership, 1994. Lifetime cert. sr. profl. in human resources. Dental asst. Donald R. Shire DDS, L.A., 1965-66; with Security Pacific Nat. Bank, Marina Del Rey, Calif., 1968-69; with First Interstate Bank, Casper, Wyo., 1971—, adminstr. asst. personnel, 1975-78, asst. v.p., asst. mgr. pers., 1978-82, v.p., dir. mktg. and pers., 1982-84, v.p., mgr. human resources, 1984-88; v.p., mgr. employee rels. First Interstate Bank Ltd., L.A., 1988-93, v.p. mgr. employee rels. Americas Region, Standard Charter Bank, 1993—, sr. v.p., 1995; instr. mktg. Am. Inst. Banking, 1983, Casper Coll., 1982. Mem. Civil Svc. Commn., City of Casper, 1983-88; bd. dirs. YMCA, 1984-87, Downtown Devel. Assn.; pres. Downtown Casper Assn. Named Bus. Woman of Yr., Bus. and Profl. Women, 1982, Young Career Woman, 1975. Mem. Nat. Assn. Bank Women, Bus. and Profl. Women (dist. dir.), Am. Soc. Pers. Adminstrn. (regional v.p., state coun. Wyo. 1987-88), Pers. and Indsl. Rels. Assn. (chmn. govt. affairs com. 1989-90, Fast Track award 1991, Pres.'s Achievement award 1993, conf. chmn. 1991, 92, dist. vice chair 1992, dist. chair 1993, 2d v.p. 1994), Fin. Women Internat. (Wyo. state chair 1986, regional edn. and tng. chair 1987, dist. coord. L.A. 1993, L.A. group chair 1994), Soc. Human Resource Mgmt. (area I v.p. 1996), St. Patrick's Parish Religious Edn. (instr. 1991-92, parish coun. 1993-94). Republican. Roman Catholic.

WOODBRIDGE, HENSLEY CHARLES, retired foreign languages educator, librarian; b. Champaign, Ill., Feb. 6, 1923; s. Dudley Warner and Ruby Belle (Mendenhall) W.; m. Annie Emma Smith, Aug. 28, 1953; 1 dau., Ruby Susan Woodbridge Jung. A.B., Coll. William and Mary, 1943; M.A., Harvard, 1946; Ph.D., U. Ill., 1950, M.S. in L.S, 1951; student, U. Nacional de Mexico, summer 1941, 45; D.Arts, Lincoln Meml. U., 1976. Corr. Worldover Press, Mexico, 1945; instr. French and Spanish U. Richmond, 1946-47; teaching asst. U. Ill., 1948-50; reference librarian Ala. Poly. Inst., 1951-53; librarian Murray (Ky.) State Coll., 1953-65; Latin-Am. bibliographer, asso. prof. fin. langs. So. Ill. U., Carbondale, 1965-71, prof., 1971-93, prof. emeritus, 1993—. Author: (with Paul Olson) Tentative Bibliography of Ibero-Romance Linguistics, 1952, Jesse Stuart: a bibliography, 1960, (with Gerald Moser) Rubén Darío y el Cojo ilustrado, 1964, (with John London and George Tweney) Jack London: a bibliography, 1966, rev. edit., 1973, Jesse Stuart and Jane Stuart: a bibliography, 1969, rev. edit., 1979, Rubén Darío: A selective critical bibliography, 1975, Rubén Darío: una bibliografía selectiva, clasificada y anotada, 1975, Benito Pérez Galdós: A selective annotated bibliography, 1975, (with David Zubatsky) Pablo Neruda: An Annotated Bibliography of Biographical and Critical Studies, 1988; co-author: Printing in Colonial Spanish America, 1976; editor Ky. Library Assn. Bull, 1959-60, Ky. Folklore Record, 1963-64, Am. Assn. Tchrs. Spanish and Portuguese-Scarecrow Press Bibliographical Series; contbg. editor: Am. Book Collector, 1965-73; assoc. editor: Hispania, 1967-81; editor, pub.: Jack London Newsletter, 1967-91; mem. editorial bd.: Modern Lang. Jour, 1971-73, Hispanic Linguistics, 1983—; co-editor: (with Dan Newberry) Basic List of Latin American Materials in Spanish, Portuguese and French, 1975; co-compiler: (with Annie Woodbridge) The Collected Short Stories of Mary Johnston, 1982, Spanish and Spanish American Literature: An Annotated Guide to Selected Bibliographies, 1983, Guide to Reference Works for the Study of the Spanish Language and Literature, 1987, 97; contbr. to: Ency. Info. and Library Scis., vol. 36, Cambridge History of Latin American Literature. Mem. Ky. Folklore Soc., Medieval Soc. Am., Cervantes Soc. Am., MLA, Am. Assn. Tchrs. Spanish and Portuguese, Bibiog. Soc. Am., Ky. Hist. Soc., Instituto de estudios madrileños, Asociación española de bibliografía, Hispanic Soc. Am. (corr.). Club: Filson. Home: 1804 W Freeman St Carbondale IL 62901-2106

WOODBRIDGE, JOHN MARSHALL, architect, urban planner; b. N.Y.C., Jan. 26, 1929; s. Frederick James and Catherine (Baldwin) W.; m. Sally Byrne, Aug. 14, 1954; children: Lawrence F., Pamela B., Diana B.; m. Carolyn Kizer, Apr. 8, 1975. B.A. magna cum laude, Amherst Coll., 1951; M.F.A. in Architecture, Princeton U., 1956. Designer John Funk, architect, San Francisco, 1957-58; designer, asso. partner Skidmore, Owings & Merrill, San Francisco, 1959-73; staff dir. Pres.'s Adv. Council and Pres.'s Temporary Commn. on Pennsylvania Ave., Washington, 1963-65; exec. dir. Pennsylvania Ave. Devel. Corp., Washington, 1973-77; lectr. architecture U. Calif., Berkeley; vis. prof. U. Oreg., Washington U., St. Louis. Co-author: Buildings of the Bay Area, 1960, A Guide to Architecture in San Francisco and Northern California, 1973, Architecture San Francisco, 1982, San Francisco Architecture, 1992. Chmn. Commn. on Architecture Episc. Ch. Recipient Fed. Design Achievement award Nat. Endowment for Arts, 1988; Fulbright scholar to France, 1951-52. Fellow AIA; mem. Nat. Trust Historic Preservation, Soc. Archtl. Historians, Phi Beta Kappa. Democrat. Episcopalian. Home and Office: 19772 8th St E Sonoma CA 95476-3803

WOODBURN, RALPH ROBERT, JR., lawyer; b. Haverhill, Mass., Nov. 3, 1946; s. Ralph Robert and Josephine Marie (McClure) W.; m. Janet M. Smith, Sept. 15, 1985. BA, Mich. State U., 1967; JD, Harvard U., 1972; LLM, Boston U., 1981. Bar: Mass. 1972, U.S. Tax Ct. 1987. Assoc. Bowers, Fortier & Lakin, Boston, 1972-76; ptnr., assoc. Haussermann, Davison & Shattuck, Boston, 1976-83; ptnr. Palmer & Dodge, Boston, 1983—; tchr. Harvard Ctr. for Lifelong Learning, Cambridge, Mass., 1986-89; chmn. Wellesley Cable Access Bd., 1993-95. Contbr. articles to Boston Bar Jour. and Estate Planning. Treas. Exeter Assn. of New Eng., Boston, 1985-89, v.p., 1989-91, pres., 1991-93. Fellow Am. Coll. Trust and Estate Counsel; mem. ABA, Boston Bar Assn. (chmn. probate legislation 1983-93), Brae Burn Country Club (Newton, Mass.), Harvard Club of Boston, Boston Probate and Estate Planning Forum (program chair 1996-97). Home: 25 Cypress Rd Wellesley MA 02181-2918 Office: Palmer & Dodge 1 Beacon St Boston MA 02108-3107

WOODBURY, ALAN TENNEY, lawyer; b. Milw., July 7, 1943; s. Isaiah Tenney and Maxine Arvilla (Hooper) W.; m. Deborah Carson Eayre, Jan.

27, 1968; children: Jeffrey Tenney, Alison Eayre. BA, Bowdoin Coll., 1965; JD, Temple U., 1968. Bar: Pa. 1968; CLU, ChFC. Atty. Fidelity Mut. Life Ins. Co., Phila., 1968-74, assoc. counsel, 1974-76, asst. v.p., assoc. counsel, 1976-78, 2nd v.p., assoc. counsel, 1978-79, 2nd v.p., sec., assoc. counsel, 1979-84; v.p., sec., assoc. counsel Fidelity Mut. Life Ins. Co., Radnor, Pa., 1984-91, sr. v.p., sec., gen. counsel, 1991-93, sr. v.p. ins. coun., 1994—. Mem. ABA, Phila. Bar Assn., Assn. Life Ins. Counsel. Republican. Office: Fidelity Mut Life Ins Co 250 King Of Prussia Rd Wayne PA 19087-5220

WOODBURY, LAEL JAY, theater educator; b. Fairview, Idaho, July 3, 1927; s. Raymond A. and Wanda (Dawson) W.; m. Margaret Lillian Swenson, Dec. 19, 1949; children: Carolyn Inez (Mrs. Donald Hancock), Shannon Margaret (Mrs. Michael J. Busenbark), Jordan Ray, Lexon Dan. BS, Utah State U., 1952; MA, Brigham Young U., 1953; PhD (Univ. fellow), U. Ill., 1954. Teaching asst. U. Ill., 1953; assoc. prof. Brigham Young U., 1954-61; guest prof. Colo. State Coll., 1962; asst. prof. Bowling Green State U., 1961-62; asso. prof. U. Iowa, 1962-65; producer Ledges Playhouse, Lansing, Mich., 1963-65; prof. speech and dramatics, chmn. dept. Brigham Young U., 1966-70, assoc. dean Coll. Fine Arts and Communications, 1969-73, dean Coll. Fine Arts and Communications, 1973-82; vis. lectr. abroad; bd. dirs. Eagle Systems Internat.; bd. dir. workshop Fedn. for Asian Cultural Promotion, Republic of China; dir. European study tour. Author: Play Production Handbook, 1959, Mormon Arts, vol. 1, 1972, Mosaic Theatre, 1976, also articles, original dramas; profl. actor PBS and feature films. Chmn. gen. bd. drama com. Young Men's Mut. Improvement Assn., 1958-61; bd. dirs. Repertory Dance Theatre; bd. dirs., chmn. ctrl. Utah ARC; chmn. Utah Alliance for Arts Edn.; mem. adv. coun. Utah Arts Festival; missionary LDS Ch., N.Y.C., 1994. With USN, 1942-46. Recipient Creative Arts award Brigham Young U., 1971, Disting. Alumni award, 1975, Tchr. of Yr. award, 1988, Excellence in Rsch. award, 1992, Disting. Svc. award, 1992. Mem. Rocky Mountain Theatre Conf. (past pres.), Am. Theatre Assn. (chmn. nat. com. royalties 1972—, mem. fin. com. 1982—), NW Assn. Univs. and Colls. (accrediting officer), Am. Theatre Assn. (v.p. Univ. and Coll. Theatre Assn.), Theta Alpha Phi, Phi Kappa Phi. Home: 1303 Locust Ln Provo UT 84604-3651

WOODBURY, MARION A., insurance company executive; b. Wilmington, N.C., 1923; m. Alice Battey Bryson; children—Sheldon, Marion A., Frank, Spencer, Alice. Student, U. N.C., 1949; LLB, Woodrow Wilson Coll., 1956. With exec. tng. program Chubb and Son, N.Y.C., 1949; asst. to pres. Bankers Fire & Marine Ins. Co., 1957, exec. v.p. to pres., 1958; v.p. Reins. Corp. of N.Y., 1959-62, exec. v.p., 1962-65, pres., 1965—, also bd. dirs.; chmn. bd., chief exec. officer, dir. United Reins. Corp. N.Y.; bd. dirs. Piedmont Mgmt. Co., Inc., Navigators Ins. Co., POHJOLA A. Ins. Corp.; trustee Coll. of Ins., 1970-75. Served with C.E. U.S. Army, 1945, PTO. Decorated Bronze Star; recipient Good Scout award Greater N.Y. Council Boy Scouts Am., 1977. Mem. Reins. Assn. Am. (chmn. 1974-75, bd. dirs.), U.S. Srs. Golf Assn. Clubs: Wall St. (gov.); Baltrusol Golf. Home: 14 Delegal Rd The Landings Savannah GA 31411 Office: Reins Corp NY 80 Maiden Ln New York NY 10038-4811

WOODBURY, MAX ATKIN, polymath, educator; b. St. George, Utah, Apr. 30, 1917; s. Angus Munn and Grace (Atkin) W.; m. Lida Gottsch, May 30, 1947; children—Carolyn, Max TenEyck, Christopher, Gregory. B.S., U. Utah, 1939; M.S., U. Mich., 1941, Ph.D., 1948; M.P.H., U. N.C., Chapel Hill, 1977. Mem. faculty U. Mich., 1947-49; mem. Inst. for Adv. Study, Princeton, N.J., 1949-50; mem. faculty Princeton U., 1950-52, U. Pa., 1952-54; prin. investigator logistics research project Office Naval Research, George Washington U., 1954-56; faculty NYU, 1956-65; prof. computer sci. Duke U., prof. biomath. Med. Ctr., 1966-88, sr. fellow Ctr. for Study of Aging and Human Devel., 1975—, sr. fellow, sr. scientist Ctr. Demographic Studies, 1985—, prof. emeritus, 1987—; pres. Biomed. Information-processing Orgn., 1961-62, Inst. for Biomed. Computer Research, 1961-71; cons. WHO, UNIVAC, CBS on computer election forecasts, 1952-62, sci. orgns., univs., govt. agys., corps. Contbr. articles to profl. jours. Served with USAAF, 1941-46, MTO. USPHS, NIH grantee, also other govt. agys., 1947—; recipient MERIT award Nat. Inst. on Aging, NIH, June 1, 1988-May 31, 1998. Fellow AAAS, Am. Statis. Assn., Inst. Math. Statistics; mem. numerous sci., profl. socs., Phi Beta Kappa, Sigma Xi, Phi Kappa Phi (inventor of GoM methodology). Home: 4008 Bristol Rd Durham NC 27707-5403 Office: Duke U Ctr Demographics 2117 Campus Dr Durham NC 27708-0408

WOODBURY, RICHARD BENJAMIN, anthropologist, educator; b. West Lafayette, Ind., May 16, 1917; s. Charles Goodrich and Marion (Benjamin) W.; m. Nathalie Ferris Sampson, Sept. 18, 1948. Student, Oberlin Coll., 1934-36; BS in Anthropology cum laude, Harvard U., 1939, MA, 1942, PhD, 1949; postgrad., Columbia U., 1939-40. Archeol. research Ariz., 1938, 39, Fla., 1940, Guatemala, 1947-49, El Morro Nat. Monument, N.Mex., 1953-56, Tehuacan, Mex., 1964; archaeologist United Fruit Co. Zaculeu Project, Guatemala, 1947-50; assoc. prof. anthropology U. Ky., 1950-52, Columbia U., 1952-58; rsch. assoc. prof. anthropology interdisciplinary arid lands program U. Ariz., 1959-63; curator archeology and anthropology U.S. Nat. Mus., Smithsonian Instn., Washington, 1963-69, acting. head office anthropology, 1965-66, chmn. office anthropology, 1966-67; prof., chmn. dept. anthropology U. Mass., Amherst, 1969-73; prof. U. Mass., 1973-81, prof. emeritus, 1981—, acting assoc. provost, dean grad. sch., 1973-74; mem. divsn. anthropology and psychology NRC, 1954-57; bd. dirs. Archaeol. Conservancy, 1979-84, Valley Health Plan, Amherst, 1981-84, Mus. of No. Ariz., 1983-90; liason rep. for Smithsonian Instn., Com. for Recovery of Archeol. Remains, 1965-69; assoc. seminar on ecol. systems and cultural evolution Columbia U., 1964-73; mem. exec. com. bd. dirs. Human Relations Area Files, Inc., New Haven, Conn., 1968-70; cons. Conn. Hist. Commn., 1970-72. Author (with A.S. Trik) The Ruins of Zaculeu, Guatemala, 2 vols., 1953, Prehistoric Stone Implements of Northeastern Arizona, 1954, Alfred V. Kidder, 1973, Sixty Years of Southwestern Archaeology, 1993; editor: (with I.A. Sanders) Societies Around the World (2 vols.), 1953, (with others) The Excavation of Hawikuh, 1966, Am. Antiquity, 1954-58, Abstracts of New World Archaeology; editor-in-chief: Am. Anthropologist, 1975-78; mem. editorial bd.: Am. Jour. Archeology, 1957-72. Mem. sch. com., Shutesbury, Mass., 1979-82; chmn. finance com. Friends of Amherst Stray Animals, 1983-85, trustee, 1991—. With USAF, 1942-45. Fellow Mus. No. Ariz., 1985. Fellow AAAS (coun. rep. Am. Anthrop. Assn. 1961-63, com. on desert and arid zones rsch. Southwest and Rocky Mountains divsn. 1958-64, vice-chair 1962-64, com. arid lands 1969-74, sec. 1970-72), Am. Anthrop. Assn. (exec. bd. 1963-66, A.V. Kidder award 1989), Archeol. Inst. Am. (exec. com. 1965-67); mem. Soc. Am. Archeology (treas. 1953-54, pres. 1958-59, chmn. fin. com. 1987-89, Fiftieth Anniversary award 1985, Disting. Svc. award 1988), Ariz. Archeol. and Hist. Soc., Archeol. Conservancy (life), Sigma Xi. Office: U Mass Dept Anthropology Machmer Hall Amherst MA 01003

WOODBURY, STEPHEN ABBOTT, economics educator; b. Beverly, Mass., Oct. 25, 1952; s. Stephen E. and Barbara (Sandberg) W.; m. Susan Pozo, May 29, 1982 (div. June 1992); 1 child, Ricardo Pozo; m. Virginia Baldwin, Dec. 7, 1996. AB, Middlebury (Vt.) Coll., 1975; MS, U. Wis., 1977, PhD, 1981. Asst. prof. of econs. Pa. State U., University Park, 1979-82; asst. prof. of econs. Mich. State U., East Lansing, 1982-88, assoc. prof. econs., 1988-94; prof. econs., 1994—; sr. economist W.E. Upjohn Inst., Kalamazoo, Mich., 1984—; dep. dir. Fed. Adv. Coun. on Unemployment Compensation, Washington, 1993-94, cons., 1994-96; cons. U. Hawaii/State of Hawaii, Honolulu, 1991-96, State of Mich. Task Force, Lansing, 1989-90, U.S. Dept. Labor, Washington, 1988, European Communities Commn., Brussels, 1987-88; vis. prof. U. Stirling, Scotland, 1992; vis. scholar Fed. Res. Bd., Washington, 1992. Author: Tax Treatment of Benefits, 1991; (with others) Access to Health Care, 1992; editor Rsch. in Employment Policy; contbr. articles to profl. jours. Recipient Rsch. grants William H. Donner Found., 1991, U.S. Dept. Health and Human Svcs., 1985, U.S. Dept. Labor, 1995, Filene Rsch. Inst., 1996, Ctr. Credit Union Rsch., U. Wis., 1997. Mem. Am. Econ. Assn., Am. Statis. Assn., Assn. for Evolutionary Econs., Econometric Soc., Indsl. Rels. Rsch. Assn., Midwest Econs. Assn. (1st v.p. 1993-94, pres.-elect 1998—), Ea. Econ. Assn., Soc. Labor Economists, Am. Law and Econs. Assn., Ctr. for Credit Union Rsch.-U. Wisc., 1997. Office: Dept Econs Marshall Hall Mich State U East Lansing MI 48824 also: WE Upjohn Inst 300 S Westnedge Ave Kalamazoo MI 49007-4630

WOODCOCK, DAVID GEOFFREY, architect, educator; b. Manchester, Eng., May 28, 1937; s. Herbert Edwin and Constance Mary (Bristol) W.; m. Kathleen Mary Bishop, Oct. 1, 1960 (dec. 1964); 1 child, Jonathan Alfred; m. Valerie Frances Gubbins, July 4, 1964; children: Frances Mary, Penelope Jane. BA with 1st class honors in Architecture, U. Manchester, 1960, D in Town Planning, 1966. Chartered architect, U.K.; registered architect, Tex. Lectr. U. Manchester, 1961; asst. prof. Tex. A&M U., College Station, 1962-66, assoc. prof., 1970-76, prof., 1976—; sr. lectr. Kent. Inst. Art & Design, Canterbury, England, 1966-70; pvt. practice, College Station, 1980—, Canterbury, 1966-70. Bd. dirs. Opera and Performing Arts Soc. Tex. A&M U., 1980-83, 88-91, pres., 1993-94, adv. bd. Hammons Sch. Architecture Drury Coll., Mo., 1990-93, Savannah (Ga.) Coll. Arts and Design/Architecture, 1987-93; active Episc. Diocese Tex. Archtl. Commn., 1987—. Recipient Rsch. Excellence award Tex. Hist. Commn., 1991, Romieniec award for archtl. edn. Tex. Sch. Architecture, 1995. Fellow AIA; mem. Royal Inst. Brit. Architecture, Assn. for Preservation Tech. Internat. bd. dirs. 1990—), Nat. Coun. for Preservation Edn. (bd. dirs.), Assn. Collegiate Schs. Architecture (regional dir. 1981-84, Disting. Prof. 1991). Avocations: drawing, creative and gifted education, choral singing. Office: Tex A&M U Dept Architecture College Station TX 77843-3137

WOODCOCK, JANET, federal official; b. Washington, Pa., Aug. 29, 1948; d. John and Frances (Crocker) W.; m. Roger Henry Miller, Nov. 16, 1981; children: Kathleen Miller, Susanne Miller. BS cum laude, Bucknell U., 1970; MD, Northwestern U., Chgo., 1977. Diplomate Am. Bd. Internal Medicine. Intern Hershey Med. Ctr./Pa. State U., 1977-78, resident in internal medicine, 1978-80, chief resident in medicine, 1980-81; fellow in rheumatology U. Calif./VA Med. Ctr., San Francisco, 1982-84; instr. medicine divsn. rheumatology and immunology VA Med. Ctr., San Francisco, 1984-85; med. officer divsn. biol. investigational new drugs Ctr. for Biologics Evaluation and Rsch./FDA, Rockville, Md., 1986-87, group leader divsn. biol. investigational new drugs, 1987-88, dep. dir. divsn. biol. investigational new drugs, 1988, dir. divsn. biol. investigational new drugs, 1988-90; dir. Ctr. for Drug Evaluation and Rsch./FDA, Rockville, Md., 1994—; acting dep. dir. Ctr. for Biologics Evaluation and Rsch., FDA, Rockville, Md., 1990-92, dir. office of therapeutics rsch. and rev., 1992-94; dir. Ctr. for Drug Evaluation and Rsch., FDA, Rockville, 1994—; instr. medicine, asst. prof. divsn. gen. internal medicine Hershey Med. Ctr./Pa. State U., 1981; analytical chemist rsch. divsn. A.B. Dick Co., Niles, Ill., 1971-73. Nat. Merit scholar Bucknell U., 1966, Pa. State scholar, 1966; Rsch. fellow Am. Rheumatism Assn.; VA Investigator grantee, 1985. Mem. Alpha Omega Alpha, Alpha Lambda Delta. Office: Dept Health & Human Svc Center Drug Evaluation & Rsch 5600 Fishers Ln Bldg Hfd-001 Rockville MD 20857-0001

WOODCOCK, JOHN ALDEN, lawyer; b. Bangor, Maine, July 6, 1950; s. John Alden Woodcock and Joan (Carlin) Nestler; m. Beverly Ann Newcombe, July 14, 1973; children: John A., Patrick C., Christopher C. AB, Bowdoin Coll., 1972; MA, U. London, 1973; JD, U. Maine, 1976. Bar: Maine 1976, U.S. Dist. Ct. Maine 1976. Assoc. Stearns, Finnegan & Needham, Bangor, 1976-80; asst. dist. atty. Penobscot County, Bangor, 1977-78; ptnr. Mitchell & Stearns, Bangor, 1980-91, Weatherbee, Woodcock, Burlock & Woodcock, Bangor, 1991—. Mem. alumni coun. Bowdoin Coll., Brunswick, Maine, 1992—, pres., 1995-96, trustee, 1996—; bd. dirs. Ea. Maine Med. Ctr., Bangor, 1980—, chmn, 1996—, Ea. Maine Healthcare, Bangor, 1989—. Master Ballou Inn of Ct.; mem. ABA, Maine State Bar Assn., Penobscot County Bar Assn. Home: 110 Main Rd N Hampden ME 04444-1404 Office: Weatherbee Woodcock Burlock & Woodcock 136 Broadway Bangor ME 04401-5206

WOODCOCK, LEONARD, humanities educator, former ambassador; b. Providence, Feb. 15, 1911; s. Ernest and Margaret (Freel) W.; m. Sharon Lee Tuohy, Apr. 14, 1978; children—Leslie, Janet, John. Ed., St. Wilfred's Coll.; student, Wayne State U., 1928-30, Walsh Inst. Accountancy, Detroit, 1928-30; numerous hon. degrees. Staff rep. internat. union UAW, 1940-46, adminstrv. asst. to pres., 1946-47, regional dir., 1947-55, internat. v.p., 1955-70, pres., 1970-77, pres. emeritus, 1977—; chief of mission with rank of amb. U.S. Liaison Office, Peking, 1977-79; amb. to People's Republic of China, 1979-81; adj. prof. U. Mich., 1981—; bd. dirs. ATC Internat. Inc., Houston, Nat. Commn. U.S. China Rels.; dynamometer operator Continental Aviation & Engring. Co., 1947. Bd. govs. emeritus Wayne State U., 1970. Mem. Am.-China Soc. (bd. dirs.). Home: 2404 Vinewood Blvd Ann Arbor MI 48104-2768

WOODCOCK, RICHARD BEVERLEY, health facility administrator; b. Leeds, Yorkshire, Eng., June 7, 1945; arrived in Can., 1948; s. Stanley Walter and Jessica Stretton (Coyne) W.; children: Matthew, Christopher, Jeffrey, Lindsay. Honors BA in Bus. Adminstrn., Waterloo (Ont.) Luth. U., 1970. Cert. hosp. adminstr. Dir. fin. Northwestern Gen. Hosp., Toronto, 1973-76; asso. adminstr. Brantford Gen. Hosp., Ont., 1976-81, pres., 1982—; sec., treas. Brantford Gen. Hosp. Found., 1977—. Fellow Am. Coll. Healthcare Execs., Can. Coll. Health Svc. Execs., Rotary (bd. dirs. Brantford chpt. 1981-84, Paul Harris fellow Rotary Internat.). Avocations: alpine skiing, boating. Office: Brantford Gen Hosp, 200 Terrace Hill St, Brantford, ON Canada N3R 1G9

WOODDELL, PHILO GLENN, fine arts educator, radio broadcaster and producer; b. Hutchinson, Kans., Sept. 3, 1941; s. Philo Davis and Jean Elise Wooddell. B of Music Edn., Southwestern Coll., Winfield, Kans., 1963; MM, Crane Sch. Music, Potsdam, N.Y., 1985; MA, NYU, 1989. Cert. in music and speech edn., N.Y. Tchr., chmn. fine arts/humanities dept. Jeffersonville (N.Y.)-Youngsville Ctrl. Sch. Dist. 1, 1965—; local host N.P.R.'s Morning Edit., WJFF-FM, prodr., host Sunday Brunch, Music of the Cinema, Music of the Stage; mem. programming and adv. bds. Radio Catskill, also pres. bd. trustees, 1991-92, v.p. bd. trustees, 1993; film music moderator Universal City, Calif.; clinician on film music N.Y. State Music Educators Assn., N.Y.C.; music and media clinician Western Heritage Mus., Glendale/Burbank, Calif.; mem. adv. com. Cities as Sch. Bldg. Leadership Team; media clinician Tisch Sch. of the Arts, N.Y.C., 1994; film music moderator UCLA, 1995; film music conf. presenter USC, L.A., 1996. Dir. profl. and semi-profl. prodns. for dinner, proscenium, exptl. and children's theatre; performed with Central City (Colo.) Opera Assn., Kansas City Starlight Theatre, Dallas Summer Musicals, N.P.R. Playhouse; shows at various Catskill resorts; vocalist with Phila. Orch., Saratoga Performing Arts Ctr., Saratoga Springs, N.Y.; voice over/narration experience; editor The Collegian; film music moderator Lowe's Theatre, N.Y.C., 1997; contbr. articles to profl. jours. Founder Sullivan County (N.Y.) Help Line; founder, bd. dirs. Sullivan County Festival of the Arts Program. Mem. Am. Guild of Variety Artists, Music Educators Nat. Conf., Am. Choral Dirs. Assn., Am. Film Inst. (charter), Arts Alliance Assn., Arts in Edn. Assn., N.Y. State United Tchrs., Sullivan County Dramatic Workshop, N.Y. State Music Educators Assn., Soc. for Preservation of Film Music, Lions Club Internat., Phi Mu Alpha Sinfonia. Home: 50 Durr Rd # 88 Jeffersonville NY 12748-0088 Office: Sta WJFF-Radio Catskill PO Box 797 Jeffersonville NY 12748-0797

WOODE, MOSES KWAMENA ANNAN, scientist, medical and chemistry educator; b. Takoradi, Ghana, June 27, 1947; came to U.S., 1981; s. Emmanuel Kwamena and Georgina Aba (Arthur) W.; m. Eunice Adjaottor, Aug. 24, 1974; children: Linda-Marie, Timothy. BS in Chemistry and Math., U. Ghana, Legon, Accra, 1971, BS in Chemistry with honors, 1972, MS in Chemistry; PhD in Chem. Crystallography, Sch. Tech. and Medicine, London, 1978. Assoc. prof. med. edn. and chemistry U. Va., Charlottesville, 1986-93, dir. Assisting Students Achieve Med. Degrees, 1987—, asst. dean, acad. support, 1988-91, assoc. dean acad. support and strategic programs, 1992—, rsch. assoc. prof. chemistry, assoc. prof. ob-gyn., 1986-93, prof. med. edn., ob-gyn. rsch. prof. chemistry, 1993—. Contbr. articles to profl. jours. Grantee NIH, 1987—, Robert Wood Johnson Found., 1988—, U.S. Dept. HHS, 1990—. Fellow Am. Inst. Chemists; mem. APHA, ACA, Am. Crystallographic Assn., Sigma Xi. Achievements include design of academic enrichment programs at high school, college and medical school levels; contribution to understanding of structure-function relationships of biologically important molecules and liquid crystals. Office: U Va Sch Medicine PO Box 446 Charlottesville VA 22902-0446

WOODEN, JOHN ROBERT, former basketball coach; b. Martinsville, Ind., Oct. 14, 1910; s. Joshua Hugh and Roxie (Rothrock) W.; m. Nellie C. Riley, Aug. 8, 1932; children: Nancy Anne, James Hugh. B.S., Purdue U., 1932; M.S., Ind. State U., 1947. Athletic dir., basketball and baseball coach Ind. State Tchrs. Coll., 1946-48; head basketball coach UCLA, 1948-75; lectr. to colls., coaches, business. Author: Practical Modern Basketball, 1966, They Call Me Coach, 1972; Contbr. articles to profl. jours. Served to lt. USNR, 1943-46. Named All-Am. basketball player Purdue U., 1930-32, Coll. Basketball Player of Yr., 1932, to All-Time All-Am. Team Helms Athletic Found., 1943, Nat. Basketball Hall of Fame, Springfield (Mass.) Coll., as player, 1960, as coach, 1970, Ind. State Baksetball Hall of Fame, 1962, Calif. Father of Yr., 1964, 75, Coach of Yr. U.S. Basketball Writers Assn., 1964, 67, 69, 70, 72, 73, Sportsman of Yr. Sports Illustrated, 1973, GTE Acad. All-Am., 1994; recipient Whitney Young award Urban League, 1973, 1st ann. Velvet Covered Brick award Layman's Leadership Inst., 1974, 1st ann. Dr. James Naismith Peachbasket award, 1974, medal of excellence Bellarmine Coll., 1985, Sportslike Pathfinder award to Hoosier with extraordinary svc. on behalf of Am. youth, 1993, GET All Am. Acad. Hall of Fame, 1994, 40 for the Age award Sports Illustrated, 1994, the 1st Frank G. Wells Disney award for role model to youth, 1995, Disting. Am. award Pres. Reagan, 1995, Svc. to Mankind award Lexington Theol. Sem., 1995, NCAA Theodore Roosevelt Sportsman award, 1995. *I have tried to live the philosophy of my personal definition of success which I formulated in the middle thirties shortly after I entered the teaching profession. Not being satisfied that success was merely the accumulation of material possessions or the attainment of a position of power or prestige, I chose to define success as "peace of mind which can be attained only through the self-satisfaction that comes from knowing you did your best to become the best that you are capable of becoming.".*

WOODFORD, ARTHUR MACKINNON, library director, historian; b. Detroit, Nov. 23, 1940; s. Frank Bury and Mary-Kirk (MacKinnon) W.; children: Mark, Amy; m. Reneé Ann Skuba, Apr. 25, 1990; stepchildren: Brandon, Christopher. Student, U. Wis., 1958-60; BA in History, Wayne State U., 1963; AM in LS, U. Mich., 1964. Libr. Detroit Pub. Libr., 1964-74; asst. dir. Grosse Pointe (Mich.) Pub. Libr., 1974-77; dir. St. Clair Shores (Mich.) Pub. Libr., 1977—. Author: All Our Yesterdays, 1969, Detroit and Its Banks, 1974, Detroit: American Urban Renaissance, 1979, Charting The Inland Seas, 1991, Tonnancour, 1994, vol. 2, 1996. With USNR, 1958-64. Mem. Mich. Libr. Assn. (v.p. 1988-89), Gt. Lakes Maritime Inst., Prismatic Club Detroit (pres. 1982), Algonquin Club (treas. 1983-93). Methodist. Avocations: tennis, bridge, reading, model shipbuilding. Home: 22401 Lakeland St Saint Clair Shores MI 48081-2323 Office: Saint Clair Shores Pub Libr 22500 E 11 Mile Rd Saint Clair Shores MI 48081-1307

WOODHOUSE, BERNARD LAWRENCE, pharmacologist, educator; b. Norfolk, Va., Aug. 14, 1936; s. Bernard L. and Marsha Ruth (Blakeney) W., June 6, 1964; children: Donna Anita, Bernadette LaVonne, Dawn Marie. BS, Howard U., 1958, MS, 1963, PhD, 1973. Instr. A&T Coll. of N.C., Greensboro, 1963-64; instr. Savannah (Ga.) State Coll., 1964-70, asst. prof., 1970-73, assoc. prof., 1973-79, prof., 1979—, dir. biology rsch. grants, 1976—, chmn. animal and welfare com., 1976-81. Mem. Savannah (Ga.) Guardsmen, sec., 1989. Grantee NIH, 1975-80, 80-87, Hoffman-La Roche, Inc., Nutley, N.J., 1976-85, 85-90. Mem. Ga. Acad. of Sci., Drug Enforcement Adminstrn, Beta Beta Beta. Democrat. Methodist. Avocation: reading. Home: 12437 Largo Dr Savannah GA 31419-2056 Office: Savannah State Coll PO Box 20353 Savannah GA 31404-9716

WOODHOUSE, DERRICK FERGUS, ophthalmologist; b. Sutton, Surrey, U.K., May 29, 1927; s. Sydney Carver and Erica (Ferguson) W.; m. Jocelyn Laira Perry, Mar. 9, 1957; children: Karen Tace, Iain Kenrick, Gillian Erica. BM, BCh., Oxford U., Eng., 1951; DO, London Coll., 1956. Intern in medicine, surgery, ophthalmology St. Thomas Hosp., Plymouth, Exeter Hosps., London, 1952-53; registrar in ophthalmology Birmingham (Eng.) Eye. Hosp., 1958-60; sr. registrar in ophthalmology Bristol (Eng.) Eye Hosp., 1960-63; cons. eye surgeon Wolverhampton & Midland Counties Eye Infirmary, Eng., 1963-89; staff opthalmologist Liverpool Hosp., NSW, Australia, 1989—. Contbr. articles to profl. jours.; author: Ophthalmic Nursing, 1980. Mem. Wolverhampton Health Authority, 1970-77; treas. Ophthalmic Nursing Bd., 1970-84, chmn., 1984-88. With RAF, 1953-57. Recipient Gold medal, Nepal Med. Assn., 1989. Fellow Royal Coll. Surgeons, Royal Soc. Medicine, Royal Coll. Ophthalmologists; mem. Irish Coll. Ophthalmologists, Brit. Computer Soc., N.Y. Acad. Scis. Mem. Soc. of Friends.

WOODHOUSE, JOHN FREDERICK, food distribution company executive; b. Wilmington, Del., Nov. 30, 1930; s. John Crawford and Anna (Houth) W.; m. Marilyn Ruth Morrow, June 18, 1955; children: John Crawford II, Marjorie Ann Woodhouse Purdy. BA, Wesleyan U., 1953; DHL, 1997; MBA, Harvard U., 1955. Bus. devel. officer Can. Imperial Bank of Commerce, Toronto, Ont., 1955-59; various fin. positions Ford Motor Co., Dearborn, Mich., 1959-64, Cooper Industries, Inc., Mount Vernon, Ohio, 1964-67; treas. Houston, 1967-69, Crescent-Niagara Corp., Buffalo, 1968-69; exec. v.p., chief fin. officer Sysco Corp., Houston, 1969-71, pres., chief operating officer, 1972-83, pres., chief exec. officer, 1983-85, CEO, 1985-96, mem. exec. and fin. coms., 1996—, chmn. bd. dirs., chmn. exec. com., 1986—; bd. dirs. Shell Oil Co., Winrock Internat.; dir. Harvard Bus. Sch. Assocs., 1995—. Chmn. Mich. 16th dist. rep. Club, 1962-64; treas. Cooper Industries Found., 1967-69; trustee Wesleyan U., 1976-92, vice-chmn., 1986-92; ruling elder Presbyn.. Ch.; bd. trustees Mt. Holyoke Coll., South Hadley, Mass., 1996—. Mem. Nat. Am. Wholesale Grocer's Assn. (bd. dirs. 1990—, vice chmn. 1992, chmn. 1994-96), Internat. Foodservice Distbrs. Assn. (bd. dirs. 1988—), Houston Soc. Fin. Analysts, Fin. Execs. Inst., Harvard Bus. Sch. Club (bd. dirs.), Sigma Chi. Avocations: backpacking, canoeing, tennis. Office: Sysco Corp 1390 Enclave Pky Houston TX 77077-2025

WOODHULL, JOHN RICHARD, electronics company executive; b. LaJolla, Calif., Nov. 5, 1933; s. John Richard Woodhull and Mary Louise (Fahey) Hostetler; m. Barbara Adams; children: Elizabeth A., John A. BS in Engring. Physics, U. Colo., 1957, MS in Applied Math., 1960. Engr. Space Tech. Labs. (now TRW Systems), Redondo Beach, Calif., 1960-63; mgr., engr. Northrop Corp., Hawthorne, Calif., 1964; mem. tech. staff Logicon, Inc., San Pedro, Calif., 1964-69, pres., chief exec. officer, Torrance, Calif., 1969—, also bd. dirs.; instr. physics U. Colo., 1959-60; bd. dirs. 1st Fed. Fin. Corp. Bd. mgrs. San Pedro (Calif.) and Peninsula YMCA; bd. dirs. Los Angeles YMCA, 1985—, Sunrise Med., Torrance, 1986—. With USN, 1956-59. Mem. Chief Execs.' Orgn., World Bus. Coun., Nat. Indsl. Security Assn. (bd. dirs. 1986—). Avocations: sailboat racing, tennis, skiing. Office: Logicon Inc 3701 Skypark Dr Ste 200 Torrance CA 90505-4712*

WOODHULL, PATRICIA ANN, artist; b. Gary, Ind., Nov. 24, 1924; d. John Joseph and Georgia Mildred (Voorhis) Harding; m. Bradley Allen Woodhull, May 8, 1948; children: Leslie, Marcia, Clarisse. BS in Clothing Design, Purdue U., 1946; life teaching credential, Calif. State U., Fullerton, 1978. Social worker County Dept. Lake County and Bartholomew County, Gary and Columbus, Ind., 1946-50; home demonstrator Pub. Svc. Co. Ind., Columbus, 1950-53; substitute tchr. Fullerton (Calif.) H.S. Dist., 1968-73; children's art and drama tchr. Fullerton Cmty. Svcs., 1973-85; children's pvt. art tchr. Fullerton, 1990-93; art tchr. Montessori Sch., Fullerton, 1990-91; art/drama tchr. creative arts program Fullerton Pub. Schs., 1972-89; founder, dir. Players Improv Theatre Group, Fullerton, Calif. One woman shows include Fullerton City Libr., 1992, William Carlos Gallery, Fullerton, 1992, 93, Whittier (Calif.) City Hall, 1993, Muckinthaler Ctr., Fullerton, 1993, Brookhurst Ctr., Anaheim, 1993, Whitier Libr. Show, 1994, L.A. Mcpl. Art Gallery, 1996, Orlando Gallery, 1996, Laguna Art Inst., 1996; exhibited in group shows at Whittier Art Gallery, 1991, Hillcrest Art Show, Creative Arts Ctr., Burbank, Calif., 1991, Bidge Gallery City Hall, L.A., 1992, The Art Store, Fullerton, 1992, Women Painters West, 1993, New England Fine Arts Inst., Boston, 1993; represented in pvt. collections. Recipient Spl. award Orange County Fair, Costa Mesa (Calif.) County Fair, 1985; 3rd pl. award Hillcrest Whittier (Calif.) Show, 1990, 2nd award West Coast Collage Show, Lancaster, Calif., 1989, Evelyn Nunn Miller award Women Painters West, Torrance, Calif., 1994. Mem. Nat. League Am. Pen Women (pres. Orange County 1993), Women Painters West, Pan Hellenic Orange County (pres. 1994), Alpha Chi Omega (pres. local chpt. 1993).

Republican. Avocations: designing knitwear, reading, music, community theatre. Home: 1519 Harmony Ln Fullerton CA 92831-2015

WOODHURST, ROBERT STANFORD, JR., architect; b. Abbeville, S.C., July 12, 1921; s. Robert Stanford and Eva (Ferguson) W.; m. Dorothy Ann Carwile, Aug. 4, 1945; 1 son, Robert Stanford III. BS in Architecture, Clemson U., 1942. Registered arch., S.C., Ga. Designer Harold Woodward, Arch., Spartanburg, S.C., 1946-47; assoc. architect F. Arthur Hazard, Arch., Augusta, Ga., 1947-54; ptnr. Woodhurst & O'Brien, Architects, Augusta, 1954-83, Woodhurst Partnership, 1983—; v.p. Southeastern Architects and Engrs., Inc., Augusta, 1964-83; lectr. history architecture N. Augusta Community Coll.; mem. nat. exam. com. Nat. Council Archtl. Regis. Bds.; pres. Ga. State Bd. Archs. Chmn. Augusta-Richmond County Planning Commn., 1966-68; trustee Hist. Augusta, Inc.; active Mayor's Adv. Com., 1965-68; mem. Augusta Bldg. Code Bd. Appeals, 1955-58. Served to capt. U.S. Army, 1942-45. Decorated Air medal with 7 oak leaf clusters; Croix de Guerre avec palms (France); prisoner ofwar, Germany. Fellow AIA (Bronze medal 1942); mem. Ga. Assn. AIA (pres. 1977, Bronze medal 1977, Rothchild Silver Medal 1987), Soc. Archtl. Historians, Nat. Council Archtl. Registration Bds., Augusta Country Club, Pinnacle Club, Elks. Democrat. Baptist. Designed and built: 1st Baptist Ch., Augusta, Univ. Hosp. Med. Ctr., Augusta, Peabody Apts. and Irvin Towers, Augusta, W. Lake Country Club, Augusta, Med. Library, Med. Coll. Ga., Library Voorhees Coll., Denmark, S.C., Ambulatory Care Ctr., Univ. Hosp., Augusta, Married Students Apartments, Med. Coll. Ga., Covenant Presbyn. Ch., Augusta, Student Ctr. Voorhees Coll., Pres.' Home Voorhees Coll., others. Home: 810 Dogwood Ln Augusta GA 30909-2704 Office: Woodhurst Partnership 607 15th St Augusta GA 30901-2601

WOODIN, MARTIN DWIGHT, retired university system president; b. Sicily Island, La., July 7, 1915; s. Dwight E. and Gladys Ann (Martin) W.; m. Virginia Johnson, Sept. 7, 1939 (dec.); children: Rebecca Woodin Johnson, Pamela Woodin Fry, Linda Woodin Middleton; m. Elisabeth Wachalik, Oct. 5, 1968. B.S., La. State U., 1936; M.S., Cornell U., 1939, Ph.D., 1941; L.H.D. (hon.), U. New Orleans, 1985. Faculty La. State U., 1941-85, prof. agrl. econs., head dept., 1957-59; dir. resident instrn. Coll. Agr., 1959-60; dean La. State U. at Alexandria, 1960-62; exec. v.p. La. State U. System, Baton Rouge, 1962-72; pres. La. State U. System, 1972-85; Cons. agr. and planning, Nicaragua, Taiwan, Thailand. Contbr. articles to profl. jours. Dep. dir. La. Civil Def. Agy., 1961-72; v.p., exec. com. United Givers Baton Rouge ; sec. La. State U. Found., 1962-72; mem. La. Constn. Revision Commn., Arts and Humanities Coun. of Greater Baton Rouge; mem. pres.'s coun. Nat. Assn. State Univs., 1972-85; mem. coun. trustees Gulf South Rsch. Inst., 1972-85; pres. Coun. So. Univs., 1975-76. With USNR, 1942-46, PTO. Named Alumnus of Yr., La. State U., 1985; named to Order of Jose Cecilio Del Valle, Republic of Honduras, 1985. Mem. Am. Agrl. Econ. Assn., Am. Mktg. Assn., VFW, Am. Legion (post comdr.), Internat. House, So. Assn. Land Grant Colls. and State Univs. (pres. 1977-78, 83-84), Elks, Rotary, Sigma Xi, Omicron Delta Kappa, Phi Kappa Phi (pres.), Beta Gamma Sigma, Phi Eta Sigma, Gamma Sigma Delta, Alpha Zeta, Pi Gamma Mu, Acacia. Presbyterian. Home: 234 Court St Baton Rouge LA 70810-4801

WOODING, WILLIAM MINOR, medical statistics consultant; b. Waterbury, Conn., Aug. 24, 1917; s. George Lee and Ella Elizabeth (Asher) W.; m. Nina C. Peaslee, May 30, 1940; children: Barbara Lee Wooding Bose, Elizabeth Ann. B Chem. Engrng. cum laude, Poly. Inst. Bklyn., 1953. Lab. asst. Am. Cyanamid Co., Stamford, Conn., 1941-44, chemist, 1945-50, rsch. chemist, 1950-56, rsch. adminstrv. svcs. coord., 1956-57; asst. chief chemist Revlon Rsch. Ctr., N.Y.C., 1957-60, assoc. rsch. dir., 1960-65; assoc. rsch. dir. Carter-Wallace, Inc., Cranbury, N.J., 1965-67, dir. tech. svcs., 1967-75; dir. statis. svcs. Carter-Wallace, Inc. and Wallace Labs., Cranbury, 1975-82; cons. med. statis. and clin. trials BioStatistics, Swanton, Vt., 1982—; instr. Stat-a-Natrix Inst., Edison, N.J., 1983-86. Author: Planning Pharmaceutical Clinical Trials, 1994. Home and Office: BioStatistics RR 1 Box 4690 Maquam Shore Swanton VT 05488-9736

WOODLAND, IRWIN FRANCIS, lawyer; b. New York, Sept. 2, 1922; s. John James and Mary (Hynes) W.; m. Sally Duffy, Sept. 23, 1954; children: Connie, J. Patrick, Stephen, Joseph, William, David, Duffy. BA, Columbia U., 1948; JD, Ohio State U., 1959. Bar: Calif. 1960, Wash., 1991, U.S. Dist. Ct. (cen. dist.) Calif. 1960, U.S. Dist. Ct. (no. dist.) Calif. 1962, U.S. Dist. Ct. (so. dist.) Calif. From assoc. to ptnr. Gibson, Dunn & Crutcher, L.A., 1959-88; ptnr. Gibson, Dunn & Crutcher, Seattle, 1988—; Bd. dirs. Sunlaw Energy Corp., Vernon, Calif. With USAF, 1942-45, ETO. Mem. ABA, Calif. Bar Assn., L.A. Bar Assn., Wash. State Bar Assn., Fed. Energy Bar Assn., Am. Mgmt. Assn., Phi Delta Phi, Jonathan Club, Bel Air Bay Club. Roman Catholic.

WOODLAND, N. JOSEPH, optical engineer, mechanical engineer; b. Atlantic City, N.J., Sept. 6, 1921. BS in Mech. Engrng., Drexel U., 1947; MME, Syracuse U., 1956. Tech. asst. to unit chief, liquid thermal diffusion project for separating uranium isotopes Manhattan Project, Oak Ridge, Tenn., 1943-46; mech. designer Burlington Industries, 1947; lectr. in mech. engrng. Drexel U., 1948-49, cons., 1987; cons. in aircraft hydraulics design, 1950; various positions at staff and sr. levels IBM Corp., 1951-87; cons., 1987—. Recipient Nat. Medal Tech. U.S. Dept. Commerce, 1992; named one of Drexel U.'s 100 Most Outstanding Alumni, 1992. Mem. Anthony J. Drexel Soc. Achievements include patent (with Bernard Silver) for Classifying Apparatus and Method, a bar code system, and the creation of the Universal Product Code system. Office: 426 Van Thomas Dr Raleigh NC 27615-5231

WOODLE, E. STEVE, transplant surgeon; b. Texarkana, Ark., Jan. 7, 1954; three children. BS summa cum laude, Tex. A&M U., 1976; MD magna cum laude, U. Tex., 1980. Diplomate Am. Bd. Surgery, Am. Coll. Surgeons. Asst. prof. surgery Washington U. Sch. Medicine, St. Louis, 1990-92; asst. prof. surgery & immunology U. Chgo., 1992—; com. mem. Ctr. for Biol. Evaluation and Rsch., FDA, Washington, 1994-97. Contbr. more than 90 articles to med. and sci. jours., also chpts. to books. Mem. Am. Soc. Transplant Surgeons, Internat. Transplantation Soc., Soc. Univ. Surgeons, Ctrl. Surg. Assn., Western Surg. Assn., Soc. U. Surgeons. Office: U Chgo Dept Surgery MC 5027 5841 S Maryland Ave Chicago IL 60637-1463

WOODLE, ROY V., services company executive; b. Bogota, Tex., June 3, 1935; s. Lee Roy and Lillie May (Herring) W.; m. Ola Faye Phillips, Jan. 26, 1956; children: Linda Kathleen Woodle Eady, Elizabeth Ann Woodle. BSME, Tex. A&M U., College Station, Tex., 1957. Various positions Gen. Dynamics Corp., San Diego, CA, 1957-74; dir. internat. ops. Gen. Dynamics Corp., St. Louis, Mo., 1974-79; v.p. mktg. Gen. Dynamics Svc. Co., San Diego, 1979-82; dir. internat. mktg. ITT, Gen. Elec., Paramus, N.J., 1982-83; v.p. Vinnell Corp., Fairfax, Va. 1983-89, sr. v.p., 1989-93, pres. & CEO, 1993—. 1st Lt. U.S. Army Res., 1957-63. Avocations: tennis, skiing, scuba. Office: Vinnel Corp 12150 Monument Dr Fairfax VA 22033-4051

WOODLEY, DAVID TIMOTHY, dermatology educator; b. St. Louis, Aug. 1, 1946; s. Raoul Ramos-Mimosa and Marian (Schlueter) W.; m. Christina Paschall Prentice, May 4, 1974; children: David Thatcher, Thomas Colgate, Peter Paschall. AB, Washington U., St. Louis, 1968; MD, U. Mo., 1973. Diplomate Am. Bd. Internal Medicine, Am. Bd. Dermatology, Nat. Bd. Internal Medicine. Intern Beth Israel Med. Ctr., Mt. Sinai Sch. Medicine, N.Y. Hosp., Cornell U. Sch. Medicine, N.Y.C., 1973-74; resident in internal medicine U. Nebr., Omaha, 1974-76; resident in dermatology U. N.C., Chapel Hill, 1976-78, asst. prof. dermatology, 1983-85, assoc. prof. dermatology, 1985-88; prof. medicine, co-chief div. dermatology Cornell U. Med. Coll., N.Y., 1988-89; prof. and vice chair dept. dermatology Stanford U., 1989-93, Northwestern U., 1993—; research fellow U. Paris, 1978-80; expert NIH, Bethesda, Md., 1983-89; prof., assoc. chmn. dermatology Stanford U Sch. Medicine, 1989-93; chmn. dermatology Sch. Medicine Northwestern U., 1993—. Contbr. chpts. to books and articles in field to profl. jours. Mem. Potomac Albicore Fleet, Washington, 1982-83, Friends of the Art Sch., Chapel Hill, 1983—, Jungian Soc. Triangle Area, Chapel Hill, 1983—. Fellow Am. Acad. Dermatology; mem. Dermatology Found., Am. Soc. for Clin. Research, Soc. Investigative Dermatology, ACP (assoc.), Assn. Physican Poets, Am. Soc. for Clin. Investigation, 1988. Home: 2626 N Lakeview Ave Apt 3003 Chicago IL 60614-1826 Office: Northwestern U Med Sch Dept Dermatology 303 E Chicago Ave Chicago IL 60611-3008*

WOODLOCK, DOUGLAS PRESTON, judge; b. Hartford, Conn., Feb. 27, 1947; s. Preston and Kathryn (Ropp) W.; m. Patricia Mathilde Powers, Aug. 30, 1969; children: Pamela, Benjamin. BA, Yale U., 1969; JD, Georgetown U., 1975. Bar: Mass. 1975. Reporter Chgo. Sun-Times, 1969-73; staff mem. SEC, Washington, 1973-75; law clk. to Judge F.J. Murray, U.S. Dist. Ct. Mass., Boston, 1975-76; assoc. Goodwin, Procter & Hoar, Boston, 1976-79, 83-84, ptnr., 1984-86; asst. U.S. atty., Boston, 1979-83; judge U.S. Dist. Ct., Boston, 1986—; instr. Harvard U. Law Sch., 1980, 81; mem. U.S. Jud. Conf. Com. on Security, Space and Facilities, 1987-95; chmn. New Boston Fed. Courthouse Bldg. Com., 1987—. Contbr. articles to profl. jours. Articles editor Georgetown Law Jour., 1973-75. Chmn. Commonwealth of Mass. Com. for Pub. Counsel Services, 1984-86, Town of Hamilton Bd. Appeals, 1978-79. Recipient Dir.'s award U.S. Dept. Justice, 1983, Thomas Jefferson award for Pub. Architecture, AIA, 1996. Mem. ABA, Mass. Bar Assn., Boston Bar Assn., Am. Law Inst., Am. Judicature Soc., Am. Bar Found, Fed. Judges Assn. (bd. dirs. 1996—). Office: US Dist Ct McCormack PO & Courthouse Rm 1502 Boston MA 02109

WOODMAN, HAROLD DAVID, historian; b. Chgo., Apr. 21, 1928; s. Joseph Benjamin and Helen Ruth (Sollo) W.; m. Leonora Becker; children—Allan James, David Edward. B.A., Roosevelt U., 1957; M.A., U. Chgo., 1959, Ph.D., 1964. Lectr. Roosevelt U., 1962-63; asst. prof. history U. Mo., Columbia, 1963-66; assoc. prof. U. Mo., 1966-69, prof., 1969-71; prof. Purdue U., West Lafayette, Ind., 1971—, Louis Martin Sears disting. prof., 1990—; chmn. Com. on Am. Studies, 1981-94. Author: Conflict and Consensus in American History, 1966, 9th rev. edit., 1996, Slavery and the Southern Economy, 1966, King Cotton and His Retainers, 1968, Legacy of the American Civil War, 1973, New South-New Law, 1995; mem. editorial bd. Jour. So. History, 1972-75, Wis. Hist. Soc., 1972-76, Bus. History Rev., 1971-77, Agrl. History, 1976-82, Am. Hist. Rev., 1981-84, Jour. Am. History, 1985-88. Served with U.S. Army, 1950-52. Recipient Otto Wirth award Roosevelt U., 1990; Woodrow Wilson Internat. Center for Scholars fellow, 1977; Social Sci. Rsch. Coun. faculty grantee, 1969-70; Nat. Humanities Ctr. Fellow, 1983-84. Mem. Am. Hist. Assn., Orgn. Am. Historians, Econ. History Assn., Agrl. History Soc. (pres. 1983-84, Everett E. Edwards award 1963), Soc. Am. Historians, Bus. History Conf. (pres. 1981-82), Ind. Assn. Historians (pres. 1983-84), So. Hist. Assn. (exec. coun. 1982-85, Ramsdell award 1965, pres. 1995-96). Home: 1100 N Grant St West Lafayette IN 47906-2460 Office: Purdue U Dept History West Lafayette IN 47907

WOODMAN, HARRY ANDREWS, retired life insurance company executive, consultant; b. Orange, N.J., June 15, 1928; s. Harry Andrews and Mildred Amelia (Woods) W.; m. Betty Jo Pulsford, July 1, 1950; children: Richard Cushman, Andrea Ellen, Lynn Adele, Thomas Gordon. BA, Amherst Coll., 1950. With N.Y. Life Ins. Co., N.Y.C., 1950-89, 2d v.p., 1968-71, v.p., 1971-89; pvt. practice underwriting, actuarial cons. Cos Cob, Conn., 1989—. With USN, 1952-53. Mem. Soc. Actuaries, Home Office Life Underwriters Assn. (former pres.). Home and Office: 58 N Old Stone Bridge Rd Cos Cob CT 06807-1510

WOODMAN, WALTER JAMES, lawyer; b. Talara, Peru, Jan. 21, 1941; s. Walter James and Nora Carmen (Wensjoe) W.; m. Ruth Meyer, Dec. 19, 1970; children: Justin Meyer, Jessica Hilary. BA, U. Miami, 1964; JD, So. Meth. U., 1967. Bar: Tex. 1967, U.S. Dist. Ct. (no. dist.) Tex. 1967, U.S. Ct. Appeals (5th cir.) 1968, U.S. Supreme Ct. 1971, U.S. Dist. Ct. (we. dist.) La. 1979, U.S. Dist. Ct. (ea. dist.) Tex. 1983, U.S. Dist. Ct. (mid. dist.) La. 1988, U.S. Dist. Ct. (ea. dist.) La. 1989. Lawyer Dallas, 1967-72, Waxahachie, Tex., 1972-79, Shreveport, La., 1979—; bd. dirs. N.W. La. Legal Svcs., Shreveport, 1993-96. Author book revs. and articles. Candidate Tex. Ho. of Reps., 1972; bd. dirs. Gov.'s Pan Am. Commn., Baton Rouge, 1993-96. Mem. North La. Civil War Roundtable. Home: Nonesuch Farm 12250 Ellerbe Rd Shreveport LA 71115 Office: 9045 Ellerbe Rd Ste 103 Shreveport LA 71106-6799

WOODMANSEE, GLENN EDWARD, employee relations executive; b. Feb. 8, 1936; s. Glenn E. and Elaine (Turnquist) W.; m. Sharon E. Horne, Sept. 5, 1959; chidlren: Lynn Ann, Thomas Edward. Student, Coe Coll., 1954-55; BS, Ariz. State U., 1960. Assoc. group mem. Prudential Ins. Co., Seattle, 1960-64; regional mgr. Blue Cross, N.Y.C., 1964-72; mgr. employee benefits McDermott Inc./Babcock & Wilcox, New Orleans, 1972-82; dir. employee relations Tidewater Inc., New Orleans, 1982-95; v.p. S&E Enterprise Co., Carriere, Miss., 1995-96. Bd. dirs. CPC Hosp., New Orleans, 1988-94; pres. Manalapan Rep. Club, Englishtown, N.J., 1977; county committeeman N.J. Rep. Party, Englishtown, 1970-77. Served to cpl. U.S. Army, 1955-57. Recipient N.Y.C. Marathon medal N.Y.C. Track Club, 1987. Mem. SAR, Am. Soc. Pers. Assocs., Bus. Coalition Health (treas. 1986-88, pres. 1988-90), Tng. and Devel. Assn. Am., Risk Ins. Mgmt. Soc., Toastmasters. Republican. Presbyterian. Club: New Orleans Athletic, South Shore Yacht. Avocations: marathon running, swimming, golf, boating. Home: 104 Pine Burr Rd Carriere MS 39426-7704

WOODRESS, JAMES LESLIE, JR., English language educator; b. Webster Groves, Mo., July 7, 1916; s. James Leslie and Jessie (Smith) W.; m. Roberta Wilson, Sept. 28, 1940. A.B., Amherst Coll., 1938; A.M., NYU, 1943; Ph.D., Duke U., 1950; LittD, U. Nebr., 1995. News editor Sta. KWK, St. Louis, 1939-40; rewriteman, editor UPI, N.Y.C., 1940-43; instr. English, Grinnell (Iowa) Coll., 1949-50; asst. prof. English, Butler U., Indpls., 1950-53; asso. prof. Butler U., 1953-58; asso. prof. English, San Fernando Valley (Calif.) State Coll., 1958-61, prof., 1961-66, chmn. dept., 1959-63, dean letters and scis., 1963-65; prof. English, U. Calif.-Davis, 1966-87, chmn. dept., 1970-74; vis. prof. Sorbonne, Paris, 1974-75, 83. Author: Howells and Italy, 1952, Booth Tarkington: Gentleman from Indiana, 1955, A Yankee's Odyssey: The Life of Joel Barlow, 1958, Dissertations in American Literature, 1957, 62, 68, Willa Cather: Her Life and Art, 1970, 75, 81, American Fiction 1900-50, 1974, Willa Cather: A Literary Life, 1987; editor: Eight American Authors, 1971, American Literary Scholarship: An Annual, 1965-69, 75-77, 79, 81, 87, Critical Essays on Walt Whitman, 1983, Cather's The Troll Garden, 1983, (with Richard Morris) Voices from America's Past, anthology, 1961-62, 75. Served to lt. AUS, 1943-46. Ford Fund for Advancement Edn. fellow, 1952-53; Guggenheim fellow, 1957-58; Fulbright lectr. France, 1962-63; Fulbright lectr. Italy, 1965-66; recipient Hubbell medal, 1985. Mem. MLA (sec. Am. Lit. group 1962-63), AAUP, Phi Beta Kappa. Address: 824 Sycamore Ln Davis CA 95616-3225 Office: U Calif Dept English Davis CA 95616

WOODRICK, ROBERT, food products executive. CEO, chmn. D W Food Ctrs., Grand Rapids, Mich. Office: D&W Food Ctrs PO Box 878 Grand Rapids MI 49588-0878*

WOODRING, DEWAYNE STANLEY, religion association executive; b. Gary, Ind., Nov. 10, 1931; s. J. Stanley and Vera Luella (Brown) W.; m. Donna Jean Wishart, June 15, 1957; children: Judith Lynn (Mrs. Richard Bigelow), Beth Ellen (Mrs. Thomas Carey). B.S. in Speech with distinction, Northwestern U., 1954, postgrad. studies in radio and TV broadcasting, 1954-57; M.Div., Garrett Theol. Sem., 1957; L.H.D., Mt. Union Coll., Alliance, Ohio, 1967; D.D., Salem (W.Va.) Coll., 1970. Asso. youth dir. Gary YMCA, 1950-55; ordained to ministry United Methodist Ch., 1955; minister of edn. Griffith (Ind.) Meth. Ch., 1955-57; minister adminstrn. and program 1st Meth. Ch., Eugene, Oreg., 1957-59; dir. pub. relations Dakotas area Meth. Ch., 1959-60, dir. pub. relations Ohio area, 1960-64; adminstrv. exec. to bishop Ohio East area United Meth. Ch., Canton, 1964-77; asst. gen. sec. Gen. Council on Fin. and Adminstrn., United Meth. Ch., Evanston, Ill., 1977-79; assoc. gen. sec. Gen. Council on Fin. and Adminstrn., 1979-84; exec. dir., chief exec. officer Religious Conf. Mgmt. Assn., 1982—; mem. staff, dept. radio svcs. 2d assembly World Coun. Chs., Evanston, 1954; vice-chmn. commn. on entertainment and program North Ctrl. Jursidictional Conf., 1968-72, chmn., 1972-76; mem. commn. on gen. conf. United Meth. Ch., 1972-93, bus. mgr., exec. dir., 1976-93, mem. divsn. interpretation, 1969-72; chmn. comm. commn. Ohio Coun. Chs., 1961-65; mem. exec. com. Nat. Assn. United Meth. Found., 1968-72; del. World Meth. Conf., London, Eng., 1966, Dublin, Ireland, 1976, Honolulu, 1981, Nairobi, 1986, Singapore, 1991, Rio de Janeiro, Brazil, 1996; exec. com. World Meth. Coun., 1986—; del. White House Conf. on Travel and Tourism, 1995; bd. dirs. Ohio East Area United Meth. Found., 1967-78, v.p., 1967-76; chmn. bd. mgrs. United Meth. Bldg., Evanston, 1977-84; lectr., cons. on fgn. travel; mem. cust. adv. bd. Red Lion/Doubletree Hotels. Creator: nationally distbd. radio series The Word and Music; producer, dir.: TV series Parables in Miniature, 1957-59. Adviser East Ohio Conf. Communications Commn., 1968-76; pres. Guild Assocs., 1971—; trustee, 1st v.p. Copeland Oaks Retirement Ctr., Sebring, Ohio, 1969-76; bd. dirs. First Internat. Summit on Edn., 1989. Recipient Cert. Meeting Profl. award, 1985, Cert. Expt. Mgr. award, 1988; named to Ky. Cols., 1989, Conv. Liaison Coun. Hall of Leaders honoree, 1994. Mem. Am. Soc. Assn. Execs., Ind. Soc. Assn. Execs. (Mtg. Planner of Yr. award 1990), Mtg. Profl. Internat., Conv. Liaison Coun. (bd. dirs., past chmn.), Def. Orientation Conf. Assn. (chaplain), Ind. Conv. Visitors Assc. (bd. dirs., 1996-99) Cert. Mtg. Profls. (bd. dirs. 1983-91), Internat. Assn. Exposition Mgmt., Found. for Internat. mtgs. (bd. dirs.), Marriott Cust. Leadsp. Forum. Home: 7224 Chablis Ct Indianapolis IN 46278-1540 Office: 1 RCA Dome St 120 Indianapolis IN 46225-1023

WOODRUFF, BRUCE EMERY, lawyer; b. Mason City, Iowa, June 23, 1930; s. Frederick Bruce and Grace (Emery) W.; m. Carolyn Clark, Aug. 18, 1956; children: David C., Douglas B., Lynn M., Daniel R. BS in Bus., U. Ill., 1952; JD, Washington U., St. Louis, 1959. Bar: Mo. 1959, D.C. Dist. Ct. (ea. dist.) Mo. 1959, U.S. Ct. Appeals (8th cir.) 1960, U.S. Supreme Ct. 1979. Assoc. Armstrong, Teasdale, Schlafly, Davis & Dicus, St. Louis, 1959-65; ptnr. Armstrong Teasdale, Schlafly & Davis (and predecessor firms), St. Louis, 1966-95, sr. counsel, 1996—; prin. counsel St. Louis C.C., 1962-89; bd. dirs. Christian Health Svcs. Devel. Corp., St. Louis, BJC Health Sys., St. Louis, Cass. Comml. Corp., Cass Bank & Trust Co., Rainbow Village, Inc.; city atty., Kirkwood, Mo., 1986. Named Kirkwood Citizen of Yr., 1983. Mem. ABA (banking law com.), Mo. Bar Assn., Bar Assn. Met. St. Louis, Am. Acad. Healthcare Attys. Republican. Presbyterian. Clubs: Algonquin (Glendale, Mo.); Noonday (St. Louis (bd. dirs. 1988-91). Avocations: golf, swimming, sailing, photography. Home: 9 Taylor Estates Kirkwood MO 63122 Office: Armstrong Teasdale Schlafly & Davis 1 Mel Nor Sq Ste 2600 Saint Louis MO 63125-5329

WOODRUFF, C(HARLES) ROY, professional association executive; b. Anniston, Ala., Sept. 27, 1938; m. Kay Carolyn Jernigan, June 26, 1962; children: Charles R. Jr., Earl David. BA, U. Ala., 1960; BD, So. Bapt. Theol. Sem., 1963, PhD in Psychology of Religion and Pastoral Care, 1966. Lic. profl. counselor, Va. Asst. pastor Ft. Mitchell Bapt. Ch., South Ft. Mitchell, Ky., 1960-63; Protestant chaplain Silvercrest Hosp., New Albany, Ind., 1963-66; dir. dept. pastoral care and edn. Bryce State Hosp., Tuscaloosa, Ala., 1966-71; assoc. prof., chaplain supr. dept. patient counseling Med. Coll. Va., Richmond, 1971-76; assoc. prof., chmn. dept. psychology of religion and pastoral care Midwestern Bapt. Theol. Sem., Kansas City, Mo., 1976-78; exec. dir. Peninsula Pastoral Counseling Ctr., Newport News, Va., 1978-88, Am. Assn. Pastoral Counselors, Washington, 1988—; lecturing fellow Interpreter's House, Lake Junaluska, N.C., 1968-78; pastoral counselor, clin. supr. Psychol. Clinic, U. Ala., Tuscaloosa, 1969-71; adj. staff mem. The Counseling Inst., Kansas City, 1976-78. Author: Alcoholism and Christian Experience, 1968; (with others) Alcohol, In and Out of the Church, 1968, Work Adjustment: The Goal of Rehabilitation, 1973, Pastoral Theology and Ministry, Key Resources, 1983, The Dictionary of Pastoral Care and Counseling, 1990; also articles. Apptd. by Gov. of Va. to Bd. Profl. Counselors, Commonwealth of Va., 1987-95 (chmn. 1993-95); mem. Nat. Mental Health Leadership Forum, 1990-93. United Meth. Ch. Gen. Bd. Christian Social Concerns grantee, 1965; So. Bapt. Theol. Sem. teaching fellow, 1965-66. Fellow Coll. Chaplains of Am. Protestant Hosp. Assn.; mem. Assn. for Clin. Pastoral Edn. (cert. supr.), Assn. Couples for Marriage Enrichment (cert.). Home: 10827 Burr Oak Way Burke VA 22015-2416 Office: Am Assn Pastoral Counselors 9504A Lee Hwy Fairfax VA 22031-2303

WOODRUFF, DONALD B., motion picture art director, production designer. Set designer: (films) Barbarosa, 1982; art dir.: (films) Ruthless People, 1986, Harry and the Hendersons, 1987, Jaws-the Revenge, 1987, Who's That Girl?, 1987, The Naked Gun: From the Files of Police Squad!, 1988, Fletch Lives, 1989, The Hunt for Red October, 1990, For the Boys, 1991, Crimson Tide, 1995, Nixon, 1996, Turbulence, 1996, Volcano, 1997, Virus, 1997. Home: 5060 E Kings Grove Somis CA 93066

WOODRUFF, FAY, paleoceanographer, geological researcher; b. Boston, Jan. 23, 1944; d. Lorande Mitchell and Anne (Fay) W.; m. Alexander Whitehill Clowes, May 20, 1972 (div. Oct. 1974); m. Robert G. Douglas, Jan. 27, 1980; children: Ellen, Katerina. RN, Mass. Gen. Hosp. Sch. Nursing, Boston, 1966; BA, Boston U., 1971; MS, U. So. Calif., 1979. Rsch. assoc. U. So. Calif., L.A., 1978-81, rsch. faculty, 1981-96; keynote spkr. 4th Internat. Symposium on Benthic Foraminifera, Sendai, Japan, 1990. Contbg. author: Geological Society of America Memoir, 1985; contbr. articles to profl. jours. Life mem. The Nature Conservancy, Washington, 1992; bd. dirs. Friends of Friendship Park, 1995-97. NSF grantee, 1986-94. Mem. Am. Geophys. Union, Geol. Soc. Am., Internat. Union Geol. Scis. (internat. commn. on stratigraphy, subcommn. on Neogene stratigraphy 1991-97), Soc. Woman Geographers (sec. So. Calif. chpt. 1990-96), Soc. Econ. Paleontologists and Mineralogists (sec., editor N.Am. Micropaleontology sect. 1988-90), Oceanography Soc., Sigma Xi. Avocation: birding. Office: U So Calif Dept Geol Scis Los Angeles CA 90089-0740

WOODRUFF, GENE LOWRY, nuclear engineer, university dean; b. Greenbrier, Ark., May 6, 1934; s. Clarence Oliver and Avie Ercilla (Lowry) W.; m. Marylou Munson, Jan. 29, 1961; children—Gregory John, David Reed. B.S. with honors, U.S. Naval Acad., 1956; M.S. in Nuclear Engring., MIT, 1963, Ph.D. in Nuclear Engring., 1966. Registered profl. engr., Wash. Asst. prof. nuclear engring. U. Wash., Seattle, 1965-70, assoc. prof., 1970-76, prof., 1976-93, chmn. dept., 1981-84, dir. nuclear engring. labs., 1973-76, dean Grad. Sch., 1984-93, prof. chem. engring. environ. studies, 1989—; vice-chair, chair-elect Grad. Record Exam., 1991-92, chair, 1992-93; cons. to govt. and industry. Contbr. numerous articles to sci. and tech. jours. Served to lt. USN, 1956-60. Mem. Nat. Soc. Profl. Engrs. (Achievement award 1977), Am. Nuclear Soc. (Achievement award 1977, chmn. honors/awards com. 1981-84, nat. program com. 1971-75, exec. com. fusion div. 1976-80, vice chmn. edn. div. 1983-84, Arthur Holly Compton award 1986), Am. Soc. Engring. Edn., Assn. Grad. Schs. (v.p./pres.-elect 1990-91, pres. 1991-92). Democrat. Home: 7423 Sunnyside Ave N Seattle WA 98103 Office: University of Washington Box 351750 Seattle WA 98195-1750*

WOODRUFF, JUDY CARLINE, broadcast journalist; b. Tulsa, Nov. 20, 1946; d. William Henry and Anna Lee (Payne) W.; m. Albert R. Hunt, Jr., Apr. 5, 1980; children: Jeffrey Woodruff, Benjamin Woodruff, Lauren Ann Lee. Student, Meredith Coll., 1964-66; B.A., Duke U., 1968. News announcer, reporter Sta. WAGA-TV, Atlanta, 1970-75; news corr. NBC News, Atlanta, 1975-76; White House corr. NBC News, Washington, 1977-83; anchor Frontline, PBS documentary series, 1983-90; corr. MacNeil-Lehrer News Hour, PBS, Washington, 1983-93; anchor and sr. corr. CNN, Washington, 1993—; mem. bd. advisors Henry Grady Sch. Journalism, U. Ga., 1979-82; bd. visitors Wake Forest U., 1982-89; mem. bd. advisors Benton Fellowship in Broadcast Journalism, U. Chgo., 1984-90, Knight Fellowship in Journalism, Stanford U., 1985—; trustee Duke U., 1985—; founding bd. dirs. Internat. Women's Media Found., 1989—. Author: This is Judy Woodruff at the White House, 1982. Mem. Commn. on Women's Health, The Commonwealth Fund. Recipient award Leadership Atlanta, Class of 1974, Atlanta chpt. Women in Comms., 1975, Edward Weintal award for excellence in fgn. policy reporting, 1987, Joan Shorenstein Barone award for series on def. issues, 1987, Helen Bernstein award for excellence in journalism N.Y. Pub. Libr., 1989, Pres.'s award Nat. Women's Hall of Fame, 1994, CableAce award for best newscaster, 1995, Allen H. Neuharth award for excellence in journalism, 1995. Mem. NATAS (Atlanta chpt. Emmy award 1975), White House Corrs. Assn. Office: Cable News Network 820 1st St NE Washington DC 20002-4243*

WOODRUFF, KATHRYN ELAINE, English educator; b. Ft. Stockton, Tex., Oct. 12, 1940; d. James Arthur and Catherine H. (Stevens) Borron; m. Thomas Charles Woodruff, May 18, 1969; children: Robert Borron, David Borron. BA, Our Lady of the Lake U., San Antonio, 1963; MFA, U. Alaska, 1969; PhD, U. Denver, 1987. Cert. tchr., Tex., Colo. English and journalism tchr. Owensboro (Ky.) Cath. High Sch., 1963-64, Grand Junction

(Colo.) Dist. 12, 1964-66; English tchr. Monroe High Sch., Fairbanks, Alaska, 1966-67; teaching asst. U. Alaska, Fairbanks, 1967-69, instr., 1969-70; instr. U. Colo., Boulder, 1979, Denver, 1988-89; instr. Regis Coll., Denver, 1987-89; asst. prof. Econs. Inst., Boulder, 1989-92; asst. prof. English Colo. Christian U., Lakewood, 1993—; tchr. Upward Bound, Fairbanks, 1968; instr. ethnic and women writers course U. Colo., Denver, 1988-93; mem. Assoc. Writing Programs; soprano Boulder Chorale, Cantabile Singers. Author: (poetry) Before the Burning, 1994; poetry readings in Colo., Tex. and Paris. Friend Chautauqua Music Festival, Boulder, 1985—; dir. 12th Annual Arts Festival, Fairbanks, 1969. Named one of Outstanding Young Women Am., 1966; nominated for Poet Laureate of Colo., 1996; grantee NEH, 1996. Mem. AAUW, MLA, Assoc. Writing Programs, Soc. Internat. Devel. UN Assn., Nat. Women's Hall of Fame. Democrat. Mem. Christian Ch. Avocations: singing, tennis, skiing, volleyball, travel. Office: Colo Christian U 180 S Garrison St Lakewood CO 80226-1053

WOODRUFF, KAY HERRIN, pathologist, educator; b. Charlotte, N.C., Sept. 22, 1942; d. Herman Keith and Helen Thelma (Tucker) Herrin; m. John T. Lyman, May 3, 1980; children: Robert, Geoffry, Carolyn. BA in Chemistry, Duke U., 1964; MD, Emory U., 1968. Diplomate Am. Bd. Pathology (trustee 1993—). Medicine and pediat. intern U. N.C., Chapel Hill, 1968-69, resident in anatomic pathology, 1969-70; chief resident in anatomic pathology, instr. U. Okla., Oklahoma City, 1970-71, fellow in electron microscopy-pulmonary pathology, instr., 1971-72; chief resident in clin. pathology U. Calif., San Francisco, 1972-74, asst. clin. prof. dept. anatomic pathology, 1974-91, assoc. clin. prof., 1991—; chief electron microscopy VA Hosp., San Francisco, 1974-75, attending clin. cons. dept. anatomic pathology, 1986—; pvt. practice, San Pablo, Calif., 1981—; pres. med. staff Brookside Hosp., San Pablo, 1994, med. dir. Regional Cancer Ctr., 1995—; assoc. pathologist Children's Hosp., San Francisco, 1979-81, St. Joseph's Hosp., San Francisco, 1977-79; cons. pathologist Lawrence Berkeley (Calif.) Lab., 1974-93; med. dir. Bay Area Tumor Inst. Tissue Network, San Pablo, 1989—; asst. clin. prof. pathology health and med. scis. program U. Calif., Berkeley and U. Calif., San Francisco Joint Med. Program, 1985-91, assoc. clin. prof., 1991—, others. Contbr. articles and abstracts to med. jours. Mem. exec. bd. Richmond (Calif.) Quits Smoking, 1986-90, Bay Area Tumor Inst., Oakland, Calif., 1987—; mem. exec. bd. Contra Costa unit Am. Cancer Soc., Walanut Creek, Calif., 1985-87, mem. profl. edn. com., 1985—, mem. pub. edn. com., 1985-86, mem. task force on breast health Calif. div., 1992-93; mem. transfusion adv. com. Irwin Meml. Blood Bank, San Francisco, 1977-83; chmn. transfusion adv. com. Alameda Contra County Blood Bank, 1989-92; commr. Calif. Bd. Med. Quality Assurance, 1978-80. Recipient young investigator award Am. Lung Assn., 1975-77; Outstanding Svc. awards Am. Cancer Soc., 1986, 87, Disting. Svc. award, 1988; Disting. Clin. Tchg. award U. Calif., San Francisco and Berkeley Joint Med. Program, 1987, Outstanding Tchg. award, 1988, Excellence in Basic Sci. Instrn. award, 1990, Excellence in Tchr. Clin. Scis. award, 1993; cert. of recognition Cmty. Svc. Richmond, 1989. Mem. AMA, Coll. Am. Pathologists (editl. bd. CAP Today 1986-90, bd. govs. 1990-96, chair coun. on practice mgmt. 1994), Am. Med. Women's Assn. (exec. bd. 1984-87, regional bd. govs. 1984-87), Am. Bd. Pathologists (trustee 1991—), No. Calif. Women's Med. Assn. (pres. 1982-84), Calif. Soc. Pathologists (bd. dirs. 1988-90), No. Calif. Oncology Group, South Bay Pathology Soc., Am. Assn. Blood Banks, Calif. Med. Assn., Alameda-Contra Costa County Med. Soc., Am. Soc. Clin. Pathology, Calif. Pathology Soc. Avocations: classical piano, bicycle touring, distance running, reading, wind surfing. Office: Brookside Hosp Dept Pathology 2000 Vale Rd San Pablo CA 94806-3808

WOODRUFF, MARTHA JOYCE, home health agency executive; b. Unadilla, Ga., Jan. 3, 1941; d. Metz Loy and Helen (McCorvey) Woodruff. BA, Shorter Coll., 1963; MA, U. Tenn.-Knoxville, 1972. Tchr., Albany H.S. (Ga.), 1963-69; instr. U. Tenn.-Knoxville, 1970-72; asst. prof. Valdosta State Coll. (Ga.), 1972-76; coord. Staff Builders, Atlanta, 1976-78; pres., owner Med. Pers. Pool, Knoxville, 1978-93; owner, pres. Priority Healthcare Svcs, Knoxville, 1993—, Pers. Pool of Knoxville, Inc., 1985-87; mem., adviser Owners Adv. Coun., Pers. Pool of Am., Ft. Lauderdale, Fla., 1980-82; active Altzheimers Assn. Mem. Nat. Coun. on Aging, Nat. Assn. for Adult Daycare, Exec. Women Internat. (bd. dirs. Knoxville chpt. 1996), East Tenn. Women's Polit. Caucus, Tenn. Assn. Home Care, Nat. Assn. Homecare, Knoxville C. of C. (com. for cost containment 1982-85), Blount County C. of C. (retirement com. 1983, mem. indsl. rels. com. 1983). Republican. Methodist.

WOODRUFF, NEIL PARKER, agricultural engineer; b. Clyde, Kans., July 25, 1919; s. Charles Scott and Myra (Christian) W.; m. Dorothy Adele Russ, June 15, 1952; children—Timothy C., Thomas S. B.S., Kans. State U., 1949, M.S., 1953; postgrad., Iowa State U., 1959. Agrl. engr. Agrl. Research Service, Dept. Agr., Manhattan, Kans., 1949-63; research leader Agrl. Research Service, Dept. Agr., 1963-75; cons. engr. Manhattan, 1975-77; civil engr. Kans. Dept. Transp., Topeka, 1977-79; prof., mem. grad. faculty Kans. State U., civil engr. facilities planning, 1979-84; mem. sci. exchange team to, Soviet Union, 1974; with W/PT Cons., 1984—. Contbr. articles to tech. jours. and books. Fellow Am. Soc. Agrl. Engrs. (Hancor Soil Water Engring. award 1975); mem. Sigma Xi, Gamma Sigma Delta. Home and Office: 12906 W Blue Bonnet Dr Sun City West AZ 85375-2538

WOODRUFF, SHIRLEY, middle school educator; b. Richmond, Calif., May 30, 1951; d. Vern LeRoy and Betty Jo (Salyer) Cole; m. Carl Woodruff, June 22, 1974; children: Dan, David, Ben, Mark, Joseph. AA, Solano C.C., Rockland, Calif., 1971; BA in Social Sci., Calif. State U., Sacramento, 1973; postgrad., Idaho State U., 1972-73; student, Contra Costa Jr. Coll., San Pablo, Calif., 1969-70; postgrad., Brigham Young U. Cert. reading specialist, secondary and elementary credentials, kindergarten endorsement, reading endorsement K-12, social studies K-12, Idaho, Calif. Tchr. grades 5 and 6, tchr. art and music Sch. Dist. 91, Idaho Falls, Idaho, 1973-74; chpt. I tchr., 1979-82; tchr. kindergarten Bonneville Joint Dist. 93, Idaho Falls; 3rd grade tchr., 1982-85; elem. tchr. Bonneville Joint Dist. 93, Idaho Falls; 9th grade reading tchr., Book Fair chmn. Sandcreek Mid. Sch., Idaho Falls, Idaho, 1992—; tchr. reading Bonneville Joint Dist. 93, Idaho Falls, 7th grade reading, geography, and lit. tchr. study skills, 1985—, mem. dist. curriculum com. lang. arts dept., 1995-96, bldg. cons. for accelerated reader program, 1996—, chairperson lang. arts dept. for state evaluations. Past editor Hi-Hopes ICIRA state newsletter; past editor Edn. Coalition Newsletter Goals 2000, Idaho Falls, 1992-93; writer ch. newsletter. Libr. Sunday sch. tchr.; chmn. Multiple Sclerosis read-a-thon Iona Elem. Sch., 1980; adv. Reading Club, Sandcreek Mid. Sch., 1990—, team leader Team of Tchrs., 1992-93, book fair chmn., 1992—; bldg. rep. East Idaho Reading Coun., 1992-95; mem. steering com. Edn. Coalition, Idaho Falls, 1991-93. Mem. NEA, Nat. Coun. Tchrs. English, Internat. Reading Assn. (Pres.'s award Idaho coun.), East Idaho Reading Coun. (rep. 1990—, membership chair, bldg. rep. 1994-95, past pres., past v.p.), Idaho Edn. Assn., Bonneville Edn. Assn. (bldg. rep. 1994-95). Home: 5511 Concord Circle Idaho Falls ID 83401-5244

WOODRUFF, THOMAS ELLIS, electronics consulting executive; b. Stockton, Calif., Feb. 8, 1921; s. Ennis Casselberry and Gracella (Scotford) W.; m. Doris Elaine Walters, Jan. 14, 1947 (div. Aug. 1962); children: Mary Ann Woodruff Mahaffy, Patricia Lee; m. Ruth Elizabeth Craik, Feb. 25, 1964; 1 child, Robert Peter; stepchildren: Gordon Lee Vickers, Barbara Ann Vickers, Mary Jean Vickers. AA, Stockton Jr. Coll., 1941; BSEE, U. Calif., Berkeley, 1943. Registered profl. engr., Calif. Engr. GE, Syracuse, N.Y., 1944-47; staff engr. Hughes Aircraft Co., Culver City, Calif., 1947-56; mgr. electronics design Sanders Assocs., Nashua, N.H., 1956-58, chief engr. preliminary design, 1958-60, mgr. spl. programs div., 1960-62, corp. dir. systems, 1962-65, v.p., gen. mgr. corp. systems group, 1965-73, v.p. antisubmarine weapons and communications, 1966-72, dir., 1968-70, sr. dir., 1970-76, v.p. gen. mgr. ocean systems group, 1972-76, v.p. sci. and tech., 1976-88, corp. cons., 1989—; v.p. Sanders Nuclear Corp., Nashua, 1966-71; mem. adv. com. Def. Intelligence Agy., Washington, 1978-83; joint adv. com. MIT Lincoln Lab., Bedford, Mass., 1988-89; cons. Superconductor Tech., Inc., Santa Barbara, Calif., 1988—, Oryx, Inc., Paramus, N.J., 1989—, Sanders/Lockheed, 1988-91; ret. 1992. Patentee, co-patentee 14 inventions in electronics for computers, control systems, video displays, submarine detection devices, others. Mem. IEEE (sr.). Republican. Avocations: skiing, photography, motorcycling, swimming. Home and Office: 8 Berkeley St Nashua NH 03060-2309

WOODRUFF, TOM, JR., special effects designer; b. Williamsport, Pa., Jan. 20, 1959; s. Thomas Howard and Shirley Joanne (Boyer) W.; m. Tami H. Spitler, Aug. 22, 1981; children: David Thomas, Taylor Jon, Connor Boyer. BA (cum laude), Lycoming Coll., 1980. Artist, technician Burman Studios, Van Nuys, Calif., 1983; co-designer, artist Stan Winston Studio, Inc., Northridge, Calif.; designer, ptnr. Amalgamated Dynamics, Inc., Chatsworth, Calif., 1988—. Designer and performer (film) Tremors, 1989, Alien III, 1990; co-designer (film) The Santa Clause, 1994, Demolition Man, 1993, Wolf, 1993; co-designer, performer (film) Pumpkinhead, 1987, Leviathan, 1988, Alien Nation, 1988, Death Becomes Her, 1992 (Academy award Visual Effects 1993), Jumanji, 1995, Mortal Kombat, 1995; dir., writer (short film) The Demon with 3 Tales, 1987; lab technician (film) Predator, 1987; artist and performer (Film) Monster Squad, 1986, The Terminator, 1985, Aliens, 1986, (TV) Amazing Stories, 1986. Office: Amalgamated Dynamics Inc 20100 Plummer St Chatsworth CA 91311-5448*

WOODRUFF, TRUMAN O(WEN), physicist, emeritus educator; b. Salt Lake City, May 26, 1925; s. Wilford Owen and Evelyn (Ballif) W.; m. Ambrosina Lydia Solaroli, Sept. 14, 1948 (dec. June 1991); m. Patricia O'Keefe Vincent, Sept. 23, 1995. AB, Harvard U., 1947; BA, Oxford (Eng.) U., 1950; PhD, Calif. Inst. Tech., 1955. Nat. scholar Harvard, 1942-44, 46-47, Sheldon traveling fellow, 1947-48; Rhodes scholar Oxford U., 1948-50; Dow Chem. Co. fellow, Howard Hughes fellow Calif. Inst. Tech., 1950-54; research asso. physics U. Ill., 1954-55; physicist Gen. Elec. Research Lab., 1955-62; prof. physics Mich. State U., 1962-85, prof. emeritus, 1985—, chmn. dept., 1972-75; sr. scientist research labs. Hughes Aircraft Co., Malibu, Calif., 1986-87; cons. in physics Los Angeles, 1987—; vis. prof. Scuola Normale Superiore, Pisa, Italy, 1982—. Contbr. articles to sci. jours. Served with USNR, 1944-46. Fulbright fellow U. Pisa, 1968-69. Fellow Am. Phys. Soc.; mem. Assn. Harvard Chemists, Phi Beta Kappa, Sigma Xi. Office: 911 E Spruce St Sequim WA 98382-3519

WOODRUFF, VIRGINIA, broadcast journalist, writer; b. Morrisville, Pa.; d. Edwin Nichols and Louise (Meredith) W.; m. Raymond F. Beagle Jr. (div.); m. Albert Plaut II (div.); 1 child, Elise Meredith. Student, Rutgers U. News corr. Sta. WNEW-TV Metromedia, N.Y.C., 1967; nat., internat. critic-at-large Mut. Broadcasting System, 1968-75; lectr. Leigh Bur., 1969-71; byline columnist N.Y. Daily Mirror, N.Y.C., 1970-71; first Arts critic Teleprompter and Group W Cable TV, 1977-84; host/producer The First Nighter N.Y. Times Primetime Cable Highlight program, 1977-84; pres., chief exec. officer Starpower, Inc., 1984-91; affiliate news corr. ABC Radio Network, N.Y.C., 1984-86; pres. Promarket People Inc., 1991-93; S.W. contbg. corr. Am. in the Morning, First Light, Mut. Broadcasting System, 1992; S.W. freelance corr. Voice of Am., USIA, 1992—; perennial critic Off-Off Broadway Short Play Festival, N.Y.C., 1984—; was 1st Woman on 10 O'Clock News, WNEW-TV, 1967. Contbg. feature writer Vis a Vis mag., 1988-91. Mem. celebrity panel Arthritis Telethon, N.Y.C., 1976. Selected episodes of First Nighter program in archives N.Y. Pub. Libr., Billy Rose Theatre Collection, Rodgers and Hammerstein Collection, Performing Arts Rsch.Ctr. Mem. Drama Desk. Presbyterian. Clubs: National Arts, Dutch Treat.

WOODRUFF, WANDA LEA, elementary education educator; b. Woodward, Okla., May 2, 1937; d. Milton Casper and Ruth Arlene (Bradshaw) Shuck; m. William Jennings Woodruff, Aug. 18, 1962; children: Teresa Kaye, Bruce Alan, Neal Wayne. BS, Northwestern State U., 1959; MA in Edn., Olivet Nazarene U., 1973. Cert. K-8th grade tchr. 2d grade tchr. Anthony (Kans.) Pub. Schs., 1959-60, transition class tchr., 1960-61, 1st grade tchr., 1961-62; 5th grade tchr. Versailles (Ky.) Pub. Schs., 1962-63; 1st grade tchr. Bradley (Ill.) Elem. Schs., 1968-93; presch. vol. Concern Ctr., Bartlesville, Okla., 1994—. Com. chmn. Bus. and Profl. Women, Anthony, 1959-62; sec. com. PTA, Anthony, 1959-63, Bradley (Ill.) PTA, 1968-93. Recipient grant for edn. First of Am. Bank, 1991-92, 92-93. Mem. Bartlesville Pilot Club Internat. (edn./patriotism chairperson 1994-95, dir. 1995-96, mem. com. Spl. Olympics 1995-96, pres-elect 1996—). Avocations: jogging, reading, baking, working with children and young people. Home: 2373 Mountain Dr Bartlesville OK 74003-6926

WOODRUFF, WILLIAM JENNINGS, theology educator; b. Vassar, Kans., Sept. 30, 1925; s. Kenneth Arthur and Carrie (Brecheisen) W.; m. Wanda Lea Shuck, Aug. 18, 1962; children: Teresa Kaye, Bruce Alan, Neal Wayne. BA, Ottawa U., 1954; MDiv, Fuller Theol. Sem., Pasadena, Calif., 1958; MRE, Asbury Theol. Sem., Wilmore, Ky., 1963, ThM, 1964; postgrad., U. Pa., 1965-68, Concordia Theol. Seminary, 1976-84, Trinity Theol. Seminary, 1993-95. Youth dir. Hyde Park EUB Ch., Wichita, 1958-59; tchr. Lenora (Kans.) Rural High Sch., 1959-60; pastor Attica (Kans.) EUB Ch., 1960-62, Jersey City EUB Ch., 1964-65, Phila. EUB Ch., 1965-68; with Olivet Nazarene U., Kankakee, Ill., 1968—, prof.; ret., 1991. Contbr. to Religious and Theol. Abstracts, 3 jours., 1968-94; contbr. articles to profl. jours. Cpl. U.S. Army, 1951-53, Republic of Korea. Mem. Evang. Theol. Soc., Evang. Tchrs. Tng. Assn., Wesleyan Theol. Soc., Near East Archaeol. Soc., Phi Delta Lambda, Theta Pi, Kappa Delta Pi. Avocations: photography, travel, camping. Home: 2373 Mountain Dr Bartlesville OK 74003-6926

WOODRUM, CLIFTON A., III, lawyer, state legislator; b. Washington, July 23, 1938; s. Clifton A. Jr. and Margaret (Lanier) W.; m. Emily Abbitt, Aug. 10, 1963; children—Robert, MeredithW. Snowden, Anne. A.B., U. N.C., 1961; LL.B., U. Va., 1964. Bar: Va. 1964, U.S. Dist. Ct. (we. dist.) Va. 1964, U.S. Ct. Appeals (4th cir.) 1968, U.S. Supreme Ct. 1970. Assoc. Dodson, Pence & Coulter, Roanoke, Va., 1964-68; ptnr. Dodson, Pence, Viar, Woodrum & Mackey, 1968-95, counsel Dodson, Pence & Viar, 1995—; mem. Va. Ho. of Dels., 1980—. Chmn. 6th Dist. Democratic Com., Va., 1972-76; mem. State Water Commn., 1981—; State Crime Commn., 1982—, chmn. 1995—; chmn. Med. Malpractice Study, Va., 1984-85. Mem. ABA, Assn. Trial Lawyers Am., Va. Bar Assn., Roanoke Bar Assn. Episcopalian. Home: 2641 Cornwallis Ave SE Roanoke VA 24014-3339 Office: Dodson Pence & Viar PO Box 1371 Roanoke VA 24007-1371

WOODRUM, PATRICIA ANN, librarian; b. Hutchinson, Kans., Oct. 11, 1941; d. Donald Jewell and Ruby Pauline (Shuman) Hoffman; m. Clayton Eugene Woodrum, Mar. 31, 1962; 1 child, Clayton Eugene, II. BA, Kans. State Coll., Pittsburg, 1963; MLS, U. Okla., 1966. Br. libr. Tulsa City-County Libr. System, 1964-65, head brs., 1965-66, head reference dept., 1966-67, chief extension, chief pub. svc., 1967-73, asst. dir., 1973-76, exec. dir., 1976-96; bd. dirs. Local Am. Bank Tulsa. Mem. editorial bd. Jour. of Library Administration. Active Friends of Tulsa Libr., Leadership Tulsa Alumni; regent UCT/RSC, Tulsa. Recipient Disting. Libr. award Okla. Libr. Assn., 1982, Leadership Tulsa Paragon award, 1987, Women in Comm. Newsmaker award, 1989, Outstanding Alumnus award U. Okla. Sch. Libr. Info. Studies, 1989, Headliner award Tulsa Press Club, 1996; inducted into Tulsa City-County Libr. Hall of Fame, 1989, Okla. Womens Hall of Fame, 1993. Mem. ALA, Pub. Libr. Assn. (pres. 1993-94), Okla. Libr. Assn. (pres. 1978-79, Disting. Libr. award 1982, Meritorious Svc. award 1996), Tulsa C. of C. Democrat. Episcopalian. Avocations: backpacking, swimming, gardening. Office: Tulsa City-County Libr 400 Civic Ctr Tulsa OK 74103-3857

WOODRUM, ROBERT LEE, executive search consultant; b. Merkel, Tex., Mar. 3, 1945; s. Bill and Norma (Shea) W.; m. Linda Mary Larkin, July 20, 1968; children: Jennifer, Michael. BA, Calif. State U., Northridge, 1967; postgrad., U. Okla., 1974. Press sec. U.S. Senate, Washington, 1977-78; dir. pub. affairs U.S. Office Personnel Mgmt., Washington, 1979-80; pres. Corp. Communications, Washington, 1980-82; v.p. Norton Simon Inc., N.Y.C., 1982-83; spl. asst. to the commr. NFL, N.Y.C., 1983-84; exec. dir. Ritz Paris Hemingway Award, 1984-87; pres. Ritz Paris Internat., 1984-86; sr. v.p. AmBase Corp., 1986-91; v.p., ptnr. Korn/Ferry Internat., N.Y.C., 1991—; advisor USIA, Washington, 1980-93, ARC, 1983, White House Vets. Com., 1979-80. Trustee N.Y.C. Meals on Wheels, Inc. Lt. comdr. USN, 1968-77. Decorated Navy Achievement medal (2). Mem. N.Y. Sky Club. Home: 6 Plumbridge Ln Hilton Head Island SC 29928-3360 Office: Korn/Ferry Internat 237 Park Ave New York NY 10017-3140

WOODS, BOBBY JOE, transportation executive; b. Frederick, Okla., June 20, 1935; s. Vivin Richard and Mattie Marie (Malone); divorced; children: Donald B., Kathryn M., David R., Lynda J. Student, U. Calif., Berkeley, 1955-56; AA, Phoenix Coll., 1955; student, Glendale (Ariz.) Coll., 1968, 75. Pres. Southwest Prorate Inc., Phoenix, 1967-95, TCAB Registration Cons., Inc., 1993—; dist. exec. Boy Scouts Am., Phoenix, 1968-76; pres. Facing E's Enterprises, Inc., Yarnell, Ariz., 1991-93. Mem. Profl. Trucking Svcs. Assn. (pres. 1989-90), Lions Club (dist. gov. 1992-93, zone chmn. 1983-84, dep. dist. gov. 1984-85, lt. gov. 1991-92, dist. sight and hearing chmn. 1985-91, Sight and Hearing Found. state hearing chmn. 1985-89). Republican. Avocations: hiking, camping, stamp collecting, computers, collecting 78 RPM records. Home: 918 W Cochise Dr Phoenix AZ 85021-2343 Office: TCAB Registration Cons 2045 W Glendale Ave Phoenix AZ 85021-7841

WOODS, CYNDY JONES, junior high educator, researcher; b. Phoenix, Oct. 26, 1954; d. Glenn Billy and Helen Marie (Harrison) Jones; m. Clifford R. Woods, Apr. 3, 1975; children: Sean, Kathleen, Connor. AA in English, St. John's Coll., 1974; BA in English, Ariz. State U., 1992, M in Secondary Edn., 1994. Cert. secondary tchr., c.c. instr., Ariz. Tchr. grades 6-8 John R. Davis Sch., Phoenix, 1993, Thomas J. Pappas Sch., Phoenix, 1994—; tchr. Glendale C.C., 1997—; adj. faculty English and lit. Rio Salado C.C., 1995—, Glendale C.C., 1997—; treas. Martin Luther Sch. Bd., Phoenix, 1985-89; presenter in field. Contbr. poetry to anthologies Dance on the Horizons, 1993, The Sound of Poetry: Best Poems of 1995, Across the Universe, 1996; contbr. articles to profl. jours. Mem. St. Francis Xavier Sch. Bd., Phoenix, 1995; v.p. City/County Child Care Bd., Phoenix, 1988-92; youth group advisor Mt. Calvary Luth. Ch., Phoenix, 1988-96; mem. SRP Ednl. Adv. Coun., 1996—; mem. Maricopa County Juvenile Cmty. Justice Com., 1997—. Mem. Ariz. Edn. Assn., Brophy Coll. Prep. Mother's Guild, Xavier Coll. Prep. Mother's Guild. Democrat. Avocations: computers, homeless issues, at-risk issues, volleyball, writing. Home: PO Box 27575 Phoenix AZ 85061 Office: Thomas J Pappas Sch 355 N 6th Ave Phoenix AZ 85003-1509

WOODS, DENNIS CRAIG, school superintendent; b. Akron, Ohio, Nov. 29, 1946; m. Janice Mary Matvey, Apr. 21, 1971; children: Gregory, Jeffrey, Mark. BA, Brown U., 1968; MA, U. Akron, 1974; postgrad., Ohio State U., 1990—. Job placement specialist Summit County Bd. Edn., Akron, 1971-72; tchr. English, athletic dir. South H.S., Akron, 1972-77; unit prin. Buchtel H.S., Akron, 1977-80; asst. prin. Firestone H.S., Akron, 1980-81, prin., 1987-90; prin. Ellet H.S., Akron, 1981-87; grad. rsch. assoc. Policy Rsch. for Ohio Based Edn., Columbus, 1990-91; asst. dir. Sch. Study Coun. of Ohio, Columbus, 1991-92; supt. Sandy Valley Local Schs., Magnolia, Ohio, 1992-96, Bay Village (Ohio) City Sch. Dist., 1996—; instructional audit team Sch. Effectiveness Trainers, Columbus, 1992—; presenter adminstr.'s acad. Middletown (Ohio) City Sch. Dist., 1994; presenter Ohio Acad. for Sch. Improvement, Columbus, 1993; site visitor Blue Ribbon Schs. Program, Washington, 1991; presenter in field. Founding mem. Sandy Valley TAP Group, Magnolia, 1993-96; advancement chair Troop 50, Boy Scouts Am., Akron, 1986-93; three gallon blood donor ARC, Akron, 1980—; trustee The Bay Village Ednl. Found.; eucharistic min. St. Raphael Ch. Lt. (j.g.) USNR, 1968-70. Recipient Secondary Prin. award Akron Secondary Prins. Assn., 1985, 89, Pyramid award Nat. Sch. Pub. Rels. Assn., 1997; E.E. Lewis fellow Ohio State U., 1991, Eikenberry scholar, 1990. Mem. ASCD, Horace Mann League, Ohio Assn. Local Supts., Ohio Sch. Bds. Assn., Ohio Inst. Effective Sch. Leadership (first cohort 1995), Am. Assn. Sch. Adminstrs., Greater Cleve. Sch. Supts. Assn., Buckeye Assn. Sch. Adminstrs. (exec. and pub. rels. com. 1995, legis. com. 1996), Sandy Valley C. of C., Bay Kiwanis Club, Touchdown Club, Phi Delta Kappa. Avocations: reading, physical fitness, ornithology. Office: Bay Village City Sch Dist 377 Dover Center Rd Bay Village OH 44140-2304

WOODS, DONNA SUE, education educator, reading consultant, state agency administrator; b. Springhill, La., Jan. 15, 1954; children: Klaten A., Matthew M., Laura E., Gabriele E. BA, La. Tech U., 1975; MEd, La. State U., 1983; EdD, Okla. State U., 1992. Cert. English, social studies, gifted edn. tchr., La.; cert. English, gifted edn. and reading tchr., Okla. Tchr. English, Grawood (La.) Christian Schs., 1979-80; tchr. spl. edn. Bossier Parish Sch. Bd., Benton, La., 1981-83, curriculum developer, 1990; tchr. gifted Curtis Elem. Sch., Bossier City, La., 1983-88; tchr. lang. arts Elm Grove (La.) Jr. High Sch., 1988-90; teaching asst., univ. rep. Okla. entry yr. assistance Okla. State U., Stillwater, 1990-92, co-dir., instr. 13th ann. reading workshop, 1991, instr. Coll. Vet. Medicine, 1991, developer, dir. student tchr. seminar, 1992; asst. prof. Coll. Edn. Northwestern Okla. State U., Alva, 1992-95; dir. reading and literacy Okla. State Dept. Edn., Oklahoma City, 1995—; adj. instr. Oklahoma City C.C., 1991-92, U. Okla., 1995—; dir. Okla. Nat. Young Readers' Day, 1994, 95-96; presenter in field. Tutor YWCA, Shreveport, La., 1975; supt. youth Sun. schs. 1st Presbyn. Ch., Edmond, Okla., 1991, youth choir dir., 1994—, youth handbells dir., 1995—. Named Favorite Tchr. of Yr., Bossier C. of C., 1987; Centennial scholar Okla. State U. Coll. Edn. Alumni Assn., 1992. Mem. Internat. Reading Assn. (conf. presenter 1996), Okla. Reading Assn. (conf. presenter 1993—), Okla. Early Childhood Tchrs. Assn. (conf. presenter 1991), Alpha Upsilon Alpha (faculty sponsor 1994-95), Kappa Delta Pi, Phi Delta Kappa. Republican. Avocations: reading, music, collecting and repairing antiques, quilting, youth work. Home: 8326 Bo Jack Houston TX 77040 Home: 8326 Bo Jack Houston TX 77040

WOODS, ELDRICK See WOODS, TIGER

WOODS, GEORGE EDWARD, judge; b. 1923; m. Janice Smith. Student, Ohio No. U., 1941-43, 46, Tex. A&M Coll., 1943, Ill. Inst. Tech., 1943; JD, Detroit Coll. Law, 1949. Sole practice, Pontiac, Mich., 1949-51; asst. pros. atty. Oakland City, Mich., 1951-52; chief asst. U.S. atty., Ea. Dist. Mich., 1953-60, U.S. atty., 1960-61; assoc., Honigman, Miller, Schwartz and Cohn, Detroit, 1961-62; sole practice, Detroit, 1962-81; judge, U.S. Bankruptcy Ct., 1981-83, U.S. Dist. Ct. (ea. dist.) Mich., Detroit, 1983—. Served with AUS, 1943-46. Fellow Internat. Acad. Trial Lawyers, Am. Coll. Trial Lawyers; mem. Fed. Bar Assn., State Bar Mich. Office: US Dist Ct 277 US Courthouse 231 W Lafayette Blvd Detroit MI 48226-2720

WOODS, GERALD WAYNE, lawyer; b. Durham, N.C., Sept. 15, 1946; m. Deborah Jordan Bates, Apr. 30, 1983; children: Paul Ellis, Katherine Jordan. BS, U. N.C., 1968; JD, Emory U., 1973. Bar: Ga. 1973, U.S. Dist. Ct. (no. dist.) Ga. 1974, U.S. Supreme Ct. 1980, U.S. Dist. Ct. (so. dist.) Ga. 1987. With retail mgmt. Sears, Roebuck & Co., Atlanta, 1968-70; asst. to exec. sec. bd. regents U. Ga. System, Atlanta, 1973-76, asst. exec. sec., 1976-78; legal advisor to pres. Med. Coll. of Ga., Augusta, 1978-90, v.p. for bus. ops., legal advisor to the pres., asst. prof. med. jurisprudence, 1990—; mem. faculty Sr. Acctg. Officers Workshop Nat. Assn. of Coll. and Univ. Bus. Officers, Myrtle Beach, S.C., 1981; lectr. law seminars and med. confs., nationwide. Contbr. articles to profl. jours. Councilman City of Augusta, 1984-95; pres. YMCA of Augusta, Inc., 1987-88; bd. dirs. Leadership Augusta, 1982-85, 94—, others; bd. dirs. Augusta Symphony, 1988-90, pres., 1990-91; mem. adv. bd. Augusta Youth Ctr.; trustee Augusta-Richmond County Pub. Libr., 1984-85; active Richmond County Dem. Exec. Com., 1983-86, Richmond County Bd. of Health, 1986—, Augusta Symphony League, 1986—; bd. dirs. Augusta Youth Ctr., 1988-93, Augusta Symphony, 1988-90, pres., 1990-91, Leadership Augusta, 1994—; chmn. Greater Augusta Arts Coun. Cultural Action Plan Steering Com., 1992; mem. air svc. task force Augusta C. of C., 1990—; mem. Cities in Sch. Inc. Bd., 1996, Southeastern Tech. Ctr. Bd., 1996. Mem. State Bar Ga. (medico-legal liaison and mental health coms. 1979, vice chmn. coll. and univ. com., sch. and coll. law sect. 1986-88), Augusta Bar Assn., Ga. Soc. Hosp. Attys., Am. Acad. Hosp. Attys., Nat. Assn. Coll. and Univ. Attys. (exec. bd. 1983-86), Nat. Health Lawyers Assn., Kiwanis (treas. Ansley club 1977, bd. dirs. 1977-78), Nat. Assn. Coll. and Univ. Bus. Officers, Forrest Hills Assn. (pres. 1982-85, bd. dirs. 1985—), U. N.C. Alumni Assn. (v.p. Augusta chpt. 1984-90), Pinnacle Club, Augusta Country Club. Avocation: photography. Office: Med Coll Ga 312 Adminstrn Bldg Augusta GA 30912

WOODS, GERALDINE PITTMAN, health education consultant, educational consultant; b. West Palm Beach, Fla.; d. Oscar and Susie (King) Pittman; m. Robert I. Woods, Jan. 30, 1945; children: Jan, Jerri, Robert, Jr. Student, Talladega Coll., 1938-40, D.Sc. (hon.), 1980; B.S. in Zoology, Howard U., 1942; M.A., Radcliffe Coll. and Harvard U., 1943, Ph.D. in Neuroembryology, 1945; D.Sc. (hon.), Benedict Coll., 1977; HHD (hon.), Howard U., 1989; LHD (hon.), Meharry Med. Coll., 1988; DSc (hon.), Fisk U., 1991, Bennett Coll., 1993. Instr. Howard U., Washington, 1945-46; pres. L.A. chpt. Jack and Jill, 1954-56; pres. Aux. to Med., Dental and Pharm.

Assn. of So. Calif., 1951-55, state pres., 1955; past mem. local met. bd. YWCA; mem. nat. adv. coun. Gen. Med. Scis. Inst. NIH, 1964-68, spl. cons., 1969-87; mem. gen. rsch. support program adv. com., div. rsch. resources NIH, 1970-73, 77-78. Mem. regional com. Girl Scouts U.S.A., 1969-75, nat. bd., 1975-78; exec. bd. Cmty. Rels. Conf. So. Calif., 1968-72; exec. com. Leadership Conf. Civil Rights, 1967-70; chmn. Def. Adv. Com. Women in Svcs., 1968; mem. air pollution manpower devel. adv. com. EPA, 1973-75; mem. fgn. svcs. officers selection bds. Dept. State, 1967; mem. Calif. Com. on Public Edn.; mem. Calif. Post Secondary Edn. Commn., 1974-78, vice chmn., 1976; chmn. bd. trustees Howard U., 1975-88; chmn. Howard U. Found., 1984-88; trustee Calif. Mus. Found., Atlanta U., 1974-86; bd. dirs. Ctr. for Ednl. Opportunity at Claremont Colls., Robert Wood Johnson Health Policy Fellowships; mem. Inst. Medicine of NAS, 1974—, Nat. Commn. for Cert. of Physicians Assts., 1974-81; initiated Minority Access to Rsch. Careers, also, Minority Biomed. Rsch. Support program NIH, 1972; co-chmn. internat. conf. Woman to Woman: Single Parenting from a Global Perspective, 1987; video Re: MARC and MBRS programs A Time for Celebration, 1987; bd. dirs. Charles R. Drew U. Medicine and Sci., 1990-93; founder Head Start, L.A., 1965 (award 1985). Named Woman of Yr. Zeta Phi Beta, 1954, one of 20 Famous Black Scientists Nabisco, 1982, Black Woman of Achievement Smithsonian Instn., 1981; recipient Meritorious Achievement award Nat. Med. Assn., Inc., 1979, Leadership Achievement award Nat. Assn. Equal Opportunity in Higher Edn., 1987, awards from Pres.'s Coun. of Youth Opportunity, Iota Phi Lambda, Nat. Pan-Hellenic Coun., Howard U. Alumni Assn., So. Calif. Nat. Assn. Colored Women, Calif. Mus. Found., Ch. Christian Fellowship, NIH, Howard U., Delta Sigma Theta, Delta Headstart, 1985, award Calif. State U., 1993, others; one of honorees Dollars and Sense mag. Salute to Am.'s Top 100 Black Business and Profl. Women, 1985; Morehouse Coll. program Rsch. Extravaganza dedicated to her, 1988; named to Gallery of Honor, Assn. Minority Health Profl. Schs., 1990. Mem. NAACP (life), Nat. Coun. Negro Women (life), Golden Key, Phi Beta Kappa, Delta Sigma Theta (pres. R & D Found. 1983-88, nat. pres. 1963-67, ann. Geraldine P. Woods sci. award by Fed. City Alumnae chpt. established in her honor given to an outstanding scientist, Geraldine Pittman Woods Headstart/State Presch. Ctr. dedicated 1993, Mary Church Terrell award 1979), Delta Sigma Theta. Congregationalist.

WOODS, GRANT, state attorney general; m. Marlene Galán; children: Austin, Lauren, Cole, Dylan. Grad., Occidental Coll., Ariz. State Coll., 1979. Atty. gen. Ariz., 1990—. Founder Mesa Boys and Girls Club. Office: Atty Gen Office 1275 W Washington St Phoenix AZ 85007-2926

WOODS, GURDON GRANT, sculptor; b. Savannah, Ga., Apr. 15, 1915; s. Frederick L. and Marion (Skinner) W. Student, Art Student's League N.Y.C., 1936-39, Bklyn. Mus. Sch., 1945-46; Ph.D. (hon.), Coll. San Francisco Art Inst., 1966. exec. dir. San Francisco Art Inst., 1955-64; dir. Calif. Sch. Fine Arts, 1955-65; prof. Adlai E. Stevenson Coll., U. Calif. at Santa Cruz, 1966-74; dir. Otis Art Inst., Los Angeles, 1974-77; asst. dir. Los Angeles County Mus. Natural History, 1977-80; Sculptor mem. San Francisco Art Commn., 1954-56; mem. Santa Cruz County Art Commn., Regional Arts Council of Bay Area. Exhibited: N.A.D., 1948, 49, San Francisco Art Assn. anns., 1952-54, Denver Mus. Anns., 1952, 53, Whitney Mus. Ann., 1953, Sao Paulo Biennial, 1955, Bolles Gallery San Francisco, 1969, 70, 72, L.A. Mcpl. Gallery, 1977, San Jose Inst. Contemporary Art (Calif.), Washington Project for the Arts retrospective, 1968-85, Washington, 1985, Retrospective Art Mus. Santa Cruz County, Calif., 1987, d.p. Fong Gallery, 1993, 94, Michael Angelo Gallery, Santa Cruz, 1995; commns. include: cast concrete reliefs and steel fountain, IBM Ctr., San Jose, Calif., fountain, Paul Masson Winery, Saratoga, Calif., McGraw Hill Pubs. (now Birkenstock), Novato, Calif.; work in permanent collection Oakland (Calif.) Mus.; papers in Archives of Am. Art, Smithsonian Instn., Washington. Recipient citation N.Y.C., 1948; prize N.A.D., 1949; Chapelbrook Found. research grantee, 1965-66; Sequoia Fund grantee, 1967; Research grantee Creative Arts Inst., U. Calif., 1968; grantee Carnegie Corp., 1968-69. Mem. Artists Equity Assn (pres. No. Calif. chpt. 1950-52, nat. dir. 1952-55). Address: 133 Seascape Ridge Dr Aptos CA 95003-5890

WOODS, HARRIETT RUTH, retired political organization president; b. Cleve., June 2, 1927; d. Armin and Ruth (Wise) Friedman; student U. Chgo., 1945; B.A., U. Mich., 1949; LLD (hon.) Webster U., 1988; m. James B. Woods, Jan. 2, 1953; children: Christopher, Peter, Andrew. Reporter, Chgo. Herald-Am., 1948, St. Louis Globe-Democrat, 1949-51; producer Star. KPLR-TV, St. Louis, 1964-74; moderator, writer Sta. KETC-TV, St. Louis, 1962-64; council mem. University City, Mo., 1967-74; mem. Mo. Hwy. Commn., 1974, Mo. Transp. Commn., 1974-76; mem. Mo. Senate, 1976-84, lt. gov. State of Mo., 1985-89; pres. Inst. for Policy Leadership, U. Mo., St. Louis, 1989-91; pres. Nat. Women's Polit. Caucus, 1991-95; dir. Federal Home Loan Mortgage Corp., 1995—; fellow inst. politics J.F. Kennedy Sch. Govt., Harvard U., 1988. Bd. dirs. LWV of Mo., 1963, Nat. League of Cities, 1972-74; Dem. nominee for U.S. Senate, 1982, 86. Jewish.

WOODS, HENRY, federal judge; b. Abbeville, Miss., Mar. 17, 1918; s. Joseph Neal and Mary Jett (Wooldridge) W.; m. Kathleen Mary McCaffrey, Jan. 1, 1943; children—Mary Sue, Thomas Henry, Eileen Anne, James Michael. B.A., U. Ark., 1938, J.D. cum laude, 1940. Bar: Ark. bar 1940. Spl. agt. FBI, 1941-46; mem. firm Alston & Woods, Texarkana, Ark., 1946-48; exec. sec. to Gov. Ark., 1949-53; mem. firm McMath, Leatherman & Woods, Little Rock, 1953-80; judge U.S. Dist. Ct. (ea. dist.) Ark., 1980—; referee in bankruptcy U.S. Dist. Ct., Texarkana, 1947-48; spl. assoc. justice Ark. Supreme Ct., 1967-74, chmn. com. model jury instrns., 1973-80; chmn. bd. Ctr. Trial and Appellate Advocacy, Hastings Coll. Law, San Francisco, 1975-76; mem. joint conf. com. ABA-AMA, 1973-78, Ark. Constl. Revision Study Commn., 1967-68. Author treatise comparative fault.; Contbr. articles to legal jours. Pres. Young Democrats Ark., 1946-48; mem. Gubernatorial Com. Study Death Penalty, 1971-73. Mem. ABA, Ark. Bar Assn. (pres. 1972-73, Outstanding Lawyer award 1975), Pulaski County Bar Assn., Assn. Trial Lawyers Am. (gov. 1965-67), Ark. Trial Lawyers Assn. (pres. 1965-67), Internat. Acad. Trial Lawyers, Internat. Soc. Barristers, Am. Coll. Trial Lawyers, Am. Bd. Trial Advocates, Phi Alpha Delta. Methodist. Home: 42 Wingate Dr Little Rock AR 72205-2556 Office: US Dist Ct PO Box 3683 Little Rock AR 72203-3683

WOODS, HOWARD JAMES, JR., civil engineer; b. Elizabeth, N.J., Oct. 11, 1955; s. Howard James and Catherine (Hurring) W. BCE cum laude, Villanova U., 1977, MCE, 1985. Registered profl. engr. N.Y., N.J., Pa., Md., N.Mex. Environ. engr. EPA, Phila., 1977-81; project engr. Johnson, Mirmiran & Thompson, Silver Spring, Md., 1981-83; dir. engring. ea. div. Am. Water Works Svc. Co., Haddon Heights, N.J., 1983-85, mgr. ops. ea. div., 1985-86, dir. planning, 1986-88, east regional mgr. ops., 1988-92; v.p. N.J. Am. Water Co., Haddon Heights, 1992-97; project rev. br. head Delaware River Basin Commn., West Trenton, N.J., 1997—; v.p. Am. Water Works Svc. Co., 1997—. Apptd. by gov. to N.J. Water Supply Adv. Coun., 1991. Named one of Oustanding Young Men Am., Jaycees, 1984, Outstanding Civil Engring. Alumnus, Grad. Sch. Villanova U., 1986; recipient John J. Gallen award Villanova U. Coll. of Engring. Tech. Achievement award. Mem. ASCE, Nat. Water Well Assn., Am. Mgmt. Assn., Am. Water Works Assn., Amnesty Internat., Villanova Club (So. N.J.), Tau Beta Pi. Democrat. Roman Catholic. Avocations: skiing, music, photography. Home: 51 Warren St Beverly NJ 08010-1323 Office: Delaware River Basin Commn PO Box 7360 West Trenton NJ 08628

WOODS, JAMES HOWARD, actor; b. Vernal, Utah, Apr. 18, 1947. Student, MIT, 1965-69. Performances include (Broadway prodns.) Borstal Boy, Trial of the Catonsville 9, Finishing Touches, Moonchildren (Theatre World award), off-Broadway prodn. Saved (Obie award, Clarence Derwent award); (films) The Visitors, 1971, Hickey and Boggs, 1972, The Way We Were, 1973, The Gambler, 1974, Night Moves, 1975, Distance, 1975, Alex & the Gypsy, 1976, The Choirboys, 1977, The Onion Field, 1979 (Golden Globe award nomination), The Black Marble, 1980, Eyewitness, 1981, Split Image, 1982, Fast-Walking, 1982, Videodrome, 1983, Against All Odds, 1984, Once Upon a Time in America, 1984, Cat's Eye, 1985, Joshua Then and Now, 1985, Salvador, 1986 (Acad. award nomination, 1987), Best Seller, 1987, Cop, 1988, The Boost, 1988, True Believer, 1989, Immediate Family, 1989, The Hard Way, 1991, Straight Talk, 1992, Diggstown, 1992, Chaplin, 1992, The Getaway, 1994, The Specialist, 1994, Curse of the Starving Class, 1994, Nixon, 1995, Casino, 1995, Ghosts of Mississippi, 1996 (Acad. award nomination); (TV miniseries) Holocaust, 1978; (TV movies) All the Way Home, 1971, Footsteps, 1972, A Great American Tragedy, 1972, Foster and Laurie, 1975, F. Scott Fitzgerald in Hollywood, 1976, The Disappearance of Aimee, 1976, Raid on Entebbe, 1977, The Gift of Love, 1978, And Your Name is Jonah, 1979, The Incredible Journey of Doctor Meg Laurel, 1979, Badge of the Assassin, 1985, Promise, 1986 (Emmy award, Golden Apple award, Golden Globe award), In Love and War, 1987 (Golden Globe award nomination), (Hallmark TV) My Name Is Bill W. (Emmy award 1989), Women & Men: Stories of Seduction, 1990, The Boys, 1991, Citizen Cohn, HBO, 1992 (Emmy nomination, Lead Actor - Miniseries, 1993), Jane's House, 1994, Indictment: The McMartin Trial, 1995 (Emmy nomination, Cable Ace nomination), The Summer of Ben Tyler, 1996 (Golden Globe nomination); guest on The Simpsons, 1994 (voice only). Mem. Acad. Motion Picture Arts and Scis., Internat. Platform Assn., Players Club, Mountaingate Country Club. Office: Guttman Assocs 118 S Beverly Dr Beverly Hills CA 90212-3003

WOODS, JAMES ROBERT, lawyer; b. San Francisco, Aug. 3, 1947; s. Robert H. and Grace (Snowhill) W.; 1 child, Heather F. AB with honors, U. Calif., Berkeley, 1969; JD, U. Calif., Davis, 1972. Bar: Calif. 1972, N.Y. 1973, U.S. Dist. Ct. (so. & ea. dists.) N.Y. 1975, U.S. Ct. Appeals (2d cir.) 1975, U.S. Dist. Ct. (no. dist.) Calif. 1984. Ptnr. LeBoeuf, Lamb, Greene & MacRae L.L.P., San Francisco, 1983—. Co-author: California Insurance Law and Practice; contbr. articles to profl. jours. Office: LeBoeuf Lamb Greene & MacRae LLP 1 Embarcadero Ctr Ste 400 San Francisco CA 94111-3619

WOODS, JAMES STERRETT, toxicologist; b. Lewistown, Pa., Feb. 26, 1940; s. James Sterrett and Jane Smith (Parker) W.; m. Nancy Fugate, Dec. 20, 1969; 1 dau., Erin Elizabeth. AB, Princeton U., 1962; MS, U. Wash., 1968, PhD, 1970; MPH, U. N.C., 1978. Diplomate Am. Bd. Toxicology. Research assoc. dept. Pharmacology Yale U. Sch. Medicine, New Haven, 1970-72; staff fellow environ. toxicology. Nat. Inst. Environ. Health Scis. br. NIH, Research Triangle Park, N.C., 1972-75, head biochem. toxicology sect., 1975-77; sr. rsch. leader environ.-occupational health risk evaluation Battelle Ctrs. for Pub. Health Rsch. and Evaluation, Seattle, 1978—; research prof. U. Wash., Seattle, 1979—. Contbr. articles to profl. jours. Served with USN, 1962-66. Scholar USPHS, 1966-70; Fellow Am. Cancer Soc., 1970-72. Mem. AAAS, APHA, Am. Assn. Cancer Rsch., Am. Soc. Pharmacology and Exptl. Therapeutics, Pacific NW Assn. Toxicologists (founding pres.), Soc. Epidemiology Rsch., Sox. Toxicology, Am. Coll. of Epidemiology. Home: 4516 55th Ave NE Seattle WA 98105-3837 Office: Battelle Research Ctr 4000 NE 41st St Seattle WA 98105-5428

WOODS, JAMES WATSON, JR., cardiologist; b. Lewisburg, Tenn., Feb. 20, 1918; s. James Watson and Sara Frances (Watson) W.; m. Marion Briner, Nov. 26, 1944; children: Diane, James Watson III, Martin Briner. B.A., U. Tenn., 1939; M.D., Vanderbilt U., 1943. Diplomate: Am. Bd. Internal Medicine. Intern, then resident in medicine U. Pa. Hosp., 1943, 44, 46-47, fellow in cardiology, 1947-48; mem. faculty U. N.C. Med. Sch., Chapel Hill, 1953—; prof. medicine U. N.C. Med. Sch., 1964-87, prof. of medicine emeritus, 1987—, chief hypertension unit, 1964—; mem. sr. attending staff N.C. Meml. Hosp. Author papers in field; contbr. chpts. to books. Served as officer M.C., USNR, 1944-46. Fellow ACP; mem. Am. Fedn. Clin. Research, Am. Clin. and Climatological Assn., Council High Blood Pressure Research, Internat. Soc. Hypertension, So. Soc. Clin. Investigation, N.C. Heart Assn. (pres. 1971-72, Bronze medallion 1970, Silver medallion 1972), Sigma Xi, Alpha Omega Alpha, Phi Eta Sigma, Phi Kappa Phi. Democrat. Presbyterian. Home: 631 Quarterstaff Rd Winston Salem NC 27104-1638

WOODS, JOE ELDON, general contractor; b. Hammon, Okla., Apr. 24, 1933; s. Joseph W. and Gertrude E. (Martin) W.; student Ariz. State U., 1955-61; O.P.M. Program Harvard U., 1984-87; m. Nina Jo Shackelford, July 5, 1952; 1 son, J. Grant. Vice-pres. Kitchell Corp., Phoenix, 1965-69; v.p. devel. Doubletree, Inc., Phoenix, 1969-78; pres., owner Joe E. Woods, Inc., Mesa, Ariz., 1977—; bd. dirs. Price-Woods, Inc., Mesa, 1985—; chmn., bd. dirs. Joe Woods Devel., Mesa, 1986—. Mem. cmty. adv. bd. Cox Comms., 1996—; Ariz. adv. bd. Liberty Mus. Inst., 1997. With U.S. Army, 1953-55, Korea. Mem. Associated Gen. Contractors, Mesa C. of C. (bd. dirs. 1983-87, chmn. 1985-86, v.p. 1984-85, pres. 1985-86), Harvard Bus. Sch. Republican. Presbyterian. Clubs: Mesa Country, White Mountain Country (Pinetop, Ariz.), Rotary, Ariz. C. of C. (bd. dirs. 1997). Avocations: golf, fishing, skiing. Office: Joe E Woods Inc 63 E Main St Ste 401 Mesa AZ 85201-7422

WOODS, JOHN ELMER, plastic surgeon; b. Battle Creek, Mich., July 5, 1929; m. Janet Ruth; children: Sheryl, Mark, Jeffrey, Jennifer, Judson. BA, Asbury Coll., 1949; MD, Western Res. U., 1955; PhD, U. Minn., 1966. Intern Gorgas Hosp., Panama Canal Zone, 1955-56, resident in gen. surgery, 1956-57; resident in gen. surgery Mayo Grad. Sch., Rochester, Minn., 1960-65, resident in plastic surgery, 1966-67; resident in plastic surgery Brigham Hosp., Boston, Mass., 1968; fellow, transplant cons. Harvard Med. Sch., Cambridge, Mass., 1969; cons. in gen. and plastic surgery Mayo Clinic, Rochester, 1969-93, vice chmn. Dept. Surgery; asst. prof. Mayo Med. Sch., Rochester, 1973-76, assoc. prof., 1976-80, prof. plastic surgery, 1980-93, Stuart W. Harrington prof. surgery; vis. prof. Yale Sch. Medicine, New Haven, 1984, Harvard Sch. Medicine, Cambridge, 1984. Contbr. over 200 articles to profl. jours.; also 26 book chpts. and 1 film. Recipient Disting. Mayo Clinician award, 1991. Mem. AMA (council on sci. affairs 1985—), ACS (grad edn. com. 1985—), Am. Bd. Med. Specialties, Am. Bd. Plastic Surgery (sec.-treas. 1985-88, chmn. 1988-89), Am. Soc. Plastic Surgeons Ednl. Fedn. (pres. 1984-85). Avocations: skiing, sailing, reading, the arts. Office: Mayo Clinic E 6-B Plummer N-10 Rochester MN 55905-0001

WOODS, JOHN WILLIAM, retired lawyer; b. Ft. Worth, Dec. 10, 1912; s. John George and Eugenia (Smith) W.; m. Gertie Leona Parker, Apr. 15, 1954. B.S., North Tex. State U., 1951, M.Ed., 1952; J.D., St. Mary's U., San Antonio, 1967; postgrad., Fresno State Coll., 1952, West Tex. State U., 1959. Bar: Tex. bar 1966. Tchr. Corcoran, Calif., 1952-53, Pampa, Tex., 1953-63; Tchr. Harlandale Sch. Dist., San Antonio, 1963-67; practicing atty. Amarillo, Tex., 1967-68; county atty. Sherman County, Tex., 1969-72, county judge, 1988, ret.; justice of peace, 1975-88; pvt. practice, Stratford, Tex., 1968-95; ret., 1995. Served to ensign USN, 1930-47, ETO. Mem. Tex. Bar Assn., 69th Jud. Bar Assn., Am. Legion, Masons, Shriners. Democrat. Mem. Disciples of Christ. Home: 2200 W 7th Ave Apt 104 Amarillo TX 79106-6773

WOODS, JOHN WILLIAM, electrical, computer and systems engineering educator, consultant; b. Washington, Dec. 5, 1943; s. John Gill and Margaret (McHugh) W.; m. Harriet Hemmerich, June 17, 1972; children: Anne, Christopher. BSEE, MIT, 1965, MSEE, 1967, PhD, 1970. Sr. rsch. engr. Lawrence Livermore (Calif.) Nat. Lab., 1973-76; asst. prof. Rensselaer Poly. Inst., Troy, N.Y., 1976-78, assoc. prof., 1978-84, prof., 1985—; vis. prof. Delft Tech. U., The Netherlands, 1985; program dir. NSF, Washington, 1987-88; assoc. dir. Ctr. for Image Processing Rsch., 1992—; cons. Kodak, Rochester, N.Y., 1985-86, Johns Hopkins Applied Physics Lab., Laurel, Md., 1987, Calian Comms. Ltd., 1990-91; co-founder Focus Interactive Tech., Inc., 1993. Co-author: Probability and Random Processes for Engineers, 1986, 2d edit., 1994; editor: Subband Image Coding, 1991; co-editor: Handbook of Visual Communications, 1995; mem. editl. bd. Graphical Models and Image Processing, 1989-93; contbg. author book chpts., articles to profl. jours. Mem. Com. Acad. Excellence, Clifton Park, N.Y., 1984. Capt. USAF, 1969-73. Grantee NSF, Air Force Office Sci. Rsch., Advanced Rsch. Projects Agy., Ctr. Advanced TV Studies, 1978—. Fellow IEEE (editl. bd. Trans. on Video Tech. 1990—); mem. IEEE Signal Processing Soc. (com. chmn. 1983-85, ednl. com. chmn. 1987-93, ad. com. mem. 1986-88, assoc. editor jour. 1979-82, co-chmn. tech. program com. 1st IEEE Internat. Conf. on Image Processing 1994, Best Paper awards 1977, 86, Meritorious Svc. award 1989, Tech. Achievement award 1993). Roman Catholic. Home: 43 Longview Dr Clifton Park NY 12065-2318 Office: Rensselaer Poly Inst ESCE Dept Troy NY 12180-3590

WOODS, LAWRENCE MILTON, airline company executive; b. Manderson, Wyo., Apr. 14, 1932; s. Ben Ray and Katherine (Youngman) W.; m. Joan Frances Van Patten, June 10, 1952; 1 dau., Laurie. B.Sc. with honors, U. Wyo., 1953; M.A., N.Y. U., 1973, Ph.D., 1975; LL.D., Wagner Coll., 1973. Bar: Mont. 1957; C.P.A., Colo., Mont. Accountant firm Peat, Marwick, Mitchell & Co. (C.P.A.'s), Billings, Mont., 1953; supervisory auditor Army Audit Agy., Denver, 1954-56; accountant Mobil Producing Co., Billings, Mont., 1956-59; planning analyst Socony Mobil Oil Co., N.Y.C., 1959-63; planning mgr. Socony Mobil Oil Co., 1963-65; v.p. North Am. div. Mobil Oil Corp., N.Y.C., 1966-67; gen. mgr. planning and econs. North Am. div. Mobil Oil Corp., 1967-69, v.p., 1969-77, exec. v.p., 1977-85, also dir.; pres., chief exec. officer, dir. Centennial Airlines, Inc., 1985-87; pres., dir. Woshakie Travel Corp., 1988—, High Plains Pub. Co. Inc., 1988—; bd. dirs. The Aid Assn. for Lutherans Mutual Funds. Author: Accounting for Capital, Construction and Maintenance Expenditures, 1967, The Wyoming Country Before Statehood, 1971, Sometimes the Books Froze, 1985, Moreton Frewen's Western Adventures, 1986, British Gentlemen in the Wild West, 1989; editor: Wyoming Biographies, 1991, Wyoming's Big Horn Basin, 1996; co-author: Takeover, 1980; editor: Wyoming Biographies, 1991; contbr.: Accountants' Encyclopedia, 1962. Bd. dirs. U. Wyo. Research Corp. Served with AUS, 1953-55. Mem. ABA, Mont. Bar Assn., Am. Inst. CPA's, Chgo. Club. Republican. Lutheran. Office: High Plains Pub Co PO Box 1860 Worland WY 82401-1860

WOODS, MARVIN, project controls engineer; b. Whiteville, Tenn., Oct. 2, 1960; s. Milton and Rebecca (Cross) W.; m. Sharon Elaine Dickson, June 5, 1983; children: Marvin Jr., Justin Marc. BS in Engring. Mgmt., U. Mo., Rolla, 1982; MBA in Mgmt., Lindenwood Coll., 1987. Cert. cost engr. Frame attendance Southwestern Bell, St. Louis, 1978; sr. engr. McDonnell Douglas Corp., St. Louis, 1983-92; performance measurement mgr. Morrison Knudsen Corp., Weldon Spring, Mo., 1992—. Coordinating advisor Jr. Achievement, St. Louis, 1988-92; v.p. North County YMCA Swim Team Parent's Club, 1992-93, pres., 1993-94; mgr. Florissant (Mo.) Athletic Assn. Baseball, 1991—; pres. New Northside Child Devel. Ctr. PTA, 1993-95. Named one of Outstanding Young Men Am., 1988. Mem. Am. Inst. Indsl. Engrs., Am. Assn. Cost Engrs., U. Mo. Rolla Alumni Assn. Avocations: baseball, bowling, golf. Home: 3844 Salida Ct Florissant MO 63034-1000 Office: MK Ferguson Co 7295 Highway 95 S # Rt 2 Saint Charles MO 63303

WOODS, NANCY FUGATE, women's health nurse, educator. BS, Wis. State U., 1968; MSN, U. Wash., 1969; PhD, U. N.C., 1978. Staff nurse Sacred Heart Hosp., Wis., 1968, Univ. Hosp., Wis., 1969-70, St. Francis Cabrini Hosp., 1970; nurse clinician Yale-New Haven Hosp., 1970-71; instr. nursing Duke U., Durham, N.C., 1971-72, from instr. to assoc. prof., 1972-78; assoc. prof. physiology U. Wash., Seattle, 1978-82, prof. physiology, 1982-84, chairperson dept. parent and child nursing, 1984-90, prof. dept. parent and child nursing, 1990—; dir. Ctr. Women's Health Rsch., U. Wash., Seattle, 1989—; Pres. scholar U. Calif., San Francisco, 1985-86; cons. USPHS, 1984-85, U. Tex., U. Mont, NIH, 1987, Oreg. Health Sci. U., 1985-87, 87-89, Nat. Ctr. Nursing, 1988, Nordic Inst. Nursing Sci., 1990, U. N.C., Chapel Hill, 1990, 91, U. Ariz., 1991, Mont. State U., 1991, Emory U., Atlanta, 1992. Contbr. articles to profl. jours. Fellow ANA, Am. Acad. Nursing; mem. AAUP, APHA, Am. Coll. Epidemiology, Soc. Menstrual Cycle Rsch. (v.p. 1981-82, pres. 1983-85), Soc. Advanced Women's Health Rsch. Office: U Wash Ctr Womens Health Rsch Sch Nursing Seattle WA 98195

WOODS, PENDLETON, college official, author; b. Ft. Smith, Ark., Dec. 18, 1923; s. John Powell and Mabel (Hon) W.; m. Lois Robin Freeman, Apr. 3, 1948; children: Margaret, Paul Pendleton, Nancy Cox. BA in Journalism, U. Ark., 1948. Editor, asst. pub. mgr. Okla. Gas & Electric Co., Oklahoma City, 1948-69; dir. Living Legends of Okla., Okla. Christian Univ., Oklahoma City, 1969-82, project, promotion dir. Enterprise Square and Am. Citizenship Ctr., 1982-92, dir. Nat. Edn. Program and Am. Citizenship Ctr., 1992—; arbitrator BBB; leader youth seminars in field. Bd. dirs. Campfire Girls Council, Okla. Jr. Symphony (past pres.), Boy Scout Council, Zoo Amphitheater of Oklahoma City, Will Rogers Centennial Commn., Greater Oklahoma City Tree Bank Found.; bd. dirs., co-founder Ctrl. Park Neighborhood Assn.; dir. Okla. for Resource Preservation; chmn. State Directional signage task force; vol. reader Okla. Libr. for the Blind; past pres. Okla. Assn. Epilepsy; past pres. Keep Okla. Beautiful; past pres. Oklahoma City Mental Health Clin.; pub. relations chmn. Oklahoma County chpt. A.R.C.; past chmn. Western Heritage award Nat. Cowboy Hall of Fame; past pres., hon. lifetime dir. Variety Health Center; dir. Am. Freedom Council; state pres. Sons Am. Revolution; exec. dir. Oklahoma City Bicentennial Commn.; mem. Okla. Disabilities Coun.; charter dir. Okla. Vets. Med. Rsch. Found.; cons. Exec. Svc. Corps; mem. Coun. Pub. Affairs. Served with AUS, WWII and Korean War; ret. col.; state historian Okla. N.G.; chmn. Oklahoma City Independence Day Parade, mem. exec. com. Oklahoma City Centennial Commn. Named Outstanding Young Man of Year, Oklahoma City Jr. C. of C., 1953; recipient Silver Beaver award Boy Scouts Am., 1963, Wokan award Okla. City Coun. Camp Fire Girls, 1968, Silver medal award of Advt. Fedn. Am., Disting. Community Service award of Neighborhood Devel. and Conservation Ctr, Gold and Silver Patrick Henry Patriotism medals of Mil. Order of the World Wars, 2 Commendation awards Am. Assn. for State and Local History; also 4 honor medals Freedoms Found., Jefferson Davis medal United Daus. of the Confederacy, Okla. Disting. Svc. medal (2), Outstanding Contbn. to Okla. Museums, Okla. Museums Assn., 1987, Outstanding Contbn. to Okla. Tourism award Okla. Dept. Tourism, 1989, 3 All Am. Community Svc. award U. Ark. Alumni Assn., 1992, 5 Who Care award KOCO-TV, 1993, Jefferson award Am. Inst. for Pub. Svc., 1993, Mayor's award in Beautification, 1994, George Washington award Youth Leadership Found., St. Augustine, Fla., 1993. Mem. Soc. Assoc. Indsl. Editors (past v.p.), Advt. Fedn. Am. (past dist. dir.), Central Okla. Bus. Communicators (past pres., hon. life mem.), Okla. Jr. C. of C. (hon. life; past internat. dir.), Okla. Distributive Edn. Clubs (hon. life), Okla. com. ESGR pub. affairs officer), Oklahoma City Advt. Club (past pres.), Words of Jesus Found. (pres.), Okla. Zool. Soc., Okla. Geneal. Soc. (past pres.), Okla. City chpt. U. Ark. Almuni Assn. (charter pres.), Okla. Lung Assn. (pub. relations com.), Okla. County chpt. Am. Cancer Soc. (dir.), Okla. Travel Industries Assn., Okla. Hist. Soc. (publ. editor), Okla. Heritage Assn. (publ. editor), Oklahoma City Beautiful (publ. editor), Okla. Safety Coun. (publ. editor), Oklahoma County Hist. Soc. (dir., past pres.), 45th Inf. Div. Assn. (past pres.), Mus. Unassigned Lands (chmn.), Mil. Order World Wars (regional comdr., Okla. City comdr., nat. staff), Oklahoma City Hist. Preservation Commn., Oklahoma City Heritage Roundtable, Greater Oklahoma City Clean and Green Coalition, Sigma Delta Chi, Kappa Sigma (nat. commr. publs), Lincoln Park Country (pres.), Am. Ex-Prisoners of War (state comdr.), Okla. Vets Coun. (chmn.). Author: You and Your Company Magazine, 1950, Church of Tomorrow, 1964, Myriad of Sports, 1971, This Was Oklahoma, 1979. Recorded Sounds of Scouting, 1969, Born Grown, 1974 (Western Heritage award Nat. Cowboy Hall Fame), One of a Kind, 1977, Countdown to Statehood, 1982, The Thunderbird Tradition, 1989, A Glimpse at Oklahoma, 1990; editor Looking Ahead. Home: 541 NW 31st St Oklahoma City OK 73118-7334

WOODS, PHILIP WELLS (PHIL WOODS), jazz musician composer; b. Springfield, Mass., Nov. 2, 1931; s. Stanley J. and Clara (Markley) W.; m. Beverly Berg, 1957 (div. 1973); children: Garth Darryl, Aimee Francesca; m. Jill Goodwin, Dec. 20, 1985; stepchildren: Allisen, Tracey Trotter. Student, Juilliard Sch., N.Y.C., 1948-52; LLD (hon.), East Stroudsberg U., 1994. Alto saxophone and clarinet with Dizzy Gillespie and Quincy Jones, alto saxophone with Benny Goodman, Gene Krupa, Thelonious Monk, Buddy Rich, Charlie Barnet, Michel Legrand, many others; leader European Rhythm Machine, 1968-73, Phil Woods Quartet, 1974-84, Phil Woods Quintet, 1984—; composer Rights of Swing, Three Improvisations, Sonata for Alto and Piano (Four Moods), The Sun Suite, I Remember, Deer Head Sketches, numerous others; recs. with own bands include Rights of Swing, 1971, Phil and Quill (3 albums with Gene Quill), Images (with Michel Legrand) (Grammy award 1976), (with Benny Carter) My Man Benny, My Man Phil, I Remember: A Tribute to Some of the Great Jazz Musicians, 1979, More Live (Grammy award 1982), At the Vanguard (Grammy award 1983), (as the Phil Woods Quintet) All Bird's Children (as Phil Woods' Little Big Band), Evolution, Real Life, Flash, Astor and Elis, Mile High Jazz; played saxophone on many other recs. including Clark Terry and Ben Webster's Happy Faces, Symbiosis by Bill Evans, A New Album with Lena Horne, Just the Way You Are with Billy Joel, Dr. Wu with Steely Dan; also played on motion picture soundtracks The Hustler, 1961, Blow-Up, 1966, Twelve Angry Men, 1957, It's My Turn, 1980, Boy In A Tree. Co-founder, bd. dirs. Delaware Water Gap (Pa.) Celebration of the Arts, 1978—. Named

New Star of 1956 Downbeat mag.; winner Down Beat Critics' Poll, 1975-79, 81-90, 92-93, 96, Down Beat Readers' Poll, 1975-95; recipient Golden Feather award for best group Phil Woods Quartet Downbeat Critics' Poll, 1978, Downbeat Readers Poll award for best acoustic group Phil Woods Quintet, 1988-91, Downbeat Critics' Poll award for best acoustic group Phil Woods Quintet, 1990, Jazz Times Readers Poll award for best alto sax, 1990, 92; elected to Am. Jazz Hall of Fame, 1994. Mem. Am. Fedn. Musicians. Internat. Assn. Jazz Educators. Avocations: reading, cooking, movies, computers. Office: PO Box 278 Delaware Water Gap PA 18327-0278

WOODS, PHYLLIS MICHALIK, elementary school educator; b. New Orleans, Sept. 12, 1937; d. Philip John and Thelma Alice (Carey) Michalik; 1 child, Tara Lynn Woods. BA, Southeastern La. U., 1967. Cert. speech and English tchr., libr. sci., La. Tchr. speech, English and drama St. Charles Parish Pub. Schs., Luling, La., elem. tchr., secondary tchr. remedial reading, Chpt. I reading specialist; Wicat tchr. coord.; tchr. cons. St. Charles parish writing project La. State U. Writing Project. Author: Egbert, the Egret, Egbert's Picnic, Egbert Visits Sammy, Angel Without Wings; songwriter; contbr. articles and poems to River Parish Guide, St. Charles Herald. Sch. rep. United Fund, St. Charles Parish Reading Assn.; parish com. mem. Young Authors, Tchrs. Who Write; active 4-H. Mem. ASCD, Internat. Reading Assn., St. Charles Parish Reading Coun., Newspaper in Edn. (chmn., historian), La. Assn. Newspapers in Edn. (state com.).

WOODS, REGINALD FOSTER, management consulting executive; b. Charleston, W.Va., Sept. 25, 1939; s. Reginald Foster and Jean Lee (Hill) W.; m. Katharine Terry Norden, May 11, 1963; children: Eric Arthur, Elizabeth Terry, Tracy Lee. BME, Cornell U., 1961, MME, 1962, MBA, 1963. Mktg. specialist Gen. Electric Co., N.Y.C., 1963-64; dir. flight equipment and facilities planning Eastern Airlines, N.Y.C., 1964-70; v.p. planning Butler Internat., Inc., Montvale, N.J., 1970, sr. v.p. fin., 1971-80, exec. v.p., 1980-86, pres., 1986-87; chmn. Mgmt. Resources Group, Inc., Saddle River, N.J., 1987-96; pres., ceo The Advantage Ptnrs., Chatham, N.J., 1992-94; bd. dirs. Benedetto, Gartland & Greene, Inc., N.Y.C., DCG Corp., Roseville, Calif., The Greenleaf Co., Cranford, N.J., pres. DCG Corp., 1994—. Mem. Ridgewood Country Club, Glenmore Country Club.

WOODS, RICHARD DALE, lawyer; b. Kansas City, Mo., May 20, 1950; s. Willard Dale and Betty Sue (Duncan) W.; m. Cecelia Ann Thompson, Aug. 11, 1973 (div. July 1996); children: Duncan Warren, Shannon Cecelia. BA, U. Kans., 1972; JD, U. Mo., 1975. Bar: Mo. 1975, U.S. Dist. Ct. (we. dist.) Mo. 1975. Assoc. Shook, Hardy & Bacon L.L.P., Kansas City, Mo., 1975-79, ptnr., 1980—; gen. chmn. Estate Planning Symposium, Kansas City, 1985-86; chair Northland Coalition, 1993. Chmn. fin. com. North Woods Ch., Kansas City, 1986-88, 93-96; mem. sch. bd. N. Kansas City Sch. Dist., 1990-97, treas., 1992-97; chmn. planned giving com. Truman Med. Ctr., 1992—; mem. Clay County Tax Increment Fin. Commn., 1990—. Fellow Am. Coll. Trust and Estate Counsel; mem. ABA, KC, Mo. Bar Assn., Kans. City Met. Bar Assn., Lawyers Assn. Kans. City (sec., v.p., pres. young lawyers sect. 1981-84), Kans. City Estate Planning Soc. (bd. dirs. 1985-88, 93-95). Democrat. Office: Shook Hardy & Bacon LLP One Kansas City Place 1200 Main St Kansas City MO 64105

WOODS, RICHARD SEAVEY, accountant, educator; b. Albion, N.Y., Mar. 1, 1919; s. Stanley Taylor and Helen Saxe (Seavey) W.; m. Dorothy Signor Blake, Dec. 19, 1945; children: David Blake, Michael Signor, Martha Seavey, Catherine Hardie. A.B., U. Rochester, 1941; M.B.A., U. Pa., 1947, Ph.D., 1957. C.P.A., Pa. Tchr. English pub. schs. Shortsville, N.Y., 1941-42; instr. accounting U. Pa. Wharton Sch., Phila., 1947-52; asst. prof. U. Pa. Wharton Sch., 1952-58, asso. prof., 1958-64, prof., 1964-87, prof. emeritus, 1987—, asso. chmn. dept., 1961-63, acting chmn., 1961-62, 75-76, chmn., 1963-69. Author: (with O.S. Nelson) Accounting Systems and Data Processing, 1961; cons. editor: Accountant's Handbook, 1970; editor, contbr.: Audit Decisions in Accounting Practice, 1973, Audit Decision Cases, 1973. Served to lt. USNR, 1942-46. Mem. Am. Accounting Assn., Am. Inst. C.P.A.s. Home: 645 Willow Valley Sq J-307 Lancaster PA 17602-4871 Office: Steinberg-Dietrich Hall Univ of Pa Philadelphia PA 19104

WOODS, ROBERT A., chemical company executive. Pres. ICI Americas Inc., Wilmington, Del.; pres. agrl. products Zeneca Inc., Wilmington, 1993—. Office: Zeneca Inc 1800 Concord Pike PO Box 15458 Wilmington DE 19850-5458

WOODS, ROBERT ARCHER, investment counsel; b. Princeton, Ind., Dec. 28, 1920; s. John Hall and Rose Erskine Heilman W.; m. Ruth Henrietta Diller, May 27, 1944; children—Robert Archer III, Barbara Diller (Mrs. Gregory Alan Klein), Katherine Heilman (Mrs. John E. Glennon), James Diller. A.B., U. Rochester, 1942; M.B.A., Harvard, 1946. Account exec. Stein Roe & Farnham (investment counsel), Chgo., 1946-53, ptnr., 1954-90; gov. Investment Co. Inst. Trustee U. Rochester; bd. dirs. Chgo. Juvenile Protective Assn., Chgo. Infant Welfare Soc., Chgo. Assn. Retarded Citizens. Served to lt. (s.g.) USNR, 1943-46. Mem. Am. Mgmt. Assn. (trustee 1973), Harvard Bus. Sch. Club Chgo. (pres. 1961), Phi Beta Kappa, Delta Upsilon. Clubs: Univ. Chgo, Chicago, Tower. Home: 470 Orchard Ln Winnetka IL 60093-4222 Office: 1 S Wacker Dr Chicago IL 60606-4614

WOODS, ROBERT EDWARD, lawyer; b. Albert Lea, Minn., Mar. 27, 1952; s. William Fabian and Maxine Elizabeth (Schmit) W.; m. Cynthia Anne Pratt, Dec. 26, 1975; children: Laura Marie Woods, Amy Elizabeth Woods. BA, U. Minn., 1974, JD, 1977; MBA, U. Pa., 1983. Bar: Minn. 1977, U.S. Dist. Ct. Minn. 1980, U.S. Ct. Appeals (8th cir.) 1980. Assoc. Moriarty & Janzen, Mpls., 1977-81, Berger & Montague, Phila., 1982-83; assoc. Briggs and Morgan, St. Paul and Mpls., 1983-84, ptnr., 1984—; adj. prof. William Mitchell Coll. Law, St. Paul, 1985; exec. com., bd. dirs. LEX MUNDI, Ltd., Houston, 1989-93, chmn. bd. 1991-92; bd. dirs. Midwest Asia Ctr., 1993-95, chmn. bd., 1994-95. Author (with others) Business Torts, 1989; sr. contbg. editor: Evidence in America: The Federal Rules in the States, 1987. Mem. ABA, Minn. State Bar Assn., Hennepin County Bar Assn., Ramsey County Bar Assn. (chmn. corp., banking and bus. law sect. 1985-87), Assn. Trial Lawyers Am., Wharton Club of Minn., Phi Beta Kappa. Home: 28 N Deep Lake Rd North Oaks MN 55127-6506 Office: Briggs & Morgan 2400 IDS Ctr 80 S 8th St Minneapolis MN 55402-2100

WOODS, ROSE MARY, former presidential assistant, consultant; b. Sebring, Ohio, Dec. 26, 1917; d. Thomas M. and Mary (Maley) W. Ed. high sch.; L.D.H., Pfeiffer Coll., 1971. With Royal China, Inc., Sebring, 1935-43, Office Censorship, 1943-45, Internat. Tng. Adminstrn., 1945-47, Herter Com. Fgn. Aid, 1947, Fgn. Service Ednl. Found., 1947-51; sec. to senator, then v.p. Nixon, 1951-61; asst. Mr. Nixon with firm Adams, Duque & Hazeltine, Los Angeles, 1961-63, firm Nixon, Mudge, Rose, Guthrie, Alexander & Mitchell, N.Y.C., 1963-68; exec. asst. to former Pres. Nixon, 1969-75; now consultant. Named 1 of 10 Women of Year Los Angeles Times, 1961, 1 of 75 Most Important Women in Am. Ladies Home Jour., 1971. Home: 1194 W Cambridge St Alliance OH 44601-2169

WOODS, SANDRA KAY, manufacturing executive; b. Loveland, Colo., Oct. 11, 1944; d. Ivan H. and Florence L. (Betz) Harris; m. Gary A. Woods, June 11, 1967; children: Stephanie Michelle, Michael Harris. BA, U. Colo., 1966, MA, 1967. Personnel mgmt. specialist CSC, Denver, 1967; asst. to regional dir. HEW, Denver, 1968-69; urban renewal rep. HUD, Denver, 1970-73, dir. program analysis, 1974-75, asst. regional dir. community planning and devel., 1976-77, regional dir. fair housing, 1978-79; mgr. ea. facility project Adolph Coors Co., Golden Colo., 1980, dir. real estate, 1981, v.p. chief environ. health and safety officer, 1982-96, v.p. strategic selling initiatives, 1996—. pres. Industries for Jefferson County (Colo.), 1985. Mem. Exec. Exchange, The White House, 1980; bd. dirs. Golden Local Devel. Corp. (Colo.), 1981-82; fundraising dir. Coll. Arts and Scis., U. Colo., Boulder, 1982-89, U. Colo. Found.; mem. exec. bd. NCCJ, Denver, 1982-94; v.p. Women in Bus., Inc., Denver, 1982-83; mem. steering com. 1984 for All Denver Women, 1983-84; mem. 10th dist. Denver br. Fed. Reserve Bd., 1990-96, chmn. bd., 1995-96; bd. dirs Nat. Jewish Hosp. 1994—. Named one of Outstanding Young Women Am., U.S. Jaycees, 1974, 78, Fifty Women to Watch, Businessweek, 1987, 92, Woman of Achievement YWCA, 1988. Chmn. Greater Denver Corp., 1991—. Mem. Indsl. Devel. Resources Council (bd. dirs. 1986-89), Am. Mgmt. Assn., Denver C. of C. (bd. dirs. 1988-96, Disting. Young Exec. award 1974, mem. Leadership Denver, 1976-77), Colo. Women's Forum, Nat. Assn. Office and Indsl. Park Developers (sec. 1988, treas. 1989), Committee of 200 (v.p. 1994-95), Phi Beta Kappa, Pi Alpha Alpha. Republican. Presbyterian. Club: PEO (Loveland, Colo.). Office: Coors Brewing Co NH 301 Golden CO 80401

WOODS, TIGER (ELDRICK WOODS), professional golfer; b. Cypress, Calif., Dec. 30, 1975; s. Earl and Kultida W. Student, Stanford U. Winner U.S. Jr. Amateur titles, 1991, 92, 93, U.S. Amateur titles, 1994, 95, 96, U.S. Amateur Championship, 1995, 96, Walt Disney World Classic, 1996, Las Vegas Invitational, 1996, NCAA Tournament, 1996. Winner Masters tournament, 1997. Youngest, first African Am., first Asian Am., and first to win Masters by largest margin of 12 strokes, 1997. Office: PGA 100 Avenue Of Champions Palm Beach Gardens FL 33418-3653

WOODS, WALTER EARL, biomedical manufacturing executive; b. Phila., Sept. 26, 1944; s. Walter Earl and Janet I. (Ferguson) W.; m. Anna Maria Gianfreda, Dec. 4, 1975; children: Jeffrey, Elaine, Roberto, Carlo. BS in Biology, Del. Valley Coll. Sci. and Agr., 1966. Pilot plant operator Shell Chem., Woodbury, N.J., 1966-67; virologist, tissue culturist 1st U.S. Med. Lab., N.Y.C. and Ft. Meade, Md., 1967-69; virologist Merck, Sharpe & Dohme, West Point, Pa., 1969-70; quality control and assurance supr. Richardson-Merrell Inc., Swiftwater, Pa., 1970-74; cons., dir. influenza vaccine mfg. Richardson-Merrell Inc., Naples, Italy, 1974-75; mgr. biol. prodn. Richardson-Merrell Inc., Swiftwater, 1976-78; mgr. biol. prodn. Connaught Labs., Inc., Swiftwater, 1978-81, dir. vaccine mfg., 1982-84, dir. mfg. resource planning, class A rating, 1984-88, dir. product devel. and mgmt., 1989-91, project dir. SAP software installation, 1997—; dir. project mgmt., chmn. HIB and Pertussis bus. groups Pasteur Mérieux Connaught, 1991-95; project dir. licensing Acellular Pertussis and Japanese Encepahlitis Vacines, 1992, HIB vaccine, 1993, licensed acP vaccine, Germany, 1994; bus. dir. for license of acellular pertussis vaccine, infant indications; mem. joint devel. com. Merck-Connaught Partnership; corp. sponsor for licensing of DTacP vaccine for infant use, 1996. Bd. dirs. Northeastern Pa. Indsl. Resource Ctr., Wilkes-Barre, Pa., 1988-91. Recipient Banting-Best award, 1989. Mem. ASM, Pharm. Mfrs., Project Mgmt. Inst., Internat. Assn. Biol. Standardization. Avocations: soccer, music, gardening, reading. Home: 53 Deerfield Way Scotrun PA 18355-9637 Office: Connaught Labs Inc PO Box 187 Swiftwater PA 18370-0187

WOODS, WALTER RALPH, retired agricultural scientist, administrator; b. Grant, Va., Dec. 2, 1931; s. John Wythe and Hazel Gladys (Hash) W.; m. Jacqulyn Rose Miller, Sept. 14, 1953; children: Neal Ralph, Diana Lyn. B.S., Murray (Ky.) State U., 1954; M.S., U. Ky., 1955; Ph.D., Okla. State U., 1957. Instr. animal sci. Okla. State U., 1956-57; asst. prof., then assoc. prof. Iowa State U., 1957-62; assoc. prof., then prof. U. Nebr., 1962-71; prof. animal sci., head dept. Purdue U., 1971-85; dean Kans. State U., Manhattan, 1985-92, dir. Agrl. Expt. Sta., 1985-92, dir. Coop. Ext. Svc., 1987-92; asst. adminstr. for regional rsch. CSRS USDA, Washington, 1993-94; acting dep. adminstr. USDA/CSREES, Washington, 1994-95. Author papers, articles in field. Bd. dirs. Ind. 4-H Found., 1979-81, Kans. 4-H Found., 1987-92; mem. leadership coun. Kans. Value Added Ctr., 1990-92; mem. exec. com. Kans. Rural Devel. Coun., 1990-93; chair Coun. Adminstrv. Head Agr., 1992, Great Plains Agr. Coun., 1990-92. Recipient Disting. Agrl. Alumni award Murray State U., 1969, Meritorious Service award Ind. Pork Producers Assn., 1975. Mem. Am. Soc. Animal Sci. (sec.-treas. Midwest sect. 1979-81, pres. Midwest sect. 1983-84). Mem. Disciples of Christ Ch. Home: 8318 Strathmore Ln Roanoke VA 24019

WOODS, WARD WILSON, JR., investment company executive; b. Ann Arbor, Mich., June 27, 1942; m. Priscilla Bacon; children: Katherine, Alexandra. BA, Stanford U., 1964. With constrn. and real estate firm, San Francisco, 1964-66, gen. mgr., 1966-67; with Lehman Bros., N.Y.C., 1967-78, ptnr., 1973-1978; mng. dir. Lehman Bros. Kuhn Loeb Inc., N.Y.C., 1973-78; sr. ptnr. Lazard Freres & Co., N.Y.C., 1978-89; pres., chief exec. officer Bessemer Securities Corp., N.Y.C., 1989—; mng. ptnr. Bessemer Holdings, L.P., N.Y.C., 1989—; bd. dirs. Freeport McMoflan Copper and Gold Co., Boise Cascade, Kelley Oil and Gas Corp., Bessemer Trust Co. Trustee Stanford U. Boys Club of N.Y.; vice-chmn. Asia Soc.; mem. Coun. on Fgn. Rels.; gov. The Nature Conservancy; bd. visitors Inst. for Internat. Studies Stanford U. Office: Bessemer Securities Corp 630 5th Ave New York NY 10111-0100

WOODS, WILLIAM ELLIS, lawyer, pharmacist, association executive; b. Ballinger, Tex., Sept. 25, 1917; s. Cary Dysart and Gertrude Mae (Ellis) W.; m. Martha Brockman, May 28, 1954. B.S., U. Tex. Sch. Pharmacy, 1938; J.D., Sch. Law, 1953. Bar: Tex. bar 1954, U.S. Supreme Ct 1957. Dir. emergency med. service Tex. State Health Dept., 1942-43, USPHS, 1943-47; asst. dir. Nat. Pharm. Survey Office, 1947-48; with Eli Lilly & Co., 1948-51; first dir. U. Tex. Pharmacy Extension Service, Austin, 1953-54; pvt. practice law Corpus Christi, Tex., 1954-58; asst. to exec. v.p. Nat. Pharm Council, N.Y.C., 1958-64; sec. Nat. Pharm Council, 1964-65; Washington rep., assoc. gen. counsel Nat. Assn. Retail Druggists, 1965-76, exec. v.p., 1976-84, hon. past pres., 1984; presenter testimony on health, pharmacy and small bus. before coms. of U.S. Congress and various fed. agys.; mem. Joint Commn. on Pharmacy Practitioners; chmn. Nat. Small Bus. Legis. Coun., 1981; pres. Nat. Drug Trade Conf., 1981; del. U.S. Pharmacopoeial Conv., 1975, 80. Contbr. articles to pharmacy pubs. Recipient Achievement Medal award Alpha Zeta Omega, 1975, Lubin Profl. Pharmacy award U. Tenn., 1982; established Wm. E. Woods Endowed Presdl. Scholarship in Law, U. Tex., 1994. Mem. ABA, Tex. Bar Assn., Law Sci. Acad., Phi Delta Phi, U. Tex. Chancellor's Coun., Nat. Assn. Execs., Univ. Club, Internat. Club, Capitol Hill Club, Can. Club (N.Y.C.). Methodist. Home: PO Box 1045 Easton MD 21601-1045

WOODS, WILLIE G., dean, English language and education educator; b. Yazoo City, Miss.; d. John Wesley and Jessie Willie Mae W. BA, Shaw U., Raleigh, N.C., 1965; MEd, Duke U., 1968; postgrad., Pa. State U., 1970, 80-82, Temple U., 1972, U. N.H., 1978, NYU, 1979, Indiana U. of Pa., 1986-88; PhD, Indiana U. of Pa., 1995. Tchr. schs. in N.C. and Md., 1965-69; mem. faculty Harrisburg (Pa.) Area Community Coll., 1969—, assoc. prof. English and edn., 1976-82, prof., 1982-94, sr. prof., 1994—, supr. Writing Ctr., 1975-78, coord. Act 101/Basic Studies Program, 1978-83, dir. Acad. Founds. program 1983-87, asst. dean academ. affairs Acad. Found. and Basic Edn. Div., 1987-89, asst. dean acad. affairs, chmn. social sci., pub. svcs. and basic edn. div., 1989-94, dean social sci., pub. svcs. and basic edn. divsn., 1994—, chmn. dirs. coun., 1981-82, acting v.p. faculty and instrn., 1996—; tchr. Community Resources Inst., 1975-90; moderator workshops, cons. in field. Asst. editor Black Conf. Higher Edn. Jour., 1980. Sec., exec. com. People for Progress, 1971-73; bd. mgrs., exec. com. Camp Curtin br. YMCA, 1971-79; bd. dirs. Alternative Rehab. Communities, 1978—; bd. mgrs. Youth Urban Svcs., Harrisburg Area YMCA, 1981-92; bd. dirs. Dauphin Residences, Inc., 1981-88. Kellogg fellow in expanding leadership diversity in cmty. coll. program, 1994-95; recipient cert. of merit for community svcs. City of Harrisburg, 1971, Youth Urban Svcs. Vol. of Yr. award, 1983, Black Student Union award Harrisburg Area Community Coll., 1984. Mem. Pa. Assn. Devel. Educators (chmn. conf. 1980, sec. 1981-82, v.p. 1986-87, pres. 1987-88), Pa. Black Conf. Higher Edn. (Outstanding Svc. award 1980, Central Region award 1982), Nat. Coun. Tchrs. English, Pa. Edn. Assn., Am. Assn. Community and Jr. Colls., Nat. Coun. on Black Am. (instl. rep. 1983—), AAUP, Alpha Kappa Alpha (Outstanding Svc. award 1983, 97, Basileus award 1984, Ida B. Wells Excellence in Media award 1994, Ivy Honor Roll of Clips award 1994), Alpha Kappa Mu, Phi Kappa Phi. Baptist. Home: 1712 Ft Patton Dr Harrisburg PA 17112-8511 Office: 3300 Cameron Street Rd Harrisburg PA 17110-2914

WOODS, WINTON D., law educator; b. Balt., Jan. 11, 1938; s. W.D. and Nancy N. W.; m. Barbara Lewis; children: Tad, Adam, Brooke, Lindsy, Jessica. AB Econ./Gov., Ind. U., 1961, JD with distinction, 1965. Bar: Ind., Ariz.; U.S. Supreme Ct. Law clk. U.S. Dist. Ct. (no. dist.) Calif., Sacramento, 1965-67; prof. law U. Ariz., Tucson, 1967—; reporter U.S. Dist. Ariz. Civil Justice Reform Act Com., 1992—; pres. Law Office Computing, Inc., 1990—; dir. Courtroom of the Future Project, U. Ariz., 1993—. Contbr. articles to profl. jours; author: The Lawyers Computer Book, 1990. Mem. bio-ethics com. UMC, Tucson, 1984-96. Recipient Fulbright award, 1979, Educator of Yr. award Internat. Comm. Industry Assn., 1996-97; fellow NEH, 1972, Nat. Inst. for Dispute Resolution, 1982. Mem. ABA, Ariz. State Bar Assn. Jewish. Avocations: computers, automobiles, photography. Office: U Ariz Coll of Law U Ariz Tucson AZ 85721

WOODSIDE, DONNA J., nursing educator; b. Ft. Wayne, Ind., Feb. 3, 1940; d. Evan Russell and Helen Bernice (High) Owens; m. Henry W. Schroeder, Nov. 28, 1959 (dec.); children: William Schroeder, Michael Schroeder; m. Robert J. Woodside, Jan. 11, 1974; children: Chris, Tracy. BSN, U. Evansville, 1970; MSN, U. Cin., 1975, EdD, 1981. Cert. diabetes educator, gerontology nurse. Staff nurse Wahiawa (Hawaii) Community Hosp., Health Profl. Agy., Cin.; instr. Bethesda Hosp. Sch. Nursing, Cin.; assoc. prof. U. Cin., 1991; pres. Concepts R & D Inc., 1989—; field nurse Willowbrook Home Health Care, Inc., 1993—. Mem. Am. Assn. Diabetes Educators, Sigma Theta Tau. Home: 2230 Oakleaf Dr Franklin TN 37064-7413

WOODSIDE, FRANK C., III, lawyer; b. Glen Ridge, N.J., Apr. 18, 1944. BS, Ohio State U., 1966, JD, 1969; MD, U. Cin., 1973. Bar: Ohio 1969, Ky. 1991, Mo. 1993, Tenn. 1993; diplomate Am. Bd. Profl. Liability Attys. Mem. Dinsmore & Shohl, Cin.; clin. prof. pediats. U. Cin., 1992—; adj. prof. law U. Cin., 1973-92. Editor: Drug Product Liability, 1985—. Fellow Am. Coll. Legal Medicine, Am. Soc. Hosp. Attys., Soc. Ohio Hosp. Attys.; mem. ABA, Ohio State Bar Assn., Fed. Bar Assn., Internat. Assn. Def. Counsel, Cin. Bar Assn., Def. Rsch. Inst. (chmn. drug and med. svc. com. 1988-91). Office: Dinsmore & Shohl 1900 Chemed Ctr 255 E 5th St Cincinnati OH 45202-4700

WOODSIDE, LISA NICOLE, academic administrator; b. Portland, Oreg., Sept. 7, 1944; d. Lee and Emma (Wenstrom) W. Student Reed Coll., 1962-65; MA, U. Chgo., 1968; PhD, Bryn Mawr Coll., 1972; cert. Harvard U. Inst. for Ednl. Mgmt., 1979; MA, West Chester U., 1994. Cert. in wellness counseling, creative energy options. Mem. dean's staff Bryn Mawr Coll., 1970-72; asst. prof. Widener U., Chester, Pa., 1972-77, assoc. prof. humanities, 1978-83, asst. dean student services, 1972-76, assoc. dean, 1976-79, dean, 1979-83; acad. dean, prof. of humanities Holy Family Coll., Phila., 1983—, v.p., dean acad. affairs, prof. humanities, 1990—; cons. State N.J. Edn. Dept., 1990; accreditor Commn. on Higher Edn., Middle States Assn., 1977-83, 94. Co-author: New Age Spirituality: An Assessment. City commr. for community rels. Chester, 1980-83; mem. Adult Edn. Council Phila. Am. Assn. Papyrology grantee Bryn Mawr Coll.; S. Maude Kaemmerling fellow Bryn Mawr Coll. Mem. Am. Assn. Higher Edn., Coun. Ind. Colls., Eastern Assn. Coll. Deans, Pa. Assn. Colls. and Tchr. Educators, AAUW (univ. rep. 1975-83), Nat. Assn. Women in C. of C., Am. Psychol. Assn., Transpersonal Assn., Audubon Soc., Phi Eta Sigma, Alpha Sigma Lambda, Psi Chi. Home: 360 Saybrook Ln # A Media PA 19086-6761 Office: Holy Family Coll Torresdale Humanities Dept Philadelphia PA 19114

WOODSIDE, ROBERT ELMER, lawyer, former judge; b. Millersburg, Pa., June 4, 1904; s. Robert E. and Ella (Neitz) W.; m. F. Fairlee Habbart, July 11, 1931 (dec.); children—William Edward, Robert James, Jane Fairlee; m. Anna C. Woodside, June 27, 1987. A.B., Dickinson Coll., 1926, LL.B., 1928, LL.D. (hon.), 1951. Bar: Pa. 1928. Practiced in Millersburg and Harrisburg, Pa., 1928-42; judge Ct. Common Pleas, Dauphin Co., 1942-51; became atty. gen. Commonwealth of Pa., 1951; judge Superior Court Pa., 1953-65; ptnr. Mette, Evans and Woodside, Harrisburg, 1965-87; ret., 1987; adj. prof. Dickinson Sch. Law, Carlisle, Pa., 1969-87; legislator Pa. State House of Reps., 1932-42, Rep. house leader, 1939, 41; mem. Joint State Govt. Commn., 1939-42; del. 16th congl. dist. Rep. Nat. Conv., 1952; chmn. Pa. Little Hoover Commn.; chmn. Pa. Council Juvenile Ct. Judges, 1947-49. Pres. bd. trustees Pa. Industrial Sch., White Hill, Pa., 1945-55; chmn. on Commn. on Constl. Revision; mem. Pa. Constl. Conv., 1967-68. Mem. Omicron Delta Kappa, Phi Kappa Sigma, Tau Kappa Alpha. Methodist. Clubs: Mason (33 deg., Shriner), Red Man, Royal Arcanum. Home: 351 Union St Millersburg PA 17061

WOOD-SMITH, DONALD, plastic surgeon; b. Sydney, Australia, June 30, 1931; s. William Frederick and Vera Mary; children: Christina Margaret, Donald William, Phillip Raynor. MB, BS, Sydney U., 1954. Diplomate Am. Bd. Plastic Surgury. Surg. resident Lewisham Hosp., Sydney, 1954-56, Royal Marsden Hosp., 1957-58; resident plastic surgery N.Y. U. Hosp. Med. Center, 1960-64, asst. and assoc. attending surgeon, 1964-92; vis. surgeon Bellevue Hosp., 1964-92; chmn. plastic surgery Manhattan Eye Ear and Throat Hosp., 1975-77; assoc. prof. plastic surgery NYU, 1977-84, prof., 1984-92; surgeon, dir. plastic surgery Manhattan Eye Ear and Throat Hosp., 1977-84; cons. plastic surgeon N.Y. Eye and Ear Infirmary, chmn. dept. plastic and reconstructive surgery, 1984—; prof. plastic surgery Columbia Presbyn. Med. Ctr., 1991—. Author: Nursing Care of the Plastic Surgery Patient, 1967, Cosmetic Facial Surgery, 1973; contbr. articles to med. jours. Fellow ACS, Royal Coll. Surgeons of Edinburgh; mem. Am. Assn. Plastic Surgeons, Am. Soc. Plastic and Reconstructive Surgeons, Am. Soc. Maxillofacial Surgeons, N.Y. Acad. Medicine, Brit. Assn. Plastic Surgeons, N.Y. Athletic Club. Republican. Office: 830 Park Ave New York NY 10021-2757

WOODSON, AL CURTIS, software company executive, software engineer; b. Phila., May 22, 1960; s. Alfred Curtis and Evelyn Gretel Woodson; m. Lenora Vinett Dunham, Aug. 25, 1990. BS in Mktg., Hampton U., 1982. Cons. J.E.S. Search Firm Inc., Atlanta, 1986; sales rep. Inacomp Computer Ctrs., Atlanta, 1986-87, desk top pub. specialist, 1987, store mgr., 1987, Apple mktg. mgr., 1987-88, Apple bus. devel. engr., 1988-89; Apple systems engr. Datagraphic, Inc., Roswell, Ga., 1989-90, product mgr. computer networking, 1990-91, mgr. product rsch. and devel., 1991-93; pres. Questeck, Ltd., Alpharetta, Ga., 1993—; speaker in field. Officer inf. U.S. Army, 1982-85. Mem. Nat. Assn. Desktop Pubs. (futrends group), Nat. Bus. Forms Assn. (ANSI X12 standards rev. com., EDI standard revs. com., non-impact com.), Xplor Internat., Omega Psi Phi. Home: 10535 Willow Meadow Cir Alpharetta GA 30202-5710 Office: Questeck Ltd Ste 401-26 10945 State Bridge Rd Alpharetta GA 30022-8164

WOODSON, BENJAMIN NELSON, III, insurance executive; b. Altoona, Kans., June 5, 1908; s. Benjamin Nelson and Mary Ola (Burke) W.; m. Grace Cook, Jan. 25, 1930 (dec. Apr. 1981); 1 child, Mary Burnett Crowell; m. Audrey Haney Watson, Apr. 1, 1983. Student pub. schs. Omaha. Stenographer, salesman, officer Mut. Trust Life Co., Chgo., 1928-37; exec. Life Ins. Mgmt. Rsch. Assocs., Hartford, Conn., 1937-44; exec. v.p. Commonwealth Life, Louisville, 1944-50; mng. dir. Nat. Assn. Life Underwriters/Life Underwriters Tng. Coun., Washington, 1950-53; pres. Am. Gen. Life, Houston, 1953-72; v.p., then pres., Am. Gen. Corp., Houston, 1954-72, chmn. chief exec. officer, 1972-78, also bd. dirs.; dir. Mitchell Energy & Devel., Houston, 1976—, Am. Capital Mutual Funds, Houston, 1969-96; ptnr., spl. counsel exec. com. John L. Wortham & Son, Houston, 1958—. CLU. Author: More Power to You, 1950; The Set of The Sail, 1968; Simple Truth, 1980, The Best of Woody, 1993; contbr. essays to Life Assn. News, 1937-95. Bd. dirs. Tex. Med. Ctr., Houston, 1981—, Up With People, Tucson, 1972—, Sch. Ins. and Fin. Svcs. Mktg., U. Houston, 1983—, regent, vice chmn. U. Houston, 1977-83; gov. Rice U., Houston, 1962-74, overseer Jones Grad. Sch. Bus., 1977-83, overseer emeritus, 1983—; founder, life trustee Houston Found. for Retarded. Named Disting. Citizen Goodwill Industries, 1973, Man of Yr., Fedn. Ins. Counsel, 1980, Houston Honoree of Yr., NCCJ, 1976; recipient Solomon Huebner Gold award, 1988. Mem. Million Dollar Round Table (life), Nat. Assn. Life Underwriters (John Newton Russell award 1963), Tex. Assn. Life Underwriters, Houston Assn. Life Underwriters, Life Underwriter Tng. Council (founder, life trustee), Life Ins. Mktg. and Research Assn., Houston C. of C. (chmn. 1972-73, named Outstanding Leader 1972). Republican. Mem. Oahu Country (Honolulu); Houston (pres. 1970-72), River Oaks Country (v.p., bd. dirs. 1978-81) Forum (founding chmn. 1979—) (Houston), Metropolitan (N.Y.C.), Woodlands Country. Home: 3711 San Felipe Rd Ste 13-G Houston TX 77019 Office: 2727 Allen Pky Ste 460 Houston TX 77019-2100

WOODSON, DARREN RAY, professional football player; b. Phoenix, Apr. 25, 1969. Student, Ariz. State U. Safety Dallas Cowboys, 1992—. Named to Sporting News NFL-All-Pro Team, 1994; selected to Pro Bowl, 1994, 96. Mem. Dallas Cowboys Super Bowl XXVII Champions, 1992, Super Bowl XXVIII, 1993. Office: Dallas Cowboys 1 Cowboys Pkwy Irving TX 75063-4945*

WOODSON, GAYLE ELLEN, otolaryngologist; b. Galveston, Tex., June 9, 1950; d. Clinton Eldon and Nancy Jean (Stephens) W.; m. Kevin Thomas Robbins; children: Nicholas, Gregory, Sarah. BA, Rice U., 1972; MD, Baylor Coll. Medicine, 1975. Diplomate Am. Bd. Otolaryngology (bd. dirs.). Fellow Baylor Coll. Medicine, Houston, 1976, Inst. Laryngology & Otology, London, 1981-82; asst. prof. Baylor Coll. Medicine, 1982-87; asst. attending Harris County Hosp. Dist., Houston, 1982-86; with courtesy staff Saint Luke's Episcopal Hosp., Houston, 1982-87; assoc. attending The Methodist Hosp., Houston, 1982-87; asst. prof. U. Calif. Med. Sch., San Diego, 1987-89; chief otolaryngology VA Med. Ctr., San Diego, 1987-92; assoc. prof. U. Calif. Sch. Med., San Diego, 1989-92; prof. otolaryngology U. Tenn., Memphis, 1993—; mem. staff Bapt. Meml. Hosps., Meth. Hosps., Le Bonheur Children's Hosp.; numerous presentations and lectures in field. Contbr. numerous articles and abstracts to med. jours., also videotapes. Fellow ACS (bd. govs.), Royal Coll. Surgeons, Soc. Univ. Otolaryngologists (pres. elect), Am. Soc. Head and Neck Surgery, Am. Laryngol. Assn., Triological Soc.; mem. AMA, Am. Acad. Otolaryngology-Head and Neck Surgery (bd. dirs. 1993-96), Am. Med. Women's Assn. (pres. Memphis br.), Soc. Head and Neck Oncologists Eng., Am. Physiol. Soc., Assn. Women Surgeons, Am. Bd. Otolaryngology (bd. dirs., residency rev. com. for otolaryngology), Am. Soc. of Head and Neck Surgeons (coun.). Office: U Tenn Dept Oto/HNS 956 Court B2-10 Memphis TN 38163

WOODSON, HERBERT HORACE, retired electrical engineering educator; b. Stamford, Tex., Apr. 5, 1925; s. Herbert Viven and Floy (Tunnell) W.; m. Blanche Elizabeth Sears, Aug. 17, 1951; children: William Sears, Robert Sears, Bradford Sears. SB, SM, MIT, 1952, ScD in Elec. Engring., 1956. Registered profl. engr., Tex., Mass. Instr. elec. engring., also project leader magnetics div. Naval Ordnance Lab., 1952-54; mem. faculty M.I.T., 1956-71, prof. elec. engring., 1965-71, Philip Sporn prof. energy processing, 1967-71; prof. elec. engring., chmn. dept. U. Tex., Austin, 1971-81, Alcoa Found. prof., 1972-75, Tex. Atomic Energy Research Found. prof. engring., 1980-82, Ernest H. Cockrell Centennial prof. engring., 1982-93, dir. Center for Energy Studies, 1973-88, assoc. dean devel. and planning Coll. Engring., 1986-87, acting dean, 1987-88, dean' chair for excellence in engring., 1988-96; ret.; staff engr. elec. engring. div. AEP Service Corp., N.Y.C., 1965-66; cons. to industry, 1956—. Author: (with others) Electromechanical Dynamics, parts I, II, III. Served with USNR, 1943-46. Recipient Fed. Engr. Yr. Awd., Nat Soc. Profl. Engr., 1990. Fellow IEEE (life, pres. Power Engring. Soc. 1978-80); mem. Am. Soc. Engring. Edn., Nat. Acad. Engring., AAAS. Achievements include patents in field. Home: 7603 Rustling Rd Austin TX 78731-1333

WOODSON, RODERICK KEVIN, professional football player; b. Fort Wayne, Ind., Mar. 10, 1965. Student, Purdue U. Cornerback Pittsburgh Steelers, 1987—. Named kick returner The Sporting News Coll. All-Am. Team, 1986, Sporting News NFL All-Pro Team, 1989, cornerback, 1990, 92, 93, NFL 75th Anniversary "All Time Team", 1994; selected Pro Bowl, 1996. Played in Pro Bowl, 1989-93. Office: Pittsburgh Steelers Three Rivers Stadium 300 Stadium Cir Pittsburgh PA 15212*

WOODSON-HOWARD, MARLENE ERDLEY, former state legislator; b. Ford City, Pa., Mar. 8, 1937; d. James and Susie (Lettrich) Erdley; m. Francis M. Howard; children: George Woodson, Bert Woodson, Robert Woodson, Daniel Woodson, David Woodson. BS, Ind. U. of Pa., 1958; MA, U. South Fla., 1968; EdD, Nova U., 1981. Prof. math. Manatee Community Coll., 1970-82, dir., Inst. Advancement, 1982-86; exec. dir. Manatee Community Coll. Foundation, 1982-86; pres. Pegasus Enterprises, Inc., 1986—; state senator Fla., 1986-90. Candidate for gov. of Fla., 1990; pres. New Coll. Libr. Assn.; past pres. Manatee Symphony. Mem. Women Owners Network, Sarasota C. of C., Kiwanis (bd. dirs.). Republican. Roman Catholic. Home: 12 Tidy Island Blvd Bradenton FL 34210-3301

WOODSWORTH, ANNE, university dean, librarian; b. Fredericia, Denmark, Feb. 10, 1941; d. Thorvald Ernst and Roma Yrsa (Jensen) Lindner; 1 child, Yrsa Anne. BFA, U. Man., Can., 1962; BLS, U. Toronto, Ont., Can., 1964, MLS, 1969; PhD, U. Pitts., 1987. Edn. libr. U. Man., 1964-65; reference libr. Winnipeg Pub. Library, 1965-67; reference libr. sci. and medicine dept. U. Toronto, 1967-68; med. librarian Toronto Western Hosp., 1969-70; research asst. to chief librarian U. Toronto, 1970-71, head reference dept., 1971-74; personnel dir. Toronto Pub. Library, 1975-78; dir. librs. York U., Toronto, 1978-83; assoc. provost for librs. U. Pitts., 1983-88, assoc. prof., 1988-91; dean Palmer Sch. Libr. and Info. Sci. L.I. U., 1991—; pres. Anne Lindner Ltd., 1974-83; bd. dirs. Population Rsch. Found., Toronto, 1980-83, Ctr. for Rsch. Libraries, 1987-88; mem. rsch. libraries adv. coun. OCLC, 1984-87. Author: The Alternative Press in Canada, 1972, Leadership and Research Libraries, 1988, Patterns and Options for Managing Information Technology on Campus, 1990, Library Cooperation and Networks, 1991, Managing the Economics of Leasing and Contracting Out Information Services, 1993, Reinvesting in the Information Job Family, 1993, The Future of Education for Librarianship: Looking Forward from the Past, 1994. Dir. Sr. Fellows Inst., 1995—; trustee L.I. Librs. Resources Coun., 1993-96. Can. Coun. grantee, 1974, Ont. Arts Coun. grantee, 1974, Coun. on Libr. Resources grantee, 1986, 88, 91, 93; UCLA sr. fellow, 1985. Mem. ALA (econ. accreditation 1990-94, councillor 1993—), Can. Assn. Rsch. Librs. (pres. 1981-83), Assn. Rsch. Librs. (bd. dirs. 1981-84, v.p. 1984-85, pres. 1985-86), Assn. Coll. and Rsch. Librs. (chmn. K.G. Saur award com. 1991-93), Assn. for Libr. and Info. Sci. Edn., N.Y. Libr. Assn., Internat. Soc., Am. Soc. Info. Sci., Archons of Colophon. Office: LI U CW Post Campus 720 Northern Blvd Greenvale NY 11548-1319

WOODWARD, C. VANN, historian; b. Vanndale, Ark., Nov. 13, 1908; s. Hugh Allison and Bess (Vann) W.; m. Glenn Boyd MacLeod, Dec. 21, 1937 (dec.); 1 child, Peter Vincent (dec.). PhB, Emory U., 1930; MA, Columbia U., 1932; PhD, U. N.C., 1937; hon. doctoral degrees, U. Ark., Brandeis U., Cambridge U., Colgate U., Columbia U., Dartmouth Coll., Dickinson Coll., Emory U., Henderson State U., Johns Hopkins U., U. Mich., U. N.C., Northwestern U., Pa. U., Princeton U., Rhodes Coll., Rutgers U., Tulane U., Washington and Lee U., William and Mary Coll. Instr. English Ga. Sch. Tech., 1930-31, 1932-33; asst. prof. history U. Fla., 1937-39; vis. asst. prof. history U. Va., 1939-40; assoc. prof. history Scripps Colls., 1940-43; assoc. prof. history Johns Hopkins U., 1946, prof., 1947-61; Commonwealth lectr. U. London, 1954; Harmsworth prof. Am. history Oxford U., 1954-55; Sterling prof. history Yale U., 1961-77, prof. emeritus, 1977—, Jefferson lectr. in humanities, 1978. Author: Tom Watson: Agrarian Rebel, 1938, The Battle for Leyte Gulf, 1947, Origins of the New South, 1951, (Bancroft prize), Reunion and Reaction, 1951, The Strange Career of Jim Crow, 1955, The Burden of Southern History, 1960, American Counterpoint, 1971, Thinking Back, 1986, The Future of the Past, 1989, The Old World's New World, 1991; editor: The Comparative Approach to American History, 1968, Responses of the Presidents to Charges of Misconduct, 1974, Mary Chesnut's Civil War, 1981 (Pulitzer prize 1982), (series) The Oxford History of the United States, 11 vols., 1982—; co-editor: The Private Mary Chesnut, 1984. Served as lt. USNR, 1943-46. Recipient Nat. Acad. Inst. Arts and Letters Lit. award, 1954, Gold medal for history, 1990, Am. Coun. Learned Socs. prize, 1962, Life Work award Am. Hist. Soc., 1986, Life Work Bobst. award, NYU, 1989; Guggenheim Found. fellow, 1946-47, 60-61. Mem. Am. Philos. Soc., Am. Acad. Arts and Letters, Am. Hist. Assn. (pres. 1969), So. Hist. Assn. (pres. 1952), Orgn. Am. Historians (pres. 1968-69, Disting Svc. award 1989), Am. Acad. Arts and Scis. (v.p. 1987-88), Brit. Academy, Royal Hist. Soc., Phi Beta Kappa. Home: 83 Rogers Rd Hamden CT 06517-3541

WOODWARD, CLINTON BENJAMIN, JR., civil engineering educator; b. El Paso, Tex., Mar. 4, 1943; s. Clinton Benjamin and Iris Elizabeth (Zant) W.; m. Willie Ann Shollenbarger, June 14, 1969 (div. June 1976); m. Deon Bennett Speir, Nov. 22, 1979; 1 child, Clinton Benjamin III. BSET, N.Mex. State U., 1976; MS, Colo. State U., 1978; MSCE, N.Mex. State U., 1984, PhD, 1986. From asst. mgr. to pres. Woodward Enterprises Co., Inc., Las Cruces, N.Mex., 1968-82; assoc. prof. N.Mex. State U., 1987—. Contbr. articles to profl. jours. With USN, 1962-66.. Mem. ASCE, Am. Soc. for Engring. Edn., Soc. for Exptl. Mechanics, Forest Products Soc., Soc. Wood Sci. and Tech. Avocations: camping, fly fishing.

WOODWARD, DANIEL HOLT, librarian, researcher; b. Ft. Worth, Oct. 17, 1931; s. Enos Paul and Jessie Grider (Butts) W.; m. Mary Jane Gerra, Aug. 27, 1954; children: Jeffrey, Peter. BA, U. Colo., 1951, MA, 1955; PhD, Yale, 1958; MSLS, Cath. U. Am., 1969. Mem. faculty Mary Washington Coll. of U. Va., 1957-72, prof. English, 1966-72, librarian, 1969-72; librarian Huntington Library, Art Collections and Bot. Gardens, San Marino, Calif., 1972-90, sr. rsch. assoc., 1990-97; ind. scholar, 1997—. Editor: The Poems and Translations of Robert Fletcher, 1970, The Ellesmere Chaucer: A New Monochromatic Facsimile, 1997; co-editor: New Ellesmere Chaucer Facsimile, Ellesmere Chaucer: Essays in Interpretation, 2 vols., 1995. Served with AUS, 1952-54. Mem. Bibliog. Soc. Am., Phi Beta Kappa, Beta Phi Mu. Home: 4 Governor's Ln Princeton NJ 08540

WOODWARD, DAVID LUTHER, lawyer, consultant; b. Alexandria, La., Mar. 18, 1942; s. Luther Washburn and Ruby Ellen (Robertson) W.; m. Adeline Myree Peterson, July 12, 1965 (div. 1971); m. Louisette Marie Forget, Nov. 12, 1973. BA, Fla. State U., 1965, JD, 1969; LLM, U. London, 1982. Bar: Fla. 1969, Okla. 1982, Tex. 1987, U.S. Dist. Ct. (mid. and so. dists.) Fla. 1971, U.S. Dist. Ct. (no. and we. dists.) Okla. 1983, U.S. Dist. Ct. (no. dist.) Tex. 1985, U.S. Dist. Ct. (ea. dist.) Wis. 1992, U.S. Ct. of Claims 1970, U.S. Ct. Appeals (fed. and D.C. cirs.) 1970, (5th and 11th cirs.) 1981, (10th cir.) 1982, (9th cir.) 1985, U.S. Tax Ct. 1970, U.S. Ct. Mil. Appeals 1970, U.S. Supreme Ct. 1973. Trial atty. USDA, Washington, 1970; asst. atty. gen. State of Fla., Tampa, 1971-73; ptnr. Rose & Woodward, Tampa, 1973-76; pvt. practice The Law Offices of David Luther Woodward, Tampa, 1976-80; appellate pub. defender State of Okla., 1980-81; instr. U. Okla. Coll. Law, Norman, 1980-81; assoc. Jones, Gungoll, Jackson, Collins & Dodd, Enid, Okla., 1982-84, Brice & Barron, Dallas, 1985-86; pvt. practice Dallas, 1986—; of counsel Kenneth R. Guest & Assocs., Dallas, 1990-91, Sapp & Madden, Dallas and Austin, 1991, Bennett & Kurtzman, Dallas, 1991-93. Contbr. articles to profl. jours. Episcopalian. Office: 222 Turtle Creek Tower 3131 Turtle Creek Blvd Dallas TX 75219-5415

WOODWARD, FREDERICK MILLER, publisher; b. Clarksville, Tenn., Apr. 15, 1943; s. Felix Grundy and Laura Henrietta (Miller) W.; m. Elizabeth Louise Smoak, Mar. 23, 1967; children: Laura Claire, Katherine Elizabeth. BA cum laude, Vanderbilt U., 1965; postgrad., Tulane U., 1965-70. Manuscript editor U.S.C. Press, Columbia, 1970-73, mktg. dir., 1973-81; dir. U. Press of Kans., Lawrence, 1981—; mem. adv. com. Kans. Ctr. for the Book, Topeka, 1987—; lectr. pub. U. Kans., Lawrence, Kans. State U., Manhattan, 1983—; book judge Western Heritage Ctr., Oklahoma City, 1988. Mem. Assn. Am. Univ. Presses (bd. dirs. 1988-91, pres. 1995-96, past pres. 1996-97), Kans. State Hist. Soc. (life), Phi Beta Kappa. Democrat. Avocations: racquetball, reading, music. Home: 2220 Vermont St Lawrence KS 66046-3066 Office: U Press Kans 2501 W 15th St Lawrence KS 66049-3905

WOODWARD, GRETA CHARMAINE, construction company executive, rental and investment property manager; b. Congress, Ohio, Oct. 28, 1930; d. Richard Thomas and Grace Lucetta (Palmer) Duffey; m. John Jay Woodward, Oct. 29, 1949; children: Kirk Jay, Brad Ewing, Clay William. Bookkeeper Kaufman's Texaco, Wooster, Ohio, 1948-49; office mgr. Holland Furnace Co., Wooster, 1948-49; acctg. clk. Columbus and So. Ohio Electric, 1949-50; interviewer, clk. State Ohio Bur. Employment Services, Columbus, 1950-51; clk. Def. Constrn. Supply Ctr. (U.S. Govt.) (formerly Columbus Gen. Depot), 1951-52; treas. Woodward Co., Inc., Reynoldsburg, Ohio, 1963—. Newspaper columnist Briarcliff News, 1960-63. Active Reynoldsburg PTA, 1960-67; Reynoldsburg United Meth. Ch.; mem. women's service bd. Grant Hosp. Avocations: bike riding, crocheting, writing poetry, stock market, water aerobics, line dancing, ballroom dancing. Office: Woodward Excavating Co Inc 7340 Tussing Rd Reynoldsburg OH 43068-4111

WOODWARD, JAMES HOYT, academic administrator, engineer; b. Sanford, Fla., Nov. 24, 1939; s. James Hoyt and Edith Pearl (Breeden) W.; m. Martha Ruth Hill, Oct. 13, 1956; children: Connie, Tracey, Wade. BS in Aero. Engring. with honors, Ga. Tech. Inst., 1962, MS in Aero. Engring., 1963, PhD in Engring. Mechanics, 1967; MBA, U. Ala.-Birmingham, 1973. Registered profl. engr., Ala. Asst. prof. engring. mechanics USAF Acad., Colo., 1965-67, assoc. prof., 1967-68; asst. prof. engring. mechanics N.C. State U., 1968-69; assoc. prof. engring. U. Ala., Birmingham, 1969-70, assoc. prof., 1973-77, prof. civil engring., 1977-89, asst. v.p., 1973-78, dean engring., 1978-84, acad. v.p., 1984-89; chancellor U. N.C., Charlotte, 1989—; dir. tech. devel. Rust Engring. Co., Birmingham, 1970-73; cons. in field. Contbr. articles to profl. jours. With USAF, 1965-68. Mem. ASCE, ASME, Am. Soc. Engring. Edn., Am. Mgmt. Assn., Sigma Xi. Methodist. Office: U NC Charlotte Office of Chancellor Charlotte NC 28223

WOODWARD, JAMES KENNETH, pharmacologist; b. Anderson, Mo., Feb. 5, 1938; s. Audley J. and Doris Evelyn (Fields) W.; A.B. in Chemistry, B.S. in Biology, S.W. Mo. State Coll., 1960; postgrad. U. Kans. (USPHS fellow) 1960-62; Ph.D. (USPHS fellow), U. Pa. Sch. Medicine, 1967; m. Kathleen Ruth Winget, June 25, 1960 (div. Nov. 1994); children—Audley J., Kimie Connette; m. Lisa Marie Stuart, Feb. 28, 1996. Pharmacologist, Stine Lab., Newark, Del., 1963-65, research pharmacologist, 1967-71; sr. research pharmacologist Merrell-Nat. Labs., Cin., 1972-73, sect. head, 1973-74, head dept. pharmacology, 1974-78; head dept. pre-clin. pharmacology Merrell Research Center, Merrell Dow Pharms., Inc., 1978-83, assoc. dir. research adminstrn. Merrell Dow Research Inst., 1983-88, dir. biol. devel. Merrell Dow Research Inst., 1988-90, dir. int. reg. affairs, 1990-93; dir. clin. cand. prep. Marion Merrell Dow, 1993, ret., 1993, cons., 1993. USPHS postdoctoral fellow U. Pa., 1967. Pres., Golf Manor Recreation Commn., Cin., 1973-75. Mem. Phila. Physiol. Soc., AAAS. Democrat. Baptist. Patentee antisecretory compounds of imidazoline series. Home: 972 Sheridan Dr Lancaster OH 43130-1923 Office: 2110 E Galbraith Rd Cincinnati OH 45237-1625

WOODWARD, KATHERINE ANNE, secondary education educator; b. Detroit, Apr. 6, 1942; d. Walter E. and Helen (Leuer) Roberts; m. Clifford Edward Woodward, July 1, 1967; children: Ted, Bob, Chris, John-Paul. BA in History, Webster U., 1964; student, St. Louis U., 1966; MA in History, Sam Houston State U., 1991. Cert. tchr., Tex., Mo. Tchr. world history Oxford (Ala.) High Sch., 1967-69; tchr. English Santa Fe Jr. High Sch., Altaloma, Tex., 1969; tchr. world history Jersey Village High Sch., Houston, 1985—. Co-founder, pres. Brazoria County Cay Care, Alvin, Tex., 1970-73; co-founder Cypress Creek Emergency Med. Svc., Houston, 1975. Named Outstanding Young Women in Am., 1976. Mem. ASCD, AAUW (pres. North Harris County 1976-77), Tex. Coun. Social Studies, Cypress-Fairbanks Coun. Social Studies (pres. 1994-95, scholarship 1990), Nat. Coun. Social Studies. Avocations: travel, reading, Dutch painting, music, boating. Office: Jersey Village High Sch 7600 Solomon St Houston TX 77040-2134

WOODWARD, KENNETH EMERSON, retired mechanical engineer; b. Washington, Oct. 30, 1927; s. George Washington and Mary Josephine (Compton) W.; m. Mary Margaret Eungard, Mar. 29, 1956; children: Stephen Mark, Kristi Lynn. BME, George Washington U., 1949, M Engring. Adminstrn., 1960; MS, U. Md., 1953; PhD, Am. U., 1973. Mech. engr. Naval Rsch. Lab., Washington, 1950-54; value engring. program mgr. Harry Diamond Labs., Washington, 1955-74; sci. adviser U.S. Army Med. Bioengring. R & D Lab., Ft. Detrick, Md., 1974-75; mech. engr. Woolcott & Co., Washington, 1975-90; ret., 1990. Author: Solar Energy Applications for the Home, 1978; contbr. over 40 articles to profl. publs. With U.S. Army, 1946-47. Recipient Dept. of the Army Decoration for Exceptional Civilian Svc., Honors Achievement award Angiology Rsch. Found., Purdue Frederick Co., Engring. Alumni Achievement award George Washington U., Washington, 1987. Mem. ASME, Am. Soc. for Artificial Internal Organs. Republican. Baptist. Achievements include 12 U.S. and 2 foreign patents, development of artifical human heart. Home: 1701 Hunts End Ct Vienna VA 22182-1833

WOODWARD, LESTER RAY, lawyer; b. Lincoln, Nebr., May 24, 1932; s. Wendell Smith and Mary Elizabeth (Theobald) W.; m. Marianne Martinson, Dec. 27, 1958; children: Victoria L. Woodward Eisele, Richard T., David M., Andrew E. BSBA, U. Nebr., 1953; LLB, Harvard U., 1957; LLD (hon.), Bethany Coll., 1974. Bar: Colo., 1957. Assoc. Davis, Graham & Stubbs, Denver, 1957-59, 60-62, ptnr., 1962—; Teaching fellow Sch. Law Harvard U., 1959-60. Bd. dirs. Bethany Coll., Lindsborg, Kans., 1966-74, 87-95, chmn., 1989-92; bd. dirs. Pub. Edn. Coalition, Denver, 1985-92, chmn., 1988-89; mem. Colo. Commn. Higher Edn., Denver, 1977-86, chmn., 1979-81. Mem. ABA, Colo. Bar Assn., Am. Law Inst. Republican. Lutheran. Home: 680 Bellaire St Denver CO 80220-4935 Office: Davis Graham & Stubbs 370 17th St Ste 4700 Denver CO 80202-5647

WOODWARD, RALPH LEE, JR., historian, educator; b. New London, Conn., Dec. 2, 1934; s. Ralph Lee and Beulah Mae (Suter) W.; m. Sue Dawn McGrady, Dec. 30, 1958; children: Mark Lee, Laura Lynn, Matthew McGrady. A.B. cum laude, Central Coll., Mo., 1955; M.A., Tulane U., 1959, PhD, 1962. Asst. prof. history Wichita (Kans.) U., 1961-62, U. S.W. La., Lafayette, 1962-63; asst. prof. history U. N.C., Chapel Hill, 1963-67; asso. prof. U. N.C., 1967-70; prof. history Tulane U., New Orleans, 1970—; head dept. history Tulane U., 1973-75, chmn. dept. history, 1986-88; dir. Tulane Summer in C. Am., 1975-78; prof. in charge Tulane Jr. Year Abroad, Paris, 1975-76; Fulbright lectr. Universidad de Chile, Universidad Catolica de Valparaiso, Chile, 1965-66, Universidad del Salvador, Universidad Nacional, Buenos Aires, 1968; vis. prof. U.S. Mil. Acad., West Point, N.Y., 1989; regional liaison officer Emergency Com. to Aid Latin Am. Scholars, 1974. Author: Class Privilage and Economic Development, 1966, Robinson Crusoe's Island, 1969, Positivism in Latin America, 1850-1900, 1971, Central America: A Nation Divided, 1976, 2d edit., 1985, Tribute to Don Bernardo de Galvez, 1979, Belize, 1980, Nicaragua, 1983, 2d edit., 1994, El Salvador, 1988, Guatemala, 1992, Rafael Carrera and the Emergence of the Republic of Guatemala, 1993 (Alfred A. Thomas Book award); editor: Central America: Historical Perspectives on the Contemporary Crises, 1988; assoc. editor: Revista del Pensamiento Centroamericano, 1975, Research Guide to Central America and the Caribbean, 1985, Encyclopedia of Latin American History and Culture, 1996; contbg. editor: Handbook of Latin American Studies, 1987-90; series editor: World Bibliographical Series, 1987—; contbr. articles to profl. jours. Served to capt. USMC, 1955-58. Recipient Alfred B. Thomas Book award Southeastern Coun. Latin Latin Am. Studies, 1994; Henry L. and Grace Doherty Found. fellow Tulane U., 1962; named La. Humanist of Yr. La. Endowment for Humanities, 1995. Mem. Am. Hist. Assn. (mem. Conf. L.Am. History, pres. 1989, mem. gen. coun. 1974-76), La. Hist. Assn., Southeastern Conf. L.Am. Studies (program chmn. 1975, pres. 1975-76), L.Am. Studies Assn., Com. on Andean Studies (chmn. 1972-73), Geography and History Acad. Guatemala. Office: Tulane U Dept History New Orleans LA 70118

WOODWARD, ROBERT FORBES, retired government official, consultant; b. Mpls., Oct. 1, 1908; s. Charles Emerson and Ella (Robertson) W.; m. Virginia Parker Cooke, Feb. 20, 1943 (dec. Jan. 1990); children: Robert Forbes, Mary Cooke. A.B., U. of Minn., 1930; student, George Washington U., 1941; LL.D., U. of Pacific, 1962. Joined U.S. Fgn. Service, 1931; vice consul at Winnipeg, Man., Can., 1932-33; student Fgn. Service Tng. Sch., Dept. of State, Washington, 1933; vice consul Buenos Aires, 1933-36; temp. vice consul Asuncion, Paraguay, 1935; 3d sec. legation and vice consul Bogota, Colombia, 1936-37; vice consul Rio de Janeiro, Brazil, 1937-38; assigned div. Latin Am. Affairs, Dept. State, Washington, 1938-42, 44; 2d sec. of embassy and consul La Paz, Bolivia, 1942-44, dep. chief mission, 1942-44; dep. chief mission Guatemala, 1944-46, Habana, 1946-47; dep. dir. Inter-Am. Affairs, Dept. State, Washington, 1947-49; assigned Nat. War Coll., 1949-50; deputy chief mission Stockholm, Sweden, 1950-52; chief fgn. service personnel Dept. State, 1952-53; dep. asst. sec. state for Inter-Am. Affairs, 1953-54; ambassador to Costa Rica, 1954-58, to Uruguay, 1958-61, to Chile, 1961, to Spain, 1962-65; asst. sec. state for Inter-Am. affairs, 1961-62; adviser to spl. negotiators (Canal Treaties with Panama), 1965-67; interim dir. Office of Water for Peace, 1967; ret., 1968; cons. Dept. State, 1968—, Research Analysis Corp., 1969—, Youth for Understanding, 1972—; acting provost Elbert Covell (Spanish-lang.) Coll., U. of Pacific, Stockton, Calif., 1970; Chmn. U.S. del. Econ. Commn. Latin Am., Santiago, Chile, 1961; vice chmn. U.S. del. Alliance for Progress Conf., Punta del Este, 1961, U.S. del. Fgn. Ministers meeting, Punta del Este, 1962; chmn. U.S. del. Internat. Red Cross Conf., Vienna, 1965; chmn. U.S. del. Conf. for Revision of OAS Charter, Panama, 1966; conducted study on Panama Canal for Dept. Army, Research Analysis Corp., 1971; conducted study on usefulness of UNESCO to U.S. for Dept. State, 1972; coordinator, chief U.S. del. to Working Group with Latin Am. and Caribbean Govts. on transnat. enterprises, 1974-75. Mem. Inter-Am. Commn. on Human Rights, 1972-76, Am. Acad. Diplomacy, Washington Inst. Fgn. Affairs. Recipient Distinguished Service award U. Minn., 1963. Mem. Met. Club, Chevy Chase Club, Sulgrave Club, Ret. Diplomatic and Consular Officers Club. Home: 1642 Avon Pl NW Washington DC 20007-2958

WOODWARD, ROBERT UPSHUR, newspaper reporter, writer; b. Geneva, Ill., Mar. 26, 1943; s. Alfred E. and Jane (Upshur) W.; m. Elsa Walsh, Nov. 25, 1989; children: Tali, Diana. B.A., Yale U., 1965. Reporter Montgomery County (Md.) Sentinel, 1970-71; reporter Washington Post, 1971-78, met. editor, 1979-81, asst. mng. editor, 1981—. Author: (with Carl Bernstein) All the President's Men, 1974, The Final Days, 1976, (with Scott Armstrong) The Brethren, 1979, Wired, 1984, Veil: The Secret Wars of the CIA, 1987, The Commanders, 1991, (with David S. Broder) The Man Who Would Be President, 1991, The Agenda: Inside the Clinton White House, 1994, The Choice, 1996. Served with USN, 1965-70. Office: Washington Post Co 1150 15th St NW Washington DC 20071-0001

WOODWARD, STEPHEN RICHARD, newspaper reporter; b. Fukuoka City, Japan, July 27, 1953; came to U.S., 1954; s. Leonard Edwin and Etsuko (Okumura) W.; m. Sandra Elizabeth Richardson, Dec. 31, 1979; children: Daniel Joseph, Elizabeth Etsuko. BA in English, Wright State U., 1975; MA in Journalism, U. Mo., 1979. Advt. coordinator Wright State U., Dayton, Ohio, 1976-77; reporter Kansas City (Mo.) Star, 1979-82; assoc. editor then editor Kansas City Bus. Jour., 1982-83; editor then gen. mgr. Portland (Oreg.) Bus. Jour., 1984-86; exec. bus. editor The Hartford (Conn.) Courant, 1986-87; editor San Francisco Bus. Times, 1987-88; bus. editor The Oregonian, Portland, 1989-93, reporter, 1993—. Recipient 1st Place Investigative Reporting award Assn. Area Bus. Publs., 1983, 1st Place Column Writing award Assn. Area Bus. Publs., 1985. Mem. Investigative Reporters and Editors Inc. Avocations: astronomy, chess, creative writing. Home: 3309 NE Irving St Portland OR 97232-2538 Office: The Oregonian 1320 SW Broadway Portland OR 97201-3411

WOODWARD, SUSAN ELLEN, economist, federal official; b. Loma Linda, Calif., June 14, 1949; d. Frank Colwin and Dollie Dorothy (O'Kane) W.; 1 child, Sonja Stenger Weissman; m. Robert E. Hall, July 20, 1995. BA in Econs., UCLA, 1970, PhD in Mgmt./Fin., 1978. Instr. U. Wash., Seattle, 1975, U. Toronto, 1975-77, UCLA, 1976-83, 84-85, U. Calif., Santa Barbara, 1977-79, U. Rochester (N.Y.), 1983-84; sr. staff economist Coun. Econ. Advisers, Washington, 1985-87; dep. asst. sec., chief economist HUD, Washington, 1987-92; chief economist SEC, Washington, 1992-95; with Cornerstone Rsch., Menlo Park, Calif., 1996—. Mem. Am. Econ. Assn. (editor 1983-87), Am. Fin. Assn. Home: 2122 California St NW # 252 Washington DC 20008-1803 also: 1682 Oak Ave Menlo Park CA 94025-5838 Office: Cornerstone Rsch 1000 El Camino Real Menlo Park CA 94025-4327

WOODWARD, THEODORE ENGLAR, medical educator, internist; b. Westminster, Md., Mar. 22, 1914; s. Lewis Klair and Phoebe Helen (Neidig) W.; m. Celeste Constance Lauve, June 24, 1938; children: William E., R. Craig, Celeste L. Woodward Applefeld. BS, Franklin and Marshall Coll., 1934, DSc (hon.), 1954; MD, U. Md., 1938; DSc (hon.), Western Md. Coll., 1950, Hahnemann U., 1993. Diplomate Am. Bd. Internal Medicine. Asst. prof. medicine U. Md. Sch. Medicine, Balt., 1946-48, assoc. prof., also dir. sect. infectious disease, 1948-54, prof., 1954-83, prof. emeritus, 1983—, chmn. dept., 1954-81; attending physician Balt. VA Med Ctr., 1949—; with Armed Forces Epidemiol. Bd., Washington, 1952-92, mem. commns., 1952-72, pres. bd., 1976-78, 80-92; mem. U.S./Japan Coop. Med. Sci. Program, Washington, 1965-95, emeritus, 1995—; disting. physician Cen. VA, Washington, 1981-87. Author: Chloramphenicol, 1958, 200 Years of Medicine in Baltimore, 1976, A History of the Department of Medicine, University of Maryland, 1807-1981, 1987, A History of Armed Forces Epidemiological Board, 1940-1990, 1990, Carroll County (Md.) Physicians of the 19th and Early 20th Centuries, 1990, The Armed Forces Epidemiological Board: The History of the Commissions, 1995; contbr. chpts. to textbooks. Life trustee Gilman Sch., Balt., 1955—. Lt. col. Medical Svc. Corp U.S. Army, 1941-46, ETO, PTO. Decorated Order of the Sacred Treasure Gold and Silver Star Govt. of Japan; recipient U.S.A. Typhus Commn. medal Dept. Def., 1945, also Exceptionally Disting. Svc. award, 1990, Outstanding Civilian Svc. medal with oak leaf cluster Dept. Army, 1981. Recipient Disting. Svc. award

AMA, 1995. Mem. ACP (master, gov. Md. regent 1969-70, James D. Bruce Meml. award 1970, Disting. Tchr. award 1992), Am. Clin. and Climatol. Assn. (pres. 1969-70), Infectious Disease Soc. Am. (pres. 1976-77, Finland award 1972, Bristol award, Kass award 1991), Inst. Medicine NAS, Elkridge Club (Towson, Md.), Mayo Fellows Assn. (hon.), Hamilton St. Club. Republican. Avocations: photography, gardening, raising wild fowl. Home: 1 Merrymount Rd Baltimore MD 21210-1908 Office: Balt VA Med Ctr 10 N Green St Baltimore MD 21210

WOODWARD, THOMAS AIKEN, lawyer; b. Beatrice, Nebr., June 28, 1933; s. Thomas Aiken and Jessie (Griggs) W.; m. Sara Hubka, Dec. 27, 1962; children: Thomas A., Hewett G. BA, U. Nebr., 1955; JD, U. Mich., 1960; LLM in Taxation, NYU, 1961. Bar: N.Y. 1961, Nebr. 1963, Pa. 1987. Ptnr. Kutak, Rock & Campbell, Omaha, 1969-87; ptnr., chmn. tax dept. Eckert, Seamans, Cherin & Mellott, Pitts., 1987-92; spl. counsel Weller, Wicks & Wallace, Pitts., 1992—. Served to lt. USN, 1955-58. Mem. ABA, N.Y. Bar Assn., Nebr. Bar Assn., Pa. Bar Assn., Allegheny County Bar Assn. Republican. Presbyterian. Office: Weller Wicks & Wallace Ste 600 Benedum Trees Bldg Pittsburgh PA 15222-1775

WOODWARD, THOMAS MORGAN, actor; b. Ft. Worth, Sept. 16, 1925; s. Valin Ridge and Francis Louise (McKinley) W.; m. Enid Anne Loftis, Nov. 18, 1950; 1 child, Enid Anne. AA, Arlington State Coll., 1948; BBA, U. Tex., 1951. Motion picture and TV actor, 1955—; numerous TV appearances include Dallas; motion pictures include The Great Locomotive Chase, 1955, Slaughter on 10th Ave., 1957, The Gun Hawk, 1962, Cool Hand Luke, 1966, The Wild Country, 1973, Which Way Is Up, 1977, Speed Trap, 1978, Battle Beyond the Stars, 1980, Girls Just Want to Have Fun, 1985, Dark Before Dawn, 1987, Gunsmoke III, 1991. With USAAF, 1944-45; to capt. USAF, 1951-53. Recipient Golden Boot award Motion Picture and TV Fund, 1988, Golden Lariat award Nat. Western Film Festival, 1988, Lifetime Achievement award in the arts Arlington Tex. Arts Coun., 1994, Lifetime Achievement award for western film acting Wild West Film Festival, 1995; named Disting. Alumnus of Arts U. Tex., 1969; inducted into the Walk of Western Stars William S. Hart Mus., L.A., 1990. Mem. Acad. Motion Picture Arts and Scis., SAR, Pi Kappa Alpha (Disting. Achievement award 1981, inducted into Order of West Range 1988).

WOODWELL, GEORGE MASTERS, ecology research director, lecturer; b. Cambridge, Mass., Oct. 23, 1928; s. Philip McIntire and Virginia (Sellers) W.; m. Alice Katharine Rondthaler, June 23, 1955; children: Caroline Alice, Marjorie Virginia, Jane Katharine, John Christopher. AB, Dartmouth Coll., 1950; AM, Duke U., 1956, PhD, 1958; DSc (hon.), Williams Coll., 1977, Miami U., 1984, Carleton Coll., 1988, Muhlenberg Coll., 1990, Duke U., 1994; Dartmouth Coll., 1996. Mem. faculty U. Maine, 1957-61, assoc. prof. botany, 1960-61; vis. asst. ecologist, biology dept. Brookhaven Nat. Lab., Upton, N.Y., 1961-67; ecologist Brookhaven Nat. Lab., 1965-67, sr. ecologist, 1967-75; founder, dir. Ecosystems Center, 1975-85; dep. and asst. dir. Marine Biol. Lab., Woods Hole, Mass., 1975-76; pres. and dir. Woods Hole Research Ctr., 1985—; chmn. Conf. on Long Term Biol. Consequences of Nuclear War, 1982-83. Editor: Ecological Effects of Nuclear War, 1965, Diversity and Stability in Ecological Systems, 1969, (with E.V. Pecan) Carbon and the Biosphere, 1973, The Role of Terrestrial Vegetation in the Global Carbon Cycle: Measurement by Remote Sensing, 1984, The Earth in Transition: Patterns and Processes of Biotic Impoverishment, 1990, (with K. Ramakrishna) Forests for the Future, 1993, (with F.T. Mackenzie) Biotic Feedbacks in the Warming of the Earth, 1995. Founding trustee Environ. Def. Fund, 1967; founding trustee Natural Resources Def. Coun., 1970, vice chmn., 1974—; founding trustee World Resources Inst., 1982-96; bd. dirs. World Wildlife Fund, 1970-84, chmn., 1980-84; bd. dirs. Conservation Found., 1975-77, Ruth Mott Fund, 1984-91, chmn., 1989-91; bd. dirs. Ctr. for Marine Conservation, 1990—; adv. com. TMI Pub. Health Fund, 1980-94. Recipient Joseph Priestley award Dickinson Coll., 1993, Hutchinson medal Garden Club of Am., 1993, Disting. Svc. award Am. Inst. Biol. Scis., 1982, Heinz Environ. prize, 1996. Fellow AAAS, Am. Acad. Arts and Scis.; mem. NAS, Brit. Ecol. Soc., Ecol. Soc. Am. (v.p. 1966-67, pres. 1977-78), Sea Edn. Assn. (bd. dirs. 1980-85), Sigma Xi. Rsch., pub. on structure and function of natural communities, biotic impoverishment, especially ecological effects of ionizing radiation, effects of persistent toxins, world carbon cycle and warming of the earth, sci. and internat. environ. affairs. Office: Woods Hole Research Ctr Box 296 13 Church St Woods Hole MA 02543-1007

WOODWORTH, RAMSEY LLOYD, lawyer; b. Syracuse, N.Y., Dec. 26, 1941; s. Woodrow Lloyd and Helen (Ramsey) W.; m. Diane Elizabeth McMillion, June 12, 1971; children: Scott, Ashley, Jeffrey. AB, Brown U., 1964; LLM cum laude, Syracuse (N.Y.) U., 1967. Bar: N.Y. 1967, D.C. 1968, U.S. Ct. Appeals (D.C. cir.) 1968. Atty., advisor FCC, Washington, 1967-68; from assoc. to ptnr. Hedrick & Lane, Washington, 1968-82; prin. Wilkes, Artis, Hedrick & Lane, Chartered, Washington, 1982—. Convenor Peace Luth. Ch., Alexandria, 1985-86. Mem. Fed. Comm. Bar Assn. (exec. com. 1986-89, chair responsibility com. 1984-86, treas. 1989-90, chmn. Fed. Commn. Bar Assn. Found. 1991-93, trustee 1991-94, Univ. Club Washington, Order of Coif. Avocation: swimming. Office: Wilkes Artis Hedrick & Lane 1666 K St NW Ste 1100 Washington DC 20006-2803

WOODY, CAROL CLAYMAN, data processing executive; b. Bristol, Va., May 20, 1949; d. George Neal and Ida Mae (Nelms) Clayman; B.S. in Math., Coll. William and Mary, Williamsburg, Va., 1971; M.B.A. with distinction (IBM Corp. fellow 1978, Stephen Bufton Meml. Ednl. Found. grantee, 1978-79), Babcock Sch., Wake Forest U., 1979; m. Robert William Woody, Aug. 19, 1972. Programmer trainee GSA, 1971-72; systems engr. Citizens Fidelity Bank & Trust Co., Louisville, 1972-75; programmer/analyst-tng. coordinator Blue Bell, Inc., Greensboro, N.C., 1975-79; supr. programming and tech. services J.E. Baker Co., York, Pa., 1979-82, fin. design supr. bus. systems Lycoming div. AVCO, Stratford, Conn., 1982-83; project mgr. Yale U., 1984—; co-owner Sign of the Sycamore, antiques; mem. Data Processing Standards Bd., 1977, CICS/VS Adv. Council, 1975; speaker Nat. Fuse Conf., 1989, Aion expert systems nat. conf., 1990, bus. sch. Coll. William & Mary, 1994. Mem. Am. Bus. Woman's Assn. (chpt. v.p. 1978-79; Merit award 1978), NAFE (founder shoreline network 1993), Assn. for System Mgmt., Assn. for Image Info. Mgmt., Project Mgmt. Inst., Network Inc. of Conn. (treas. 1996-97), Delta Omicron (alumni pres. 1973-75, regional chmn. 1979-82). Republican. Presbyterian. Author various manuals, contbr. article to profl. jour. Home: PO Box 1450 Guilford CT 06437-0550 Office: PO Box 208276 175 Whitney Ave New Haven CT 06520-8276

WOODY, DONALD EUGENE, lawyer; b. Springfield, Mo., Mar. 10, 1948; s. Raymond D. and Elizabeth Ellen (Bushnell) W.; m. Ann Louise Ruhl, June 5, 1971; children: Marshall Wittmann, Catherine Elizabeth. BA in Polit. Sci. with honors, U. Mo., 1970, JD, 1973. Bar: Mo. 1973, U.S. Dist. Ct. (we. dist.) Mo. 1973, U.S. Ct. Appeals (8th cir.) 1973, U.S. Supreme Ct. 1987. Assoc. Neale, Newman & Bradshaw, Springfield, 1973-74; ptnr. Taylor, Stafford & Woody, Springfield, 1974-82, Taylor, Stafford, Woody, Cowherd & Clithero, Springfield, 1983-93, Taylor, Stafford, Woody, Clithero & Fitzgerald, Springfield, 1993—. Editor U. Mo. Law Rev., 1973. Chmn. county campaign U.S. senator Thomas Eagleton, Springfield, 1980; committeeman Greene County Dem. Party, Springfield, 1984-86; cons. Children's Home Mayors commn., Springfield, 1985. Mem. ABA, Springfield Metro Bar Assn. (sec. 1977-80, precedure com. 1986, bd. dirs. 1991-93, pres.-elect 1995, pres. 1996), Assn. Trial Lawyers Am., Springfield C. of C. (chmn. performing arts com. 1980-84), Order of Coif, Phi Delta Phi. Avocations: fishing, growing roses, bicycling, running. Home: 1421 S Ginger Blue Ave Springfield MO 65809-2260 Office: Taylor Stafford Woody Clithero & Fitzgerald 3315 E Ridgeview St Ste 1000 Springfield MO 65804-4083

WOODY, JOHN FREDERICK, secondary education educator; b. Indpls., Apr. 27, 1941; s. Ralph Edwin and Crystal Oleta (Thomas) W.; m. Nancy Ann Henry, July 7, 1963; children: Michael, Laura. BS in Secondary Sch. Teaching, Butler U., 1963, MS in Edn., 1967, adminstrn. lic., 1979, postgrad., 1991—; postgrad., UCLA, 1980-82, Ind. U., 1990, U. Amsterdam, The Netherlands, 1985, Mont. State U., 1993, Purdue U., 1994. Tchr. Pub. Sch. 90, Indpls., 1963-66, Broad Ripple High Sch., Indpls., 1966-89; tchr., head social studies dept. Arlington H.S., Indpls., 1989—. Author: (resource kits for hist. events) Cram, Inc., 1976-81, (filmstrips) Lowe Sheldrew, 1976-81; contbr. articles to profl. jours. and sch. materials. Sponsor Rep. Nat. Com., 1982—; deacon Heritage Bapt. Ch., 1983—; mem. U.S. Congress German Bundestag Select Com. Ind., 1986-93. Fulbright scholar U.S. Info. Agy., 1985. Mem. ASCD, Nat. Coun. Social Studies, Ind. Coun. Social Studies, Arlington Acad. Com. Avocations: reading, writing, swimming, lifting weights. Home: 7362 Woodside Dr Indianapolis IN 46260-3137 Office: Arlington High Sch 4825 N Arlington Ave Indianapolis IN 46226-2401

WOODY, MARY FLORENCE, nursing educator, university administrator; b. Chambers County, Ala., Mar. 31, 1926; d. Hugh Ernest and May Lillie (Gilliland) W.; diploma Charity Hosp. Sch. Nursing, 1947; BS, Columbia U., 1953, M.A., 1955. Staff nurse Wheeler Hosp., Lafayette, Ala., 1947-48; polio nurse Willard Parker Hosp., N.Y.C., 1949; staff nurse, supr. VA Hosp., Montgomery, Ala., 1950-53; faculty mem., field supr., nursing dept. Tchrs. Coll., Columbia U., N.Y.C., 1955-56; asst. dir. nursing Emory U. Hosp., clin. asst. prof. Emory U. Sch. Nursing, Atlanta, 1956-68; asst. dir., dir. nursing Grady Meml. Hosp., Atlanta, 1968-79; founding dean, prof. Sch. Nursing, Auburn (Ala.) U., 1979-84; assoc. dir., dir. nursing Emory U. Hosp., Atlanta, 1984-93; interim dean Sch. Nursing, Emory U., 1992-93; chmn. Ga. Statewide Master Planning Com. for Nursing and Nursing Edn., 1971-75; faculty preceptor patient care adminstrn. Sch. Public Health, U. Minn., 1977-79; mem. bd. dirs. Wesley Woods Found. & Long Term Hosp., 1994—. Recipient Spl. Recognition, 5th Dist. and Ga. Nurses Assn., 1978, 93, Disting. Achievement in Nursing Svc. award Columbia U. Tchrs. Coll. Alumni Assn., 1992, Jane Van de Vrede Outstanding Svc. to Citizens of Ga. award Ga. League Nursing, Cert. Spl. Recognition award Ga. Nurses Assn., 1993. Fellow Am. Acad. Nursing (charter); mem. Am. Nurses Assn., Nat. League Nursing, Am. Heart Assn., Emory U. Nell Hodgson Woodruff Sch. Nursing Alumni Assn. (hon. 1994), Sigma Theta Tau. Democrat. Chmn. bd. dirs. Am. Jour. Nursing Co., 1978-83. Address: 907 Lenox Hill Ct Atlanta GA 30324-2957

WOOG, DOUG, collegiate ice hockey coach; m. Janice; children: Amy, Steve, Dan. BS in Edn., U. Minn., 1967; MEd, Coll. St. Thomas. Hockey player U.S. Nat. Team, 1967; head soccer coach, asst. hockey and baseball coach South St. Paul H.S., 1968-71; coach jr. hockey St. Paul Vulcans, Minn. Jr. Stars, 1971-77; coach west team (gold medalists) U.S. Olympic Festival, Colorado Springs, 1978; head hockey coach South St. Paul H.S., 1978-87; head coach ice hockey U. Minn., Mpls., 1985—; chmn. nat. skating com. USA Hockey; head coach U.S. Nat. Jr. Hockey Team, 1985, U.S. Select 17 Team, 1989. Chair Wakota Area Bd. South St. Paul area; vol. Make-A-Wish Found. Mem. St. Paul C. of C., St. Paul Coaches Assn. (past pres.). Office: U Minn 516 15th Ave SE Rm 270 Minneapolis MN 55455-0120

WOOG, JOHN J., eye plastic surgeon; b. Jamaica, N.Y., Feb. 28, 1958; m. Mary Anna Woog. BS, Pa. State Univ., 1978; MD, Thomas Jefferson Univ., 1980. Diplomate Am. Bd. Ophthalmology. Co-dir. Eye Plastics & Orbit Svc. Mass. Eye & Ear Infirmary, Boston, 1985-88; pvt. practice ophthalmology Sloane, Kraut, & Finkelstein, Brookline, Mass., 1985-89, Ophthalmic Cons. Boston, 1989—; dir. Eye Plastics & Orbit Svc. New England Medical Ctr., Boston, 1988-94, co-dir. Eye Plastics & Orbit Svc., 1994—; assoc. clinical prof. Tufts Univ. Sch. Medicine, Boston, 1994—; clinical instr. Harvard Medical Sch., 1989—; bd. dirs. Ophthalmic Cons. Boston, 1989—, Boston Eye Surgery & Laser Ctr., 1992—. Sect. editor: Principles & Practices of Ophthalmology, Eye Plastics, 1994. Fellow Am. Acad. Ophthalmology (Honor award 1994), Am. Soc. Ophthalmic Plastic & Reconstructive Surgery (Rsch. award 1985). Office: Ophthalmic Cons Boston 50 Staniford St Fl 6 Boston MA 02114-2517

WOOLAM, GERALD LYNN, surgeon; b. Lubbock, Tex., Apr. 16, 1937; s. Rawson Harp and Christine Leta (Rampy) W.; m. Nan Kelly, Feb. 28, 1959; children—Kelly Ann, Gerald Lynn, Gregory Alan. B.A., Tex. Tech. U., 1958; M.D., Baylor U., 1962. Diplomate Am. Bd. Surgery. Intern Parkland Meml. Hosp., Dallas, 1962-63; resident gen. surgery Mayo Clinic and Mayo Grad. Sch. Medicine, U. Minn., Rochester, 1963-67; chief resident asso. in surgery Mayo Clinic and Mayo Grad. Sch. Medicine, U. Minn., 1967-68; practice medicine specializing in surgery Lubbock, 1968—; assoc. clin. prof. surgery Tex. Tech. U. Sch. Medicine, 1972-74, clin. prof., 1975—, prof., interim chmn. dept. surgery, 1980-81. Contbr. articles to profl. jours. Bd. dirs. Community Concert Assn. of Lubbock, 1968-71, 1st United Meth. Ch., Lubbock, 1970-75, 76—, South Plains Health Systems, 1976-81; trustee West Tex. Found., 1971-74. Served with USNR, 1954-62. Recipient Outstanding Clin. Prof. award Tex. Tech. U., 1977. Fellow ACS; mem. AAAS, Priestley Soc. (dir. 1970-73, pres. 1981-82), Lubbock Surg. Soc. (pres. 1972), AMA, Lubbock-Crosby-Garza County Med. Soc. (treas., exec. com. 1971—, pres. 1986), Osler Soc., Am. Cancer Soc. (pres. Lubbock unit 1972-73, pres. Tex. div. 1978-79, nat. del. 1980-88, nat. dir. 1988—), Am. Heart Assn. (pres. Lubbock County div. 1973-74), Tex. Surg. Soc., Soc. Surgery Alimentary Tract, Soc. for Surg. Oncology, Central Assn. Dentists and Physicians, So. Surg. Assn., Sigma Xi, Phi Chi, Alpha Omega Alpha, Phi Kappa Phi, Phi Eta Sigma, Alpha Epsilon Delta. Home: 4007 69th St Lubbock TX 79413-5945 Office: 3702 21st St Lubbock TX 79410-1230

WOOLARD, EDGAR S., JR., chemical company executive; b. Washington, N.C., Apr. 15, 1934; s. Edgar Smith and Mamie (Boone) W.; m. Peggy Harrell, 1956; children: Annette, Lynda. BS, N.C. State U., 1956. Indsl. engr. DuPont, Kinston, N.C., 1957-59, group supr. indsl. engring., 1959-62, supr. mfg. sect., 1962-64, planning supr., 1964-65; staff asst to prodn. mgr. DuPont, Wilmington, Del., 1965-66; product supr. DuPont, Old Hickory, Tenn., 1966-69, engring. supt., 1969-70; asst. plant mgr. DuPont, Camden, S.C., 1970-71; plant mgr. DuPont, Kinston, S.C., 1971-73; dir. products mktg. div. DuPont, Wilmington, Del., 1973-75, mng. dir. textile mktg. div., 1975-76, mgr. corp. plans dept., 1976-77, gen. dir. products and planning div., 1977-78, gen. mgr. textile fibers, 1978-81, v.p. textile fibers, 1981-83, exec. v.p., 1983-85, vice chmn., 1985-87, pres., COO, 1987-89, chmn., CEO, 1989-96, chmn., 1996—; bd. dirs. N.C. Textile Found., Citicorp. Trustee Med. Ctr. Del., N.C. State U., Winterthur Mus. Lt. U.S. Army. Recipient Internat. Palladium medal Soc. Chimie Industrille (Am. sect.), 1995. Office: DuPont 1007 Market St Wilmington DE 19801-1227

WOOLARD, WILLIAM LEON, lawyer, electrical distributing company executive; b. Bath, N.C., Aug. 26, 1931; s. Archie Leon and Pearl Irene (Boyd) W.; m. Virginia Harris Stratton, June 17, 1961; children: William Leon Jr., Margaret Anne. AB, Duke U., 1953, LLB, JD, 1955. Bar: N.C. 1955, U.S. Dist. Ct. (we. and mid. dists.) N.C. 1960. Claims analyst Md. Casualty Co., Charlotte, N.C., 1955-56; dist. mgr. Chrysler Corp., Charlotte, 1956-60; ptnr. Jones, Hewson & Woolard, Charlotte, 1960-86, of counsel, 1986—; pres. Armature Winding Co., Inc., Charlotte, 1970—, also bd. dirs.; v.p. Power Products Mfg. Co., Charlotte, 1970—, also bd. dirs. Mem. adminstrv. bd. 1st United Meth. Ch., Charlotte, 1961-78, trustee, 1984-87; trustee Lawyers Ednl. Found., Charlotte, 1970-78; bd. dirs. Christian Rehab. Ctr., Charlotte, 1972-73, N.C. Eye and Human Tissue Bank, Winston-Salem, 1978-79. Recipient Order of Civil Merit Moran award Republic of Korea, 1990, Disting. Svc. medal Republic of China, 1990, Medal of Friendship Pope John Paul II, 1990, Humanitarian Citizen of Merit medal Republic of China, 1990, Humanitarian medal France, 1990, Outstanding Svc. medal Mayor of Paris, 1990, numerous others; Angier B. Duke scholar Duke U., 1949-53; Carnegie Found. fellow Duke U., 1951-52, Melvin Jones fellow Lions Found., 1978. Mem. ABA, N.C. Bar Assn., N.C. State Bar Assn., 26th Jud. Dist. Bar Assn., Am. Judicature Soc., Lions (pres. Charlotte Cen. Club 1972-73, pres., trustee ednl. found. 1973-87, dist. gov., chmn. coun. govs. internat. orgn. 1978-79, internat. bd. dirs. 1981-85, Ambassador of Goodwill award 1983, internat. 3d v.p. 1986-87, 2d v.p. 1987-88, 1st v.p. 1988-89, internat. pres. 1989-90, immediate past pres. 1990-91, chmn. bd. trustee 1990-91), Masons, Shriners, Phi Kappa Sigma, Delta Theta Phi. Avocations: collecting antique and rare books, opera, boating, fishing. Home: 638 Hempstead Pl Charlotte NC 28207-2320 Office: PO Box 32277 Charlotte NC 28232-2277

WOOLDREDGE, WILLIAM DUNBAR, health facility administrator; b. Salem, Mass., Oct. 27, 1937; s. John and Louise (Sigourney) W.; m. Johanna Marie; children: John, Rebecca Wistar. BA, Colby Coll., 1961; MBA, Harvard U., 1964. Staff assoc. Sun Oil Co., Phila., 1964-67; treas. Ins. Co. N.Am., Phila., 1967-72; treas. B.F. Goodrich Co., Akron, Ohio, 1972-84, sr. v.p., 1978-79, exec. v.p., chief fin. officer, mem. mgmt. com., 1979-84; chief fin. officer, exec. v.p., dir. Belden & Blake Corp., North Canton, Ohio, 1984-89; sr. v.p., chief fin. officer, dir. Belden & Blake Oil Prodn., Inc., 1984-89; prin. dir. Carleton Group, Cleve., 1989-92; CFO, COO, v.p. King's Med. Co., Hudson, Ohio, 1993—, also bd. dirs.; pres. Hudson Econ. Devel. Corp. Bd. dirs. Salvation Army, North Park Coll. and Seminary; trustee Children's Hosp. Med. Ctr., Akron. With U.S. Army, 1956-58. Mem. Fin. Execs. Inst. Episcopalian. Club: Country of Hudson. Home: 100 Sunset Dr Hudson OH 44236-2925 Office: King's Med Co 1920 Georgetown Rd Hudson OH 44236-4060

WOOLDRIDGE, DEAN EVERETT, engineering executive, scientist; b. Chickasha, Okla., May 30, 1913; s. Auttie Noonan and Irene Amanda (Kerr) W.; m. Helene Detweiler, Sept. 1936; children—Dean Edgar, Anna Lou, James Allan. A.B., U. Okla., 1932, M.S., 1933; Ph.D., Calif. Inst. Tech., 1936. Mem. tech. staff Bell Telephone Labs., N.Y.C., 1936-46; co-dir. research and devel. labs Hughes Aircraft Co., Culver City, Calif., 1946-52, v.p. research and devel., 1952-53; pres., dir. Ramo-Wooldridge Corp., Los Angeles, 1953-58, Thompson Ramo Wooldridge, Inc., Los Angeles, also Cleve., 1958-62; research assoc. Calif. Inst. Tech., 1962-79. Author: The Machinery of the Brain, 1963, The Machinery of Life, 1966, Mechanical Man, 1968, Sensory Processing in the Brain, 1979, also articles. Recipient Citation of Honor Air Force Assn., 1950, Raymond E. Hackett award, 1955, Westinghouse Sci. Writing award AAAS, 1963, Disting. Svc. Citation U. Okla, Disting. Alumnus award Calif. Inst. Tech., 1983. Fellow AAAS, Am. Acad. Arts and Sci., Am. Phys. Soc., IEEE, AIAA; mem. Nat. Acad. Scis., Nat. Acad. Engring., Calif. Inst. Assocs., Am. Inst. Physics, Phi Beta Kappa, Sigma Xi, Tau Beta Pi, Phi Eta Sigma, Eta Kappa Nu. Address: 4545 Via Esperanza Santa Barbara CA 93110-2319

WOOLDRIDGE, PATRICE MARIE, marketing professional, martial arts and meditation educator; b. Chgo., June 3, 1954; d. Charles E. and Marlys E. (Kuehn) Reardon; m. Patrick Wooldridge, June 27, 1981. AS, Moraine Valley Coll., 1974; BA, Govs. State U., 1976, MA, 1977; MBA, Loyola U., Chgo., 1983. Community prof. Govs. State U., University Park, Ill., 1977-78; counselor, social worker Bloom Twp. High Sch., Chicago Heights, Ill., 1977-78; market analyst Dr. Scholl Footcare, Chgo., 1978-79; supr. consumer rsch. Unocal, Schaumburg, Ill., 1979-84; group rsch. dir. Tatham-Laird & Kudner, Chgo., 1984-87; v.p., assoc. dir. strategic planning & rsch. Bayer Bess Vanderwarker Advt., Chgo., 1987-90; v.p. dir. qualitative svcs. Goldring/MIL Rsch., 1990-91; pres. Wooldridge Assocs., Inc., Chgo., 1991—; instr. dancing, 1969-89; instr. T'ai Chi the Sch. of T'ai Chi Chuan, N.Y.C., 1986—; instr. Arica the Arica Inst., N.Y.C., 1978—. Performer The Anawim Players, Chgo., 1985—; treas. Karma Thegsum Choling, Chgo., 1987-97; bd. dirs. Illustrated Theatre Co., Chgo., 1987, The Human Process, Chgo., 1992—, Tai Chi Found., Inc., 1994—; adv. bd. N.W. Suburban Boy Scouts, Schaumburg, 1984. Mem. Am. Mktg. Assn., Qualitative Rsch. Cons. Assn., Union of Concerned Scientists, The Planetary Soc. Home and Office: 1717 W Rascher Ave Chicago IL 60640-1117

WOOLDRIDGE, WILLIAM CHARLES, lawyer; b. Miami, Fla., Feb. 24, 1943; s. Clarence Edward and Easter Marguerite (Souders) W.; m. Joyce L. Norton, June 15, 1968; children: William Charles, John Michael. BA, Harvard U., 1965, LLB, U. Va., 1969. Bar: Va. 1969. Atty., Norfolk and Western Ry. Co., 1973-82; with Norfolk So. Corp., 1982-89, v.p. dept. law. 1996—.Pres. John Marshall Found., Richmond, Va., 1992-94; pres. Norfolk Hist. Soc., 1994-96. Served to capt. JAGC, U.S. Army, 1969-73. Mem. ABA, Va. Bar Assn. Republican. Office: Norfolk So Corp 3 Commercial Pl Norfolk VA 23510-2108

WOOLERY-ANTILL, MYRA JO, pediatric clinical nurse specialist; b. Balt., Jan. 20, 1959; d. James Elmer and Myra Eileen (Hoover) Woolery; m. Forrest Denver Antill, Feb. 14, 1982. BSN, U. Md., Balt., 1981; M of Nursing, U. Wash., 1986. Cert. pediatric oncology nurse, PALS. Clin. nurse Johns Hopkins Hosp., Balt., 1981-84; pediatric home care nurse Staff Builders, Balt., 1984; rsch. asst. U. Wash., Seattle, 1985; staff nurse Swedish Med. Ctr., Seattle, 1986-87; clin. nurse specialist NIH, Bethesda, Md., 1987—. Contbr. chpts. to books; contbr. articles to profl. newsletters and jours. Vol., planning com. Camp Goodtimes, Seattle, 1985-87; nurse Camp Fantastic, Front Royal, Va., 1991, 94, 95, 96, Camp Sunshine, Front Royal, 1994. Named one of Outstanding Young Women in Am., 1986; Am. Cancer Soc. scholar, 1985-86. Mem. Assn. Pediatric Oncology Nurses (cert., practice chair 1991-93, mem. FDA working group 1991-94, Pres.' Cert. of Appreciation 1993, hon. bd. mem. Nat. Capitol chpt. 1988-89, sec. 1989-91, pres. 1991-95), Assn. for Care of Children's Health, Oncology Nurses Assn., Sigma Theta Tau. Home: 5638 Carville Ave Baltimore MD 21227-3927 Office: NIH 9000 Rockville Pike Bethesda MD 20814-1436

WOOLEVER, NAOMI LOUISE, retired editor; b. Williamsport, Pa., Sept. 17, 1922; d. Samuel Bruce and Kathryn Elizabeth (Schmidt) W. B.S., Pa. State U., 1944, M.A., 1966, postgrad., 1974-76. Reporter, women's editor Gazette & Bulletin, Williamsport, 1944-53; women's editor Sun-Gazette, Williamsport, 1953-72, assoc. city editor, 1972-74; prof. journalism Williamsport Area Community Coll., 1974-76; nat. editor, mng. editor Grit Pub. Co., Williamsport, 1976-81, editor in chief, 1981-88; career cons. high sch. and coll. journalism classes, Pa. Contbr. articles to profl. jours. Named Woman of Yr., Williamsport Univ. Women, 1967. Mem. Pa. Women's Press Assn. (pres. 1960-62, Pa. Newswoman of Yr. 1958), Nat. Fedn. Press Women (bd. dirs. 1960-62), Soroptimist Club (pres. Williamsport chpt. 1958-60), Univ. Women's Club (pres. 1961-63), Friends of James V. Brown Libr., Williamsport Country Club, Williamsport Woman's Club, Lycoming County Hist. Soc., Clio Club (pres. 1991-93), Phi Kappa Phi, Kappa Tau Alpha, Zeta Tau Alpha. Republican. Mem. United Methodist Ch. Avocations: music, duplicate bridge, photography, sports. Home: 326 N Montour St Montoursville PA 17754-1832

WOOLF, KENNETH HOWARD, Architect; b. N.Y.C., Aug. 19, 1938; s. Howard Walter and Elizabeth Ann (Levy) W.; B Arch., Cornell U., 1961; m. Elizabeth Adair Rainwater, July 3, 1965; children—Robert Gregg, Susan Adair, Jennifer Adair. Staff architect Look & Morrison, Architects, Pensacola, Fla., 1965-72; pvt. practice architecture, Pensacola, 1972—; instr. architecture Pensacola Jr. Coll., part-time 1967-76. Chmn., Pensacola Archtl. Rev. Bd., 1970-81; mem. Gulf Breeze Planning Bd., 1976-78; chmn. Pensacola City Bd. Adjustment and Appeals, 1995—. Served with USN, 1961-65. Named Jaycee of Yr., 1970. Mem. AIA (sec. N.W. Fla. chpt. 1976-77, 1977-78, pres. N.W. Fla. 1979-81; Comml. Design Honor award 1975). Prin. works include: Coca-Cola Bottling Co. Plant, Pensacola, 1974, 3 profl. office bldgs. towers, Pensacola, 1976, 84, 92, Bapt. Hosp. addition, 1977, The Village, Housing for Elderly, 1978, 81, Azalea Trace Retirement Cmty. Complex, 1980, Northview Cmty. 1981, Coca-Cola Bottling Plant, Beaumont, Tex., 1983, Episcopal Day Sch., Pensacola, 1993. Mem. AIA (sec. N.W. Fla. chpt. 1976-77, 77-78, pres. N.W. Fla. 1979-81, Comml. Design Honor award 1975), Rotary. Episcopalian. Home: 15 N Sunset Blvd Gulf Breeze FL 32561-4051 Office: 100 W Gadsden St Pensacola FL 32501-3910

WOOLF, MICHAEL E., lawyer; b. Phoenix, Mar. 17, 1949. BS, Ariz. State U., 1971, JD cum laude, 1974. Bar: ariz. 1974. Ptnr. O'Connor, Cavanagh, Anderson, Killingsworth & Beshears, P.A., Phoenix. Mem. ABA, Maricopa County Bar Assn., State Bar Ariz. Office: O'Connor Cavanagh Anderson Killingsworth & Beshears PA 1 E Camelback Rd Ste 1100 Phoenix AZ 85012-1656

WOOLF, NANCY JEAN, neuroscientist, educator; b. Ft. Sill, Okla., July 27, 1954; d. Lee Allen and Rachel Christine (Sedjo) W.; m. Larry Lee Butcher, Dec. 24, 1983; children: Lawson Frederick, Ashley Ellen. BS, UCLA, 1978, PhD, 1983. Grad. researcher UCLA, 1979-83, asst. rsch. neuroscientist, 1984-92, adj. assoc. prof., 1992—, assoc. rsch. neuroscientist, 1992—. Contbr. some 40 articles to various sci. publs. Recipient Colby prize Sigma Kappa Found., Indpls, 1990; named Woman of Yr. Coll. of the Desert, Palm Desert, Calif., 1976. Mem. AAAS, Assn. Acad. Women (Grad. Woman of Yr. UCLA 1983), Soc. for Neurosci. Achievements include compilation of complete map of central nervous system neurons that utilize the neurotransmitter acetylcholine; MAP-2 alterations with classical conditioning, model of synaptic changes with mammalian memory trace. Office: U Calif Dept Psychology 405 Hilgard Ave Los Angeles CA 90095-9000

WOOLF, WILLIAM BLAUVELT, retired association executive; b. New Rochelle, N.Y., Sept. 18, 1932; s. Douglas Gordon and Katharine Hutton (Blauvelt) W. A.A., John Muir Jr. Coll., 1951; student, U. Calif. at Berkeley, 1951; B.A., Pomona Coll., 1953; M.A., Claremont (Calif.) Grad. Sch., 1955; Ph.D., U. Mich., 1960. Instr., asst. prof., asso. prof. U. Wash., Seattle, 1959-68; assoc. sec., dir. adminstrn. AAUP, Washington, 1968-79; mng. editor Math. Revs., Am. Math. Soc., Ann Arbor, Mich., 1979-90, acting exec. editor, 1984-85; assoc. exec. dir. Am. Math. Soc., Providence, 1990-96. Bd. dirs. Nat. Child Research Center, Washington, 1975-77; trustee Friends Sch., Detroit, 1985-90, treas., 1986-90. Fulbright Research fellow U. Helsinki, Finland, 1963-64. Fellow AAAS; mem. ACLU (life, treas. Washington 1966-68, bd. dirs. Washtenaw County and Mich. State 1989-90, bd. dirs. R.I. State 1993-95, treas. 1994-95), Am. Math. Soc., Math. Assn. Am. Quaker. Home: 275 Pond Rd Port Townsend WA 98368

WOOLFENDEN, JAMES MANNING, nuclear medicine physician, educator; b. L.A., Nov. 8, 1942. BA with distinction, Stanford U., 1964; MD, U. Wash., 1968. Diplomate Am. Bd. Nuclear Medicine (chmn. credentials com. 1993-94, vice-chmn. examinations com. 1993-95, chmn. exam. com. 1995-96, sec. 1994-96, chmn. 1996—), Nat. Bd. Med. Examiners; lic. physician Calif., Ariz., Wash. Med. intern L.A. County-U. So. Calif. Med. Ctr., 1968-69; med. resident West L.A. VA Med. Ctr., 1969-70; nuclear medicine resident L.A. County-U. So. Calif. Med. Ctr., 1972-74; from asst. prof. radiology to assoc. prof. radiology U. Ariz., Tucson, 1974-84, prof. radiology, 1984—; mem. med. staff Univ. Med. Ctr., Tucson, 1974—; cons. VA Med. Ctr., 1974—; cons. med. staff Tucson Med. Ctr., 1975—, Carondelet St. Joseph's Hosp., 1974—, St. Mary's Hosp., Tucson, 1976-90; mem. Nat. Cancer Inst. site visit team NIH, 1976, mem. NHLB Inst. site visit team NIH, 1976, mem. diagnostic radiology study sect., 1993—, chmn., 1995—; mem. med. liaison officer network EPA, 1983—; cons.-tchg. med. staff Kino Comty. Hosp., 1984-94; med. officer Clin. Ctr., NIH, Bethesda, 1984-85; mem. Ariz. Cancer Ctr., U. Ariz., 1988—, sr. clin. scientist Univ. Heart Ctr., 1990—; Ariz. bd. regents U. Ariz. Presdl. Search Com., 1990-91; chmn. Ariz. Atomic Energy Commn., 1979-80, Ariz. Radiation Regulatory Hearing Bd., 1981—; bd. dirs. Calif. Radioactive Materials Mgmt. Forum, 1989—, chmn.-elect, 1993-94, chmn., 1994-95, Western Forum Edn. in Safe Disposal of Low-Level Radioactive Waste, 1990—, vice chmn., 1991-92, chmn., 1992-94. Manuscript reviewer: Noninvasive Med. Imaging, 1983-84, Jour. Nuclear Medicine, 1985—, Investigative Radiology, 1989-94, Archives of Internal Medicine, 1990—; contbr. book chpts.: Diagnostic Nuclear Medicine, 2d edit., 1988, Adjuvant Therapy of Cancer, 1977, Fundamentals of Nuclear Medicine, 1988, others; contbr. articles and book revs. to profl. publs. Mem. Am. Heart Assn. Coun. on Cardiovasc. Radiology. Maj. U.S. Army, 1970-72, Vietnam. Fellow Am. Coll. Nuclear Physicians (long range planning com. 1981-83, govt. affairs com. 1984—, exec. com. 1987-91, sec. 1989-91, parliamentarian 1991-95, treas. 1996—, mem. publs. com. 1993—, chmn. publs. com. 1993-94, and many others); mem. AMA (diagnostic and therapeutic tech. assessment reference panel 1982—), Am. Fedn. Clin. Rsch., Am. Nuc. Soc., Soc. Nuclear Medicine (com. on audit 1992—, bd. trustees 1992-96, ho. dels. 1996—, fin. com. 1996—, Bronze medal for sci. exhibit 1984, bd. dirs., sec.-treas. So. Calif. chpt. 1993-95, pres.-elect 1995-96, pres. 1996—), Assn. Univ. Radiologists, Pima County Med. Soc., Radiol. Soc. N.Am. Office: Ariz Health Scis Ctr 1501 N Campbell Ave Tucson AZ 85724-0001

WOOLFORD, DONNELL, professional football player; b. Balt., Jan. 6, 1966. Student, Clemson U. Cornerback Chgo. Bears, 1989—. Named to Sporting Coll. All-Am. Team, 1988, to Pro Bowl Team, 1993. Office: Chgo Bears Halas Hall 2550 N Washington Rd Lake Forest IL 60045*

WOOLHISER, DAVID ARTHUR, hydrologist; b. LaCrosse, Wis., Jan. 21, 1932; s. Algie Duncan and Blanche Lenore (Jasperson) W.; m. Kathryn Brown, Apr. 21, 1957; children: Carl David, Curt Fredric, Lisa Kathryn. B.S. in Agr., U. Wis.-Madison, 1955, BSCE, 1955, PhD, 1962; MS, U. Ariz., 1959. Instr. U. Ariz., Tucson, 1955-58; hydraulic engr. Agrl. Research Service, USDA, Madison, Wis., 1959-61, Columbia, Mo., 1961-63; asst. prof. Cornell U., Ithaca, N.Y., 1963-67; research hydraulic engr. Agrl. Research Service, Ft. Collins, Colo., 1967-81, Tucson, 1981-91, collaborator, 1991-92; vis. scientist Inst. Hydrology, Wallingford, Eng., 1977-78; vis. prof. Imperial Coll., London, 1977-78; faculty affiliate Colo. State U., 1967-84; adj. prof. U. Ariz., 1981-92; vis. prof. Va. Poly. Inst. and State U., 1992; sr. rsch. sci. Colo. State U., 1993-94, faculty affiliate, 1994—; vis. prof. U. Córdoba, Spain, 1993-94, 96. Contbr. articles to profl. jours. Recipient Disting. Svc. citation Coll. engring. U. Wis.-Madison, 1991. Fellow Am. Geophys. Union (Robert E. Horton award 1983); mem. NAE, ASCE (Hunter Rouse Lectr. 1994, Arid Lands Hydraulic Engring. award 1988), Office: 1631 Barnwood Dr Fort Collins CO 80525-2069

WOOLLAM, JOHN ARTHUR, electrical engineering educator; b. Kalamazoo, Mich., Aug. 10, 1939; s. Arthur Edward and Mildred Edith (Hakes) W.; children: Catherine Jane, Susan June. BA in Physics, Kenyon Coll., 1961; MS in Physics, Mich. State U., 1963, PhD in Solid State Physics, 1967; MSEE, Case Western Res. U., 1978. Rsch. scientist NASA Lewis Rsch. Ctr., Cleve., 1967-80; prof. U. Nebr., Lincoln, 1979—, dir. Ctr. Microelectronic and Optical Materials Rsch., 1988—; pres. J.A. Woollam Co., Inc., Lincoln, 1987—. Editor Jour. Applied Physics Com., 1979-94. Grantee NASA, NSF, USAF, Advanced Rsch. Projects Agy. Fellow Am. Phys. Soc.; mem. Am. Vacuum Soc. (chmn. thin film divsn. 1989-91). Office: U Nebr Dept Elec Engring 209NWSEC Lincoln NE 68588-0511

WOOLLEN, EVANS, architectural firm executive; b. Indpls., Aug. 10, 1927; s. Evans Jr. and Lydia (Jameson) Ritchey; m. Nancy Clarke Sewell, July 16, 1955 (dec. 1992); children: Ian, Malcolm Sewell. BA, Yale U., 1952, MArch, 1952. Lic. architect Ind., Ala., Conn., Del., Ill., Ky., La., Maine, Mass., N.C., Ohio, Tenn. Chmn. Woollen, Molzan & Ptnrs., Indpls., 1955—; resident Am. Acad. in Rome, spring 1996. Architect Pilot Ctr., Cin. (Nat. HUD 1975), St. Marys Coll. Libr. (Nat. AIA-ALA 1983), Grainger Libr., U. Ill., Urbana, Wartburg Coll. Libr., Waverly, Iowa, Asbury Coll. Libr., Wilmore, Ky. Mem. bd. Ind. State Welfare Bd., 1956-59, Art Assn., 1956-66, Indpls. Capital Improvement Bd., 1965-69. With Signal Corps U.S. Army, 1946-47. Resident Am. Acad. in Rome, 1996. Fellow AIA. Democrat. Address: 43 W 43rd St Indianapolis IN 46208-3721 Office: Woollen Molzan & Ptnrs Inc 47 S Pennsylvania St Indianapolis IN 46204-3622

WOOLLEY, CATHERINE (JANE THAYER), writer; b. Chgo., Aug. 11, 1904; d. Edward Mott and Anna L. (Thayer) W. AB, UCLA, 1927. Advt. copywriter Am. Radiator Co., N.Y.C., 1927-31; freelance writer, 1931-33; copywriter, editor house organ Am. Radiator & Standard San. Corp., N.Y.C., 1933-40; desk editor Archtl. Record, 1940-42; prodn. editor SAE Jour., N.Y.C., 1942-43; pub. relations writer NAM, N.Y.C., 1943-47; condr. workshop on juvenile writing Truro Ctr. for Arts, 1977, 78, 92, Cape Cod Writers Conf., 1990, 91, 92; instr. writing for juveniles Cape Cod Writers Conf., 1965, 66, 92. Author: juvenile books (under name Catherine Woolley) I Like Trains, 1944, rev., 1965, Two Hundred Pennies, 1947, Ginnie and Geneva, 1948, paperback edit., 1988, David's Railroad, 1949, Schoolroom Zoo, 1950, Railroad Cowboy, 1951, Ginnie Joins In, 1951, David's Hundred Dollars, 1952, Lunch for Lennie, 1952 (pub. as L'Incontentabile Gigi in Italy), The Little Car That Wanted a Garage, 1952, The Animal Train and Other Stories, 1953, Holiday on Wheels, 1953, Ginnie and the New Girl, 1954, Ellie's Problem Dog, 1955, A Room for Cathy, 1956, Ginnie and the Mystery House, 1957, Miss Cathy Leonard, 1958, David's Campaign Buttons, 1959, Ginnie and the Mystery Doll, 1960, Cathy Leonard Calling, 1961, paperback edit., 1988, Look Alive, Libby!, 1962, Ginnie and Her Juniors, 1963, Cathy's Little Sister, 1964, paperback edit., 1988, Libby Looks for a Spy, 1965, The Shiny Red Rubber Boots, 1965, Ginnie and the Cooking Contest, 1966, paperback 1979, Ginnie and the Wedding Bells, 1967, Chris in Trouble, 1968, Ginnie and the Mystery Cat, 1969, Libby's Uninvited Guest, 1970, Cathy and the Beautiful People, 1971, Cathy Uncovers a Secret, 1972, Ginnie and the Mystery Light, 1973, Libby Shadows a Lady, 1974, Ginnie and Geneva Cookbook, 1975, adult book Writing for Children, 1990, paperback, 1990; (under name Jane Thayer) The Horse with the Easter Bonnet, 1953, The Popcorn Dragon, 1953, rev. edit. 1989, Where's Andy?, 1954, Mrs. Perrywinkle's Pets, 1955, Sandy and the Seventeen Balloons, 1955, The Chicken in the Tunnel, 1956, The Outside Cat, 1957, English edit., 1958, 83, Charley and the New Car, 1957, Funny Stories To Read Aloud, 1958, Andy Wouldn't Talk, 1958, The Puppy Who Wanted a Boy, 1958, rev., 1986, paperback edition, 1988, French translation Le Petit Chien Qui Voulait Un Garcon, 1991, The Second-Story Giraffe, 1959, Little Monkey, 1959, Andy and His Fine Friends, 1960, The Pussy Who Went To the Moon, 1960, English edit., 1961, A Little Dog Called Kitty, 1961, English edit., 1962, 75, The Blueberry Pie Elf, 1961, English edit., 1962, revised edit., 1994, Spanish edit., 1995, Andy's Square Blue Animal, 1962, Gus Was a Friendly Ghost, 1962, English edit., 1971, Japanese edit., 1982, A Drink for Little Red Diker, 1963, Andy and the Runaway Horse, 1963, A House for Mrs. Hopper; the Cat that Wanted to Go Home, 1963, Quiet on Account of Dinosaur, 1964, English edit., 1965, 74, paperback edit., 1988, Emerald Enjoyed the Moonlight, 1964, English edit., 1965, The Bunny in the Honeysuckle Patch, 1965, English edit., 1966, Part-Time Dog, 1965, English edit. 1966, The Light Hearted Wolf, 1966, What's a Ghost Going to Do?, 1966, English edit. 1972, Japanese edit., 1982, The Cat that Joined the Club, 1967, English edit. 1968, Rockets Don't Go To Chicago, Andy, 1967, A Contrary Little Quail, 1968, Little Mr. Greenthumb, 1968, English edit., 1969, Andy and Mr. Cunningham, 1969, Curious, Furious Chipmunk, 1969, I'm Not a Cat, Said Emerald, 1970, English edit. 1971, Gus Was A Christmas Ghost, 1970, English edit. 1973, Japanese edit., 1982, Mr. Turtle's Magic Glasses, 1971, Timothy And Madam Mouse, 1971, English edit., 1972, Gus And The Baby Ghost, 1972, English edit. 1973, Japanese edit., 1982, The Little House, 1972, Andy and the Wild Worm, 1973, Gus Was a Mexican Ghost, 1974, English edit. 1975, Japanese edit., 1982, I Don't Believe in Elves, 1975, The Mouse on the Fourteenth Floor, 1977, Gus Was a Gorgeous Ghost, 1978, English edit., 1979, Where Is Squirrel?, 1979, Try Your Hand, 1980, Applebaums Have a Robot, 1980, Clever Raccoon, 1981, Gus Was a Real Dumb Ghost, 1982, Gus Loved His Happy Home, 1989; contbr. stories to juvenile anthologies in U.S., Great Britain, France, Germany, and Holland, sch. readers, juvenile mags. Trustee Truro Pub. Libraries, 1974-84; Mem. Passaic (N.J.) Bd. Edn., 1953-56, Passaic Redevel. Agy., 1952-53; pres. Passaic LWV, 1949-52. Named mem. N.J. Literary Hall of Fame, 1987; recipient Phantom Friends Lifetime Achievement award, 1992. Mem. Authors League Am., Friends of Truro Libraries, Truro Hist. Soc., Amnesty Internat. U.S.A., Kenilworth Soc. Democrat. Home: PO Box 71 Truro MA 02666-0071

WOOLLEY, DONNA PEARL, timber and lumber company executive; b. Drain, Oreg., Jan. 3, 1926; d. Chester A. and Mona B. (Cheever) Rydell; m. Harold Woolley, Dec. 27, 1952 (dec. Sept. 1970); children: Daniel, Debra, Donald. Diploma, Drain High Sch. Sec. No Life Ins. Co., Eugene, Oreg., 1943-44; sec., bookkeeper D & W Lumber Co., Sutherlin, Oreg., 1944, Woolley Logging Co. & Earl Harris Lumber Co., Drain, 1944-70; pres. Woolley Logging Co., 1970—, Smith River Lumber Co., 1970—, Mt. Baldy Mill, 1970-81, Drain Plywood Co., 1970-81, Woolley Enterprises, Inc., Drain, 1973—, Eagle's View Mgmt. Co., Inc., Eugene, 1981—. Bd. dirs. Oreg. Cmty. Found., Portland, Oreg., 1990—, Wildlife Safari, Winston, Oreg., 1986; trustee emeritus U. Oreg. Found., Eugene, 1979—; trustee Linfield Coll. Found., McMinnville, Oreg., 1990—; v.p. Oreg. Trail coun. Boy Scouts Am., Eugene, 1981—; exec. dir. World Forestry Ctr., Portland, 1991—. Recipient Pioneer award U. Oreg., 1982, Econ. and Social Devel. award Soroptimist Club, 1991. Mem. Oreg. Women's Forum, Pacific Internat. Trapshooting Assn., Amateur Trapshooting Assn., Eugene C. of C. (bd. dirs. 1989-92), Arlington Club, Town Club (bd. dirs., pres.), Sunnydale Grange, Cottage Grove/Eugene Rod & Gun Club. Republican. Avocations: golf, travel. Office: Eagle's View Mgmt Co Inc 1399 Franklin Blvd Eugene OR 97403-1979

WOOLLEY, GEORGE WALTER, biologist, geneticist, educator; b. Osborne, Kans., Nov. 9, 1904; s. George Aitcheson and Nora Belle (Jackson) W.; m. Anne Geneva Collins, Nov. 2, 1936; children: George Aitcheson, Margaret Anne, Lawrence Jackson. B.S., Iowa State U., 1930; M.S., U. Wis., 1931, Ph.D., 1935. Fellow U. Wis., 1935-36; mem. staff Jackson Meml. Lab., Bar Harbor, Maine, 1936-49; bd. dirs. Jackson Meml. Lab., 1937-49, v.p. bd., 1943-47, asst. dir. and sci. adminstr., 1947-49, vis. research assoc., 1949—; mem. chief div. steroid biology Sloan-Kettering Inst., N.Y.C., 1949-58, prof. biology, 1949-58; prof. biology Sloan-Kettering Inst. div. Cornell U. Med. Coll., Ithaca, N.Y., 1951—, chief div. human tumor exptl. chemotherapy, 1958-61, chief div. tumor biology, 1961-66; assoc. scientist Sloan-Kettering Inst. Cancer Research, 1966—; health sci. adminstr., program coordinator, head biol. scis. sect. Nat. Inst. Gen. Medical Scis., NIH, 1966-85; cons. Nat. Edn. Service U.S., Washington, 1961—; spl. cons. to Nat. Cancer Inst., NIH, 1956—; Mem. Expert Panel on Carcinogenicity, unio intern. contra cancerum, 1962—; mem. panel com. on growth NRC, 1945-51; mem. several internat. med. congresses. Author chpts. in med. books; mem. editorial bd. Jour. Nat. Cancer Inst., 1947-50. Trustee Dalton Schs., N.Y.C. Fellow AAAS, N.Y. Acad. Sci.; mem. Am. Mus. Natural History, Nat. Sci. Tchrs. Assn. (cons. 1961—), Am. Assn. Cancer Research (dir. 1951-54), Am. Soc. Human Genetics, Mt. Desert Island Biol. Lab., Soc. Exptl. Biology and Medicine, Am. Inst. Biol. Scis., Am. Assn. Anatomists, Am. Genetic Assn., Wis. Acad. Arts Sci. and Letters, Jackson Lab. Assn., Genetics Soc. Am., Environ. Mutagen Soc., Sigma Xi. Clubs: Bar Harbor, Bar Harbor (Maine) Yacht. Achievements include advanced research, teaching and administration in genetics, from the beginnings of the field to present; contributions to fields of cancer, virology, endocrinology and molecular biology. Home: 5301 Westbard Cir Apt 336 Bethesda MD 20816-1427

WOOLLEY, MARGARET ANNE (MARGOT WOOLLEY), architect; b. Bangor, Maine, Feb. 4, 1946; d. George Walter and Anne Geneva (Collins) W.; m. Gerard F. Vasisko, June 22, 1985. BA, Vassar Coll., 1969; MArch, Columbia U., 1974. Registered architect, N.Y. Urban designer Mayor's Office Lower Manhattan Devel., 1974-76, Mayor's Office Devel., N.Y.C., 1976-78; project mgr. Office Econ. Devel., N.Y.C., 1978-81, dep. dir. design and engring., 1981-83; dep. dir. design N.Y.C. Pub. Devel. Corp., 1983-85, asst. v.p. design, 1985-86, v.p. design, 1986-91; v.p. design N.Y.C. Econ. Devel. Corp., 1991-94; dep. program dir. corrections program unit N.Y.C. Dept. Design and Constrn., 1996—; mem. N.Y. State Licensing Bd. Architecture, 1994—; mem. archtl. registration examination com. Nat. Coun. Archtl. Registration Bds., 1995—. Mem. assoc. bd. regents L.I. Coll. Hosp., Bklyn., 1982-93, mem. planning and devel. com., 1983-93; pres. assoc. bd. regents, 1988-89. William Kinne Fellows scholar, 1973. Mem. AIA (bd. dirs. N.Y.C. chpt. 1988-90, nat. pub. architects steering com. 1993-95), N.Y. State Assn. Architects (bd. dirs. 1990-92), Heights Casino Club, Vassar Club, Jr. League. Home: 135 Willow St Brooklyn NY 11201-2255

WOOLLEY, MARY ELIZABETH, research administrator; b. Chgo., Mar. 16, 1947; John Joseph and Ellen Louise (Bakke) McEnerney; m. John Stuart Woolley, Dec. 6, 1969 (div. 1985); children: George Newsom, Nora Ellen; m. Michael Howland Campbell, Jan. 1, 1989. BS, Stanford U., 1969; MA, San Francisco State U., 1972; postgrad., U. Calif., San Francisco and Berkeley, 1974-75. Assoc. dir. Inst. Epidemiology and Behavioral Medicine, San Francisco, 1979-81; adminstr. Med. Rsch. Inst. of San Francisco, 1981-82, v.p., adminstr., 1982-86, v.p., exec. dir., 1986-90; pres. Research! Am., Alexandria, Va., 1990—; cons. in fin. and mgmt. NIH, Bethesda, Md., 1984-92; adj. faculty U. Calif. Sch. Pub. Health, Berkeley, 1983-92, mem. Dean's adv. coun., 1995—; founding mem. Whitehead Inst. Bd. Assocs., 1995—; lectr. to profl. assns.; bd. dirs. The Lovelace Inst., 1997—. Editor Jour. of Soc. Rsch. Adminstrs., 1986-89, mem. editl. rev. bd., 1989-95; mem. editl. bd. Jour. Women's Health, 1992—, Sci. Comm., 1994—; contbr. articles and editls. to profl. jours. Bd. dirs. Kensington (Calif.) Edn. Found., 1986-89, Enterprise for H.S. Students, 1990-92; mem. capital campaign com. Calif. Shakespeare Festival, 1989-91, v.p. Med. Rsch. Assns. Am., 1993-95; bd. advisors Friends of Cancer Rsch., 1996—. Recipient Silver Touchstone award Am. Hosp. Assn., 1994, Disting. Svc. award Columbia Coll. Physicians and Surgeons, 1994. Mem. AAAS, Assn. Ind. Rsch. Insts. (pres.-elect 1987-89, pres. 1989-90), Soc. Rsch. Adminstrs. (bd. dirs. 1986-90, bd. advisors 1990-93, Hartford-Nicholson Svc. award 1990, Disting. Contbn. to Rsch. Adminstrn. award, 1993), Calif. Biomedical rsch. Assn. (bd. govs. 1986-90), Md. Gov.'s Commn. on Women's Health, 1993-96. Democrat. Office: Research! Am 1522 King St Alexandria VA 22314-2717

WOOLLIAMS, KEITH RICHARD, arboretum and botanical garden director; b. Chester, Eng., July 17, 1940; s. Gordon Frank and Margaret Caroline W.; m. Akiko Narita, Apr. 11, 1969; children: Frank Hiromi, Angela Misako. Grad., Celyn Agrl. and Hort. Inst., North Wales, 1955; student, U. Liverpool, various horticultural insts., 1956-59; Kew Cert., Royal Bot. Gardens, Kew, U.K., 1963. Cert. Horticulture Union Cheshire and Lancs. Insts., 1955, Royal Hort. Soc., 1956, 57, 58, Nat. Cert. Horticulture, 1958, Cert. Arboriculture, 1962. Supt. field sta. U. London Queen Mary Coll., Brentwood, Essex, Eng., 1963-65; horticulturist Horizons Ltd., Bermuda, 1965-67; dept. forests, supt. botanic gardens Papua, New Guinea, 1967-68; instr. Eng. staff indsl. cos., Japan, 1968-71; supt., horticulturist Nat. Tropical Bot. Garden, Kauai, Hawaii, 1971-74; horticulturist Waimea Arboretum and Botanical Garden, Haleiwa, Hawaii, 1974-80, dir., 1980—; mem. Pacific islands plant recovery coordinating com. U.S. Fish and Wildlife Svc., 1993—; mem. Hawaii Rare Plant Restoration Group, 1991—. Contbr. articles to profl. jours., New Royal Hort. Soc. Dictionary of Gardening, 1992. Field assoc. botany Bishop Mus., Honolulu, 1981—; bd. dirs. Friends of Honolulu Bot. Gardens, 1980-96; v.p., founder Waimea Arboretum Found., 1977—; bd. dirs. Condominium Estate, Wahiawa, Hawaii, 1990—. Mem. Am. Assn. Botanical Gardens and Arboreta, Am. Hort. Soc., Hawaii Audubon Soc., Hawaiian Botanical Soc. (pres. 1979), Internat. Assn. Plant Taxonomists, Royal Hort. Soc., Kew Guild. Avocations: fishing, home repairs, music, reading, travel. Office: Waimea Arboretum & Bot Garden 59-864 Kamehameha Hwy Haleiwa HI 96712-9406

WOOLLING, KENNETH RAU, internist; b. Indpls., Mar. 6, 1918; s. Kenneth Kaarta and Marie May (Rau) W.; m. Catherine Margaret McColl, Mar. 20, 1948; children: Kenneth Rau Jr., Mary Catherine. BA magna cum laude, Butler U., 1939; postgrad., Harvard U., 1939-40; MD, Ind. U., 1943; MS in Medicine, U. Minn., 1951. Diplomate Nat. Bd. Med. Examiners, Am. Bd. Internal Medicine, Am. Bd. Cardiovascular Disease. Intern Indpls. City Hosp. (now Wishard Meml.), Indpls., 1943-44; resident in internal medicine Marion County Gen. Hosp., Indpls., 1947; fellow, first asst. internal medicine Mayo Found., Rochester, Minn., 1948-52; mem. med. staff, mem. tchg. staff postgrad. med. edn. Marion County Gen. Hosp. (name now Wishard Meml. Hosp.), Indpls., 1952—; founder, dir., peripheral vascular diseases clinic Indpls City & Marion County Gen. Hosp. (now Wishard Meml.), Indpls., 1952-68; pvt. practice internal medicine and cardiovascular diseases Indpls, 1952—; founder, dir. peripheral vascular diseases clinic Meth. Hosp., Indpls., 1967-72, founder, dir. vascular lab., 1970-73, mem. med. staff, tchr. staff postgrad. med. edn., 1952—; mem. staff St. Vincent Hosp., St. Francis Hosp. and Winona Meml. Hosp., Indpls., 1952—; charter mem. med. adv. com. Butler U., Indpls, 1956—. Contbr. articles to profl. jours., 1950—. Capt. Med. Corps U.S. Army, 1944-46. Fellow Am. Coll. Chest Physicians, Coun. on Clin. Cardiology Am. Heart Assn., 1963. Fellow ACP, Am. Coll. Angiology (gov. state of Ind. 1979-80); mem. AMA (50 Yr. award 1993), SAR, Am. Soc. Internal Medicine, Am. Diabetes Assn., Ind. Diabetes Assn., Am. Fedn. for Clin. Rsch., N.Y. Acad. Med. Scis., North Ctrl. Clin. Soc., Mayo Cardiovascular Soc., Ind. Hist. Soc., Res. Officers Assn., Am. Legion, Shriners, Masons (Scottish Rite and Mystic Tie Lodge), Contemporary Club of Indpls., Indpls. Athletic Club, Highland Golf and Country Club, Phi Delta Theta (50 yr. award 1985), Phi Kappa Phi, Phi Chi. Presbyterian. Office: PO Box 80192 Indianapolis IN 46280-0192

WOOLLS, ESTHER BLANCHE, library science educator; b. Louisville, Mar. 30, 1935; d. Arthur William and Esther Lennie (Smith) Sutton; m. Donald Paul Woolls, Oct. 21, 1953 (div. Nov. 1982); 1 son, Arthur Paul. AB in Fine Arts, Ind. U., 1958, MA in Libr. Sci., 1962, PhD in Libr. Sci., 1973. Elem. libr. Hammond Pub. Schs., Ind., 1958-65, libr. coord., 1965-67; libr. coord. Roswell Ind. Schs., N.Mex., 1967-70; prof. libr. sci. U. Pitts., 1973—; exec. dir. Beta Phi Mu, 1981-95. Author: The School Library Media Manager, 1995, So You're Going to Run a Library, 1995, Ideas for School Library Media Centers, 1996; editor: Continuing Professional Education and IFLA: Past, Present, and a Vision for the Future, 1993. Fulbright scholar, 1995-96; recipient disting. svc. award Pa. Sch. Librs. Assn., 1993. Mem. ALA (mem. coun. 1985-89, 91-94, 95—), Am. Assn. Sch. Librs. (bd. dirs. 1983-88, pres. 1993-94, disting. svc. award 1997), Pa. Learning Resources Assn. (pres. 1984-85), Internat. Assn. Sch. Librs. (bd. dirs. 1991—), Internat. Fedn. Libr. Assns. (mem. standing com. sch. librs. sect. 1991—, editor continuing profl. edn. roundtable newsletter). Home: 270 Tennyson Ave Pittsburgh PA 15213-1416 Office: U Pitts Sch Info Scis 135 N Bellefield Ave Pittsburgh PA 15213-2609

WOOLSEY, DAVID ARTHUR, leasing company executive; b. Oakland, Calif., Nov. 27, 1941; s. Stanley Arthur Woolsey and Jane Bernadette (Gallagher) Woolsey-Weyler; m. Kathleen Marie McDonnell, June 26, 1965; children: Anne C., Matthew J., Jane K. BS, U. San Francisco, 1963; MBA, U. Calif., Berkeley, 1965. Mgr. lease and spl. projects financing Kaiser Aluminum & Chem. Corp., Oakland, Calif., 1965-68; v.p. U.S. Leasing Internat., Inc., San Francisco, 1968-78; exec. v.p. GATX Capital Corp., San Francisco, 1978, exec. v.p., 1982-88, also bd. dirs.; COO, Orix U.S.A. Corp., 1988—, also bd. dirs. Mem. Equipment Leasing Assn. Am., Orinda Country Club (Cali, pres. 1981), Commonwealth Club (Calif), Bohemian Club, Univ. Club N.Y. Republican. Roman Catholic. Home: 58 The Knoll Orinda CA 94563-1523 Office: ORIX USA Corp 780 3rd Ave New York NY 10017-2024

WOOLSEY, FREDERICK WILLIAM, retired journalist, music critic; b. Miles City, Mont., Oct. 7, 1919; s. Fred W. and Louise (Gaylord) W.; m. Mary Lou Hubbard, Apr. 27, 1957 (dec. June 1976); m. Jane R. Towery, Oct. 15, 1983. B.J., U. Mo., 1943. Radio news writer Sta. KXOK, St. Louis, 1943; telegraph desk The Times, Shreveport, La., 1946; reporter, features writer Nashville Tennessean, 1947-55, night city editor, 1955; reporter, rewrite desk Louisville Times, 1956-65, music critic, 1960-85; feature writer Courier-Jour. Sunday mag., 1965-85. Author: radio series Tall Tales of Tenn; folklore, Sta. WSM, Nashville, 1954-55; contbr. articles to journalism anthologies. Mem. Louisville Human Rights Com., 1960; chmn. pub. rels. com. City-County Human Rels. Commn., 1961-62; mem. Ky. Civil Liberties Union, 1956—; bd. dirs. Louisville Urban League, 1958-68, Widowed Persons Svc., 1978-80, Louisville Chamber Music Soc., 1982—, U. Louisville Libr. Assocs.; co-founder, exec. bd. Friends of U. Louisville Sch. Music, 1991-93. With USAF, 1943-46. Recipient certificate of merit for mag. writing Am. Bar Assn., 1974. Democrat. Episcopalian. Home: 2416 Dundee Rd Louisville KY 40205-2047

WOOLSEY, JOHN MUNRO, JR., lawyer; b. N.Y.C., Apr. 22, 1916; s. John M. and Alice B. (Bacon) W.; m. Ledlie Laughlin, Dec. 27, 1948; children: John, Alice, Henry, Mary. B.A., Yale U., 1938, LL.B., 1941. Bar: N.Y. 1941, Mass. 1947. Assoc. Debevoise, Stevenson, Plimpton & Page, N.Y.C., 1941-42; with Bd. Econ. Warfare, Washington, 1942; with firm Herrick & Smith and predecessor firms, Boston, 1946-86, ptnr., 1956-83, of counsel, 1984-86; of counsel Palmer & Dodge, 1986—; with Office of U.S. Chief of Counsel, Nürnberg Trials, Germany, 1945-46. Former pres. Trustees of Reservations, Shady Hill Sch. Served to lt. USNR, 1942-46. Decorated Order of White Lion (Czechoslovakia). Mem. Am. Antiquarian Soc., Am. Law Inst., Tavern Club, Century Club (N.Y.C.). Office: Palmer & Dodge One Beacon St Boston MA 02108

WOOLSEY, LYNN, congresswoman; b. Seattle, Nov. 3, 1937. BA, U. San Francisco, 1980. Mem. 103rd-105th Congresses from 6th Calif. dist., 1993—; mem. Ho. Reps. coms. on budget, & econ. & edn l. opportunity. Office: US House of Reps 439 Cannon Bldg Washington DC 20515-0506*

WOOLSEY, R. JAMES, lawyer; b. Tulsa, Sept. 21, 1941; s. Robert James and Clyde (Kirby) W.; m. Suzanne Haley, Aug. 15, 1965; children—Robert Nathaniel, Daniel James, Benjamin Haley. B.A. with great distinction, Stanford U., 1963; M.A. (Rhodes scholar), Oxford (Eng.) U., 1965; LL.B., Yale U., 1968. Bar: Calif. bar 1969, D.C. bar 1970. Program analyst Office Sec. Def., Washington, 1968-70, NSC, Washington, 1970; gen. counsel Com. Armed Services, U.S. Senate, 1970-73; assoc. firm Shea & Gardner, Washington, 1973-77; ptnr. Shea & Gardner, 1979-89; ambassador and U.S. rep. to negotiation on conventional armed forces in Europe, 1989-91; ptnr. with Shea & Gardner, 1991-93; dir. Central Intelligence, Washington, 1993-95; ptnr. Shea & Gardner, 1995—; undersec. of navy, 1977-79; advisor U.S. del. SALT, Helsinki and Vienna, 1969-70. Mem. Pres.'s Commn. on Strategic Forces, 1983-84, Fed. Ethics Law reform, 1989; Blue Ribbon Commn. on Defense Mgmt., 1985-86; del.-at-large Soviet Arms Talks, Geneva, 1983-86; trustee Stanford U., 1972-74, Regent Smithsonian Instution, 1989-93; dir. Martin Marietta, 1991-93, British Aerospace Inc., 1992-93, Fairchild Industries, 1984-89, Titan Corp., 1983-89, DynCorp, 1988-89, USF&G, 1995—, Sun Healthcare Group, Inc., 1995—, Yurie Systems, Inc., 1996—. Served with U.S. Army, 1968-70. Mem. Council Fgn. Relations, Phi Beta Kappa. Presbyterian. Office: Shea & Gardner 1800 Massachusetts Ave NW Washington DC 20036-1806

WOOLSEY, ROBERT EUGENE DONALD, mineral economics, mathematics and business administration educator; b. Fort Worth, Oct. 31, 1936; s. Eugene Ralph W. and Ruby Ruth (White) Binder Woolsey; m. Ronita Elaine Packer, Sept. 17, 1958; children: Wysandria W.W., Darrell E. B.A., U. Tex., 1959, M.A., 1967, Ph.D., 1969. Staff mem. Sandia Corp., Albuquerque, 1966-68; assoc. dir. Computer Center U. Tex., Austin, 1968-69; assoc. prof. math. Colo. Sch. Mines, Golden, 1969-72, prof. math., 1972-74, prof. mineral econs., 1974-79, prof., head dept., 1979-81, MAPCO Found. prof., 1981-84, prof., program dir. Ops. Rsch./Mgmt. Sci. program divsn. econs. & bus., 1988—; vis. coll. Colo. Women's Coll., Denver, 1979-81; adj. prof. U. Waterloo, Ont., Can., 1972—, Instituto Technologico de Monterrey, Nuevo Leon, Mexico, 1974—, U. Witwatersrand, Johannesburg, S. Africa, 1984—; vis. prof. dept. engring. U.S. Mil. Acad., West Point, N.Y., 1986-87; prof. core faculty Walden U., 1990—; bd. dirs. Southland Energy Corp., Tulsa, New Tech. Devel. Co., Inc., Vancouver, B.C., Can. Author: Operations Research for Immediate Application, 1975, Applied Management Science, 1980; editor: Transactions of the Institute of Industrial Engineering, 1981-84, Production and Inventory Management, 1984—, Interfaces, 1975-82, Jour. Ops. Mgmt., 1986-87; contbr. articles to profl. jours. Pres. Rocky Mountain Fire Brigade, Inc., Golden, Colo., 1972-83. Served to capt. USAF, 1959-62. Named tchr. of yr. Standard Oil Ind., 1972, 96; recipient 1st Harold Larnder Meml. prize Can. Operational Rsch. Soc., 1986, Disting. Civilian Svc. medal U.S. Dept. Army, 1987, Comdrs. medal, 1991, Outstanding Civilian Svc. medal, 1995; named Hon. Col. 115 Engr. Regiment U.S. Army, 1987. Fellow Am. Inst. Decision Sci. (v.p. 1981-83); mem. Inst. Mgmt. Scis. (council 1976-78, pres. 1986-87), Inst. Indsl. Engrs. (sr. mem., editor 1981-84), Ops. Rsch. Soc. Am. (editor 1975-82), Newcomen Soc. Republican. Episcopalian. Home: 1826 Smith Rd Golden CO 80401-1756 Office: Colo Sch Mines Divsn Econs & Bus Golden CO 80401

WOOLSTON-CATLIN, MARIAN, psychiatrist; b. Seattle, Jan. 20, 1931; d. Howard Brown and Katharine Nichols (Dally) Woolston; m. Randolph Catlin Jr., July 5, 1959; children: Laura Louise, Jennifer Woolston, Randolph III. BA cum laude, Vassar Coll., 1951; MD, Harvard U., 1955. Diplomate Nat. Bd. Medicine. Intern and resident in medicine Children's Hosp., Boston, 1956; resident in psychiatry Mass. Mental Health Ctr., Boston, 1957-59; fellow in child psychiatry Tavistock Clin., London, 1961; commonwealth fellow in child psychiatry Harvard U. at Gaebler Children's Unit, Waltham, Mass., 1975-78, clin. instr. psychiatry, 1978-79; pvt. practice Wellesley Hills, Mass., 1978-91, Medfield, Mass., 1991—; clin. instr. psychiatry Harvard U. at Mass. Mental Health Ctr., Boston, 1957-59, 78-82, Tufts U. at Mass. Mental Health Ctr., 1957-59; mem. exec. bd. Parents' and Children's Svcs., Boston, 1983-86. Designer H.H. Hunnewell Meml. Garden for New England Flower Show Mass. Hort. Soc., 1975 (Ames Cup award). Mem. exec. bd. Ext. Divsn. New Eng. Conservatory Music, 1972-75; charter mem. reuse com. Medfield State Hosp., 1992—. Fellow Am. Acad. Child and Adolescent Psychiatry; mem. AMA, Am. Psychiat. Assn., Mass. Psychiat. Assn., Mass. Med. Soc., Boston Vassar Club (exec. bd. 1963-75), Hills Garden Club Wellesley (exec. bd. and design chief 1973-75). Episcopalian. Avocations: landscape design, sculpting. Home and Office: 314 North St Medfield MA 02052-1204

WOON, PAUL SAM, technical executive; b. Shanhai, China, July 1, 1942; s. Ramon L. and Rita C. (Wu) W.; m. Lin-Sun Juan, Dec. 7, 1973; children: Audrey Hui, Eric Chih. BS, U. Iowa, 1965, MS, 1968; PhD, U. Akron, 1974. Rsch. chemist clin. rsch. ctr. U. Iowa, Iowa City, 1965-68; rsch. chemist PPG Industries, Barberton, Ohio, 1968-71; instr. dept. chemistry Cuyahoga Coll., Cleve., 1972-73; staff rsch. assoc. Appleton (Wis.) Papers-NCR, 1974-76; rsch. mgr. Kimberly-Clark Corp., Neenah, Wis., 1976-81, rsch. dir., 1981-87; sr. rsch. dir. Kimberly-Clark Corp., Roswell, Ga., 1987-90, dir. nonwovens internat., 1990-95; v.p. product and materials devel. Asia-Pacific Region Kimberly Clark Corp., Bangkok, Thailand, 1995—; chmn. minority retention and recruitment com. Kimberly-Clark Corp., 1989-91. Contbr. articles to profl. jours.; patentee in field. Named Indsl. fellow U. Akron, 1971-74. Mem. Orn. Chinese-Ams. (pres. Ga. chpt. 1993). Avocations: coins and stamp collections, oriental antiques collection. Office: Kimberly-Clark Corp 1400 Holcomb Bridge Rd # 100/4 Roswell GA 30076-2190

WOOSLEY, RAYMOND, pharmacology and medical educator; b. Ky., Oct. 2, 1942; m. Julianne B. BS, Western Ky. U., 1964; PhD, U. Louisville, 1967; MD, U. Miami, 1973. Med. lic. Tenn. 1976, D.C. 1988. Intern, resident Vanderbilt U. Hosp., Nashville, 1973-76; sr. pharmacologist, dir. rsch. Meyer (Glaxo) Labs., Ft. Lauderdale, Fla., 1968-71; instr. dept. medicine, pharmacology Vanderbilt U., Nashville, 1976-77, asst. prof., 1977-79, assoc. prof., 1979-84, assoc. dir. clin. rsch. ctr., 1981-88, prof., 1984-88; prof. pharmacology, medicine, chmn. dept. pharmacology Georgetown U. Sch. Medicine, Washington, 1988—, also chief divsn. clin. pharmacology, 1988-94; dir. Inst. for Cardiovascular Scis., Washington, 1995—; researcher in field. Author: Clinical Application of Zinc Metabolism, 1975, Cardiovascular Pharmacology and Therapeutics, 1994; contbr. chpts. to books and articles to profl. jours. NIH Predoctoral fellow NIH, 1964-67, postdoctoral fellow U. Louisville, 1967-68, Vanderbilt U., 1976-77, Am. Coll. Clin. Pharmacology fellow, 1974; Ogden scholar Western Ky. U., 1960-64; recipient Cancer Devel. award in Clin. Pharmacology Pharm. Mfrs. Assn. Found., 1977-80. Fellow Am. Coll. Clin. Pharmacology, Am. Coll. Physicians, Am. Heart Assn. (coun. clin. cardiology 1985—); mem. Am. Soc. Pharmacology & Exptl. Therapeutics (clin. pharmacology exec. com. 1981-92), Am. Fedn. Clin. Rsch., Am. Soc. Clin. Pharmacology and Therapeutics (Rawls-Palmer award 1990), Am. Bd. Clin. Pharmacology, Assn. Med. Sch. Pharmacology (pres. 1996—). Office: Georgetown U Sch Medicine Dept Pharmacology 3900 Reservoir Rd NW Washington DC 20007-2195

WOOSLEY, STANFORD EARL, astrophysicist; b. Texarkana, Tex., Dec. 8, 1944; s. Homer Earl and Wanda Faye (Fisher) W.; m. Susan Marie Haas, Aug. 8, 1993. BA in Physics, Rice U., 1966, PhD in Space Sci., 1971. Rsch. assoc. Rice U., Houston, 1971-73; cons. Law Liv. Nat. Lab, 1973—; rsch. fellow in physics Kellogg Radiation Lab. Calif. Tech., Pasadena, Calif., 1973-75; asst. prof. U. Calif., Santa Cruz, 1975-78, assoc. prof., 1978-83, prof. astronomy and astrophysics, 1983—, chmn. dept., 1984-87, 89-91; sci. adv. com. Inst. Theoretical Physics, Santa barbara, 1991-94. Editor: High Energy Transients, 1984, Supernova, 1991, Nuclear Astrophysics, 1993; contbr. over 170 articles to profl. jours. Grantee NASA, NSF, Calif. Space Inst., 1977—. Fellow Am. Phys. Soc.; mem. Am. Astron. Soc. (coun. 1990-93, chair com. to aid astronomy in the FSU). Achievements include research into the lives and deaths of massive stars and supernova, nucleosynthesis and x-ray and gamma ray bursts. Home: 115 Auburn Ave Santa Cruz CA 95060-6231 Office: U Calif Astronomy Dept Santa Cruz CA 95064

WOOSNAM, IAN HAROLD, professional golfer; b. St. Martins, Shropshire, U.K., Mar. 2, 1958; s. Harold and Joan Woosnam; m. Glendryth Mervyn Pugh, Nov. 12, 1983; children: Daniel Ian, Rebecca Louise, Ami Victoria. Ed., St. Martins Modern Sch. Profl. golfer, 1976—; tournament winner News of the World under 23 match-play, 1979, Cacharel under 25 Championship, 1982, Swiss Open, 1983, Silk Cut Masters, 1983, Scandinavian Enterprise Open, 1984, Zambian Open, 1985, Lawrence Batley TPC, 1986, 555 Kenya Open, 1986, Hong Kong Open, 1987, Jersey Open, 1987, Cepsa Madrid Open, 1987, Bell's Scottish Open, 1987, 90, Lancome Trophy, 1987, 93, Suntory World Match-Play Championship, 1987, 90, World Cup (Wales) Team and Individual, 1987, Million Dollar Challenge, 1987, Volvo PGA Championship, 1988, Carrols Irish Open, 1990, 91, 92, Epson Grand Prix, 1990, U.S. Masters, 1991, USF&G Classic, 1991, PGA Grand Slam of Golf, 1991, World Cup Individual, 1991, Murpheys English Open, 1993, Air France Cannes Open, 1994, Brit. Masters, 1994, Johnnie Walker Classic, 1996, Scottish Open, 1996, German Open, 1996, Heineken Classic, 1996; ranked 1st Sony world rankings, 1991, Ryder Cup Team Mem., 1983, 85, 87, 89, 91, 93, 95. Avocations: snooker, sports, water skiing.

WOOSTER, ROBERT, history educator; b. Beaumont, Tex., Aug. 27, 1956; s. Ralph Ancil and Edna Lee (Jones) W.; m. Catherine Cox, 1992. BA, Lamar U., 1977, MA, 1979; PhD, U. Tex., 1985. Scholar in residence Tex. State Hist. Assn., Liberty, 1985-86; asst. prof. Corpus Christi (Tex.) State U., 1986-90, assoc. prof., 1990-95, prof., 1995—. Author: Soldiers, Sutlers and Settlers (Bates award 1987), U.S. Military and Indian Policy, 1988, History of Fort Davis, 1990, Nelson A. Miles and The Twilight of the Frontier Army, 1993; editorial adv. bd. Southwestern Hist. Quar., Austin, Tex., 1989—. Dep. dir. U.S. Mil. Acad./ROTC fellowship U.S. Mil. Acad., West Point, N.Y., 1990. Mem. Tex. State Hist. Assn., Western Hist. Assn., Orgn. Am. Historians. Democrat. Home: 4600 Ocean Dr Apt 708 Corpus Christi TX 78412-2543 Office: Texas A&M Univ 6300 Ocean Dr Corpus Christi TX 78412-5503

WOOSTER, WARREN S(CRIVER), marine science educator; b. Westfield, Mass., Feb. 20, 1921; s. Harold Abbott and Violet (Scriver) W.; m. Clarissa Pickles, Sept. 13, 1948; children: Susan Wooster Allen, Daniel, Dana. Sc.B., Brown U., 1943; M.S., Calif. Inst. Tech., 1947; Ph.D., UCLA, 1953. From research asst. to prof. Scripps Instn. Oceanography, U. Calif., 1948-73; dir. UNESCO Office Oceanography, 1961-63; dean Rosenstiel Sch. Marine Atmospheric Sci., U. Miami, 1973-76; prof. marine studies and fisheries U. Wash., Seattle, 1976-91, prof. emeritus, 1992; dir. Inst. Marine Studies U. Wash., 1979-82. Contbr. to books, profl. jours. Served with USNR, 1943-46. Fellow Am. Geophys. Union, Am. Meterol. Soc.; mem. Sigma Xi. Office: U Wash Sch Marine Affairs 3707 Brooklyn Ave NE Seattle WA 98105-6715

WOOTAN, GERALD DON, osteopathic physician, educator; b. Oklahoma City, Nov. 19, 1944; s. Ralph George and Corrinne (Loafman) W. BA, Ctrl. State U., Edmond, Okla., 1970, BS, 1971, MEd, 1974; MB, U. Okla., Oklahoma City, 1978; DO, Okla. State U., 1985. Dir. mfg. engring. lab. GE, Oklahoma City, 1965-70; counseling psychologist VA Hosp., Oklahoma City, 1970-76; physician asst. Thomas (Okla.) Med. Clin., 1978-81; pvt. practice, Jenks, Okla., 1986—; intern Tulsa Regional Med. Ctr., 1985-86; assoc. prof. Okla. State U. Coll. Osteo. Medicine, 1986-95, with Springer Clinic, 1995—; sec. Springer Clinic Inc., Tulsa, 1990-91; chmn. gen. practice quality assurance Tulsa Regional Med. Ctr., 1989-91; v.p. New Horizons Counseling Ctr., Clinton, Okla., 1977-81; sr. aviation med. examiner FAA, Tulsa, 1991—; pres. S.W. Diagnostics, Inc., Tulsa, 1989-91, Okla. Edn. Found. Osteo. Medicine, Tulsa, 1988-89; pres., trustee Tulsa Long Term Care Authority. Contbr. articles to profl. jours.; patentee for human restraint. Advancement chmn., chmn. Eagle bd. rev. Boy Scouts Am., Tulsa, 1987-88; trustee Tulsa Long Term Care Authority, 1988-91; trustee Tulsa Community Found. for Indigent Health Care, Inc., 1988-91. With USN, 1962-64. Named Clin. Preceptor of Yr., U. Okla., 1980, Outstanding Alumni award Okla. State U. Coll. Osteo. Medicine, 1990. Mem. Am. Osteo. Assn., Okla. Osteo. Assn., Tulsa Dist. Osteo. Soc. (pres. 1991-92), Am. Acad. Physician Assts., Am. Coll. Gen. Practitioners, Okla. Acad. Gen. Practitioners (pres.), Am. Coll. Osteo. Family Physicians (bd. cert. 1993, pres. Okla. chpt. 1993-94), Okla. State U. Coll. Osteo. Medicine Alumni Assn. (pres. 1988-89). Avocations: scuba diving, aviation medicine. Home: 4320 E 100th St Tulsa OK 74137-5305 Office: Springer Clinic 324 W Main St Jenks OK 74037-3747

WOOTEN, CECIL AARON, religious organization administrator; b. Laurel, Miss., June 3, 1924; s. Cecil A. and Alice (Cox) W.; m. Helen Moss, Apr. 4, 1947; children: Michael, Margaret, Martin, Marsha, Mark. B.S. in Mech. Engring, U. Ala., 1949. With CBI Industries, 1941—, bd. dirs., 1965-83; mng. dir. CBI Constructors Ltd., London, 1957-62; mgr. (Houston sales dist.), 1962-64; v.p., mgr. corp. services Oak Brook, Ill., 1968-69; sr. v.p.-gen. sales mgr., 1969-78; sr. v.p. comml. devel. Chgo. Bridge & Iron Co. (subs. CBI Industries), 1978-79; sr. v.p. corp. adminstrn. CBI Industries, Oak Brook, 1980-83; dir. devel. Christian Family Services, Gainesville, Fla., 1983-86, Denver Ch. of Christ, 1986-88, Boston Ch. of Christ, 1988-92; pres. Internat. Chs. of Christ, Inc., L.A., 1994—; bd. dirs. Oak Brook (Ill.) Bank. Former trustee Elmhurst (Ill.) Coll.; former bd. sponsors Good Samaritan Hosp., Downers Grove, Ill. Served to 1st lt. AUS, 1943-46. Mem. ASME, Nat. Soc. Profl. Engrs. Lodge: Rotary. Home: 1340 Cherokee Ct Camarillo CA 93010-3660 Office: Internat Chs of Christ 3530 Wilshire Blvd Ste 1750 Los Angeles CA 90010-2362

WOOTEN, FRANK THOMAS, research facility executive; b. Fayetteville, N.C., Sept. 24, 1935; s. Frank Thomas and Katherine (McRae) W.; m. Linda Walker, July 14, 1962; children: Laurin Walker, Patrick Thomas, Ashley Tripp. BSEE, Duke U., 1957, PhD, 1964. Engr. Corning Glass Works, Raleigh, N.C., 1964-66; engr. Research Triangle Inst., Research Triangle Park, N.C., 1966-68, mgr. biomed. engring., 1968-75, exec. asst. to pres., 1975-80, v.p., 1980-89, pres., 1989—. Contbr. articles on semiconductors and biomed. engring. to profl. publs., 1966-83; patentee semiconductors tech. Bd. dirs. N.C. Biotech. Ctr., 1989—, MCNC, 1989-94; corp. mem. Nat. Inst. Statis. Scis., 1990—. Served to lt. (j.g.) USN, 1957-59. Shell fellow, 1961; recipient Disting. Engring. Alumnus award Duke U., 1991. Mem. IEEE, Assn. for Advancement Med. Instrumentation (chmn. com. on aerospace tech. 1971-77), Ballistic Missile Def. Orgn. (tech. application rev. panel 1990-94). Baptist. Office: Research Triangle Inst PO Box 12194 3040 W Cornwallis Rd Research Triangle Park NC 27709

WOOTEN, FREDERICK (OLIVER), applied science educator; b. Linwood, Pa., May 16, 1928; s. Frederick Alexander and Martha Emma (Guild) W.; m. Jane Watson MacPherson, Aug. 30, 1952; children: Donald, Bartley. BS in Chemistry, MIT, 1950; PhD in Chemistry, U. Del., 1955. Sr. scientist Lawrence Livermore (Calif.) Lab., 1957-72; prof. applied sci. U. Calif., Davis, 1972—, chmn. designated emphasis in computational sci., 1989—; vis. prof. physics Drexel U., Phila., 1964, Chalmers Tech. H.S., Goteborg, Sweden, 1967-68, Heriot-Watt U., Edinburgh, Scotland, 1979, Trinity Coll., Dublin, Ireland, 1986, Mich. State U., East Lansing, 1993, Boston U., 1996; vis. scholar in math. U. Mass., Amherst, 1991; staff physicist All-Am. Engring. Co., Wilmington, Del., 1955-57; chmn. applied sci. U. Calif., Davis, 1973-93, chmn. designated emphasis in computational sci., 1989—; cons. in field. Author: Optical Properties of Solids, 1972. Mem. AAAS, Am. Phys. Soc., N.Y. Acad. Scis., Sigma Xi. Home: 2328 Alameda Diablo Diablo CA 94528 Office: Univ Calif Dept Applied Sci Davis CA 95616

WOOTEN-BRYANT, HELEN CATHERINE, academic administrator; b. Houston, Feb. 24, 1940; d. Johnny Clement and Roberta (Glenn) Steward. BS in Elem. Edn., Prairie View A&M U., 1962, MEd in Adminstrn. and Supervision, 1966. Cert. elem. tchr. Tchr. Chgo. Bd. Edn., 1962-83; prin. Vanderpoel Magnet Sch. Humanities, Chgo., 1984—. Communion minister St. James Cath. Ch. Mem. Nat. Women of Achievement (pres. Chgo. chpt. 1988—, Excellence award 1988), Chgo. Prin. Assn., Prairie View A&M U. Alumni Assn. (founder, pres. Chgo. chpt., 1987—), Sigma Gamma Rho (pres. 1981-83, chairwoman cen. regional nominating com. 1982-84, chairwoman polit. action com. 1985—, Karrie Regional award 1980, Outstanding Pres. award Chgo. Alumnae chpt., 1987, Fred Hampton Inst. award 1990). Republican. Roman Catholic. Avocations: golf, bridge. Office: Vanderpoel Magnet Sch Humanities 9510 S Prospect Ave Chicago IL 60643-1220

WOOTTEN, THOMAS FRANKLIN, criminal justice administrator; b. Orlando, Fla., Jan. 13, 1931; s. John Franklin and Betty (Shadburn) W.; m. Ruth Marie Raiman, Sept. 26, 1953 (div. 1978); m. Heidi Herbold, Apr. 12, 1978. AB in Clin. Psychology, Ohio State U., 1953, postgrad., 1958-59; postgrad., Nova U., 1977-82. Comdr. USN, 1949, active duty at sea and overseas, 1949-76, ret., 1976; mgmt. adminstr. Office Commonwealth Atty., Virginia Beach, Va., 1977-79; pres., CEO Inst. Applied Polygraph Sci., Virginia Beach, 1979-82; undersheriff Portsmouth (Va.) Sheriff's Office, 1982-93; co-chair Va. Polygraph Adv. Bd., Va. Dept. Commerce, 1988-96. Decorated Legion of Merit (valor), Air Medal, Nat. Honor medal Republic of Vietnam. Mem. VFW, Am. Polygraph Assn. (various coms. 1976—, chair stds. and ethics 1985-86, co-chair accreditation com. 1991-92), Am. Assn. Police Polygraphists, Am. correctional Assn., Nat. Sheriff's Assn., Internat. Assn. Chiefs Police, Navy League, U.S. Power Squadron, Sons Confederate Vets., U.S. Naval Inst., Pi Kappa Alpha, Psi Chi. Republican. Avocations: yachting, photography, marksmanship, genealogical research. Home: 2228 Windward Shore Dr Virginia Beach VA 23451-1728

WOOTTON, JOHN FRANCIS, physiology educator; b. Penn Yan, N.Y., May 31, 1929; s. John Edenden and Margaret Eliza (Smith) W.; m. Joyce Albertine Mac Mullen, Aug. 28, 1959; children: J. Timothy, David M., Barbara H., Bruce C. BS, Cornell U., 1951, MS, 1953, PhD, 1960. Grad. rsch. asst. Cornell U., Ithaca, N.Y., 1956-60; post doctoral fellow U. Coll., London, 1960-62; from asst. prof. to assoc. prof. dept. physiology Cornell U., 1962-70, prof. dept. physiology, 1970—, assoc. dean Grad. Sch., 1980-83; grad. faculty rep. field of physiology Cornell U., 1990-92, 93-97, acting chmn. dept. physiology, 1997—; vis. scientist MRC Molecular Biology, Cambridge, Eng., 1969-70, Nat. Inst. Med. Rsch., London, 1985-86, 92-93; teporary sr. rsch. assoc. Stanford (Calif.) U., 1977-78. Contbr. articles to profl. jours. 1st lt. USAR, 1954-56. Rsch. and Travel grantee NIH, USDA Burroughs Wellcom Fund, Med. Rsch. Coun., Cornell Biotech. Program. Mem. AAAS, Am. Soc. Biochemistry, Molecular and Cell Biology, Am. Chem. Soc., Biophys. Soc., Protein Soc., Sigma Xi (v.p., pres. Cornell chpt.). Avocations: travel, choral singing, gardening, art, fishing. Office: Cornell U Dept Physiology T8-022 Veterinary Rsch Tower Ithaca NY 14853-5908

WORACHEK, SUSAN, music educator; b. Bloomington, Ind., Feb. 18, 1952; m. James Allen Worachek, July, 1978; children: Jennifer Ann, Sarah Elizabeth. BS, Miami U., 1974; MEd, Xavier U., 1981. Cert. tchr., Ohio. Music educator Norwood (Ohio) Pub. Schs., 1974-85; gifted students educator P.A.G.E., Inc., Cin., 1992-94; coord. musical arts Cin. Hills Christian Acad., 1995—. Dist. chmn. cultural arts contest Valley Area Coun. PTA, Cin, 1990-93, advisor, 1990-91; chmn. bd. Christian edn. Messiah Luth. Ch., Cin., 1993—; mem. supt.'s adv. coun. Princeton Bd. Edn., Cin., 1993—; mem. bus. adv. com. Glendale Elem. Sch., Cin., 1993—, pres. No. Hills Piano Tchr's. Forum, 1991-93, Glendale PTA, 1993-95; judge Ohio Fedn. Music Clubs, Cin., 1986-94. Mem. Glendale Lyceum, Village Gardeners, Delta Omicron. Avocations: tennis, bridge, people, music. Office: Cin Hills Christian Acad 11300 Snider Rd Cincinnati OH 45249-2222

WORBOYS, ROGER DICK, communications executive; b. Syracuse, N.Y., Sept. 1, 1947; s. Carl Stape and Dorothy Elsa (Dick) W.; m. Mary Lee Tasker, Nov. 27, 1971; children: Thomas, Elizabeth. Bachelors degree, Alfred U., 1969; M in Bus., U. N.H., 1971. Asst. dir. residences U. N.H., Durham, 1971; mgr.- regional mgr. Continental Cablevision, Boston, 1974-86; v.p. ops. Simmons Comm., Stamford, Conn., 1986-88, Insight Comm., Glasgow, Scotland, N.Y.C., 1988-95, Bresnan Comms., White Plains, N.Y., 1996—; sec. bd. Simmons Comm., Stamford, 1986-88. Chair Pub. Sch. Tech. Adv., Dover, N.H. Mem. Portsmouth N.H. C. of C. (pres.), Rotary Internat. (bd. dirs.). Roman Catholic. Avocations: recreational bike riding, hiking, climbing. Office: Bresnan Comms 709 Westchester Ave White Plains NY 10604-3103

WORCESTER, ANNE PERSON, sports association executive; married. Degree in Econs. with honors, Duke U., 1982. Tournament coord. racquet sports divsn. Internat. Mgmt. Group, 1983-84; dir. corp. sales Lipton Championships, 1985-86, head corp. sales Phila. men's tennis tournament, 1986-87; tournament mgr. tennis events Lipton Championships, Spain, 1987-88; dir. worldwide ops. Va. Slims Tennis, 1988-91; mng. dir. Women's Tennis Coun., 1991-94; CEO WTA Tour, 1994—. Named one of Most Powerful Women in Tennis, Tennis Week Mag., 1993, one of Power 25, Racquet Mag., 1994, 95. Office: WTA Tour 1266 E Main St Ste 4 Stamford CT 06902-3546*

WORCESTER, DONALD EMMET, history educator, author; b. Tempe, Ariz., Apr. 29, 1915; s. Thomas Emmet and Maud (Worcester) Makemson; m. Barbara Livingston Peck, July 5, 1941; children: Barbara Livingston and Elizabeth Stuart (twins), Harris Eugene. AB, Bard Coll., 1939; MA, U. Calif., 1940, PhD, 1947. Lectr. Calif. Coll. Agr., Davis, 1946, U. Calif., 1947; asst. prof. U. Fla., 1947-51, assoc. prof., 1951-55, head dept., 1955-59, prof. history, 1955-63; chmn. dept. history Tex. Christian U., 1963-72, Lorin A. Boswell prof. history, 1971-80, Ida and Cecil Green emeritus tutor, 1981-94; vis. prof. U. Madrid, 1956-57; chmn. bd. Univ. Press Mgrs., 1961-63. Author: The Interior Provinces of New Spain, 1786, 1951, (with Wendell G. Schaeffer) The Growth and Culture of Latin America, 1956, 2d edit., 1971, Sea Power and Chilean Independence, 1962, Spanish edit., 1971, The Three Worlds of Latin America, 1963, (with Maurice Boyd) American Civilization, 1964, (with Robert and Kent Forster) Man and Civilization, 1965, Makers of Latin America, 1966, Brazil: From Colony to World Power, 1973; editor: Forked Tongues and Broken Treaties, 1975, Bolivar, 1977, The Apaches: Eagles of the Southwest, 1979, German edit., 1982, The Chisholm Trail: High Road of the Cattle Kingdom, 1981, Pioneer Trails West, 1985, The Spanish Mustang: From the Plains of Andalusia to the Prairies of Texas, 1986, The Texas Cowboy, 1986, The Texas Longhorn: Relic of the Past, Asset of the Future, 1987, (fiction) The War in the Nueces Strip, 1989, A Visit from father and other Tales of the Mojave, 1990, Brazos Scout, 1991, Man on Two Ponies, 1992, Gone to Texas, 1993, Western Horse Tales, 1994; also children's books; mng. editor: Hispanic Am. Hist. Rev, 1960-65; editor TCU Monographs in History and Culture, 1966-73; mem. editl. bd. The Am. West. Served to lt. comdr. USNR, 1941-45. Recipient Golden Spur award Western Writers Am., 1975, 80; C.L. Sonnichsen Book award, 1985. Mem. Western Hist. Assn. (v.p. 1973-74, pres. 1974-75), Western Writers Am. (v.p. 1972-73, pres. 1973-74, Saddleman award 1988), N.Mex. Hist. Soc., Westerners Internat. (dir. 1975-80, pres. 1978, 79), Tex. Inst. Letters, Phi Beta Kappa, Phi Alpha Theta (pres. 1960-62). Home: 9321 Bear Creek Rd Aledo TX 76008-4004 Office: Texas Christian U Dept History Fort Worth TX 76129

WORD, ELIZA SWITZER, critical care nurse, administrator; b. Staunton, Va., June 3, 1946; d. Emily Virginia Switzer; m. Herman Lee Word, Nov. 7, 1972; 1 child, Herman Lee. Diploma, Roanoke (Va.) Meml. Hosp., 1966; BSN, Lynchburg (Va.) Coll., 1988. Nurse VA Med. Ctr., Salem, Va., Community Hosp., Roanoke, Roanoke Meml. Hosp.; critical care nurse VA Med. Ctr., Salem, nurse mgr. oper. rm. Mem. ANA. Home: 2611 Hillendale Dr NW Roanoke VA 24017-1115

WORDEN, ALFRED MERRILL, former astronaut, research company executive; b. Jackson, Mich., Feb. 7, 1932; s. Merrill Bangs and Helen Crowell) W.; m. Jill Lee Hotchkiss, July 9, 1982; children: Merrill Ellen, Alison Pamela, Tamara Lynn. BS, U.S. Mil. Acad., 1955; MS in Aeros., Astronautical and Instrumentation Engring., U. Mich., 1963, DSc in Astronautical Engring., 1972. Commd. 2nd lt. USAF, 1955, advanced through grades to lt. col., 1971; stationed at Andrews AFB, Md., 1956-61, U. Mich., 1961-63, Farnborough, Eng.; with RAF, 1963-65; instr. Aerospace Rsch. Pilots Sch., Edwards AFB, Calif., 1965-66; astronaut Manned Spacecraft Ctr., NASA, Houston, 1966-72; command module pilot Apollo XV, 1971; sr. aerospace engr., test pilot, dir. systems studies divsn. Ames Rsch. Ctr., Moffett Field, Calif., 1972-75, ret., 1975; v.p. High Flight Found., Colorado Springs, Colo., 1975—; pres. MW Aerospace, Inc., 1985—, Jet Electronics and Tech., Inc., 1990-93; staff v.p. BF Goodrich Aerospace, Brecksville, Ohio, 1993—. Author: poetry Hello Earth-Greetings from Endeavour, 1974; children's book A Flight to the Moon, 1974. Bd. dirs. Boys' Clubs Am., Palm Beach County, Salvation Army. Inducted into Mich. Aviation Hall of Fame, 1990. Mem. AIAA, Soc. Exptl. Pilots, Am. Astron. Soc., Explorers Club, Circumnavigators Club. Episcopalian (sr. warden 1969-71). Office: BF Goodrich Rsch Ctr 9921 Brecksville Rd Brecksville OH 44141-3201

WORDEN, ELIZABETH ANN, artist, comedy writer, singer; b. Karnes City, Tex., Nov. 8, 1954; d. Alan Walker and Mary Paralee (Long) W. BS in Comms., U. Tex., 1977. Disc jockey, newsperson KMMK Radio, McKinney, Tex., 1978, KPBC Radio, Irving, Tex., 1979-80, KDNT Radio, Denton, Tex., 1980-81, KJIM Radio, Ft. Worth, 1981-82, KPBC Radio, Irving, 1983, KRYS Radio, Corpus Christi, Tex., 1984; owner Worden Industries, Corpus Christi, Tex. Executed paintings for Am. Embassy, Bogota, Colombia; one-woman shows include Art Ctr., Corpus Christi, 1990; exhibited in group shows at Tex. A&M, corpus Christi, 1986, 92, Galeria Chapparal, Corpus Christi, 1988, New Eng. Fine Art Inst., Boston, 1993, Am. Embassy, Bogota; paintings in pvt. collections throughout the country. Mem. Art Ctr. Corpus Christi. Mem. Tex. Fine Arts Assn., Nat. Assn. Fine Artists. Avocations: writing fiction and poetry, acting, photography, reading. Home and Office: Worden Industries 3842 Brookhill Dr Corpus Christi TX 78410-4404

WORDEN, KATHARINE COLE, sculptor; b. N.Y.C., May 4, 1925; d. Philip Gillette and Katharine (Pyle) Cole; m. Frederic G. Worden, Jan. 8, 1944; children: Rick, Dwight, Philip, Barbara, Katharine. Student Potters Sch., Tucson, 1940-42, Sarah Lawrence Coll., 1942-44. Sculptor; works exhibited Royce Galleries, Galerie Francoise Besnard (Paris), Cooling Gallery (London), Galerie Schumacher (Munich), Selected Artists Gallery, N.Y.C., Art Inst. Boston, Reid Gallery, Nashville, Weiner Gallery, N.Y.C., Boston Athanaeum, House of Humor and Satire, Gabrovo, Bulgaria, 1983, Newport Bay Club, 1984; pvt. collections Grand Palais (Paris), Dakar and Bathurst, Africa; dir. Stride Rite Corp., 1980-85; occupational therapist psychopathic ward Los Angeles County Gen. Hosp., 1953-57; Headstart vol., Watts, Calif., 1965-67; tchr. sculpture Watts Towers Art Center, 1967-69; participant White House Women Doers Luncheon meeting, 1968; dir. Cambridgeport Problem Center, Cambridge, Mass., 1969-71; mem. Jud. Nominating Commn., 1976-79; bd. overseers Boston Mus. Fine Arts, 1980-83; bd. govs. Newport Seamens Ch. Inst., 1989-91; trustee Comm. Rsch., Miami, Fla., 1960-69, chmn. bd., 1966-69; trustee Newport Art Mus., 1984-86, 92-94, Jamestown Cmty. Theatre, 1994-97, Newport Health Found., 1986-91, Hawthorne Sea Fund, 1990-93; bd. dirs. Boston Center for Arts, 1976-80, Child and Family Svcs. of Newport County, 1983-90, 91-97. Mem. Common Cause (Mass. adv. bd. 1971-72, dir. 1974-75), Mass. Civil Liberties Union (exec. bd. 1973-74, dir. 1976-77). Home: 24 Fort Wetherill Rd Jamestown RI 02835-2908

WORDEN, WILLIAM MICHAEL, city agency administrator, preservation consultant; b. Detroit, Nov. 4, 1942; s. Scott Buell and Virginia Alexandra (Moynihan) W.; m. Barbara Williams, Mar. 27, 1976. Student, Ohio U., 1961-63; BA in Art History, Ohio State U., 1967, postgrad., 1967-68. Sole propr. William M. Worden, Organbuilder, Detroit, 1970-76; adminstrv. coord. Detroit Urban Conservation Project, Wayne State U., Detroit, 1976-77; staff dir. Historic Designation Adv. Bd. of Detroit, 1977—; bd. dirs. Mich. Historic Preservation Network, 1988-96, sec., 1988-95, chmn., 1995-96; bd. dirs. Steamship Hist. Soc. Am., 1994—; planner, tour guide for hist. ch. and organ tours Detroit Hist. Soc., 1976—; mem. bd. advisors nat. Trust for Hist. Preservation, 1978-87, advisor emeritus; pres. The Steamer Columbia Found.; owner, operator Nat. Historic Landmark steamboat. Editor-in-chief Steamboat Bill, 1997—; contbr. articles to profl. jours. Trustee Cass Cmty. Meth. Ch., Detroit, 1988-93; bd. dirs., corp. sec. Maintenance Ctrl. for Srs., Detroit, 1981-85; bd. dirs., sec., pres. Indian Village Assn., Detroit, 1977-82; bd. dirs., sec. Gt. Lakes Maritime Inst., 1959-74; mem. archtl. rev. com. Roman Cath. Archdiocese of Detroit, 1993—. Recipient Career Civil Servant award Am. Soc. Pub. Adminstrn., 1985, Testimonial resolution Detroit City Coun., 1985, Samaritan of the Yr. award Most Holy Trinity Ch., 1986. Mem. AIA (hon. affiliate), Organ Hist. Soc., numerous orgns. in preservation and maritime history. Roman Catholic. Avocations: antiques, maritime history, music. Office: Historic Designation Adv Bd 204 City County Bldg Detroit MI 48226

WORDSMAN, ELIZABETH SCHMITT, senior manager print production; b. Milw., Mar. 1, 1955; d. Paul E. and Dorothy A. (Rehmer) Schmitt; m. Arthur Wordsman, Dec. 29, 1986. BFA, Boston U., 1981. Advt. mgr. Brills Inc., Milw., 1983-85; prodn. mgr. in tng. Allied Graphics Arts, N.Y.C., 1985-87; acct. supr. Bel-Aire Assoc., N.Y.C., 1987-88; cons. Bloomingdale's, N.Y.C., 1988-89; sales promotion prodn. dir. Lord & Taylor, N.Y.C., 1989-95; sr. mgr. print purchasing and prodn. Avon Products, N.Y.C., 1995—; judge Gravure Assn. of Am. Golden Cylinder awards, 1996. Recipient Gold Ink award Printing & Pub. Exec., 1992, 93, 96, Rose Achievement award Lord & Taylor, 1993. Mem. Direct Mktg. Assn., Gravure Assn. of Am. Office: Avon Products 1251 Avenue Of The Americas Fl 5 New York NY 10020-1104

WORDSWORTH, JERRY L., wholesale distribution executive; b. 1944. With MBM, Rocky Mount, N.C., 1966—, chmn., pres., CEO. Office: MBM PO Box 800 Rocky Mount NC 27802*

WORELL, JUDITH P., psychologist, educator; b. N.Y.C.; d. Moses and Dorothy Goldfarb; m. Leonard Worell, Aug. 11, 1947 (div.); children: Amy, Beth, Wendy; m. H.A. Smith, Mar. 23, 1985. BS magna cum laude, Queens Coll., 1950; MA, Ohio State U., 1952, PhD in Clin. Psychology, 1954; DHL (hon.), Colby-Sawyer Coll., 1993. Research assoc. Iowa Psychopathic Hosp., Iowa City, 1957-59; research assoc. Okla. State U., 1960-66; asst. prof. U. Ky., Lexington, 1969-71; assoc. prof. U. Ky., 1971-75, prof. ednl. and counseling psychology, 1976—, dir. counseling psychology tng. program, 1980-93, chairperson dept. ednl. and counseling psychology, 1993—. Author: (with C.M. Nelson) Managing Instructional Problems, 1981; (with W.E. Stilwell) Psychology for Teachers and Students, 1981; Psychological Development in the Elementary Years, 1982; (with Fred Danner) The Adolescent as Decision-maker: Applications to Development and Education, 1989; (with Pam Remer) Feminist Perspectives in Therapy: An Empowerment Model for Women, 1992; (with N. Johnson) Feminist Visions in Psychology: Education, Research, and Practice, 1997; assoc. editor Jour. Cons. and Clin. Psychology, 1976-79, mem. editorial bd., 1984-89; assoc. editor Psychol. Women Quar., 1984-89, editor, 1989-95; mem. editorial bd. Sex Roles, 1984—, Psychol. Assessment, 1991-97, Clin. Psychology Rev., 1991-97, Women and Therapy, 1992—; cons., reviewer 10 jours.; contbr. articles to profl. jours. Named U. Ky. Campus Woman of Yr., 1976, Outstanding Univ. Grad. prof., 1991, Disting. Ky. psychologist, 1990; USPHS fellow, 1953; NIMH rsch. grantee, 1962-69. Fellow APA (pres. Clin. Psychology of Women 1986-88, chmn. com. state assn. rels. 1982-83, fellow selection divsn. 35 com. 1983-84, policy and planning bd. 1989-92, publs. and communications bd. 1992—, chair 1996—, chair jours. com., pres. divsn. psychology of woman 1997—, Disting. Leader for Women in Psychology 1990), Ky. Psychol. Assn. (pres. 1981-82, rep. at large 1995—), Southeastern Psychol. Assn. (exec. coun. mem.-at-large, pres.-elect 1993-94 pres. 1994-95), Am. Women in Psychology, Phi Beta Kappa. Home: 3892 Gloucester Dr Lexington KY 40510-9729 Office: U Ky Dept Ednl and Counseling Psychology 235 Dickey Hall Lexington KY 40506

WORENKLEIN, JACOB JOSHUA, lawyer; b. N.Y.C., Oct. 1, 1948; s. Abraham and Cela (Zyskind) W.; m. (div.); children: David, Daniel, Laura; m. Cindy Sternkler, Feb. 26, 1995. BA, Columbia U., 1969; MBA, JD, NYU, 1973. Bar: N.Y. 1974. From assoc. to ptnr. Milbank, Tweed, Hadley & McCloy, N.Y.C., 1973-93, chmn. firm planning com., 1988-90, exec. com., 1990-93, sr. advisor to exec. com., 1993-94; mng. dir., group head of global project fin. group Lehman Bros., N.Y.C., 1993-96; mng. dir., head project fin, commodity fin., export fin. Soc. Gen., N.Y.C., 1996—; mem. investment banking mgmt. com. Lehman Bros., 1993-96; mem. adv. coun. Amoco Power Resources Corp., 1995—; adj. prof. fin. NYU Stern Sch. of Bus. Mem. editl. bd. Jour. Project Fin., 1996—; contbr. articles to profl. jours. Pres. Old Broadway Synagogue, N.Y.C., 1978—; trustee Fedn. Jewish Philanthropies, N.Y.C., 1984-86; bd. overseers United Jewish Appeal-Fedn. Jewish Philanthropies, 1987, chmn. lawyers divsn. major gifts, 1989-91, chmn. lawyers divsn., 1991-93, bd. dirs., 1991—; trustee Jewish Cmty. Rels. Coun. N.Y., 1995—. Office: Soc Gen 1221 Avenue Of The Americas New York NY 10020-1001

WORK, BRUCE VAN SYOC, business consultant; b. Monmouth, Ill., Mar. 20, 1942; s. Robert M. and Evelyn (Rusken) W.; m. Janet Kay Brown, Nov. 12, 1966; children: Bruce, Terra. B.A., Monmouth Coll., 1964; B.S., U. Mo.-Rolla, 1966; postgrad., U. Chgo., 1978-79. Registered profl. engr., Ill. Various mgmt. positions Midcon Corp. (and subs.), 1966-79; pres. Indsl. Fuels Corp., Troy, Mich., 1979-85, Costain Coal Inc., Troy, Mich., 1985-89; pvt. practice small bus. cons., 1989-92; bus. cons. Wallis Oil Co., 1992—. Mem. various coms. Cuba United Meth. Ch. Mem. Detroit Athletic Club, Forest Lake Country Club, Blue Key. Office: 1732 Lakeshore Dr Cuba MO 65453-9684 *One of the keys to success is to treat everyone as you would like to be treated, equally and with respect. People are the key to your success.*

WORK, CHARLES ROBERT, lawyer; b. Glendale, Calif., June 21, 1940; s. Raymond P. and Minna M. (Fricke) W.; m. Linda S. Smith, Oct. 4, 1965 (div.); children: Matthew Keehn, Mary Lucila Landis, Benjamin Reed; m. Veronica A. Haggart, Apr., 1985, 1 child, Andrew Haggart. BA, Wesleyan U., 1962; JD, U. Chgo., 1965; LLM, Georgetown U., 1966. Bar: D.C. 1965, Utah 1965. Asst. U.S. atty. D.C., 1966-73; dep. adminstr. law enforcement assistance adminstrn., U.S. Dept. Justice, 1973-75; ptnr. Peabody, Lambert & Meyers, Washington, 1975-82, McDermott, Will & Emery, Washington, 1982—. Recipient Rockefeller Pub. Service award 1978. Mem. D.C. Bar (pres. 1976-77). Office: McDermott Will & Emery 1850 K St NW Washington DC 20006-2213

WORK, HENRY HARCUS, physician, educator; b. Buffalo, Nov. 11, 1911; s. Henry Harcus and Jeannette (Harcus) W.; m. Virginia Codington, Oct. 20, 1945 (dec. Nov. 1991); children—Henry Harcus III, David Codington, William Bruce, Stuart Runyon. A.B., Hamilton Coll., Clinton, N.Y., 1933; M.D., Harvard, 1937. Intern, resident Boston Children's Hosp., 1937-40, Emma P. Bradley Home Providence, 1940, Buffalo Children's Hosp., 1940-42, N.Y. Hosp., 1945-47; psychiat. services adviser, chief U.S. Children's Bur., Washington, 1948-49; assoc. prof. pediatrics U. Louisville, 1949-55; mem. faculty UCLA, 1955-72, prof. psychiatry and pub. health, 1966-72; chief profl. svcs. Am. Psychiat. Assn., Washington, 1972-83; clin. prof. George Washington U., Georgetown U., Uniformed Svcs. U. of Health Scis., U. Md., 1973—. Author: A Guide to Preventive Child Psychiatry, 1965, Minimal Brain Dysfunction: A Medical Challenge, 1967, Psychiatric Emergencies in Childhood, 1967, Crisis in Child Psychiatry, 1975, also articles. Served to capt. AUS, 1942-45. Recipient Simon Wile Award, Amer. Acad. of Child and Adolescent Psychiatry, 1994. Mem. So. Calif. Psychiat. Assn. (pres. 1966-67), Am. Orthopsychiat. Assn. (v.p. 1968-69), Am. Coll. Psychiatry (sec.-gen. 1979-93), Group for Advancement of Psychiatry (pres. 1982-85). Home: 4986 Sentinel Dr Apt 504 Bethesda MD 20816

WORK, JANE MAGRUDER, professional society administrator; b. Owensboro, Ky., Mar. 30, 1927; d. Orion Noel and Willie May (Stallings) Magruder; m. William Work, Nov. 26, 1960; children: Paul MacGregor, Jeffrey William. BA, Furman U., 1947; MA, U. Wis., 1948; PhD, Ohio State U., 1959. Dir. radio U. South Miss., Hattisburg, 1948-51; pub. relations assoc. Ohio Fuel Gas Co./Columbia Gas, Columbus, 1952-62; adj. prof. communications Pace U., N.Y.C., 1963-75; dir. speechmodule ERIC, Washington, 1975-76; mgr. orgn. liaison, dir. legis. analysis Nat. Assn. Mfgs., Washington, 1977-84, asst. v.p. legis. analysis, 1984-87, v.p. legis. analysis, 1987-93, v.p. mem. comm., 1993—; adv. bd. public affairs NYU Grad. Bus. Sch., 1983-87; adv. bd. Proedn. Mag., 1984-87; cons. IBM, Xerox, 1963-77. Contbr. articles to profl. jours. Transition team Consumer Product Safety Commn., Washington, 1979-80; mem., chmn. No. Va. Pvt. Industry Council, Fairfax County, 1979-85; co-chair Va. Gov.'s Employment & Tng. Task Force, Richmond, 1983; active in other civic activities. Named to Acad. Women Achievers YWCA, 1987. Mem. Future Homemakers of Am. (bd. dirs. 1985-88), Issue Mgmt. Assn. (bd. dirs. 1985-88), Nat. Assn. Industry-Edn. Coop. (bd. dirs. 1983—), Am. Soc. Assn. Execs. (rsch. adv. com. 1989-97), Speech Communication Assn. (sect. chmn. 1980-82), The Planning Forum (bd. dirs. Capital chpt. 1990-93), World Future Soc. (steering network 1993 Gen. Assembly), Alpha Psi Omega (hon.), Pi Kappa Delta (hon.). Republican. Presbyterian. Avocations: gardening, tennis. Home: 6245 Cheryl Dr Falls Church VA 22044-1809 Office: Nat Assn Mfrs Ste 1500 1331 Pennsylvania Ave NW Washington DC 20004-1703

WORK, WILLIAM, retired association executive; b. Ithaca, N.Y., Aug. 10, 1923; s. Paul and Helen Grace (Nicholas) W.; m. Jane Noel Magruder, Nov. 26, 1960; children—Paul Magregor, Jeffrey William. AB, Cornell U., 1946; MA, U. Wis., 1948, PhD, 1954; D Arts (hon.), Eastern Mich. U., 1986; LLD (hon.), Emerson Coll., 1987. Cert. assn. exec. Instr., asso. dir theatre Purdue U., 1948-50; from instr. to prof., dir. theatre Eastern Mich. U., 1951-63; exec. sec. Speech Communication Assn., Annandale, Va., 1963-88, ret., 1988; mem. faculty U. Wis., 1950-51, So. Ill. U., 1959; cons., reader, review panelist U.S. Office Edn., 1966-71; del. White House Conf. Children, 1970; pres. Alliance Assn. Advancement Edn., 1977, Coun. Communication Socs., 1974-77; past. mem. AAAS, AAUP, Internat. Communication Assn., Internat. Inst. Communications. Contbr. articles, revs. profl. jours. Mem. Mich. Cultural Commn., 1959-60; mem. Hastings-on-Hudson (N.Y.) Bd. Edn., 1972-75. Recipient Alex Drier award, 1962. Mem. Phi Kappa Phi. Democrat. Unitarian. *If, as George Santayana wisely noted, those who cannot remember the past are condemned to repeat it, then it must be equally true that those who fail to prepare for the future are condemned to endure it.*

WORKMAN, GEORGE HENRY, engineering consultant; b. Muskegon, Mich., Sept. 18, 1939; s. Harvey Merton and Bettie Jane (Meyers) W.; Asso. Sci., Muskegon Community Coll., 1960; B.S.E., U. Mich., 1966, M.S.E., 1966, Ph.D., 1969; m. Vicki Sue Hanish, June 17, 1967; children—Mark, Larry. Prin. engr. Battelle Meml. Inst., Columbus, Ohio, 1969-76; pres. Applied Mechanics Inc., Longboat Key, Fla., 1976—; instr. dept. civil engring. Ohio State U., 1973, 82. Served with USN, 1961-64. Named Outstanding Undergrad. Student, Engring. Mechanics dept. U. Mich., 1965-66, Outstanding Grad. Student, Civil Engring. dept., 1968-69. Registered profl. engr., Ohio. Mem. Am. Acad. of Mechanics, ASME, Sigma Xi, Chi Epsilon, Phi Kappa Phi, Phi Theta Kappa. Congregationalist. Contbr. tech. papers to nat. and internat. confs. Home and Office: 3431 Bayou Ct Longboat Key FL 34228-3028

WORKMAN, JEROME JAMES, JR., chemist; b. Northfield, Minn., Aug. 6, 1952; s. Jerome James and Louise Mae (Sladek) W.; m. Rebecca Marie Zittel, Aug. 3, 1974; children: Cristina Louise, Stephannie Michelle, Daniel Jerome, Sara Marie, Michael Timothy. BA with honors, St. Mary's U., Winona, Minn., 1976, MA, 1980; PhD, Columbia Pacific U., San Rafael, Calif., 1984; postgrad., Columbia U., 1990-91. Prin. Workman & Assocs., Mankato, Minn., 1980-82; pres. Biochem. Cons., Mankato, Minn., 1982-84; sr. chemist Technicon Instruments, Tarrytown, N.Y., 1984-87; supervising scientist Bran & Luebbe/Technicon, Tarrytown, 1987; sr. scientist Hitachi Instruments, Danbury, Conn., 1987-89; mgr. tech. support NIR Systems/Perstorp Analytical, Silver Spring, Md., 1989-90, mgr. mktg., 1990-92, dir. mktg., 1992-93; assoc. advisor Inst. Textile Tech., Charlottesville, Va., 1992—; prin. scientist Perkin Elmer Corp., Norwalk, Conn., 1993-96; rsch. fellow Kimberly-Clark Corp., Analytical Sci. & Tech., Neenah, Wis., 1996—; instr. Fedn. Analytical Chemistry and Spectroscopy Socs.; external examiner U. Guelph, Ont., Can., 1993-94, mem. steering com. and rep. indsl. adv. bd. Ctr. for Process Analytical Chemistry 1993—. Author: Introduction to Near-Infrared Spectroscopy, 1995; contbr. to book: Near-Infrared Analysis, 1991; co-author: Statistics in Spectroscopy, 1991, (series) Chemometrics in Spectroscopy; editor: The Process Pages for NIRnews, Internat. Com. for Near Infrared Spectroscopy, 1993—; co-editor: The Academic Press Handbook of Molecular Spectroscopy, 1995-96; contbg. editor Spectroscopy Mag.; editl. adv. bd. for Spectroscopy, 1995—, Applied Spectroscopy Reviews, 1995—, Lab. Robotics and Automation, 1995—, Wiley-Intersci. Series in Lab. Automation, 1993; process editor: Jour. of Near Infrared Spectroscopy, 1995—; contbr. articles to profl. jours. Recipient Heart of Gold award Minn. affiliate Am. Heart Assn., 1984; Am. Heart Assn. H.N. and H.B. Shapira scholar, 1971, 72; NSF grantee, 1977, 78. Fellow Royal Soc. Chemistry U.K., Am. Inst. Chemists; mem. ASTM (exec. com., vice-chair main com. on molecular spectroscopy, chmn. quantitative practice working group, chair subcom. on process analyzers), Am. Chem. Soc. (instr. course on Practical Near-IR Analysis), Soc. for Applied Spectroscopy, Coun. Near-Infrared Spectroscopy (pres.), Joint Com. Atomic and Molecular Phys. Data (chmn. UV-VIS,, exec. coun.), Nat. Honor Soc., Sigma Xi, Delta Epsilon Sigma. Achievements include research in near infrared dispersive instrumentation, statistics and chemometrics. Office: Analytical Sci & Tech Kimberly-Clark Corp 2100 Winchester Rd Neenah WI 54956

WORKMAN, KAYLEEN MARIE, special education educator; b. Paola, Kans., Aug. 25, 1947; d. Ralph I. and Pearl Marie (Shults) Platz; m. John Edward Workman, Aug. 10, 1980; children: Andrew Ray, Craig Michael. BS in Edn., Emporia State U., 1969, MS in Edn., 1983. Tchr. English/speech Lincoln (Kans.) High Sch., 1969-70, substitute tchr., 1970-71; substitute tchr. Hudson (Wis.) Sch. Dist., 1971-72; tchrs. aide learning disabilities Park Forest South (Ill) Jr. High Sch., 1977-78; learning disabilities/English instr. George York Sch., Osawatomie, Kans., 1978-97; supr. Loose Ends Clown Troop, 1988-91; presenter in field. Author of poems. Com. mem., sec. Cub Scouts, Osawatomie, 1987-88, com. mem. Boy Scouts Am., 1988-91, sec., 1990-91; forensics judge Osawatomie H.S. Forensics Team, 1991-92; hunter's safety instr. Osawatomie Sportsman's Club, 1982-86; mem. Osawatomie Cmty. Band, 1990-92. Mem. Osawatomie-NEA (v.p. 1982-83, 93-94, pres. 1983-84, 94-95, sec. 1986), Kans.-NEA (Sunflower uniserv adminstrv. bd. 1985, Sunflower uniserv coord. coun.), Learning Disabilities Assn., Delta Kappa Gamma. Avocations: hunting, fishing, collecting Santa Clauses, writing poetry, shopping.

WORKMAN, MARGARET LEE, state supreme court justice, chief justice; b. May 22, 1947; d. Frank Eugene and Mary Emma (Thomas) W.; m. Edward T. Gardner III; children: Lindsay Elizabeth, Christopher Workman, Edward Earnshaw. AB in Polit. Sci., W.Va. U., 1969, JD, 1974. Bar: W.Va. 1974. Asst. counsel to majority, pub. works com. U.S. Senate, Washington, 1974-75; law clk. 13th jud. cir., W.Va. Ct., Charleston, 1975-76, judge, 1981-88; pvt. practice Charleston, 1976-81; justice W.Va. Supreme Ct. Appeals, Charleston, 1989—, chief justice, 1993, 97. Advance person for Rosalyn Carter, Carter Presdl. Campaign, Atlanta, 1976. Democrat. Episcopalian. Office: State Supreme Ct 317 Strader Rd Charleston WV 25311-1579

WORKMAN, NORMAN ALLAN, accountant, graphic arts consultant; b. Boston, Apr. 20, 1918; s. William Horace and Estelle Emily (Hanlon) W.; m. Harriet Patricia Banfield, Aug. 1, 1946; children: Stephen, Mark, Brian, Patricia. Student, Coll. William and Mary, 1938-39; BS in Econs. magna cum laude, Bowdoin Coll., 1941. CPA, Oreg. Staff acct. Lybrand Ross Bros. & Montgomery, Boston, 1941-43, Whitfield Stratford & Co., Portland, Oreg., 1946-51; ptnr. Workman, Shephard & Co., CPAs, Portland, 1951-60; sole practitioner Portland, 1961—. Newsletter columnist Good Impressions, 1993—. Chmn. bd. Sylvan Sch., Portland, 1956-57; pres. Doernbecher Children's Hosp. Found., Portland, 1963-85, Bowdoin Club Oreg., Portland, 1963—; trustee Oreg. Episcopal Schs., Portland, 1974-76. Lt. (j.g.) Supply Corps, USNR, 1944-46. Mem. AICPA, Inst. Mgmt. Accts. (pres. Portland chpt. 1954-55), Oreg. Soc. CPA's, Pacific Printing and Imaging Assn., Arlington Club, Multnomah Athletic Club, Phi Beta Kappa. Avocations: bird hunting, fishing, horticulture. Home: 4381 SW Fairview Blvd Portland OR 97221-2709 Office: 1750 SW Skyline Blvd Portland OR 97221-2533

WORKMAN, ROBERT PETER, artist, cartoonist; b. Chgo., Jan. 27, 1961; s. Tom Okko and Virginia (Martin) W. Freelance artist Chgo.; artist Villager Newspaper, Chgo., 1991—; instr. St. Xavier Coll., Chgo., 1985; cartoonist Bridge View News, Oak Lawn, Ill., 1983-89, Village View Pubs., Oak Lawn, 1989; artist Villager News, 1991; TV art dir. Media-In-Action, Oak Lawn; lectr. Oxford U., Eng.; substitute tchr. Morgan Pk. Acad., Chgo.; artist-in-residence Chgo. Pub. Libr.; featured voice Am. Radio, 1992; exhibitor Seville Spain Am. Pavilion, Expo 92, Seville, 1992, Royal Acad. Arts Exhbn., 1995. Author: (cartoon strip) Cypher, 1983-89; Sesqui Squirrel Coloring Book, 1982, Sesqui Squirrel History of Chicago, 1983, (artists' books) Sesqui Squirrel History of the Constitution, Sesqui Squirrel Presents How Columbus Discovered America; author: (novel) Angels of Doom; artworks and books in collections of 87 mus. and librs. and pvt. collections, including Smithsonian, Art Inst. Chgo., Daley Br. Libr., Chgo., Ill. Exec. Mansion Mus., Sesquicentennial Archives Chgo. Pub. Libr. (awards and honors), The Vatican Libr., Rome, Bodleian Libr. U. Oxford, Eng., Mt. Greenwood Br. Pub. Libr. Chgo., Ill. Collection, Libr. Nat. Mus. Am. Art, Nat. Portrait Gallery. Mem. nat. adv. bd. Am. Security Coun., Boston, Va.; originator Kennedy Pk. Libr., Chgo. Featured in Artist's mag., 1990; recipient Resolution City Coun. Chgo., 1992. Mem. Am. Watercolor Soc., No. Ill. Newspaper Assn., Art Inst. Chgo. (freelancer 1991), Artists' Resource Trust Ft. Wayne Mus. Art, Ridge Art Assn., VFW, S.W. Archdiocesan Singles, Friends Oxford U., Alumni Sch. Art Inst. Chgo., KC. Roman Catholic. Home and Office: 2509 W 111th St # 2E Chicago IL 60655-1325

WORKMAN, WILLIAM DOUGLAS, III, former mayor; b. Charleston S.C., July 3, 1940; s. William Douglas, Jr. and Rhea (Thomas) W.; BA, The Citadel, 1961; grad. U. S.C., 1962; m. Marcia Mae Moorhead, Apr. 23, 1966 (div. Dec. 1995); children: William Douglas IV, Frank Moorhead; m. Patti Gage Fishburne Marks, June 22, 1996; stepchildren: Gage Russell Marks, Barnwell Johnson Marks, Kemp Fishburne Marks. Reporter, Charleston News & Courier, 1965-66, Greenville (S.C.) News, 1966-70; tchr., adminstr., dean allied health scis. Greenville Tech. Coll., 1967-75; exec. asst. to Gov. of S.C., Columbia, 1975-78; mktg. exec. Daniel Internat. Corp., Greenville, 1978-90, dir. of facilities Fluor Daniel, 1991-93; v.p. S.C. ops. Piedmont Natural Gas, 1994—; mayor City of Greenville, 1983-95. Chmn. Greenville County Rep. Conv., 1980, 82, 87, 89, 91, S.C. 4th Congl. Dist. Rep. Conv., 1980, 82, 84; chmn. S.C. Rep. Conv., 1984, 89, vice chmn., 1982, 87; Rep. nominee U.S. Congress 4th Dist. S.C., 1986; mem. S.C. Adv. Commn. on Intergovtl. Rels., 1990-96; bd. dirs. S.C. Appalachian Coun. of Govts., 1991-95; mem. Mcpl. Assn. S.C. 1981-95 (bd. dirs., 1990-95, pres., 1993-94); trustee Sch. Dist. Greenville County, 1969-75, also vice chmn.; bd. dirs. YMCA Camp Greenville, 1973-83, 90-95, chmn., 1975; chmn. S.C. Health Coordinating Coun., 1976-78; founder S.C. Literacy Assn., treas., 1969-73; mem. Greenville City Council, 1981-83; mem. Southern Growth Policies Bd., 1992-95. Served with AUS, 1962-64; ret. lt. col. USAR. Decorated Army Commendation medal with 2 oak leaf clusters; named Outstanding State Chmn., S.C. Jaycees, 1969; Order of Palmetto, 1978. Mem. Res. Officers Assn., Assn. U.S. Army, Am. Legion, Southea. Gas Assn., Nat. Mgmt. Assn. (mgr. yr. award Greenville chpt. 1985), Newcomen Soc. (co-chmn. S.C. com.), S.C. Downtown Devel. Assn. (bd. dirs.), Greenville Country Club, Greenville-Piedmont Citadel Club (past pres.), Greenville City Club (bd. dirs.), Poinsett Club, Greenville adv. bd. Nat. Bank of S.C., Carolina Yacht Club. Home: 30 Craigwood Rd Greenville SC 29607-3652 Office: PO Box 1905 Greenville SC 29602-1905

WORLEY, BLAND WALLACE, banker; b. Kinston, N.C., Aug. 14, 1917; s. Bland W. and Ida Ruth (Gooding) W.; m. Ada Harvey, June 28, 1941; children: Anne, Ada, Bland W. B.S., U. N.C., 1938; grad. exec. program, 1955; grad., Grad. Sch. Banking, Rutgers U., 1954. Insp. Hooper Holmes Bur., Greensboro, N.C., 1938-39; mgr. CIT Corp., Salisbury, N.C., 1939-42; mgr. time payment dept. Wachovia Bank & Trust Co., High Point, N.C., 1946-50; v.p., also High Point office exec. Wachovia Bank & Trust Co., 1951-56; sr. v.p. charge Wachovia Bank & Trust Co. (Greensboro operations), 1956-69; exec. v.p. charge statewide banking div. Wachovia Bank & Trust Co., Winston-Salem, N.C., 1969-70, also dir.; vice-chmn., dir., 1970-75; past trustee Wachovia Realty Investments; former CEO, dir. Barclays Am. Corp., chmn., 1976-84; dir., chmn. First Fed. Savs. & Loan Assn., Charlotte, N.C.; dir. Culp Inc., High Point, N.C.; past vol. chmn. for N.C. U.S. Savs. Bond Program. Past chmn. nat. exec. com. for vol. state chmn. 1969-77; pres. Greater Greensboro United Fund, 1975-77; past treas., mem. nat. exec. bd. Boy Scouts Am., 1970-85; past bd. dirs. N.C. Citizens Assn.; bd. dirs. N.C. Coun. Mgmt. and Devel., 1979-84; bd. dirs., past pres. Bus. Found. of N.C.; trustee, former chmn. bd. trustees Greensboro Coll.; past trustee Atlantic Christian Coll., Wilson, N.C.; past bd. visitors Guilford Coll., Greenboro; trustee U. N.C., Charlotte, 1981-85. Named High Point Young Man of Yr., 1953, Outstanding Young Businessman N.C., 1958; recipient Silver Beaver, Silver Antelope, Silver Buffalo awards Boy Scouts Am., Disting. Citizens award N.C. Citizens for Bus. and Industry, 1987. Mem. N.C. Bankers Assn. (past pres.), Nat. Consumer Fin. Assn., Greensboro C. of C. (past pres., disting. citizen award 1968), Greater Charlotte C. of C. (chmn. 1980-81), Piedmont Club, Old Town Country Club. Home: 1244 Arbor Rd Apt 232 Winston Salem NC 27104-1136

WORLEY, GORDON ROGER, retail chain financial executive; b. Arlington, Nebr., Oct. 13, 1919; s. Carl H. and Zella E. (Ludwig) W. B.S., U. Nebr., 1945; M.B.A., Northwestern U., 1956. C.P.A., Ill. With Aldens, Inc., Chgo., 1940-67; asst. treas. Aldens, Inc., 1956-57, v.p., treas., 1957-67; v.p., controller Gamble-Skogmo, Inc., Mpls., 1967; v.p. fin. Montgomery Ward & Co., Inc., 1967-68; exec. v.p. fin. Montgomery Ward & Co., Inc., Chgo., 1975-83; also dir.; v.p. fin. Marcor Inc., Chgo., 1968-75; also dir. Marcor Inc.; dir. Signature Fin./Mktg. Inc., Montgomery Ward Ins. Group, Ill. Power Co., Decatur, Axia, Inc, Stein, Roe & Farnham Funds, Am. Mgmt. Systems, Inc., Arlington, Va. Bd. dirs. Northwestern Meml. Hosp.; trustee Garrett-Evang. Theol. Sem., chmn., 1984-89, mem. and vice chmn. Ill. Capital Devel. Bd., 1973-77; mem. Nat. Commn. on Electronic Fund Transfers, 1975-77. Served with USAAF, 1943-46. Mem. Conf. Bd. Coun. of Fin. Execs., Fin. Execs. Inst., Nat. Retail Mchts. Assn., Execs. Club, Econ. Club, Mid-Am. Club, Chgo. Club, Oak Park Country Club, Hole-In-The-Wall Club (Naples, Fla.). Methodist.

WORLEY, JANE LUDWIG, lawyer; b. Reading, Pa., Sept. 4, 1917; d. Walter Schearer and Marion Grace (Johns) L.; m. Floyd Edwin Worley, Oct. 30, 1946 (dec. Jan. 1982); children: Laetitia Anne, Thomas Allen, Christopher Ludwig. AB, Bryn Mawr Coll., 1938; JD, Temple U., 1942. Bar: Pa. 1943, U.S. Dist. Ct. (ea. dist.) Pa. 1980, U.S. Supreme Ct. 1968. Assoc. Richardson Moss & Richardson, Reading, 1943-48; pvt. practice Wernersville, Pa., 1948—; sec., bd. dirs. Worley Lumber Co. Inc., Wernersville, 1955—. Sec. Friends of Reading Mus. Art, 1986-91; sec. Berks County chpt.

ARC, 1986-87, v.p., 1987-91. Mem. ABA, Pa. Bar Assn., Berks County Bar Assn., DAR, Jr. League Reading. Republican. Mem. United Ch. of Christ. Avocations: antique and art collecting, travel. Office: 551 W Penn Ave Wernersville PA 19565-1417

WORLEY, LLOYD DOUGLAS, English language educator; b. Lafayette, La., Sept. 11, 1946; s. Albert Stiles and Doris (Christy) W.; m. Maydean Ann Mouton, Apr. 4, 1966; children: Erin Shawn, Albert Stiles II. BA, U. SW La., 1968, MA, 1972; PhD, So. Ill. U., 1979. Ordained priest, Liberal Cath. Ch. Tchr. Lafayette H.S., 1969-74; vis. asst. prof. dept. English So. Ill. U., Carbondale, 1979-80; asst. prof. dept. English Pa. State U., DuBois, 1980-87; assoc. prof., assoc. dir. composition dept. English U. No. Colo., Greeley, 1987-88, prof. dept. English, 1988—; acting dir. Writing Component Ctr. Basic Skills, So. Ill. U., 1980. Editor: Ruthven Literary Bull., 1988-92; contbr. book chpts., articles. Rector Parish of St. Albertus Magnus, sec-treas. Am. Province; provost Am. Clerical Synod Chpt. Decorated Knight Bachelor of Yugoslavia, 1996, Hereditary Knight of San Luigi, 1996, Knight Cmdr. Order of Merit St. Angilbert, 1993, Prelate Comdr. Order of Noble Companions of Swan, 1993, Grand Chamberlain, 1995, Knight Order of Guadalupe, 1995, Knight Comdr. Justice Sovereign Order St. John, Knight Grand Cross of Bear of Alabona, 1995; created hereditary Baron, Royal and Serene House of Alabona-Ostrogojsk et de Garama, HRSH Prince William I, created Count Palatine of Maxalla, 1996. Fellow Philalethes Soc.; mem. ASCD, Internat. Assn. for Fantastic in Arts (divsn. head Am. Lit. 1987-93), Lord Ruthven Assembly (pres. 1988-94, founding pres. emeritus 1994), Conf. Coll. Composition and Commn., Nat. Coun. Tchrs. English, Am. Conf. Irish Studies, Sigma Tau Delta (bd. dirs. 1990-96, high plains regent various states 1992-96), Masons (century lodge #190), Order of DeMolay (chevalier, cross of honor, legion of honor), Knights Holy Sepulchre (Sov. Grand Master), Rose Croix Martinist Order (pres. premier nat. coun.). Democrat. Office: 2644 11th Ave # D-109 Greeley CO 80631-8441

WORLEY, MARVIN GEORGE, JR., architect; b. Oak Park, Ill., Oct. 10, 1934; s. Marvin George and Marie Hyancinth (Donahue) W.; B.Arch., U. Ill., 1958; m. Maryalice Ryan, July 11, 1959; children—Michael Craig, Carrie Ann, Alissa Maria. Project engr. St. Louis area Nike missile bases U.S. Army C.E., Granite City, Ill., 1958-59, architect N.Cen. div. U.S. Army C.E., Chgo., 1960; architect Yerkes & Grunsfeld, architects, Chgo., 1961-65, asso., 1965; asso. Grunsfeld & Assos., architects, Chgo., 1966-85.; prin. Marvin Worley Architects, Oak Park, Ill., 1985—. Dist. architect Oak Park Elementary Schs., Dist. 97, 1973-80. Mem. Oak Park Community Improvement Commn., 1973-75; mem. exec. bd. Oak Park Council PTA, 1970-73, pres., 1971-72. Served with AUS, 1959. Mem. AIA (corporate), Chgo. Assn. Commerce and Industry, Oak Park-River Forest C. of C. Office: 37 South Blvd Oak Park IL 60302-2777

WORLEY, ROBERT WILLIAM, JR., lawyer; b. Anderson, Ind., June 13, 1935; s. Robert William and Dorothy Mayhew (Hayler) W.; m. Diana Lynn Matthews, Aug. 22, 1959; children: Nathanael, Hope Hillegas. BS in Chem. Engring., Lehigh U., 1956; LLB, Harvard U., 1960. Bar: Conn. 1960, Fla. 1977, U.S. Supreme Ct. 1966. Assoc. then ptnr. Cummings & Lockwood, Stamford, Conn., 1960-91; gen. counsel Consol. Asset Recovery Corp. sub. Chase Manhattan Corp., Bridgeport, Conn., 1991-94; v.p., sr. assoc. counsel The Chase Manhattan Bank, N.Y.C., 1994—. Mem. trustees com. on bequests and trusts Lehigh U., 1979—; mem. Conn. Legis. Task Force on Probate Court System, 1991-93; chmn. Greenwich Arts Council, 1981-82; v.p., bd. dirs. Greenwich Choral Soc., 1962-77, 80, mem., 1960-95; bd. dirs. Greenwich Ctr. for Chamber Music, 1981-85, Greenwich Symphony, 1986-89; commr. Greenwich Housing Authority, 1972-77; past mem. Republican Town Com. Greenwich; mem. bldg. com. for sr. ctr. Greenwich Bd. Selectmen, 1980-81. Served to capt. JAGC, AUS, 1965. Mem. Conn. Bar Assn. (exec. com. probate sect. 1980), Fla. Bar Assn., Stamford Bar Assn. (sec.), Greenwich Bar Assn. Republican. Christian Scientist. Club: Landmark, Harvard Boston. Home: 316 Sound Beach Ave Old Greenwich CT 06870-1932 Office: The Chase Manhattan Bank Legal Dept 39th Flr 270 Park Ave New York NY 10017-2014

WORMAN, HOWARD JAY, physician, educator; b. Paterson, N.J., May 21, 1959; s. Louis and Dora (Rubin) W. BA, Cornell U., 1981; MD, U. Chgo., 1985. Diplomate Am. Bd. Internal Medicine. Intern N.Y. Hosp., N.Y.C., 1985-86, resident, 1986-87; guest investigator Rockefeller U., N.Y.C., 1987-90; asst. prof. Mt. Sinai Sch. Medicine, N.Y.C., 1990-94; asst. attending physician Mt. Sinai Hosp., N.Y.C., 1990-94; asst. prof. Coll. Physicians and Surgeons Columbia U., N.Y.C., 1995—; asst. attending physician Presbyn. Hosp., N.Y.C., 1995—. Mem. editl. bd. Hepatology, Frontiers in Biosci.; contbr. articles to profl. jours. Recipient Physician-Scientist award NIH, 1987-92; Charles E. Culpeper scholar in Med. Scis., 1994-95. Mem. AAAS, ACP, Am. Chem. Soc., Am. Fedn. Clin. Rsch. (Trainee award in clin. rsch. 1989, Henry Christian award 1990), Am. Soc. Cell Biology, Am. Assn. Study of Liver Diseases, N.Y. Acad. Scis. (vice chmn. biol. scis. sect. 1992-93, chmn. 1993-94), Hon. Order Ky. Cols., Phi Beta Kappa. Democrat. Jewish. Avocations: music, reading. Office: Columbia U Coll Physicians & Surgeons 630 W 168th St New York NY 10032-3702

WORMAN, LINDA KAY, nursing administrator; b. Buffalo, N.Y., Sept. 28, 1959; d. Robert Kindig and Winifred (Hostetter) W. BSN, Emory U., 1980; MPH, U. N.C., 1986. RN; cert. lactation cons.; cert. advanced nursing adminstr. Staff nurse SICU U. Hosp., Cleve., 1980-81; staff nurse labor and delivery Med. Ctr., Columbus, Ga., 1981; dep. prin. tutor Macha (Africa) Mission Hosp., 1981-85; staff nurse neurosci. ICU Duke U. Hosp., Durham, N.C., 1985-86; nurse mgr. maternal-child Woodland (Calif.) Meml. Hosp., 1986-88; nurse mgr. obstetrics Pa. State U. Hosp., Hershey, 1988-94; v.p. nursing svcs. Jersey Shore (Pa.) Hosp., 1994-96; dir. maternal-child health Newton (N.J.) Meml. Hosp., 1996—. Rape and domestic violence crisis vol. Harrisburg YWCA, 1992-94. Mem. Am. Orgn. of Nurse Execs., Pa. Perinatal Assn. (bd. dirs. 1989-94). Home: 8 Yetter Rd Newton NJ 07860 Office: Newton Meml Hosp 175 High St Newton NJ 07860-1004

WORMAN, RICHARD W., insurance company executive, state senator; b. Noble County, Ind., July 3, 1933; s. William D. and Leah M. W.; m. Marna Jo Neuhouser, Sept. 29, 1951; children—Terry Jo, Renny, Denny, Rex, Tammy. Buyer, Neuhouser Poultry, Leo, Ind., 1951-53; salesman Allen Dairy, Ft. Wayne, Ind., 1953-57; with Nationwide Ins. Co., Columbus, Ohio, 1957-88, dist. sales mgr.; owner Securance Ins., 1990—; mem. Ind. Ho. of Reps., 1972-76, Ind. Senate, 1978—; trustee, assessor County of Allen, Ind., 1970-72. C.L.U. Mem. Life Underwriters Assn., Republican. United Methodist. Clubs: Lions (past pres.), Mason (past master), Shriner, Elks, Optimist. Office: PO Box 320 Leo IN 46765-0320

WORMWOOD, RICHARD NAUGHTON, retired naturalist; b. Old Forge, N.Y., May 21, 1936; s. F. Earl Hill-Wormwood and Eleanor Bardou-Naughton; m. Michele Gano-Kenney (div.); children: Anneene, Chauncey; m. Donna Rhodes-Harrington, Jan. 30, 1983; one stepchild, Melissa Harrington Goucher. Student, Rochester Inst. Tech., 1955, Harper Coll., 1956, Russell Sage Coll., 1957, New Paltz Art Coll., 1958, N.Am. Sch. Conservation, 1972-74, N.Y. State Police Acad., 1974, Herkimer C.C., 1977-78. Dir. Tailored Ski Instruction, 1965-79; interpretive naturalist Adirondack Naturalist Explorations, Warrensburg, N.Y., 1980-91; with Adirondack Park Agency, Newcomb, N.Y., 1991; miniature craftsman Adirondack Rustic Miniatures, Brant Lake, N.Y., 1991-96; with Omni/Sagamore, Lake George, N.Y., 1992-93; Wormwood Wild Ventures/Adirondack Eco-tour Adventure Guides, Lake George, N.Y., 1994-96; with Adirondack Wilderness Cmty. Sch., 1997; gadfly Pro Ski Instructors of Am., 1965-68. Author: Wilderness Option, 1979, Adirondak Frontier, 1982, Finding Sasquatch, 1982, Adirondack Naturalist, 1989, The End of You: The Ecological Drowning of American Civilization, 1997, The End of You, The Environmental Drowning of America, 1997. Civil rights activist, Greenwich Village, Mexico City, 1957; founder Adirondack Naturalist Fellowship, 1991, Conservatory of Naturism, 1995. Avocations: wilderness walking and canoeing, nature photography and videography, landscape design.

WORNER, THERESA MARIE, physician; b. Breckenridge, Minn., Feb. 19, 1948; d. William Daniel and Elizabeth (Stelten) W.; m. Martin Herbst, Mar. 24, 1979. AB, St. Theresa Coll., 1970; MD, U. Minn., 1974. Diplomate Am. Bd. Internal Medicine. Rotating intern Kings County Hosp., Bklyn., 1974-75, resident medicine, 1975-77; fellow VA Med. Ctr., Bronx, N.Y., 1977-78; chief med. sect. Alcoholism treatment program VA Med. Ctr., Bronx, 1978-87; asst. prof. medicine Mt. Sinai Sch. Medicine, N.Y.C., 1984-87; mem. faculty Postgrad. Ctr., 1985-90; physician in charge alcoholism svcs. L.I. Coll. Hosp., Bkyn., 1987-92; assoc. prof. clin. medicine SUNY, Health Sci. Ctr., Bkyn., 1988—; dir. rsch. 32BJ Health Fund, 1992—; clin. assoc. prof. Pub. Health Cornell U. Med. Coll., 1996—; pres./founder Alcohol. Info, 1995—; advisor Patient Care Mag., 1984—; cons. REA, 1996—. Referee Hepatology, 1986, Jour. Study Alcohol, 1984—, Substance Abuse, 1992—, Alcoholism: Clinical and Exptl. Rsch., 1992—, Drug and Alcohol Dependence, 1993—, Drug Therapy, 1994—, Addiction, 1996—; contbr. numerous articles to profl. jours. Active Bronx Bot. Garden, Mus. Modern Art, Met. Mus. Art, Mus. Natural History, Bklyn. Mus. Art, Turtle Bay Civic Assn., Bklyn. Lyric Opera, Empire State Opera, Amato Opera. Grantee Child Welfare Adminstrn., 1991, 92, 93; recipient Physicians Recognition award AMA, 1984, 89, 91, 96, Cert. of Merit Govt. Employees Ins. Co., 1986, PACT Intern Site award, 1991, 92. Fellow ACP; mem. AAAS, Am. Med. Soc. on Alcoholism and Other Drug Dependence, Am. Soc. Internal Medicine, Am. Assn. for Study Liver Diseases (Travel award 1978), N.Y. Acad. Scis., Rsch. Soc. on Alcoholism, Internat. Soc. Biologic Rsch. in Alcoholism. Home: 322 E 50th St New York NY 10022-7902 Office: Rsch Dept 32BJ Health Fund 13th fl 101 Avenue Of The Americas New York NY 10013-1933

WORRELL, ALBERT CADWALLADER, forest economics educator; b. Phila., May 14, 1913; s. Pratt Bishop and Bertha May (Cadwallader) W.; m. Helen Haffner Diefendorf, July 31, 1937; children: Kathleen Worrell Weigel, Frederick Strayer, Nancy WorrellShumaker. B.S., U. Mich., 1935, M.F., 1935, Ph.D., 1953. Asso. prof. U. Ga., 1947-55; asso. prof. Yale, 1955-63, prof. forest econs., 1963-67; Edwin Weyerhaeuser Davis prof. forest policy, 1967-83, Edwin W. Davis prof. emeritus, 1983—; forest economist U.N. Econ. Commn. for Latin Am., Santiago, Chile, 1960-61; guest prof. U. Freiburg, Germany, 1970. Author: Economics of American Forestry, 1959, Principles of Forest Policy, 1970, Unpriced Values, 1979. Mem. Soc. Am. Foresters. Home: 134 Meadowbrook Dr Nacogdoches TX 75964-6568

WORRELL, ANNE EVERETTE ROWELL, newspaper publisher; b. Surry, Va., Mar. 7, 1920; d. Charles Gray and Ethel (Roache) Rowell; student Va. Intermont Coll., 1939, LittD (hon.), 1991; student U. Richmond, 1965; m. Thomas Eugene Worrell, Sept. 12, 1941; 1 son, Thomas Eugene. Founding stockholder Worrell Newspapers Inc., 1949, v.p., dir., 1969-73; pres. Bristol Newspapers, Inc., Va., pubs. Bristol Herald-Courier, Bristol Va.-Tennessean, 1979—; v.p., sec. Worrell Investment Co., Charlottesville, Va. Pres., Bristol Jr. League, 1959; bd. dirs. The Corp. for Thomas Jefferson's Poplar Forest Found., Friends of Bacon's Castle; trustee Va. Hist. Soc., Va. Intermont Coll., 1973—, Preservation Alliance Va., Assn. for the Preservation of Va. Antiquities, Va. Hist. Soc.; active State Rev. Bd., Bayly Mus. Named Outstanding Alumna, 1981. Mem. DAR (Shadwell chpt.), Nat. Trust for Hist. Preservation. Clubs: Contemporary, Farmington Country. Episcopalian. Home: Seven Sunset Circle Farmington Charlottesville VA 22901 Office: Pantops PO Box 5386 Charlottesville VA 22905-5386 also: Bristol Newspapers Inc 320 Morrison Blvd Bristol VA 24201-3812

WORRELL, AUDREY MARTINY, geriatric psychiatrist; b. Phila., Aug. 12, 1935; d. Francis Aloysius and Dorothy (Rawley) Martiny; m. Richard Vernon Worrell, June 14, 1958; children: Philip Vernon, Amy Elizabeth. MD, Meharry Med. Coll., 1960. Diplomate Am. Bd. Psychiatry and Neurology. Intern Misericordia Hosp., Phila., 1960-61; resident SUNY-Buffalo Affiliated Hosp., 1961-63, Buffalo Psychiat. Ctr., 1963-64; dir. capitol region Mental Health Ctr., Hartford, Conn., 1974-77; acting regional dir. Region IV, State Dept. Mental Health, 1976-77; asst. chief psychiatry VA Med. Ctr., Newington, Conn., 1977-78, acting chief psychiatry, 1978-79, chief psychiatry, 1978-80; dir. Capitol Regional Mental Health Facilities, Hartford, Conn., 1980-87; clin. prof. psychiatry U. Conn., 1981-87; commr. State Dept. Mental Health, Hartford, 1981-86; CEO and med. dir. Vista Sandia Hosp., Albuquerque, 1986-88; dir. consultation liason Lovelace Med. Ctr., Albuquerque, 1988-89, geriatric psychiatry, 1989-93, dir. geriatric psychiatry Charter Hosp., Albuquerque, 1993-96, St. Joseph Med. Sys., Albuquerque, 1994—; pvt. practice, 1996—. Contbr. articles to profl. jours. Bd. dirs. Transitional Services, Buffalo, 1973-74, ARC, Buffalo, 1973-74, Child and Family Services, Hartford, 1972-73; co-chmn. United Way/Combined Health Appeal, State of Conn., 1983, 84; active Child Welfare Inst. Adv. Bd., Hartford, 1983—, Conn. Prison Bd., Hartford, 1984-85. Recipient Leadership award Conn. Council Mental Health Ctrs., 1983; Outstanding Contbn. award to Health Services YWCA, Hartford, 1983; chmn. Gov.'s Task Force on Mental Health Policy, 1982-85; mem. Gov.'s Task Force on Homeless, 1983-85. Mem. New Eng. Mental Health Commrs. Assn., Am. Med. Women's Assn., Conn. Assn. Mental Health and Aging, Conn. Coalition for Homeless Inc., Conn. Rehab. Assn., Am. Assn. Psychiat. Adminstrs., Am. Hosp. Assn., AMA, Am. Orthopsychiat. Assn., Am. Pub. Health Assn., Assn. Mental Health Adminstrs., Hosp. and Community Psychiatry Service, Corporators of Inst. of Living of Hartford, Am. Psychiat. Assn., Conn. Psychiat. Soc., NASMHPD (sec., bd. dirs. 1982-86), Am. Coll. Psychiatrists, Am. Coll. Mental Health Adminstrs.

WORRELL, BILLY FRANK, health facility administrator; b. Columbia, Ala., Oct. 12, 1939; s. Beachum Worrell and Madeline (Scott) Wells; children: Jon, Kevin, Heather; m. Lorna Faye Jones, Nov. 26, 1991. A in Bus., Thomas Coll., Thomasville, Ga., 1978; BS magna cum laude, Albany State Coll., 1990, MBA, 1991; MS, LaSalle U., 1995, PhD, 1996. Registered respiratory therapist, respiratory care profl., arterial blood gas technician, neo-natal advanced life support technician. Electrician USN, 1957-60, Newport News (Va.) Shipbldg., 1960-63; mfg. mgr. Lockheed Aircraft, Marietta, Ga., 1963-70, Champion Homes, Thomasville, Ga., 1970-74; salesman Cadillac dealership Thomasville, 1974-76; estimator Knight-Dodson Constrn. Co., Thomasville, 1976-78; adminstr. Ga. Army Nat. Guard, Thomasville, 1978-84; ret., 1984; allied health mgr. Phoebe Putney Meml. Hosp., Albany, 1988-93; dir. cardiopulmonary dept. Mitchell County Hosp., Camilla, Ga., 1994-95; dir. cardiopulmonary contract svcs. Sumter County Hosp., Americus, Ga., 1995—. Columnist newspaper column Lee County Ledger, 1990; actor film and plays. Vol. Salvation Army, Thomasville, 1978-83, Sr. Citizens Group, Thomasville, 1980-83, Kidney Found., Thomasville, 1980-85. Mem. Nat. Bd. Respiratory Care, Ga. Respiratory Care, Toastmasters. Republican. Avocations: guitar, singing, reading, photography, restoring old cars. Home: 1142 Philema Rd S Leesburg GA 31763-9314 Office: Sumter County Hospital Americus GA 31709

WORRELL, CYNTHIA LEE, bank executive; b. Moncton, N.B., Can., May 27, 1957; came to U.S., 1979; d. Ronald William and Audrey Helen (Crothers) Jones; m. Geoffrey H. Worrell, Sept. 1, 1979; children: Lindsay Andrea, Geoffrey Andrew, Ashley Taylor. Student, U. New Brunswick, Fredericton, 1979. Lic. real estate broker, Mass., Pa., Calif. Instr. New Brunswick C.C., Fredericton, N.B., Can., 1978-79, Massasoit C.C., Brockton, Mass., 1981-82, Brockton Cmty. Schs., 1981-82; regional mgr. and instr. Worldwide Ednl. Services, Clifton, N.J.; procedures and documentation analyst Capital Blue Cross, Harrisburg, Pa., 1985; v.p., br. mgr. Comfed Mortgage Co., Inc., Mass., 1985-90; sr. residential loan officer Bank of Am., Santa Clara, Calif., 1990-92; regional sales mgr., asst. v.p. Shearson Lehman Mortgage, San Jose, Calif., 1992-93; br. mgr. Cypress Fin., San Jose, 1993-94, PNC Mortgage Corp. Am., San Jose, 1994—; program dir. worldwide Ednl. Svcs., Taunton, Mass., 1995; area prodn. mgr. Plymouth Mortgage Co., Foxborough, Mass., 1995-96, Ameriquest Mortgage, Hingham, Mass., 1996-97; br. mgr. Bank United of Tex. Commonwealth United Mortgage, West Bridgewater, Mass., 1996—; br. mgr. Nat. City Mortgage-Commonwealth United Mortgage, 1997—; guest spkr. numerous trade shows, real estate bd. seminars, cmty. workshops, stress mgmt. personal profiles, motivational speaking and workshops; instr. mortgage banking Calif. State U., Hayward, 1994—; mem. adv. bd., instr., outside cons. Calif. State U. Ext. divsn., 1993-95; cert. trainer Carlson Learning Co., 1993—; trainer in diversity, conflict resolution, sexual harassment, and time mgmt.; cmty. trainer WCR, BPW, Old Colony Vocat. Sch., Wareham H.S., Wareham Mid. and Elem. Schs., Wareham Supts. Office, Fall River Sch. Dist., Old Rochester Jr. and Sr. H.S., Bristol County Tng. Consortium, and Transitional Assistance, Bridgewater Cmty., Wareham Foster Parents, Wareham Decas Sch., 1996—. Mem. editl. bd. Mortgage Originator, 1995; contbr. articles to profl. jours. Vol. Handi Kids, Bridgewater, Mass., 1985-90, Fremont/Newark YMCA youth basketball and soccer; mem. Forest Park PTA, Self-Def. Inst. Tae Kwon Do Club; donor Berwick Boys Club; bd. dirs. Wareham Childcare; mem. adv. coun. Wareham H.S.; trustee Le Lycée Internat. de la Nouvelle Angleterre, Inc., Boston, 1997. Named to IBC 200 Women of Achievement, 1991-92, ABI 2000 Notable Women, 1991-92,ABI Personalities of Am., 1992, Internat. Order of Merit, 1992, The World Found. of Successful Women, 1992, Outstanding Young Women in Am., 1984, 88. Mem. NAFE, Mass. Mortgage Bankers Assn., Data Entry Mgmt. Assn., Middleboro C. of C., Wareham Bus. and Profl. Women's Club (v.p. program dir.), Taunton Area C. of C., Toastmasters, Plymouth Bd. Realtors, Bristol County Bd. Realtors, Women's Coun. of Realtors, Bristol County C. of C. Republican. Avocations: swimming, golf, horseback riding, curling. Home: 7 Kingwood St Wareham MA 02571-2828 Office: Commonwealth United Mortgage 700 W Center St Ste 1 West Bridgewater MA 02379

WORRELL, RICHARD VERNON, orthopedic surgeon, college dean; b. Bklyn., June 4, 1931; s. John Elmer and Elaine (Callender) W.; BA, NYU, 1952; MD, Meharry Med. Coll., 1958; m. Audrey Frances Martiny, June 14, 1958; children: Philip Vernon, Amy Elizabeth. Intern Meharry Med. Coll., Nashville, 1958-59; resident gen. surgery Mercy-Douglass Hosp., Phila., 1960-61; resident orthopedic surgery State U. N.Y. Buffalo Sch. Medicine Affiliated Hosps., 1961-64; resident in orthopedic pathology Temple U. Med. Ctr., Phila., 1966-67; pvt. practice orthopedic surgery, Phila., 1964-68; asst. prof. acting head div. orthopedic surgery U. Conn. Sch. Medicine 1968-70; attending orthopedic surgeon E.J. Meyer Meml. Hosp., Buffalo, Millard Fillmore Hosp., Buffalo, VA Hosp., Buffalo, Buffalo State Hosp.; clin. instr. orthopedic surgery SUNY, Buffalo, 1970-74; chief orthopedic surgery VA Hosp., Newington, Conn., 1974-80; asst. prof. surgery (orthopedics) U. Conn. Sch. Medicine, 1974-77, assoc. prof., 1977-83, asst. dean student affairs, 1980-83; prof. clin. surgery SUNY Downstate Med. Ctr., Bklyn., 1983-86; dir. orthopedic surgery Brookdale Hosp. Med. Ctr., Bklyn., 1983-86; prof. of orthopedics U. N.Mex. Sch. of Medicine, 1986—, prof., vice chmn. dept. orthopaedics, 1997—; dir. orthopedic oncology U. N.Mex. Med. Ctr., 1987—; mem. med. staff U. N.Mex. Cancer Ctr., 1987—; chief orthopedic surgery VA Med. Ctr., Albuquerque, 1987—; cons. in orthopedic surgery Newington (Conn.) Children's Hosp., 1968-70; mem. sickle cell disease adv. com. NIH, 1982-86. Bd. dirs. Big Bros. Greater Hartford. Served to capt. M.C., U.S. Army Res., 1962-69. Diplomate Am. Bd. Orthopedic Surgery, Nat. Bd. Med. Examiners. Fellow ACS, Am. Acad. Orthopedic Surgeons, Royal Soc. Medicine, London; mem. AMA, Am. Orthopaedic Assn., Am. Soc. Clin. Pathologists, Orthopedic Rsch. Soc., Internat. Soc. Orthopedic Surgery and Traumatology, N.Mex. Soc. Clin. Oncology, Internat. Fedn. Surg. Colls. (assoc.), Alpha Omega Alpha. Office: U NMex Sch Medicine Albuquerque NM 87131-5296

WORSECK, RAYMOND ADAMS, economist; b. Providence, Mar. 25, 1937; s. Wilford Howe and Florence Marie (Dillmann) W.; m. Mary Elizabeth Lottes, July 15, 1972; children: Andrew Wilford, David Edward. BS in Math., St. Louis U., 1959, MA in Econs., 1970. Registered rep. N.Y. Stock Exchange. Commodity analyst Longstreet-Abbott & Co., St. Louis, 1959-65, dir. basic rsch., 1965-67; sr. price analyst Doane Agrl. Svc., St. Louis, 1967-69; dir. commodity rsch. A.G. Edwards & Sons, Inc., St. Louis, 1969-85, mgr. econ. rsch., 1985—, chief economist, 1989—. Mem. Am. Econs. Assn., Nat. Assn. Bus. Economists (chpt. pres. 1984-85), Fin. Analysts Soc. (bd. govs. St. Louis chpt. 1994-95), St. Louis Com. on Fgn. Rels., Futures Industry Assn. (nat. pres. rsch. divsn. 1983-84), Pub. Securities Assn. (econs. adv. com.), St. Louis Soc. Fin. Analysts (bd. govs.). Avocations: history, music, cycling. Home: 331 Elm Valley Dr Saint Louis MO 63119-4574 Office: AG Edwards & Sons Inc 1 N Jefferson Ave Saint Louis MO 63103-2205

WORSHAM, BERTRAND RAY, psychiatrist; b. Atkins, Ark., Feb. 14, 1926; s. Lewis Henry and Emma Lavada (Burris) W.; m. Margaret Ann Dickson, June 4, 1947 (div. 1960); children: Eric Dickson, Vicki Gayle; m. Lynne Ellen Reynolds, Aug. 27, 1976; children: Mary Ellen Clarice, Richard Andrew (dec.). BA, U. Ark., 1951; MD, U. Ark., Little Rock, 1955. Intern Hillcrest Med. Ctr., Tulsa, 1955-56; resident in psychiatry Menninger Sch. Psychiatry, Topeka, 1956-59; pvt. practice, 1959-78; clin. instr. U. Okla. Sch. Medicine, 1965-78; coord. drug and alcohol treatment unit Washington D.C. VA Med. Ctr., 1978-84; med. dir. Norman divsn. Okla. State Vets. Ctr., 1984-89; psychiat. cons. Comty. Counselling Ctr., Oklahoma City, 1989—; cons. Oklahoma City Vets. Hosp., 1959-72, State Dept. Pub. Health, 1960-65; dir. Cmty. Mental Health Ctr., Shawnee, Okla., 1965-72; mem. staff Coyne Campbell Hosp., 1960-78, Bapt. Med. Ctr., 1960-78, Mercy Health Ctr., 1960-78, Deaconess Hosp., 1963-78, Dr.'s Gen. Hosp., 1963-78, Presbyn. Hosp., 1962-78, U. Health Sci. Ctr., 1962-78, Children's Meml. Hosp., 1968-78, Oklahoma City VA Hosp., 1960-78, Washington D.C. Va. Hosp., 1978-84, Okla. Vets. Ctr., Norman, 1984-89. Mem. Civil Disaster Com., Oklahoma City, 1966, USN League, Okla., 1972—. With USAF, 1944-46; capt. USNR, 1957-66, ret. Fellow Menninger Found., Charles F. Menninger Found.; mem. AMA, Am. Psychiat. Assn. (Okla. dist. br. 1959-78, 84—), Assn. Mil. Surgeons of U.S., Ret. Officers Assn., World Fedn. for Mental Health, Internat. Platform Assn., Washington Psychiat. Assn., No. Va. Mental Health Assn., Masons (32 degree). Republican. Episcopalian. Avocations: golf, church activities. Home: 9915 N Kelley Ave Oklahoma City OK 73131-2022 Office: Comty Counseling Ctr 1140 N Hudson Ave Oklahoma City OK 73103-3918 *Man's ability to do goal-directed work is his greatest asset. And as results add together he more nearly approaches an infinitely profound civilization.*

WORSLEY, JAMES RANDOLPH, JR., lawyer; b. Rocky Mount, N.C., July 28, 1924; s. James Randolph and Helen Marie (Killian) W.; m. Cornelia Cheston, Feb. 11, 1956; children: Cornelia Worsley Newell, Julia Worsley Neilson, Charlotte Cheston Worsley. BS, E. Carolina U., 1944; postgrad., Harvard U., 1944-45, LLB, 1949. Bar: N.C. 1949, D.C. 1949. Assoc. Klagsbrunn, Hanes & Irwin, Washington, 1949-54; ptnr. Ober, Kaler, Grimes & Shriver (and predecessor firm), Washington, 1955-94, coun., 1995—. Chmn. Md. Potomac Water Authority, 1969-71, Montgomery County (Md.) Charter Revision Commn., 1967; mem. pastoral coun. Archdiocese of Washington, 1975-78; bd. dirs. Madeira Sch., Greenway, Va., 1975-81. Fellow Am. Bar Found.; mem. Chevy Chase Club, Met. Club. Democrat. Roman Catholic. Avocations: sailing, tennis. Home: 11 Quincy St Chevy Chase MD 20815-4226 Office: Ober Kaler Grimes & Shriver 1401 H St NW Ste 500 Washington DC 20005-2110

WORTH, GARY JAMES, communications executive; b. Berkeley Township, N.J., Dec. 13, 1940; s. Melvin Raymond and Viola Vista (Landis) W. Student, Trenton State Coll., 1964, Palm Beach Jr. Coll., 1958-59. Dir. sta. relations MBS, Inc., N.Y.C., 1972; v.p. sta. relations MBS, Inc., 1972; exec. v.p. MBS, Inc., Washington, 1972-79; mem. exec. com. MBS, Inc., 1978-79; v.p. Mut. Reports, Inc., Washington, 1972-79; dir. Mut. Reports, Inc., 1972-79; v.p., dir. WCFL, Inc., Chgo., 1979, Mut. Radio N.Y., Inc., N.Y.C., 1979; pres. Robert Wold Co. Inc. and subs. Wold Communications, Inc., L.A., 1980-85, also dir.; pres., chief exec. officer, dir. WesternWorld Inc. and subs. WesternWorld TV, L.A., 1986-93, The Video Tape Co., North Hollywood, Calif., 1987-93; sec. dir. WesternWorld Video Inc., L.A., 1986-87; CEO Starcom Television Svcs., Inc., 1993—96; chmn., CEO Starcom Entertainment, Inc., 1993—; CEO Starcom Mgmt. Svcs. Inc., 1993—. Producer, dir.: USAF movie Assignment McGuire. Served to capt. USAF, 1960-66, Vietnam. Decorated Air Force Commendation medal, Armed Forces Expeditionary medal; recipient Chief Herbert H. Almers Meml. award Bergen County (N.J.) Police Acad., 1972. Mem. Nat. Assn. Broadcasters, Nat. Assn. TV Program Execs., Nat. Informercial Mktg. Assn. Methodist.

WORTH, GEORGE JOHN, English literature educator; b. Vienna, Austria, June 11, 1929; came to U.S., 1940, naturalized, 1945; s. Adolph and Theresa (Schmerzler) W.; m. Carol Laverne Dinsdale, Mar. 17, 1951; children: Theresa Jean (Wilkinson), Paul Dinsdale. AB, U. Chgo., 1948, MA, 1951; PhD, U. Ill., 1954. Instr. English U. Ill., Urbana, 1954-55; faculty U. Kans., Lawrence, 1955—, assoc. prof., 1962-65, prof. English lit., 1965-95; prof. emeritus English, 1995—; asst. chmn. dept. U. Kans., Lawrence, 1961-62, assoc. chmn., 1962-63, acting chmn., 1963-64, chmn., 1964-79. Author: James Hannay: His Life and Work, 1964, William Harrison Ainsworth, 1972, Dickensian Melodrama, 1978, Thomas Hughes, 1984, Great Expectations: An Annotated Bibliography, 1986; editor: (with Harold Orel) Six

Studies in Nineteenth Century English Literature and Thought, 1962, The Nineteenth Century Writer and His Audience, 1969, (with Edwin Eigner) Victorian Criticism of the Novel, 1985. Mem. AAUP, MLA, Dickens Fellowship, Internat. Assn. U. Profs. English, Dickens Soc., Midwest Victorian Studies Assn., Rsch. Soc. for Victorian Periodicals. Office: U Kans Dept English Wescoe Hall Lawrence KS 66045-2115

WORTH, IRENE, actress; b. Nebr., June 23, 1916. B.Edn., U. Calif. at Los Angeles, 1937; pupil, Elsie Fogarty, London, 1944-45. Formerly tchr. Debut as Fenella in: Escape Me Never, N.Y.C., 1942; Broadway debut as Cecily Harden in: The Two Mrs. Carrolls, 1943; London debut in The Time of Your Life, 1946; following roles, mostly on London stage, include Anabelle Jones in Love Goes to Press, 1946; Ilona Szabo in: The Play's The Thing, 1947; as Eileen Perry in: Edward my Son, 1948; as Lady Fortrose in: Home is Tomorrow, 1948; as Mary Dalton in: Native Son, 1948; title role in: Lucrece, 1948; as Olivia Raines in: Champagne for Delilah, 1949; as Celia Coplestone in: The Cocktail Party, 1949, 50; various roles with Old Vic Repertory Co., London, including Desdemona in Othello; Helena in Midsummer Night's Dream and Lady Macbeth in Macbeth; also Catherine de Vausselles in: The Other Heart, tour to S. Africa, 1952; as Portia in: The Merchant of Venice, 1953; found. mem. Shakespeare Festival Theatre, Stratford, Ont., Can., 1953; as Helena in: All's Well That Ends Well; Queen Margaret in: Richard III, London; appeared as Frances Farrar in: A Day by the Sea, 1953-54; leading role in: The Queen and the Rebels, 1955, Hotel Paradiso, 1956; as Mary Stuart, 1957, The Potting Shed, 1958; Albertine Prine in: Toys in the Attic, 1960 (Page One award); mem., Royal Shakespeare Co., 1962-64; including world tour King Lear, 1964; star: Tiny Alice, N.Y.C., 1964, Aldwych, 1970; Noel Coward trilogy Shadows of the Evening; Hilde in: A Song at Twilight; Anna-Mary in: Come into the Garden Maud (Evening Standard award); Hesione Hushabye in: Heartbreak House (Variety Club Gt. Britain award 1967); Jocasta in: Oedipus, 1968; Hedda in: Hedda Gabler, 1970; with internat. Co., Theatre Research, Paris and Iran, 1971; leading role in: Notes on a Love Affair, 1972; Mme. Arkadina in: The Seagull, 1973; Gertrude in: Hamlet; Mrs. Alving in: Ghosts, 1974; Princess Kosmonopolis in: Sweet Bird of Youth, 1975-76 (Jefferson award, Tony award); Lina in: Misalliance, 1976; Mme. Ranevskaya in: The Cherry Orchard, 1977 (Drama Desk award); Kate in: Old Times, 1977, After the Season, 1978, Happy Days, 1979, Eyewitness, 1980, Coriolanus, 1988, Lost In Yonkers, (Tony award, 1991), Valentina in The Bay at Nice-Royal Nat. Theatre, 1986, Irene Worth's Edith Wharton on tour, 1994 "A Weeks Worth" Almeida Theatre, 1996, Melbourne Festival, 1996; films include; role of Leonie in: Orders to Kill, 1958 (Brit. Film Acad. award), The Scapegoat, 1958, King Lear, 1970, Nicholas and Alexandra, 1971, Rich Kids, 1979, Eyewitness, 1981, Death Trap, 1982, Fast Forward, 1985, Lost in Yonkers, 1993, also numerous radio, TV appearances, Eng., Can., U.S., including; Stella in: The Lake; Ellida Wangel in: The Lady from the Sea (Daily Mail Nat. TV award), also Candida, Duchess of Malfi, Antigone, Prince Orestes, Variations on a Theme, The Way of the World, The Displaced Person; (with Brit. Broadcasting Co.) Coriolanus, 1984; poetry recitals, recs.; (recipient Whitbread Anglo-Am. award outstanding actress 1967). Decorated comdr. Brit. Empire (hon.). Address: Internat Creative Mgmt care Sam Cohn 40 W 57th St Fl 6 New York NY 10019-4001*

WORTH, MARY PAGE, mayor; b. Balt., Jan. 23, 1924; d. Christian Allen and Margaret Pennington (Holbein) Schwarzwaelder; m. William James Worth, Nov. 4, 1947 (dec. May 1986); children: Margaret Page, William Allen, John David III. Student, Ladycliff Coll., Highland Falls, N.Y., 1941-42, Abbott Sch. Art, Washington, 1942-44. Selectman Town of Searsport, Maine, 1973-75; mayor City of Belfast, Maine, 1986—; recreation chmn. Town of Searsport, 1970-72. Del. Rep. State Conv., Maine, 1970-94; pres. Searsport Reps., 1974-76; active ARC Overseas Assn., 1976—; pres. Searsport C. of C., 1976-79; mem. exec. bd. Waldo County Com. for Social Action, Belfast, 1986—; mem. Abnacki coun. Girl Scouts U.S.; tutor Literacy Vols. Am.; recreation specialist ARC, Camp Haugen, Japan, 1946-47; bd. dirs. RSVP-Walto County, Heat Start Waldo County; vol. tchr. Sch. for Blind, Cholon, Republic Vietnam, 1959-61, Am. Sch. at Saigon, Republic Vietnam, 1959-61; club dir. USAF Spl. Svcs., Ft. Meyer, Va., 1962-63, U.S. Army Spl. Svcs., Ft. Belvoir, Va., 1963-64; mem. Congresswoman Olympia Snow's Mpcl. Adv. Bd.; town chair Rep. Party; mem. adv. Belfast History Project. Mem. DAR (officer Maine 1986—), Internat. Platform Assn., Ret. Officers Assn. (life), 11th Airborne Assn./511th Parachute Infantry Regiment Korea War Vets. Assn., Waldo County Humane Soc. (pres. 1990—), Waldo County Law Enforcement (v.p. 1990—), VFW Aux., Am. Legion Aux., Belfast Garden Club (parliamentarian 1984—), Rotary (bd. govs. com. Maine St. '90). Avocations: Great Dane breeding, antiques. Home: 5 Seaside Dr Belfast ME 04915-1235 Office: City of Belfast Mayor's Office 71 Church St Belfast ME 04915-6208

WORTH, MELVIN H., surgeon, educator; b. Norwich, Conn., July 14, 1930; s. Melvin H. and Stella E. (Cline) W.; m. Alice Tenzer, May 17, 1953; children: Nancy, David. AB, Clark U., 1950; MD, NYU, 1954. Diplomate Am. Bd. Surgery. Intern Bellevue Hosp., N.Y.C., 1954-55, resident, 1957-61, dir. trauma svc., 1966-79; dir. surgery S.I. U. Hosp., N.Y.C., 1979—; assoc. prof. NYU, N.Y.C., 1968-69; prof. clin. surgery SUNY, Bklyn., 1979—; prof. surgery Uniformed Svc. U. Health Sci. Ctr., 1996—; chmn. trauma designation com. N.Y.C. Emergency Med. Svc., 1990; mem. Office of Profl. Med. Conduct of N.Y. State, 1983—. Vice chmn. N.Y. State Health Rev. and Planning Coun., 1988-95. Capt. USMC, 1955-57. Fellow ACS, Am. Coll. Gastroenterology; mem. Internat. Soc. Surgery, Soc. Am. Gastrointestinal Endoscopic Surgeons, Am. Assn. for Surgery of Trauma, Assn. Acad. Surgery, Soc. Critical Care Medicine, Assn. Surg. Edn., N.Y. Surg. Soc. (pres. 1989), Alpha Omega Alpha. Home: 3003 Van Ness St NW Washington DC 20008-4809 Office: Staten Island U Hosp 475 Seaview Ave Staten Island NY 10305-3436

WORTHAM, DEBORAH LYNNE, school system director, principal; b. Chgo., May 13, 1949; d. Leon Cabot and Bessie (Summers) Smith; m. Chester Hopes Wortham, Jan. 29, 1972; children: Shelley Sharon, Chester Hopes III. BS, U. Wis., 1972; MS, Morgan State U., 1981. Tchr., reading tchr., support tchr. Balt. City Pub. Schs., 1972-87, asst. prin., 1988-90, prin. Samuel Coleridge Taylor Sch., 1990-94, dir. efficacy, 1994—; program facilitator Balt. Schs.-Johns Hopkins U., 1987-88; dean of edn. Higher Dimensions Learning Ctr., Balt., 1985—. Author: Teaching by Signs and Wonders, 1992. Recipient Mayor's Citation for Volunteerism, Balt., 1982, Am. Best Elem. Sch. for Significant Improvement award Redbook Mag., 1993, 95; cited Administrator's Class Act, Channel ll TV, Balt., 1991. Mem. ASCD, Phi Delta Kappa, Alpha Kappa Alpha. Democrat. Pentecostal. Office: Balt City Pub Schs Bd Edn 200 E North Ave Baltimore MD 21202-5910

WORTHAM, THOMAS RICHARD, English language educator; b. Liberal, Kans., Dec. 5, 1943; s. Tom and Ruth (Cavanaugh) W. AB, Marquette U., 1965; PhD, Ind. U., 1970. From asst. prof. to assoc. prof. UCLA, 1970-82, prof., 1982—, vice-chmn. and dir. undergrad. studies, 1993-97, chmn. dept., 1997—; vis. prof. Am. lit. U. Warsaw, Poland, 1976-77; sr. rsch. fellow Am. Coun. of Learned Socs., 1983-84. Editor: James Russell Lowell's The Biglow Papers: A Critical Edition, 1977, Letters of W. D. Howells, vol. 4, 1892-1901, 1983, The Early Prose Writings of William Dean Howells, 1853-1861, 1990; asst. editor Nineteenth-Century Fiction, 1971-75, mem. adv. bd., 1976-83, co-editor, 1983-86; co-editor Nineteenth-Century Literature, 1986-95, editor, 1995—; mem. editl. bd. The Collected Works of Ralph Waldo Emerson, 1996—. Regent's faculty fellow in the humanities U. Calif., 1971; travel grantee Nat. Endowment for the Humanities, 1985-86, 88-89; grants-in-aid of rsch. Am. Philos. Soc., 1976, 81. Mem. MLA Am. (Norman Foerster prize com. of Am. Lit. sect. 1973, chmn. Pacific coast region, com. on manuscript holdings of Am. Lit. sect. 1972-78, mem. Hubbell prize com. of Am. Lit. sect. 1989-91), Am. Studies Assn., Ralph Waldo Emerson Soc. (bd. dirs. 1992-95), Assn. for Document Editing, Internat. Assn. Univ. Profls. English. Episcopalian. Avocations: breeding and training Arabian horses. Office: U Calif Dept English 405 Hilgard Ave Los Angeles CA 90095-9000

WORTHEN, JOHN EDWARD, academic administrator; b. Carbondale, Ill., July 15, 1933; s. Dewey and Annis Burr (Williams) W.; m. Sandra Damewood, Feb. 27, 1960; children: Samantha Jane, Bradley Edward. BS in Psychology (Univ. Acad. scholar), Northwestern U., 1954; MA in Student Pers. Adminstrn., Columbia U., 1955; EdD in Adminstrn. in Higher Edn. (Coll. Entrance Exam. Bd. fellow), Harvard U., 1964; PhD (hon.), Yeungnam U., Daegu, Korea, 1986. Dean of men Am. U., 1959-61; dir. counseling and testing and asst. prof. edn., 1963-66, asst. to provost and asst. prof., 1966-68, acting provost and v.p. acad. affairs, 1968, assoc. provost for instrn., 1969, v.p. student affairs, 1970-75, v.p. student affairs and adminstrn., 1976-79; pres. Ind. U. of Pa., 1979-84, Ball State U., Muncie, Ind., 1984—; cons. to public schs. Aviator USN, 1955-59. Mem. Am. Assn. Counseling and Devel., Ind. C. of C., Ind. Bus. Modernization and Tech. Corp., First Merchants Corp., Rotary Internat., Phi Delta Kappa, Kappa Delta Pi (dir.).

WORTHEY, CAROL, composer; b. Worcester, Mass., Mar. 1, 1943; d. Bernard Krieger and Edith Lilian (Cramer) Symonds; m. Eugene Worthey III, June 1969 (div. 1980); 1 child, Megan; m. Raymond Edward Korns, Sept. 21, 1980. BA in Music Composition, Columbia U., 1965; grad., Dick Grove Sch. Music., L.A., 1979; grad. filmscoring prog., UCLA, 1978; music studies with Darius Milhaud, Walter Piston, Elliot Carter, Vincent Persichetti, Grant Beglarian, Karl Korte, Otto Luening, Eddy Lawrence Manson, Dick Grove; studied, RISD, 1948-54, Columbia U., 1965. Sr. composer, arranger Celebrity Ctr. Internat. Choir, Hollywood, Calif., 1985—. Composer, arranger The Hollywood Chorale; composer ballets Athena, 1963, The Barren, 1965, piano works performed in France, Italy, Germany, Canada, U.S., Eng. by Mario Feninger, 1992, Pastorale, performed in Mex., 1994, Neighborhood of the Heart, 1994, (choir) Unquenchable Light, 1993, (film score) The Special Visitor, 1992; compositions performed at Aspen Music Festival, 1963, Carnegie Hall, 1954, Dorothy Chandler Pavilion, 1986-89; appeared as singer-songwriter L.A. Songwriter's Showcase, 1977; arranger Merv Griffin Show, 1981, The Night Before Christmas, L.A. Children's Theater, 1988-91, Capistrano Valley Symphony, 1994, Very Old Merry Old Christmas, Dorothy Chandler Pavilion, 1994, Judge, 1994; (CD) David Arkenstone Return of the Guardian, 1996; composer, lyricist, librettist full-length musical The Envelope Please, 1988; author: Treasury of Holiday Music, 1992, (poems) The Lonely Wanderer Comes Home, 1994; art work exhibited RISD, 1952, Folk and Art Mus., L.A., 1975, 1st Internat. Art Exhibit Celebrity Ctr. Pavilion, 1992; cable tv show: Neighborhood of the Heart, 1995, 96. Vol. performer various childcare ctrs., old folks homes, etc.; judge Composer's Competition, Inner City Cultural Ctr., 1995, 96. Recipient Silver Poet award World of Poetry, 1987, 2nd place winner, 1st BarComposers and Songwriters Competition for "Fanfare for Joy & Wedding March", 1990, Golden Poet award World of Poetry, 1992. Mem. Nat. Assn. Composers, USA, Broadcast Music Inc., Nat. Acad. Songwriters, Songwriters and Composers Assn., Toastmasters Internat. (Competent Toastmaster 1996), Film Adv. Bd. Jewish. Avocations: gourmet cooking, films, macrame, creative writing, calligraphy.

WORTHING, CAROL MARIE, minister; b. Duluth, Minn., Dec. 27, 1934; d. Truman James and Helga Maria (Bolander) W.; children: Gregory Alan Beatty, Graydon Ernest Beatty. BS, U. Minn., 1965; MDiv, Northwestern Theol. Seminary, 1982; DMin, Grad. Theol. Found., Notre Dame, Ind., 1988; MBA in Ch. Mgmt., Grad. Theol. Found., Donaldson, Ind., 1993. Secondary educator Ind. (Minn.) Sch. Dist., 1965-78; teaching fellow U. Minn., 1968-70; contract counselor Luth. Social Svc., Duluth, 1976-78; media cons. Luth. Media Svcs., St. Paul, 1978-80; asst. pastor Messiah Luth. Ch., Fargo, N.D., 1982-83; vice pastor Messiah Luth. Ch., Fargo, 1983-84; assoc. editor Luth. Ch. Am. Ptnrs., Phila., 1982-84; editorial assoc. Luth. Ptnrs. Evang. Luth. Ch. Am., Phila. and Mpls., 1984—; parish pastor Resurrection Luth. Ch., Pierre, S.D., 1984-89; assoc. pastor Bethlehem Luth. Ch., Cedar Falls, Iowa, 1989-90; exec. dir. Ill. Conf. Chs., Springfield, 1990-96, Tex. Conf. of Chs., 1996—; mem. pub. rels. and interpretation com. Red River Valley Synod, Fargo, 1984-86, mem. ch. devel., Pierre, 1986-87; mem. mgmt. com. office comm. Luth. Ch. in Am., N.Y.C., Phila., 1984-88; mem. mission ptnrs. S.D. Synod, 1988, chmn. assembly resolutions com., 1988; mem. pre-assembly planning com., ecumenics com., chmn. resolutions com. N.E. Iowa Synod, 1989-90; mem. ch. and society com., 1990-96; ecumenical com., 1995-96; Luth. Ecumenical Rep. Network, 1995-96; Cen. and So. Ill. Synod, 1996—, S.W. Tex. Synod; nat. edn. cons. Am. Film Inst., Washington, 1967-70; chaplain state legis. bodies, Pierre, 1984-89. Author: Cinematics and English, 1967, Peer Counseling, 1977, Tischrede Lexegete, 1986, 88, 90, Way of the Cross, Way of Justice Walk, 1987, Introducing Collaboration as a Leadership Stance and Style in an Established Statewide Conference of Churches, 1993. Co-facilitator Parents of Retarded Children, 1985; bd. dirs. Countryside Hospice, 1985; cons. to adminstrv. bd. Mo. Shores Women's Ctr., 1986. Mem. NAFE, Nat. Assn. Ecumenical Staff (chair of site selection com. 1991-92, chair of scholarship com. 1993-94, mem. profl. devel. com. 1993-94, chair program planning com. 1996, bd. dirs. 1995-96), Pierre-Ft. Pierre Ministerium (v.p. 1986-87, pres. 1987-88). Democrat. Avocations: writing prose and poetry, concerts, theater, art, photography. Home: 3816 S Lamar Blvd #3302 Austin TX 78704 Office: Tex Confs Chs 1033 La Posada Dr Ste 225 Austin TX 78752-3824 *Ecumenism is, I believe, about full coherence between our ecclesiology and our ethics. The Spirit of God calls the church to come together for a compassionate purpose: to respond to all who suffer, so that the world might be transformed into God's own vision of peace, justice, and love.*

WORTHINGTON, GEORGE RHODES, retired naval officer; b. Louisville, July 11, 1937; s. William Bowman and Elizabeth (Frost) W.; m. Sydna Anne Alexander, Mar. 28, 1981 (div. Oct. 1990); children: Rhodes Ballard, Graham Rankins, Greer Anne. BS, U.S. Naval Acad., 1961; postgrad., USMC, Quantico, Va., 1975-76, Nat. War Coll., 1978-79. Commd. ensign USN, 1961, advanced through grades to rear adm., 1989; communications officer USS Halsey Powell USN, San Diego, 1961-63, flag lt., aide comdr. cruiser-destroyer Flotilla Seven, 1963-65; exec. officer Underwater Demolition Team Eleven USN, Coronado, Calif., 1965-68; ops. officer USS Strong USN, Charleston, S.C., 1969-71; exec. officer Naval Spl. Warfare Group USN, Saigon, Vietnam, 1971-72; comdg. officer Seal Team One USN, Coronado, 1972-74; naval attache Def. Attache Office USN, Phnom Penh, Cambodia, 1974-75; comdg. officer Undersea Warfare Group One USN, Coronado, 1976-78; program sponsor Office of Chief of Naval Ops. USN, Washington, 1979-85; comdr. Naval Spl. Warfare Group One Naval Spl. Warfare Group One, Coronado, 1985-87; chief of staff Spl. Ops. Command Europe USN, Stuttgart, Fed. Republic Germany, 1987-88; dep. asst. sec. of def. (spl. ops.) Def. Dept., Washington, 1988-89; comdr. Naval Spl. Warfare Command, Coronado, 1989-92; mktg. agent, cons. PIDEAC Inc., Coronado, 1992—; cons. IFG Ltd., Vantage Systems, Inc., Burdeshaw Assoc., Inc., WarRoom Rsch., LLC; v.p. IBD, Inc. Decorated D.S.M., Legion of Merit (2), Def. Superior Svc. medal, Meritorious Svc. medal, Navy Combat Action ribbon. Mem. TROA (past chpt. pres.), Mayflower Soc. D.C., Naval Acad. Alumni Assn., Naval Inst., (past pres.), Navy League San Diego, MILMEC, Army-Navy Club, Army-Navy Country Club. Republican. Episcopalian. Avocations: masters swimming, skiing, sport parachuting. Address: 11000 Adella Ave # 4 Coronado CA 92118

WORTHINGTON, JANET EVANS, academic director, English language educator; b. Springfield, Ill., Jan. 30, 1942; d. Orville Ray and Helen May (Tuxhorn) Evans; m. Gary H. Worthington; children: Rachael Allene, Evan Edmund, Adam Nicholas Karl. Student, Blackburn Coll., 1960-62; BA in English Lang. and Lit., U. Chgo., 1965; MA in English, U. Iowa, 1969; PhD in English Edn., Fla. State U., 1977; postgrad., W. Va. Inst. Tech., 1981-82, Rensselaer Poly. Inst., 1984. Teaching. fellow Fla. State U., Tallahassee, 1971-72, grad. assistant, 1972-73; coord. lang. arts rsch. Piedmont Schs. Project, Greer, S.C., 1973-76; English instr. Woodrow Wilson High Sch., Beckley, W.Va., 1976-77; Reading specialist, adj. instr. in English W. Va. Inst. Tech., Montgomery, W.Va., 1977-78; asst. prof. W.Va. Inst. Tech., Montgomery, 1979-82, assoc. prof., 1983-87, prof. English, 1987-88; dir. W.Va. Inst. Tech., Oak Hill, 1988-90; tech. writing program coord. Community and Tech. Coll. W.Va. Inst. Tech., Montgomery, 1983-88; dir. continuing edn. Nicholls State U., Thibodaux, La., 1990—; tech. writing cons., various bus., 1986—, Dept. of Mines, State of W.Va., 1980-81; reading cons. Dept of Mines, 1980-81, Mt. Hope (W.Va.) High Sch., 1980-81, Reading Tchrs. Study Group, Kanawha County, W.Va., 1981-83; project mgr. Dept. of Mines, State of W.Va., 1981-83, Dept. of Nat. Resources, State of W.Va., 1984-85; involved in curriculum devel. for various depts., W.Va. Inst. Tech., 1973-90, Raleigh County Schs., Beckley, W.Va., Piedmont Schs. Project, Greer, S.C., English and reading instr. Upward Bound Program, W.Va. Inst. Tech., 1980-85; adj. instr. W.Va. Coll. Grad. Studies, 1979, 81, 83. Author (with William Burns): Practical Robotics: Systems, Interfacing, and Applications, 1986, (with A.B. Somers): Candles and Mirrors: Response Guides for Teaching Novels and Plays in Grades Six through Twelve, 1984, Response Guides for Teaching Children's Books, 1979; editorial bd.: W.Va. Community Coll. Jour.; reviewer: Macmillan Pub. Co. texts, 1985; editor: Diamond Shamrock, 1985; co-producer, host (TV series): About the Author; contbr. numerous articles to profl. jours.; participated in numerous presentations. Mem. W.Va. Community Coll. Assn.; bd.dirs., Curtain Callers, 1979-89, Fayette Fine Arts Coun., 1986-87; promotions chair, W.Va. Children's Book award com., 1984-85. Mem. AAUW (recording sec. 1983-85, pres. 1985—), Assn. for Tchrs. of Tech. Writing, Nat. Assn. for Devel. Edn., Soc. for Tech. Comm. Home: 112 E Garden Dr Thibodaux LA 70301-3750 Office: Nicholls State U Continuing Edn PO Box 2011 Thibodaux LA 70310

WORTHINGTON, J.B., business executive. Dir. strategic planning Kerr-McGee Corp., Oklahoma City, Okla. Office: Kerr-McGee Corp PO Box 25861 Oklahoma City OK 73125

WORTHINGTON, MELVIN LEROY, minister, writer; b. Greenville, N.C., June 17, 1937; s. Wilbur Leroy and Alma Lee (Braxton) W.; m. Anne Katherine Wilson, Sept. 12, 1959; children: Daniel Edward, Lydia Anne. Diploma, Imperial Detective Acad., Cin., 1965; B.Bibl.Edn., Columbia Bible Coll., S.C., 1959; B.Th., Luther Rice Sem., Jacksonville, Fla., 1967, B.Div., 1969, M.Th., 1970, D.Th., 1974; M.Ed., Ga. State U.-Atlanta, 1979. Ordained to ministry, Central Conf. Free Will Baptists, 1957. Pastor Union Chapel Free Will Bapt. Ch., Chocowinity, N.C., 1959-62, Palmetto Free Will Bapt. Ch., Vanceboro, N.C., 1959-62, First Free Will Bapt. Ch., Darlington, S.C., 1962-66, Wesconnett Free Will Bapt. Ch., Jacksonville, Fla., 1967; pastor First Free Will Bapt. Ch., Amory, Miss., 1967-72, Albany, Ga., 1972-79; exec. sec. Nat. Assn. Free Will Bapt., Inc., Nashville, 1979—, chmn. Sunday Sch. bd., 1975-77, asst. moderator, 1977-79, chmn. grad. study com., 1976-77; clk. S.C. State Assn. Free Will Bapt., Florence, 1966-67; asst. moderator Ga. State Assn. Free Will Bapt., Moultrie, 1973-74, moderator, 1975-79; pres. Ga. Bible Inst., Albany, 1978. Editor in chief: Contact mag., 1979—, author editorial, 1980—; contbr. articles to profl. jours. Adv. bd. Nat. Fedn. Decency, 1985; nat. bd. dirs. Christian Leaders for Responsible TV, 1986. Mem. Evang. Press Assn., Religious Conf. Mgmt. Assn. (dir. 1983, v.p. 1986, pres. 1989-92), Nashville C. of C., Future Farmers Am. (N.C. Farmer degree 1955, Am. Farmer degree 1957). Democrat. Home: 3308 Timber Trail Dr Antioch TN 37013-1011 Office: Nat Assn Free Will Bapt Inc 5233 Mount View Rd Antioch TN 37013-2306 *The basic principle which has guided, governed and guarded my life has been a burning desire to find, follow and finish the will of God.*

WORTHINGTON, PATRICIA, elementary education educator; b. Mineola, N.Y., Sept. 25, 1948; d. George Edward and Thelma (Carson) Donnelly; m. Michael Worthington, July 16, 1977. BS, Parsons Coll., Fairfield, Iowa, 1970; postgrad., Morningside Coll., Davenport, Iowa, Drake U. Cert. tchr., Iowa. Elem. tchr. Gilmore City (Iowa) Bradgate Comunity Sch., 1970—; co-chmn. Phase III, Iowa Dept. Edn.; chairperson for Cmty. Svc. Grant, 1996. Career edn. grantee, 1977, Roy J. Carver grantee Nat. Geog. Kids Network, 1990. Mem. Iowa Edn. Assn. (past sec.-treas., pres.). Home: 2014 W River Dr Humboldt IA 50548-2634 Office: 412 S E Ave Gilmore City IA 50541

WORTHINGTON, WALTER THOMAS, career military officer; b. Kinston, N.C., Jan. 5, 1940; s. Anthony Pelt and Mary Alma (Wilson) W.; m. Marilyn Jane Sutton, Apr. 11, 1964; 1 child, Charles Anthony. BS, East Carolina Coll., 1963. Commd. officer USAF, advanced through grades to major gen.; dir. joint ops. planning & execution sys. project group USAF, MacDill AFB, Fla., 1986-87, dep. dir. employment U.S. Transportation Command, 1987-88; comdr. 836th Air Divsn. USAF, Davis-Monthan AFB, Ariz., 1988-90; vice comdr. 12th Air Force & U.S. Southern Air Forces USAF, Bergstrom AFB, Tex., 1990-92; dep. comdr. in chief, chief of staff U.S. Southern Command USAF, Quarry Heights, Panama, 1992-94; comdr. Air Force Security Assistance Ctr. USAF, Wright-Patterson AFB, Ohio, 1994—. Mem. Air Force Assn., Air War Coll. Assn., Order of Daedalians. Avocations: golf, reading, flying. Home: 430 Metzger Dr Wright Patterson AFB OH 45433

WORTHLEY, HAROLD FIELD, minister, educator; b. Brewer, Maine, Nov. 3, 1928; s. Herbert Morrison and Aline May (Field) W.; m. Barbara Louise Bent, June 25, 1955; children—Susan Louise Field, Laura May, David Bruce. A.B., Boston U., 1950, M.A., 1951; S.T.B., Harvard Div. Sch., 1954, S.T.M., 1956, Th.D., 1970. Ordained to ministry United Ch. of Christ, 1954. Minister Congl. chs., Maine, N.H., Mass., 1951-62; assoc. prof. religion and chaplain Wheaton Coll., Norton, Mass., 1963-77; exec. sec., archivist Congl. Christian Hist. Soc., Boston, 1971—; librarian Congl. Library, Boston, 1977—; editor Bull. of Congl. Library, 1976—, Hist. Intelligencer, 1980-86. Author: Inventory of the Records of the Particular Churches of Massachusetts, 1620-1805, 1970; contbr. articles to profl. jours. Fellow Pilgrim Soc., Congl. Christian Hist. Soc.; mem. United Ch. of Christ Hist. Council. Home: 14 Mansfield Ave Norton MA 02766-2212 Office: The Congregational Libr 14 Beacon St Boston MA 02108-3704

WORTHY, JAMES CARSON, management educator; b. Midland, Tex., Jan. 8, 1910; s. James Arthur and Minnie (Gressett) W.; m. Mildred Leritz, June 20, 1934; 1 dau., Joan (Mrs. Robert Wood Tullis). Student, Northwestern U., 1929-33; AB, Lake Forest Coll., 1952, LLD (hon.), 1961; LLD, Chgo. Theol. Sem., 1960; LittD (hon.), Sangamon State U., 1991. Employment mgr. Schuster & Co., Milw., 1936-38; mem. personnel staff Sears, Roebuck & Co., Chgo., 1938-50; dir. employee relations Sears, Roebuck & Co., 1950-53, asst. to chmn. bd., 1955, vice pres. pub. relations, 1956-61; v.p. Cresap, McCormick & Paget, 1962-72; prof. Sangamon State U., Springfield, Ill., 1972-78; prof. J.L. Kellogg Grad. Sch. Mgmt. Northwestern U., Evanston, Ill., 1978-96, prof. emeritus, 1996—; asst. dep. adminstr. NRA, Washington, 1933-36; asst. sec. commerce, 1953-55; Industry mem. spl. panel WSB, 1952; mem. President's Com. on Govt. Contracts, 1953-55, President's Commn. on Campaign Costs, 1961-62; Mem. Ill. Bd. of Higher Edn., 1967-69. Bd. dirs. Nat. Merit Scholarship Corp., 1958-63; mem. exec. bd. Indsl. Relations Research Assn., 1952-54; pres. Sears-Roebuck Found., 1956-61; trustee Chgo. Theol. Sem., 1953-73; dir. Selected Am. Shares, 1961-79,Comml. Credit Co., 1975-81, Control Data Corp., 1979-87, William C. Norris Inst., 1987—; co-chmn. Ill. Citizens for Eisenhower-Nixon, 1952; pres. United Rep. Fund of Ill., 1959-60; mem. Nat. Rep. Finance Com., 1958-60; del. Rep. Nat. Conv., 1960; pres. Republican Citizens League Ill., 1961-62. Fellow Acad. Mgmt. (Dean of Fellows 1987-90), Internat. Acad. Mgmt.; mem. Commercial Club, Univ. Club (Chgo.), Indian Hill Club (Winnetka, Ill.). Congregationalist. Home: 23 Calvin Cir Evanston IL 60201-1911 Office: Northwestern U JL Kellogg Grad Sch Mgmt Evanston IL 60201

WORTHY, K(ENNETH) MARTIN, lawyer; b. Dawson, Ga., Sept. 24, 1920; s. Kenneth Spencer and Jeffrie Pruett (Martin) W.; m. Eleanor Vreeland Blewett, Feb. 15, 1947 (dec. July 1981); children: Jeffrie Martin, William Blewett; m. Katherine Teasley Jackson, June 17, 1983. Student, The Citadel, 1937-39; B.Ph., Emory U., 1941, J.D. with honors, 1947; MBA cum laude, Harvard U., 1943. Bar: Ga. 1947, D.C. 1948. Assoc. Hopkins & Sutter (formerly Hamel & Park), Washington, 1948-51, ptnr., 1952-69, 72-90, sr. counsel, 1991—; asst. gen. counsel Treasury Dept., 1969-72; chief counsel IRS, 1969-72; dir. Beneficial Corp., 1977-96, emeritus, 1996—; mem. Nat. Coun. Organized Crime, 1970-72; cons. Justice Dept., 1972-74. Author: (with John M. Appleman) Basic Estate Planning, 1957; contbr. articles to profl. jours. Del. Montgomery County Civic Fedn., 1951-61, D.C. Area Health and Welfare Coun., 1960-61; mem. coun. Emory U. Law Sch., 1976—, chmn., 1993-95; trustee Chelsea Sch., 1981—, St. John's Coll., Annapolis, Md. and Santa Fe, 1987-93, 95—, Sherman Found., Newport Beach, Calif., 1991—, Ga. Wildness Inst., 1997—; chmn. dept. fin. Episcopal Diocese, Washington, 1969-70; fellow Aspen Inst., 1982-92. Capt. AUS, 1943-46, U.S. Army, 1951-52. Recipient Army Commendation Ribbon, 1945, Treasury Exceptional Svc. award and medal, 1972, IRS Commrs. award, 1972, Disting. Alumnus award Emory U., 1992. Fellow Am. Bar Found., Am. Coll. Tax Counsel (bd. regents 1980-88, chmn. 1985-87), Atlantic Coun. (counselor); mem. ABA (coun. taxation sect. 1965-69, 72-75, chmn. 1973-74, del. Nat. Conf. Lawyers and CPAs 1981-87, ho. of dels. 1983-89, chmn. audit com. 1985-90), Fed. Bar Assn. (nat. coun. 1969-72, 77-79), Ga. Bar Assn., D.C. Bar, Am. Law Inst., Nat. Tax Assn., Am. Tax Policy Inst. (trustee 1989—), Chevy Chase Club, Met. Club, Sea Island Club, Harvard

Club N.Y.C., Phi Delta Theta, Phi Delta Phi, Omicron Delta Kappa. Home: PO Box 30264 189 W Gascoigne 18th Ave Sea Island GA 31561 Office: Hopkins & Sutter 888 16th St NW Fl 7 Washington DC 20006-4103

WORTHY, PATRICIA MORRIS, municipal official, lawyer; b. Fort Benning, Ga., May 28, 1944; d. Walter and Ruby Mae (Lovett) Morris. AA, Queensborough Community Coll., 1964; BA, Bklyn. Coll., 1966; JD, Howard U., 1969. Bar: D.C. 1971. Trial atty. NLRB, Washington, 1969-71; dep. gen. counsel ACTION, Washington, 1971-74; assoc. Dolphin, Branton, Stafford & Webber, Washington, 1974-77; dep. asst. sec. for regulatory functions HUD, Washington, 1977-80; adj. prof. Howard U. Sch. Law, 1979-92; chmn. D.C. Pub. Service Commn., 1980-91, Washington Met. Area Transit Commn., 1980-91; chief of staff Office of Mayor Sharon Pratt Kelly, Washington, 1991-92; prof. law Howard U., Washington, 1992—; bd. dirs. Yankee Energy System, Inc.; chmn. D.C. Jud. Nomination Commn.; mem. adv. bd. Afro-Am. Datanamics, Inc. Bd. dirs. Nat. Black Child Devel. Inst., 1975-80, Anacostia Econ. Devel. Corp., 1970-74; chmn. Occupl. Safety and Health Bd., Washington, 1979-80; trustee WETA-TV Channel 26, 1984-94. Mem. ABA, Nat. Conf. Black Lawyers, Nat. Conf. Bar Examiners (multistate profl. responsibility com. 1986-89), World Peace Through Law (chairperson young lawyers sect. 1973-75). Office: Howard U Sch Law Van Ness & Connecticut Ave NW Washington DC 20001

WORTLEY, GEORGE CORNELIUS, government affairs consultant, investor; b. Syracuse, N.Y., Dec. 8, 1926; s. George C. and Arlene (Hirsh) W.; m. Barbara Jane Hennessy, May 13, 1950; children: George C. IV, Ann Wortley Lavin, Elizabeth Wortley Ring. B.S., Syracuse U., 1948. Newspaper pub., pres. Manlius Pub. Corp., Fayetteville, N.Y., 1950-92; pres. Nat. Editorial Found., 1968-73; mem. 97th-100th Congresses from 27th N.Y. Dist., 1981-89, mem. Banking, Fin. and Urban Affairs com., mem. Select Com. on Aging, Select Com. on Children, Youth and Family; pvt. bus. cons., investor Washington, 1989—, Sunrise Holdings, Inc., Washington, 1993—; pres. Am. Newspapers Reps., 1966-68. Pres. Hiawatha coun. Boy Scouts Am., 1972-75; mem. Nat. Commn. on Hist. Publs. and Records, 1977-80, Fayetteville Sr. Citizen Housing Commn., 1977-80; mem. allocations com. United Way of Ctrl. N.Y., 1979-81; mem. pub. rels. com. St. Camillus Health Care Ctr., 1971-78; mem. fed. legis. com. Am. Lung Assn., 1974-77; bd. dirs. Crouse-Irving Meml. Hosp. Found., 1975-87, pres. 1979-81; bd. dirs. Am. Heart Assn., N.Y., 1960-80, chmn. pub. rels. com., 1970-74, chmn. legis. com. 1977, mem. fund raising adv. com., 1974-79; trustee Cazenovia Coll., 1981-94; bd. dirs. Onondaga Hist. Assn., 1980-90; dir. Global Leadership Inst., 1987—. Served with MMR, USNR, WWII. Recipient Silver Beaver award Boy Scouts Am., 1973, Silver Antelope award, 1981. Mem. Nat. Newspaper Assn. (legis. com. 1976-80), Greater Syracuse C. of C. (dir. 1979-81), Upstate Coun. Indsl. Editors, LeMoyne Coll. Pres.'s Assocs., Syracuse U. Alumni Asn. (nat. treas. 1973-77), Chavaliers du Testabin, Cosmos Club, Century Club, Georgetown Club, Lions, KC, Kappa Sigma (pres. 1957-59). Republican. Roman Catholic. Office: 1350 I St NW Ste 200 Washington DC 20005-3305

WORTMAN, RICHARD S., historian, educator; b. N.Y.C., Mar. 24, 1938; s. Joseph R. and Ruth (Nacht) W.; m. Marlene Stein, June 14, 1960; 1 child, Leonie. B.A., Cornell U., 1958; M.A., U. Chgo., 1960, Ph.D., 1964. Instr. history U. Chgo., 1963-64, asst. prof., 1964-69, asso. prof., 1969-76, prof., 1976-77; prof. history Princeton U., 1977-88, dir. Russian studies, 1982-88; prof. history Columbia U., 1988—; trustee Nat. Council for Soviet and Eastern European Research, 1983-89; sr. fellow Harriman Inst., 1985-86. Author: The Crisis of Russian Populism, 1967, The Development of a Russian Legal Consciousness, 1976, (with Leopold Haimson and Ziva Galili) The Making of Three Russian Revolutionaries: Voices from the Menshevik Past, 1987, Scenarios of Power: Myth and Ceremony in Russian Monarchy, vol. I, 1995. Social Sci. Research Council grantee, 1975-76; Guggenheim fellow, 1981-82. Mem. Am. Assn. Advancement Slavic Studies (pres. Mid-Atlantic Slavic Conf. 1982-83), AAUP., Am. Hist. Assn. Home: 410 Riverside Dr Apt 91 New York NY 10025-7924

WORTMANN, DOROTHY WOODWARD, physician; b. Easton, Pa., Mar. 14, 1945; d. Robert Simpson III and Esther (Thomas) Woodward; m. Robert Lewis Wortmann, June 14, 1969; children: Jonathan Thomas, William Lewis. BA, Mount Holyoke Coll., 1967; MD, U. Kans. Sch. Medicine, 1971. Diplomate Am. Bd. Pediatrics, subspecialty pediat. rheumatology. Clin. instr. pediatrics Med. Coll. Wis., Milw., 1979-80, instr. pediatrics, 1980-82, asst. prof. pediatrics, 1982-92; assoc. clin. prof. pediatrics East Carolina U. Sch. Medicine, Greenville, N.C., 1993—; med. dir. rheumatology Children's Hosp. Wis., Milw., 1980-92. chair for juvenile arthritis and mem. pub. and patient svcs. com. Arthritis Found., Milw., 1981-92; med. adv. bd. Lupus Found., Milw., 1983-92. Recipient Disting. Svc. award Arthritis Found., 1991. Fellow Am. Acad. Pediatrics (mem. exec. coun. for rheumatology 1993—), Am. Coll. Rheumatology (mem. sect. pediat. rheumatology); mem. N.C. Med. Soc. Office: East Carolina U. Sch Medicine Dept Pediatrics Brody Med Scis Bldg Greenville NC 27858

WORZEL, JOHN LAMAR, geophysicist, educator; b. West Brighton, S.I., N.Y., Feb. 21, 1919; s. Howard Henry and Marie Alma (Wilson) W.; m. Dorothy Crary, Nov. 22, 1941; children: Sandra, Howard, Richard, William P. B.S. in Engring. Physics, Lehigh U., 1940; M.A. in Geophysics (grad. resident scholar), Columbia U., 1948, Ph.D., 1949. Research assoc. Woods Hole (Mass.) Oceanographic Inst., 1940-46; geodesist Columbia U., N.Y.C., 1946-48; research assoc. Columbia U., 1948-49, instr. geology, 1949, asst. prof., 1950-52, assoc. prof., 1952-57, prof., 1957-72; asst. dir. Lamont Geol. Obs., Palisades, N.Y., 1951-64; acting dir. Lamont Geol. Obs., 1964-65, assoc. dir., 1965-72; prof., dep. dir. earth and planetary scis. div. Marine Biomed. Inst., U. Tex. Med. Br., Galveston, 1972-74; acting dir. geophys. lab. Marine Sci. Inst., 1974-75, dir. geophys. lab., 1975-79; also prof. geol. sci. dept. U. Tex. at Austin, 1972-79; adj. prof. Rice U., 1974-78; ret., 1979; Bd. dirs. Palisades Geophys. Inst., 1970—, treas., 1970-74, pres., 1974—. Bd. dirs. Rockland County council Boy Scouts Am., 1964-72. Recipient USN Meritorious Pub. Service citation Dept. of Navy, 1964; Guggenheim Found. fellow, 1963. Fellow Internat. Assn. Geodesy, Am. Geophys. Union, Geol. Soc. Am.; mem. Soc. Exploration Geophysicists (chmn. com. 1974-76, v.p. 1978-79), Pi Mu Epsilon, Tau Beta Pi. Republican. Lutheran. Research on gravity and seismic refraction and reflection at sea, sound transmission of sea water. Home: Apt A-308 8117 Blue Heron Dr E Wilmington NC 28405

WÖSSNER, MARK MATTHIAS, business executive; b. Berlin, Oct. 14, 1938; m. Anna Hvastija, Mar. 30, 1991. Dr. Ing., Tech. U., Karlsruhe, Germany, 1968. Mgmt. asst. Bertelsmann, Gütersloh, Germany, 1968; with tech. works mgmt. Bertelsmann/Mohndruck, Gütersloh, Germany, 1970, tech. dir., 1972, gen. mgr., 1974; exec mem. Bertelsmann, Gütersloh, 1976, bd. dir., dep. chmn., 1981, chmn., CEO, 1983. Office: Bertelsmann AG Zentrale Offentlichkeitsarbeit, Postfach 111, D-33311 Gutersloh Germany

WOSZCZYK, WIESLAW RICHARD, audio engineering educator, researcher; b. Czestochowa, Poland, Jan. 9, 1951; arrived in Can., 1974; s. Waclaw Konstanty and Krystyna Maria (Malek) W.; m. Trudy Elizabeth Erickson, Dec. 28, 1978; children: Jake, Magda. MA, State Acad. Music, Warsaw, Poland, 1974; PhD, Chopin Acad., Warsaw, 1984. Rsch. asst. McGill U., Montreal, Can., 1974-75; recording engineer Basement Recording Co. Inc., N.Y.C., 1975-76; sound dir. Harry Belafonte Enterprises Inc., N.Y.C., 1977; chief engr. Big Apple Recording Studios, N.Y.C., 1976-78; asst. prof. McGill U., Montreal, 1978-84, chmn. grad. studies in sound recording, 1979—, assoc. prof., 1984-91, full prof., 1991—; tech. dir. McGill Records, Montreal, 1987—; owner, cons. Sonologic Registered, Montreal, 1988—; chmn. internat. conf. TV Sound Today and Tomorrow, 1991; vis. prof. Bang and Olufsen A/S, Denmark, 1994. Recording engr. over 50 records and films, 1975-85; prodr. over 30 compact discs, 1985—; mem. rev. bd. Jour. Audio Engring., 1992; contbr. articles to profl. jours. Recipient Grand Prix du Disque award Can. Coun. for Arts, 1978, Bd. Govs. award Audio Engring. Soc., 1991; Major Rsch. SSHRC grantee Rsch. Coun. Can., 1986, 93; Indsl. grantee Sony Classical, 1992, Bruel & Kjaer, 1991. Mem. Audio Engring. Soc. (gov., chmn. membership com. 1991—), Acoustical Soc. Am., Sigma Xi. Roman Catholic. Achievements include 3 patents on audio transducers; major rsch. on the design and application of transducers for music recording, auditory design in sound recording, multi-channel sound recording, reprodn. and audio-visual interactions. Office: McGill U Faculty Music, 555 Sherbrooke St W, Montreal, PQ Canada H3A 1E3

WOTIZ, JOHN HENRY, chemist, educator; b. Ostrava, Czech Republic, Apr. 12, 1919; came to U.S., 1939, naturalized, 1944; s. Berthold B. and Bertha (Kauder) W.; m. Kathryn Erdody, Feb. 23, 1945; children: Anita, Karen, Vivian. Student, Czech Polytechnicum, Prague, 1937; B.S., Furman U., 1941; M.S., U. Richmond, 1943; Ph.D., Ohio State U., 1948. Instr. U. Pitts., 1948-50, asst. prof., 1950-54, assoc. prof., 1954-57; group leader research center Diamond Alkali Co., Painesville, Ohio, 1957-59; sr. group leader Diamond Alkali Co., 1959-62; prof., chmn. chemistry dept. Marshall U., Huntington, W.Va., 1962-67, So. Ill. U., Carbondale, 1967-68; prof. So. Ill. U., 1968-89, prof. emeritus, 1989—; Nat. Acad. Scis. vis. prof., USSR, 1969, Eastern Europe, 1972; vis. prof., lectr., East Asian and Pacific Ocean countries, 1974, Japan, 1982, Gt. Britain, Fed. Republic Germany, Norway, Sweden, Czechoslovakia, Poland, Hungary, 1987, Peoples Republic China, 1988, Can., India, 1990; past cons. Air Reduction Co., Watson Standard Co.; pres. Glenview Press, Carbondale, Ill. Editor: The Kekulé Riddle: A Challenge for Chemists and Psychologists, 1993. contbr. articles to profl. jours. Served as lt., Chem. Corps AUS, 1946-48. Recipient Univ. gold medal Vysoká Škola Báňská in Ostrava, Czech Republic, 1992. Mem. Am. Chem. Soc. (chmn. div. history of chemistry 1979-80, chmn. of So. Ill. Section, 1992, bd. dirs. Ctr. for History of Chemistry, Internat. Dexter award for outstanding contbns. to history of chemistry 1982), History of Sci. Soc., AAUP, Am. Contract Bridge League, Sigma Xi. Unitarian-Universalist. Home: 903 S Glenview Dr Carbondale IL 62901-2438

WOTRING, MELANIE JEAN See HASTINGS, MELANIE

WOTT, JOHN ARTHUR, arboretum and botanical garden executive, horticulture educator; b. Fremont, Ohio, Apr. 10, 1939; s. Arthur Otto Louis and Esther Wilhelmina (Werth) W.; children: Christopher, Timothy, Holly. BS, Ohio State U., 1961; MS, Cornell U., 1966, PhD, 1968. Mem. staff Ohio State Coop. Extension Svc., Bowling Green, 1961-64; rsch. asst. Cornel U., Ithaca, N.Y., 1964-68; prof. Purdue U., West Lafayette, Ind., 1968-81; prof. Ctr. Urban Horticulture U. Wash., Seattle, 1981—; assoc. dir. Ctr. Urban Horticulture U. Wash., Seattle, 1990-93; dir. arboreta Washington Park Arboretum, Seattle, 1993—. Contbr. numerous papers to profl. jours. Mem. Am. Soc. Horticultural Sci. (com. chmn. 1967-82), Am. Assn. Botanic Gardens and Arboreta, Internat. Plant Propagators Soc. (pres. 1984, sec.-treas. 1985—). Avocations: music, antiques. Office: Washington Park Arboretum U Wash Box 358010 Seattle WA 98195-8010

WOUK, HERMAN, writer; b. N.Y.C., May 27, 1915; s. Abraham Isaac and Esther (Levine) W.; m. Betty Sarah Brown, Dec. 9, 1945; children: Abraham Isaac (dec.), Nathaniel, Joseph. AB with gen. honors, Columbia U., 1934; LHD (hon.), Yeshiva U., 1954; LLD (hon.), Clark U., 1960; LittD (hon.), Am. Internat. Coll., 1979; PhD (hon.), Bar-Ilan U., 1990, Hebrew U., 1997. Writer radio programs for various comedians N.Y.C., 1935; asst. writer weekly radio scripts comedian Fred Allen, 1936-41; Presdl. cons. to U.S. Treasury, 1941; vis. prof. English Yeshiva U., 1952-57; scholar-in-residence Aspen Inst. Humanistic Studies, 1973-74. Author: novels: Aurora Dawn, 1947, The City Boy, 1948, Slattery's Hurricane, 1949, The Caine Mutiny, 1951 (Pulitzer Prize award for fiction 1952), Marjorie Morningstar, 1955, Youngblood Hawke, 1962, Don't Stop the Carnival, 1965, The Winds of War, 1971, War and Remembrance, 1978, Inside, Outside, 1985 (Washingtonian Book award 1986), The Hope, 1993, The Glory, 1994; dramas: The Traitor, 1949, The Caine Mutiny Court-Martial, 1953; comedy: Nature's Way, 1957; non-fiction: This is My God, 1959; screenplays for TV serials: The Winds of War, 1983, War and Remembrance, 1986. Trustee Coll. of V.I., 1961-69; bd. dirs. Washington Nat. Symphony, 1969-71, Kennedy Ctr. Prodns., 1974-75. Exec. officer U.S.S. Southard USNR, 1942-46, PTO. Recipient Richard H. Fox prize, 1934, Columbia U. medal for Excellence, 1952, Alexander Hamilton medal, 1980, U. Calif.-Berkeley medal, 1984, Golden Plate award Am. Acad. Achievement, 1986, USN Meml. Found. 'Lone Sailor' award, 1987, Yad Vashem KaZetnik award, 1990. Mem. Naval Res. Assn., Dramatists Guild, Authors Guild, Internat. Platform Assn. (Ralph Waldo Emerson award 1981), PEN. Jewish. Clubs: Bohemian (San Francisco); Cosmos, Metropolitan (Washington); Century Assn. (N.Y.C.). Office: care BSW Literary Agy 3255 N St NW Washington DC 20007-2845

WOVSANIKER, ALAN, lawyer, educator; b. Newark, Mar. 19, 1953; s. Harold and Sally (Gooen) W.; m. Susan Orme, Aug. 23, 1987. AB, Brown U., 1974; JD, Harvard U., 1977. Bar: N.J. 1977. Law clk. to presiding judge U.S. Dist. Ct. N.J., Camden, 1977-78; ptnr. Lowenstein, Sandler, Kohl, Fisher & Boylan, P.A., Roseland, N.J., 1978—; adj. prof. Seton Hall Law Sch., 1988-91, Rutgers U. Law Sch., 1989—; chmn. dist. ethics com. Supreme Ct. Contbr. articles to profl. jours. Mem. exec. com. N.J. chpt. Anti-Defamation League. Mem. Essex County Bar Assn. (chmn. banking law com. 1994—, trustee 1996—). Office: Lowenstein Sandler Et Al 65 Livingston Ave Roseland NJ 07068-1725

WOYCZYNSKI, WOJBOR ANDRZEJ, mathematician, educator; b. Czestochowa, Poland, Oct. 24, 1943; came to U.S., 1970; s. Eugeniusz and Otylia Sabina (Borkiewicz) W.; m. Elizabeth W. Holbrook; children: Lauren Pike, Gregory Holbrook, Martin Wojbor. MSEE, Wroclaw (Poland) Poly., 1966; PhD in Math., Wroclaw U., 1968. Asst. prof. Inst. Math. Wroclaw U., 1968-72, assoc. prof., 1972-77; prof. dept. math. Cleve. State U., 1977-82; prof., chmn. dept. math. and stats. Case Western Res. U., Cleve., 1982-91, dir. Ctr. for Stochastic and Chaotic Processes in Sci. and Tech., 1989—; rsch. fellow Inst. Math. Polish Acad. Scis., Warsaw, 1969-76; postdoctoral fellow Carnegie-Mellon U., Pitts., 1970-72; vis. assoc. prof. Northwestern U., Evanston, Ill., 1976-77; vis. prof. Aarhus (Denmark) U., 1972, U. Paris, 1973, U. Wis., Madison, 1976, U. S.C., 1979, U. N.C., Chapel Hill, 1983-84, Gottingen (Germany) U., 1985, 91, 96, U. NSW, Sydney, Australia, 1988, Nagoya (Japan) U., 1992, 93, 94, U. Minn., Mpls., 1994. Dep. editor in chief: Annals of the Polish Math. Soc., 1973-77; assoc. editor Chemometrics Jour., 1987-94, Probability and Math. Stats., 1988—, Annals of Applied Probability, 1989-96, Stochastic Processes and Their Applications, 1993—; co-editor: Martingale Theory and Harmonic Analysis in Banach Spaces, 1982, Probability Theory and Harmonic Analysis, 1986, Nonlinear Waves and Weak Turbulence, 1993, Nonlinear Stochastic PDE's: Hydrodynamic Limit and Burgers' Turbulence, 1995, IN a Reporter's Eye: The Life of Stefan Bonach, 1996, Stochastic Models in Geosystems, 1997; author: (monograph) Martingales and Geometry in Banach Spaces I, 1975, part II, 1978; co-author: Random Series and Stochastic Integrals: Single and Multiple, 1992, Distributions in the Physical and Engineering Sciences, vol. 1, Distributional and Fractal Calculus, Integral Transforms and Wavelets, 1997. Rsch. grantee NSF, 1970, 71, 76, 77, 81, 87—, Office of Naval Rsch., 1985-96. Fellow Inst. Math. Stats.; mem. Am. Math. Soc., Am. Statis. Assn., Polish Math. Soc. (Gt. prize 1972), Polish Inst. Arts and Scis., Racquet Club East, Rowfant Club. Roman Catholic. Avocations: tennis, music, skiing, sailing, rare books collecting. Home: 3296 Grenway Rd Cleveland OH 44122-3412 Office: Case Western Res U Dept Statistics Cleveland OH 44106

WOYSKI, MARGARET SKILLMAN, retired geology educator; b. West Chester, Pa., July 26, 1921; d. Willis Rowland and Clara Louise (Howson) Skillman; m. Mark M. Woyski, June 19, 1948; children: Nancy Elizabeth, William Bruno, Ronald David, Wendelin Jane. BA in Chemistry, Wellesley (Mass.) Coll., 1943; MS in Geology, U. Minn., 1945, PhD in Geology, 1946. Geologist Mo. Geol. Survey and Water Resources, Rolla, 1946-48; instr. U. Wis., Madison, 1948-52; lectr. Calif. State U., Long Beach, 1963-67; lectr. to prof. Calif. State U., Fullerton, 1966-91, assoc. dean Sch. Natural Sci. and Math., 1981-91, emeritus prof., 1991—. Contbr. articles to profl. jours.; author lab. manuals; editor guidebooks. Fellow Geol. Soc. Am. (program chmn. 1982); mem. South Coast Geol. Soc. (hon. pres. 1974), Mineral Soc. Am. Home: 1843 Kashlan Rd La Habra CA 90631-8423

WOYTHAL, CONSTANCE LEE, psychologist; b. Milw., Nov. 6, 1954; d. Gerald Clarence and Shirley Estelle (Gross) W.; m. John Francis Neisius, Mar. 20, 1982; children: Adam, Abby. BS, U. Wis., Milw., 1976; MS in Edn., U. Wis., River Falls, 1978; postgrad., Alfred Adler Inst., Chgo., 1980, George Williams Coll., 1984, Marquette U., 1984, Cardinal Stritch Coll., 1987, Wis. Sch. Profl. Psychology, 1990. Lic. sch. psychologist, Wis.; nat. cert. sch. psychologist. Psychologist Sch. Dist. of Marshfield, Wis., 1978-81, Sheboygan County Handicapped Children's Edn. Bd., Sheboygan Falls, Wis., 1981-91; devel. coord. wellness program Sheboygan County Handicapped Children's Edn. Bd., Plymouth, Wis., 1984—; psychologist Plymouth (Wis.) Joint Sch. Dist., Plymouth, Wis., 1991—; workshop facilitator Marshfield Clinic, 1981; cons. wellness lifestyle program Sch. of Sheboygan County, 1985—; lectr. profl. groups; mem. profl. adv. bd. Children with Attention Deficit Disorder (ChADD), 1992-93. Bd. dirs. Family Connections, 1988-90. Mem. APA (student affiliate), NASP, Nat. Wellness Assn., N.Am. Soc. Adlerian Psychologists, Wis. Sch. Psychology Assn., Sheboygan Wellness Assn. (bd. dirs. 1982-88), Mental Health Assn. Avocations: swimming, singing, hiking, cross country skiing, stereophile. Home: 859 Chaplin Ct Plymouth WI 53073-1012 Office: Riverview Mid Sch Riverview Cir Plymouth WI 53073

WOYTOWITZ, PETER JOHN, mechanical engineer; b. Balt., Nov. 9, 1953; s. Peter John and Anna Mae (Zink) W.; m. Cristina Guevarra, Oct. 12, 1985; children: Christopher John, Phillip Charles. BSME, U. Md., 1976; MS in Engring., Santa Clara U., 1980; degree of engr., Stanford U., 1985; PhD, Santa Clara U., 1993. Registered profl. engr. Calif. Stress engr. Boeing Comml. Airplane Co., Seattle, 1977-78; engr. rsch. & devel. Ford Aerospace and Communications Corp., Palo Alto, Calif., 1978-83; sr. engr. Anamet Labs., Inc., San Carlos, Calif., 1983-85; sr. mech. engr. Failure Analysis Assocs., Menlo Park, Calif., 1985-93; v.p., prin. engr. Engring. Mechanics Tech., San Jose, Calif., 1993—; lectr. San Jose State U., 1985-88, 93—, Santa Clara (Calif.) U., 1993—; book reviewer McGraw-Hill, 1993; jour. reviewer Mechanism & Machine Theory, 1993. Co-author: Optimization of Structural Systems, 1991. Mem. ASME (v.p. student chpt. 1975), AIAA, Am. Acad. Mechs., Pi Tau Sigma. Roman Catholic. Home: 318 Farley St Mountain View CA 94043-4422 Office: Engring Mechanics Tech 4340 Stevens Creek Blvd Ste 166 San Jose CA 95129-1147

WOZNIAK, DEBRA GAIL, lawyer; b. Rockford, Ill., Oct. 3, 1954; d. Richard Michael and Evalyn Louise Wozniak. BA, U. Nebr., 1976, JD, 1979. Bar: Nebr. 1980, Iowa 1980, Ill. 1982. CPCU. Asst. legal counsel Iowa Ho. of Reps., Des Moines, 1980-81; mng. atty. Rapp & Gilliam, Des Moines, 1981; from asst. counsel to counsel and asst. dir. Alliance of Am. Insurers, Schaumburg, Ill., 1981-87; from asst. counsel to counsel StateFarm Ins. Cos., Bloomington, Ill., 1987—. Mem. Nebr. Bar Assn., Iowa Bar Assn. Avocation: antiques. Office: State Farm Ins Cos One State Farm Plz Bloomington IL 61710

WOZNIAK, DONALD RICHARD, information systems executive; b. Buffalo, Dec. 30, 1953; s. Bernard Alexander and Virginia Worthem (Trost) W.; m. Carol Andrea Wolff, Dec. 27, 1975; children: Gregory Alan, Sarah Candace. BA, SUNY, Buffalo, 1975. Cert. sys. profl. Assn. for Sys. Mgmt. Data processing ops. mgr. Donn Corp., Westlake, Ohio, 1976-78; sr. programmer/analyst The City Bank Co., Lorain, Ohio, 1978-79; info. sys. dir. Nat. Assn. Coll. Stores, Oberlin, Ohio, 1979-93, Bonne Bell, Inc., Lakewood, Ohio, 1993—; mem. Book Industry Sys. Adv. Com., N.Y.C., 1980-93, Internat. Std. Book Number Adv. Bd., N.Y.C., 1981-92; chair Book Industry Sys. Adv. Com., N.Y.C., 1985. Contbr. articles to profl. jours. Recipient Award of Excellence, Am. Soc. Assn. Execs., 1989. Mem. Common, Workshop Players Theatre (bd. dirs.). Avocations: theatre arts, racquetball. Office: Bonne Bell Inc 1006 Crocker Rd Westlake OH 44145-1031

WOZNIAK, RICHARD MICHAEL, SR., retired city and regional planner; b. rural Fullerton, Nebr., Nov. 28, 1928; s. Theo Charles and Monica (Lesiak) W.; m. Evalyn Louise Pickett, Sept. 9, 1951; children: Debra, Karen, Richard Michael, Steve. BS, Iowa State U., 1954. Cert. landscape architect. Landscape architect Rockford (Ill.) Nurseries, 1954-55; landscape architect, city planner Harland Bartholomew & Assocs., St. Louis, 1955-58; sr. planner Springfield/Sangamon County Regional Planning Commn., Springfield, Ill., 1958-60; city planner City of Omaha, 1960-64; owner, cons. Richard M. Wozniak & Assocs., Fremont, Nebr., 1964-74; exec. v.p. Mits Kawamoto & Aassocs., Omaha, 1974-76; owner, planning cons., racher Richard M. Wozniak & Assocs., Long Pine, Nebr., 1976-84; dir. planning and community devel. City of Norfolk (Nebr.)/Madison County, 1984-97; ret., 1997; cons. to more than 45 cities and counties in Ill., Mich. and Nebr., 1955-84; v.p., pres. Nebr. State Bd. Landscape Architects, Lincoln, 1967-84; treas. Nat. Coun. Landscape Architecture Bds., 1976. Author numerous studies and reports, comprehensive plans; designer land planning for parks and subdivs. With U.S. Army, 1946-49, USAFR, 1954-68. Recipient numerous awards. Mem. Am. Planning Assn. (charter), Am. Inst. Cert. Planners (charter), Nebr. Assn. County Ofcls. (v.p., pres. 1985-91), Am. Legion, Nebr. Planning and Zoning Assn. Avocations: woodworking, farming, fishing, sculpturing. Home: RR 1 Box 410 Madison NE 68748-9746

WRAASE, DENNIS RICHARD, utilities company executive, accountant; b. Washington, Mar. 15, 1944; s. Richard Harold and Esther Morelle (Cowan) W.; m. Cecilia Anne Kirby, Dec. 30, 1987; children: Richard Reid, Elisabeth Kirby. BS, U. Md., 1966; MS, George Washington U., 1975. CPA, Md. Acct. Exxon Corp., Balt., 1966-70; fin. analyst Exxon Corp., Houston, 1970-74; mgr. fin. systems Potomac Electric Power Co., Washington, 1974-78, asst. comptr., 1978-81, dir. computer and gen. svcs., 1981-83, comptr., 1983-92, v.p., 1986-89, sr. v.p., 1989—; CFO, 1996—; CEO Potomac Capital Investment, 1996—. Pres. Olney Jaycees, Md., 1978; bd. dirs., v.p. Nat. Capital area Boy Scouts Am., Washington, 1987—, Better Bus. Bur., Washington Bd. Trade. With USAR, 1967-73. Mem. Am. Inst. CPAs, Fin. Execs. Inst. Democrat. Lutheran. Office: Potomac Electric Power Co 1900 Pennsylvania Ave NW Rm 800 Washington DC 20068-0001

WRAY, BETTY BEASLEY, allergist, immunologist, pediatrician; b. Ga., 1935. MD, Med Coll. Ga., 1960. Diplomate Am. Bd. Allergy and Immunology, Am. Bd. Clin. Lab. Immunology. Intern Talmadge Meml. Hosp., Augusta, Ga., 1960-61, resident in pediatrics, 1962, 64-65, fellow in pediatric allergy, 1966-68; staff mem. U. Hosp., Augusta, Ga., 1974—; staff mem. Med. Coll. Ga.; Augusta, Ga., 1979—, prof. pediatric medicine, chief allergy and immunology; vice-chair dept. pediats. Mem. Am. Acad. Allergy and Immunology, Am. Acad. Pediatrics, Am. Coll. Allergy and Immunology, So. Med. Assn. Office: Med Coll of Georgia Cj # 141 Augusta GA 30912

WRAY, CECIL, JR., lawyer; b. Memphis, Nov. 19, 1934; s. Thomas Cecil and Margaret (Malone) W.; m. Gilda Gates, Sept. 11, 1964; children: Christopher A., Kathleen Wray Baughman. Student, U. Va., 1952-53; BA magna cum laude, Vanderbilt U., 1956; LLB, Yale U., 1959. Bar: Tenn. 1959, N.Y. 1961, U.S. Supreme Ct. 1964. Registered counseil juridique, France, 1978-82. Law clk. to justice Tom C. Clark U.S. Supreme Ct., Washington, 1959-60; assoc. Debevoise & Plimpton, N.Y.C., 1960-67, ptnr., 1968-96, of counsel, 1997—; resident ptnr. Debevoise & Plimpton, Paris, 1976-79; adj. prof. N.Y. Law Sch., 1997—. Co-author: Innovative Corporate Financing Techniques, 1986. Pres. Search & Care, Inc., N.Y.C., 1981-87, Episcopal Charities, N.Y.; vestryman St. James' Ch., N.Y.C., 1982-87, warden, 1988-94; trustee Fondation des Etats-Unis, Paris, 1976-79; bd. dirs. East Side Community Ctr., Inc., Hudson Highlands Music Festival; mem. bd. fgn. parishes Episcopal Ch., 1995—; mem. Adirondack coun. Hudson Highlands Land Trust. Fellow Am. Coll. Investment Counsel (trustee 1981-86, pres. 1983-84); mem. ABA, Am. Law Inst., Assn. Bar City N.Y., Coun. Fgn. Rels., Ausable Club (St. Huberts, N.Y.), Union Club, Century Club, Order of Coif, Phi Beta Kappa. Episcopalian. Home: 47 E 88th St New York NY 10128-1152 Office: Debevoise & Plimpton 875 3rd Ave New York NY 10022-6225

WRAY, GAIL MILLER, government agency administrator, environmentalist; b. Milw., Feb. 23, 1939; d. Frederic C. Miller and Adele E. (Kanaley) O'Shaughnessy; children: Jennifer, Edward, Hillary. BA in Polit. Sci., Trinity Coll., Washington, 1961; spl. degree, Montessori Soc., Chgo., 1963. Office mgr., asst. plant mgr. Americology Can Co., 1978-81; recycling dir. Village of Shorewood, Wis., 1981-89; recycling coord. U.S. EPA, Washington, 1989-91; chair Presidential Coun. on Fed. Recycling and Procurement Policy, Washington, 1991-94; apptd. by gov. Wis. as exec. dir. Wis. Recycling Market Devel. Bd., 1994—. Polit. affairs chair Jr. League of Am., 1976-77; founder Shorewood (Wis.) Conservation Com., 1980; chair LWV Nat. Resources Portfolio, 1987-86, pres. Greater Milw. LWV, 1980-82; mem. program com. Pub. Policy Forum, Milw., 1985-89; founder and pres. Associated Recyclers of Wis., 1987-89; bd. dirs. Midwest Recycling Coalition. Recipient Cert. Appreciation Am. Field Svc. Internat./Inter-cultural., People on the Move award, Milw. Bus. Jour., 1988, Nat. Govs. Assn. Recognition award, 1990; Named to Most Interesting People, Milw. Mag., 1990. Mem.

Worldwide Women in the Environment (chair EPA Forum 1989-94, bd. dirs.), Friends of UN Environment Program, Nat. Recycling Coalition (market devel. com.). Roman Catholic. Avocations: sports, animal owner, travel. Home: 12144 N Ridge Rd Mequon WI 53092-1025

WRAY, GERALDINE SMITHERMAN (JERRY WRAY), artist; b. Shreveport, La., Dec. 15, 1925; d. David Ewart and Mary Virginia (Hoss) Smitherman; m. George Downing Wray, June 24, 1947; children: Mary Virginia Hill, Deanie Galloway, George D. Wray III, Nancy Armistead. BFA with honors, Newcomb Art Sch., Tulane U., 1946. One woman shows include Don Batman Gallery, Kansas City, Mo., 1982, Gallery II, Baton Rouge, 1985, McNeese Coll., Lake Charles, La., 1987, Dragonfly Gallery, Shreveport, La., 1987, Barnwell Garden and Art Ctr., Shreveport, 1988, 95, Southdown Mus., Houma, La., 1989, La. State U., Shreveport, 1991, WTN Radio Station, Shreveport, 1993, The Cambridge Club, Shreveport, 1993, Centerary Coll., 1993, Northwestern State U., Natchitoches, La., 1995, Goddard Mus., Ardmore, Okla., 1996, Art Buyers Caravan, Atlanta, 1996, Lockhaven (Pa.) U., 1996, Billingsley Gallery, Pensacola, Fla., 1996, Casa D'Ante, Shreveport, La., 1996, N.E. State U., Monroe, La., 1977, Art Expo, N.Y.C., 1997; Group shows include Watercolor USA Springfield., Mo., 1988, Waddell's Gallery, Shreveport, 1988, 91, Water Works Gallery, Dallas, 1990, Southwestern Watercolor Show, 1991 (D'Arches award), Masur Mus. Exhibition (honorable mention 91, 92), , Bossier Art Ctr., Bossier City, La., 1992, Irving Art Assn. (honorable mention), 1992, Leon Loard Gallery, Montgomery, Ala., 1993, Ward-Nasse Gallery, N.Y.C., 1993, 97, Soc. Experimental Artists Internat. (1st. place, honorable mention), 1993, Palmer Gallery, Hot Springs, Ark., 1994, Art Expo, N.Y.C., 1996, Billinglsey Gallery, Pensacola, Fla., 1996, Casa D'Arte, Shreveport, 1996, Art Buyers Caravan, Atlanta, 1996, The Wall Gallery, Savannah, Ga., 1997, Backwoods Gallery, El Dorado, Ark., 1997, Art Effects Gallery, Merian, Pa., Stecoto Gallery, Macon, Ga., 1997, Visual Inspirations, Newton, N.J., 1997, Whithum Gallery, Dayton, Ohio, 1997. Art chmn. Jr. League, Shreveport, 1955-60; bd. dirs. Holiday-in-Dixie Cotillion, Shreveport, 1974-76. Mem. Nat. Assn. Women Artists, Nat. Watercolor Soc. (signature mem. 1994, 96), Southwestern Watercolor Soc. (signature mem. 1991), La. Watercolor Soc. (signature mem. 1990), La. Artists Inc. (elected mem.). Episcopalian. Avocation: tennis. Home: 573 Spring Lake Dr Shreveport LA 71106-4603

WRAY, GILDA GATES, foundation administrator; b. Washington, Jan. 15, 1943; d. Samuel Eugene and Philomene (Asher) Gates; m. Cecil Wray, Jr., Sept. 11, 1964; children: Christopher, Kathleen Wray Baughman. BA cum laude, Smith Coll., 1964; MA in Internat. Affairs, Columbia U., 1966. Exec. dir. Horizon Concerts, N.Y.C., 1981-87; from program officer to sr. program officer Charles Hayden Found., N.Y.C., 1987-92, v.p., 1992—, trustee, 1993—; bd. dirs. Hudson Valley Shakespeare Festival; mem. rels. com. N.Y. Regional Assn. Grantmakers, 1990-93. Trustee Brearley Sch., N.Y.C., 1979-88, Yorkville Civic Coun., N.Y.C., 1979-81; bd. mgrs. N.Y. Jr. League, 1973-76, 79-81; chmn. grants com. St. James Ch., N.Y.C., 1979-87, mem .gov. com. Babcock-Michel Fund, 1988-92; mem. adv. bd. DeKay Found., N.Y.C., 1991—; mem. gov. bd. Fgn. Policy Assn., N.Y.C., 1982-90; trustee Adirondack Mus., 1994—. Mem. Cosmopolitan Club (bd. govs. 1992-95). Episcopalian. Avocations: hiking, tennis, skiing, gardening, reading. Office: Charles Hayden Found One Bankers Trust Plz 130 Liberty St New York NY 10006-1105

WRAY, ROBERT, lawyer; s. George and Ann (Moriarty) W.; m. Lila Keogh (dec.); children: Jennifer, Edward, Hillary. BS, Loyola U., 1957; JD, U. Mich., 1960. Bar: D.C., Ill. 1960. Assoc. Hopkins & Sutter, Chgo., 1964-69; gen. counsel Agy. for Internat. Devel., 1969-71; sr. counsel TRW, Inc., 1972-73, Export-Import Bank of the U.S., 1974-79; prin. Robert Wray Assocs., 1979-86; internat. ptnr. Pierson, Ball & Dowd, 1986-87; prin. Robert Wray Assocs., 1988—; spec. counsel Graham & James, 1988—. Recipient medal of superior honor Dept. of State. Mem. ABA, Fed. Bar Assn., Am. Soc. Internat. Law, Internat. Bar Assn., Coun. for Excellence in Govt., Bretton Woods Com., Met. Club, Talbot Country Club, Annapolis Yacht Club. Office: Robert Wray Assocs 2000 M St NW Washington DC 20036-3307

WRAY, THOMAS JEFFERSON, lawyer; b. Nashville, July 17, 1949; s. William Esker and Imogene (Cushman) W.; m. Susan Elizabeth Wells, Aug. 19, 1972; children: William Clark, Caroline Kell. BA, Emory U., 1971; JD, U. Va., 1974. Bar: Tex. 1974, U.S. Dist. Ct. (so., no. and ea. dists.) Tex. 1976, U.S. Ct. Appeals (5th and 11th cirs.) 1976, U.S. Supreme Ct. 1987. Assoc. Fulbright & Jaworski, L.L.P., Houston, 1974-82; ptnr. Fulbright & Jaworski, Houston, 1982—. Mem. ABA, Houston Bar Assn., Houston Mgmt. Lawyers Forum (chmn. 1981-82), Houston Club, Briar Club, Phi Beta Kappa. Republican. Episcopalian. Home: 3662 Ella Lee Ln Houston TX 77027 Office: Fulbright & Jaworski 1301 Mckinney St Ste 5100 Houston TX 77010-3095

WREFORD, DAVID MATHEWS, magazine editor; b. Perth, Australia, Dec. 17, 1943; emigrated to Can., 1966; s. Peter Mathews and Mary Lichfield (Edquist) W.; m. Donna Diane Campbell, Sept. 28, 1970; children—Elizabeth Mary, Catherine Anne. B.Sc. in Agr. with honours, U. Western Australia, 1966. Field editor Southam Bus. Publns. Ltd., Winnipeg, Man., Can., 1967-73; field editor Country Guide, Public Press Ltd., Milton, Ont., 1973-75; editor Country Guide, United Grain Growers Ltd., Winnipeg, 1975—. Mem. Man. Inst. Agrologists, Agrl. Inst. Can., Canadian Fedn. Farm Writers and Broadcasters. Mem. Ch. of Eng. Home: 294 Elm St, Winnipeg, MB Canada R3M 3P3 Office: United Grain Growers Ltd, PO Box 6600, Winnipeg, MB Canada R3C 3A7 also: Toronto-Dominion Centre 25th Fl, 201 Portage Ave, Winnipeg, MB Canada R3C 3A7

WREGE, JULIA BOUCHELLE, tennis professional, physics educator; b. Charleston, W.Va., Apr. 11, 1944; d. Dallas Payne and Mary Louise (Hagan) Bouchelle; m. Douglas Ewart Wrege, July 13, 1968; children: Dallas Ewart, Shannon Bouchelle. B.S. in Physics, Ga. Inst. Tech., 1965, M.S. in Physics, 1967. Systems analyst GE Apollo Systems, Daytona Beach, Fla., 1967-68; med. scientist Space Instruments Research, Atlanta, 1968-70; head tennis profl. Riverside Tennis Club, Atlanta, 1971-72, Am. Adventures, Roswell, Ga., 1972-75, Hampton Farms Tennis Club, Marietta, Ga., 1975-79; head women's tennis coach Ga. Inst. Tech., Atlanta, Ga., 1979-86, 91-92; v.p. Sirius Software, Inc., 1988—; instr. physics So. Coll. Tech., 1990—; stadium chmn., umpire, referee USTA, Atlanta, 1977—. Author: Tournament Manual, 1977, 3d edit., 1989; co-developer software TMS Tennis Tournament, 1989. Pres. Dickerson Mid. Sch. Parent-Tchr.-Student Assn., Marietta, Ga., 1982-85. Named Umpire of Yr., Ga. Tennis Assn., 1978, So. Tennis Assn., 1978; Ga. Tennis Coach of Yr., Assn. Intercollegiate Athletics for Women-Ga. Tennis Coaches Assn., 1981, 82, 83; named to Ga. Tech. Athletic Hall of Fame, 1997. Mem. U.S. Profl. Tennis Assn. (pres. 1980), U.S. Tennis Assn., Intercollegiate Tennis Coaches Assn., Ga. Tennis Assn. (pres. 1976-81, 94—, v.p. 1974-76, 91-92), Atlanta Lawn Tennis Assn., Atlanta Profl. Tennis Assn., Alpha Xi Delta, Sigma Pi Sigma. Republican. Episcopalian. Home: 1366 Little Willeo Rd Marietta GA 30068-2135

WREN, HAROLD GWYN, arbitrator, lawyer, legal educator; b. Big Stone Gap, Va., May 19, 1921; s. James H. and Jessie M. (Reeve) W.; m. Beryl E. Bird, Nov. 20, 1948; children: James H., II, Geoffrey G. A.B., Columbia U., 1942, LL.B., 1948; J.S.D., Yale U., 1957. Bar: N.Y. 1948, Okla. 1956, Tex. 1959, Ky. 1983. Assoc. firm Willkie Farr & Gallagher, N.Y.C., 1948-49; assoc. prof. law U. Miss., Oxford, 1949-54; prof. law U. Okla., Norman, 1954-57, So. Meth. U., Dallas, 1957-65, Boston Coll., 1965-69; dean, prof. law Lewis and Clark Law Sch., Portland, Oreg., 1969-72, U. Richmond, Va., 1972-76; prof. law U. Louisville, 1976-91, dean, 1976-81; arbitrator Am. Arbitration Assn., 1958—, Fed. Mediation and Conciliation Service, 1958—; of counsel Voyles and Johnson, P.S.C., Louisville, 1991—. Author: Creative Estate Planning, 1970, Problems in Corporate Changes, 1958, Problems in Texas Estates, 1961, (with Gabinet and Carrad) Tax Aspects of Marital Dissolution, 1987, (with Glascock) The Of Counsel Agreement, 1991. Served to capt. USNR, 1942-80. Fulbright scholar, 1953-54. Fellow Am. Coll. Trust and Estate Counsel, Am. Coll. Tax Counsel, Am. Bar Found. (life); mem. ABA, Louisville Bar Assn., Conversation Club, Order of Coif, Phi Beta Kappa, Phi Kappa Phi. Democrat. Episcopalian. Home: 5944 Ashwood Bluff Dr Louisville KY 40207-1269 Office: 730 W Main St Ste 480 Louisville KY 40202-2641

WREN, ROBERT JAMES, aerospace engineering manager; b. Moline, Ill., May 12, 1935; m. Jordis Wren; children: James, Patrick, Kiley. BSCE, U. Tex., 1956; MSCE, So. Meth. U., 1962; doctoral candidate, U. Houston. Registered profl. engr. Tex. Engring. aide Ctrl. Power and Light Co., Corpus Christi, 1954; sta. clk. City of Austin (Tex.) Power Plant, 1954-55; assoc. engr., hydraulic engr. U.S. Bur. of Reclamation, Austin, 1955-57; structural test engr. Gen. Dynamics, Ft. Worth, 1957-62; sr. structural dynamics engr., mgr. vibration and acoustic test facility NASA-Manned Spacecraft Ctr., Houston, 1962-63, 63-66, head exptl. dynamics sect., 1965-70; mgr. Apollo Spacecraft 2TV-1 CSM Test Program, 1966-68, Apollo Lunar Module-2 Drop Test Program, 1968-70; mgr. structural design space sta., space base, lunar base, mars mission NASA-Manned Spacecraft Ctr., Houston, 1970-73; mgr. structural design and devel., space shuttle carrier aircraft-747 NASA Johnson Space Ctr., Houston, 1973-74, mgr. structural div. space shuttle payload systems, 1974-84; mgr. engring. directorate for space shuttle payload safety NASA-Johnson Space Ctr., Houston, 1984-94, alternate chmn. space shuttle payload safety review panel, 1990—, mgr. engring. dir. vehicle and payload flight sys. safety, 1994—. Pres. Friendswood Little League Baseball, 1980-83; bd. dirs. Bay Area YMCA, Houston, 1982—, chmn., 1983-84. Recipient Sustained Superior Performance award NASA, Personal Letter of Commendation, George Low NASA Apollo Program, Outstanding Svc. award NASA, Group Achievement awards NASA; Paul Harris fellow Rotary. Mem. Space Ctr. Rotary (dir., treas., sec., v.p. 1979-85, pres. 1985-86, Rotary dist. 5890/govt. rep. 1986-87, area coord. 1987-89, zone leader 1988-89, gov.'s aide 1989-90, chmn. dist. assembly 1989-90, 93-94, fin. com. 1989-91, Rotary Nat. award for Space Achievement Found./co-founder, bd. dirs. 1984—), Rotary World Health Found. Plastic Surgery for Children (co-founder, bd. dirs. 1985—), Rotary Space Meml. Found. (co-founder, bd. dirs. 1986—). Methodist. Avocations: snow and water skiing, running, scuba diving, tennis, sailing. Home: PO Box 1466 Friendswood TX 77549-1446 Office: NASA Johnson Space Ctr Houston TX 77058

WRENN, JAMES JOSEPH, East Asian studies educator; b. New Haven, Conn., July 7, 1926; s. James Joseph and Mariea (Enright) W.; m. Harriet Huddleston Calhoun, July 7, 1953; children: Annemarie Wrenn-Bessmer, James Joseph, Michael Enright, Christopher David. BA, Yale U., 1953, PhD, 1964. Lectr. in Chinese Grad. Sch., Yale U., New Haven, 1961-62, Brown U., Providence, 1962-64; asst. prof. Brown U., 1964-67, assoc. prof. linguistics, 1967-73, prof., 1974-91, co-chmn. East Asian Studies, 1987-95, dir. Ctr. for Lang. Studies, 1987-90, prof. emeritus, 1996. Contbr. articles to profl. jours. Platoon sgt. USMCR, 1944-46, PTO, 1950-52, Korea. Fgn. area fellow Ford Found., Republic of China, 1958-59. Mem. AAUP, MLA, Am. Council Tchrs. Fgn. Langs., Assn. Asian Studies, Chinese Lang. Tchrs. Assn. Club: Faculty. Home: 22 Rhode Island Ave Providence RI 02906-5506 Office: Brown U Brown Sta Box 1850 Providence RI 02912

WRIGHT, ALFRED GEORGE JAMES, band symphony orchestra conductor, educator; b. London, June 23, 1916; came to U.S., 1922, naturalized, 1936; s. Alfred Francis and Elizabeth (Chapman) W.; m. Bertha Marie Farmer, Aug. 6, 1938; children: Adele Marie Wright Needham, Cynthia Elaine Wright Williams; m. Gladys Violet Stone, June 28, 1953. BA, U. Miami, 1937, MEd, 1947; PhD (hon.), Troy State U., 1980. Dir. music Miami Sr. High Sch., 1938-54; prof., head dept. bands Purdue U., Lafayette, Ind., 1954-85; founder, condr. U.S. Coll. Wind Band Tours, 1971—; pres. Internat. Music Tours, Inc.; v.p., exec. sec. Music Tour Svcs., Inc.; dir. prerace pageant Indpls. 500 Mile Automobile Race, 1957-82; mem. adv. coun. Performing Arts Abroad, 1972—; chmn. N.Am. Band Dirs. Coordinating Commn., 1974-75, Nat. H.S. Honors Band, 1975-76, 77—; jury World Music Contest, Holland, 1974, 70, 81, 85; bd. dirs. 500 Festival Assocs., 1961-81; founder, chmn. bd. dirs. Hall of Fame Disting. Band Condrs.; pres. All Am. Hall of Fame Band Found.; chmn. bd., CEO John Philip Sousa Meml. Found., 1979—. Founding condr., Purdue U. Symphony Orch., 1971-81; Author: The Show Band, 1957, Marching Band Fundamentals, 1963, Bands of the World, 1970; marching band editor: Instrumentalist mag, 1953-81; contbr. articles to profl. mags. Mem. bd. advisors Internat. Music Festivals, 1989; bd. dirs. World Assn. Wind Bands and Ensembles Found., 1991-94. Decorated Star of the Order John Philip Sousa; recipient Disting. Svc. award Purdue U., 1993. Mem. Nat. Band Assn. (founder, pres. 1960-63, hon. life pres. 1973), Coll. Band Dirs. Nat. Assn., Am. Sch. Band Dirs. Nat. Assn., Japan Marching Band Assn. (hon. bd. dirs. 1971-77), Big Ten Band Dirs. Assn. (pres. 1977), Am. Bandmasters Found. (bd. dirs. 1987-89), Am. Bandmasters Assn. (pres. 1979-80), Nat. Acad. Wind and Percussive Arts (founder, chmn. 1961-81), Phi Mu Alpha, Kappa Kappa Psi (Disting. Svc. award 1981), Phi Beta Mu. Home and Office: 345 Overlook Dr West Lafayette IN 47906-1249

WRIGHT, ANDREW, English literature educator; b. Columbus, Ohio, June 28, 1923; s. Francis Joseph and Katharine (Timberman) W.; m. Virginia Rosemary Banks, June 27, 1952; children: Matthew Leslie Francis, Emma Stanbery. A.B., Harvard U., 1947; M.A., Ohio State U., 1948, Ph.D., 1951. Prof. English lit. U. Calif., San Diego, 1963—; chmn. dept. lit. U. Calif., 1971-74; dir. U. Calif. Study Center, U.K. and Ireland, 1980-82; vis. prof. U. Queensland, Australia, 1984, Colegio de la Frontera Norte, San Antonio del Mar, Baja, Calif., 1991-92. Author: Jane Austen's Novels: A Study In Structure, 1953, Joyce Cary: A Preface to His Novels, 1958, Henry Fielding: Mask and Feast, 1965, Blake's Job: A Commentary, 1972, Anthony Trollope: Dream and Art, 1983; Fictional Discourse and Historical Space, 1987; contbg. author numerous books, articles to profl. jours.; editorial bd. Nineteenth Century Fiction, 1964-86. Bd. dirs. Calif. Coun. Humanities, 1983-87. Guggenheim fellow, 1960, 70; Fulbright Sr. Research fellow, 1960-61. Fellow Royal Soc. Lit.; mem. MLA, Jane Austen Soc., Athenaeum (London), Trollope Soc., Santayana Soc., Phi Beta Kappa. Home: 7227 Olivetas Ave La Jolla CA 92037-5335 Office: U Calif San Diego Dept Lit La Jolla CA 92093-0410

WRIGHT, ANTONY POPE, research chemist; b. Charlottesville, Va., Apr. 28, 1943; s. David McCord and Caroline J. (Jones) W.; m. Judith A. Brown, Apr. 26, 1975; children: Christopher W., David M., Simon K., Amy E. BSc, McGill U., Montreal, Que., Can., 1963; PhD, U. Wis., 1973. Chemist Stauffer Wacker Silicones, Adrian, Mich., 1967-70; scientist Dow Corning Corp., Midland, Mich., 1973—; vis. fellow U. Durham, Eng., 1989-90. Contbr. chpt. to book. Lt. (j.g.) USNR, 1963-67. Fellow Royal Soc. Chemistry; mem. Am. Chem. Soc. Achievements include patents in fields of catalysis, organofluorine and organosilane/silicone products and synthesis; co-discovery of the Wright West Rearrangement in Organosilicon Chemistry, the telomerization of diiodochlordtrifluorethylene in organofluorine chemistry. Home: 7300 N Jefferson Rd Rhodes MI 48652-9602 Office: Dow Corning Corp PO Box 995 Midland MI 48686

WRIGHT, BARBARA EVELYN, microbiologist; b. Pasadena, Calif., Apr. 6, 1926; d. Gilbert Munger Wright and Leta Luella (Brown) Deery. AB, Stanford U., 1947, MA, 1948, PhD, 1951. Biologist NIH, Bethesda, Md., 1953-61; assoc. biochemist Mass. Gen. Hosp., Boston, 1961-69; asst. prof. microbiology Harvard Med. Sch., Boston, 1966-75, assoc. prof., 1975-82; rsch. dir. Boston Biomed. Rsch. Inst., 1967-82; rsch. prof. divsn. biol. scis. U. Mont., Missoula, 1982—; dir. Stella Duncan Rsch. Inst., Missoula, 1982—; cons. Miles Lab., Elkhart, Ind., 1980-84. Author: Critical Variables in Differentiation, 1973; editor: Control Mechanisms in Respiration and Fermentation, 1963; contbr. articles to profl. jours. Grantee NIH, NSF, 1991-96. Mem. AAAS (pres. Pacific divsn. 1984-85), Am. Soc. for Microbiology (Nat. Found. for Microbiology lectr. 1970, divsnl. lectr. 1978), Am. Soc. Biol. Chemists. Avocations: board sailing, skiing, kayaking. Home: 1550 Trotting Horse Ln Missoula MT 59804-5870 Office: Divsn. Biol. Scis. U Mont DBS Missoula MT 59812

WRIGHT, BETH SEGAL, art historian, educator; b. N.Y.C., July 23, 1949; d. Ben and Ella (Litvack) Segal; m. Woodring Erik J. Wright, Sept. 5, 1971; children: Benjamin, Joshua. AB cum laude, Brandeis U., 1970; MA, U. Calif., Berkeley, 1972, PhD, 1978. Instr. Mountain View Coll., Dallas, 1978-82; lectr. U. Tex., Dallas, 1980-81, Tex. Christian U., Ft. Worth, 1981; asst. prof. U. Tex., Arlington, 1984-88, assoc. prof., 1988—; adj. and vis. asst. prof. art history U. Tex., Arlington, 1981-84. Contbr. articles to Art Bull., Arts Mag., Nouvelles de l'Estampe, Clio, others. Kress Found. hon. traveling fellow, 1975-76; NEH Travel to Collections grantee, Paris, 1987, 93; U. Tex. Arlington Rsch. Enhancement grantee, Paris, 1990, 93, Coll. Art Assoc. Meiss grant, 1996. Mem. Société de l'Histoire de l'Art Française (contbr. articles to bull.), Am. Soc. for 18th-Century Studies, Coll. Art Assn., Midwest Art History Soc. (bd. dirs. 1990-93).

WRIGHT, BETTY REN, children's book writer; b. Wakefield, Mich., June 15, 1927; d. William and Revena Evelyn (Trezise) W.; m. George Albert Frederiksen, Oct. 9, 1976. BA, Milw.-Downer Coll., 1949. With Western Pub. Co., Inc., 1949-78, mng. editor Racine Editl., 1967-78. Author numerous juv. and jr. novels, including The Doll House Murders, 1983, Christina's Ghost, 1985, The Summer of Mrs. MacGregor, 1986, A Ghost in the Window, 1987, The Pike River Phantom, 1988, Rosie and the Dance of the Dinosaurs, 1989, The Ghost of Ernie P., 1990, A Ghost in the House, 1991, The Scariest Night, 1991, The Ghosts of Mercy Manor, The Ghost of Popcorn Hill, 1993, The Ghost Witch, 1993, A Ghost Comes Calling, 1994, Out of the Dark, 1995, Haunted Summer, 1996, Too Many Secrets, 1997, also numerous picture and ednl. books; contbr. fiction to mags. Recipient Alumni Svc. award Lawrence U., 1973, Lynde and Harry Bradley Maj. Achievement award, 1997, numerous awards for books including Mo. Mark Twain award, 1986, 96, Tex. Bluebonnet award, 1986, 88, Young Readers award Pacific N.W. Libr. Assn., 1986, Reviewer's Choice Booklist, Ala. Young Readers award, 1987, Ga. Children's Choice award, 1988, Ind. Young Hoosier Book award, 1989, 96, Children's Choice Book/Internat. Reading Assn.—CBC, 1984, S.C. Children's Choice award, 1995, Okla. Sequoyah Children's Choice award, 1988, 95. Mem. AAUW, Allied Authors, Coun. for Wis. Authors (juv. book award 1985, 96), Phi Beta Kappa. Avocations: reading, travel. Home and Office: 6223 Hilltop Dr Racine WI 53406

WRIGHT, BOB, broadcasting executive; b. Rockville Center, N.Y., Apr. 23, 1943; m. Suzanne Werner, Aug. 26, 1967; children: Kate, Christopher, Maggie. A.B. in History, Coll. Holy Cross, 1965; LL.B., U. Va., 1968. Bar: N.Y. 1968, Va. 1968, Mass. 1970, N.J. 1971. With Gen. Electric Co., 1969-70, 73-80, gen. mgr. plastics sales dept., 1978-80; law sec. to chief judge U.S. Dist. Ct., N.J., 1970-73; pres. Cox Cable Communications, Atlanta, 1980-83; exec. v.p. Cox Communications, 1980-83; v.p., gen. mgr. housewares, audio and cable TV ops. GE, 1983-84; pres., chief exec. officer GE Fin. Svcs. Inc., 1984-86, NBC, N.Y.C., 1986—. Office: NBC Inc 30 Rockefeller Plz New York NY 10112*

WRIGHT, BURTON, sociologist; b. Detroit, Jan. 31, 1917; s. Burton and Hazel Marie (Thomas) W.; A.A., C.Z. Coll., 1944; B.A., U. Wash., Seattle, 1947, M.A., 1949; Ph.D., Fla. State U., 1972; m. Marie Fidelis Gallivan, Jan. 26, 1942; children: Burton III, Catherine Margaret (dec.). Enlisted U.S. Navy, 1937, commd. and advanced through grades to comdr., 1957; dir. Naval Res. Recruiting, 1960-64; ret., 1964; mem. faculty U. Wash., 1947-49, Northwestern U., summers 1956-59, George Washington U., Washington, 1954-60, Rollins Coll., Winter Park, Fla., 1966-69; cons. Ford Found., 1951, Dept. Air Force, 1955, U.S. Army Chem. Corps, 1956; prof. dept. sociology U. Central Fla., Orlando, 1972-82, prof. emeritus, 1982-89; ret., 1989; vis. prof. Troy State U., Dothan; dir. Am. Sociol. Assn. Nat. Honors Program, 1981-89. Decorated Navy Commendation medal. Fellow Am. Anthrop. Assn.; mem. Am. Sociol. Assn. (membership com. 1983-86), Soc. Psychol. Study Social Problems, AAUP, Am. Acad. Arts and Scis., Soc. Study Social Problems, So. Sociol. Soc., North Central Sociol. Soc. Roman Catholic. Club: Univ. (Winter Park). Author: (with John P. Weiss and Charles M. Unkovic) Perspective: An Introduction to Sociology, 1975; (with Vernon Fox) Criminal Justice and the Social Sciences, 1978; (with John P. Weiss) Social Problems, 1980. Home: 502 Dunleith Blvd Dothan AL 36303-2936

WRIGHT, C. T. ENUS, former college administrator; b. Social Circle, Ga., Oct. 4, 1942; s. George and Carrie Mae (Enus) W.; m. Mary Stephens, Aug. 9, 1974. B.S., Fort Valley State U. (Ga.), 1964; M.A., Atlanta U., 1967; Ph.D., Boston U., 1977. Tchr., Ga. Pub. Schs., Social Circle, 1965-67; mem. faculty Morris Brown Coll., Atlanta, 1967-73, div. chmn., 1973-77; program dir., asst. provost Eastern Wash. U., Cheney, 1977-81; v.p. academic affairs Talladega Coll. (Ala.), 1981-82; pres. Cheyney U. Pa., Cheyney, 1982-85; v.p. and provost Fla. Meml. Coll., 1985-89; exec. dir. Internat. Found. and Coord. African-African Am. Summit, 1989—; cons. and lectr. in field. Author: (booklet) The History of Black Historical Mythology, 1980; contbr. articles to profl. jours. Commnr., Wash. Pub. Broadcasting, Olympia, 1980-84; exec. com. Boy Scouts Am., Phila., 1982—. Human Relations scholar, 1969, Nat. Teaching fellow Boston U., 1971. Mem. Am. Assn. Colls. and Univs. (coms. 1982—), Am. Hist. Assn. (coms. 1970—), Assn. Study Afro-Am. Life & History (coms. 1965—), Nat. Assn. Equal Opportunity in Higher Edn. (coms. 1982—), NEA (coms. 1965—). Am. Baptist. Clubs: Lions (Cheyney, Wash. (v.p. 1979-81)); Tuscan; Atlanta Constitution. Office: Intl Found 5122 E Shea Blvd Apt 2098 Scottsdale AZ 85254-4679

WRIGHT, CALEB MERRILL, federal judge; b. Georgetown, Del., Oct. 7, 1908; s. William Elwood and Mary Ann (Lynch) W.; m. Katherine McAfee, Nov. 29, 1937; children: Thomas Merrill, William Elwood, Scott McAfee, Victoria. BA, Del. U.; LLB, Yale U., 1933. Bar: Del. 1933. Solo practice Georgetown, 1933-55; U.S. dist. judge Del. Dist., 1955-57, chief judge, 1957-73, sr. judge, 1973—. Mem. Del., Sussex County bar assns., Am. Judicature Soc., Am. Law Inst., Kappa Alpha. Republican. Presbyterian. Club: Wilmington. Home: Cokesbury Village C20 726 Loveville Rd Hockessin DE 19707-1515 Office: US Dist Ct 844 N King St # 34 Wilmington DE 19801-3519

WRIGHT, CAMERON HARROLD GREENE, electrical engineer; b. Quincy, Mass., Jan. 21, 1956; s. Frederick Herman Greene and Dorothy Louise (Harrold) W.; m. Robin Michele Rawlings, May 14, 1988. BSEE summa cum laude, La. Tech. U., 1983; MSEE, Purdue U., 1988; PhD, U. Tex., 1996. Registered profl. engr., Calif. Commd. 2d lt. USAF, 1983, advanced through grades to major, 1995; avionics design engr. USAF Avionics Lab., Wright-Patterson AFB, Ohio, 1983-86; divsn. chief space test range space divsn. USAF, L.A. AFB, 1988-90, dir. advanced satellite systems, 1990-91; instr. elec. engring. USAF Acad., Colorado Springs, 1991-93, asst. prof., 1996—; mem. exec. com. Nat. Aerospace and Electronics Conf., Dayton, Ohio, 1983-86; bd. dirs. Rocky Mountain Bioengring. Symposium. Contbr. articles to profl. jours.; reviewer profl. jours.; co-author, editor: An Introduction to Electrical Engineering, 1994. Coord. tech. career motivation Dayton Sch. Dist., 1983-86; speaker engring. careers Colorado Springs Middle Sch., 1991-93; vol. computer/network cons. Project Transitions Hospice, Austin, Tex., 1995-96. Mem. IEEE (sr.), Air Force Assn. (life, dir. L.A. Young Astronaut program 1988-91, Officer of Yr. 1991), Am. Soc. for Engring. Edn. Achievements include development of unique process to detect incoming missile warheads for Strategic Defense Initiative, robotic laser system for eye surgery. Office: Dept Elec Engring 2354 Fairchild Dr Ste 2f6 U S A F Academy CO 80840-6236

WRIGHT, CATHY HESS, secondary education educator; b. Battle Creek, Mich., Oct. 28, 1958; d. Robert Jr. and Eleanore Coulter (Kelley) Hess; m. Eugene Stephen Wright III, May 29, 1993; 1 child, Cody Stephen. BFA, Fla. State U., 1980, MFA, 1982. Profl. artist-in-residence, instr. Montgomery (Ala.) Ballet, 1983-90, Ala. Dance Theatre, Montgomery, 1990-93; founding dance dept. head Carver Creative and Performing Arts Magnet H.S., Montgomery, 1983—, lead tchr., 1996—; adj. instr. Auburn U., Montgomery, 1983-89; com. mem. Gov. Folsom's subcom. on edn. reform, Montgomery, 1994; mem. dance grant selection com. Ala. State Coun. on Arts, Montgomery, 1987, 89, mem. spkr. bur., 1988-89; bd. cons. Ala. Alliance for Arts Edn., Montgomery, 1995-96. Choreographer (dance) Comic Relief, 1988, (First Prize award), Opiate, 1989 (First Prize award). Mem. steering com. Nat. High Sch. Dance Festival, 1992—. Recipient Am. Tchr. award honor in dance Walt Disney Corp., 1992; choreographic fellow Ala. State Coun. on the Arts, 1988, Artist-in-Edn. fellow Nat. Endowment for the Arts & Coun. for Basic Edn., 1995-96; named one of 1000 Outstanding Women of the Nineties, Mirabella Mag., 1994. Mem. NEA, Assn. for Supervision and Curriculum Devel., Nat. Dance Assn.-Am. Alliance for Health, Physical Edn., Recreation and Dance, Ala. Edn. Assn., Ala. State Assn. for Health, Physical Edn., Recreation and Dance (Dance Educator of Yr. 1990-91), Kappa Delta Pi. Avocations: reading, snow skiing, exercise, cooking. Office: Booker T Washington Magnet HS 632 S Union St Montgomery AL 36104-5836

WRIGHT, CHARLES ALAN, law educator, author; b. Phila., Sept. 3, 1927; s. Charles Adshead and Helen (McCormack) W.; m. Mary Joan Herriott,

July 8, 1950 (div. Jan. 1955); 1 child, Charles Edward; m. Eleanor Custis Broyles Clarke, Dec. 17, 1955; children: Henrietta, Cecily; stepchildren: Eleanor Custis Clarke, Margot Clarke. BA, Wesleyan U., Middletown, Conn., 1947; LL.B., Yale U., 1949; LHD (hon.), Episcopal Theol. Sem. S.W., 1992. Bar: Minn. 1951, Tex. 1959. Law clk. to Hon. Charles E. Clark, U.S. Ct. Appeals (2d cir.), New Haven, 1949-50; asst. prof. law U. Minn., Mpls., 1950-53, assoc. prof., 1953-55; assoc. prof. law U. Tex., Austin, 1955-58, prof., 1958-65, McCormick prof., 1965-80, Bates prof., 1980—; Arthur Goodhart vis. prof. legal sci. Cambridge (Eng.) U., 1990-91, Hayden W. Head regents chair, 1990-91; vis. prof. U. Pa., 1959-60. Harvard U., 1964-65, Yale U., 1968-69; vis. fellow Wolfson Coll., Cambridge U., 1984; reporter study div. of juridstiction between state and fed. cts. Am. Law Inst., 1963-69; mem. adv. com. on civil rules Jud. Conf. U.S., 1961-64, standing com. on rules of practice and proc., 1964-76, 87-93; cons., counsel for Pres., 1973-74; mem. com. on infractions NCAA, 1973-83, chmn., 1978-83, chmn. adminstrv. rev. panel, 1993-94; mem. permanent com for Oliver Wendell Holmes Devise, 1975-83; mem. Commn. on Bicentennial of U.S. Constn., 1985-92. Author: Wright's Minnesota Rules, 1954, Cases on Remedies, 1955, (with C.T. McCormick and J.H. Chadbourn) Cases on Federal Courts, 9th edit., 1992, Handbook of the Law of Federal Courts, 5th edit., 1994, (with H.M. Reasoner) Procedure-The Handmaid of Justice, 1965, Federal Practice and Procedure: Criminal, 2d edit., 1982, (with A.R. Miller) Federal Practice and Procedure: Civil, 1969-73, 2d edit. (with A.R. Miller and M.K. Kane), 1983—, 2d edit. (with A.R. Miller and R.L. Marcus), 1994, (with A.R. Miller and E.H. Cooper) Federal Practice and Procedure: Jurisdiction and Related Matters, 1975-82, 2d edit., 1986—, (with K.W. Graham and V.J. Gold) Federal Practice and Procedure: Evidence, 1977—; mem. editorial bd. Supreme Ct. Hist. Soc. Yearbook, 1987-93—. Trustee St. Stephen's Episc. Sch., Austin, Tex., 1962-66, St. Andrew's Episc. Sch., Austin, 1971-74, 77-80, 81-84, chmn. bd., 1973-74, 79-80; trustee Capitol Broadcasting Assn., Austin, 1966—, chmn. bd., 1969-90; trustee Austin Symphony Orch., 1966—, mem. exec. com., 1966-70, 72-83, 86—; trustee Austin Choral Union, 1984-90, Austin Lyric Opera Soc., 1986—; bd. dirs. Am. Friends of Cambridge (Eng.) U., 1994—. Hon. fellow Wolfson Coll. Cambridge U., 1986—. Mem. ABA (commn. on standards jud. adminstrn. 1970-77), AAAS, Am. Law Inst. (coun. 1969—, 2d v.p. 1987-88, 1st v.p. 1988-92, pres. 1993—), Am. Bar Found. (Rsch. award 1989), Inst. Jud. Adminstrn., Am. Judicature Soc., Philos. Soc. Tex., Am. Friends Cambridge U. (bd. dirs. 1994—), Country Club, Tarry House Club, Headliners Club, Ridge Harbor Yacht Club, Barton Creek Lakeside Club (Austin), Century Club, Yale Club (N.Y.C.), Mid Ocean Club (Bermuda). Republican. Episcopalian. Avocations: reading and reviewing mysteries, railroads, fishing, coaching Legal Eagles (intramural touch football team). Home: 5304 Western Hills Dr Austin TX 78731-4822 Office: U Tex Sch Law 727 E 26th St Austin TX 78705-3224

WRIGHT, CHARLES EDWARD, lawyer; b. Portland, Oreg., Mar. 21, 1906; s. Archibald Robert and Grace May (Springer) W.; m. Elisabeth Knowlton Strong, Oct. 28, 1937; children—Frederick Pares, Hilda Wright Rhodes, Elisabeth Wright Ritchie. A.B., Yale U., 1929, LL.B., 1932. Assoc. firm Platt, Platt, Fales, Smith & Black, Portland, 1933-37; sr. atty. Seattle regional office SEC, 1937-43; practice in Portland, 1943—; partner firm Bullivant, Wright, Johnson, Pendergrass and Hoffman, 1947-90; ptnr. Bullivant, Houser, Bailey, Pendergrass & Hoffman, 1990-94; retired, 1994. Bd. dirs. Portland Jr. Symphony; trustee, v.p. Catlin Hillside Schs. Mem. ABA, Oreg. Bar Assn., Am. Judicature Soc., Travelers Aid Soc. (dir. 1946), Portland Art Assn. (past dir.), Oreg. Yale Alumni Assn. (pres. 1961), City Club (past dir.), Class Coun. Yale 1929. Home: 7226 NW Penridge Rd Portland OR 97229-6806

WRIGHT, CHARLES PENZEL, JR., English language educator; b. Pickwick Dam, Tenn., Aug. 25, 1935; s. Charles Penzel and Mary Castleman (Winter) W.; m. Holly McIntire, Apr. 6, 1969; 1 child, Luke Savin Herrick. B.A., Davidson (N.C.) Coll., 1957; M.F.A., U. Iowa, 1963; postgrad., U. Rome, 1963-64. Mem. faculty U. Calif., Irvine, 1966-83; prof. English U. Calif., 1976-83; mem. faculty U. Va., Charlottesville, 1983—; Fulbright vis. prof. N.Am. lit. U. Padua, Italy, 1968-69; disting. vis. prof. U. Degli Studi, Florence, Italy, 1992. Author: The Dream Animal, 1968, The Grave of the Right Hand, 1970, The Venice Notebook, 1971, Hard Freight, 1973, Bloodlines, 1975, Colophons, 1977, China Trace, 1977, Wright: A Profile, 1979, The Southern Cross, 1981, Country Music: Selected Early Poems, 1982, The Other Side of the River, 1984, Zone Journals, 1988, Halflife, 1988, Xionia, 1990, The World of the 10,000 Things, 1990, Chickamauga, 1995, Quarter Notes, 1995, Black Zodiac, 1997; trans.: The Storm and Other Poems (Eugenio Montale), 1978, Orphic Songs (Dino Campana), 1984. Served with AUS, 1957-61. Recipient Pen Translation Prize, 1979, Nat. Book award for poetry, 1983, citation in poetry Brandeis U. Creative Arts Awards, 1987, Merit medal Am. Acad. and Inst. Arts and Letters, 1992, Ruth Lilly Poetry prize, 1993, Lenore Marshall Poetry prize, 1996; Fulbright scholar, 1963-65; Guggenheim fellow, 1976, Ingram Merrill fellow, 1980, 93. Mem. Fellowship of So. Writers, Am. Acad. Arts and Letters. Home: 940 Locust Ave Charlottesville VA 22901-4030 Office: English Dept Univ Va Charlottesville VA 22901

WRIGHT, CHARLES SPAULDING, II, writer, communications consultant; b. Traverse, Mich., Apr. 13, 1955; s. Charles Spaulding and Carol (McManus) W.; m. Debra Lynn Memmer, June 20, 1981; children: Katherine, Sarah, Zachary. AA, Northwestern Mich. Coll., Traverse City, Mich., 1981; BS, Western Mich. U., 1983. Coord. supr. Traverse Bay Area Sch. Dist., 1977; announcer, producer Interlochen (Mich.) Arts Acad., 1977; gen. mgr. Sta. WNMC-AM and FM, Traverse City, 1977-79; archtl. news reporter McGraw-Hill, Dearborn, Mich., 1985-86; community editor Pioneer Publs., Big Rapids, Mich., 1987-88; freelance writer North Channel, Southfield, Mich., 1988-91; pres. Northwind Cons., Southfield, Mich., 1991-92; writer, cons. CSW Enterprises, Traverse City, 1991-95; cons. Spec Assocs., 1996—; cons. McCann-Dumont & Assocs., Ferndale, Mich., 1990-96; reporter numerous articles on constrn., design, police beat, human interest, 1985-88; rep. Com. for a Responsible Fed. Budget, Southfield, Mich., 1995. Author: Public Affairs in N.W. Michigan, 1980. Pub. affairs dir. Blue Star Found., Birmingham, Mich., 1990-91; philanthropist Children's Make-A-Wish Found., Village Assn., Southfield, 1990—; del-at-large Rep. Party Planning Com., 1996. Scholar Western Mich. U., 1983; recipient Cert. Appreciation Pres. of U.S., 1980, HHS, 1980, 96, 97, Cert of Appreciation, Pres. Clinton, 1996. Mem. Smithsonian Inst., Libr. of Congress (charter mem.); founding mem. Libr. Congress Archives. Roman Catholic. Avocations: reading, golfing, sailing, collecting first edition books, fishing.

WRIGHT, CHATT GRANDISON, academic administrator; b. San Mateo, Calif., Sept. 17, 1941; s. Virgil Tandy and Louise (Jeschien) W.; children from previous marriage: Stephen Brook, Jon David, Shelley Adams; m. Janice Teply, Nov. 28, 1993. Student, U. Calif., Berkeley, 1960-62; BA in Polit. Sci., U. Calif., Davis, 1964; MA in Econs., U. Hawaii, 1968. Instr. econs. U. Hawaii, Honolulu, 1968-70; mgr. corp. planning Telecheck Internat., Inc., Honolulu, 1969-70; economist State of Hawaii, Honolulu, 1970-71; adminstr. manpower City & County of Honolulu, 1971-72; bus. adminstr., dean. Hawaii Pacific U., Honolulu, 1972-74, v.p., 1974-76, pres., 1976—. Mem. City and County of Honolulu Manpower Area Planning Commn., 1976-82; mem. Mayor's Salary Commn. City of County of Honolulu, 1977-80; mem. Honolulu City Ethics Commn., 1978-84; em. City and County of Honolulu Labor Market Adv. Coun., 1982-84; bd. dirs. Hawaii Econ. Devel. Corp., 1980-84; trustee Queen's Med. Ctr., Honolulu, 1986-92, Honolulu Armed Svcs. YMCA, 1984-86, Hawaii Maritime Ctr., 1990-92; chmn. bd. trustees Hist. Hawaii Found., 1995-96, mem., 1990-96; mem. adv. bd. Cancer Rsch. Ctr. Hawaii, 1987; trustee St. Andrew's Priory Sch., 1994—; bd. dirs. Hawaii Visitors Bur., 1995—; mem. adv. bd. HCEE, 1996—; bd. dirs. Downtown Improvement Assn., 1988-96, Outrigger Duke Kahanamoku Found., 1996—, Hawaii Opera Theatre, 1997—; mem. Hawaii Execs. Coun., 1996—; bd. govs. Hawaii Med. Libr., 1989-92; mem. adv. bd. Aloha coun. Boy Scouts Am., 1991—; trustee Molokai Gen. Hosp., 1991-92. With USN, 1967-80. Recipient Pioneer award Pioneer Fed. Savs. Bank, 1982. Mem. Am. Assn. Higher Edn., Assn. Governing Bds. Univs. and Colls., Japan-Am. Soc. Honolulu, Social Sci. Assn., Nat. Assn. Intercollegiate Athletics (vice chair NAIA coun. of pres. 1994, mem. NAIA coun. of pres. 1985—), Hawaii Joint Coun. Econ. Edn. (bd. dirs. 1982-88), Western Coll. Assn. (exec. com. 1989-92), Hawaii Assn. Ind. Colls. and Univs. (chmn. 1986), Hawaii C. of C., Sales and Mktg. Execs. Club Honolulu, Outrigger Canoe Club, Pacific Club (Honolulu), Plaza Club (bd. govs. 1992—), Oahu Country Club, Waialae Country Club, Rotary (Paul Harris fellow 1986). Republican. Episcopalian. Avocations: hunting, fishing, reading, travel. Office: Hawaii Pacific U Office Pres 1166 Fort Street Mall Honolulu HI 96813-2708 also: Hawaii Pacific Univ Gallery 1164 Bishop St Honolulu HI 96813

WRIGHT, CLIFFORD SIDNEY, accounting educator; b. New Orleans, Mar. 7, 1943; s. Samuel H.P. and Winifred (Vonderhaar) W.; m. Jane Eniz Truch, Aug. 2, 1969; children: Mark, Christopher, Erin. BA, BS, U. New Orleans, 1967; MBA, Loyola U., 1970; JD, Northwestern Calif. Sch. Law, 1990. CPA, La. Mgr. FNBC, New Orleans, 1967-70; prof. bus. Xavier U., New Orleans, 1970—; pvt. practice, Metairie, La., 1970—. Deacon Archdiocese of New Orleans, 1987—; bd. dirs. Hospice, Metairie, 1996, St. Vincent de Paul Soc., Metairie, 1996. Mem. AICPA, La. Soc. CPAs, Am. Acctg. Assn., Nat. Acctg. Assn., Nat. Soc. Pub. Accts., Assn. Govt. Accts. Democrat. Roman Catholic. Avocations: running, music, travel. Home: 3716 Fran St Metairie LA 70001 Office: Xavier U La 7325 Palmetto St New Orleans LA 70125-1056

WRIGHT, CONNIE SUE, special education educator; b. Nampa, Idaho, Aug. 26, 1943; d. Ruel Andrew and Renabel Carol (Graham) Farwell; m. Roger R. Wright, July 5, 1968; 1 child, Jodi C. BA, N.W. Nazarene Coll., 1967; MA in Spl. Edn., Boise State U., 1990. Cert. elem. tchr. grades kindergarten through 8th, cert. spl. edn. tchr. grades kindergarten through 12th, Idaho. Tchr. 3rd and 4th grades Vallivue Sch. Dist. 139, Caldwell, Idaho, 1967-69; tchr. 2nd grade Nampa Sch. Dist. 131, 1969-70; tchr. 3rd grade Caldwell Sch. Dist. 132, 1970-73; tchr. spl. edn. grades kindergarten through 3rd Hubbard Elem. Sch., Kuna (Idaho) Joint Sch. Dist. 3, 1985-92; tchr. adolescents CPC Intermountain Hosp. of Boise, 1992-93; tchr. spl. edn. Pioneer Elem. Sch., Meridian, Idaho, 1993—; mem. Internat. Edn. Conf. Between Russia and U.S., 1994. Libr. Horizon's Reading Coun., 1990-91. Named Tchr. Yr. Pioneer Elem. Sch., 1994-95. Mem. Coun. for Exceptional Children, Coun. for Learning Disabilities, Internat. Reading Assn. (Idaho coun.), Delta Kappa Gamma Soc. Internat. (Omicron chpt.). Avocations: reading, doll making, computers.

WRIGHT, DANIEL, wine specialist, consultant; b. Hull, Yorkshire, Eng., June 24, 1931; came to U.S., 1971; s. Edwin Vincent and Agnes Mary (Paden) W.; m. Agnes Macdonald Doull, July 9, 1955 (div. 1977); children: Oliver Hamish, Alistair Louis, Edwina Moira, William Joseph, Jeffrey Peter. Diploma in hotel and catering ops.-mgmt., Westminster Tech. Coll., London, 1952. Trainee, asst. mgr. wine dept. Fortes & Co., Hoteliers, London, 1952-57; tech. mgr. Asher Storey & Co., wine shippers, London, 1958; wine mgr. St. James Bonded Warehouses, London, 1958-64; gen. mgr. wine and spirits dept. Hunt Edmonds Brewery, Banbury, Oxford, Eng., 1964-68; wine and spirit contr. Vaux Brewery, Sunderland, Durham, Eng., 1968-71; corp. wine dir. Ga. Crown Distbg. Co., Atlanta, 1978-89; wine specialist, cons. Jax Beer & Wine (formerly Greens Beer & Wine Stores), Atlanta, 1990-97; mem. adv. bd. Atlanta Wine Festival, 1981—, judge wine competitions, 1981—. Bd. dirs. Park North Homeowners Assn., Atlanta, 1986-88; chief judge Atlanta Wine Festival, 1991. With Brit. Army, 1949-51. Fellow Brit. Bottlers Inst.; mem. Chaine des Rotisseurs (chevalier Atlanta 1977—), Companions of Beaujolais. Avocations: mycology, tennis, walking, studying languages. Home: 6709 Park Ave NE Atlanta GA 30342-2366

WRIGHT, DAVID BURTON, retired newspaper publishing company executive; b. Fowler, Ind., Aug. 29, 1933; s. Claude Matthew and Rose Ellen (Lavelle) W.; m. Geraldine F. Gray, May 9, 1964; children—David Andrew, Anne Kathleen. A.B., Wabash Coll., 1955. C.P.A., Ind. Audit staff George S. Olive & Co. C.P.A.s, Indpls., 1958-63, mgmt. cons., 1963-65; controller Herff Jones Co., Indpls., 1965-69, corp. controller, asst. sec., 1970-71; asst. bus. mgr. Indpls. Newspapers Inc., 1971-77, asst. sec., treas., 1975-93, bus. mgr., 1977-93, v.p., 1982-93; asst. sec., treas. Central Newspapers Inc., Indpls., 1975-79, sec., treas., 1979-89; asst. sec., treas. Muncie Newspapers Inc., Ind., 1975-93; mem. St. Francis Hosp. Adv. Bd., Indpls., 1983—. Sec. St. Francis Hosp. Adv. Bd., 1986-87, v.p., 1987-91, pres., 1991-93. Served with U.S. Army, 1956-58. Mem. Ind. Assn. CPAs, Indpls Econ. Club, KC. Roman Catholic. Home: 6713 Forrest Commons Blvd Indianapolis IN 46227-2396

WRIGHT, DAVID L., food and beverage company executive; b. Wenatchee, Wash., Mar. 12, 1949; s. Franklin Sven and Mary Elizabeth (Collins) W.; m. Karen Sue Rice, Mar. 28, 1981; children: Kara, Erin, Jonathan, Anna Catherine. BA, U. Calif., Davis, 1971. Chief of rsch. dept. of benefit payments State of Calif., Sacramento, 1972-75; profl. staff mem. com. on agr. U.S. Ho. Reps., Washington, 1975-77; adminstrv. asst. Rep. William C. Wampler, Washington, 1977-81; spl. asst. for legis. affairs to Pres. The White House, Washington, 1981-84; dir. govt. affairs Pepsico Inc., Purchase, N.Y., 1984-87; v.p., govt. affairs Pepsico, Inc., Purchase, N.Y., 1987—; vice chair Pub. Affairs Coun., Washington, 1995—. Dir., v.p. Nat. Conf. State Legislatures Found., Denver, 1989-96. Capt. USAR, 1971-79. Mem Capitol Hill Club, Redding Country Club. Republican. Office: Pepsico Inc 700 Anderson Hill Rd Purchase NY 10577-1403

WRIGHT, DAVID RAY, secondary school educator; b. Lampasas, Tex., Oct. 31, 1953; s. James Arlen and Peggy Pauline (Hail) W.; m. Marion Kay Hewitt, Nov. 9, 1989; children: Rebecca Jane, Gregory Neill. BS, S.W. Tex. State U., 1976; postgrad., Baylor U., 1989-90. Cert. tchr., Tex. Tchr./coach Copperas Cove (Tex.) I.S.D., 1976—; supt. adv. com. Copperas Cove I.S.D., 1987-89, 96-97, profl. consultation com.. 1989-90; test devel. advisor TAAS Instr. Objectives for Wellness, Tex. Edn. Agy., Austin, 1993. Actor: (motion picture) Gilbert Grape, 1993; dancer/actor: (motion picture for TV) Another Pair of Aces, 1991, Seduction in Travis County, 1992, Big T, 1992; singer Bluegrass Gospel Band; mem. First Bapt. Players Drama group. Recipient Excellence in Teaching award Killeen Daily Herald, 1987; tchr. of the Yr. award Copperas Cove Vets. of Foreign Wars, Post 8577, 1991. Mem. Nat. Dance Assn., AAHPERD, Tex. Assn. of Health, Phys. Edn., Recreation, and Dance (clinician State Convs. 1991, 93, chair Phys. Edn. Pub. Info. Com. 93-94), Tex. Clogging Coun., Lloyd Shaw Found., Country Song and Dance Found., Western Swing Hall of Fame. Baptist. Home: 1608 E Robertson Ave Copperas Cove TX 76522-3175

WRIGHT, DEIL SPENCER, political science educator; b. Three Rivers, Mich., June 18, 1930; s. William Henry and Gertrude Louise (Buck) W.; m. Patricia Mae Jaffke, Aug. 22, 1953; children: David C., Mark W., Matthew D., Lois L. BA, U. Mich., 1952, M in Pub. Adminstrn., 1954, PhD, 1957. Asst. prof. polit. sci. Wayne State U., Detroit, 1956-59; from asst. to assoc. prof. U. Iowa, Iowa City, 1959-67; assoc. prof. U. Calif., Berkeley, 1965-66; prof. U. N.C., Chapel Hill, 1967-83, alumni disting. prof., 1983—; Carl Hatch vis. prof. U. N.Mex., Albuquerque, 1987; adj. prof. U. Okla., Norman, 1972—; lectr. USIA, Washington, various dates; cons. Office Mgmt. and Budget, Washington, 1979-80. Author: Understanding Intergovernmental Relations, 3d edit., 1988; editor: Federalism and Intergovernmental Relations, 1984, Globalization and Decentralization, 1996; contbr. over 100 articles to various polit. sci. and pub. adminstrn. jours. Mem. dir's. adv. com. NIH, Bethesda, Md., 1970-74, N.C. Coun. on State Goals and Policies, Raleigh, 1973-77, N.C. State Internship Coun., Raleigh, 1985-93. Internat. Inst. Mgmt. research fellow, Berlin, 1977. Fellow Nat. Acad. Pub. Adminstrn.; mem. AAAS, Am. Polit. Sci. Assn., Am. Soc. Pub. Adminstrn., Midwest Polit. Sci. Assn., Policy Studies Orgn., So. Polit. Sci. Assn. (pres. 1981-82). Republican. Methodist. Lodge: Rotary (bd. dirs. Chapel Hill club 1981, 84, 90). Home: 204 Velma Rd Chapel Hill NC 27514-7641 Office: U North Carolina Dept Polit Sci Campus Box 3265 Chapel Hill NC 27599-3265

WRIGHT, DONALD CONWAY, editorial cartoonist; b. Los Angeles, Jan. 23, 1934; s. Charles C. and Sally (Olberg) W.; m. Rita Rose Blondin, Oct. 1, 1960 (dec. June 1968); m. Carolyn Ann Jay, Feb. 5, 1969. Student, Fla. pub. schs. Staff photographer, copy boy Miami News, Fla., 1952-56, graphics editor, 1958-60, polit. cartoonist, 1960-63, editorial cartoonist, 1963—; with The Palm Beach Post, West Palm Beach, Fla., 1989—; syndicated by Washington Star Syndicate, 1970, N.Y. Times Syndication Sales Service, 1976-82, Chgo. Tribune Co. Syndicate, 1982—; prod. animated cartoons for nat. TV distbn. Newsweek Broadcasting Service, 1978, for "Sunday" Today Show, NBC, 1987, 88; lectr. Miami-Dade Community Coll., 1985. Author: Wright On!, 1971, Wright Side Up, 1981; co-author: Gang of Eight, 1985; exhibited in one-man shows at Inst. for Contemporary Art, Fla. State U., Tallahassee, 1982, Lowe Art Mus., U. Miami, Coral Gables, Fla., 1979, U. Miami Lowe Art Mus., 1968; group show, Dayton, Ohio, 1969; represented in permanent collection Syracuse U., N.Y.; created theme artwork From the Hip (Dino De Laurentiis), 1987. Bd. overseers Emerson Coll., Boston U., 1976-79; AUS 1956-58. Recipient Outstanding Young Man in Communications Media award Young Democrats Fla., 1965, award Nat. Cath. Press, 1965, citation Freedoms Found., Valley Forge, Pa., 1966, Pulitzer prize, 1966, 80, Sch. Bell award Fla. Edn. Assn., 1968, Grenville Clark Editorial Page Cartoon award The Stanley Found. Iowa, 1969, Scripps-Howard Edward J. Meeman Conservation award Scripps-Howard Found., 1971, 1st place award Fla. Better Newspaper Daily Contest Fla. Press Assn., 1972, 1st prize Population Inst. Cartoon Contest Awards, N.Y.C., 1975, Editorial Category award Population Inst. Cartoon Contest Awards, N.Y.C., 1975, Nat. Headliner award Press Club Atlantic City, N.J., 1980, Tom Wallace award Inter Am. Press Assn., 1983, 86, 90, Robert F. Kennedy Meml. Journalism award, Washington, 1983, 88, 1st recipient Cox Newspapers award, 1988, David Brinkley award Barry U., 1989. Mem. Overseas Press Club Am. (awards 1969, 72, 80, 82, 85, 92), Nat. Cartoonists Soc. (Reuben award 1985, 86), Soc. Profl. Journalists (award for disting. svc. in journalism 1978, 90). Democrat. Office: The Palm Beach Post 2751 S Dixie Hwy West Palm Beach FL 33405-1233*

WRIGHT, DONALD EUGENE, retired librarian; b. Boulder, Colo., July 25, 1930; s. Kelley E. and Iva Bell (Winkle) W.; m. Verna Venetta Vorpahl, June 18, 1953 (dec.); children: Sara, Amy, John Kelley. A.B., U. Colo., 1952; A.M., U. Denver, 1953. Library asst. U. Colo., 1948-52, Denver Pub. Library, 1952; reference asst. Ft. Wayne (Ind.) Pub. Library, 1953, Detroit Pub. Library, 1953-56; dir. N. Platte (Nebr.) Pub. Library, 1956-58; library cons. Nebr. Pub. Library Commn., 1958-60; asst. dir. Lincoln (Nebr.) City Libraries, 1960-61; dir. project to aid small pub. libraries ALA, 1961-63, exec. sec. reference services div., 1963-64, exec. sec. trustee assn., 1963-64; chief bur. library services Conn. Dept. Edn., 1964-65; assoc. state librarian, also chief library devel. Ill. State Library, Springfield, 1965-67; librarian Evanston (Ill.) Pub. Library, 1967-92; adminstrv. librarian Niles (Ill.) Pub. Library Dist., 1992-93; ret., 1993; interim dir. OakPark (Ill.) Pub. Libr., 1995-96; Chmn. Gov. Nebr. Conf. Library Trustees, 1958; co-chmn. for Ill. White House Conf. on Library and Info. Svc., 1977-78, vice chmn. nat. task force, 1985, nat. transition team, 1992. Contbr. profl. jours. Mem. Nebr. Library Assn. (bd. dirs. 1958-61, pres. elect 1961), ALA (life, pres. library adminstrn. div. 1978-79), Ill. Library Assn. (pres. 1972). Presbyterian. Clubs: Rotary; University (Evanston). Home: 1715 Chancellor St Evanston IL 60201-1513

WRIGHT, DONALD FRANKLIN, newspaper executive; b. St. Paul, July 10, 1934; s. Floyd Franklin and Helen Marie (Hansen) W.; m. Sharon Kathleen Fisher, Dec. 30, 1960; children: John, Dana, Kara, Patrick. BME, U. Minn., 1957, MBA, 1958. With Mpls. Star & Tribune Co., 1958-77, research planning dir., then ops. dir., 1971-75, exec. editor, 1975-77; exec. v.p., gen. mgr. Newsday, Inc., L.I., 1977-78, pres., chief operating officer, 1978-81; pres., chief operating officer Los Angeles Times, 1981-87; sr. v.p. Times Mirror Co., Los Angeles, 1988—. Hon. mem., former vice chmn. bd. trustees Claremont Grad. Sch. and Univ. Ctr.; vice chmn., past chmn. L.A. Area coun. Boy Scouts Am., 1989—, v.p. western region, past pres. area IV; bd. dirs. Assocs. Calif. Inst. Tech., U. Minn. Found.; past bd. dirs. United Way Long Island, Calif.;. Mem. Am. Newspaper Pubs. Assn. (past chmn. telecom. com. and prodn. mgmt. com.), U. Minn. Alumni Assn., City Club Bunker Hill. Presbyterian. Office: Times Mirror Co Times Mirror Sq Los Angeles CA 90053

WRIGHT, DOUGLAS TYNDALL, former university administrator, civil engineer; b. Toronto, Oct. 4, 1927; s. George C. and Etta (Tyndall) W.; B.A.Sc. with honors in Civil Engring, U. Toronto, 1949; M.S. in Structural Engring, U. Ill., 1952; Ph.D. in Engring, U. Cambridge, 1954; D.Eng. (hon.), Carleton U., 1967; LL.D. (hon.), Brock U., 1967, Concordia U., 1982; D.Sc. (hon.), Meml. U. Nfld., 1969; DHL (hon.), Northeastern U., 1985, U. Waterloo, 1995; D.Univ. (hon.), Strathclyde U., Glasgow, 1989; D de L'Université, Compiegne U., France, 1991; D Univ. (hon.), Université de Sherbrooke, 1992; DSc, McMaster U., 1993, Queen's U., 1993; LLD (hon.), U. Waterloo, 1995. Lectr. dept. civil engring. Queen's U., 1954-55, asst. prof., 1955-58, assoc. prof., 1958; prof. civil engring. U. Waterloo, 1958-67, chmn. dept. civil engring., 1958-63, dean engring., 1959-66; chmn. Ont. Com. on Univ. Affairs Govt. of Ont., 1967-72; chmn. Ont. Commn. Post-Secondary Edn., Toronto, 1969-72, dep. provincial sec. for social devel., 1972-79; dep. minister culture and recreation, 1979-80; pres. U. Waterloo, Ont., 1981-93; prof. engring. U. Waterloo, Ont., 1981—; vis. prof. Universidad Nacional Autónoma de Mexico, 1964, 66, Université de Sherbrooke, 1966-67; cons. engr. Netherlands and Mexican Pavilions Expo, 1967, Olympic Sports Palace, Mexico City, 1968, Ont. Place Dome and Forum, 1971; tech. advisor Toronto Skydome, 1984-92; dir. ElectroHome Ltd., Bell Can., London Life Ins. Co., London Ins. Group, Com Dev Ltd., Geometrica Inc., Visible Decisions, Inc., Meloche, Monnex, Inc., Goeken Group Inc., Can. Inst. for Advanced rsch., RIM Ltd., London Guarantee Ins. Co.; mem. Premier's Coun. on Sci. and Tech., Ont., 1985-91, Prime Min.'s Nat. Adv. Bd. for Sci. and Tech., 1985-91; Can. rep. Coun. for Internat. Inst. Applied Sys. Analysis, Laxenburg, Austria; Prime Min.'s personal rep. to Coun. Mins. of Edn., 1990-91. Contbr. articles to profl. jours. Bd. dirs. African Students Found., Toronto, 1961-66; bd. dirs. Ont. Curriculum Inst., 1964-67; bd. govs. Stratford Shakespearian Festival, 1984-86, mem. senate, 1987. Athlone fellow, 1952-54; named Officer of Order of Can., 1991, Chevalier L'Ordre National du Mérite of France, 1992; recipient Gold medal Ont. Profl. Engrs., 1990, Can. Engrs. Gold Medal award Can. Coun. Profl. Engrs., 1992, Engineering Institute of Canada, Sir John Kennedy Medal Award, 1995. Fellow ASCE, Can. Acad. Engring., Engring. Inst. Can. (del. Engrs. Coun. Profl. Devel., N.Y.C. 1961-70); mem. Assn. Profl. Engrs. Province Ont., Internat. Assn. Bridge and Structural Engring., Internat. Assn. Shell Structures, Can. Assn. Latin Am. Studies, Am. Acad. Mechanics, Can. Inst. Internat. Affairs, Can. Inst. Pub. Adminstrn. Clubs: Royal Can. Yacht, Univ. (Toronto). Office: U Waterloo, Engring Dept, Waterloo, ON Canada N2L 3G1

WRIGHT, DOUGLASS BROWNELL, judge, lawyer; b. Hartford, Conn., May 30, 1912; s. Arthur Brownell and Sylvia (Stephens) W.; m. Jane Hamersley, Sept. 24, 1938; children: Jane C., Douglass B., Hamersley S., Elizabeth B., Arthur W. A.B., Yale U., 1933; LL.B., Hartford Coll. Law, 1937. Bar: Conn. 1937. Legal dept. Aetna Life Ins. Co., 1937-39; partner Davis, Lee, Howard & Wright, Hartford, 1939—; lectr. law U. Conn., 1946—; asst. state's atty. State of Conn., 1952-59; judge Conn. Circuit Court, 1959-65, Conn. Superior Ct., 1965—; leader orch. Judge Wright and the Four Wrongs. Author: Connecticut Law of Torts, 1956, Connecticut Legal Forms, 5 vols., 1958, Connecticut Jury Instructions, 3 vols., 1960, 76. Sec., dir. Captioned Films for the Deaf, Inc.; bd. dirs., pres. Am. Sch. for Deaf, 1942—; trustee Hartt Mus. Found., 1949—, Good Will Boys Club Hartford, 1950—; regent U. Hartford; bd. dirs. Vis. Nurse Assn., Newington Home for Crippled Children, Hartford Times Farm, Loomis Sch.; incorporator Conn. Inst. for Blind. Served as lt. USNR, 1942-45. Mem. Phi Beta Kappa, Psi Upsilon. Conglist. Clubs: University (Hartford), Hartford Golf (Hartford), Hartford Tennis (Hartford), 20th Century (Hartford); Coral Beach and Tennis (Bermuda); Hillsboro (Pompano Beach, Fla.). Home: 275 Steele Rd Apt 114A West Hartford CT 06117-2751 Office: 95 Washington St Hartford CT 06106-4406

WRIGHT, EARL JEROME, pastor, bishop; b. Altheimer, Ark., Dec. 10, 1929; s. Frank Lee and Emma Ophelia (Tillman) W.; m. Geraldine Marvel Miller, Aug. 16, 1952; children: Earl Jerome, Michael Ellis, Marvel Sheryl. Grad., William Tyndale Bible Coll., Detroit, 1953; DDiv (hon.), Trinity Hall Div. Sch., 1961. Ordained min. Ch. of God in Christ, 1953. Postal clk. U.S. Post Office, Detroit, 1952-67; pastor Miller Meml. Ch. of God in Christ, Detroit, 1963—; bishop 2d Eccles. Jurisdiction S.W. Mich., Detroit, 1985—; chair adv. com. Bd. of Bishops, 1986—; chmn. ways and means com. Gen. Assembly, 1991—; nat. sec. youth dept. United Nat. Auxs. Conv., 1970-76, nat. registrar, 1976-82. Mem. exec. bd. dirs., NAACP, Detroit, 1983-87; mem. bd. dirs. FEMA, Detroit, 1983—; vice chmn. Mayor's Clergy Com., Detroit, 1987-91. Avocations: fishing, health spa activities, bike riding, horseback riding. *

WRIGHT, ERNEST MARSHALL, physiologist, consultant; b. Belfast, Ireland, June 8, 1940; came to U.S., 1965; BSc, U. London, 1961, DSc, 1978; PhD, U. Sheffield, Eng., 1964. Research fellow Harvard U., Boston, 1965-66; from asst. prof. to full prof. physiology UCLA Med. Sch., 1967—, chmn. dept. physiology, 1987—; cons. NIH, Bethesda, Md., 1982—, Senator Jacob K. Javits neurosci. investigator, 1985. Office: UCLA Sch Med Dept Physiology 10833 Le Conte Ave Los Angeles CA 90095-3075

WRIGHT, EUGENE ALLEN, federal judge; b. Seattle, Feb. 23, 1913; s. Elias Allen and Mary (Bailey) W.; m. Esther Ruth Ladley, Mar. 19, 1938; children: Gerald Allen, Meredith Ann Wright Morton. AB, U. Wash., 1935, JD, 1937; LLD, U. Puget Sound, 1984. Bar: Wash. 1937. Assoc. Wright & Wright, Seattle, 1937-54; judge Superior Ct. King County, Wash., 1954-66; v.p., sr. trust officer Pacific Nat. Bank Seattle, 1966-69; judge U.S. Ct. Appeals (9th cir.), Seattle, 1969—; acting municipal judge, Seattle, 1948-52; mem. faculty Nat. Jud. Coll., 1964-72; lectr. Sch. Communications, U. Wash., 1965-66, U. Wash. Law Sch., 1952-74; lectr. appellate judges' seminars, 1973-76, Nat. Law Clks. Inst., La. State U., 1973; chmn. Wash. State Com. on Law and Justice, 1968-69; mem. com. on appellate rules Jud. Conf., 1978-85, mem. com. on courtroom photography, 1983-85, com. jud. ethics, 1984-92, com. Bicentennial of Constn., 1985-87. Author: (with others) The State Trial Judges Book, 1966; also articles; editor: Trial Judges Jour., 1963-66; contbr. articles to profl. jours. Chmn. bd. visitors U. Puget Sound Sch. Law, 1979-84; mem. bd. visitors U. Wash. Sch. Law, 1989—; bd. dirs. Met. YMCA, Seattle, 1955-72; lay reader Episc Ch. Served to lt. col. USAR, 1941-46, col. Res., ret. Decorated Bronze Star, Combat Inf. badge; recipient Army Commendation medal, Disting. Service award U.S. Jr. C. of C., 1948, Disting. Service medal Am. Legion. Fellow Am. Bar Found.; mem. ABA (coun. div. jud. adminstrn. 1971-76), FBA (Disting. Jud. Svc. award 1984), Wash. Bar Assn. (award of merit 1983), Seattle-King County Bar Assn. (Spl. Disting. Svc. award 1984), Appellate Judges Conf., Order of Coif, Wash. Athletic Club, Rainier Club, Masons (33 deg.), Shriners, Delta Upsilon (Disting. Alumni Achievement award 1989), Phi Delta Phi. Office: US Ct Appeals 9th Cir 902 US Courthouse 1010 5th Ave Seattle WA 98104-1130

WRIGHT, FAITH-DORIAN, artist; b. Bklyn., Feb. 9, 1934; d. Abraham and Molly (Janoff) J.; children: Jordan Merritt, Igrid-beth. BS, NYU, 1955, MA, 1958; postgrad., Pratt and Parsons Sch. of Design. Works exhibited in Kathryn Markel Gallery, N.Y.C., 1981, 92, Cumberland Gallery, Nashville, 1981, 92, Barbara Gillman Gallery, Miami, 1982, Hand and Hand Gallery, 1985, 86, Suzanne Gross, Phila., 1986, 87, Gallery Four, Alexandria, Va., 1986, 87, 88, Henri Gallery, Washington, 1986, 87, 88, 89. 90. 91. 92. 93. 94, Benton Gallery, Southampton, 1986, 87, 88, 89, 91, 92, 93, King Stephen Mus., Hungary, 1987, Nat. Gallery Women in the Arts, 1987, 88, 90, 91, 92, Ruth Volid Gallery, Chgo., 1990, James Gallery, Pitts., 1990, Aart Vark Gallery, Phila., 1990, Merrill Chase Gallery, Chgo., 1990, 91, 92, Guild Hall Mus., East Hampton, N.Y., 1991, Joy Berman Gallery, Phila., 1992, Ctr. for Book Arts, N.Y.C., 1992, Barnard-Biederman Fine Arts, N.Y.C., 1994, Arlene Bujese Gallery, East Hampton, 1994, 95, 96, Stoney Brook U., 1994, Harper Collins Exhbn. Space, 1995, Ctr. for Book Arts, 1996, arlene bujese, 1997, Galerie Cargo, Paris, 1997, N.Y. State Mus., Albany, 1997; permanent collections Nat. Postal Art Mus., Ottawa, Can., Nat. Inst. Design, Ahmedabad, India, Fine Arts Acad., New Delhi, India, Mus. Modern Art, N.Y.C., Nat. Mus. Women in the Arts, Washington, D.C., Israel Mus., Jerusalem, Brenau Coll., Grainsville, Ga. Blue Cross, Blue Shield, Phila., Mc Donald's, Oakbrook, Ill., The Hyatt Collection, Chgo., Guild Hall Mus., Saul, Ewing, Reineck & Saul, Phila., Shevick, Ravich, Koster, Tobin, Clark, N.J., Sidley & Austin, L.A., Catalano & Sparber, N.Y.; contbr. critical essays to various periodicals. Mem. Women in Arts, Women's Caucus for Arts, Artists Equity, Visitation Bd. of Met. Mus.-Rockefeller Connection. Address: 300 E 74th St New York NY 10021-3712

WRIGHT, FRANK GARDNER, newspaper editor; b. Moline, Ill., Mar. 21, 1931; s. Paul E. and Goldie (Hicks) W.; m. Barbara Lee Griffiths, Mar. 28, 1953; children: Stephen, Jeffrey, Natalie, Gregory, Sarah. B.A., Augustana Coll., Rock Island, Ill., 1953; postgrad., U. Minn., 1953-54. Suburban reporter Mpls. Star, 1954-55; with Mpls. Tribune, 1955-82, N.D. corr., 1955-56, Mpls. City Hall reporter, 1956-58, asst. city editor, 1958-63, Minn. polit. reporter, 1963-68, Washington corr., 1968-72, Washington bur. chief, 1972-77, mng. editor, 1977-82; mng. editor/news Mpls. Star and Tribune, 1982-84, assoc. editor, 1984—; juror for Pulitzer Awards, 1983-84. Chmn. Golden Valley Human Rights Commn., 1965-67; Bd. dirs. Luth. Social Services, Washington. Recipient several Page 1 awards Twin Cities Newspaper Guild, 1950's, 60's, Worth Bingham prize Worth Bingham Meml. Fund, 1971; runnerup Raymond Clapper award for Washington correspondence, 1971; Outstanding Achievement award Augustana Alumni Assn., 1977; citation for excellence in internat. reporting Overseas Press Club, 1985; Minn. SPJ/SDX 1st Place Page One award for in-depth reporting, 1988, MWAP award Human Interest Reporting, 1995. Mem. Am. Newspaper Guild (chmn. Mpls. unit 1961-67, editorial v.p. Twin Cities 1963-67), Minn. AP Editors Assn. (pres. 1981), Phi Beta Kappa. Home: 4912 Aldrich Ave S Minneapolis MN 55409-2353 Office: 425 Portland Ave Minneapolis MN 55415-1511

WRIGHT, FRANZ, poet, writer, translator; b. Vienna, Austria, 1953. Translator, author of introduction Rainer Maria Rilke, The Unknown Rilke, 1990; translator modern and contemporary French and German poets; author: (poems) Tapping the White Cane of Solitude, The Earth Without You, Eight Poems, 1981, The One Whose Eyes Open When You Close Your Eyes, 1982, No Siege Is Absolute, 1983, Going North in Winter, 1986, Entry in an Unknown Hand, 1989, Midnight Postscript, 1990, And Still the Hand Will Sleep in Its Glass Ship, 1990, Rorschach Test, 1995, The Night World and the Word Night, 1993; represented in anthologies; contbr. articles to profl. publs. Recipient Witter Bynner Prize for Poetry, 1995, PEN/Voelcker award, 1996; NEA fellow, 1985, 92, Guggenheim fellow, 1989, Whiting fellow, 1991. Office: 38 Francis St Everett MA 02149-4814

WRIGHT, GEARLD LEWIS, mayor, retired educator; b. Lyman, Wyo., Feb. 22, 1933; s. Alton and Ida Mabel (Jensen) W.; m. Lila Lynn Florence, July 16, 1953; children: Jeri Lynn, Alan Kay, Lori Marie, Daryl Wilmer, Merlin Craig, Craig Alton. Diploma in secondary instr., Brigham Young U., 1961, diploma in provisional counseling, 1961. Educator Granite Sch. Dist., Salt Lake City, 1961-87, retired, 1987; mayor West Valley City, Utah; mem. exec. com. Coun. of Govts., Utah Econ. Devel. Corp. Utah, trustee; mem. Pub. Safety Com., Econ. Devel. Com., Utah League Cities, Towns Policy Com., Govs Task Force on Weapons, Nat. League Cities Transp. and Comms. Com., U.S. Conf. Mayors Criminal and Social Justice Com., transp. and comms. com. Pres. Hunter Coun.; mem. Joh Short Feasibility Study Com.; rep. Salt Lake County Assn. Cmty. Couns.; past pres. Jackson Hole Home Owners Assn., Conf. Salt Lake Valley Mayors; active PTA, PTSA; parents adv. com. mem. Primary Children's Med. Ctr., spl. coms., organizer Family Living Seminar; sec., treas. Joseph Thompson Family Orgn.; past. chmn., com. mem. Westfest Internat. Festival. Recipient Dist. Merit award Westview Scouting Dist., West Valley, Utah, 1986. Mem. Wasatch Front Regional Coun. (bd. dirs.). Avocations: sports, history, religion, travel. Home: 5432 Janette Ave West Valley City UT 84120 Office: West Valley City 3600 Constitution Blvd West Valley City UT 84119-3720

WRIGHT, GEORGE CULLEN, electronics company executive; b. Anderson, S.C., June 28, 1923; s. Benjamin Norman and Essie Floride (Cole) W.; m. Kathleen Ashe, Oct. 19, 1947; children: Carol Ann (Mrs. John C. Marquardt), George Cullen, Florenda Jean, William Norman. BS, Clemson U., 1948. Asst. supt. Duke Power Co., 1949-56; city mgr. Gaffney, S.C., 1956-60; v.p. mktg. Hubbard & Co., Chgo., 1960-65; dir. Methode Electronics, Inc., Rolling Meadows, Ill., 1956—; v.p., dir. Anchor Coupling Co., Inc., Libertyville, Ill., 1973-76; pres., dir. Exec. Extension & Ventures, Inc., Barrington, Ill., 1976-78, White Marlin Marine, Inc., Anderson, S.C., 1976-86, Piedmont Corp., 1986—. Patentee in field. Pres. Barrington East Ass., 1968-70. Served with USAF, 1942-45. Mem. AIEE Electron Industry Assn., Am. Mgmt. Assn. Lodges: Rotary, Sertoma (pres. 1963-65). Home: 224 Jolly Rd Townville SC 29689-3540

WRIGHT, GLADYS STONE, music educator, composer, writer; b. Wasco, Oreg., Mar. 8, 1925; d. Murvel Stuart and Daisy Violet (Warren) Stone; m. Alfred George Wright, June 28, 1953. BS, U. Oreg., 1948, MS, 1953. Dir. bands Elmira (Oreg.) U-4 High Sch., 1948-53, Otterbein (Ind.) High Sch., 1954-61, Klondike High Sch., West Lafayette, Ind., 1962-70, Harrison High Sch., West Lafayette, 1970-84; organizer, condr. Musical Friendship Tours, Cen. Am., 1967-79; v.p., condr. U.S. Collegiate Wind Band, 1975—; bd. dirs. John Philip Sousa Found. 1984—; chmn. Sudler Cup, 1986—, Sudler Flag, 1982; pres. Internat. Music Tours, 1984—. Key to the City, Taxco, Mex., 1975. Editor: Woman Conductor, 1986—; composer: marches Big Bowl and Trumpets and Tabards, 1987; contbg. editor: Informusica (Spain). Bd. dirs. N. Am. Wildlife Park, Battleground, Ind. 1985. Recipient Medal of the order John Philip Sousa Found., 1988, Star of Order, 1991; 1st woman guest conductor U.S. Navy Band, Washington D.C., 1961, Goldman Band, N.Y.C., 1958, Kneller Hall Band, London, 1975, Tri-State Music Festival Massed Orch., Band, Choir, 1985; elected to Women Bd. Dirs. Hall of Fame of Disting. Women Conductor, 1994. Mem. Am. Bandmasters Assn. (bd. dirs. 1993, 1st woman mem.), Women Band Dirs. Nat. Assn. (founding pres. 1967, sec. 1985, recipient Silver Baton 1974, Golden Rose 1990, Hall of Fame 1995), Am. Sch. Band Dirs. Assn., Nat. Band Assn. (Citation excellence 1970), Tippecoanoe Arts Fedn. (bd. dirs. 1986-90), Tippecanoe Fife and Drum Corps. (bd. dirs. 1984), Daughters of Am. Revolution, Col. Dames-Pre Quitanen Chpt., New England Women, Tau Beta Sigma (Outstanding Svc. to Music award 1970), Phi Beta Mu (1st hon. women mem. 1972), North Am. Wildlife Park (bd dirs, 1990—). Avocations: historic preservation, environ. activities.

WRIGHT, GORDON BROOKS, musician, conductor, educator; b. Bklyn., Dec. 31, 1934; s. Harry Wesley and Helen Philomena (Brooks) W.; m. Inga-Lisa Myrin Wright, June 13, 1958 (div. 1979); children: Karin-Ellen Sturla, Charles-Eric, Daniel Brooks. MusB, Coll. Wooster, 1957; MA, U. Wis., 1961; postgrad., Salzburg Mozarteum, 1972, Loma Linda U., 1979; studied with, René Leibowitz, Carl Melles, Wilfred Pelletier, Herbert Blomstedt, Hans Swarowsky. Founder, music dir. Wis. Chamber Orch., 1960-69; music dir. Fairbanks (Alaska) Symphony Orch., 1969-89; prof. music Univ. Alaska, Fairbanks, 1969-89, prof. emeritus, 1989—; founder, music dir. Arctic Chamber Orch., Fairbanks, 1970-89; exec. dir. The Reznicek Soc., Indian, Alaska, 1982—. Guest condr. Philharmonia Hungarica, Philomusica London, Norwegian Radio Orch., Orch. St. Luke's, Anchorage Symphony Orch., Musashino Orch., Tokyo, Tohoku Orch., Sendai, Japan; composer: Suite of Netherlands Dances, 1965, Six Alaskan Tone Poems, 1974, Symphony in Ursa Major, 1979 (Legis. award 1979), 1984 Overture, Scott Joplin Suite, 1987, Toccata Festiva, 1992; columnist Alaska Advocate. Founder, bd. dirs. No. Alaska Environ. Ctr., Fairbanks, 1971-78. Served as pvt. AUS, 1957-59. Mem. Am. Musicol. Soc., Royal Musical Assn., Am. Symphony Orch. League, Condr.'s Guild, Arturo Toscanini Soc., Am. Fedn. Musicians, Royal Mus. Assn., Sierra Club (lchmn. Fairbanks Group 1969-71), Friends of Earth-Alaska (bd. dirs. 1978—), Wilderness Soc., Audubon Soc., Alaska Conservation Soc. (editor Rev. 1971-78), Ctr. for Alaskan Coastal Studies (bd. dirs. 1982—). Avocations: hiking, kayaking, collecting books, photography. Home: HC 52 Box 8899 Indian AK 99540-9604

WRIGHT, GORDON PRIBYL, management, operations research educator; b. Crosby, Minn., May 18, 1938; s. Kenneth Eugene and Verla Emily (Pribyl) W.; m. Judith Ann Hill, Aug. 19, 1961; 1 dau., Teresa Ann. B.A., Macalester Coll., 1960; M.A., U. Mass., 1963; Ph.D., Case Western Res. U., 1967. Systems analyst Conn. Gen. Life Ins. Co., Bloomfield, 1960-61; instr. dept. math. U. Mass., 1961-63; statistician, mgmt. scis. group Goodyear Tire & Rubber Co., Akron, Ohio, 1963-64; instr., research asst., ops. research dept. Case Inst. Tech., Cleve., 1964-67; asst. prof. dept. indsl. engring. and mgmt. scis. Technol. Inst., Northwestern U., 1967-70; assoc. prof. mgmt. and statistics Krannert Grad. Sch. Mgmt. and Sch. of Sci., Purdue U., West Lafayette, Ind., 1970-75; assoc. dean Krannert Grad. Sch. Mgmt. and Sch. of Sci., Purdue U., 1979-84, dir. prof., 1982—, Krannert disting. prof., 1982—, dir. of research, 1985-89, dir. doctoral programs, 1985-89; prof., chmn. mgmt., dir. profl. programs Krannert Grad. Sch. Mgmt., Purdue U., 1978-79; Basil Turner prof. mgmt. Purdue U., 1987—; vis. prof. bus. adminstrn. and stats. Amos Tuck Sch. Bus. Adminstrn., Dartmouth Coll., 1976-77; vis. prof. Bradley U.; vis. prof. mgmt. sci. Grad. Sch. Mgmt. UCLA, 1984-85; cons. Okamura Mfg. Co., Yokohama, Japan. Author: (with David G. Olson) Designing Water Pollution Detection Systems, 1974, (with Andrew B. Whinston and Gary J. Koehler) Optimization of Leontief Systems, 1975, (with Herbert M. Moskowitz) An Experiential Approach to Management Science, 1975, Introduction to Management Science, 1979, Statistics for Business and Economics, 1982, (with Frank M. Bass) Stochastic Brand Coice and Brand Switching: Theory Analysis and Description, 1980; contbr. (with Frank M. Bass) articles on ops. research and mgmt. to profl. jours. Served with USAF Res., 1961-67. Recipient Salgo-Noren Found. award for outstanding teaching in bus. adminstrn., 1975; NSF research grantee, 1968-70; Dept. Transp. research grantee, 1972-74; HEW research grantee, 1969-70; Sloan Found. research grantee, 1972-75; Fulbright scholar to Ger., 1986; Vis. Erskine fellowship U. Canterbury, New Zealand, 1985. Mem. Ops. Research Soc. Am., Inst. Mgmt. Scis., Sigma Xi, Beta Gamma Sigma. Home: 136 Seminole Dr West Lafayette IN 47906-2116 Office: Krannert Sch Mgmt Purdue U West Lafayette IN 47907

WRIGHT, GWENDOLYN, art center director, writer, educator; b. Chgo., May 14, 1946; d. William Kemp and Mary Ruth (Brown) W.; m. Paul Rabinow, Nov. 18, 1980 (div. 1982); m. Thomas Bender, Jan. 14, 1985; children: David, Sophia. BA, NYU, 1969; MArch, U. Calif., Berkeley, 1974, PhD, 1980. Assoc. prof. Columbia U., N.Y.C., 1983-87, prof., 1988—; dir. Buell Ctr. for Study Am. Architecture, N.Y.C., 1988-92; cons. Fulbright Scholars, Coun. Internat. Exch. Scholars, Washington, 1988-91. Author: Building the Dream: A Social History of Housing in America, 1980, Moralism and the Model Home, 1981, The History of History in American Schools of Architecture, 1990, The Politics of Design in French Colonial Urbanism, 1991. Fellow Ford Found., 1979-80; Stanford Inst. for Humanities, 1982-83, Mich. Inst. for Humanities, 1991, Getty Ctr. for History of Art and the Humanities, 1992—. Fellow Soc. Am. Historians, N.Y. Inst. for Humanities; mem. Soc. Archtl. Historians, Coll. Art Assn., Am. Hist. Assn., Orgn. Am. Historians. Democrat. Home: 54 Washington Mews New York NY 10003-6608 Office: Columbia U Avery Hall New York NY 10027

WRIGHT, HAROLD STANLEY, lawyer; b. Honolulu, Nov. 9, 1918; s. Harold Stanley Wilkinson and Julia (Wright) Gilman; m. June McCormack, Aug. 16, 1953; children: Barry H., Kirby M., Julie A. BA, U. Hawaii, 1943; JD, Harvard U., 1949. Bar: Hawaii 1949, U.S. Dist. Ct. Hawaii 1949, U.S. Ct. Appeals (9th cir.) 1952. Assoc. Smith Wild Beebe & Cades, Honolulu, 1949-52; ptnr. Cades Schutte Fleming & Wright, Honolulu, 1952—. Chmn. Pacific War Meml. Commn., Honolulu, 1973-75. Maj. U.S. Army, 1941-46, PTO. Mem. ABA, Hawaii Bar Assn. Office: Cades Schutte Fleming & Wright 1000 Bishop St Honolulu HI 96813-4212

WRIGHT, HARRY, III, retired lawyer; b. Lima, Ohio, Apr. 27, 1925; s. Harry Jr. and Marjorie (Riddle) W.; m. Louise Forbes Taylor, Dec. 15, 1956; children: Harry IV, Whitaker Wilson, Priscilla W. Nicholson. Student, The Citadel, 1942-43; B.S., U. Ky., 1948; LL.B., Harvard, 1951. Bar: Ohio 1951. With Porter, Wright, Morris & Arthur, Columbus, 1951—; ptnr. Porter, Wright, Morris & Arthur, 1956-88, of counsel, 1988-95, ret., 1995; adj. prof. law Japan Law Ctr., 1986. Mem. adv. bd. Salvation Army, 1958-74; pres. bd. trustees Six Pence Sch., Columbus, 1965-75; trustee Bradford Coll., 1957-75, pres. bd., 1972-74; trustee Columbus Acad., 1975-81, pres. bd., 1978-80; trustee Columbus Coun. World Affairs, 1979-82 Opera/Columbus, 1980-88, 89-95, Ballet Met., 1987-91; trustee Green Lawn Cemetery, 1992—, Neighborhood Ho., 1993—. With USAF, 1943-46. Mem. ABA (chmn. gen. practice sect. 1976-77, ho. of dels. 1978-87), Ohio Bar Assn. (Supreme Ct. Commn. on CLE 1988-94), Columbus Bar Assn., Columbus Club, Rocky Fork Hunt and Country Club. Episcopalian. Home: 292 N Drexel Ave Columbus OH 43209-1429 Office: 41 S High St Columbus OH 43215-6101

WRIGHT, HARRY FORREST, JR., retired banker; b. Woodbury, N.J., Nov. 9, 1931; s. Harry Forrest and Bertha (Strumpfer) W.; m. Lorraine Catherine McLaughlin, Oct. 16, 1954; children: Harry Forrest III, Lonni Caryn, Gregory William, Douglas Carl. Student, Temple U., 1949-50, Am. Inst. Banking, 1950-52; accounting certificate, Wharton Sch., U. Pa., 1960, asso. degree, 1962. Clk. First Nat. Bank, Phila., 1951-60; asst. comptroller, then asst. v.p. First Pa. Co., 1960- 64; v.p. Md. Nat. Bank, Balt., 1964-66; v.p., comptroller Md. Nat. Bank, 1966-70, sr. v.p., comptroller, 1970-73, exec. v.p., 1973-81, sr. exec. v.p., 1981-89, also bd. dirs., ret., 1989; v.p., treas. Md. Nat. Corp., 1974-77, sr. v.p., 1977-83; exec. v.p., chief fin. officer MNC Fin., Inc., 1983-88, ret., 1989; treas., dir. Md. Nat. Optimation Svcs., Inc., 1969-76, chmn., 1976-79; sec. Md. Switch, Inc., 1976-79; treas., dir. Manab Properties, Inc.; pres., dir. 10 Light St. Corp., 1973-82; affiliate Property Tax Cons., San Diego, 1990—. Treas. Cub Scouts Am., Severna Park, Md., 1965-66, St. Martin's Kindergarten, 1967-72, Bayberry Hill Property Owners Assn., 1985—; bd. dirs. Greater Balt. chpt. Nat. Found. March of Dimes, 1972-89, v.p., 1977-79, pres., 1979-81, chmn., 1981-84; bd. dirs. Nat. Coun. Vols., 1983-85, 89-95, Nat. Fin. Task Force, 1989-95; bd. dirs. Md. Sch. for Blind, 1975—, v.p., 1981-88, pres., 1988-94, chmn. bd., 1994—; chmn. Richard E. Hoover Commn. for Low Vision and Blindness at Greater Balt. Med. Ctr., 1990-92, treas., 1992—. Mem. Bank Adminstrn. Inst. (pres. Balt. 1970-71, state dir. 1971-73, dist. dir. 1977-79), Fin. Execs. Inst. (dir. 1976-78), Sigma Kappa Phi. Club: Mchts. (Balt.) (bd. dirs. 1974-87, v.p. 1976-79, pres. 1979-82). Home and Office: 1314 Saint Josephs Ct Crownsville MD 21032-2129 *Success in life is not measured in material wealth, but in diversity of accomplishment, contribution to social good, and respect from peers, subordinates, and superiors alike. The greatest joys are in children and grandchildren and their growth and achievements, and in teaching them continually to strive harder to be successful and happy.*

WRIGHT, HASTINGS KEMPER, surgeon, educator; b. Boston, Aug. 28, 1928; s. Donald M. and Lucia (Durand) W.; m. Nancy E. Howell, June 19, 1954; children: Mark, Kenneth, Barbara, Donald. AB, Harvard U., 1950, MD, 1954, MA, 1973. Diplomate: Am. Bd. Surgery. Intern Univ. Hosps. Cleve., 1954, resident, 1957-61; asst. prof. surgery Western Res. U., Cleve., 1961-66; assoc. prof. surgery Med. Sch. Yale U., New Haven, 1967-72, prof. Med. Sch., 1972-95; prof. surgery emeritus, 1995—; chief gen. surgery Yale-New Haven Hosp., 1968-79, asst. chief surgery, 1979-95. Author: Complications of GI Surgery, 1972; asst. chief editor Archives of Surgery, Chgo., 1977-89. Capt. U.S. Army, 1955-57. Fellow ACS, Am. Surg. Assn.; mem. Soc. Univ. Surgeons (program dir. 1972), Am. Gastroent. Assn., Soc. Surgery Gastrointestinal Tract. Republican. Episcopalian. Clubs: Mory's Assoc. (New Haven); Yale (N.Y.C.). Home: 35 Wood Rd Branford CT 06405-4935 Office: Yale U Med Sch Dept Surgery 333 Cedar St New Haven CT 06510-3206

WRIGHT, HELEN KENNEDY, professional association administrator, publisher, editor, librarian; b. Indpls., Sept. 23, 1927; d. William Henry and Ida Louise (Crosby) Kennedy; m. Samuel A. Wright, Sept. 5, 1970; 1 child, Carl F. Prince II (dec.). BA, Butler U., 1945, MS, 1950; MS, Columbia U., 1952. Reference libr. N.Y. Pub. Libr., N.Y.C., 1952-53, Bklyn. Pub. Libr., 1953-54; reference libr., cataloger U. Utah, 1954-57; libr. Chgo. Pub. Libr.; asst. dir. pub. dept. ALA, Chgo., 1958-62, editor Reference Books Bull., 1962-85, asst. dir. for new product planning, pub. svcs., 1985—, dir. office for libr. outreach svcs., 1987-90, mng. editor yearbook, 1988—. Contbr. to Ency. of Careers, Ency. of Libr. and Info. Sci., New Book of Knowledge Ency., Bulletin of Bibliography, New Golden Book Ency. Recipient Louis Shores/Oryx Pr. award, 1991. Mem. Phi Kappa Phi, Kappa Delta Pi, Sigma Gamma Rho. Roman Catholic. Home: 1138 W 111th St Chicago IL 60643-4508 Office: ALA 50 E Huron St Chicago IL 60611-2729

WRIGHT, HELEN PATTON, professional society administrator; b. Washington, Jan. 15, 1919; d. Raymond Stanton and Virginia (Mitchell) Patton; m. James Skelly Wright, Feb. 1, 1945 (dec. 1988); 1 son, James Skelly; m. John H. Pickering, Feb. 3, 1990. Student, Sweet Briar Coll., 1936-38; grad., Washington Sch. Secretaries, 1939, Am. U., 1989. Tchr. Washington Sch. Secs., N.Y.C., 1939-40; sec. The White House, 1941-43, Am. Embassy, London, 1943-45; asst. to exec. dir. Senate Atomic Energy Com., 1946-47. Author: My Journey Recollections of the First Seventy Years, 1995. V.p., mem. budget and admissions com. United Fund New Orleans, 1960-62; chmn. met. div., campaign; v.p. Dept. Pub. Welfare, Orleans Parish and City New Orleans, 1960-62, Milne Asylum for Destitute Orphan Boys, New Orleans, 1958-62; mem. bd. New Orleans Social Welfare Planning Coun., 1954-62, New Orleans Cancer Soc., 1958-60; v.p. Juvenile Ct. Adv. Com. New Orleans, 1961; successively sec., v.p., pres. Parents' Assn. Metairie Park Country Day Sch., 1956-59; v.p. La. Assn. Mental Health, 1960-62; del. dir. to Nat. Assn. Mental Health, 1960-62; bd. mem. Washington Health and Welfare Coun., 1962-64, Hillcrest Children's Ctr., Washington, 1963-69, D.C. Mental Health Assn., 1962-72, 73-76; bd. dirs. Hospice Care of D.C., 1981-88, 90-96, pres., 1986-88; mem. adv. bd. civil commitment project Nat. Ctr. for State Cts., 1981; bd. dirs. Nat. Assn. Mental Health, 1960-66, 67-74, sec., 1968-70, pres.-elect, 1970-71, pres., 1972-73, cons. on assn. film, 1972; mem. Commn. on Mentally Disabled, Am. Bar Assn., 1973-80; mem. adv. bd. Alzheimer's Assn. Greater Washington chpt., 1996; chmn. altar guild Christ Ch. Cathedral, New Orleans, 1960, Little Sanctuary of St. Albans Sch., Washington, 1965; pres. Altar Guild, St. Alban's, Chgo., 1976, 77; chmn. Washington com. Nat. Cathedral Assn., 1976-79, trustee, 1976-90, sec., 1977, v.p., 1980-83, trustee emeritae, 1997; bd. dirs. Nat. Ctr. Voluntary Action; mem. task panel Mental Health Problems, Scope and Boundaries, Pres.'s Commn. Mental Health, 1977; mem. tech. rev. com. Md. Psychiat. Rsch. Ctr., 1979-81. Address: 5317 Blackstone Rd Bethesda MD 20816-1822

WRIGHT, HERBERT E(DGAR), JR., geologist; b. Malden, Mass., Sept. 13, 1917; s. Herbert E. and Annie M. (Richardson) W.; m. Rhea Jane Hahn, June 21, 1943; children—Richard, Jonathan, Stephen, Andrew, Jeffrey. AB, Harvard U., 1939, MA, 1941, PhD, 1943; DSc (hon.), Trinity Coll., Dublin, Ireland, 1966, U. Minn., 1996; PhD (hon.), Lund U., Sweden, 1987. Instr. Brown U., 1946-47; asst. prof. geology U. Minn., Mpls., 1947-51, asso. prof., 1951-59, prof., 1959-74, Regents' prof. geology, ecology and botany, 1974-88; dir. Limnological Research Center, 1963-90. Served to maj. USAAF, 1942-45. Decorated D.F.C., Air medal with 6 oak leaf clusters; recipient Pomerance award Archeol. Inst. Am., 1985, Ann. award Sci. Mus. Minn., 1990; Guggenheim fellow, 1954-55, Wenner-Gren fellow, 1954-55. Fellow AAAS, Geol. Soc. Am. (Ann. award archeol. divsn. 1989, Disting. Career award geology and geomorphology divsn. 1992), Soc. Am. Archeology (Fryxell award 1993); mem. NAS, Ecol. Soc. Am., Am. Soc. Limnology, Oceanography, Am. Quaternary Assn. (Career award 1996), Arctic Inst., Brit. Ecol. Soc. Research on Quaternary geology, paleoecology, paleolimnology and environ. archaeology in Minn., Wyo., Sweden, Yukon, Labrador, Peru, eastern Mediterranean. Home: 1426 Hythe St Saint Paul MN 55108-1423 Office: U of Pillsbury 221 Pillsbury Hall 310 Pillsbury Dr SE Minneapolis MN 55455-0219

WRIGHT, HUGH ELLIOTT, JR., association executive, writer; b. Athens, Ala., Nov. 20, 1937; s. Hugh Elliott and Martha Angeline (Shannon) W. A.B., Birmingham-So. Coll., 1959; M.Div., Vanderbilt U., 1962, D.Ministry, 1967; postgrad., Harvard U., 1963. Ordained to ministry Methodist Ch., 1963; pastor Baxter (Tenn.) Meth. Ch., 1963-64; assoc. pastor Waverly Pl. Ch., Nashville, 1965-66; field sec. Tenn. Heart Assn., Nashville, 1964-65; editorial asst. Motive mag., Nashville, 1965-67; Protestant-Orthodox editor Religious News Service, N.Y.C., 1967-75; research fellow Auburn Theol. Sem., N.Y.C., 1976; editor project on mediating structures and public policy Am. Enterprise Inst., 1979-80; coordinator project on ch., state and taxation NAt. Conf. of Christians and Jews, N.Y.C., 1980-83; v.p. for program NCCJ, N.Y.C., 1983-88, sr. v.p., dep. to pres., 1988-91; program cons. N.Y.C., 1992—; cons. Hartford Sem. Found., 1972, United Meth. Bd. Global Ministries, 1975-78, 92—, United Meth. Communications, 1979-81, Nat. Congress for Cmty. Econ. Devel., 1996—; bd. dirs. Internat. Coun. Christians and Jews, DePaul Coll. Law Ctr. on Ch. State Rels., Nat. Coun. Chs. Com. on Religious Liberty, Nat. Coun. Religious and Pub. Edn. Host: Challenge to Faith, Sta. WOR, 1973-77; author: (with R. Lecky) Can These Bones Live, 1969, The Big Little School, 1971, (with R. Lynn) Go Free, 1973, Challenge to Mission, 1973, (with Juanita Wright) Viewers Guide to Six American Families, 1977, (with Howard Butt) At the Edge of Hope, 1978, (with Douglas McGaw) A Tale of Two Congregations, 1980, Holy Company: Christian Heroes and Heroines, 1980, RNS Reporting...Sixty Years of Religious News Service, 1993; editor: (with Robert Lecky) Black Manifesto: Religion, Racism and Reparations, 1969. Recipient award Birmingham Council Indsl. Editors, 1959, Founders medal Vanderbilt U., 1962, Shepherd prize Vanderbilt, 1962, Religious Heritage of Am. award in journalism, 1972, Asso. Ch. Press Feature Article award, 1980. Mem. Authors League and Guild, Am. Acad. Religion, Phi Beta Kappa, Sigma Delta Chi, Alpha Tau Omega, Alpha Psi Omega, Eta Sigma Phi. Democrat. Home: 1346 Midland Ave Bronxville NY 10708-6840 Office: 475 Riverside Dr Ste 1356 New York NY 10115-0122

WRIGHT, IRVING SHERWOOD, physician, retired educator; b. N.Y.C., Oct. 27, 1901; s. Harry J. and Cora Ann (Hassett) W.; m. Grace Mansfield Demarest, Oct. 15, 1927; children: Barbara Mansfield, Alison Sherwood; m. Lois Elliman Findlay, Oct. 31, 1953. A.B., Cornell U., 1923, M.D., 1926. Diplomate: Am. Bd. Internal Medicine (mem. adv. bd. 1940-49), subcert. in cardiovascular diseases. Intern N.Y. Post Grad. Med. Sch. and Hosp. of Columbia, 1927-29, asst. and assoc. vis. physician, 1929-39, prof. clin. medicine, dir. and exec. officer dept. medicine, 1939-46; asst. physician Bellevue Hosp. (Cornell Div.), 1931-34, assoc., 1934-37; assoc. prof. Cornell Med. Coll. and assoc. attending physician N.Y. Hosp., 1946-48; prof. clin. medicine Cornell Med. Coll., 1948-68, emeritus clin. prof., 1968—; attending physician Drs. Hosp., N.Y.C., 1934-80, N.Y. Hosp., 1948-80; investigator into biomed. problems of aging; hon. staff dept. medicine N.Y. Hosp., 1980—; physician Met. Opera, 1935-62; dir. medicine Cornell Div.) Welfare Hosp. Chronic Disease, 1937-40 (1st pres. its med. bd. 1937-39), cons. physician, 1940-46; cons. to Orange Meml. Hosp., East Orange, N.J., Monmouth Meml. Hosp., Long Branch, N.J., Hackensack (N.J.) Hosp., Mt. Vernon (N.Y.) Hosp.; chief of med. service Army and Navy Gen. Hosp., Hot Springs (Ark.) Nat. Park, 1942-43; cons. in medicine U.S. Army, 6th Service Command, 1944-45, 9th Service Command, 1945; coordinator health survey Am. prisoners of war from Far East, 1945; chmn. Internat. Com. on Blood Clotting Factors, 1954-63, sec. gen., 1963-68; chmn. com. on cerebral vascular diseases NIH, 1961-65; mem. Pres.'s Comm. Heart Disease, Cancer and Stroke, 1966-68; nat. chmn. Commn. Heart Disease Resources, 1968-76. Author and editor numerous books on cardiovascular diseases.; Editor-in-chief: Modern Medical Monographs; Contbr. articles to med. jours. Chmn. Josiah Macy, Jr. Found. Conf. Blood Clotting, 1947-52; Trustee Cornell U., 1960-65. Served as lt. comdr. USNR, 1935-39; lt. col. to col. AUS, 1942-46; civilian cons. in medicine to surgeon gen. U.S. Army, 1946-74; mem. civilian adv. com. to sec. navy, 1946-47. Recipient Albert and Mary Lasker award Am. Heart Assn., 1960, Gold Heart award, 1958, Disting. Service award, 1976; Irving Sherwood Wright professorship in geriatrics at Cornell U. Med. Coll., 1976. Fellow Royal Coll. Physicians (London), ACP (regent, pres. 1965-66, pres. emeritus 1987—), Acad. Medicine (chmn. geriatrics sect. 1976-79, outstanding Contbns. to Sci. and Medicine award medal 1986); mem. Am. Assn. Physicians, AMA (chmn. sect. exptl. med. and therapeutics 1939-40), Am. Heart Assn. (chmn. sect. for study peripheral circulation 1939-40, mem. exec. com., bd. dirs. 1935-57, pres. 1952-53, mem. Nat. Adv. Heart Council 1954-58, 60-61), Cornell U. Med. Coll. Alumni Assn. (pres 1953), NRC (sub-com. cardiovascular diseases 1947-51), Am. Soc. Clin. Investigation, Soc. Exptl. Biology and Medicine, N.Y. Acad. Scis., Am. Geriatrics Soc. (pres. 1971-72, Henderson award 1970, Thewlis award 1974), Am. Fedn. for Aging Research (founding pres. 1980-86, AFAR Distinction award 1987), Harvey Soc., Sigma Xi, Alpha Omega Alpha; corr. mem. of Acad. Columbian de Ciencas Exactas Fisico-Quimicas Y Naturales (Bogota); hon. mem. Royal Soc. Medicine of London, med. socs. Brazil, Chile, Peru, Argentina, Cuba, Switzerland, Sweden and USSR; also hon. faculty of U. Chile. Presbyn (bd. sessions 1935-36). Club: St. Nicholas Society (N.Y.). Home: 25 E End Ave New York NY 10028-7052 *My aim in life has been to improve the quality of medical care in the fields of internal medicine, geriatric cardiovascular diseases by research, teaching at undergraduate, graduate, and international levels, the development of standards and guidelines, and the application of the best of modern knowledge to the care of patients. In light of the technology of recent years I have placed particular emphasis on the role of a primary physician for the patient, who will apply his scientific knowledge with compassion and an understanding of the total illness-including the social and emotional aspects of the patient's problem rather than his disease alone. This, as I see it, is the challenge of the modern physician.*

WRIGHT, JAMES DAVID, sociology educator, writer; b. Logansport, Ind., Nov. 6, 1947; s. James Farrell and Helen Loretta (Moon) W.; m. Christine Ellen Stewart, July 25, 1987; children: Matthew James, Derek William. BA, Purdue U., 1969; MS, U. Wis., 1970, PhD, 1973. Cert. specialist social policy and evaluation rsch. Asst. prof. sociology U. Mass., Amherst, 1973-76, assoc. prof., 1976-79, prof., 1979-88; Favrot prof. human rels. Tulane U., New Orleans, 1988—. Author/co-author: The Dissent of the Governed, 1976, Under the Gun, 1983, The State of the Masses, 1986, Homelessness and Health, 1987 (commendation Nat. Press Club 1988), Address Unknown: Homeless in America, 1989, The Greatest of Evils: Urban Poverty and the Urban Underclass, 1993, others; editor: (book series) Social Institutions and Social Change, 1984—, (jour.) Social Sci. Rsch. Jour., 1978—; contbr. numerous articles, essays, book chpts. to profl. publs. Mem. Am. Sociol. Assn., Soc. for Study Social Problems. Democrat. Avocations: cooking, gardening, travel.

WRIGHT, JAMES EDWARD, judge; b. Arlington, Tex., Jan. 15, 1921; s. James Robert and Clairette (Smith) W.; m. Eberta Adelaide Slataper, June 25, 1946; 1 child, Patricia Diane Wright Rogers. JD, U. Tex., 1949. Bar: Tex. 1949. Practice in Ft. Worth, 1949-69; city atty. Arlington, 1951-61; judge 141st Dist. Ct., Ft. Worth, 1970-88, sr. dist. judge, 1988—. Served with USAAF, World War II. Paul Harris fellow, 1981; named Disting. Alumnus U. Tex.-Arlington, 1982; named to Mil. Sci. Dept. Hall of Honor, U. Tex.-Arlington, 1985. Fellow Tex. Bar Found. (life); mem. ABA, Ft. Worth-Tarrant County Bar Assn. (pres. 1958-59), Tex. Bar Assn., Sons of the Rep. of Tex., Rotary (pres. Downtown Ft. Worth club 1966-67), Masons (32 deg.), Shriners, Phi Alpha Delta. Methodist. Home: 717 Briarwood Blvd Arlington TX 76013-1502

WRIGHT, JAMES EDWARD, dean, history educator; b. Madison, Wis., Aug. 16, 1939; s. Donald J. and Myrtle (Hendricks) W.; m. Joan Bussah, Sept. 3, 1962 (div.); children: James J., Anne Marie, Michael J.; m. Susan DeBevoise, Aug. 18, 1984. BS, Wis. State U., 1964; MS, U. Wis., 1966, PhD, 1969; MA (hon.), Dartmouth Coll., 1980. From asst. prof. to assoc. prof. history Dartmouth Coll., Hanover, N.H., 1969-80, prof. history, 1980—, assoc. dean faculty, 1981-85, dean faculty, 1989-97, acting pres., 1995, provost, 1997—; sr. historian U. Mid Am., Lincoln, Nebr., 1976-77; humanist-in-residence Colo. Humanities Coun., Georgetown, 1975. Author: Galena Lead District, 1966, Politics of Populism, 1974, Progressive Yankees, 1987; author, co-editor: Great Plains Experience, 1978. Trustee Kimball Union Acad., Meriden, N.H., 1990-94; dir. Sherman Fairchild Found., Greenwich, Conn., 1991—; chair Hanover Dem. Town Com., 1970-74. Cpl. USMC, 1957-60. Danforth fellow, 1964-69, Guggenheim fellow, 1973-74, Charles Warren fellow Harvard U., 1980-81. Mem. Orgn. Am. Historians (chair film, media com. 1983-85), Western History Assn. (chair Caughey prize 1986-87), Phi Beta Kappa (hon.). Home: 7 Quail Dr Etna NH 03750-4404 Office: Dartmouth College Provost Hanover NH 03755

WRIGHT, J(AMES) LAWRENCE, lawyer; b. Portland, Oreg., Apr. 12, 1943; s. William A. and Esther M. (Nelson) W.; m. Mary Aileene Roche, June 29, 1968; children: Rachel, Jonathan, Christopher. BBA, Gonzaga U., 1966, JD, 1972; LLM, NYU, 1977. Bar: Wash. 1972, U.S. Ct. Mil. Appeals 1974, U.S. Tax Ct. 1976, U.S. Supreme Ct. 1976. Prin. Halverson & Applegate, P.S., Yakima, Wash., 1972-74, 77—. Mem. St. Elizabeth Hosp. Found., Yakima, 1986-89, Yakima Meml. Hosp. Found., 1990—; pres. fin. bd. St. Paul's Cathedral, Yakima, 1979—; mem. fin. coun. Diocese of Yakima, 1994—; v.p. Apple Tree Racing Assn., 1986-87; bd. dirs. Capital Theatre, Yakima, 1985-95. Capt. U.S. Army, 1966-68, 74-76. Mem. ABA, Wash. Bar Assn., Yakima County Bar Assn., Rotary. Roman Catholic. Avocations: tennis, golf. Office: Halverson & Applegate PS PO Box 22730 311 N 4th St Yakima WA 98907-2715

WRIGHT, JAMES ROSCOE, chemist; b. White Hall, Md., July 7, 1922; s. James Grover and Rose Adele (Hulshart) W.; m. Blanca Zulema Guerrero, June 4, 1950; children: James Alfred, Ronald Keith. B.S. in Edn., Md. State U., Salisbury, 1946; B.S., Washington Coll., 1948; M.S., U. Del., 1949, Ph.D. in Chemistry, 1951; grad., Program Mgmt. Devel., Harvard, 1967, Fed. Execs. Inst., U. Va., 1972. Asst. prof. Trinity U., San Antonio, 1951-52; research chemist S.W. Research Inst., San Antonio, 1951-52, Chevron Research Corp., Richmond, 1952-60; with Nat. Bur. Standards, 1960—; chief bldg. research div., 1967-72, dir. center bldg. tech., 1972-74; dep. dir. Inst. for Applied Tech., 1974-76, acting dir., 1976-78; dep. dir. Nat. Engring Lab., 1978-85; head U.S. del. industralized bldg. to, USSR, 1969; U.S. del. Internat. Union Testing and Rsch. Labs. for Materials and Structures, 1969-74, 75-85, mem. bur., 1970-73, 74-78, 79—, pres., 1971-72, v.p., 1979-82, pres., 1982-85, hon. mem., 1985—; mem. bldg. rsch. adv. bd. NRC, 1976-80; vice chmn., mem. exec. com. U.S. nat. com. Internat. Coun. Bldg. Rsch., Studies and Documentation, 1969-73; rep. Nat. Bur. Standards to Fed. Constrn. Coun., 1967-70; mem. fire coun. Underwriters Labs., 1969-73; mem. U.S.-Egypt working group Tech. Rshc. and Devel., 1976-80; hon. mem. Producers Coun.; guest worker Nat. Bur. Standards, 1985-88; dir., treas. St. Mark Elderly Housing Corp., 1987—; mem. Smithsonian Exhibit Group, 1989—. Author. Served as officer AUS, 1943-46, ETO. Decorated Bronze Star, Purple Heart, Combat Infantry Badge; recipient Gold medal award for exceptional svc. Dept. Commerce, 1975. Mem. Am. Chem. Soc. (emeritus), ASTM (dir. 1977-80, chmn. com. on soc. devel. 1979-80), Chem. Soc. Washington (chmn. auditing com. 1965-66, chmn. profl. rels. and status com. 1964, chmn. long-range planning com. 1967, assoc. editor Capital Chemist 1963-65), Buick Club Am. (bd. dirs. Washington chpt. 1991—, pres. 1990—), Sigma Xi, Kappa Alpha. Patentee in field. Home: 6204 Lone Oak Dr Bethesda MD 20817-1744

WRIGHT, JANE COOKE, physician, educator, consultant; b. N.Y.C., Nov. 30, 1919; d. Louis T. and Corinne (Cooke) W.; m. David D. Jones. A.B., Smith Coll., 1942; M.D. with honors, N.Y. Med. Coll., 1945; Dr. Med. Scis., Women's Med. Coll. Pa., 1965; Sc.D., Denison U., 1971. Intern Bellevue Hosp., N.Y.C., 1945-46, resident, 1946, mem. staff, 1955-67; resident Harlem Hosp., 1947, chief resident, 1948; clin. Cancer Rsch. Found., Harlem Hosp., 1949-52; dir., 1952-55; mem. staff Harlem Hosp., 1949-55; practice medicine specializing in clin. cancer chemotherapy N.Y.C.; mem. faculty dept. surgery Med. Ctr., N.Y. U., N.Y.C., 1955-67; adj. assoc. prof. Med. Ctr., N.Y. U., 1961-67, also dir. cancer chemotherapy services research, 1955-67; prof. surgery N.Y. Med. Coll., N.Y.C., 1967-87, prof. surgery emeritus, 1987—, assoc. dean, 1967-75; mem. staff Manhattan VA Hosp., 1955-67, Midtown, Met., Bird S. Color, Flower-Fifth Ave. Hosps., all N.Y.C., 1967-79, Westchester County Med. Center, Valhalla, N.Y., 1971-87, Lincoln Hosp., Bronx, N.Y., 1979-87; cons. Health Ins. Plan of Greater N.Y., 1962-94; cons. Blvd. Hosp., 1963—, St. Luke's Hosp., Newburgh, N.Y., 1964—; pelvic malignancy rev. com. N.Y. Gynecol. Soc., 1965-66, St. Vincent's Hosp., N.Y.C., 1966—, Dept. Health, Edn. and Welfare, 1968-70, Wyckoff Heights Hosp., N.Y.C., 1969—, NIH, 1971—, others; adv. bd. Skin Cancer Found. Contbr. articles to profl. jours. Mem. Manhattan coun. State Commn. Human Rights, 1949—, Pres.'s Commn. Heart Disease, Cancer and Stroke, 1964-65, Nat. Adv. Cancer Coun. NIH, 1966-70, N.Y. State Women's Coun., 1970-72; bd. dirs. Medico-CARE, Health Svcs. Improvement Fund Inc.; trustee Smith Coll., Northampton, Mass., 1970-80. Recipient numerous awards, including; Mademoiselle mag. award, 1952; Lady Year award Harriet Beecher Stowe Jr. High Sch., 1958; Spirit Achievement award Albert Einstein Sch. Medicine, 1965; certificate Honor award George Gershwin Jr. High Sch., 1967; Myrtle Wreath award Hadassah, 1967; Smith medal Smith Coll., 1968; Outstanding Am. Women award Am. Mothers Com. Inc., 1970; Golden Plate award Am. Acad. Achievement, 1971; Exceptional Black Scientists Poster Ciba Geigy, 1980. Fellow N.Y. Acad. Medicine; mem. Nat. Med. Assn. (edit. bd. jours.), Manhattan Ctrl. Med. Soc., N.Y. County Med. Soc. (nominating com.), AMA, AAAS, Am. Assn. Cancer Rsch. (dir. Rsch. Salute 1971-74), N.Y. Acad. Scis., N.Y. Cancer Soc., Internat. Med. and Rsch. Found. (v.p.), Am. Cancer Soc. (dir. div.), N.Y. Cancer Soc. (pres. 1970-71), Am. Soc. Clin. Oncology (sec. treas. 1964-67), Contin Soc., Sigma Xi, Lambda Kappa Mu, Alpha Omega Alpha. Club: The 400 (N.Y. Med. Coll.). Address: 315 W End Ave New York NY 10023-8158

WRIGHT, JEFF REGAN, civil engineering educator; b. Spokane, Wash., Nov. 25, 1950; s. Harold U. and Gail Virginia (Hodgson) W.; m. Delores Jeanne Finch, Sept. 14, 1972; children: Kelly Hodgson, Myka Kristine. BA, U. Wash., 1975, BS, 1976, MSCE, 1977; PhD, Johns Hopkins U., 1982. Asst. prof. civil engring. Purdue U., West Lafayette, Ind., 1982-86, assoc. prof., 1986-90; prof., 1990—; dir. Ind. Water Resources Rsch. Ctr. Purdue U., West Lafayette, Ind., 1989—; v.p. OMTEK Engring., West Lafayette, 1986—. Author: Civil and Environmental Systems Engineering, 1996, Expert Systems Applications to Urban Planning, 1989; contbr. numerous articles to profl. publs. Mem. ASCE (editor-in-chief Jour. Infrastructure Sys.), Ops. Rsch. Soc. Am., Inst. Mgmt. Scis. Office: Purdue U WRRC Sch Civil Engring West Lafayette IN 47907-1284

WRIGHT, JEFFREY, actor. stage appearances include (with Arena Stage, Washington D.C.) Les Blancs, She Stoops to Conquer, Juno and the Paycock (with Yale Repertory) Search and Destroy, Playboy of the West Indies, Daylight in the Exile, N.Y. Shakespeare Festival prodn. of Othello, Millennium Approaches, 1993, Angels in America: Perestroika, 1994 (Antoinette Perry award for Featured Actor in a Play 1994); T.V. appearances include The Young Indiana Jones Chronicles, Seperate But Equal; films include Presumed Innocent, 1990, Jumpin' at the Bone Yard, 1991, Basquiat, 1996, Critical Care, 1997. *

WRIGHT, JERRY JAYE, physical education educator; b. Richmond, Ind., July 30, 1944; s. Robert Evan and Janet W. (Jay) W.; m. Mary Lee Cathey, Dec. 27, 1980. AA, Art Acad., Cin., 1964; BA, Saginaw Valley State U., 1974; MEd, Bowling Green State U., 1976; PhD, The Ohio State U., 1980. Illustrator Advt. Svcs., Richmond, Ind., 1964-71; asst. baseball coach Bowling Green (Ohio) State U., 1974-75; asst. baseball and basketball coach Saginaw (Mich.) Valley State U., 1975-77; asst. prof. U. No. Iowa, Cedar Falls, 1980-81, U. Wis., Milw., 1981-86; head tennis coach Penn State U., Altoona, Pa., 1986-91; assoc. prof. Penn State U., Altoona, 1986—; chair dept. exercise and sports sci. sport historian Penn State U., Altoona, 1989—. Author: Phys. Educator Jour., 1986, Jour. of Sport History, 1988, Strategies Jour., 1991, 1992, Baseball Rsch. Jour., 1992, The National Pastime, 1993, Encyclopedia of Major League Baseball Teams, 1993, Nine: A Journal of Baseball History and Social Policy Perspectives, 1994, 95, 96, Canadian Journal of the History of Sport, 1994, International Journal of the History of Sport, 1994, Baseball's First Stars, 1996. Sport historian Blair County Hist. Soc., Altoona, 1989—. Sgt. U.S. Army, 1965-67. Mem. North Am. Soc. for Sport History, Orgn. for Am. Historians, Soc. for Am. Baseball Rsch., Am. Alliance for Phys. Edn., Phys. Edn. in Higher Edn. Avocations: coll. sport memorabilia, baseball cards, tennis, golf, sport historian rsch. Office: Pa State U 3000 Ivyside Park Altoona PA 16601-3760

WRIGHT, JESSE HARTZELL, psychiatrist, educator; b. Altoona, Pa., Sept. 21, 1943; s. Jesse H. and Marion (Stone) W.; m. Susanne Judy Wright, July 9, 1967; children: Andrew, Laura. BS, Juniata Coll., 1965; MD, Jefferson Med. Coll., 1969; PhD, U. Louisville, 1976. Diplomate Am. Bd. Psychiatry and Neurology, Am. Bd. Med. Examiners; lic. psychiatrist, Ky. Asst. prof. U. Louisville, 1975-79, assoc. prof., 1979-87, prof., 1987—; clin. dir. Norton Psychiat. Clinic, Louisville, 1975-83, med. dir., 1983—; resident in psychiatry U. Mich., Ann Arbor, 1970-73; cons. Our Lady of Peace Hosp., Louisville, 1978—, Bapt. Hosp., Louisville, 1979—, Jewish Hosp., Louisville, 1987—. Author first multimedia computer program for psychotherapy, chpts. to books; contbr. articles to prof. jours. Fellow APA; mem. Ky. Psychiat. Assn. (sec. 1979-80, v.p. 1980-81, pres. 1982-83). Avocations: gardening, running, theater, skiing. Home: 15 Indian Hills Trl Louisville KY 40207-1532 Office: Norton Psychiat Clinic 200 E Chestnut St Louisville KY 40202-1822

WRIGHT, JOHN, classics educator; b. N.Y.C., Mar. 9, 1941; s. Henry and Dorothy (Chaya) W.; m. Ellen Faber, June 16, 1962; children: Jennifer, Emily. B.A., Swarthmore Coll., 1962; M.A., Ind. U., 1964, Ph.D., 1971. Instr. classics U. Rochester, 1968-72, asst. prof., 1972-75; asso. prof. Northwestern U., Evanston, Ill., 1975-77; prof. Northwestern U., 1977-83, John Evans prof. Latin lang. and lit., 1983—, chmn. dept., 1978—. Author: The Play of Antichrist, 1967, Dancing in Chains: The Stylistic Unity of the Comoedia Palliata, 1974, The Life of Cola de Rienzo, 1975, Essays on the Iliad: Selected Modern Criticism, 1978, Plautus: Curculio, Introduction and Notes, 1981, rev. edit., 1993, Ralph Stanley and the Clinch Mountain Boys: A Discography, 1983, The Five-String Banjo Stanley Style, 1984, rev. edit. (Clyde Pharr) Homeric Greek: A Book for Beginners, 1985, It's the Hardest Music in the World to Play: The Ralph Stanley Story in His Own Words, 1987, Traveling the High Way Home: Ralph Stanley and the World of Traditional Bluegrass Music, 1993; album Everything She Asks For, 1993; columnist: Banjo Newsletter; contbr. articles to profl. jours. Fellow Am. Acad. Rome, 1966-68; Nat. Endowment Humanities Younger humanist fellow, 1973-74; named to Honorable Order of Ky. Colonels; recipient songwriting prize Santa Fe Bluegrass and Old Time Music Festival, 1996. Mem. Am. Acad. in Rome Soc. of Fellows, Am. Philol. Assn., Ill. Classical Conf., Petronian Soc., Met. Opera Guild, Chgo. Area Bluegrass Assn., Minn. Bluegrass and Old-Time Music Assn., Internat. Bluegrass Music Assn. (Print Media Personality of Yr. 1994), BMI, Nat. Acad. Recording Arts and Scis. Club: Ralph Stanley Fan. Home: 1137 Noyes St Evanston IL 60201-2633 Office: Northwestern U Dept Classics Evanston IL 60208-2200

WRIGHT, JOHN, film editor. Editor films (with Graeme Clifford and Garth Craven) Convoy, 1978, Separate Ways, 1981, Only When I Laugh, 1981, Frances, 1982, Mass Appeal, 198, Explorers, 1985, (with Mark Roy Warner and Edward A. Warschilka) The Running Man, 1987, Gleaming the Cube, 1989, (with Dennis Virkler) The Hunt for Red October, 1990 (Acad. award nomination for best film editing 1990), (with Steve Mirkovich) Teenage Mutant Ninja Turtles II: The Secret of the Ooze, 1991, Last Action Hero, 1993, Speed, 1994 (Acad. award nomination for best film editing 1994), Die Hard with A Vengeance, 1995, Broken Arrow, 1996, The Rock, 1996; editor TV movies Heartsounds, 1984, My Name Is Bill W., 1989, Sarah, Plain and Tall, 1991. Office: Broder Kurland Webb Uffner Agency 9242 Beverly Blvd Ste 200 Beverly Hills CA 90210-3710*

WRIGHT, JOHN COLLINS, chemistry educator; b. Oak Hill, W. Va., Aug. 5, 1927; s. John C. and Irene (Collins) W.; m. Margaret Ann Cyphers, Sept. 11, 1949; children: Jeffrey Cyphers, John Timothy, Curtis Scott, Keith Alexander. B.S., W.Va. Wesleyan Coll., 1948, LL.D. (hon.), 1974; Ph.D., U. Ill., 1951; D.Sc. (hon.), U. Ala., 1979, W.Va. Inst. Tech., 1979. Research chemist Hercules, Inc., 1951-57; mem. faculty W.Va. Wesleyan Coll., 1957-64; asst. program dir. NSF, 1964-65; dean Coll. Arts and Scis., No. Ariz. U., 1966-70, W.Va. U., Morgantown, 1970-74; vice chancellor W.Va. Bd. Regents, Charleston, 1974-78; pres. U. Ala., Huntsville, 1978-88, prof. chemistry, 1988—; interim pres. W.Va. Coll. Grad. Studies, Institute, 1975-76; hon. research asso. Univ. Coll., London, Eng., 1962-63; cons. NSF, 1965—, Army Sci. Bd., U.S. Army, 1979-82. Served with USNR, 1945-46. Mich. fellow Center Study Higher Edn., U. Mich., 1965-66. Mem. AAAS, NSTA. Office: 4724 Panorama Dr SE Huntsville AL 35801-1215

WRIGHT, JOHN MACNAIR, JR., retired army officer; b. L.A., Apr. 14, 1916; s. John MacNair and Ella (Stradley) W.; m. Helene Tribit, June 28, 1940; children: John MacNair III, Richard Kenneth. B.S., U.S. Mil. Acad., 1940; grad., Airborne Sch., 1947, Strategic Intelligence Sch., 1948; advanced course, Inf. Sch., 1951, Command and Gen. Staff Coll., 1953; M.B.A., U. So. Calif., 1956; grad., Army Logistics Mgmt. Sch., 1957, Advanced Mgmt. Program, U. Pitts., 1959, Nat. War Coll., 1961, Army Aviation Sch., 1965; M.S. in Internat. Affairs, George Washington U., 1973. Enlisted U.S. Army, 1935, comd. 2d. lt., 1940, advanced through grades to lt. gen., 1970; comdr. Battery Wright Corregidor, P.I., 1942; with intelligence div. War Dept. Gen. Staff, 1946-48; mil. attache Am. embassy, Paraguay, 1948-50; bn. comdr. 508th Airborne Regtl. Combat Team, 1951-52; asst. chief of staff for pers. 7th Inf. Div., Korea, 1953, asst. chief staff logistics, 1954; assigned office U.S. Army Chief of Staff, 1956-60; chief staff 8th Inf. Div., 1961-62, asst. chief staff plans and ops. 7th Corps, 1962-63, asst. chief staff plans and ops. 7th Army, 1963-64, asst. div. comdr. 11th Air Assault Div., 1964-65; asst. div. comdr. 1st Cav. Div. (Airmobile) Vietnam, 1965-66; assigned office asst. Chief Staff Force Devel., 1966-67; comdg. gen. U.S. Army Inf. Ctr., 1967-69; comdt. U.S. Army Inf. Sch., 1967-69; comdg. gen. 101st Airborne Div. (Airmobile), Vietnam, 1969-70; controller of the Army Washington, 1970-72; ret., 1973. Dir. R&D Boy Scouts Am., 1973, nat. dir. program, 1974-77, nat. dir. program support, 1977-78; nat. dir. exploring, 1978-81, mem. nat. exploring com., 1981—; pres. Chattahoochee (Ga.) coun. Boy Scouts Am., 1968-69, mem. exec. bd. region 5, 1967-69; mem. nat. coun., 1964-73; tech. adviser Vietnamese Boy Scout Assn., 1965-66; Regent for Life Nat. Eagle Scout Assn., 1988—; exploring chmn. five nations dist. Calif. Inland Empire Coun., 1992—. Decorated D.S.M. with 2 oak leaf clusters, Silver Star with oak leaf cluster, Legion of Merit with oak leaf cluster, D.F.C., Bronze Star with oak leaf cluster, Air medal with 59 oak leaf clusters, Army Commendation medal, Prisoner of War medal, Purple Heart with oak leaf cluster, Combat Inf. badge, Master Parachutist, Sr. Army Aviator, numerous area and campaign ribbons, fgn. decorations; recipient Silver Beaver award Boy Scouts Am., 1961, Silver Antelope award, 1969, Distinguished Eagle Scout award, 1971, Disting. Svc. award Founders and Patriots Am., 1988, Freedoms Found. at Valley Forge Hon. medal, 1992; elected Army Aviation Hall of Fame, 1986. Mem. Assn. U.S. Army, Army Aviation Assn. Am. (pres. 1974-76), 101st Airborne Divsn. Assn., 1st Cavalry Divsn. Assn., SAR (pres. Tex. Soc. 1987-88, pres. Inland Empire chpt. 1992-93, Silver Good Citizenship medal 1984, 87, Meritorious Svc. medal 1986, Patriot, Liberty and Gold Good Citizenship medals 1988), Ret. Officers Assn., West Point Soc., Mil. Order World Wars (Patrick Henry award 1986, 90, comdr. Dallas chpt. 1985-86, vice comdr. dept. ctrl. Calif. 1991-92, comdr. Inland Empire chpt. 1992-93), Nat. Gavel Soc., Nat. Order Founders and Patriots of Am. (sec.-gen. 1986-88, gov. gen. 1988-90, councillor gen. Calif. Soc. 1990-95), Soc. Descendants of Colonial Clergy, Flagon and Tchr. Soc., Soc. Colonial Wars (lt. gov. Calif. soc. 1992—, gov. 1997-98), Sons of the Revolution in State of Calif. (pres. 1993-94), Soc. War of 1812 (dist. dep. pres. gen. 1991—, v.p. Calif. soc. 1993-94, pres. 1994-95), Nat. Huguenot Soc., Soc. Sons and Daus. of Pilgrims, Order Ams. Armorial Ancestry, Soc. Descendents Founders of Hartford, Old Plymouth Colony Descendents, Mil. Order of the Loyal Legion of the U.S., Mil. Order Fgn. Wars of the U.S. (pres. Calif. Soc. 1996-97), Hereditary Order of First Families of Mass., Masons, Shriners, Sojourner, Phi Kappa Phi, Beta Gamma Sigma, Alpha Kappa Psi. Prisoner of war of Japanese, 1942-45. Home: 21227 George Brown Ave Riverside CA 92518-2880

WRIGHT, JOHN PEALE, retired banker; b. Chattanooga, Mar. 27, 1924; s. Robert T. and Margaret (Peale) W.; m. Ruth Garrison, Sept. 11, 1948; children: Margaret Shapard, John Peale, Ruth Garrison, Mary Ivens. Student, Davidson Coll., 1941-43, U. N.C., 1943; B.S. in Phys. Sci, U. Chgo., 1944; M.B.A., Harvard U., 1947. With Am. Nat. Bank & Trust Co., Chattanooga, 1947-82; pres. Am. Nat. Bank & Trust Co., 1962-82, also dir.; dir. spl. projects Third Nat. Corp., Nashville, 1983-85; chmn. bd., dir. Third Nat. Bank of Anderson County, 1980-84. Served to lt. USAAF, 1943-46. Mem. Robert Morris Assocs. (pres. 1968-69), Tenn. Bankers Assn. (bd. dirs., pres. 1973-74). Presbyterian (elder, treas.). Home: PO Box 1667 Santa Rosa Beach FL 32459-1667

WRIGHT, JOHN ROBERT, pathologist; b. Winnipeg, Man., Can., Aug. 18, 1935; came to U.S., 1961, naturalized, 1968; s. Ross Grant and Anna Marie (Crispin) W.; m. Deanna Pauline Johnson, June 25, 1960; children—Carolyn Deanna, David John. M.D. with honors, U. Man., 1959. Diplomate: Am. Bd. Pathology. Intern Winnipeg Gen. Hosp., 1959-60, resident, 1960-61; resident Balt. City Hosp., 1961-63, Buffalo Gen. Hosp., 1963-64; teaching fellow in medicine U. Man., 1960-61; instr. in pathology, Buswell fellow SUNY-Buffalo, 1965-67, prof. pathology, chmn. dept. pathology, 1974-96, interim dean medicine, v.p. clin. affairs, 1997—; asst. chief pathology Balt. City Hosps. and; asst. prof. Johns Hopkins U., 1967-74; cons. Roswell Park Meml. Inst., 1975—, bd. visitors, 1981—, interim dir., 1985-86, chmn. bd. visitors, 1987—. Recipient Louis A. and Ruth Siegel Teaching award SUNY-Buffalo, 1977, 78, 88, Deans award SUNY, 1987. Mem. AMA, AAAS, Coll. Am. Pathologists, Am. Soc. Investigative Pathologists, Am. Soc. Clin. Pathologists, U.S. and Can. Acad. Pathology, Assn. Pathology Chairmen (pres. 1994-96), Am. Heart Assn., Alpha Omega Alpha. Research in amyloidosis and aging, pathology of amyloidosis, characterization of clin. amyloid syndromes. Home: 46 Wynngate Ln Williamsville NY 14221-1840 Office: SUNY 173 Cass Ave Buffalo NY 14206-1915

WRIGHT, JOHN SPENCER, school system administrator; b. Washington, May 8, 1948; s. Clarence S. and Florence (Nagel) W.; m. Debra Kim Buck, Aug. 4, 1973; 1 child, Deanna Michelle. BA in Econs., U. Va., 1969, MEd in Secondary Adminstrn., 1971, EdD in Adminstrn. and Supervision, 1976. Cert. social studies tchr., prin., supt., fin. officer, N.C.; registered sch. bus. adminstr. Tchr. govt. and social studies Lane H.S., Charlottesville, Va., 1969-72, spl. asst. to prin., 1972-74; supr. Sch. Gen. Learning Charlottesville H.S., 1974-75; exec. dir. Va. Assn. Sch. Execs., Charlottesville, 1976-78; prin. E.C. Glass H.S., Lynchburg, Va., 1978-82; dir. bus. svcs. Lynchburg Pub. Schs., 1982-86, dir. fin. and planning svcs., 1986; asst. supt. bus. and fin. svcs. Greensboro (N.C.) Pub. Schs., 1986-90, assoc. supt. human and fin. resources, 1990-93; assoc. supt. adminstrv. svcs. Guilford County (N.C.) Schs., 1993—; investigating probation officer 8th Regional Juvenile and Domestic Rels. Ct., Charlottesville, 1970-71; grad. asst., teaching asst. Sch. Edn., U. Va., 1975-76; rsch. asst. Tayloe Murphy Inst., U. Va., 1975-76; asst.

prof. Grad. Sch. Edn., U. Va., 1976-78; part time asst. prof. Grad. Sch. Edn., U. Va., 1978-80; adj. prof. U. Va., Sch. Continuing Edn., 1983, 86. Co-author: Charlottesville Change Project: Year End Report, 1974; editor: Developments in School Law, 1976-78; contbr. articles and reviews to profl. jours. Bd. dirs. Triad Sickle Cell Anemia Found.; past bd. dirs. Presbyn. Home and Family Svcs., Inc.; past v.p. deductible fund Local Govt. Ins. Funds, Greensboro, Guilford, N.C., past pres. liability fund; mem. N.C. Profl. Rev. Com., 1993—; mem. N.C. Profl. Practices Commn., 1996—; mem. Com. 100, Greensboro Human Rels. Commn. Mem. ASCD, Am. Assn. Sch. Adminstrs., Am. Assn. Sch. Pers. Adminstrs., Assn. Sch. Bus. Officials, Southeastern Assn. Sch. Bus. Officials, N.C. Assn. Sch. Bus. Officials (legis. com., past region chmn., vice-chair and mem. state exec. com.), Edn. Law Assn., Sch. Edn. Found. (dean's coun. U. Va.), Distributive Edn. Clubs Am. (hon. life), Greensboro C. of C. (govtl. affairs coun., minority/women bus. devel. coun.), U. Va. Alumni Assn. (former class agt.), Va. Student Aid Found., Leadership Greensboro Alumni Assn., Greensboro Civitans (v.p. 1993-94, bd. dirs. 1994-96), Human Resources Mgmt. Assn. Greensboro (bd. dirs. 1997—), Phi Delta Kappa (former chpt. treas.), Kappa Delta Pi, others. Presbyterian. Home: 4610 Charlottesville Rd Greensboro NC 27410-3655 Office: Guilford County Schools PO Box 880 Greensboro NC 27402-0880

WRIGHT, JON ALAN, physicist, researcher; b. Tacoma, Wash., Jan. 18, 1938; s. Edward S. and Peggy (Hawley) W.; m. Barbara McCulley, Jan. 27, 1962; children: Jeffrey, Allison, Dana. BS, Cal Tech, 1959; PhD in Physics, U. Calif., Berkeley, 1965. Staff physicist Aerospace Corp., L.A., 1965; postdoctoral physicist U. Calif., San Diego, 1965-67; prof. physics U. Ill., Urbana, 1967-82; dir. Ctr. for Studies of Non-Linear Dynamics, San Diego, 1982—; rsch. physicist U. Calif., San Diego, 1990—; vis. prof. U. Utrecht, Netherlands, 1976; vis. assoc. prof. Stanford U., Palo Alto, Calif., 1973. Contbr. tech. papers to profl. jours. Achievements include specialization in nonlinear dynamics, nonlinear waves, semiclassical methods, ocean waves and remote sensing of ocean. Office: INLS U Calif 0402 San Diego CA 92093-0402

WRIGHT, JOSEPH ROBERT, JR., corporate executive; b. Tulsa, Sept. 24, 1938; s. Joe Robert and Ann Helen (Cech) W. B.S., Colo. Sch. Mines, 1961; M.I.A., Yale U., 1964. Vice pres. Booz, Allen & Hamilton, 1965-71; dep. dir. Bur. Census, Dept. Commerce, 1971-72; dep. adminstr. Social and Econ. Statis. Adminstrn., 1972-73, acting asst. sec. econ. affairs, 1973; asst. sec. adminstr. Dept. Agr., 1973-76; pres. Citicorp Retail Inc. and Retail Consumer Services Inc., N.Y.C.; v.p. Citicorp, Inc., 1976-81; dep. sec. Dept. Commerce, Washington, 1981-82; dep. dir. Office Mgmt. and Budget, Washington, 1982-88; chmn. Pres.'s Council on Integrity and Efficiency, 1982-89; chmn. Pres.'s Coun on Mgmt. Improvement, 1984-89; dir. Office Mgmt. and Budget, 1988-89; exec. v.p., vice chmn. W.R. Grace & Co., N.Y.C., 1989-94; chmn. Grace Environ., Inc., 1989-94, Avic Group Internat., 1995—, Jefferson Ptnrs., 1995—; bd. dirs. Travelers Corp., 1990—, Harcourt, Brace, Jovonavich, Inc., 1990-91, W.R. Grace & Co., 1989-91, Canonie Environ., Inc., 1989-94, Grace Energy, Inc., 1990-94, Productora de Papeles, S.A., 1991-94, La Posta Recycling Ctr., Inc., 1992-94, Nat. Assn. Mfg.; bd. advs. Baker & Taylor, 1992—, Netmatics, 1996—, Deswell Industries, Inc., 1995—, Ardshiel, Inc., 1990-94; fed. co-chmn. Coastal Plains Regional Commn., 1981-82, Four Corners Regional Commn., 1981-82, New Eng. Regional Commn., 1981-82, Old West Regional Commn., 1981-82, Pacific N.W. REgional Commn., 1981-82, S.W. Border Regional Commn., 1981-82; ptnr. Gulfstream Capital, 1995—, Austin Trading Co., 1995—. Mem. adv. bd. Coun. for Excellence in Govt., 1988-96, The Jefferson Group, 1993—; trustee Hampton U., 1990—. 1st lt. AUS, 1963-65. Recipient Pres.'s Citizens award and medal, 1989; named Govt. Exec. of Yr., Govt. Computer News Mag., 1988, medal disting. achievement Colo. Sch. Mines, 1985. Mem. Young Pres. Orgn., Nat. Acad. Pub. Adminstrn., Colo. Sch. Mines Alumni Assn., Pres.'s Export Coun., Chief Execs. Orgn., World Bus. coun., Reagan Alumni Assn., Palm Beach (Fla.) Golf and Polo Club, Banyon Country Club (Fla.), Sky Club (N.Y.C.). Home: 2 Ocean Ln Lake Worth FL 33462-3337 Office: 2100 W Sample Rd Ste 300 Pompano Beach FL 33064 also: Jefferson Capital 1341 G St NW Washington DC 20005 also: Avic Group Internat 599 Lexington Ave New York NY 10022

WRIGHT, JUDITH MARGARET, law librarian, educator; b. Jackson, Tenn., Aug. 16, 1944; d. Joseph Clarence and Mary Catherine (Key) Wright; m. Mark A. Johnson, Apr. 17, 1976; children—Paul, Michael. B.S., Memphis State U., 1966; M.A., U. Chgo., 1971; J.D., DePaul U., 1980. Bar: Ill. 1980. Librarian Oceanway Sch., Jacksonville, Fla., 1966-67; program dir. ARC, South Vietnam, 1967-68; documents and reference librarian D'Angelo Law Library, U. Chgo., 1970-74, reference librarian, 1974-77, dir., lectr. in law, 1980—; mem. adv. bd. Legal Reference Svcs. Quar., 1981—. Mem. ABA, Am. Assn. Law Libraries, Chgo. Assn. Law Libraries. Democrat. Methodist. Home: 5525 S Harper Ave Chicago IL 60637-1829

WRIGHT, KATIE HARPER, educational administrator, journalist; b. Crawfordsville, Ark., Oct. 5, 1923; d. James Hale and Connie Mary (Locke) Harper; BA, U. Ill., 1944; MEd, 1959; EdD, St. Louis U., 1979; m. Marvin Wright, Mar. 21, 1952; 1 dau., Virginia K. Jordan. Elem. and spl. edn. tchr. East St. Louis (Ill.) Pub. Schs., 1944-65, dir. Dist. 189 Instructional Materials Program, 1965-71, dir. spl. edn. Dists. 188, 189, 1971-77, asst. supt. programs, 1977-79; interim supt. East St. Louis Sch. Dist. 189, 1993-94; adj. faculty Harris/Stowe State Coll., 1980; mem. staff St. Louis U., 1989—; interim supt. Dist. 189 Schs., 1994—; cons. to numerous workshops, seminars in field; mem. study tour People's Republic of China, 1984. Mem. Ill. Commn. on Children, 1973-85, East St. Louis Bd. Election Commrs.; pres. bd. dirs. St. Clair County Mental Health Center, 1970-72, 87— (award 1992); bd. dirs. River Bluff coun. Girl Scouts U.S., 1979—, nat. bd. dirs., 1981-84; bd. dirs. United Way, 1979—, Urban League, 1979—, Provident Counseling Ctr., 1995—; pres. bd. trustees East St. Louis Pub. Library, 1972-77; pres., bd. dirs. St. Clair County Mental Health Ctrs., 1987; adv. bd. Magna Bank; charter mem. Coalition of 100 Black Women; mem. coordinating council ethnic affairs Synod of Mid-Am., Presbyn. Ch. U.S.A; charter mem. Metro East Links Group; charter mem. Gateway chpt. The Links, Inc.; Ill. Minority/Female Bus. Coun., 1991—; mem. State of Ill. Corrections Sch. Bd. Author: Delta Sigma Theta/East St. Louis Chapter History, 1992. Recipient Lamp of Learning award East St. Louis Jr. Wednesday Club, 1965, Outstanding Working Woman award Downtown St. Louis, Inc., 1967, Ill. State citation for ednl. document Love is Not Enough, 1974, Delta Sigma Theta citation for document Good Works, 1979, Girl Scout Thanks badge, 1982, award Nat. Coun. Negro Women, 1983, Community Svc. award Met. East Bar Assn., 1983, Journalist award Sigma Gamma Rho, Spelman Coll. Alumni award, 1990, A World of Difference award, 1990, 91, Edn. award St. Louis YWCA, 1991, SIU-E-Kimmel award, 1991, St. Clair County Mental Health award, 1992, Gateway East Metropolitan Ministry Dr. M.L. King award, 1993, Nat. Coun. Negro Women Black Women Leader of the Year, 1995, Disting. Alumni award U. Ill., 1996; named Woman of Achievement, St. Louis Globe Democrat, 1974, Outstanding Adminstr. So. region Ill. Office Edn., 1975, Woman of Yr. in Edn. St. Clair County YWCA, 1987, Nat. Top Lady of the Yr., 1988; named to Vashon High Sch. Hall of Fame, 1989, Citizen Ambassador, South Africa, 1996. Mem. Am. Libraries Trustees Assn. (regional v.p. 1978-79, 92, nat. sec. 1979-80), Ill. Commn. on Children, Mensa, Council for Exceptional Children, Top Ladies of Distinction (pres. 1987-91, nat. editor 1991—, journalism award 1992, Media award 1992), Delta Sigma Theta (chpt. pres. 1960-62), Kappa Delta Pi (pres. So. Ill. U. chpt. 1973-74), Phi Delta Kappa (Service Key award 1984, chpt. pres. 1984-85), Iota Phi Lambda, Pi Lambda Theta (chpt. pres. 1985-87). Republican. Presbyterian. Club: East St. Louis Women's (pres. 1973-75). Contbr. articles to profl. jours.; feature writer St. Louis Argus Newspaper, 1979—. Home: 733 N 40th St East Saint Louis IL 62205-2138

WRIGHT, KENNETH BROOKS, lawyer; b. Whittier, Calif., June 5, 1934; s. Albert Harold and Marian (Schwey) W.; m. Sandra Beryl Smith, June 20, 1959; children: Margo Teresa, Daniel Brooks, John Waugh. B.A. cum laude, Pomona Coll., 1956; J.D., Stanford U., 1960. Bar: Calif. 1961, U.S. Supreme Ct. 1979. Assoc., then ptnr. Lawler, Felix & Hall, 1961-77; ptnr. Morgan, Lewis & Bockius, Los Angeles, 1978—; teaching team leader Nat. Inst. Trial Advocacy, 1978-80; mem. governing com. Calif. Continuing Edn. of Bar, 1973-77, chmn., 1975-76; nat. panel arbitrators Am. Arbitration Assn., 1970—; lectr. ABA Sect. Litigation Nat. Inst., 1979-86; bd. dirs. L.A. Internat. Comml. Arbitration Ctr. Chmn. bd. editors: Am. Bar Jour, 1977-81. Pres. Pomona Coll. Alumni Assn., 1970-71; pres. parent tchr. coun. Campbell Hall Sch., 1973-74, bd. dirs., 1976—, vice chmn., 1994—; counsel Vol. League San Fernando Valley, 1979-81; chmn. sect. adminstrn. of justice Town Hall of Calif., 1970-71; sr. warden Episcopal Ch., 1973-74. Served with U.S. Army, 1956-57. Mem. ABA (dir. programs litigation sect. 1977-81, mem. coun. 1982-88, mem. standing com on comm. 1978-88, chmn. 1987-88, chmn. sect. book pub. com. 1986-89, pres. fellows young lawyers 1985-86, bd. dirs. 1980-89), Internat. Bar Assn., Assn. Bus. Trial Lawyers (chair com. alt. dispute resolution 1991-93, bd. dirs. 1993-96), Am. Law Inst., Am. Bar Found., Am. Bd. Trial Advs., So. Calif. Def. Counsel, Def. Rsch. Inst., State Bar Calif. (mem. gov. com. continuing edn. of the bar 1972-77, chmn. 1975-76), Conf. Barristers (exec. com. 1966-69, 1st v.p. 1969), L.A. County Bar Assn. (com. on judiciary 1981-83, chmn. continuing legal edn. adv. com. 1989-91, vice-chmn. continuing legal edn. com. 1991-93, bd. dirs. L.A. Lawyers 1989-94), L.A. County Bar Found. (bd. dirs., trustee 1993—, mem. exec. com. internat. sect. 1996—), U.S. Supreme Ct. Hist. Soc., Jonathan Club, Chancery Club, Phi Beta Kappa. Republican. Avocations: skiing, tennis. Home: 3610 Longridge Ave Sherman Oaks CA 91423-4918 Office: Morgan Lewis & Bockius 801 S Grand Ave Fl 22 Los Angeles CA 90017-4613

WRIGHT, KENNETH OSBORNE, retired astronomer; b. Ft. George, B.C., Can., Nov. 1, 1911; s. Charles Melville and Agnes Pearl (Osborne) W.; m. Margaret Lindsay Sharp, Sept. 25, 1936 (dec. June 1969); 1 child, Nora Louise Wright Osborne; m. Jean May MacLachlan, Mar. 21, 1970. B.A., U. Toronto, Ont., Can., 1933, M.A., 1934; Ph.D., U. Mich., 1940; D.Sc. (hon.), Nicholas Copernicus U., Torun, Poland, 1973. With Dominion Astrophys. Obs., Victoria, B.C., 1936-84, asst. dir., 1960-66, dir., 1966-76, guest worker, 1976-84; hon. prof. physics U. Victoria, 1965-80, bd. govs., 1973-75; lectr. U. B.C., 1943-44; spl. lectr. in astronomy U. Toronto, 1959-60; research asso. Mt. Wilson and Palomar Obs., 1962; chmn. asso. com. on astronomy NRC Can., 1972-74. Decorated Can. Centennial medal. Fellow Royal Soc. Can.; mem. Internat. Astron. Union, Am. Astron. Soc., Can. Astron. Soc., Royal Astron. Soc. Can. (Gold medal 1933), Royal Astron. Soc., Astron. Soc. Pacific., Round Table, Rotary. Mem. United Ch. of Can. Research, publs. in field. Home: #202 1375 Newport Ave, Victoria, BC Canada V8S 5E8

WRIGHT, KENNETH WESTON, pediatric ophthalmologist; b. L.A., Oct. 25, 1950; s. Harvey Weston and Mary Jo W.; m. Donna Marie; children: Jamie, Matthew, Michael, Lisa, Andrew. BA, Calif. Lutheran Coll., 1972; MD, Boston U., 1977. Intern Harbor Gen. Hosp./UCLA, 1978; resident Doheny Eye Inst., L.A., 1978-81; fellow in pediat. ophthalmology Johns Hopkins Hosp., Balt., 1981, Children's Hosp. Nat. Medicine, Washington, 1982; assoc. prof. U. So. Calif., L.A., 1982-92; pvt. practice, 1992-94; head pediat. ophthalmology/strabismus Cleve. Clinic Found., 1994-97; pvt. practice L.A., 1997—. Author, editor: Textbook of Ophthalmology, 1996; editor: Pediatric Ophthalmology & Strabismus, 1995; contbr. articles to profl. jours. NIH grantee. Fellow Am. Acad. Pediatrics, Am. Acad. Ophthalmology (com.); mem. Am. Assn. Pediat. Ophthalmology/Strabismus, Wilmer Resident Assn. Avocations: surfing, tennis. Office: Am Eye Inst 8635 W 3rd St Los Angeles CA 90048-6101

WRIGHT, KIETH CARTER, librarian, educator; b. Billings, Mont., Nov. 11, 1933; s. Donald DeWitt and Isabella Sarah W.; children from previous marriage: Cynthia Jean, Elizabeth Anne. BA, Willamette U., 1955; MDiv, Union Theol. Sem., N.Y.C., 1958; MS In Libr. Scis, Columbia U., 1968, D of Libr. Scis., 1972. Chaplain intern Big Spring (Tex.) State Hosp., 1958-59; pastoral care worker N.C. Bapt. Hosp., Winston-Salem, N.C., 1960-64; adminstr. Nat. Council Chs., N.Y.C., 1964-70; librarian Gallaudet U., Washington, 1972-75; mem. faculty Cath. U. Am., Washington, 1976; dean Dept. Libr. and Info. Studies U. Md., College Park, 1977-79; chmn. dept. libr. sci. and ednl. technology Sch. Edn. U. N.C., Greensboro, 1980-86, prof. Sch. Edn., 1986—. Author: Library and Information Services for Handicapped Individuals, 1979, 3d edit., 1989, Workstations and Local Area Networks for Libraries, 1990, Serving Disabled, 1991, The Challenge of Technology, 1993, Computer-related Technologies in Library Operation, 1995. Office Edn. grantee, 1992-94. Mem. ALA. Home: 1605 Bearhollow Rd Greensboro NC 27410-3501 Office: U NC Sch Edn Greensboro NC 27412-5001

WRIGHT, LAURALI R. (BUNNY WRIGHT), writer; b. Saskatoon, Sask., Can., June 5, 1939; d. Sidney Victor and Evelyn Jane (Barber) Appleby; m. John Herbert Wright, Jan. 6, 1962 (separated 1986); children: Victoria Kathleen, Johnna Margaret. Student, Carleton U., 1958-59, U. B.C., 1960, 62-63, U. Calgary, 1970-71, Banff Sch. Fine Arts, 1976; MA, Simon Fraser U., Burnaby, B.C., Can., 1995. Reporter Saskatoon Star-Phoenix, 1968-69, Calgary Albertan, 1969-70; reporter, columnist Calgary Herald, 1970-76, 1970-76, asst. city editor, 1976-77; freelance writer Calgary, 1977—. Author: (novels) Neighbours, 1979 (New Alta. novelist award Alta Culture and Multiculturalism 1978), The Favorite, 1982, Among Friends, 1984, The Suspect, 1985 (Edgar Allen Poe award Mystery Writers Am. 1986), Sleep While I Sing, 1986, Love in the Temperate Zone, 1988, A Chill Rain in January, 1989 (Arthur Ellis award Crime Writers Can. 1990), Fall From Grace, 1991, Prized Possessions, 1993, A Touch of Panic, 1994, Mother Love, 1995, Strangers Among Us, 1996. Mem. Writers Union Can., Authors' Guild of U.S., Internat. P.E.N., Mystery Writers of Am., Authors League Am., Periodical Writers Assn. Can., Writers Fedn. B.C. Avocations: gardening, reading, movies, theater, concerts, jogging. Office: Virginia Barber Lit Agy Inc 101 Fifth Ave New York NY 10003-1008*

WRIGHT, LAWRENCE A., federal judge; b. Stratton, Maine, Dec. 25, 1927; m. Avis Leahy, 1953; children: Michael, David, James, Stephen, Douglas. BA, U. Maine, 1953; JD, Georgetown U., 1956; LLM, Boston U., 1962. Bar: D.C. 1956, Maine 1956, Mass. 1968, Vt. 1971. Sr. trial counsel chief counsel office IRS, Boston, 1958-69; tax commr. State of Vt., 1969-71; ptnr. Gravel, Shea & Wright Ltd., Vt., 1971-84; judge U.S. Tax Ct., Washington, 1984—. Commr. U.S. Battle Monuments Commn., 1982-84. 2d lt. U.S. Army, 1945-48; ret. col. JAG, USAR, 1978. Decorated Legion of Merit, others. Home: 1844 Northbridge Ln Annapolis MD 21401-6575 Office: US Tax Ct 400 2nd St NW Washington DC 20217-0001

WRIGHT, LINDA JEAN, manufacturing company executive; b. Chgo., Dec. 14, 1949; d. Eugene F. and Rosemary Margaret (Kiley) Kemph; m. Kelly W. Wright, Jr., Feb. 1979 (div. 1984); m. Samuel Neuwirth Klewans, Aug. 28, 1986 (div. 1991). Student Loretto Heights Coll., 1967-69, U. Ill., 1970-71. Asst. to v.p. Busey 1st Nat. Bank, Urbana, 1969-72; spa mgr., supr. sales tng. Venus and Apollo Health Club, San Antonio, 1973-76; owner Plant Shop, San Antonio, 1976-77; with Enterprise Bank, Falls Church, Va., 1977-84, comml. lending officer, 1978-84, sr. v.p., 1979-84, corp. sec. of bd. dirs., 1980-84; pres., CEO Fairfax Savs. Bank, 1984-87, Bankstar, N.A. (formerly Bank 2000 of Reston, N.A.), 1988-90; v.p. Ryan-McGinn Inc., Arlington, Va., 1991-95; v.p. Bethlehem Corp., 1995—; bd. dirs. INOVA Inst. Rsch. and Edn., 1990-94. Apptd. pub. ofcl., chmn. Va. Small Bus. Fin. Authority, Richmond, 1984-88; trustee Inova Health System, 1992-95; mem. exec. com. Fairfax-Falls Ch., United Way, United Way Capital Area, Washington, 1984-85; Fairfax County Spl. Task Force, 1986; bd. dirs. Fairfax Com. of 100, 1993-95; mem., bd. dirs. Hospice No. Va., Arlington, 1985-86, chmn. No. Va. Local Devel. Corp., 1986; mem. oper. bd. Fairfax Hosp., 1987-94; pres. No. Va. Transp. Alliance, 1987-92; bd. dirs. Va. Found. for Rsch. and Econ. Edn., 1989-91, No. Va. coun. Am. Heart Assn., 1989-94. Mem. Fairfax County C. of C. (dir., v.p., pres. 1987-88), Nat. Assn. Bank Women (chmn. No. Va. group 1980-81), Fairfax Hunt Club, Tower Club (bd. govs. 1989-95). Roman Catholic. Avocations: aviation, fox hunting.

WRIGHT, MARSHALL, retired manufacturing executive, former diplomat; b. El Dorado, Ark., July 14, 1926; s. John Harvey and Helen Vaughan (Williams) W.; m. Mable Olean Johnson, Sept. 12, 1950 (dec. June 1989); children: William Marshall, Jefferson Vaughan; m. Lind Groseclose Vaughan, Mar. 31, 1990. Student, U. Ark., 1946-48, Cornell U., 1957-58; B.S. in Fgn. Service, Georgetown U., 1951. Joined U.S. Fgn. Service, 1953; vice consul Egypt, 1953-55; adminstrv. officer Can., 1956; econ. officer Burma, 1958-60; polit. officer Thailand, 1966-67; spokesman for State Dept., 1964-66; country dir. for Philippines, 1969; sr. mem. NSC, 1967-68, dir. long range planning, 1970-72; asst. sec. state for congl. relations, 1972-74; sr. fellow Nat. War Coll., 1969-70; v.p. govt. affairs Eaton Corp., 1974-76, v.p. pub. affairs, 1976-80, v.p. corp. affairs, 1980-91. Chmn. Cleve. ARC; trustee Cleve. Orch., Cleve. Inst. Music; chmn. Cleve. Com. Fgn. Rels.; vice chmn. Govtl. Rsch. Inst.; mem. Conf. Bd. Pub. Affairs Rsch. Coun., MAPI, Pub. Affairs Coun.; bd. dirs. Cleveland Town Hall, Bus. Industry Polit. action Com. With USMC, 1944-46. Recipient Meritorious Service award State Dept., 1966, Distinguished Service award, 1972. Mem. Am. Fgn. Svc. Assn., Columbia Country Club, Met. Club, Dacor, Mayfield Country, Union, Moss Creek Golf Club. Home (summer): 304 Corning Dr Cleveland OH 44108-1014 Home (winter): Moss Creek Plantation 80 Toppin Dr Hilton Head SC 29926

WRIGHT, MARTHA HELEN, elementary education educator; b. Leesburg, Fla., Nov. 6, 1955; d. Richard and Helene (McRae) Wright; children: Robert L., Micah R. BS, Bethune-Cookman Coll., 1977. Cert. tchr., Fla. Payroll clk. Inland Container Corp., Orlando, Fla., 1978; computer operator So. Bell Telephone, Orlando, 1978-79; tchr. 4th and 5th grades Orange County Pub. Schs., Orlando, 1979-80; homeparent Health Rehab. Svcs., Orlando, 1980-81; elem. tchr. Pinar Elem. Sch., Orlando, 1981-83, Central Ave Elem. Sch., Kissimmee, Fla., 1983—; program coord. U. Ctrl. Fla., Orlando, summer 1990; program dir. Frontline Outreach, Inc., Orlando,. summers 1984-89; youth counselor The Pvt. Industry Coun., Orlando, summers 1991-92. Author plays; poet; choreographer dance recital. Inner city tutor Frontline Outreach, summer 1987; founder Adopt-A-Grandparent, Kissimmee, 1986—; dir., creator UN Day/Cultural Awareness, 1991-92. Recipient Community Svc. award Walt Disney World, 1991, 92, Youth Group Vol. of Yr. award Beverly Enterprises, 1993, Teacherrrific award Walt Disney Co., 1996-97, other awards. Avocations: writing, playing piano, reading, choreography, modern dance, and motivational speaking. Home: PO Box 1370 Orlando FL 32802-1370

WRIGHT, MARY DORIS, physician; b. Wendell, N.C., Dec. 12, 1943; d. Roosevelt and Olivia (Baker) W. BS, N.C. Coll., Durham, 1966; MD, Howard U., Washington, 1974; postgrad., Johns Hopkins U., 1990-92. Diplomate family practice, occupational medicine, preventive medicine; lic. physician, D.C., N.Y., Pa., N.C., Md. Intern, resident Howard U. Hosp., Washington, 1974-77; biologist Nat. Cancer Inst., NIH, Bethesda, Md., 1967-70; asst. med. dir. Shaw Cmty. Health Ctr., Washington, 1978-81; clinic dir. Bell and William Med. Assocs., Phila., 1977-78; emergency medicine physician Hadley Meml. Hosp., Washington, 1980-81; chief med. officer adminstrv. medicine U.S. EPA, Washington, 1981-85; chief med. officer adminstrv. and occupational medicine U.S. Govt. Printing Office, Washington, 1985-90; med. officer D.C. Gen. Hosp., Washington, 1990—; pres., CEO M.D.W. Healthcare Group, Inc., Silver Springs, Md., 1981—; mem. courtesy staff Providence Hosp., Washington, family practice staff Sibley Hosp., Washington. With USPHS, 1977-78. Recipient Nat. Med. Fellowship tuition award, 1970-72. Mem. AMA, APHA, Nat. Med. Asn., Am. Acad. Fed. Civil Svcs. Physician's Assn., D.C. Med. Soc., Med Chi, Beta Kappa Chi. Avocations: home decorating, reading, gourmet cooking.

WRIGHT, MARY JAMES, multimedia instructional designer; b. Charlottesville, Va., Aug. 20, 1946; d. Harry Beech and Virginia Allen (Root) James; m. Paul Sims Wright, July 26, 1969; children: Christopher Brennan, Keith Allen. BA summa cum laude, Mary Washington Coll., 1968; MA, Northwestern U., 1969; postgrad., Trinity Coll., 1981, Gallaudet U., 1991. Instr. drama and speech Mary Washington Coll., Fredericksburg, Va., 1969-71, Charles County Community Coll., La Plata, Md., 1973-79; arts and media coord. Charles County Arts Coun., La Plata, 1973-82, Gen. Smallwood Mid. Sch., Indian Head, Md., 1980-82, No. Va. Community Coll., Annandale, 1982-84; computer-based learning specialist USDA Grad. Sch., Washington, 1984-85, U.S. Army Engr. Sch., Ft. Belvoir, Va., 1985-87, Battelle Meml. Inst., Columbus, Ohio, 1987-88; videodisc designer Kendrick & Co., Washington, 1988-90; instrnl. design mgr. The Discovery Channel, Bethesda, Md., 1990-93; instnl. design mgr., writer Edunetics Corp., Arlington, Va., 1994-97; interactive multimedia designer and developer Smart House, Ltd. Partnership, Upper Marlboro, Md., 1990; project mgr., instl. designer Toby Levine Comms., Inc., 1990-97; exec. editor Time-Life Edn., Alexandria, Va., 1997—. Author, dir.: Story-Theatre for Children, 1979; contbr. articles to profl. jours.; pub. videodiscs, CD-ROMS, Web sites and classroom guides for nat. media products for PBS, Discovery Channel, Nat. Geographic, Edunetics Corp. Pres. Am. Christian Television System of No. Va., Action for Women, Charles County AAUW; sign lang. interpreter Deaf Ministry. Nat. Danforth fellow 1969; recipient Achievement award Dept. of Army, 1986, Kendrick & Co., 1989; recipient Outstanding Arts Programming award Md. Dept. Parks and Recreation, 1980, Silver and Bronze Cindy awards (Cinema in Industry and Edn.), 1992, Red Ribbon Am. Film & Video Assn. Festival, Special Gold Jury award Houston Internat. Film Festival, 1992, Gold award Nebr. Interactive Media, 1993. Mem. ASCD, Internat. Interactive Courseware Soc. (Mark of Excellence award 1992), Assn. for Devel. Computer-Based Instrn. Systems (coord. spl. interest groups D.C. chpt. 1989-90), No. Va. Registry Interpreters for the Deaf, Mortar Bd., Alpha Psi Omega, Alpha Phi Sigma. Home: 4302 Rolling Stone Way Alexandria VA 22306-1225 Office: Time-Life Inc 2000 Duke St Alexandria VA 22314-3414

WRIGHT, MAX, information processing executive, consultant, youth leadership corporate training executive; b. Windsor, England, June 14, 1954; came to the U.S., 1989; s. Harold Edwin and Sheila Doreen (Young) W.; 2 children: Robyn, Devan Lucien. Electronics tech. Electricity Supply Commn., Germiston, South Africa, 1972-74, R. Muller, Johannesburg, South Africa, 1974-75; svc. mgr., sr. technician OKTV, George, South Africa, 1975-77; field engr. Burroughs Machines, Johannesburg, 1978-79; systems analyst Sidha Assocs. (Pty.) Ltd., Johannesburg, 1980-84, mng. dir., 1984-88; v.p. Arisoft, Inc., Fairfield, Iowa, 1989-97, pres., 1997—. Contbr. articles to profl. jours. Tchr. Transcendental meditation, 1979—; treas. South African Assn. Age of Enlightenment, 1980-87; founder, pres. Life Force, Inc., 1994—. Mem. T'ai Chi Assn. South Africa, Fairfield T'ai Chi Assn. (founding instr. and dir. 1992—). Avocations: Transcendental meditation, T'ai Chi Ch'uan, peaceful warrior training. Office: Arisoft Software PO Box 2198 Fairfield IA 52556-8198

WRIGHT, MICHAEL KEARNEY, public relations executive; b. Durham, N.C., Apr. 23, 1928; s. Wilburn Kearney and Roberta Audrey (Lee) W. BS, N.C. Cen. U., 1951; MS, Columbia U., 1954. Actor, singer, dancer Broadway and TV, 1951-60; dir. edn. Am. Cancer Soc., N.Y.C., 1960-69; dir. audio/visual edn. Media Medica, Inc., N.Y.C., 1969; dir. N.Y. office McFadden, Strauss & Irwin Inc., N.Y.C., 1970-75; v.p. ICPR, N.Y.C., 1975-77; sr. v.p. Stone Assocs., N.Y.C., 1977-85; pres. The Wright Co., N.Y.C., 1985; v.p. The Lippin Group, N.Y.C., 1985—; pub. rels. cons. Nuclear Rsch. Assocs., New Hyde Park, N.Y., 1967-69. Bd. dirs. CSC Repertory Co., N.Y.C., 1988-89; counsellor 1st Ch. of Religious Sci., N.Y.C., 1981-96, Alcoholics Anonymous, N.Y.C., 1970—; lectr. Sci. of Mind, N.Y.C., 1988-96; supporter ASPCA, Humane Soc., Morris Dees and others. With U.S. Army, 1946-47. Mem. NATAS, Am. Film Inst., Smithsonian Assocs., Actors' Equity Assn., N.Y. City Ctr., Alpha Kappa Mu, Beta Kappa Chi. Avocations: collector old movies on videos, weightlifting. Home: 200 E 36th St Apt 11G New York NY 10016-3648

WRIGHT, MICHAEL WILLIAM, wholesale distribution, retailing executive; b. Mpls., June 13, 1938; s. Thomas W. and Winifred M. Wright. B.A., U. Minn., 1961, J.D. with honors, 1963. Ptnr. Dorsey & Whitney, Mpls., 1966-77; sr. v.p. Supervalu Inc., Mpls., 1977-78; pres., chief operating officer Super Valu Stores, Inc., Mpls., 1978—, chief exec. officer, 1981—, chmn., pres. and CEO, 1982—; bd. dirs., past chmn. Fed. Res. Bank, Mpls.; bd. dirs. Norwest Corp., Honeywell, Inc., The Musicland Group, Shopko, Inc., S.C. Johnson & Co., Inc., Cargill, Inc., Internat. Ctr. for Cos. of the Food Trade and Industry, Food Mktg. Inst., Nat. Am. Wholesale Grocers Assn., Inc.; vice chmn. Food Mktg. Inst. 1st lt. U.S. Army, 1964-66. Office: Supervalu Inc PO Box 990 Minneapolis MN 55440*

WRIGHT, MILDRED ANNE (MILLY WRIGHT), conservator, researcher; b. Athens, Ala., Sept. 9, 1939; d. Thomas Howard and Anne Louise (Ashworth) Speegle; m. William Paul Wright, Nov. 20, 1965; children: Paul Howard, William Neal. BS in Physics, U. Ala., Tuscaloosa, 1963. Rschr. in acoustics Wyle Labs., Huntsville, Ala., 1963-64; tchr. physics, English Huntsville H.S., 1964-67; ptnr. Flying Carpet Oriental Rugs, Florence, Ala., 1974—; adj. mem. faculty U. North Ala., Florence, 1988, lectr. Inst. for Learning in Retirement, 1991—. Columnist Times Daily,

1992—; photojournalist, writer River Views Mag., 1993—; contbr. articles to profl. jours. (1st pl. award 1986, 87). Pianist, organist Edgemont Meth. Ch., Florence, 1987-90 (Outstanding Svc. award 1990); mem. steering com. Melton Hollow Nature Ctr., Florence, 1990—, Design Ala., Florence, 1991, River Heritage Discovery Camp, 1993-95; mem. River Heritage Com., Florence, 1991—; accompanist Shoals Boy Choir, Muscle Shoals, Ala., 1992-93; bd. dirs. Heritage Preservation, Inc., Capital award, 1992, pres., 1990-92, 96-97, treas., 1995-96, Tenn. Valley Hist. Soc., pres., 1991-95, Ala. Preservation Alliance, treas., 1993-96, Florence Main Street program, 1992-94, Maud Lindsay Free Kindergarten, Frank Lloyd Wright Rosenbaum House Found., Inc., 1992—, Gen. Joseph Wheeler Home Found., 1994—, treas. 1995-97, newsletter editor, 1995—; (merit award, 1996) Southeastern Mus. Assn.; sec. Friends of the Ala. Archives, 1995—; mem. adv. coun. Human Environ. Scis. Dept.; mem. Coby Hall steering com. U. North Ala., 1992—, Kennedy-Douglas Ctr. Arts; adv. bd. Old Cahawba of Ala., 1996—; adv. bd. Waterloo Mus., 1995—, Florence Children's Mus., 1995-96. Recipient Disting. Svc. award Ala. Hist. Commn., 1991, Merit award Ala. Preservation Alliance, 1995, Southeastern Muss. Assn., 1996. Mem. Ala. Writers' Conclave (Creative Works award 1986, 87), Ala. Hist. Assn., Ala. Archeol. Soc., Natchez Trace Geneal. Soc., Colbert County Hist. Landmarks Found., Nat. Trust for Hist. Preservation, Tennessee Valley Art Assn. (exhibit chmn. 1996—), La Grange Living History Assn., Trail of Tears Assn., Firenze Club (past pres., pres. 1996—), Optimist Club, Sigma Pi Sigma. Avocations: bridge, photography, travel, discovering old buildings, gardening. Home: PO Box 279 Florence AL 35631-0279

WRIGHT, MINTURN TATUM, III, lawyer; b. Phila., Aug. 7, 1925; s. Minturn T. and Anna (Moss) W.; m. Nonya R. Stevens, May 11, 1957; children: Minturn T., Richard S., Robert M., Marianne F. BA, Yale U., 1949; LLB, U. Pa., 1952. Bar: Pa. 1953, U.S. Ct. Appeals (3d cir.) 1953, U.S. Supreme Ct. 1962. Law clk. U.S. Ct. Appeals (3d cir.), 1952-53; assoc. Dechert, Price & Rhoads, Phila., 1953-61, ptnr., 1961-95, chmn., 1982-84; bd. dirs. Penn Va. Corp., Phila. Contributionship, Vector Security Co. Inc., Cotiga Devel. Co.; vis. prof. U. Pa. Law Sch., 1965-69, 93—. Contbr. articles to profl. jours. Trustee Acad. Nat. Scis. Phila., 1958—, chmn., 1976-81, vice chmn., 1995—; trustee Hawk Mountain Sanctuary Assn., chmn. bd. dirs., 1992—, Rare Ctr., The Nature Conservancy (Pa. chpt.). Served with U.S. Army, 1943-46. Mem. ABA, Pa. Bar Assn., Phila. Bar Assn., Nat. Coal Lawyers Assn., Eastern Mineral Law Assn. (trustee), Phila. Club, Milldam Club. Episcopalian. Office: Dechert Price & Rhoads 4000 Bell Atlantic Tower 1717 Arch St Philadelphia PA 19103-2713

WRIGHT, MURIEL DEASON See WELLS, KITTY

WRIGHT, NORMAN HAROLD, lawyer; b. N.Y.C., Mar. 7, 1947; s. Donald H. and Georgianna (Reinert) W.; m. Julie K. Angert, May 29, 1971; children: Zane H., Anne V. BS in Engring., U. Toledo, 1969; JD, Creighton U., 1978. Bar: Nebr. 1978, U.S. Ct. Appeals (8th cir.) 1978, U.S. Supreme Ct. 1989. Engr. E.I. DuPont de Nemours & Co., Inc., Columbus, Ohio, 1969-72, El Paso, Tex., 1972-75; assoc. Fraser, Stryker, Vaughn, Meusey, Olson, Boyer & Bloch, P.C., Omaha, 1978-83, ptnr., 1984—; dir. Nebr. Tax Rsch. Coun., Lincoln, 1989—. Author: Nebraska Legal Forms, Real Estate, 1983. Chmn. bd. Am. Diabetes Assn., Omaha, 1991; bd. trustees Trinity Cathedral Episcopal Ch., Omaha, 1986-89. Mem. ABA, Nebr. Bar Assn., Inst. Property Taxation, Nebr. Tax Forum, Cosmopolitan Club (sec. 1990-92, pres. 1995). Republican. Episcopalian. Avocations: golf, skiing, baseball. Home: 8910 Frances St Omaha NE 68124-2041 Office: Fraser Stryker Vaughn Meusey Olson Boyer & Bloch PC 409 S 17th St Ste 500 Omaha NE 68102-2609

WRIGHT, SIR (JOHN) OLIVER, retired diplomat; b. U.K., Mar. 6, 1921; m. Lillian Marjory Osborne, Sept. 19, 1942; children: Nicholas, John, Christopher. Ed., Solihull Sch., Christ's Coll., Cambridge, Eng.; D.H.L. (hon.), U. Nebr., 1983; LL.D., Rockford Coll., 1984. Joined Diplomatic Service, 1945; Brit. ambassador to Denmark, 1966-69, to Fed. Republic Germany, 1975-81, to U.S., 1982-86; vis. prof. U.S.C.; Tobin Lewin vis. prof. Wash. U., St. Louis. Trustee Brit. Mus., 1986-91; bd. dirs. Brit. Council; chmn. Anglo-Irish Encounter, 1986-91. With Royal Navy, 1941-45. Decorated D.S.C., knight grand cross Royal Victorian Order, knight grand cross Order of St. Michael and St. George, grand cross German Order of Merit; named hon. fellow Christ's Coll., 1981; Clark fellow, Cornell U., 1987. Mem. German C. of C. London (pres.). Club: Travellers' (London). Avocations: theatre; gardening.

WRIGHT, PETER MELDRIM, lawyer; b. Charlottesville, Va., Apr. 10, 1946; s. David McCord and Caroline Wallace (Jones) W.; m. Astrid Gabriella Mercedes Sandberg, June 4, 1972; children: David Habersham, Christian Langdon. AB, U. Ga., 1967, JD, 1972. Bar: Ga. 1972, U.S. Dist. Ct. (no. dist.) Ga. 1972. Assoc. Jones, Bird & Howell, Atlanta, 1972-77, ptnr., 1977-82; ptnr. Alston & Bird, Atlanta, 1982—. Author: A Survey of State Blue Sky Laws Applicable to Tax Exempt Bonds, 1987, Long Term Care Facilities, Chapter 7 of Health Care Corporate Law—Facilities and Transactions, 1996. Sec. Atlanta coun. Soc. Colonial Wars in Ga., 1975-88, dep. gov., 1989-91; mem. Soc. Cin. Ga., Savannah, historian, 1996—. Mem. ABA, Ga. Bar Assn., Atlanta Bar Assn., Nat. Assn. Bond Lawyers (chmn. blue sky laws and legal investment law coms. 1982-85, bd. dirs. 1985-86), Ga. Hist. Soc. (bd. curators 1993-94, sec. 1994—), Oglethorpe Club (Savannah, Ga.), St. Andrew's Soc. Savannah. Home: 3502 Woodhaven Rd NW Atlanta GA 30305-1011 Office: Alston & Bird 1 Atlantic Ctr 1201 W Peachtree St NW Atlanta GA 30309-3400

WRIGHT, PHILIP LINCOLN, zoologist, educator; b. Nashua, N.H., July 9, 1914; s. Clarence H. and Avis (Dary) W.; m. Margaret Ann Halbert, July 21, 1939 (dec. 1988); children: Alden H., Philip L., Ann E. Wright Dwyer; m. Hedwig G. Tourangeau, Dec. 28, 1989. B.S., U. N.H., 1935, M.S., 1937; Ph.D., U. Wis., 1940. Instr. to assoc. prof. zoology U. Mont., 1939-51, prof., 1951-85, emeritus prof., 1985—, chmn. dept. zoology, 1956-69, 70-71; on leave South Africa, 1970; Maytag vis. prof. zoology Ariz. State U., 1980. Author: (with W.H. Nesbitt) Records of North American Big Game, 8th edit., 1981, How to Score Big Game Trophy Heads, 1985; assoc. editor: Jour. Mammalogy, 1956-64; editor gen. notes and revs., 1966-68; contbr. numerous articles on mammalogy and ornithology. Fellow AAAS; mem. Am. Soc. Zoologists, Am. Soc. Mammalogists, Mont. Acad. Scis. (pres. 1957), Soc. for Study Reprodn., Am. Ornithol. Union, Cooper Ornithol. Soc., Wildlife Soc. (editorial bd. jour. Wildlife Mgmt. 1966-68), Explorers Club, Sigma Xi, Phi Sigma, Gamma Alpha. Club: Boone and Crockett (chmn. panel judges 16th award program, hon. mem. 1984, Sagamore Hill medal 1996).

WRIGHT, RANDOLPH EARLE, retired petroleum company executive; b. Brownsville, Tex., Dec. 22, 1920; s. William Randolph and Nelle Mae (Earle) W.; m. Elaine Marie Harris, May 9, 1943; 1 son, Randolph Earle. B.S., U. Tex., 1942. With Texaco Inc., 1946-82; mgr. gas div. Texaco Inc., Houston, 1968-70; gen. mgr. producing dept. Texaco Inc., 1970-71, v.p. gas dept., 1971-82; v.p., sr. officer Texaco Inc., Houston, 1972-80; past pres., dir. Sabine Pipe Line Co.; v.p., asst. to pres. Texaco U.S.A., 1980-82, ret., 1982; past v.p. Texaco Mineral Co.; past chmn. engring. found. adv. council U. Tex., Austin. Past mem. exec. bd. Sam Houston Area council Boy Scouts Am.; past bd. dirs., past pres. Jr. Achievement S.E. Tex.; past bd. dirs. Houston Symphony Soc., Tex. Research League, Houston C. of C.; past trustee U. St. Thomas; trustee S.W. Research Inst. Served with USNR, World War II. Mem. Tex. Research League. Clubs: Lakeside.

WRIGHT, RICHARD JOHN, business executive; b. Bklyn., June 17, 1951; s. David Francis and Mary Catherine W.; m. Linda Marie Green, May 24, 1975; children: Sean, Bridget. B.S. in Physics with honors, Bates Coll., 1973; M.B.A., Rutgers U., 1974. C.P.A. Mgr. Coopers & Lybrand, N.Y.C., 1975-81; chief fin. officer Drexel Burnham Lambert, N.Y.C., 1981-92; pres., dir. DP Investments G.P. Corp., N.Y.C., 1992—; pres. DPI-A Corp., N.Y.C., 1992—, DPI-B Corp., N.Y.C., 1992—; mng. dir. Viking Group, Ltd., Whittredge Capital, L.P. Trustee Mount Desert Island Biol. Lab. Mem. AICPA, Fin. Exec. Inst., N.Y. State Soc. CPAs, Williams Club, Spring Lake Bath and Tennis Club. Office: DP Investments GP Corp 450 Lexington Ave New York NY 10017-3911

WRIGHT, RICHARD NEWPORT, III, civil engineer, government official; b. Syracuse, N.Y., May 17, 1932; s. Richard Newport and Carolyn (Baker) W.; m. Teresa Rios, Aug. 23, 1959; children—John Stannard, Carolyn Maria, Elizabeth Rebecca, Edward Newport. B.C.E., Syracuse U., 1953, M.C.E. (Parcel fellow), 1955; Ph.D., U. Ill., 1962. Jr. engr. Pa. R.R., Phila., 1953-55; instr. civil engring. U. Ill., Urbana, 1957-62; asst. prof. U. Ill., 1962-65, assoc. prof., 1965-70, prof., 1970-74, adj. prof., 1974-79; chief structures sect. Bldg. Research div. U.S. Bur. Standards, Washington, 1971-72; pres. Internat. Council for Bldg. Research, Studies and Documentation, 1983-86; dep. dir. tech. Ctr. Bldg. Tech., 1972-73, dir., 1974-91; dir. Bldg. and Fire Rsch. Lab., 1991—. Contbr. articles to profl. jours. Pres. Montgomery Village Found., 1989-90, bd. dirs., 1985—. Served with AUS, 1955-57. Named Fed. Engr. of Yr. Nat. Soc. Profl. Engrs., 1988. Fellow ASCE, AAAS. Home: 20081 Doolittle St Montgomery Village MD 20879-1354 Office: Dept of Commerce Nat Inst Standards & Tech Bldg and Fire Research Labs Gaithersburg MD 20899

WRIGHT, RICHARD OSCAR, III, pathologist, educator; b. La Junta, Colo., Aug. 9, 1944; s. Richard O. Sr. and Frances R. (Curtiss) W.; m. Bernale Trout, May 31, 1969; children: Lauren Diane, Richard O. IV. BS in Biology, Midwestern State U., 1966; MS in Biology, U. Houston, 1968; DO, U. Health Sci., 1972. Cert. anatomic pathology and lab. medicine Am. Osteo. Bd. Pathology. Sr. attending pathologist Normandy Met. Hosps., St. Louis, 1977-81; sr. attending pathologist Phoenix (Ariz.) Gen. Hosps., 1981-97, dir. med. edn., 1989-92, 96—; clin. asst. prof. pathology Coll. Osteo. Medicine, Pomona, Calif., 1985—; dir. labs., chmn. dept. John C. Lincoln Hosp., Deer Valley, 1997—; dir. med. edn., chmn. dept. pathology, dir. labs. John C. Lincoln Hosp., Deer Valley, Ariz., 1997—; clin. instr. pathology Ohio U. Coll. Osteo. Medicine, Athens, 1976-77; clin. asst. prof. pathology Kirksville (Mo.) Coll. Osteo. Medicine, 1985-87; vis. lectr. pathology New Eng. Coll. Osteo. Medicine, Biddeford, Maine, 1989-92; cons. pathologist Phoenix (Ariz.) Indian Med. Ctr., 1992-94; adv. bd. Inter Soc. Coun. Pathology, Chgo., 1992—. Active Ariz. Rep. Party, Phoenix, Rep. Nat. Coun., Washington; precinctman Dist. 18 Maricopa County, Ariz., 1996, Madison Heights Precinct, 1996; chmn. bd. trustees Phoenix (Ariz.) Gen. Hosp., 1994-95; ex-occicio, trustee, 1995-97; trustee John C. Lincoln Found., 1997—; mem. found. adv. coun. Lincoln Health Found.-Phoenix Gen. Hosp. Osteo. Endowment Fund. Recipient Mead-Johnson award Nat. Osteo. Assn., 1975. Fellow Am. Osteo. Coll. Pathologists (pres. 1989-90, bd. govs. 1984-91), Coll. Pathologists, Coll. Am. Pathologists, Am. Soc. Clin. Pathologists; mem. Ariz. Osteo. Med. Assn. (del. dist. 2 ho. of dels.), Ariz. Soc. Pathologists, Century Club Alumni Assn., AAAS, Alpha Phi Omega, Rho Sigma Chi, Psi Sigma Alpha. Presbyterian. Office: Anatomic Pathology Assoc 19829 N 27th Ave Phoenix AZ 85027-4001

WRIGHT, ROBERT, broadcast executive. Office: NBC 30 Rockefeller Plz Fl 52 New York NY 10112*

WRIGHT, ROBERT JOSEPH, lawyer; b. Rome, Ga., Dec. 13, 1949; s. Arthur Arley and Maude T. (Lacey) W.; m. Donna Ruth Bishop, Feb. 18, 1972; children: Cynthia Ashley, Laura Christine. BA cum laude, Ga. State U., 1979; JD cum laude, U. Ga., 1983. Bar: Ga. 1983, U.S. Dist. Ct. (no. dist.) Ga. 1983, U.S. Dist. Ct. (mid. dist.) Ga. 1985. Assoc. Craig & Gainer, Covington, Ga., 1983-84, Heard, Leverett & Adams, Elberton, Ga., 1984-86; gen. counsel Group Underwriters, Inc., Elberton, 1987—. Editorial staff Ga. Jour. Internat. and Comparative Law, 1981-82. Mem. State Bar Ga. (sec. legal econs. sect. 1987-88, chmn. legal econs. sect. 1988-90), Order of the Coif, Masons, Phi Alpha Delta. Baptist. Home: 1030 E Canyon Creek Ct Watkinsville GA 30677-1500

WRIGHT, ROBERT PAYTON, lawyer; b. Beaumont, Tex., Feb. 15, 1951; s. Vernon Gerald and Huberta Read (Nunn) W.; m. Sallie Chesnutt Smith, July 16, 1977; children: Payton Cullen, Elizabeth Risher. AB, Princeton U., 1972; JD, Columbia U., 1975. Bar: Tex. 1975. Ptnr. Baker & Botts, L.L.P., Houston, 1975—. Author: The Texas Homebuyer's Manual, 1986. Mem. Am. Coll. Real Estate Lawyers, State Bar Tex. (chmn. coun. real estate, probate, trust law sect. 1994-95), Houston Bar Assn. (chmn. real estate sect. 1989-90), Tex. Coll. Real Estate Lawyers, Houston Real Estate Lawyers Coun., Houston Club (mem. com. young mems. 1987). Episcopalian. Office: Baker & Botts LLP 910 Louisiana St Houston TX 77002-4916

WRIGHT, ROBERT ROSS, III, law educator; b. Ft. Worth, Nov. 20, 1931; m. Susan Webber; children: Robert Ross IV, John, David, Robin. BA cum laude, U. Ark., 1953, JD, 1956; MA (grad. fellow), Duke U., 1954; SJD (law fellow), U. Wis., 1967. Bar: Ark. 1956, U.S. Supreme Ct. 1968, Okla. 1970. Instr. polit. sci. U. Ark., 1955-56; mem. firm Forrest City, Ark., 1956-58; partner firm Norton, Norton & Wright, Forrest City, 1959; asst. gen. counsel, asst. sec. Crossett Co., Ark.; atty. Crossett div. Ga.-Pacific Corp., 1960-63; asst. sec. Pub. Utilities Co., Crossett, Triangle Bag Co., Covington, Ky., 1960-62; mem. faculty law sch. U. Ark., 1963-70; asst. prof., dir. continuing legal edn. and research, then asst. dean U. Ark. (Little Rock div.), 1965-66, prof. law, 1967-70; vis. prof. law U. Iowa, 1969-70; prof. U. Okla., 1970-77; dean U. Okla. (Coll. Law); dir. U. Okla. (Law Center), 1970-76; vis. prof. U. Ark., Little Rock, 1976-77; Donaghey Disting. prof. U. Ark, 1977—; vis. disting. prof. U. Cin., 1983; Ark. commr. Nat. Conf. Commrs. Uniform State Laws, 1967-70; past chmn. Com. Uniform Eminent Domain Code; past mem. Com. Uniform Probate Code, Ark. Gov.'s Ins. Study Commn.; chmn. Gov. Commn. on Uniform Probate Code; chmn. task force joint devel. Hwy. Research Bd.; vice chmn. Okla. Jud. Council, 1970-72, chmn., 1972-75; chmn. Okla. Center Criminal Justice, 1971-76. Author: Arkansas Eminent Domain Digest, 1964, Arkansas Probate Practice System, 1965, The Law of Airspace, 1968, Emerging Concepts in the Law of Airspace, 1969, Cases and Materials on Land Use, 3d edit., 1982, supplement, 1987, 4th edit., 1991, Uniform Probate Code Practice Manual, 1972, Model Airspace Code, 1973, Land Use in a Nutshell, 1978, 2d edit., 1985, 3d edit., 1994, The Arkansas Form Book, 1979, 2d edit., 1988, Zoning Law in Arkansas: A Comparative Analysis, 1980; contbr. numerous articles to legal jours. Mem. Little Rock Planning Commn., 1978-82, chmn., 1982. Named Ark. Man of Year Kappa Sigma, 1958. Fellow Am. Law Inst., Am. Coll. Probate Counsel (acad.); mem. ABA (chmn., exec. coun. gen. practice, solo and small firm sect., former chmn. new pubs. editl. bd., sect. officers conf., ho. of dels. 1994—), Ark. Bar Assn. (exec. coun. 1985-88, ho. of dels., life mem., chmn. eminent domain code com., past mem. com. new bar ctr., past chmn. preceptorship com., exec. com. young lawyers sect.), Okla. Bar Assn. (past vice-chmn. legal internship com., former vice-chmn. gen. practice sect.), Pulaski County Bar Assn., Ark. Bar Found., U. Wis. Alumni Assn., Duke U. Alumni Assn., U. Ark. Alumni Assn., Order of Coif, Phi Beta Kappa, Phi Alpha Delta, Omicron Delta Kappa. Episcopalian. Home: 249 Pleasant Valley Dr Little Rock AR 72212-3170 Office: U Ark Law Sch 1201 Mcalmont St Little Rock AR 72202-5142

WRIGHT, ROBERT THOMAS, JR., lawyer; b. Detroit, Oct. 4, 1946; s. Robert Thomas and Jane Ellen (Blandin) W.; m. Diana Feltman, June 8, 1994; children: Sarah Allison, Jonathan Brian. BA in History and Polit. Sci., U. N.C., 1968; JD, Columbia U., 1974. Bar: Fla. 1974. Assoc. Paul & Thomson, Miami, Fla., 1974-77; assoc. Mershon, Sawyer, Johnston, Dunwoody & Cole, Miami, 1977-81, ptnr., 1981-95; ptnr. Shutts & Bowen, Miami, 1995—. Pillar United Way, Dade County, Fla., 1988, 89, 90, 91, 92, 93, 94, 95, 96. 1st lt. U.S. Army, 1968-71. Mem. ABA, Fla. Bar, Dade County Bar Assn. Avocations: golf, rugby, African cichlids. Home: 11095 SW 84th Ct Miami FL 33156 Office: Shutts & Bowen 201 S Biscayne Blvd Ste 1500 Miami FL 33131-4328

WRIGHT, RODNEY H., architect; b. Valparaiso, Ind., June 2, 1931; s. George and Lena May (Cahoon) W.; m. Sydney Sullivan Goelitz, Feb. 16, 1966; children by previous marriage: Weston, Julie-An; stepchildren: Louise Goelitz, Ann Marie Goelitz, Thomas Goelitz. Grad. high sch. With various archtl. firms, 1953-60, pvt. practice architecture, 1960—; architect Hawkweed Group Ltd., Chgo., 1978-85; sole propr. Rodney Wright, Architect; lectr Northwestern U., 1971; keynote speaker First Solar Symposium, Sao Paulo, Brasil, 1976; presenter 1987 European Conf. on Architecture, Munich, 1st/2d conf. How Successful Directors Manage, 1986-93; speaker for various child care mtgs. and workshops. Author: Hawkweed, 1975, Passive Solar House Book, 1980, Urban Brickyard, Saving Energy Serving Children, 1993. Bd. dirs. Lake County Urban League, 1961-69, chmn., 1961-65; bd. dirs. Uptown Devel. Ctr., Chgo., 1969-73. With U.S. Army, 1950-53. Design fellow Nat. Endowment for Arts, 1975; recipient award U. Wis./Early Childhood Edn. Conf. Fellow AIA (chpt. dir. 1971, co-chmn. task force 1 1969-72, mem. nat. com. community devel. ctrs. 1970-72). Pioneer in design of passive solar and superinsulated bldgs. Research design of child care environments, including use of color, equipment, natural nonpolluting materials. Address: RR 4 Box 175A Osseo WI 54758-8962

WRIGHT, ROSALIE MULLER, magazine and newspaper editor; b. Newark, June 20, 1942; d. Charles and Angela (Fortunata) Muller; m. Lynn Wright, Jan. 13, 1962; children: James Anthony Meador, Geoffrey Shepard. BA in English, Temple U., 1965. Mng. editor Suburban Life mag., Orange, N.J., 1960-62; assoc. editor Phila. mag., 1962-64, mng. editor, 1969-73; founding editor Womensports mag., San Mateo, Calif., 1973-75; editor scene sect. San Francisco Examiner, 1975-77; exec. editor New West mag., San Francisco and Beverly Hills, Calif., 1977-81; features and Sunday editor San Francisco Chronicle, 1981-87, asst. mng. editor features, 1987-96; v.p. and editor-in-chief Sunset Mag, Menlo Park, Calif., 1996—; tchr. mag. writing U. Calif., Berkeley, 1975-76; participant pub. procedures course Stanford U., 1977-79; chmn. mag. judges at conf. Coun. Advancement and Support of Edn., 1980, judge, 1984. Contbr. numerous mag. articles, critiques, revs., Compton's Ency. Mem. Am. Assn. Sunday and Feature Editors (treas. 1984, sec. 1985, 1st v.p. 1986, pres. 1987), Am. Newspaper Pubs. Assn. (pub. task force on minorities in newspaper bus. 1988-89, Chronicle minority recruiter 1987-94), Internat. Women's Forum, Women's Forum West (bd. dirs. 1993—, sec. 1994), Western Pub. Assn., Am. Soc. Mag. Editors. Office: Sunset Magazine 80 Willow Rd Menlo Park CA 94025-3661 *Keep a sharp eye out for talent, recognize it and reward it, and everyone profits.*

WRIGHT, SCOTT OLIN, federal judge; b. Haigler, Nebr., Jan. 15, 1923; s. Jesse H. and Martha I. Wright; m. Shirley Frances Young, Aug. 25, 1972. Student, Central Coll., Fayette, Mo., 1940-42; LLB, U. Mo., Columbia, 1950. Bar: Mo. 1950. City atty. Columbia, 1951-53; pros. atty. Boone County, Mo., 1954-58; practice of law Columbia, 1958-79; U.S. dist. judge Western Dist. Mo., Kansas City, from 1979. Pres. Young Democrats Boone County, 1950, United Fund Columbia, 1965. Served with USN, 1942-43; as aviator USMC, 1943-46. Decorated Air medal. Mem. ABA, Am. Trial Lawyers Assn., Mo. Bar Assn., Mo. Trial Lawyers Assn., Boone County Bar Assn. Unitarian. Clubs: Rockhill Tennis, Woodside Racquet. Lodge: Rotary (pres. Columbia 1965). Office: US Dist Ct US Courthouse 811 Grand Blvd Ste 741 Kansas City MO 64106-1909

WRIGHT, STEPHEN CHARLES, financial planner; b. Troy, N.Y., Dec. 26, 1951; s. Gilbert E. and Gwendolyn (Johnson) W.; m. Michelle Ratuszny, Apr. 20, 1974; children: Leslie William, Alexandra Elizabeth. BS, Cornell U., 1973. CFP. Pvt. practice, 1973-82; asst. v.p. E.F. Hutton, Glens Falls, N.Y., 1982-88; 2nd v.p. Shearson Lehman Hutton, Saratoga Springs, N.Y., 1988-90; v.p. investments Paine Webber, Glens Falls, N.Y., 1990—, retirement planning cons., 1994—. Guest radio talk shows Economy and the Market, 1992. Asst. Boy Scouts Am., Greenwich, N.YH., 1991-92; dir. Washington County chpt. Am. Cancer Soc., Cambridge, N.Y., 1986-90. Recipient All Am. Team award Am. Funds Group, L.A., 1990, 91, 92, 93, 94, 95. Mem. Inst. Cert. Fin. Planners, Cornell Friends of Astronomy, , Cornell U. Alumni Assn., Elks, Kiwanis (program chmn. 1989-95), Alpha Zeta. Avocations: skiing, horses, astronomy, family. Home: RR 2 Box 81 Greenwich NY 12834-9417 Office: Paine Webber PO Box 2841 Glens Falls NY 12801-6841

WRIGHT, STEPHEN GAILORD, civil engineering educator, consultant; b. San Diego, Aug. 13, 1943; s. Homer Angelo and Elizabeth Videlle (Ward) W.; m. Ouida Jo Kennedy; children: Michelle, Richard. BSCE, U. Calif., Berkeley, 1966, MSCE, 1967, PhD CE, 1969. Prof. civil engring. U. Tex., Austin, 1969—. Contbr. numerous tech. papers & research reports, 1969—. Mem. ASCE. Republican. Presbyterian. Home: 3406 Shinoak Dr Austin TX 78731-5739 Office: U Tex Dept Civil Engring Austin TX 78712

WRIGHT, SUSAN WEBBER, judge; b. Texarkana, Ark., Aug. 22, 1948; d. Thomas Edward and Betty Jane (Gary) Webber; m. Robert Ross Wright, III, May 21, 1983; 1 child, Robin Elizabeth. BA, Randolph-Macon Woman's Coll., 1970; MPA, U. Ark., 1972, JD with high honors, 1975. Bar: Ark. 1975. Law clk. U.S. Ct. Appeals 8th Circuit, 1975-76; asst. prof. law U. Ark.-Little Rock, 1976-78, assoc. prof., 1978-83, prof., 1983-90, asst. dean, 1976-78; dist. judge U.S. Dist. Ct. (ea. dist.) Ark., Little Rock, 1990—; vis. assoc. prof. Ohio State U., Columbus, 1981, La. State U., Baton Rouge, 1982-83; mem. adv. com. U.S. Ct. Appeals 8th Circuit, St. Louis, 1983-88. Author: (with R. Wright) Land Use in a Nutshell, 1978, 2d edit., 1985; editor-in-chief Ark. Law Rev., 1975; contbr. articles to profl. jours. Mem. ABA, Ark. Bar Assn., Pulaski County Bar Assn., Am. Law Inst., Ark. Assn. Women Lawyers (v.p. 1977-78). Episcopalian. Office: US Courthouse 600 W Capitol Ave Ste 302 Little Rock AR 72201-3323

WRIGHT, THEODORE OTIS, forensic engineer; b. Gillette, Wyo., Jan. 17, 1921; s. James Otis and Gladys Mary (Marquiss) W.; m. Phyllis Mae Reeves, June 21, 1942 (div. 1968); children: Mary Suzanne, Theodore Otis Jr., Barbara Joan; m. Edith Marjorie Jewett, May 22, 1968; children: Marjorie Jane, Elizabeth Carter. BSEE, U. Ill., 1951, MS in Engring., 1952; postgrad., Air Command and Staff Coll., 1956-57, UCLA, 1958. Registered profl. engr. Wash. 2d lt. U.S. Air Force, 1942-65, advanced through grades to lt. col., 1957, ret., 1965; dep. for engring. Titan SPO, USAF Sys. Command, L.A., 1957-65; rsch. engr. The Boeing Co., Seattle, 1965-81; pres. The Pretzelwich, Inc., Seattle, 1981—; cons., forensic engr. in pvt. practice Bellevue, Wash., 1988—; adj. prof. U. Wash., Greenriver Jr. Coll., both 1967-68. Contbr. articles to nat. and internat. profl. jours. Decorated Purple Heart, Air medal. Mem. NSPE (v.p. western region 1985-87), ASTM (com. E-43 metric practice 1988—), Nat. Coun. Weights and Measures, Wash. Soc. Profl. Engrs. (state pres. 1981-82, Disting. Svc. award 1980, Engr. of Yr. 1996, Columbia award 1996), U.S. Metric Assn. (life, cert. advanced metrication speciallist), Am. Nat. Metric Coun. (bd. dirs. 1978-94), Air Force Assn. (charter life, state pres. 1974-76, 90-91, Jimmy Doolittle fellow 1975), Order of Daedalians (life), Eta Kappa Nu, Pi Mu Epsilon, Tau Beta Pi. Democrat. Presbyterian. Avocations: flying, photography, classical music, archaeology. Home: 141 140th Pl NE Bellevue WA 98007-6939

WRIGHT, THEODORE PAUL, JR., political science educator; b. Pt. Washington, N.Y., Apr. 12, 1926; s. Theodore Paul and Margaret (McCarl) W.; m. Susan Jane Standfast, Feb. 18, 1967; children: Henry Sewall, Margaret Standfast, Catherine Berrian. BA magna cum laude, Swarthmore Coll., 1949; MA, Yale U., 1951, PhD, 1957. Instr. govt. Bates Coll., Lewiston, Maine, 1955-57; asst. prof., 1957-64, assoc. prof., 1964-65; assoc. prof. polit. sci. Grad. Sch. Public Affairs, SUNY, Albany, 1965-71, prof., 1971-95; prof. emeritus SUNY, Albany, 1995—. Author: American Support of Free Elections Abroad, 1964; contbr. articles on Indian Muslims and Pakistan to profl. jours., chpts. to books. Trustee Am. Inst. Pakistan Studies, 1973-82. Served with USNR, 1944-46. Carnegie intern Indian civilization U. Chgo., 1961-62; Fulbright rsch. prof. India, 1963-64; Am. Inst. Indian Studies rsch. fellow India, 1969-70; Am. Coun. Learned Socs. grantee on South Asia in London, 1974-75; Am. Inst. Pakistan Studies/Fulbright rsch. fellow, Pakistan, 1983-84, Fulbright lectr., 1990-91. Mem. South Asian Muslim Studies Assn. (pres. 1988—), Assn. Asian Studies (chmn. N.Y. Conf. on Asian Studies 1988-89), Dutch Settlers Soc. of Albany (pres. 1988-90), Adirondack Mountain Club, Phi Beta Kappa (chpt. pres. 1992-93), Phi Delta Theta. Republican. Unitarian. Home: 27 Vandenburg Ln Latham NY 12110-1190 Office: SUNY Albany Grad Sch Pub Affairs Milne Hall Albany NY 12222

WRIGHT, THEODORE ROBERT FAIRBANK, biologist, educator; b. Kodaikanal, Tamil Nadu, India, Apr. 10, 1928; s. Horace Kepler and Adelaide Caskey (Fairbank) W.; m. Eileen Marie Yongen, Jan. 6, 1951. ABin Biology, Princeton U., 1949; MA in Biology, Wesleyan U., 1954; PhD in Zoology, Yale U., 1959. Asst. professor biology Johns Hopkins U., Balt., 1959-65; assoc. prof. biology U. Va., Charlottesville, 1965-75, prof. biology, 1975-95; prof. emeritus, 1995—; vis. scientist Max Planck Inst. for Biology, Tubingen, 1975-76, Devel. Biology Ctr., U. Calif., Irvine, 1982. Editor: The Genetics and Biology of Drosophila, vol. 2a-c, 1978, vol. 2d, 1980, Genetic Regulatory Hierarchies in Development, 1990; co-editor: Advances in Genetics, 1988-92. With U.S. Army, 1950-52. NIH postdoctoral fellow

Max Planck Inst. for Biology, Tubingen, Fed. Republic Germany, 1958-59; NSF grantee, 1967-72, 90-93; NIH grantee, 1972-93; Am. Cancer Soc. grantee, 1988-90. Fellow AAAS; mem. AAUP, Genetics Soc. Am., Soc. for Devel. Biology, Va. Acad. Sci., Sigma Xi. Office: U Va Dept Biology Gilmer Hall Charlottesville VA 22903-2477

WRIGHT, THOMAS PARKER, computer science educator; b. Springfield, Mo., July 3, 1924; s. James Lewis and Vesta Marie (Parker) W.; m. Elizabeth Jane Smith; children from previous marriages: Jeffrey, Kathleen, Thomas, Ramona, Karen. BA in Math., Henderson State U., 1948; MA in Math., La. State U., 1962. Math., sci. tchr. Hondo (N.Mex.) Union H.S., 1950-53; prin. Westridge (Ark.) H.S., 1954-55; math. tchr. Santa Ana (Calif.) Unified Sch. Dist., 1955-63; math., computer instr. Santa Ana Coll., 1963-71; adminstrv. dean Rancho Santiago CC., Santa Ana, 1971-79; art gallery mgr. Lahaina (Hawaii) Galleries, Inc., 1979-80; pres. Maui Fine Arts, Inc., Kihei, 1981—; computer sci. instr. Maui C.C., Kahului, Hawaii, 1983-94; sys. programmer Santa Ana Coll., 1966-71, Maui C.C., 1983-94; software cons. Babcock Electronics, Costa Mesa, Calif., 1964-66; multi-media and internet software developer Maui C.C., 1994-95; dir. Maui Ednl. Tech. R & D Devel. Ctr. World Wide Web, 1995-97. Author computer programs; one man show Maui Community Coll., 1989; exhibited in group shows at Art Maui, 1984, 86, 89. Pres. Santa Ana Tchrs. Assn., 1960, Santa Ana Coll. Faculty Assn., 1965. 1st lt. USMCR, 1944-46, 50-52. Mem. U. Hawaii Profl. Assembly, NEA. Republican. Presbyterian. Avocations: water color and acrylic painting, computer art, ocean fishing, photography. Home: 811 S Kihei Rd Apt 3L Kihei HI 96753-9086 Office: Maui Rsch and Tech Ctr 590 Lipoa Pkwy Kihei HI 96753-6900

WRIGHT, THOMAS WILLIAM DUNSTAN, architect; b. Rome, Jan. 12, 1919; s. Charles Will and Helen Bree (Dunstan) W.; m. Penelope Ladd, Aug. 6, 1942 (dec. June 1988); children: Peter W.D., Felicity Wright Evans, Allegra; m. Anita Robbins Gordon, Dec. 30, 1995. AB, Harvard U., 1941, MArch, 1950. Designer Joseph Saunders (architect), Alexandria, Va., 1950; assoc. Leon Brown (architect), Washington, 1950-53; ptnr. firm Brown and Wright, Washington, 1953-80; sole propr. Thomas W. D. Wright, FAIA, Architects, 1980—; pres. Wright & Rubin Architects, P.C., 1985-89, Wright & Heyne Architects, 1990-91; prin. Thomas W.D. Wright, FAIA, Washington, 1991—; past mem. Old Georgetown bd. U.S. Commn. Fine Arts; past 1st v.p. D.C. Commn. Arts; past mem. D.C. Commrs. Planning and Urban Renewal Adv. Council; arbitrator Am. Arbitration Assn. Served to lt. comdr. USNR, 1941-46. Am. Sabre Fencing champion, gold medallist sr. age group (70-74); mem. U.S. Sr. Fencing Team, gold medallist sabre 70, 1995. Fellow AIA (past pres. Washington Met. chpt., past nat. chmn. com. on Nat. Capital City, past mem. com. on design, com. on housing); mem. Soc. Archtl. Historians, Nat. Assn. Intergroup Relations Ofcls., Nat. Assn. Housing and Redevel. Ofcls., Nat. Com. against Discrimination in Housing, ACLU. Democrat. Clubs: Cosmos (Washington), Harvard (Washington). Home: 7500 Exeter Rd Bethesda MD 20814-6108 Office: 1400 20th St NW Washington DC 20036-5906 *Since the essential origin of creativity is knowing the sources, then the fundamental source of design is the human being—its body, its mind, its senses and reactions, individually and collectively.*

WRIGHT, VERNON HUGH CARROLL, bank executive; b. Bronxville, N.Y., Sept. 24, 1942; s. Dudley Hugh and Helen Margurite (Carroll) W. m. Lucy Hiss Babb, June 7, 1966; children: Dudley Hugh II, Katherine Babb. BS in acctg., U. Balt., 1969. Sr. v.p. Maryland Nat. Bank, Balt., 1969-90, 91, MNC Fin., Balt., 1990-91; vice chmn., chief corporate fin. officer MBNA Am. Bank, N.A., Newark, Del., 1991—; bd. dirs. MBNA Am. Bank, Wilmington, Del. exec. v.p., chief corp. fin. officer MBNA Corp. With USN, 1962-66. Avocations: farming, teaching. Office: MBNA Am Bank 1100 N King St Wilmington DE 19884-0785

WRIGHT, WALTER AUGUSTINE, III, business and corporate lawyer; b. Newton, Mass., Feb. 9, 1957; s. Walter A. Jr. and Charlotte T. (Doucette) W.; m. Elizabeth A. Heger, July 4, 1981; children: John Walter, Gregory, Charlotte, Sarah. BA magna cum laude, Tufts U., 1979, MA in Polit. Sci., 1980; JD magna cum laude, Boston Coll., Newton, 1983. Bar: Mass. 1983, U.S. Dist. Ct. Mass. 1983, U.S. Ct. Appeals (1st cir.) 1983. Owner, mgr. Wright Contracting, Needham, Mass., 1976-81; dir. corp. rels. Gen. Scis. Corp., Needham, 1979-81; assoc. Rich May Bilodeau & Flaherty, P.C., Boston, 1983-90, mem., shareholder, v.p., 1990—; chmn. bd. Alberca, Inc., Boston, 1992-93; chmn., pres. MapleCrest Group, Inc., Needham Heights, Mass., 1993—; mng. gen. ptnr. MapleCrest Fund I, Boston; sec. e data resources, inc.; sec. Bioshelters, Inc., 1996—; asst. sec. EV Environ., Inc., 1991—; asst. sec. SR Rsch., Inc., 1996, Hunter Environ. Svcs., Inc., 1988-91, Weber Group, Inc., Thunder House, Inc., Weber Europe, Ltd.; cons., investor numerous start-up cos.; mem. IGI, LLC, 1966—. Sec., mem. State Adv. Com. for Spl. Edn.; advisor Mass. Dept. Edn., Boston, 1974-76; mem. Needham Sch. Com., 1978-81; mem. Needham Dem. Town Com.; bd. dirs. Needham Little League, 1993-96; founder Rookie League, 1993-95; mem. St. Bartholomew Pastoral Coun., 1991-94; didr. Needham Baseball, 1993—; cons. numerous polit. campaigns. Named Exch. Club New England Youth of Yr., 1975; recipient award for dedicated svc. Needham Sch. Com., 1981; honors scholar Tufts U., 1974-80, Adelman scholar, 1982. Mem. ABA (bus. law sect.), Mass. Bar Assn., Village Club (svc. award 1992), New Eng. Youth of Yr. Exch. Club, Assn. for Corp. Growth. Roman Catholic. Avocations: venture capital/investment banking, public speaking, political and business consulting, baseball, family. Home: 121 Thornton Rd Needham MA 02192-4354 Office: Rich May Bilodeau & Flaherty 294 Washington St Boston MA 02108-4608

WRIGHT, WILEY REED, JR., lawyer, retired judge, mediator; b. Seattle, Jan. 31, 1932; s. Wiley Reed and Gertrude Ellen (Datson) W.; m. Sally Harrison Clarke, 1955 (div. 1963); children: Wiley III, Margaret, Andrew; m. Roberta Hostinsky, Oct. 18, 1963; children: Cathryn, Amy, Susan. BS in Commerce, Washington and Lee U., 1954, LLB, 1956. Bar: Va. 1956, U.S. Dist. Ct. (ea. dist.) Va. 1956, U.S. Ct. Appeals (4th cir.) 1956, U.S. Supreme Ct. 1993. Law clk. to hon. judge U.S. Dist. Ct., Alexandria, Va., 1958-59; ptnr. Clarke, Richard, Moncure & Whitehead, Alexandria, 1959-68; judge corp. and cir. cts. Alexandria, 1968-79, chief judge cir. ct., 1979-84; ptnr. Hazel & Thomas P.C., Alexandria, 1984-96; mem. at large Va. State Bar Coun., 1984-90; mem. Jud. Coun. Va., 1982-84, vice chmn. jud. conf. Va., 1980-82. Assoc. editor: Virginia Circuit Judges Benchbook, 1987. Legal counsel to Alexandria C. of C., 1984-88. 1st lt. U.S. Army, 1956-58. Fellow Am. Bar Found., Va. Law Found.; mem. ABA, Va. Bar Assn., Alexandria Bar Assn., 4th Cir. Conf., George Mason Inns of Ct., Boyd-Graves Conf., Phi Delta Phi, Omicron Delta Kappa. Avocations: boating, fishing, biking. Home: PO Box 358 Lively VA 22507 Office: Jams/Endispute 700 11th St NW Ste 450 Washington DC 20001-4507

WRIGHT, WILLARD JUREY, lawyer; b. Seattle, Feb. 25, 1914; s. Raymond Garfield and Elizabeth (McPherson) W.; m. Alice Ostrander, Dec. 27, 1939 (dec. Dec. 1969); children: Susan, Alice, Rosemary, Raymond Garfield II; m. Katharyn Stubbs Little, July 18, 1970; children: Anne, Gwendolyn, Kathy. AB with honors, Princeton, 1936; cert., Woodrow Wilson Sch. Pub. and Internat. Affairs, 1936; JD with honors, U. Wash., 1939; grad., Navy. Lang. Sch., U. Colo., 1944. Bar: Wash. 1939, U.S. Dist. Ct. 1939, U.S. Ct. Appeals (9th cir.) 1958, U.S. Supreme Ct. 1958. Editor Wash. Law Rev., 1937-39; practice of law Wash., 1939—; partner Wright, Innis, Simon & Todd, Seattle, 1939-69, Davis, Wright, Todd, Riese & Jones, 1969-85; counsel Davis Wright & Jones, 1986-89, Davis Wright Tremaine, Seattle, 1990—; spl. asst. atty. gen. State of Wash., 1953; acting prof. fed. income taxation U. Wash. Law Sch., 1956; pres. Assoc. Vintners, Inc., 1979-81; pres. 1223 Spring St. Owners Assn., 1986-93; officer, dir. or gen. counsel various U.S. bus. corps.; chmn. King County Rep. Rules Com., 1950-58; chmn. 37th Dist. Rep. Orgn., 1949-52; del. Rep. Nat. Conv., Chgo., 1952. Contbr. articles to profl. jours. Trustee Seattle Found., 1954-63, pres., 1961-63, Seattle Com. Fgn. Rels., 1959-62, Lakeside Sch., 1938-67, pres., 1951-55, hon. trustee, 1967—; trustee Princeton U., 1957-61; vis. com. U. Wash. Coll. Bus. Adminstrn., 1963-70, U. Wash. Law Sch., 1974-78; pres. U. Wash. Ann. Fund, 1973-74, U. Wash. Law Sch. Found., 1974-75; trustee Helen Bush Parkside Sch., 1946-63, pres., 1959-62; dir. Seattle Times Co., 1968-89; mem. governing bd. Univ. Hosp., Seattle, 1978-87, chmn., 1980-82; sec., trustee Seattle Art Mus., 1958-88, hon. trustee, 1988—; vestryman Epiphany Episcopal Ch., 1959-64, 68-70, 73-76, 89-92, sr. warden 1970, 74-76, chancellor 1976-95, trustee ch. pension fund, N.Y., 1970-76. Lt. USNR, 1943-46. Recipient Vivian Carkeek prize U. Washington Law Sch., 1939, Disting. Svc. award Lakeside Sch., 1964, Bishop's Cross Diocese of Olympia, 1977, Crown award Epiphany Episcopal Ch., 1994, Disting. Alumnus award Lakeside Sch., 1980. Fellow Am. Bar Found., Am. Coll. Trust and Estate Counsel; mem. ABA, Wash. State Bar Assn. (chmn. real estate, probate and trusts sect. 1958-61), Seattle-King County Bar Assn. (trustee 1955-58, 64-67, pres. 1966-67), Am. Judicature Soc., Nat. Assn. Estate Planning Councils (dir. 1969-71), Estate Planning Council Seattle (pres. 1968-69, dir.), Alumni Assn. U. Wash. Law Sch. (pres. 1957-58), Seattle World Affairs Council (charter trustee, sec. 1949-57), Urban League Seattle (trustee 1956-60, 68-70, pres. bd. trustees 1956-58), Order of Coif, Princeton Quadrangle Club (pres. 1935-36), Seattle Golf Club (sec., trustee 1968-71), Phi Delta Phi. Home: 1630 43rd Ave E # 1022 Seattle WA 98112-3222 Office: Davis Wright Tremaine Century Sq Seattle WA 98101

WRIGHT, WILLIAM BIGELOW, financial executive; b. Rutland, Vt., Dec. 21, 1924; s. Earl Smith and Christine (Bigelow) W.; m. Polly Pardee, Aug. 27, 1949; children: Christine, Henry, John, Lucy. Graduated, Phillips Exeter Acad., 1943; AB, Princeton U., 1950. With Chubb & Son, N.Y.C., 1950-53; various positions Am. Internat. Group, N.Y.C., Havana, Tokyo, Seoul, Hong Kong, 1953-57; asst. to the pres. Johnson & Higgins, Caracas, Venezuela, 1957-63; pres. Marble Bank, Rutland, 1968-83; chmn. bd. Marble Bank, Marble Fin. Corp., Rutland, 1983-94; mem. adv. bd. Marble divsn. Albank, Rutland, 1994—; bd. dirs. Bunbury Co., Princeton, N.J. V.p. Windham Found., Grafton, Vt.; sch. commr. City of Rutland, 1966-75; chmn. Vt. Blue Cross and Blue Shield, 1980-83; pres. Northeast chpt. 10th Mountain Divsn. Assn., 1993-95; trustee Green Mountain Coll., Poultney, Vt., 1973—; pres. Princeton Alumni Assn. of Vt., 1989—; trustee Calvin Coolidge Meml. Found., Plymouth, Vt., 1992—. With U.S. Army, 1943-46; ETO. Mem. Ivy Club (Princeton, N.J.), Princeton Club N.Y.C., Alumni Coun. Princeton U. (exec. com. 1992-95, v.p., exec. com. Class of '47 1992—). Republican. Congregationalist. Avocations: skiing, golfing, sailing, traveling. Home: 15 Cream Hill Rd Rutland VT 05701-9802 Office: Albank Marble Divsn PO Box 978 Rutland VT 05702-0978

WRIGHT, WILLIAM COOK, archivist, historian, researcher; b. Jersey City, July 11, 1939; s. Harry Cook and Edna Margarita (Tompkins) W. BA, Gettysburg Coll., 1961; MA, U. Del., 1965, PhD, 1971. Tchr. Salem (N.J.) High Sch., 1961-65; adj. instr. U. Del., Newark, 1968-70; assoc. dir. N.J. Hist. Commn., Trenton, 1970-76; head Bur. Archives and History N.J. State Libr., Trenton, 1976-83; dir. Div. Archives and Records Mgmt., N.J. State Dept., Trenton, 1983-85; chief Bur. Records Mgmt., Trenton, 1985-89, ret., 1989; coord. state hist. records adv. bd. Nat. Hist. Publs. and Records Commn. 1976-87; mem. adv. com. for papers of William Livingston; sec. N.J. State Records Com., 1976-85, chmn., 1985; mem. adv. bd. dirs. N.J. Archives Series, 1971-86; mem. region 2 adv. coun. Nat. Archives and Records Svc., 1976-77; mem. adv. com. N.J. Newspaper Project, 1983-85, state rev. com. for hist. sites, 1976-79; mem. implementation and planning com. N.J. Supreme Ct., 1982. Author monograph: The Secession Movement in the Middle Atlantic States, 1972; compiler Directory of N.J. Newspapers, 1765-1970; contbr. articles and book revs to profl. jours. Mem. Lawrence Twp. Cultural and Heritage Adv. Com., 1989-92, chmn., 1991. Recipient Award of Recognition N.J. Hist. Commn., 1992. Mem. Acad. Cert. Achivists (cert.), N.J. Hist. Soc. Home: 10 Windsor Ct Sewell NJ 08080-2815

WRIGHT, WILLIAM EVAN, physician; b. N.Y.C., Aug. 1, 1946; s. Samuel and Frances Elnora (Perpente) W.; m. Diana Claire Dryer, Aug. 15, 1970; children: Jason William, Elizabeth Garland, Edwin Samuel. BA in Music, U. Rochester, 1968; MD, U. Pa., 1972; MPH, U. Utah, 1979; MS in Physiology, Harvard U., 1980. Diplomate Am. Bd Internal Medicine, Am. Bd. Preventive Medicine, Am. Bd. Occupl. Medicine, Am. Bd. Ind. Med. Examiners; ACOEM cert. med. rev. officer; cert. FAA med. examiner. Intern LDS Hosp., Salt Lake City, 1972-73, resident, 1973-75; resident U. Utah Med. Ctr., Salt Lake City, 1978-79, Harvard Sch. Pub. Health, Boston, 1979-80; asst. prof. U. So. Calif., L.A., 1980-86; med. dir. U.S. DEA, Arlington, Va., 1986-96; program mgr., site med. dir. DynCorp, Reston, Va., 1991-96; regional med. dir. Md. Office of CORE, Boston, 1996—; cons. in field. Contbr. articles to profl. jours. Maj. U.S. Army, 1975-77. Fellow Am. Coll. Physicians, Am. Coll. Occupational and Environ. Health; mem. Alpha Omega Alpha. Avocation: performing music. Home: 6801 Wemberly Way Mc Lean VA 22101

WRIGHTON, MARK STEPHEN, chemistry educator; b. Jacksonville, Fla., June 11, 1949; s. Robert D. and Doris (Cutler) W.; children: James Joseph, Rebecca Ann. BS, Fla. State U., 1969; PhD, Calif. Inst. Tech., 1972; DSc (hon.), U. West Fla., 1983. Asst. prof. chemistry MIT, Cambridge, 1972-76, assoc. prof., 1976-77, prof., 1977-95, Frederick G. Keyes prof. chemistry, 1981-89, head dept. chemistry, 1987-90, Ciba-Geigy prof. chemistry, 1989-95, provost, 1990-95; prof., chancellor Washington U., St. Louis, 1995—; bd. dirs. Cabot Corp., Ionics, Inc., Helix Tech. Corp., OIS (Optical Imaging Sys.), Inc. Author: Organometallic Photochemistry, 1979; editor books in field; cons. editor, Houghton-Mifflin. Trustee Mo. Bot. Garden, St. Louis Symphony, St. Louis Art Mus., St. Louis Sci. Ctr., Mary Inst. Country Day Sch.; bd. dirs. United Way Greater St. Louis. Recipient Herbert Newby McCoy award Calif. Inst. Tech., 1972, Disting. Alumni award, 1992, E.O. Lawrence award Dept. Energy, 1983, Halpern award in photochemistry, N.Y. Acad. Scis., 1983, Fresenius award Phi Lambda Upsilon, 1984, Dreyfus tchr.-scholar, 1975-80; Alfred P. Sloan fellow, 1974-76, MacArthur fellow, 1983-88. Fellow AAAS; mem. Am. Acad. Arts and Scis., Am. Chem. Soc. (award in pure chemistry 1981, award in inorganic chemistry 1988), Electrochem. Soc. Office: Washington Univ Office of Chancellor 1 Brookings Dr # 1192 Saint Louis MO 63130-4862

WRIGHT-RIGGINS, AIDSAND F., III, religious organization executive. Exec. dir. ABC Bd. of Nat. Ministries, Valley Forge, Pa. Office: ABC Bd of Nat Ministries PO Box 851 Valley Forge PA 19482-0851*

WRINKLE, JOHN NEWTON, lawyer; b. Chattanooga, July 31, 1929; s. John Stuart and Anne (Ownbey) W.; m. Louise Rucker Agee, Feb. 1, 1958; children: Anne Blair, Margaret Rucker. BA, Vanderbilt U., 1951; LLB, Yale U., 1955. Bar: Ala. 1955, U.S. Dist. Ct. (no. dist.) Ala. 1956, U.S. Ct. Appeals (5th cir.) 1958, U.S. Ct. Appeals (11th cir.) 1981, U.S. Tax Ct. 1957. Assoc. White, Bradley, Arant, All & Rose, Birmingham, Ala., 1955-63; ptnr. Bradley, Arant, Rose & White, 1963-92, counsel, 1993—; coord. prelaw students Birmingham So. Coll., 1989—. Trustee Birmingham Symphony Assn., 1970-79, 80-83, Episcopal Found. Jefferson County, 1994—; mem. bd. advisors St. Andrew's Sewanee Sch., 1985—. With USAF, 1951-52. Disting. fellow Birmingham-Southern Coll., 1995—. Fellow Am. Coll. Trust and Estate Counsel; mem. ABA, So. Employee Benefits Conf. (steering com. 1970-73), Birmingham Bar Assn., Assn. of Bar of City of N.Y., Birmingham Com. Fgn. Rels., Redstone Club, Mountain Brook Club, Country Club of Birmingham, Summit Club, Knickerbocker Club (N.Y.C.), Yale Club (N.Y.C.), Phi Beta Kappa, Phi Alpha Delta. Episcopalian. Home: 2 Beechwood Rd Birmingham AL 35213-3914 Office: Bradley Arant Rose & White 2001 Park Pl Ste 1400 Birmingham AL 35203-2700

WRIST, PETER ELLIS, pulp and paper company executive; b. Mirfield, Eng., Oct. 9, 1927; came to U.S., 1956; s. Owen and Evelyn (Ellis) W.; m. Mirabelle Harley, Sept. 3, 1955; children: Denise Wrist Parson, Philip, Lydia Wrist Schweizer, Richard; m. Kathryn Idelson. BA, Cambridge (Eng.) U., 1948, MA, 1952; MS, London U., 1952; cert. advanced mgmt. program, Harvard U., 1967; DSc (hon.), U. B.C., 1993. Rsch. physicist Brit. Paper & Bd. Industry Rsch. Assn., Kenley, Eng., 1949-52, Que. North Shore Paper Co., Baie Comeau, Can., 1952-56; rsch. physicist Mead Corp., Dayton, Ohio, 1956-60, assoc. dir. rsch., 1960-61, dir. rsch., 1961-66, mgr. rsch. and engring., 1966-68, v.p. rsch. and engring., 1968-72, v.p. tech., 1972-83; exec. v.p. Pulp and Paper Research Inst. Can., Pointe Claire, Que., 1983-86; pres., chief exec. officer Pulp and Paper Rsch. Inst. Can., Pointe Claire, Que., 1986-94, dep. chmn. bd., 1994-95; ret., 1994; chmn. prize selection com. Marcus Wallenberg Found.; chmn. Nat. Coun. for Air and Stream Improvement, 1972-75; past mem., chmn. rsch. adv. com. Inst. Paper Chemistry, 1971-83. Contbr. articles to profl. jours. Fellow Tech. Assn. Pulp and Paper Industry (bd. dirs. 1971-74, v.p. 1975-77, pres. 1977-79, Engring. award 1969, Gold medal 1983); mem. Can. Pulp and Paper Assn. (tech. sect., Howard Smith award 1954, Weldon Gold medal 1956, John S. Bates Meml. Gold medal 1997), N.Y. Acad. Sci. Avocations: sailing, gardening. Home: 7778 SE Country Estates Way Jupiter FL 33458-1042

WRISTON, KATHRYN DINEEN, lawyer, business executive; b. Syracuse, N.Y.; d. Robert Emmet and Carolyn (Bareham) Dineen; m. Walter B. Wriston, Mar. 14, 1968; 1 stepchild. Student, U. Geneva, 1958-59; BA cum laude, Smith Coll., 1960; LLB, U. Mich., 1963. Bar: N.Y.1964, U.S. Ct. Appeals (2nd cir.) 1964, U.S. Supreme Ct. 1968. Assoc. Shearman & Sterling, N.Y.C., 1963-68; bd. dirs. Northwestern Mut. Life Ins. Co., mem. ins. products and mktg. com., 1986-89, mem. audit com., 1989—, mem. investment and fin. policy com., 1989-95; bd. dirs. Santa Fe Energy Resources, Inc., mem. audit com., 1990—, chmn., 1990-93, 95—, mem. nominating com., 1990—; trustee Fin. Acctg. Found., 1992—, mem. selection com., 1992-95, mem. audit com., 1992-96, chmn., 1993-96, chmn. devel. com., 1996—, mem. fin. com., 1994—, mem. exec. com., 1996—; mem. task force on timely fin. reporting guidanace Fin. Acctg. Stds. Bd., 1982-83, mem. bd. agenda adv. com., 1981-85, mem. process and structure com., 1981-85, chmn., 1983-85, mem. adv. coun., 1981-85; mem. exec. com. CPR Inst. for Dispute Resolution, 1994—; bd. dirs. Waccamaw Corp., mem. audit stkoption, comp. coms.; bd. dirs. The Stanley Works, mem. public policy and fin. and pension coms., 1996—, chmn. audit com., 1997—, mem. execution com., 1997—. Mem. vis. com. U. Mich. Law Sch., 1973—; trustee Fordham U., Bronx, N.Y., 1971-77, 78-81, vice chmn. bd. trustees, 1980-81, mem. student affairs com., 1971-77, chmn., 1974-77, mem. faculty affairs com., 1978-81, mem. grievance com., 1971-77, 78-81, mem. com. on law sch., 1978-81; mem. ea. region selection panel Pres. Commn. on White House Fellowships, 1981-83, chmn., 1982-83; mem. bus. com. Nat. Ctr. for State Cts., 1982-88; bd. overseers Rand Inst. for Civil Justice, 1985-93; trustee John A. Hartford Found., 1991—, mem. grant com., 1991—, vice chmn., 1992—, mem. evaluation com., 1991—, mem. audit com., 1992—, chmn., 1993—, sec., 1996—; active Gov. Wilson's N.Y. Little Hoover Commn., 1974. Mem. ABA, Nat. Assn. Accts., Practicing Law Inst. (exec. 1976—, mem. programs and publs. com., chmn. 1979—, mem. membership com. 1976—, chmn. 1977-79, mem. nominating com. 1978, 81-85, v.p., 1985—, mem. bar rev. courses 1978-79, mem. fin. com. 1989—, mem. Am. Law Inst./ABA subcom. on Am. law network 1989-91), Fin. Women's Assn. N.Y., N.Y. County Lawyers Assn. (legal aid com. 1972-76), N.Y. State Bar Assn., Assn. Bar City N.Y.

WRISTON, WALTER BIGELOW, retired banker; b. Middletown, Conn., Aug. 3, 1919; s. Henry M. and Ruth (Bigelow) W.; m. Barbara Brengle, Oct. 24, 1942 (dec.); 1 dau., Catherine B.; m. Kathryn Ann Dineen, Mar. 14, 1968. B.A. with distinction, Wesleyan U., Middletown, Conn., 1941; LL.D., Wesleyan U., 1984; postgrad., Ecole Francaise Middlebury, Vt., 1941, Am. Inst. Banking, 1946; M.A., Fletcher Sch. Internat. Law and Diplomacy, 1942; LL.D., Lawrence Coll., 1962, Tufts U., 1963, Brown U., 1969, Columbia U., 1972, Morehouse Coll., 1985; D.C.S., Pace U., 1974, St. John's U., 1974; D.H.L., Lafayette Coll., 1975; LL.D., Fordham U., 1977, Hamilton Coll., 1996; D.C.S., NYU, 1977. Officer spl. div. Dept. State, Washington, 1941-42; jr. insp. comptrollers div. Citibank (N.A.), 1946-50, asst. cashier, 1950-52, asst. v.p., 1952-54, v.p., 1954-58; sr. v.p., 1958-60, exec. v.p., 1960-67, pres., 1967-70, chmn., 1970-1984, also dir.; bd. dirs. York Internat. Corp., Tandem Computers Inc., United Meridan Corp., ICOS Corp., AEA Investors Inc., Cygnus, Inc., WMNB Acquisitions Corp., Vion Pharms., Inc.; trustee Rand Corp., 1973-83; mem. Nat. Commn. on Productivity, 1970-74, Nat. Commn. for Indsl. Peace, 1973-74; chmn. Pres.' Econ. Policy Adv. Bd., 1982-89. Author: Risk and Other Four-Letter Words, 1986, The Twilight of Sovereignty, 1992. Life gov. N.Y. Hosp.; trustee Manhattan Inst. for Policy Rsch. Inc. Served with AUS, 1942-46. Mem. Bus. Coun., Links Club, Univ. Club, River Club, Sky Club, Met. Club (Washington), Palm Beach Bath and Tennis Club, Ocean Club Fla. Office: 425 Park Ave Fl 3 New York NY 10022-3506

WROBLE, ARTHUR GERARD, lawyer; b. Taylor, Pa., Jan. 21, 1948; s. Arthur S. and Sophia P. Wroble; m. Mary Ellen Sheehan, Nov. 19, 1977; children: Sophia Ann, Sarah Jean, Stacey Margaret. BSBA with honors, U. Fla., 1970, MBA, 1971, JD, 1973. Bar: Fla. 1973, U.S. Ct. Appeals (5th cir.) 1974, U.S. Ct. Appeals (11th cir.) 1981, U.S. Dist. Ct. (so. dist.) Fla. 1974, U.S. Dist. Ct. (mid. dist.) Fla. 1982, U.S. Dist. Ct. (no. dist.) Fla. 1986, U.S. Army Ct. Mil. Rev. 1989, U.S. Ct. Mil. Appeals, 1990, U.S. Supreme Ct., 1976. Ptnr. Burns, Middleton, Farrell & Faust (now Steel, Hector, Davis, Burns & Middleton), Palm Beach, Fla., 1973-82; ptnr. Wolf, Block, Schorr & Solis, Cohen, Phila. and West Palm Beach, Fla., 1982-87, Scott, Royce, Harris & Bryan, P.A., Palm Beach, 1987-89, Grantham and Wroble, P.A., Lake Worth, 1989-92; prin. Arthur G. Wroble, P.A., West Palm Beach, 1992—; mem. 15th Jud. Cir. Ct. Nominating Commn., 1979-83; mem. U. Fla. Law Ctr. Council, 1981-84, U.S. Magistrate Merit Selection Panel, So. dist. Fla., 1987; mem. adv. bd. alternative sentencing program Palm Beach County Pub. Defender's Office; adj. instr. bus. law Coll. of Boca Raton (now Lynn U.), 1988. Contbr. articles to profl. jours.; bd. dirs. Girl Scouts U.S., 1996—. Served to lt. col. JAG, USAR, 1990-91. Named Eagle Scout, Boy Scouts Am., 1962. Mem. ABA, Fla. Bar (bd. govs. young lawyers sect. 1979-83, bd. govs. 1985-89), Palm Beach County Bar Assn. (pres. young lawyers sect. 1978-79, bd. dirs. 1979-81, sec.-treas. 1981-83, pres. 1984-85), Fla. Bar Found. (bd. dirs. 1990-93), Fla. Assn. Women Lawyers, Fla. Council Bar Assn. Pres. (bd. dirs. 1986-92), Guild Cath. Lawyers Diocese Palm Beach, Inc. (pres. 1980-81, bd. dirs. 1981—), Monsingnor Jeremiah P. O'Mahoney Outstanding Lawyer award 1993), Legal Aid Soc. Palm Beach County, Inc. (bd. dirs. 1981—), Univ. Fla. Alumni Assn. Palm Beach County Club (pres. 1983-84), Kiwanis (pres. 1980-81, pres. West Palm Beach found. 1989—, dir. 1981—, Citizen of Yr. 1994), KC (grand knight 1978-79). Roman Catholic. Home: 7645 Clarke Rd West Palm Beach FL 33406-8709 Office: 1615 Forum Pl West Palm Beach FL 33401-2320

WROBLE, LISA ANN, writer, educator; b. Dearborn, Mich., June 17, 1963; d. Robert Frank and Ruth Marie (Schiller) W. Diploma, Inst. Children's Lit., 1983; BA cum laude, Ea. Mich. U., Ypsilanti, 1985. Cert. ESL tchr.; cert. ltd. profl. class B cert., Libr. Mich. Asst. editor cmty. rels. Vets. Adminstrn., Ann Arbor, Mich., 1983-85; prodn. coord. Cmty. Crier Newspaper/COMMA Graphics, Plymouth, Mich., 1985-86; proofreader Valassis Inserts, Livonia, Mich., 1986-89; tech. writer Nat. TechTeam, Dearborn, Mich., 1989-90; freelance writer Plymouth, 1990—; part-time publicist Garden City (Mich.) Osteopathic Hosp., 1990-91; creative writing instr. Cmty. Edn. Plymouth (Mich.)-Canton Schs., 1992-93; part-time libr. asst. Redford (Mich.) Twp. Dist. Libr., 1996—; writing instr. Elderwise Program, Ypsilanti, Mich., 1996-97. Author: (7 book series) Kids Throughout History, 1996; contbg. editor Metroparent, 1991-93; contbg. tech. writer Facilities Planning News, 1993—; book reviewer The ALAN Rev., 1993—; contbr. articles, essays and sects. to reference books, multi-media CD ROMs and textbooks. Tutor Cmty. Literacy Coun., Plymouth, 1989-93; vol. spkr. in schs. Recipient Reading Tutor award Cmty. Literacy Coun., 1991, 92, 93. Mem. Soc. Childrens Book Writers and Illustrators (adv. com. Mich. chpt. 1993-94), Nat. Writers Assn. (vol. critiquer 1989-93), Childrens Lit. Assn., Livonia Writers Group. Republican. Roman Catholic. Avocations: swimming, photography, drawing, cross country skiing, cooking.

WROBLESKI, JEANNE PAULINE, lawyer; b. Phila., Feb. 14, 1942; d. Edward Joseph and Pauline (Popelak) W.; m. Robert J. Klein, Dec. 3, 1979. BA, Immaculata Coll., 1964; MA, U. Pa., 1966; JD, Temple U., 1975. Bar: Pa. 1975. Pvt. practice law, Phila., 1975—; ptnr. Kohn, Swift & Graf, P.C., Phila.; lectr. on bus. law Wharton Sch., Phila. Mem. Commn. on Women and the Legal Profession, 1986-89; v.p. Center City Residents' Assn. Eisenhower Citizen Amb. del. to Soviet Union. Bd. dirs. South St. Dance Co., Women in Transition; bd. dirs., mem. exec. com. Temple Law Alumni; del. to Moscow con. on law and econ. coop., 1990; del. to jud. conf. for 3d cir. U.S. Ct. Appeals, 1991; mediator U.S. Dist. Ct. (ea. dist.) Pa., 1996. Rhea Liebman scholar, 1974. Mem. AAUW, ABA, Pa. Bar Assn., Phila. Bar Assn. (chmn. women's rights com. 1986, com. on jud. selection and reform 1986-87, chmn. appellate cts. com. 1992, bus. cts. task force), Pa. Acad. Fine Arts, Nat. Mus. Women in the Arts, Am. Judicature Soc., Jagiellonian Law Soc., Alpha Psi Omega, Lambda Iota Tau. Democrat. Clubs: Lawyers, Founders, Peale, Penn. Office: Kohn Swift & Graf PC 2400 One Reading Ctr 1101 Market St Philadelphia PA 19107-2934

WROBLEY, RALPH GENE, lawyer; b. Denver, Sept. 19, 1935; s. Matthew B. and Hedvig (Lyon) W.; m. Madeline C. Kearney, June 13, 1959; children:

Kirk Lyon, Eric Lyon, Ann Lyon. BA, Yale U., 1957; JD, U. Chgo., 1962. Bar: Mo. 1962. With Bell Telephone Co., Phila., 1957-59; assoc. Stinson, Mag & Fizzell, Kansas City, Mo., 1962-65, mem. 1965-88; ptnr. Bryan, Cave, McPheeters & McRoberts, Kansas City, 1988-92; ptnr., exec. com. Blackwell, Sanders, Matheny, Weary & Lombardi, 1992—. Bd. dirs. Human Resources Corp., 1971; mem. Civic Coun. Kansas City, 1986—; chmn. Pub. Housing Authority of Kansas City, 1971-74; vice chmn. Mayor's Adv. Commn. on Housing, Kansas City, 1971-74; bd. govs. Citizens Assn., 1965—, vice chmn., 1971-75, chmn., 1978-79; bd. dirs. Coun. on Edn., 1975-81, v.p., 1977-79; bd. dirs., pres. Sam E. and Mary F. Roberts Found., 1974-96; trustee Clearinghouse for Mid Continent Founds., 1977-96, chmn. 1987-89; bd. dirs. Bus. Innovation Ctr., 1984-91, vice-chmn. 1987-91, adv. bd. dirs., 1993—, Midwest Regional Adv. Bd. Inst. Internat. Edn., 1989-93, Internat. Trade Assn., 1989-92, v.p., 1990; former chmn. bd. dir. Mid-Am. Coalition on Healthcare, 1991-95. Mem. Mo. Bar Assn. Republican. Presbyterian (elder). Club: Yale (pres. 1969-71, outstanding mem. award 1967). Home: 1015 W 67th Ter Kansas City MO 64113-1942 Office: 2300 Main St Kansas City MO 64108-2416

WROBLOWA, HALINA STEFANIA, electrochemist; b. Gdansk, Poland, July 5, 1925; came to U.S., 1958, naturalized, 1970; MSc, U. Lodz (Poland), 1949; PhD, Warsaw Inst. Tech., 1958; 1 dau., Krystyna Wrobel-Knight. Chmn. dept. prep. studies U. Lodz, 1950-53; adj. Inst. for Phys. Chemistry, Acad. Scis., Warsaw, Poland, 1958-60; dep. dir. electrochemistry lab. Energy Inst., U. Pa., Phila., 1960-67, dir. electrochemistry lab., 1968-75; prin. research scientist Ford Motor Co., Dearborn, Mich., 1976-91; pvt. practice cons., 1991—; chmn. Gordon Rsch. Conf. on Electrochemistry, 1983. Served with Polish Underground Army, 1943-45. Decorated Mil. Silver Cross of Merit with Swords. Mem. Electrochem. Soc., Internat. Electrochem. Soc., Mensa, Sigma Xi. Contbr. chpts. to books, articles to profl. jours., patent lit.

WRONA, PETER ALEXANDER, structural engineer; b. Cracow, Poland, Feb. 19, 1955; came to U.S., 1970; s. Wlodzimierz Stefan and Anna Maria (Czech) W.; m. Bernadette Maria Waskowska, Oct. 9, 1984; 1 child, Marie. BS in Civil Engring., U. Calif., Berkeley, 1976, MS in Structural Engring., 1980. Registered profl. engr., Calif.; lic. pvt. pilot. Staff engr. Bechtel Power Corp., San Francisco, 1977-79; project engr. S. Medwadowski Cons. Engrs., San Francisco, 1980-82, 85-87; cons. Bechtel Power Corp., San Francisco, 1982-83; sr. engr. Forell and Elsesser Engrs., San Francisco, 1983-85; project engr. C.H. Wells & Assocs., San Mateo, Calif., 1987-88; assoc. Dasse Design Inc., San Francisco, 1988-96; prin. Wrona Structural Engrs., San Francisco, 1995—; pres., bd. dirs. Polam Fed. Credit Union, Redwood City, Calif., 1986—; cert. vol. engr. Office of Emergency Svcs., State of Calif., 1986—. Bd. dirs., treas. Skyview Homeowners Assn., Hayward, Calif., 1986-89. Mem. ASCE, Structural Engrs. Assn. No. Calif. (mem. continuing edn. com. 1984-86), Internat. Assn. for Shell and Spatial Structures, Chi Epsilon. Avocations: flying, sailing, skiing. Home: 28091 Ziele Creek Dr Hayward CA 94542-2425 Office: Wrona Structural Engrs 111 New Montgomery St San Francisco CA 94105

WRONG, DENNIS HUME, sociologist, educator; b. Toronto, Nov. 22, 1923; s. Humphrey Hume and Mary Joyce (Hutton) W.; m. Elaine L. Gale, Nov. 24, 1949 (div. Oct. 1965); 1 child, Terence Hume; m. Jacqueline Conrath, Mar. 26, 1966. BA, U. Toronto, 1945; PhD, Columbia U., 1956. Tchr. Princeton U., 1949-50, Rutgers U., 1950-51, U. Toronto, 1954-56, Brown U., 1956-61; mem. grad. faculty New Sch. Social Research, 1961-63; prof. sociology, chmn. dept. Univ. Coll., NYU, 1963-65; prof. sociology NYU, 1966-94, prof. emeritus, 1994—; vis. prof. U. Nev., 1965-66; vis. fellow Oxford U., 1978, European U. Inst., 1996-97. Author: American and Canadian Viewpoints, 1955, Population, 1956, 59, Population and Society, 1961, 67, 77, Skeptical Sociology, 1976, Power: Its Forms, Bases and Uses, 1979, 88, 95, Class Fertility Trends in Western Nations, 1980, The Problem of Order: What Unites and Divides Society, 1994, 95; editor: Social Research, 1961-64, (with Harry L. Gracey) Readings in Introductory Sociology, 1967, 72, 77, Contemporary Sociology: A Journal of Reviews, 1972-74, Max Weber, 1970; mem. editl. bd. Dissent, 1966—; contbg. editor Partisan Rev., 1981-87. Guggenheim fellow, 1984-85, Woodrow Wilson Internat. Ctr. for Scholars fellow, 1991-92. Mem. Am. Sociol. Assn., Eastern Sociol. Soc. Home: 144 Drakes Corner Rd Princeton NJ 08540-7519 Office: NYU Dept Sociology Washington Sq N New York NY 10003

WRONSKI, STANLEY PAUL, education educator; b. Mpls., Apr. 8, 1919; s. John and Katherine (Kotvis) W.; m. Geraldine Breslin, May 27, 1943; children: Linda A., Mary Jo Tewinkel, Sandra J., John S., Paul S. BS in Edn., U. Minn., 1942, MA, 1947, PhD, 1950. Counselor Bur. Vet. Affairs U. Minn., Mpls., 1946-47, instr. Coll. Edn., 1948-49; tchr. Marshall High Sch., Mpls., 1947-48; asst. prof. Ctrl. Wash. Coll., Ellensburg, 1950-51; from asst. to assoc. prof. Boston U., 1951-57; from assoc. prof. to prof. Mich. State U., East Lansing, 1957-84, prof. emeritus, 1984—; advisor Ministry of Edn., Bangkok, Thailand, 1964-66; pres. New Eng. Assn. Social Studies Tchrs., Boston, 1955-56, Mich. Coun. for Social Studies, 1960-61, Nat. Coun. for Social Studies, 1974. Co-author: Teaching Social Studies in High School, 1958, 73, Modern Economics, 1964, School and Society, 1964, Social Studies and Social Sciences, 1986. Active U.S. Nat. Commn. for UNESCO, Washington, 1974-76, mil. adv. coun. Ctr. for Def. Info., Washington, 1988—; pres. Greater Lansing UN Assn., 1986-88, chair Mich. UN at Fifty Planning Com., 1995. Comdr. USN, 1942-64. Recipient Internat. Educator award Pacific Rim Consortium, 1992, Glen Taggart award Mich. State U., 1995; named Outstanding Social Studies Educator, Social Studies Tchr. Jour., 1981. Mem. NEA (life), Nat. Peace Found. (charter), Univ. Club (charter). Avocations: golf, reading, volunteer work. Home: 4520 Chippewa Dr Okemos MI 48864-2008 Office: Mich State U Coll Edn Erickson Hall East Lansing MI 48824

WROTH, JAMES MELVIN, former army officer, computer company executive; b. Lincoln, Nebr., Feb. 2, 1929; s. Charles M. and Reba (Sharp) W.; m. Donna Mae Benson, June 4, 1951 (dec.); children: Mark, David S., Mary E. Bannon; m. Molly B. Mullan, June 15, 1975; stepchildren: Edward H. Mullan (dec.), Philip C. Mullan. B.S., U. Nebr., 1951; M.B.A., Syracuse U., 1963; postgrad., F.A. Sch., 1957, Command and Gen. Staff Coll., 1962, Armed Forces Staff Coll., 1967, Army War Coll., 1968; grad., Advanced Mgmt. Program, Harvard, 1972. Commd. 2d lt. U.S. Army, 1951, advanced through grades to brig. gen., 1973; 40th inf. divsn. Korea, 1952-53; instr. A.A.A. Sch., Ft. Bliss, Tex., 1954-56; with 3d Inf. Div., Ft. Benning, Ga. and, Germany, 1957-61, Office Chief of Staff, U.S. Army, 1963-66; comdg. officer 1st Bn. 31st Arty., Korea, 1967; exec. asst. to asst. sec. Army, 1968-70; exec. officer I Field Force Vietnam Arty., 1970; comdg. officer 52d Arty. Group, Vietnam, 1971; with Office Dep. Chief Staff for Personnel, Dept. Army, 1972-75; comdg. gen. VII Corps Arty. and Augsburg Germany Mil. Community, 1975-77; comdr. 2d ROTC region, Ft. Knox, Ky., 1977-79; ret., 1979; v.p., dir. mgmt. scis. ops. Gen. Research Corp., McLean, Va., 1979-82; group v.p Info. Systems & Network Corp., Bethesda, Md., 1982-93; chmn., pres. J-Tech, Inc., White Stone, Va., 1993—. Trustee Washington Adventist Hosp. Found., 1989-93. Decorated D.S.M., Legion of Merit, Bronze Star, Air Medal with V device, Army Commendation medal; Vietnamese Gallantry Cross with palm.; Recipient John J. Pershing award, 1951, 40 and 8 award, 1951, F.A. Assn. award, 1950. Mem. Nat. Soc. Pershing Rifles (past nat. comdr.), Alpha Kappa Psi, Beta Gamma Sigma. Home: 286 Breezy Pt Dr White Stone VA 22578-9802 Office: PO Box 1287 White Stone VA 22578-1287

WROTH, L(AWRENCE) KINVIN, lawyer, educator; b. Providence, July 9, 1932; s. Lawrence Counselman and Barbara (Pease) W.; m. Susan Collins, May 2, 1958 (div. 1972); children: Ann K., Caroline D., Eliza H.; m. Deborah Bethell, Aug. 10, 1972; 1 dau., Katharine L.; stepchildren—John H., David H., Elizabeth T. and Sarah B. Zobel. B.A., Yale U., 1954; LL.B., Harvard U., 1960. Bar: Mass. 1960, Maine 1974. Teaching fellow, asst. prof. law Dickinson Sch. Law, 1960-62; rsch. assoc. Harvard U., 1962-64; assoc. prof. law U. Maine Sch. Law, Portland, 1964-66; prof. U. Maine Sch. Law, 1966-96; assoc. dean Sch. Law U. Maine, 1977-78, acting dean, 1978-80, dean, 1980-90; dean, prof. Vt. Law Sch., 1996—; rsch. fellow Charles Warren Center Studies in Am. History, Harvard U., 1968-74; cons. civil and probate procedure, profl. and jud. responsibility, and ct.-bar rels. Maine Supreme Jud. Ct., 1967-96; cons. civil, probate, and criminal procedure and evidence Vt. Supreme Ct., 1969—. Author: (with R.H. Field and V.L. McKusick) Maine Civil Practice, 2d edit., 1970; editor-in-chief: Province in Rebellion, 1975; editor: (with H.B. Zobel) Legal papers of John Adams, 1965; reporter: Vermont Rules of Civil Procedure, 1971, Vermont Rules of Criminal Procedure, 1974, Maine Rules of Probate Procedure, 1980, (with J. Dooley) Vermont Rules of Evidence, 1982, Maine Code of Judicial Conduct, 1993, Vermont Code of Judicial Conduct, 1994. Pres. Greater Portland Landmarks, Inc., 1966-69, adv. trustee, 1969-85; adv. coun. Nat. Trust Hist. Preservation, 1967-70; bd. dirs. Maine Bar Found., 1983-89, sec., 1983-86, v.p., 1987, pres., 1988, fellow, 1991; bd. dirs. Pine Tree legal Assistance Inc., 1985-96; mem. bd. dirs. Nat. Assn. IOLTA Programs, Inc., 1988-90; bd. dirs. Portland Symphony Orch., 1990, v.p. for ops. and resources, 1991-95, pres., 1995-96; mem. Maine Commn. on Legal Needs, 1989-90, Commn. to Study Future of Maine's Cts., 1991-93. Recipient Littleton-Griswold prize Am. Hist. Assn., 1966, Howard H. Dana award Maine Bar Found., 1991, Justice Louis Scolnik award Maine Civil Liberties Union, 1992, Herbert Harley award Am. Judicature Soc., 1994. Fellow Am. Bar Found.; mem. ABA, Maine Bar Assn. (Disting. Svc. award 1990), Am. Law Inst., Vermont Bar Assn., Colonial Soc. Mass., Mass. Hist. Soc. Office: Vt Law Sch Chelsea St PO Box 96 South Royalton VT 05068

WRUBLE, BERNHARDT KARP, lawyer; b. Wilkes-Barre, Pa., Mar. 21, 1942; s. Maurice and Ruth Yvonne (Karp) W.; m. Judith Marilyn Eyges, Nov. 16, 1968 (div. 1987); children: Justine, Vanessa, Alexis; m. Jill Diamond, Nov. 24, 1990; children: Mattia, Austin. BA in Polit. Sci., Williams Coll., Williamstown, Mass., 1963; LLB, U. Pa., 1966; postgrad., NYU, 1972-74, Harvard U., 1978. Bar: U.S. Dist. Ct. (so. dist.) N.Y. 1969, U.S. Dist. Ct. (ea. dist.) N.Y. 1972, U.S. Ct. Appeals (2d cir.) 1972, U.S. Supreme Ct. 1972, U.S. Ct. Appeals (7th cir.) 1974, U.S. Ct. Appeals (D.C. and 4th cirs.) 1984, U.S. Ct. Appeals (5th cir.) 1985, U.S. Ct. Appeals (11th cir.) 1986. Law clk. to presiding judge U.S. Ct. Appeals (3d cir.), 1966-67; assoc. Simpson, Thacher & Bartlet, N.Y.C., 1968-73; ptnr. Simpson, Thatcher & Bartlett, N.Y.C., 1974-77; prin. dep. gen. counsel U.S. Dept. Army, Washington, 1977-79; dir. Office Govt. Ethics, Washington, 1979; exec. asst. to sec. and dep. sec. U.S. Dept. Energy, Washington, 1979-81; dir. Pres.'s Interagy. Coal Export Task Force, Washington, 1980-81; ptnr. Verner, Liipfert, Bernhard, McPherson and Hand, Washington, 1981—. Bd. dirs. Epilepsy Found. Am., 1983, chmn., 1991. Mem. ABA, D.C. Bar Assn., N.Y. State Bar Assn., Williams Coll. Alumni Assn. (pres. Washington chpt. 1986-91), Williams Coll. Soc. Alumni Assn. (exec. com. 1988-91). Democrat. Office: Verner Liipfert Bernhard McPherson and Hand 901 15th St NW Ste 700 Washington DC 20005-2327

WRUBLE, BRIAN FREDERICK, investment firm executive; b. Kalamazoo, Apr. 18, 1943; s. Milton and Rose Muriel (Nathanson) W.; m. Susan Roberta Shifrin, June 23, 1968 (div. Oct. 1984); children: Amy Carolyn, Jordan Todd; m. Kathleen Wilson Bratton, Apr. 20, 1985; 1 child, Henrietta Zane Bratton. BEE, Cornell U., 1965, MEE, 1966; MBA with distinction, NYU, 1976. Field engr. Sperry Corp., Lake Success, N.Y., 1966-69; v.p. Alliance One Instl. Services, Inc., N.Y.C., 1970-76, H. C. Wainwright and Co., Inc., N.Y.C., 1976-77, Wainwright Securities, Inc., N.Y.C., 1977; v.p., co-mgr. fundamental equities research Smith Barney, Harris Upham & Co., N.Y.C., 1977-79; exec. v.p. chief fin. ops. Equitable Life Assurance Soc. U.S., N.Y.C., 1979-92; chmn., pres., chief exec. officer Equitable Capital Mgmt. Corp., N.Y.C., 1985-92; chief investment officer Equitable Life Assurance Soc. U.S., N.Y.C., 1991-92; pres. chief oper. officer, dir. Delaware Mgmt. Holdings, Inc., 1992-95; pres., CEO The Delaware Group, 1992-95; pres., chief oper. officer Delaware Mgmt. Co., 1992-95; chmn. Delaware Distributors, Inc., 1992-95; chmn., chief exec. officer Delaware Svc. Co., Inc., 1992-95; gen. ptnr. Odyssey Ptnrs., L.P., N.Y.C., 1995—; chmn., pres. Equitable Realty Assets Corp., Atlanta, 1983-92; v.p., dir. TELMARI, Inc., N.Y.C., 1982-83, Equitable Variable Life Ins. Co., 1987-92; chmn. Equico Capital Corp., N.Y.C., 1984-92, CEO Equitable Gen. of Okla., Oklahoma City, 1985-86; bd. dirs. Advanced System Applications Inc., 1985-87, Frye Copysystems Inc., N.Y.C., 1988-90, Supermkts. Gen. Corp., 1990-92, The Jackson Lab., Inc., 1990—; trustee Equitable Retirement Plans, N.Y.C., 1980-86, Inst. Advanced Study, 1992—; gov. Assn. Investment Mgmt. and Rsch., 1992—; pres. Hudson River Trust, 1991-92, Equitable Funds, 1991-92. Vice chmn. Boys Choir of Harlem, N.Y.C., 1984-92; bd. dirs. Harlem Youth Devel. Found., 1989-92, Corp. Ptnrs. Phila. Art Mus., 1992-95, vice chmn., 1993-95; bd. govs. Jerome Levy Econ. Inst., 1990—. Recipient Heroes award Boys Choir Harlem, 1990, Founders award, 1993. Mem. IEEE, Assn. Investment Mgmt. and Rsch., N.Y. Soc. Security Analysts, Inst. CFAs (CFA, vice chmn. 1993-94, chmn. 1994-95, bd. trustees rsch. found. 1994-95, assoc. editor CFA Digest 1983—), Phila. C. of C. (bd. dirs. 1992-95, mem. exec. com. 1993-95). Republican. Jewish. Avocations: running, skiing, sailing, amateur radio. Office: Odyssey Ptnrs LP 31 W 52nd St New York NY 10019-6118

WRUCK, ERICH-OSKAR, retired foreign language educator; b. Gr. Kroessin/Pomerania, Germany, Oct. 29 1928; came to U.S., 1952, naturalized, 1954; s. Erich Albert and Erna (Kroening) W.; m. Esther Emmy Schmidt, Oct. 3, 1953; children: Eric Gordon, Karin Esther, Krista Elisabeth. BA magna cum laude, Rutgers U., 1959, MA, 1961, PhD, 1969. Asst. instr. Rutgers U., New Brunswick, N.J., 1959-62; asst. prof. Davidson (N.C.) Coll., 1962-69, assoc. prof., 1969-73, prof., chmn. dept. German, 1983-87, dir. Davidson abroad program, Marburg, Germany, 1966-67, 71-72, jr. year abroad program, Wuerzburg, Germany, 1986-87, 89-92; ret. 1994. Served to 1st lt. U.S. Army, 1953-57, to col. USAR, 1986. Recipient Meritorious Service medal Dept. Army, 1983, 86, 88; inducted into Arty. OCS Hall of Fame, 1996; Henry Rutgers scholar. Mem. Goethe Gesellschaft, Freies Deutsches Hochstift, Schiller Gesellschaft, Goethe Soc. of N. Am. (charter), Soc. for German Am. Studies, Julius Maximilians medal U. Wuerzburg, 1987. Republican. Lutheran. Avocations: painting, photography, soaring, skiing, running.

WRUCKE-NELSON, ANN C., elementary school educator; b. Mankato, Minn., Nov. 5, 1939; d. G.F. and Dorothy (Thomas) Wrucke; children: Chris, Dor-Ella. BS, Mankato State U., 1961; MLA, So. Meth. U., 1974; postgrad., U. Minn., 1963, Tex. Woman's U.; EdD in Early Childhood Edn., Tex. Woman's U., 1992. Cert. elem., kindergarten, bilingual-ESL, history tchr., Tex. Tchr. Rochester (Minn.) Pub. Schs., Christ the King Sch., Dallas; dir., tchr. Norway Christian Presch., Dallas; Every Student Learns Lang. program kindergarten tchr. Dallas Ind. Sch. Dist.; tchr. summer session Tex. Woman's U., 1991; presenter in field. Producer video: A Year of Language Learning, 1990. Sunday sch. tchr. Holy Trinity Ch. Recipient Tchr. of Yr. award, 1989, Tex. TESOL scholarship, 1994; Bill Martin Literacy Conf. scholar; named ESL Tchr. of Yr., 1991. Mem. Assn. for Childhood Edn. Internat., So. Assn. on Children Under Six, Tchrs. English to Speakers Other Lang., Tex. Tchrs. English to Speakers Other Lang., Dallas Assn. for Edn. of Young Child.

WU, GARY G., petroleum engineer, consultant; b. Beijing, People's Republic of China, Oct. 28, 1960; came to U.S., 1985; s. Baoshan Wu and Fengzi Yu; m. Ding Zhu, Dec. 27, 1992; children: Woody, Andrew. BS in Petroleum, China Petroleum U., Beijing, 1982; MS in Petroleum, U. Tex., 1988, PhD in Petroleum, 1992. Registered profl. engr., Tex. Process engr. China Oil Devel. Co., Beijing, 1982-83; project mgr. China Nat. Offshore Oil Co., Beijing, 1983-85; rsch. asst. U. Tex., Austin, 1986-90; rsch. engr. Texaco Inc., Houston, 1990-91; rsch. asst. U. Tex., Austin, 1991-92; project scientist Texaco Inc., Houston, 1992—; cons. U. Tex., Austin, 1993-94. Contbr. articles to profl. jours. and procs. Mem. Soc. Petroleum Engrs. (assoc. mem., chmn. student chpt. 1988-89, author procs. 1994). Achievements include research in geochemical modeling software "Netreac," PC-Windows software "Simtools." Avocations: skiing, soccer, swimming, micro-computers. Home: 19831 Emerald Springs Houston TX 77094 Office: Texaco-EPTD 3901 Briarpark Dr Houston TX 77042-5301

WU, GUOYAO, animal science, nutrition and physiology educator; b. China, July 28, 1962; s. Fanjiu Wu and Meixiao Huang; m. Yan Chen, Aug. 7, 1995; 1 child, Neil David. BS in Animal Sci., South China Agrl. U., 1982; MS in Animal Nutrition, Beijing (People's Republic of China) Agrl. U., 1984; MS in Animal Biochemistry, U. Alberta, Can., 1986, PhD in Animal Biochemistry, 1989; postgrad. in metabolism/diabetes, McGill U., Mont., Can., 1989-91; postgrad. in biochemistry, Meml. U. Nfld., Can., 1991. Grad. teaching asst. U. Alberta, 1985-88; postdoctoral rschr. Royal Victoria Hosp., McGill U., 1989-91, Meml. U. Newfoundland, 1991; asst. prof. dept. animal sci. and faculty nutrition Tex. A&M U., College Station, 1991-96; assoc. prof. Tex. A&M U., 1996—. Reviewer Amino Acids, Am. Jour. Clin. Nutrition, Am. Jour. Physiology, Analytical Biochemistry, Biochimica et Biophysica Acta, Can. Jour. Physiology and Pharmacology, Diabetes, Diabetologia, Gene, Jour. Animal Sci., Jour. Nutrition, Jour. Nutritional Biochemistry, Jour. Cellular Physiology, Metabolism,, Poultry Sci., Can. Diabetes Assn., Med. Rsch. Coun. Can., U. Toronto Banting and Best Ctr., Can.; editl. advisor Biochem. Jour., 1993-97; mem. editl. bd. Jour. Nutrition, 1997—; contbr. articles to profl. jours. Grantee Tex. A&M U., 1992—, Ajinomoto Inc., Japan, 1992, USDA, 1992—, Houston Livestock Show and Rodeo, 1992-95, Am. Heart Assn., 1995—; nat. scholarship for grad. studies abroad Ministry Edn. China, 1984-86, grad. tchg. assistantship U. Alta., 1985-88, dissertation fellowship, 1989, Ctr. Rsch. Fund award, 1988, Andrew Stewart Grad. prize, 1989, U. Alberta, Can. Rsch. Inst. fellowship Royal Victoria Hosp., 1988, fellowship Can. Diabetes Assn., 1989, Med. Rsch. Coun. Can. fellow, 1989-91. Mem. AAAS, Am. Diabetes Assn., Am. Inst. Nutrition, Am. Physiol. Soc., Am. Soc. Animal Sci., Biochem. Soc. U.K., Can. Soc. Nutritional Scis., Juv. Diabetes Found. Internat. (grantee 1992-94). Home: 4707 Shoal Creek Dr College Station TX 77845 Office: Tex A&M Univ Dept Animal Sci College Station TX 77843

WU, HARRY PAO-TUNG, librarian; b. Jinan, Shandong, China, May 1, 1932; came to U.S., 1960; s. James Ching-Mei and Elizabeth Hsiao (Lu) W.; m. Irene I-Len Sun, June 23, 1961; children: Eva Pei-Chen, Walter Pei-Liang. BA, Nat. Taiwan U., Taipei, 1959; student Ohio State U., 1962; MLS, Kent State U., 1966.. Archive and library asst. Taiwan Handicraft Promotion Center, Taipei, 1959-60; student asst. Kent State U. Library, 1960-61; reference librarian Massillon (Ohio) Pub. Library, 1964-65, acting asst. dir., 1965, asst. dir., head adult services, 1966; dir. Flesh Pub. Library, Piqua, Ohio, 1966-68; dir. St. Clair County Library System, Port Huron, Mich., 1968-96; founder and dir. Blue Water Library Fedn., Port Huron, 1974—; pres. Mich. Library Film Circuit, Lansing, 1977-79; mem. St. Clair County Literacy Project Com., 1986-96; bd. dirs. Blue Water Reading Coun., 1987-88, Mich. Waterways council Girl Scouts U.S.A., Port Huron, 1985-86; bd. dirs. United Way St. Clair County, Mich., 1990-91; bd. trustees Libr. Mich., 1992-95. Mem. Am., Mich. (chmn. library systems roundtable 1974-75) library assns., Am. Mgmt. Assn., Assn. Ednl. Communications and Tech., Detroit Suburban Librarians Roundtable, Chinese-Am. Librarians Assn. Clubs: Port Huron Internat. (pres. 1988), Rotary (dir. 1972-74, 88-90, Paul Harris fellow 1988). Home: 1518 Holland Ave Port Huron MI 48060-1511 Office: 210 Mcmorran Blvd Port Huron MI 48060-4014

WU, HSIU KWANG, economist, educator; b. Hankow, China, Dec. 14, 1935; came to U.S., 1952, naturalized, 1963; s. Kao Cheng and Edith (Huang) W.; m. Kathleen Gibbs Johnson, Aug. 17, 1968. Grad., Lawrenceville Sch., 1954; A.B., Princeton U., 1958; M.B.A., U. Pa., 1960, Ph.D., 1963. Prof., group coordinator fin., econs. and internat. bus. Boston U., 1968-72; prof., chmn. fin., econs. and legal studies faculty U. Ala., 1972-81, Lee Bidgood prof. fin. and econs., 1978-97, Ala. Banker Edn. Found. Banking Chair prof., 1973-78; econ. adviser Office of Comptroller of Currency, U.S. Treasury, 1966-69, 75-80; dir. Ala. Fed., 1984-88; dir. SECOR Bank FSB, 1988-93, chmn. bd., 1992-93; cons. instl. investor study SEC, 1969-70; mem. com. examiners undergrad. program for counseling and evaluation test in bus. Ednl. Testing Service, 1971, 77. Co-editor: Elements of Investments, 2d rev. edit, 1972; Contbr. articles to law and econ. jours. Sloan Faculty fellow Sloan Sch. Mgmt., Mass. Inst. Tech., 1965-66. Mem. Am. Econ. Assn., Am. Fin. Assn., Am. Statis. Assn., Fin. Mgmt. Assn. Home: 3201 Old Barn Ct Ponte Vedra Beach FL 32082

WU, JAMES CHEN-YUAN, aerospace engineering educator; b. Nanking, China, Oct. 5, 1931; came to U.S., 1953, naturalized, 1963; s. Chien Lieh and Cheng-Ling (Hsia) W.; m. Mei-Ying Chang, Sept. 7, 1957; children—Alberta Yee-Hwa, Norbert Mao-Hwa. Student, Nat. Taiwan (Formosa) U., 1949-52; BS, Gonzaga U., 1954; postgrad., Columbia U., 1954; MS (univ. fellow), U. Ill., 1955, PhD, 1957. Engr. Wah Chang Corp., N.Y.C., 1954; researcher Mass. Inst. Tech. at Cambridge, 1957; asst. prof. Gonzaga U., Spokane, Wash., 1957-59; research specialist Douglas Aircraft Co., 1959-65, group leader, 1960-61, supr., 1961-62, br. chief, 1963-65; prof. aerospace engring. Ga. Inst. Tech., 1965—; cons. N.Am. Aviation Co., Geophys. Tech. Corp., European Atomic Energy Commn., Ispra, Italy, European Atomic Energy Commn. (research center), U.S. Army Research Office, Durham, S.C. Contbr. articles to profl. jours. Chmn. bd. dirs. Chinese-Am. Inst. Recipient profl. achievement award Douglas Aircraft Co., 1963, Outstanding Tchrs. award Gonzaga U., 1959; Assoc. fellow Am. Inst. Aeros. and Astronautics. Mem. Am. Soc. Engring. Sci. (founding), Soc. Indsl. and Applied Math. (vice-chmn. Pacific N.W. 1958-59), Am. Astron. Soc. (sr.), Am. Phys. Soc., Nat. Assn. Chinese Ams. (pres. Atlanta chpt.), Sigma Xi, Tau Beta Pi, Sigma Alpha Nu. Office: Sch Aerospace Engring Georgia Inst Tech 48967 Ventura Dr Fremont CA 94539-8045

WU, LI-PEI, banker; b. Changhwa, Taiwan, Sept. 9, 1934; came to U.S., 1968; s. Yin-Su and Chiao-Mei (Hsiao) W.; m. Jenny S. Lai, Mar. 24, 1963; children: George T., Eugene Y. BA, Nat. Taiwan U., 1957; MBA, Kans. State U., Ft. Hays, 1969; Comml. Banking Exec. Program, Columbia U., 1974. Staff acct., asst. controller, asst. v.p., v.p. Nat. Bank Alaska, Anchorage, 1969-73, v.p. controller, 1973-76, sr. v.p. chief fin. officer, 1976-78; chmn. exec. com. Alaska Nat. Bank of the North, Anchorage, 1978-79, chief adminstrv. officer, 1979-80, pres., 1980-81; pres., chief exec. officer Gen. Bank, Los Angeles, 1982-84, chmn., pres, chief exec. officer, 1984—; fin. cons. alaska '84, 1981-82, Western Airlines, Los Angeles, 1981-82, Microsci. Internat. Corp., San Jose, Calif., 1986-87; bd. dirs. Simons, Li & Assocs., Ft. Collins, Colo. Pres. Taiwanese United Fund, 1991. Recipient Outstanding Entrepreneur award Nat. Assn. Investment Cos. Mem. Taiwanese Am. Citizens League (life mem., pres.). Avocations: reading, sports. Office: Gen Bank 800 W 6th St Los Angeles CA 90017-2704

WU, NELSON IKON, art history educator, author, artist; b. Peking, China, June 9, 1919; came to U.S., 1945, naturalized, 1956; s. Aitchen K. and Lu-Yü (Yang) W.; m. Mu-lien Hsüeh, Dec. 1, 1951; children: Chao-ming, Chao-ting, Chao-ping, Chao-ying. B.A., Nat. Southwest Asso. U., Kunming, China, 1942; M.A., Yale U., 1949, Ph.D., 1954. Instr. Nat. S.W. Asso. U. Kunming, China, 1942-43; asst. prof. history of art San Francisco State Coll., 1954-55; instr. Yale U., 1955-59, asst. prof., 1959-65; prof. history of art and Chinese culture Washington U., St. Louis, 1965-68, Edward Mallinckrodt Disting. Univ. prof., 1968-84, emeritus, 1984—, chmn. dept. art and archaeology, 1969-70; founder-adviser Asian Art Soc. Washington U., St. Louis, 1972—; fellow Davenport Coll., Yale, 1956-65; vis. prof. Tokyo U., 1972; Founder art festivals Yenling Yeyuan Picnic, 1952-65, Ashiya Seminar, Japan, 1966-67. Cinematographer, assoc. dir., editor motion picture The Flop, 1952; dir., writer music The Finger Painting of Wu Tsai-yen, 1955; author: (pseudonym Lu-ch'iao): Wei-yang Ko (Song Never to End, voted Most Profoundly Influential Book of 1950's by readers of China Times, 1991), 1959 (over 50 printings), Tung Ch'i-ch'ang: Apathy in Government and Fervor in Art, 1962, Chinese and Indian Architecture: City of Man, Mountain of God, and Realm of Immortals, 1963 (Italian and German transls.), Jen-tzu Tales, 1974, over 20 printings, Ch'an-ch'ing-shu, 1975, over 10 printings; contbg. author: Renditions, 1976, (with Kohara and Ch'en) Hsu/Wei and Tung Ch'i-ch'ang, Tokyo, 1978, Chinese garden design Yanling Yeyuan, 1951—; contbr. to Artibus Asiae, 1966, River Styx, 1980, 81, 82, St. Louis Post-Dispatch, 1988, China Times, 1988, 89, 92, 95, China Times Weekly, 1992, United Daily News, 1995, 96; adv. editor Tsing-hua Jour. Chinese Studies, 1982—; exhibited at Faculty Show, Washington U., 1985, St. Louis Art Mus., 1985; featured on PBS show Living Treasures, 1987. Trustee Yale-in-China Assn., 1959-65; hon. trustee Nankai Sch., Tientsin, China, 1993. Tsing-hua Research fellow, 1954-55; Morse fellow Yale, 1958-59; Am. Council Learned Socs. fellow, 1958-59; Guggenheim Found. fellow, 1965-66; Fulbright research scholar, 1965-67; research scholar Kyoto U., Japan, 1965-67; Nat. Endowment for Humanities sr. fellow, 1972; New Haven Art Festival Lit. award, 1960; Calligraphy prize Ashiya, Japan, 1966; Living Treasures plaque St. Louis Older Adult Services and Info. System, 1985; hon. in Taipei, Taiwan at a conf. on contemporary Chinese lit., 1990. Mem. St. Louis Chinese Soc. (pres. 1969-70), League of Chinese Americans (dir. 1974-77). Home: 6306 Waterman Ave Saint Louis MO 63130-4707

WU, PAN, electrical engineer; b. Hefei, Anhui, China, Dec. 12, 1955; came to U.S., 1983; s. S.H. and S.W. (Pan) Wu; m. Li Yan, July 25, 1983; children: Patrick, Leo. BSEE, U. Sci. and Tech. of China, Hefei, 1982; MSEE, Oreg. State U., Corvallis, 1987; PhD in Elec. Engring., Portland State U., 1993. Grad. asst. Portland (Oreg.) State U., 1987-91, adj. instr., 1990; sr. design engr. Intel Corp., Aloha, Oreg., 1991-94; mem. tech. staff Bell Labs., Lucent Techs., Allentown, Pa., 1994—; cons. Top-Vu Tech. Inc., New Brighton, Minn., 1990-91. Contbr. articles to profl. jours. Bd. dirs. Lehigh Valley chpt. Orgn. Chinese Ams. Textronix Found. fellow, Beaverton, Oreg., 1991, Jorgenson scholar for sci. Portland State U., 1992. Mem. IEEE, Eta Kappa Nu. Achievements include the design of the GaAs and CMOS transconductance amplifiers and transdonductance-C filters in the early stage; and patents for research and development of the CPU of Intel's 100 MHz Pentium microprocessor and the cable interface chips in AT&T's communications systems. Office: Lucent Tech Bell Labs 555 Union Blvd Rm 23r-143G Allentown PA 18103-1229

WU, RAY JUI, biochemistry educator; b. Peking, China, Aug. 14, 1928; came to U.S., 1949, naturalized, 1961; s. Hsien and Daisy (Yen) W.; m. Christina Chan, Aug. 11, 1956; children: Albert, Alice. B.S., U. Ala., 1950; Ph.D., U. Pa., 1955. Asso. mem. Pub. Health Research Inst. City of N.Y., 1957-66; asso. prof. biochemistry, molecular and cell biology Cornell U., Ithaca, N.Y., 1966-72; prof. Cornell U., 1972—, chmn. sect., 1975-79; vis. rsch. scientist Stanford U., 1965-66; NSF sr. fellow MRC Lab., Cambridge, Eng., 1971; vis. assoc. prof. MIT, 1972. Contbr. chpts. to books, articles to profl. jours. NIH grantee, 1960—; NSF grantee, 1967—; Am. Cancer Soc. grantee, 1976—; Rockefeller Found grantee, 1985—. Mem. Am. Soc. Biol. Chemists, Am. Chem. Soc., AAAS, Academia Sinica, Internat. Soc. Plant Molecular Biology. Democrat. Home: 111 Christopher Cir Ithaca NY 14850-1701 Office: Cornell U Biotechnology Bldg Ithaca NY 14853

WU, SENG-CHAI, financial planner, life insurance agency official; b. Amoy, Fuchian, China, Oct. 19, 1930; came to U.S., 1954; s. Eng-Hwa and Lian-Hoe (Iu) W.; m. Evelyn M. Mangaser, Sept. 9, 1975; children: Patrick O., Michael L., Andrew J. BA, Union Coll., Lincoln, Nebr. CLU; ChFC. Sales rep., also regional sales mgr. Home Health Edn. Svc., Richardson, Tex., 1959-68; sales rep., mgr. Met. Life Ins. Co., N.Y.C., 1968-85; sales mgr. Met. Life Ins. Co., Arcadia, Claremont, Calif., 1982-85; fin. cons. Fin. Design, Rancho Cucamonga, Calif., 1985—; gen. agy. mgr. Franklin Fin. Svcs. Corp., Springfield, Calif., 1988—, Amerus Life, Des Moines, 1991—. Active Philippines and Chinese Assn., Dallas, 1969-75; nominated to participate LIMRA Internat. Rsch. Mem. Pomona Valley Life Underwriter Assn., Arrowhead CLU Assn. Republican. Adventist. Avocations: volleyball, photography, gardening, walking. Home: 10988 Wilson Ave Alta Loma CA 91737-2438

WU, TAI TE, biological sciences and engineering educator; b. Shanghai, China, Aug. 2, 1935; m. Anna Fang, Apr. 16, 1966; 1 son, Richard. M.B., B.S., U. Hong Kong, 1956; B.S. in Mech. Engring, U. Ill., Urbana, 1958; S.M. in Applied Physics, Harvard U., 1959, Ph.D. in Engring. (Gordon McKay fellow), 1961. Rsch. fellow in structural mechanics Harvard U., 1961-63; rsch. fellow in biol. chemistry Harvard U. (Med. Sch.), 1964, rsch. assoc., 1965-66; rsch. scientist Hydronautics, Inc., Rockville, Md., 1962; asst. prof. engring. Brown U., Providence, 1963-65; asst. prof. biomath. Grad. Sch. Med. Scis., Cornell U. Med. Coll., N.Y.C., 1967-68; assoc. prof. Grad. Sch. Med. Scis., Cornell U. Med. Coll., 1968-70; assoc. prof. physics and engring. scis. Northwestern U., Evanston, Ill., 1970-73, prof., 1973-74, prof. biochemistry and molecular biology and engring. scis., 1973-85, acting chmn. dept. engring. scis., 1974, prof. biochem., molecular biology, cell biology and biomed. engring., engring. scis., applied math., 1985-94, prof. biochemistry, molecular biology, cell biology, biomed. engring., 1994—. Author: (with E.A. Kabat and others) Variable Regions of Immunoglobulin Chains, 1976, Sequences of Immunoglobulin Chains, 1979, Sequences of Proteins of Immunological Importance, 1983, Sequences of Proteins of Immunological Interest, 1987, 5th edit., 1991; editor: New Methodologies in Studies of Protein Configuration, 1985; contbr. articles to profl. jours. Recipient progress award Chinese Engrs. and Scientists Assn. So. Calif., Los Angeles, 1971; C.T. Loo Scholar, 1959-60; NIH Research Career Devel. awardee, 1974-79. Mem. Am. Soc. Biochem. & Molecular Biology, Biophys. Soc., Chgo. Assn. Immunology, Sigma Xi, Tau Beta Pi, Pi Mu Epsilon. Office: Dept Biochem Molecular & Cell Biology Northwestern U Evanston IL 60208

WU, TAI TSUN, physicist, educator; b. Shanghai, China, Dec. 1, 1933; came to U.S., 1950, naturalized, 1964; s. King Ching and Wei Van (Tsang) W.; m. Sau Lan Yu, June 18, 1967. B.S., U. Minn., 1953; S.M., Harvard U., 1954, Ph.D., 1956. Jr. fellow Soc. Fellows Harvard U., 1956-59, asst. prof., 1959-63, assoc. prof., 1963-66, Gordon McKay prof. applied physics, 1966—, prof. physics, 1994—; mem. Inst. Advanced Study, Princeton, 1958-59, 60-61, 62-63; vis. prof. Rockefeller U., 1966-67; sci. assoc. Deutsches Elektronen-Synchrotron, Hamburg, Ger., 1970-71, 82-83; Kramers prof. U. Utrecht, Netherlands, 1977-78; sci. assoc. CERN, Geneva, Switzerland, 1977-78, 86—. Author: (with Ronold W.P. King) Scattering and Diffraction of Waves, 1959, (with Barry M. McCoy) Two-Dimensional Ising Model, 1973, (with Ronold W.P. King, Glenn S. Smith and Margaret Owens) Antennas in Matter: Fundamentals, Theory and Applications, 1981, (with Hung Cheng) Expanding Protons: Scattering at High Energies, 1987, (with Raymond Gastmans) The Ubiquitous Photon: Helicity Method for QED and QCD, 1990, (with Ronold W.P. King and Margaret Owens) Lateral Electromagnetic Waves: Theory and Applications to Communications, Geophysical Exploration, and Remote Sensing, 1992. Recipient Alexander von Humboldt award, 1985; Putnam scholar, 1953; fellow A.P. Sloan Found., 1960-66; fellow NSF, 1966-67; Guggenheim Found., 1970-71. Mem. Am. Acad. Arts and Sci., Sigma Xi, Eta Kappa Nu, Tau Beta Pi. Home: 35 Robinson St Cambridge MA 02138-1403 Office: Harvard U Physics Dept 204B Pierce Hall Cambridge MA 02138-2901 *A person's strength is, simultaneously, his weakness.*

WU, TUNG, curator, art historian, art educator, artist; b. Foochow, Fukien, China, Dec. 10, 1940; came to U.S., 1965; s. Chin-Wen and Jingrong (Chen) W.; m. Ying Chin, July 16, 1974. BA, Normal U., Taipei, Taiwan, 1962; postgrad., U. Mich., 1967-70, Harvard U., 1979—. Rsch. asst. Nat. Palace Mus., Taichung, Taiwan, 1962-65; with photography archive U. Mich., 1966-68; rsch. asst. Cleve. Mus. Art, 1968; Ford Found. curatorial intern Nelson-Atkins Mus. Art, Kansas City, Mo., 1969; rsch. fellow Mus. Fine Arts, Boston, 1971-79, asst. curator, 1980-84, assoc. curator, 1985-86, curator Asian art, 1986-92, Matsutaro Shoriki curator Asian art, 1992—; teaching asst. U. Kans., Lawrence, 1969, Harvard U., 1978; vis. lectr. Harvard U., Cambridge, Mass., 1975, Emmanuel Coll., Boston, 1992, Simmons Coll., Boston, 1993; advisor Chinese Inst. Am., N.Y.C., 1985—, Chinese Cultural Found., San Francisco, 1985-87; cons. Project Emperor-One, Boston, 1983-86; panelist mus. program NEA, 1995. Mem. Nat. Com. on U.S.-China Rels., Washington, 1985—; mem. Nat. Devel. Seminar Taipei, 1989, 92, Nat. Edn. Reform, Taipei, 1994; advisor dept. Asian trade art Peabody Mus., Salem. Mass., 191—; trustee W.A. Compton Found. Oriental Arts. Fellow Nat. Mus. History, Taipei, 1984—; grantee Freer Found. U. Mich., 1968, Ford Found., Kansas City, 1969, Smithsonian Instn., Washington, 1978. Mem. Taoist Soc. Japan, Soc. Chinese Kunqu Opera, Soc. Chinese Calligraphy. Office: Mus Fine Arts Asiatic Dept 465 Huntington Ave Boston MA 02115-5523

WU, WAYNE WEN-YAU, artist; b. Tachia, Taiwan, Republic of China, Oct. 5, 1935; s. K.C. Kau and Chin-Fong (Chen) W.; m. Amy Hsueh, Dec. 25, 1961; children: Ingrid, Judy, David. BA in Fine Arts, Taiwan Normal U., 1959. Supr. art edn. ctr. Taichung (Taiwan) Libr., 1970-74; instr. fine arts dept. Taiwan Normal U., Taipei, 1973-74; instr. paintings Hunter Mus. of Art, Chatanooga, Tenn., 1980-92; artist, paintings instr. Wayne Wu's Art Studio, Atlanta, 1994—. Represented in 20 solo shows including Taiwan Mus. of Art, 1995, and over 100 group shows. Mem. Am. Watercolor Soc. Home: 2415 Hamptons Passage Alpharetta GA 30005-7411

WU, WILLIAM LUNG-SHEN (YOU-MING WU), aerospace medical engineering design specialist, foreign intelligence analyst; b. Hangchow, Chekiang Province, China, Sept. 1, 1921; came to U.S., 1941, naturalized, 1955; s. Sing-Chih and Mary (Ju-Mei) Wu. AB in Biochemistry, Stanford U., 1943, MD, 1946; MS in Chemistry and Internal Medicine, Tulane U., 1955; diploma, U.S. Naval Sch. Aviation Medicine, Pensacola, Fla., 1956, USAF Sch. Aviation Medicine, USAF Aerospace Med. Ctr., 1961; cert. of tng. in aviation medicine, U. Calif., Berkeley, 1962, 1964. Diplomate Am. Bd. Preventive Medicine, Am. Bd. Internal Medicine, Am. Bd. Psychiatry, Am. Bd. Pathology. Gen. rotating intern U. Iowa Hosps., Iowa City, 1945-46; resident Lincoln (Nebr.) Gen. Hosp., 1946-47, resident in pathology, 1947-48; resident in pathology Bryan Meml. Hosp., Lincoln, 1947-48; fellow, instr. in internal medicine Tulane U., New Orleans, 1948-54; asst. vis. physician Charity Hosp. and Hutchinson Meml. Teaching and Diagnostic and Cancer Detection Clinics, New Orleans, 1948-51, vis. physician, 1951-54; staff physician Holderman (Army) Hosp., Napa, Calif., 1958; staff physician Aviation Space and Radiation Med. Group Gen. Dynamics/Convair, San Diego, 1958-61; aerospace med. specialist, med. monitor for Life Sciences Sect. Gen. Dynamics/Astronautics, San Diego, 1961-65; aerospace med. and bioastronautics specialist Lovelace Found. for Med. Edn. and Rsch., Albuquerque, 1965-68; staff physician Laguna Honda Hosp., San Francisco, 1968-74; ret.; staff physician Kaiser-Permanente Hosp. all-night med. clinic, San Francisco, 1971-73; safety rep. and med. examiner U.S. Civil Aeronaut. Adminstrn., 1959; med. examiner Fed. Aviation Adminstrn., 1961; expert witness in forensic medicine and/or medicolegal jurisprudence for cts. Author 8 books and 100 tech. papers in field. Active mem. Planning, Rsch. and Devel. Commn. Redwood City; bd. dirs. Legal Aid Soc. Santa Clara County, U.S. Congl. Adv. Bd., Am. Security Coun. Found., Little House Sr. Multipurpose Ednl. Ctr.; Life Fellow Royal Soc. of Lichtenstein, Zurich, Switzerland, Oxford Club (N.Y. and Fla.), Royal Coll. of Heraldry. Comdr., flight surgeon M.C., USN, 1954-57. Recipient Gold medal Internat. Inst. Cmty. Svc., 1976, J. Edgar Hoover Gold Disting. Pub. Svc. award Am. Police Hall of Fame, 1991, Albert Einstein Bronze medal Universal Intelligence Data Bank Am., 1986, Cambridge Gold medal, Dedication Insignia. Fellow San Diego Biomed. Rsch. Inst. (bd. dirs. 1961-65, sec. of fellows 1961-62, chmn. of fellows 1963), Inst. Environ. Scis. (chmn. specifications and standards com.), AIAA (mem. nominating com. San Diego sect., plant rep. life sci. sect. 1963-65); mem. IEEE (vice chmn. San Diego chpt. profl. tech. group on biomed. electronics 1962-65), N.Y. Acad. Scis., Internat. Univ. Found. (hon. pres.), Internat. Acad. Found. (hon. registrar-sec.), Computer Club, Sigma Xi, U.S. Naval Inst. (life), Naval League of U.S. West-pac (life), Conss. Nat. Resource Ctr. Network. Achievements include research of theroetical aspects of cold catalyzed hydrogen fusion nuclear-rocket warm super-conductor hyper-magnetic, hydrogen-fusion space stations; patentee S(RAM-PANT)S. Home: 250 Budd Ave Apt 219 Campbell CA 95008-4061

WU, YING CHU LIN SUSAN, engineering company executive, engineer; b. Beijing, June 23, 1932; came to U.S., 1957; d. Chi-yu and K.C. (Kung) Lin; m. Jain-Ming Wu, June 13, 1959; children: Ernest H., Albert H., Karen H. BSME, Nat. Taiwan U., 1955; MS in Aero. Engring., Ohio State U., 1959; PhD in Aeros., Calif. Inst. Tech., 1963. Sr. engr. Elecro-Optical Systems, Inc., Pasadena, Calif., 1963-65; asst. prof. aero. engring. U. Tenn. Space Inst., Tullahoma, 1965-67, assoc. prof., 1967-73, prof., 1973-88; adminstr. Energy Conversion R&D Programs, Tullahoma, 1981-88; pres., chief exec. officer ERC, Inc., Tullahoma, 1987—; presdl. appointee adv. bd. Nat. Air and Space Mus., Smithsonian Inst., 1993—. Contbr. over 90 articles to profl. jours. Mem. Better Sch. Task Force, Tullahoma, 1985-86; founding mem. Tullahoma Edn. Found. for Excellence; trustee Rochester Inst. Tech., 1992-94; mem. adv. com. NASA Aeronautics, 1994—. Recipient Chancellor's Rsch. award U. Tenn., 1978, Outstanding Educator of Am. award, 1973, 75; Amelia Earhart fellow, 1958, 59, 62, Plasmadynamics and Lasersaward Am. Inst. of Aeronautics and Astronautics, 1994. Fellow ASME, AIAA (assoc., chmn. Tenn. sect., H.H. Arnold award 1984, Plasmodynamics and Lasers award 1994); mem. Soc. Women Engrs. (life mem., achievement award 1985), Rotary, Sigma Xi (chmn. U. Tenn. Space Inst. club). Office: ERC Inc PO Box 417 Tullahoma TN 37388-0417 Address: 111 Lakewood Dr Tullahoma TN 37388-5227

WUBAH, DANIEL ASUA, microbiologist; b. Accra, Ghana, Nov. 6, 1960; came to U.S., 1984; s. Daniel Asua and Elizabeth Bruba (Appoe) W.; m. Judith A. Dadson, Dec. 17, 1993; children: Vera, Ewura Abena. BSc with honors, DipEd, U. Cape Coast, Ghana, 1984; MS, U. Akron, 1988; PhD, U. Ga., 1990. Cert. in hazardous waste site ops. and emergency response health and safety. Postdoctoral fellow U.S. EPA Rsch. Lab., Athens, Ga., 1991-92; asst. prof. Towson (Md.) U., 1992-97, assoc. prof., 1997—. Contbr. articles to profl. publs. Sec. African Students Union, U. Ga., Athens, 1988; v.p. Ghana Soc. of Athens, Ga., 1989. Recipient Paul Acquarone award U. Akron, 1985, Palfrey award U. Ga., 1989, Ruska award Southeastern Electron Microscopy Soc., 1989; Faculty Rsch. grantee Towson State U., 1992; grantee NSF, 1993, USDA, 1994. Mem. AAAS, Mycological Soc. of Am., Am. Soc. Microbiology, Med. Mycological Soc. of Am., Internat. Soc. for Human and Animal Mycology, Sigma Xi (pres. Towson chpt. 1996-97). Episcopalian. Achievements include first description of the resting stage of anaerobic zoosporic fungi from rumen; first isolation of rumen zoosporic fungi from nature; description of a novel morphological development in rumen fungus; demonstration that hitherto fungi belonging to different species were the same. Home: 28 Stable Run Ct Foxridge MD 21133 Office: Towson State U Dept Biol Scis Towson MD 21204

WUDL, FRED, chemistry educator; b. Cochabamba, Bolivia, Jan. 8, 1941; came to U.S., 1958; s. Robert and Bertha (Schorr) W.; m. Linda Raimondo, Sept. 2, 1967. BS, UCLA, 1964, PhD, 1967. Postdoctoral rsch. fellow Harvard U., 1967-68; asst. prof. dept. chemistry SUNY, Buffalo, 1968-72; mem. tech. staff AT&T Bell Labs., Murray Hill, N.J., 1972-82; prof. chemistry and materials U. Calif., Santa Barbara, 1982—. Recipient arthur C. Cope scholar award Am. Chem. Soc., 1993, Award for Chemistry of Materials, 1996, Natta medal Italian Chem. Soc., 1994, Wheland medal U. Chgo., 1994. Fellow AAAS. Office: U Calif Dept Chemistry Santa Barbara CA 93106

WUDUNN, SHERYL, journalist, correspondent; b. N.Y.C., Nov. 16, 1959; d. David and Alice (Mark) W.; m. Nicholas D. Kristof, Oct. 8, 1988. BA, Cornell U., Ithaca, N.Y., 1981; MBA, Harvard U., 1986; MPA, Princeton U., 1988. Lending officer Bankers Trust Co., N.Y.C., 1981-84; intern reporter Wall St. Jour., L.A., 1986; bus. reporter South China Morning Post, Hong Kong, 1987; corr. N.Y. Times, Beijing, 1989-93, Tokyo, 1995—. Co-author: China Wakes, 1994. Recipient Pulitzer Prize for fgn. reporting, 1990, George Polk award L.I. U., N.Y., 1990, Hal Boyle award Overseas Press Club, 1990. Avocations: aerobics, singing. Office: NY Times Asahi Shumbun Bldg, 3-2 Tsukiji 5-chome, Chuo-ku Tokyo 104-11, Japan Office: NY Times 229 W 43rd St New York NY 10036-3913

WUEBBELS, THERESA ELIZABETH, visual art educator; b. Breese, Ill., Nov. 8, 1950; d. Wilson Theodore and Selma Maria (Haake) W. BA, Notre Dame Coll., St. Louis, 1972; postgrad., Boston Coll., 1976-79, Pembroke State U., 1988. Teaching nun Sch. Sisters of Notre Dame, St. Louis, 1969-80; art tchr. Cathedral Sch., Belleville, Ill., 1972-76, Sacred Heart Sch., Fort Madison, Iowa, 1976-80; missionary sister Little Sisters of Jesus, 1980-87; art tchr. Balden County Schs., Clarkton, N.C., 1989—; visual art tchrs. coord. Bladen County Schs., Elizabethtown, N.C., 1991—; bd. dirs. N.C. Alliance for Arts. Coord. Celebration of the Arts Festival for Bladen County, 1992—; task force mem. founding Clarkton Sch. Discovery, Clarkton, N.C., 1993-94. Named Tchr. of Yr. Clarkton Sch. of Discovery, 1992-93, 93-94, 94-95. Mem. N.C. Art Edn. Assn., Nat. Art Edn. Assn., Visual Art Guild. Roman Catholic. Avocations: fossils, shells, pottery, cats, nature. Home: 653 Poe Elkins Rd Clarkton NC 28433-7243 Office: Clarkton Sch Discovery PO Box 127 Clarkton NC 28433-0127

WUENSCH, BERNHARDT JOHN, ceramic engineering educator; b. Paterson, N.J., Sept. 17, 1933; s. Bernhardt and Ruth Hannah (Slack) W.; m. Mary Jane Harriman, June 4, 1960; children: Stefan Raymond, Katrina Ruth. SB in Physics, MIT, 1955, SM in Physics, 1957, PhD in Crystallography, 1963. Rsch. fellow U. Bern, Switzerland, 1963-64; asst. prof. ceramics MIT, Cambridge, 1964-69, assoc. prof. ceramics, 1969-74, prof., 1974—, TDK chair materials sci. and engring., 1985-90, dir. Ctr. Materials Sci. and Engring., 1988-93, acting dept. head dept. materials sci. and engring., 1980; vis. prof. Crystallographic Inst., U. Saarland, Fed. Republic Germany, 1973; physicist Max Planck Institut für Festkorperforschung, Stuttgart, Fed. Republic Germany, 1981; mem. U.S. nat. com. for crystallography NRC, NAS, 1980-82, 89-94; mem. N.E. regional com. for selection of Marshall Scholars, 1970-73, chmn., 1974-80. Co-editor: Modulated Structures, 1979, Neutron Scattering in Materials Science, 1995; adv. editor Physics and Chemistry of Minerals, 1976-85; assoc. editor Can. Mineralogist, 1978-80; editor Zeitschrift fuer Kristallographie, 1981-88. Ford Found. postdoctoral fellow, 1964-66. Fellow Am. Ceramic Soc. (Outstanding Educator award 1987), Mineral. Soc. Am.; mem. Am. Crystallographic Assn., Mineral. Assn. Can., Materials Rsch. Soc., Electrochem. Soc. Episcopalian. Home: 190 Southfield Rd Concord MA 01742-3432 Office: MIT 77 Massachusetts Ave Rm 13-4037 Cambridge MA 02139-4301

WUERL, DONALD W., bishop; b. Pittsburgh, Nov. 12, 1940; s. Francis J. and Mary A. (Schiffhauer) W. BA, Cath. U. Am., 1962; MA, Cath. U. Am., Rome, 1963; ThM, Pontifical Gregorian U., Rome, 1967; ThD, Pontifical U. St. Thomas, Rome, 1974; DD (hon.), Duquesne U., 1989, Washington and Jefferson Coll., 1990; HLD (hon.), La Roche Coll., 1990; LHD (hon.), St. Vincent Coll., 1992. Ordained priest Roman Cath. Ch., 1966. Asst. pastor, parochial vicar St. Rosalia Ch., Pitts., 1967-69; sec. to Cardinal John Wright Congregation for Clergy, Rome, 1969-79; vice-rector St. Paul Sem., Pitts., 1980-81, rector, 1981-85; Ord. aux. bishop of Seattle, titular bishop of Rosmarkaeum, 1986, bishop of Pittsburgh, 1988—; sec. to Bishop of Pitts., 1967-69; lectr. Duquesne U., Pitts., 1968-69, 80-85, Pontifical U. St. Thomas, 1975-79; lectr. adult theology program Diocese of Pitts., 1967-69, dir. Inst. Continuing Edn. for Priests, 1982-84, assoc. gen. sec., 1985; ofcl. Congregation for Clergy, Rome, 1969-79; mem. alumni bd. govs. Cath. U. Am., 1977-84, vice-pres. for religious, 1981-82; exec. sec. to Papal rep. for Study of Sems. in U.S., 1982-85. Author: The Forty Martyrs, 1971, Fathers of the Church, 1975, The Catholic Priesthood Today, 1976, A Visit to the Vatican, 1981, The Church and Her Sacraments: Making Christ Visible, 1990; co-author: The Teaching of Christ: A Catholic Catechism for Adults, 1976, rev., 1984, 91, abridged, 1979, study guide, 1977, A Catholic Catechism, 1986; contbg. author: New Catholic Ency.; contbr. articles to religion publs.; author religious cassette programs. Recipient Disting. Pennsylvanian award Gannon U., 1989, Brotherhood award NCCJ, 1991, Treee of Life award Jewish Nat. Fund, 1992, Disting. Alumni award Cath. U. Am., 1992; named Vectors/Pitts. Man of Yr. in religion, 1988. Mem. Am. Cath. Hist. Assn., Cath. Theol. Soc. Am., Fellowship Cath. Scholars, Acad. Romana Universale, Phi Kappa Theta (Man of Achievement award 1988). Office: Diocese of Pitts 111 Blvd Of The Allies Pittsburgh PA 15222-1613*

WUHL, CHARLES MICHAEL, psychiatrist; b. N.Y.C., Sept. 24, 1943; s. Isadore and Sali (Ackner) W.; m. Gail; children—Elise, Amy. M.D., U. Bologna, 1973. Diplomate Am. Bd. Psychiatry and Neurology. Intern, N.Y. Med. Coll., 1975-76, resident in psychiatry, 1976-77; fellow in child psychiatry Columbia Presbyn. Med. Center, 1977-78; practice medicine specializing in psychiatry and child psychiatry, Englewood, N.J., 1978—; attending staff, mem. faculty N.Y. Med. Coll.; psychiatrist NYU, also asst. clin. prof. psychiatry NYU Sch. Medicine. Contbr. to Psychosocial Aspects of Pediatric Care, 1978, World Book Ency., 1980—. Mem. Am. Psychiat Assn., AMA, Am. Acad. Child Psychiatry. Office: 163 Engle St Englewood NJ 07631-2530

WULBERT, DANIEL ELIOT, mathematician, educator; b. Chgo., Dec. 17, 1941; s. Morris and Anna (Greenberg) W.; children: Kera, Noah. BA, Knox U., 1963; MA, U. Tex., Austin, 1964, PhD, 1966. Research assoc. U. Lund (Sweden), 1966-67; asst. prof. U. Wash., Seattle, 1967-73; prof. U. Calif.-San Diego, La Jolla, 1973—; vis. prof. Northwestern U., Evanston, Ill., 1977. Contbr. articles in field. Office: U Calif San Diego Dept Math # 0112 La Jolla CA 92093

WULF, JANIE SCOTT MCILWAINE, gifted and talented education educator; b. Smithfield, Va., Mar. 30, 1934; d. Porter O'Brien and Claire (Bennett) Scott; m. Harro Biner Wulf, Sept. 22, 1962; children: Susan, Thomas, Katherine, Jane. BS, Longwood Coll., Farmville, Va., 1955; MEd in Guidance, George Mason U., Fairfax, Va., 1975; postgrad., U. Va. Cert. home econs., upper elem. tchr., guidance counselor, g/t cert., Va. Tchr. kindergarten Faith Luth. Day Sch., Arlington, Va.; tchr. home econs. Annandale H.S., Fairfax; tchr. sci. Chesterfield County Pub. Schs., Chester; tchr. English gifted and talented edn. Fairfax County Pub. Schs., Fairfax, also mid. sch. team leader, 1990-91; team leader, supervising tchr. Fairfax County Frost Sch., 1990-95, 96-97. Mem. Va. Edn. Assn., Va. Assn. Tchrs. English, Va. Mid. Sch. Assn., Am. Fedn. Tchrs., Fairfax County Fedn. of Tchrs.

WULF, JEROLD W., manufacturing executive; b. 1931. Degree in architecture, U. Minn., 1954. Field svc. rep. Andersen Corp., Bayport, Minn., 1958-59; field sales rep. Andersen Corp., Rayport, Minn., 1959-61, sales tng. mgr., 1961-64, sales adminstrn. mgr., 1964-70, mgr. rsch. and product devel., 1970-90, pres., 1990—, CEO, 1992—, also bd. dirs.; chmn. bd. dirs. Dashwood Industries Ltd., Centralia, Ont.; pres. R. Laflamme & Freres, Inc., Quebec; bd. dirs., exec. com. Nat. Wood Window and Door Assn., chmn.; bd. dirs. Firstar Corp. Minn. N.A., Firstar Stillwater, Minn. Bank NA. Bd. regents St. Croix Luth. High Sch. Lt. USN, 1954-58. Mem. Passive Solar Industries Coun., Nat. Fenestration Coun., ASTM, ASHRAE, Nat. Coun. Housing Industry, Glazing Industry Code Coun. (past chmn., pres.). Office: Andersen Corp 100 4th Ave N Bayport MN 55003-1058

WULF, MELVIN LAWRENCE, lawyer; b. N.Y.C., Nov. 1, 1927; s. Jacob and Vivian (Hurwitz) W.; m. Deirdre Howard, Dec. 18, 1962; children: Laura Melissa, Jane Miranda. B.S., Columbia U., 1952, LL.B., 1955. Bar: N.Y. 1957. Asst. legal dir. ACLU, 1958-62, legal dir., 1962-77; Distinguished vis. prof. Hofstra Law Sch., 1975, spl. prof. law, 1976-77; mem. firm Clark Wulf & Levine, 1978-83, Beldock, Levine & Hoffman, 1983—. Author articles. Served to lt. (j.g.) USNR, 1955-57. Ford Found. fellow, 1967. Home: 340 Riverside Dr New York NY 10025-3423 Office: 99 Park Ave New York NY 10016-1601

WULF, WILLIAM ALLAN, computer information scientist, educator; b. Chgo., Dec. 8, 1939; s. Otto H. and Helen W. (Westermeier) W.; m. Anita K. Jones, July 1, 1977; children: Karin, Ellen. BS, U. Ill., 1961, MSEE, 1963; PhD in Computer Sci., U. Va., 1968. Prof. computer sci. Carnegie-Mellon Univ., Pitts., 1968-81; chmn., chief exec. officer Tartan Labs., Pitts., 1981-87; AT&T prof. computer sci. Univ. Va., Charlottesville, 1988—; asst. dir. Nat. Sci. Found., Washington, 1988-90; pres. Nat. Acad. of Engring., Washington, 1996—; bd. dirs. Baker Engrs., Beaver, Pa.; cons. various computer mfrs. Author: Fundamental Structures of Computer Science, 1981. Bd. dirs. Pitts. High Tech. Coun., 1982-88; trustee Charles Babbage Inst. Fellow IEEE, AAAS, Assn. Computing Machinery (coun.); mem. NAE, Am. Acad. Arts & Scis. Avocations: woodworking, photography. Office: Nat Acad Engring 2101 Constitution Ave NW Washington DC 20418-0007

WULF, WILLIAM ARTHUR, lawyer; b. Mpls., Apr. 11, 1945; s. Robert W. and Margaret A. (Rogers) W.; m. Kathleen D. Inzeo, Jan. 4, 1969; children: Robert, Amy, Paula, Maureen. BS in History, U. Wis., 1967; JD, Marquette U., 1971. Bar: Wis. 1971, U.S. Dist. Ct. (we. dist.) Wis. 1971, U.S. Dist. Ct. (ea. dist.) Wis. 1994. Part-time city atty. City of Merrill, 1971-75; assoc. Sazama & Wulf, S.C., Merrill, 1971-79; pvt. practice Merrill, 1979-83; ptnr. Ament, Wulf & Frokjer S.C., Merrill, 1983—; cert. trial specialist Nat. Bd. Trial Advocacy. Past chmn. United Way; bd. dirs. local hosp. found. fund. With USNG, 1969-75. Mem. Nat. Orgn. Social Security Reps., State Bar Wis., Lincoln County Bar Assn. (past sec.-treas., v.p., pres.), Optimists, KC. Roman Catholic. Avocations: skiing, sailing, golf. Office: Ament Wulf & Frokjer PO Box 626 Merrill WI 54452

WÜMPELMANN, KNUD AAGE ABILDGAARD, clergyman, religious organization administrator; b. Odense, Denmark, Aug. 7, 1922; s. Heinrich Christian and Helga P.P. (Abildgaard) W.; m. Karen M. Petersen, Aug. 23, 1947; children: Jørgen, Mogens. BD, Cen. Bapt. Theol. Sem., Kansas City, Kans., 1953, MRE, 1954; DD (hon.), William Jewell Coll., Liberty, Mo., 1985. Ordained to ministry Bapt. Union Denmark, 1948. Asst. pastor Jetsmark Bapt. Ch., Denmark, 1947-50; asst. pastor Købner Meml. Ch., Copenhagen, 1950-55, min., 1955-64; gen. sec. Bapt. Union Denmark, Copenhagen, 1964-80; sec., treas. European Bapt. Fedn., Copenhagen, 1980-89; regional sec. for Europe Bapt. World Alliance, Copenhagen, 1980-89; pres. Bapt. World Alliance, McLean, Va., 1990-95. Author: Vi tror, 1966; editor: Baptistsamfundene i Rwanda-Burundi, 1968. Recipient Disting. Svc. award Ctrl. Bapt. Theol. Sem., Scroll of Honor, Bapt. Theol. Sem., Rüschlikon-Zürich, Switzerland, 1991. Home: Villavej 8, DK-4340 Toelloese

Denmark Office: Bapt World Alliance 6733 Curran St Mc Lean VA 22101-3804

WUNDER, CHARLES C(OOPER), physiology and biophysics educator, gravitational biologist; b. Pitts., Oct. 2, 1928; s. Edgar Douglas and Annabel (Cooper) W.; m. Marcia Lynn Barnes, Apr. 4, 1962; children: E(dgar) Douglas, David Barnes, Donald Charles. A.B. in Biology, Washington and Jefferson Coll., 1949; M.S. in Biophysics, U. Pitts., 1952, Ph.D. in Biophysics, 1954. Assoc. U. Iowa, Iowa City, 1954-56, asst. prof. physiology and biophysics, 1956-63, assoc. prof. physiology and biophysics, 1963-71, prof. physiology and biophysics, 1971—; cons. for biol. simulation of weightlessness U.S. Air Force, 1964; vis. scientist Mayo Found., Rochester, Minn., 1966-67. Author: Life into Space: An Introduction to Space Biology, 1966; also chpts., numerous articles, abstracts. Recipient Research Career Devel. award NIH, 1961-66; AEC predoctoral fellow U. Pitts., 1951-53; NIH spl. fellow, 1966-67; grantee NIH, NASA. Mem. Am. Physiol. Soc., The Biophys. Soc. (charter), Aerospace Med. Assn., Iowa Acad. Sci. (chmn. physiology sect. 1971-72, 83-84, 96-97, co-chmn. 1982-83, 95-96), Soc. Exptl. Biology and Medicine, Am. Soc. Biomechanics (founding), Aerospace Physiologist Soc., Iowa Physiol. Soc. (pres. 1996-97). Presbyterian. Achievements include the establishment of chronic centrifugation as an approach for investigating gravity's role as a biological determinant. Home: 702 W Park Rd Iowa City IA 52246-2425 Office: U Iowa BSB Iowa City IA 52242

WUNDERLICH, ALFRED LEON, artist, art educator; b. Salem, Oreg., June 26, 1939; s. Joseph Anthony and Anna Margaret (Meyer) W.; children: Annelise, Jonathan Resor. Cert., Cooper Union, 1961; B.F.A., Yale U., 1962, M.F.A., 1968. Dir. visual studies program Hopkins Ctr., Dartmouth Coll., Hanover, N.H., 1965-66; asst. prof. art Hopkins Ctr., Darmouth Coll., Hanover, N.H., 1966-74; assoc. prof. R.I. Sch. of Design, Providence, 1983-94; prof. R.I. Sch. of Design, Providence, 1994—; adj. lectr. Hunter Coll. CUNY, 1973, adj. prof., vis. artist Pahlavi U., Shiraz Iran, 1978, vis. artist U. Edinburgh, Scotland, Edinburgh Internat. Arts Festival, 1973, Kansas City Art Inst., Art Inst. Chgo., Ohio State U., 1986, Carnegie Mellon U., 1987, Moscow State U., 1991, Ariz. State U., 1995; fine arts advisor Inst. for Internat. Edn.; mem. U.S. Art in Space team, met with Soviet Artists Union team, Moscow, 1990; owner, artistic dir. GAS-523 project to fly aboard NASA Space Shuttle, 1997. One-man shows Dartmouth Coll., 1969, Kyoto, Japan, 1969, Pahlavi U., 1978, Kwanghow Mus., Canton, China, 1979, Chang-tu Mus., Szechwan, China, 1978, MIT, 1981, Swarthmore Coll., 1985, Knoerdler Gallery, N.Y.C., 1995, 97; group exhbns. Harvard U. 1995, MIT 1996, also numerous other group exhbns.; represented in permanent collections Mus. Modern Art, N.Y.C., Art Inst. Chgo., Yale U. Art Gallery, Nat. Gallery Scotland, 1st Nat. Bank Boston, Dartmouth Coll., Smithsonian-Cooper Hewitt Mus., Stanford U. Art Mus., also others. Recipient Bocour Color award, 1960; Yale ALumni fellow, 1962-63; Yaddo fellow, 1973; Dartmouth Faculty fellow, 1968; Fulbright grantee to India, 1963-64; Dartmouth Coll. research grantee, 1970-72; SUNY research grantee, 1983. Home: 151 Pratt St Providence RI 02906-1412 Office: RISD 2 College St Providence RI 02903-2717

WUNDERLICH, BERNHARD, physical chemistry educator; b. Brandenburg, Germany, May 28, 1931; came to U.S., 1954, naturalized, 1960; s. Richard O. and Johanne (Wohlgefahrt) W.; m. Adelheid Felix, Dec. 28, 1953; children: Caryn Cornelia, Brent Bernhard. Student, Humboldt U., Berlin, Germany, 1949-53, Goethe U., Frankfurt, Germany, 1953-54, Hastings Coll., 1954-55; Ph.D., Northwestern U., 1957. Instr. chemistry Northwestern U., Evanston, Ill., 1957-58; instr. chemistry Cornell U., Ithaca, N.Y., 1958-60, asst. prof., 1960-63; assoc. prof. phys. chemistry Rensselaer Poly. Inst., Troy, N.Y., 1963-65, prof. phys. chemistry, 1965-88, prof. emeritus, 1988—; prof. chemistry U. Tenn., Knoxville, 1988—; Disting. scientist div. chemistry Oak Ridge Nat. Lab., 1988—; cons. E.I. duPont de Nemours Co., 1963-88; dir. Lab. for Advanced Thermal Analysis; rsch. in solid state of linear high polymers. Author: Macromolecular Physics, Vol. 1, 1973, Vol. 2, 1976, Vol. 3, 1980, Thermal Analysis, 1990; author computer and audio courses on Crystals of Linear Macromolecules and Thermal Analysis; contbr. over 450 articles to profl. jours.; mem. editl. bd. Chemistry, 1965-68, Makromolekulare Chemie, Jour. Thermal Analysis; mem. adv. bd. Jour. Polymer Sci., Macromolecules, 1984-88, Polymers for Advanced Tech., Macromolecular Sci., Phys. Recipient Humboldt award, 1987-88, award for applied chem. thermodynamics Swiss Soc. for Thermal Analysis and Calorimetry, 1993, TA Instruments award Internat. Conf. Thermal Analysis and Calorimetry, 1996. Fellow Am. Phys. Soc., N.Am., Thermal Analysis Soc. (Mettler award in thermal analysis 1971); mem. Am. Chem. Soc. Home: 200 Baltusrol Dr Knoxville TN 37922-3707 Office: U Tenn Dept Chemistry Knoxville TN 37996

WUNDERLICH, RENNER, film producer, cinematographer; b. St. Louis, May 5, 1947; s. Harry Joseph and Erlynne (Renner) W.; m. Margaret Lazarus; children: Michael, Matthew. BA, Boston Coll., 1968. Prodr., dir., cinematographer, editor Cambridge (Mass.) Documentary Films, 1974—; freelance videographer and sound tech. NBC, ABC, CBS, PBS, BBC and ind. prodrs., 1984—. Prodr., dir., cinematographer, editor: (TV show) Mr. Goodman, 1972-73, (documentaries) Taking Our Bodies Back, 1974, Rape Culture, 1975, Eugene Debs and the American Movement, 1977, Killing Us Softly, 1978, Pink Triangles, 1982, Calling the Shots, 1982, 91, The Last Empire, 1986, Still Killing Us Softly, 1987, Hazardous Inheritance, 1991, Not Just a Job, 1991, Life's Work, 1993, Defending Our Lives, 1993 (Academy Award, Best Documentary Short Subject 1994). Recipient Silver Hugo award Chgo. Internat. Film Festival, 1972, Red Ribbon award Am. Film and Video Festival, 1983, 92, 1st Pl. award Nat. Coun. Family Rels. Film and Video Festival, 1984, 93, Blue Ribbon award Am. Film and Video Festival, 1986, 87, 91, Bronze Apple award Nat. Ednl. Film and Video Festival, 1988, 1st Pl. award Chicagoland Ednl. Film and Video Festival, 1988; Chris award Columbus Internat. Film Festival, PASS award Nat. Coun. Crime and Delinquency, 1993, Silver Apple award Nat. Ednl. Film and Video Festival, 1991, Cert. of Merit, AAAS, 1991, Silver placque Chgo. Internat. Film Festival, 1993, Outstanding Film of Yr. award New England Film and Video Festival, 1993, Exceptional Merit in Media award Nat. Women's Polit. Caucus, 1994. Mem. Acad. Motion Picture Arts and Scis. Avocation: electric cars. Office: Cambridge Documentary Films PO Box 385 Cambridge MA 02139*

WUNDERMAN, JAN DARCOURT, artist; b. Winipeg, Man., Can., Jan. 22, 1921; d. Rene Paul and Georgette Marie (Guionet) Darcourt; m. Frank Joseph Malina, 1938 (div. 1945); m. Lester Wunderman (div. 1967); children: Marc, Geroge, Karen Renee. BFA, Otis Art Inst., L.A., 1942. One man show Easthampton Guild Hall, L.I., 1977, Denise Bibro Fina Art Gallery, N.Y.C., 1997; two man show Denise Bibro Fine ARt Gallery, 1996; represented in numerous permanent pub., corp. and pvt. collections including Zimmerli Mus., Nat. Assn. of Women Artists, Rutgers U., 1994. Recipient Ohashi award Pan Pacific Exhbn., Tokyo and Osaka, 1962, Emily Lowe award 1965, J.J. Akston Found. prize, 1965, Canaday Meml. prize, 1979, Marian De Solo Mendes prize, 1981, Charles Horman Meml. prize, 1983, Amelia Peabody award Nat. Assn. Women, 1991, Grumbacher Gold medal of honor, 1992, Doris Kreindler award 1992. Mem. Nat. Assn. Women Artists (medal of honor 1966, Marcia Brady Tucker award 1965, E. Holzinger prize 1966, Jane C. Stanley prize 1977, Marge Greenblatt award 1990, Amelia Peabody award 1991, Solveig Stomsoe Palmer prize 1997), Am. Soc. Contemporary Artists (corr. sec. 1977-78, Bocour award 1980, Elizabeth Erlanger Meml. award 1990, Kreindler award 1992), Contemporary Artists Guild (rep. by Denise Bibro Fine Art N.Y.C.). Avocations: history, travel. Studio: 41 Union Sq W Rm 516 New York NY 10003-3208

WUNNICKE, BROOKE, lawyer; b. Dallas, May 9, 1918; d. Rudolph von Falkenstein and Lulu Lenore Brooke; m. James M. Wunnicke, Apr. 11, 1940; (dec. 1977); 1 child, Diane B. BA, Stanford U., 1939; JD, U. Colo., 1945. Bar: Wyo. 1946, U.S. Dist. Cty. Wyo. 1947, U.S. Supreme Ct. 1958, Colo. 1969. Pvt. practice law, 1946-56; ptnr. Williams & Wunnicke, Cheyenne, Wyo., 1956-69; of counsel Calkins, Kramer, Grimshaw & Harring, Denver, 1969-73; chief appellate dep. atty. Dist. Atty's Office, Denver, 1973-86; of counsel Hall & Evans L.L.C., Denver, 1986—; adj. prof. law U. Denver Coll. of Law, 1978—; lectr. Internat. Practicum Inst. Denver, 1978—; panelist Judicial Resolutions. Author: Ethics Compliance for Business Lawyers, 1987; co-author: Standby Letters of Credit, 1989, supplement, 1995, Corporate Financial Risk Management, 1992, Legal Opinion Letters Formbook, 1994, UCP 500 and Standby Letters of Credit-Special Report, 1994, Standby and Commercial Letters of Credit, 1996; columnist Letters of Credit Report; contbr. articles to profl. jours. Pres. Laramie County Bar Assn., Cheyenne, Wy., 1967-68; Dir. Cheyenne C. of C., Cheyenne, Wy., 1965-68. Recipient awards for Outstanding Svc., Colo. Dist. Attys. Coun., 1979, 82, 86, Disting. Alumni award U. Colo. Sch. of Law, 1986, 93, Lathrop Trailblazer award Colo. Women's Bar Assn., 1992, William Lee Knous award U. Colo., 1997, Eleanor P. Williams award disting. svc. in legal profession, 1997. Fellow Colo. Bar Found. (hon.); mem. ABA, Wyo. State Bar, Denver Bar Assn. (life; trustee 1977-80), Colo. Bar Assn. (life), Am. Arbitration Assn. (nat. panel, regional panel large complex cases), William E. Doyle Inn of Ct. (hon.), Order of Coif, Phi Beta Kappa. Republican. Episcopalian. Avocations: reading, writing, teaching, lecturing. Office: Hall & Evans L L C 1200 17th St Denver CO 80202-5835

WUNSCH, BONNIE RUBENSTEIN, fraternal organization executive; b. Shreveport, La., Feb. 7, 1961; d. David Ochs and Marilyn Sue (Goldstein) Rubenstein; m. Alan V. Wunsch. BBA, Emory U., Atlanta, 1983. Office adminstr. Sanger-Harris, Dallas, 1983-85; asst. buyer Sanger-Harris, 1985-87, Foley's, Houston, 1987-88; exec. dir. Alpha Epsilon Phi Sorority, Stamford, Conn., 1988—; province dir., pledge programming chmn. Alpha Epsilon Phi Sorority, 1985-87, nat. v.p. collegiate chpts., 1987-88; dir. devel. Alpha Epsilon Phi Found., 1992—; mem. Fraternity Ins. Purchasing Group, 1991—, bd. dirs., 1994—. Contbr. articles to profl. jours. Tchr. religious sch. Temple Israel, Columbus, 1989-95, pres. young adults congregation, 1991-93, bd. dirs., 1990-93, bd. dirs. sisterhood, 1991-95, also mem. dues revision com. and recruitment com., search com., ritual com. Mem. Assn. Frat. Advisors, Ctrl. Office Execs. Assn. (sec. 1993-94), Frat. Execs. Assn. (bus. mgr. 1993-94), Nat. Coun. Jewish Women (exec. bd. 1996—), Order of Omega, Women's Am. ORT (activities chmn. 1986-87). Republican. Jewish. Avocations: needlework, reading, cooking, travel. Home: 1 E Hayestown Rd Unit 67 Danbury CT 06811-2515 Office: Alpha Epsilon Phi 111 Prospect St # 2 Stamford CT 06901-1208

WUNSCH, CARL ISAAC, oceanographer, educator; b. Bklyn., May 5, 1941; s. Harry and Helen (Gellis) W.; m. Marjory Markel, June 6, 1970; children—Jared, Hannah. S.B., MIT, 1962, Ph.D., 1967. Asst. prof. phys. oceanography MIT, Cambridge, 1967-70; assoc. prof. MIT, 1970-75, prof., 1975-76, Cecil and Ida Green prof., 1976—, Sec. of Navy rsch. prof., 1985-89, head dept. earth and planetary scis., 1977-81; sr. vis. fellow U. Cambridge, Eng., 1969, 74-75, 81-82; sr. vis. scientist Geophys. Fluid Dynamics Lab., Princeton, 1993-94; vis. rschr. CNES/CNRS, Toulouse, France, 1994; cons. NSF, NAS, JPL. Author: The Ocean Circulation Inverse Problem, 1996; co-author: Ocean Acoustic Tomography, 1995; assoc. editor Jour. Phys. Oceanography, 1977-80, Revs. of Geophysics and Space Physics, 1981-85; co-editor: Evolution of Physical Oceanography, 1981; editor Cambridge U. Press Monographs on Mechanics and Applied Mathematics, 1984-88; contbr. articles to profl. jours. Recipient Tex. Instruments Found. Founders prize, 1975, Huntsman prize Bedford Inst. Oceanography and Govt. of N.S., Can., 1988, Pub. Svc. medal NASA, 1993, Fulbright sr. scholar, 1981-82; Guggenheim fellow, 1981-82. Fellow Am. Geophys. Union (James R. Macelwane award 1971, Maurice Ewing medal 1990), Am. Meterol. Soc., Royal Astron. Soc., Am. Acad. Arts and Scis.; mem. NAS (chmn. bd. ocean studies 1991-94), Soc. Indsl. and Applied Math., Oceanography Soc. Home: 78 Washington Ave Cambridge MA 02140-2708 Office: Dept Earth Atmospheric & Planetary Scis MIT Cambridge MA 02139

WUNSCH, JAMES STEVENSON, political science educator; b. Detroit, Sept. 27, 1946; s. Richard Ellis and Jane Rolston (Stevenson) W.; m. Lillian C. Richards, Mar. 29, 1969 (div. Feb. 1983), 1 child, Kathryn; m. Mary Gayle Gundlach, Aug. 19, 1983; children: Hallie, Hannah. BA, Duke U., 1968; MA, Ind. U., 1971, PhD, 1974. Rsch. fellow U. Ghana, Accra, 1971-72; asst. prof. Creighton U., Omaha, 1974-78, assoc. prof., 1978-86, prof. polit. sci., 1986—, chmn. dept., 1983-93, 96—; social sci. analyst and cons., Ghana, Liberia, Kenya, Sudan, Thailand, Philippines, USAID, Washington, 1978-80; vis. assoc. prof. Ind. U., Bloomington, 1985-86; sr. project mgr. Assocs. in Rural Devel., Burlington, Vt., 1987-88, cons., Bangladesh, Zambia, Nigeria, South Africa, Swaziland, Botswana, 1985—; USIA Disting. lectr., South Africa, 1993. Author: The Failure of the Centralized State, 1990, (monograph) Rural Development, Decentralization and Administrative Reform, 1988; contbr. articles to profl. jours., chpts. to books. Bd. dirs. Omaha Symphony Chorus, 1977-78, Nebr. Choral Arts Soc., 1982-96, Voices of Omaha, 1982-85, Trinity Cathedral, Omaha, 1980-83; participant Leadership Omaha, 1982-83; mem. Omaha Com. Fgn. Rels., 1975-95; mem. govt. affairs com. Greater Omaha C. of C., 1980-85; mem. issues and interests com. Nebr. Rep. party, 1984-88. Recipient R.F. Kennedy Quality Tchg. award Creighton U., 1985, Burlington No. award, 1992, Dean's award for excellence in tchg., 1994; rsch. award NSF, NEH, USAID, USIA; Fulbright-Hays fellow in Ghana, 1971-72, Internat. Affairs fellow N.Y. Coun. Fgn. Rels., 1978-79. Mem. ASPA, Am. Polit. Sci. Assn., Midwest Polit. Sci. Assn., African Studies Assn., Internat. Studies Assn., Phi Beta Kappa, Pi Sigma Alpha, Phi Beta Delta. Republican. Episcopalian. Avocations: vocal music, camping, cross-country skiing. Home: 1631 N 53rd St Omaha NE 68104-4947 Office: Creighton U Dept Polit Sci 30th And California Omaha NE 68178

WUNSCH, KATHRYN SUTHERLAND, lawyer; b. Tipton, Mo., Jan. 30, 1935; d. Lewis Benjamin and Norene Marie (Wolf) Sutherland; m. Charles Martin Wunsch, Dec. 22, 1956 (div. May 1988); children: Debra Kay, Laura Ellen. AB, Ind. U., 1958, JD summa cum laude, 1977; postgrad., Stanford (Calif.) U., 1977. Bar: Calif. 1977, U.S. Dist. Ct. (no. dist.) Calif. 1977. Founder Wunsch and George, San Francisco, 1989-93, Kathryn Wunsch and Assoc. Counsel, San Francisco, 1993—. Articles editor Ind. U. Law Rev., 1975-76. Mem. ABA, Calif. Bar Assn. (bus. law prof., real property and trusts sect.), San Mateo County Bar Assn., Nat. Assn. Women Bus. Owners (pres. San Francisco chpt. 1992-93), San Francisco Opera Guild, City Club, Phi Beta Kappa (v.p. no. calif. 1995—), Psi Chi. Republican. Avocations: collecting fine art and antiques, theater, opera, gardening, hiking. Office: Ste 3320 701 Welch Rd Bldg 3320 Palo Alto CA 94304-1705

WUNTCH, PHILIP SAMUELS, journalist, film critic; b. Austin, Tex., Aug. 2, 1945; s. David and Lillian (Samuels) W.; m. Mimi West, Apr. 27, 1986. BA in Journalism, So. Meth. U., 1968. Journalist, entertainment writer Dallas Times Herald, 1968-69; entertainment writer Dallas Morning News, 1969-74, film critic, 1974—. Contbr. articles to World Book Year Book, 1981—. Avocation: constant reading. Office: Dallas Morning News PO Box 655237 Dallas TX 75265-5237

WUORINEN, CHARLES PETER, composer; b. N.Y.C., June 9, 1938; s. John Henry and Alfhild (Kalijarvi) W. BA, Columbia U., 1961, MA, 1963; DMus (hon.), Jersey City State Coll., 1971. Lectr. Columbia U., 1964-65, instr., 1965-69, asst. prof., 1969-71, co-dir. Group Contemporary Music, 1962—; vis. lectr. Princeton U., 1967-68, New Eng. Conservatory, 1968-71, Yale U., 1983; adj. lectr. U. South Fla., 1971-72; faculty Manhattan Sch. Music, 1972-79, U. So. Calif., 1981; artistic dir., chmn. Am. Composers Orch., 1973-87; composer-in-residence Ojai Festival, 1975, Santa Fe Chamber Music Festival, 1993; San Francisco Symphony, 1984-89; condr. Cleve. Orch., 1976, Finnish Radio Orch., 1979, Helsinki Philharm., 1979; disting. prof. Rutgers U., 1984—; vis. prof. SUNY, Buffalo, 1989-94, NYU, 1990. Author: Simple Composition; mem. editorial bd. Perspectives of New Music; bd. mem. Composers Recs. Inc., 1962-89; composer numerous works including Music for Orchestra, 1956, Be Mery All That Be Present, mixed chorus, 1957, Concert for Four Trombones, 1960, Madrigale Spirituale, 1960, Turetzky Pieces, 1960, Evolutio: organ, 1961, Evolution Transcripta for chamber orch., 1961, Tiento Sobre Cabezon, 1961, Concert for Double Bass Alone, 1961, Trio No. 1 for flute, cello and piano, 1961, Invention for percussion quintet, 1962, Octet, 1962, Duuiensela for cello and piano, 1962, Bearbeitungen über das Glogauer Liederbuch, 1962, The Prayer of Jonah, 1962, 2d Flute Trio: Piece for Stefan Wolpe, 1962, Chamber Concerto for cello and 10 players, 1963, Piano Variations, 1963, Flute Variations, 1963, Composition for violin and 10 instruments, 1964, Chamber Concerto for flute and 10 players, 1964, Orchestral and Electronic Exchanges, 1965, Composition for oboe and piano, 1965, Chamber Concerto for oboe and 10 players, 1965, Super Salutem for male voices and instruments, 1964, Piano Concerto, 1966, The Bells for carillon, 1966, Bicinium, 2 oboes, 1966, Janissary Music for 1 percussionist, 1966, Harpsichord Divisions, 1966, Making Ends Meet for piano four-hands, 1966, John Bull: Salve Regina Versus Septem, 1966, Duo for violin and piano, 1967, The Politics of Harmony: A Masque, 1967, String Trio, 1968, Flute Variations II, 1968, Time's Encomium (electronic), 1969, Adapting to the Times for cello and piano, 1969, The Long and the Short for violin, 1969, Contrafactum for orch., 1969, Nature's Concord trumpet and piano, 1969, Piano Sonata, 1969, Ringing Changes for percussion, 1970, A Song, 1970, Tuba Concerto, 1970, A Message to Denmark Hill, 1970, Cello Variations, 1970, String Quartet, 1971, Canzona for 12 instruments, 1971, Grand Bamboula for string orch., 1971, Amplified Violin Concerto, 1972, Harp Variations, 1972, Bassoon Variations, 1972, Violin Variations, 1972, On Alligators for 8 instruments, 1972, Speculum Speculi for 6 players, 1972, Third Trio for flute, cello and piano, 1973, 12 Short Pieces for piano, 1973, Grand Union for cello and drums, 1973, Arabia Felix for 6 Instruments, 1973, Second Piano Concerto, 1974, Fantasia for violin and piano, 1974, Reliquary for Igor Stravinsky for orch., 1975, The W. of Babylon (opera), 1975, TASHI, 1975, Hyperion for 12 instruments, 1975, Cello Variations 2, 1975, 2d Piano Sonata, 1976, Percussion Symphony, 1976, The Winds, 1977, Fast Fantasy for cello and piano, 1977, Archangel for trombone and string quartet, 1977, Six Pieces for violin and piano, 1977, Six Songs for two voices, Wind Quintet, Self Similar Waltz for piano, Ancestors for chamber ensemble, 1978, Two-Part Symphony, 1978, Archaeopteryx for bass trombone and chamber ensemble, 1978, The Magic Art, A Masque for chamber orch, 1979, Fortune for 4 instruments, 1979, 2d String Quartet, 1979, The Celestial Sphere for chorus and orch., 1979, Psalm 39 for baritone and guitar, 1979, Percussion Duo, 1979, Joan's for 5 instruments, 1979, Blue Bamboula for piano, 1980, Capriccio for piano, 1981, Horn Trio, 1981, Short Suite for orch., 1981, Trio for bass instruments, 1981, New York Notes for 6 players, 1982, Mass, 1982, Divertimento for alto sax and piano, 1982, Divertimento for string quartet, 1982, Spinoff for violin, double bass and congas, 1983, Trio for violin, cello and piano, 1983, Third Piano Concerto, 1983, Rhapsody for violin and orch., 1984, Concertino, 1984, Crossfire for orch., 1984, Movers and Shakers for orch., 1984, Bamboula Squared for orch. and computer-generated sound, 1984, Natural Fantasy for organ, 1985, Horn Trio Continued, 1985, Trombone Trio, 1985, Prelude to Kullervo for tuba and orch., 1985, Double Solo for Horn Trio, 1985, Fanfare for the Houston Symphony, 1986, The Golden Dance for orch., 1986, Third Piano Sonata, 1986, Third String Quartet, 1987, Galliard for chamber orch., 1987, Bamboula Beach for orch., 1987, FIVE: Concerto for amplified cello and orch., 1987, Sonata for violin and piano, 1988, Bagatelle for piano, 1988, Ave Christe for piano, 1988, Another Happy Birthday for orch., 1988, Machault Mon Chou for orch., 1988, String Sextet, 1989, Twang for soprano and piano, 1989, A Solis Ortu for chorus, 1989, Genesis for chorus and orch., 1989, Astra for orch., 1990, Delight of the Muses for orch., 1991, Missa Brevis, 1991, A Winter's Tale for Soprano and Six Instruments, 1992, Microsymphony, 1992, Missa Renovata for Chorus and Orch., 1992, Saxophone Quartet, 1992, Concerto for Saxophone Quartet and Orch., 1993, The Mission of Virgil for orch., 1993, Percussion Quartet, 1994, Piano Quintet, 1994, Christes Crosse, 1994, Lightenings VIII, 1994, Guitar Variations, 1994, Sonata for Guitar and Piano, 1995, The Great Procession, 1995, Katz Fugue for piano, 1995, Windfall for band, 1994, Schoenberg Op. 31 Variations, (remade for two pianos, 1996), The River of Light (for string orch. and percussion, 1996), Epithalamium (for two trumpets, 1997). Recipient Philharmonic Young Composers award, 1954; Bennington Composers Conf. scholar, 1956-60; Bearns prize, 1958-59, 61; MacDowell Colony fellow, 1958; Alice M. Ditson fellow, 1959; Arthur Rose teaching fellow, 1960; Broadcast Music-Student Composers award, 1959, 61, 62, 63; Lili Boulanger Meml. award, 1963; Festival fellow Santa Fe Opera, 1962; Festival fellow World's Fair Music and Sound, 1962; commd. by Koussevitzky Found., 1964, Berkshire Music Center, 1963, Fromm Found., 1963-71, Ford Found., 1962, Orch. of Am., 1958, Columbia U., 1956, Washington and Lee U., 1964, Fine Arts Quartet, 1969, Naumberg Found., 1971, U. South Fla., 1972, Nat. Opera Inst., 1973, Light Fantastic Players, 1973, N.Y. State Council on the Arts, 1974, N.Y. Philharm., 1974, Balt. Chamber Music Soc., 1974, Buffalo Philharm., 1974, Ojai Festival, 1974, Contemporary Chamber Ensemble, 1974, TASHI, 1974, Beethoven Festival, Bonn, 1978, Albany Symphony, 1981, San Francisco Symphony, 1984, 86, 88, 89, Cleve. Orch., 1984, Balt. Symphony, 1984, Houston Symphony, 1986, N.Y.C. Ballet, 1987, 90, Libr. of Congress, 1988, New World Symphony, 1987, Chamber Music Soc. Lincoln Ctr., 1989, 92, Am./Soviet Youth Orch., 1990, Phila. Orch., 1992, Beethorenhalle Orch., Bonn Mönchengladbach and Ludwig Forum, Germany; grantee Nat. Inst. Arts and Letters, 1967, Nat. Endowment Arts, 1974, 76; Guggenheim fellow, 1968, 72; Ingraham Merrill fellow, 1972, Rockefeller Found. fellow, 1979, 80, 81, John D. and Catherine T. MacArthur fellow, 1986-91; recipient Pulitzer prize, 1970, Brandeis U. creative arts award, 1970, Creative Artists Pub. Svc. award, 1976; Arts and Letters award Finlandia Found., 1976, Koussevitzky Internat. Rec. award, 1970, 72. Mem. AAAS, AAAL, Am. Soc. Univ. Composers, Am. Composers Alliance (bd. dirs.), Am. Music Ctr. (bd. dirs.), Internat. Soc. Contemporary Music (bd. dirs.), Am. Acad. Arts and Scis., Phi Beta Kappa. Office: care Howard Stokar Mgmt 870 W End Ave New York NY 10025-4948

WURLITZER, FRED PABST, physician, surgeon; b. San Francisco, Dec. 26, 1937; s. Raimund Billings and Pauline (Pabst) W.; m. Lee Jones Wurlitzer (div. Jan. 1991); children: Ricky, Arnisha, Susan, Elena; m. Ann Marie Allan, June 2, 1992; children: Melanie, Heather, Gregory. BA, Stanford U., 1960; MD, U. Cin., 1965; MBA, Golden Gate U., 1985. Diplomate Am. Bd. Gen. Surgery. Intern, resident Highland-Almeda County Hosp., 1965-67; resident in surgery UCLA Sch. Medicine/VA Hosp., 1967-60; fellow in surg. oncology U. Tex./M.D. Anderson Hosp., Houston, 1970-71; instr. surgery U. So. Calif., Los Angeles, 1971-73; physician Pasadena (Calif.) Tumor Inst., 1971-73, San Mateo (Calif.) Med. Clinic, 1973-77; physician in pvt. practice Burlingame, Calif., 1977-84; vol. surgeon various hosps., 1989-93; pres. Wurlitzer Properties, Burlingame, 1976—. Contbr. articles to profl. jours. Comdr. USPHS, 1992—. Recipient Acknowledgement of Outstanding Svc. award Am. Cancer Soc., 1974, Disting. Svc. award Health Vols. Overseas, 1994. Fellow ACS; mem. AMA, Soc. Head and Neck Surgeons, Southwestern Surg. Congress, So. Med. Assn. Unitarian. Avocations: skiing, tennis. Home: 18289 Briarswood Kemp TX 75143

WURMAN, RICHARD SAUL, architect; b. Phila., Mar. 26, 1935; s. Morris Louis and Fannie (Pelson) W.; m. Gloria Nagy; children: Joshua, Reven, Vanessa, Anthony. BArch (T.P. Chandler fellow), U. Pa., MArch with highest honors; DFA (hon.), U. of the Arts, 1994; LHD (hon.), Art Ctr College of Design, 1995. Mem. faculty N.C. State U., Raleigh, 1962-64, 77, Washington U., St. Louis, 1965, Princeton U., 1965-67, Cambridge (Eng.) U., 1967-68, N.Y.C. program Cornell U., 1968-70, CCNY, 1968-70, UCLA, 1976, U. So. Calif., 1976; prof. architecture, dean Sch. Environ. Design, Calif. State Poly. U., Pomona; chmn. dept. Otis/Parsons, Los Angeles; with Archtl. Office Louis I. Kahn, London, 1960-62; chmn. dept. environ. design Otis Parsons Calif.; crwnding dir. Group Environ. Edn., 1968; bd. dirs. Internat. Design Conf., Aspen, Colo., 1970—, chmn., 1972; co-chmn. 1st Fed. Design Assembly, 1973; trustee Center Bldg. Edn. Programs, 1976—; dep. dir. Phila. Office Housing and Community Devel., 1977; bd. dirs., chmn., creative dir. TED Confs.-Tech. Entertainment Design Conf., 1984—, Kobe, Japan, 1992, Monterey, Calif., 1994—, Med. Comm. Conf., Charlestown, S.C., 1995; pres. Access Press Ltd., The Understanding Bus., 1981-91; designer exhbns., cons. in field; vis. scholar MIT, 1993—, RISD, 1995—. Author 53 books including The Notebooks and Drawings of Louis I. Kahn, The Nature of Recreation, Urban Atlas, Man Made Philadelphia, Aspen Visible, Our Man Made Environment; also author 27 vols. ACCESS travel and info. guidebook series; editor: What Will Be Has Alway Been: The Words of Louis I. Kahn, Information Anxiety, Follow the Yellow Brick Road, The Wall Street Journal Guide to Understanding Money and Markets, Fortune Guide to Understanding Personal finance, 1992, USAtlas, 1990, N, The Newport Guide, 1995, Information Architects, 1996, C, The Charleston Guide, 1997; DE contbr. articles to profl. jours.; retrospective exhbn. AXIS Design Gallery, Tokyo, 1991. Recipient Thornton Oakley medal, 1954, Arthur Spayd Brookes Gold medal, 1958, Kevin Lynch award MIT, 1991, Stars of Design award and Chrysler award for innovation in design Pacific Design Ctr., 1996, Chrysler award for Innovation in Design, 1996; Graham fellow, 1966, 76; T.P. Chandler fellow, 1968; fellow Guggenheim Found., 1969; fellow Rockefeller Bros. Fund, 1972; fellow Nat. Endowment Arts, 1970, 73, 74, 76, 79-80; fellow World Econ. Forum, Davos, Switzerland, 1994—; grantee Fels Found., 1970; grantee Ednl. Facilities Lab., 1972, 74; grantee Rohm & Haas Co., 1976. Fellow AIA (medal 1958); mem. Am.

Inst. Graphic Artists (v.p., bd. dirs. 1985), Alliance Graphique Internat. Address: The Orchard 180 Narragansett Ave Newport RI 02840-6929

WURMFELD, SANFORD, artist, educator; b. N.Y.C., Dec. 6, 1942; s. Charles Jacob and Esther (Witzling) W.; m. Rella Stuart-Hunt, Dec. 11, 1971; children: Jeremy Philip, Treva. BA in Art with honors, Dartmouth Coll., 1964; ind. study, Rome, 1964-65. Lectr. Hunter Coll., N.Y.C., 1967-72, asst. prof., 1972-77, assoc. prof., 1977-80, chmn. dept. art, 1978—, prof. art, 1980—; vis. artist lectr. Calif. State Coll., Hayward, Cooper Union, N.Y., Bard Coll., Arondale-on-Hudson, N.Y., Livingston Coll., New Brunswick, N.J., 1973, SUNY, Fredonia, 1971, Drexel U., Phila., 1970, Whitney Mus., 1982, Met. Mus. Art, 1987, Princeton U., 1990, The Slade Sch. U. Coll., London, 1991, Chelsea Coll. Art, London, 1991, Whitney Mus., 1992, Hochschule der Kurst, Berlin, 1995, Simon Fraser U., Vancouver, 1996, U. Victoria, B.C., 1996, Acad. Minerva, Netherlands, Glasgow (Scotland) Sch. of Art, 1997. One man shows include Susan Caldwell Gallery, Inc., N.Y., 1978, Bard Coll. Invitational Exhibit, 1977, Susan Caldwell Gallery, 1976-77, Galarie Denise Rene, 1974, Rockefeller Meml. Gallery, Fredonia, N.Y., 1971, Tibor de Nagy Gallery, 1968, Bryant Park, N.Y., Fischbach Gallery, 1969; group shows include Mus. Modern Art, N.Y., 1968, Grank Palais, Paris, 1968, Kunsthaus, Zurich, 1968, Tate Gallery, London, 1968, Ft. Worth Art Ctr., 1969, Galerie de Gestlo, Kunstfair, Basel Switzerland, 1970, 72, Columbia Film Festival, 1973, Galerie Denise Rene, 1974, Hopkins Ctr. Galleries, 1974, Lehigh U., 1976, Susan Caldwell Gallery, 1977-79, Toni Birckhard Gallery, Cin., 1980, Carnegie Internat., 1983, Shangha Exhbn. Hall Shanghai, China, 1986, Long Beach Mus. of Art, Calif., 1989, William Paterson Coll. of N.J., 1990, Hallwells Contemporary Arts Ctr., Buffalo, 1991, Louis Stern Fine Arts, L.A., 1995, Andre Zarre Gallery, N.Y., 1996, others; represented in permanent collections at Met. Mus. Art., N.Y., Guggenheim Mus., N.Y., SUNY, Fredonia, Cen. Trust Co., Cin., Am. Telephone and Telegraph, N.Y., Baxter Travenol Labs., Deerfield, Ill., Gen. Electric Corp., Fairfield, Conn., Sprengler Mus., Hanover, Fed. Republic of Germany, City of Hannover, Fed. Republic of Germany, Shreve, Lamb, & Harmon Corp., N.Y., Silkscreeners Guild, W. Ger., Warner Nat. Corp., Cin., U. N.C., William Hayes Ackland Meml. Art Ctr., Chapel Hill, others; contbr. articles to profl. jours. Recipient Ames award Dartmouth Coll., 1964; fellow Guggenheim Found., 1974, Nat. Endowments for the Arts Individual Artist's, 1987-88; CUNY faculty rsch. grantee. Home: 18 Warren St New York NY 10007-1066 Office: Hunter Coll Dept Art 695 Park Ave New York NY 10021-5024

WURMSER, LEON, psychiatry educator; b. Jan. 31, 1931; m. Zdenka Koudela; 3 children. MD, U. Zurich, Basel, Switzerland, 1955; student in Psychiatric Tng., U. Basel, 1957-61; student in Psychoanalytic Tng., Balt.-D.C. Inst., 1966-75. Various adminstrv., teaching and clin. positions, Sheppard Pratt, Balt., 1962-65, Sinai Hosp., Balt., 1966-69, Johns Hopkins U. Hosp., Balt., 1969-71, U. Md., Balt., 1971-83; clin. prof. Psychiatry U. W.Va., Morgantown, from 1983; prof. psychiatry, dir. alcohol and drug abuse program U. Md., 1977-83. Author: Raubmörder and Rauber Kriminalistik, 1959, The Mask of Shame, 1981, The Hidden Dimension, 1978, Flucht vor dem Gewissen, 1987, Die Zerbrochene Wirklichkeit, 1988, Die Maske der Scham, 1990, Das Ratsel des Masochismus, 1993; editor: (with G. Balis et al) Psychiatric Foundations of Medicine, 1978; mem. editorial bd. Substance Abuse Treatment, Forum der Psychoanalyse, Psychoanalytisches Jahrbuch; contbr. some 300 articles to profl. jours. Recipient Lewis B. Hill award Balt.-D.C. Inst. Psychoanalysis, 1975, award for Pioneering Excellence and Achievement, Am. Mental Health Found., 1979-80, Egnér prize for achievement in anthropol. psychology and philosophy, 1997; named Outstanding Tchr. in Psychiatry, U. Md., 1978-79. Fellow Am. Psychiat. Assn. (life); mem. Swiss Med. Assn., Swiss Psychiat. Assn., Am. Psychoanalytic Assn. (cert.), Czech Psychoanalytic Soc. (hon.). Home: 904 Crestwick Rd Towson MD 21286-3319 Office: 200 E Joppa Rd Towson MD 21286-3150

WÜRSIG, BERND GERHARD, marine biology educator; b. Barsinghausen, Hanover, Fed. Republic of Germany, Nov. 9, 1948; s. Gerhard Paul and Charlotte Annemarie (Yorkowski) W.; m. Melany Anne Carballeira, Nov. 19, 1969; children: Kim, Paul. BS, Ohio State U., 1971; PhD, SUNY, Stony Brook, 1978. Postdoctoral researcher U. Calif., Santa Cruz, 1978-81; prof. Moss Landing (Calif.) Marine Labs., 1981-89; dir. Marine Mammal Lab. Tex. A&M U., Galveston, 1989—; govt. cons. Minerals Mgmt. Service, Washington, 1980—. Contbr. articles to profl. jours.; contbr. seven-part miniseries to TV on lives of dolphins, dolphin problems induced by humans, also Discovery Channel show on Life of B. Würsig; co-author: The Hawaiian Spinner Dolphin, 1994, Whales, Dolphins and Porposes, 1995. Recipient Dean's award for excellence in teaching, 1986, Alban-Heiser award for excellence in Tex. conservation rsch. Zool. Soc. Houston, 1991, Student Body award for most effective tchr. Tex. A&M U., 1994-95. Mem. Marine Mammal Soc. (pres. 1991-93), N.Y. Acad. Scis., Soc. Cryptozoology, Am. Behavior Soc., Am. Mus. Natural History, Soc. Archimedes. Club: Explorers (N.Y.C.) (fellow of research). Avocations: photography, diving, airplane piloting, skiing, hiking. Home: 2304 Dixie Woods Dr Pearland TX 77581-5744 Office: Tex A&M U Marine Mammal Rsch Program 4700 Avenue U Bldg 303 Galveston TX 77551-5923

WURSTER, CHARLES FREDERICK, environmental scientist, educator; b. Phila., Aug. 1, 1930; s. Charles Frederick and Helen B. (Schmittberger) W.; m. Eva M. Tank-Nielsen, Aug. 26, 1970; children: Steven Hadley, Nina F., Erik Frederick. SB, Haverford Coll., 1952; MS, U. Del., 1954; PhD, Stanford U., 1957. Teaching asst. U. Del., 1952-54; research asst. Stanford U., 1954-57; Fulbright fellow Innsbruck, Austria, 1957-58; research chemist Monsanto Research Corp., 1959-62; research assoc. biol. scis. Dartmouth Coll., 1962-65; asst. prof. biol. scis. SUNY, Stony Brook, 1965-70; assoc. prof. environ. scis. Marine Scis. Rsch. Ctr., 1970-94, prof. emeritus, 1994—; vis. prof. Macquarie U., Sydney, Australia, 1988; founding trustee, sec., mem. exec. com. Environ. Def. Fund, Inc., 1967—; mem. adminstr's. pesticide policy adv. com. EPA, 1975-78. Contbr. numerous articles to profl. publs. Fellow AAAS; mem. Defenders of Wildlife (dir. 1975-84, 87-96), Nat. Parks and Conservation Assn. (trustee 1970-79). Research on DDT, PCBs, other chlorinated hydrocarbons, effects on phytoplankton, birds; relationship between environmental sciences and public policy; instrumental in banning several insecticides, including DDT, Dieldrin and Aldrin. Ecol. tourism. Office: SUNY Marine Scis Research Ctr Stony Brook NY 11794-5000

WURSTER, DALE ERWIN, pharmacy educator, university dean emeritus; b. Sparta, Wis., Apr. 10, 1918; s. Edward Emil and Emma Sophia (Steingraeber) W.; m. June Margaret Peterson, June 16, 1944; children: Dale Eric, Susan Gay. BS, U. Wis., 1942, PhD, 1947. With faculty U. Wis. Sch. Pharmacy, 1947-71, prof., 1958-71; prof., dean N.D. State U. Coll. Pharmacy, 1971-72, U. Iowa Coll. Pharmacy, Iowa City, 1972-84, prof., 1972—, interim dean, 1991-92, dean emeritus, 1984—; George B. Kaufman Meml. lectr. Ohio State U., 1968; cons. in field; phys. sci. adminstr. U.S. Navy, 1960-63; sci. adv. Wis. Alumni Rsch. Found., 1968-72; mem. revision com. U.S. Pharmacopoeia, 1961-70, pharmacy rev. com. USPHS, 1966-72. Contbr. articles to profl. jours., chpts. to books; patentee in field. With USNR, 1944-46. Recipient Superior Achievement citation Navy Dept., 1964, merit citation U. Wis., 1976; named Hancher Finkbine Medallion Prof. U. Iowa, 1984; recipient Disting. Alumni award U. Wis. Sch. Pharmacy, 1984. Fellow Am. Assn. Pharm. Scientists (founder, sponsor Dale E. Wurster Rsch. award 1990—, Disting. Pharm. Sci. award 1991); mem. Am. Assn. Colls. Pharmacy (exec. com. 1964-66, chmn. conf. tchrs. 1960-61, vis. scientist 1963-70, recipient Disting. Educator award 1983), Acad. Pharm. Scis. (exec. com. 1967-70, chmn. basic pharmaceutics sect. 1965-67, pres. 1975, Indsl. Pharm. Tech. award 1980), Am. Pharm. Assn. (chmn. sci. sect. 1964-65, Rsch. Achievement award 1965), Wis. (Disting. Service award 1971), Iowa Pharmacists Assn. (Robert G. Gibbs award 1983), Wis. Acad. Scis., Arts and Letters, Soc. Investigative Dermatology, Rumanian Soc. Med. Sci. (hon.), Am. Found. Pharm. Edn. (bd. grants 1987-92), Ea. Va. Med. Sch. Contraceptive Rsch. and Devel. Program (tech. adv. com. 1989—), Am. Assn. Pharm. Scientists (Disting. Scientist award 1991), Sigma Xi, Kappa Psi (past officer), Rho Chi, Phi Lambda Upsilon, Phi Sigma. Home: 16 Brickwood Knls NE Iowa City IA 52240-9144

WURTELE, CHRISTOPHER ANGUS, paint and coatings company executive; b. Mpls., Aug. 25, 1934; Valentine and Charlotte (Lindley) W.; m. Heather Campbell (div. Feb. 1977); children: Christopher, Andrew, Heidi; m. Margaret Von Blon, Aug. 21, 1977. BA, Yale U., 1956; MBA, Stanford U., 1961. V.p. Minn. Paints, Inc. (merged with Valspar Corp. 1970), Mpls., 1962-65, exec. v.p., 1965, pres., CEO, 1973-96, chmn., 1996—; dir. Gen. Mills Inc., Donaldson Co., Bemis Co., IDS Mutual Fund Group. Mem. adv. coun. Grad. Sch. Bus. Stanford U.; bd. dirs. Bush Found., Walker Art Ctr. With USN, 1956-59. Mem. Am. Bus. Conf., Mpls. Club, Nat. Paint & Coatings Assn. (bd. dirs.). Episcopalian. Home: 2409 E Lake Of The Isles Pky Minneapolis MN 55405-2479 Office: Valspar Corp 1101 S 3rd St Minneapolis MN 55415-1211

WURTELE, MORTON GAITHER, meteorologist, educator; b. Harrodsburg, Ky., July 25, 1919; s. Edward Conrad and Emily Russell (Gaither) W.; m. Zivia Syrkin, Dec. 31, 1942; children—Eve Syrkin, Jonathan Syrkin. S.B., Harvard, 1940; M.A., UCLA, 1944, Ph.D., 1953. Asst. prof. meteorology Mass. Inst. Tech., Cambridge, 1953-58; asso. prof. meteorology U. Calif. at Los Angeles, 1958-64, prof., 1964—, chmn. dept., 1971-76; vis. prof. U. Buenos Aires, 1962, U. Jerusalem, 1965; cons. in field. Prin. contbr.: Glossary of Meteorology; co-editor: Progress in Desert Research; contbr. articles to profl. jours. Trustee Univ. Corp. for Atmospheric Rsch.; pres., dir. Sage Resources, Inc. With USNR, 1940-41. Fulbright grantee, 1949-50, 65; NATO sr. fellow, 1961-62. Fellow Am. Meteorol. Soc.; mem. Am. Profs. for Peace in Middle East (nat. exec. 1974—), Royal Meteorol. Soc., Am. Geophys. Union, Phi Beta Kappa, Sigma Xi. Club: Harvard So. Calif. Home: 432 E Rustic Rd Santa Monica CA 90402-1114 Office: UCLA Meterology Dept Los Angeles CA 90095-1565

WURTMAN, JUDITH JOY, research scientist; b. Bklyn., Aug. 4, 1939; d. Alexander Mordecai and Jeanette Teicher Hirschhorn; m. Richard Jay Wurtman; children: Rachael, David. BA, Wellesely (Mass.) Coll., 1959; MA in Biology Edn., Harvard U., 1960; PhD, George Washington U., 1973. Tchr. Malden Sch. System, 1959-60; rsch. asst. Microbiol. Assocs., Bethesda, Md., 1962-67; exhibit researcher Boston Mus. Sci., 1973-74; asst. prof. Newton (Mass.) Coll., 1974-76; postdoctoral fellow dept. nutrition MIT, Cambridge, 1976-78, rsch. scientist dept. nutrition, dept. brain and cognitive sci., 1987—; mem. scientific adv. bd. NutriSystem, Phila., 1988-89, Interneuron Pharms., Boston, 1989—; bd. dirs. Walden Labs. Author: Eating Your Way Through Life, 1979, The Carbohydrate Craver's Diet, 1983, The Carbohydrate Craver's Diet Cookbook, 1984, Managing Your Mind and Mood Through Food, 1987; editor: Nutrition and the Brain (8 vols.), 1983—, The Serotonin Solution, 1996. Mem. Am. Inst. Nutrition, Am. Dietitic Assn., Am. Soc. for Clin. Nutrition, Boston Soc. Psychiatry and Neurology, Soc. for Light Treatment and Biol. Rhythms, Sigma Xi (MIT chpt.). Office: MIT Dept of Brain and Cognitive Scis E25-604 Cambridge MA 02139

WURTMAN, RICHARD JAY, physician, educator, inventor; b. Phila., Mar. 9, 1938; s. Samuel Richard and Hilda (Schreiber) W.; m. Judith Joy Hirschhorn, Nov. 15, 1959; children: Rachael Elisabeth, David Franklin. AB, U. Pa., 1956; MD, Harvard U., 1960. Intern Mass. Gen. Hosp., 1960-61, resident, 1961-62, fellow medicine, 1965-66, clin. assoc. in medicine, 1985—; research assoc., med. research officer NIMH, 1962-67; mem. faculty MIT, Cambridge, 1967—, prof. endocrinology and metabolism, 1970-80, prof. neuroendocrine regulation, 1980-84, Cecil H. Green disting. prof., 1994—; dir. Clin. Rsch. Ctr., MIT, Cambridge, 1985—; prof. neuroscience MIT, 1984-94; lectr. medicine Harvard Med. Sch., 1969—; prof. Harvard-MIT Divsn. Health Scis. and Tech., 1978—; sci. dir. Ctr. for Brain Scis. and Metabolism Charitable Trust, 1981—; invited prof. U. Geneva, 1981; Sterling vis. prof. Boston U., 1981; mem. small grants study sect. NIMH, 1967-69, preclin. psychopharmacology study sect., 1971-75; behavioral biology adv. panel NASA, 1969-72; coun. basic sci. Am. Heart Assn., 1969-74; rsch. adv. bd. Parkinson's Disease Found., 1972-80, Am. Parkinson's Disease Assn., 1978—; com. phototherapy in newborns NRC-Nat. Acad. Scis., 1972-74, com. nutrition, brain devel. and behavior, 1976, mem. space applications bd., 1976-82; mem. task force on drug devel. Muscular Dystrophy Assn., 1980-87; chmn. life scis. adv. com. NASA, 1979-82; chmn. adv. bd. Alzheimer's Disease Assn., 1981-84; assoc. neuroscis. rsch. program MIT, 1974-82; chmn. life scis. adv. bd. USAF, 1985—; Bennett lectr. Am. Neurol. Assn., 1974; Flexner lectr. U. Pa., 1975; founder, chmn. sci. adv. bd. Interneuron Pharms., Inc., 198—; Hans Lindler Meml. lectr. Weizmann Inst., 1993. Author: Catecholamines, 1966; (with others) The Pineal, 1968; editor: (with Judith Wurtman) Nutrition and the Brain, Vols. I and II, 1977, Vols. III, IV, V., 1979, Vol. VI, 1983, Vol. VII, 1986, Vol. VIII, 1990, also numerous other articles and books; mem. editl. bd. Endocrinology, 1967-73, Jour. Pharmacology and Exptl. Therapeutics, 1968-75, Jour. Neural Transmission, 1969-88, Neuroendocrinology, 1969-72, Metabolism, 1970-80, Circulation Research, 1972-77, Jour. Neurochemistry, 1973-82, Life Scis., 1973-81, Brain Rsch., 1977—. Recipient Alvarenga prize and lectureship Phila. Coll. Physicians, 1970, CIBA-Geigy Drew award in Biomed. Rsch., 1982, Roger Williams award in Preventive Nutrition, 1987, Roger J. Williams award in Preventive Medicine, 1989, NIMH Merit award, 1989—, Internat. Prize for Modern Nutrition, 1989, Hall of Fame Disting. Alumni award Ctrl. H.S. Phila., 1992; Disting. lectr. Purdue U., 1984; Rufus Cole lectr., Rockefeller U., 1985; Pfizer lectr. NYU Med. Sch., 1985; Grass Fedn. lectr. U. Ga., 1985, Alan Rothballer Meml. lectr., N.Y. Med. Coll., Valhalla, N.Y., 1989, Gretchen Kerr Green lectr in the neuroscis., 1989; Wellcome Vis. Prof. Washington State U., Pullman, 1989; Julius Axelrod Disting. lectr. in neurosci., CUNY, 1990, Sigma Tau Found. lectr. on aging, Rome, 1990, Disting. lectr. in neurosci. La. State U., 1991, McEwen lectr. Queen's U., Ont., 1991; Plenary lectr. 3d Internat. Symposium on Microdialysis, 1993; Hans Lindner Meml. lectr. Weizmann Inst., 1993. Mem. Am. Soc. Clin. Investigation, Endocrine Soc. (Ernst Oppenheim award 1972), Am. Physiol. Soc., Am. Soc. Biol. Chemists, Am. Soc. Pharmacology and Exptl. Therapeutics (John Jacob Abel award 1968), Am. Soc. Neurochemistry, Soc. Neuroscis., Am. Soc. Clin. Nutrition, Am. Inst. Nutrition (Osborne & Mendel award 1982). Club: Harvard (Boston). Achievements include some 40 U.S. patents on new treatments for diseases and conditions; invention of melatonin (melzone) for promoting sleep, and of dexfenfluramine (redux) for treating obesity. Home: 300 Boylston St Boston MA 02116-3923 Office: Mass Inst Tech 45 Carleton St # E25-604 Cambridge MA 02142-1323

WURTZ, ROBERT HENRY, neuroscientist; b. St. Louis, Mar. 28, 1936; s. Robert Henry and Alice Edith (Popplwell) W.; m. Sally Smith, Dec. 20, 1958 (div.); children: William, Erica; m. Emily Otis, Apr. 23, 1983. AB, Oberlin Coll., 1958; PhD, U. Mich., 1962. Rsch. assoc. Com. for Nuclear Info., St. Louis, 1962-63; fellow Sch. Medicine, Washington U., 1962-65; rsch. psychologist NIH, Bethesda, Md., 1965-66, physiologist, 1966-78, chief lab. sensorimotor rsch., 1978—; vis. scientist Cambridge U., Eng., 1975-76. Editor: Neurobiology of Saccadic Eye Movement, 1989. Recipient Karl Spencer Lashley award Am. Philos. Soc., 1995. Fellow AAAS; mem. NAS, Am. Acad. Arts and Scis., Soc. Neurosci. (pres. 1991), Am. Physiol. Soc., Assn. for Rsch. in Vision and Opthalmology, Soc. Exptl. Psychologists. Office: NIH Nat Eye Inst 9000 Rockville Pike Bethesda MD 20814-1436

WURTZEL, ALAN HENRY, television executive; b. N.Y.C., Jan. 29, 1947; s. Sam and Bernice (Weinstein) W.; m. Susan Warner, Dec. 20, 1970; children: Joanna, Caroline. BA, CUNY, Queens, 1967; MA, U. Mich., 1969; PhD, NYU, 1974. Asst. prof. Queens Coll. of CUNY, N.Y.C., 1970-75, U. Ga., Athens, 1975-78; mgr. social research ABC-TV, N.Y.C., 1978-81, v.p. broadcast standards and practices, 1981-88, sr. v.p. mktg. and research services, 1988-1993, sr. v.p. news mag. and longform programming, 1993—; sr. v.p. news mag. and longform programming Good Morning America, 1995—. Author: Television Production, 1978, 4th edit., 1995. Office: ABC News 47 W 66th St New York NY 10023-6201

WURTZEL, ALAN LEON, retail company executive; b. Mount Vernon, N.Y., Sept. 23, 1933; s. Samuel S. and Ruth (Mann) W.; m. Irene C. Rosenberg, Oct. 9, 1988; children from previous marriage: Judith Halle, Daniel Henry, Sharon Lee. AB, Oberlin Coll., 1955; postgrad., London Sch. Econ., 1955-56; LLB cum laude, Yale, 1959. Bar: Conn. 1959, D.C. 1960, Va. 1968. Law clk. Chief Judge David L. Bazelon, U.S. Ct. Appeals, D.C., 1959-60; assoc. Fried, Frank, Harris, Shriver & Kampelman, Washington, 1960-65; legisl. asst. to Senator Joseph Tydings, 1965-66; with Cir. City Stores, Inc. (formerly Wards Co., Inc.), Richmond, 1966—, v.p., 1968-70, pres., 1970-83, chief exec. officer, 1973-86, chmn., 1983-94; vice chmn., 1994—; pres. NATM Buying Corp., 1978-86; pres. Operation Independence, 1987-88; bd. dirs. Office Depot, Inc., Boca Raton, Fla., 1989-96, Dollar Tree Stores, Norfolk, Va., Nat. Alliance of Bus., Washington; mem. Nat. Skills Stds. Bd. Bd. visitors Va. Commonwealth Ednl. U., 1985-92; trustee Oberlin Coll., 1989-96; dir. Washington Ednl. Television Assn., 1989-95; pres. Jewish Community Fedn., Richmond, 1983-85. Mem. Va. State Bd. Edn., Gov.'s Econ. Adv. Coun. Office: 2134 R St NW Washington DC 20008-1907 Office: Cir City Stores Inc 9950 Mayland Dr Richmond VA 23233-1463

WURZBERGER, BEZALEL, psychiatrist; b. Medias, Romania, June 28, 1945; came to U.S., 1967; s. Joshua and Isabella (Fulop) W.; m. Gladys Schmidt, Mar. 19, 1971; children: Tamar, David. BA, Columbia U., 1972; MD, Nat. U., Tegucigalpa, Honduras, 1982. Diplomate, Am. Bd. Psychiatry and Neurology. Intern North Gen. Hosp., N.Y.C., 1982-83; resident in psychiatry Creedmoor Psychiat. Ctr., Queens Village, N.Y., 1983-86; clin. psychiat. fellow N.Y. Med. Coll., Valhala, N.Y., 1986-87; staff psychiatrist Glens Falls (N.Y.) Hosp., 1987-92, chmn. dept. psychiatry, 1993—; med. dir., Samaritan Counseling Ctr., Keene, N.Y., 1987—; psychiat. cons., Uihlein Mercy Ctr., Lake Placid, N.Y., 1988—. V.p. Jewish Community Tegucigalpa, 1978-80; bd. dirs. Congregation Shaarey Tefily, Glens Falls, 1989—, v.p., 1993-96, pres., 1996—. Sgt. Israeli Air Force, 1964-67. Mem. AMA, Am. Psychiat. Assn., Soc. Liaison Psychiatry, Acad. Psychosomatic Medicine, Honduran Coll. Physicians. Office: Glens Falls Hosp 80 Park St Glens Falls NY 12801-4413

WURZBURGER, WALTER SAMUEL, rabbi, philosophy educator; b. Munich, Germany, Mar. 29, 1920; s. Adolf W. and Hedwig (Tannenwald) W.; m. Naomi C. Rabinovitz, Aug. 19, 1947; children—Benjamin W., Myron I., Joshua J. BA, Yeshiva U., 1944, DD (hon.), 1987; MA, Harvard U., 1946, PhD, 1951. Ordained rabbi, 1944. Rabbi Congregation Chai Odom, Boston, 1944-53, Shaarei Shomayim Congregation, Toronto, Ont., Can., 1953-67; rabbi Shaaray Tefila Congregation, Lawrence, N.Y., 1967-94, Rabbi emeritus, 1994—; editor Tradition, N.Y.C., 1961-87; columnist Toronto Telegram, 1957-67; adj. assoc. prof. philosophy Yeshiva U., 1967-80, adj. prof., 1980—. Author: Ethics of Responsibility, 1994; editor: A Treasury of Tradition, 1967; contbg. editor Sh'ma; contbr. articles to profl. jours., chpts. to books, Ency. Judaica, Ency. of Religion, Ency. of Bioethics. Mem. exec. com. United Jewish Welfare Funds of Toronto, 1965-67; past chmn. commn. on adoptions, synagogue commn., trustee Fedn. Jewish Philanthropies N.Y.; bd. dirs. Union Orthodox Jewish Congregations Am.; chmn. com. on interreligious affairs Synagogue Coun. Am., 1973-75, 83-87, pres., 1981-83, hon. pres., 1983-85; mem. interfaith com. United Community Funds of Toronto, 1960-67; v.p. synagogue commn. Fedn. Philanthropies, 1973-75; mem. nat. adv. com. United Jewish Appeal Am., 1971-78. Recipient Nat. Rabbinic Leadership award Union Orthodox Jewish Congregations Am., 1983, Samuel Belkin Lit. award Yeshiva Coll. Alumni Assn., 1994. Mem. Rabbinical Coun. Am. (past pres.), Rabbinical Coun. Can. (past pres.). Home: 138 Hards Ln Lawrence NY 11559-1315

WURZEL, LEONARD, retired candy manufacturing company executive; b. Phila., Feb. 4, 1918; s. Maurice L. and Dora (Goldberg) W.; m. Elaine Cohen, Aug. 18, 1949; children—Mark L., Lawrence J. B.S., Washington and Jefferson Coll., 1939; M.B.A., Harvard, 1941. With Loft Candy Corp., Long Island City, N.Y., 1946-64; v.p. Loft Candy Corp., 1949-56, exec. v.p., 1956-57, pres., 1957-64, dir., 1949-64; chmn., dir. Calico Cottage Candies, Inc., 1964-94; ret., 1994; mayor Village of Sands Point, N.Y., 1989—. Capt. Adj. Gen.'s Dept., AUS, 1941-46. Decorated Bronze Star. Mem. Assn. Mfrs. Confectionery and Chocolate (bd. dirs., past pres., chmn.), Candy Chocolate and Confectionery Inst. (bd. dirs., treas.), Retail Confectioners Internat. (bd. dirs., past pres.). Home: 25 Woodland Dr Sands Point NY 11050-1136 Office: Tibbits Ln Sands Point NY 11050-0109

WURZEL, MARY V., past association executive; b. Newport, R.I., July 17, 1918; d. William James and Mary Josephine (Dennis) Veach; m. Edward Milton Wurzel, Sept. 2, 1945; children: William D., David L., Edward Michael, Donald J., James D. BA, Brown U., 1939. Pres. Ex-Ptnrs. of Servicemen/Women for Equality, Alexandria, Va., 1984-90, 92-94. Docent Kennedy Ctr.; alumni chair Brown U., Providence, R.I.; Navy Arlington Lady. Home: 203 Yoakum Pkwy # 903 Alexandria VA 22304-3723

WUSSLER, ROBERT JOSEPH, broadcasting executive, media consultant; b. Newark, Sept. 8, 1936; s. William and Anna (MacDonald) W.; children: Robert Joseph, Rosemary, Sally, Stefanie, Christopher, Jeanne. BA in Communication Arts, Seton Hall U., 1957, LLD (hon.), 1976; LLD (hon.), Emerson Coll., 1976. With CBS News, N.Y.C., 1957-72; v.p., gen. mgr. Sta. WBBM-TV, Chgo., 1972-74; v.p. CBS Sports, N.Y.C., 1974-76, pres., 1977-78; pres. Sta. CBS-TV, N.Y.C., 1976-77, Pyramid Enterprises Ltd., N.Y.C., 1978-80; exec. v.p. Turner Broadcasting System Inc., Atlanta, 1980-87, sr. exec. v.p., from 1987, bd. dirs.; pres. Atlanta Sports Teams, Inc., 1981-87; pres., chief exec. officer COMSAT Video Enterprises, Inc., Washington, 1989-92; pres. Wussler Group, 1992—; chmn. bd. dirs. Nat. Acad. TV Arts and Scis., 1986-90; bd. dirs. Atlanta Hawks Ltd., Atlanta Braves Nat. League Baseball Club, Inc.; co-owner Denver Nuggets, NBA, 1989-92. Bd. regents Seton Hall U., 1978-84; trustee Marymount Manhattan Coll., 1977-81. Recipient Emmy awards, numerous other nat. and internat. news and sports awards. Mem. Dirs. Guild Am., Internat. Radio and TV Soc., Ariz. Heart Inst., Cable Advt. Bur., Nat. Cable TV Assn. (satellite network com.), European Broadcasting Union. Roman Catholic.

WUSTENBERG, WENDY WIBERG, public affairs specialist, consultant; b. Faribault, Minn., Sept. 30, 1958; d. George Lyman and Ruth Elizabeth (Morris) Wiberg; m. William Wustenberg, Nov. 11, 1989; children: Russell Morris, Lauren Ruth. BA in Journalism, U. Minn., 1977-83. Dir. comms., press sec. Office Gov. Quie, St. Paul, 1980-83; sr. prodr. news and pub. affairs Twin Cities Pub. TV, St. Paul, 1983-88; chief of staff Minn. House Reps., St. Paul, 1990; CFO, mng. ptnr. Issue Strategies Group, St. Paul, 1988-92; cons. Wustenberg and Assocs., Farmington, MN, 1992—; trustee Farmington Sch. Bd., 1993—; dir. Cmty. Action Coun., Apple Valley, Minn., 1991-93; pres. SOAR, Inc., Rosemount, Minn., 1990—; adj. prof. Metro. State U., St. Paul, 1986—; lobbyist State of Minn., St. Paul, 1992—. Author: Families and Sexuality, 1983; creative dir.: (avt. campaign) Environmental Trust Fund, 1988 (Assn. Trends award 1988); contbr. articles to profl. jours. Minn. exec. dir. Bush/Quayle Campaign, Bloomington, 1992; trustee The Carpenter Found. and Carpenter Nature Ctr., 1995—; bd. dirs. U. Minn. Coll. Liberal Arts Alumni Bd., 1996—. Recipient Nat. Promotion award Corp. for Pub. Broadcasting, Washington, 1986, 87, Local Documentary and Outreach award, 1987, J.C. Penney award U. Mo. Journalism Sch., 1987; finalist TV Acad. awards Nat. Acad. TV Arts and Scis., N.Y.C., 1986; named Adult Educator of Yr., Mo. Valley Assn. Adult Edn., 1986; named Disting. Alumni, U. Minn., 1994. Mem. Minn. Sch. Bds. Assn. (del.), Minn. Alumni Assn., Order Eastern Star. Republican. Avocations: equestrian training, gardening, golf, furniture restoration, cooking.

WYANT, CORBIN A., newspaper publisher; m. Donna Lee Humphrey, Oct. 5, 1963; children: Mrs. Blair Milliken, Corbin W., Beth Ashley. BA, Bucknell U., 1958; student Grad. Sch. Journalism, Pa. State U., 1973-74. Reporter/photographer Daily Leader-Times, Kittanning, Pa., 1958-69, advt. sales rep., circulation mgr., 1960-61, co-pub., gen. mgr., 1961-73; pres. Daily Dispatch, Douglas, Ariz., 1965-73; pub. Daily Herald News, Punta Gorda, Fla., 1974-76; v.p., gen. mgr. Naples (Fla.) Daily News, 1977-85, pub., 1985—, pres., 1986—. Former treas. and founder Mental Health Clinic Armstrong County, Pa.; former bd. dirs. Mental Health and Mental Retardation Assn. Armstrong and Ind. Counties, Med. Ctr. Hosp., Punta Gorda, Fla.; former chmn. Armstrong County Airport Authority; former v.p., bldg. chmn. YMCA Charlotte County; elder First Presbyn. Ch., Naples, Fla.; asst. coach Babe Ruth Baseball, Naples, 1983; coach Little League, Nples, 1979; bd. dirs. Naples Philharm., Inc., 1987—, Cmty. Concert Assn., 1978-84; mem. adv. bd. Salvation Army, Naples, 1987—; v.p. Collier Cultural Ctr., Inc., 1978-82, YMCA Collier County, 1977-87. Mem. Fla. Press Assn. (bd. dirs. 1986-92, pres. 1993-94, chmn. 1994-95), Fla. Newspaper Advt. Network (founder, bd. dirs. 1987—), Econ. Devel. Coun. Collier County (bd. dris. 1995—), Edison Cmty. Coll. Endowment Corp. (bd. dirs. 1994—), Gulf Coast Sailing Assn., Collier Athletic Club, Forum Club Collier County (pres. 1988-89), Rotary (pres. Naples 1982-83). Office: Naples Daily News PO Box 7009 Naples FL 34102-6237

WYATT, DORIS FAY CHAPMAN, English language educator; b. Del Rio, Tex., July 12, 1935; d. Cecil Cornelius and Lola Wade (Veazey) Chapman;

m. Jimmy Trueman Wyatt, June 2, 1956 (div. Nov. 1977); children: Abra Natasha Smith, Kent Colin Wyatt, Garrett Bret Wyatt. BS in Edn., S.W. Tex. State U., 1956; MA in English, U. North Tex., 1969; MA in Counseling, East Tenn. State U., 1983. Cert. profl. tchr. career ladder III, Tenn.; cert. marriage and family therapist. Elem. tchr. Clover Pk. Pub. Schs., Tacoma, 1957-58; jr. high reading tchr. Levelland (Tex.) Pub. Schs., 1964-67; tchr. English Denton (Tex.) Pub. Schs., 1967-70; tchr. reading & English Vets. Upward Bound, East Tenn. State U., Johnson City, 1981-87; tchr. English Johnson City (Tenn.) Pub. Schs., 1970-97; beauty cons. Mary Kay Cosmetics, Johnson City, 1971-95; adj. faculty mem. Tusculum Coll., Greeneville, Tenn., 1993—; pine plantation owner. Area dir. People-to-People Student Ambassador Program, Washington County, Tenn., 1975-94, tchr.-leader, Johnson City, 1974-84. Named to Nat. Dean's list, 1982-83. Mem. NEA (del. to nat. convs. 1989, 90), AAUW, Johnson City Edn. Assn. (pres., bd. dirs. 1989-90), Tenn. Edn. Assn. (resolutions com. 1990, 91, 92, del. to state conv. 1989, 90), Nat. Coun. Tchrs. English, Alpha Delta Kappa (pres. 1994-96), Phi Kappa Phi. Democrat. Methodist. Avocations: people, travel, photography, reading. Home: 1805 Sundale Rd Johnson City TN 37604-3023 Office: Johnson City Pub Schs Sci Hill High Sch John Exum Pky Johnson City TN 37604-4553

WYATT, EDWARD AVERY, V, city manager; b. Petersburg, Va., Nov. 1, 1941; s. Edward Avery and Martha Vaughan (Seabury) W.; AS in Bus. Bluefield Coll.; BS in Bus., Pub. Adminstrn., Va. Poly. Inst., 1964; M.Commerce, U. Richmond, 1969; MA in Polit. Sci., Appalachian State U., 1977; m. Regina Helen Stec, Aug. 23, 1969; children: Edward Avery VI, Stephen Alexander, Kent Seabury. Chief gen. svc., City of Petersburg, Va., 1966-67, asst. to city mgr., Petersburg, 1967-70; city mgr., Washington, N.C., 1970-73, Morganton, N.C., 1973-78, Greenville, N.C., 1978-82, Fairfax, Va., 1982-91, Wilson, N.C., 1991—; adj. lectr. George E. Mason U. Bus. Sch., 1985-86; bd. dirs. Electricities of N.C.; commr. Ea. N.C. Mcpl. Power Agy. Chmn. N.C. Code Ofcls. Qualification Bd., 1980-82; mem. adv. bd. Wilson Salvation Army, 1992—; bd. dirs. Wilson United Fund. Served with USNG and USAR, 1964-70. Paul Harris fellow Rotary Internat.; Dennis Duffey Meml. award Fairfax Police Youth Club. Mem. ASPA (ea. N.C. chpt.), Internat. City Mgmt. Assn. (endowment com., chair 1991-92, coun. mgr. Flan task force, 1993-94), Va. Local Govt. Mgmt. Assn. (pres. 1989-90), N.C. City/ County Mgmt. Assn., Ea. N.C. C. of C. (mem. exec. com., vice chair mcpl. membership), Soc. Cincinnati in Va., Descendants of Francis Epes of Va. (v.p.), Wilson Rotary. Contbr. numerous articles to profl. jours. and newsletters. Home: 1307 Waverly Rd NW Wilson NC 27896 Office: City of Wilson PO Box 10 Wilson NC 27896-0010

WYATT, FOREST KENT, university president; b. Berea, Ky., May 27, 1934; s. Forest E. and Almeda (Hymer) W.; m. Janice Collins, Mar. 4, 1956; children: Tara Janice Wyatt Mounger, Elizabeth Pharr Wyatt Mitchell. BS in Edn., Delta State U., Cleveland, Miss., 1956; MEd, U. So. Miss., 1960; EdD, U. Miss., 1970; postgrad., Harvard Inst. Ednl. Mgmt., 1975. Instr., coach Univ. Mil. Sch., Mobile, Ala., 1956-60; tchr., adminstr. Bolivar County dist. schs., Cleveland, Miss., 1960-64; alumni sec. Delta State U., 1964-69, adminstrv. asst. to pres., dir. adminstrv. services, asso. prof. edn., 1969-75, pres., 1975—; dir. Grenada Bank. Contbr. articles to profl. jours. Past bd. dirs. United Givers Fund, Cleveland Beautification Commn.; past bd. dirs., past v.p. Miss. Com. for Humanities, Delta Area coun. Boy Scouts Am. Friends of State Libr. Commn.; past chmn. Indsl. Devel. Found.; past pres. Cleveland Crosstie Arts Coun.; past trustee So. Bapt. Theol. Sem.; past bd. dirs. Miss. Econ. Coun.; past pres. Gulf South Conf.; bd. dirs. Southeastern Regional Vision for Edn. With U.S. Army, 1957-58. Recipient Kossman award for Outstanding Community Svc. C. of C., 1987. Mem. Miss. Assn. Educators, Am. Coun. on Edn. (mem. com. on govtl. rels.), Am. Coun. on Tchrs. Edn., Miss. Assn. Sch. Adminstrs., Am. Assn. State Colls. and Univs. (chmn. athletic com., com. governance, com. profl. devel. task force on athletics), NCAA (coun., past chmn. student-athlete adv. com., pres's. commn., gender equity com., exec. dir. search com., chmn. athletics cert. study com. divsn. II), Miss. Assn. Colls. (past pres.), So. Assn. Colls. and Schs. (Commn. on Colls.), Inter-Alumni Coun., Cleve. C. of C. (past pres.), Cleve. Country Club (dir.), Lions, Phi Delta Kappa, Omicron Delta Kappa, Kappa Delta Pi. Address: Delta State U Cleveland MS 38733

WYATT, GERARD ROBERT, biology educator, researcher; b. Palo Alto, Calif., Sept. 3, 1925; came to Can., 1935; s. Horace Graham and Mary Aimee (Strickland) W.; m. Sarah Silver Morton, Dec. 19, 1951 (dec. Mar. 1981); children—Eve Morton, Graham Strickland, Diana Silver; m. Mary Evelyn Rogers, Mar. 16, 1985. B.A., U. B.C., Can., 1945; postgrad. U. Calif.-Berkeley, 1946-47; Ph.D., Cambridge U., 1950. Research scientist Can. Dept. Agr., Sault Ste. Marie, Ont., 1950-54; asst. prof. biochemistry Yale U., New Haven, 1954-60, assoc. prof., prof. biology, 1960-73; prof. biology Queen's U., Kingston, Ont., 1973-94, prof. emeritus, 1994—; sci. dir. Insect Biotech Can., 1990-93. Contbr. articles to profl. jours. Guggenheim fellow, 1956; Killam Research fellow, 1985. Fellow Royal Soc. Can.; mem. Can. Soc. Cell Biology, Am. Entomol. Soc. Avocation: natural history. Home: 114 Earl St, Kingston, ON Canada K7L 2H1 Office: Queen's Univ, Dept Biology, Kingston, ON Canada K7L 3N6

WYATT, JAMES FRANK, JR., lawyer; b. Talladega, Ala., Dec. 1, 1922; s. James Frank and Nannie Lee (Heaslett) W.; m. Rosemary Barbara Slone, Dec. 21, 1951; children: Martha Lee, James Frank III. B.S., Auburn U., 1943; J.D., Georgetown U., 1949, postgrad., 1950. Bar: D.C. 1949, Ala. 1950, Ill. 1953, U.S. Supreme Ct 1953. Atty. Office Chief Counsel, IRS, 1949-51; tax counsel Universal Oil Products Co., Des Plaines, Ill., 1951-63; asst. treas. Universal Oil Products Co., 1963-66, v.p. fin., treas., 1966-75; treas. CF Industries, Inc., Long Grove, Ill., 1976-78; v.p. fin., treas. CF Industries, Inc., 1978-82; assoc. Tenney & Bentley, 1983-85, Arnstein, Gluck, Lehr, Barron & Milligan, 1985-88; pvt. practice, 1989—; dir. 1st Nat. Bank, Des Plaines. Village trustee, Barrington, Ill., 1963-75; bd. dirs. Buehler YMCA, Barrington Twp. Republican Orgn., 1963—; pres. Barrington Area Rep. Workshops, 1962-63. Served to capt., Judge Adv. Gen. Corps AUS, 1944-47. Mem. Tax Execs. Inst. (v.p. 1965-66, chpt. pres. 1961-62), Fed., Am., Chgo. bar assns., Barrington Home Owners Assn. (pres. 1960-61), Newcomen Soc., Assn. U.S. Army, Scabbard and Blade, Phi Delta Phi, Sigma Chi. Episcopalian. Clubs: Barrington Hills Country; Economics, University (Chgo.). Home: 625 Concord Pl Barrington IL 60010-4508 Office: 200 Applebee St Barrington IL 60010-3063

WYATT, JAMES LESLIE, III, university president; b. Aug. 24, 1945; m. Jeanne Cogburn, 1968; children: Cathey and Will (twins), Betsy. BA, Abilene Christian U., 1968; BFA, U. Tex., Austin, 1969, MFA, 1971, PhD in Edn., 1974. Asst. dean Coll. Fine Arts, instr. art U. Tex., Austin, 1971-75, assoc. dean Coll. Fine Arts, asst. prof. art, 1975-77; dean Coll. Fine Arts, assoc. prof. U. Ark., Little Rock, 1977-83, vice chancellor for univ. advancement, assoc. prof. art, 1983-88; vice chancellor for exec. affairs, prof. art history U. Miss., 1988-95; pres. Ark. State U., State University, 1995—; speaker and presenter in field. Exhibited art work in solo shows at Gardner Galley, Abilene, Tex., 1969, Huntington Gallery, U. Tex., 1970, The Clean Well-Lighted Place Gallery, Austin, 1971; group shows include DuBose Gallery, Houston, Contemporary Gallery, Dallas, U. Ark. Little Rock; contbr. articles to profl. jours. Recipient awards, fellowships and grants. Office: Ark State U PO Box 10 State University AR 72467-0010*

WYATT, JAMES LUTHER, drapery hardware company executive; b. Williamsburg, Ky., May 13, 1924; s. Jesse Luther and Grace Edwina (Little) W.; m. Barbara Christman, Aug. 28, 1946; children—Linda Lou, William Charles Christman (dec.). B.S., U. Ky., 1947, M.S., 1948; Sc.D., Mass. Inst. Tech., 1952. Registered profl. engr., Ohio, Pa. Devel. engr. titanium div. Nat. Lead Co., Sayreville, N.J., 1948-50; tech. mgr., head, dept. metall. engring., mgr. new products Horizons, Inc., Cleve., 1953-57; cons., asso. Booz, Allen & Hamilton, N.Y.C., 1957-61; v.p. program devel. Armour Research Found., Chgo., 1961-63; v.p. new product devel. Joy Mfg. Co., Pitts., 1963-67; v.p. corp. devel. Nat. Gypsum Co., Buffalo, 1967-69, Max Factor & Co., Hollywood, Calif., 1969-71; pres. Wyatt & Co., 1971—, Jimbabs, Inc., 1983—, Ambassador Industries, Inc., Los Angeles, 1988—; U.S. del. 1st World Metall. Congress. Contbr. tech., mgmt. papers to profl. lit. Mem. Pompano Beach Power Squadron, adminstr. officer, 1991, exec. officer, 1992, comdr., 1993; chmn. bd. trustees Meth. Ch., 1992, mem. fin. com., 1993, mem. adminstrv. bd.; bd. dirs., v.p. Golden Harbour Homeowners Assn., 1997—. Lt. col. USAAF, 1942-46. Mem. AIME, Am. Soc. Metals, Sigma Phi Epsilon, Alpha Chi Sigma. Clubs: Econs. (Chgo.), Execs. (Chgo.); Univ. (N.Y.C.); Calif. Yacht. Patentee in field. Home: 510 NE Golden Harbour Dr Boca Raton FL 33432-2942 Office: Bunker Hill Twr 510 Golden Harbour Dr Boca Raton FL 33432-2942

WYATT, JOE BILLY, academic administrator; b. Tyler, Tex., July 21, 1935; s. Joe and Fay (Pinkerton) W.; m. Faye Hocutt, July 21, 1956; children: Joseph Robert, Sandra Faye. B.A., U. Tex., 1956; M.A., Tex. Christian U., 1960. Systems engr. Gen. Dynamics Corp., 1956-65; mgr. Digital Computer Lab., 1961-65; dir. computer ctr., assoc. prof. computer sci. U. Houston, 1965-72; dir. Office Info. Tech. Harvard U., 1972-76, sr. lectr. computer sci., 1972-82, v.p. adminstrn., 1976-82; chancellor Vanderbilt U., Nashville, 1982—; mem. faculty Kennedy Sch. of Harvard U., 1976-82; bd. dirs., chmn. com. on math/sci., Am. Coun. of Edn.; bd. dirs. Reynolds Metals Co., SONAT Corp., Advanced Networking and Sys. Corp. Author (with others) Financial Planning Models for Colleges and Universities, 1979; editor-in chief: Jour. Applied Mgmt. Systems, 1983; contbr. articles to profl. jours.; patentee in field of data processing. Trustee Harvard U. Press, 1976-83, pres., 1975-76, chmn. bd., 1976-79; trustee EDUCOM, Princeton, N.J., 1973-81, Leadership Nashville, 1983-93; bd. dirs. Nashville Inst. Arts, 1982-83, Ingram Industries, 1990—; chmn. adv. com. IST, NSF, 1978-85; vice chmn. bd. Mass. Tech. Devel. Corp., Boston, 1977-83; mem. Coun. Competitiveness; fellow Gallaudet Coll., 1981-83; mem. alumni bd. dirs. Harvard Bus. Sch., 1982-92. Recipient award for exemplary leadership CAUSE, Hilton Head, S.C., 1982, Nat. Tree of Life award Jewish Nat. Fund, 1988; named Outstanding Tennessean Gov. of Tenn., 1986. Fellow AAAS; mem. IEEE, Assn. Am. Univs. (chair exec. com. 1990-91), Hosp. Corp. Am. (bd. dirs. 1984-89), Nat. Assn. Ind. Colls. and Univs. (policy bd. 1980-82), Am. Coun. edn. (chair adv. com. on tech. edn. 1980-81, bd. dirs. 1990-92), Assn. Computing Machinery (pres. Dallas and Ft. Worth chpt. 1963-65), U. Rsch. Assn. (bd. trustees 1988—), So. U. Rsch. Assn., Inc. (chmn. coun. pres. 1988-89), Bus. Higher Edn. Forum (exec. com. 1990-93), Aircraft Owners and Pilots Assn., Nashville C. of C. (bd. dirs. 1983-86, pres.-elect 1995), Experimental Aircraft Assn. (pres. adv. com.), Govt. Univ. Industry Rsch. Roundtable, Sigma Xi, Beta Gamma Sigma, Phi Beta Kappa (hon.), Harvard Club (N.Y.C.). Methodist. Office: Vanderbilt U Office of Chancellor 211 Kirkland Hall Nashville TN 37240*

WYATT, JOSEPH LUCIAN, JR., lawyer, author; b. Chgo., Feb. 21, 1924; s. Joseph Lucian and Cecile Gertrude (Zadico) W.; m. Marjorie Kathryn Simmons, Apr. 9, 1954; children: Daniel, Linn, Jonathan. AB in English Lit. with honors, Northwestern U., 1947; LLB, Harvard U., 1949. Bar: Calif. 1950, U.S. Dist. Ct. (cen. dist.) Calif. 1950, U.S. Ct. Appeals (9th cir.) 1950, U.S. Tax Ct., U.S. Supreme Ct. 1965. Assoc. firm Brady, Nossaman & Walker, Los Angeles, 1950-58; ptnr. Brady, Nossaman & Walker, L.A., 1958-61; pvt. practice L.A., 1961-71; sr. mem. Cooper, Wyatt, Tepper & Plant, P.C., L.A., 1971-79; of counsel Beardsley, Hufstedler & Kemble, L.A., 1979-81; ptnr. Hufstedler & Kaus, L.A., 1981-95; sr. of counsel Morrison & Foerster, L.A., 1995—; mem. faculty Pacific Coast Banking Sch., Seattle, 1963-92, Southwestern Grad. Sch. Banking, 1988-89; adviser Am. Law Inst., 1988—, Restatement, Trusts 3d, 1988—. Author: Trust Administration and Taxation, 4 vols., 1964—; editor: Trusts and Estates, 1962-74. Lectr. continuing legal edn. programs, Calif. and Tex.; trustee Pacific Oaks Coll. and Children's Sch., 1969-97; counsel, parliamentarian Calif. Democratic party and presdl. conv. dels., 1971—; mem. Calif. State Personnel Bd., 1961-71, v.p., 1963-65, pres., 1965-67; bd trustees Calif. Pub. Employees Retirement System, 1963-71. Served with USAAF, 1943-45. Fellow Am. Coll. of Trust and Estate Counsel; mem. ABA, Internat. Acad. Estate and Trust Law (treas. 1990-96), Am. Law Inst., Calif. State Bar Assn. (del. state conf. 1956, 62-67), L.A. Bar Assn. (trustee 1956). Democrat. Christian Scientist. Avocations: poetry, fishing. Home: 1119 Armada Dr Pasadena CA 91103-2805

WYATT, LESLIE, academic administrator; m. Jeanne Cogburn; children: Cathey, Will, Betsy. BA, Abilene Christian U.; BFA in Studio Graphic Arts, U. Tex., MFA in Mus. Edn., PhD in Edn. Assoc. dean Coll. Fine Arts U. Tex.; vice chancellor univ. advancement, dean Coll. Fine Arts U. Ark., Little Rock; vice chancellor exec. affairs U. Miss.; pres. Ark. State U., 1995—. Bd. dirs. Jonesboro Indsl. Devel. Corp., United Way of Jonesboro; chmn. St. Bernards Regional Med. Ctr. Heart Walk. Mem. Greater Jonesboro C. of C. (bd. dirs.). Office: Office of Pres PO Box 10 State University AR 72467

WYATT, OSCAR SHERMAN, JR., energy company executive; b. Beaumont, Tex., July 11, 1924; s. Oscar Sherman Sr. and Eva (Coday) W.; m. Lynn Sakowitz; children: Carl, Steven, Douglas, Oscar Sherman III, Brad. BS in Mech. Engring., Tex. Agrl. and Mech. Coll., 1949. With Kerr-McGee Co., 1949, Reed Roller Bit Co., 1949-51; ptnr. Wymore Oil Co., 1951-55; founder Coastal Corp., Corpus Christi, Tex., 1955; now chmn. bd. Coastal Corp., Houston. Trustee DeBakey Med. Found.; founding mem., bd. stewards Tex. Aviation Hall of Fame. Served with USAAF, World War II. Office: Coastal Corp Coastal Tower 9 E Greenway Plz Houston TX 77046

WYATT, RICHARD JED, psychiatrist, educator; b. Los Angeles, June 5, 1939; children: Elizabeth, Christopher, Justin. BA, Johns Hopkins U., 1961, MD, 1964; MD (hon.), Ctrl. U. Venezuela, 1977. Intern in pediat. Western Res. U. Hosp., Cleve., 1964-65; resident in psychiatry Mass. Mental Health Ctr., Boston, 1965-67; with NIMH, 1967—, asst. dir. intramural rsch., 1977-87, chief neuropsychiatry br., chief Neurosci. Ctr., 1972—; clin. prof. psychiatry Stanford U. Med. Sch., 1973-74, Duke U. Med. Sch., 1975—, Uniformed Svcs. Sch. Medicine, 1980—, Columbia U., 1987—; practice medicine specializing in psychiatry Washington, 1968—; cons. Psychiatry Shelter Program for the Homeless, Columbia U., 1987—; mem. sci. adv. bd. Nat. Alliance for Rsch. Schizophrenia and Depression, 1991. Mem. editl. bd. Advances in Neurosci., 1989, Harvard Rev. Psychiatry, 1992; assoc. prodr. PBS spls. To Paint the Stars, Moods in Music. Recipient A.E. Bennett award Soc. Biol. Psychiatry, 1971, Psychopharm. award APA, 1971, Superior Achievement award USPHS, 1980, Dean award Am. Coll. Psychiatrists, McAlpin Rsch. Achievement award Nat. Mental Health Assn., 1986, Media award for To Paint the Stars, 1991, Arthur P. Noyes award Commonwealth of Pa., 1986, Arieti award Am. Acad. Psychoanalysts, 1989, Robert L. Robinson award for Moods in Music, 1990, Mental Health Bell Media award for Moods in Music, Mental Health Assn. Atlanta, 1991. Fellow Am. Psychiat. Assn., Am. Coll. Neuropsychopharmacology (Efron award 1983); mem. AMA, Washington Psychiat. Assn. Office: NIMH Neurosci Ctr Rm 536 WAW Bldg St Elizabeth Hosp Washington DC 20032-2698

WYATT, ROBERT LEE, IV, lawyer; b. Las Cruces, N.Mex., Mar. 9, 1964; s. Robert Lee III and Louise Carole (Bard) W.; m. Vicki Harris Wyatt. BS, Southeastern Okla. State U., 1986; JD, U. Okla., 1989. Bar: Okla. 1989, U.S. Dist. Ct. (we. dist.) Okla. 1990, U.S. Ct. Appeals (10th cir.) 1990, U.S. Dist. Ct. (no. dist.) Okla. 1991, U.S. Ct. Appeals (8th cir.) 1991, U.S. Supreme Ct. 1993. Intern Okla. State Bur. Investigation, Oklahoma City, 1988-89, guest lectr., 1989; dep. spl. counsel Gov. of Okla., 1995; atty. Jones, Wyatt & Roberts, Enid, Okla., 1989—. Mem. ABA (mem. criminal & litigation sects.), Okla. Bar Assn. (mem. ins., family and litigation sects.), Garfield County Bar Assn., Okla. Criminal Def. Lawyers Assn., Nat. Inst. for Trial Advocacy, Nat. Assn. Criminal Defense Lawyers, Phi Delta Phi, Alpha Chi. Democrat. Baptist. Home: 2430 Sherwood Dr Enid OK 73703 Office: Jones Wyatt & Roberts 114 E Broadway Ave Enid OK 73701-4126

WYATT, ROBERT ODELL, journalism educator; b. Jackson, Tenn., Feb. 7, 1946; s. Odell and Sera Mae (Mebane) Wyatt. BA, U. of the South, 1968; MA, Northwestern U., 1970, PhD, 1973; MS, U. Tenn., 1977. From asst. to assoc. prof. U. Tenn., Nashville, 1973-79; assoc. prof. Mid. Tenn. State U., Murfreesboro, 1979-84, prof., 1984—, dir. Office Communication Rsch., 1989—; vis. prof. comm. U. Caen, France, 1994; cons. in comm.; mem. Pulitzer Prize Jury, 1980, 85, 91, 93, chair jury, 1985, 91, 93; rsch. cons. Freedom Forum First Amendment Ctr., Vanderbilt U.; bd. trustees Seabury-Western Theol. Sem., Evanston, Ill., 1996—. Author: Free Expression and the American Public, 1991 (Sigma Delta Chi award for rsch. on journalism 1992); editor book sect. The Nashville Tennessean, 1978-93; contbr. articles to profl. jours. Mem. Soc. Profl. Journalists, Assn. for Edn. in Journalism and Mass Comm., Internat. Comm. Assn., Am. Assn. Pub. Opinion Rsch., Speech Comm. Assn. Democrat. Episcopalian. Home: 2008 Hackberry Ln Nashville TN 37206-1823 Office: Middle Tenn State U PO Box 391 Murfreesboro TN 37133-0391

WYATT, RUSSELL SCOTT, optician; b. Kew Gardens, N.Y., July 27, 1948; s. William Douglas and Margaret Mae (Anderson) W.; divorced. BA, U. Pitts., 1970; AS in Vision Care Technology, Miami Dade Cmty. Coll., 1980. Cert. optician Fla. State Bd., 1980. Optician Pearl Vision, Miami, 1980-82, Royal Optical, Mary Esther, Fla., 1987-90, Optiworld, Mary Esther, Fla., 1990-93, White Wilson Med., Ft. Walton Beach, Fla., 1993—. Table tennis tchr. YMCA and Destin (Fla.) Cmty. Ctr., 1992. With USN, 1982-86. Fellow Nat. Acad. Opticianry. Republican. Presbyterian. Avocations: golf, bowling, table tennis, aerobics, weight training. Home: 1318 Lewis Turner Blvd #18 Fort Walton Beach FL 32547 Office: White Wilson Med Ctr PA 1005 Mar Walt Dr Fort Walton Beach FL 32547-6707

WYATT, WILSON WATKINS, JR., finance association and public relations executive; b. Louisville, Dec. 3, 1943; s. Wilson Watkins Sr. and Anne (Duncan) W.; m. Jane Clay, Aug. 15, 1964 (dec. 1975); children: Carol, Wilson III, Sarah Wyatt. Student, U. of the South, 1961-65. Reporter The Courier-Jour., Louisville, 1965-67; pub. rels. account exec. Doe-Anderson Advt., Louisville, 1967-68; account exec. Zimmer-McClaskey-Lewis, Louisville, 1968-70; ptnr. Bennett & Wyatt Pub. Rels., Louisville, 1970-71; state rep., vice chair appropriations and revenue com. Ky. Gen. Assembly, Frankfort, 1969-71; exec. dir. Louisville Cen. Area Inc., 1971-77; dir. corp. affairs and communications Brown & Williamson Tobacco Corp., Louisville, 1977-82; v.p. pub. policy BATUS Inc., Washington, 1982-86; v.p. corp. affairs BATUS Inc., Louisville, 1986-90; sr. v.p. corp. affairs PNC Fin. Corp., Pitts., 1990-92; sr. v.p. corp. comm. and govt. rels. The Travelers Cos., Hartford, 1992-94; exec. dir., CEO Am. Acad. of Actuaries, Washington, 1995—; lead U.S. def. pub. rels. activities against hostile takeover for B.A.T. Industries, U.K., 1989-90; chmn. Travelers Found., 1991-94, Travelers Good Govt. Com., 1992-94. Mem. youth adv. com. Atlantic Inst., 1967-68; del. North Atlantic Treaty Assn. Young Leaders Conf., 1967; chmn. Leadership Effort for All Dems., Ky., 1967-68; regional campaign coord. for Robert F. Kennedy, Ky.-Ind., 1968; mem. Pres.'s Forum, Washington, 1988-91; trustee Conn. Policy Econ. Commn., 1992-95; mem. exec. com. Hartford Downtown Coun., 1992-94; mem. adv. bd. Dem. Leadership Coun., Washington; mem. Am. Savings Edn. Campaign U.S. Dept. Labor, 1996. Named one of Outstanding Young Men in Am., Ky. Jaycees, 1973. Mem. The Vice Pres.'s Forum, Pub. Affairs Rsch. Coun. (conf. bd. 1986-95), Assn. Chief Execs. Coun., Pub. Affairs Coun. (bd. dirs. 1982—, exec. com. 1982-86), Speakers Club (Washington), Greater Hartford C. of C. (exec. com. 1992-94), Hartford Stage (bd. dirs. 1993-95), Congl. Country Club, City Club, Louisville Country Club, Congl. Country Club (Bethesda, Md.), City Club, Louisville Country Club. Avocations: boating, photography, writing, tennis. Home: 8116 Autumn Gate Ln Bozman MD 20817

WYATT-BROWN, BERTRAM, historian, educator; b. Harrisburg, Pa., Mar. 19, 1932; s. Hunter and Laura Hibbler (Little) Wyatt-B.; m. Anne Jewett Marbury, June 30, 1962; children: Laura (dec.), Natalie. BA, U. of South, 1953, LLD (hon.), 1985; BA with honours, King's Coll., Cambridge (Eng.) U., 1957, MA, 1961; PhD, Johns Hopkins U., 1963. Faculty Colo. State U., Ft. Collins, 1962-64, U. Colo., Boulder, 1964-66, Case Western Res. U., Cleve., 1966-83; prof. history Case Western Res. U., 1974-83; Richard J. Milbauer prof. history U. Fla., Gainesville, 1983—; Fleming lectr. La. State U., Baton Rouge, 1995; vis. prof. U. Wis.-Madison, 1969-70. Author: Lewis Tappan and the Evangelical War Against Slavery, 2d edit., 1971, Southern Honor: Ethics and Behavior in the Old South, 1982, paperback edit., 1983, Yankee Saints and Southern Sinners, 1985, paperback edit., 1990, Honor and Violence in the Old South, 1986; The House of Percy: Honor, Melancholy and Imagination in a Southern Family, 1994, 96, The Literary Percys: Family History, Gender, and the Southern Imagination, 1994; editor: The American People in the Antebellum South, 1973, Southern Biography Series, 1995—; contbr. articles to profl. jours. Served to lt. USNR, 1953-55. Grantee Am. Philos. Soc., 1968-69, 72-73, NEH, summer 1975; Guggenheim fellow, 1974-75; assoc. Woodrow Wilson Internat. Ctr. Scholars, 1975; fellow Davis Ctr. Princeton U., 1977-78, NEH fellow, 1985-86, NEH fellow Nat. Humanities Ctr., 1989-90; recipient Ramsdell award So. Hist. Assn., 1971, History prize Ohio Acad. History, 1983, ABC/Clio, 1989, Jefferson Davis Meml. prize for History, 1983; finalist Am. Book award and Pulitzer prize for History, 1983; Commonwealth Fund lectr. Univ. Coll., London, 1985, Lamar lectr. Mercer U., 1993, Webb lectr. U. Tex., Arlington, 1994. Mem. Orgns. Am. Historians (exec. coun. 1990-93), Soc. Am. Historians, So. Hist. Assn. (exec. coun. 1994—), Soc. for History Early Am. Republic (pres. 1995-96), Phi Beta Kappa, Phi Alpha Theta (History prize 1983). Episcopalian. Home: 3201 NW 18th Ave Gainesville FL 32605-3705

WYCHE, BRADFORD WHEELER, lawyer; b. Greenville, S.C., Feb. 22, 1950; s. C. Thomas and Harriet Durham (Smith) W.; m. Carolyn Diane Smock, July 1, 1978; children: Charles Denby Smock, Jessica Kaye. AB in Environ. Sci., Princeton U., 1972; MS in Natural Resource Mgmt., Yale U., 1974; JD, U. Va., 1978. Bar: S.C. 1978, U.S. Dist. Ct. S.C. 1978, U.S. Ct. Appeals (4th cir.) 1978; cert. civil mediator. Ptnr. Wyche, Burgess, Freeman & Parham, Greenville, 1979—. Contbr. articles to profl. jours. Mem. S.C. Gov.'s Coun. on Natural Resources, Columbia, 1983-84, Pendleton Place, Greenville, 1984-88, S.C. Coastal Coun., 1986-95; pres. Warehouse Theatre, Greenville, 1982-83, Greenville's Symphony Assn., 1989-90; chair Greenville Cmty. Found., 1994. Mem. S.C. Bar Assn. (vice chmn. ADR sect. 1996), Upstate Mediation Network (pres. 1996). Avocations: tennis, piano, whitewater kayaking. Home: 312 Raven Rd Greenville SC 29615-4248 Office: Wyche Burgess Freeman & Parham PO Box 728 44 E Camperdown Way Greenville SC 29602

WYCHE, CYRIL THOMAS, lawyer; b. Greenville, S.C., Jan. 28, 1926; C. Granville and Mary (Wheeler) W.; m. Harriet Smith, June 19, 1948; children: Sara McCall, Bradford Wheeler, Mary Frances. BE, Yale U., 1946; LLB, U. Va., 1949; LLD (hon.), Clemson U., 1997, Furman U., 1997. Bar: S.C. 1948, U.S. Dist. Ct. S.C. 1950, U.S. Ct. Appeals (4th cir.) 1952, U.S. Ct. Claims 1964, U.S. Supreme Ct. 1970. Ptnr. Wyche, Burgess, Freeman & Parham, P.A., Greenville, S.C., 1948—. Pres., bd. dirs. YMCA, Greenville, 1960; pres. Greenville Little Theatre, 1965, Arts Festival Assn., Greenville, 1970, Greenville Community Corp., 1976—; bd. dirs. Greater Greenville C. of C., 1980. Served with USN, 1943-46. Named Environmentalist of Yr., State of S.C., 1979; recipient Conservation award Gulf Oil Corp., 1983, Alexander Calder award, 1996, Oak Leaf award The Nature Conservancy, 1996, Order of the Palmetto award S.C. Gov., 1996. Mem. ABA, S.C. Bar Assn., Greenville County Bar Assn., Am. Judicature Soc. Presbyterian. Avocations: skiing, scuba diving, piano, tennis, white water canoeing. Office: Wyche Burgess Freeman & Parham 44 E Camperdown Way PO Box 728 Greenville SC 29602

WYCHE, MADISON BAKER, III, lawyer; b. Albany, Ga., Aug. 11, 1947; s. Madison Baker Jr. and Merle (McKemie) W.; m. Marguerite Jernigan Ramage, Aug. 7, 1971; children: Madison Baker IV, James Ramage. BA, Vanderbilt U., 1969, JD, 1972. Bar: Ga. 1972, ZU.S. Dist. Ct. (mid. dist.) Ga. 1972, U.S. Ct. Appeals (5th cir.) 1973, S.C. 1976, U.S. Dist. Ct. S.C. 1977, U.S. Ct. Appeals (4th cir.) 1977, U.S. Supreme Ct. 1980, U.S. Ct. Appeals (11th cir.) 1981, U.S. Dist. Ct. (no. dist.) Ga. 1995. Assoc. Perry, Walters, Lippitt & Custer, Albany, 1972-76, Thompson, Ogletree & Deakins, Greenville, S.C., 1976-77, Ogletree, Deakins, Smoak & Stewart, Greenville, 1977-80; ptnr. Ogletree, Deakins, Nash, Smoak & Stewart, Greenville, 1980—; bd. dirs. Happy Ho., Inc., Albany. Co-incorporator, sec. State of Tenn. Intercollegiate State Legislature, Nashville, 1967-69; state sec.-treas. Coll. Young Dems., Nashville, 1968; mem. employer and employee rels. com. N.C. Citizens for Bus. and Industry, Raleigh, 1984-97; mem. United Way Greenville, vestry Christ Episcopal Ch., Greenville, 1981-85. Capt. U.S. Army, 1969-77. Recipient Eagle Scouts award Boy Scouts Am., 1961. Mem. ABA, S.C. Bar Assn. (unauthorized practice of law com. 1977-95, chmn. 1982-86, 87-92, ho. of dels. 1991—, nominating com. 1992-95, CLE divsn., chmn. seminars subcom. 1995—), Ga. Bar Assn., Atlanta Bar Assn., Indsl. Rels. Rsch. Assn., S.C. Def. Trial Lawyers Assn., St. Andrews Soc. Upper S.C. (bd. dirs. 1979-81, v.p. 1986-87, pres. 1988-90), Palmetto Soc. (bd. dirs.), Rotary (bd. dirs. 1982-84, Paul Harris fellow 1986), Commerce Club of Greenville (bd. dirs. 1990—), Phi Delta Phi. Office: Ogletree Deakins Nash Smoak & Stewart PO Box 2757 Greenville SC 29602-2757

WYCHE, MARGUERITE RAMAGE, realtor; b. Birmingham, Ala., May 30, 1950; d. Raymond Crawford and Marguerite Getaz (Taylor) Ramage; m. Madison Baker Wyche III, Aug. 7, 1971; children: Madison Baker IV, James Ramage. BA cum laude, Vanderbilt U., 1972. Lic. broker, S.C., also cert. real estate specialist, grad. Real Estate Inst. Real estate agt. Slappey Realty Co., Albany, Ga., 1973-76, McCutcheon Co., Greenville, S.C., 1973-76; real estate agt. Furman Co., Greenville, 1985-87, broker's assoc., 1987-95; v.p., broker in charge The Furman Co. Residential LLC, Greenville, 1995—; v.p. The Furman Co. Residential LLC, 1996; bd. dirs. Multiple Listing Svc., 1997. Bd. dirs. Christ Ch. Episcopal Sch., Greenville, 1979-82, 86-89, chmn. bd. visitors, 1992-93; bd. dirs., cmty. v.p. Jr. League of Greenville, 1983, state pub. affairs chair S.C. Jr. League, 1984; mem. Greenville Cmty. Planning Coun., 1983; bd. dirs., chmn. long range planning com. Meals on Wheels, Greenville, 1990-93; mem. Palmetto Soc.-United Way of Greenville, 1992—; mem. elves workshop com. Children's Hosp., Greenville, 1992-93; mem. Greenville Tech. Found. Bd., 1995—, Met. Arts Coun., 1996—, Endowment Corp. Christ Ch., 1996—, Mayor's Task Force, 1996—. Mem. Greenville Bd. Realtors, Million Dollar Club (life), Vanderbilt Alumni Assn., Christ Ch. Episcopal Sch. Alumni Assn. (pres., bd. dirs. 1980-81), Mortar Board, Delta Delta Delta. Republican. Episcopalian. Avocations: golf, skiing, gardening, hiking, travel. Home: 134 Rockingham Rd Greenville SC 29607-3621 Office: The Furman Co 252 S Pleasantburg Dr Ste 100 Greenville SC 29607-2547

WYCHE, SAMUEL DAVID, sportscaster; b. Atlanta, GA, Jan. 5, 1945; m. Jane Wyche; children—Zak, Kerry. B.A., Furman U., 1966; Masters degree, U. S.C. Profl. football player Continental Football League, Wheeling Ironmen, 1966; profl. football player Cin. Bengals, 1968-70, Washington Redskins, 1971-73, Detroit Lions, 1974-75, St. Louis Cardinals, 1976, Buffalo Bills, 1976; owner sporting goods store, Greenville, S.C., 1974-92; asst. coach San Francisco 49ers, 1979-82; head coach Ind. U., Bloomington, 1983, Cin. Bengals, 1984-91, Tampa Bay (Fla.) Buccaneers, 1992-95; sports analyst NBC Sports, Tampa, 1996—, co-host NFL Live Pre-Game Show. Named Coach of Yr. NFL, 1988. Office: Sam Wyche Inc 413 Stony Rd Landrum SC 29356-3341

WYCKOFF, E. LISK, JR., lawyer; b. Middletown, N.J., Jan. 29, 1934; m. Elizabeth Ann Kuphal; children: Jenny Adele, Edward Lisk III. BA, Duke U., 1955; JD, U. Mich., 1960. Ptnr. Kramer, Levin, N.Y.C.; lectr. Practising Law Inst., 1970—, World Trade Inst., various profl. and bus. orgns. in U.S. and abroad; spl. counsel N.Y. Bankers Assn., 1974—; counsel N.Y. State Senate Com. Housing and Urban Renewal, 1969-71, N.Y. State Senate Com. Judiciary, 1963-64, Com. Affairs of the City of N.Y., 1962; mem. N.Y.C. Mayor's Taxi Study Commn., 1967. Directing editor, commentator West's McKinney's Forms on Estates and Trusts, 1974—; mng. editor, 1982-84; commentator McKinney's Not-For-Profit Corp. law, 1995—; contbr. articles to profl. jours. Bd. dirs. 1652 Wyckoff House and Assn., Inc., 1982—; trustee Soc. for Preservation of L.I. Antiquities, 1988—, N.Y.C. Hist. House Trust, 1993—, Inner-City Scholarship Fund., Inc. 1993—, The Bard Ctr. Bard Coll., 1994—, Goodspeed Opera Co., 1996—; trustee, pres. Homeland Found., 1989—; bd. advisors Wildlife Conservation Soc., 1993—; mem. Concilium Socalium to Vatican Mus., 1991—; papal hon. Knight Commr. of Order of St. Gregory The Great, 1995. Fellow Am. Coll. Trust and Estate Counsel, Am. Bar Found.; mem. ABA (chair com. on internat. property, estate and trust of law sect. real property, probate and trust law, taxation 1991—), Internat. Fiscal Assn., Internat. Bar Assn., N.Y. State Bar Assn. (exec. com. tax sect., chmn. com. income taxation estates and trusts 1976-80, com. internat. estate planning 1980—), Assn. of Bar of City of N.Y., Holland Soc. Club, St. Nicholas Soc. Club, Knickerbocker Club, Racquet and Tennis Club (N.Y.C.), Mashomack Fish and Game Preserve Club (Pine Plains, N.Y.), Essex Yacht Club (Conn.), N.Y. Yacht Club. Avocations: tennis, sailing. Office: Kramer Levin 919 3rd Ave New York NY 10022

WYCLIFF, NOEL DON, journalist, newspaper editor; b. Liberty, Tex., Dec. 17, 1946; s. Wilbert Aaron and Emily Ann (Broussard) W.; m. Catherine Anne Erdmann, Sept. 25, 1982; children: Matthew William, Grant Erdmann. BA, U. Notre Dame, 1969. Reporter Houston Post, 1970-71, Dayton (Ohio) Daily News, 1972-73, Seattle Post-Intelligencer, 1978, Dallas Times-Herald, 1978-79, Chgo. Sun-Times, 1981-85; reporter, editor Chgo. Daily News, 1973-78; editor N.Y. Times, N.Y.C., 1979-81, editorial writer, 1985-90; dep. editor editorial page Chgo. Tribune, 1990-91, editor editorial page, 1991—; occasional instr. journalism Columbia Coll., Chgo., Roosevelt U., Chgo. Finalist for Pulitzer prize in editl. writing, 1996; Woodrow Wilson fellow, 1969. Mem. Am. Soc. Newspaper Editors (Disting. Writing award for editls. 1997), Nat. Assn. Black Journalists, Nat. Assn. Minority Media Execs. Roman Catholic. Office: Chicago Tribune 435 N Michigan Ave Chicago IL 60611

WYCOFF, ROBERT E., petroleum company executive; b. Tulsa, 1930; married. B.S.M.E., Stanford U., 1952, M.S.M.E., 1953. With Atlantic Richfield Co., L.A., 1953—, various engring. and mgmt. positions, 1957-70, mgr. western region Internat. div., 1971-73, v.p., resident mgr. Alaska region N.Am. Producing div., 1973-74, corp. planning v.p., 1974-77, sr. v.p. planning and fin., 1977-80, exec. v.p., 1980-84, chief corp. officer, 1984, vice chmn., 1985, pres. emeritus, 1986-93, also dir.; chmn. Lyondell Petrochem. Co., Houston. Mem. ASME, Am. Petroleum Inst. Office: Atlantic Richfield Co PO Box 2579 515 S Flower St Los Angeles CA 90071*

WYCOFF, WILLIAM MORTIMER, lawyer; b. Pitts., Jan. 1, 1941; s. William Clyde and Margaret (Shaffer) W.; m. Deborah Seyl, Jan. 25, 1963; children: Ann Richardson, Pieter Claesen. AB, Cornell U., 1963; JD, Northwestern U., 1966. Bar: Pa. 1967, U.S. Ct. Appeals (3d cir.) 1967), U.S. Dist. Ct. (we. dist.) Pa. 1967. Assoc., now ptnr. Thorp Reed and Armstrong, Pitts., 1966—. Pres. Children's Home Pitts., 1976-78, 86-88, now bd. dirs.; pres. Pressley Ridge Schs., Pitts., 1988-90, now bd. dirs.: pres. Pressley Ridge Found.; pres., bd. dirs. Pitts. Dance Coun., 1991-94; trustee Pitts. Cultural Trust, 1991-94. Fellow Am. Coll. Trial Lawyers; mem. Acad. Trial Lawyers Allegheny County. Avocations: photography, skiing, biking, hiking, golf. Office: Thorp Reed and Armstrong One Riverfront Ctr 20 Stanwix St Pittsburgh PA 15222-4801

WYDEN, RON, senator; b. Wichita, Kans., May 3, 1949; s. Peter and Edith W.; m. Laurie Oseran, Sept. 5, 1978; 1 child, Adam David. Student, U. Santa Barbara, 1967-69; A.B. with distinction, Stanford U., 1971; J.D., U. Oreg., 1974. Campaign aide Senator Wayne Morse, 1972, 74; co-founder, co-dir. Oreg. Gray Panthers, 1974-80; dir. Oreg. Legal Services for Elderly, 1977-79; instr. gerontology U. Oreg., 1976, U. Portland, 1980, Portland State U., 1979; mem. 97th-104th Congresses from 3d Oreg. dist., Washington, D.C., 1981-96; U.S. Senator from Oreg., 1996—. Recipient Service to Oreg. Consumers award Oreg. Consumers League, 1978, Citizen of Yr. award Oreg. Assn. Social Workers, 1979, Significant Service award Multnomah County Area Agy. on Aging, 1980; named Young Man of Yr. Oreg. Jr. C. of C., 1980. Mem. Am. Bar Assn., Iowa Bar Assn. Democrat. Jewish. Office: 259 Russell Senate Bldg Washington DC 20510

WYDICK, RICHARD CREWS, lawyer, educator; b. Pueblo, Colo., Nov. 1, 1937; s. Charles Richard and Alice (Marsh) W.; m. Judith Brandli James, 1961; children—William Bruce, Derrick Cameron. B.A., Williams Coll., 1959; LL.B., Stanford U., 1962. Bar: Calif. bar 1962. Asso. firm Brobeck, Phleger & Harrison, San Francisco, 1966-71; mem. faculty U. Calif. Law Sch., Davis, 1971—; prof. law U. Calif. Law Sch., 1975—, dean, 1978-80. Author: Plain English for Lawyers, 3d edit., 1994. Served to capt. USAR, 1962-66. Office: Sch Law U Calif Davis CA 95616

WYDRA, FRANK THOMAS, healthcare executive; b. Republic, Pa., May 11, 1939; s. Frank T. and Anne M. (Kois) W.; m. Karen Branch, June 24, 1961; children: Denise Lee, Sheryl Lynn, Frank Thomas III. BS in Mgmt., U. Ill., 1961. V.p. Allied Supermarkets, Inc., Detroit, 1967-75; sr. v.p. HGH Health System, Detroit, 1975-85; pres. Radius Health Care Sysytems, Inc., Detroit, 1983-85; cons. Birmingham, Mich., 1985-88; exec. v.p. The Chi Group, Ann Arbor, Mich., 1988-91; owner IRI, Mgmt. Cons., Detroit, 1991—; lectr. various profl. groups; bd. dirs. Mich. Health Systems Inc., Saber-Salisbury Assocs. Inc., Midwestern Health Ctr., MultiCare Med. Inc., RHS Inc. Author: Learner Controlled Instruction, 1980, (with others) Hospital Survival Guide, 1984, The Cure, 1992; creator 2 mgmt. games Performulations, 1978, The Dynamics of Power and Authority, 1981; contbr. articles to profl. jours. Personnel program advisor Mich. State U. Sch. Labor Relations, 1979-83; chmn. new programs Wayne County Community Coll., Detroit, 1979-80; bd. dirs. Detroit Metro Youth Found., 1980-83, State Mich. Health Occupations Council, Lansing, 1982-85. Capt. U.S. Army, 1961-63. Recipient numerous awards ASTD, Nat. Soc. Performance and Instrn., Mich. SOc. Instructional Tech., Supermarket Inst. Mem. Am. Hosp. Assn., Planning Soc. of Am. Hosp. Assn., Hosp. Personnel Adminstrs. Assn. (pres. 1981-82, numerous awards), Am. Mgmt. Assn., Am. Soc. Hosp. Pers.Adminstrs. (bd. dirs. 1981-83), Mich. Soc. Instrnl. Tech. (life, pres. 1973-74), Mich. Hosp. Assn., Employers Assn. Detroit (bd. dirs. 1982-85), Detroit Athletic Club. Avocations: writing, sailing. Home: 1001 W Glengarry Cir Bloomfield Hills MI 48301-2223

WYER, JAMES INGERSOLL, lawyer; b. Denver, June 9, 1923; s. William and Katherine (Rolfe) W.; m. Joan Best Connelly, Aug. 13, 1960; children: Joan Connelly Tatnall, Peter Ford, June Wyer Nugent. B.A., Yale U., 1945, LL.B., 1949. Bar: N.Y. 1950, N.J. 1987. Assoc. Dewey, Ballantine, Bushby, Palmer & Wood, N.Y.C., 1949-56, Am. Cyanamid Co., Wayne, N.J., 1956; v.p., gen. counsel Am. Cyanamid Co., 1973-86; of counsel St. John & Wayne, Newark, 1987—; bd. dirs. TherMold, Inc., William Penn Life Ins. Co. N.Y., PharmGenics, Inc. Bd. dirs. Nat. Legal Ctr. for the Pub. Interest. Served with USNR, 1943-46. Mem. Assn. Gen. Counsel (1st v.p. 1982-84, pres. 1985-86), ABA, Assn. of Bar of City of N.Y., Atlantic Legal Found. (chmn. 1986—). Republican. Clubs: Jupiter Island (Hobe Sound, Fla.); Seabright (N.J.) Beach, Seabright Lawn, Tennis and Cricket (Rumson, N.J.); Coral Beach and Tennis (Bermuda), Hobe Sound (Fla.) Yacht. Office: St John & Wayne 2 Penn Plz E Newark NJ 07105-2246

WYER, PETER CHARLES, emergency physician; b. Delhi, N.Y., July 16, 1943; s. Robert Selden and Wilhelmina (Sebesta) W.; m. Judith Ann Sholdebrand, Mar. 10, 1976. BS, Columbia U., 1970; MD, U. Pa., 1974. Diplomate Am. Bd. Emergency Medicine. Attending emergency medicine physician Wyckoff Hghts. Med. Ctr., Bklyn., 1979-92; pvt. practice Bronx, N.Y., 1981-92; asst. prof. emergency medicine N.Y. Med. Coll., Valhalla, N.Y., 1992—; asst. clin. prof. emergency medicine Columbia Presbyterian Med. Ctr., N.Y.C., 1997—; rsch. dir. dept. emergency medicine Lincoln Hosp., 1996-97. Pres. Coalition of Comty. of Physicians, Bronx, N.Y., 1990-91. Fellow Am. Coll. Emergency Physicians, N.Y. Acad. Medicine; mem. Soc. Acad. Emergency Medicine, Bronx County Med. Soc. (pres. 1995-96). Avocation: classical pianist.

WYETH, ANDREW, artist; b. Chadds Ford, Pa., July 12, 1917; s. Newell Converse and Carolyn (Bockius) W.; m. Betsy Merle James, May 15, 1940; children: Nicholas, James Browning. Educated pvt. tutors; DFA (hon.), Colby Coll., Maine, 1954, Harvard U., 1955, Dickinson Coll., 1958, Swarthmore Coll., 1958, Nasson Coll., 1963, U. Md., U. Del., Northeastern U., Temple U., 1964; LHD (hon.), Tufts U., 1963; DFA (hon.), Princeton U., 1965; LHD (hon.), Franklin and Marshall Coll., 1965, Lincoln U., 1966, Amherst Coll., 1967; DFA (hon.), Bowdoin Coll., 1970; LHD (hon.), Ursinus Coll., 1971; DFA (hon.), U. Pa., 1972; LHD (hon.), West Chester U., 1984; DFA (hon.), Dartmouth Coll., 1984, Bates Coll., 1987; LHD (hon.), U. Vt., 1988. Artist, landscape painter, 1936—; first one-man show William Macbeth Gallery, N.Y.C., 1937, first solo exhbn. ever held in White House, 1970, first exhbn. by living Am. artist Royal Acad. Arts, London, 1980; exhibited Doll & Richards, Boston, 1938, 40, 42, 44, Cornell U., 1938, Macbeth Gallery, 1938, 41, first tempera show, 1943, 45, Currier Gallery, Manchester, N.H., 1939, room of watercolors, Art Inst. Chgo., 1941; room at Realist and Magic Realist show, Mus. Modern Art, N.Y.C., 1943; one-man exhbn., M. Knoedler & Co., N.Y.C., 1953, 58, Mass. Inst. Tech., Cambridge, 1960, Fogg Art Mus., William Farnsworth Library and Mus., 1963, Helga Pictures at numerous art museums, other univs. and museums; also exhbns. Arnot Mus., Elmira, N.Y., 1986, Seibu-Pisa, Tokyo, 1986, Kenesaw (Ga.) Mus. Art, 1986, Thomasville (Ga.) Art Ctr., 1987, Acad. of the Arts of USSR, Leningrad, 1987, Acad. of the Arts USSR, Moscow, 1987, Nat. Gallery of Art, Washington, 1987, Corcoran Gallery Art, Washington, 1987, An American Vision: Three Generations of Wyeth Art, various mus., 1987, Dallas Mus. Art, 1987, Mus. Fine Arts, Boston, 1988, Terra Mus. Am. Art, Chgo., 1988, Mus. Fine Arts, Houston, 1988, Setagaya Art Mus., Tokyo, 1988, L.A. County Mus. Art, L.A., 1988, Palazzo Reale, Milan, Italy, 1988, Fitzwilliam Mus., Cambridge, Eng., 1988, Fine Arts Mus. San Francisco, 1988, Brandywine River Mus., Chadds Ford, Pa., 1988, Detroit Inst. Arts, k1989, Sezon Mus. Art, Tokyo, 1991, Heckscher Mus., Huntington, N.Y., 1989, Gilcrease Mus., Tulsa, 1989, Portland (Maine) Mus. Art, 1989, Nukaga Gallery, Japan, 1990, Marcelle Fine Art Inc., N.Y.C., 1990, Takuji Kato Modern Art Mus., Tokyo, 1991, Takuji Kato Modern Art Mus., Chichibu City, Japan, 1991, Jacksonville (Fla.) Art Mus., 1992, Portland (Maine) Mus. Art, 1993, Farnsworth Art Mus., Rockland, Maine, 1994, San Francisco Mus. Modern Art, 1995, Charles and Emma Frye Art Mus., 1995; represented in permanent collections Met. Mus. Art, Nat. Gallery Art. Awarded 1st prize Wilmington Soc. Fine Arts, 1939, Obrig prize Am. Watercolor Soc., 1945, award of Merit, Am. Acad. Arts and Letters and Nat. Inst. Arts and Letters, 1947, 1st prize in watercolor Nat. Acad., 1946, Gold medal Nat. Inst. Arts and Letters, 1965, George Walter Dawson Meml. medal Phila. Watercolor Club, 1957, Mellon Gold medal of Achievement Pa. Artists Exhibit, Ligonier Valley, Pa., 1958, Arts Festival award and Citation for bringing dignity to Am. art Phila. Mus. Art, 1959, Percy M. Owens Meml. award Fellowship of Pa. Acad. Fine Arts, Phila., 1960, Presdl. Medal of Freedom, 1963, citation LaSalle Coll., Phila., 1965, Gold medal of honor Pa. Acad. Fine Arts, 1966, Carnegie Inst. award, award for excellence 1st award recognize outstanding performance in arts, Washington Coll., Chestertown, Md., 1976; Gold medal Nat. Arts Club, 1978, first Am. artist awarded Presdl. award Gold Congl. medal, 1988. Mem. Am. Watercolor Soc. (certificate of merit 1962), Nat. Inst. Arts and Letters, Soviet Acad. Arts (hon.), Academie des Beaux-Arts, Chester County Art Assn. (dir.), Audubon Soc. (dir.), N.Y. Watercolor Soc., Wilmington Soc. Fine Arts, Phila. Watercolor Club (dir.), Washington Watercolor Club (dir.), Balt. Watercolor Club (dir.), Am. Acad. Arts and Letters. (Nat. Academician elect May 1945, Gold medal preeminence in painting 1965), Am. Acad. Arts and Scis., Royal Soc. Painters and Watercolours (London). Office: care Frank E Fowler PO Box 247 Lookout Mountain TN 37350-0247*

WYETH, JAMES BROWNING, artist; b. Wilmington, Del., July 6, 1946; s. Andrew and Betsy (James) W.; m. Phyllis Overton Mills, Dec. 12, 1968. Privately tutored. One man shows include: M. Knoedler & Co., N.Y.C., 1966, William A. Farnsworth Mus., Rockland, Maine, 1969, Coe Kerr Gallery, N.Y.C., 1974, Brandywine River Mus., Chadds Ford, Pa., 1974, Joslyn Art Mus., Omaha, 1976, Pa. Acad. Fine Arts, 1980, Greenville County Art Mus., Greenville, S.C., 1981, Amon Carter Mus., Ft. Worth, 1981, Anchorage Fine Arts Mus., 1983; touring exhbn. An American Vision: Three Generations of Wyeth Art, various mus. worldwide, 1987—. Mem. stamp adv. com. U.S. Postal Service, 1969—; mem. Nat. Endowment for Arts, 1972—; bd. govs. Nat. Space Inst., 1975—. Served with Del. Air N.G., 1966-71. Office: care James Graham & Sons 1014 Madison Ave New York NY 10021-0103*

WYGANT, FOSTER LAURANCE, art educator; b. Dayton, Ohio, Oct. 30, 1920; s. Harold F. and M. Esther (Weber) W.; m. Rae E. Hoyt, 1 child, Nancy Laura. Profl. diploma, Juilliard Sch. Music, 1942; B.A., Columbia U., 1949, M.A., 1956, Ed.D., 1959; postgrad., Am. Art Sch., Art Students League, 1951-53. Clarinetist Dallas Symphony and free-lance clarinetist N.Y.C., 1945-47, publicity, fund-raising positions, and free-lance artist, 1952-56, tchr. art, pub. schs., 1956-59; asst. prof. Montclair State Coll., N.J., 1959-63, assoc. prof., 1963-68; prof. art edn. U. Cin., 1968-87, chmn. dept., 1968-84, dir. Sch. Art Edn. and Art History, 1984-86, emeritus prof., 1987—; vis. sr. lectr. Leeds Coll. Art, Eng., 1966; regional chmn. Scholastic Awards Program, 1968-84; chmn. Action for Arts in Ohio Schs., 1974-75. Author: Art in American Schools in the Nineteenth Century, 1983, School Art in American Culture 1820-1970, 1993; editor, prin. author: Standards for Art Teacher Preparation Programs, 1979, Principles, Purposes and Standards for School Art Programs, 1982; contbr. numerous articles to profl. jours. Served with U.S. Army, 1941-45. N.Y. State and Juilliard Sch. Music scholar, 1939-41; Kellogg Found. fellow Columbia U., 1955-56. Mem. Nat. Art Assn. (nat. dir. higher edn. divsn. 1975-79, Recognition award 1980, Disting. Svc. award 1982, Disting. fellow 1995), Ohio Art Edn. Assn. (pres. 1972-74), Seminar for Rsch. in Art Edn., Coun. for Policy Studies in Art Edn., Am. Fedn. Musicians. Home: 3562 Interwood Ave Cincinnati OH 45220-1824

WYGOD, MARTIN J., pharmaceuticals executive; b. N.Y.C.. BS, N.Y.U., 1961. Chmn., pres., chief exec. officer Medco Containment Inc., Montvale, N.J., 1983-94; chmn. Synetic, Inc., Elmwood Park, N.J., 1994—. Office: Synetic Inc 669 River Dr # 2 Elmwood Park NJ 07407-1361

WYKES, EDMUND HAROLD, retired insurance company executive; b. Newcastle-on-Tyne, Eng., July 19, 1928; s. Cyril Edmund and Sylvia (Glover) W.; m. Joan Nightingale, Oct. 1, 1955; children—Julie, Christopher. LL.B., Durham U., 1949; postgrad., Gibson and Weldon Coll. Law, 1953. Bar: Ont. 1958. Solicitor H.E. Ferens & Son, Durham City, Eng., 1953-57; sec., counsel Imperial Life Assurance Co. of Can., Toronto, 1971-77, gen. counsel, sec., 1977-80, v.p., gen. counsel, sec., 1980-91, v.p., sec., 1991-93; ret., 1993. Solicitor Supreme Ct. Eng., 1953. Served with RAF, 1949-51. Mem. English Law Soc., Assn. Life Inst. Counsel, Am. Soc. Corp. Secs. Inc. Home: 86 Wimbleton Rd, Etobicoke, ON Canada M9A 3S5

WYKOFF, FRANK CHAMPION, economics educator; b. Oakland, Calif., Feb. 20, 1942; s. Victor Clifton and Clarisse (Champion) W.; m. Jane Pierpont Humphreys, Sept. 11, 1965; children: Victor Clifton, Elisabeth Pierpont. AB, U. Calif., Berkeley, 1963, MA, 1965, PhD, 1968. Instr. U. Calif., Berkeley (part-time), 1964-68, 74; prof. econs. Pomona Coll., Claremont, Calif., 1968—, Elden Smith prof., 1979—; dir. Ctr. for Study of Economics; vis. prof. U. B.C., Vancouver, 1976-77; fin. economist U.S. Treasury Dept., Washington, 1972-73; cons., 1973-81; instr. U. Wis.-Madison, 1971; speaker Found. for Am. Communications, 1982—; expert cons. GAO, Washington, 1980—; acad. dean Found. For Am. Comms., 1997—. Author: Macroeconomics, 1981, Understanding Economics Today, 1986, 5th edit., 1996; editor Econ. Inquiry Jour., 1989-96. Faculty fellow GAO, 1980; fellow Brookings Instn., 1972-73, NSF, 1976; faculty fellow Haynes Found., 1969, 71; fellow Ford Found., 1968, 70. Mem. Am. Econ. Assn., Western Econ. Assn., Inst. on Advanced Econs. for Journalists (dir. FACS). Home: 1001 Richmond Dr Claremont CA 91711-3351 Office: Pomona Coll Econ Inquiry 109 Seaver North 645 N College Ave Claremont CA 91711-4412

WYLAN, BARBARA, artist; b. Providence, 1933; divorced; children: Andrea, Brock. BFA, R.I. Sch. of Design, Providence, 1955; studied with Donald Stoltenberg, Claude Croney, Murray Wentworth, Ruth Wynn, Charles Movalli, Dong Kingman. Tchr. watercolor workshops; juror various exhbns. 25 one-person shows; exhibited widely in more than 100 group shows including Watercolor USA (Springfield award 1982), Nat. Soc. Painters in Casein and Acrylic 38th Ann., Nat. Arts club, N.Y.C. (Dr. David Soloway award 1991); works owned by numerous pvt., corp. and instnl. collectors including Fine Arts Mus. of the South.; represented by Market Barn Gallery, Falmouth, The Spectrum of Am. Artists and Craftsmen, Brewster, Hyannis, Nantucket, Newport, West Palm Beach. Mem. Nat. Soc. Painters in Casein and Acrylic, Watercolor USA Honor Soc., New Eng. Watercolor Soc., Copley Soc. Boston.

WYLAND (ROBERT), artist; b. Detroit, 1956. Owner Wyland Galleries. Prin. works 66 murals worldwide including Whaling Wall, Laguna Beach, Calif., 1977, Whaling Wall XXXIII, Hawaii, 1992, Planet Ocean, Hawaii, 1992, Whaling Wall, Oracle, Ariz., 1996. Office: 5757 Wilshire Blvd Ste 460 Los Angeles CA 90036-3684

WYLE, EWART HERBERT, clergyman; b. London, Sept. 12, 1904; s. Edwin and Alice Louise (Durman) W.; B.A., U. Louisville, 1930; B.D., Lexington Theol. Sem., 1933; postgrad. Louisville Presbyn. Theol. Sem., Temple U., 1933-35; D.D., Tex. Christian U., 1953; m. Prudence Harper, June 12, 1959; 1 son, Ewart Herbert. Ordained to ministry Christian Ch., 1935; pastor First Ch., Palestine, Tex., 1935-37, First Ch., Birmingham, Ala., 1937-41, First Ch., Tyler, Tex., 1944-54, Country Club Ch., Kansas City, Mo., 1954-59; minister Torrey Pines Ch., La Jolla, Calif., 1959-79, minister emeritus, 1979—. Bd. dirs. Scripps Meml. Hosp., pres., 1980-81. Served as chaplain, maj., AUS, 1941-44. Mem. Mil. Order World Wars, Am. Legion, Tau Kappa Epsilon, Pi Kappa Delta. Clubs: Masons (32 deg.), Shriners, Rotary, LaJolla Beach and Tennis. Home: 8850 N La Jolla Scenic Dr La Jolla CA 92037-1608

WYLE, FREDERICK S., lawyer; b. Berlin, Germany, May 9, 1928; came to U.S., 1939, naturalized, 1944; s. Norbert and Malwina (Mauer) W.; m. Katinka Franz, June 29, 1969; children: Susan Kim, Christopher Anthony, Katherine Anne. B.A. magna cum laude, Harvard U., 1951, LL.B., 1954. Bar: Mass. 1954, Calif. 1955, N.Y. 1958. Teaching fellow Harvard Law Sch., 1954-55; law clk. U.S. Dist. Ct., No. Dist. Calif., 1955-57; assoc. firm Paul, Weiss, Rifkind, Wharton & Garrison, N.Y.C., 1957-58; pvt. practice San Francisco, 1958-62; spl. asst. def. rep. U.S. del. to NATO, Paris, 1962-63; mem. Policy Planning Council, Dept. State, Washington, 1963-65; dep. asst. sec. def. for European and NATO affairs Dept. Def., Washington, 1966-69; v.p. devel., gen. counsel Schroders, Inc., N.Y.C., 1969-71; atty., cons. Schroders, Inc., 1971-72; chief exec. officer Saturday Rev. Industries, Inc., San Francisco, 1972-76; individual practice law San Francisco, 1976—; internat. counsel to Fed. States Micronesia, 1974-82; cons. Rand Corp., Dept. of Def., Nuclear Regulatory Commn.; trustee in bankruptcy, receiver various corps since 1974. Contbr. to: Ency. Brit, 1972, also articles in profl. publs., newspapers. Served with AUS, 1946-47. Mem. World Affairs Coun., Internat. Inst. Strategic Studies, Phi Beta Kappa. Office: 28th Flr 3 Embarcadero Ctr Ste 28 San Francisco CA 94111-4003

WYLIE, EVAN BENJAMIN, civil engineering educator, consultant, researcher; b. Donavon, Sask., Can., Jan. 14, 1931; came to U.S., 1950; s. Mansel and Florence (Riddell) W.; m. Frances Eleanor Miller, Feb. 4, 1955; children—Brian Douglas, Scott Cameron, Karen Louise. B.S. in Civil Engring., U. Denver, 1953; M.S. in Civil Engring., U. Colo., 1955; Ph.D. in Civil Engring., U. Mich., 1964. Registered profl. engr., Mich. Engr. Ford Motor Co. of Can., Toronto, Ont., 1956-59; asst. prof. civil engring. U. Denver, 1959-62; asst. prof. civil engring. U. Mich., Ann Arbor, 1965-66, assoc. prof. civil engring., 1966-70, prof. civil engring., 1970—, chmn. dept. civil engring., 1987-90, chmn. dept. civil and environ. engring., 1991-94. Author: (with V.L. Streeter) Hydraulic Transients, 1967, Fluid Mechanics, 1975, 8th edit., 1985, Fluid Transients, 1978, Fluid Transients in Systems, 1993. Fellow ASME, ASCE; mem. Am. Soc. Engring. Edn., Internat. Assn. Hydraulic Rsch. Republican. Avocations: tennis; skiing; woodworking. Home: 4684 Mulberry Woods Cir Ann Arbor MI 48105-9778 Office: Univ Mich Dept Civil Environ Engring Ann Arbor MI 48109-2125

WYLIE, MARY EVELYN, psychiatrist, retired anesthesiologist, educator; b. Huntington, W.Va., Jan. 28, 1947; d. Herman E. and Charlotte (Toney) Smith; m. John K. Ostlund, June 14, 1987; 1 child, Sarah Johnson. BS in Biology, U. Ill., Chgo., 1973, MD, 1977. Diplomate Am. Bd. Anesthesiology. Intern Northwestern U. Med. Ctr., Chgo., 1977-78, resident in anesthesiology, 1978-80; fellow in adult and pediatric cardiac anesthesia Tufts-New Eng. Med. Ctr., Boston, 1980-81; anesthesiologist Waltham (Mass.)-Weston Hosp., 1981-88, Boston City Hosp., 1988-90, Presbyn. Univ. Hosp., Pitts., 1991—; asst. prof. anesthesiology Boston U. Med. Sch., 1988-90, U. Pitts. Med. Sch., 1991-93; resident in psychiatry Western Psychiatric Inst. and Clinic/U. Pitts. Med. Ctr., 1996—; NIMH Rsch. Fellow in late-life mood and anxiety disorders. Mem. AMA, Pa. Med. Soc., Am. Soc. Anesthesiologists, Pa. Soc. Anesthesiologists,Pa. Psychiat. Soc., Am. Psychiatric Assn. Baha'i. Avocation: ballroom dancing. Office: Western Psychiatric Inst and Clinic Dept Anesthesia 3811 Ohara St # 740 Bt Pittsburgh PA 15213-2593

WYLLIE, PETER JOHN, geologist, educator; b. London, Feb. 8, 1930; came to U.S., 1961; s. George William and Beatrice Gladys (Weaver) W.; m. Frances Rosemary Blair, June 9, 1956; children: Andrew, Elizabeth (dec.), Lisa, John. B.Sc. in Geology and Physics, U. St. Andrews, Scotland, 1952, B.Sc. with 1st class honours in Geology, 1955, Ph.D. in Geology, 1958, D.Sc. (hon.), 1974. Glaciologist Brit. W. Greenland Expdn., 1950; geologist Brit. N. Greenland Expdn., 1952-54; asst. lectr. geology U. St. Andrews, 1955-56; research asst. geochemistry Pa. State U., State College, 1956-58, asst. prof. geochemistry, 1958-59, asso. prof. petrology, 1961-65, acting head, dept.

geochemistry mineralogy, 1962-63; research fellow chemistry Leeds (Eng.) U., 1959-60, lectr. exptl. petrology, 1960-61; prof. petrology geochemistry U. Chgo., 1965-77, Homer J. Livingston prof., 1978-83, chmn. dept. geophys. scis., 1979-82, master phys. scis. collegiate div., asso. dean coll., asso. dean phys. scis. div., 1972-73; chmn. div. geol. and planetary scis. Calif. Inst. Tech., Pasadena, 1983-87, prof. geology, 1987—; chmn. commn. exptl. petrology high pressures temperatures Internat. Union Geol. Scis.; mem. adv. panel earth scis. NSF, 1975-78, chmn. adv. com. earth scis. div., 1979-82; mem. U.S. Nat. Com. on Geology, 1978-82; mem. U.S. Nat. Com. Internat. Union Geodesy and Geophysics, 1980-84, U.S. Nat. Com. Geochemistry, 1981-84; chmn. com. on objectives in solid-earth scis. NRC, 1988-93; hon. prof. China U. Geoscis., Beijing, 1996. Author: The Dynamic Earth, 1971, The Way the Earth Works, 1976; editor: Ultramafic and Related Rocks, 1967; chmn. editorial & writing com. Solid-Earth Sciences and Society, 1993; editor Jour. Geology, 1967-83; editor-in-chief Minerals Rocks (monograph series), 1967—. Served with RAF, 1948-49. Heavyweight boxing champion RAF Scotland, 1949; recipient Polar medal H.M. Queen Elizabeth, Eng., 1954; Quantrell award, 1979; Wollaston medal Geol. Soc. London, 1982, Abraham-Gottlob-Werner-Medaille German Mineral. Soc., 1987. Fellow Am. Acad. Arts and Sci., Royal Soc. London, Edinburgh Geol. Soc. (corr.), Mineral Soc. Am. (pres. 1977-78, award 1965), Am. Acad. Scis. (fgn. assoc.), Am. Geophys. Union, Indian Geophys. Union (fgn.), Nat. Acad. Sci. India (fgn.), Russian Acad. Scis. (fgn.), Russian Mineral. Soc. (fgn., hon.), Indian Nat. Sci. Acad. (fgn.), Academia Europaea (fgn.), Geol. Soc. Am.; mem. Mineral. Soc. Gt. Britain and Ireland (hon.), Internat. Mineral Assn. (2d v.p. 1978-82, 1st v.p. 1982-86, pres. 1986-90), Internat. Union of Geodesy and Geophysics (v.p. 1991-95, pres. 1995-99), Chinese Acad. Scis. (fgn. mem.). Office: Calif Inst Tech Geol Planetary Scis 17 # 25 Pasadena CA 91125

WYLLY, BARBARA BENTLEY, performing arts association administrator; b. Bala-Cynwyd, Pa., June 10, 1924; d. William Henry and Virginia (Barclay) Bentley; m. William Beck Wylly, Apr. 26, 1947; children: Virginia Wylly Johnson, Barbara L., Thomas C. II. A, Briarcliff Jr. Coll., 1943. Pres. bd. dirs. Hillside Hosp. Inc., Atlanta, 1982, mem. adv. coun., 1982—; pres. Atlanta Symphony Assocs., 1975-76, mem. adv. bd., 1976—; chmn. bd. dirs. Ctr. for Puppetry Arts, Atlanta, 1988—. Republican. Episcopalian. Avocations: walking, reading, music. Home: 940 Foxcroft Rd NW Atlanta GA 30327-2622 Office: Ctr Puppetry Arts 1404 Spring St NW Atlanta GA 30309-2820

WYLY, CHARLES JOSEPH, JR., corporate executive; b. Lake Providence, La., Oct. 13, 1933; s. Charles Joseph and Flora (Evans) W.; m. Caroline Denmon; children: Martha, Charles Joseph III, Emily, Jennifer. B.S., La. Tech. U., 1956. Sales rep. IBM Service Bur. Corp., 1956-64; v.p. Wyly Corp., Dallas, 1964-65, exec. v.p., 1965-69, pres., 1969-73, chmn. exec. com., 1973-76, dir., 1964-76; chmn. bd. Earth Resources Co., 1968-80; vice chmn. bd. dirs. USACafes, Inc. (Bonanza Internat., Inc.), 1968-89, Sterling Software, Inc., Michaels Stores, Inc.; chmn. Tex. High-Speed Rail Authority, 1990-91, Maverick Capital, 1990-96. Mem. Pres.'s Advisory Council on Mgmt. Improvement, 1970-73; vice-chmn. Devel. Council So. Methodist U. Found. Sci. and Engring., 1970-71; Mem. Republican Nat. Fin. Com., 1970—; Bd. dirs. Dallas County United Way Fund; pres. Dallas Theater Center., 1972-79. Mem. Am. Mgmt. Assn., Pi Kappa Alpha, Omicron Delta Kappa, Delta Sigma Pi, Beta Gamma Sigma. Clubs: City, Crescent, Park City, Brookhollow (Dallas). Office: 300 Crescent Ct Ste 1200 Dallas TX 75201

WYMAN, DAVID SWORD, historian, educator; b. Weymouth, Mass., Mar. 6, 1929; s. Hollis Judson and Ruth (Sword) W.; m. Mildred Louise Smith, Sept. 13, 1950; children: James Nayler, Teresa Carol. AB, Boston U., 1951; EdM, Plymouth State Coll., 1961; AM, Harvard U., 1962, PhD, 1966; DHL (hon.), Hebrew Union Coll. Jewish Inst. Religion, 1986, Yeshiva U., 1988. Various positions, 1951-57; tchr. pub. schs. Tilton, N.H., 1957-60; tchr. pub. high sch. Penacook, N.H., 1960-61; prof. history U. Mass., Amherst, 1966-91, Josiah DuBois prof. history, 1986-91, Josiah DuBois prof. emeritus, 1991—, chmn. Judaic Studies Program, 1977-78, 82-84; acad. advisor Simon Wiesenthal Ctr., L.A., 1983—; nat. coun. Nat. Christian Leadership Conf. for Israel, 1986, numerous radio and TV appearances; historian advisor to films. Author: Paper Walls: America and the Refugee Crisis, 1938-41, 1968, The Abandonment of the Jews: America and the Holocaust, 1941-45, 1984 (Anisfield-Wolf award 1984, Stuart Bernath award 1984, Theodore Saloutos book award 1984, Present Tense Lit. award 1984, Boston Hadassah Myrtle Wreath award 1985, Nat. Jewish Book award 1985); editor: America and the Holocaust, 13 vols. documents, 1989-90, The World Reacts to the Holocaust, 1996; contbr. articles to profl. jours., chpts. to books. Recipient Chancellor's medal, U. Mass., 1986, Achievement award Isaac M. Wise Temple, Cin. 1986, Humanitarian award Bklyn. Holocaust Meml. Com., 1986; elected to Boston U. Collegium Disting. Alumni, 1986; Woodrow Wilson fellow, 1961-62, 65-66; grantee Social Sci. Rsch. Coun., 1969-70, Am. Coun. Learned Socs., 1969-70, Charles Warren Ctr. at Harvard U., 1969-70. Mem. Soc. for Am. Baseball Rsch., N.H. Hist. Soc., Friends Hist. Assn., Phi Beta Kappa. Avocations: baseball, greyhounds as pets, local N.H. history. Home: 61 Columbia Dr Amherst MA 01002-3105

WYMAN, JAMES THOMAS, petroleum company executive; b. Mpls., Apr. 9, 1920; s. James Claire and Martha (McChesney) W.; m. Elizabeth Winston, May 6, 1950; children: Elizabeth Wyman Wilcox, James Claire, Steven McChesney. Grad., Blake Prep. Sch., Mpls., 1938; B.A., Yale U., 1942. With Mpls. Star and Tribune, 1946-50; advt. mgr. Super Valu Stores, Inc., Eden Prairie, Minn., 1951-54; store devel. mgr. Super Valu Stores, Inc., 1955-56, gen. sales mgr., 1956-57, sales v.p., 1957-60, dir., 1959-87, exec. v.p., 1961-64, pres., chief exec. officer, 1965-70, chmn. exec. com., 1970-76, ret., 1976; chmn. bd., bd. dirs. Marshall & Winston, Inc. Served to lt. (s.g.) USNR, World War II. Clubs: Minneapolis; Woodhill Country (Wayzata). Home: 2855 Woolsey Ln Wayzata MN 55391-2752 Office: 1105 Foshay Tower Minneapolis MN 55402

WYMAN, JAMES VERNON, newspaper executive; b. Brockton, Mass., Nov. 17, 1923; s. George Dewey and Christine Laverne (Skinner) W.; m. Viola Marie Bousquet, June 24, 1950; children: J. Vernon, Douglas Phillip, Carolyn Anne. Student, Northeastern U., Boston, 1946-48; BS in Journalism, Boston U., 1951. From staff to dep. exec. editor Providence Jour.-Bull., 1951-88, v.p., exec. editor, 1989-95, ret., 1995. Served with AUS, 1942-46, PTO. Recipient Yankee Quill award, 1989, Disting. Alumni award Boston U. Coll. of Comm. Alumni Bd., 1996. Mem. New Eng. AP News Execs. Assn. (past pres.), AP Mng. Editors Assn., New Eng. Soc. Newspaper Editors, Acad. New Eng. Journalists (past dir.), New Eng. Newspaper Assn., Sigma Delta Chi (past pres. New Eng. chpt.). Roman Catholic. Home: PO Box 7511 Cumberland RI 02864-4914 *Success comes in many packages and is gauged in myriad ways. But it must be most rewarding when it can be measured in terms of simple, effective service to others—in terms of sincere endeavors to foster hope and to ignite the human spirit in those around you.*

WYMAN, L. PILAR, indexer; b. Beirut, Nov. 14, 1964; d. Samuel Haynes and Laura Pilar (Garzon) W.; m. Peter John McMenamin, Nov. 4, 1991; children: Leith Maria, Hugh Haynes. BA, St. John's Coll., 1986. Typist Editl. Svcs., Annapolis, Md., 1983-86, assoc. indexer, 1989-93; chief indexer Wyman Indexing, Annapolis, 1990—; instr. basic indexing USDA Grad. Sch., 1996—. Author: (booklet) Indexing FAQ, 1994; contbr. articles, letters, and indexes to profl. publs. Minority grad. fellow NSF, 1987. Mem. Soc. for Tech. Comm., Am. Med. Writers Assn., Am. Soc. Indexers (chair Washington chpt. 1995-96). Democrat. Episcopalian. Avocations: sailing, reading, parenting, travel. Office: Wyman Indexing 1240L Gemini Dr Annapolis MD 21403

WYMAN, LOUIS CROSBY, judge, former senator, former congressman; b. Manchester, N.H., Mar. 16, 1917; s. Louis Eliot and Alice Sibley (Crosby) W.; m. Virginia Elizabeth Markley, Aug. 20, 1938; children—Jo Ann, Louis Eliot. B.S. with honor, U. N.H., 1938; LL.B. cum laude, Harvard U., 1941. Bar: Mass. bar 1941, N.H. bar 1941, D.C. bar 1947, Fla. bar 1957. Asso. firm Ropes, Gray, Best, Coolidge & Rugg, Boston, 1941-42; mem. firm Wyman, Starr, Booth, Wadleigh & Langdell, Manchester, N.H., 1949-52; gen. counsel to U.S. Senate investigating com., 1946; sec. to U.S. Senator Styles Bridges, 1947; counsel to joint congl. com. on Fgn. Econ. Cooperation, 1948-49; atty. gen. N.H., 1953-61; legis. counsel to gov. N.H., 1961; partner Wyman, Bean & Stark, Manchester, 1957-78; asso. justice Superior Ct. N.H., 1978—; mem. 88th, 90th-94th congresses from 1st dist. N.H., mem. com. appropriations, subcom. on def.; apptd. U.S. senator, 1974; chmn. N.H. Commn. on Interstate Cooperation; mem. Jud. Council of N.H.; chmn. Nat. Com. on Internal Security, 1958-61. Served as lt. USNR, 1942-46. Fellow Am. Coll. Trial Lawyers; mem. ABA (chmn. standing com. jurisprudence and law reform 1961-63), Mass. Bar Assn., N.H. Bar Assn., Fla. Bar Assn., D.C. Bar Assn., Nat. Assn. Attys. Gen. U.S. (pres. 1957-58), Phi Kappa Phi, Theta Chi, Kappa Delta Pi. *In a mixed up world each person needs a goal—something he or she can strive for, work toward and measure progress against. Mine has always been to try to help make this world a better place to live for all—with dignity, privacy, security and reasonable comforts. Toward greater progress in this goal I forsook the practice of law for years of public service during which it was more clearly possible to do much for people. Less money but more action if you will. Throughout everything in life it is vital to believe in something greater than man alone and to seek guidance from prayer. Faith that sincere effort will be rewarded, if not in this life in the next, also helps.*

WYMAN, RALPH MARK, corporate executive; b. Usti, Czechoslovakia, Feb. 7, 1926; came to U.S., 1941, naturalized, 1946; s. Hans and Stella (Parnas) W.; m. Lotte Ann Novak, Oct. 25, 1947; 1 dau., Leslie Andrea Wyman Cooper. Student, Upper Can. Coll., 1942, Bucknell U., 1942-43; B.S. in Bus. Adminstrn., NYU, 1945; postgrad., Columbia U., 1945-46. Asst. mgr. export dept. Liebermann Waelchi & Co., Inc., N.Y.C., 1946-47; trainee White Weld Co. (investment brokers), 1947-48; v.p. H.O. Canfield Co., 1948-65, vice chmn. bd., 1965-79, dir., 1953-79; dir. Pantasote Inc., 1960-89, vice chmn. bd., 1967-89; mng. partner United Eagle Mgmt. Co., Eagle Mgmt. Co., 1960-95; pres. Veritas Co., 1960—; dir., chmn. Eagle Capital Internat. LLC, 1985—; dir., vice chmn. Affiliate Artists, Inc., 1971-88. Pres. Panwy Found.; bd. dirs. United Way of Greenwich, 1980-86; bd. dirs. Kids in Crisis, Greenwich, 1993—, sec., 1995; trustee Princeton Theol. Sem., 1976—, vice chmn., 1997—. Mem. Greenwich Country Club, Lambda Chi Alpha. Presbyterian (elder, trustee Synod of N.E. 1974-76). Home: 34 Baldwin Farms North Greenwich CT 06831 Office: Greenwich Office Park 9 10 Valley Dr Greenwich CT 06831

WYMAN, RICHARD THOMAS, information services consultant; b. Wilmington, Del., June 4, 1951; s. William Harper and Marian Kathryn (Bode) W. Pa. State U., 1969-71, Def. Language Inst., 1974-75, Control Data Inst., Dallas, 1979. Enlisted U.S. Army, 1971, served to staff sgt., 1979; data ctr. mgr. thrift svcs. divsn. ADP Inc., Dallas, 1979-80; support mgr. Electronic Data Sys., Inc., Dallas, 1980-85, info. modeling analyst, 1985-90; pres. Strategic InfoSource, Plano, Tex., 1991-93; sr. cons. The SABRE Group, Ft. Worth, 1993-97; assoc. Perot Sys. Corp., Richardson, Tex., 1997—; rep. 101st Airborne Divsn. Nat. Conf. Skill Maintenance, Ft. Meade, Md., 1977. Author: (spl. course) U.S. Army Intelligence, 1978-79. Co-chmn. sub-com. City Bond Referendum Com., Plano, 1990; mem. City of Plano Historic Landmark Com., 1993—, vice chmn. 1996, chmn. 1996—. Recipient Army Commendation medal, 1978, 79, Vol. Svc. award, Office of Mayor, Plano, 1990. Home: 717 Kipling Dr Plano TX 75023 Office: Perot Sys Corp 3000 Telecom Pkwy Richardson TX 75082

WYMAN, RICHARD VAUGHN, engineering educator, exploration company executive; b. Painesville, Ohio, Feb. 22, 1927; s. Vaughn Ely and Melinda (Ward) W.; m. Anne Fenton, Dec. 27, 1947; 1 son, William Fenton. B.S., Case Western Res. U., 1948; M.S., U. Mich., 1949; Ph.D., U. Ariz., 1974. Registered profl. engr., Nev.; registered geologist, Ariz., Calif.; lic. water right surveyor, Nev. Geologist N.J. Zinc Co., 1949, 52-53, Cerro de Pasco Corp., 1950-52; chief geologist Western Gold & Uranium, Inc., St. George, Utah, 1953-55, gen. supt., 1955-57, v.p., 1957-59; pres. Intermountain Exploration Co., Boulder City, Nev., 1959-93; tunnel supt. Reynolds Electric & Engring. Co., 1961-63, mining engr., 1965-67; asst. mgr. ops. Reynolds Electric and & Engring. Co., 1967-69; constrn. supt. engr. Sunshine Mining Co., 1963-65; lectr. U. Nev., Las Vegas, 1969-73, assoc. prof., 1973-80, dept. chmn., 1976-80, prof., 1980-92, prof. emeritus, 1992—, chmn. dept. civil and mech. engring., 1984-90, chmn. dept. civil and environ. engring., 1990-91; mineral rep. Ariz. Strip Adv. Bd., 1976-80, U.S.B.L.M.; mem. peer rev. com. Nuclear Waste Site, Dept. Energy, Las Vegas, 1978-82; pres. Ariz. Juno Resources, Boulder City, 1980-83, v.p., 1990—; pres. Wyman Engring. Cons., 1987—; cons. Corp. Andina de Fomento, Caracas, Venezuela, 1977-78; v.p. Comstock Gold, Inc., 1984-93; program evaluator Accreditation Bd. for Engring. and Tech., 1995—. Contbr. articles to profl. jours. Sec. Washington County Republican Party, Utah, 1958-60; del. Utah Rep. Conv., 1958-60; scoutmaster Boy Scouts Am., 1959-69. Served with USN, 1944-46. Fellow ASCE (edn. divsn. 1990, local rep. nat. conv. Las Vegas 1990), Soc. Econ. Geologists (life); mem. AIME (chmn. So. Nev. sect. 1971-72, dir. 1968—, sec.-treas. 1974-92, chmn. Pacific S.W. Minerals Conf. 1972, gen. chmn. nat. conv. 1980, Disting. Mem. award 1989), Assn. Engring. Geologists (dir. S.W. sect. 1989-91), Am. Inst. Minerals Appraisers, Nev. Mining Assn. (assoc.), Assn. Ground Water Scientists and Engrs., Arctic Inst. N.Am. (life), Am. Soc. Engring. Edn., Soc. for History of Discoveries, Sigma Xi (pres. Las Vegas sect. 1986-91), Phi Kappa Phi (pres. U. Nev. Las Vegas chpt. 100 1982-83), Sigma Gamma Epsilon. Congregationalist. Home: 610 Bryant Ct Boulder City NV 89005-3017 Office: Wyman Engring PO Bxo 60473 Boulder City NV 89006-0473

WYMAN, WILLIAM GEORGE, musician; b. London, Oct. 24, 1936; m. Mandy Smith (div. 1992); 1 child from previous marriage, Stephen; m. Suzanne Accosta, Apr. 1993; children: Katharine, Jessica. Owner Ripple Records, Ripple Music, Ripple Publs., Ripple Prodns.; owner Sticky Fingers restaurant, London. Bassist with musical group, The Rolling Stones, 1962-92; albums include: 12 x 5, 1964, The Rolling Stones Now, 1965, Out of Our Heads, 1965, December's Children, 1965, Big Hits, 1966, Aftermath, 1966, Got Live If You Want It, 1967, Between the Buttons, 1967, Their Satanic Majesties Request, 1967, Flowers, 1967, Beggar's Banquet, 1968, Through the Past Darkly, 1969, Let it Bleed, 1969, Get Yer Ya Yas Out, 1970, Sticky Fingers, 1971, Hot Rocks: 1964-1971, 1972, Exile on Main Street, 1972, More Hot Rocks (Big Hits & Fazed Cookies), 1972, Goats Head Soup, 1973, It's Only Rock n' Roll, 1974, Made in the Shade, 1975, Metamorphosis, 1975, Black and Blue, 1976, Love You Live, 1977, Some Girls, 1978, Sucking in the Seventies, 1981, Tattoo You, 1981, Still Life, 1981, Undercover, 1983, Rewind: 1971-1984, Between the Sheets, 1985, Dirty Work, 1986, Emotional Rescue, 1988, Steel Wheels, 1989, Flashpoint, 1991, Voodoo Lounge, 1994, (with Charlie Watts, Andy Fairweather-Low, Chris Rea, Paul Rogers, Jimmy Page) Willie and the Poor Boys, 1985, (with Gary Brooker) Willie and the Poor Boys Live, 1985, Left the Rolling Stones, 1995, numerous others; solo recs. include Stone Alone, Monkey Grip, Bill Wyman, Stuff; films Sympathy for the Devil, 1970; Gimme Shelter, 1970, Ladies and Gentlemen the Rolling Stones, 1974, Let's Spend the Night Together, 1982, Digital Dreams, 1983, Rolling Stones in IMAX Larger Than Live; composer: (soundtrack) Green Ice; author: photographs Chagall Mediterrané, 1984, (with Ray Coleman) Stone Alone: The Story of a Rock 'n' Roll Band, 1991; contbr. photographs to Chagall's World. Avocations: archeology, writing. Address: care Ripple Prodns Ltd, 344 Kings Rd, London SW3 5UR, England*

WYMORE, LUANN COURTNEY, education educator; b. Kansas City, Mo., Feb. 22, 1942; d. Clifford Willis and Lola (Moore) Courtney; m. George Philip Wymore, Dec. 27, 1964; children: Courtney, Kristin, Ryan. BA, William Jewell Coll., 1964; MA, U. Mo., Kansas City, 1969; PhD, Mo. U., 1989. Cert. elem., biology, Englisy tchr., Mo. Elem. tchr. Sch. Dist. North Kansas City, Mo., 1964-69; assoc. prof. elem. edn. Mo. Valley Coll., Marshall, 1989—; presenter in field. Contbr. articles to profl. jours. Leader Girl Scouts U.S.A., Slater, Mo., 1980's, 4-H Club, Orearville, Mo., 1980's. Mem. ASCD, PEO, Internat. Reading Assn. Democrat. Avocations: reading, piano, organ, travel. Home: 820 Rich St Slater MO 65349-1258 Office: Mo Valley Coll 500 E College St Marshall MO 65340-3109

WYNAR, BOHDAN STEPHEN, librarian, author, editor; b. Lviv, Ukraine, Sept. 7, 1926; came to U.S., 1950, naturalized, 1957; s. John I. and Euphrosina (Doryk) W.; m. Olha Yarema, Nov. 23, 1992; children: Taras, Michael, Roxolana, Yarynka. Diplom-Volkswirt Econs., U. Munich, Germany, 1949, Ph.D., 1950; M.A., U. Denver, 1958. Methods analyst, statistician Tramco Corp., Cleve., 1951-53; freelance journalist Societ Econs., Cleve., 1954-56; adminstrv. asst. U. Denver Librs., 1958-59, head tech. svcs. div., 1959-62; assoc. prof. Sch. Librarianship, U. Denver, 1962-66; dir. div. libr. edn. State U. Coll., Geneseo, N.Y., 1966-67; dean Sch. Libr. Sci. State U. Coll., Geneseo; prof. State U. Coll., 1967-69; pres. Libraries Unlimited Inc., 1969—. Author: Soviet Light Industry, 1956, Economic Colonialism, 1958, Ukrainian Industry, 1964, Introduction to Bibliography and Reference Work, 4th edit, 1967, Introduction to Cataloging and Classification, 8th edit, 1992, Major Writings on Soviet Economy, 1966, Library Acquisitions, 2d edit, 1971, Research Methods in Library Science, 1971, Economic Thought in Kievan Rus', 1974; co-author: Comprehensive Bibliography of Cataloging and Classification, 2 vols., 1973, Ukraine: A Bibliographic Guide to English Language Publications, 1990; editor Ukrainian Quar., 1953-58, Preliminary Checklist of Colorado Bibliography, 1963, Studies in Librarianship, 1963-66, Research Studies in Library Science, 1970—, Best Reference Books, 3d edit., 1985, 4th edit., 1992, Colorado Bibliography, 1980; gen. editor: American Reference Books Ann., 1969—; editor: ARBA Guide to Subject Encyclopedias and Dictionaries, 1985, ARBA Guide To Biographical Dictionaries, Reference Books in Paperback, An Annotated Guide, 2d edit., 1976, 3rd edit., 1991, Dictionary of Am. Library Biography, 1978, Ukraine-A Bibliographic Guide to English-Language Publications, 1990, International Writings of Bohdan S. Wynar 1949-1992, 1993, Recommended Reference Books for Medium-Sized and Small Libraries, 1981—; co-editor, contbr. Ency. Ukraine, 1955—;editor Library Sci. Ann., 1984-90. Bd. dirs., mem. exec. bd. ZAREVO, Inc. Mem. ALA (pres. Ukrainian Congress com. br., Denver 1976), Colo. Library Assn., N.Y. Library Assn., Am. Assn. Advancement Slavic Studies (pres. Ukrainian Research Found. 1976-90), AAUP, Ukranian Hist. Assn. (exec. bd.), Sevčenko Societe Scientifique (Paris), Ukrainian Acad. Arts and Scis. (N.Y.C.). Office: Librs Unltd Inc 6931 S Yosemite St Englewood CO 80112-1415

WYNDRUM, RALPH W., JR., communications company executive; b. N.Y.C., Apr. 20, 1937; s. Ralph W. and Virginia M. (Woolley) W.; m. Meta Schmidt, Apr. 23, 1960; children: Dorothy, Jeanne, Ralph, Joan. B.S., Columbia U., 1959, M.S. in Elec. Engring., 1960, M.S. in Bus. Adminstrn., 1978; Sc.D., NYU, 1963. Mem. tech. staff Bell Labs., Murray Hill, N.J., 1963-65; supr. exploratory circuit design Bell Labs., 1965-69; head loop transmission tech. dept. Bell Labs., Holmdel and Whippany, N.J., 1969-79; head advanced loop transmission systems dept. Bell Labs., Whippany, 1979-87, head internat. loop systems dept., 1987, dir. systems analysis ctr., 1987-90, dir. quality process ctr., 1990-92, dir. quality, engring., software and techs., 1993-94; v.p. AT&T World Svcs., 1994—, dir. process engr. ctr., 1995—; v.p. tech. AT&T Labs., 1996—; adj. prof. N.J. Inst. Tech., 1965, Stevens Inst. Tech., 1980-88. Contbr. articles to profl. jours. Fellow IEEE (bd. dirs. 1988-90, v.p. pubs. 1990-91, President's Leadership award 1991); mem. IEEE Comm. Soc. (chmn. conf. bd. 1981-87), Sigma Xi, Eta Kappa Nu, Beta Gamma Sigma. Republican. Roman Catholic. Patentee in field. Home: 35 Cooney Ter Fair Haven NJ 07704-3001 Office: AT&T Labs Rm 3L324 Holmdel NJ 07733

WYNER, AARON DANIEL, mathematician; b. N.Y.C., Mar. 17, 1939; s. Alvin and Mary (Jacobson) W.; m. Nusha Zukerman, June 9, 1963; children—Tamar, Abraham, Dena, Yael. BS, Queens Coll., 1960, Columbia U., 1960; MS, Columbia U., 1961, PhD, 1963. Asst. prof. elec. engring. Columbia U., 1963; mem. tech. staff Bell Labs., Murray Hill, N.J., 1963-96, head comm. analysis rsch. dept., 1974-93, disting. mem. tech. staff, 1996—; adj. and vis. prof. Columbia U., Polytech. U., Technion, Haifa, Israel, Weizmann Inst. Sci., Rehovot, Israel., Princeton U. Assoc. editor: IEEE Transactions on Info. Theory, 1970-72, editor-in-chief, 1983-86. Guggenheim Found. fellow, 1966. Fellow IEEE (past pres. Info. Theory Soc., Centennial medal 1984, Claude Shannon award), AAAS; mem. Internat. Sci. Radio Union (chmn. U.S. comm. on signals and sys. 1987-90, vice-chmn. internat. commn. 1990-93), Nat. Acad. Engring. Patentee in field. Home: 43 Glenview Rd South Orange NJ 07079-1061 Office: Bell Labs 600 Mountain Ave New Providence NJ 07974-2008

WYNER, JUSTIN L., laminating company executive; b. Boston, Aug. 6, 1925; s. Rudolph H. and Sara G. Wyner; m. Genevieve Gloria Geller, July 3, 1955; children: George Michael, Daniel Mark, James Henry. BS cum laude, Tufts Coll., 1946; MBA, Harvard U., 1948. Chmn. bd. Shawmut Mills div. R.H. Wyner Assocs., West Bridgewater, Mass. Mem. Brookline Rep. Town Com., 1964—; trustee Beth Israel Hosp., Boston, 1966-96, mem. fin. com., 1972-80; trustee Temple Israel, Boston, 1964—, pres., 1979-82, chmn. bd. mgrs., 1983-94; trustee Am. Jewish Hist. Soc., 1987—, pres., 1992—; trustee Hebrew Coll., 1967—, chmn. cultural affairs com., 1977-78, trustee Temple Kehillath Israel, 1967—; trustee Combined Jewish Philanthropies, Boston, 1966-96, bd. mgrs., 1989—; trustee Roxbury Latin Sch., 1985-89; moderator Town of Brookline, Mass., 1970-82, 91-94, chmn. fin. com., 1961-64; nat. chmn. Reps. for Eugene McCarthy, 1968; chmn. Brookline United Fund, 1960; pres. Jewish Community Rels. Coun., 1971-73, mem. adminstrv. com., 1967—; dir. Brookline Taxpayer's Assn., 1956-61, Brookline Community Coun., 1957-61; gov. Hebrew Union Coll.-Jewish Inst. Religion, 1987-92; bd. dirs. Mass. div. Am. Cancer Soc., 1987—; pres. Hebrew Free Loan Soc. Boston, 1972-88; active various other civic and religious orgns.; exec. com. bd. overseers Beth Israel Deaconess Hosp., 1996—; dir. Ctr. for Jewish History, 1996—. Mem. Nat. Assn. for Textile Tech. (nat. bd. govs. 1970-73), Nat. Knitwear Mfrs. Assn. (past dir., bd. dirs., present hon. life dir.), New Bedford Yacht Club, Harvard (Boston and N.Y.C.), Belmont Country Club, Thorny Lea Golf Club, Norfolk Trout. Avocations: sailing, amateur radio, golf. Home: 830 Newton St Chestnut Hill MA 02167-2643 Office: Shawmut Mills 208 Manley St West Bridgewater MA 02379-1044

WYNER, YEHUDI, composer, pianist, conductor, educator; b. Calgary, Alta., Can., June 1, 1929; s. Lazar and Sarah Naomi (Shumiatcher) Weiner; m. Nancy Joan Braverman, Sept. 16, 1951 (div. 1967); children: Isaiah, Adam, Cassia; m. Susan M. Davenny, June 15, 1967. Diploma, Juilliard Sch. Music, 1946; A.B., Yale U., 1950, B.Mus., 1951, M.Mus., 1953; M.A., Harvard U., 1952. Vis. assoc. prof. Hofstra Coll., 1959; lectr. Queens Coll., N.Y.C., 1959-60; instr. Hebrew Union Coll., N.Y.C., 1957-59; music dir. Westchester Reform Temple, N.Y.C., 1959-68; asst. prof. theory Yale U., 1963-69, assoc. prof. theory, 1969-77, chmn. composition dept., 1969-73; prof. music SUNY, Purchase, 1978-89, dean music, 1978-82; faculty Berkshire Music Ctr., 1975-85; faculty Tanglewood Music Ctr. (formerly Berkshire Music Ctr.), 1975—; vis. prof. composition Cornell U., 1987 Ziskind vis. prof. composition Brandeis U., 1987-88, Walter Naumburg prof. composition, dir. contemporary ensemble, 1989—; vis. prof. Harvard U., 1991-93, 96-97. Mus. dir., New Haven Opera Soc., 1968-77, Turnau Opera Assn., 1961-64; mem., Bach Aria Group, 1968—; composer-condr., Tanglewood, 1961; composer-in-residence, Santa Fe Chamber Music Festival, 1982, Am. Acad. in Rome, spring 1991; composer: Two Chorale Preludes for Organ, 1951, Partita for Piano, 1952, Dance Variations for Wind Octet, 1953, rev., 1959, Psalm 143, chorus, 1952, Sonata for Piano, 1954, Concert Duo for Violin and Piano, 1955-57, Dedication Anthem, 1957, Serenade for Seven Instruments, 1958, Passover Offering, 1959, Three Informal Pieces for Violin and Piano, 1961, Friday Evening Service for Cantor, Chorus, Organ, 1963, Incidental Music for play The Old Glory, 1964, Torah Service with Instruments, 1966, Da Camera for Piano and Orch, 1967, Cadenza for Clarinet and Harpsichord, 1969, De Novo for cello and small ensemble, 1971, Liturgy for the High Holidays, 1971, Three Short Fantasies for Piano, 1963-71, Songs, 1950-79, Canto Cantabile for Soprano and Concert Band, 1972, music for play The Mirror, 1972-73, Memorial Music for Soprano and 3 Flutes, 1971-73, Intermedio for Soprano and String Orchestra, 1974, Wedding Music, 1976, Dances of Atonement for Violin and Piano, 1976, Fragments from Antiquity; 5 songs for soprano and symphony orch., 1978; Piano Quartet, 1980, All the Rage for flute and piano, 1980; Processionals and Marches, 1979, 80, Tanz and Maissele, 1981, On This Most Voluptuous Night, 1982, Passage for 7 Instruments, 1983, Wind Quintet, 1984, String Quartet, 1985, Composition for Viola and Piano, 1987, Toward the Center for piano, 1988, Sweet Consort for flute and piano, 1988, Leonardo Vincitore for 2 sopranos, string bass and piano, 1988, O To Be a Dragon, four songs for women's chorus and piano, 1989, Trapunto Junction for brass trio and percussion, 1991, Changing Time for small ensemble, 1991, New Fantasies for piano, 1991, Amadeus' Billiard for small ensemble, 1991, Il Cane Minore for 2 clarinets and bassoon, 1992, Wedding Dances: From the Notebook of Suzanne de Venné, 1993, Post Fantasies for Piano, 1993, Prologue and Narrative for cello and orch., 1994, Song Cycle for soprano, baritone and piano, Restaurants, Wines-Bistros, Shrines, 1994, More Fantasies for Piano, 1994, Lyric Harmony for orch., 1995, Praise Ye the Lord for soprano and ensemble, 1996, A Mad Tea Party for soprano, 2 baritones, flute, violin, cello and piano, 1996, Epilogue for Orch., 1996. Recipient Inst. Arts and Letters grant, 1961, Brandeis Creative Arts award, 1963; commns. from Yale U.,

1958, Mich. U., 1959, Fromm Found., 1960, Koussevitzky Found. at Library Congress, 1960, Ford Found., 1971, Yale Band, Yale Repertory Theater, Cantilena Chamber Players, Aeolian Chamber Players, Santa Fe Chamber Music Festival, Collage of Boston, N.Y. Woodwind Quintet, Frank Taplin project, NEA Consortium, Boston Symphony Chamber Players, Atlantic Sinfonietta, Carnegie Hall Am. Composers Orch., RNCM Manchester Internat. Cello Festival; Rome Prize fellow, 1953-56; Alfred E. Hertz fellow U. Calif., 1953-54; Guggenheim fellow, 1960, 76-77; NEA grantee, 1976. Mem. Internat. Soc. Contemporary Music (mem. bd.), Am. Composers Alliance (exec. bd.), Am. Music Center (exec. bd.). Office: Music Dept Brandeis U Waltham MA 02254

WYNETTE, TAMMY, singer; b. Red Bay, Ala., May 5, 1942; d. William Hollis Pugh; m. George Jones, Sept. 1968 (div.); m. George Richey, 1978; children: Gwen, Jackie, Tina. Former beauty operator. Rec. artist Epic Records, 1967—; regular appearances on Grand Ole Opry; tours U.S., Can., Europe; recs. include: Womanhood, Stand By Your Man, 1975, Run Woman Run, 1970, Woman to Woman, 1974, Womanhood, 1978, Crying In The Rain, 1981, Sometimes When We Touch, 1985, From the Bottom of my Heart, 1986, Higher Ground, 1987, Next To You, 1989, Heart Over Mind, 1990, Best Loved Hits, 1991, (with others) Tears of Fire: The 25th Anniversary Collection, 1992; author autobiography Stand By Your Man, 1982; TV appearances include: (TV movie) Stand by Your Man, 1981; host The Acad. Country Music's 20th. Anniversary Reunion, 1986, The 25th Ann. Acad. Country Music Awards, 1990, The Legends of Country Music, 1994; films include From Nashville with Music, 1969. Named Female Vocalist of Year Country Music Assn., 1968, 69, 70.

WYNGAARDEN, JAMES BARNES, physician; b. East Grand Rapids, Mich., Oct. 19, 1924; s. Martin Jacob and Johanna (Kempers) W.; m. Ethel Vredevoogd, June 20, 1946 (div. 1977); children: Patricia Wyngaarden Fitzpatrick, Joanna Wyngaarden Gandy, Martha Wyngaarden Krauss, Lisa Wyngaarden Rolland, James Barnes Jr. Student, Calvin Coll., 1942-43, Western Mich. U., 1943-44; MD, U. Mich., 1948; DSc (hon.), U. Mich. and Med. Coll. of Ohio, 1984, U. Ill., 1985, George Washington U., 1986; PhD (hon.), Tel Aviv U., 1987; DSc. (hon.), U. S.C., West Mich. U., 1989. Diplomate: Am. Bd. Internal Medicine. Intern Mass. Gen. Hosp., Boston, 1948-49; resident Mass. Gen. Hosp., 1949-51; vis. investigator Pub. Health Rsch. Inst., N.Y.C., 1952-53; investigator NIH, USPHS, Bethesda, Md., 1953-56; asso. prof. medicine and biochemistry Duke U. Med. Sch., 1956-61, prof., 1961-65; vis. scientist Inst. Biologie-Physicochemique, Paris, 1963-64; prof., chmn. U. Pa. Med. Sch., 1965-67; physician-in-chief Med. Svc. Hosp. U. PA., Phila., 1965-67; Frederic M. Hanes prof., chmn. dept. medicine Duke U. Sch. of Medicine, Durham, N.C., 1967-82; physician-in-chief Med. Svc. Duke U. Hosp., Durham, 1967-82; chief of staff Duke U. Hosp., Durham, 1981-82; dir. NIH, Bethesda, MD, 1982-89; assoc. dir. life scis. Office of Sci. and Tech. Policy, Exec. Office of Pres., The White House, 1989-90; dir. Human Genome Orgn., 1990-91; fgn. sec. NAS, 1990-94; prof. medicine, assoc. vice chancellor for health affairs Duke U., Durham, N.C., 1990-94, ret., 1994; mem. staff VA, Durham County Hosps.; sr. assoc. dean internat. med. programs U. Pa., Phila., 1995—; cons. Office Sci. and Tech. Exec. Office of Pres., 1966-72; Mem. Pres.'s Sci. Adv. Com., 1972-73; mem. Pres.'s Com. for Nat. Medal of Sci., 1977-80; mem. adv. com. biology and medicine AEC, 1966-68; mem. bd. sci. counselors NIH, 1971-74; mem. adv. bd. Howard Hughes Med. Inst., 1969-82; mem. adv. council Life Ins. Med. Research Fund, 1967-70; adv. bd. Sci. Yr., 1977-81; vice chmn. Com. on Study Nat. Needs for Biomed. and Behavioral Research Personnel, NRC, 1977-81; bd. dirs. Hybridon Corp., Human Genome Scis., Magainen Pharm. Author: (with W.N. Kelley) Gout and Hyperuricemia, 1976; mem. editorial bd. Jour. Biol. Chemsitry, 1971-74, Arthritis and Rheumatism, 1959-66, Jour. Clin. Investigation, 1962-66, Ann. Internal Medicine, 1964-74, Medicine, 1963-90; editor: (with J.B. Stanbury, D.S. Fredrickson) The Metabolic Basis of Inherited Disease, 1960, 66, 72, 78, 83, (with O. Sperling and A. DeVries) Purine Metabolism in Man, 1974, (with L.H. Smith, Jr.) Cecil Textbook of Medicine, 16th edit., 1982, 19th edit., 1992. Bd. dirs. Royal Soc. Medicine Found., 1971-76, The Robert Wood Johnson Found. Clin. Scholar Program, 1973-78. Ensign USNR, 1943-46; sr. surgeon USPHS, 1951-56, rear adm. USPHS, 1982-90. Recipient Borden Undergrad. Research award, U. Mich., 1948, N.C. Gov.'s award for sci., 1974, Disting. Alumnus award We. Mich. U., 1984, Robert Williams award Assn. Profs. Medicine, 1985, Dalton scholar in medicine, Mass. Gen. Hosp., 1950, Richard Schweiker Excellence in Govt. award, 1985, Fedn. of Am. Socs. of Exptl. Biology Pub. Svc. award, 1989, Humanitarian award Nat. Orgn. for Rare Diseases, 1990; Royal Coll. Physicians fellow, 1984. Mem. Am. Rheumatism Assn., Am. Fedn. Clin. Research, So. Soc. Clin. Investigation (pres. 1974, founder's medal 1978), ACP (John Phillips Meml. award 1980), Am. Soc. Clin. Investigation, AAAS, Am. Soc. Biol. Chemists, Assn. Am. Physicians (councillor 1973-77, pres. 1978), Endocrine Soc., Nat. Acad. Scis., Royal Acad. Scis. Sweden, Am. Acad. Arts and Sci., Inst. Medicine, Sigma Xi. Democrat. Presbyterian. Club: Interurban Clinical (Balt.). Avocations: tennis, skiing, painting.

WYN-JONES, ALUN (WILLIAM WYN-JONES), software developer, mathematician; b. Tremadoc, Gwynedd, Great Britain, Aug. 15, 1946; came to U.S., 1976; s. Goronwy Wyn and Mai Jones; m. Jocelyn Ripley, July 29, 1977; 1 stepchild, Electra Truman. BSc with honors, U. Manchester, U.K., 1968; MSc, Univ. Coll. London, 1970. Rsch. engr. Marconi-Elliott Computer Labs., Borehamwood, U.K., 1970-71; asst. tutor math. Poly. North London, 1971-72; programmer CRC Info. Systems, Ltd., London, 1972-76; mgr. devel. Warner Computer (now Warner Ins.), N.Y.C., 1976-80; pres., owner, developer Wallsoft Systems, Inc., N.Y.C., 1982-92, Integrity Systems Corp., N.Y.C., 1980-94; software cons. investment banking divsn. Goldman, Sachs & Co., N.Y.C., 1994—; invited speaker at profl. confs. Author, co-author computer software. Recipient Byte Award Distinction Byte Editors and Columnists, 1988, Readers Choice award Data Based Advisor Readers, 1990, 91. Mem. AAAS, Am. Math. Soc., Math. Assn. Am.s. Methodist. Achievements include development of template programming in automatic code generation. Home: 609 Columbus Ave Apt 14D New York NY 10024-1436

WYNN, ALBERT RUSSELL, congressman; b. Phila., Sept. 10, 1951; m. Jessie Jackson, Jan. 14, 1994; 1 child, Gabrielle. BS, U. Pitts., 1973; student, Howard U.; JD, Georgetown U., 1979. Intern African Regional Affairs, U.S. State Dept., 1972-73; exec. dir. consumer protection divsn. Prince George's County, 1977-81; mem. Md. Ho. of Dels., 1982-86; lawyer Albert R. Wynn & Assocs., 1982-86; mem. Md. State Senator from Dist. 25, 1986-92, 103d-105th Congresses from 4th Md. Dist., Washington, 1993—; regional Dem. whip, mem. commerce com.; mem. banking & fin. svcs com., internat. rels. com., Patuxent Inst. reform task force, 1988—, joint com. econ. devel. strategy, 1989—; del. Dem. Nat. Conv. 1984, 88,96; pres. Metro. Washington coun. consumer agenices. Mem. NAACP legal assistance program, coalition on black affairs, voter registration, edn. coalition, gov.'s task force drunk & drugged driving; 1st vice chmn. legis. black caucus; chmn. Prince George's County black elected officials alliance. Mem. J. Franklin Bourne Bar Assn., Kappa Alpha Psi (past pres.). Democrat. Baptist. Home: 526 Truman Dr Largo MO 20772 Office: US Ho of Reps 407 Cannon Bldg Washington DC 20515-1404

WYNN, BRUCE, physician assistant; b. Evarts, Ky., Oct. 9, 1948; s. Sylvan and Ruby Evelyn (Cox) W.; m. Margaret Elaine Beard, Sept. 13, 1968; children: Bruce Clinton, Bradley James. Cert. physician asst., Med. U. S.C., 1976. Cert. physician asst. Nat. Commn. on Cert. of Physician's Assts., Ga. Chief cardiopulmonary therapy Redmond Park Hosp., Rome, Ga., 1974-75; physician asst. Robert T. Connor, M.D., Rome, 1975-84, Rome (Ga.) Gen. Practice, 1984—. Active Gideon Internat., Rome, 1983. Sgt. USMC, 1968-72. Fellow Am. Acad. Physicians' Assts., Ga. Assn. Physicians' Assts. (regional liaison Health Svc. Area region 2 1979-80). Avocations: numismatics, gardening, carpentry, hunting. Home: 7 Glenrise Terrace NW Rome GA 30165 Office: Rome Gen Practice 101 John Maddox Dr Rome GA 30165-1419

WYNN, COY WILTON, journalist; b. Prescott, Ark., Aug. 9, 1920; s. Ota Gilbert and Kate (Ward) W.; m. Leila Birbari, June 2, 1947. B.A., La. Coll., Pineville, 1941; M.A., La. State U., 1942. Chmn. dept. journalism Am. U., Cairo, Egypt, 1945-47; dir. div. journalism Lehigh U., Bethlehem, Pa., 1947-50; free-lance writer Middle East, 1950-51; corr. AP, Beirut, Lebanon, 1951-55; bur. chief AP, Cairo, 1955-61; corr. Time mag., Rome, 1962-74; chief bur. Time mag., Cairo, 1974-78; chief Rome Bur. Time mag., 1979-85, cons. on Vatican affairs, 1985-91, ret., 1991. Author: Nasser of Egypt: The Search for Dignity, 1959, Keepers of the Keys, 1988; also articles. Former mem. Associazione della Stampa Estera in Italia; former hon. trustee John Cabot U., Rome. Named to Hall of Fame Sch. Mass. Comms. La. State U. Roman Catholic. Clubs: American (Rome) (past pres.). Home: 52 Viale Liegi, Rome Italy 00198

WYNN, JOHN CHARLES, clergyman, retired religion educator; b. Akron, Ohio, Apr. 11, 1920; s. John Francis and Martha Esther (Griffith) W.; m. Rachel Linnell, Aug. 27, 1943; children: Mark Edward, Martha Lois Borland, Maryan Kay Ainsworth. BA, Coll. Wooster, 1941; BD, Yale U., 1944; MA, Columbia U., 1963, EdD, 1964; DD, Davis and Elkins Coll., 1958. Ordained to ministry Presbyn. Ch., 1944. Student asst. pastor Trinity Luth. Ch., New Haven, 1943-44; assoc. minister First Presbyn. Ch., Evanston, Ill., 1944-47; pastor El Dorado, Kans., 1947-50; dir. family edn. and research United Presbyn. Bd. Christian Edn., Phila., 1950-59; prof. Colgate Rochester/Bexley Hall/Crozer Theol. Sem., 1959-85, prof. emeritus, 1985—; pvt. practice family therapy; adj. prof. U. Rochester, San Francisco Theol. Sem., St. Bernard's Sem., Wesley Theol. Sem.; postdoctoral fellow Cornell U., 1973-74, St. John's U., 1980; lectr. Sch. Continuing Edn. Johns Hopkins U.; mem. summer faculty Union Theol. Sem., N.Y.C.; del. study conf. World Coun. Chs., 1953, 57, 64, 65, 67, 75, 80; lectr. 5 univs., Republic of South Africa, 1968; chmn. com. on sexuality in human cmty. U.P. Ch.; vol. mem. chaplaincy staff Charlestown Care Ctr., Balt. Author: How Christian Parents Face Family Problems, 1955, Pastoral Ministry to Families, 1957, Families in the Church, A Protestant Survey, 1961, Christian Education for Liberation and Other Upsetting Ideas, 1977, Family Therapy in Pastoral Ministry, 1982 (rev. and expanded as Family Therapy in Pastoral Ministry: Counseling for the Nineties, 1991), The Family Therapist, 1987; Editor: Sermons on Marriage and Family Life, 1956, Sex, Family and Society in Theological Focus, 1966, Sexual Ethics and Christian Responsibility, 1970; Contbr. articles to mags. and religious jours. Bd. dirs. Presbyn. Life, Planned Parenthood League Rochester and Monroe County, Family Service Rochester, Pastoral Counseling Ctr. Fellow Am. Assn. Marriage and Family Therapy (approved supr.); mem. Religious Edn. Assn., Nat. Coun. Chs. of Christ in U.S.A. (chmn. com. family life 1957-60), Nat. Coun. Family Rels., Family Svc. Assn. Am., Rochester Coun. Chs. (dir.). Address: 717 Maiden Choice Ln Apt 523 Catonsville MD 21228-6116

WYNN, KARLA WRAY, artist, agricultural products company executive; b. Idaho Falls, Idaho, Oct. 1, 1943; d. Wiliam and Elma (McCowin) Lott; m. Russell D. Wynn, June 7, 1963 (div. 1996); children: Joseph, Jeffrey, Andrea. Student, Coll. of Holy Names, 1962-63, Providence Coll. Nursing, 1962-63; BFA, Idaho State U., 1989; postgrad., Alfred U., 1993. Co-owner R.D. Wynn Farms, American Falls, Idaho, 1963-96, office mgr., 1975-84; co-owner Redi-Gro Fertilizer Co., American Falls, 1970-96, office mgr., 1980-84; pres. Lakeside Farms, Inc. (name now Redi-Gro Fertilitzer Inc.), American Falls, 1975-96; artist, 1990—; owner Blue Heron, Pocatello, Idaho, 1991-96. Watercolor paintings and ceramic clay sculptures exhibited at various art shows and galleries. Buddhist.

WYNN, ROBERT E., retired career officer, electronics executive; b. Dallas, Jan. 31, 1942; s. Wendell W. and Thelma (Smart) W.; m. Lavenia K. Davis, Mar. 25, 1972; children: Leslie, Lauren. Bachelors degree, West Point, 1964; MEE, U. Tenn., 1971. Commd. 2d lt. U.S. Army, 1964, advanced through grades to commdg. gen., 1990; chief comm. Ops. Divsn. 5th Signal Command, Heidelberg, Germany, 1979-81; chief of staff 5th Signal Command, Worms, Germany, 1984-85; chief plans and programs, dep. chief staff Ops. and Plans DCS for OPS and PLANS, Washington, 1981-84; comdr. 2d Signal Brigade, Mannheim, Germany, 1986-88, U.S. Army Info. Systems Command/Tng. Doctrine Command, Ft. Monroe, Va., 1988-90; commdg. gen. 7th Signal Command, Ft. Ritchie, Md., 1990-92, U.S. Army Info. Systems Engring. Command, Ft. Huachuca, Ariz., 1992—; ret., 1995; mgr. C3 sys. Raytheon E-Systems Inc., Richardson, Tex., 1995—. Decorated Bronze Star, Legion of Merit, Silver Order of Mercury. Mem. Assn. U.S. Army Assn. Grads. (life), Armed Forces Comm. and Electronics Assn. (life, bd. dirs.), Sky Soldier (life, 173d airborne brigade), Signal Corps Regiment (life). Avocations: golf, tennis. Home: 703 Laredo Cir Allen TX 75002-5444

WYNN, ROBERT LOUIS, II, state government official, business owner; b. Greensboro, N.C., Jan. 2, 1954; s. Robert L. and Margaret L. (Howerton) W.; m. Millie J. Jones, May 28, 1983. BA in Polit. Sci., U. N.C., 1976; JD, U. Mich., 1979. Bar: Mich.; lic. real estate broker, N.C., Wis. Atty. UAW Legal Svcs., Detroit, 1979-80; legis. analyst Wis. State Sen., Madison, 1981-83; asst. to pres. Guilford Coll., Greensboro, N.C., 1984-85; dir. minority bus. Wis. Dept. Devel., Madison, 1985—; owner, pres. C.P. Industries, Inc., Madison, 1992-95; bus. instr. Madison Bus. Coll., 1983-85; pres. Robert Wynn and Assocs., Madison, 1987—; bd. dirs. Dancy and Assocs., Virginia Beach., Va., Minority Bus. Mgmt. Seminars, Madison. Pub., author: (newsletter) Minority Bus. Devels., 1985-90. Trustee Madison Jr. Coll. of Bus., 1992—; founder, pres. Robert and Margaret H. Wynn Meml. Scholarship Fund, Greensboro, 1982—, Madison Area Investment Club, 1987-90; bd. dirs. Colorlines Found., Milw., 1990-92; mem. Leadership Greensboro, 1985; coord. Robert L. Wynn Golf Tournament, 1983—; pres. South Ctrl. Wis. Regional Coun. Investment Clubs. Recipient John Motley Morehead scholarship Morehead Found., U. N.C., 1972-76, Wis. Minority Small Bus. Advocate of Yr., SBA, 1991, Minority Bus. Achievement award Wis. Supplier Devel. Coun., 1991. Mem. Wis. Black State Employees (fundraising com. 1992—), Madison Golfers Alliance (pres.), Kappa Alpha Psi (treas. Madison chpt. 1991-94). Avocations: stock investing, current events, golf, bridge, skiing. Office: Wis Dept Devel PO Box 7970 Madison WI 53707-7970

WYNN, ROBERT RAYMOND, retired engineer, consultant; b. Omaha, Mar. 4, 1929; s. Horace Oscar and Yvonne Cecil (Witters) W.; m. Joann Elizabeth Swicegood, June 28, 1974; children: Kay, William, Frederick, Andrew, Emma, Lawrence, Robert. Diploma in Nuclear Engring., Capitol Radio Engring. Inst., 1964; BSEE, Pacific Internat. Coll. Arts and Scis., 1964; AA in Bus. Adminstrn., Allen Hancock Coll., 1969; MSEE, Pacific Internat. Coll. Arts and Scis., 1971; MSMS, West Coast U., 1975, ASCS, 1985; BSCS, U. State of N.Y., 1985. Registered profl. engr., Calif. Meteorologist United Air Lines, Calif., 1949-53; engring. planner Aircraft Tools Inc., Inglewood, Calif., 1953-55; field service engr. N. Am. Aviation, Inglewood, Calif., 1955-59; R&D engr. Carstedt Research Inc., N. Long Beach, Calif., 1959-60; test engr. Martin Marrietta Corp., Vandenburg AFB, Calif., 1960-64; project engr. Fed. Electric Corp., Vandenburg AFB, Calif., 1965-69; systems engr. Aeronutronic Ford Corp., Pasadena, Calif., 1970-75; MTS Jet Propulsion Lab., Pasadena, Calif., 1975-83; engring. mgr. Space Com., Redondo Beach, Calif., 1983-84; engring. specialist Boeing Service Inc., Pasadena, 1984-86; cons., mem. tech. staff Jet Propulsion Lab., Pasadena, 1986-96; ret., 1996; instr. computer sci. and CAD, Jet Propulsion Lab., 1980-82. With USAAF, 1946. Mem. Calif. Soc. Profl. Engrs., Exptl. Aircraft Assn. (pres. Lompoc chpt. 1968), Am. Legion Rep. (life), W. Coast U. Alumni Assn. Democrat. Avocations: model airplane design and constrn., flying, camping. Home: PO Box 26316 Prescott Valley AZ 86312-6316

WYNN, SHERRI LORRAINE, educational administrator; b. Indpls., July 9, 1953; d. Clay M. and Norma L. (Price) Mace; m. James Stephen Wynn, Aug. 19, 1972; children: Shea, Shawn, Shannon. BS in Edn., Ind. U., Indpls., 1975, MS in Spl. Edn., 1988; EdS in Sch. Adminstrn., Ind. U., Bloomington, 1994, EdD in Sch. Adminstrn., 1997. Cert. tchr., adminstr., Ind. Tchr. MSD Warren Twp., Indpls., 1973-78; tchr. spl. edn. Blue River Spl. Edn. Coop., Shelbyville, Ind., 1986-88; tchr. Indpls. Pub. Schs., 1988-93, dir. spl. project, 1991-93; dist. site coord. modern red schoolhouse project Hudson Inst., 1993—; coord. Modern Red Schoolhouse edn. reform project Beech Grove (Ind.) City Schs., 1993-96; prin. MSD Warren Twp., Indpls., 1996—; assoc. faculty Ind. U., Bloomington, 1992; mem. adv. bd. Organized Assn. Southside Indpls. Schs., 1992—; univ. liaison U. Indpls., 1992—, assoc. mem. faculty, 1993; presenter in field. Author: What Parent Think About Outcome-Based Education, 1997. Bd. dirs. New Palestine (Ind.) Community Libr., 1982-84, Indian Creek Christian Ch., Indpls., 1986—. Grantee Community Leaders Allied for Superior Schs., Ameritech Super Sch., 1991—, Ind. Dept. Edn. Mem. ASCD, Coun. Exceptional Children, Kappa Delta Pi, Phi Delta Kappa, Alpha Lambda Delta. Avocations: quilting, reading, counted cross-stitch, bread making. Home: 6718 Bloomfield Dr Indianapolis IN 46259-1234

WYNN, SUSAN RUDD, physician. BS, Tex. A&M U., 1979, MD, 1981; postgrad., Mayo Grad. Sch. Medicine, 1981-84, 84-86. Diplomate Am. Bd. Pediatrics, Am. Bd. Allergy and Immunology; lic. Tex. Assoc. cons. dept. pediatrics Mayo Clinic, Rochester, Minn., 1987; pvt. practice, allergy and clin. immunology Fort Worth (Tex.) Allergy and Asthma Assocs., 1988—; instr. in pediatrics, Mayo Med. Sch., 1986-87; presenter in field. Contbr. articles to profl. jours. Bd. visitors Scott and White Clinic, 1994—; adv. bd. M. D. Anderson Physicians, 1992-94. Recipient Disting. Student award Tex. A&M U., 1975, Residents' award Northwest Pediatric Soc., 1984, Leon Unger award Am. Coll. Allergists, 1985, Geigy Fellowship Am. Coll. Allergists, 1987, travel grants; named to Outstanding Young Women of Am., 1989. Mem. AMA (chair med. student sect. 1980-81, chair com. on women in medicine 1987-89), Mayo Assn. of Fellows (treas. 1984-85), Mayo Alumni Assn. (exec. com. 1983-87, 95—), The Mayo Alumnus (adv. bd. 1983-87), Tarrant County Med. Soc. (bd. dirs. 1990—, v.p. 1994-95, pres.-elect 1995-96, pres. 1996-97), Minn. Med. Assn. (trustee 1984-85), Tex. Med. Assn. (vice spkr. 1997—, various coms.), Am. Acad. Pediats., Am. Coll. Allergy and Immunology (bd. regents 1994—), Alpha Omega Alpha, Alpha Zeta, others. Office: 5929 Lovell Ave Fort Worth TX 76107-5029

WYNN, THOMAS JOSEPH, judge, educator; b. Chgo., Aug. 30, 1918; s. Phillip H. and Delia B (Madden) W.; m. Bernadette L. Lavelle, Apr. 17, 1948; children: Thomas Joseph, John P. AB, DePaul U., 1941, JD, 1942. Bar: Ill. 1942. Spl. investigator Phoenix & Murphy, Chgo., 1942; pvt. practice law Chgo., 1946-59; ptnr. Wynn & Ryan, Chgo., 1959-79; assoc. judge Cir. Ct. Cook County, Ill., 1979-83, judge chancery div. mechanic's lien sect., 1983-96, retired, 1996; lectr. bus. law Latin Am. Inst., Chgo., 1946-47; mem. faculty Coll. Commerce, DePaul U., Chgo., 1947—, assoc. dean Evening div., 1957-73, prof., 1972-79, part-time faculty, 1979-83, adj. prof. bus. law, 1983—; asst. atty. gen. Ill., 1957-58; bd. dirs., gen. counsel Suburbanite Bowl, Inc., 1958-79; gen. legal counsel Chgo. Consortium Colls. and Univs., GM Tool Corp.; pres., bd. dirs. Metroplex Leasing and Financing, Inc. Candidate for alderman Chgo. City Coun., 1951; candidate for judge Mcpl. Ct. Chgo., 1956; exec. sec., bd. dirs. Ill. Good Govt. Inst., 1958-79; mem. adv. bd. to dean Coll Law DePaul U., 1992—. Ensign-lt. (S.G.) USNR, 1942-46. Mem. Ill. Bar Assn., Chgo. Bar Assn. (mem. arbitration and alternative dispute resolution com., civil practice coms., mem. internat. law com., mem. judiciary com., mem. cir. ct. com.), Ill. Judges Assn. (com. mandatory arbitration alt. dispute resolution, com. pubs.), Assn. Univ. Evening Colls. (past chmn.), Am. Bus. Law Assn. (pres. 1972-73), Am. Real Estate and Urban Econs. Assn., Chgo. Area Evening Deans and Dirs. Assn., U.S. Adult Edn. Assn., Ill. Adult Edn. Assn., Am. Right-of-Way Assn. (advisor chmn., nat. ednl. com., 1963-64), St. Vincent DePaul Soc., DePaul Law Alumni Assn. (past pres.), Smithsonian Inst., Pres.'s Club, (DePaul U. 1986—), Blue Key, Gamma Eta Gamma, Beta Gamma Sigma, Delta Mu Delta. Home: 27592 W Cuba Rd Barrington IL 60010-2770

WYNNE, BRIAN JAMES, former association executive, consultant; b. N.Y.C., Dec. 2, 1950; s. Bernard and Dolores (Doyle) W. Student, Institute des Sciences Politiques, Paris, 1970-71; BA, Coll. Holy Cross, 1972; MA, U. So. Calif., 1974. Staff Exec. Cons., Inc., McLean, Va., 1974-76; prin., 1976-78; exec. dir. Indsl. Designers Soc. Am., Washington, 1978-88; cons. to various non-profit orgns.; dir. Worldesign 85, founder Worldesign Found. Mem. Am. Soc. Assn. Execs., Indsl. Designers Soc. Am. (hon.), Phi Sigma Iota. Home: 5200 N Ocean Blvd Fort Lauderdale FL 33308-3019

WYNNE, JOHN OLIVER, newspaper, broadcast and cable executive; b. Norfolk, Va., July 6, 1945; s. Oliver Jr. and Margaret (Klasman) W.; m. Susan Stribling (Snodgrass), Dec. 23, 1972; children: John Oliver Jr., Lee Stribling (dec.), Bradford Annan. BA, Princeton U., 1967; JD, U. Va., 1971. Bar: Va. 1971. Atty. Willcox, Savage, Lawrence, Dickson & Spindle, Norfolk, 1971-74; corp. sec. Landmark Comm., Inc., Norfolk, 1974-77, v.p. broadcast and cable, 1977-78; v.p., gen. mgr. Sta. KNTV-TV subs. Landmark Comm., Inc., Norfolk; pres. broadcasting and video enterprises Landmark Comm., Inc., 1980-90, COO, pres. newspapers and broadcasting group, 1990-91, pres., CEO, 1991—; chmn. The Weather Channel, 1981—, The Travel Channel, 1992—. Trustee Norfolk Acad., 1980—, Va. Found. for Ind. Colls., 1990—; chmn. Jr. Achievement, Norfolk, 1987, Capital Campaign South Hampton Rds. United Way, Norfolk, 1986; mem. State Coun. Higher Edn. for Va., 1993-94; mem. bd. dirs. Tidewater Scholarship Found., 1988—; reg. chmn. Leadership Giving 8-State South Region for Princeton University's 250th Anniv., 1995—. Mem. Nat. Cable TV Assn. (bd. dirs. 1988—), Harbor Club. Episcopalian. Club: Harbor (Norfolk). Avocations: golf, tennis, skiing, walking, reading. Office: Landmark Communications Inc 150 W Brambleton Ave Norfolk VA 23510-2018

WYNNE, JOHNNY CALVIN, university dean, plant breeding researcher; b. Williamston, N.C., May 17, 1943; s. James Harry and Rachel Loraine (Ayers) W.; m. Diane Louise Sawyer, 1961 (div. Feb. 1989); children: Debbie Ann, Donna Carol; m. Jacqueline Crawford Creech, Nov. 25, 1989; children: John Christopher, James Alexander. BS, N.C. State U., 1965, MS, 1968, PhD, 1974. Instr. crop sci. dept. N.C. State U., Raleigh, 1968-74, asst. prof., 1974-78, assoc. prof., 1978-83, prof., 1983-91, acting tchg. adminstr., 1987-89, head dept., 1989-91, assoc. dean, dir. N.C. agr. rsch. svc., 1992—. Recipient rsch. award Nat. Peanut Coun., 1992. Fellow AAAS, Am. Peanut Rsch. and Edn. Soc. (pres. 1990, Bailey award 1977); mem. Crop Sci. Soc. Am., Coun. for Agrl. Sci. and Tech., So. Assn. Expt. Sta. Dirs. (chmn. 1994), Sigma Iota Rho. Office: N Carolina State Univ PO Box 7643 Raleigh NC 27695

WYNNE, LINDA MARIE, administrative assistant, artist; b. N.Y.C., Nov. 10, 1950; d. Thomas Lauren Flake and Sally Gaudiosi; m. Michael Francis Wynne, Jan. 9, 1973 (div. Apr. 1985); 1 child, Michael Thomas. AA, Borough of Manhattan C.C., 1972. Stock person S&A Stores, Queens, N.Y., 1966-69; part-time bookkeeper Bohack Corp., Queens, N.Y., 1970-72; sr. teller, tng. specialist Union Dime Savs. Bank, N.Y.C., 1973-77; adminstrv. asst. Eagle Elec. Mfg., N.Y.C., 1983-84, Castle Oil Corp., Harrison, N.Y., 1985-91, Prisma Group, N.Y.C., 1992-93, Misco Enterprises, N.Y.C., 1994-95, Concord Comm., Woodside, N.Y., 1995—. Exhibited in group shows at Oliver Art Studio, 1979-89, The Emerging Collector, 1987, All Queens Women, 1991, Cultural Environ., 1991; exhibited in outdoor shows at Big Six Towers, 1983, Friends of the Mineola Libr., 1983-89, Joseph Bulova Sch., 1990, 40th St. Festival, 1991, The Sunnyside Found. Fall Festival, 1988-91, Sunnyside Gardens Cmty. Assn. Inc., 1989, 90, 91, Gateway, 1988-91, Bowne Park, 1991, 93, 94, Queens Bot. Garden, 1990, 91, Floral Park Art League, 1991, Mineola's Performing Art Weekend, 1988-91, Alliance of Queens Artists, 1991, Washington Square Outdoor Art Exhibit, 1988, 89, 90. Avocations: reading, exercising (1st prize Ladies Body Building), theatre and movie goer, travel.

WYNNE, LYMAN CARROLL, psychiatrist; b. Lake Benton, Minn., Sept. 17, 1923; s. Nels Wind and Ella C. (Pultz) W.; m. Adele Rogerson, Dec. 22, 1947; children: Christine, Randall, Sara, Barry, Jonathan. War certificate, Harvard, 1943, MD, 1947, PhD in Social Psychology, 1958; MD (hon.), Oulu U., Finland, 1989. Med. intern Peter Bent Brigham Hosp., Boston, 1947-48; grad. fellow social relations dept. Harvard, 1948-49; resident neurology Queen Square Hosp., London, Eng., 1950; resident psychiatry Mass. Gen. Hosp., Boston, St. Elizabeth's Hosp., Washington, also NIMH, 1951-54; psychoanalytic tng. Washington Psychoanalytic Inst., 1954-60, teaching analyst, 1965-72; cons., investigator WHO, 1965—; staff NIMH, 1954-57, chief sect. family studies, 1957-61, chief adult psychiatry br., 1961-72; mem. faculty Washington Sch. Psychiatry, 1956-72; prof. U. Rochester Sch. Medicine and Dentistry, 1971—, chmn. dept. psychiatry, 1971-77, dir. div. family programs, 1971-83; psychiatrist-in-chief Strong Meml. Hosp., Rochester, N.Y., 1971-77; vis. lectr. Am. U., Beirut, Lebanon, 1963-64. Chmn. bd. dirs. Family Process; mem. editorial adv. bd. Jour. Nervous and Mental Diseases; sr. editor: The Nature of Schizophrenia, 1978; editor: The State of the Art in Family Therapy Research; co-editor: Psychosocial Intervention in Schizophrenia, 1983, Children at Risk for Schizophrenia, 1984, The Language of Family Therapy, 1985; sr. editor Systems Consultation, 1986. Chmn. AAMFT Rsch. & Edn. Found., 1992-94. Med. dir. USPHS, 1961-72; mem. NRC, 1969-72. Recipient Commendation medal USPHS, 1965; Hofheimer prize Am. Psychiat. Assn., 1966; Frieda Fromm-

Reichmann award Am. Acad. Psychoanalysis, 1966; Meritorious Service medal USPHS, 1966; Stanley Dean award Am. Coll. Psychiatrists, 1976; McAlpin Research Achievement award, 1977, Disting. Achievement in Family Therapy Research, Am. Family Therapy Assn., 1981; Disting. Research Achievement award Assn. Marriage and Family Therapy, 1982, Disting. Profl. Contbn. award Am. Assn. for Marriage and Family Therapy, 1985, Disting. Contbn. to Family Therapy award Am. Family Therapy Assn., 1989. Fellow Am. Psychiat. Assn. (life), Am. Acad. Psychoanalysis; mem. Am. Psychosomatic Soc. (mem. council 1969-72), Psychiat. Research Soc., Western N.Y. Psychoanalytic Soc. (pres. 1986-87), Am. Coll. Psychoanalysts, Am. Family Therapy Assn. (pres. 1986-87), Am. Assn. for Marriage and Family Therapy (bd. dirs. 1992-94), Am. Psychoanalytic Assn., Assn. for Clin. Psychosocial Rsch. (coun. 1984-91). Home: 17 Tobey Brk Pittsford NY 14534-1819 Office: Strong Meml Hosp Rochester NY 14642-8409

WYNNE-EDWARDS, HUGH ROBERT, entrepreneur, scientist; b. Montreal, Que., Can., Jan. 19, 1934; s. Vero Copner and Jeannie Campbell (Morris) W.-E.; married; children from previous marriages: Robin Alexander, Katherine Elizabeth, Renée Elizabeth Lortie, Krista Smyth, Jeannie Elizabeth, Alexander Vernon. B.Sc. with 1st class honors, U. Aberdeen, Scotland, 1955; M.A., Queen's U., 1957, Ph.D., 1959; D.Sc. (hon.), Meml. U., 1975. Registered profl. engr. B.C., 1995—. With Geol. Survey Can., 1958-59; lectr. Queen's U., Kingston, Ont., 1968-72, asst. prof., then assoc. prof., 1961-68, prof., head dept. geol. scis., 1968-72; prof., then Cominco prof., head dept. geol. scis. U. B.C., Vancouver, 1972-77; asst. sec. univ. br. Ministry of State for Sci. and Tech., Ottawa, 1977-79; sci. dir. Alcan Internat. Ltd., Montreal, 1979-80, v.p. R&D, chief sci. officer, 1980-89; CEO Moli Energy Ltd., Vancouver, 1989-90; pres. Terracy Inc., Vancouver, 1989—; sci. advisor Teck Corp., Vancouver, 1989-91; pres., CEO B.C. Rsch. Inc., Vancouver, 1993-97, exec. chmn., 1997—; chmn. Silvagen Inc., 1996—; advisor Directorate Mining and Geology, Uttar Pradesh, India, 1964, Grenville project Que. Dept. Natural Resources, 1968-72; vis. prof. U. Aberdeen, 1965-66, U. Witwatersrand, Johannesburg, South Africa, 1972; UN cons., India, 1974, SCITEC, 1977-78; mem. sci. adv. com. CBC, 1980-84; mem. Sci. Coun. Can., 1983-89, Nat. Adv. Bd. on Sci. and Tech., 1987; indsl. liaison com. UN Ctr. for Sci. and Tech. in Devel., 1982-84; vice chmn. tech. adv. group Bus. Coun. for Sustainable Devel., Geneva, 1991; mem. Nat. Biotech. Adv. Coun., 1995—. Bd. dirs. Royal Victoria Hosp., Montreal, 1984-89; dir. Soc. Quebecoise d'initiatives petroliére, 1983-87; dir. CS Resources Ltd., 1993—; dir. Atomic Energy Can. Ltd., 1996—. Decorated officer Order of Can., 1991; recipient Spendiarov prize 24th Internat. Geol. Congress, Montreal, 1972. Fellow Can. Acad. Engring., Royal Soc. Can.; mem. Can. Rsch. Mgmt. Assn. (vice chmn. 1982-84, chmn. 1984-85, assn. medal 1987), Univ. Club (Montreal). Mem. United Ch. Avocations: tennis, skiing, carpentry. Office: Terracy Inc, 2030 27th St, West Vancouver, BC Canada V7V 4L4 also: BC Rsch Inc, 3650 Wesbrook Mall, Vancouver, BC Canada V6S 2L2

WYNSTRA, NANCY ANN, lawyer; b. Seattle, June 25, 1941; d. Walter S. and Gaile E. (Cogley) W. BA cum laude, Whitman Coll., 1963; LLB cum laude, Columbia U., 1966. Bar: Wash. 1966, D.C. 1969, Ill. 1979, Pa. 1984. With appellate sect., civil div. U.S. Dept. Justice, Washington, 1966-67; TV corr.-legal news Stas. WRC, NBC and Stas. WTOP, CBS, Washington, 1967-68; spl. asst. Corp. Counsel, Washington, 1968-70; dir. planning and rsch. D.C. Superior Ct., Washington, 1970-78; spl. advisor White House Spl. Action Office for Drug Abuse Prevention, Washington, 1973-74; fellow Drug Abuse Coun., 1974-75; chief counsel Michael Reese Hosp. and Med. Ctr., Chgo., 1978-83; exec. v.p., gen. counsel Allegheny Health Edn. and Rsch. Found., Pitts., 1983—; pres., chief exec. officer Allegheny Health Svcs. Provider's Ins. Co., 1989—; assoc. prof. Sch. of Urban and Pub. Affairs Carnegie Mellon U., 1985—, Allegheny U. Health Scis., 1991—; cons. to various drug abuse programs, 1971-78; bd. overseers Whitman Coll., 1993—. Mem. ABA, Nat. Health Lawyers Assn. (bd. dirs. 1985-91, 92-97, 97—, chair publs. com. 1989-91, audit com. 1991-92, treas. 1992-93, 95-96, exec. com. 1992—, edn. fund com., 1992-93, mem. nominating com. 1992-93, sec. 1993-95, treas. 1995-96, pres.-elect 1996-97, pres. 1997—), Am. Soc. Hosp. Attys., others. Presbyterian. Author: Fundamentals of Health Law; contbr. articles to profl. jours. Office: Allegheny Health Edn & Rsch Found 120 5th Ave Ste 2900 Pittsburgh PA 15222-3001

WYRICK, CHARLES LLOYD, JR., publisher, writer, editor; b. Greensboro, N.C., May 5, 1939; s. Charles Lloyd and Edythe Ellen (Ellis) W.; m. Constance Micheffe Hooper, Aug. 22, 1964; children—Charles Lloyd, III, Christopher Conrad Hooper. B.A., Davidson (N.C.) Coll., 1961; M.F.A., U. N.C., 1967. Instr. Stephens Coll., Columbia, Mo., 1964-66; asst. head programs div. Va. Museum, Richmond, 1966-68; exec. dir. Assn. Preservation Va. Antiquities, Richmond, 1968-70; pres. Research & Restoration, Inc., Richmond, 1970-73; dir. Del. Art Mus., Wilmington, 1973-79, Gibbes Mus. Art, Charleston, S.C., 1980-86; pres. Wyrick & Co., Charleston, 1986—, Dixie Media, Inc., Charleston, 1989—; editor, pub. "Omnibus", 1989-94; mem. Richmond Commn. Archt. Rev., 1969-72, New Castle County (Del.) Hist. Rev. Bd., 1975-88, also vice chmn.; mem. Bd. Archtl. Rev. City of Charleston, 1988-94, chmn., 1992-94; mem. Charleston Consortium on Higher Edn.; cons. in field. Author: "The 17th Street Market", 1972; contbr. articles to profl. jours. Bd. visitors Davison Coll., 1974-77; chmn. Econs. of Amenities City of Charleston, 1978, S.C. Coastal Conservation League, 1989-94; bd. dirs. Charleston Area Arts Coun., 1989-91, Friends of Charleston County Courthouse, 1989-94, Pub. Art Trust, 1988-90; adv. com. S.C. Dept. Natural Resources, 1992—. Recipient 1st award spl. column writing Va. Press Assn., 1973. Mem. Assn. Am. Pubs., Pubs. Assn. of South (bd. dirs. 1990-92, pres. 1991-92), S.C. Acad. Authors (bd. dirs. 1990-92), Carolina Yacht Club. Home: 34 Legare St Charleston SC 29401-2336 Office: 1-A Pinckney St Charleston SC 29401-2626

WYRICK, DANIEL JOHN, science/health textbook editor, science specialist; b. Oakland, Calif., May 22, 1952; s. Charles Truman and Thelma Lillian (White) W.; m. Christine Evelyn Ingels, Nov. 10, 1972; children: Aimee, Emilie. BA, Pacific Union Coll., 1977, MA, 1984. Cert. tchr., Calif. Tchr. Pine Hills Jr. Acad., Auburn, Calif., 1977-81; prin., tchr. Fort Bragg (Calif.) Seventh Day Adventist Elem. Sch., 1981-85; sci. tchr. Lodi (Calif.) Adventist Elem. Sch., 1985-89; sci./health textbook editor N.Am. Div. of Seventh Day Adventist, Silver Spring, Md., 1989-95; sci. specialist Lodi Adventist Elem. Sch., 1995—. Co-author: Life series sci./health textbooks, 1993—, Every Friday, 1987. Youth leader Fairmont Seventh Day Adventist Ch., Lodi, 1986-91, ch. elder, 1988; youth leader English Oaks Seventh Day Adventist Ch., Lodi, 1991-93, ch. elder, 1991—; mem. Lodi Acad. Sch. Bd., 1992-95. Mem. Nat. Sci. Tchrs. Assn., Calif. Sci. Tchrs. Assn., Calif. Assn. Pvt. Schs. Republican. Avocations: fishing, camping, photography, outdoor education. Office: Lodi Acad 1230 S Central Ave Lodi CA 95240-5907

WYRICK, PRISCILLA BLAKENEY, microbiologist; b. Greensboro, N.C., Apr. 28, 1940; d. Carnie Lee and Prestine (Blakeney) W. BS in Med. Tech., U. N.C., Chapel Hill, 1962; MS in Bacteriology, U. N.C., 1967, PhD in Bacteriology, 1971. Technologist Clin. Microbiology Lab., N.C. Meml. Hosp., Chapel Hill, 1962-64; asst. supr. Clin. Microbiology Lab., N.C. Meml. Hosp., 1964-65, supr., 1965-66; sci. staff fellow Nat. Inst. Med. Rsch., Mill Hill, London, 1971-73; asst. prof. dept. microbiology U. N.C. Sch. Medicine, Chapel Hill, 1973-79; assoc. prof. U. N.C. Sch. Medicine, 1979-88, prof., 1988—. Grantee, NIH. Mem. Am. Acad. Microbiology, Am. Soc. Microbiology (pres. N.C. br. 1981-82, chmn. div. gen. med. microbiology 1981-82), AAAS, Soc. Infectious Diseases, Sigma Xi. Office: U NC Sch Medicine CB 7290 816 FLOB Chapel Hill NC 27599

WYRSCH, JAMES ROBERT, lawyer, educator, author; b. Springfield, Mo., Feb. 23, 1942; s. Louis Joseph and Jane Elizabeth (Welsh) W.; m. B. Darlene Wyrsch, Oct. 18, 1975; children: Scott, Keith, Mark, Brian, Marcia. BA, U. Notre Dame, 1963; JD, Georgetown U., 1966; LLM, U. Mo., Kansas City, 1972. Bar: Mo. 1966, U.S. Ct. Appeals (8th cir.) 1971, U.S. Supreme Ct. 1972, U.S. Ct. Appeals (10th cir.) 1974, U.S. Ct. Appeals (5th cir.) 1974, U.S. Ct. Mil. & Appeals 1978, U.S. Ct. Appeals (6th cir.) 1982, U.S. Ct. Appeals (11th cir.) 1984, U.S. Ct. Appeals (7th cir.) 1986, U.S. Ct. Appeals (4th cir.) 1990. Assoc. Wyrsch, Hobbs, Mirakian, & Lee, P.C. and predecessors, Kansas City, Mo., 1970-71, of counsel, 1972-77, ptnr., 1978—, pres., sharehlder, 1988—; adj. prof. U. Mo., 1981—; mem. com. instrns. Mo. Supreme Ct., 1983—. Capt. U.S. Army, 1966-69; named to Who's Who in Kansas City Law, Kansas City Bus. Jour., 1991, 1994; recipient Joint Svcs. Commendation medal U.S. Army, 1969, U. Mo. Kansas City Svc. award Law Found., 1991-92. Fellow Am. Coll. Trial Lawyers, Am. Bar Found.; mem. ABA, Am. Arbitration Assn. (panel arbitrators), Mo. Bar Assn. (vice chmn. criminal law com. 1978-79), Kansas City Bar Assn. (chmn. anti-trust com. 1981), Assn. Trial Lawyers Am., Am. Bd. of Trial Advocates (adv.), Nat. Assn. Criminal Def. Attys., Mo. Assn. Criminal Def. Attys. (sec. 1982), Phi Delta Phi, Country Club of Blue Springs, Kansas City Club. Democrat. Roman Catholic. Co-author: Missouri Criminal Trial Practice, 1994; contbr. articles to profl. jours. Home: 1501 NE Sunny Creek Ln Blue Springs MO 64014-2044 Office: Wyrsch Hobbs Mirakian & Lee PC 1101 Walnut St Fl 13 Kansas City MO 64106-2134

WYRTKI, KLAUS, oceanography educator; b. Tarnowitz, Germany, Feb. 7, 1925; came to U.S., 1961; s. Wilhelm and Margarete (Pacharzina) W.; m. Helga Kocher, June 6, 1954 (div. 1970); children: Undine, Oliver; m. Erika Maassen. PhD magna cum laude, U. Kiel, Germany, 1950. With German Hydrographic Inst., Hamburg, 1950-51; German Rsch. Coun. postdoctoral rsch. fellow U. Kiel, 1951-54; head Inst. Marine Rsch., Djakarta, Indonesia, 1954-57; sr. rsch. officer, then prin. rsch. officer div. fisheries and oceanography Commonwealth Sci. and Indsl. Rsch. Orgn., Sydney, Australia, 1958-61; assoc. rsch. oceanographer, then rsch. oceanographer Scripps Instn. Oceanography, U. Calif., 1961-64; prof. oceanography U. Hawaii, Honolulu, 1964—; chmn. North Pacific Expt., 1974-80, com. on climate changes and ocean Internat. Assn. Phys. Scis. of the Oceans; mem. Spl. Com. on Ocean Rsch. Working Group on Prediction of El Nino, Sci. Working Group on Topography Expt., panel on climate and global change NOAA. Author: El Nino—The Dynamic Response of the Equatorial Pacific Ocean to Atmospheric Forcing, 1975; editor: Oceanographic Atlas of the International Indian Ocean Expedition, 1988; mem. editl. bd. Jour. Phys. Oceanography, 1971-79. Recipient Excellence in Rsch. award U. Hawaii, 1980, Rosenstiel award U. Miami, 1981. Fellow Am. Geophys. Union (Maurice Ewing medal 1989), Am. Meteorol. Soc. (Harald Ulrick Sverdrup Gold medal 1991), Deutsche Meteorologische Gesellschaft (Albert Defant medal 1992). Office: U Hawaii 1000 Pope Rd Honolulu HI 96822-2336

WYSCHOGROD, EDITH, philosophy educator; b. N.Y.C.; d. Morris and Selma Shurer; m. Michael Wyschogrod, Mar. 6, 1955; children: Daniel, Tamar. AB, Hunter Coll., 1957; PhD, Columbia U., 1970. Prof. philosophy Queens Coll., Flushing, N.Y., 1967-92; J. Newton Rayzor prof. philosophy and religious thought Rice U., Houston, 1992—. Author: Emmanuel Levinas: The Problem of Ethical Metaphysics, 1974, Spirit in Ashes, 1985, Saints and Postmodernism, 1990; co-editor: Lacan and Theological Discourse, 1989. Nat. Humanities Ctr. fellow, 1981, Woodrow Wilson Ctr. fellow, 1987-88, Guggenheim fellow, 1995-96. Mem. Am. Acad. Religion (pres. 1992-93). Office: Rice University PO Box 1892 6100 South Main Houston TX 77005

WYSE, LOIS, advertising executive, author; b. Cleve., 1928; d. Roy B. Wohlgemuth and Rose (Schwartz) Weisman; m. Marc Wyse (div. 1980); m. Lee Guber (dec. 1988). Pres. Wyse Advt. Inc., N.Y.C., 1951—; bd. dirs. Ctr. for Comm.; ptnr. City & Co. Author 60 books; contbg. editor Good Housekeeping; syndicated columnist Wyse Words. Trustee Beth Israel Med. Ctr., N.Y.C. Mem. Woman's Forum, PEN. Office: Wyse Advt Inc 22 W 23rd St New York NY 10010-5211

WYSE, ROGER EARL, physiologist; b. Wauseon, Ohio, Apr. 22, 1943. BS in Agr., Ohio State U., 1965; MS, Mich. State U., 1967, PhD in Crop Sci., 1969. Fellow Mich. State U., 1969-70; plant physiologist Agr. Rsch. Svc. USDA, 1970-86; dean of rsch. Cook Coll. Rutgers U., 1986-92; dean, dir. Coll. Agr. and Life Sci. U. Wis., Madison, 1992—. Recipient Arthur Flemming award, 1982. Mem. AAAS, Am. Soc. Plant Physiol., Am. Soc. Agronomy, Am. Soc. Crop Sci. Office: Univ of Wisconsin Wisconsin Agr Experiment Sta 140 Agricultural Hall Madison WI 53706

WYSE, ROY, labor union administrator; b. Sept. 18, 1932; m. Pat Wyse; 5 children. With assembly plant Ford Motor Co., Liberty, Mo., from 1951; with UAW, 1951—, sec. Local 249, 1972-79, internat. rep., regional auditor, 1979-86, asst. dir. Region 5, 1986-89, dir. Region 5, 1989-95, nat. sec.-treas., 1995—, also dir. nat. aerospace dept., 1995—. Past mem., past pres. Orick (Mo.) Bd. Edn.; mem. Orrick City Coun. Address: UAW Pub Rels & Pubs Dept 8000 E Jefferson Ave Detroit MI 48214-3963*

WYSE, WILLIAM WALKER, lawyer, real estate executive; b. Spokane, Wash., July 20, 1919; s. James and Hattie (Walker) W.; m. Janet E. Oswalt, Jan. 30, 1944; children: Wendy L., Scott C., Duncan E. AB, U. Wash., 1941; JD, Harvard U., 1948. Bar: Oreg. 1948. Pvt. practice Portland; ptnr. Stoel, Rives, Boley, Jones & Gray, 1953-88; pres. Wyse Investment Svcs., 1988—; past dir. Treasureland Savs. and Loan Assn.; past trustee, sec. Pacific Realty Trust; past trustee Holladay Park Plaza. Bd. dirs. Cmty. Child Guidance Clinic, 1951-57, pres., 1956-57; chmn. ctrl. budget com. United Fund, 1958-60; 1st v.p. United Good Neighbors; chmn. bd. dirs. Portland Sch. Bd., 1959-66; bd. dirs. Oreg. Symphony Soc., 1965-74, 93—, pres., 1968-70; pres. Tri-County Cmty. Coun., 1970-71; bd. dirs. Portland Mental Health Assn.; bd. dirs., sec. Oreg. Parks Found. Mem. ABA, Oreg. Bar Assn., Multnomah County Bar Assn., Am. Coll. Real Estate Lawyers, Univ. Club, Arlington Club, Portland City Club (past gov.), Wauna Lake Club, Delta Upsilon. Republican. Presbyterian. Home: 3332 SW Fairmount Ln Portland OR 97201-1446 Office: 806 SW Broadway Portland OR 97205-3333

WYSER-PRATTE, JOHN MICHAEL, lawyer; b. Paris, Sept. 4, 1936; came to U.S., 1950; s. Eugene John and Marguerite (von Prattes) W.-P.; m. Jean Doughty Templeton, Aug. 22, 1964 (div. Jan. 1976); children: Michèle Marguerite, Renée Christine; m. Maryse Sislian, Jan. 23, 1976; 1 child, Anne Catherine. BA, Coll. of the Holy Cross, 1958; JD, Georgetown U., 1963; cert. in internat. law studies, U. Geneva, 1964, Institut Universitaire des Hautes Etudes Internationales. Bar: N.Y. 1965, U.S. Ct. Appeals (2d crct.) 1974, U.S. Dist. Ct. (so. and ea. dists.) N.Y. 1975. Assoc. Coudert Bros., N.Y.C., 1964-71, ptnr., 1972-86; ptnr. Schnader, Harrison, Segal & Lewis, N.Y.C., 1987-95, Ross & Hardies, N.Y.C., 1995—; rsch. asst. Inst. for Internat. Trade Law, Georgetown U. Law Ctr., 1962-63; guest lectr., seminar speaker local C. of C.s, France, 1986—; guest speaker ann. Round Table Groupement des Industries Françaises Aéronautiques et Spatiales, Paris, 1986-92. Capt. USMC, 1958-62, USMCR, 1962-71. Schulte Zur Hausen fellow, 1963-64. Mem. ABA, Union Internationale des Avocats, Assn. Bar City of N.Y., French-Am. C. of C. (U.S.), Paris Am. Club. Republican. Roman Catholic. Office: Ross & Hardies Park Ave Towers 65 E 55th St New York NY 10022-3219

WYSK, RICHARD A., engineering educator, researcher; b. Holyoke, Mass., Sept. 22, 1948; s. Stanley and Sophia Dorothy (Mazurowski) W.; m. Caryl Lynne Ray, Jan. 18, 1969; children: Richard Patrick, Rebecca Jeanne, Robyn Caryl. BS in Indsl. Engring. & Ops. Rsch., U. Mass., 1972, MS in Indsl. Engring. & Ops. Rsch., 1973; PhD in Indsl. Engring., Purdue U., 1977. Prodn. control mgr. Gen. Electric, Erie, Pa., 1973-75; rsch. analyst Caterpillar Tractor, Inc., Peoria, Ill., 1975-76; assoc. prof. Va. Polytechnic Inst., Blacksburg, 1977-83; prof. Pa. State U., State College, 1983-90; dir. Inst. Mfg. Systems, College Station, 1990-94; Royce Wisenbaker chair Tex. A&M U., College Station, 1990-94; William Lionhard chair in engring. William Leonhard chair in engring., State College, 1995—. Co-author: A Study Guide for the P.E. in I.E., 1982, An Intro to Automated Proc. Plan., 1985, Modern Manufacturing Process Engineering, 1989, Computer-aided Manufacturing, 1991 (Book-of-the-Yr. award Inst. Indsl. Engrs. 1992, E. Eugene Merchant Mfg. Textbook award Soc. Mfg. Engrs. 1992). Pks. commr. Montgomery County Pks. & Recreation, Blacksburg, 1982-83; adv. mem. Inst. Systems Rsch. U. Md., 1991-95. With U.S. Army, 1969-71, Vietnam. Decorated Army Commendation medal with 2 oak leaf clusters. Fellow Inst. Indsl. Engrs. (chpt. pres. 1990—, Region III Award of Excellence 1982, D. Baker award 1993); mem. Soc. Mfg. Engrs. (sr., Outstanding Young Mfg. Engr. 1981), Engring. Accreditation Commn. (commr. 1990-92), Sigma Xi. Avocations: racquetball, basketball. Office: Pa State U 207 Hammond Bldg State College PA 16802-1401

WYSLOTSKY, IHOR, engineering company executive; b. Kralovane, Czechoslovakia, Dec. 22, 1930; s. Ivan and Nadia (Alexiew) W.; came to U.S., 1958, naturalized, 1961; M.E., Sch. Aeros., Buenos Aires, Argentina, 1955; m. Marta Farion, 1983; children: Katria, Bohdan, Roman, Alexander. Design engr. Kaiser Industries, Buenos Aires, 1955-58; cons. design engr., Newark, 1959-64; chief engr. Universal Tool Co., Chgo., 1964-69; pres. CBC Devel Co., Inc., Chgo., 1969-74; pres. TEC, Inc., Chgo., 1972-83; pres. REDEX Corp., 1983-89, chmn. 1993—; engring. adviser to bd. Biosystems Insts., Inc., La Jolla, Calif. Co-founder Ukrainian Univ. Studies, U. Ill.; co-founder, pres. Am. Ukrainian Bus. Coun., 1991-93; mem. Ukrainian working com. Ctr. Strateqic Internat. Studies, Washington. Vis. com. mem. Harvard U. Mem. Packaging Inst. U.S.A., Am.-Israeli C. of C. (v.p.), Brit. Engring. Assn. River Plate. Mgmt. adv. bd. Modern Plastics Publs. Patentee in field. Home: 6133 N Forest Glen Ave Chicago IL 60646-5015 Office: 860 E State Pkwy Schaumburg IL 60173-4529

WYSNEWSKI, ROY EDWARD, physicist; b. Cin., Aug. 24, 1935; m. Barbara Elaine Brennan, Sept. 19, 1957 (div. Sept. 1976); David, Donna Sue Wysnewski DeGuzman, Daniel; m. Judith Elizabeth Bates, Mar. 18, 1978. BS in Physics/Math., U. Cin., 1959. Asst. engr. GE Co., Evandale, Ohio, 1956-57, nuclear physicst, 1959-61; physicist Hercules Powder Co., Cumberland, Md., 1961-63; chief radiographer Gen. Dynamics Corp., San Diego, 1963-65; sr. tech. specialist GAF Corp., Binghamton, N.Y., 1965-80, DuPont Co., Wilmington, Del., 1980-83; tech. mgr. Fuji NDT Sys., Roselle, Ill., 1983—; instr. video: Fundamentals of Film Interpretation, 1987. Author: (copyright) Energy Level for Film Substitution, 1994. Mem. Zoning Bd. Appeals, Conklin, N.Y., 1968-72. Fellow Am. Soc. for Non-Destructive Testing; mem. ASTM (E-7 Cert. of Appreciation 1996). Democrat. Avocations: meteorology, gardening, reading. Home and Office: 5785 Beaurivage Ave Sarasota FL 34243

WYSOCKI, ANNETTE B., nurse scientist, educator; b. Raleigh, N.C., Dec. 31, 1954; d. Robert Joseph and Frances (Overton) W.; m. John Nussbaum, May 2, 1987. BSN, East Carolina U., 1978, MSN, 1980; PhD, U. Tex., 1986. Cert. med.-surg. nurse. Staff nurse U. Va., Charlottesville, 1978-79, Seton Med. Ctr., Austin, Tex., 1981-86; rsch. and teaching asst. U. Tex., Austin, 1982-84; sr. rsch. assoc. U. Tex. Southwestern Med. Ctr., Dallas, 1986-87; NIH postdoctoral rsch. fellow U. Tex., Dallas, 1987-89, Cornell U. Med. Coll., N.Y.C., 1989-91; adj. asst. prof. NYU, N.Y.C., 1991—; rsch. asst. prof., dir. nursing rsch. NYU Med. Ctr., N.Y.C., 1991—. Mem. editorial bd. Wounds: A Compendium of Clin. Rsch. and Practice; contbr. articles to profl. jours. Vol. Girl Scouts U.S.A. Am. Nurses Found. scholar; grantee NIH, 1988-91, 93—, Nat. Inst. Nursing Rsch., Am. Nurses Found., 1984-85. Mem. AAAS, Am. Soc. Cell Biology, N.Y. Acad. Scis., Wound Healing Soc., Soc. Investigative Dermatology, Assn. Oper. Rm. Nurses, Sigma Theta Tau. Avocations: hiking, camping, gardening, sailing. Office: NYU Med Ctr PHL-875 550 1st Ave New York NY 10016-6481

WYSOCKI, BOLESLAW A(NTONI), psychologist, educator; b. Poland, June 10, 1912; s. Wladyslaw and Wiktoria (Mizia) Wysocki; student U. Cracow, U. Edinburgh (Scotland), Cambridge (Eng.) U., Oxford (Eng.) U., 1932-48; Ph.D., U. London (Eng.), 1954. Came to U.S., 1952, naturalized, 1958. Dir. edn. Ministry Edn., Gt. Britain, 1948-52; counselor, tchr. Marquette U., Milw., 1952-55; assoc. prof. psychology Alliance (Pa.) Coll., 1955-57, Merrimack (Mass.) Coll., 1957-60, Regis (Mass.) Coll., 1960-62; prof. psychology Newton (Mass.) Coll., 1962-75, Boston Coll., 1975—. Clin. work mental instns., 1952—. Served as mil. psychologist Polish Army, 1943-48. Mem. Am., Mass., Brit. psychol. socs., Polish Inst. Arts and Scis. in Am., AAUP. Contbr. articles to profl. jours. Home: 240 Brattle St Cambridge MA 02138-4628 Office: Boston Coll Dept Psychology Mcguinn Hall Chestnut Hill MA 02167

WYSS, DAVID ALEN, financial service executive; b. Ft. Wayne, Ind., Nov. 14, 1944; s. Alen G. and Anne W. (Winicker) W.; m. Grace H. Hawes, June 11, 1966; children: Sarah J., Alen D. BS, MIT, 1966; PhD, Harvard U., 1971. Economist Fed. Res., Washington, 1970-74, sr. economist, 1975-77; advisor Bank Eng., London, 1974-75; sr. staff economist Council Econ. Advisers, Washington, 1977-79; v.p. DRI Ltd., London, 1979-83; rsch. dir. DRI/McGraw Hill, Lexington, Mass., 1983—. Contbr. numerous articles to profl. jours. Mem. Am. Econ. Assn., Am. Statis. Assn., Nat. Assn. Bus. Economists. Office: DRI/McGraw Hill 24 Hartwell Ave Lexington MA 02173-3103

WYSS, JOHN BENEDICT, lawyer; b. Evanston, Ill., Nov. 23, 1947; s. Walther Erwin and Caroline Nettie (Benedict) W.; m. Joanne P. Comstock, Oct. 22, 1994; children: John Christian, Kirsten Dunlop. BS in Physics summa cum laude, Stanford U., 1969; JD, Yale U., 1972. Bar: Calif. 1972, D.C. 1974, U.S. Supreme Ct. 1976. Trial atty. antitrust div. U.S. Dept. Justice, Washington, 1972-74; assoc. Kirkland & Ellis, Washington, 1974-78, ptnr., 1978-83; ptnr. Wiley, Rein & Fielding, Washington, 1983—. Mem. ABA, Phi Beta Kappa. Office: Wiley Rein & Fielding 1776 K St NW Washington DC 20006-2304

WYSS, NORMA ROSE TOPPING, counselor, supervisor, educator, writer; b. Wautoma, Wis., Jan. 7, 1919; d. Eugene Leonard Topping and Sylvia Maude (Attoe-Dumond) Topping Schubert; m. Werner Oscar Wyss; children: Werner Oscar II (dec.), Christine Camille (dec.), Melanie Rose (dec.), Sylvia Ann (dec.). Diploma, Waushara Normal, 1939; BA in Elem. Edn., Fla. State U., 1949, MS, 1960; postgrad., U. Md., 1964; PhD in Social Change and Counselling, Walden U., 1986; grad., Inst. Children's Lit., West Redding, Conn., 1993. Cert. employment counselor and supr. Tchr. Hoeft Sch., Berlin, Wis., 1939-40, Escambia County Sch. Bd., Pensacola, Fla., 1946-66; area I counselor supr. Fla. State Dept. of Labor, Pensacola and Tallahassee, 1966-79; freelance writer N.Y.C., 1986-90; field interviewer Arbitron, Laurel, Md., 1985-88; counselor Career Mgmt. Specialists, 1994-95. Author: Core Counseling: The Christian Faith and the Helping Relationship: A Paradigm of Social Change, 1990; children's short stories. Communicant mem., usher, greeter, cantor, pre-marriage counselor, good shepherd co-chmn. Luth. Ch. of the Resurrection, Pensacola, Fla. Mem. Am. Counseling Assn., Nat. Assn. Ret. Tchrs., Escambia Educators (life), Fla. Ret. Educators (life), DAR (treas. Pensacola chpt. 1988-90, Alpha Delta Kappa (1st pres. Fla. Alpha chpt. 1953), Kappa Delta Pi. Democrat. Avocations: conchology, reading, playing organ, water color, oil painting. Office: 92B-2600 W Michigan Ave Pensacola FL 32526

WYTON, ALEC, composer, organist; b. London, Aug. 3, 1921; came to U.S., 1950, naturalized, 1968; s. Gilbert and Jessie (Burrage) W.; m. Mary Thornton Broman; children: Vaughan, Richard, Patrick, Christopher. B.A., Oxford U., 1945, M.A., 1949; Mus.D. (hon.), Susquehanna (Pa.) U., 1970. Asst. organist Christ Church Cathedral, Oxford U., 1943-46; organist St. Mathews Ch., Northampton, Eng., 1946-50, Christ Church Cathedral, St. Louis, 1950-54, Cathedral St. John the Divine, N.Y.C., 1954-74, St. James's Ch., N.Y.C., 1974-87, St. Stephen's Ch., Ridgefield, Conn., 1987-96; chair dept. music Manhattan Sch. Music, 1984-93; adj. prof. music Union Theol. Sem., N.Y.C., 1960-73; chmn. dept. ch. music Manhattan Sch. Music, 1984-93; coord. standing commn. on ch. music Episcopal Ch., 1974-85. Composer numerous pieces.; Contbr. articles to profl. jours. Served with Brit. Army, 1941-42. Fellow Royal Coll. Organists, Am. Guild Organists (hon. fellow, pres. 1964-69), Royal Canadian coll. Organists, Royal Acad. Music, Royal Sch. Ch. Music. Republican. Episcopalian. Home: 15 Summit Ln Ridgefield CT 06877-4042

WYVILL, J. CRAIG, research engineer, program director; b. Washington, May 8, 1951; s. Andrew J. and Rach. C. Wyvill; m. Peggy T. Wyvill. BSME, Ga. Tech, 1973; MBA, Ga. State U., 1981. Registered profl. engr., Ga., Va. Energy sys. engr. Union Carbide Corp., Charleston, W.Va., 1973-75; project officer EPA, Washington, 1975-79; rsch. engr. Ga. Tech Rsch. Inst., Atlanta, 1979—, dir. agrl. tech. rsch. program, 1982-94, dir. office food industry programs, 1994—. Mem. ASME, Soc. Mfg. Engrs. (chpt. chmn. 1990, 93-94), Inst. Food Technologists, Ga. Agribus. Coun. Office: Ga Tech Rsch Inst Marc Bldg Rm 335 Atlanta GA 30332-0823

XENAKIS, STEPHEN NICHOLAS, psychiatrist, army officer; b. Washington, July 5, 1948; s. Stanley Steve and Mary Alexandria (Poulos) X.; m. Mary Elizabeth Boddie, Jan. 19, 1974; children: Nicholas John, Lea Elizabeth. AB, Princeton U., 1970; MD, U. Md., Balt., 1974; postgrad., Balt.-D.C. Psychoanalytic Inst., 1972-75, Armed Forces Staff Coll., 1984-85, U.S. Army War Coll., 1989-90. Diplomate Am. Bd. Psychiatry and

Neurology. Commd. U.S. Army, 1972, advanced through grades to brig. gen., 1994; resident U. Md., Balt., 1974; intern Letterman Army Med. Ctr., Presidio of San Francisco, 1974-75, resident in psychiatry, 1975-78; fellow in child and adolescent psychiatry Letterman Army Med. Ctr., U. Calif., San Francisco, 1978-80; chief dept. psychiatry Darnell Army Community Hosp., Ft. Hood, Tex., 1980-82; div. surgeon 1st Cav. Div., Ft. Hood, Tex., 1982-84; chief child, adolescent, family psychiatry Eisenhower Army Med. Ctr., Ft. Gordon, Ga., 1985-86, dep. comdr. clin. svcs., dir. med. edn., 1986-89; comdr. Blanchfield Army Community Hosp., 1990-93; project mgr. AMEDD Vanguard, Fairfax, Va., 1993, TRICARE S.E., Augusta, Ga., 1994-95; cmdg. gen. Southeast Regional Command Eisenhower Army Med. Ctr., Ft. Gordon, Ga., 1995—; clin. prof. Uniformed Svcs. of Health Scis., Bethesda, Md., 1985—, Med. Coll. of Ga., Augusta, 1985—; lectr., author Porter Lecture, 1989. Contbr. articles to profl. jours. Bd. dirs. Augusta Regional AIDS Coun., 1987-89. Fellow Am. Acad. and Adolescent Psychiatry, Am. Psychiat. Assn., Am. Coll. Physician Execs., Assn. Mil. Surgeon U.S. Greek Orthodox. Office: Commander Eisenhower Army Med Ctr Fort Gordon GA 30905

XIE, GANQUAN, mathematician, computational geophysical scientist, educator; b. Changsha, Hunan, People's Republic of China, July 2, 1943; s. Shuming Xie and Sumen Liu; m. Jianhua Li, Sept. 29, 1969; children: Feng, Lee. BCS, Hunan U., ChangSha City, 1966; PhD, SUNY, 1984; postdoctoral rsch., Courant Inst. Math., 1984-86. Asst. prof. Hunan Computer Research Inst., 1967-80; vice-chmn. Soc. Computational Math., Hunan, 1979-81; postdoctoral research Courant Inst. Math., N.Y.C., 1984—; prof., dir. Hunan Computer Rsch. Tech. Inst., 1987-88; staff scientist Lawrence Berkely Nat. Lab., 1991—; chmn. Chinese Computational Math. Soc., 1986-88; vis. rscher SUNY, 1989; vis. prof. KSU, 1990. Mem. editorial com. Jour. Computational Math., Beijing, 1987-88; inventor in field; contbr. to profl. jours. Nat. Sci. Found. grantee, 1986-87, recipient Chinese Scientific prize, 1978. Mem. N.Y. Acad. Scis., Soc. Indsl. Applied Math., Soc. of Exploration Geophysicists, Am. Geophys. Union. Avocations: applied math., numerical inverse tomography of the seismic exploration and electromagnetic exploration. Home: 1413 Glendale Ave Berkeley CA 94708-2027 Office: Lawrence Berkeley Nat Lab Bldg 90 Earth Scis Divsn Berkeley CA 94720

XIN, LI, physiologist; b. Shenyang, Liaoning, People's Republic of China, June 14, 1955; came to U.S., 1989; s. Zhili and Huiming (Wang) X.; m. Huizhong Peng; 1 child, Ryan Xin. MD, China Med. U., Shenyang, Liaoning, People's Republic of China, 1982, MS, 1988. Instr. dept. physiology China Med. U., Shenyang, Liaoning, People's Republic of China, 1983-86, asst. prof. dept. physiology, 1987-89; rsch. asst. prof. dept. physiology U. Tenn., Memphis, 1989-91; rsch. assoc. dept. pharmacology Temple U., Phila., 1992-96, assoc. scientist dept. pharmacology, 1996—; coun. standing mem. Youth Scientists Soc., Shenyang, 1988—. Contbr. articles to profl. jours. Recipient Prize for Excellent Paper, Chinese Physiol. Soc., 1985, Visiting fellowship Boehringer Ingelheim Fonds Found. for Basic Rsch. in Medicine, 1989. Mem. AAAS, Am. Physiol. Soc., N.Y. Acad. Scis., Soc. for Neurosci., Sigma Xi. Achievements include rsch. on ctrl. control of body temperature regulation, integration by preoptic anterior hypothalamus of brain under both physiol. and pathological conditions as well as actions of pharmacological agts.; mediation of endogenous neuropeptides in analgesic and body temperature responses to opioids. Home: 114 E Cuthbert Blvd # A-3 Westmont NJ 08108-1848 Office: Temple U Dept of Pharmacology 3420 N Broad St Philadelphia PA 19140-5104

XIONG, JEAN Z., artist, consultant; b. Beijing, China, Nov. 1, 1953; came to U.S., 1983.; d. Xian-Li and Zhang Yao (Zhu) Xiong; m. Charles C. Feng, Apr. 12, 1989. Grad., Shu Zhou (China) Inst., 1977; MFA, Acad Art Coll., San Francisco, 1986. Freelance artist/instr. Beijing, 1978-81; design artist First Impressions Advt., Reno, 1986; computer artist Visual Dynamics, San Francisco, 1988-89, Mediagenic, Menlo Park, 1989-91; leader artist Tecmagik Inc., Redwood City, Calif., 1992-94; computer artist Electronic Arts, San Mateo, Calif., 1995—; cons. entertainment software devel., Calif., 1991-92, 94-95; artist Electronic Arts, San Mateo, 1995—. One-woman shows San Francisco, 1984, 85, Monterey, Calif., 1984; exhbns. in Hong Kong, China, 1979, 80, 81. Recipient prize of Excellence Nat. Youth Artist Assn., 1980, Artist Assn., Hong Kong, 1981; scholar Acad. Art Coll., 1983-86. Mem. Mus. Modern Art, Tradtional Chinese Inst. (Beijing). Office: 2000 De Anza Blvd San Mateo CA 94402-3915

XU, LEI, computer scientist, educator; b. DuYun, China, Apr. 17, 1959; s. ShuiYuan and DieRan (Yue) X.; m. AiPing Zhan, July 3, 1984; 1 child, TianYi. B in Engring., Harbin Inst. Tech., China, 1981; MEng., Tsinghua U., Beijing, 1984, PhD, 1987. Postdoctoral fellow dept. math. Peking U., Beijing, 1987-88, assoc. prof. dept. math., 1988-92; sr. rsch. assoc. dept. info. tech. Lappeenranta (Finland) U. Tech., 1989-90; rsch. assoc. dept. computer sci. Concordia U., Montreal, 1990-91; vis. scientist Robotics Lab. Harvard U., Cambridge, Mass., 1991-92; postdoctoral assoc. dept. cognition and brain MIT, Cambridge, 1992-93; sr. lectr. dept. computer sci. The Chinese U. of Hong Kong, 1993-96, prof. dept. computer sci., 1996—; prof. Info. Sci. Ctr. and Nat. Lab. of Perception Peking U., 1992—; chmn., mem. numerous tech. coms. acad. confs.; presenter in field. Assoc. editor IEEE Trans. Neural Networks, 1994—, Neural Networks, 1994—, Internat. Jour. Neural Sys., 1993—, Neurocomputing, 1995—; adv. editor Neurocomputing Surveys, 1996—; contbr. over 180 articles to acad. jours., conf. procs. Recipient Fok Ying Tung Edn. Found. prize, 1988, Young Scientists prize Beijing Assn. Sci. and Tech., 1988, Chinese Nat. Nature Sci. award Chinese Sci. and Tech. Coun., 1994, Leadership award Internat. Neural Network Soc., 1995. Mem. IEEE (sr.), N.Y. Acad. Scis., Am. Assn. for the Advancement of Sci., Asia Pacific Neural Network Assembly (v.p. 1994-96, pres. 1996—), Internat. Assn. Pattern Recognition (tech. com. on neural networks 1993—), Sigma Xi. Avocations: Chinese classical poetry, Chinese chess, travel, mountain climbing, history. Office: Chinese U Hong Kong Dept Computer Sci, HSN ENG Bldg Rm 1006, Sha Tin Hong Kong

XUE, LAN, engineering educator; b. Beijing, China, June 25, 1959; s. Futang and Jingmei (Yu) X.; m. Xiaoping Li, Apr. 3, 1985; 1 child, Dyland Mooching. BSME, Changchun Inst. Optics, 1982; MS in Tech. Systems Mgmt., SUNY, Stony Brook, 1986, MS in Policy and Mgmt., 1987; PhD in Engring. and Pub. Policy, Carnegie Mellon U., 1991. Instr., researcher Changchun (People's Republic of China) Inst. Optics, 1982-85; rsch. and teaching asst. SUNY, Stony Brook, 1985-87, Carnegie Mellon U., Pitts., 1987-91; asst. prof. George Washington U., Washington, 1991—; assoc. prof., asst. dir. Devel. Rsch. Acad. 21st Century Tsinghua U., Beijing, 1996—; cons. Capital Iron & Steel Co., Beijing, 1993, Tangshan (China) Iron & Steel Co., 1993, The World Bank, 1994, NIST, 1994-95; lectr. in field. Contbr. articles to profl. jours. Dilthy fellow George Washington U., 1993; recipient Pride award George Washington U., 1995, Stephen Lee award Carnegie Mellon U., 1991, Short Term Enrichment Program award AAAS, 1989, Chinese Econ. Rsch. fellowship Washington Ctr. for China Studies, 1996. Mem. IEEE Soc. on Engring. Mgmt., Chinese Econ. Soc., Chinese Profl. Forum (pres. 1993-94), Tech. Transfer Soc. (bd. dirs. 1994-95), Inst. Mgmt. Sci., Am. Soc. for Engring. Edn., Chinese Assn. for Sci. and Tech. (pres. Washington chpt. 1995-96). Avocations: reading, table tennis, tai-chi, travel. Office: George Washington U Dept Engring Mgmt Washington DC 20052 Office: Tsinghua U, Devel Rsch Acad, 100084 Beijing China

YABLANS, FRANK, film company executive, motion picture producer; b. N.Y.C., Aug. 27, 1935; s. Morris and Annette Y.; m. Ruth Edelstein, Dec. 21; children: Robert, Sharon, Edward. Student, CCNY, U. Wis. Salesman, Warner Bros., 1956-58; br. mgr. Walt Disney Prodns., 1958-66; v.p. Filmways Prodns., 1966-69; successively v.p. sales, v.p. marketing, exec. v.p., pres. Paramount Pictures Corp., N.Y.C., 1969-75; pres. Frank Yablans Presentations, Inc., N.Y.C., 1975—; dir. Dirs. Co., Cinema Internat. Corp.; chmn. bd. MGM/UA Entertainment Co., 1983-85; founder Northstar Entertainment, 1985—; pres. Epic Records, 1989—; pres., chief exec. officer Nova Internat. Films, Inc. Films include Silver Streak, 1976, The Other Side of Midnight, 1977, The Fury, 1978, (also co-author screen play) North Dallas Forty, 1979, Mommie Dearest (producer, co-author screen play), Monsignore, 1982, The Star Chamber, 1983, Kid Co, 1983, Boy and Cell, 1989, Lisa, 1990. Chmn. entertainment div. Fedn. Jewish Philanthropies; bd. dirs. Boys' Clubs Am., Will Rogers Hosp.; trustee Am. Film Inst. Served with AUS, 1954-56. Decorated commendatore Repubblica Italiana. Mem. Variety Club Internat. (chmn.), Motion Picture Assn. (dir.). Club: Fairview Country. Office: Epic Productions Inc 4640 Lankershim Blvd Ste 600 North Hollywood CA 91602-1845*

YABLON, JEFFERY LEE, lawyer; b. Chgo., June 28, 1948; s. Robert R. and Faye I. (Goldberg) Y.; m. Jean C. LaPrade, Apr. 17, 1983. BA with honors, U. Wis., 1970; JD, Stanford U., 1973. Bar: Calif. 1974, D.C. 1975. Law clk. to Judge Cynthia Holcomb Hall, U.S. Tax Ct., Washington, 1973-75; Fulbright scholar U. Florence, Italy, 1975-76; assoc. Covington & Burling, Washington, 1976-80, Lee, Toomey & Kent, Washington, 1980-82; assoc. Shaw, Pittman, Potts & Trowbridge, Washington, 1982-84, ptnr., 1984—. Contbr. articles to legal jours. Bd. dirs. Am. Friends Hebrew U., Washington, 1991—. Mem. ABA, State Bar Calif., D.C. Bar. Jewish. Office: Shaw Pittman Potts & Trowbridge 2300 N St NW Washington DC 20037-1122

YABLON, LEONARD HAROLD, publishing company executive; b. N.Y.C., June 3, 1929; s. Philip A. and Sarah (Herman) Y.; children: Scott Richard, Bonnie Michele. BS, L.I. U., 1950; MBA, CCNY, 1969. CPA, N.Y. Acct., 1950-63; exec. v.p., dir. Forbes Inc., N.Y.C., 1963—; pres. Sangre de Cristo Ranches, Fiji Forbes; v.p. Forbes Investors Adv. Inst.; pres. Forbes Trinchera; sec.-treas. Forbes Found.; pres. Forbes Europe. Home: Pleasant Ridge Rd Harrison NY 10528 Office: 60 5th Ave New York NY 10011-8802

YABLUN, RONN, secondary education educator, small business owner; b. Chgo., July 11, 1950; s. Sidney and Phyllis (Bender) Y.; m. Anna Yablun, Dec. 17, 1977 (div. Jan. 1987); children: Melissa, Alex, Mark, William. BS in Edn., No. Ill. U., 1972. Cert. tchr., Ill., Calif. Tchr. art Page Sch., Beverly Hills, Calif., 1977-78; tchr. math. Calif. Prep. Sch., Encino, 1978-80; dir. of instruction The Reading Game, Encino, 1980-83; tchr. math. and computers Northridge (Calif.) Jr. High Sch., 1983—, math. dept. chairperson, 1991—; owner, dir. Mathamazement, Tarzana, Calif., 1983—; leadership sponsor Northridge Jr. H.S., 1985-88, pentathlon coach, 1985-89, theatrical dir., 1989—, dean of students, 1995-96. Contbr. articles to jours.; author: How to Develop Your Child's Gifts and Talents in Math, Mathamazement. GTE fellow, 1989; grantee L.A. Unified Schs.; recipient Outstanding Classroom Tchr. award L.A. Unified Schs.. 1989. Mem. NEA, United Tchrs. L.A. (chpt. chmn. 1994-96), Calif. Tchrs. Assn., Phi Kappa Sigma (sec., social chmn.). Avocation: choreographer, director. Office: Mathamazement 6047 Tampa Ave Ste 303 Tarzana CA 91356-1157

YACKEL, JAMES WILLIAM, mathematician, academic administrator; b. Sanborn, Minn., Mar. 6, 1936; s. Ewald W. and Marie E. (Heydlauff) Y.; m. Erna Beth Seecamp, Aug. 20, 1960; children: Jonathan, Juliet, Carolyn. BA, U. Minn., 1958, MA, 1960, PhD, 1964. Rsch. instr. dept. math. Dartmouth Coll., Hanover, N.H., 1964-66; asst. prof. dept. stats. Purdue U., West Lafayette, Ind., 1966-69, from assoc. prof. to prof., 1969-76, assoc. dean sci., 1976-87; vice chancellor acad. affairs Purdue U. Calumet, Hammond, Ind., 1987-90, chancellor, 1990—; rsch. mathematician Inst. Def. Analysis, Washington, 1969. Author: Applicable Finite Mathematics, 1974; editor Statistical Decision Theory, 1971; contbr. articles to profl. jours. Fellow AAAS; mem. Am. Math. Soc., Math. Assn. Am., Inst. Math. Stats. Research on Ramsey's theorem and finite graphs, stochastics processes, density estimation. Office: Purdue U Calumet Office of Chancellor Hammond IN 46323

YACKLE, ALBERT REUSTLE, aeronautical engineer; b. Willow Grove, Pa., May 13, 1922; s. Albert J. and Marion D. (Reustle) Y.; m. Ruth E. Everett, Sept. 18, 1948; children: Linda McCann, Tom, Brad. BS in Mech. Engring. Aeronautical Option, Pa. State U., 1943. Registered profl engr., Calif. Structures engr. Ea. Aircraft, 1944; structures engr. Kellett Aircraft Corp., 1946-48, chief structures engr., 1950-60; structures engr. Chase Aircraft, 1948-50; advanced design and program mgr. Lockheed Aircraft Corp., 1960-91; ret., 1991; cons. Huntington Med. Rsch. Inst., Pasadena, Calif., 1991-96. Contbr. tech. papers to profl. jours. Lt. (j.g.) USN, 1944-46. Recipient Lockheed Spl. Achievement awards, 1976, 77, 79, 87; inducted into H.S. Hall of Fame, 1996. Fellow (assoc.) AIAA; mem. Am. Helicopter Soc. Achievements include 2 patents in rigid rotor helicopters. Home: 5105 Quakertown Ave Woodland Hills CA 91364-3538

YACKLEY, LUKE EUGENE, head nurse, mental health nurse; b. Elmhurst, Ill., Apr. 20, 1950; s. Lawrence E. and Patricia Anne (Neumann) Y.; m. Teresa D. Thompson, Apr. 27, 1973; children: Gregory Scott, Julia Ann, Timothy Kevin, Kathleen Mary. BA in Sociology, Quincy (Ill.) U., 1972; AA in Nursing, Kankakee (Ill.) C.C., 1977; BSN, U. Md., 1991, MS, 1994. RN, Md. Mental health specialist Dept. Mental Health, Manteno, Ill., 1974-78; staff nurse acute psychiatry Vets. Adminstrn., Perry Point, Md., 1978-82, head nurse addictions, 1982—. Scoutmaster Boy Scouts Am., Charlestown, Md., 1993-97, scouter 1985—; Lector, Eucharistic min. Good Shepherd Parish, Perryville, Md., 1987—; adviser for explorer post Boy Scouts Am., Perry Point, 1993—; h.s. sports ofcl. NEMOA, Harford County, Md., 1982—. Recipient Outstanding Performance award VA Med. Ctr., 1987, Team Building award, 1992. Roman Catholic. Avocations: scouting, officiating, camping, backpacking. Home: 1616 Carpenters Point Rd Perryville MD 21903-2009 Office: Substance Abuse Treatment Program 22H VA Med Ctr Perry Point MD 21902

YACKTMAN, DONALD ARTHUR, financial executive, investment counselor; b. Chgo., Sept. 12, 1941; s. Victor and Matilda (Chamberlain) Y.; m. Carolyn I. Zuppann, June 15, 1965; children:Donald, Stephen, Jennifer, Melissa, Brian, Robert, Michael. BS, U. Utah, 1965; MBA, Harvard U., 1967. Chartered investment counselor. Trainee, Continental Bank, Chgo., 1967-68; assoc. Stein Roe & Farnham, Chgo., 1968-74, ptnr., 1974-82; pres. Selected Am. Shares; sr. v.p. Prescott Asset Mgmt., 1982-92; pres. Yacktman Asset Mgmt. Co. and Yacktman Fund, 1992—; first v.p. N.W. Suburban coun. Boy Scouts Am., 1984-96; young men's pres. Ch. Jesus Christ Latter Day Saints. Mem. Fin. Analysts Soc. Office: Yacktman Asset Mgmt Co 303 W Madison St Ste 1925 Chicago IL 60606-3308

YACOB, YOSEF, lawyer, economist; b. Dire Dawa, Harar, Ethiopia, Nov. 12, 1947; s. Yacob and Egziaraya (Osman) Zanios; m. Betsy Ann Boynton; children: Sarah Ann, Matthew Yosef, Ezra Yosef, Jarred Yosef, Rachel Helen. BA, Linfield Coll., 1971; JD, Lewis and ClarkU., 1974. Bar: Oreg. 1975, U.S. Dist. Ct. Oreg. 1979, U.S. Ct. Appeals (9th cir.) 1980. Rschr. criminal justice State of Oreg., Salem, 1974, sr. administrv. analyst, 1974-76; adjudications specialist, legal counsel, law enforcement coun. Office of the Gov. State of Oregon, Salem, 1976-78; chief administrv. law judge State of Oregon, Milwaukie, 1978-83, dir. hearings, appeals, 1982-84; mng. atty. Hyatt Legal Services, Clakamas, Oreg., 1984-86; pres., sr. ptnr. Yacob & Assocs. P.C., Clackamas, 1986-93; dir. gen. for legal affairs, gen. counsel Ministry of Fgn. Affairs, Govt. of Ethiopia, 1993—. Co-author: Evaluation of Multwomah County District Attorney's High Impact Project, 1978. Avocations: alpine skiing, nordic skiing, water skiing, reading. Home: 6885 SW Montgomery Way Wilsonville OR 97070-6739 Office: Yacob & Assocs PC Northwest Legal Svcs 6885 SW Montgomery Way Wilsonville OR 97070-6739

YACOUB, IGNATIUS I., university dean; b. Dwar Taha, Syria, Jan. 5, 1937; came to U.S. 1978; s. Immanuel and Martha (Kharma) Y.; m. Mary Haddad, Sept. 14, 1961; children—Hilda, Lena, Emile. A.B., Middle East Coll., Beirut, Lebanon, 1960; M.A., Pacific Union Coll., Angwin, Calif., 1964; Ph.D., Claremont Grad. Sch., Calif., 1976. Dean studies Middle East Coll., Beirut, Lebanon, 1967-73, 75-78; dir. dept. edn. Afro-Mideast div. Seventh-Day Adventist Ch., 1970-73, dir. dept. pub. affairs, 1975-78; prof., chmn. dept. bus. econs. Southwestern Union Coll., Keene, Tex., 1978-80; prof., chmn. dept. bus. and econs. Loma Linda U., Riverside, Calif., 1980-86, dean Sch. of Bus. and Mgmt., 1986-90; prof. mgmt., 1995—; dean Sch. Bus. and Mgmt., La Sierra U., Riverside, Calif., 1990-95; prof. adminstrn. and mgmt. Loma Linda (Calif.) U., 1995—; bd. dirs. Riverside Nat. Bank. Mem. Exec. 2000 Coun. Riverside Cmty. Hosp. Found., 1991-95. Recipient Gov.'s Appreciation award, Lions Club, Lions Club award, Beirut, cert. Appreciation Exec. 2000 Coun., 1994, 95, Cert. of Appreciation Claremont Grad. Sch. Alumni Coun., 1996, Mentemoreles Univ. Mex., 1992, 94. Mem. Am. Mgmt. Assn., Acad. Mgmt., Greater Riverside C. of C. (Svc. award 1995), Corona C. of C. Seventh-day Adventist. Home: 2722 Litchfield Dr Riverside CA 92503-6213

YACOWITZ, HAROLD, biochemist, nutritionist; b. N.Y.C., Feb. 17, 1922; s. Louis and Clara (Kurtzberg) Y.; m. Ann Ruth Barnett, Dec. 31, 1941; children: Caryn R., Richard S., Suzanne Yacowitz Dragan. BS, Cornell U., 1947, M in Nutritional Sci., 1948, PhD, 1950. Rsch. biochemist Parke-Davis Inc., Detroit, 1950-51; assoc. prof. Ohio State U., Columbus, 1951-55; head nutrition rsch. dept. Squibb Inst. for Med. Rsch., New Brunswick, N.J., 1955-59; dir. rsch. Nopco Chem. Co. Inc., Harrison, N.J., 1959-61, Amburgo Co. Inc., Phila., 1961-80; rsch. assoc. Fairleigh Dickinson U., Madison, N.J., 1961-80; pres., dir. rsch. Dr. H. Yacowitz & Co., Piscataway, N.J., 1961—, Animal Identification & Marking Systems Inc., Piscataway, 1982-97; pres. Peninsula Investment & Devel. Inc., Cambridge, Md., 1961—; pres., bd. dirs. rsch. Drug Delivery Devices Inc., Piscataway, 1991—. Contbr. articles to profl. jours.; patentee in field. Leader Boy Scouts Am., Ithaca, N.Y., 1946-50, Piscataway, 1955-59. With U.S. Army, 1943-46, ETO, PTO. Grange League Fedn. fellow Cornell U., 1947-48, Robert Gould rsch. fellow, Cornell U., 1949-50, Coun. on Arteriosclerosis fellow Am. Heart Assn., 1970. Fellow N.Y. Acad. Scis. (chmn. sect. biology and medicine 1972-76); mem. Am. Chem. Soc., Am. Inst. Nutrition, Am. Assn. Lab. Animal Scientists, Exptl. Investors Club (New Brunswick, pres. 1955-59). Jewish. Avocations: gardening, sailing, fishing, swimming. Office: Drug Delivery Devices Inc 221 2nd Ave Piscataway NJ 08854-3519

YADALAM, KASHINATH GANGADHARA, psychiatrist; b. Bangalore, India, Dec. 17, 1954; came to U.S., 1980; s. Gangadhara N. and Ramarathna G. (Daglur) Y.; m. Jyothi Kashinath, Feb. 26, 1981; children: Akhila, Adithya. MD, Kasturba Med. Coll., Manipal, India, 1977. Diplomate, Am. Bd. Psychiatry and Neurology. Resident in psychiatry U. Nebr., Omaha, 1980-83; clin. fellow psychopharmacology Med. Coll. Pa., Phila., 1983-84; instr. Med. Coll. Pa., 1984-85, asst. prof., 1985-89, dir. neuropsychiatry clinic, 1987-91, assoc. prof., 1989-91; med. dir. Diagnostic and Consultation Ctr. Med. Coll. of Pa.; assoc. dir. The Neuropsychiat. Clinic of La., 1991-96, med. dir., 1996—; med. dir. Schizophrenia Diagnostic and Consultation Ctr., 1990. Author: (with others) Drug Induced Dysfunction in Psychiatry, 1992; contbr. articles to med. jours. Grantee, NIMH, 1987; recipient Young Investigator award, Internat. Congress Schizophrenia Rsch., Balt., 1987, Young Scientist award Winter Workshop on Schizophrenia, Badgastein, Austria, 1990. Mem. Am. Psychiat. Assn., Am. Coll. Clin. Pharmacology, Nat Alliance of the Mentally Ill. Hindu. Avocations: table tennis, chess, squash, fitness. Office: 2829 4th Ave Ste 150 Lake Charles LA 70601-7887

YAFFA, JACK BER, healthcare administrator, educator; b. Camden, N.J., Apr. 28, 1941; s. Harry and Rose (Plotkin) Y.; m. Phyllis P. Pollack, June 21, 1964; children: Andrew, Samuel, Jodi, Gregory. BA, U. Richmond, 1963, MD, 1968. Cert. Am. Bd. Surgery; cert. Fla. Bd. Med. Examiners, Va. Bd. Med. Examiners. Surg. intern U. Miami (Fla.) Med. Ctr., 1968-69, surg. resident, 1969-73, chief resident in surgery, 1972-73; pvt. practice in gen.-vascular surgery Miami, 1973-95; assoc. chief of staff ambulatory care Miami VA Med. Ctr., 1995—; asst. prof. clin. surgery U. Miami Med. Sch., 1995—; chief med. officer Oakland Park Outpatient Clinic, Dept. VA Med. Ctr.; asst. chief of surgery Bapt. Hosp. Miami, 1978-79, chief of surgery, 1980-81, 91-93, chief of cardiac surgery, 1982-84, chief of trauma surgery, 1983, chmn. peripheral vascular lab., 1982-83, chief of staff, 1984-88, adminstrv. dir. critical care, 1988-92; active staff South Miami Hosp.; mem. governing bd. emergency med. svcs. tng. U. Miami Sch. Medicine, 1989-95. Fellow ACS (gov.-at-large 1990, bd. govs. 1991-96, instr. advanced trauma life support 1981-93, mem. state com. trauma 1985-93, sec.-treas. Miami chpt. 1983-85, pres. Miami chpt. 1985-87, councilor Miami chpt. 1990-92); mem. AMA, Fla. Med. Assn. (com. on emergency med. svcs., coun. on hosp. med. staffs), Fla. Surg. Soc. (bd. dirs. 1990—), South Fla. Noninvasive Vascular Soc., Miami Surg. Soc., Jackson Surg. Soc., Dade County Med. Assn., Soc. Laparendoscopic Surgeons, Southeastern Surg. Congress, So. Med. Congress (assoc. councilor 1989), Surg. Hist. Soc. Jewish. Avocations: boating, fishing. Office: Miami VA Med Ctr 1201 NW 16th St Miami FL 33125-1624

YAFFE, BARBARA MARLENE, journalist; b. Montreal, Que., Can., Mar. 4, 1953; d. Allan and Ann (Freedman) Y.; m. Wilson E. Russell, Aug. 30, 1985. Student, McGill U., 1970-73; BA, U. Toronto, 1974; B in Journalism, Carleton U., 1974. Reporter Montreal Gazette, 1975-76, Toronto Globe and Mail, 1976-79; reporter, columnist Toronto Globe and Mail, Halifax, N.S., 1979-81; TV bur. chief CBC-TV, St. Johns, Nfld., 1981-84, Edmonton, Alta., 1983; reporter Toronto Globe and Mail, St. John's, 1984-86; editor Sunday Express, St. John's, 1987-88; editor Vancouver Sun, 1988-93, columnist, 1993—. Recipient Gov. Gen.'s award Roland Michener Found., 1977. Jewish. Office: c/o Vancouver Sun, 2250 Granville St, Vancouver, BC Canada V6H 3G2

YAFFE, DAVID PHILIP, lawyer; b. Waukegan, Ill., Jan. 31, 1952; s. Robert M. Yaffe and Ruth David Rickard; m. Deborah Miriam Passow Yaffe, December 26, 1976; children: Andrea, Alicia. BA, Johns Hopkins U., 1974; JD with honors, George Washington U., Washington, 1977. Bar: Va. 1977, D.C. 1978, U.S. Ct. Appeals (4th cir.) 1978, U.S. Ct. Appeals (9th cir.) 1982. Assoc. Duncan & Allen, Washington, 1977-83, ptnr., 1983-96, mng. ptnr., 1988-94; mem. Van Ness Feldman, P.C., Washington, 1996—. Contbr. articles to profl. jours. Nat. chair Second Decade Soc., Johns Hopkins U., Balt., 1993-94; co-pres. Agudus Achim Congregation, Alexandria, Va., 1993-95. Mem. ABA (sect. on nat. resources, energy and environ. law, vice chmn. electric power com. 1993—), Fed. Energy Bar Assn. Avocation: golf. Home: 4528 Sleaford Rd Annandale VA 22003

YAFFE, JAMES, author; b. Chgo., Mar. 31, 1927; s. Samuel and Florence (Scheinman) Y.; m. Elaine Gordon, Mar. 1, 1964; children: Deborah Ann, Rebecca Elizabeth, Gideon Daniel. Grad., Fieldston Sch., 1944; B.A. summa cum laude, Yale U., 1948. Prof. Colo. Coll., Colo. Springs, 1968—; dir. gen. studies Colo. Coll., 1981—. Author: Poor Cousin Evelyn, 1951, The Good-for-Nothing, 1953, What's the Big Hurry?, 1954, Nothing But the Night, 1959, Mister Margolies, 1962, Nobody Does You Any Favors, 1966, The American Jews, 1968, The Voyage of the Franz Joseph, 1970, So Sue Me!, 1972, Saul and Morris, Worlds Apart, 1982, A Nice Murder for Mom, 1988, Mom Meets Her Maker, 1990, Mom Doth Murder Sleep, 1991, Mom Among the Liars, 1992, My Mother the Detective, 1997; play The Deadly Game, 1960, (with Jerome Weidman) Ivory Tower, 1967, Cliffhanger, 1985; also TV plays, stories, essays, revs. Served with USNR, 1945-46. Recipient Nat. Arts Found award, 1968. Mem. P.E.N., Authors League, Writers Guild of Am., Dramatists Guild, A.A.U.P., Mystery Writers of Am., Phi Beta Kappa. Jewish. Club: Elizabethan (Yale). Avocations: music, bridge, movies. Address: 1215 N Cascade Ave Colorado Springs CO 80903-2303 Office: Colo Coll Off Dir Gen Studies Colorado Springs CO 80903

YAFFE, PETER MARC, public policy consultant, gas industry executive; b. Phila., May 31, 1948; s. Joseph X. and Silvia (Fishbein) Y.; m. Christine Ann Phillips, Nov. 12, 1988; children: Elizabeth Ann, Spencer Phillips. BA, U. Miami, 1970; postgrad., Inst. Orgnl. Mgmt., 1985, Harvard U.-MIT, 1993, Temple U., 1996. Spl. asst. to gov. Commonwealth of Pa., Harrisburg, 1971-77; adminstr. Greater Phila. Partnership, 1977-80; cons. Pub. Mgmt. Cons., Inc., Phila., 1981; spl. asst. to mayor for legis. City of Phila., 1982-84; v.p. govt. affairs Phila. C. of C., Harrisburg, 1985-86; spl. asst. to sec. of labor and industry Commonwealth of Pa., Harrisburg, Pa., 1987-88; dir. govt. affairs Waste Mgmt., Inc., Morrisville, Pa., 1988—; region v.p. govt. and pub. affairs Waste Mgmt., Inc., Bensalem, Pa., 1990—, group v.p. govt. and pub. affairs, 1992-95; group v.p. govt. and pub. affairs The Yaffe Group, Wyndmoor, Pa., 1995—; cons. Phila. Gas Works, 1997—. Mem. McCarthy for Pres. Com., Washington, 1968, Shapp for Gov. Com., Pa., 1970, McGovern for Pres. Com., Washington, 1972, Carter/Mondale Election Com., Washington, 1976, Bill Green for U.S. Senate Com., Pa., 1976, State Govt. Affairs Coun., 1990-95; polit. dir. Kennedy for Pres. Com., Pa., 1980; Broward County (Fla.) polit. dir. Carter/Mondale Re-Election Com., 1980; exec. dir. Pa. Dem. State Com., Harrisburg, 1982, 86; spl. asst. to chmn. Dem. Nat. Com., Washington, 1984; Pa. chmn. White House conf. on Youth, 1971; bd. dirs. Nat. Coun. State Commn. on Children and Youth, 1976. Recipient Community Svc. award Chapel of the Four Chaplins, Phila., 1978. Mem. N.J. Solid Waste Mgmt. Assn. (steering com. 1988-95), Md./Del. Nat. Solid Waste Mgmt. Assn. (steering com. 1989-95), Pa. Waste Industry Assn. (steering com. 1988-95), Va. Waste Industry Assn. (steering com. 1988-95). Home: 8115 Eastern Ave Wyndmoor PA 19038-7943 Office: 800 W Montgomery Ave Philadelphia PA 19122

YAFFE, STUART ALLEN, physician; b. Springfield, Ill., July 6, 1927; m. Natalie, 1952; children: Scott, Kim Yaffe Schoenburg. BS cum laude, U. Alaska, 1951; MD, St. Louis U., 1956. Diplomate Am. Bd. Family Practice. Intern St. Louis CIty Hosp., 1956-57, resident, 1957-58; physician pvt. practice, 1958—; clin. assoc. prof. So. Ill. U. Sch. Medicine., Springfield, 1971—; ptnr. Springfield Clinic, 1989—. With U.S. Army, 1945-47. Mem. AMA, Am. Acad. Family Physicians, Ill. Acad. Family Physicians, Ill. State Med. Soc., Sangamon County Med. Soc. Office: 1100 Centre West Dr Springfield IL 62704-2100

YAFFE, SUMNER JASON, pediatrician, research center administrator, educator; b. Boston, May 9, 1923; s. Henry H. and Ida E. (Fisher) Y.; m. Anita Yaffe; children: Steven, Kris, Jason, Noah, Ian, Zachary. A.B., Harvard U., 1945, M.A., 1950; M.D., U. Vt., 1954. Diplomate Am. Bd. Pediatrics. Intern Children's Hosp., Boston, 1954-55, resident, 1955-56; resident in pediatrics St. Mary's Hosp., London, 1956-57; instr. pediatrics Stanford U., Palo Alto, Calif., 1959-60, asst. prof., 1960-63; assoc. prof. pediatrics SUNY-Buffalo, 1963-66, prof., 1966-75, adj. prof. biochem. pharmacology, 1968-75, acting chmn. dept. pediatrics, 1974-75; prof. pediatrics and pharmacology U. Pa., Phila., 1975-81; dir. Ctr. for Research for Mothers and Children, NIH, Bethesda, Md., 1981—; clin. prof. pediatrics Georgetown U. Med. Ctr., 1986, Johns Hopkins Hosp., 1986; attending physician Palo Alto-Stanford Hosp., 1959-63; attending physician Children's Hosp., Buffalo, 1963-75, Phila., 1975-81; vis. prof. pharmacology Karolinska Inst., Stockholm, 1969-70; dir. Pediatric Renal Clinic, Stanford Med. Ctr., 1960-63; dir. newborn nursery service Palo Alto-Stanford Hosp., 1960-63, program dir. Clin. Research Ctr. for Premature Infants, 1962-63; dir. Clin. Research Ctr. for Children Children's Hosp., Buffalo, 1963-70, dir. Poison Control Ctr., 1967-75, dir. div. clin. pharmacology, Phila., 1975-81; program cons. Nat. Inst. Child Health and Human Devel., NIH, 1963-71, mem. tng. grant com., 1963-65, mem. reproductive biology com., 1965-67; mem. adv. panel on maternal and child health WHO, Geneva, 1970—; liaison rep. drug research bd. NRC, 1971-75, com. on drug dependence, 1972-75, mem. com. on problems of drug safety, 1972-75; mem. adv. panel in pediatrics U.S. Pharmacopeia, 1970—, in toxicology, 1974-75; cons. Am. Found. for Maternal and Child Health, Inc., 1973—; pres. Maternal and Child Health Research Found., Children's Hosp., 1974—; Wall Meml. lectr. Children's Hosp., Washington, 1968—; Dr. W.E. Upjohn lectr. Can. Med. Assn., 1974; Louisville pediatric lectr. Sch. Medicine U. Louisville, 1974; William N. Creasy vis. prof. clin. pharmacology SUNY, 1976; advisor Internat. Childbirth Assn. Greater Phila., 1979-83; guest lectr. Dept. Pediatrics Georgetown U. Hosp., Washington, 1988—; lectr. in pediatrics Johns Hopkins Sch. Medicine, Balt., 1988—. Author: Clinics in Perinatology, 1974, Drug Assessment: Criteria and Methods, 1979, Pediatric Pharmacology, 1980, 2d edit. 1992; co-author: (with R. Galinsky) Clinical Therapeutics, 1978; editor: (with R. H. Schwartz) Drug and Chemical Risks to the Fetus and Newborn, 1980, (with G.G. Briggs, T.W. Bodendorfer, R.K. Freeman) Drugs in Pregnancy and Lactation, A Reference Guide to Fetal and Neonatal Risk, 1983, 2d edit., 1986, 4th edit., 1994, (J.V. Aranda) Pediatric Phyarmacology, 2nd edit., 1993; mem. editorial bd. Pediatric Alert, 1977—, Pharmacology, 1977—, Devel. Pharmacology and Therapeutics, 1979-95; mem. editorial adv. bd. Drug Therapy, 1979—; cons. editor Clin. Pharmacokinetics, 1977; co-editor Developmental Pharmacology, 1979-94; contbr. chpts. to profl. books., articles to profl. jours. Served with U.S. Army, 1943-44. Recipient Lederle Med. Faculty award Lederle Found., 1962; Fulbright scholar, 1956-57. Fellow Acad. Pharm. Scis.; mem. AMA (com. on drugs 1963-68), Am. Acad. Pediatrics (chmn. com. on drugs 1967-76), AAUP, Am. Coll. Clin. Pharmacology and Chemotherapy, Am. Fedn. for Clin. Rsch., Am. Pediatric Soc., Am. Pharmaceutics Assn., Am. Pub . Health Assn., Am. Soc. for Clin. Pharmacology and Therapeutics (chmn. sect. on pediatric pharmacology 1977-83), Am. Soc. Pharmacology and Exptl. Therapeutics, Fedn. Am. Socs. for Exptl. Biology, Perinatal Rsch. Soc., Soc. for Pediatric Research, Sigma Xi, Alpha Omega Alpha. Home: 6417 Tilden Ln Rockville MD 20852-3742 Office: Nat Inst of Child Health & Human Devel 6100 Executive Blvd Bethesda MD 20892-7510

YAGER, HUNTER, advertising executive; b. Bklyn., Sept. 29, 1929; s. Jules and Lucille (Kornblum) Y.; m. Gertrude Kathryn Johnson, Feb. 17, 1960; children—Leslie Jeanne, Andrew Hunter, Phoebe Hildreth. BA, N.Y. U., 1950; MBA, Harvard U., 1955. Copywriter Donahue & Coe, Inc., N.Y.C., 1951-53; account exec. Foote, Cone & Belding, N.Y.C., 1955-58; account exec., account supr., v.p., mgmt. supr., exec. v.p. mgmt. com. Grey Advt., Inc., N.Y.C., 1958-85; dir. Grey Advt., Ltd., Can., 1970-79; mktg. and advt. cons., 1985—; dir. Vicorp Restaurants, Inc., 1996—; instr. mktg. NYU, 1961-62. Dir., sec., mem. exec. com., devel. com., mktg. com. Chamber Music Soc. of Lincoln Ctr., 1986-90; dir., mktg. com. Manhattan Theatre Club, 1987-92; bd. dirs., pres. West Lyon Farm Condominium Assn., Greenwich, Conn., 1985-90; v.p. Powder Mill Owners Assn., Londonberry, Vt.; bd. dirs. Harvard Bus. Sch. Club, Fairfield County, 1986-91; trustee exec. bd. Manchester Music Festival, 1993-95. Mem. Camp Rising Sun Alumni Assn., Harvard Bus. Sch. Alumni Assn. (bd. dirs. 1993-96), Harvard Club. Home: West Fields RR 2 Box 3190 Manchester VT 05255

YAGER, JOHN WARREN, retired banker, lawyer; b. Toledo, Sept. 16, 1920; s. Joseph A. and Edna Gertrude (Pratt) Y.; m. Dorothy W. Merki, July 25, 1942; children: Julie M., John M. AB, U. Mich., 1942, JD, 1948. Bar: Ohio 1948. Pvt. practice law Toledo, 1948-64; trust officer Toledo Trust Co., 1964-69; v.p., trust officer Fifth Third Bank, 1969-91; sec. First Ohio Bancshares, Inc., 1980-85; ret. Pres. Toledo Met. Park Dist., 1971-85, Neighborhood Health Assn., 1974-75, councilman, Toledo, 1955-57, 60-61, mayor, 1958-59; bd. dirs. Toledo-Lucas County Library, 1968-70, Riverside Hosp., Downtown Toledo Assn.; past pres. Toledo Legal Aid Soc., Toledo Council Chs., Toledo Mcpl. League, Econ. Opportunity Planning Assn., Toledo, Com. on Relations with Toledo, Spain. Maj. USMC, 1942-46, 50-52. Decorated Bronze Star; named one of 10 Outstanding Young Men in Toledo, 1952, 54, 55. Mem. Toledo Bar Assn., Delta Tau Delta. Home: 29301 Bates Rd Perrysburg OH 43551-3808

YAGER, JOSEPH ARTHUR, JR., economist; b. Owensville, Ind., Apr. 14, 1916; s. Joseph Arthur and Edna (Pratt) Y.; m. Virginia Estella Beroset, Sept. 2, 1938; children: Thomas, Martha. A.B., U. Mich., 1937, J.D., 1939, M.A., 1940; grad., Nat. War Coll., 1955. Economist OPA, 1942-44; economist State Dept., 1946-47, chief China research br., 1949-50; chief div. research for State Dept., Far East, 1952-57; attaché U.S. consulate gen., Canton, China, 1947-48; consul U.S. consulate gen., Hong Kong, 1950-51; econ. counselor Taipei, 1957-59; dep. chief of mission, 1959-61; dir. Office Chinese Affairs, 1961, Office East Asian Affairs, 1961-63; mem. Policy Planning Council, 1963-66, vice chmn., 1966-68; dep. dir. internat. and social studies div. Inst. Def. Analyses, 1968-72; sr. fellow Brookings Instn., 1972-83, guest scholar, 1983-86; resident cons. Sci. Applications Internat. Corp., 1986-89, sr. fellow, 1989-96; cons., 1996—. Author: Transforming Agriculture in Taiwan, 1988, Prospects for Nuclear Weapons Proliferation in a Changing Europe, 1992; co-author: Energy and U.S. Foreign Policy, 1974, New Means of Financing International Needs, 1978, Military Equation in Northeast Asia, 1979, Nonproliferation and U.S. Foreign Policy, 1980, International Cooperation in Nuclear Energy, 1981, Energy Balance in Northeast Asia, 1984, Energy Policy Experience of Asia Countries, 1987. Served in AUS, 1944-45. Mem. Phi Delta Phi, Delta Tau Delta. Home: 10006 Woodhill Rd Bethesda MD 20817-1218

YAGER, VINCENT COOK, banker; b. Chgo., June 15, 1928; s. James Vincent and Juanita (Cook) Y.; m. Dorothy Marie Gallagher, Sept. 28, 1957; children: Susan Marie, Sheila Ann. BA, Grinnell Coll., 1951. Asst. cashier Chgo. Nat. Bank, 1954-60, Harris Trust & Savs. Bank, Chgo., 1960-63; v.p. comml. loan dept. Madison Bank & Trust, Chgo., 1963-68; v.p. fin. Cor-Plex Internat. Corp., Chgo., 1968-70; pres., chief exec. officer, dir. First Nat. Bank of Blue Island, Ill., 1970-89; pres., CEO Great Lakes Fin. Resources, Inc., Matteson, Ill., 1982-96, also bd. dirs. Mem. adv. bd. St. Francis Hosp., Blue Island, others. With U.S. Army, 1951-53, ETO. Mem. Robert Morris Assocs. (pres. chpt. 1981-82), Bankers Club of Chgo. (pres.). Mem. United Ch. of christ. Clubs: Midlothian Country; Econ. of Chgo. Lodge: Rotary. Home: 1032 S Rand Rd Villa Park IL 60181-3145 Office: 1st Nat Bank Blue Island 13057 Western Ave Blue Island IL 60406-2418

YAGIELA, JOHN ALLEN, dental educator; b. Washington, July 23, 1947; s. Stanley and Kathryn Marie (Gilkeson) Y.; m. Dolores Jean Mitchell, Mar. 21, 1970; children: Gregory, Leanne. Student, U. Calif., Riverside, 1965-67; DDS, UCLA, 1971, postgrad., 1982-83; PhD in Pharmacology, U. Utah, 1975. Diplomate Am. Dental Bd. Anesthesiology. Asst. prof. dentistry Emory U., Atlanta, 1975-78, assoc. prof., 1978-82; assoc. prof. UCLA, 1982-83, prof., 1983—, assoc. dean acad. and adminstrv. affairs, 1984-89; cons. Astra Pharm. Products Inc., Worcester, Mass., 1982—, VA Wadsworth divsn., L.A., 1983-92, Gen. Med. Co., L.A., 1988—, ADA, Chgo., 1991—. Co-author: Regional Anesthesia of the Oral Cavity, 1981, Local Anesthesia of the Oral Cavity, 1995; co-editor: Pharmacology and Therapeutics for Dentistry, 3d edit., 1989; editor Anesthesia Progress, 1990-95, The Pulse, 1996—; contbr. articles on dental therapeutics to profl. jours. Recipient Award of Achievement Am. Coll. Dentists, 1971; Regents scholar UCLA, 1968-71; Alpha Omega award, 1971. Fellow Am. Dental Soc. Anesthesiology; mem. ADA, AAAS, Internat. Assn. Dental Rsch. (sec.-treas. PTTG group 1984-88, pres.-elect 1989-90, pres. 1990-91), Am. Assn. Dental Schs. (chmn. pharmacology therapeutics sect. 1983), Am. Soc. Dentist Anesthesiolgists (v.p. 1995-97, pres.-elect 1997—), Omicron Kappa Upsilon. Methodist. Avocations: photography, hiking, scuba diving. Home: 23918 Stagg St West Hills CA 91304-6114 Office: UCLA Sch Dentistry Ctr for Health Scis Los Angeles CA 90095

YAGODA, HARRY NATHAN, system engineering executive; b. Bklyn., May 19, 1936; s. Hyman and Sylvia (Yoskowitz) Y.; m. Myrna Rita Hirschel; children: Michelle Robin, Randi Noelle. BSEE, CUNY, 1958; MSEE, NYU, 1960; PhDEE, Poly. U. N.Y., 1963. Registered profl. engr. 19 states including N.Y., N.J., Calif. Mem. tech. staff AT&T Bell Labs., Whippany, N.J., 1958-62; assoc. prof. engrng. Poly. U. N.Y., Bklyn., 1962-70; pres. Computran Systems Corp., Hackensack, N.J., 1970—. Named Disting. Alumnus, Poly. U. N.Y., 1980. Fellow Inst. Transp. Engring. (bd. dirs. 1982-84). Home: 2077 Center Ave Ph A Fort Lee NJ 07024-4905 Office: Computran Systems Corp 100 1st St Hackensack NJ 07601-2124

YAGYU, KUNIYOSHI, surgeon; b. Asa, Japan, Nov. 3, 1950; s. Yukihiko and Kazuko (Murata) Y.; m. Noriko Ohara, Dec. 8, 1985; children: Mitsuyoshi, Eriko. MD, U. Tokyo, 1976, DMS, 1986. Intern U. Tokyo Hosp., 1976-77, sr. resident, 1981-82, assoc., 1982-86, instr., 1989-93, asst. prof., 1993-97; staff dept. surgery Tokyo Welfare Pension Hosp., 1977-79; staff dept. surgery Japanese Red Cross Med. Ctr., Tokyo, 1979-81, chief cardiovasc. surgery, 1997—; staff surgeon Kanagawa Children Med. Ctr., Yokohama, Japan, 1986-87; scholar Alexander von Humboldt Found. Hannover (Germany) Med. Sch., 1987-89. Co-author: Surgical Diagnosis, 1988, Current Therapy in Cardiovascular Disease, 1994, 96. Recipient Tech. award Nikkei BP Inc., 1996, Silver Disting. Svc. Order, Japanese Red Cross Soc., 1996; grantee-in-aid for sci. rsch. Ministry of Edn., Sci. and Culture, Japan, 1990, 92. Mem. N.Y. Acad. Sci., AAAS, Transplantation Soc., Am. Heart Assn., Internat. Soc. for Artificial Organs, Internat. Soc. for Heart and Lung Transplantation. Avocations: jogging, skiing, painting, sculpture. Home: 2-21-3 Ekoda Aoba-ku, Yokohama 225, Japan Office: Japanese Red Cross Med Ctr, Cardiovasc Sgy, 4-1-22 Hiroo, Shibuya-ku, Tokyo 150, Japan

YAHR, MELVIN DAVID, physician; b. N.Y.C., Nov. 18, 1917; s. Isaac and Sarah (Reigelhaupt) Y.; m. Felice Turtz, May 9, 1948; children—Carol, Nina, Laura, Barbara Anne. A.B., N.Y. U., 1939, M.D., 1943. Diplomate: Am. Bd. Psychiatry and Neurology (pres.). Intern Lenox Hill Hosp., N.Y.C., 1943-44; resident Lenox Hill Hosp., also Montefiore Hosp., Bronx, N.Y., 1947-48; staff Columbia, 1948-73, asso. prof. clin. neurology, 1957-62, prof. neurology, 1962-70, H.H. Merritt prof. neurology, 1970-73, asst. dean grad. medicine, 1959-67, assoc. dean, 1967-73; asst. neurologist N.Y. Neurol. Inst., 1948-53, assoc. attending neurologist, 1953-60, attending neurologist, 1960-73; Goldschmidt prof. neurology, chmn. dept. neurology Mt. Sinai Med. Center, 1973-92; Aidekman Family Prof. Neurological Rsch., 1992—; exec. dir. Parkinson's Disease Found., 1957-73; panel neurologist N.Y.C. Bd. Edn., 1958-59; mem. com. evaluation drugs in neurology NIH, 1959-60, panel mem. neurol. study sect., 1959-80; mem. com. revisions U.S. Pharmacopea. Assoc. editor: Internat. Jour. Neurology; editor-in-chief Jour. Neural Transmission, 1989—; Archives Neurology, 1964-89. Fellow Am. Acad. Neurology, N.Y. Acad. Medicine, Harvey Soc.; mem. A.M.A. (chmn. com. neurol. disorders in industry), Am. Neurol. Assn. (sec.-treas. 1959-68, pres. 1969), Assn. Research Nervous and Mental Disease, N.Y. State Neurol. Soc., New York County Med. Soc., Am. Epilepsy Soc., Eastern Assn. Electroencephalographers. Office: Mt Sinai School of Med City U Clin Ctr Rsch Parkinson's 5 E 98th St # 1139 New York NY 10029-6501

YALCINTAS, M. GÜVEN, medical physicist; b. Milas, Turkey, Apr. 11, 1946; came to U.S., 1968; s. Kazim and Samiye Yalcintas; 1 child, Banu. BS in Physics, Ankara U., 1967; MS in Health Physics, U. Rochester, 1971, PhD in Med. Physics, 1974. Dir. EGE MEd. Sch., Izmir, Turkey, 1975-76, EMI Med., Chgo., 1976-77; group leader Oak Ridge (Tenn.) Nat. Lab., 1977-88; dir. tech. transfer Lockheed Martin, Oak Ridge, 1988-93, dir. tech. transfer of environ. techs., 1993-96; pres. Applied Profls., 1996—; adj. prof. radiation biology Tenn. Tech U.; adj. prof. environ. scis. Tusculcum Coll., adv. bd. environ. sci. program. Contbr. articles to profl. jours. Lt. Turkish Army, 1975-76. Mem. Am. Nuclear Soc. chmn. 1986—, newsletter editor), East Tenn. Health Physics Assn., Health Physical Soc. Avocations: soccer, chess, writing, boating, skiing. Home: 208 Toqua Greens Dr Loudon TN 37774-2588 Office: Lockheed Martin Box 2003 MS 7172 Oak Ridge TN 37831-7172

YALDEN, MAXWELL FREEMAN, Canadian diplomat; b. Toronto, Ont., Can., Apr. 12, 1930; s. Frederick and Marie (Smith) Y.; m. Janice Shaw, Jan. 28, 1952; children: Robert, Cicely (dec.). B.A., Victoria Coll., U. Toronto, 1952; M.A., U. Mich., 1954, Ph.D., 1956; D.U. (hon.), U. Ottawa, 1982. With Can. Dept. External Affairs, 1956-69, asst. undersec. state, 1969-73, dep. minister communications, 1973-77, commr. ofcl. langs., 1977-84; Can. amb. to Belgium and Luxembourg, 1984-87; chief Can. Human Rights Comms., Ottawa, 1987-96; apptd. UN Human Rights Com., 1996—. Office: 52 Crichton St, Ottawa, ON Canada K1M 1V7

YALE, JEFFREY FRANKLIN, podiatrist; b. Derby, Conn., Jan. 18, 1943; s. Irving and Bernice (Blume) Y.; m. Lenore Bernsley, Apr. 23, 1987; children: Brian Joseph, Andrew Malcolm, Owen Slade. Student, U. Fla., 1960-62; D of Podiatric Medicine, Ill. Coll. Podiatric Medicine, 1966. Diplomate Am. Bd. Podiatric Surgery, Am. Bd. Podiatric Orthopedics, Am. Bd. Med. Quality Assurance and Utilization Rev. Surg. resident Highland Gen. Hosp., Oakland, Calif., 1966-67; capt. U.S. Army Med. Svc., Fort Ord, Calif., 1967-71; instr. masters level Quinnipiac Coll., Hamden, Conn., 1981; cons. surgeon VA Med. Ctr., West Haven, Conn., 1982—; chmn. podiatric surgery Griffin Hosp., Derby, Conn., 1974—; assoc. clin. prof. U. Osteo. Health Scis., Des Moines, 1982—; chmn. Podiatric Medicine Test Com. Nat. Bd. Podiatric Med. Examiners, 1977-94; pres. Ct. Examining Bd. in Podiatry, 1979, Am. Acad. Podiatric Sports Medicine, 1986; pres. Yale Podiatry Group, P.C., Ansonia, Conn., 1976—; bd. dirs. Podiatry Ins. Co. Am., Brentwood, Tenn., also chmn. underwriting com.; editl. adv. bd. Am. Podiatric Med. Assn., 1992-95. Author: Firm Footings For the Athlete, 1984, The Arthritic Foot, 1984, Yale's Podiatric Medicine, 3d edit., 1987; contbr. numerous sci. articles to profl. jours. Corporator Griffin Hosp., Derby, Conn., 1982. Capt. U.S. Army, 1967-71. Fellow Am. Acad. Podiatric Sports Medicine, Am. Assn. Hosp. Podiatrists, Am. Coll. Foot and Ankle Surgeons; mem. New Haven County Podiatric Med. Assn., Conn. Podiatric Med. Assn., Am. Podiatric Med. Assn., Conn. Pub. Health Assn., Am. Pub. Health Assn. Jewish. Avocations: marble collecting, swimming, gardening. Home: 18 Inwood Rd Woodbridge CT 06525-2558 Office: Yale Podiatry Group PC 364 E Main St Ansonia CT 06401-1904

YALE, SEYMOUR HERSHEL, dental radiologist, educator, university dean, gerontologist; b. Chgo., Nov. 27, 1920; s. Henry and Dorothy (Kulwin) Y.; m. Muriel Jane Cohen, Nov. 6, 1943; children: Russell Steven, Patricia Ruth. B.S., U. Ill., 1944, D.D.S., 1945, postgrad., 1947-48. Pvt. practice of dentistry, 1945-54, 56—; asst. clin. dentistry U. Ill., 1948-49, instr. clin. dentistry, 1949-53, asst. prof. clin. dentistry, 1953-54, assoc. prof. dept. radiology Coll. Dentistry, 1956, prof., head dept. Coll. Dentistry, 1957-65, adminstrv. asst. to dean Coll. Dentistry, 1961-63, asst. dean Coll. Dentistry, 1963-64, acting dean Coll. Dentistry, 1964-65, dean, 1965-87, dean emeritus, 1987—; also mem. grad. faculty dept. radiology Coll. Medicine U. Ill., Chgo., prof. dentistry and health resources mgmt. Sch. Pub. Health, 1987—; sr. dental dir. Dental Care Plus Mgmt. Corp., Chgo.; pres., dir. dental edn. Dental Care Plus Mgmt. Ednl. Svcs., Ltd.; health care facilities planner; dir. tng. Dental Technicians Sch., U.S. Naval Tng. Ctr., Bainbridge, md., 1954-56; mem. subcom. 16 Nat. Com. on Radiation Protection; mem. Radiation Protection Adv. Bd., State of Ill., 1971, City of Chgo. Health Sys. Agy.; founder Ctr. for Rsch. in Periodontal Disease and Oral Molecular Biology, 1977; organizer, chmn. Nat. Conf. on Hepatitis-B in Dentistry, 1982; organizer, dir. Univ. Taskforce Primary Health Care Project, U. Ill., Chgo.; chmn. U. Ill.-U. Stockholm-U. Gothenberg Conf. on Geriatrics, 1985; dir. planning AMVETS/UIC Tchg. Nursing Home Project, 1987-91; co-sponsor 1st Egyptian Dental Congress, 1984; adj. prof. Ctr. for Exercise Sci. and Cardiovasc. Rsch., Northeastern Ill. U., Chgo., 1991, Northwestern U. Sch. Dentistry Divsn. Behavioural Scis., Evanston, Ill., 1996—. Editor-in-chief Dental Care Plus Mgmt. Digest, 1995—. Bd. dirs., co-benefactor (with wife) World Heritage Mus., U. Ill., Urbana, 1985; mem. Hillel Bd., U. Ill.-Chgo.; life mem. (with wife) Bronze Circle of Coll. Liberal Arts, U. Ill., Urbana; mem. (with wife) Pres.' Council, U. Ill. Recipient centennial research award Chgo. Dental Soc., 1959; Distinguished Alumnus award U. Ill., 1973; Harry Sicher Meml. Lecture award Am. Coll. Stomologic Surgeons, 1983. Fellow Acad. Gen. Dentistry (hon.), Am. Coll. Dentists; mem. Ill. Dental Soc. (mem. com. on radiology), Chgo. Dental Soc., Internat. Assn. Dental Rsch., Am. Acad. Oral Roentgenology, Am. Dental Assn., Odontographic Soc. Chgo. (Award of Merit 1982), Council Dental Deans State Ill. (chmn.), N.Y. Acad. Scis., Gerontol. Soc. Am., Pierre Fauchard Acad. (Man of Yr. award Ill. sect. 1988), Am. Pub. Health Assn., Gerontol. Soc. Am., Omicron Kappa Upsilon, Sigma Xi, Alpha Omega (hon.). Established (with wife) collection of Coins of Ottoman Empire and Related Mohammedan States and supplemental antique map collection at World Heritage Mus. Home: 155 N Harbor Dr Chicago IL 60601-7364 Office: 25 E Washington St Chicago IL 60602

YALEN, GARY N., insurance company executive; b. N.Y.C., May 17, 1942; s. Sidney Leo and Mildred (Epstein) Y.; m. Rena Lynn Gear, Nov. 3, 1968; children—Robert, Lesley. BEE, Rensselaer Poly. Inst., 1964; MBA, U. Mich., 1965. Chartered fin. analyst. Mktg. engr. N.Y. Telephone Co., N.Y.C., 1965-69; security analyst Merrill Lynch, N.Y.C., 1969-74; security analyst Irving Trust Co., N.Y.C., 1974-80, research dir., 1980-83, sr. v.p., chief investment officer, 1983-87, exec. v.p., 1987-89; exec. v.p. Bank of N.Y., 1989-90; chief investment officer, exec. v.p. Fortis Asset Mgmt. (formerly Amev), 1990-95; pres., chief investment officer Fortis Advisers, 1995—. Served with U.S. Army, 1966-68, Vietnam. Mem. N.Y. Soc. Security Analysts, Beta Gamma Sigma. Avocations: golf, bridge. Home: 175 Nancy Ln Wyckoff NJ 07481-2522 Office: Fortis Advisers One Chase Manhattan Plz New York NY 10005

YALMAN, ANN, magistrate, lawyer; b. Boston, June 9, 1948; d. Richard George and Joan (Osterman) Y. BA, Antioch Coll., 1970; JD, NYU, 1973. Trial atty. Fla. Rural Legal Svcs., Immokalee, Fla., 1973-74; staff atty. EEO, Atlanta, 1974-76; pvt. practice Santa Fe, N.Mex., 1976—; part time U.S. magistrate, N. Mex., 1988-96. Commr. Met. Water Bd., Santa Fe, 1986-88. Mem. N.Mex. Bar Assn. (commr. Santa Fe chpt. 1983-86). Home: 441 Calle La Paz Santa Fe NM 87501-2821 Office: 304 Catron St Santa Fe NM 87501-1806

YALOW, ROSALYN SUSSMAN, medical physicist; b. N.Y.C., N.Y., July 19, 1921; d. Simon and Clara (Zipper) Sussman; m. A. Aaron Yalow, June 6, 1943; children: Benjamin, Elanna. A.B., Hunter Coll., 1941; M.S., U. Ill., Urbana, 1942, Ph.D., 1945; D.Sc. (hon.), U. Ill., Chgo., 1974, Phila. Coll. Pharmacy and Sci., 1976, N.Y. Med. Coll., 1976, Med. Coll. Wis., Milw., 1977, Yeshiva U., 1977, Southampton (N.Y.) Coll., 1978, Bucknell U., 1978, Princeton U., 1978, Jersey City State Coll., 1979, Med. Coll. Pa., 1979, Manhattan Coll., 1979, U. Vt., 1980, U. Hartford, 1980, Rutgers U., 1980, Rensselaer Poly. Inst., 1980, Colgate U., 1981, U. So. Calif., 1981, Clarkson Coll., 1982, U. Miami, 1983, Washington U., St. Louis, 1983, Adelphi U., 1983, U. Alta. (Can.), 1983, SUNY, 1984, Tel Aviv U., 1985, Claremont (Calif.) U., 1986, Mills Coll., Oakland, Calif., 1986, Cedar Crest Coll., Allentown, Pa., 1988, Drew U., Madison, N.J., 1988, Lehigh U., 1988; L.H.D. (hon.), Hunter Coll., 1978; DSc. (hon.), San Francisco State U., 1989, Technion-Israel Inst. Tech., Haifa, 1989; DSc (hon.), Med. Coll. Ohio Toledo, 1991; L.H.D. (hon.), Sacred Heart U., Conn., 1978, St. Michael's Coll., Winooski Park, Vt., 1979, Johns Hopkins U., 1979, Coll. St. Rose, 1988, Spertus Coll. Judaica, Chgo., 1988; D. honoris causa, U. Rosario, Argentina, 1980, U. Ghent, Belgium, 1984; D. Humanities and Letters (hon.), Columbia U., 1984; DSc (hon.), Fairleigh Dickinson U., 1992, Conn. Coll., 1992, Smith Coll., Northampton, Mass., 1994, Union Coll., Schenectady, 1994. Diplomate: Am. Bd. Scis. Lectr., asst. prof. physics Hunter Coll., 1946-50; physicist, asst. chief radioisotope service VA Hosp., Bronx, N.Y., 1950-70, chief nuclear medicine, 1970-80, acting chief radioisotope service, 1968-70, sr. med. investigator emeritus; research prof. Mt. Sinai Sch. Medicine, CUNY, 1968-74, Disting. Service prof., 1974-79, Solomon A. Berson Disting. prof.-at-large, 1986—; Disting. prof.-at-large Albert Einstein Coll. Medicine, Yeshiva U., 1979-85, prof. emeritus, 1986—; chmn. dept. clin. scis. Montefiore Med. Ctr., Bronx, 1980-85; cons. Lenox Hill Hosp., N.Y.C., 1956-62, WHO, Bombay, 1978; sec. U.S. Nat. Com. on Med. Physics, 1963-67; mem. nat. com. Radiation Protection, Subcom. 13, 1957; mem. Pres.'s Study Group on Careers for Women, 1966-72; sr. med. investigator VA, 1972-92, sr. med. investigator emeritus, 1992—. Co-editor: Hormone and Metabolic Research, 1973-79; editorial adv. council: Acta Diabetologica Latina, 1975-77, Ency. Universalis, 1978—; editorial bd.: Mt. Sinai Jour. Medicine, 1976-79, Diabetes, 1976, Endocrinology, 1967-72; contbr. numerous articles to profl. jours. Bd. dirs. N.Y. Diabetes Assn., 1974. Recipient VA William S. Middleton Med. Research award, 1960; Eli Lilly award Am. Diabetes Assn., 1961; Van Slyke award N.Y. met. sect. Am. Assn. Clin. Chemists, 1968; award A.C.P., 1971; Dickson prize U. Pitts., 1971; Howard Taylor Ricketts award U. Chgo., 1971; Gairdner Found. Internat. award, 1971; Commemorative medallion Am. Diabetes Assn., 1972; Bernstein award Med. Soc. State N.Y., 1974; Boehringer-Mannheim Corp. award Am. Assn. Clin. Chemists, 1975; Sci. Achievement award AMA, 1975; Exceptional Service award VA, 1975; A. Cressy Morrison award N.Y. Acad. Scis., 1975; sustaining membership award Assn. Mil. Surgeons, 1975; Distinguished Achievement award Modern Medicine, 1976; Albert Lasker Basic Med. Research award, 1976; La Madonnina Internat. prize Milan, 1977; Golden Plate award Am. Acad. Achievement, 1977; Nobel prize for physiology/medicine, 1977; citation of esteem St. John's U., 1979; G. von Hevesy medal, 1978; Rosalyn S. Yalow Research and Devel. award established Am. Diabetes Assn., 1978; Banting medal, 1978; Torch of Learning award Am. Friends Hebrew U., 1978; Virchow gold medal Virchow-Pirquet Med. Soc., 1978; Gratum Genus Humanum gold medal World Fedn. Nuclear Medicine or Biology, 1978; Jacobi medallion Asso. Alumni Mt. Sinai Sch. Medicine, 1978; Jubilee medal Coll. of New Rochelle, 1978; VA Exceptional Service award, 1978; Fed. Woman's award, 1961; Harvey lectr., 1966; Am. Gastroenterol. Assn. Meml. lectr., 1972; Joslin lectr. New Eng. Diabetes Assn., 1972; Franklin I. Harris Meml. lectr., 1973; 1st Hagedorn Meml. lectr. Acta Endocrinologica Congress, 1973; Sarasota Med. award for achievement and excellence, 1979; gold medal Phi Lambda Kappa, 1980; Achievement in Life award Ency. Brit., 1980; Theobald Smith award, 1982; Pres.'s Cabinet award U. Detroit, 1982; John and Samuel Bard award in medicine and sci. Bard Coll., 1982; Disting. Research award Dallas Assn. Retarded Citizens, 1982, Nat. Medal Sci., 1988; Abram L. Sachar Silver Medallion Brandeis U., Waltham, Mass., 1989, Disting. Scientist of Yr. award ARCS, N.Y.C., 1989, Golden Scroll award The Jewish Advocate, Boston, 1989, spl. award Clin. Ligand Assay Soc., Washington, 1988, numerous others. Fellow N.Y. Acad. Scis. (chmn. biophysics div. 1964-65), Am. Coll. Radiology (asso. in physics), Clin. Soc. N.Y. Diabetes Assn.; mem. Nat. Acad. Scis., Am. Acad. Arts and Scis., Am. Phys. Soc., Radiation Research Soc., Am. Assn. Physicists in Medicine, Biophys. Soc., Soc. Nuclear Medicine, Endocrine Soc. (Koch award 1972, pres. 1978), Am. Physiol. Soc., (hon.) Harvey Soc., (hon.) Med. Assn. Argentina, (hon.) Diabetes Soc. Argentina, (hon.) Am. Coll. Nuclear Physicians, (hon.) The N.Y. Acad. Medicine, (hon.) Am. Gastroent. Assn., (hon.) N.Y. Roentgen Soc., (hon.) Soc. Nuclear Medicine, Phi Beta Kappa, Sigma Xi, Sigma Pi Sigma, Pi Mu Epsilon, Sigma Delta Epsilon, Tau Beta Pi. Office: VA Hosp 130 W Kingsbridge Rd Bronx NY 10468-3992

YALOWITZ, KENNETH SPENCER, ambassador; b. Chgo., May 28, 1941; s. Henry and Audrey (Socol) Y.; m. Judith Gold, 1963; 1 child, Andrew Seth. BS, U. Wis., 1962; MA in Polit. Sci., Columbia U., 1964;

cert., Russian Inst., 1965. Career fgn. svc. officer Sr. Fgn. Svc. U.S. Dept. State, 1966—; fgn. affairs analyst Bur. Intelligence and Rsch. Dept. State, 1966-68, with Arms Control and Disarmament Agy., 1969-71; econ. officer at U.S. Embassy Dept. State, Moscow, 1975-77; comml. attache at embassy Dept. State, The Hague, The Netherlands, 1977-80; dep. dir. Office Internat. Econ Affairs, Bur. Internat. Orgn. Affairs Dept. State, Washington, 1980-82; dep. dir. econ. affairs Office of Soviet Union Affairs Dept. State, 1982-84, econ. counselor U.S. Mission to NATO, 1985-88, dir. Office of Australia and New Zealand Affairs, Bur. East Asian and Pacific Affairs, 1989-91; min. counselor for econ. affairs U.S. Embassy Dept. State, Moscow, 1991-93, acting dep. chief of mission U.S. Embassy, 1992-93; U.S. amb. to Belarus Fgn. Svc., Dept. State, Minsk, 1994—; congl. fgn. affairs fellow Am. Polit. Sci. Assn., 1985; with Bur. East/West Trade Dept. Commerce, 1973-75; area studies chmn. for the states of the former Soviet Union Sch. Area Studies Fgn. Svc. Inst., Washington, 1993-94; vis. prof. internat. rels. Indsl. Coll. of the Armed Forces, 1988. Woodrow Wilson fellow Woodrow Wilson Nat. Fellowship Found., 1962. Mem. Am. Fgn. Svc. Assn., Am. Polit. Sci. Assn. Office: US Amb Belarus US Dept State Washington DC 20521-7010*

YAMADA, KENNETH MANAO, cell biologist; b. Mpls., Sept. 18, 1944; s. Paul Manao and Masaye (Uriu) Y.; m. Susan Jane Sleeper, July 1, 1973. BA in Biol. Scis., Stanford U., 1966, PhD in Biol. Scis., 1971, MD, 1972. Intern Mary's Help Hosp./Seton Med. Ctr., Daly City, Calif., 1972-73; commd. lt. USPHS, 1974, advanced through grades to capt., 1982—; sect. chief Nat. Cancer Inst., Bethesda, Md., 1980-90; lab. chief Nat. Inst. Dental Rsch., Bethesda, Md., 1990-96, br. chief, 1996—; mem. NIH Cell Biology Study Sect., 1979-83; mem. external adv. com. Howard U. Cancer Rsch. Ctr., 1979-88; co-chmn. Gordon Conf. on Fibronectin, 1982; Stadtler lectr. U. Tex. Sys. Cancer Ctr., M.D. Anderson Hosp., 1988; Swerling lectr. Dana-Farber Cancer Inst., Harvard Med. Sch., 1988. Contbr. more than 250 articles to profl. jours. Postdoctoral fellow U. Oreg., Dept. Biology, Eugene, 1973-74; recipient Eli Luke and Jacob David Rsch. award, 1972. Fellow AAAS; mem. Am. Soc. Cell Biology (coun. mem. 1992-95), Am. Soc. Biochemistry and Molecular Biology, Internat. Soc. Matrix Biology (coun. mem. 1994—), Southeastern Cancer Rsch. Assn. (bd. dirs. 1980-83), Soc. Devel. Biology, Phi Beta Kappa (Undergrad. Rsch. award), Sigma Xi. Office: Natl Inst of Dental Rsch Bldg 30 Rm 421 30 Convent Dr Bethesda MD 20892-4370

YAMADA, SHINICHI, mathematician, computer scientist, educator; b. Nagoya, Japan, Jan. 10, 1937; s. Umekichi and Nami (Kawashima) Y.; m. Atsuyo Yamamoto, Oct. 10, 1964; 1 child, Atsushi. BSc, U. Tokyo, 1959, DSc, 1988; SM, Harvard U., 1970. System analyst Nippon Univac Co., Tokyo, 1959-70, tech. advisor, 1970-90; lectr. Keio U., Tokyo, 1980-85, Waseda U., Tokyo, 1982—, Chiba U., 1989—, Hiroshima U., 1993; lectr. Hirosaki U., Japan, 1993, 95, prof. dept. info. sci., 1990-93; prof. dept. info. scis. Sci. U. Tokyo, 1993—, chair dept. info. scis., 1996—. Author: Sciences of Information Processing, 1984, Micro-Prolog Collection, 1986, Kowalski Logic for Problem Solving, 1987, Encyclopedia of Artificial Intelligence, 1988, Encyclopedia of Computer Systems, 1989, Handbook of Theoretical Computer Sciences, 1994, Encyclopedia of Mathematical Information Sciences, 1996. Mem. editorial staff Info. Processing Soc. Japan, 1983-87; contbr. articles to profl. jours. Mem. IEEE, Am. Math. Soc., Math. Soc. Japan, Assn. Symbolic Logic, Soc. Indsl. and Applied Math., Harvard Club of Japan. Home: 821-19 Nishi-Fukai, Nagareyama-Shi Chiba 270-01, Japan Office: Sci U Tokyo Dept Info Sci, Yamasaki 2641 Noda City, Chiba 278, Japan

YAMADA, TOSHIKATSU AUGUSTINE, academic administrator, mechanical engineer; b. Nagoya, Aichi, Japan, Jan. 23, 1923; s. Etsujiro and Yuki (Takeuchi) Y.; m. Chizuko Shirota, Nov. 22, 1956; children: Takahisa, Chieko. B in Engring., Nagoya (Japan) U., 1948, D in Engring., 1977. Asst. Nagoya (Japan) U., 1963-66; asst. prof. Toyota Coll. Tech., Japan, 1966-70, prof., 1970-87; pres. Aichi Coll. Tech., Gamagori, Japan, 1987—. Author: Milling With Plain Milling Cutters, 1977, Under The Beautiful Purple-Blue Flag, 1987. Mem. ASME, Japan Soc. Mech. Engrs., Gamagori (Japan) Internat. Assn. (dir. 1992—, v.p. 1994—). Avocations: classical music, tea ceremonies, bird watching, Judo. Home: 3-8-10 Wakamuzu, Chikusa Nagoya 464, Japan Office: Aichi Coll Tech, 50-2 Manori Nishihasama, Aichi Gamagori 443, Japan

YAMAGUCHI, KRISTI TSUYA, ice skater; b. Hayward, Calif., July 12, 1971; d. Jim and Carole (Doi) Y. Gold medalist, Figure Skating Albertville Olympic Games, 1992; U.S. Skating champion, 1992, World Skating champion, 1991, 1992, World Junior champion, 1988, world profl. figure skating champion, 1994. Recipient Women First award YWCA, 1993. Avocations: tennis, rollerblading, reading, and dancing. Address: IMG c/o Yuki Saegusa 22 E 71st St New York NY 10021*

YAMAGUCHI, MICHAEL JOSEPH, prosecutor. Bar: Calif. 1978. U.S. atty. U.S. Dept. Justice, San Francisco, 1980—. Office: US Attys Office Box 36055 450 Golden Gate Ave San Francisco CA 94102*

YAMAGUCHI, YUKIO, chemistry research scientist; b. Hiroshima, Japan, Feb. 22, 1941; came to U.S., 1970; s. Tameo and Miyuki (Kodama) Y.; m. Masako Iwamura, Aug. 3, 1994. BE, Kyushu U., Fukuoka, Japan, 1964, ME, 1966; PhD, U. Tex., Austin, 1978. Research assoc. Kyushu U., Fukuoka, 1966-70; postdoctoral fellow U. Tex., Austin, 1979-80; postdoctoral fellow U. Calif. and Lawrence Berkeley Lab., Berkeley, 1980-82, chemistry rsch. scientist, 1982-87; chemistry rsch. scientist U. Ga., Athens, 1987—. Author: (with Y. Osamura, J.D. Goddard and H.F. Schaefer) A New Dimension to Quantum Chemistry: Analytic Derivative Methods in Ab Initio Molecular Electronic Structure Theory; contbr. articles to profl. jours. Mem. Am. Chem. Soc., Chem. Soc. of Japan. Avocations: reading, travel, swimming. Office: U Ga Ctr Computational Quantum Chem Athens GA 30602

YAMAKAWA, ALLAN HITOSHI, academic administrator; b. San Francisco, Oct. 18, 1938; s. Victor Tadashi and Alice Tsugie (Sato) Y.; m. Nancy Ann Habel, Apr.17, 1977 (div. Mar 1987); children: Bryan Allan, David Scott. BS, Roosevelt U., 1962, MEd, 1970. Tech. svcs. dir. audio visual libr. Roosevelt U., Chgo., 1958-60; dean, exec. dir. Ency. Britannica Schs., Inc., Chgo., 1960-67; curriculum svcs. dir. Field Enterprises Newspaper Div., Chgo., 1967-70; edn. svcs. dir. Chgo. Tribune Co., 1970-76; tng. svcs. dir. Dialogue Systems Inc., N.Y.C., 1976-79; orgn. devel. dir. U. Ill., Chgo., 1979—; cons., trainer Can. Daily Newspaper Pub. Assn., Toronto, 1973-84, Am. Newspaper Pub. Found., Reston, Va., 1972-80, Gifted Students Found. Dallas, 1974-75; cons. Cedars Sinai Med. Ctr., Beverly Hills, Calif., 1983—, W. K. Kellogg Found., 1987—. Author: Handbooks of Teaching Methods, 1974, Communicate, 1975, Catalysts For Change, 1976, Evaluation of Senior Administrators, 1994; patentee experiential learning method. Instr. ARC, Chgo., 1954-85; bd. dirs. Edison Regional Gifted Ctr. Sch., Chgo., pres., 1989-93; dist. program chmn. Boy Scouts Am., 1985—. Mem. ASTD, ASCD, Soc. Programmed and Automated Learning, Toastmasters (pres. 1974-76). Avocations: photography, computer programming, electronics, pyrotechnics, film production. Office: Univ Ill 1524(G) W Pratt Blvd Chicago IL 60626

YAMAKAWA, DAVID KIYOSHI, JR., lawyer; b. San Francisco, Jan. 25, 1936; s. David Kiyoshi and Shizu (Negishi) Y. BS, U. Calif., Berkeley, 1958, JD, 1963. Bar: Calif. 1964, U.S. Supreme Ct. 1970. Prin. Law Offices of David K. Yamakawa Jr., San Francisco, 1964—; dep. dir. Cmty. Action Agy., San Francisco, 1968-69; dir. City Demonstration Agy., San Francisco, 1969-70; mem. adv. coun. Calif. Senate Subcom. on the Disabled, 1982-83, Ctr. for Mental Health Svcs., Substance Abuse and Mental Health Svcs. Adminstrn. U.S. Dept. Health and Human Svcs., 1995—; chmn. cmty. residential treatment system adv. com. Calif. Dept. Mental Health, 1980-85, San Francisco Human Rights Commn., 1977-80; pres. Legal Assistance to the Elderly, 1981-83; 2d v.p. Nat. Conf. Social Welfare, 1983—; v.p. Region IX, Nat. Mental Health Assn., 1981-83; vice-chmn. Mt. Zion Hosp. and Med. Ctr., 1986-88; bd. dirs. United Neighborhood Ctrs. of Am., 1977-83, ARC Bay Area, 1988-91, Goldman Inst. on Aging, 1993—, v.p., 1994-96, vice-chmn., 1996—; bd. trustees Mt. Zion Med. Ctr., U. Calif., San Francisco, 1993—; chmn. bd. trustees United Way Bay Area, 1983-85; chief fin. officer Action for Nature, Inc., 1987—; v.p. Friends of Legal Assistance to the Elderly, 1984—; bd. dirs. Ind. Sector, 1986-92, Friends of the San Francisco Human Rights Commn., 1980—, CFO, 1980-85, vice chmn., 1985-94, CFO, 1994—, La Madre de los Pobres, 1982—, v.p., 1994—, Nat. Concilio Am., 1987—, Legal Coun., 1996—, legal coun., 1996—, Hispanic Community Found. of the Bay Area, 1989—, legal coun., 1989—; bd. dirs. Non-Profit Svcs., Inc., 1987—, sec., 1987-90, chmn., 1990—; pres. Coun. Internat. Programs, San Francisco, 1987-89, pres. Internat. Inst. of San Francisco, 1990-93; mem. citizens adv. com. San Francisco Hotel Tax Fund Grants for the Arts Program, 1991—. Recipient John B. Williams Outstanding Planning and Agy. Rels. vol. award United Way of the Bay Area, 1980, Mortimer Fleishhacker Jr. Outstanding Vol. award United Way, 1985, Spl. Recognition award Legal Assistance to the Elderly, 1983, Commendation award Bd. Suprs. City and County of San Francisco, 1983, cert. Honor, 1985, San Francisco Found. award, 1985, 1st Mental Health Awareness award Mental Health Assn. San Francisco, 1990; David Yamakawa Day proclaimed in San Francisco, 1985. Mem. ABA (Liberty Bell award 1986). Office: 582 Market St Ste 410 San Francisco CA 94104-5305

YAMAMOTO, JOE, psychiatrist, educator; b. Los Angeles, Apr. 18, 1924; s. Zenzaburo and Tomie (Yamada) Y.; m. Maria Fujitomi, Sept. 5, 1947; children: Eric Robert, Andrew Jolyon. Student, Los Angeles City Coll., 1941-42, Hamline U., 1943-45; B.S., U. Minn., 1946, M.B., 1948, M.D., 1949. Asst. prof. dept. psychiatry, neurology, behavioral sci. U. Okla. Med. Center, 1955-58, asst. prof., 1958-60; assoc. prof. dept. psychiatry U. So. Calif. Sch. Medicine, Los Angeles, 1961-69; prof. U. So. Calif. Sch. Medicine, 1969-77, co-dir. grad. edn. psychiatry, 1963-70; prof. UCLA, 1977-94, emeritus prof., 1994—; dir. Psychiat. Outpatient Clinic, Los Angeles County-U. So. Calif. Med. Center, 1958-77; dir. adult ambulatory care services UCLA Neuropsychiat. Inst., 1977-88, chief Lab. for Cross Cultural Studies. Contbr. articles in field to profl. jours. Served to capt., M.C. U.S. Army, 1953-55. Fellow Am. Psychiat. Assn. (life), Pacific Rim Coll. Psychiatrists, Am. Acad. Psychoanalysis (trustee, mem. exec. com., pres. 1978-79), Am. Coll. Psychiatrists, Am. Orthopsychiat. Assn. (pres.-elect 1993-94, pres. 1994-95, past pres.), Am. Assn. for Social Psychiatry (trustee 1981-84, v.p. 1984-86); mem. So. Calif. Psychoanalytic Inst. and Soc. (pres. 1972-73), Soc. for Study of Culture and Psychiatry, Group for Advancement Psychiatry (bd. dirs. 1992-94), Kappa Phi, Alpha Omega Alpha. Office: UCLA Neuro-psychiat Inst 760 Westwood Plz Los Angeles CA 90024-8300 *Learning about the diverse peoples of America, I have been fascinated with how we can be Asian, Hispanic, Black, European, and Native American and still identify with our national values. We value our freedom, individual rights and our ability to be someone different but equal. In mental health also there is a need for recognition of cultural differences and the need of treatment response to the individual.*

YAMAMOTO, KAORU, psychology and education educator; b. Tokyo, Mar. 28, 1932; came to U.S., 1959; s. Saburo and Hideko (Watanabe) Y.; m. Etsuko Hamazaki, Apr. 6, 1959 (div. 1986); m. Carol-Lynne Moore, Oct. 4, 1986; children: Keita Carey Moore, Kiyomi Lynne Moore. BS in Engring., U. Tokyo, 1953; MA, U. Minn., 1960, PhD, 1962. Engr. Toppan Printing Co., Tokyo, 1953; engr., rsch. chemist Japan Oxygen Co., Tokyo, 1954-57, 58-59; asst. prof. Kent (Ohio) State U., 1962-65; from asst. to assoc. prof. U. Iowa, Iowa City, 1965-68; prof. Pa. State U., University Park, 1968-72, Ariz. State U., Tempe, 1972-87, U. Colo., Denver, 1987—; vis. prof. U. Minn., Mpls., 1974, Simon Fraser U., Burnaby, B.C., Can., 1984, U.Victoria, B.C., 1986, U. Wash., Seattle, 1987, Zhejiang Normal U., Jinhua, China, 1991; Fulbright lectr. U. Iceland, 1985. Author: The Child and His Image, 1972, Their World, Our World, 1993; author, editor: 6 books; co-author: Beyond Words, 1988; editor Am. Ednl. Rsch. Jour., 1972-75, Ednl. Forum, 1984-92; contbr. chpts. to books and articles to profl. jours. Landsdowne scholar U. Victoria, 1985. Fellow APA; mem. Am. Sociol. Assn., Am. Anthrop. Assn., Motus Humanus. Avocations: winter sports, travel, classical music, reading. Office: U Colo Denver Box 106 PO Box 173364 Denver CO 80217-3364

YAMAMOTO, KEITH ROBERT, molecular biologist, educator; b. Des Moines, Feb. 4, 1946. BS, Iowa State U., 1968; PhD, Princeton U., 1973. Asst. prof. biochemistry U. Calif., San Francisco, 1976-79, assoc. prof., 1979-83, prof., 1983—, vice chmn. dept., 1985—, dir. biochemistry and molecular biology program, 1988—; mem. genetic biology rev. panel NSF, Washington, 1984-87; chmn. molecular biology study sect. NIH, Bethesda, Mdf., 1987-90, mem. nat. adv. coun. for human genome rsch., 1990-91. Co-author: Gene Wars: Military Control over the New Genetic Technologies, 1988; co-editor: Transcriptional Regulation, 1992 ; assoc. editor Jour. Molecular Biology, 1988—, editor Molecular Biology of the Cell, 1991—. Mem. Com. for Responsible Genetics, Boston, 1989—; testifier hearings on biol. warfare com. on govtl. affairs U.S. Senate, Washington, 1989. Recipient Gregory Pincus medal Worchester Found. for Exptl. Biology, 1990; Dreyfus tchr.-scholar, 1982-86. Fellow Am. Acad. Arts and Scis.; mem. AAAS, NAS (panel on sci. responsibility and conduct of rsch. 1990-91), Protein Soc., Am. Soc. for Cell Biology (coun. 1991-92), Am. Soc. for Biochemistry and Molecular Biology (publs. com. 1990-93), Am. Soc. for Devel. Biology. Home: 332 Douglass St San Francisco CA 94114-2452 Office: U Calif San Francisco Dept Biochemistry 513 Parnassus Ave San Francisco CA 94122-2722*

YAMAMOTO, MICHAEL TORU, journalist; b. San Francisco, July 9, 1960; s. Harry Naoto and Noriko (Yoshitomi) Y.; m. Marianne Chin, Oct. 9, 1993. BA Psychology, San Francisco State U., 1981, BA Journalism, 1981. Editor San Francisco State U. Phoenix, 1980; news editor Hayward (Calif.) Daily Rev., 1979-80, Long Beach (Calif.) Press-Telegram, 1981; nat. desk editor L.A. Times, 1981-85; night news editor L.A. Times, Washington, 1986-87, investigative projects editor, 1988; dep. city editor San Francisco Chronicle, 1989-92, exec. projects editor, 1993, city editor, 1993-95; mng. editor news CNET, San Francisco, 1996—; adj. prof. Am. U., Washington, 1987, Calif. State U. at Northridge, Calif., 1984-85; vis. faculty mem. Am. Press Inst., Reston, Va., 1994, Poynter Inst. for Media Studies, St. Petersburg, Fla., 1995, San Francisco Unified Sch. Dist., 1994; fellow Coro Found., San Francisco, 1990-91. Recipient Dow Jones Newspaper Fund scholarship, Princeton, N.J., 1980. Mem. Asian Am. Journalism Assn., White House Corr. Assn., Soc. Profl. Journalists., World Affairs Coun. Office: CNET 150 Chestnut St San Francisco CA 94111-1004

YAMANE, GEORGE MITSUYOSHI, oral diagnosis and radiology educator; b. Honolulu, Aug. 9, 1924; s. Seigi and Tsuta (Moriwaki) Y.; m. Alice Matsuko Nemoto, July 6, 1951; children: Wende Michiko, Linda Keiko, David Kiyoshi. Student, U. Hawaii, 1944; A.B., Haverford Coll., 1946; D.D.S., U. Minn., 1950, Ph.D., 1962. Teaching, research asst. U. Hawaii, Honolulu, 1943-44; teaching asst. div. oral pathology, oral diagnosis Sch. Dentistry, U. Minn., Mpls., 1951-53; asst. prof. oral pathology Coll. Dentistry U. Ill., Chgo., 1957-59; dir. tissue lab. Sch. Dentistry U. Wash., Seattle, 1960-63; asst. prof. oral pathology Sch. Dentistry U. Wash., 1959-63; grad. faculty mem. U. Minn., Mpls., 1963-70; prof., chmn. div. oral diagnosis, oral medicine and oral roentgenology U. Minn., 1963-70; prof., chmn. dept. oral diagnosis and radiology Dental Sch. Univ. of Medicine and Dentistry of N.J., 1970-83; prof. dept. biodental sci. Dental Sch. Coll. of Medicine and Dentistry of N.J., 1983-88, assoc. dean research and postgrad. programs, 1976-79, dir. div. oral and pathobiology, 1988-92, prof. dept oral pathology, biology and diagnosis sci., 1988-92, prof. emeritus, 1992—; cons. Children's Orthopedic Hosp. and Med. Ctr., Seattle, 1960-63, VA Hosp., American Lake, Wash., 1961-63, Mpls., 1964-70; cons. Minn. State Dept. Health, 1965-70, Wyo. State Bd. Health, 1966-70. Contbr. articles to med. and dental jours. Served with AUS. USPHS fellow, 1953-55; recipient Nell S. Talbot Instructorship award Coll. Dentistry U. Ill., 1958; Excellence in Teaching award U. Medicine and Dentistry N.J., 1984, Exceptional Merit award U. Medicine and Dentistry N.J., 1986. Fellow Am. Acad. Oral Pathology, AAAS, Am., Internat. colls. dentists, N.J. Acad. Medicine; mem. Am. Dental Assn., Orgn. Tchrs. Oral Diagnosis (sec.-treas. 1970-73, pres. 1974-75), Am. Acad. Periodontology, Internat. Assn. Dental Research, Am. Assn. Dental Schs., Sigma Xi (pres. Newark chpt. 1985), Omicron Kappa Upsilon, Xi Psi Phi.

YAMANE, STANLEY JOEL, optometrist; b. Lihue, Kauai, Hawaii, Mar. 13, 1943; s. Tooru and Yukiko (Miura) Y.; m. Joyce Mitsuko Tamura; children—Stanley Tooru Aiichi, Karen Margaret. B.S. in Optometry, Pacific U., 1966, O.D., 1966. Diplomate Am. Acad. Optometry. Practice optometry Waipahu, Hawaii, 1967-73; ptnr. with Dr. Dennis M. Kuwabara, 1973-81; ptnr. Drs. Kuwabara & Yamane, Optometrists, Inc., Waipahu, 1981-91; with br. office Drs. Kuwabara & Yamane, Optometrists, Inc., Honolulu; with DBA Eye Care Assocs. of Hawaii, Honolulu, 1989-91; dir. profl. affairs Vistakon, Inc., 1991-92; v.p. profl. affairs Vistakon Inc., 1992—, chair global profl. affairs coun., 1996—; lectr., cons. in field; sec.-treas. Hawaii Bd. Examiners in Optometry, 1975-76, v.p., 1976-78, pres., 1978-80; mem. adj. faculty Coll. Optometry, Pacific U., 1977-91, Pa. Coll. Optometry, 1981-91, So. Coll. Optometry, 1982-91, U. Mo., St. Louis, 1990-91; bd. dirs. Hawaii Vision Svc. Plan, 1984-91. Cons. editor Optometric Mgmt. Jour., 1981-91, Contact Lens Forum Jour., 1987-91, editor, 1991; contbr. articles to profl. jours. Bd. mgrs. Leeward Oahu Br. YMCA, 1967-70, Hi-Y advisor, 1967-71, mem. Century Club, 1967-91, bd. mgrs. West Oahu Br., 1971-78, gen. chmn. sustaining membership, 1976; 2d v.p. August Ahrens Elem. Sch. PTA, 1969; mem. Leeward Mental Health Adv. Council, 1975-76, Friends of Waipahu Cultural Garden Park Found., 1976—, Aloha council Boy Scouts Am., 1976-91; mem. bus. adv. council Waipahu High Sch., 1976-81, Parent-Tchr.-Community Adv. Council, 1978-80; bd. dirs. Central/Leeward unit Am. Cancer Soc., 1977-80, pub. edn. dir., 1978-79, v.p., 1979-80, founder, chmn. Celebrity Auction, 1980, dir. Oahu Baseline Survey, 1978; bd. dirs. Barbers Point council Navy League Am., 1981-85; profl. bd. advisors U. Houston Inst. for Contact Lens Research. Recipient Merit award Nat. Eye Research Found., 1974, Disting. Service award, 1976. Fellow Am. Acad. Optometry (cornea and contact lens diplomate, vice chair cornea and contact lens sect. 1992-94, chair cornea and contact lens sect. 1994—, sec., 1990-92, vice chair ethics com. 1991-92, corp. support for Jour. com. 1981, chair diplomate awards com. 1988-90), AAAS, Am. Optometric Assn. (ann. congress del. 1978, pub. health com. 19738, optometric paraoptometric personnel com. 1978-79, contact lens project team 1979-80, task force on R&D 1984-87, contact lens sect. coun. 1988-92, sec., 1989-90, vice chair 1990-91, chair elect 1991-92, numerous coms.), Leeward Oahu Jaycees (Disting. Service award 1969, Top Outstanding Young Man award 1975), Hawaii State Jaycees, Am. Optometric Found. (bd. dirs. 1981-91 , chmn. task force clin. research 1981-83, nominations com. 1982, treas. 1985-86, sec., 1987-88, pres.-elect, 1988-89, pres. 1989-90), Am. Pub. Health Assn., Better Vision Inst., Coll. Optometrists in Vision Devel., Hawaii Optometric Assn. (corr. sec. 1968-70, state newsletter editor 1968-70, rec. sec. 1971, 2d v.p. 1972, pres. 1974-75; Man of Yr. 1975, Optometrist of Yr. 1979), Internat. Optometric & Optical League, Internat. Soc. Contact Lens Rsch., Brit. Contact Lens Assn., Japan Contact Lens Acad., Nat. Assn. of the Professions, Nat. Eye Research Found. (fellow Internat. Orthokeratology sect.; editorial bd. Contacto Jour. 1979, contact lens cert. com. 1981-85), Nat. Fedn. Ind. Bus., Optometric Cons. in Contact Lens Optometric Extension Program Found. (chmn. study group 1969-70, state dir. 1971-73), Optometric Hist. Soc., Optometric Polit. Action Coms., Soc. Contact Lens Specialists, Hawaii Assn. Children with Learning Disabilities, Hawaii Assn. Intellectually Gifted Children (pub. relations chmn. 1st Ann. State Conf. 1975, legis. lobbyist 1975-76), Waipahu Bus. Assn. (bd. dirs. 1974-78, chmn. pub. relations 1974-75, legis. lobbyist 1974-75, pres. 1974-75), Nat. Acad. Practice in Optometry (mem.-at-large on exec. com., disting. practitioner in optometry). Democrat. Baptist. Home: 8609 Autumn Green Dr Jacksonville FL 32256-9560 Office: Vistakon Inc Vp Profl Affairs 4500 Salisbury Rd Ste 300 Jacksonville FL 32216-0954

YAMARONE, CHARLES ANTHONY, JR., aerospace engineer, consultant; b. Bronxville, N.Y., Oct. 30, 1936; s. Charles Anthony and Mildred (La Manna) Y.; m. Catherine MacMullan, May 31, 1957; children: Charles Anthony III, Thomas, Stephen, Mark, James. BSEE, Manhattan Coll., 1958. Design engr. Gen. Precision Inc., Pleasantville, N.Y., 1958-62; engr. supr. Jet Propulsion Lab., Calif. Inst. Tech., Pasadena, 1962-69, sect. mgr., 1969-76, data processing mgr., 1976-80, project mgr., 1980—. Recipient Astronautique medal Assn. Aeronautique et Astronautique de France, 1992, medal Ctr. Nat. d'Etudes Spatiales, 1994, Outstanding Leadership medal NASA, 1993. Mem. Am. Geophys. Union, Am. Inst. for Advancement of Science. Office: Jet Propulsion Lab Topex Project Office 4800 Oak Grove Dr Pasadena CA 91109-8001*

YAMASAKI, YUKUZO, lawyer; b. Yamaguchi, Japan, Oct. 12, 1924; s. Bunsaburo and Yasuko (Ueda) Y. m. Keiko Furubayashi, Aug. 15, 1961; children: Takao, Chiyo. BA, Tokyo U., 1952; M of Comparative Law, So. Meth. U., 1965. Assoc. Shozawa & Nagashima (name now Nagashima & Ohno), Tokyo, 1961-72; trainee Kaye,Scholer,Fierman, Hayes & Handler, N.Y.C., 1965-66; sr. ptnr. Yamasaki Law & Patent Office, Tokyo, 1972—. Author: Digest of Japanese Patent Infringement Cases 1966-68, 1970; contbr. articles to Jour. of Assn. Internat. pour Protection Propriété Indsl. Mem. Indsl. Property Coun. of the Patent Office, Tokyo, 1991-96. Recipient commendation Ministry Internat. Trade Industry. Mem. First Tokyo Bar Assn., Japanese Bar Assn. (chmn. intellectual property com. 1989-90), Patent Attys. Assn. of Japan, Inter-Pacific Bar Assn. (chmn. intellectual property com. 1991-93), Japanese Br. Assn. Internat. Protection Propriété Indsl. (councillor, commendation 1986). Home: 2-20-21 Higashi, Kunitachi Tokyo 186, Japan Office: Yamasaki Law & Patent Office, 1-11-28 Nagatacho, Chiyoda-ku Tokyo 100, Japan

YAMATO, KEI C., international business consultant; b. Honokaa, Hawaii, Sept. 21, 1921; s. Kango and Shizuka (Tanaka) Y.; children: Karen, Marla, Kei Tracy. BA, U. Hawaii, 1946; LLD, Yale, 1950; DD, World Christianship Ministries, 1994. Ordained to ministry Ind. Universal Ch. of God, 1994. Pres. Internat. Bus. Mgmt. Co., 1950; founder Pacific-Asia Bus. Council, 1950; pres. Orchids of Hawaii Internat., Inc., 1951, Polynesian Products, Inc., Holiday Promotions Internat., Inc., 1952, Orchawaii Internat. Travel Corp., 1962, Pacific Area Landscaping, Inc., 1970—, Hawaii Hort. Enterprises, Inc., 1970—, Agrisystems, Inc., 1971-95; minister Ind. Universal Ch. God, Honolulu, 1995—; v.p., dir. Sperry & Hutchison Travel Awards, Inc., 1964, Copley Internat. Corp., 1967; all N.Y.C.; pres. Internat. Cons. Co., 1968, Asia-Pacific Corp., 1968; chmn. Asia Internat. Group of Cos., Asia Internat. Cons.; mng. dir. Internat. Cons. Assocs., 1993; universal cons. svcs. God's Universal Ch. and Ministries. Bd. dirs. Internat. Execs. Assn., World Trade Club N.Y.C., Sales Execs. Club N.Y.C.; mem. Regional Export Expansion Council, U.S. Dept. Commerce; organizer Asia Pacific Inst.; pres. Saudi Arabia Pacific Asia Bus. Council, Arab Asian Assocs. Served to 1st lt. AUS, World War II, ETO. Decorated Silver Star, Purple Heart with 2 oak leaf clusters. Mem. Advt. Club N.Y.C., Nat. Indsl. Conf. Bd., Profl. Mgmt. Cons. Assn. Am., Sales Promotion Execs. Assn., Chgo. Execs. Club, Sales and Marketing Execs. Internat., N.Y. Hort. Soc., Asia Soc., Japan Soc., Am. Mgmt. Assn. (lectr.), 442d Regimental Combat Team Assn., Landscape Contractors Assn. Hawaii, Gen. Contractors Assn. Hawaii, Friends East-West Center, East-West Philosophers Conf., Hawaii Assn. Nurserymen, Hawaii Bot. Soc., Honolulu Execs. Assn., U. Hawaii Alumni Assn., Navy League, Nat. Fedn. Ind. Bus., Am. Assn. Nurserymen, Pacific Area Travel Assn., Assn. U.S. Army, Hawaii Visitors Bur., Hawaii C. of C., U.S. Arab C. of C., Saudi Arabia Bus. Council. Clubs: Rotary, Bankers. Home: PO Box 781 Honolulu HI 96808

YAMAYEE, ZIA AHMAD, engineering educator, dean; b. Herat, Afghanistan, Feb. 2, 1948; came to U.S., 1974; s. Sayed and Merjan Ahmad. BSEE, Kabul (Afghanistan) U., 1972; MSEE, Purdue U., 1976, PhD, 1978. Registered profl. engr., Calif., Wash. Mem. faculty of engring. Kabul U., 1978; engr. Systems Control, Inc., Palo Alto, Calif., 1979-81; sr. engr. Pacific N.W. Utilities, Portland, Oreg., 1981-83; assoc. prof. elec. engring. Clarkson U., Potsdam, N.Y., 1983-85; assoc. prof. Gonzaga U., Spokane, 1985-87, dean Sch. Engring., 1988—; prof., chair elec. engring. dept. U. New Orleans, 1987-88; part-time rsch. engr. La. Power and Light Co., New Orleans, 1987-88; sr. cons. Engring. and Cons. Svcs., Spokane, 1989—. Contbr. articles, reports to profl. jours. Bd. dirs. Wash. State Math., Engring. Sci. Achievement, Seattle, 1989—; mem. Spokane Intercollegiate Rsch. and Tech. Inst. Adv. Coun., 1990—. NSF grantee. Mem. Am. Soc. Engring. Edn., IEEE (sr.). Office: University of Portland 5000 N Willamette Blvd Portland OR 97203-5743

YAMIN, DIANNE ELIZABETH, judge; b. Danbury, Conn., June 4, 1961; d. Raymond Joseph and Linda May (Bucko) Goetz; m. Robert Joseph Yamin, Sept. 3, 1988; children: Samantha Blythe, Rebecca Anne. AB, Lehigh U., 1983; JD, Mercer U., 1986. Bar: Conn. 1986, U.S. Dist. Ct. Conn. 1989. Lawyer Gerald Hecht & Assocs., Danbury, 1986-92; judge State Conn., Danbury, 1991—; atty. Yamin & Yamin, Danbury, 1992—; chmn. ethics com. Conn. Probate Assembly, 1994—; mem. Conn. Coun. on Adoptions, 1992—, Conn. Probate Assembly, 1991—. Bd. dirs. Big Bros./Big Sisters, Danbury, 1987-94; dir. Lions Club Danbury, 1993-94; dir. Conn. Brass Soc., Inc., 1991—, Friends of Tarrywile Park, Inc., Danbury, 1993—; dir. Danbury Music Ctr., 1996—. Recipient outstanding young citizen award Conn. Jaycees, 1994, pro bono award Conn. Legal Svcs., 1993; named as one of 21 Young Lawyers Leading Us into the 21st Century, ABA Mag., 1995. Mem. ABA, Conn. Bar Assn., Conn. Health Lawyers Assn., Danbury Bar Assn, Omicron Delta Kappa. Republican. Roman Catholic. Avocations: ballet, volunteerism, travel, outdoor activities. Home: 8 Johnson Dr Danbury CT 06811-2927 Office: 155 Deer Hill Ave Danbury CT 06810-7726

YAMIN, MICHAEL GEOFFREY, lawyer; b. N.Y.C., Nov. 10, 1931; s. Michael and Ethel Y.; m. Martina Schaap, Apr. 16, 1961; children: Michael Jeremy, Katrina. AB magna cum laude, Harvard U., 1953, LLB, 1958. Bar: N.Y. 1959, U.S. Dist. Ct. (so. dist.) N.Y., U.S. Dist. Ct. (ea. dist.) N.Y., U.S. Ct. Appeals (2d cir.) 1966, U.S. Supreme Ct. 1967. Assoc. Weil, Gotshal & Manges, N.Y.C., 1958-65; sr. ptnr. Colton, Hartnick, Yamin & Sheresky, N.Y.C., 1966-93; sr. ptnr. Kaufmann, Feiner, Yamin, Gildin & Robbins, LLP, N.Y.C., 1993—. Bd. trustees Gov.'s Com. Scholastic Achievement, 1976—; chmn. Manhattan Community Bd. 6, 1986-88, mem., 1974-88; mem. Manhattan Borough Bd., 1986-88; bd. trustees Rockland County Soc. Prevention of Cruelty to Children, 1979—. Served as lt. USNR, 1953-55, Korea. Mem. ABA, N.Y. State Bar Assn., Assn. Bar City N.Y., Fed. Bar Coun., Am. Fgn. Law Assn. (Am. Branch), Internat. Law Assn., Societe de Legislation Comparee, Internat. Bar Assn. Clubs: Harvard Faculty (Cambridge, Mass.); Harmonie, Harvard (N.Y.C.) (trustee N.Y. Found. 1981—, sub-chmn. schs. and scholarships com. 1972-93, bd. mgrs. 1985-88, 93—, chair house com. 1992-95, v.p. 1995—), Harvard Alumni Assn. (elected dir. 1995—). Office: 777 3rd Ave New York NY 10017

YAMMINE, RIAD NASSIF, oil company executive; b. Hammana, Lebanon, Apr. 12, 1934; s. Nassib Nassif and Emilie (Daou) Y.; came to U.S., 1952, naturalized, 1963; m. Beverly Ann Hosack, Sept. 14, 1954; children: Kathleen Yammine Gross, Cynthia Yammine Rotman, Michael. BS in Petroleum Engring., Pa. State U., 1956; postgrad. Advanced Mgmt. Program, Harvard U., 1977. Registered profl. engr., Ohio. Engr. Trans-Arabian Pipe Line Co., Saudi Arabia, 1956-61; with Marathon Pipe Line Co., 1961-75, mgr. Western div., Casper, Wyo., 1971-74, mgr. Eastern div., Martinsville, Ill., 1974-75; mktg. ops. div. mgr. Marathon Oil Co., 1975-83; pres. Marathon Pipeline Co., 1983-84; v.p. supply and transp. Marathon Petroleum Co., 1984-88, dir., 1984-90; pres. EMRO Mktg. Co., 1988—; bd. dirs. Marathon Oil Co.; also officer, bd. dirs. various subs. Patentee in field. Trustee, Wright State Univ. Found.; past trustee, Fisk U. Mem. ASME, Am. Petroleum Inst., Springfield and Clarck C. of C. (bd. dirs.). Republican. Club: Findlay Country. Home: 200 Penbrooke Dr Findlay OH 45840-8301 Office: 539 S Main St Findlay OH 45840-3242 also: 500 Speedway Dr Enon OH 45323-1056

YAMNER, MORRIS, lawyer; b. Passaic, N.J., Sept. 5, 1938; s. Sam and Edna (Halpern) Y.; 1 child, Laura; m. Gail Garber, Oct. 23, 1975; children: Amy, Lisa. BS in Bus., Ohio State U., 1959; JD, Georgetown U., 1962. Bar: N.J. 1962, N.Y. 1983. Law sec. Superior Ct., Somerville, N.J., 1962-63; dep. atty. gen. Atty. Gen. Office, Trenton, N.J., 1963-66; ptnr. Cole, Yamner & Bray, Paterson, N.J., 1966-90, Sills, Cummis, Newark, 1990—. Bd. dirs. Jewish Fedn., Clifton, N.J., 1985—, YM/YMHA, 1980—. Mem. Daus. of Miriam (bd. dirs. 1985—), Preakness Hills Country Club (bd. dirs. 1992—). Office: Sills Cummis 1 Riverfront Plz Newark NJ 07102-5401

YAN, CHONG CHAO, pharmacology, toxicology and nutrition researcher; b. Qing Jiang, Jiangsu, China, Oct. 16, 1963; came to the U.S., 1993; s. Mao Liang Yan and Gui Ying Ding; m. Yun Sun, July 28, 1988; 1 child, Jenny. BSc, Nanjing (China) Med. Coll., 1985; MS, Chinese Acad. Preventive Med., Beijing, 1988, MD/PhD, 1992. Rsch. fellow dept. metabolism and pathol. biochemistry Inst. Superiore di Sanità, Rome, 1990-92; rsch. fellow dept. gastroenterology U. Modena, Italy, 1992-93; rsch. assoc. dept. pharmacology U. Ariz., Tucson, 1993-95, asst. sci. investigator dept. pharmacology, 1995—; rschr. Chinese Acad. Preventive Medicine, Beijing, 1985-90; rschr. Nutrition Inst. Internat., Inc., 1996—; dir. Nutrition Inst. Internat., Inc., 1996—. Contbr. articles to profl. jours. Mem. Internat. Soc. Toxinology, Soc. Exptl. Biology and Medicine, Soc. Toxicology. Avocations: driving, swimming, table tennis, volleyball. Office: Univ Ariz Dept Pharmacology Tucson AZ 85724-1969

YANAGISAWA, SAMUEL TSUGUO, electronics executive; b. Berkeley, Calif., Feb. 18, 1922; s. Jusaku George and Mitsuyo (Mochizuki) Y.; m. Fernande Gerardine Renar, July 10, 1952; children: Shane Henry, Steven Kim, Ian Gerard. B.S. with honors in Elec. Engring., U. Calif.-Berkeley, 1942. Product line mgr. Machlett Labs. Inc., Springdale, Conn., 1943-63; v.p. ops. Warnecke Electron Tubes, Inc., Des Plaines, Ill., 1963-67; with Varo Inc., Garland, Tex., 1968-87, pres., 1971-84, chief exec. officer, 1974-85, chmn., 1976-87, also bd. dirs., ret., 1987; pres. Yanagisawa & Assocs., Dallas, 1989—; dir. Republic Bank, Garland; mem. Army Sci. Bd., 1986-90. Contbr. articles to profl. jours.; patentee electron devices. bd. dirs. So. Meth. U. Found. for Sci. and Engring.; mem. adv. coun., chmn. bd. visitors McDonald Obs., U. Tex., Austin; mem. adv. coun. Communities Found. of Tex.; bd. dirs. Dallas Council on World Affairs; adv. coun. Sch. Engring. U. Tex. at Dallas. Served to lt. AUS, 1945-46. Mem. IEEE (sr.), AAAS, Am. Def. Preparedness Assn., U.S. Night Vision Assn., Soc. Info. Display, Am. Electronic Assn., Am. Vacuum Soc., Assn. U.S. Army, Assn. Old Crows, Japanese Am. Citizens League, Nat. Japanese Am. Hist. Soc., Phi Beta Kappa, Sigma Xi, Tau Beta Pi, Eta Kappa Nu. Office: Yanagisawa & Assocs 7708 Chalkstone Dr Dallas TX 75248-5320

YANCEY, ASA GREENWOOD, SR., physician; b. Atlanta, Aug. 19, 1916; s. Arthur H. and Daisy L. (Sherard) Y.; m. Carolyn E. Dunbar, Dec. 28, 1944; children: Arthur H. II, Carolyn L., Caren L., Asa Greenwood Jr. BS, Morehouse Coll., 1937, ScD (hon.), 1991; MD, U. Mich., 1941; ScD (non.), Howard U., 1991. Diplomate Am. Bd. Surgery. Intern City Hosp., Cleve., 1941-42; resident Freedmen's Hosp., Washington, 1942-45, U.S. Marine Hosp., Boston, 1945; instr. surgery Meharry Med. Coll., 1946-48; chief surgery VA Hosp., Tuskegee, Ala., 1948-58; chief surgery of Hughes Spalding Pavilion, 1958-72; pvt. practice specializing in surgery Atlanta, 1958-86; med. dir. Grady Meml. Hosp., Atlanta, 1972-89; mem. staff Hughes Spalding Hosp., St. Joseph Hosp., Emory U. Hosp., up to 1986-88; asst. prof. surgery Emory U., 1958-72, assoc. prof., 1972-75, prof. surgery, 1975-86, prof. emeritus, 1986—, assoc. dean Emory U. Sch. Medicine, 1972-89; clin. prof. surgery Morehouse Sch. Medicine, 1985—. Contbr. articles to profl. jours. Mem. Atlanta Bd. Edn., 1967-77, Fulton-De Kalb Hosp. Authority; trustee Body for Grady Meml. Hosp., 1989-93. 1st lt. M.C., AUS, 1942. Fellow ACS, Am. Surg. Assn.; mem. Nat. Med. Assn. (1st v.p. 1989-90, trustee 1960-66, editorial bd. jour. 1964-80), Inst. Medicine of NAS, So. Surg. Assn. Baptist. Home and Office: 2845 Engle Rd NW Atlanta GA 30318-7216

YANCEY, ELEANOR GARRETT, retired crisis intervention clinician; b. Ga., Oct. 24, 1933; adopted d. Overton LaVerne Garrett; m. Robert Grady Yancey, Nov. 10, 1961 (div. Apr. 1968); children: Katherine La Verne, David Shawn. Student, High Mus. Art Inst., 1952-53, Ga. State U., 1953-55, 78; BA, La Grange Coll., 1957. Social worker, case worker Fulton County Dept. Family and Children's Svcs., Atlanta, 1957-61; asst. tchr. Atlanta (Ga.) Bd. Edn., 1973-85; mental health crisis intervention clinician Dekalb County Bd. Health, Decatur, 1985-95, acting dir. crisis intervention, 1988-90; ret., 1995. Performed summer stock, 1969-70. Performed summer stock with Rogers & Co., 1969, 70; band booster pres. Henry Grady H.S., Atlanta, 1977-78, v.p. PTA, 1978-79; pres. PTA Morningside Elem. Sch., Atlanta, 1977; grand juror Dekalb County, Decatur, 1983; active Sesquicentennial Celebration of Ala. Statehood. Mem. Kappa Kappa Iota (Lambda chpt. state pres. 1987-88, Eta pres. local chpt. 1992-97). Democrat. Avocations: drawing, gardening, travel, music. Home: 3425 Regalwoods Dr Doraville GA 30340-4019

YANCEY, JIMMIE ISAAC, marketing professional; b. Ripley, Miss., Dec. 11, 1935; s. Charlie Edward and Overa (Wilbanks) Y.; m. Jonell Smith, Mar. 1, 1958; children: Angela Jo, Jamie Lorraine, Cynthia Overa, Melanie Ann. BS, Miss. State U., 1963, MBA, 1966. Editor univ. rels. Miss. State. U., Starkville, 1963-65, editor coll. bus., 1965-66; editor Miss. Extension Svc., Starkville, 1966-67, Nat. Cotton Coun., Memphis, 1967-71; pub. rels. dir. Cotton Inc., Raleigh, N.C., 1971, Am. Soybean Assn., Hudson, Iowa, 1971-78; gen. mgr. Prog. Farmer Network, Starkville, 1978-86; owner, mgr. Yancey Agrl. Network, Starkville, 1986—; mktg. cons. Wyffel's Hybrids, Inc., Atkinson, Ill., 1987-93. Bd. dirs. Agri-Bus. Edn. Found.; sr. adv. com. Coll. Bus. and Industry, Miss. State U. Mem. Nat. Agrl. Mktg. Assn., (pres. 1986-87, Meritorious Svc. award 1986), Nat. Assn. Farm Broadcasters, Am. Advt. Fedn., Starkville C. of C. (venture capital com. 1990), Am. Soybean Assn. (Mertorious Svc. award 1974, Broadcaster of Yr. 1984), Hudson C. of C. (pres. 1972, Iowa chpt.), Nat. Alliance of Ind. Corp. Cons., Miss. Rotary, Pres.'s Club. Presbyterian. Avocations: gardening, fishing.

YANCEY, RICHARD CHARLES, investment banker; b. Spokane, Wash., May 28, 1926; s. George R. and M. Ruth (Yenney) Y.; m. Mary Anne Shaffer, Feb. 5, 1956; children: Leslie, Jennifer, Richard C. Jr. BA in Econs., Whitman Coll., Walla Walla, Wash., 1949; MBA with distinction, Harvard U., 1952. Assoc. Dillon, Read & Co. Inc., N.Y.C, 1952-63; v.p. Dillon, Read & Co., Inc., N.Y.C., 1963-75, mng. dir., 1975-89, dir., 1990; sr. adv., 1992; ret. Dillon, Read & Co., Inc., N.Y.C., 1992; bd. dirs. Composite Group Mut. Funds, Spokane, Wash., Ad Media Ptnrs., Inc., N.Y.C., The Score Bd., Inc., Cherry Hill, N.J., Capmac Holdings, Inc., N.Y.C., Fiberite, Inc., Tempe, Ariz., Czech and Slovak Am. Enterprise Fund, Greenwich, Conn. ; former mem. partnership bd. Whittle Comms. L.P., Knoxville, Tenn. Former bd. overseers Whitman Coll.; former trustee, former pres. Plymouth Ch. of Pilgrims, Bklyn.; former trustee N.Y. Infirmary-Beekman Downtown Hosp. Served with USNR, 1944-46, PTO. Mem. N.Y. Soc. Security Analysts, Harvard Club, Met. Club, N.Y.C., Pilgrims of the U.S. Republican. Home: 42 Monroe Pl Brooklyn NY 11201-2603 Office: Dillon Read & Co Inc 535 Madison Ave Fl 15 New York NY 10022-4212

YANCEY, WALLACE GLENN, retired insurance company executive; b. Langdale, Ala., Sept. 8, 1930; s. Wallace Odell and Nellie Leigh (Roughton) Y.; m. Betty Jo Carden, June 1, 1956; children—Angela, Susan, Reed. B.S. in Bus. Adminstrn., Auburn U., 1956. Sales rep. Arkwright Mut. Ins. Co. (formerly Arkwright-Boston Ins. Co.), Birmingham, Ala., 1957-59; sales rep. Arkwright Mut. Ins. Co. (formerly Arkwright-Boston Ins. Co.), Atlanta, 1960-61; br. mgr. Arkwright Mut. Ins. Co. (formerly Arkwright-Boston Ins. Co.), N.Y.C., 1961-64; regional sales mgr. Arkwright Mut. Ins. Co. (formerly Arkwright-Boston Ins. Co.), Atlanta, 1964-68; v.p. mktg. Arkwright Mut. Ins. Co. (formerly Arkwright-Boston Ins. Co.), Waltham, Mass., 1975-79, sr. v.p., 1979-88, exec. v.p., 1988—; v.p., gen. mgr. Hobbs Group, Inc. (formerly Hobbs Brook Agy., Inc.), Waltham, 1969-75, pres., chief exec. officer, 1985—; pres., chief exec. officer HPR Ltd., Bermuda, Arkwright Mgmt. Corp, Hamilton, Bermuda; exec. v.p. Arkwright Mut. Ins. Co., Waltham, 1988-95. Comdr. Acton Minutemen, Mass., 1978-79; bd. dirs. Acton Youth Hockey Assn., 1973-75. Served with USN, 1948-52, Korea. Republican. Congregationalist. Home: 92 Southbay Rd Indian Pt Georgetown ME 04548 Office: Arkwright Mut Ins Co 225 Wyman St Waltham MA 02154-1209

YANCHYSHYN, MADELYN, poet, writer; b. Mt. Holly, N.J., Aug. 16, 1939; d. Frank and Andunnina (Yaniro) Panico; m. Harry A. Tomasko, Aug. 26, 1962 (div. June, 1971); children: Denise, Daryla; m. John P. Yanchyshyn, Apr. 23, 1973; children: Rochelle, Jacob. Grad. high sch., Burlington, N.J.; cert., Burlington County Inst. Tech. Operator N.J. Bell Telephone Co., Burlington, 1957-61; office mgr. Posteraro & Co., Willingboro, N.J., 1962-70; sec./cashier Delrando Diner, Riverside, N.J., 1970-75; poet Roebling, N.J., 1985—; writer Roebling, 1994—. Author: Pending Calamity Hovers America, 1995, Enlightened Journey, 1995, Lifes's Inspirational Poems, 1995, Poetic Footsteps for Children, 1997, America Through Annals of Time, 1997; contbr. Treasured Poems of America, 1993, The Space Between, 1994, Poetic Voices of Am., 1995, Am. Poetry Annual, 1995, Best Poems of '95, 1995. Recipient Golden Poet award World of Poetry Bd. Dirs., 1986, award of merit cert., 1985, Editor's Choice award Nat. Libr. Poetry, 1994. Mem. Internat. Soc. Poets (Poet of Merit award 1994), Deborah Found., Song Writers Club, Palm Beach Guild of the Fla. Philharms. Avocations: composing lyrics, music, writing.

YANCIK, JOSEPH JOHN, government official; b. Mt. Olive, Ill., Dec. 1, 1930; s. Joseph John and Anna (Gubach) Y.; m. Rosemary Panich, Feb. 19, 1955; children—Geri Anne, Ellen Marie. BS, U. Ill., 1954; MS in Mining Engring., Mo. Sch. Mines, 1956; PhD, U. Mo., Rolla, 1960. Mining research engr. St. Joe Lead Co., Bonne Terre, Mo., 1955-58; mgr. research and devel. Monsanto Co., St. Louis, 1960-70; asst. dir. mining U.S. Bur. Mines, Washington, 1970-77; v.p. research Nat. Coal Assn., Washington, 1977-82; pres. Bituminous Coal Research, Inc., Washington, 1980-82; dir. Coal Export Office U.S. Dept. Commerce, Washington, 1982-84; dir. Office of Energy Internat. Trade Adminstrn., Washington, 1984-95; pvt. practice Mc Lean, 1995—; cons. energy in internat. trade and investment; dir. energy affairs U.S.-Russia Bus. Coun., Washington, 1996—. Contbr. articles to profl. jours. Served with C.E. U.S. Army, 1950-52. Recipient Alumni Achievement award U. Mo.-Rolla, 1975, Silver Medal award U.S. Dept. Commerce, 1986, Gold Medal award Dept. Commerce, 1992. Mem. Cosmos Club (Washington). Roman Catholic. Home and Office: 1703 James Payne Cir Mc Lean VA 22101-4223

YANCURA, ANN JOYCE, library director; b. Ft. Smith, Ark., Oct. 1, 1943; d. John Michael and Elizabeth Ann (Grcevic) Traub; m. Nicholas Daniel Yancura, Dec. 26, 1966; children: Daniel, Elizabeth. BA, U. Akron, 1965; MLS, Kent (Ohio) State U., 1982. Tchr. Akron Pub. Schs., 1966-70; mgr. SCM Corp., Strongsville, Ohio, 1982-85; exec. dir. Nola Regional Libr., Youngstown, Ohio, 1985-90, McKinley Meml. Libr., Niles, Ohio, 1990—. Bd. dirs. Info. Access, Foster City, Calif., 1993—; mem. Niles Hist. Soc., 1990—, Leadership Mahoning Valley, 1996-97. Named Outstanding Grad., Kent State U./Crawford Bindery, 1982, Boss of the Yr., Am. Bus. Women, 1992, Outstanding Cmty. Leader, Youngstown Vidicator, 1993; recipient Recognition award Friends of Libr., Niles, 1992. Mem. ALA (mem. coms.), Ohio Libr. Assn. (bd. dirs., mem. coun.), Ohio Mus. Assn., Pub. Libr. Assn. (mem. coms.), Niles C. of C. (bd. dirs. 1991-94), Niles Rotary (bd. dirs. 1990—, Outstanding Svc. award 1992, 93, 94), Beta Phi Mu. Republican. Roman Catholic. Avocations: reading, travel, gardening. Home: 2180 Brittainy Oaks Trail Warren OH 44484 Office: McKinley Meml Libr 40 N Main St Niles OH 44446-5004

YANCY, WILLIAM SAMUEL, pediatrician; b. Pittsboro, Miss., Aug. 17, 1939; s. Lester Truman and Maxyne (Lindsay) Y.; m. Susan Elizabeth Guest, June 19, 1965; children: Amy Yancy Lee, William Samuel Jr., James Michael. BA, Duke U., 1961, MD, 1965. Resident in pediatrics Duke U. Med. Ctr., Durham, N.C., 1965-66, 67-68; resident in pediatrics, then fellow in adolescent medicine U. Rochester (N.Y.) Med. Ctr., 1966-67, 70-71; pediatrician Durham Pediatrics, 1971—; dir. adolescent medicine tng. program Duke U. Med. Ctr., 1971—, dir. behavioral pediat. tng. program, 1978-90, assoc. clin. prof. psychiatry, 1982—, clin. prof. pediatrics, 1984—; dir. pediat. tng. program Durham Regional Hosp., 1977-80, med. coun., 1980-86, chmn. dept. pediatrics, 1980-86, chmn. nursery com., 1986— ; pediatrician Duke U. Affiliated Physicians, 1995—; bd. mem. Am. Bd. Pediatrics, 1992—; chmn. Coalition for Healthy N.C. Youth, 1991-95; editl. bd. Jour. Devel. and Behavioral Pediatrics, 1984—. Bd. dirs. Child Advocacy Commn. Durham, 1973-76, 79-85, pres. 1973-74; bd. dirs. Durham Cmty. Guidance Clinic, 1974-76; N.C. State Coordinating Coun., Raleigh, 1994-95; vestry St. Stephen's Episcopal Ch., Durham, 1985-87, 95—. Lt. cmdr. U.S. Navy, 1968-70. Fellow Am. Acad. Pediatrics, Soc. Adolescent Medicine (exec. sec.-treas. 1978-83, pres. 1985-86, chmn. fin. com. 1989-93); mem. AMA, Internat. Assn. Adolescent Health, Soc. Devel. & Behavioral Pediatrics (pres. 1984-85), N.C. Pediat. Soc. (chmn. com. on adolescents 1989—), Beta Omega Sigma, Omicron Delta Kappa. Avocations: stamp collecting, writing, golf. Home: 59 Kimberly Dr Durham NC 27707 Office: Durham Pediatrics 2609 N Duke St Ste 801 Durham NC 27704-3048

YANDELL, CATHY MARLEEN, foreign language educator; b. Anadarko, Okla., Dec. 27, 1949; d. Lloyd O. and Maurine (Dunn) Y.; m. Mark S. McNeil, Sept. 7, 1974; children: Elizabeth Yandell McNeil, Laura Yandell McNeil. Diplome d'etudes, Inst. des Professeurs de Français à l'Etranger, Sorbonne, 1970; BA, U. N.Mex., 1971; MA, U. Calif., Berkeley, 1973, PhD, 1977. Teaching asst. U. Calif., Berkeley, 1971-75, acting instr., 1976-77; asst. prof. Carleton Coll., Northfield, Minn., 1977-83, assoc. prof., 1983-89, prof. French, 1989—; chair comm. on the status of women Carleton Coll., Northfield, 1983-85, ednl. policy com., 1985-86, 96-97, romance langs. and lits., 1990-94, pres. of faculty, 1991-94, Bryn-Jones disting. tchg. prof. humanities, 1996—. Co-author: Vagabondages: Initiation à la litt. d'expression française, 1996; contbr. to Art & Argumentation: The Sixteenth Century Dialogue, 1993, French Texts/American Contexts: French Women Writers, 1994, Montaigne: A Collection of Essays, Vol. 4, Language and Meaning, 1995; editor: Pontus de Tyard's Solitaire Second, ou prose de la musique, 1980; contbr. articles to profl. jours. Active exec. com., then mem. Amnesty Internat., Northfield, 1980—. Regents' Travelling fellow U. Calif. at Berkeley, 1975-76; Faculty Devel. grantee Carleton Coll., 1988, 91; NEH Rsch. fellow., 1994-95. Mem. MLA (del. 1989-92). Democrat. Avocations: dance, music, hiking, biking, cross-country skiing. Home: 514 5th St E Northfield MN 55057-2220 Office: Carleton College 1 N College St Northfield MN 55057-4001

YANDERS, ARMON FREDERICK, biological sciences educator, research administrator; b. Lincoln, Nebr., Apr. 12, 1928; s. Fred W. and Beatrice (Pate) Y.; m. Evelyn Louise Gatz, Aug. 1, 1948; children: Mark Frederick, Kent Michael. A.B., Nebr. State Coll., Peru, 1948; M.S., U. Nebr., 1950, Ph.D., 1953. Research asso. Oak Ridge Nat. Lab. and Northwestern U., 1953-54; biophysicist U.S. Naval Radiol. Def. Lab., San Francisco, 1955-58; asso. geneticist Argonne (Ill.) Nat. Lab., 1958-59; with dept. zoology Mich. State U., 1959-69; prof., asst. dean Mich. State U. (Coll. Natural Sci.), 1963-69; prof. biol. scis. U. Mo., Columbia, 1969—, dean Coll. Arts and Scis., 1969-82, research prof., dir. Environ. Trace Substances Research Ctr., 1983-93, dir. Alzheimer's Disease and Related Disorders Program, 1994—; research prof., dir. Environ. Trace Substances Research Ctr. and Sinclair Comparative Medicine Research Farm, Columbia, 1984-94; prof. emeritus, 1994—; Trustee Argonne Univs. Assn., 1965-77, v.p., 1969-73, pres., 1973, 76-77, chmn. bd., 1973-75; bd. dirs. Coun. Colls. Arts and Scis., 1981-82; mem. adv. com. environ. hazards VA, Washington, 1985—, chmn. sci. coun., 1988—, chmn. of com., 1990—. Contbr. articles to profl. jours. Trustee Peru State Coll., 1992—. Served from ensign to lt. USNR, 1954-58. Recipient Disting. Svc. award Peru State Coll., 1989. Fellow AAAS; mem. AAUP (Robert W. Martin acad. freedom award 1971), Am. Inst. Biol. Sci., Environ. Mutagen Soc., Genetics Soc. Am., Radiation Research Soc., Soc. Environ. Toxicology and Chemistry. Home: 2405 Ridgefield Rd Columbia MO 65203-1531 Office: U of Mo 521 Clark Hall Columbia MO 65211

YANDLE, STEPHEN THOMAS, law school dean; b. Oakland, Calif., Mar. 7, 1947; s. Clyde Thomas and Jane Walker (Hess) Y.; m. Martha Anne Welch, June 26, 1971. BA, U. Va., 1969, JD, 1972. Bar: Va. 1972. Asst. dir. admissions U. Va. Law Sch., Charlottesville, 1972-76; from asst. to assoc. dean Northwestern U. Sch. Law, Chgo., 1976-85; assoc. dean Yale U. Law Sch., New Haven, 1985—; bd. dirs. The Access Group. Bd. dirs. The Access Group, 1996—. Served to capt. U.S. Army, 1972. Mem. Law Sch. Admission Coun. (programs, edn. and prelaw com. 1978-84), Assn. Am. Law Schs. (chmn. legal edn. and admissions sect. 1979, nominations com. 1987, chmn. adminstrn. of law schs. sect. 1991), Nat. Assn. for Law Placement (pres. 1984-85, co-chmn. Joint Nat. Assn. com. on placement 1986-88), New Haven Legal Assistance Assn. (bd. dirs., treas.). Office: Yale Law Sch Sch Law PO Box 208215 New Haven CT 06520-8215

YANEY, GEORGE, history educator; b. Teaneck, N.J., Oct. 30, 1930; s. Arthur J. and Frances (Levings) Y.; m. Ann Hinrichs, June 7, 1952; children: Brian, Dale, Carolyn, Tara. B in Mgmt. Engring., Rensselaer Poly. Inst., 1952; MA, U. Colo., 1956; PhD, Princeton U., 1961. Instr. Coll. Wooster, Ohio, 1957-58; prof. history U. Md., College Park, 1960-92, prof. emeritus, 1992—. Author: Systematization of Russian Government, 1973, Urge to Mobilize, 1982, World of the Manager, 1994. Served to capt. USMC, 1952-54, Korea. Rsch. fellow Harvard U., 1969-70, fellow Slavic Rsch. Ctr., U. Hokkaido, Japan, 1990-91; Fulbright grantee, 1975, 77, 85, Internat. Rsch. Exchanges Bd. grantee 1965, 75, 77, 85, 89. Home: 7303 Baylor Ave College Park MD 20740-3001 Office: Univ of Maryland Dept Of History College Park MD 20742

YANG, BAIYIN, adult education educator; b. Changshu, Jiangsu, China, Mar. 17, 1962; came to U.S., 1992; s. Zongde Yang and Feng Ying Gu; m. Xiaoping Lu, Dec. 14, 1987; children: Zhuowei, Zhuoyu. BS, Nanjing U., 1982; M Continuing Edn., U. Sasktchewan, Can., 1992; PhD, U. Ga., 1996. Lectr. The Chinese Acad. Scis., Nanjing, 1982-87, coord. tng. and devel., 1987-90; computer lab. advisor U. Saskatchewan, Saskatoon, 1990-92; stat. cons. U. Ga., Athens, 1993-96; asst. prof. adult edn. Auburn (Ala.) U., 1996—; rsch. asst. U. Ga., 1992-96, tchg. asst. summer 1992; rsch. asst. U. Saskatchewan, 1990-91. Contbr. articles to profl. jours. Mem. APA, Am. Ednl. Rsch. Assn., Am. Assn. Adult and Continuing Edn., ASTD, Kapp Delta Pi. Office: Dept Vocat & Adult Edn Auburn U Auburn AL 36849

YANG, CHAO YUH, chemistry educator; b. Pingtung, Taiwan, May 8, 1939; came to U.S., 1982; s. Shang-Sheng and Kuei-Mei (Lee) Y.; m. Manlan Lou Yang; children: Tseming, Tseliang, Thomas. BS, Tamkang U., Taipei, Taiwan, 1962; MS, Georg-August U., Goettingen, Germany, 1970, PhD, 1973. Tchr. Chiatung Agr. High Sch., Pingtung, Taiwan, 1963-64; chemist Kuantu Glass Plant, Taipei, 1964-68; postdoctoral fellow dept. molecular biology Max-Planck Inst. for Exptl. Medicine, Goettingen, 1973-75, scientist dept. immunochemistry, 1975-82; asst. prof. biochemistry Baylor Coll. Medicine, Houston, 1982-89, asst. prof. dept. medicine, 1983-86, rsch. assoc. prof. dept. medicine, 1986-90, rsch. assoc. prof. dept. biochemistry, 1989-91, rsch. prof. medicine, 1990—, 1990-95; rsch. prof. biochemistry, 1991-95, prof. medicine and biochemistry, 1995—; dir. peptide core Nat. Rsch. and Demonstration Ctr. in Arteriosclerosis, Baylor Coll. Medicine, 1984-96, mem. internal adv. com., 1986-96; mem. organizing com. 10th Internat. Conf. on Methods in Protein Structure Analysis, Snowbird, Utah, 1994; mem. sci. com. 7th Internat. Conf. on Methods in Protein Sequence Analysis, Berlin, 1988, 8th Internat. Conf., Sweden, 1990; reviewer grants Biomed. Rsch. rev. Com., Nat. Inst. on Drug Abuse, NSF, Washington; lectr. in field. Reviewer papers for Jour. Chromatography, Jour. Lipid Rsch., Jour. Protein Chemistry, Molecular and Cellular Biochemistry, Biochemistry, Arteriosclerosis; contbr. numerous articles to profl. jours. Pres. Taiwanese Am. Citizens League of Houston, 1988-90, Taiwanese Am. Assn. of Houston, 1985-86. Grantee NIH, 1986-96, Meth. Hosp. Found., 1988-91, AHA, 1985-87, 87-90, BRSG Funds, 1982-83. Home: 4102 Levonshire Dr Houston TX 77025-3915 Office: Baylor Coll Medicine 6565 Fannin St Houston TX 77030-2704

YANG, CHEN NING, physicist, educator; b. Hefei, Anhwei, China, Sept. 22, 1922; married, 1950; 3 children. BSc, SW Assoc. U., China, 1942; PhD in Physics, U. Chgo., 1948; DSc (hon.), Princeton U., 1958, Polytech. Inst. Bklyn., 1965, U. Wroclaw, 1974, Gustavus Adolphus Coll., 1975, U. Md., 1979, U. Durham, Eng., 1979, Fundan U., China, 1984, Eidg Technische Hochschule, Switzerland, 1987, Moscow State U., 1992. Instr. physics U. Chgo., 1948-49; mem. Inst. Advanced Study, Princeton, N.J., 1949-66, prof., 1955-66; Albert Einstein prof. physics, dir. inst. theoretical physics SUNY, Stony Brook, 1966—; disting. prof.-at-large Chinese U., Hong Kong; trustee Woods Hole Oceanographical Inst., 1962-78, Rockefeller U., 1970-76, Salk Inst., 1978-79; mem. governing coun. Courant Inst. Math. Sci., 1963—; mem. sci. adv. com. IBM, 1966-71; chmn. divsn. particles & fields Internat. Union Pure & Applied Physics, 1972-76; chmn., fachbeirat Max Planck Inst. Physics, Munich, 1980-83. Recipient Bower Achievement in Sci. award and prize Franklin Inst., 1994, Nobel prize in Physics, 1957, Rumford prize, 1980, Nat. medal sci., 1986, Liberty award, 1986, Benjamin Franlin medal, 1993. Mem. NAS (chmn. panel theoretical physics 1965, chmn. physics surv. com. 1965), Am. Philosophical Soc., Royal Spanish Acad. Sci., Polish Acad. Sci., Royal Soc. London, Russian Acad. Sci. Achievements include research in theoretical physics. Office: SUNY Stony Brook Inst Theoretical Phys Stony Brook NY 11794-3840

YANG, EDWARD S., electrical engineering educator; b. Nanking, Peoples Republic of China, Oct. 16, 1937; s. Joseph L. and York-Shih (Lung) Y.; m. Ruth Chu; children: David K., Grace S. BS, Nat. Cheng-Kung U., Taiwan, 1957; MS, Okla. State U., 1961; PhD, Yale U., 1966. Engr. IBM Corp., Poughkeepsie, N.Y., 1961-63; asst. prof. elec. engring. Columbia U., N.Y.C., 1965-70, assoc. prof., 1970-75, prof., 1975—, chmn. dept., 1987-89, 93-96; prof., chair of microelectronics U. Hong Kong, 1997—. Author: Fundamental Semiconductor Devices, 1978, Microelectronic Devices, 1988; contbr. over 150 articles to profl. jours. Fellow IEEE. Office: Columbia U Dept Of Elec Engring New York NY 10027

YANG, HENRY T., university chancellor, educator; b. Chungking, China, Nov. 29, 1940; s. Chen Pei and Wei Gen Yang; m. Dilling Tsui, Sept. 2, 1966; children: Maria, Martha. BSCE, Nat. Taiwan U., 1962; MSCE, W.Va. U., 1965; PhD, Cornell U., 1968; D honoris causa, Purdue U., 1996. Rsch. engr. Gilbert Assocs., Reading, Pa., 1968-69; asst. prof. Sch. Aeros. and Astronautics, Purdue U., West Lafayette, Ind., 1969-72, assoc. prof., 1972-76, prof., 1976-94, Neil A. Armstrong Disting. prof., 1988-94, sch. head, 1979-84; dean engring. Purdue U., 1984-94; chancellor U. Calif., Santa Barbara, 1994—; mem. sci. adv. bd. USAF, 1985-89; mem. aero. adv. com. NASA, 1985-89; mem. engring. adv. com. NSF, 1988-91; mem. mechanics bd. visitors ONR, 1990-93; mem. def. mfg. bd. DOD, 1988-89, def. sci. bd., 1989-91; mem. acad. adv. bd. Nat. Acad. Engring., 1991-94; mem. tech. adv. com. Pratt & Whitney, 1993-95; bd. dirs. Allied Signal; mem. Naval Rsch. Adv. Com., 1996—. Recipient 12 Best Tchg. awards Purdue U., 1971-94, Centennial medal Am. Soc. Engring. Edn., 1993. Fellow AIAA, ASEE; mem. NAE, Academia Sinica. Home: University Calif University House Santa Barbara CA 93106 Office: U California Chancellors Office Santa Barbara CA 93106

YANG, RALPH TZU-BOW, chemical engineering educator, researcher; b. Chung King, China, Sept. 18, 1942; came to U.S., 1965, naturalized, 1976; s. Chen Pei and Wei (Gee) Y.; m. Frances H. Chang, Dec. 23, 1972; children: Michael, Robert. BS, Nat. Taiwan U., 1964; MS, Yale U., 1968, PhD, 1971. Rsch. assoc. Argonne Nat. Lab., Ill., 1972-73; sci. Aluminum Co. of Am., Pitts., 1973-74; group leader Brookhaven Nat. Lab., Upton, N.Y., 1974-78; assoc. prof. SUNY, Buffalo, 1978-82, prof., 1982—, chmn. chem. engring. dept., 1990-95; Praxair prof. chem. engring., chair, 1993-95, prof., chmn. chem. engring. dept. U. Mich., 1995—; cons. in field. Author: Gas Separation by Adsorption Processes, 1987; editor Imperial Coll. Press, 1996—; contbr. articles to profl. jours. Patentee in field. Rsch. grantee NSF, 1980—, Dept. Energy, 1980—, Alcoa Found., 1979-81. Fellow Am. Inst. Chem. Engring. (William H. Walker award for excellence in contbn. to chem. engring. lit., 1991, Inst. award for excellence in gases tech. 1996); mem. Am. Chem. Soc. (Ind. Engring. Chem. Rsch. jour. adv. bd. 1991-93), Am. Carbon Soc. (adv. bd. 1985—), Am. Soc. Engring. Edn., Internat. Adsorption Soc. (adv. bd. Jour. of Adsorption 1993—), Adsorption Sci. and Tech. (adv. bd. 1986—). Office: U Mich Dept Chem Engring Ann Arbor MI 48109

YANG, SHANG FA, biochemistry educator; b. Tainan, Taiwan, Nov. 10, 1932; came to U.S., 1959, naturalized, 1971; s. Chian-Zuei and En-Liu (Lu) Y.; m. Eleanor Shou-yuan, Sept. 16, 1964; children: Albert, Bryant. BS, Nat. Taiwan U., 1956, MS, 1958; PhD, Utah State U., 1962. Rsch. assoc. U. Calif., Davis, 1962-63, NYU Med. Sch., N.Y.C., 1963-64, U. Calif.-San Diego, La Jolla, 1964-65; asst. biochemist U. Calif.-Davis, 1966-69, assoc. biochemist, 1969-74, prof., biochemist, 1974-94, chmn., 1989-90, prof. emeritus, 1994—; prof. Hong Kong U. Sci. & Tech., 1994-96; v.p. Academia Sinica, Taipei, 1997—; vis. prof. U. Konstanz, Germany, 1974, Nat. Taiwan U., Taipei, 1983, U. Cambridge, Eng., 1983, Nagoya U., Japan, 1988-89. Assoc. editor Jour. Plant Growth Regulation, 1981-94; mem. editl. bd. Plant Physiology, 1974-92, Plant Cell Physiology, 1987-91, Plant Physiology and Biochemistry, 1988—, Acta Phytophysiologica Sinica, 1988-93. Recipient Campbell award Am. Inst. Biol. Sci., 1969; Guggenheim fellow, 1982; recipient Internat. Plant growth Substance Assn. Research award, 1985, Wolf prize agriculture, 1991, Outstanding Rsch award Am. Soc. Horticultural Sci., 1992. Mem. NAS, Academia Sinica, Am. Soc. Biochemistry and Molecular Biology, Am. Soc. Plant Physiologists (chmn. Western sect. 1982-84). Home: 1118 Villanova Dr Davis CA 95616-1753 Office: Academia Sinica, Nanking, Taipei 11529, Taiwan

YANG, WEN-CHING, chemical engineer; b. Taipei, Taiwan, Nov. 11, 1939; came to U.S., 1964; s. Ting-Lien and Ho (Lee) Y.; m. Rae Tien, Aug. 24, 1968; children: Evonne R., Peter T. BSChemE, Nat. Taiwan U., Taipei, 1962; MSChemE, U. Calif., Berkeley, 1965; PhD in Chem. Engring., Carnegie Mellon U., 1968. Sr. engr. rsch. and devel. ctr. Westinghouse Electric Co., Pitts., 1968-76, fellow engr., 1976-93, adv. engr. sci. and tech. ctr., 1993—; instr. U. Pitts., 1980, 83; chair rsch. rev. panel Office Fossil Energy, Dept. Energy, Washington, 1990. Author: (with others) Encyclopedia of Fluid Mechanics, 1986, 92; editor spl. vol. Powder Tech. jour., 1987; contbr. over 80 papers to sci. jours. Lt. Army Tank Corp., 1962-63. Fellow AIChE (programming chair and sec. group 3, editor 5 symposium series vols. 1987-88, 92-93, sec. particle tech. forum 1993—, Fluidized Processes Recognition award 1993, George Westinghouse Signature award of excellence 1995); mem. Am. Chem. Soc., Chinese Am. Chem. Soc. (pres. Pitts. chpt. 1994), Orgn. Chinese Am. Achievements include patents in field; development of widely-used correlations and design equations in pneumatic transport and fluidization areas. Avocations: Chinese calligraphy, painting, tennis, gardening. Home: 236 Mount Vernon Dr Export PA 15632-9035 Office: Westinghouse Electric Co Sci & Tech Ctr 1310 Beulah Rd Pittsburgh PA 15235-5068

YANG, XIANGZHONG, research scientist, administrator, educator; b. Weixian, Hebei, China, July 31, 1959; came to U.S., 1983; s. Wukui Yang and Fengrong Zhang; m. Xiuchun Tian, Jan. 5, 1986; 1 child, Andrew Chun. BS in Animal Sci. with honors, Beijing Agrl. U., 1982; diploma, Nanjing (China) Agrl. U., 1982; MS in Reproductive Physiology, Cornell U., 1986, PhD in Reproductive Physiology, 1990. Rsch. asst. Cornell U., Ithaca, N.Y., 1983-89, lab. program coord., 1987-90, postdoctoral fellow, 1990-91, sr. rsch. assoc., dir. Embryo Engring. Program, 1992-96; assoc. prof., head Transgenic Animal Facility, Biotech Ctr./Animal Sci., U. Conn., Storrs, 1996—; adj. prof. Beijing Agrl. U., 1992—; adj. prof. Cornell U., 1996—; hon. prof. Chinese Acad. Agrl. Scis., Beijing, 1991—, Beijing Agrl. U., 1992—, Xinjiang (China) Acad. Animal Scis., 1993—; dir. China-Cornell Fellowship Programs, Ithaca, 1992-96; dir. China Bridges Internat., Storrs, 1996—; chmn. local arrangement com. Reprodn. in Farm Animals Symposium, Ithaca, 1992; mem. internat. program com. Ann. M.C. Chang Meml. Conf., 1992; cons. sci. dir. Baylor Ctr. Reproductive Health, Dallas, 1993-94; cons. Gencyme Transgenics, Inc., Framingham, Mass., 1993—, PPL Therapeutics, Blacksburg, Va.; assoc. prof. dept. animal sci. U. Conn., Storrs. Author: Biotechnology of Preimplantational Embroys, 1993; editor-in-chief Agr. Scis. Overseas, 1990-94; contbr. numerous articles to sci. jours., abstracts, tech. papers to conf. procs. Grantee CU Biotech, 1993—, EAIC Inc., 1993—, USDA, 1991-94, 92-95, 96-98, Rockefeller Found., 1991-95, 92-95, Rockefeller Found., 1991-95, 92-97, 97—, Lingnan Found., 1995-97, 97-99, Vet Sch., 1993-94, 94-96, Transpharm. Inc., 1994—, Baylor U., 1994-96, Genzyme Transgenic Corp., 1996—; fellow China State Edn. Commn., 1983-85, Cornell U. Grad. Sch., 1985; recipient 1st place award Nat. Entrance Exam. Graduate Study, Beijing Agrl. U., 1981. Mem. Internat. Embryo Transfer Soc. (edn. com. mem. 1992-94), Soc. Study of Reproduction (com. chair 1991-93), The N.Y. State Acad. of Scis., Chinese Agrl. Assn. Students and Scholars (founder, pres. 1988-89, conf. chair 1989), Am. Fertility Soc., Chinese Soc. and Tech. Assn., Sigma Xi.

YANG, YANG, research scientist; b. Kaohsiung, Taiwan, Nov. 7, 1958; came to U.S., 1985; s. Shun-Wen and Huang-Yin Yang; m. Danmei Lee, May 30, 1987. BS in Physics, Nat. Cheng Kung U., 1982; MS in Physics, U. Mass., 1988, PhD in Physics, 1992. Rsch. asst. U. Mass., Lowell, 1989-91; rsch. assoc. U. Calif., Riverside, 1991-92; rsch. scientist UNIAX Corp., Santa Barbara, Calif., 1992-96; prof. UCLA, 1997—. Contbr. articles to profl. jours. Mem. Am. Phys. Soc., Material Rsch. Soc. Office: UCLA Dept Materials Sci/Engring Los Angeles CA 90095-1595

YANG, YUEH SAM, electronics company executive; b. Taipei, Taiwan, Rep. of China, Jan. 14, 1952; s. K.L. and Y.Y. (Liu) Y.; m. Laura Hsu Yang, Aug. 5, 1978; children: Rick Yang, Stephen Yang. BS, National Tsing Hua U., 1974; MS, U. Cin., 1977; PhD, U. Tex., Austin, 1981. Prin. rsch. engr. Arco Oil & Gas Co., Plano, Tex., 1981-91; pres. Galaxy Elec. Co., Richardson, Tex., 1991—. Home: 6335 Pineview Rd Dallas TX 75248 Office: Galaxy Elec Co 201 E Arapaho Rd Richardson TX 75081-2720

YANG, ZHEN, research scientist; b. Shenyang, Liaoning, People's Republic of China, Aug. 16, 1959; came to U.S., 1992; s. Gue-Fu Yang and Jing-Ren Han; m. Su-Ling Lu, Aug. 10, 1986; 1 child, Lu-Ning. BS in Pharm. Chemistry, Shenyang Coll. Pharmacy, 1982, MS in Pharm. Chemistry, 1986; PhD in Organic Chemistry, Chinese U. of Hong Kong, 1992. Asst. engr. Pharm. Factory of Baoto, Inner Mongolia Autonomous Region, China, 1982-83; teaching asst. pharm. dept. Shenyang Coll. Pharmacy, 1986-89; rsch. asst. Chinese U. of Hong Kong, 1989, teaching asst., 1989-92; rsch. scientist Scripps Rsch. Inst., La Jolla, Calif., 1992-95; asst. prof. Scripps Rsch. Inst., La Jolla, 1995—. Contbr. articles to profl. jours. Fellow Hong Kong Jockey Club, 1989-92. Achievements include total synthesis of taxol, total synthesis of brevetoxin B, Zaragozic acid and epothilane B. Home: 3717 Nobel Dr Apt 1106 San Diego CA 92122-4533 Office: The Scripps Rsch Inst Dept Chemistry MB 10A 10666 N Torrey Pines Rd La Jolla CA 92037-1027

YANKAUER, ALFRED, physician, educator; b. N.Y.C., Oct. 12, 1913; s. Alfred Sr. and Teresa (Loewy) Y.; m. Marian Wynn, May 22, 1948; children: Kenneth and Douglas (twins). BA, Dartmouth Coll., 1934; MD, Harvard U., 1938; MPH, Columbia U., 1947. Diplomate Am. Bd. Pediatrics, Am. Bd. Preventive Medicine and Pub. Health. Health officer N.Y.C. Dept. Health, 1947-50; asst. commr. of health Rochester (N.Y.) Health Bur., 1950-52; dir. MCH Bur. N.Y. State Dept. Health, Albany, 1952-61; WHO prof. child health Madras (India) Med. Sch., 1957-59; regional advisor Pan-Am. Health Orgn./WHO, Washington, 1961-66; sr. rsch. assoc. Sch. of Pub. Health Harvard U., Boston, 1966-73; prof. family and community health and pediatrics Med. Sch. U. Mass., Worcester, 1973—; asst. prof. health Cornell U. Med. Coll., N.Y.C., 1947-50; med. dir. pediatric nurse practitioner program Mass. Gen.Hosp./Northeastern U. Coll. of Nursing, Boston, 1972-79. Editor Am. Jour. Pub. Health, 1975-90; contbr. over 200 articles to profl. jours. Mem. health adv. com. Pub. Affairs Assn., N.Y.C., 1980-88; bd. dirs. Am. Social Health Commn., Research Triangle Park, N.C., 1984-90, chmn. rsch. adv. com., 1990—. Maj., M.C., U.S. Army, 1941-45, ETO. Fellow Am. Acad. Pediatrics (Jop Lewis Smith award 1979); mem. APHA (Excellence award 1990), Mass. Pub. Health Assn. (Lemuel Shatluck award 1987). Democrat. Office: U Mass Med Ctr 55 Lake Ave N Worcester MA 01655-0002

YANKEE, MARIE, educator, publishing executive; m. J.R. Yankee, June 6, 1956; children: Michael, David, Stephen, Jennifer. Diploma Montessori edn., Montessori Inst. Am., 1968; MS, Southeastern U., Greenville, S.C., 1980, PhD, 1981. Chief exec. officer The Fernhaven Studio, Los Angeles, 1966—, Montessori Ednl. Environment, Los Angeles, 1974—, Yankee Montessori Mfg., L.A., 1980-86; pres. Internat. Montessori Inst. Tchr. Ednl. Programs, Sage, Calif., 1980—; rsch. editor Edn. Systems Pub., L.A., 1982—; dir. EEI, Inc., L.A., 1987—; cons. Calif. pub. schs., 1976; prof. Univ. Coll. Vancouver. Author: Montessori Curriculum, 1985, Reading Program, 1981, Science for Preschool, 1981, Geography for Preschool, 1982. Mem. Am. Montessori Soc., Montessori Inst. Am. Home: 38395 Trifone Rd Hemet CA 92544-9693 Office: PO Box 890944 Temecula CA 92589-0944

YANKWICH, PETER EWALD, chemistry educator; b. L.A., Oct. 20, 1923; s. Leon Rene and Helen (Werner) Y.; m. Elizabeth Pope Ingram, July 14, 1945; children: Alexandra Helen Yankwich Capps, Leon Rene II, Richard Ingram. BS, U. Calif., Berkeley, 1943, PhD, 1945. Mem. sci. staff Radiation Lab., U. Calif., Berkeley, 1944-48; faculty U. Calif., 1947-48; mem. faculty U. Ill., Urbana, 1948-88, prof. chemistry, 1957-88; head div. phys. chemistry U. Ill., Urbana, 1962-67, v.p. acad. affairs, 1977-82; Mem. Adv. Coun. on Coll. Chemistry, 1961-68; NSF Sr. Postdoctoral fellow, 1960-61, exec. officer Directorate for Sci. and Engring. Edn., 1985-90, Directorate for Edn. and Human Resources, 1990-92, sr. staff assoc., 1992—. Mem. Urbana Bd. Edn., 1958-73. Fellow AAAS, Am. Phys. Soc.; mem. Am. Chem. Soc. (chmn. phys. chemistry div. 1971-72, chem. edn. planning and coordinating com. 1974-77, chmn. edn. commn. 1977-81, bd. dirs. 1982-91), Phi Beta Kappa, Sigma Xi. Home: 4512 4th Rd N Arlington VA 22203-2343

YANNAS, IOANNIS VASSILIOS, polymer science and engineering educator; b. Athens, Apr. 14, 1935; s. Vassilios Pavlos and Thalia (Sarafoglou) Y.; m. Stamatia Frondistou (div. Oct. 1984); children: Tania, Alexis. AB, Harvard U., 1957; SM, MIT, 1959; MS, Princeton U., 1965, PhD, 1966. Asst. prof. mech. engring. MIT, Cambridge, 1966-68, duPont asst. prof., 1968-69, assoc. prof., 1969-78, prof. polymer sci. and engring. dept. mech. engring., 1978—, prof., dept. materials sci. and engring., 1983—; prof. Harvard-MIT Div. Health Scis. and Tech., Cambridge, 1978—; vis. prof. Royal Inst. Tech., Stockholm, 1974. Mem. editorial bd. Jour. Biomed. Materials Rsch., 1986—, Jour. Materials Sci. Materials Medicine, 1990—, Tissue Engineering, 1994—; contbr. over 100 tech. articles. to profl. jours.; 13 patents in field. Recipient awards for design of first successful artificial skin for treatment of massively burned patients, including Founders award Soc. for Biomaterials, 1982, Clemson award Soc. for Biomaterials, 1992, Fred O. Conley award Soc. Plastics Engrs., 1982, award in medicine and genetics Sci. Digest/Cutty Sark, 1982, Doolittle award Am. Chem. Soc., 1988; fellow Pub. Health Svc., Princeton U., 1963, Shriners Burns Inst., Mass. Gen. Hosp., Boston, 1980-81. Fellow Am. Inst. Chemists, Am. Inst. Med. and Biol. Engrs. (founding mem.), Biomaterials Sci. and Engring.; mem. Inst. Medicine of Nat. Acad. Scis. Office: MIT Bldg 3-332 77 Massachusetts Ave Cambridge MA 02139-4301

YANNI, JOHN MICHAEL, pharmacologist; b. St. Mary's, Pa., Nov. 3, 1952; s. John Paul and Regina (Emmert) Y.; m. Nancy Jane Reedy, Sept. 22, 1979; children: Susan Elizabeth, Jennifer Ruth, Steven Reedy. BS, Allegheny Coll., 1974; MS, Va. Commonwealth U., 1979, PhD, 1982. Biologist A.H. Robins Co., Richmond, Va., 1980-82, sr. rsch. biologist, 1982-86, rsch. assoc., 1986-88; group leader Eastman Kodak Co., Rochester, N.Y., 1988-90; asst. dir. Alcon Labs., Inc., Fort Worth, 1990-92, dir., 1992-93, sr. dir., 1993—. Contbr. articles to profl. jours. Alden scholar Allegheny Coll., 1974. Mem. Am. Soc. Pharmacology and Exptl. Therapeutics, N.Y. Acad. Sci., Assn. for Rsch. in Vision and Ophthalmology, Soc. for Leukocyte Biology. Achievements include patents in area of allergy; described thromboxane A2's muco-secretory effect; identified antiallergic potential of Arylalkly-heterocyclic amines; discovered potential drugs (patanol, emedine) for treatment of ocular allergy; described secretory response of human conjunctival and choridal mast cells. Office: Alcon Labs Inc 6201 South Fwy Fort Worth TX 76134-2001

YANNUZZI, WILLIAM A(NTHONY), conductor; b. Balt., July 30, 1934; s. Carmine and Maria Rosaria (Capparelli) Y. A.B. cum laude, Johns Hopkins U., 1957, M.A., 1958; M.A., St. Johns Coll., Santa Fe, 1969. Tchr. French Balt. City Coll., 1958-66; mem. faculty Peabody Conservatory, 1977—. Asst. condr., Balt. Opera Co., Inc., 1962-73; music dir., 1973—. Served with U.S. Army, 1951-54. Mem. Phi Beta Kappa. Office: Balt Opera Co Inc 1202 Maryland Ave Baltimore MD 21201-5512

YANOFF, ARTHUR SAMUEL, artist, art therapist; b. Boston, May 9, 1939; s. Jack and Sheila (Molensky) Y.; m. Carol Marie Meider (div.); 1 child, Lenya Alexis; m. Joan Elizabeth Zito, Jan. 10, 1977; 1 child, Almaisa Marishka. Student, Mus. Sch. of Fine Arts, Boston, 1958-61; studied with Jason Berger, Brookline, Mass., 1962-65. Instr. children's summer art program Temple Beth Jacob, Concord, N.H., 1969; art design cons. Lillabulero Press, Northwood Narrows, N.H., 1967-74; art therapist for emotionally disturbed children N.H. Hosp., Concord, 1967-74; designer therapeutic program for children with learning disabilities N.H. Hosp., Northwood Narrows, 1970-71; art instr. adult edn. program Coe-Brown Acad., Northwood, N.H., 1972; instr. Manchester Inst. Art, Concord, N.H., 1973-74, art therapist, 1975—. Author: The Paste-Up Autobiography: A Visual Memoir; An Approach to Psychotherapy and Remedial Teaching, 1973; del. to N.H. Bicentennial Com., 1974-75; one-man shows include Brooks Sch., N. Andover, Mass., 1966, B.E.L. Gallery, Westport, Conn., 1972, Boston Ctr. for Arts, 1974, Addison Gallery of Am. Art, Andover, Mass., 1974, New Hampton Sch., N.H., 1976, Ithaca House Gallery, N.Y., 1976, Mus. of Fine Arts, Boston, 1983, Babson Coll., Wellesley, Mass., 1983, Currier Gallery of Art, Manchester, N.H., 1985, Concordia Coll., Bronxville, N.Y., 1986, Symposium '88 Le Centre D'Art, Baie-St-Paul, Quebec, Prix, Rene Richard; exhibited in painting series including The Teaching of Isaac Luria, New Engl. Coll. Gallery, Henniker, N.H., 1995, Yeshiva U. Mus., N.Y.C., 1996-97; represented in pub. collections including Mus. of Fine Arts, Boston, Addison Gallery of Am. Art, Andover, Mass., New Hampton Sch., N.H., N.H. Commn. on Arts, Concord, N.H. Savs. Bank, Concord, Hampshire Coll., Amherst, Mass., Babson Coll., Wellesley, Mass., MFA/Hines Indsl. Found., Cambridge, Mass., Rose Art Mus., Brandeis U., Waltham, Mass., Currier Gallery of Art, Manchester, Le Centre D'Art, Baie-St-Paul, Quebec, Chabad House Lubavitch of N.H., Manchester, Detroit Inst. Arts, Mus. Art, Ft. Lauderdale, Fla., Concordia Coll. Gallery, Bronxville, N.Y., Temple Beth Shalom, Santa Fe; exhibited in numerous shows in Mass., Va., N.H., Maine, Sante Fe, L.A. Meml. Found. Jewish Culture fellow, N.Y.C., 1989-90; recipient grant Max and Anna Levinson Found. and Ctr. for Jewish Culture and Creativity, 1996. Mem. Boston Painters and Sculptors, Am. Art Therapy Assn., N.H. Art Assn., Livestock Guard Dog Assn. Hampshire Coll., Am. Southdown Breeders Assn., N.H. Sheep and Wool Growers Assn., Greater Boston Kerry Blue Terrier Club (participant sheep guarding project). Jewish. Avocations: study and evaluate terriers and other dogs for predator control and livestock protection. Home: PO Box 233 50 Lenox Rd West Stockbridge MA 01266 Office: 6 Melrose St Boston MA 02116-5510

YANOFF, MYRON, ophthalmologist; b. Phila., Dec. 21, 1936; s. Jacob and Lillian S. (Fishman) Y.; m. Karin Michelle Lindblad, Aug. 8, 1980; 1 dau., Alexis A.; children by previous marriage: Steven L., David A., Joanne M. A.B., U. Pa., 1957; M.D., 1961. Prof. ophthalmology and pathology U. Pa. Med. Sch., Phila.; William F. Norris and George E. de Schweinitz prof. ophthalmology, chmn. dept., dir. Scheie Eye Inst., 1977-86; chmn., prof. ophthalmology Allegheny U. of the Health Scis., Phila., 1988—; 1st exchange vis. prof. U. Vienna, 1992. Author: Ocular Pathology, Textbook of Ophthalmology; contbr. articles to profl. jours. Served to maj. M.C. USAR. Recipient Humboldt award, 1988. Mem. Am. Ophthalmic Soc., Verhoeff Soc., Am. Acad. Ophthalmology (Sr. Honor award 1995). Office: Allegheny Univ Dept Ophthalmology Broad & Race Sts Philadelphia PA 19102

YANOFSKY, CHARLES, biology educator; b. N.Y.C., Apr. 17, 1925; s. Frank and Jennie (Kopatz) Y.; m. Carol Cohen, June 19, 1949, (dec. Dec. 1990); children: Stephen David, Robert Howard, Martin Fred; m. Edna Crawford, Jan. 4, 1992. BS, CCNY, 1948; MS, Yale U., 1950, PhD, 1951, DSc (hon.), 1981; DSc (hon.), U. Chgo., 1980. Rsch. asst. Yale U., 1951-54; asst. prof. microbiology Western Res. U. Med. Sch., 1954-57; mem. faculty Stanford U., 1958—, prof. biology, 1961—, Herzstein prof. biology, 1966—. career investigator Am. Heart Assn., 1969-95. Served with AUS, 1944-46. Recipient Lederle Med. Faculty award, 1957; Eli Lilly award bacteriology, 1959; U.S. Steel Co. award molecular biology, 1964; Howard Taylor Ricketts award U. Chgo., 1966; Albert and Mary Lasker award, 1971; Townsend Harris medal Coll. City N.Y., 1973; Louisa Gross Horwitz prize in biology and biochemistry Columbia U., 1976; V.D. Mattia award Roche Inst., 1982; medal Genetics Soc. Am., 1983; Internat. award Gairdner Found., 1985; named Passano Laureate Passano Found., 1992. Mem. NAS (Selman A. Waksman award in microbiology 1972), Am. Acad. Arts and Scis., Genetics Soc. Am. (pres. 1969, Thomas Hunt Morgan medal 1990), Am. Soc. Biol. Chemists (pres. 1984), Royal Soc. (fgn. mem.), Japanese Biochem. Soc. (hon.). Home: 725 Mayfield Ave Stanford CA 94305-1016 Office: Stanford U Dept Of Biological Sci Stanford CA 94305

YAO, ANDY SHUNCHI, computer science educator; b. Toufen, Taiwan, Republic of China, Mar. 24, 1956; s. Weilu and Tinmay (Huang) Y.; m. Feng-Yi Chen Apr. 4, 1997; children: Wesley R., Addison R. AA in Elec. Engring., Ming Hsin Engring. Coll., Taiwan, Rebublic of China; BS in Computer Sci., Old Dominion U., MS in Computer Sci.; PhD in Computer Sci., Kennedy Western U. Sr. sys. analyst IMS, Rockville, Md., 1984-91; assoc. prof. U. Md., College Park, 1990—; prof. Montgomery Coll., Rockville, 1985—. Avocations: singing, writing. Home: 11619 Paramus Dr North Potomac MD 20878 Office: Montgomery Coll 51 Mannakee St Rockville MD 20850-1101

YAO, DAVID DA-WEI, engineering educator; b. Shanghai, China, July 14, 1950; came to U.S., 1983, naturalized, 1990; s. William Kang-Fu and Nancy Yun-Lan (Lu) Y.; m. Helen Zhi-Heng Chen, Jan. 31, 1979; children: Henry, John. MASc, U. Toronto, Ont., Can., 1981, PhD, 1983. Assoc. prof. systems engring. Harvard U., Cambridge, Mass., 1986-88; asst. prof. indsl. engring. and ops. rsch. Columbia U., N.Y.C., 1983-86, prof., 1988—, Thomas Alva Edison prof., 1992—; acad. visitor AT&T Bell Labs., Holmdel, N.J., 1989, T.J. Watson Rsch. Ctr., IBM, Yorktown, N.Y., 1990—. Co-author: Monotone Structure in Discrete-Event Systems, 1994; editor: Stochastic Modeling and Analysis of Manufacturing Systems, 1994; contbr. more than 100 articles to sci. jours. including Maths. Ops. Rsch., Jour. of Assn. Computing Machinery, Advances in Applied Probability, 1983—. Recipient Presdl. Young Investigator award NSF, Washington, 1987-92, Guggenheim fellow John Simon Guggenheim Meml. Found., N.Y.C., 1991-92. Mem. IEEE, Soc. Indsl. and Applied Math., Ops. Rsch. Soc. Am. (George Nicholson prize 1983). Achievements include development of theory of algebraic structures in discrete-event systems, theory of stochastic convexity and its applications in queuing networks, stochastic network models for computer integrated manufacturing systems, methodologies in the optimization and control of stochastic discrete-event systems. Home: 1261 Underhill Ave Yorktown Heights NY 10598-5718 Office: Columbia U EOR 302 Mudd Bldg New York NY 10027-6699

YAO, HILDA MARIA HSIANG, banker, strategic planner; b. Honolulu, Sept. 11, 1956; d. Hsin-Nung and Dorothy Wen (Wu) Y. BA cum laude, U. Pacific, 1975; MA, U. Wis., 1976. Ops. analyst Visa Internat., San Mateo, Calif., 1977-80; sr. product mgr. Bank of Am., San Francisco, 1980-81, asst. v.p., strategic planner Calif. electronic banking div., 1981-84, v.p., div. strategic planner U.S. wholesale svcs. world banking div., 1984-85, v.p., head dealer corp. svcs., 1985-89, v.p., dir. retail banking adminstrn., 1989-90, v.p., CFO internat. pvt. banking divsn., 1990-92, v.p., dir., deputy mgr. internat. investment svcs., 1992-93, v.p., head fiduciary policy, 1993-95, sr. v.p., dir. pvt. banking, trust and investment mgmt., 1995—. Bd. regents U. Pacific, Stockton, Calif., 1984-85, 91—; treas. pres.'s jr. adv. coun. Bank of Am., 1982-83; active exec. com. Campaign for Wis., 1991—; bd. dirs. U. Wis. Found., 1995—; bd. visitors Coll. of Letters and Sci. U. Wis., Madison, 1995—; mem. adv. bd. program in medicine and philosophy Calif. Pacific Med. Ctr., San Francisco, 1993—; mem. Pacific Coun. on Internat. Policy, 1996—; mem. China study group Pacific Coun. on Internat. Policy and Rand Corp., 1996—; hon. avisor China Soc. for People's Friendship Studies, 1992—. U. Wis. fellow, 1975-76, alumni fellow U. Pacific, 1983, Outstanding Young Alumna award U. Pacific, 1989. Mem. Nat. Vehicle Leasing Assn. (treas. 1988-89), World Affairs Counc., Calif. Acad. Scis., Commonwealth Club Calif., Bank Am. Club, Bankers Club San Francisco, World Trade Club, Univ. Club, The Mus. Soc., Calif. Legion of Honor, Bascom Hill Soc. U. Wis., President's Circle U. Pacific, Nat. Soc. Hist. Preservation, 1841 Club-Punahou Sch., Odyssey Club. Avocations: Shakespeare, opera, languages, swimming, golf. Home: Gramercy Towers 1177 California St San Francisco CA 94108-2212 Office: Bank of Am 50 California St Ste 1300 San Francisco CA 94111

YAO, JAMES TSU-PING, civil engineer; b. Shanghai, China, July 7, 1933; came to U.S. 1953; s. C.C. and Mae Jane (Wang) Y.; m. Anna Lee, June 14, 1958; children: Tina Lee, Timothy H.J., Shana Lynn. BSCE, U. Ill., 1957, MSCE, 1958, PhD, 1961. Registered profl. engr. Tex., N.Mex. Postdoctoral preceptor Columbia U., N.Y.C., 1964-65; asst. prof. civil engring. U. N.Mex., Albuquerque, 1961-64, assoc. prof., 1965-69, prof., 1969-71; prof. Purdue U., W. Lafayette, Ind., 1971-88, asst. head dept. civil engring., 1983-88, asst. dean grad. sch., 1984-87; prof. Tex. A&M U., College Station, 1988—, head dept. civil engring., 1988-93, Carolyn S. and Tommie E. Lohman prof. engring. edn., 1996—. Editor Jour. Structural Engring., 1990-92. Recipient Max Planck Rsch. award Alexander Von Humboldt Found., 1990, Civil Engring. Disting. Alumnus award, U. Ill., Urbana, 1991, Centennial medallion Am. Soc. Engring. Edn., 1993. Fellow ASCE (State-of-the-Art of Civil Engring. award 1973, 83, Alfred M. Freudenthal medal 1990, Richard R. Torrens award 1992, Pres.'s medal 1995). Avocations: volleyball, paperfolding. Office: Tex A&M Univ Dept Civil Engring College Station TX 77843-3136

YAO, TITO GO, physician; b. Manila, May 30, 1943; came to U.S., 1970, naturalized, 1984; s. Vicente and Sin Keng (Go) Y.; M.D., Far Eastern U., Manila, 1969; m. Lilia Ytem, July 3, 1976; children—Robert James, Richard. Diplomate Am. Bd. Pediatrics, Am. Bd. Quality Assurance. Intern, Evang. Deaconess Hosp., Milw., 1970-71; resident in pediatrics T.C. Thompson Children's Hosp., Chattanooga, 1971-72, Methodist Hosp., Bklyn., 1972-73; fellow St. Christopher Hosp. Children, Phila., 1973-74, Cook County Children's Hosp., Chgo., 1974-75; dir. GSK Med. Center, Chgo., 1976—, chmn. Loretto Hosp. dept. pediatrics, 1988—; dir. RJ Med. Center, Chgo., 1980—; mem. staff Norwegian Am. Hosp., Loretto Hosp., St. Anthony's Hosp. Fellow Am. Acad. Pediatrics, Am. Coll. Utilization Rev. Physicians; mem.

AMA (Physician Recognition award 1973—), Assn. Philippine Physicians Practicing in Am., Ill. Med. Assn., Am. Assn. Individual Investors, Chgo. Med. Soc., Chgo. Pediatric Soc. Office: 5351 W North Ave Chicago IL 60639-4350 also: 5140 W Chicago Ave Chicago IL 60651-2903

YAPLE, HENRY MACK, library director; b. Vicksburg, Mich., May 30, 1940; s. Henry J. and Pauline B. (Spencer) Y.; m. Marilyn Lou Bales, Dec. 31, 1971; children: Sean H., Kendra S. BA in English with hons., Kalamazoo Coll., 1963; MA, U. Idaho, 1966; postgrad., U. d'Aix-Marseille, France, 1965-66, U. Toronto, 1966-69; MLS, W. Mich. U., 1972. Order libr. Mich. State U., E. Lansing, 1972-74, humanities bibliographer, 1974-78; acquisitions libr. U. Wyo., Laramie, 1978-87; libr. dir. Whitman Coll., Walla Walla, Wash., 1987—; Mem. Wyo. Coun. for the Humanities, 1982-86. U. Toronto scholar, 1966-69; Rotary fellow, 1965, 66; U. Wyo. rsch. grantee, 1982, 86. Mem. ALA, Wyo. Libr. Assn. (pres. 1984-85), Nat. Ski Patrol System (sr. patroller 1978-95, nat. #6946 1988), Wash. Libr. Assn., Northwest Assn. of Pvt. Colls. and U. Librs. (pres. 1987-88, 94-95), Rotary (Walla Walla), Beta Phi Mu. Avocations: book collecting, skiing, kayaking. Home: 1889 Fern St Walla Walla WA 99362-9393 Office: Whitman Coll Office Libr 345 Boyer Ave Walla Walla WA 99362-2067

YARAR, BAKI, metallurgical engineering educator; b. Adana, Turkey, Feb. 28, 1941; came to U.S., 1980; s. Salih and Sidika Yarar; m. Ruth G. Yarar; children: Deniz, Defne. BSc in Chemistry, Mid. East Tech. U., Ankara, Turkey, 1965, MSc in Chemistry, 1966; PhD in Surface Chemistry, U. London, 1969; DIC in Mineral Tech., Imperial Coll. London, 1969. Instr. Mid. East Tech. U., 1970-71, asst. prof., 1971-76, assoc. prof., 1976-79; vis. prof. U. B.C., Vancouver, Can., 1979-80; assoc. prof. Colo. Sch. of Mines, Golden, 1980-86, prof., 1986—; pvt. practice cons. in mineral processing, worldwide, 1980—. Author chpts. to books, over 120 papers; editor books; mem. editl. bd. 4 jours. Lt. Turkish Army, 1970-71. Holder numerous awards and certificates of recognition. Mem. Soc. Mining Engrs. (chmn. fundamental com. 1989), Am. Chem. Soc., Materials Rsch. Soc., Sigma Xi (life, pres. CSM chpt.). Achievements include pioneering work in selective flocculation; invention of the gamma floation process; patent for superconductivity meter device. Home: 13260 Braun Rd Golden CO 80401-1643 Office: Colo Sch Mines Dept Metal Engring Golden CO 80401

YARBOROUGH, WILLIAM CALEB, former professional stock car race driver; b. Timmonsville, S.C., Mar. 27, 1939. Named Grand Nat. Champion Nat. Assn. Stock Car Auto Racing, 1976. Winner Atlanta 500, 1967, 68, 74, Cam 2 Motor Oil 400, 1977, Capital City 400, 1976, Carolina 500, 1975, Daytona 500, 1968, 77, 83, 84, Mason-Dixon 500, 1969, Nat. 500, 1973, So. 500, 1968, 73, 74, 78, Va. 500, 1974, 77, Wilkes 400, 1974, Winston Western 500, 1974; champion Winston Cup, 1976-78, many others. Office: care Nat Assn Stock Car Auto Racing 1801 Volusia Ave Daytona Beach FL 32114-1215 Address: Cale Auto Sports 9617 Dicksie Rd Charlotte NC 28208*

YARBOROUGH, WILLIAM GLENN, JR., military officer, forest farmer, defense, aerospace and international business executive; b. Rock Hill, S.C., June 21, 1940; s. William Glenn and Bessie (Rainsford) Y.; m. Betsy Gibson, Jan. 24, 1969; children: Bill, Clinton, Frank, Elizabeth. BS, U. S.C., 1961, MBA, 1969; postgrad. Command and Gen. Staff Coll., 1970, Naval War Coll., 1979, Colgate-Darden Grad. Bus. Sch., U. Va., 1983. Commd. to U.S. Army, advanced through grades to col., 1980; co. and troop comdr. and squadron staff officer, Vietnam, Europe, 1961-71, strategist, Washington, 1971-73, chief of assignments, Office Personnel Mgmt., Mil. Personnel Ctr., Washington, 1973-76; comdr. 1st Squadron, 1st Cavalry, Europe, 1976-78; chief of staff and spl. asst. to chief of staff 1st Armored Div., Europe, 1978; br. chief Office of Chief of Staff, Washington, 1979-80; exec. to dep. commanding gen. Material Devel. and Readiness Command, Washington, 1980-81; mil. dep. for asst. sec. for research, devel. and acquisition, Washington, 1981-85; army mktg. dir. Grumman Corp., Bethpage, N.Y., 1990-93; corp. v.p. Allied Rsch. Corp., Vienna, Va., 1993—; bd. dirs. Carleton Techs. Decorated Silver Star, Bronze Star medal with 4 oak leaf clusters and V device, Purple Heart. Mem. Assn. U.S. Army (George Washington chpt., v.p. membership), Am. Legion, Armed Forces Communications and Electronics Assn., U.S. Army Armor Assn., SAR, Am. Def. Preparedness Assn. (bd. dirs. N.Y. chpt.), Nat. Guard Assn., Res. Officer Assn., Purple Heart VFW Soc., Army-Navy Club, Army Navy Country Club, Belle-Meade Country Club, Tower Club. Home: PO Box 115 Thomson GA 30824-0115 also: 1453 Wrightsboro Rd Thomson GA 30824-7347 also: 604 Pompano Rd Edisto Island SC 29438-3119 Office: Allied Rsch Corp 8000 Towers Crescent Dr Ste 750 Vienna VA 22182-2700

YARBOROUGH, WILLIAM PELHAM, writer, lecturer, retired army officer, consultant; b. Seattle, May 12, 1912; s. Leroy W. and Addessia (Hooker) Y.; m. Norma Mae Tuttle, Dec. 26, 1936; children: Norma Kay (dec.), William Lee, Patricia Mae. BS, U.S. Mil. Acad., 1936; grad., Command and Gen. Staff Coll., 1944, Brit. Staff Coll., 1950, Army War Coll., 1953. Commd. 2nd lt. U.S. Army, 1936, advanced through grades to lt. gen., 1968, ret., 1971; various assignments U.S. Army, U.S., Philippines and ETO, 1936-42; exec. officer Paratroop Task Force, North Africa, 1942; comdr. 2d Bn., 504th Par. Inf. Regt., 82d Airborne Div., Sicily invasion, 1943, 509th Parachute Inf., Italy and France, 1943-44; comdg. officer 473 Inf., Italy, 1945; provost marshal 15th Army Group, ETO, 1945, Vienna Area Command and U.S. Forces, Austria, 1945-47; mem. staff, faculty U.S. Army Info. Sch., 1948-49; operations officer, gen. staff Joint Mil. Assistance Adv. Group, London, Eng., 1951-52; mem. faculty Army War Coll., 1953-56, 57; dep. chief Mil. Assistance and Adv. Group, Cambodia, 1956-57; comdg. officer 66th CIC Group, Stuttgart, Germany, 1958-60, 66th M.I. Group, Stuttgart, 1960; comdg. gen. U.S.A. Spl. Warfare Ctr.; also comdt. U.S. Army Spl. Warfare Sch., Ft. Bragg, 1961-65; sr. mem. UN Command Mil. Armistice Commn., Korea, 1965; asst. dep. chief staff DCSOPS for spl. operations Dept. Army, Washington; chmn. U.S. delegation Inter-Am. Def. Bd., Joint Brazil U.S. Def. Commn., Joint Mexican-U.S. Def. Commn.; Army mem. U.S. sect. permanent Joint Bd. on Def., Can.-U.S. Def. Commn., Washington, 1965; asst. chief of staff intelligence Dept. Army Washington, 1966-68; comdg. gen. I Corps Group, Korea, 1968-69; chief staff, also dep. comdr.-in-chief U.S. Army, Pacific, Hawaii, 1969-71. Contbr. Internat. Mil. and Def. Ency., 1993, MacMillan Ency. of the Am. Mil., 1994; William P. Yarborough collection papers and artifacts donated to Mugar Meml. Librs., Boston U. Decorated Disting. Svc. medal with three oak leaf clusters, Silver Star, Legion of Merit with three oak leaf clusters, Bronze Star, Joint Svc. Commendation medal with oak leaf clusters, Croix de Guerre with Palm (France), Cross for Valor and Diploma (Italy), Order of Merit Second Class (Korea), Order of Ulchi (Korea). Fellow Co. Mil. Historians, Explorers Club; mem. Kiwanis Club. Home: 160 Hillside Rd Southern Pines NC 28387-6727

YARBRO, ALAN DAVID, lawyer; b. Huntington, W.Va., Sept. 16, 1941; s. John David and Bernice (Bulette) Y.; m. Lee Merryman Myers, July 1961; children: Wendy, Jennifer, Caroline. AB magna cum laude, Harvard U., 1962, LLB cum laude, 1966. Bar: Md. 1966, U.S. Ct. Appeals (4th cir.) 1966, U.S. Dist. Ct. Md. 1966. Assoc. Venable Baetjer & Howard, Balt., 1966-72, ptnr., 1973-96; gen. counsel Mercantile Bankshares Corp., 1996—. Trustee Children's Hosp., Balt., 1986—, pres. W.S. Baer Corp., 1990—; bd. dirs. The Park Heights St. Acad., Balt., 1986-89. Fellow Am. Bar Found., Md. Bar Found.; mem. ABA, Md. Bar Assn., Bar Assn. of Balt. (chmn. ethics com. 1988-89).

YARBRO, BILLY RAY, elementary school educator, basketball coach; b. Linden, Tenn., Mar. 22, 1957; s. Nashel and Melvina (Vaughn) Y.; m. Diane Wynn, Feb. 2, 1982 (div. June 1990); children: Crystal, Lindsey; 1 stepchild, Lisa Wynn; m. Darlene Johnson, May 26, 1993; 1 stepchild, Crystal Brooks. BS, Freed Hardeman U., 1979; MA, Austin Peay U., 1988. Cert. tchr., Tenn. Tchr. Pope Elem. Sch., Linden, 1980-83, prin., 1983-87; asst. prin. Linden Elem. Sch., 1987-89, phys. edn. tchr., 1989-90, math. tchr., basketball coach, 1990—. Mem. Perry County Edn. Assn. (pres. 1990-92). Mem. Ch. of Christ. Avocations: playing and umpiring baseball, softball and basketball. Home: PO Box 359 Linden TN 37096-0359 Office: Linden Elem College St Linden TN 37096

YARBRO, JAMES WESLEY, financial executive; b. Woodbury, Tex., Mar. 30, 1920; s. Daniel Fore and Annie Belle (Hunt) Y.; m. Mary Elise Alderdice, Aug. 17, 1944; children: Suzanne Elise, James Wesley Jr., Rosemary. BS, North Tex. State Coll., 1940. CPA, Tex. Instr. high sch. Crane, Tex., 1940-42; aviator USN, South Pacific Theater, 1942-45; internal revenue agt. U.S. Treasury Dept., Ft. Worth, 1946-51; asst. sec.-treas., tax mgr. So. Prodn. Co., Ft. Worth, 1951-57; with Tex. Pacific Coal & Oil Co., Ft. Worth, 1957-63, fin. v.p., bd. dirs., 1959-63; fin. v.p. King Resources Co., Denver, 1963-66; fin. v.p., sec.-treas. Western Co. N.Am., Ft. Worth, 1967-69; pvt. practice fin. svc. Ft. Worth, 1969-88; ret., 1988. Lt. USNR, 1942-45. Mem. AICPAs, Tex. Soc. CPAs, Ind. Petroleum Assn. Am., Petroleum Club Ft. Worth, Rotary. Christian Ch. Home: 1417 Westover Ln Fort Worth TX 76107-3547

YARBROUGH, MARTHA CORNELIA, music educator; b. Waycross, Ga., Feb. 8, 1940; d. Henry Elliott and Jessie (Sirmans) Y.; B.M.E., Stetson U., 1962; M.M.E., Fla. State U., 1968, Ph.D., 1973. Choral dir. Ware County High Sch., Waycross, Ga., 1962-64, Glynn Acad., Brunswick, Ga., 1964-70; asst. choral dir. Fla. State U., 1970-72; cons. in music Muscogee County Sch. Dist., Columbus, Ga., 1972-73; cons. in tchr. edn. Psycho-Edno. Cons., Inc., Tallahassee, 1972-73; asst. prof. music edn., dir. univs. choruses and oratorio soc. Syracuse U., 1973-76, assoc. prof. music edn., 1976-83, prof., 1983-86, acting asst. dean Coll. Visual and Performing Arts, 1980-82, acting dir. Sch. Music, 1980-82, chmn. music edn., 1982-86; prof. music La. State U., Baton Rouge, 1986—, coordinator music, edn., 1986—, Haymon prof. of Music, 1995—; artist in residence Sch. Music U. Ala., Tuscaloosa, 1989-90. Chair exec. com. Music Edn. Rsch. Coun., 1992-94. Mem. Music Educators Nat. Conf. (sr. rschr. award, 1996), N.Y. State Sch. Music Assn., Am. Ednl. Research Assn., Soc. Research Music Edn. (mem. exec. com. 1988-90, program chair 1990-92, chair, 1992-94), AAUP, Pi Kappa Lambda, Phi Beta, Kappa Delta Pi. Co-author: Competency-Based Music Education, 1980; mem. editorial com. Jour. Research in Music Edn.; contbr. articles to profl. jours., chpts. in books. Office: Sch Music La State U Baton Rouge LA 70803

YARD, RIX NELSON, former athletic director; b. Ocean County, N.J., July 1, 1917; s. George Rix and Lena (Nelson) Y.; m. Adra Gehrett, Sept. 12, 1941; children: Rix Nelson, Constance. BS, U. Pa., 1941, MS, 1947, EdD, 1956. Tchr. Swissvale (Pa.) High Sch., 1946; instr., asst. football coach, head basketball coach Denison U., 1947-49, chmn. dept. phys. edn., dir. athletics, lacrosse coach, 1953-63; asst. football coach U. Pa., 1949-53; dir. athletics Tulane U., 1963-76, prof. phys. edn., 1968-82, prof. emeritus, 1982—, dir. club and intramural sports, 1976-82, also adminstr. phys. edn. major program. Pres. New Orleans Football Hall of Fame, 1965-76; Vice pres. Granville (Ohio) Bd. Edn., 1961-63; asst. fire chief Granville Vol. Fire Co., 1958-63; mem. Granville Zoning Com., 1961; Bd. dirs. New Orleans chpt. A.R.C. Served with USNR, 1941-46; ret. capt. Res. Named Nat. Lacrosse Coach of Yr., 1963; named to Sports Hall of Fame Denison U., 1983, Ohio Lacross Hall of Fame, 1995. Mem. Nat. Collegiate Athletic Assn. (chmn. TV com. 1958, 60, rep. to Sugar Bowl 1964-78, chmn. ins. com. 1971-76, chmn. acad. and testing requirements com.), Nat. Assn. Coll. Dirs. Athletics (exec. com.); (named to Hall of Fame 1977); Mem. Navy League (dir. New Orleans chpt.). Club: New Orleans Quarterback (dir. 1967-78). Home: 6 Roberts Landing Dr Poquoson VA 23662-1026

YARDE, RICHARD FOSTER, art educator; b. Boston, Oct. 29, 1939; s. Edgar St. Clair and Enid (Foster) Y.; m. Susan Donovan, July 8, 1967; children: Marcus, Owen. BFA in Painting cum laude, Boston U., 1962, MFA, 1964. Asst. prof. art Boston U., 1965-71; assoc. prof. art Wellesley Coll., 1971-76; vis. assoc. prof. Amherst Coll., 1976-77, Mt. Holyoke Coll., 1980-81; vis. artist Mass. Coll. Art, 1977-91; prof. art U. Mass., Boston, 1981-90, Amherst, 1990—; visual arts panelist Mass. Coun. Art and Humanities, 1976-78; bd. overseers Inst. Contemporary Art, Boston, 1991—. Exhibited in one-man shows Studio Mus. in Harlem, San Diego Mus., Balt. Mus., Smith Coll. Mus. Art, Northampton, Mass., 1997; exhibited in group shows Newport (R.I.) Art Mus., NAD, Mass. Cultural Coun. Recipient Alumni award for disting. contbn. to arts Boston U., 1987, Chancellor's award for disting. scholarship U. Mass., Boston, 1984, Acad. award in art Am. Acad. Arts and Letters, 1995, Disting. Tchg. award U. Mass. Amherst, 1997; Nat. Endowment for Arts fellow, 1976, other awards. Office: U Mass Amherst care Arts Dept Fine Arts Ctr Amherst MA 01003

YARDIS, PAMELA HINTZ, computer consulting company executive; b. N.Y.C., Sept. 23, 1944; d. Edward F. and Isabella (Sawers) Hintz; m. J.A. Yardis, Apr. 2, 1966 (div. July 1980); children: Bradley, Brent, Tricia, Todd, Ryan, Kara, Melissa. BA, Bethany Coll., 1966; MA, Columbia U., 1983, MEd, 1983. Cert. mgmt. cons. Tchr. Yonkers (N.Y.) Pub. Schs., 1966-68; cons. PHY, Inc., Stamford, Conn., 1978-83; account exec. Mgmt. Systems, Stamford, 1982-84; sr. account exec., cons. Mgmt. Dynamics, Yonkers, 1984-86; v.p. GMW Assn., Inc., N.Y.C., 1986-87; pres. Chestnut Hill Cons. Group, Inc., Stamford, 1987—. Chmn. Mayor's Commn. Prevention Youth Drug and Alcohol Abuse, Stamford, 1986-91; mem. Dem. Cen. Com., Stamford, 1984—; bd. dirs., pres. Alcohol and Drug Coun., Inc., Conn. Communities for Drug Free Youth, Childcare, Inc., Youth Shelter. Recipient Gov.'s Cmty. Svc. award, 1988, Golden Rule award J.C. Penney, Bravo award YWCA, 1992, Women of Enterprise award SBA & Avon, Inc., 1993, Sacian award S.W. Area Commerce and Bus., 1994. Mem. Women in Mgmt. (v.p. 1986-88, Ann. Recognition award), Data Processing Mgmt. Assn., Advt. Rsch. Found., Inst. Mgmt. Cons. (pres. Fairfield Westchester chpt. 1990-93, chmn. 1993-94, fellow 1995, nat. bd. dirs., chmn. 1993-95), Sales and Mktg. Execs. (bd. dirs.). Presbyterian. Avocations: travel, camping, politics. Home: 125 Chestnut Hill Rd Stamford CT 06903-4029 Office: Chestnut Hill Cons Group PO Box 15755 Stamford CT 06901-0755

YARDLEY, JOHN FINLEY, aerospace engineer; b. St. Louis, Feb. 1, 1925; s. Finley Abna and Johnnie (Patterson) Y.; m. Phyllis Steele, July 25, 1946; children: Kathryn, Robert, Mary, Elizabeth, Susan. B.S., Iowa State Coll., 1944; M.S., Washington U., St. Louis, 1950. Structural and aero. engr. McDonnell Aircraft Corp., St. Louis, 1946-55, chief strength engr., 1956-57; project engr. Mercury spacecraft design, 1958-60; launch ops. mgr. Mercury and Gemini spacecraft, Cape Canaveral, Fla., 1960-64; Gemini tech. dir. Mercury and Gemini spacecraft, 1964-67; v.p., dep. gen. mgr. Eastern div. McDonnell Douglas Astronautics, 1968-72, v.p., gen. mgr., 1973-74, pres., 1981-88, sr. corp. v.p., 1989, ret.; assoc. adminstr. for manned space flight NASA, Washington, 1974-81. Served to ensign USNR, 1943-46. Recipient Achievement award St. Louis sect. Inst. Aerospace Scis., 1961, John J. Montgomery award, 1963, Pub. Service award NASA, 1963, 66 ; profl. achievement citation Iowa State Coll., 1970, Spirit of St. Louis medal, 1973, Alumni citation Washington U., 1975, Disting. Achievement citation Iowa State U., 1976, Presdl. citation as meritorious exec. Sr. Exec. Service, 1980, NASA Disting. Service medal, 1981, Goddard Meml. trophy, 1983, Achievement award Washington U. Engring. Alumni, 1983, Elmer A. Sperry award, 1986; named Engr. of Yr. NASA, 1982; Von Karman Astronautics Lectureship award, 1988. Fellow AIAA (Goddard award 1982), Am. Astronautical Soc. (Space Flight award 1978); mem. Internat. Acad. Astronautics, NASA Alumni League (bd. dirs.), Nat. Acad. Engring., Nat. Space Club (bd. govs.), Tau Beta Pi, Phi Kappa Phi, Phi Eta Sigma, Phi Mu Epsilon. Presbyterian. Home: 14319 Cross Timbers Ct Chesterfield MO 63017-5718

YARDLEY, JONATHAN, journalist, columnist; b. Pitts., Oct. 27, 1939; s. William Woolsey and Helen (Gregory) Y.; m. Rosemary Roberts, June 14, 1961 (div. 1975); children: James Barrett, William W. II.; m. Susan L. Hartt, Mar. 23, 1975. AB, U. N.C., Chapel Hill, 1961; DHL (hon.), George Washington U., 1987. Writer N.Y. Times, 1961-64; editorial writer, book editor Greensboro (N.C.) Daily News, 1964-74; book editor Miami (Fla.) Herald, 1974-78, Washington Star, 1978-81; book critic, columnist Washington Post, 1981—. Author: Ring: A Biography of Ring Lardner, 1977, Our Kind of People: The Story of an American Family, 1989, Out of Step: Notes from a Purple Decade, 1991, States of Mind: A Personal Journey Through the Mid-Atlantic, 1993, Misfit: The Strange Life of Frederick Exley, 1997; editor: My Life as Author and Editor (H.L. Mencken), 1993, Selected Stories (Ring Lardner), 1997. Recipient Pulitzer prize for criticism, 1981, Disting. Alumnus award U. N.C., 1989; Nieman fellow in journalism Harvard U., 1968-69. Episcopalian. Home: 223 Hawthorne Rd Baltimore MD 21210-2503 Office: Washington Post 1150 15th St NW Washington DC 20071-0001

YARED, GABRIEL, composer; b. Lebanon, 1949. Composer, orchestrator, 1973—. Composer for Johnny Hallyday, Charles Aznavour, Gilbert Becaud, Mireille Mathieu, Sylvie Vartan, Tania Maria, Francoise Hardy, (filmography) Sauve Qui Peut La Vie, 1979, Nemo, 1984, Beyond Therapy, 1987, Agent Trouble, 1987, Clean and Sober, 1988, Tennessee Nights, 1989, Romero, 1989, Vincent and Theo, 1990, Map of the Human Heart, 1992, Marmottes Les, 1993, Wings of Courage, 1995, English Patient, 1996 (Golden Globe award 1996, AA nomination 1996). Office: Gorfaine-Schwartz 3301 Barham Blvd Ste 201 Los Angeles CA 90068*

YARED, LINDA S., mechanical engineer; b. East Grand Rapids, Mich., July 31, 1952; d. Fozee S. and Penny (Bassler) Y. BS in Mech. Engring., U. Md., 1987. Sr. tech. rep. Xerox Corp., Rosslyn, Va., 1979-84; sr. engr. Mack Trucks, Allentown, Pa., 1987-90, Allied Signal Braking Systems, South Bend, Ind., 1990-95; project engr. Tri/Mark Corp., New Hampton, Iowa, 1995—. Patentee in field. Mem. ASME, NOW (treas. 1994), Soc. Automotive Engrs. (sec. 1988-90), Soc. Women Engrs. Avocation: dog obedience training. Office: Tri/Mark Corp Indsl Park New Hampton IA 50659

YARGER, SAM JACOB, dean, educator; b. Pontiac, Mich., Oct. 8, 1937; s. Ralph And Eva L. (Little) Y.; m. Gwen Polk (div. 1982); 1 child, Mark Alan; m. Sally K. Mertens. BS in Elem. Edn., Eastern Mich. U., 1959; MA in Sch. Psychology, U. Mich., 1962; PhD in Ednl. Psychology, Wayne State U., 1968. Asst. prof. Oakland (Mich.) Community Coll., 1967-68, U. Toldeo, 1968-71; assoc. prof. Syracuse (N.Y.) U., 1971-77, prof., 1977-84, assoc. dean, 1980-84; dean, prof. U. Wis., Milw., 1984-92, U. Miami, Fla., 1992—; rschr. Assessment Pre-Vocat. Skills Mentally Retarded Youth, 1964-65, Tchr. Attitude Change in REls. to Program Input, 1968, Leader Behavior in a Task Oriented Setting in Relation to Group Activity, 1968, Attitudes Inner-City Residents Toward Ednl. Programs and Tchrs., 1970, Dimensions Tchr. Ctr. Movement in Am. Edn., 1972-75, Dimensions Field Derived Content in Tchr. Edn. Programs, 1973-75, Nat. Study Inservice Edn., 1976-77, Nat. Study Preservice Edn., 1976-77, Nat. Study Preservice Edn., 1976-77, Nat. Study Federally-Funded Tchr. Ctr., 1979-82, Nat. Study Tchr. Edn., 1985-94; developer, dir. tchr. edn. programs, various U.S. locations; mem., chmn. various univs. coms.; cons., spkr. in field. Author: Improving Teacher Education, 1978, Documenting Success - A Guidebook for Teacher Centers, 1979, Inservice Teacher Education, 1980; author monographs; contbr. articles to profl. jours., chpts. to books. Mem. Am. Ednl. Rsch. Assn. (assoc. editor 1983-85, chair elect Orgn. Instl. Affiliates 1994-95), Am. Assn. Colls. for Tchr. Edn. (bd. dirs. 1984-87, exec. com. 1985-87). Office: U Miami Sch Edn PO Box 248065 Coral Gables FL 33124-8065

YARINGTON, CHARLES THOMAS, JR., surgeon, administrator; b. Sayre, Pa., Apr. 26, 1934; s. C.T. and Florence (Hutchinson) Y.; m. Barbara Taylor Johnson, Sept. 28, 1963; children: Leslie Anne, Jennifer Lynne, Barbara Jane. AB, Princeton, 1956; MD, Hahnemann Med. Coll., 1960; grad., Army Command and Gen. Staff Coll., 1969, Air War Coll., 1973, Indsl. Coll. Armed Forces, 1974. Intern Rochester (N.Y.) Gen. Hosp., 1960-61; resident Dartmouth Hosp., 1961-62, U. Rochester Strong Meml. Hosp., 1962-65; instr. otolaryngology U. Rochester Sch. Medicine, 1962-65; asst. prof. surgery W.Va. U. Sch. Medicine, 1967-68; assoc. prof., chmn. dept. otorhinolarygology U. Nebr. Med. Center, 1968-69, prof., chmn. dept. otorhinolarygology, 1969-74; clin. prof. otolaryngology U. Wash., Seattle, 1974—; clin. prof. surgery Uniformed Services U. Health Scis., Bethesda, 1985—; chief otolaryngology Virginia Mason Med. Ctr., Seattle, 1978-88, 92-95, chief dept. surgery, 1988-91; surgeon Mason Clinic, Seattle, 1996—; Cons. Surg. Gen. USAF, Hunter Group Med. Mgmt. Cons., 1996—; pres. Virginia Mason Rsch. Ctr., Seattle, 1983-85; trustee Mason Clinic, 1988-91; adv. coun. Nat. Inst. Neurol. Diseases, Communicative Diseases, Stroke of NIH, Bethesda, Md., 1986-90; bd. dirs. Virginia Mason Hosp., Mirginia Mason Med. Ctr., bd. govs., 1989—. Author books and articles in field.; Mem. editorial bd. Aviation, Space, Environ. Med. Jour., Otol. Clinics of N. Am., Mil. Medicine, Otolaryngology-Head and Neck Surgery. Trustee Seattle Opera Assn., 1983-89. Maj., M.C. AUS, 1965-67; brig. gen. USAF Res., to 1986. Decorated D.S.M., Legion of Merit; named Commdr. Venerable Order St. John (Gt. Britain), Companion with Star, Order Orthodox Hospit, Republic of Cypress; recipient Sir Henry Wellcome medal, 1984. Fellow ACS, Royal Soc. Medicine, Am. Acad. Otolaryngology (Barraquer Meml. award 1968, mem. standing com., bd. govs. 1982-88, Honor award 1974); mem. AMA, Am. Broncho-Esophagological Assn. (council, treas. 1982-86, pres. 1987-88), Am. Laryngol. Assn., Pacific Coast Soc. Ophthalmology and Otolaryngology (coun., pres. 1987-88), Soc. Med. Cons. to Armed Forces, Am. Soc. Head and Neck Surgery, N.W. Acad. Head and Neck Surgery (pres. 1984-86), Am. Soc. Otology, Rhinology and Laryngology (v.p. 1992-93), Res. Officers Assn. (pres. Seattle chpt., nat. officer), Pan-Pacific Surg. Assn., Sons of Revolution (pres. Wash. 1985-87), Internat. Power Boat Assn. (officer), Seattle Yacht Club, Princeton Quadrangle Club, RAF Club (London), Cosmos Club (Washington), Rainier Club (Seattle), Sigma Xi. Office: Mason Clinic 1100 9th Ave Seattle WA 98101-2756

YARIV, AMNON, electrical engineering educator, scientist; b. Tel Aviv, Israel, Apr. 13, 1930; came to U.S., 1951, naturalized, 1964; s. Shraga and Henya (Davidson) Y.; m. Frances Pokras, Apr. 10, 1972; children: Elizabeth, Dana, Gabriela. B.S., U. Calif., Berkeley, 1954, M.S., 1956, Ph.D., 1958. Mem. tech. staff Bell Telephone Labs., 1959-63; dir. laser research Watkins-Johnson Co., 1963-64; mem. faculty Calif. Inst. Tech., 1964—, Thomas G. Myers prof. elec. engring. and applied physics, 1966—; chmn. bd. ORTEL Inc. Author: Quantum Electronics, 1967, 75, 85, Introduction to Optical Electronics, 1971, 77, 89, Theory and Applications of Quantum Mechanics, Propagation of Light in Crystals. Served with Israeli Army, 1948-50. Recipient Pender award U. Pa., Harvey prize Technion, Israel, 1992. Fellow IEEE (Quantum Electronics award 1980), Am. Optical Soc. (Ives medal 1986), Am. Acad. Arts and Scis.; mem. NAS, NAE, Am. Phys. Soc. Office: 1201 E California Blvd Pasadena CA 91125-0001

YARKONY, GARY MICHAEL, physician, researcher; b. N.Y.C., May 22, 1953; m. Kirsten Kohlmeyer; children: Judith, Rachel, Seth, Lauren. BA in Biology, SUNY, Buffalo, 1974; MD, SUNY, Syracuse, 1978; Master in Mgmt., Northwestern U., 1994. ;. Intern, then resident in physical medicine, rehab. Northwestern U., Chgo., 1978-81, chief resident dept. rehab. medicine, 1980; asst. dir. head trauma program Rehab. Inc. Chgo., 1981-84, attending staff, 1981-94; v.p. clin. program devel. Schwab Rehab. Hosp., Chgo., 1994—; clin. prof. sect. orthopaedic surgery and rehab. medicine U. Chgo. Med. Ctr., 1995—, clin. prof. dept. surgery and neurology, 1995—; attending physician Northwestern Meml. Hosp., Chgo., 1984-94; assoc. prof. dept. rehab. medicine Northwestern U. Med. Sch., 1985-94; adj. prof. Pritzker Inst. for Med. Engring., Ill. Inst. Tech., 1991—; dir. rehab. Midwest Regional Spinal Cord Injury Care Sys., Chgo., 1984-94. Contbr. articles to profl. jours. and chpts. to book. Fellow Am. Acad. Physical Medicine and Rehab.; mem. Assn. Academic Physiatrists, Am. Spinal Injury Assn., Internat. Med. Soc. Paraplegia, Internal Rehab. Medicine Assn., Phi Beta Kappa, Phi Eta Sigma. Office: Schwab Rehab Hosp 1401 S California Ave Chicago IL 60608-1612

YARLAGADDA, RAMBABU VENKATA, financial manager; b. Vijayawada, Andhra, India, July 16, 1959; came to U.S., 1982; s. Bhagat Singh and Kumdwati (Machineni) Y.; m. Rama Devi Ratakonda, May 21, 1987; children: Jay Kiran, Tara. BSChemE, Regional Engring., Rourkela, India, 1981; MSChemE, Ill. Inst. Tech., 1983; MBA, U. Chgo., 1988. Fin. ops. analyst Beatrice U.S. Food Corp., Chgo., 1984-86; cons. Beatrice Splty. Products, Inc., Chgo., 1986-87; acting controller E-II Food Spltys., Inc., Oakbrook Terrace, Ill., 1987-88, cons., 1988-89; zone fin. mgr. Taco Bell Corp., Elmhurst, Ill., 1989-90; mgr. planning Pepsi-Cola Co., Somers, N.Y., 1990-91, group mgr. planning, 1991-94; controller Sara Lee Meat Group, Sara Lee Corp., Memphis, 1994-95; v.p. fin., CFO Living Books, San Francisco, 1995-96; v.p. svcs. bus., CFO Narrative Comm. Corp., Los Altos, Calif., 1996—. Mem. Am. Inst. Chem. Engrs. Hindu. Avocations: horseback riding, reading, camping. Home: 109 Secluded Pl Lafayette CA 94549

YARLOW, LORETTA, art museum director; b. N.Y.C., Sept. 26, 1948; d. Albert and Sylvia (Seligsohn) Y.; m. Gregory Salzman, June 5, 1977; children: Nina, Alexander. BA, Sarah Lawrence Coll., 1970; EdM, Harvard U.,

1971. Curator Inst. Contemporary Art, Boston, 1972-74; co-dir. Yarlow/Salzman Gallery, Toronto, Ont., Can., 1974-84; dir./curator Art Gallery York U., Toronto, 1988—. Office: Art Gallery York U, 4700 Keele St, North York, ON Canada M3J 1P3

YARMOLINSKY, ADAM, law educator; b. N.Y.C., Nov. 17, 1922; s. Avrahm and Babette (Deutsch) Y.; m. Harriet Leslie Rypins, 1945 (div. 1981); children: Sarah Franklin, Tobias, Benjamin Levi, Matthew Jonas; m. Jane Cox Vonnegut, 1984 (dec.); m. Sarah Ames Ellis, 1990. AB, Harvard U., 1943; LLB, Yale U., 1948. Bar: N.Y. 1949, D.C. 1952; U.S. Supreme Ct. 1955. Law clk. to Judge C.E. Clark U.S. Ct. Appeals (2d cir.), 1948-49; assoc. Root, Ballantine, Harlan, Bushby & Palmer, N.Y.C., 1949-50; law clk. to Justice Stanley Reed U.S. Supreme Ct., 1950-51; assoc. Cleary, Gottlieb, Friendly & Ball, Washington, 1951-55; dir. Washington office Fund for the Republic, Inc., 1955-56, sec., 1956-57; pub. affairs editor Doubleday & Co., Inc., 1957-59; cons. pvt. founds., 1959-60, spl. asst. sec. of def., 1961-64; dep. dir. Pres.'s. Anti-Poverty Task Force, 1964; chief U.S. Emergency Relief Mission to Dominican Republic, 1965; prin. dep. asst. sec. def. for internat. security affairs, 1965-66; prof. law Harvard U.; mem. inst. politics John F. Kennedy Sch. Govt., 1966-72; (on leave, 1970-72); chief exec. officer Welfare Island Devel. Corp., 1971-72; Ralph Waldo Emerson univ. prof. U. Mass., 1972-77; counselor ACDA, 1977-79; of counsel Fort & Schlefer, Washington, 1979—; prof. policy scis. grad. program U. Md. Balt. County, Balt., 1985-93, acting provost, 1986-87, provost, 1987-93; regents prof. pub. policy U. Md. System, 1993—; lectr. Am. U. Law Sch., 1951-56, Yale U. Law Sch., 1958-59; adj. prof. Georgetown U. Law Ctr., 1984-85; cons. Office Tech. Assessment, 1974-77; mem. gov.'s adv. coun. Mass. Comprehensive Health Planning Agy., 1972-76; nat. adv. com. Inst. for Rsch. on Poverty, 1972-77; mem. Governing Coun. Wye Faculty Seminar; moderator Aspen Inst. Exec. Seminars, 1976—, Troutbeck Ednl. Leadership Program, 1984—, Oxford Aspen Seminars, 1986-89. Author: Recognition of Excellence, 1960, The Military Establishment, 1971, Paradoxes of Power, 1983; editor: Case Studies in Personnel Security, 1955, Race and Schooling in the City, 1980; editor: (with Nicholas Farnham) Rethinking Liberal Education, 1995; spl. corr. The Economist, London, 1956-60; contbr. articles to profl. jours. Trustee Bennington Coll., 1984—, chmn., 1986-88; trustee Robert F. Kennedy Meml., Vera Inst. Justice, 1967—, New Directions Edn. Fund, 1979-82, Ctr. for Nat. Policy, 1984—, Am. Sch. Tangiers, 1979-89, Ocean Rsch. and Edn. Soc., 1980-85, Coalition for Nat. Svc., 1986—, Coun. Econ. Priorities, 1990-93, Hospice Care of D.C., 1990-97, Ind. Sector, 1980-84, 89-95, 96—, chmn. gov. rels. com., 1989-92, vice chmn. bd., 1994-95; chmn. bd. Com. for Nat. Security, 1986-91; chmn. bd. Lawyers Alliance for World Security, 1995—; trustee PACT, 1995—. Recipient Disting. Pub. Svc. medal Dept. Def., 1966. Fellow Am. Acad. Arts and Scis.; mem. Nat. Acad. Social Ins., Assn. Bar City of N.Y. (chmn. coms. sci. and law 1984-87), Am. Law Inst. (life), Hudson Inst., Internat. Inst. Strategic Studies, Nat. Acad. Social Ins., Inst. Medicine of NAS (charter mem., coun. 1970-77, com. on human rights 1978-89), Coun. on Fgn. Rels., Century Club (N.Y.C.), Cosmos Club. Office: UMBC 1000 Hilltop Cir Baltimore MD 21250-0001

YARNALL, D. ROBERT, JR., entrepreneur, investor; b. Phila., Feb. 11, 1925; s. D. Robert and Elizabeth (Biddle) Y.; m. Rie Gabrielsen, June 24, 1954 (dec. Oct. 1980); children: Joan, Sara, Kristina; m. Anne Gates, July 3, 1982; stepchildren—Sarah, Michael, Amy Gates. B.M.E., Cornell U., 1948. Mech. engr. Westinghouse Electric Co., Phila., 1947; dir. relief mission to Poland Am. Friends Service Com., 1948-49; with Yarnall Waring Co. (name changed to Yarway Corp. 1965), Phila., 1949-86, v.p., 1957-62, pres., chief exec. officer, 1962-78, chmn. bd., 1968-86; founder, chmn. bd. Envirite Corp., Plymouth Meeting, Pa., 1975—; dir. James G. Biddle Co., Plymouth Meeting, Pa., 1957-78, chmn. bd., 1976-78; dir. Fed. Res. Bank of Phila., 1965-72, dep. chmn., 1971-72; dir. S.K.F. Industries, King of Prussia, Pa., Quaker Chem. Co., Phila., Meritor Fin. Group (PSFS), Keystone Internat. Inc., Houston; Cons. UN Indsl. Devel. Orgn. mission to, Indonesia, 1968; exec.-in-residence on faculty Centre d'Etudes Industrielles, Geneva, Switzerland, 1971-72; Bd. dirs. World Affairs Council, Pa., 1957-61, 64-68, 74—, chmn. bd., 1978-80. Trustee Internat. House, Phila., chmn., 1972-76; trustee U. Pa., 1981—, Phila Art Mus., 1978—, Greater Phila. Partnership, 1975—; trustee St. John's Coll., Annapolis, Md., 1975-86, vice chmn., 1978-82; bd. dirs. Pa. Environ. Council, 1976—, WHYY, Phila., Greater Phila. First Corp., 1984-86, Chestnut Hill Hosp., 1986—. Served with Am. Field Service with Brit. Army, World War II. Mem. ASME, Chief Execs. Orgn. Clubs: Philadelphia, Union League, Divotee Golf (Phila.). Home: 6706 Springbank Ln Philadelphia PA 19119-3713 Office: Envirite Corp Plymouth Meeting PA 19462

YARNELL, JEFFREY ALAN, regional credit executive; b. Columbus, Ohio, Oct. 23, 1941; s. Russell Lester and Grace Wilma (Adams) Y.; m. Carroll Ginevra Meier, July 6, 1982; children: Natalie, Brian. Student, Ohio State U., 1963. Cert. credit exec. Nat. Assn. Credit Mgmt. Teller Huntington Nat. Bank, Columbus, Ohio, 1965-66; credit mgr. janitrol divsn. Midland Ross, Columbus, 1966-68; asst. credit mgr. Marlite divsn. Masonite, Dover, Ohio, 1968-72; v.p., gen. credit mgr. wholesale fl. coverings Carson Pirie Scott, Chgo., 1972-88; regional credit mgr. Ga.-Pacific Corp., Des Plaines, Ill., 1988—; bd. dirs. Chgo.-Midwest Credit Mgmt. Assn., 1991-94. Author: Credit Manual, 1978. Advisor Jr. Achievement, Dover, Ohio, 1969-70; mem. Toastmasters Internat., Columbus, Ohio, 1965-67; councilor Boy Scouts Am., Palos Heights, Ill., 1980-81. With USNR, 1963-65. Mem. Chgo.-Midwest Credit Mgmt. Assn. (bd. dirs. 1991-94). Republican. Lutheran. Avocations: golf, skiing, chess, reading, stock market analysis, bowling. Office: Ga Pacific Corp PO Box 105144 4100 Wild Wood Pkwy Atlanta GA 30348

YARNELL, MICHAEL ALLAN, lawyer; b. Chgo., Sept. 10, 1944; s. Howard Winfred and Mary Elizabeth (Card) Y.; m. Karen Alice Hockenyos, June 12, 1971 (div. Mar. 1994); children: Sarah Munro, Jacob Rainey; m. Kristina Louise Renshaw, July 17, 1996. BS, Ariz. State U., 1967; JD with honors, U. Ill., 1971. Bar: Ariz. 1971. Ptnr. Streich, Lang, Weeks & Cardon, Phoenix, 1971-91, also bd. dirs.; mem. Myers, Barnes & Jenkins, Phoenix, 1991; judge Maricopa County Superior Ct., Phoenix, 1991—. Author: Ins and Outs of Foreclosure, 1981, 9th edit., 1996; projects editor Law Rev. U. Ill. Law Forum, 1970; contbr. articles to profl. jours. Chairperson Phoenix Children's Theatre, 1987. 1st lt. U.S. Army, 1971-72, Korea. Fellow Ariz. Bar Found.; mem. ABA, Am. Judicature Assn., Maricopa Bar Assn., State Bar Ariz. (Outstanding Contbn. to Continuing Legal Edn. award 1988), Order of Coif, Phi Kappa Phi. Republican. Avocations: computers, small boat sailing, white water rafting. Office: Maricopa County Superior Ct 101 W Jefferson St Phoenix AZ 85003-2206

YARNELL, RICHARD ASA, anthropologist; b. Boston, May 11, 1929; s. Sidney Howe and Floy Mae (Wilson) Y.; m. Meredith Jean Black; children—Karen Lyn, Anne Chesson, William Sidney, Susan Lynn. Student, Tex. A&M Coll., 1946-47; B.S., Duke U., 1950; M.A., U. N.Mex., 1958; Ph.D., U. Mich., 1963. Mem. faculty Emory U., Atlanta, 1962-71, asso. prof., 1967-71; mem. faculty U. N.C., Chapel Hill, 1971—, prof. anthropology, 1975-94, prof. emeritus, 1994—. Contbr. papers, reports to profl. jours., books. With USAF, 1951-55. Fellow AAAS; mem. Soc. for Econ. Botany, Soc. Ethnobiology, Southeastern Archaeol. Conf., Soc. Am. Archaeology (Fryxell medal 1992). Office: U NC Dept Anthropology Clb 3115 Chapel Hill NC 27514

YAROSEWICK, STANLEY J., academic administrator, physicist; b. Epping, N.H., Sept. 10, 1939. BS, U. N.H., 1961; MS, Clarkson Coll. Tech., 1963, PhD in Physics, 1966. Asst. prof. physics Clarkson Coll. Tech., Potsdam, N.Y., 1966-69, assoc. prof. physics, 1969-74; prof. physics West Chester (Pa.) Univ., 1974-87, v.p. acad. affairs, provost, 1987-94, interim pres., 1991-92; pres. Keene (N.H.) State Coll., 1994—. Mem. Am. Assn. Physics Tchrs., Am. Assn. State Colls. and Univs. Office: Keene State Coll 229 Main St Keene NH 03435-0001*

YARROW, ANDREW LOUIS, writer, journalist, educator, international relations consultant; b. Washington, June 11, 1957; s. Leon Jay and Marian Jeannette (Radke) Y. BA, UCLA, 1979; MA, Princeton U., 1981; MPA, Harvard U., 1994. Reporter N.Y. Times, N.Y.C., 1981-92; prof. Am. Univ., Washington, 1994—; spl. asst. to sec. labor U.S. Dept. Labor, Washington, 1995—; internat. rels. cons. World Bank, Washington, 1994-95, UN. Author: Latecomers: Children of Parents Over 35, 1991; contbr. articles to profl. jours. and popular mags. Recipient fellowship Inst. for Internat. Edn., Eng., 1979, Visitors Program award European Union, Brussels, 1993, Rsch. grant Govt. France, 1992-93. Mem. Phi Beta Kappa. Democrat. Avocations: photography, creative writing. Home: 1845 47th Pl NW Washington DC 20007 Office: US Dept Labor Washington DC 20210

YARROW, PETER, folksinger; b. N.Y.C., May 31, 1938. B.A., Cornell U. Mem. group: Peter, Paul, and Mary, 1962—, also solo performer, recording artist, Warner Bros.: albums with Peter, Paul, and Mary include: Peter, Paul, and Mary, Moving, In the Wind, In Concert, A Song Will Rise, See What Tomorrow Brings, Peter, Paul, and Mary Album, Album 1700, Late Again, Peter, Paul & Mommy, 10 Years Together: The Best Of, Reunion, Peter, Paul & Mommy, Too (Emmy nominee 1993), No Easy Walk to Freedom, Lifelines; solo album: Peter, 1972, That's Enough for Me, 1973, Hard Times, 1975, Love Songs, 1975; on Broadway appearance: Peter, Paul, and Mary "From Bleecker to Broadway", 1986; TV spls. include: Reunion, Holiday Concert, Peter, Paul & Mommy, Too, Lifelines (PBS). Bd. dirs. Newport Folk Found., Kerrville (Tex.) Folk Festival, Ctr. for Global Edn., Augsberg Coll.; chmn. bd. trustees Telluride Inst., 1997. Recipient Emmy nominee for "Puff the Magic Dragon", 1979, Citizen Action Leadership award, Vista, 1979, Alfred Lowenstein award, 1982, Hospice Care of R.I. award, 1987, Nat. Emergency Civil Liberties Com. award, 1988, Interlochen Disting. Alumnus Arts award, 1992, Conn. Hospice award, 1993, Grammy award for prodr. Peter Paul & Mommy, too, 1994, Kate Wolf Meml. award for the World Folk Music Assn., 1994.

YARWOOD, DEAN LESLEY, political science educator; b. Decorah, Iowa, Mar. 17, 1935; s. Harold Nicholas and Elsie Mabel (Roney) Y.; m. Elaine Delores Bender, Sept. 2, 1956; children: Lucinda, Kent, Keith, Douglas, Dennis. BA, Iowa U., 1957; MA, Cornell U., 1961; PhD, U. Ill., 1966. Tchr. social studies, acting jr. high prin. Mid-Prairie Community Sch., Wellman, Iowa, 1957-59; asst. prof. Coe Coll., Cedar Rapids, Iowa, 1963-66, U. Ky., Lexington, 1966-67; asst. prof. U. Mo., Columbia, 1967-70, assoc. prof., 1970-78, prof., 1978—, dir. grad. studies dept. polit. sci., 1970-72, 88, 94-97, chmn. dept. polit. sci., 1988-91, Frederick A. Middlebush prof. polit. sci., 1992-95. Editor: The National Administrative System: Selected Readings, 1971, Public Administration, Politics, and the People: Selected Readings for Managers, Employees and Citizens, 1987; author, co-author numerous articles in polit. sci. jours. Recipient Bradish Meml. scholarship, 1953-57, Iowa Merit scholarship, 1956-57, Woodrow Wilson fellowship, 1959-60, James Garner fellowship, 1961-62, Woodrow Wilson Dissertation fellowship, 1962-63. Mem. Am. Soc. Pub. Adminstrn. (chmn. sect. on pub. adminstrn. edn. 1986-87, publs. com. 1986-89, com. on orgnl. rev. and evaln. 1995-97, Ctrl. Mo. chpt. coun. 1979-80, pres. 1980-81, ex-officio mem. coun. 1981-83), Am. Polit. Sci. Assn., Midwest Polit. Sci. Assn., So. Polit. Sci. Assn., Mo. Polit. Sci. Assn. (v.p. 1990-91, pres. 1991-92), Mo. Inst. for Pub. Adminstrn. (coun. 1976-77, v.p. 1977-78, pres. 1978-79), Phi Beta Kappa. Home: 304 Mumford Dr Columbia MO 65203-0230 Office: U Mo Dept Polit Sci 314 Professional Bldg Columbia MO 65211

YARYAN, RUBY BELL, psychologist; b. Toledo, Apr. 28, 1938; d. John Sturges and Susan (Bell) Y.; m. John Frederick Buenz, Jr., Dec. 15, 1962 (div. 1968). AB, Stanford U., 1960; PhD, U. London, 1968. Lic. clin. psychologist; diplomate Am. Bd. Psychology. Rsch. dir., univ. radio and tv U. Calif., San Francisco, 1968-70; dir. delinquency coun. U.S. Dep. Justice, Washington, 1970-73; evaluation dir. Office of Criminal Justice Planning, Sacramento, Calif., 1973-76; CAO project mgr. San Diego (Calif.) County, 1977-92; dir. devel. svcs. Childhelp USA, Woodland Hills, Calif., 1992-94; rsch. coord. Neuropsychiat. Inst. and Hosp. UCLA, 1986-87; exec. dir. Centinela Child Guidance Clinic, Inglewood, Calif., 1987-89; clin. dir. Nat. Found. Emotionally Handicapped, North Hills, Calif., 1990-93; pvt. practice Beverly Hills, Calif., 1973—; psychologist Sr. Psychology Svcs., North L.A. County, 1994—; cons. White House Conf. Children, Washington, 1970; mem. Nat. Adv. Com. Criminal Justice Standards and Goals, Washington, 1973; clin. affiliation UCLA Med. Ctr. Contbr. articles to profl. jours.; chpts. to books and monographs in field. Chair Human Svcs. Commn., City of West Hollywood, Calif., 1986; first vice-chair United Way/Western Region, L.A., 1988; mem. planning-allocations-rsch. coun. United Way, San Diego, 1980-82. Grantee numerous fed., state and local govt. orgns. Mem. Am. Psychol. Assn., Western Psychol. Assn., Calif. Psychol. Assn., Am. Orthopsychiat. Assn., Am. Profl. Soc. on Abuse of Children, Phi Beta Kappa. Episcopalian. Avocations: painting, music, theatre, writing, reading. Office: 337 S Beverly Dr Ste 107 Beverly Hills CA 90212-4307

YASHER, MICHAEL, accountant; b. United, Pa., Aug. 17, 1928; s. Michael and Mary (Sasik) Y.; m. Margaret Jean Wallace, June 23, 1946 (dec. July 12, 1987); 1 child, Michael. BS, Penn State U., 1956; diploma, Air Command & Staff Coll., 1972, Nat. Defense U., 1977; MA, Ctrl. Mich. U., 1983. CPA, D.C.; cert. profl. contract mgr., D.C. Enlisted USAF, 1948; commd. 1st lt. U.S. GAO, Washington, 1960, advanced through grades to col., 1982; ret. USAF, 1988; mem. appropriations com. U.S. House of Reps., 1978-79; acct. to the comptroller U.S. Air Materials Command, 1979-83; acct., cons. E. K. Williams Co., Silver Spring, Md., 1985—. Contbr. numerous papers and articles to profl. publs. Treas. Boy Scouts Am., Rockville, Md., 1970s; bd. dirs. Sr. Softball Assn., Montgomery County, Md., 1993-94; pres. Leisure World (Md.) Billiards Club, 1994-96, treas. 1997; commr., organizer Senior Softball League, 1994, Montgomery County, Md., 1994; participant Nat. Sr. Olympics, San Antonio, 1995, Tucson, 1997. Col. USAF, 1948-88, Korea. Recipient Bronze medal for softball Md. Sr. Olympics, 1992, 1993, 96, Gold medal, 1994, Bronze medal for volleyball, 1993, 1995, 96, Silver medal for Softball, 1995, Meritorious Svc. award U.S.G.A.O., 1975, Data Systems Design Ctr. Outstanding Officer Mobilization Augmentee, 1978, 14 military decorations and others. Mem. AICPA, Res. Officers Assn., Billiards Club, Am. Legion. Democrat. Roman Catholic. Avocations: coin collecting, sports. Home: 15107 Interlachen Dr Apt 318 Silver Spring MD 20906-5625 Office: E K Williams Co 1700 Elton Rd Silver Spring MD 20903-1747

YASHON, DAVID, neurosurgeon, educator; b. Chgo., May 13, 1935; s. Samuel and Dorothy (Cutler) Y.; children—Jaclyn, Lisa, Steven. B.S. in Medicine, U. Ill., 1958, M.D., 1960. Diplomate Am. Bd. Neurol. Surgery. Intern U. Ill., 1961, resident, 1961-64, asst. in neuroanatomy, 1960; clin. instr. neurosurgery U. Chgo., 1965-66; asst. prof. neurosurgery Case Western Res U., Cleve., 1966-69; assoc. prof. neurosurgery Ohio State U., Columbus, 1969-74, prof., 1974-89, prof. emeritus, 1989—; mem. staff St. Ann's Hosp., Children's Hosp., Park Med. Ctr.; cons. Med. Research and Devel. Command, U.S. Army; mem. Neurology B Study Sect NIH. Author: Spinal Injury; contbr. articles to med. jours. Served as capt. U.S. Army, 1960-68. Fellow Royal Coll. Surgeons Can. (cert.), A.C.S.; mem. AMA, Am. Physiol. Soc., Congress Neurol. Surgeons, Am. Assn. Anatomists, Canadian, Ohio neurosurg. socs., Am. Assn. Neurol. Surgeons, Research Soc. Neurol. Surgeons, Acad. Medicine Columbus and Franklin County, Soc. for Neurosci., Soc. Univ. Surgeons, Am. Acad. Neurology, Assn. for Acad. Surgery, Am. Acad. Neurol. Surgery, Am. Assn. for Surgery of Trauma, Central Surg. Soc., Ohio Med. Soc., Columbus Surg. Soc., Sigma Xi, Alpha Omega Alpha. Office: Park Med Ctr 1492 E Broad St Ste 1201 Columbus OH 43205-1546

YASNYI, ALLAN DAVID, communications company executive; b. New Orleans, June 22, 1942; s. Ben Z. and Bertha R. (Michalove) Y.; BBA, Tulane U., 1964; m. Susan K. Manders; children: Benjamin Charles, Evelyn Judith, Brian Mallut. Free-lance exec. producer, producer, writer, actor and designer for TV, motion picture and theatre, 1961-73; producer, performer The Second City; dir. fin. and adminstrn. Quinn Martin Prodns., Hollywood, Calif., 1973-76, v.p. fin., 1976-77, exec. v.p. fin. and corp. planning, 1977; vice chmn., CEO QM Prodns., Beverly Hills, Calif., 1977-78, chmn. bd., CEO, 1978-80; pres., CEO The Synapse Communications Group, Inc., 1981—; exec. dir., adj. prof. U. So. Calif. Entertainment Tech. Ctr., 1994—; participant IC IS Forum, 1990-95; exec. prodr. first live broadcast combining Intelsat, Intersputnik, The Voice of Am., and The Moscow World Radio Svc., 1990; resource guest Aspen Inst. Exec. Seminars, 1990; chmn. bd. dirs. Found. of Global Broadcasting, Washington, 1987-93. Trustee Hollywood Arts Coun., 1980-83; exec. v.p., trustee Hollywood Hist. Trust, 1981-91; bd. dirs. Internat. Ctr. for Intergative Studies, N.Y.C., 1988-92; bd. dirs. Asthma and Allergy Foun. Am., 1981-85. Logistical combat officer U.S. Army, 1964-66, Viet Nam. Named to Tulane U. Hall of Fame. Mem. Acad. TV Arts and Scis., Inst. Noetic Scis., Hollywood Radio and TV Soc., Hollywood C. of C. (dir., vice-chmn. 1978-93), Screen Actors Guild, Assn. Transpersonal Pyschology (keynote speaker 1988). Office: 4132 Fulton Ave Sherman Oaks CA 91423-4340

YASSIN, ROBERT ALAN, museum administrator, curator; b. Malden, Mass., May 22, 1941; s. Harold Benjamin and Florence Gertrude (Hoffman) Y.; m. Marilyn Kramer, June 9, 1963; children: Fredric Giles, Aaron David. BA (Rufus Choate scholar), Dartmouth Coll., 1962; postgrad., Boston U., 1962-63; M.A., U. Mich., 1965, postgrad. (Samuel H. Kress Found. fellow), 1968-70, Ph.D. candidate, 1970; postgrad (Ford Found. fellow), Yale U., 1966-68. Asst. to dir. Mus. Art U. Mich., 1965-66, asst. dir., 1970-72, asso. dir., 1972-73, acting dir., 1973, instr. dept. history of art, 1970-73; co-dir. Joint Program in Mus. Tng., 1970-73; chief curator Indpls. Mus. Art, 1973-75, 87-89, acting dir., 1975, dir., 1975-89; exec. dir. Tucson Mus. Art, 1990—; adj. prof. Herron Sch. Art Ind. U./Purdue U., 1975-89. Contbr. to mus. publications. Mem. Ariz. Hist. Soc., Ariz. Mus. Assn., Tucson Mus. Assn., Tucson Arts Coalition., Tucson Downtown Adv. Coun. Mem. Am. Assn. Mus. (bd. dirs. Internat. Coun. Mus. 1986-89), Assn. Art Mus. Dirs., Coll. Art Assn. Am., Intermus. Conservation Assn. (chmn. exec. com. 1977-78), Tucson C. of C. (cultural affairs com., econ. devel. com.), Nat. Trust Historic Preservation, Rotary. Jewish. Home: 3900 N Calle Casita Tucson AZ 85718-7204 Office: Tucson Mus Art 140 N Main Ave Tucson AZ 85701-8218

YASTOW, SHELBY, lawyer. Sr. v.p., gen. counsel, sec. McDonald's Corp., Oak Brook, Ill. Office: Mc Donalds Corp Campus Office Bldg 1 Crok Dr Hinsdale IL 60521*

YASTRZEMSKI, CARL MICHAEL, former baseball player, public relations executive; b. Southampton, N.Y., Aug. 22, 1939; m. Carolann Casper, Jan. 30, 1960. Student, Notre Dame U.; B.S. in Bus. Adminstrn., Merrimack Coll. Second baseman, shortstop Raleigh (N.C.), Carolina League, 1959; outfielder Mpls. (Am. Assn.), 1960; left fielder Boston Red Sox (Am. League), 1961-83, cons., instr., 1983—; with Eaton Vance Corp., Boston, 1968—, Kahn's & Co. (subs. Sara Lee Corp.), Cincinnati, 1978—. Chosen most valuable player Carolina League, 1959; chosen most valuable player Am. League, 1967; inducted into Baseball Hall of Fame, 1989. Mem. Am. League All-Star Team, 1963, 65-77, 79, 83. Office: Eaton Vance Corp 24 Federal St Fl 5 Boston MA 02110-2507*

YASUDA, HIROTSUGU KOGE, chemical engineering professor; b. Kyoto, Japan, Mar. 24, 1930; s. Mitsuo and Kei (Niwa) Y.; m. Gerda Lisbeth Schmidtke, Apr. 6, 1968; children: Ken Eric, Werner Akira, Lisbeth Kay. BSChemE, Kyoto U., 1953; MS in Polymer Chemistry, SUNY, Syracuse, 1959, PhD in Polymer and Phys. Chemistry, 1961. Rsch. assoc. Ophthalmic Plastic Lab., Mass. Eye & Ear Infirmary, Boston, 1962-63; head biomaterial sect. eye rsch. Cedar-Sinai Med. Ctr., L.A., 1963-65; vis. scientist Royal Inst. Tech., Stockholm, 1965-66; sr. chemist Rsch. Triangle Inst., Rsch. Triangle Pk., N.C., 1966-72, mgr. Polymer Rsch. Lab., 1972-78; prof. chem. engring. U. Mo., Rolla, 1978-88, dir. Thin Films Inst., 1974-88; prof. chem. engring. U. Mo., Columbia, 1988—, chmn. dept., 1988-90, dir. Ctr. for Surface and Plasma Techs., 1989—. Author: Plasma Polymerization, 1985. Home: 1004 Lake Point Ln Columbia MO 65203-2900 Office: U Mo Ctr for Surface Sci and Plasma Tech Columbia MO 65211

YASUFUKU, SACHIO, electrical engineer, educator; b. Qingdao, China, Nov. 11, 1929; (parents Japanese citizens); s. Kozo and Takie (Suematsu) Y.; m. Yoko Kikutani, Dec. 16, 1958. BS, Nagoya (Japan) U., 1952, D Engring., 1979. Rschr. Furukawa Electric Co., Ltd., Yokohama, Japan, 1952-63, prodn. engr., 1963-65; rsch. leader Furukawa Electric Co., Ltd., Hiratsuka, Japan, 1965-72; sr. specialist Toshiba Corp. Yokohama, Kawasaki, Japan, 1972-79, chief specialist, 1979-89; adj. prof. Tokyo Denki U., 1989—. Contbr. articles to profl. publs.; patentee in field. Recipient nat. award for invention Japan Inst. Invention and Innovation, 1963, 23 nat. awards for progress of elec. machinery Japan Elec. Mfrs. Assn. , 1974. Fellow IEEE (sec. Tokyo chpt. Elec. Insulation Soc. 1980-83, chmn. 1984-86, regional editor Elec. Insulation mag. 1988-91, contbg. editor 1992—); mem. AAAS, N.Y. Acad. Scis. Roman Catholic. Avocation: travel. Home: 520 3-1 Higashi Kugenuma, Fujisawa Kanagawa 251, Japan Office: Tokyo Denki U, 2-2 Nishiki-cho Kanda, Chiyoda-ku Tokyo 101, Japan

YATES, ALBERT CARL, academic administrator, chemistry educator; b. Memphis, Sept. 29, 1941; s. John Frank and Sadie L. (Shell) Y.; m. Ann Young; children: Steven, Stephanie, Aerin Alessandra, Sara Elizabeth. B.S., Memphis State U., 1965; Ph.D., Ind. U., 1968. Research assoc. U. So. Calif., Los Angeles, 1968-69; prof. chemistry Ind. U., Bloomington, 1969-74; v.p. research, grad. dean U. Cin., 1974-81; exec. v.p., provost, prof. chemistry Washington State U., Pullman, 1981-90; pres. Colo. State U., Fort Collins, 1990—; chancellor Colo. State U. System, Fort Collins, 1990—; mem. grad. record exam. bd. Princeton (N.J.) U., 1977-80, undergrad. assessment program council, 1977-81; cons. NRC, 1975-82, Office End., HEW, 1978-80; mem. exec. council acad. affairs NASULGC, 1983-87, ACE, 1983-87,. nat adv. council gen. med. scis. NIH, 1987—. Contbr.: research articles to Jour. Chem. Physics; research articles to Phys. Rev.; research articles to Jour. Physics, Phys. Rev. Letters, Chem. Physics Letters. Served with USN, 1959-62. Recipient univ. and State honors and awards. Mem. Am. Phys. Soc., Am. Chem. Soc., AAAS, Nat. Assn. State Univs. and Land Grant Colls. (mem. exec. council academic affairs), Am. Council Edn. (mem. exec. com. academic affairs), Sigma Xi, Phi Lambda Upsilon. Home: 1744 Hillside Dr Fort Collins CO 80524-1965 Office: Colo State U 102 Administration Bldg Fort Collins CO 80523*

YATES, CHARLES RICHARDSON, former arts center executive; b. Atlanta, Sept. 9, 1913; s. Presley Daniel and Julia (Richardson) Y.; m. Dorothy Malone, May 20, 1944; children: Dorothy Y. Kirkley, Charles R., Sarah F., J. Comer. B.S. with honors, Ga. Inst. Tech., 1935. With 1st Nat. Bank Atlanta, 1935-47, asst. v.p., 1940-47; with Joshua L. Baily & Co., Inc., Atlanta, 1947-60; v.p. Joshua L. Baily & Co., Inc., 1956-60; v.p. finance Atlantic Coast Line R.R. Co. and L. & N. R.R. Co., 1960-67; v.p. Seaboard Coast Line R.R. Co., 1967-71, v.p. finance, 1971-73; v.p. finance L. & N. R.R. Co., 1967-73; pres. Atlanta Arts Alliance, 1973-83; trustee Profile Fund I, Sacramento; dir. Technology Park/Atlanta. Trustee Ga. Tech. Found., Woodruff Arts Ctr. Served with AUS, 1941-42; lt. USNR, 1942-46. Mem. Ga. C. of C. (dir., pres. 1965-67), East Lake Golf Club (pres. 1995—), Augusta Nat. Club (sec.), Atlanta Athletic Club, Peachtree Golf Club, Capital City Club, Royal and Ancient Golf Club. Episcopalian.

YATES, DAN CHARLES, insurance company official; b. Spring Valley, Ill., Oct. 14, 1952; s. Earl John Jr. and Charlotte Elaine (Sandberg) Y.; m. Margaret Mary McBride, Mar. 1, 1980; 1 child, Keith. B Bus. in Fin., Western Ill. U., 1977. CPCU. Claims adjuster G.A.B. Bus. Svcs., Kansas City, Mo., 1978-80; claims mgr. Dodson Group, Kansas City, 1980—; mem. conf. com. Property Loss Rsch. Bur., Schaumburg, Ill., 1994-96, vice chair, 1994-95, chair, 1995-96; chair legal subcom. of the western regional adv. com. of property Loss Rsch. Bur., 1996; adv. coun. midwest region Nat. Assn. Ind. Ins. Adjusters, 1986-89, mem. Credit Com. for Bee Dee Co. Credit Union, 1992— (pres., chair 1994—). Vol. Jr. Achievement. With U.S. Army, 1972-74. Mem. Kansas City Property Claims Assn. (pres. 1992). Avocations: bowling, basketball, blood donor. Office: Dodson Group 9201 State Line Rd Kansas City MO 64114-3234

YATES, DAVID JOHN C., chemist, researcher; b. Stoke-on-Trent, Staffordshire, Eng., Feb. 13, 1927; came to U.S., 1958; s. Eric John and Beatrice Victoria (Street) Y.; m. Natalie Chmelnitsky, June 22, 1983. B.S. with honors, U. Birmingham, U.K., 1949; Ph.D., U. Cambridge, Eng., 1955, Sc.D., 1968. Rsch. physicist Kodak Labs., Wealdstone, London, 1949-50; rsch. chemist Brit. Ceramic Rsch. Assn., Stoke-on-Trent, 1950-51; rsch. assoc. dept. colloid sci. U. Cambridge, 1951-58; lectr. Sch. Mines and dept. chemistry Columbia U., N.Y.C., 1958-60; sr. rsch. fellow Nat. Phys. Lab., Teddington, U.K., 1960-61; rsch. assoc. corp. labs. Exxon Rsch. and Engring., Annandale, N.J., 1961-86; rsch. prof. dept. of chem. engring. Lafayette Coll., Easton, Pa., 1986-87; rsch. prof. dept. materials sci. Rutgers U., Piscataway, N.J., 1987-88; cons. San Diego, 1988—. Contbr. over 70 articles to profl. jours., chpts. to books; 13 U.S. patents, numerous fgn. patents. Fellow Inst. of Physics (U.K.), Royal Soc. Chemistry (U.K.), N.Y. Catalysis Club (chmn. 1966-67). Club: N.Y. Catalysis (chmn. 1965-66). Avocations: photography, bicycling, gliding, travel, sports cars.

YATES, ELIZABETH (MRS. WILLIAM MCGREAL), author, editor; b. Buffalo, Dec. 6, 1905; d. Harry and Mary (Duffy) Y.; m. William McGreal, Nov. 6, 1929. Grad., Franklin Sch., Buffalo, Oaksmere, Mamaroneck, N.Y.; student, London (Eng.); Litt.D. (hon.), Aurora Coll., 1965, Ripon Coll., 1970, Rivier Coll.; L.H.D. (hon.), Eastern Bapt. Coll., 1966, U. N.H., 1967, New Eng. Coll., 1972, Franklin Pierce Coll., 1981. Staff mem. U. Conn., U. Ind., U. Colo., U. N.H. writers confs., 1948—; staff mem. Christian Writers and Editors Conf., Green Lake, Wis., 1957—; Mem. gov.'s State Libr. Commn. Author: High Holiday, 1938, Hans and Frieda, 1938, Gathered Grace, 1939, Climbing Higher, 1939, Quest in the Northland, 1940, Haven for the Brave, 1941, Under the Little Fir, 1941, Around the Year in Iceland, 1942, Patterns on the Wall, 1942, Mountain Born, 1943, Wind of Spring, 1944, The Young Traveller in the U.S.A, 1946, Nearby, 1947, Once in the Year, 1947, Beloved Bondage, 1948, Amos Fortune, Free Man, 1950, Guardian Heart, 1950, Children of the Bible, 1950, Brave Interval, 1952, A Place For Peter, 1952, Hue and Cry, 1953, Rainbow Round the World, 1954 (Jane Addams children's book award Women's Internat. League for Peace and Freedom 1955), Prudence Crandall, Woman of Courage, 1955, The Carey Girl, 1956, Pebble in a Pool, The Widening Circles of Dorothy Canfield Fisher's Life, 1958 (reissued as The Lady from Vermont 1971), The Lighted Heart, 1960, The Next Fine Day, 1961, Someday You'll Write, 1962, Sam's Secret Journal, 1963, Carolina's Courage, 1963, Howard Thurman, Portrait of a Practical Dreamer, 1964, Up the Golden Stair, 1966, Is There a Doctor in the Barn, 1966, With Pipe, Paddle and Song, 1968, New Hampshire, 1969, On that Night, 1969, Sarah Whitcher's Story, 1971, Skeezer, Dog with a Mission, 1972, The Road Through Sandwich Notch, 1973, We, The People, 1974, A Book of Hours, 1976, Call It Zest, 1977, The Seventh One, 1978, My Diary, My World, 1981, Silver Lining, 1981; My Widening World, 1983, One Writer's Way, 1984, Sound Friendships, 1987, Spanning Time, 1996, Editor: Piskey Folk, 1941, Doll Who Came Alive, 1941, 72, Joseph, 1947, The White Ring, 1949, The Christmas Story, 1949, Your Prayers and Mine, 1954, Sir Gibbie, 1962; Contbr. book revs., articles, essays, interviews to periodicals. Trustee Town Library, Peterborough, N.H.; bd. dirs. N.H. Assn. for Blind. Recipient N.Y. Herald Tribune Spring Festival award, 1943, 50, Newbery medal, 1951, William Allen White award, 1953, Sarah Josepha Hale award, 1970, N.H. Gov.'s award of distinction, 1982, Pettee medal U. N.H., 1994. Mem. Delta Kappa Gamma (Pettee medal 1994). Address: Box 295 149 E Side Dr Concord NH 03301-5475

YATES, ELLA GAINES, library consultant; b. Atlanta, June 14, 1927; d. Fred Douglas and Laura (Moore) Gaines; m. Joseph L. Sydnor (dec.); 1 child, Jerri Gaines Sydnor Lee; m. Clayton R. Yates (dec.). A.B., Spelman Coll., Atlanta, 1949; M.S. in L.S, Atlanta U., 1951; J.D., Atlanta Law Sch., 1979. Asst. br. librarian Bklyn. Pub. Library, 1951-54; head children's dept. Orange (N.J.) Pub. Library, 1956-59; br. librarian E. Orange (N.J.) Pub. Library, 1960-69; med. librarian Orange Meml. Hosp., 1967-69; asst. dir. Montclair (N.J.) Pub. Library, 1970-72; asst. dir. Atlanta-Fulton Pub. Library, 1972-76, dir., 1976-81; dir. learning resource ctr. Seattle Opportunities Industrialization Ctr., 1982-84; asst. dir. adminstrn. Friendship Force, Atlanta, 1984-86; state librarian Commonwealth of Va., 1986-90; library cons. Price Waterhouse, 1991; adv. bd. Library of Congress Center for the Book, 1977-85; cons. in field; vis. lectr. U. Wash., Seattle, 1981-83; mem. Va. Records Adv. Bd., 1986-90; mem. Nagara Exec. Bd., 1987-91. Contbr. to profl. jours. Vice chmn. N.J. Women's Coun. on Human Rels., 1957-59; chmn. Friends Fulton County Jail, 1973-81; bd. dirs. United Cerebral Palsy Greater Atlanta, Inc., 1979-81 Coalition Against Censorship, Washington, 1981-84, YMCA Met. Atlanta, 1979-81, Exec. Women's Network, 1979-82, Freedom To Read Found., 1979-85, Va. Black History Mus., Richmond, 1990-91; sec., exec. dir. Va. Libr. Found. Bd., 1986-90. Recipient meritorious svc. award Atlanta U., 1977, Phoenix award City of Atlanta, 1980, Serwa award Nat. Coalition 100 Black Women, 1989, Black Caucus award, 1989, disting. svc. award Clark-Atlanta U., 1991, ednl. support svc. award Tuskegee Airmen, 1993; named profl. woman of yr. NAACP N.J., 1972, outstanding chum of yr., 1976; named outstanding alumni Spelman Coll., 1977, named to alumni hall of fame, 1995. Mem. ALA (exec. bd. 1977-83, commn. freedom of access to info.), NAACP, Southeastern Libr. Assn., Nat. Assn. Govt. Archives and Records Adminstrn. (exec. bd. 1987-91), Delta Sigma Theta. Baptist. Home and Office: 1171 Oriole Dr SW Atlanta GA 30311-2424

YATES, ELSIE VICTORIA, retired secondary English educator; b. Newport, R.I., Dec. 16, 1916; d. Andrew James and Rachel Agnes (Sousa) Tabb; m. George Herman Yates, July 12, 1941 (div. Apr. 1981); children: Serena, George Jr., Michael, Elsie French, David. AB in English and History, Va. Union U., 1938; postgrad., U. R.I., 1968-73, Salve Regina U., 1968-73. Life cert. in secondary English and reading specialist, R.I. Reading specialist grades 7 and 8 title I Newport (R.I.) Sch., 1971-74, secondary English educator, 1975-87; ret., 1987. Mem. adult com. Young Life, Newport, 1981-93; active Newport (R.I.) Substance Abuse Force, 1989-93; chmn. multicultural curriculum com. New Visions for Newport (R.I.) Schs., 1991-94; mem. edn. com. Swinburne Sch., Newport, 1992-94; active Equity in Edns. Com.-Concerned Citizens Group. Recipient Outstanding Ednl. Contbn. Under Title I award U.S. Office Edn., Bur. Sch. Sys., 1976, Presdl. citation Nat. Edn. Assn. R.I., 1987, Appreciation for Svc. award Cmty. Bapt. Ch., Newport, 1988, Outstanding Svc. award in field of edn. to the youth in cmty. Queen Esther Chpt. 2, Newport, 1992. Mem. NAACP (life), R.I. Ret. Tchrs. Assn., Newport Ret. Tchrs. Assn. Baptist. Avocations: reading, handicrafts, community activities. Home: 8 Bayside Ave Apt A Newport RI 02840-1321

YATES, ELTON G., retired petroleum industry executive; b. Slidell, La., July 31, 1935; s. Elton O. and Leona E. (Sollberger) Y.; m. Jo Ellen Levy, Apr. 11, 1955; children—Sherlyn, Michele, Steven. B.S. in Petroleum Engring, La. State U., 1957. Petroleum engr. Texaco Inc., various locations, 1957-68; dist. engr. Texaco Inc., Corpus Christi, Tex., 1968-70; div. devel. engr. Texaco Inc., Houston, 1970-71; coordinator joint ops. Texaco Inc., N.Y.C., 1971-75; pres., gen. mgr. Texaco Iran, London, 1975-77; asst. gen. mgr. producing Eastern Hemisphere Texaco Inc., N.Y.C., 1977-78; gen. mgr. producing Harrison, N.Y., 1978-79, corp. v.p., dept. head producing, 1979-82; div. pres. Texaco Oil Trading and Supply, 1981-82; pres. Texaco Middle East/Far East, 1982-84, Texaco Latin Am./West Africa, 1984-87; corp. sr. v.p. Texaco Inc., White Plains, N.Y., 1987-94, ret., 1994; bd. dirs. numerous Texaco Inc. Co. subs., Coast Guard Found.; former dir. Arabian Am. Oil Co.; dir. Caltex Corp. and Amoseas. Mem. dean's adv. coun. Coll Engring. La. State U. Elected to La. State U. Coll. Engring. Hall of Distinction. Mem. Soc. Petroleum Engrs. of AIME, 25 Yr. Club of Petroleum Industry, Country Club of N.C., Country Club of Darien (Conn.), Country Club of Pinehurst (N.C.), Phi Epsilon Tau. Presbyterian.

YATES, ISABEL MCCANTS, city council member; b. Winnsboro, S.C., Oct. 1, 1924; d. Charles Spencer and Isabel Elliott (Gooding) McCants; m. Eugene Wilson Yates, June 30, 1948; children: Eugene W., Mackie Yates Hempel, Carolyn Yates Cunningham, Elliott Glenn. BA, U. S.C., 1944; MA, Ohio State U., 1945; postgrad., U. Ky., 1964-78. English tchr. Spartanburg (S.C.) H.S., 1945-46; English instr. U. S.C., Columbia, 1946-48, Newberry (S.C.) Coll., 1948-49; ptnr. retail dress shop Track Two, Midway, Ky., 1973-78; sec., ptnr. Merit Tours and Convention Planning, Lexington, Ky., 1981-90; 4th dist. coun. mem. Lexington-Fayette Urban County Govt., 1992—. Contbr. articles to profl. jours. Bd. vice chmn. Lexington Philharm. Soc., 1974-75; bd. chmn. Environ. Commn., Lexington, 1980-82, Lexington Directions, 1985-87, Arts and Heritage Festival, Lexington, 1989-90, U. Ky. Ctr. on Aging Found., Lexington, 1989-92; v.p. Nat. Am. Mothers, Inc., Am. Mothers, Inc., Waldorf Astoria, N.Y., 1989-91; chair devel. coun. Midway (Ky.) Coll., 1991-93. Named Ky. Mother of Yr., Ky. Mother's Assn., Elizabethtown, Ky., 1981, Outstanding Women of Lexington Chpt. Beta Sigma Phi, 1984, Outstanding Vol. Fund Raiser, Nat. Soc. Fund-Raising Execs., 1990; recipient Woman of Achievement award YWCA, Lexington, 1989, Campaign Cabinet award United Way, Lexington, 1989. Mem. Ky. Ednl. TV (adv. bd.), Lexington Jr. League (adv. bd.), Lexington Arts and Cultural Coun. (co-chair fund raising 1992-95), Friends of McConnell Springs (mem., founder, bd. chair 1993-96), New Century Lexington (bd. mem. 1995-96). Democrat. Methodist. Avocations: tennis, reading, traveling. Home: 717 Malabu Dr Lexington KY 40502-3338 Office: Lexington-Fayette Urban County Govt 200 E Main St Lexington KY 40507-1315

YATES, JAY REESE, physician; b. Brigham City, Utah, Apr. 17, 1949; s. Jay A. and Audrene (Harper) Y.; m. Colleen Ostice, Sept. 3, 1970; children: York, Tyson, Cameron, Britney, Breck. BS, U. Utah, 1971, MD, 1975. Diplomate Am. Bd. Family Practice. Intern Providence Hosp., Southfield, Mich., 1975-76, resident, 1976-78; staff physician Tanner Clinic, Layton, Utah, 1978—, bd. dirs., 1985—, pres., 1992—; pres. Humana Hosp. Davis North, Layton, 1984-86. Mem. Am. Acad. Family Practice, Utah Med. Assn., Davis County Med. Assn. (pres. 1990). Baptist. Avocations: golf, skiing, water skiing, racquetball, reading. Office: Tanner Clinic 2121 Robins Dr Layton UT 84041-1131

YATES, JERE EUGENE, business educator, management consultant; b. Memphis, Apr. 4, 1941; s. Emmett Eugene and Naomi Christine (Whitfield) Y.; m. Carolyn Kay Hall, June 8, 1962; children: Camille, Kevin, Brian. BA, Harding U., 1963, MTh, MA, 1966; PhD, Boston U., 1968. Instr. Harding U., Searcy, Ark., 1967-69; prof. bus. Pepperdine U., Malibu, Calif., 1969—; cons. Hughes Aircraft Co., L.A., 1973—, Allied-Signal Corp., North Hollywood, Calif., 1985-90, Pacific Physican Svcs., 1988-96, Med Ptnrs./Mullikin, 1996—. Author: Managing Stress, 1979 (membership book award, 1979); contbr. articles to profl. jours. Mem. AAUP, Acad. Mgmt., UCP/Spastic Children's Found. (bd. dirs., exec. com.), Orgnl. Behavior Teaching Soc., North Ranch Country Club. Republican. Mem. Ch. of Christ. Office: Pepperdine U Business Dept 24255 Pacific Coast Hwy Malibu CA 90263-0001

YATES, JOHN MELVIN, ambassador; b. Superior, Mont., Nov. 25, 1939; s. Leon Glen and Violet May (McPheeters) Y.; m. Peggy Maureen Simpson, Mar. 26, 1961 (dec. Apr. 1986); children: Catherine Diener, John Simpson, Maureen Cole, Paul Marion, Leon Gregory; m. Mary Barbara Carlin, Jan. 30, 1988. A.B., Stanford U., 1961; M.A., Fletcher Sch. Law and Diplomacy, 1962, M.A.L.D., 1963, Ph.D., 1972. Fgn. service officer U.S. Dept. State, Washington, 1964—, Algiers, Algeria, 1964-66, Blantyre, Malawi, 1967-68, Bamako, Mali, 1969-71, New Delhi, India, 1973-75, Ankara, Turkey, 1975-77, Libreville, Gabon, 1977-80, Washington, 1971-73, 80-82; U.S. amb. to Republic of Cape Verde U.S. Dept. State, 1983-86; counselor for polit. affairs U.S. Dept. State, Manila, 1986-89; dep. chief of mission U.S. Dept. State, Lagos, Nigeria, 1989-91; dep. chief of mission U.S. Dept. State, Kinshasa, Zaire, 1991-93, chief of mission, 1993-95; amb. to Republic of Benin U.S. Dept. State, Cotonou, 1995—. Recipient Presdl. award for sustained superior accomplishment in conduct of fgn. policy. Mem. Am. Fgn. Service Assn. Office: Cotonou Dept State Washington DC 20521-2120

YATES, JOHN THOMAS, JR., chemistry educator, research director; b. Winchester, Va., Aug. 3, 1935; s. John Thomas and Kathryn (Barnett) Y.; m. Kerin Joyce Narbut, Oct. 18, 1958; children: Geoffrey, Nathan. BS, Juniata Coll., 1956; PhD, MIT, 1960. Asst. prof. chemistry Antioch Coll., Yellow Springs, Ohio, 1960-63; NRC fellow, research chemist Nat. Bur. Standards, Washington, 1963-66; R.K. Mellon prof. chemistry U. Pitts., 1982—, dir. Surface Sci. Ctr., 1982—; co-dir. materials rsch. ctr. U. Pitts., 1994, R.K. Mellon prof. chemistry and physics, 1994—. Co-author: The Surface Scientist's Guide to Organometallic Chemistry, 1987; co-editor: Vibrational Spectroscopy of Molecules on Surfaces, 1987, Chemical Perspectives of Microelectronic Materials, Vol. 131; assoc. editor: Studies in Surface Science and Catalysis, 1986; series editor: Methods of Surface Characterization, 1987; bd. editors Ann. Rev. Phys. Chemistry, 1983-85, Jour. Phys. Chemistry, 1983-88, Jour. Chem. Physics, Jour. Catalysis, Chem. Revs., Langmuir, Surface Sci., Applications of Surface Sci., Accounts Chem. Rsch.; assoc. editor Langmuir; contbr. revs. and articles to profl. jours.; inventor desorption spectrometer, 1981. Sherman Fairchild Disting. scholar Calif. Inst. Tech., 1977-78; recipient Silver medal Dept. Commerce-Nat. Bur. Stds., 1973, Stratton award, 1981, Gold medal Dept. Commerce Nat. Bur. Stds., 1981, Pres.'s Disting. Rsch. award U. Pitts., 1989, Proctor & Gamble award, 1989, Alexander von Humboldt Sr. Rsch. award, 1994. Fellow Am. Phys. Soc. (bd. dirs. divsn. chem. physics 1991—, chmn. divsn. chem. physics 1989), Am. Vacuum Soc. (chmn. surface sci. divsn. 1973, 92, trustee 1975, bd. dirs. 1982-85, M.W. Welch award 1994, fellow 1994); mem. NAS, Am. Chem. Soc. (chmn. divsn. colloid and surface chemistry, Langmuir lectr. 1979, Kendall award in colloid of surface chemistry 1986, Morley prize Cleve. chpt. 1990, Peter Deloye lectr. Cornell U. 1993). Office: U Pitts Surface Sci Ctr Dept Chemistry Pittsburgh PA 15260

YATES, KEITH LAMAR, retired insurance company executive; b. Bozeman, Mont., Oct. 29, 1927; s. Thomas Bryan and Altha (Norris) Y.; m. Dolores Hensel, Aug. 30, 1948; children: Thomas A., Molly Yates McIntosh, Richard A., Nancy Yates Sands, Penny Dannielle Yates, Pamela Yates Beeler. BA, Eastern Wash. State U., 1953. Salesman Ancient Order United Workmen, Spokane, Wash., 1952-53, sales mgr., 1953-56, corp. sec., 1956-73; corp. sec. Neighbors of Woodcraft, Portland, Oreg., 1973-89, pres., 1989-92; ret., 1992. Author: Life of Willie Willey, 1966, The Fogarty Years, 1972, History of The Woodcraft Home, 1975, An Enduring Heritage, 1992. Pres. Wash. State Christian Mens Fellowship, Seattle, 1965-67; pres. Met. Area Assn. Christian Chs., 1981-83; mem. regional bd. Christian Chs. Oreg., 1990-94. Command sgt.-maj., ret., 1987; served with USN, USAF, USANG, 1946-87. Mem. Wash. State Frat. Cong., (cert. Commendation 1969, sec. 1957-68, pres., mem. exec. bd., chmn. conv. program advt. com. 1960-73), Oreg. State Frat. Cong. (Outstanding Frat. 1975-76, Spl. Appreciation award 1984, Frat. Family of Yr. 1986, sec. 1975-87, pres., mem. exec. bd. 1974—), Nat. Fraternal Congress Am. (conv. arrangement com. 1964, 90, publicity com. 1964, 65, 68, 90, credentials com. 1970, 77, 78, pres. press & pub. rels. sec. 1971-72, pub. rels. com. 1971-73, chmn. 1972, co-chmn. press and pub. rels. frat. seminar 1972, frat. monitor com. 1974-75, mem. com. 1975-76, family life com. 1978-80, constitution com. 1980, pres. state frat. congs. sec. 1981-82, historian 1987—, Washington County's Disting. Patriot, 1988), Portland Ins. Acctg. and Statis. Soc. Assn. Records Mgrs. and Adminstrs. (Oreg. chpt.), Portland C. of C., Wash. Ins. Coun., Wash. Claims Assn., Seattle Underwriting Assn. Home: 29860 SW Buckhaven Rd Hillsboro OR 97123-8821

YATES, LEIGHTON DELEVAN, JR., lawyer; b. Atlanta, Sept. 4, 1946; s. Leighton Delevan and Stella Louise (Hill) Y.; m. Phyllis Jeanne Hummer, Dec. 22, 1968; children: Leighton Delevan III, Lauren Jeanne. BA, Hampden-Sydney Coll., Va., 1968; JD with high honors, U. Fla., 1973. Bar: Fla. 1974, U.S. Dist. Ct. (middle dist.) Fla. 1975. Assoc. Maguire, Voorhis & Wells, P.A., Orlando, Fla., 1974-77, shareholder, 1978—, dept. chmn., 1985-90, exec. com., 1990-94; dir. Hubbard Constrn. Co., Winter Park, Fla.; adminstrv. dir. SunTrust Bank, Ctrl. Fla., Orlando, 1990—. Exec. editor U. Fla. Law Rev., 1973. Mem. Fla. Bd. Bar Examiners, 1992—, vice chmn., 1995-96, chmn. 1996—; chmn. Ctrl. Fla. Blood Bank, 1995—, vice chmn., 1976-95; chmn. Orlando Opera Co., 1994, pres., 1993. Mem. ABA, Fla. Bar Assn., Orange County Bar Assn., Univ. Club of Orlando, Country Club of Orlando, Order of the Coif, Omicron Delta Kappa, Phi Kappa Phi. Republican. Presbyterian. Avocations: scuba diving, fishing, music, reading. Home: 3218 S Osceola Ave Orlando FL 32806-6251 Office: Maguire Voorhis & Wells PA 200 S Orange Ave Ste 3000 Orlando FL 32801-3440

YATES, MICHAEL FRANCIS, management consultant; b. N.Y.C., Feb. 9, 1946; s. John Berchmans and Jane Ann (Gretz) Y.; m. Christine Mary Dallos, Jan. 14, 1967; children—Erik Michael, Alison; BA, U. Buffalo, 1968. Mgmt. trainee, dept. mgr. Sears, Roebuck & Co., Buffalo, 1968-69; cons. Rothman & D'Alessandro, Inc., N.Y.C., 1969-71; sr. cons. Martin & Segal & Co., Inc., N.Y.C., 1971-75, A.S. Hansen, Inc., N.Y.C., 1975-78; exec. v.p. A.M. D'Alessandro & Co., Inc., North Haledon, N.J., 1978-81; mng. dir., Alexander & Alexander Consulting Group, Inc., Lyndhurst, N.J., 1981-97; pres. Michael F. Yates & Co., Inc., Glen Gardner, N.J., 1997—. Pres. Lincoln Sch. PTA, 1975-77; chmn. Bethlehem Twp. Econ. and Indsl. Devel. Bd., 1980-83; pres. Bethlehem Twp. Republican Club, mem. Hunterdon County com.; mem. Republican Nat. Com. Mem. Am. Mgmt. Assn., Am. Compensation Assn., Soc. Human Resource Mgmt., Adminstrv. Mgmt. Soc., Aircraft Owners and Pilots Assn. Office: 519 Lannon Ln Glen Gardner NJ 08826-3817

YATES, NORRIS WILLIAM, JR., lawyer; b. Alamo Heights, Tex., July 6, 1926; s. Norris William and Maggie Barkley (Curry) Y.; m. Mary Hutchings Spencer, Dec. 30, 1947 (div. Aug. 1949); 1 child, William Spencer; m. Jimmie Carolyn Cook, Sept. 17, 1955; children: Victoria Carolyn Marullo, Rebecca Elizabeth Yates Bird. BA in Econs., Tex. A&M U., 1950; JD, U. Tex., 1957. Bar: U.S. Ct. of Military Appeals, 1963, U.S. Supreme Ct., 1964, Tex., 1957. Asst. to mgr. rates and tariffs Slick Airways, Inc., San Antonio, 1950; assoc. Beckmann, Stanard, Wood, Barrow & Vance, San Antonio, 1957-60; pvt. practice San Antonio, 1960-67, 83—; asst. criminal dist. atty., chief civil sect. Bexar County Dist. Atty.'s Office, San Antonio, 1967-82; mcpl. ct. judge City of San Antonio, 1966-67. Editor The Subpoena, 1958-59. Exec. com. Bexar County Dem. Party, San Antonio. Cpl. U.S. Army, Airborne Infantry, 1944-46, ETO; 1st lt. USAF, 1951-55, B-29 Bomber Pilot, Korea, lt. col. USAFR, ret. 1978. Decorated Bronze Star medal, combat infantry badge, glider badge, pilot's wings, three battle stars. Mem. Daedalians, USAF Pilot Class 52-George Assn. (recording sec.), 307th Bomb Group/Wing Inc. (pres.), Toastmasters (past pres., Disting. Dist. Gov. 1969-70, Disting. Toastmaster 1984, Presdl. citation 1992), Masons (past master, 32 degree), San Antonio A&M Club (dir.). Democrat. Presbyterian. Avocations: travel, photography. Home: 2118 Kenilworth Blvd San Antonio TX 78209

YATES, PATRICIA ENGLAND, employment company executive; b. Sparta, Tenn., Sept. 18, 1958; d. Edsel and Gladys Mary (Garland) England; m. Dennis Eugene Yates, Nov. 30, 1990. BS in Home Econs., Tenn. Tech. U., 1982. Purchasing sec. Porelon, Inc., Cookeville, Tenn., 1982-87; buyer purchasing dept. Tenn. Tech. U., Cookeville, Tenn., 1987-88; dir. pers. J & S Constrn. Co., Inc., Cookeville, 1988-93; placement coord. Holland Employment (formerly Putnam Employment Svc. Inc.), Cookeville, 1993-95; svc. specialist Hamilton-Ryker Co., Shelbyville, Tenn., 1995—; dir. projects Nat. and Internat. Issues Rsch., Sparta, Tenn., 1982—. Mem. Nat. Exch. Club, Profl. Secs. Internat. (chpt. v.p. 1997), Bus. and Profl. Women's Orgn. (treas. 1990, 2d v.p. 1992, Finalist Young Careerist 1994), U.C. Soc. Resource Mgmt. (treas. 1993), Internat. Platform Assn. Avocations: reading, theater, drama, landscaping, needle work. Office: The Hamilton-Ryker Co 100 Public Square Shelbyville TN 37160

YATES, PETER, director, producer; b. Ewshoot, Surrey, England, July 24, 1929; s. Robert L. and Constance Yates; m. Virginia Pope; 3 children. Student, Royal Acad. of Dramatic Art. Entered film industry, 1956. Films directed: Summer Holiday, 1962, One Way Pendulum, 1964, Robbery, 1966, Bullitt, 1968, John and Mary, 1969, The Hot Rock, 1971, The Friends of Eddie Coyle,1972, for Pete's Sake, 1973, The Deep, 1976, Krull, 1982, Eleni, 1985, Suspect, 1987, An Innocent Man, 1989, The Run of the Country, 1995; dir., producer Murphy's War, 1970, Mother, Jugs and Speed, 1975, Breaking Away, 1979 (nominated Acad. award 1980), Eyewitness, 1980, The Dresser, 1983 (nominated Acad. award 1984), The House on Carroll Street, 1986, Year of the Comet, 1991, Roommates, 1994. Mem. Acad. Motion Pictures Arts & Scis., Dirs. Guild Am., Garrick Club. Address: Dirs Guild Am 7920 Sunset Blvd Los Angeles CA 90046*

YATES, ROBERT DOYLE, anatomy educator; b. Birmingham, Ala., Feb. 28, 1931; s. James William, Jr. and Mildred (Doyle) Y.; m. Jane Congleton, 1955; children: Robert Lee, Pamela C. BS, U. Ala., 1954, MS, 1956, PhD, 1959. Student anatomy dept. U. Ala., Birmingham, postdoctoral fellow, 1959-60; with U. Tex., Galveston, 1961-72; prof. anatomy Tulane U. Med. Sch., New Orleans, 1972—, chmn. dept. anatomy, 1972—; vis. investigator Harvard U. Med. Sch., Boston, 1962-63, Yale U. Med. Sch., New Haven, 1965-67. Mem. editorial bd.: Am. Jour. Anatomy, Anat. Record; contbr. articles to profl. jours. and chpts. to books. Vestryman Trinity Episc. Ch., Galveston, 1965-68; vestryman, jr. warden Trinity Episc. Ch., New Orleans, 1985-89, sr. warden, 1989-92. With inf. U.S. Army, 1960-61. Recipient numerous awards NIH, 1965-72, Research Career Devel. award, Golden Apple teaching award AMA Student Assn., 1971. Mem. Am. Assn. Anatomists (chmn. nominating com. 1980, sec.-treas. 1988-96), Internat. Fedn. Assn. Anatomists (treas. 1989-96), Assn. Anatomy Cell Biology and Neurobiology Chairpersons (sec.-treas. 1976—), Am. Soc. Cell Biology. Republican. Avocations: tennis, stained glass, beveled glass, hunting. Office: Tulane U Sch of Medicine 1430 Tulane Ave New Orleans LA 70112-2699

YATES, SIDNEY RICHARD, congressman, lawyer; b. Chicago, Ill., Aug. 27, 1909; s. Louis and Ida (Siegel) Y.; m. Adeline Holleb, June 24, 1935; 1 child, Stephen R. Ph.B., U. Chgo., 1931, J.D., 1933. Bar: Ill. bar 1933. Practiced as sr. mem. Yates & Holleb; asst. atty. Ill. State Bank Receiver, 1935-37; asst. atty. gen. attached as traction atty. Ill. Commerce Commn., 1937-40; mem. 80th-87th, 89th-105th Congresses from 9th Dist. Ill., 1949-62, 1965—; ranking minority mem. Appropriations subcoms. on the Interior; U.S. del. UN Trusteeship Council with rank of ambassador. Served to lt. USN, 1944-46. Recipient Joseph Henry medal Smithsonian Instn., 1995. Mem. Am., Ill. State, Chgo. bar assns., Am. Vets. Com., Chgo. Council Fgn. Relations, Decalogue Soc. Lawyers. Democrat. Jewish. Clubs: City, Bryn Mawr Country. Office: US House of Reps 2109 Rayburn House Bldg Washington DC 20515-1309*

YATSEVITCH, GRATIAN MICHAEL, retired army officer, diplomat, engineer; b. Kiev, Russia, Nov. 16, 1911; s. Michael Gratian and Margaret (Thomas) Y.; A.B., Harvard U., 1933, M.A., 1934, postgrad. (J.B. Woodworth fellow), 1935-40; m. Barbara Stewart Franks, July 2, 1973; children by previous marriage—Gael Yatsevitch McKibben, Peter, Kara, Gratian. Mining engr. Zlot Mines Ltd., also Beshina Gold Mines Ltd. of London in Yugoslavia, 1935-40, mgr. gold mine, 1936-40; commd. 2d lt. field arty.-U.S. Army, 1933, advanced through grades to col., 1951; chief cannon and aircraft armament br. devel. prodn. cannon, Office of Chief of Ordnance, 1940-45; mil. attache, Moscow, 1945-46; U.S. del. Allied Control Comm., Sofia, Bulgaria, 1946-47; mil. attache, Sofia, 1947-49; attache and spl. asst. to U.S. Amb., Turkey, 1952-53, Iran, 1957-63; sr. staff officer, Washington, 1950-52, 53-57; ret., 1969; hon. chmn. Star Trading and Marine Co., Washington; econ. cons. Middle E. Decorated Legion of Merit with oak leaf cluster. Clubs: Met. (Washington); Carlton, Lansdowne (London); Camden Yacht. Contbr. articles on arty. and mineral. subjects to mags. Home: Easterly Shermans Pt Camden ME 04843 Office: 1050 17th St NW Ste 450 Washington DC 20036-5519

YATVIN, JOANNE INA, school superintendent; b. Newark, Apr. 17, 1931; d. John and Mary Edna (Cohen) Goldberg; m. Milton Brian Yatvin, June 8, 1952; children: Alan, Bruce, Lillian, Richard. Ba, Douglass Coll., 1952; MA, Rutgers U., 1962; PhD, U. Wis., 1974. Cert. sch. adminstr. Tchr. Hamburg (N.J.) Pub. Schs., 1952-53, New Brunswick (N.J.) Pub. Schs., 1953-55, Mayaguez (P.R.) Schs., 1958-59, Milltown (N.J.) Pub. Schs., 1959-62, East Brunswick (N.J.) Pub. Schs., 1962-63; tchr., prin. Madison (Wis.) Met. Sch. Dist., 1963-88; supt. Cottrell Sch. Dist., Boring, Oreg., 1988—; adv. bd. mem. Big Books Mag., 1990-91; cons. various sch. dists. Author: Learning Language Through Communication, 1986, (monograph) A Whole Language Program for a Whole School, 1991; contbr. chpts. in books and articles to profl. jours. Recipient Excellence in Print award Washington Edpress, 1987, Disting. Elem. Edn. Alumni award U. Wis., 1988; named Elem. Prin. of Yr. Wis. Dept. Edn., 1985, Wis. State Reading Assn., 1985. Mem. ASCD, Internat. Reading Assn., Nat. Coun. Tchrs. English (chair com. on ctrs. excellence 1986-89), Nat. Middle Sch. Assn., Oreg. Reading Assn., Oreg. Coun. Tchrs. English, Phi Delta Kappa. Home: 5226 SW Northwood Ave Portland OR 97201-2832 Office: Cottrell Sch Dist 36225 SE Proctor Rd Boring OR 97009-9719

YAU, KEVIN KAM-CHING, astronomer; b. Hong Kong, July 11, 1959; came to U.S., 1992; s. Ching-Fat and Ping-Kiu (Leung) Y.; m. Florence Wai-Chung Liu, Aug. 22, 1987; children: Stephanie, Cherrymay. BS in Physics, U. Liverpool, Eng., 1982; MS in Astrophysics, U. Durham, Eng., 1984, PhD in Astronomy, 1988. Sr. rsch. asst. U. Durham, 1987-92; postdoctoral fellow Jet Propulsion Lab., Pasadena, Calif., 1992-94, mem. tech. staff, 1994—. Co-author: Halley's Comet in History, 1985; contbr. articles to profl. jours. Rsch. scholar U. Durham, 1984-87; awardee Victor Nadarov Fund, Royal Astron. Soc., 1983. Fellow Royal Astron. Soc.; mem. Internat. Astron. Union, Am. Astron. Soc. Achievements include expert status on the long-term motion of cometary orbits; successfully determining the past orbit of comet Halley and Swift-Tuttle and identified their returns from hist. records back to 200 B.C.; co-discoverer of the 164 BC return of Halley's comet from Babylonian clay tablets; world authority on the application of early astronomical observations to solve contemporary problems in astronomy. Office:

Jet Propulsion Lab MS 230-101 4800 Oak Grove Dr Pasadena CA 91109-8001

YAU, STEPHEN SIK-SANG, computer science and engineering educator, computer scientist, researcher; b. Wusei, Kiangsu, China, Aug. 6, 1935; came to U.S., 1958, naturalized, 1968; s. Pen-Chi and Wen-Chum (Shum) Y.; m. Vickie Liu, June 14, 1964; children: Andrew, Philip. BS in Elec. Engring, Nat. Taiwan U., China, 1958; MS in Elec. Engring, U. Ill., Urbana, 1959, PhD, 1961. Asst. prof. elec. engring. Northwestern U., Evanston, Ill., 1961-64, assoc. prof., 1964-68, prof., 1968-88, prof. computer scis., 1970-88, Walter P. Murphy prof. Elec. Engring. and Computer Sci., 1986-88, also chmn. dept. computer scis., 1972-77; chmn. dept. elec. engring. and computer sci. Northwestern U., 1977-88; prof. computer and info. sci., chmn. dept. U. Fla., Gainesville, 1988-94; prof. computer sci. and engr., chmn. Ariz. State U., 1994—; conf. chmn. IEEE Computer Conf., Chgo., 1967; symposium chmn. Symposium on feature extraction and selection in pattern recognition Argonne Nat. Lab., 1970; gen. chmn. Nat. Computer Conf., Chgo., 1974, First Internat. Computer Software and Applications Conf., Chgo., 1977; Trustee Na. Electronics Conf., Inc., 1965-68; chmn. organizing com. 11th World Computer Congress, Internat. Fedn. Info. Processing, San Francisco, 1989; gen. co-chmn. Internat. Symposium on Autonomous Decentralized Systems, Japan, 1993, gen. chmn., Phoenix, 1995. Editor-in-chief Computer mag., 1981-84; assoc. editor Jour. Info. Scis., 1983—; editor IEEE Trans. on Software Engring., 1988-91; contbr. numerous articles on software engring., distributed and parallel processing systems, computer sci., elec. engring. and related fields to profl. publs.; patentee in field. Recipient Louis E. Levy medal Franklin Inst., 1963, Golden Plate award Am. Acad. of Achievement, 1964, The Silver Core award Internat. Fedn. Info. Processing, 1989, Spl. award, 1989. Fellow IEEE (mem. governing bd. Computer Soc. 1967-76, pres. 1974-75, dir. Inst. 1976-77, chmn. awards com., 1996—; Richard E. Merwin award Computer Soc. 1981, Centennial medal 1984, Extraordinary Achievement 1985, Outstanding Contbn. award Computer Sci. Soc. 1985), AAAS, Franklin Inst.; mem. Assn. for Computing Machinery, Am. Fedn. Info.-Processing Socs. (mem. exec. com. 1974-76, 79-82, dir. 1972-82, chmn. awards com. 1979-82, v.p. 1982-84, pres. 1984-86; chmn. Nat. Computer Conf. Bd. 1982-83), Am. Soc. Engring. Edn., Sigma Xi, Tau Beta Pi, Eta Kappa Nu, Pi Mu Epsilon. Office: AZ State U PO Box 875 406 Tempe AZ 85287-5406

YAU, TE-LIN, corrosion engineer; b. Ton-Chen, Anhuei, China, Apr. 9, 1945; s. Chiu-Ho and Chih (Yang) Y.; m. Jue-Hua Tsai, Mar. 19, 1979; children: Kai-Huei, Ian-Huei, Jean-Huei. BS in Engring. Sci., Cheng Kung U., Taiwan, 1969; MS in Engring. Sci., Tenn. Technol. U., 1972; PhD in Metall. Engring., Ohio State U., 1979. Mech. engr. Taiwan Shipbuilding Corp., Keelung, Taiwan, 1970-71; chief corrosion engr. Wah Chang, Albany, Ore., 1979—; cons. Fontana Corrosion Ctr., Ohio State U., Columbus, 1979. Author: ASTM STP, 1984, 85, 86, 90, 92, 95, 96, ASM Metals Handbook, 1987, ASM Stress Corrosion Cracking, 1992; contbr. over 60 articles to profl. jours. Mem. Nat. Assn. Corrosion Engrs. Internat. (chmn. T-5A-38 task group on reactive metals 1993-96), Electrochem. Soc., TAPPI, Sigma Xi. Achievements include a patent on novel liquid metal seal on zirconium or hafnium reduction apparatus; devel. of new applications for reactive metals, improving the performance of reactive metals by employing metall., electrochem. and mech. techs. Home: 1445 Belmont Ave SW Albany OR 97321-3765 Office: Wah Chang Albany 1600 Old Salem Rd NE Albany OR 97321-4548

YAVITZ, BORIS, business educator and dean emeritus; b. Tbilisi, USSR, June 4, 1923; came to U.S., 1946, naturalized, 1950; s. Simon and Miriam (Mindlin) Y.; m. Irene Bernhard, July 17, 1949; children—Jessica Ann, Judith, Emily. M.A., Cambridge (Eng.) U., 1943; M.S., Columbia U., 1948, Ph.D., 1964. Economic cons. Jewish Agy. for Palestine, N.Y.C., 1948-49; mgmt. cons. Werner Mgmt. Cons., Larchmont, N.Y., 1949-54; owner, mgr. Simbar Devel. Corp., N.Y.C., 1954-61; faculty Columbia U., N.Y.C., 1964-94; prof. mgmt. Columbia U., 1964-94; dean Columbia U. (Grad. Sch. Bus.), 1975-82, Paul Garrett prof. pub. policy and bus. responsibility, 1982-94; dep. chmn., dir. Fed. Res. Bank N.Y., 1976-82; dean emeritus, Paul Garrett prof. emeritus Columbia U., 1994—; prin. Lear, Yavitz & Assocs. L.L.C., 1995—; bd. dirs. J.C. Penney Co. Inc., Barnes Group Inc., Israel Discount Bank of N.Y., Crane Co., Medusa Corp.; trustee Am. Assembly, N.Y.C., 1975-82; vice chmn. The Inst. for the Future, 1984—; bd. govs. Media and Soc. Seminars, 1983-84; mem. nat. adv. coun. W. Averill Harriman Inst. Advanced Study of Soviet Union, 1983—; chmn. Nat. Assn. Corp. Dirs. Blue Ribbon Commn. on Corp. Governance. Author books; contbr. articles in field to profl. jours. Served to lt. British Royal Navy, 1943-46. Mem. ASME, Inst. Mgmt. Sci. Home and Office: Old Canoe Place Rd Hampton Bays NY 11946

YAWN, DAVID MCDONALD, journalist; b. Knoxville, Tenn., Aug. 11, 1956; s. McDonald Yawn and Eva (Taylor) Quinn; m. Cathy Whitmire, Sept. 8, 1990. BA in Print Journalism, U. Miss., 1981. Staff writer Clarksdale (Miss.) Press Register, 1982-85; sr. staff writer Memphis Bus. Jour., 1985-97; sr. comms. specialist Fed. Express Corp., Memphis, 1997—; one of 3 Am. journalists invited to take econ. tour of Germany, 1995, France, 1995, The Netherlands, 1997. Editor: In the Shadow of the Wall, The Partnering Paradigm, Sane Investing for the Non-Financial; contbg. editor internat. for Cotton Farming mag.; cons. editor Guild Binder Press Book publs., 1993—. Active Memphis Long Range Econ. Devel. Planning Com. Named one of Outstanding Young Men Am., 1984, 89; recipient Sch. Bell award Miss. Assn. Educators, 1983. Mem. Soc. Profl. Journalists (Mid South chpt. Award of Excellence 1995), Nat. Assn. Real Estate Editors. Republican. Presbyterian. Avocations: karate, photography, travel, jazz music, architecture. Home: 1082 Kings Park Rd Memphis TN 38117-5434 Office: Memphis Bus Jour 88 Union Ave Ste 102 Memphis TN 38103-5100

YAWORSKI, JOANN, reading skills educator; b. Phillipsburg, N.J., Oct. 11, 1956; d. Michael and Cecilia (Ruchala) Y. BA, Pa. State U., 1977; MEd, Millersville U., 1982; postgrad., U. Houston, 1984, Lehigh U., 1988-90; PhD, SUNY, Albany, 1996. Cert. tchr. Russian lang., Russian area studies, reading specialist, elem edn., Tex., N.J., Pa., N.Y. Reading tutor Ephrata (Pa.) Sr. H.S., 1980-81; tchr. Am. History/World Cultures Linden Hall Sch., Lititz, Pa., 1981-82; tchr., Russian lang. Spring Branch Sch. Dist., Houston, Tex., 1982-85; dir. devel. reading Green Mountain Coll., Poultney, Vt., 1989-95; instr. dept. reading U. Albany (N.Y.), SUNY, 1995-96; ind. reading, rsch. cons., 1996—; asst. prof. Augusta (Ga.) State U., 1997—; presenter 28th, 29th and 30th ann. confs. Coll. Reading and Learning Assn. Mem. U.S. Figure Skating Assn. Democrat. Roman Catholic. Avocations: instructing skiing and ice skating, precision team ice skating, ice dancing, ballet. Office: Augusta State U Devel Studies Dept 2500 Walton Way Augusta GA 30904-2200

YAWORSKY, GEORGE MYROSLAW, physicist, technical and management consultant; b. Aug. 4, 1940; s. Myroslaw and Mary (Yaworsky) Y.; m. Zenia Maria Smishkewych, Sept. 9, 1972; 1 child, Maria Diana. BS in Physics, Rensselaer Poly. Inst., 1962, MBA, 1977, PhD in Physics, 1979; MS in Physics, Carnegie-Mellon U., 1964. Physicist Republic Steel Research Ctr., Independence, Ohio, 1966-68; tech. and mgmt. cons. in ops. research, mktg. analyses, computer modeling, sci. programming and other areas to state govt., pvt. cos., 1972-81; internat. tech. assessment and analysis cons. EG&G Inc., Rockville, Md., 1981-82; program dir.-computer integrated mfg. Eagle Research Group, Arlington, Va., 1982-83; prin. investigator high volume mfg. Sci. Applications, Inc., McLean, Va., 1983-84; cons. computer integrated mfg., design of experiments, quality engring., materials sci., tech. transfer, defense conversion, Eastern Europe bus. ventures, internat. bus. and mgmt., 1984—; mem. U.S. del. to Coordinating Com. for Multilateral Export Controls, Paris, 1982; adj. assoc. prof. biomed. engring., U. Tenn., Memphis, 1992—. Contbr. articles to profl. jours.; guest book reviewer, author and contbr. Recipient Physics Teaching award Rensselaer Poly. Inst., 1971; John Huntington scholar; Rensselaer Alumni scholar. Mem. N.Y. Acad. Scis., Robotics Internat. of Soc. Mfg. Engrs. (sr.), Computer and Automated Systems Assn. of Soc. Mfg. Engrs. (sr., chmn. Greater Washington chpt. 1985-93), Am. Phys. Soc., Am. Assn. Physics Tchrs., Am. Prodn. and Inventory Control Soc., AAAS, Rensselaer Alumni Assn., Sigma Xi. Home and Office: 5121 Clinton Rd Alexandria VA 22312-2117

YBARRA, KATHRYN WATROUS, systems engineer; b. Middletown, Conn., Aug. 7, 1943; d. Claude Philip Jr. and C. Lyle (Crook) Watrous; m. Norman L. Adams (div.); children: Cynthia Anne Leonard, Suzette Mae Gross, Daniel Joseph Adams; m. Raul M. Ybarra, Dec. 11, 1976; stepchildren: Esther Ingram, Yolanda Ybarra, Lisa Ybarra. BA in Computer Sci., U. Tex., 1985. Scientific programmer Tracor, Inc., Austin, 1978-86; tech. staff engr. Honeywell, Inc. Comml. Avionics, Phoenix, 1986—. Mem. Friends of Phoenix Libr., v.p. Juniper chpt., 1996-97. Mem. RTCA (spl. com. # 147, Traffic Alert and Collision Avoidance Sys. II, chair requirements working group 1991—, leadership citation 1995), IEEE Computer Soc. Roman Catholic. Achievements include 5 patents for algorithms related to aircraft tracking systems for collision avoidance. Home: 3360 W Phelps Rd Phoenix AZ 85023

YEAGER, CAROLINE HALE, radiologist, consultant; b. Little Rock, Sept. 5, 1946; d. George Glenn and Crenor Burnelle (Hale) Y.; m. William Berg Singer, July 8, 1978; children: Adina Atkinson Singer, Sarah Rose Singer. BA, Ind. U., Bloomington, 1968; MD, Ind. U., Indpls., 1971. Diplomate Am. Bd. Radiology; med. lic. State of Calif. Intern Good Samaritan Hosp., Los Angeles, 1971-72; resident in radiology King Drew Med. Ctr. UCLA, Los Angeles, 1972-76; dir. radiology Hubert Humphrey Health Ctr., Los Angeles, 1976-77; asst. prof. radiology UCLA, Los Angeles, 1977-84; asst. prof. radiology King Drew Med. Ctr. UCLA, Los Angeles, 1977-85, dir. ultrasound, 1977-84; ptnr. pvt. practice Beverly Breast Ctr., Beverly Hills, Calif., 1984-87; cons. Clarity Communications, Pasadena, Calif., 1981—; pvt. practice radiology Claude Humphrey Health Ctr., 1991-93; dir. sonograms and mammograms Rancho Los Amigos Med. Ctr., 1993-94; trustee Assn. Teaching Physicians, L.A., 1976-81; cons. King Drew Med. Ctr., 1984, Gibraltar Savs., 1987, Cal Fed. Inc., 1986, Medical Faculty At Home Professions, 1989—, Mobil Diagnostics, 1991-92, Xerox Corp., 1990-91, Frozen Leopard, Inc., 1990-91. Author: (with others) Infectious Disease, 1978, Anatomy and Physiology for Medical Transcriptionists, 1992; contbr. articles to profl. jours. Trustee U. Synagogue, Los Angeles, 1975-79; mem. Friends of Pasadena Playhouse, 1987-90. Grantee for innovative tng. Nat. Fund for Med. Edn., 1980-81. Mem. Am. Inst. Ultrasound in Medicine, L.A. Radiology Soc. (ultrasound sect.), Nat. Soc. Performance and Instrn. (chmn. conf. Database 1991, publs. L.A. chpt. 1990, info. systems L.A. chpt. 1991, dir. adminstrn. L.A. chpt. 1992, Outstanding Achievement in Performance Improvement award L.A. chpt. 1990, bd. dirs. 1990-93, Pres. award for Outstanding Chpt. 1992, v.p. programs 1993), Stanford Profl. Women L.A. Jewish. Avocations: geneology, writing, humor. Home and Office: 3520 Yorkshire Rd Pasadena CA 91107-5440

YEAGER, CHARLES WILLIAM, lawyer, newspaper publisher; b. Frederick, Md., Sept. 18, 1921; s. Ralph A. and Ina Jane (Nuckles) Y.; m. Charlotte L. Matthews, Nov. 26, 1958; children: Gretchen A. Murphy, Kristin A. Bridge, Charles W. Yeager Jr., Matthew R. Yeager. BA, W.Va. U., 1943; LLB, U. Va., 1948. Bar: W.Va. 1948, Fla. 1969, U.S. Supreme Ct. 1968. Ptnr. Steptoe & Johnson, Charleston, W.Va., 1948-93; of counsel Rose and Atkinson, Charleston, 1993—. Pub., editor The Nicholas CHronicle. Maj. U.S. Army, 1942-46. Democrat. Office: Nicholas Chronicle 603 Church St Summersville WV 26651-1411

YEAGER, ERNEST BILL, physical chemist, electrochemist, educator; b. Orange, N.J., Sept. 26, 1924; s. Ernest Frederick and Olga (Wittwer) Y. BA, Montclair State Coll., N.J., 1945; LLD (hon.), Montclair State Coll., 1983; MS in Chemistry, Case Western Res. U., 1946; PhD in Phys. Chemistry, Western Res. U., 1948. Instr. Case Western Res. U., 1948-51, asst. prof., 1951-56, assoc. prof., 1956-58, prof. chemistry, 1958-83, Frank Hovorka prof. chemistry, 1983-90, prof. emeritus, 1990—, acting chmn. dept. chemistry, 1964-65, chmn. dept. chemistry, 1969-72, chmn. faculty senate, 1972-73; dir. Case Ctr. for Electrochem. Scis. (now called Ernest B. Yeager Ctr. for Electrochem. Scis.), 1976-91; vis. prof. U. Southampton, Eng., 1968; cons. Union Carbide Corp., 1954-85, Inst. Def. Analyses, 1963-66, 91-92, NASA, 1964-68, Argonne Nat. Lab., 1965-67, Gen. Motors Corp., 1969-76, Eveready Battery Co., 1985-93; mem. com. undersea warfare NRC, 1961-73; adv. bd. Office Critical Tables, 1964-69, mem. phys. scis. div., 1968-73; mem. power panel Advanced Research Project Agy., 1972-75; chmn. Gordon Research Conf. Electrochemistry, 1966; mem. internat. commn. electrochemistry Internat. Union Pure and Applied Chemistry, 1971-76; mem. vis. com. Brookhaven Nat. Lab., 1979-81; mem. adv. com. on USSR-Eastern Europe Nat. Acad. Sci., 1979-85; mem. com. on battery materials tech. Nat. Materials Adv. Bd., 1980-81, mem. com. on fuel cells, 1981-83; mem. rev. com. chem. tech. div. Argonne Nat. Lab., 1984-88; mem. com. on electrochem. aspects of energy conservation and prodn. Nat. Materials Adv. Bd. NRC, 1985-86; mem. advanced fuel cell working group Dept. Energy, 1984; mem. com. on electrochem. aspects of energy conservation and prodn. of the nat. materials adv. bd. NRC, 1985-86; mem. NSF com. for internat. programs., 1988-91; mem. bd. visitors Chemistry Div. Office of Naval Rsch., 1988-90. Editor: Transactions of the Symposium on Electrode Processes, 1959, 66, Techniques of Electrochemistry, Vol. I, 1972, Vol. II, 1973, Vol. III, 1977, Comprehensive Treatise of Electrochemistry, Vol. I, 1980, Vols. II, III, IV, 1981, Vols. V, VI,VII, 1983, Vols. VIII, IX, X, 1984, Electrochemistry in Industry: New Directions, 1982; mem. editorial bd. Jour. Advanced Energy Conversion, 1964-66; sect. editor Electrochem. Acta, 1972-76; contbr. articles to profl. jours. Elder area Presbyn. ch. Coffin fellow 1947-48, NATO sr. fellow, 1968; recipient Ann. Tech. award Cleve. Tech. Socs. Coun., 1954, Ann. award Chem. Professions, 1967-68, Ann. Alumni citation Montclair State Coll., 1968, Commendation cert. USN, 1972; named Case Ctr. for Electrochem. Scis. renamed Ernest B. Yeager Ctr. for Electrochem. Scis. in his honor, 1994. Fellow AAAS; mem. AAUP, Acoustical Soc. Am. (v.p. 1969-70, Biennial award), Electrochem. Soc. (hon., v.p. 1962-65, pres. 1965-66, Acheson medal 1980, Heise award Cleve. sect. 1965, de Nora medal 1992), Am. Chem. Soc. (Morley medal 1981), Soc. Applied Spectroscopy (pres. Cleve. chpt. 1953-54), Internat. Soc. Electrochemists (hon., v.p. 1967-69, pres. 1969-70), Optical Soc. Am., Chem. Soc. London, Sigma Xi (pres. Case Western Res. U. chpt. 1959-60). Home: Judson Gardenview Apt 117 1801 Chestnut Hills Dr Cleveland OH 44106

YEAGER, GEORGE MICHAEL, investment counsel executive; b. Pelham Manor, N.Y., Sept. 5, 1934; s. Harold Caldwell and Marybelle Alden (Glos) Y.; m. Barbara Gow, July 7, 1962; children: Scott Alden, Kathryn Gow. AB, Dartmouth Coll., 1956, MBA, 1957. Adminstrv. asst. Fed. Res. Bank N.Y, 1957-59; v.p. Yeager & Anderson, Inc., N.Y.C., 1959-60; pres. Yeager, Wood & Marshall, Inc., N.Y.C., 1960—. Mem. Assn. Investment Mgmt. & Rsch., Investment Counsel Assn. Am. (gov.), N.Y. Soc. Security Analysts, Univ. Club, Econ. Club, U.S. Global Leaders Growth Fund (pres. 1995—), Internat. Soc. Financial Analysts Employee Benefits Inst., Mill Reef Club, Siwanoy Country Club. Home: 2 Elm Rock Rd Bronxville NY 10708-4904 Office: 630 5th Ave Ste 2910 New York NY 10111-0100

YEAGER, JANICE SKINNER, library director; b. Corbin, Ky., July 3, 1945; d. Raymond and Eula (Reeves) Skinner; m. Thomas A. Yeager, Nov. 11, 1988. BA, Berea Coll., 1966; MLS, U. Ky., 1969. Cert. libr., Ind. Extension libr. Rock County Libr. Systems, Janesville, Wis., 1969-71; serial bibliographer Ohio State U. Librs., Columbus, 1971-74; adminstr. Arrowhead Libr. System, Janesville, 1974-85; asst. dir. Monroe County Pub. Libr., Bloomington, Ind., 1985-91, assoc. dir. support svcs., 1991—; adj. instr. Ind. U., Bloomington, 1987. Mem. ALA (coun. 1995—), AAUW (named to ednl. found. program 1985, pres. Bloomington br. 1989-91), Ind. Libr. Fedn. (sec. 1990-91, bd. dirs. 1992—), South Cen. Ind. Pers. Assn. (sec. 1987, pres. 1988), Stone Hills Libr. Network (pres. 1990-91), Network Career Women (sec. 1986), Pub. Libr. Assn. (pres. pub. libr. sys. sect. 1982-83). Office: Monroe County Pub Libr 303 E Kirkwood Ave Bloomington IN 47408-3534

YEAGER, JOSEPH HEIZER, JR., lawyer; b. Indpls., Jan. 8, 1957; s. Joseph Heizer and Marilyn Virginia (Hillyard) Y.; m. Candance A. Grass, June 2, 1984; children: Samuel, Henry. AB cum laude, Harvard U., 1979; JD cum laude, Ind. U., 1983. Bar: Ind. 1983, U.S. Dist. Ct., (so. and no. dist.) Ind. 1983, U.S. Ct. Appeals (7th cir.) 1986, U.S. Supreme Ct. 1996. Dir. ops. Penn and Schoen Assocs., N.Y.C., 1979-80; assoc. Baker & Daniels, Indpls., 1983-89, ptnr., 1990—. Pres. Indpls. Legal Aid Soc., 1992-94; chmn. Indpls. Com. for UNICEF, 1986-91; mem. Indpls. Com. for Fgn. Affairs, 1986-91. Mem. Ind. Bar Assn., Indpls. Bar Assn. (litigation sect. exec. com. 1985-86, 1996—). Democrat. Office: Baker & Daniels 300 N Meridian St Ste 2700 Indianapolis IN 46204-1750

YEAGER, MARK L., lawyer; b. Chgo., Apr. 7, 1950. BA, U. Mich., 1972; JD, Northwestern U., 1975. Bar: Ill. 1975, Fla. 1985. Ptnr. McDermott, Will & Emery, Chgo., 1975—. Mem. ABA (vice-chmn. Robinson-Patman Act com.).

YEAGER, MYRON DEAN, English language educator, business writing consultant; b. Evansville, Ind., Oct. 27, 1950; s. Robert Paul and Sarah Mazol (Hunt) Y. BA, Grace Coll., 1972; MA, Purdue U., 1974, PhD, 1980. Cert. tchr., Calif. Assoc. prof. Grace Coll., Winona Lake, Ind., 1976-84, Chapman U., Orange, Calif., 1984—; cons. numerous firms, 1980—; faculty chmn. Chapman U., Orange, 1991-92, dept. chmn., 1990-93; dept. chmn. Grace Coll., Winona Lake, 1981-84. Author: (chpt.) Business Writing, 1989; contbr. articles to profl. jours. and mags. Recipient UCLA Clark postdoctoral fellowship, 1982, David Ross fellowship Purdue U., 1980, Valerie Seudder award for outstanding tchg., 1992. Mem. ACLU, AAUP, Am. Soc. Eighteenth-Century Studies, Johnson Soc. Western Region, Assn. Bus. Communication, Phi Beta Delta. Office: Chapman Univ 333 N Glassell St Orange CA 92866-1011

YEAGER, PHILLIP CHARLES, transportation company executive; b. Bellevue, Ky., Nov. 15, 1927; s. Ferd A. and Helen (Koehler) Y.; m. Joyce E. Ruebusch, June 2, 1951; children: David P., Debra A. Yeager Jensen, Mark A. BA, U. Cin., 1951. Warehouse mgr. Pure Carbonic Co., Cin., 1950-52; trace clk., rate clk., asst. office mgr. Pa. R.R., Chgo., 1952-56; salesman Pa. R.R., Kansas City, Mo., 1956-59; asst. dir. Trailvan Pa. R.R., Phila., 1959-65; div. sales mgr. Pa. R.R., Milw., 1965-68; dir. Trailvan Penn-Ctrl. R.R., N.Y.C., 1968-71; pres. Hub City Terminals, Chgo., 1971-85; chmn. The Hub Group, Chgo., 1985—; also bd. dirs.; bd. dirs. 30 Hubcity terminals. Cpl. U.S. Army, 1946-47. Recipient Achievement award Intermodal Transp. Assn., 1991, Harry E. Salzberg medallion for outstanding achievement in transp.; named Chgo. Transp. Man of Yr., Chgo. Transp. Assn., 1990. Mem. N.Y. Traffic Club, Chgo. Traffic Club. Republican. Lutheran. Avocations: golf, biking, swimming. Office: The Hub Group Inc 377 E Butterfield Rd Ste 700 Lombard IL 60148-5659*

YEARGIN-ALLSOPP, MARSHALYN, medical epidemiologist, pediatrician; b. Greenville, S.C., May 17, 1948; d. Grady Andrew and Willie Mae (Blocker) Yeargin; m. Ralph Norman Allsopp, Apr. 5, 1975; children: Timothy Chandler, Whitney Marisha. Student Bennett Coll., 1964-66; BA, Sweet Briar Coll., 1968; MD, Emory U., 1972. Diplomate Am. Bd. Pediatrics. Intern Montefiore Hosp., Bronx, N.Y., 1972-73, resident, 1973-75; instr. pediatrics Albert Einstein Coll. Medicine, Bronx, 1975-77, asst. prof. pediatrics, 1977-78, 80-81; pediatrician Montefiore-Morrisania Comprehensive Health Care Ctr., Bronx, 1975-78, Louise Wise Adoption Agy., N.Y.C., 1975-80, Children's Evaluation and Rehab. Ctr., Rose F. Kennedy Ctr., Bronx, 1980-81; officer USPHS, 1981—, comdr., 1983—; epidemiologic intelligence surveillance officer birth defects br. Ctrs. for Disease Control, Atlanta, 1981-83, preventive medicine resident, 1982-84, med. epidemiologist, 1984—; pediatric cons. Clayton County Early Intervention Program, Jonesboro, Ga., 1983—; med. dir. Easter Seal Presch. Program, Atlanta, 1981-83; physician Com. on Handicapped, N.Y.C., 1979-81, United Cerebral Palsy Program, Bronx, 1980-81. Bd. overseers Sweet Briar Coll., 1981-89; bd. dirs. Neighborhood Arts Ctr., Atlanta, 1984-87; mem. prevention edn. com. Retarded Citizens, Atlanta, 1984-96; mem. fundraising campaign Greater Atlanta YWCA, 1985; bd. trustees Pace Acad., 1986—; co-chmn. Minority Atlanta Families in Ind. Schs., Inc., 1986—; chair, Bd. dirs. profl. adv. com. Cerebral Palsey Ctr., REACH, Inc., Atlanta, 1988—; mem. State of Ga. Interagy. Coun. for Edn. of the Handicapped Act., 1988-96; mem. sci. adv. bd. Nat. Alliance for Autism Rsch. Recipient Disting. Alumna award, Sweet Briar Coll., 1992. Fellow Am. Acad. Pediatrics, Am. Acad. Cerebral Palsy and Devel. Medicine; mem. AMA, Atlanta Med. Assn., Jack and Jill of Am., Phi Beta Kappa, Delta Sigma Theta. Office: Ctrs for Disease Control 4770 Buford Hwy NE Atlanta GA 30341-3717

YEARIAN, MASON RUSSELL, physicist; b. Lafayette, Ind., July 5, 1932; married; three children. BS, Purdue U., 1954; MS, Stanford U., 1956, PhD in Physics, 1961. Rsch. assoc. physics U. Pa., 1959-61; from asst. prof. to assoc. prof. Stanford (Calif.) U., 1961-71, prof. physics, 1971—, dir. High Energy Physics Lab., 1973-95. Office: Stanford U WW Hanson Exptl Physics Lab Stanford CA 94305-4085*

YEARLEY, DOUGLAS CAIN, mining and manufacturing company executive; b. Oak Park, Ill., Jan. 7, 1936; s. Bernard Cain and Mary Kenny (Howard) Y.; m. Elizabeth Anne Dunbar, Feb. 8, 1958; children: Sandra, Douglas Jr., Peter, Andrew. BMetE, Cornell U., 1958; postgrad., Harvard U., 1968. Engr. welding Gen. Dynamics, Groton, Conn., 1958-60; dir. rsch., project engr. Phelps Dodge Copper Products, Elizabeth, N.J., 1960-68; mgr. ops. Phelps Dodge Internat. Co., N.Y.C., 1968-71; v.p. ops. Phelps Dodge Tube Co., L.A., 1971-73; exec. v.p. Phelps Dodge Cable and Wire Co., Yonkers, N.Y., 1973-75; pres. Phelps Dodge Brass Co., Lyndhurst, N.J., 1975-79; pres. Phelps Dodge Sales Co., N.Y.C., 1979-82, v.p. mktg., 1979-82; sr. v.p. Phelps Dodge Corp., N.Y.C., 1982-87, exec. v.p., 1987-89, chmn., CEO, 1989-91; chmn., pres., CEO Phelps Dodge Corp., Phoenix, 1991—, also bd. dirs.; bd. dirs. USX Corp., Pitts., J.P. Morgan and Co., Inc. and Morgan Guaranty Trust Co., N.Y.C., Lockheed Martin Corp., Calabasas, Calif., So. Peru Copper Co. Mem. Ariz. Econs. Coun., 1989—, Conf. Bd., 1989—; bd. dirs. Am. Grad. Sch. Internat. Mgmt., 1990-92, Phoenix Symphony, 1988-94; chmn. Arts Coalition, 1989-90; trustee Phoenix Art Mus., 1994—. Mem. Nat. Elec. Mfrs. Assn. (bd. dirs. 1983-92), Internat. Copper Assn. (bd. dirs. 1987—, chmn. 1990—), Am. Mining Congress (vice chmn.), Nat. Mining Assn. (chmn.), Copper Devel. Assn. (chmn. 1989-93, dir. 1993—), Nat. Assn. Mfrs. (bd. dirs. 1988-94), Bus. Roundtable, Bus. Coun., Skyu Club, Echo Lake Country Club, Paradise Valley Country Club, Ariz. Club, Blind Brook Country Club. Republican. Congregationalist. Avocations: tennis, golf, classical music. Home: 8201 N Via De Lago Scottsdale AZ 85258-4215 Office: Phelps Dodge Corp 2600 N Central Ave Phoenix AZ 85004-3050

YEARWOOD, TRISHA, country music singer, songwriter; b. Monticello, Ga., 1964; m. Chris Latham (div.); m. Robert Reynolds, May 21, 1994. Degree in Music Bus., Belmont Coll. Intern MTM Records, demo singer, commercial jingles singer; recording artist MCA Records. Albums include Trisha Yearwood, 1991 (platinum), Hearts in Armor, 1992 (Grammy nomination: Best Country Female Vocal, 1994 for "Walkaway Joe"), The Song Remembers When, 1993, Thinkin' About You, 1995, Everybody Knows, 1996; back-up vocalist Garth Brooks albums; opening act Garth Brooks Tour, 1991; TV appearances on TNN American Music Shop. Named Best New Country Artist by Am. Music Awards, 1992, Top New Female Vocalist by Acad. Country Music, 1992; first female in country music history to have debut single reach #1 on charts with She's in Love with the Love, 1991. Office: MCA Records Internat 70 Universal City Plz Universal Cty CA 91608-1011*

YEATES, ZENO LANIER, retired architect; b. Atlanta, Jan. 9, 1915; s. Zeno Epps and Louise (Ames) Y.; m. Elsie Lankford, June 12, 1947; children—Zeno Ames, Arthur Lankford, Laura. B.S. in Civil Engring, Miss. State U., 1937; B.Arch., U. Pa., 1942, M.Arch., 1976. Asso. J. Frazer Smith & Assos., Memphis, 1947-57; partner Zeno Yeates & Assos., Memphis, 1957-63; pres. Yeates & Gaskill, Inc. (Architects), Memphis, 1963-79, Yeates Gaskill Rhodes (Architects, Inc.), 1980-85; ret., 1983; chmn. Tenn. Br. Arch. and Engring. Examiners, 1963-67; vol. Internat. Exec. Svc. Corp.; designer 11 hosps. in S.Am., Ctrl. Am., Eastern Europe. Fellow AIA (dir. 1975-77); mem. Tenn. Soc. Architects (pres. 1958), Constrn. Specifications Inst. Presbyterian. Clubs: Kiwanis (Memphis), Univ. (Memphis). Home: 2992 Gardens Way Memphis TN 38111-2647

YEATMAN, HARRY CLAY, biologist, educator; b. Ashwood, Tenn., June 22, 1916; s. Trezevant Player and Mary (Wharton) Y.; m. Jean Hansford Anderson, Nov. 24, 1949; children—Henry Clay, Jean Hansford. A.B., U. N.C., Chapel Hill, 1939, M.A., 1942, Ph.D., 1953; student, Cornell U., summer 1937. Asst. prof. biology U. of South, Sewanee, Tenn., 1950-54; asso. prof. U. of South, 1954-60, prof., 1960—, Kenan prof., 1980—, chmn. dept., 1972-76, elderhostel tchr., 1987-88; vis. prof. marine biology Va. Inst.

Marine Sci., Gloucester Point, summer 1967; cons. Smithsonian Instn., Sci. Applications, Inc., La Jolla, Calif., Ctrs. for Disease Control, Atlanta, WHO, Ecol. Analysts, Inc., Balt., Duke Power Co., Charlotte, N.C. Contbr. articles to profl. jours. Served with AUS, 1942-46. Gen. Edn. Bd. fellow, 1941-42; Brown Found. fellow, 1984. Fellow AAAS; mem. Soc. Systematic Biology (charter), Soc. Limnology and Oceanography (charter), Soc. Ichthyology and Herpetology, Tenn. Acad. Sci., Am. Micros. Soc., Am. Ornithologists Union, Tenn. Ornithol. Soc., Tenn. Archeol. Soc., Nat. Speleological Soc., Blue Key, Phi Beta Kappa, Sigma Xi, Omicron Delta Kappa, Sigma Nu. Republican. Episcopalian. Home: Jumpoff Rd PO Box 356 Sewanee TN 37375 Office: Woods Lab Sewanee TN 37383-1000

YEATMAN, HOYT, special effects expert, executive. BA, UCLA, 1977. Mem. spl. effects crews for various movies; mem. animation and spl. effects teams NBC-TV, N.Y.C.; mem. prodn. team Paramount Pictures; co-founder, v.p., supr. visual effects Dream Quest Images, Simi Valley, Calif.; guest speaker, U.S. and overseas. Visual effects works include: (TV) Laugh-In Spls., Buck Rogers, Battlestar Gallactica, (movies) Close Encounters of the Third Kind, The Abyss (Oscar 1989), Star Trek: The Motion Picture, (projects) Michael Jackson's Moonwalker, John Badham's Blue Thunder, Short Circuit, Steven Spielberg's Amazing Stories; also dir. TV commls. for Proctor & Gamble, Taco Bell. Office: Dream Quest Images 2635 Park Center Dr Simi Valley CA 93065-6209*

YEATON, CECELIA E(MMA), healthcare administration executive; b. Suffern, N.Y., Sept. 7, 1939; d. Cornelius and Marguerite Augusta (von Lueck) Schoolcraft; m. M. Bruce Yeaton, June 30, 1961; 1 child, Cecily Marguerite (dec.). BA, U. Maine, 1961. Diplomate Am. Coll. Health Care Execs. Adminstr. asst. Roger Williams Hosp., Providence, R.I., 1974-75; office mgr. radiology Hillcrest Hosp., Pittsfield, Mass., 1875-79, dir. quality assurance/risk mgmt., 1980-88; asst. adminstr. Univ. Hosp., Bklyn., 1988—; cons. Dalton (Mass.) Nursing Home, Inc., 1985-87; chief reference svcs. Western Conn. U. Libr., Danbury, Conn.; asst. dir. Mary C. Wheeler Sch., Providence. Active Ind. Women's Forum, Sisters in Crime, N.Y. Mem. Ind. Women's Forum, Mass. Soc. Hosp. Risk Mgmt. (bd. dirs. 1984-88, pres. 1986-87), Am. Soc. Healthcare Risk Mgmt. (edn. com. 1985-86), Greater N.Y. Hosp. Assn. (regional adv. group 1993—), Am. Coll. Healthcare Execs., Metro. Healthcare Adminstrs. Assn., Am. Soc. Quality Control. Republican. Episcopalian. Avocations: short story and essay writing, cooking, watercolors. Office: Univ Hosp 445 Lenox Rd Box 23 Brooklyn NY 11203

YEATS, ROBERT SHEPPARD, geologist, educator; b. Miami, Fla., Mar. 30, 1931; s. Robert Sheppard and Carolyn Elizabeth (Rountree) Y.; m. Lillian Eugenia Bowie, Dec. 30, 1952 (dec. Apr. 1991); children: Robert Bowie, David Claude, Stephen Paul, Kenneth James, Sara Elizabeth; m. Angela M. Hayes, Jan. 7, 1993. B.A., U. Fla., 1952; M.S., U. Wash., 1956, PhD, 1958. Registered geologist, Oreg., Calif. Geologist, petroleum exploration and prodn. Shell Oil Co., Ventura and Los Angeles, Calif., 1958-67; Shell Devel. Co., Houston, 1967; assoc. prof. geology Ohio U., Athens, 1967-70; prof. Ohio U., 1970-77; prof. geology Oreg. State U., Corvallis, 1977—; prof. oceanography Oreg. State U., 1991—, chmn. dept., 1977-85; geologist U.S. Geol. Survey, 1968, 69, 75; Glomar Challenger scientist, 1971, co-chief scientist, 1973-74, 78; mem. Oreg. Bd. Geologist Examiners, 1981-83; chmn. Working Group 1 Internat. Lithosphere Program, 1987-90; mem. geophysics study com. NRC, 1987-94; chmn. task force group on paleoseismology Internat. Lithosphere Program, 1990—; chmn. subcom. on Himalayan active faults Internat. Geol. Correlation Program, Project 206, 1984-92; researcher on Cenozoic tectonics of So. Calif., Oreg., New Zealand and Himalaya; active faults of Calif. Transverse Ranges, deep-sea drilling in Ea. Pacific; vis. scientist N.Z. Geol. Survey, 1983-84, Geol. Survey of Japan, 1992, Inst. de Phys. du Globe de Paris, 1993. Mem. Ojai (Calif.) City Planning Commn., 1961-62, Ojai City Council, 1962-65. 1st lt. U.S. Army, 1952-54. Named Richard H. Jahns Disting. Lectr. in Engring. Geology, 1995; Ohio U. rsch. fellow, 1973-74; grantee NSF, U.S. Geol. Survey. Fellow AAAS, Geol. Soc. Am. (chmn. structural geology and tectonics divsn. 1984-85, Cordilleran sect. 1988-89, assoc. editor bull. 1987-89); mem. Am. Assn. Petroleum Geologists (Outstanding Educator award Pacific sect. 1991), Am. Geophys. Union, Seismol. Soc. Am., European Union of Geoscis., Oreg. Acad. Sci. Home: 1654 NW Crest Pl Corvallis OR 97330-1812 Office: Oreg State U Dept Geoscis Corvallis OR 97331

YEAW, MARION ESTHER, retired nurse; b. Chgo., June 13, 1926; d. Clarence Yates and Olga Sophia (Gorling) Y. BSN, U. Mich., 1949; MEd, Mills Coll., Oakland, Calif., 1965. Cert. tchr. in nursing, Calif. Staff nurse U. Mich. Hosp., Ann Arbor, 1949-51; instr. pediatric nursing Kaiser Found. Sch. Nursing, Oakland, 1951-76, 1976-78; instr. pediatric nursing Contra Costa Community Coll., San Pablo, Calif., 1976-78, Merritt C.C., Oakland, Calif.; dir. staff devel. Waters Edge Inc., Alameda, Calif., 1978-89; retired, 1989. Mem. AAUW, LWV, Bus. and Profl. Women's Club (Woman of Achievement award 1988), Alumnae Assn. U. Mich. Sch. Nursing, Mills Coll. Alumni Assn. Lutheran. Home: 1601 Broadway # 6 Alameda CA 94501-3050

YEAZEL, KEITH ARTHUR, lawyer; b. Fayetteville, N.C., Feb. 14, 1956; s. Russell E. and Barbara E. (Weaver) Y.; m. Deborah M. MacDonald, Aug. 30, 1986. BA, Ohio State U., 1983; JD, Capital U., 1989. Bar: Ohio 1989, U.S. Dist. Ct. (so. dist.) Ohio 1989, U.S. Ct. Appeals (6th cir.) 1990, U.S. Supreme Ct. 1992. Law clk. to judge George C. Smith U.S. Dist. Ct., Columbus, Ohio, 1988-89; prin. Keith A. Yeazel, Atty. at Law, Columbus, 1989—. Mem. ABA, Ohio Bar Assn., Columbus Bar Assn., Nat. Assn. Criminal Def. Lawyers, Ohio Assn. Criminal Def. Lawyers, Order of Curia. Republican. Lutheran. Office: 65 S 5th St Columbus OH 43215-4307

YEAZELL, RUTH BERNARD, English language educator; b. N.Y.C., Apr. 4, 1947; d. Walter and Annabelle (Reich) Bernard; m. Stephen C. Yeazell, Aug. 14, 1969 (div. 1980). BA with high honors, Swarthmore Coll., 1967; MPhil (Woodrow Wilson fellow), Yale U., 1970, PhD, 1971. Asst. prof. English Boston U., 1971-74, UCLA, 1975-77, assoc. prof., 1977-80, prof., 1980-91, Yale U, 1991—, dir. grad. studies, 1993—, Chace family prof., 1995—, dir. Horace Walpole Libr., 1996—. Author: Language and Knowledge in the Late Novels of Henry James, 1976, Death and Letters of Alice James, 1981, Fictions of Modesty: Women and Courtship in the English Novel, 1991; assoc. editor Nineteenth-Century Fiction, 1977-80; editor: Sex, Politics, and Science in the 19th Century Novel, 1986, Henry James: A Collection of Critical Essays, 1994. Woodrow Wilson fellow, 1967-68, Guggenheim fellow, 1979-80, NEH fellow, 1988-89, Pres.'s Rsch. fellow U. Calif., 1988-89. Mem. MLA (exec. coun. 1985-88), English Inst. (supervising com. 1983-86). Office: Yale U Dept English New Haven CT 06524

YEE, ALBERT HOY, retired psychologist, educator; b. Santa Barbara, Calif., June 14, 1929; children: Lisa Diane, Hoyt Brian, Cynthia Rae. B.A., U. Calif., Berkeley, 1952; M.A., San Francisco State U., 1959; Ed.D., Stanford U., 1965. Post-doctoral research fellow U. Oreg., Eugene, 1966-67; assoc. prof. edn. U. Wis., Madison, 1967-70, prof., 1970-73; prof. ednl. psychology, dean grad. studies and research Calif. State U., Long Beach, 1973-79, originating founder Grad. Ctr., 1974; prof. edn. U. Mont., 1979-83, dean Sch. Edn., 1979-82; sr. lectr. psychology Chinese U. of Hong Kong, 1985-89; dean, prof. psychology Am. Coll., Singapore; sr. lectr. psychology Nat. U., Singapore, 1989-90; dir. program U. Md., Hongkong, 1990; disting. vis. prof. ednl. psychology spl. adviser coll. grad. studies and internat. programs Marist Coll., 1990-92; prof. ednl. psychology Fla. Internat. U., Miami, 1992-94; chmn. 1st Fed. Adv. Com. for Asian and Pacific Island Ams., Bur. Census, 1976-81. Author: Man, Society and the World, 1968; coauthor: Comprehensive Spelling Instruction: Theory, Research and Application, 1971; editor: Social Interaction in Educational Settings, 1971, Perspectives on Management Systems Approaches to Education: A Symposium, 1973, Search for Meaning, 1984, A Study on Possible Future Developments for Hong Kong: Strategic Planning and Innovations, 1985, A People Misruled: Hong Kong and the Chinese Stepping-Stone Syndrome, 1989, 2d edit., 1992; editor: East Asian Higher Education: Traditions and Transformatinos, 1994. With AUS, 1952-55, Korea, Japan. Recipient Civic Commendation Madison, 1973; sr. Fulbright lectr. Tokyo and Tamagawa Univs., Japan; also 1st Fulbright scholar to People's Republic China, 1972. Fellow AAAS, Nat. Conf. Research in English, Am. Psychol. Assn. , Am. Psychol. Soc.; mem. Calif. Coll. and Univ. Faculty Assn. (founder 1961), Chinese Hist. Soc. Am. and Orgn. of Chinese Americans (Bicentennial speaker), Asian-Am. Psychol. Assn. (pres. 1979-82, jour. editor 1981-82), Western Mont. Stanford Alumni Club (founding pres. 1997—). Home: 3822 Lincoln Rd Missoula MT 59802-3039

YEE, ALFRED ALPHONSE, structural engineer, consultant; b. Honolulu, Aug. 5, 1925; s. Yun Sau and Kam Ngo (Lum) Y.; m. Janice Ching (div.); children: Lailan, Mark, Eric, Malcolm, Ian; m. Elizabeth Wong, June 24, 1975; children: Suling, Trevor, I'Ling. BSCE, Rose Hulman Inst. Tech., 1948, Dr. of Engring. (hon.), 1976; MEng in Structures, Yale U., 1949. Registered profl. engr., Hawaii, Calif., Guam, Fla., Tex., Minn., Ohio., Northern Mariana Islands. With civil engring. dept. Dept. Pub. Works, Terr. of Hawaii, Honolulu, 1949-51; structural engr. 14th Naval Dist., Pearl Harbor, Hawaii, 1951-54; pvt. practice structural engring. cons. Honolulu, 1954-55; structural engring. cons. Park & Yee Ltd., Honolulu, 1955-60; pres. Alfred A. Yee & Assocs. Inc., Honolulu, 1960-82; v.p., tech. adminstr. Alfred. A. Yee div. Leo A. Daly, Honolulu, 1982-89; pres. Applied Tech. Corp., Honolulu, 1984—. Patentee in concrete tech., land and sea structures; contbr. articles to profl. jours. Served with U.S. Army, 1946-47. Named Engr. of Yr., Hawaii Soc. Profl. Engrs., 1969, one of Men Who Made Marks in 1970, Honolulu, 1970. Fellow Yale Engring. Assn., PCI; mem. Nat. Acad. Engring., Prestressed Concrete Inst. (Martin P. Korn award 1965), NSPE, Soc. Naval Architects and Marine Engrs., Fla. Engring. Soc., Internat. Assn. Bridge and Structural Engring., Post-Tensioning Inst., ASCE (hon.), Am. Concrete Inst. (hon.). Avocations: golfing, swimming. Office: 1441 Kapiolani Blvd Ste 810 Honolulu HI 96814-4404

YEE, DAVID, chemist, pharmaceutical company executive; b. Albany, N.Y., Sept. 26, 1948; s. Fook On and King Sau (Seto) Y.; m. Vivien Chee-Nan Yeo, May 11, 1974; children: Daniel Ming-dao, Peter Ming-de. BS (cum laude), Rensselaer Polytech. Inst., 1970; MS, Cornell U., 1973, PhD, 1978. Fellow Max Planck Inst. for Exptl. Medicine, Göttingen, Germany, 1978-80; rsch. assoc. Harvard U., 1980-85; rsch. dir. Advance Biofactures Corp., Lynbrook, N.Y., 1985—. Contbr. articles to profl. jours. including Analytical Chemistry, Jour. of Molecular Evolution, Biochemistry, Hoppe-Seyler's Zeitschrift für Physiologische Chemie, FEBS Letters, European Jour. Biochemistry; patentee in field. Mem. AAAS, Am. Chem. Soc., Am. Sci. Affiliation, N.Y. Acad. Scis. Office: 35 Wilbur St Lynbrook NY 11563-2358

YEE, ROBERT DONALD, ophthalmologist; b. Beijing, China, Feb. 21, 1945; came to U.S., 1947, naturalized, 1947; s. James and Marian Y.M. (Li) Y.; m. Linda Margaret Neil, June 28, 1968; children—Jillian Neil, Allison Betram. A.B., Harvard U., 1966, M.D., 1970. Diplomate Am. Bd. Ophthalmology. Intern, U. Rochester, N.Y., 1970-71; resident in ophthalmology Jules Stein Eye Inst., UCLA, 1971-74; fellow in neuro-ophthalmology Nat. Eye Inst., Bethesda, Md., 1974-76; chief ophthalmology Harbor-UCLA Med. Ctr., Torrance, Calif., 1976-78; asst. prof. ophthalmology Sch. Medicine, UCLA, 1976-78, assoc. prof., 1978-82, prof., 1982-87; prof., chmn. dept. ophthalmology Ind. U. Sch. Medicine, Indpls., 1987—; mem. residency rev. com. for ophthalmology Accrediation Coun. for Grad. Med. Edn., 1995—. Mem. editorial bd. Investigative Ophthalmology and Visual Sci., 1982—, von Graefe's Archives of Ophthalmology, 1983-89. Author numerous med. research papers. Served as lt. comdr. USPHS, 1974-76. Fulbright scholar, 1966; NIH grantee, 1976—; Dolly Green Research scholar, 1984-86; Feldman endowed chair ophthalmology UCLA, 1984-87. Fellow ACS, Am. Acad. Ophthalmology; mem. Assn. Rsch. in Vision and Ophthalmology (chmn. eye movement sect. 1981, 87, trustee 1996—), Am. Ophthal. Soc., Ind. Acad. Ophthalmology, Chinese Am. Ophthal. Soc. (pres. 1996—), Ind. Med. Soc., Indpls. Ophthal. Soc., Phi Beta Kappa, Alpha Omega Alpha. Office: Ind U Med Ctr 702 Rotary Cir Indianapolis IN 46202-5133

YEE, STEPHEN, airport executive. Adminstrv. asst. health dept. City of L.A., 1958-63, sr. adminstrv. asst. dept. airports, 1963-72, fed. aid coord., 1972-75, project mgr., 2d level roadway and terminal improvements, airport facilities planner, 1975-83, staff asst. to bd. airport commrs., 1983-85, airport mgr. L.A. Internat. Airport, 1985—. Office: Los Angeles Intl Airport Los Angeles Dept of Airports 1 World Way Los Angeles CA 90045-5803*

YEGGE, ROBERT BERNARD, lawyer, college dean emeritus, educator; b. Denver, June 17, 1934; s. Ronald Van Kirk and Fairy (Hill) Y. A.B. magna cum laude, Princeton U., 1956; M.A. in Sociology, U. Denver, 1958, J.D., 1959. Bar: Colo. 1959, D.C. 1978. Ptnr. Yegge, Hall and Evans, Denver, 1959-78; with Harding Shultz & Downs successor to Nelson and Harding, 1979—; prof. U. Denver Coll. Law, 1965—, dean, 1965-77, dean emeritus, 1977—; asst. to pres. Denver Post, 1971-75; v.p., exec. dir. Nat. Ctr. Preventive Law, 1986-91. Author: Colorado Negotiable Instruments Law, 1960, Some Goals; Some Tasks, 1965, The American Lawyer: 1976, 1966, New Careers in Law, 1969, The Law Graduate, 1972, Tomorrow's Lawyer: A Shortage and Challenge, 1974, Declaration of Independence for Legal Education, 1976. Mng. trustee Denver Ctr. for Performing Arts, 1972-75; chmn. Colo. Coun. Arts and Humanities, 1968-80, chmn. emeritus, 1980—; mem. scholar selection com. Henry Luce Found., 1975—; Active nat. and local A.R.C., chmn. Denver region, 1985-88; trustee Denver Symphony Soc., Inst. of Ct. Mgmt., Denver Dumb Friends League, 1992—, Met. Denver Legal Aid Soc., 1994—, Colo. Acad.; trustee, vice chmn. Nat. Assembly State Arts Agys.; vice chmn. Mexican-Am. Legal Edn. and Def. Fund, 1970-76. Recipient Disting. Svc. award Denver Jr. C. of C., 1965; Harrison Tweed award Am. Assn. Continuing Edn. Adminstrs., 1985, Alumni Faculty award U. Denver, 1993. Mem. Law and Soc. Assn. (life, pres. 1965-70), ABA (chmn. lawyers conf. 1987-88, chmn. accreditation commn. for legal assistant programs 1980-90, standing com. legal assts. 1987-92, standing com. delivery legal svcs. 1992-95, com. on Gavel award 1995—, del. to jud. adminstrn. coun. 1989-95, Robert B. Yegge award 1996), Colo. Bar Assn. (bd. govs. 1965-77), Denver Bar Assn., D.C. Bar Assn., Am. Law Inst., Am. Judicature Soc. (bd. dirs. 1968-72, 75-85, Herbert Harley award 1985), Am. Acad. Polit. and Social Sci., Am. Sociol. Soc., Assn. Am. Law Schs., Order St. Ives, Phi Beta Kappa, Beta Theta Pi, Phi Delta Phi, Alpha Kappa Delta, Omicron Delta Kappa. Home: 3472 S Race St Englewood CO 80110-3138 Office: Harding Shultz & Downs 1200 17th St Ste 1950 Denver CO 80202-5835

YEGGY-DAVIS, GERALDINE MARIE, elementary reading and special education educator; b. Riverside, Iowa, July 25, 1922; d. Henry Clair and Mary Maurine Yeggy; m. Henry Louis Davis, Dec. 28, 1976. BA, Marycrest Internat. U., Davenport, Iowa, 1947; MA, U. Detroit, 1970; postgrad., UCLA; Ednl. Specialist degree, Western Ill. U., 1976; PhD in Reading Edn., La Salle U., 1995. Cert. permanent tchr., ednl. adminstr., reading specialist, learning disabilities, Iowa. Primary tchr. numerous sch. systems, including, Davenport, Ottumwa, Iowa, Ft. Madison, Des Moines, Mpls., Rock Island, Ill.; reading specialist, primary tchr. Chpt. I, Davenport Community Schs.; tchr. spl. edn. Child Devel., Inc., Milan, Ill.; pres. Child Devel. Inc., Milan, Ill.; administrator C.O.P.E. Tutoring Sch. Inc., Milan, Ill., 1996—; workshop presenter curriculum of perceptual/conceptual experiences program; adminstr. C.O.P.E. Tutorial School Inc. for primary children with learning disabilites, Milan Ill., bd. dirs., pres. Contbr. numerous publs. for children. Bd. dirs. Quad-Cities Spl. Persons Encounter Christ (S.P.E.C.); active Illowa Dog Trainers. Recipient Ind. U. Sch. Project award for Effective Teaching of Reading, 1983, Golden Apple award Scott County, 1991; fellow Wall St. Jour., 1964. Mem. NEA, ASCD, Ill. ASCD, Nat. Coun. Tchrs. English, Internat. Reading Assn., Ill. State Edn. Assn., Iowa Reading Assn., Miss. River Band Reading Assn., Nat. Learning Disabilities Assn., Ill. Learning Disabilities Assn., Early Childhood Edn. Assn., Nat. Coun. Tchrs. Math. Home: 509 33rd Ave W Milan IL 61264-3753 Office: COPE Tutoring Sch Inc Annex Bldg 3 124 3rd Ave W Milan IL 61264-2440

YEGIAN, RICHARD, real estate executive. BSME, Harvey Mudd Coll., 1985; MCE, MBA, Northwestern U., 1986. Co-founder Admiral Devel. Co., Burbank, Calif., 1986—; pres., CEO Admiral Realty, Glendale, Calif., 1989—. Mem. Mensa. Office: Admiral Realty 100 N Brand Blvd 2d Fl Glendale CA 91203-2614

YEGULALP, TUNCEL M., mining engineer, educator; b. Konya, Turkey, Nov. 5, 1937; came to U.S., 1963; s. Faik Suleyman and Selma Safiye (Karatay) Y.; m. Sevinc Guneri, July 5, 1963; children—Ali, Serdar. B.S., Tech. U., Istanbul, 1961; D.Engring. Sci., Columbia U., 1968. Mining engr. M.T.A., Ankara, Turkey, 1961-63, chief feasibility studies group, 1971; research engr. Mobil Research, Paulsboro, N.J., 1967-69; chief systems cons. Sisag Ltd., Ankara, 1971-72; asst. prof. Columbia U., N.Y.C., 1972-75, assoc. prof. Henry Krumb Sch. Mines, 1975-85, prof., 1985—; dir. N.Y. Mining and Mineral Resources Inst. Rsch., 1987—; elected permanent mem. U.S. del. World Mining Congress, 1993. Author articles in field. Served to 2d lt. C.E. Turkish Army, 1969-71. Internat. AEC fellow, Vienna, 1963; Krumb fellow, Columbia U., 1964, Campbell fellow, 1965. Mem. AIME, Inst. Mgmt. Scis., Ops. Research Soc. Am., Turkish Studies Assn., Sigma Chi. Moslem. Office: Columbia U 805-1 SWM New York NY 10027

YEH, CHAI, electrical engineer, educator; b. Hangchow, China, Sept. 21, 1911; came to U.S., 1933, naturalized, 1956; s. Yun Ching and Ai Hwa (Ho) Y.; m. Ida Chiang, June 20, 1936; children—Yin, Jen. B.S., Chekiang U., Hangchow, 1931; Ph.D., Harvard U., 1936. Prof. elec. engring. Pei Yang U., Tientsin, China, 1936-37, Tsing Hwa U., Peking, China, 1937-48; chmn. dept. elec. engring. Tsing Hwa U., 1945-47; vis. prof. elec. engring. U. Kans., 1948-56; prof. elec. and computer engring. U. Mich., Ann Arbor, 1956-81, prof. emeritus, 1981-97. Author: Handbook of Fiber Optics, Theory and Applications, 1990, Applied Photonics, 1994; contbr. articles to profl. jours. Elected to Internat. Directory Disting. Leadership, 1994. Mem. IEEE, Sigma Xi. Home: 1111 Alvarado Ave Apt F 364 Davis CA 95616-5918 Office: U Mich Dept Engring Ann Arbor MI 48109

YEH, GEORGE CHIAYOU, engineering company executive; b. Chiayi City, Taiwan, Oct. 3, 1926; came to U.S., 1953; s. Chinshyang and Teauchai (Auyang) Woo; m. Lillian Rueieng How, Dec. 27, 1957; children: Bryan V., Katherine A., Christine J., Maximillian S. BS, Nat. Taiwan U., Taipei, 1950; DEng., U. Tokyo, 1953; MS, U. Toronto, Ont., Can., 1955, PhD, 1957. Lectr. Japan Tech. Fedn., Tokyo, 1952-53; assoc. prof. chem. engring. Auburn (Ala.) U., 1957-61; assoc. prof. chem. engring. Villanova (Pa.) U., 1961-63, prof. chem. engring., 1963-91, prof. emeritus, 1991—, asst. v.p. academic affairs, dir. rsch. and patent affairs, 1973-79; pres. Thermodyne Corp., Newtown Square, Pa., 1992—, Hammo Inc., Newtown Square, 1992—; dir. rsch. Rising Sun Engring. Co., Ala., 1958-61; cons. Thiele Kaoline Co., Ga., 1959-62, Ingersol-Rand Co., N.Y., 1975-78; prin. investigator NASA, Tex., 1967-73. Contbr. articles to profl. jours.; patentee (77) in field, U.S. and fgn. countries. Mem. bd. overseers Soc. of Friends, Westtown, 1968—; bd. dirs. Westtown Sch., 1984-85. Recipient Cert. of Appreciation NASA, 1968, 69, 70, Meritorious Svc. award United Inventors and Scientists Am., 1976, Letters of Appreciation White House & Nuclear Power Regulatory Commn., 1979. Fellow Am. Inst. Chemists (chmn. 1972-76, Meritorious Svc. award 1972), Tau Beta Pi (Disting. Engr. award 1968). Avocations: oil painting, gardening, Bonsai. Office: Thermodyne Corp PO Box 442 Newtown Square PA 19073-1012

YEH, GREGORY SOH-YU, physicist, educator; b. Shanghai, Peoples Republic of China, Apr. 11, 1933; came to the U.S., 1953; BS, Holy Cross U., 1957; MS, Cornell U., 1960; PhD, Case Inst. Tech., Cleve., 1966. Rsch. physicist Goodyear, Akron, Ohio, 1960-61; sr. rsch. physicist Gen. Tire, Akron, 1961-64; asst. prof. U. Mich., Ann Arbor, 1967-69, assoc. prof., 1969-72, prof., 1972—; vis. scientist Ford Motor Co., Dearborn, Mich., 1970, Dow Corning, Midland, Mich., 1981; vis. prof. U. Calif., Berkeley, 1982, U. Ulm, Germany, 1973, 83. Avocations: photography, skiing. Office: U Mich Physics Dept Dow Bldg 3042 Ann Arbor MI 48109

YEH, JOHN, reproductive endocrinologist; b. Taipei, Taiwan, Oct. 24, 1956; s. Yun-Chi and Hsing-Wu (Tseng) Y. AB, Harvard U., 1979; MD, U. Calif., San Diego, 1983. Intern, resident Beth Israel Hosp., Boston, 1983-87; fellow Brigham & Women's Hosp., Boston, 1987-89, staff reproductive endocrinologist, 1989—, dir. rsch. reproductive endocrinology, 1993—; instr. Harvard Med. Sch., Boston, 1987-91, asst. prof., 1991-95, assoc. prof., 1995—. Author: Legal Aspects of Infertility, 1991; contbr. articles to profl. jours. NIH Reproductive Scientist Devel. award, 1989-91, Clin. Investigator award, 1993. Fellow Am. Coll. Ob-Gyn. (Searle-Richardson award 1991); mem. Am. Fertility Soc. (Assoc. Mem.'s Prize Paper 1988, 91), Soc. Reproductive Endocrinologists (assoc.), The Endocrine Soc., Soc. for Gynecologic Investigation. Achievements include research in role of peptide growth factors in etiology of female reproductive tract diseases. Office: Dept Ob-Gyn Dept Ob-Gyn 640 Jackson St Saint Paul MN 55101-6110

YEH, K. H., bank executive; b. Taipei, Taiwan, Republic of China, Feb. 1, 1932; m. Hsiu-Mei Yeh Tsang. BA, Nat. Taiwan U., 1954. Exec. v.p. Hwa Nan Comml. Bank, Ltd., Taiwan, 1955-81; pres. Banking Inst. Republic China, 1981-88; CEO Fin. Info. System Group Ministery Fin., Taiwan, 1984-88; pres. Chang Hwa Comml. Bank Ltd., Taiwan, 1988-94; chmn. Taipeibank, Taipei, 1994—. Author: Theory and Practice of Lending Management, 1980; editor: Practice of Bank's Consumer Loan, 1983. Recipient Disting. Fin. Staffer award Ministry Fin., Taipei, 1974. Mem. Banker's Assn. Taiwan (chmn. 1988-92), Banker's Assn. Taipei (chmn. 1992-97), Taiwan U. Alumni Assn. (mng. dir. Taipei chpt. 1994), Taiwan U. Alumni Club, Taipei Yuen-Shan Club. Home: 3 Fl No 432 Chi Lin Rd, Taipei 104, Taiwan Office: Taipeibank, 50 Sec 2 Chung Shan N Rd, Taipei 104, Taiwan

YEH, PAUL PAO, electrical and electronics engineer, educator; b. Sung Yang, Chekiang, China, Mar. 25, 1927; came to U.S., 1956, naturalized, 1963; s. Tsung Shan and Shu Huan (Mao) Y.; m. Beverley Pamela Eng, May 15, 1952; children: Judith Elaine, Paul Edmond, Richard Alvin, Ronald Timothy, Cheryl Chuan-Hang. Student, Nat. Cen. U., Nanking, China, 1946-49; BSEE, U. Toronto (Ont., Can.), 1951; MSEE, U. Pa., 1960, PhD, 1966. Registered profl. engr., Ont. Design engr. Can. Gen. Electric Co., Toronto, 1951-56; asst. prof. SUNY, Binghamton, 1956-57; sr. engr. H.K. Porter, ITE & Kuhlman, Phila. and Detroit, 1957-61; assoc. prof. N.J. Inst. Tech., Newark, 1961-66; supr. rsch. and devel. N.Am. Rockwell, Anaheim, Calif., 1966-70; sr. R&D engr. Lockheed Advanced Devel. Co., Burbank, Calif., 1970-72, 78-89; mem. tech. staff The Aerospace Corp., El Segundo, Calif., 1972-78; chief scientist Advanced Systems Rsch., Pasadena, Calif., 1989—; cons. Consol. Edison Co., N.Y.C., 1963-64, Pub. Svc. Elec. and Gas Co. N.J., 1965-66, Zhejiang Sci. and Tech. Exch. Ctr. with Fgn. Countries, 1995—; sr. lectr. State U. Calif., Long Beach, 1967-73; vis. prof. Chung Shan Inst. Sci. and Tech., 1989-92, Tsinghua U., 1993—, S.E. U., 1994—, Zhejiang U., 1994—; cons. prof. Northwestern Poly. U., 1993—, Shanghai U., 1994—; hon. prof. Beijing U. Aeros. and Astronautics, 1993—, Zhejiang U. Sci. and Tech., 1994—; rschr. power sys. design and control, 1951-66; investigator R&D Stealth tech. electronic warfare, avionics, IR/EO Tech, nuclear hardening, anti-submarine warfare. Recipient Achievement award for anti-submarine warfare/magnetic anomaly detection sys. Lockheed Corp. Mem. IEEE (sr., life), Nat. Mgmt. Assn. (life), Am. Def. Preparedness Assn., Assn. Old Crows, Chinese Am. Engring./Sci. Assn. So. Calif. (pres. 1969-71), Nat. Ctrl. U. Alumni Assn. (pres. 1977), Nat. Security Indsl. Assn., Beijing Assn. for Sci. and Tech. Exchs. with Fgn. Countries, (hon. dir.), Assn. Profl. Engrs. of Ont., N.Y. Acad. Scis., Air Force Assn., Zhejiang Assn. for Sci. and Tech. Exchs. with Fgn. Countries (advisor), Armed Forces Comms. and Electronics Assn., U.S. Naval Inst., Assn. U.S. Army. Republican. Presbyterian. Achievements include patent for Non-Capacitive Transmission Cable. Home: 5555 Via De Campo Yorba Linda CA 92887-4916 Office: Advanced Systems Rsch Inc 33 S Catalina Ave Ste 202 Pasadena CA 91106-2426

YEH, RAYMOND WEI-HWA, architect, educator; b. Shanghai, China, Feb. 25, 1942; came to U.S., 1958, naturalized, 1976; s. Herbert Hwan-Ching and Joyce Bo-Ding (Kwan) Y.; m. Hsiao-Yen Chen, Sept. 16, 1967; children—Bryant Po Yung, Clement Chung-Yung, Emily Su-Yung. B.A., U. Oreg., 1965, B.Arch., 1967; M.Arch., U. Minn., 1969. Cert. Nat. Coun. Archtl. Registration Bds.; registered architect, Okla., Calif., Hawaii. Draftsman, designer various archtl. firms, 1965-68; design architect Ellerbe Architects, St. Paul, 1968-70; v.p., dir. design Sorey, Hill, Binnicker, Oklahoma City, 1973-74; prin. architect Raymond W.H. Yeh & Assos., Norman, Okla., 1974-80; asst. prof. to prof. U. Okla., Norman, 1970-79; head dept. architecture, prof. Calif. Poly. State U., San Luis Obispo, 1979-83; dean Coll. Architecture U. Okla., Norman, 1983-92; prin. architect W.H. Raymond Yeh, Norman, 1983-93; dean sch. architecture U. Hawaii at Manoa, Honolulu, 1993—; profl. adviser Neighborhood Conservation and Devel. Center, Oklahoma City, 1977 79. Works include: St. Thomas More U. Parish and Student Center, Norman, Summit Ridge Center Retirement Community, Harrah, Okla., (recipient Nat. Design award Guild Religious

Architecture 1978). Nat. Endowment for Arts fellow, 1978-79. Fellow AIA (dir., pres. Okla. chpt. 1986, design awards, nat. com. chmn. 1989); mem. Calif. Coun. Archtl. Edn. (dir., pres. 1982-83), Okla. Found. for Architecture (founding chair bd. 1989-90), Asian Soc. Okla. (award of Excellence 1992). Presbyterian. Office: U Hawaii Manoa Sch Architecture Honolulu HI 96822

YEH, TSUNG, orchestral conductor; b. Shanghai, People's Republic China, May 17, 1950; came to U.S., 1981; s. Zu-Jiu and Ren-Qing (Zhang) Ye; m. Sau-Lan Wong, Apr. 8, 1983; 1 child, Mona. B. Music, The Mannes Coll. Music, 1983; postgrad., Yale U., 1983-84. Exxon/Arts Endowment condr. St. Louis Symphony Orch., 1984-87; prin. condr. St. Louis Youth Orch., 1986-87; resident condr. Fla. Orch., Tampa and St. Petersburg, Fla., 1987-89; music dir., condr. South Bend (Ind.) Symphony Orch., 1988—; prin. guest condr. Albany (N.Y.) Symphony Orch., 1991—; guest condr. Rochester (N.Y.) Philharm., 1987, Minn. Orch., Mpls., 1987, Traverse (Mich.) Symphony Orch., 1989, Taiwan (Republic of China) Symphony Orch., 1989, San Francisco Symphony Orch., 1989, Albany (N.Y.) Symphony Orch., 1990, Taipei (Republic of China) Symphony Orch., 1991, Hong Kong Philharm. Orch., 1991. Mem. Fischoff Chamber Music Assn. (bd. dirs. 1989—), Am. Symphony Orch. League, Conductors' Guild. Office: South Bend Symphony Orch 120 W La Salle Ave South Bend IN 46601-1313*

YEH, WILLIAM WEN-GONG, civil engineering educator; b. Szechwan, China, Dec. 5, 1938; s. Kai-Ming and Der-Chao (Hu) Y.; m. Jennie Pao, Mar. 25, 1967; children: Michael, Bobby. B.S.C.E., Nat. Cheng-Kung U., Taiwan, 1961; M.S.C.E., N.Mex. State U., 1964; Ph.D. in Civil Engring., Stanford U., 1967. Acting asst. prof. Stanford U., 1967; asst. research engr. UCLA, 1967-69, asst. prof. civil engring., 1969-73, assoc. prof., 1973-77, prof., 1977—, chmn. dept., 1985-88; cons. Office of Hydrology, UNESCO, Paris, 1974, Jet Propulsion Lab., Pasadena, Calif., 1975-78, U.S. Bur. Reclamation, Phoenix, 1977-81, Dept. Water and Power, São Paulo, Brazil, 1981-83, Rockwell Internat., 1983-88, U.S. AID, 1987-91, Met. Water Dist. of So. Calif., 1989—. Contbr. numerous articles to scholarly jours. Recipient Disting. Faculty award UCLA Engring. Alumni Assn., 1975; recipient Engring. Found. Fellowship award United Engring. Trustees, 1981, numerous research grants including NSF, 1967—. Fellow Am. Geophys. Union (Robert E. Horton award 1989), ASCE (hon., editor Jour. Water Resources Planning and Mgmt. 1988-93, Julian Hinds award 1994); mem. Am. Water Resources Assn. Home: 822 Hanley Ave Los Angeles CA 90049-1914 Office: U Calif 5732 B BH 405 Hilgard Ave Los Angeles CA 90095-9000

YELENICK, MARY THERESE, lawyer; b. Denver, May 17, 1954; d. John Andrew and Maesel Joyce (Reed) Y. B.A. magna cum laude, Colo. Coll., 1976; J.D. cum laude, Georgetown U., 1979. Bar: D.C. 1979, U.S. Dist. Ct. D.C. 1980, U.S. Ct. Appeals (D.C. cir.) 1981, N.Y. 1982, U.S. Dist. Ct. (so. and ea. dists.) N.Y. 1982, U.S. Supreme Ct. 1992, U.S. Ct. Appeals (5th cir.) 1995. Law clk. to presiding justices Superior Ct. D.C., 1979-81; ptnr. Chadbourne & Parke, N.Y.C., 1981—. Editor Jour. of Law and Policy Internat. Bus., 1978-79. Mem. Phi Beta Kappa. Democrat. Roman Catholic. Home: 310 E 46th St New York NY 10017-3002 Office: Chadbourne & Parke 30 Rockefeller Plz New York NY 10112

YELLEN, JANET LOUISE, government official, economics educator; b. Bklyn., Aug. 13, 1946; d. Julius and Anna Ruth (Blumenthal) Y.; m. George Arthur Akerlof, July 8, 1978; 1 child, Robert Joseph. BA in Econs. summa cum laude, Brown U., 1967; PhD, Yale U., 1971. Asst. prof. econs. Harvard U., Cambridge, Mass., 1971-76; lectr. London Sch. Econs. and Polit. Sci., Washington, 1978-80; asst. prof. econs. Sch. Bus. Adminstrn., U. Calif., Berkeley, 1980-82, assoc. prof., 1982-85, prof. Haas Sch. Bus., 1985—, Bernard T. Rocca Jr. prof. internat. bus. and trade, 1992—; cons. div. internat. fin., Bd. Govs. of FRS, Washington, 1974-75, economist trade and fin. studies sect., 1977-78, mem., 1994-97; chair coun. econ. advisers The Cabinet, Washington, 1997—; rsch. fellow MIT, Cambridge, 1974; cons. Congl. Budget Office, 1975-76, mem. panel econ. advisers, 1993—; rsch. affiliate Yale U., New Haven, 1976; mem. adv. panel in econs. NSF, 1977-78, 91-92; mem. Brookings Panel on Econ. Activity, 1987-88, 90-91, sr. adviser, 1989—; Yrjö Jahnsson Found. lectr. on macroecon. theory, Helsinki, 1977-78; mem. Coun. on Fgn. Rels., 1976-81. Author: (monograph) (with Arrow and Shavell) The Limits of the Market in Resource Allocation, 1977; assoc. editor Jour. Econ. Perspectives, 1987-91; contbr. articles to profl. jours. Hon. Woodrow Wilson fellow, 1967, grad. fellow NSF, 1967-71, Guggenheim fellow, 1986-87; grantee NSF, 1975-77, 90-94. Mem. Am. Econ. Assn. (adv. com. to Pres. 1986-87, nominating com. 1988-90), Phi Beta Kappa. Home: 3201 Leland St Chevy Chase MD 20815 Office: 314 Old Exec Office Bldg 17th & Pennsylvania Ave NW Washington DC 20502 also: The Cabinet Old Exec Office Bldg NW Washington DC 20501

YELLEN, JOHN EDWARD, archaeologist; b. N.Y.C., Nov. 1, 1942; s. Julius and Ruth (Blumenthal) Y.; m. Alison Spence Brooks, Dec. 21, 1971; children: Elizabeth Spence, Alexander Brooks. BA, Hobart Coll., 1964; MA, Harvard U., 1966, PhD, 1974. Predoctoral fellow Smithsonian Inst., Washington, 1971-72, postdoctoral fellow, 1972-73, rsch. assoc., 1973-77; program dir. NSF, Washington, 1977-92, archaeology program dir., 1993—. Author: Archaeological Approaches to the Present, 1977; co-editor: Experimental Archeology, 1977. Pres. Sousa Neighborhood Assn., Washington, 1991. Grantee Nat. Geog. Soc., 1973, NSF, 1975-77. Fellow Explorers Club (chair exploration com. 1996—); mem. Internat. Union Pre and Proto-Historic Scis. (exec. com. 1991—), Paleoanthropology Soc. (founder), Harvard Club. Achievements include ethnographic and archaeological research in Botswana, archaeological research in Zaire, Ethiopia. Home: 810 E St SE Washington DC 20003

YELLEN, LINDA, film director, writer, producer; b. Forest Hills, N.Y., July 13; d. Seymour and Bernice (Mittelman) Y. BA magna cum laude, Barnard Coll.; MFA in Film, Columbia U., PhD in Lang., Lit. and Communications. Mem. film faculty Columbia U., N.Y.C., Barnard Coll., Yale U., CUNY; prin. Chrysalis-Yellen Prodns., Inc., N.Y.C., 1982—; pres. The Linda Yellen Co., N.Y.C., 1988—; represented by William Morris Agy. Producer, dir.: (films) Prospera; Come Out, Come Out; Looking Up, 1978; exec. producer (film) Everybody Wins, 1989; producer, dir., co-writer (film) Prisoner Without a Name, Cell Without A Number, NBC-TV, 1984 (Peabody award, Writers Guild nominee for best screenplay); exec. producer, producer (CBS network spls.): Hard Hat and Legs, 1980; Mayflower: The Pilgrims Adventure, 1979; Playing For Time, 1981 (Emmy award for best dramatic spl., Peabody award, Christopher award); exec. producer, producer, co-writer (CBS network spl.) The Royal Romance of Charles and Diana, 1982; exec. producer, producer (TV movies): Second Serve: The Renee Richards Story, CBS-TV, 1986 (Luminous award), Liberace, CBS-TV, 1988; exec. producer Hunt for Stolen War Treasures, syndicated TV, 1989, Sweet Bird of Youth, NBC-TV, 1989; dir., writer, prodr. Chantilly Lace, 1993, Parallel Lives, 1994, The End of Summer, 1995, (Showtime); contbr. articles to N.Y. Times, Village Voice, Interview, Hollywood Reporter. Mem. Dirs. Guild Am. (exec. council), Writers Guild Am., Acad. TV Arts and Scis., Women in Film.*

YELLIN, VICTOR FELL, composer, music educator; b. Boston, Dec. 14, 1924; s. Mendl and Sarah (Fell) Y.; m. Isabel Joseph, May 26, 1948; 1 son, David. A.B. cum laude, Harvard U., 1949, A.M., 1952, Ph.D., 1957. Teaching fellow Harvard U., Cambridge, Mass., 1952-56; asst. prof. NYU, N.Y.C., 1956-58, assoc. prof., 1961-64, prof., 1964—; asst. prof. Williams ., Williamstown, Mass., 1958-60; assoc. prof. Ohio State ., Columbus, 1960-61; coordinator N.Y. Metro-Fulbright-Hayes Vis. Scholars, 1978-82; mem. editorial adv. bd. Am. Music. Composer: (opera) Abaylar, 1974 (song cycle) Dark of the Moon, 1986; conductor: Mrs. H.H.A. Beach's Grand Mass in E-flat, N.Y.C., 1982; author: Chadwick, Yankee Composer, 1990, Bye Bye Blues Variations for Violin and Piano, Tully Hall, N.Y.C., 1992; contbr. articles in Early Melodrama in Am., The Aethiop, Orchestral Restoration, Am. Music, 1996. Served with U.S. Army, 1943-46, ETO. Recipient grant Nat. Endowment Humanities, 1978. Mem. Am. Musicol. Soc., Sonneck Soc. Office: NYU 100 Washington Sq E New York NY 10003-6688

YELTON, ELEANOR O'DELL, retired reading specialist; b. Maryville, Tenn., Jan. 21, 1929; d. Rondie Bliss and Maxie (Williams) O'Dell; m. Doran Yelton, Aug. 26, 1951; children: Doran II, Marshall, David, Holly. BS, East Tenn. State U., 1951. Cert. tchr., Fla. Tchr. Rozelle Sch., Memphis, 1952-55; tchr. English Clay High Sch., Green Cove Springs, Fla., 1963-66, reading specialist, 1986-96; reading specialist The Bolles Sch., Jacksonville, Fla., 1966-84; chair adv. coun. Clay High Sch., Green Cove Springs, 1991-92. Author: (newsletters) PERKS, 1990 (Secondary Reading Coun. Fla. award 1991), Parents' Link, 1993. Mem. Internat. Reading Assn., Fla. Reading Assn., Secondary Reading Coun. Fla., Clay County Acad. Excellence, Clay County Reading Coun. (founder Books for Babies program Humana Hosp. 1990, pres. 1990-91, Literacy award 1995). Avocations: traveling, reading, computers. Home: 3977 Susan Dr Green Cove Springs FL 32043

YELVERTON, DEBORAH SUE, middle school art educator; b. Wilson, N.C., Mar. 17, 1956; d. George Elliott and Hadilene (Coley) Yelverton. BS, Atlantic Christian Coll., 1978. Cert. art educator, N.C. Tchr. art Frink Jr. High Sch., LaGrange, N.C., 1978-79, Wayne County Schs., Goldsboro, N.C., 1979—; mem. judge panel Youth Art Month Art Exhibit, Raleigh, N.C., 1983, mem. Youth Art Month Com., 1982-84; judge panelist Western N.C. Scholastic Arts Competition, Greensboro, 1990, Seymour Johnson AFB Adult Divsn. Arts/Crafts Contest, Goldsboro, 1988-94, 95; mem. Wayne County Mid. Sch. Task Force, Goldsboro, 1990-91. Group photography exhibits include Wayne County Artists that Teach, 1985, N.C. Black/White Photography Travel Exhibit, 1980. Grantee Arts in Schs. program, Cmty. Arts Coun. Wayne County, 1987-88, 89-90; recipient Zeno Spence Art Educator award, 1996; named Outstanding Young Educator Goldsboro Jaycees, 1994. Mem. Nat. Art Edn. Assn., N.C. Art Edn. Assn. Avocations: music, photography, collecting unicorns, dancing. Home: 2601 Cashwell Dr Apt H Goldsboro NC 27534-4253 Office: Ea Wayne Mid Sch 3518 Central Heights Rd Goldsboro NC 27534-8027

YEMMA, JOHN, newspaper editor. Fgn. editor Boston Globe. Office: Globe Newspaper Co 135 Morrissey Blvd Boston MA 02107*

YEN, HENRY CHIN-YUAN, computer systems programmer, engineer, consulting company executive; b. Mpls., Apr. 18, 1958; s. James and Elizabeth Y.; m. Michele Calen, Oct. 8, 1988; children: Andrew, Matthew. Sr. systems programmer Grumman Data Systems Corp., Bethpage, N.Y., 1978-83; mgr. Data Ctr. On-Line Software Internat., Inc., Ft. Lee, N.J., 1983-85, lead systems programmer, 1985-88; v.p. The Galamery Co., Inc., Del., 1988—, Aegis Info. Systems, Inc., Del., 1989—; bd. dirs. Personal Computer Systems Corp. Mem. IEEE, Assn. Computing Machinery, Nat. Sys. Programmers Assn., Mensa. Avocations: bicycling, profl. musician. Home: PO Box 802 Hicksville NY 11802-0802 Office: Aegis Info Systems Inc PO Box 730 Hicksville NY 11802-0730

YEN, SAMUEL S(HOW)-C(HIH), obstetrics and gynecology educator, reproductive endocrinologist; b. Beijing, Feb. 22, 1927; s. K.Y. and E.K. Yen; children: Carol Amanda, Dolores Amelia, Margaret Rae. BS, Cheeloo U., China, 1949; MD, U. Hong Kong, 1954, DSc, 1980. Diplomate Am. Bd. Ob-Gyn (bd. examiners 1973-78), Am. Bd. Reproductive Endocrinology (bd. examiners 1976-82). Intern Queen Mary Hosp., Hong Kong, 1954-55; resident Johns Hopkins U., Balt., 1956-60; assoc. prof. reproductive biology Case Western Res. U., Cleve., 1970—; prof. ob-gyn U. Calif., San Diego, 1972-83, chmn. dept. reproductive medicine, 1972-83, prof. reproductive medicine, 1983—; dir. reproductive endocrinology U. Calif. Med. Ctr., San Diego, 1983—, W.R. Persons chair, 1987; assoc. dir. obstetrics Univ. Hosp., Cleve., 1968-70; DeGroof lectr., 1987; Van Campenhaut lectr. Can. Fertility and Andrology Soc., 1995. Editor: Reproductive Endocrinology Physiology, Pathophysiology and Clinical Management, 1978, 2d rev. edit., 1986, 3d edit., 1991; mem. editorial bd. Endocrine Revs., 1984—. Recipient Axel Munthe Found. award, 1982, Simpson medal U. Edinburgh, Scotland, 1996; Oglebay fellow, 1968-69. Fellow Royal Coll. Ob-Gyn., Royal Coll. Obstetricians and Gynecologists (ad eundem, London); mem. NAS Inst. Medicine, Assn. Am. Physicians, Soc. for Gynecol. Investigation (pres. 1981, Disting. Scientist award 1992), Endocrine Soc. (Rorer Clin. Investigator award 1992). Office: U Calif-San Diego Reproductive Medicine # 0633 La Jolla CA 92093-0633*

YEN, SHERMAN, applied behavior analyst, educator, substance abuse treatment specialist; b. Peking, China, Aug. 4, 1934; came to U.S., 1956; s. C. H. Yen and Pei Wang. PhD, Catholic U. Am., 1969. Prof. psychology Essex Community Coll., Balt., 1970—; pres. Applied Rsch. and Mgmt., Inc., Owings Mills, Md., 1987—; exec. dir. Alcohol and Drug Treatment, Inc., Owings Mills, Md., 1988—; adj. assoc. prof. psychology Loyola Coll., Balt., 1980—; mem. MD. State Coun. Alcohol and Drug Abuse, Balt., 1987—. Mem. APA, Assn. Behavior Analysis. Roman Catholic. Office: Applied Rsch & Mgmt Inc PO Box 133 Owings Mills MD 21117-0133

YEN, TEH FU, civil and environmental engineering educator; b. Kun-Ming, China, Jan. 9, 1927; came to U.S., 1949; s. Kwang Pu and Ren (Liu) Y.; m. Shiao-Ping Siao, May 30, 1959. BS, Cen. China U., 1947; MS, W.Va. U., 1953; PhD, Va. Poly. Inst. and State U., 1956; hon. doctoral degree, Pepperdine U., 1982, Internat. U. Dubna, Russia, 1996. Sr. research chemist Good Yr. Tire & Rubber Co., Akron, 1955-59; fellow Mellon Inst., Pitts., 1959-65; sr. fellow Carnegie-Mellon U., Pitts., 1965-68; assoc. prof. Calif. State U., Los Angeles, 1968-69; assoc. prof. U. So. Calif., 1969-80, prof. civil engring. and environ. engring., 1980—; hon. prof. Shanghai U. Sci. and Tech., 1986, U. Petroleum, Beijing, 1987, Daqing Petroleum Inst., 1992; cons. Universal Oil Products, 1968-76, Chevron Oil Field Rsch. Co., 1968-75, Finnigan Corp., 1976-77, GE, 1977-80, United Techs., 1978-79, TRW Inc., 1982-83, Exxon, 1981-82, DuPont, 1985-88, Min. Petroleum, Beijing, 1982—, Biogas Rsch. Inst.-UN, Chengdu, 1991. Author numerous tech. books; contbr. articles to profl. jours. Recipient Disting. Svc. award Tau Beta Pi, 1974, Imperial Crown Gold medal, Iran, 1976, Achievement award Chinese Engring. and Sci. Assocs. So. Calif., 1977, award Phi Kappa Phi, 1982, Outstanding Contbn. honor Pi Epsilon Tau, 1984, Svc. award Republic of Honduras, 1989, award in Petroleum Chem. Am. Chem. Soc., 1994, Kapitsa Gold medal Russian Fedn., 1995. Fellow Royal Chem. Soc., Inst. Petroleum, Am. Inst. Chemists; mem. Am. Chem. Soc. (bd. dirs. 1993, councillor, founder and chmn. geochemistry divsn. 1979-81, Chinese Acad. Scis. (standing com.), Acad. Scis. Russian Fedn. (academician, fgn. mem.). Home: 2378 Morslay Rd Altadena CA 91001-2716 Office: U So Calif University Park KAP 224A Los Angeles CA 90089

YEN, WILLIAM MAO-SHUNG, physicist; b. Nanking, Kiangsu, China, Apr. 5, 1935; came to U.S., 1952; s. Wanli and Jane Hsanlin (King) Y.; m. Delane Robinson, Aug. 16, 1968 (div. May 1974); m. Laurel Frances Curtis, Aug. 18, 1978; 1 child, Jane Luhsan Bess. BS, U. Redlands, 1956; PhD, Washington U., 1962. Rsch. assoc. Stanford (Calif.) U., 1962-65; asst. prof. U. Wis., Madison, 1965-68, assoc. prof., 1968-72, prof., 1972-90, ret., 1990; Graham Perdue prof. U. Ga., Athens, 1986—; cons. Lawrence Livermore (Calif.) Nat. Labs., 1975-84, Argonne (Ill.) Nat. Labs., 1976-82, Rosemount Corp., Eden Prairie, Minn., 1988—, Chromonix LLD, Beverly Hills, Mich., 1995—. Editor: Laser Spectroscopy of Solids I, 1981, II, 1988, Dynamical Processes in Disordered Solids, 1989; contbr. more than 190 articles to scholarly and profl. jours. Washington U. fellow, 1960, J.S. Guggenheim Found. fellow, 1979, Fulbright Sr. fellow, 1995; recipient Sr. U.S. Scientist award A.V. Humboldt Found., 1985, 90; named hon. prof. U. St. Antonio de Abad, Cusco, Peru, 1983, hon. prof. Inst. Physics, Acad. Sinica, 1995. Fellow AAAS, Am. Physical Soc., Optical Soc. Am.; mem. Electro Chem. Soc., Materials Rsch. Soc., Ceramics Soc. Am., Sigma Xi. Achievements include pioneering establishment of laser spectroscopy as a tool to study optical properties of solids. Home: 180 River Oak Way Athens GA 30605-2677 Office: U Ga Dept Physics and Astronomy Athens GA 30602

YENKIN, BERNARD KALMAN, coatings and resins company executive; b. Columbus, Ohio, Dec. 2, 1930; s. Abe I. and Eleanore G. (Weiner) Y.; m. Miriam Schottenstein, Mar. 31, 1957; children: Leslie Mara, Jonathan, Allison Katsev, Amy. BA, Yale U., 1952; MBA, Harvard U., 1954. V.p. Yenkin-Majestic Paint Corp., Columbus, 1968-77, pres., 1977-85, chmn. bd., 1985—. Pres. Columbus Jewish Fedn., 1980-82, Pro Musica Chamber Orch., Columbus, 1983-85, Columbus Torah Acad., 1977-79; bd. v.p. Jewish Ednl. Svc. N.Am., N.Y.C., 1991-95. Recipient Mayor's award for Vol. Svc. City of Columbus, 1984, Young Leadership award Columbus Jewish Fedn., 1965. Mem. Yale Club of Cen. Ohio (pres. 1979-81), Yale Club of N.Y., Athletic Club (Columbus). Office: Yenkin-Majestic Industries 1920 Leonard Ave Columbus OH 43219-2514

YEO, RON, architect; b. Los Angeles, June 17, 1933; s. Clayton Erik and Rose G. (Westman) Y.; m. Birgitta S. Bergkvist, Sept. 29, 1962; children: Erik Elov, Katarina Kristina. B.Arch., U. So. Calif., 1959. Draftsman Montierth & Strickland (Architects), Long Beach, Calif., 1958-61; designer Gosta Edberg S.A.R. Arkitekt, Stockholm, 1962; partner Strickland & Yeo, Architects, Garden Grove, Calif., 1962-63; pres. Ron Yeo, Architect, Inc., Corona del Mar, Calif., 1963—; cons., lectr. in field. Archtl. works include Garden Grove Civic and Community Center, 1966, Hall Sculpture Studio, 1966, Garden Grove Cultural Center, 1978, Gem Theater, 1979, Festival Amphitheatre, 1983, Los Coyotes Paleontol. Interpretive Ctr., 1986. Mem. Orange County Planning Commn., 1972-73, 1975-76; chmn. Housing and Community Devel. Task Force, 1978, Orange County Fire Protection Planning Task Force, City of Newport Beach City Arts Commn., 1970-72; pres. Orange County Arts Alliance, 1980-81. Fellow AIA; mem. Constrn. Specifications Inst. Democrat. Office: Ron Yeo FAIA Architect Inc 500 Jasmine Ave Corona Del Mar CA 92625-2308

YEO, RONALD FREDERICK, librarian; b. Woodstock, Ont., Can., Nov. 13, 1923; s. Frederick Thomas and Jugertha Aleda (Vansickle) Y.; m. Margaret Elizabeth Horsley, Oct. 12, 1953; children: Joanne, Peter. BA, U. Toronto, 1948, BLS, 1966; LLD (hon.), U. Regina, 1990. Mgr. book dept. Am. News Co., Toronto, 1948-53; sales mgr., dir. Brit. Book Service, Toronto, 1953-63; mgr. trade div. Collier-Macmillan Can., Ltd., Toronto, 1963-65; pub. services coordinator North York (Ont.) Pub. Library, 1966-71; chief librarian Regina (Sask.) Pub. Library, 1971-88; mem. Nat. Library Adv. Bd., 1982-87, chmn., 1986-87. Served with RCAF, 1942-45. Recipient Silver Jubilee medal, 1977. Mem. Can. Libr. Assn. (pres. 1978-79), Can. Assn. Pub. Librs. (chmn. 1975-76), Sask. Libr. Assn., Adminstrs. of Large Pub. Librs. (chmn. 1973-74), Kiwanis (pres. Regina chot. 1981-82).

YEOMANS, DONALD KEITH, astronomer; b. Rochester, N.Y., May 3, 1942; s. George E. and Jessie (Sutherland) Y.; m. Laurie Robyn Ernst, June 20, 1970; children: Sarah, Keith. BA, Middlebury (Vt.) Coll., 1964; MS, U. Md., 1967, PhD, 1970. Supr. Computer Scis. Corp., Silver Spring, Md., 1973-76; rsch. astronomer Jet Propulsion Lab., Pasadena, Calif., 1976-92, supr., 1993—; discipline specialist Internat. Halley Watch, 1982-89; prin. investigator NASA Comet Mission, 1987-91, Near-Earth Asteroid Rendezvous Mission, 1994—. Author: Comet Halley: Once in a Lifetime, 1985, The Distant Planets, 1989, Comets: A Chronological History of Observation, Science, Myth, and Folklore, 1991. Recipient Space Achievement award AIAA, 1985, Exceptional Svc. medal NASA, 1986, Achievement award Middlebury Coll. Alumni, 1987; named NASA/JPL Sr. Rsch. Scientist, 1993. Mem. Internat. Astron. Union, Am. Astron. Soc., Astron. Soc. Pacific. Democrat. Presbyterian. Avocations: tennis, history of astronomy. Office: Jet Propulsion Lab 4800 Oak Grove Dr # 301-150G Pasadena CA 91109-8001

YEOMANS, DONALD RALPH, Canadian government official, consultant; b. Toronto, Ont., Can., Mar. 25, 1925; s. Ralph and Louise (Weismiller) Y.; m. Catherine Simpson Williams, May 13, 1950; children: Patricia Ann, Nancy Louise, Jane Elizabeth. B.A.Sc., U. Toronto, 1947. Registered profl. engr., Ont.; cert. mgmt. acct. Mem. Bur. of Govt. Orgns., Ottawa, Ont., 1962-64; dep. sec. Treasury Bd., Ottawa, 1964-69; asst. dep. minister Dept. Supply and Services, Ottawa, 1969-75; assoc. exec. dir. Anti-Inflation Bd., Ottawa, 1975-76; asst. dep. minister Dept. Nat. Health-Welfare, Ottawa, 1976-77; commr. Correctional Services of Can., Ottawa, 1977-85; chmn. Tariff Bd., 1985-89; spl. advisor Can. Jud. Centre, 1989-92; mem. bd. govs. Carleton U., 1980-93, chmn., 1989-91; spl. advisor Royal Com. Govt. Orgns., 1961, Royal Com. Fin. Accountability, 1977; assoc. Cons. and Audit Can., 1992—; exec. counsellor Pub. Svc. Commn., 1990-95; cons. to govt. and industry, 1990—; mem. bd. govs. Can. Comprehensive Audit Found., 1989-94; mem. ind. adv. com. Auditor Gen. Can., 1989-95; chmn. Coun. Adminstrv. Tribunals, 1986; chmn. Coun. Chairs Ont. Univs., 1991-93; mem. Expert Com. on AIDS in Prisons, 1992-94; chmn. awards com. Am. Correctional Assn., 1992—. Recipient Centennial medal Govt. Can., 1967, Jubilee medal Govt. Can., 1977, E.R. Cass award Am. Corr. Assn., 1991; Australian Commonwealth fellow, 1985. Fellow Soc. Mgmt. Accts. Can (pres. 1977); mem. Assn. State Correctional Adminstrs (pres. 1983), Inst. Pub. Adminstrn. Can. (pres. 1974). Clubs: Five Lakes (pres. 1975); Canadian (Ottawa, pres. 1978). Home and Office: 310 Clemow Ave, Ottawa, ON Canada K1S 2B8

YEOMANS, RUSSELL ALLEN, lawyer, translator; b. Vancouver, B.C., Can., May 13, 1944; came to U.S., 1951; s. Douglas Allen and Mabel Jean (Maguire) Y.; m. Minako Hara, July 7, 1981; children: Megumi Kay, Ken Douglas. BA, U. Calif., Berkeley, 1966, postgrad.; LLB, U. Ottawa, Ont., Can., 1985; LLM, U. Wash., 1986; postgrad., Hiroshima (Japan) U., York U., Toronto, 1990-92. Bar: N.Y. 1988, Calif. 1992; called to Ont. bar, 1991. Mem. rsch. dept. Japan External Trade Orgn., San Francisco, 1967-69; translator Sec. State, Ottawa, Ont., 1971-73, 84-85; head fgn. trade dept. Tanaka Shoji, Hiroshima, Japan, 1973-76; head tchr. Brit. Japan, Tokyo, 1977-81; fgn. law cons. Tokyo Aoyama Law Office, 1986-88; assoc. Baker & McKenzie, Toronto, 1989-91, L.A., 1991-92; pvt. practice, Rancho Palos Verdes, Calif., 1992-93; ptnr. Sanders and Yeomans, Torrance, Calif., 1993-94; pvt. practice Rancho Palos Verdes, Calif., 1994—; legal adv. Seicho-No-Ie Internat. Hdqs., Tokyo. With USN, 1961-65. Mem. N.Y. State Bar Assn., York Bar Assn., Law Soc. Upper Can., C. of C., Indonesian Bus. Soc., U. Calif. Berkeley Alumni Assn., U. Wash. Law Alumni Assn., Tokyo Can. Club (v.p., pres. 1987-89). Home: 6746 Los Verdes Dr Palos Verdes Peninsula CA 90275-5528 Office: PO Box 3214 Palos Verdes Peninsula CA 90274-9214

YEOSOCK, JOHN JOHN, army officer; b. Wilkes-Barre, Pa., Mar. 18, 1937; s. John A. and Elizabeth B. (Petras) Y.; m. Betta Lynn Hoffner, July 20, 1960; children—John John, Elizabeth John. BS in Indsl. Engring., Pa. State U., 1959; MS in Ops. Rsch., U.S. Naval Postgrad. Sch., Monterey, Calif., 1969; postgrad., Nat. War Coll., 1976. Commd. officer U.S. Army, 1959, advanced through grades to lt. gen.; brigade comdr. 194th Armored Brigade, Ft Knox, Ky., 1978-80; chief of staff 1st Cavalry div. U.S. Army, Ft. Hood, Tex., 1980-81, asst. div. comdr., 1983-84; project mgr. Saudi N.G., Riyadh, Saudi Arabia, 1981-83; dep. chief of staff ops. Forces Command., Atlanta, 1984-86; comdr. 1st Cavalry Div., Ft. Hood, 1986-88; asst. dep. chief of staff for ops. The Pentagon, Washington, 1988-89; comdr. 3d Army and dep. comdg. gen. Forces Command, Ft. McPherson, Ga., 1989—&; comdr. U.S., U.K., French Army Forces, Kuwaiti Theater Ops., Desert Storm, Saudi Arabia, 1990-91; internat. cons., 1993—. Decorated D.S.M. (3), Legion of Merit (2), Bronze Star, French Legion of Honor, King Faisal award Class II, King Abdul Aziz medal Class II (Saudi Arabia), Combat Infantryman badge; recipient Nat. Vets. award, 1994, AUSA Inspiration award Atlanta, 1992; named Outstanding Engring. Alumnus, Pa. State U., 1990, Disting. Alumni, 1992, Disting. Alumnus, Valley Forge Mil. Acad., 1994; named to Pi Kappa Phi Hall of Fame. Mem. Wilkes-Barre C. of C. (hon., Achievement award 1991). Home: 411 Taberon Rd Peachtree City GA 30269-3215

YEP, WALLEN LAI, import/export company executive, author; b. Stockton, Calif., July 23, 1943; s. Hong Wey and Kim Chin Gee Y.; m. Yong Sun Hwang, June 12, 1970; 1 child, Lisa Suk Kyung. AA, Coll. of San Mateo, 1972; BA, Calif. State U., San Francisco, 1975; certificate in contract administrn., U. Calif., Berkeley, 1975; MBA, Golden Gate U., 1977. Cert. profl. cons. to mgmt. Nat. Br. Profl. Mgmt. Cons. Contract price analyst U.S. Army Procurement Agy., Korea, 1969; base supply supr. AAEOI, Korea, 1970-71; staff-advisor In-Change Group, Korea, 1971; administrv. svcs. supr. Far West Lab., San Francisco, 1971-74; assoc. administr. Met. Transp. Commn., Berkeley, 1974-84; prin. W. Yep Internat. Cons., Piedmont, Calif., 1985—; instr. Asian mktg. and internat. bus. mgmt. Lincoln U., 1978-83; guest panelist East Indian experience in N. Am. symposium U. Calif., Berkeley, So. East Asian Studies, 1978; speaker internat. symposium econ. cooperation and fgn. trade, Taiyuan, Shanxi Province, China, 1984; internat. speaker in field. Author: Occupational Certification and Licensing Handbook, 1978, Hidden Fallacies of Foreign Market Data, 1979, Financial Status of the PRC, Wage Differentials in PRC, Consumer Value Analysis, Who Are You, 1994, Sequel, 1994, Man Before Adam, 1995, Rule of the Serpent, 1997, As Petals Fall, 1997, The War with the Spirits, 1996, Another Day, 1997. Co-chmn. North Beach Chinatown Youth Svcs. Ctr., 1977-86; hon. adv. bd. Mission Coaltion, 1977-79; pres.

Internat. Ctr. Tech. Assistance and Devel.; adv. East Bay Local Devel. Corp., 1977; mem. Oakland (Calif.) Unified Sch. Dist. Affirmative Action Purchasing adv. com. , 1978; mem. Pres. adv. bd. West Coast Christian Coll., 1983; Presdl. invitation to be del. Calif.-White House/Nat. Gov.'s conf. fgn. trade and export promotion, Seattle, 1979. Served with U.S. Army, 1967-69. Named Outstanding Young Men of Am. Jaycees, 1980; recipient Citizen of the Day award KABL Radio, 1978. Mem. Nat. Assn. Purchasing Mgmt. (cert. purchasing mgr.), No. Calif. Purchasing Mgmt. Assn., Oakland World Trade Assn., Assn. of MBA Execs., Calif., Golden Gate Alumni Assns., Nat. Contract Mgmt. Assn. (cert. profl. contracts mgr.). Office: PO Box 21011 Piedmont CA 94620-1011

YERGIN, DANIEL HOWARD, writer, consultant; b. Los Angeles, Feb. 6, 1947; s. Irving H. and Naomi Y.; m. Angela Stent, Aug. 10, 1975; children: Alexander George, Rebecca Isabella. BA with first class honors, Cambridge U., Eng., 1968, MA, 1970, PhD, 1974; PhD (hon.), U. Mo., 1980, U. Houston, 1994. Contbg. editor New York mag., 1968-70; research fellow Harvard U., Cambridge, Mass., 1974-76; lectr. bus. sch. Harvard U., 1976-79, lectr. Kennedy Sch. Govt., 1979-83; research assoc. Harvard U., Cambridge, 1983—; pres. Cambridge Energy Research Assoc., Cambridge, 1982—, also chmn., sec. energy task force on strategic energy R&D; mem. policy adv. com. Program on U.S.-Japan Rels., Harvard U.; mem. bd. energy experts Dallas Morning News; mem. internat. panel advisors Asia-Pacific Petroleum Conf.; fellow World Econ. Forum, Davos. Author: Shattered Peace: The Origins of the Cold War and the National Security State, 1977, rev. edit., 1990, The Prize: Epic Quest for Oil, Money and Power, 1991 (Pulitzer Prize for non-fiction 1992); co-author: Cold War, 1977, Energy Future, 1979, Global Insecurity, 1982, Future of Oil Prices: Perils of Prophecy, 1984, Russia 2010: And What It Means for the World, 1993; contbg. editor Atlantic Monthly, 1977-83. Mem. adv. bd. Solar Energy Rsch. Inst., Golden, Colo., 1979-81; sec. Energy Adv. Bd. Fellow Univ. Consortium for World Order Studies, 1974-75, Rockefeller Found., 1975-79, German Marshall Fund, 1980-81; Marshall scholar Cambridge U., 1974. Fellow Atlantic Inst. Internat. Affairs; mem. PEN, Lehrman Inst. (assoc.), Coun. on Fgn. Rels., Nat. Petroleum Coun., Internat. Assn. for Energy Econs., Am. Hist. Assn., Am. Polit. Assn., Royal Inst. Internat. Affairs, Assn. Marshall Scholars (bd. dirs. 1988-91), U.S. Energy Assocs. (bd. dirs.), Offshore No. Seas Found. Internat. Coun., The Nature Conservancy (Last Great Places com.), Yale Club (N.Y.C.), Harvard Club (N.Y.C.). Office: Cambridge Energy Rsch Assocs 20 University Rd Ste 450 Cambridge MA 02138-5756

YERKES, DAVID NORTON, architect; b. Cambridge, Mass., Nov. 5, 1911; s. Robert Mearns and Ada (Watterson) Y.; m. Catharine Noyes, Oct. 7, 1939 (dec. 1969); 1 dau., Catharine; m. Sarah Hitchcock Satterlee, July 9, 1972. B.A., Harvard U., 1933; M.F.A., Yale U., 1935. Draftsman, designer Chgo. and Washington, 1937-39, Deigert & Yerkes and Assos., Washington, 1945-69, David N. Yerkes & Assos., Washington, 1970-80, Yerkes, Pappas and Parker, 1980-83; Mem. panel archtl. advisers Nat. Commn. Fine Arts, 1961-63, 79-82; vice chmn. Presdl. Inaugural Parade Com., 1965. Prin. works include Voice of America Studios, Washington, 1958, Nat. Arboretum Hdqrs. Bldg. Am. Embassy, Somalia, also Madeira Sch. Auditoriu, 1969; 4 stas. Washington subway sys., 1971-81, hdqrs., Nat. Trust Historic Preservation, Washington, 1977, suite, Time, Inc., Washington, 1980, also various schs., labs; paintings exhibited in New Eng. and Washington. Served to capt. AUS, 1943-45. Firm recipient numerous regional and nat. awards; recipient Kemper award AIA, 1972. Fellow AIA (bd. dirs. 1965-68, v.p. 1968-69, chmn. nat. honor awards jury 1966, chmn. Reynolds Meml. award jury 1969, pres. found. 1974-76). Home: 1527 30th St NW Washington DC 20007-3088

YERKES, SUSAN GAMBLE, newspaper columnist; b. Evanston, Ill., Sept. 5, 1959; d. Charles Tyson and Darthea (Campbell) Higgins. BA in Liberal Arts (hon.), U. Austin, 1974; MA in Mass Comms., Wichita State U., 1976. Pub. affairs dir. anchor KAKE-TV, Wichita, Kans., 1977-81; freelance writer pub. rels. YS Comms. Global, 1981-84; metro columnist San Antonio Light, 1986-93; lifestyle columnist S.A. Express News, San Antonio, 1993—; radio TV host WOAI-AM, San Antonio, 1993—; nat. assn. broadcast editls., Boston, 1978-81. Recipient 1st Place Column Writing Nat. Press Women, 1988. Mem. Internat. Women's Forum, Women in Comm., Pub. Rel. Soc. Am., Rotary, Phi Beta Kappa. Episcopalian. Avocations: horseback riding, travel, reading, friends, the Internet. Home: 7711 Broadway # 29B San Antonio TX 78209 Office: San Antonio Express News Ave E 3rd St San Antonio TX 78205

YERMAN, FREDRIC WARREN, lawyer; b. N.Y.C., Jan. 8, 1943; s. Nat W. and Tina (Barotz) Y.; m. Ann R. Rochlin, May 31, 1965; children: Emily, Deborah. BA, CUNY, 1963; LLB, Columbia U., 1966. Bar: N.Y. 1967. Assoc. Kaye, Scholer, Fierman, Hays & Handler, N.Y.C., 1966-74, ptnr., 1974—, chmn. exec. com., 1990-92; bd. dirs. Lawyer's Com. for Civil Rights under Law, N.Y. Bd. dirs. United Way Tri-State, N.Y., Legal Aid Soc., N.Y.C.; chmn. Jewish Bd. Family and Children Svcs., N.Y.C., 1994—. Fellow Am. Coll. Trial Lawyers. Home: 31 Sheridan Rd Scarsdale NY 10583-1523 Office: Kaye Scholer Fierman Hays & Handler 425 Park Ave New York NY 10022-3506

YERUSHALMI, YOSEF HAYIM, historian, educator; b. N.Y.C., May 20, 1932; s. Leon and Eva (Kaplan) Y.; m. Ophra Pearly, Jan. 4, 1959; 1 child, Ariel. BA, Yeshiva U., 1953; M in Hebrew Lit., Jewish Theol. Sem. Am., 1957, DHL (hon.), 1987; MA, Columbia, 1961, PhD, 1966; MA (hon.), Harvard, 1970; LHD (hon.), Hebrew Union Coll., 1996; PhD (hon.), U. Haifa, Israel, 1997. Instr. Jewish history Rutgers U., New Brunswick, N.J., 1963-66; asst. prof. Hebrew and Jewish History Harvard U., 1966-70, prof., 1970-78, Jacob E. Safra prof. Jewish history and Sephardic civilization, 1978-80, chmn. dept. near eastern langs. and civilizations, 1978-80; mem. Ctr. for Israel and Jewish Studies Columbia U., N.Y.C., 1980—. Author: From Spanish Court to Italian Ghetto: isaac Cardoso, A Study in Seventeenth-Century Marranism and Jewish Apologetics, 1971, Haggadah and History, 1975, The Lisbon Massacre of 1506, 1976, Zakhor: Jewish History and Jewish Memory, 1982, Freud's Moses: Judaism Terminable and Interminable, 1991, Ein Feld in Anatot: Versuche uber judische Geschichte, 1993, Diener von Königen und nicht Diener von Dienern: Einige Aspekte der politischen Geschichte der Juden, 1995; author (in Hebrew): Spinoza on the Survival of the Jews, 1983; contbr. articles to profl. publs. on Spanish and Portuguese Jewry and history of psychoanalysis; chmn. publs. com. Jewish Publ. Soc., 1972-84; pres. Leo Baeck Inst., 1986-91. Bd. dirs. Conf. Jewish Social Studies, Psycho analytic Research and Devel. Fund, Editorial Bd., History and Memory. Recipient Newman medal CUNY, 1975, Nat. Jewish Book award, 1983, 92,Ansley award Columbia U. Press, 1968, medal of achievement in history Nat. Found. for Jewish Culture,1995; Kent fellow, 1963, travel fellow Nat. Found. for Jewish Culture, 1964, fellow NEH, 1976-77, Rockefeller fellow in humanities, 1983-84, Guggenheim fellow, 1989-90; Carl Friedrich von Siemens Stiftung fellow (Munich), 1996-97. Fellow Am. Acad. Jewish Research, Am. Acad. Arts and Scis., Academia Portuguesa da História (hon.). Home: 450 Riverside Dr New York NY 10027-6821 Office: Columbia U 511 Fayerweather Hall 116th St & Broadway New York NY 10027

YESAWICH, PETER CHARLES, advertising executive; b. Ithaca, N.Y., Oct. 28, 1950; s. Paul Joseph Jr. and Elizabeth (Larkin) Y.; divorced; children: Peter Charles, Paul Christopher. BS, Cornell U., 1972, MS, 1974, PhD, 1976; AMP, Yale U., 1994. Dir. rsch. Robinsons, Inc., Orlando, Fla., 1976-78, v.p., 1978-81, exec. v.p., 1981-83; pres., CEO Yesawich, Pepperdine & Brown, Orlando, 1983—; vis. assoc. prof. Cornell U., Ithaca, 1977—, U. Ctrl. Fla., Orlando, 1988—; chmn. Pope Tourism Inst., Orlando, 1988-90. Contbr. articles to profl. jours. Recipient World Travel award Am. Assn. Travel Editors, 1985, Silver Medal award Am. Assn. Advt. Agys., 1992, Adrian award Hospitality Sales and Mktg. Assn. Internat., 1993; named Author of Yr. Cornell Quar., 1986. Mem. Cornell Hotel Soc., Am. Hotel & Motel Assn., Caribbean Hotel Assn., Hotel Sales Mktg. Assn., Am. Mktg. Assn. Avocations: jogging, writing. Office: Yesawich Pepperdine & Brown Ste 600 1900 Summit Tower Orlando FL 32810-5912

YESILADA, BIROL ALI, political science educator; b. Nicosia, Cyprus, Aug. 12, 1956; came to U.S., 1971; s. Ali and Sermin (Mustafa) Y.; m. Susan Diana Lesea, Aug. 20, 1980; children: Sermin, Selin. AB, U. Calif., Berkeley, 1977; MA, San Francisco State U., 1979; PhD, U. Mich., 1984. Vis. asst. prof. U. Mo., Columbia, 1984-85, asst. prof., 1985-91; vis. asst. prof. Middle East Tech. U., Ankara, Turkey, 1987-88; vis. rsch. specialist State Planning Orgn., Ankara, Turkey, 1987-88; assoc. prof. U. Mo., Columbia, 1991—, chair dept. polit. sci., 1994—; pres. Oceania Corp., 1992—; cons. State Planning Orgn., Ankara, 1987-88, Libr. of Congress, Washington, 1988-92, Coun. on Fgn. Rels., N.Y.C., 1990-91, U.S. State Dept. Fgn. Svc. Inst., 1995—, Nat. Intelligence Coun., Washington, 1996-97, U.S. Inst. Peace, 1996; chair internat. studies adv. com. U. Mo., Columbia, 1992-94. Author, co-editor: Agrarian Reform in Reverse: The Food Crisis in the Third World, 1987, The Political and Socioeconomic Transformation of Turkey, 1993; co-author: The Emerging European Union, 1996; mem. editl. bd. Cyprus Rev. Jour., 1987—, New Perspectives on Turkey, 1987-95; contbr. articles to profl. jours. Bd. dirs. U. Mo. Peace Studies, Columbia, 1988-92; adv. bd. Constl. Studies Found. Mo., 1996—. Rsch. fellow Am. Coun. Learned Socs. and Social Sci. Rsch. Coun., 1987, Fulbright-Hays, 1982, Turkish Econ. and Social Studies Found. of Eczacibasi Holding, 1995, William T. Kemper fellow for tchng. excellence U. Mo. and Commerce Bank, 1996; recipient Purple Chalk Tchg. Excellence award U. Mo., Columbia Arts and Scis. Coll., 1991; rsch. bd. grantee U. Mo., 1996. Mem. Am. Polit. Sci. Assn., European Cmty. Studies Assn., Middle East Studies Assn., Columbia Rotary Club, Golden Key Honor Soc. Muslim. Avocations: jogging, swimming, camping, stamp collecting, ballroom dancing. Home: 1700 Princeton Dr Columbia MO 65203-1851

YESLOW, ROSEMARIE, real estate professional; b. Detroit; d. Karl E. and Madeline E. (Paret) Norberg; widowed; children: Bradford (dec.), Tod, Eric (dec.), Mark. Student, U. Miami, 1947-49; AA in Journalism, Broward Jr. Coll., 1972; student, Fla. Atlantic U., 1973-75; grad., Realtor Inst., 1995. Ins. agt. Wittenstein Ins. Agy., Hollywood, Fla., 1965-75; owner, operator The Karl Motel/Apartments, Hallandale, Fla., 1980—; realtor/assoc. The Keyes Co., Hollywood, 1990-93; realtor, assoc. Ebby Halliday Real Estate, Dallas, 1993—; real estate investor, Hollywood, 1960—. Contbr. articles to profl. jours. Edn. v.p. Nat. Coun. Jewish Women, Hollywood, 1960-66; unit and dept. chmn. LWV, Ft. Lauderdale, Fla., 1960-72; edn. chmn. Dem. Exec. Com., Broward County, Fla., 1976-78; mem. planning and zoning bd. City of Hallandale, 1988-92. Recipient Sch. Bell award Fla. Edn. Assn., 1966. Mem. Nat. Assn. Realtors, Hollywood Bd. Realtors, Hallandale Adult Cmty. Ctr. (adv. com., Cert. of Appreciation 1989), Hallandale Citizens United, Hallandale C. of C. (bd. dirs. 1987-92, Small Bus. Person of Yr. award 1990), Sierra Club. Democrat. Jewish. Avocations: camping, reading, hiking, swimming. Home: 4247 Throckmorton St Dallas TX 75219-2206 Office: Ebby Halliday Real Estate 8333 Douglas Ave Ste 100 Dallas TX 75225-5811

YESTON, MAURY, composer, lyricist, educator; b. Jersey City, Oct. 23, 1945; s. David and Frances (Haar) Y.; m. Anne Sheedy, 1982; children: Jake, Max. BA, Yale U., 1967, PhD, 1974; MA, Clare Coll., Cambridge (Eng.) U., 1972. Assoc. prof. dept. music Yale U., New Haven, 1974-82, dir. undergrad. studies in music, 1976-82; tchr. BMI Mus. Theatre Workshop, 1982—. Composer, lyricist: off-Broadway play Cloud 9 - Music, 1981; Broadway play Nine - The Musical, 1982 (Tony award 1982, Grammy award nominee 1982, Drama Desk award 1982), One Two Three Four Five, 1987, Grand Hotel, 1989 (Tony award nominee 1990), (rec.) Goya: A Life in Song, 1989, December Songs, 1990, Phantom, 1991; composer: Movement for Cello and Orchestra, 1967; author: The Stratification of Musical Rhythm, 1975; author, editor: Readings in Schenker Analysis, 1977. Recipient BMI award, 1982, 89. Office: Flora Roberts 157 W 57th St New York NY 10019-2210*

YETMAN, LEITH ELEANOR, academic administrator; b. Kellits, Clarendon, Jamaica, West Indies; came to U.S., 1967; d. 2nd child of 12 children of Percival Augustus and Grace Elizabeth (Anderson) Y.; m. Noel W. Miller, Apr. 8, 1961 (div. 1977); children: Donovan, Jo-Ann, Kirk, Lori-Anne; adopted children: LaFara, Samantha, Brandon Ryan. Attended, Bethlehem Teachers Coll., St. Elizabeth, Jamaica, 1960; BSC, Baruch Coll., 1976; MA, Columbia U., 1978. Cert. tchr., N.Y. Legal sec. various law firms, N.Y.C., 1969-76; instr. Taylor Bus. Inst., N.Y.C., 1977-79; founder, pres., dir. N.Y. Inst. Bus. Tech., N.Y.C., 1981—. Founder Grace Inst. Bus. Tech., Bklyn., 1996. Recipient Outstanding Achievement award Baruch Coll. Alumni Assn., 1989; Leith E. Yetman Day proclaimed June 1, 1994 by Manhattan Borough Pres. Mem. Better Bus. Bur. N.Y.C. Office: NY Inst Bus Tech 401 Park Ave S New York NY 10016-8808

YETT, FOWLER REDFORD, mathematics educator; b. Johnson City, Tex., Oct. 18, 1919; s. James William, Sr. and Rebecca Jane (Stribling) Y.; BS in Chem. Engring. (Univ. scholar), U. Tex., Austin, 1943, MA in Math., 1952; PhD, Iowa State U., 1955; m. Mary Sue Lytle, June 17, 1945 (div. 1977); children: Jane Marie, Rebecca Yett Root, Mary Wester Yett Research chemist, research chem. engr. Manhattan Project, U. Chgo 1943-44, Richland, Wash., 1944-45, Dow Chem. Co., Freeport, Tex., 1945; owner, mgr. Camera Supplies of Houston, 1946-49; teaching fellow math. U. Tex., Austin, 1949-52, asst. prof., 1956-65; instr. math. Iowa State U., Ames, 1952-55; asst. prof. math. Long Beach (Calif.) State Coll., 1955-56; prof. math. U. So. Ala., Mobile, 1965-89, chmn. dept., 1965-68; sr. rsch. engr. N.Am. Aviation, Inc., Downey, Calif., summers 1956-57, 59; faculty rsch. assoc. Boeing Co., Seattle, summer 1958; pres. Dr. Fowler Redford Yett & Daus., Inc., Solar, Inc.; founder Dr. Fowler Redford Yett's World Acad. of Faith, Health Langs. and Scis. Active all Lyndon Baines Johnson election campaigns, 1937-68. Mem. Am. Math. Soc., Tau Beta Pi, Omega Chi Epsilon, Phi Lambda Upsilon, Phi Eta Sigma, Pi Mu Epsilon. Methodist (tchr. Sunday sch. 1970-71). Home: 660 Merritt Dr Mobile AL 36609-6026

YEUNG, ALBERT TAK-CHUNG, civil engineering educator; b. Hong Kong, July 13, 1959; came to U.S., 1984; s. Siu-Hung and Pui-Chan (Lip) Y.; m. Kitman Iris Luk, Jan. 16, 1986; children: Loren Wayne, Ernest Hayes. BSc in Engring., U. Hong Kong, 1982; MS, U. Calif., Berkeley, 1985, PhD, 1990. Registered profl. engr., Tex., civil engr., Hong Kong; chartered engr., U.K. Engring. asst. T.H. Chuah & Assocs. Cons. Engrs., Singapore, 1980, Geotech. Control Office, Hong Kong, 1981; staff engr. Binnie & Ptnrs. Internat., Hong Kong, 1982-83, staff resident engr., 1984; lectr. Haking Wong Tech. Inst., Hong Kong, 1983-84; rsch. asst. U. Calif., Berkeley, 1985, 86, 87-89, grad. student instr., 1985-87; rsch. asst. Lawrence Berkeley Lab., 1989; asst. prof. civil engring. Northeastern U., Boston, 1990, Tex. A&M U., College Station, 1991—; asst. rsch. engr. Tex. Transp. Inst., College Station, 1991—; pres. Albert T. Yeung Geotech. Engr., College Station, 1992—; faculty advisor Hong Kong Student Assn., Tex. A&M U., College Station, 1991—, Asian Am. Assn., 1992-94; spkr. H.S. JETS Club, 1991—. Lead editor: Vertical and Horizontal Deformations of Foundations and Embankments, 2 vols., 1994; co-author: Laboratory Soil Testing for Engineers, 3rd edit., 1994; asst. editor-in-chief: Practice Periodical of Hazardous, Toxic, and Radioactive Waste Management/ASCE, 1996—; contbr. articles to profl. jours. Earth Tech. Corp. fellow, Long Beach, Calif., 1987-89; rsch. grantee Tex. Advanced Tech. Program, Tex. Higher Edn. Coord. Bd., Austin, 1992, 94, Tex. Dept. Transp. Coop. Rsch. Program, Austin, 1992, Gulf Coast Hazardous Substance Rsch. Ctr., Beaumont, Tex., 1992, Nat. Coop. Hwy. Rsch. Program, Transp. Rsch. Bd., NRC, Washington, 1993, Energy Resources Program, Tex. A&M U. Sys., 1993; recipient Rsch. Initiation award NSF, Washington, 1992, Select Young Faculty award Tex. Engring. Exptl. Sta., 1993. Fellow The Geological Soc., mem. AAUP, ASTM (mem. com. D18 on soil and rock and com. D34 on mixed waste 1993—), ASCE (editl. bd. Jour. Geotech. Engring. 1994—, publs. com. geotech. engring. divsn. 1994—, environ. geotech. com. engring. divs. 1992—, sec. Tex. sect. geotech. com. 1993-94, vice chmn. Tex. sec. geotech. com. 1994-95, chair 1995-96, groundwater com., environ. engring. divs., Arthur Casagrande Profl. Devel. award 1996, Tex. section ASCE Civil Engring. Paper award 1996), Am. Soc. Surface Mining and Reclamation (com. on containment and mitigation of toxic mine waste 1994—), Am. Soc. Engring. Edn. (Dow Outstanding New Faculty award 1994, chair environ. engring. divs. 1993-94), Internat. Soc. Soil Mechanics and Found. Engring., Hong Kong Instn. of Engrs. (prize 1981, Kumagai prize 1994), Clay Mineral Soc., Inst. of Civil Engrs. Achievements include use of electrokinetics to extract contaminants from fine-grained soil, use of electrophoresis of clay particles to seal leaks in geomembrane liners, use of cone penetration technology to detect and delineate subsurface contamination, use of waste tire chips for highway earth structure construction, use of long-term ground anchors for retaining structures. Avocations: travel, photography, gardening, sports, collecting. Office: Tex A&M U Dept Civil Engring College Station TX 77843-3136

YEUNG, EDWARD SZESHING, chemist; b. Hong Kong, Feb. 17, 1948; came to U.S., 1965; s. King Mai Luk and Yu Lung Yeung; m. Anna Kunkwok Seto, Sept. 18, 1971; children: Rebecca Tze-Mai, Amanda Tze-Wen. AB magna cum laude, Cornell U., 1968; PhD, U. Calif., Berkeley, 1972. Instr. chemistry Iowa State U., Ames, 1972-74; asst prof. Iowa State U., 1974-77, assoc. prof, 1977-81, prof. chemistry, 1981-89, disting. prof., 1989—. Contbr. articles to profl. jours. Alfred P. Sloan fellow, 1974-76; recipient Am. Chem Soc. award in Analytical Chemistry, 1994. Fellow AAAS; mem. Soc. Applied Spectrosci. (Lester Strock award 1990), Am. Chem. Soc. (award in chem. instrumentation 1987, award in analytical chemistry 1994). Home: 1005 Jarrett Cir Ames IA 50014-3937 Office: Iowa State U Gilman Hall Ames IA 50011

YGLESIAS, HELEN BASSINE, author, educator; b. N.Y.C., Mar. 29, 1915; d. Solomon and Kate (Goldstein) Bassine; m. Bernard Cole, 1938 (div. 1950); children: Tamar Cole, Lewis Cole; m. Jose Yglesias, Aug. 19, 1950 (div. 1992); 1 child, Rafael. Student pub. schs.; LHD (hon.), U. Maine, 1996. Literary editor Nation Mag., 1965-70; adj. assoc. prof. writing Columbia Sch. Arts, N.Y.C., 1973—; vis. prof. creative writing Writers Workshop, U. Iowa, Iowa City, 1980. Author: (novels) How She Died (Houghton Mifflin award), 1972, Family Feeling, 1976, Sweetsir, 1981, The Saviors, 1987, (non-fiction) Starting: Early, Anew, Over and Late, 1978, Isabel Bishop, 1989. Home: HC 64 Box 2075 Brooklin ME 04616-9713

YHOUSE, PAUL ALAN, manufacturing executive; b. Grand Rapids, Mich., June 23, 1949; s. Keith E. and Elaine (Laraway) Y.; m. Elizabeth Orlyk, Aug. 21, 1971. BBA, U. Mich., 1971. With Arthur Andersen & Co., various locations, 1971-76, mgr., 1976-82, ptnr., 1982-91; sr. v.p., CFO Holnam Inc., Dundee, Mich., 1991-93; pres., CEO, 1993—. Active adv. bd. Paton Acctg. Ctr., U. Mich., Ann Arbor. Mem. AICPA (chmn. healthcare com. 1980-91), Fin. Execs. Inst., Mich. Anssn. CPAs. Office: Holnam Inc 6211 Ann Arbor Rd Dundee MI 48131-9527

YIANNIAS, NANCY MAGAS, municipal official; b. Kalamazoo, Feb. 1, 1936; d. George A. and Irene (Callas) Magas; m. Andrew Chris Yiannias, Oct. 20, 1968; 1 child, Chris Andrew. BA, Western Mich. U., 1957; MPH, U. Mich., 1963. Registered sanitarian, Ill. Health educator Stickney Pub. Health Dist., Burbank, Ill., 1966-72, Chgo. Heart Assn., 1972-73; health coord. Village of Elk Grove, Ill., 1974—. Mem. bd. counselors Alexian Bros. Med. Ctr., Elk Grove Village, 1977—. Mem. APHA, Ill. Pub. Health Assn. (sec. 1981), Soc. Pub. Health Educators, Ill. Soc. Pub. Health Educators (mem. program planning com. 1966), Ill. Environ. Health Assn., N.W. Suburban Access to Care Assn. Home: 1521 Manor Ln Park Ridge IL 60068-1541 Office: Elk Grove Village Dept Health 901 Wellington Ave Elk Grove Village IL 60007-3456

YIELDING, K. LEMONE, physician; b. Auburn, Ala., Mar. 25, 1931; s. Riley Lafayette and Bertie (Dees) Y.; m. Lerena Wade Hauge, Dec. 7, 1973; children: K. Lemone, Michael Lafon, Teresa Louise, Riley Lafayette, Katrina Elizabeth, Elaine Louise Blodgett, Laura Carlen Blodgett. BS, Ala. Poly. Inst., 1949; MS, U. Ala., 1952, MD, 1954. Intern U. Ala. Med. Center, 1954-55; clin. assoc. Nat. Inst. Arthritis and Metabolic Diseases, NIH, 1955-57, sr. investigator, 1958-64; resident med. service USPHS Hosp., Balt., 1957-58; adj. asst. prof. medicine Georgetown U. Med. Sch., 1958-64; cons. USPHS, 1964-68, 75—; prof. biochemistry, assoc. prof. medicine, chief lab. molecular biology U. Ala. Med. Ctr., Birmingham, 1964-80; prof., chmn. dept. anatomy, prof. medicine U. So. Ala. Coll. Medicine, Mobile, 1980-87; dean grad. sch. U. Tex. Med. Br., Galveston, 1987-95, dean emeritus, 1995—; cons. Am. Heart Assn., Arthritis Found., NIH, NASA. Contbr. to profl. jours., books. Served with USPHS, 1955-64. Grantee USPHS, Am. Cancer Soc., Nat. Found.-March of Dimes, U.S. Army, Am. Inst. Cancer Research. Mem. Am. Soc. Biol. Chemistry, Am. Assn. Cancer Research, Am. Assn. Photobiology, Assn. Research Vision and Ophthalmology, Soc. Exptl. Biology and Medicine, Am. Soc. Pharm. and Exptl. Therapeutics, Am. Assn. Pathologists, So. Soc. Clin. Investigation, Am. Assn. Anatomy, Soc. Toxicology, Sigma Xi.

YIH, CHIA-SHUN, fluid mechanics educator; b. Kweiyang, Kweichow, China, July 25, 1918; s. Ting-Jian and Wan-Lan (Shiao) Y.; m. Shirley Gladys Ashman, Feb. 17, 1949; children: Yiu-Yo, Yuen-Ming David, Weiling Katherine. BS, Nat. Central U., 1942; MS, U. Iowa, 1947, PhD, 1948. Instr. Nat. Kweichow U., 1944-45; instr. math. U. Wis., 1948-49; lectr. U. B.C., 1949-50; assoc. prof. Colo. State U., 1950-52; rsch. engr. U. Iowa, 1952-54, assoc. prof., 1954-56; assoc. prof. U. Mich., Ann Arbor, 1956-58; prof. U. Mich., 1958-68, Stephen P. Timoshenko Disting. univ. prof. fluid mechanics, 1968-88, S.P. Timoshenko Disting. univ. prof. emeritus, 1988—; grad. rsch. prof. U. Fla., 1987-90, grad. rsch. prof. emeritus, 1990—; vis. prof. U. Paris, U. Grenoble, France, 1970-71; Henry Russel lectr. U. Mich., 1974; lectr. Chinese Acad. Sci., Beijing, 1981, von Kármán Inst., Brussels, 1981, Internat. Ctr. of Theoretical Physics, Trieste, Italy, 1994, Cheng Kung U., Tainan, Taiwan, 1995; G.I. Taylor lectr. U. Fla., 1992; hon. prof. U. Hong Kong, 1996—; cons. Huyck Felt Co., 1960-64; trustee Rocky Mountain Hydraulic Lab., 1976-85; attaché de recherche in math. French Govt., 1951-52. Author: Dynamics of Nonhomogeneous Fluids, 1965, Fluid Mechanics, An Introduction to the Theory, 1969, 79, 88, Stratified Flows, 1980; editor: Advances in Applied Mechanics, 1970-82; mem. editl. bd. Advances in Applied Mechanics, 1983—, Physics of Fluids, 1969-72, SIAM Jour. Applied Math., 1971-72, Ann. Revs. of Fluid Mechanics, 1969-72, Advances in Mechanics of China, 1988—, Acta Mechanica Sinica, 1992—, Applied Math. and Mechanics, to 1989, Jour. Hydrodynamics, to 1989; contbr. articles to profl. jours. Recipient Achievement award Chinese Inst. Engrs. N.Y., 1968, Achievement award Chinese Engrs. and Scientists Assn. So. Calif., 1973, Sr. Scientist award Humboldt Found., Fed. Republic Germany, 1977-78, Theodore von Kármán medal ASCE, 1981, Stephen S. Attwood award U. Mich., 1984; sr. postdoctoral fellow NSF, 1959-60, Guggenheim fellow, 1964. Fellow Am. Phys. Soc. (chmn. exec. com. fluid dynamics divsn. 1973-74, Fluid Dynamics prize 1985, Otto Laporte award 1989); mem. U.S. Nat. Acad. Engring., Academia Sinica, Sigma Xi, Pi Mu Epsilon, Tau Beta Pi, Phi Kappa Phi. Home: 3530 W Huron River Dr Ann Arbor MI 48103-9417 Home (winter): 4084 NW 23d Cir Gainesville FL 32605

YIM, SOLOMON CHIK-SING, civil engineering educator, consultant; b. Hong Kong, Sept. 11, 1952; came to U.S., 1972; s. Fuk-Ching and San-Chan (Leung) Y.; m. Lenore S. Hata, Aug. 27, 1983; children: Rachel L., Joshua A. BSCE, Rice U., 1976; MSCE, U. Calif., Berkeley, 1977, MA in Math., 1981, PhD in Civil Engring., 1983. Registered profl. engr., Oreg. Rsch. asst. U. Calif., 1976-83, vis. lectr., 1983-84, vis. assoc. prof., 1993-94; sr. rsch. engr. Exxon Prodn. Rsch. Co., Houston, 1984-87; asst. prof. civil engring. Oreg. State U., Corvallis, 1987-91, assoc. prof., 1991-97, prof., 1997—; cons. engr., 1977—; mem. ship structures com. NRC, 1990-96; mem. grad. fellowship com. in sci. and engring. Dept. Def., 1989-96; sr. vis. scientist Norwegian Coun. for Sci. and Indsl. Rsch., Trondheim, 1994. Fellow Office Naval Rsch., 1988-91; sr. faculty rsch. fellow USN, 1993. Mem. ASCE (publ. com. 1993-96, editl. bd. 1996—), ASME, Soc. Naval Architecture and Marine Engrs., Internation Soc. Offshore and Polar Engrs. (charter, conf. tech. program com. 1992—). Achievements include research in nonlinear stochastic dynamics and chaos of ocean systems, in nonlinear response of structures to earthquakes. Office: Oreg State U Apperson Hall 202 Corvallis OR 97331

YIN, BEATRICE WEI-TZE, medical researcher; b. Taipei, Taiwan, Mar. 9, 1959; came to U.S., 1970; d. Chuan Keun and Ming Hsien (Huang) Y. BS, CUNY, Flushing, 1982, MS, 1988. Rsch. asst. Meml. Sloan-Kettering Cancer Ctr., N.Y.C., 1982—. Inventor Monoclonal antibodies to human gastrointestinal cancers, 1992. Avocations: readings, travel, gardening. Office: Meml Sloan Kettering Cancer Ctr 1275 York Ave New York NY 10021-6007

YIN, FANG-FANG, medical physicist, educator; b. Ningbo, Zhejiang, China, Sept. 14, 1958; came to U.S., 1985; s. Shisheng Yin and Xiaoxian Ma; m. Li Sun, Feb. 14, 1986; children: Moli Yin, Lucy Yin. BS, Zhejiang U., 1982; MS, Bowling Green (Ohio) State U., 1987; PhD, U. Chgo., 1992. Cert.

medical physicist Am. Bd. Radiology. Lectr. Industry U. of East China, Shanghai, 1982-85; grad. asst. Bowling Green State U., 1985-87; rsch. asst. U. Chgo., 1987-88, researcher, 1989-91; asst./med. physicist U. Rochester, N.Y., 1992-93; sr. instr./med. physicist U. Rochester, 1994—, asst. prof./med. physicist, 1994—; chief Oncologic Imaging Rsch. Lab., Rochester, 1994—. Contbr. articles to profl. jours.; patentee for automated method and system for the detection and classification of abnormal lesions and parenchymal distortions in med. images. Recipient Overman Summer fellowship Bowling Green State U., 1986; rsch. grantee Am. Cancer Soc., 1994, The Whitaker Found., 1995-98. Mem. Am. Assn. Physicists in Medicine. Avocations: tennis, ping pong. Office: Univ Rochester 601 Elmwood Ave # 647 Rochester NY 14642-0001

YIN, GERALD ZHEYAO, technology and business executive; b. Beijing, Jan. 29, 1944; came to U.S., 1980; s. Huaixing and Halumi Yin; m. Junling June Yen; 1 child, John Chengjian. BS in Chem. Physics, U. Sci. & Tech. China, Beijing, 1967; postgrad., Beijing U., 1978-80; PhD in Chemistry, UCLA, 1984. Process engr. Lanzhou Oil Refinery, Lanzhou, People's Republic of China, 1968-73; mgr. research staff Chinese Acad. Sciences, Lanzhou, 1973-78; sr. process engr. Intel Corp. Santa Clara TD, Santa Clara, Calif., 1984-86; mgr., staff engr. Lam Rsch. Corp., Rsch. & Devel., Fremont, Calif., 1986-91; mng. dir. Etch New Product, Santa Clara, Calif., 1991—; chief tech. officer Etch Group, gen. mgr. Silicon Etch divsn.; v.p. Applied Materials, Inc., Santa Clara, 1991—. Author: Introducing Orthogonal Design to Semiconductor Industry, 1985; inventor Rainbow oxide etcher, 200mm enhanced Electron Cyclotron Resonance reactor, High Density plasma source for Dielectric Etch (IPS) and Decoupled Plasma Source and reactors for Conductor Etches (DPS). Recipient Nat. Acad. award People's Republic of China, 1979, Nat. Acad. Invention award, People's Republic of China, 1980. Mem. Electrochem. Soc., Am. Chem. Soc., Am. Vacuum Soc., Silicon Valley Chinese Engring. Assn. (founder, first pres.). Achievements include 12 U.S., Japanese and German patents, 30 patent applications pending. Office: Applied Materials Inc 3320 Scott Blvd # 1114 Santa Clara CA 95054-3101

YIN, SHIH-JIUN, biochemist; b. Hsuchow, China, Nov. 27, 1946; arrived in Taiwan, 1949; s. Shau-Chian and Hwei-Shan (Wu) Y.; m. Yung-Mei Chen, June 21, 1969; children: Ho-An, Chih-An. BS in Botany, Nat. Chung-Hsing U., Taichung, Taiwan; MS in Biochemistry, Nat. Def. Med. Ctr., Taipei, 1974; PhD in Biochemistry, Ind. U., 1984. Teaching asst. Nat. Chung-Hsing U., Taichung, 1970-72; asst. researcher Tri-Svc. Gen. Hosp., Taipei, 1974-78; from instr. to assoc. prof. Nat. Def. Med. Ctr., Taipei, 1978-88, prof., biochemistry dept., 1989—, biochemistry dept. head, 1990-96; chief biochemistry rsch. lab. Tri-Svc. Gen. Hosp., Taipei, 1984-97; vis. scientist Karolinska Inst., Stockholm, 1989; vis. prof. Ind. U. Sch. Medicine, Indpls., 1992; speaker in field. Contbr. articles to profl. jours. Lt. Taiwan Air Force, 1969-70. Recipient Excellent Rsch. award Nat. Sci. Coun., 1990-91. Mem. AAAS, Chinese Biochem. Soc. (editl. bd. 1992-96), Rsch. Soc. on Alcoholism, Internat. Soc. for Biomed. Rsch. on Alcoholism, European Soc. for Biomed. Rsch. on Alcoholism. Nationalist Party. Avocations: reading, music, hiking, overseas travel. Home: Ln 24 Alley 5 # 75 2F, Ting-Chow Rd 3d Sect, Taipei 100, Taiwan Office: Nat Def Med Ctr Dept Biochem, PO Box 90048, Taipei 100, Taiwan

YING, JOHN L., manufacturing executive; b. Shanghai, Chiang-Su, People's Republic of China, June 15, 1948; came to U.S., 1970; s. D.C. and W.T. (Ma) Y.; m. Cynthia C. Chen, Apr. 7, 1981; children: Janice, Jonathan. BS, Tatung Inst. Tech., Taipei, Taiwan, 1969; MS, Poly. Inst. Bklyn., 1972; Profl. Engrs. Degree, Columbia U., N.Y.C., 1974. Application engr. Summit Engring Co., Taipei, 1969-70; asst. to pres. James Betesh Import Co., N.Y.C., 1972-73; strategic planner GM, Detroit, 1973-79; asst. to pres. Lawless Detroit Diesel Corp., City of Industry, Calif., 1979-81; pres., chief exec. officer Cen. Power Products, Inc., Liberty, Mo., 1981—, also bd. dirs.; bd. dirs. Cen. Mfg., Inc., Grandview, Mo., USA-China C. of C. Dir. adv. bd. Mark Twin Banks, Kansas City, Mo.; mem. Clay County (Mo.) Econ. Devel. Coun., 1984—; mem. Rep. Senatorial Inner Circle, Washington, 1985—. Recipient Outstanding Minority Bus. Enterprise award Minority Bus. Devel. Agy., Kansas City/Washington, 1986. Mem. USA-China C. of C., Kansas City Club, Hallbrook Country Club.

YIP, CECIL CHEUNG-CHING, biochemist, educator; b. Hong Kong, June 11, 1937; emigrated to Can., 1955; m. Yvette Fung, Oct. 15, 1960; children: Christopher, Adrian. B.Sc., McMaster U., Can., 1959; Ph.D., Rockefeller U., 1963. Research assoc. Rockefeller U., N.Y.C., 1963-64; asst. prof. U. Toronto, Ont., Can., 1964-68, assoc. prof., 1968-74, prof., 1974—, Charles H. Best prof. of med. rsch., 1987-93; chair Banting and Best dept. med. rsch. U. Toronto, Ont., 1990-95; vice-dean rsch. U. Toronto, 1992—. Contbr. sci. articles to publs. Recipient Charles H. Best prize Can. Hoechst Diabetes Workshop, 1972. Mem. AAAS, Am. Soc. Biol. Chemists, Can. Biochem. Soc. Home: 125 Melrose Ave, Toronto, ON Canada M5M 1Y8 Office: Banting and Best Dept Med Rsch, 112 College St, Toronto, ON Canada M5G 1L6

YNTEMA, MARY KATHERINE, retired mathematics educator; b. Urbana, Ill., Jan. 20, 1928; d. Leonard Francis and M. Jean (Busey) Y. BA in Math., Swarthmore Coll., 1950; MA in Math., U. Ill., 1961, PhD in Math., 1965. Tchr., secondary math. Am. Coll. for Girls, Istanbul, Turkey, 1950-54, Columbus (Ohio) Sch. for Girls, 1954-57; computer programmer MIT Lincoln Lab., Lexington, Mass., 1957-58; tchr., secondary math Roundup (Mont.) High Sch., 1959-60; asst. prof. math U. Ill., Chgo., 1965-67; asst. prof. computer sci. Pa. State U., University Park, 1967-71; assoc. prof. to prof. math. Sangamon State U., Springfield, Ill., 1971-91; ret., 1991. Avocation: enjoyment of nature.

YOAKAM, DWIGHT, country western musician; b. Pikeville, Ky., 1956. Albums include Guitars, Cadillacs, Etc. Etc., 1985, Hillbilly Deluxe, 1987, Buenas Noches From A Lonely Room, 1988, Just Lookin' for a Hit, 1989, If There Was a Way, 1990, This Time, 1993, Dwight Live, 1995, Gone, 1996; duet with Buck Owens Streets of Bakersfield, 1988 (No. 1 single); co-prodr. stage appearance Southern Rapture, 1993; appeared in Roswell, Showtime cable feature, 1994, Sling Blade, feature film, 1996. Named Top Male Vocalist by Acad. Country Music, 1986; recipient Grammy award for best country vocal performance by male for Ain't That Lonely Yet, 1993, also 14 nominations; Premiere Performance acting award Motion Picture Club, 1996.

YOCAM, DELBERT WAYNE, software products company executive; b. Long Beach, Calif., Dec. 24, 1943; s. Royal Delbert and Mary Rose (Gross) Y.; m. Janet McVeigh, June 13, 1965; children—Eric Wayne, Christian Jeremy, Elizabeth Janelle. B.A. in Bus. Adminstrn., Calif. State U.-Fullerton, 1966; M.B.A., Calif. State U., Long Beach, 1971. Mktg.-supply changeover coordinator Automotive Assembly div. Ford Motor Co., Dearborn, Mich., 1966-72; prodn. control mgr. Control Data Corp., Hawthorne, Calif., 1972-74; prodn. and material control mgr. Bourns Inc., Riverside, Calif., 1974-76; corp. material mgr. Computer Automation Inc., Irvine, Calif., 1976-78; prodn. planning mgr. central staff Cannon Electric div. ITT, World hdqrs., Santa Ana, Calif., 1978-79; exec. v.p., COO Apple Computer, Inc., Cupertino, Calif., 1979-91; pres., COO, dir. Tektronix Inc., Wilsonville, Oreg., 1992-95; chmn., CEO Borland Internat., Inc., Scotts Valley, Calif., 1996—; ,em. faculty Cypress Coll., Calif., 1972-79; bd. dirs. Adobe Sys Inc., Mountain View, Calif., 1991—, Oracle Corp., Redwood Shores, Calif., 1997—, AST Rsch., Inc., Irvine, Calif., 1992-95, Integrated Measurement Sys. Inc., Beaverton, Oreg., 1995-97, Castelle, Inc., Santa Clara, Calif., 1995-96, Sapiens Internat. Corp., 1995—, Boomtown, Inc., Verdi, Nev., 1995—, Raster Graphics, Inc., San Jose, Calif., 1995—, Xircom, Inc., Thousand Oaks, Calif., 1996—; vice chmn. Tech. Ctr. Innovation, San Jose, Calif., 1989-90. Mem. Am. Electronics Assn. (nat. bd. dirs. 1988-89), Control Data Corp. Mgmt. Assn. (co-founder 1974), L.A. County Heart Assn. (active 1966).

YOCHELSON, BONNIE ELLEN, museum curator, art historian; b. Buffalo, Nov. 6, 1952; d. Samuel and Kathryn (Mersey) Y.; m. Paul Lewis Shechtman, Sept. 3, 1972; children: Emily, Anna. BA in History, Swarthmore Coll., 1974; MA, NYU, 1979, PhD, 1985. Asst. curator dept. prints and drawings Nat. Gallery Art, Washington, 1979-81; lectr. dept. art history U. Pa.q, Phila., 1985-87; curator prints and photographs Mus. of the City of N.Y., 1987-91, cons. curator, 1991—; faculty M of Photography program Sch. Visual Arts, N.Y.C., 1988—; adj. assoc. prof. dept. art history NYU, 1987. Mem. Coll. Art Assn.

YOCHELSON, ELLIS L(EON), paleontologist; b. Washington, Nov. 14, 1928; s. Morris Wolf and Fannie (Botkin) Y.; m. Sally Witt, June 10, 1950; children: Jeffrey, Abby, Charles. BS, U. Kans., 1949, MS, 1950; PhD, Columbia U., 1955. Paleontologist U.S. Geol. Survey, 1952-85, scientist emeritus, 1991; biostratigrapher, specializing in Paleozoic gastropods and minor classes of extinct mollusks; lectr. night sch. George Washington U., 1962-65; rsch. assoc. dept. paleobiology Smithsonian Instn., Washington, 1965—; lectr. Univ. Coll., U. Md., 1966-74; rsch. assoc. Smithsonian Instn., 1967—; lectr. U. Del., 1981; vis. prof. U. Md., 1986-87; organizer N.Am. Paleontol. Conv., 1969, editor proc., 1970-71; Co-editor: Essays in Paleontology and Stratigraphy, 1967; editor: Scientific Ideas of G.K. Gilbert, 1980; editorial bd. Nat. Geog. Rsch. and Exploration; contbr. numerous articles to profl. jours. Co-editor: Essays in Paleontology and Stratigraphy, 1967; editor: Scientific Ideas of G.K. Gilbert, 1980; contbr. numerous articles to profl. jours. Fellow AAAS (chmn. sect. E 1971); mem. Soc. Systematic Zoology (sec. 1961-66, councilor 1973), Internat. Paleontol. Assn. (treas. 1972-76), Paleontol. Soc. (pres. 1976), History of Earth Scis. Soc. (sec.-treas. 1982-85, sec. 1986-87, pres. 1989), N.Am. Paleontol. Conv. (sec.), Smithsonian Instn. (150th Anniversary com.), Sigma Xi. Office: Smithsonian Instn E-305A Mus Natural History Washington DC 20560

YOCHEM, BARBARA JUNE, sales executive, lecturer; b. Knox, Ind., Aug. 22, 1945; d. Harley Albert and Rosie (King) Runyan; m. Donald A. Yochem (div. 1979); 1 child, Morgan Lee; m. Don Heard, Dec. 12, 1987. Grad. high school, Knox, Ind., 1963. Sales rep. Hunter Woodworks, Carson, Calif., 1979-84, sales mgr., 1984-87; sales rep. Comml. Lumber and Pallet, Industry, Calif., 1987-92; owner By By Prodns., Glendora, Calif., 1976—. Author: Barbara Yochem's Inner Shooting; contbr. articles to profl. jours. Head coach NRA Jr. Olympic Shooting Camp, 1989-94; foster parent, 1992-94. Recipient U.S. Bronze medal U.S. Olympic Com., 1976, World Bronze medal U.S. Olympic Com., 1980; nominated Calif. Trapshooting Hall of Fame, 1994. Avocation: trapshooting. Address: By By Prodns 19045 Sorrel Dr Apple Valley CA 92308

YOCHUM, PHILIP THEODORE, retired motel and cafeteria chain executive; b. Quakertown, Pa., Sept. 20, 1924; s. Theodore J. and Margaret (Scheetz) Y.; m. Connie Petrillose, June 23, 1947; children: Cynthia, Philip Theodore. B.S. in Hotel Adminstrn., Cornell U., 1948. Engaged in hotel and restaurant work Quakertown, Pa.; engaged in hotel and restaurant work Ithaca, N.Y., 1948-51; various positions to regional mgr. Slater System, Inc., Balt., 1951-57; asst. v.p. ops. A.L. Mathias Co., Towson, Md., 1957-59; v.p. A.L. Mathias Co., 1959-61, exec. v.p., 1961-65; exec. v.p. (merger A.L. Mathias Co. and Servomation Corp. 1964); pres. Servomation Mathias, Inc. (merger into Servomation Corp., 1974), 1965-74, regional mgr. for food service mgmt. and vending, 1974-76; also dir.; dir. corp. devel. S & S Enterprises (operating Golden Plough Restaurants in Md. and N.J.), 1977-80; dist. mgr. Canteen Corp., Landover, Md., 1980-81; v.p., gen. mgr. Davis Bros., Inc., Hdqrs. Atlanta, 1981-91. Trustee Food Service Execs. Assn. Edn. Trust Fund. Served with AUS, World War II, ETO. Decorated Purple Heart. Mem. Internat. Food Service Execs. Assn. (Food Exec. of Year award Balt. br. 1972, 1990, city chmn. So. region, sec., publicity chmn. Atlanta br.), Food Service and Lodging Inst. (dir.), Cornell Soc. Hotelmen, Ga. Hospitality and Travel Assn., Nat. Restaurant Assn. Home: 158 77th St Avalon NJ 08202-1019

YOCK, ROBERT JOHN, federal judge; b. St. James, Minn., Jan. 11, 1938; s. William Julius and Erma Idella (Fritz) Y.; m. Carla Marie Moen, June 13, 1964; children: Signe Kara, Torunn Ingrid. B.A., St. Olaf Coll., 1959; J.D., U. Mich., 1962; postgrad., U. Strasbourg, France, 1961, Old Dominion Coll., 1964-65, U. Minn., 1966-67. Bar: Minn. 1962, U.S. Supreme Ct. 1965, D.C. 1972. Asso. Thomas, King, Swenson & Collatz, St. Paul, 1966-69; chief counsel Nat. Archives, Office Gen Counsel, GSA, Washington, 1969-70, exec. asst. to adminstr., 1970-72; asst. gen. counsel GSA, 1972-77; trial judge U.S. Ct. Claims, Washington, 1977-82; judge U.S. Claims Ct., Washington, 1982-92, U.S. Ct. Fed. Claims, Washington, 1992—. Served with JAGC USN, 1962-66. Mem. ABA, Minn., Fed., D.C. Bar Assns. Home: 4200 Webster Ct Annandale VA 22003-3424 Office: US Ct Fed Claims 717 Madison Pl NW Washington DC 20005-1011*

YOCKIM, JAMES CRAIG, state senator, oil and gas executive; b. Williston, N.D., Feb. 13, 1953; s. Daniel and Doris (Erickson) Y.; children: Jenna, Ericka. BSW, Pacific Luth. U., 1975; MSW, San Diego State U., 1979. Caseworker Dyslin Boys Ranch, Tacoma, 1975-77; landman Fayette Oil & Gas, Williston, 1980-82; head caseworker, program dir. Pyslin Boys Ranch, 1979-80; owner Hy-Plains Energy, Williston, 1982-87; city fin. commr. City of Williston, 1984-88; therapist Luth. Social Svcs., Williston, 1983-95; senator N.C. State Senate, 1986—; owner James C. Yockim Resources, Williston, 1987—. Dir. Bethel Luth. Found., 1993—; del. N.D. Dem. Conv., 1984, 86, 88, 90, 92, 94, 96; dist. chmn. Dem. Party, Williston, 1988; caucus chmn. Dem. Caucus N.D. State Senate; mem. N.D. Legis. Coun., 1997—. Recipient Ruth Meiers award N.D. Mental Health Assn., 1989, Legislator of Yr. award N.D. Children's Caucus, 1989; named Outstanding Young North Dakotan N.D. Jaycees, 1988. Mem. NASW. Avocations: racquetball, softball, golf. Home: 1123 2nd Ave E Williston ND 58801-4302 Office: 322 Main Ste 202 PO Box 2344 Williston ND 58802-2344

YOCUM, CHARLES FREDRICK, biology educator; b. Storm Lake, Iowa, Oct. 31, 1941; s. Vincent Cary and Olive Lucille (Cammack) Y.; m. Patricia Joan Bury, Jan. 1, 1981; 1 son, Erik Charles. BS, Iowa State U., 1963; MS, Ill. Inst. Tech., 1968; PhD, Ind. U., 1971. Research biochemist Ill. Inst. Tech. Research Inst., Chgo., 1963-68; grad. fellow Ind. U., Bloomington, 1968-71; postdoctoral fellow Cornell U., Ithaca, N.Y., 1971-73; asst. prof. U. Mich., Ann Arbor, 1973-77, assoc. prof., 1978-82, prof. biol. scis. and chemistry, 1983—, chmn. dept. biology, 1985-91; vis. prof. Mich. State U., East Lansing, 1980-81; cons. NSF, Washington, 1982—. Editorial bd. Plant Physiology, Photosynthesis Research, Biochimica et Biophysica Acta.; contbr. articles to various publs. Fulbright fellow, 1996; rsch. grantee NSF, 1978—, USDA, 1978—; recipient Henry Russel award U. Mich., 1977. Mem. AAAS, Am. Chem. Soc., Am. Soc. Plant Physiologists, Am. Soc. Biol. Chemists, Am. Soc. Photobiology. Avocations: classical music, travel. Office: Dept Biology Univ of Mich Ann Arbor MI 48109-1048

YOCUM, HARRISON GERALD, horticulturist, botanist, educator, researcher; b. Bethlehem, Pa., Apr. 2, 1923; s. Harrison and Bertha May (Meckes) Y. BS, Pa. State U., 1955; MS, Rutgers U., 1961. Horticulture instr. U. Tenn., Martin, 1957-59; biology tchr., libr. asst. high schs., El Paso, Tex., 1959-60; rsch. asst. geochronology lab. U. Ariz., Tucson, 1960-67, rsch. asst. environ. rsch. lab., 1969-76; landscaping supt. Tucson Airport Authority, 1976-82; instr. Pima C.C., Tucson, 1976—. Contbr. articles to profl. jours. Founder Tucson Bot. Gardens, 1964. Mem. Am. Hort. Soc., Men's Garden Club Tucson (pres. 1991), Tucson Cactus & Succulent Soc. (pres. 1991, 92), Internat. Palm Soc. (charter), El Paso Cactus and Rock Club, Tucson Gem and Mineral Soc., Old Pueblo Lapidary Club, Deming Mineral Soc., Nat. Geog. Soc., Ariz.-Sonora Desert Mus., Huachuca Vigilantes, Penn State Alumni Assn., Pa. Club Tucson, Fraternal Order Police Assocs., N.Am. Hunting Club (life), Boyce-Thompson Arboretum, Shriners, Masons, Scottish Rite. Lutheran. Home: 1628 N Jefferson Ave Tucson AZ 85712-4204

YODAIKEN, RALPH E., pathologist, occupational medicine physician; b. Johannesburg, Republic of South Africa, 1928. BS, U. Witwatersrand, Republic of South Africa, 1956; MPH, Johns Hopkins U., 1976. Diplomate Am. Bd. Pathology, Am. Bd. Forensic Medicine. Intern Coronation Hosp., Johannesburg, 1956-57; resident U. Witwatersrand Med. Ctr., 1957-58, Johannesburg Gen. Hosp., 1958; assoc. pathologist Buffalo Gen. Hosp., 1965-67; mem. staff Cin. Gen. Hosp., 1968-71; rsch. assoc. Johns Hopkins U. Sch. Hygiene and Pub. Health, Balt., 1976—; sr. staff mem. Nat. Inst. Occupational Safety and Health, Washington, 1977—, chmn. sr. adv. staff, 1983; dir. office occupational medicine Occupational Safety and Health Adminstrn., U.S. Dept. Labor, Bethesda, 1983-91, sr. med. advisor, 1991—; lectr. U. Witwatersrand, 1958-63; adj. asst. prof. pathology, SUNY Buffalo, 1963-67; adj. assoc. prof. U. Cin., 1968-71; adj. prof., adj. assoc. prof. medicine Emory U., Atlanta, 1971-75; adj. clin. prof. George Washington U., 1975—; with Johns Hopkins Sch. Hygiene and Pub. Health; clin. prof. preventive medicine uniformed svcs. U. Health Scis. Served to lt. Israeli Army, 1948-50. Fellow Coll. Am. Pathologists, Am. Coll. Occupational and Environ. Health.

YODER, ANNA MARY, reading educator; b. Iowa County, Iowa, Nov. 14, 1933; d. Kores M. and Sadie Rebecca (King) Y. BS in Elem. Edn., Ea. Mennonite U., 1959; MA in Linguistics, Hartford Sem. Found., 1968; MA in Curriculum and Instruction, U. Tenn., 1975; postgrad., U. Iowa, 1975-81. Tchr. Am. Sch., Tegulcigalpa, Honduras, 1969-70, Escuela Internat. Sch., San Pedro Sula, Honduras, 1970-75; tchr. bilingual Muscatine (Iowa) Cmty. Schs., 1977-78, tchr., supr. title I, 1978-79; tchr. Escuela Internat. Sch., 1979-80; tchr. home room Muscatine Cmty. Schs., 1980-87, reading tchr., 1987—; nat. dir. adult educators Alfalit Spanish wun of Lit, Honduras, 1963-69. Author/editor: Pre-Cartilla de Alfalit, 1968. Mem. Sisters Cities, Muscatine, 1994, bd. dirs., 1995—. Mem. NEA, Assn. Childhood Edn. Internat., Internat. Reading Assn., Reading Recovery Coun. N.Am. (tchr. 1995—). Avocations: cats, reading, quilts, volunteer activities. Office: Jefferson Sch 1000 Mulberry Ave Muscatine IA 52761-3925

YODER, BRUCE ALAN, chemist; b. Seward, Nebr., Apr. 29, 1962; s. Elwood John and Elda Raye (Stutzman) Y. BS in Chemistry, Wayne State Coll., 1983. Lab. technician Wayne (Nebr.) State Coll., 1982-83; lab. technician Harris Labs., Lincoln, Nebr., 1984, chemist, 1984; scientist Dorsey Labs., Lincoln, 1984-86, scientist A, 1986-88; product stability analyst Sandoz Pharms., Lincoln, 1988-89, Sandoz Rsch. Inst., Lincoln, 1989-91; mgr. lab. computer ops. Sandoz Pharms., Lincoln, 1991-97; pres., CEO Data Mgmt. Svcs., Inc., Lincoln, 1997—. Mem. Lancaster County Young Reps., Lincoln, 1988—, co-chmn., 1990-91, pres., 1991-93; mem. Nebr. Fedn. Young Reps., 1988—, mem. exec. com., 1990—; mem. exec. com. Lancaster County Rep. Party, 1990—; mem. Def. Adv. Com. Lancaster County, 1992—; mem. Lincoln Mayor's Cmty. Cabinet, 1992-93; mem. Lincoln City Charter Revision Commn., 1994—; trustee Wayne State Coll. Found., 1991—; advisor Jr. Achievement, 1993—. Recipient Dwight M. Frost, MD award for Overcoming a Phys. Disability Immanuel Rehab. Ctr., 1993, Verdi Smith award for outstanding voluntary contbns. to Lancaster County Rep. Party, 1995-96, First Dist. Outstanding Vol. award Nebr. Reps., 1996-97. Mem. Am. Inst. Chemists, Am. Chem. Soc., Jaycees. Mennonite. Achievements include design of a sample holder for solid dosage forms when using a hunter color instrument, design of a new computer system for Sandoz Pharmaceuticals laboratory computer operations. Home: 2240 Winding Way Lincoln NE 68506-2846 Office: Sandoz Pharms 10401 Highway 6 Lincoln NE 68517-9704

YODER, EDGAR PAUL, education educator; b. Millersburg, Ohio, June 20, 1946; s. Albert Daniel Yoder and Ella Marie (Bontrager) Erb; m. Deborah Jean Barnhart, June 12, 1971; children: Scott, Suzan. BSA, Ohio State U., 1968, MS, 1972, PhD, 1976. Cert. tchr., counselor, prin., Ohio, Va. Tchr. agr. and sci. Conotton Valley Schs., Bowerston, Ohio, 1968-69, East Holmes Schs., Berlin, Ohio, 1969-72; curriculum specialist Ohio State U., Columbus, 1972-74, project dir., 1974-76; asst. prin. Montgomery County Schs., Blacksburg, Va., 1976-77; asst. prof. Va. Poly. Inst. and State U., Blacksburg, 1977-78; asst. prof. Pa. State U., University Park, 1978-84, assoc. prof. tchr. edn., 1984-94, prof., 1994—, interim dept. head, 1995—; cons. Poland Ministry Edn., Warsaw, 1994, Swaziland Ministry Agr., Mbane, 1985, 87, U. Peredenyia, Kandy, Sri Lanka, 1984. Author text: Ag Supplies and Services, 1974, (with others) Undergraduate Education in Agriculture, 1989, also chpt. to book. Chmn. community svc. Sertoma Internat., Columbus, 1975; asst. dir. Va. HSA Assn., Blacksburg, 1978; sect. chmn. Am. Heart Assn., State College, Va., 1981; pres. Ferguson Twp. PTO, State College, 1983-84; bd. dirs. RAFT Drug Rehab. Ctr., Radford, 1976-78, Nat. Future Farmers Am., Alexandria, Va., 1981-83. Recipient Hon. Degree, Nat. Future Farmers Am., 1983. Mem. Nat. Assn. Coll. Tchrs. Agr. (pres., teacher fellow 1987, Regional Outstanding Teaching award 1992), Am. Assn. Agr. Educators (legis. chmn. 1985), Am. Assn. Ednl. Rsch. Assn., Am. Vocat. Edn. Rsch. Assn., Assn. Internat. Agr. and Extension Edn., Phi Delta Kappa, Gamma Sigma Delta (Teaching award of Merit 1987). Avocations: collecting sports memorabilia, restoring antiques, classic cars. Office: Penn State U Coll Agricultural Scis University Park PA 16802

YODER, EDWIN MILTON, JR., columnist, educator, editor, writer; b. Greensboro, N.C., July 18, 1934; s. Edwin M. and Mytrice M. (Logue) Y.; m. Mary Jane Warwick, Nov. 1, 1958; children: Anne Daphne, Edwin Warwick. B.A., U. N.C., 1956; BA, MA (Rhodes scholar), Oxford (Eng.) U., 1958; D.H.L. (hon.), Grinnell Coll., 1980, Elon Coll., 1986; DLitt (hon.), U. N.C., 1993, Richmond Coll., London. Editorial writer Charlotte (N.C.) News, 1958-61; editorial writer Greensboro Daily News, 1961-64, assoc. editor, 1965-75; asst. prof. history U. N.C., Greensboro, 1964-65; editorial page editor Washington Star, 1975-81; syndicated columnist Washington Post Writers Group, 1982-97; prof. journalism and humanities Washington and Lee U., 1992—. Author: Night of the Old South Ball, 1984, The Unmaking of a Whig, 1990, Joe Alsop's Cold War, 1995, The Historical Present, 1997; contbr. articles to periodicals. Recipient awards editorial writing N.C. Press Assn., 1958, 61, 66, Walker Stone award Scripps-Howard Found., 1978, Pulitzer prize editorial writing, 1979; Disting. Alumnus award U. N.C., Chapel Hill, 1980. Mem. Nat. Conf. Editorial Writers, Am. Soc. Newspaper Editors. Democrat. Episcopalian. Home: 4001 Harris Pl Alexandria VA 22304-1720

YODER, FREDERICK FLOYD, fraternity executive; b. Wilkinsburg, Pa., Oct. 7, 1935; s. Floyd Elvin and Mary Viola (Stahl) Y. B.S. in Journalism, Ohio U., 1957. Mem. hdqrs. staff Sigma Chi, Evanston, Ill., 1957—, coordinator chpt. visitation and installations program, 1964-72, leadership tng. adminstr., 1962-76, editor mag., 1972-91, dir. comm., 1991-93, dir. alumni participation and cmty. svc., 1994—. Editor The Norman Shield, 1973-91, Sigma Chi Membership Directory, 1977, 87, 97; contbr. articles to interfrat. jours. Served with AUS, 1958. Mem. Coll. Frat. Editors Assn. (past pres., Varner Outstanding Frat. Communicator award, Ford Outstanding Svc. award), Chgo. Headline Club, Soc. Profl. Journalists, Omicron Delta Kappa. Home: 2603 Sheridan Rd Evanston IL 60201-1752 Office: 1714 Hinman Ave Evanston IL 60201-4517

YODER, HATTEN SCHUYLER, JR., petrologist; b. Cleve., Mar. 20, 1921; s. Hatten Schuyler and Elizabeth Katherine (Knieling) Y.; m. Elizabeth Marie Bruffey, Aug. 1, 1959; children: Hatten Schuyler III, Karen Marianne. AA, U. Chgo., 1940, SB, 1941; student, U. Minn., summer 1941; PhD, Mass. Inst. Tech., 1948; D honoris causa, U. Paris VI, 1981; DEngring. (hon.), Colo. Sch. of Mines, 1995. Petrologist Geophys. Lab., Carnegie Instn., Washington, 1948-71, dir., 1971-86, dir. emeritus, 1986—; cons. Los Alamos (N.Mex.) Nat. Lab., 1972—; trustee The Cutter Trust, 1992—. Author: Generation of Basaltic Magma, 1976; editor: The Evolution of the Igneous Rocks: Fiftieth Anniversary Perspectives, 1979; co-editor Jour. of Petrology, 1959-69; assoc. editor Am. Jour. Sci, 1972-90; contbr. articles to sci. jours. Trustee The Cutler Trust, 1992—; bd. advisors Coll. of Democracy of the Nat. Grad. U., founders com. 1985, exec. com./sec.-treas. 1995—). Served to lt. comdr. USNR, 1942-58. Naval Expedition to Siberia, 1945-46. Recipient Bicentennial medal Columbia U., 1954, A.G. Werner medal German Mineral Soc., 1972; named to Disting. Alumni Hall of Fame, Lakewood (Ohio) H.S., 1990; mineral yoderite named in his honor. Fellow Geol. Soc. Am. (coun. 1966-68, A.L. Day medal 1962), Geol. Soc. London (hon. Wollaston medal 1979), Geol. Soc. South Africa (du Toit lectr. 1987), Am. Acad. Arts and Scis., Mineral. Soc. Am. (coun. 1962-64, 69-73, pres. 1971-72, MSA award 1954, Roebling medal 1992), Am. Geophys. Union (pres. volcanology, geochemistry and petrology sect. 1962-64); mem. NAS (chmn. geology sect. 1973-76, A.L. Day prize and lectr. 1972), Mineral Soc. London (hon., Hallimond lectr. 1979), Geol. Soc. Finland, Russian Mineral Soc. (hon.), Geochem. Soc. (organizer, founding mem., coun. 1956-58), Am. Chem. Soc., Mineral Assn. Can., Washington Acad. Sci., Geol. Soc. Washington, Chem. Soc. Washington, French Soc. Mineralogy and Crystallography (hon.), Am. Philos. Soc. (coun. 1983-85, 94-97), Pub. Mems. Assn. of Fgn. Svc. (bd. dirs. 1993-96, v.p. 1994), History of Earth Scis. Soc. (pres. 1995-96, sec.-treas., bd. advisors Coll. of Democracy Nat. Grad. U.), SAR, Sigma Xi, Phi Delta Theta (Golden Legion award). Home: 6709 Melody Ln Bethesda MD 20817-3152 Office: Geophys Lab 5251 Broad Branch Rd NW Washington DC 20015-1305

YODER, JOHN CLIFFORD, producer, consultant; b. Orrville, Ohio, Jan. 30, 1927; s. Ray Aquila Yoder and Dorothy Mildred (Hostetler) Yoder Hake; m. Alice Vigger Andersen, Mar. 2, 1963 (div. Nov. 1992); children: Gorm Clifford, Mark Edward. BA in Philosophy and Polit. Sci., Ohio Wesleyan U., 1951. Prodn. supr. Sta. WFMJ-TV, Youngstown, Ohio, 1954-62; producer Sta. NBC-TV, Chgo., 1964-72; ind. producer cons. Evanston, Ill., 1972—. Producer radio program Conversations From Wingspread, 1972-90 (George Foster Peabody Broadcasting award 1974, Ohio State award 1978, Freedoms Found. Honor medal 1978); appeared in film The Untouchables, 1994, TV program Missing Persons, 1993. Pub. rels. and pub. info. com. Chgo. Heart Assn. (Meritorious Svc. award 1978); electronic media advisor The White House, Washington, 1972; bd. dirs. Youngstown (Ohio) Sumphony Soc., 1959-63, Youngstown Playhouse, 1952-63, Bensenville (Ill.) Home Soc. 1985-89. With USAF, 1945-47 PTO. Recipient Disting. Svc. award Inst. Medicine of Chgo. 1971. Mem. Am. Fedn. Television & Radio Artists, , Nat. Acad. TV Arts and Scis., Screen Actors Guild, Midwest Pioneer Broadcasters, Soc. Profl. Journalists, Mus. Broadcast Comms., Masons, Am. Legion, Chgo. Headline Club. Avocations: tennis, golfing, sailing, fishing, reading. Home: 720 Noyes St Apt D 2 Evanston IL 60201-2848

YODER, MARIANNE ELOISE, software developer, consultant; b. Phoenix, Ariz.; d. William Amber and Maryanne King; m. William Ernest Yoder, Dec. 26, 1977. BSN, U. San Francisco, 1972; MS, U. Ariz., 1982, PhD, 1989. RN, Ariz. Nurse U.S. Navy, 1971-80, 91; grad. teaching asst. U. Ariz., Tucson, 1980-82; faculty U. Ariz., Tucson, Nev., 1982-85; grad. rsch. assoc. U. Ariz., Tucson, 1985-90; faculty, dir. coll. health profl. Computer Learning Ctr. No. Ariz. U., Flagstaff, Ariz., 1990-92; software developer Flagstaff, Ariz., 1992-96, Carson City, Nev., 1996—; chair Ariz. state commn. nursing rsch., 1992-96; chair of PILOT group, Assn. Devel. of Computer-Based Instructional Systems, Columbus, Ohio, 1990-92. Author: Software Integration Plan Introduction to Nursing Diagnosis, 1992, 2nd edit., 1993, contbg. author: Computer Applications in Nursing Education and Practice, 1993; contbr. articles to profl. jours. Vol. Flagstaff Pub. Libr., 1993-96. Recipient Pioneer in Nursing Edn. Informatics award Nurse Educator's Microworld & Fuld, 1994, Meritorious Tchg. Asst. award U. Ariz. Found., 1987. Mem. NLN (exec. bd. 1993-97), N.Y. Acad. of Scis., WEB Soc., Sigma Xi, Sigma Theta Tau (treas. 1970-71), Pi Lambda Theta. Avocations: quilting, skiing, puzzle-making. Home and Office: 631 Roundup Rd Carson City NV 89701-7615

YODER, MYRON EUGENE, secondary school educator; b. Reading, Pa., Oct. 28, 1953; s. Robert W. and Carmen D. (Keinard) Y.; m. Debra Kuper, Dec. 27, 1975; children: Joshua B., Rebecca A. BE cum laude, Kutztown U., 1976; Masters Equavalency, Pa. Dept. Edn., 1979; MEd cum laude, Kutztown U., 1981. Cert. secondary social studies tchr., Pa. With maintenance ride repair Dorney Pk, Allentown, Pa., 1968-72; postal asst. Lehigh County U.S. P.O. SCF180, Allentown, 1972-73; insp. Fairtex Mills, Allentown, 1973-74; correctional officer Lehigh County Prison, Allentown, 1974-76; emergency prison counselor Lehigh County Prison, 1979-84; mgr., supr. Hosp. Cen. Svcs., Allentown, 1976; tchr., dept. chmn., curriculum coord. Allentown Sch. Dist., 1976—; tchr. trainer Ctr. for Civic Edn., Bicentennial Commn., Calabasas, Calif., 1987—, Temple U. LEAP, 1987—; sch. coord. Boy Scouts Am. Awareness Post, Allentown, 1989—; scholar Pa. Humanities Coun., Phila., 1991; Pa. Congl. Dist. 15 coord. for We the People Citizen and Constn. Program, 1992—; apptd. commr. Pa. Profl. Standards and Practices Commn.; mem. social studies student standards devel. team Pa. Dept. Edn., 1996; mem. assessment and student standard exercise devel. team Social Studies State Collaborative, 1996. Photographer (Kinisa Local award 1980, 83); computer programmer Class Dues Record Keeper, 1987-88 (1st dist., 2nd regional runner-up computer learning award), Study Hall Record Keeper, 1988 (1st dist., 2nd regional award); contbr. articles to profl. publs. Chmn. Borough of Emmaus Operation Homecoming, 1991; discussion leader Pa. Humanities Coun., Emmaus, 1992, Allenton, 96; com. mem. Allentown Columbus Quincentenary, 1991, Allentown Black History Month Com., 1990-91; coord. We the People program Pa. Congl. Dist. 15; bd. dirs. Jr. Achievement of Lehigh Valley, 1993, Korea/Vietnam Meml. Nat. Ednl. Ctr., 1993. Recipient Applied Econs. Tchr. Yr. award Jr. Achievement of Lehigh Valley, 1990, 93, Jr. Achievement Applied Econs. Tchr. of Yr. for Pa. award, 1991, Pa. DAR Am. History Tchr. of Yr. award, 1993, Nat. Soc. DAR Am. History medal, 1993, cooperating Tchr. award Kutztown U., 1994, SAR Silver Good Citizenship medal, 1994; selected by Jr. Achievement to travel to Soviet Union to train Soviet tchrs. in using Jr. Achievment applied econs., 1991; finalist Pa. Tchr. of Yr., 1995. Mem. NEA, Nat. Coun. Social Studies, Pa. Coun. Social Studies (Outstanding Secondary Social Studies Tchr. 1992), Pa. State Edn. Assn. (internat. rels. com. region chmn. 1987, vice chmn. state com., 1996-97, tchr. trainer student assessment tng. cadre), Lehigh Valley Coun. Social Studies, Lehigh U. Coll. Edn. Alumni Coun. (Outstanding Tchr. award 1992), Allentown Edn. Assn. (v.p. 1991-96), Kiwanis. Republican. Lutheran. Avocation: photography. Office: Louis E Dieruff H S 815 N Irving St Allentown PA 18103-1832

YODER, PATRICIA DOHERTY, public relations executive; b. Pitts., Oct. 30, 1939; d. John Addison and Calmela Grace (Conti) Doherty; children: Shari Lynn, Wendy Ann. BA, Duquesne U., 1961. Press sec. U.S. Ho. of Reps., 1965-69; dir. office of pub. info. City of Ft. Wayne, 1973-76; asst. mgr. pub. and corp. comm. Mellon Bank N.A., Pitts., 1977-79; v.p. pub. affairs Am. Waterways Operators Inc., Washington, 1980-83; sr. v.p., gen. mgr. 1983-86, exec. v.p., dir. internat. banking, 1989-91, Hill and Knowlton Inc., Pitts.; sr. v.p. corp. and pub. affairs PNC Bank, Pitts., 1987-89; v.p., mgr. corp. pub. rels. and advt. GE Capital, Stamford, Conn., 1991-95; corp. v.p. pub. affairs and comm. GTE Corp., Stamford, 1995-96. Trustee Shadyside Hosp., Pressley Ridge Sch., Pitts., Ellis Sch.; bd. dirs. Children's Mus., Civic Light Opera, Pitts. Ballet Theatre. Recipient Outstanding Woman Bus. & Industry, 1988, Disting. Alumna award Duquesne U., 1996. Mem. Pitts. Field Club, Duquesne Club, Indian Harbor Yacht Club, Century Club of Disting. Duquesne U. Alumni. Roman Catholic. Home: 13 Brownhouse Rd Old Greenwich CT 06870-1502

YODER, RONDA ELAINE, nursing educator; b. Indpls., Oct. 7, 1963; d. Charles Stewart and Sarah Angeline (Pfaff) Bower; m. Robert Paul Yoder, July 22, 1989; children: Robert Andrew, Sarah Elizabeth. BSN, Pensacola Christian Coll., 1985; MSN, Ind. U., Indpls., 1988; DSN, U. Ala., Birmingham, 1994. Emergency staff nurse Westview Hosp., Indpls., 1986-88, West Fla. Regional Med. Ctr., Pensacola, 1988-89; DON Pensacola Christian Coll., 1988-93, mem. nursing faculty, 1993—. Mem. Sigma Theta Tau. Home: 1245 Langley Ave Pensacola FL 32504-8038

YODER, RONNIE A., judge; b. Knoxville, Tenn., July 10, 1937; s. Raymond Abraham and Veryl Hope (Hostetler) Y.; m. Shirley Mae Grimes, June 28, 1961; children: Susan Elizabeth, Mary Amanda, Elizabeth Anne, John Anthony Gerhard. BA in Polit. Sci. with honors, U. Va., 1958, JD, 1961. Bar: Va. 1961, N.Y. 1963, D.C. 1965, U.S. Dist. Ct. D.C. 1965, U.S. Dist. Ct. (so. dist.) N.Y. 1969, U.S. Ct. Claims 1964, U.S. Supreme Ct. 1968. Assoc. Mudge Rose Guthrie & Alexander, N.Y.C. and Washington, 1962-70; of counsel Zuckert Scoutt & Rasenberger, Washington, 1970-72, ptnr., 1972-75; adminstrv. law judge U.S. Dept. Labor, Washington, 1976, CAB, Washington, 1976-84, U.S. Dept. Transp., Washington, 1985—; adminstrv. law judge Nat. Transp. Safety Bd., 1979-80, Maritime Adminstrn., 1983, 86-88, FDIC, 1982-83, SBA, 1983, FAA, 1985—, Fed. Hwy. Adminstrn., 1985—, Fed. R.R. Adminstrn., 1993-95, Rsch. and Spl. Programs Adminstrn., 1991—, Surface Transp. Bd., 1996—. Mem. editorial bd. U. Va. Law Rev., 1959-61; contbr. articles to profl. jours. Sec., co-counsel Capital Headstart, 1966-68; narrator Lincoln Commn., 1985, 86; mem. permanent jud. commn. Nat. Capital Presbytery, 1985-91. Rockefeller fellow, 1961. Mem. ABA (jud. divsn. coun. 1994-95, exec. com. nat. conf. adminstrv. law judges 1980-83, 85-89, 90-96, sec. 1991-92, vice chmn. 1992-93, chmn.-elect 1993-94, chmn. 1994-95, mem. Nat. Ctr. for State Cts. working group on asbestos litigation govt. employees sect. 1982-84, parliamentarian 1991-92, 96-97, reporter Model Code Jud. Conduct for Fed. Adminstrv. Law Judges 1989, adminstrv. law sect. com. on internat. and comparative adminstrv. law, sect. of sect. officers chmn. task force on participation in profl. assns. by govt. employees 1991-92, vice chmn. social security com. sr. lawyers sect. 1996—), FBA, Am. Judicature Soc., Fed. Adminstrv. Law Judges Conf. (exec. com. 1976-81, 85, 87), Nat. Assn. Adminstrv. Law Judges, Va. Bar Assn. (bd. govs. adminstrv. law sect.), Am. Judges Assn., D.C. Bar Assn., SAR, Phi Beta Kappa, Phi Eta Sigma. Home: 1400 Summit Ave Alexandria VA 22302-2735 Office: Dept Transp 400 7th St SW Rm 9228 Washington DC 20590-0001

YODER, SARA ANN, emergency nurse; b. Allensville, Pa., Oct. 24, 1932; d. David E. and Katie E. (Yoder) Y.; m. John R. Yoder, May 11, 1957; children: Edna M., Jennifer R. Diploma, Lewistown Hosp. Sch. Nursing, Pa., 1956. RN, CEN. Oper. rm. nurse Lewistown Hosp., Pa., 1956-58, obstetrics nurse, 1959-65, house supr., 1965-72, nurse emergency dept., 1972—. Mem. Emergency Nurses Assn. (treas. Seven Mountains chpt. 1992-94), Mennonite Health Assn. Republican. Avocations: knitting, reading. Home: 88 Water St Allensville PA 17002

YODER, STANLEY JONAS, orthopedic surgeon; b. Belleville, Pa., Aug. 13, 1938; s. Moses Aaron and Kathryn Barbara Y.; children: Stanley Phillip, Julie Beth. BA, Goshen (Ind.) Coll., 1960; MD, Jefferson Med. Coll., Phila., 1964. Diplomate Am. Bd. Orthop. Surgery. Intern Geisingermedica Ctr., Danville, Pa., 1964-65, resident, 1968-72; orthop. surgeon Billings (Mont.) Clinic, 1972-78, Centre Orthop., State College, Pa., 1978-93, U. Orthop. & Sports Medicine Ctr., State College, Pa., 1993—; cons. Mont. Ctr. Handicapped, Billings, 1976-78; team physician Rocky Mountain Coll., Billings, 1973-78; chief of staff Rehab. Hosp., Pleasan Gap, Pa., 1986-92. Pres. Boalsburg (Pa.) Village Conservancy, 1989. Lt. comdr USPHS, 1965-68. Fellow Am. Acad. Orthop. Surgeons; mem. Pan Pacific Surg. Assn., Pa. Med. Soc., Centre County Med. Soc. (pres. 1978—), Interstate Orthop. Soc., Ea. Orthop. Assn. Republican. Mennonite. Avocations: gardening, hiking, fishing. Home: 404 W Main St Boalsburg PA 16827 Office: Univ Orthop & Sports Medicine Ctr 101 Regent Ct State College PA 16801-7965

YODOWITZ, EDWARD J., lawyer; b. N.Y.C., 1943. BS, Long Island U., 1965; JD, U. Balt., 1969. Bar: N.Y. 1972. Mem. Skadden, Arps, Slate, Meagher & Flom, N.Y.C. Mem. ABA. Office: Skadden Arps Slate Meagher & Flom 919 3rd Ave New York NY 10022

YOE, HARRY WARNER, retired agricultural economist; b. Martinsburg, W. Va., Oct. 20, 1912; s. Horace George and Mary Morrow (Van Metre) Y.; m. Barbara Virginia Fultz, Mar. 22, 1936; children—Harry Warner, Robert Boyd, Paul Michael. B.S., W. Va. U., 1935, grad. study, 1940. Agriculturist U.S. Dept. Agr., Red House Homesteads, W. Va., 1935-38; dir. spl. project U.S. Dept. Agr., Princeton, W.Va., 1938-40; dist. supr. Farm Security Adminstrn. U.S. Dept. Agr., Morgantown, W. Va., 1940-42; econ. cons. Supreme Comdr. Allied Power, Tokyo, Japan, 1947-51; agrl. adminstr. Inter-Am. Affairs, 1951-53; dir. div. Western S.A., ICA, 1953-57; dir. USOM to Haiti, 1957-61, ICA West Indies and Eastern Caribbean Mission, Port-of-Spain, Trinidad, W.I., 1961-62; with AID, Dept. State, Wash., 1962-64; dir. AID mission Georgetown, British Guiana, 1964-68; assoc. mem. firm, dir. econs. and planning div. Miller-Warden-Western, Inc., 1968-69; dir., v.p. Hoskins-Western-Sonderegger, Inc., 1969-82; ret., 1982. Author: Fisheries Cooperatives in Japan, 1950. Served from lt. (j.g.) to comdr. USNR, 1942-46. Recipient commendation for econ. rehab. Yokohama area, Japan U.S. Army, 1946, meritorious award for econ. reforms Japanese Fishing Industry, 1951; spl. commendation ICA, 1953; superior honor award AID, 1967. Mem. Rotary, Alpha Zeta, Pi Kappa Alpha. Episcopalian. Home: RR 3 Martinsburg WV 25401-9803

YOERGER, ROGER RAYMOND, agricultural engineer, educator; b. LeMars, Iowa, Feb. 17, 1929; s. Raymond Herman and Crystal Victoria (Ward) Y.; m. Barbara M. Ellison, Feb. 14, 1953; 1 child, Karen Lynne; m. Laura M. Summitt, Dec. 23, 1971; stepchildren—Daniel L. Summitt, Linda Summitt Canull, Anita Summitt Smith. B.S., Iowa State U., 1949, M.S., 1951, Ph.D., 1957. Registered profl. engr., Ill. Instr., asst. prof. agrl. engring. Iowa State U., 1949-56; assoc. prof. Pa. State U., 1956-58; prof. U. Ill., Urbana, 1959-85; head agrl. engring. dept. U. Ill., 1978-85, prof. emeritus, 1985—. Contbr. articles to profl. jours. Patentee in field. Mem. Ill. Noise Task Force, 1974-80. Fellow Am. Soc. Agrl. Engrs. (Massey-Ferguson medal 1989); mem. Am. Soc. Engring. Edn., Phi Kappa Phi (dir. fellowships, dir. 1971-83, pres.-elect 1983-86, pres. 1986-89), Rotary. Roman Catholic. Home: 107 W Holmes St Urbana IL 61801-6614 Office: 1304 W Pennsylvania Ave Urbana IL 61801-4726

YOGANATHAN, AJIT PRITHIVIRAJ, biomedical engineer, educator; b. Colombo, Sri Lanka, Dec. 6, 1951; came to U.S., 1973; s. Ponniah and Mangay (Navaratnam) Y. BSChemE with honors, Univ. Coll., U. London, 1973; PhDChemE, Calif. Tech. U., 1978. Engring. asst. Shell Oil Refinery, Stanlow, Eng., 1972; teaching asst. Calif. Inst. Tech., 1973-74, 1976, rsch. fellow, 1977-79; asst. prof. Ga. Inst. Tech., 1979-83, assoc. prof., 1983-88, chmn. bioengring. com., 1984-88, prof. chem. engring., 1988-94, dir. Bioengring. Ctr., 1989—, prof. mech. engring., 1989-94, co-dir. Emory U.-Ga. Tech. Biomed. Tech. Ctr., 1992—, Regents prof., 1994—; adj. assoc. prof. U. Ala., 1985—. Founding fellow Am. Inst. Med. & Biol. Engring., 1992; recipient Edwin Walker prize Brit. Inst. Mech. Engrs., 1988, Humboldt fellowship, 1985, Am. Heart Assn.-Ga. Affiliate Rsch. Investigatorship award, 1980-83, Calif. Inst. Tech. fellowship, 1973-77, Goldsmid Medal and prize Univ. Coll., 1973, 72, Brit. Coun. scholarship, 1971-73. Mem. AICE, ASME, Biomed. Engring. Soc., Am. Soc. Echocardiography (dir. 1987-91). Office: Sch of Chem Engring Ga Tech U Atlanta GA 30332

YOH, HAROLD LIONEL, JR., engineering, construction and management company executive; b. Bryn Mawr, Pa., Dec. 12, 1936; s. Harold Lionel and Katherine (Hulme) Y.; m. Mary Michael Milus, June 20, 1959; children: Harold Lionel III, Michael Hulme, Karen Bogart, Jeffrey Milus, William Courtlandt. B.S. in Mech. Engring, Duke, 1958; M.B.A., U. Pa., 1962. Vice pres. H.L. Yoh Co. subs. Day & Zimmerman, Inc., Phila., 1960-63, sr. v.p. div. mgr., 1963-64, pres., 1964-76; v.p. adminstrn. Day & Zimmermann, Inc., Phila., 1961-69, sec., 1966-70, v.p., treas., 1969-76, vice chmn., chief exec. officer, 1976-80, chmn. bd., chief exec. officer, 1980—; also bd. dirs. Day & Zimmermann, Inc.; past pres., past dir. Nat. Tech. Services Assn.; bd. dirs. Continental Bancorp. Greater Phila First Corp. and several other privately held cos. Bd. dirs. Phila. Coll. Arts, Bryn Mawr Civic Assn., Phila. Indsl. Devel. Corp., The Haverford Sch.; past chmn. bd. dirs. Pop Warner Little Scholars; past Pa. State chmn. U.S. Savs. Bonds.; chmn. dean's council Sch. Engring. Duke U., chmn. univ. Greater Phila. Area Capital Campaign; Mid-Atlantic regional chmn. U.S. Olympics. Named Ambassador City of Phila., Silver Knight of D&Z Lone Star chpt. Mgmt. Nat. Mgmt. Assn., 1979-80; recipient Blue Devil award Duke U., Disting. Alumnus award Duke U., Robert Morris award Boy Scouts Am. Mem. ASME, Am. Def. Preparedness Assn. (dir.), Phila. C. of C. (chmn., dir.), Young President's Orgn. (internat. dir.), Phila. Pres.' Orgn., Chief Execs. Orgn., Navy League (life), Newcomen Soc., World Bus. Council, Sigma Nu. Republican. Episcopalian. Clubs: Union League, Phila. Country (Phila.); Merion Golf (Ardmore, Pa.); University (Washington); Seaview Country (N.J.). Avocations: golf, fishing. Home: 116 Summit House West Chester PA 19382-6518 Office: Day & Zimmermann Inc 1818 Market St Philadelphia PA 19103-3638*

YOHALEM, HARRY MORTON, lawyer; b. Phila., Jan. 21, 1943; s. Morton Eugene and Florence (Mishnun) Y.; m. Martha Caroline Remy, June 9, 1967; children: Seth, Mark. BA with honors, U. Wis., 1965; JD cum laude, Columbia U., 1969, M in Internat. Affairs., 1969. Bar: N.Y. 1969, D.C. 1981, Calif. 1992, U.S. Supreme Ct. 1985. Assoc. Shearman & Sterling, N.Y.C., 1969-71; asst. counsel to gov. State of N.Y., Albany, 1971-73, counsel office planning svcs., 1973-75; asst. gen. counsel FEA, Washington, 1975-77; mem. staff White House Energy Policy and Planning Office, Washington, 1977; dep. gen. counsel for legal svcs. Dept. Energy, Washington, 1978-80, dep. under sec., 1980-81; ptnr. Rogers & Wells, Washington, 1981-91; gen. counsel Calif. Inst. Tech., Pasadena, 1991—. Editor comments Columbia Jour. Transnat. Law, 1967-68, rsch. editor, 1968-69. Prin. Coun. for Excellence in Govt., Washington, 1990—; pres. Opera Bel Canto, Washington, 1984-87; mem. Lawyers Com. for Arts, Washington, 1981-88; mem. adv. bd. Pasadena Conservatory of Music, Calif., 1994—. Harlan Fiske Stone scholar Columbia U., 1967, 69. Mem. ABA, Calif. Bar Assn., D.C. Bar Assn. Athenaeum, Phi Kappa Phi. Home: 1060 Stoneridge Dr Pasadena CA 91105-2844 Office: Calif Inst Tech 4800 Oak Grove Dr JPL 180-305 Pasadena CA 91109

YOHN, DAVID STEWART, virologist, science administrator; b. Shelby, Ohio, June 7, 1929; s. Joseph Van and Agnes (Tryon) Y.; m. Olivetta Kathleen McCoy, June 11, 1950; children: Linda Jean, Kathleen Ann, Joseph John, David McCoy, Kristine Renee. B.S., Otterbein Coll., 1951; M.S., Ohio State U., 1953, Ph.D., 1957; M.P.H., U. Pitts., 1960. Research fellow, scholar in microbiology Ohio State U., Columbus, 1952-56, prof. virology Coll. Veterinary Medicine, 1969-95, prof. emeritus, 1995—, dir. Comprehensive Cancer Ctr., 1973-88, dep. dir. Comprehensive Cancer Ctr., 1988-94, dir. emeritus Comprehensive Cancer Ctr., 1994—; research assoc., asst. prof. microbiology U. Pitts., 1956-62; assoc. cancer research scientist Roswell Park Meml. Inst., Buffalo, 1962-69; mem. nat. med. and sci. adv. com. Leukemia Soc. Am., 1970-91, trustee, 1971-91; pres. Ohio Cancer Research Assocs., 1982—; mem. cancer research centers rev. com. Nat. Cancer Inst., 1972-77. Pres. bd. deacons North Presbyn. Ch., Williamsburg, N.Y., 1967-68. Recipient Pub. Service award Lions, 1968. Mem. Am. Assn. Cancer Rsch., Am. Soc. Microbiology, Am. Assn. Immunologists, Internat. Assn. Comparative Rsch. on Leukemia and Related Diseases (sec.-gen. 1974-95), Ohio Valley-Lake Erie Assn. Cancer Ctrs. (sec. 1978-95), Sertoma (pres. 1992-93, chmn. bd. dirs. 1993-94, Dist. Sertoman of Yr. award 1987). Home: 974 Willow Bluff Dr Columbus OH 43235-5047 Office: Ohio State U Comprehensive Cancer Ctr 300 W 10th Ave Ste 1132 Columbus OH 43210-1240

YOHN, WILLIAM H(ENDRICKS), JR., federal judge; b. Pottstown, Pa., Nov. 20, 1935; s. William H. and Dorothy C. (Cornelius) Y.; m. Jean Louise Kochel, mar. 16, 1963; children: William H. III, Bradley G., Elizabeth J. AB, Princeton U., 1957; JD, Yale U., 1960. Bar: Pa. 1961, U.S. Dist. Ct. D.C. 1961. Ptnr. Wells Campbell Reynier & Yohn, Pottstown, 1961-71; mem., chmn. coms. Pa. House of Reps., Harrisburg, 1968-80; ptnr. Binder Yohn & Kalis, Pottstown, 1971-81; judge Montgomery County Ct. of Common Pleas, Norristown, Pa., 1981-91, U.S. Dist. Ct., ea. dist., Pa., 1991—; asst. D.A., Montgomery County D.A. Office, 1962-65; instr. Am. Inst. of Banking, 1963-66. Bd. dirs. Greater Pottstown Drug Abuse Prevention Program, 1970-76, Pottstown Meml. Med. Ctr., 1974-95, chmn., 1984-95. Cpl. USMCR, 1960-66. Mem. Pa. Bar Assn., Montgomery Bar Assn. (bd. dirs. 1967-70). Republican. Office: US Dist Ct 3809 US Courthouse 601 Market St Philadelphia PA 19106-1713

YOKEN, MEL B(ARTON), French language educator, author; b. Fall River, Mass., June 25, 1939; s. Albert Benjamin and Sylvia Sarah (White) Y.; m. Cynthia Stein, June 20, 1976; children: Andrew Brett, David Ryan, Jonathan Barry. B.A., U. Mass., 1960, Ph.D., 1972; M.A.T., Brown U., 1961. Instr. French U. Mass., Dartmouth, 1966-72, asst. prof., 1972-76, assoc. prof., 1976-81 prof., 1981—, dir. French summer study program French Inst., 1981-88; vis. prof. Wheaton Coll., 1987, U. of Montreal, 1981-88, translator New Bedford Superior Ct., New Bedford, Mass., 1985—, Fall River Superior Ct., Fall River, Mass., 1985—; mem. nominating com. Nobel prize for lit., 1972—. Pres. Friends of Fall River Pub. Libr., 1972-80, pres. bd. dirs., 1972-80; pres. New Bedford Pub. Libr., 1980-82, Am. Field Svc., 1985—. Recipient Disting. Svc. award City Fall River, 1974, 80, Excellence in Teaching French award, 1984, 85, Gov.'s citation, 1986, Nat. Disting. Leadership award, 1990, Dist. Svc. award Mass. Foreign Lang. Assn., 1992, Medaille de Vermeil du Rayonnement de la Langue Française, L'Academie Francaise, 1993; Mel Yoken Day proclaimed by Mayor of New Bedford, 1990; Govt. of Que. grantee, 1981-85, 87-89, Can. Embassy grantee, 1986, 87, Southeastern Mass. U. grantee, 1985, 89, 90. Mem. MLA (life), Am. Assn. Tchrs. French (life), Am. Coun. Tchrs. Fgn. Langs., Middlebury Amicale (life), N.E. MLA (coord. 1987-91), New Eng. Fgn. Lang. Assn., Mass. Fgn. Lang. Assn. (bd. dirs. 1985-90, disting. svc. award 1992), N.Y. State Assn. Fgn. Lang. Tchrs., Internat. Platform Assn., Francophone Assn. (v.p. 1990—), Fall River C. of C., Brown U. Alumni Assn. (rep.), Richelieu Internat. Universal Manuscript Soc. (v.p. 1993—). Author: Claude Tillier, 1976, Speech is Plurality, 1978, Claude Tillier (1801-44): Fame and Fortune in His Novelistic Work, 1978, Entretiens Quebecois I, 1986, Entretiens Quebecois II, 1989, Letters of Robert Molloy, 1989, Festschrift in Honor of Stowell Goding, 1993, Entretiens Quebecois III, 1997; contbr. articles to profl. jours. Avocations: traveling, languages, baseball, postcards, meteorology. Home: 261 Carroll St New Bedford MA 02740-1412 Office: U Mass Dartmouth Lang Dept Old Westport Rd North Dartmouth MA 02747-2512

YOKLEY, RICHARD CLARENCE, fire department administrator; b. San Diego, Dec. 29, 1942; s. Clarence Ralph and Dorothy Junese (Sackman) Y.; m. Jean Elizabeth Liddle, July 25, 1964; children: Richard Clarence II, Karin Denise Yokley Dillard. Student, San Diego City Coll., 1967; AS, Miramar Coll., 1975; student, London Fire Brig. Tng. Acad., 1994, Fire Svc. Coll., Eng., 1994. Cert. fire officer, fire instr., Calif. Disc jockey Sta. KSDS-FM, San Diego, 1966-67; bldg. engr. Consolidated Systems, Inc., San Diego, 1968-72; with Bonita-Sunnyside Fire Dept., Calif., 1972—; ops. chief Bonita-Sunnyside Fire Dept., 1991-93, maintenance officer, 1993—; med. technician Hartson Ambulance, San Diego, 1978-80, Bay Gen. Hosp. (now Scripps Hosp.), Chula Vista, Calif., 1980-83, EMT-D Sea World of San Diego, 1997—; chmn. South Bay Emergency Med. Svc., 1988. Contbr. articles to jours., newspapers and mags. Asst. curator Firehouse Mus., San Diego, 1972-89, docent, 1990-93; scoutmaster troop 874 Boy Scouts Am., Bonita, Calif., 1978-79. With USAF, 1962-66. Recipient Heroism and Community Svc. award Firehouse Mag., N.Y.C., 1987, Star News Salutes award Chula Vista Star News, 1987, Golden Svc. award San Diego County Credit Union, 1988. Mem. Internat. Assn. Firefighters (pres. local chpt. 1981-82), Calif. State Firefighters Assn. (dep. dir. so. divsn. 1994—), Calif. Fire Mechanics, San Diego County Fire Prevention Officers (v.p. 1984, pres. 1985), Bonita Bus. and Profl. Assn. (bd. dirs. 1991-93, Historian award 1987), Fire Mark Cir. of the Ams. (dir. 1994—), Smokey Bear Collectors Assn. (co-founder, dir. 1995—), South Bay Commn., Bonita Hist. Mus. (co-founder 1986), Sport Chalet Dive Club (v.p. 1991). Republican. Methodist. Avocations: scuba diving, visit fire departments of foreign countries, collect fire memorabilia, snow skiing. Office: Bonita-Sunnyside Fire Dept 4900 Bonita Rd Bonita CA 91902-1725

YOKUBAITIS, ROGER T., lawyer; b. Wharton, Tex., Jan. 9, 1945. Attended, St. Louis U.; BA, JD, U. Houston, 1969. Bar: Tex. 1969. Ptnr. Carmody & Yokubaitis, L.L.P., Houston. Mem. ABA, Houston Bar Assn., State Bar of Tex., Houston Bankruptcy Conf., Am. Bankruptcy Inst. Office: Carmody & Yokubaitis LLP 5718 Westheimer Rd Ste 1010 Houston TX 77057-5732

YOLEN, JANE, author; b. N.Y.C., Feb. 11, 1939; d. Will Hyatt and Isabelle (Berlin) Y.; m. David Wilber Stemple, Sept. 2, 1962; children: Heidi Elisabet, Adam Douglas, Jason Frederic. B.A., Smith Coll., 1960; M.Ed., U. Mass., 1978; LL.D. (hon.), Coll. of Our Lady of the Elms, 1980. Asst. editor This Week mag., 1960; mem. staff Saturday Rev., 1960; asst. editor Gold Medal Books, 1961, Rutledge Press, 1961-63; asst. juvenile editor A.A. Knopf, Inc., 1963-65; free-lance writer, 1965—; lectr. dept. edn. Smith Coll., 1979-84; editor Jane Yolen books, imprint Harcourt Brace Jovanovich, 1988-97; tchr. writers confs. Centrum, Cape Cod Writers Conf., Soc. Children's Book Writers, U. Mass.; mem. Mass. Council on Arts, 1974. Author: Pirates in Petticoats, 1963, The Witch Who Wasn't, 1964, The Emperor and the Kite, 1968, Writing Books for Children, 1973, The Girl Who Cried Flowers, 1974, The Hundredth Dove, 1978, The Dream Weaver, 1979, Commander Toad in Space, 1980, The Gift of Sarah Barker, 1981, Touch Magic, 1981, Dragon's Blood, 1982, Tales of Wonder, 1983, Heart's Blood, 1984, Cards of Grief, 1984, Dragonfield, 1985, Merlin's Booke, 1986, The Lullabye Songbook, 1986, Ring of Earth, 1986, Favorite Folktales From Around the World, 1986, Piggins, 1987, Owl Moon, 1987, Three Bears, 1987, A Sending of Dragons, 1987, The Devil's Arithmetic, 1988, Sister Light/Sister Dark, 1988, White Jenna, 1989, Dove Isabeau, 1989, Baby Bear's Bedtime Book, 1990, Tam Lin, 1990, Bird Watch, 1990, Sky Dogs, 1990, Wizard's Hall, 1991, All those Secrets of the World, 1991, Wings, 1991, Hark! A Christmas Sampler, 1991, Encounter, 1992, Briar Rose, 1992, Letting Swift River Go, 1992, What Rhymes with Moon, 1993, Welcome to the Greenhouse, 1993, Honkers, 1993, Here There Be Dragons, 1993, Grandad Bill's Song, 1994, Good Griselle, 1994, The Girl in the Golden Bower, 1994, Old Dame Counterpane, 1994, Old Macdonald's Songbook, 1994, Here There Be Unicorns, 1994, Beneath the Ghost Moon, 1994, The Wild Hunt, 1995, Ballad of the Pirate Queens, 1995, And Twelve Chinese Acrobats, 1995, Water Music, 1995, Among Angels, 1995, Here They Be Witches, 1995, O. Jerusalem, 1996, Welcome to the Sea of Sand, 1996, Passager, 1996, Hobby, 1996, Sacred Places, 1996, Here There Be Angels, 1996, Milk and Honey, 1996, Meet The Monsters, 1996, Once Upon Ice, 1997, Merlin, 1997, Child of Faerie, 1997, Twelve Impossible Things Before Breakfast, 1997, Miz Berlin Walks, 1997, Nocturne, 1997, also others. Mass. del. Democratic Nat.

Conv., 1972; town coordinator Robert Drinan's campaign, 1970; chmn. bd. trustees Hatfield (Mass.) Library, 1978-83. Mem. Soc. Children's Book Writers (bd. dirs. 1974—), Children's Lit. Assn. (bd. dirs. 1977-79), Sci. Fiction Writers Am. (pres. 1986-88), Nat. Assn. for Preservation and Perpetuation of Storytelling, Authors Guild, Bay State Writers Guild, Western New Eng. Storytellers Guild (founder), Mystery Writers Am., Horror Writers Am., Authors Guild. Democrat. Jewish/Quaker. Home: 31 School St Hatfield MA 01038-9701

YOLLICK, BERNARD LAWRENCE, otolaryngologic surgeon; b. Toronto, Mar. 24, 1922; came to U.S., 1949; s. Samuel and Beatrice (Roth) Y.; m. Liny L. Pajgin, 1947; children: Ingrid, Eric Lyf. Sr. Matriculation, Harbord Collegiate Inst., Toronto, 1939; MD, U. Toronto, 1945. Diplomate Am. Bd. Surgery, Am. Bd. Otolaryngology. Intern Sunnybrook Hosp., toronto, 1945-46; resident D.C. Gen. Hosp., Washington, 1950, St. Louis County Hosp., Clayton, Mo., 1952-53; Am. Cancer Soc. fellow M.D. Anderson Cancer Hosp., Houston, 1953-54; resident in pathology Cook County Hosp., Chgo., 1949; surgeon Houston, 1953-59; fellowship in otolaryngology VA Hosp., Dallas, 1960-63; asst. prof. anatomy Baylor Med. Sch., Houston, 1953-59; assoc. prof. anatomy U. Tex. Dental Sch., Houston, 1953-59, Baylor Coll. Dentistry, Dallas, 1987-90; mem. staff Children's Med. Ctr., Dallas, 1990—; mem. staff, chief dept. otolaryngology St. Paul Med. Ctr., Dallas, 1990-97; cons. Tex. Workers Compensation Ins. Fund, 1996—; mem. staff Vets. Adminstrn. Hosp., Dallas, 1990—. Contbr. articles to profl. jours. Served to capt. Royal Can. Army Med. Corps, 1942-45. Recipient fellowship Am. Cancer Soc., 1953. Fellow Am. Coll. Surgeons; mem. Tex. Otolaryn. Assn. (pres. 1979).

YOLTON, JOHN WILLIAM, philosopher, educator; b. Birmingham, Ala., Nov. 10, 1921; s. Robert Elgene and Ella Maude (Holmes) Y.; m. Jean Sebastian, Sept. 5, 1945; children: Karin Frances Yolton Griffith, Pamela Holmes Yolton Smith. BA with honors, U. Cin., 1945, MA, 1946; postgrad., U. Calif., Berkeley, 1946-50; DPhil (Fulbright fellow), Balliol Coll., Oxford, Eng., 1952; LL.D. (hon.), York U., 1974; D.Litt. (hon.), McMaster U., 1976. Vis. lectr. philosophy Johns Hopkins U., 1952-53; asst. prof. Princeton U., 1952-57; assoc. prof. Kenyon Coll., 1957-61; prof. U. Md., 1961-63; prof. philosophy York U., Toronto, 1963-78; chmn. dept. York U., 1963-73, acting dean grad. studies, 1967-68, acting pres., 1973-74; prof. philosophy Rutgers U., New Brunswick, N.J., 1978—; dean Rutgers Coll., Rutgers U., 1978-85, John Locke prof. history of philosophy, 1989-92, prof. emeritus philosophy, 1992—; cons. Bertrand Russell Archives, McMaster U., 1973-86. Author: John Locke and the Way of Ideas, 1956, Metaphysical Analysis, 1967, Locke and the Compass of Human Understanding, 1970, Thinking Matter, 1983, Perceptual Acquaintance from Descartes to Reid, 1984, Locke and French Materialism, 1991, Perception and Reality, 1996, other books; gen. editor Clarendon Edit. of Works of John Locke, Oxford U. Press, 1984-92, Blackwell's Companion to the Enlightenment, 1992, Locke Dictionary (Blackwell), 1993, Library of the History of Ideas, 1989—; Concerning Education, 1989, 5 books in field; mem. edtl. bd. jours. in field; v.p., bd. dirs. Jour. of the History of Ideas, 1991—; contbr. articles to profl. jours. Mem. N.J. Com. for Humanities, 1978-85, treas., 1980-85. Am. Council Learned Socs. fellow, 1960-61; Can. Council fellow, 1968-69. Mem. Mind Assn., Can. Philos. Assn., Am. Soc. for 18th Century Studies, Hume Soc.

YONDA, ALFRED WILLIAM, mathematician; b. Cambridge, Mass., Aug. 10, 1919; s. Walter and Theophelia (Naruscewicz) Y.; B.S., U. Ala., 1952, M.A. in Math., 1954; m. Mary Jane McManus, Dec. 19, 1949 (dec.); children—Nancy, Kathryn, Elizabeth, John; m. Peggy A. Terrel, June 22, 1975. Mathematician rocket research Redstone Arsenal, Huntsville, Ala., 1953, U.S. Army Ballistic Research Labs., Aberdeen, Md., 1954-56; instr. math. U. Ala., Tuscaloosa, 1954, Temple U., Phila., 1956-57; asso. scientist, research and devel. div. Avco Corp., Wilmington, Mass., 1957-59; sr. mem. tech. staff RCA, Camden, N.J., 1959-66; mgr. computer analysis and programming dept. Raytheon Co. space and information systems div., Sudbury, Mass., 1966-70, mgr. software systems lab., 1969-70, prin. engr. missiles systems div., 1970-73; mgr. systems analysis and programming GTE Govt. Systems Corp., 1973-77, mgr. software engring. Atlantic ops., 1977-82, sr. mem. tech. staff Command Control & Communications Sector, 1983-91; software systems engr. Yonda Software Systems Cons., 1991—. Pres., Milford Area Assn. Retarded Children, 1970-74; vice-chmn. fin. com. Town of Medway, 1973; bd. dirs. Blackstone Valley Mental Health and Retardation Area , 1970-76; trustee Medway Libraries, 1973-82, chmn., 1974-81. Served with USAAF, 1943-46. Hon. fellow Advanced Level Telecommunications Tng. Center, Ghaziabad, India, 1981. Registered profl. engr. Mem. AAAS, IEEE, Math. Assn. Am., N.Y. Acad. Scis., Sigma Xi, Phi Eta Sigma, Pi Mu Epsilon (pres. Ala. chpt. 1953-54), Sigma Pi Sigma. Contbr. articles to profl. jours. Office: 12 Sunset Dr Medway MA 02053-2008

YONG, RAYMOND NEN-YIU, civil engineering educator; b. Singapore, Apr. 10, 1929; naturalized, 1966; s. Ngim Djin and Lucy (Loh) Y.; m. Florence Lechensky, July 8, 1961; children—Raymond T.M., Christopher T.K. BA in Math. and Physics, Washington and Jefferson Coll., 1950; BS, MIT, 1952; MS, Purdue U., 1954; MEngring., McGill U., Montreal, Que., Can., 1958, PhD, 1960. Mem. faculty McGill U., 1959-95, prof. civil engring., 1965-72, William Scott prof. civil engring. and applied mechanics, 1972-95; dir. Geotech Rsch. Ctr., 1973-95; assoc. mem. Ctr. for Medicine, Ethics and Law McGill U., 1991-95; adj. prof. civil engring. U. Fla., Gainesville, 1984—; adj. rsch. prof. civil engring. Carleton U., Ottawa, 1990; disting. rsch. prof. U. Wales, Cardiff, 1995—; sr. sci. dir. Geoenviron. Engring. Rsch. Ctr., Cardiff Sch. Engring., U. Wales,1995. Author: Soil Properties and Behavior, 1975 (Japanese edit. 1977), Introduction to Soil Behavior, 1966 (Japanese edit. 1974), Vehicle Traction Mechanics, 1985, Principles of Contaminant Transport in Soils, 1992 (Japanese edit. 1995). Decorated chevalier Ordre National du Que., 1985; recipient Killam prize Can. Coun., 1985, ASTM Charles B. Dudley award, 1988, Can. Environ. Achievement award, Lifetime Achievement Environment Can., 1991. Fellow Royal Soc. Can., Engring. Inst. Can., Can. Soc. for Civil Engring.; mem. ASCE, ASTM (Charles B. Dudley award 1988), Inst. Civil Engrs., Soc. Rheology, Clay Minerals Soc., Internat. Soc. Terrain-Vehicle Systems (pres. 1993—), Can. Geotech. Soc. (R.F. Legget award 1993). Office: McGill U Dept Civil Engring, and Applied Mechanics, 817 Sherbrooke St w, Montreal, PQ Canada H3A 2K6

YONKER, RICHARD AARON, rheumatologist; b. Phila., Aug. 8, 1952. BA, George Washington U., 1974; DO, Coll. Osteopathic Medicine, 1978. Diplomate Am. Bd. Internal Medicine, Am. Bd. Rheumatology. Rheumatologist Sarasota (Fla.) Arthritis Ctr., 1984—. Fellow Am. Coll. Rheumatology; mem. Am. Osteopathic Assn., Fla. Med. Assn., Fla. Osteopathic Med. Assn., Fla. Rheumatology Soc., Sarasota County Med. Soc. Office: Sarasota Arthritis Ctr 3500 S Tamiami Trl Sarasota FL 34239-6026

YONKMAN, FREDRICK ALBERS, lawyer, management consultant; b. Holland, Mich., Aug. 22, 1930; s. Fredrick Francis and Janet Dorothy (Albers) Y.; m. Kathleen VerMeulen, June 9, 1953 (div. Sept. 22, 1980); children: Sara, Margriet, Nina.; m. Barbara Anne Sullivan, Aug. 22, 1981; 1 child, Fredrick Ryan. BA, Hope Coll., Holland, 1952; JD, U. Chgo., 1957. Bar: N.Y. 1958, Mass. 1968, D.C. 1984. With Winthrop, Stimson, Putnam & Roberts, N.Y.C., 1957-64; sec., gen. counsel Reuben H. Donnelley Corp., N.Y.C., 1964-66, Dun & Bradstreet, Inc., N.Y.C., 1966-68; lawyer Sullivan & Worcester, Boston, 1968-72; gen. counsel Am. Express Co., N.Y.C., 1972-78; exec. v.p. Am. Express Co., 1975-80; pres. Buck Cons., N.Y.C., 1980-81; mgmt. cons., psychoanalyst, 1981—; counsel Peabody, Lambert & Myers, Washington, 1983-84; chmn. Outward Bound, Inc., Garrison, N.Y., 1980-81; mem. bd. and chmn. audit com. Kennecott Corp., 1978-81; adj. prof. law Georgetown U., 1976-78; chmn. Georgetown Internat. Law Inst., 1980-81; vis. com. U. Chgo. Law Sch., 1980-82. Bd. dirs. Washington Campus Program, 1976-81; With AUS, 1952-54. Recipient Silver Anniversary award Nat. Coll. Athletic Assn., 1977. Mem. ABA, N.Y. State Bar Assn., Mass. Bar Assn., Rsch. Soc. for Process Oriented Psychology (Zurich) (diplomate), Union Club (Boston). Presbyterian. Home: 300 Taconk Rd Greenwich CT 06831

YONTZ, KENNETH FREDRIC, medical and chemical company executive; b. Sandusky, Ohio, July 21, 1944; s. Kenneth Willard and Dorothy (Kromer) Y.; m. Jean Ann Marshall, July 21, 1962 (div. Aug. 1982); children: Terri, Christine, Michael, Jennifer; m. Karen Glojek, July 7, 1984 (wid. Dec. 1994); m. Karen Mc Diarmid, Jan. 10, 1997. BSBA, Bowling Green State U., 1971; MBA, Eastern Mich. U., 1979. Fin. planning mgr. Ford Motor Co., Rawsonville, Mich., 1970-74; fin. mgr. Chemetron Corp., Chgo., 1974-76, pres. fire systems div., 1976-80; pres. electronics div. Allen Bradley Co., Milw., 1980-83, group. pres. electronics, 1983-85, exec. v.p., 1985-86; chmn. bd., pres., chief exec. officer Sybron Corp., Milw., 1986—, also bd. dirs.; bd. dirs. Playtex Corp., N.Y.C., Birg Electronics, St. Louis, Thomson Minwax Co., N.J. Bd. dirs. Boys and Girls Club; founder Karen Youtz Womens Cardiac Awareness Ctr. Mem. Nat. Assn. Mfrs. (bd. dirs.), Bluemound Country Club, Milw. Athletic Club, The Milw. Club (bd. dirs.), Montclair Golf Club, Vintage Club (Indian Wells, Calif.). Roman Catholic. Office: Sybron Corp 411 E Wisconsin Ave Milwaukee WI 53202-4409 *Positive results are seldom achieved from negative thoughts.*

YOO, JAMES H., radiation oncologist, nuclear medicine physician; b. South Korea, Dec. 13, 1941; came to U.S., 1968; s. Ki S. and Ki O. (Lee) Y.; m. Esther Cha Yoo, Sept. 3, 1968; children: James, Thomas, Andrew. BSE, Seoul (Korea) Nat. U., 1964, MSE, 1968; PhD, Tex. Tech. U., 1971; MD, U. Tex., San Antonio, 1982. Diplomate Am. Bd. Radiology, Am. Bd. Nuclear Medicine. Pediatric intern U. Tex. Health Sci. Ctr., San Antonio, 1982-83, resident in nuclear medicine, 1983-87; resident in radiation oncology Temple U./Tufts Med. Sch.-New Eng. Med. Ctr., Boston, 1987-90; asst. staff physician City of Hosp Med. Ctr., Duarte, Calif., 1990-91; staff radiation oncologist dept. vets. affairs East Orange (N.J.) Med. Ctr., 1991—; rsch. staff physician ECOG, 1992—, mem. Radiation Oncology sect., 1995—. Chmn., pres. Korean Ednl. Com., N.Y. and N.J., 1995—; chmn. bd. dirs. Hankook Coll., 1995—; elder Korean Bahn Sok Ch., Livingston, N.J., 1993—. Maj. M.C. USAR, 1983-95. Fellow N.J. Acad. Medicine; mm. ASTRO. Presbyterian. Avocations: hiking, jogging, aerobics. Office: East Orange VA Med Ctr 385 Tremont Ave East Orange NJ 07018-1095

YOOD, HAROLD STANLEY, internist; b. Plainfield, N.J., Feb. 23, 1920; s. Raphael and Netta (Newcorn) Y.; m. Helen H. Hull, Nov. 8, 1941; children: Pamela, Patricia Yood Herskovitz, Paula Yood Peterson, Andrew H. BA, U. Va., 1940, MD, 1943. Intern Syracuse (N.Y.) U. Med. Ctr., 1943; pvt. practice Plainfield, N.J., 1946-91; med. dir. Cen. Jersey Individual Physicians Assn.; staff dept. medicine Muhlenberg Hosp., 1946—, pres. staff, 1980-86, cons., 1991-95, emeritus, 1995—. Contbr. articles to Jour. Med. Soc. N.J., Communication for Ciba, others. Bd. govs. Muhlenberg Regional Med. Ctr., 1980-86, exec. com.; trustee, v.p. United Way Plainfield/Fanwood, 1975-81; bd. dirs. United Way Union County, 1978-81; pres. Jewish Community Ctr., Plainfield, 1970-71; v.p. Jewish Fedn. Cen. N.J., 1971-73, Cen. N.J. Jewish Home for Aged, 1973-80. Capt. M.C. AUS, 1944-45, ETO. Decorated Purple Heart, Combat Med. badge, Combat Glider badge. Fellow Am. Coll. Gastroenterology (sr.), Am. Coll. Angiology (ret.), Internat. Coll. Angiology (ret.); mem. AMA, Med. Soc. N.J. (governing coun. hosp. med. staff sect. 1983-92, chmn. 1988-90; trustee 1989-90), Union County Med. Soc., Plainfield Area Med. Assn., Am. Coll. Physician Execs., Lions (life). Office: CJIPA 1133 Park Ave Plainfield NJ 07060-3006 *Enjoyment in my profession, pleasure in relationship with patients, a belief in the necessity for civic and community volunteer involvement, a commitment to support causes that aid the unfortunate and do no harm to individuals.*

YOON, JI-WON, virology, immunology and diabetes educator, research administrator; b. Kang-Jin, Chonnam, Korea, Mar. 28, 1939; came to U.S., 1965; s. Baek-In and Duck-Soon (Lee) Y.; m. Chungja Rhim, Aug. 17, 1968; children: John W., James W. MS, U. Conn., 1971, PhD, 1973. Sr. investigator NIH, Bethesda, Md., 1978-84; prof., chief div. virology U. Calgary, Alta., Can., 1984—, prof., assoc. dir. diabetes rsch. ctr., 1985-90, prof., dir. diabetes rsch. ctr., 1990—; mem. edit. bd. Annual Review Advances Present Rsch. Animal Diabetes, 1990—, Diabetes Rsch. Clin. Practice, 1989—; scientific coord. 10th Internat. Workshop on Immunology Diabetes, Jerusalem, 1989-90; sr. investigator NIH, 1976-84. Contbg. author: Current Topics in Microbiology and Immunology, 1990, Autoimmunity and Pathogenesis of Diabetes, 1990; contbr. articles to New England Jour. Medicine, Jour. Virology, Sci., Nature, The Lancet, Jour. Diabetes. Rsch. fellow Sloan Kettering Cancer Inst., 1973-74, Staff fellow, Sr. Staff fellow NIH, 1974-76, 76-78; recipient NIH Dir. award, 1984, Heritage Med. Scientist award, Alberta Heritage Found. Med. Rsch., 1984, Lectrship. award, 3d Asian Symposium Childhood Diabetes, 1989, 8th Annual Meeting Childhood Diabetes, Osaka, Japan, 1990, 9th Korean/Can. Heritage award, 1989. Mem. Am. Soc. Immunologists, Am. Diabetes Assn., Am. Soc. Microbiology, N.Y. Acad. Sci., Soc. Virology, Internat. Diabetes Fedn. Baptist. Achievements include first isolation of diabetogenic virus from patients with recent onset of IDDM; first demonstration of prevention of virus-induced diabetes by vaccination with nondiabetogenic virus in animals; discovery that autoimmune IDDM can be prevented by depletion of macrophages in autoimmune diabetic NOD mice, certain viral glycoproteins (rubella virus E2 glycoprotein) can induce organ-specific autoimmune disease; research on molecular identification of diabetogenic viral gene in animal models, discovery of a nontoxic organic compound with no side effects that completely prevents type I diabetes in NOD mice, discovery that bacterial superantigens such as staphylococcal enterotoxins (SEC1, SEC3) can prevent autoimmune type I diabetes by activation of CD4+ suppressor T cells in NOD mice; research on the role of cloned T-Cells in the pathogenesis of autoimmune Type I Diabetes at cellular and molecular level. Home: 206 Edgeview Dr NW, Calgary, AB Canada T3A 4W9 Office: Julia McFarlane Diabetes Rsch Ctr, 3330 Hospital Dr NW, Calgary, AB Canada T2N 4N1

YOON, SEWANG, engineering executive; b. Chinhae, Korea, July 28, 1949; came to U.S., 1975; s. Jah Choon and In Soon (Chung) Y.; m. Youngok Byun, Mar. 12, 1975; children: Janice J., Stella J. BS, Seoul (Korea) Nat. U., 1971; MS, UCLA, 1977, PhD, 1980. Mgr. R&D M/A-COM, PHI, Torrance, Calif., 1980-89; v.p. tech. Amonix Inc., Torrance, 1989—. Recipient Meritorious Paper award GOMAC-86, 1986, R & D 100 award for silicon photovoltaic cell, R&D Mag., 1994. Mem. IEEE (assoc.), Sigma Xi. Achievements include design, manufacture and commercialization of a point focus type concentrator solar cell with a record efficiency of 25.5% at 250X concentration, using a point contact cell concept. Office: Amonix Inc 3425 Fujita St Torrance CA 90505-4018

YORBURG, BETTY (MRS. LEON YORBURG), sociology educator; b. Chgo., Aug. 27, 1926; d. Max and Hannah (Bernstein) Gitelman; m. Leon Yorburg, June 23, 1946; children: Harriet, Robert. PhB, U. Chgo., 1945, MA, 1948; PhD, New Sch. Social Rsch., 1968. Instr., Coll. New Rochelle, 1966-67; lectr. City Coll. and Grad. Center, City U. N.Y., 1967-69, asst. prof., 1969-73, assoc. prof. sociology dept., 1973-77, prof., 1978—; rsch. asst. Prof. Clifford Shaw, Chgo. Area Project, 1946-47. Author: Utopia and Reality, 1969, The Changing Family, 1973, Sexual Identity: Sex Roles and Social Change, 1974, The New Women, 1976, Introduction to Sociology, 1982, Families and Societies, 1983, Family Relationships, 1993, Sociological Reality, 1995. Mem. AAAS, Am. Sociol. Assn., Ea. Sociol. Assn., Am. Coun. Family Rels., N.Y. Acad. Scis. Home: 20 Earley St Bronx NY 10464-1512 Office: CCNY Sociology Dept 138th Convent Ave New York NY 10031-9127

YORDAN, CARLOS MANUEL, foreign service officer; b. P.R., Nov. 27, 1925; s. Nicholas and Octavia (Baez) Y.; m. Hilda Bordas, Aug. 16, 1946; 1 son, Carlos Manuel. Student, Gregg Bus. Coll., 1940-42; M.A. in Polit. Sci., U. Chgo. (corr.), 1960, M.A. in Am. History, 1962. Joined U.S. Fgn. Service, 1947; chief clk. engring. dept. Unifruitco, Dominican Republic, 1944-47; adminstrv. officer State Dept., Santo Domingo, Dominican Republic, 1947-50, Quito, Ecuador, 1950-52; 2d sec., vice consul State Dept., Lima, Peru, 1953-55, Rangoon, Burma, 1956-58, London, 1958-60, Budapest, Hungary, 1960-61, Washington, 1961-65; 1st sec., consul State Dept., Warsaw, Poland, 1965-67, West Berlin, 1967-70, Dublin, 1970-73, Brasilia, Brazil, 1973-77; counselor embassy Santo Domingo, Dominican Republic, 1977-81. Mem. Fgn. Svc. Assn., Royal Dublin Soc., Am. Soc. Natural History, Country Tennis Ctr. Sarasota (Fla.), Tournament Players Club Prestancia. Office: 3697 Gleneagle Dr Sarasota FL 34238-2812

YORINKS, ARTHUR, children's author, writer, director; b. Roslyn, N.Y., Aug. 21, 1953; s. Alexander and Shirley (Kron) Y.; m. Adrienne Berg, Oct. 23, 1983. Writer, tchr. performer Am. Mime Theatre, 1969-79; instr. theatre arts Cornell U., Ithaca, N.Y., 1972-79; assoc. dir. New Works Project, N.Y.C., 1977—; founder, artistic dir. Moving Theatre, N.Y.C., 1979; founder, assoc. artistic dir. The Night Kitchen, N.Y.C., 1990—. Author: (children's books) Sid and Sol, 1977, The Magic Meatballs, 1979, Louis the Fish, 1980 (Sch. Libr. Jour. Best Book Yr. Citation 1980), It Happened in Pinsk, 1983 (Booklist Children's Editor's Choice 1984, Biennale of Illustration plaque 1985), Hey, Al, 1986 (ALA Notable Book citation 1986, Caldecott medal 1987, Ky. Bluegrass award 1988), Bravo Minski, 1988 (Sch. Libr. Jour. Best Book Yr. Citation 1988), Company's Coming, 1988 (ALA Notable Book citation 1986), Oh, Brother, 1989 (Sch. Libr. Jour. Best Book Yr. Citation 1989), Ugh, 1990 (Sch. Libr. Jour. Best Book Yr. citation 1990), Christmas in July, 1991, Whitefish Will Rides Again, 1994, The Miami Giant, 1995, Frank & Joey Go To Work, 1996, Frank & Joey Eat Lunch, 1996, (plays) Six, 1973, The Horse, 1978, Crackers, 1979, The King, 1980, Kissers, 1980, Piece for a Small Cafe, 1981, Piece for a Larger Cafe, 1982, So, Sue Me, 1994, It's Alive!, 1995; (opera librettos) Leipziger Kerzenspiel, 1984, The Juniper Tree, 1985 (music by Philip Glass), The Fall of the House of Usher, 1988 (music by Philip Glass), (screenplay) Sid and Sol, 1982, It's a Miracle, 1991, Usher, 1991, Making Scents, 1993, Frank & Joey Eat Lunch, 1996, Frank and Joey Go to Work, 1996. Office: The Night Kitchen 10 E 53rd St New York NY 10022-5244*

YORK, DONALD GILBERT, astronomy educator, researcher; b. Shelbyville, Ill., Oct. 28, 1944; s. Maurice Alfred and Virginia Maxine (Huntwork) Y.; m. Anna Sue Hinds, June 12, 1966; children: Sean, Maurice, Chandler, Jeremy. BS, MIT, 1966; PhD, U. Chgo., 1971. Rsch. asst. Princeton (N.J.) U., 1970-71, rsch. assoc., 1971-73, rsch. astronomer, 1973-78, sr. rsch. astronomer, 1978-82; assoc. prof. U. Chgo., 1982-86, prof., 1986-92, Horace B. Horton prof. astronomy and astrophysics, 1992—; dir. Apache Point Obs., Astrophys. Rsch. Consortium, Seattle, 1984—, Sloan Digital Sky Survey, 1990—. Contbr. articles to profl. jours. Recipient Pub. Svc. award NASA, 1976; grantee NASA, 1978—, NSF, 1984—. Mem. Internat. Astron. Union, Am. Astron. Soc. (publs. bd. 1980-83). Republican. Avocations: squash, white water canoeing, science history, religion history. Office: 5640 S Ellis Ave Chicago IL 60637-1433

YORK, E. TRAVIS, academic administrator, former university chancellor, consultant; b. Mentone, Ala., July 4, 1922; s. E. Travis and Leila (Hixon) Y.; m. Vermelle Cardwell, Dec. 26, 1946; children: Lisa Carol, Travis Loften. B.S., Auburn U., 1942, M.S., 1946, D.Sc. (hon.), 1982; Ph.D. (research fellow 1946-49), Cornell U., 1949; postgrad., George Washington U., 1957-59; D.Sc. (hon.), U. Fla., 1984, Ohio State U., 1996. Assoc. prof. agr. N.C. State Coll., 1949-52, prof., 1952-56, head dept. agronomy, 1953-56; Eastern dir. Am. Potash Inst., 1956-59; dir. Ala. Extension Service, Auburn U., 1959-61; adminstr. Fed. Extension Service, U.S. Dept. Agr., 1961-63; provost for agr. U. Fla., 1963-67, v.p. agrl. affairs, 1967-73, exec. v.p., interim pres., 1973-74, Disting. Svc. prof., 1988—; chancellor State U. System of Fla., 1975-80, chancellor emeritus, 1980—. Mem. Am. Food for Peace Coun., 1961-62, Freedom from Hunger Com., 1961-62, Pres.'s. Panel Vocat. Edn., 1961-62; chmn. coun. grad. edn. in agrl. scis. So. Regional Edn. Bd., 1964-66, mem., 1975-80, exec. com., 1978-80, mem. pres. coun., Pres.' Sci. Adv. Coun. Task Force on World Food Problems, 1966-67; mem. senate, exec. com. Nat. Assn. State Univs. and Land Grant Colls., 1967-70; mem. Edn. Commn. of States, 1975-79, steering com., 1977-79, treas., exec. com., 1978-79; bd. dirs. Nat. 4-H Svc. Com., 1963-75, AV Med. Corp., Sante Fe, 1987-96; trustee, bd. dirs Hlth Improvement Inc mem., 1996—, mem. exec. com. Nat. 4-H Found., 1968-73; mem.-at-large nat. coun. Boy Scouts Am., 1962-75; dir., pres. Alpha Gamma Rho Edn. Found., 1965-72; bd. dirs. Nat. Ctr. for Voluntary Action, 1970-74; mem. Bd. for Internat. Food and Agrl. Devel., 1980-86, chmn., 1983-86; trustee Escuela Agricola Panamericana, 1980-88, Found. for Agronomic Rsch., 1980-92; tech. adv. com., cons. Group for Internat. Agrl. Rsch., 1983-89; trustee Agronomic Sci. Found., 1989-92. Officer AUS, 1943-45. Recipient B.B. Comer award excellence natural sci. Auburn U., 1942; disting. svc. award Fla. Vet. Med. Assn., 1966; Nat. 4-H Alunbi award, 1967; George Washington honor medal award Freedoms Found., 1967; nat. ptnr. in 4-H award, 1970; disting. faculty award U. Fla., Fla. Blue Key, 1972; E.T. York, Jr. disting. svc. award U. Fla., 1973; honors medal U. Fla. Acad. Scis., 1974; E.T. York svc. award Fla. Bd. Regents, 1983, disting. svc. award Am. Farm Bur., 1991, Rotary Internat., 1994; named to Fla. Agrl. Hall of Fame, 1990, Ala. Agrl. Hall of Honor, 1995, Internat. Adult and Continuing Edn. Hall of Fame, 1996; designated as Great Floridian, Fla. History Assn., 1997. Fellow AAAS, Am. Soc. Agronomy, Soil Sci. Soc. Am., AM. Crop Sci. Soc.; mem. Am. Soc. Hort. Sci. (hon.), Assn. So. Agrl. Scientists (pres. 1968), Blue Key, Rotary (dist. gov. 1981-82, svc. above self award 1993), Sigma Xi, Phi Kappa Phi, Alpha Zeta, Gamma Sigma Delta (internat. disting. svc. award 1973), Omicron Delta Kappa, Phi Delta Kappa, Epsilon Sigma Phi, Alpha Gamma Rho (named to Hall of Fame 1982). Methodist. Address: 4020 SW 78th St Gainesville FL 32608-3608

YORK, ELIZABETH JANE, innkeeper; b. Camden, N.J., July 27, 1934; d. Charles Evans and Christine (Taggart) Yorke; m. Anthony Neil Gaeta, April 2, 1960 (div. Jan. 1986); children: Gregory, Anthony, Anne. BA, Wheaton (Ill.) Coll., Ill., 1957; postgrad., U. N.C., 1957-58. Owner Designing Woman, Minot, Mass., 1976-81; broker Vin Doyle Real Estate, Scituate, Mass., 1978-81; owner, innkeeper The Four Chimneys, Nantucket Island, Mass., 1981-90; gen. mgr. The Roberts House Group, Nantucket Island, Mass., 1992-95; writer, 1995—; cons. in field. Group dir. Scituate Newcomers Club, 1976-81; vol. Hosp. Thrift Shop, Nantucket, 1982—, Second Shop, Nantucket, 1982—; mem. Nantucket Conservation Found. Mem. Nantucket C. of C., Cape Cod C. of C., Nantucket Hist. Soc., Nantucket Lodging Assn., Atheneum, Hospice. Republican. Episcopalian. Club: Cliffside Beach. Avocations: sailing, antiques, books, travel. Home: 2275 Nauset Rd North Eastham MA 02651 Home and Office: PO Box #1450 North Eastham MA 02651

YORK, GARY ALAN, lawyer; b. Glendale, Calif., Aug. 29, 1943; m. Lois York, 1987; 1 child, Jonathan Alan. BA, Pomona Coll., 1965; LLB, Stanford U., 1968. Bar: Calif. 1969. Ptnr. Dewey Ballantine, L.A., 1985-95, Buchalter, Nemer, Fields & Younger, L.A., 1995—; instr. law sch. UCLA, 1968-69. Bd. editors Stanford Law review, 1966-68. Mem. ABA (chmn. real estate fin. com., real property probate and trust sect. 1987-89, chmn. usury com. 1992-93), L.A. County Bar Assn. (chmn. real estate fin. sect. 1993-96), State Bar of Calif., Am. Coll. Real Estate Lawyers. Office: Buchalter Nemer Fields & Younger 601 S Figueroa St Los Angeles CA 90017-5704

YORK, HERBERT FRANK, physics educator, government official; b. Rochester, N.Y., Nov. 24, 1921; s. Herbert Frank and Nellie Elizabeth (Lang) Y.; m. Sybil Dunford, Sept. 28, 1947; children: David Winters, Rachel, Cynthia. AB, U. Rochester, 1942, MS, 1943; PhD, U. Calif., Berkeley, 1949; DSc (hon.), Case Inst. Tech., 1960; LL.D., U. San Diego, 1964, Claremont Grad. Sch., 1974. Physicist Radiation Lab., U. Calif., Berkeley, 1943-58, assoc. dir., 1954-58; asst. prof. physics dept. U. Calif., Berkeley, 1951-54, assoc. prof., 1954-59, prof., 1959-61; dir. Lawrence Radiation Lab., Livermore, 1952-58; chief scientist Advanced Rsch. Project Agy., U.S. Dept. Def., 1958; dir. advanced rsch. projects divsn. Inst. for Def. Analyses, 1958; dir. def. rsch. and engring. Office Sec. Def., 1958-61; chancellor U. Calif.-San Diego, 1961-64, 70-72, prof. physics, 1964—, chmn. dept. physics, 1968-69, dean grad. studies, 1969-70, dir. program on sci., tech. and pub. affairs, 1972-88; dir. Inst. Global Conflict and Cooperation, 1983-88, dir. emeritus, 1988—; amb. Comprehensive Test Ban Negotiations, 1979-81; trustee Aerospace Corp., Inglewood, Calif., 1961-87; mem. Pres.'s Sci. Adv. Com., 1957-58, 64-68, vice chmn., 1965-67; trustee Inst. def. Analysis, 1963-96; gen. adv. com. ACDA, 1962-69; mem. Def. Sci. Bd. , 1977-81; spl. rep. of sec. def. at space arms control talks, 1978-79; mem. coun. nat. labs. Pres. U. Calif., 1991—; mem. task force future nat. labs. Sec. Emergy, 1994-95; cons. Stockholm Internat. Peach Rsch. Inst.; rschr. in application atomic energy to nat. def. problems of arms control and disarmament, elem. particles. Author: Race to Oblivion, 1970, Arms Control, 1973, The Advisors, 1976, Making Weapons, Talking Peace, 1987, Does Strategic Defense Breed Offense?, 1987, (with S. Lakoff) A Shield in the Sky, 1989, Arms and the Physicist, 1994; also numerous articles on arms or disarmament; bd. dirs. Bull. Atomic Scientists. Trustee Bishop's Sch., La Jolla, Calif., 1963-65. Recipient E.O. Lawrence award AEC, 1962; Guggenheim fellow, 1972. Fellow Am. Phys. Soc. (forum on physics and soc. award 1976, Leo Szilard award 1994), AAAS; mem. Internat. Acad. Astronautics, Fedn. Am. Scientists (chmn. 1970-71, exec. com. 1969-76, 95—, pub. svc. award 1992), Pugwash Movement 1969—, Phi Beta Kappa, Sigma

Xi. Home: 6110 Camino De La Costa La Jolla CA 92037-6520 Office: U Calif-San Diego Mail Code 0518 La Jolla CA 92093

YORK, JAMES MARTIN, judge; b. Abilene, Tex., Feb. 22, 1939; s. James Orville and Hazel Mae (Martin) Y.; m. Sandra L. Zunker, June 5, 1959 (div. 1967); children: Debra Lynn, James Martin Jr.; m. Nora Darlene Buechman, Nov. 3, 1972; 1 child, Victoria Lee. Student, Baylor U., 1957-60, LLB, 1962. Bar: Tex. 1962. Atty. Matthew & Matthews, Dallas, 1962-63, Ross, Banks, May & Cron, Houston, 1963-64, Law Offices of Fred W. Moore, Houston, 1964-65; pvt. practice Houston, 1965-94. Sect. editor Baylor Law Rev., 1962. State Rep. primary candidate Rep. Party, Houston, 1970; del.-at-large Rep. State Conv., Houston, 1971; Rep. primary cand. for judge 310th Dist. Ct., 1994; coach Westbury Nat. Little League, Houston, 1967, Voss West Little League, Houston, 1969, 70; apptd. assoc. judge 246th Dist. Ct., 1995. Named Boss of Yr. Houston Assn. Legal Secs., 1973. Mem. Rotary Club of Houston, Inwood Forest Golf Club, Houston Bar Assn., State Bar of Tex., Baylor Alumni Assn., Baylor Lettermen's Assn. Baptist. Avocations: golf, swimming, reading. Office: 246th Dist Ct 7th Fl Family Law Ctr 1115 Congress St Houston TX 77002-1927

YORK, JAMES ORISON, real estate executive; b. Brush, Colo., June 27, 1927; s. M. Orison and Marie L. (Kibble) Y.; m. Janice Marie Sjoberg, Aug. 1, 1959; children: Douglas James, Robert Orison. Student, U. Calif. at Berkeley, 1945-46; B.A. cum laude, U. Wash., 1949. Teaching fellow U. Wash., Seattle, 1950-52; econ. research analyst Larry Smith & Co. (real estate), Seattle and N.Y.C., 1953-60; partner Larry Smith & Co. (real estate), Seattle, 1960-66; pres. Larry Smith & Co. (real estate), San Francisco, 1966-71; pres., chief exec. officer R.H. Macy Properties, N.Y.C., also sr. v.p. planning and devel., dir. R.H. Macy & Co., Inc., 1971-88; pres. James York Assocs. (real estate), 1988—; dir. HRE Properties, Inc.; trustee Corp. Property Investors; chmn., N.Y.C. retail div. Am. Cancer Soc. Contbg. author: Shopping Towns-USA, 1960. Trustee ICSC Ednl. and Rsch. Found. With USNR, 1945-47. Recipient Disting. Alumnus award U. Wash., 1989. Mem. Am. Soc. Real Estate Counselors, Urban Land Inst., Internat. Real Estate Fedn., Internat. Council Shopping Centers, Phi Beta Kappa, Lambda Alpha. Episcopalian. Clubs: Olympic (San Francisco); American Yacht (Rye, N.Y.); Corinthian Yacht (Seattle); Union League (N.Y.C.); Knights of Malta, Order St. John, Washington Athletic (Seattle), Royal Victoria (B.C.) Yacht. Home and Office: 4 Riverstone Laguna Niguel CA 92677-5309

YORK, JAMES WESLEY, JR., theoretical physicist, educator; b. Raleigh, N.C., July 3, 1939; s. James Wesley and Mary Smedes (Poyner) Y.; m. Betty Louise Mattern, Aug. 19, 1961; children: Virginia York Setzer, Guilford Mattern. B.S. with high honors in Physics, N.C. State U., Raleigh, 1962, Ph.D. in Physics, 1966. Asst. prof. N.C. State U., Raleigh, 1965-68; rsch. assoc. Princeton (N.J.) U., 1968-69, lectr., 1969-70, asst. prof., 1970-73; assoc. prof. U. N.C., Chapel Hill, 1973-77, prof. dept. physics, 1977-89, Agnew H. Bahnson, Jr. disting. prof. physics, 1989—, dir. Inst. Field Physics, 1984-90; vis. asst. prof. U. Md., College Park, 1972; prof. associe U. Paris, 1976; vis. scientist Harvard U., Cambridge, 1977; vis. prof. U. Tex., Austin, 1979, 87; spkr. Internat. Symposium on Methods of Differential Geometry in Physics and Mechanics, Warsaw, Poland, 1976; Alfred Schild Meml. lectr. U. Tex., 1979; del. Seventh Internat. Congress on Math. Physics, Boulder, Colo., 1983, Tex. Symposium on Relativistic Astrophysics, Jerusalem, 1984, Marcel Grossman Meeting, Rome, 1985, 97, NATO Advanced Study Inst., Les Houches, France, 1982, Huelva, Spain, 1992, Paris, 1992, Banff, Can., 1992, other internat. and nat. meetings; co-organizer sci. meetings including Neutron stars and pulsars, Princeton, 1969, Space-time dynamics, Aspen Ctr. for Theoretical Physics, 1981, Classical Problems in Gravitation, 1990, Cosmic Censorship, 1992; mem. com. of visitors physics divsn. NSF, 1991; plenary lectr. Fifth Can. Conf. on Gen. Relativity and Astrophysics, Waterloo, 1993, Directions in Gen. Relativity, College Park, Md., 1993, Pacific Coast Gravity Mtg., Salt Lake City, 1996, hon. physics chmn. Cornelius Lanczos Internat. Centenary, Raleigh, N.C., 1993. Mem. editorial bd. Jour. Math. Physics, 1989-92; contbr. chpts. to books, articles to sci. jours. Decorated Companion of St. Patrick, 1960; recipient 3d prize Gravity Rsch. Found. Essay award, 1975; Ford Found. fellow, 1962-65; Battelle Found. grantee, 1967, NSF postdoctoral fellow, 1969-70, Nat. Rsch. Com. France grantee, 1976, NSF grantee, 1974—, travel grantee, 1971, 76, 83, 84; U.S.A.-Israel Binat. Sci. Found. grantee, 1987-90, 90-93; recipient Disting. Alumnus award, 1997. Fellow Am. Phys. Soc.; mem. AAAS, Internat. Soc. Gen. Relativity and Gravitation, Rotary, Sigma Xi, Phi Kappa Phi, Tau Beta Pi, Sigma Pi Sigma, Pi Mu Epsilon, Phi Eta Sigma. Episcopalian. Avocations: literature, music, sports. Office: U NC Dept Physics and Astronomy Chapel Hill NC 27599-3255

YORK, JOSEPH RUSSELL, media production technician; b. Royal Center, Ind., Oct. 19, 1940; s. William Russell and Naomi (Wellman) Y.; Student Olivet Nazarene Coll., until 1965; BS, Ball State U. student, 1980, MS, 1982; m. Teresa Luanne Ping, June 15, 1963; children: Sherra JoAnn, Kerra SuzAnn, Darren Joseph, Terra LeAnn. Photojournalist, Danville (Ill.) Comml. News, 1961-62, Kankakee (Ill.) Daily Jour., 1963; motion picture dir., editor Calvin Prodns., Inc., Kansas City, Mo., 1965-71, Communico, Inc., St. Louis, 1971-73; editing supr. Premier Film & Rec. Co., Inc., St. Louis, 1973—; producer, dir. TV programming Kans. Fish and Game Commn., 1983—; owner, operator Trinity Prodns., St. Louis, 1963-83; pres. York's Foto Express, Inc., 1986—; asst. libr., prof. humanities and lit. Pratt C.C., 1988—; dir. med. svcs. audio support systems and spl. events Olivet Nazarene U., Bourbonnais. Ill., 1990—; owner, pres. EQ Audio, 1996—, J. York-Wooden Games & Recreation, 1996—, COuntry Custom Cabinets and Classic Coach Investment Autos. Pastor Ch. of the Nazarene, Selma, Ind. Recipient 1st Pl. award U.S. Indsl. Film Festival, 1972; 2d Pl. award Festival of Ams.-V.I., 1977. Mem. Profl. Photographers Am., Photomarketing Assn. Internat.; Golden Key Nat. Honor Soc. Home: 140 S Country Ct Bourbonnais IL 60914-2113 Office: 140 S Country Ct Bourbonnais IL 60914-2113

YORK, MICHAEL (MICHAEL YORK-JOHNSON), actor; b. Fulmer, Eng., Mar. 27, 1942; s. Joseph Gwynne and Florence Edith (Chown) Johnson; m. Patricia McCallum, Mar. 27, 1968. BA with honors in English, Univ. Coll., Oxford U. (Eng.), 1964; DFA (hon.), U. So. Calif. Created Chevalier de l'ordre Nat. des Arts Et Letter (France) 1995, Created Officer of the Order of the British Empire (OBE),1996. Profl. debut with Dundee Repertory Theatre, Scotland, 1964; mem. Nat. Theatre Co., London, 1965-66; TV film or miniseries appearances include: Much Ado About Nothing, The Forsyte Saga, Rebel in the Grave, True Patriot, Jesus of Nazareth, 1977, A Man Called Intrepid, 1979, The Phantom of the Opera, 1983, The Master of Ballantrae, 1984, Space, 1985, The Far Country, 1985, Are You My Mother, 1986, Ponce de Leon, 1987, Till We Meet Again, 1989, The Road to Avonlea, 1991, Gardens of the World, 1993; The Four Minute Mile, The Lady and the Highway Man, 1988, The Heat of the Day, 1988, The Hunt for Stolen War Treasure, 1989, The Night of the Fox, 1990, The Magic Paintbrush, 1993, David Copperfield's Christmas, 1994, Teklab, 1994, Fall From Grace, 1994, Not of This Earth, 1995, Duel of Hearts, September, 1995, A Young Connecticut Yankee in King Arthur's Court, 1995, Danielle Steele's The Ring, 1996, True Women, 1997, (TV series) Knots Landing, 1987, SeaQuest, 1995, The Naked Truth, 1995, Babylon 5, 1995, The Ring, 1996, (un coup De Baguette Magique) True Women, 1997, Sliders, 1997; stage appearances include: Any Just Cause, 1967, Hamlet, 1970, Broadway prodns. of Outcry, 1973, Ring Round the Moon, 1975, Bent, 1980, Cyrano de Bergerac, 1981, Whisper in the Mind, 1990, The Crucible, 1991, Someone Who'll Watch Over Me, 1993, Nora, 1993, Ira Gershwin at 100, 1996; appeared in motion pictures including: The Taming of the Shrew, 1966, Accident, 1966, Red and Blue, 1967, Smashing Time, 1967, Romeo and Juliet, 1967, The Strange Affair, 1967, The Guru, 1968, Alfred the Great, 1968, Justine, 1969, Something for Everyone, 1969, Zeppelin, 1970, La Poudre D'Escampette, 1971, Cabaret, 1971, England Made Me, 1971, Lost Horizon, 1972, The Three Musketeers, 1973, Murder on the Orient Express, 1974, Great Expectations, 1974, Conduct Unbecoming, 1974, The Four Musketeers, 1975, Logan's Run, 1976, Seven Nights in Japan, The Last Remake of Beau Geste, 1977, The Island of Dr. Moreau, 1977, Fedora, 1977, The Riddle of the Sands, 1978, Final Assignment, 1980, The White Lions, Success is the Best Revenge, 1984, Dawn, 1985, Vengeance, 1986, The Secret of the Sahara, 1987, Imbalances, 1987, Lethal Obsession, 1987, Midnight Cop, 1988, The Return of the Musketeers, 1989, The Long Shadow, 1991, Eline Vere, 1991, Wide Sargasso Sea, 1991, Rochade, 1991, Discretion Assured, Shadow of a Kiss, 1993, Gospa, 1994, Good Vibrations, 1997, Goodbye America, 1997, Austin Powers, Dark Planet, 1997, (film) The Treat, 1997; radio performances The Dark Tower, 1977, (recipient Peabody award), A Matter of Honor, 1986, Babbitt, 1987, The Crucible, 1988, Are You Now, UTZ, 1989, McTeague, 1992, Make and Break, 1993; recs. include: Mere Christianity, 1982, Anna Karenina, 1985, Don Quixote, 1986, The King Must Die, 1988, British Rock: The First Wave, UTZ, 1989, The Modigliani Scandal, 1989, The Mummy, 1989, Candide, 1989, The Vampire Lestat, 1989, The Berlin Stories, 1990, The Remains of the Day, 1990, City of Joy, 1991, Beyond Love, 1991, Memories, Dreams, Reflections, 1991, A Poet's Bible, 1992, Einstein's Dreams, 1993, Accidentally on Purpose, 1993, The English Patient, 1993, Fortune's Favorite, 1993, The Three Musketeers, 1993, Paradise Lost, 1993, The Book of Psalms, 1994, The Book of Virtues, 1994, The Magic Paw-Paw, 1994; contbr. (books) The Courage of Conviction, 1985, Voices of Survival, 1987; author: Accidentally on Purpose, 1992; (recording) The Rubaiyat of Omar Khayyam, 1995, Aesop's Fables, 1995, The Poetry of Edgar Allen Poe, 1995, The Hunting of the Snark, Caesar's Women, 1996, Treasure Island, 1996, (Grammy Nomination) The Wind in the Willows, 1996, Rose, 1996, Daily Word, 1997. Chmn. Calif. Youth Theatre. Avocations: travel, music, art. Office: GML 3500 W Olive Ste 1400 Burbank CA 91505

YORK, MICHAEL CHAREST, librarian; b. Newton, Mass., Jan. 2, 1947; s. Richard Francis and Frances Winship (Thibaut) Y.; m. Carol Roberts, June 26, 1982; 1 child, Michael Bradley. BA, U. N.H., 1971; MS, La. State U., 1972; MBA, Plymouth State Coll., 1990. Ref. libr. Ithaca (N.Y.) Coll., 1973-77; asst. dir. libr. Castleton (Vt.) State Coll., 1977-81; libr. dir. Merrimack Valley Coll., Manchester, N.H., 1981-85, U. N.H., Manchester, 1985-91; univ. libr. U. N.H., Durham, 1991-95; libr. dir. Colby-Sawyer Coll., New London, N.H., 1996—. Mem. ALA, New Eng. Libr. Assn. (pres. 1988-89), N.H. Libr. Assn., N.H. State Libr. Adv. Coun. Avocations: sailing, skiing, woodworking. Home: 15 Catamount Rd Goffstown NH 03045-2700 Office: Colby-Sawyer Coll 100 Main St New London NH 03257-4612

YORK, RICHARD TRAVIS, art dealer; b. Nashville, Oct. 22, 1950; s. James Samuel and Jeane (Townes) Y. BA, Vanderbilt U., 1972. Dir. Am. art Hammer Galleries, N.Y.C., 1974-76; in charge Am. dept. M. Knoedler & Co., N.Y.C., 1976-77; assoc. Hirschl & Adler Galleries, N.Y.C., 1977-81; dir., owner Richard York Gallery, N.Y.C., 1981—. Author: (exhbn. catalogs) American Folk Art, 1977, The Eye of Steiglitz, 1978 (Arlis award), Buildings Architecture in American Modernism, 1980, Ellen Day Hale, 1981 (Arlis award), The Natural Image: Plant Forms in American Modernism, 1982, An American Gallery, 1986, vols. I & II, 1987, III & IV, 1988, V, 1989, VI, 1990, VII, 1992, Charles G. Shaw: Abstractions of the Thirties, 1987, Will Henry Stevens: A Modernist's Response to Nature, 1987, Joseph Stella: The Tropics, 1988, Joseph Goldyne: Twenty Years of Work, 1992, American Paintings from the Collection of James H. Ricau, 1993, Modernism at the Salons of America, 1922-1936, 1995, California: One-hundred Forty Years of Art Produced in the State, 1996. Mem. art adv. com. Colby Coll., 1990-94; mem. art adv. panel IRS, 1991—. Mem. Art Dealers Assn. Am. (bd. dirs. 1992-95), William Cullen Bryant Fellows, Met. Mus. of Art, N.Y.C. Office: Richard York Gallery 21 E 65th St New York NY 10021-6524

YORK, SHIRLEY MARIE, artist; b. Aurora, Ill., Aug. 25, 1923; d. John Frederick and Beulah Mary (Noack) Vockrodt; m. Herman Maxwell Grimwood, 1947 (div. Feb. 1959); children: Sherry Lynn, Jon Frederick; m. John Garth York, June 12, 1959. Student, Chgo. Art Inst., 1943, U. Chgo., 1944; BAF, U. N.Mex., 1945; student, Inst. of Fine Arts, Mexico City, 1960. Mosaic glass artist; worked with archtl. firms in Tex. and Okla. Artist: Italian glass mosaics, 1960-78; commd. artist in Tex., Okla., Ill., N.Y., Costa Rica, Mexico; represented in pvt. collections in U.S., Mexico and Europe. Recipient purchase award N.Mex. Arts Divsn., Office of Cultural Affairs, Santa Fe, 1995. Mem. AAUW. Avocations: writing, poetry.

YORK, THEODORE ROBERT, consulting company executive; b. Mitchel Field, N.Y., May 4, 1926; s. Theodore and Helen (Zierak) Y.; m. Clara Kiefer, Jan. 3, 1952; children: Theodore R. II, Sharon L., Scott K., Krista A. Jarman. BS, U.S. Mil. Acad., 1950; MBA, George Washington U., 1964; MPA, Nat. U., 1984. Commd. 2d lt. USAF, 1950, advanced through grades to col., 1970, ret., 1974; pres. T. R. York Cons., Fairfax, Va., 1974-79, T. R. Cons., San Diego, 1979-85, ULTRAPLECS Intelligent Bldgs., Sandy, Utah, 1991—; dir. Software Productivity Consortium, Herndon, Va., 1985-90. Mem. Loudoun County Rep. Com., Leesburg, Va., 1990-91. Decorated DFC, Air medal (5), Meritorius Svc. medal, Joint Svcs. Commendation medal, Air Force Commendation medal (5). Mem. Internat. Facilities Mgmt. Assn., Intelligent Bldgs. Inst. (advisor), Instituto Mexicana Del Edificios Intelegente (hon.), Office Planners and Users Group, Shriners, Masons. Avocations: computers, electronics. Office: ULTRAPLECS Intelligent Bldg 1289 S Bluff View Dr Sandy UT 84092-5922 *Success is measured in terms of help from others. I believe in building a team to manage any project. Always use the word "we" and forget the word "I" when addressing a successful project and loyalty will follow.*

YORK, TINA, painter; b. Germany, Feb. 9, 1951. Student, Sch. Mus. Fine Arts, Boston, 1967-71; studied with, George Dergalis, Wayland, Mass., 1967-75; BA cum laude, Brandeis U., 1978; postgrad., N.Y. Med. Coll., 1980-83. Solo exhbns. include Gallery of Contemporary Art, Provincetown, Mass., 1969, Springfield (Mass.) Art Assn., 1971, Copley Soc., Boston, 1972, 73, Boston U., 1974, Mendler Gallery, Rockport, Mass., 1974, Cambridge (Mass.) Art Assn., 1975, Ames Gallery, N.Y.C., 1976, Gallery Seven, Boston, 1977, Brandeis U., Waltham, Mass., 1978, Rue Oker Gallery of Art, Sturbridge, Mass., 1979, Art Collectors Gallery, N.Y.C., 1981, 153 Gallery, Inc., N.Y.c., 1982, Creative Concepts, L.A., 1984, Alpha Contemporary Exhibits, L.A., 1985, Darraby Gallery, L.A., 1986, 8th St. Gallery, L.A., 1986, Koplin Gallery, L.A., 1987, Galerie Beverly Hills, Calif., 1988, Convention Ctr., Rome, 1988, Merck, Sharpe & Dohme, Rahway, N.J., 1988, Erlgangen Kultur Borse, Germany, 1989, Arwell Gallery, Laguna, Calif., 1989, Deutsch-Amerikanisches Inst., Regensburg, Germany, 1990, Art in Pub. Bldgs., Nuremberg, Germany, 1990, Art Expo, N.Y.C., 1990, Amerikahaus, Nuremberg, 1990, Art 5, Nuremberg, 1990, Dresdner Bank, Nuremberg, 1990, Studio Gallery, North Hollywood, Calif., 1991, 92, La Foire Internat d'Art Contemporain, Paris, 1992, Herbstmesse, Frankfurt, Germany, 1992, Kunstforum Internat., Aachen, Germany, 1993, Ambiente, Frankfurt, 1993, NASA Ames Rsch. Ctr., Moffett Field, Calif., 1994, NASA Johnson Space Ctr., Houston, 1995; group exhbns. include Brockton (Mass.) Art Assn., 1969, Scituate (Mass.) Arts Festival, 1969, Temple Beth Elohim Arts Festival, Newton, Mass., 1969, Temple Shalom Arts Festival, Medford, Mass., 1969, Auburndale (Mass.) Congregational Ch. Art Exhibit, 1969, others. Office: Postfach 730146, 8500 Nurnberg 73, Germany

YORK, VERMELLE CARDWELL, real estate broker and developer; b. Evergreen, Ala., Jan. 30, 1925; d. Frederick Lofton and Emmie Mildred (Pitts) Cardwell; m. E. Travis York, Jr., Dec. 26, 1946; children: Lisa, Travis. BS, Auburn U., 1946. Pres. Tralisa Corp., Gainesville, Fla., 1966-87, sec., treas., 1988-94; sec., treas. Caret Corp., Gainesville, Fla., 1979-86, pres., 1987—. Mem. devel. com. Harn Mus., Gainesville, Fla., 1990-96, Hospice House, Gainesville, 1992-96; co-chair March of Dimes, Gainesville, 1995, Red Ribbon Campaign, 1989, 90. Recipient President's Medallion, U. Fla., 1980; named Woman of Distinction Santa Fe C. C., 1988. Mem. The Heritage Club (mem. amb. com. 1991-96), P.E.O. (pres. 1989-90), Surfside N. Club, (dir. 1988-91), Gainesville Women's Forum (membership chair 1994-96), DAR, Phi Kappa Phi. Avocations: genealogy. Home: 4020 SW 78th St Gainesville FL 32608 Office: Caret Corp 4020 SW 78th St Gainesville FL 32608-3608

YORKE, JAMES ALAN, chaos mathematician; b. Beijing, Aug. 3, 1941; married; three children. Car, Columbia U., 1963; PhD in Math., U. Md., 1966. From rsch. assoc. to rsch. assoc. prof. Inst. Phys. Sci. and Technology/U. Md., College Park, 1966-72, rsch. prof. math., 1972—; Guggenheim fellow, 1980-81, disting. prof., 1995—; dir. Inst. for Physical Scis., and Tech., 1988—. Mem. AAMS, Am. Math. Soc., Math. Assn. Am., Soc. Indsl. and Applied Math. Office: University of Maryland Inst for Phys Science & Tech College Park MD 20472

YORKE, MARIANNE, lawyer, real estate executive; b. Ridley Park, Pa., Nov. 4, 1948; d. Joseph George and Catherine Veronica (Friel) Y. BA, West Chester U., 1971; JD, Temple U., 1980; MS, U. Pa., 1987. M in Corp. Real Estate, Internat. Assn. Corp. Real Estate Execs., 1996. Bar: Pa. 1981, N.Y. 1992. Mgr. CIGNA Corp., Phila., 1982-85, asst. dir., Phila., 1985-89; v.p. Chase Manhattan Bank, N.Y.C., 1989-92; real estate dir. Johnson & Johnson, 1992—; real estate atty. Garfinkel & Volpicelli, Phila., 1980-82; prin., mng. ptnr. Yorke/Eisenman, Real Estate, Phila., 1976-89, prin., mng. ptnr. Yorke/Mac Lachlin Real Estate, Phila, 1989—; lectr. Women in the Arts, 1982-90; guest speaker Wharton Sch. Bus. Class of 1989, U. Pa., grad. sch. arts and scis. Class of 1990. Contbr. articles to profl. jours. Solicitor Pa. Ballet, Phila., 1983-90, United Way, Phila., 1983-90; mem. steering com. U. Pa., 1986-90, dir. alumni assn., 1987-90; mem. adv. com. for econ. devel. Luth. Settlement House Adv, 1986-88; bd. dirs. Hamilton Townhouse Assn., Phila., 1988-90, chmn. ins. com., 1989-90, 718 Broadway, Inc., N.Y.C., 1990-94, Johnson Health Care Svcs. Recipient Live for Life award Johnson Health Mgmt., 1995. Mem. ABA (forum on constrn. 1982-90), Pa. Bar Assn. (condominium and zoning coms. 1982-90), Assn. of Bar of City of N.Y. (sects. on internat. law and real property law 1992-94), Phila. Bar Assn., Phila. Women Real Estate Attys., Nat. Assn. Corp. Real Estate Execs. (internat. coun. 1984—, comml. coun. 1984—), Internat. Atty's Roundtable, Women's Law Caucus, Phi Alpha Delta. Independent. Roman Catholic. Home: The Admiralty 55 Ocean Ave Apt 4C Monmouth Beach NJ 07750-1367 Office: Johnson & Johnson 1 Johnson And Johnson Plz New Brunswick NJ 08933-0001

YORKIN, BUD (ALAN YORKIN), producer, director; b. Washington, Pa., Feb. 22, 1926; s. Maurice A. and Jessie (Sachs) Y.; children: Nicole, David. BS in Elec. Engring., Carnegie-Mellon U., 1948; postgrad. in English Lit., Columbia U., 1951; LHD, Washington and Jefferson Coll., 1974. ptnr. Tandem Prodns., Inc., L.A., 1959-74. With engring. staff, NBC, N.Y.C., 1949-50, stage mgr., NBC, 1950-52; assoc. dir. Colgate Comedy Hour, 1952-53; dir. TV shows including Dinah Shore Show, Tony Martin Show, Ernie Ford Show, George Gobel Show, N.Y.C. and L.A., 1948-52; writer, producer, dir. An Evening With Fred Astaire, 1958, Another Evening With Fred Astaire, 1959, Jack Benny spls., 1959; exec. producer TV series All in the Family, 1971-79, Sanford and Son, 1972-77, Maude, 1972-78, Good Times, 1974-79, Diff'rent Strokes, 1978-86, What's Happening, 1976-79, Carter Country, 1977-79, Archie Bunker's Place, 1980-83, The Night They Raided Minsky's, Cold Turkey, Deal of the Century, Blade Runner, also numerous spls.; dir. (films) Come Blow Your Horn, 1965, Never Too Late, 1966, Divorce, American Style, 1967, Inspector Clouseau, 1968; producer, dir. (films) Start the Revolution Without Me, 1970, The Thief Who Came to Dinner, 1971, Twice in a Lifetime, 1985, Arthur on the Rocks, 1988, Love Hurts, 1990, Intersection, 1993. Trustee Am. Film Inst., Mus. Contemporary Art, L.A., Carnegie-Mellon U., Am. Heart Assn., UCLA. Recipient several Emmy awards, Sylvania award, Look award, Dirs. Guild award, Harvard Lampoon's Golden Jester award, Peabody award. Mem. TV Acad. Arts and Scis. (past gov.), Dirs. Guild Am. (gov.). Office: Bud Yorkin Prodns Inc 345 N Maple Dr Ste 206 Beverly Hills CA 90210-3856

YORSZ, STANLEY, lawyer; b. Norwich, Conn., June 5, 1953; s. Stanley and Helen (Chimilewski) Y.; m. Margaret A. McLean, June 14, 1986. BA, Colgate U., 1975; JD, Dickinson U., 1978. Bar: Pa. 1978, U.S. Dist. Ct. (we. dist.) Pa. 1978, U.S. Ct. Appeals (3d cir.) 1980, U.S. Supreme Ct. 1980. Law clk. to judge Pa. Superior Ct., Pitts., 1978-80; assoc. Buchanan Ingersoll P.C., Pitts., 1980-86, ptnr., 1986—. Editor comments Dickinson Law Rev., 1978. Mem. ABA, Allegheny County Bar Assn., Pa. Bar Assn., Rivers Club. Roman Catholic. Avocations: tennis, squash, golf. Office: Buchanan Ingersoll PC 1 Oxford Ctr 301 Grant St Pittsburgh PA 15219

YORTY, SAMUEL, lawyer, former mayor; b. Lincoln, Nebr., Oct. 1, 1909; s. Frank Patrick and Johanna (Egan) Y.; m. Elizabeth Hensel, Dec. 1, 1938 (dec. Fev. 1984; 1 son, William Egan (dec. Oct. 1983); m. Gloria Haig, June 8, 1986. Student law sch., Southwestern U., U. So. Calif., U. Calif. Extension. Bar: Calif. bar 1939. Since practiced in Los Angeles; mem. 82d Congress from 14th Dist. Calif., 83d Congress from 26th Dist. Calif.; mayor Los Angeles, 1961-73; Mem. Calif. State Assembly, 1936-40, 49-50. Served to capt. USAAF, 1942-45. Decorated Encomineda medal Spain; comdr. Finnish Lion; Nat. Order So. Cross Brazil; comdr.'s cross German Order Merit; Gt. Silver Insignia of Honor with Star Austria; Order Civil Merit Korea; Knight Legion of Honor France; Order Homayoun medal Iran; Order Sun of Peru. Republican. Home and Office: 3100 Padre Blvd South Padre Island TX 78597

YOSELOFF, JULIEN DAVID, publishing company executive; b. N.Y.C., June 25, 1941; s. Thomas and Sara (Rothfuss) Y.; m. Darlene Starr Carbone, Aug. 6, 1967; children—Michael Ian, Anthony Alexander. B.A., U. Pa., 1962; student, London Sch. Econs., 1962-63; MA, Rutgers U., 1994. With A.S. Barnes and Co., Inc., Cranbury, N.J., 1963-80; dir. Associated Univ. Presses, Inc., 1966—; pres. Rosemont Pub. and Printing Corp., 1985—. Served with AUS, 1964. Mem. Phi Beta Kappa Assocs., Phi Beta Kappa, Pi Sigma Alpha. Avocations: amateur radio, photography. Office: 440 Forsgate Dr Cranbury NJ 08512

YOSELOFF, THOMAS, publisher; b. Sioux City, Iowa, Sept. 8, 1913; s. Morris and Sarah (Rabinowitz) Y.; m. Sara Rothfuss, Apr. 30, 1938; children: Julien David, Mark Laurence; m. Lauretta Sellitti, Apr. 23, 1964; 1 dau., Tamar Rachel. A.B., U. Iowa, 1934; Litt.D. (hon.), Bucknell U., 1982; L.H.D. (hon.), Fairleigh Dickinson U., 1982. Chmn. Rosemont Pub. & Printing Corp., 1969—, Associated Univ. Presses, 1969—, Golden Cockerel Press, London, 1979—. Author: A Fellow of Infinite Jest, 1946, (with Lillian Stuckey) Merry Adventures of Till Eulenspiegel, 1944, Further Adventures of Till Eulenspiegel, pub. 1957, The Time of My Life, 1979; Editor: Seven Poets in Search of an Answer, 1944, Voyage to America, 1961, Comic Almanac, 1963, The Man from the Mercury, 1986. Pres. Center for War/Peace Studies, 1977-91. Recipient award of merit Bucknell U., 1975, award of merit U. Del., 1987. Mem. Phi Beta Kappa, Sigma Delta Chi, Delta Sigma Rho. Home: Box 289 68 Cedar Dr Colts Neck NJ 07722-1672 Office: 440 Forsgate Dr Cranbury NJ 08512

YOSHIKI-KOVINICK, MARIAN TSUGIE, author; b. L.A., Feb. 17, 1941; d. Eddie Junichi and Teruko Ruth (Kawamoto) Yoshiki; m. Philip Peter Kovinick, June 17, 1973. BA, U. So. Calif., 1963; MA, Azusa Pacific U., 1980. Tchr. Pasadena (Calif.) Unified Sch. Dist., 1964-66, Centinela Valley Union H.S. Dist., Lawndale, Calif., 1966-83; freelance writer, rschr. L.A., 1983—. Rschr., cons. for various exhbns.: The Woman Artist in the American West, 1976, California Light, 1990, Guy Rose, American Impressionist, 1995; rschr. for books: Elsie Palmer Payne, 1990, American Scene Painting, 1991; co-author: The Encyclopedia of Women Artists of the American West, 1997; transcriber: Oral History of American Artists, Archives of American Art, Smithsonian Instn., 1995—. Democrat. Avocations: calligraphy, crocheting, needlepoint, gardening, photography. Home and Office: 4735 Don Ricardo Dr Los Angeles CA 90008

YOSHINO, GEORGE, food products executive; b. Kennewick, Wash., June 25, 1928; s. Frank H. and Kazuye (Hada) Y.; m. Frances T. Kaku, Dec. 29, 1951 (div. 1979); children: Jean Frances, Frankie Jo, Michael Stanton, Harry Walter; m. Marguerite Shirley Mosley, Dec. 8, 1990. Grad. high sch., Weiser, Idaho. Owner Yoshino Farms, Quincy, Wash., 1948—; pres. Columbia Growers Inc, Quincy, 1956-62, Yoshino Western, Inc., Quincy, 1962-68, Wyco, Inc., Seattle, 1968-74; asst. sr. v.p. U & I Inc., Pasco, Wash., 1974-79; dir., gen. mgr. Spad Distributing, Inc., Pasco, 1979-86; pres. Century 21 Products, Inc., Pasco, 1987—; bd. dirs. Pacific One NA; exec. bd. Benton-Franklin Govtl. Conf., 1993—; dir. Assoc. Wash. Bus. Mem. City Coun. Quincy, 1964-66; bd. dirs. Columbia Basin Commn., Olympia, Wash., 1964-68; dir. Associated Wash. Bus., 1994—; dir. exec. com. Benton Franklin Regional Coun., 1993—. Mem. Produce Mktg. Assn., Associated Wash. Bus. Republican. Office: Century 21 Products Inc 1917 N 2nd Ave Pasco WA 99301-3722

YOSHIUCHI, ELLEN HAVEN, childbirth educator; b. Newark, Apr. 15, 1949; d. Michael Joseph and Adeline V. (Lindblom) Haven; m. Takeshi Yoshiuchi, Dec. 1, 1973; children: Teri Takumi, Niki Noboru. BA summa cum laude, CUNY, 1980; M Profl. Studies in Human Rels., N.Y. Inst. Tech., 1991. Cert. bereavement svcs. counselor. Pvt. practice childbirth edn., 1983-89; program asst. parent/family edn. St. Luke's/Roosevelt Hosp. Ctr., N.Y.C., 1989-93, mem. faculty parent/family edn. program, 1990—; mem. faculty Family Ctr. at Riverdale Neighborhood House, Bronx, N.Y., 1991-

96; faculty mem. The Greater N.Y. March of Dimes, N.Y.C., 1996—; mem. perinatal bereavement com. St. Luke's/Roosevelt Hosp. Ctr., N.Y.C., 1989-95. Editor ASPO/N.Y.C. News, 1983-86; contbr. articles to profl. jours. Bd. trustees Pan Asian Repertory Theatre, N.Y.C., 1996—. Fellow Am. Coll. Childbirth Educators; mem. Internat. Childbirth Edn. Assn., N.Y. State Perinatal Assn., Am. Soc. for Psychoprophylaxis in Obstetrics/Lamaze (cert. tchr., pres. N.Y.C. chpt. 1987-91, nominating com. 1991-93, dir. ednl. program 1991-93).

YOSHIZUMI, DONALD TETSURO, dentist; b. Honolulu, Feb. 18, 1930; s. Richard Kiyoshi and Hatsue (Tanouye) Y.; BS, U. Hawaii, 1952; DDS, U. Mo., 1960, MS, 1963; m. Barbara Fujiko Iwashita, June 25, 1955; children: Beth Ann E., Cara Leigh S., Erin Yuri. Clin. instr. U. Mo. Sch. Dentistry, Kansas City, 1960-63; pvt. practice, Santa Clara, Calif., 1963-70, San Jose, Calif., 1970—. With USAF, 1952-56. Mem. Am. Dental Assn., Calif. Dental Assn., Santa Clara County Dental Soc., Omicron Kappa Upsilon, Delta Sigma Delta. Contbr. articles to profl. jours. Home: 5054 Parkfield Ave San Jose CA 95129-3225 Office: 2011 Forest Ave San Jose CA 95128-4813

YOSHIZUMI, TERRY TAKATOSHI, medical physicist; b. Osaka, Japan, July 2, 1949; came to U.S., 1975; s. Akira and Fumie Yoshizumi; m. Rebecca P. Peterson; 1 child, Alexander J. BS, Ehine U., Japan, 1973; MS, UCLA, 1975, U. Cin., 1977; PhD, U. Cin., 1980. Rsch. fellow Sloan-Kettering Inst., N.Y.C., 1980-81; chief radiation safety officer The Bklyn. Hosp., 1981-82; instr. U. Cin., 1982-83; asst. prof. W.Va. U., Morgantown, 1983-87, Howard Univ. Coll. Medicine, Washington, 1987-90; radiation safety officer Va. Conn. Health Care Sys., 1990—; assoc. rsch. scientist Yale U. Sch. of Medicine, New Haven, 1991-96, lectr., 1996—. Author: (with others) Physics of Nuclear Medicine, 1984; contbr. articles to profl. jours. including Physics Medicine and Biology, Jour. of Nuclear Medicine, Nuclear Med. Biology, Health Physics. Sloan-Kettering Ins./Cornell Grad. Sch. Med. Scis. postdoctoral fellow, 1980-81, Soc. Nuclear Medicine student rsch. fellow, 1980; U. Cin. scholar, 1975-80. Mem. Am. Coll. Radiology, Health Physics Soc., Am. Assn. of Physicists in Medicine. Office: VA Conn Healthcare Sys 950 Campbell Ave West Haven CT 06516-2770

YOSKIN, JON WILLIAM, II, insurance company executive; b. Phila., Oct. 16, 1939; s. Lewis William and Louise (Houck) Y.; m. Dorothea James, Sept. 25, 1961 (div. Mar. 1992); children: Nicholas, Dorothea, Maurice P.; m. Elizabeth Anne Groves, Sept 26, 1992. Pvt. practice Phila., 1959-74; sr. v.p. Mid. Atlantic Gen. Investment Co., Phila., 1974-80; exec. v.p. Transatlantic Life Assurance Co., Phila., 1980-85, Meritor Life Ins. Co., Phila., 1985-88; owner, CEO Tri-Arc Fin. Svcs., Phila., 1988—; chmn., CEO Magellan Ins. Co. Ltd., Bermuda, Bermuda, 1996—; bd. dirs. Nat. Media Corp. Bd. dirs. Concerto Soloist, Phila., 1990-92, Phila. Commn. to End. Homelessness, 1995—; mem. Spl. Olympics Adv. Com. Mem. Nat. Assn. Life Underwriters, Nat. Assn. Ins. Brokers (bd. dirs.), Profl. Assn. Ins. Agts., Sons of Am. Revolution, Mil. Order Loyal Legion of U.S. Republican. Episcopalian. Avocation: big game hunting. Home: 1606 Pine St Philadelphia PA 19103-6711 Office: Tri-Arc Fin Svcs PO Box 6745 983 Old Eagle School Rd Ste 616 Wayne PA 19087

YOSKOWITZ, IRVING BENJAMIN, lawyer, manufacturing company executive; b. Bklyn., Dec. 2, 1945; s. Rubin and Jennie Y.; m. Carol L. Magil, Feb. 11, 1973; children: Stephen M., Robert J. BBA, CCNY, 1966; JD, Harvard U., 1969; postgrad., London Sch. Econs., 1971-72. Bar: N.Y. 1970, D.C. 1970, Conn. 1982. Programmer IBM, East Fishkill, N.Y., 1966; systems analyst Office Sec. Def., Washington, 1969-71; asso. firm Arnold & Porter, Washington, 1972-73; atty. IBM, 1973-79; regional counsel IBM, Bethesda, Md., to 1979; dep. gen. counsel United Technologies Corp., Hartford, Conn., 1979-81; v.p. and gen. counsel United Technologies Corp., 1981-86, sr. v.p., gen. counsel, 1986-90, exec. v.p., gen. counsel, 1990—; bd. dirs. BBA Group, PLC, 1995—. Mem. editorial bd. Harvard Law Rev., 1968-69. With U.S. Army, 1969-71. Knox fellow, 1971-72. Mem. ABA, Am. Corp. Counsel Assn. (bd. dirs. 1982-85), Assn. Gen. Counsels. Office: United Techs Corp United Techs Bldg Hartford CT 06101

YOST, LYLE EDGAR, farm equipment manufacturing company executive; b. Hesston, Kans., Mar. 5, 1913; s. Joseph and Alma (Hensley) Y.; m. Erma Martin, July 31, 1938; children: Byron, Winston, Susan, Cameron. B.S. B.A, Goshen Coll., 1937; postgrad., U. Ind., 1940. With St. Joseph Valley Bank, Elkhart, Ind., 1938-41; tchr. Wakarusa (Ind.) High Sch., 1942-45; founder Hesston Corp., Kans., 1947, pres., 1949-83; now chmn. bd. Hesston Corp.; ret., 1991. Bd. dirs., past pres. Farm and Indsl. Equipment Inst.; mem. Gov.'s Com. for Ptnrs. for Progress Kans.-Paraguay; chmn. com. establishing creamery in Uruguay, 1967; mem. State Dept. cultural del. to USSR, 1967; past chmn. pres.'s adv coun. Hesston Coll. (Kans.); chmn. Prince of Peace Chapel, Aspen, Colo. Named Farmarketing Man of Year Nat. Agrl. Advt. and Marketing Assn., 1969; Kansan of Achievement in Bus., 1972; Kansan of Year, 1974. Mem. Alpha Kappa Psi (hon.). Home: 123 Kingsway Hesston KS 67062-9271 Office: PO Box 909 Hesston KS 67062-0909

YOST, NICHOLAS CHURCHILL, lawyer; b. Washington, Aug. 15, 1938; s. Charles Woodruff and Irene Ravitch (Oldakowska) Y.; m. Sandra Moore Rennie; children: Robert, Scott, Daniel. AB, Princeton U., 1960; LLB, U. Calif., Berkeley, 1963. Bar: Calif. 1964, U.S. Supreme Ct. 1972, D.C. 1978. Dep. atty. gen. adminstrv. law Calif. Dept. Justice, 1965-69; counsel Calif. State Environ. Quality Study Coun., 1969-71; dep. atty. gen. in charge environ. unit Calif. Dept. Justice, 1971-77; gen. counsel Coun. Environ. Quality, Exec. Office of Pres., Washington, 1977-81; vis. scholar Environ. Law Inst., Washington, 1981-82; sr. atty. Ctr. for Law in Pub. Interest, Washington, 1982-85; ptnr. Dickstein, Shapiro & Morin, Washington, 1985-94, Sonnenschein Nath & Rosenthal, San Francisco, 1994—; U.S. dir. legal and adminstrv. aspects of environ. protection agreement between U.S. and USSR, 1977-81; dir. Pres.'s Task Force on Global Resources and Environ., 1980-81; mem. U.S. Del. to UN Conf. Environ. and Devel., Rio, 1992; mem. Calif. EPA Blue Ribbon Commn. on a Unified Environ. Statute, 1994—. Contbr. articles to profl. jours. Capt. U.S. Army, 1963-65. Recipient Nat. Environ. Quality award Natural Resources Coun. Am., 1996. Mem. ABA (chmn. standing com. on environ. law 1989-91), State Bar Calif. (chmn. com. on environ. 1975-76), D.C. Bar Assn. (co-chmn. environ., energy and natural resources sect. 1985-86, 88-89), Environ. Law Inst. (bd. dirs. 1986-92), UN Assn. L.A. (v.p. 1969-71), UN Assn. Washington (bd. dirs. 1987-93). Home: 901 Powell St Apt 8 San Francisco CA 94108-2024 Office: Sonnenschein Nath 685 Market St Ste 10 San Francisco CA 94105-4202

YOST, PAUL ALEXANDER, JR., foundation executive, retired coast guard officer; b. Phila., Jan. 3, 1929; s. Paul Alexander Sr. and Jeanne Moore (Bailey) Y.; m. Jan Worth, June 2, 1951; children: Linda L., Paul Alexander III, David J., Lisa L., Christopher J. BS, USCG Acad., 1951; MS, U. Conn., 1959; MA, George Washington U., 1964; grad., Naval War Coll., 1964. Commd. ensign USCG, 1951, advanced through grades to adm., 1986; comdr. 8th dist. USCG, New Orleans, 1978-81; chief staff hdqrs. USCG, Washington, 1981-84; comdr. 3d dist., maritime Atlantic def. zone, and Atlantic area USCG, N.Y.C., 1984-86; commandant USCG, Washington, 1986-90, ret., 1990; pres. James Madison Found., Washington, 1990—. Decorated D.S.M. with gold star, Silver Star, Legion of Merit combat "V" with gold star, Meritorious Service Medal. Office: James Madison Meml Fellowship Found 2000 K St NW Washington DC 20006-1809

YOST, WILLIAM ALBERT, psychology educator, hearing researcher; b. Dallas, Sept. 21, 1944; s. William Jacque and Gladys (Funk) Y.; m. Lee Prater, June 15, 1969; children—Kelley Ann, Alyson Leigh. B.A., Colo. Coll., 1966, DSc (hon.), 1997; Ph.D., Ind. U., 1970. Assoc. prof. psychology U. Fla., Gainesville, 1971-77; dir. sensory physiology and perception program NSF, Washington, 1982-83; prof. psychology Loyola U., Chgo., 1977-89, dir. Parmly Hearing Inst., 1977—, prof. hearing scis., 1990—, dir. interdisciplinary neurosci. minor, 1997—; adj. prof. psychology and otolarynogology Loyola U., Chgo., 1990—; individual expert bio-acoustics Am. Nat. Stds. Inst., 1983—; mem. study sect. Nat. Inst. Deafness and Other Communication Disorders, 1990-94; mem. hearing bioacoustics and biomechanics com. Nat. Rsch. Coun., 1992—. Author: Fundamentals of Hearing, 1977, 84, 94; editor (with others) New Directions in Hearing Science, 1985, Directional Hearing, 1987, Auditory Processing of Complex Sounds, 1987, Classification of Complex Sounds, 1989, Psychoacoustics, 1993; assoc. editor Auditory Neurosci., 1994—; ad hoc reviewer NSF, Air Force Office Sci. Rsch., Office Naval Rsch., 1981—; contbr. chpts. to books, articles to profl. jours. Pres. Evanston Tennis Assn., Ill., 1984, 90. Grantee NSF, 1974—, NIH, 1975—, AFOSR, 1983—. Fellow AAAS, Acoustical Soc. Am. (assoc. editor jour. 1984-91, chair tech. com. 1990—), Am. Speech-Lang.-Hearing Assn.; mem. NAS (exec. com. on hearing bioacoustics, biomechanics 1981-87, chmn. 1993-97), Assn. Rsch. in Otolaryngology (sec.-treas. 1984-87, pres.-elect 1987-88, pres. 1988-89), Acoustics Soc. Am. (chair com. psychol. and physiol. acoustics 1990—), Nat. Inst. Deafness and Other Comm. Disorders (task force, rev. panel 1990-94, chmn. 1994), Am. Auditory Soc. (exec. bd. 1993-98). *I am fortunate that I am in an occupation that is so much fun. Teaching and research are very enjoyable. Most days for me are fun.*

YOTHER, ANTHONY WAYNE, critical care nurse, nurse manager; b. Anniston, Ala., Jan. 30, 1964; s. Johnny Wayne and Carol Sue (Bradshaw) Y. BSN, Jacksonville State U., 1987; MSN, U. Ala., Birmingham, 1992; MS in Health Care Policy and Adminstrn., Mercer U., 1994. Cert. med.-surg. nursing, med.-surg. clin. specialist, nursing adminstrn., adult critical care nursing, pediatric adv. life support. ICU mgr. Grady Health Sys., Atlanta, 1994—. Mem. ANA (cert.), AACCN (cert.), Am. Heart Assn., Ga. Nurses Assn., Laurleen B. Wallace Coll. Nursing Alumni Assn. (v.p. 1988-90, pres. 1990-92), U. Ala.-Birmingham Alumni Assn., Mercer U. Alumni Assn., Jacksonville State U. Alumni Assn., Sigma Theta Tau Internat.

YOTHER, MICHELE, publisher; b. Atlanta, Aug. 25, 1965; d. Carole (Spence) Marsh; m. Michael B. Yother, Mar. 17, 1990; 1 child, Christina Michele. BA in acctg. cum laude, Ga. State U., 1990. Asst. v.p. Bank Am., Atlanta, 1986-90; pres. Gallopade Pub. Group, Atlanta, 1990—; pres. Carole Marsh Family Interactive Multimedia, 1993—. Pub. over 2500 children's books, computer disks and activities. Equifax Bus. scholar Ga. State U., 1989. Mem. Women's Nat. Book Assn. (bd. dirs. 1994-95), Bank Am. Club (pres. 1989), Golden Key. Methodist. Home: 359 Milledge Ave SE Atlanta GA 30312-3238 Office: Gallopade Pub Group 359 Milledge Ave SE Ste 100 Atlanta GA 30312-3238

YOUMAN, ROGER JACOB, editor, writer; b. N.Y.C., Feb. 25, 1932; s. Robert Harold and Ida (Kellner) Y.; m. Lillian Frank, June 22, 1958; children: Nancy, Laura, Joshua, Andrew. B.A., Swarthmore Coll., 1953. Desk asst. CBS News, N.Y.C., 1953; program editor TV Guide, N.Y.C., 1956; regional editor TV Guide, Memphis, 1956-57, Houston, 1957; asst. programming editor TV Guide, N.Y.C., 1957-60; assoc. editor TV Guide, Radnor, Pa., 1960-65, asst. mng. editor, 1965-72, mng. editor, 1972-76, exec. editor, 1976-79, 80-81, co-editor, 1981-90, editor, 1990-93; editor Panorama, 1979-80; editl. dir. TV Guide On Screen, 1993-96; freelance writer, editorial cons., 1996—; del. U.S.-Soviet Bilaterial Info. Talks, 1988, 90. Author: How Sweet It Was, The Television Years; contbr. articles to various publs. Served with AUS, 1954-55. Home: 752 Mancill Rd Wayne PA 19087-2043

YOUMANS, JULIAN RAY, neurosurgeon, educator; b. Baxley, Ga., Jan. 2, 1928; s. John Edward and Jennie Lou (Milton) Y.; children—Reed Nesbit, John Edward, Julian Milton. B.S., Emory U., 1949, M.D., 1952; M.S., U. Mich., 1955, Ph.D., 1957. Diplomate: Am. Bd. Neurol. Surgery. Intern U. Mich. Hosp., Ann Arbor, 1952-53; resident in neurol. surgery U. Mich. Hosp., 1953-55, 56-58; fellow in neurology U. London, 1955-56; asst. prof. neurosurgery U. Miss., 1959-62, assoc. prof., 1962-63; assoc. prof. Med. U. S.C., 1963-65, prof., 1965-67, chief div. neurosurgery, 1963-67; prof. U. Calif., Davis, 1967-91; prof. emeritus, 1991—; chmn. dept. neurosurgery U. Calif., 1967-82; cons. USAF, U.S. VA, NRC. Editor: Neurological Surgery, 1973; contbr. articles to profl. jours. No. vice chmn. Republican State Central Com. of Calif., 1979-81. Served with U.S. Navy, 1944-46. Mem. ACS (bd. govs. 1972-78), Congress of Neurol. Surgeons (exec. com. 1967-70), Am. Acad. Neurology, Am. Assn. Neurol. Surgeons, Am. Assn. Surgery of Trauma, Pan-Pacific Surg. Assn., Western Neurosurg. Soc., Neurosurg. Soc. Am., Soc. Neurol. Surgeons, Soc. Univ. Neurosurgeons, N. Pacific Soc. Neurology and Psychiatry, Royal Soc. Medicine, Am. Trauma Soc., U.S. C. of C., Bohemian Club, Sutter Club, Capital Club of Sacramento, Rotary. Republican. Episcopalian. Office: 502 Mace Blvd Ste 10 Davis CA 95616-4338

YOUMANS, WILLIAM BARTON, physiologist; b. Cin., Feb. 3, 1910; s. Charles Trimble and Lucy May (Gardiner) Y.; m. Cynthia McCreary Holbrook, Nov. 24, 1932; children: William Barton, Carol Anne, Charles Gilbert. BS, Western Ky. State Coll., Bowling Green, 1932; MS, Western Ky. State Coll., 1933; PhD, U. Wis., 1938; MD, U. Oreg., 1944. Intern Henry Ford Hosp., Detroit, 1944-45; instr. biology Western Ky. U., Bowling Green, 1932-35; rsch. asst. physiology U. Wis., Madison, 1935-36; instr. physiology U. Wis., 1936-38; instr. physiology to assoc. prof. physiology U. Oreg. Med. Sch., Portland, 1938-42; prof. physiology U. Oreg. Med. Sch., 1942-46, head physiology dept., 1946-52; prof. and chmn. dept. physiology U. Wis., Madison, 1952-71; prof. physiology U. Wis., 1971-76, prof. emeritus, 1976—; mem. physiology study sect. USPHS, 1952-56, mem. tng. grant and fellowship rev. panels, 1956-60, 60-64. Author: Nervous and Neurohumoral Regulation of Intestinal Motility, 1949, Hemodynamics in Failure of the Circulation, 1951, Basic Medical Physiology, 1952, Fundamentals of Human Physiology, 1957, others; contbr. articles to profl. jours. Recipient Meritorious Achievement award, U. Oreg. Med. Sch. Alumni Assn., 1967, Emeritus Faculty award, U. Wis. Med. Alumni Assn., 1985. Fellow AAAS; mem. Am. Physiol. Soc., Am. Soc. Pharmacology and Exptl. Therapeutics, Am. Heart Assn., Alpha Omega Alpha, Phi Sigma, Gamma Alpha. Avocations: tenor banjo, gardening, camping. Home: 118 Klahanie View Ln Port Angeles WA 98363-8300

YOUNG, ALICE, lawyer; b. Washington, Apr. 7, 1950; d. John and Elizabeth (Jen) Y.; m. Thomas L. Shortall, Sept. 22, 1984; children: Amanda, Stephen. AB magna cum laude, Yale U., 1971; JD, Harvard U., 1974. Bar: N.Y. 1975. Assoc. Coudert Bros., N.Y.C., 1974-81; mng. ptnr. Graham & James, N.Y.C., 1981-87; ptnr. Milbank, Tweed, Hadley & McCloy, N.Y.C., 1987-93; ptnr., chair Asia Pacific Practice (U.S.) Kaye, Scholer, Fierman, Hays & Handler, N.Y.C., 1994—; mem. Coun. on Fgn. Rels., 1977—. Contbr. articles to profl. jours. Trustee Aspen (Colo.) Inst., 1988—, Pan-Asian Repertory Theatre, N.Y.C., 1987-90, Lingnan Found., N.Y.C., 1984-91, Asia/Pacific Coun. of The Nature Conservancy, 1995—; mem. bus. com. Met. Mus. Art, N.Y.C., 1989-94, Nat. Com. on U.S.-China Rels., 1993—, U.S.-China Bus. Coun., 1993—, Com. of 100, 1993—, dir. 1995—; mem. bd. overseers visitation com. to Law Sch., Harvard U., 1994—, chair subcom. on grad. program Harvard U., 1996. Named one of 40 Under 40 Crain's Bus., N.Y.C., 1989; Bates fellow Yale U., 1970, NDFL fellow Harvard U., 1967-68; recipient Star award N.Y. Women's Agenda, 1992. Mem. ABA, N.Y. State Bar Assn. (fgn. investment com.), Assn. Bar City N.Y. (spl. com. on rels. with Japanese bar, Union Internat. des Avocats), Nat. Asian Pacific Am. Bar Assn., Asian Am. Bar Assn. N.Y., Harvard Law Sch. Assn. N.Y.C. (trustee 1990-94), Japan Soc. (sec. 1989—), Asia Soc. (pres.'s coun. 1984—). Office: Kaye Scholer Fierman Hays & Handler 425 Park Ave New York NY 10022-3506

YOUNG, ALINE PATRICE, controller; b. Sacramento, Nov. 8, 1957; d. Rene Francis and Patricia May (Taylor) LeFevre; 1 child, Daniel Alan Young. AA, Fullerton Coll., 1979; BA, Calif State U., Fullerton, 1981; MBA, Pepperdine U., 1988. Mgmt. devel. program Gen. Electric Credit, Anaheim, Calif., 1981-83; credit mgr. Kwikset/Emhart, Anaheim, Calif., 1983-88, Avery Dennison, Azusa, Calif., 1988-90; contr., fin. mgr. Avery Dennison, Monrovia, Calif., 1990-92, site mgr., contr., 1992-95; dir. bus. process transformation Allied Signal Inc., Torrance, Calif., 1995—. Chairperson Vision 95 Lutheran High Sch., Orange, Calif., 1993. Mem. Am. Mgmt. Assn., Inst. Mgmt. Accts. Republican. Methodist. Avocations: skiing, reading, dancing. Office: Allied Signal Aerospace M/Stor 38-2 2525 W 190th St Torrance CA 90504-6002

YOUNG, ANDREA C., communications executive; b. Rochester, N.Y., June 21, 1952; d. Vito Anthony and Mary Christine (Ruta) Calzone; m. Dennis Young, Jan. 4, 1989. BA in Music, Psychology, SUNY, Oswego, 1974. Media buyer Grey Advt., Los Angeles, 1976-77; media dir. Pickwick Internat., Los Angeles, 1977-79; regional coordinator MCA Distbg., Inc., Los Angeles, 1979-80; dir. Franklin Music div. Young Entertainment, Atlanta, 1980-84; v.p. Young Systems, Ltd., Atlanta, 1984-90, pres., 1990—; bd. dirs., pres. KAJX Aspen Pub. Radio. Mem. Nat. Assn. Rec. Merchandisers (assoc., chmn. trade show com. 1997), Ga. Exec. Women's Network. Avocations: skiing, rollerblading, radio DJ, silversmithing. Address: PO Box 133 Aspen CO 81612 Office: Young Systems Ltd 6185 Buford Hwy Ste C100 Norcross GA 30071-2303

YOUNG, ANDREW BRODBECK, lawyer; b. Phila., Feb. 8, 1907; s. Edward E. and Estelle (Brodbeck) Y.; m. Olive C. Sherley, Apr. 22, 1933; children: Andrew Oliver (dec.), Sherley (Mrs. Paul A. Hollos). A.B., Princeton U., 1928; LL.B., Harvard U., 1931. Bar: Pa. 1931. Ptnr. Stradley, Ronon, Stevens & Young, Phila., 1985-95, assoc., 1995—; v.p., bd. dirs. W.W. Interests (formerly Warren Webster & Co.); bd. dirs. Welex Inc., Holmes Investment Co., Phila.; lectr. finance U. Pa., 1939-66; lectr. various tax insts., 1953-81; mem. Mayor's Com. Exec. and Elective Salaries Phila. City Govt., 1959, Mayor's Com. Port Promotion Phila., 1959-63; mem. adv. coun. Phila. Cmty. Renewal Program, 1964-66; chmn., dir. Phila. Indsl. Devel. Corp., 1963-68, pres., 1963-70, chmn., 1970-86; mem. Mayor's Tax Study Commn., 1960, mem. Commr. Internal Revenue's Adv. Group, 1965; voting trustee Phila. Belt Line Ry. Co. Chmn. bd. trustees Mary Jacobs Meml. Libr. Found., Rocky Hill, N.J.; trustee Lovett Found., Michael Bruder Found., Frank Michaels Scholarship Found., Penjerdel Found.; mem. coun. pres.'s advisers LaSalle Coll., 1969-74. With Surgeon Gen.'s Office, AUS, 1942-45. Fellow Am. Bar Found.; mem. ABA (mem. ho. of dels. 1966-70, mem. council tax sect. 1958-70, chmn. sect. 1963-65), Pa. Bar Assn., Am. Law Inst. (tax adv. group, corps.-stockholders project 1957-59), Am. Coll. Tax Counsel, Am. Law Inst. (estate and gift tax project 1964-67), Phila. C. of C. (pres. 1958-60, chmn. bd. 1960-62, dir.), Am. Arbitration Assn. (nat. panel arbitrators), Phi Beta Kappa. Republican. Episcopalian. Clubs: Philadelphia, Sunday Breakfast, Sunnybook Golf, Tunkhannock Creek Assn., Penn, Wilderness, Anglers. Home: 613 Foulkeways Gwynedd PA 19436-1024 Office: 2600 One Commerce Sq 2005 Market St Philadelphia PA 19103-7042

YOUNG, ANN ELIZABETH O'QUINN, historian, educator; b. Waycross, Ga.; d. James Foster and Pearl Elizabeth (Sasser) O'Quinn; student Shorter Coll.; BA, MA, U. Ga., PhD, 1965; m. Robert William Young, Aug. 18, 1968; children: Abigail Ann, Leslie Lynn. Asst. prof. history Kearney (Nebr.) State Coll. (name now U. Nebr. at Kearney 1991), 1965-69, assoc. prof., 1969-72, prof., 1972—; participant Inst. on Islam, Middle East and World Politics, U. Mich., summer 1984, Coun. on Internat. Ednl. Exch., London, 1990, NEH Seminar NYU, 1993, faculty senate mem., 1985—, sec. 1993-94, pres., 1995-96. Mem. NEA, PEO, Phi Alpha Theta, Delta Kappa Gamma (chpt. pres. 1978-79), Phi Mu. Republican. Presbyterian. Contbg. author Dictionary of Georgia Biography; contbr. articles to profl. revs. Office: U Nebr at Kearney Dept History Kearney NE 68849-1285

YOUNG, ARTHUR PRICE, librarian, educator; b. Boston, July 29, 1940; s. Arthur Price and Marion (Freeman) Y.; m. Patricia Dorothy Foss, June 26, 1965; children: John Marshall, Christopher Price. BA, Tufts U., 1962; MA in Tchg., U. Mass., 1964; MSLS, Syracuse U., 1969; PhD, U. Ill., 1976. Head reader svcs., social sci. bibliographer SUNY-Cortland, 1969-72; rsch. assoc. U. Ill. Libr. Rsch. Ctr., Urbana, 1972-75; asst. dean pub. svcs., assoc. prof. U. Ala., Tuscaloosa, 1976-81; dean librs., prof. U. R.I., Kingston, 1981-89; dir. Thomas Cooper Libr., U. S.C., Columbia, 1989-93; sr. fellow UCLA, 1991; dir. librs., mem. adj. faculty dept. history No. Ill. U., DeKalb, 1993—; mem. adj. faculty Syracuse (N.Y.) U., 1970-71, Rosary Coll., River Forest, Ill., 1994—; pres. Consortium R.I. Acad. and Rsch. Librs., 1983-85; mem. bd. govs. Univ. Press New England, 1987-89; mem. exec. bd. Ill. Libr. Computer Sys. Orgn., 1995—; chair Coun. Dirs. State Univ. Librs., 1994-95. Author: Books for Sammies: American Library Association and World War I, 1981, American Library History: A Bibliography of Dissertations and Theses, 1988, Higher Education in American Life, 1636-1986: A Bibliography of Dissertations and Theses, 1988, Cities and Towns in American History: A Bibliography of Doctoral Dissertations, 1989, Academic Libraries: Research Perspectives, 1990, Religion and the American Experience, 1620-1900: A Bibliography of Doctoral Dissertations, 1992, Religion and the American Experience, the Twentieth Century: A Bibliography of Doctoral Dissertations, 1994; editl. bd. various jours. Chair Coun. of Dirs. Ill. State Univ. Librs., 1994-95. Served to capt. USAF, 1964-68. Recipient Berner Nash award U. Ill., 1976. Mem. ALA (chmn. editorial bd., chair Libr. Rsch. Seminar I, 1996), Assn. Coll. and Rsch. Librs. (publs. in librarianship 1982-88, chmn. Jesse H. Shera Endowment Fund com. 1991-94), S.C. Libr. Assn. (chmn. libr. adminstrn. sect. 1991-92), Assn. Rsch. Librs. (scholarly commn. com. 1991-93), Orgn. Am. Historians, Am. Hist. Assn., Phi Kappa Phi, Beta Phi Mu, Phi Delta Kappa. Episcopalian. Home: 912 Borden Ave Sycamore IL 60178-3200

YOUNG, BARBARA, psychiatrist, psychoanalyst, psychiatry educator, photographer; b. Chgo., Oct. 27, 1920; d. William Harvey and Blanche (DeBra) Y. AB, Knox Coll., 1942; MD, Johns Hopkins U., 1945; grad., Balt. Psychoanalytic Inst., 1955. Intern Univ. Hosps., Iowa City, Iowa, 1945-46, asst. resident in neurologh, 1945-47; asst. resident in psychiatry Phipps Clinic, Johns Hopkins U. Hosp., Balt., 1947-49; staff psychiatrist Perry Point (Md.) VA Hosp., 1949-51; practice medicine specializing in psychiatry/psychoanalysis Balt., 1951—; instr. Johns Hopkins U., 1953-69, asst. prof. psychiatry, 1969—; asst. prof. emeritus, photographer, 1958—; lectr. dept. psychiatry Johns Hopkins U.; lectr. Lucy Daniels Found., Carey, N.C., local psychiat. and social orgns. Works represented in Mus. Modern Art, N.Y.C., Balt. Mus. Art, Santa Barbara (Calif.) Mus. Art, Eastman House, Rochester, N.Y., Yale U. Gallery of Art; photographer: The Plop-A-Lop Tree, 1995. Mem. Am. Psychoanlytic Assn., Am. Psychiat. Assn., Balt.-Washington Soc. for Psychoanalysis. Democrat. Address: 5307 Herring Run Dr Baltimore MD 21214-1937

YOUNG, BARNEY THORNTON, lawyer; b. Chillicothe, Tex., Aug. 10, 1934; s. Bayne and Helen Irene (Thornton) Y.; m. Sarah Elizabeth Taylor, Aug. 31, 1957; children: Jay Thornton, Sarah Elizabeth, Serena Taylor. BA, Yale U., 1955; LLB, U. Tex., 1958. Bar: Tex. 1958. Assoc. Thompson, Knight, Wright & Simmons, Dallas, 1958-65; ptnr. Rain, Harrell, Emery, Young & Doke, Dallas, 1965-87; mem. firm Locke Purnell Rain Harrell (A Profl. Corp.), 1987—; bd. dirs. Jones-Blair Co. Mem. adv. coun. Dallas Cmty. Chest Trust Fund, Inc., 1964-66; bd. dirs. Mental Health Assn. Dallas County, Inc., 1969-72, Trammell Crow Family Found., 1984-87; trustee Hockaday Sch., Dallas, 1971-77, 90—, chmn., 1994-96, Dallas Zool. Soc., 1986-92, Lamplighter Sch., Dallas, 1976—, chmn., 1983-86, St. Mark's Sch., Dallas, 1970—, pres., 1976-78, The Found. for Callier Ctr. and Comm. Disorders, 1988—, Friends of Ctr. for Human Nutrition, 1988—, Shelter Ministries of Dallas Found., 1993—, Dallas Hist. Soc., 1993—; mem. Yale Devel. Bd., 1984-91. Fellow Tex. Bar Found., Dallas Bar Found.; mem. ABA, Tex. Bar Assn., Dallas Bar Assn., Am. Judicature Soc., Order of Coif, Phi Beta Kappa, Pi Sigma Alpha, Phi Gamma Delta, Phi Delta Phi, Dallas Country Club., Petroleum Club (Dallas), Yale Club (Dallas, N.Y.C.). Home: 6901 Turtle Creek Blvd Dallas TX 75205-1251 Office: Locke Purnell Rain Harrell 2200 Ross Ave Dallas TX 75201

YOUNG, BETTY MAE, special education educator; b. Winona, Miss., Sept. 27, 1957; d. Robert Wall and Pearlie Mae (McCarrell) Y. BS in Edn., Jackson State U., 1978, MS in Edn., 1979. Cert. Nat. Reach Trainer. Tchr. Unified Sch. Dist. 501, Topeka, 1980—; first asst. coach volleyball Jardine Mid. Sch., Topeka, 1986—, advisor to leader base team, 1987-96, spl. svcs. rep. sch. site adv. coun., 1992—, head track coach 1990—, tng. team multicultural curriculum, 1991—, staff devel. trainer 1992—, rep. spl. edn. component outcomes based staff devel. tng. team, 1992, dept. head spl. edn. Named Disting. Mid. Sch. Tchr., Selection Com., Topeka, 1990-91; recipient Bldrs. award Topeka Pks. and Recreation, 1991. Mem. NEA (chpt. v.p. 1991-93), Topeka Alliance Black Sch. Educators (memberships chairperson 1990—, conv. chairperson 1993, Disting. Black Educator 1993, pres. elect 1994—), Kansans of Color (planning com. 1992-96). Avocations: reading, exercising, shopping, decorating, social activities. Home: PO Box 4274 Topeka KS 66604-0274 Office: Jardine Mid Sch 260 SW 23rd St Topeka KS 66611

YOUNG, BETTYE JEANNE, retired secondary education educator; b. Chgo., Nov. 2, 1929; d. Frank M. Forbish and Mary Bernice (Phillips) Lunde; m. Dale Eugene Young, July 22, 1950; 1 child, Debra Jeanne. AA, Vallejo Jr. Coll., 1964; BA in History, Dominican Coll., 1968. Tchr. North

Star Elem., Anchorage, 1978; tchr. Inlet View Elem., Anchorage, 1978-82, tchr.-in-charge, 1979-82; tchr. Ctrl. Jr. High Sch., Anchorage, 1982—, chair social studies dept., 1994-95; vol. tchr. reading and math. Anacortes Elem. Sch., 1997—; chairperson N.W. Accreditation for Ctrl. Jr. High Sch., 1983; mem. Supt.'s Apprasal Com., Anchorage, 1983-85, Anchorage Sch. Dist.'s Talent Bank, 1979-93, Social Studies Curriculum Com., 1979-95, exec. bd. State Coun. Social Studies, 1990-92; chair social study dept. Ctrl. Jr. H.S., 1994—, established youth ct. Author: Thematic Approach to U.S. History, 1989 (Merit award Alaska State Dept.), Immigration Unit for U.S. History, 1988 (Merit award Alaska State Dept.), others in field. Voter registrar, Anchorage, 1984; del. Rep. Caucus, Fairbanks, Alaska, 1984; facilitator marriage seminars, Anchorage, 1989-90; mem. Ch. choir, music dept., Anchorage, 1978-93; mem. adv. bd. Law Related Edn., Anchorage, 1993-94; bd. dirs. Alaska Jr. Coll., 1993-94; vol. reading and math. tchr. elem. schs.; vol. Anacortes Aux. Patrol Police, 1995—. Named Tchr. of Month Anchorage Sch. Dist., 1981; recipient Jr. Achievement Appreciation award, Project Bus., 1987-92, Support of Social Studies award, Alaska Dept. Edn., 1991, 92; grantee Law Related Edn. Fed. Govt., ABA, 1990-94. Mem. NEA, Anchorage Edn. Assn. (chair instrnl. profl. devel. 1984-85), Anchorage Area Social Studies Coun. (sec. 1983-84, v.p. 1988-90, pres. 1990-92), Nat. Coun. Social Studies, Alaska Coun. Social Studies (secondary tch. of the yr. 1991), Phi Delta Kappa (Cook Inlet chpt., v.p. 1990-92), Delta Kappa Gamma. Avocations: travel, camping, motorcycle riding, reading, writing. Home: 3909 W 6th St Anacortes WA 98221-1295 Office: Ctrl Jr High Sch 1405 E St Anchorage AK 99501-5047

YOUNG, BRYANT COLBY, football player; b. Chicago Heights, Ill., Jan. 27, 1972. Student, Notre Dame U. Defensive tackle San Francisco 49ers, 1994—. Named to Pro Bowl, 1996. Office: care San Francisco 49ers 4948 Centennial Blvd Santa Clara CA 95054-1229*

YOUNG, BRYANT LLEWELLYN, lawyer, business executive; b. Rockford, Ill., Mar. 9, 1948; s. Llewellyn Anker and Florence Ruth Y. AB, Cornell U., 1970; JD, Stanford U., 1974. Bar: Calif. 1974, Nev. 1975, D.C. 1979. Law clk. U.S. Dist. Ct. (no. dist.) Calif., San Francisco, 1974-75; assoc. Dinkelspiel, Pelavin, Steefel & Levitt, San Francisco, 1975-77; White House fellow, spl. asst. to sec. HUD, Washington, 1977-78, spl. asst. to sec., 1978-79, acting dep. exec. asst. for ops. Office of Sec., 1979; dep. gen. mgr. New Community Devel. Corp., 1979, acting gen. mgr., 1979-80; mgmt. cons. AVCO Corp., 1980; spl. asst. to chmn. bd. and chief exec. officer U.S. Synthetic Fuels Corp., Washington, 1980-81, project dir., 1981; pres. Trident Mgmt. Corp., San Francisco, 1981-87; of counsel Pelavin, Norberg, Harlick & Beck, San Francisco, 1981-82, ptnr., 1982-87; mng. ptnr. bus. section Carroll, Burdick & McDonough, San Francisco, 1987-90; founding ptnr. Young, Vogl & Harlick, San Francisco, 1990-93, Young, Vogl, Harlick, Wilson & Simpson, LLP, San Francisco, 1993—; pres. Young Enterprises, Inc., 1995—. Mem. pub. affairs com. San Francisco Aid Retarded Citizens, Inc., 1977; U.S. co-chmn. New Towns Working Group, U.S.-USSR Agreement on Cooperation in Field of Housing and Other Constrn., 1979-80; treas., bd. dirs. White House Fellows Found., 1980-84; prin. Coun. Excellence in Govt., Washington, 1986-94; mem. adv. com. Nat. Multi-Housing Coun., 1987-92; mem. Ross Sch. Found., 1994—, sec., 1995—; mem. bd. dirs. Marin AIDS Project, 1996—, sec., 1997—. Mem. ABA (real property, trust and probate law sects. 1975-96), White House Fellows Assn. (chmn. ann. meeting 1979, del. China 1980), Am. Field Svc. Returnees Assn., Can.-Am. C. of C. No. Calif. (v.p., bd. dirs. 1992—), Chile-Calif. Found. (mem. exec. com., bd. dirs. 1993-96). Office: 425 California St Ste 2500 San Francisco CA 94104-2210

YOUNG, C. CLIFTON, judge; b. Nov. 7, 1922, Lovelock, Nev.; m. Jane Young. BA, U. Nev., 1943; LLB, Harvard U., 1949. Bar: Nev. 1949, U.S. Dist. Ct. Nev. 1950, U.S. Supreme Ct. 1955. Justice Nev. Supreme Ct., Carson City, 1985—, chief justice, 1989-90. Office: Nev Supreme Ct 201 S Carson St Carson City NV 89701-4702

YOUNG, C. W. (BILL YOUNG), congressman; b. Harmarville, PA, Dec. 16, 1930; m. Beverly Young; children: Robert, Billy, Patrick. Mem. Fla. Legislature, 1960-70, 92nd-105th Congresses from 10th dist. Fla., 1971—, Fla. Constn. Revision Commn., 1965-67; chmn. So. Hwy. Policy Com., 1966-68; mem. Electoral Coll., 1968; mem. appropriations com., chmn. sub-com. Def., Labor, HHS and Edn. Fla. Legislature. Named Most Valuable Senator, Capitol Press Corps, 1969. Methodist. Office: US Ho Reps 2407 Rayburn Ho Office Bldg Washington DC 20515-0910

YOUNG, CAPRICE YVONNE, municipal official; b. Palo Alto, Calif., Oct. 11, 1965; d. Michael G. and Nancy (Schwartz) Y. BA in History with Stats., Yale U., 1988; MPA in Pub. Fin., U. So. Calif., 1991. Coro Pub. Policy fellow Coro Found., 1988-89; dir. tng. Liaison Citizen Program, L.A., 1989-90; chief mgmt. analyst, fin. and adminstrn. L.A. County Transp. Commn., 1990-93; special asst. to CEO Met. Transp. Authority, 1993-94; asst. deputy mayor City of L.A., 1994-97; mgmt. cons. IBM Global Svcs., 1997—. Author: Local Youth Group Programs, 1985, Giving Sanctuary, 1986. Gant rev. panel mem. fund for a Just Soc., 1992—; bd. sec. Liaison Citizen Program, 1990-94; 2d v.p. SFV Mental Health Ctr., 1993-96; bd. dirs. Hollygrove, 1993—. Mem. Govt. Fin. Officers' Assn., Am. Soc. Pub. Adminstrn., Yale Club So. Calif. Avocations: sailing, scuba. Home: 3750 Lankershim Blvd Los Angeles CA 90068-1220 Office: City of L A 17th Fl 355 S Grand Ave Los Angeles CA 90071

YOUNG, CHARLES EDWARD, university chancellor; b. San Bernardino, Calif., Dec. 30, 1931; s. Clayton Charles and Eula May (Walters) Y. AA, San Bernardino Coll., 1954; AB, U. Calif., Riverside, 1955; MA, UCLA, 1957, PhD, 1960; DHL (hon.), U. Judaism, L.A., 1969. Congl. fellow Washington, 1958-59; adminstrv. analyst Office of the Pres., U. Calif., Berkeley, 1959-60; asst. prof. polit. sci. U. Calif., Davis, 1960; asst. prof. polit. sci. UCLA, 1960-66, assoc. prof., 1966-69, prof., 1969—, asst. to chancellor, 1960-62, asst. chancellor, 1962-63, vice chancellor, adminstrn., 1963-68, chancellor, 1968—; bd. dirs. Intel Corp., Acad. TV Arts and Sci. Found.; cons. Peace Corps., 1961-62, Ford Found. on Latin Am. Activities, 1964-66; mem. bd. govs. L.A. Met. Project. Mem. Knight Found. Commn. on Intercollegiate Athletics, Calif. Coun. on Sci. and Tech., Town Hall of Calif., Carnegie Comm. Task Force on Sci. and Tech. and the States, Pacific Coun. on Internat. Policy, NCAA Pres.'s Commn., Coun. for Govt.-Univ.-Industry Rsch. Roundtable and the Nat. Rsch. Coun. Adv. Bd.-Issues in Sci. and Tech., Nat. Com. on U.S.-China Rels., chancellor's assocs. UCLA, coun. trustees L.A. Ednl. Alliance for Restructuring Now; past chair. Assn. Am. Univs., Nat. Assn. State Univs. and Land-Grant Colls.; past co-chair Calif. Campus Compact; mem. adminstrv. bd. Internat. Assn. Univs.; bd. govs. Found. Internat. Exchange Sci. and Cultural Info. by Telecom., The Theatre Group Inc.; v.p. Young Musicians Found.; bd. dirs. L.A. Internat. Visitors Coun., Greater L.A. Energy Coalition, L.A. World Affairs Coun.; trustee UCLA Found. With USAF, 1951-52. Named Young Man of Year Westwood Jr. C. of C., 1962; recipient Inter-Am. U. Cooperaton award Inter-Am. Orgn. Higher Edn., Neil H. Jacoby Internat. award UCLA Student Ctr., 1987, Edward A. Dickson Alumnus of Yr. award UCLA Alumni Assn., 1994, Disting. Svc. award U. Calif. Riverside Alumni Assn., 1996, Treasure of L.A. award L.A. Ctrl. City Assn., 1996, Albert Schweitzer Leadership award Hugh O'Brien Youth Found., 1996; hon. fellow UCLA Coll. Letters and Sci., 1996. Fellow AAAS. Office: UCLA Office of Chancellor 405 Hilgard Ave Los Angeles CA 90095-9000

YOUNG, CHARLES RANDALL, software professional; b. Phila., Dec. 18, 1950; s. Charles Calvin and Henrietta Emma (Sorber) Y.; m. Mary Frances Hoey, June 8, 1973. BS with honors in Math., Drexel U., 1973; MS in Computer and Info. Sci., Ohio State U., 1975. Programmer coop Princeton (N.J.) Time Sharing Svcs., 1969-71; grad. tchg. asst. Ohio State U., Columbus, 1973-75; compiler programmer Burroughs, Paoli, Pa., 1975-76; simulation programmer Sperry, Blue Bell, Pa., 1976-78, computer security lead programmer, designer, 1978-84, operating sys. group mgr., 1984-89; disk program devel. mgr. Unisys, Blue Bell, Pa., 1989-91, compiler and posix program mgr., 1991-93, open/oltp program mktg. mgr., 1993-94, superserver and internet product and mktg. mgr., 1995—. Contbr. articles to profl. jours. Mem. IEEE, Assn. Shareware Profls. Reformed Episcopal. Avocations: swimming, opera, church bass soloist, tennis. Home: 412 Norristown Rd Ambler PA 19002-2737 Office: Unisys PO Box 500 Blue Bell PA 19424-0001

YOUNG, CHRISTOPHER, composer. Scores include (films) The Dorm That Dripped Blood, 1982, Robbie, 1982, The Power, 1983, Savage Hunter, 1984, Highpoint, 1984, Wheels of Fire, 1984, Avenging Angel, 1984, Def-Con 4, 1985, Wizards of the Lost Kingdom, 1985, Barbarian Queen, 1985, Nightmare on Elm Street Part II: Freddy's Revenge, 1985, Godzilla 1985, 1985, Torment, 1986, Getting Even, 1986, Invaders from Mars, 1986, Trick or Treat, 1986, Hellraiser, 1987, Flowers in the Attic, 1987, The Telephone, 1987, Bat-21, 1988, Haunted Summer, 1988, Hellbound: Hellraiser II, 1988, The Fly II, 1989, Hider in the House, 1989, Bright Angel, 1991, The Five Heartbeats, 1991, The Vagrant, 1992, The Dark Half, 1992, Rapid Fire, 1992, Jennifer Eight, 1992, Sliver, 1993, Dream Lover, 1994, Murder in the First, 1995, (TV movies) American Harvest, 1987, Last Flight Out, 1990, Max and Helen, 1990, Murder in the First, 1994, Judicial Consent, 1995, Tales From the Hood, 1995, Species, 1995, Virtuosity, 1995, Copycate, 1995, Unforgettable, 1996, Norma Jean and Marilyn, 1996, Head Above Water, 1996, Set it Off, 1996, Murder at 1600, 1997, The Flood, 1997. Address: 1422 Abbot Kinney Blvd Venice CA 90291-3741

YOUNG, DALE LEE, banker; b. Palmyra, Nebr., Mar. 13, 1928; s. Mike P. and Grace (Clutter) Y.; m. Norma Marie Shalla, June 18, 1950; children—Shalla Ann, Philip Mike. B.B.A., U. Nebr., 1950. With FirsTier Bank N.A. (formerly First Nat. Bank & Trust Co.), Lincoln, Nebr., 1950-91, cashier, 1966-91, v.p., 1966-76, exec. v.p., 1976-92; sec. ISCO, Inc., Lincoln, 1991—, also bd. dirs.; bd. dirs. Woodmen Accident and Life Co.; sec., bd. dirs. Leasing Corp. Treas. Lincoln City Library Found.; Treas., mem. exec. com. Nebr. Republican Com., 1968—; bd. dirs., v.p. Lincoln Symphony; bd. dirs. Lincoln Community Services, ARC, Lincoln Found.; trustee Bryan Meml. Hosp., 1976-80; mem. Lincoln City Coun., 1991—. Served with AUS, 1946-48, 50-51. Mem. Nebr. Art Assn., Omaha-Lincoln Soc. Fin. Analysts, Lincoln C. of C. (pres.), Theta Xi. Presbyterian. Clubs: Nebraska, Lincoln Country, Univ. Home: 2627 Park Ave Lincoln NE 68502-4023 Office: PO Box 81008 Lincoln NE 68501-1008

YOUNG, DAVID MICHAEL, biochemistry and molecular biology educator, physician; b. Bluffton, Ind., Oct. 11, 1935; s. Eli and Ruth (Comer) Y.; m. Diane Tangeman, Dec. 28, 1957 (div. 1971); children: Peter Michael, Amy Katherine; m. Lucia Virginia Patat, Sept. 2, 1972; children: David Michael II, Allison Amelia. B.S., Duke U., 1957, M.D., 1959. Diplomate: Nat. Bd. Med. Examiners. Intern pediatrics dept. Duke U. Med. Ctr., Durham, N.C., 1958-60; staff scientist Lab Cellular Physiology and Metabolism Nat. Heart Inst., NIH, 1960-62; vis. scientist McCollum-Pratt Inst., Johns Hopkins U., Balt., 1962-63, asst. prof. biology, 1963-64; asst. prof. Harvard U. Med. Sch., Boston, 1965-72, assoc. prof. Biol. chemistry, 1972-79, tutor biochem. scis., 1966-76, mem. grad. program for advanced study in immunology, 1971-76, assoc. chmn. div. med. scis., chmn. program for cell biology, 1972-76; head Lab Phys. Biochemistry Mass. Gen. Hosp., Boston, 1965-79; prof. biochemistry U. Fla. Coll. Medicine, Gainesville, 1979—, prof. medicine, 1979-86, chmn. dept. biochemistry and molecular biology, 1979-81, prof. molecular biology, 1981-86, prof. pediatrics, 1986—; mem. cell physiology study sect. NIH, Bethesda, Md., 1978-82, sect. chmn., 1980; acad. assoc. Nichols Inst., San Juan Capistrano, Calif., 1976—; vis. prof. biology Johns Hopkins U., 1994, 95. Editor-in-chief: Jour. Molecular and Cellular Biochemistry, 1983—; patentee nerve growth factor, nerve growth factor antibody. Served to sr. surgeon USPHS, 1959-63. USPHS spl. fellow, 1962; recipient career devel. award USPHS, 1967-72; NIHresearch grantee, 1964—; grantee John A. Hartford Found., 1968-73. Fellow AAAS; mem. Am. Soc. Biol. Chemists, Am. Chem. Soc., Biophys. Soc., Am. Soc. for Clin. Investigation, Am. Heart Assn. (research allocations com. 1976-79), Am. Soc. for Cell Biology, Alpha Omega Alpha. Home: 2106 NW 27th Ter Gainesville FL 32605-3873 Office: Dept Biochemistry and Molecular Biology Coll Medicine U Fla Gainesville FL 32610

YOUNG, DAVID NELSON, media and business consultant; b. Baton Rouge, Nov. 12, 1953; s. Nelson Joseph and Agnes (LeBlanc) Young; m. Michéle Marie-Therese Bedél, May 7, 1979; children: Jason, Jessica. Student, La. State U., 1972, U. S.W. La., 1975. News editor Gonzales (La.) Weekly, 1976-77; prs. D.N. Young & Assocs., Inc., Gonzales, Washington, Moscow, 1977—; organizer Soviet/Am. Culinary Exch., 1989, Soviet/Am. High Sch. Basketball Excha., 1990; cons. in field. Host, Ascension Jour. TV Show. Bd. dirs. Ascension Cancer/Leukemia Soc., Gonzales, 1978—, Ctr. for Russian/Am. Bus., Washington, 1992; organizer Soviet/Am. High Sch. Basketball Exch.; nat. committeeman La. Dem. Ctrl. Com., 1996. Recipient Best-in-Depth Reporting award La. Newspaper Assn., 1984, Appreciation award USIA, 1988, Sovincentr Medal Honor, Moscow World Trade Ctr., 1988. Mem. East Ascension Genealogical Soc. (pres. 1980-81), East Ascension Sportsman League. Roman Catholic. Avocations: reading, computing, cooking. Office: Young Communications Group LLC 203 W Ascension St Gonzales LA 70737-2803

YOUNG, DAVID POLLOCK, humanities educator, author; b. Davenport, Iowa, Dec. 14, 1936; s. Cecil T. and Mary Ella (Pollock) Y.; m. Chloe Hamilton, June 17, 1963 (dec. Feb. 1985); children—Newell Hamilton, Margaret Helen; m. Georgia L. Newman, Dec. 31, 1989. B.A., Carleton Coll., 1958; M.A., Yale, 1959, Ph.D., 1965. Faculty dept. English Oberlin Coll., 1961—, prof., 1973—, Longman prof. of English, 1986—; Translator. Author: Something of Great Constancy: the Art of "A Midsummer Night's Dream", 1965, Sweating Out the Winter, 1969, The Heart's Forest: Shakespeare's Pastoral Plays, 1972, Boxcars, 1973, Work Lights: 32 Prose Poems, 1977, Rilke's Duino Elegies, 1978, The Names of A Hare in English, 1979, (with Stuart Friebert) A Field Guide to Contemporary Poetry and Poetics, 1980, Four T'ang Poets, 1980, (with Stuart Friebert and David Walker) Valuable Nail: Selected Poems of Günter Eich, 1981, (with Dana Hábová) Interferon, or On Theater, Poems by Miroslav Holub, 1982, (with Keith Hollaman) Magical Realist Fiction, 1984; editor: (with Stuart Friebert and David Walker) Field: Contemporary Poetry & Poetics, (with Stuart Friebert) The Longman Anthology of Contemporary American Poetry, 1983, Foraging, 1986, Troubled Mirror: A Study of Yeats's The Tower, 1987, Sonnets to Orpheus, Rainer Maria Rilke, 1987, THe Heights of Macchu Picchu, 1987, Earthshine, 1988, Five T'ang Poets, 1990, The Action to the Word: Structure and Style in Shakespearean Tragedy, 1990, (with Dana Hábová) Vanishing Lung Syndrome Poems by Miroslav Holub, 1990, The Planet on the Desk: Selected and New Poems, 1960-90, 1991, Shakespeare's Middle Tragedies: New Century Views, 1992, The Book of Fresh Beginnings: Selected Poems of Rainer Maria Rilke, 1994, Night Thoughts and Henry Vaughan, 1994, (with Stuart Friebert) Models of the Universe, an Anthology of the Prose Poem, 1995; editor: FIELD, Contemporary Poetry and Poetics, 1969—, contbr. poetry to lit. publs. Recipient U.S. award Internat. Poetry Forum, 1969, Ohio Individual Artist award, 1990; Guggenheim fellow, NEA fellow. Office: Oberlin Coll Dept English Oberlin OH 44074*

YOUNG, DAVID WILLIAM, accounting educator; b. L.A., Feb. 8, 1942; s. William Albert and Hilda Mary (Cook) Y.; m. Ernestine M.L. Van Schaik, Oct. 4, 1968 (div. 1975); m. Francesca Michela Larson, Jan. 28, 1984; children: Christian William, Anthony Edwin. BA, Occidental Coll., 1963; MA, UCLA, 1966; D in Bus. Adminstrn., Harvard U., 1977. Systems engr. IBM, Glendale, Calif., 1963-64; asst. to pres. Lundberg Survey, Inc., Hollywood, Calif., 1964-66; program economist U.S. AID, El Salvador, 1966-69; cons. Thomas Goldsmith & Assoc., Cambridge, Mass., 1969-71; mng. dir. Commonwealth Mgmt. Sys., Cambridge, 1971—; assoc. prof. mgmt. Harvard U. Sch. Pub. Health, Boston, 1976-85, cons. faculty mem., 1985—; prof. acctg. and control Boston U. Sch. Mgmt., 1985—, chmn. dept. acctg., 1986-91, dir. acctg. MBA program, 1989-93, dir. inst. acctg. rsch. and edn., 1989-93, dir. health care mgmt. program, 1991-94; prin. The Crimson Group, Cambridge, 1994—; vis. prof. mgmt. control Instituto de Estudios Superiores de la Empresa, Barcelona, Spain, 1984. Author: The Managerial Process in Human Service Agencies, 1979, Financial Control in Health Care, 1984, The Hospital Power Equilibrium, 1985, Management Control in Nonprofit Organizations, 1984, 88, 94, Introduction to Financial and Management Accounting: A User Perspective, 1994; contbr. articles to profl. jours. Trustee Roxbury Comprehensive Cmty. Health Ctr., 1983-86, Art Inst., Boston, 1990-96, Mass. Eye and Ear Infirmary, Boston, 1990-92, Symmes Hosp., Arlington, 1993-94, The Atrium Sch., 1995-97, Youville Hosp., 1997—; commr., chair Mass. Hosp. Payment Sys., 1992-95. Milton Fund fellow Harvard Med. Sch., 1984. Mem. Am. Acctg. Assn., Am. Econ. Assn. Democrat. Office: Boston U Sch Mgmt 595 Commonwealth Ave Boston MA 02215-1704

YOUNG, DER-LIANG FRANK, civil engineering educator, researcher; b. Chia-Yi, Taiwan, Jan. 4, 1946; s. Wu-Shang and Lee-Rang (Lee) Y.; m. Ching-Ju Yu, Aug. 29, 1971; children: Jacqueline, James. BS, Nat. Taiwan U., 1968, MS, 1971; MS, Calif. Inst. Tech., 1972; PhD, Cornell U., 1976. Registered profl. engr., Ill. Rsch. assoc. Cornell U., Ithaca, N.Y., 1975-76; sr. engr. Harza Engrng. Co., Chgo., 1976-81, Nortech Engrng. Co., Irvine, Calif., 1981-83; sr. mem. tech. staff Rockwell Internat., Canoga Park, Calif., 1983; assoc. prof. Nat. Taiwan U., 1983-84, prof., 1984—; vis. assoc. prof. Nat. Taiwan U., 1978-79, dir. Hydraulic Rsch. Lab., 1985-91; adj. prof. Centry U., Beverly Hills, Calif., 1982-83; vis. expert Sinotech Engrng. Corp., Taipei, 1991-92; examiner Dept. Examination, Taipei, 1988-97; cons. to Gov., Taipei County Govt., 1989-97; advisor Nat. Sci. and Tech. Mus., Kaohsiung, Taiwan, 1986-94. Contbr. articles to books and profl. jours. Judge Outstanding Youth Medal Award, Taipei, 1990-91. Served to 2d lt. Chinese Army, 1968-69. Recipient Disting. Rsch. award Nat. Sci. Coun. Republic of China, 1992—, Disting. Leadership award Am. Biog. Inst., 1989. Mem. Internat. Assn. for Hydraulic Rsch. (coun. Asian and Pacific div. 1988-95), Am. Geophys. Union, Chinese Inst. Civil and Hydraulic Engrs. (coun. water resources engring. 1985-96). Avocations: swimming, hiking, baseball, fishing, reading. Office: Nat Taiwan U Dept Civil Engring, 1 sec 4 Roosevelt Rd, 10617 Taipei Taiwan

YOUNG, DONALD ALAN, physician; b. Oakland, Calif., Feb. 8, 1939; s. Leo Alan and Pearl Anita (Walker) Y.; children: Jennifer, Karen. B.A., U. Calif., Berkeley, 1960, M.D., 1964. Diplomate Am. Bd. Internal Medicine. Intern, then resident in internal medicine U. Calif. Hosp., San Francisco, 1964-66; resident in internal medicine Parkland Hosp., Dallas, 1966-67; fellow chest diseases U. Calif. Hosp., San Francisco, 1967-68; mem. staff Palo Alto (Calif.) Med. Clinic, 1970-75; med. dir. Am. Lung Assn., 1975-77; scholar adminstrv. scholars program VA, Washington, 1977-80; dep. dir. policy Bur. Program Policy, Health Care Financing Adminstrn. HHS, Washington; exec. dir. Prospective Payment Assessment Commn., Washington, 1984—; clin. instr. U. Calif. Med. Sch., San Francisco, 1968-70, Stanford U. Med. Sch., 1970-75. Trustee Vt. Lung Center; bd. dirs. Mid-Md. Lung Assn. Served with M.C. AUS, 1968-70. Decorated Commendation medal.; Recipient Borden award, 1964. Home: 5495 Vantage Point Rd Columbia MD 21044-2637 Office: 300 7th St SW Suite 301B Washington DC 20024

YOUNG, DONALD E., congressman; b. Meridian, Calif., June 9, 1933; m. Lula Fredson; children—Joni, Dawn. AA, Yuba Jr. Coll., 1952; BA ., Chico (Calif.) State Coll., 1958. Former educator, river boat capt.; mem. Fort Yukon City Council, 6 years, mayor, 4 years; mem. Alaska Ho. of Reps., 1966-70, Alaska Senate, 1970-73, 93rd-104th Congresses from Alaska, 1973—; mem. transp. & infrastructure com., chmn. resources com. With U.S. Army, 1955-57. Republican. Episcopalian. Office: US House of Representatives 2111 Rayburn Bldg Ofc B Washington DC 20515-0201

YOUNG, DONALD FREDRICK, engineering educator; b. Joplin, Mo., Apr. 27, 1928; s. Oral Solomon and Blanche (Trent) Y.; m. Gertrude Ann Cooper, Apr. 15, 1950; children: Michael, Pamela, Susan, Christopher, David. B.S., Iowa State U., 1951, M.S., 1952, Ph.D., 1956. Research engr. AEC Ames Lab., 1952-55; asst. prof. Iowa State U., Ames, 1955-58, assoc. prof., 1958-61, prof. engrng. sci. and mechanics, 1961-74, Anson Marston Disting. prof. engrng., 1974—. Author: Introduction to Applied Mechanics, 1972, (with others) Essentials of Mechanics, 1974, (with others) Fundamentals of Fluid Mechanics, 1990, 2d edit., 1994, A Brief Introduction to Fluid Mechanics, 1997; contbr. articles to profl. jours. Recipient Outstanding Tchr. award Standard Oil, 1971, Faculty citation Iowa State Alumni Assn., 1972, Spl. Recognition award Iowa State U. Rsch. Found., 1988, David R. Boylan Eminent award for rsch., 1995. Fellow ASME (chmn. bioengrng. div. 1973-74); mem. Am. Heart Assn., Am. Soc. Engrng. Edn., Pi Tau Sigma, Pi Mu Epsilon, Phi Kappa Phi, Sigma Xi. Home: 2042 Prairie Vw E Ames IA 50010-4558 Office: Iowa State U 3023 Black Engr Ames IA 50010

YOUNG, DONALD STIRLING, clinical pathology educator; b. Belfast, N. Ireland, Dec. 17, 1933; s. John Stirling and Ruth Muir (Whipple) Y.; m. Silja Meret; children: Gordon, Robert, Peter. MB, ChB, U. Aberdeen, Scotland, 1957; PhD in Chem. Pathology, U. London, 1962. Terminable lectr. materia medica U. Aberdeen, 1958-59; fellow Postgrad. Med. Sch., U. London, 1959-62, registrar, 1962-64; vis. scientist NIH, Bethesda, Md., 1965-66; chief clin. chemistry service NIH, 1966-77; head clin. chemistry sect. Mayo Clinic, Rochester, Minn., 1977-84; prof. pathology and lab. medicine U. Pa., 1984—; dir. William Pepper Lab. Hosp. of U. Pa., 1984—; past bd. dirs. Nat. Com. Clin. Lab. Standards. Co-editor: Drug Interference and Drug Metabolism in Clinical Chemistry, 1976, Clinician and Chemist, 1979, Chemical Diagnosis of Disease, 1979, Drug Measurement and Drug Effects in Laboratory Health Science, 1980, Interpretation of Clinical Laboratory Tests, 1985, Effects of Drugs on Clinical Laboratory Tests, 1995, Effects of Preanalytical Variables on Clinical Laboratory Tests, 1996. Recipient Dir.'s award NIH, 1977, Gerard B. Lambert award, 1974-75, MDS Health Group award Can. Soc. Clin. Chemists, 1978; Roman lectr. Australian Assn. Clin. Biochemists, 1979; Jendrassik award Hungarian Soc. Clin. Pathologists, 1985, ATB award Italian Soc. Clin. Biochemistry, 1987. Mem. Am. Assn. Clin. Chemistry (J.H. Roe award Capital sect. 1973, Bernard Gerulat award N.J. sect. 1977, Ames award 1977, Van Slyke award N.Y. met. sect. 1985, J.G. Reinhold award Phila. sect. 1993, past pres.), Internat. Fedn. Clin. Chemists (past pres.), Acad. Clin. Lab. Physicians and Scientists (past exec. com.), Assn. Clin. Biochemists (Ciba-Corning lectr. 1985). Achievements include research in clinical chemistry, optimized use of the clinical laboratory. Home: 1116 Remington Rd Wynnewood PA 19096-4045 Office: Hosp U Pa 3400 Spruce St Philadelphia PA 19104

YOUNG, DOUGLAS, Canadian government official; b. Tracadie, Sept. 20, 1940. Min. transport Canada, 1993-1996, min. human resources development, 1996-97, min. nat. def., min. vet. affairs, 1996—. Provincial first elected to N.B. Legislature g.e., 1978, reelected g.e., 1982, 87; apptd. Min. Fisheries and Aquaculture, 1987; elected to the House of Commons g.e., 1988. Office: Human Resource Devel Nat Def Hdqs, 101 Colonel By Dr, Ottawa, ON Canada K1A 0K2 also: House Commons, Ottawa, ON Canada K1A 0A6

YOUNG, DOUGLAS REA, lawyer; b. Los Angeles, July 21, 1948; s. James Douglas and Dorothy Belle (Rea) Y.; m. Terry Forrest, Jan. 19, 1974; 1 child, Megann Forrest. BA cum laude, Yale U., 1971; JD, U. Calif.-Berkeley, 1976. Bar: Calif. 1976, U.S. Dist. Ct. (no. dist.) Calif. 1976, U.S. Ct. Appeals (6th and 9th cirs.) 1977, U.S. Dist. Ct. (cen. dist.) Calif. 1979, U.S. Dist. Ct. Hawaii, U.S. Supreme Ct. 1982. Law clk. U.S. Dist. Ct. (no. dist.) Calif., San Francisco, 1976-77; assoc. Farella, Braun & Martel, San Francisco, 1977-82, ptnr., 1983—; spl. master U.S. Dist. Ct. (no. dist.) Calif., 1977-78, 88, 96; mem. Criminal Justice Act Def. Panel no. dist. Calif.; mem. faculty Calif. Continuing Edn. of Bar, Berkeley, 1982—, Nat. Inst. Trial Advocacy, Berkeley, 1984—, Practicing Law Inst., 1988—, Hastings Coll. of Advocacy, 1985—, adj. prof., 1990; vis. lectr. law Boalt Hall/U. Calif., Berkeley, 1986; judge pro tem San Francisco Mcpl. Ct. 1984—, San Francisco Superior Ct., 1990—. Author: (with Purver and Davis) California Trial Handbook, 2d ed., (with Hon. Richard Byrne, Purver and Davis), 3d edit., (with Purver, Davis and Kerper) The Trial Lawyers Book, (with Hon. Eugene Lynch, Taylor, Purver and Davis) California Negotiation and Settlement Handbook; contbr. articles to profl. jours. Bd. dirs. Berkeley Law Found., 1977-79, chmn., 1978-79; bd. dirs. San Francisco Legal Aid Soc., pres., 1993—, Pub. Interest Clearinghouse, San Francisco, chmn., 1987—, treas. 1988—; chmn., Attys. Task Force for Child Children, Legal Services for Children, 1987—, mem. State Bar Appeciate Law Adv. Commn., 1994—. Recipient award of appreciation Berkeley Law Found., 1983. Mem. ABA (Pro Bono Pub. award 1992), San Francisco Bar Assn. (founding chmn. litigation sect. 1988-89, award of appreciation 1989, bd. dirs. 1990-91), Calif. Acad. Appellate Lawyers, Lawyers Club San Francisco. Democrat. Office: Farella Braun & Martel 235 Montgomery St Ste 3000 San Francisco CA 94104-3117

YOUNG, DWIGHT WAYNE, ancient civilization educator; b. Lambert, Okla., Dec. 15, 1925; s. Maurice Leonard and Freda Flora (Polson) Y.; m. Barbara Louise Pirtle, May 25, 1946; children: Terry Wayne, Cecilia Ann. B.A. magna cum laude, Hardin-Simmons U., Abilene, Tex., 1949; Th.M. Dallas Theol. Seminary, 1956; Ph.D., Dropsie Coll., 1955; postgrad.,

Brown U., 1959-60. Asst. prof. Brandeis U., Waltham, Mass., 1958-63, assoc. prof., 1963-67, 69-72, prof., 1972-87, prof. emeritus, 1987—; cons. Harper & Row Pubs., N.Y.C., 1958-60; vis. prof. Hebrew U., Jerusalem, Israel, 1965, Cornell U., Ithaca, N.Y., 1967-69; chief editor Pirtle Polson Pubs., Gloucester, Mass., 1980—. Author: Coptic Manuscripts from the White Monastery: Works of Shenute, 1993; editor: Studies Presented to Hans Jakob Polotsky, 1981, The Future of Coptic Studies, 1978; contbr. numerous articles and revs. on ancient civiliations to profl. jours. Served with USMC, 1943-46. Recipient Solomon award in Hebrew, Dallas Theol. Seminary, 1951; fellow in Arabic, U. Mich., 1960. Mem. Internat. Assn. for Coptic Studies. Home: 5555 N Sheridan Rd Apt 1102 Chicago IL 60640-1624 Office: Brandeis U Dept Nr Ea Studies South St Waltham MA 02154

YOUNG, EDWIN HAROLD, chemical and metallurgical engineering educator; b. Detroit, Nov. 4, 1918; s. William George and Alice Pearl (Hicks) Y.; m. Ida Signe Soma, June 25, 1944; children—David Harold, Barbara Ellen. B.S. in Chem. Engring, U. Detroit, 1942; M.S. in Chem. Engring, U. Mich., 1949, M.S. in Metall. Engring, 1952. Chem. engr. Wright Air Devel. Center, Dayton, Ohio, 1942-43; instr. U. Mich., Ann Arbor, 1946-52; asst. prof. U. Mich., 1952-56, assoc. prof., 1956-59, prof. chem. and metall. engring., 1959-89, prof. emeritus chem. and metall. engring., 1989—; Mem. Mich. Bd. Registration for Profl. Engrs., 1963-78, chmn., 1969-70, 72-73, 75-76; mem. Mich. Bd. Registration for Architects, 1963-78. Author: (with L.E. Brownell) Process Equipment Design, 1959; contbr. articles to profl. jours. Dist. commr. Boy Scouts Am., 1961-64; mem. Wolverine coun., 1965-68. With USNR, 1943-46, to capt. Res. ret., 1978. Fellow ASME, ASHRAE, Am. Inst. Chemists, Am. Inst. Chem. Engrs. (Donald Q Kern award 1979), Engring. Soc. Detroit; mem. Am. Chem. Soc., Am. Soc. Engring. Edn., Nat. Soc. Profl. Engrs. (pres. 1968-69, award 1977), Mich. Soc. Profl. Engrs. (pres. 1962-63, Engr. of Year award 1976), Mich. Assn. of Professions (pres. 1966, Distinguished award 1970), Nat. Council Engring. Examiners, Naval Res. Assn., Res. Officers Assn., Sigma Xi, Tau Beta Pi, Phi Kappa Phi, Phi Lambda Upsilon, Alpha Chi Sigma. Republican. Baptist. Home: 609 Dartmoor Rd Ann Arbor MI 48103-4513

YOUNG, EDWIN S. W., federal agency official; b. Honolulu, Nov. 13, 1943; s. Hoon Kwan and Clara (Lee) Y.; m. Joan Tay, May 19, 1978. BA, U. Hawaii, 1966; MBA, U. Utah, 1975; MS, U. So. Calif., 1983. Asst. gen. mgr. Royal Men's Shops, Inc., Honolulu, 1973-75; mgmt. analyst U.S. Gen. Acctg. Office, Denver and Honolulu, 1976-83; audit mgr. USAF Audit Agy., L.A., 1983-84, 87-90; fgn. svc. officer Dept. State, 1984-87; with Office of Insp. Gen., Office Policy & Program Rev., Washington, 1984-87; divsn. dir., asst. dir., dir. prodn. Naval Audit Svc. Western Region, Vallejo, Calif., 1990-95; desk officer, planning and policy dir. Naval Audit Svc., Washington, 1995; regional inspector gen. for auditing U.S. Small Bus. Adminstrn., L.A., 1995—, rep. World Affairs Coun. So. Calif., 1995—; U.S. govt. rep. Pacific and Asian Affairs Coun., Honolulu, 1978-83; USN audit svc. rep. World Affairs Coun. No. Calif. 1990-95; exec. dir. The Asian-Am. Found. Phoenix 1990—; SBA rep. World Affairs Coun., So. Calif. Community coord. Kailua Neighborhood Bd., Honolulu, 1978-83; area rep. Urban Mass Transit Authority, Honolulu, 1978-83; active John F. Kennedy Ctr. for Arts, Corcoran Gallery Art, L.A. County Mus. Art, San Francisco DeYoung Mus. Art. Capt. USAF, 1966-72. Recipient Commendation awards U.S. Gen. Acctg. Office, 1980, USAF Audit Agy., 1983, 88, 90, USAF Acctg. and Fin. Ctr., 1984, U.S. Naval Audit Svc. award 1992, 94, 95. Mem. Assn. Govt. Accts., Soc. Mil. Compts., Inst. Internal Auditors, Nat. Geog. Soc., Chinese C. of C., World Affairs Council, Smithsonian Inst. Roman Catholic. Avocations: photography, skiing, swimming, tennis, snorkeling.

YOUNG, ELIZABETH BELL, consultant; b. Franklinton, N.C., July 2, 1929; d. Joseph H. and Eulalia V. (Miller) B.; m. Charles A. Young, Nov. 27, 1964. BA, N.C. Cen. U., 1948, MA, 1950; PhD, Ohio State U., 1959. Cert. speech pathologist; cert. audiologist. Chairperson dept. English Barber Scotia Coll., Concord, N.C., 1949-52; dir. speech area, prof. Talladega (Ala.) Coll., 1954-56; dir. speech clinic, prof. Va. State U., Petersburg, 1956-57; prof. Fla. A&M U., Tallahassee, 1959; chmn. dept. English Fayetteville (N.C.) State U., 1959-63; speech pathologist, rsch. asst. Howard U. Sch. Dentistry, Washington, 1963-64; prof., chairperson dept. English U. Md.-East Shore, Princess Anne, Md., 1965-66; prof., supr. Speech Clinic Cath. U. Am., Washington, 1966-79; congl. staff aide U.S. Ho. of Reps., Washington, 1981-82, 88-90; prof. speech U. D.C., Washington, 1983-84; cons. nat. and local orgns. Washington, 1985-88, 90—; lectr. over 250 speeches, seminars and workshops; speechwriter, cons. Nat. Assn. Equal Opportunity in Higher Edn., Washington, 1990. Contbr. articles to profl. jours. Fundraiser, pub. rels. polit. candidates, 1963-90; mem. bd. United Negro Coll. Fund, 1970-80, D.C. Gen. Hosp. Handicapped Intervention Program, 1970-91. Recipient Citations and Certs. of Achievement community and nat. orgns., 1959-90. Fellow Am. Speech-Lang.-Hearing Assn.; mem. Pub. Mems. Assn. (bd. mem. 1980-91), Ohio State U. Alumni Assn., N.C. Cen. U. Alumni Assn. Democrat. Baptist. Avocations: reading, collecting sculpture of foreign countries, travel, writing, public speaking.

YOUNG, ESTELLE IRENE, dermatologist; b. N.Y.C., Nov. 2, 1945; d. Sidney D. and Blanche (Krosney) Young. BA magna cum laude, Mt. Holyoke Coll., 1963; MD, Downstate Med. Ctr., 1971. Intern, Lenox Hill Hosp., N.Y.C., 1971-72, resident in medicine, 1972-73; resident in dermatology Columbia Presbyn. Hosp., N.Y.C., 1973-74, NYU Med. Ctr., 1974-75, Boston U. Hosp., 1975-76; asst. dermatologist Harvard U. Health Services, Cambridge, Mass., 1975-76; assoc. staff mem. dermatology Boston U. Med. Ctr., 1976-77; practice medicine specializing in dermatology, Petersburg, Va., 1976—; mem. staff Poplar Springs Hosp., 1976—, Southside Regional Med. Ctr. (formerly Petersburg Gen. Hosp.), 1976—, Cen. State Hosp., 1984—; clin. instr. dept. dermatology Med. Coll. Va., 1976—, asst. clinic prof., 1988-94, assoc. clin. prof., 1994—; sec. med. staff Petersburg Gen. Hosp., 1982—. Fellow Am. Acad. Dermatology; mem. Va. Med. Soc., Va. Dermatology Soc., Tidewater Dermatology Soc. (pres. 1982-83), Physicians for Social Responsiblity Soc., Tidewater Physicians for Social Responsibility (pres. 1990—), Internat. Physicians for Prevention of Nuclear War, Southside Va. Med. Soc., Sigma Xi. Contbr. articles to profl. jours. Home: 2319 Monument Ave Richmond VA 23220-2603 Office: 612A S Sycamore St Petersburg VA 23803-5828

YOUNG, EVERETT J., management consultant, agricultural economist; b. Webberville, Mich., Mar. 14, 1913; s. J.P. and Ullie Jospehine (Sigourney) Y.; m. Irene Elizabeth Olick, June 18, 1949. BS in Agrl., Mich. State U., 1939, MBA, 1960. Field rep. Mich. Fam Bur., Lansing, Mich., 1940-45; asst. exec. sec. Mich. Assn. Farmer Coops., Lansing., 1945-55; advisor mktg. U.S. State Dept., Washington, 1955-57; mktg. specialist Mich. Dept. Agrl., Lansing, 1957-58; mgr. Dairy Assn. Retail Inds., Detroit, 1961-63; ast. dir. Agrl. Coop. Devel. Internat., Washington, 1968-69; appraiser County of Eaton, Charlotte, Mich., 1974-83; farm mgr. pvt. practice, Charlotte, 1972—; cons. E. Jay Young Mktg., Detroit, 1962-68, Experience, Inc., Mnpls., 1969-70, Internat. Devel. Svcs., Washington, 1971-72; chief of party Internat. Coop. Devel. Assn., 1969-70; mgr. two farms. Author: Agricultural Cooperative, 1952; (USDA Aid Pub.) Food Mktg. in Developing Countries, 1970. Bd. dirs. Episc. Westrn Diocese Mich., Kalamazoo, 1978-82; exec. com. Eaton County Rep. Club, Charlotte, 1983. Recipient Bishop's cross Episc. Ch., Kalamazoo, 1978. Mem. Internat. Assn. Agrl. Economists, Am. Foreign Svc. Assn., Circumnavigators Club, Shriner, Patriarch Mich. State U., Knights Templar, Lansing Farmers Club. Republican. Methodist. Avocations: travel, organ, French lang. Home: 539 Lansing St Charlotte MI 48813-1163

YOUNG, FRANCIS ALLAN, psychologist; b. Utica, N.Y., Dec. 29, 1918; s. Frank Allan and Julia Mae (McGowen) Y.; m. Judith Wadsworth Wright, Dec. 21, 1945; children—Francis Allan, Thomas Robert. B.S., U. Tampa, 1941; M.A., Western Res. U., 1945; Ph.D., Ohio State U., 1949. Instr. Wash. State U., Pullman, 1948-50; asst. prof. Wash. State U., 1950-56, assoc. prof., 1956-61, prof. psychology, 1961-88, dir. primate rsch. ctr., 1957-88, prof., dir. emeritus, 1988—; vis. prof. ophthalmology U. Oreg., Portland, 1964; asst. dir. U. Wash. Regional Primate Ctr., dir. primate field sta., 1966-68; vis. prof. pharmacology U. Uppsala (Sweden) Med. Sch., 1971; vis. prof. optometry U. Houston, 1979-80. Editor: (with Donald B. Lindsley) Early Experience and Visual Information Processing in Perceptual and Reading Disorders, 1970; contbr. chpts. to books, numerous articles to profl. jours. Named Disting. Psychologist State of Wash., Wash. Psychol. Assn., 1973; recipient Paul Yarwood Meml. award Calif. Optometric Assn., 1978; Apollo award Am. Optometric Assn., 1980; Nat. Acad. Sci.-NRC sr. postdoctoral fellow in physiol. psychology U. Wash., 1956-57; research grantee NSF, 1950-53; research grantee USAF, 1965-72; research grantee NIH, 1960-78. Home: 344 NW Webb St Pullman WA 99163-3150 Office: Wash State U Psychology Dept Pullman WA 99164-1170

YOUNG, FRANK EDWARD, former federal agency administrator, religious organization administrator; b. Mineola, N.Y., Sept. 1, 1931; s. Frank E. and Erma F. Y.; m. Leanne Hutchinson, Oct. 20, 1956; children: Lorrie, Debora, Peggy, Frank, Jon. MD, SUNY, 1952; PhD, Case Western Res. U., 1959; DSc (hon.), Roberts Wesleyan Coll., 1983, Houghton Coll., 1984, SUNY, 1986, L.I. U., 1986, Western Bapt. Coll., 1988. Asst. prof. pathology Western Res. U., Cleve., 1962-65; assoc. mem. microbiology Scripps Clinic & Rsch. Found., LaJolla, Calif., 1965-68; assoc. prof. biology U. Calif., San Diego, 1967-70; mem. microbiology & exptl. pathology Scripps Clinic & Rsch. Found., LaJolla, Calif., 1968-70; prof. microbiology and chmn. dept., prof. pathology and radiation biology and biophysics U. Rochester, N.Y., 1970-79, dir. Med. Ctr., 1979-81, dean Sch. Medicine and Dentistry, 1979-84, v.p. for health affairs, 1981-84; commr. FDA, Rockville, Md., 1984-89, dep. asst. sec. for health sci. and environ., 1989-93; dir. office emergency preparedness, 1993—; now with Adult Ministries, Bethesda, Md.; U.S. rep. WHO exec. bd., Geneva, 1985-88; bd. dirs. High Tech., Rochester, N.Y., 1983-84. Contbr. numerous articles on cloning, gene mapping, gene shuttle vectors, 1970-84; initiator Fed. Regulations rules to increase access to exptl. drugs to desperately ill, 1987-88. Lectr. Christian orgns., 1970—; mem. United Way, Rochester, N.Y., 1982-84, N.Y. State Statutory Adv. Com. on DNA, Albany, N.Y., 1978. Recipient sec.'s spl. citation Dept. Health and Human Svcs., 1989, Surgeon Gen.'s Exemplary Svc. medal, 1988, Disting. Svc. medal Pub. Health Svc., 1986, Edward Mott award, 1985, Surgeon Gen.'s Medallion, 1992. Mem. Inst. Medicine of NAS, AAAS, Am. Acad. Microbiology (bd. govs.). Avocations: fishing, boating, yard work. Office: Adult Ministries 5500 River Rd Bethesda MD 20816*

YOUNG, FRANK MITCHELL, musical theater producer; b. Pasadena, Tex., May 22, 1940. Student, U. Tex., 1958, U. Houston, 1960; BA, UCLA, 1963. Asst. condr., singer, stage mgr. Houston Grand Opera, 1963-75; stage mgr. Washington Opera, 1968-71; founder, pres., CEO, Theater Under Stars, Houston, 1971—; exec. dir. 5th Avenue Mus. Theatre Co., Seattle, 1989—. Debut in Carmen, Houston Grand Opera, 1958; producer 200 mus. prodns., 1968— including 23 Houston premieres, 8 world premieres and 1 Am. premiere. Mem. Nat. Alliance for Mus. Theatre (pres.), Tex. Non-Profit Theatres, Houston Theater Alliance (v.p.), Houston Cultural Arts Council (theater panel). Office: Theater Under the Stars 4235 San Felipe St Houston TX 77027-2901

YOUNG, FRANKLIN, nutritional biochemistry educator, researcher; b. Beijing, China, Feb. 1, 1928; came to U.S., 1950, naturalized, 1967; s. Andrew On-Yin and Helen (Loh) Y.; m. Kathlina Patanella. Student U. Shanghai, 1946-48; AB, Mercer U., 1951; BS, U. Fla., 1952, M. Agr., 1954, PhD, 1960. Cert. nutrition specialist. Grad. research fellow U. Fla., Gainesville, 1958-60; post doctoral research fellow, 1960-61; research assoc. Bowman Gray Sch. Medicine, Winston-Salem, N.C., 1961-65, research instr., 1965-66; assoc. prof. U. Hawaii, Honolulu, 1968-83; prof. nutritional biochemistry, chmn. and researcher cardiovascular diseases and hypertension U. Utah, Salt Lake City, 1983-85; prof. nutritional biochemistry West Chester U., Pa., 1985—. Contbr. articles to profl. jours. Mem. Am. Inst. Nutrition, Sigma Xi, Gamma Sigma Delta (charter mem., treas. 1970-71), Phi Kappa Phi, Phi Sigma. Office: West Chester U Dept Health West Chester PA 19383

YOUNG, GENEVIEVE LEMAN, publishing executive, editor; b. Geneva, Sept. 25, 1930; came to U.S., 1945, naturalized, 1968; d. Clarence Kuangson and Juliana Helen (Yen) Y.; m. Cedric Sun, 1955 (div. 1972); m. Gordon Parks, Aug. 26, 1973 (div. 1979). BA (Wellesley Coll. scholar), Wellesley Coll., 1952. Asst. editor Harper & Row (pubs.), N.Y.C., 1960-62; editor Harper & Row (pubs.), 1962-64, asst. mng. editor, 1964-66, mng. editor, 1966-70; exec. editor J.B. Lippincott Co., N.Y.C., 1970-77; v.p. J.B. Lippincott Co., 1972-77; sr. editor Little, Brown & Co., N.Y.C., 1977-85; editor-in-chief Lit. Guild Am., N.Y.C., 1985-88; v.p., editorial dir. Bantam Books, N.Y.C., 1988-92. Alumna trustee Phillips Acad., Andover, Mass., 1975-78, class agt., 1979-85; mem. Wellesley Bus. Leadership Coun., 1989—; mem. Youth Counseling League, 1986—, pres., 1989-96, mem. com. of 100, 1991-93; mem. Literacy Vols. N.Y.C., 1992—, sec., 1996—; mem. Andover Devel. Bd., 1993—; trustee Jewish Bd. Family and Children's Svcs., 1996—. Recipient Alumna Achievement award Wellesley Coll., 1982, Matrix award, 1988. Mem. Assn. Am. Pubs. (exec. coun. gen. pub. div. 1975-78, 85-87, freedom to read com. 1972-75), Women's Media Group (pres. 1981-82, 2d v.p. 1994-95), Century Assn. Home: 30 Park Ave New York NY 10016-3801

YOUNG, GEORGE BERNARD, JR., professional football team executive; b. Balt., Sept. 22, 1930; s. George Bernard and Frances Marie (Kauders) Y.; m. Kathryn M.L. Reddington, Sept. 4, 1965. A.B., Bucknell U., 1952; M.B.A., Loyola U., Balt., 1967; CASE, Johns Hopkins U., 1971. Tchr. history, head football coach Calvert Hall High Sch. and Balt. City Coll., 1953-68; asst. dir. player personnel Balt. Colts, 1968-70, offensive line coach, 1970; dir. player personnel, 1971-73, offensive coordinator, line coach, 1973-74; dir. profl. scouting Miami (Fla.) Dolphins, 1975-79; gen. mgr. N.Y. Football Giants, 1979—, now also v.p. Democrat. Roman Catholic. Office: NY Giants Giants Stadium East Rutherford NJ 07073*

YOUNG, GEORGE CRESSLER, federal judge; b. Cin., Aug. 4, 1916; s. George Philip and Gladys (Cressler) Y.; m. Iris June Hart, Oct. 6, 1951; children: George Cressler, Barbara Ann. A.B., U. Fla., 1938, LL.B., 1940; postgrad., Harvard Law Sch., 1947. Bar: Fla. 1940. Practice in Winter Haven, 1940-41; asso. firm Smathers, Thompson, Maxwell & Dyer, Miami, 1947; adminstrv., legislative asst. to Senator Smathers of Fla., 1948-52; asst. U.S. atty. Jacksonville, 1952; partner firm Knight, Kincaid, Young & Harris, Jacksonville, 1953-61; U.S. dist. judge No., Middle and So. dists. Fla., 1961-73; chief judge Middle Dist., 1973-81, sr. judge, 1981—; Mem. com. on adminstrn. fed. magistrates system Jud. Conf. U.S., 1973-80. Bd. dirs. Jacksonville United Cerebral Palsy Assn., 1953-60. Served to lt. (s.g.) USNR, 1942-46. Mem. Rollins Coll. Alumni Assn. (pres. 1968-69), ABA (spl. com. for adminstrn. criminal justice), Fla. Bar Assn. (gov. 1960-61), Jacksonville Bar Assn. (past pres.), Am. Judicature Soc., Am. Law Inst., Order of Coif, Fla. Blue Key, Phi Beta Kappa, Phi Kappa Phi, Phi Delta Phi, Sigma Alpha Epsilon. Home: 2424 Shrewsbury Rd Orlando FL 32803-1334 Office: US Dist Ct 635 US Courthouse 80 N Hughey Ave Orlando FL 32801-2231

YOUNG, GEORGE H., III, investment banker; b. Washington, D.C., Feb. 10, 1959; s. George H. Jr. and Jeanne Marie (Collins) Y.; m. Adina Chouequet, Oct. 12, 1996. BA in Internat. Rels. with honors, Brown U., 1982; MPhil in Internat. Rels., Magdalene Coll., U. Cambridge, Eng., 1983; MPPM, Yale U., 1987. Assoc. cons. Bain & Co., Boston, 1983-85; assoc. CS First Boston, N.Y.C., 1987-90, v.p., 1990-91, dir., 1992-94; White House fellow U.S. Dept. Treasury, Washington, 1991-92; sr. v.p. Lehman Bros., N.Y.C., 1994-96, mng. dir., 1996—; spkr. in field. Vol. Ch. of the Holy Trinity, N.Y.C., 1990—; application reader White House Fellows Commn., N.Y.C., 1993—; mem. alumni coun. exec. com., co-chair budget and fin. com. Phillips Acad., Andover, Mass., 1994—. Mem. Coun. Fgn. Rels., Assn. of U.S. Army, Harrow Sch. Assn., Oxford & Cambridge Univ. Club, Yale Golf Club. Roman Catholic. Home: 21 E 22nd St Apt 10F New York NY 10010 Office: Lehman Bros 3 World Fin Ctr New York NY 10285

YOUNG, GORDON ELLSWORTH, composer, organist; b. McPherson, Kans., Oct. 15, 1919; s. Benjamin Warden and Rose Esther (Johnson) Y. Mus.B., Southwestern Coll., 1940, Mus.D., 1960; attended, Curtis Inst. Music, 1944-46; studies with Powell Weaver, Kansas City Conservatory; studies with Joseph Bonnet, Paris. Organist First Meth. Ch., Tulsa, 1940-44; staff organist Radio Sta. KVOO, 1941-44; music writer Tulsa Daily World, 1942-44; organist First Presbyn. Ch., Lancaster, Pa., 1944-48; faculty, glee club dir. Franklin and Marshall Coll., 1946-47; organist Arch St. Presbyn. Ch., Phila., 1949-50, First Presbyn. Ch., Detroit, 1952-72; concert artist. Composer numerous organ, choir, solo voice and instrumental works; performer in 12 fgn. countries; contbr. to Bapt. Hymnal, 1991, Seventh-Day Adventist Hymnal, Hymns for the Family of God; compositions performed and recorded by Christopher Parkening, Feike Asma, Mormon Tabernacle Choir, Crystal Cath. Choir on EMI-Angel, Philips, Goth, Word and Bonneville record labels. Recipient Special Tribute award State of Mich., biographical tribute Nat. Fedn. Music Clubs, 1992. Mem. ASCAP (several awards), Am. Guild of Organists (life, hon.). Republican. Presbyn. Office: PO Box 256 Detroit MI 48231-0256 *A positive attitude in all things makes the whole difference between success and failure in a career.*

YOUNG, GRACE MAY-EN, pediatrician; b. Pitts.. AB, Harvard U., 1977; MD, Columbia U., 1981. Diplomate Am. Bd. Pediat. Emergency Medicine, Am. Bd. Pediat. Asst. prof. pediat. George Washington U. Sch. Medicine, Washington, 1986-90, NYU Sch. Medicine, N.Y.C., 1990-93; assoc. prof. pediat. U. Md. Sch. Medicine, Balt., 1993—. Office: Univ Md Med Ctr Pediat Emergency Dept 22 S Greene St # N1w45 Baltimore MD 21201-1544 Address: 9308 Elmhirst Dr Bethesda MD 20814

YOUNG, GWYNNE A., lawyer; b. Durham, N.C., 1950. AB, Duke U., 1971; JD, U. Fla., 1974. Bar: Fla. 1974. Asst. state atty. 13th Judicial Cir., Fla.; mem. Carlton, Fields, Ward, Emmanuel, Smith & Cutler P.A., Tampa, Fla.; instr. U. Fla. Coll. Law, 1974. Exec. editor U. Fla. Law Review, 1973-74. Pres. Jr. League Tampa, Inc., 1985-86; bd. dirs. Assn. Jr. Leagues, Inc., 1987-89, Duke U. Nat. Alumni Assn., 1993—. Fellow Am. Bar Found.; mem. ABA... Office: Carlton Fields Ward Emmanuel Smith & Cutler PA 1 Harbour Pl 777 S Harbour Island Blvd Tampa FL 33602

YOUNG, HARRISON, II, software development and marketing executive; b. Bklyn., Feb. 11, 1944; s. Harrison and Bobbie Aline (King) Y.; m. Shirley Gene Stanfield, Aug. 31, 1967 (div. Sept. 21, 1992); children: Melanie Marie, Tracy Lea; m. Emelie Martha Mannweiler, Dec. 18, 1993. BBA, Pacific Western U., L.A., 1990; MBA, U. Leicester, Eng., 1993. Cert. computer profl. Sr. systems rep. Info. Systems divsn. RCA, Houston, 1967-70; sr. scientist and program mgr. Tetra Tech Inc., San Diego, 1970-74; co-founder, exec. v.p. and sr. program mgr. Atlantic Analysis Corp., Norfolk, Va., 1974-85; program mgr. Comarco Inc., Anaheim, Calif., 1985-86, v.p., divsn. gen. mgr., 1986-87; pres. Washington-based subs. Comarco Inc., 1987-88; pres., CEO, dir. Comarco Inc., Anaheim, 1985-90; pres., CEO Tetra Tech Systems Integration subsidiary Honeywell, San Diego, 1990-92; pres., COO JWK Internat. Corp., Annandale, Va., 1992-94; pres., CEO Advanced Programming Concepts, Austin, Tex., 1994—. Bd. dirs. Blue Cross Blue Shield of Va., 1976-81. With USN, 1961-67. Mem. Am. Mgmt. Assn., Armed Forces Comms. and Electronics Assn., Nat. Contract Mgmt. Assn., Data Processing Mgmt. Assn., Instrumentation Soc. Am. Avocations: boating, computers, foreign travel. Home: 12633 Pony Ln Austin TX 78727 Office: Advanced Programming Concepts 7004 Bee Caves Rd Austin TX 78746-5065

YOUNG, HENRY E., medical educator; b. Dayton, Ohio, Dec. 5, 1951; s. Henry O. and Lucille M. Y.; m. Valerie E. Achorn, May 16, 1976; 1 child, Katherine. BS in Biology, Ohio State U., 1974; MS in Zoology, U. Ark., 1977; PhD, Tex. Tech. U., 1983. Instr.biochemistry Rush-Presbyn.-St. Luke's Med. Ctr., Chgo., 1987-88; asst. prof. anatomy Mercer U. Sch. Medicine, Macon, Ga., 1988-95, asst. prof. surgery, 1988-94, assoc. prof. anatomy, pediatrics, 1995—. Inventor in field. NIH Postdoctoral fellow biochemistry Case Western Res. U., Cleve., 1983-85, Muscular Dystrophy Assn. postdoctoral fellow, 1985-87; recipient Hooding award Excellence in Teaching and Rsch. Mercer U. Med. Sch., 1993, 94. Mem. Nat. Coun. Adoptable Children, Ga. Coun. Adoptable Children. Avocations: reading, lapidary, stain glass, singing. Home: 195 Ashton Dr Macon GA 31220 Office: Mercer U Sch Medicine 1550 College St Macon GA 31201-1554

YOUNG, HOWARD SETH, chemist, researcher; b. Birmingham, Ala., July 7, 1924; s. Tilden Hendricks and Annie Lou (McGaugh) Y.; m. Anne Reid Maven, Aug. 29, 1945; children: Alice McGaugh, Glenn Reid, Margaret Reid, George Maven, Ralph Hendricks, Elizabeth Anne, Joan McGaugh. BS in Chemistry, Birmingham Southern Coll., 1942; PhD, Brown U., 1948. Chemist Tenn. Eastman Co., Kingsport, 1948-51, sr. rsch. chemist, 1951-62, rsch. assoc., 1963-67, sr. rsch. assoc., 1967-70, dir. engring. rsch., 1970-74; dir. phys. and analytical chemistry rsch. Eastman Chems. Div., Kingsport, 1976-84, asst. dir. rsch., 1984-85, dir. rsch., 1985-89, ret., 1989. Contbr. articles to profl. jours.; patentee in field. Served to corp. U.S. Army, 1945-46. Mem. Am. Chem. Soc., Sigma Xi. Avocations: reading, walking, birdwatching. Home: 1909 E Sevier Ave Kingsport TN 37664-3231

YOUNG, HOWARD THOMAS, foreign language educator; b. Cumberland, Md., Mar. 24, 1926; s. Samuel Phillip and Sarah Emmaline (Frederick) Y.; m. Carol Osborne, Oct. 5, 1949 (div. 1966); children—Laurie Margaret, Jennifer Anne; m. Jennifer Bunker, July 15, 1966 (div. 1980); m. Edra Lee Airheart, May 23, 1981; 1 child, Timothy Howard. B.S. summa cum laude, Columbia U., 1950, M.A., 1952, Ph.D., 1954. Lectr. Columbia U., N.Y.C., 1950-54; asst. prof. Romance langs. Pomona Coll., Claremont, Calif., 1954-60; assoc. prof. Pomona Coll., Claremont, 1960-66, Smith prof. Romance langs., 1966—; vis. prof. Middlebury Program in Spain, Madrid, 1986-87, U. Zaragoza, 1967-68; chief reader Spanish AP Ednl. Testing Service, Princeton, 1975-78, chmn. Spanish lang. devel. commn., 1976-79; mem. fgn. lang. adv. commn. Coll. Bd., N.Y.C., 1980-83; mem. West Coast selection commn. Mellon Fellowships for Humanities, Princeton, 1984-86, European selection com., 1987, 90. Author: The Victorious Expression, 1964, Juan Ramón Jiménez, 1967, The Line in the Margin, 1980; editor: T.S. Eliot and Hispanic Modernity, 1995; contbr. numerous articles and book revs. to profl. jours. Dir. NEH summer seminar for Sch. tchrs., 1993. Served with USNR, 1944-46, ETO. Fellow Del Amo Found., 1960-61, NEH, 1975, 89-90; Fulbright fellow; 1967-68; Rockefeller Study Ctr. scholar, 1976. Mem. MLA, Assn. Tchrs. Spanish and Portuguese, Am. Comparative Lit. Assn., Acad. Am. Poets, Assn. Lit. Scholars and Critics. Home: 447 W Redlands Ave Claremont CA 91711-1638 Office: Pomona Coll Modern Romance Dept 550 Harvard Ave Claremont CA 91711-6380

YOUNG, HUGH DAVID, physics educator, writer, organist; b. Ames, Iowa, Nov. 3, 1930; s. Hugh Surber and Nellie Sibella (Peters) Y.; m. Alice Carroll, June 25, 1960; children: Gretchen Carroll, Rebecca Susan. BS in Physics, Carnegie-Mellon U., 1952, MS in Physics, 1953, PhD in Physics, 1959, BFA in Music, 1972. From instr. to assoc. prof. physics Carnegie-Mellon U., Pitts., 1956-77; prof. Carnegie-Mellon U., 1977—; head dept. natural scis. Margaret Morrison Carnegie Coll., Carnegie-Mellon U., 1962-67, acad. coordinator, lectr. modern engring. mgrs. program, 1966-82; vis. assoc. prof. physics U. Calif., Berkeley, 1967-68, vis. prof. physics, 1974; asst. organist St. Paul's Cathedral, Pitts., 1978-82. Author: Statistical Treatment of Experimental Data, 1962, Fundamentals of Mechanics and Heat, 2d edit., 1974, Fundamentals of Optics and Modern Physics, 2d edit., 1976; (with Sears and Zemansky) College Physics, 7th edit., 1990, University Physics, 9th edit., 1996. Bd. dirs. Renaissance and Baroque Soc., 1980-86. Recipient Ryan Tchg. award Carnegie Inst. Tech., 1965, Doherty award for excellence in edn. Carnegie Mellon U., 1997. Mem. Am. Assn. Physics Tchrs., Am. Phys. Soc., Am. Guild Organists (assoc.). Democrat. Avocations: organ, rock climbing. Home: 5746 Aylesboro Ave Pittsburgh PA 15217-1412 Office: Carnegie-Mellon Univ Dept Physics Pittsburgh PA 15213

YOUNG, J. A., bishop. Bishop of N.W. Okla. Ch. of God in Christ, Lawton. Office: Ch of God in Christ PO Box 844 Lawton OK 73501*

YOUNG, J. LOWELL, soil chemist, biologist; b. Perry, Utah, Dec. 13, 1925; s. I.A. and Elzada (Nelson) Y.; m. Ruth Ann Jones, Sept. 15, 1950; children: Gordon, LoAnn, Colene, Kathryn. BS, Brigham Young U., 1953; PhD, Ohio State U., 1956. Rsch. asst. Ohio Agrl. Expt. Sta., Columbus, 1953-56, postdoctoral fellow, 1956-57; chemist Agrl. Research Service USDA, Corvallis, Oreg., 1957-64, rsch. chemist, 1964-78; asst. prof. Oreg. State U., Corvallis, 1957-63, assoc. prof., 1963-78, prof. soil sci., 1978-90, Courtesy prof. soil sci., 1990—; rsch. chemist Horticultural Crops Rsch. Unit USDA, Corvallis, 1978-88; collaborator Horticultural Crops Rsch. Unit U.S. Dept. Agrl., Corvallis, 1988-91. Contbr. articles to profl jours. Served with USAAF, 1944-46. Mem. AAAS, Internat. Soil Sci. Soc., Internat. Humic Substances Soc., Soil Sci. Soc. of Am. (officer 1972-75, assoc. editor jour. 1975-80), Am. Soc. Agromony (officer western 1966-72), Western Soc. Soil Sci. (officer 1966-71), Inst. for Alternative Agrl. Office: Oreg State U Crops & Soil Sci Dept Corvallis OR 97331

YOUNG, JACK ALLISON, financial executive; b. Aurora, Ill., Dec. 31, 1931; s. Neal A. and Gladys W. Young; m. Virginia Dawson, Jan. 24, 1959; children: Amy D., Andrew A. BS in Journalism, U. Ill., 1954. CLU; chartered fin. cons.; registered security rep. Advt. writer Caterpillar Tractor Co., 1956-58; ins. agent Equitable Life Assurance Soc., St. Geneva, Ill., 1958—, ins. broker, 1972—; pres. Jack A. Young and Assocs., 1978—; pres. Creative Brokerage, Inc., 1982—; pres., gen. securities prin. Chartered Planning, Ltd.; past trustee Equitable CLU Assn.; past chmn. Equitable Nat. Agents Forum. Bd. dirs. Tri-City Family Services, 1975-83, pres., 1979-81; trustee Delnor-Community Health System, 1985—, chmn., 1988-91; bd. dirs. St. Charles Ctr. Phys. Rehab., 1991—; chmn., pres. Delnor-Community Health Care Found., 1986-88; dir. Kane County Bar Found., Inc., 1997—. Served to lt. (j.g.), USN, -56. Named to Equitable Hall of Fame, 1978. Mem. Million Dollar Round Table (life), Am. Soc. C.L.U.s, Am. Coll. C.L.U. Golden Key Soc., Fox Valley Estate Planning Council, Internat. Assn. for Fin. Planning, Inc., Aurora Assn. Life Underwriters (past pres., nat. committeeman), Nat. Assn. Securities Dealers (registered prin.). Club: Geneva Golf (pres. 1994). Home: 18 Campbell St Geneva IL 60134-2732 Office: 28 N Bennett St Geneva IL 60134-2207

YOUNG, JACQUELINE EURN HAI, state legislator; b. Honolulu, May 20, 1934; d. Paul Bai and Martha (Cho) Y.; m. Harry Valentine Daniels, Dec. 25, 1954 (div. 1978); children: Paula, Harry, Nani, Laura; m. Everett Kleinjans, Sept. 4, 1988. BS in Speech Pathology, Audiology, U. Hawaii, 1969; MS in Edn., Spl. Edn., Old Dominion U., 1972; advanced cert., Loyola Coll., 1977; PhD in Communication, Women's Studies, Union Inst., 1989. Dir. dept. speech and hearing Md. Sch. for the Blind, Balt., 1975-77; dir. deaf-blind project Easter Seal Soc. Oahu, Hawaii, 1977-78; project dir. equal ednl. opportunity programs Hawaii State Dept. Edn., Honolulu, 1978-85, state ednl. specialist, 1978-90; state rep. dist. 20 Hawaii State Legislature, Honolulu, 1990-92, state rep. dist. 51, 1992-94; vice-speaker Hawaii Ho. of Reps., Honolulu; apptd. to U.S. Dept. Ef. Adv. Commn. on Women in the Svc.; cons. spl. edn. U.S. Dept. Edn., dept. edn. Guam, Am. Samoa, Ponape, Palau, Marshall Islands, 1977-85; cons. to orgns. on issues relating to workplace diversity; adj. prof. commn., anthopology, mgmt. Hawaii Pacific U. TV producer. 1st v.p. Nat. Women's Polit. Caucus, 1988-90; chair Hawaii Women's Polit. Caucus, 1987-89; bd. dirs. YWCA Oahu, Kalihi Palama Immigrant Svc. Ctr., Hawaii Dem. Movement, Family Peace Ctr.; appointee Honolulu County Com. on the Status of Women, 1986-87; mem. Adv. Coun. on Family Violence. Recipient Outstanding Woman Leader award YWCA of Oahu, 1994, Pres.'s award Union Inst., 1993, Fellow of the Pacific award Hawaii-Pacific U., 1993, Headliner award Honolulu chpt. Women in Commn., 1993. Mem. Soroptimist Internat. (Kailua chpt.), Orgn. Women Leaders, Kailua C. of C., Korean C. of C., Kook Min Hur, Sierra Club, Korean Univ. Club. Home: 212 Luika Pl Kailua HI 96734-3237

YOUNG, JAMES EARL, ceramics educator, educational administrator; b. Chgo., Dec. 20, 1922; s. James Alexander and Ellen (Chedister) Y.; children: Hugh Parker, Katherine Sue. BS, U. Ill., 1948; PhD, State U. N.Y. Coll. Ceramics Alfred U., 1962. Ceramic engr. Republic Steel Co., Chgo., 1948-52; ceramic engr. Armour Research Found., Chgo., 1952-55; research supr. Structural Clay Research Found., Geneva, Ill., 1955-57; research fellow State U. N.Y. Coll. Ceramics at Alfred U., 1957-61, asst. prof., 1961-63, assoc. prof., 1963-67, prof., chmn. dept., 1967-70; dean Coll. Arts and Scis., Rutgers U., Camden, N.J., 1970-73; provost Rutgers U., Newark, 1973-82; exec. dir. Commn. on State Colls. of N.J., 1982-84; prof. Rutgers U., 1984—. Contbr. articles to tech. jours. Served with AUS, 1943-46. Am. Council Edn. fellow acad. adminstrn., 1966-67. Mem. Am. Ceramic Soc. Home: 130 Kingsberry Dr Somerset NJ 08873-4309 Office: PO Box 909 Piscataway NJ 08855-0909

YOUNG, JAMES EDWARD, lawyer; b. Painesville, Ohio, Apr. 20, 1946; s. James M. and Isabel P. (Rogers) Y. BBA, Ohio U., 1968; JD, Ohio State U., 1972. Bar: Ohio 1972; Law clk. to chief judge U.S. Ct. Appeals, Nashville, 1972-73; chief counsel City of Cleve., 1980-81, law dir., 1981-82; assoc. Jones, Day, Reavis & Pogue, 1973-79, ptnr., 1983—. Office: Jones Day Reavis & Pogue 901 Lakeside Ave E Cleveland OH 44114-1116

YOUNG, JAMES FRED, college president; b. Burnsville, N.C., Nov. 11, 1934; s. James Ray and Nina (Briggs) Y.; m. Phyllis Elizabeth Johnson, Apr. 15, 1962; children: Alan James, David Barden, Jane Elizabeth. AA, Mars Hill Coll., 1954; BS, Wake Forest U., 1956; MEd, U. N.C., 1957; EdD, Columbia U., 1964. Tchr. Micaville (N.C.) High Sch., 1957-58; research asst. Columbia U., 1959; prin. Enfield Sch., Halifax County, N.C., 1959-61; asst. supt. Halifax County (N.C.) Schs., 1961-64, Burlington (N.C.) City Schs., 1964-68; supt. Lynchburg (Va.) public schs., 1968-71; dep. supt. public instr. Commonwealth of Va., Richmond, 1971-73; pres. Elon Coll., Elon College, N.C., 1973—; chmn. bd. N.C. Nat. Bank, Burlington.; Bd. dirs. Burlington Day Sch., 1974—, Appalachian Regional Edn. Lab., Charleston, W.Va., 1972-73; chmn. Gov.'s Task Force on Financing Standards of Quality for Public Schs. in Va., 1972-73; sec. exec. com. Ind. Coll. Fund N.C., 1976-78; mem. exec. com. United Ch. of Christ Council for Higher Edn., 1977—. Served with AUS, 1958. Mem. N.C. Edn. Assn. (pres. Halifax County unit 1960-61, Burlington unit 1967-68), N.C. Assn. Ind. Colls. and Univs. (sec. exec. com. 1978—, chmn. 1985-89), Nat. Assn. Intercollegiate Athletics (pres.'s adv. coun. 1977—, com. on eligibility and acad. standards, chmn. coun. pres.'s 1988-90), Internat. Assn. Univ. Pres. (v.p. southeastern region), Alamance County C. of C. (dir. 1974-75). Club: Rotary. Office: Elon Coll Office of Pres E Haggard Ave PO Box 398 Elon College NC 27244-9344*

YOUNG, JAMES HARVEY, historian, educator; b. Bklyn., Sept. 8, 1915; s. W. Harvey and Blanche (DeBra) Y.; m. Myrna Goode, Aug. 25, 1940; children: Harvey Galen, James Walter. B.A., Knox Coll., 1937, D.H.L., 1971; M.A., U. Ill., 1938, Ph.D., 1941; D.Sc., Rush U., 1976. Mem. faculty Emory U., 1941-84, prof. history, 1958-80, Charles Howard Candler prof. Am. social history, 1980-84, prof. emeritus, 1984—, chmn. dept., 1958-66; vis. assoc. prof. Columbia U., 1949-50; mem. nat. adv. food and drug council FDA, 1964-67; mem. Consumers Task Force, White House Conf. on Food, Nutrition and Health, 1969; mem. history life scis. study sect. NIH, 1970-73, 79-80, 91-93, chmn., 1992-93; vis. lectr. Am. Assn. Colls. Pharmacy Vis. Lectrs. Program, 1970-73; cons.-panelist NEH, 1970-83; cons. in history Centers for Disease Control; advisor Am. Coun. Sci. and Health; Logan Clendening lectr. U. Kans. Med. Ctr., 1973; Samuel X. Radbill lectr. Phila. Coll. Physicians, 1978; Beaumont lectr. Yale U., 1980; vis. hist. scholar Nat. Library Medicine, 1986; Harold J. Lawn lectr. U. Minn., 1990; David L. Cowen lectr. Rutgers U., 1990; James Campbell lectr. Rush U., 1992; Waring lectr. Med. U. S.C., 1993. Author: The Toadstool Millionaires, 1961, The Medical Messiahs, 1967, expanded edit., 1992, American Self-Dosage Medicines, An Historical Perspective, 1974, Pure Food: Securing the Federal Food and Drugs Act of 1906, 1989, American Health Quackery: Collected Essays, 1992; editor: (with W.A. Beardslee and T.J.J. Altizer) Truth, Myth and Symbol, 1962, (with T.L. Savitt) Disease and Distinctiveness in the American South, 1988. Served with AUS, 1943-45. FDA rsch. appointee, 1977-85; Carnegie Rsch. grantee, 1947, USPHS grantee, 1960-65, Nat. Libr. Medicine grantee, 1990-94; Faculty fellow Fund Advancement Edn., 1954-55, Social Sci. Rsch. Coun. fellow, 1960-61, Guggenheim fellow, 1966-67. Mem. Am. Hist. Assn., So. Hist. Assn. (pres. 1982), Orgn. Am. Historians, Soc. Am. Historians, Am. Assn. History of Medicine (coun., Fielding H. Garrison lectr. 1979, William H. Welch medal 1982, Continuing Lifetime Achievement award 1992), Am. Inst. History of Pharmacy (coun., hon. pres. 1993-95, Edward Kremers award 1962), Phi Beta Kappa, Sigma Xi, Phi Kappa Phi, Omicron Delta Kappa, Phi Alpha Theta. Congregationalist. Home: 272 Heaton Park Dr Decatur GA 30030-1027

YOUNG, JAMES JULIUS, university administrator, former army officer; b. Fort Ringgold, Tex., Nov. 28, 1926; s. John Cooper and Violet Thelma (Ohl) Y.; m. June Agnes Hillstead, Dec. 17, 1948; children: Robert Michael, Steven Andrew, Patrick James, Mary Frances. B.S., U. Md., 1960; M.H.A., Baylor U., 1962; Ph.D. in Hosp. and Health Adminstrn, U. Iowa, 1969. Commd. 2d lt. U.S. Army, 1947, advanced through grades to brig. gen., 1977; comdr., med. ops. officer, dir. tng. field med. units in European Command, 1949-53; comdr. Mil. Med. Leadership Sch., 1953-54; med. advisor (Nationalist Army of China), 1955-57; asst. adminstr. Fitzsimons Army Med. Center, 1957-60; med. plans and ops. officer (US Forces), Korea, 1962-63; sr. field med. instr., chief field med. service Med. Field Service Sch., 1963-66; dir. health care orgn. and mgmt. analysis Office of Surgeon Gen., 1969-71; dir. med. plans and ops. directorate Office of the Surgeon, Military Assistance Command, Vietnam, 1971-72; exec. officer, chief adminstrv. services Silas Hays Army Hosp., 1973-74; military health analyst, military health care study OMB, Exec. Office of Pres., 1974-76; dep. dir. resources mgmt. and cons. for health care adminstrn. Office of Surgeon Gen., 1976-77; chief Med. Services Corps, U.S. Army and; dir. resources mgmt. Office of Surgeon Gen., 1977-81; ret., 1981; instr. U. Iowa, 1967-69; asst. prof., preceptor Baylor U., 1973-74; vice chancellor for health affairs W.Va. Bd. Regents, Charleston, 1982-87; dean sch. of allied health scis. U. Tex. Health Sci. Ctr., San Antonio, 1987-90, interim dean Sch. Medicine, 1988-89, dean Sch. Medicine, 1989—; cons. to Min. of Health, Republic of Vietnam, 1971-72; adj. prof. Baylor U., 1977-81, George Washington U., 1975-76, W.Va. U., 1986; prof. U. Tex. health Sci. Ctr., San Antonio, 1989—. Contbr. articles to profl. jours. Decorated D.S.M., Legion of Merit, Meritorious Service medal and; others; recipient Walter Reed medallion for service, 1981; Army Med. Dept. medallion for contribution to health service, 1981. Mem. APHA, Coun. Deans, Assn. of Am. Med. Colls., Assn. Mil. Surgeons (chmn. med. svc. sect. 1978), Assn. U.S. Army, Interagy. Inst. Fed. Health Execs., Phi Kappa Tau. Roman Catholic. Home: 1610 Anchor Dr San Antonio TX 78213-1943 Office: U Tex Health Sci Ctr Office Of Dean Med Sch San Antonio TX 78284

YOUNG, JAMES MORNINGSTAR, physician, naval officer; b. Massillon, Ohio, Oct. 28, 1929; s. Ralph Louis and Pauline Louise (Morningstar) Y.; m. Bettylu Jones, July 3, 1952; children: Anne Christine, Mark Andrew, Patricia Jane, Elizabeth Lynne, Judith Pamela, Claudia Dianne; m. Mariette M. Aubuchon, Oct. 11, 1970; children: Gretchen Camille, Jason Paul. AB, Duke U., 1951, MD, 1955. Diplomate Am. Bd. Internal Medicine. Intern Bethesda Naval Hosp., 1955-56, asst. dir. tissue bank, 1956-58, resident, 1958-61; commd. lt. (j.g.) USN, 1955, advanced through grades to lt. comdr., 1961, promoted to temporary rank capt., 1963; White House physician to Presidents Kennedy and Johnson, Washington, 1963-66; staff Oakland (Calif.) Naval Hosp., 1966-69; chief medicine Naval Hosp. Boston, Chelsea, Mass., 1969-74; med. officer Naval Air Sta., South Weymouth, Mass., 1974-75; assoc. clin. prof. medicine Boston U. Sch. Medicine, 1969-75; v.p. med. affairs Mass. Blue Shield/Blue Cross, 1975-87; lectr. Harvard Sch. Pub. Health, 1987-90; sr. advisor Beijing Coll. Traditional Chinese Medicine, 1987-88; med. advisor U.S.-China People's Friendship Assn., Washington, 1988-90; cons. USPHS, Office Asst. Sec. for Health, Nat. Ctr. for Health Svcs., Rsch. and Health Care Tech. Assessment, HHS, 1985-90; v.p. for med. affairs Greenery Rehab. Group, Inc., 1988-90; assoc. med. dir. New. Eng. Rehab. Hosp., 1992-95, chief medicine, 1992-95. Contbr. articles to med. publs. Decorated knight comdr. with star Equestrian Order of the Holy Sepulchre of Jerusalem; named Disting. Citizen of Washington H.S., Massillon, Ohio, 1993. Fellow ACP, AMA, Alpha Omega Alpha, Omicron Delta Kappa, Beta Omega Sigma, Sigma Alpha Epsilon. Home: 77 Harvey Mill Rd Lee NH 03824

YOUNG, JAY ALFRED, chemical safety and health consultant, writer, editor; b. Huntington, Ind., Sept. 8, 1920; s. Jacob Phillip and Marie (Skully) Y.; m. Anne Elizabeth Neff, June 29, 1942 (dec. June 1962); children: John, Paul, Cecelia, Michael, Joseph, Andrea, Therese, Gregory, Thomas, Lucy, Margaret, Antonia; m. Mary Ann Owens, Aug. 15, 1962; children: James, Laurence; 4 stepchildren. BS, Ind. U., 1939; AM, Oberlin Coll., 1940; PhD, U. Notre Dame, 1950. Chief chemist Asbestos Mfg. Co., Huntington, Ind., 1941-42; ordnance engr. U.S. War Dept., Washington, 1942-44; from instr. to prof. chemistry King's Coll., Wilkes-Barre, Pa., 1949-69; vis. prof. Carleton U., Ottawa, Ont., Can., 1969-70, Fla. State U., Tallahassee, 1975-77; Hudson prof. Auburn (Ala.) U., 1970-75; mgr. tech. publs. Chem. Mfrs. Assn., Washington, 1977-80; chem. safety and health cons. Silver Spring, Md., 1980—; pro bono cons. OSHA, EPA, Consumer Product Safety Commn., Washington, 1980—; invited lectr. chem. edn. and chem. health and safety U.S., Can., Mex., Brazil, Argentina, Chile, Great Britain, Norway, France, Italy, India, Indonesia, Australia, New Zealand, Japan, 1963—. Author: Practice in Thinking, 1958, Elements of General Chemistry, 1960, Chemical Concepts, 1963, Selected Principles of Chemistry, 1963, Arithmetic for Students of Science, 1968, Instructor's Guide for Chemistry, a Cultural Approach, 1971, Study Guide for General Chemistry, 1974, Fire!, 1977, Actions and Reactions, 1978, Chemistry, A Human Concern, 1978, Kitchen Chemistry, 1980, Electron Microscopy Safety Handbook, 1985; co-author: Study Guide for Continental Classroom Chemistry, NBC/TV, vols. I and II, 1959, 60, Keys to Chemistry, 1973, Chemistry Preparation Laboratory, 1973, Keys to Oxidation-Reduction, 1974, Things that Last, 1977, Principles of Laboratory Safety (with videotape), 1980, OSHA Hazard Communication Regulations, 1984, Chemical Safety Manual for Small Businesses, 1st edit., 1989, 2d edit., 1992, Developing a Chemical Hygiene Plan, 1990; editor: Guidelines and Recommendations for the Preparation and Continuing Education of Secondary School Teachers of Chemistry, 1977, Improving Safety in the Chemical Laboratory: A Practical Guide, 1st edit., 1989, 2d edit., 1992 (also contbr.), Safety in Academic Chemistry Laboratories, 6th edit., 1995; co-editor: Health Chemistry Laboratory Experiments, 1987, Handbook of Chemical Health and Safety, 1997 (also contbr.); contbr. and cons. numerous books; contbr. Encyclopedia Britannica, and over 100 articles to profl. jours. Tech. resource person to media and expert witness of chem. hazards, precautions, transp. incidents involving chems.; mem. NSF Coll. Chemistry Commn., 1962-68. Lt. USNR, 1944-46. Recipient Disting. Chemistry Alumnus award U. Notre Dame, 1968, Excellence in Chemistry Teaching award Mfg. Chemists Assn., 1970. Fellow AAAS; mem. Am. Chem. Soc. (councilor 1963-87, policy com. 1970-81, sec. divsn. chem. edn. 1969-78, chmn. divsn. chem. health and safety 1979-80, chem. health and safety award 1991). Roman Catholic. Avocations: wood and metalworking, gardening. Home and Office: 12916 Allerton Ln Silver Spring MD 20904-3105

YOUNG, JAY MAITLAND, product manager health care products; b. Louisville, Nov. 26, 1944; s. Clyde Dudley and Olive May (Tyas) Y. BA in Chemistry and Math magna cum laude, Vanderbilt U., 1966; MS in Biochemistry, Yale U., 1967, MPhil in Phys. Chemistry, 1968, PhD in Chemistry, 1971. Asst. prof. chemistry Bryn Mawr (Pa.) Coll., 1970-76; rsch. biochemist Abbott Labs., Abbott Park, Ill., 1977-78; project mgr. physiolog. diagnostics Abbott Labs., Abbott Park, 1978-80, project mgr. cancer product devel., 1980-82, internat. clin. specialist sci. affairs, 1982-85, clin. project mgr. physiol. diag. quality and sci. support, 1986-90, staff quality assurance and sci. support, 1990-93, fertility, pregnancy, thyroid mgr., quality and sci. support, 1993-95; fertility, pregnancy, thyroid, cancer mgr., product quality assurance Abbott Labs., Abbott Park, 1995—; cons. Inst. for Cancer Rsch., Fox Chase, Phila., 1974, vis. scientist, 1975-76; honors examiner Swarthmore Coll., 1973, 74; mem. vis. evaluation com., 1975; presenter to med. groups on cancer markers, viral hepatitis and epidemiology of AIDS, 1982-84. Contbr. articles to profl. jours.; patentee in med. field. Predoctoral fellow NSF, Yale U., 1966-70; postdoctoral fellow, NIH, U. Oxford, 1971-72; grantee NSF, NATO Travel grant, U. Salford, Eng., 1974. Mem. Am. Med. Writers Assn. Office: Abbott Labs Dept 9FK AP31 200 Abbott Park Rd Abbott Park IL 60064-3501

YOUNG, JEANETTE COCHRAN, corporate planner, reporter, analyst; b. Franklin, Ind., Mar. 12, 1953; d. Charles Morris and Marjorie Elizabeth (Rohrbaugh) Cochran; m. William Alan Young, Aug. 18, 1979 (div. 1994); children: Kathryn Elizabeth, Stephen Robert. BA, De Pauw U., 1975; MBA, U. Pa., 1977. Fin. analyst Eli Lilly & Co., Indpls., 1977-79; sr. fin. analyst Samsonite, Denver, 1980, Honeywell Test Instruments divsn., Denver, 1980-82; prin. analyst Fluor Corp., Sugar Land, Tex., 1982-86; sr. fin. analyst Caterpillar, Joliet, Ill., 1989-90, Texaco Chem. Co., Houston, 1990-93; coord. planning, budget Texaco, Inc., Houston, 1993—; asst. to pres. Texaco USA, Houston, 1996. Mem. ARC, Arapahoe County, Colo., 1982; vol. United Way of Tex. Gulf Coast, 1996—. Mem. NAFE, AAUW, Am. Mgmt. Assn. Avocations: travel, reading. Office: Texaco 1111 Bagby St Houston TX 77002-2551 also: Texaco PO Box 4325 Houston TX 77210-4325

YOUNG, JEFFRY, psychologist, gerontologist, educator, statistician; b. Harvey, Ill., Aug. 23, 1952; s. Harold Joyce and Marion June Young. Student, St. Patrick's Coll., Mountain View, Calif., 1971-73; BA in Philosophy & Psychology, San Jose State U., 1977, MA in Gen. Psychology, 1978; PhD in Pub. Affairs, Claremont (Calif.) Grad. Sch., 1986. Coord., rsch. assoc. Ctr. for Applied Social Rsch. Claremont Grad. Sch., 1979-86; postdoctoral intern, behavioral scis. svc. sect. L.A. Police Dept., 1986-87; assoc. dir. Ruby Gerontology Ctr. Calif. State U., Fullerton, 1988-91, dir. Gerontology Rsch. Inst., 1989-92, rsch. prof. Sch. Humanities and Social Scis., 1986-93; assoc. dir. Roybal Inst. for Applied Gerontology Calif. State U., L.A., 1991-94, dir. Gerontology Rsch. Ctr., 1991-94; dir. advocacy and demonstration projects Nat. Asian Pacific Ctr. Aging, Seattle, 1994-97; rsch. dir. Puget Sound Coun. Sr. Citizens, 1996—; gen. mgr. Sound Rsch. Assoc., Rollingbay, Wash., 1997—; adj. asst. prof. Sch. Gerontology, U. So. Calif., L.A., 1991-94; adj. prof. dept. psychology Calif. State U., L.A., 1991-94; co-prin. investigator Alzheimer's Outreach Project Nat. Inst. on Aging, UCLA, 1992-95; cons. health resources and svcs. adminstrn. Alzheimer's Demonstration project East L.A., Calif., 1992-94; project dir. Alzheimer's Disease Rsch. Ctr., Nat. Inst. on Aging, U. So. Calif. and U. Calif., Irvine, 1991-94; dir. Adminstrn. Aging Project, 1994—; prin. investigator Agy. Health Care Policy and Rsch., 1995; facilitator White House Conf. on Aging, 1995; mem. tech. adv. com. Assn. Asian Pacific Health Care Orgns., 1996. Author abstracts, monographs, and articles. Chair adv. bd. com. Rancho Los Amigos Med. Ctr., Downey, Calif., 1993—; touch judge uni. div. So. Calif. Rugby Football Union, 1988-91; pres. Meals on Wheels of Fullerton, Calif., 1993-94; chmn. instl. rev. bd. Calif. State U., L.A., 1994. Recipient Cert. of Recognition, L.A. Police Dept., 1987, Points of Light award, 1992, others; named to Outstanding Young Men of Am., 1986. Mem. APA, Am. Psychol. Soc., Gerontol. Soc. Am., Am. Evaluation Assn. (charter mem.), Am. Bd. Forensic Examiners, N.Am. Mycological Soc. (life), Cascade Sports Collectors Assn., Phi Beta Delta, Sigma Phi Omega (life). Roman Catholic. Avocations: mycology, rare books, rugby, Nordic skiing, microscopy. Home: PO Box 4627 Rollingbay WA 98061-0627

YOUNG, JERRY WESLEY, animal nutrition educator; b. Mulberry, Tenn., Aug. 19, 1934; s. Rufus William and Annie Jewell (Sweeney) Y.; m. Charlotte Sullenger, July 8, 1959; children: David, Jeretha. BS, Berry Coll., 1957; MS, N.C. State U., 1959, PhD, 1963. Asst. prof. Iowa State U., Ames, 1965-70, assoc. prof., 1970-74, prof. in animal sci. & biochemistry, 1974—. Contbr. articles to profl. jours. Postdoctoral fellow NIH, 1963-65. Mem. Am. Dairy Sci. Assn. (Outstanding Dairy Nutrition Rsch. 1987), Am. Inst. Nutrition, Am. Soc. Animal Sci., Am. Chem. Soc., Sigma Xi, Phi Kappa Phi, Gamma Sigma Delta. Baptist. Office: Iowa State U 313 Kildee Hall Ames IA 50010

YOUNG, JESS R., physician; b. Fairfield, Ill., Feb. 4, 1928; s. Edgar S. and Clara B. (Musgrave) Y.; m. Gloria Wynn, July 10, 1953; children—James C., Patricia A. BS, U. Steubenville, 1951; MD, St. Louis U., 1955. Intern Highland Alameda County Hosp., Oakland, Calif., 1955-56; resident in internal medicine Cleve. Clinic Hosp., 1956-59, mem. staff dept. peripheral vascular disease, 1959—, chmn. dept., 1976-97. Co-author: Leg Ulcer, 1975, Peripheral Vascular Diseases, 1991, 1996; contbr. articles to profl. jours., chpts. to books. Served with AUS, 1946-47. Mem. AMA, Am. Heart Assn. (stroke council), Am. Coll. Cardiology, Internat. Cardiovascular Soc., ACP, Am. Fedn. Clic. Research, Ohio Soc. Internal Medicine, Soc. for Vascular Medicine and Rsch., Inter-Urban Club. Methodist. Home: 1503 Burlington Rd Cleveland OH 44118-1216 Office: 9500 Euclid Ave Cleveland OH 44195-0001

YOUNG, JOAN CRAWFORD, advertising executive; b. Hobbs, N.Mex., July 30, 1931; d. William Bill and Ora Maydelle (Boone) Crawford; m. Herchelle B. Young, Nov. 23, 1971 (div.). BA, Hardin Simmons U., 1952; postgrad. Tex. Tech. U., 1953-54. Reporter, Lubbock (Tex.) Avalanche-Jour., 1952-54; promotion dir. Sta. KCBD-TV, Lubbock, 1954-62; account exec. Ward Hicks Advt., Albuquerque, 1962-70; v.p. Mellekas & Assocs., Advt., Albuquerque, 1970-78; pres. J. Young Advt., Albuquerque, 1978—. Bd. dirs. N.Mex. Symphony Orch., 1970-73, United Way of Greater Albuquerque, 1985-89; bd. trustees N.Mex. Children's Found., 1994-96. Recipient Silver medal N.Mex. Advt. Fedn., 1977. Mem. N.Mex. Advt. Fedn. (bd. dirs. 1975-76), Am. Advt. Fedn., Greater Albuquerque C. of C. (bd. dirs. 1984), Albuquerque Petroleum Club (membership chmn. 1992-93, bd. dirs. 1993—, sec. 1994-95, v.p. 1995-97, pres. 1997—). Republican. Author: (with Louise Allen and Audre Lipscomb) Radio and TV Continuity Writing, 1962. Office: 1638 Tierra Del Rio NW Albuquerque NM 87107-3242

YOUNG, JOANN ELIZABETH, veterinarian; b. Ware, Mass., July 2, 1953; D. Gordon Charles and Barbara Ann (Robinson) Y.; m. Jerome Peter Lang, May 24, 1986. AAS, SUNY, 1973; BSN, Boston U., 1985; DVM, Wash. State U., 1994. Lic. Vet. Wash., Mont., Maine. Vet. tech. Westboro (Mass.) Animal Hosp., 1973-78, Berkshire Vet. Hosp., Pittsfield, Mass., 1979-82; admitting officer U. Mass. Med. Ctr., Worcester, Mass., 1978-79; RN Ruidoso (N. Mex.) Hondo Valley Hosp., 1985-86, Group Health Ctrl. Hosp., Seattle, 1986-87, SE Wash. Home Health and Hospice, Pullman, 1988-90; vet. Colfax (Wash.) Vet. Hosp., 1994—. Mem. AVMA, Wash. State Vet. Med. Assn. Democrat. Roman Catholic. Avocations: horseback riding, gardening, travel. Home: 302 Old Moscow Rd Pullman WA 99163-8832 Office: Colfax Vet Hosp 1715 N Oak St Colfax WA 99111-9704

YOUNG, JOHN ALAN, electronics company executive; b. Nampa, Idaho, Apr. 24, 1932; s. Lloyd Arthur and Karen Eliza (Miller) Y.; m. Rosemary Murray, Aug. 1, 1954; children: Gregory, Peter, Diana. BSEE, Oreg. State U., 1953; MBA, Stanford U., 1958. Various mktg. and fin. positions Hewlett Packard Co. Inc., Palo Alto, Calif., 1958-63, gen. mgr. microwave divsn., 1963-68, v.p. electronic products group, 1968-74, exec. v.p., 1974-77, COO, 1977-78, pres., 1977-92, CEO, 1978-92; ret., 1992; bd. dirs. Wells Fargo Bank, Wells Fargo and Co., Chevron Corp., SmithKline Beecham Plc. Affymetrix, Inc., Shaman Pharms. Inc., Ciphergen, Novell, Inc.; chmn. Smart Valley, Inc., Lucent Technologies. Chmn. ann. fund Stanford U., 1966-73, nat. chmn. corp. gifts, 1973-77, mem. adv. coun. Grad. Sch. Bus., 1967-73, 75-80, Univ. trustee, 1977-87; bd. dirs. Mid-Peninsula Urban Coalition, 1971-80, co-chmn., 1983-85; chmn. Pres.'s Commn. on Indsl. Competitiveness, 1983-85, Nat. Jr. Achievement, 1983-84; pres. Found. for Malcolm Baldrige Nat. Quality Award; mem. Adv. Com. on Trade Policy and Negotiations, 1988-92. With USAF, 1954-56. Mem. Nat. Acad. Engring., Coun. on Competitiveness (founder, founding chair computer systems policy project 1986), Bus. Coun. (co-chair pres. com. of adcisors on sci. & tech. 1993—).

YOUNG, JOHN EDWARD, lawyer; b. Tulsa, July 11, 1935; s. Russell Edward and Frances Lucille (Wetmore) Y.; m. Mary Moore Nason, Dec. 27, 1966; children: Cynthia Nason, Abigail Brackett. BS with honors, Calif. Inst. Tech., 1956; LLB magna cum laude, Harvard U., 1959. Bar: N.Y. 1961, U.S. Dist. Ct. (so. dist.) N.Y. 1973. Assoc. Cravath, Swaine & Moore, N.Y.C., 1960-67, ptnr., 1968-95; resident ptnr. Cravath, Swaine & Moore, Paris, 1971-73, London, 1990-95. Editor Harvard Law Rev., 1958-59. Trustee Internat. Sculpture Ctr., 1997—, Royal Oak Found., 1997—, Sir John Soone's Mus. Found., 1997—; gov. Am. Crafts Mus., 1997—. Sheldon Traveling fellow Harvard U., 1959-60. Mem. ABA, N.Y. State Bar Assn., Assn. of Bar of City of N.Y., Century Assn., Harvard Club of N.Y.C., City Univ. Club London. Democrat. Episcopal. Home: 1088 Park Ave New York NY 10128-1132 Office: Cravath Swaine & Moore 825 8th Ave New York NY 10019-7416

YOUNG, JOHN HARDIN, lawyer; b. Washington, Apr. 25, 1948; s. John D. and Laura Virginia (Gwathmey) Y.; m. Mary Frances (Farley) Crosby. AB, Colgate U., 1970; JD, U. Va., 1973; BCL, Oxford U., Eng., 1976. Bar: Va. 1973, D.C. 1974, U.S. Dist. Ct. (ea. dist.) Va. 1974, U.S. Dist. Ct. D.C. 1974, Internat. Trade Ct. 1974, U.S. Ct. Fed. Claims 1974, U.S. Ct. Appeals (4th, Fed. and D.C. cirs.), U.S. Supreme Ct. 1977, U.S. Dist. Ct. Md. 1989. Ptnr. Porter Wright Morris & Arthur, Washington, 1988-92, of counsel, 1992—; gen. counsel The Smoot Corp., 1992—; mem. adv. bd. Antitrust Bull., Jour. Antiturst Law and Econs.; mem. U.S. Sec. State's adv. com. Pvt. internat. Law, 1987-95; chmn. Va. Retirement Sys. Rev. Bd., 1990-94; asst. atty. gen. Commonwealth of Va., 1976-78; mem. master plan task force City of Alexandria, Va., 1987-88, mem. budget and fiscal affairs adv. com., 1989-91; moderator Alexandria Forum, 1993—, Fedn. Forum/TV channel 10, 1989-91; gen. counsel CAPAccess, 1992-96. Contbr. articles to profl. jours. and books on litigation, evidence and trial tactics. Gen. counsel Dem. Party of Va., 1993—, state counsel, 1989-92, state counsel dem. predsl. campaign, 1980-96; counsel Gov. Wilder recount, 1989, Gov. Glendenning recount, 1995; nat. chair DNC Conf. of Dem. Counsel, 1995-96; mem. exec. com. DNC Nat. Lawyers Coun., 1992—. Mem. ABA (vice-chair 1997-98, coun. 1986-89, adminstrv. law sect., chmn. trade regulation and competition com., 1983-86, chair CLE com. 1991-94, chair dispute resolution com.

1994—), Am. Law Inst., George Mason Am. Inn of Ct. (master, counselor 1996—), Hon. Soc. Mid. Temple U.K., Comml. Bar Assn. U.K. (overseas mem.), Am. Inns of Ct., Temple Bar Found. (founding mem., dir.), Phi Alpha Theta (history honors). Episcopalian. Home: 5146 Woodmire Ln Alexandria VA 22311-1301 Office: 5201 Leesburg Pike Ste 1100 Falls Church VA 22041-3203

YOUNG, JOHN WATTS, astronaut; b. San Francisco, Sept. 24, 1930; s. William H. Y.; m. Susy Feldman; children by previous marriage: Sandra, John. BS in Aero. Engring, Ga. Inst. Tech., 1952; D Applied Sci. (hon.), Fla. Technol. U., 1970; LLD (hon.), Western State U., 1969; DSc (hon.), U. S.C., 1981, Brown U., 1983. Joined USN, 1952, advanced through grades to capt.; test pilot, program mgr. F4 weapons systems projects, 1959-62; then maintenance officer Fighter Squadron 143, Naval Air Sta., Miramar, Calif.; chief astronaut office Flight Ops. Directorate, 1975-87, spl. asst. dir. JSC for engring. ops., safety, 1987-96, comdr. 54-hour, 36-orbit 1st flight of Shuttle Space, 1981, and 10 day orbital shuttle 1st flight Space Lab., 1983, assoc. dir. tech. JSC, 1996—. Decorated DFC (3), D.S.M. (2); recipient NASA Disting. Svc. medal (3), NASA Exceptional Svc. medal (2), NASA Engring. Achievement medal, 1988, NASA Outstanding Leadership medal, 1992, NASA Outstanding Achievement medal, 1994, Congl. Space medal of honor, 1981; named Disting. Young Alumni Svc. award Ga. Tech. Acad. Disting. Engrs., 1994; named to Nat. Aviation Hall of Fame, 1988. Fellow Am. Astronautical Soc. (Flight Achievement award 1972, 81, 83, Space Flight award 1993), Soc. Exptl. Test Pilots (Iven Kincheloe award 1972, 81), AIAA (HAley Astronautics award 1973, 82, 84); mem. Sigma Chi. Astronaut NASA, made 1st two-man 3 orbit flight, Gemini 3, Mar. 1965, Gemini 10 3 day flight, 1966, Apollo 10 8-day flight lunar landing dress rehearsal, 1969, Apollo 16 11 day lunar landing and surface exploration, 1972; dir. space shuttle br., astronaut office, 1973-75. Office: NASA Johnson Space Ctr Houston TX 77058

YOUNG, JOHNNY, foreign service officer; b. Savannah, Ga., Feb. 6, 1940; s. John A. and Eva (Grant) Y.; m. Angelena V. Clark, Sept. 23, 1967; children: David John, Michelle Jeanine. B.S. cum laude in Bus., Temple U., 1966. Chief acct. procurement dept. City of Phila., 1960-67; budget officer Am. Embassy, Tananarivo, Madagascar, 1967-69, gen. services officer, Conakry, Guinea, 1970-72, Nairobi, Kenya, 1972-74; adminstrv. officer, Doha, Qatar, 1974-77, Bridgetown, Barbados, 1977-79, adminstrv. counselor, Amman, Jordan, 1983-85, The Hague, Netherlands, from 1985; career counselor Dept. State, Washington, 1979-81, exec. dir., from 1981; ambassador to Sierra Leone, Freetown, 1990—. Ambassador's rep. Am. Club, Amman, 1983—, Am. Community Sch. Bd., Amman, 1983—. Recipient Group Meritorious award State Dept., 1970, Meritorious Honor, 1975, Cash and Meritorious award, 1983, Meritorious Step Increase award, 1984. Mem. Municipal Fin. Officers Assn. Democrat. Roman Catholic. Office: Am Embassy Lome Togo US Dept State Washington DC 20521-2300*

YOUNG, JON NATHAN, archeologist; b. Hibbing, Minn., May 30, 1938; s. Robert Nathan Young and Mary Elizabeth (Barrows) Roy; m. Karen Sue Johnson, June 5, 1961 (div. May 1980); children: Shawn Nathan, Kevin Leigh; m. Tucker Heitman, June 18, 1988 (div. Apr. 1996). BA magna cum laude, U. Ariz., 1960, PhD, 1967; MA, U. Ky., 1962. Archeologist Nat. Park Svc. Southwest Archeol. Ctr., Globe and Tucson, Ariz., 1967-75; exec., camp dir. YMCA of Metro. Tucson, 1976-77; asst. dir. Kit Carson Meml. Found., Taos, N.Mex., 1978; co-dir. Las Palomas de Taos, 1979; archeologist Nat. Forest Svc., Carson Nat. Forest, Taos, 1980—; exec. order cons. U.S. Sec. Interior, 1973-75. Author: The Salado Culture in Southwestern Prehistory, 1967; co-author: Excavation of Mound 7, 1981, First-Day Road Log in Tectonic Development of the Southern Sangre de Cristo Mountains, 1990. Advisor Boy Scouts Am.; active YMCA White Rag Soc.; mem. Kit Carson Hist. Mus. Grantee NEH, 1978; Ariz. Wilson Found., NSF, Ky. Rsch. Found. fellow, 1960-62; Baird Found., Bausch and Lomb, Elks; recipient cert. merit USDA, 1987, 89. Fellow AAAS, Am. Anthrop. Assn., Explorers Club, Royal Anthrop. Inst.; mem. Current Anthropology (assoc.), Ariz. Archaeol. and Hist. Soc., Ariz. Hist. Soc., Ctr. Anthropol. Studies, Coun. on Am.'s Mil. Past, Friends of Taos Pub. Libr., Kit Carson Hist. Mus., New Mex. Heritage Preservation Alliance, Soc. Hist. Archaeology, Soc. Am. Archaeology, Harwood Found., Millicent Rogers Mus., Taos Archaeol. Soc., San Juan County Mus. Assn., Taos County Hist. Soc. (bd. dirs.), Sigma Xi, Phi Beta Kappa, Alpha Kappa Delta, Phi Kappa Phi, Delta Chi. Home: PO Box 2207 Taos NM 87571-2207 Office: Nat Forest Svc Suprs Office 208 Cruz Alta Rd Taos NM 87571-5983

YOUNG, JOSEPH H., federal judge; b. Hagerstown, Md., July 18, 1922; s. J. Edgar and Mabel K. (Koser) Y.; m. Doris Oliver, Sept. 6, 1947; children: Stephen A., William O., J. Harrison. A.B., Dartmouth Coll., 1944; LL.B., U. Va., 1951. Bar: Md. 1951. Assoc. firm Marbury Miller & Evans, Balt., 1951-52; assoc. firm Piper & Marbury, Balt., 1952-58, ptnr., 1958-71, mng. ptnr., 1968-71; judge U.S. Dist. Ct. Md., from 1971, now sr. judge; instr. Johns Hopkins U. (McCoy Coll.), 1954-62. Bd. dirs. Legal Aid Soc. Balt., 1958-71, CICHA (Health Appeal), 1964-71; bd. dirs. exec. com. Md. div. Am. Cancer Soc., 1958—, chmn. div. bd. dirs. 1969-71, bd. dirs. 1966—, chmn. nat. svcs. com. 1970-73, chmn. exec. com. 1976-77, dir.-at-large 1973-83, vice-chmn. nat. bd. 1975-77, chmn. nat. bd. 1977-80, chmn. pub. issues com. 1981-83, past officer dir. 1983-90, hon. life mem. 1990—, chmn. world-wide fight com. 1987-90, also mem. trust adv. bd.; mem. oncology adv. coun. Johns Hopkins U.; chmn. com. on campaign orgn. & pub. edn. Internat. Union Contra Cancer, Geneva, Switzerland, 1981-90, mem. fin. com., 1990—, chmn. 1993—, exec. com. 1993—. Decorated Bronze Star, Purple Heart. Recipient Disting. Service Award Am. Cancer Soc., 1983; Dartmouth Coll. Alumni award, 1983; James Ewing Soc. award, 1983. Mem. 4th Circuit Jud. Conf., Assn. Alumni Dartmouth Coll. (pres. 1984-85). Republican. Presbyterian (elder, deacon, trustee). Clubs: Hamilton Street, Rule Day, Lawyers Round Table. Office: US Dist Ct 101 W Lombard St Ste 720 Baltimore MD 21201-2609

YOUNG, JOSEPH LAURIE, architecture educator; b. Huntsville, Tex., Sept. 23, 1924; s. Benjamin Wiley and Margaret (Cater) Y. BArch, U. Tex., 1950; MArch, Ga. Inst. Tech., 1955. Registered architect S.C. Teaching fellow U. Tex., Austin, 1948-50; prof. emeritus architecture Clemson U., S.C., 1950—, Univ. marshall, 1985-88; Hayes Fulbright fellow Middle East Tech. U., Ankara, Turkey, 1963-64; cons. to bus.; artist drawings of hist. bldgs., 1950—; faculty advisor, 1956—; resident prof. Charles E. Daniel Clemson U. Centre Bldg. Rsch. and Urban Study, Genova, Italy, 1985-86, 88-89; dir. Clemson U. Ctr. for Archtl. Study, Coll. of Charleston, S.C., 1988. Elder Ft. Hill Presbyn. Ch. With USNR, 1943-46. Recipient Student Adviser award Clemson U., 1989. Fellow AIA (pres. S.C. chpt. 1971-72, Svc. awards 1969, 71, bd. dir. S.C. chpt. 1966-69); mem. S.C. AIA, Tiger Brotherhood, Rotary Internat., Tau Sigma Delta, Sigma Alpha Epsilon, Rotary (Paul Harris fellow). Home: 705 Clemson House PO Box 712 Clemson SC 29631

YOUNG, JOSEPH LOUIS, artist; b. Pitts., Nov. 27, 1919; s. Louis and Jennie (Eger) Y.; m. Millicent Goldstein, June 19, 1949; children: Leslie Sybil, Cecily Julie. Grad., Westminster Coll., New Wilmington, Pa., 1941, D. Litt., 1960; Edwin Austin Abbey mural painting scholar, 1949; grad., Boston Mus. Sch. Fine Arts, 1951; Albert H. Whitin traveling fellow, Am. Acad. in Rome, 1951-52. Newspaperman Pitts. and N.Y.C., 1941-43; lectr. Tufts Coll., 1949; painting instr. Boston Mus. Sch., 1950; Idylwild Arts Found., 1959, Brandeis Camp Inst., 1962-74; founder, dir. Joseph Young Mosaic Workshop, 1953—; founding chmn. dept. archtl. arts Brooks Santa Barbara (Calif.) Sch. Fine Arts, 1969-75; head mus. exhibits Bowers Mus., Santa Ana, Calif., 1977-78; head visual arts CETA program, City of Los Angeles, 1978-80; organized internat. sculpture competition for city of Huntington Beach, Calif., 1974; art cons. Allied Arts Commn., City of Huntington Beach, 1973-74; cons. Art in Public Bldgs. Program, Calif. Arts Council, 1976-77; field adminstr. CCA/CETA Program, Los Angeles; Invited prin. speaker at nat. convs. A.I.A., Am. Craftsmen Council, 4th Congress I.A.P.A., 7th Nat. Sculpture Conf., Council of Am., U. Kans.; lectr. Rome, Venice, Florence (as guest) Italian govt., 1959. Restoration of mosaics from Greek and Roman periods and Della Robbia sculpture, 1972-73; author: A Course in Making Mosaics, 1957, Mosaics, Principles and Practice, 1963, also articles in profl. jours.; pub. mural painting bibliography, 1946; asso. founding editor: Creative Crafts mag, 1960-64; concept and design: ART$MARKET, 1979; work featured 16mm documentary film The World of Mosaic; true fresco, oil and mosiac mural commns. in, Boston, Chgo., Pitts., Los Angeles, survey govt. sponsored mural painting programs, 1951; one man show, Pitts. Arts and Crafts Center, 1950, Falk-Raboff Gallery, Los Angeles, 1953, ten year retrospective exhbn. archtl. art work, Desert Mus., Palm Springs, Calif., 1963, Calif. council A.I.A. Fine Arts Architecture Exhbn., 1964, Nat. Gold Medal Exhbn. of N.Y. Archtl. League, 1951, Platt Gallery, Bel Air, Calif., 1996; work reproduced in numerous books, mags., newspapers throughout the world; invited to submit designs for Nebr. State Capitol murals, paintings and mosiacs in numerous pvt. collections; executed mosiac murals Los Angeles Police Facilities Bldg., 1955, Don Bosco Tech. High Sch., 1956, Temple Emanuel, 1957, Southland Shopping Center, 1958, Our Lady of Lourdes Ch., 1959, Cameo residence, Beverly Hills, Calif., 1961, Santa Barbara Stock Exchange, 1960, St. Martins Ch., La Mesa, Calif., 1966, stained glass windows, liturgical art program, Congregation Beth Sholom, San Francisco, 1966, West Apse of Nat. Shrine of Immaculate Conception, Washington, 1966, mosiac arch, Eden Meml. Park, San Fernando, Calif., 1960; commd. to execute mural, Los Angeles County Hall of Records, Shalom Meml. Park, Chgo., B.V.M. Presentation Ch., Midland, Pa., 1961, Hollenbeck Police Sta., Los Angeles, 1963, Beth Emet Temple, Anaheim, Calif., 1963, Temple Sinai, Glendale, Calif., 1963, Sinai Temple, Los Angeles, 1963, Valley Beth Israel, Sun Valley, Calif., 1964, Beth Tikvah, Westchester, Calif., 1964, Belmont High Sch., Los Angeles, 1972; commd. to design and execute 14 bas-relief concrete-mosaic murals for exterior of, Math. Scis. Bldg. at UCLA, bronze sculpture, La Mirada (Calif.) Civic Theatre, 1979; did liturgical art programs for, Congregation B'nai B'rith, Santa Barbara, Temple Beth Torah, Alhambra, Temple Beth Ami, West Covina, Temple Menorah, Redondo Beach, Temple Solael, Canoga Park, Temple Bamidbar, Lancaster, Temple Beth Jacob, Redwood City (all Calif.), other congregations in Calif., concrete bas reliefs, Southgate County Pub. Library, 1973, mosaics for, St. Mary of Angels, Hollywood, Calif., 1973, Triforium polyphonoptic, kinetic tower, Los Angeles Mall, 1969-75; multimedia presentations for, 400th Anniversary Michelangelo, Italian Trade Commn., Casa de Maria, Santa Barbara, Hancock Coll., Santa Maria, Los Angeles County Mus. Art, U. Calif., Los Angeles and Irvine., designs for Holocaust Monument for Pan-Pacific Park in Los Angeles won national competition and dedicated in 1992; appointed to City of West Hollywood Arts Commn.; chmn. Fine Arts Bd., U. of Judaism, L.A.; completed cycle of Stained Glass windows for Ventura County Jewish Community Ctr. devoted to theme of Seven Days of Creation, 12 tribes stained glass for Temple Beth Israel, West Hollywood, Calif., 1991; work subject of restrospective exhbn. at the Jewish Community Galleries, 1986; commd. projects now represented by Yanov & Gold, Ltd. of Los Angeles, Calif.; chapel design Heritage Pointe, Mission Viejo, Calif. Served with USAAF, 1943-46. Recipient Nat. Army Arts contest award, 1945; Huntington Hartford Found. fellow, 1952-53; named Cavaliere della Republica Italiana, 1975. Fellow Internat. Inst. Arts and Letters (life); mem. Nat. Soc. Mural Painters (nat. v.p. 1969—), Artists Equity Assn. (pres. So. Calif. chpt. 1956, nat. v.p. 1960), Calif. Confedn. Arts (founding pres. 1976). Home and Studio: Art in Architecture 7917 1/2 Norton Ave Los Angeles CA 90046-5204

YOUNG, KATHERINE ANN, education educator; b. Castleford, Idaho, Apr. 9, 1941; d. Ross and Norna (Scully) Stoner; m. Virgil Monroe Young, Dec. 20, 1964; 1 child, Susan Annette. BS in Elem. Edn., U. Idaho, 1965; MEd, Ea. Washington U., 1969; EdD, Utah State U., 1980. Cert. advanced elem. tchr., Idaho. Tchr. spl. edn. Coeur d'Alene (Idaho) Sch. Dist., 1965-66; tchr. elem. grades Coeur d' Aleue (Idaho) Sch. Dist., 1966-67, Boise (Idaho) Sch. Dist., 1967-88; assoc. prof. edn. Boise State U., 1988-93, prof., coord. elem. edn., 1993—; dir. Alliance of Idaho Geographers/Nat. Geographic Soc., 1993—. Co-author: (resource book) The Story of Idaho Author's, 1977, The Story of Idaho Guide and Resource Book, 1993; author: The Utah Activity Book, 1980, Constructing Buildings, Bridges, and Minds, 1993; cons., contbr. (nat. edn. jour.) Learning, 1991—. Named Idaho Tchr. of Yr., State Dept. of Edn., Boise, 1983; invited to luncheon at White House, Pres. Ronald Reagan, Washington, 1983; Recipient Outstanding Young Educator award Boise Jaycees, 1983; profiled in Idaho Centennial pub., 1990; travel to Japan grantee Rocky Mountain Region Japan Project, 1990. Mem. ASCD, Nat. Coun. for Social Studies, Idaho Law Found., Alliance Idaho Geographers (state coord.). Avocations: travel, reading. Office: Boise State U Dept Tchr Edn 1910 University Dr Boise ID 83725-0001

YOUNG, KEITH LAWRENCE, lawyer; b. Chgo., Jan. 15, 1953; s. Lawrence E. and June E. (Verboomen) Y.; m. Wendy A. Kollross; children: Kyle W., Lauren E., Taylor H. BS, Iowa State U., 1974; JD, Ill. Inst. Tech., 1977. Bar: Ill. 1977, U.S. Dist. Ct. (no. dist.) Ill. 1977, U.S. Ct. Appeals (7th cir.) 1977. Pvt. practice law Chgo., 1977—; assoc. Anesi, Ozmon & Lewin, Chgo., 1977-79, James Demos Ltd., Chgo., 1979-80; ptnr. Lambruschi Young & Assocs., Chgo., 1980-87. Mem. ATLA, Ill. Bar Assn., Chgo. Bar Assn., Ill. Trial Lawyers Assn. Office: 333 W Wacker Dr Chicago IL 60606-1220

YOUNG, KENNETH EVANS, educational consultant; b. Toronto, Ont., Can., Mar. 21, 1922; s. John Osborne Wallace and Gwendolyn May (Evans) Y.; m. Mae Catherine Wittenmyer, July 1, 1945; 1 child, Bruce Kenneth. AB, San Francisco State Coll., 1943; MA, Stanford U., 1947, PhD, 1953; LLD (hon.), U. Nev., 1972. Instr. journalism and speech San Francisco State Coll., 1946-48; instr. journalism and English Calif. State Poly. Coll., San Luis Obispo, 1949-50; from asst. prof. to acting dean Coll. Arts and Scis. Kellogg-Voorhis Campus, Pomona, 1951-57; dean faculty U. Alaska, College, 1957-59; fellow in coll. adminstrn. U. Mich., Ann Arbor, 1959-60; exec. v.p. U. Nev., Reno, 1960-64; pres. SUNY, Cortland, 1964-68; v.p., dir. Washington office Am. Coll. Testing Program, 1968-75; pres. Council on Postsecondary Accreditation, Washington, 1975-80; exec. dir. Nat. Univ. Continuing Edn. Assn., Washington, 1980-84; dir. Inst. for Learning in Retirement, Am. U., Washington, 1984-89; sr. assoc., cons. Diane U. Eisenberg Assocs., Washington, 1984-95; chmn. Evans-McCan Group, 1996—. Prin. editor: Understanding Accreditation, 1983; contbr. articles to profl. jours. Sgt. U.S. Army, 1943-45. Republican. Home: 4200 Cathedral Ave NW Apt 512 Washington DC 20016-4912

YOUNG, KEVIN, track and field athlete. Olympic track and field participant Barcelona, Spain, 1992. Recipient 400m Hurdles Gold medal Olympics, Barcelona, 1992; world recorder holder in 400m hurdles. Office: US Olympic Com 1750 E Boulder St Colorado Springs CO 80909-5724 Address: 13010 Bethany Rd Alpharetta GA 30201-1052*

YOUNG, LAURA, dance educator, choreographer; b. Boston, Aug. 5, 1947; d. James Vincent and Adelaide Janet Young; m. Anthony Charles Catanzaro, Sept. 26, 1970 (div. Nov. 1981); m. Christopher Edward Mehl, Aug. 23, 1987. Grad. high sch., Cohasset, Mass. Dancer Met. Opera Ballet, N.Y.C., 1971-73; dancer Boston Ballet Co., 1963-65, prin. dancer, 1965-71, 73-89, ballet mistress, 1989-91; guest tchr. Dance Tchrs. Club Boston, 1978-82, Dance Masters Assn., 1979, 90, 92, 93, Walnut Hill Sch., Natick, Mass., 1984-87, 90-91; asst. dir. Boston Ballet II, 1984-86, tchr., dir., 1986-96, dir. summer dance program, 1986-94; 1st hon. mem. Dance Masters Assn., Chpt. 5, 1992; mem. faculty Boston Conservatory, 1990-94; prin. Boston Ballet Sch., 1993—. Choreographer (ballets) Occasional Waltzes, 1984, Albinoni Suite, 1986, Champ Dances, 1987, A Place of Sound and Mind, 1988, Deadlock, 1989, Rumpelstiltskin, 1989. Recipient Leadership award Greater Boston C. of C., 1987; named Disting. Bostonian, Boston's 350th Jubilee Com., 1980. Mem. Am. Guild Mus. Artists, Dance Masters Am. (hon.). Office: Boston Ballet Co 19 Clarendon St Boston MA 02116-6107

YOUNG, LAURENCE RETMAN, biomedical engineer, educator; b. N.Y.C., Dec. 19, 1935; s. Benjamin and Bess (Retman) Y.; m. Joan Marie Fisher, June 12, 1960; children—Eliot Fisher, Leslie Ann, Robert Retman. A.B., Amherst Coll., 1957; S.B., MIT, 1957; S.M., Mass. Inst. Tech., 1959, Sc.D., 1962; Certificat de License (French Govt. fellow), Faculty of Sci. U. of Paris, France, 1958. Registered profl. engr., Mass. Engr. Sperry Gyroscope Co., Great Neck, N.Y., 1957; engr. NASA Instrumentation Lab., MIT, 1958-60, asst. prof. aero. and astronautics, 1962-67, assoc. prof., 1967-70, prof., 1970—, payload specialist spacelab life sci., 1991-93; Apollo Program prof., chair in astronautics MIT, Cambridge, 1995—; prof. Baylor Coll. Medicine, Houston, 1996—; dir. Nat. Space Biomed. Rsch. Inst., 1997—; summer lectr. U. Ala., Huntsville, 1966-68; lectr. Med. Sch. Harvard U., 1970-78; mem. tng. com. biomed. engring. NIH, 1971-73; mem. com. space medicine and biology Space Sci. Bd., NAS, 1974-77, chmn. vestibular panel summer study of life scis. in space, 1977; mem. com. engring. and clin. care NAE, 1970; mem. Air Force Sci. Adv. Bd., 1979-85; mem. Air Force Studies Bd., NRC, 1982, Aeros. and Space Engrs. Bd., 1982-87; mem. NRC Com. on Space Sta., 1987, 1991—, Com. on Human Exploration Space, 1990, Com. on Human Factors, 1990—; CHABA coun. NASA Task Force on Sci. Uses of Space Sta., 1982-85; vis. prof. Swiss Fed. Inst. Tech., Zurich, 1972-73, Conservatoire Nationale des Arts and Metiers, Paris, 1972-73, Stanford U., 1987-88; vis. scientist Kantonsspital Zurich, 1972-73; prin. investigator vestibular expts. on Spacelabs—1, SLS-1, 2 and D-1, 1977—; cons. Applied Sci. Lab., NASA, Gulf & Western, Link div. Singer Co., Boeing, Lockheed, others; payload specialist Space Shuttle STS-58 (Spacelab SLS-2), NASA Johnson Space Ctr., 1992—. Contbg. author: chpt. on vestibular system Medical Physiology, 1974, Handbook of Physiology, 1983, Encyclopedia of Neuroscience, 1987; editorial bd. chpt. on vestibular system Internat. Jour. Man-Machine Studies, 1966-75, Neurosci., 1976-92; contbr. numerous articles to profl. jours. Recipient Pub. Service Group Achievement award NASA, 1984; Exceptional Civilian Service award U.S. Air Force, 1985. Fellow IEEE (Franklin V. Taylor award 1963, First Ann. Space Life Sci. lectr. 1990), AIAA (Dryden lectr. 1981), Aerospace Medical Assn. (Jeffries Medical Rsch. award 1992), Aerospace Human Factor Assn. (Paul Hensen award 1995), U.S. Ski Assn. (award of merit 1976), Explorers Club; mem. NAE, Inst. Medicine, Am. Physiol. Soc. (1st lectr. in aerospace life scis. 1990), Biomed. Engring. Soc. (founding/charter mem., dir. 1972-75, pres. 1979-80, Alza lectr. 1984), Aerospace Med. Assn., ASTM (com. on snow skiing 1975—, chmn. 1988-93), Internat. Soc. Skiing Safety (bd. dirs. 1977-85), Internat. Fedn. Automatic Control (tech. com. biomed. engring. 1975-85), AIAA (working group for simulator facilities 1976-80), Nat. Acad. Engrs., Inst. Medicine, Internat. Acad. Astronautics, Barany Soc., Cosmos Club, Explorers Club, Tau Beta Pi. Home: 8 Devon Rd Newton MA 02159-1648 Office: MIT Man-Vehicle Lab Rm 37-219 Cambridge MA 02139

YOUNG, LAWRENCE, electrical engineering educator; b. Hull, Eng., July 5, 1925; arrived in Can., 1955; naturalized, 1972; s. Herbert and Dora Y.; m. Margaret Elisabeth Jane, Jan. 5, 1951. B.A., Cambridge U., 1946, Ph.D., 1950, Sc.D., 1963. Asst. lectr. Imperial Coll., London, 1952-55; mem. research staff B.C. Research Council, 1955-63; assoc. prof. U. B.C., Vancouver, 1963-65, prof. dept. elec. engring., 1965-90, prof. emeritus, 1990—. Author: Anodic Oxide Films, 1961; contbr. articles to profl. jours. Recipient Callinan award Dielectrics div. Electrochemical Soc., 1983, Can. Electrochem. Gold medal, 1990. Fellow IEEE, Royal Soc. Can. Office: Dept Electrical Engineering, U BC, Vancouver, BC Canada V6T 1W5

YOUNG, LEO, electrical engineer; b. Vienna, Austria, Aug. 18, 1926; came to U.S., 1953, naturalized, 1958; s. Samuel and Marie Y.; m. Fay Merskey, Jan. 4, 1953 (dec. May 1981); children—Philip Michael, Sarah Anne, Joseph David; m. Ruth Breslow, Jan. 2, 1983. BA, Cambridge U., 1946, MA, 1950; MS, Johns Hopkins U., 1956, D.Engring. (Westinghouse-B.G. Lamme grad. scholar), 1959, D.H.L. (hon.), 1989. Lab. mgr. Decca Radar, Ltd., Surbiton, Eng., 1951-53; adv. engr. Westinghouse Electric Corp., Balt., 1953-60; staff scientist, program mgr. Stanford Research Inst., Menlo Park, Calif., 1960-73; staff cons., asso. supt. Naval Research Lab., Washington, 1973-81; dir. research Office of Undersec. for Def. Research and Engring., Dept. Def., 1981-94; cons. to dir. def. rsch. and engring. Dept. Def., 1994—; bd. dirs. Filtronic-Comtek (U.K.); mem. NSF delegation to Japan, 1995; chair NSF Rev. Panel on Critical Techs., 1997. Author: Microwave Filters, 1964, Systems of Units in Electricity and Magnetism, 1969, Advances in Microwaves, Vols. 1-8, 1966-74, Everything You Should Know About Pensions Plans, 1976; also articles. Fellow AAAS, IEEE (pres. 1980, pres. Microwave Soc. 1969, Microwave prize 1963, Microwave Career award 1988, Disting. Contbns. to Engring. Professionalism IEEE-USA 1993, Pinnacle award 1995); mem. Sigma Xi. Patentee in field. *It has been my goal to serve the public and my belief that engineering and science improve the quality of life. I have enjoyed doing engineering research and am fortunate in receiving recognition.*

YOUNG, LIONEL WESLEY, radiologist; b. New Orleans, Mar. 14, 1932; s. Charles Henry and Ethel Elsie (Johnson) Y.; m. Florence Inez Brown, June 24, 1957; children: Tina Inez, Lionel Thomas, Owen Christopher. BS in Biology, St. Benedict's Coll., Atchison, Kans., 1953; MD, Howard U., 1957. Diplomate Am. Bd. Radiology. Intern Detroit Receiving Hosp., Wayne State Univ. Coll. of Medicine, 1957-58; resident Strong Meml. Hosp., U. Rochester (N.Y.) Med. Ctr., 1958-61; pediatric radiologist, assoc. prof. radiology and pediatrics U. Rochester Med. Ctr., 1965-75; prof. radiology and pediatrics U. Pitts., 1975-86; dir. radiology and pediatrics Children's Hosp. of Pitts., 1980-86; chmn. radiology Children's Hosp. Med. Ctr. of Akron (Ohio), 1986—, Children's Hosp. and Northeastern Ohio U. Coll. Medicine, Rootstown, 1987—; pres. Akron Pediatric Radiologists, 1986—. Lt. comdr. USN, 1961-63. Mem. Am. Coll. Radiology (mem. coun., steering com.), Soc. for Pediatric Radiology. Democrat. Roman Catholic. Avocation: music. Office: Division of Pediatric Radiology Loma Linda Univ Children's Hosp 11234 Anderson St Loma Linda CA 92354-2804*

YOUNG, LUCY CLEAVER, physician; b. Wheeling, W.Va., Aug. 8, 1943. BS in Chemistry, Wheaton Coll. (Ill.), 1965; MD, Ohio State U., 1969. Diplomate Am. Bd. Family Practice, Bd. of Ins. Medicine. Rotating intern Riverside Meth. Hosp., Columbus, Ohio, 1969-70; resident Trumbull Meml. Hosp., Warren, Ohio, 1970-71; practice medicine specializing in family practice, West Chicago, Ill., 1971-73, Paw Paw and Mendota, Ill., 1973-78; co-founder and med. dir. Wholistic Health Ctr. of Mendota, 1976-78; asst. med. dir. Met. Life Ins. Co., Gt. Lakes Head Office, Aurora, Ill., 1979-80; med. dir. Commonwealth Life Ins. Co., Louisville, 1980-85; assoc. prof. U. Ill. Abraham Lincoln Sch. Medicine, 1976-79; faculty monitor MacNeal Meml. Hosp. Family Practice Ctr. (Ill.), 1979-80; faculty preceptor U. Louisville Family Practice Dept., 1981-85; Locum Tenens Family Practice for Kron Med. Corp. of Chapel Hill, N.C., 1986-89; physician Red Bird Mission & Med. Ctr., Beverly, Ky., 1989-90; family practice floater Ochsner Clinic satellites, New Orleans, 1990—; clin. faculty preceptor La. State U. Sch. Medicine, 1992—; mem. staffs Ctrl. DuPage Hosp., Winfield, Ill., 1971-73, Mendota Cmty. Hosp., 1973-80, Ochsner Found. Hosp., New Orleans, 1991—. Vol. Red Bird Med. Ctr., 1985—; part-time worship coord. Hosanna Luth Ch., Mandeville, La., 1996—. Fellow Am. Acad. Family Practice; mem. Christian Med. and Dental Soc. (del. to House 1995—). Home: PO Box 0730 Madisonville LA 70447-0730 Office: Ochsner Clinic Family Medicine Dept 2005 Veterans Blvd Metairie LA 70002

YOUNG, MALCOLM EUGENE, JR., social studies secondary educator; b. Sulphur Springs, Tex., Sept. 27, 1943; s. Malcolm Eugene Sr. and Cleo Lessie (Wilson) Y.; m. Frances Jeane Tatum, Aug. 27, 1966; children: Robert, Kerri, Scott. BS, Howard Payne U., 1967; MEd, North Tex. State U., 1969. Lic. tchr., Tex. Tchr., coach Travis Jr. High Sch., Irving, Tex., 1967-69, MacArthur High Sch., Irving, 1969-71, North Jr. High Sch., Richardson, Tex., 1971-72, Westwood Jr. High Sch., Richardson, 1972-75; tchr., coach J.J. Pearce High Sch., Richardson, 1975-78, tchr., 1978—. Tchr. participant Close Up, Washington, 1989, Law-Related Edn. Summer Inst., Austin, 1993, 96, 97; sponsor, participant Close Up-Citizen Bee regional competition, Dallas, 1990-95. Taft Seminar for Tchrs. fellow, Austin, Tex., 1995. Mem. Nat. Coun. Social Studies, Assn. Tex. Profl. Educators, Tex. Coun. Social Studies, Richardson Assn. Tex. Profl. Educators. Methodist. Avocations: leather work, hunting, fishing, camping. Office: Richardson Ind Sch Dist 1600 N Coit Rd Richardson TX 75080-2805

YOUNG, MARGARET ALETHA MCMULLEN (MRS. HERBERT WILSON YOUNG), social worker; b. Vossburg, Miss., June 13, 1916; d. Grady Garland and Virgie Aletha (Moore) McMullen; BA cum laude, Columbia Bible Coll., 1949; grad. Massey Bus. Coll., 1958; MSW, Fla. State U., 1965; postgrad. Jacksonville U., 1961-62, Tulane U., 1967; m. Herbert Wilson Young, Aug. 19, 1959. Dir. Christian edn. Eau Claire Presbyn. Ch., Columbia, S.C., 1946-51; tchr. Massey Bus. Coll., Jacksonville, Fla., 1954-57, office mgr., 1957-59; social worker, unit supr. Fla. div. Family Svcs., St. Petersburg, 1960-66, dist. casework supr., 1966-71; social worker, project supr., program supr. Project Playpen, Inc., 1971-81, pres. bd., 1982-83, cons., 1986-89; pvt. practice family counselor, 1982—; mem. coun. Child Devel. Ctr., 1983-89; mem. transitional housing com., Religious Community Svcs., 1984-90. Mem. Acad. Cert. Social Workers, Nat. Assn. Social Workers (pres. Tampa Bay chpt. 1973-74), Fla. Assn. for Health and Social Services (pres. chpt. 1971), Nature Conservancy, Eta Beta Rho. Democrat. Presbyn.

Rotary Ann (pres. 1970-71). Home: Presbyterian Home CMR 13 201 W 9th North St Summerville SC 29483-6721

YOUNG, MARGARET CHONG, elementary education educator; b. Honolulu, May 8, 1924; d. Henry Hon Chin and Daisy Kyau (Tong) Chong; m. Alfred Y.K. Young, Feb. 21, 1948; children: Robert S.W., Richard S.K., Linda S.K. EdB, 5th yr. cert., U. Hawaii, 1945. Cert. tchr., Hawaii. Tchr. Waipahu (Hawaii) Elem. Sch., Manoa Housing Sch., Hawaii Dept. Edn., Honolulu, Pauoa Elem. Sch., Honolulu. Author: And They Also Came, History of Chinese Christian Association, Hawaii's People From China; contbr. numerous articles to profl. jours. Ch. sch. tchr., supt. United Ch. Christ-Judd St. Grantee San Francisco State Coll. Mem. NEA, Hawaii State Tchrs. Assn., Hawaii Congress of Parents and Tchrs. (hon. life mem.), Kappa Kappa Iota (Disting. Educator award 1986-87), Delta Kappa Gamma (internat.).

YOUNG, MARILYN RAE, mayor, former school system adminstrative secretary; b. Muskegon, Mich., Dec. 29, 1934; d. Albert Henry Cribley and Mildred Ida (Johnson) Raby; m. Peter John Young, May 21, 1955; children: Pamela Lynn Young-Walker, Lane Allen. Grad. high sch., Calumet City, Ill., 1952. Dep. pub. fiduciary Yuma County, Ariz., 1979-83; adminstrv. sec. Yuma Sch. Dist. One, 1983-95; councilman City of Yuma, 1990-93, mayor, 1993—. Pres. bd. dirs. Behavioral Health Svcs. of Yuma, 1979-90; vice chmn. Yuma Planning and Zoning Commn., 1985-89; v.p. bd. dirs. Children's Village, Yuma, 1983-89; lay leader Trinity United Meth. Ch., 1986-95; grad. Yuma Leadership Inc., 1985, treas. bd. dirs., 1986-89; participant Ariz. Women's Town Hall, 1989-93, various Yuma County Town Halls, 1987-93; adv. bd. mem. Friends of KAWC; chmn. Yuma Pub. Safety Police Bd., 1990—, Yuma Fire Pub. Safety Bd., 1990—, Yuma Youth Leadership Com., 1991-95; mem. allocation panel United Way, 1991-93; charter mem. Friends of Roxaboxen; active H.S. Ad Hoc Com., 1991-97; exec. bd. mem. Yuma Met. Planning Orgn., 1990—, Western Ariz. Coun. of Govts., 1990—; corp. bd. dirs. Greater Yuma Econ. Devel., 1990-95; hon. chmn. Yuma County San Luis Rio Colo. Commn., 1990—; mem. Nat. League of Cities FAIR Com., 1990—, FAIR steering com., 1997—, Binational Border Health Task Force, 1990—, resolution com. League of Ariz. Cities and Towns, 1990—, mem. com. U.S. Conf. of Mayors, 1990—. Mem. Yuma County C. of C. (mem. mil. affairs com. 1988-90). Avocations: community involvement, reading, travel, needlework. Home: 1288 W 18th St Yuma AZ 85364-5313 Office: City of Yuma 180 W 1st St Yuma AZ 85364-1407

YOUNG, MARVIN OSCAR, lawyer; b. Union, Mo., Apr. 4, 1929; s. Otto Christopher and Irene Adelheide (Barlage) Y.; m. Sue Carol Mathews, Aug. 23, 1952; children: Victoria Leigh, Kendall Marvin. A.B., Westminster Coll., 1951; J.D., U. Mich., 1954; LLD, Westminster Coll., 1989. Bar: Mo. 1954. Practice law firm Thompson, Mitchell, Thompson Douglas, St. Louis, 1954-55, 57-58; atty. Mo. Farmers Assn., Columbia, 1958-67; exec. v.p. First Mo. Corp., Columbia, 1965-68; v.p. ops. MFA-Central Coop., Columbia, 1967-68; v.p., gen. counsel, sec. Peabody Coal Co., St. Louis, 1968-82; gen. counsel Peabody Holding Co., Inc., St. Louis, 1983-85; also dir., sec. subs. and affiliates Peabody Coal Co.; ptnr. Gallop, Johnson & Neuman, St. Louis, 1986—, chmn. corp. dept., 1988-90, chmn. energy dept., 1990—; city atty. Warson Woods, Mo., 1990—; speaker at legal insts. Assoc. editor Mich. Law Rev., 1953-54; contbr. articles to profl. jours. Pres. Warson Woods PTA, 1974-75; trustee Met. Sewer Dist. St. Louis, 1974-80, chmn. 1978-80; mem. Mo. Energy Coun., 1973-77, Mo. Environ. Improvement and Energy Resources Athority, 1983-87, vice chmn. 1986-87; trustee Eastern Mineral Law Found., 1983—; pres. Alumni Assn. Westminster Coll., Fulton, Mo., 1978-80, trustee coll., 1977—, exec. com., 1978—, chmn. 1986-90; chmn. Churchill Meml. and Libr., Fulton, 1992—; mem. Chancellor's Coun. Adv. Bd. U. of Mo., St. Louis, 1992—; mem. lawyers adv. coun. Gt. Plains Legal Found., Kansas City, Mo., 1976-84; mem. Rep. Com. Boone County, Mo., 1962-68, chmn. legis. dist. com., 1962-64, 66-68; alt. del. Rep. Nat. Conv., 1968; pres. Clayton Twp. Rep. Club, 1973-77; sr. warden Episc. Ch., 1988-89. Served to capt. USAF, 1955-57. Recipient alumni award of merit, 1972; Churchill fellow, 1990; named Coal Lawyer Yr. Nat. Coal Assn., 1994. Mem. ABA, Mo. Bar Assn., Bar Assn. Met. St. Louis, Barristers Soc., Round Table Club of St. Louis, John Marshall Rep. Lawyers Club (pres. 1977), Mo. Athletic Club, Rotary (bd. dirs. St. Louis club 1993-95), Masons, Order of Coif. Home: 555 Flanders Dr Saint Louis MO 63122-1617 Office: Gallop Johnson & Neuman LC 101 S Hanley Rd Ste 1600 Saint Louis MO 63105-3406

YOUNG, MARY ELIZABETH, history educator; b. Utica, N.Y., Dec. 16, 1929; d. Clarence Whitford and Mary Tippit Y. B.A., Oberlin Coll., 1950; Ph.D. (Robert Shalkenbach Found. grantee, Ezra Cornell fellow), Cornell U., 1955. Instr. dept. history Ohio State U., Columbus, 1955-58; asst. prof. Ohio State U., 1958-63, assoc. prof., 1963-69, prof., 1969-73; prof. history U. Rochester, N.Y., 1973—; cons. in field. Author: Redskins, Ruffleshirts, and Rednecks: Indian Allotments in Alabama and Mississippi, 1830-1860, 1961; co-editor, contbr.: The Frontier in Americal Development: Essays in Honor of Paul Wallace Gates, 1969. Recipient Pelzer award Miss. Valley Hist. Assn., 1955, Award Am. Studies Assn., 1982, Ray A. Billington award, 1982; Social Sci. Research Council grantee, 1968-69. Mem. Am. Hist. Assn., Orgn. Am. Historians, Soc. for Historians of the Early Am. Republic, Am. Antiquarian Soc. Home: 2230 Clover St Rochester NY 14618-4124 Office: U Rochester Dept History Rochester NY 14627

YOUNG, MARY SEAN, actress; b. Louisville; m. Robert Andre Lujan; 1 child: Rio Kelly Lujan. Grad., Interlochen Arts Acad., Mich., 1978. Actress: (feature films) Jane Austen in Manhattan, 1980, Stripes, 1981, Blade Runner, 1982, Young Doctors in Love, 1982, Dune, 1984, Baby - Secret of the Lost Legend, 1985, No Way Out, 1987, Wall Street, 1987, The Boost, 1988, Cousins, 1989, Fire Birds, 1990, A Kiss Before Dying, 1991, Once Upon a Crime, 1992, Love Crimes, 1992, Fatal Instinct, 1993, Ace Ventura: Pet Detective, 1994, Even Cowgirls Get the Blues, 1994, Dr. Jekyll and Ms. Hyde, 1995, The Proprietaire, 1995; TV appearances include Under the Biltmore Clock, Tender Is the Night, Blood and Orchids, 1986, Blue Ice, 1994, Witness to the Execution, 1994, Mirage, 1995, Evil Has a Face, 1996, Everything to Gain, 1996, Gun, 1997. Office: Shonderosa Productions PO Box 20547 Sedona AZ 86341

YOUNG, MATT NORVEL, JR., university chancellor emeritus; b. Nashville, Oct. 5, 1915; s. Matt Norvel and Ruby (Morrow) Y.; m. Helen Mattox, Aug. 31, 1939; children: Emily Lemley, Matt Norvel III, Marilyn Stewart, Sara Jackson. BA, Abilene Christian U., 1936; MA, Vanderbilt U., 1937, PhD, 1943; LHD, Calif. Coll. Medicine, 1964; LLD, Lubbock Christian U., 1982, Pepperdine U., 1987. Min. College Ch. of Christ, Lipscomb U., 1941-43, Broadway Ch. Christ, Lubbock, Tex., 1944-57; pres. Pepperdine U., L.A., 1957-71, chancellor, 1971-84, chancellor emeritus, 1985—, also regent.; chmn. bd. dirs. 21st Century Christian Pub. Co., Nashville; bd. dirs. Imperial Bank, L.A.; co-founder Lubbock Christian U., 1957, Lubbock Children's Home, 1953, Tex. Tech. U. Bible chair, 1950. Author: History of Christian Colleges, 1949, The Church is Building, 1956; co-founder: 21st Century Christian mag., 1938, editor, pub., 1945-76; editor Power for Today, 1955-70, Preachers of Today, Vol. I, 1952, Vol. II, 1959, Vol. III, 1964, Vol. IV, 1970, Vol. V, 1982, Churches of Today, Vol. I, 1960, Vol. II, 1969, Stress is a Killer, 1978. Bd. govs. L.A. County Mus. Natural History, 1960—, trustee, 1970—; bd. dirs. Nat. Coun. on Alcoholism, 1981-83, Calif. M-2 Prisoner Rehab. Assn., 1986-90, Forest Lawn Meml. Parks, Christian Higher Edn. Found.; vice chmn. bd. Union Rescue Mission. Recipient George Washington medal Freedom Found., 1962, 64. Mem. L.A. Area C. of C. (bd. dirs.), Phi Delta Kappa. Clubs: Bohemian, California. Lodge: Rotary. Home: 24420 Tiner Ct Malibu CA 90265-4705 Office: Pepperdine U 24255 Pacific Coast Hwy Malibu CA 90263-0001

YOUNG, MAURICE ISAAC, mechanical and aerospace engineering educator; b. Boston, Feb. 10, 1927; s. Joseph J. and Alice (Lifshitz) Y.; m. Eleanor Cooper, Sept. 25, 1954; children: Rochelle, Gerald, Rosalind. Student, Worcester Poly. Inst., 1944-45; PhB, U. Chgo., 1949, BS, 1949; MA, Boston U., 1950; PhD, U. Pa., 1960. Sr. dynamics engr. Bell Aircraft Corp., Buffalo, 1951-52; Sr. dynamics engr. Bell Aircraft Corp., Ft. Worth, 1952-53; group engr. Jacobs Aircraft Engine Co., Pottstown, Pa., 1953-54; prin. tech. engr. Piasecki Helicopter and Aircraft Corp., Morton, Pa., 1954-56, Phila., 1956-58; sr. engring. specialist communications and weapons div. Philco Corp., Phila., 1958-61; mgr. applied mechanics Philco Corp., 1958-61; mgr. helicopter research and advanced tech. Vertol Div. Boeing Co., Phila., 1961-68; prof. mech. and aerospace engring. U. Del., 1968-88, prof. emeritus, 1988; mem. internat. organizing com. for modeling and simulation Internat. Assn. Sci. and Tech. for Devel., 1982; cons. Vigyan Rsch. Assocs., Hampton, Va., 1988-90; also cons. in field; NASA-Am. Soc. Engring. Edn. faculty fellow, NASA Langley Rsch. Ctr., 1987. Mem. editorial bd. Powered Lift Aircraft, 1975-83. Served with USAAF, 1946-47. DuPont Faculty fellow, 1969-70; U.S. Army grantee, 1971-76. Fellow AIAA (assoc.); mem. Soc. Engring. Sci., Sigma Xi. Home: 852 Brompton Ct Newport News VA 23608-9344

YOUNG, MERWIN CRAWFORD, political science educator; b. Phila., Nov. 7, 1931; s. Ralph Aubrey and Louise (Merwin) Y.; m. Rebecca Conrad, Aug. 17, 1957; children: Eva Colcord, Louise Conrad, Estelle Merwin, Emily Harriet. BA, U. Mich., 1953; postgrad., Inst. Hist. Rsch. U. London, 1955-56, Inst d'Etudes Politiques, U. Paris, 1956-57; Ph.D., Harvard U., 1964. Asst. prof. polit. sci. U. Wis., Madison, 1963-66, assoc. prof., 1966-69, prof., 1969—, Rupert Emerson prof., 1983; H. Edwin Young prof., 1994; chmn. African Studies Program U. Wis., Madison, 1964-68, chmn. dept. polit. sci., 1969-72, 84-87, assoc. dean Grad. Sch., 1968-71, acting dean Coll. Letters and Sci., 1992-93; vis. prof. Makerere U. Coll., Kampala, Uganda, 1965-66; dean Faculty of Social Sci. Nat. U., Lubumbashi, Zaire, 1973-75; Fulbright prof. U. Dakar, Senegal, 1987-88. Author: Politics in the Congo, 1965, The Politics of Cultural Pluralism, 1976 (Herskovits prize 1977, Ralph Bunche prize 1979), Ideology and Development in Africa, 1982, The African Colonial State in Comparative Perspective, 1994 (Gregory Luebbert prize 1995); co-author: Cooperatives and Development, 1981, The Rise and Decline of the Zairian State, 1985; editor: The Rising Tide of Cultural Pluralism: The Nation-State at Bay?, 1993. Served to 1st lt. U.S. Army, 1953-55. Social Sci. Rsch. fellow, 1967-68, Ford Faculaty fellow, 1967-68, Guggenheim Found. fellow, 1972-73; vis. fellow Inst. for Advanced Study, Princeton, 1980-81; fellow Woodrow Wilson Internat. Ctr. for Scholars, 1983-84. Mem. Am. Polit. Sci. Assn., African Studies Assn. (pres. 1982-83, Disting. Africanist award 1990). Home: 639 Crandall St Madison WI 53711-1836 Office: U Wis Dept Polit Sci North Hall 1050 Bascom Mall Madison WI 53706-1316

YOUNG, MICHAEL C., allergist, immunologist, pediatrician; b. Chgo., July 10, 1953; s. Koon C. and Siu Fun (Hui) Y.; m. Karen Lee Young, Apr. 7, 1979; 1 child, Liane. AB cum laude, Harvard Coll., 1975; MD, Yale U., 1979. Diplomate Am. Bd. Allergy and Immunology, Am. Bd. Pediatrics, Nat. Bd. Med. Examiners. Resident pediatrics Children's Hosp., Boston, 1979-82, fellow in allergy and immunology, 1982-84, asst. in medicine (immunology), attending physician, 1984—; clin. instr. pediatrics Harvard Med. Sch., Boston, 1984—; mem. active staff South Shore Hosp., South Weymouth, Mass., 1985—. Contbr. articles to profl. jours. Recipient Nat. Rsch. Svc. award NIH, 1982-84. Fellow Am. Coll. Allergy and Immunology (Parke Davis Allergy Fellows award 1983), Am. Acad. Allergy and Immunology, Am. Coll. Chest Physicians, Am. Acad. Pediatrics; mem. New Eng. Soc. Allergy, Mass. Allergy Soc. (pres. 1992-94), Mass. Med. Soc. Office: South Shore Allergy & Asthma Specialists 851 Main St South Weymouth MA 02190-1612

YOUNG, MICHAEL KENT, lawyer, educator; b. Sacramento, Nov. 4, 1949; s. Vance Lynn and Ethelyn M. (Sowards) Y.; m. Suzan Kay Stewart, June 1, 1972; children: Stewart, Kathryn, Andrew. BA summa cum laude, Brigham Young U., 1973; JD magna cum laude, Harvard U., 1976. Bar: Calif. 1976, N.Y. 1985. Law clk. to Judge Benjamin Kaplan, Supreme Jud. Ct. Mass., Boston, 1976-77; law clk. to Justice William H. Rehnquist, U.S. Supreme Ct., Washington, 1977-78; assoc. prof., prof., Fuyo prof. Japanese law Columbia U., N.Y.C., 1978—; dir. Ctr. Japanese Legal Studies Ctr. for Korean Legal Studies, N.Y.C., 1985—; dir. Program Internat. Human Rights and Religious Liberties Columbia U., N.Y.C., 1995—; dep. legal advisor U.S. Dept. State, Washington, 1989-91, dep. under sec. for econ. affairs, 1991-93, amb. for trade and environ. affairs, 1992-93; vis. scholar, mem. law faculty U. Tokyo, 1978-80, 83; vis. prof. Waseda U., 1989; chmn. bd. advisors Japan Soc.; spl. counsel select subcom. arms transfers to Bosnia U.S. Ho. of Reps., 1996; mem. steering com. Law Profs. for Dole, 1996; POSCO Rsch. Inst. fellow, 1993—; counsel subcom. on transfer of Iranian arms to Bosnian Muslims U.S. Ho. of Reps., 1996. Fellow Japan Found., 1979-80; Fulbright fellow, 1983-84. Mem. Coun. Fgn. Rels. Mem. LDS Ch. Avocations: skiing, scuba diving, photography.

YOUNG, MICHAEL WARREN, geneticist, educator; b. Miami, Fla., Mar. 28, 1949; s. Lloyd George and Mildred (Tillery) Y.; m. Laurel Ann Eckhardt, Dec. 27, 1978; children: Natalie, Arissa. BA, U. Tex., 1971, PhD, 1975. NIH postdoctoral fellow Stanford (Calif.) U. Med. Sch., 1975-77; asst. prof. genetics The Rockefeller U., N.Y.C., 1978-83, assoc. prof., 1984-88, prof., 1988—; head Rockefeller unit NSF Sci. and Tech. Ctr. Biol. Timing, 1991—; investigator Howard Hughes Med. Inst., N.Y.C., 1987-96; adv. panel on genetic biology NSF, Washington, 1983-87; spl. advisor Am. Cancer Soc., N.Y.C., 1985—; spl. reviewer genetics study sect. NIH, Bethesda, Md., 1990—, cell biology study sect., 1993—. Contbr. articles to profl. jours. Meyer Found. fellow, N.Y.C., 1978-83. Fellow N.Y. Soc. Fellows; mem. AAAS, Genetics Soc. Am., Am. Soc. Microbiologists, N.Y. Acad. Scis., Harvey Soc. Achievements include research on transposable DNA elements, molecular genetics of nerve and muscle development, biological clocks, molecular control of circadian rhythms. Home: 51 Greenwoods Rd Old Tappan NJ 07675 Office: The Rockefeller Univ 1230 York Ave New York NY 10021-6307

YOUNG, MILTON EARL, retired petroleum production company executive; b. San Angelo, Tex., Dec. 3, 1929; s. Edward Earl and Annie Mae (North) Y.; m. Clara Louise Sens, June 1, 1957; children—Vanessa, Bradley. A.A., San Angelo Coll., 1950; B.S. in Petroleum Engring, U. Tex., 1953. Various positions Continental Oil Co., 1953-73; v.p. for prodn., drilling, engring. Tesoro Petroleum Corp., San Antonio, 1973-74, sr. v.p., 1974-85, group v.p. exploration and prodn., 1985-86, retired, 1986. Served with USNR, 1948-49. Mem. Soc. Petroleum Engrs. Republican. Lutheran. Home: 1802 Frazar Rd Sealy TX 77474-8439

YOUNG, MORRIS, electrical engineering consultant; b. Alexandria, Egypt, Aug. 28, 1937; came to U.S., 1949; s. Nessim and Anna Yahia; m. Susan Slater, Dec. 22, 1962; children: Bruce Leonard, Amy Ellen. Student, CUNY, 1953-58, 63-67. Assoc., chief elec. engr. I.M. Robbins P.C., 1973-94; v.p. Joseph R. Loring & Assocs., N.Y.C., 1994—; with Nassau Tech. Svcs., Wantagh, N.Y., 1995—; sr. elec. engr. Burrwood Engring. & Design. Trustee bd. edn. Wantagh Schs., dist. liaison to B.O.C.E.S., chmn. subcom. citizen's adv. com. for capital improvement project, budget adv. com., guest lectr. in indsl. arts dept.; appointee Nassau County Exec. Francis Purcell's Task Force; officer L.I. Planning Coun.; coach, mgr., Am. league pres. Wantagh Little League; chmn. cub pack 185 Boy Scouts Am.; v.p. Wantagh/Seaford Homeowners Assn.; mem. L.I. R.R. Commuter's Coun.; vol. Friends in Svc. to Humanity; bd. dirs. Temple Beth Emeth, Hewlett. Mem. Nat. Soc. Archtl. Engrs., Wantagh Rep. Club, Am. Legion, Jewish War Vets. of the U.S. Home: 3452 Beltagh Ave Wantagh NY 11793-2552 Office: Data Power Systems 4 Haynes Ave West Islip NY 11795

YOUNG, NANCY, lawyer; b. Washington, Dec. 3, 1954; d. John Young and Byounghye Chang; m. Paul Brendan Ford, Jr., May 28, 1983; children: Paul Brendan III, Ian A., Hunter Chang Young, Jade Augustine Young. BA, Yale U., 1975, MA, 1976; JD, Columbia U., 1979. Bar: N.Y. 1981. Assoc. Simpson Thacher & Bartlett, N.Y.C., 1979-82, Richards O'Neil & Allegaert, N.Y.C., 1982-86; ptnr., chair internat. practice group Richards & O'Neil, N.Y.C., 1986—; lectr. Am. corp. and securities law Tokyo U. Faculty of Law, 1992; bd. dirs. Tsumura Internat. Inc. Contbr. articles to legal publs. Named Internat. Woman of Yr., 1992-93. Mem. ABA (co-chmn. conf. minority ptnrs in corp. majority law firms 1992), Asian-Am. Bar Assn., Assn. Bar of City of N.Y., Internat. Bar Assn., Am. Fgn. Law Assn., Coun. on Fgn. Rels., Fgn. Policy Assn. (bd. govs.), Yale U. Alumni Assn. (bd. govs. 1989-92), Columbia U. Law Sch. Assn. (bd. dirs. 1991-92), Columbia U. Alumni Assn. (bd. dirs. 1991-92), Internat. Lawyers Club, Yale Club N.Y. (bd. dirs. 1996—). Home: One East End Ave New York NY 10021 Office: Richards & O'Neil 885 3rd Ave New York NY 10022-4834

YOUNG, NANCY HENRIETTA MOE, elementary education educator; b. Athens, Ohio, June 25, 1936; d. Charles N. Moe and Mary E. (Sams) Moe-Oyler; m. Henry O. Young, May 13, 1956; children: Pamela Sue Young Paustenbach, Patrick H. BA in Elem. Edn., Ohio U., 1973, degree in elem. edn., 1983. Tchr. 3rd grade Berne Union Sch., Sugar Grove, Ohio, 1968-86, tchr. 4th grade, 1987-94, head dept., 1992-94; tchr. 8th grade English and reading Berne Union Mid. Sch., Sugar Grove, Ohio, 1995-96, 6th grade English, reading and sci. tchr., 1996-97. Jennings scholar Capital U., 1980-81. Mem. NEA, Ohio Edn. Assn., Berne Union Edn. Assn. Republican. Mem. 1st Ch. of God. Avocations: music, reading, traveling, family. Home: 2410 Blue Valley Rd SE Lancaster OH 43130-9019 Office: Berne Union Middle Sch 506 N Main St Sugar Grove OH 43155-9500

YOUNG, NEIL, musician, songwriter; b. Toronto, Ont., Can., Nov. 12, 1945; m. Pegi Young; children: Ben, Amber; 1 child (with Carrie Snodgrass), Zeke. Formed rock group Buffalo Springfield (with Stephen Stills), with group until 1968; solo performer, also joined group Crosby, Stills & Nash (became Crosby, Stills, Nash & Young), 1969-70, 74-75; as solo artist and with bank Crazy Horse, 1968-69, 70—. Albums include (with Crosby, Stills, Nash & Young) Déja Vu, 1970, Four-Way Street, 1971, So Far, 1974, American Dream, 1988; (solo albums) Neil Young, 1969, After the Goldrush, 1970, Harvest, 1972, Journey Through the Past, 1972, Time Fades Away, 1973, On the Beach, 1974, Zuma, 1975, American Stars 'n' Bars, 1977, Decade, 1977, Comes a Time, 1978, Hawks and Doves, 1980, Reactor, 1981, Trans, 1983, Neil and The Shocking Pink: Everybody's Rocking, 1983, Old Ways, 1985, Landing on Water, 1986, Freedom, 1989, Harvest Moon, 1992, (4 Grammy nominations), Lucky Thirteen, 1993, Unplugged, 1993; (with Crazy Horse) Everybody Knows This is Nowhere, 1969, Tonight's the Night, 1975, Rust Never Sleeps, 1979, Live Rust, 1979, Life, 1987, Ragged Glory, 1990, Weld, 1991, Arc, 1991, Arc Weld, 1991, Sleeps With Angels, 1994; (with Buffalo Springfield) Buffalo Springfield Again, 1967, Last Time Around, 1968, Retrospective, 1969; (with the Bluenotes) This Note's For You, 1988; (with Stills-Young Band) Long May You Run, 1976; (with The Stray Gators) Time Fade Away; Tony and Susan Alamo christian Foundation Orchestra and Chorus, 1995; (with others) Mirror Ball, 1995, Journey Through the Past, 1995, Old Ways; composed film soundtrack Journey Through the Past, 1973, Where the Buffalo Roam, 1980, Human Highway, 1982; writer, dir., performer film Rust Never Sleeps. Academy award nominee, Best Original Song, 1993 (for "Philadelphia" from Philadelphia). Office: Warner Bros Reprise Records 75 Rockefeller Plz New York NY 10019*

YOUNG, OLIVIA KNOWLES, retired librarian; b. Benton, Ark., Sept. 3, 1922; d. Wesley Taylor and Med Belle (Crawford) Knowles; m. Calvin B. Young, Oct. 6, 1951; 1 child, Brigham Taylor. BA, Tenn. Tech. U., 1942; BS in Libr. Sci., George Peabody Coll. for Tchrs., 1946. Head periodicals and documents dept. Peabody Coll. Library, Nashville, 1946-49; area librarian U.S. Army, Austria, 1949-51; librarian Cairo Pub. Library, Ga., 1955-57, Caney Fork Regional Library, Sparta, Tenn., 1957-58; chief librarian Fort Stewart Ft. Stewart (Ga.) U.S. Army, 1959-63; dir. Watauga Regional Library, Johnson City, Tenn., 1963-70; dir. devel. and extension Tenn. State Library and Archives, Nashville, 1971-82, state librarian and archivist, 1982-85; ret., 1985. Mem. Tenn. Library Assn. (treas. 1970, Honor award 1985), Southeastern Library Assn., ALA, Boone Tree Library Assn. (pres. 1968). Methodist. Club: Altrusa (sec. 1967). Home: PO Box 160444 San Antonio TX 78280-2644

YOUNG, ORAN REED, political scientist, educator; b. Yonkers, N.Y., Mar. 15, 1941; s. John A. and Eleanor (Wiggin) Y.; children: Linda Katrin, Naomi Frankel. AB, Harvard U., 1962; MA, Yale U., 1964, PhD, 1965. Mem. staff Hudson Inst., 1962-64; rsch. assoc. Harvard, 1965; prof. polit. sci. Princeton, 1966-71; prof. govt. U. Tex., Austin, 1972-76; prof. govt. and politics U. Md., College Park, 1976-82; co-dir. Ctr. for No. Studies, 1980-82, dir., 1983-86, sr. fellow, 1986—; sr. fellow Dickey Ctr.; dir. Inst. Arctic Studies, Inst. Internat. Environ. Governance; rsch. prof. govt., prof. environ. studies Dartmouth Coll., 1987—; mem. polar rsch. bd. NRC, 1989—; U.S. del. Internat. Arctic Sci. Com., 1993—. Author: The Intermediaries: Third Parties in International Crises, 1967, Systems of Political Science, 1968, (with others) Neutralization and World Politics, 1968, The Politics of Force: Bargaining During International Crises, 1968, (with others) Political Leadership and Collective Goods, 1971, Bargaining: Formal Theories of Negotiation, 1975, Resource Management at the International Level, 1977, Compliance and Public Authority, A Theory with Applications to International Politics, 1979, Natural Resources and the State: The Political Economy of Resource Management, 1981, Resource Regimes: Natural Resources and Social Institutions, 1982, International Cooperation: Building Regimes for Natural Resources and the Environment, 1989; co-author: The Age of the Arctic: Hot Conflicts and Cold Realities, 1989, Global Environmental Changes: Understanding the Human Dimensions, 1992, Arctic Politics: Conflict and Cooperation in the Circumpolar North, 1992, Polar Politics: Creating International Environment Regimes, 1993, International Governance: Protecting the Environment in a Stateless Society, 1994, The International Political Economy and International Institutions, 1996; Global Environmental Change and International Governance, 1996, Global Governance: Drawing Insight from the Environmental Experience, 1997, Creating Regimes, 1997; sr. editor: World Politics, 1968-76; mem. editl. bd. Internat. Orgn., 1968-76, 90-95. Chmn. com. on the human dimensions of global change NRC, 1989-95; mem. sci. steering com. Human Dimensions of Global Change Programme, 1995; mem. PI IHDP Core project Instnl. Dimensions of Global Change, 1997—. Mem. Internat. Studies Assn., Am. Soc. Polit. and Legal Philosophy, Pub. Choice Soc., Am. Polit. Sci. Assn., Cosmos Club. Home: PO Box 1594 Norwich VT 05055-1594 Office: Dartmouth Coll 6214 Steele Hall Hanover NH 03755-3560

YOUNG, PATRICK, writer, editor; b. Ladysmith, Wis., Oct. 19, 1937; s. Rodney and Janice (Wolf) Y.; m. Leah Ruth Figelman, Oct. 8, 1966; 1 child, Justine Rebecca. BA, U. Colo., 1960. Reporter UPI, Washington, 1961-62; journalist USN, 1963-64; staff writer Nat. Observer, Silver Spring, Md., 1965-77; free-lance writer Laurel, Md., 1977-79; mem. sr. staff Pres.'s Commn. on the Accident at Three Mile Island, Washington, 1979; chief sci. and med. writer Newhouse News Svc., Washington, 1980-88; editor Sci. News, Washington, 1988-95; ind. writer, editor, cons., 1995—; sci. writer in residence U. Wis., 1986. Author: Asthma and Allergies, 1980, Drugs and Pregnancy, 1987, Schizophrenia, 1988; co-author: Keeping Young Athletes Healthy, 1991. With USN, 1963-64. Recipient Howard W. Blakeslee award Am. Heart Assn., 1971, Sci. Writing award in physics and astronomy Am. Inst. Physics, 1974, James T. Grady award Am. Chem. Soc., 1977. Mem. Nat. Assn. Sci. Writers, Nat. Press Club.

YOUNG, PAUL ANDREW, anatomist; b. St. Louis, Oct. 3, 1926; s. Nicholas A. and Olive A. (Langford) Y.; m. Catherine Ann Hofmeister, May 14, 1949; children—Paul, Robert, David, Ann, Carol, Richard, James, Steven, Kevin, Michael. B.S., St. Louis U., 1947, M.S., 1953; Ph.D., U. Buffalo, 1957. Asst. in anatomy U. Buffalo, 1953, instr. anatomy, 1957; asst. prof. anatomy St. Louis U., 1957, asso. prof., 1966, prof., 1972—, chmn. dept., 1973—. Author: (with B.D. Bhagat and D.E. Biggerstaff) Fundamentals of Visceral Innervation, 1977, (with P.H. Young) Basic Clinical Neuroanatomy, 1996, also computer assisted neurological anatomy tutorials; contbr. articles to profl. publs. Recipient Golden Apple award Student AMA, 1974, Teaching award Acad. Sci. St. Louis, 1993. Mem. Am. Assn. Anatomists, Am. Assn. Clin. Anatomists, Soc. Neurosci., Sigma Xi, Alpha Omega Alpha. Office: St Louis U Dept Anatomy & Neurobiology 1402 S Grand Blvd Saint Louis MO 63104-1004

YOUNG, PAUL RAY, medical board executive, physician; b. Fairfield, Nebr., June 27, 1932; s. Earl Edward and Louisa May (Saunders) Y.; m. Irene Marie Gray (div. 1971); children: Michael, Susan, Jean, James; m. Faye Elizabeth Hall, Oct. 28, 1972. BA, U. Nebr., Lincoln, 1953; MD, U. Nebr., Omaha, 1958. Diplomate Am. Bd. Family Practice. Intern Rsch. Hosp., Kansas City, Mo., 1958-59; pvt. practice, Raytown, Mo., 1961-67; dir. continuing med. edn. Rsch. Hosp., Kansas City, Mo., 1967-71; assoc. prof. family practice U. Mo. Coll. Medicine, Columbia, 1971-75; chmn. dept. U. Nebr. Coll. Medicine, 1975-80, U. Tex. Med. Br., Galveston, 1980-88; dep. dir. Am. Bd. Family Practice, Lexington, Ky., 1988-90, exec. dir., 1990—; mem. RRC for Family Practice, Chgo., 1976-87, chmn., 1979-87. Founding editor Family Practice Recert., 1979, Jour. Am. Bd. Family Practice, 1987.

Pres. Nicholas J. Piscano Meml. Found., Lexington, 1990—. Capt. M.C., USAF, 1959-61. Fellow Am. Acad. Family Physicians; mem. Soc. Tchrs. Family Practice (bd. dirs. 1970-72), Alpha Omega Alpha. Office: Am Bd Family Practice Inc 2228 Young Dr Lexington KY 40505-4219

YOUNG, PETER ROBERT, librarian; b. Washington, Aug. 13, 1944; s. Ju Chin and Jane Kathrine (Lybrand) Y.; m. Mary Sue Townsend, Mar. 25, 1978; children: Kathryn, Timothy; children from previous marriage: Robert, Jonathan. AB Philosophy, Coll. Wooster, Ohio, 1966; grad., George Washington U., 1967; MSLS Libr. Svc., Columbia U., 1968. Adminstrv. libr. Am. U. Libr., Washington, 1968; head cataloger, reference libr. Franklin & Marshall Coll. Libr., Lancaster, Pa., 1971-74; asst. libr. pub. svcs. Rice U. Librs., Houston, Tex., 1974-76; asst. dir. Grand Rapids (Mich.) Pub. Libr., 1978; sales support libr. CL Systems Inc., Newtonville, Mass., 1976-78, libr. systems analyst, 1978-80; customer svcs. officer Cataloging Distbn. Svc. Libr. Congress, Washington, 1980-84, asst. chief Marc edit. divsn., 1984-85, chief Copyright Cataloging divsn., 1985-88; dir. acad. info. svcs. The Faxon Co., Westwood, Mass., 1988-89, dir. Faxon Inst. Advanced Studies Scholarly and Sci. Communication, 1989-90; exec. dir. U.S. Nat. Commn. Librs. and Info. Sci., Washington, 1990—; exec. bd. Fed. Libr. and Info. Ctr. com., 1993—; adv. bd. Highsmith Press, 1991—; co chair libr. stats. standard revision com. Nat. Standards Info. Office, 1989-93; libr. adminstrs. devel. program U. Md.; implementation task force libr. data Nat. Ctr. Edn. Stats. U.S. Office Edn., 1988, adv. coun. edn. stats. Office Edn. Rsch, and Improvement, 1990—; lectr. in field. Edit. bd. Serials Review, 1990—; contbr. articles to profl. jours. With U.S. Army, 1968-70, Vietnam. Mem. ALA (pub. policy for pub. librs. com. 1993—, com. rsch. and stats. 1990—, various coms., assns.), Chinese Am. Libr. Assn. (chair pub. rels. com. 1987-88, pres. 1989-90), Ont. Libr. Assn. (planning com., del. mem.), U.S. Nat. Commn. Librs. and Info. Sci. (stats. task force 1988-89). Office: Natl Commission on Libraries 1110 VErmont Ave NW Ste 820 Washington DC 20005-3522

YOUNG, PHILIP HOWARD, library director; b. Ithaca, N.Y., Oct. 7, 1953; s. Charles Robert and Betty Irene (Osborne) Y.; m. Nancy Ann Stutsman, Aug. 18, 1979. BA, U. Va., 1975; PhD, U. Pa., 1980; MLS, Ind. U., 1983. Asst. prof. history Appalachian State U., Boone, N.C., 1980-82; reference asst. Lilly Library, Ind. U., Bloomington, 1982-83; adminstr., info. specialist Ind. Corp. for Sci. & Tech., Indpls., 1983-85; dir. Krannert Meml. Library, U. Indpls., 1985—. Mem. Am. Library Assn., Ind. Libr. Fed., Archaeological Inst. Am., Phi Beta Kappa, Phi Alpha Theta, Beta Phi Mu. Democrat. Methodist. Home: 1944 Patton Dr Speedway IN 46224-5355 Office: U Indpls Krannert Meml Libr 1400 E Hanna Ave Indianapolis IN 46227-3630

YOUNG, PHYLLIS CASSELMAN, music educator; b. Milan, Kans., Oct. 20, 1925; d. Phillip James and Velma (Stewart) Casselman; m. James M. Young, July 14, 1945 (dec. Sept. 1991). MusB with high honors, U. Tex., 1949, MusM, 1950. Tchr. string instruments Kansas City (Kans.) Pub. Schs., 1951-52; prof. cello and string pedagogy U. Tex., Austin, 1953—; dir. U. Tex. String Project, Austin, 1958-93; Parker C. Fielder Regents prof. music U. Tex., Austin, 1991—; presenter numerous workshops and master classes, 1976—. Author: Playing the String Game, 1978, The String Play, 1986; also articles. Mem. Am. String Tchrs. Assn. (state pres. 1972-74, nat. pres. 1978-80, Nat. citation 1974, 82, Disting. Svc. award 1984), European String Tchrs. Assn., Music Educators Nat. Conf., Suzuki Assn. Ams., Tex. Music Educators Assn. Home: 7304 W Rim Dr Austin TX 78731-2043 Office: Sch Music Univ Tex Austin TX 78712

YOUNG, RALPH ALDEN, soil scientist, educator; b. Arickaree, Colo., July 14, 1920; s. Edmond Birdsall and Lottie Opal (Payne) Y.; m. Helen Augusta Claudon, Aug. 28, 1942; children—Gregg, Gayle. B.S., Colo. State U., 1942; M.S., Kans. State U., 1947; Ph.D., Cornell U., 1953. Instr. soils Kans. State U., 1947-48; asst. prof. soils N.D. State U., 1948-50, 53-55, asso. prof., 1955-59, prof., 1959-62; vis. soil chemist U. Calif. at Davis, 1962-63; prof. soil sci., chmn. div. plant, soil and water sci. U. Nev., Reno, 1963-75; assoc. dir. Nev. Agrl. Expt. Sta., 1975-82; prof. soil sci. U. Nev., 1982-84, prof. emeritus, 1985—. Contbr. articles to profl. jours. Served to capt. AUS, 1943-46. Fellow AAAS; mem. Soil Conservation Soc. Am. (pres. chpt. 1968), Am. Soc. Agronomy, Soil Sci. Soc. Am., Western Soil Sci. Soc. (pres. 1972-73), Sigma Xi, Alpha Zeta, Gamma Sigma Delta, Phi Kappa Phi. Home: 2229 Stagecoach Rd Grand Junction CO 81503-2614

YOUNG, RAYMOND ALLEN, chemist, educator. BS in Wood Products Engring., SUNY, Syracuse, 1966, MS in Paper Chemistry, 1968; PhD in Wood and Polymer Chemistry, U. Wash., 1973. Process supr. Kimberly-Clark Corp., Niagara Falls, N.Y., 1968-69; vis. scientist Swedish Forest Products Lab., Stockholm, 1972-73; postdoctoral fellow, staff scientist Textile Rsch. Inst., Princeton, N.J., 1973-74; prof. wood and polymer chemistry dept. forestry U. Wis., Madison, 1975—; cons. UN, USAID, NATO, Rome, Shell Oil, London, Kimberly-Clark Corp., Union Carbide Corp., Grain Processing Corp., Stone & Webster Engrings. Cons., Thatcher Plastics Co., Biodyne Chems., Resource Mgmt. Assocs.; expert witness various law firms. Author: Cellulose: Structure, Modification and Hydrolysis, 1986, Modified Cellulosics, 1978, Introduction to Forest Science, 2d edit., 1990, Paper and Composites from Agro-Based Resources, 1996; contbr. chpts. to books, articles to profl. jours.; patentee infield. Fulbright scholar Royal Inst. Tech., Stockholm, 1972; recipient Sr. Fulbright Rsch. award Aristotelian U., Thessaloniki, Greece, 1989, Sci. Exchange award to Romania Nat. Acad. Sci., 1990. Mem. Am. Chem. Soc. (publicity chmn. Cellulose Paper and Textile divsn. 1980-82, student coord. 1992-95), Internat. Acad. Wood Sci. Office: Dept Forestry U Wis Madison WI 53706

YOUNG, RAYMOND GUINN, music educator; b. Morrilton, Ark., Dec. 21, 1932; s. Theodore T. and Vida Mae (Guinn) Y.; m. Barbara Ann Woolcox, Aug. 29, 1953 (div. Nov. 1986); children: Steven Cary, Dale, Michael, Rae Ann; m. Joan Arno, Nov. 20, 1994. MusB, U. Mich., 1955, MusM, 1956. Band dir. Trenton (Mich.) High Sch., 1956-61; asst. band dir., instr. trombone and euphonium U. So. Miss., Hattiesburg, 1961-68, dir. bands, 1968-72; dir. bands La. Tech. U., Ruston, 1972-85, head dept. mus., 1972-88, prof. music, 1988-91; dir. orch. Ruston Civic Symphony, 1975-80; condr. USA Honor Bands, Honolulu, 1975-88; soloist Tokyo Kosei Wind Orch., 1985. Dir. choir Univ. Presbyn. Ch., Ruston, 1973-85. Mem. Am. Bandmaster Assn., La. Bandmaster Assn. (Bandmaster of Yr. 1983), Nat. Band Assn., Coll. Band Dirs. Nat. Assn., Ruston Antique Car Assn. (pres. 1984, 85), Phi Beta Mu, Phi Mu Alpha Sinfonia, Kappa Kappa Psi, Sigma Alpha Iota. Lodge: Masons (illustrious master 1969, 70). Home: 149 Sherlock Herring Rd Purvis MS 39475-3150

YOUNG, RAYMOND HENRY, lawyer; b. Boston, Sept. 28, 1927; s. Raymond H. and Clara Elms (Oakman) Y.; m. Louisa Breda, Sept. 1, 1951; children: Christopher, Pamela, Amy. AB, Yale U., 1947, LLB, 1950. Bar: Mass. 1951. Assoc. Warner, Stackpole, Stetson & Bradlee, Boston, 1950-52; pvt. practice Boston, 1952-64; ptnr. Young & Bayle, Boston, 1964—. Mem. ABA (past sec. sect. real property, probate and trust law, mem. commn. legal problems of the elderly), Am. Coll. Trust and Estate Counsel (mem. joint editorial bd. for uniform probate code), Am. Law Inst. (advisor for restatement property 3d donative transfers), Nat. Commn. on Nat. Probate Ct. Standards, Internat. Acad. Trust and Estate Law (past pres.), Mass. Bar Assn., Boston Bar Assn. (past pres.), Boston Estate Planning Coun. (past pres., Estate Planner of Yr. award 1991), Boston Probate and Estate Planning Forum. Home: 122 Garfield St Watertown MA 02172-4916 Office: Young & Bayle 150 Federal St Boston MA 02110

YOUNG, REBECCA LEE, special education educator; b. Muncie, Ind., June 22, 1950; d. Norman Lee and Evelyn Faye (Mann) Hofherr; m. James Paul Young, Feb. 21, 1974; children: Evelyn Kaye, Jason Paul. BS, Ball State U., 1975; MS, St. Francis Coll., Ft. Wayne, Ind., 1985. Cert. screener for scotopic sensivity syndrome. Tchr. severe and profound Carlin Park Elem. Sch., Angola, Ind., 1975-80; tchr. learning disabled Lakeland High Sch., La Grange, Ind., 1980—; tchr.-multi-categorical class Parkside Elem. Sch., La Grange, 1991—; tchr. presch. handicapped Sch. Opportunity, LaGrange, summer 1987; insvc. presenter, 1987—; mem. Lakeland Tech. Com., 1992-95, Parkside Tech. Com., 1992—. Vol. instr. Lakeland Band Camp, 1986-88; bd. dirs. Lakeland Band Boosters, 1986-89, Human Rights Com., La Grange, 1987—; mem. Lakeland Tech. Com., 1992—. Mem. ASCD, Coun. for Exceptional Children, Ind. Tchrs. Assn., Ind. Computer Educators, Lakeland Edn. Assn. (tech. com. 1992), Delta Kappa Gamma (chmn. scholarship com. 1985—), Sigma Alpha Iota, Learning Disabilities Assn. (Parkside child study team 1990—). Avocations: playing flute, reading, swimming. Home: 353 Parkway St Lagrange IN 46761-1603 Office: Parkside Elem Sch 1 LeMaster Cir Lagrange IN 46761

YOUNG, REBECCA MARY CONRAD, state legislator; b. Clairton, Pa., Feb. 28, 1934; d. Walter Emerson and Harriet Averill (Colcord) Conrad; m. Merwin Crawford Young, Aug. 17, 1957; children: Eve, Louise, Estelle, Emily. BA, U. Mich., 1955; MA in Teaching, Harvard U., 1963; JD, U. Wis., 1983. Bar: Wis. 1983. Commr. State Hwy. Commn., Madison, Wis., 1974-76; dep. sec. Wis. Dept. of Adminstrn., Madison, 1976-77; assoc. Wadsack, Julian & Lawton, Madison, 1983-84; elected rep. Wis. State Assembly, Madison, 1985—. Translator: Katanga Secession, 1966. Supr. Dane County Bd., Madison, 1970-74; mem. Madison Sch. Bd., 1979-85. Recipient Wis. Register Deeds Assn. Cert. of Appreciation for Leadership, 1995, Wis. NOW Feminist of Yr. award, 1996, Eunice Zoghlin Edgar Lifetime Achievement award ACLU, 1996, Recognition award Dem. Party of Dane County, 1996. Mem. LWV. Democrat. Avocations: board games, hiking. Home: 639 Crandall St Madison WI 53711-1836 Office: State Legislature-Assembly PO Box 8953 Madison WI 53708-8953

YOUNG, RICHARD ALAN, publishing company executive; b. Oak Park, Ill., Mar. 17, 1935; m. Carol Ann Schellinger, June 28, 1958; children: Steven, Karen, Christopher. Student, Colo. Sch. Mines, 1954-56; B.A., U. Iowa, 1958. Chief engr. Cardox Corp., Chgo., 1958-61; asst. chief engr. Goodman Mfg. Co., Chgo., 1961-63; plant and environ. engr. Signode Corp., Glenview, Ill., 1963-68; editor Pollution Engring. Tech. Pub. Co., Barrington, Ill., 1968-81; exec. dir. Nat. Registry of Environ. Profls., 1988—; pub. Cahners Pub. Co., Des Plaines, Ill., 1990-95; dj. prof. George Williams Coll.; mcpl. pollution control adviser and enforcement officer for 24 cities and state govts; ofcl rep. and pollution control expert U.S. Govt. at tech. transfer meetings. Editor 26 books on environ. engring.; pollution engring.; series editor, Marcel Dekker Inc., N.Y.C.; Contbr. articles to profl. jours. Recipient Jesse H. Neal certificate for outstanding editorial writing Am. Bus. Press, Inc., 1971, Outstanding Service award Western Soc. Engrs., Charles Ellet award as Most Outstanding Engr. of Yr. 1970; Environ. Quality award EPA, 1976. Mem. Internat. Assn. for Pollution Control (dir.), Assn. Local Air Pollution Control Ofcls., Am. Soc. Bus. Press Editors (Editl. Excellence award 1980, Design Excellence award 1982), Am. Inst. Plant Engrs. (past nat. chmn. environ. quality), Internat. Congress Environ. Profls. (mng. dir.), Nat. Inst. Hazardous Materials Mgmts. (dir. 1984-88, cert. hazardous materials mgr.), Soc. Environ. Mgmt. & Tech. (nat. dir.). Patentee in field.

YOUNG, RICHARD WILLIAM, corporate director; b. Ridgewood, N.Y., Oct. 17, 1926; s. Charles Michael and Louise Margaret (Baust) Y.; m. Sheila deLisser, Sept. 11, 1949; children: Christine, Noreen, Brian, Eileen. A.B., Dartmouth Coll., 1946, A.M., 1947; Ph.D., Columbia U., 1950. Sr. rsch. chemist Chemotherapy div. Am. Cyanamid Co., Conn., 1950-56, group leader pesticide chems. Agrl. div., 1956-58, dir. chem. Agrl. div., 1958-60, dir. chem. rsch. cen. rsch. div., 1960-62; asst. dir. rsch. Polaroid Corp., Cambridge, Mass., 1962-69, v.p., 1963-69, sr. v.p. rsch. and devel., 1969-72, sr. v.p., pres. Internat. div., 1972-80, exec. v.p., dir. worldwide mktg., 1980-82; pres. Houghton Mifflin Co., Boston, 1982-85; chmn., CEO Mentor O & O, Inc., Norwell, Mass., 1985-92; bd. dirs. Bay State Milling Corp., Quincy, Mass., Instron Corp., Canton, Mass., Oceantrawl Inc., Seattle, Mentor Corp., Santa Barbara, Calif. Patentee in field. Chmn. bd. trustees Regis Coll., Weston, Mass.; trustee Mass. Eye and Ear Infirmary, Boston, 1963-90, Trinitas Found., Quincy; mem. corp. Northeastern U., Boston, 1960-92. Mem. Am. Chem. Soc. Home: 100 Royalston Rd Wellesley MA 02181-1244 Office: Trinitas Found 100 Congress St Quincy MA 02169-0906

YOUNG, ROBERT A., III, freight systems executive; b. Ft. Smith, Ark., Sept. 23, 1940; s. Robert A. and Vivian (Curtis) Y.; m. Mary Carleton McRae; children—Tracy, Christy, Robert A. IV, Stephen. BA in Econs., Washington and Lee U., 1963. Supr. terminal ops. Ark. Best Freight, Ft. Smith, 1964-65; pres. Data-Tronics Inc, Ft. Smith, 1965-67; sr. v.p. Nat. Bank of Commerce, Dallas, 1967-70; v.p. fin. Ark. Best Corp., Ft. Smith, 1970-73, exec. v.p., 1973, pres., chief operating officer, 1973-88, chief exec. officer, 1988—; pres. ABF Freight Systems, Inc., Ft. Smith, 1979-94; bd. dirs. First Nat. Bank, Ft. Smith, Mosler Corp., Hamilton, Ohio. Pres. United Way, Ft. Smith, 1981; vice chmn. bd. dirs. Sparks Regional Med. Ctr., Ft. Smith, 1995; chmn. bd. trustees Ark. Coll.; bd. dirs. ATA Found., Inc., Ft. Smith Boys Club; chmn. bd. trustees Lyon Coll. Recipient Silver Beaver award Boy Scouts Am. Mem. Am. Trucking Assn. (vice chmn.), Ark. State C. of C. (pres., bd. dirs., chmn.), Phi Delta Theta. Presbyterian. Home: Ark Best Corp PO Box 10048 Fort Smith AR 72917-0048 Office: ABF Freight Systems Inc 3801 Old Greenwood Rd Fort Smith AR 72903-5937 also: Ark Best Corp 3801 Old Greenwood Rd Fort Smith AR 72903

YOUNG, ROBERT ANTHONY, association director; b. Syracuse, N.Y., May 21, 1943; s. Frank A. and Grace (Farnett) Y. BS, Le Moyne Coll., 1965; MS, Long Beach State Coll., 1966. Exec. dir. Cystic Fibrosis Found., Syracuse, 1974-75; dir. pub. rels. & programs Am. Heart Assn., New Orleans, 1975-76; dir. programs La. State Bar Assn., New Orleans, 1976-84; exec. dir. Am. Coll. Trial Lawyers, Irvine, Calif., 1984—. With USAF, 1966-67. Mem. Am. Soc. Assn. Execs., Nat. Assn. Bar Execs. (leadership award 1986, chmn's. award pub. rels. sect. 1984). Avocations: travel, golf, tennis. Office: Am Coll of Trial Lawyers 8001 Irvine Center Dr Ste 960 Irvine CA 92618-2921

YOUNG, ROBERT CRABILL, medical researcher, science facility administrator, internist; b. Columbus, Ohio, 1940. MD, Cornell U., 1965. Diplomate Am. Bd. Internal Medicine, subspecialty bds. hematology and med. oncology. Intern N.Y. Hosp., N.Y.C., 1965-66, resident, 1966-67; sr. resident Yale-New Haven Med. Ctr., 1969-70; sr. investigator, attending physician med. br. Nat. Cancer Inst., Bethesda, Md., from 1971, chief med. br., 1974-88; pres. Fox Chase Cancer Ctr., Phila., 1988—; clin. prof. medicine Georgetown U., from 1974, assoc. prof., 1976-84; clin. prof. medicine George Washington U., 1984—; bd. Sci. Advisors, NCI, 1996—; bd. Nat. Cancer Policy, 1997—. Assoc. editor Jour. Clin. Oncology; chmn. editl. bd. Oncology Times. Sr. surgeon USPHS, 1967-69. Fellow ACP; mem. Am. Soc. Hematology, Am. Assn. Cancer Rsch., Am. Soc. Clin. Oncology (pres. 1990), Am. Cancer Soc. (bd. dir. 1995—). Office: Fox Chase Cancer Ctr 7701 Burholme Ave Philadelphia PA 19111-2412

YOUNG, ROBERT DONALD, physicist, educator; b. Chgo., Apr. 20, 1940; s. Robert Joseph and Nellie Y.; children: Robert Gerald, Jennifer Ann Young Rolinski; m. BJ Marymont, Feb. 14, 1981; 1 child, Emily Marymont. BS in Physics, Ill. Inst. Technology, 1962; MS in Physics, Purdue U., 1965, PhD in Physics, 1967. Devel. engr. Western Elec., Cicero, Ill., 1962; process engr. Nat. Video Corp., Chgo., 1963; asst. prof. physics Ill. State U., Normal, 1967-73, assoc. prof., 1974-78, prof., 1979—, dir. rsch. Coll. Arts and Scis., 1994-95, assoc. v.p. for rsch., dean grad. studies, 1995-97, chair dept. physics, 1997—; adj. prof. physics U. Ill., Urbana, 1986-97. Contbr. articles to Proceedings Nat. Acad. Sci., Ann. Rev. Biophysics, Phys. Rev. Letters, Chemica Scripta, Jour. Phys. Chemistry, Jour. Chem. Physics, Computers in Physics, Physical Rev., Biophysical Jour. Named Researcher of Yr., Ill. State U., 1989. Mem. Am. Phys. Soc., Am. Chem. Soc., Biophys. Soc., Am. Assn. Physics Tchrs. Achievements include research on glassy properties of proteins, usage of computer techniques in physics education, individualized modular approach in physics education. Home: 4 Turner Rd Normal IL 61761-4218 Office: Ill State Univ Physics Dept Normal IL 61790-8756

YOUNG, ROGER AUSTIN, natural gas distribution company executive; b. Boston, Feb. 2, 1946; s. Robert Harris McCarter and Gloria Bond (Tenney) Y.; m. Linda Furste, Sept. 6, 1975; children: Catherine Simms, Geoffrey Furste. B.A., Princeton U., 1968. Systems analyst Orange and Rockland Utilities, Inc., Spring Valley, N.Y., 1968-72; asst. v.p. Bay State Gas Co., Boston, 1972-75, v.p., 1975-80; exec. v.p. Bay State Gas Co., Canton, Mass., 1980-81; pres. Bay State Gas Co., Westborough, Mass., 1981-90, pres., chief exec. officer, 1990-96; chmn., bd. dirs., CEO, 1996—; chmn., bd. trustees, mem. exec. com. Inst. Gas Tech.; regional bd. dirs. Baybanks, Inc. Bd. dirs. New Eng. Council. Mem. Am. Gas Assn., New Eng. Gas Assn. (bd. dirs., chmn. 1984-85), Newcomen Soc., Associated Gas Distbrs. Congregationalist. Clubs: The Country (Brookline, Mass.); Colonial (Princeton, N.J.). Home: 125 Mill St PO Box 95 Sherborn MA 01770 Office: Bay State Gas Co 300 Friberg Pky Westborough MA 01581-3900

YOUNG, ROLAND FREDERIC, III, lawyer; b. Norway, Maine, Apr. 8, 1954; s. Roland Frederic Jr. and Marylyn May (Bartlett) Y.; m. Dona Davis Gagliano, Aug. 18, 1979; children: Meghan, Wesley, Taylor. AB, Cornell U., 1976; JD, U. Conn., 1979. Bar: Conn. 1979, U.S. Dist. Ct. Conn., U.S. Tax Ct., U.S. Ct. Appeals (2d cir.). Lectr. Hartford (Conn.) Grad. Ctr., Hartford, Conn., 1992—; ptnr. Howard, Kohn, Sprague & FitzGerald, Hartford, Conn., 1984-91, O'Brien, Tanski, Tanzer & Young, Hartford, Conn., 1991—; lectr. Hartford Grad. Ctr., 1991—. Author (seminar booklet) Confidentiality of Med. Records, 1989, Limiting Damages, 1990; co-author (seminar booklet) Med. Malpractice in Conn., 1992; editor Conn. Risk Mgmt. Assn., 1986—. Mem. Am. Acad. Hosp. Attys. (chmn. publs. and programs subcom., tchg. hosps.), Def. Rsch. Inst., Inc., Am. Soc. Law and Medicine, Nat. Assn. Health Law Attys., Am. Coll. Healthcare Execs., Conn. Bar Assn., Conn. Def. Lawyers Assn., Conn. Hosp. Assn., Hartford County Bar Assn. (medico-legal liaison com.). Avocations: tennis, skiing, golf. Office: O'Brien Tanski Tanzer and Young City Place II 16th Fl Hartford CT 06103

YOUNG, RONALD FARIS, commodity trader; b. Schenectady, Dec. 17, 1939; s. James Vernon and Dorothy (Girod) Y.; m. Anne Randolph Kendig, Feb. 23, 1963; children: Margaret Randolph Reynolds, Anne Corbin. B.A., U. Va., 1962; M.B.A., Harvard U., 1966. Grain trader Continental Grain Co., 1966-70; pres. Conti-Commodities, Chgo., 1970; v.p. commodity sales DuPont, Glore Forgan, Chgo., 1971-72; self-employed commodity trader Chgo. Bd. Trade, 1972-78; ind. trader Va. Trading Co., 1978-90, pres., 1978-84, dep. chmn., 1984-89; pres. Randolph Ptnrs., Ltd., 1983-91; chmn. bd. Chgo. Bd. Trade, 1978, dir., 1975-77, 80. Bd. dirs. Princeton Fund, 1981-82, Lake Forest Hosp., 1981-84, Lake Forest Country Day Sch., 1981-86. Served with USMCR, 1959-65. Mem. Casino Club, Racquet Club (bd. dirs. 1989—), Onwentsia Club (Lake Forest, Ill., bd. dirs. 1981-90, pres. 1991-93), Everglades Cub (Palm Beach, Fla.), Bath and Tennis Club (Palm Beach, Fla.). Republican. Episcopalian. Home: 1448 N Lake Shore Dr Chicago IL 60610-1625 Office: 141 W Jackson Blvd Unit 1520A Chicago IL 60604-3001

YOUNG, ROY ALTON, university administrator, educator; b. McAlister, N.Mex., Mar. 1, 1921; s. John Arthur and Etta Julia (Sprinkle) Y.; m. Marilyn Ruth Sandman, May 22, 1950; children: Janet Elizabeth, Randall Owen. BS, N.Mex. A&M Coll., 1941; MS, Iowa State U., 1942, PhD, 1948; LLD (hon.), N.Mex. State U., 1978. Tchg. fellow Iowa State U., 1941-42, instr., 1946-47, Indsl. fellow, 1947-48; asst. prof. Oreg. State U., 1948-50, assoc. prof., 1950-53, prof., 1953—, head dept. botany and plant pathology, 1958-66, dean rsch., 1966-70, acting pres., 1969-70, v.p. rsch. and grad. studies, 1970-76, dir. Office for Natural Resources Policy, 1986-90; chancellor U. Nebr., Lincoln, 1976-80; mng. dir., pres. Boyce Thompson Inst. Plant Rsch., Cornell U., Ithaca, N.Y., 1980-86; mem. Commn. on Undergrad. Edn. in Biol. Scis., 1963-68; mem. Gov.'s Sci. Coun., 1987-90; cons. State Exptl. Stas. divsn. USDA; chmn. subcom. plant pathogens, agriculture bd. NAS-NRC, 1965-68; mem. exec. com. study on problems of pest control, 1972-75; mem. exec. com. Nat. Govs.' Coun. on Sci. and Tech., 1970-74; mem. U.S. com. man and biosphere UNESCO, 1973-82; mem. com. to rev. U.S. component Internat. Biol. Program, NAS, 1974-76; mem. adv. panel on postdoctoral fellowships in environ. sci. Rockefeller Found., 1974-78; bd. dirs. Pacific Power & Light Co., 1974-91, PacifiCorp., 1984-91, Boyce Thompson Inst. for Plant Rsch., 1975-93, Boyce Thompson Southwestern Arboretum, 1981-92, Oreg. Grad. Inst., 1987-94; mem. adv. com. Directorate for Engring. and Applied Sci., NSF, 1977-81; mem. sea grant adv. panel, 1978-80; mem. policy adv. com. Office of Grants, USDA, 1985-86. Trustee Ithaca Coll., 1982-89. Lt. USNR, 1943-46. Recipient Disting. Svc. award Oreg. State U., 1978. Fellow AAAS (exec. com. Pacific div. 1963-67, pres. div. 1971), Am. Phytopathology Soc. (pres. Pacific div. 1957, chmn. spl. com. to develop plans for endowment 1984-86, bd. dirs. 1986-88); mem. Oreg. Acad. Sci., Nat. Assn. State Univs. and Land Grant Colls. (chmn. coun. for rsch. policy and adminstrn. 1970, chmn. standing com. on environment and energy 1974-82, chmn. com. on environment 1984-86), Sigma Xi, Phi Kappa Phi, Phi Sigma, Sigma Alpha Epsilon. Home: 3605 NW Van Buren Ave Corvallis OR 97330-4950

YOUNG, RUSSELL DAWSON, physics consultant; b. Huntington, N.Y., Aug. 17, 1923; s. C. Halsey and Edna (Dawson) Y.; m. Carol Vaughn Jones, Aug. 14, 1954; children: Bessmarie, Gale, Janet, Shari. BS in Physics, Rensselaer Poly. Inst., Troy, N.Y., 1953; PhD in Physics, Pa. State U., 1959. Rsch. assoc. Pa. State U., State College, 1959-61; project leader Nat. Bur. Stds., Gaithersburg, Md., 1961-73, chief optics and micrometrology, 1973-78; chief mech. processing div. Nat. Bur. Stds., Gaithersburg, 1975-80, ind. sys. div. chief, 1980-81, chief mech. prodn. div., 1980-81; pres. R.D. Young Cons., Pasadena, Md., 1981—. Contbr. articles to profl. jours.; inventor in field of instrumentation. 1st lt. Signal Corps, U.S. Army, 1943-46. Recipient Edward V. Condon award Dept. Commerce, 1974, Silver medal 1979, Gaede-Langmuir award 1994, Presdl. citation 1986, Washington Acad. Scis. award 1988. Fellow Internat. Inst. Prodn. Engring. Rsch., Nat. Inst. Standards and Tech.; mem. Am. Vacuum Soc. Avocation: boating. Home: 852 Riverside Dr Pasadena MD 21122-1730

YOUNG, SCOTT ALEXANDER, television journalist, author; b. Man., Can., Apr. 14, 1918; s. Percy Andrew and Jean Ferguson Y.; m. Edna Blow Ragland, June 18, 1940; children: Robert, Neil; m. Astrid Carlson Mead, May 20, 1961; children: Deirdre, Astrid; m. Margaret Burns Hogan, May 9, 1980. Grad. high sch.; LittD honoris causa, Trent U., Can., 1990. Columnist Toronto (Ont., Can.) Globe and Mail, 1957-69, 71-80; sports editor Toronto Telegram, 1969-71; TV writer and personality, 1957—. Author: Red Shield in Action, 1949, Scrubs on Skates, 1952, reissue, 1985, Boy on Defense, 1953, reissue, 1985, (novel) The Flood, 1956, HMCS, Text for Gilbert Milne's Photos, 1960 (with Astrid Young) (biography) O'Brien, 1967, Silent Frank Cochrane, 1973, (with Punch Imlach) Hockey is a Battle, 1969, (with George Robertson), (novel) Face-Off, 1971, Clue of the Dead Duck, 1962, reissue, 1981, Boy at the Leaf's Camp, 1963, reissue, 1985 (with Astrid Young) (novel) Big City Office Junior, 1964, Scott Young Sports Stories, 1965, The Leafs I Knew, 1966, We Won't Be Needing You, Al, and Other Stories, 1968, (with Leo Cahill) Goodbye Argos, 1973, War on Ice, 1976, Canada Cup of Hockey 1976, 1976 (with Margaret Hogan) Best Talk in Town, 1980 (with Conn Smythe) Memoirs of the Late Conn Smythe, 1981 (with Punch Imlach) Heaven and Hell in the NHL, 1982, (novel) That Old Gang of Mine, 1982, Neil and Me, 1984, 2nd edit., 1997, (biography) Hello Canada, 1985, Gordon Sinclair-A Life and Then Some, 1987, (novel) Murder in a Cold Climate, 1988, Face-Off in Moscow, 1989, 100 Years of Dropping the Puck, 1989, (short stories) Home for Christmas, 1989, The Boys of Saturday Night, 1990, (with Alan Eagleson) Power Play, 1991, (novel) The Shaman's Knife, 1993, (autobiography) A Writer's Life, 1995, short stories in several anthologies. Mem. Province Ont. Royal Commn. Violence in Communications Industry, 1975-77. Served with Royal Canadian Navy, World War II. Recipient Can. Nat. Newspaper award, 1959, Wilderness award for TV script, 1963, U.S. Eclipse award, 1971; named to NHL Hall of Fame, 1988, Man. Hockey Hall of Fame, 1992. Address: 331 Bland, Cavan, ON Canada L0A 1C0

YOUNG, SCOTT THOMAS, business management educator; b. Oak Park, Ill., Dec. 28, 1949; s. Thomas Menzies and Grace (Butler) Y.; children: Reginald, Galen. BA, U. Ga., 1974; MBA, Ga. Coll., 1982; PhD, Ga. State U., 1987. Prof. U. Utah, Salt Lake City, 1987—, chmn. mgmt. dept., 1994-97, assoc. dean David Eccles Sch. Bus.; mgmt. cons. to numerous orgns.; lectr., speaker, cons. on ops., quality and project mgmt. Author: Managing Global Operations; contbr. numerous articles to profl. jours. Founder MITSI Awards. With U.S. Army, 1971-73. Decorated Commendation medal; grantee Nat. Assn. Purchasing Mgmt., 1986. Mem. Decision Sci. Inst., Acad. Mgmt., Prodn. and Ops. Mgmt. Soc. Avocation: marathon running. Office: U Utah David Eccles Sch Bus Salt Lake City UT 84112

YOUNG, SONIA WINER, public relations director, educator; b. Chattanooga, Tenn., Aug. 20, 1934; d. Meyer D. and Rose (Demby) Winer; m. Melvin A. Young, Feb. 24, 1957; 1 child, Melanie Anne. BA, Sophie Newcomb Coll., 1956; M in Ednl. Psychology, U. Tenn.-Chattanooga, 1966. Cert. speech and hearing specialist Am. Speech and Hearing Assn. Speech therapist Chattanooga-Hamilton County Speech and Hearing Ctr., 1961-66, ednl. psychology, 1966-78; staff psychologist Chattanooga Testing and Counseling Services, 1978-80; ins. rep. Mut. Benefit Life Ins. Co., Chattanooga, 1980-84; columnist Chattanooga Times, 1982-84; cmty. affairs reporter Sta. WRCB-TV, Chattanooga, 1983-84; pub. relations and promotions dir. Purple Ladies, Inc., Chattanooga, 1984—; cons. psychology Ga. Dept. Human Resources, also Cheerhaven Sch., Dalton, 1970-78; adj. prof. psychology U. Tenn.-Chattanooga, 1971-80, adj. prof. dept. theatre and speech, 1988—; pres. Speak Out; bd. dirs. M. Young Comm., Vol. Ctr., 1995—, Arthritis Found., 1995—; spl. projects dir. Chattanooga State Technical C.C., 1995—. Contbg. editor Chattanooga Life and Leisure Mag. Pres. Chattanooga Opera Guild, 1973-74, Chattanooga Opera Assn., 1979-80; bd. dirs., sec. Chattanooga-Hamilton County Bicentennial Libr., 1977-79; pres. Little Theatre of Chattanooga, 1984-90, bd. dirs., 1974—; v.p. Girls Club, Chattanooga, 1979-80; bd. dirs. March of Dimes, 1988; Chattanooga Symphony Guild, Mizpah Congregation, Chattanooga Area Literacy Council, Chattanooga Cares, 1993—, Tourist Devel. Agy., 1990—; mem. alumni council U. Tenn.-Chattanooga; mem. selection com. Leadership Chattanooga, 1984-86; sec. Allied Arts Greater Chattanooga, 1978-80, residential campaign chmn., 1985; bd. dirs. Chattanooga Ctr. for the Dance, Ptnrs. for Acad. Excellence, 1987—, Chattanooga Mental Health Assn., 1988; chmn. March of Dimes Mother's March, 1988, One of a Kind-the Arts Against AIDS-Chattanooga Cares, 1993, 94; co-chair Am. Heart Assn. Gala, 1994, chmn., 1995; chair Little Theatre Capital Campaign, 1995; chmn. Galactic Gala fundraiser Chatanooga State Coll., 1996. Recipient Disting. Citizens award City of Chattanooga, 1975, Steakley award Little Theatre Chattanooga, 1982, Pres. award, 1991, 92, Vol. of Yr., 1995, Woman of Distinction award Am. Lung Assn., 1995, Vol. of Yr. award, 1995, Vol. of Yr. award Chattanooga Cares, 1995. Mem. Phi Beta Kappa (pres. Chattanooga chpt. 1978-79). Jewish. Home: 1025 River Hills Cir Chattanooga TN 37415-5611 Office: U Tenn Theatre & Speech Dept 615 Mccallie Ave Chattanooga TN 37403-2504

YOUNG, STEVEN, professional football player; b. Salt Lake City, Oct. 11, 1961. JD, Brigham Young, 1993. With L.A. Express, USFL, 1984-85, Tampa Bay Buccaneers, 1985-87; quarterback San Francisco 49ers, 1987—; NFL MVP, 1992, NFL Player of the Year, 1994. Organized, manages the Forever Young Found. benefitting Bay Area & Utah youth-oriented charities. Davey O'Brien Award, 1983, All-America team quarterback, The Sporting News, 1983; Named NFL's Top-rated quarterback, 1991, named NFL MVP The Sporting News, 1992, NFL All-Pro team quarterback, The Sporting News, 1992, Bay Area Sports Hall of Fame Profl. Athlete of the Year, 1992, Superbowl MVP, 1994. Played in Pro Bowl 1992, 93; highest rated passer NFL, 1991-93. Office: San Francisco 49ers 4949 Centennial Blvd Santa Clara CA 95054-1229*

YOUNG, SUSAN EILEEN, elementary education educator; b. New Haven, Aug. 8, 1956; d. James William and Rosemary Ann (Drotar) Tobin; m. Randy Harold Young, May 17, 1986; 1 child, Sarah Elizabeth. BA, Annhurst Coll., 1978; postgrad., George Mason U., 1988-91. Cert. tchr., Conn., Va. Tchr. St. Mary Sch., Branford, Conn., 1978-81, Holy Spirit Sch., Annandale, Va., 1990-92; tchr. asst. West Gate Sch., Manassas, Va., 1994-97; substitute tchr. Fairfax (Va.) Sch. System, Prince William County (Va.) County Sch. System, Diocese of Arlington Schs., 1987-90; home tutor, Dale City, Va., summer 1991. Vol. Spl. Olympics, Denver, 1983. With USN, 1983-87. Mem. ASCD, Internat. Reading Assn., Kappa Delta Pi, Phi Delta Kappa. Roman Catholic. Avocations: piano, sports, crafts, reading. Office: West Gate Sch 8031 Urbanna Rd Manassas VA 20109-3135

YOUNG, THOMAS HARLAN, lawyer; b. Bethlehem, Pa., Dec. 13, 1946; s. Harlan A. and Dorothy E. (Kelchner) Y.; m. Karen L. Rogers, Oct. 30, 1987. BS in Chem. Engring., U. Pa., 1968; JD, Georgetown U., 1972. Bar: Va. 1972, Ill. 1973, Colo. 1980, U.S. Ct. Appeals (fed. cir.) 1977. Examiner U.S. Patent Office, Washington, 1968-70; law clk. U.S. Dept. Interior, Washington, 1970-72, U.S. Dist. Ct. Del., Wilmington, 1972-73; ptnr. Kirkland & Ellis, Chgo., 1973-79, Rothgerber, Appel, Powers & Johnson, Denver, 1980-96, Dorsey & Whiterey, Denver, 1996—; cons., Solar Energy Rsch. Inst., Lakewood, Colo., 1979-80; adj. prof. Colo. Law Sch. Contbr. to profl. publs. Mem. ABA, Va. Bar Assn., Ill. Bar Assn., Colo. Bar Assn. (ethics com.), Denver Athletic Club. Republican. Mem. United Ch. of Christ. Avocation: running. Home: 5500 Hawthorn Cir Littleton CO 80121-2137 Office: Dorsey & Whiterey 370 17th St Ste 4400 Denver CO 80202-1370

YOUNG, THOMAS WADE, journalist; b. Raleigh, N.C., Jan. 16, 1962; s. Bobby Wade and Harriett Thomas (Daniel) Y.; m. Kristen Lucille Gooch, June 7, 1986. BA, U. N.C., 1983, MA, 1987. Part time announcer WCBQ Radio, Oxford, N.C., 1979-83; reporter, news anchor WDNC Radio, Durham, N.C., 1984-86; writer, prodr., editor AP, Washington, 1987—. Author of short stories and essays. With Air N.G. Mem. Radio and TV Corr. Assn. Baptist. Avocations: licensed pilot, cert. scuba diver. Home: 1524 Mount Eagle Pl Alexandria VA 22302-2120 Office: AP Broadcast Svcs 1825 K St NW Washington DC 20006-1202

YOUNG, TOMMIE MORTON, social psychology educator, writer; b. Nashville. BA cum laude, Tenn. State U., 1951; MLS, George Peabody Coll. for Tchrs., 1955; PhD, Duke U., 1977; postgrad. U. Okla., 1967, U. Nebr., 1968. Coord., Young Adult Program, Lucy Thurman br. YWCA, 1951-52; instr. edn. Tenn. State U., Nashville, 1956-59; instr., coord. media program Prairie View Coll. (Tex.), 1959-61; asst. prof. edn., assoc. prof. English, dir. IMC Ctr., U. Ark.-Pine Bluff, 1965-69; asst. prof. English and edn., dir. learning lab., N.C. Central U., Durham, 1969-74; prof., dir./chairperson libr. media svcs. and dept. ednl. media, dir. Afro-Am. Family Project, N.C. Agrl. and Tech. State U., Greensboro, 1975—; adj. prof. langs., lit. and philosophy, dir. schs. history project Tenn. State U., Nashville, 1994—; dir. workshops, grants; pres., dir. Ednl. Cons. Svcs. Author: Afro American Genealogy Sourcebook, 1987, Oral Histories of Former All-Black Public Schools, 1991, After School Programs for At-Risk Youth and Their Families, 1994, Sable Scenes, 1996; contbr. poem to Poetry: American Heritage; contbr. rsch. papers, articles to profl. jours. Nat. chmn. Com. to Re-Elect the Pres.; past sec. Fedn. Colored Women's Clubs; bd. dirs. Southwestern div. ARC, Nashville area, 1994—, dir. Volun-Teens; chairperson learning resources com. Task Force Durham Day Care Assn.; bd. dirs., chairperson schs. div. Durham County Unit Am. Cancer Soc.; past mem. adv. bd., bd. dirs. YMCA, Atlanta; chair Guilford County Commn. on Needs of Children; bd. advisors NIH, N.C. Coun. of the Arts; mem. Guilford County Involvement Coun.; chmn. N.C. adv. com. U.S. Civil Rights Com.; mem. exec. planning com. Greensboro; hon. staff mem. 54th Legis. Dist., Nashville, 1996. Recipient awards ARC, 1968, 73, NAACP, 1973, HEW, 1978, U.S. Commn. on Civil Rights, 1982; named Disting. Alumni Tenn. State U., 1994. Mem. AAUW (honor award 1983, pres. Greensboro br., chairperson internat. rels. com.), ALA (divsn. coll. and rsch. librs., past chair), NAACP (life, 1st v.p. Durham br., exec. bd. Greensboro br., dir. parent edn./child advocacy program, Woman of Yr. 1992), NEA, Assn. Childhood Ednl. Internat., Comparative and Internat. Edn. Assn., Archives Assoc., Internat. Platform Assn., Nat. Hist. Soc., Greensboro Jr. League (community adv. bd. 1991—), African Am. Gen. Soc. Tenn. (founder 1994), Zeta Phi Beta (chairperson polit. action com. eastern region, nat. grammateus, Polit. and Civic Svc. award 1974, Outstanding Social-Polit. Svc. award 1982, Woman of Yr. 1977), Commn. on Status of Women (Woman of Achievement 1991), Phi Kappa Phi (Disting. Alumni award Tenn. State U. 1994, Disting Alumni NAFEO award, 1995, Carl Rowan-Oprah Winfrey lectr. Tenn. State U., 1995, Excellence in Journalism award SPJ, 1995, info. officer 1996). Home: PO Box 17648 Nashville TN 37217-0684

YOUNG, TZAY Y., electrical and computer engineering educator; b. Shanghai, China, Jan. 11, 1933; came to U.S., 1958; s. Chao-Hsiung and Chiu-Ming (Chu) Y.; m. Lily Liu, Dec. 27, 1965; children: Debbie Chia-Pei, Arthur Chia-Kai. BS, Nat. Taiwan U., Taipei, 1955; MS, U. Vt., 1959; DEng, Johns Hopkins U., 1962. Rsch. assoc. Johns Hopkins U., Balt., 1962-63; mem. tech. staff Bell Labs., Murray Hill, N.J., 1963-64; asst. prof. Carnegie-Mellon U., Pitts., 1964-68, assoc. prof., 1968-74; prof. elec. and computer engring. U. Miami, Coral Gables, Fla., 1974—, acting chmn. dept., 1988-91, chmn. dept., 1991—; sr. postdoctoral rsch. assoc. NAS, NASA, Goddard Space Flight Ctr., Md., 1972-73. Author: (with T.W. Calvert) Classification, Estimation and Pattern Recognition, 1974; editor: (with K.S. Fu) Handbook of Pattern Recognition and Image Processing, 1986; editor: Handbook of Pattern Recognition and Image Processing, vol. 2, Computer Vision, 1994; also numerous articles. Rsch. grantee NSF, NASA, FHTIC, also indsl. grants. Fellow IEEE (assoc. editor Trans. Computers 1974-76; editorial bd. Trans. Pattern Analysis and Machine Intelligence 1979-84, adv. bd. 1984-90); mem. Sigma Xi, Eta Kappa Nu, Omicron Delta Kappa. Office: U Miami Dept Elec & Computer Engring Coral Gables FL 33124

YOUNG, VERNON ROBERT, nutrition, biochemistry educator; b. Rhyl, Wales, Nov. 15, 1937; came to U.S., 1961; married, 1966; 5 children. BS, U. Reading, 1959; diploma in agr., Cambridge U., 1960; PhD in Nutrition, U. Calif., Davis, 1965; MD (hon.), Uppsala U., Sweden, 1997. Lectr. nutritional biochemistry MIT, Cambridge, Mass., 1965-66, asst. prof. physiology chemistry, 1966-72, assoc. prof., 1972-76, prof. nutritional biochemistry, 1976—; program mgmt. human nutrition competitive rsch. grants program USDA, 1980-81; assoc. program dir. MIT Clin. Rsch. Ctr., Cambridge, Mass., 1985-87; biochemist dept. surgery Mass. Gen. Hosp. & Harvard Med. Sch., Boston, 1987—; sr. vis. scientist USDA Human Nutrition Ctr. Aging, Tufts U., 1988—. Recipient Rank prize in Nutrition, 1989, Recipient of the Bristol-Myers Squibbs/Mead Johnson award of Nutrition, 1995. Mem.IOM/NAS, Am. Inst. Nutrition (Mead Johnson award 1973, Borden award 1982), Am. soc. Clin. Nutrition (McCollum award 1987), Nutrition Soc., Gerontology Soc. Am., Am. Chem. Soc. Office: MIT Lab Human Nutrition Rm E17-434 50 Ames St Cambridge MA 02139

YOUNG, VIRGIL M., education educator; b. Santa Rosa, Calif., Sept. 24, 1936; s. Virgil M. and Vesta May (Huyett) Williams; stepson Louis H. Young; m. Katherine Ann Young, Dec. 20, 1964; 1 child, Susan Annette. BS, U. Idaho, 1958, EdD, 1967. Cert. advanced secondary sch., sch. supt., Idaho. Tchr. Moscow (Idaho) Sch. Dist.; adminstrv. asst. to supt. Coeur d'Alene (Idaho) Sch. Dist.; prof. emeritus Boise (Idaho) State U. Author: (elem., jr. high textbook) The Story of Idaho, 3 editions; co-author: The Story of the Idaho Guide and Resource Book, 1993. Capt. USAR. Mem. N.W. Assn. Tchr. Educators (past pres.), Idaho Assn. Colls. Tchr. Edn. (past pres.), Phi Delta Kappa (past pres.).

YOUNG, WILLIAM BENJAMIN, special education educator; b. Wichita, Kans., Jan. 30, 1929; s. Ernest William and Florence Belle (McCann) Y.; m. La Vona P., Feb., 1949 (div. 1973); children: Lynda, David, Timothy; m. Patricia Sue Reber, Aug., 1974. Student, Southwestern Coll., Winfield, Kans., 1947-48; B in Gen. Edn., U. Omaha, 1961; MS in Pers. Counseling, Miami U., Oxford, Ohio, 1965; PhD in Exceptional Edn., Adminstrn. and Counseling, Ohio State U., 1972. Cert. elem. and secondary adminstr., tchr., counselor, psychologist, psychometrist, spl. edn., mental retardation, learning disabled/behavior disordered, emotionally handicapped, Ind.; cert. K-12 guidance counselor and edn. leadership, Fla.; lic sexologist, flight instr.; lic. Coast Guard capt. Enlisted USAF, 1948; dir. commd. 2nd lt. commd. 2d lt., 1955; advanced through grades to capt. USAF, 1960, ret., 1966; numerous teaching and counseling positions as civilian, 1966-91; co-owner, instr. Ft. Wayne (Ind.) Ground Schs., 1984-88; marriage and family counselor, pvt. practice, 1966-91; tchr., counselor, behavior specialist Broward County Schs., Ft. Lauderdale, Fla., 1989—; cons., internat. presenter/lectr. learning and behavior problems; adj. prof. grad. spl. edn. Nova U. Mem. ACA, Coun. for Exceptional Children, Coun. Behavior Disorders, Fla. Counseling Assn., 32 degree Masons. Avocations: flying, sailing, traveling, golf, swimming. Home: 2548 Gulfstream Ln Fort Lauderdale FL 33312-4704

YOUNG, WILLIAM DAVID, computer scientist; b. Albuquerque, Nov. 22, 1953; s. Youree Harold and Alma Catherine (Callahan) Y. BS in Math. with honors, U. Tex., 1975, BA in Philosophy with high honors, 1976, MA in Philosophy, 1976, MA in Computer Sci., 1980, PhD in Computer Sci., 1988; postgrad., U. Notre Dame, 1976-77. Rsch. engring. sci. asst., systems analyst U. Tex., Austin, 1978-87; computing rsch. sci. Computational Logic, Inc., Austin, 1987-88, sr. computing rsch. sci., 1988—, also bd. dirs.; part-time instr. Austin C.C., 1978-80, Southwest Tex. State U., San Marcos, 1980-81, 83-86; rsch. sci. Honeywell Secure Computing Tech. Ctr., St. Anthony, Minn., 1984-87; invited lectr., presenter, speaker in field; publ. chair Computer Security Workshop III, 1990, IV, 1991; chmn. panel Symposium Software Analysis, Testing and Verification, 1991, program com., 1991; organizer, chmn. panel computer security founds. Computer Security Workshop II, 1989; bd. dirs. Computational Logic, Inc. Mem. editl. bd. Jour. Computer Security; contbr. articles to profl. jours. papers in field. Mem. IEEE, Assn. Computing Machienry, Abelian Group Investment Club (pres. 1992-96), Phi Beta Kappa, Phi Eta Sigma, Pi Mu Epsilon, Upsilon Pi Epsilon. Home: 2208 Lindell Ave Austin TX 78704-5131 Office: Computational Logic Inc 1717 W 6th St Ste 290 Austin TX 78703-4777

YOUNG, WILLIAM F., legal educator; b. 1925. B.A., U. Tex., 1947, LL.B., 1949. Bar: Tex. 1949. Grad. fellow Harvard U., 1951-52; prof. U. Tex., 1949-56, Columbia U., 1956-95, emeritus, 1966. Mem. Am. Law Inst., Order of Coif. Office: Columbia U Sch Law 435 W 116th St New York NY 10027-7201

YOUNG, WILLIAM GLOVER, federal judge; b. Huntington, N.Y., Sept. 23, 1940; s. Woodhull Benjamin and Margaret Jean (Wilkes) Y.; m. Beverly June Bigelow, Aug. 5, 1967; children: Mark Edward, Jeffrey Woodhull, Todd Russell. A.B., Harvard U., 1962, LL.B., 1967. Bar: Mass. 1967, U.S. Supreme Ct. 1970. Law clk. to chief justice Supreme Jud. Ct., Mass., 1967-68; spl. asst. atty. gen. Mass., 1969-72, chief legal counsel to gov., 1972-74; asso. firm Bingham, Dana and Gould, Boston, 1968-72; ptnr. Bingham, Dana and Gould, 1975-78; assoc. justice Superior Ct., Commonwealth of Mass., Boston, 1978-85; judge U.S. Dist. Ct. Mass., Boston, 1985—; lectr. part time Harvard Law Sch., 1979-90, Boston Coll. Law Sch., Boston U. Law Sch. Served to capt. U.S. Army, 1962-64. Mem. Am. Law Inst., Mass. Bar Assn., Boston Bar Assn., Harvard Alumni (pres. 1976-77). Office: US Dist Ct Rm 1903 McCormack PO & Courthouse Boston MA 02109

YOUNGBERG, ROBERT LOVETT, psychologist; b. Lynn, Mass., Jan. 9, 1962; s. Robert Curtis and Maureen Timothea (Lovett) Y.; m. Denise Ann Dunne; 1 child, Cassidy Ann. BS, Boston Coll., 1984, MA, 1986; PhD, Temple U., 1995. Sr. clinician Choate Hosp. Crisis Team, Woburn, Mass., 1986-88; rsch. specialist U. Pa. Med. Sch., Phila., 1989-91; clin. fellow McLean Hosp. Harvard Med. Sch., Belmont, Mass., 1993-95, Mass. Gen. Hosp./Harvard Med. Sch., 1994-96, Lahey Clinic, Burlington, Mass., 1996—. Recipient scholarship Boston Coll. Alumni Assn., 1984-86; grantee Found. for Cognitive Therapy and Rsch., U. Pa., 1991. Fellow Am. Counseling Assn.; mem. APA (assoc.), Am. Assn. Suicidology. Roman Catholic. Home: 24 Long Dr Westborough MA 01581-3642 Office: McLean Hosp Mill St Belmont MA 02106

YOUNGBERG, ROBERT STANLEY, principal, consultant; b. Chgo., Apr. 21, 1932; s. Holger Raymond and Eva Boyd (Carr) Y.; m. Catherine Jane Fitzpatrick, June 19, 1954; children: Kevin, Melissa, Margo Jenkins, Brian. BS, U. Ill., 1954; MEd, Wayne State U., 1959; PhD, U. Mich., 1975. Tchr. Hanneman-Herman-Dixon, Detroit, 1956-62; counselor Barbour Jr. High/Ruddman Jr. High Sch., Detroit, 1962-67, Redford High Sch., Detroit, 1967-70; prin. mid. sch. Novi, Mich., 1970-79, prin. high sch., 1979-92; pvt. practice edn. cons. Clearwater, Fla., 1992—; site evaluator secondary recognition program U.S. Dept. Edn., Mich. Dept. Edn., 1988-97; immigration and customs inspector U. S. Dept. Justice, 1961-64; summer camp dir. Mich. and Wis., 1965-70; cons. in field. Chmn. citizens adv. com. Sch. Facilities, Detroit, 1958-59; chmn. Citizens Adv. Com. on Mid. Schs., Novi, 1972-74, Citizens Adv. Com. on Humanities and Arts, 1975, Great Cities Sch. Improvement Project, Detroit, 1962-64, Dist. Curriculum Coun., Novi, 1972-80; bd. dirs. Youth Assistance Bd., Novi, 1975-79; site vis. North Ctrl. Assn., 1968-91; bus. cons. Mgmt. Style for Retail Merchants, Novi, 1988-91. With U.S. Army, 1954-56. Mem. Mich. Assn. Sch. Adminstrs., Mich. Assn. Secondary Sch. Prins., Nat. Assn. Secondary Sch. Prins., Nat. ASCD, Kensington Valley Activities Conf. (bd. dirs.), Phi Delta Kappa. Avocations: physical fitness, senior games, racquetball, basketball, track and field events. Office: 2427 Bond Ave Clearwater FL 33759-1204

YOUNGBLOOD, ELAINE MICHELE, lawyer; b. Schenectady, N.Y., Jan. 9, 1944; d. Roy W. and Mary Louise (Read) Ortoleva; m. William Gerald Youngblood, Feb. 14, 1970; children: Flagg Khristian, Megan Michele. BA, Wake Forest Coll., 1965; JD, Albany Law Sch., 1969. Bar: Tex. 1970, U.S. Dist. Ct. (no. dist.) Tex. 1971, U.S. Dist. Ct. (so. dist.) Tex. 1972, Tenn. 1978, U.S. Dist. Ct. (mid. dist.) Tenn. 1978. Assoc. Fanning & Harper, Dallas, 1969, Crocker & Murphy, Dallas, 1970-71, McClure & Burch, Houston, 1972-75, Brown, Bradshaw & Plummer, Houston, 1975-76; ptnr. Seligmann & Youngblood, Nashville, 1977-88; atty. Law Offices of Elaine M. Youngblood, Nashville, 1988-94; of counsel Ortale, Kelley Herbert & Crawford, 1994—. Mem. Com. for Women in Govt., Dallas, 1969-71, Law Day com. of Dallas Bar Assn., 1970-71. Mem. ABA, Tex. Bar Assn., Tenn. Bar Assn., Nashville Bar Assn. (fee dispute com. 1990—, vice chmn. 1996, chmn. 1997, CLE com. 1996, L.A.W. 1996—, bd. dirs. 1996, treas., 1997, blvd. bolt com. 1996, publicity), Tenn. Trial Lawyers Assn., Nat. Assn. Women Lawyers, Phi Beta Pi, Cable Club of Nashville (charter), Davidson County Rep. Women's Club. Republican. Episcopalian. Address: PO Box 198985 200 Fourth Ave N Fl 3 Noel Pl Nashville TN 37219-8985

YOUNGBLOOD, JOHNNY RAY, pastor; m. Joyce Terrell; 3 children. Grad., Dillard U., D of Ministry (hon.), 1993; MDiv, Colgate-Rochester Sem.; D of Ministry, United Theol. Sem., Dayton, Ohio, 1990; DD (hon.), Boston U., 1993; LHD (hon.), SUNY, 1994. Sr. pastor St. Paul Cmty. Bapt. Ch., Bklyn., 1975—; organizer Eldad-Medad Men's Bible study class St. Paul Cmty. Bapt. Ch., 1987—, sponsor Father's Day Weekend Conf., 1991—, Nehemiah Housing Project, Bklyn. Samuel D. Proctor fellow; book celebrating the life of ministry of Dr. Youngblood, Upon This Rock: The Miracles of A Black Church, authored by Samuel G. Freedman, 1993; chronicled in N.Y. Times, The Charlie Rose Show, CBS Sunday Morning News, ABC's World New Tonight, NBC Nightly News, The McCreary Report, 20/20, and others; recognized in Congl. Record. Office: St Paul Cmty Bapt Ch 859 Hendrix St Brooklyn NY 11207-7901*

YOUNGBLOOD, RICHARD NEIL, columnist; b. Minot, N.D., May 9, 1936; s. Edward Anthony and Helen (Condo) Y.; m. Adele Henley, May 4, 1957 (div. 1983); children: Kent Jay, Ruth Adele, Beth Alise; m. Mary Dinneen, July 14, 1984. BA, U. N.D., 1958. Reporter Grand Forks (N.D.) Herald, 1955-63; reporter Mpls. Star Tribune, 1963-67, asst. city editor, 1967-69, bus./fin. editor, 1969-84, columnist, 1984—. Recipient Excellence award in bus. and fin. journalism John Handcock Mut. Life, 1974; named Newspaper Farm Editor of Yr. Newspaper Farm Editors of Am., 1965. Avocations: reading, crossword puzzles, boating. Office: Mpls Star Tribune 425 Portland Ave Minneapolis MN 55415-1511

YOUNG-BRUEHL, ELISABETH, philosophy educator, psychoanalyst; b. Elkton, Md., Mar. 3, 1946; d. Herbert Gibbons Young and Lois (Williams) Sutton. BA, New Sch. for Social Rsch., 1968, MA, 1974, PhD, 1974. Prof. philosophy Wesleyan U., Middletown, Conn., 1974-91; prof. psychology Haverford (Pa.) Coll., 1992—. Author: Freedom and Karl Jaspers Philosophy, 1981, Hannah Arendt, 1982, Anna Freud, 1988, Mind and The Body Politic, 1989, Freud on Women, 1990, Creative Characters, 1991, Global Cultures, 1994, The Anatomy of Prejudices, 1996. NEH fellow, 1984-85, Guggenheim Found. fellow, 1986-87. Mem. Authors Guild. Democrat. Office: Haverford Coll Haverford PA 19041

YOUNGDAHL, JAMES EDWARD, lawyer; b. Mankato, Minn., Nov. 17, 1926; s. Benjamin Emanuel Lincoln and Livia (Bjorkquist) Y.; children: Jay Thomas Armstrong, Jan Kristi, Lincoln Anders Morton, Sara Lise. Student, Washington U., St. Louis, 1944-45; AB, U. Mo., 1947; LLB, U. Ark., 1959. Bar: Ark. 1959. Field sec. League for Indsl. Democracy, N.Y.C., 1947-48; nat. rep., asst. regional dir. Amalgamated Clothing Workers Am.-CIO and AFL-CIO, St. Louis, Paducah, Ky., New Orleans, 1948-56; since practiced in Little Rock, Memphis, New Orleans and Albuquerque; ptnr. McMath, Leatherman, Woods & Youngdahl, 1959-68, Youngdahl & Larrison, 1968-80, Youngdahl & Youngdahl P.A., 1980—, Youngdahl, Sadin & McGowan, 1985—; instr. labor law U. Ark. Sch. Law, 1963, 69-71, U. Ark. Sch. Law (Ark. Law Sch.), 1964-66; mem. arbitration services adv. com. Fed. Mediation and Conciliation Service, 1978-84. Editor-in-chief: Ark. Law Rev, 1958-59; contbg. editor: Ark. Advocate, 1972-74; contbr. articles to profl. jours. Vice chmn. New Orleans Forum, 1953-54; pres. Ark. Assn. for Mental Health, 1960-61; chmn. Ark. adv. com. U.S. Commn. on Civil Rights, 1962-65; mem. exec. com. So. Regional Council, 1969-74; mem. nat. exec. bd. Workers Def. League, 1965-75; bd. dirs. Voter Edn. Project, Inc., 1971-74. Home: 2046 Royal St New Orleans LA 70116 Office: 2929 Coors Blvd NW Ste 100 Albuquerque NM 87120-1272 also: Ste 1805 124 W Capitol Little Rock AR 72203

YOUNGER, BETTY NICHOLS, social worker; b. Cleve., 1927; d. Manson E. and Esther L. (McDonald) Nichols; m. Paul A. Younger, 1952 (dec. Mar. 1969); children: Deborah, Rebekah, Sarah, Martha. BA, Otterbein Coll., 1949; MS in Social Adminstrn., Western Res. U., 1951. Cert. social worker, Mich.; diplomate Am. Bd. Examiners in Clin. Social Work. Family and youth worker East Harlem Protestant Parish, N.Y.C., 1951-52; organizer, parent worker Fidelity Presch., Cleve., 1955, 58-60; community worker YWCA, Cleve., 1966-67; organizer, dir. Community United Headstart, Cleve., 1965; social worker Children's Hosp., Columbus, Ohio, 1968, Mt. Sinai Hosp., Chgo., 1972-73, Billings Hosp. U. Chgo., 1973; supr. Ill. Masonic Med. Ctr., Chgo., 1974-79; counselor Barry County Substance Abuse, Hastings, Mich., 1981-82; organizer, dir. Love, Inc., Barry County, Mich., 1983-84; mgr. Cir. Pines Ctr., Delton, Mich., 1984-85; therapist Family & Child Svcs., Jackson, Mich., 1986, Livonia (Mich.) Counseling Ctr., 1986-89; pvt. practice Shumard Counseling, Livonia, 1988-91, Cambridge Counseling, Livonia, 1991-93, Tapestry Counseling, Ann Arbor, 1991-93; tchr. Schoolcraft Coll., Livonia, 1987—; bus. ptnr. Creating Results, Ann Arbor, Mich., 1990—. Mem. ACLU, NOW, Women's Internat. League Peace and Freedom, Sierra Club. Avocations: travel, writing and photography, pottery, cooking, gardening.

YOUNGER, JUDITH TESS, lawyer, educator; b. N.Y.C., Dec. 20, 1933; d. Sidney and Kate (Greenbaum) Weintraub; m. Irving Younger, Jan. 21, 1955; children: Rebecca, Abigail M. B.S., Cornell U., 1954; J.D., NYU, 1958; LL.D. (hon.), Hofstra U., 1974. Bar: N.Y. 1958, U.S. Supreme Ct 1962, D.C. 1983, Minn. 1985. Law clk. to judge U.S. Dist. Ct., 1958-60; asso. firm Chadbourne, Parke, Whiteside & Wolff, N.Y.C., 1960-62; mem. firm Younger and Younger, and (successors), 1962-67; adj. asst. prof. N.Y. U. Sch. Law, 1967-69; asst. atty. gen. State of N.Y., 1969-70; assoc. prof. Hofstra U. Sch. Law, 1970-72, prof., assoc. dean, 1972-74; dean, prof. Syracuse Coll. Law, 1974-75; dep. dean, prof. law Cornell Law Sch., 1975-78, prof. law, 1975-85; vis. prof. U. Minn. Law Sch., Mpls., 1984-85, prof., 1985—; of counsel Popham, Haik, Schnobrich & Kaufman, Ltd., Mpls., 1989-95; cons. NOW, 1972-74, Suffolk County for Revision of Its Real Property Tax Act, 1972-73; mem. N.Y. Gov.'s Panel To Screen Candidates of Ct. of Claims Judges, 1973-74; mem. Minn. Lawyers' Profl. Responsibility Bd., 1991-93. Contbr. articles to profl. jours. Trustee Cornell U., 1973-78. Mem. ABA (council legal edn. 1975-79), Am. Law Inst. (adv. restatement property 1982-84), AAUP (v.p. Cornell U. chpt. 1978-79), N.Y. State Bar Assn., Assn. of Bar of City of N.Y., Minn. Bar Assn. Home: 3520 W Calhoun Pky Minneapolis MN 55416-4657 Office: U Minn Law Sch Minneapolis MN 55455

YOUNGERMAN, JACK, artist, sculptor; b. Louisville, Mar. 25, 1926; s. Guy Arthur and Margaret Anne (Everhart) Y.; m. Delphine Seyrig, July 3, 1950; 1 son, Duncan Pierre. Student, U. N.C., 1944-46; B.A., U. Mo., 1947; postgrad., Ecole des Beaux Arts, Paris, 1947-48. instr. Yale U., New Haven, 1974-75, Hunter Coll., N.Y.C., 1981—, Sch. Visual Arts, N.Y.C., 1981—. One-man shows include Betty Parsons Gallery, N.Y.C., 1958, 60, 61, 64, 65, 68, Paris, 1951, 62, 63, Milan, 1965, Los Angeles, 1963, Worcester Art Mus., 1965, MIT, 1966, Galerie Adrien Maeght, Paris, 1966, Phillips Collections, Washington, 1968, Galerie Denise Rene, Galerie Rive Gauche, Paris, 1973, Pace Gallery, N.Y.C., 1971, 73, 75, Central Park, N.Y.C., 1981, Washburn Gallery, N.Y.C., 1981, 84-87, Guggenheim Mus., 1986, Heland Wetterling Gallery, Stockholm, 1989; exhibited in group shows at Carnegie Internat., 1958, 61, Mus. Modern Art, 1959, Corcoran Mus., Washington, 1958, 63, 79, Kimura Gallery, Tokyo, 1960, Whitney Mus., 1960, 65, 74, 77, 88, 89, Guggenheim Mus., 1961, 64, 66, 81, 82, 86, 88, Art Inst. Chgo., 1962, Mus. Bousmans van Beuningen, Rotterdam, The Netherlands, 1966, Jewish Mus., N.Y.C., 1967, 68, 69, Carnegie Instn., 1971, Hirshhorn Mus., 1980, Haus der Kunst, Munich, W.Ger., 1981, Nat. Gallery Art, Washington, 1981, 83, 89, Found. Nat. des Artes Graphiques et Plastiques, Paris, 1983, Mus. Fine Arts, Budapest, Hungary, 1985, L.A. County Mus. Art, 1986, U.S. Embassy,

Moscow, 1988, Szepmuveszeti Muzem, Budapest, 1988, Nat. Gallery of Art, Washington, D.C., 1989, Whitney Mus., N.Y.C., 1989, Ferie Internacional de Arte Contemporaneo, Madrid, Spain, 1991; represented in permanent collections, Mus. Modern Art, N.Y.C., Knox-Albright Mus., N.Y.C., Worcester Art Mus., Smithsonian Instn., Washington, Whitney Mus., Corcoran Mus., Carnegie Inst. Mus. Art, Phillips Collections, Washington, La. Mus. Modern Art, Humlebach, Denmark, New Sch. for Social Rsch., Olympic Sculpture Park, Seoul, S. Korea, Solomon R. Guggenheim Mus., N.Y.C., Univ. Art Mus., Berkeley, Calif., Vassar Coll., Poughkeepsie, N.Y., Yale U. Art Ctr., New Haven, Conn.; stage designs Histoire de Vasco, Paris, 1956; stage design Deathwatch, N.Y.C., 1958. Recipient Nat. Council Arts and Sci., 1966; NEA fellow, 1972; Guggenheim Found. fellow, 1977. Address: PO Box 508 2003 Scuttlehole Rd Bridgehampton NY 11932-0508 Office: Washburn Gallery 20 W 57th St New York NY 10019-3917*

YOUNGKEN, HEBER WILKINSON, JR., former university administrator, pharmacy educator; b. Phila., Aug. 13, 1913; s. Heber Wilkinson and Clara (Eastman) Y.; m. Daphne Goodwin, Mar. 28, 1942; children: John R., Richard C. A.B., Bucknell U., 1935; B.S., Mass. Coll. Pharmacy, 1938; M.S., U. Minn., 1940, Ph.D., 1942; student, Harvard Grad. Sch., 1938-39; DSc (hon.), U. R.I., 1992. Asst. biology and pharmacognosy Mass. Coll. Pharmacy, 1935-39; teaching asst. pharmacognosy Coll. Pharmacy, U. Minn., 1939-42; from. instr. to prof. pharmacognosy U. Wash., Seattle, 1942-57; chmn. dept., dir. med. plant lab. U. Wash., 1946-57; prof. pharmacognosy, dean Coll. Pharmacy, U. R.I., 1957-81, v.p. acad. affairs, 1967-68, provost health sci. affairs, 1969-81; vis. prof. U. London, 1970, U. Cairo, Egypt, 1977, 79, 81, 85. Author: (with R. Pratt) Pharmacognosy, 2d edit, 1956, Organic Chemistry in Pharmacy, 1949, Natural Products in Pharmacy; also numerous papers in field. Mem. R.I. Health Care Coordinating Coun., R.I. Gov.'s Justice Commn.; pres. R.I. Health Sci. Edn. Coun., 1976-77; chmn. sect. pharmacognosy/natural products Acad. Pharm. Scis., 1976-77; bd. dirs. R.I. Soc. for Prevention Blindness, Health Data Resources, Inc., R.I. Search; bd. dirs. URI Found., pres. 1984-87. With USNR, 1943-46; now capt. Res. Recipient Edwin L. Newcomb award research pharmacognosy Am. Found. Pharm. Edn., 1951. Fellow Am. Pharm. Assn., Am. Assn. Coll. Pharmacy, AAAS; mem. Soc. Exptl. Biology and Medicine, N.Y. Acad. Sci., Am. Soc. Hosp. Pharmacists, R.I. Pharm. Assn. (Toxicology award 1964, Man of Yr. award 1979, Bowl of Hygeia award 1989), Am. Coll. Apothecary, Soc. Econ. Botany, R.I. Soc. Hosp. Pharmacists, Am. Soc. Pharmacognosy (pres. 1970), Rotarian Club, Sigma Xi, Phi Kappa Phi, Phi Sigma, Rho Chi, Kappa Psi, Phi Kappa Psi. Baptist. Home: 188 Oakwoods Dr Wakefield RI 02879-2533 Office: U RI Coll Pharmacy Kingston RI 02881

YOUNG LIVELY, SANDRA LEE, nurse; b. Rockport, Ind., Dec. 31, 1943; d. William Cody and Flora Juanita (Carver) Thorpe; m. Kenneth Leon Doom, May 4, 1962 (div. 1975); children: Patricia, Anita, Elizabeth, Melissa, Kenny. AS, Vincennes U., 1979, student, U. So. Ind., 1987—. Nursing aide, nurse Forest Del Nursing Home, Princeton, Ind., 1975-80; charge nurse Welborn Bapt. Hosp., Evansville, Ind., 1979-80, 82-83; staff nurse Longview Regional Hosp., Tex., 1980-82; dir. home health Roy H. Laird Meml. Hosp., Kilgore, Tex., 1984-86; med. post-coronary nurse Mercy Hosp., Owensboro, Ky., 1987, Dept. of Corrections charge nurse, Branchville Tng. Ctr., Tell City, Ind, 1987-90; charge nurse dept. mental health Evansville (Ind.) State Hosp., 1990—; staff nurse, asst. dir. Leisure Lodge Home Health, Overton, Tex., 1983-84. Grantee Roy H. Laird Meml. Hosp., 1986. Mem. NAFE, Menniger Found., Vincennes U. Alumni Assn., Internat. Platform Assn. Avocations: writing, research, cake decorating, house plants. Home: Rt 1 PO Box 1831 B Jefferson TX 75657 Office: Evansville State Hosp 3400 Lincoln Ave Evansville IN 47714-0147

YOUNGMAN, HENNY, comedian; m. Sadie Cohen (dec.); children: Gary, Marilyn. Appeared regularly on: radio show Kate Smith, during 1930's, now nightclub and concerts comedian; appears on TV; appeared in: TV series Henny and Rocky, 1955, Joey and Dad, 1975; film Silent Movie, 1976, History of the World, Part I, 1981, The Comeback Trial, 1982, Goodfellows, 1990; recs. include Take My Album...Please, 1978, 128 Greatest Jokes, In Concert, 1987, Bits & Pieces, 1992; author 10 books including: How Do Youe Like ME So Far?, Take My Wife Please, 400 Travelins Salesmen's Jokes, 500 All Time Greatest One-Liners, Don't Put My Name on This Book, Take My Life, Please, Big Book of Insults, 1995, Big Big Book of Insults. Office: care of Peter Mallon 8051 Shalom Dr Spring Hill FL 34606-6939 *Life should be like a one liner--good to the last word.*

YOUNGMAN, OWEN RALPH, newspaper executive; b. Chgo., Apr. 24, 1953; s. Ralph Elmer and Charlotte Earldine (Ottoson) Y.; m. Linda Ann Erlandson, Aug. 24, 1975. Sportswriter Ashtabula Star-Beacon, Ohio, 1969-71; office clerk Chgo. Tribune, 1971-73, transcriber, 1973-75, copy editor, slotman, 1976-79, copy chief, news editor, 1979-83, dep. sports editor, 1984-86, assoc. met. editor, 1986-88, assoc. features editor, 1988-90, dep. fin. editor, 1990-91, assoc. mng. editor, 1991-93, features editor, 1993-95, mng. editor, features, 1995, dir. interactive media, 1996—. Mem. Newspaper Assn. Am. New Media Fedn. (bd. dirs.), Am. Soc. Newspaper Editors, President's Club of North Park Coll., Arts Club of Chgo. Avocations: philately, vocal and instrumental music. Home: 40 Kenmore Ave Deerfield IL 60015-4750 Office: Chicago Tribune 435 N Michigan Ave Chicago IL 60611

YOUNGNER, JULIUS STUART, microbiologist, educator; b. N.Y.C., Oct. 24, 1920; m. Tula Liakakis, 1943 (dec. 1963); children—Stuart, Lisa; m. Rina C. Balter, Aug. 3, 1964. BA, NYU, 1939; MS, U. Mich., 1941, ScD, 1944. Diplomate: Am. Acad. Microbiology. Teaching asst. dept. microbiology Sch. Medicine, U. Mich., 1941-43, instr., 1946-47; scientist Nat. Cancer Inst., Bethesda, Md., 1949; asst. prof. Virus Research Lab., U. Pitts., 1949-56, asso. prof. dept. microbiology, Sch. Medicine, 1956-60, prof., 1960—; chmn. dept. microbiology Virus Research Lab., U. Pitts. (Sch. Medicine), 1966-85, chmn. dept. microbiology, biochemistry, and molecular biology, 1985-89, Disting. Svc. prof., 1989—; vis. prof. dept. microbiology, Faculty Medicine U. Athens, Greece, 1963; F.G. Novy meml. lectr. Sch. Medicine, U. Mich., 1965; nat. lectr. Found. for Microbiology, 1972-73; 6th ann. Lippard meml. lectr. Coll. Physicians and Surgeons, Columbia U., 1980; mem. study sect. virology and rickettsiology USPHS, NIH, 1965-69; mem. bd. sci. councilors Nat. Inst. Allergy and Infectious Diseases, 1970-74, chmn., 1973-74, mem. task force on virology, 1976-77; mem. clin. a fellowship study sect. NIH, 1979-80; mem. adv. group to microbiology program Am. Inst. Biol. Scis., 1970-73; asso. mem. commn. on influenza Armed Forces Epidemiol. Bd., Dept. Def., 1959-69, mem., 1970-73; com. .on biomed. research and research tng. Am. Assn. Med. Colls., 1973-75; cons. to surgeon gen. Dept. Army, 1973-76. Contbr. chpts. to books, articles to sci. jours. Referee Macy faculty scholar award program Josiah Macy, Jr., Found., 1977; mem. study group immunology and infectious diseases Health Research Services Found., 1959-79, chmn., 1978-79; mem. microbiology and virology study group Am. Cancer Soc., 1981-85, chmn., 1985. Served with U.S. Army, 1944-46; with USPHS, 1947-49. E.I. du Pont de Nemours & Co. ednl. aid grantee, 1973. Fellow Hellenic Soc. Microbiology and Hygiene (hon. fgn.); mem. AAAS, AAUP, Am. Soc. Microbiology (chmn. sect. T 1981—, mem. com. med. microbiology and immunology, bd. pub. and sci. affairs 1981—), Am. Soc. Virology (pres.-elect 1985-86, pres. 1986-87), Soc. for Gen. Microbiology, Am. Assn. Immunologists, Infectious Diseases Soc. Am., Assn. Med. Microbiology Chmn. (pres.), Am. Acad. Microbiology (bd. govs. 1985-91), Am. Type Culture Collection (trustee 1992-95, vice chmn. 1996—, chmn. bd. sci. dirs. 1995—), Internat. Soc. Interferon and Cytokine Rsch. (hon.). Office: U Pitts Dept Molecular Genetics & Biochemistry Pittsburgh PA 15261

YOUNGQUIST, WALTER LEWELLYN, consulting geologist; b. Mpls., May 5, 1921; s. Walter Raymond and Selma Regina (Knock) Y.; m. Elizabeth Salome Pearson, Dec. 11, 1943; children: John, Karen, Louise, Robert. BA, Gustavus Adolphus Coll., St. Peter, Minn., 1942; MSc, U. Iowa, 1943, PhD, 1948. Registered profl. geologist, Oreg. Jr. geologist U.S. Geol. Survey, 1943-44; rsch. assoc. U. Iowa, Iowa City, 1945-48; asst. prof. geology U. Idaho, Moscow, 1948-51; sr. geologist Internat. Petroleum Co., Talara, Peru, 1951-54; prof. geology U. Kans., Lawrence, 1954-57, U. Oreg., Eugene, 1957-66; cons. geologist Minerals dept. Exxon Corp., Houston, 1968-73; geothermal cons. Eugene Water & Electric Bd., 1973-92; ind. cons. Eugene, 1992—. Author: Investing in Natural Resources, 1980, Mineral Resources and the Destinies of Nations, 1990, GeoDestinies, 1997; co-author: Ordovician Cephalopod Fauna of Baffin Island, 1954. Ensign, USNR, 1944-45. Recipient Lowden Prize in Geology, U. Iowa, 1943. Fellow AAAS, Geol. Soc. Am.; mem. Am. Assn. Petroleum Geologists, Geothermal Resources Coun., N.W. Energy Assn., N.Y. Acad. Scis. Lutheran. Avocations: fly-tying, photography, fishing. Office: PO Box 5501 Eugene OR 97405-0501

YOUNGS, DIANE CAMPFIELD, learning disabilities specialist, educator; b. Margaretville, N.Y., Feb. 16, 1954; d. Richard Maxwell and Charlotte June (Rickard) Campfield; m. William H. Youngs, June 30, 1984. BS in Edn., SUNY, Geneseo, 1976, MS in Edn., 1977. Tchr. educable mentally retarded Tompkins-Seneca-Tioga Bd. Coop. Ednl. Svcs., Ithaca, N.Y., 1978-80; tchr. learning disabled Joint Svcs. for Spl. Edn., Mishawaka, Ind., 1980—; assoc. faculty Ind. U.-South Bend Grad. Sch. Edn., 1996—; mem. Task Force for Reorgn. Spl. Edn., Mishawaka, 1990-91; coord. Tiny Talkers Summer Speech/Lang. Camp, 1994—. Mem. Coun. for Exceptional Children, Learning Disabilities Assn., Coun. for Learning Disabilities, Kappa Delta Pi, Psi Iota Xi. Republican.

YOUNGS, JACK MARVIN, cost engineer; b. Bklyn., May 2, 1941; s. Jack William and Virginia May (Clark) Y.; B in Engring., CCNY, 1964; MBA, San Diego State U., 1973; m. Alexandra Marie Robertson, Oct. 31, 1964; 1 child, Christine Marie. Mass properties engr. Gen. Dynamics Corp., San Diego, 1964-68, rsch. engr., 1968-69, sr. rsch. engr., 1969-80, sr. cost devel. engr., 1980-81, cost devel. engring. specialist, 1981-95; prin. estimator Martin Marietta Astronautics, 1994-95; estimating adminstr. Lockheed Martin Astronautics, 1995-96; prin., owner Youngs Group, 1996—. Dist. dir. Scripps Ranch Civic Assn., 1976-79; pres. Scripps Ranch Swim Team, 1980-82; dir., 1986-87; judge Greater San Diego Sci. and Engring. Fair, 1981-92. Mem. Princeton U. Parents Assn. Recipient 5th place award World Body Surfing Championships, 1987, 6th place award, 1988. Mem. AIAA, N.Y. Acad. Scis., Alumni Assn, CUNY, Bklyn. Tech. H.S. Alumni Assn., Inst. Cost Analysis (cert., charter mem., treas. Greater San Diego chpt. 1986-90), Soc. Cost Estimating and Analysis (cert. cost estimator/analyst, pres. San Diego chpt. 1990-91), Internat. Soc. Parametric Analysts (bd. dirs. San Diego chpt. 1987-90), Nat. Mgmt. Assn. (space systems divsn. charter mem. 1985, award of honor Convair chpt. 1975), Assn. MBA Execs., San Diego State U. Bus. Alumni Assn. (charter mem. 1986), Convair Alumni Assn., Scripps Ranch Swim and Racquet Club (dir. 1977-80, treas. 1978-79, pres. 1979-80), Beta Gamma Sigma, Chi Epsilon, Sigma Iota Epsilon. Lutheran. Research in life cycle costing and econ. analysis. Office: 11461 Tribuna Ave San Diego CA 92131-1907

YOUNGS, WILLIAM ELLIS, motion picture engineer, projectionist; b. Miami, Fla., Apr. 30, 1916; s. Edward Ray and Maude Myrtle (Burd) Y.; m. Mary Helen Still, Aug. 28, 1948; 1 child, Renee Helen. Student, Nat. Radio Inst., 1952. Film technician Washington Motion Picture Co., 1934-35, U.S. Dept. State, Washington, 1948-53; night service mgr. MGM Film Exchange, Washington, 1936-41; mgr., projectionist Calvert Theatre, Prince Frederick, Md., 1941-42; research asst. Exec. Office of the President, Washington, 1942; photo lab technician Office War Info., Washington, 1942-43; br. chief, advisor film and equipment USIA, Washington, 1953-78; engr., projectionist Motion Picture Assn. Am., Washington, 1979-94; advisor Stephens Coll., Columbia, Mo., 1973-75. Columnist Falls Church (Va.) Sun-Echo, 1953-55. Pres. Greenway Downs Civic Assn., Falls Church, 1953-54; pres. Second (Indian Head) Div. Assn. D.C. br., 1953-57; hon. recruiter USN, 1984. With U.S. Army, 1943-45, ETO. Fellow Soc. Motion Picture and TV Engrs. (life; nat. membership chmn. 1969, Outstanding Svc. award 1979); mem. Washington Film and Video Coun. (life; pres. 1967-68), Univ. Film and Video Assn., SAR (pres. Fairfax Resolves 1991-92, Va. ofcl. photographer, nat. mem. mag. adv. com. SAR/DAR liaison com. 1990—, historian 1993-94, editor 1994—, Meritorious Svc. medal 1991, Va. medal, 1994, Pres. Gen.'s citation for Disting. Svc. and Silver Good Citizenship medal 1994, Patriot medal 1996),. Presbyterian. Avocations: photography, pub. relations, hist. and tech. writing. Home: 1436 Mayflower Dr Mc Lean VA 22101-5614

YOUNGWOOD, ALFRED DONALD, lawyer; b. N.Y.C., Apr. 27, 1938; s. Milton and Lillian (Ginsburg) Y.; m. Judith Goldfarb, June 24, 1963; children: Jonathan David, Stephen Michael. BA magna cum laude, Yale U., 1959; LLB magna cum laude, Harvard U., 1962. Bar: N.Y. 1962, D.C. 1970, U.S. Tax Ct. 1964, U.S. Ct. Appeals (2d cir.) 1969. Law clk. to judge U.S. Dist. Ct. N.Y., 1962-63; assoc. Paul, Weiss, Rifkind, Wharton & Garrison, N.Y.C., 1964-70, ptnr., 1970—. Fulbright scholar, London, 1963-64. Fellow Am. Coll. Tax Counsel; mem. ABA, N.Y. State Bar Assn. (chmn. tax sect. 1978-79, exec. com. 1971—, ho. of dels. 1979-80), Assn. of Bar of City of N.Y. Home: 1125 Park Ave New York NY 10128-1243 Office: Paul Weiss Rifkind Wharton 1285 Ave Of The Americas New York NY 10019-6028

YOUNIE, WILLIAM JOHN, special education educator, researcher; b. Boston, July 25, 1932; s. Edward Younie; m. Anne Marie Ring, Sept. 8, 1956; children: Anne Elizabeth, John William. BS in Edn., Boston Tchr.'s Coll., 1953; MEd, Tufts U., 1954; EdD, Columbia U., 1959. Cert. elem. edn., handicapped and learning disabilities tchr., sch. counselor, N.J. Tchr. elem. Delmar (N.Y.) Pub. Schs., 1954-55, Deer Park (N.Y.) Schs., 1955-56; children's libr. Agnes Russel Columbia U., N.Y.C., 1956-57; tchr. Yonkers (N.Y.) Pub. Schs., 1957-59; dir. edn. Southbury (Conn.) Tng. Sch., 1959-63; assoc. prof. Tchr.'s Coll. Columbia U., N.Y.C., 1963-70; dept. chair, prof. William Paterson Coll., Wayne, N.J., 1970—; cons. Fedn. of the Handicapped, N.Y.C., 1965-70, Abilities Inc., Albertson, N.Y., 1967-70, Elwyn (Pa.) Inst., 1968-84, Vineland (N.J.) Tng. Sch., 1985-89. Author: Introduction to Work Study Programs, 1965, Instructional Approaches to the Slow Learner, 1966, (with others) The World of Rehabilitation, 1970, Basic Speech Improvement, 1975; icon paintings, photograph exhibits at Paramus (N.J.) Cmty. Sch., Paramus Pub. Libr., Art Gallery of Loyola Coll., Md., William Paterson Coll., Wayne. Com. chmn. Boy Scouts Am., Southbury, 1959-63; bd. dirs. State Gov.'s Coun. on Mental Retardation, Tenton, N.J., 197071, N.J. Spl. Edn. Instnl. Med. Ctr., Clifton, N.J., 1975-76; mem. adv. bd. Edison State Coll., 1990—, acad. coun., 1993—. Named Educator of the Yr., Morris chpt. ARC, 1990, N.J. State Assn. for Retarded Citizens, 1990; Fulbright fellow People's Republic of China, 1988. Fellow Am. Assn. on Mental Retardation; mem. Coun. for Exceptional Children (pres. Featherstown chpt. 1978). Avocations: woodworking, painting, photography, model railroads, brewerania collecting. Home: 307 South Dr Paramus NJ 07652-4812 Office: William Paterson Coll 300 Pompton Rd Wayne NJ 07470-2103

YOUNT, DAVID EUGENE, physicist, educator; b. Prescott, Ariz., June 5, 1935; s. Robert Ephram and Jeannette Francis (Judson) Y.; m. Christel Marlene Notz, Feb. 22, 1975; children—Laura Christine, Gregory Gordon, Steffen Jurgen Robert, Sonja Kate Jeannette. B.S. in Physics, Calif. Inst. Tech., 1957; M.S. in Physics, Stanford U., 1959, Ph.D. in Physics, 1963. Instr. Princeton U., 1962-63, asst. prof. physics, 1963-64, Minn. Mining and Mfg. fellow, 1963; NSF postdoctoral fellow U. Paris, Orsay, France, 1964-65; rsch. assoc. Stanford Linear Accelerator Ctr. Stanford U., 1965-69; assoc. prof. U. Hawaii, 1969-73, prof., 1973—, chmn. dept. physics and astronomy, 1979-85, acting asst. v.p. for acad. affairs, 1985-86, v.p. rsch. and grad. edn., 1986-95. Author: Who Runs the University: The Politics of Higher Education in Hawaii, 1985-92, 96. Mem. Am. Phys. Soc., Undersea and Hyperbaric Med. Soc., Am. Chem. Soc., U.S. Tennis Assn., Sigma Xi. Republican. Lutheran. Achievements include development (with J. Pine) of first high-energy positron beam, (with others) of SLAC two-meter streamer chamber; discovery (with others) of rho (1600) and psi (3772) mesons; development and experimental verification of theoretical model describing the nuclei which initiate bubble formation in aqueous media, including blood and tissue. Home: 5468 Opihi St Honolulu HI 96821-1924 Office: U Hawaii 2505 Correa Rd Honolulu HI 96822-2219 *Actualizing my potential is the central theme of my life. I have the potential to work, to play, to learn, to love, to teach, and to understand. These are not conscious goals so much as forces which motivate my behavior. I work very hard, not for success, but because fulfillment requires an effort. I try to be honest, not as a goal, but because dishonesty interferes with learning, loving, teaching and understanding. I enjoy children, not because I'm an affectionate adult, but because I see that we are involved in the same process.*

YOUNT, GEORGE STUART, paper company executive; b. L.A., Mar. 4, 1949; s. Stanley George and Agnes (Pratt) Y.; m. Geraldine Marie Silvio, July 18, 1970; children: Trisha Marie, Christopher George. Postgrad., Harvard U., 1983-86. Mgmt. trainee Fortifiber Corp., L.A., 1969-71, asst. to v.p. ops., 1971-75, adminstrv. v.p., treas., sec., 1975-85, exec. v.p., sec., CFO, bd. dirs., 1985-90, chmn., CEO, 1991—; pres., dir. Fonzia Corp., 1993—; bd. dirs. Stanwall Corp., pres., 1989—; bd. dirs. Thompson & Co. Ins. Svcs., Pasadena, Calif., 1996—; past pres. Hollister Ranch Cattle Coop., Gaviota, Calif., 1986-88; bd. dirs. Consol. Media Corp., Pasadena, Calif., Electrocel Tech. Sys., Santa Fe Springs, Calif. Team leader L.A. United Way, 1981-86; bd. dirs. Big Bros. Greater L.A., 1984-87, L.A. coun. Boy Scouts Am., 1992—; mem. Young Pres. Orgn., 1991, forum moderator, 1993-95, chpt. forum officer, 1997—. Mem. Am. Paper Inst. (dir. 1993—, splty. coaters and extrusion sect. 1990—), Nat. Assn. Corp. Dirs., Harvard Bus. Club So. Calif., Harvard Owner/Pres. Mgmt. Program Club, Jonathan Club (L.A.), Rotary (bd. dirs. L.A. club 1992-94), Internat. Wine and Food Soc. Avocations: scuba diving, electronics, cattle ranching, computers. Office: Fortifiber Corp 1001 Tahoe Blvd Incline Village NV 89451-9309

YOUNTS, SANFORD EUGENE, university administrator; b. Davidson County, N.C., Aug. 29, 1930; m. Ruth Wilson; children—Gregory Sanford, Leslie Joan. B.S., N.C. State U., 1952, M.S., 1955; Ph.D., Cornell U., 1957. Asst. prof. agronomy U. Md., College Park, 1957-59; eastern agronomist Am. Potash Inst., 1959-60; assoc. prof. N.C. State U., Raleigh, 1960-64; southern regional dir. Potash Inst. N.Am., 1964-67, v.p., 1967-69; dir. rural devel. ctr. U. Ga., Tifton, 1969-72; v.p. for services U. Ga., Athens, 1972—. Editor: (with others) Potassium in Agriculture, 1966, monographs on soil fertility; contbr. articles to profl. jours. Co-chmn., bd. trustees Ctr. for PVO/Univ. Collaboration in Devel., Cullowhee, N.C.; chmn. State Heart Fund Campaign, Ga., 1983, 84; chmn. bd. trustees South-East Consortium, Chapel Hill, N.C., 1981. Named Outstanding Prof., N.C. State U., 1963, Disting. Alumnus, N.C. State U. Coll. Agr. and Life Scis.; recipient Order of May Decoration, Argentine Govt., 1994. Fellow Soil Sci. Soc. Am., Am. Soc. Agronomy, Crop Sci. Soc. Am.; mem. AAAS, Phi Kappa Phi. Lodge: Kiwanis (pres. 1976, disting. pres. 1977). Office: U Ga 300 Old College Athens GA 30602

YOUPA, DONALD G., broadcast executive. BA in Polit. Sci., Rutgers U., 1959. Exec. dir., v.p. Sears-Roebuck Found., Chgo.; v.p. devel. KCET, L.A., 1978-80, sr. v.p. mktg. and devel., 1980-87, exec. v.p., 1987-94, exec. v.p., COO, 1994—. Office: KCET 4401 W Sunset Blvd Los Angeles CA 90027-6017

YOURZAK, ROBERT JOSEPH, management consultant, engineer, educator; b. Mpls., Aug. 27, 1947; s. Ruth Phyllis Sorenson. BCE, U. Minn., 1969; MSCE, U. Wash., 1971, MBA, 1975. Registered profl. engr., Wash., Minn. Surveyor N.C. Hoium & Assocs., Mpls., 1965-68, Lot Surveys Co., Mpls., 1968-69; site layout engr. Sheehy Constrn. Co., St. Paul, 1968; structural engring. aide Dunham Assocs., Mpls., 1969; aircraft and aerospace structural engr., program rep. Boeing Co., Seattle, 1969-75; engr., estimator Howard S. Wright Constrn. Co., Seattle, 1976-77; dir. project devel. and adminstrn. DeLeuw Cather & Co., Seattle, 1977-78; sr. mgmt. cons. Alexander Grant & Co., Mpls., 1978-79; mgr. project systems dept., project mgr. Henningson, Durham & Richardson, Mpls., 1979-80; dir. project mgmt., regional offices Ellerbe Assocs., Inc., Mpls., 1980-81; pres. Robert Yourzak & Assocs., Inc. Mpls., 1982—; lectr. engring. mgmt. U. Wash., 1977-78; lectr., adj. asst. prof. dept. civil and mineral engring. and mech./indsl. engring. Ctr. For Devel. of Tech. Leadership, Inst. Tech.; mgmt. scis. dept. Sch. Mgmt. U. Minn., 1979-90, 1996—; bd. adv. inst. tech., 1989-93; founding mem., membership com., mem. Univ. of Minn. com. Minn. High Tech. Coun., 1983-95; speaker in field. Author: Project Management and Motivating and Managing the Project Team, 1984. Chmn. regional art group experience Seattle Art Mus., 1975-78; mem. Pacific N.W. Arts Council, 1977-78, ex-officio adviser Mus. Week, 1976; bd. dirs. Friends of the Rep. Seattle Repertory Theatre, 1973-77; mem. Symphonics Seattle Symphony Orch., 1975-78. Scholar Boeing Co., 1967-68, Sheehy Constrn. Co., summer 1967. Named An Outstanding Young Man of Am., U.S. Jaycees, 1978. Fellow Project Mgmt. Inst. (cert. project mgmt. profl., speaker, founding pres. 1985, chmn., adv. com. 1987-89, bd. dirs. 1984-86, program com. chmn. and organizing com. mem. Minn. chpt. 1984, speaker, project mgr. internat. mktg. program 1985-86, chmn. internat. mktg. standing com. 1986, long range and strategic planning com. 1988-93, chmn., 1992, v.p. pub. rels. 1987-88, ex-officio dir. 1989, 1992, internat. pres. 1990, chmn. bd. 1991, ex-officio chmn. 1992, internat. bd. dirs., chmn. nominating com. 1992, chmn., exec. dir. selection com., 1996-97); mem. ASTD (So. Minn. chpt.), Am. Cons. Engrs. Coun. (peer reviewer 1986-89), Am. Arbitration Assn. (mem. Mpls. panel of constrn. arbitrators), Minn. Surveyors and Engrs. Soc., ASCE (chmn. continuing edn. subcom. Seattle chpt. 1976-79, chmn. program com. 1978, mem. transp. and urban planning tech. group 1978, Edmund Friedman Young Engr. award 1979, chmn. continuing edn. subcom. 1979-80, chmn. energy com. Minn. chpt. 1980-81, bd. dir. 1981-89, sec. 1981-83, v.p. profl. svcs. 1983-84, v.p. info. svcs. 1984-85, pres. 1986-87, past pres. 1987-89, fellow 1988—, speaker), Inst. Indsl. Engrs. (pres. Twin Cities chpt. 1985-86, chmn. program com. 1983-84, bd. dirs. 1985-88, awards com., chmn. 1984-89, speaker), Cons. Engrs. Council Minn. (chmn. pub. rels. com. 1983-85, vice chmn., 1988, chmn., 1989, program com. chmn. Midwest engrs. conf. and exposition 1985-90, speaker, Honor award 1992), Inst. Mgmt. Cons. (cert. mgmt. cons.), Mpls. Soc. Fine Arts, Internat. Facility Mgmt. Assn., Am. Soc. Engring. Edn., Rainer Club (co-chmn. Oktoberfest), Sierra Club, Chowder Soc., Mountaineers, North Star Ski Touring, Chi Epsilon (life). Office: 7320 Gallagher Dr Ste 325 Minneapolis MN 55435-4510

YOUSEF, MONA LEE, psychotherapist; b. N.Y.C., May 16, 1964; d. Mohamed Moawad and Myra (Schansinger) Y. BS in Human Devel. and Family Studies, Cornell U., 1986; MSW, NYU, 1991. Cert. social worker, HIV counselor, N.Y.; cert. master addictions counselor. Coord. People with AIDS buddy program Home Care Am., N.Y.C., 1987-88; rsch. asst. Gay Men's Health Crisis, N.Y.C., 1988; caseworker AIDS assessment program Gouverneur Hosp., N.Y.C., 1989; support group facilitator Body Positive, N.Y.C., 1989-92; clin. social worker mental health clinic Lower Eastside Svc. Ctr., N.Y.C., 1991-93; clin. social worker alcoholism outpatient dept. Manhattan Bowery Corp., N.Y.C., 1993-95; psychotherapist Counseling Ctr., Morris Heights Health Ctr., Bronx, N.Y., 1995—; pvt. practice psychotherapy, N.Y.C., 1993—. Contbg. writer PWA Coalition Newsline. Participant AIDS walk Gay Men's Health Crisis, N.Y.C. Mem. NASW, Acad. Cert. Social Workers, Am. Assn. Grief Counselors, N.Y. State Soc. for Clin. Social Work, Assn. for Death Edn. and Counseling, Stuyvesant H.S. Alumni Assn., Psi Chi (life). Democrat. Avocations: dancing, reading, writing, cooking, fitness. Office: 168 5th Ave Frnt 2N New York NY 10010-5910

YOUSUFF, SARAH SAFIA, physician; b. Binghampton, N.Y., Dec. 8, 1960; d. Mohamed and Razia (Sivaramasastry) Y.; m. Donald John Sudy, Aug. 7, 1993. BA in Zoology, U. Tex., Austin, 1982; MD, U. Tex., 1988. Diplomate Am. Bd. Anesthesiology, Am. Bd. Pain Medicine. Fellow in med. mgmt. U. N.C., Chapel Hill, 1992-93; resident in anesthesiology U. Wash., Seattle, 1988-92; staff anesthesiologist Krōn Med., Research Triangle Park, N.C., 1992-94; med. dir. dept. anesthesiology Southwest Hosp., Little Rock, Ark., 1994-96; pres. Southwest Anesthesia Assocs., Little Rock, 1994-95; ptnr. Pain Cons. Ark., 1995—; dir. Southwest Pain Mgmt. Clinic, Little Rock, 1995—. capt. USAR, 1990—. Mem. AMA, Am. Soc. Anesthesiology, Am. Coll. Physician Execs., Ark. Med. Soc., Pulaski County Med. Soc., Internat. Spinal Injection Soc., Internat. Assn. for Study of Pain, Am. Acad. of Pain Medicine, Am. Soc. of Regional Anesthesia. Avocations: photography, international travel, computers, international healthcare. Home: 18 Edenfield Cv Little Rock AR 72212-2667 Office: Southwest Pain Mgmt Clinic 11401 Interstate 30 Little Rock AR 72209-7042

YOUTCHEFF, JOHN SHELDON, physicist; b. Newark, Apr. 16, 1925; s. Slav Joseph and Florence Catherine (Davidson) Y.; A.B., Columbia, 1949, B.S., 1950; Ph.D., U. Calif. at Los Angeles, 1953; m. Elsie Marianne, June 17, 1950; children: Karen Janette, John Sheldon, Mark Allen, Heidi Mary Anne, Lisa Ellen. Ops. analyst Gen. Electric Co., Ithaca, N.Y., 1953-56, cons. engr. Missile & Space Div., Phila., 1956-64, mgr. advanced reliability programs, 1964-72; mgr. reliability and maintainability Litton Industries, College Pk., Md., 1972-73; program mgr. U.S. Postal Service Hdqrs., Washington, 1973—; instr. U. Pa., 1965-66, Villanova U., 1957—. Served to lt. USAAF, 1943-46; to comdr. USNR, 1946—. Registered profl. engr., Calif., D.C. Fellow AAAS, British Interplanetary Soc., Am. Inst. Aero. and Astronautics (asso.); mem. IEEE (sr.), Ops. Research Soc., Research Soc. Am., Am. Math. Soc., Am. Physics Soc., Am. Chem. Soc., Am. Astron. Soc., Am. Geol. Soc., Nat. Soc. Profl. Engrs., Engring. and Tech. Socs. Council Del. Valley (speakers bur.), Res. Officers Assn., Am. Legion. Roman Catholic. Clubs: Explorers (N.Y.C.), Optimists Internat. (pres. Valley Forge chpt. 1970-71). Holder 3 U.S. patents; contbr. articles to profl. jours. and proc. Home: 1400 S Joyce St Apt 540 Arlington VA 22202-1822 Office: L'Enfant Plz Washington DC 20260

YOVICH, DANIEL JOHN, educator; b. Chgo., Mar. 5, 1930; s. Milan D. and Sophie (Dorociak) Y.; m. Anita Barbara Moreland, Feb. 7, 1959; children: Daniel, Amy, David, Julie Ann. Ph.B., DePaul U., 1952; M.A., Governors State U., 1975, M.S., 1976. Cert. reality therapist, cert. profl. mgr., PMA instr. Formulator Nat. Lead Co., 1950-52, 56-59; researcher Montgomery Ward, Chgo., 1959-62; tech. dir. Riley Bros., Inc., Burlington, Iowa, 1962-66, Mortell Co., Kankakee, Ill., 1966-70; exec. dir. Dan Yovich Assos., 1970-79; asst. prof. Purdue U., Hammond, Ind., 1979-84, assoc. prof., 1984-90, prof., 1990—; instr. Army Security Agy. Sch., 1954-56; instr. Napoleon Hill Acad., 1965-66; cons. Learning House, Inc., 1964—; instr. Kankakee C. C. Continuing Edn., 1976; assoc. Hill, Zediker & Assocs. Psychologists, Kankakee, 1975-79; mem adv. bd. Nat. Congress of Inventor Orgns., 1984. Author: Applied Creativity; prdr., moderator: (program) Careers Unlimited, Sta. WCIU-TV, Chgo., 1967; contbr. articles to profl. jours. Mem. community adv. council Governors State U., 1978. Served to 1st lt. AUS, 1952-56. Recipient Outstanding Citizen Award News Pub. Co. Am., 1971, Outstanding Tchr. award Purdue U., 1980, 82, 83, Faculty Service award Nat. U. Continuing Edn. Assn., 1984, Disting. Service award Purdue U.-Calumet Alumni Assn., 1988, Arthur Young award Venture Mag., 1988. Mem. World Future Soc., Nat. Mgmt. Assn., Am. Soc. Tng. and Devel., Am. Soc. Profl. Supervision (exec. sec. 1986), Inventors and Entrepreneurs Soc. Ind. (founder, exec. dir. 1984), Global Intuition Network, Internat. Creativity Network, Infantry Officer Cand. Sch. Alumni Assn. (life), Napoleon Hill Found., Inst. Reality Therapy, Inst. Contemporary Living, Soc. Am. Inventors (life), Am. Legion, K.C. Patentee game Krypto, coating Sanitane. Home: 6736 Waveland Ave Hammond IN 46323-1444 Office: Purdue U (Calumet) 2200 169th St Hammond IN 46323-2068

YOVICICH, GEORGE STEVEN JONES, civil engineer; b. Belgrade, Yugoslavia, June 2, 1929; s. Steven and Draginja (Djurdjevic) Y.; m. Sofija Sckulic, Feb. 3, 1960; 1 son, Steven. B.S. in Civil Engring, High Tech. Sch., Belgrade; M.S.C.E., U. Darmstadt, Germany, 1956; Ph.D. in Bus. and Adminstrn, U. Fla. Registered profl. engr., Ill. and other states. Civil engr. Hollabird & Root, Chgo., 1956-58; bridge engr. Div. Hwys. Ill. Dept. Transp., Chgo., 1958-70; v.p.-project mgr. Arcadia Internat. & Co., Skokie, Ill., 1956-70, chmn. bd., pres., 1970—; chmn. bd. Arcadia Engring. Internat. Inc.; pres. Arcadia Internat. Inc., 1974—; v.p. Hoppmann & Assocs. Inc., Evanston, Ill., 1987—; projects mgr. Midwest, Granite Constrn. Co.; Prof. structural engring. Northwestern U.; prof. math. and structural engring. U. Ill. at Chgo. and Urbana; v.p. Arcadia Nat. Builders; mem. bd. trustees Mchts. Funds Bank, Internat. Bank, Miami, Fla. Legis. asst., mem. hwys. com., mem. traffic safety com., utilities com., r.r. and aviation com., welfare com., Ill. Ho. of Reps., 1970—; advisor Internat. Parliment for Safety and Peace, UN; bd. dirs. Oakton C.C., Skokie, Sch. Dist. 68, Skokie. Maj. AUS, 1954-56. Mem. ASCE, Registered Profl. Engrs. Soc.

YOVITS, MARSHALL CLINTON, computer and information science educator, university dean; b. Bklyn., May 16, 1923; s. Louis Frederick and Rebecca (Gerber) Y.; m. Anita S. Friedman, Aug. 2, 1952; children: Bruce J., Mara F., Steven. B.S., Union Coll., Schenectady, 1944, M.S., 1948; M.S., Yale U., 1949, Ph.D., 1951. Sr. physicist John Hopkins U., 1951-56; physicist electronics br. Office Naval Rsch., Washington, 1956, head info. systems br., 1956-62; dir. Naval Analysis Group, 1962-66; prof., chmn. dept. computer and info. sci. Ohio State U., 1966-78, prof., 1978-79; prof. computer and info. sci. Sch. of Sci., Ind. U., Purdue U., Indpls., 1980—, dean., 1980-88; prof. emeritus Ind. U., Purdue U., Indpls., 1993—; gen. chmn. Computer Sci. conf. NSF, 1973. Editor: (with Scott Cameron) Self-Organizing Systems, Proc. Interdisciplinary Conf., 1960, Large-Capacity Memory Techniques for Computing Systems, 1961 (with George T. Jacobi, Gordon D. Goldstein) Self-Organizing Systems, 1962, (with D.M. Gilford, R.H. Wilcox, E. Staveley, H.D. Lerner) Research Program Effectiveness, 1966, Advances in Computers, Vol. 11, 1971; editor: series Advances in Computers, Vols. 13-40; contbr. rsch. articles to profl. jours. AEC fellow, 1950-51, Indpls. Ctr. Advanced Rsch. fellow, 1988-89; recipient Navy Superior Civilian Service award, 1964; Navy Outstanding Performance award, 1961. Fellow AAAS (chmn. coun. sect. T 1985-88, chmn. 1996—), IEEE (computer soc. chmn. awards com. 1989, bd. govs. 1988-89, computer pioneer award 1990), Assn. for Computing Machinery (coun., gen. chmn. computer sci. conf. 1982), EDUCOM (nominating com.), Sigma Xi. Home: 9016 Dewberry Ct Indianapolis IN 46260-1527

YOW, KAY, university athletic coach. Head coach N.C. State U., Raleigh, 1975—. Office: NC State U Box 8501 Case Athletics Ctr Raleigh NC 27695-8501

YOW, THOMAS SIDNEY, III, college administrator; b. Raleigh, N.C., July 12, 1943; s. Thomas Sidney Jr. and Christine (Southerland) Y.; m. Julia Lee Bryson; children: Robert, Steve. BA, Meth. Coll., 1966; MDiv, Duke U., 1971, EdD, 1982; DD, Meth. Coll., 1989. Dir. admissions, fin. aid Meth. Coll., Fayetteville, N.C., 1973-77; asst. to pres. Louisburg (N.C.) Coll., 1977-85; pres. Martin Meth. Coll., Pulaski, Tenn., 1985-91, Young Harris (Ga.) Coll., 1991—; bd. dirs. Towns County Bank, Hiawassee, Ga. Bd. dirs. Blue Ridge EMC, Young Harris, Ga., 1994—, Cub Scouts, Louisburg, 1977; mem. commn. on colls. SACS, 1994—; mem. nat. adv. com. Atlanta Com. Olympic Games, 1992-96; mem. Ga. Student Fin. Commn., 1996—. Paul Harris fellow, 1988; Olympic torchbearer, 1996. Mem. Ga. Pvt. Coll. Assn. (pres. 1996—), Towns County C. of C. (bd. dirs. 1992-95). Office: Young Harris Coll Young Harris GA 30582

YRIGOYEN, CHARLES, JR., church denomination executive; b. Phila., Dec. 9, 1937; s. Charles and Erma Mae (Suters) Y.; m. Jeanette Alice Brittingham, Dec. 13, 1958; children: Debra Jean, Charles III. BS in Econs., U. Pa., 1959; BD, Lancaster (Pa.) Theol. Sem., 1962; ThM, Ea. Bapt. Theol. Sem., Phila., 1964; PhD, Temple U., 1973; DD (hon.), Albright Coll., 1987. Ordained to ministry United Meth. Ch., 1960. Pastor various chs. Meth. Ch., Pa., 1958-66; campus min. Meth. Ch., Phila., 1966-68; chaplain, prof. religion Albright Coll., Reading, Pa., 1968-82; gen. sec. Gen. Com. on Archives and History, United Meth. Ch., Madison, N.J., 1982—; vis. scholar Union Theol. Sem., N.Y.C., 1980, adj. prof., 1982-93; adj. prof. ch. history Drew U., Madison, 1982—; adj. prof. Moravian Theol. Sem., Bethlehem, Pa., 1994—; mem. exec. com. World Meth. Coun., 1986—; bd. dirs. Wesley Works Editl. Project. Author: Acts for Our Time, 1987, John Wesley: Holiness of Heart and Life, 1996; editor: Reformed and Catholic, 1978, Catholic and Reformed, 1979, Historical Dictionary of Methodism, 1996, Meth. History Jour., 1982—. Trustee Ocean City (N.J.) Tabernacle Assn., Epworth (England) Old Rectory. Masland fellow Union Theol. Sem., 1975, 80. Mem. World Meth. Hist. Soc. (gen. sec. 1987—), Wesley Hist. Soc., Wesleyan Theol. Soc., Am. Soc. Ch. History, Charles Wesley Soc. Republican. Home: 2 Hemlock Ln Morristown NJ 07960-6774 Office: Gen Com on Archives and History PO Box 127 Madison NJ 07940

YSSELDYKE, JAMES EDWARD, psychology educator, research center administrator; b. Grand Rapids, Mich., Jan. 1, 1944; 2 children. Student in psychology, Calvin Coll., 1962-65; BA in Psychology, Biology, Western Mich. U., 1966; MA in Sch. Psychology, U. Ill., 1968, PhD, 1971. Lic. consulting psychologist, Minn. Tchr. spl. edn Kent County Juvenile Ct. Ctr., Grand Rapids, 1966-67; research asst. U. Ill. Inst. Research on Exceptional Children, 1969-70, teaching asst. dept. ednl. psychology, 1970; sch. psychology intern Oakland County Schs., Pontiac, Mich., 1970-71; asst. prof. sch. psychology Pa. State U., 1971-75, assoc. prof., 1975; assoc. prof. U. Minn., Mpls., 1975-79, prof., 1979-91, dir. Inst. Research on Learning Disabilities, 1977-83, dir. Nat. Sch. Psychology Inservice Tng. Network, 1977-83; dir. sch. psychology program U. Minn., 1987-93, dir. Nat. Ctr. on Ednl. Outcomes, 1991—; advisor, cons. and researcher in field. Author: (with J. Salvia) Assessment in Special and Remedial Education, 1985, 6th edit., 1995, (with B. Algozzine and M. Thurlow) Critical Issues in Special and Remedial Education, 1992, Strategies and Tactics for Effective Instruction, 1997, (with S.L. Christenson) The Instructional Environment System II, 1993, (with B. Algozzine) Special Education: A Practical Approach for Teachers, 1995; editor: Exceptional Children, 1984-90; assoc. editor: The School Psychologist, 1972-75, mem. editorial bd., cons. editor numerous jours.; contbr. chpts. to books and articles to jours. Dir. Nat. Ctr. on ednl. outcomes, 1991—. Recipient Disting. Teaching award U. Minn., 1988; fellow NIMH, 1967-69; grantee in field. Fellow APA (Lightner Witmer award 1973); mem. ASCD, APA, Am. Ednl. Rsch. Assn., Coun. for Exceptional Children (Rsch. award 1995), Nat. Assn. Sch. Psychologists, Coun. for Ednl. Diagnostic Svcs. Office: Nat Ctr on Ednl Outcomes 350 Elliott Hall 75 E River Rd Minneapolis MN 55455-0280

YTTREHUS, ROLV BERGER, composer, educator; b. Duluth, Minn., Mar. 12, 1926; s. Chris and Petra (Andal) Y. BA, U. Minn., Duluth, 1950; MusM, U. Mich., 1953; studies with Goffredo Petrassi, Acad. Santa Cecilia, Rome, 1962; studies with Nadia Boulanger, Paris, 1954-55; studies with Roger Sessions, Princeton, N.J., 1957-60; studies with, Aaron Copland, Tanglewood, 1958. Instr. music U. Mo., Columbia, 1963-68; asst. prof. Purdue U., West Lafayette, Ind., 1968-69; assoc. prof. U. Wis., Oshkosh, 1969-77; prof. Rutgers U., New Brunswick, N.J., 1977-96; prof. emeritus, 1996—; recorded with Composers Recs., Inc., 1st Edition Records, Centaur Records; lectr. Internat. Ferienkurse Für Neue Musik, Darmstadt, Germany, 1994. Composer: Music for Winds, Percussion and Viola, 1961, Expressioni Per Orchestra, 1962, Music for Winds, Percussion, Cello and Voices, 1969, Quintet, 1973, Sextet, 1974, Gradus Ad Parnassum, 1979, Sonata for Percussion and Piano, 1983, Explorations for Solo Piano, 1985, Sonata for Cello and Piano, 1988, Raritan Variation (solo piano), 1989, Symphony No. 1, 1995, Espressioni per Orchestra for Philharm. Orch., Augsburg, Germany, 1996. Served with USN, 1944-46, PTO. Recipient award Minn. Fedn. Music Clubs, 1957, Margaret Lee Crofts award, Tanglewood, Mass., 1958, award N.J. Coun. on Arts, 1989; Fulbright scholar, 1954, scholar Govt. of Italy, 1960-62; fellow Composers Conf., 1971, 72, 75; grantee Nat. Endowment for Arts, 1976. Mem. Internat. Soc. Contemporary Music (bd. dirs. 1979—), Am. Composers Alliance (rec. award 1985), Composers Guild N.J. (pres. 1985-92). Avocation: reading. Home: One Woods Circle East Brunswick NJ 08816

YU, AITING TOBEY, engineering executive; b. Chekiang, China, Jan. 6, 1921; came to U.S., 1945, naturalized, 1955; s. H.K. and A. (Chow) Y.; m. Natalie Kwok, Nov. 10, 1951; children: Pamela, Leonard T. BS, Nat. Cen. U., Chungking, China, 1943; SM, MIT, 1946; PhD, Lehigh U., 1949; MBA, Columbia U., 1972. Registered profl. engr., Fla. Asst. prof. engring. NYU, 1949-51; design engr. Hewitt-Robins Inc., 1951-54, chief design engr., 1955-58, engring. mgr., 1958-59; dir. systems engring. Hewitt-Robins Inc., Totowa, N.J., 1967-68, v.p. ops., 1968-71; tech. dir. West S.Am. Overseas Corp., N.Y.C., 1959-67; prin. A.T. Yu Cons. Engrs., 1971-72; co-founder, chmn. Orba Corp., Mountain Lakes, N.J., 1972—, now chmn. emeritus. Contbr. articles to profl. jours; patentee in field. Recipient nat. outstanding engring. achievement awards by ASCE, NSPE, AIME, ASME. Mem. NAE, AIME (chmn. minerals processing div., SME pres. 1986), NSPE, Nat. Acad. Forensic Engrs., Nat. Acad. Engring., Sigma Xi. Home: 962 Gullane Dr Cypress Run Tarpon Springs FL 34689 Office: Orba Corp 1250 W Sam Houston Pkwy S Houston TX 77042-1913

YU, ANTHONY C., religion and literature educator; b. Hong Kong, Oct. 6, 1938; came to U.S., 1956, naturalized, 1976; s. P.C. and Norma (Au) Y.; m. Priscilla Tang, Sept. 18, 1963; 1 son, Christopher Dietrich. B.A., Houghton Coll., 1960; S.T.B., Fuller Theol. Sem., 1963; Ph.D., U. Chgo., 1969, DLitt, 1996. Instr. U. Ill.-Chgo., 1967-68; asst. prof. U. Chgo., 1968-74, assoc. prof., 1974-78, prof., 1978-88, Carl Darling Buck disting. svc. prof. humanities Div. Sch., Dept. East Asian Langs., Comparative Lit. and Civilizations, English, 1988—; assoc. vis. prof. Ind. U., Bloomington, 1975; Whitney J. Oates short-term vis. fellow Princeton U., 1986; Disting. vis. prof. Faculty of Arts, U. Alta., Can., 1992; mem. joint com. on study Chinese civilization Am. Coun. Learned Socs., 1980-86, bd. dirs., 1986-94; regional chmn. Mellon Fellowship in Humanities, 1982-92; bd. dirs. Ill. Humanities Coun., 1995—; vis. prof. dept. religion Chinese U. Hong Kong, 1997. Asst. editor Jour. Asian Studies, 1975-78; co-editor Jour. Religion, 1980-89; author, editor: Parnassus Revisited, 1973; editor, translator: The Journey to the West, 4 vols., 1977-83, Essays on The Journey to the West and Other Studies (in Chinese), 1989; co-editor (with Mary Gerhart) Morphologies of Faith: Essays on Religion and Culture in Honor of Nathan A. Scott, Jr., 1990. Recipient Gordon J. Laing prize, 1983; Danforth fellow, 1960-67; Guggenheim fellow, 1976-77; NEH translation grantee, 1977-82; Am. Coun. Learned Socs. sr. fellow, 1986-87; Masterworks Study grante NEH Seminar for Pub. Sch. Tchrs., 1992. Mem. MLA, Assn. for Asian Studies, Am. Acad. Religion (bd. dirs. 1995—), Am. Comparative Lit. Assn., Assn. Lit. Scholars and Critics, Milton Soc. Am., The Arts Club. Home: 950G N Clark St Chicago IL 60610 Office: U Chicago 1025 E 58th St Chicago IL 60637-1509

YU, GEORGE TZUCHIAO, political science educator; b. London, May 16, 1931; s. Wangteh and Ying (Ho) Y.; m. Priscilla Chang, Aug. 11, 1957; children: Anthony, Phillip. A.B., U. Calif., Berkeley, 1954, M.A., 1957, Ph.D., 1961. Asst. prof. polit. sci. U. N.C., Chapel Hill, 1961-65; assoc. prof. polit. sci. U. Ill., Urbana, 1965-70; prof. U. Ill., 1970—, head dept., 1987-92, dir. Ctr. for East Asian and Pacific Studies, 1992—, dir. grad. studies, 1981-85; vis. sr. lectr. polit. sci. Univ. Coll., Nairobi, 1968; chair U.S.-China African Studies Exchange Com., 1985—. Author: The Chinese Anarchist Movement, 1961, 65, Party Politics in Republican China, 1966, China and Tanzania, 1970, China's African Policy, 1975, Intra-Asian International Relations, 1977, Modern China and Its Revolutionary Process, 1985, American Studies in China, 1993, China in Transition, 1994, Asia's New World Order, 1997. Grantee Social Sci. Rsch. Coun., 1967-68, 70-71, NEH, 1978-81, 84-86, Earhart Found., 1976-77, 81-83, 88, Ford Found., 1985-87, 89, 92. Mem. Assn. Asian Studies, African Studies Assn. Office: 702 S Wright St Urbana IL 61801-3631

YU, JEN, medical educator; b. Taipei, Taiwan, Jan. 23, 1943; came to U.S., 1969; s. Chin Chuan and Shiu Lan (Lin) Y.; m. Janet Chen, June 16, 1973; children—Benjamin, Christopher. M.D., Nat. Taiwan U., 1968; Ph.D. in Physiology, U. Pa., 1972. Diplomate Am. Bd. Phys. Medicine and Rehab. Intern. Phila. Gen. Hosp., 1972-73; resident in phys. medicine and rehab. Hosps. U. Pa., 1973-75; asst. prof. dept. phys. medicine and rehab. U. Pa. Sch. Medicine, Phila., 1975-76, U. Tex. Health Sci. Ctr., San Antonio, 1976-79, assoc. prof., 1979-81; prof. dept. phys. medicine and rehab. U. Calif.-Irvine Coll. Medicine, 1981-82, prof., chmn. dept. phys. medicine and rehab., 1982—. Contbr. articles to med. jours. Mem. Am. Acad. Phys. Medicine and Rehab., Am. Congress Rehab. Medicine, Assn. Acad. Physiatrists, Am. Assn. Anatomists, Soc. for Neurosci. Office: U Calif Irvine Med Ctr Dept Phys Medicine & Rehab 101 The City Dr S Orange CA 92868-3201

YU, JESSICA, director, producer, writer, editor. Bd. dirs. Internat. Documentary Assn. Assoc. prodr. Home Base: A Chinatown Callen Heinlenville, Sour Death Balls, 1993, Rose Kennedy: A Life to Remember, Maya Lin: A Strong Clear Vision (Acad. award for best feature documentary 1995), 1994, Breathing Lessons: The Life and Work of Mark O'Brien (Acad. award for best documentary short subject), 1996, (TV) Men of Re-enaction; guest appearances The Jon Stewart Show, The Other Side, Good Day L.A. Recipient Edward R. Murrow award Skeptics Soc., 1995. Office: Pacific News Svc 450 Mission St Rm 506 San Francisco CA 94105

YU, KITSON SZEWAI, computer science educator; b. Toishan, Kwangtung, China, Apr. 4, 1950; came to U.S., 1969; s. Ho Yee and Yin Sang (Chan) Y.; m. Mabel Griseldis Wong, July 15, 1972; 1 child, Robin Roberta Emily. BS, Troy State U., 1974, MS, 1977, BS, 1980. Cert. systems profl.; cert. data processing educator. V.p. Troy (Ala.) Computer Ctr., 1976-81; computer instr. Tory State U., 1980-81, Linn Benton Community Coll., Albany, Oreg., 1981—; dir. real estate program Linn Benton Community Coll., 1985—; mng. broker Kitson Realty, Corvallis, Oreg., 1975—. Vice pres. econ. devel. Daleville C. of C., Ala., 1976; dir. Corvalis Youth Symphony, 1990-93. Mem. Data Processing Mgmt. Assn. (bd. dirs. at large 1982-93, v.p. 1984-85, pres. 1985-86), Greater Albany Rotary (treas. 1985—), Corvallis Multiple Listing Exch. (bd. dirs. 1990-94), Gamma Beta Phi. Home: 2768 NW Wintergreen Pl Corvallis OR 97330-3550 Office: Linn Benton C C 6500 Pacific Blvd SW Albany OR 97321-3755 *Personal philosophy: Ask, when appropriate; Aid, when appreciated.*

YU, ROBERT KUAN-JEN, biochemistry educator; b. Chungking, China, Jan. 27, 1938; came to U.S., 1962; m. Helen Chow, July 1, 1972; children: David S., Jennifer S. BS, Tunghai U., Taiwan, 1960; PhD, U. Ill., 1967; Med.ScD. (hon.), Tokyo, 1980; MA (hon.), Yale U., 1985. Rsch. assoc., instr. Albert Einstein Coll. Medicine, Bronx, 1967-72; asst. prof. Yale U., New Haven, 1973-75, assoc. prof., 1975-82, prof., 1983-88; prof. biochemistry, chmn. dept. Med. Coll. Va. Va. Commonwealth U., Richmond, 1988—; mem. study sect. NIH, Washington, 1980-84; mem. Bd. Lab. Svcs., Va., 1994—. Editor: Gangioside Structure Function and Biomedical Potential, 1984, New Trends in Ganglioside Research, 1988; contbr. over 500 articles to profl. publs. Josiah Macy scholar, 1979; grantee NIH, 1975—; recipient Va. Outstanding Scientist of Yr. award, 1995, Jacob Javits award NIH, 1984-91, Alexander von Humboldt award, 1990. Mem. AAAS, Am. Soc. Cell Biology, Am. Soc. Neurochemistry (mem. coun. 1983-86, 91—), Internat. Soc. Neurochemistry, Soc. Neurosci., Am. Soc. Biochemistry and Molecular Biology, Am. Chem. Soc., N.Y. Acad. Sci. Home: 306 Cheswick Ln Richmond VA 23229-7660 Office: Va Commonwealth Univ Medical College Virginia Richmond VA 23298-0614

YU, ROGER HONG, physics educator; b. Shanghai, China, Apr. 19, 1960; came to U.S., 1987; s. Rei Qian and Wei-Zen (Zhang) Y.; m. Ting Shi, Sept. 8, 1990; children: William S., John S. BS, Shanghai U. Sci. & Tech., 1982; MS, U. Mo., 1987; PhD, Mont. State U., 1990. Lectr. physics Shanghai U. Sci., 1982-85; teaching asst. U. Mo., Kansas City, 1985-86, rsch. asst., 1986-87; teaching asst. Mont. State U., Bozeman, 1987-88, rsch. asst., 1988-90; prof. physics Ctrl. Wash. U., Ellensburg, 1990—, dist. prof. rsch., chmn. dept. physics, 1997—. Contbr. articles to profl. jours.; referee Phys. Rev. B. Mem. Am. Phys. Soc., Acoustic Soc. Am., Coun. Undergrad. Rsch., Associated Western Univs. (rsch. and edn. com.). Office: Ctrl Wash U Dept Physics Ellensburg WA 98926

YU, VICTOR LIN-KAI, physician, educator; b. Mpls., Jan. 9, 1943; s. Robert S.H. and Victoria (Hsiao) Y.; m. Deborah Lin, June 19, 1971; children: Chen Ming, Kwan Ting. BA, Carleton Coll., 1965; MD, U. Minn., 1970. Internship and residency U. Colo., Denver, 1970-72; residency Stanford U., Palo Alto, Calif., 1974, postdoctoral fellow, 1975-77; prof. medicine U. Pitts., 1978—; chmn. bd. sci. counselors NIH, 1986-92; chief infectious disease sect. VA Med. Ctr., Pitts., 1981—; disting. lectr. Am. Soc. Microbiology, 1988; Malia lectr. Southside Hosp., 1992; Berris lectr. U. Toronto, 1993; Rubin lectr. Berkshire AHEC. Contbr. rsch. on Legionnaires' disease to sci. publs. Recipient Disting. Rsch. award Am. Legion, 1982, Health Svcs. Rsch. Found., 1984; named disting. scientist Chinese Med. Soc., Taipei, Taiwan, 1988; recipient Gold medal for Outstanding Contbn. to Sci., Fed. Exec. Bd., 1993, Citation of Merit, Allegheny County, Pa., 1993. Fellow ACP; mem. Orgn. Chinese Ams. (officer Pitts. sect. 1978—). Home: 87 Longue Vue Dr Pittsburgh PA 15228-1538 Office: U Pitts Divsn Infectious Disease 501 Kaufmann Bldg Pittsburgh PA 15213

YU, YI-YUAN, mechanical engineering educator; b. Tienjin, China, Jan. 29, 1923; came to U.S., 1947, naturalized, 1962; s. Tsi-Chi and Hsiao-Kung (Wang) Y.; m. Eileen Hsiu-Yung Wu, June 14, 1952; children: Yolanda, Lisa. BS, Tienjin U., 1944; MS, Northwestern U., 1950, PhD, 1951. Prof. mech. engring. (Poly Inst. Bklyn.), 1957-66; cons. engr. Gen. Electric Space Div., Valley Forge, Pa., 1966-70; Disting. prof. aero. engring. (Wichita State U.), 1972-75; mgr. components and analysis Rockwell Internat., Rocketdyne, , Canoga Park, Calif., 1975-79, exec. engr. Energy Systems, 1979-81; dean engring. N.J. Inst. Tech., Newark, 1981-85, prof. mech. engring., 1981-93, prof. emeritus, 1993—, rsch. prof., 1996-97; vis. prof. Cambirdge U., 1960; advisor Middle East Tech. U., Ankara, Turkey, 1966; lectr. Gen. Electric Co., 1963-73; mem. ad hoc com. on dynamic analysis USN, 1968-69; cons. internat. adv. panel Chinese U. Devel. Project, 1983, David W. Taylor Naval Ship Rsch. and Devel. Ctr., 1987-88; cons. Atty. Gen.'s Office State N.J., 1982-84. Contbr. Handbook of Engineering Mechanics, 1962; author: Vibrations of Elastic Plates, 1996. Guggenheim fellow, 1959-60; Air Force Office Sci. Research grantee, 1956-66; NASA grantee, 1967-69, 74-75. Fellow AIAA (assoc.), ASME (life); mem. Am. Soc. Engring. Edn., Am. Soc. for Composites, Am. Acad. Mechanics (chmn. com. mech. edn. 1993-94), Sigma Xi, Phi Kappa Phi, Pi Tau Sigma, Tau Beta Pi. Presbyterian. Home: 24 Gordon Rd Essex Fells NJ 07021-1604 Office: 323 King Blvd Newark NJ 07102 *At the end of each day, let everyone of us ask the question: Have I done the best I can this day to make the world a better place to live for myself and for my fellow human beings? As long as the answer is yes, it does not matter whether one is a teacher, farmer, worker, businessperson or homemaker.*

YUAN, JUNYING, medical educator, researcher; b. Shanghai, China. BS, Fudan U., Shanghai, 1982; PhD in Neurosci., Harvard U., 1989. Postdoctoral trainee in devel. biology MIT, 1989-90; instr. medicine Harvard U., 1990-91, asst. prof. medicine and program in neurosci., 1992-96, asst. prof. cell biology and program in neurosci., 1996—; asst. geneticist Cardiovasc. Rsch. Ctr. Mass. Gen. Hosp., 1990-96. Mem. editl. bd. Current Biology, 1996; ad hoc reviewer NIH Human Embryology and Devel. 2 Study Sect., 1995, regular reviewer, 1996—; patentee in field; contbr. articles to profl. jours.; presenter in field. Recipient Wilson S. Stone Meml. award MD Anderson Cancer Ctr. U. Tex., 1994, Established Investigator award Am. Heart Assn., 1996—; Ryan fellow Harvard Med. Sch., 1985-89. Office: Harvard Med Sch Dept Cell Biology 240 Longwood Ave Boston MA 02115-5701

YUAN, SHAO WEN, aerospace engineer, educator; b. Shanghai, China, Apr. 16, 1914; came to U.S., 1934, naturalized, 1954; s. Ti An and Chieh-huang (Chien) Y.; m. Hui Chih Hu, Nov. 5, 1950. B.S., U. Mich., 1936; M.E., Stanford U., 1939; M.S., Calif. Inst. Tech., 1937, Ph.D., 1941. Rsch. engr. Glenn Martin Co., 1942-43; chief of rsch. Helicopter div. McDonnell Aircraft Corp., 1943-45; instr. Washington U., St. Louis, 1944-45; adj. prof. Poly. Inst. Bklyn., 1946-49, assoc. prof., 1949-54, prof., 1954-57; ptnr. von Kármán, Yuan & Arnold Assocs., 1955-63; prof. aerospace engring. U. Tex., 1958-68; prof., chmn. mech. engring. div. George Washington U., 1968-78, chmn. civil, mech. and environ. dept., 1973-78, 80-81, prof. emeritus, 1984; pres. RISE, Inc., 1977-85; Canadair Chair prof. U. Laval, Can., 1957-58; chmn. adv. com. Joint Inst. for Advancement of Flight Sci., 1970-84; hon. prof. Zhejiang U., 1987—; cons. Edo Aircraft Corp., Aerojet Corp., Cornell Aero. Lab., Dept. of Interior, Oak Ridge Nat. Lab., N.Am., Aviation, Inc., Fairchild-Hiller Corp., McDonnell-Douglas Corp., The World Bank; hon. adviser Nat. Center Research of China, Taiwan, 1958-68; chmn., founder 1st U.S.-China Conf. on Energy, Resources, and Environment, 1982; founder Consortium of Univs. for Promoting Grad. Aerospace Studies, 1984; founder Disting. Lecture Series on Founds. of Aerospace Research and Devel., 1986. Author: Foundations of Fluid Mechanics, 1967; Contbr. to: High Speed Aerodynamics and Jet Propulsion series, 1959, Energy, Resources, and Environment: Procs. at 1st U.S.-China Conf., 1982. Recipient Outstanding Achievements award George Washington U., 1981; named Outstanding Educator of Am., 1970, Outstanding Chinese American, 1983. Fellow AAAS, AIAA; mem. ASME (life), Am. Soc. Engring. Edn., Soc. Engring. Sci. (bd. dirs. 1973-78, pres. 1977), Torchbearers Caltech, Founding Grant Soc. of Stanford U. (charter), John Montieth Soc. of U. Mich. (charter), Sigma Xi, Phi Kappa Phi, Phi Tau Phi, Sigma Gamma Tau, Pi Tau Sigma, Tau Beta Pi, Tau Xi Sigma. Achievements include patents in field. Home: 1400 Geary Blvd Apt 1505 San Francisco CA 94109-6570 *As engineers and scientists, we are concerned with that "something beyond"; consequently, the utmost achievement of an engineer is to create what has never been, for the improvement of quality of life.*

YUAN, SIDNEY WEI KWUN, cryogenic engineer, consultant; b. Hong Kong, July 30, 1957; came to U.S., 1975; s. Chia Chi and Tso Tak (Wong) Y.; m. Katherine K.Y. Dai, Sept. 8, 1981; children: Jacquelyn Kate, Chrystal Sidney. BSc, UCLA, 1980, MSc, 1981, PhD, 1985. Rsch. asst. UCLA, 1980-81, rsch. engr., 1981-85, teaching asst., 1984-85; rsch. scientist Lockheed Missiles & Space Co., Palo Alto, Calif., 1985-96, BEI Electronics, Sylmar, Calif., 1996—; cons. Toyo Sanso Inc., Japan, 1990—, Applied Aerotek Inc., 1991—, Compliance Engring. and Tech., 1992—, Applied Scis. Labs., 1992—; lectr. fundamentals of superconductivity UCLA, 1989. Contbr. over 40 articles on cryogenics, thermodynamics, heat and mass transport to profl. jours. Recipient Nat. Excellence Recognition award Space Found., 1985, Superior Performance Team award Lockheed, 1990. Mem. AIAA (Engr. of Yr. award 1991), Am. Inst. Chem. Engrs. (Indsl.

Rsch. award 1994), Cryogenic Soc. Am. (vice chmn. no. Calif.), Sigma Xi, Tau Beta Pi. Republican. Avocations: table tennis, go. Home: 2255 29th St Santa Monica CA 90405-2007 Office: 13100 Telfair Ave San Fernando CA 91342-3573

YUAN, XIAO-JIAN, medical researcher, educator; b. Xintian, Hunan, People's Republic of China, May 9, 1963; s. Tian-Lin Yuan and Li-Hua Chen. MD, Suzhou (China) Med. Coll., 1983; PhD in Physiology, Peking Union Med. Coll., Beijing, 1993; postgrad., U. Md., 1993. Intern Suzhou Med. Coll. Hosp., 1982-83; resident Lanzhou (China) Med. Coll. Hosp., 1983-84; mem. sci. cadre Office Sci. and Tech. Gansu Environ. Protection Bur., Lanzhou, 1984; rsch. assoc. dept. environ. medicine Gansu Inst. Environ. Scis., Lanzhou, 1984-85; postdoctoral fellow dept. physiology and medicine U. Md. Sch. Medicine, Balt., 1988-93, rsch. asst. prof. dept. physiology, 1993-96, rsch. asst. prof. divsn. pulmonary and critical care med., 1993-96, asst. prof., 1996—; lectr. in field; ad hoc reviewer grant applications NIH, 1995—, study section mem. Am. Heart Assn., 1995-97; ad hoc reviewer rsch. grant applications Wellcome Trust (London), 1995, U.S. Dept. Vets. Affairs, 1995. Author: Olympic Complete Words, 1988; editorial asst. Gansu Assn. Environ. Scis., 1984-85; contbr. articles to profl. jours. Parker B. Francis fellow, 1994-97. Mem. AAAS, Am. Heart Assn. (Md. affiliate rsch. fellow 1990-92, grantee 1990-92, 93-95, 96—, Cournand and Comroe Young Investigator award 1995, Best Abstract award 1996), Am. Physiol. Soc. (Giles F. Filley Meml. award 1995, Rsch. Career Enhancement award 1995), Am. Thoracic Soc., Biophys. Soc., Chinese Assn. Physiol. Sci. (editorial asst. 1987-88), Soc. Chinese Bioscientists in Am. (Dr. C.W. Dunker award 1993). Home: 30 Jones Valley Circle Baltimore MD 21209 Office: U Md Sch Medicine Div Pulmonary Medicine 10 S Pine St # 800 Baltimore MD 21201-1116

YUAN TSEH LEE, chemistry educator; b. Hsinchu, Taiwan, China, Nov. 29, 1936; came to U.S., 1962, naturalized, 1974; s. Tsefan and Pei (Tasi) L.; m. Bernice Wu, June 28, 1963; children: Ted, Sidney, Charlotte. BS, Nat. Taiwan U., 1959; MS, Nat. Tsinghua U., Taiwan, 1961; PhD, U. Calif., Berkeley, 1965. From asst. prof. to prof. chemistry U. Chgo., 1968-74; prof. emeritus U. Calif., Berkeley, 1974—, also former prin. investigator Lawrence Berkeley Lab. Contbr. numerous articles on chem. physics to profl. jours. Recipient Nobel Prize in Chemistry, 1986, Ernest O. Lawrence award Dept. Energy, 1981, Nat. Medal of Sci., 1986, 90, Peter Debye award for Phys. Chemistry, 1986; fellow Alfred P. Sloan, 1969-71, John Simon Guggenheim, 1976-77; Camille and Henry Dreyfus Found. Tchr. scholar, 1971-74, Harrison Howe award, 1983. Fellow Am. Phys. Soc.; mem. NAS, AAAS, Am. Acad. Arts and Scis., Am. Chem. Soc. Office: U Calif Dept Chemistry Berkeley CA 94720*

YUDOF, MARK G., law educator, academic administrator; b. Phila., Oct. 30, 1944; s. Jack and Eleanor (Parris) Y.; m. Judith Lynn Gomel, July 11, 1965; children: Seth Adam, Samara Lisa. BA, U. Pa., 1965, LLB, 1968. Bar: Pa. 1970, U.S. Supreme Ct. 1974, U.S. Dist. Ct. (we. dist.) Tex. 1975, U.S. Ct. Appeals (5th cir.) 1976, Tex. 1980. Law clk. to judge U.S. Ct. Appeals (5th cir.), 1968-69; assoc. gen. counsel to ABA study FTC, 1969; research assoc. Harvard Ctr. Law and Edn., 1969-70, sr. staff atty., 1970-71; lectr. Harvard Grad. Sch. Edn., 1970-71; asst. prof. law U. Tex., Austin, 1971-74, prof., 1974—, assoc. dean, 1979-84, James A. Elkins Cent. Chair in Law, 1983-97, dean, 1984-94, exec. v.p., provost, 1994-97, John Jeffers Rsch. Chair in Law, 1991-94; pres. U. Minn., 1997—; of counsel Pennzoil vs. Texaco, 1987; mem. adv. bd. Inst. for Transnat. Arbitration, 1988—, Am. Jour. Edn., 1991—; chmn. bd. contbrs. to Tex. Lawyer, 1988—; mem. nat. bd. contbrs. Am. Lawyer Newspapers Group, Inc., 1988—; mem. telecomm. infrastructure fund bd. State of Tex. Author: When Government Speaks, 1983 (Scribes Book award 1983, cert. merit ABA 1983), (with others) Educational Policy and the Law, 1992, (with others) Gender Justice, 1986. Mem. Tex. Gov.'s Task Force on Sch. Fin., 1989-90, Tex. Gov.'s Select Com. on Edn., 1988; bd. dirs. Freedom to Read Found., 1989-91; mem. adv. bd. Austin Diagnostic Clinic Cmty., 1989-95; mem. Austin Cable Commn., 1981-84, chmn., 1982; mem. nat. panel on sch. desegregation rsch. Ford Found., 1977-80; mem. state exec. com. Univ. Interscholastic League, 1983-86; mem. rsch. adv. com. Ctr. for Policy Rsch. in Edn., 1985—; bd. dirs. Jewish Children's Regional Svc., 1980-86, Austin Diagnostic Med. Ctr., 1995—; mem. Gov.'s Select Task Force on Pub. Edn., 1995—; mem. Telecomms. Infrastructure Fund Bd., State of Tex., 1995—. Recipient Teaching Excellence award, 1975, Most Meritorious Book award Scribes, 1983, Humanitarian award Austin region NCCJ, 1988, Antidefamation League Jurisprudence award, 1991; fellow Queen Mary and Westfield Coll., U. London. Fellow Tex. Bar Found., Am. Bar Found.; mem. ABA (legal edn. and admissions to bar sect. 1984—), Am. Law Inst., Tex. Bar Assn., Assn. Am. Law Schs. (chmn. law and edn. sect. 1983-84, mem. exec. com. 1988-90), Univ. Club, Headliners Club, Met. Club. Avocation: collecting antique maps. Office: U Tex Exec Vice Pres/Provost MAI 201 Austin TX 78712

YUE, AGNES KAU-WAH, otolaryngologist; b. Shanghai, Peoples Republic China, Dec. 1, 1947; came to U.S., 1967; d. Chen Kia and Nee Yuan (Ying0 ; m. Gerald Kumata, Sept. 25, 1982; children: Julie, Allison Benjamin. BA, Wellesley Coll., 1970; MD, Med. Coll. Pa., 1974; postgrad., Yale U., 1974-78. Intern Yale-New Haven Hosp., 1974-75, resident, 1975-78; fellow U. Tex. M.D. Anderson Cancer Ctr., Houston, 1978-79; asst. prof. U. Wash., Seattle, 1979-82; physician Pacific Med. Ctr., Seattle, 1979-90; pvt. practice Seattle, 1991—. Fellow Am. Acad. Otolaryngology, Am. Coll. Surgeons; mem. Northwest Acad. Otolaryngology. Avocations: sailing, opera, profl. voice, cooking. Office: 1801 NW Market St Ste 410 Seattle WA 98107-3909

YUE, ALFRED SHUI-CHOH, metallurgical engineer, educator; b. China, Nov. 12, 1920; s. Choy Noon-woo and Sze Man-hun (Tom) Y.; m. Virginia Chin-wen Tang, May 21, 1944; children: Mary, Raymond Yuan, John, Ling Tsao, David, Nancy Chang. B.S., Chao-tung U., 1942; M.S., Ill. Inst. Tech., 1950; Ph.D., Purdue U., 1956. Assoc. engr. Taiwan Aluminum Co., 1942-47; instr. Purdue U., 1952-56; research engr. Dow Chem. Co., Midland, Mich., 1956-62; sr. mem. Lockheed, Palo Alto Research Lab., 1962-69; now cons.; prof. engring. and applied sci. U. Calif., Los Angeles, 1969—; hon. prof. Xian Jiao-tong U., China, 1980; cons. LTV Aerospace Co., Lockheed Missile & Space Co., Atlantic Richfield Co.; Sec.-gen. Chinese Culture Assn. in U.S.A., 1967, also; bd. dirs. Chinese scholar to U.S.A. Fellow AIAA (assoc.); mem. AAAS, AIME, Am. Soc. Metals, Materials Rsch. Soc., Sigma Xi, Sigma Pi Sigma, Tau Beta Pi, Phi Tau Phi (pres. 1978-82).

YUECHIMING, ROGER YUE YUEN SHING, mathematics educator; b. Mauritius, Feb. 25, 1937; s. James and Marie Yuechiming; m. Renée Bethery, Nov. 9, 1963; children: Françoise, Marianne, Isabelle. BSc with 1st class honours, U. Manchester, Eng., 1964, PhD, 1967. Asst. U. Strasbourg, France, 1967-69; lectr. math. U. Paris VII, 1970—; participant math. confs. and seminars in numerous countries; referee various math. jours. Contbr. over 80 articles on ring theory to sci. jours. of numerous countries. Mem. French Math. Soc., Am. Math. Soc., London Math. Soc., Belgian Math. Soc. Achievements include introduction of concept of p-injective modules, new approaches in ring and module theory leading to a better understanding of von Neumann regular rings, V-rings, self-injective rings and generalizations. Home: 38 rue du Surmelin, 75020 Paris France Office: U Paris VII Unité Mixte de Rsch, 9994 CNRS 2 Pl Jussieu, 75251 Paris France

YUELYS, ALEXANDER, former cosmetics company executive; b. Bronx, N.Y., Aug. 12, 1926; s. Dionisyus and Anastasia (Stathes) Y.; m. Nicoletta Lardas, Dec. 9, 1950; 1 son, Jordan. B.A., Hunter Coll., 1950. C.P.A., N.Y. With Arthur Young, 1952-56, Haskins & Sells, 1950-52; with Fabergé, Inc., N.Y.C., 1956-83, exec. v.p., chief fin. officer, dir.; dir. Brut Prodns., Inc., Am. Stage Co. Bd. dirs. St. Michael's Home for Aged, v.p., 1984—. Served with USAAF, 1945-46. Mem. Fin. Execs. Inst., Nat. Assn. Accountants. Home: PO Box 836 Alpine NJ 07620-0836

YUEN, BENSON BOLDEN, airline management consultant, software executive; b. Hong Kong, Nov. 20, 1960; came to U.S., 1968; s. Eugene Howard and Janet (Chan) Y. BSBA in Fin. summa cum laude, U. Cen. Fla., 1983. Mgr. market planning and automation Fla. Express, Inc., Orlando, 1983-85, dir. pricing, 1986-87; dir. customer svc. Seabrook Mktg., Inc., Houston, 1988-91, v.p. customer svc., 1992-94; v.p. consulting svcs. PROS Strategic Solutions, Inc., Houston, 1994-96, sr. v.p. mktg. and consulting svcs., 1996—; cons. airline revenue mgmt., mktg. automation, bus. mgmt., sys. devel. and bus. process engring. to more than 50 airlines and industry-related firms world wide. Designer (software) Passenger Revenue Forecast and Optimization System, 1989, Group Revenue Optimization and Management System Version 3, 1990-94, Version 4, 1995—, Holiday Mgmt. Module, Network Pricing Analysis Sys., Hub Complex Optimization. Avocations: travel, music. Office: PROS Strategic Solutions 3223 Smith St Ste 100 Houston TX 77006-6623

YUILL, THOMAS MACKAY, academic administrator, microbiology educator; b. Berkeley, Calif., June 14, 1937; s. Joseph Stuart and Louise (Dunlop) Y.; m. Ann Warnes, Aug. 24, 1960; children: Eileen, Gwen. BS, Utah State U., 1959; MS, U. Wis., 1962, PhD, 1964. Lab. officer Walter Reed Army Inst. Rsch., Washington, 1964-66; med. biologist SEATO Med. Research Lab., Bangkok, Thailand, 1966-68; asst. prof. U. Wis.-Madison, 1968-72, assoc. prof., 1972-76, prof., 1976—, dept. chmn., 1979-82, assoc. dean., 1982-93; dir. Inst. Environ. Studies, 1993—; cons. NIH, Bethesda, 1976-86; chmn. Viral Diseases Panel, U.S.-Japan Biomed. Scis. Program, 1979-86, Am. Com. Arbovirology, 1982—; bd. dirs. Cen. Tropical Agrl. Res. Teaching, Turrialba, Costa Rica, 1988-96. Contbr. chpts. to books, articles to profl. jours. Served to capt. U.S. Army, 1964-66. Recipient grants state and fed. govts., 1968—. Mem. Orgn. Tropical Studies (pres. 1979-85), Wildlife Disease Assn. (treas. 1980-85, pres. 1985-87, editl. bd. 1989-96), Am. Soc. Tropical Medicine and Hygiene (mem. editl. bd. 1984-96), Am. Soc. Microbiology, Am. Soc. Virology, Wildlife Soc., Sigma Xi. Avocations: flying; cross-country skiing; music. Office: U Wis Inst Environ Studies 40 Science Hall 550 N Park St Madison WI 53706-1404

YULE, JOE, JR. See ROONEY, MICKEY

YULISH, CHARLES BARRY, public affairs executive; b. Cleve., Oct. 14, 1936; s. Isadore and Shirley Yulish; m. Barbara Pearlman, Aug. 22, 1973 (div. 1995); 1 child, Alexi Jules-Nicholas; m. Cynthia Brown Fleek, Oct. 28, 1995. AA in Govt., U. Fla., 1957; BS in Polit. Sci., Kent State U., 1959; MPA, Maxwell Sch., Syracuse U., 1961; postgrad., NYU, 1961-63, New Sch. Social Rsch., 1963-64. Spl. projects officer AEC, Washington and N.Y.C., 1961-63; pub. affairs mgr. Atomic Indsl. Forum, N.Y.C., 1963-66; pres., chief exec. officer Charles Yulish Assocs. Inc., N.Y.C., 1966-83; exec. v.p. Wesley, Brown & Bartle Inc., N.Y.C., 1984-87; vice chmn., ptnr. Holt, Ross & Yulish, Edison, N.J., 1988-92; exec. v.p., mng. dir. E. Bruce Harrison Co., Washington, 1993-95; v.p. corp. comm. U.S. Enrichment Corp., Bethesda, Md., 1995—; bd. dirs. Intermedia News and Feature Svcs. Writer, dir. (film) Energy: We Have the Choices, 1978 (Golden Eagle award); editor: Hard vs. Soft Energy Paths, 1980; author over 60 articles on classical music. Founder, bd. dirs. Serge Koussevitsky Archives Soc., N.Y.C., 1977; bd. dirs. Imperial Russia Hist. Soc., 1986, U.K. and U.S. Friends of Benjamin Franklin. Maxwell fellow Syracuse U., 1960. Mem. Internat. Assn. Pub. Participation Practitioners, Pub. Rels. Soc. Am., Counselors Acad., Soc. Profl. Mgmt. Cons. (cert.). Home: 1438 Q St NW Washington DC 20009-3808

YUN, DANIEL DUWHAN, physician, foundation administrator; b. Chinjoo, Korea, Jan. 20, 1933; came to U.S., 1959, naturalized, 1972; s. Kapryong and Woo Im Yun; m. Rebecca Sungja Choi, Apr. 13, 1959; children: Samuel, Lois, Caroline, Judith. BS, Coll. Sci. and Engring., Yon-Sei U., 1954, MD, 1958; student U. Pa., 1963, PhD Barrington U., 1995. Intern, Quincy (Mass.) City Hosp., 1960; resident and fellow Presbyn.-U. Pa. Med. Ctr., Phila., 1961-65; med. dir. Paddon Meml. Hosp., Nfld., Labrador, Can., 1965-66; dir. spl. care unit Elkins Park (Pa.) Hosp., 1967-79; founder, pres. Philip Jaisohn Meml. Found., Inc., Elkins Park, Pa., 1975-85, also med. dir., trustee; clin. prof. medicine U. Xochicalco, 1978; faculty Med. Coll. Pa.-Hahnemann U. Mem. Bd. Asian Studies Found., U.S. Senatorial Bus. Adv. Bd.; mem. home safety com. Mayor's Commn. on Svcs. to Aging, Phila.; trustee United Way of Southeastern Pa., co-founder Rep. Presdl. Task Force; mem. U.S. Congl. Adv. Bd.; cons. on Korean affairs Phila. City Coun.; hon. mem. adv. coun. Peaceful Unification Policy of Korea; chmn. bd. Korean-Am. Christian Broadcasting of Phila.; mem. Phila. Internat. City Coord. Com.; commr. Pa. Human Rels. Commn., 1991—; founder, pres. Korean Heritage Found., 1991—; amb. City of Phila., 1991. Recipient Phila. award-Human Rights award, 1981, Disting. Community Svc. award Phila. Dist. Atty., 1981, medal of Merit Presdl. Task Force, 1981, Medal of Nat. Order, Republic of Korea, 1984, Nat. Dong Baek medal Republic of Korea, 1987, award City Coun. Phila., 1987, Gov.'s Pa. Heritage awards, 1990, commendation award Pa. Senate, 1991, award Asian Law Ctr., 1991, Republican Senatorial Medal of Freedom, 1994; named to Legion of Honor, The Chapel of Four Chaplains, named Amb. City of Phila., 1991. Mem. AMA, Am. Soc. Internal Medicine, Am. Coll. Cardiology, Am. Heart Assn. (mem. council on clin. cardiology), Pa. Med. Soc., Phila. County Med. Soc., Royal Soc. Health, Am. Coll. Internat. Physicians, World Med. Assn., Fedn. State Med. Bds., Am. Law Enforcement Officers' Assn., Am. Fedn. Police, Internat. Culture Soc. Korea (hon.), Am. Soc. Contemporary Medicine and Surgery. Home: 3903 Somers Dr Huntingdon Valley PA 19006-1913 Office: 60 Township Line Rd Elkins Park PA 19027-2220

YUN, HSING, head religious order; b. Chiangtu, Chiangsu, China, July 22, 1917; came to the U.S., 1980s.; s. Cheng-bao Lee and Yu-ying Liu. Student, Ch'i-hsia Vinaya Sch., 1941, Chiao-shan Buddhist Coll., 1948; PhD (hon.), Oriental U., L.A., 1978. Dir. Hua-ts'ang Temple, Nanjing, China, 1949; Buddhist missionary Lei-yin Temple, Ilan, Taiwan, 1952-66; abbot Fo Kuang Shan, Kaohsiung, Taiwan, 1967-85; master Fo Kuang Shan, Kaohsiung, 1986-91; pres. Hsi Lai U., L.A., 1991—, Buddha's Light Internat. Assn., L.A., 1992—. Avocations: Buddhist lectures and writings.

YUN, JAMES KYOON, electrical engineer; b. Andong, South Korea, Oct. 26, 1965; came to U.S., 1973; s. Joh Kyong and Karen Suk (Kim) Y. BSEE, U. Ill., 1987, MSEE, 1989. System engr. GE Co., Syracuse, N.Y., 1989-91, software engr., 1991-93; software engr. Martin Marietta Corp., Syracuse, 1993-95; sr. mem. engring. staff Lockheed Martin Corp., Moorestown, N.J., 1995—; cons. Silver Knight Co., Liverpool, N.Y., 1994—. Inventor seal indicator. Mem. IEEE, Assn. for Computing Machinery, Tau Beta Pi, Eta Kappa Nu.

YUN, SAMUEL, minister, educator; b. Ulsan, Republic of Korea, June 19, 1958; came to U.S., 1984; s. Eungoh and Chanho (Kim) Y.; m. Kyungim Martha Mah, Jan. 10, 1984; children: Miriam, Joseph, Michelle, John. BTh, Yonsei U., Seoul, Republic of Korea, 1980, MTh, 1984; MA in Religion, U. Dubuque, 1985; ThM, Harvard U., 1987; postgrad., Boston U., 1987-96. Ordained to ministry Korean Presbyn. Ch. in Am., 1987. Preacher Carmel-Peniel Presbyn. Ch., Rewey, Wis., 1984-85; assoc. pastor, dir. edn. Korean Presbyn. Ch. in Boston, Cambridge, Mass., 1985-88; pastor The Peace Ch., Brockton, Mass., 1988-90, Korean Presbyn. Garden Ch., Hackensack, N.J., 1990-93, Princeton (N.J.) Glory Presbyn. Ch., 1993—; prof., dean acad. affairs Presbyn. Theol. Sem. in Am., Corona, N.Y., 1986-95; sec. gen. Coun. Korean Chs. in New Eng., Boston, 1989-90; rec. sec. Coun. Korean Chs. in N.J., 1991-93; adj. prof. New Brunswick Theol. Seminary, 1994—. Author: Living the Word, 1990, Living the Prayer, 1994; translator The Black Gold and Isram, 1985. Mem. Am. Acad. Religion, Soc. Bibl. Lit. Home: 9 Sayre Dr Princeton NJ 08540-5804 Office: 115 Sand Hills Rd Monmouth Junction NJ 08852-3109

YUND, GEORGE EDWARD, lawyer; b. Chgo., Apr. 15, 1952; s. Carl George and Rae Alnola (Stimpert) Y.; m. Cynthia Ann Buehler, June 16, 1973; children: Laura, Jeffrey, Brian. BA, Ohio State U., 1974; JD, U. Mich., 1977. Bar: Ohio 1977, U.S. Dist. Ct. (so. dist.) Ohio 1977, U.S. Ct. Appeals (4th and 6th cirs.) 1978, U.S. Supreme Ct. 1991. Assoc. Frost & Jacobs, Cin., 1977-84, ptnr., 1984—; counsel to Nat. Assn. Profl. Baseball Leagues, Inc., St. Petersburg, Fla., 1988—. Mem. ABA, Ohio Bar Assn., Cin. Bar Assn. Office: Frost & Jacobs 2500 PNC Ctr 201 E 5th St Cincinnati OH 45202-4117

YUNE, HEUN YUNG, radiologist, educator; b. Seoul, Korea, Feb. 1, 1929; came to U.S., 1966; s. Sun Wook and Won Eun (Lee) Y.; m. Kay Kim, Apr. 12, 1956; children: Jeanny Kim, Helen Kay, Marc Eany. MD, Severance Med. Coll., Seoul, 1956. Lic. physician, Republic of Korea, Ind.; diplomate Am. Bd. Radiology, Korean Bd. Radiology. Intern Presbyn. Med. Ctr., Chonju, Korea, 1956-57, resident in surgery, 1957-60; resident in radiology Vanderbilt U. Hosp., Nashville, 1960-63, instr. radiology, 1962-64; chief radiology Presbyn. Med. Ctr., Chonju, Korea, 1964-66; from asst. to assoc. prof. radiology Vanderbilt U. Med. Sch., Nashville, 1966-71; prof. radiology Ind. U. Sch. Medicine, Indpls., 1971—, John A. Campbell prof. radiology, 1991-94, John A. Campbell prof. radiology emeritus, 1994—, dir. residency program, 1985-94, prof. otolaryngology, head and neck surgery, 1992-94, prof. otolaryngology, head and neck surgery emeritus, 1994—; vis. prof. Yonsei U. Coll. Medicine, Seoul, 1985, Ajou U. Coll. of Medicine, Suwon, 1995-96; active staff Ind. U. Hosps., 1971—, Indpls. VA Hosp., 1971—, Wishard Meml. Hosp., 1971—. Editorial reviewer Am. Jour. Roentgenology, 1975—, Radiology, 1985—, Jour. Vascular and Interventional Radiology, 1989—; contbr. articles to profl. jours. Ordained elder Presbyn. Ch. Capt. Rep. of Korea Army, 1951-55. Decorated Bronze Star, U.S. Army, Wharang medal for meritorious mil. svc., Rep. of Korea Army. Fellow Am. Coll. Radiology; mem Assn. Univ. Radiologists, Radiol. Soc. N.Am., Am. Roentgen Ray Soc., Alpha Omega Alpha, others. Avocations: painting, photography, music appreciation, golf, travel. Home: 2887 Brook Vista Carmel IN 46032-4096 Office: Ind U Med Ctr 500 N University Blvd Indianapolis IN 46202-5253

YUNGINGER, JOHN W., allergist. Exec. sec. Am. Bd. Allergy and Immunology, Phila. Office: Am Bd Allergy and Immunology 3624 Market St Philadelphia PA 19104-2675*

YUNICH, ALBERT MANSFELD, physician; b. Ruvno, Russia, June 15, 1909; s. Max A. and Bessie (Feldman) Y.; arrived in U.S., 1911; B.A., Cornell U., 1931, M.D., 1935; Sc.D. (hon.), Albany Med. Coll., 1985; m. Mary Lynn Aronson, June 9, 1935. Intern, Albany Med. Center Hosp., 1935-36, resident, 1936-39; fellow in gastroenterology Mt. Sinai Hosp., N.Y.C., 1939-40; instr. medicine Albany Med. Coll., 1940-42, asst. clin. prof. gastroenterology, 1942-52, assoc. clin. prof., 1952-65, clin. prof. gastroenterology, 1967-76, clin. prof. gastroenterology emeritus, 1977—, sr. physician, gastroenterologist Albany Med. Center Hosp.; cons. gastroenterology St. Peter's Hosp., VA Hosp., Albany. V.p. Albany Symphony Orch., 1960-64; mem. exec. com. Albany County unit Am. Cancer Soc., 1974-78; chmn. Mary and Gene Sarazen Scholarship Fund, Siena Coll., 1978; trustee Nat. Jewish Hosp., Denver, 1965-75. Diplomate Am. Bd. Internal Medicine and Gastroenterology. Fellow Am. Coll. Gastroenterology (life); mem. Albany County Med. Soc., Med. Soc. State N.Y., AMA, Am. Coll. Gastroenterology, Am. Soc. Internal Medicine, Pan-Am. Med. Assn., Alpha Omega Alpha. Jewish. Clubs: Fort Orange, Colonie Country. Contbr. articles to med. jours. Home: Heritage Rd # 222 Guilderland NY 12084-9314 Office: Albany Med Coll Albany NY 12208

YUNIS, JORGE JOSE, anatomy, pathology, and microbiology educator; b. Sincelejo, Colombia, Oct. 5, 1933; s. José and Victoria (Turbay) Y.; m. Malvina Torbay, Jan. 15, 1994; children by previous marriage: George, Olga, Karl, Amira, Omar. MD, Complutense U., Madrid, 1956, PhD, 1957. Gen. practice medicine Barranquilla, Colombia, 1957-59; resident in clin. pathology U. Minn., Mpls., 1959-62, resident in anat. pathology, 1962-64, mem. faculty, 1965-89, prof., 1969-89, dir. grad. studies of lab. medicine, 1969-74, dir. grad. studies of pathology, 1972-74, chmn. human genetics com. for health scis., 1972-77; mem. faculty Hahnemann U., Phila., 1989-92, prof. dept. neoplastic diseases, 1989-92, vice chmn., assoc. dir. Inst. for Cancer and Blood Diseases, 1989-92, dir. Human Genetics and Molecular Biology Div., 1989-92, prof. dept. pathology, 1991-92; prof. depts. anatomy, pathology, microbiology & immunology Thomas Jefferson U. Med. Coll., Phila., 1993—; dir. cancer biol., dept. anatomy, pathology, cell biology Thomas Jefferson U. Med. Coll., Phila., 1993—; vis. prof. numerous univs. Author: Human Chromosome Method, 1965, 75, Biochemical Methods in Red Cell Genetics, 1969, Molecular Pathology, 1975, New Chromosomal Syndromes, 1977, Molecular Structure Human Chromosomes, 1977, Esencia Humana, 1995, Así es la Vida, 1997; contbr. more than 250 articles to profl. jours. Named Clin. Prof. of Yr. Harvard Med. Sch., 1987; honored by Colombian Parliament, Bogota, 1986, 93, Colombian Med. Schs. Assn., 1993. Mem. Leukemia Soc. Am. (trustee 1983-88), Colombian Acad. Medicine. Avocations: poetry, literature, photography. Office: Jefferson Med Coll 1020 Locust St Philadelphia PA 19107-6731

YURCHENCO, HENRIETTA WEISS, ethnomusicologist, writer; b. New Haven, Mar. 22, 1916; d. Edward and Rebecca (Bernblum) Weiss; m. Basil Yurchenco, June 1936 (div. 1955); 1 child, Peter; m. Irving Levine, 1965 (div. 1979). Student, Yale U., 1935-36; student piano scholarship, Mannes Coll. Music, 1936-38. Radio producer WNYC, WBAI, others, 1939-69; writer, critic, tchr., folk music editor Am. Record Guide and Musical Am., 1959-70; prof. music Coll. City N.Y., 1962-86, Bklyn. Coll., 1966-69, New Sch. for Social Research, 1961-68; co-dir. project for study of women in music, Grad. Ctr. CUNY. Author: A Fiesta of Folk Songs From Spain and Latin America, 1967, A Mighty Hard Road: A Biography of Woody Guthrie, 1970, !Hablamos! Puerto Ricans Speak, 1971; contbr. articles to profl. jours.; 11 field recs. from Mexico, P.R., John's Island, S.C., Guatemala, Ecuador, Morocco, issued by Libr. Congress, Folkways, Nonesuch, Folkways/Smithsonian Global Village; collections in Libr. Congress, Discoteca Hebrew U., Jerusalem, Arais Montana Inst., Madrid, Inst. Nacional Indigenista, Mexico City. Recipient grants-in-aid Am. Philos. Soc., 1954, 56, 57, 65, 67, 89, grants-in-aid CUNY Faculty Research Fund, 1970, 83, 87; NEH grantee, 1984. Mem. Internat. Council Traditional Music (com. on women's studies), Soc. Ethnomusicology, Soc. Asian Music, Sonneck Soc., Internat. Assn. Study of Popular Music, Am. Musicologists Soc. Research in folk, tribal and popular music for Library of Congress, Mexico, Guatemala, P.R., Spain, Morocco, Balearic Islands, John's Island, S.C., Ireland, 1941-83. Home: 360 W 22nd St New York NY 10011-2600 Office: 139th St And Convent Ave New York NY 10031

YURCHUCK, ROGER ALEXANDER, lawyer; b. Amityville, N.Y., June 9, 1938; s. Alexander and Ella Marie (Munley) Y.; m. Sally Ward, Apr. 14, 1961 (div. 1972); children: Scott, Lauren; m. Susan Holland, June 1, 1985. AB cum laude, Northwestern U., 1959; LLB, Harvard U., 1962. Bar: Ohio 1962. Assoc. Vorys, Sater Seymour and Pease, Columbus, Ohio, 1962-68, ptnr., 1969-71, 73—; ptnr. Cin. office Vorys, Sater Seymour and Pease, 1984—; v.p., gen. counsel Fed. Home Loan Mortgage Corp., Washington, 1971-73; vice chmn., bd. dirs. Securities Investors Protection Corp., Washington, 1982-88. Del. Rep. Nat. Conv., 1980, 84. Mem. ABA, Fed. Bar. Assn., Ohio Bar Assn., Phi Beta Kappa. Republican. Episcopalian. Clubs: Queen City (Cin.). Office: Vorys Sater Seymour and Pease 221 E 4th St Cincinnati OH 45202-4124

YURCISIN, JOHN, church official; m. Ann Popovich, July 16, 1944; 1 child, Ann Melanie. Grad., N.J. State Coll., 1940, Christ the Saviour Sem., 1944. Ordained, 1944. Asst. pastor St. John's Ch., Hawk Run, Pa.; administr. St. Mary's Ch., Clarence, Pa.; pastor Sts. Peter and Paul Ch., Windber, Pa., 1944-52, Christ the Saviour Parish, Johnstown, Pa., 1952; diocesan chancellor; dean Cathedral Parish, Christ the Saviour Sem., 1951-75; elevated to dignity of Protopresbyter, 1962; prof. Orthodox Christian ethics, Carpatho-Russian history and lang., Ch. Slavonic Christ the Saviour Sem.; vicar gen. Am. Carpatho-Russian Orthodox Diocese, 1990—. Editor The Ch. Messenger, 1949-65, A.C.R.Y. Ann. and Ch. Almanac.; contbr. numerous articles and leaflets in field. Decorated Czech. Orthodox Ch.; Carpatho-Russian Studies chair named in his honor. Mem. Orthodox Soc. of Am. Office: 964 Village Brook Way Columbus OH 43235-5033*

YURIKO (YURIKO KIKUCHI), dancer, choreographer; b. San Jose, Calif.; m. Charles Kikuchi, 1946. Student, UCLA, Martha Graham Sch. Mem. Martha Graham Dance Co., 1944-67; dir., founder Yuriko Dance Co., 1967-74; assoc. artistic dir. Martha Graham Dance Co., 1991—; artistic dir. dance company Time and Talents Club, Bombay, 1974; organizer Modern Dance Sch., Ctr. Internat. de la Danse, Paris, 1975; resident guest tchr., modern dance cons. Ballet Nacional de Cuba, 1976; ind. modern dance choreographer Warsaw Weiklki Classic Ballet Co., 1977, 78, Australian Dance Theater's Concert at Adelaide Festival of the Arts, 1978; guest tchr., choreographer Akar Modern Dance Co., Switzerland, 1981; guest tchr. Nat. U. Costa Rica, Nat. Ballet of Mexico, Martha Graham Sch. Contemporary Dance; guest artist and tchr. various cities including London, Paris, Mexico City, Zurich, Tokyo and Cologne, Germany. Dancer premiere prodns. Appalachian Spring, Cave of the Heart, Dark Meadow, Embattled Garden, Clytemnestra; appeared on Broadway as Eliza in The King and I, 1951; performed feature role The Small House of Uncle Thomas, Sandhog, Flower

Drug Song; dir., re-staged Broadway prodn. of The King and I, 1977, London prodn., 1979, dir. Toyko prodn., 1978; dir. Madame Butterfly. Recipient Bessie award N.Y. Dance and Performance, 1991; grantee N.Y. State Arts Coun., Nat. Endowment for the Arts; Guggenheim fellow for choreography, 1968; commissioned to choreograph and perform Judith Symphony. Office: c/o Catherine Gaffigan #44L 400 W 43rd St Apt 44L New York NY 10036-6318

YURKO, JOSEPH ANDREW, chemical engineer; b. Youngstown, Ohio, Mar. 30, 1955; s. Joseph George and Virginia Mary (Cossentino) Y.; m. Valerie Ann Congdon, Sept. 9, 1992; children: Andrew Dale, Laura Ann. B in BioEngring. Sci., Cleve. State U., 1981, B in Chem. Engring., 1981. Lic. profl. engr. Tex. Structural draftsperson HK Ferguson Co., Cleve., 1974-76, architectural draftsperson, 1976-77, process design engr., 1981-84; chem. engr. Chemical Data Systems, Inc., Oxford, Pa., 1984-85; tech. sales engr. Autoclave Data Systems, Inc., Erie, Pa., 1985-86; sr. process design engr. Morrison Knudsen Corp., Cleve., 1987—, process start up engr., 1988-95; cons. EI Dupont de Nemours and Co., Wilmington, Del., 1985-86, Mobil Oil Rsch. Ctr., Princeton, N.J., 1985-86, SmithKline French Labs., Phila., 1985-86, Anheuser-Busch Cos., St. Louis, Dow Corning, Midland Mich., 1996; spkr. in field. Author: (manuals) Aseptic Filtration Tech. Operating Procedure, 1990, Waste Stream Evaporator Tech. Operating Procedure, 1991, Clean-in-Place Process Tech. Operating Procedure, 1992, Viobin Sci. Proten Labs. Pancreatin, Heparin and Blood Processes, 1995; editor: (manual) Natural Water Carbonation Tech. Ops., 1992. Coach track Cath. Youth Orgn. St. Bridgets Cath. Ch., Parma, Ohio, 1977; campaigner Multiple Sclerosis Soc., Cleve., 1978; counselor Soc. Cripplied Children Cuyahoga County, Strongsville, 1979. Mem. Am. Inst. Chem. Engrs. (sec. Cleve. chpt. 1988-89, vice chair Del. Valley chpt. 1986-87), Food Pharm. and Bioengring. Div., Am. Chem. Soc, Cleve. Engring. Soc., Internat. Soc. Pharm. Engring. Republican. Methodist. Achievements include proposed process conversion of carbon dioxide emissions into oxygen and hydroponically grown products for Anheuser-Busch Inc.; ultraviolet photographic study of particle motion in fluid dynamic study of new Autoclave Engrs. microclave reactor with catalyst basket and internals for heterogeneous catalysis, proposition of ceramically encapsulated metallic beads impregnated with catalyst for novel reactor designed to contain catalyst in magnetic zone. Home: 19099 Hunt Rd Strongsville OH 44136-8415 Office: Morrison Knudsen Corp MK Ferguson Plaza 1500 W 3rd St Cleveland OH 44113-1453

YURKO, RICHARD JOHN, lawyer; b. Ottawa, Ont., Can., Oct. 30, 1953; came to U.S., 1960; s. Michael and Catherine (Ewanishan) Y.; m. Martha S. Faigen, Apr. 18, 1982; children: Nathan, Daniel. AB summa cum laude, Dartmouth Coll., 1975; JD cum laude, Harvard U., 1979. Bar: Mass. 1979, U.S. Dist. Ct. Mass. 1980, U.S. Ct. Appeals (1st cir.) 1980. Law clk. to Judge James L. King, U.S. Dist. Ct. for So. Dist. Fla., Miami, 1979-80; assoc. Bingham, Dana & Gould, Boston, 1980-85; assoc. Widett, Slater & Goldman, P.C., Boston, 1985-87, shareholder, 1987-92, chmn. litigation dept., 1989-91, hiring ptnr., 1992; shareholder Hutchins, Wheeler & Dittmar, Boston, 1992-94, chmn. litigation dept., 1992-94; shareholder Yurko & Perry, P.C., Boston, 1995—. Contbr. articles to legal jours. Mem. ABA, Mass. Bar Assn., Boston Bar Assn. (chmn. antitrust com.), Phi Beta Kappa. Home: 56 Old Colony Rd Wellesley MA 02181-2844 Office: Yurko & Perry P C 100 City Hall Plz Boston MA 02108-2105

YUROW, JOHN JESSE, lawyer; b. Washington, Jan. 30, 1931; s. Louis and Lauretta (Jedeikin) Y.; m. Bette Hilary Troshinsky, Aug. 1, 1953; children—Michael Jay, Gary Alan, Diane Ruth Yurow Beckwith, Lois Anne. A.B., George Washington U., 1953, J.D., 1958. Bar: D.C. 1958, Mich. 1961. Trial atty. Office Regional Counsel, IRS, Detroit, 1958-62; assoc. Arent, Fox, Kintner, Plotkin & Kahn, Washington, 1962-68, ptnr., 1969—; professorial lectr. in law George Washington U., Washington, 1974-76. Past mem. editorial bd. George Washington U. Law Rev.; contbr. articles on tax subjects to profl. publs. Served with U.S. Army, 1953-55. Mem. D.C. Bar Assn. (chmn. taxation div. 1977-78), ABA, Fed. Bar Assn. (chmn. taxation com. 1972-73), Order of Coif, Phi Delta Phi. Democrat. Club: Indian Spring Country (Silver Spring, Md.). Lodge: B'nai B'rith. Avocations: tennis; travel. Home: 931 Clintwood Dr Silver Spring MD 20902-1724 Office: Arent Fox Kintner Plotkin & Kahn 1050 Connecticut Ave NW Washington DC 20036

YURSO, JOSEPH FRANCIS, engineering manager; b. Hazleton, Pa., July 5, 1930; s. Joseph James and Anna (Payne) Y.; m. Helen Elizabeth Michel, Dec. 17, 1955 (dec. Aug. 1988); children: Joseph Michael, Joanne Elizabeth; m. Barbara Lee Bergen, Apr. 17, 1993. BSME, Pa. State U., 1952; MSME, U.S. Naval Postgrad. U., 1960; hon. degree, Carnegie Mellon U., 1973. Registered profl. engr., Va., Conn. Commd. ens. USN, 1955, advanced through grades to capt., 1975; planning and quality assurance officer, supr. shipbldg. USN, Groton, Conn., 1967-71; ship maintenance officer to comdr. in chief Atlantic Fleet USN, Norfolk, Va., 1971-75; dep. CEO to supr. of shipbldg. conversion and repair USN, Newport News, Va., 1975-77; prodn. officer Norfolk Naval Shipyard USN, Portsmouth, Va., 1977-79; supr. of shipbldg., CEO USN, Groton, Conn., 1979-81; shipyard comdr., CEO Portsmouth Naval Shipyard USN, 1981-84, ret., 1984; group mgr., chief engr. Q.E.D. Sys., Inc., Virginia Beach, Va., 1986-96, dir. tech. devel., 1996—; sr. investigator Naval Sea Sys. Command, Washington, 1974-75, 78-79, 83-84. Contbg. author: Naval Engineering and American Sea Power, 1989; contbr. to profl. publs. Pres. Atlantic Fleet Credit Union, Norfolk, 1974-79, Emmanuel Luth. Ch., Virginia Beach, 1985-87. Recipient Legion of Merit. Mem. ASME, Am. Soc. Naval Engring. (chmn. tidewater sect. 1990-91, mem. nat. coun. 1990-92, Presdl. award 1991, 92, Frank G. Law award 1994, nat. v.p. 1993—, nat. pres. 1997—), Am. Soc. Quality Control (vice chmn. 1991-92, chmn. 1992-95, Presdl. award 1992), Soc. Naval Archs. and Marine Engrs. (chmn. programs 1991-92). Achievements include providing leadership in improving industrial performance of Portsmouth Naval Shipyard, to improve utilization of fleet/U.S. Navy maintenance facilities, introduction of new concepts of quality assurance to U.S. Navy shipbuilding and repair. Home: 4629 Player Ln Virginia Beach VA 23462-4639

YURT, ROGER WILLIAM, medical educator, physician; b. Louisville, June 8, 1945; s. Albert William and Mary Louise (McGrath) Y.; m. Joan A. Terry, Sept. 3, 1971; children: Jennifer, Daniel, Gregory. BS in Biology, Loyola U., New Orleans, 1967; MD, U. Miami, 1972. Diplomate Nat. Bd. Med. Examiners. Intern Parkland Meml. Hosp.-Southwestern Med. Sch., U. Tex.-Dallas, 1972-73, resident in surgery, 1973-74; postdoctoral fellow in medicine Robert B. Brigham Hosp.-Harvard U. Med. Sch., Boston, 1974-77; postdoctoral trainee NIH, 1975-77; resident in surgery, then chief resident in surgery N.Y. Hosp.-Cornell Med. Ctr., N.Y.C., 1977-79, acting dir. Burn Ctr., dir. rsch., 1982-83, dir. Trauma Ctr., 1992—, prof. surgery, 1982-92, prof. surgery, 1992—, The Johnson & Johnson Disting. prof. surgery, 1995—, vice chmn. dept. surgery Cornell U. Med. Coll., 1987—, acting chmn., 1991-93, dir. Burn Ctr., 1995—; acting surgeon-in-chief, The N.Y. Hosp., 1991-93; clin. asst. prof. surgery Uniformed Services U. of Health Sci., Bethesda, Md., 1980-82; clin. asst. prof. gen. surgery Health Sci. Ctr., U. Tex.-San Antonio, 1981-82; chmn. burn com., mem. bd. dirs. Regional Emergency Med. Services of N.Y., 1982-84, mem. trauma ctr. adv. com., 1984—, chmn., 1995—, N.Y. Bklyn. ACS Com. Trauma, 1994—; dir. Mulhearn Research Lab., N.Y.C., 1982—. Editor: Infections in Surgery, 1981-88; contbr. articles to med. jours. Served to maj. M.C., U.S. Army, 1979-82. Grantee United Health Found., 1968-69, NIH, 1984-87; fellow Sch. Medicine, U. Miami, summer 1969-71, USPHS, 1973-75; Irma Hirschl Trust Career Scientist award, 1984-88. Mem. Am. Surg. Assn. Surg. Infection Soc. (charter, chmn. membership com., sec. 1987-90, pres. 1991-92), Assn. Acad. Surgery, Soc. Univ. Surgeons, Internat. Surg. Soc., Am. Assn. for Surgery of Trauma, Ea. Assn. for Surgery of Trauma, Alpha Omega Alpha, Omicron Delta Kappa. Roman Catholic. Office: Cornell U Medical Coll 1300 York Ave New York NY 10021-4805

YUSPEH, ALAN RALPH, lawyer; b. New Orleans, June 13, 1949; s. Michel and Rose Fay (Rabenovitz) Y.; m. Janet Horn, June 8, 1975. B.A., Yale U., 1971; M.B.A., Harvard U., 1973; J.D., Georgetown U., 1978. Bar: D.C. 1978. Mgmt. cons. McKinsey & Co., Washington, 1973-74; adminstrv. asst., legis. asst. Office of U.S. Senator J. Bennett Johnston, Washington, 1974-78; atty. Shaw, Pittman, Potts & Trowbridge, Washington, 1978-79, Ginsburg, Feldman, Weil and Bress, Washington, 1979-82; gen. counsel Com. on Armed Services-U.S. Senate, Washington, 1982-85; ptnr. Preston, Thorgrimson, Ellis & Holman, Washington, 1985-88, Miller & Chevalier, Washington, 1988-91, Howrey & Simon, Washington, 1991—. Editor Law and Policy in Internat. Business jour., 1978-79, Nat. Contract Mgmt. Jour., 1988-92; assoc. editor Pub. Contract Law jour., 1987-91. Chmn. bd. of ethics, City of Balt., 1988-96, mem. planning commn., 1996—. 1st lt. USAR, 1971-77. Home: 1812 South Rd Baltimore MD 21209-4506 Office: Howrey & Simon 1299 Pennsylvania Ave NW Washington DC 20004-2400

YUSSOUFF, MOHAMMED, physicist, educator; b. Cuttack, India, Aug. 14, 1942; came to U.S., 1991; s. Haji and Nurunnisa Fakhruddin; m. Farhana Begum, Apr. 6, 1969; children: Ashraf, Zeenat, Mustafa. MSc, Delhi U., 1963; PhD, Indian Inst. Tech., Kanpur, 1967. Prof. physics Indian Inst. Tech., Kanpur, 1967-90; vis. prof. physics Mich. State U., East Lansing, 1991—; vis. scientist U. Köln, Germany, 1972-74, U. Western Ont., London, Can., 1990-91; Humboldt scientist Atomic Energy Agy, Jülich, Germany, 1979-81; vis. prof. U. Konstanz, Germany, 1986-89; guest scientist Ford Rsch., Dearborn, Mich., 1991—; mem. com. physics examination Pub. Svc. Commn., Delhi, India, 1976-86, rsch. grants Univ. Grants Commn., Delhi, 1985-90; bd. dirs. Aligarh (India) Muslim U., 1989-90; dir. Internat. Sch. on Band Structure, Indian Inst. Tech., 1986. Editor: Electronic Band Structure and Its Applications, 1987, The Physics of Materials, 1987; developer of Slow Pace program for teaching sci. and engring. to deficient students with poor social, econ. or sch. backgrounds; patentee for monitoring the catalytic converters in cars, U.S., 1996. Mem. Am. Phys. Soc., Internat. Ctr. Theoretical Physics (assoc.). Islam. Achievements include pioneering work on theory of freezing, theory of disordered systems, chanelling, clusters, electronic structure, ionic conductors, exhaust gas sensors, superconductors, zeolites, and foundations of quantum theory. Home: 31011 Grandview St Westland MI 48186-5065 Office: Mich State Univ Dept Physics East Lansing MI 48824-1116 also: Ford Motor Co Scientific Rsch Lab Dearborn MI 48121-2053

YUSTER-FREEMAN, LEIGH CAROL, publishing company executive; b. Trenton, N.J., July 23, 1949; d. Leon Carl and Helen Loretta (Wisniewski) Markiewicz; m. Charles Yuster (div. Apr. 1985); stepchildren: Sarah, Elizabeth, Jared, Alexandra; m. Richard N. Freeman; 1 child, Jessica Lee Freeman. Profl. dancer, 1967-71; editor R.R. Bowker, N.Y.C., 1971-72, ISBN agy. editorial coord., 1972-78, editorial coord., 1978-79, mgr., AV svcs., 1979-81, mgr., data sources, 1981-83, sr. product mgr., 1983-85, exec. editor, mng. editor, 1985-87, dir. product enhancements, 1987-88, dir. product devel., pub. Ulrich's Database, 1989-90; assoc. pub. Bowker Bus. Rsch., A&I Pub. R.R. Bowker, New Providence, N.J., 1990-91, also pub. Ulrich's Database, 1990-91, pub. Broadcasting & Cable Yearbook, 1991-97, v.p. database pub., 1996—; mng. dir. Reed Reference Pub., New Providence, 1992-94, v.p. bibliographies, 1994-96, v.p. directories, 1996; v.p. Database Publishing R.R. Bowker, New Providence, 1996—; ptnr. Eagle Bakery, Trenton, N.J., 1991-92. Recipient Climate of Excellence award, Cahners Pub. Co., Newton, Mass., 1987, Cert. of Appreciation, Consortium of Univ. Film Ctrs., Kent, Ohio, 1986. Mem. ALA, NAFE, Consortium of Coll. and Univ. Media Ctrs., Actors Equity Assn. Democrat. Jewish. Avocations: gardening, dancing, music, kinesiology, community services. Home: 19 Theodora Dr Hillsborough NJ 08876

YUZEITIS, JAMES RICHARD, information specialist; b. Chgo., Nov. 11, 1942; s. Stanley J. and Amy B. (English) Y.; m. Susan C. London, Oct. 7, 1967; children: Timothy, David, Amy. BA in Econs., Loyola U., Chgo., 1965, MS in Personnel Mgmt., 1968. Personnel adminstr. Chgo. Police Dept., 1965-67; personnel asst. McDonald's Corp., Chgo., 1967-69; ops. trainee McDonald's Corp., Washington, 1969-70; personnel mgr. McDonald's Corp., Detroit, 1970-72; licensing mgr. McDonald's Corp., Columbus, Ohio, 1972-73; internat. personnel cons. McDonald's Corp., Oakbrook, Ill., 1973-80, dir. of human resources, 1980-86, dir. human resources devel., 1986-91; pres. Quality Surveys, Inc., Big Timber, Mont., 1991—; cons. Ronald McDonald Children's Charities, Chgo., 1986-88. Cons. and vol. Ronald McDonald Houses, Chgo., 1987; vol. Crazy Mont. Mus. Soc., Big Timber, 1991-92; bd. dirs. Pioneer Med. Ctr., Big Timber, 1993—. Recipient medal of Merit Cath. Youth Orgn., Chgo., 1960. Mem. Soc. for Human Resource Mgmt., Human Resource Planning Soc., Indsl. Rels. Rsch. Soc. Avocations: ranch mgmt., fishing, music. Home: PO Box 1244 Big Timber MT 59011-1244 Office: Quality Surveys Inc PO Box 1089 Big Timber MT 59011-1089

YZAGUIRRE, RAUL HUMBERTO, civil rights leader; b. San Juan, Tex., July 22, 1939; s. Ruben Antonio and Eva Linda (Morin) Y.; m. Audrey H. Bristow, Jan. 2, 1965; children: Regina Dolores, Raul Humberto, Elisa Almalinda, Roberto Hayse, Rebecca Morin, Benjamin Ruben. Student, U. Md., 1963-64; B.S., George Washington U., 1968. Registered med. technologist. Student and community activist, 1963-65; active War on Poverty, 1969-74; founder, exec. dir. Interstate Research Assocs (Hispanic cons. firm), Washington, 1969-73; v.p. Center for Community Change, Washington, 1974; community organizer in S.Tex., 1974; pres. Nat. Council of La Raza, Washington, 1974—; lectr. Harvard U., U. Notre Dame, U. Tex., others.; commr. U.S. Nat. Commn. for UNESCO, 1983—; chmn. bd. dirs. Associated SW Investors, 1976—. Co-chmn. Nat. Urban Coalition, 1975-83; co-chmn. Working Com. on Concerns of Hispanics and Blacks, 1979—, sec. ind. sector, 1983-84; sec., chmn. Forum of Nat. Hispanic Orgns., 1976-79; chmn. adv. com. I.N.S.; former trustee Common Cause; co-founder, chmn. Nat. Neighborhood Coalition, 1977—; immediate past chair Ind. Sector; bd. dirs. Enterprise Found., Nat. Dem. Insts. Served with USAF, 1959-62. Recipient Rockefeller Public Service award, 1979, Common Cause Pub. Service award, 1986; fellow Inst. Politics John F. Kennedy Sch. Govt. Mem. Am. GI Forum, Hispanic Assn. Corp. Responsibility (co-founder, chmn. bd. dirs.). Democrat. Roman Catholic. Office: Nat Coun La Raza 1111 19th St NW Ste 1000 Washington DC 20036-3622 *The civil rights struggle of the 80's will be the transformation of America to a truly pluralistic society where cultural differences will not only be tolerated, but indeed valued.*

YZERMAN, STEVE, professional hockey player; b. Cranbrook, B.C., Can., May 9, 1965. With Detroit Red Wings, 1983—. Recipient Lester B. Pearson award, 1988-89; named Sporting News NHL Rookie of Yr., NHL All-Rookie Team, 1983-84, 1988-93. Youngest person ever to play in NHL All-Star game, 1984; mem. Stanley Cup Champions, 1997. Office: Detroit Red Wings 600 Civic Center Dr Detroit MI 48226-4408*

ZABANAL, EDUARDO OLEGARIO, lawyer; b. Legazpi City, Albay, The Philippines, Aug. 8, 1952; came to U.S., 1986; s. Jose Agas and Maria Soledad (Olegario) Z.; m. Leorosie Rebodos Nabor, June 18, 1983; children: Shalimar Rosary, Angelica Almira, Regina Tatiana, Lorelei Blossom, Eduardo Olegario. BA, Aquinas U., The Philippines, 1972; BL, U. The Philippines, 1978. Bar: Hawaii 1990, The Philippines 1979, U.S. Dist. Ct. Hawaii 1990. Assoc. Pacis & Reyes, Manila, 1979-86; pvt. practice Honolulu, 1990—. Contbr. articles to profl. jours. Bd. dirs. Kahaluu Neighborhood Bd., Honolulu, 1991-93; active Filipino Coalition for Solidarity, Honolulu, 1991—. Recipient recognition among Disting. Filipinos in Oahu, FIL-AM Courier, 1995. Mem. ABA, Assn. Trial Lawyers Am., Hawaii State Bar Assn., Hawaii Filipino Lawyers Assn., Integrated Bar The Philippines, Philippine Bar Assn., Filipino C. of C. Hawaii. Roman Catholic. Avocations: jogging, travel, reading. Home: 1031 Nuuanu Ave Apt 404 Honolulu HI 96817-5602

ZABEL, EDWARD, economist, educator; b. Orange, N.J., Oct. 17, 1927; s. Otto and Helen (Katzenberger) Z.; m. Norma Nicholson, June 23, 1956; children: Jeffrey, David, Richard. B.A., Syracuse (N.Y.) U., 1950; M.A., Princeton U., 1953, Ph.D., 1956. Research asst. Princeton U., 1954-56; economist Rand Corp., Santa Monica, Calif., 1956-58; mem. faculty U. Rochester, N.Y., 1958-81; prof. econs. U. Rochester, 1967-81; prof. econs. U. Fla., Gainesville, 1981-83, Matherly prof. econs. and decision scis., 1983—; assoc. editor Mgmt. Sci., 1969-73; bd. editors Applied Econs., 1973—, Applied Econs. Letters, 1993—. Contbr. articles to profl. jours. Served with AUS, 1945-47. Ford Found. fellow, 1964-65; NSF rsch. grantee, 1960-81. Mem. Am. Econ. Assn., Econometric Soc., Internat. Soc. Inventory Rsch., Western Econ. Assn., Inst. mgmt. Scis., AAUP, Phi Beta Kappa. Democrat. Home: 1926 NW 27th St Gainesville FL 32605-3863 Office: U Fla Dept Econs Gainesville FL 32611

ZABEL, SHELDON ALTER, lawyer, law educator; b. Omaha, Apr. 25, 1941; s. Louis Julius and Anne (Rothenberg) Z.; m. Roberta Jean Butz, May 10, 1975; children: Andrew Louis, Douglas Patrick, Robert Stewart Warren. AB cum laude, Princeton U., 1963; JD cum laude, Northwestern U., 1966. Bar: Ill. 1966, U.S. Supreme Ct. 1976. Law clk. to presiding justice, Ill. Sup. Ct., 1966-67; assoc. Schiff, Hardin & Waite, Chgo., 1967-73, ptnr., 1973—; instr. environ. law Loyola U., Chgo. Mem. bd. dirs. Chgo. Zool. Soc. Mem. ABA, Chgo. Bar Assn., Chgo. Coun. Lawyers, Order of Coif. Jewish. Clubs: Union League, Metropolitan (Chgo.). Avocations: skiing, squash. Office: Schiff Hardin & Waite 7200 Sears Tower 233 S Wacker Dr Chicago IL 60606-6306

ZABEL, VIVIAN ELLOUISE, secondary education educator; b. Randolph AFB, Tex., July 28, 1943; d. Raymond Louis and Dolly Veneta (Lyles) Gilbert; m. Robert Lee Zabel, Feb. 18, 1962; children: René Lynne, Robert Lee Jr., Randel Louis, Regina Louise. BA in English and Speech, Panhandle State U., 1977; postgrad., U. Ctrl. Okla., 1987-92. Cert. tchr., Okla. Tchr. English, drama, speech, debate Buffalo (Okla.) H.S., 1977-79; tchr. English, drama, speech Schulter (Okla.) H.S., 1979-80; tchr. English Morris (Okla.) H.S., 1980-81; tchr. speech, drama, debate Okla. Christian Schs., Edmond, 1981-82; tchr. English, drama, debate, speech/debate coach Braman (Okla.) H.S., 1982-83; debate coach Pawhuska (Okla.) H.S., 1983-84; tchr. English, French, drama, speech and debate coach Luther (Okla.) H.S., 1984-95; tchr. debate, forensics, yearbook, newspaper, English, competitive speech Deer Creek H.S., Edmond, Okla., 1995—; dir. drama Nazarene Youth Impact Team, Collinsville, Okla., 1979-81; tchr. h.s. Sun. sch. class Edmond Ch. of Nazarene, 1991-94; mem. cmty.-sch. rels. com. Luther Pub. Schs., 1991-92, supt.'s adv. com., 1992-94. Editor Potpourri mag., 1975-77; author poetry, short stories. Adult supr. Texas County 4-H, Adams, Okla., 1975-77; double diamond coach NFL; adjudicator and tournament dir. qualifying OSSAA Tournaments. Recipient Disting. Svc. award NFL, 1994, Editor's Choice award for poetry, 1997, Tchr. of Excellence, 1996. Mem. Nat. Debate Coaches Assn., Nat. Fedn. Interscholastic Speech and Debate Assn., Okla. Speech Theatre Communications Assn., Okla. Tchrs. English. Republican. Nazarene. Home: 2912 Rankin Ter Edmond OK 73013-5344 Office: Deer Creek HS 6101 NW 206th St Edmond OK 73003-9365 *Children are our future, yet we are living in an age of throw-away children. We must find a way to save these children, to give them purpose, training, and love so that they have a promising future, and so will we.*

ZABRISKIE, JOHN L., healthcare and agricultural products manufacturing company executive; b. 1940. -. With Merck & Co., Inc., Whitehouse Station, N.J., 1965-93, past exec. v.p., past pres. mfg. divsn.; chmn., CEO Upjohn Co., Kalamazoo, 1993-95, also bd. dirs.; pres., CEO Pharmacia & Upjohn, Inc., Windsor, U.K., 1995—. Office: Pharmacia & Upjohn, Inc, 67 Alma Rd, Windsor Berkshire SL4 3HD, England

ZABSKY, JOHN MITCHELL, engineering executive; b. Joplin, Mo., Apr. 18, 1933; s. Joseph Anthony and Joan (Lucas) Z. AS, Joplin Jr. Coll., 1953; BSME, U. Mo., 1956; MSME, U. Kans., 1965. Profl. engr., Mo. System engr. Bendix KCD, Kansas City, Mo., 1958-62; rsch. engr. Rocketdyne, Neosho, Mo., 1962-65, Boeing Co., Huntsville, Ala., 1965-66; prin. rsch. engr., scientist Honeywell Inc., St. Paul, 1966-71; chief engr. Pressure Tank & Pipe Fabrication Co., Nashville, 1971-72, Engring. for Industry, Danville, Va., 1972-73; area mgr. fluid machinery Dresser Adv. Tech. Ctr., Irvine, Calif., 1973-85; v.p. ops. ATI, Laguna Niguel, Calif., 1985-93; pres. Cytoprobe, San Diego, 1993-94, v.p. ops., 1994-95; cons. Oral Care Products, L.A., 1990-92, Kleenair Sys., Inc., Irvine, Calif., 1995—. Patentee in field. Pres. Mpls.-St. Paul Singletons, 1969-72. Mem. AIAA, ASME, Mo. Soc. Profl. Engrs., Soc. Mfg. Engrs. Home: 3640C S Main St Santa Ana CA 92707-5720

ZACEK, JOSEPH FREDERICK, history educator, international studies consultant, East European culture and affairs specialist; b. Stickney, Ill., Dec. 18, 1930; s. Joseph and Emilie (Dvorak) Z.; m. Judith Ellen Cohen (div. 1975); 1 child, Natalie Ann; m. Jane Perlberg Shapiro; stepchildren: Leslie Helen, Peter Carl. BA summa cum laude, U. Ill., Champaign-Urbana, 1952, MA in History, 1953, PhD in History, 1962; cert., Columbia U. Inst. on East Cen. Europe, 1962. Asst. prof. history Occidental Coll., L.A., 1962-65; asst. prof., dir. Russian & East European Programs UCLA, 1965-68; assoc. prof. SUNY at Albany, 1968-71, dir. Russian & East European Programs, 1968-77, 91-92, prof., 1971—, chair dept. history, 1974-77; mem. selection com. for East Europe Internat. Rsch. and Exch. Bd., Princeton, N.J., 1978-81; nat. bd. cons. NEH, Washington, 1975—; vis. scholar IREX Comenius U., Bratislava, and Charles U., Prague, Czechoslovakia, 1973, Columbia U., 1977-78, U. Ill, Champaign-Urbana, 1987. Author: Palacky: The Historian as Scholar and Nationalist, 1970; editor, co-author: Frantisek Palacky, 1798-1876: A Centennial Appreciation, 1981, The Enlightenment and the National Revivals in Eastern Europe, 1983, The Intimate Palacky, 1984; also numerous periodical articles and chpts. in multi-authored books. With M.I., U.S. Army, 1954-57. Fgn. Area Tng. fellow Ford Found., Columbia U., 1960-62, Sr. Humanities fellow Rockefeller Found., 1977-78, fellow Russian Rsch. Ctr. Harvard U., 1986-91; rsch. grantee Am. Coun. Learned Soc./Soc. Sci. Rsch. Coun., 1965, Am. Philos. Soc., 1968; recipient Comenius medal Govt. of Czech and Slovak Fed. Republic, 1992, Medal of Comenius Pedagogical Inst. in Prague, 1992, Josef Hlávka medal of Czechoslovak Acad. of Scis. in Prague, 1992; also other grad. and postdoctoral awards and grants. Mem. Am. Hist. Assn., Am. Assn. for Advancement Slavic Studies, Czechoslovak History Conf., Slovak Studies Assn., Consortium on Revolutionary Europe, Assn. for Study of Ethnicity and Nationalism, Phi Beta Kappa. Avocations: travel, gardening, music. Office: SUNY Dept History Albany NY 12222

ZACHARIAS, DAVID ALEXANDER, career military officer; b. Lansing, Mich., Jan. 26, 1952; s. Heinz Zacharias and Geraldine Rose (Hoover) Nicholas; m. Dana Lynn Hawkins, Sept. 19, 1992; children: Devon Alexandra, Darin Laryssa. BSEE, U.S. Naval Acad., Annapolis, Md., 1974. Commd. U.S. Navy, 1974, advanced through grades to capt.; damage control asst. USS Bergall U.S. Navy, Norfolk, Va., 1975-79; ops. officer, navigator, weapons officer USS Pintado U.S. Navy, San Diego, 1979-83; command and control officer Comsubpac U.S. Navy, Pearl Harbor, Hawaii, 1984-86, exec. officer USS Bremerton, 1986-89; prof. joint edn. Armed Forces Staff Coll. U.S. Navy, Norfolk, 1989-92; commanding officer USS Indpls. U.S. Navy, Pearl Harbor, 1992-94; ops. officer Comcrudesgru One U.S. Navy, San Diego, 1994—. Home: 141 F Ave Coronado CA 92118-1211 Office: Comcrudesgru One Uss Constellation # 64 FPO AP 96635-2780

ZACHARIAS, DONALD WAYNE, academic administrator; b. Salem, Ind., Sept. 28, 1935; s. William Otto and Estelle Mae (Newlon) Z.; m. Tommie Kline Dekle, Aug. 16, 1959; children: Alan, Eric, Leslie. BA, Georgetown (Ky.) Coll., 1957, LLD (hon.), 1983; MA, Ind. U., 1959, PhD, 1963. Asst. prof. communication and theatre Ind. U., 1963-69; assoc. prof. U. Tex., Austin, 1969-72; prof. U. Tex., 1972-79, asst. to pres., 1974-77; exec. asst. to chancellor U. Tex. System, 1978-79; pres. Western Ky. U., 1979-85, Miss. State U., 1985—; bd. dirs. First Fed. Savs. & Loan Assn., Bowling Green, Ky., Inst. for Tech. Devel., Sanderson Farms, Inc., Miss. econ. Coun. Author: In Pursuit of Peace: Speeches of the Sixties, 1970. Bd. dirs. Greenview Hosp.; pres. Southeastern Conf., 1989-91. With U.S. Army, 1959-60. Named Mississippian of Yr. Data Processing Mgmt. Assn.; recipient Teaching award Ind. U. Found., 1963, Cactus Teaching award U. Tex., 1971, Justin Smith Morrill award U.S. Dept. Agriculture, 1992. Mem. Inst. Tech. Devel. (bd. dirs. 1985-92), Nat. Assn. State Univs. and Land-Grant Colls. (exec. com. 1990-92), Phi Kappa Phi (pres. 1978). Democrat. Episcopalian. Office: Miss State U Office of Pres PO Box J Mississippi State MS 39762

ZACHARIASEN, FREDRIK, physics educator, consultant; b. Chgo., June 14, 1931; s. William Houlder and Ragni (Durban-Hansen) Z.; m. Nancy Walker, Jan. 27, 1957; children—Kerry, Judith. B.S., U. Chgo., 1951; Ph.D., Calif. Inst. Tech., 1956. Instr. MIT, Cambridge, 1955-56; research physicist U. Calif.-Berkeley, 1956-57; asst. prof. physics Stanford U., Calif., 1957-60; prof. Calif. Inst. Tech., Pasadena, 1960—; assoc. dir. Los Alamos Nat. Lab., 1982-83. Author: Structure of Nucleons, 1960; Hadron Physics, 1973; Sound Fluctuation, 1979. Sloan fellow, 1960-64; Guggenheim fellow, 1970. Home: 2235 Villa Heights Rd Pasadena CA 91107-1142 Office: Calif Inst Tech 1201 E California Blvd Pasadena CA 91125-0001

ZACHEM, HARRY M., oil company executive; b. Ironton, Ohio, Aug. 14, 1944; s. Charles Russell and Millie (Norris) Z.; children: Nancy Kathryn, Mary Elizabeth. BA, U. Ky., 1968; A.M.P., Harvard U., 1985. Supr. Ky. State Govt., Frankfort, 1968-71; sales rep. Ashland Oil Inc., Balt., 1972-74; pub. relations rep. Ashland Oil Inc., Ashland, Ky., 1974-75; Washington rep. Ashland Oil Inc., 1975-81, v.p. fed. govt. relations, 1981-86; adminstrv. v.p. Ashland Oil Inc., Ashland, 1986-88; sr. v.p. external affairs Ashland, Inc., 1988—. bd. dirs. Danny Thompson Leukemia Found., Sun Valley, Idahom, 1996—; mem. global adv. coun. Thunderbirds-Am. Grad. Sch. Internat. Mgmt., Phoenix, 1996—. Mem. Nat. Assn. Mfrs. (bd. dirs. 1992—). Episcopalian. Avocations: golf, sailing. Office: Ashland Inc PO Box 391 Ashland KY 41105-0391

ZACHER, VALERIE IRENE, interior designer; b. Woodland, Calif., Dec. 12, 1942; d. Albert Richard and Laura Ruth (Mast) Z.; m. William Robert Wallace, June 14, 1964 (div. Oct. 1968); 1 child, Jason Zachery Wallace. BA in Polit. Sci., Stanford U., 1964; AS in Interior Design, West Valley Coll., 1982; cert. TESL, U. Calif. Santa Cruz, Santa Clara, 1994. Owner, operator Artefactorage, Fresno, Calif., 1968-77; owner, designer Viz a Viz, Los Gatos, Calif., 1978-82; facilities project mgr. Nat. Semiconductor, Santa Clara, Calif., 1982-85; project supr. Mervyns, Hayward, Calif., 1985-86; interior designer, project mgr. Charles Schwab & Co., San Francisco, 1986-87; small bus. advisor US Peace Corps, Gaborone, Botswana, 1987-89, Swedish Coop. Ctr., Gaborone, 1989-90; English tchr. YCC Am. Club, Yokohama, Japan, 1992-93; interior design cons. Los Gatos, 1993—; design/facilities cons. Octel Comm. Corp., Milpitas, Calif., 1994—; interior designer Am. Cancer Soc. Designers Showcase, 1994, 95, 96. Mem. Internat. Facilities Mgrs. Assn. Avocations: gourmet cooking, gardening, travel. Home and Office: 16721 Madrone Ave Los Gatos CA 95030-4120

ZACHERT, MARTHA JANE, retired librarian; b. York, Pa., Feb. 7, 1920; d. Paul Rodes and Elizabeth Agnes (Lau) Koontz; m. Edward G. Zachert, Aug. 25, 1946; 1 child, Lillian Elizabeth. AB, Lebanon Valley Coll., 1941; MLS, Emory U., 1953; DLS, Columbia U., 1968. Asst. Enoch Pratt Free Library, Balt., 1941-46; head librarian Wood Research Inst., Atlanta, 1947; sch. librarian DeKalb (Ga.) County Schs., 1950-52; head librarian, prof. history of pharmacy So. Coll. Pharmacy, Mercer U., Atlanta, 1952-63; instr. Ga. State Coll., 1962-63, Emory U., summers 1955-59, 1956-57, 59-60; mem. faculty Library Sch., Fla. State U., 1963-78, prof., 1973-78; prof. Coll. Librarianship U. S.C., Columbia, 1973-74, 78-84; vis. fellow Brit. Library, 1980; cons. So. Regional Med. Library, Emory U., 1976-77, Nat. Library Medicine, 1977, others. Assoc. editor: Jour. Library History, 1966-71, 73-76; mng. editor, 1971-73; cons. editor: Jour. Library Adminstrn., 1979-86; contbr. numerous articles to profl. jours. Fellow Med. Libr. Assn.; mem. ALA, Spl. Librs. Assn. (past pres. Fla. chpt., spl. citation 1977, Hall of Fame 1985), Southwestern Libr. Assn. (Hall of Fame 1985), Am. Printing History Assn., Beta Phi Mu (pres. 1974-75). Home and Office: 2018 W Randolph Cir Tallahassee FL 32312-3349

ZACHERT, VIRGINIA, psychologist, educator; b. Jacksonville, Ala., Mar. 1, 1920; d. R.E. and Cora H. (Massee) Z. Student, Norman Jr. Coll., 1937; AB, Ga. State Woman's Coll., 1940; MA, Emory U., 1947; PhD, Purdue U., 1949. Diplomate: Am. Bd. Profl. Psychologists. Statistician Davison-Paxon Co., Atlanta, 1941-44; research psychologist Mil. Contracts, Auburn Research Found., Ala. Poly. Inst.; indsl. and research psychologist Sturm & O'Brien (cons. engrs.), 1958-59; research project dir. Western Design, Biloxi, Miss., 1960-61; self-employed cons. psychologist Norman Park, Ga., 1961-71, Good Hope, Ga., 1971—; rsch. assoc. med. edn. Med. Coll. Ga., Augusta, 1963-65, assoc. prof., 1965-70, rsch. prof., 1970-84, rsch. prof. emeritus, 1984—, chief learning materials divsn., 1973-84, faculty senate, 1976-84, acad. coun., 1976-82, pres. acad. coun., 1983, sec., 1978; mem. Ga. Bd. Examiners Psychologists, 1974-79, v.p., 1977, pres. 1978; adv. bd. Comdr. Gen. ATC USAF, 1967-70; cons. Ga. Silver Haired Legislature, 1980-86, senator, 1987-93, pres. protem, 1987-88, pres., 1989-93, rep., spkr. protem, 1993-96, spkr., 1997—, Nat. Silver-Haried Congress rep., 1995—, spkr. 1997—; govs. appointee White House Conf. on Aging, 1971, 96, Ga. Coun. on Aging, 1988-96; U.S. Senate mem. Fed. Coun. on the Aging, 1990-93; senator appointee White House Conf. on Aging, 1995; Ga. Health Decision's appointee to Ga. Coalition for Health, 1996—. Author: (with P.L. Wilds) Essentials of Gynecology-Oncology, 1967, Applications of Gynecology-Oncology, 1967. Del. White House Conf. on Aging, 1981, 95. Served as aerologist USN, 1944-46;aviation psychologist USAF, 1949-54. Fellow AAAS, Am. Psychol. Assn.; mem. AAUP (chpt. pres. 1977-80), Sigma Xi. (chpt. pres. 1980-81). Baptist. Home: 1126 Highland Ave Augusta GA 30904-4628 Office: Med Coll Ga Dept Ob-Gyn Augusta GA 30912 *It's really quite simple—I find, if I wish to be understood or heard, that simplicity is necessary but not ever easy. Simplicity is basic, essential and always the major factor in my search for truth.*

ZACHMEYER, RICHARD FREDERICK, administrator; b. Rochester, N.Y., Apr. 21, 1942; s. Paul Arlo and Dorothy Cecilia (McLean) Z.; m. Christine Pittinaro, Oct. 16, 1982. BS, SUNY, Brockport, 1982; MS, U. Ky., 1985. Program mgr. Ky. Coalition Career Leisure Devel., Lexington, 1984-85, project dir., programs mgr., 1986-89; project coord., training dir. U. Ky., Lexington, 1985-86; exec. dir. Catskill Ctr. Independence, Oneonta, N.Y., 1989—; co-founder, officer Leatherstocking Life Skills Inst., Oneonta, 1992—; cons. City of Miami, Fla., 1986-88, U.S. Dept. Edn., Washington, 1992—, Vacation Resorts Internat., Hyannis, Mass., 1993—, Nat. Ins. Disability Rehab. Rsch., Washington, 1994—; co-founder Officer Coalition Ind. Living, N.Y., 1993—. Author: Effect of a Specialized Training Workshop on Attitudes of Special Educators Toward Disabled Persons, 1987; co-author: Access to Leisure, 1988, Preparing for Transition, 1989. Mem. adult svcs. planning coun. Fayette County Govt., Lexington, 1986-89; mem. extended sch. year planning Fayette County Schs., Lexington, 1986-89; mem. Ams. With Disabilities Act compliance Oneonta Pub. Transit, 1993—, Otsego County (N.Y.) Govt., 1994—. Avocations: music, painting, travel. Home and Office: Catskill Ctr Independence PO Box 1274 Oneonta NY 13820

ZACHOS, KIMON STEPHEN, lawyer; b. Concord, N.H., Nov. 20, 1930; s. Stephen and Sophia (Bacogiannis) Z.; m. Anne Colby, July 5, 1959; children: Ellen, Elizabeth, Sarah. BA, Wesleyan U., 1952; JD, NYU, 1955; LLM, Boston U., 1968; LLD (hon.), N.H. Coll., 1992, St. Anselm Coll., 1994. Bar: N.H. 1955, U.S. Dist. Ct. N.H. 1957, U.S. Supreme Ct. 1963. Ptnr. Sheehan, Phinney, Bass & Green, Manchester, N.H., 1957—; White House fellow, spl. asst. to atty. gen. Nicholas deB. Katzenbach, Washington, 1965-66; bd. dirs. New Eng. Tel., Bank of Ireland 1st Holdings Inc., Citizens Bank N.H., Hitchiner Mfg. Co., Inc., also others. Dep. speaker N.H. Ho. Reps., 1969-74; active various charitable and ednl. orgns. Named Man of Yr., Manchester C. of C., 1985, Disting. Citizen, Boy Scouts Am., 1987, Bus. Leader of Yr., New Hampshire Assn. C of C., 1994; recipient Brotherhood award NCCJ, 1966, Disting. Alumnus award, Wesleyan U., 1997. Mem. ABA, N.H. Bar Assn. Republican. Greek Orthodox. Avocation: stamp collecting. Home: 2093 Elm St Manchester NH 03104-2316 Office: Sheehan Phinney Bass & Green 1000 Elm St Manchester NH 03101-1730

ZACHRY, HENRY BARTELL, JR., construction company executive; b. 1933; married. BSCE, Tex. A&M U., 1954. With H.B. Zachry Co., San Antonio, 1957—, pres., chief exec. officer, 1965-86, chmn., dir., 1984—. Office: H B Zachry Co PO Box 21130 527 W Logwood San Antonio TX 78221-1810 also: Zachry Inc 527 Logwood Ave San Antonio TX 78221-1738*

ZACK, ARNOLD MARSHALL, lawyer, mediator, arbitrator; b. Lynn, Mass., Oct. 7, 1931; s. Samuel George and Bess Ethel (Freedman) Z.; m. Norma Eta Wilner, Aug. 10, 1969; children: Jonathan Samuel, Rachel Anne. AB, Tufts Coll., 1953; LLB, Yale U., 1956; MPA, Harvard U., 1961. Asst. to Saul Wallen (arbitrator), 1956-63; cons. UN Mission to Congo, 1960, U.S. Peace Corps, 1961-63, Labor Dept., 1962-79, Pres.'s Study Commn. on Nat. Service Corps, 1962-63, U.S. AID, 1963—, Friedrich Ebert Stiftung, 1963-64, Nat. Center for Dispute Settlement, 1968-76; vis. Fulbright lectr. Haile Selassie U., Addis Ababa, 1963-64; referee Nat. R.R.Adjustment Bd., 1964—; mem. faculty Harvard U. Trade Union Program, 1985—; dir.Labor-Mgmt. Inst., Am. Arbitration Assn., 1966-68; full time mediator/arbitrator, Boston, 1968—; bd. dirs. ctr. for socio-legal studies faculty of law U. Natal, 1986-92; mem. Fgn. Svc. Labor Rels. Bd., 1982-84, Presdl. Emergency Bds. 221 and 222; chair Presdl. Emergency Bd. 232; cons. Internat. Labor Orgn., 1961—; chair Essential Industries Dipute Settlement Bd. Bermuda, 1993—; chair Essential Svcs. Dispute Settlement Bd., Bermuda, 1996—; vis. lectr. Yale Law Sch., 1995—; permanent arbitrator, Am. Airlines & APA, IAM, TWA and Air Line Pilots Assn., TWA and IAM; Yale U. and Fedn. Univ., Procter & Gamble and Ind. Oil and Chem. Workers, Commonwealth Mass., Capital ABC and NABET. Author: Labor Training in Developing Countries, 1964, Ethiopia's High Level Manpower-Analysis and Projections, 1964, Handbook on Grievance Arbitration in the Public Sector, 1974, Handbook on Fact Finding and Arbitration in the Public Sector, 1974, Grievance Arbitration, A Practical Guide, 1977; (with R. Bloch) Arbitration of Discipline and Discharge Cases, 1979, (with R. Bloch) The Agreement in Negotiation and Arbitration, 1983; 2nd Edition, 1995— Arbitration in Practice, 1984, Mediation in the Public Sector, 1985, Grievance Arbitration: Cases on the Merits in Discipline Discharge and Contract Interpretation, 1989, Handbook on Grievance Arbitration: Issues on Procedure and Ethics, 1992; contbr. articles to profl. jours. Recipient Whitney North Seymour medal for oustanding contbn. to arbitration, 1980, Cushing Gavin award, 1986, Mildred Spaulding award, 1987, Disting. Svc. award for arbitration of labor-mgmt. disputes, 1989. Fellow African Studies Assn.; mem. Nat. Acad. Arbitrators (treas. 1972-75, bd. govs. 1977-79, v.p. 1980-82, pres. 1994-95, pres. Rsch. and Edn. Found. 1989-91), Am. Arbitration Assn., Indsl. Rels. Rsch. Assn., Internat. Soc. for Labor Law and Social Security (bd. dirs.), Harvard Club (Boston), Yale Club (N.Y.C.). Address: 170 W Canton St Boston MA 02118-1216

ZACK, DANIEL GERARD, library director; b. Waukegan, Ill., Oct. 1, 1943; s. Raymond Gerard and Rosanna Marie (Atkinson) Z.; m. Mary Frances Anthony, Aug. 25, 1966; children: Jennifer Lee, Rebecca Jane. BA in Psychology, Western Ill. U., 1967; MS in Libr. Sci., U. Ill., 1975. Editor IBM Corp., Rochester, Minn., 1968-70, Memorex Corp., Mpls., 1970-74; rsch. assoc. Libr. Rsch. Ctr. U. Ill., Urbana, 1974-75; asst. dir. Portage County Pub. Libr., Stevens Point, Wis., 1976-78; dir. Burlington (Iowa) Pub. Libr., 1978-87, Gail Borden Pub. Libr., Elgin, Ill., 1987—. Trustee Batavia (Ill.) Pub. Libr., 1997—; founder Friends of Ill. Libr., 1990, bd. dirs. 1990—. Mem. ALA, ACLU, Ill. Libr. Assn. (mgr. pub. libr. forum 1991-92, exec. bd. dirs. 1992-95, pub. policy com. 1995—), Pub. Libr. Assn. (intellectual freedom com. 1993-96), Kiwanis. Office: Gail Borden Pub Libr Dist 200 N Grove Ave Elgin IL 60120-5505

ZACK, STEVEN JEFFREY, master automotive instructor; b. Middletown, Conn., Oct. 12, 1955; s. Mathias Charles and Sylvia Ann (Berkowitz) Z. AAS, Williamsport Area C.C., 1976. Cert. EPA instr. Automotive technician Bob Sharp Nissan, Danbury, Conn., 1976-79; svc. engr. Ingersoll Rand, Painted Post, N.Y., 1979-85; tech. svc. rep. Chrysler Motor Corp., Metairie, La., 1985-87; automotive instr. Hartford (Conn.) Tech. Inst., 1988-92; master automotive instr. SPX/Automotive Diagnostics, Kalamazoo, Mich., 1992—, EPA/Coalition Safer Cleaner Vehicles, Albany, 1994—; tng. cons. Conn. DMV, North Haven, 1994—; coun. cons. Coalition Safer Cleaner Vehicles/Coun. of Automotive Trainer, Lisle, Ill., 1995—; master instr. EPA/Coalition Safer Cleaner Vehicles, Albany, N.Y., 1994—. Author: (book) Automotive Diagnostic Maps, 1995, (manuscript) Electronic Combustion Graph, 1993; patentee electric car heat exchanger motor. Mem. Coalition for Safer Cleaner Vehicles. Avocation: God. Home: PO Box 293 Deep River CT 06417-0293

ZACKHEIM, ADRIAN WALTER, editor; b. N.Y.C., Sept. 19, 1951; s. Albert Alex and Mary Elizabeth (Cooper) Z.; m. Sarah Babst Parsons, Sept. 1, 1985; children: Adrian Alex, David Parsons. BA, Grinnell Coll., 1973; MA, U. Toronto, Ont., Can., 1975. Editor St. Martins Press, N.Y.C., 1977-79; editor Doubleday & Co., Inc., N.Y.C., 1979-84, sr. editor, 1984-85; sr. editor William Morrow & Co., Inc., N.Y.C., 1986-89, sr. editor, v.p., 1989-90, exec. editor, v.p., 1990-91, editorial dir., v.p., 1991-94; pub. dir., v.p. HarperBus, 1994-97; exec. editor, v.p. Harper Collins, 1994-97, pub. HarperBus., sr. v.p. Harper Collins adult trade, 1997—. Office: Harper Collins 10 E 53rd St New York NY 10022-5244

ZACKHRAS, RUBEN, Marshallese government official. Minister of finance Govt. of the Marshall Islands, Majuro. Office: Ministry of Finance PO Box D Cabinet Bldg Majuro MH 96960*

ZACKS, GORDON BENJAMIN, manufacturing company executive; b. Terre Haute, Ind., Mar. 11, 1933; s. Aaron and Florence Melton (Spurgeon) Z.; married; children: Catherine E., Kimberly A. B.A., Coll. Commerce, Ohio State U. With R.G. Barry Corp., Pickerington, Ohio, 1955—, exec. v.p., 1964-65, pres., 1965—, chmn. bd., 1979—, now also chief exec. officer, chmn. Mem. Nat. Republican Senatorial Com.; hon. chmn. United Jewish Appeal; bd. dirs. numerous Jewish orgns., locally and nationally. Mem. Chief Exec. Officer Orgn., Am. Mgmt. Assn. Republican. Home: 140 N Parkview Ave Columbus OH 43209-1436 Office: R G Barry Corp 13405 Yarmouth Dr NW Pickerington OH 43147-8493 also: PO Box 129 Columbus OH 43216-0129

ZACKS, SUMNER IRWIN, pathologist; b. Boston, June 29, 1929; s. David and Rose Z.; m. Marilyn Garfinkel, June 28, 1953; children—Nancy Alice, Charles Matthew, Susan Esther. B.A. cum laude, Harvard Coll., 1951, M.D. magna cum laude, 1955; M.A. (hon.), U. Pa., 1975, Brown U., 1977. Diplomate Am. Bd. Pathology. Intern Mass. Gen. Hosp., Boston, 1956; resident Mass. Gen. Hosp., 1956-58; teaching fellow Harvard U., 1956; asst. prof. pathology U. Pa., 1962-64, assoc. prof., 1964-71, prof., 1971-76; prof. pathology Brown U., 1976-89, chmn. pathology, 1977-82; pathologist in chief Miriam Hosp., Providence, R.I., 1976-88, ret., 1989. Author: The Motor Endplate, 1964, 74, Atlas of Neuropathology, 1971; contbr. chpts. to books and articles to profl. jours. Served to capt. USAR, 1958-60. Fellow Am. Coll. Pathology; mem. Histochem. Soc. (sec. 1965-68), Am. Coll. Pathologists, Assn. Am. Pathologists, Am. Soc. Cell Biology, Am. Soc. Neuropathologists, Internat. Acad. Pathology, Sigma Xi.

ZAENGLEIN, WILLIAM GEORGE, JR., lawyer; b. Orange, N.J., Jan. 31, 1929; s. William George Sr. and Elsie May (Traenkle) Z.; m. Elizabeth J. Skinner, Dec. 18, 1954; 1 son, William George, III; m. Joyce A. Moffit, Oct. 18, 1968; 1 son, Eric Hunter. B.A., Yale U., 1952, J.D., 1955. Bar: D.C. 1957, Calif. 1969, U.S. Dist. Ct. (cen. dist.) Calif. 1969. With gen. counsel's office GSA, 1956-59; contract adminstr. Lear Siegler Corp., 1959-63; sr. contract adminstr. Northrop Corp., 1963-66; legal asst. law firm Orange, Calif., 1966-69; v.p., corp. counsel First Am. Title Ins. Co., The First Am. Fin. Corp., Santa Ana, Calif., 1969-77; v.p., sec., corp. counsel First Am. Title Ins. Co., 1977-91; v.p., sec., counsel The First Am. Fin. Corp., 1977-91; retired, 1991; dir. First Am. Trust Co., 1976—. Mem. Orange County Bar Assn., Am. Soc. Corporate Secs., Yale Club of So. Calif., Phi Delta Phi, Chi Phi. Office: First Am Fin Corp 114 E 5th St Santa Ana CA 92701-4642

ZAENTZ, SAUL, motion picture producer; b. Passaic, N.J.. Producer films: One Flew Over the Cuckoo's Nest, 1975 (Oscar for Best Picture), Three Warriors, 1977, Lord of the Rings, 1978, Amadeus, 1984 (Oscar for Best Picture), The Unbearable Lightness of Being, 1988, At Play in the Fields of the Lord, 1991, The English Patient, 1996 (Academy Award for Producer Best Picture, Irving G. Thalberg award 1996); exec. producer The Mosquito Coast, 1986. Office: Saul Zaentz Co 2600 10th St Berkeley CA 94710-2522

ZAFFARONI, ALEJANDRO C., biochemist, medical research company executive; b. Montevideo, Uruguay, Feb. 27, 1923; came to U.S., 1944; s. Carlos and Luisa (Alfaro) Z.; m. Lyda Russomanno, July 5, 1946; children—Alejandro A., Elisa. B., U. Montevideo, 1943; Ph.D. in Biochemistry, U. Rochester, 1949; Doctorate (hon.), U. Republic, Montevideo, 1983; M.Divinity, Cen. Bapt. Seminary, 1987. Dir. biochem. research Syntex S.A., Mexico City, 1951-54, v.p., dir. research, 1954-56; exec. v.p., dir. Syntex Corp., Palo Alto, Calif., 1956-68; pres. Syntex Labs. Inc., Palo Alto, Calif., 1962-68, Syntex Research, Palo Alto, Calif., 1962-68; founder, co-chmn. ALZA Corp., Palo Alto, Calif., 1968—, also CEO; founder, mem. policy bd. and exec. com. DNAX Research Inst. of Molecular and Cellular Biology, Inc., Palo Alto, Calif., 1980—, chmn., 1980-82; founder, chmn., chief exec. officer Affymax, N.V., Palo Alto, 1989—; chmn. Internat. Psoriasis Research Found., Palo Alto; incorporator Neuroscis. Research Found. MIT, Brookline, Mass.; bd. govs. Weizmann Inst. Sci., Rehovot, Israel; mem. pharm. panel of com. on tech. and internat. econs. and trade issues Nat. Acad. Engrng. Office of Fgn. Sec. and Assembly of Engrng., Washington; hon. prof. biochemistry Nat. U. Mex., 1957, U. Montevideo, 1959. Contbr. numerous articles to profl. jours.; patentee in field. Recipient Barren medal Barren Found., Chgo., 1974; Pres.'s award Weizmann Inst. Sci., 1978; Chem. Pioneer award Am. Inst. Chemists, Inc., 1979, National Medal of Technology, 1995. Fellow Am. Acad. Arts and Scis., Am. Pharm. Assn.; mem. AAAS, Am. Chem. Soc., Am. Found. Pharm. Edn., Am. Inst. Chemists, Inc., Am. Soc. Biol. Chemists, Inc., Am. Soc. Microbiology, Am. Soc. Pharmacology and Exptl. Therapeutics, Biomed. Engrng. Soc., Calif. Pharmacists Assn., Internat. Pharm. Fedn., Internat. Soc. Chronobiology, Internat. Soc. Study of Biol. Rhythms, Soc. Exptl. Biology and Medicine, Sociedad Mexicana de Nutricion y Endocrinologia, Biochem. Soc. Eng., Endocrine Soc., Internat. Soc. Research in Biology of Reproduction, N.Y. Acad. Scis., Christian Legal Soc. (Mo. bd. dirs. 1973—), Tau Kappa Epsilon (internat. pres. 1953-57). *

ZAFFIRINI, JUDITH, state senator; b. Laredo, Tex., Feb. 13, 1946; d. George and Nieves Pappas; m. Carlos Zaffirini, 1965; 1 child, Carlos Jr. BS, U. Tex., 1967, MA, 1970, PhD, 1978. Committeewoman Tex. State Dem. Exec. Com., 1978-84; mem. Tex. State Senate, 1987—, pres. pro tempore, 1997, chair health and human svcs. com.; del. Dem. Nat. Conv., 1980, 84. Recipient Medal of Excellence Nat. League United Latin Am. Citizens, 1987, Jose Maria Morelos y Pavon Medal of Merit for leadership in strengthening U.S.-Mex. rels., 1987, George Washington Medal of Excellence for Individual Achievement Freedoms Found. at Valley Forge, 1988; named Woman of Achievement Tex. Press Women, 1980, Gov. of Tex. for a Day, Apr. 19, 1997; inductee Nat. Hispanic Hal of Fame, 1987. Democrat. Roman Catholic. Home: PO Box 627 Laredo TX 78042-0627 Office: 1407 Washington St Laredo TX 78040-4411

ZAFREN, HERBERT CECIL, librarian, educator; b. Balt., Aug. 25, 1925; s. Morris and Sadie Mildred (Edlavitch) Z.; m. Miriam Koenigsberg, Feb. 11, 1951; children: Ken, Edie. AB, Johns Hopkins U., 1944, postgrad., 1946-49; diploma, Balt. Hebrew Coll., 1944, LittD (hon.), 1969; AM in Libr. Sci, U. Mich., 1950. Jr. instr. Johns Hopkins U., Balt., 1947-49; bibliog. searcher Law Libr. U. Mich., Ann Arbor, 1949-50; libr. Hebrew Union Coll.-Jewish Inst. Religion, Cin., 1950-91, prof. Jewish bibliography, 1968-95, prof. emeritus, 1996—; exec. dir. Am. Jewish Periodical Ctr., Cin., 1956-80, co-dir., 1980-96, dir., 1996—; dir. librs. Cin., L.A., N.Y.C., Jerusalem, 1966-94; dir. emeritus librs. Hebrew Union Coll.-Jewish Inst. Religion, Cin., 1994—; mem. exec. bd. Jewish Book Coun. Am., 1979-96. Editor Studies in Bibliography and Booklore, 1953—, Bibliographica Judaica, 1969—; compiler: A Gathering of Broadsides, 1967. With USN, 1944-46. Mem. ALA, Assn. Jewish Librs. (founder, nat. pres. 1965-66), World Coun. on Jewish Archives (v.p. 1977-81), Assn. Jewish Studies, Spl. Librs. Assn. (pres. Cin. chpt. 1953-54), Coun. Archives and Rsch. Librs. in Jewish Studies (pres. 1974-78, 89-91), Am. Hist. Assn., Israel Bibliophiles, World Union Jewish Studies, AAUP (chpt. pres. 1964-68), Grolier Club (N.Y.C.), Phi Beta Kappa, Beta Phi Mu. Office: Hebrew Union Coll- Jewish Inst Religion 3101 Clifton Ave Cincinnati OH 45220-2404

ZAGARE, FRANK COSMO, political science educator; b. Bklyn., June 7, 1947; s. Domenick Joseph and Josephine Ann (Stager) Z.; m. Patricia M. Sclafani, May 26, 1974; children: Catherine, Ann, Elizabeth. BA, Fordham U., 1969; MA, NYU, 1972, PhD, 1977. Asst. prof. Boston U., 1978-87; assoc. prof. SUNY, Buffalo, 1987-91, prof., 1991—, chmn. dept. polit. sci., 1991-94, 96—. Author: Game Theory, 1984, Dynamics of Deterrence, 1987; contbr. articles to profl. publs. MIT/Harvard fellow 1984; grantee U.S. Inst. Peace, 1989-90, NSF, 1992-94, 96—. Mem. Am. Polit. Sci. Assn. (coun. mem. conflict processes sect. 1986-89), Internat. Studies Assn., Midwest Polit. Sci. Assn. Home: 123 Morris Ave Buffalo NY 14214-1609 Office: SUNY Buffalo 520 S Park Ave Buffalo NY 14204-2626

ZAGEL, JAMES BLOCK, federal judge; b. Chgo., Mar. 4, 1941; s. Samuel and Ethel (Samuels) Z.; m. Margaret Maxwell, May 27, 1979. BA, U. Chgo., 1962, MA in Philosophy, 1962; JD, Harvard U., 1965. Bar: Ill. 1965, U.S. Dist. Ct. (no. dist.) Ill. 1965, U.S. Supreme Ct. 1970, U.S. Ct. Appeals (7th cir.) 1972. Asst. atty. gen. criminal justice divsn. State of Ill., Springfield, 1970-77; chief prosecuting atty. Ill. Jud. Inquiry Bd., Springfield, 1973-75; exec. dir. Ill. Law Enforcement Commn., Springfield, 1977-79; dir. Ill. Dept. Revenue, Springfield, 1979-80, Ill. Dept. State Police, Springfield, 1980-87; judge U.S. Dist. Ct. (no. dist.) Ill., Chgo., 1987—. Co-author: Criminal Law and Its Administration, 1989, Cases and Comments on Criminal Procedure, 1992. Named Outstanding Young Citizen, Chgo. Jaycees, 1977 ; recipient Disting. Service Merit award Assn. Commerce and Industry, 1983. Mem. Chgo. Bar Assn., Jud. Conf. of U.S. (codes of conduct com. 1987-92). Office: US Dist Ct 219 S Dearborn St Ste 2188 Chicago IL 60604-1801

ZAGER, RONALD I., chemist, consultant; b. N.Y.C., Dec. 27, 1934; s. Joseph and Theodora Zager; m. Judith Ellen Bilt, Dec. 24, 1961 (div. July 1975); children: Scott Lawrence, Joseph Daniel; m. Anne Coykendall Chase, 1995. BS, Bklyn. Coll., 1955; MS in Chemistry, Stevens Inst. Tech., 1969. Chemist Charles Pfizer & Co., N.Y.C., 1956-58, Halocarbon Products, Hackensack, N.J., 1958-66; devel. chemist Tenneco Chems., Garfield, N.J., 1966-71; sr. chemist Givaudan Corp., Clifton, N.J., 1971-77; tech. dir. Internat. Flavors and Fragrances, Union Beach, N.J., 1977-88; cons. Highlands, N.J., 1988-92, Glen, N.H., 1993—; overseas tech. cons. Unistar Program, UN, 1992. Mem. Am. Chem. Soc., Assn. Cons. Chemists and Chem. Engrs. (v.p. 1990-92, pres. 1993-94). Achievements include research in aroma chemicals and organic fluorocarbons. Office: Ronald Zager Assocs Box 1200 85 Glen Ledge Rd Glen NH 03838

ZAGNOLI, ROLAND CANDIANO, management and marketing consultant, pharmacist; b. Highland Park, Ill., Nov. 6, 1931; s. Valerio Walter and Maria Adalgisa (Solignani) Z.; m. Virginia Louise Rizzo, Oct. 7, 1961; children: Roland Christopher, Lisa Louise, Regina Marie, Laurette Rene, Annia Lynn. BS in Pharmacy, U. Mich., 1955; MBA, Harvard U., 1957; LLB, LaSalle Extension U., 1963. RPh, Fla.; registered consulting pharmacist, Fla. Tech. & adminstrv. rotation trainee Abbott Labs., Inc., North Chgo., 1957-59, corp. product mgr., 1959-63; dir. product mgmt. & new mktg. devel. Ross pediatric div. Abbott Labs., Inc., Columbus, Ohio, 1963-65; dir. product mgmt. internat. div. Abbott Labs., Inc., North Chgo., 1965-67; dir. mktg. & sales diagnostics div. Abbott Labs., Inc., North Chgo. & Los Angeles, 1967-70; dual mgr. Amp-Vial project & mfg. hosp. div. Abbott Labs., Inc., North Chgo. & Rocky Mountain, N.C., 1970-73; pres., gen. mgr. Health Care Industries, Inc., Michigan City, Ind., 1973-76, pres., chmn. bd., chief exec. officer, 1976-81; pres., chief exec. officer M/PIC Cons., Deltona, Fla., 1982—, Med. Inventors Corp., Orlando, Fla., 1988—; charter mem. Pharmacy Advancement Com. U. Mich., 1976-91; mem. Cen. Fla. Inventors Coun., Orlando, 1984-89; charter mem., bd. advisors Southtech Growth Fund, Ltd., Orlando, 1988-89; advisor Internat. Med. Techs., Winter Springs, Fla., 1989-92. Inventor Dye Pharm. Chem. (tablets dye-coating stability), 1958; patentee, 1959. Charter mem. Cen. Fla. Coun. High Tech., Orlando, 1984-94; gen. chmn. Notre Dame Parish Festival, Michigan City, 1977-79; pres. Evans Scholars Alumni, 1961-62; mem., cons. Mktg. & Mgmt. Ctrl. Fla. Innovation, Corp. 1995—; fund raiser various orgns. Evans Scholar of Yr. Western Golf Assn., 1954; won 8 golf tournament weekend championships at 7 sites in 4 states; William Douglas McAdams fellow, 1955-57. Mem. Am. Pharm. Assn., Ctrl. Fla. Soc. Hosp. Pharmacists, Fla. Soc. Hosp. Pharmacists, Cen. Fla. Pharmacy Assn. (v.p. 1990-91), Fla. Pharmacy Assn., Assn. Univ. Tech. Mgrs., Walnut Hill Country Club (Columbus), Pottawattamie Country Club (Michigan City), Kiwanis, Rotary, Phi Eta Sigma, Rho Chi. Home and Office: 1936 Saxon Blvd Deltona FL 32725

ZAGON, LAURIE, artist, writer, color consultant; b. N.Y.C., Feb. 4, 1950; d. Jerome and Janet (Rabinowitz) Z.; m. Joseph Sorrentino, Dec. 21, 1991. BFA, Md. Inst. Coll. Art, 1971; MFA, Syracuse U., 1973. Asst. prof. Art CUNY, N.Y.C., 1973-87; color cons. Fieldcrest/Cannon, N.Y.C., 1987-88; nat. speaker Am. Soc. Interior Designers, Washington, 1993—; color, art therapist, Flagstaff, Ariz., 1996, Big Brothers/Big Sisters No. Ariz., 1996. Illustrator (book) It's Never Too Late to Have a Happy Childhood, 1989; one-woman shows include The Nat. Arts Club, N.Y.C., 1989, Gallery 1757, Laguna Beach, Calif., 1991; group exhibits include John Szoke Gallery, N.Y.C., Helio Galleries, N.Y.C., CUNY Abstract Show of Shanghai, China,

1986, L.A. Mcpl. Gallery, 1993, Phoenix Airport Galleries, 1996; co-author: Power of Color, 1995. Color/art therapist for AIDS Children, L.A. Children's Hosp., 1994—; color/art therapist for recovering addicts Capo by the Sea, Dana Point, Calif., 1991, Martin Luther Hosp., Anaheim, 1990; active painting workshops for the terminally ill, 1995—. Home and Office: 1107 Fair Oaks Ave # 147 South Pasadena CA 91030-3311

ZAGOREN, ALLEN JEFFREY, surgeon; b. Bklyn., May 17, 1947; s. Max and Harriett (Feldman) Z.; m. Gail Marie Sarcinella, Feb. 20, 1977. BA in Biology, Hofstra U., 1969; DO, Phila. Coll. Osteo. Medicine, 1975. Diplomate Am. Bd. Osteo. Surgery, Nat. Bd. Examiners Osteo.-Med. Surgery. Intern Stratford (N.J.) div. John F. Kennedy Meml. Hosp., 1975-76; resident Cherry Hill (N.J.) Med. Ctr., 1976-80; assoc. prof. surgery U. Medicine and Dentistry, Piscataway, N.J., 1980-82; practice osteo. medicine specializing in surgery Des Moines, 1982—, Capitol Hill Surgery, Des Moines, 1994—; mem. staff Mercy Hosp. Med. Ctr., Des Moines; practice osteo. medicine specializing in surgery Capitol Hill Surgery, Des Moines; chmn. dept. surgery Des Moines Gen. Hosp., 1985-91, Madison County Meml. Hosp., Winterset, Iowa; adj. prof. surgery and nutrition U. Osteo. Medicine; assoc. prof. pharmacy Drake U.; lectr. in field; mem. Nat. Bd. Examiners in Osteo. Medicine and Surgery; mem. surg. rev. com. Bd. Med. Examiners of Iowa, 1996—; med. dir. Wound Care Ctr., 1996, program dir. gen. surgery residency, 1993—. Contbr. articles to profl. jours.; creator videotapes (with others). Bd. dirs. Des Moines Gen. Hosp. Found., sec., 1986-95; active Iowa Found. for Med. Care, Nutritional Coun. Iowa; chmn. bd. dirs. Des Moines Gen. Found., 1991-94; trustee Tiffereth Israel Synagogue, 1992. Grantee SKF Labs., Phila., 1986, Norwich (N.Y.) Eaton Labs., 1986, Ross Labs., 1995-97. Fellow Am. Coll. Osteo. Surgeons (rsch., nutritional support, visual aids coms., chair rsch. com. 1991-92, 1st Prize awards 1982, 83), Am. Coll. Nutrition, Internat. Coll. Surgeons; mem. Am. Osteo. Soc., Am. Soc. Gastrointestinal Endoscopy, Iowa Osteo. Med. Assn. (pres. 1994-95, chmn. constrn. and v.p. bylaws coms. 1992, trustee), Polk County Med. Soc. (treas. 1991-93), Am. Soc. Parenteral and Enteral Nutrition (bd. dirs. 1986, chmn. various coms.), Rhoades Rsch. Found., Iowa and Nebr. Soc. Parenteral and Enteral Nutrition (pres. 1990-92), Iowa Health Leadership Consortium (CEO com.), Smithsonian Instn., Airplane Owners and Pilots Assn., Iowa Nebr. Nutrition Soc. (pres. 1990-92). Jewish. Avocations: flying, golf, swimming, skiing, writing. Office: Capitol Hill Surgery 1300 Des Moines St Des Moines IA 50309-5547

ZAGOREN, JOY CARROLL, health facility director, researcher; b. N.Y.C., Oct. 31, 1933; d. Murray Morris and Celia (Donner) Rossman; m. Robert H. Zagoren, June 29, 1958 (div. 1988); children: Glenn, Robin; m. Robert Henry Chester, Apr. 1, 1988; children: Peter, Lisabeth, Melinda, Cecily, Kate. BS, NYU, 1957; MS, Adelphi U., 1969; PhD with distinction, NYU, 1981. Sec. sch. faculty Great Neck (N.Y.) Pub. Schs., 1957-71; rsch. scientist Inst. Psychobiol. Studies, Queens Village, N.Y., 1968-71; rsch. assoc. Albert Einstein Coll. Medicine, Bronx, N.Y., 1971-84; asst. prof. Sch. Medicine SUNY, Stony Brook, 1984-86; dir. Seriatum, N.Y.C., 1991—; ptnr. Winter Tree Collection; chmn. Esrath Nashim Hosp., 1986—; med. bd. dirs. Sarah Herzog Meml. Hosp., 1994—. Editor: The Node of Ranvier, 1984; contbr. articles to profl. jours. Chair Peace Corps Svc. Coun., Tri-State, 1965-75; pres. Kidney Found. L.I., N.Y., 1965-77; v.p. United Cmty. fund L.I., 1970-83; bd. dirs. Jerusalem Mental Health Ctr., N.Y.C., 1986—; mem. med. bd. dirs. Sarah Herzog Meml. Hosp., hon. chair dinner, 1995, chair dinner, 1996. Recipient post doctoral fellowship NIH, 1982-84, svc. awards Kidney Found., Kiwanis, and others, 1970-87; named Disting. Alumnus of Yr., Adelphi U., 1986. Mem. AAAS, ACA, N.Y. Acad. Sci., Am. Assn. Neuropathology, Esrath Nashim Hosp. (chairperson 1986—, apptd. med. bd. dirs. 1994. Democrat. Jewish. Avocations: art, literature, piano, swimming, gardening. Home: 405 E 82nd St New York NY 10028-6038 Office: Seriatum PO Box 396 Livingston Manor NY 12758-0396

ZAGORIA, SAM D(AVID), arbitrator, author, educator; b. Somerville, N.J., Apr. 9, 1919; s. Nathan and Rebecca (Shapiro) Z.; m. Sylvia Bomse, Dec. 21, 1941; children: Paul, Marjorie Zagoria Isacks, Ronald. BL in Journalism, Rutgers U., 1941. With New Brunswick (N.J.) Daily Home News, 1940-41, N.J. Def. Coun., Trenton, 1941-42; Fed. Office Govt. Reports, Newark, 1942; reporter Washington Post, 1946-55; adminstrv. asst. to Senator Clifford P. Case, Washington, 1955-65; mem. NLRB, Washington, 1965-69; dir. Labor-Mgmt. Rels. Svc. U.S. Conf. of Mayors, Washington, 1970-78; mem. U.S. Consumer Product Safety Commn., 1978-84; ombudsman Washington Post, 1984-86; arbitrator, writer, 1986—; Fulbright lectr., Copenhagen, 1987; vis. prof. Fla. Atlantic U., Boca Raton, 1988-91; adj. prof. Wake Forest U., Winston-Salem, N.C., 1993—. Author: Public Workers, Public Unions, 1972, The Ombudsman: How Good Governments Handle Citizens' Grievances, 1988. Campaign mgr. reelection Senator Case, 1960; campaign mgr. race for gov., former Sec. of Labor James P. Mitchell, 1961. With USAAF, 1942-45. Nieman fellow Harvard, 1954. Mem. Common Cause, Nat. Consumers League, Rutgers U. Alumni Assn. Jewish. Home and Office: 2864 Wynfield Crossing Ln Winston Salem NC 27103-6597 also: 3101 S Ocean Blvd Apt 622 Highland Beach FL 33487-2524

ZAGORIN, JANET SUSAN, professional development director; b. Lakewood, N.J.; d. Irving C. and Dorothy (Tarshish) Z. BA, Douglass Coll., 1975; MLS, Rutgers U., 1977. Asst. law libr. N.J. Atty. Gen., Trenton, 1977-78; head of reference sect. Cardozo U. Law Sch., N.Y.C., 1978-79; law and legis. svcs. libr. FTC, Washington, 1979-81; dir. of reference Paul Weiss Rifkind, N.Y.C., 1981-82; libr. dir. Riker Danzig Scherer & Hyland, Morristown, N.J., 1982; libr., profl. devel. dir. Baker & McKenzie, N.Y.C., 1982-96; dir. practice devel. Stroock & Stroock & Lavan LLP, N.Y.C., 1996—. Mem. ABA (vice chmn. standing com. Law Libr. Congress 1995-96, chmn. 1996—), Fin. Women's Assn. (mem. bd. dirs. 1993-95), Bus. Women's Network, Am. Assn. Law Librs. (chair fgn. comparative internat. law com. 1990-91, vice chair pvt. law librs. 1990-91, chair 1991—, chair com. on recruitment 1991), Spl. Librs. Assn., Hadassah.

ZAGORIN, PEREZ, historian, educator; b. Chgo., May 29, 1920; s. Solomon Novitz and Mildred (Ginsburg) Z.; m. Honoré Desmond Sharrer, May 29, 1947; 1 son, Adam. A.B., U. Chgo., 1941; A.M., Harvard U., 1947, Ph.D., 1952. Various positions OWI, U.S. Govt., U.P. Syndicate, CIO, 1942-46; instr. Amherst Coll., 1947-49; lectr. Vassar Coll., 1951-53; from asst. prof. to prof. history McGill U., 1955-65; prof. U. Rochester, 1965—, Joseph C. Wilson prof. history, 1982-90, Joseph C. Wilson prof. history emeritus, 1990—, chmn. dept., 1968-69, acting chmn. dept., 1988-89; vis. prof. Johns Hopkins, 1964-65; Amundsen vis. prof. U. Pitts., 1964; William Andrews Clark Meml. Library prof. UCLA, 1975-76; Thompson lectr. history Vassar Coll., 1987. Author: A History of Political Thought in the English Revolution, 1954, The Court and the Country, 1969, Culture and Politics from Puritanism to the Englightenment, 1980, Rebels and Rulers 1500-1660, 2 vols., 1982, Ways of Lying: Dissimulation, Persecution, and Conformity in Early Modern Europe, 1990, Milton Aristocrat and Rebel: The Poet and His Politics, 1992; co-editor: Philosophy Science and Religion in England 1640-1700, 1991, Guide to Historical Literature, 1994; contbr. numerous articles in hist. jours.; mem. editorial bd. Jour. of the History of Ideas. Sheldon traveling fellow Harvard U., 1949-50, Fulbright fellow 1949-50, faculty rsch. fellow Social Sci. Rsch. Coun., 1958-59, 61-62, sr. rsch. fellow Folger Shakespeare Libr., 1964-65, fellow Inst. Advanced Study, Princeton, N.J., 1972-73, sr. fellow Nat. Humanities Ctr., 1978-79, fellow Ctr. Advanced Study in Behavioral Scis., 1983-84, Edgar F. Shannon Ctr. for Advanced Studies fellow U. Va., 1994—. Fellow Royal Hist. Soc., Am. Acad. Arts and Scis.; mem. Am. Hist. Assn. (chmn. Gershoy and Schuyler prize com. 1982-84). Home: 2990 Beaumont Farm Rd Charlottesville VA 22901 Office: U Rochester Dept History Rochester NY 14627

ZAHARIA, ERIC STAFFORD, developmental disabilities program administrator; b. Pomona, Calif., Aug. 24, 1948; s. Edgar A. and Dorothy (Stafford) Z.; m. Caryle Koentz, Dec. 23, 1967; children: Tye W., Tieg A. BA, Pomona Coll., 1970; MEd, U. Ariz.-Tucson, 1973; PhD, George Peabody Coll., 1978; postgrad., Govt. Execs. Inst. U. N.C., Chapel Hill, 1981. Mental retardation worker Ariz. Tng. Program, Tucson, 1970-71, unit dir., 1971-73; dir. residential svcs. Willmar State Hosp., (Minn.), 1973-76; rsch. asst. Inst. on Mental Retardation and Intellectual Devel., Nashville, 1976-78; dir. mental retardation program svcs. Dept. Mental Health/Mental Retardation, State of Tenn., Nashville, 1978-79; dir. Caswell Ctr., Kinston, N.C., 1979-86; program adminstr. Colo. Div. of Devel. Disabilities, Denver, 1986-90; dir. Utah divsn. Svcs. for People with Disabilities, Salt Lake City, 1990-95; ind. cons. Park City, Utah, 1995—; mem. adj. faculty East Carolina U., Greenville, 1979-86; bd. dirs. Neuse Enterprises Inc., Kinston. Chmn. Big Bros./Sisters Kinston Inc., 1980-83; mem. N.C. Coalition for Community Svc., 1982-85. Mem. Am. Assn. Mental Retardation, Nat. Assn. Supts., Pub. Residential Facilities, Assn. Retarded Citizens, Kinston C. of C. (bd. dirs. 1983-86). Home: 8010 Juniper Dr Park City UT 84060-5370 Office: 120 N 200 W Salt Lake City UT 84103-1550

ZAHL, PAUL FRANCIS MATTHEW, dean; b. N.Y.C., May 24, 1951; m. Mary McLean Cappleman, Dec. 29, 1973; children: John Arthur, David William Franklin, Simeon McLean. Student, U. N.C., 1968-70; AB magna cum laude, Harvard Coll., 1972; MPhil in Theology, U. Nottingham, Eng., 1975; diploma in pastoral studies, St. John's Theol. Coll., Nottingham, 1975; ThD, Eberhard-Karls-Univ., Tübingen, Germany, 1994. Ordained min. Protestant Episcopal Ch., 1976. Deacon in tng. Good Shepherd Episcopal Ch., Silver Spring, Md., 1975-76; curate Grace Ch., N.Y.C., 1976-82; rector St. Mary's Ch., Scarborough, N.Y., 1982-88, St. James' Ch., Charleston, S.C., 1988-92; fellow Episcopal Ch. Found., 1993-95; dean Cathedral Ch. of the Advent, Birmingham, Ala., 1995—; tchr. Gen. Theol. Sem., N.Y.C., 1979-82, The King's Coll., Briarcliff Manor, N.Y., 1985-88, Coll. Charleston, S.C., 1990-92, U. Tübingen, Germany, 1992-93; vis. scholar Wycliffe Hall, Oxford, Eng., 1994-95. Author: Who Will Deliver Us?, 1983, Die Rechtfertigungslehre Ernst Kasemanns, 1996; columnist The Anglican Digest, 1986—; contbr. articles to profl. jours. Mem. Phi Beta Kappa. Office: Cath Church of the Advent 2017 6th Ave N Birmingham AL 35203-2701

ZAHN, CARL FREDERICK, museum publications director, designer, photographer; b. Louisville, Mar. 9, 1928; s. Fred Joseph and Myrtle (Fulks) Z.; m. Betty Jane Woodrow, Nov. 18, 1950 (div. July 1977); children: Lisa, Karen, Richard; m. Felicitas Magdalena Fuhlrott, July 30, 1979. BA, Harvard Coll., 1948. Asst. in conservation Fogg Art Mus., Cambridge, Mass., 1949-50; with art dept. Benton & Bowles Inc., N.Y.C., 1950-51; design asst. Inst. Contemporary Art, Boston, 1951-56; dir. publs. Mus. Fine Arts, Boston, 1956—; also dir. exhbns., 1995-96, ret., 1997. exhibitions include: Addison Gallery Am. Art, Andover, Mass., 1959, Am. Inst. Graphic Arts, N.Y.C., 1960—, Rose Art Mus. Brandeis U., Waltham, Mass., 1969; author: Introduction to Hermann Zapf and His Design Philosophy, 1987; co-author Weston's Westons: Portraits and Nudes, 1989. Mem. Am. Inst. Graphic Arts (v.p. 1971-72), Soc. Printers, Bund Deutscher Buchkünstler, Mink Meadows Golf Club, East Chop Tennis Club (bd. dirs. 1970-72), Longwood Cricket Club. Home: 39 Cedarwood Rd Jamaica Plain MA 02130-3021 also: 1808 Par Pl Sarasota FL 34240

ZAHN, DONALD JACK, lawyer; b. Albany, N.Y., Oct. 24, 1941; s. Jerome and Clara (Zinsher) Z.; m. Laurie R. Hyman, Aug. 19, 1966; children: Lawrence, Melissa. AB, NYU, 1963; LLB, Union U., 1966; LLM in Taxation, NYU, 1967. Bar: N.Y. 1966, U.S. Dist. Ct. (no. dist.) N.Y. 1966, U.S. Tax Ct. 1969, U.S. Ct. Appeals (2d cir.) 1970, Tex. 1972, U.S. Ct. Appeals (5th and 11th cirs.). Assoc., Bond, Schoeneck and King, Syracuse, N.Y., 1967-71; ptnr. Haynes and Boone, Dallas, 1971-82, Akin, Gump, Strauss, Hauer & Feld, Dallas, 1982-92; assoc. prof. internat. taxation, fed. income taxation, bus. assns., corp. taxation Tex. Wesleyan Sch. Law, Irving, Tex., 1992—; adj. lectr. Baylor U. Sch. of Law Fed. Income Taxation, 1995; vis. prof. U. San Diego Sch. of Law Grad. Taxation Program, 1996, 97; adj. prof. Sch. Law, So. Meth. U., Dallas, 1972-87, 90-91. Trustee, sec. mem. exec. and fin. com., nominating com. Greenhill Sch., Addison, Tex., 1980-90; trustee, chmn. budget com., mem. fin. com. Jewish Fedn. Greater Dallas, 1978-89; trustee, chmn. Found. Jewish Fedn., Dallas, 1980-89; trustee, v.p., pres. Dallas chpt. Am. Jewish Com., 1980-92; mem. Tex. World Trade Council, 1986-87, Dallas Mayor's Internat. Com. Mem. State Bar Tex. (sec. 1982-83, chmn. tax sect. 1984-85, newsletter taxation sect. editor 1980-81), Internat. Bar Assn., Internat. Comte (N. Tex. commn.), Southwestern Legal Found. (adv. bd., treas. Internat. and Comparative Law Ctr., lectr. Acad. in Internat. Law), N.Y. State Bar Assn. Jewish. Office: Tex Wesleyan U Sch of Law 2535 E Grauwyler Rd Irving TX 75061-3410

ZAHN, TIMOTHY, writer; b. Chgo., Sept. 1, 1951; s. Herbert William and Marilou (Webb) Z.; m. Anna L. Romo, Aug. 4, 1979; 1 child, Corwin Jame. BA, Mich. State U., 1973; MA, U. Ill., 1975. Author: The Blackcollar, 1983, A Coming of Age, 1984, Cobra, 1985, Spinneret, 1985, Blackcollar: The Backlash Mission, 1986, Cobra Strike, 1986, Triplet, 1987, Deadman Switch, 1988, Cobra Bargain, 1988, Warhorse, 1990, Heir to Empire, 1991, Dark Force Rising, 1992, Star Wars: The Last Command, 1993, Conquerors' Pride, 1994, Conquerors' Heritage, 1995, Conquerors' Legacy, 1996; aso. sci. fiction short stories. Recipient Hugo award nomination for short story World Sci. Fiction Conv., 1983, Hugo award for best novella Cascade Point, 1984, Hugo award nomination short story, 1985. Office: c/o Bantam Books Inc 1540 Broadway New York NY 10036-4039

ZAHND, RICHARD HUGO, professional sports executive, lawyer; b. N.Y.C., July 22, 1946; s. Hugo and Rose (Genovese) Z.; m. Phyllis Beth Workman, Aug. 13, 1978; children: Andrew Richard, Melissa Dawn. A.B., NYU, 1968, J.D., 1971. Bar: N.Y. 1972. Assoc. Paul, Weiss, Rifkind, Wharton & Garrison, N.Y.C., 1971-74; staff atty. Madison Square Garden Corp., N.Y.C., 1974-75; v.p. legal affairs Madison Square Garden Center, Inc., N.Y.C., 1975-79; v.p., gen. counsel Madison Square Garden Corp., N.Y.C., 1979-86; v.p. N.Y. Knickerbockers Basketball Club, N.Y.C., 1979-86, N.Y. Rangers Hockey Club, N.Y.C., 1979-86; ptnr. Morrison & Foerster, N.Y.C., 1986-91; sr. v.p., gen. counsel NHL Enterprises, L.P., N.Y.C., 1992—. Served to capt. U.S. Army, 1972. John Norton Pomeroy scholar NYU Law Sch., 1969; Mortimer Bishop scholar NYU Law Sch., 1969; Judge Jacob Markowitz scholar NYU Law Sch., 1970; recipient Am. Jurisprudence prize NYU Law Sch., 1969. Episcopalian. Office: 1251 Ave Americas Fl 46 New York NY 10020

ZAHNER, MARY ANNE, art educator; b. Dover, Ohio, Mar. 30, 1938; d. Alfred James and Anna Elizabeth (Stewart) Riggle; m. Gordon Dean Zahner, Aug. 27, 1960 (dec. Mar. 1967); 1 child, Anne Colette; m. John Charles Opalek, Aug. 21, 1982. BFA, Ohio U., 1960, MA, 1969; PhD, Ohio State U., 1987. Cert. tchr., Ohio. Instr. art Springfield Twp. Schs., Akron, Ohio, 1960-61, Logan (Ohio) High Sch., 1961-62; instr. art Dover High Sch., 1967-68, chair art dept., 1969-71; teaching asst. Ohio State U., Columbus, 1980-82; from instr. art edn. to asst. prof. U. Dayton, 1971-80, asst. prof., 1982-91, assoc. prof., 1991—; mem. faculty rights, governance and svc. com. U. Dayton, 1992-93, mem. arts series com., 1995—, mem. Higher Edn. Steering Com. Ohio Dept. Edn., 1995, mem. exec. bd. Western Regional Profl. Devel. Ctr., 1996—; reviewer Harcourt, Brace, 1993-94, Prentice Hall Inc., 1996-97. Author: (chpt.) The History of Art Education: Proceedings from the Second Pa. State Conference, 1989; group exhibn. includes Westbeth Gallery, N.Y., 1995. Sec. Kettering (Ohio) Arts Coun., 1990, mem., 1988-93; mem. discretionary support com. Miami Valley Arts Coun., Dayton, 1992; coord. 3d congl. art contest sponsored by Tony P. Hall, Dayton, 1993, 94, 95; mem.-at-large edn. com. Culture Works: The Arts and Culture Alliance of the Miami Valley, 1996—; mem. exec. bd. Western Regional Profl. Devel. Ctr., 1996—. Recipient Best of Show award Canton Art Inst., 1969, Inst. Faculty award The Ohio Partnership for the Visual Arts, 1989. Fellow Ohio Art Edn. Assn. (mem. editl. bd. Ohio Art Edn. Jour. 1986—, editor newsletter Artline 1988, workshop coord. 1992, 97, cons. tchr. insvc. for Dayton Pub. Schs. 1995, Outstanding Art Tchr. western dist. 1992, 96); mem. ASCD, Nat. Art Edn. Assn., Assn. Tchr. Educators, Ohio Alliance for Arts Edn., Univ. Coun. for Art Edn., Phi Delta Kappa, Phi Kappa Phi, Delta Kappa Gamma. Democrat. Presbyterian. Avocations: music, theater, physical fitness. Home: 4429 Wilmington Pike Kettering OH 45440-1934 Office: U Dayton 114 Rike Ctr Dayton OH 45469-1690

ZAHRLY, JANICE HONEA, management educator; b. Ft. Payne, Ala., Sept. 27, 1943; d. John Wiley and Lillian (McKown) Honea. BA, U. Fla., 1964; MBA, U. Ctrl. Fla., 1980; PhD, U. Fla., 1984. Tchr. Hope Mills (N.C.) H.S., 1964-65, Satellite Beach (Fla.) H.S., 1965-69; realtor-assoc. WD Webb Realty, Melbourne, Fla., 1969-70; realtor Aero Realty, Melbourne, 1970-72, Albert J. Tuttle, Realtor, Melbourne, 1972-74; mktg. mgr. Cypress Woods Devel., Orlando, Fla., 1974-76; regional campaign mgr. Pres. Ford Com., 1976; ednl. researcher Peace Corps, Korea, 1976-78; rsch. analyst, tech. writer Rsch. Sys. Inc., Orlando, 1979-80; rsch. asst., lectr. U. Fla., Gainesville, 1980-84; asst. prof. Wayne State U., Detroit, 1984-89; assoc. prof. Old Dominion U., Norfolk, Va., 1989-94, U. N.D., Grand Forks, 1994—; mem. Melbourne Bd. Realtors, 1969-76, orientation chair, 1972, pub. rels. chair, 1973, civic affairs chair, 1973, grievance com., 1975; cons. Wayne County Retarded Persons Assn., Detroit, 1985, Gov.'s Conf. on Women Entrepreneurs, Mich., 1986, Oakland County AAUW Conf. on Women, Mich., 1987, 88, Coll. Bus. and Pub. Adminstrn. Inst. of Mgmt., Old Dominion U., Norfolk, 1990, U.S. Army Corps Engrs., Norfolk, 1990; presenter in field. Contbr. chpts. to books, articles to profl. jours. and procs. Vol. Tidewater AIDS Crisis Task Force, Norfolk, 1990-93, bd. dirs., 1990-92, v.p., 1991, rec. sec., 1992; mem. occupational adv. com. Brevard County Mental Health Ctr., Fla., 1973-74; mem. Brevard County Libr. Bd., 1973-74; bd. dirs. Fla. Dist. 12 Mental Health Bd., 1973-74, sec. 1973-74; bd. dirs. Alachua County Crisis Ctr., Gainesville, 1982-84, chair, 1983-84; vol. Open Door, Detroit, 1986-89; bd. dirs. United Way Grand Forks area, 1996—; pres. bd. dirs. Cherry Arms Condominium Assn., 1996—. Recipient Best Paper award Midwest Soc. for Human Resources/Indsl. Rels., 1989, F.W. Lawrence award U. N.D., 1996; rsch. fellow Fed. Mogul Corp., 1987-88; rsch. grantee Wayne State U., 1985-89, Old Dominion U., 1990, U. N.D., 1995, 96. Mem. AAUW (bd. dirs. 1974-75), Acad. Mgmt., Assn. for Rsch. on Nonprofit Orgns./Vols., So. Mgmt. Assn., Hampton Rds. Gator Club (co-founder, treas. 1989-91), Alpha Omicron Pi (bd. dirs. alumnae chpt. 1969-73, v.p. 1969-73). Avocations: travel, writing fiction, photography, music. Home: 3424 Cherry St Apt A1 Grand Forks ND 58201-7692

ZAHUMENY, JANET MAE, secondary education educator; b. Rahway, N.J., Mar. 23, 1945; d. Richard Evans and Elsie Mae (Walling) Franklin; m. Edward Zahumeny, Dec. 21, 1966 (div. 1987); 1 child, Carole Ann. BA, Newark State Coll., 1967; MEd, William Paterson Coll., 1990; MA, Kean Coll., 1994. Cert. secondary tchr., N.J. Math. tchr. Hunterdon Cen. High Sch., Flemington, N.J., 1967-68; math., computer tchr. Roselle Park (N.J.) High Sch., 1968—; instr. computers Roselle Park Adult Sch., 1987-88; instr. computer tech. William paterson Coll., 1992—, U. Calif., Berkeley, 1995—; cons. Gray's Appraisal, Cranford, N.J., 1987; textbook editor Prentice Hall, 1989; computer group asst. Bell Labs., Whippany, N.J., summers 1972-73; chmn. Dist. Computer Study Com., 1988; in-svc. tchr. tng., 1988—; 8th grade computer coord., 1988-89; mem. Mid. State Evaluation Team, 1972, 82, 85; liaison com. RPHS, 1985—, dist. tech. com., 1996—; cooperating tchr. Kean Coll., 1990—, Montclair State U.; adminstrv. asst. to v.p. Alpha Wire, summer 1991—; participant Computing Inst., 1983, Woodrow Wilson Inst., 1991, 96, NSF Inst., 1991; mem. Key Curriculum Press Profl. Devel. Team, 1993—; webmaster, Roselle Pk., N.J. Home Page, 1995—. Mem. Web Site editl. bd. William Paterson Coll. Inst. for Tech. in Math. Active Crandford PTA, Roselle Park PTSA; cons. Roselle Park Web Site. Named Outstanding Acad. Tchr., Cittone Inst., Edison, N.H., 1988, Outstanding Tchr., N.J. Gov.'s Recognition Program, 1989, Outstanding Computer/Math. Tchr. Tandy Techs., 1991; recipient Grad. Scholarship Kean Coll., Union, N.J., 1992, Computer Grant award 1993, Presdl. award for excellence in math. tchg., 1994, 95. Mem. NEA, Nat. Coun. Tchrs. Math., Assn. Math. Tchrs. N.J., N.J. Edn. Assn., Roselle Park Edn. Assn., N.J. Assn. for Ednl. Tech., WPC Inst. for Tech. in Math., Mensa, Kean Coll. Alumni Assn., William Paterson Coll. Alumni Assn., Cranford Mcpl. Alliance, Papermill Playhouse Theater Guild, Pi Lambda Theta, Kappa Delta Pi, Phi Kappa Phi. Avocations: computers, embroidering, sailing, bowling, bridge. Office: Roselle Park High Sch 185 W Webster Ave Roselle Park NJ 07204-1617

ZAIDI, IQBAL MEHDI, biochemist, scientist; b. Bijnor, India, June 30, 1957; s. Iqbal Haider and Habib (Zehra) Z.; m. Nuzhat Shikoh, Jan. 2, 1993; 1 child, Shan Zehra. BS in Chemistry with honors, Aligarh M. U., 1976, MS in Biochemistry, 1978, PhD in Biochemistry, 1984. Cert. in radiation. Rsch. fellow Indsl. Toxicology Rsch. Ctr., Lucknow, India, 1979-83; rsch. affiliate N.Y. State Health Dept., Albany, 1984-91; scientist Applied Biosystems div. Perkin Elmer Corp., Foster City, Calif., 1991—. Contbr. articles to profl. jours. Mem. AAAS, Am. Chem. Soc. (biochem. tech. div. 1992—), Shia Assn. Bay Area, N.Y. Acad. Scis. Avocations: photography, swimming, travel, natural history. Office: Perkin Elmer Corp Applied Biosystems Divsn 850 Lincoln Centre Dr Foster City CA 94404-1128

ZAILLIAN, STEVEN, screenwriter, director; b. Calif., Jan. 30, 1953. BA, San Francisco State U., 1975. Scripts include: The Falcon and the Snowman, 1985, Awakenings, 1990 (Acad. award nominee for best adapted screenplay, 1990), Jack the Bear, 1993, Schindler's List, 1993 (Acad. award best adapted screenplay 1993); co-writer (with Donald Stewart and John Milius) Clear and Present Danger, 1994; scriptwriter, dir.: Searching for Bobby Fisher, 1993.

ZAIMAN, JOEL HIRSH, rabbi; b. Chgo., Mar. 10, 1938; s. Solomon and Ruth (Levy) Z.; m. Ann Shanok, July 1, 1959; children: Elana Beth, Sarina, Ari Lev. BS, DePaul U., 1957; Master of Hebrew Letters, Jewish Theol. Sem., N.Y.C., 1962. Assoc. rabbi Temple Emanu-El, Providence, 1962-73, sr. rabbi, 1973-80; sr. rabbi Chizuk Amuno Congregation, Balt., Md., 1980—; pres. Balt. Bd. Rabbis, 1985-87; 1st v.p. Synagogue Coun. Am., 1988, pres., 1989-91. Contbr. articles to profl. jours. Chmn. edn. com. Solomon Schecter Day Sch., Balt., 1983; bd. dirs. Balt. Bd. Jewish Edn., Md. Commn. on Hereditary and Congenital Disorders, Assoc. Jewish Charities and Welfare Fund, Levindale Hebrew Geriat. Ctr. and Hosp., Balt., 1984—, long range planning com.; v.p. Balt. Jewish Coun., 1992-94, pres., 1994-96; chancellors rabbinic cabinet Jewish Theol. Sem.; bd. dirs., patient care adv. com. Sinai Hosp., 1991; bd. dirs., chmn. program com. Inst. Christian and Jewish Studies; adv. coun. Md. Health Care Decisions Act, 1994—. Fellow Pearlstone Inst. Jewish Living (program planning com.); mem. Rabbinical Assembly (exec. council, long range planning com.), United Synagogue Commn. Jewish Edn. (chmn.), Md. Jewish Hist. Soc. (bd. dirs.), Associated Jewish Fedn. Balt. (bd. dirs. 1991—). Home: 7912 Winterset Ave Baltimore MD 21208-3109 Office: Chizuk Amuno Congregation 8100 Stevenson Rd Baltimore MD 21208-1866

ZAIMAN, K. ROBERT, dentist; b. Cin., Oct. 19, 1944; s. Noboru Gary and Toshiko (Matsuyama) Z.; m. Kimberly Ann Sass, Nov. 6, 1976; children: Kara Jean, Matthew Robert. Student, Creighton U., Omaha, 1962-64, DDS, 1968. Asst. prof. Creighton U. Sch. Dentistry, Omaha, 1971-73, assoc. prof., 1973-75; pvt. practice dentistry Omaha, 1971—. Past v.p., bd. dirs. Japanese-Am. Citizens League, Omaha, 1977-86; mem. bd. elders King of Kings Luth. Ch., 1990-95. Lt. comdr. USN, 1964-71. Fellow Acad. Gen. Dentistry (pres. 1976-77, nat. del. 1971-76), Acad. Continuing Edn.; mem. ADA, Omaha Dist. Dental Soc. (treas. 1980-85, bd. dirs. 1968-92), Nebr. Dental Assn. (del. 1971—), Omaha Study Club (pres.), Delta Sigma Delta (pres. 1973-74). Office: 10841 Q St Ste 109 Omaha NE 68137-3543

ZAISER, KENT AMES, lawyer; b. St. Petersburg, Fla., June 10, 1945; s. Robert Alan and Marion (Brown) Z. AB Duke U., 1967; postgrad. U. Calif.-Berkeley, 1971; JD, U. Fla., 1972. Bar: Fla. 1973, U.S. Dist. Ct. (no. dist.) Fla. 1974, U.S. Supreme Ct. 1978, U.S. Dist. Ct. (so. dist.) Fla. 1980, U.S. Dist. Ct. (mid. dist.) Fla. 1981, U.S. Ct. Appeals (11th cir.) 1981. Rsch. aide Fla. Supreme Ct., Tallahassee, 1973-75, adminstrv. asst. to chief justice, 1975-76; asst. gen. counsel Fla. Dept. Natural Resources, Tallahassee, 1976-80; asst. atty. gen. Fla. Dept. Legal Affairs, Tallahassee, 1980-85; dep. gen. counsel S.W. Fla. Water Mgmt. Dist., Brooksville, 1985-89, gen. counsel, 1989-92; ptnr. Foley and Lardner, Tallahassee, 1992-93; prin. Kent A. Zaiser, P.A., Tallahassee, 1994—; cons. Fla. State Cts. Adminstr., Tallahassee, 1975. Contbg. author: Environmental Regulation and Litigation in Florida, 1980-84. Campaign chmn. Vince Fechtel for State Rep. of Fla., Leesburg, 1972. Mem. Tallahassee Bar Assn., Jefferson County Bar Assn. Democrat. Episcopalian. Club: Governors. Home: 3286 Longleaf Rd Tallahassee FL 32310-6406 Office: PO Box 6045 Tallahassee FL 32314-6045

ZAITZEFF, ROGER MICHAEL, lawyer; b. Detroit, June 25, 1940; s. Peter and Mary (Fedchenia) Z.; m. Amine Erma Wefali, Jan. 30, 1970; children: Zachary, Natasha, Zoe, Peter. BA with high honors and high distinction, U. Mich., 1962; MA with distinction, U. Calif., Berkeley, 1963, JD, 1969. Bar: N.Y. 1970, U.S. Dist. Ct. (so. dist.) N.Y. 1975, U.S. Ct. Appeals (2nd cir.) 1975, D.C. 1985. Assoc. Seward & Kissel, N.Y.C., 1969-77, ptnr., 1977-94; ptnr. Latham & Wakins, N.Y.C., 1994—. Contbr. articles to U. Fla. Law Rev., The Bus. Lawyer, Internat. Bus. Lawyer, Touro Law Rev., Internat. Tax and Bus. Lawyer, Nat. Law Jour. Mem. Tribar Opinion Com., 1990-93.

Heller grantee U. Mich., 1962. Mem. ABA, Internant. Bar Assn., Assn. of Bar of City of N.Y., N.Y. State Bar Found., Southwestern Legal Found. (adv. bd.), N.Y. County Lawyers Assn. (spl. com. legal opinions in comml. transactions), Phi Beta Kappa. Office: Latham & Watkins 885 3rd Ave New York NY 10022-4834

ZAJAC, JACK, sculptor, painter; b. Youngstown, Ohio, Dec. 13, 1929; s. John and Elizabeth Z.; m. Corda Eby, Sept. 19, 1956; children: Aaron John, Christian Rafael. Student, Scripps Coll., 1949-53, Am. Acad., in Rome, 1954-55, 57-58, 58-59. prof. art U. Calif., Santa Cruz. One-man shows include San Diego Mus., 1975, Pub. Gardens, Orveito, 1976; works shown in group exhbns. Pitts. Internat., 1955-65, Biennale di Roma, 1968, Stephen Wirtz Gallery, San Francisco, 1984, represented in permanent collections Mus. Modern Art, N.Y.C., Whitney Mus., Hirshorn Mus., Forum Gallery, N.Y.C.. Rome Prize fellow, 1954; Guggenheim fellow, 1959; Am. Acad. Arts and Letters grantee, 1958. Fellow Am. Acad. in Rome; mem. NAD.

ZAJAS, J. JONATHAN R., management consulting company executive, principal; b. Buffalo, Oct. 10, 1954; s. Michael A.A. and Janet J. (Rusch) Z. BA in Humanities, English, Bus. Edn., Canisius Coll. Buffalo, 1975; BS in Liberal Arts, SUNY, Albany, 1977; MA in Humanities, Philosophy, Ethics, Calif. State U., Dominguez Hills, 1976; MBA in Mgmt. and Mktg., U. Tex., Edinburg, 1979; D in Bus. Adminstrn. in Mgmt., Calif. Western U., 1980; MBA in Acctg., Tex. State U., Alpine, 1982; PhD, U. Wyoming, 1985; MA in Profl. Counseling, Liberty U. Va., 1993. Cert. personnel cons., Nat. Assn. Pers. Cons.; cert. profl. supt., prin./supr., Tex.; cert. sch. dist. adminstr., tchr., counselor, N.Y.; accredited prof. in human resources; cert. mediator, arbitrator, Better Bus. Bur.; mem. nat. panel arbitrators Am. Arbitration Assn. Tchr. bus., English N.Y. and Tex. Sch. Dists., 1974-80; city adminstr., CFO City of Port Isabel, Tex., 1979-81; asst. prof., MBA dir., chmn. bus. adminstrn. programs Sul Ross State U. Ctr., Alpine and Del Rio, Tex., 1981-86; from vis. assoc. to prof. mgmt. Mt. St. Mary Coll., Newburgh, N.Y., 1989-90; pres., dir., sr. cons. The Corp. Mgmt. Group, Del Rio and Nashville, 1984—; sr. prof. bus. adminstrn. U. Mary Hardin Baylor, Belton, Tex., 1992-94; sch. prin., dir. guidance Clymer (N.Y.) Ctr. Sch., 1994-96; mediator, arbitrator BBB Western N.Y., Jamestown, 1995—; mem. adv. bd. Future Bus. Leaders Am., Clymer, 1994—; sr. mgmt. cons., cons./advisor Border Fed. Credit Union, Del Rio, 1983-85; comml. arbitrator, mem. nat. panel arbitrators Am. Arbitration Assn., N.Y.C., Dallas, 1984-95. Author, editor: Our Moments of Time, 1979 (Excellence in Writing award 1980), A Comparative Analysis of Interpersonal Communication, Leadership and Motivational Styles Among C.E.O.'s, 1981, The Total Career and Life Portfolio: A Guide for Your Success, 1996, The Wee Little Pigs: An Economic Fable, 1997, Jeremy Brown's Womderful Surprise, 1997, The Pooch that Loves to Mooch, 1997; thers; co-author: (with O. Church) Applying Telecommunications and Technology from a Global Business Perspective, 1997 (Guest Editor's award 1995); author, editor: The Marketing of Executives & Career Development Success, 1995; spl. editor, Exec. Devel. jours., 1995; contbr. articles to profl. jours. Mem. adv. New Compact for Learning Coun., Clymer Ctrl. Sch. Dist. Wide Com., 1994—; co-chair, advisor to San Antonio chpt. Cert. Employee Benefits Specialist Bd., 1991; chair, co-chair econ. devel. coun. S.W. Tex. Comm. for Higher Edn., Del Rio, 1987-89; mem. adv. bd., chair fund raising com. Youth For Christ Ministry, Brownsville, Tex., 1978-80. Recipient Outstanding Martial Artist of Yr. award U.S. Profl. Martial/Artist Assn., 1975, Outstanding Tchr. of Yr. award U.S. Profl. Martial/Artist Assn., 1976, Master Tchrs. award for Leadership Excellence, Master Tchrs. Coun., 1995, Cert. of Appreciation for Leadership and Svc., Future Bus. Leaders Am., 1995, 96. Mem. Inst. Cert. Profl. Mgrs. (cert. profl. mgr.), Am. Assn. Christian Counselors (charter, profl., assoc.), Nat. Honor Soc., Phi Kappa Phi. Avocations: public speaking, creative writing, hiking, water sports, aerobics.

ZAJICEK, JERONYM, music educator; b. Krasne, Brezno, Czechoslovakia, Nov. 10, 1926; came to U.S., 1952; s. Frantisek Zajicek and Emilie (Lauterkranz) Zajickova. Student, Charles U., Prague, Czechoslovakia, 1946-49; MusB, Roosevelt U., 1957, MusM, 1958; studies with K.B. Jirak, Paul A. Pisk; PhD, Charles U., Prague, 1990. Music program dir. for Czechoslovak sect. Radio Free Europe, Munich, 1950-52; prof. theory and composition Loop Coll., Chgo., 1964-96. Composer numerous works including Clarinet Sonata, 1958, Sinfonietta for Large Orch., 1958, Cello Sonata, 1975; recorded Concertino for Flute and String Orch., 1963, Willie Schwegler Flute and Cologne Radio Orch., String Quartet, 1963, Pater Noster for mixed chorus, 1996, Sonatina for flute, clarinet and bassoon, 1996. Oliver Ditson fellow, 1956, 57; 1st prize Internat. Soc. for Contemporary Music (Chgo. chpt. 1964). Roman Catholic. Home: 4230 Prescott Ave Lyons IL 60534-1537 Office: Harold Washington Coll 30 E Lake St Chicago IL 60601-2403

ZAJONC, ROBERT B(OLESLAW), psychology educator; b. Lodz, Poland, Nov. 23, 1923; came to U.S., 1949, naturalized, 1953; s. Mieczyslaw and Anna (Kwiatkowska) Z.; m. Donna Benson, June 20, 1953 (div. 1981); children: Peter Clifford, Michael Anton, Joseph Robert; m. Hazel Markus, May 25, 1982; 1 child, Krysia Courcelle Rose. Ph.D., U. Mich., 1955; Dr. hon. causa, U. Louvain, 1984, U. Warsaw, 1989. Asst. prof. psychology U. Mich., 1955-60, assoc. prof., 1960-63, prof., 1963-94, Charles Horton Cooley Disting. prof. psychology, 1983-94, rsch. scientist Inst. for Social Rsch., 1960-83, dir., 1989; prof. psychology Stanford (Calif.) U., 1994—; directeur d'études Maison des Sciences de L'Homme, Paris, 1985-86; vis. prof. U. Oxford, 1971-72. Author: Social Psychology: An Experimental Approach, 1965; editor: Animal Social Psychology, 1970; assoc. editor: Jour. Personality and Social Psychology, 1960-66. Guggenheim fellow, 1978-79; Fulbright fellow, 1962-63; recipient Disting. Prof. award of social sci., 1983. Fellow AAAS (co-recipient Psychol. prize 1976), APA (Disting. Sci. Contbrn. award 1978), Japan Soc. Promotion of Sci., N.Y. Acad. Scis.; mem. Soc. for Exptl. Social Psychology (Disting. Scientist award 1986), Polish Acad. Scis. (fgn.). Office: Stanford U Dept Psychology Jordan Hall Stanford CA 94305

ZAK, ROBERT JOSEPH, lawyer; b. Steubenville, Ohio, July 29, 1946; s. Joseph and Pearl (Munyas) Z.; m. Kristy Hubbard Winkler, Sept. 13, 1980; children: Elizabeth Adele, Robert Joseph Jr., Barbara Ann. BS, W.Va. U., 1968, JD, 1975. Bar: W.Va. 1975, U.S. Dist. Ct. (so. dist.) W.Va. 1975, U.S. Dist. Ct. (no. dist.) W.Va. 1989, U.S. Ct. Appeals (4th cir.) 1990. Staff atty. Pub. Svc. Commn. of W.Va., Charleston, 1975-76; assoc. Preiser & Wilson L.C., Charleston, 1976-81, ptnr., 1981-85; sr. ptnr. Zak & Assocs., Charleston, 1985—; hearing examiner W.Va. Bd. Regents, Charleston, 1987-90; spl. asst. atty. gen. State of W.Va., Charleston, 1980-87; chmn. civil svc. commn. City of Charleston, 1987-90; mem. State of W.Va. Worker's Compensation Appeals Bd., Charleston, 1991—. With U.S. Army, 1969-71, Vietnam. Fellow Am. Acad. Matrimonial Lawyers; mem. Order of Barristers. Republican. Presbyterian. Office: Zak & Assocs 607 Ohio Ave Charleston WV 25302-2228

ZAKANITCH, ROBERT RAHWAY, artist; b. Elizabeth, N.J., May 24, 1935; s. Andrew and Mary Z. Student, Newark (N.J.) Sch. Fine and Indsl. Art, 1954-57. vis. artist, lectr. Sch. Art Inst. Chgo., 1976, U. Calif., San Diego, 1974; lectr. numerous univs. One man shows include Henri Gallery, Alexandria, Va., 1965, Reese Palley Gallery, N.Y.C., 1970, 71, Cunningham Ward, N.Y.C., 1973, 74, Holly Solomon Gallery, N.Y.C., 1977, Robert Miller Gallery, N.Y.C., 1978, 79, 81, 84, 85, 88, Galerie Liatowitsch, Basel, Switzerland, 1978, Galerie Rudolf Zwirner, Cologne, Fed. Republic Germany, 1979, Daniel Templon Gallery, N.Y.C., 1980, Bruno Bischofberger Gallery, Zurich, 1980, James Mayor Gallery, London, 1981, Marcus Gallery, 1984, Inst. Contemporary Art, Phila., 1981, Akira Ikeda Gallery, Nagoya, Japan, 1981, Daniel Templon Gallery, Paris, 1982, 87, 91, McIntosh-Drysdale Gallery, Washington, 1983, Harcus Gallery, Boston, 1984, 87, 89, Delahunty Gallery, Dallas, 1984, Helander/Rubinstein Gallery, Palm Beach, Fla., 1985, 89, Asher Faure Gallery, L.A., 1985, Yares Gallery, Scottsdale, Ariz., 1987, Sidney Janis Gallery, N.Y.C., 1990, Jason McCoy Gallery, N.Y.C., 1994, 1995 (John Simon Guggenheim fellowship grant), Guild Hall, East Hampton, N.Y., 1995, Hirschl & Adler, N.Y.C., 1995, others; group shows include Franklin Gallery, Cornell U., 1978, Va. Mus. Fine Arts, 1979, Palais des Beaux-Arts, Brussels, 1979, Inst. Contemporary Art, U. Pa., 1979, New Mus., N.Y., 1979, Galerie Daniel Templon, Paris, 1980, Nat. Gallery Art, Washington, 1980, Indpls. Mus. Art, 1980, San Francisco Art Inst., 1980, Whitney Mus. Am. Art, N.Y., 1981, Jacksonville Art Mus., 1981, Galeria Civica, Italy, 1982, Mus. Fine Arts, Boston, 1982, Fay Gold Gallery, Atlanta, 1982, High Mus. Art, Atlanta, 1983, Meml. Art Gallery, Rochester, N.Y., 1983, Kuntsmus., Luzern, 1983. Served with U.S. Army, 1958-60. John Simon Guggenheim fellowship grant, 1995. Studio: 119 N 11th St Brooklyn NY 11211

ZAKARIAN, ALBERT, lawyer; b. Pawtucket, R.I., May 3, 1940; m. Barbara Ann Zakarian, May 28, 1967; children: Adam, Dana. BA, Trinity Coll., 1962; LLB, Columbia U., 1965. Bar: Conn. 1965, U.S. Dist. Ct. Conn. 1965, U.S. Ct. Appeals (2nd cir.) 1971. Assoc. Day, Berry & Howard, Hartford, Conn., 1968-75, ptnr., 1975—; panelist Conn. Alt. Disp. Resolution, Ctr. for Pub. Resources, 1988—; co-chair Fed. Spl. Masters Program for Dist. of Conn. . Contbr. articles to profl. jours. Mem. town com. Simsbury (Conn.) Dems., 1974-86; chmn. Simsbury Human Rels. Commn., 1985. Capt. JAGC USAF, 1965-68, Vietnam. Decorated Bronze Star. Fellow Am. Coll. Trial Lawyers, Am. Bar Found.; mem. Nat. Bd. Trial Advocacy, Am. Bd. Trial Advs. (pres. Conn. chpt. 1997—), Conn. Bar Assn. (chmn. civil justice sect. 1979-82, fed. judiciary com.), Hartford County Bar Assn. (pres. 1985-86). Democrat. Office: Day Berry & Howard Cityplace Hartford CT 06103

ZAKARIAN, JOHN J., journalist; b. Jerusalem, Oct. 26, 1937; came to U.S., 1957; s. Ivan and Arsha (Aghabekian) Z.; m. Kay Holder, Sept. 14, 1963; children—Paul, David. B.S. in Journalism, So. Ill. U., 1961; M.A. in Mass Communication, U. Iowa, 1965. Reporter AP, Chgo., 1961; reporter Register-Mail, Galesburg, Ill., 1962-64; legis. corr., editorial editor Lindsay-Schaub Newspapers, Decatur, Ill., 1965-69; assoc. editor Herald Traveler, Boston, 1970-71; editorial writer Post-Dispatch, St. Louis, 1971-77; editor editorial page Hartford Courant, Conn., 1977—. Named Alumnus of Yr., So. Ill. U., Carbondale, 1972; recipient Walker Stone Editorial Writing award Scripps-Howard Found., Cin., 1984, 1st prize for Editls. New England Associated Press, 1986, Citation for Excellence Overseas Press Club Am., 1987, Tom Wallace award for Interpretative Commentary Inter Am. Press Assn., 1989; Nieman fellow Harvard U., 1968-69, Am. Leadership Forum, Fellow, founder Hartford and Houston, 1984-85. Mem. Nat. Conf. Editorial Writers (pres. 1976), Am. Soc. Newspaper Editors (mem. internat. press com.). Mem. Armenian Orthodox Ch. Avocations: tennis; chess; gardening; mountain climbing. Office: Hartford Courant 285 Broad St Hartford CT 06115-2500*

ZAKHEIM, DOV SOLOMON, economist, government official; b. Bklyn., Dec. 18, 1948; s. Zvi Hirsh and Bella (Rabinowitz) Z.; BA summa cum laude, Columbia U., 1970; student London Sch. Econs., 1968-69; DPhil, Oxford U., 1974; m. Barbara Jane Portnoi, Aug. 20, 1972 (div. 1990); children: Keith Samuel, Roger Israel, Scott Elisha; m. Deborah Bing Lowy, May 26, 1991. Rsch. fellow St. Antony's Coll., U. Oxford, Eng., 1974; asst. to mng. dir. U.K. br. Internat. Credit Bank Geneva, 1974-75; asso. analyst Nat. Security and Internat. Affairs, Congl. Budget Office, Washington, 1975-78, prin. analyst, 1978-81; spl. asst. to asst. sec. def. (internat. security policy) Dept. Def., 1981-82, spl. asst. to under sec. def. (policy), 1982-83; asst. under sec. def. (policy and resources), 1983-85; dep. undersec. def. for planning and resources, 1985-87; exec. v.p. System Planning Corp., Arlington, Va., 1987-90, corp. v.p., 1990—; CEO SPC Internat. Inc., 1988—; cons. to sec. def. and under sec. def. (policy), 1987-93, ABC News, 1991; adj. prof. Nat. Def. U., 1992, Columbia U., 1995-96, Yeshiva U., 1995-96; guest lectr. War Coll., others. Contbr. articles to profl. jours. V.p. S.E. Hebrew Congregation, Silver Spring, Md., 1978-80; bd. dirs. Yeshiva H.S. of Greater Washington, 1979-82, Young Israel Shomrai Emunah, 1983-85; hon. bd. dirs. Hebrew Acad. of Greater Washington, 1980-82; bd. deps. of Brit. Jews, 1971-72; mem. Chief Rabbi's Chaplaincy Bd., U.K., 1971-72; mem. U.S. Commn. for Preservation of Am.'s Heritage Abroad, 1991-95. Recipient Dirs.'s Award for outstanding svc. Congressional Budget Office, 1979, Disting. Pub. Service medal, Dept. Def., 1986, Bronze Palm to Disting. Pub. Svc. medal Dept. Def. 1987; NSF fellow, 1970-73; Columbia Coll. Kellett fellow, 1974. Mem. Council Fgn. Relations, Internat. Inst. Strategic Studies, U.S. Naval Inst., Royal Inst. Internat. Affairs (U.K.), Soc. Govt. Economists, Phi Beta Kappa. Club: Columbia, Capitol Hill, United Oxford and Cmbridge U. Contbr. articles to profl. jours. Home: 817 Lamberton Dr Silver Spring MD 20902-3038 Office: System Planning Corp 1500 Wilson Blvd Arlington VA 22209-2404

ZAKI, ABDELMONEIM EMAM, dental educator; b. Cairo, Egypt, Dec. 18, 1933; came to U.S., 1959; naturalized, 1976; s. Emam Badr El Din and Fatima Hussein (Kamel) Z. DDS, Cairo U., 1955, MS in Radiology, 1958; MSc in Dentistry, Ind. U., Indpls., 1962; PhD in Anatomy, U. Ill., Chgo., 1969. Dental surgeon Demonstration Tng. Ctr., Qalyb, Egypt, 1955-59; instr., then asst. prof. Cairo U., 1962-67; rsch. asst., assoc. U. Ill., Chgo., 1967-69, asst. prof., 1970-72, assoc. prof., 1972-75, prof. dentistry, 1975—, head dept. oral biology, 1994-96; sr. investigator, Nat. Inst. Dental Rsch., Bethesda, Md., 1981-82; cons., Cairo U., Alexandria U., Tanta U., all in Egypt, 1976—. Author: Human Dentition, 1965, rev. edit., 1967; contbr. numerous articles and abstracts to dental publs. Mem. Arab-Am. Anti-Discriminatin Com., Washington. Fellow Internat. Coll. Dentists; mem. Am. and Internat. Assns. Dental Rsch. (officer Chgo. chpt. 1982-97), Am. Assn. Anatomists, Electron Microscope Soc. Am., N.Y. Acad. Scis., Chgo. Acad. Sci., Egyptian-Am. Club Chgo., Arab Am. Univ. Grads., Chgo. Health Club, Sigma Xi. Moslem. Office: U Ill Chgo 801 S Paulina St Chicago IL 60612-7210

ZAKIM, DAVID, biochemist; b. Paterson, N.J., July 10, 1935; s. Sam and Ruth (Sorokin) B.; m. Nancy Jane Levine, June 12, 1957 (div. 1976); children: Michael, Eric, Thomas; m. Dagmar Auralia Stanke, July 30, 1978; children: Tamara, Robert. AB in Chemistry, Cornell U., 1956; MD summa cum laude, SUNY, Bklyn., 1961. Diplomate Am. Bd. Internal Medicine. Intern N.Y. Hosp., N.Y.C., 1961-62, asst. resident, 1962-63, fellow, 1963-65; asst. prof. to prof. medicine and pharmacology U. Calif., San Francisco, 1968-83; Vincent Astor Disting. prof. medicine Cornell U. Med. Coll., N.Y.C., 1983—; prof. biochemistry Cornell U. Grad. Sch. Med. Sci., 1983—. Contbr. over 150 articles to profl. jours.; editor: Hepatology: A Textbook of Liver Disease, 1982, 3rd edit., 1996, Disorders of Acid Secretion, 1991; editor series: Current Topics in Gastroenterology, 1985; editor Gastroenterology Medicine Today, 1992—. Capt. U.S. Army, 1965-68. Named Disting. Alumnus, SUNY-Bklyn., 1986. Mem. Am. Assn. Physicians, Am. Soc. Biol. Chemists, Biophysics Soc. Achievements include patent on fusion of proteins with lipid vesicles; demonstration of the lipid-dependence of UDP-glucuronyl transferase; elucidation of mechanism for uptake of fatty acids and bilirubin into cells. Home: 15 Cole Dr Armonk NY 10504-3004 Office: Cornell U Med Coll Medicine-Gastroenterology 1300 York Ave New York NY 10021-4805

ZAKIN, JACQUES LOUIS, chemical engineering educator; b. N.Y.C., Jan. 28, 1927; s. Mordecai and Ada Davies (Fishbein) Z.; m. Laura Pienkny, June 11, 1950; children: Richard Joseph, David Fredric, Barbara Ellen, Emily Anne, Susan Beth. B in Chem. Engring., Cornell U., 1949; MSChemE, Columbia U., 1950; DEng. Sci., NYU, 1959. Chem. engr. Flintkote Research Labs., Whippany, N.J., 1950-51; research technologist, research dept. Socony-Mobil, Bklyn., 1951-53, sr. research technologist, 1953-56, supervising technologist, 1959-62; assoc. prof. chem. engring. U. Mo., Rolla, 1962-65; prof. U. Mo., 1965-77, dir. minority engring. program, 1974-77, dir. women in engring. program, 1975-77; chmn. dept. chem. engring. Ohio State U., Columbus, 1977-94, Helen C. Kurtz prof. chem. engring., 1994—; chmn. sci. manpower and resources com. Coun. Chem. Rsch., 1984-86, mem. governing bd., 1986-89; exec. com., 1988-89; mem. adv. bd. State of Ohio Alternative Fuels, 1992-93; vis. prof. Technion, 1968-69, 94-95, Hebrew U., 1987. Co-editor: Proc. Turbulence Symposium, 1969, 71, 73, 75, 77, 79, 81, 83; contbr. articles to profl. jours.; patentee in field. Mem. bd. dirs. Rolla Community Concert Assn., 1966-77, 2d v.p., 1975-77; bd. dirs. Ozark Mental Health Assn., 1976-77; trustee Ohio State Hillel Found., 1981-84, treas., 1984-89, pres., 1989-92; trustee Congregation Beth Tikvah, 1983; bd. trustees Columbus Jewish Fedn., 1989-92; co-chmn. Academics and Scientists for Soviet Refuseniks. With USNR, 1945-46. Recipient Outstanding Rsch. award U. Mo., 1970, Josef Hlavka Meml. medal Czechoslovakian Acad. Sci., 1992, Clara M. and Peter L. Scott Faculty award for excellence in engring. edn., 1996; named Outstanding Educator of Yr., Ohio Soc. Profl. Engrs., 1994, Tech. Person of Yr., Columbus Tech. Coun., 1987; Am. Chem. Soc. Petroleum Rsch. Fund Internat. fellow, 1968-69, Socony-Mobil Employee Incentive fellow NYU, 1956-59, Sr. Fulbright Rsch. fellow Technion, 1994-95. Fellow Am. Inst. Chem. Engrs.; mem. Am. Chem. Soc., Soc. of Rheology, Am. Soc. Engring. Edn., Sigma Xi, Phi Lambda Upsilon, Phi Eta Sigma, Alpha Chi Sigma, Tau Beta Pi, Phi Kappa Phi. Jewish. Patentee in field. Office: Ohio State U 140 W 19th Ave Columbus OH 43210-1110

ZAKKAY, VICTOR, aeronautical engineering educator, scientist; b. Baghdad, Iraq, Sept. 8, 1927; came to U.S., 1946, naturalized, 1956; s. Haron and Massouda Isac (David) Zakkai. B.Ae.E., Poly Inst. Bklyn., 1952, M.Ae.E., 1953, Ph.D.Ae.E., 1959. Research assoc. prof. Poly Inst. Bklyn., 1962-64; assoc. prof. aeronautics NYU, Bronx, 1964-65, prof. aero. and astron. engring., asst. dir. Aero. Lab., 1965-73; prof. applied sci., dir. Antonio Ferri Labs. NYU, Westbury, N.Y., 1973, 75—; chmn. dept. applied sci. NYU, N.Y.C., 1977-84, Astor prof. aero. sci., 1980—; cons. TRW Environ. Engring., Research Triangle Park, N.C., 1980-81, Advanced Tech. Labs., Westbury, 1977-81, b.v. Neratoom, The Hague, Netherlands, 1981—. Editor: (with Olfe) Supersonic Flow, Chemical Processes and Radiation Transfer, 1963; contbr. articles to profl. jours. Mem. AIAA, Sigma Xi, Tau Beta Pi, Sigma Gamma Tau. Home and Office: NYU Barney Building 34 Stuyvesant St New York NY 10003-7506

ZAKSHESKE, MARK RICHARD, treasurer; b. Erie, Pa., Apr. 16, 1956; s. Vernon F. and Ruth M. (Merski) Z.; m. Heidi Widmar, July 18, 1981; children: Jennifer, Joseph, Julia. BS, John Caroll U., 1978; MBA, Loyola Coll., 1993. CPA, Ohio. Internal auditor Ameritrust, Cleve., 1978-79, Eaton Corp., Cleve., 1979-80; sr. internal auditor Marshall Field, Cleve., 1980-81; contr. Standard Products Co., Goldsboro, N.C., 1981-88, Haskell of Pitts., Verona, Pa., 1988-90, Stone Indsl., College Park, Md., 1990-95; treas. Precision Products Group, Inc., Rockford, Ill., 1995-96; CFO Modern Metal Products Co., Rockford, 1996—. Treas. Our World Underwater, 1996—. Mem. Fin. Mgmt. Assn., KC (warden 1988-94). Republican. Roman Catholic. Avocations: scuba diving, running. Home: 7241 Sentinel Rd Rockford IL 61107-5503 Office: Modern Metal Products Co 726 Beacon St Loves Park IL 61111-5904

ZALAZNICK, SHELDON, editor, journalist; b. Bronx, N.Y., Aug. 6, 1928; s. Samuel and Esther Leah (Schneiderman) Z.; m. Vera Altobelli, Apr. 4, 1953; 1 dau., Andrea. B.A., Univ. Coll. N.Y. U., 1948; M.A., Tchrs. Coll. Columbia, 1950. Tchr. English Benjamin Franklin High Sch., N.Y.C., 1950-52; assoc. editor Newsweek mag., 1952-56; v.p. Manning Pub. Relations Co., 1956-59; sr. editor Forbes mag., 1959-63, mng. editor, 1976-89; founding editor New York mag. sect. N.Y. Herald Tribune, N.Y.C., 1963-64; Sunday editor N.Y. Herald Tribune, 1964-66; staff writer Gen. Learning Corp., 1966-67; assoc. editor Fortune mag., 1967-69; v.p., editorial dir. New York mag., 1969-76. Home: 458 W 246th St Bronx NY 10471-3330

ZALDASTANI, GUIVY, business consultant; b. Tbilisi, Republic of Georgia, Nov. 1, 1919; arrived in Paris, 1925, came to U.S., 1948, naturalized 1953; s. Soliko and Mariam (Hirsely) Z.; m. Meredeth Fowler, May 1956 (div. Jan. 1982); children: Nicholas, Tamara, Nina; m. Micheline de Bievre, May 12, 1984; 1 child, Brian O'Connell. License en Droit, Sorbonne U., Paris, 1945, Diplome d'Etudes Superieures en Droit, 1946; MBA, Harvard U., 1951. Dept. mgr., buyer Federated Dept. Stores, Boston, 1957-62; pres. Finishing Touch, Boston, 1962-80, Ryan & Elliott Internat. Real Estate, Boston, 1980-83, Zaldastani Cons., Boston, 1982—; vis. prof. Tbilisi Tech. U. Editor Voice of Free Georgia, 1951-65, Iveria, 1970-80, periodical in Georgian lang. Cons. Ho. of Reps. crimes of Krushchev, 1960; pres. Georgian Youth Assn., Paris, 1942-47; charter mem. Rep. Presdl. Task Force, Washington, 1980; co-chmn. Harvard Bus. Sch. Reunion, Cambridge, 1961, 76, 86, 96. Served to lt. French Marines, 1940-41. Elected Hon. Citizen, Rep. Georgia, 1997. Mem. Georgian Assn. in U.S. (pres. 1966-74, bd. dirs. 1974-95), Harvard Club (N.Y.C. and Boston), Sommerset Club (Boston), Harvard Faculty Club (Boston), Cercle de l'Union Interalliée (Paris), Univ. Club (Boston). Republican. Avocations: piano, reading, travel. Home: 85 E India Row Apt 12F Boston MA 02110-3397

ZALDASTANI, OTHAR, structural engineer; b. Tbilisi, Republic of Georgia, Aug. 10, 1922; came to U.S., 1946; naturalized, 1956; s. Soliko Nicholas and Mariam Vachnadze (Hirsely) Z.; m. Elizabeth Reily Bailey, June 22, 1963; children: Elizabeth, Anne, Alexander. Diplome D'Ingenieur, Ecole Nationale des Ponts et Chaussees, Paris, 1945; Licencie es Scis., Sorbonne, Paris, 1946; MS in Geotech. Engring., Harvard U., 1947, DSc in Aerodynamics, 1950. Registered profl. engr., Mass., R.I., Tenn., Mo., N.H. Mem. faculty Harvard U., Cambridge, Mass., 1947-50; ptnr. Nichols, Norton and Zaldastani, Boston, 1952-63; pres. Nichols, Norton and Zaldastani, Inc., Boston, 1964-76, Zaldastani Assocs., Inc., Boston, 1976-88, chmn., 1988—; Gordon McKay vis. lectr. structural mechanics Harvard U., 1961; trustee, 1st v.p. Mass. Constrn. Industry Bd., 1973-76; mem. Mass. Designer Selection Bd., 1976-80. Contbg. author: Advances in Applied Mechanics, vol. 3, 1953. Patentee sound absorbing block, prestressed concrete beam and deck system. Trustee Wheelock Coll., Boston, 1975-81, mem. corp., 1984—; trustee Boston U. Med. Ctr., 1976—; trustee Brooks Sch., North Andover, Mass., 1986—. Recipient awards from various orgns. and agys. including Prestressed Concrete Inst., Cons. Engrs. Coun. New Eng., Am. Inst. Steel Constrn., Concrete Reinforcing Steel Inst., Dept. Transp., Am. Concrete Inst. Fellow ASCE (Ralph W. Horne award), AIAA (assoc.), Am. Concrete Inst.; mem. Georgian Assn. in the U.S. (pres. 1958-65), Sigma Xi, Harvard Club, Harvard Faculty Club (Cambridge), Somerset Club (Boston), Country Club (Brookline, Mass.), Rolling Rock Club (Ligonier, Pa.). Home: 70 Suffolk Rd Chestnut Hill MA 02167 Office: Zaldastani Assocs Inc 7 Water St Boston MA 02109-4511

ZALESKI, BRIAN WILLIAM, chiropractor; b. Trenton, N.J., Oct. 27, 1962; s. Joseph Rudolph and Roseline (Moore) Z.; m. Petra Gertrude Tucker, Apr. 10, 1983; children: Natasha Reneé, Tatyana Amber. Student, Def. Lang. Inst., Monterey, Calif., 1980-81; BS, Palmer Coll., 1992, D of Chiropractic, 1992. Indsl. disability evaluator, Calif.; qualified med. evaluator, Calif. Grad. rschr. Palmer Coll. of Chiropractice, Davenport, Iowa, 1991-92; chiropractor Peninsula Spinal Care, Daly City, Calif., 1992; chiropractor Creekside Family Chiropractic, Vacaville, Calif., 1992—, Suisun City, Calif., 1996—; prin. investigator, presenter Internat. Conf. on Spinal Manipulation, 1992. Editor Napa Solano Chiropractor, 1996—. Baseball umpire Iowa High Schs., Davenport, 1989-92, Men's Sr. League, Davenport, 1989-91, No. Calif. Umpires Assn., San Mateo, Calif., 1992; mem. adv. bd. Solano Serve Our Srs. Recipient scholarship Internat. Chiropractors Assn., 1989, 90, Cecil M. Grogan scholarship Palmer Internat. Alumni Assn., 1991, Alma Nielsen scholarship Internat. Chiropractors Assn. Aux., 1991, Student Rsch. grant Palmer Coll. Chiropractic, 1992; named to Dean's List, 1991-92. Mem. Internat. Chiropractors Assn. (coun. on chiropractic pediatrics), Calif. Chiropractic Assn. (net masters com., ins. rels. com., webmaster home pages sect.), Assn. for History of Chiropractic, Palmer Internat. Alumni Assn., Napa/Solano Chiropractic Soc. (pres., editor), Masons, Delta Sigma Chi, Chi Rho Theta. Republican. Office: Creekside Family Chiropractic 3000 Alamo Dr Ste 108 Vacaville CA 95687-6345 also: Creekside Family Chiropractic 411 Main St Ste C Suisun City CA 94585

ZALESKI, JAMES VINCENT, electronics executive; b. Kenosha, Wis., Oct. 8, 1943; s. Louis Edward and Lena Louise (Bellotti) Zalewski; m. Beverly Rae Neumann, Nov. 8, 1969. BBA, U. Wis., 1966, BSME, 1966, MS, 1967. Project engr. AC Electronics div. GM, Milw., 1968-73; ops. mgr. Applied Computer Sci., Inc., Milw., 1970-72; sect. mgr. Delco Electronics div. GM, Santa Barbara, Calif., 1973-84, dept. mgr., 1984-85, chief engr., 1985-87; pres., chief exec. officer Vetronix Corp., Santa Barbara, Calif., 1984—; chief exec. officer Vetronix Japan, Ltd., Kawagoe, Japan, 1990—; pres., chief exec. Vetronix Sales Corp., Santa Barbara, CA, 1997—; pres., CEO Vetronix Sales Corp., 1997—. Contbr. articles to profl. jours.; patentee in field. Named Entrepreneur of Yr. Greater L.A. Inc. mag., 1995. Mem. Soc. Automotive Engrs., Evans Scholars Assn., Mensa. Avocation: backpacking. Office: Vetronix Corp 2030 Alameda Padre Serra Santa Barbara CA 93103

ZALESKI, JAN FRANCISZEK, biochemist; b. Bytom, Poland, Feb. 3, 1949; came to U.S., 1979; s. Stanislaw and Maria (Fliska) Z.; m. Margaret M. Toczkowska, Dec. 28, 1971; children: Marta, Monika. MS in Biochemistry, U. Warsaw, Poland, 1971, PhD in Biochemistry, 1978. Rsch. assoc., asst. prof., assoc. prof. U. Warsaw Inst. Biochemistry, 1971-82; vis. scientist Roswell Park Meml. Inst., Buffalo, 1979-82; assoc. scientist Okla. Med. Rsch. Found., Oklahoma City, 1982-85; rsch. assoc. U. Pa. Med. Sch., Phila., 1985-88; vis. scientist Great Lakes Lab., Buffalo, 1988; rsch. assoc.

prof. Rutgers U. Sch. Pharmacy, New Brunswick, N.J., 1989—; cons. J.A. Haley Vets. Hosp., Tampa, 1985, Great Lakes Lab., Buffalo, 1988, Wyeth-Ayerst Rsch., Princeton, 1994. Contbr. articles to profl. jours., chpts. to books. Co-recipient awards Ministry Sci. and Higher Edn., Warsaw, 1978, Polish Acad. Scis., Warsaw, 1979. Mem. Internat. Soc. Study of Xenobiotics, Am. Soc. Biochemistry and Molecular Biology. Avocations: antique and modern prints collecting, photography, basketball, gardening. Office: Rutgers U Lab Cell & Biochem Toxicology 41 Gordon Rd Piscataway NJ 08854-5945

ZALESKI, JEAN, artist; b. Birkirkara, Malta; d. John M. and Carolina (Micallef) Busuttil; children: Jeffrey, Philip, Susan. Student, Art Students League, N.Y.C., 1955-58, New Sch., N.Y.C., 1967-69, Moore Coll. Art, Phila., 1970-71, Parsons Sch. Design, N.Y.C., 1974-75, Pratt Inst., N.Y.C., 1976-77. Dir. art Studio 733, Great Neck, N.Y., 1963-67; sr. art instr. Hussian Coll. Art, Phila., 1970-71; dir. Naples (Italy) Art Studio, 1972-74; corp. sec. Women in The Arts, N.Y.C., 1974-75, exec. coord., 1976-78; adj. lectr. Bklyn. Coll., 1974-75, Hofstra U., 1977-82, Cooper Union, 1986—. One-woman shows include: Adelphi U., 1975, Women in Arts Gallery, N.Y.C., 1975, Il Gabbiano Gallery, Naples, 1973, Wallnuts Gallery, Phila., 1971, Neikrug Gallery, N.Y.C., 1970, Alonzo Gallery, N.Y.C., 1979, 80, Va. Ctr. for Creative Arts, Sweet Briar, 1981, Hodgell Galleries, Sarasota, Fla., 1982, 83, Elaine Starkman Gallery, N.Y.C., 1986, Romano Gallery, Barnegat Light, N.J., 1987, 88, Citicorp Ctr., N.Y.C., 1988-89, Z Gallery, N.Y.C., 1991, Sweet Briar Coll., Va., 1993, Trinity Coll., Hartford, 1996; group exhbns. include Art U.S.A., N.Y.C., 1969, Internat. Art Exhbn., Cannes, France, 1969, Frick Mus., Pitts., 1970, NAD, N.Y.C., 1970-71, Phila. Mus. Art, 1971, Am. Women Artists, Palazzo Vecchio, Florence, 1972, Internat. Women's Arts Festival, Milan, Italy, 1973 (Gold medal), Bklyn. Mus., 1975, Sweet Briar Coll., 1977, CUNY, 1978, Va. Ctr., 1988, Mus. Hudson Highlands, 1982, Pace U. Gallery, N.Y.C., 1982, Bayly Mus., Charlottesville, Va., 1986, Allbright Knox Mus., Buffalo, 1986, E. Starkman Gallery, N.Y.C., 1987, Nabisco, 1989, Queens Coll., N.Y., 1991-92, Mus. City of N.Y., 1993; author: Winged Spirits, 1995; co-author COW/LINES, 1983; represented in permanent collections N.Y. Pub. Library, Met. Mus. Art, Va. Ctr. for Creative Arts, Nat. Mus. Women in Arts, Mus. of City of N.Y., Nat. Mus. Malta; vis. artist, critic various colls. and univs., 1976—. Ragdale fellow, 1986—, Va. Ctr. for Creative Arts fellow, 1976-96, Tyrone Guthrie Ctr. fellow, 1991; grantee NEA, 1982, Artists Space, 1988; recipient Susan B. Anthony award NOW, 1986. Mem. Artists Equity, Women in the Arts, Manhattan Pl. Health Club. Democrat. Roman Catholic. Avocations: music, theater, writing.

ZALEZNIK, ABRAHAM, psychoanalyst, management specialist, educator; b. Phila., Jan. 30, 1924; s. Isadore and Anna (Appelbaum) Z.; m. Elizabeth Ann Aron, June 24, 1945; children: Dori Faith, Ira Harry. AB in econs., Alma Coll., 1945, DLitt (hon.), 1992; MBA, Harvard U., 1947, DCS, 1951; grad., Boston Psychoanalytic Soc. and Inst., 1965. Research asst. Harvard U. Grad. Sch. Bus. Adminstrn., 1947-48, instr., 1948-51, asst. prof., 1951-56, assoc. prof., 1956-61, prof., 1961—, Cahners-Rabb prof. social psychology of mgmt., 1967-83, Konosuke Matsushita prof. leadership, 1983-90, Konosuke Matsushita prof. leadership emeritus, 1990—; research fellow Boston Psychoanalytic Soc. and Inst., 1965-68, mem. faculty, 1972—; pvt. practice psychoanalysis Boston, 1968—; cons. to mgmt.; chmn. bd. King Ranch, Ogden Corp.; bd. dirs. Ardco, Inc., Timberland Co., Freedom Comms., Inc., Am. Greetings, Butchers, Inc., Grossman, Inc. Author: Human Dilemmas of Leadership, 1966, (with Manfred F.R. Kets de Vries) Power and the Corporate Mind, 1975, The Managerial Mystique, 1989, An Executive Guide to Motivating People, 1990, Learning Leadership, 1992; contbr. articles to profl. jours. Trustee Beth Israel Hosp., Boston, 1968—. Served with USN, 1942-46. Mem. Boston Psychoanalytic Soc., Am. Psychoanalytic Assn. (cert.), Am. Sociol. Assn., Tavern Club (Boston), Belmont Country Club (Mass.). Home: 170 N Ocean Blvd Palm Beach FL 33480 Office: Harvard University Business School Boston MA 02163 also: King Ranch Inc 2 Pennsylvania Plz New York NY 10121

ZALINSKI, EDMUND LOUIS GRAY, insurance executive, mutual funds and real estate executive, investor; b. Salt Lake City, Aug. 18, 1915; s. Edward Robins and Agnes (de Schweinitz) Z.; m. Matilde Eleanor Mittendorf, July 15, 1939; children: Nancy Zalinski Johnson, Matilde Zalinski Davidson, Susanne Zalinski Williams. AB, Cornell U., 1937; MBA, Harvard, 1938; PhD summa cum laude, NYU, 1944. Mgr. sales offices N.Y. Life Ins. Co., 1938-47, asst. v.p., 1951-52, 2d v.p., 1953-54, v.p., 1954-55; instr. NYU, 1944-46; 1st mng. dir. Life Underwriter Tng. Coun., 1947-51, founder, life trustee, 1947-97; exec. v.p. Nat. Assn. Life Underwriters, 1949-51; v.p., chmn. agy. com. John Hancock Mut. Life Ins. Co., Boston, 1955-57; pres., CEO Life Ins. Co. N.Am., 1957-71; pres, dir. INA Life Ins. Co. N.Y., 1968-72; v.p., dir. INA Properties, Inc., INA Trading Corp., Phila. Investment Corp.; dir., chmn. exec. com. Bryn Mawr Trust Co., 1963-88; chmn. Greit Realty Trust, 1966-79; bd. dirs. leasing cos.; bd. dirs. Transwall Corp., B.G. Balmer Co., Integra Life Scis. Corp.; mem. adv. coun. Underwriter Edn. and Tng., 1947-50, Joint Com. on Mmgt. Tng., 1948-51; mem. rsch. adv. com. Life Inst. Agy. Mgmt. Assn., 1951-57; Huebner Found. lectr. Am. Coll., Bryn Mawr, Pa., 1956; mem. vis. com. Grad. Sch. Bus. Adminstrn., Harvard Coll., NYU; trustee Am. Coll. Life Underwriters, 1954-72, chmn. mgmt. edn. com., 1957-72, also chmn. devel. com.; treas., founder, chmn. Life Underwriters Tng. Coun., 1947—, life trustee, 1968—. Author publs. relating to field. Trustee, mem. exec. com., v.p. Phila. Mus. Art, 1965-72; bd. dirs. Bur. Mcpl. Rsch., Phila.; bd. dirs., chmn. exec. com. Pa. Economy League, 1963-72. Recipient Huebner Gold Medal award for professionalism in fin. edn. and tng. Am. Coll., 1993. Mem. Life Inst. Assn. Am. (dir. 1970-72), Ins. Fedn. Pa. (dir., chmn. 1970-72), Newcomen Soc., Loyal Legion, SAR, Cornell Club Phila. (dir.), Harvard Bus. Sch. Club Phila. (past pres.), Merion Cricket Club, Palmbrook Country Club. Home: 100 Grays Ln Apt 401 Haverford PA 19041-1754 also: 9701 W Sandstone Dr Sun City AZ 85351-2058 Office: 410 Lancaster Ave Haverford PA 19041-1329

ZALINSKY, SANDRA H. ORLOFSKY, school counselor; b. Elizabeth, N.J., July 11, 1959; d. Marion E. (Carrajat) Orlofsky; m. Thomas J. Zalinsky, Apr. 12, 1985. BA in Math. & Sci. Edn., Glassboro State Coll., 1981; MA in Adminstrn., Jersey City State Coll., 1985, MA in Counseling, 1990; EdD in Child & Youth Studies, Nova Southeastern U., 1994. Nat. cert. sch. counselor; master addictions counselor. Sr. cam counselor Brick (N.J.) Recreation Dept., 1978-81; tchr. high sch. math. and sci. Brick (N.J.) Twp. Bd. Edn., 1981-88; counselor, cons. pvt. agys., Ocean County, N.J., 1988—; counselor high sch. Brick Twp. Bd. Edn., 1988—; dept. head guidance Brick Twp. H.S., 1995—; speaker in field. Mem. ASCD (nat. cert. counselor), N.J. Counseling Assn., N.J. Sch. Counselors Assn., N.J. Edn. Assn. (sch. rep. 1981—), Skippers Cove Yacht Club, Phi Delta Kappa. Avocations: sailing, scuba diving, photography, tennis, travel. Home: 20 Davey Jones Way Waretown NJ 08758-2106 Office: Brick Twp Bd Edn 101 Hendrickson Ave Brick NJ 08724-2574

ZALIOUK, YUVAL NATHAN, conductor; b. Haifa, Israel, Feb. 10, 1939; s. Israel Nahum and Ahuda (Nathanson) Z.; m. Susan Marlys Davies, May 5, 1972; children: Eyal, Adam, Tamar. LL.B., Hebrew U., Jerusalem, 1964; student, Rubin Acad. Music, Jerusalem, 1960-63, Guildhall Sch. Music, London, 1965-67. Founder YZ Enterprises, Inc., Maumee, Ohio; apptd. music dir., condr. Raanana Symphonette Orch., Israel, 1996. Condr. Royal Ballet of London, 1966-70; music dir. Opera Studio, Paris, 1973-74, Haifa Symphony, 1975-77; interim chief condr. Edmonton (Alta., Can.) Symphony Orch., 1980-81; music dir., condr. Toledo Symphony Orch., 1980-89, condr. laureate, 1989—; music dir., condr. Raanana Symphonette Israel, 1996—. Recipient 1st prize Am.-Israel Cultural Found. Competition, 1965; 2d prize Internat. Condrs. Competition, Besancon, France, 1966; 1st prize Internat. Condrs. Competition, Besancon, 1967; 1st prize for progressive programming ASCAP, 1984, Entrepreneur of Yr. award, 1992; winner Mitropoulos Condrs. Competition, N.Y.C., 1970. Jewish. Club: Rotary. Office: YZ Enterprises Inc 1930 Indian Wood Cir Maumee OH 43537-4001*

ZALK, ROBERT H., lawyer; b. Albert Lea, Minn., Dec. 1, 1944; s. Donald B. and Juliette J. (Erickson) Z.; m. Ann Lee Anderson, June 21, 1969; children: Amy, Jenna. BA, Carleton Coll., 1966; JD, U. Minn., 1969. Bar: Minn. 1969, U.S. Dist. Ct. Minn. 1969. Atty. Popham, Haik, Schnobrich, Kaufman & Doty, Mpls., 1969-72, No. States Power Co., Mpls., 1972-73, Wright, West & Diessner, Mpls., 1973-84, Fredrikson & Byron P.A., Mpls., 1984-94, Zalk & Assocs., Mpls., 1994-95, Zalk & Eayrs, Mpls., 1995—. Fellow Am. Acad. Matrimonial Lawyers bd. mgrs. Minn. chpt. 1989-92), Minn. State Bar Assn. (co-chmn. maintenance guideline com. 1991-94), Hennepin County Bar Assn. (co-chmn. family law sect. 1990-91). Office: Zalk & Eayrs PA Sunset Ridge Bus Park 5861 Cedar Lake Rd S Minneapolis MN 55416-1481

ZALL, PAUL MAXWELL, retired English language educator, consultant; b. Lowell, Mass., Aug. 3, 1922; s. Nathan and Bertha (Rubin) Z.; m. Elisabeth Weisz, June 21, 1948; children: Jonathan, Barnaby, Andrew. BA, Swarthmore Coll., 1948; AM, Harvard U., 1950, PhD, 1951. Teaching fellow Harvard U., 1950-51; instr. Cornell U., 1951-55, U. Oreg., 1955-56; research editor Boeing Co., 1956-57; asst. prof. Calif. State Coll., Los Angeles, 1957-61; asso. prof. Calif. State Coll., 1961-64, prof. English, 1964-86; research scholar, cons. to library docents Huntington Library, San Marino, Calif., 1986-96; acting chmn. dept. Calif. State Coll., 1969-71; cons. in report writing, proposal preparation and brochures to industry and govt. agys., 1957—. Author: Elements of Technical Report Writing, 1962, Hundred Merry Tales, 1963, Nest of Ninnies, 1970, Literary Criticism of William Wordsworth, 1966, (with John Durham) Plain Style, 1967, Simple Cobler of Aggawam in America, 1969; (with J.R. Trevor) Proverb to Poem, 1970, Selected Satires of Peter Pindar, 1971, Comical Spirit of Seventy Six, 1976, Ben Franklin Laughing, 1980; (with J.A.L. Lemay) Autobiography of Benjamin Franklin, 1981; (with Leonard Franco) Practical Writing, 1978, Norton Critical Edition of Franklin's Autobiography, 1986, Abe Lincoln Laughing, 1983, 95; (with E. Birdsall) Descriptive Sketches, 1984, Mark Twain Laughing, 1985, Being Here, 1987, George Washington Laughing, 1989, Franklin's Autobiography: Model Life, 1989, Founding Mothers, 1991, Becoming American, 1993, Lincoln's Legacy, 1994, Wit and Wisdom of the Founding Fathers, 1996, Blue and Gray Laughing, 1996. Pres. Friends of South Pasadena Library, 1967-70. Served with USAAF, 1942-45, ETO. Am. Philos. Soc. fellow, 1964, 66; John Carter Brown Libr. rsch. grantee, Huntington Libr. rsch. grantee, fellow, 1993. Home: 1911 Leman Ln South Pasadena CA 91030-4628 Office: Huntington Libr San Marino CA 91108

ZALL, ROBERT ROUBEN, food scientist, educator; b. Lowell, Mass., Dec. 6, 1925; s. Samuel and Sarah (Cohen) Z.; m. Mollie Leah Wiseblood, June 8, 1949; children—Linda Zall Sheffield, Judy Zall Kusek, Jonathan J. B.S., U. Mass., 1949, M.S., 1950; Ph.D., Cornell U., 1968. Gen. mgr. Grandview Dairies, Bklyn. and Arkport, N.Y., 1950-66; dairy industry cons. Ithaca, N.Y., 1966-68; dir. research prodn. Crowley Foods Co., Binghamton, N.Y., 1968-71; prof. food sci. Cornell U., 1971-92; prof. emeritus, 1992—; past trustee Milk Industry Pension and Welfare Fund; dairy industry cons., project dir. EPA-Industry demonstration whey processing plant. Author: (with Bela G. Liptak) Environmental Engineers Handbook, 1972; co-contbr. to Food Processing Waste Management, 1979, Food Processing, 15 vols., 1979, Dairy Microbiology, 1981, rev. edit., 1990; contbr. numerous articles to profl. jours., popular mags. Served with AUS, 1944-46. Recipient Cert. Appreciation EPA, 1975, 79; Howard B. Marlott award N.Y. State Milk and Food Sanitarians. Mem. Internat. Assn. Milk, Food and Environ. Sanitarians, Internat. Dairy Fedn., Inst. Food Technologists, Am. Soc. Agrl. Engrs., Masons, Phi Kappa Phi. Patentee automatic cleaning apparatus, stabilization of milk and improved cheese yield, Rennin-like enzymes from clams, a process for preserving fish and microbial production of acetaldeyde. Home: 54 Woodcrest Ave Ithaca NY 14850-6241 Office: Cornell U Dept Food Sci Stocking Hall Ithaca NY 14853-7201 *Most people I know, never made a success of themselves by just working forty hours a week. It takes hard work, the love of a good wife, and the willingness to accept challenges.*

ZALLEN, HAROLD, corporate executive, scientist, former university official; b. Boston, Apr. 7, 1926; s. Joseph and Lillian L. (Stahl) Z.; m. Eugenia Malone, Aug. 23, 1959. BS in Pharmacy, Northeastern U., Boston, 1951; EdM in Sci. and Math., Boston U., 1954; MS in Organic Synthetic Medicinal Chemistry, Purdue U., 1959, PhD in Analytical Medicinal Chemistry and Nucleonics, 1960. Registered pharmacist, Mass. With USAAF, 1943-46, combat flier, sgt. 487th bomb group, 839th bomb squadron; commd. 1st lt. U.S. Army, 1955, advanced through grades to col., 1986; ret.; mgr. Shoppers World Pharmacy, Inc., Framingham, Mass., 1951-53; asst. prof. phys. sci. Portia Law Sch. Calvin Coolidge Coll., Boston, 1952-54; tchr. physics and chemistry Natick (Mass.) High Sch., 1955-56; grad. instr., asst. radiol. control officer Purdue U., Lafayette, Ind., 1957-58; assoc. prof. chemistry Coll. Pharmacy Mercer U., Atlanta, 1960-61; assoc. prof. to prof., head dept. radiol. scis., dir. Office Radiol. Safety Auburn U., Ala., 1961-66; specialist phys. sci. rsch. div. higher edn. rsch. Bur. Rsch., U.S. Office Edn., 1966-67, head curriculum higher edn. rsch., 1967; head instructional sci. equipment program, assoc. program dir., then dir. spl. projects program NSF, Washington, 1967-72; asst. dean, dir. rsch. and grad. studies Okla. State U., Stillwater, 1972-73, prof. chemistry, 1972-73, rsch. prof. biochemistry and molecular biology, 1973-75; assoc. v.p. for adminstrn. and fin., chief adminstrv. officer Health Scis. Ctr. Campus U. Okla., Oklahoma City and Tulsa, 1973-75; assoc. v.p. for systems planning, procedure devel. and spl. projects, cen. adminstrn. U. Okla., Norman, from 1975; exec. v.p. Acad. World Inc., 1975—; pres., CEO Malone, Zallen & Assocs. div. AcaWorld Corp., Greenville, N.C.; v.p., dir. nuclear div. Vachon, Nix & Assocs., Atlanta; pres., chief exec. officer Computer Profls. Inc., Computer Distbrs. Corp.; pres. Malone Group Internat., Columbus, Ga.; sci. advisor Litton Corp./Army Rsch. Inst. 1991, Omega Tng. Group Inc./GIAT Industries, France, 1992—, Wetzel Internat., Inc., 1994—; chmn. bd. dirs. Cons. Unltd., Columbus, Ga.; analytical chemist Communicable Diseases Ctr. USPHS, Atlanta, 1962; spl. lectr. Radiobiology Inst., NSF, 1963-64; mem. Pres.'s Sci. and Technol. Adv. Commn., Washington; bd. dirs. Internat. Sci. and Engring. Fairs, Sci. Svc., Inc., 1973-85; v.p. Okla. Coll. Osteo. Medicine and Surgery, Tulsa; cons. Okla. State Regents for Higher Edn.; Gov. N.C. primary alt. to So. States Energy Bd., 1984-90, mem. exec. com. bd., 1986; cons. in field. Author 4 books in field, 1986-89; editor, pub. Jour. Internat 6800 Computer Ctr.; contbr. numerous articles to profl. jours. Republican candidate N.C. Gen. Assembly, 1986. Recipient Mayoralty cert. of merit for outstanding svc. and Key to City, City of New Orleans, 1973, Most Outstanding Alumni award Northeastern U., 1996; GE sci. fellow Union U., Schenectady, NY., 1955, fellow Purdue Rsch. Found., 1958, Elks Cancer Soc., 1959, Am. Cancer Soc., 1960. Mem. Am. Chem. Soc. (bd. dirs., chmn. Auburn sect. 1966), Am. Soc. Engring. Edn. (long range planning com.), Nat. Coun. Univ. Adminstrs., Soc. Rsch. Adminstrs. (pres. So. sect. from 1974, chmn. publs. com.), Health Physics Soc., Greenville (N.C.) Area C. of C. (chmn. rsch.), Columbus Club, Rotary (chmn. bull. com. Auburn 1963, bd. dirs. Auburn 1964, bd. dirs. Stillwater 1972-73, Greenville 1981-86, charter pres. Greenville, N.C. Morning club 1986, Paul Harris fellow), MAsons (32 degree), Shriners, Sigma Xi, Phi Lambda Upsilon, Rho Chi, Phi Delta Kappa, Delta Sigma Theta, Beta Phi (past nat. sec.). Baptist. Office: Malone Group Internat PO Box 8767 Columbus GA 31908-8767

ZALOZNIK, ARLENE JOYCE, oncologist, army officer; b. Pitts., Jan. 30, 1948; d. Ernest and Frances Elizabeth (Augustin) Z. BS, Carlow Coll., 1969; MS, Duquesne U., 1972; MD, Med. Coll. Pa., 1976. Diplomate Am. Bd. Internal Medicine, Am. Bd. Oncology. Commd. U.S. Army, 1976, advanced through grades to col.; intern then resident in hematology and oncology Madigan Army Med. Ctr., Tacoma, 1976-77; fellow in hematology and oncology Fitzsimons Army Med. Ctr., Aurora, Colo., 1979-81, staff oncology, 1981-82, asst. chief med. oncology, 1982-84, chief hematology and oncology, 1984-86; chief hematology and oncology Brooke Army Med. Ctr., Ft. Sam Houston, Tex., 1986—; asst. dep. for health policy U.S. Army, Washington; clin. instr. dept. medicine U. Colo. Health Sci. Ctr., 1982-86. Contbr. articles to books and profl. jours. and publs. Active profl. edn. com. Aurora-Adams Unit Am. Cancer Soc., 1983-86, pres., 1983-86, also active Colo. div., 1984-86. Fellow ACP; mem. AMA, Am. Coll. Physician Execs., Am. Soc. Clin. Oncology, Assn. Mil. Surgeons. Home: 9808 Brixton Ln Bethesda MD 20817 Office: Office Asst Dep for Health Policy The Pentagon Rm 2E591 Washington DC 20130

ZALTA, EDWARD, otorhinolaryngologist, physician; b. Houston, Mar. 2, 1930; s. Nouri Louis and Marie Zahde (Lizmi) Z.; m. Carolyn Mary Gordon, Oct. 8, 1971; 1 child, Ryan David; children by previous marriage: Nouri Allan, Lori Ann, Barry Thomas, Marci Louise. BS, Tulane U., 1952, MD, 1956. Diplomate Am. Bd. Quality Assurance and Utilization Rev. Physicians. Intern Brooke Army Hosp., San Antonio, 1956-57; resident in otolaryngology U.S. Army Hosp., Ft. Campbell, Ky., 1957-60; practice medicine specializing in otolaryngology Glendora, West Covina and San Dimas, Calif., 1960-82; ENT cons. City of Hope Med. Ctr., 1961-76; mem. staff Foothill Presbyn.; past pres. L.A. Found. Community Svc., L.A. Poison Info. Ctr., So. Calif. Physicians Coun., Inc.; founder, chmn. bd. dirs. CAPP CARE, INC.; founder Inter-Hosp. Coun. Continuing Med. Edn.; mem. bd. trustees U.S. Pharmacopeial Convention, Inc. Author: (with others) Medicine and Your Money; mem. editorial staff Managed Care Outlook, AAPPO Jour., Med. Interface; mem. editl. adv. bd. Inside Medicaid Managed Care, Disease Management News; contbr. articles to profl. jours. Pres. bd. govs. Glendora Unified Sch. Dist., 1965-71; mem. Calif. Cancer Adv. Coun., 1967-71, Commn. of Californias, L.A. County Commn. on Economy and Efficiency. Served to capt. M.C. AUS, 1957-60. Recipient Award of Merit Order St. Lazarus, 1981. Mem. AMA, Calif. Med. Assn., Am. Acad. Otolaryngology, Am. Coun. Otolaryngology, Am. Assn. Preferred Provider Orgns. (past pres.), Am. Coll. Med. Quality, L.A. County Med. Assn. (pres. 1980-81), Kappa Nu, Phi Delta Epsilon, Glendora CountryClub, Centurion Club, Sea Bluff Beach and Racquet Club; Center Club (Costa Mesa, Calif.), Pacific Golf Club (San Juan, Capistrano). Republican. Jewish. Home: 3 Morning Dove Laguna Niguel CA 92677-5331 Office: West Tower 4000 Macarthur Blvd Ste 10000 Newport Beach CA 92660-2526

ZALUTSKY, MORTON HERMAN, lawyer; b. Schenectady, Mar. 8, 1935; s. Albert and Gertrude (Daffner) Z.; m. Audrey Englebardt, June 16, 1957; children: Jane, Diane, Samuel. BA, Yale U., 1957; JD, U. Chgo., 1960. Bar: Oreg. 1961. Law clk. to presiding judge Oreg. Supreme Ct., 1960-61; assoc. Hart, Davidson, Veazie & Hanlon, 1961-63, Veatch & Lovett, 1963-64, Morrison, Bailey, Dunn, Cohen & Miller, 1964-69; prin. Morton H. Zalutsky, P.C., 1970-76; ptnr. Dahl, Zalutsky, Nichols & Hinson, 1977-79, Zalutsky & Klarquist, P.C., Portland, Oreg., 1980-85, Zalutsky, Klarquist & Johnson, Inc., Portland, 1985-94; Zalutsky & Klarquist, P.C., Portland, 1994—; instr. Portland State U., 1961-64, Northwestern Sch. of Law, 1969-70; assoc. prof. U. Miami Law Sch.; lectr. Practising Law Inst., 1971—, Oreg. State Bar Continuing Legal Edn. Program, 1970, Am. Law Inst.-ABA Continuing Legal Edn. Program, 1973—, 34th, 37th NYU ann. insts. fed. taxation, So. Fed. Tax Inst., U. Miami Inst. Estate Planning, Southwestern Legal Found., Internat. Foun. Employee Benefit Plans, numerous other profl. orgns.; dir. A-E-F-C Pension Plan, 1994—. Author: (with others) The Professional Corporation in Oregon, 1970, 82; contbg. author: The Dentist and the Law, 3d edit.; editor-in-chief (retirement plans) Matthew Bender's Federal Tax Service, 1987—; contbr. to numerous publs. in field. Mem. vis. com. U. Chgo. Law Sch. Mem. ABA (vice chair profl. svcs. 1987-89, mem. coun. tax sect. 1987-89, spl. coord. 1980-85), Am. Law Inst., Am. Bar Retirement Assn. (trustee, bd. dirs., vice chair 1990-91, chair 1991-92), Multnomah County Bar Assn., Am. Tax Lawyers (charter mem.), Oreg. Estate Planning Coun. Jewish. Home: 3118 SW Fairmount Blvd Portland OR 97201-1466 Office: 215 SW Washington St Fl 3D Portland OR 97204-2636

ZAMAN, MUSHARRAF, civil engineering educator; b. Rajshahi, Bangladesh, Mar. 8, 1952; came to U.S., 1979; s. Md. Gias Uddin and Jahanara Begum; m. Afroza Khanam, Aug. 7, 1981; children: Jessica, Ashiq. MSCE, Carleton U., Can., 1979; PhDCE, U. Ariz., 1982. Registered profl. engr., Okla. Lectr. civil engring. U. Engring. and Tech., Dhaka, Bangladesh, 1975-76; rsch. assoc. Asian Inst. Tech., Bangkok, 1976-77; grad. tchg. asst. Carleton U., Ottawa, Can., 1977-79; rsch. asst. Va. Tech., Blacksburg, 1979-81; rsch. assoc. U. Ariz., Tucson, 1981-82; asst. prof. U. Okla., Norman, 1982-88, assoc. prof., 1988-93, prof., 1993—; faculty advisor Bangladesh Student Assn., U. Okla., Norman, 1983—, Muslim Student Assn., 1990—; summer faculty fellow Argonne (Ill.) Nat. Lab., 1986; v.p. geotech. Consortium Internat., Oklahoma City, 1992-94; co-organizer U.S.-Can. Geomechanics Workshop, 1992. Co-editor Internat. Jour. for Numerical and Analytical Methods in Geomechanics (application briefs); assoc. editor Jour. Petroleum Sci. and Engring.; contbr. articles to European Jour. Mechanics, Computer Methods in Applied Mechanics and Engring., Internat. Jour. Numerical Analytical Met. Geomech., Internat. Jour. Petroleum Sci. and Engring., Applied Math. Modelling, ASME Jour. Applied Mechanics, ASME Jour. Energy Resources Tech., Jour. Geotech. Engring. divsn. ASCE, Jour. Engring. Mechanics divsn. ASCE, Jour. Transp. Engring. divsn. ASCE, Arabian Jour. Sci. and Engring., Transp. Rsch. Record. Mem. ASCE (mem. deep found. com. 1987—), Internat. Assn. Computer Methods and Advances in Geomechanics (co-chmn. internat. conf. 1992-94, co-editor newsletter 1989—, mem. internat. adv. com. 9th conf., bd. dirs. 1996—), Am. Rock Mechanics Assn. (founding mem.). Home: 501 Starbrook Ct Norman OK 73072-4722 Office: U Okla 202 W Boyd St Rm 334 Norman OK 73019-1024

ZAMBIE, ALLAN JOHN, lawyer; b. Cleve., June 9, 1935; s. Anton J. and Martha (Adamski) Z.; m. Nancy Hall, Sept. 22, 1973. Student, Ohio U., 1953-54; B.A., Denison U., 1957; LL.B., Western Res. U. (now Case Western Res. U.), 1960. Bar: Ohio bar 1960. Asso. firm Hribar and Conway, Euclid, Ohio, 1961-63; staff atty. The Higbee Co., Cleve., 1963-67; asst. sec. The Higbee Co., 1967-69, sec., 1969-74, v.p.-sec., 1974-88, gen. counsel, 1978-88; v.p., sec., gen. counsel The Lamson & Sessions Co., Cleve., 1989-94; of counsel Conway, Marken, Wyner, Kurant & Kern Co., LPA, Cleve., 1994-95; v.p.-sec. John P. Murphy Found., Cleve., 1996—. Trustee Cleve Music Sch. Settlement, pres. bd. trustees, 1980-82, treas. 1996—; past trustee N.E. Ohio affiliate Am. Heart Assn., 1969-96. Served with AUS, 1960-61. Mem. Ohio Bar Assn., Cleve. Bar Assn., Am. Soc. Corporate Secs. (nat. v.p. 1977—). Home: 2953 Litchfield Rd Cleveland OH 44120-1738 Office: Terminal Tower Ste 924 Tower City Ctr Cleveland OH 44113-2203

ZAMBITO, RAYMOND FRANCIS, oral surgeon, educator; b. N.Y.C., Nov. 9, 1926; s. John and Lucy (Mecca) Z.; m. Dorothy M. Sikoryak, Apr. 23, 1960; children: Mary Lucille, Paul Michael, Christine Marie, John Raymond, Michael Sikoryak, Peter Ignatius. Student, Bklyn. Coll., 1943-44; B.S., U. Scranton, 1948; DDS, NYU, 1953, cert. in oral surgery, 1956; MA in Adminstrn. in Higher Edn., Columbia U., 1968, EdD, 1978; MBA in Health Care Mgmt., Adelphi U., 1978; DSc honoris causa, Seton Hall U., 1994. Diplomate Am. Bd. Oral and Maxillofacial Surgery. Intern in oral surgery Kings County Hosp. Ctr., Bklyn., 1956-57; resident in gen. anesthesiology Jewish Chronic Disease Hosp., Bklyn., 1957; resident in oral surgery and anesthesiology Cook County Hosp., Chgo., 1957-59; practice gen. dentistry Kings Park, N.Y., 1953-55, Chgo., 1958-59; oral surgery Bklyn., 1959-61, Williston Park, N.Y., 1961-66, N.Y.C., 1966-68, Jamaica, N.Y., 1968—; asst. dept. of oral and maxillo-facial surgery U. Ill. Coll. Dentistry, 1958-59; instr. Sch. of Dental and Oral Surgery, Columbia U., N.Y.C., 1961-66; chief of svc. in dept. dentistry St. Francis Hosp., Roslyn, N.Y., 1963-66; cons. in oral surgery and dental dept. adminstrn., 1975-85; asst. attending oral surgeon Kings County Hosp. Ctr., Bklyn., 1959-62; attending oral surgeon L.I. Jewish Med. Ctr., New Hyde Park, N.Y., 1962-71; asst. attending oral surgeon Queens Hosp. Ctr., Jamaica, N.Y., 1964-65; assoc. attending oral surgeon Elmhurst (N.Y.) Gen. Hosp. 1965-66; attending oral surgeon and dir. dentistry and oral surgery Lincoln Hosp., 1966-68; asst. prof. of dental surgery Albert Einstein Coll. of Medicine, Yeshiva U., 1966-68, asst. clin. prof., 1968-73; oral surgeon-in-charge Cath. Med. Ctr. of Bklyn., 1968—; cons. in oral and maxillo-facial surgery St. Joseph's Hosp. and Med. Ctr., Paterson, N.J., 1976—; asst. prof. dept. oral surgery and anesthesiology Fairleigh Dickinson U. Sch. of Dentistry, Hackensack, N.J., 1971-72, prof., 1972-89, coordinator dir. hosp. dentistry, 1972-89; adj. assoc. prof. of clin. pharmacy and dentistry Bklyn. Coll. of Pharmacy, 1976-77; cons. oral surgeon Suffolk State Sch., Melville, N.Y., 1965-71; dir. Spl. Dental Clinic for the Handicapped, Bur. of the Handicapped, Cath. Charities, Bklyn., 1973-75; mem. Cath. Med. Mission Bd., Mission OAAC Surgery, Dominican Rep., 1991—, summers 92-96. Co-editor: Hospital Dental Practice, A Manual, 1978, Immunology and Infectious Diseases of the Mouth, Head, and Neck, 1991, Manual of Dental Therapeutics, 1991; editor-in-chief Jour. Hosp. Dental Practice, 1973-80; contbr. articles on oral surgery and dental edn. to profl. jours. Lectr. Christian Life Communities movement to secondary schs. and colls., various states, 1962—; tchr. confrat. religious classes, 1964-85; mem. parish coun. St. Gertrude's Roman Cath. Ch., Bayville, N.Y., 1969-72, chmn., 1971-72; founder, chmn. Fedn. Lay Orgns., Diocese of Rockville Centre, 1968-72; pres. David Park Civic Assn., 1966-67; couns. Nat. Coun. Cath. Men, Washington, 1967-72. With USN, 1944-46, capt. Dental Corps, USNR ret. Decorated knight Order of Malta in U.S.; grantee HEW, 1967-70, 85-88. Fellow Am. Coll. of Dentists, Internat. Coll. Dentists, Am. Pub. Health Assn., Am. Dental Soc. of Anesthesiology, L.I. Acad. of Odontology; mem. Am. Soc. of Oral and Maxillofacial Surgeons, Am. Dental Assn. (mem. rev.

com. coun. on hosp. and instnl. dental svcs. 1975—, cons. coun. on dental edn. 1973—), N.Y. State Soc. of Oral Surgeons (alt. del. to Am. Soc. Oral Surgeons), Am. Acad. Oral Pathology, Am. Acad. of History of Dentistry, N.Y. State Dental Soc. of Anesthesiology (pres. 1964), Am. Assn. Of Hosp. Dentists, Cath. Dentists Guild (pres. 1955-56), Am. Hosp. Assn. (mem. coun. on profl. svcs. 1976-78), Am. Coll. Oral and Maxillo Facial Surgeons (v.p. 1976-79), Christian Med. Soc., Internat. Assn. of Oral Surgeons, Nat. Fedn. of Christian Life Communities (pres. nat. fedn. 1971-73), del. to internat. gen. assembly in Rome, 1967, Dominican Republic, 1970), Omicron Kappa Upsilon. Home: 603 Bayville Rd Locust Valley NY 11560-1207 Office: Cath Med Ctr Bklyn and Queens 88-25 153rd St Jamaica NY 11432-3731

ZAMBOLDI, RICHARD HENRY, lawyer; b. Kittanning, Pa., Nov. 22, 1941; s. Henry F. and Florence E. (Colligan) Z.; m. Maria Therese Reiser, Aug. 12, 1967; children: Elizabeth M., Richard H. Jr., Margaret B. BBA, St. Bonaventure U., 1963; JD, Villanova U., 1966. Bar: U.S. Dist. Ct. (we. dist.) Pa. 1966, Pa. 1968, U.S. Ct. Appeals (3d cir.) 1970, U.S. Supreme Ct. 1981. Law clk. U.S. Dist. Ct. (we. dist.) Pa., Pitts., 1966-67; atty. Nat. Labor Rels. Bd., Pitts., 1967-68; assoc. Kanehann & McDonald, Allentown, Pa., 1968-69; ptnr. Elderkin Martin Kelly Messina & Zamboldi, Erie, Pa., 1969-90; atty. Knox McLaughlin Gornall & Sennett, Erie, 1990—; Author (student articles) Villanova Law Rev., 1964-65, editor, 1965-66. Mem. Pa. Bar Assn., Erie County Bar Assn. Republican. Roman Catholic. Home: 6206 Lake Shore Dr Erie PA 16505 Office: Knox McLaughlin Gornall & Sennett 120 W 10th St Erie PA 16501-1410

ZAMBONE, ALANA MARIA, special education educator; b. Vineland, N.J., Sept. 17, 1952; d. L. Alan and Joyce (Bernero) Z. AB in Spl. Edn., U. N.C., Chapel Hill, 1974; MS in Human Devel. Liaison, George Peabody Coll. Tchrs., 1978; PhD in Spl. Edn., Vanderbilt U., 1984. Cert. spl. edn., visual impairments, mental retardation, N.C. Tchr., counselor Orange County Assn. for Retarded Citizens, Chapel Hill, N.C., 1973-74; lead tchr. Shelbyville-Bedford (Tenn.) County Adult Svc. Ctr., 1974; program coord. Dickson (Tenn.) County Adult Svcs., 1974-75; dept. head, habilitative svcs. CloverBottom Devel. Ctr., Nashville, Tenn., 1975-76; exec. dir. Waves, Inc. Adult Svcs., Fairview, Tenn., 1976-77; from vocat. cons. to liaison, Peabody Tchrs. Coll. Vanderbilt U., 1977-80; chairperson, bd. dirs. Residential Svcs., Inc., Nashville, 1976-80; asst. prof., coord., dept. curriculum N.C. State U., Raleigh, N.C., 1981-84; coord. and asst. prof., div. spl. edn. Minot (N.D.) State U., 1984-86; coord. internat. outreach svcs. Hilton-Perkins Internat. Program Perkins Sch. for the Blind, Watertown, Mass., 1989-94; assoc. prof., dir. Inst. for Visually Impaired Pa. Coll. Optometry, Phila., 1994—; nat. cons. Am. Found. for the Blind, N.Y.C., 1986-89; adj. asst. prof. div. spl. edn., Columbia U., 1987—; co-dir. model infant/toddler program, sch. medicine, U. N.C., Chapel Hill, 1983-84; bd. dirs. N.D. Coun. for the Arts; adv. bd. Blind Babies Found.; mem. adv. com. Robert E. Miller, Inc., Community Residential Svcs. for Disabled Children; bd. dirs. Specialized Svcs. for Children, Inc.; sch. edn. rep. to fac. N.C. State U., sch. edn. fac. sec., among others. Grantee Busch Found., N.D. Coun. Arts, Nat. Coun. on the Arts, Dean's Grant Program, Burlington/No. Found., Kate B. Reynolds Found., Nat. Rural Spl. Edn. Consortium, U.S. Office Human Devel. Svcs., U.S. Office of Spl. Edn. Mem. Council for Exceptional Children (past dir. div. visual handicaps), Assn. for Retarded Citizens, Assn. for Persons with Severe Handicaps, Am. Assn. Mental Deficiency, Am. Assn. for Applied Behavior Analysis, Nat. Assn. for Parents of the Visually Impaired, Internat. Assn. for the Edn. of the Deaf-Blind, Assn. for the Edn. and Rehab. of the Blind and Visually Impaired (pre-sch. div., multihandicaps div., chairperson elect multiple disabilities div.). Avocation: scuba diving. Office: Pa Coll Optometry 1200 W Godfrey Ave Philadelphia PA 19141-3323

ZAMBONI, HELEN ATTENA, lawyer, international telecommunications executive; b. Tuxedo, N.Y., Oct. 29, 1951; d. Frank Joseph and Janet Edwards (Johnson) Z.; m. Steve I. Rosen, Jan. 2, 1982. BA cum laude, Mount Holyoke Coll., 1973; JD cum laude, Syracuse U. Coll. of Law, 1977. Title officer Ticor Title Guarantee, Rochester, N.Y., 1977-79; assoc. atty. Underberg & Kessler, Rochester, 1980-82, Phillips, Lytle, Hitchcock et al, Rochester, 1982-83; corp. atty. Frontier Corp., Rochester, 1983-84; sr. corp. atty. Rochester Telephone, Rochester, 1984-85, mng. atty., 1985-93, acting gen. counsel, 1993-94, corp. counsel, 1994-96; pres. internat. ops., 1996—. Dir. YMCA of Greater Rochester, 1986—, Career Devel. Svcs., 1992—; mem. capital campaign com. Syracuse U. Coll. of Law, 1994—. Avocations: gardening, reading, old houses. Home: 25 Spring St Avon NY 14414-1330 Office: Frontier Corp 180 S Clinton Ave Rochester NY 14646-0001

ZAMECNIK, PAUL CHARLES, oncologist, medical research scientist; b. Cleve., Ohio, Nov. 22, 1912; m.; 3 children. AB, Dartmouth Coll., 1933; MD, Harvard U., 1936; DSc (hon.), U. Utrecht, 1966, Columbia U., 1971, Harvard U., 1982, Roger Williams Coll., 1983, Dartmouth Coll., 1988, U. Mass., 1994. Resident Huntington Meml. Hosp. Harvard U., Boston, MA, 1936-37; intern. U. Hosps., Cleve., Ohio, 1938-39; Moseley traveling fellow Carlsberg Labs. Harvard U., Copenhagen, 1939-40; Finney-Howell fellow Rockefeller Inst., 1941-42; instr., assoc. prof. Harvard U., 1942-56, Collis P. Huntington prof., 1956-79; dir. J.C. Warren Labs., 1956-79; chmn. exec. com. Dept. Medicine Harvard U., 1956-61; emeritus prof. oncological medicine Sch. Medicine, 1979—; prin. sci. Worcester Found. Experimental Biology, 1979—; physician Mass. Gen. Hosp., 1956-79, hon. physician, 1979—; vis. fellow dept. chemistry Calif. Tech. U., 1952; vis. Commonwealth scholar in chemistry U. Cambridge, 1962. Recipient Warren Triennial prize, 1946, 50, James Ewing award, 1962, Borden award, 1965, Am. Cancer Soc. Nat. award, 1968, Passano award, 1970, Nat. medal of sci. NSF, 1991, Hudson Hoagland award, 1992, City of Medicine award, Durham, N.C., 1995, Enterprize 2000 award City of Worcester, Mass., 1996, Lasker award, 1996. Mem. NAS, Am. Acad. Arts and Sci., Am. Soc. Biol. Chemists, Am. Assn. Cancer Rsch. (pres. 1964-65), Assn. Am. Physicians, Interurban Club, Peripatetic Club. Office: Worcester Found Exptl Biology 222 Maple Ave Shrewsbury MA 01545-2732

ZAMES, GEORGE DAVID, electrical engineer, educator; b. Poland, Jan. 7, 1934; s. Sam Simha and Leona Z.; m. Eva Eisenfarb, July 21, 1964; children: Ethan, Jonathan. B of Engring., McGill U., 1954; ScDEE, MIT, 1960. Asst. prof. MIT, 1960-65, Harvard U., 1962-63; sr. scientist NASA, Cambridge, Mass., 1965-71; vis. prof. Technion, Haifa, Israel, 1972-74; prof. elec. engring. McGill U., Montreal, 1974—, Macdonald chmn. elec. engring., 1983—. Assoc. editor So. Indsl. and Applied Math. Jour. on Control, 1968-84, Systems and Control Letters, 1981-84, Internat. Math. Assn. Jour. Math. Control and Info., 1983—, Math. of Control Signals and Systems, 1987—; editor at large Jour. Robust and Non-linear Control, 1990—; contbr. articles to profl. jours. Athlone fellow Imperial Coll., London U., 1954-56, Resident rsch. assoc. NAS, 1966-67, Guggenheim fellow, 1965-66, Killam fellow, 1984-86, Sr. fellow Can. Inst. Advanced Rsch., 1984—; recipient Brit. Assn. medal McGill U., 1954, Outstanding Paper award Am. Automatic Control Coun., 1968, classic Paper citation Inst. Sci. Info., 1981, Outstanding Paper award Control Sys. Soc., 1977, 80, 82, 86, Isaac Walton Killam prize for sci., Can., 1995, Rufus Oldenburger medal ASME, 1996. Fellow IEEE (Control Sci. Field award 1985), Royal Soc. Can. Home: 4996 Circle Rd, Montreal, PQ Canada H3W 1Z7 Office: McGill U Dept Elec Engring, 3480 University St, Montreal, PQ Canada H3A 2A7

ZAMIR, FRANCES ROBERTA (FRANCES ROBERTA WEISSSWEDE), principal; b. Bklyn., Nov. 6, 1944; d. Martin and Jean (Roskosky) Swede. BA in English, Calif. State U., Northridge, 1967, MA in Spl. Edn., 1975; MA in Ednl. Adminstrn., Calif. State U., L.A., 1987. Credential adminstrv. svcs., std. elem, spl. edn.-learning handicapped, Calif; cert. resource specialist. Childrens' ctr. tchr. L.A. Unified Sch. Dist., 1966-68, elem. tchr., 1968-76, spl. edn. tchr., 1976-80, resource specialist tchr., 1980-86, mentor tchr., 1984-86, program specialist/region advisor, 1986-90, asst. prin., 1990-96; owner, ptnr. Best Bet Ednl. Therapy/Tutoring Referral Svc., 1979-81; cons. Academics Plus Tutoring Referral Svc., 1984-86; asst. prof. resource specialist cert. program Calif. State U., Dominguez Hills, 1987-90; instr. early and regular edn. credential program UCLA, 1990—; mem. Cluster 5 Instructional Cabinet LAUSD, 1996—; mem. asst. prin. steering com. L.A. Unified Sch. Dist., Region C, 1992-93; adminstr. portfolio documentation subcom. Adminstrv. Tng. Acad., 1991; sch. site rev. coms. Calif. State Dept. Edn., 1985-87, ad hoc com. on quality indicators, 1985. Mem. Speakers Bur. Commn. on Jews with Disabilities, 1985-86, Assoc. Adminstrs. L.A. Rep. Coun., elem. asst. prin. rep., 1992-94; so. Calif. regional rep. Calif. Assn. Program Specialists, 1988-90. Mem. NEA, Assoc. Adminstrs., L.A. Rep. Coun. (elem. asst. prin. rep. 1992-94), Friends of Calif. State, Calif. Assn. Program Specialists (so. Calif. regional rep. 1988-90), Calif. Assn. Sch. Adminstrs. (spl. edn. com. L.A. chpt. 1985-86, 87-88), Calif. Assn. Resource Specialists (state v.p. and conf. chair 1993-94, state pres. 1984-85, bd. dirs. 1983-86), Calif. Tchrs. Assn., Women in Ednl. Leadership, Kappa Delta Pi, Phi Delta Kappa. Office: L A Unified Sch Dist 450 N Grand Ave Los Angeles CA 90012-2123

ZAMMIT, JOHN P., financial planner; b. N.Y.C., May 11, 1942; s. John G. and Farla (Rudolph) Z.; children: Karen M., Christine B. BA, Hunter Coll., 1972; MS, L.I. U., 1976; adminstrn. cert., Emporia U., 1979. Investigator Equifax, N.Y.C., 1965-67; agent N.Y. Life Ins. Co., N.Y.C., 1967-76; elem. sch. tchr. L.I., N.Y., 1976-77; elem. prin. Olpe, Kans., 1977-78, Buffalo, Minn., 1978-79; mgr. Kraun & Assocs., St. Paul, 1978-79; pres., owner Midwest Adv. Svc. Inc., St. Paul, 1979-95. Contbr. articles to profl. jours. With USMC, 1960-64. Avocations: public speaking, creative writing, investment club, psychology. Home and Office: Midwest Advisory Svc Ste 102 1028 Cherry Laurel Ln Dallas TX 75211-6820

ZAMMIT, JOSEPH PAUL, lawyer; b. N.Y.C., May 19, 1948; s. John and Farla (Rudolph) Z.; m. Dorothy Therese O'Neill, June 6, 1970; children: Michael, Paul, Brian. AB, Fordham U., 1968; JD, Harvard U., 1971; LLM, NYU, 1974. Bar: N.Y. 1972, U.S. Dist. Ct. (so. and ea. dists.) N.Y. 1973, U.S. Ct. Appeals (2d cir.) 1973, U.S. Supreme Ct. 1978, U.S. Dist. Ct. (no. dist.) N.Y. 1983, U.S. Ct. Appeals (11th cir.) 1987. Assoc. Reavis & McGrath, N.Y.C., 1971-74; asst. prof. law St. John's U., Jamaica, N.Y., 1974-76, assoc. prof., 1976-78; assoc. Reavis & McGrath, N.Y.C., 1978-79, ptnr., 1979-88; ptnr. Fulbright & Jaworski L.L.P. (formerly Fulbright Jaworski & Reavis McGrath), N.Y.C., 1989—; adj. assoc. prof. St. John's U., Jamaica, 1979-83, adj. prof., 1984—; mem. panel computer arbitrators Am. Arbitration Assn., N.Y.C., 1977—. Bd. editors Computer Law Strategist, 1987—; contbr. articles to profl. jours. Mem. ABA, N.Y. State Bar Assn., Assn. of Bar of City of N.Y. (chmn. com. on computer law 1995—, chmn. comml. liability subcom. 1981-87), Computer Law Assn., Phi Beta Kappa. Office: Fulbright & Jaworski LLP 666 5th Ave New York NY 10103-0001

ZAMMITT, NORMAN, artist; b. Toronto, Ont., Can., Feb. 3, 1931. AA, Pasadena City Coll., 1957; MFA, Otis Art Inst., Los Angeles. One-man shows include Felix Landau Gallery, L.A., 1962, 66, 68, L.A. County Mus. Art, 1977, Corcoran Gallery, Washington, 1978, Flow-Ace Gallery, 1984, Loma Linda U., Riverside, Calif., 1987, Elysium Studio 13, L.A., 1995, 96; included in group shows at L.A. County Mus. Art, 1987, Haags Gemeentemus. Arts, The Hague, 1987, Bronx Mus. Arts, N.Y., 1987, Ace Contemporary Exhbns., L.A., 1988; represented in permanent collections at Libr. of Congress, Corcoran Gallery, Nat. Gallery, Hirschhorn Collection, Washington, Mus. Modern Art, N.Y.C., L.A. County Mus. Modern Art, San Francisco Mus. Modern Art, Larry Aldrich Found. Mus., Conn., Rowland Inst. Sci., Cambridge, Mass., Seattle Art Mus., Stanford U. Hosp., Palo Alto, Calif.; also represented in pvt. collections. Guggenheim fellow, 1968; Pollock-Krasner grantee, 1991. Home: 233 N Wilson Ave Pasadena CA 91106-1422

ZAMORA, MARJORIE DIXON, retired political science educator; b. Farm Randolph, N.Y., Nov. 8, 1933; d. Wendell Hadley and Jessie (Mercer) Dixon; m. Cornelio Raul Zamora, Dec. 20, 1969; 1 child, Daniel Cornelio. BA, Earlham Coll., 1956; MA, U. Ill., 1968; postgrad., U. Ill., Chgo., 1989—. Tchr. Ridge, Sch., Godsman Sch., Stenson Sch., various cities, 1956-62; with U.S. Peace Corps, tchr. Palmares High Sch., Costa Rica, 1963-64; reporter Lerner Newspaper, Chgo., 1965; dormitory counselor U. Ill., Urbana, 1966-68, 86; instr. Chgo. City Coll., 1968-69; prof. polit. sci. Moraine Valley C.C., Palos Hills, Ill., 1969-94, prof. emeritus, 1994—; researcher, Univ. Ill., Chgo., 1985-88. Contbr. articles on Costa Rican polit. bus. cycle and economy, land reform to various publs. in U.S., Cen. Am. Campaign dir. Polit. State Legis., 1974-76. Mem. AAUW, Western Springs Bank and Orch. Assn. (pres. 1990-91), Am. Assn. Retired Persons, State Cmty. Coll. Retirees Assn., Kiwanis (LaGrange, Ill.). Mem. Soc. of Friends. Avocations: skiing, swimming, writing fiction, nonfiction, symphonic music, scuba. Home: 3820 Lawn Ave Western Springs IL 60558-1141

ZAMPARELLI, ELSA MARIA JOHANNA ELISABETH, costume designer, art director; b. Dec. 8, 1944; d. Jan Albertus and Maria Johanna (de Jeu) Van de Bovenkamp; m. Robert G. Zamparelli, Aug. 12, 1968 (div. Aug. 1985); m. Steve Kenneth Irish, Aug. 10, 1991; children: André, Mark, Alicia. Costume and set designer: (TV) The Bold and the Beautiful (Emmy award best set decoration 1993, 94); (films) Dances With Wolves (Acad. award nomination 1991), The Last of the Mohicans (Brit. Acad. award nomination 1992), Ace Ventura: When Nature Calls, 1995. Office: Smith Gosnell Nicholson & Assoc PO Box 1166 1515 Palisades Dr Pacific Palisades CA 90272

ZAMPIELLO, RICHARD SIDNEY, metals and trading company executive; b. New Haven, May 7, 1933; s. Sidney Nickolas and Louise Z.; B.A., Trinity Coll., 1955; M.B.A., U. Bridgeport, 1961; m. Helen Shirley Palsa, Oct. 10, 1961; 1 son, Geoffrey Richard. With Westinghouse Elec. Corp., Pitts., 1955-64; exec. v.p. Ullrich Copper Corp., subs. Foster Wheeler, Kenilworth, N.J., 1964-71; sr. v.p. Gerald Metals, Inc., Stamford, Conn., 1971-85; group v.p. Diversified Industries Corp., St. Louis, 1985-90; pres. Plume and Atwood Brass Mill div. Diversified Industries Corp., Thomaston, Conn., 1985-90; pres. Upstate Metals Corp., Canastota, N.Y., 1990—. Mem. ASME, Soc. Mfg. Engrs., AIME. Clubs: Yale, Mining (N.Y.C.); Lake Waramug Country (Washington, Conn.), Washington Country. Home: Woodbury Rd Washington CT 06793-1814 Office: 20 E Main St Waterbury CT 06702-2302

ZANAKIS, STEVE H., management science/information systems educator; b. Athens, Greece, Nov. 16, 1940; came to U.S., 1968; m. Helen Avagianou, 1968; children: Aliki, Christina, Helena. BS in Mech./Elec. Engring., Nat. Tech. U., Athens, 1964; MBA, Pa. State U., 1970, MS in Stats., 1972, PhD in Bus. Adminstrn., 1973. Registered engr., Greece. Indsl. engr. Greek Productivity Ctr., Athens, 1967-68; asst. prof. indsl. engring. and systems analysis W.Va. Coll. Grad. Studies, Charleston, 1972-76, assoc. prof. and dir. indsl. engring. and systems analysis, 1976-80; assoc. prof. mgmt. Coll. of Bus. Adminstrn. Fla. Internat. U., Miami, 1980-82, prof. and founding chmn. dept. decision scis. and info. systems, 1982-86, prof. decision scis. and info. systems., 1986—; cons. Union Carbide Corp., W.Va. Dept. Hwys., Charleston Area Med. Ctr., Key Pharm. Ryder, U.S. Acad. for Ednl. Devel.; instr. exec. mgmt. devel. programs, U.S., Europe, S.Am. Author: Production Operations Management Software for IBM, PC, 1989, Production Planning and Scheduling, 1984, Engineering Economy, 1975, Optimization in Statistics, 1983, Stat-ez: An Easy to Use Statistical Software, 1987, Decision Support System for Conflict Resolution and Strategy Selection, 1991, Decision Support System for Stock Market Trading & Portfolio Management; guest editor Mgmt. Sci. Jour., 1983, European Jour. Ops. Rsch., 1986; assoc. editor Decision Scis. Jour., 1990—; contbr. numerous articles to profl. jours. Recipient Fla. Bd. Regents Teaching award, 1994, Fla. Internat. U. Awards for excellence in research, 1993, teaching, 1991, outstanding achievement, 1990 and svc., 1986; State of Fla. Hwy. Adminstrn. Rsch. grantee, 1984-85, Fed. grantee, 1976-77. Mem. Inst. for Ops. Rsch. & Mgmt. Sci., Decision Scis. Inst., Tech. Chamber of Greece. Greek Orthodox. Office: Fla Internat U Dept Decision Scis/Info Sys Miami FL 33199

ZANARDELLI, JOHN JOSEPH, healthcare services executive; b. Monongahela, Pa., July 27, 1950; s. John and Linda (Lazzari) Z.; m. Suzanne King, Jan. 29, 1972; children: Brandon John, Stephen William, Robyn Lynn. AA, Community Coll. Allegheny Cty, Pitts., 1970; AS in Acctg., Community Coll. Allegheny Cty., Pitts., 1991; BS in Edn., California U. Pa., 1972; MPH, U. Pitts., 1979, cert. acct., 1994. Rsch. asst. grad. sch. pub. health U. Pitts., 1973-78; adminstrv. resident Ctrl. Med. Ctr. and Hosp., Pitts., 1978-79; vice chmn., sec., dir. Allegheny Mountain Health Enterprises, Inc, Oil City, Pa., 1985-88; exec. v.p. Oil City Area Health Ctr., Inc., 1979-88; exec. v.p., chief oper. officer Grane Healthcare, Inc., Pitts., 1988-90; adminstr., chief oper. officer Southwood Psychiat. Hosp., Inc., Pitts., 1990-91; exec. dir. Allegheny divsn. Presbyn. Sr.Care, Pitts., Pa., 1991-92; exec. dir., CEO, United Meth. Svcs. for Aging, 1993—; preceptor health adminstrn. program grad. schs. in pub. health and bus. U. Pitts., 1980—; pres. HCPP, Inc., Pitts., 1983—. Fellow Am. Coll. Healthcare Execs. Home: 2997 Greenwald Rd Bethel Park PA 15102-1615 Office: Asbury Heights 700 Bower Hill Rd Pittsburgh PA 15243-2040

ZAND, DALE EZRA, business management educator; b. N.Y.C., July 22, 1926; m. Charlotte Edith Rosenfeld, Oct. 16, 1949; children—Fern, Mark, Karen, Jonathan, Matthew. BEE, Cooper Union, 1945; MBA, NYU, 1949, PhD, 1954. Asst. to v.p. Spector Bags, 1947-49; v.p. Glo-Cold Co., 1949-50; mem. faculty N.Y. U. Stern Sch. Bus., 1950—, prof. mgmt., 1963—, chmn. dept., 1968—; cons. to industry, 1951—; Bd. dirs. Newfield Exploration Co., Nat. Tng. Labs. Inst. Applied Behavioral Sci. Author: Information, Organization, and Power, 1981, The Leadership Triad, 1997, also articles. Served with USNR, 1945. Ford Found. fellow, 1959-60. Mem. Am. Psychol. Soc., Inst. Mgmt. Sci., Acad. Mgmt., Internat. Assn. Applied Social Scientists. Office: NYU Stern Sch Bus 40 W 4th St # T7 16 New York NY 10012-1106

ZANDE, RICHARD DOMINIC, civil engineering firm executive; b. Battle Creek, Mich., Apr. 29, 1931; s. Dominic and Maria O. (Bombassei) Z.; m. Marilyn Sue Love, Feb. 15, 1958; children: Michael, Michelle, Brent, Patrick. BSCE, Mich. State U., 1955. Registered profl. engr. Ohio, Fla., Ky., W.Va., Mich., Pa., Ind., Ill., N.J., S.C. Prin. Martin & Zande, Columbus, Ohio, 1966-68; chief exec. officer R.D. Zande & Assoc., Columbus, 1968—, Zande Environ. Svc., Columbus, 1988—, Zande-Garrod, Inc., Cin., 1990—; bd. dirs. Franklin County Solid Waste Mgmt. Authority, Columbus, 1985-87; mem. engring. adv. bd. Ohio State U., Columbus, 1988—; mem. small bus. adv. com. Cleve. Fed. Res. Bank, 1992—. Bd. dirs. St. Stephen's Community House, Columbus, 1988—, Bus. Exec. Coun. for the Ctr. for Applied and Profl. Edn., Franklin U., 1990-92, Purchasing Procedures Task Force City of Columbus, Jr. Achievement, 1989-92; dir. small bus. solicitations United Way. Mem. ASCE, NSPE, Ohio Assn. Cons. Engrs., Am. Cons. Engrs. Coun., Greater Columbus Devel. Com., Columbus C. of C. (bd. dirs. 1987-92). Roman Catholic. Home: 901 Bluffview Dr Columbus OH 43235-1776 Office: RD Zande & Assocs Inc 1237 Dublin Rd Columbus OH 43215-7000

ZANDER, ALVIN FREDERICK, social psychologist; b. Detroit, Oct. 13, 1913; s. Hugo Helmuth and Frieda Wilhemenia (Miesler) Z.; m. Patience Clare, Dec. 19, 1939; children—Constance, Christopher, Judith; m. Marion Cranmore, Aug. 11, 1980 (dec. May 1997). BS, U. Mich., 1936, MS in Pub. Health, 1937, PhD, 1942. Asst. dir. research service Boy Scouts Am., N.Y.C., 1943-45; asst. prof. psychology Springfield (Mass.) Coll., 1946-47; prof. psychology, dir. Research Center for Group Dynamics, U. Mich., Ann Arbor, 1959-79; asso. v.p. U. Mich., 1973-80. Author: Group Dynamics, 1953, 3d edit., 1968, Motives and Goals in Groups, 1971, revised edit., 1996, Groups at Work, 1977, Making Groups Effective, 1982, 2d edit., 1994, The Purposes of Groups and Organizations, 1985, Effective Social Action by Community Groups, 1990, Making Boards Effective, 1993. Served with USPHS, 1944-46. U. Chgo. fellow, 1938-39; Fulbright fellow. Oslo, Norway, 1957-58; Japanese Govt. fellow, 1980-81; Gen. Edn. Bd. fellow U. Iowa, 1942. Mem. Am. Psychol. Assn. (div. sec.), Am. Psychol. Soc., Soc. Psychol. Study Social Issues (pres.), Soc. Exptl. Social Psychology. Home: 2841 Ptarmigan Dr # 4 Walnut Creek CA 94595-3136

ZANDER, GAILLIENNE GLASHOW, psychologist; b. Bklyn., Apr. 7, 1932; d. Saul and Anna (Karasik) G.; m. A.J. Zander, Aug. 5, 1952; children: Elizabeth L., Caroline M., Catherine A. MusB, U. Wis., 1953, MS, 1970; PhD, Marquette U., 1984. Diplomate Am. Bd. Forensic Examiners. Music tchr. Wis. Sch. Systems, 1953-65; psychol. asst. Vernon Psychol. Labs., Chgo., 1965-70; psychologist Milw. Pub. Schs., 1970-92, CESA 19, Kenosha, Wis., 1977-78; pvt. practice psychology Milw., 1980—. Fellow Am. Orthopsychiat. Assn.; mem. APA, Wis. Psychol. Assn., Psychologists Assn. in Milw. Pub. Schs. (rep., v.p., pres.), Am. Acad. Pain Mgmt. (diplomate). Home: 13750 Carson Ct Brookfield WI 53005-4989 also: Cooper Resource Ctr 20860 Watertown Rd Waukesha WI 53186-1872

ZANDER, GLENN R., airline company executive; b. 1951. Joined TWA, Mt. Kisco, N.Y., 1971—, from various mgmt. positions to v.p. and overseas contr., 1971-87, sr. v.p. fin., CFO, 1987—, co-CEO, 1992—. Office: care Aloha Airlines PO Box 30028 Honolulu HI 96820

ZANDER, JANET ADELE, psychiatrist; b. Miles City, Mont., Feb. 19, 1950; d. Adelbert William and Valborg Constance (Buckneberg) Z.; m. Mark Richard Ellenberger, Sept. 16, 1979; 1 child, Evan David Zander Ellenberger. BA, St. Olaf Coll., 1972; MD, U. Minn., 1976. Diplomate Am. Bd. Psychiatry and Neurology. Resident in psychiatry U. Minn., Mpls., 1976-79, fellow in psychiatry, 1979-80, asst. prof. psychiatry, 1981—; staff psychiatrist St. Paul (Minn.) Ramsey Med. Ctr., 1980—, dir. edn. in psychiatry, 1980—, dir. inpatient psychiatry, 1986—; vice chair Dept. Psychiatry St. Paul Ramsey Med. Ctr., 1991-96; bd. dirs. Perry Assurance. Contbr. research articles to sci. jours. Sec. Concentus Musicus Bd. Dirs., St. Paul, 1981-89; mem. property com. St. Clement's Episcopal Ch., St. Paul, 1985. Mem. Am. Psychiat. Assn., Am. Med. Women's Assn., Minn. Psychiat. Soc. (ethics com. 1985-87, women's com. 1985-87, coun. 1994-96), Minn. Med. Assn., Ramsey County Med. Soc. (bd. dirs. 1994-96). Democrat. Avocations: singing, skiing. Home: 230 Crestway Ln West Saint Paul MN 55118-4424 Office: St Paul Ramsey Med Ctr 640 Jackson St Saint Paul MN 55101-2502

ZANE, BILLY, actor. Appeared in films Back To The Future, 1985, Critters, 1986, Dead Calm, 1989, The Case of the Hillside Strangler, 1989, Back To The Future Part II, 1989, Memphis Belle, 1990, Blood and Concrete I.R.S., 1991, Orlando, 1992, Sniper, 1993, Tombstone, 1993, Only You, 1994, Tales From The Crypt Presents Demon Knight, 1995, Danger Zone, 1995, Head Above Water, 1996, The Phantom, 1996. Office: Creative Artists Agy 9830 Wilshire Blvd Beverly Hills CA 90212*

ZANE, RAYMOND J., lawyer, state senator; b. Woodbury, N.J., July 23, 1939; s. Clarence R. and Veronica (Levy) Z.; children—Marybeth, Raymond II, Kenneth. B.S. in Bus. Adminstrn., St. Joseph's U., 1965; J.D., Rutger's U., 1974. Bar: N.J. 1974, N.Y. 1989. Freeholder, Gloucester County, Woodbury, N.J., 1971-73; mem. N.J. Senate, 1973—, dep. asst. minority leader. Mem. N.J. Bar Assn., Gloucester County Bar Assn. Home: 509 Sharp Dr Mickleton NJ 08056-1441 Office: 39 S Broad St Woodbury NJ 08096-7920 also: NJ State Senate State Capital Trenton NJ 08608

ZANETTA, JOSEPH MICHAEL, university administrator, lawyer; b. Jamestown, N.Y., Apr. 26, 1953; s. Joseph A. and Freda (Felanzo) Z.; m. Ellen L. Leggett, June 2, 1979; 1 child, Samuel Leggett Zanetta. BS, Cornell U., 1975, JD, 1978. Bar: N.Y. 1980. Mem. Hartley & Fessenden, Attys., Jamestown, 1978-79; devel. officer Cornell U., Ithaca, N.Y., 1979-82; assoc. dir. maj. gifts Tufts U., Medford, Mass., 1982-83; dir. devel. Belmont Hill Sch., Belmont, Mass., 1983-86; exec. dir. external affairs Sch. Bus. Adminstrn. U. So. Calif., L.A., 1986-93; v.p. advancement Whittier (Calif.) Coll., 1993—; chmn. Pasadena Enterprise Ctr. Sec.-treas. Lord Found. of Calif., L.A., 1988-93. Mem. Coun. for Advancement and Support of Edn. (chair nat. confs. 1990, 92), Univ. Club of L.A. (bd. dirs. 1991—), Phi Kappa Phi (bd. dirs. 1991—). Roman Catholic. Avocations: golf, swimming, travel. Home: 391 S Parkwood Ave Pasadena CA 91107-5037 Office: Whittier College 13406 Philadelphia St Whittier CA 90601-4446

ZANETTI, JOSEPH MAURICE, JR., corporate executive; b. San Francisco, Aug. 3, 1928; s. Joseph Maurice and Lillian Mary (Solari) Z.; m. Marilyn Ruth Parker, Aug. 11, 1956; children: Pamela, Gregory, Geoffrey, Regina. BA, Saint Mary's Coll., 1950; postgrad., U. Calif., Berkeley, 1950-51, 53-55, 56-57; postgrad. in Edn., San Francisco State Coll., 1955-56. Cert. secondary tchr., Calif. Tchr. Piedmont (Calif.) High Sch., 1956-57, Pleasant Hill (Calif.) High Sch., 1957-58; supr. Sandia Labs., Albuquerque, 1958-64; mktg. dir. Ednl. Research Assocs., Albuquerque, 1964-66; exec. asst. Sandia Labs., Albuquerque, 1966-73; pres. U. of Albuquerque, Albuquerque, 1973-75; dir. area devel. Pub. Svc. Co. of N.Mex., Albuquerque, 1975-86; pres., chmn. bd. dirs. Rio Grande Trading Co. Inc., Albuquerque, 1986-88; pres. Foresight, Inc., Albuquerque, 1988-90; v.p. Summa Med. Corp., Albuquerque, 1988-91; sr. v.p. Summa Med. Corp., Vienna, Va., 1991-92; v.p. Systems Support Agy. Inc., Vienna, Va., 1992-93; pres. Complexus, Inc., Albuquerque, N.Mex., 1993—; cons. Pub. Service Co. N.Mex., Albuquerque, 1986-88; ; pres. N.Mex. Internat. Trade and Investment Council Inc., Albuquerque, 1984-89; active Adv. Bd. Coll. and U. Partnership Program, Memphis, 1984—. Chmn. adv. bd. N.Mex. Mus. Natural History, Albuquerque, 1985-90; vice chmn., bd. govs. Albuquerque Tech. Vocat. Inst., 1971-77; mem. Bd. Edn., Albuquerque Pub. Schs., 1971-77. Capt. USNR, 1948-83. Mem. Res. Officers Assn. (life), Resource Devel. Com., Albuquerque Pub. Schs. (chmn.). Republican. Roman Catholic.

ZANETTI, RICHARD JOSEPH, editorial director; b. Weehawken, N.J., Mar. 22, 1939; s. Mario and Lucille (Coco) Z.; m. Norma Diane Nesheim, June 28, 1969; children: Joseph, Michael. BSChemE, Bucknell U., Lewisburg, Pa., 1961, MSChemE, 1964. Technologist Mobil Oil Corp., Bklyn., 1964-66; co-founder ASD Arts, Boston, 1979; dept. editor Chem. Wk. Mag., N.Y.C., 1980-84; assoc. editor Chem. Engring. Mag., N.Y.C., 1984-88, editor-in-chief, 1988—; editl. dir. Chem. Info. Svcs., N.Y.C., 1991—; lectr. in field. Producer, dir. documentary film: Standups, 1979. Cons. Manhattan Coll., Riverdale, N.Y., 1989—. 1st lt. U.S. Army, 1964-65. Recipient Hammer award Nat. Performance Rev. Mem. Chemist Club, Am. Bus. Press Club, Tau Beta Pi, Omicron Delta Kappa. Avocations: fiction writing, fishing, stamp collecting. Office: McGraw Hill 1221 Ave Of The Americas New York NY 10020-1001

ZANGERLE, JOHN A., lawyer; b. Lakewood, Ohio, Jan. 24, 1942. BA, Haverford Coll., 1964; JD, Case Western Res. U., 1967. Bar: Ohio 1967. Ptnr. Baker & Hostetler, Cleve. Office: Baker & Hostetler 3200 Nat City Ctr 1900 E 9th St Cleveland OH 44114-3401

ZANNA, MARTIN THOMAS, physician; b. Mpls., Apr. 2, 1947; s. Peter J. and Mary L. (Peck) Z. AB, Harvard U., 1969, MPH, 1976; MD, U. Minn., 1973. Diplomate Am. Bd. Preventive Medicine. Resident in pub. health N.J. State Dept. Health, 1974-77, acting dir. chronic disease svcs., 1976-79, dir. chronic disease svcs., 1979-81; med. adminstr. Fla. Dept. Health and Rehab. Svcs., Tallahassee, 1981-82; med. cons. N.J. Medicaid, Trenton, 1982—, chief med. cons., 1990-96; med. cons. N.J. State Dept. Health and Sr. Svcs., 1996—; mem. Fla. Cancer Coun., 1981-82, Fla. Bd. Med. Examiners, 1982; mem. N.J. Hypertension Study Group, 1977-81; chmn. grad. med. edn. com. N.J. State Dept. Health, 1993—. Participant Fla. Gov.'s Mission to Haiti, 1982; mem. divsn. profl. edn. Am. Cancer Soc., 1976-81. Fellow Am. Coll. Preventive Medicine; mem. Am. Pub. Health Assn., Harvard Club (Boston), Harvard Faculty Club (Cambridge). Home: # 11 201 Salem Ct Apt 11 Princeton NJ 08540-7039 Office: NJ State Dept Health & Sr Svcs CN 722 Trenton NJ 08625-0722

ZANNIERI, NINA, museum director; b. Summit, N.J., Feb. 1, 1955; d. Angelo Joseph and Louise Mary (Brumm) Z.; m. Douglas M. Vogel, Oct. 29, 1994. BA, Boston Coll., 1977; postgrad., Coll. of William & Mary, 1977-78; MA, Brown U., 1980. Curatorial asst. R.I. Hist. Soc., Providence, 1980-81, asst. curator, 1981-83, curator, 1983-86; dir. Paul Revere Meml. Assn., Boston, 1986—. Gen. editor: (exhbn. catalog) Paul Revere: The Man Behind the Myth, 1988; collaborator: (house guide) A Most Magnificent Mansion; project dir.: (exhbn. catalog) Let Virtue Be A Guide To Thee, 1983. Bd. dirs. Freedom Trial Found., Boston, Slater Mill Hist. Site, Pawtucket, R.I. Mem. Am. Assn. Mus.'s, New Eng. Mus. Assn. (curators com. 1984-86, bd. dirs. 1988-96), Am. Assn. State and Local History, Phi Beta Kappa. Office: Paul Revere Meml Assn The Paul Revere House 19 North Sq Boston MA 02113-2405

ZANOT, CRAIG ALLEN, lawyer; b. Wyandotte, Mich., Nov. 15, 1955; s. Thomas and Faye Blanch (Sperry) Z. AB with distinction, U. Mich., 1977; JD cum laude, Ind. U., 1980. Bar: Ind. 1980, Mich. 1981, U.S. Dist. Ct. (so. dist.) Ind. 1980, U.S. Dist. Ct. (no. dist.) Ind. 1981, U.S. Ct. Appeals (6th cir.) 1985, U.S. Dist. Ct. (ea. dist.) Mich. 1987, U.S. Dist. Ct. (we. dist.) Mich. 1990. Law clk. to presiding justice Allen County Superior Ct, Ft. Wayne, 1980-81; ptnr. Davidson, Breen & Doud P.C., Saginaw, Mich., 1981—. Mem. ABA, Mich. Bar Assn., Ind. Bar Assn., Saginaw County Bar Assn. Roman Catholic. Home: 547 S Linwood Beach Rd Linwood MI 48634-9432 Office: Davidson Breen & Doud PC 1121 N Michigan Ave Saginaw MI 48602-4762

ZANOTTI, JOHN PETER, broadcasting company executive; b. L.A., June 12, 1948; m. Claudia Jean Haskell, Aug. 8, 1970; children: Jeffrey, Laura, Mark, Christina. AB cum laude, U. So. Calif., 1970; JD magna cum laude, Ariz. State U., 1974. Assoc. corp. dept./pub. fin. O'Melveny and Myers, L.A., 1974-78; corp. dir. legal Harte-Hanks Comms. Inc., San Antonio, 1978-79, asst. sec., 1979-80, v.p. legal, sec., 1980-83; pres. Harte-Hanks Mktg./Cen. Group, Cin., 1983-84; asst. to pres. newspaper divsn. Gannett Co., Inc., Rosslyn, Va., 1984-85; pres., pub. The Cin. Enquirer, 1985-90; CEO, exec. v.p. Phoenix (Ariz.) Newspapers, Inc., 1990-91; pub. The Ariz. Republic, The Phoenix Gazette, 1990-91; pres. TV group Gt. Am. Broadcasting Co., 1991-92, pres., COO, 1992-93; CEO, pres. Citicasters Inc. (formerly Gt. Am. Comms. Co.), Cin., 1993-96. Contbr. articles to profl. jours. Trustee Children's Hosp. Med. Ctr., 1989-90, 94—, Johnny Bench Scholarship Fund, 1987-90, 91—, Taft Mus., 1992-93, Xavier U., 1989-90; bd. dirs. Neediest Kids of All, 1986-90, 91—, Ariz. State U. Law Soc., 1990-94; internat. bd. dirs. Just Say No, 1991-92; mem. Walter Cronkite Sch. Journalism and Telecomm. Endowment Com., Ariz. State U., 1990-91, Cin. Bus. Com., 1987-90, Phoenix-40, 1990-91; bd. advisors U. Cin. Coll. Bus. Adminstrn., 1988-90; co-chmn. Last Resort Scholarship Fund, Cin. Youth Collaborative, 1989-90. Mem. Assn. for Maximum Svc. TV, Inc. (bd. dirs. 1992—), Nat. Assn. Broadcasters (bd. dirs. 1994—), TV Operators Caucus, Inc. (bd. dirs. 1993—), State Bar Calif., State Bar Tex., Greater Cin. C. of C. (bd. trustees 1988-90), Cin. Country Club, Commonwealth Club, Queen City Club. Office: American Financial 1 E 4th St Fl 2 Cincinnati OH 45202-3717

ZANOTTI, MARIE LOUISE, hospital admininstrator; b. Pitts., May 3, 1954; d. Louis Charles and Josephine Rose (Antoniello) Z. BS, U. Pitts., 1976; M of Pub. Health, Yale U., 1980. Adminstrv. asst. Presbyn.-Univ. Hosp., Pitts., 1980-82; dir. Meml. Hosp. Burlington County, Mt. Holly, N.J., 1982-85; accoc. hosp. dir. The Milton S. Hershey Med. Ctr.-Univ. Hosp., Hershey, Pa., 1985-92; assoc. hosp. dir. Latrobe (Pa.)Area Hosp., 1993; workshop presenter Healthcare Fin. Mgmt. Assn., 1988-89. Active Hershey Bus. Assn., 1988—; bd. dirs. Ronald McDonald House, 1991-92, Chestnut Ridge chpt. ARC, 1993—, Med. Alliance Ins. Network, Ltd., 1993—, Latrobe Area C. of C., 1996—. Fellow Am. Coll. Healthcare Execs.; mem. Healthcare Adminstrs. Group (pres. 1989), Hosp. Assn. Pa., Hosp. Coun. Western Pa., Latrobe Area C. of C., Exec. Women Westmoreland County, Yale U. Hosp. Adminstrn., Latrobe Country Club. Avocations: performing arts, sports. Home: 111 Mara Lago St Greensburg PA 15601-9593 Office: Latrobe Area Hosp 121 W 2nd Ave Latrobe PA 15650-1068

ZANUCK, RICHARD DARRYL, motion picture company executive; b. Beverly Hills, Calif., Dec. 13, 1934; s. Darryl F. and Virginia (Fox) Z.; m. Lili Gentle; children: Virginia, Janet; m. Linda Harrison, Oct. 26, 1969; children: Harrison Richard, Dean Francis; m. Lili Fini, Sept. 23, 1978. Grad., Harvard Mil. Acad., 1952; B.A., Stanford, 1956. Story, prodn. asst. Darryl F. Zanuck Prodns., 1956, v.p., 1956-62; president's prodn. rep. 20th Century-Fox Studios, Beverly Hills, 1962-63; v.p. charge prodn. 20th Century-Fox Studios, 1963-69, pres., 1969-71, dir., 1966-71; chmn. 20th Century-Fox Television, Inc.; sr. exec. v.p. Warner Bros., Inc., 1971-72; co-founder, pres. Zanuck/Brown Co., 1972-88; founder, pres., owner The Zanuck Co., 1989—. Producer: The Sting, 1973 (Acad. award), Jaws, 1975, Jaws 2, 1978, The Island, 1980, Neighbors, 1982, The Verdict, 1983, Cocoon, 1985, Target, 1985, Cocoon, the Return, 1988, Driving Miss Daisy, 1989 (Acad. award, Irving G. Thalberg award 1991), Rush, 1991, Rich in Love, 1992, Clean Slate, 1993, Wild Bill, 1995, Mulholland Falls, 1996. Nat. chmn. Fibrosis Assn., 1966-68; mem. organizing com. 1984 Olympics; trustee Harvard Sch. 2d lt. U.S. Army. Named Producer of Yr., Nat. Assn. Theatre Owners, 1974, '85, Producers Guild Am., 1989; recipient Irving Thalberg award, 1991, Lifetime Achievement award, Producers Guild Am., 1993. Mem. Acad. Motion Picture Arts and Scis. (bd. govs.), Screen Producers Guild, Phi Gamma Delta. Office: Zanuck Co 202 N Canon Dr Beverly Hills CA 90210-5302*

ZAPAPAS, JAMES RICHARD, pharmaceutical company executive; b. Martinsville, Ind., July 15, 1926; s. James K. and Bertha (Gardner) Z.; m. Patricia A. Ryan, Aug. 30, 1947; children: Marianne Zapapas McGriff, Patricia Zapapas Parry, Gail Zapapas Rodecker, James R., Carol, Julie. BS in Pharmacy, Purdue U., 1947, ScD hon., 1979. Dir. dry products ops. Eli Lilly & Co., Indpls., 1967-70, dir. pers., 1970-73, dir. pers. and pub. rels., 1973-74, v.p. prodn. ops., 1974-75, group v.p., dir., 1976-77, pres. Elizabeth Arden Inc., 1975-76, chmn. bd., 1977-87, ret., 1987; bd. dir., group v.p. Eli Lilly & Co., 1976-86; bd. dir. Am. United Life. Republican. Roman Catholic. Home: 5025 Plantation Dr Indianapolis IN 46250-1638

ZAPEL, ARTHUR L., book publishing executive; b. Chgo., 1921; m. Janet Michel (dec.); children: Linda (dec.), Mark, Theodore, Michelle; m. Cynthia Rogers Pisor, 1986; stepchildren: Dawn, Anthony. BA in English, U. Wis., 1946. Writer, prodr. Westinghouse Radio Stas.; film writer Galbreath Studios, Ft. Wayne; creative dir. Kling Studios, Chgo., 1952-54; writer, prodr. TV commls. J. Walter Thompson Advt., Chgo., 1954-73, v.p. TV and radio prodn., 1954-73; founder, pres. Arthur Meriwether, Inc., 1973-83; pres. Meriwether Pub. Ltd., 1969-90, chmn., 1990-97; pres. Westcliffe (Colo.) Ctr. for the Arts. Illustrator: 'Twas the Night Before, The Jabberwock; created game A Can of Squirms; wrote plays for ednl. use in schs. and chs.; supr. editing and prodn. 1200 plays and musicals, 1970-95; exec. editor 74 books on theater skills for secular and religious use. Founding pres. Art Students League of Colorado Springs, 1992; past pres. Colo. Springs Symphony Coun.; past bd. dirs. Colorado Springs Opera Festival. Recipient numerous awards Freedoms Found., Valley Forge, Art Dirs. Club N.Y., Art Dirs. Chgo., Hollywood Advt., 1960-67, Gold Records Radio Ad Bur., 1959-60, XV Festival Internat. Du Film Publicitaire Venise, 1968, Gold Camera award U.S. Indsl. Film Festival, 1983, Dukane award, 1983, Gold award Houston Internat. Film Festival, 1984. Office: Meriwether Pub Ltd 885 Elkton Dr Colorado Springs CO 80907-3557

ZAPF, HERMANN, book and type designer; b. Nuremberg, Germany, Nov. 8, 1918; s. Hermann and Magdalene (Schlamp) Z.; m. Gundrun von Hesse, Aug. 18, 1951; 1 child, Christian Ludwig. Freelance designer, 1938—; type dir. D. Stempel AG, type foundry, Frankfurt, Fed. Republic of Germany, 1947-56; design cons. Mergenthaler Linotype Co., N.Y.C. and Frankfurt, 1957-74; cons. Hallmark Internat., Kansas City, Mo., 1966-73; v.p. Design Processing Internat. Inc., N.Y.C., 1977-86; prof. typographic computer programs Rochester (N.Y.) Inst. Tech., 1977-87; chmn. Zapf, Burns & Co., N.Y.C., 1987-91; instr. lettering Werkkunstschule, Offenbach, Fed. Republic Germany., 1948-50; prof. graphic design Carnegie Inst. Tech., 1960; instr. typography Technische Hochschule, Darmstadt, Fed. Republic Germany, 1972-81. Author: William Morris, 1948, Pen and Graver, 1952, Manual Typographicum, 1954, 68, About Alphabets, 1960, 70, Typographic Variations, 1964, Orbis Typographicus, 1980, Hora fugit/Carpe diem, 1984, Hermann Zapf and His Design Philosophy, 1987, ABC-XYZapf, 1989, Poetry Through Typography, 1993, August Rosenberger, 1996; designer types, Palatino, Melior, Optima, ITC Zapf Chancery, ITC Zapf Internat., Digiset, Marconi, Digiset Edison, Digiset Aurelia, Pan-Nigerian, URW-Roman and San Serif, Renaissance Roman. Hon. curator Computer Mus., Boston. Recipient Silver medal Brussels, 1962, 1st prize typgoraphy Biennale Brno, Czechoslovakia, 1966, Gold medal Type Dirs. Club, N.Y., Frederic W. Goudy award Inst. Tech. Rochester, 1969, Silver medal Internat. Book Exhbn., Leipzig, 1971, Gold medal, 1989; Johannes Gutenberg prize Mainz, Fed. German Republic, 1974, Gold medal Museo Bodoniano, Parma, Italy, 1975, J.H. Merck award, Darmstadt, 1978, Robert Hunter Middleton award, 1987, Euro Design award, 1994, Wadim Lazursky award, Acad. of Graphic Arts, Moscow, 1996; named hon. citizen State of Tex., 1970, hon. royal designer for industry. Mem. Royal Soc. Arts, Am. Math. Soc., Alliance Graphique Internationale, Bund Deutscher Grafik Designer, Internat. Gutenberg Gesellschaft; hon. mem. Type Dirs. Club N.Y.C., Soc. Typographique de France (Paris), Soc. Typographic Arts (Chgo.), Double Crown Club (London), Soc. Scribes and Illuminators (London), Friends of Calligraphy (San Francisco), Soc. Printers (Boston), Soc. Graphic Designers Can., Bund Deutscher Buchkünstler, Grafiska Inst. (Stockholm), Typophiles, Alpha Beta Club (Hong Kong), Soc. of Calligraphy (L.A.), Wynkyn de Worde Soc. (London), Monterey Calligrapher's Guild, Washington Calligraphers Guild, Eesti Kalligraafide Koondis (Tallinn, Estonia), Typographers Internat. Assn., Art Dirs. Club Kansas City, Assocs. Stanford U. Librs., Alcuin Soc. (Vancouver), Goudy Internat. Ctr., Brno Biennale Assn., Gamma Epsilon Tau.

ZAPFFE, NINA BYROM, retired elementary education educator; b. Independence, Mo., Aug. 17, 1925; d. Richmond Douglas and Nina Belle (Howell) Byrom; m. Robert Glenn Fessler, June 25, 1946 (dec. June 1947); 1 child, Robert Glenn Fessler Zapffe; m. Fred Zapffe, July 1, 1952; children: Paul Douglas, Carl Raymond. BA, So. Meth. U., 1946. Fin. sec. Tyler St. Meth. Ch., Dallas, 1948-49; tchr. Dallas Ind. Sch. Dist., 1949-52, Norman (Okla.) Pub. Schs., 1966-74; cert. chief reader for GED Writing Skills Test Part II GED Testing Svc., Am. Coun. on Edn., Washington, 1990—; adv. com. (Learning Skills Ctr.) Moore-Norman Vocat.-Tech. Sch., 1988—. Adv. bd. Norman Salvation Army, 1978-90; organizer, historian Norman Salvation Army Womens Auxiliary, 1983—, Norman Literacy Coun., 1976—; organizing com., past pres. Norman Interfaith Coun., 1974-93; organizing com., past treas. Friends of the Norman Libr., 1979—; mem. McFarlin Meml. United Meth. Ch., pres., historian 2-in-1 Sunday Sch. class, 1996, lay leader, 1980-81. Named to Literacy Hall of Fame Pioneer Libr. Sys., Norman, 1995. Mem. DAR (vice regent Black Beaver chpt. 1996), Nat. Soc. Daus. 1812 (state treas. 1996), Old Regime Study Club (sec. 1996), Coterie Club (pres. 1996), Delta Delta Delta Alumnae. Republican. Avocation: genealogy. Home: 2717 Walnut Rd Norman OK 73072-6940

ZAPP, ROBERT LOUIS, electronic test engineer; b. Columbus, Ohio, Apr. 19, 1946; s. Robert Louis and Harriet Evelyn (Miller) Z.; m. Mary Louise Appl, May 1, 1971; children: Christine, Robert. AD in Electronic Engring. Tech., DeVry Inst., 1974; BS in Electronic Engring. Tech., Franklin U., 1984. Electronic technician Battelle Meml. Inst., Columbus, 1973-84; quality control test engr. Liebert Corp., Worthington, Ohio, 1984-87, quality control engr., 1987-94, electronics test engr., 1994—. Big brother Big Bro. Assn., 1968-74. With USAF, 1965-69. Mem. Am. Soc. Quality Control, Am. Legion. Roman Catholic. Avocations: computer programming, electronics, camping, fishing, bowling. Home: 322 Demorest Rd Columbus OH 43204-1125

ZAPPA, GAIL, record producer; m. Frank Zappa; children: Moon, Dweezil, Ahmet, Diva. Recipient (with Frank Zappa) Best Recording Package-Boxed Grammy award for Frank Zappa's Civilization, Phaze III, 1996. Office: ICA PO Box 5265 North Hollywood CA 91616

ZAPPALA, STEPHEN A., state supreme court justice; b. 1932; s. Frank and Josephine Zappala. B.A., Duquesne U.; LL.B., Georgetown U., 1958. Bar: Pa. 1958. Solicitor Allegheny County, Pitts., 1974-76; judge Ct. of Common Pleas-Allegheny County, 1980-82; assoc. justice Pa. Supreme Ct., 1982—. Served with U.S. Army. Office: Pa Supreme Ct 2802 Grant Bldg Grant St Pittsburgh PA 15219-2202*

ZAPPE, JOHN PAUL, city editor, educator; b. N.Y.C., July 30, 1952; s. John Paul and Caroline (Pikor) Z.; m. Siobhan Bradshaw, May 30, 1982. AA, Dutchess Community Coll., Poughkeepsie, 1971; BA, Marist Coll., 1973; JD, Syracuse (N.Y.) U., 1978. Reporter Poughkeepsie Jour., 1973-75, Nev. State Jour., Reno, 1979-80; freelance reporter Am. Media Bold, Oakland, Calif., 1981-83; reporter Press-Telegram, Long Beach, Calif., 1983-88, city editor, 1988-97, webmaster PT Connect, 1995-97, mgr. new media, 1997—; tchr. Syracuse U., 1976-78, Calif. State U., 1985-87; cons. Am. Media Bold, 1981-83. Chmn. Local 69 Newspaper Guild, Long Beach, 1984-87. Mem. Investigative Editors and Reporters. Office: Press-Telegram 604 Pine Ave Long Beach CA 90844-0003

ZAR, JERROLD H(OWARD), academic administrator, biology educator, statistician; b. Chgo., June 28, 1941; s. Max and Sarah (Brody) Z.; m. Carol Bachenheimer, Jan. 15, 1967; children: David Michael, Adam Joseph. BS, No. Ill. U., 1962; MS, U. Ill., Urbana, 1964, PhD, 1967. NSF fellow marine sci. Duke U. Marine Lab., Beaufort, N.C., 1965; research assoc. dept. zoology U. Ill., Urbana, 1967-68; asst. prof. dept. biol. scis. No. Ill. U., DeKalb, 1968-71; assoc. prof. No. Ill. U., 1971-78, prof., 1978—, chmn. dept. biol. scis., 1978-84, assoc. provost grad. studies and research, dean Grad. Sch., 1984—; vis. scientist Argonne Nat. Lab., 1974; cons. EPA, also other govt. agys. and industries; founder, dir. ENCAP, Inc., 1974-93. Author: Biostatistical Analysis, 1974, 2d edit., 1984, 3d edit., 1996. NIH fellow U. Ill. Urbana, 1965-67. Fellow AAAS; mem. Am. Inst. Biol. Scis., Am. Ornithologists Union, Am. Physiol. Soc., Am. Statis. Assn., Biometric Soc., Cooper Ornithol. Soc., Am. Soc. Zoologists, Ecol. Soc. Am. (cert. sr. ecologist), Nat. Assn. Biol. Tchrs., Nat. Assn. Environ. Profls. (cert. environ. profl.), Wilson Ornithol. Soc. Office: No Ill U Off Dean Grad Sch De Kalb IL 60115-2864

ZARA, LOUIS, author, editor; b. N.Y.C., Aug. 2, 1910; s. Benjamin and Celia (Glick) Rosenfeld; m. Bertha Robbins, Sept. 23, 1930; children: Paul, Philip, Daniel; m. Marlene Brett, Mar. 22, 1958; m. Helen Dillman, Aug. 7, 1987. Student, Hebrew Theol. Coll., 1926-27; ed., Crane Coll., 1927-30, U. Chgo., 1930-31. Chmn. Walt Whitman Fellowship, 1940; Vice pres. Ziff Davis Pub. Co., Chgo., N.Y.C., 1946-61; editor-in-chief Masterpieces, 1950-51, dir. gen. book div., 1959-61; pres. Pub.'s Cons., Inc., N.Y.C., 1955-56, Internat. Communications Corp., N.Y.C., 1955-56; editor in chief gen. trade div. Follett Pub. Co., N.Y.C., 1962-65; editor in chief Mineral Digest, 1969-77; creative dir. George Jensen, Inc., 1974-77; cons. Astro Minerals Ltd., 1968-83. Author: novels Blessed is the Man, 1935, Give Us This Day, 1936, Some for the Glory, 1937, This Land is Ours, 1940, Against This Rock, 1943, Ruth Middleton, 1946, Rebel Run, 1951, In the House of the King, 1952, Blessed is the Land, 1954, Dark Rider, 1961; non-fiction Jade, 1969, Locks and Keys, 1969; also stories, scenarios, radio scripts, dramas, Twentieth Century Fox Scenario, 1936, ABC radio-TVshow Stump the Authors, 1945-46; scripts Scattergood Baines, 1941; contbr. fiction, essays and articles to mags. and anthologies, including O'Brien Best Short Stories of 1940. Recipient essay medal Internat. Benjamin Franklin Soc., 1930, Prose award Chgo. Found. Lit., 1940, Daroff Meml. fiction award, 1955. Fellow Royal Numis. Soc., Am. Numis. Soc.; mem. Authors Guild, Melville Soc., Overseas Press Club, Mineral Soc. Am., Macdowell Colony Fellows, Appraisers Soc. Am. (bd. dirs. 1980-87, pres. 1988-90, hon. life 1994), Nat. Commn. Anti-Defamation League (hon. life). Home: 141 E 56th St New York NY 10022-2709

ZARANKA, WILLIAM F., academic administrator, author; b. Elizabeth, N.J., Dec. 22, 1944; s. William A. and Anne M. (Paulauska) Z.; m. Ruth Annalea Falchero; children: Jacob, Philip. BA, Upsala Coll., 1966; MA, Purdue U., 1968; PhD, U. Denver, 1974. Instr. Purdue U., West Lafayette, Ind., summer 1969; asst. prof. U. Pa., Phila., 1975-78; teaching fellow U. Denver, 1969-71, instr. English., 1969-71, 74-75, asst. prof., dir. creative writing, 1978-84, dean arts and humanities, 1984-89, provost, 1989—. Author: The Branx X Anthology of Poetry, 1981, The Brand X Anthology of Fiction, 1983, (poetry) A Mirror Driven through Nature, 1981, Blessing, 1986. Fellow Breadd Loaf Writers Conf., 1981. Roman Catholic. Avocation: astronomy. Office: U Denver Office of Provost 2199 S University Blvd Denver CO 80210-4711*

ZARATE, ANN GAIRING, academic administrator, lawyer; b. Oak Park, Ill., Oct. 28, 1959; d. Donald Albert and Beverly Jean (Eppink) Gairing; m. Eugene Anthony Zarate, Oct. 5, 1985; children: Anthony Michael, Melissa Ann. BA in Comm. magna cum laude, Tulane U., 1982; JD, Cleve. State U., 1985. Bar: Ohio. Atty. Seymour Gross, Assoc., Cleve., 1985; adminstr. endowment trusts Case Western Res. U., Cleve., 1986-91; dir. devel. Salvation Army, Cleve., 1991-92; exec. dir. and asst. v.p. univ. advancement U. North Ala. Found., Florence, 1992—. Mem. Jr. women's com. Cleve. Playhouse, 1989-92. Mem. AAUW, Leadership Shoals/Shoals C. of C., Florence Rotary Club, Alpha Lambda Delta. Avocations: travel, cooking, weight lifting, swimming. Office: Univ North Ala Found PO Box 5059 Florence AL 35630

ZARAZOGA, DANIEL, professional boxer; b. Mexico City, Dec. 11, 1959. Named WBC Super Bantamweight Champion, 1985, 1988-90, 91-92, 95. Achievements include record of 53 wins, 7 losses, and 3 ties, with 27 knock-outs. Office: c/o Consejo Mundial de Boxeo, Genova 33 Despacho # 503, 06600 Mexico City Mexico

ZARB, FRANK GUSTAVE, insurance brokerage executive; b. N.Y.C., Feb. 17, 1935; s. Gustave and Rosemary (Antinora) Z.; m. Patricia Koster, Mar. 31, 1957; children: Krista Ann, Frank, Jr. B.B.A., Hofstra U., 1957, M.B.A., 1962, L.H.D., 1975. Trainee Cities Service Oil Co., N.Y.C., 1957-62; gen. partner Goodbody & Co., N.Y.C., 1962-69; exec. v.p. CBWL-Hayden Stone, Inc. (investment banking), N.Y.C., 1969-71; asst. sec. U.S. Dept. Labor, Washington, 1971-72; exec. v.p. Hayden Stone, Inc., N.Y.C., 1972-73; assoc. dir. Office of Mgmt. and Budget, Washington, 1973-74; asst. to Pres. for Energy Affairs U.S., 1974-77; adminstr. Fed. Energy Adminstrn., Washington, 1974-77; adv. U.S. Congress, 1977-78; gen. ptnr. Lazard Freres & Co., N.Y.C., 1977-88; chmn., pres. chief exec. officer Smith, Barney, Harris, Upham & Co., Inc., N.Y.C., 1988-93; vice chmn., group chief exec. The Travelers Inc., N.Y.C., 1993-94; chmn., pres., CEO Alexander & Alexander Svcs. Inc., N.Y.C., 1994—; bd. dirs. CS First Boston, Inc., Coun. on Fgn. Rels.; former chmn. N.Y. Stock Exch. Nominating Com. Author: The Stockmarket Handbook, 1969, Handbook of Financial Markets, The Municipal Bond Handbook. Mem. bd. trustees Gerald R. Ford Found.; mem. and former chmn. bd. trustees Hofstra U. Recipient Disting. Scholar award Hofstra U., 1974; bus. sch. named in his honor Hofstra U. Mem. Coun. Fgn. Rels. *

ZARCONE, MICHAEL JOSEPH, experimental physicist, consultant; b. Danbury, Conn., Dec. 10, 1950; s. Michael Joseph Zarcone and Mary Elizabeth Belardinelli; children from previous marriage: Cassandra Marie, Sally Marie; m. Sheila Candelario, Feb. 21, 1981; children: Michael Joseph, Christopher Michael. BS in Physics, Fairfield U., 1973; MS in Physics, N.Mex. Inst. Mining and Tech., 1984; PhD in Physics, U. Conn., 1989. Rsch. asst. Radon Lab., Socorro, N.Mex., 1983-84, VandeGraaff Accelerator Lab., Storrs, Conn., 1985-89; physics instr. Cen. Conn. State U., New Britain, 1989-90; accelerator tech. fellow Brookhaven Nat. Lab., Upton, N.Y., 1990-91, asst. physicist, 1991-93, physics assoc. II, 1993—; dir. prodn., cons. Corning Costar Corp., Upton, 1994—; coord. environ. safety and health Corning Costar Corp., 1996—; cons. Corning. Contbr. articles to profl. jours. including Phys. Rev. A, Nuclear Instruments and Methods in Phys. Rsch., Physics Rev. Letters, Atmospheric Environment, Semiconductor Internat. Mem. AAAS, Am. Phys. Soc., Sigma Xi. Avocations: mountain climbing, hiking. Home: 17 Jones St East Setauket NY 11733 Office: Brookhaven Nat Lab Bldg 901A Upton NY 11973

ZARE, RICHARD NEIL, chemistry educator; b. Cleve., Nov. 19, 1939; s. Milton and Dorothy (Amdur) Z.; m. Susan Leigh Shively, Apr. 20, 1963; children: Bethany Jean, Bonnie Sue, Rachel Amdur. BA, Harvard, 1961; postgrad., U. Calif., Berkeley, 1961-63; PhD (NSF predoctoral fellow), Harvard, 1964; DS (hon.), U. Ariz., 1990, Northwestern U., 1993, ETH, Zürich, 1993. Postdoctoral fellow Harvard, 1964; postdoctoral research asso. Joint Inst. for Lab. Astrophysics, 1964-65; asst. prof. chemistry Mass. Inst. Tech., 1965-66; asst. prof. dept. physics and astrophysics U. Colo., 1966-68, assoc. prof. physics and astrophysics, asso. prof. chemistry, 1968-69; prof. chemistry Columbia, 1969-77, Higgins prof. natural sci., 1975-77; prof. Stanford U., 1977—, Shell Disting. prof. chemistry, 1980-85, Marguerite Blake Wilbur prof. chemistry, 1987—, prof. physics, 1992—; cons. Aeronomy Lab., NOAA, 1966-77, radio standards physics divsn. Nat. Bur. Standards, 1968-77, Lawrence Livermore Lab., U. Calif., 1974—, SRI, Internat., 1974—, Los Alamos Sci. Lab., U. Calif., 1975—; fellow adjoint Joint Inst. Lab. Astrophysics, U. Colo.; mem. IBM Sci. Adv. Com., 1977-92; chmn. commn. on phys. scis., math. and applications Nat. Rsch. Coun., 1992-95; chmn. bd. dirs. Annual Revs., Inc., 1995—; rschr. and author publs. on laser chemistry and chem. physics. editor Chem. Physics Letters, 1982-85; contbr. and rschr. articles on laser chemistry and chem. physics to profl. jours. Recipient Fresenius award Phi Lambda Upsilon, 1974, Michael Polanyi medal, 1979, Nat. Medal Sci., 1983, Spectroscopy Soc. Pitts. award, 1983, Michelson-Morley award Case Inst. Tech. Case We. Res. U., 1986, ISCO award for Significant Contbns. to Instrumentation for Biochem. Separations, 1990, Ea. Analytical Symposium award, 1996, Exceptional Sci. Achievement award NASA, 1997; nonresident fellow Joint Inst. for Lab. Astrophysics, 1970—, Alfred P. Sloan fellow, 1967-69, Christensen fellow St. Catherine's Coll., Oxford U., 1982, fellow Stanford U., 1984-86; Bing Fellowship Teaching award, 1996; named Calif. Scientist of Yr., 1997.$D96, Calif. Scientist of Yr., 1997. Fellow AAAS, Calif. Acad. Scis. (hon.); mem. NAS (mem. coun., Chem. Scis. award 1991), Nat. Scis. Bd., Am. Acad. Arts and Scis., Am. Phys. Soc. (Earle K. Plyler prize 1981, Irving Langmuir prize 1985), Am. Chem. Soc. (Harrison Howe award Rochester chpt. 1985, Remsen award Md. chpt. 1985, Kirkwood award Yale U. chpt. 1986, Willard Gibbs medal Chgo. chpt. 1990, Peter Debye award in phys. chemistry 1991, Linus Pauling medal 1993, The Harvey prize 1993, Dannie-Heineman Preis 1993, Analytical Chemistry Divsn. award in chem. instrumentation 1995), Am. Philos. Soc., Chem. Soc. London, Phi Beta Kappa. Office: Stanford U Dept Chemistry Stanford CA 94305-5080

ZAREFSKY, DAVID HARRIS, academic administrator, communication studies educator; b. Washington, June 20, 1946; s. Joseph Leon and Miriam Ethel (Lewis) Z.; m. Nikki Sheryl Martin, Dec. 23. 1970; children: Beth Ellen, Marc Philip. BS, Northwestern U., 1968, MA, 1969, PhD, 1974. Instr. communication studies Northwestern U., Evanston, Ill., 1968-73, asst. prof., 1974-77, assoc. prof., 1977-82, prof., 1982—, chmn. dept., 1975-83, assoc. dean Sch. Speech, 1983-88, dean, 1988—. Author: President Johnson's War on Poverty, 1986 (Winans-Wichelns award 1986), Lincoln, Douglas and Slavery, 1990 (Winans-Wichelns award 1991), Public Speaking: Strategies for Success, 1996; co-author: Contemporary Debate, 1983; editor: Rhetorical Movement, 1993; co-editor: American Voices, 1989, Contemporary American Voices, 1992; contbr. articles to profl. jours. Recipient Best Article award So. Speech Communication Assn., 1985, Midwest Forensic Assn., 1988; named Debate Coach of the Year Georgetown U., 1973, Emory U., 1972. Mem. AAUP, Speech Comm. Assn. (pres. 1993, dist. scholar award 1994), Ctrl. State Comm. Assn. (pres. 1986-87), Am. Forensic Assn. (Svc. award 1989), Delta Sigma Rho-Tau Kappa Alpha (Svc. award 1986), others. Democrat. Jewish. Avocations: stamp collecting, reading, travel. Office: Northwestern U 1905 Sheridan Rd Evanston IL 60208-0820

ZAREM, ABE MORDECAI, management consulting executive; b. Chgo., Mar. 7, 1917; s. I.H. and Lea (Kaufman) Z.; m. Esther Mariam Moskovitz, Oct. 4, 1941; children: Janet Ruth, David Michael, Mark Charles. B.S. in Elec. Engring, Ill. Inst. Tech., 1939, LL.D. (hon.), 1968; M.S. in Elec. Engring, Calif. Inst. Tech., 1940, Ph.D., 1944; LL.D., U. Calif. at Santa Cruz, 1967. Design engr. very high voltage power transmission system Allis Chalmers Rsch. div., 1944; initiator, group mgr. Microtime & Electro Optical Phys. Rsch., U.S. Naval Test Sta., 1945-48; assoc. dir., mgr. L.A. div. Stanford Rsch. Inst., 1948-56; mem. faculty UCLA, 1956-61; founder, chmn., pres. Electro-Optical Systems, Inc., Pasadena, Calif., 1956-67; v.p. Xerox Corp., L.A., 1963-67, sr. v.p., dir. corp. devel., bd. dirs., 1967-69; mgmt. and engring. cons., 1969-79; founder, chmn. Xerox Devel. Corp., L.A., 1975-80; chmn. strategic bus. planning, techno-econ. and venture capital, pres., owner Abe M. Zarem & Co., 1981—; founder, mng. dir., Frontier Assoc., 1980—; mem. adv. com. competitive tech. program State of Calif., 1989; mem. Calif. Coun. Sci. and Tech., chmn. advanced sci. & tech. programs com. Author: Utilization of Solar Energy, 1963. Traffic and parking commr. City of Beverly Hills, 1971-72, planning commr., 1972-73; Bd. dirs. Music Center Opera Assn., Los Angeles, 1968—; nat. trustee City of Hope; trustee Calif. Inst. Arts, 1973-76. Named Outstanding Young Elec. Engr. in U.S. Eta Kappa Nu, 1948; One of America's Ten Outstanding Young Men U.S. Jr. C. of C., 1950; recipient Albert F. Sperry medal Instrument Soc. Am., 1969. Fellow AIAA, IEEE; sci. mem. (a founder) Solar Energy Soc.; mem. Nat. Acad. Engring. Inventor World's fastest high-speed camera, automatic oscillograph. Home: 9640 Lomitas Ave Beverly Hills CA 90210-3333 *I have always had a Vision, Mission & Series of Strategic Objectives - The principal one having been instilled by loving parents & family who encouraged me. I was born to identify talent and to challenge it to do more than it would have done if it had not met me. I am mentor and tormentor. I build and stretch people.*

ZAREMBA, THOMAS EDMUND MICHAEL BARRY, biology educator; b. Detroit, May 6; s. Edmund Julius Thiel and Ethel Grace (Barry) Z. Ed. Oakland U., Rochester, Mich., U. Detroit, Wayne State U. Tchr., Center Line (Mich.) Public Schs., Livonia (Mich.) Public Schs.; instr. biol. scis. Wayne State U., Detroit, 1974—. Mem. Mich. Eye Bank, Nat. Trust Historic Preservation, Internat. Friends Van Cliburn, Met. Opera Guild, Friends of Detroit Symphony Orch., Founders Soc., Detroit Inst. Arts, Internat. Platform Assn., Detroit Sci. Ctr., Friends for Orch. Hall, Tex. Funeral Dirs. Assn., Orch. Hall Assocs.; bd. dirs. Van Cliburn Found, Inc., Detroit Grand Oprea Assn., 9th Ann. Internat. Piano Competition. Mem. AAAS, Nat. Funeral Dirs. Assn., Mich. Funeral Dirs. Assn., Am. Film Inst. (sponsor), Nat. Trust Hist. Preservation, Wayne State U. Alumni Assn., Oakland U. Alumni Assn. Roman Catholic. Clubs: Scarab (life, bd. dirs.), Players (Detroit). Office: 217 Farnsworth St Detroit MI 48202-4018

ZAREMBKA, PAUL, economics educator; b. St. Louis, Apr. 17, 1942. BS, Purdue U., 1964; MS, U. Wis., 1967, PhD, 1967. Asst. prof. U. Calif., Berkeley, 1967-72; vis. prof. Heidelberg (Fed. Republic Germany) U., 1970-71, Gottingen (Fed. Republic Germany) U., 1972; assoc. prof. SUNY, Buffalo, 1973-76, prof., 1976—, dir. grad. studies dept. econs., 1995—; sr. rsch. officer Internat. Labor Office, Geneva, 1974-77; researcher Louis Pasteur U., Strasbourg, France, 1978-79; Fulbright-Hayes lectr. Coun. Internat. Exchange of Scholars, Poznan, Poland, 1979. Author: Toward a Theory of Economic Development, 1972; editor: Frontiers in Econometrics, 1974, Research in Political Economy, 1977—; co-editor: Essays in Modern Capital Theory, 1976; contbr. articles to profl. publs. Active Buffalo Ctr. chpt. exec. bd. United Univ. Professions, 1981—, pres., 1991-95, grievance officer acad., 1995—; active AFL-CIO Buffalo Labor Coun., 1982-83, 96—, Commn. on Quality Edn. in Buffalo in the 1990s, 1990-91; mem. subcom. on capital appropriations City of Buffalo, 1990—, citizens adv. com., 1997—, chmn. subcom. on city reorgn., 1997—; bd. dirs. United Parents, 1991-94; chair Labor Party, Buffalo, 1996. NSF grantee, 1969-72. Office: SUNY Dept Econs 415 Fronczak Hall Buffalo NY 14260

ZAREMSKI, MILES JAY, lawyer; b. Chgo., Aug. 16, 1948; s. Samuel and Ann (Levine) Z.; m. Elena Cinthia Resnik, July 19, 1970; children: Jason Lane, Lauren Devra. BS, U. Ill., 1970; JD, Case Western Res. U., 1973. Bar: Ill. 1973, U.S. Dist. Ct. (no. dist.) Ill. 1973, U.S. Ct. Appeals (7th cir.) 1973, U.S. Supreme Ct. 1977, U.S. Ct. Appeals (8th cir.) 1988, U.S. Dist. Ct. Nebr. 1996. Spl. asst. state's atty. Lake County, Ill., 1980-82; ptnr., co-chair health care practice group Rudnick & Wolfe, Chgo., 1995—; asst. prof. med. jurisprudence U. Health Scis./Chgo. Med. Sch., 1991—; arbitrator, mandatory arbitration programs Cook and Lake Counties, Ill., 1990—. Editor: Medical and Hospital Negligence, 4 vols., 1988, supplement, 1993, 95-97; contbr. chpts. in books and articles to profl. jours.; author: Reengineering Healthcare Liability Litigation, 1997. Oversight com. law sch. Case Western Res. U., Cleve., 1985—, bd. dirs., 1996—; mem. exec. com. law sch. ctr for health care Loyola U., Chgo., 1987-89; mem. lakefront commn. City of Highland Park, Ill., 1982-84; bd. dirs., officer Regional Organ Bank Ill., Chgo., 1986-91; bd. dirs. The Lambs, Libertyville, Ill., 1982-84, Jocelyn Ctr. for Mental Health, 1994-96. Named one of Outstanding Young Men in Am., U.S. Jaycees, 1979. Fellow Am. Coll. Legal Medicine (assoc. in law 1973-91, chair legal com. 1996—, editl. bd. Jour. Legal Medicine 1981—, bd. dirs.); mem. ABA (various coms. tort and ins. practice sect., vice chmn. 1979-90, chmn. med. and law com. 1984-85, editor-in-chief Forum 1979-81, spl. com. on med. profl. liability 1985, 91-95, editl. bd. Forum on Health Law 1989-91)), Ill. Bar Assn. (1st and 3d prizes 1978-79), Lake County Bar Assn., Am. Soc. Law and Medicine (editor-in-chief 1981-83, bd. editors 1983-86), Am. Acad. Hosps. Attys., Am. Soc. Writers on Legal Subjects (scribes), Nat. Health Lawyers Assn., Ill. Assn. Hosps. Attys. Jewish. Avocations: baseball, soccer, coaching athletic teams. Office: Rudnick & Wolfe 203 N La Salle St Ste 1800 Chicago IL 60601-1225 *Success is a journey; not a destination. "A man may make many mistakes but he isn't a failure until he starts blaming someone else." John R. Wooden.*

ZARET, BARRY LEWIS, cardiologist, medical educator; b. N.Y.C., Oct. 3, 1940; s. Irving Z. and Beatrice (Fader) Zaret; m. Myrna Zimmerman, June 23, 1963; children: Adam L., Elliot C., Owen M. B.S., Queens Coll., 1962; M.D., NYU, 1966; M.A., Yale U., 1982. Diplomate: Am. Bd. Internal Medicine. Intern Bellevue Hosp., N.Y.C., 1966-67, resident, 1967-79; research fellow John Hopkins U., Balt., 1969-71; asst. prof. medicine Yale U., New Haven, 1973-76, assoc. prof. medicine and diagnostic radiology, 1976, chief sect. cardiology, 1978—, assoc. prof. medicine and diagnostic radiology, 1980-82, prof. medicine and diagnostic radiology, 1982-84; Robert W. Berliner prof. medicine Yale U., 1984—, assoc. chair clin. affairs dept. internal medicine, 1994—; mem. staff Yale-New Haven Med. Ctr. Mem. editorial bd. Am. Jour. Cardiology, 1977—, Jour. Am. Coll. Cardiology, 1986-91, 92—, Jour. Cardiac Imaging, 1986—, Circulation, 1993; assoc. editor: Yearbook of Nuclear Medicine, 1980-95; editor-in-chief Jour. Nuclear Cardiology, 1993—; contbr. articles to profl. jours. Recipient Casimir Funk award Soc. Mil. Surgeons, 1973; recipient Herrman Blumgart Pioneer award New Eng. chpt. Soc. Nuclear Medicine, 1978. Fellow Am. Coll. Cardiology, Coun. Clin. Cardiology, Am. Heart Assn., Coun. Circulation, Am. Heart Assn., Am. Physiology Soc.; mem. Am. Soc. Clin. Investigation, Am. Fedn. Clin. Rsch., Assn. Am. Physicians, Soc. Nuclear Medicine, Am. Soc. Nuclear Cardiology, Assn. Univ. Cardiologists, Assn. Profs. Cardiology (pres. 1992), Phi Beta Kappa, Alpha Omega Alpha, Interurban Clin. Club. Jewish. Home: 15 Cassway Rd Woodbridge CT 06525-1214 Office: Yale U Sch Medicine 333 Cedar St # 3fmp New Haven CT 06510-3206

ZARICZNYJ, BASILIUS, orthopedic surgeon; b. Ukraine, Aug. 31, 1924; came to U.S., 1951; s. Alex and Maria (Kostiw) Z.; m. Stefania Pidburny, Aug. 21, 1954; children: Marta, Stephanie Christine, Andrea Maria, Mark B. MD, U. Bonn, Germany, 1951; MD (hon.), Odessa State Med. U., Ukraine, 1996. Diplomate Am. Bd. Orthopedic Surgery. Resident St. Luke's Hosp., Chgo., 1954-56, Univ. Hosps., Oklahoma City, 1955-56; fellow in orthopedics Northwestern U., Chgo., 1957; asst. prof. Sch. Medicine U. Okla., Oklahoma City, 1957-58; orthopedic surgeon Springfield, Ill., 1958—; clin. prof. Sch. Medicine So. Ill. U., Springfield, Ill., 1973-85, acting chmn. divsn. orthopedic surgery, 1972-75, chief sports medicine sect., 1975-82, program chmn. sports injury symposium, 1977-79, 82, 83; mem. sports medicine com. Ill. State Med. Soc., 1979-80; chmn. dept. orthopedic surgery St. John's and Meml. Hosps., Springfield, 1970-79; program chmn. Med. Congress of World Fedn. of Ukrainian Med. Assn., Dniepropetrovsk, 1994, Odessa, Ukraine, 1996; presenter Am. Acad. Orthopedic Surgeons, Miami, Fla., 1961, N.Y., 1969, San Francisco, 1971, Washington, 1972, Las Vegas, 1973, 77, Anaheim, Calif., 1983, Chgo. Orthopedic Soc., 1967, 76, O'Donoghue Okla. Orthopedic Alumni Assn., Oklahoma City, 1972, 75, 78, Internat. Soc. for Orthopedic Surgery and Traumatology, XII World Congress, Tel Aviv, 1972, Copenhagen, 1975, Kyoto, Japan, 1978, So. Ill U. Sch. Medicine, Springfield, 1977, 79, 80, 82, Ill. State Orthopedic Soc., Chgo., 1978, ACS, Chgo., 1979, Am. Orthopedic Soc. for Sports Medicine, Atlanta, 1980, Big Sky, Mont., 1980,, Lake Tahoe, Nev., 1981, Clin. Orthopedic Soc., Chgo., 1987, World Fedn. Ukrainian Med. Assn., Kiev, Ukraine, 1990, U. Lviv, Ukraine, 1990, 11th Congress of Orthopedic Surgeons of Ukraine, Kharkiv, 1991, Congress of World Fedn. of Ukrainian Med. Assn., Kharkiv, 1992, Dniprepetrovsk, 1994, Odessa, 1996, Ukraine, among others. Mem. editl. bd. Jour. Ukrainan Med. Assn. N.Am., 1977-95; contbr. articles to profl. jours. and med. textbooks. Fellow Am. Acad. Orthopedic Surgery; mem. AMA, Ill. Orthopedic Soc., Internat. Soc. Orthopedic Surgery and Traumatology, Am. Orthopedic Soc. for Sports Medicine, Internat. Soc. of the Knee, Mid-Am. Orthopedic Assn., Ukrainian Acad. and Profl. Assn. Pres. 1985-89), Sangamon County Med. Soc., Chgo. Orthopedic Soc. Avocations: golfing, walking, chess. Home and Office: 125 Oakmont Dr Springfield IL 62704-3118

ZARINS, BERTRAM, orthopaedic surgeon; b. Latvia, June 22, 1942; came to U.S., 1946, naturalized, 1956; s. Richard Arthur and Maria (Rozenbergs) Z. AB in Chemistry, Lafayette Coll., 1963; MD, SUNY, Syracuse, 1967. Diplomate Am. Bd. Orthop. Surgery. Clin. instr. orthop. surgery Harvard Med. Sch., Boston, 1976—, asst. clin. prof., 1982—; orthop. surgeon Mass. Gen. Hosp., Boston, 1982-95; assoc. clin. prof. Harvard Med. Sch., Boston, 1995—; chief sports medicine unit Mass. Gen. Hosp., Boston, 1982—; team physician Boston Bruins Hockey Team, 1976—; chmn. edn. com. Sports Medicine Coun., U.S. Olympic Com., 1980-92; team physician New England Patriots football team, 1982—; head physician USA Olympic teams XIV Winter Olympic Games, Sarajevo, Yugoslavia, 1984. Contbr. articles to profl. jours. Team physician N.E. Revolution profl. soccer team, 1996—. Lt. comdr. M.C., USNR, 1973-75. Fellow ACS, Am. Acad. Orthop. Surgeons (chmn. com. on sports medicine 1993—), Am. Coll. Sports Medicine; mem. AMA, Internat. Arthroscopy Assn. (bd. dirs. 1991-95), Arthroscopy Assn. N.Am., N.Am. Trauma Assn. (pres. 1977), Internat. Soc. of the Knee, Am. Shoulder and Elbow Surgeons, Herodicus Soc., Brookline (Mass.) Country Club, Somerset Club. Office: Mass Gen Hosp Ambulatory Care Ctr Ste 514 Boston MA 02114

ZARINS, CHRISTOPHER KRISTAPS, surgery educator, vascular surgeon; b. Tukums, Latvia, Dec. 2, 1943; came to U.S., 1946; s. Richard A. and Maria (Rozenbergs) Z.; m. Zinta Zarins, July 8, 1967; children: Daina, Sascha, Karina. BA, Lehigh U., 1964; MD, Johns Hopkins U., 1968. Surgery residency U. Mich., Ann Arbor, 1968-74; asst. prof. surgery U. Chgo., 1976-79, assoc. prof. surgery, 1979-82, prof. surgery, 1983-93, chief of vascular surgery, 1978-93; prof. surgery, chmn. divsn. vascular surgery Stanford (Calif.) U., 1993—, acting chmn. dept. of surgery, 1995—. Author: Essays In Surgery, 1986, Atlas of Vascular Surgery, 1988; editor Jour. of Surg. Rsch., 1982-95; contbr. articles to profl. jours. Pres. Latvian Med. Found., Boston, 1991. Lt. comdr. USN, 1974-76. Grantee NIH, NSF. Mem. Am. Surg. Soc., Soc. for Clin. Surgery, Soc. for Vascular Surgery, Internat. Soc. for Cardiovascular Surgery, Soc. of Univ. Surgeons, Latvian Nat. Acad. of Scis., Latvian Vascular Surg. Soc. (pres. 1989). Avocations: triathlons, skiing. Office: Stanford U Med Ctr Divsn Vascular Surgery 300 Pasteur Dr # H3630 Stanford CA 94305-5450

ZARKIN, HERBERT, retail company executive. Exec. vice-pres. Zayre Corp., Framingham, Mass., until 1986; pres. Zayre Corp., HomeClub subs., Framingham, Mass., 1986-88; chmn. Zayre Corp., Zayre Stores div., Framingham, Mass., 1988—; pres., CEO Waban Inc, Natick. Office: Waban 1 Mercer Rd Natick MA 01760-2400*

ZARLE, THOMAS HERBERT, academic administrator. BS, Springfield Coll., 1963; MA, Ohio U., 1965; PhD, Mich. State U., 1970; MPH, Harvard U., 1978. V.p. instl. advancement Bentley Coll., Waltham, Mass., until 1988; pres. Aurora U., Ill., 1988—. Office: Aurora U Office of Pres 347 S Gladstone Ave Aurora IL 60506-4877*

ZARO, BRAD A., research company executive, biologist; b. San Jose, Calif., Dec. 4, 1949; s. Raymond J. and Irene R. Z.; children: Amy C., Kristen E. BA in Zoology, San Jose State U., 1974, MA in Biology, 1981. Chemist, Dept. Drug Metabolism Syntex Rsch., Inc., Palo Alto, Calif., 1976-78, chemist II, Dept. Drug Metabolism, 1978-81, chemist III, Dept. Drug Metabolism, 1981-84, clin. rsch. assoc. I, Inst. of Clin. Medicine, 1984-85, clin. rsch. assoc. II, Inst. of Clin. Medicine, 1985-87, sen. clin. rsch. assoc., Inst. of Clin. Medicine, 1985-87; sen. clin. rsch. assoc. Triton Biosciences, Inc., Alameda, Calif., 1988, mgr. clin. trials, 1988; pres. Clinimetrics Rsch. Assoc., Inc., San Jose, 1988—. Contbr. articles to scholarly jours. Mem. Am. Coll. Clin. Pharmacology, Am. Assoc.'s for the Advancement of Sci., Assoc.'s of Clin. Pharmacology, Prof. Tech. Cons's. Democrat. Roman Catholic. Avocations: scuba diving, skiing, flying airplanes. Office: Clinimetrics Rsch Assocs 2025 Gateway Pl Ste 132 San Jose CA 95110-1005

ZARR, MELVYN, lawyer, law educator; b. Worcester, Mass., Aug. 29, 1936; m. Gail Sclar, Aug. 29, 1971. A.B., Clark U., 1958; LL.B., Harvard U., 1963. Bar: Mass. bar 1964, Maine bar 1973. Staff atty. NAACP Legal Def. & Edn. Fund, Inc., N.Y.C., 1963-69; co-dir. Mass. Law Reform Inst., Boston, 1970-73; prof. law U. Maine, 1973—; U.S. magistrate, Portland, Maine, 1977-82. Mem. Am. Law Inst. Home: 19 Mckinley Rd Falmouth ME 04105-1913 Office: U Maine Sch Law 246 Deering Ave Portland ME 04102-2837

ZARRELLA, ARTHUR M., superintendent; b. Providence, July 30, 1936; s. Joseph and Flora (Santoro) Z.; m. Ann Miletta, Aug. 19, 1960; children: Matthew, Mark, Chris, Paul. BS, U. R.I., 1960; D of Pedagogy (hon.), R.I. Coll., 1985. Cert. bus. edn., history, social studies, guidance and counseling, critic tchr., secondary sch. prin., secondary sch. asst. prin., supt. of schs. Tchr. bus. edn. Cranston High Sch. West, 1961-62; tchr. bus. edn. Mt. Pleasant High Sch., 1962-65, tchr. social studies, 1965-68; social studies dept. head Ctrl. High Sch., 1968-70, guidance dept. head, 1970-72, student rels. adminstr., 1972-76, prin., 1976-87; prin. Classical H.S., 1987-88, acting asst. supt. for secondary edn., 1988-89, asst. supt. for secondary edn., 1989-90, asst. supt. secondary edn./dep., 1990—, acting supt. schs., 1991-92, supt. of schs., 1992—; asst. coach track and field Mt. Pleasant H.S., 1961-64, head coach track and field, 1964-69; tchr. Brown U., 1970, Providence Coll., 1973-74, 74-75, 86—, advisor adminstrv. internship program, 1976-82; tchr. R.I. Coll., 1980, 82, 95—, social worker practicum supervision U. R.I., 1976-78; advisor adminstrv. internship program Harvard U., 1985-86; cons. The Inst. for Ednl. Leadership, Inc., Hartford, 1985; presenter in field, many others. Contbr. articles to profl. jours. Bd. dirs. Mt. Pleasant Little League, 1973-76, treas., 1973-75, pres., 1976; bd. dirs. West End Community Assn., 1976-89, Wiggins Village Tenants Assn., 1980—, Young Vols. of R.I., 1982-84, Urban Edn. Ctr., 1982—, R.I. Leadership Acad., 1983-85, Keep Providenc Beautiful, 1984-85, Providence Edn. Fund, 1985-88, West End Community Ctr., 1986-90, Todd Morsilli Fund, 1987—, chairperson, 1989-91; scholarship chairperson Italian Am. Sports Hall of Fame, 1988-89; others. With USNG, 1959-65. Recipient Delta Sigma Theta Sorority's Comty. Svc. award, 1986, Mayor's citation for comty. svc., 1989, R.I. Ho. of Reps. citation for comty. svc., 1989, Gov.'s citation for comty. svc., 1989, R.I. Senate citation for comty. svc., 1989, Youth Dirs. Assn. Comty. Svc. award, 1989, NAACP Edn. award, 1989, R.I. Ho. of Reps. citation for commitment to substance abuse programs, 1991, Mayor's Citizen citation, 1991, Roberto Clemente Citizen award, 1991, Excellence in Edn. award U. R.I. Alumni Assn., 1996; fellow Danforth Found., 1994—, Annenberg fellow, 1994—. Mem. Nat. Assn. Secondary Sch. Prins., R.I. Assn. Secondary Sch. Prins., R.I. Sch. Adminstrs. Assn., Barnard Club. Roman Catholic. Home: 80 Waller St Providence RI 02908-3822 Office: Dept Supt of Schs 797 Westminster St Providence RI 02903-4018

ZARRO, JANICE ANNE, lawyer; b. Newark, June 30, 1947; d. Samuel James and Elma Dora (Monaco) Z.; m. Bobby C. Wood. BA, Rutgers U., 1969; JD, IIT-Chgo.-Kent Coll. Law, 1973. Bar: Pa. 1974. Counsel jud. com. U.S. Ho. Reps., Washington, 1973-77; profl. staff mem. counsel labor and human resources com. U.S. Senate, Washington, 1977-80; dir. Avon Products, Inc., N.Y.C., 1980-81; dir. Avon Products, Inc., Washington, 1982-86, v.p., 1986-90; pres. The Novus Group, Inc., 1990-92; dir. fed. affairs Mallinckrodt Med., 1992—, v.p., 1993-94; v.p. govt. affairs Worldwide Mallinckrodt Inc., 1994—; gen. counsel Nat. Italian-Am. Found., 1989-96, chair bd. trustees, 1996—; mem. Bus. Govt. Rels. Coun., Washington, 1987—. Past chmn. Nat. Capital chpt. Multiple Sclerosis Soc. Recipient Leadership Recognition award Nat. Women's Econ. Alliance, 1984. Mem. ABA, Pa. Bar Assn. Home: 6A W Chapman St Alexandria VA 22301-2502

ZARROW, PHILIP M., electronic assembly process consultant; b. Paterson, N.J., Apr. 9, 1953; s. Frank T. and Barbara E. (Strassman) Z.; m. Golda A. Lechner; children: Joel, Rosalee. BS in Bus. Adminstrn., Rider Coll., 1975. Applications engr./mktg. specialist Argus Internat., Hopewell, N.J., 1975-76; sales engr. Tooltronics, Inc., Glendale, Calif., 1976-78; sales engr., dist. mgr. Universal Instrument Corp., Irvine, Calif., 1978-81; western regional mgr. Test Systems Inc., Tempe, Ariz., 1981-82, Trilog, Inc., Irvine, 1982-83; product mgr., western regional mgr. Excellon-Micronetics, Torrance, Calif., 1983-87; product mgr. Vitronics Corp., Newmarket, N.H., 1987-92; mgr. tech. devel. GSS/Array Tech., San jose, Calif., 1992-94; pres., cons. ITM, Inc., Durham, N.H., 1993—; co-founder, cons. Synergistek Assocs., Round Lake Beach, Ill., 1991-92; dir. ITM, Inc., 1993—, pres., CEO, 1995—; assoc. cons. Teltech, Mpls., 1994—. Co-author: SMT Glossary-Terms & Definitions, 1994; columnist, tech. corr. Circuits Assembly Mag., 1995—, mem. editl. adv. bd, 1993-95, tech. corr., 1995—; contbr. articles to profl. jours. Mem. ISHM, Surface Mount Tech. Assn. (bd. dirs. 1988-91, Mem. Distinction award 1995), Surface Mount Tech. Equipment Mfg. Assn. (chair reflow com. 1990-92). Achievements include research and development of surface mount technology assembly processes; particular expertise in reflow soldering processes, equipment and technology, and component placement; development of reflow and placement equipment classification method and related terminology. Office: ITM Inc PO Box 921 Durham NH 03824

ZARTMAN, DAVID LESTER, animal sciences educator, researcher; b. Albuquerque, July 6, 1940; s. Lester Grant and Mary Elizabeth (Kitchel) Z.; m. Micheal Aline Plemmons, July 6, 1963; children: Kami Renee, Dalan Lee. BS, N.Mex. State U., 1962; MS, Ohio State U., 1966, PhD, 1968. Jr. ptnr. Marlea Guernsey Farm, Albuquerque, 1962-64; grad. rsch. assoc. Ohio State U., Columbus, 1964-68; asst. prof. dairy sci. N.Mex. State U., Las Cruces, 1968-71, assoc. prof., 1971-79, prof., 1979-84; prof., chmn. dept. Ohio State U., Columbus, 1984—; pres. Mary K. Zartman, Inc., Albuquerque, 1976-84; cons. Bio-Med. Electronics, Inc., San Diego, 1984-89, Zartemp, Inc., Northbrook, Ill., 1990, Recom Applied Solutions, 1993—, Am. Registry of Profl. Animal Scientists, 1996—. Contbr. articles to profl. jours.; patentee in field. Recipient State Regional Outstanding Young Farmer award Jaycees, 1963, Disting. Rsch. award N.Mex. State U. Coll. Agr. and Home Econs., 1983; named one of Top 100 Agr. Alumni, N.Mex. State U. Centennial, 1987; spl. postdoctoral fellow NIH, New Zealand, 1973; Fulbright-Hayes lectr., Malaysia, 1976. Fellow AAAS; mem. Am. Dairy Sci. Assn., Am. Soc. Animal Sci., Dairy Shrine Club, Ohio Extension Profs. Assn., Poultry Sci. Assn., Am., Ohio Farm Bur., Sigma Xi, Gamma Sigma Delta, Alpha Gamma Rho (1st Outstanding Alumnus N.Mex. chpt. 1985), Alpha Zeta, Phi Kappa Phi. Home: 7671 Deer Creek Dr Columbus OH 43085-1551 Office: Ohio State U 2029 Fyffe Rd Columbus OH 43210-1007

ZARWYN, BERTHOLD, physical scientist; b. Vienna, Austria, Aug. 22, 1921; came to U.S., 1949, naturalized, 1955; s. Joseph and Bronislawa Regina (Unger) Z.; M.E., Gliwice, Poland, 1946; Sc.D., Munich (W. Ger.) U., 1947; Ph.D., N.Y.U., 1954; Engring. Sc.D., Columbia, 1963. Project engr. Curtiss-Wright Corp., Woodridge, N.J., 1951-55; staff scientist AMF Corp., N.Y.C., 1955-57; chief scientist Link Aviation Co., Binghamton, N.Y., 1957-58; head research staff Am. Bosch-Arma Corp., Garden City, N.Y., 1958-63; corp. cons. Cutler-Hammer Corp., Deer Park, N.Y., 1963-65; chief engr. Bell Aerosystems Corp., Niagara Falls, N.Y., 1965-66; sr. cons. Mitre Corp., Bedford, Mass., 1966-68; spl. asst. to commanding gen., acting chief engr. Hdqrs. U.S. Army Materiel Command, Arlington, Va., 1968-71, chief phys. scis. br., U.S. Army Devel. and Readiness Command, Alexandria, Va., 1971-75, phys. scientist U.S. Army Harry Diamond Labs., Washington, 1975-78; chief system analysis br. U.S. Army Elec. Rsch. and Devel. Command, Adelphi, Md., 1978-79, chief tech. divsn., 1979-81, asst. tech. dir., 1981-85; spl. asst. to dep. chief of staff for tech. and program mgmt. U.S. Army Lab. Command, Adelphi, 1985-87, pres. Pan-Tech. Corp., 1987—; adj. faculty, lectr., cons. in field; dir. Film Microelectronics Co. Inc., Burlington, Mass., 1965-67. Mem. IEEE, Am. Phys. Soc., N.Y. Acad. Scis., Sigma Xi. Editorial bd. Bavarian Soc. Engrs., 1947-49; translation panel Russian Jour. Applied Math. and Mechanics with Pergamon Inst., 1956-57. Inventor nuclear gyroscope, microwave holography, other items. Home and Office: Pan-Tech Corp 11211 S Military Tr # 4312 Boynton Beach FL 33436-7234

ZARZOUR, ROBIN ANN, special education educator; b. Parma, Ohio, Apr. 14, 1964; d. Robert Halim and Rosalie Frances (Ezzie) Z. AAS in Early Childhood Edn., Cuyahoga C.C., 1985; BS in Spl. Edn., Cleve. State U., 1990, MA in Early Childhood Spl. Edn., 1993. Early childhood spl. edn. aide Middleburg Spl. Presch., Middleburg Heights, Ohio, 1983-86; counselor Camp Sunshine, Parma, Ohio, 1986-88; early childhood spl. religious tchr. St. Charles, Parma, Ohio, 1988-89; early childhood spl. edn. tchr. Parma City Sch. System, 1990—. Mem. Cleve. Assn. Mid. Ea. Orgn., 1992—. Recipient Tchr. of Yr. award Cuyahoga Spl. Edn. Svc. Ctr., 1993—. Mem. Coun. for Exception Children, Parma Edn. Assn. (union bldg. rep. 1992—). Democrat. Roman Catholic. Avocations: golf, working out, movies, music.

ZASLAVSKY, ROBERT, secondary school educator; b. Phila., Feb. 26, 1942; s. Harry and Sally (Zwick) Z.; div.; 1 child, Cordelia Helena. AB in Philosophy, English Lit., Temple U., 1964; MA in Philosophy, New Sch. Social Rsch., 1969, PhD in Philosophy, 1978; postgrad., Cabrini Coll., 1989—. Substitute tchr. math. and English Phila. Bd. Edn., 1964; caseworker Phila. Dept. Pub. Assistance, 1964-65, N.Y.C. Dept. Welfare, 1965-68; instr. philosophy Villanova U., 1971-73; instr. philosophy of art Immaculata Coll., 1975; libr. interlibr. loan and reference Bryn Mawr (Pa.) Coll., 1973-86; exec. producer, on-air performer, camera oper. Studio 9 Video Prodns., 1986—; adj. instr. English and religion, student tchr. adviser Cabrini Coll., 1990; instr. lit. Main Line Sch. Night, 1991-95; instr. humanities Akiba Hebrew Acad., Merion Station, Pa., 1990-96; instr. English Marine Mil. Acad., Harlingen, Tex., 1997—; job counselor Kingston (N.Y.)

Community Ctr., 1968; presenter seminars; guest lectr. Greek lit. Bryn Mawr Coll., 1976-78, Villanova U., 1978-81; assoc. Greater Phila. Philosophy Consortium, 1983-86; instr. Rittenhouse Acad., 1989, Haverford Twp. Adult Sch., 1989, Valley Forge Mil. Acad., 1989-90; instr. Elderhostel program Cabrini Coll., 1990, 91, Valley Forge Hist. Soc., 1991. Contbr. articles, revs. to lit. publs. Mem. ASCD, Nat. Coun. Tchrs. English, Ind. Sch. Tchrs. Assn. (classical langs. div.), Pa. State Edn. Assn., The American Classical League, Mystery Writers Am., Core Knowledge Fdn. Home: 2115 E Vinson # 5107 Harlingen TX 78550 Office: Marine Mil Acad 320 Iwo Jima Blvd Harlingen TX 78550-3627

ZASLOW, JEFFREY LLOYD, syndicated columnist; b. Phila., Oct. 6, 1958; s. Harry and Naomi (Weintraub) Z.; m. Sherry Lynn Margolis, July 4, 1987; children: Jordan Danielle, Alexandra Nicole, Eden Gabrielle. BA with honors, Carnegie-Mellon U., 1980. Reporter/columnist The Orlando (Fla.) Sentinel, 1980-83; staff writer The Wall St. Jour., Chgo., 1983-87; columnist The Chgo. Sun Times, 1987—, USA Weekend mag., 1995—. Author: (with others) You Can Do Something About AIDS, 1988, Tell Me All About It, 1990, Take It from Us, 1994, Talk of Fame, 1997; contbr. feature articles to The N.Y. Times, Reader's Digest, Phila. Inquirer, Boston Globe, Cosmopolitan mag., Glamour, Bus. Week, others; writer of liner notes for singer Don McLean's double-live album, 1983; numerous appearances on TV including ABC's Nightline with Ted Koppel, Good Morning Am., NBC's Today Show, CBS This Morning, Oprah Winfrey Show, The Larry King Show, NBC's Tonight Show, CBS's Saturday Night with Connie Chung; subject of articles in Time, Newsweek, People, Life, Washington Post, others. Jewish. Achievements include organizing annual reader-participation programs providing school supplies and holiday gifts for 28,000 needy children in Chicago; annual Zazz Bash for singles raises money for Chicago charities. Office: Chgo Sun-Times Inc 401 N Wabash Ave Ste 320 Chicago IL 60611-5644

ZASSENHAUS, HILTGUNT MARGRET, physician; b. Hamburg, Ger., July 10, 1916; came to U.S., 1952, naturalized, 1957; d. Julius and Margret Z. Diploma of Scandinavian Langs., U. Hamburg, 1938; MD, U. Copenhagen, 1952; MD (hon.), Goucher Coll., Towson State U., U. Notre Dame, 1975, U. Md., 1984, Washington Coll., Md., 1984, Western Coll. Md., 1987, U. Md., Balt. County, 1988. With German Dept. Justice, Berlin, 1941-45; secret relief action for Scandinavian polit. prisoners; organizer relief action for German orphans German Dept. Justice, 1945-48; intern, then resident in internal medicine Balt. City Hosp., 1952-54; pvt. practice specializing in internal medicine Balt., 1954—; med. bd. Greater Balt. Med. Center; appointed mem. Md. Council Humanities, 1979—; del. Med. and Chirurgical Faculty of State of Md., 1985-89. Author: biography On Guard in The Dark, 1948; autobiography Walls (Christopher award as best book of year 1975, Best Book of Yr . Book Assn. Evang. Ch. Germany 1981); subject of documentary Woman of Courage, 1989; also articles, essays. Trustee White Rose Found., N.Y., 1988; bd. dirs. Roland Park Country Sch., GBMC, Balt., 1985; bd. dirs. Greater Balt. Medf. Ctr., 1986,; trustee The White Rose Found., N.Y.C., 1988; apptd. hon. senator U. Hamburg, 1990. Decorated knight St. Olav's Order 1st class (Norway); Order Dannebrog 1st class (Denmark), Bundesverdienstkreuz 1st class (Fed. Republic Germany); recipient Danish Red Cross medal, 1948, Norwegian Red Cross medal, 1948, 86, Gold Meml. medal Senate of City of Hamburg, Fed. Republic Germany, 1986, Community Service award Med. Assn. Md., 1986, Gold medal U. Hamburg, 1990; named Outstanding Woman of Year in Balt. County AAUW, 1976; nominated for Nobel Peace Prize, 1974; named to Md. Women's Hall of Fame, 1986; subject of documentary It Mattered to Me, produced by ITV, Yorkshire TV (Eng.), 1981; apptd. hon. sen. U. Hamburg, Fed. Republic Germany, 1990. Mem. Physicians for Social Responsibility (bd. dirs.), Balt. County Med. Soc. Address: 7028 Bellona Ave Baltimore MD 21212-1111 *I know that one person can make the difference. That gives me hope that the walls of hate and prejudice separating man from man one day will fade so that people will cease destroying each other and join to serve life.*

ZATKO, PATRICIA ANN, nursing administrator, geriatrics nurse; b. Buffalo, July 18, 1943; d. Vincent and Florence (Cybulski) Lipka; m. Steven Paul Zatko, Jan. 9, 1965 (dec. Mar. 1984); children: Julie Ann, Steven Paul II, John Vincent. LPN, Boces, 1979; ADN, Trocaire Coll., 1986; BSN magna cum laude, SUNY, Buffalo, 1991. Practical nurse Erie County Med. Ctr., Buffalo, 1979-86, gen. duty nurse, 1986-88, quality rev. nurse, 1988-91, case mgr., 1991—, nursing researcher, 1992. Vol. outreach com. Our Lady of the Blessed Sacrament Ch., Depew, N.Y., 1985—, lector, 1986—, Eucharistic min., bereavement com., grief support group; sec. Citizens for a Greener Depew, 1991, 92; vol. Benedict House. Recipient award Nat. Assn. Counties, 1992, 96. Mem. N.Y. State Nurses Assn. (award 1986), Quality Assurance of Hospice Buffalo, Sigma Theta Tau. Democrat. Roman Catholic. Avocations: crafts, reading, volunteer work, church work. Home: 223 French Rd Depew NY 14043-2162 Office: Erie County Med Ctr 462 Grider St Buffalo NY 14215-3021

ZATKOFF, LAWRENCE P., federal judge; b. 1939; m. Nancy L. Chenhall; four children. BSBA, U. Detroit, 1962; JD cum laude, Detroit Coll. Law, 1966. Bar: Mich., U.S. Supreme Ct. Mem. corp. personnel staff Chrysler Corp., 1962-66; asst. prosecuting atty. Macomb County, Mich.; with Moll, Desenberg, Purdy, Glover & Bayer, Detroit, 1966-68; ptnr. LaBarge, Zatkoff & Dinning, Roseville, 1968-78; probate judge Macomb County, 1978-82; judge Macomb County Cir. Ct., 1982-87, U.S. Dist. Ct. (ea. dist.) Mich., 1986—; part-time faculty Detroit Coll. Law; mem. rep. assembly Mich. State Bar, mem. spl. com. on grievances; appointed assoc. govt. appeal agt. SSS, 1969-72. Guest lectr., past mem. scholarship ball com. Macomb County Community Coll.; citizen's adv. bd. Macomb-Oakland Regional Ctr., 1978-79; ex officio mem. Macomb County Youthscope; adv. bd. Met. Detroit chpt. March of Dimes; trustee St. Joseph Hosp. of Mt. Clemens; mem. Selfridge Air NG Base Community Council; Rep. candidate 12th dist. U.S. Congress Mich., 1976, party treas. 12 dist. 1975, exec. com., 1975, chmn. Macomb County exec. com., 1976, del. several nat. and regional Rep. Convs., Macomb County campaign coordinator for U.S. Sen. candidate Marvin Esch, 1976. Mem. ABA, Fed. Bar Assn., Mich. Bar. Assn., Macomb County Bar. Assn. (dir., treas. Young Lawyers sect., past probate ct. liason to bd. dirs., mem. cir. ct. liason com.), Detroit Bar Assn., Am. Judicare Soc., Am. Arbitration Assn., Nat. Orgn. Legal Problems of Edn., Nat. Council Juvenile and Family Ct. Judges, Mich. Probate and Juvenile Ct. Judges Assn. (mental health com.), Nat. Coll. Probate Judges, Mich. Judges Assn., VFW (legal case rep. 1976, spokesman Vietnamese Embassy Paris 1976, judge Voice of Democracy programs 1975, state wide scholarships judge, Voice of Democracy awards 1975, 76, Americanism award 1976, Spl. Recognition award 1978). Clubs: 100, Macomb County 300, Rep. Majority (charter). Office: US Dist Ct 707 US Courthouse 231 W Lafayette Blvd Detroit MI 48226-2720*

ZATLIN, GABRIEL STANLEY, physician; b. N.Y.C., Dec. 5, 1935; s. Samuel and Bernice (Morgenstern) Z.; m. Linda M. Gertner, Dec. 29, 1959 (div. 1973); children: Jonathan Reid, Andrew Evan; m. Lorna G. Schofield, May 14, 1983; 1 child, Sarah Schofield. BS, U. Miami, Coral Gables, Fla., 1956; MD, Washington U., St. Louis, 1960. Diplomate Am. Bd. Pediatrics, Am. Bd. Family Practice. Intern St. Louis Children's Hosp., 1960-61, resident, 1961-62; resident Children's Hosp. Med. Ctr., Boston, 1965-66, Downstate Med. Ctr., Bklyn., 1979-81; Epidemiologist Ctrs. for Disease Control, Atlanta, 1962-64; pvt. practice Atlanta, 1966-73; cons. Pertamina, Jakarta, Indonesia, 1974-76; field dir. African Health Trng. Project, Yaounde, Cameroun, 1976-77; assoc. dir. Brown U. Health Svcs., Providence, 1977-79; asst. prof. Downstate Med. Ctr., Bklyn., 1981-82; assoc. dir. St. Mary Hosp. Family Practice, Hoboken, N.J., 1982-88; dir. St. Mary Hosp. Family Practice, 1988-92; clin. assoc. prof. Downstate Med. Ctr., Bklyn., 1992-95, dir. family practice residency program, 1993-95; faculty family practice residency program Beth Israel Hosp., 1995—; clin. asst. prof. Albert Einstein Sch. Medicine. Contbr. articles to profl. jours.; cons. Resident/Staff Physician jour., 1985—, VIS jour., 1986—. With USPHS, 1962-64. Fellow Am. Acad. Pediatrics; mem. Am. Acad. Family Practice, Soc. for Adolescent Medicine. Avocations: gardening, fencing. Office: Inst for Urban Family Prac 16 E 16th St New York NY 10003-3105

ZATUCHNI, GERALD IRVING, physician, educator; b. Phila., Oct. 5, 1933; s. Samuel and Minnie (Pollack) Z.; m. Bette Ruth Christine, June 15, 1958; children: Cheryl Lee, Bettina, Mimi. AB, Temple U., 1954, MD, 1958, MSc, 1965. Diplomate Am. Bd. Obstetrics and Gynecology. Intern Walter Reed Army Hosp, Washington, 1958-59; residency in ob-gyn Temple U. Med. Ctr., Phila., 1962-65; gen. practice medicine Phila., 1965-66; staff assoc. Population Council, N.Y.C., 1966-69; resident advisor Population Council, New Dehli, 1969-71; cons. World Health Orgn., Geneva, 1971-73; regional advisor Population Council, Tehran, Iran, 1973-75; assoc. med. dir. Population Council, N.Y.C., 1975-76; prof. ob-gyn. Northwestern U., Chgo., 1977—; cons. Medico-Legal, 1982—; bd. dirs. Fertility Research Northwestern U. Author books; editor numerous books, jours. Served to capt. USMC, 1958-62. Recipient Phillip Williams prize Phila. Ob. Soc., 1964, Babcock Surg. prize Temple U., 1965; Fertility Research grantee, U.S. Govt., 1981. Fellow Am. Coll. Ob-Gyn.; mem. Soc. Advancement Contraception (pres. 1986). Avocations: painting, sailing, golf, tennis. Office: Prentice Women's Hosp 680 N Lake Shore Dr Ste 1000 Chicago IL 60611-4451

ZAUNER, CHRISTIAN WALTER, university dean, exercise physiologist, consultant; b. Phila., July 21, 1930; s. Philip Walter and Margaret Helen (Gilmor) Z.; m. Betty Ann Schwenk, Feb. 1, 1957; children: Beth, Ward, Joe. BS, West Chester State, 1956; MS, Syracuse U., 1957; PhD, So. Ill. U., 1963. Asst. prof. Temple U., Phila., 1963-65; prof. phys. edn. and medicine U. Fla., Gainesville, 1965-84; dir. Sports Medicine Inst., Mt. Sinai Med. Ctr., Miami Beach, Fla., 1984-87; chmn. exercise sci. Oreg. State U., Corvallis, 1987-94; dean health and human performance East Carolina U., Greenville, N.C., 1994—; cons. in exercise rehab. Hosp. Corp. Am.; cons. in sports medicine State of Kuwait, Arab Gulf; cons. sport sci. curriculum Ministry Edn., Thailand. Contbr. numerous articles to various profl. jours. Served with USN, 1951-54. Grantee U. Fla., 1971, Am. Scandinavian Foun., 1971, Fla. Blue Key, 1978, Nat. Acad. Sci., 1985-86, 88, 90, 94. Fellow Am. Coll. Sports Medicine; mem. Am. Physiol. Soc., N.Y. Acad. Scis., AAHPERD, Sigma Chi. Democrat. Roman Catholic. Office: East Carolina U Sch Health & Human Performance Greenville NC 27858-4353

ZAUSNER, L. ANDREW, lawyer; b. Plainfield, N.J., May 1, 1949; s. Sol and Beatrice (Summer) Z; m. Nancy J. Zausner, Aug. 10, 1990; children: L. Alexander, Samantha Rae. B.A., Boston U., 1971; M.B.A., U. Pa., 1975, J.D., 1975. Bar: Pa. 1975, D.C. 1979, U.S. Supreme Ct. 1979. Mem. firm Blank, Rome, Comisky & McCauley, Phila., 1975-77; atty., adv. legislation Fed. Energy Adminstrn., Washington, 1977; spl. asst. to acting gen. counsel Dept. Energy, Washington, 1977-78; exec. asst. to dep. sec. Dept. Energy, 1978-79; dir. govt. relations Pennzoil Co., 1979-82, v.p. govt. relations, 1982-85; ptnr. Webster & Sheffield, 1985-90, Dickstein, Shapiro, Morin & Oshinsky, LLP, Washington, 1990—; bd. dirs. Dauphin Deposit Corp., Harrisburg, Pa., chmn. trust and investment com. Home: 8909 Abbey Ter Potomac MD 20854-5434 Office: 2101 L St NW Ste 800 Washington DC 20037-1526

ZAVARIN, EUGENE, forestry science educator; b. Sombor, Yugoslavia, Feb. 21, 1924; came to U.S., 1950; s. Alexey K. and Iya A. (Shepkin) Z.; m. Valentina S. Kusubov, July 15, 1956; children: Ksenya, Sergey, Michael, Nina, Mavrick. BS, U. Goettingen, Fed. Republic Germany, 1949; PhD, U. Calif., Berkeley, 1954. Sr. lab. technician U. Calif., Berkeley, 1952-54; asst. specialist Forest Products Lab., Richmond, Calif., 1954-57, asst. forest product chemist, 1957-62, assoc. forest product chemist, 1962-68, forest product chemist, 1968—; lectr. wood chemistry U. Calif., Berkeley, 1962-75, prof. forestry, 1975-92; prof. forestry emeritus, 1992—; Reviewer grant proposals NSF. Mem. editorial adv. bd. Jour. Wood Chemistry and Tech.; contbr. articles to profl. jours.; writer short stories; translator theater plays into Russian. Fellow NIH, Institut de Chimie des Substances Naturelle, Gif-sur-Yvette, France, 1963; NSF grantee, 1965-67, USDA grantee, 1986-88. Fellow Internat. Acad. Wood Sci.; mem. Am. Chem. Soc., Sigma Xi. Republican. Avocations: travel, gardening, photography. Home: 280 Edgehill Way San Francisco CA 94127-1005 Office: U Calif Forest Products Lab 1301 S 46th St Richmond CA 94804-4600

ZAVATSKY, MICHAEL JOSEPH, lawyer; b. Wheeling, W.Va., Dec. 15, 1948; s. Mike and Mary (Mirich) Z.; m. Kathleen Hanson, May 28, 1983; children: David, Emily. BA in Internat. Studies, Ohio State U., 1970; MA in Polit. Sci., U. Hawaii, 1972; JD, U. Cin., 1980. Bar: Ohio 1980, U.S. Dist. Ct. (so. dist.) Ohio 1981, U.S. Ct. Appeals (6th cir.) 1985, U.S. Supreme Ct. 1989. Ptnr. Taft, Stettinius & Hollister, Cin., 1980—; adj. prof. in trial practice and immigration law U. Cin., 1986—. Trustee Internat. Visitors Ctr., Cin., 1984-86; bd. dirs. Cin. Charter Com., 1988-91; bd. dirs., mem. steering com. Leadership Cin., 1994-96. Capt. USAF, 1973-77. William Graham fellow U. Cin., 1979, East West Ctr. fellow U. Hawaii, 1970. Mem ABA, Ohio Bar Assn., Cin. Bar Assn., Am. Immigration Lawyers Assn. (chmn. Ohio chpt. 1987-88, 90-93), Potter Stewart Inn of Ct., Order of Coif. Home: 3820 Eileen Dr Cincinnati OH 45209-2013 Office: 1800 Star Bank Ctr Cincinnati OH 45202

ZAVON, MITCHELL RALPH, physician; b. N.Y.C., May 9, 1923; s. Irving and Claire (Gutterman) Z.; m. Betty Berthold, June 24, 1976; children by previous marriage: Peter, Dan, Juliet, Barbara. Student, Cornell U., 1940-43, Harvard U., 1943-44; M.D., Boston U., 1945-49; postgrad. Duke U., 1951-52, U. Cin., 1956-58. Diplomate Am. Bd. Med. Examiners, Am. Bd. Preventive Medicine, Am. Bd. Indsl. Hygiene. Intern, Wilson Meml. Hosp., Johnson City, N.Y.; surgeon USPHS, Washington, 1950-56; from instr. to asst. clin. prof. U. Cin., 1952-74, from asst. prof. to clin prof. Industrial medicine, 1956-71; asst. health commr. Cin. Health Dept., 1956-74; med. dir. Ethyl Corp., Baton Rouge, 1974-76; dir. health Occidental Chem. Corp., Niagara Falls, N.Y., 1976-86; pres., med. dir. Agatha Corp., 1968—; mem., cons., del. Threshold Limits Com., 1962-87; mem., cons. Biol. Indeces Com., 1982-96; mem. cons. staffs Niagara Falls Meml. Hosp, pres. Place-to-Be, 1978-83; mem. cons. staff Mt. St. Mary's Hosp., 1980-94; med. dir. Buffalo Union Occupl. Health Ctr., 1996—. Contbr. articles to profl jours. Bd. dirs. HART; mem. Cincinnatus Assocs., 1969-7, Bd. Health Niagara County, N.Y., 1994—, pres., 1997. Fellow APHA, Am. Coll. Occupl. and Environ. Medicine, Am. Indsl. Hygiene Assn.; mem. AMA, AAAS, Am. Assn. Adv. Scis., NY. State Med. Soc., Niagara County Med. Soc.; Am. Conference on Govtl. Indsl. Hygienists. Unitarian. Office: Agatha Corp 4497 Lower River Rd Lewiston NY 14092-1056 Other: PO Box 58425 Cincinnati OH 45258-0425

ZAWACKI, BRUCE EDWIN, surgeon, ethicist; b. Northampton, Mass., Dec. 6, 1935. BS, Coll. of the Holy Cross, 1957; MD, Harvard U., 1961; MA, U. So. Calif., 1986. Diplomate Am. Bd. Surgery. Dir. burn study br. U.S. Army Inst. Surg. Rsch., San Antonio, 1968; gen. surgeon So. Calif. Permanente Med. Group, Panorama City, 1969-71; dir. burn ctr. L.A. County and U. So. Calif. Med. Ctr., L.A., 1971—; assoc. prof. surgery U. So. Calif. Sch. Medicine, L.A., 1975—; assoc. prof. religion U. So. Calif. Sch. Religion, L.A., 1992—; chair ethics resource com. LAC and U. So. Calif. Med. Ctr., L.A., 1988—. Contbr. articles to profl. jours. Served to maj. U.S. Army, 1967-68. Mem. Am. Burn Assn. (2d v.p., bd. trustees 1992-93; Harvey Stuart Allen Disting. Svc. award 1996), Soc. for Health and Human Values, L.A. Surg. Soc., Internat. Soc. for Burn Injuries. Achievements include first to describe the natural history of reversible burn injury, the independence of burn hypermetabolism from evaporative water loss and an autonomous role for burn patients without precedent for survival. Office: LAC & USC Med Ctr 1200 N State St Rm 12-650 Los Angeles CA 90033-4525

ZAWADA, EDWARD THADDEUS, JR., physician, educator; b. Chgo., Oct. 3, 1947; s. Edward Thaddeus and Evelyn Mary (Kovarek) Z.; m. Nancy Ann Stephen, Mar. 26, 1977; children: Elizabeth, Nicholas, Victoria, Alexandra. BS summa cum laude, Loyola U., Chgo., 1969; MD summa cum laude, Loyola-Stritch Sch. Medicine, 1973. Diplomate Am. Bd. Internal Medicine, Am. Bd. Nephrology, Am. Bd. Nutrition, Am. Bd. Critical Care, Am. Bd. Geriatrics, Am. Bd. Clin. Pharm., Am. Bd. Forensic Examiners. Intern UCLA Hosp., 1973, resident, 1974-76; asst. prof. medicine UCLA, 1978-79, U. Utah, Salt Lake City, 1979-81; assoc. prof. medicine Med. Coll. Va., Richmond, 1981-83; assoc. prof. medicine, physiology & pharmacology U. S.D. Sch. Medicine, Sioux Falls, 1983-86, Freeman prof., chmn. dept. Internal Medicine, 1987—, chief div. nephrology and hypertension, 1983-88, pres. univ. physician's practice plan, 1992—; chief renal sect. Salt Lake VA Med. Ctr., 1980-81; asst. chief med. service McGuire VA Med. Ctr., Richmond, 1981-83. Editor: Geriatric Nephrology and Urology, 1984; contbr. articles to profl. publs. Pres. Minnehaha div. Am. Heart Assn., 1984-87, pres. Dakota affiliate Am. Heart Assn., 1989-91. VA Hosp. System grantee, 1981-85, 85-88; Health and Human Svcs. grantee Pub. Health Scvs. Rsch. Adminstrn. Bureau Health Profl., 1993—. Fellow ACP, Am. Coll. Chest Physicians, Am. Coll. Nutrition, Am. Coll. Clin. Pharmacology, Internat. Coll. Angiology, Am. Coll. Angiology, Am. Coll. Clin. Pharmacology, Am. Coll. Forensic Examiners, Royal Soc. Medicine; mem. Internat. Soc. Nephrology, Am. Soc. Nephrology, Am. Soc. Pharmacology and Exptl. Therapeutics, Am. Physiol. Soc., Am. Inst. Nutrition, Am. Soc. Clin. Nutrition, Am. Geriatric Soc., Westward Ho Country Club. Democrat. Roman Catholic. Avocations: golf, tennis, skiing, cinema, music. Home: 2908 S Duchess Ave Sioux Falls SD 57103-4826 Office: U SD Sch Medicine 1400 W 22nd St Sioux Falls SD 57105-1505

ZAWINUL, JOSEF, bandleader, composer, keyboardist, synthesist; b. Vienna, Austria, July 7, 1932; came to U.S., 1959; s. Josef and Maria (Hameder) Z.; m. Maxine Byars, Mar. 16, 1964; children—Anthony, Erich, Ivan. Student, Realgymnasium, Vienna, 1945-49, Vienna Conservatory Music, 1942-47; Dr. honoris Causa, 1969. Appeared with Vienna Radio Orch., 1952-58, Maynard Ferguson, 1959; mem. Fatty George Band, 1956-58; accompanist Dinah Washington, 1959-61, Joe Williams, 1961; mem. Cannonball Adderley Quintet, 1961-70; recs. with Miles Davis include Bitches Brew, In a Silent Way; founder own group Weather Report, 1970-85, Zawinul Syndicate, 1985—; recs. include: Weather Report, Vitous, 1971, I Sing the Body Electric, 1972, Tale Spinnin', Black Market, 1974, Heavy Weather, 1977, Mr. Gone, 1978,Mysterious Traveler, Night Passage, Sportin Life, Weather Report with Jaco Pastorius, 1981, This is This, 1986, (with Miles Davis), In a Silent Way, 1969, Bitches Brew, 1970, (with Salifkeita) Amen, 1992, (solo) Dialects, Zawinul, (with Zawinul Syndicate) Immigrants, Black Water, 1989, Lost Tribes. Recipient Jazz Record of Year award 5 of 8 albums, 1973-78; named Best Synthesizer player Downbeat mag., 1984, 85, 89. Address: Internat Music Network 2 Main St # Fl4 Gloucester MA 01930-5726

ZAWISTOWSKI, STEPHEN LOUIS, psychologist, educator; b. Lackawanna, N.Y., July 28, 1955; s. Louis Henry and Alice Theresa (Bartus) Z.; m. Jane Elaine Clark, May 26, 1979; 1 child, Matthew. BA, Canisius Coll., 1977; AM, U. Ill., 1979, PhD, 1983. Vis. asst. prof. Ind. U., Bloomington, 1983-84, postdoctoral fellow, 1984-85; asst. prof. St. John's U., N.Y.C., 1985-88; sr. v.p. ASPCA, N.Y.C., 1988—. Co-author: Animal Rights Handbook, 1990; co-editor: For Kids Who Love Animals, 1991; contbg. editor Animal Watch Mag.; co-exec. prodr. (film) Question of Respect, 1990 (Silver Apple award 1990); mem. bd. editors Psychologists for the Ethical Treatment of Animals, 1988-95; founding co-editor Jour. Applied Animal Welfare Sci.; contbr. articles to profl. jours. Scoutmaster Boy Scouts Am., S.I., 1988—; asst. coach S.I. Youth Soccer, 1986-95; bd. dirs. Nat. Coun. on Pet Population Study and Policy, v.p., 1995-96, pres., 1996-97; mem. steering com. N.Y. State Watchable Wildlife Program. Recipient Stan Lesny scholarship Kosciuszki Found., 1977, U. Ill. Grad. fellowship, 1977, Postdoctoral fellowship NSF, 1984; named Psychologist of Yr., Psychologists for Ethical Treatment of Animals, 1989. Mem. Animal Behavior Soc., Order of Arrow, Sigma Xi. Achievements include research in genetics and animal learning, animal behavior and welfare. Office: ASPCA 424 E 92nd St New York NY 10128-6804

ZAX, LEONARD A., lawyer; b. Paterson, N.J., July 16, 1950; s. Harry and Shirley Jeanne (Hollander) Z.; m. Helen Kemp, May 25, 1980; children: David Hollander, Laura Alexandra. BA, U. Chgo., 1971; M of City Planning, Harvard U., 1975, JD, 1975. Bar: N.J. 1978, D.C. 1978. Spl. asst. to gen. counsel HUD, 1975-76, spl. asst. to sec. HUD, 1976-77; lectr., mem. faculty Harvard U., Cambridge, Mass., 1977-78; assoc. Fried, Frank, Harris, Shriver & Kampelman, Washington, 1977-82, ptnr., 1982-95; ptnr. Latham & Watkins, 1995—, also chmn. real estate group; co-chmn. Mayor's Downtown Housing Commn., Washington, 1986-89, D.C. Enterprise Zones Study Commn., 1986-89; D.C. Downtown Interactive Retail Task Force, 1996—; co-chmn. Washington adv. com. Asian Real Estate Assn., Washington, 1991-92. Contbg. author Nat. Law Jour., L.A. Times, Harvard Law Bull., Real Estate Fin. Jour., Urban Land, Washington Business Jour., Washington Post; editor: Real Estate and the RTC: A Guide to Asset Purchases and Contracting, Urban Land Inst., 1990. Trustee Nat. Bldg. Mus., D.C. Preservation League, 1988-95, Greater Washington Rsch. Ctr.; mem. Fannie Mae Nat. Adv. Coun., 1994-95; Harvard U. Adv. Com. on Real Estate Devel., 1990-92. Mem. ABA (chmn. com. on housing and urban devel. law 1986-89, steering com. representation of the Homeless Project 1988-91, governing bd. forum com. affordable housing and community devel. 1991-94), D.C. Bar Assn., Urban Land Inst., Nat. Multi Housing Coun. (mem. nat. realty com.). Home: 4511 28th St NW Washington DC 20008-1035 Office: Latham & Watkins Ste 1300 1001 Pennsylvania Ave NW Washington DC 20004-2505

ZAX, MELVIN, psychologist, educator; b. Cambridge, Mass., Apr. 14, 1928; s. Joseph and Sadie (Kirshner) Z.; m. Ruth Leah Vogel, Apr. 23, 1977; children: Jeffrey S., David B., Jonathan B. A.B., Boston U., 1951, A.M., 1952; Ph.D., U. Tenn., 1955. Clin. psychologist U. Tenn., Knoxville, 1955-56; staff psychologist St. Elizabeths Hosp., Washington, 1956-57; asst. prof. psychology U. Rochester, N.Y., 1957-62, assoc. prof. psychology, 1962-67, prof., 1967-93, prof. emeritus, 1993—; pvt. practice, 1973—; chmn. exptl. and spl. tng. rev. com. NIMH, 1970-71. Author: (with G. Stricker) Patterns of Psychopathology, 1963, (with E.L. Cowen) Abnormal Psychology: Changing Conceptions, 1972, (with G.A. Specter) An Introduction to Community Psychology, 1974, (with M. Nichols) Catharsis in Psychotherapy, 1977; editor: (with Stricker) The Study of Abnormal Behavior: Selected Readings, 1964, (with Cowen and E.A. Gardner) Emergent Approaches to Mental Health Problems, 1967, (with D. Dorr and J. Bonner) The Psychology of Discipline, 1983; adv. editor Jour. Cons. and Clin. Psychology, 1965-81; contbr. articles to profl. jours. Served with AUS, 1946-47. NIMH spl. research fellow Psykologisk Inst., Copenhagen, 1966-67. Fellow Am. Psychol. Assn.; mem. Eastern Psychol. Assn., AAUP, Phi Beta Kappa, Sigma Xi, Phi Kappa Phi. Home: 27 Sky Ridge Dr Rochester NY 14625-2167 Office: 625 Panorama Trl Bldg 2 Rochester NY 14625-2432

ZAYAS-BAZAN, EDUARDO, foreign language educator; b. Camagüey, Cuba, Nov. 17, 1935; came to U.S., 1962, naturalized, 1969; s. Manuel Eduardo and Aida Modesta (Loret de Mola); m. Carolyn M. Novak, Sept. 12, 1987; children: Eduardo, Elena María. Dr. en Derecho, U. Nat. José, 1958; MS, Kans. State Tchrs.' Coll., 1966. Social worker Cuban Refugee Asst. Program, 1962-64; Spanish tchr. Plattsmouth High Sch., 1964-65, Topeka West High Sch., 1965-66; Spanish instr. Appalachian State U., 1966-68; asst. prof. East Tenn. State U., Johnson City, 1968-73; assoc. prof. East Tenn. State U., 1973-79, prof, 1979—, chmn. fgn. lang. dept., 1973-93. Author: (with P. Ferreiro) Como dominar la redacción, 1989, (with G. Fernández de la Torriente) Cómo aumentar su vocabulario 3, Cómo escribir cartas eficaces, 1989, (with N.A. Humbach and José B. Fernández) Nuestro mundo, 1990, (with José Fernández) !Arriba!, 1993, (with Carolyn M. Novak) No se equivoque con el inglés, 1993, El inglés que usted no sabe que sabe, Primera y Segunda Serie, 1993; editor: (with Anthony G. Lozano) Del amor a la revolución, 1975, (with L. Suárez) De aquí y de allá, 1980, (with G. J. Fernández Así somos, 1983; translator: Secret Report on Cuban Revolution, 1981. Pres. Sister Cities Internat., Johnson City, 1971-76. Recipient Disting. Faculty award E. Tenn. State U., 1978. Mem. ACTFL, AAUSC, Am. Assn. Tchrs. Spanish and Portuguese (pres. 1985), Tenn. Fgn. Lang. Teaching Assn. (pres. 1980, Jacqueline Elliott award 1989), Nat. Assn. Cuban-Am. Educators (pres. 1991-93, chair bd. dirs. 1994—), Sigma Delta Pi (Premio Martel 1984), Pi Delta Phi. Home: 2310 David Miller Rd Johnson City TN 37604-3510 Office: East Tenn State U Dept Fgn Langs Johnson City TN 37614

ZAYEK, FRANCIS MANSOUR, bishop; b. Manzanillo, Cuba, Oct. 18, 1920; s. Mansour and Mary (Coury) Z. Student, St. Joseph's Catholic U., Beirut, 1938; D.D., U. Propagation of Faith, 1947, Ph.D., 1947; D.C.L., Lateran U., 1951. Ordained priest Roman Catholic Ch., 1946; rector Maronite Cathedral of Holy Family, Cairo, 1951-56; Oriental sec. to Vatican Apostolic Internunciature; mem. Archdiocesan Tribunal, 1951-56; promoter of justice Sacred Roman Rota, 1956-58; prof. Oriental canon law Internat. Coll. St. Anselm, Rome, 1958-60, Lateran U., Rome, 1960-61; aux. bishop to Cardinal James De Barros Camera; archbishop of Rio de Janeiro, 1962;

consecrated maronite bishop, 1962; titular bishop of Callinicum, maronite bishop Rio de Janeiro, 1962-64; presided over First Ann. Maronite Conv., Washington, 1964; first maronite exarch of U.S.A., 1966—, first eparch of St. Maron of Detroit, 1972-77, first eparch of St. Maron of Bklyn., 1977—, given title of archbishop, 1982. Decorated knight comdr. Equestrian Order of Holy Sepulchre of Jerusalem; recipient medal of merit Govt. of Republic Italy, 1966. Address: Eparch of St Maron 294 Howard Ave PO Box 010-360 Staten Island NY 10301*

ZAZULA, BERNARD MEYER, physician administrator; b. Bklyn., July 7, 1941; s. Harry and Clara (Serchuk) Z.; m. Elise Hoch, Aug. 2, 1966; children: Rona, Harold. BA, Yeshiva Coll., 1961; MD, Albert Einstein Coll., 1965; MPH, Columbia U., 1976. Diplomate Nat. Bd. Med. Examiners, Am. Bd. Preventive Medicine; med. lic., N.Y.; cert. in pub. health and gen. preventive medicine. Intern, resident in pediats. Kings County Hosp., Bklyn., 1965-68; sub-dist. med. officer of health Ministry of Health, Jerusalem, 1971-73; dist. health officer N.Y.C. Dept. Health, 1973-74, dir. Bur. for Handicapped Children, 1975-86; med. dir. Medicaid program N.Y.C. Human Resources Adminstrn., 1986—; hon. staff Flushing (N.Y.) Hosp., 1989-93; tchg. staff Wyckoff Heights Hosp., Queens, N.Y., 1993—. Mem., bd. dirs. Queens Valley Homeowners' Civic Assn., Flushing, 1985-91, Young Israel of Kew Gardens Hills, N.Y., 1983-91. Maj. U.S. Army, 1968-70, Vietnam. Fellow N.Y. Acad. Medicine; mem. APHA, Queens County Med. Soc. (pres. 1995-96), Med. Soc. State of N.Y. (chmn. ethics com. 1992—), Alumni Assn. Albert Einstein Coll. Medicine (nat. pres. 1991-93), mem. bd. trustees, 1996—. Jewish. Avocations: travel, walking, reading. Home: 144-05 70th Rd Flushing NY 11367 Office: Med Assistance Program 330 W 34th St New York NY 10001-2406

ZBACNIK, RAYMOND ERIC, process engineer; b. Cleve., June 28, 1951; s. Eric Victor and Jeanette Beatrice (Brock) Z. BSChE, Purdue U., 1973; MEChE, Manhattan Coll., 1977; postgrad., Stevens Inst. Tech., 1977-78, Ind. U., Purdue U., 1985. Process engr. Foster Wheeler Corp., Livingston, N.J., 1974-78, sr. process engr., 1979-81, process supr., 1981-84; process engr. Norton Co., Stow, Ohio, 1988-90, Babcock & Wilcox, Barberton, Ohio, 1990—. Mem. AIChE, Am. Chem. Soc., Instn. Chem. Engrs., N.Y. Acad. Scis., World Apostolate of Fatima. Roman Catholic. Avocations: prayer, reading, hiking, writing. Home: 4388 Millburn Ave Stow OH 44224-2879 Office: Babcock & Wilcox Utility & Environ Power Divsn 20 S Van Buren Ave Barberton OH 44203-3522

ZBIEGIEN, ANDREA, religious education educator, consultant, educational administrator; b. Berea, Ohio, May 12, 1944; d. Leopold and Anna Meri (Voskovich) Z. BS in Edn., St. John Coll., 1969; MS in Edn., John Carroll U., 1973; MDiv, Grad. Theol. Union, 1986, D of Ministry, 1988. Tchr. jr. h.s. Diocese of Cleve., 1964-76, instr. dept. religious edn., 1971-82, dir. religious edn., 1976-82; diocesan dir. religious edn. Diocese of Toledo, 1982-87; instr. Dept. Christian Formation Diocese of Savannah, Ga., 1987—; dir. religious edn. Diocese of Savannah, 1987—; substitute tchr., Cleve., also Brunswick, Ga., 1976—; cons. Benziger Pub. co., Ohio, 1971-78, Our Sunday Visitor Pubs., 1978-90, Silver, Burdett & Ginn, Savannah, Charleston, St. Augustine, 1988—; adj. prof. St. John U. Grad. Theol. Sem., summers 1978—. Author: RCIA: Parish Team Formation, 1987; producer, author: (videos) RCIA: Parish Team Formation, 1987; contbr. articles to profl. jours. Facilitator Bishop's Task Force Action for a Change, Cleve., 1969-72; adv., facilitator Systematic Techniques of Effective Parenting, Huron County, Ohio, 1982-87; adv. Commn. on Children and Youth, Glynn County, Ga., 1989—; vol. Medicine for World's Poor. Recipient scholarship KC, Cleve., 1961-69. Mem. AAUW, NCCL, YWCA, Nat. Assn. of Pastoral Coords. and Dirs., Nat. Cath. Edn. Assn., Sisters for Christian Cmty., Ind. Order of Foresters, Golden Isles Fiberarts Guild. Avocations: fiberarts, creative writing, oil painting and sketching. Home: 707A Newcastle St Brunswick GA 31520-8012 Office: SFX Christian Formation Ctr 1116 Richmond St Brunswick GA 31520-7545

ZDANIS, RICHARD ALBERT, academic administrator; b. Balt., July 15, 1935; s. Albert Francis and Elsie (Kral) Z.; m. Barbara Rosenberger, June 5, 1955; children: Michael Richard, Carole Lynn. BA, Johns Hopkins U., 1957, PhD in Physics, 1960. Rsch. assoc. Princeton (N.J.) U., 1960-61, instr., 1961-62; asst. prof., then assoc. prof. Johns Hopkins U., Balt., 1962-69, prof., 1969-88, assoc. provost, 1975-79, v.p. for adminstrv. svcs., 1977-79, vice provost, 1979-88; provost Case Western Res. U., Cleve., 1988—; cons. Naval Ordnance Lab., 1967-68, 69-74. Bd. dirs. Great Lakes Mus., Cleve. Edn. Found., 1990-96, Cleve. chpt. ARC, N.E. Ohio Coun. on Higher Edn.; mem. governing coun. Ohio LINK, 1994—. Mem. AAAS, Am. Phys. Soc., Associated Univs. Inc. (bd. dirs.), Assn. Univs. for Rsch. in Astronomy (bd. dirs.). Office: Case Western Reserve Univ Office of Provost 10900 Euclid Ave Cleveland OH 44106-1712

ZEAMER, RICHARD JERE, engineer, executive; b. Orange, N.J., May 13, 1921; s. Jay and Margery Lilly (Herman) Z.; m. Jean Catherine Hellens, July 8, 1944 (div. 1966); children: Audrie Dagna, Richard Warwick, Geoffrey Hellens; m. Theresa Elizabeth Taborsky, Mar. 27, 1969; children: Emily Elizabeth, Charlotte Anne. BSME, MIT, 1943, MSCE, 1948; PhD in Mech. Engring., U. Utah, 1975. Registered profl. engr., Utah. Civil engr. Morton C. Tuttle, Boston, 1949-53; process design engr. Nekoosa Edwards Paper Co., Port Edwards, Wis., 1953-55; process engr. W.Va. Pulp and Paper Co., Luke, Md., 1955-60; rocket engr., supr. Allegany Ballistics Lab., Rocket Ctr., W.Va., 1960-65; engring. supr. Hercules Powder Co., Magna, Utah, 1965-69; engr. structures, heat, flow, combustion & failure analysis Hercules Rocket Plant, Magna, 1969-83; project engring. mgr. Hercules Aerospace Div., Magna, 1983-89; pres., mgr. Applied Sci. Assocs., Salt Lake City, 1989—; chmn. policy studies UN Assn. Utah, 1990—; project leader world problem analyses, 1990—. Contbr. papers, articles, reports to profl. pubis. Judge sci. fair, Salt Lake County, Utah, 1985—; chmn. citizens policy panel Utah chpt. UN Assn., U.S.A., N.Y.C., 1990—; mem. Utah State Hist. Soc., Salt Lake City, 1968-91, Mil. History Soc. Utah, Salt Lake City, 1990—. 1st lt. U.S. Army, 1943-46. Recipient commendation for presentation on world population problem Utah's Forum on Global Environ., 1992. Fellow AIAA (astronautics assoc.); mem. Cons. Engrs. Coun. Utah (article award 1992), League Utah Writers, Wasatch Mountain Club (hike leader 1987—). Achievements include patent for improved artillery ammunition, successful application of engineering approach to analysis of history. Home and Office: Applied Sci Assocs 843 13th Ave Salt Lake City UT 84103-3327

ZEBROSKI, EDWIN LEOPOLD, consulting engineer; b. Chgo., Apr. 1, 1921; s. Peter Paul and Sophie (Rydz) Z.; m. Gisela Karin Rudolph, Sept. 6, 1969; children: Lars, Zoe, Susan, Peggy. BS, U. Chgo., 1941; PhD, U. Calif., Berkeley, 1947. Registered prof. engr., Calif. Project engr. Gen. Electric Co., Schenectady, N.Y., 1947-53; mgr. devel. engring. Gen. Electric Co., San Jose, Calif., 1958-73; mgr. engring. SRI Internat., Menlo Park, Calif., 1954-58, dir. systems and materials dept., 1974-79; dir. nuclear safety analysis ctr. EPRI, Palo Alto, Calif., 1979-81; v.p. engring. INPO, Atlanta, 1981-83; chief nuclear scientist EPRI, 1983-87; dir. risk mgmt. svcs. APTECH Engring. Svcs., Sunnyvale, Calif., 1988—; vis. prof. Purdue U., West Lafayette, Ind., 1977-78; cons. OTA, Washington, 1980, 82-83, Dept. Energy, Washington, 1985-90, panels Nat. Rsch. Coun., 1990—, Electricite de France, 1986-87, Dept. Interior, Washington, 1987-89, EPRI, Palo Alto, 1988-94, Acad. Sci., USSR, 1987, Juelich Lab., Germany, 1988; mem. commn. engring. edn. NRC, Washington, 1970-73. Contbr. chpts. to books, numerous articles to profl. jours.; patentee in field. Pres. bd. Unitarian Ch., Palo Alto, 1967-68. Recipient Charles A. Coffin award Gen. Electric Co., Schenectady, 1954. Fellow AAAS, Am. Nuclear Soc. (bd. exec. com. 1969-71), Am. Inst. Chemists; mem. NAE (chmn. energy com. 1984-86, chmn. mem. com. 1986-87, policy com. 1995-96), Am. Phys. Soc., Soc. for Risk Analysis. Avocations: safety and risk management, decision analysis, music, writing. Office: APTECH Engring Svcs 1282 Reamwood Ave Sunnyvale CA 94089-2233

ZEBROWITZ, LESLIE ANN, psychology educator; b. Detroit, Nov. 8, 1944; d. Aaron Harry and Esther (Milgrom) Z.; m. A. Verne McArthur (div. July 1988); children: Caleb Jonathan McArthur, Loren Zachary McArthur. BA, U. Wis., 1966; MS, Yale U., 1968, PhD, 1970. Asst. prof. psychology Brandeis U., Waltham, Mass., 1970-76, assoc. prof., 1976-82, prof., 1982—, chmn. dept., 1986-91; Manuel Yellen prof. social rels. Brandeis U., Waltham, 1989—; vis. scholar Henry Murray Rsch. Ctr. Radcliffe Coll., Cambridge, Mass., 1991-92, vis Erskine fellow, U. Canterbury, 1996; program dir. social psychology, NSF, Arlington, Va., 1994-95. Author: Social Perception, 1991, Reading Faces, 1997; contbr. numerous articles to sci. jours. Ford. Found. faculty fellow, 1973-74; NIMH rsch. grantee, 1975-81, 87—. Fellow Am. Psychol. Assn.; mem. Am. Psychol. Soc. (charter), Soc. for Exptl. Social Psychology, Ea. Psychol. Assn., Phi Beta Kappa. Office: Brandeis U Dept Of Psychology Waltham MA 02254

ZECCA, JOHN ANDREW, retired association executive; b. Bklyn., June 18, 1914; s. Joseph and Elvira (Orsi) Z.; m. Jean Ann Scott, June 27, 1964; 1 son, John Andrew. Student, Heffley Queensboro Coll., Ridgewood, N.Y., 1931, N.Y. U., 1933-36. Auditor ASCE, 1936-50, comptroller, 1950-60; registered rep. Goodbody & Co., 1960-61; pvt. cons. practice, 1961-64; sec., gen. mgr. United Engring. Trustees, 1965-81; trustee Engring. Index, Inc., 1967-81; sec. Engring. Found., 1965-81. John Fritz Medal Bd. Award, 1965-81; Daniel Guggenheim Medal Bd. Award, 1965-81. Mem. East Side Assn., ASCE, Council Engring. and Sci. Soc. Execs., Am. Soc. Assn. Execs. Home: 15 Hillside Ter Suffern NY 10901-2104

ZECHMAN, DAVID MARK, hospital administrator, educator; b. Cleve., Jan. 31, 1956; s. Richard Lee Zechman and Marilyn Ann Molter; m. Rhonda Dale Lovett, Aug. 20, 1977; children: Audra, Alyssa. BS, Miami U., Oxford, Ohio, 1977; postgrad. studies in Respiratory Therapy, Northwestern U. Med. Sch., Chgo., 1983; M in Pub. Adminstrn., Cleve. State U., 1989. Biology tchr. and coach St. Bridget Sch., Cleve., Ohio, 1982; respiratory therapist St. Luke's Hosp., Cleve., 1982-83; supr. respiratory therapy Fairview Hosp., Cleve., 1983-85; supr., clin. instr. respiratory therapy Metrohealth Med. Ctr., Cleve., 1985-86, staff devel. instr., 1986-87, mgmt. specialist dermatology, renal hemodialysis, 1987-89, acting adminstrv. dir. dept. medicine, 1989, mgr. divsn. cardiology, 1989-91; adminstrv. dir. cardiovascular svcs. St. Vincent Med. Ctr., Toledo, Ohio, 1991-92; adminstr. Mid-Am. Heart Inst. St. Lukes/Shawnee Mission Health System, Kansas City, Mo., 1992—; mem. Nat. Fin. Com. United Network for Organ Sharing; faculty presenter Am. Coll. Cardiovascular Adminstrs., Boston, 1991, Anaheim, Calif. 1991, Mpls., Atlanta, 1993. H.S. Sunday sch. tchr., youth group advisor, 1989—; bd. dirs. Kansas City chpt. Am. Heart Assn., 1994—; cmty. youth softball coach, 1994—; bd. dirs. Blue Valley Christian Ch., chmn. pastor rels. com., 1995-96; mem. Kansas City Urban League Multicultural Leadership Devel. Inst., 1997. Mem. Am. Coll. Healthcare Execs. (assoc.), Am. Soc. Cardiovascular Profls./ Soc. Cardiovascular Mgmt. (v.p., bd. dirs.), Nat. Cardiovascular Network Exec Com. Avocations: volleyball, basketball, golf, running. Office: St Luke's Hosp 4400 Wornall Rd Kansas City MO 64111-3238

ZECKHAUSER, RICHARD JAY, economist, educator; b. Phila., Nov. 1, 1940; s. Julius Nathaniel and Estelle (Borgenicht) Z.; m. Nancy Mackell Hoover, Sept. 9, 1967; children: Bryn Gordon, Benjamin Rennell. A.B., Harvard U., 1962, Ph.D., 1969. Jr. fellow Soc. Fellows Harvard U., 1965-68, mem. faculty, 1968—, prof. polit. econ. Kennedy Sch., 1972—, now Frank P. Ramsey prof. polit. economy; bd. dirs. Recovery Engring., Inc., Johnson-Grace Co., Comm. Group Ins., founder, bd. dirs. Niederhoffer, Cross & Zeckhauser, 1968-84. Co-author: A Primer for Policy Analysis, 1978, Demographic Dimensions of the New Republic, 1981; editor or co-editor: Benefit-Cost and Policy Analysis, 1974, What Role for Government, 1982, Principals and Agents: The Structure of Business, 1985, Am. Soc. Pub. and Pvt. Responsibilities, 1986; Privatization and State-Owned Enterprise: Lessons from the United Kingdom, Canada and the United States, 1988, Strategy and Choice, 1991, Wise Choices, Games, Decisions, and Negotiations, 1996. contbr. more than 150 articles to profl. jours. Fellow Econometric Soc., Assn. for Pub. Policy and Mgmt., Am. Acad. Arts and Scis. Champion numerous regional and nat. contract bridge competitions. Home: 138 Irving St Cambridge MA 02138-1929 Office: Harvard U John F Kennedy Sch Govt 79 Jfk St Cambridge MA 02138-5801

ZEDILLO PONCE DE LEÓN, ERNESTO, president of Mexico; b. Mexico City, Apr. 27, 1951; s. Rodolfo Zedillo Castillo and Martha Alicia Ponce de Leon; m. Nilda Patricia Velasco Nuñez; children: Ernesto, Emiliano, Carlos, Nild Patricia, Rodrigo. Student, Instituto Politécnico Nacional, Bradford U., U. Colo.; MA, Yale U., 1977, PhD, 1981. With Partido Revolucionario Institucional, 1971—, Instituto de Estudios Políticos, Económicos y Sociales; econ. rschr. Dirección Gen. de Programación Económica y Social; lectr. Colegio de Mex., 1978-80; dep. mgr. finance and econ. rsch., advisor to bd. dirs. Banco de Mex.; dep. sec. for planning and budget Govt. Mex., Mexico City, 1985-88, sec. for planning and budget, 1988-92, sec. public edn., 1992-93, pres., 1994—; campaign mgr. presdl. nominee Luis Donald Colosio Partido Revolucionario Institucional, 1993-94. Campaign mgr. Luis Donaldo Colosio. Office: Office of Pres, Patio de hono 20 Piso, Mexico City 06067, Mexico*

ZEDLER, JOY BUSWELL, ecological sciences educator; b. Sioux Falls, S.D., Oct. 15, 1943; d. Francis H. and Charlotte (Johnson) Buswell; m. Paul H. Zedler, June 26, 1965; children: Emily and Sarah (twins). BS, Augustana Coll., 1964; MS, U. Wis., 1966, PhD, 1968. Instr. U. Mo., Columbia, 1968-69; prof. San Diego State U., 1969—; mem. Nat. Wetland Tech. Com., Water Sci. Tech. Bd. Nat. Rsch. Coun., 1991-94; dir. Pacific Estuarine Rsch. Lab., 1985—, Coastal and Marine Inst., 1991-93; gov. bd. The Nature Conservancy, 1995—. Author: Ecology of Southern California Coastal Wetlands, 1982, Salt Marsh Restoration, 1984; co-author: A Manual for Assessing Natural and Restored Wetlands, 1990, Ecology of Tijuana Estuary, 1992, Tidal Wetland Restoration, 1996. Fellow San Diego Natural History Mus.; mem. Ecol. Soc. Am. (mem. pub. affairs com. 1988-90), Soc. Wetlands Scientists, Am. Assn. Limnology and Oceanography, Soc. Ecol. Restoration. Achievements include pioneering studies of impacts of freshwater inflows to coastal wetlands in southwestern U.S. and Australia; contributions to understanding of coastal wetland functioning; development of methods for improving restoration projects in coastal wetlands; identification of shortcomings of ongoing coastal wetland restoration programs. Office: San Diego State U Biology Dept San Diego CA 92182-4615

ZEDROSSER, JOSEPH JOHN, lawyer; b. Milw., Jan. 24, 1938; s. Joseph and Rose (Zollner) Z. AB, Marquette U., 1959; LLB, Harvard U., 1963. Bar: N.Y. 1964, U.S. Dist. Ct. (so. dist.) N.Y. 1966, U.S. Dist. Ct. (ea. dist.) N.Y. 1971, U.S. Ct. Appeals (2d cir.) 1971, U.S. Ct. Appeals (D.C. Cir.) 1975, U.S. Supreme Ct. 1975. Assoc. William G. Mulligan, N.Y.C., 1964-67, Christy, Bauman, Frey and Christy and successors, N.Y.C., 1967-71; dir. community devel. unit Bedford-Stuyvesant Community Legal Svcs. Corp., N.Y.C., 1971-73; assoc. atty. fed. defender svcs. unit Legal Aid Soc., N.Y.C., 1973-74; asst. atty. gen. Environ. Protection Bur., N.Y. State Dept. Law, N.Y.C., 1974-80; regional counsel EPA, N.Y.C., 1980-82; assoc. prof. St. John's U. Sch. Law, N.Y.C., 1982-86; ptnr. Rivkin, Radler, Dunne & Bayh, Uniondale, N.Y., 1986-89, Breed, Abbott & Morgan, N.Y.C., 1989-93, Whitman Breed Abbott & Morgan, N.Y.C., 1993-95; v.p. CPR Inst. for Dispute Resolution, N.Y.C., 1996. Lectr., contbr. to course handbooks for courses sponsored by Practicing Law Inst. and other assns. Lt. USNR, 1965-74, USAR, 1963-65. Mem. ABA, Assn. of Bar of City of N.Y., N.Y. State Bar Assn. (mem. Environ. Law Sect. Exec. Com.), Alpha Sigma Nu. Roman Catholic. Home: 45 East End Ave Apt 11F New York NY 10028

ZEFF, OPHELIA HOPE, lawyer; b. Oak Park, Ill., Aug. 19, 1934; d. Bernard Allen and Esther (Levinsohn) Gurvis; m. David Zeff, Dec. 29, 1957 (div. 1983); children: Sally Lyn Zeff Propper, Betsy Zeff Russell, Ellen, Adam; m. John Canterbury Davis, Sept. 18, 1987. BA, Calif. State U., 1956; JD, U. Pacific, 1975. Bar: Calif. 1975. Reporter Placerville (Calif.) Mountain Dem., 1956-57, Salinas Californian, 1957-59; corr. Modesto (Calif.) Bee, 1962-64; atty. ALRB, Sacramento, 1975-76, Yolo County Counsel, Woodland, Calif., 1976-78, Law Office of O.H. Zeff, Woodland, 1978-85; employee rels. officer Yolo County, 1985-87; ptnr. Littler, Mendelson, Fastiff, Tichy & Mathiason, Sacramento, 1987—. Mem. Vallejo (Calif.) Sch. Bd., 1971-74, pres., 1974; mem. Woodland Libr. Bd., 1982; v.p. LWV, Vallejo, 1972; mem. LWV, Sacramento, 1987—. Recipient Am. Jurisprudence Lawyer Coop. Pub., 1974. Mem. Sacramento County Bar, Sacramento Women Lawyers, Indsl. Rels. Assn. No. Calif., Traynor Soc. (life). Democrat. Jewish. Avocations: hiking, skiing, biking, reading, traveling. Office: Littler Mendelson Fastiff Tichy & Mathiason 400 Capitol Mall Fl 16 Sacramento CA 95814

ZEFF, STEPHEN ADDAM, accounting educator; b. Chgo., July 26, 1933; s. Roy David and Hazel (Sex) Z. B.S., U. Colo., 1955, M.S., 1957; M.B.A., U. Mich., 1960, Ph.D., 1962; D in Econs. honoris causa, Turku Sch. Econs. and Bus. Adminstrn., Finland, 1990. Instr. U. Colo., 1955-57; teaching fellow, instr. U. Mich., 1958-61; asst. prof. acctg. Tulane U., New Orleans, 1961-63, assoc. prof., 1963-67, prof., 1967-77, W.R. Irby prof., 1977-78; prof. acctg. Rice U., 1978-79, Herbert S. Autrey prof., 1979—; prof. acctg. U. Limburg, The Netherlands, 1992-95; vis. assoc. prof. U. Calif.-Berkeley, 1964-65, U. Chgo., 1966; vis. prof. Instituto Tecnológico y de Estudios Superiores de Monterrey, Mex., 1969, Victoria U., Wellington, New Zealand, 1976, Harvard U., 1977-78, Northwestern U., 1982, 83, U. Tex.-Austin, 1986, Free U. Amsterdam, 1990, 91, U. Nijenrode, 1994—; spl. lectr., hon. sr. Fulbright scholar Monash U., Australia, 1972. Author: Uses of Accounting for Small Business, 1962, American Accounting Association, Its First 50 Years, 1966, Forging Accounting Principles in Five Countries: A History and an Analysis of Trends, 1972, Forging Accounting Principles in Australia, 1973, Forging Accounting in New Zealand, 1979, Company Financial Reporting: A Historical and Comparative Study of the Dutch Regulatory Process, 1992; editor: Business Schools and the Challenge of International Business, 1968, Asset Appreciation, Business Income and Price-Level Accounting: 1918-1935, 1976, The Accounting Postulates and Principles Controversy of the 1960s, 1982, The U.S. Accounting Profession in the 1890s and Early 1900s, 1988; co-editor: Essays in Honor of William A. Paton: Pioneer Accounting Theorist, 1979, Sourcebook on Accounting Principles and Auditing Procedures 1917-1953, 1984, Milestones in the British Accounting Literature, 1996, Accounting Research, 1948-58, 1996, Readings and Notes on Financial Accounting, 5th edit., 1997; book rev. editor Acctg. Rev., 1962-66, editor, 1977-82; rev. editor Acctg. Horizons, 1995-97; founder, editor Boletín Interamericano de Contabilidad, 1968-71; contbr. articles to profl. jours. Mem. Am. Acctg. Assn. (dir. edn. 1969-71, pres. 1985-86, named Outstanding Acctg. Educator 1988), European Acctg. Assn. (exec. com. 1981—), Tex. Soc. CPAs (hon.), Am. Econ. Assn., Inst. Mgmt. Accts., Fin. Execs. Inst., AAUP. Club: Harvard (N.Y.C.). Home: 4545 Acacia St Bellaire TX 77401-3701 Office: Rice University MS 531 6100 Main St Houston TX 77005-1827

ZEFFIRELLI, FRANCO, theater and film director; b. Florence, Italy, Feb. 12, 1923; s. Ottorino Corsi and Alaide Cipriani. Attended, U. Architecture, Florence.; DHL, U. San Diego, 1980; PhD, U. Tel Aviv, 1993. Actor in Crime and Punishment, 1946, Euridyce, 1947; appeared in film Onorevole Angelina, 1948; set designer for various prodns. of Luchino Visconti, 1949-52, A Streetcar Named Desire, The Three Sisters; dir. (films) The Taming of the Shrew, 1966, Romeo and Juliet, 1967, Brother Sun, Sister Moon, 1971, Filumena Marturano, 1977, The Champ, 1979, Endless Love, 1981, I Pagliacci, 1981, La Traviata, 1982, Cavalleria Rusticana, 1986, Otello, 1986, The Young Toscanini, 1988, Hamlet, 1990, Sparrow, 1993, Jane Eyre, 1996, (ballet) Swan Lake, 1985; co-screenwriter, dir.(film) Hamlet, 1990; TV dir. Giorni Di Distruzione, 1966, Fidelio conducted by Leonard Bernstein, 1970, Missa Solemnis of Beethoven conducted by Wolfgang Sawallisch in Basilica of St. Peter in presence of Pope Paul VI, 1970, Jesus of Nazareth (epic film), 1976; numerous operas including Cenerentola, La Scala, 1953, I Pagliacci, 1959, Cavalleria Rusticana, 1959, Lucia Di Lammermoor, Covent Garden, 1959, La Boheme, La Scala, 1963, Falstaff, Met. Opera, 1964, Tosca, Covent Garden, 1965, Norma, Paris Opera, 1965, Anthony and Cleopatra, Met. Opera, 1966, Otello, Met. Opera, 1972, Don Giovanni, Staatsoper, Vienna, 1972, Un Ballo in Maschera, La Scala, 1972, Otello, La Scala, 1976, Carmen, Staatsoper, Vienna, 1978, La Traviata, 1979, 83, Tosca, Met. Opera, 1985, Turandot, 1987, Don Giovanni, 1990, Don Carlo, La Scala, 1992, Aida, Rome Opera, 1993, Carmen, Arena Diverona, 1995, Carmen, Met, 1996, Aida, New Nat. Theatre, Tokyo, 1997; theater dir. Romeo and Juliet, Old Vic Co., London, 1960, Othello, Stratford-on-Avon, Eng., 1961, Camille, Winter Garden Theatre, N.Y.C., 1962, Who's Afraid of Virginia Woolf?, Festival del Teatro, Venice, and Paris, 1963, Romeo and Juliet, Verona, Italy, Paris, Vienna, Austria, Rome and Milan, Italy, Moscow and Leningrad, 1964, Hamlet, 1964, After The Fall, 1965, Much Ado About Nothing, Old Vic Theatre, 1965, La Lupa, Florence, Rome, Vienna, Zurich, Switzerland, Paris, London and Moscow, 1965, A Delicate Balance, 1966, Black Comedy, 1967, Venti Zecchini D'Oro, 1968, Due Piu Due Non Fanno Quattro, 1969, Sabato, Doemnica, Lunedi, Nat. Theatre, London, 1973, The Dead City, Italy, 1975, Lorenzaccio, Comedie Française, Paris, 1976, Filumena Marturano, Lyric Theatre, London, 1977; author: Zeffirelli by Zeffirelli, 1986. Recipient Liberty award, 1986. Mem. Dirs. Guild Am. Roman Catholic. Address: Via Lucio Volumnio 37, 00178 Rome Italy

ZEFFREN, EUGENE, toiletries company executive; b. St. Louis, Nov. 21, 1941; s. Harry Morris and Bess (Dennis) Z.; m. Steccia Leigh Stern, Feb. 2, 1964; children: Maryl Renee, Bradley Cruvant. AB, Washington U., 1963; MS, U. Chgo., 1965, PhD, 1967. Research chemist Procter & Gamble Co., Cin., 1967-75, sect. head, 1975-77, assoc. dir., 1977-79; v.p. R & D, Helene Curtis, Inc., Chgo., 1979-95; pres. Helene Curtis USA, Chgo., 1995-96, corp. sr. v.p., 1996—. Co-author: The Study of Enzyme Mechanisms, 1973; contbr. articles to profl. jours.; patentee in field of enzymes and hair care. Mem. AAAS, Am. Chem. Soc., Soc. Cosmetic Chemists, Cosmetic Toiletry and Fragrance Assn. (sci. adv. com. 1979-95, vice chmn. 1984-88, chmn. 1988-90, bd. dirs. 1996—), Indsl. Rsch. Inst., Omicron Delta Kappa. Republican. Jewish. Avocations: tennis, swimming, skiing, reading adventure and espionage novels. Office: Helene Curtis Inc 325 N Wells St Chicago IL 60610-4705

ZEGARELLI, EDWARD VICTOR, retired dental educator, researcher; b. Utica, N.Y., Sept. 9, 1912; s. Frank Anthony and Maria Josephine (Ambrusiello) Z.; m. Irene Marie Ceconi, June 17, 1939; children: Edward V., David J., Philip E., Peter J. AB, Columbia U., 1934, DDS, 1937, DSc (hon.), 1983; MS, U. Chgo., 1942. Staff Sch. Dental and Oral Surgery, Columbia U., 1937-78, asst. instr., then successively instr., asst. prof., asso. prof., head diagnosis and roentgenology, 1947-58, chmn. com. dental research, 1956-78, Dr. Edwin S. Robinson prof. dentistry, 1958, prof. dentistry, dir. div. stomatology, 1958-78, acting dean, 1973, dean, 1974-78, dean emeritus, 1979—; Edward V. Zegarelli prof. dentistry, 1993—; chmn. sect. hosp. dental services Columbia-Presbyn. Med. Center; dir. and attending dentist dental service Presbyn. Hosp., 1974-79, also mem. exec. com. of med. bd., 1974-76; police surgeon N.Y.C., 1968-89; chmn. exam. com. N.E. Regional Bd. Dental Examiners, 1969-90; cons. VA, Washington; Weisberger Meml. lectr. Harvard U., 1969, Mershon Meml. lectr., 1970, Ralph L. Spaulding Meml. lectr., 1972; deans com. Montrose VA Hosp.; cons. East Orange, Kingsbridge VA hosps., Westchester Med. Ctr., Valhalla, N.Y., USPHS, Phelps Meml. Hosp., Tarrytown, N.Y., Vassar Bros. Hosp., Poughkeepsie, Bur. Medicine, FDA, Council on Dental Therapeutics; area cons. VA; cons.-lectr. U.S. Naval Dental Sch., Bethesda, Md., 1970-78; pres. N.Y. State Bd. Dental Examiners, 1970-71; chmn. exam. rev. com. N.E. Regional Bd. Dental Examiners, 1969-90; Samuel Charles Miller Meml. lectr., 1976; mem. council deans Am. Assn. Dental Schs., 1973-79; mem. postgrad. edn. com. N.Y.C. Cancer Com.; mem. profl. edn. and grants com. N.Y.C. div. Am. Cancer Soc., 1963-73; chmn. panel on drugs in dentistry NAS, NRC, FDA; mem. N.Y. State Health Research Council, N.Y. Commn. on Health Manpower; chmn. bd. govs. (dental) Gen. Health Ins., N.Y.C. Contbg. author: The Thyroid, Medical Roentgenology, Current Pediatric Therapy, Cancer of Head and Neck; author: (with others) Pharmacotherapeutics of Oral Disease, 1964, Clinical Stomatology, 1966, Diagnosis of Diseases of Mouth and Jaws, 1969, 2d edit., 1978; also articles on mouth, jaw bone disease. Bd. dirs. Hist. Soc. Tarrytowns, 1983, United Way Tarrytowns, 1983, YMCA of Tarrytowns, 1984, Phelps Meml. Hosp. Hospice Agy, 1986. Recipient Austin Sniffen medal 9th Dist. Dental Soc., 1961; Columbia U. Dental Alumni Research award, 1963; Jarvie-Burkhart medal N.Y. Dental Soc., 1970; Samuel J. Miller medal Am. Acad. Oral Medicine, 1976; Henry Spenadel award 1st Dist. Dental Soc., 1979; Man of Yr. award C. of C. Tarrytowns and Irvington, 1983; Man of Achievement award Americans for Italian Migration, 1984; named Disting. Practitioner mem. Nat. Acads. Practice, 1986. Fellow Am. Coll. Dentists (William J. Gies medal 1981), N.Y. Acad. Dentistry, Internat. Coll. Dentists, 9th Dist. Dental Soc.; mem. Am. Acad. Oral Pathology, Am. Assn. for Cancer Edn. (charter), Am. Assn. Dental Examiners (Dentist Citizen of Yr. award 1978), Orgn. Tchrs. Oral Diagnosis, N.Y. Acad. Scis., N.Y. Dental Soc. (chmn. council sci. research 1956-71), Greater N.Y. Acad. Prosthodontics (hon.), Guatemala Dental Soc. (hon.), Am. Dental Assn. (mem. council dental therapeutics 1963-69, vice chmn. 1969), Columbia Dental Alumni Assn., William Jarvie Research Soc., Internat. Assn. Dental Research, AAAS, Nat.

Italian-Am. Found., Sigma Xi (chpt. pres. 1974-76), Omicron Kappa Upsilon (sec. treas. Columbia chpt. 1944-57, pres. 1959-60), Sigma Phi Alpha., Knight Malta. Lodge: Rotary (pres. 1985-86) (Tarrytown). Home: 120 Gory Brook Rd Tarrytown NY 10591

ZEHE, ALFRED FRITZ KARL, physics educator; b. Farnstaedt, Halle, Germany, May 23, 1939; came to Mexico, 1990; s. Alfred and Lina Olga (Kuhnt) Z.; m. Ruth Schorrig, July 30, 1960; children: Axel, Peter. MSc, U. Leipzig, Germany, 1964, D of Natural Scis., 1969, Habilitation, 1974; D honoris causa, U. Puebla, Mexico, 1980. Researcher U. Leipzig, 1964-68, asst. prof., 1968-71, assoc. prof., 1971-75; prof. Tech. U. Zwickau, Germany, 1975-80, Tech. U. Dresden, Germany, 1980-91; prof. physics U. Puebla, 1991—; dir. dept. math. and scis. Tech. U. Zwickau, Germany, 1975-76; dir. dept. exptl. solid-state physics U. Puebla, 1977-80; dir. vacuum-physics chair Tech. U. Dresden, 1980-90, INTERCONSULT, Mex., Germany, 1994—. Author: Zehe-Roepke Rule for Electromigration, 1985, Microelectronics and ASIC's design, 1994, Industrial Metrology, 1995, Vacuum Technologies, 1996; editor: Fisica y Tecnologia de Semiconductores, 1982, Compendio Tecnológico para la Práctica Industrial, 1994—; contbr. articles to profl. jours.; patentee in field. Recipient Cincuentenario medal of honor U. PUebla, 1989, Disting. Prof. award Inst. Superior de Informatica, Santo Domingo, 1991; named Disting. Citizen, City Coun., Puebla, 1990. Mem. Phys. Soc. Germany, Phys. Soc. Mex., Math. Soc. Republic Dominicana, Acad. Materials Scis. Mex., Acad. Scis. Republic Dominicana, N.Y. Acad. Scis. Avocations: music, travel, science. Home: Schillerstr 19, 01326 Dresden Germany Office: U Autonoma de Puebla, Apartado Postal # 1505, 72000 Puebla Mexico

ZEHL, OTIS GEORGE, optical physicist; b. Elizabeth, N.J., July 9, 1946; s. Otis George and Elizabeth Theresa (Blehart) Z.; m. Ellen Mayo Hummel, May 18, 1985; 1 child, Elizabeth. BA in Physics with high honors, Rutgers U., 1968; PhD in Physics, U. Md., 1978. Teaching asst. grad. physics lab. U. Md., College Park, Md., 1971-73; doctoral rsch. asst. solid state physics U. Md., Md., 1973-78; sr. scientist Amecom Litton Systems, Md., 1979-91; sr. optical physicist Sachs Freeman Assn., Landover, Md., 1991-95; cons., 1995—; dir. Planning Design Implementation, Inc., Vienna, Va., 1987-92. Contbr. articles to profl. jours. Dir. Rosslyn Children's Ctr., Arlington, Va., 1991—. With U.S. Army, 1969-71. Supporter Friends of the Libraries-Rutgers, 1991—. Achievements include co-invention and five patents in areas of acousto-optics and electro-optics; tech. mgmt. and contbr. to state of art Bragg cell fabrication and test; rsch. and devel. of optical components to def. system; devel. fiber optic and interferometric sensor systems. Home: 10113 Windy Knoll Ln Vienna VA 22182-1542

ZEHNER, LEE RANDALL, biotechnologist, research director; b. Darby, Pa., Mar. 15, 1947; s. Warren L. and Alycia G. (Van Riper) Z.; m. Susan D. Hovland, June 23, 1973; children: Adam, Erica. BS in Chemistry, U. Pa., 1968; PhD in Organic Chemistry, U. Minn., 1973. Sr. rsch. chemist Arco Chem. Co., Glenolden, Pa., 1973-78; rsch. group leader Ashland Chem. Co., Dublin, Ohio, 1978-82; mgr. organic rsch. W.R. Grace & Co., Clarksville, Md., 1982-85; dir. biotech. programs Biospherics Inc., Beltsville, Md., 1985—, v.p. sci. svcs., 1991—. Author various tech. publs.; patentee in field. Mem. AIChE, Am. Chem. Soc., Inst. Food Technologists, Am. Mgmt. Assn., N.Y. Acad. Scis. Avocations: swimming, computers, chess. Home: 131 Brinkwood Rd Brookeville MD 20833-2304 Office: Biospherics Inc 12051 Indian Creek Ct Beltsville MD 20705-1261

ZEHR, CLYDE JAMES, church administrator; b. Valley Ctr., Kans., Oct. 4, 1934; s. John Wesley and Anna Mae (Carithers) Z.; m. Leona Mae Zehr, Nov. 23, 1957; children: Karen Elaine, Mark Wesley. BS, U. Kans., 1957; ThM, Western Evang. Sem., Portland, Oreg., 1961; MBA, Seattle U., 1976. Ordained to ministry Evang. Meth. Ch., 1961. Structural engr. Boeing Co., Seattle, 1957-59; pastor Rockwood Evang. Meth. Ch., Portland, 1961-63; missionary OMS Internat., Seoul, Republic of Korea, 1964-80; dir. Christian Leadership Seminars, Kent, Wash., 1980-82; supt. N.W. dist. Evang. Meth. Ch., Kent, 1982-86; gen. supt. Evang. Meth. Ch., Wichita, Kans., 1986-94; N.W. dist. supt. Evang. Meth. Ch., Seattle, 1995—. Author: Study Notes on Leadership, 1982, The Innovator/Administrator Conflict, 1986, Focus on Effectiveness, 1990. Republican. Office: Evang Meth Ch NW Dist Office PO Box 75673 Seattle WA 98125-0673

ZEHRING, KAREN, information executive; b. Washington, Dec. 5, 1945; d. Robert William Zehring and Gretchen (Lorenz) Proos; m. George Lang, 1970 (div. 1979); m. Peter Frank Davis, June 10 1979 (div. 1995); children: Jesse, Antonia. BA, U. Denver, 1967; postgrad., Yale U., 1967-68. Assoc. pub. mktg. and sales Instl. Investor Systems, Inc., N.Y.C., 1968-74; co-owner, co-creator Café des Artistes Restaurant, N.Y.C., 1975-79; owner, pub. The Corp. Fin. Letter, N.Y.C., 1976-78; group dir. planning and devel. Bus. Week mag., N.Y.C., 1977-78; owner, pub., exec. editor Corp. Fin. Sourcebook The Corp. Fin. Bluebook, N.Y.C., 1979-84; chmn., pres., pub., editor-in-chief Corp. Fin. mag., N.Y.C., 1986-90; cons. Karen Zehring & Assocs., Castine, Maine, 1990-94; mng. ptnr. Creative Devel. Ptnrs., N.Y.C., 1995—. Mem. The Women's Forum, Am. Soc. Mag. Editors, Vt., N.H. Direct Mktg. Assn. Unitarian.

ZEHRING, PEGGY JOHNSON, artist; b. Hutchinson, Kans., Jan. 4, 1941; d. Phillip E. and Bernice (Ashley) Johnson; m. R. David Zehring, July 27, 1963; children: Lisa, Geoff. BS, U. Kans., 1963; BA, U. Ill., 1977. Instr. Bellevue (Wash.) C.C., 1979-93, Sch. Visual Concepts, Seattle, 1985-86, Seattle Ctrl. C.C., 1987—, North Seattle C.C., 1987—, Coupeville (Wash.) Art Ctr., 1993—; juror and lectr. Eastside Assn. Fine Art, Mercer Island Visual Arts League, Nat. League Am. Artists & Pen Women; lectr. Women Painters of Washington, Bellevue Art Mus., N.W. Watercolor Soc. One-woman shows include King County Arts Commn., Seattle, Blake Gallery, Seattle, Bellevue (Wash.) C.C., PACCAR, Bellevue, Pacific N.W. Bell, Seattle, U. Ill., Chgo.; exhibited in group shows at COCA Annual, Seattle, Seattle Art Mus. Sales & Rental Gallery, LewAllen Fine Art, Santa Fe, Bellevue Art Mus., Diablo Valley Coll., Elizabeth Prince Gallery, Prescott, Ariz.; represented in selected collections City of Lynnwood, Wash., Pacific NW Bell, PACCAR, Delitte, Haskins & Sells, Opti-Copy, Kansas City, Harper & Assocs., Bellevue and numerous other pvt. collections; work published in The Artistic Touch I and II, The Encyclopedia of Living Artists. Recipient First Place award Ariz. Internat., Snowgrass Art Inst., Cashmere, Wash., Kans. State Fair, Hutchinson, Honorable Mention award W. Wash. State Fair; named finalist Pierce County Libr. Project, Gig Harbor, Wash. Home: PO Box 967 LaVeta CO 81055

ZEICHNER, OSCAR, historian, educator; b. N.Y.C., Jan. 2, 1916; s. Joseph and Lena (Schaeffer) Z.; m. Florence Koenigsberg, June 27, 1942; children: Barbara Ann, Carolyn Sue. B.A. cum laude, CCNY, 1936; M.A., Columbia U., 1938, Ph.D., 1946. Mem. faculty CCNY, 1936—, prof. history, 1960-76, prof. emeritus, 1976—, asst. dean in charge grad. studies Coll. Liberal Arts and Sci., 1957-63, asso. dean in charge Coll. Liberal Arts and Sci., 1963-68, dean grad. studies CCNY (Coll. Liberal Arts and Sci.), 1968-72; assoc. dean grad. studies CUNY, 1963-68. Author: Connecticut's Years of Controversy, 1750-76, 1949, 70; editorial bd.: Connecticut Am. Revolution Bicentennial Series Publs.; contbr. articles to profl. jours. Recipient hon. mention J.H. Dunning prize Am. Hist. Assn., 1946. Mem. Assn. for Study Conn. History (pres. 1975-76), Phi Beta Kappa (pres. Gamma chpt. 1971-72). Home: 5500 Fieldston Rd Bronx NY 10471-2533

ZEIDENSTEIN, GEORGE, population educator; b. Pitts., July 29, 1929; s. Max and Sophia (Cohen) Z.; m. Sondra F. Auerbach, Jan. 25, 1953; children: Laura, Louis Peter. B.A., U. Pitts., 1951; J.D. cum laude, Harvard U., 1954. Bar: N.Y. 1954. Pvt. practice N.Y.C., 1954-65; vol. lawyer Lawyers Constl. Def. Com., Holly Springs, Miss., 1964; partner firm Spear and Hill, 1962-65; country dir. Nepal Kathmandu, Peace Corps, 1965-68; regional dir. designate Office E. Asia and Pacific, Washington, 1968; pres. Bklyn. Linear City Devel. Corp., N.Y.C., 1968-69; sr. program officer Asia and Pacific Ford Found., 1969-71, dep. head Asia and Pacific, 1971-72; rep. Ford Found., Bangladesh, 1972-76; pres., trustee Population Council, N.Y.C., 1976-93; disting. fellow Harvard Ctr. Population and Devel. Studies, Cambridge, Mass., 1993—; chmn. Himalayas coun. Asia Soc., 1970-72; assoc. seminar tradition and change in South and S.E. Asia, Columbia U., 1971-73, assoc. seminar on tech. and pub. issues, 1981-85; coun. Overseas Devel. Coun., 1979-93; chmn. Appraisal Group Global Com. Parliamentarians on Population and Devel., 1985-86; bd. visitors Grad. Sch. Pub. Health, U. Pitts., 1988—; advisor to chair Ind. Commn. on Population and Quality of Life, 1993-95. Vice chmn. bd. trustees, chmn. program com. Save the Children Fedn., 1991-95, Internat. Ctr. Rsch. on Women, 1993—; chmn. Internat. HIV/AIDS Alliance, 1993—; bd. dirs. Earthforce, 1993-95; active Britton Woods Com., 1992—. Decorated knight comdr. Order of Lion (Finland, Senegal). Home: 795 East St N Goshen CT 06756-1130 Office: Harvard Ctr Population Devel Studies 9 Bow St Cambridge MA 02138-5103

ZEIDLER, FRANK P., former association administrator, mayor, arbitrator, mediator, fact-finder; b. Milw., Sept. 20, 1912; s. Michael and Clara (Nitschke) Z.; m. Agnes Reinke; children: Clara, Dorothy, Michael, Anita, Mary, Jeannette. Student, Marquette U., 1930, U. Wis. Extension Div., 1930-70, U. Chgo., 1937; LLD (hon.), U. Wis., 1958, St. Olaf Coll., 1988; LHD (hon.), Carthage Coll., 1983, Mt. Mary Coll., 1993, U. Wis.-Milw., 1990. Dir. Milw. Pub. Schs., 1941-48; mayor City of Milw., 1948-60; dir. Wis. Dept. Resource Devel., 1963-64; sec. emeritus Pub. Enterprise Com.; mem. U.S. nat. comm. UNESCO, 1953, 56, 59. Author: Shakespeare's plays in modern verse. Pres. Ctrl. North Cmty. Coun.; past pres., co-editor newsletter Greater Milw. UN Assn., pres.; nat. chmn. Socialist Party U.S.A., 1973-83; Socialist Party candidate for Pres. U.S., 1976; convenor Dem. Socialist Conf.; past pres. Luth. Social Action Conf.; bd. dirs. Goethe House, Milw., Milw. Theol. Inst.; mem. exec. coun. Luth. Ch. Am., 1980-82; hon. mem. cabinet Interfaith Conf. Greater Milw.; chmn. Norman Thomas Inst. for Peace and Social Justice. Named One of 10 Outstanding Young Men, Nat. Jr. C. of C., 1949; recipient Eugene V. Debs award, 1977. Mem. Milw. World Federalist Assn. (bd. dirs.), Nat. Model R.R. Assn. (founder). Home: 2921 N 2nd St Milwaukee WI 53212-2411

ZEIEN, ALFRED M., consumer products company executive; b. N.Y.C., Feb. 25, 1930; s. Alphonse and Betty (Barthelemy) Z.; m. Joyce Valerie Lawrence, Dec. 26, 1952; children—Scott, Grey, Claudia. B.S., Webb Inst.; M.B.A. postgrad., Harvard U. Group v.p. Gillette Co., Boston, 1973-74, sr. v.p., 1978-81, vice chmn., 1981-90, pres., 1990-91, chmn., chief exec. officer, 1991—; div. gen. mgr. Braun AG, Frankfurt, Federal Republic of Germany, 1974-76, chmn. bd., 1976-78; bd. dirs. Polaroid Corp., Cambridge, Mass., Repligen Corp., Cambridge, Raytheon Corp., Lexington, Mass., Bank of Boston, Mass. Mut. Ins. Co., Springfield. trustee Univ. Hosp., Boston, 1983—. Avocations: sailing; tennis. Home: 300 Boylston St Boston MA 02116-3923 Office: Gillette Co Prudential Towers Bldg Boston MA 02199

ZEIFANG, DONALD P., lawyer; b. Niagara Falls, N.Y., Apr. 13, 1936. BA, U. Notre Dame, 1960; JD, Georgetown U., 1963. Bar: D.C. 1965. Law clk. to Hon. John J. Sirica U.S. Dist. Ct. (D.C. dist.), 1963-65; ptnr. Baker & Hostetler, Washington. Mem. ABA, D.C. bar, Fed. Comm. Bar, Nat. Assn. Broadcasters (v.p. 1973-80, sr. v.p. 1976-80 govt. rels.). Office: Baker & Hostetler 1050 Connecticut Ave NW Washington DC 20036

ZEIGEN, SPENCER STEVEN, architect; b. Bklyn., Oct. 11, 1924; s. David and Ethel (Katz) Z.; m. Mildred Weinman, Dec. 27, 1952 (dec. Sept. 1992); children: Steven, Scott; m. Lillian Glogau, Oct. 10, 1993; children: Jordan Glogau, Laurence Glogau, Alexander Glogau. BFA suma cum laude, U. Pa., 1952. Registered architect, N.J. Arch. Leo Fischer Arch., South Orange, N.J., 1952-54, Frank Grad Sons Arch., Newark, 1954-64; staff arch. Rutgers State U., New Brunswick, N.J., 1964-74; pvt. practice Highland Park, N.J., 1974-78, Jamesburg, N.J., 1978—; arch. Collins, Uhl, Hoisington, Anderson Arch., Princeton, N.J., 1978-80, Brown Hale Arch., Newark, 1980-82; dir. arch. Brown & Mathews, Fords, N.J., 1982-86; bd. arch. High Rise Condominiums, Fort Lee, N.J., 1982-89; cons. roofing expert Kipcon, Inc., Highland Park, 1988—, bldg. materials analyst, 1988—; instr. arch. Newark Coll. Engring., 1963-69. Prin. works include N.J. Divsn. Motor Vehicles Testing Facilities, N.J. Cultural Ctr., Rutgers U. Ednl. Facilities. Bd. dirs. Whittingham Homeowners Assn., Jamesburg, N.J., 1990-93. Sgt. USAF, 1942-46. Mem. Am. Soc. Arch., Am. Soc. Planners. Democrat. Jewish. Avocations: bridge, tennis, bocci, reading, drawing. Home and Office: 19 Winthrop Rd Jamesburg NJ 08831-2603

ZEIGER, HERBERT EVAN, JR., neurosurgeon; b. Landgale, Ala., Aug. 23, 1949; s. H. Evan Sr. and Imogene (Morris) Z.; m. Margaret Swift Shook, Feb. 25, 1984; children: H. Evan III, Ashley Shook, Douglas Shook. BA, Samford U., 1971; MD, U. Ala., 1974. Diplomate Am. Bd. Neurol. Surgery. Intern Carraway Meth. Med. Ctr., Birmingham, 1975-76; resident Washington U. Med. Sch./ Barnes Hosp., St. Louis, 1976-81; attending neurosurgeon Carraway Meth. Med. Ctr., Birmingham, Ala., 1987—; pres. med. staff, 1992-93, 96, 97; assoc. prof. neurosurgery U. Ala., Brimingham, 1981-87; attending neurosurgeon, chmn. dept. neurosurgery Norwood Clinic, Brimingham, 1987—. Author: Stroke and the Extracranial Vessels, 1983; contbr. articles to profl. jours. Bd. dirs. Ala. Family Alliance, Birmingham, 1989—, Children's Harbor, Birmingham, 1993-96, Salvation Army, Birmingham, 1990—. Fellow U. Western Ont. London, Can., 1981. Fellow Am. Coll. Surgeons; mem. Am. Assn. Neurol. Surgeons, So. Neurosurg. Soc., Neurosurg. Soc. Ala (pres. 1988-90), Birmingham Surg. Soc., Congress Neurol. Surgeons, Jefferson County Med. Soc. (pres. 1997), Rotary (fellow com. 1990). Presbyterian. Avocations: flying, running, family, trout fishing, sailing. Home: 3009 Canterbury Ln Birmingham AL 35223 Office: Norwood Clinic Inc 1528 Carraway Blvd Birmingham AL 35234-1911

ZEIGER, LARRY See KING, LARRY

ZEIGER, SCOTT LESLIE, commercial theater executive; b. Bklyn., Sept. 25, 1960; s. Martin Zeiger and Phyllis Roberta Miller Iampieri; m. Kathleen Marie Ryan, Dec. 4, 1988; 1 child, Joshua Ryan. BA, U. Fla., 1982. Regional mktg. dir. Ringling Bros. Barnum and Bailey Circus, Washington, 1983; dir. mktg. Pace Theatrical Group, Houston, 1983-86, v.p., 1986-89, exec. v.p., 1989-91; pres. Pace Theatrical Group, N.Y.C., 1991—. Exec. prodr.: The Who's Tommy, 1993 (5 Tony awards). Adv. com. Houston Downtown Theatre Dist., 1986-93; bd. dirs. Story Theatre, Ft. Lauderdale, Fla., 1993—. Mem. League of Am. Theatres and Prodrs. (exec. com. 1992—, bd. govs. 1988-92). Jewish. Avocations: travel, exercise, music. *

ZEIGLER, BERNARD PHILLIP, electrical and computer engineering educator; b. Montreal, Que., Can., Mar. 5, 1940; came to U.S., 1962; naturalized, 1985; s. Maurice and Sylvia (Filger) Z.; m. Rebecca Robinson, May 1964 (div. 1984); children: Bianca, Noemi; m. Christine Dymek, Aug. 1985; 1 child, Claire. B in Engring. Physics, McGill U., 1962; MEE, MIT, 1964; PhD in Computer Sci., U. Mich., 1969. Asst. prof. computer sci. U. Mich., Ann Arbor, 1970-73, assoc. prof. computer sci., 1973-75; vis. scientist Weizman Inst. Sci., Israel, 1975-80; prof. computer sci. Wayne State U., Detroit, 1981-85; prof. elec. and computer engring. U. Ariz., Tucson, 1985—. Author: Theory of Modelling and Simulation, 1976, Multifacetted Modelling and Discrete Event Simulation, 1984, Object-Oriented Simulation of HierarchialModular Models, 1990, Objects and Systems, 1996. With USAF, 1995—. Research grantee, NSF, 1982—, NASA, 1987—. Fellow IEEE. Office: U Ariz Dept ECE Tucson AZ 85721

ZEIGLER, EARLE FREDERICK, physical education-kinesiology educator; b. N.Y.C., Aug. 20, 1919; s. Clarence Mattison and Margery Christina (Beyerkohler) Shinkle; m. Bertha M. Bell, June 25, 1941; children—Donald H., Barbara A. AB, Bates Coll., 1940; AM, Yale U., 1944, PhD, 1951; LLD, U. Windsor, 1975; DSc, U. Lethbridge, Alta, Can., 1997. Assoc. phys. dir., aquatic dir. Bridgeport (Conn.) YMCA, 1941-43; instr. German U. Conn., Storrs, 1943-47; coach, instr. phys. edn. Yale U., 1943-49; asst. prof. U. Western Ont. (Can.), London, 1949-50; prof., chmn. dept. phys., health and recreation edn. U. Western Ont. (Can.), 1950-56, assoc. prof. Sch. Edn.; supr. phys. edn. and athletics U. Mich., Ann Arbor, 1956-63; chmn. dept. phys. edn. Sch. Edn. U. Mich., 1961-63; prof. dept. phys. edn. for men Coll. Phys. Edn., U. Ill., Urbana, 1963-72; head dept. phys. edn. for men, chmn. grad. dept. Coll. Phys. Edn., U. Ill., 1964-68; prof. dept. phys. and health edn. U. Western Ont., London, 1971-89, prof. emeritus, 1989—; dean U. Western Ont. (Faculty of Phys. Edn.), 1972-77. Author: A History of Professional Preparation for Physical Education in the United States, 1951, Administration of Physical Education and Athletics, 1959, The Case Method Approach: An Instructional Manual, 1959, Philosophical Foundations for Physical, Health, and Recreation Education, 1964, A Brief Introduction to the Philosophy of Religion, 1965, (with H.J. VanderZwaag) Physical Education: Progressivism or Essentialism, 1968, Problems in the History and Philosophy of Physical Education and Sport, 1968, (with M.L. Howell and M. Trekell) Research in the History and Philosophy of Physical Education and Sport, 1971, Personalizing Physical Education and Sport Philosophy, 1975, Physical Education and Sport Philosophy, 1977, Issues in North American Physical Education and Sport, 1979, Decision-Making in Physical Education and Athletics, 1982, (with G.W. Bowie) Management Competency Development in Sport and Physical Education, 1983, Ethics and Morality in Sport and Physical Education, 1984, (with J. Campbell) Strategic Market Planning: An Aid to the Evaluation of an Athletics/Recreation Program, 1984 , Assessing Sport and Physical Education: Diagnosis and Projection, 1986, (with G. Bowie and R. Paris) Competency Development in Sport and Physical Education Management, 1988, (with A. Mikalachki and G. Leyshon) Change Process in Sport and Physical Education Management, 1988, Introduction to Sport and Physical Education Philosophy, 1989, Sport and Physical Education: Past, Present, Future, 1990, Professional Ethics for Sport Managers, 1992, Critical Thinking for the Professions of Health, Physical Education, Recreation, and Dance, 1994, A Selected, Annotated Bibliography of Completed Research on Management Theory and Practice in Physical Education and Athletics to 1972, 1995, (with G.W. Bowie) Developing Management Competency in Sport and Physical Education, 1995; author, editor: A History of Sport and Physical Education to 1900, 1973, A History of Physical Education and Sport in the United States and Canada, 1975, (with M.J. Spaeth) Administrative Theory and Practice in Physical Education and Athletics, 1975, History of Physical Education and Sport, 1979, rev. edit., 1988, Physical Education and Sport: An Introduction, 1982, Physical Education and Kinesiology in North America: Professionalism and Scholarly Foundations, 1994; contbr. articles to profl. jours. Recipient Outstanding Tchr. award U. Western Ont., 1987, Disting. Svc. award Internat. Soc. Comparative Phys. Edn. and Sport, 1988; inducted into Univ. Western Ont.'s Wall of Wrestling Fame, 1991, Univ. Western Ont.'s W Club Hall of Fame, 1995; named first Human Movement Scis. and Edn. scholar U. Memphis, 1994. Fellow Am. Acad. Kinesiology and Phys. Edn. (pres. 1981-82, Hetherington award 1989); mem. AAHPERD (Alliance scholar 1977-78, Disting. Svc. award 1979, Honor award 1981, Gulick award 1990), Philosophy Edn. Soc., Internat. Assn. Profl. Schs. Phys. Edn., Can. Assn. Health, Phys. Edn. and Recreation (v.p. 1955-56, v.p. 1983-85, honour award 1975, spl. presentation citation 1986), Am. Philos. Assn., Nat. Assn. Phys. Edn. in Higher Edn., N.Am. Soc. Sport History (life), Philosophic Soc. for Study of Sport (pres. 1974-75), N.Am. Soc. for Sport Mgmt. (founding mem., hon. past pres. 1986-87), Canadian Profl. Schs. Conf. (pres. 1953-55), Ont. Recreation Assn. (v.p. and dir. 1955-56), Soc. Municipal Recreation Dirs. Ont. (Honor award 1956), Phi Epsilon Kappa (life). N.Am. Soc. Sport Mgmt. created the Annual Earle Zeigler Lecture, 1988. Home: 105 8560 Currie Rd, Richmond, BC Canada V6Y 1M2 also: 1177 Sudden Valley Bellingham WA 98226-4818 *Ever since the Platonic tradition split what we once before believed to be a unified organism into mind and body, and then Christianity added a spiritual dimension that shattered a unified concept of the organism even further, purposeful human movement in sport, dance, play, and exercise has been regarded as inferior to so-called intellectual attainments. My life purpose is to work toward redressing that imbalance by promoting a type of education that restores the Greek Classical Ideal.*

ZEIGLER, L(UTHER) HARMON, political science educator; b. Savannah, GA., Mar. 9, 1936; s. Luther H. and Sarah Louise (Betts) Z.; m. Patricia Lynn Duffy, Dec. 20, 1956; children: Michael, Amanda. BA, Emory U., 1957; MA, U. Ill., 1958, PhD, 1960. Asst. prof. Fla. State U., Tallahassee, 1960-61, Emory U., Atlanta, 1961-63, U. Ga., Athens, 1963-64; assoc. prof. U. Oreg., Eugene, 1964-67, prof. dept. polit. sci., 1967-85, chmn., 1982-85; Philip M. Phibbs disting. prof. Am. politics U. Puget Sound, Tacoma, Wash., 1985-92; affiliate prof. U. Wash., 1986-92. Author: The Irony of Democracy, 1970, 10th edit., 1996, Governing American Schools, 1974, Professionals Versus the Public: Attitudes, Commnication and Response in Local School Districts, 1980, American Politics in the Media Age, 1983, Women, Public Opinion and Politics: The Changing Attitudes of American Women, 1984, Pluralism, Corporatism and Confucianism, 1988, The Political Community, 1990, Political Parties in Industrial Democracies, 1992. Fellow Ford Found., 1969; Guggenheim fellow, 1969-70; Fulbright-Hays grantee W. Germ., 1977; sr. scholar Australia, 1978. Mem. Am. Polit. Sci. Assn.

ZEIGLER, VICKI LYNN, pediatrics nurse; b. Hampton, S.C., May 26, 1961; d. Richard Jackson and Miriam Banner (Smith) Z.; m. Paul Crawford Gillette, Feb. 1, 1992. BSN, Med. U. of S.C., 1982, MSN, 1991. RN, S.C.; cert. spl. competency in cardiac pacing for non-physicians N.Am. Soc. Pacing and Electrophysiology. Staff nurse pediatrics Med. U. S.C., Charleston, 1983-85, nurse clinician pediatric cardiology, 1985-91, pediatric arrhythmia/pacemaker case mgr., 1992-94, pediatric arrhythmia nurse specialist, 1994-96; pediat. arrhythmia case mgr. Cook Children's Med. Ctr., Ft. Worth, 1996—; BLS instr. Am. Heart Assn., Columbia, S.C. Contbr. articles to profl. jours. Recipient Young Investigator award Sigma Theta Tau. Mem. AACN, Assn. for Care of Children's Health, North Am. Soc. of Pacing and Electrophysiology, Am. Heart Assn. Coun. of Cardiovascular Nursing, Sigma Theta Tau. Republican. Avocations: sailing, auto racing, reading. Office: Cook Childrens Med Ctr Cardiology Dept 801 7th Ave Fort Worth TX 76104-2733

ZEILE, FRED CARL, oceanographer, meteorologist; b. Phila., Nov. 3, 1950; s. Fred Carl Jr. and Catherine Elizabeth (Wolfrum) Z.; children: Kirche Leigh, Alicia Elizabeth; m. Ingrid Elizabeth Leyrer, Dec. 17, 1988. BS in Oceanography, U.S. Naval Acad., 1973; MS in Meteorology and Oceanography, Naval Postgrad. Sch., 1979; MA in Nat. Security & Strategic Studies, Naval War Coll., 1991. Commd. ensign USN, 1973, advanced through grades to comdr., 1988; meteorologist USS Inchon, Norfolk, Va., 1979-81; oceanography instr. U.S. Naval Acad., Annapolis, Md., 1981-83; commanding officer Oceanographic Unit 4 USNS Chauvenet, Indonesia, 1984-85; dep. asst. chief staff for emerging systems Comdr. Naval Oceanography Command, Stennis Space Center, Miss., 1987-90; commanding officer Naval Oceanography Command Facility, Keflavik, Iceland, 1990-92; tactical oceanography br. head Office of Oceanographer of Navy, Washington, 1992-93; bus. area mgr. Analysis & Technology, Inc., Bay St. Louis, Miss., 1993—. Mem. VWF (life), Am. Meteorol. Soc., Marine Tech. Soc. (chmn. Gulf Coast chpt. 1994), Masons (master Mason), Sigma Xi. Republican. Lutheran. Avocations: fishing, golf. Home: 101 Brushfire Ln Slidell LA 70458-5567 Office: Analysis & Tech Inc 321 Shieldsboro Sq Bay Saint Louis MS 39520-2823

ZEILIG, NANCY MEEKS, magazine editor; b. Nashville, Apr. 28, 1943; d. Edward Harvey and Nancy Evelyn (Self) Meeks; m. Lanny Kenneth Fielder, Aug. 20, 1964 (div. Dec. 1970); m. Charles Elliot Zeilig, Jan. 6, 1974 (div. Dec. 1989); 1 child, Sasha Rebecca. BA, Birmingham-So. Coll., 1964; postgrad., Vanderbilt U., 1971-73. Editorial asst. Reuben H. Donnelley, N.Y.C., 1969-70; asst. editor Vanderbilt U., Nashville, 1970-74; editor U. Minn., St. Paul, 1975; asst. editor McGraw-Hill Inc., Mpls., 1975-76; mng. editor Denver mag., 1976-80; editor Jour. Am. Water Works Assn., Denver, 1981—. Editor, co-pub.: WomanSource, 1982, rev. edit., 1984; contbr. articles to consumer mags. Co-chair arts adv. com. Denver Sch. Arts, 1994-96. Avocations: travel, reading British and Am. fiction, cooking. Subject of NBC News documentary Women Like Us, 1980. Office: Jour Am Water Works Assn 6666 W Quincy Ave Denver CO 80235-3011

ZEILINGER, ELNA RAE, elementary educator, gifted-talented education educator; b. Tempe, Ariz., Mar. 24, 1937; d. Clayborn Eddie and Ruby Elna (Laird) Simpson; m. Philip Thomas Zeilinger, June 13, 1970; children: Shari, Chris. BA in Edn., Ariz. State U., 1958, MA in Edn., 1966, EdS, 1980. Bookkeeper First Nat. Bank of Tempe, 1955-56; with registrar's office Ariz. State U., 1956-58; piano tchr., recreation dir. City of Tempe; tchr. Thew Sch., Tempe, 1958-61; elem. tchr. Mitchell Sch., Tempe, 1962-74, intern prin., 1976, personnel intern, 1977; specialist gifted edn. Tempe Elem. Schs., Tempe, 1977-86; elem. tchr. Holdeman Sch., Tempe, 1986-89; tchr. grades 1-12 and adult reading, lang. arts, English Zeilinger Tutoring Svc., 1991—; grad. asst. edn. adminstrn., Iota Workshop coordinator Ariz. State U., 1978; presenter Ariz. Gifted Conf., 1978-81; condr. survey of gifted programs, 1980; reporter public relations Tempe Sch. Dist., 1978-80, Access com. for gifted programs, 1981-83. Author: Leadership Role of the Principal in Gifted Programs: A Handbook, 1980; Classified Personnel Handbook, 1977, also reports, monographs and paintings. Mem. Tempe Hist. Assn., liaison, 1975; mem. Tempe Art League; mem. freedom train com. Ariz. Bicentennial Commn., 1975-76; bd. dirs. Maple Property Owners Assn., 1994—;

storyteller Tempe Hist. Mus., 1997—. Named Outstanding Leader in Elem. and Secondary Schs., 1976' Ariz. Cattle Growers scholar, 1954-55; Elks scholar, 1954-55; recipient Judges award Tempe Art League, 1970, Best of Show, Scottsdale Art League, 1976. Democrat. Congregationalist.

ZEILINGER, PHILIP THOMAS, aeronautical engineer; b. David City, Nebr., Feb. 13, 1940; s. Thomas Leroy and Sylvia Dorothy Zeilinger; m. Elna Rae Simpson, June 13, 1970; children: Shari, Chris. AS, Wentworth Mil. Acad., Lexington, Mo., 1959; BSME, Kans. U., 1962. Estimator, engr. Reynolds Electronics and Engring. Co., El Paso, Tex., 1966-68; accessories coord. ITI Garrett, Phoenix, 1974-79, cntrl. access engr., 1968—, controls coord. ITEC, 1983-84, integrated support specialist ITEC, 1984-86, mgr. systems software light helo turbine engring. co. div., 1986-91, FAA designated engr. rep. engine div., 1991—; chmn. Light Helicopter Turbine Engine Company Computer Aided Acquistion and Logistics Working Group. V.p. Indsl. Devel. Authority, Tempe, Ariz., 1979-84; pres. Univ. Royal Garden Homes Assn., Tempe, 1984-90. 1st lt. U.S. Army, 1962-66. Recipient Vol. Svc. award City of Tempe, 1984, Grand Cross of Color, Internat. Order of Rainbow Girls, 1978. Mem. AIAA, Aircraft Owners and Pilots Assn., Explt. Aircraft Assn. (v.p. chpt. 228 1974-79), Masons (master 1990-92, chmn. statewide picnic 1992, Mason of the Yr. 1992). Democrat. Unitarian. Achievements include patent for Airesearch/Garrett. Home: 760 N Sycamore Pl Chandler AZ 85224-6925 Office: 111 S 34th St Phoenix AZ 85034-2802

ZEILLER, WARREN, former aquarium executive, consultant; b. Weehawken, N.J., Nov. 11, 1929; s. Arthur Herman and Ruth (Preusser) Z.; m. Judith Marion Ricciardi, May 27, 1961; children: Dianne Leigh, Todd Kiersted. B.Sc. in Animal Husbandry, Colo. A&M Coll., 1955; M.A. in Bus., Mich. State U., 1957. Mgmt. trainee Grand Union Co., 1956-58; corp. sec., salesman Art Zeiller Co., Inc., Allendale, N.J., 1958-60; salesman Joseph Abraham Ford Co., Miami, Fla., 1960; with Miami Seaquarium, 1960-85, curator, 1962-85, v.p., gen. mgr., 1977-85, ret., 1985; pres. Images of Art, Inc., Coral Gables, Fla.; exec. dir. Tropical Everglades Visitor Assn., 1988—; lectr., cons. bus., mktg., tourism; TV appearances. Author: Tropical Marine Invertebrates of Southern Florida and the Bahama Islands, 1974, Tropical Marine Fishes of Southern Florida and the Bahama Islands, 1975, Introducing the Manatee, 1992; contbr. articles to profl. jours. Treas. Jr. Orange Bowl Com., 1984-85; mem. adv. bd. Coral Gables War Meml. Youth Ctr., 1973-93, pres., 1981-83; mem. Gov.'s tourism adv. coun. Fla. Hospitality Industry Coun., 1983-84; bd. dirs. Dade Marine Inst.; bd. dirs., pres. Humane Soc. Greater Miami, Inc., 1993-94. Served with USN, 1951-55. Mem. Fla. Attractions Assn. (v.p. 1981-82, pres. 1982-83), Mus. and Art Center, Colo. State U. Alumni Assn., Sigma Chi. Republican. Methodist. Club: Rotary (pres. Coral Gables 1978-79). Patentee surg. cast and cast removal saw. Home: 5016 SW 72nd Ave Miami FL 33155-5529

ZEISEL, GLORIA, real estate company executive; b. Braddock, Pa., June 21, 1920; d. Max and Rachel (Kaufman) Sperling; m. Henry Israel Zeisel, Feb. 1, 1942; children: Cheryl Kramer, Elliot, Howard, Debra Moed. Student, Bklyn. Coll. Pres., founder Adolph Schreiber Sch., Monsey, N.Y., 1954; sec., treas., dir. HiTech Mfg. Co., N.J., 1992—; sec., treas., dir. Real Estate Cos., N.Y., N.J., Fla., 1975—. Founder, life mem. Cmty. Synagogue Monsey, 1954—; founder, bd. trustees Holocaust Ctr., Spring Valley, N.Y., 1988—; bd. govs. Good Samaritan Hosp., Suffern, N.Y., co-chmn. showcase, 1994; vol. United Jewish Appeal. Recipient Outstanding Citizen of Jewish Cmty. Ramapo Town Bd., 1994. Mem. Amit Women Nat. Orgn. (life), Brandies Women Nat. Orgn. (life), Israel Bond Orgn. (bd. dirs., bd. trustees). Home: 18 Hilltop Pl Monsey NY 10952

ZEISEL, STEVEN H., nutritionist, educator; b. N.Y.C., July 16, 1950. BS in Life Sci., MIT, 1971; MD, Harvard Med. Sch., 1975; PhD in Nutrition, MIT, 1980. Asst. Children's Hosp., Boston, 1980-81; asst. prof. pathology and pediatrics Boston U. Sch. Medicine, 1982-87, assoc. prof., 1987-90, prof., 1990; prof. dept. pediatrics U. N.C., Chapel Hill, 1990—, prof., chair dept. nutrition, 1990—; chair med. edn. com. Am. Soc. Clin. Nutrition, 1995-96; chair joint membership com. AIN/ASCN, 1992-94; mem. study sect. Clin. Nutrition Rsch. units NIH, 1993-95; del. Assn. AMCCAS, 1991-96. Editor-in-chief Jour. Nutritional Biochemistry. Mem. Am. Soc. Nutritional Scis., Am. Soc. Clin. Nutrition, Am. Soc. Parenteral and Enteral Nutrition, Am. Coll. Nutrition, Am. Pub. Health Assn., Soc. Pediatric Rsch. Office: UNC Dept Nutrition # 7400 Sch Pub Health/Sch Medicine 2212 McGavran Greenberg Hal Chapel Hill NC 27599-7400

ZEISLER, RICHARD SPIRO, investor; b. Chgo., Nov. 28, 1916; s. Erwin Paul and Ruth Henrietta (Spiro) Z. B.A., Amherst Coll., 1937; postgrad., Harvard U., 1937-38; M.Div., Va. Theol. Sem., 1941. Religious work, 1941-47; owner Richard S. Zeisler & Co. (investments), N.Y.C., 1948—. Bd. dirs. Chamber Music Soc., Lincoln Center, 1969—, Skowhegan Sch. Painting and Sculpture, 1983—; trustee Mus. Modern Art, 1979—, mem. com. on painting and sculpture, 1972—, architecture and design com., 1989—; trustee, former v.p. Jewish Bd. Family and Children's Services, N.Y.C., 1951—; past pres. Am. Jewish Com. (N.Y. chpt.); past co-chmn. NCCJ (N.Y. chpt.); mem. com. for dance collection, past chmn. N.Y. Pub. Library, 1967—; mem. creative arts commn. Brandeis U., 1958-94; mem. art adv. com., past chmn. Mt. Holyoke Coll., 1963—; fellow Pierpont Morgan Library, 1963—; governing life mem. Art Inst. Chgo., 1977—, mem. com. on 20th century painting and sculpture, 1981—; life fellow Met. Mus., 1969—; mem. Manhattan Inst., 1990—; mem. adv. coun. Princeton (N.J.) Art Mus., 1993—. Mem. N.Y. Soc. Security Analysts, Am. Coun. on Germany, Asia Soc., U.S.-New Zealand Coun., Ams. Soc., Century Assn. Club (N.Y.C.), Univ. Club (N.Y.C.), Grolier Club (N.Y.C.), Arts Club (Chgo.), Reform Club (London), Econ. of N.Y. Home and Office: 980 Fifth Ave New York NY 10021-0126

ZEIT, RUTH MAE, foundation administrator; b. N.Y.C., May 13, 1945; d. Albert Joseph and Gertrude (Goldberg) Janover; children: Rachael Miriam, Rebecca Madeleine. BA, U. Pa., 1967, postgrad., 1969-70; postgrad., Temple U., 1967-69. Teaching fellow Temple U., Phila., 1967-69, U. Pa., Phila., 1969-70; dir. piano music studio Phila., 1969—; pres. Lupus Found. Del. Valley, Ardmore, Pa., 1983—; Mem. Winner's Ball com. Lupus Found. of Del. Valley, Ardmore, 1986-87, presiding officer, bd. dirs., med. adv. bd., 1983—, prin. organizer Ednl. Symposia, 1983—, prin. organizer patient support groups, 1983—; organizer Lupus Loop Fundraising Marathon Walk/Run; lectr. Prin. coordinator Lupus Found. of Del. Valley Newsletter, 1983—. Liaison with Phila. Mayor Ed Rendell, liaison between Julius Erving and Children's Hosp. of Phila.; coord. Julius Erving Lupus Rsch. Fund; target chmn. Undergrad. Admissions Secondary Sch. Com., U. Pa. Mem. Am. Coll. of Musicians, Sigma Delta Gamma, Music Tchrs. Nat. Assn., Pa. Music Tchrs. Assn. Democrat. Jewish. Avocations: piano, theatre, symphony, movies. Home: 1640 Oakwood Dr Apt W-122 Narberth PA 19072-1232 Office: Lupus Found Delaware Valley 44 W Lancaster Ave Ardmore PA 19003-1339

ZEITLIN, BRUCE ALLEN, cryogenics technology executive; b. N.Y.C., July 31, 1943; s. Lester and Rae (Benson) Z.; m. Amy Joy Kozan, Aug. 29, 1965; children: Laurence, Jessica, Andrea. BS, Rensselaer Poly. Tech., 1965; MS, Stevens Inst. Tech., 1968. Scientist Airco Cen. Rsch. Lab., Murray Hill, N.J., 1965-70; tech. dir. Magnetic Corp. of Am., Waltham, Mass., 1970-72; v.p. IGC/Advanced Supercondrs., Waterbury, Conn., 1985-95, Intermagnetics Gen. Corp., Latham, N.Y., 1986-95; corp. v.p., gen. mgr. APD Cryogenics, a subsidiary of Intermagnetics, Allentown, Pa., 1995—; bd. dirs. Alsthom Intermagnets SA, Paris. Patentee in field. Mem. Am. Phys. Soc. Avocation: astronomy. Office: APD Cryogenics Inc 1833 Vultee St Allentown PA 18103-4742

ZEITLIN, EUGENIA PAWLIK, educator, librarian, writer; b. N.Y.C., Jan. 29; d. Charles and Pauline (Klimowski) Pawlik; m. Herbert Zakary Zeitlin, July 3, 1949; children: Mark Clyde, Joyce Therese Zeitlin Harris, Ann Victoria, Clare Katherine. BA in English, Bklyn. Coll., 1945; MA in English, NYU, N.Y.C., 1951; MALS, Rosary Coll., 1968. Teaching credential N.Y., Ariz., Calif., Ill. English tchr. Sea Cliff, L.I., N.Y., 1945-47; English, math. tchr. Merrick (N.Y.) Sch. Dist., 1948-49; English tchr. Wilson Sch. Dist., Phoenix, 1949-50; counselor West Phoenix (Ariz.) High Sch., 1953-56; asst. prof. English Wright Coll., Chgo., 1965-66; asst. prof. English, asst. to v.p. curriculum and instrn. Oakton C.C., Des Plaines, Ill., 1970-76; libr. Pasadena City Coll., L.A. C.C. Dist., L.A., 1979-91, City of L.A., 1984—. Contbr. articles to profl. jours. Named Northridge City Employee of Yr., 1986. Mem. AAUW (br. pres. Lancaster, Calif. 1958-60), Thoreau Soc. (life), Beta Phi Mu. Avocations: freelance writing and editing, book collecting. Home: 20124 Phaeton Dr Woodland Hills CA 91364-5633

ZEITLIN, HERBERT ZAKARY, retired college president, private pilot; b. N.Y.C., Nov. 14, 1919; s. Leonard and Martha Josephine (Soff) Z.; m. Eugenia F. Pawlik, July 3, 1949; children: Mark Clyde, Joyce Therese Zeitlin Harris, Ann Victoria, Clare Katherine. BS, NYU, 1947, MA, 1949; EdD, Stanford U., 1956. Tchr. Mepham High Sch., Bellmore, N.Y., 1946-47, Nassau County Vocat. Edn. Extension Bd., Mineola, N.Y.; electronics instr., adj. faculty Mephan C.C., 1946-49; tchr., counselor, dir. testing Phoenix Union High Sch. and Coll. Dist., 1949-57; dean eve. coll., prin. high sch. Antelope Valley Union High Sch. and Coll. Dist., Lancaster, Calif., 1957-62; dean instrn. Southwestern Coll., Chula Vista, Calif., 1962-64; pres., supt. Triton Coll., River Grove, Ill., 1964-76; pres., dean West L.A. Coll., 1976-80; pres. Trident Consultants, L.A., mgmt. cons., 1976—; adj. faculty Ariz. State U., Flagstaff, 1953-55, No. Ill. U., DeKalb, 1971-76, U. Calif., Santa Barbara, 1979. Author: The Incredible Triton College Story; editor in field. Pres. Antelope Valley Breeze & Sage, 1959-60, Bob Vivant Homeowners Assn., 1982-84; mayor Upper Woodland Hills, Calif. Served with USAAF, 1942-46. Recipient spl. commendation Chgo. Tribune, spl. commendation Richard Ogilvie, former gov. Ill.; Adminstr. of Yr. award Triton Coll. Faculty Assn., 1974; Spl. Achievement award for visionary accomplishment Ill. Sch. Adminstrs. Assn., 1976. Mem. Ariz. Vocat. Guidance Assn. (pres. 1951-52), Ariz. State Vocat. Assn., Antelope Valley Rotary (pres. 1962), Maywood Ill. Rotary (pres. 1972-73). Home: 20124 Phaeton Dr Woodland Hills CA 91364-5633 Office: Paramount Properties 21731 Ventura Blvd Woodland Hills CA 91364-1845 *I always felt that being the president of an organization, having held 16 presidencies in my lifetime, was like being the quarterback on the football team. You had a choice of running with the ball and taking some bruises or passing it to someone who should score. I was lucky most of the time in selecting some very fine receivers.*

ZEITLIN, MARILYN AUDREY, museum director; b. Newark, July 14, 1941; d. Sidney M. and Theresa Feigenblatt) Litchfield; widowed; children: Charles C. Sweedler, Milo Sweedler. Student, Vanderbilt U., 1963-65; AB in Humanities, Harvard U., 1966, MA in Teaching of English, 1967; postgrad., Cornell U., 1971-74. Dir. Ctr. Gallery, Bucknell U., Lewisburg, Pa., 1975-78; Freedman Gallery, Albright Coll., Reading, Pa., 1978-81, Anderson Gallery, Va. Commonwealth U., Richmond, 1981-87; curator, acting co-dir. Contemporary Arts Mus., Houston, 1987-90; exec. dir. Washington Projects for the Arts, 1990-92; dir. Univ. Art Mus., Ariz. State U., Tempe, 1992—; juror Dallas Mus. of Arts, McKnight Awards, Mpls.; grant evaluator IMS; grant evaluator, panelist NEH; lectr., cons. in field. Editor, contbr. essays to art publs. Bd. dirs. Cultural Alliance Washington; curator, commr. for U.S. for 1995 Venice Biennale. Samuel H. Kress fellow, 1972-73. Mem. Assn. Coll. and Univ. Mus. and Galleries (v.p. 1986-88), Am. Assn. Mus., Coll. Art Assn. (U.S. commr. Venice Biennale 1995). Office: Ariz State U Art Mus PO Box 872911 Tempe AZ 85287-2911

ZEITLIN, MAURICE, sociology educator, author; b. Detroit, Feb. 24, 1935; s. Albert J. and Rose (Goldberg) Z.; m. Marilyn Geller, Mar. 1, 1959; children: Michelle, Carla, Erica. BA cum laude, Wayne State U., 1957; MA, U. Calif., Berkeley, 1960, PhD, 1964. Instr. anthropology and sociology Princeton (N.J.) U., 1961-64, research assoc. Ctr. Internat. Studies, 1962-64; asst. prof. sociology U. Wis.-Madison, 1964-67, assoc. prof., 1967-70, prof., 1970-77, dir. Ctr. Social Orgn., 1974-76; prof. sociology UCLA, 1977—, also research assoc. Inst. Indsl. Relations; vis. prof. polit. sci. and sociology Hebrew U., Jerusalem, 1971-72. Author: (with R. Scheer) Cuba: An American Tragedy, 1963, 1964, Revolutionary Politics and the Cuban Working Class, 1967, 1970, The Civil Wars in Chile, 1984, (with R.E. Ratcliff) Landlords and Capitalists, 1988, The Large Corporation and Contemporary Classes, 1989; (with J. Stepan-Norris) Talking Union, 1996; Latin Am. editor Ramparts mag., 1967-73; editor-in-chief: Political Power and Social Theory, 1980-90; mem. editorial adv. bd. The Progressive mag., 1985-96; editor: (with J. Petras) Latin America: Reform or Revolution?, 1968, American Society, Inc., 1970, 1977, Father Camilo Torres: Revolutionary Writings, 1972, Classes, Class Conflict, and the State, 1980, How Mighty a Force?, 1983, Insurgent Workers: The Origins of Industrial Unionism, 1987. Chmn. Madison Citizens for a Vote on Vietnam, 1967-68; chmn. Am. Com. for Chile, 1973-75; mem. exec. bd. U.S. Com. for Justice to Latin Am. Polit. Prisoners, 1977-84; mem. exec. com. Calif. Campaign for Econ. Democracy, 1983-86. Ford Found. fellow, 1965-67, 70-71; Guggenheim fellow, 1981-82; NSF grantee, 1981, 82; recipient Project Censored award Top Censored Story, 1981; named to Ten Best Censored list, 1978. Mem. Am. Sociol. Assn. (governing council 1977-80, Disting. Contbn. Scholarship award in Pol. Sociology 1992, 96). Internat. Sociol. Assn. (editorial bd. 1977-81), Latin Am. Studies Assn., Orgn. Am. Historians. Democrat. Jewish. Office: UCLA Haines 237 405 Hilgard Ave Los Angeles CA 90095-9000 *Personal philosophy: "If I am not for myself who will be? and when I am for myself, what am I?" Hillel, the Elder.*

ZEKMAN, PAMELA LOIS (MRS. FREDRIC SOLL), reporter; b. Chgo., Oct. 22, 1944; d. Theodore Nathan and Lois Jane (Bernstein) Z.; m. Fredric Soll, Nov. 29, 1975. B.A., U. Calif. at Berkeley, 1965. Social worker Dept. Public Aid Cook County, Chgo., 1965-66; reporter City News Bur., Chgo., 1966-70, Chgo. Tribune, 1970-75, Chgo. Sun-Times, 1975-81; investigative reporter Sta. WBBM-TV, Chgo., 1981—. Recipient Pulitzer Prize awarded to Chicago Tribune for gen. local reporting on vote fraud series, 1973; Community Service award for vote fraud series UPI, 1972; Feature Series award for nursing home abuses series AP, 1971; Pub. Service award for slumlord series UPI, 1973; Newswriting award AP, 1973; In Depth Reporting award for police brutality series AP, 1974; Investigative Reporting awards Inland Daily Press Assn., 1974, 78; Investigative Reporting award for series on city waste AP, 1975; Pulitzer Prize for pub. service for series on hosp. abuses, 1976; Investigative Reporting award for series on baby selling, 1976; Pub. Service award for series on currency exchange abuses UPI, 1976; Investigative Reporting award for series on abuses in home for retarded children AP, 1977; Soc. Midland Authors Golden Rake award; UPI Public Service award; Ill. AP award; Nat. Headliners Club award; Sweepstakes award for Mirage Tavern investigative project, 1978; Nat. Disting. Service award for series on med. abuses in abortion clinics Sigma Delta Chi, 1979; named Journalist of Yr. No. Ill. U., 1979; recipient George Foster Peabody Broadcasting award, 1982, 85, RTNDA Investigative Reporting award, 1983, DuPont Columbia award 1982, 87. Office: WBBM-TV 630 N Mcclurg Ct Chicago IL 60611-4495*

ZEKMAN, TERRI MARGARET, graphic designer; b. Chgo., Sept. 13, 1950; d. Theodore Nathan and Lois (Bernstein) Z.; m. Alan Daniels, Apr. 12, 1980; children: Jesse Logan, Dakota Caitlin. BFA, Washington U., St. Louis, 1971; postgrad, Art Inst. Chgo., 1974-75. Graphic designer (on retainer) greeting cards and related products Recycled Paper Products Co., Chgo., 1970—, Jillson Roberts, Inc., Calif.; apprenticed graphic designer Helmuth, Obata & Kassabaum, St. Louis, 1970-71; graphic designer Container Corp., Chgo., 1971; graphic designer, art dir., photographer Cuerden Advt. Design, Denver, 1971-74; art dir. D'Arcy, McManus & Masius Advt., Chgo., 1975-76; freelance graphic designer Chgo., 1976-77; art dir. Garfield Linn Advt., Chgo., 1977-78; graphic designer Keiser Design Group, Van Noy & Co., Los Angeles, 1978-79; owner and operator graphic design studio Los Angeles, 1979—. Recipient cert. of merit St. Louis Outdoor Poster Contest, 1970, Denver Art Dirs. Club, 1973.

ZELANSKI, PAUL JOHN, art educator, author; b. Hartford, Conn., Apr. 13, 1931; s. John and Sofie (Berkowski) Z.; m. Annette Harding, June 30, 1965; children: John, Noemi, Ruth. Cert., The Cooper Union, 1955; BFA, Yale U., 1957; MFA, Bowling Green (Ohio) State U., 1958. Instr. art North Tex. State U., Denton, 1958-61; prof. art U. Conn., Storrs, 1962—; artist McDowell Art Colony, Peterborough, N.H.; advisor Permanent Pigments; panelist studio talk show Sta. WGHB, Boston, 1963-68; cons. Binnery & Smith; Getty lectr. North Tex. State U., 1989; vis. artist Inst. of Art of Krakow, Poland, 1990, Acad. Visual Arts, Maastricht, 1994; co-chair 3 Nations Student Project, Eng., The Netherlands, USA. Author: Design Principles and Problems, 1984, 2nd edit., 1995, Shaping Space, 1987, 2nd edit., 1995, The Art of Seeing, 1988, 3d edit., 1994, 4th edit., 1997, Color, 1989, 2nd edit., 1995; contbr. articles to profl. jours. Mem. com. silver anniversary U. Conn. Sch. Fine Arts, 1985; bd. dirs. Yale U. Art Sch. Alumni Assn., 1979-80. Cpl. U.S. Army, 1952-54. Accademia Italia fellow, 1977. Fellow Am. Commputing Machinery; mem. Computer Art and Design Edn. (chartered), Silvermine Guild Artists, New Eng. Artist Assn. (bd. dirs. 1966-76), Textbooks Authors Am. Roman Catholic. Avocation: reading. Home: 17 Cowles Rd West Willington CT 06279-1705 Office: U Conn # U99 Storrs Mansfield CT 06268

ZELAZO, NATHANIEL K., engineering executive; b. Lomza, Poland, Sept. 28, 1918; came to U.S., June, 1928; s. Morris and Ida (Kachorek) Z.; m. Helene Fishbein-Ret, June 27, 1943 (dec. 1996); children—Ronald Elliott, Annette Renee Middleton. B.S., CUNY, 1940; postgrad., Columbia U., 1940-42, 52-55; M.S.M.E., U. Wis., 1957, DE (hon.), 1986; D. Engring., Milw. Sch. Engring., 1983. Registered profl. engr., Wis., D.C. Vice pres. Norden Ketay (United Tech.), N.Y.C., 1952-55; dir. research devel. Avionics div. J. Oster Corp., Racine, Wis., 1955-59; pres., chief officer Astronautics Corp. Am., Milw., 1959-84, chief exec. officer, 1984—; chmn. bd. Astronautics C.A. Ltd., 1988—, Kearfott Guidance and Navigation Corp., Wayne, N.J., 1988—; v.p. Fgn. Sales Corp., St. Thomas, V.I., 1988—; dir. Astronautics-Kearfott ElectroAutomatica (AKE), St. Petersburg, Russia. Regent emeritus Milw. Sch. Engring., 1984, bd. dirs., 1980—; mem. engring. adv. coun. Marquette U., Milw., 1984, mem. Pres.'s Exec. Senate; mem. Greater Milw. Com. Recipient Employer of Yr. award Dept. Def., 1982, Billy Mitchell Meml. award Air Force Assn., 1977, Small Businessman of Yr. award SBA, 1966, Disting. Svc. award U. Wis., Madison, 1985, ECE Centennial medal U. Wis. Madison, 1991, High Tech. Exporter of Yr. award Wis. Dept. Devel., 1989, Entrepreneur of Yr. award in high tech. Arthur Young, Inc., 1989, Wis. Mfr. of Yr. Spl. award Redlin Browne & Co., 1990, Gov.'s New Product award Wis. Soc. Profl. Engrs., 1993; honoree NCCJ, 1990; named Engr. of Yr., 1985, Engrs. and Scientists Milw. Mem. AIAA, IEEE (Centennial medal 1984), Nat. Soc. Profl. Engrs., Am. Soc. Naval Engrs., Am. Helicopter Soc., Engrs. and Scientists of Milw., Inc., Physics Club Milw., Air Force Assn., Navy League U.S., Am. Technion Soc. (Albert Einstein award 1982), Wis. Clubs: Wisconsin, Milw. Yacht. Avocations: music; sailing; skiing. Home: 1610 N Prospect Ave Milwaukee WI 53202-2491 Office: Astronautics Corp Am 4115 N Teutonia PO Box 523 Milwaukee WI 53201-0523

ZELBY, LEON WOLF, electrical engineering educator, consulting engineer; b. Sosnowiec, Poland, Mar. 26, 1925; came to U.S., 1946, naturalized, 1951; s. Herszel and Helen (Wajnryb) Zylberberg; m. Rachel Kupfermintz, Dec. 28, 1954; children: Laurie Susan, Andrew Stephen. BSEE, Moore Sch. Elec. Engring., 1956; MS, Calif. Inst. Tech., 1957; PhD, U. Pa., 1961. Registered profl. engr., Pa., Okla. Mem. staff RCA, Hughes R & D Labs., Lincoln Lab., MIT, Sandia Corp., Argonne (Ill.) Nat. Labs., Inst. for Energy Analysis; mem. faculty U. Pa., 1959-67, assoc. prof., 1964-67; assoc. dir. plasma engring. Inst. Direct Energy Conversion, 1962-67; prof. U. Okla., Norman, 1967-95, dir. Sch. Elec. Engring., 1967-95; ret., 1995; cons. RCA, 1961-67, Moore Sch. Elec. Engring., 1967-68, also pvt. firms. Editor Tech. and Soc. mag., 1990-93; contbr. articles on energy-associated problems and issues to profl. jours. With AUS, 1946-47. Cons. Electrodynamic Corp. fellow Calif. Inst. Tech., 1957, Mpls.-Honeywell fellow U. Pa., 1957-58, Harrison fellow, 1958. Mem. IEEE, Franklin Inst., Sigma Xi, Tau Beta Pi, Eta Kappa Nu, Pi Mu Epsilon, Sigma Tau, Phi Kappa Phi. Home: 1009 Whispering Pines Dr Norman OK 73072-6912 *To learn as much, and to experience as much as possible, without harm to others; read, study, vary professional and recreational activities within constraints of the system.*

ZELBY, RACHEL, realtor; b. Sosnowiec, Poland, May 6, 1930; came to U.S., 1955; d. Herschel Kupfermintz and Sarah Rosenblatt; m. Leon W. Zelby, Dec. 28, 1954; children: Laurie Susan, Andrew Stephen. Student, U. Pa., 1955, Realtors' Inst., Norman, Okla., 1974; grad., Realtors Inst., Oklahoma City, 1978. Lic. realtor, broker, Okla.; cert. residential specialist, Okla. Realtor, broker, ptnr. Realty World Norman Heritage, 1973-81; realtor, broker Century 21 Parker Real Estate, Norman, 1981—, residential specialist, 1986—. Mem. Jr. Svc. League, Norman, 1980—; charter mem. Assistance League Norman, 1970—; bd. dirs. Juvenile Svcs., Inc., Norman, 1975-76; bd. viss. Coll. Fine Arts U. Okla., 1992—. Mem. Nat. Assn. Realtors, Norman Bd. Realtors, Women's Coun. Realtors (treas. 1985), U. Okla. Women's Assn. (past pres.), Norman C. of C., LWV. Avocations: aerobics, contract bridge, theatre, music, travel. Home: 1009 Whispering Pines Dr Norman OK 73072-6912 Office: Century 21 Parker Real Estate 319 W Main St Norman OK 73069-1312

ZELDES, JACOB DEAN, lawyer; b. Galesburg, Ill., Dec. 10, 1929; s. Louis Herman and Sophia Ruth (Koren) Z.; m. Nancy S. Zeldes, Aug. 23, 1953; children: Stephen, Kathryn, Amy. BS, U. Wis., 1951; LLB, Yale U., 1957. Bar: Conn. 1957, U.S. Dist. Ct. Conn. 1958, U.S. Ct. Appeals (2nd cir.) 1959, U.S. Supreme Ct. 1960, U.S. Tax Ct. 1966. Ptnr. Zeldes Needle & Cooper PC, Bridgeport, Conn. Lt. (j.g.) USNR, 1951-53, Korea. Fellow Am. Bar Found., Am. Coll. Trial Lawyers; mem. ABA Assn. Profl. Responsibility Lawyers, Conn. Bar Assn. (lawyer to lawyer dispute resolution com., spl. counsel Conn. Ho. of Reps., select com. to investigate impeachment of probate judge 1985), Conn. Trial Lawyers Assn., Assn. Trial Lawyers of Am., Nat. Assn. Criminal Def. Lawyers, Conn. Criminal Def. Lawyers Assn., Bridgeport Bar Assn. Democrat. Jewish. Avocations: swimming, hiking, travel. Office: Zeldes Needle & Cooper PC 5th Flr 1000 Lafayette Blvd Fl 5 Bridgeport CT 06604-4725

ZELDIN, RICHARD PACKER, publisher; b. Worcester, Mass., Aug. 7, 1918; s. M. and Virginia (Gealt) Z.; m. Virginia Graves, Nov. 25, 1950; children—Elizabeth Ann, Richard Shepherd. BS, West Chester U., Pa., 1942; grad. exec. program bus. adminstrn., Columbia U., 1966. Gen. mgr. profl. and reference book div. McGraw-Hill Book Co., Inc., 1948-68; v.p., publishing dir. Litton Ednl. Pub. Co., Inc., 1968-70; pres. R.R. Bowker Co., 1970-76, Xerox Coll. Pub., Xerox Individualized Pub., 1970-76;; pub. John Wiley & Sons, Inc., 1976-83; v.p. Moseley Assocs. Inc., N.Y.C., 1983—; sec.-treas. sci., tech. and med. book pubs. group Assn. Am. Pubs., 1966-70; mem. adv. com. comml. publs. AEC, 1966-70. Author: A Tennis Guide to the USA, 1980, Business Forms on File, 1984, Personal Forms on File, 1984. Served to lt. USNR, 1942-46. Recipient Disting. Alumni award West Chester U., 1974. Mem. Info. Industry Assn. (sec. 1973—), IEEE, Am. Soc. Info. Sci., Soc. for Scholarly Pub. Clubs: Dutch Treat (N.Y.C.), Pubs. Lunch (N.Y.C.). Home: 20 Fairfield Dr Tinton Falls NJ 07724-3114 Office: Moseley Assocs Inc 342 Madison Ave New York NY 10016-0601

ZELEN, MARVIN, statistics educator; b. N.Y.C., June 21, 1927; m. Thelma Geier, Sept. 10, 1950; children: Deborah, Sandra. BS, CCNY, 1949; MS, U. N.C., 1951; PhD, Am. U., 1957; MA (hon.), Harvard U., 1977. Stat. eng. lab. Nat. Bureau of Standards, 1952-61; assoc. prof. Univ. Md., 1960-61; head, stat. and applied Math. section Nat. Cancer Inst., 1963-66; leading prof. State Univ., Buffalo, N.Y.C., 1967-77; pres. Frontier Sci. and Tech. Rsch. Found., Boston, 1975—; chmn. dept. biostats. Dana Farber Cancer Inst., Boston, 1977—; prof. Harvard U. Sch. Pub. Health, Boston, 1977—; chmn. dept. biostat. Harvard U., 1980-90; vis. prof. Univ. Wis., 1961-63, vis. assoc. prof. Univ. Calif., 1958. Sgt. U.S. Army, 1945-46. Fulbright scholar, 1965-66. Fellow Am. Acad. Arts and Sci., AAAS, Inst. Math. Stats., Am. Statis. Assn.; mem. Internat. Stats. Inst. Home: 230 Eliot St Chestnut Hill MA 02167-1447 Office: Harvard Sch Pub Health 677 Huntington Ave Boston MA 02115-6028

ZELENY, MARJORIE PFEIFFER (MRS. CHARLES ELLINGSON ZELENY), psychologist; b. Balt., Mar. 31, 1924; d. Lloyd Armitage and Mable (Willian) Pfeiffer; BA, U. Md., 1947; MS, U. Ill., 1949, postgrad., 1951-54; m. Charles Ellington Zeleny, Dec. 11, 1950 (dec.); children: Ann Douglas, Charles Timberlake. Vocational counseling psychologist VA, Balt., 1947-48; asst. U. Ill. at Urbana, 1948-50, research asso. Bur. Research, 1952-53; chief psychologist dept. neurology and psychiatry Ohio State U. Coll. Medicine, Columbus, 1950-51; research psychologist, cons., Tucson, Washington, 1954—. Mem. Am., D.C. psychol. assns., AAAS, Southeastern Psychol Assn., DAR, Nat. Soc. Daus. Colonial Wars, Nat. Soc. Colonial Dames XVII Century, Nat. Soc. Descendants of Early Quakers, Nat. Soc. Daus. of Am. Colonists, Nat. Soc. Dames of Ct. of Honor, Nat. Soc. U.S. Daus. of 1812, Mortar Bd., Delta Delta Delta, Sigma Delta Epsilon, Psi Chi,

Sigma Tau Epsilon. Roman Catholic. Home: 6825 Wemberly Way Mc Lean VA 22101-1534

ZELEVAS, SHARON ROSE, art history educator, lawyer; b. Chgo., Aug. 1; d. John Andrew and Stella Regina (Swik) Z. BS with honors in Psychology, Loyola U., Chgo., 1975; MA in Museology, No. Ill. U., 1977; MA in History of Art and Culture, Rosary Coll., Florence, Italy, 1981; JD, John Marshall Law Sch., Chgo., 1986. Mgmt. cons. Hartford (Conn.) Ins. Group, 1977-79; archivist, curator mus. and hist. collection ADA, Chgo., 1981-83; mus. intern Nat. Gallery of London, 1987; tax specialist Coopers and Lybrand, Chgo., 1987-89; rsch. assoc. Uffizi Gallery and Bargello Mus., Florence, 1989; prof. law St. Xavier U., Chgo., 1990-91; prof. art history Triton Coll., River Grove, Ill., 1990—; pres. ZeLeVas & Assocs., Internat. and Domestic Tax Counsel, Chgo., 1993—; cons. Abrams Pub., N.Y.C., 1993—; reviewer, critic Blackwell Pubs., London, 1991—, McGraw-Hill, Inc., N.Y.C., 1995—. Author: Giovanni Domenico Tiepolo's Divertimenti Per Li Regazzi, 1981; curator (Pfaelzer Collection Exhibit) Form and Unform: A Search for Unity, 1976. Harvard U. Ctr. for Renaissance Studies vis. fellow Villa I Tatti, Florence, 1979, 80, 89; Anabel Mack Taylor scholar, 1979, 80. Mem. Coll. Art Assn., Internat. Ctr. of Medieval Art, Advocates Soc., Phi Alpha Delta (vice-justice 1985-86). Roman Catholic. Home: 4858 S Kildare Ave Chicago IL 60632-4430 Office: Triton Coll Dept Fine Arts 2000 N 5th Ave River Grove IL 60171-1907

ZELIFF, WILLIAM H., JR., former congressman; b. June 12, 1936; m. Sydna Zeliff. BS, Univ. Conn. Exec. DuPont Co., 1959-76; mem. 102nd-104th Congresses from 1st dist. N.H., 1991-96; owner Christmas Farm Inn, 1996—; chmn. govt. reform & oversight subcom. on Nat. Security, Internat. Affairs & Criminal Justice; mem. transp. & infrastructure com., small bus. com. Served U.S. Army. Protestant. Office: Christmas Farm Inn PO Box CC Jackson NH 03846*

ZELIKOW, HOWARD MONROE, management and financial consultant; b. Bklyn., Apr. 17, 1934; s. Herman and Mae (Rebell) Z.; m. Doris Brown, June 10, 1956 (div. Aug. 1987); children—Lori Ann Zelikow Florio, Daniel M.; m. Marcie Peskin Rosenblum, Dec. 12, 1987. BA, Dartmouth Coll., 1955, MBA, Amos Tuck Sch., 1956. Acct., Ernst & Ernst, N.Y.C., 1956-61; controller Kratter Corp., N.Y.C., 1961-64; mgr. J.H. Cohn, C.P.A.s, Newark, 1964-65; ptnr. Zelikow & Rebell, CPA's, N.Y.C., 1965-70; v.p. Oxbow Constrn. Corp., Port Washington, N.Y., 1970-76; exec. v.p., treas., chief fin. officer Progressive Ins. Cos., Mayfield Village, Ohio, 1976-87; prin. ZKA Assocs., Cleve., 1987—; ptnr. Kayne Anderson & Co., L.A., 1988—; bd. dirs. Fin. Security Assurance Holding LTD, N.Y.C., Queensway Fin. Holdings Ltd., Toronto, The Right Start Inc., Westlake, Calif. Trustee, Village of Great Neck Estates, Great Neck, N.Y., 1975-76. Mem. AICPA, Fin. Execs. Inst., Oakwood Club, Hillcrest Club, Phi Beta Kappa. Jewish. Home: 10118 Empyrean Way Los Angeles CA 90067 Office: ZKA Assocs Investment Mgmt 1800 Avenue Of The Stars Los Angeles CA 90067-4212

ZELIN, JEROME, retail executive; b. Bklyn., Dec. 24, 1930; s. Isidore and Ida (Roffman) Z.; m. Muriel Altsher, Dec. 18, 1955; children—Dorothy, Michael, Steven. BS magna cum laude, N.Y.U., 1952. Acct. Seymour Schwartz CPA, 1954-57; partner firm Schwartz, Zelin & Weiss CPAs, N.Y.C., 1958-61; vice chmn., pres., exec. v.p., treas., financial v.p., dir. Unishops, Inc. (retail co.), Jersey City, 1961-74; exec. v.p. Masters, Inc., Westbury, N.Y., 1974—. Trustee Temple Sholom of Flatbush. Served with AUS, 1952-54. Mem. N.Y. Soc. CPAs, Am. Inst. CPAs, Beta Gamma Sigma, Tau Alpha Omega. Jewish. Home: 225 Arkansas Dr Brooklyn NY 11234-6901

ZELINSKI, JOSEPH JOHN, engineering educator, consultant; b. Glen Lyon, Pa., Dec. 30, 1922; s. John Joseph and Lottie Mary (Oshinski) Z.; m. Mildred G. Sirois, July 22, 1946; children: Douglas John, Peter David. BS, Pa. State U., 1944, PhD, 1950. Grad. fellow Pa. State U., University Park, 1946-50; project supr. applied physics lab. Johns Hopkins U., Silver Spring, Md., 1950-58; staff scientist Space Tech. Labs. (now TRW, Inc.), Redondo Beach, Calif., 1958-60; head chem. tech. div. Ops. Evaluation Group MIT, Cambridge, 1960-62; prin. rsch. scientist Avco Everett (Mass.) Rsch. Lab., 1962-64; prof. mech. engring. Northeastern U., Boston, 1964-85, prof. emeritus, 1985—; pres. World Edn. Resources, Ltd., Tampa, Fla., 1984—; cons. Avco Everett Rsch. Lab., 1964-71, Pratt & Whitney Aircraft, East Hartford, Conn., 1966-70, Modern Electric Products and Phys. Scis. Co., Inc., Boston, 1980-82, Morrison, Mahoney and Miller, Boston, 1984; vice-chmn., chmn. exec. com. Univ. Grad. Coun., Northeastern U., Boston, 1980-84, dir. mech. engring. grad. program, 1982-85; del. 4th World Conf. Continuing Engring. Edn., Beijing China People to People, Spokane, Wash., 1989. Contbr. articles to profl. jours. Prin. Confraternity Christian Doctrine, Andover, Mass., 1961-64; pres. Andover Edn. Coun., 1962-64; vice chmn. Dem. Town Com., Boxford, Mass., 1980-84. Lt. (j.g.) USNR, 1943-46, PTO. Mem. AAAS, ASME, Am. Chem. Soc., N.Y. Acad. Scis., Combustion Inst. Democrat. Roman Catholic. Achievements include U.S. and foreign patents for coal combustion system for magnetohydrodynamic power generation, for fuel-cooled combustion systems for jet engines flying at high Mach numbers; prediction of optical observables of re-entry vehicles from analysis of decomposition mechanisms of heat-shield materials; invention of high-temperature furnace for production of crystalline graphite; development and verification of a design method for ramjet combustors. Home: Hunters Green 9207 Jubilee Ct Tampa FL 33647-2511

ZELINSKY, DANIEL, mathematics educator; b. Chgo., Nov. 22, 1922; s. Isaac and Ann (Ruttenberg) Z.; m. Zelda Oser, Sept. 23, 1945; children: Mara Sachs, Paul O., David. BS, U. Chgo., 1941, MS, 1943, PhD, 1946. Rsch. mathematician applied math group Columbia U., N.Y.C., 1941-43; instr. U. Chgo., 1943-44, 46-47; Nat. Rsch. Coun. fellow Inst. Advanced Study, Princeton, N.J., 1947-49; from asst. to assoc. prof. dept. math. Northwestern U., Evanston, Ill., 1949-60, prof., 1960-93, prof. emeritus, 1993—, acting chmn. math. dept., 1959-60, chmn., 1975-78; vis. prof. U. Calif. Berkeley, 1960, Fla. State U., Tallahassee, 1963, Hebrew U., Jerusalem, 1970-71, 85, others; vis. scholar Tata Inst., 1979; mem. various coms. Northwestern U.; lectr. in field. Author: A First Course in Linear Algebra, 1968, rev. edit., 1973; contbr. articles to profl. jours. Fulbright grantee Kyoto U., 1955-56, grantee NSF, 1958-80; Guggenheim fellow Inst. Advanced Study, 1956-57, Indo-Am. fellow, 1978-79. Fellow AAAS (mem. nominating com. sect. A 1977-80, chmn. elect sect. A 1984-85, chmn. 1985-86, retiring chmn. 1986-87), Am. Math. Soc. (mem. coun. 1961-67, editor Transactions of A.M.S. 1961-67, mem. various coms., mem. editorial bd. Notices of A.M.S. 1983-86, chmn. editorial bds. com. 1989, chmn. ad hoc com. 1991-92). Jewish. Home: 613 Hunter Rd Wilmette IL 60091-2213 Office: Northwestern U Dept Math Evanston IL 60208

ZELINSKY, PAUL O., illustrator, painter, author; b. Evanston, Ill., Feb. 14, 1953; s. Daniel and Zelda B. (Oser) Z.; m. Deborah M. Hallen, Dec. 31, 1981; children: Anna H., Rachel L. BA summa cum laude, Yale U., 1974; MFA in Painting, Tyler Sch. Art, 1976. Art instr. San Diego State U., 1976; freelance illustrator/author, 1977—. Illustrator: Ralph S. Mouse, 1982, Dear Mr. Henshaw, 1993, More Rootabagas, 1993, Swamp Angel, 1994; illustrator, adapter: Rumpelstiltskin; illustrator, adapter, designer: The Wheels on the Bus, 1990. Recipient Caldecott Honor for Hansel & Gretel, 1985, Rumpelstiltskin, 1987, Swamp Angel, 1995, Best Illustrated Book N.Y. Times Book Rev., N.Y.C., 1981, 85, 94. Mem. Graphic Artists Guild, Children's Illustrators and Authors (charter), Soc. Children's Book Writers and Illustrators, Phi Beta Kappa. Avocations: cooking, reading, child care.

ZELIS, ROBERT FELIX, cardiologist, educator; b. Perth Amboy, N.J., Aug. 5, 1939; s. Felix Andrew and Rita Marie (Jurasz) Z.; m. Gail Ann Heelon, Sept. 10, 1960; children: Robert Felix, Kathleen, Karen, David. B.S. cum laude, U. Mass., 1960; M.D. with honors, U. Chgo., 1964. Diplomate: Am. Bd. Internal Medicine (cardiovascular disease). Intern, then asst. resident in medicine Beth Israel Hosp., Harvard U. Med. Sch., 1964-66; clin. asso. (lt. comdr. USPHS) cardiology br. Nat. Heart Inst., NIH, Bethesda, Md., 1966-68; mem. faculty U. Calif. Med. Sch., Davis, 1968-74; asst. asso. prof. medicine U. Calif. Med. Sch., 1972-74, chief lab. clin. physiology, 1968-74, asst. chief sect. cardiovascular medicine, 1970-74; prof. medicine and cellular/molecular physiology Milton S. Hershey (Pa.) Med. Center, Pa. State U. Coll. Medicine, 1974—, chief div. cardiology, 1974-84, dir. cardiology research, 1984—. Editor: The Peripheral Circulations, 1975; co-editor: Calcium Blockers, 1982; mem. editorial bd. Annals Internal Medicine, 1976-79, Am. Jour. Physiology, 1976-79, Circulation, 1979-82, Am. Heart Jour., 1980-90, Am. Jour. Cardiology, 1983-86, Jour. C.V. Pharmacology, 1991—, Jour. Am. Coll. Cardiology, 1994—; contbr. articles to med. jours. Walter S. Barr fellow, 1960-64; recipient Borden Research award, 1964, Palmer award for Faculty Mentoring Pa. State U., 1997. Fellow A.C.P., Am. Coll. Chest Physicians, Am. Coll. Cardiology (gov. Eastern Pa. 1977-80); mem. Am. Fedn. Clin. Research (pres. 1977-78), Am. Soc. Clin. Investigation (nat. council 1981-85, v.p. 1984-85), Am. Physiol. Soc., Assn. Am. Physicians, Assn. Univ. Cardiologists, Am. Soc. Pharmacology and Exptl. Therapeutics, Am. Heart Assn. (nat. fellow councils circulation, arteriosclerosis, clin. cardiology and epidemiology, v.p. for community programs 1979-81, award of merit 1983 v.p., exec. com. Pa. 1976-79, pres. Pa. affiliate 1979-80, Charles T. Mears Humanitarian award 1984), Western Soc. Clin. Research, Sigma Xi, Alpha Omega Alpha, Phi Eta Sigma. Roman Catholic. Home: 227 Homestead Rd Hershey PA 17033-1328 Office: MS Hershey Med Ctr Cardiology Divsn Box 850 Hershey PA 17033

ZELLER, CLAUDE, physicist, researcher; b. Aulnay, France, Dec. 11, 1940; came to U.S., 1976; m. Elisabeth Kreib, 1962 (div. 1967); 1 child, Frédéric: m. Florence Labour, Oct. 14, 1967; children: Caroline, Elisabeth. PhD, Univ. Nancy, France, 1968. Rsch. physicist Univ. Nancy, France, 1968-76; visiting rsch. faculty Univ. Pa., Phila., 1976-79; sr. physicist Pitney Bowes R&D, Norwalk, Conn., 1979-84, mgr. applied physics, 1984-91; fellow Pitney Bowes, Shelton, Conn., 1992—; adv. bd. CNRS, Paris, 1969-71; sec. scientific bd. Univ. Nancy, 1971-76; cons. Bruker-Spectrospin, Wissembourg, France, 1970-75. Contbr. 78 articles to profl. jours. Recipient sr. fellowship, NATO, 1976. Mem. IEEE, N.Y. Acad. Scis., Am. Phys. Soc., Appalachian Mountain Club, Soc. for Imaging Sci. and Tech., U.S. Jaycees, L'Union Alsacienne (v.p.), Am. Soc. Le Souvenir Français. Roman Catholic. Achievements include pioneer work in electron beam X-Ray microanalysis, early design of soft cast steel electro-magnet yoke for NMR applications, development of advanced materials such as high electrical conductivity intercalated graphite fibers composite materials and very high magnetic permeability amorphous fibers, investigation of the interferences of electronic articles surveillance systems with pacemakers and reporting to international regulatory commissions; 6 patents. Home: 97 Fan Hill Rd Monroe CT 06468-1831 Office: Pitney Bowes Inc 35 Waterview Dr Shelton CT 06484-4301

ZELLER, FRANCIS JOSEPH, dean; b. Chgo., July 31, 1943; s. Charles Joseph and Erma J. (Kile) Z.; m. Frances Joan McGrath, Aug. 3, 1968; children: Patrick, Brian. BA in English, Lewis U., 1967; MA in Edn. Adminstrn., No. Ill. U., 1970, EdD in Edn. Adminstrn., 1983. Chmn. Robert Frost Jr. High Sch., Schaumburg, Ill., 1967-69; asst. bus. mgr. Park Ridge (Ill.) Elem. Sch., 1970-71; bus. mgr. Barrington (Ill.) High Sch., 1971-73; dean bus. svcs. Illinois Valley Community Coll., Oglesby, Ill., 1973—. Contbr. articles to profl. jours. Mem. adv. com. state Univ. Retirement System, Champaign, Ill., 1983-90. Named Outstanding Life Rotarian La Salle (Ill.) Rotary Club, 1976. Mem. NEA, Ill. C.C. Chief Fin. Officers (bd. dirs. 1984-87, chair 1993-95), Ill. Assn. Sch. Bus. Ofcls. (past pres., life mem. 1972—). Internat. Assn. Sch. Bus. Ofcls. (chair comm. col. com.), Ottawa C. of C., Golden Triangle Club, Art Inst. Chgo., Delta Sigma Pi. Avocations: tennis, cross-country skiing, bicycling. Office: Ill Valley Cmty Coll 815 N Orlando Smith St Oglesby IL 61348-9692

ZELLER, JOSEPH PAUL, advertising executive; b. Crestline, Ohio, Mar. 19, 1940; s. Paul Edward and Grace Beatrice (Kinstle) Z.; m. Nancy Jane Schmidt, June 17, 1961; children: Laurie, Joe. BA, U. Notre Dame, 1962; MFA, Ohio U., 1963. Mgr.radio/television Drewrys Ltd. USA, Inc., South Bend, Ind., 1963-64; media supr. Tatham-Laird & Kudner, Chgo., 1964-67; v.p. assoc. media dir. J. Walter Thompson Co., Chgo., 1967-77; v.p. media dir, v.p. Campbell-Mithun, Chgo., 1977-80; sr. v.p., dir. media, fin., chmn. media coun. D'Arcy Masius Benton & Bowles, Chgo., 1980-96, sr. v.p., 1996—; chmn. Z Prop, 1986—; dir. circle Desert Caballeros Mus., 1994-96. Pres. Amateur Hockey Assn. Ill., 1985. Mem. Broadcast Pioneers, Chgo. Advt. Club, Moose. Roman Catholic. Avocations: amateur hockey, country music.

ZELLER, KENNETH J., state official. Commr. Dept. Labor, Indpls. Office: Rm W195 402 W Washington St Ste W195 Indianapolis IN 46204-2742

ZELLER, MICHAEL EDWARD, physicist, educator; b. San Francisco, Oct. 8, 1939; s. Edward Michael and Marie (Eschen) Z.; m. Linda Marie Smith, June 12, 1960; children: Jeffrey, Daniel. B.S., Stanford U., 1961; M.S., UCLA, 1964, Ph.D., 1968. Research assoc. UCLA, 1968-69; instr. physics Yale U., New Haven, 1969-70, asst. prof., 1970-76, assoc. prof., 1976-82, prof., 1982—, chmn., 1989-95, Henry Ford II prof., 1996—. Recipient DeVane medal Phi Beta Kappa, 1980. Fellow Am. Phys. Soc.; mem. N.Y. Acad. Sci., Sigma Xi, Sigma Pi Sigma. Democrat. Jewish. Home: 135 Newton Rd Woodbridge CT 06525-1534 Office: Yale U Physics Dept 260 Whitney Ave New Haven CT 06511-7208

ZELLER, MICHAEL EUGENE, lawyer; b. Queens, N.Y., June 19, 1967; s. Hans Ludwig and Geri Ann (Schottenstein) Z. BA, Union Coll., 1989; JD, Temple Law Sch., 1992; LLM magna cum laude, U. Hamburg, Germany, 1994. Bar: N.Y. 1992, U.S. Dist. Ct. (so. and ea. dists.) N.Y. 1995, N.C. 1996. Fgn. intern Bryan Gonzalez Vargas y Gonzalez Baz, Mexico City, 1990; student law clerk Hon. Jane Cutler Greenspan, Phila., 1990-91; fgn. clerk DROSTE, Hamburg, 1991, fgn. assoc., translator, 1992-94; freelance translator Charlotte, N.C., 1995—; assoc. Internat. and Corp. Law Group of Moore & Van Allen PLLC, Charlotte, 1995—; vol. atty. Children's Law Ctr. Mem. Charlotte World Affairs Coun., Charlotte Mayor's Internat. Cabinet; bd. dirs. Alemannia Soc. Recipient scholarship Fedn. German/Am. Clubs, 1987. Mem. ABA, N.Y. State Bar Assn., N.C. Bar Assn., Mecklenburg County Bar Assn., Gewerblicher Rechtsschutz und Urheberrecht e.V., European Am. Bus. Forum, Am. Translators Assn. Avocations: singing, theater, golf, fictional writing. Office: 100 N Tryon St Fl 47 Charlotte NC 28202-4000

ZELLER, MICHAEL JAMES, psychologist, educator; b. Des Moines, Dec. 3, 1939; s. George and Lila (Fitch) Z. BS, Iowa State U., 1962, MS, 1967. Instr. psychology Mankato (Minn.) State U., 1967-73, asst. prof. psychology, 1974-89, assoc. prof. psychology, 1990—; mem. social sci. edn. coun. Mankato State U., 1976—; ednl. cons. Random House, Scott Foresman, West Pub. Editor: Test Item File to Accompany Introduction to Psychology, 6th edit., 1992; co-author: Test Item File to Accompany Introduction to Psychology, 5th edit., 1989, Test File for Psychology, 3d edit., 1988, Unit Mastery Workbook, 1st edit., 1974, 2d edit., 1976, Test Item File to Accompany Psychology, 1st edit., 1974, 2d edit., 1976, Psychology: A Personal Approach, 1st edit., 1982, 2d edit., 1984; contbr. chpts. to books. With USAR, 1964-70. Mem. APA, Minn. Psychol. Assn., Inter-Faculty Orgn., Midwestern Psychol. Assn., Psi Chi (award 1988). Achievements include development and research on educational materials, methods of instruction and career opportunities for psychology majors. Home: PO Box 1958 Mankato MN 56002-1958 Office: Mankato State U Dept of Psychology MSU 35 PO Box 8400 Mankato MN 56002

ZELLERBACH, WILLIAM JOSEPH, retired paper company executive; b. San Francisco, Sept. 15, 1920; s. Harold Lionel and Doris (Joseph) Z.; m. Margery Haber, Feb. 25, 1946; children: John William, Thomas Harold, Charles Ralph, Nancy. B.S., Wharton Sch., U. Pa., 1942; grad., Advanced Mgmt. Program, Harvard U., 1958. With Crown Zellerbach Corp. and subs., 1946-85; officer, dir. Crown Zellerbach Corp., 1960-85. Mem gen. adv. com. fgn. assistance programs AID, 1965-68; pres. Zellerbach Family Fund. Served as lt. USNR, 1942-46. Mem. Nat. Paper trade Assn. (pres. 1970). Clubs: Villa Taverna (San Francisco), Presidio Golf (San Francisco), Pacific Union (San Francisco), Commonwealth (San Francisco); Peninsula Country (San Mateo, Calif.). Office: 120 Montgomery St Ste 2100 San Francisco CA 94104-4324

ZELLIOT, ELEANOR MAE, history educator; b. Des Moines, Oct. 7, 1926; d. Ernest A. and Minnie (Hadley) Z. BA, William Penn Coll., 1948; MA, Bryn Mawr (Pa.) Coll., 1949; PhD, U. Pa., 1969. Assoc. editor The Am. Friend, Richmond, Iowa, 1950-58; tchr. Scattergood Sch., West Branch, Iowa, 1958-60; editor Pendle Hill Pubs., Wallingford, Pa., 1960-62; acting instr., asst. prof. U. Minn., Mpls., 1966-69; researcher South Asia Hist. Atlas, Mpls., 1966-69; from asst. prof. to assoc. prof. Carleton Coll., Northfield, Minn., 1969-79; prof. Carleton Coll., Northfield, 1979-97, dept. chair, 1989-92, Laird Bell prof., 1993-97; pres. Midwest Conf. on Asian Affairs, 1996-97. Author: From Untouchable to Dalit, 1992, 96; editor: Experience of Hinduism, 1988, (jour. issue) Marathi Sampler, 1982; contbr. articles to profl. jours. Mem. Dem. Farmer Labor Party, Minn., LWV. Fellowship NEH, 1987, Fulbright, 1992. Mem. Minn. Consortium for South Asia, Am. Inst. of Indian Studies (v.p. 1994-97, bd. trustees, fellowship 1985, 89), Assoc. Colls. of Midwest, India Studies, Assn. of Asian Studies. Mem. Soc. of Friends. Avocations: walking, cooking. Office: Carleton Coll Northfield MN 55057

ZELLMAN, ANDE, editor; b. New Haven, Sept. 6, 1952; s. Seymour Zellman and Lillian Shapiro. BS, Boston U., 1974. Features editor Boston Phoenix, 1978-82; mag. editor Dallas Times Herald, 1982; asst. mag. editor Boston Globe, 1983-85, mag. editor, 1985-94, assoc. editor media devel., 1994-96; assoc. editor New Media, 1996—; N.E. judge Livingston Awards (journalism), N.Y., 1988—. Mem. Sunday Mag. Editors Assn. (pres. 1988-90). Office: Boston Globe Mag 135 Morrissey Blvd Boston MA 02107

ZELLNER, ARNOLD, economics and statistics educator; b. Bklyn., Jan. 2, 1927; s. Israel and Doris (Kleiman) Z.; m. Agnes Marie Sumares, June 20, 1953; children—David S., Philip A., Samuel N., Daniel A., Michael A. AB, Harvard, 1949; PhD, U. Calif. at Berkeley, 1957; PhD (hon.), U. Madrid, 1986, U. Lisbon, 1991. Asst., then assoc. prof. econs. U. Wash., 1955-60; Fulbright vis. prof. Netherlands Sch. Econs., Rotterdam, 1960-61; assoc. prof., then prof. econs. U. Wis., 1961-66; H.G.B. Alexander disting. service prof. econs. and statistics U. Chgo., 1966-96, prof. emeritus, 1996—; dir. H.G.B. Alexander Rsch. Found., 1973-96; cons. Battelle Meml. Inst., 1964-71; vis. rsch. prof. U. Calif., Berkeley, 1971, 96; Trustee Nat. Opinion Rsch. Corp., 1973-80; bd. dirs. Nat. Bur. Econ. Rsch., 1980—, seminar leader NSF-NBER Seminar on Bayesian Inference in Econometrics and Stats., 1970-95; vis. prof. Am. U., Cairo, 1997, Hebrew U., 1997. Co-author: Systems Simulation for Regional Analysis, 1969, Estimating the Parameters of the Markov Probability Model, 1970; author: Bayesian Inference in Econometrics, 1971, Basic Issues in Econometrics, 1984, Bayesian Analysis in Econometrics and Statistics: The Zellner View and Papers, 1997; editor: Economic Statistics and Econometrics, 1968, Seasonal Analysis of Economic Time Series, 1978; assoc. editor: Econometrica, 1962-68; co-editor: Studies in Bayesian Econometrics and Statistics, 1975, Jour. Econometrics, 1972—, founding editor ASA Jour. Bus. and Econ. Stats., 1983; contbr. articles to profl. jours. Pres. Leonard J. Savage Meml. Trust Fund, Chgo., 1977—. Served with AUS, 1951-53. Fellow AAAS, Am. Acad. Arts and Scis., Econometric Soc., Am. Statis. Assn. (pres. elect 1990—, pres. 1991—, chmn. bus. and econs. sect. 1980, chmn. Bayesian statis. sci. sect. 1993); mem. Am. Econ. Assn., Internat. Statis. Inst., Internat. Soc. Bayesian Anaysis (co-pres. 1993, pres. 1994-96), Soc. Actuaries (trustee, rsch. found., 1994—). Avocations: travel, golf, tennis. Home: 5628 S Dorchester Ave Chicago IL 60637-1722 Office: U Chgo Grad Sch Bus 1101 E 58th St Chicago IL 60637-1511

ZELLNER, KENNETH KERMIT, elementary education educator; b. Allentown, Pa., Sept. 4, 1945; s. Mellis Myron and Thelma Amanda (Bortz) Z.; m. Jean Elizabeth Welsh, June 24, 1978; children: Todd Benjamin, Amanda Elizabeth. BS, Kutztown U., 1967, MEd, 1971. Cert. elementary and secondary edn., environ. edn., supervision elementary edn., Pa. Tchr. Parkland Sch. Dist., Allentown, 1967—, environ. lab. cons., 1980-97; cooperating tchr. East Stroudsburg (Pa.) U., 1973-97, Lehigh U., Bethlehem, Pa., 1992-94, sci. camp instr. SMART Ctr., 1993-94; faculty mentor Pa. Gov.'s Sch. of Excellence for Teaching Pa. Dept. Edn., Harrisburg, 1992. Contbr. articles to profl. jours. Mem. little Lehigh watershed curriculum task force Wildlands Conservancy, Emmaus, Pa., 1984-97; mem. newspapers in edn. adv. coun. Allentown Morning Call, 1988-89. Recipient Presdl. Award for Excellence in Sci. and Math. Teaching NSF, 1992, Regional Catalyst award for Excellence in Sci. Teaching Chem. Manufacturers Assn., 1994, Nat. Educators award Milken Family Found., 1994, Congrl. Citation for Outstanding Sci. Teaching Pa. Ho. of Reps., 1994. Mem. Pa. Sci. Tchrs. Assn., Nat. Sci. Tchrs. Assn., Coun. for Elem. Sci. Internat., Assn. Presdl. Awardees in Sci. Teaching, Soc. Elem. Presdl. Awardees, Masons (worshipful master 1985). Republican. Lutheran. Avocations: woodworking, antique and classic cars, snow skiing. Home: 9022 Reservoir Rd Germansville PA 18053-2731 Office: Kernsville Sch 5051 Kernsville Rd Orefield PA 18069-2321

ZELMANOWITZ, JULIUS MARTIN, mathematics educator, university administrator; b. N.Y.C., Feb. 20, 1941; s. Morris and Tillie (Holtz) Z.; m. Joan R. Traubel, June 24, 1962; 1 child, Dawn Michèle. AB, Harvard U., 1962; MS, U. Wis., 1963, PhD, 1966. Asst. prof. U. Calif., Santa Barbara, 1966-73, assoc. prof., 1973-77, prof. maths., 1977—, assoc. vice chancellor acad. affairs, 1985-87, assoc. vice chancellor acad. personnel, 1988—; assoc. prof. Carnegie-Mellon U., Pitts., 1970-71; vis. asst. prof. UCLA, 1969-70, vis. assoc. prof. 1973-74; vis. prof. U. Rome, 1977, McGill U., Montreal, Quebec, 1982-83, 87-88, U. Munich, 1983, 88. Contbr. articles to profl. jours. Sr. rsch. grantee Italian Nat. Rsch. Coun., Rome, 1977, Palermo, 1988; named Milw. Prof. of Maths. The Technion, Haifa, Israel, 1979; Fulbright sr. fellow, Munich, 1983. Mem. Am. Math. Soc., Math. Assn. Am. Home: 3215 Laurel Canyon Rd Santa Barbara CA 93105-2015 Office: U Calif Dept Math Santa Barbara CA 93106

ZELNICK, CARL ROBERT, Congressional correspondent; b. N.Y.C., Aug. 9, 1940; s. David Isadore and Lillian (Ostrow) Z.; m. Pamela Margaret Sharp, Dec. 30, 1967; children: Eva Michal, Dara Yael, Marni Ruth. B.S., Cornell U., 1961; LL.B., U. Va., 1964. Bar: N.Y. 1965, D.C. 1966. Law assoc. H. Charles Ephraim, Washington, 1966-67; corr./columnist Anchorage Daily News, 1968-76; Assoc. editor Environmental Law Reporter, 1971-72; spl. corr. Christian Sci. Monitor, 1973-77; corr./bur. chief Nat. Pub. Radio, Washington, 1972-76; exec. editor Frost/Nixon Interviews, Washington, 1976-77; dir. news coverage ABC-TV, Washington, 1977-81; dep. bur. chief ABC News, Washington, 1981-82; Moscow bur. chief, corr. ABC News, 1982-84; corr. ABC News, Israel, 1984-86; ABC News Pentagon corr. Washington, 1986-94. Author: Backfire--A Reporter Looks at Affirmative Action, 1996; contbr. articles to newspapers and mags. Served with USMC, 1964-65. Recipient Gavel awards Am. Bar Assn., 1969, 74, Du Pont award Columbia U. Sch. Journalism, 1984, Emmy award, 1984, 92. Mem. Council on Fgn. Relations, Radio and TV Corrs. Assn., Internat. Inst. for Strategic Studies, Washington Press Club, Phi Epsilon Pi, Phi Delta Phi. Jewish. Office: ABC News Washington Bureau 1717 Desales St NW Washington DC 20036-4401

ZELNICK, STRAUSS, entertainment company executive; b. Boston, June 26, 1957; s. Allan Zelnick and Elsa Lee Strauss; m. Wendy Belzberg, 1990; children: Cooper, Lucas. BA summa cum laude, Wesleyan U., Middletown, Ct., 1979; MBA, Harvard U., 1983, JD cum laude, 1983. Bar: N.Y. 1984. Dir. internat. TV Columbia Pictures Internat. Corp., N.Y.C., 1983-85, v.p. internat. TV, 1985-86; sr. v.p. corp. devel. Vestron Inc., Stamford, Conn., 1986-87, exec. v.p., 1987, pres., chief oper. officer, 1988-89; pres., chief oper. officer Twentieth Century Fox, L.A., 1989-93; pres., CEO Crystal Dynamics, Palo Alto, Calif., 1993-95; pres., CEO, BMG Entertainment N.Am., N.Y.C., 1995—. Trustee Wesleyan U., 1992—; mem. contemporary arts coun. Mus. Modern Art, 1989, Young Pres. Orgn.; chmn. Covenant House Calif., 1992-95; bd. dirs. Covenant House, N.Y.C., 1995—. Mem. N.Y. State Bar Assn., Harvard Club, Phi Beta Kappa. Avocations: squash, sailing, skiing. Office: BMG Entertainment NA 1540 Broadway New York NY 10036-4039

ZELON, LAURIE DEE, lawyer; b. Durham, N.C., Nov. 15, 1952; d. Irving and Doris Miriam (Baker) Z.; m. David L. George, Dec. 30, 1979; children: Jeremy, Daniel. BA in English with distinction, Cornell U., 1974; JD, Harvard U., 1977. Bar: Calif. 1977, U.S. Ct. Appeals (9th cir.) 1978, U.S. Supreme Ct. 1989. Assoc. Beardsley, Hufstedler & Kemble, L.A., 1977-81; assoc. Hufstedler, Miller, Carlson & Beardsley, L.A., 1981-82, ptnr., 1983-88; ptnr. Hufstedler, Miller, Kaus & Beardsley, L.A., 1988-90, Hufstedler, Kaus & Ettinger, L.A., 1990-91, Morrison & Foerster, L.A., 1991—; mem. Calif. Assembly, 1993—. Editor-in-chief: Harvard Civil Rights-Civil Liberties Law Rev., 1976-77; contbg. author: West's California Literary Forms: Civil Procedure Before Trial, 1996. Vol. atty. ACLU of So. Calif., L.A.,

1977—; bd. dirs. N.Y. Civil Liberties Union, 1973-74. Mem. ABA (chmn. young lawyers divsn. pro bono project 1981-83, delivery and pro bono projects com. 1983-85, subgrant competition-subgrant monitoring project 1985-86, chair standing com. on lawyers pub. svc. responsibility 1987-90, chair law firm pro bono project 1989-91, standing com. legal aid and indigent defendants 1991—, chair 1993—, mem. ho. dels. 1993—), Calif. Bar Assn. (bd. dirs. appellate project 1995—, chair commn. on access to justice 1997), L.A. County Bar Assn. (trustee 1989-91, v.p. 1992-93, sr. v.p. 1993-94, pres.-elect 1994-95, pres. 1995-96, fed. cts. and practices com. 1984-93, vice chmn. 1987-88, chmn. 1988-89, chmn. judiciary com. 1991-92, chair real estate litigation subsect. 1991-92), Women Lawyers Assn. L.A., Calif. Women Lawyers Assn. Democrat. Office: Morrison & Foerster 555 W 5th St Ste 3500 Los Angeles CA 90013-1080

ZEMAN, JAROLD KNOX, history educator; b. Semonice, Czechoslovakia, Feb. 27, 1926; emigrated to Can., 1948, naturalized, 1955; s. Jaroslav and Jaroslava (Potuckova) Z.; m. Lillian Koncicky, June 18, 1951; children: Miriam, Dagmar, Timothy, Janice. Grad., Charles U., Prague, 1948, Th.Cand., 1948; B.D., Knox Coll., U. Toronto, Ont., Can., 1952; Dr.Theol., U. Zurich, Switzerland, 1966; DD (hon.), McMaster U., Hamilton, Ont., 1985, Acadia U., Wolfville, N.S., 1994. Ordained to ministry Baptist Ch., 1950; pastor in Toronto and Villa Nova, Ont., 1949-59; sec. dept. Can. missions Bapt. Conv., Toronto, 1959-68; prof. ch. history Acadia U., Wolfville, N.S., Can., 1968-91, dir. Ctr. for Bapt. and Anabapt. Studies, 1991-97; vis. prof. Bapt. Theol. Sem., Ruschlikon, Switzerland, 1965, 84, Mennonite Sem., Elkhart, Ind., 1976-77, Regent Coll., Vancouver, B.C., 1979, Gordon-Conwell Theol. Sem., Boston, 1983, Moravian Theol. Sem., Bethlehem, Pa., 1984, Ontario Theol. Sem., Toronto, 1986, 92; guest lectr., U.S., Can.; mem. religious adv. com. CBC. Author: God's Mission and Ours, 1963, The Whole World At Our Door, 1964, The Anabaptists and the Czech Brethren in Moravia, 1526-1628: A Study of Origins and Contacts, 1969, The Hussite Movement and the Reformation in Bohemia, Moravia and Slovakia, 1350-1650, 1977, Baptist Roots and Identity, 1978, Renewal of Church and Society, 1984, Open Doors: Baptists in Canada 1950-90, 1992; co-author: Baptists in Canada 1760-1990: A Bibliograhpy, 1989; numerous articles.; editor: The Believers' Church in Canada, 1979, Baptists in Canada, 1980, Costly Vision, 1988. Mem. Bapt. Fedn. Can. (pres. 1979-82), Am. Hist. Assn., Am. Soc. Ch. History, Soc. Reformation Research, Can. Soc. Ch. History, Czechoslovak Soc. Arts and Scis. Home: PO Box 164, Wolfville, NS Canada B0P 1X0 Office: Acadia U, Wolfville, NS Canada B0P 1X0

ZEMANIAN, ARMEN HUMPARTSOUM, electrical engineer, mathematician; b. Bridgewater, Mass., Apr. 16, 1925; s. Parsegh and Filor (Paparian) Z.; m. Edna Odell Williamson Zemanian, July 12, 1958; children: Peter, Thomas, Lewis, Susan. BEE, CCNY, 1947; ScD in Engring., NYU, 1953; prof. honoris causa, Dubna (Russia) U., 1996. Registered profl. engr., N.Y. Tutor CCNY, 1947-48; engr. The Maintenance Co., N.Y.C., 1948-52; from asst. to assoc. prof. NYU, 1952-62; prof. SUNY, Stony Brook, 1962-83, leading prof., 1983--. Author: Distribution Theory and Transform Analysis, 1965, Generalized Integral Transformations, 1968, Realizability Theory for Continuous Linear Systems, 1972, Infinite Electrical Networks, 1991, Transfiniteness for Graphs, Electrical Networks and Random Walks, 1996; co-author: Electronics, 1961; editor and co-founder (rsch. jour.) Circuits, Systems and Signal Processing, 1982—. NSF faculty fellow in sci., 1975-76; recipient Sci. award Armenian Students Assns. Am., 1982; Academician (fgn. mem.) Armenian Acad. Scis., 1990, Academician (fgn. mem.) Armenian Acad. Engrs., 1994. Fellow IEEE, Am. Math. Soc., Russian Acad. Natural Scis. (fgn. mem.; Kapitsa Gold medal 1996), Sigma Xi, Tau Beta Pi, Eta Kappa Nu. Democrat. Presbyterian. Office: SUNY Engring Dept Stony Brook NY 11794-2350

ZEMANS, JOYCE PEARL, art historian, arts administrator; b. Toronto, Ont., Can., Apr. 21, 1940; m. Frederick H. Zemans; children: Deborah, David, Marcia. BA, U. Toronto, 1962, MA in Art History, 1966. Co-chair dept. art history Ont. Coll. Art, Toronto, 1970-71, chair dept. liberal arts, 1973-75; chair dept. visual arts York U., Toronto, 1975-81, assoc. prof., 1975-95, univ. prof., 1995—, dean faculty fine arts, 1985-88, co-dir. MBA program in arts and media adminstrn., faculty adminstrv. studies, 1994—, Robarts chair in Can. studies, 1995-96; dir. Can. Coun., Ottawa, Ont., 1989-92. Author: (book) Jock Macdonald, 1986; (catalogue) J.W.G. Macdonald: The Inner Landscape, 1981, Christopher Pratt, 1985, Kathleen Munn and Edna Tacon: New Perspectives on Modernism, 1989; (career series) Art, 1971; contbr. articles to profl. jours. Bd. dirs. Nat. Coun. Art Adminstrn., 1979-82. Mem. Can. Assn. Fine Art Deans (exec.), Internat. Coun. Fine Art Deans (bd. dirs. 1985-89), Internat. Assn. Art Critics, Univ. Art Assn. Can., Coll. Art Assn., Comité International de l'histoire de l'art, Can., Laidlaw Found. (pres.), Am. Assn. Arts Adminstrn. Educators. Office: York U, Faculty of Fine Arts, Toronto, ON Canada M3J 1P3

ZEMECKIS, ROBERT L., film director; b. Chgo., 1952; m. Mary Ellen Trainor. Ed., U. So. Calif. Cinema Sch. Dir.: (films) I Wanna Hold Your Hand, 1978, Used Cars, 1980, Romancing the Stone, 1984, Back to the Future, 1985, Back to the Future, Part II, 1989, Who Framed Roger Rabbit?, 1988, Back to the Future, Part II, 1989, Back to the Future, PartIII, 1990, Death Becomes Her, 1992, Forrest Gump, 1994 (Best Dir. Acad. award), Contact, 1996; co-screenwriter: 1941, 1979, Trespass, 1992; exec. prodr. : The Public Eye, 1992. Mem. Dirs. Guild Am. Office: care Gelfand Rennert & Feldman 1880 Century Park E Ste 900 Los Angeles CA 90067-1609 also: CAA 9830 Wilshire Blvd Beverly Hills CA 90212-1804 also: South Side Amusement Bugalow 127 100 Universal City Plz Universal City CA 91608*

ZEMEL, JAY NORMAN, electrical engineer, educator; b. N.Y.C., June 26, 1928; s. Leo and Miriam Esther (Schwartz) Z.; m. Jacqueline Eva Lax, July 21, 1950; children: Alan Raymond, Babette Sharon, Andrea Melanie. B.S., Syracuse U., 1949, M.S., 1953, Ph.D., 1956; M.A. (hon.), U. Pa., 1971. Supervisory research physicist U.S. Naval Ordnance Lab., 1954-66; RCA prof. solid state electronics U. Pa., 1966-93, H. Nedwill Ramsey prof. sensor techs., 1993-96, H. Nedwill Ramsey prof. emeritus, 1996—, chmn. dept. elec. engring., 1973-77, dir. Ctr. for Chem. Electronics, 1979-85, dir. Ctr. for Sensor Tech., 1985-89; vis. prof. Nat. Poly. Inst. Mex., 1971, U. Tokyo, 1978, Naval Research Lab., 1977-78, U. Neuchatel, Switzerland, 1987, U. N.C., Charlotte, 1991-92; vis. scientist Instituto Elettronica dello Stato Solido-Centro Nazionale dela Reserca, Rome, 1985; dir. Advanced Study Inst. on Non-destructive Evaluation in Semi-condr. Materials and Devices NATO, 1978, dir. Advanced Study Inst. on Chemically Sensitive Electronic Devices, 1980; mem. com. on sci. and the arts Franklin Inst. Editor in chief: Thin Solid Films, 1972-90; contbr. articles to profl. jours. Recipient Meritorious Civilian Service award Navy Dept., 1958, Sustained Superior Performance award, 1960. Fellow IEEE. Home: 223 Meetinghouse Rd Jenkintown PA 19046-2906 Office: U Pa Moore Sch Elec Engring Philadelphia PA 19104-6314

ZEMEL, NORMAN PAUL, orthopedic surgeon; b. Bklyn., Oct. 15, 1939; s. Nathan M. and Mary (Sklarevsky) Z.; m. Mary P. Kane. BSN, Rutgers U., 1961; MD, Thomas Jefferson Med. Sch., 1965. Bd. cert. orthopedic surgery with added qualification in hand surgery Am. Bd. Orthopaedic Surgery. Orthopaedic surgery resident Northwestern U., Chgo., 1969-73; hand surgery fellow Boyes Hand Fellowship, L.A., 1973-74; hand surgery physician Boyes, Stark, Ashworth, L.A., 1974-88, Kerlan-Jobe Orthopaedic Clinic, Inglewood, Calif., 1989—; clin. assoc. prof. dept. orthopaedics U. So. Calif. Sch. Medicine, L.A., 1977—. Contbr. chpts. to books and articles to profl. jours. Lt. USNR, 1966-68, Vietnam. Mem. ACS, Am. Acad. Orthopaedic Surgery (bd. councilors), Am. Soc. for Surgery of the Hand, Western Orthopaedic Assn. (pres. L.A. chpt. 1993-94), Soc. Internat. de Orthopedique et de Traumatologie. Avocations: walking, reading, photography. Office: Kerlan-Jobe Orthopaedic Clinic 501 E Hardy St Ste 300 Inglewood CA 90301-4026

ZEMKE, WILLIAM A., farm management educator; b. Pulcifer, Wis., Nov. 26, 1938; s. Alfred E. and Geneva A. (Bergner) Z.; m. Sharon Joy Anderson, Dec. 2, 1961; 1 child, William A. Jr. BS in Agrl. Edn., U. Wis., River Falls, 1960, MS in Agrl. Edn., 1972. Artificial inseminator Badger Breeders, Shawano, Wis., 1960-62; farm loan officer Prodn. Credit Assn., Antigo, Wis., 1965-66; vocat. agrl. Lake Holcombe, Wis., 1966-71; teaching asst. U. Wis., River Falls, 1971-72; instr. farm mgmt. Northeast Wis. Tech. Coll., Green Bay, 1972-1997; retired, 1997; dir. State Bank Kewaunee (Wis.), 1987—, Kewaunee Area Scholars Inc., 1989—. Author: Farm Business Analysis, 1975, Financial Management Tools, 1993, Feed Economics and Dairy Decision Making Tools, 1996, 300 Farm Business Management Computer Spreadsheet Programs, 1986-96. Sec. Kewaunee Lions, 1991, pres. 1996-97; mem. Am. Legion, Kewaunee, 1972-92. With U.S. Army, 1962-65. Mem. NAt. Vocat. Agrl. Tchrs. Assn., NAt. Farm Ranch Bus. Mgmt. Edn. Assn., Wis. Assn. Vocat. Agrl. Instrs., Wis. Vocat. Assn., Wis. Edn. Assn. Lutheran. Avocations: hunting, fishing, woodworking, horticulture. Home: N1302 Lakeshore Rd Kewaunee WI 54216-9584 Office: Northeast Wis Tech Coll PO Boc 19042 2740 W Mason St Green Bay WI 54307

ZEMM, SANDRA PHYLLIS, lawyer; b. Chgo., Aug. 18, 1947; d. Walter Stanley and Bernice Phyllis (Churas) Z. BS, U. Ill., 1969; JD, Fla. State U., 1974. Bar: Ill. 1975, Fla. 1975. With fin. dept. Sinclair Oil, Chgo., 1969-70; indsl. rels. advisor Conco Inc., Mendota, Ill., 1970-72; assoc. Seyfarth, Shaw, Fairweather & Geraldson, Chgo., 1975-82, ptnr., 1982—. Bd. dirs. Chgo. Residential Inc., 1993-97, pres., 1994-97; mem. Art Inst. Round Table, Chgo., 1993-94. Mem. Ill. State Bar Assn., Fla. State Bar Assn., Univ. Club Chgo. (bd. dirs. 1991-94). Office: Seyfarth Shaw 55 E Monroe St Chicago IL 60603-5701

ZEMMER, JOSEPH LAWRENCE, JR., mathematics educator; b. Biloxi, Miss., Feb. 23, 1922; s. Joseph Lawrence and Hazel (Quint) Z.; m. Joan Kornfield, June 28, 1950; children—Joel Alan, Rachel Lee, Judith Louise. B.S., Tulane U., 1943, M.S., 1947; Ph.D., U. Wis., 1950. Mem. faculty U. Mo., Columbia, 1950—, prof. math., 1961—, chmn. dept., 1967-70, 73-76, prof. emeritus, 1987—; Fulbright lectr. Osmania U., Hyderabad, India, 1963-64. Contbr. articles to profl. jours. Served with AUS, 1944-46. Mem. Am. Math. Soc., Math. Assn. Am. (chmn. Mo. 1960-61), Can. Math. Soc., Phi Beta Kappa, Sigma Xi. Home: 701 Glenwood Ct Columbia MO 65203-2832 Office: U Mo Dept Mathematics Columbia MO 65211

ZEMPLENYI, TIBOR KAROL, cardiologist; b. Part Lupča, Czechoslovakia, July 16, 1916; came to U.S., 1968, naturalized, 1974; s. David Dezider and Irene (Pollak) Z.; m. Hana Bendová, Aug. 13, 1952; 1 son, Jan. MD, Charles U., Prague, Czechoslovakia, 1946, Docent Habilit., 1966; CSc. (PhD), Czechoslovak Acad. Sci., 1960, DSc., 1964. Clin. asst. with dept medicine Prague Motol Clinic, 1946-52; head atherosclerosis rsch. Inst. for Cardiovascular Rsch., Prague, 1952-68; assoc. prof. medicine Charles U., 1966-68; assoc. prof. medicine U. So. Calif., L.A., 1969-75, prof., 1975-92, prof. emeritus, 1992—; attending physician L.A. County- U.So. Calif. Med. Ctr. Author: Enzyme Biochemistry of the Arterial Wall, 1968; editl. bd. Atherosclerosis, 1962-75, Cor et Vasa, 1993—; adv. bd. Advances in Lipid Rsch., 1963-66; contbr. articles to numerous profl. jours. WHO fellow for study in Sweden and Gt. Britain, 1959. Fellow Am. Heart Assn., Am. Coll. Cardiology; mem. Western Soc. for Clin. Rsch., Longevity Assn. (mem. sci. bd.), European Atherosclerosis Group, Italian Soc. for Atherosclerosis (hon.). Office: 3400 Loadstone Dr Sherman Oaks CA 91403-4512

ZEMTSOV, ALEXANDER, dermatology and biochemistry educator; b. Baku, USSR, Nov. 9, 1959; came to U.S., 1977; s. Ilya and Marya (Dubinsky) Z.; m. Tali Giveon, Oct. 17, 1987; children: Raquel Karen, Gregory Ethan. BA magna cum laude, Temple U., 1981; MSc, U. Pa., 1982; MD with honors, NYU, 1986. Diplomate Am. Bd. Dermatology. Intern, then resident Cleve. Clinic Hosp. Found., 1989-90; assoc. prof. biochemistry and molecular biology Ind. U. Sch. Medicine, Muncie, 1995—. Editor Skin Rsch. and Tech. Jour.; contbr. articles to profl. jours. and books. Recipient Am. Soc. Dermatol. Surgery award, 1989; Cert. Appreciation, Ohio Dermatol. Soc., 1990. Fellow Am. Acad. Dermatology, Am. Contact Dermatitis Soc.; mem. Soc. Magnetic Resonance, Internat. Soc. for Digital Imaging of Skin (pres.), Kiwanis. Jewish. Avocations: stamp collecting, hiking, swimming. Office: University Dermatology Ctr 2525 W University Ave Ste 402 Muncie IN 47303-3409

ZEN, E-AN, research geologist; b. Peking, China, May 31, 1928; came to U.S., 1946, naturalized, 1963; s. Hung-chun and Heng-chi'h (Chen) Z. AB, Cornell U., 1951; MA, Harvard U., 1952, PhD, 1955. Research fellow Woods Hole Oceanographic Inst., 1955-56, research asso., 1956-58; asst. prof. U. N.C., 1958-59; geologist U.S. Geol. Survey, 1959-80, rsch. geologist, 1981-89; adj. rsch. prof. geology U. Md., 1990—; vis. assoc. prof. Calif. Inst. Tech., 1962; Crosby vis. prof. MIT, 1973; Harry H. Hess sr. vis. fellow Princeton U., 1981; counselor 28th Internat. Geol. Congress. 1986-89. Contbr. articles to profl. jours. Recipient Maj. John Coke medal Geol. Soc. London, 1992, Outstanding Contbn. to Pub. Understanding of Geology award Am. Geol. Inst., 1994, Thomas Jefferson medal Va. Mus. Natural History Found., 1996. Fellow AAAS, Am. Acad. Arts and Scis., Geol. Soc. Am. (councillor 1985-88, v.p. 1991, pres. 1992, Day medal 1986), Mineral. Soc. Am. (coun. 1975-77, pres. 1975-76, Roebling medal 1991); mem. NAS, Geol. Soc. Washington (pres. 1973), Mineral. Assn. Can. Office: U Md Dept Geology College Park MD 20742

ZENBOPWE, (WALTER CADE), III, artist, musician, singer, actor; b. N.Y.C.; s. Walter Cade and Helen (Henderson) Brehon. Student, Arts Students League, Inst. Modern Art. Appeared in (plays) Amen Corner, Hatful of Rain, Jim Pavone & the Buzz Bomb, Mary Mary, Don't Bother I Can't Cope, Harlequinade, The Story of Ulysses, Mateus, Which Way America, Poetry Now Subway Cinema, (films) Cotton Comes to Harlem, Education of Sonny Carson, Claudine, Now, Angel Heart, The Wiz, FX, (T.V.) Joe Franklin Show, Positively Black, Soul, Sammy Davis Telethon, June Rolands, Musical Chairs, Big Blue Marble; one man shows include: Ocean County Coll., 1977, Jackson State U., 1980, Phoenix Gallery, Atlanta, 1982, Olin Mus. Art, Bates Coll., Maine, 1993, others; 2-man shows include: Manchester Inst. Arts and Scis., 1968, Lewiston-Auburn Coll., Maine, 1993, others; 3 man shows include: Suffolk Community Coll., 1987; group shows include Whitney Mus., 1971, Corcoran Gallery, 1972, Black Expo, N.Y.C., 1973, Miss. Mus. Fine Art, 1991, Roanoke (Va.) Mus. Fine Art, 1982, Tampa Mus., 1982, Hunter Mus. Art, 1983, Tucson Mus. Art, 1983, New Eng. Fine Arts Inst., Maine, 1993, Lewiston-Auburn Coll., 1994; represented in permanent collections Fine Arts Mus. South, Bruce Mus., Virginia Beach Art Mus., Rockefeller Found., Peter A. Juley and son Collection, Smithsonian Inst. Nat. Mus. Am. Art, others. Recipient numerous awards for paintings, 1978—, including best in show award Las Olas Art Festival, 1980, Arts Festival Atlanta, 1981, Bruce Mus., 1983, 84, 94, 1st prize, Fine Arts Mus. South, 1982. Mem. SAG, Artists Equity. Avocations: boating, motorcycling, martial arts, fencing. Home and Studio: 172-03 119th Ave Jamaica NY 11434

ZENG, XUEGANG, telecommunications engineer, engineering educator; b. Linxia, Gansu, China, Nov. 11, 1963; s. Guangyao Zeng and Yufen Yang; m. Shaohong Wang, Feb. 2, 1988; 1 child Xi Zeng. BSEE, Northwestern Poly. U., China, 1984, MSEE, 1987; PhD in Electrical Engring., Xidian U., China, 1990. Postdoctoral rsch. U. of Electronic Sci. and Tech. of China, Chengdu, 1990-92, assoc. prof. electrical engring., 1992-95, prof., 1995—; rsch. fellow U. Bradford, England, 1993-94; sr. rschr. Ill. Inst. of Tech., Chgo., 1995-96; sr. telecomms. engr. Compact Software, Inc., Paterson, N.J., 1996—; vis. scholar The Chinese U. of Hong Kong, 1993; reviewer Inst. of Elec. Engrs. procs. and letters, England, 1992—, ACTA electronica sicina, China, 1992—. Editor-in-chief conf. proc., 1992; contbr. articles to profl. jours.; inventor analysis method for nonlinear circuits software, 1994. Named One of 10 most outstanding young persons The Govt. of Sichuan, China, 1995; recipient top-grade achievement award in sci. and tech. The Nat. Edn. Com. of China, 1995; Royal Soc. fellow, London, 1993; Croucher Found. scholar, Hong Kong, 1992. Mem. MTT Soc. of IEEE, N.Y. Acad. of Scis., Chinese Inst. of Electronics (sr.). Avocations: badminton, swimming, music. Office: U Electronic Sci and Tech, Lab 570, Sichuan Chengdu 610054, China also: Compact Software Inc 201 McLean Blvd Paterson NJ 07504

ZENG, ZHAO-BANG, geneticist, educator; b. Wuhan, China, Dec. 8, 1957; came to the U.S., 1986; s. Guangming and Yulan (Ni) Z.; m. Jia Ma, Sept. 9, 1983; 1 child, Jiemin. BS, Huazhong Agrl. U., 1981; PhD, U. Edinburgh, 1986. Asst. lectr. Huazhong Agrl. U., Wuhan, 1982-83; postdoctoral rsch. assoc. N.C. State U., Raleigh, 1986-90, vis. asst. prof., 1990-91, rsch. asst. prof., 1992-94; rsch. assoc. prof., 1994—; adj. prof. Hunzhong Agrl. U., Wuhan, China, 1995—. Assoc. editor Genetics, 1994—, Theoretical Population Biology, 1995—; contbr. articles and revs. to profl. jours. Grantee NIH, 1990—, NSF, 1993—, USDA, 1994—. Mem. Am. Soc. Genetics, Soc. for Study Evolution, Biometric Soc., Phi Kappa Phi, Sigma Xi. Avocations: computer games, jogging, classical music, reading. Home: 112 Kirkfield Dr Cary NC 27511-6815 Office: NC State U Dept Statistics Box 8203 Raleigh NC 27695

ZENGER, JOHN HANCOCK, retired publishing company executive; b. Salt Lake City, Nov. 13, 1931; s. John H. and L. (Hancock) Z.; m. Dixie Robison, June 1, 1955 (div. 1978); children: Mark R., Robin, Todd R., Blake R., Mitchell R., Drew R.; m. Holly Olsen, June 29, 1979; stepchildren: Roger, Kirk, Lori, Michael. BS, Brigham Young U., 1955; MBA, UCLA, 1957; D in Bus. Adminstrn., U. So. Calif., Los Angeles, 1963. Asst. prof. Grad Sch. Bus. U. So. Calif., L.A., 1966-67; exec. v.p. Blanfield-Smith and Co., Pasadena, Calif., 1965-67; v.p. human resources Syntex Corp., Palo Alto, Calif., 1967-77; pres. Zenger-Miller Inc., Cupertino, Calif., 1977-92; group v.p. Times Mirror Co., San Jose, 1992-97; ret. Chmn. Palo Alto Human Rels. Coun., 1961-66. Ford Found. fellow, 1962-63; recipient Disting. Svc. award Brigham Young U., 1983; named to Human Resources Devel. Hall of Fame, 1994. Mem. Am. Soc. Tng. and Devel., Brigham Young U. Alumni Assn. (pres. 1981). Republican. Mormon. Avocation: magic. Home: 175 Luzern Rd Midway UT 84049-1268

ZENNER, NICO, air transportation executive; b. Gent, Belgium, Aug. 1, 1964. BS in Commerce and Consular Sci., EHSAL, Brussels, 1989. Regional mgr. Sabena, Singapore, 1991; regional mgr. Sabena, Thailand, 1992; gen. mgr. Sabena, Can., 1993; asst. gen. mgr. Sabena, N.Y.C., 1993—.

ZENNER, SHELDON TOBY, lawyer; b. Chgo., Jan. 11, 1953; s. Max and Clara (Goldner) Z.; m. Ellen June Morgan, Sept. 2, 1984; children: Elie, Nathaniel. BA, Northwestern U., 1974, JD, 1978. Bar: U.S. Dist. Ct. (no. dist.) Ill. 1978. Assoc. Shadur, Krupp & Miller, Chgo., 1978-80; law clk. to judge U.S. Dist. Ct. (no. dist.) Ill., Chgo., 1980-81; asst. U.S. atty., dep. chief spl. prosecutions div. No. Dist. of Ill., Chgo., 1981-89; ptnr. Katten Muchin & Zavis, Chgo., 1989—; adj. faculty Medill Sch. Journalism, Northwestern U., 1982-89, Sch. of Law, 1986—; instr. Nat. Inst. Trial Attys., 1989—. Mem. Phi Beta Kappa. Office: Katten Muchin & Zavis 525 W Monroe St Chicago IL 60661-3629

ZENOWITZ, ALLAN RALPH, government official; b. Queens Village L.I., N.Y., Apr. 18, 1928; s. Ralph and Ann Louise (Brickman) Z. Student, Trinity Coll., 1947-49; spl. studies, Yale U., 1947, Harvard U., 1948; grad., U.S. Army Armor Sch., 1950; spl. studies, U. Va., 1955, U.S. Naval War Coll., U.S. Army War Coll., Nat. Def. Univ., U.S. Army Command and Gen. Staff Coll.; BA in Govt. and Internat. Rels., U. Conn., 1960; JD, New Eng. Sch. Law, 1964; grad., U.S. Army Quatermaster Sch., 1966, U.S. Army Logistics Mgmt. Coll., 1970. Congl. intern, 1946-47; New Eng. area mgr. F.G. Ludwig Inc., Hartford, Conn., 1953-54; dir. ARZ Pub. Relations and Devel., Hartford, Conn., 1955-56; mgmt. exec. Saks Fifth Ave, N.Y.C., 1956-57; dir. spl. situations Fred Gaertner Jr. & Assoc., mgmt. engrs., bus. cons., N.Y.C., 1957-60; aide to gov. of Mass., 1961-62; state dir. Mass. Civil Def. Agy., Office Emergency Preparedness, 1965-71; chmn. Mass. Emergency Communications Commn.; mem. Mass Radiol. Adv. Protection Coun.; chmn. Mass. Gov's Water Emergency Adv. Com., 1965-71, Mass. Emergency Energy Com., 1970-71; regional dir. U.S. Office of Civil Def., 1971-72, U.S. Def. Civil Preparedness Agy., 1972-79; dir. resources mgmt. Fed. Emergency Mgmt. Agy., Washington, 1980-81, dir. fed. plans, 1981-82, chief Nat. Defense Exec. Res., 1982-83; sr. policy advisor Nat. Emergency Tng. Ctr., 1983-88; spl. asst. for hazardous material mgmt. Office Sec. Def., Washington, 1988-93; sr. policy advisor, exec. officer Fed. Emergency Mgmt. Agy., Washington, 1994—; mem. exec. com. Christian A. Herter chair in internat. relations; mem. policy com. Boston Fed. Exec. Bd., 1971-79; mem. U.S.-Can Civil Emergency Adv. Com., 1971-79; chmn. adv. council New Eng. Sch. Law, Law Enforcement Legal Edn. Program; del. NATO sr. civil emergency com., 1972; cons. Republican Nat. Com., 1964-65; adj. prof. New Eng. Sch. Law, 1965-71; chmn. Dept. Defense Fire Protection Coordinating Com., 1988-91. Mem. Mass. Rep. State Com., 1964-65; mem. Great Barrington Rep. Town Com., 1964-65. Served as 1st lt. AUS, 1950-52; served to col. AUS, brig. gen. (ret.). Recipient White House Citation for outstanding pub. svc., 1967, Disting. Svc. award Dept. Def., 1971, 91; decorated Commendation medal U.S. Army 1966, 1968, Meritorious Svc. medal U.S. Army, 1976, Legion of Merit U.S. Army, 1977, Conspicious Svc. medal, 1974, 94; charter mem. Sr. Exec. Svc. U.S. Govt., 1979. Mem. Am. Acad. Polit. Sci., Am. Polit. Sci. Assn., Am. Soc. Internat. Law,Nat. Emergency Mgmt. Assn. (pres. 1969-70, exec. com. 1968-71, hon. pres. 1971—), Am. Soc. Pub. Adminstrn., U. Conn. Alumni Assn. (pres. greater Washington chpt. 1983-90), Army and Navy Club (Washington). Home: 2555 Pennsylvania Ave NW Washington DC 20037-1613 also: 20 Berkshire Hts Rd Great Barrington MA 01230 Office: 500 C St SW Washington DC 20024-2523

ZENTMYER, GEORGE AUBREY, plant pathology educator; b. North Platte, Nebr., Aug. 9, 1913; s. George Aubrey and Mary Elizabeth (Strahorn) Z.; m. Dorothy Anne Dudley, May 24, 1941; children: Elizabeth Zentmyer Dossa, Jane Zentmyer Fernald, Susan Dudley. A.B., UCLA, 1935; M.S., U. Calif., 1936, Ph.D., 1938. Asst. forest pathologist U.S. Dept. Agr., San Francisco, 1937-40; asst. pathologist Conn. Agrl. Expt. Sta., New Haven, 1940-44; asst. plant pathologist to plant pathologist U. Calif., Riverside, 1944-62, prof. plant pathology, 1962—, prof. emeritus, 1981—, faculty rsch. lectr., 1964, chmn. dept., 1968-73, trustee, 1993-94; cons. NSF, Trust Ty. of Pacific Islands, 1964, 66, Commonwealth of Australia Forest and Timber Bur., 1968, AID, Ghana and Nigeria, 1969, Govt. South Africa, 1980, Govt. Israel, 1983, Govt. Western Australia, 1983, Ministry Agriculture and U. Cordoba, Spain, 1989, Govt. Costa Rica, 1993; mem. NRC panels, 1968-73. Author: Plant Disease Development and Control, 1968, Recent Advances in Pest Control, 1957, Plant Pathology, An Advanced Treatise, 1977, The Soil-Root Interface, 1979, Phytophthora Cinnamomi and the Diseases it Causes, 1980, Phytophthora: Its Biology, Taxonomy, Ecology and Pathology, 1983, Ecology and Management of Soilborne Plant Pathogens, 1984, Compendium of Tropical Fruit Diseases, 1994; assoc. editor: Ann. Rev. of Phytopathology, 1971—, Jour. Phytopathology, 1951-54, internat. editl. bd. Internat. Jour. Pest Mgmt., 1990—, also jour. articles. Bd. dirs. Riverside YMCA, 1949-58, Friends of Mission Inn, 1981—, pres., 1991-93, Calif. Mus. Photography, 1988—; pres. Town and Gown Orgn., Riverside, 1962; bd. dirs. Riverside Hospice, 1982-85, pres., 1984-85; bd. dirs. Friends U. Calif. Riverside Botanic Garden, 1985-89, 91-95, pres., 1987-89; bd. trustees U. Calif. Riverside Found., 1993-94. Recipient award of honor Calif. Avocado Soc., 1954, spl. award of honor, 1981; recipient Emeritus Faculty award U. Calif., Riverside, 1991, UCLA Alumnus award, 1996; Guggenheim fellow, Australia, 1964-65, NATO sr. sci. fellow, Eng., 1971; NSF rsch. grantee, 1963, 68, 71, 74, 78; Bellagio scholar Rockefeller Found., 1985. Fellow AAAS (pres. Pacific div. 1974-75), Am. Phytopath. Soc. (pres. 1966, pres. Pacific eiv. 1955, found. bd. dirs. 1987—, v.p. 1991—, award of merit Caribbean div. 1972, award of distinction 1983, Lifetime Achievement award Pacific div. 1991), Explorers Club; mem. NAS, Mycol. Soc. Am., Am. Inst. Biol. Scis., Bot. Soc. Am., Internat. Avocado Soc. (hon.), Brit. Mycol. Soc., Australasian Plant Pathology Soc., Philippine Phytopath. Soc., Indian Phytopath. Soc., Assn. Tropical Biology, Internat. Soc. Plant Pathology (councilor 1973-78), Pacific Assn. Tropical Phytopathology, Internat. Avocado Soc. (hon.), Sigma Xi, Gamma Sigma Delta. Home: 708 Via La Paloma Riverside CA 92507-6403

ZENTNER, ANNE DIENER, flutist; b. Rochester, N.Y., Oct. 13, 1948; d. Frederick William and Alma Mary (Bastian) Diener; m. Miles Zentner, June 28, 1996; 1 child from previous marriage, Katherine Anne. BMus, Juilliard Sch., 1970, MS, 1971. Prin. flutist L.A. Philharm. Orch., 1971—; instr. flute U. So. Calif., L.A., 1990—; vis. prof. flute Rice U., Houston; instr. master classes, L.A., Santa Barbara, Wyo., Fla., Tojo Sch., Tokyo. Solo performances with orch. include (West Coast premiere) Bernstein "Halil," 1983, (world premiere) Stucky Concerto for 2 flutes and orch., 1995, Bach Brandenburg Concertos with P. Zukerman, Mozart Complete Works for Flute and Orch.; featured soloist L.A. Philharm. recs.: Debussy "Afternoon of a Faun," Leinsdorf, Ravel "Daphnis & Chloe." Recipient Bronze medal Competition Internat., Geneva, Switzerland, 1973. Office: LA Philharm Orch 135 N Grand Ave Los Angeles CA 90015

ZENTZ, PATRICK JAMES, artist, rancher; b. Cando, N.D., Jan. 22, 1947; s. Clifford Wayne and Sybil Mae (Dehrer) Z.; m. Susan Grace Hedley, Dec.

7, 1968; children: Keenan, Jesse, Tyson. BA in Biology, Westmont Coll., 1969; MFA in Sculpture, U. Mont., 1974. juror Nev. State Coun. on the Arts Grants Program, Las Vegas, 1989, Nev. State Coun. on the Arts, Artists Fellowship Program, Reno, 1990, Wash State Commn. on the Arts, Olympia, 1992; artist adv. task force Western States Arts Fedn., Portland, 1991; del. Japan-Am. Grassroots Summit, Tokyo and Kyoto, Japan; vis. artist program U. Ill., Carbondale, 1994; lectr. in field. Exhibited in group shows Western State Arts Found., Bklyn. Mus., 1986, No. Ariz. U., 1987, Mont. State U., 1987, Washington Project for the Arts, 1987, Curtis Ctr., Phila., 1987, Aspen Art Mus., 1988, Missoula Mus. of the Arts, 1989, Beall Park Art Ctr., Bozeman, Mont., 1989, John Michael Kohler Art Ctr., 1989, Henry Art Gallery, U. Wash., Seattle, 1989, Seattle Art Mus., 1989, The Ctr. on Contemporary Art, Seattle, 1990, Hockaday Ctr. for the Arts, Kalispell, Mont., Contemporary Arts Mus., Houston, 1990, Boulder Art Ctr., 1991, U. Mont., 1992, Beam Art Gallery, U. Nev., 1992, Internat. Sculpture Ctr., Phila., 1992, Cheney Cowles Mus., Spokane, Wash., 1994, San Antonio Mus. of Art, 1994, Rubelle & Norman Schaffer Gallery, Pratt Inst., Bklyn., 1994, Boise Art Mus., 1995, Neuberger Mus. of Art, SUNY, Purchase, 1997; represented in permanent collections U. Med. Ctr. U. Wash., Seattle, 1990, Richard Tam Alumni Ctr. U. Nev., Las Vegas, 1991, Snake River Correctional Instn., Ontario, Oreg., 1993, Yellowstone Art Mus., Billings, Mont., 1992, Western State Hosp., Ft. Steilecom, Wash., 1993, Salt Palace, Salt Lake City, 1994, TRI-MET Westside Light Rail Sys., Portland, 1995, Mus. of Fine Art, U. Mont., Missoula, 1997. Grantee Art Matters, Inc., 1988, LEF Found., 1992; fellowship Nat. Endowment for the Arts, 1990.

ZEO, FRANK JAMES, health products company professional; b. Springfield, Mass., Jan. 9, 1910; s. Michael and Jennie (Acquavella) Z.; m. Dorothea Louise Duncan, June 27, 1942; children: Virginia D. Kriz, Cynthia J. Newell. AB, Yale U., 1932; postgrad., Syracuse U., 1935-37. Cons. Pub. Adminstrn. Svc., Chgo. and Boston, 1938-40; cons. Mass. Taxpayers Found., Boston, 1940-58, exec. v.p., 1959-71; cons. mgmt./pub. affairs Boston, 1971—; ind. distributor Changes Internat. Inc., Ft. Walton Beach, Fla., 1996—. Bd. dirs. Greater Boston Salvation Army Bd., 1970—, Exec. Svc. Corps of New Eng., Boston, Operation Able, Boston, 1982—; chmn. Nat. Taxpayers Conf., Boston, 1970-71; trustee John Hancock Variable Series Trust I, Boston, 1968—; New Eng. peer support coord. Elizabeth Campbell Peer Support Program, Manly, N.S.W., Australia; bd. dirs. Ron Burton Tng. Village, Hubbardston, Mass., 1991—; hon. trustee East Boston Savs. Bank, 1971—, Mass. Taxpayers Found., Boston, 1985—. Lt. Col. USAF, 1942-45. Decorated Legion of Merit; recipient Founder's award Salvation Army. Mem. Govtl. Rsch. Assn. (hon.), Coun. Mem. Yale Club of Boston, Rotary (past pres. Boston club). Congregationalist. Avocations: photography, music, fishing, walking, writing. Home: 90 Naugus Ave Marblehead MA 01945-1552 Office: Change Internat Inc 90 Naugus Ave Marblehead MA 01945-1552

ZEPEDA, ENRIQUE E., V, lawyer; b. Mexico City, June 20, 1963; came to U.S., 1993; s. Enrique and Rosalba (Vazquez) Z.; m. Silvia Ceballos, Jan. 22, 1994. JD, U. Nat. Autonoma de Mex., Mexico City, 1994. Cert. lawyer Ministry Edn. Mex. Assoc. gen. dir. Bufete Zepeda Trujillo, Mexico City, 1982-93; vice consul, assoc. legal attaché Office Atty. Gen. Mex., Consulate Gen. of Mex., San Antonio, 1993—. Office: Office Atty Gen Mex 100 W Houston St Ste 1441 San Antonio TX 78205-1457

ZEPF, THOMAS HERMAN, physics educator, researcher; b. Cin., Feb. 13, 1935; s. Paul A. and Agnes J. (Schulz) Z. BS summa cum laude, Xavier U., 1957; MS, St. Louis U., 1960, PhD, 1963. Asst. prof. physics Creighton U., Omaha, 1962-67, assoc. prof., 1967-75, prof., 1975—, acting chmn. dept. physics, 1963-66, chmn., 1966-73, 81-93, coord. allied health programs, 1975-76, coord. pre-health scis. advising, 1976-81; cons. physicist VA Hosp., Omaha, 1966-71; vis. prof. physics St. Louis U., 1973-74; program evaluator Am. Coun. on Edn., 1988—. Contbr. articles and abstracts to Surface Sci., Bull. Am. Phys. Soc., Proceedings Nebr. Acad. Sci., The Physics Tchr. jour., others. Recipient Cert. Recognition award Phi Beta Kappa U. Cin. chpt., 1953, Disting. Faculty Svc. award Creighton U., 1987, Excellence in Teaching award Creighton U., 1997. Mem. AAAS, Am. Phys. Soc., Am. Assn. Physics Tchrs. (pres. Nebr. sect. 1978), Nebr. Acad. Sci. (life, chmn. physics sect. 1985—), Internat. Brotherhood Magicians, Soc. Am. Magicians (pres. assembly #7, 1964-65), KC, Sigma Xi (Achievement award for rsch. St. Louis chpt. 1963, pres. Omaha chpt. 1993-94), Sigma Pi Sigma. Roman Catholic. Office: Creighton U Dept Physics Omaha NE 68178 *The real magic we all have at our disposal - not trickery, not pseudoscience, not spells and incantations - is our ability to comprehend our world, to understand how things behave. Through science we can use that understanding to predict outcomes and exert a measure of control over nature. It's a sacred trust. It makes the scientist a kind of modern day magician.*

ZERBS, STEPHEN TAYLOR, telecommunications development engineer; b. Churdan, Iowa, May 5, 1946; s. Hobert Frank and LaVon Monica (Mantz) Z.; m. Patricia Lynn Tvrdik, Mar. 28, 1976; children: Rick Andrew, Steve Matthew. AAS in Electronics Tech., Iowa State U., 1967; BS, U. Nebr., 1984, cert. advanced mgmt., 1995; MBA in Global Tech., Tufts U., 1995. Engring. assoc. Western Elec., Omaha, Nebr., 1967-82; planning engr. Western Elec./AT&T, Omaha, 1983-91; sr. engr. AT&T/Lucent Technologies, Omaha, 1992—. Inventor and patentee in field with numerous U.S. and Fgn. Patents. Elected mem. Sanitary Improvement Dist. 29, Gretna, Nebr., 1980-82. Recipient Outstanding Recognition Jr. Achievement Omaha, 1969. Mem. IEEE, Tel. Pioneers Am., Am. Legion (assoc.). Office: Lucent Techs 120th and I Streets Omaha NE 68137

ZERELLA, JOSEPH T., pediatric surgeon; b. Youngstown, Ohio, Mar. 7, 1941; s. Atilio and Ann (Capuzello) Z.; m. Diana Isabelle Talbot, Aug. 5, 1967; children—Ann, Michael, Mark. B.S., Northwestern U., 1962, M.D., 1966. Diplomate Am. Bd. Surgery, Am. Bd. Pediatric Surgery. Intern Med. Coll. Wis., Milw., 1966-67, resident in surgery, 1967-68, 70-73; tng. fellow in pediatric surgery Children's Hosp. Med. Ctr., Cin., 1973-75; staff pediatric surgeon Phoenix Children's Hosp., 1975—; Phoenix, 1975—; pvt. practice medicine specializing in pediatric surgery, Phoenix, 1975—; mem. staff Good Samaritan Hosp., Phoenix, 1975—, sect. chief pediatric surgery, 1979—; mem. staff St. Joseph's Hosp., Phoenix, 1975—, sect. chief pediatric surgery, 1980—; Contbr. articles to profl. jours. Served as capt. U.S. Army, 1968-70. Fellow ACS, Am. Acad. Pediatrics, Am. Pediatric Surg. Assn., Pacific Assn. Pediatric Surgeons. Roman Catholic. Office: Saguaro Children's Surgery Ltd 1301 E Mcdowell Rd Ste 100 Phoenix AZ 85006-2605

ZERETZKE, FREDERICK FRANK H., artist, educator; b. Milw., July 4, 1919; s. Herman and Hertha Hildegarde (Riebow) Z.; m. Marian Louise Elfers, Dec. 7, 1942; children: Frederick J., David L., Mary J., John E. Student, Milw. Art Inst., 1938-39, Layton Sch. of Art, Milw., 1940-41, Rockford (Ill.) Coll., 1947. Art tchr. Burpee Art Gallery, Rockford, Ill., 1946-48; mural artist People's Real Estate Agy., Rockford, 1958, Grace Luth. Ch., Loves Park, Ill., 1960, Swedem House, Rockford, 1972; artist oil meml. young girl First United Presbyn. Ch., Greeley, Colo., 1963; mural artist Linos, Rockford, 1974; art tchr. pvt. studio, Rockford, Ill., 1968-78; art. tchr. pvt. studio, Burlington, Wash., 1978—; artist and tchr. art in nat. def. Camp Callan, San Diego, 1942-43, Rock Valley Coll., Rockford, Ill., 1970-77, Skagit Valley Coll., Mt. Vernon, Wash., 1978-80; water color instr. Daniel Smith Art, Seattle, 1994, 95. Exhibited in Z Studio, Burlington, Vt., Departures Gallery, Anacortes, Wash., 1996; also group shows in art galleries, Wis., Calif., Wash., Ill., Elements Gallery, Bellingham, Wash., 1988-90, Fox Glove Art Gallery, Mt. Vernon, Wash., 1989—, Twisted Willow Gallery, Mt. Vernon, 1993—, Arts and Frame Gallerie, Canyon Lake, Calif., 1993, Arts Coun. Snohomish County, Everett, Wash., 1993; executed mural in Hadamar, Germany, 1945, Lino's Italian REstaurant, Rockford, Ill.; pvt. collections include Joseph Stroyan 1978-91, North Whidbey Inn, Oak Harbor, Wash., Kenney Fellers 1990-95 Timbers Restaurant, Sedro-Woolley, Wash., Pastor Karsten Baalson 1983-95. Sec. Loves Park (Ill.) Zoning Bd., 1949-56; mem. Skagit Human Rights Task Force to Protect Fundamental Human Rights Guaranteed in Constitution of U.S., 1996. With U.S. Army, 1941-45, ETO. Scholar Milw. Art Inst., 1939, Layton Sch. Art, 1940; awarded commission for design for Swedish Tour of Sveas Soner Chorus of Rockford, 1965; named Artist of Yr. Winnebago County, 1974. Mem. Tamaroa Water Color Soc. Rockford (hon. lifetime, founder, pres. 1964), Skagit Art Assn. (pres. 1987-88). Mem. Unitarian Ch. Avocations: photography, psychology, travel, hiking, outdoor life. Home: 722 Peterson Rd Burlington WA 98233-2656

ZERIN, JAY M., lawyer; b. Bklyn., Dec. 9, 1938; s. Samuel and Ruth (Skolsky) Z.; children: Samuel, Jon. BS, 1960; JD, Bklyn. Law Sch., 1963. Staff atty. Greater N.Y. Savs. Bank, Bklyn., 1963-65; asst. dist. atty. Kings County Dist. Atty., Bklyn., 1965-69; ptnr. Zerin & Cooper Attys., Bklyn. and N.Y.C., 1969-93; sec. Care Claim Svcs. Ltd., Pomona, N.Y., 1994—, GM Premium Fin. Corp., Pomona, N.Y., 1996—. Recipient Disting. Svc. award Pres. of U.S., 1976. Mem. N.Y. State Bar Assn., Kings County Def. Bar Assn. (v.p. 1969-87), Rotary Club of Nanuet (bd. dirs.), Ramapough Sportsman Club. Republican. Jewish. Avocations: reading, hunting. Office: Northside Plz 978 Route 45 Pomona NY 10970-3521

ZERIN, STEVEN DAVID, lawyer; b. N.Y.C., Oct. 1, 1953; s. Stanley Robert and Cecilie Paula (Goldberg) Z.; children: Alexander James, J. Oliver. BS, Syracuse U., 1974; JD, St. Johns U., 1977. Bar: N.Y. 1978, U.S. Dist. Ct. (so. dist.) N.Y. 1985, U.S. Supreme Ct. 1986. Assoc. Gladstein & Isaac, N.Y.C., 1981-82, Sperry, Weinberg, Wels, Waldman & Rubenstein, N.Y.C., 1982-85; ptnr. Wels & Zerin, N.Y.C., 1985—. Trustee, mem. bd. govs. Daytop Village. Mem. ABA (exec. mem. and lectr. family law sect.), N.Y. State Bar Assn. (exec. com. family law sect.), Assn. of Bar of City of N.Y. Democrat. Home: 12 East 88th St New York NY 10128 Office: Wels & Zerin 600 Madison Ave Fl 22 New York NY 10022-1615

ZERNER, MICHAEL CHARLES, chemistry and physics educator, consultant, researcher; b. Boston, Jan. 31, 1940; s. Maurice Bernard and Blanche (Deutsch) Z.; m. Anna Gunilla Fojerstam, May 5, 1966; children: Erik Mark, Emma Danielle. BS, Carnegie Mellon Inst., 1961; MA, Harvard U., 1962, PhD, 1966; postdoctoral U. Uppsala, (Sweden), 1968-70. Asst. prof. U. Guelph (Ont., Can.), 1970-74, assoc. prof., 1974-80, prof., 1980-82, adj. prof., 1982-87; prof. chemistry and physics U. Fla., Gainesville, 1981—, chmn. dept. chemistry, 1988-94; cons. in theoretical chemistry; co-organizer Internat. Sanibel Symposium on Theoretical Chemistry, 1983—. Served to capt. U.S. Army, 1966-68. Recipient cert. U.S. Army Materials Command, 1975, Humboldt prize, 1991-94, Achievement award Internat. Soc. Quantum Bio., 1986; named Fulbright Disting. Prof., 1987; NIH fellow, 1968-70; Grantee NSF, Nat. Sci. and Engring. Rsch. Coun. of Can., Office Naval Rsch. Fellow AAAS, Am. Inst. Physics; mem. Am. Chem. Soc., Sigma Xi, others. Patentee in photoconduction and polymer sci.; co-editor Procs. Internat. Conf. Quantum Chemistry and Internat. Conf. Quantum Biology and Pharmacology, 1978—; Internat. Congress Quantum Chemistry, 1983—; editor Adv. Quantum Chemistry; assoc. editor Internat. Jour. Quantum Chemistry; contbr. pubs. to profl. lit. Office: U Fla Dept Of Chemistry Gainesville FL 32611

ZERNIAL, SUSAN CAROL, education educator; b. L.A., July 2, 1948; d. Gus Edward and Gladys Elizabeth (Hale) Z. BA, Calif. State U., Long Beach, 1973; MA, Calif. State U., 1975; EdD, U. San Francisco, 1992. Cert secondary and elementary tchr.; libr. credential. Libr. Clovis (Calif.) Unified Schs., 1975-78; media specialist Anaheim (Calif.) Union High Sch. Dist., 1975; libr. Benicia (Calif.) Unified Sch. Dist., 1978-80; tchr. Atascadero (Calif.) Unified Schs., 1985-93; adj. prof. Edn. Adams State Coll., Alamosa, Colo., 1993—; acquisitions editor Librs. Unltd./Tchrs. Ideas Press, Englewood, Colo. Recipient Scholarship, Calif. Assn. Sch. Librs., 1974. Mem. ASCD, Am. Rsch. Assn., Phi Delta Kappa. Avocations: camping, hiking, reading, writing. Home: 8547 E Arapahoe Rd # J-152 Englewood CO 80112-1430

ZERVAS, NICHOLAS THEMISTOCLES, neurosurgeon; b. Lynn, Mass., Mar. 9, 1929; s. Themistocles and Demetra P. (Stasinopoulos) Z.; m. Thalia Poleway, Feb. 15, 1959; children—T. Nicholas, Christopher Louis, Rhea. A.B., Harvard U., 1950; M.D., U. Chgo., 1954. Intern N.Y. Hosp., 1955; resident in neurology Montreal Neurol. Inst., 1956; resident in neurosurgery Mass. Gen. Hosp., Boston, 1958-62; fellow in stereotaxic cerebral surgery U. Paris, 1960-61; asst. attending surgeon, asso. neurosurgery Jefferson Med. Coll., Phila., 1962-67; asso. prof. surgery Harvard U., 1971-77; also chief neurosurg. service Beth Israel Hosp., Boston, 1967-77; prof. surgery Harvard U., 1977—; also chief neurosurg. service Mass. Gen. Hosp., 1977—; Higgins prof. neurosurgery Harvard U., 1987—. Contbr. numerous articles to sci. jours. Chmn. Mass. Coun. Arts and Humanities, 1983-91; trustee Boston Symphony Orch., 1990—, vice chmn., 1993—, pres., 1994. Capt. M.C. AUS, 1956-58. Fellow Am. Acad. Arts and Scis.; mem. Am. Acad. Neurol. Surgery (pres. 1990-91), Am. Assn. Neurol. Surgeons, Soc. Neurol. Surgeons, Am. Neurol. Assn., Am. Bd. Neurol. Surgery (chmn. 1990-91), Inst. Medicine Nat. Acad. Scis., Sigma Xi. Home: 100 Canton Ave Milton MA 02186-3507 Office: Mass Gen Hosp 32 Fruit St Boston MA 02114-2620

ZERZAN, CHARLES JOSEPH, JR., gastroenterologist; b. Portland, Oreg., Dec. 1, 1921; s. Charles Joseph and Margaret Cecelia (Mahony) Z.; BA, Wilamette U., 1948; MD, Marquette U., 1951; m. Joan Margaret Kathan, Feb. 7, 1948; children: Charles Joseph, Michael, Kathryn, Paul, Joan, Margaret, Terrance, Phillip, Thomas, Rose, Kevin, Gregory. Commd. 2d. lt., U.S. Army, 1940, advanced through grades to capt., 1945, ret., 1946, re-enlisted, 1951, advanced through grades to lt. col., M.C., 1965; intern Madigan Gen. Hosp., Ft. Lewis, Wash., 1951-52; resident in internal medicine Letterman Gen. Hosp., San Francisco, 1953-56, Walter Reed Gen. Hosp., Washington, 1960-61; chief of medicine Rodriquez Army Hosp., 1957-60, U.S. Army Hosp., Fort Gordon, Calif., 1962-65; chief gastroenterology Fitzsimmons Gen. Hosp., Denver, 1965-66; chief profl. services U.S. Army Hosp., Ft. Carson, Colo., 1967-68; dir. continuing med. edn. U. Oreg., Portland, 1968-73; ptnr. Permanente Clinic, Portland, 1973—; assoc. clin. prof. medicine U. Oreg., 1973—; individual practice medicine, specializing in gastroenterology, Portland, 1968-92; staff Northwest Permanente, P.C., ret., 1996, dir., 1980-83. Mem. Portland Com. Fgn. Rels., 1996—, bd. dirs., 1994—. Decorated Legion of Merit, Army Commendation medal with oak leaf cluster; Meritorious Alumnus award Oreg. Health Scis. U., 1990. Diplomate Am. Bd. Internal Medicine. Fellow A.C.P.; mem. Am. Gastroenterol. Assn., Oreg. Med. Assn. (del. Clackamas County), Ret. Officers Assn. Republican. Roman Catholic. Home and Office: 6364 SE Mcnary Rd Portland OR 97267-5119

ZETTER, LOIS C., personal manager; b. Boston, Jan. 6, 1939; d. Oscar and Pauline (Krasnov) Z.; m. Walter S. Unterseher, Sept. 25, 1988. BA in Theatre Arts cum laude, Brandeis U., 1960. Prin. LeMond/Zetter Mgmt. Inc., L.A., Carson City, Nev., 1971—. Appeared in plays Fiddler on the Roof, How To Succeed in Business Without Really Trying, Ben Bagley's Cole Porter Revue; assoc. prodr. (film) Moment By Moment; co-prodr. (TV series) Cover Up, Dads; prodn. cons. (films) Grease, Blow Out, Urban Cowboy; managed careers of John Travolta, Patrick Swayze, Katherine Helmond, Mickey Rourke, Mark Harmon, etc. Donor Aid for AIDS, Brandeis U., Friendly Hand Found., The Pacific Ctr., Gaucher Disease Found. Recipient Spirit award Brandeis U., 1995. Mem. Acad. TV Arts and Scis., Conf. Personal Mgrs., Women in Film. Office: LeMond/Zetter Mgmt Inc 5570 Old Us Highway 395 N Carson City NV 89704-9584

ZEUGNER, JOHN FINN, history educator, writer; b. N.Y.C., Oct. 7, 1938; s. Orland Kump and Ethel (Finn) Z.; m. Alice Chatfield Valentine, Sept. 7, 1968; children: Emily Valentine, Maxwell Finn, Laura Ruth. A.B., Harvard U., 1959; M.A., Fla. State U., 1968, Ph.D., 1971. Night mgr. Beach Cart, Sarasota, Fla., 1960-67; asst. prof. history Worcester Poly. Inst., Mass., 1971-74; assoc. prof. Worcester Poly. Inst., 1974-82, prof., 1982—; Fulbright lectr. Osaka U., Kobe U., Japan, 1976-78; vis. prof. Keio U., Tokyo, 1981-83; Bryant Drake guest prof. Kobe Coll., Japan, 1994-95. Contbr. articles, short stores to profl. publs. Served with USCG, 1961-62. Named Paris Fletcher Disting. Prof. Humanities, Worcester Poly. Inst., 1985; grantee NEA, 1970. Mem. Orgn. Am. Historians, Soc. Historians Am. Fgn. Rels., Soc. Historians Tech. Avocations: tennis; chess. Home: 31 William St Worcester MA 01609-2313 Office: Worcester Poly Inst Humanities & Arts Dept Worcester MA 01609

ZEUSCHNER, ERWIN ARNOLD, investment advisory company executive; b. Freiburg, Germany, Nov. 17, 1935; came to U.S., 1936; s. Reinhold Hermann and Helene Barbara (Maas) Z.; m. Christa Elfreide Ellmers, June 20, 1959 (dec. Aug., 1971); children—Peter Erwin, Suzanne Christina, Andrea Ellmers; m. Margaret Anne Finn, Mar. 25, 1972; 1 dau., Elizabeth Nora. B.A. in Econs., Queens Coll., 1957; M.B.A. in Fin, NYU, 1964. Sr. v.p. Chase Manhattan Bank, N.Y.C., 1970-72; sr. v.p., dir. Chase Investors Mgmt. Corp., 1972-80; sr. v.p. Chase Manhattan Corp., 1970-80; ptnr. David J. Greene & Co. (investment advs.), N.Y.C., 1980—. Trustee Marymount Manhattan Coll., 1997. Served to capt. USAF, 1958-60. Mem. N.Y. Soc. Security Analysts (dir.). Home: 1 Middle Dr Manhasset NY 11030-1414 Office: 599 Lexington Ave New York NY 10022-6030

ZEVNIK-SAWATZKY, DONNA DEE, litigation coordinator; b. Tulsa, Dec. 15, 1946; d. Robert Joseph Z. and Dorothy Dee (Robertson) Zink; m. Kenneth Sawatzky, May 30, 1965; children: K. Brian, Kaira D. Student, U. Ctrl. Okla., 1977, Okla. State U., 1984. Cert. AIDS educator, State of Okla., 1995-97. Sec. Farmers Ins. Co., Oklahoma City, 1974-80; office mgr. S.A.F.E., Inc., Oklahoma City, 1980-83; jr. acct. Southeast Exploration Corp., Oklahoma City, 1983-84; acct. Young Bros., Inc., Oklahoma City, 1984-88, The Denman Co., Inc., Oklahoma City, 1988-89; litigation coord. ACLU Okla., Oklahoma City, 1994—; bd. dirs. ACLU Okla., 1995—. Author and illustrator: That Place--Otherwhere, 1994, Something for Otherwhere, 1995; author: At Our House, 1979-83; columnist Putnam City-N.W. News, Warr Acres, Okla., 1979-83; designer stage sets Miss Warr Acres Pageant, 1971-88. Bd. dirs. Miss Warr Acres (Okla.) Pageant, 1984-88, Warr Acres C. of C., 1981-85; treas. ACLU of Okla., 1995—, bd. dirs., 1994—; child welfare advocate Okla. State Dept. Human Svcs., Oklahoma City, 1987-89; coord. AIDS clinic Triangle Assn., Oklahoma City, 1994-97. Named Honorary Mayor of Warr Acres, 1971, Super Citizen, 1973, Outstanding Vol. Okla. State Dept. Human Svcs., 1988; recipient Svc. award Warr Acres C. of C., 1979, Legis. Commendation State of Okla., 1988, numerous Okla. Newspaper Column of Month awards Okla. Press Assn., Oklahoma City, 1981-82. Mem. ACLU (Exec. Dir. Vol. Svc. award 1996), Amnesty Internat., The Interfaith Alliance, Pflag, Human Rights Campaign, Okla. Coalition to Abolish the Death Penalty. Democrat. Methodist. Avocations: painting, writing, photography, family. Office: 3012 N Lee Ave Ste A Oklahoma City OK 73103-1017

ZEVON, SUSAN JANE, editor; b. N.Y.C., July 23, 1944; d. Louis and Rhea (Alter) Z. BA, Smith Coll., 1966. Asst. editor trends and environments House & Garden, N.Y.C., 1970-80; account supr. Jessica Dee Communications, N.Y.C., 1981-84; editor architecture House Beautiful, N.Y.C., 1985—. Author: Inside Architecture, 1997, (with others) Decorating On The Cheap, 1984. Mem. Archtl. League N.Y., Smith Coll. N.Y. Club (v.p. 1987-88, pres. 1988-89). Avocations: films, lit., gymnastics, art. Office: House Beautiful 1700 Broadway New York NY 10019-5905

ZEVON, WARREN, singer, songwriter; b. Chgo., Jan. 24, 1947; m. Crystal Zevon (div.); 1 child, Ariel; 1 child from previous marriage, Jordan. Folksinger, writer commls., pianist with Everly Bros., 1970-73; albums include Wanted Dead or Alive, 1970, Warren Zevon, 1976, Excitable Boy, 1978 (gold record), Bad Luck Streak in Dancing School, 1980, Stand in the Fire, 1980, The Envoy, 1982, Sentimental Hygiene, 1987, Transverse City, 1989, (with Hindu Love Gods) Hindu Love Gods, 1990, Mr. Bad Example, 1991, Learning to Flinch, 1993, A Quiet Normal Life (the best of Warren Zevon), 1993, Mutineer, 1995, I'll Sleep When I'm Dead: The Warren Zevon Anthology, 1996, (with others) Wanted Dead or Alive, 1996; composer: When Johnny Strikes up the Band, Hasten Down the Wind, Werewolves of London, Poor Poor Pitiful Me, Play It All Night Long, Roland the Headless Thompson Gunner. Office: Elektra Entertainment 75 Rockefeller Plz New York NY 10019*

ZEYEN, RICHARD JOHN, plant pathology educator; b. Mankato, Minn., Jan. 17, 1943; s. Clifford John and Eleanor Otilla (Laase) Z.; m. Anita Kozan, June 25, 1967 (div. 1971); m. Carol Breese Van Why, Dec. 10, 1984. Dir. EM facility Minn. Agrl. Exptl. Sta., St. Paul, 1971—; asst. prof. plant pathology U. Minn., St. Paul, 1973-75, assoc. prof., 1976-83, prof., 1983—; cons. Minn. Pollution Control Agy. Contbr. articles to profl. jours. Underwood fellow Agr., Food and Rsch. Coun., U.K., 1993; NATO Scientific Exch. Program fellow, Wales, U.K., 1990-95. Mem. AAAS, Am. Phytopathol. Soc. (chmn. various coms. 1967—), Microscopy Soc. Am., Minn. Microscopy Soc. (past officer, bd. dirs., pres. 1981-82), Mankato State U. Alumni Assn. (bd. dirs. 1974-77), Sigma Xi. Achievements include analytical electron microscopy, X-ray microanalysis applications to biolog. specimens; molecular and biochem. regulation genetically controlled plant disease resistance; plant viruses, their vectors; cytochemistry diseased plants. Office: U Minn Dept Plant Pathology 495 Borlaug Hall Buford Cir Saint Paul MN 55108

ZHAN, STEVE Q., optical engineer, researcher; b. Jiangxi, China, Oct. 1, 1963; s. Liqiang and Ruosu (Liu) Z.; m. Qing Lin, June 24, 1991; 1 child, Youjiu. BS, Zhejiang U., Hangzhou, China, 1982; MS, Tianjin (China) U., 1987; PhD, Kobe (Japan) U., 1994. R&D engr. Huazhong Precinct Instrument Factory, Hubei, China, 1982-84; chief engr. ALP Corp., Osaka, 1993-96; v.p. Laser Video Projection, Inc., Overland Park, Kans., 1996—. Contbr. articles to profl. jours. Mem. Soc. of Photographic Instrumentation Engrs. Avocations: computer programming, optical information processing, optical system designing, laser engineering. Office: Laser Video Projection Inc 8897 Lenexa Dr Overland Park KS 66214-3240

ZHANG, CHARLES C., financial planner; b. Shanghai. M in Econs., Western Mich. U., 1991; PhD candidate, LaSalle U. ChFC; CFP; CLU. Sr. fin. advisor Am. Express Fin. Advisors, Inc., Kalamazoo, 1991—. Mem. Am. Soc. CLU and ChFC, Inst. cert. Fin. Planners, Internat. Assn. Fin. Planning. Office: Am Express Fin Advisors Inc 5136 Lovers Ln Ste 200 Portage MI 49002-1518

ZHANG, HEPING, biostatistician; b. Duchang, Jiangxi, China, Nov. 16, 1963. BS, Jiangxi Normal U., Nanchang, 1982; MS, Huazhong Normal U., Wuhan, 1986; PhD, Stanford U., 1991. Lectr. Jiangxi Normal U., Nanghang, 1982-87; asst. prof. Yale U., New Haven, Conn., 1992—. Mem. Am. Statis. Assn., Inst. Math. Stats., Internat. Statis. Inst. Achievements include research in recursive partitioning and its applications in health sciences; design issues in mapping QTL in humans; research in the analysis of MRI imaging data. Office: Yale Univ Sch of Medicine Dept Epidemiology & Pub Health 60 College St New Haven CT 06510-3210

ZHANG, JIANPING, electrical engineering educator, researcher; b. Rugao, China, June 26, 1960; s. D. and N. (Min) Z.; m. Zhiping Fan, Feb. 14, 1987; 1 child, Yifan. BS, Nanjing Normal U., China, 1982; MS, Beijing U. Posts and Telecom., 1987, PhD, 1990. Tchg. asst. Nanjing Normal U., 1982-84; tchg. asst., rsch. assoc. Beijing U. Posts and Telecom., 1984-90; asst. prof. S.E. U., China, 1990-92; Humboldt Rsch. fellow Technische U. Berlin, 1992-94; rsch. assoc. Northwestern U., Evanston, Ill., 1994—; sec. gen. Jiangsu Comm. Inst., 1990-92. Author: (chpt.) Optical Processes in Microcavities, 1996; inventor in field; contbr. articles to profl. jours. Recipient Hon. award Chinese Govt., 1989, Sci. and Tech. Achievement award Chinese Govt., 1990; rsch. fellow Alexander von Humboldt Found., Germany, 1992. Mem. IEEE, Optical Soc. Am. Avocations: riding bicycles, table tennis. Office: Northwestern Univ Elec Engring Computer Sci 2145 Sheridan Rd Evanston IL 60208-0834

ZHANG, JINGWU, immunologist; b. Shanghai, Feb. 2, 1956; arrived in Belgium, 1986; s. Yuzeng and Xiochin Zhang; m. Ying Chin, Feb. 19, 1986; children: Linda, Peter. MD, Shanghai (China) Med. U., 1984; DSc, U. Brussels, 1990. Lic. MD. Rsch. fellow Dr. Willems Inst., Diepenbeek, Belgium, 1986-90, head dept., 1990—; rsch. assoc. Harvard Med. Sch., Boston, 1991-92; vis. prof. Baylor Coll. Medicine, Houston, 1993; prof. Limburgs U. Ctr., Diepenbeek, 1994—, Shanghai Med. U., 1995. Contbr. articles to profl. jours.; patentee in field. Recipient Rsch. award Am. Multiple Slcerosis Soc., 1990, Achievement award Belgian Soc. Clin. Immunology, 1993, Internat. award Assn. Malattie Rare, 1994. Mem. AAAS, N.Y. Acad. Scis., European Immunology Fedn., Am. Assn. Immunologists. Avocations: painting, music, sports. Office: Baylor Coll Medicine Dept Neurology Houston TX 77030

ZHANG, XIAODONG, computer science educator and researcher; b. Beijing, China, July 16, 1958; came to the U.S., 1983; s. Min and Yishan

(Jiang) Z.; m. Yan Meng, July 20, 1985; 1 child, Simon. BS, Beijing (China) Poly. U., 1982; MS, U. Colo., 1985, PhD, 1989. Rsch. asst. Beijing (China) Poly. U., 1982-83, Environ. Rsch. Lab., Boulder, Colo., 1983-85, U. Colo., Boulder, 1985-89; tech. staff Toplogix Inc., Denver, 1989; asst. prof. U. Tex., San Antonio, 1989-92, assoc. prof., 1993-97, chair computer sci., 1993, dir. high performance computing and software lab., 1993-97; prof. Coll. William and Mary, Williamsburg, Va., 1997—; vis. scientist Rice U., 1990-91; guest prof. Wuhan U., China, 1995-97; guest rsch. prof. U. Sci. and Tech. of China, 1997—; adv. panelist NSF, 1995, 96, 97; program chair 4th Internat. Workshop on Modeling, Analysis and Simulation of Computer and Telecomm. Systems; keynote spkr. 8th Internat. Conf. on Parallel and Distributed Computer Sys., 1996; co-founder, v.p. YABI, Inc., 1996—. Co-author: Multiprocessor Performance, 1994; editor Jour. of Parallel Computing, 1994-95; contbr. articles to profl. jours. Recipient Disting. Rsch. Achievement award U. Tex., 1993, Best Paper award 9th Internat. Conf. on Supercomputing, 1995; grantee NSF, 1990—, Southwestern Bell, 1992-97, USAF, 1993-97, AFOSR, 1995—, ONR, 1995—. Mem. IEEE (sr.; chmn. tech. com. on supercomputing applications, disting. visitor, program coms., program com. 7th Symposium on Parallel and Distributed Processing 1995, 8th Symposium, 1996, 4th Internat. Symposium on High Performance Computer Arch. 1997, mem. steering com. Supercomputing '96, '97, High Performance Computing Asia '97), Assn. Computing Machinery (nat. lectr., program coms., program com. 10th Internat. Conf. on Supercomputing), Soc. Indsl. and Applied Math. Office: Coll William and Mary Computer Sci Williamsburg VA 23187

ZHANG, XIAO-FENG, power system engineer, researcher; b. Sichuan, Peoples Republic of China, Aug. 8, 1951; came to U.S., 1988; d. Yong-Qing and Lan (Li) Z.; m. Paul McEntire, June 22, 1996; 1 child, John. BS in EE, Taiyuan Engring. Inst., Shanxi, 1976; MS in EE, Electric Power Rsch. Inst., 1983. Power engr. Jinchong Dist. Power Bur., Shanxi, 1976-80; power system engr. EPRI, Beijing, 1983-88, Systems Control, Palo Alto, Calif., 1988-89; sr. power engr. Empros Systems Internat., Plymouth, Minn., 1989-93; cons. Pacific Gas & Elec. Co., San Ramon, Calif., 1993-94; sr. engr. ABB Systems Control, Santa Clara, Calif., 1995—. Contbr. articles to profl. jours. Recipient 1st prize EPRI of China, 1985, 2d prize Ministry of Electric Power, Beijing, 1986, 3d prize Chinese Nat. Com., 1987. Mem. Power Engring. Soc. IEEE (sr.), Computer Soc. IEEE. Avocations: travel, swimming, table tennis, photography. Home: 1523 Johnson Ave San Jose CA 95129-4714 Office: ABB Systems Control 2550 Walsh Ave Santa Clara CA 95051-1315

ZHANG, YONG-HANG, electrical engineering educator; b. Nanjing, Jiangsu, China, May 8, 1959; came to U.S., 1991; s. Ru-Ying and Aili (Wang) Z.; m. Zhiruo Shuai, May 2, 1985; 1 child, Elisa Tiannuo. MSc, Inst. Semicondrs., Beijing, 1987; D rer. nat., Stuttgart (Germany) U., 1991. Teaching asst. Nanjing Normal U., 1982-84; rschr. Max-Planck-Inst. for Solid States, Stuttgart, 1988-91; asst. rsch. engr. U. Calif., Santa Barbara, 1991-93, Hughes Rsch. Labs, Malibu, Calif., 1993-96; assoc. prof. elec. engring. dept. Ariz. State U., Phoenix, 1996—; referee Phys. Rev. B. Contbr. 1 book chpt. and articles to Phys. Rev. B., Applied Physics, Applied Physics Letters, over 41 papers to refereed internat. jours. Mem. IEEE, Am. Phys. Soc. Office: Ariz State U Elec Engring Dept Tempe AZ 85287

ZHANG, YOUXUE, geology educator; b. Huarong County, Hunan, China, Sept. 17, 1957; came to U.S., 1983; s. Zaiyi Zhang and Dezhen Wu; m. Zhengjiu Xu; children: Dan, Ray. BS in Geol. Scis., Peking U., Beijing, 1982; MA in Geol. Scis., Columbia U., 1985, MPhil, 1987, PhD in Geol. Scis., 1989. Grad. rsch. asst. Columbia U., N.Y.C., 1983-88; postdoctoral fellow Calif. Inst. Tech., 1988-91; asst. prof. geology U. Mich., Ann Arbor, 1991—. Contbr. articles to profl. jours. Named Young Investigator, NSF, 1994. Mem. Am. Geophys. Union, Geochem. Soc. (F.W. Clarke medal 1993), Mineral. Soc. Am., Sigma Xi. Office: Dept Geol Sci U Mich Ann Arbor MI 48109-1063

ZHANG WEI-QIANG, dancer. Grad. with highest honors, Beijing Dance Acad., 1979; postgrad., Houston Ballet Acad. Prin. dancer Beijing Dance Acad. Ballet Co., 1981-84, Ctrl. Ballet of China, 1984-92, Royal Winnipeg (Man., Can.) Ballet, 1992—; guest artist Houston Ballet, Star Dancers Ballet, Japan, Asami Maki Ballet Co., Universal Ballet Co. of Korea, The Hong Kong Ballet, Goh Ballet, Can., Gala performance in memory of Anton Dolin, London, 1984, 2nd Internat. Ballet Competition Gala, Paris, 1986, 2d Aoyama Ballet Festival, Tokyo, 1988, Gala performance in memory of Prix de Lausanne, Tokyo, 1989, Japan Ballet Festival, Tokyo, 1989, 91, 92, and numerous other festivals and galas. Prin. roles include Giselle, Don Quixote, Swan Lake, Nutcracker, Raymonda, La Fille Mal Gardee, Coppelia, The Leaves Are Fading, The Afternoon of the Faun, Scotch Symphony, Allegro Brillante, Romeo & Juliet, Sleeping Beauty. Recipient Bronze medal 2nd Internat. Ballet Competition, Jackson, Miss., 1982, 2nd prize 4th World Ballet Competition, Osaka, Japan, 1984, Bronze medal 5th Moscow Internat. Ballet Competition, 1985, Highest Honor award 1st Nat. Ballet Competition, Beijing, 1985. Office: Royal Winnipeg Ballet, 380 Graham Ave, Winnipeg, MB Canada R3C 4K2*

ZHAO, JIAN HUI, electrical and computer engineering educator; b. Nanping, Fujian, China, Aug. 2, 1959; came to U.S., 1983; s. Yumao Zhao and Su Qing Chen; m. Menghan Pan, Apr. 28, 1992. BS in Physics, Amoy U., China, 1982; MS in Physics, U. Toledo, 1985; PhD in E.E., Carnegie Mellon U., 1988. Rsch. asst. Nonlinear Optics Lab. U. Toledo, Ohio, 1983-85; rsch. asst. Solid State Elec. Lab. Carnegie Mellon U., Pitts., 1985-88; asst. prof. electric and computer engring. dept. Rutgers U., New Brunswick, N.J., 1988-93, assoc. prof. electric and computer engring. dept., 1993—; cons. Army Rsch. Lab., Ft. Monmouth, 1991—, Westinghouse, Pitts., NZ Applied Techs., Boston. Contbr. numerous articles to profl. jours. Henry Rutgers fellow Rutgers U., New Brunswick, N.J., 1989, 90; recipient Initiation award NSF, 1990, Best Teaching Performance award Rutgers Eta Kappa Nu, 1991. Mem. IEEE (sr.), Am. Phys. Soc., Materials Rsch. Soc., N.Y. Acad. Sci. Achievements include patents for InP/InGaAsP optoelectronic high speed thyristor, an AlGaAs/GaAs-based optothyristor for ultra-high power switching, field effect real space transfer transistor, electrical tunable superlattice detector for wavelength division demultiplexing applications. Office: Rutgers Univ Elec & Computer Engring Dept Brett & Bowser Rds Box 909 Piscataway NJ 08855

ZHAO, LI, fine arts company executive, teacher, consultant; b. Tianjin, China, Mar. 16, 1958; came to U.S., 1984; d. Robert Yunnian Chao and Qizhen Cao; m. Shiyi Zhang, Aug., 1984 (div. 1987); m. Kenneth Lloyd Schoolland, Aug. 8, 1988 (div. 1994); 1 child, Kenli Dulcinea. BA, Foreign Lang. Inst., Tianjin, China, 1983; MA, U. Minn., 1987; Mgmt. Sci. (Japanese), Japan-Am. Inst. Mgmt. Sci., Honolulu, 1988; MS in Japanes Bus. Study, Chaminade U., Honolulu, 1988. Steel mill worker Guang Xi, China, 1969-78; tchr. Liu-Zhou Steel Mill High Sch., Guang Xi, 1978; translator, researcher China Dept. Transp., Beijing, 1983-84; teaching asst. U. Minn., Mpls., 1985-87; intern trainee Tobu Dept. Store, Tokyo, Japan, 1988; pres. Schoolland Internat., 1988—; sales mgr. trainee Duty Free Shops, Honolulu, 1989-92; gen. mgr. Double-Eye Hawaii, Honolulu, 1989-92, 1989—; gen. mgr. Tianjin Victor Entertainment Co. Ltd., Tianjin, China, 1994—. Editor: (newsletters) Double-Eye News, 1989-92, Libertarian Party Hawaii News, 1991-93. Chmn. membership com. U.S.-China People's Friendship Assn., 1988-89; mem. legis. com. Small Bus. Hawaii; bd. dirs. Libertarian Party Hawaii, 1992. Recipient Model Citizen award Mpls. Police Dept., 1992; named Outstanding Grad. Student, U. Minn., 1992. Mem. Am. Mktg. Assn. (bd. dirs.), Am. Soc. Interior Designers, Sales and Mktg. Execs. of Honolulu, Honolulu Japanese C. of C. (chair com.), Honolulu Acad. Art, Japan-Am. Assn. Hawaii, Assn. Hawaii Artists (corr. sec.), Chinese C. of C. Honolulu. Avocations: writing, reading, swimming, dancing, travel.

ZHAO, MEISHAN, chemical physics educator, researcher; b. Shanxian, Shandong, People's Republic of China, Nov. 5, 1958; came to U.S., 1984; s. Zhong Chen Zhao and Ming Rong Zhang; m. Linlin Cai, Sept. 2, 1983; children: Fang, Yuan, Nan. MS in Physics, U. Minn., 1986, PhD in Chem. Physics, 1989. Lectr. physics S.E. U. China, Nanjing, 1982-84; teaching asst., rsch. asst. U. Minn., Mpls., 1984-89; rschr. James Franck Inst. U. Chgo., 1990—. Contbr. articles to profl. jours. Mem. AAAS, Am. Phys. Soc. (internat. editl. bd. Internal. Physics Edn., Chinese ed., 1991-92), N.Y. Acad. Sci. Home: 5642 S Drexel Ave Chicago IL 60637-1418 Office: Univ Chgo James Franck Inst 5640 S Ellis Ave Chicago IL 60637-1433

ZHENG, LISA LIQING, computer consultant; b. Xian, China, May 11, 1966; came to U.S., 1990; d. Youzhong Zheng and Siuping Huang. BSEE, Huazhong U. Sci. and Tech., 1988; MSEE, Purdue U., 1992. Asst. engr. Inst. Electronics Chinese Acad. Scis., Beijing, 1988-90; electronics engr., sys. programmer Computer Graphics, Corp., Indpls., 1992-94; programmer Bertelsmann Music Group, Inc., Indpls., 1994-96; computer cons. SEI Info. Tech., Chgo., 1996—. Avocations: traveling, philately, swimming, bicycling, cooking.

ZHENG, MAGGIE (XIAOCI), materials scientist, vacuum coating specialist; b. Shanghai, Apr. 21, 1949; came to U.S., 1986; d. George and Helen (Chou) Cheng; 1 child, Dee. BS in Physics, Qufu Normal U., Shangdong, China, 1981; MSEE, U. Sci. and Tech. China, Beijing, 1984; MS in Materials Sci., U. Wis., 1988, PhD in Materials Sci., 1991. Lectr. Tsinghua U., Beijing, 1984-86; assoc. scientist United Techs., East Hartford, Conn., 1991-92; staff scientist Pratt & Whitney, TALEN, Rocky Hill, Conn., 1992-93; materials and coating process engr. Chromalloy Turbine Techs., Middletown, N.Y., 1993-94; engr. GE Power Generation, Schenectady, N.Y., 1995—; rsch. asst. U. Wis., Madison, 1986-91. Contbr. articles in profl. pubs.; patentee in field. Mem. NAFE, Am. Metal Soc., Minerals, Metals and Materials Soc. Office: GE Power Generation Bldg 55 Rm 103 1 River Rd Schenectady NY 12345

ZHOU, HUANCHUN, chemist, administrator; b. Shanghai, Oct. 1, 1939; came to U.S., 1985; s. Qingyun and Wanxian (Hu) Z.; m. Qingliang Li, Sept. 5, 1967; 1 child, Fugang. BS equivalent, Fudan U., China, 1962; MS, Shanghai U. Tech., China, 1981; PhD equivalent, U. Fla., 1990. Engr. Wuxi Oil Pump Factory, Jiangsu, China, 1962-67; laborer, analytical technician Wuxi Oil Pump Factory, 1968-74, analytical tech., 1974-76; faculty Shanghai U. Tech., 1982-84; rschr. dept. chemistry U. Fla., Gainesville, 1985-91; chemist Fla. Dept. Agr., 1991—; chem. lab. chief Wuxi Oil Pump Factory, 1963-66; chmn. sect. chem. analysis Wuxi Sci-Tech. Assn., 1963-66; lectr. to 201st Am. Chem. Soc. Meeting, 1991. Corr. editor: Jour. Chem. Analysis and Phys. Test, 1964-66; contbr. articles to profl. jours. Co-grantee Office of Naval Rsch., 1991. Achievements include research in determination of phosphorus together with other 6 elements in chrome steel in one solution by using a nonoxidizing acid first in world; searched out of the direct and quantitative relationship between solubility and charges and radii of ions first in world; promotion of simple natural sieve method to prove infinity of prime twins and derivation of simple and most accurate formula in world to estimate number of prime twins; discovered relationship between phase graphs and differential thermal analysis curves; co-developer chemical polymerization polyaniline and polypyrrole on Langmuir-Blodgett trough; discovered method to monitor polymerizations by Langmuir-Blodgett computerized techniques. Home: 7517-C Pitch Pine Cir Tampa FL 33617

ZHOU, KANG-WEI, physics educator; b. Zhongxian, Sichuan, China, June 21, 1935; s. Cheng-Han Zhou and Zhi-Fang Xiong; m. Shi-Fang Dai, Sept. 24, 1961; 1 child, Zhou Bing. B Physics, Sichuan U., Chengdu, China. Asst. lectr. Inner Mongolia U., Huhehaote, China, 1961-71; technician Chengdu 1st radio factory, 1971-78; asst. lectr. Sichuan U., 1979-80, lectr., 1981-85, assoc. prof., 1986-92, prof. physics, 1993—. Author: Diferential and Integral Calculus, 1987; contbr. articles to profl. jours. Recipient sci./tech. award Nat. Edn. Com. of China, 1990, Govt. Sichuan, 1993. Mem. AAAS, Chinese Ctr. of Advanced Sci. and Tech., Internat. Ctr. for Materials Physics, Acad. Sinica, Am. Phys. Soc. Avocations: music, touring. Office: Dept Physics, Sichuan Univ, Chengdu 610064, China

ZHOU, MING DE, aeronautical scientist, educator; b. Zhejiang, China, June 26, 1937; s. Pin Xiang and Ang Din (Xia) Z.; m. Zhuang Yuhua, Aug. 12, 1936; children: Zhengyu, Yan Zhuang. BS, Beijing U. Aeros.-Astronautics, 1962; MS, Northwestern U. Tech., 1967; PhD, Internat. Edn. Rsch. Found., 1992. Tchr. Harbin (China) U. Tech., 1962-64, 67-73; from lectr. to prof. Nanjing (China) U. Aeronautics and Astronautics, 1973-86, 86—; dean bd. postgrad. studies Nanjing (China) U. Aeros. and Astronautics, 1985-89; nationally qualified PhD advisor China, 1989—; rsch. scientist U. Ariz., Tucson, 1991-93, rsch. prof., 1993—; vis. scholar Cambridge (England) U., 1980-82; guest scientist Inst. Exptl. Fluid Mechanics, Göttingen, Germany, 1983-84, 85, 87; sr. vis. scientist Tech. U. Berlin, 1988, 90; rsch. assoc. U. So. Calif., L.A., 1989-90. Author: (with others) Viscous Flows and Their Measurements, 1988, (with others) Introduction to Vorticity and Vortex Dynamics, 1992; mem. edit. com. Chinese Jour. Exptl. Mechanics, 1986-89; contbr. articles to Jour. Fluid Mechanics, Physics of Fluids, Aero. Jour. U.K., Experiments in Fluids, AIAA Jour., Chinese Jour., Aeronautics. Co-recipient Nat. award Progress in Sci. and Tech. first class, Peoples Republic of China, 1985. Mem. AIAA (sr.), Am. Phys. Soc., Chinese Soc. Aeronautics, Chinese Soc. Mechanics (mem. acad. group exptl. fluid mechanics 1986-89), Chinese Soc. Aerodynamic Rsch. (acad. group unsteady flow and vortex control 1985-89). Achievements include patent for techniques and device of artificial boundary layer transition.

ZHU, AI-LAN, opera singer; b. Nanjing, Jiang Su, Peoples Republic of China, Nov. 29, 1956; came to U.S., 1984; d. De-Chang Zhu and Shu-hua Tsao; m. Chai-Lun Yueh, Oct. 30, 1982. MusB, Cen. Conservatory Music, Beijing, 1977; Artist Diploma in Opera, Hartt Sch of Music, U. Hartford, 1986. Appeared in leading opera houses of N.Am.; leading soprano in Tex. Opera Theater, Houston, 1987, Va. Opera Assn., Norfolk, 1987, Met. Opera, 1988, Opera Theater St. Louis, 1989, PepsiCo Summerfare and European tour, N.Y., 1989, Lyric Opera of Boston, 1990, Glyndebourne Opera Festival, 1990, 91, Lyric Opera of Kansas City, 1990, Caramoor Festival, N.Y., 1990, Chautauqua Opera and Orch., 1990, Opera Pacific, L.A., 1991, Minn. Opera, 1992, Opera Co. Phila., 1992, Mich. Opera Theater, 1993, Austin Lyric Opera, 1993, 94—, Scottish Opera, 1994, Conn. Opera, 1995, Atlanta Opera, 1995, Conn. Opera, 1995, 96, Shanghai Symphony, 1996, Austin Lyric Opera, 1997, San Antonio Symphony, 1997, San Diego Opera, 1997; European tour Pelléas et Mélisande, 1992-93; concert singer Chautauqua (N.Y.) Instn., 1987, Liederkranz Found., N.Y.C., 1989; recital The Theatre Musical de Paris, Chatelet, 1991; concert tour with Sherrill Milnes, Beijing, China, 1993. Finalist Luciano Pavarotti internat. vocal competition, Opera Cos. Phila., 1985; recipient 1st prize Sigma Alpha Iota vocal competition, Chautauqua, N.Y., 1986, 5th prize Liederkranz Found. vocal competition, N.Y.C., 1989. Mem. Am. Guild Mus. Artists. Home: 51 King Philip Dr West Hartford CT 06117-2140 Office: John J Miller 801 W 181st St Apt 20 New York NY 10033-4518

ZHU, YONG, research scientist; b. Shanghai, Oct. 30, 1947; s. Shuping Chu and Zhiping Wang; m. Shaokui Wang, Apr. 22, 1977; 1 child, Shenke. B of Engr., East China Inst. Chem. Tech., Shanghai, 1981; postgrad., Tianhin Inst. Textile Engring., 1982; PhD in Organic Chemistry, U. Ill., 1992. Laborer Qingdao (China) Cigarette Manufacture, 1968-72; rsch. asst. Qingdao Inst. Light Industry, 1972-77; asst. prof., head dept. Shandong Inst. Textile Engring., China, 1983-87; vis. scientist U. Ill., Urbana, 1987-88, tchg./rsch. asst., 1988-92, postdoctoral rsch. assoc., 1992-93; scientist Procter and Gamble Far East, Kobe, Japan, 1993-95, Procter and Gamble Co., Cin., 1995—; cons. Qingdao Manufacture of Dyeing Auxiliaries, 1983-87, Jiaonan (China) Manufacture of Fragrances, 1984-87. Contbr. articles to profl. jours. Recipient Edn. scholarship Chinese Edn. Assn., 1987. Mem. Am. Chem. Soc. (vol. in pub. outreach 1991-95), Inter-Am. Photochem. Soc., Chinese Color-Optical Soc., Shandong Textile Engring. Assn. Avocations: sports (volleyball, swimming), music (violin, social dance), travelling.

ZHUKOV, YURI, ballet dancer; b. Leningrad, Russia. Student, A.Y. Vaganova Sch. Choreography, Leningrad. With Kirov Ballet; soloist San Francisco Ballet, 1989-92, prin. dancer, 1992—. Appeared in ballets Nutcracker, Serenade, The Four Temperaments, Handel-a Celebration, The Sleeping Beauty, Swan Lake, Aurora Polaris, Menuetto, The Four Seasons, Variations de Ballet, Vivaldi Concerto Grosso, Dreams of Harmony, The End, Dark Elegies, Rodin, Job, Cinderella, Giselle, Scotch Symphony. Office: San Francisco Ballet 455 Franklin St San Francisco CA 94102-4438*

ZHUO, MIN, neurobiology educator; b. Xia Pu, People's Republic of China, Nov. 25, 1964; came to U.S., 1988; s. Zi-Jing and Wan-Ru (Huang) Z.; m. Kelly Bin Wei, Apr. 27, 1993; 1 child, Morgan Zhuo. BS, Chinese Inst. Sci. Tech., 1985; MS, Shanghai Inst. Physiology, 1987; PhD, U. Iowa, 1992. Vis. scientist U. Iowa, 1988-89; postdoctoral fellow Columbia U., N.Y.C., 1992-93; rsch. assoc. Howard Hughes Med. Inst. Columbia U., 1993-95, Stanford U., 1995-96; asst. prof. dept. anesthesiology Washington U., St. Louis, 1996—. Contbr. articles and abstracts to profl. jours. Recipient first award NIH. Mem. Soc. for Neurosci., Internat. Assn. for Study of Pain (Travel award 1990), Am. Pain Soc. (Travel awards 1990, 91, 92), AAAS. Avocations: painting, fishing, biking, dancing. Office: Washington U Dept Anesthesiology Campus Box 8054 Saint Louis MO 63110-1093

ZIADEH, FARHAT J., Middle Eastern studies educator; b. Ramallah, Palestine, Apr. 8, 1917; s. Jacob and Nimeh Farah Z.; m. Suad Salem, July 24, 1949; children—Shireen, Susan, Rhonda, Deena, Reema. B.A., Am. U., Beirut, 1937; LL.B., U. London, 1940. Bar: Barrister-at-law Lincoln's Inn 1946. Instr. Princeton U., 1943-45, lectr. Oriental studies, 1948-54, asst. prof., 1954-58, asso. prof., 1958-66; magistrate Govt. of Palestine, 1947-48; editor Voice of Am., USIA, 1950-54; prof. U. Wash., Seattle, 1966—; prof., chmn. dept. Near Eastern lang. and lit. U. Wash., 1970-82, dir. Ctr. Arabic Study Abroad, 1983-89; adj. prof. U. Wash. Law Sch., 1978-87, prof. emeritus, 1987—;. Author: Reader in Modern Literary Arabic, 1964, Lawyers, The Rule of Law and Liberalism in Modern Egypt, 1968, Property Law in the Arab World, 1979; contbr. articles to profl. jours. Mem. Middle East Studies Assn. (pres. 1979-80), Am. Oriental Soc. (past pres. western br.), Am. Research Center in Egypt (past bd. govs., exec. com.), Am. Assn. Tchrs. Arabic (past pres.). Eastern Orthodox. Office: Univ Wash Mid Eastern Studies Dept Seattle WA 98195

ZIAVRAS, SOTIRIOS GEORGE, computer and electrical engineer, educator; b. Athens, Jan. 2, 1962; came to the U.S., 1984; s. George Spyros and Sofia George Z. Diploma in elec. engring., Nat. Tech. U., 1984; MS, Ohio U., 1985; DSc, George Washington U., 1990. Rschr. Riso (Denmark) Nat. Lab., 1983; teaching and rsch. asst. Ohio U., Athens, 1984-85; disting. grad. teaching asst. George Washington U., Washington, 1985-89, rsch. asst., 1986; assoc. prof. N.J. Inst. Tech., Newark, 1990—; rschr. Walter Reed Army Inst. Rsch., Silver Spring, Md., 1987-88; rsch. asst. U. Md., College Park, 1988-89; vis. prof. George Mason U., Fairfax, Va., 1990. Contbr. articles to profl. jours.; assoc. editor: Pattern Recognition Jour., 1994—. Recipient Rsch. Initiation award NSF, 1991, New Millenium Computing Point Design award NSF/DARPA, 1996. Mem. IEEE (sr.), Assn. for Computing Machinery, N.Y. Acad. Scis. (adv. bd. CIS sect. 1994—), Eta Kappa Nu. Achievements include development of class of high-performance, low-cost interconnection networks for massively parallel computers called reduced hypercubes; introduction of class of multilevel architectures for high-performance multiresolution image analysis, design of an NSF/Darpa-funded New Millennium Computing Parallel Computer for PetaFLOPS performance by 2007. Office: NJ Inst Tech Elec Computer Engring Dept Newark NJ 07102

ZIBART, MICHAEL ALAN, wholesale book company executive; b. Nashville, Mar. 12, 1947; s. Alan Walter and Joy (Hughes) Z.; m. Margaret Anne Boyd, Dec. 27, 1976; children: Emily Joy, Mary Claire. B.A., Vanderbilt U., 1969. Mgmt. trainee Zibart Bros. Books, Nashville, 1961-69; property mgr. Pollack Co., Nashville, 1966-69; buyer Ingram Book Co., Nashville, 1970-75, mgr. trade dept., 1976, v.p., 1976-85, exec. v.p., 1985-88; founder, pres. ProMotion, Inc., Nashville, 1988—. Author: Almanac on Bookselling, 3d edit., 1980; pub. (monthly book review) BookPage. Office: ProMotion Inc 2501 21st Ave S # 5 Nashville TN 37212-5626

ZICHEK, MELVIN EDDIE, retired clergyman, educator; b. Lincoln, Nebr., May 5, 1918; s. Eddie and Agnes (Varga) Z.; A.B., Nebr. Central Coll., 1942; M.A., U. Nebr., 1953; D.Litt., McKinley-Roosevelt Ednl. Inst., 1955; m. Dorothy Virginia Patrick, May 28, 1942; 1 dau., Shannon Elaine. Ordained to ministry Christian Ch., 1942; minister Christian chs., Brock, Nebr., 1941, Ulysses, Nebr., 1942-43, Elmwood, Nebr., 1943-47, Central City, Nebr., 1947-83, ret., 1983; rural tchr., Merrick County, Nebr., 1937-40; prin. Alvo (Nebr.) Consol. High Sch., 1943-47; supt. Archer (Nebr.) Pub. Schs., 1948-57; head dept. English and speech Central City (Nebr.) High Sch., 1957-63; supt. Marquette (Nebr.) Consol. Schs., 1963-79. Served as chaplain's asst. AUS, 1942. Mem. Grand Island Ret. Tchrs. Assn. Republican. Home: 2730 N North Rd Grand Island NE 68803-1143

ZICHEK, SHANNON ELAINE, secondary school educator; b. Lincoln, Nebr., May 29, 1944; d. Melvin Eddie and Dorothy Virginia (Patrick) Z. AA, York (Nebr.) Coll., 1965; BA, U. Nebr., Kearney, 1968; postgrad., U. Okla., Edmond, 1970, 71, 72, 73, 74, 75, U. Nebr., Kearney, 1980, 81, 82, 89, 92. Tchr. history and English, NW High Sch., Grand Island, Nebr., 1948—. Republican. Christian. Home: 2730 N North Rd Grand Island NE 68803-1143

ZICK, JOHN WALTER, retired accounting company executive; b. Highland Park, Ill., Sept. 21, 1925; s. Walter Ernest and Helen Ann (Wiedenhoeft) Z.; m. Mary Ann Sutter, Dec. 11, 1948; children: Sharon, Catherine, John W. B.S., Northwestern U., 1948. With Price Waterhouse, Chgo., 1948-73, N.Y.C., 1973-86; partner Price Waterhouse, 1960-86, partner in charge N.Y.C. office, 1973-76, regional mng. partner, 1976-78, co-chmn., ops., dept. sr. partner, 1978-86. Bd. dirs. Mid-Am. chpt. ARC, 1968-73, Medic Alert Found. U.S., 1994—; founding mem., elder Winnetka (Ill.) Presbyterian Ch., 1956-67; bd. auditors New Trier Twp., Ill., 1969-73; trustee Carnegie Hall Soc. and Corp., 1980—; mem. corp. Greenwich Hosp. Assn., 1980-89. Served with USN, 1943-46. Mem. AICPA (treas. and dir. 1974-77), Ill. Soc. CPAs (pres. 1971-72). Clubs: Pine Valley Golf; Union League (N.Y.C.); Blind Brook; Burning Tree (Washington).

ZICK, LEONARD OTTO, accountant, manufacturing executive, financial consultant; b. St. Joseph, Mich., Jan. 16, 1905; s. Otto J. and Hannah (Heyn) Z.; student Western State U., Kalamazoo; m. Anna Essig, June 27, 1925 (dec. May 1976); children: Rowene (Mrs. A.C. Neidow), Arlene (Mrs. Thomas Anton), Constance Mae (Mrs. Hilary Snell), Shirley Ann (Mrs. John Vander Ley) (dec.); m. Genevieve Evans, Nov. 3, 1977 (dec. Nov. 1996). Sr. ptnr. firm Zick, Campbell & Rose Accts. and predessor firms, South Bend, Ind., 1928-48; sec.-treas. C. M. Hall Lamp Co., Detroit, 1948-51, pres. 1951-54, chmn. bd., 1954-56; pres., treas., dir. Allen Electric & Equipment Co. (now Allen Group, Inc.), Kalamazoo, 1954-57, pres., treas., dir. The Lithibar Co. (now Lithibar-Matik, Inc.), Holland, Mich., 1957-61; fin. v.p., treas., dir., chmn. bd. Crampton Mfg. Co., 1961-63; mgr. corp. fin. dept. Manley, Bennett, McDonald & Co., Detroit, 1963-68; mgr. Leonard O. Zick & Assocs., Holland, 1968-88; former dir. Eberhard's Foods, Inc., Grand Rapids. Former mem. Mich. Rep. Cen. Com.; trustee YMCA Found., Clearwater, Fla., Adm. Richard E. Byrd Ctr., Boston; vice chmn. Army-Navy Munitions Bd., 1941-42, asst. to vice chmn. War Prodn. Bd., 1941-43. Mem. Nat. Assn. Accts. (past nat. v.p., dir.), Mich. Self Insurers Assn. (past pres.), Fin. Execs. Inst., Stuart Cameron McLeod Soc. (past pres.), Union League (Chgo.), Rotary (Paul Harris fellow), Holland Country Club. Lutheran. Home: 360 W 40th St Apt 312 Holland MI 49423-4674

ZICKEL, JOHN, mechanical engineering educator; b. Munich, Germany, Feb. 9, 1919; came to U.S., 1937; s. Fred and Nadja (Blau) Z.; m. Hannah Mary Siegel, Nov. 27, 1942; children—Mark D., Robin J. BSME, Lehigh U., 1948, MS in Math., 1949; PhD in Applied Math., Brown U., 1953. Registered profl. engr., Calif. Structural specialist GE, Schenectady, N.Y. and San Jose, Calif., 1952-58; mgr. structural rsch. Aerojet Gen., Sacramento, 1958-67; prof. mech. engring. Calif. State U.-Sacramento, 1967-91, chmn. dept., 1981-91; cons. in field. Author: Structural Aspects of Nuclear Power Plants, 1958; Product Liability Prevention, 1977. Patentee isotensoid pressure vessel. Served to 1st lt. U.S. Army, 1941-45. Fellow ASME (local chmn. 1972-79); mem. Am. Soc. Engring. Edn., Soc. Automotive Engrs. (Teetor fellow 1978), Soc. Exptl. Mechanics, Sigma Xi, Tau Beta Pi. Club: Am. Contract Bridge League (pres. 1965-68) (Sacramento). Home: 6063 Ranger Way Carmichael CA 95608-1836

ZIEBARTH, E. WILLIAM, news analyst, educator; b. Columbus, Wis., Oct. 4, 1910; s. John and Priscilla (Conrad) Z.; m. Elizabeth Herreid, Dec. 16, 1939; 1 son, John Thomas. B.S., U. Wis., 1933, Ph.M., 1934; Ph.D., U. Minn., 1948, D.H.L. (hon.), 1985. Staff U. of Air, WHA, U. Wis., 1934; instr. speech U. Minn., 1936; acting gen. mgr. sta. WLB, 1944, asso. prof., chmn. dept. speech, 1948, prof., chmn. dept. speech and theatre arts, 1949—, dean summer session, 1954—, dean gen. extension div., 1963-64; dean Coll. Liberal Arts, 1964, interim pres., 1974; cons. for TV World Affairs, 1954; founder, also dir. Min. Sch. of Air, 1938; prodn. mgr. WCCO-CBS, 1945, news analyst, 1947-52, exec. cons., 1948; ednl. dir. central div. CBS network, 1946, cons., 1948-51, spl. fgn., corr., internat. affairs analyst, Scandinavia, So. and Western Europe, 1949, fgn. corr., internat. broadcaster, Scandinavia, Western Europe, Western Asia, 1950, Asiatic analysis, Tokyo, Japan, 1952; exec. v.p., interim gen. mgr. KTCA-TV, KTCI-TV, 1976; exec. v.p., gen. mgr. Twin City Area Pub. TV Corp., 1976-77; radio edn. cons. Hill Found. award study in Soviet Union, 1958, 68; bd. dirs. Midwest Ednl. Television Corp.; trustee Twin City Area TV Corp.; co-chmn. feasibility research Pan-Pacific-Mainland Edn. and Communication Expt. by Satellite, Honolulu, Tokyo, Hong Kong, 1973. Author Six Classic Plays for Radio and How to Produce Them, published in, 1940; contbr.: articles to profl. jours. Mass Media editor Speech Monographs, 1951-53; cons. editor: articles to profl. jours. Central States Speech Jour. Dir. Hennepin County Tb Assn., Minn. Tb and Pub. Health Assn.; mem. Gov.'s Youth Commn.; mem. Nat. Commn. on Arts and Scis. Joint winner nat. Peabody award, 1948; recipient citation Nat. English Council, 1949; Radio Council award for distinguished news analysis, 1952, for significant contbns. internat. understanding, 1951; first award Nat. Inst. Edn. by Radio for news interpretation, 1952; Best Commentator award AFTRA, 1955; joint winner Peabody award, internat. affairs, 1960; Nat. Peabody award, 1972; Blakeslee award Nat. Heart Assn., 1972; Mitchell V. Charnley award for Outstanding Contbns. to Broadcast Journalism, 1982; Outstanding Individual award Speech-Communication Assn., 1979; N.W. Area Found. fellow to People's Republic of China, 1976. Mem. Nat. Assn. Edn. by Radio, Fgn. Policy Assn., Minn. Hist. Soc., Nat. Adult Edn. Assn., Nat. Assn. Ednl. Broadcasters and Telecasters, Nat. Soc. Study Communication (Radio council, mass media com.), Central States Speech Assn., Chi Phi, Phi Kappa, Delta Sigma Rho, Phi Delta Kappa, Psi Chi, Alpha Epsilon Rho, Delta Phi Lambda, Lambda Alpha Psi. Clubs: Hesperia, Greyfriars, Campus, Univ. St. Paul. Home: 1666 Coffman St Apt 325 Saint Paul MN 55108-1340 Office: N-231 Psychology Elliott Hall # U Minn Minneapolis MN 55455

ZIEBARTH, ROBERT CHARLES, management consultant; b. Evanston, Ill., Sept. 12, 1936; s. Charles A. and Marian (Miller) Z.; m. Patience Arnold Kirkpatrick, Aug. 28, 1971; children—Dana Kirkpatrick, Scott Kirkpatrick, Christopher, Nicholas. A.B., Princeton, 1958; M.B.A., Harvard, 1964. With Bell & Howell Co., Chgo., 1964-73; treas., chief fin. officer Bell & Howell Co., 1969-73; mgmt. cons. Ziebarth Co., 1973—; mem. dirs. adv. bd. Arkwright Boston Ins. Co., devel. com. Nat. Assn. Ind. Schs.; bd. dirs. M.B.A. Resources, Inc., Telemedia, Inc., Corp. Resources, Inc., Nordemann Grimm Inc. Assoc. Community Renewal Soc., Citizens Coun. Gateway House; mem. Ill. Bd. Higher Edn., Ill. Joint Edn. Commn.; trustee Choate Sch.; trustee, pres. Latin Sch.Chgo., Chgo. Maternity Ctr.; bd. dirs. Harvard Bus. Sch. Fund, U.S.O., Inc., Prentice Women's Hosp., Northwestern Meml. Corp., Found. for Reproductive Rsch. and Edn., Endowments Inc., Bond Portfolio Endowments Inc. Served to lt. USNR, 1958-62. Mem. Naval Hist. Found., Art Inst. Chgo., Chgo. Hist. Soc., Mus. Modern Art. Presbyn. Clubs: Mid-Am. (Chgo.), Racquet (Chgo.), Saddle and Cycle (Chgo.), Economic (Chgo.), Executives (Chgo.). Office: PO Box 4569 Ketchum ID 83340-4569

ZIEGAUS, ALAN JAMES, public relations executive; b. Bremerton, Wash., May 8, 1948; s. Alan Moon and Dorothy (Lamont) Z.; m. Constance Jean Carver, 1972; children: Jennifer, Ashley. BJ, San Diego State U., 1970. Staff writer San Diego Tribune, 1972-77; exec. asst. San Diego City Council, 1977-78; v.p. Gable Agy., San Diego, 1978-80; pres. Stoorza, Ziegaus & Metzger, San Diego, 1980—. Mem. planning com. County San Diego, 1980-82; mem. sewage task force City of San Diego, 1986-88, civil svc. com., 1992—; trustee armed forces YMCA, San Diego, 1984—. Recipient Best Investigative Series award AP, 1975. Mem. San Diego Press Club (Best News Story award 1973). Home: 12351 Brassica St San Diego CA 92129-4127 Office: Stoorza Ziegaus & Metzger 225 Broadway Fl 18 San Diego CA 92101-5005*

ZIEGENHAGEN, DAVID MACKENZIE, healthcare company executive; b. Mpls., May 25, 1936; s. Elmer Herbert Ziegenhagen and Margaret Ruth (Mackenzie) Kruger; m. Mary Ange Kinsella, Nov. 26, 1966 (div. Dec. 1982); children: Marc, Eric. BA, U. Minn., 1962. Assoc. dir. Thailand Peace Corps, Bangkok, 1963-65; Thailand program officer Peace Corps, Washington, 1966-67; dir. Western Samoa Peace Corps, Apia, 1967-70; exec. dir. Mental Health Assn. Minn., Mpls., 1970-76; co-founder, pres. Current Newspapers, Inc., Burnsville, Minn., 1975-84; sr. program officer The St. Paul Found., 1982-84; pres. DMZ Assocs., St. Paul, 1983—; exec. dir. Minn. Bd. Med. Practice, St. Paul, 1985-88; CEO, pres. Stratis Health, Bloomington, Minn., 1988—; field dir. Am Refugee Com., Bangkok, 1979; dir. Health Edn. Rsch. Found., St. Paul, 1993—; mem. Citizens League, Mpls., 1975—, dir., 1988-95; mem. Adminstrs. in Medicine, Washington, 1985-88; dir. Walk-In Counseling Ctr., Mpls., 1990—, Ctr. for Clin. Quality Evaluation, Washington, 1990—. Mem. Nat. Mental Health Staff Coun. (pres. 1970-76). Avocations: travel, international development, arts. Office: Stratis Health 2901 Metro Dr Ste 400 Minneapolis MN 55425-1529

ZIEGENHORN, ERIC HOWARD, lawyer, legal writer; b. Independence, Mo., Oct. 17, 1957. AB in Econs. with honors, U. Mo., 1979; JD, U. Calif., Berkeley, 1983. Bar: Calif. 1983, Kans. 1986, Mo. 1987. Atty. Law Offices of Richard A. Goodman, Oakland, Calif., 1983-86, Lewis, Rice & Fingersh, Overland Park, Kans., 1986-87; pvt. practice, legal writer Kansas City, Mo., 1987—; sr. staff atty. Midland Loan Svcs., 1991-96. Author: (3-vol. set) Missouri Legal Forms, 1992. Mem. Mo. Bar Assn., Calif. Bar Assn.

ZIEGLER, DANIEL MARTIN, chemistry educator; b. Quinter, Kans., July 6, 1927; s. Anton T. and Clara (Weissbeck) Z.; m. Mary Alice Weir, Aug. 19, 1952; children: Daniel L., Paul W., Mary Claire, James M. BS in Chemistry, St. Benedicts Coll., 1949; PhD in Chemsitry, Loyola U., 1955; postdoctoral, U. Wis., 1955-58. Asst. prof. Inst. Enzyme Rsch. U. Wis., Madison, 1958-61; asst. prof. chemistry U. Tex., Austin, 1961-62, assoc. prof. chemistry, 1962-69, prof. chemistry, 1969—, Roger J. Williams Centennial prof. in biochemistry, 1990—. Editor jour. Biol. Chemistry, 1979-83, 85-90, 93—; mem. editl. bd. Analyt. Biochemistry, 1989-91, Arch. Biochem. Biophys., 1966-71; contbr. articles to profl. jours. Recipient Bernard B. Brodie award Am. Soc. Pharmacol. Exptl. Therapy, 1990, Alexander von Humboldt award, Germany, 1991; estab. investigator Am. Heart Assn., 1960-65. Mem. Internat. Soc. for the Study of Xenobiotics (hon. life). Home: 6704 Shoal Creek Blvd Austin TX 78757-4379 Office: U Tex Dept Chemistry/Biochemistry Austin TX 78712

ZIEGLER, DEWEY KIPER, neurologist; b. Omaha, May 31, 1920; s. Isidor and Pearl (Kiper) Z.; Mar. 30, 1954; children: Amy, Laura, Sara. BA, Harvard U., 1941, MD, 1945. Diplomate Am. Bd. Psychiatry and Neurology (bd. dirs. 1974-83, exec. com. 1978-82). Intern in medicine Boston City Hosp., 1945-46; asst. resident then chief resident in neurology N.Y. Neurol. Inst.-Columbia U. Coll. Physicians and Surgeons, 1948-51; resident in psychiatry Boston Psychopathic Hosp., 1951-53; asst. chief neurol. service Montefiore Hosp., N.Y.C.; and asst. prof. neurology Columbia U., 1953-55; asst. prof. U. Minn., 1955-56; asso. clin. prof. U. Kans. Med. Sch., 1956-64, chief dept. neurology, 1968-85; prof. U. Kans. Med. Center, 1964-89, prof. emeritus, 1989—; cons. Social Security Adminstrn., 1975—; mem. com. on certification and co-certification Am. Bd. Med. Specialties, 1979-82. Author: In Divided and Distinguished Worlds, 1942; Contbr. numerous articles to profl. jours. Served to lt., j.g., M.C. USNR, 1946-48. Fellow Am. Acad. Neurology (pres. 1979-81, v.p. 1972-73); mem. AMA, Am. Neurol. Assn., Am. Epilepsy Soc. Jewish. Home: 8347 Delmar Ln Shawnee Mission KS 66207-1821 Office: Kans U Med Center 3900 Rainbow Blvd Kansas City KS 66103-2918

ZIEGLER, DONALD EMIL, chief federal judge; b. Pitts., Oct. 1, 1936; s. Emil Nicholas and Elizabeth (Barclay) Z.; m. Claudia J. Chermak, May 1, 1965; 1 son, Scott Emil. B.A., Duquesne U., 1958; LL.B., Georgetown U., 1961. Bar: Pa. 1962, U.S. Supreme Ct. 1967. Practice law Pitts., 1962-74; judge Ct. of Common Pleas of Allegheny County, Pa., 1974-78; judge U.S. Dist. Ct. (we. dist.) Pa., Pitts., 1978-94, chief judge, 1994—. Treas. Big Bros. of Allegheny County, 1969-74. Mem. ABA, Pa. Bar Assn., Allegheny County Bar Assn., Am. Judicature Soc., St. Thomas More Soc. Democrat. Roman Catholic. Club: Oakmont Country. Office: US Post Office & Courthouse 6th Fl Courtroom 12 7th & Grant Sts Pittsburgh PA 15219

ZIEGLER, DONALD ROBERT, accountant; b. Lancaster, Pa., Nov. 15, 1932; s. John Jacob and Esther Mae (McKelly) Z.; m. Suzanne Foster, children: D. Rand, Scott F., Kurt J. B.S. in Econ. Acctg., Franklin and Marshall Coll., 1954. CPA, Pa. Mgr., sr. staff mem. Price Waterhouse, Phila., 1954-67, ptnr. 1967-92, sr. practice ptnr., 1978-92, mng. ptnr. Mid-Atlantic area, 1985-88; vice chmn. Southeast Region, 1988-92; mem. policy bd. Price Waterhouse, N.Y.C., 1980-88, mem. mgmt. com., 1986-92. Author: (with others) Managing and Accounting for Inventories, 1980. Contbg. author various books in field. Trustee Franklin and Marshall Coll., 1983—, alumni exec. coun., 1979-83, devel. com., exec. com. 1995—, chmn. audit com., 1989—, Phila. alumni coun.; trustee Pa. Ballet, 1988-92, 94-95, devel. and fin. coms., vice chmn. bd. trustees, 1989-92, chmn. exec. com., 1989-91. With U.S. Army, 1955-57. Recipient Outstanding Soldier award U.S. Army, 1955, Disting. Svc. Alumni medal Franklin and Marshall Coll, 1991. Mem. AICPA (auditing standards com. 1973-76, chmn. subcom. fraud 1976-80), Pa. Inst. CPAs (Phila. chpt. exec. coun.). Clubs: Rehoboth Beach Country Club; Phila. Aviation (bd. govs. and treas. 1969-90), Royal Blackheath Golf (U.K.). Home: RD 1 700 N Trooper Rd Norristown PA 19403-4502 Office: Price Waterhouse LLP 30 S 17th St Philadelphia PA 19103-4021

ZIEGLER, EARL KELLER, minister; b. Sheridan, Pa., Mar. 4, 1929; s. Abraham Hoffman and Rhoda Bucher (Keller) Z.; m. Vivian Zug Snyder, Aug. 12, 1951; children: Karen Louise Miller, Randall Earl, Doreen Kay Creighton, Michael Wayne, Konnae Ziegler Berces, Sulien Nicodemus. BA, Elizabethtown (Pa.) Coll., 1951; MDiv, Bethany Theol. Sem., Chgo., 1954; DDiv, Lancaster (Pa.) Theol. Sem., 1982. Ordained to ministry Ch. of the Brethren, 1950. Pastor Woodbury (Pa.) Congregation, Pa., 1954-60, Black Rock Ch. of Brethren, Brodbecks, Pa., 1960-70, Mechanic Grove Ch. of Brethren, Quarryville, Pa., 1970-83, Atlantic N.E. Dist. Exec., Harrisburg, Pa., 1983-89, Lampeter (Pa.) Ch. of the Brethren, 1989—; moderator Ch. of the Brethren, Elgin, Ill., 1993-94; moderator various dists., Pa., 1959—; mem. Gen. Bd., Ch. of Brethren, 1975-80; chmn. Parish Ministerial Commn., 1979-80; dir. Family Life Inst., 1961, 64, mem. Nat. Korean Cons. Com., 1988-91, Denominational Structure Com., 1990-91, others; adj. prof. ch. history Evang. Sem., Myerstown, Pa., 1988—. Author: Divorce Among the Church of the Brethren Clergy, 1981; contbr. articles to profl. jours. Pres. Manheim Elem. PTA, 1964-65; trustee Elizabethtown Coll., 1965-83; dir. Community Choir, Lineboro, Md., 1966-70; dir. Solanco Community Men's Chorus, Quarryville, 1976-83. Recipient Alumni citation, Elizabethtown Coll. Alumni Assn., 1964, award for Outstanding Ch. Planting in Azua Province of Dominican Republic, 1990, Award of Appreciation, Germantown Ch. of Brethren, 1990. Mem. Lampeter Willow St. Ministerium (pres. 1989-91). Republican. Office: Ch of the Brethren Gen Offices 1451 Dundee Ave Elgin IL 60120-1674 *"You shall have what your faith expects," were the words of Jesus to two blind men. These words challenge the potential within each of us, a faith that conquers, a spirit that soars. Between the possible and the impossible is the measure of one's will.**

ZIEGLER, EKHARD ERICH, pediatrics educator; b. Saalfelden, Austria, Apr. 12, 1940; children: Stefan, Gabriele, Lena. M.D., U. Innsbruck, Austria, 1964. Diplomate: Am. Bd. Pediatrics. Intern U. Innsbruck, 1966-67, resident in pediatrics, 1967-68 70-71, resident in pharmacology, 1964-66, asst. dept. pediatrics, 1970-73; vis. instr. pediatrics U. Iowa, Iowa City, 1968-70, asst. prof. pediatrics, 1973-76, assoc. prof., 1976-81, prof., 1981—; mem. nutrition study sect. NIH, 1988-92. Recipient Nutrition award Am. Acad. Pediactrics, 1988. Mem. Am. Soc. Clin. Nutrition, Soc. Pediatric Research, Soc. Exptl. Biology and Medicine, N.Am. Soc. Pediatric Gastroenterology, Midwest Soc. Pediatric Research, Am. Pediatric Soc., The Nutrition Soc., N.Y. Acad. Scis., Am. Acad. Pediatrics. Club: Univ. Athletic (Iowa City). Office: U Iowa Dept Pediatrics Iowa City IA 52242

ZIEGLER, JACK (DENMORE), cartoonist; b. N.Y.C., July 13, 1942; s. John Denmore and Kathleen Miriam (Clark) Z.; m. Jean Ann Rice, Apr. 20, 1968 (div. 1995); children: Jessica, Benjamin, Maxwell; m. Kelli Joseph, Aug. 1996. B.A. in Communication Arts, Fordham U., 1964. Free-lance cartoonist N.Y.C., 1972—; cartoonist The New Yorker, N.Y.C., 1974—. Author: Hamburger Madness, 1978, Filthy Little Things, 1981, Marital Blitz, 1987, Celebrity Cartoons of the Rich and Famous, 1987, Worst Case Scenarios, 1990, Mr. Knocky, 1993; illustrator: (children's books) Lily of the Forest, 1987, Flying Boy, 1988, Annie's Pet, 1989, Eli and the Dimplemeyers, 1994 (adult books) Waiting Games, 1983, The Joy of Stress, 1984, That's Incurable!, 1984, Modern Superstitions, 1985, The No-Sex Handbook, 1990, There'll Be a Slight Delay, 1991, Byte Me!, 1996. Mem. Cartoonists Assn. (founding mem.), The Glory Boys, Nat. Cartoonists Soc. Democrat.

ZIEGLER, JOHN AUGUSTUS, JR., lawyer; b. Grosse Pointe, Mich., Feb. 9, 1934; s. John Augustus and Monnabell M. Ziegler; divorced; children: John Augustus III, Laura, Lisa, Adeline. AB, U. Mich., JD, 1957. Bar: Mich. 1957. Since practiced in Detroit; assoc. Dickinson, Wright, McKean & Cudlip, 1957-65, ptnr., 1965-68; ptnr. Parsons, Tennent, Hammond, Hardig & Ziegelman, 1969-70, Ziegler, Dykhouse & Wise, 1970-77; pres. Nat. Hockey League, 1977-92, chmn. bd. govs., 1976-78; of counsel Dickinson, Wright, Moon, Van Dusen & Freeman, Detroit, 1992—. Office: 1 Detroit Ctr 500 Woodward Ave Ste 4000 Detroit MI 48226-3423 also: 375 Park Ave Ste 2004 New York NY 10152-2099

ZIEGLER, JOHN BENJAMIN, chemist, lepidopterist; b. Rochester, N.Y., Jan. 2, 1917; s. John Benjamin Sr. and Sarah Jeanette (Murrell) Z.; m. Dorothy Mary Zucker, June 29, 1946 (dec. July 1985); children: Katherine Lois, Jeffrey Benjamin, Conrad Lawrence. BS in Chemistry, U. Rochester, 1939; MS in Chemistry, U. Ill., 1940, PhD in Organic Chemistry, 1946. Cert. chemist. Jr. chemist Merck & Co., Inc., Rahway, N.J., 1940-43; spl. rsch. asst. U. Ill., Urbana, 1943-46; chemist J.T. Baker Chem. Co., Phillipsburg, N.J., 1946-48; assoc. chemist CIBA Pharm. Co., Summit, N.J., 1948-51, sr. chemist, 1951-53, supr. labs., 1953-64, mgr. process rsch. lab., 1964-69; dir. chem. devel. CIBA-GEIGY Pharm. Co., Summit, 1969-75, dir. process rsch., 1975-76, sr. staff scientist, 1976-80; ret.; bus. adminstr. sci. dept. Seton Hall U., South Orange, N.J., 1980-82. Contbr. articles to profl. jours.; patentee in field. Chmn. com. Union county Tech. inst., 1963; past mem. N.J. Coun. R & D; reserved list, scientific and tech. personnel, war manpower commn., 1944. Mem. Am. Chem. Soc., Lepidoptera Rsch. Found., Lepidopterists' Soc. (exec. coun., past treas., other offices), Assn. for Tropical Lepidoptera, Internat. Sci. Collectors' Assn. (vice chmn. exec. coun. 1993—, exec. dir. 1995—), Patronymic in Zool. Nomenclature: Genus Ziegleria (K. Johnson Insecta, Lepidoptera, Lycaenidae 1993), Alpha Chi Sigma (pres. Zeta chpt. 1945-46), Phi Lambda Upsilon, Sigma Xi. Republican. Achievements include Hon. Patronymic in Zool. Nomenclature. Avocations: lepidoptera rsch., tennis, hiking, reading, current events. Home: 64 Canoe Brook Pky Summit NJ 07901-1434

ZIEGLER, R. W., JR., lawyer, consultant; b. Pitts.; children: Caroline, Gretchen, Jeremy, Benjamin, Phoebe, Polly. Student, Carnegie Tech., U. Pitts.; JD, Duquesne U., 1972. Bar: Pa. 1972, Calif. 1981, U.S. Ct. Appeals (3d cir.) 1977, U.S. Dist. Ct. (we. dist.) Pa. 1972, U.S. Supreme Ct. 1977, U.S. Tax Ct. 1978, Calif. 1982, U.S. Dist. Ct. (no. dist.) Calif. 1982, U.S. Ct. Appeals (9th cir.) 1982. Ptnr. Ziegler & Ombres, Pitts., 1973-79; pres. Ziegler Ross Inc., San Francisco, 1979—; lectr. for Bar Assns. Author: Law Practice Management; editor: Law Office Guide in Computing. Mem. ABA, Am. Mgmt. Assn., Pa. State Bar Assn., Calif. State Bar Assn. Office: 1350 Bayshore Hwy Ste 690 Burlingame CA 94010-1815

ZIEGLER, RAYMOND STEWART, retired architect; b. Colorado Springs, Colo., Aug. 18, 1919; s. Edwin L. and Grace (Stewart) Z.; m. Jolene Baddeley, Aug. 22, 1942; children: John, Richard. Student, Ecole De Beaux Arts, Atelier Winslow, U. Calif., San Francisco Archtl. Club. Ptnr. Allison, Rible, Robinson and Ziegler, Architects, Los Angeles, 1958-69; exec. dir., v.p. Allison, Rible, Robinson and Ziegler an asso. group of Leo A Daly Co., 1969-74; ptnr. Raymond Ziegler Partnership, Architects, 1974-77; pres., chmn. bd. Ziegler Kirven Parrish Architects, 1978-84; pvt. cons. practice Altadena, Calif., 1984-96; ret., 1996; mem. Calif. adv. bd. Office Architecture and Constrn., 1968-77, chmn., 1971; vis. prof. sch. architecture U. Hawaii, 1987. Bd. dirs. L.A. Beautiful, 1974-77, 80-86, v.p., 1984, pres., 1985-86, pres.'s coun., 1987-89; bd. dirs. Soc. for Prevention Blindness, 1974-76; hon. lifetime dir. San Gabriel Valley unit Am. Cancer Soc., 1978—, chmn. campaign adv. bd., 1979-80; mem. Untied Way Health Ptnrs. Coun., 1982-85; mem. L.A. County Arhitects Evaluation Commn., 1984-97; chmn. profl. practice sect. com. for 1989 licensing exam. Calif. Bd. Archtl. Examiners. 1st lt. inf. AUS, World War II. Fellow AIA (treas. So. Calif. chpt. 1968-69, bd. dirs. Calif. coun. 1968-69, trustee Ins. Trust of Calif. coun. 1977-81, chmn. 1980-81, bd. dirs. Pasadena and Foothill chpt. 1984, treas. 1985-86); mem. Archtl. Guild (bd. dirs.), Design Profls. Safety Assn. (dir. 1979-85), L.A. C. of C. (bd. dirs. 1972-77), Hist. Soc. Soc. Calif. (bd. dirs. 1982-84, 86-91), Masons, Rotary. Home: 1276 Sunnyoaks Cir Altadena CA 91001-1543

ZIEGLER, RICHARD FERDINAND, lawyer; b. Elizabeth, N.J., Aug. 1, 1949; m. Carolyn Lewis; children: Anna B., David A., Andrew P. D-J. BA in History summa cum laude, Yale u., 1971; JD magna cum laude, Harvard U., 1975. Bar: N.Y. 1976, U.S. Dist. Ct. (so. and ea. dists.) N.Y. 1976, U.S. Dist. Ct. (ea. dist.) Mich. 1982, U.S. Supreme Ct. 1984, U.S. Dist. Ct. (no. dist.) N.Y. 1987. Law clk. to judge U.S. Dist. Ct. (so. dist.), N.Y.C., 1975-76; assoc. Paul, Weiss, Rifkind, Wharton & Garrison, N.Y.C., 1976-77; asst. U.S. atty. U.S. Dept. Justice (so. dist.) N.Y., N.Y.C., 1977-80; assoc. Cleary, Gottlieb, Steen & Hamilton, N.Y.C., 1980-83, ptnr., 1983—. Mem. ABA, Assn. Bar City of N.Y., Fed. Bar Coun., N.Y. State Bar Assn. (chmn. com. on profl. ethics).

ZIEGLER, ROBERT OLIVER, special education educator; b. Cullman, Ala., Sept. 6, 1939; s. Mary Catherine (Taylor) McDonald; adopted Edgar and Kathryn Ziegler; m. Gladys L. Friese, May 3, 1962 (div. Jan. 1970); children: Robert, Edgar, Lesha, Kathy. BS, U. Ala., Tuscaloosa, 1961, MA, 1964, PhD, 1970. Cert. spl. edn. tchr., sch. counselor, music tchr., Ga. Band dir. Phillips Jr. H.S., Mobile, Ala., 1961-62, Wiggins (Colo.) H.S., 1962-63, Eastwood Jr. H.S., Tuscaloosa, 1963-65, McAdory H.S., McCalla, Ala., 1966-70, Calera (Ala.) H.S., 1971-72; prof. music edn. Tift Coll., Forsyth, Ga., 1972-78; jr. H.S. counselor Clayton County Schs., Jonesboro, Ga., 1978-80; elem. sch. counselor Rockdale County Schs., Conyers, Ga., 1980-82; spl. edn. tchr. Henderson Jr. H.S., Jackson, Ga., 1982-87; spl. edn. tchr. Clayton County Schs., Jonesboro, Ga., 1987-92, gen. music tchr., 1996—; spl. edn. tchr. City Schs. of Decatur, Ga., 1992-96; elem. sch. music tchr. Clayton County Schs., 1996—; clarinetist Mobile (Ala.) Symphony Orch., 1961-62; vis. lectr. Stillman Coll., Tuscaloosa, Ala., 1970-71; prof. grad. sch. Mercer U., Macon, 1972-74; vis. lectr. in music Wesleyan Coll., Macon, Ga., 1975-76; acting head music dept. Tift Coll., Forsyth, Ga., 1976-77; curriculum cons. South Metro Psychoednl. Ctr., Atlanta City Schs., 1989. Contbr. articles to profl. publs. Minister of music, choir dir. United Meth. Ch., 1961-90, lay leader, 1989-94; mem. South Metro Concert Band, Morrow, Ga., 1978—, Tara Wind Band, Jonesboro, Ga., 1987-88. Recipient Cert. of Appreciation United Meth. Ch., 1990, Spl. Mission Recognition award United Meth. Women, 1983; U. Ala. grantee, 1960-61;. Mem. Profl. Assn. Ga. Educators (bldg. rep. 1994-96), Soc. for Preservation and Encouragement of Barber Shop Quartet Singing in Am. (founding, co-dir. Fayetteville chpt. 1990). Avocations: tennis, ragtime piano playing, singing gospel music. Home: 2669 Jodeco Dr Jonesboro GA 30236-5311 Office: Clayton County Schs 500 Highway 138 W Jonesboro GA 30238-2222

ZIEGLER, RONALD LOUIS, association executive, former government official; b. Covington, Ky., May 12, 1939; s. Louis Daniel and Ruby (Parsons) Z.; m. Nancy Lee Plessinger, July 30, 1960; children: Cynthia Lee Charas, Laurie Michelle Albright. Student, Xavier U., 1957-58; BS, U. So. Calif., 1961; DSc (hon.), Mass. Coll. Pharmacy, 1989, L.I. U., 1993. With Procter & Gamble Distbg. Co., 1961; account rep. J. Walter Thompson Co., 1962-68; press aide Calif. Rep. Central Com., 1961-62; press aide to Richard Nixon in Calif. gubernatorial campaign, 1962; press aide staff Richard Nixon, 1968-69; press sec. to Pres. Nixon, 1969-74, asst. to, 1973-74; mng. dir., sr. v.p. internat. services Syska and Hennessy, Inc., Washington, 1975-80; pres. Nat. Assn. Truck Stop Operators, Alexandria, Va., 1980-87; pres., chief exec. officer Nat. Assn. Chain Drug Stores, Alexandria, 1987—; mem. nat. adv. bd. U. Okla.; adv. coun. Pharm. Found. U. Tex. Bd. dirs. Nat. Coun. on Patient Info. and Edn., Nat. Conf. on Pharm. Assns., Richard Nixon Libr. and Birthplace. Mem. Am. Soc. Assn. Execs., Nat. Retail Fedn. (bd. dirs.), Pharmacists Against Drug Abuse, Assn. White House Press Secs., Nat. Orgn. Rare Disorders, Sigma Chi Alumni. Office: Nat Assn Chain Drug Stores 413 N Lee St Alexandria VA 22314-2301

ZIEGLER, WILLIAM, III, diversified industry executive; b. N.Y.C., June 26, 1928; s. William and Helen (Murphy) Z.; m. Jane Elizabeth Troy, Feb. 22, 1952; children: Melissa Jane, William Troy, Peter Martin, Cynthia Curtis, Helen Matilda, Karl Huttig. B.A., Harvard U., 1950; M.B.A., Columbia U., 1962. Pres. Hay Island Holding Corp., N.Y.C., 1959-64; chmn. bd., CEO Swisher Internat. Group Inc., 1995—; chmn. bd., dir. Swisher Internat. Group Inc. Pres. E. Matilda Ziegler Found. for Blind; sec. Matilda Ziegler Pub. Co. for Blind; bd. dirs. Maritime Aquarium. Lt. USNR, 1952-54. Clubs: N.Y. Yacht, Noroton (Conn.) Yacht. Home: 161 Long Neck Point Rd Darien CT 06820-5815 Office: 20 Thorndal Cir Darien CT 06820-5421

ZIEGLER, WILLIAM ALEXANDER, lawyer; b. N.Y.C., July 15, 1924; s. William Alexander and Sally (Cootes) Z.; m. Glenn Crawley, Feb. 10, 1950; children: Richard S., Daryl A. Henning, Susan G. Barrows, W. Thomas. A.B., Harvard U., 1944, J.D., 1949. Bar: N.Y. 1949, U.S. Tax Ct. 1950, U.S. Dist. Ct. (so. dist.) N.Y. 1949, U.S. Dist. Ct. (ea. dist.) N.Y. 1957, U.S. Dist. Ct. (no. dist.) Ohio 1973, U.S. Dist. Ct. (ea. dist.) Mich. 1983, U.S. Ct. Apppeals (1st cir.) 1963, U.S. Ct. Appeals (2d cir.) 1957, U.S. Ct. Appeals (3d cir.) 1986, U.S. Ct. Appeals (4th cir.) 1979, U.S. Ct. Appeals (5th cir.) 1987, U.S. Ct. Appeals (6th cir.) 1984, U.S. Ct. Appeals (7th cir.) 1992, U.S. Ct. Appeals (8th cir.) 1981, U.S. Ct. Appeals (9th cir.) 1973, U.S. Ct. Appeals (10th and 11th cirs.) 1983, U.S. Ct. Appeals (D.C. cir.) 1972, U.S. Supreme Ct. 1972. Assoc. Sullivan & Cromwell, N.Y.C., 1949-56, ptnr., 1957-89; bd. dirs. H.W. Wilson Co., Std. Comml. Corp.; sec. bd. dirs., chmn. exec. com. Engring. Info., Inc.; sec., bd. dirs. H.W. Wilson Found. Mem. Assn. Bar City N.Y., Fgn. Policy Assn. (bd. dirs.), Riverside Country Club (Mont.), Harvard Club of N.Y.C., Harvard Club Fairfield County (bd. dirs.). Office: 125 Broad St New York NY 10004-2400

ZIEHLER, TONY JOSEPH, insurance agent; b. Anderson, Ind., June 20, 1936; s. Joseph Anthony and Julie Ann (Kette) Z.; m. Alice Mae Pattison, Apr. 2, 1956 (div. 1972); children: Susan Z. Brown, Kathryn Z. Dwyer, Jane Z. Bee, Patricia Z. Koty, Michael; m. Barbara Buys Wood, Feb. 28, 1981; stepchildren: David Wayne Wood, Brent Douglas Wood. BSBA, U. Ariz., 1958. CLU. Prin. Ziehler Ins. Group, LLC, Tucson, 1958—. Employee edn. chmn. So. Ariz. Div. Am. Cancer Soc.; co-chmn. Medic-Alert Found., Pima County, Ariz.; chmn. Tucson Festival Soc.; mem. Salpointe High Sch. Found., others. Recipient William Wisdom award U. Ariz., Tucson, 1958. Mem. Greater Tucson Assn. Life Underwriters (pres. 1963-64, Agt. of Yr. 1975), Ariz. Assn. Life Underwriters (pres. 1970-71, Agt. of Yr. 1980), So. Ariz. CLU Soc. (pres. 1968-69), Salvation Army (pres. adv. bd. 1984-85), Univ. of Ariz. Found. (mem. planned giving com.), Rotary, (com. chmn.), Tucson Conquistadores (pres. 1985-86), Los Charros del Desierto, Golden Key Soc., MIllion Dollar Round Table, others. Republican. Avocations: travel, trail riding, Belgian draft horses, mountain hiking, sports. Home: 6000 E Calle De Vita Tucson AZ 85750-1957 Office: 6420 E Broadway Blvd Ste B102 Tucson AZ 85710-3536

ZIELINSKI, PAUL BERNARD, grant program administrator, civil engineer; b. West Allis, Wis., Sept. 9, 1932; s. Stanley Charles and Lottie Charlotte (Pliskiewicz) Z.; m. Monica Theresa Beres, July 13, 1957; children: Daniel Paul, Gregory John, Robert Mathias, Sarah Anne. BSCE, Marquette U., 1956; MS, U. Wis., 1961, PhD, 1965. Registered profl. engr., Wis., S.C. Asst. instr. engring. mechanics Marquette U., Milw., 1956-59, asst. prof., 1964-67; instr. civil engring. U. Wis., Madison, 1959-64; from asst. prof. to prof. Clemson (S.C.) U., 1967-78, prof. environ. and systems engring., 1978-82, prof. civil engring., 1982-90, prof. emeritus, 1991—; dir. S.C. Water Resources Rsch. Inst., Clemson, 1978-90; assoc. dir. associateship grant program Nat. Rsch. Coun., Washington, 1990—; cons. Am. Pub. Works Assn., Chgo., 1973-76, Nat. Coun. Examiners of Engring. and Surveying, Clemson, 1973—. Chmn. Clemson City Planning Commn., 1971-74; ex-officio mem. S.C. Water Resources Commn., Columbia, 1978-90. Mem. ASCE, Am. Soc. for Engring. Edn., Sigma Xi. Roman Catholic. Home:

2111 Wisconsin Ave NW Apt 717 Washington DC 20007-2278 Office: Nat Rsch Coun 2201 Constitution Ave NW Washington DC 20037-2907

ZIEMANN, G. PATRICK, bishop; b. Pasadena, Calif., Sept. 13, 1941. Attended, St. John's Coll. and St. John's Sem., Camarillo, Calif., Mt. St. Mary's Coll., L.A. Ordained priest Roman Cath., 1967. Titular bishop, aux. bishop Diocese Santa Rosa, Obba, 1986-92; bishop Diocese Santa Rosa, Santa Rosa, Calif., 1992—. Office: Chancery Office PO Box 1297 547 B St Santa Rosa CA 95401*

ZIEMER, RODGER EDMUND, electrical engineering educator, consultant; b. Sargeant, Minn., Aug. 22, 1937; s. Arnold Edmund and Ruth Ann (Rush) Z.; m. Sandra Lorann Person, June 23, 1960; children: Mark Edmund, Amy Lorann, Norma Jean, Sandra Lynn. B.S., U. Minn., 1960, M.S., 1962, Ph.D., 1965. Registered profl. engr., Mo. Research asst. U. Minn., Mpls., 1960-62; research assoc. U. Minn., 1962; prof. elec. engring. U. Mo., Rolla, 1968-83; prof. elec. engring. U. Colo., Colorado Springs, 1984—, chmn. dept. elec. engring., 1984-93; cons. Emerson Electric Co., St. Louis, 1972-84, Mid-Am. Regional Coun., Kansas City, Mo., 1974, Motorola, Inc., Scottsdale, Ariz., 1980-84, Martin Marietta, Orlando, 1980-81, TRW, Colorado Springs, summer, 1985, Sperry, Phoenix, 1986, Pericle Communications, summer, 1994, Motorola, Schaumburg, 1995. Author: Principles of Communications, 1976, 2d edit., 1985, 3d edit., 1990, 4th edit., 1995, Signals and Systems, 1983, 2d edit., 1989, 3rd edit., 1993, Digital Communications and Spread Spectrum Systems, 1985, Introduction to Digital Communication, 1992, Introduction to Spread Spectrum Communications, 1995, Elements of Engineering Probability and Statistics, 1997; editor: IEEE Jour. on Selected Areas in Communications, 1989, 92, 95, IEEE Communications Mag., 1991. Served to capt. USAF, 1965-68. Scholar Western Electric, 1957-59; trainee NASA, 1962-65. Fellow IEEE; mem. Am. Soc. Engring. Edn., Armed Forces Communications and Electronics Assn., Sigma Xi, Tau Beta Pi, Eta Kappa Nu. Lutheran. Home: 8315 Pilot Ct Colorado Springs CO 80920-4412 Office: Univ Colo PO Box 7150 Colorado Springs CO 80933-7150

ZIENTARA, SUZANNAH DOCKSTADER, insurance company executive; b. Wichita, Kans., Oct. 1, 1945; d. Ralph Walter and Patricia Ann (Harvey) Dockstader; m. Larry Henry Zientara, Oct. 18, 1975; 1 child, Jillian Sue Zientara Cox. Student, U. Kans., 1963-64; BS in Bus. Edn., Ft. Hays State U., 1968; MEd in Secondary Guidance and Counseling, U. Mo., St. Louis, 1973. CLU. Sec. to supt. Wichita Pub. Schs., 1968-69; tchr. bus. edn. Wichita Heights High Sch., 1969-71, Lindbergh High Sch., St. Louis, 1971-72, Holman Jr. High Sch., St. Louis, 1972-75; guidance counselor Pattonville Heights Jr. High Sch., St. Louis, 1975-79; tchr. data processing Lawrence (Kans.) High Sch., 1979-85; ins. agt. State Farm Ins. Cos., Lawrence, 1985-90; agy. mgr. State Farm Ins. Cos., Tulsa, 1990-95; agy. field exec. State Farm Ins. Cos., Topeka, 1995—; mem. Regional Mgr. Coun., Tulsa, 1992-93; participant Purdue Profl. Mgmt. Inst., West Lafayette, Ind., 1993. Author: Introduction to Data Processing, 1983. Mem. Williams Edn. Fund, U. Kans. Named Outstanding Young Woman of Am., 1974. Mem. Am. Soc. CLU's and ChFC's, USTA, Am. Ski Assn., Topeka C. of C., U. Kans. Alumni Assn., PEO, Shawnee Country Club, Mortar Bd., Pi Omega Pi. Republican. Episcopalian. Avocations: tennis, golf, snow skiing, bridge, music. Home: 3637 SW Kings Forest Rd Topeka KS 66610-1553 Office: State Farm Ins Cos 2930 SW Wanamaker Dr Ste 6 Topeka KS 66614-4116

ZIENTY, FERDINAND BENJAMIN, chemical company research executive, consultant; b. Chgo., Mar. 21, 1915; s. Albert Frank and Rose Cecelia (Przypyszny) Z.; BS, U. Ill., 1935; MS, U. Mich., 1936, PhD, 1938; m. Claylain Lorraine Cawiezell, Apr. 14, 1945; children: Jane Zienty Wheeler, Donald Ferd. Research chemist organic chems. div. Monsanto Co., St. Louis, 1938-40, research group leader, 1940-47, asst. dir. research, 1947-50, asso. dir. research, 1950-56, dir. research, 1956-60, dir. advanced organic chems. research, 1960-64, mgr. research and devel., 1964-79, dir. chemistry bio med program, 1979-83, dir. research Health Care div., 1983, cons., 1983—, v.p. research George Lueders & Co. subs. Monsanto Co., St. Louis, 1968-70. Recipient Hodel, Saltiel, Hodel prize for scholarship, 1935, Sesquicentennial award U. Mich., 1967, Disting. Alumnus award U. Mich. Coll. Pharmacy, 1981, Loyalty award U. Ill. Alumni Assn., 1997. Fairchild scholar, 1935, Frederick Stearns fellow, 1936-37. Fellow AAAS, N.Y. Acad. Scis., Acad. Scis. of St. Louis (trustee); mem. Am. Chem. Soc., Am. Inst. Chem. Engrs., Am. Pharm. Assn., Inst. Food Technologists, Mo. Acad. Sci., Soc. Chem. Industry (London). Clubs: Triple A Country, Univ. Club. St. Louis. Contbr. articles to profl. jours. Patentee in field. Home and Office: 850 Rampart Dr Saint Louis MO 63122-1644

ZIERDT, CHARLES HENRY, microbiologist; b. Pitts., Apr. 24, 1922; s. Conrad Henry and Nancy Leora (Harshberger) Z.; m. Margaret May Wise, June 1, 1942 (div. 1962); children—Charles Henry, Jr., Carolyn, Douglas, Richard; m. Willadene Smith, Sept. 30, 1967. B.S., Pa. State U., 1943; M.S., U. Mich., 1945; Ph.D., George Washington U., 1967. Rsch. assoc. Parke-Davis & Co., Detroit, 1945-48; microbiologist Henry Ford Hosp., Detroit, 1948-53, USPHS, Detroit, 1953-56; rsch. microbiologist NIH, Bethesda, Md., 1956—. Scientist sponsor U. Md., 1975—; instr. Found. Advanced Edn. Scis., Bethesda, 1978—. Author: Glucose Nonfermenting Gram Negative Bacteria in Clinical Microbiology, 1978; Non-fermentative Gram Negative Rods: Laboratory Identification and Clinical Aspects, 1985; McGraw-Hill Yearbook of Science and Technology, 1986; Diagnostic Procedures for Bacterial Infections, 1987; contbr. over 100 articles to profl. jours. Patentee in field. Active PTA. Fellow Am. Acad. Microbiology; mem. Am. Soc. Microbiology (chpt. pres. 1976), U.S. Fedn. Culture Collections (membership chmn. 1985), Avanti Owners Assn. Internat., Mensa, Model A Ford Club of Am. (Fairfax, Va. chpt. pres. 1985), Model T Ford Club Internat., Antique Auto Club Am. (pres. Sugar Loaf Mountain region 1997), Sigma Xi. Republican. Achievements include the classification and pathogenesis of Blastocystis Hominis, an intestinal protozoan parasite of man. Avocations: gardening; antique car restoration, church historian. Home: 4100 Norbeck Rd Rockville MD 20853-1869 Office: NIH Bethesda MD 20816

ZIERDT, JOHN GRAHAM, JR., transportation company executive; b. Warner Robbins, Ga., July 22, 1943; s. John Graham and Elizabeth (Matthews) Z.; m. Regina Astor, June 18, 1966; children: John III, Karen, Michael. BS in Engring., U.S. Mil. Acad., 1966; MS in Engring., Ariz. State U., 1972. Commd. 2d lt. U.S. Army, 1966, advanced through grades to brig. gen., 1991; battalion comdr. 702d Maintenance Battalion U.S. Army, Camp Casey, Korea, 1984-85; brigade comdr. 46th Support Group U.S. Army, Ft. Bragg, N.C., 1988-89, comdg. gen. 1st Corps Support Command, 1989-91; dir. logistics U.S. Army Forces Command U.S. Army, Atlanta, 1991-95; ret. U.S. Army, 1995; pres., CEO TransCor Am., Inc., Nashville, 1995—. Author: Acquisition Management: The Role and The Reality, 1987. Decorated Legion of Merit with 2 oak leaf clusters, Bronze Star with oak leaf cluster, Disting. Svc. medal; Nat. security fellow Kennedy Sch. Govt., Harvard U., 1986-87. Republican. Roman Catholic. Home: 516 Midway Cir Brentwood TN 37027-5179 Office: TransCor Am Inc 1510 Fort Negley Blvd Nashville TN 37203-5037

ZIERING, WILLIAM MARK, lawyer; b. New Britain, Conn., Feb. 4, 1931; s. Jacob Max and Esther (Freedman) Z.; m. Harriet Koskoff, Aug. 20, 1958 (div. Sept. 1993); 1 son, Benjamin. B.A., Yale U., 1952; J.D., Harvard U., 1955. Bar: Conn. 1955, Calif. 1962. Assoc. Koskoff & McMahon, Plainville, Conn., 1959-60; sr. trial atty. SEC, San Francisco, 1960-65; pvt. practice law San Francisco, 1965—; ptnr. Bremer & Ziering, 1972-77; instr. Golden Gate U. Law Sch., San Francisco, 1968-75. Vice pres., bd. dirs. Calif. League Handicapped, 1972—. Served to comdr. USNR, 1955-58. Mem. ABA, Calif. Bar Assn., San Francisco Bar Assn. (past chmn. securities, corps. and banking), Navy League (dir.). Club: Commonwealth. Home: 440 Davis Ct Apt 620 San Francisco CA 94111 Office: 4 Embarcadero Ctr Ste 3400 San Francisco CA 94111-4187

ZIERLER, NEAL, retired mathematician; b. Balt., Sept. 17, 1926; s. Joseph Nathan and Betsey (Levie) Z.; m. Betty Matsumoto, Dec. 26, 1950 (div. 1981); children: Robert Eugene, Joan Mariye, Ann M. AB, Johns Hopkins U., 1945; AM, Harvard U., 1949, PhD, 1959. Mathematician, physicist Ballistic Rsch. Labs., Aberdeen, Md., 1951; mem. tech. staff instrumentation lab. MIT, Cambridge, Mass., 1952-54; mem. tech. staff Lincoln Lab. MIT, Lexington, Mass., 1954-60; supr. info. processing group of jet propulsion lab. Calif. Inst. Tech., Pasadena, 1960-61; sr. scientist ARCON Corp., Lexington, 1961-62; head sub-dept. process analysis MITRE Corp., Bedford, Mass., 1962-65; tech. staff Ctr. for Comm. Rsch. Inst. Def. Analysis, Princeton, N.J., 1965-96. Patentee error-detecting and -correcting devices; contbr. articles to profl. jours. Lt. USN, 1944-46. Fellow IEEE; mem. Am. Math. Soc., Math. Assn. Am. Avocations: tennis, skiing, photography. Office: Inst Def Analysis Ctr Communications Rsch Thanet Rd Princeton NJ 08540-3699

ZIEROLF, MARY LOUISE, nurse anesthetist; b. Lima, Ohio, Dec. 12, 1946; d. Charles Peter and Agatha Cecilia (Jackman) Z. Diploma in nursing, St. Rita's Sch. Nursing, Lima, Ohio, 1967; diploma in anesthesia, Cin. Gen. Hosp., 1971; BS in Edn., U. Cin., 1974. RN, Ohio; cert. nurse anesthetist; cert. CPR instr., neonatal resuscitation. Staff nurse operating rm. St. Rita's Hosp., Lima, 1967-69; staff anesthetist, invsc. coord. Mercy Anesthesia Assocs Inc/Anesthesia & Intensive Care Cons, Cin., 1971—; staff anesthetist, specialist in obstet. anesthesia McCullough-Hype Hosp., Oxford, Ohio, 1993-96; staff anesthetist Mercy Fairfield, 1996—, Intensive Care Consultants, Inc.; vis. lectr. Coll. Nursing, U. Cin., 1990-92; lectr. anesthesia in 3d world countries, 1992. Author papers. Mem. anniversary program to Russia, People to People/Citizen Amb. Program, Seattle, 1991, participant in 1st CRNA anesthesia exch. of tech. and sci. info. in China, 1989; active taking monthly blood pressures Fairfax (Ohio) Sr. Citizens, 1988—. Named one of Outstanding Young Women of Am., 1976. Mem. Am. Assn. Nurse Anesthetists, Ohio State Assn. Nurse Anesthetists (bd. dirs. 1981-83, 92—, pres. Greater Cin. Ednl. Dist. 1991—, chair fall Osana meeting 1995—, co-chair fall meeting 1997, sec. 1996-97), Am. Bus. Woman's Assn. (pres. 7 Hills chpt. 1982—, Woman of Yr. 1982), U. Cin. Alumni Assn., Gen. Hosp. Sch. Nurse Anesthesia Alumni. Roman Catholic. Avocations: reading, traveling, volunteer work for needy and elderly. Home: 6 West Knoll Fairfield OH 45014 Office: Mercy Hosp Anderson 7500 State Rd Cincinnati OH 45255-2439

ZIESE, NANCYLEE HANSON, social worker; b. Sioux City, Iowa, July 26, 1938. BA in Sociology, Morningside Coll., 1960; MSW, U. Iowa, 1982, cert. in aging studies, 1986. Social worker Florence Crittenton Home, Sioux City, 1960-65, L.A. County, 1965; social worker, supr. Polk County Dept. Social Welfare, Des Moines, 1966-69; social worker, community liaison Tommy Dale Meml., Sioux City, Iowa, 1977-79; dir. internships Briar Cliff Coll., Sioux City, 1981-83; dir. continuing edn. Coe Coll., Cedar Rapids, Iowa, 1983-85; exec. dir. Profl. Women's Network, Cedar Rapids, 1985-87; pvt. practice WOMANPLACE Counseling, Cedar Rapids, 1985-87; adoption coord. Hillcrest Family Svcs., Cedar Rapids, 1987—; bd. dirs. Young Parent's Network M.E.L.D., Cedar Rapids, 1988—, pres., 1994-96 ; cons. projects related to community improvement, recycling. Contbr. articles to newspapers. Bd. mem., v.p. Sioux City Sch. Bd., 1978-83; bd. mem., pres. Friends of Iowa Pub. TV, 1978-88, Family Svc., Boys and Girls Home, Sioux City, 1973-81; steering bd. Iowa Women's Polit. Caucus, 1987-93, pres., 1992-93; chair Iowa Women's Caucus Rsch. and Edn. Ctr., 1994; bd. dirs. commn. mem. Episcopal Diocese Iowa-Human Needs; chair Birth Defects Inst. Adv. Com., Iowa Inter-Agy. Adoption Coalition; bd. mem. Linn County Adolescent Pregnancy Prevention Coalition, treas. 1992-96, Young Parents Network, 1988—, pres. 1994-96, Friends of Iowa Commn. on Status of Women; mem. steering com. ERA Iowa 1992, 1991—; mem. gov.'s com. adoption reform in Iowa, 1993, 94, lt. gov.'s com. spl. needs adoption in Iowa, 1994; bd. dirs., pub. policy chair AAUW, 1995—; v.p. Iowa Breast Cancer Action; cons. med. ethics com. for In-Vitro Fertilization Adoption program, U. Iowa, 1995; Frequent spkr. on adoption and Women's Issues. Recipient Outstanding Svc. awards Sioux City C. of C., 1976, Siouxland Arts Coun., 1977; named Woman of the Yr., Linn County, Cedar Rapids, Iowa, 1995. Mem. NASW, Profl. Women's Network Cedar Rapids (bd. mem.), mem. Rotary Internat. Republican. Episcopalian. Avocations: women's movement, human needs, reading, walking. Office: Hillcrest Family Svcs 205 12th St SE Cedar Rapids IA 52403-4028

ZIETLOW, RUTH ANN, reference librarian; b. Richland Center, Wis., Apr. 5, 1960; d. James Eldon and Dixie Ann (Doudna) Z.; m. David Robert Voigt, Aug. 22, 1992; 1 child, Eleanor Ruth. BA in English, U. Nebr., 1987; MA in Libr. Studies, U. Wis., 1990; cert. in info. sys., U. St. Thomas, St. Paul, 1995. English instr. Guangzhou (China) English Lang. Ctr. Zhongshan U., 1987-88; adminstrv. asst. Helm Group, Lincoln, Nebr., 1988-89; circulatio supr. Sch. Edn. U. Wis., Madison, 1990-91; libr. specialist St. Paul Pub. Libr., 1991-92; reference librarian coordinator extention library svcs. U. St. Thomas, 1991—. Author manual: Electronic Communication and Information Resources Manual, 1995. Mem. Am. Soc. Info. Sci. (jobs chair Minn. chpg. 1996—). Avocations: gardening, reading. Office: U St Thomas O'Shaughnessey-Frey Libr 2115 Summit Ave Saint Paul MN 55105-1048

ZIFCHAK, WILLIAM C., lawyer; b. 1948. BA, Harvard U., 1970; JD, Columbia U., 1973. Bar: N.Y. 1974, U.S. Ct. Appeals (2d cir.) 1975, U.S. Ct. Appeals (3d cir., D.C. cir.) 1983, U.S. Dist. Ct. (so. dist.) N.Y. 1984. Ptnr., co-chair dept. labor and employment law Kaye, Scholer, Fierman, Hays & Handler, N.Y.C; planning com. NYU Ann. Nat. Conf. Labor, 1991—. Contbr. articles to profl. jours. Mem. ABA (sect. labor and employment law 1975—, subcom. antitrust, RICO and labor rels. law), Assn. Bar City of N.Y. (sec. com. labor and employment law 1984-87), N.Y. State Bar (comml.-fed. litig. sect. co-chair labor and employment law com. 1995—). Office: Kaye Scholer Fierman Hays & Han 425 Park Ave New York NY 10022-3506

ZIFF, LARZER, English language educator; b. Holyoke, Mass., Oct. 2, 1927; s. Isadore Menden and Sara (Rosenbloom) Z.; m. Ruth Rosalind Geisenberger; children—Joshua, Oliver, Joel, Abigail. Student, Middlebury Coll., 1945-47; M.A., U. Chgo., 1951, Ph.D., 1955; M.A. (hon.), U. Oxford, Eng., U. Pa. Prof. English U. Calif., Berkeley, 1956-73; univ. lectr. Oxford U., Eng., 1973-78; prof. English U. Pa., 1978-81; Caroline Donovan prof. English Johns Hopkins U., Balt., 1981—, chair dept., 1991-95; dir. U. Calif. Edn. Abroad Program, U.K., Ireland, 1969-71; cons. and lectr. in field. Author: The Career of John Cotton, 1962; The American 1890's, 1968; Puritanism in America, 1973; Literary Democracy, 1981; Writing in the New Nation, 1991; also articles, essays in profl. jours.; mem. editorial bds. including ELH, 1981—. Recipient numerous awards for excellence in English including Christian Gauss award, the American 1890's, 1967; Fulbright fellow, 1959-60, fellow Am. Coun. Learned Socs., 1963-64, Newberry Libr., 1964, NEH, 1967-68, Guggenheim fellow, 1977-78, Woodrow Wilson Internat. Ctr. for Scholars, 1986-87; Fulbright Disting. Sr. Lectr., 1993. Fellow Am. Acad. Arts and Scis., Soc. Am. Historians; mem. MLA, Am. Antiquarian Soc., Am. Studies Assn. Office: Johns Hopkins U Dept English Baltimore MD 21218

ZIFF, MORRIS, internist, rheumatologist, educator; b. N.Y.C., Nov. 19, 1913; s. Benjamin and Ethel (Seldowitz) Z.; m. Jacqueline Mae Miller, Dec. 10, 1978; children: Edward B., David R. BS, NYU, 1934, PhD, 1937, MD, 1948. Intern Bellevue Hosp., N.Y.C., 1948-49, resident in internal medicine, 1949-50, attending physician, 1950-58; asst. prof. medicine NYU, 1954-57, assoc. prof., 1957-58; Ashbel Smith prof. internal medicine U. Tex. Health Sci. Ctr., Dallas, 1958-84, Ashbel prof. emertus internal medicine, 1984—, Morris Ziff prof. rheumatology, 1982—; dir. Harold C. Simmons Arthritis Rsch. Ctr., Dallas, 1983-84; attending physician Parkland Meml. Hosp., Dallas, 1958—; mem. med. staff Zale-Lipshy Univ. Hosp., Dallas, 1989—; cons. Dallas VA Hosp., Brooke Army Hosp., 1964-75, William Beaumont Army Hosp., 1965-76. Contbr. over 250 articles to sci. jours., chpts. to books. Recipient Heberden medal Heberden Soc. London, 1964, Rsch. Career award USPHS, 1962-84, Marchman award Dallas So. Med. Soc., 1968, Disting. Svc. award Arthritis Found., 1968, Disting. Alumni Sci. award NYU, 1966, Carol Nachman prize in rheumatology, 1974, World Internat. Conf. on Inflammation prize, 1986, Rheuma medal Asutrian Soc. Rheumatology, 1996. Fellow ACP; mem. Assn. Am. Physicians, Am. Soc. Clin. Investigation, Am. Assn. Immunologists, Am. Coll. Rheumatology (master, Bunim medal 1982, Gold medal 1988), N.Y. Acad. Medicine (Klemperer medal 1991), Harvey Soc., Phi Beta Kappa, Sigma Xi, Alpha Omega Alpha. Home: 11116 Pinocchio Dr Dallas TX 75229-4031 Office: U Tex Health Sci Ctr Health Sci Ctr 5323 Harry Hines Blvd Dallas TX 75235-7208

ZIFF, PAUL, philosophy educator; b. N.Y.C., Oct. 22, 1920; m. Loredana Vanzetto; 3 children. BFA, Cornell U., 1949, PhD, 1951. Instr. philosophy U. Mich., Ann Arbor, 1952-53; from instr. to asst. prof. Harvard U., Cambridge, Mass., 1953-59; from asst. prof. to assoc. prof. U. Pa., 1959-63; prof. U. Wis., 1964-68, U. Ill., Chgo., 1968-70; Kenan prof. U. N.C., Chapel Hill, 1970-88, prof. emeritus, 1988—; chmn. bd. dirs. Chapel Hill Ctr. Linguistic Rsch.; cons. in field. Contbr. articles to profl. jours. Paul Ziff chair installed in his honor U. N.C., 1994; festschrift Language, Mind and Art pub. in his honor, 1994; grantee Rockefeller Found., spring 1955, Guggenheim Found., Rome, 1962-63. Office: Chapel Hill Ctr for Philosophic Linguistic Rsch 1309 Brigham Rd Chapel Hill NC 27514-3402

ZIFF, WILLIAM BERNARD, JR., retired publishing executive; b. June 24, 1930; s. William B. and Amelia (Morton) Z.; m. Tamsen Ann Kojis, 1987; children from previous marriage: Dirk Edward, Robert David, Daniel Morton. BA, Rutgers U., 1951; postgrad., Heidelberg U., 1952-53, U. Madrid, 1952-53. Ptnr., then owner and chmn. Ziff Davis Pub. Co., N.Y.C., until 1984; pub. chmn. Ziff Communication Corp., N.Y.C., 1987-93; ret., 1993. Office: Ziff Bros Investments 153 E 53rd St New York NY 10022-4611

ZIFFREN, KENNETH, lawyer; b. Chgo., June 24, 1940. BA, Northwestern U., 1962; JD, UCLA, 1965. Bar; Calif. 1967. Law clerk to Chief Justice Warren, 1965-66; ptnr. Ziffren, Brittenham, Branca & Fischer, L.A. Mem. ABA, State Bar Calif., L.A. County Bar Assn., Beverly Hills Bar Assn., L.A. Copyright Soc. (pres. 1977-78). Office: Ziffren Brittenham Branca & Fischer 2121 Ave Of Stars Fl 32 Los Angeles CA 90067-5010*

ZIGLAR, JAMES W., former federal official, lawyer, investment banker; b. Pascagoula, Miss., Dec. 8, 1945; married; 3 children. BA, George Washington U., 1968, JD, 1972. Bar: Va. 1972, D.C. 1973, N.Y. 1975, Ariz. 1977. Staff asst. Senator James Eastland, Washington, 1964-71; spl. asst. Dept. of Justice, Washington, 1971-72; law clk. to assoc. justice Harry Blackmun U.S. Supreme Ct., Washington, 1972-73; assoc. Mudge, Rose, Guthrie et al, N.Y.C., 1973-77; ptnr. O'Connor, Cavanagh, Anderson et al, Phoenix, 1977-80; sr. v.p. dept. pub. fin. Dillon, Read & Co., N.Y.C., 1980-84; mng. dir. Paine Webber, Inc., Washington, 1984-86, 90—; asst. sec. Dept. of Interior, Washington, 1987-88; mng. dir. Drexel Burnham Lambert Inc., N.Y.C., 1989-90. Bar: Va. 1972, D.C. 1973, N.Y. 1975, Ariz. 1977. Office: Paine Webber Inc 919 18th St NW Ste 650 Washington DC 20006-5503

ZIGLER, EDWARD FRANK, psychologist, educator; b. Kansas City, Mo., Mar. 1, 1930; s. Louis and Gertrude (Gleitman) Z.; m. Bernice Gorelick, Aug. 28, 1955; 1 child, Scott. BA, U. Mo.-Kansas City, 1954; PhD, U. Tex., 1958; MA (hon.), Yale, 1967; DSc (hon.), Boston Coll., 1985; LHD (hon.), Bank St. Coll. Edn., 1989, U. New Haven, 1991, St. Joseph Coll., 1991; PhD (hon.), U. Mo., 1993, CUNY, 1995; Hon. degree, CUNY, 1995; LLD (hon.), Gonzaga U., 1995. Psychol. intern Worcester (Mass.) State Hosp., 1957-59; asst. prof. psychology U. Mo., 1958-59; mem. faculty Yale U., 1959—, prof. psychology and child study center, 1967—, Sterling prof., 1976—, dir. child devel. program, 1961-76, chmn. dept. psychology, 1973-74; head psychology sect. Yale Child Study Center, 1967—; dir. Bush Center in Child Devel. and Social Policy, 1977—; chief Children's Bur. NEW, Washington, 1970-72; cons. in field, 1962—; mem. nat. steering com. Project Head Start, 1965-70, chmn. 15th anniversary Head Start com., 1980; mem. nat. adv. com. Nat. Lab. Early Childhood Edn., 1967-70; nat. rsch. adv. bd. Nat. Assn. Retarded Children, 1968-73; nat. rsch. coun. Project Follow-Through, 1968-70; chmn. adv. com. Vietnamese Children's Resettlement, 1975; mem. Pres.'s Com. on Mental Retardation, 1980; joint appointee Yale U. Sch. Medicine, 1982—, chmn. Yale Infant Care Leave Commn., 1983-85, Parents as Tchrs., 1986—; mem. adv. com. Head Start Quality and Expansion, 1993; mem. adv. com. on svcs. for families with infants and toddlers HHS, 1994. Author, co-author, editor books and monographs; contbr. articles to profl. jours. Served with AUS, 1951-53. Recipient Gunnar Dybwad Disting. scholar in behavioral and social sci. award Nat. Assn. Retarded Children, 1964, 69, Social Sci. Aux. award, 1962, Alumni Achievement award U. Mo., 1965, Alumnus of Yr. award, 1972, C. Anderson Aldrich award Am. Acad. Pediatrics, 1985, Nat. Achievement award Assn. for Advancement of Psychology, 1985, Dorothea Lynde Dix Humanitarian award for svc. to handicapped Elwyn Inst., 1987, Sci. Leadership award Joseph P. Kennedy Jr. Found., 1990, Mensa Edn. and Rsch. Found. award for excellence, 1990, Nat. Head Start Assn. award, 1990 Founders award, 1995, Bldg. dedication Edward Zigler Head Start Ctr., 1990, As They Grow award in edn. Parents mag., 1990, Excellence in Edn. award Pi Lambda Theta, 1991, Friend of Edn. award Conn. Edn. Assn., 1991, Loyola-Mellon Social Sci. award 1991, Pres.'s award Conn. Assn. Human Svcs., 1991, Harold W. McGraw, Jr. prize in edn., 1992, Disting. Achievement in Rsch. award Internat. Assn. Sci. Study of Mental Deficiency, 1992, Disting. Svc. award Coun. Chief State Sch. Officers, 1993, Outstanding Fed. Leadership in Support of Head Start Rsch., Adminstrn. on Children, Youth and Families, 1993, Child and Family Advocacy award Parents as Tchrs. Nat. Ctr., 1994, Nat. Distinction award U. Pa. Edn. Alumni Assn., 1994, Disting. Fellow award So. Conn. State U. chpt. Phi Delta Kappa; named Hon. Commr. Internat. Yr. of Child, 1979. Fellow Am. Orthopsychiat. Assn. (Blanche F. Ittleson award 1989, pres. 1993-94), APA (pres. divsn. 7, 1974-75, G. Stanley Hall award 1979, award for disting. contbns. to psychology in pub. interest 1982, Nicholas Hobbs award 1985, award for disting. profl. contbns. to knowledge 1986, Edgar A. Doll award 1986, award for disting. contbn. to cmty. psychology and cmty. mental health 1989; pres.-elect divsn. 37 1997); mem. Inst. Medicine of NAS, AAAS, Am. Acad. Mental Retardation (Career Rsch. award 1982), Soc. Psychol. Study Social Issues (Kurt Lewin Meml. award 1995), Zero to Three (Dolley Madison award 1995), P.R. Head Start Assn. (Outstanding Leadership award 1995). Home: 177 Ridgewood Ave North Haven CT 06473-4442 Office: Yale U Dept Psychology PO Box 208205 2 Hillhouse Ave New Haven CT 06520-8205

ZIKAKIS, JOHN P., consultant, educator, researcher, biochemist; b. Piraeus, Greece, Sept. 16, 1933; came to U.S., 1958; s. Philip J. and Salome J. (Moshou) Z.; m. Kiki K. Matrozos, Aug. 29, 1958; 1 child, Salome J. Assoc. engr., Pythagoras Coll., Piraeus, 1956; BA, U. Del., 1965, MS, 1967, PhD, 1970. Third merchant marine engr. Onassis Shipping Enterprises, Ltd., London, 1956-58; lab. asst. DuPont de Nemours and Co., Newark, Del., 1959-61; research asst. U. Del., Newark, 1965-70, asst. prof. animal sci. dept., 1970-75, assoc. prof. animal sci. dept., 1975-81, prof. animal sci. dept., coll. marine studies, 1981-89; acad. indust. consultant, 1986—; prof. food sci. U. Del., Newark, 1987-89, prof. emeritus, 1989; v.p. United Chitotechnologies, Inc., Newark, 1989-93; cons. U. Thessaloniki, Greece, 1972-80; vis. prof. U. Panama, 1984-85, sci. advisor, 1985-89; sci. advisor Govt. of Greece, 1972-74; organizer numerous nat. and internat. sci. confs. and symposia over past 23 yrs. Author: Chitin, Chitosan and Related Enzymes, 1984, Advances in Chitin and Chitosan, 1992; mem. editorial bd. Jour. Agr. Food Chemistry, 1983-86; contbr. over 125 articles to profl. jours. Patentee in field. Trustee Riverside Hosp., Wilmington, Del., 1977-84; pres. bd. dirs. Maison Grande Condominium Assn., Inc., Miami Beach, Fla., 1990-92; bd. dirs. Holy Trinity Greek Orthodox Ch., Wilmington, 1971-73; pres. bd. govs. Commondore Condominium Assn., Ft. Lauderdale, Fla., 1993-94. 1st lt. Greek Air Force, 1952-56. Sr. Fulbright scholar, U. Panama, 1984-85; recipient Gold medal and cert. U. Patra, 1973, cert. recognition, commendation for excellence in rsch., edn., pub. svc. Pres. of U. Del., 1977. Mem. AAAS, Am. Chem. Soc. (historian div. agrl. and food chemistry 1980-84, chmn. pub. rels. com. 1980-85, chmn. disting. svc. award com. 1987-88, co-founder, editor div. agrl. and food chemistry membership directory 1980-86, chmn. div. agrl. and food chemistry 1986-87, Disting. Svc. award 1991), N.Y. Acad. Scis., Del. Acad. Sci., Inst. Food Technologists, Am. Inst. Biol. Sci., Am. Chitosci. Soc. (co-founder, trustee, pres. 1989—), Am. Dairy Sci. Assn., Sigma Xi. Avocations: tennis, sailing, swimming, gymnastics, travel. Office: 307 SE 14th St Fort Lauderdale FL 33316-1929

ZIKMUND, BARBARA BROWN, minister, seminary president, church history educator; b. Ann Arbor, Mich., Oct. 16, 1939; d. Henry Daniels and Helen (Langworthy) Brown; m. Joseph Zikmund II, Aug. 26, 1961; 1 child, Brian Joseph. BA, Beloit Coll., 1961; BDiv, Duke U., 1964, PhD, 1969; D in Div (hon.), Doane Coll., 1984, Chgo. Theol. Sem., 1985, Ursinus Coll., 1989. Ordained to ministry United Ch. of Christ, 1964. Instr. Albright Coll., Reading, Pa., 1966-67, Temple U., Phila., 1967-68, Ursinus Coll., Collegeville, Pa., 1968-69; asst. prof. religion studies Albion Coll., Mich., 1970-

75; asst. prof. ch. history, dir. studies Chgo. Theol. Sem., 1975-80; dean and assoc. prof. ch. history Pacific Sch. Religion, Berkeley, Calif., 1981-85, dean and prof. ch. history, 1985-90; pres. Hartford (Conn.) Sem., 1990—; chmn. United Ch. of Christ Hist. Coun., 1983-85, mem. coun. for ecumenism, 1983-89; mem. Nat. Coun. Chs. Commn. on Faith and Order, 1979-87, World Coun. of Chs. Programme Theol. Edn., 1984-91, Nat. Coun. Chs. Working Group on Inter-Faith Rels., 1992—, World Orgn. Confs. Theol. Instns., sec. treas. 1992—; bd. dirs. Mechanics Savings Bank. Author: Discovering the Church, 1983; editor: Hidden Histories in the UCC, 1984, vol. 2, 1987; (with Manschreck) American Religious Experiment, 1976; mem. editorial bd. Jour. Ecumenical Studies, 1987—, Mid-Stream, 1991—; contbr. articles to profl. jours. Mem. City Coun., Albion, Mich., 1972-75; elector Wadsworth Atheneum, 1994—, corporator St. Francis Hosp., 1994—; pres. Greater Hartford Consortium for Higher Edn., 1994—. Woodrow Wilson fellow, 1964-66; NEH grantee, 1974-75; vis. scholar Schlesinger Libr. Women's History, Radcliffe Coll., 1988-89. Mem. Assn. Theol. Schs. (v.p. 1984-86, pres. 1986-88, issues implementation grantee 1983-84), Am. Soc. Ch. History (council 1983-85, pres. elect 1995—), Internat. Assn. Women Ministers (v.p. 1977-79), AAUW (v.p. 1973-75), Greater Hartford C. of C. (bd. dirs. 1992-95). Democrat. Office: Hartford Sem Office of Pres 77 Sherman St Hartford CT 06105-2260

ZIKORUS, ALBERT MICHAEL, golf course architect; b. Needham, Mass., Apr. 9, 1921; s. Walter Peter and Rose Mary (Smith) Z.; m. Charlene Bradstreet Aldrich; 1 child, Michael; m. Joan Gayle Boone, 1979. Student, Mass. State Coll., 1941. Greenskeeper Ould Newbury Golf Course, Newburyport, Mass., 1942, Wellesley (Mass.) Golf Course, 1946, Woodbtidge (Conn.) Golf Course, 1948-51; assoc. William F. Mitchell Architect, 1951-52, Orin E. Smith Architect, Southington, Conn., 1953-58. Designed Tunxis Plantation Country Club, Farmington, Conn., Twin Hills Country Club, Longmeadow, Mass., Timberlin Golf Course, Berlin, Conn., Tashua Golf Course, Trumbull, Conn., Segalla Country Club, Amenia, N.Y., others. Sgt. USAF, 1942-46. Mem. Am. Soc. Golf Course Architects. Avocations: swimming, fishing, hiking, hunting, golf. Home/Office: PO Box 187 Canaan ME 04924-0187 Office: PO Box 187 Canaan ME 04924-0187

ZILBERT, ALLEN BRUCE, education educator, computer consultant; b. Bronx, N.Y., May 26, 1957; s. Murray and Perla Z.; m. Barbara Dale Palley, July 1, 1984; children: Heather Robynne, Jared Lee. BA in Econ., CUNY, 1978; MBA, St. Johns U., 1980, advanced profl. cert., 1982; MEd in Adminstrv. Computer Systems Edn., Columbia U., 1986, EdD, 1988; postgrad., Kennedy-Western U., 1995—. Instr. bus. computer info. systems & quantitative methods Hofstra U., Hempstead, N.Y., 1981-83; asst. prof. info. systems Pace U. Sch. Computer Sci. and Info. Systems, N.Y.C., 1983-89; dir. ancillary systems Advanced Med. Systems, Rockville Ctr., N.Y., 1989-90; asst. prof. mgmt. Long Island U. Sch. Bus., Coll. Mgmt., Brookville, N.Y., 1990-94; asst. prof. mgmt. info. sys. Sy Syms Sch. Bus., David Zysman prof. of mgmt. info. sys. Yeshiva U., N.Y.C., 1994—; mem. curriculum com. Pace U. Sch. Computer Sci. and Info. Sys., 1983-89; chmn. personal computer resources com. Advanced Med. Sys., 1989-90; mem. campuswide computer com. L.I. U., 1991-94, chmn., 1993-94, chmn. scholarship awards com., 1990-91; assembly collegiate schs. bus. curriculum planning com. Coll. Mgmt., 1993-94, chmn. computer needs, usage and stds. com., 1990-93, chmn. mgmt. dept. computer com., chmn. scholar awards com., 1992-93; book and software reviewer. Contbr. articles to profl. jours. Mem. IEEE, Assn. for Computer Tng. and Support, Assn. for Computing Machinery, Data Processing Mgmt. Assn., Internat. Assn. for Computer Info. Sys., Internat. Assn. Mgmt., Info. Resources Mgmt. Assn.

ZILLY, THOMAS SAMUEL, federal judge; b. Detroit, Jan. 1, 1935; s. George Samuel and Bernice M. (McWhinney) Z.; divorced; children: John, Peter, Paul, Luke; m. Jane Greller Noland, Oct. 8, 1988; stepchildren: Allison Noland, Jennifer Noland. BA, U. Mich., 1956; LLD, Cornell U., 1962. Bar: Wash. 1962, U.S. Ct. Appeals (9th cir.) 1962, U.S. Supreme Ct. 1976. Ptnr. Lane, Powell, Moss & Miller, Seattle, 1962-88; judge U.S. Dist. Ct. (we. dist.) Wash., Seattle, 1988—; judge pro tem Seattle Mcpl. Ct., 1972-80. Contbr. articles to profl. jours. Mem. Cen. Area Sch. Council, Seattle, 1969-70; scoutmaster Thunderbird Dist. council Boy Scouts Am. Seattle, 1976-84; bd. dirs. East Madison YMCA. Served to lt. (j.g.) USN, 1956-59. Recipient Tuahku Dist. Service to Youth award Boy Scouts Am., 1983. Mem. ABA, Wash. State Bar Assn., Seattle-King County Bar Assn. (treas. 1979-80, trustee 1980-83, sec. 1983-84, 2d v.p. 1984-85, 1st v.p. 1985-86, pres. 1986-87). Office: US Dist Ct 410 US Courthouse 1010 5th Ave Seattle WA 98104-1130

ZILVERSMIT, DONALD BERTHOLD, nutritional biochemist, educator; b. Hengelo, Holland, July 11, 1919; came to U.S., 1939, naturalized, 1950; s. Herman and Elizabeth (DeWinter) Z.; m. Kitty Fonteyn, June 28, 1945; children: Elizabeth Ann, Dorothy Susan, Sarah Jo. Student, U. Utrecht, Holland, 1936-39, DSc in Phys. Scis. (hon.), 1980, BS, U. Calif., Berkeley, 1940, PhD, 1948. Mem. faculty U. Tenn. Med. Coll., 1948-66, prof., 1956-66; prof. nutrition, prof. biochemistry, molecular and cell biology divs. nutritional sci. and biol. scis. Cornell U., 1966—, prof. emeritus, 1990—; vis. prof. U. Leiden, Holland, 1961-62, Mass. Inst. Tech., 1972-73; vis. fellow Australian Nat. U., Canberra, Australia, 1966; vis. lectr. Venezuela Inst. Sci. Investigations, 1977; career investigator Am. Heart Assn., 1959-89; editor Jour. Lipid Research, 1958-62, Circulation Research, 1962-67, 68-74, Circulation, 1960-65, Biochim. Biophysica Acta, 1969-79, Arteriosclerosis, 1980-90; editor Procs. Soc. Exptl. Biology and Medicine, 1975-87, mem. adv. council, 1978-81; cons. NIH. Editor-in-chief: Jour. of Lipid Research, 1958-61; adv. bd., 1962-72; Contbr. articles to profl. jours. Recipient Borden award, 1976, Disting. Achievement in Nutrition Rsch. award Bristol-Myers Squibb, 1990. Fellow Am. Inst. Nutrition; mem. AAAS, NAS, Am. Physiol. Soc., Am. Soc. Biol. Chemists, Coun. on Arteriosclerosis, Am. Heart Assn. (exec. bd. 1968-70, G. Lyman Duff Meml. award 1978), Soc. Exptl. Biology and Medicine, N.Y. Acad. Scis., Philosophy of Sci. Assn., Soc. Lit. and Sci., Phi Beta Kappa, Sigma Xi. Office: Cornell U Div Nutritional Scis Ithaca NY 14853

ZILVETI, CARLOS BENJAMIN, preventive medicine physician, pediatrician; b. Sucre, Bolivia, June 14, 1928; came to U.S., 1956; s. Carlos and Marina (De La Reza) Z.; m. Halina J. Daszewski, Sept. 8, 1957 (div. Sept. 1976); 1 child: Carlos Joseph III; m. Vita Palazzolo, Sept. 5, 1987. BS, Sacred Heart Coll., Sucre, Bolivia, 1946; MD, U. San Francisco Xavier, Sucre, Bolivia, 1954; MPH, Yale U., 1966. Physician in rural medicine Bolivian Power Co., La Paz, 1955; intern in pediats. and gen. medicine Hosp. Obrero V.P.E., La Paz, 1956; asst. resident in pediats. St. Luke's Hosp., Meml. Cancer Ctr., Woman's Hosp., N.Y.C., 1957-58, Hosp. of St. Raphael, New Haven, Conn., 1958-59; pvt. practice New Haven, Conn., 1960-63; dir. maternal-child health New Haven Dept. Health, 1964-74; regional med. officer South and Ctrl. Am. Peace Corps, Bogota, Colombia, 1975-76; regional med. officer West Africa Peace Corps, Liberia, Ghana, Togo, 1976-79; chief environ. medicine Wilford Hall Med. Ctr. USAF, San Antonio, 1979-83, cons. preventive and occupl. medicine, 1983-91; ret. USAF, 1991, cons. aerospace-preventive medicine; cons. FDA, HEW, Washington, 1966-75; cons. to Headstart Am. Acad. Pediats., Stanford-Norwalk, Conn., 1968-75; regional med. officer, sci. attache West Africa U.S. Dept. State. Contbr. articles to profl. jours. Chmn. gov.'s task force Conn. State Dept. HEalth, Hartford, 1969-75. Fellow Am. Acad. Pediats. (emeritus), Am. Coll. Preventive Medicine; mem. APHA, AMA, New Eng. Pub. Health Assn., Conn. Acad. Preventive Medicine, Am. Occupl. Med. Assn. Avocations: long distance swimming, tennis, golf, international travel, classical music. Home: 9222 Dover Ridge San Antonio TX 78250-3557

ZIMA, MICHAEL DAVID, lawyer; b. St Louis, Aug. 13, 1968; s. Marvin Walter Z. BA, U. Mich., 1990; JD, Ind. U., 1993. Atty. Dist. Coun. IRS, Jacksonville, Fla., 1993—. Author: (short story) The Brook, 1994, The Play, 1994. Mem. Ind. State Bar. Avocations: tennis, golf, basketball, waterskiing, writing. Home: 8787 Southside Blvd # 918 Jacksonville FL 32256 Office: Dist Counsel IRS 400 W Bay St Rm 564 Jacksonville FL 32202-4410

ZIMAND, HARVEY FOLKS, lawyer; b. N.Y.C., Aug. 28, 1928; s. Savel and Gertrude (Folks) Z.; m. Ingeborg Rockosch, 1963 (div. 1980); children—Patricia Folks, Stephanie Folks; m. Noel French, Apr. 30, 1983. B.A., Colgate U., 1950; postgrad., Oxford U., Eng., 1950; M.A., U. Chgo., 1951; postgrad., Columbia U., 1952-53; LL.B., Yale U., 1957. Bar: N.Y. 1957. Rapporteur Council for Fgn. Relations, N.Y.C., 1952-53; atty. Dept. Navy, Washington, 1956-70; ptnr. Kelley Drye & Warren, N.Y.C., 1970—; dir. Toronto-Dominion Trust Co., N.Y.C. Bd. dirs. Virginia Day Nursery, N.Y.C., 1980-84. Served to cpl. U.S. Army, 1951-53. Fellow N.Y. Bar Found., Am. Coll. Probate Counsel; mem. ABA, N.Y. State Bar Assn., Assn. Bar City of N.Y., Estate Planning Council. Republican. Episcopalian. Clubs: Yale (N.Y.C.); Randolph Mountain (N.H.). Home: 120 E 81st St New York NY 10028-1428 Office: Kelley Drye & Warren LLP 101 Park Ave New York NY 10178

ZIMBALIST, EFREM, III, publishing company executive. BA in Econs., Harvard U., 1968, MBA, 1972. Sr. engagement mgr. McKinsey and Co., Inc., L.A., 1972-77; chmn., CEO, Correia Art Glass, Inc., 1977-92; asst. to group v.p. newspapers Times Mirror, N.Y.C., 1992-93, v.p. strategic devel., 1995; pres., CEO, Times Mirror Mags., Inc., N.Y.C., 1995—; bd. dirs. Cheniere Energy; trustee Hartford Courant Founds. Mem. nat. coun. House Ear Inst.; chmn. emeritus bd. trustees Robert Louis Stevenson Sch. Officer M.I., U.S. Army, 1969-70, Vietnam. Office: Times Mirror Mags Inc Two Park Ave New York NY 10016-5695

ZIMBARDO, PHILIP GEORGE, psychologist, educator, writer; b. N.Y.C., Mar. 23, 1933; s. George and Margaret (Bisicchia) Z.; m. Christina Maslach, Aug. 10, 1972; children: Zara, Tanya; 1 son by previous marriage, Adam. AB, Bklyn. Coll., 1954; MS, Yale U., 1955, PhD, 1959; hon. degree, U. Peru, 1996, Pacific Grad. Sch. Psychology, 1996. Asst. prof. psychology Yale U., New Haven, 1959-61, NYU, N.Y.C., 1961-67; vis. assoc. prof. psychology Columbia U., N.Y.C., 1967-68; prof. psychology Stanford (Calif.) U., 1968—; pres. P.G. Zimbardo, Inc., San Francisco. Author: Cognitive Control of Motivation, 1969, Canvassing or Peace, 1970, Psychology and You, 1976, Shyness, What It Is, What To Do About It, 1977, Influencing Attitudes and Changing Behavior, rev. edit., 1977, The Shyness Workbook, 1979, A Parent's Guide to the Shy Child, 1981, The Psychology of Attitude Change and Social Influence, 1991, Psychology and Life, rev. edit., 1996. Pres. Montclair Ter. Assn., 1975—; sr. project advisor Exploratorium, 1993; host, writer, gen. acad. advisor PBS-TV series Discovering Psychology, 1987-90. Ctr. for Advanced Study of Behavioral Scis. fellow, 1971; recipient Peace medal Tokyo Police Dept., 1972, City Medal of Honor, Salamanca, Spain, Disting. Tchr. award Am. Psychol. Found., 1975. Mem. APA (Presdl. citation Discovery Psychology series 1994), AAAS, AAUP, Internat. Congress Psychology, Western Psychol. Assn. (pres. 1983), Ea. Psychol. Assn., Calif. Psychol. Assn. (Disting. Contbn. to Rsch. award 1978), Can. Psychol. Assn., Soc. for Psychol. Study of Social Issues, Soc. for Clin. and Exptl. Hypnosis, Sigma Xi, Phi Beta Kappa, Psi Chi. Roman Catholic. Home: 25 Montclair Ter San Francisco CA 94109-1517 Office: Stanford U Psychology Dept Stanford CA 94305 *One of the few virtues of growing up in a poor urban ghetto is the realization that people are the most important resource we have—to be used wisely, well and as often as possible. The second is the tempering of book learning by street wits. The third is to value a career that allows me to contribute to improving the quality of our lives through research and teaching.*

ZIMENT, IRWIN, medical educator; b. England, 1936. MB BChir, Cambridge U., 1961. Intern, resident England, 1961-64, USA, 1964-65; resident Bronx Mcpl. Hosp. Ctr., 1965-66; dir. respiratory therpay Harbor Gen. Hosp., Torrance, Calif., 1968-75; chief medicine Olive View-UCLA Med. Ctr., 1975—, med. dir., 1994-97; prof. medicine UCLA Sch. Medicine, 1980—. Contbr. articles to profl. jours. Infectious Disease fellow Wadsworth VA Hosp., L.A., 1966-68. Mem. Am. Thoracic Soc. (clin. problems assembly chmn. 1981-82, resp. bd. med. advisors 1986-90), Am. Coll. Chest Physicians (mem. editl. bd.), Nat. Assn. Med. Dir. Respiratory Care (founding mem., vice pres. 1978, treas. 1979-81, bd. dirs. 1983-89), Calif Thoracic Soc. (pres. 1980-81, various coms. 1970-85), L.A. Lung Assn. (various coms. 1969-86). Office: Olive View-UCLA Med Ctr Dept of Med Rm 2B-182 14445 Olive View Dr Sylmar CA 91342-1495

ZIMERING, MARK BERNARD, endocrinologist, researcher; b. St. Paul, Feb. 7, 1955; s. Ruben and Sabina (Sczwarz) Z.; m. Laurie Ellen Friedlander, May 26, 1984; chidren: Yvette Francine, Jeffrey Hale. AB, Harvard Coll., 1977; PhD, Yeshiva U., 1983, MD, 1984. Diplomate Am. Bd. Internal Medicine. Internal medicine intern, resident Hennepin County Med. Ctr., Mpls., 1984-86; med. staff fellow NIH, Bethesda, Md., 1986-90; assoc. prof. medicine UMDNJ/Robert Wood Johnson Med. Sch., New Brunswick, N.J., 1991—; staff endocrinologist Vets. Affairs Med. Ctr., Lyons, N.J., 1990—; co-chmn. N.J. State Vets. Health Adminstrn. Diabetes Adv. Com., East Orange, 1995-96. Contbr. articles to profl. jours.; reviewer Jour. Clin. Endocrinology & Metabolism, 1994-96. Awarded grants in aid Merck Rsch. Labs., Rahway, N.J., 1991-97. Mem. AAAS, The Endocrine Soc., The Am. Diabetes Assn. Avocation: playing and coaching soccer. Office: Vets Affairs Med Ctr Med Svc Lyons NJ 07939

ZIMET, CARL NORMAN, psychologist, educator; b. Vienna, Austria, June 3, 1925; came to U.S., 1943, naturalized, 1945; s. Leon and Gisela (Kosser) Z.; m. Sara F. Goodman, June 4, 1950; children: Andrew, Gregory. BA, Cornell U., 1949; PhD, Syracuse U., 1953; postdoctoral fellow, Standard U., 1953-55. Diplomate in clin. psychology Am. Bd. Profl. Psychology (trustee 1966-74). Instr., then asst. prof. psychology and psychiatry Yale U., 1955-63; mem. faculty U. Colo. Med. Center, 1963—, prof. clin. psychology, 1965—, head div., 1963—; Mem. Colo. Bd. Psychol. Examiners, 1966-72, Colo. Mental Health Planning Commn., 1964-66; mem. acad. adv. com. John F. Kennedy Child Devel. Center, U. Colo., 1966—; chmn. Council for Nat. Register of Health Service Providers in Psychology, 1975-85, pres., mem. exec. bd. div. psychotherapy, 1970—; chair exec. com. Assn. Psychol. Internship Ctrs., 1988-91. Bd. editors: Jour. Clin. Psychology, 1962—, Jour. Clin. and Cons. Psychology, 1964-73, Psychotherapy, 1967—, Profl. Psychology, 1969-75. With USNR, 1943-46. Recipient Disting. Service award Colo. Psychol. Assn., 1976. Fellow APA (council reps. 1969-72, 73—, bd. dirs. 1985-88, Disting. award for profl. contbn. 1987, div. psychotherapy and div. clin. psychology), Soc. Personality Assessment (pres. 1975-76, bd. dirs., chair gen. psychol. services 1987—); mem. Am. Acad. Clin. Psychology (pres. 1993—), Denver Psychoanalytic (trustee 1968-71), Am. Group Psychotherapy Assn., Med. Sch. Profs. Psychology (pres. 1992-94). Home: 4325 E 6th Ave Denver CO 80220-4939

ZIMET, LLOYD, psychologist, health planner, educator; b. Bklyn., Oct. 5, 1951; s. Victor R. and Marcia (Sorkin) Z. BA, Whittier (Calif.) Coll., 1973; MA, U. Md., 1983, PhD, 1984; MPH, NYU, 1989. Head basketball coach Aarhus (Denmark) U., 1973-78, 80-82, 85-86; resident dir. U. Md., College Park, 1978-80; sports supr. Montgomery County (Md.) Dept. of Recreation, 1978, 82-84; dir. health promotion Optimal Fitness Inc., N.Y.C., 1986-91; internat. cons. cmty. and occupational health, 1991—; dir. edn. AIDS Ctr. of Queens (N.Y.) County, 1989-90; dir. Patricia Manning Meml. Fund childhood cancer Am. Cancer Soc., Queens, 1988-95; mem. AIDS adv. com. N.Y.C. Bd. of Edn., 1989-90; mem. adv. bd. Adolescent Health Network, Queens, 1989-90; keynote speaker NYU Health Edn. Alumni, 1990, USPHS Region II Conf., 1991. Bd. govs. U.S. Amateur Boxing Fedn., Colorado Springs, Colo., 1988-91; bd. dirs. Met. Amateur Boxing Fedn., N.Y.C., 1988-91; mem. USA Boxing Nat. Scholarship com., 1984-88. Fellow Soc. Pub. Health Educators; mem. APHA, APA.

ZIMKAS, CHARLES PATRICK, JR., space foundation director; b. Scranton, Pa., Sept. 8, 1940; s. Charles Zimkas Sr. and Margaret (Bakunas) Sullick; m. Ursula Frediel Marten; children: Robert L., Uwe F., Michael P., Brian David. Enlisted USAF, advanced through grades to chief master sgt., 1958; dep. chief of staff, personnel adminstrv. div. Aerospace Def. Command, Colorado Springs, Colo., 1971-74; exec. to dep. chief of staff personnel Aerospace Def. Command, Colorado Springs, 1975-80; chief of adminstrn. Air Forces Iceland, Keflavik, 1974-75; first sr. enlisted advisor USAF Space Command, Colorado Springs, 1980-84; ret., 1984; dir. regional devel. Noncommissioned Officers Assn., San Antonio, 1984-86; dir. ops. U.S. Space Found., Colorado Springs, 1986—. Named Air Force Outstanding Airman of Yr., 1978; recipient Air Force Legion Merit. Mem. Noncommd. Officers Assn. (bd. dirs. 1978-84, chmn. bd. dirs. 1982-84, Order of Sword award 1978, Excalibur award 1979), Air Force Assn. (pres. Lance P. Sijan chpt., medal of merit 1990, 94, exceptional svc. award 1996). Home: 729 Drew Dr Colorado Springs CO 80911-2606 Office: US Space Found 2860 S Circle Dr Ste 2301 Colorado Springs CO 80906-4107

ZIMM, BRUNO HASBROUCK, physical chemistry educator; b. Woodstock, N.Y., Oct. 31, 1920; s. Bruno L. and Louise S. (Hasbrouck) Z.; m. Georgianna S. Grevatt, June 17, 1944; children: Louis H., Carl B. Grad., Kent (Conn.) Sch., 1938; A.B., Columbia U., 1941, M.S., 1943, Ph.D., 1944. Research assoc. Columbia U., 1944; research assoc., instr. Polytech. Inst. Bklyn., 1944-46; instr. chemistry U. Calif. at Berkeley, 1946-47, asst. prof., 1947-50, assoc. prof., 1950-51; vis. lectr. Harvard U., 1950-51; research assoc. research lab. Gen. Electric Co., 1951-60; prof. chemistry U. Calif., San Diego, 1960-91, prof. emeritus, 1991—. Assoc. editor: Jour. Chem. Physics, 1947-49; adv. bd.: Jour. Polymer Sci, 1953-62, Jour. Bio-Rheology, 1962-73, Jour. Biopolymers, 1963—, Jour. Phys. Chemistry, 1963-68, Jour. Biophys. Chemistry, 1973—. Recipient Bingham Medal Soc. Rheology, 1960, High Polymer Physics prize Am. Phys. Soc., 1963; Kirkwood medal Yale U., 1982. Mem. Biophys. Soc., Am. Soc. Biol. Chemists and Molecular Biologists, Am. Chem. Soc. (Baekeland award 1957), Nat. Acad. Scis. (award in Chem. Scis. 1981), Am. Acad. Arts and Scis., Am. Phys. Soc.

ZIMMAR, GEORGE PETER, publishing executive, psychology educator; b. Chgo., Dec. 31, 1937; s. Peter George and Sofia (Kanellis) Z.; m. Doulie J. Pappas; children: Sofia Corrine, Peter David George. BS in Psychology, Roosevelt U., 1960, MS in Exptl. Psychology, 1961; PhD in Neurosci., SUNY, Buffalo, 1966; postgrad., MIT, 1968. Rsch. assoc. Northwestern U. Med. Sch., Chgo., 1960-61; instr. psychology SUNY, Buffalo, 1962-64; asst. prof. Grinnell (Iowa) Coll., 1965-69; prof., chmn. dept. Briarcliff Coll., Briarcliff Manor, N.Y., 1970-77; editor Praeger Pubs., N.Y.C., 1978-81; sr. editor CBS Pub. Group/Elsevier, N.Y.C., 1981-88; editor-in-chief Rowman & Littlefield Pubs., Totowa, N.J., 1988-89; sr. editor Springer-Verlag, N.Y.C., 1989-92; pres. Youth Edn. Systems, Inc., Scarborough, N.Y., 1985—, also chmn. bd. dirs.; adj. prof. Pace U., Pleasantville, N.Y., 1977, NYU, 1991—; v.p., bd. dirs. McGraw Learning Labs. Inc., Dobbs Ferry, N.Y., 1970-774; bd. dirs. Psychosocial Press, Madison, Conn. Author: Chronology of Wars, 1989; contbr. articles to profl. jours. Pres. Ch. of Our Saviour, Rye, N.Y., 1981-82, bd. dirs., 1973—; capital campaign officer Hackley Sch., Tarrytown, N.Y., 1988; bd. trustees Soc. Preservation Greek Heritage, Washington, 1997—. Hillman fellow Roosevelt U., 1961, Sloan Found. fellow, 1968; Cattell grantee Grinnell Coll., 1967. Mem. APA, Am. Psychol. Soc. (charter), Cognite Sci. Soc., Sigma Xi. Greek Orthodox. Office: Youth Edn Systems Inc Scarborough Station Briarcliff Manor NY 10510

ZIMMER, DONALD WILLIAM, coach professional athletics, former professional baseball manager; b. Cin., Jan. 17, 1931; s. Harold Lesley and Lorraine Bertha (Ernst) Z.; m. Jean Carol Bauerle, Aug. 16, 1951; children: Thomas Jeffrey, Donna Jean. Student pub. schs., Cin. Baseball player Dodger Farm Clubs, 1949-54, Bklyn. Dodgers, 1954-57, Los Angeles Dodgers, 1958-59, Chgo. Cubs, 1960-61, N.Y. Mets, 1962, Cin. Reds, 1962, Los Angeles Dodgers, 1963, Washington Senators, 1963-65, Toei Flyers, Tokyo, 1966; mgr. Cin. Reds Farm Clubs, Knoxville and Buffalo, 1967, Indpls., 1968; mgr. San Diego Padre Farm Clubs, Key West, Fla., 1969, Padre Farm Club, Salt Lake City, 1970; coach Montreal Expos, Que., Can., 1971; mgr. San Diego Padres, 1972-73; coach Boston Red Sox, 1974-76, mgr., 1976-80; mgr. Tex. Rangers, 1981-82; coach N.Y. Yankees, 1983, 86, 96—, Chgo. Cubs, 1984, 85, 86, San Francisco Giants, 1987; mgr. Chgo. Cubs, 1988-91; coach Boston Red Sox, 1992, Colo. Rockies, Denver, 1993-95; mem. minor league All-Star Teams, Hornell, N.Y., 1950, Elmira, N.Y., 1951, Mobile, Ala., 1952, St. Paul, 1953; player World Series teams 1955, 56, 59, coach 1975, 96. Recipient Bill Stern award NBC, 1949; named St. Paul Rookie of Yr., 1953; mem. All Star Team, 1961, 78, 81, 90; named Nat. League Mgr. of Yr. 1989. Mem. Profl. Baseball Players Am. (life), Old Time Ball Players Wis. Office: care NY Yankees Yankees Stadium Bronx NY 10451

ZIMMER, JOHN HERMAN, lawyer; b. Sioux Falls, S.D., Dec. 30, 1922; s. John Francis and Veronica (Berke) Z.; student Augustana Coll., Sioux Falls, 1941-42, Mont. State Coll., 1943; LLB, U. S.D., 1948; m. Deanna Langner, 1976; children by previous marriage: Mary Zimmer Quinlin, Robert Joseph, Judith Maureen Zimmer Rose. Bar: S.D. 1948. Pvt. practice, Turner County, S.D., 1948—; of counsel Zimmer, Duncan & Cole, Parker, S.D., 1992—; states atty. Turner County, 1955-58, 62-64; asst. prof. med. jurisprudence U. S.D.; minority counsel U.S. Senate Armed Services Com. on Strategic and Critical Materials Investigation, 1962-63; chmn. Southeastern Council Govts., 1973-75; mem. U. S.D. Law Sch. adv. council, 1973-74. Chmn. Turner County Rep. Com., 1955-56; mem. S.D. Rep. adv. com., 1959-60; alt. del. Rep. Nat. Conv., 1968; pres. S.D. Easter Seal Soc., 1986-87. Served with AUS, 1943-46; PTO. Decorated Bronze Star, Philippine Liberation ribbon. Mem. ABA, Fed., S.D. (commr. 1954-57) Bar Assns., Assn. Trial Lawyers Am., S.D. Trial Lawyers Assn. (pres. 1967-68), VFW, Am. Legion, Elks, Shrinters, Phi Delta Phi. Home: RRI PO Box 640 Parker SD 57053 Office: Zimmer & Duncan Law Bldg PO Box 550 Parker SD 57053-0547

ZIMMER, LAWRENCE WILLIAM, JR., sports announcer; b. New Orleans, Nov. 13, 1935; s. Lawrence W. Sr. and Theodora (Ahrens) Z.; m. Dawn M. Caillouet, June 4, 1955 (div. June 1972); children: Larry III, Tracey; m. Brigitte Bastian, Nov. 17, 1972. Student, La. State U., 1953-55; BJ, U. Mo., 1957. Sports dir. KFRU Radio, Columbia, Mo., 1960-66; asst. mgr. programming WAAM Radio, Ann Arbor, Mich., 1966-71; sportscaster, sports dir. KOA Radio, Denver, 1971—. Bd. mem. Colo. Ski Mus. and Hall of Fame, Vail, 1981—, Opera Colo., Denver, 1985—. 1st lt. U.S. Army, 1958-60. Named Colo. Sportscaster of the Yr., Nat. Sportscasters and Sportswriters Assn., Salisbury, N.C., 1988, 90, 91, Broadcaster of the Yr., Colo. Broadcaster's Assn., Denver, 1995. Avocations: skiing, jogging, opera. Office: KOA Radio 1380 Lawrence St Ste 300 Denver CO 80204-2055

ZIMMER, PAUL JEROME, publisher, editor, poet; b. Canton, Ohio, Sept. 18, 1934; s. Jerome Francis and Louise Celina (Surmont) Z.; m. Suzanne Jane Koklauner, Apr. 4, 1959; children: Erik Jerome, Justine Mary. BA, Kent State U., 1959. Assoc. dir. U. Pitts. Press, 1967-78; dir. U. Ga. Press, Athens, 1978-84, U. Iowa Press, Iowa City, 1984—. Author: (poetry) Family Reunion, 1983 (AAAL award 1985), The Great Bird of Love, 1989 (award Nat. Poetry Series 1989), Big Blue Train, 1993, Crossing to Sunlight: Selected Poems, 1996. With U.S. Army, 1954-55. Avocation: collecting antique photography. Home: 730 E College St Iowa City IA 52240 Office: U Iowa Press 119 W Park Rd Iowa City IA 52246-2307

ZIMMER, RICHARD ALAN, lawyer; b. Newark, N.J., Aug. 16, 1944; s. William and Evelyn (Schlank Rader) Z.; m. Marfy Goodspeed, Dec. 27, 1965; children: Carl William, Benjamin Goodspeed. BA, Yale U., 1966, LLB, 1969. Bar: N.Y. 1971, U.S. Dist. Ct. (so. and ea. dists.) N.Y. 1974, N.J. 1975, U.S. Dist. Ct. N.J. 1975, U.S. Supreme Ct. 1980. Assoc. Cravath, Swaine and Moore, N.Y.C., 1969-75; gen. atty. Johnson & Johnson, New Brunswick, N.J., 1976-91; mem. N.J. Gen. Assembly, 1982-87, chmn. state govt. com., 1986-87; mem. N.J. Senate, 1987-91, 102nd-103rd Congresses from 12th N.J. dist., Washington, D.C., 1991-96; with Dechert Price & Rhoads, Princeton, 1997—; lectr. in pub. and internat. affairs Woodrow Wilson Sch., Princeton U., 1997—. Treas. Hunterdon Hospice, Flemington, N.J., 1984-86, Hunterdon Med. Ctr. Capital Campaign, 1997; chmn. Citizens for a Better N.J., 1997—. Mem. ABA, N.J. State Bar Assn., Hunterdon County Bar Assn. Republican. Home: Locktown-Flemington Rd Flemington NJ 08822-9541 Office: Dechert Price & Rhoads Princeton Pike Corp Ctr POB 5218 Princeton NJ 08543

ZIMMER, WILLIAM HOMER, JR., retired insurance company executive; b. Cin., Mar. 3, 1930; s. William Homer and Esther Caroline (Krueger) Z.; m. Virginia Louise Avey, June 27, 1951; children: William H. III, Amy Zimmer Schneider. BSBA, Ohio State U., 1952. Staff asst. Cin. Gas & Electric Co., 1952, asst. treas., treas.-sec., v.p. fin., sr. v.p. fin.; vice chmn. Cin. Fin. Corp., 1981-95; ret., 1995; bd. dirs. Alltel Corp., Little Rock. Former trustee Bethesda Hosp. Mem. The Oaks (Sarasota, Fla.), Western Hills Country Club, Double Eagle Country Club (Galena, Ohio), Queen City Club, Masons (33 deg.). Presbyterian. Avocations: golf, fishing, travel. Home: 5883 Countryhills Dr Cincinnati OH 45233-1727

ZIMMERLY, JAMES GREGORY, lawyer, physician; b. Longview, Tex., Mar. 25, 1941; s. George James and Irene Gertrude (Kohler) Z.; m. Nancy Carol Zimmerly, June 11, 1966; children: Mark, Scott, Robin; m. Johanna

Bross Huffer, Feb. 14, 1991. BA, Gannon Coll., 1962; MD, U. Md., 1966, JD, 1969; MPH, Johns Hopkins U., 1968. Bar: Md. 1970, D.C. 1972, U.S. Ct. Mil. Appeals 1973, U.S. Supreme Ct. 1973. Ptnr. Acquisto, Asplen & Morstein, Ellicott City, Md., 1970—. Chmn. dept. legal medicine Armed Forces Inst. Pathology, 1971-91; prof. George Washington U., 1972-80; adj. prof. law Georgetown U. Law Ctr., 1972—, Antioch Sch. Law, 1977-80; assoc. prof. U. Md. Sch. Medicine, 1973—; mem. sci. adv. bd. Armed Forces Inst. Path., 1997—; cons. Dept. Def., Dept. Justice, HHS, VA, 1971-91. Fellow Am. Acad. Forensic Scis., Am. Coll. Legal Medicine, (pres. 1980-81), Am. Coll Preventive Medicine; mem. ABA, Md. Bar Assn., Am. Soc. on Law and Medicine, Am. Coll. Emergency Physicians, Md. Med. Soc. Editor: Legal Aspects of Medical Practice, 1978-88, Jour. Legal Medicine, 1975-78, Md. Med. Jour., 1977-88, Lawyers' Med. Ency., 1980-90, chrmn. bd. dirs. Baltimore Rh Lab., 1984—, Med. Dir. Monumental Life Ins. Co., 1994—, chrmn. Am. Coll. Legal Med. Fdn., Bd. Dirs., 1996—. Home: 6300 Old National Pike Bluestone Overlook Boonsboro MD 21713 Office: Monumental Life Ins Co 2 E Chase St Baltimore MD 21202-2505

ZIMMERMAN, AARON MARK, lawyer; b. Syracuse, N.Y., Jan. 28, 1953; s. Julius and Sara (Lavine) Z. B.S., Syracuse U., 1974, J.D., 1976. Bar: N.Y. 1977, Pa. 1977, D.C. 1978, S.C. 1978, Fla. 1978, U.S. Dist. Ct. S.C. 1978, U.S. Dist. Ct. (no. dist.) N.Y. Corp. atty., asst. sec. Daniel Internat. Corp., Greenville, S.C., 1977-79; ptnr. Abend, Driscoll & Zimmerman, 1979-81; Zimmerman Law Office, Syracuse, 1981—. Bd. dirs. Syracuse Friends Ametuer Boxing, 1982-92. Mem. Am. Arbitration Assn. (arbitrator), Workers Compensation Com. N.Y. State Bar (exec. com. 1984—), Workers Compensation Assn. of Cen. N.Y. (charter mem., dir., treas. 1980-95), N.Y. State Bar, S.C. State Bar, D.C. State Bar, Fla. State Bar, ABA. Lodge: Masons. Home: 602 Standish Dr Syracuse NY 13224-2018 Office: 117 S State St Syracuse NY 13202-1103

ZIMMERMAN, ANITA ELOISE, elementary education educator; b. Wilkes-Barre, Pa., Apr. 27, 1954; d. Edward Martin and Ada Eloise (Jacoby) Mushal; m. Jeffrey Zimmerman, June 19, 1976. BS in Elem. Edn./Early Childhood Edn., Coll. Misericordia, 1976; M Equivalency, various univs., State of Pa., 1986. Cert. elem. edn. and early childhood edn. tchr., Pa. Tchr. third grade Hunlock Creek (Pa.) Elem. N.W. Area Sch. Dist., 1976—; Rif co-coord. Hunlock Elem. PTO, 1978—, newsletter coord., 1978—, numerous offices to pres. 1992—; tchr. mentor N.W. Area Sch. Dist., Shickshinny, Pa., 1989. Pianist Roaring Brook Bapt. Ch., 1980—, asst. organist, 1980—, asst. music dir., 1980—. Recipient Encouragement of Outstanding Young Writers award Luzerne County Poetry Soc., Wilkes-Barre, 1990. Mem. N.W. Area Edn. Assn. (rep. 1986-87). Republican. Avocations: pianist, vocal soloist, organist, reading, author children's plays. Office: Hunlock Creek Elem RR 1 Hunlock Creek PA 18621-9801

ZIMMERMAN, BERNARD, judge; b. Munich, Bavaria, Fed. Republic Germany, May 31, 1946; came to U.S., 1949; s. Sam and Roza (Spodek) Z.; m. Grace L. Suarez, Oct. 23, 1976; children: Elizabeth, Adam, David, Dara Bylah. AB, U. Rochester, 1967; JD, U. Chgo., 1970. Bar: Calif. 1971, La. 1971, U.S. Supreme Ct. 1975, U.S. Dist. Ct. (no., ea., cen. and so. dists.) Calif., U.S. Dist. Ct. (ea. dist.) La., U.S. Ct. Appeals (9th cir.). Law. clk. chief judge U.S. Dist. Ct. (ea. dist.) La., New Orleans, 1970-71; asst. prof. law La. State U., Baton Rouge, 1971-72; ptnr. Pillsbury, Madison & Sutro, San Francisco, 1972-95; legal cons. 3d Constnl. Conv. Commonwealth of the No. Mariana Islands, Northern Mariana Islands, 1995; U.S. magistrate judge U.S. Dist. Ct. (no. dist.) Calif., 1995—; dep. pub. defender City of San Francisco, 1975; arbitrator U.S. Dist. Ct., San Francisco, AAA; judge pro tem San Francisco Superior and Mcpl. Cts. Bd. dirs., mem. exec. com. San Francisco Lawyers' Com. on Urban Affairs, 1984-95, treas., 1987; mem. regional bd. Anti-Defamation League, 1989-95. Mem. Phi Beta Kappa. Democrat. Jewish. Club: Olympic (San Francisco). Office: 450 Golden Gate Ave San Francisco CA 94102

ZIMMERMAN, BERNARD, investment banker; b. Bklyn., Dec. 7, 1932; s. Jacob and Pearl (Schechner) Z.; BBA, City Coll. N.Y., 1954; MBA, NYU, 1957; m. Joyce M. Singer, Dec. 24, 1960; children: Wayne Jay, Ellen Holly. CPA, N.Y. Fin. exec. consumer products Spartans Industries, Inc., N.Y.C., 1961-65; sr. v.p. Scheinman, Hochstin, and Trotta, Inc., N.Y.C., 1965-72; pres. Bernard Zimmerman and Co., Inc., 1972—, Beacon Hill Mgmt., Inc., 1994—; sr. v.p. corp. fin. Gruntal & Co., Inc., 1983-84; pres., chmn. bd., pres. St. Lawrence Seaway Corp., Indpls., 1985-93, fin. cons.; sr. v.p. The Zimmerman Group, Inc., 1991-96; chmn. bd. dirs., pres. Beacon Hill Mutual Fund, Inc., Boston, 1994-97; liquidating trustee Unity Buying Svc. Co. Liquidating Trust, Hicksville, N.Y.; bd. dirs. Sbarro, Inc., Commack, N.Y.; fin. cons. Beautiful Visions-U.S.A., Ltd., Bethpage, N.Y. Bd. dirs. Inst. Cancer Rsch. and Molecular Medicine, Thomas Jefferson U., Phila.; trustee Sharro Family Found., Commack, 1993—; mem. Nat. Assn. Corp. Dir. Blue Ribbon Commn. on Corp. Greviance-Best Practice Coun., 1997. With AUS, 1955-57. Mem. N.Y. State Soc. CPAs, Am. Arbitration Assn., N.Y. Road Runners Club. Home and Office: 18 High Meadow Rd Weston CT 06883-2946

ZIMMERMAN, BRYANT KABLE, retired lawyer; b. Mt. Morris, Ill., Nov. 19, 1922; s. Milo D. and Hazel G. (Kable) Z.; m. Harriet Bong, Jan. 20, 1946; children: Paula, Keith, Craig. A.B., Augustana Coll., 1946; student, Washington U., St. Louis, 1942-43; LL.B., Harvard U., 1948. Bar: Calif. 1949. Assoc. counsel McCutchen, Doyle, Brown & Enersen, San Francisco, 1949-63; v.p., gen. counsel FrancoWestern Oil Co., Bakersfield, Calif., 1963-65; sr. v.p., sec., chief legal officer, dir. Guy F. Atkinson Co., South San Francisco, Calif., 1965-88; of counsel Pettit & Martin, San Francisco, 1988-95. Bd. dirs., v.p. Rep. Alliance, 1965-74; bd. dirs., sec. Atkinson Found., 1967-88; trustee Willamette U., 1978-90; chmn. Nat. Constrn. Employers Coun., 1985-86, Californians for Compensation Reform, 1984-88; chmn. Coun. on Multiemployer Pension Security, 1983-86; pres. United Meth. Found., 1991-97. With USAAF, 1942-46. Mem. Nat. Constructors Assn. (bd. dirs. 1980-83, chmn. 1983). Home: 75 Del Monte Dr Hillsborough CA 94010-6226

ZIMMERMAN, DON, film editor. Prodns. include: Coming Home, 1978, Heaven Can Wait, 1978, Uncle Joe Shannon, 1978, Being There, 1979, A Change of Seasons, 1980, Barbarosa, 1982, Rocky III, 1982, Best Friends, 1982, Staying Alive, 1983, Teachers, 1984, Rocky IV, 1985, Cobra, 1986, Over the Top, 1986, Fatal Beauty, 1987, Everybody's All-American, 1988, The Package, 1989, Navy Seals, 1990. Office: The Gersh Agy 232 N Canon Dr Beverly Hills CA 90210-5302*

ZIMMERMAN, DON CHARLES, plant physiologist, biochemist; b. Fargo, N.D., Feb. 27, 1934. BS, N.D. State U., 1955, MS, 1959, PhD in Biochemistry, 1964. Rsch. chemist sci. and edn. adminstrn. agrl. rsch. USDA, 1959—, ctr. dir. argl. rsch. svc., 1988—; asst. prof. N.D. State U., 1964-69, adj. prof. biochemistry, 1969—. Mem. AAAS, Am. Soc. Plant Physiology. Office: No Dakota Univ USDA Red River Vly Agrl Rsch Ctr Univ Sta PO Box 5677 Fargo ND 58105

ZIMMERMAN, D(ONALD) PATRICK, lawyer; b. Albany, N.Y., Mar. 20, 1942; s. Bernard M. and Helen M. (Eshelman) Z. Student Lawrenceville Sch., 1960; BA, Rollins Coll., 1964; JD, Dickinson Sch. Law, 1967. Bars: Pa. 1968, U.S. Supreme Ct. 1971. Atty., Legal Aid, 1968-69; pub. defender, Lancaster County, Pa., 1969-72; sole practice, Lancaster, Pa., 1974—; instr. Ct. Common Pleas for Constables, 1976—; solicitor Lancaster County Dep. Sheriff Assn., 1977—, Lancaster County Constable Assn., 1975—; instr. sheriff's dept. Lancaster County for Dep. Sheriffs, 1978—; of counsel to Dep. Sheriff Assn. Pa., 1979-81; spl. counsel Pa. State Constables Assn., 1981; chmn. Bd. Arbitrators Lancaster County, 1975-81; spl. counsel Legislative Com. to Constable Assn. Pa., 1982; mem. pastoral coun. St. Anthony's Catholic Ch., 1995—. Recipient Ofcl. Commendation of Merit, Lancaster County Sheriff's Dept., 1979, Ofcl. Commendation of Merit Fraternal Order Police State Lodge 66, 1985, Outstanding Svc. award, 1987, Disting. Service award Fraternal Order State Police Pa., 1987, Outstanding Leadership award, 1988. Mem. ABA, Am. Trial Lawyers Assn., Pa. Bar Assn., Lancaster County Bar Assn. Author: The Pennsylvania Landlord and Tenant Handbook, 1982, revised edit., 1993; contbr. articles to profl. jours. Office: 214 E King St Lancaster PA 17602-2977

ZIMMERMAN, EARL ABRAM, physician, scientist, educator, neuroendocrinology researcher; b. Harrisburg, Pa., May 5, 1937; s. Earl Beckley and Hazel Marie (Myers) Z. B.S. in Chemistry, Franklin and Marshall Coll., 1959; M.D., U. Pa., 1963. Diplomate Am. Bd. Psychiatry and Neurology, Am. Bd. Internal Medicine. Intern Presbyn. Hosp., N.Y.C., 1963-64, resident, 1964-65; resident Neurol. Inst. CPMC, N.Y.C., 1965-68, research fellow endocrinology, 1970-72; asst. prof. to prof. neurology Columbia U., N.Y.C., 1972-85; prof., chmn. dept. neurology Oreg. Health Sci. U., Portland, 1985—; dir. neurology Helen Hayes Hosp., Haverstraw, N.Y., 1982-83. Mem. editl. bd. Jour. Histochem. Cytochemistry, 1980-85, 87, Neuroendocrinology, 1985-88, Annals of Neurology, 1985-91, Western Jour. Medicine, 1993—, Jour. Clin. Endocrinal Metabolism, 1995—; contbr. numerous articles to profl. jours. Maj. USAF, 1968-70. Rsch. grantee NIH, 1977—. Mem. Am. Neurol. Assn. (program chmn. 1980-82), Am. Acad. Neurology (Wartenber lectr. 1985), Endocrine Soc. Democrat. Mem. United Ch. of Christ. Avocations: woodworking; gardening; theatre; music; art; skiing; tennis. Office: Oreg Health Sci U Dept Neurology 3181 SW Sam Jackson Park Rd Portland OR 97201-3011

ZIMMERMAN, EDWIN MORTON, lawyer; b. N.Y.C., June 11, 1924; s. Benjamin and Tobie (Fuchs) Z.; m. Caroline Abbot, July 3, 1956; children: Sarah Abbot, Lyle Benjamin, Miriam Appleton. AB, Columbia U., 1944, LLB, 1949. Bar: N.Y. 1949, D.C. 1969, U.S. Supreme Ct 1969. With Hoover Commn. Reorgn. Exec. Br., 1948; law clk. to Hon. Stanley F. Reed U.S. Supreme Ct., 1950-51; law clk. to Judge Simon H. Rifkind U.S. Dist. Ct., 1949-50; pvt. practice law N.Y.C., 1951-59; prof. law Stanford U., 1959-69; with Justice Dept., 1965-69, asst. atty. gen. charge antitrust div., 1968-69; mem. Covington & Burling, Washington, 1969—; Mem. coun. Adminstrv. Conf. U.S., 1975-78; mem. mfg. studies bd. Nat. Acad. Sci., 1983-87. Trustee Textile Mus., 1983—, pres. bd. trustees, 1987-96; mem. Folger Poetry Bd., 1990—; mem. adv. bd. Partisan Rev., 1996—. 1st lt. AUS, 1944-46. Mem. ABA, Assn. of Bar of City of N.Y., Am. Law Inst., Coun. Fgn. Rels., Phi Beta Kappa. Home: 1820 Kalorama Sq NW Washington DC 20008-4022 Office: Covington & Burling PO Box 7566 1201 Pennsylvania Ave NW Washington DC 20004-2401

ZIMMERMAN, EVERETT LEE, English educator, academic administrator; b. Lancaster, Pa., Dec. 9, 1936; s. Amos Wanner and Anna (Sensenig) Z.; m. Muriel Laden, Apr. 28, 1963, children: Andrew, Daniel. BA, Bob Jones U., 1958; MA, Temple U., 1961, PhD, 1966. Lectr. Temple U., Phila., 1961-62; instr. Rutgers U., Camden, N.J., 1962-66, asst. prof., 1966-69; asst. prof. U. Calif., Santa Barbara, 1969-72, assoc. prof., 1972-80, prof. English, 1980—, dean, 1988-89. Author: Defoe and the Novel, 1975, Swift's Narrative Satires, 1983, The Boundaries of Fiction, 1996; also articles. Dem. committeeman, Phila., 1965-66. Jr. Faculty fellow, 1971, Humanities Inst. fellow, 1975 U. Calif.; NEH grantee, 1986; Guggenheim fellow, 1989-90. Mem. MLA, Am. Soc. 18th Century Studies. Home: 1822 Prospect Ave Santa Barbara CA 93103-1950 Office: U of Calif Dept Of English Santa Barbara CA 93106

ZIMMERMAN, GAIL MARIE, medical foundation executive; b. Fort Wayne, Ind., June 23, 1945; d. Albert Douglas and Aina Dorothy (Johnson) Z. B.A., U. Puget Sound, 1967. Intelligence analyst CIA, Washington, 1970-72; research asst. Arthur Young & Co., Portland, Oreg., 1972-74; emergency med. service planner Marion-Polk-Yamhill Counties, Salem, Oreg., 1975-76; health cons. Freedman Assocs., Portland, Oreg., 1976-77; legis. asst. U.S. Senator Bob Packwood, Portland, 1977-78; exec. dir. Nat. Psoriasis Found., Portland, 1979—; mem. dermatology panel U.S. Parmacopoeial Conv., 1985-94; lay rep. Nat. Inst. Arthritis, Musculoskeletal and Skin Disease, NIH, 1990-94. Founding bd. dirs. Nat. Abortion Rights Action League, Portland, 1977; pres. bd. dirs. Oreg. Common Cause, Portland, 1977-78. Democrat. Avocations: tennis; flute. Office: Nat Psoriasis Found 6600 SW 92nd Ave Ste 300 Portland OR 97223-7195

ZIMMERMAN, GEORGE OGUREK, physicist, educator; b. Poland, Oct. 20, 1935; s. Charles and Carolin Olga (Fisher) Z.; m. Isa Kaftal, Oct. 4, 1964. B.S., Yale U., 1958, M.S., 1959, Ph.D. (Univ. Wilson fellow 1959-60, D.N. Clark fellow 1959-61), 1963. Research assoc. Yale U., 1962-63; asst. prof. physics Boston U., 1963-68, assoc. prof., 1968-74, prof., 1974—, assoc. chmn. dept. physics, 1971-72, chmn. dept., 1973-83, chmn. faculty coun., 1985-86, dir. honors program in sci. and engring. for HS students, 1978—; mem. staff Nat. Magnet Lab., Cambridge, Mass., 1964, vis. scientist, 1964-70; assoc. physicist U. Calif., San Diego, 1973; vis. scientist Brookhaven Nat. Lab., 1980; vis. scholar Harvard U., 1988, Kamerling Onnes Laboratorium, Leiden, The Netherlands, 1988; pres. Zerres Corp.; participant numerous physics teaching improvement programs for secondary sch. tchrs. and students. Contbr. articles on low temperature physics, phase transitions and superconductivity to profl. jours.; patentee in field. Rsch. Corp. grantee, 1964-65, Air Force Office Sci. Rsch. grantee, 1966-86, NSF grantee, 1975—. Mem. Am. Phys. Soc., N.Y. Acad. Scis., AAAS, Phi Beta Kappa, Sigma Xi. Home: 566 Commonwealth Ave Boston MA 02215-2520 Office: Boston U Dept Physics Boston MA 02215 *Administration is easier than science because in administration one can create one's own reality, while in science reality is unalterable.*

ZIMMERMAN, GIDEON K., minister; b. Lehr, N.D., Aug. 18, 1920; m. Eleanor Pekrul; children: Paul, Mark (dec.), Thomas. Diploma, N.Am. Baptist Sem., Rochester, N.Y., 1943; B.A., Wesley Coll., U. N.D., 1951; postgrad., Bethany Bibl. Sem., 1958-59, Chgo. Lutheran Sem., 1959-61; B.D., N.Am. Bapt. Sem., Sioux Falls, S.D., 1960, D.D. Pastor First Bapt. Ch., Auburn, Mich., 1943-47, Grace Bapt. Ch., Grand Forks, N.D., 1947-51, Temple Bapt. Ch., Milw., 1951-55; gen. sec. dept. Christian edn. N. Am. Bapt. Conf., 1955-68, exec. sec., 1968-79, estate planning counselor, 1979-85. Home: 3721 Bardstown Rd Apt 308 Louisville KY 40218-2261

ZIMMERMAN, HAROLD SAMUEL, retired state senator, newspaper editor and publisher, state administrator; b. Valley City, N.D., June 1, 1923; s. Samuel Alwin and Lulu (Wylie) Z.; m. Julianne Williams, Sept. 12, 1946; children—Karen, Steven, Judi Jean (dec.). B.A., U. Wash., 1947. News editor Sedro-Woolley (Wash.) Courier-Times, 1947-50; editor, pub. Advocate, Castle Rock, Wash., 1950-57; pub. Post-Record, Camas, Wash., 1957-80; assoc. pub., columnist, 1980; assoc. pub., columnist, dir. Eagle Publs., Camas, 1980-88. Mem. Wash. Ho. of Reps., 1967-80; mem. Wash. Senate, 1981-88, Wash. State Environ. Hearings Bd., Lacey, 1988-93. Served with USAAF, 1943-46. Mem. Grange, Sigma Delta Chi, Sigma Chi. Republican. United Methodist. Clubs: Lions, Kiwanis.

ZIMMERMAN, HAROLD SEYMOUR, elementary school educator; b. Bklyn., June 3, 1928. BA, Bklyn. Coll., 1950; MA, So. Ill. U., Edwardsville, 1970; postgrad., various, 1950-90. 8th grade English, Social Studies, Reading tchr. Sherwood Day Sch., Chesterfield, Mo., 1956-64; 7th grade core curriculum, English, Social Studies tchr. Nipher Jr. High Sch., Kirkwood, Mo., 1964-70; 7th grade Social Studies, team teaching tchr. Brittany Woods Sch., University City, Mo., 1971-91; tchr. Russian lit. OASIS, 1995; tchr. Russian Art Oasis, 1996; adj. prof. Russian studies Lindenwood Coll., St. Charles, Mo., 1975—, Washington U., 1972-91; participant 1st U.S./Russia Joint Conf. on Edn., 1994; cons. in field. Author: Facing Issues of Family Living; contbr. articles to profl. jours. Chairperson bd. trustees Indian Meadows subdivsn., Olivette, Mo.; chairperson Youth Commn., Olivette; vol. OASIS, St. Louis Zoo. Mem. NEA, ASCD, Mo. Edn. Assn., Nat. Coun. Social Studies (spl. interest groups psychology, tchr. edn., religion in schs.), Mo. Geog. Alliance Tchr. Cons., People to People, World Coun. of Affairs, Bus. for Russia. Home: 450 E Lockwood Ave Webster Groves MO 63119 *My goal in life is, and was to meet my potential to use for the service of others; a religious commitment.*

ZIMMERMAN, HELENE LORETTA, business educator; b. Rochester, N.Y., Feb. 26, 1933; d. Henry Charles and Loretta Catherine (Hobert) Z. BS, SUNY, Albany, 1953, MS, 1959; PhD, U. N.D., 1969. Cert. records mgr. Bus. tchr., chmn. bus. dept. Williamson (N.Y.) Cen. Sch., 1953-69; asst. prof. U. Ky., Lexington, 1969-70; assoc. prof. bus. Cen. Mich. U., Mt. Pleasant, 1970-74, prof., 1974—. Author General Business, 1977; contbg. author to records mgmt. text book, 1987. Sec. Isabella County Christmas Outreach, Mt. Pleasant, 1983—. Mem. Assn. Records Mgmt. and Adminstrn., Inst. Cert. Records Mgrs. (sec. 1985-89, exam. devel. com. 1993—), Internat. Soc. Bus. Edn. (internat. v.p. English speaking nations 1986-88), Nat. Bus. Edn. Assn., Mich. Bus. Edn. Assn. (bd. dirs. 1985-90, 95—, pres. 1988-89), AAUW (pres. 1984-86), Delta Kappa Gamma (state pres. 1987-89, internat. fin. com. 1990-94, internat. ad hoc com. on tech. 1996—). Avocations: travel, crafts. Office: Ctrl Mich U Grawn # 337 Mount Pleasant MI 48859

ZIMMERMAN, HOWARD ELLIOT, chemist, educator; b. N.Y.C., July 5, 1926; s. Charles and May (Cohen) Z.; m. Jane Kirschenheiter, June 3, 1950 (dec. Jan. 1975); children: Robert, Steven, James; m. Martha L. Bailey Kaufman, Nov. 7, 1975 (div. Oct. 1990); m. Peggy J. Vick, Oct. 1991; stepchildren: Peter and Tanya Kaufman. B.S., Yale U., 1950, Ph.D., 1953. NRC fellow Harvard U., 1953-54; faculty Northwestern U., 1954-60, asst. prof., 1955-60; assoc. prof. U. Wis., Madison, 1960-61; prof. chemistry U. Wis., 1961—, Arthur C. Cope and Hilldale prof. chemistry, 1975—; chmn. 4th Internat. Union Pure and Applied Chemistry Symposium on Photochemistry, 1972; organizer, chmn. Organic Photochemistry Symposium at Pacifichem 95, Honolulu, 1995. Author: Quantum Mechanics for Organic Chemists, 1975; mem. editorial bd.: Jour. Organic Chemistry, 1967-71, Molecular Photochemistry, 1969-75, Jour. Am. Chem. Soc., 1982-85, Revs. Reactive Intermediates, 1984-89; contbr. articles to profl. jours. Recipient Halpern award for photochemistry N.Y. Acad. Scis., 1979, Chem. Pioneer award Am. Inst. Chemists, 1986, Sr. Alexander von Humboldt award, 1988, Hilldale award U. Wis., 1988-89, 90. Mem. NAS, Am. Chem. Soc. (James Flack Norris award 1976, Arthur C. Cope Scholar award 1991), Chem. Soc. London, German Chem. Soc., Inter-Am. Photochemistry Assn. (co-chmn. organic div. 1977-79, exec. com. 1979-86), Phi Beta Kappa, Sigma Xi. Home: 1 Oconto Ct Madison WI 53705-4925 Office: U Wis Chemistry Dept 1101 University Ave Madison WI 53706-1322

ZIMMERMAN, HYMAN JOSEPH, internist, educator; b. Rochester, N.Y., July 19, 1914; s. Philip and Rachel (Marine) Z.; m. Kathrin J. Jones, Feb. 28, 1943; children: Philip M., David J., Robert L., Diane E. AB, U. Rochester, 1936; MA, Stanford U., 1938, MD, 1943. Diplomate Am. Bd. Internal Medicine. Intern Stanford (Calif.) U. Hosp., 1942-43; asst. resident in medicine Gallinger Mcpl. Hosp. divsn. George Washington U., Washington, 1946-47, chief resident in medicine, 1947-48, clin. instr. in medicine, 1948-51, prof. Sch. Medicine, 1965-68, 71-79, prof. medicine, gastroenterology Sch. Medicine, 1986-89, prof. emeritus, 1989—; asst. chief of med. svc. VA Hosp., Washington, 1949-51; chief of med. svc. VA Hosp., Omaha, 1951-53, Chgo., 1953-57; chief of liver and metabolic rsch. lab. VA Hosp., Washington, 1965-68; chief of med. svc. VA Hosp., Boston, 1968-71; chief of med. svc. VA Hosp., Washington, 1971-78, sr. clinician, 1978-80, disting. physician, 1984-89; disting. scientist Armed Forces Inst. Pathology, Washington, 1989—; asst. prof. medicine Coll. Medicine U. Nebr., Omaha, 1951-53; assoc. prof. of medicine Coll. of Medicine U. Ill., Chgo., 1953-57; prof., chmn. dept. medicine Chgo. Med. Sch., 1957-65; chmn. dept. of medicine Mt. Sinai Hosp., Chgo., 1957-65; prof. of medicine Sch. of Medicine Boston U., 1968-71; clin. prof. Sch. of Medicine Georgetown U., Washington, 1971-78; sr. clinician VA Hosp., Washington, 1978—; clin. prof. medicine Howard U., 1971-78, Uniformed Svcs. U. Health Scis., 1978—; cons. Clin. Ctr. NIH, Bethesda, 1965—, USN Med. Ctr., Bethesda, 1965—; vis. prof., lectr. numerous hosps. and univs. Author: Hepatotoxicity, 1978; contbr. numerous articles to med. jours.; contbg. editor numerous med. pubs. Maj. AUS, 1943-46. Recipient William Beaumont award for clin. rsch., 1981, Disting. Achievement award Am. Assn. for Study Liver Disease, 1986, gold medal Can. Liver Found., 1989. Fellow ACP (mastership 1993); mem. AMA (mem. coun. on drugs, mem. gastroenterology panel 1968-70), AAAS, AAUP, Am. Soc. Clin. Pharmacology and Therapeutics, Am. Fedn. for Clin. Rsch., Am. Diabetes Assn., Endocrine Soc., Asian-Pacific Assn. for Study of Liver Diseases, Am. Soc. Clin. Investigation, N.Y. Acad. Scis., Cen. Soc. Clin. Rsch., Soc. for Exptl. Biology and Medicine, Am. Gastroenterol. Assn. (named Disting. Educator 1990), Drug Info. Assn., Cosmos Club, Sigma Xi, Alpha Omega Alpha. Home: 7913 Charleston Ct Bethesda MD 20817-1421 Office: Armed Forces Inst Path Hepatic Dept Washington DC 20306-6000

ZIMMERMAN, JAMES ROBERT, radiologist, engineer; b. Dearborn, Mich., Dec. 26, 1960; s. Carl Edward and Mary Kathleen (Devlin) Z. B Mech. Engring., GM Engring. and Mgmt. Inst., Flint, Mich., 1984; MD, U. Miss., Jackson, 1990. Bd. cert. in diagnostic radiology. Resident in surgery Roanoke (Va.) Meml. Hosps., 1990-92; resident in radiology U. Miss. Med. Ctr., 1992-96; radiologist Upson Regional Med. Ctr., Thomaston, Ga., 1996—. Contbr. articles to med. jours. Mem. Rep. Task Force, Washington, 1994. Mem. AMA, Radiol. Soc. N.Am., Am. Roentgen Ray Soc., So. Med. Assn. Roman Catholic. Avocations: golf, biking, running. Home: 619 Kingston Rd Thomaston GA 30286 Office: Upson Regional Med Ctr 801 W Gordon St Thomaston GA 30286

ZIMMERMAN, JEAN, lawyer; b. Berkeley, Calif., Dec. 3, 1947; d. Donald Scheel Zimmerman and Phebe Jean (Reed) Doan; m. Gilson Berryman Gray III, Nov. 25, 1982; children: Charles Donald Buffum and Catherine Elisabeth Phebe (twins); stepchildren: Alison Travis, Laura Rebecca, Gilson Berryman. BSBA, U. Md., 1970; JD, Emory U., 1975. Bar: Ga. 1975, D.C. 1976, N.Y. 1980. Asst. mgr. investments FNMA, Washington, 1970-73; assoc. counsel Fuqua Industries Inc., Atlanta, 1976-79; assoc. Sage Gray Todd & Sims, N.Y.C., 1979-84; assoc. counsel J. Henry Schroder Bank & Trust Co., N.Y.C., 1984-85, asst. gen. counsel, 1986, assoc. gen. counsel, 1987; assoc. gen. counsel, asst. sec. IBJ Schroder Bank & Trust Co., N.Y.C., 1988-90, chief counsel, sec., 1991-93, sr. v.p., gen. counsel, sec., 1993—; asst. sec. IBJ Schroder Bus. Credit Corp., N.Y.C., 1987-90, bd. dirs., sec., 1991-95, sr. v.p., gen. counsel, sec., bd. dirs., 1996—; sr. v.p., gen. counsel, sec., bd. dirs. Innovest Capital Mgmt., Inc., N.Y.C., 1997—; sr. v.p., gen. counsel, sec. Innovest Corp., N.Y.C., 1997—; asst. sec. IBJ Schroder Banking Corp., N.Y.C., 1989-90, chief counsel, sec., 1991-93; asst. sec. IBJ Schroder Internat. Bank, Miami, Fla., 1989-90, sec., 1991—; asst. sec. IBJS Capital Corp., N.Y.C., 1988-90, sec., 1991—; sec. Bonaght Corp., N.Y.C., 1991—; chief legal officer, sec. Execution Svcs., Inc., N.Y.C., 1991-93. Founder, officer ERA Ga., Atlanta, 1977-79; bd. dirs. Ct. Apptd. Spl. Advs., 1988-94. Named one of Outstanding Atlantans, 1978-79. Mem. ABA, Assn. of Bar of City of N.Y., Ga. Assn. Women Lawyers (bd. dirs. 1977-79), Am. Soc. Corp. Secs., Inc., LWV, DAR. Republican. Office: IBJ Schroder Bank & Trust Co 1 State St New York NY 10004-1505

ZIMMERMAN, JO ANN, health services and educational consultant, former lieutenant governor; b. Van Buren County, Iowa, Dec. 24, 1936; d. Russell and Hazel (Ward) McIntosh; m. A. Tom Zimmerman, Aug. 26, 1956; children: Andrew, Lisa, Don and Ron (twins), Beth. Diploma, Broadlawns Sch. of Nursing, Des Moines, 1958; BA with honors, Drake U., 1973; postgrad., Iowa State U., 1973-75. RN, Iowa. Asst. head nurse maternity dept. Broadlawns Med. Ctr., Des Moines, 1958-59, weekend supr. nursing svcs., 1960-61, supr. maternity dept., 1966-68; instr. maternity nursing Broadlawns Sch. Nursing, 1968-71; health planner, community rels. assoc. Iowa Health Systems Agy., Des Moines, 1978-82; mem. Iowa Ho. Reps., 1982-86; lt. gov., Senate pres. State of Iowa, 1987-91; cons. health svcs., grant writing and continuing edn. Zimmerman & Assocs., Des Moines, 1991—; dir. patient care svcs. Nursing Svcs. of Iowa, 1996—; ops. dir. Medlink Svcs., Inc., Des Moines, 1992-96; dir. nurses Nursing Svcs. of Iowa, 1996—. Contbr. articles to profl. jours. Mem. advanced registered nurse practioner task force on cert. nurse mid-wives Iowa Bd. Nursing, 1980-81, Waukee, Polk County, Iowa Health Edn. Coord. Coun., Iowa Women's Polit. Caucus, Dallas County Women's Polit. Caucus; chmn. Des Moines Area Maternity Nursing Conf. Group. 1969-70, task force on sch. health svcs. Iowa Dept. Health, 1982, task force health edn. Iowa Dept. Pub. Instruction, 1979, adv. com. health edn. assessment tool, 1980-81, Nat. Lt. Govs., chair com. on Agrl. and Rural Devel., 1989; Dallas County Dem. Cen. Com., 1972-84; bd. dirs. Waukee Cmty. Sch. Bd., 1976-79, pres. 1978-79; bd. dirs. Iowa PTA, 1979-83, chairperson Health Com., 1980-84; mem. steering com. ERA, Iowa, 1991-92; founder Dem. Activist Women's Network (DAWN), 1992. Mem. ANA, LWV (health chmn. met. Des Moines chpt.), Iowa Nurses Assn., Iowa League for Nursing (bd. dirs. 1979-83), Family Centered Childbirth Edn. Assn. (childbirth instr., advisor), Iowa Cattleman's Assn., Am. Lung Assn. (bd. dirs. Iowa 1988-92), Dem. Activist Women's Network (founder 1992). Mem. Christian Ch. Avocations: gardening, sewing, reading, bridge, breeding British White cattle. Office: Zimmerman & Assocs 7630 Ashworth Rd West Des Moines IA 50266-5859

ZIMMERMAN, JOHN H., communications company executive; b. Akron, Ohio, Oct. 3, 1932; s. Erle C. and Agnes R. (Lower) Z.; m. LaVonne A. Robertson, July 25, 1953; children: Rebecca Zimmerman Brown, J. Jeffrey, Amy Leigh Zimmerman Larimore. B.A. in Econs., Colgate U., 1954; M.B.A., Kent State U., 1962. Dir. labor relations Firestone Tire and Rubber Co., Akron, Ohio, 1975-78, v.p. employee relations, 1978-82; sr. v.p. human resources MCI Communications, Washington, 1982-95; human resource cons., 1996—; adj. prof. Kent State U., 1963-66, U. Akron, 1970-72; mem. U.S. Gov. Commn. on Achieving Necessary Skills, 1990-92; mem. adv. coun. Ctr. for Workplace Excellence; mem. Work Readiness Adv. Com. V.p. Akron-Canton Regional Airport Bd. Trustees, 1981-82; active Nat. Com. Vietnam POW Reemployment, 1972-73; mem. adv. bd. Nat. Urban League, N.Y.C., 1972-83, U. Akron Ctr. Econ. Edn., 1981-82; Nat. Alliance Businessmen Bd., 1973-82; mem. adv. bd. Sch. Bus. and Pub. Mgmt., George Washington U., 1987-96; trustee Akron Gen. Med. Ctr., 1981-82, Akron YMCA, 1980-82; chmn. Summit County Pers. Rev. Commn., 1970. Mem. Am. Mgmt. Assn. (mem. HR adv. coun. 1986-93, chair 1991-93, bd. trustees 1991-93), Phi Beta Kappa. Presbyterian. Home: 7272 Evans Mill Rd Mc Lean VA 22101-3423

ZIMMERMAN, JOSEPH FRANCIS, political scientist, educator; b. Keene, N.H., June 29, 1928; s. John Joseph and May Veronica (Gallagher) Z.; m. Margaret Bernardette Brennan, Aug. 2, 1958; 1 child, Deirdre Ann. BA, U. N.H., 1950; MA, Syracuse U., 1951, PhD, 1954. Instr. govt. Worcester Poly. Inst., 1954-55, asst. prof., 1955-57, assoc. prof., 1957-62, prof., 1962-65; lectr. Clark U., Worcester, Mass., 1957-65; prof. polit. sci. SUNY, Albany, 1965—; staff dir. N.Y. State Joint Legis. Com. Transp., 1967-68, rsch. dir., 1968-73; rsch. dir. N.Y. State Select Legis. Com. Transp., 1977-82, Legis. Commn. on Critical Transp. Problems, 1982-95. Author: State and Local Government, 1962, The Massachusetts Town Meeting: A Tenacious Institution, 1967, The Federated City: Community Control in Large Cities, 1972, Pragmatic Federalism, The Reassingment of Functional Responsibility, 1976, (with Frank W. Prescott) The Politics of the Veto of Legislation in New York, 1980, The Government and Politics of the Empire State, 1981, Local Discretionary Authority, 1981, (with Deirdre A. Zimmerman) The Politics of Subnational Governance, 1983, State-Local Relations: A Partnership Approach, 1983, 2d edit., 1995 (CHOICE award as outstandin acad. book, 1984), Participatory Democracy: Populism Revived, 1986, Federal Preemption: The Silent Revolution, 1990, Contemporary American Federalism, 1992, (with Wilma Rule) United States Electoral System: Their Impact Upon Women and Minorities, 1992, (with Wilma Rule) Electoral Systems in Comparative Perspective: Their Impact on Women Minorities, 1994, Curbing Unethical Behavior of Government, 1994, Interstate Relations: The Neglected Dimension of Federalism, 1996, The Recall: Tribunal of the People, 1997; contbr. articles to profl. publs. Pres. Citizens' Plan E Assn., Worcester, 1960-62, Citizens for Neighborhood Improvement Worcester, 1957-59. Served to capt. USAF, 1951-53. Named 1 of 3 Outstanding Young Men Worcester Jr. C. of C., 1959, 61, 1 of 3 Outstanding Young Men Mass, Jr. C. of C., 1961, disting. citizen award Nat. Conf. on Govt., 1986. Mem. Am. Polit. Sci. Assn., Am. Soc. Public Adminstrn., Nat. Mcpl. League. Roman Catholic. Club: German-Am. Social. Home: 82 Greenock Rd Delmar NY 12054-4414 Office: SUNY Grad Sch Public Affairs 135 Western Ave Albany NY 12203-1011

ZIMMERMAN, JUDITH ROSE, elementary art educator; b. Youngstown, Ohio, Jan. 17, 1945; d. Emery and Josephine Leona (Terlecki) Ference; m. William Carl Zimmerman, Jr., Nov 27, 1965; children: Shawn, William III. BFA in Art Edn., Kent State U., 1977, MEd in Curriculum and Instruction, 1992. Cert. art tchr., Ohio. Elem. art tchr. Sandy Valley Sch. Dist., Magnolia, Ohio, 1977—; instr. art Massillon (Ohio) Art Mus. Adv. com. Edn. Enhancement Partnership Coun., Canton, Ohio, 1992; active Little Art Gallery, 1992, Massillon Art Mus. Mem. NEA, Nat. Art Edn. Assn., Ohio Edn. Assn., Ohio Art Edn. Assn. (chairperson east cen. divsn. 1985-90, elem. divsn. 1989-91, Art Educator of Yr. 1983, Featured Art Tchr. of Month 1990), Ohio Alliance for Art Edn., Canton Art Inst. (Art Educator of Yr. 1992), Phi Delta Kappa (newsletter editor McKinley chpt.). Roman Catholic. Avocations: reading, tennis, music, oil painting, walking. Home: 802 Lucille Ave SW North Canton OH 44720-2820 Office: Sandy Valley Sch Dist RR 2 Magnolia OH 44643-9802

ZIMMERMAN, KATHLEEN MARIE, artist; b. Floral Park, N.Y., Apr. 24, 1923; d. Harold G. and Evelyn M. (Andrade) Z.; m. Ralph S. Iwamoto, Nov. 23, 1963. Student, Art Students League, N.Y.C., 1942-44, Nat. Acad. Sch. Fine Arts, N.Y.C., 1944-47, 50-54. tchr. drawing and painting Midtown Sch. Art, N.Y.C., 1947-52. Illustrator: (with Ralph S. Iwamoto) Diet for a Small Planet, 1971; one woman shows include Westbeth Gallery, N.Y.C., 1973, 74, St. Mary's Coll., St. Mary's City, Md., 1990; exhibited in group shows at Woodstock Art Gallery, N.Y., 1945, Nat. Arts Club, N.Y.C., 1948-56, 84, Emily Lowe Award Show, 1951, Contemporary Arts Gallery, N.Y.C., 1952, 60, Allied Artists Ann., N.Y.C., 1956, 78, 80-91, 93-96, Art USA, 1958, Village Art Ctr., 1956-61, ACA Gallery, 1958, 59, Studio Gallery, 1957-60, City Center Gallery, 1960, Janet Nessler Gallery, N.Y.C., 1961, Silvermine Guild, Conn., 1962, Pioneer Gallery, Cooperstown, N.Y., 1962, 63, Audubon Artists Anns., N.Y.C., (various shows) 1963-96, NAD, (16 shows) 1969-97, Nat. Assn. Women Artists Anns., N.Y.C., 1957-85, 87-97, Women Artists Award Winners Show, N.Y.C., 1974, Am. Watercolor Soc., N.Y.C., 1975-78, 80, Cheyenne (Wyo.) Western Galleries, 1975, 76, 77, Edward-Dean Mus., Cherry Valley, Calif., 1975, 76, 77, Frye Mus., Seattle, 1975, 76, 77, Boise Gallery Art, 1975, Central Wyo. Mus. Art, 1975, 76, Willamette U., 1975, Yellowstone Art Ctr., Billings, Mont., 1975, Utah State U., 1975, Applewood Art Gallery, Colo., 1976, Charleston Art Gallery, W.Va., 1976, Kent State U., 1976, Cin. Art Club, 1976, Martello Mus., Key West, Fla., 1976, Buecker Gallery, N.Y.C., 1976, Anchorage Fine Arts Mus., 1976, Davis and Long Gallery, N.Y.C., 1977, Butler Inst. Am. Art, 1978, Washington Square East Gallery, NYU, 1979, Internat. Festival Women Artists, Copenhagen, 1980, City Gallery, N.Y.C., 1981, Bergen Community Mus., Paramus, N.J., 1983, Kenkeleba Gallery, N.Y.C., 1985, Adelphi Univ., Garden City, N.Y., 1987, Lotos Club, N.Y.C., 1987, Temperance Hall Gallery, Bellport, N.Y., 1987, Monmouth Mus., Lincroft, N.J., 1987, Marbella Gallery, N.Y.C., 1989, Knickerbocker Artists, 1990, Brownstone Gallery, N.Y.C., 1993, Viridian Gallery, N.Y.C., 1995, Sundance Gallery, Bridgehampton, N.Y., 1996, Mcpl. Art Ctr., Athens, Greece, 1996, ISE Art Found., N.Y.C., 1996; represented in permanent collections, Butler Inst. Am. Art, Youngstown, Ohio, Sheldon Swope Art Gallery, Terre Haute, Ind., Lauren Rogers Mus. Art, Laurel, Miss., U. Wyo. Art Mus., Laramie, U. Miami Lowe Art Mus., Coral Gables, Fla., N.C. Mus. Art, Raleigh, Swarthmore Coll., Pa., Erie Art Ctr. (Pa.), Nat. Acad. Design, N.Y.C.; bibiography James Mellow, N.Y. Times Art Review, 1973, Hilton Kramer, N.Y. Times Review, 1977, Helen A. Harrison, N.Y. Times Review, 1987; contbr. bibliography to Gerald F. Brommer's The Art of Collage, 1978, Christopher Schink's Mastering Color & Design in Watercolor, 1981, John and Joan Digby's The Collage Handbook, 1985, David Ferry's "Painting Without a Brush", 1992, Gerald F. Brommer's Collage Techniques, 1994. John F. and Anna Lee Stacey scholar, 1954. Mem. NAD (Henry Ward Ranger Fund purchase prize 1976, 82, cert. of merit 1980, L.G. Sawyer prize 1988, Ogden Pleissner Meml. award 1991, William A. Paton prize 1993), Audubon Artists (John Wenger Meml. award 1978, Ralph Fabri medal 1981, J&E Liskin Meml. award 1987, Dick Blick award 1994), Am. Watercolor Soc. (Barse Miller Meml. award 1976), Nat. Assn. Women Artists (14 prizes 1957—), Allied Artists Am. (silver medal 1981, 91, Jane Peterson award 1985, Creative Watercolor prize 1989), N.Y. Artists Equity Assn. (Dr. Maury Leibovitz award 1985). Home: 463 West St Apt 1110A New York NY 10014-2040

ZIMMERMAN, LOUIS SEYMOUR, lawyer; b. Houston, Mar. 17, 1949; s. Robert Eugene and Rosalind (Pincoffs) Z.; m. Janet Whaley, Aug. 9, 1975; children: Patrick, Thomas, Frank. BA, Williams Coll., 1971; JD, U. Tex., 1974. Bar: Tex. 1974, U.S. Dist. Ct. (so. and we. dists.) Tex. 1974, D.C. 1974, U.S. Ct. Appeals (5th, 11th and D.C. cirs.) 1974. Law clk. to Hon. judge Owen Cox U.S. Dist. Ct., Corpus Christi, Tex., 1974-76; assoc. Fulbright & Jaworski, Houston, 1976-82; ptnr. Fulbright & Jaworski, Washington, 1983-86, Austin, Tex., 1986—. Office: Fulbright & Jaworski 600 Congress Ave Ste 2400 Austin TX 78701-3238

ZIMMERMAN, LYDIA, community health nurse, retired; b. McMinnville, Oreg., Jan. 12, 1929; d. Frederick H. and Anna Katarina (Beisel) Koch; m. Howard C. Zimmerman, July 14, 1956; children: Sylvia, Angela, Joan, Garth. Diploma in nursing, Emanuel Hosp. Sch. Nursing, Portland, Oreg., 1949; BSN, U. Wash., 1953; cert. sch. nurse practitioner, UCLA, 1977. RN, Calif.; cert. pub. health nurse; cert. family life educator, sch. nurse. Asst. supr., head nurse surg. Emanuel Hosp., Portland, Oreg., 1949-50; coll. nurse Linfield Coll., McMinnville, Oreg., 1951-52; public health nurse I, sch. nurse, counselor high sch. Lane County Health Dept., Eugene, Oreg., 1953-57, staff nurse, asst. supr. maternal-child, mental health, 1958-63; public health nurse Lucas County Health Dept., Toledo, Ohio, 1967-69; private nurse Shafter, Calif., 1972-74; sch. nurse Rosedale Sch. Dist., Bakersfield, Calif., 1974-76, Beardsley Sch. Dist., Bakersfield, Calif., 1974-80, Panama-Buena Vista Union Sch. Dist., Bakersfield, Calif., 1974-96; ret., 1996; lctr. Bakersfield Coll., Calif. State Coll., Bakersfield. Mem. APHA, NEA, AAUW, Am. Acad. Nurse Practitioners, Calif. Tchrs. Assn., Nat. Assn. Sch. Nurses (Calif. rep. 1986-87, 87-88), Calif. Sch. Nurses Orgn., Kern County Sch. Nurses Orgn. (co-founder, pres. 1981-83, 91-92), Sex Info. and Edn. Coun. U.S., Nat. Coun. on Family Rels., Ctr. Sci. in Pub. Interest, Calif. Assn. Neurologically Handicapped Children, Assn. Children with Learning Disabilities, Learning Disabilities Assn. Am. (co-founder, pres. Kern County chpt. 1972-74, 76-78, 88-96, past pres., program chairperson 1997), Am. Hist. Soc. Germans from Russia, Sigma Theta Tau Internat. Congregationalist.

ZIMMERMAN, MARLIN U., JR., chemical engineer; b. Akron, Ohio, Aug. 2, 1923; s. Marlin Ulrich and Helen (Nelson) Z. BChemE, Johns Hopkins U., 1944; MBA, Harvard U., 1966. Registered profl. engr., Ohio. Jr. engr. Standard Oil Co. (Ohio), Cleve., 1944-46, engr., 1946-48, sr. engr., 1948-49; process engr. Lima (Ohio) refinery Standard Oil Co. (Ohio), 1949-50; group engr. Standard Oil Co. (Ohio), Cleve., 1951-55, group supr., 1956-60, supr. process sys. sect., 1961-63, head acrylonitrile task force, 1961, tech. specialist, 1964-66; mgr. long term planning Norton Co., Worcester, Mass., 1966-69; cons. John Van Der Valk & Assocs., N.Y.C., 1970-73; pvt. practice cons. chem. engr. ammonia-urea Hackensack, N.J., 1974—; head task force to help commercialize Sohio acrylonitrile process. Contbr. articles to profl. jours. Baker scholar, 1966. Mem. AIChE, Johns Hopkins Club, Tudor and Stuart Club, Tau Beta Pi, Beta Theta Pi. Methodist. Achievements include patent for process improvement of Tosco shale process for oil recovery, patent for pig handling for gasoline blender meter testing loop, others. Avocations: travel, photography, reading, investing, computer programming. Home and Office: 229 Union St Hackensack NJ 07601

ZIMMERMAN, MARTIN E., financial executive; b. Chgo., Jan. 28, 1938; s. Joseph and Sylvea Zimmerman; m. Rita Kalifon, June 20, 1961 (div. 1992); children: Jacqueline, Adam. BSEE, MIT, 1955-59; MBA in Fin., Columbia U., 1961. Dir. market research Nuclear-Chgo., Inc. div. G.D. Searle & Co., 1964-67; pres. Telco Mktg. Services, Inc., Chgo., 1967-74; pres., chmn., chief exec. officer Linc Group, Inc., Chgo., 1975—; pres., CEO Linc Anthem Corp., 1994-96—. Contbr. numerous articles on leasing to profl. mags. Bd. overseers Columbia U. Grad. Sch. Bus.; trustee Mus. Contemporary Art, Chgo., Ravenswood Med. Ctr., Chgo. Capt. U.S. Army, 1961-63. McKinsey scholar, Kennecott Copper fellow Columbia U., 1959-61. Mem. Equipment Lessors Assn. (bd. dirs.). Clubs: University, Mid-Am. (Chgo.). Avocations: fishing, hunting, skiing, amateur radio. Home: 100 E Bellevue Pl Apt 26D Chicago IL 60611-1125 Office: The Linc Group Inc 303 E Wacker Dr Ste 1000 Chicago IL 60601-5212

ZIMMERMAN, MICHAEL DAVID, state supreme court chief justice; b. Chgo., Oct. 21, 1943; s. Elizabeth Porter; m. Lynne Mariani (dec. 1994); children: Evangeline Albright, Alessandra Mariani, Morgan Elisabeth. BS, U. Utah, 1966, JD, 1969. Bar: Calif. 1971, Utah 1978. Law clk. to Chief Justice Warren Earl Burger U.S. Supreme Ct., Washington, 1969-70; assoc. O'Melveny & Myers, L.A., 1970-76; assoc. prof. law U. Utah, 1976-78, adj. prof. law, 1978-84, 89—; of counsel Kruse, Landa, Zimmerman & Maycock, Salt Lake City, 1978-80; spl. counsel Gov. of Utah, Salt Lake City, 1978-80; ptnr. Watkiss & Campbell, Salt Lake City, 1980-84; assoc. justice Supreme Ct. Utah, Salt Lake City, 1984-93, chief justice, 1994—; co-moderator Justice Soc. Program of Snowbird Inst. for Arts and Humanities, 1991, 92; moderator, Tanner lecture panel dept. philosophy U. Utah, 1994—; faculty Judging Sci. Program Duke U., 1992; bd. dirs. Conf. of Chief Justices, 1995—. Note editor: Utah Law Rev., 1968-69; contbr. numerous articles to legal publs. Mem. Project 2000, Coalition for Utah's Future, 1985-96; trustee Hubert and Eliza B. Phibard Found., Rowland-Hall St. Mark's Sch. Named Utah State Bar Appellate Ct. Judge of Yr., 1988; recipient Excellence in Ethics award, Ctr. for Study of Ethics, 1994; participant Justice and Soc. Program of Aspen Inst. for Humanistic Studies, 1988, co-moderator, 1989; Awareness Day Found. fellow. Fellow Am. Bar Found.; mem. ABA (faculty mem. judges' seminar 1993), Am. Law Inst., Utah Bar Assn., Salt Lake County Bar Assn., Jud. Conf. U.S. (adv. com. civil rules 1985-91), Utah Jud. Coun. (supreme ct. rep. 1986-91), chair 1994—, Utah Constnl. Revisions Commn., Snowbird Inst. for Arts and Humanities (bd. dirs., 1989—), Am. Inns of Ct. VII, Am. Judicature Soc. (bd. dirs. 1995—), Order of Coif, Phi Kappa Phi. Office: Utah Supreme Ct 332 State Capitol Building Salt Lake City UT 84114-1202*

ZIMMERMAN, MICHAEL GLENN, marketing and communications executive; b. Charlotte, N.C., Nov. 22, 1957; s. Glenn Calvin and Phyllis Ann (Miller) Z.; m. MaryBeth O'Neill, Sept. 2, 1989; children: Abbey Marie, Maggie Kathleen. BA in Journalism, Ohio State U., 1980. Acct. supr. Paul Werth Assocs., Columbus, Ohio, 1980-84; acct. mgr. Watt, Roop & Co., Cleve., 1984-85, sr. acct. mgr., 1985-87, v.p., 1987-89, sr. v.p., 1989-92, exec. v.p., dir. client svcs., 1992—; mem. mktg. com. Cleve. regional office Ohio State U., 1990—. Mktg. com. United Way Cuyahoga County, Cleve., 1990—; trustee, devel. chmn., v.p. Ctr. for Mental Retardation, Cleve., 1991—; small bus. alliance Rock & Roll Hall of Fame, Cleve., 1992—. Mem. Am. Advt. Fedn. (Addy award 1989), Pub. Rels. Soc. Am. (Silver Anvil award 1988, 92), Hermit Club Cleve., Elyria Country Club. Republican. Avocations: Ohio State football, arts, travel, gourmet cooking/dining, golf. Home: 3143 Clark Pky Westlake OH 44145-4642 Office: Watt Roop & Co 1100 Superior Ave E Cleveland OH 44114-2518

ZIMMERMAN, NANCY PICCIANO, library science educator; b. Jeannette, Pa., July 29, 1951; d. Daniel Joseph and Helen Elizabeth (Lipinski) Picciano; m. Lee W. Zimmerman, Aug. 10, 1974; children: Matthew, Renée. BA in English, Carlow Coll., Pitts., 1973; MLS in Libr. Sci., U. Pitts., 1974; MS in Computer Edn. and Cognitive Sys., U. North Tex., 1992; PhD in Libr. and Info. Studies, Tex. Woman's U., 1992. Lic. libr. media specialist, K-12, lang. arts/English 7-12. Libr. media specialist Fairfield (Calif.)-Suisun Sch. Dist., 1976-78; reference libr. Pikes Peak Libr. Dist., Colorado Springs, Colo., 1983; libr. media specialist North Pole (Alaska) H.S., 1984-85, Prince William County Schs., Woodbridge, Va., 1985-89; dir. info. retrieval lab. Tex. Woman's U., Denton, 1989-91; adj. prof., rsch. assoc. U. North Tex., Denton, 1991-92; asst. prof. Sch. Info. and Libr. Studies SUNY, Buffalo, 1993—. Nat. stroke and turn ofcl. U.S. Swimming, 1985—. Recipient ALISE rsch. grant award, 1994. Mem. ALA (chair Libr. Rsch. Round Table 1995-96), Am. Assn. Sch. Librs. (treas. 1996—), Internat. Assn. Sch. Librs., N.Y. Libr. Assn., Phi Delta Kappa, Beta Phi Mu (nat. exec. coun. 1994—). Office: SUNY at Buffalo Sch Info & Libr Studies 534 Baldy Hall Box 601020 Buffalo NY 14260-1020

ZIMMERMAN, PAUL ALBERT, retired college president, minister; b. Danville, Ill., June 25, 1918; s. Albert Carl and Hanna Marie (Haffner) Z.; m. Genevieve Emmaline Bahls, June 11, 1944; children—Karmin (Mrs. Raymond Philp), Thomas. Student, Concordia Coll., Ft. Wayne, Ind., 1936-39; B.A., Concordia Sem., St. Louis, 1941, M.Div., 1944; M.A., U. Ill., 1947, Ph.D., 1951; D.D., Concordia Sem., Springfield, Ill., 1975; LLD (hon.), Concordia Coll., Ann Arbor, Mich., 1994. Prof. theology and sci. Bethany Coll., Mankato, Minn., 1944-53; prof. Concordia Tchrs. Coll., Seward, Nebr., 1953-54; pres. Concordia Tchrs. Coll., 1954-61, Concordia Luth. Jr. Coll., Ann Arbor, Mich., 1961-73, Concordia Coll., River Forest, Ill., 1973-83, ret., 1983; pastor St. Luke's Luth. Ch., Harrison, Mich., 1983-88. Author and editor: Darwin, Evolution and Creation, 1959, Rock Strata and the Bible Record, 1971, Creation, Evolution and God's Word, 1972. Chmn. Washtenaw County Red Cross, 1968-70; pres. Ann Arbor Found., 1970-71; mem. Citizens Com. Study Taxation, Ann Arbor, 1972; mem. adv. bd. St. Joseph Mercy Community, 1969-72; chmn. Luth. Ch. Mo. Synod's Bd. for Mission Services, 1982-92, Mission Task Force, 1990-91, adminstrv. asst. pres. Mo. Synod, 1972-73, 93-94, mem. curriculum commn. bd. higher edn., 1963-73, mem. task force constl. revision Mo. Synod, chmn. com. adjudication procedures Mo. Synod, Mo. Synod com. on structure, 1995—. Fellow Creation Rsch. Assn. Lutheran. Home: 2798 Princeton Dr Traverse City MI 49684-9131

ZIMMERMAN, RAYMOND, retail chain executive; b. Memphis, TN, 1933; married. V.p. Service Mdse. Co., Inc., Nashville, from 1959, pres., 1973-1981, chmn., 1981—, now also chief exec. officer, also bd. dirs. Office: Service Merchandise Co Inc 7100 Service Merchandise Dr Brentwood TN 37027-2927*

ZIMMERMAN, RICHARD ANSON, food company executive; b. Lebanon, Pa., Apr. 5, 1932; s. Richard Paul and Kathryn Clare (Wilhelm) Z.; m. Nancy J. Cramer, Dec. 27, 1952; children: Linda Joan, Janet Lee. BA in Commerce, Pa. State U., 1953; LLD, Lebanon Valley Coll., 1992. Asst. sec. Mellon Bank, Harrisburg, Pa., 1956-58; with Hershey (Pa.) Foods Corp., 1958—, asst. to pres., 1965-71, v.p., 1971-76, pres., chief oper. officer, 1976-84, pres., 1984-85, CEO, 1984-95, chmn., 1985-94; ret., 1994; bd. dirs. Lance, Inc., Westvaco Corp., Eastman Kodak Co. Trustee Pa. State U., United Theol. Sem.; mem. United Way Am. Lt USN, 1953-56. Recipient Alumni fellow award Pa. State U., 1978, Disting. Alumni award Pa. State U., 1987, N.C.C.J. Nat. Brotherhood award, 1988. Mem. Alumni Assn. Pa. State U. (pres. 1982-83), Hershey Country Club, Masons, Rotary (pres. Hershey 1973-74), Phi Kappa Psi. Methodist. Office: Hershey Foods Corp PO Box 810 Hershey PA 17033-0810

ZIMMERMAN, RICHARD GAYFORD, journalist; b. Springfield, Ohio, Sept. 3, 1934; s. Charles Ballard and Dorothy Cubitt (Gayford) Z. B.F.A. cum laude, Wittenberg U., 1956; M.A., Am. U., 1958. Freelance writer and polit. cartoonist, 1959-61; wire editor Urbana (Ohio) Daily Citizen, 1960-61; state house corr. Horvitz Newspapers, Mansfield, Lorain, Dover and Willoughby, Ohio, 1962-64, Dayton (Ohio) Jour. Herald, 1964-67; chief state house bur. Cleve. Plain Dealer, 1967-71, reporter Washington bur., 1971-72, chief Washington bur., 1972-77, nat. corr., 1978-85; freelance writer Africa, 1977. Co-author: Ohio Politics, 1994; contbr. articles to various publs. Served with USAF, 1961-62. Recipient award Ohio A.P., 1971, 83, award Ohio Legis. Corrs. Assn., 1968, 69. Mem. Ohio Press Club (trustee 1969), Nat. Press Club (sec. 1974-75, vice chmn. bd. govs. 1975-76, chmn. speakers com. 1979-80, chmn. house com. 1986-88, chmn. forum com. 1990-91, Washington Corr. award 1982, Lifetime Svc. award 1995), Ohio Legis. Corrs. Assn. (v.p. 1969-70), Beta Theta Pi. Home: 125 10th St SE Washington DC 20003-3922

ZIMMERMAN, ROBERT ALLEN See DYLAN, BOB

ZIMMERMAN, ROGER JOSEPH, fishery biologist; b. Alice, Tex., Dec. 2, 1941; s. Walter George and Laura Virgie (Heine) Z.; m. Domenica Marie DeCaro, Dec. 28, 1976; children: Kathryn, Robert. BS in Biology, Tex. A&I Coll., 1966, MA in Biology and Geology, 1969; PhD in Marine Scis., U.P.R., Mayaguez, 1979. Tchg. asst. biology dept. U. South Fla., Tampa, 1971; rsch. assoc. marine sci. dept. U. South Fla., St. Petersburg, 1971-73; rsch. assoc. P.R. Nuclear Ctr. U. P.R., 1974-75, grad. fellow, 1975-78, marine benthic ecologist Ctr. for Energy & Environ. Rsch., 1978-81; fishery ecologist fishery mgmt. divsn. NOAA/NMFS Galveston (Tex.) Lab., 1981-91, divsn. chief fishery ecology divsn., 1991-93, lab. dir., 1993—; rsch. fellow U.S. Nat. Mus. Natural History, Smithsonian Instn., Washington and Harbor Beach, Fla., summer 1975, 76; vis. instr. marine biology dept. Tex. A&M U., Galveston, summer 1988, 89; vis. instr. biology dept. Corpus Christi (Tex.) State U., 1986; tchg. asst. biology U. South Fla., 1970; lectr.-counselor Tex. A&I U., 1969, lab. coord., tchg. asst., 1968-69; OAS and U.S. AID advisor to Instuto de Pesca de Ecuador, 1985-88; mem. com. coastal ocean estuarine habitat rsch. planning com. NOAA 1987, sci. adv. com., 1989; chair predator-prey com. S.E. Fisheries Sci. Ctr., 1990-91; coord. climate and global change ecol. sys. and dynamics work group NMFS, 1990, spl. asst. to office of sr. scientist, 1990; mem. sci. adv. com. Galveston Bay project Nat. Estuary Program, 1993-94, mem. mgmt. com. Corpus Christi project, 1994-95; acting dir. SEFSC Galveston lab., 1993; bd. dirs. Gulf of Mex. regional marine rsch. program NMFS-SEFSC, 1992-93; rep. programs on coastal fisheries and estuarine ecology SERSC, 1992-95; cons. advisor in field; adj. wildlife and fisheries dept. and biology dept. Tex. A&M U., dept. biology Corpus Christi State U., dept. marine scis. La. State U., 1985-89, dept. biology U. Houston, 1983-85; presenter workshops in field. Reviewer for jours. in field, including Fishery Bull., Contbns. to Marine Sci., Marine Ecology Progress Series, Jour. Exptl. Marine Biology and Ecology, Marine Biology, Bull. Marine Sci., Jour. Wetlands Ecology and Mgmt., Estuaries, Coastal and Shelf Sci., also various proposals; editl. reviewer SEFSC Galveston Lab., 1984—; contbr. numerous articles to profl. publs.; author abstracts, revs. in field. Mem. Estuarine Rsch. Fedn., Gulf Estuarine Rsch. Soc., Crustacean Soc., Am. Fisheries Soc., Assn. Marine Labs. of the Caribbean. Office: Nat Marine Fisheries Svc SE Fisheries Sci Ctr 4700 Avenue U Galveston TX 77551-5923

ZIMMERMAN, SOL SHEA, pediatrician; b. N.Y.C., June 25, 1948; s. Isaac and Estera (Berkowicz) Z.; m. Diana F. Zimmerman, Aug. 8, 1971; children: Jeffrey, Steven, Andrew. AB, Columbia U., 1968; MD, NYU, 1972. Diplomate Am. Bd. Pediats.; pediat. critical care medicine. Intern dept. pediats. NYU-Bellevue Hosp. Ctr., N.Y.C., 1972-73, resident dept. pediats., 1973-75, chief resident dept. pediats., 1977-78, asst. prof. clin. pediats., 1978-83, assoc. prof. clin. pediats., 1983—, dir. pediat. critical care medicine, 1978—, assoc. dir. dept. pediats., 1985—; pres. Pediat. Assocs. N.Y.C., P.C., 1978—. Editor, author: (textbook) Critical Care Pediatrics, 1985. Chmn. com. on heart, health in the young N.Y.C. affiliate Am. Heart Assn., 1987-93. Maj. USAF MC, 1975-77. Fellow Am. Acad. Pediats., Am. Coll. Chest Physicians, Critical Care Medicine; mem. N.Y. Soc. Pediat. Critical Care Medicine (v.p. 1989-91, pres. 1991-93), Alpha Omega Alpha. Office: Pediat Assocs of NYC PC 317 E 34th St New York NY 10016-4974

ZIMMERMAN, THOM JAY, ophthalmologist, educator; b. Lincoln, Ill., Oct. 5, 1942; s. Kenneth Earl and Georgia Rosemary (Taylor) Z.; m. Tinker Steiner; 1 child, Jessica. BS in Zoology, U. Ill., 1964; MD, U. Ill., Chgo., 1968; PhD in Pharmacology, U. Fla., 1976. Diplomate Nat. Bd. Med. Examiners, Am. Bd. Ophthalmology. Intern St. Lukes Hosp., Chgo., 1968-69; resident U. Fla. Coll. Medicine, Dept. Ophthalmology, Gainesville, 1971-74, corneal fellow, 1974-75, glaucoma fellow, 1976-77; acting chmn. dept. ophthalmology La. State U., New Orleans, 1977; assoc. prof. ophthalmology and pharmacology Ochsner Clinic, New Orleans, 1977-79; prof. pharmacology and toxicology U. Louisville, 1986—, prof., chmn. dept. ophthalmology, 1986—; ophthalmic cons. (glaucoma) USPHS Hosp., New Orleans, 1977-82; cons. Nat. Adv. Eye Council and NEI, 1983; U.S. rep. for exec. com. Pan-Am. Glaucoma Soc., 1983-85; chmn. glaucoma symposium of Nat. Soc. to Prevent Blindness, 1988; guest lectr. numerous profl. socs. and confs. Author 6 books and numerous editorials; contbr. sci. articles to profl. jours.; mem. editorial bd. Jour. Continuing Edn. in Ophthalmology, 1977—, Annals of Ophthalmology, 1978—, Advances in Therapy, 1986—; contbr. book chpts., abstracts. Served with USPHS, 1969-71. Recipient Will F. Lyon award Presbyn.-St. Lukes Hosp., 1969; Robert E. McCormick scholar Research to Prevent Blindness Inc., 1978; grantee Nat. Eye Inst., 1978-84, 85-86; delivered Culler Meml. lecture, Ohio State U., 1986. Fellow Am. Coll. Clin. Pharmacology; mem. AMA (Physician's Recognition award 1971, 73, 75, 77, 79, 81, 83), Assn. for Research in Vision and Ophthalmology, Am. Soc. for Clin. Pharmacology and Therapeutics, Am. Soc. Contemporary Ophthalmology, Internat. Glaucoma Congress, Am. Acad. Ophthalmology, La.-Miss. Ophthalmology Soc., Research to Prevent Blindness Ophthalmologic Assn., So. Med. Assn., Can. Implant Soc., Ky. Med. Assn., Ky. Acad. Eye Physicians and Surgeons, Louisville Acad. Ophthalmology, Jefferson County Med. Soc., Alpha Omega Alpha. Home: 389 Mockingbird Valley Rd Louisville KY 40207-1337 Office: Univ of Louisville Dept Ophthalmology 301 E Muhammad Ali Blvd Louisville KY 40202-1511

ZIMMERMAN, WILLIAM EDWIN, newspaper editor and publisher; b. Bklyn., Feb. 2, 1941; s. George and Ruth (Edelbaum) Z.; m. Teodorina Bello, Dec. 13, 1969; 1 child, Carlota Pastora. BA, Queens Coll., 1962. Pres. Guarionex Press, Ltd., N.Y.C., 1979—; with Am. Banker, N.Y.C., 1962-82, editor, sr. v.p., 1982-89; editor in chief Banking Week, 1986-89; dep. editor. Sunday Bus. sect., The N.Y. Times, 1989; spl. projects editor, editor Student Briefing Page Newsday, L.I., N.Y., 1989—. Author: How to Tape Instant Oral Biographies, 1979, A Book of Questions to Keep Thoughts and Feelings, 1984, Make Beliefs, 1987, Life Lines: A Book of Hope, 1990, The Little Book of Joy, 1995, Dogmas: Simple Truths from a Wise Pet, 1995, Make Beliefs for Kids of All Ages, 1996, A Book of Sunshine, 1997, Personal Wisdom, 1997, Cat-e-chisms: Feline Answers to Life's Big Questions, 1997. Mem. Am. Oral History Assn., N.Y. Fin. Writers Assn., Am. Soc. Bus. Writers, Overseas Press Club, Deadline Club, Am. Soc. Bus. Press Editors, Dowtown Athletic Club, N.Y. Athletic Club, Sigma Delta Chi. Democrat. Jewish. Office: Newsday Inc 2 Park Ave New York NY 10016-5675

ZIMMERMAN, WILLIAM ROBERT, entrepreneur, engineering based manufacturing company executive; b. Cleve., May 11, 1927; s. Irving and Ella (Berger) Z.; m. Nancy Owen, 1963 (div. 1970); 1 child, Amanda; m. Eileen Samuelson, Nov. 11, 1979. BS, MIT, 1948, MS, 1949. Cons. Kurt Salmon Assocs., Washington, 1949-50, A.T. Kearney and Co., Chgo., 1950-52; mill mgr. Am. Envelope Co., West Carrollton, Ohio, 1952-56; exec. v.p. Avery Internat., Pasadena, Calif., 1956-67; pres. Swedlow, Inc., Garden Grove, Calif., 1967-73, Monogram Industries, Inc., Santa Monica, Calif., 1973-78; bd. dirs. Bentley Mills Industry, Calif., Moorhouse Industries, Fullerton, Calif. Council pres. Boy Scouts Am., Painesville, Ohio, 1957-62; exec. com. Jr. Achievement So. Calif., Los Angeles, 1975-77; trustee Los Angeles County Mus. Nat. History, 1987—, Harvey Mudd Coll., Claremont, Calif., 1983—. Republican. Clubs: Calif. (Los Angeles); Valley Hunt, Annendale (Pasadena). Avocations: tennis, jogging. Office: Zimmerman Holdings Inc 2600 Mission St San Marino CA 91108-1676

ZIMMERMANN, GERHARDT, conductor; b. Van Wert, Ohio, June 22, 1945; s. Ervin and Ethel Jane (Allen) Z.; m. Sharon Marie Reher, Mar. 17, 1974; children: Anna Marie, Peter Karl Irum. MusB, Bowling Green State U.; MFA, U. Iowa; student, with James Dixon, Leopold Sipe, Flora Contino, Richard Lert. Tchr. in Genoa (Ohio) Pub. Schs., 1967-70; condr. orch. Augustana Coll., Rock Island, Ill., 1971-72; music dir. Clinton (Iowa) Symphony Orch., 1971-72; asst. prof. music, condr. orchs. Western Ill. U., Macomb, 1972-74; asst. condr. St. Louis Symphony Orch., 1974-78, assoc. condr., 1978-82; music dir., condr. St. Louis Youth Orch., 1975-82, Canton Symphony Orch., 1980—, N.C. Symphony Orch., Raleigh, 1982—; guest condr. Recipient 2d Prize Georg Solti Conducting Competition 1973. Mem. Am. Symphony Orch. League, Nat. Acad. Rec. Arts and Scis., Phi Mu Alpha Sinfonia. Office: NC Symphony Orch Meml Auditorium PO Box 28026 Raleigh NC 27611-8026*

ZIMMERMANN, JOHN, financial consultant; b. Milw., June 10, 1937; s. Elmer Harry and Norman Wihelmina (Bergmann) Z.; m. Mary Sue Lankford, Apr. 9, 1959; children: Elizabeth, John Mark. B.B.A., U. Wis., Milw., 1964; M in Banking, Rutgers U., 1984. CPA, Wis., Ga. Audit mgr./research Price Waterhouse & Co., Milw., 1964-73, N.Y.C., 1971-73; asst. v.p., controller First Nat. Bank of Atlanta, 1973-74, v.p., controller, 1974, group v.p., controller, 1974-77, sr. v.p., controller, 1977-84; sr. v.p., controller First Atlanta Corp., 1985-86; exec. v.p., chief operating officer Enterprise Bank Network Inc., Atlanta, 1986-88; cons. to fin. instns., 1990—; bd. dirs. Vinings (Ga.) Bank and Trust, Monogram Credit Card Bank Ga. (subs. GE). Chmn. three yr. capital expansion campaign New Sch., Atlanta, 1984-87, bd. dirs., 1989-91, 94—, also treas.; v.p. adminstrn., fin. and labor United Way Atlanta, 1984-86, mem. goal setting com., 1982, bd. dirs., 1986-88. With USAF, 1955-59. Named Tinker AFB Airman of Quarter, USAF, 1956. Mem. AICPA, Fin. Execs. Inst. (pres. Atlanta chpt. 1982-83, so. area dir. 1985-87), Ga. Soc. CPAs, Wis. Soc. CPAs, Atlanta Athletic Club, Yacht Club. Office: 2160 Fairfax Dr Alpharetta GA 30004-1475

ZIMMERMANN, JOHN PAUL, plastic surgeon; b. Milw., Mar. 9, 1945; s. Paul August and Edith Josephine (Tutsch) Z.; m. Bianca Maria Schaldach, June 13, 1970; cbildren: Veronica, Jean-Paul. BS in Biology, Chemistry, Marquette U., 1966; MD, Med. Coll. Wis., 1970. Diplomate Am Bd. Plastic Surgery. Internship surgery Stanford U. Sch. of Medicine, Calif., 1970-71, residency in gen. surgery, plastic & reconstructive surgery, 1974-79; flight surgeon USAF, 1971-73; fellowship head & neck surgery Roswell Park Meml. Cancer Inst., Buffalo, N.Y., 1977; pvt. practice Napa, Calif., 1979—; dir. Aesthetic Surgery Ctr. of Napa Valley, Calif., 1993—; clinical asst. prof. of plastic surgery Stanford U. Sch. of Medicine, Calif., 1993—; bd. dirs. Interplast, Palo Alto, Calif. (pres., bd. dirs. 1991-94, chmn. bd. dirs. 1994-95). Mem. Am. Soc. Plastic & Reconstructive Surgeons, Am. Soc. Aesthetic Plastic Surgeons, Lipoplasty Soc., Calif. Soc. Plastic Surgeons (bd. dirs.), Calif. Med. Assn., Napa County Med. Assn. Republican. Roman Catholic. Avocations: sailing, golf, direct care of indigent patientsthrough Interplast. Office: 3344 Villa Ln Ste 10 Napa CA 94558

ZIMMERMANN, T. C. PRICE, historian, educator; b. Bryn Mawr, Pa., Aug. 22, 1934; s. R.Z. and Susan (Goodman) Z.; m. Margaret Upham Ferris. BA, Williams Coll., 1956, Oxford U., 1958; MA, Oxford U., 1964; AM, Harvard U., 1960, PhD, 1964. Asst. prof. Reed Coll., Portland, Oreg., 1964-67, assoc. prof., 1967-73, prof. history, 1973-77, chmn. dept. history, 1973-75; v.p. acad. affairs Davidson (N.C.) Coll., 1977-86, Charles A. Dana prof. History, 1986—; mem. Oreg. Com. for Humanities NEH, 1971-77; mem. Region 14 selection com. Woodrow Wilson Nat. Fellowship Found., Princeton, N.J., 1967-70. Author: Paolo Giovio: The Historian and the Crisis of Sixteenth-Century Italy, 1995 (Helen and Howard R. Marraro Book prize Am. Hist. Assn. 1996, Presdl. Book award Am. Assn. for Italian Studies 1997); co-editor of collected works of Paolo Giovio, 1985; contbr. articles to profl. jours. Pres. Am. Alpine Club, N.Y.C., 1979-82, bd. dirs., 1975-83; bd. dirs. Charlotte Opera Assn., N.C., 1980-82, N.C. Outward Bound Sch., Morgantown, 1978-81; bd. advisors Lowell Obs., 1988-93; mem. Rome Prize Jury (Post-Classical Humanistic Studies) Am. Acad. in Rome, 1993. Danforth fellow, 1956-62, Fulbright fellow, Italy, 1962-64, Villa "I Tatti" fellow Harvard U. Ctr., 1970-71; Am. Council of Learned Socs. fellow, N.Y.C., 1975-76. Mem. Am. Hist. Assn., Renaissance Soc. Am., Sixteenth Century Studies Conf., Soc. Italian Hist. Studies, Am. Assn. Italian Studies, Phi Beta Kappa. Office: Davidson College PO Box 1719 Davidson NC 28036-1719

ZIMMERMANN, WARREN, former foreign service officer; b. Phila., Nov. 16, 1934; s. Albert Walter and Barbara (Shoemaker) Z.; m. Corinne Roosevelt Robinson Chubb, Apr. 18, 1959; children: Corinne Alsop, Warren Jr., Elizabeth Zimmermann Metcalfe. BA, Yale U., 1956; BA/MA, Cambridge U., Eng., 1958. Joined Office Fgn. Svc., 1961; consular and polit. officer Am. Embassy, Caracas, Venezuela, 1962-64; student Serbo-Croation lang. Fgn. Svc. Inst., 1964-65; polit. officer Am. Embassy, Belgrade, Yugoslavia, 1965-68; Soviet policy analyst Bur. Intelligence & Rsch., Dept. State, 1968-70; speechwriter to sec. of state Dept. State, Washington, 1970-73; student Russian lang. Fgn. Svc. Inst., Dept. State, 1973; dep. chief, polit. sect. Am. Embassy, Moscow, 1973-75; spl. asst. policy planning Bur. European Affairs, Dept. State, 1975-77; counselor polit. affairs Am Embassy, Paris, 1977-80; dep. chmn. U.S. del. Madrid Conf. Security and Cooperation in Europe, 1980-81; dep. chief mission Am. Embassy, Moscow, 1981-84; dep. U.S. del. with rank of amb. negotiations on nuclear/space arms race with Soviet Union, Geneva, 1985-86; chmn. U.S. del. with rank of amb. Vienna meeting Conf. on Security and Cooperation in Europe, 1986-89; amb. to Yugoslavia, 1989-92; dir. Bur. Refugee Programs Dept. State, Washington, 1992-94; sr. fellow Rand Corp., 1994; sr. fellow Rand, 1994, sr. cons., 1995—; disting. fellow New Sch. Social Rsch., 1994—; professorial lectr. Johns Hopkins Sch. Advanced Internat. Studies, 1994-96; disting. fellow Sch. Pub. Affairs, U. Md., 1995; Kathryn and Shelby Cullom Davis prof. columbia U., 1996—; vis. fellow coun. Fgn. Rels., N.Y.C., 1984-85; chief U.S. del. negotiations Hotline Upgrade Agreement with Soviet Union, 1983-84; Carnegie tchg. fellow Yale U., 1958-59. Author: Origins of a Catastrophe: Yugoslavia and Its Destroyers, 1996. With U.S. Army, 1959. Mem. Coun. Fgn. Rels., Internat. Inst. Strategic Studies. Democrat. Avocations: history, tennis, skiing, fishing. Home: 96 Interpromontory Rd Great Falls VA 22066

ZIMMETT, MARK PAUL, lawyer; b. Waukegan, Ill., July 4, 1950; s. Nelson H. Zimmett and Roslyn (Yastrow) Zimmett Grodzin; m. Joan Robin Urken, June 11, 1972; children: Nora Helene, Lili Eleanor. BA, Johns Hopkins U., 1972; JD, NYU, 1975. Bar: N.Y. 1976, U.S. Dist. Ct. (so. and ea. dists.) N.Y. 1976, U.S. Dist. Ct. (no. dist.) Calif. 1980, U.S. Ct. Appeals (2d cir.) 1980, U.S. Supreme Ct. 1981, U.S. Ct. Appeals (5th cir.) 1986, U.S. Ct. Appeals (9th cir.) 1988. Assoc. Shearman & Sterling, N.Y.C., 1975-83, ptnr., 1984-90; adj. assoc. prof. internat. law NYU, 1986-88. Author: Letters of Credit, New York Practice Guide Business and Commercial Law, 1990; contbr. articles to profl. jours. Mem. ABA (subcom. on letters of credit, com. on uniform comml. code sect. bus. law), N.Y. State Bar Assn., Assn. of Bar of City of N.Y., N.Y. County Lawyers Assn. (com. on bus. bankruptcy law), Citizens Union. Democrat. Jewish. Office: 126 E 56th St New York NY 10022-3613

ZIMMIE, THOMAS FRANK, civil engineer, educator; b. Scranton, Pa., Jan. 24, 1939; s. Thomas and Stella Josephine (Price) Z.; m. Patricia Joyce Kelly, June 8, 1962 (div. 1979); 1 child, David Thomas; m. Judith Anne Braden, July 13, 1989. BSCE, Worcester Poly. Inst., 1960; MSCE, U. Conn., 1962, PhD in Geotech. Engring., 1972. Registered profl. engr., N.Y., Conn. Staff engr. Union Carbide Corp. (Linde div.), Buffalo, 1964-68; profl. engr. Town of Mansfield, Conn., 1968-72; ptnr. Wang and Zimmie Cons., Troy, N.Y., 1973-80; v.p. Arch Engring. Cons., Troy, 1984-88; program dir. NSF, Washington, 1988-90; pres., CEO Civrotech Cons. Engrs., Inc., Troy, 1993—; mem. faculty dept. civil engring Rensselaer Poly. Inst., Troy, 1973—; postdoctoral researcher Norwegian Geotech. Inst., Oslo, 1972-73; geotech. engr. N.Y. Dept. Environ. Conservation, Albany, 1983-85; town engr. Town of North Greenbush, N.Y., 1985-88. Editor: Permeability and Groundwater Contamination, 1981. 1st lt. U.S. Army, 1962-64. Mem. ASCE (Outstanding Svc. award 1986, 87), ASTM (Spl. Svc. award 1980, Charles Dudley award 1984), Transp. Rsch. Bd., Am. Rd. and Transp. Builders Assn. Achievements include research in environmental geotechnology. Home: 39 Zelenke Dr Wynantskill NY 12198-8627 Office: Rensselaer Poly Inst Civil Engring Dept Soil Mechanics Lab Troy NY 12180

ZIMNY, MARILYN LUCILE, anatomist, educator; b. Chgo., Dec. 12, 1927; d. John and Lucile Ruth (Andryske) Z. BA, U. Ill., 1948; MS, Loyola U., Chgo., 1951, PhD, 1954. Asst. prof. anatomy La. State U. Med. Ctr., New Orleans, 1954-59, assoc. prof., 1959-64, prof., 1964-75, prof., acting head, 1975-76, prof., head, 1976—, acting dean sch. grad. studies, 1989-90, dean sch. grad. studies and vice-chancellor for academic affairs, 1990—; vis. prof. anatomy U. Costa Rica Sch. Medicine, 1961, 62; chmn. La. Edn. Quality Support Fund Planning Com., State of La., Bd. Regents, 1993—; mem. So. Regional Edn. Bd., Regional Consortium of State higher Edn. Health Affairs Ofcls., 1993—. Grantee, NIH, 1958-72, 88-89, Arthritis Found., 1969-72, Schlieder Ednl. Found., 1972-75, Frost Found., 1975-78, NSF, 1982-83. Mem. AAAS, Am. Assn. Anatomists (mem. exec. com. 1981-85, program sec. 1990-94), Am. Physiol. Soc., Assn. Anatomy Chmn. (pres. 1983), Electron Microscopic Soc. Am., Am. Assn. Dental Schs. (sect. anat. scis.), Assn. Rsch. in Vision and Ophthalmology, Am./Internat. Assn. Dental Rsch., Omicron Kappa Upsilon, Alpha Omega Alpha. Home: 3330 Esplanade Ave New Orleans LA 70119-3132 Office: La State U Med Ctr Resource Ctr New Orleans LA 70112 *My appreciation for people has been a major factor in attaining my professional goals. Other factors include perseverance in the face of challenge, decision-making, warranted aggressiveness, mental curiosity and dealing openly with friends and colleagues.*

ZIMNY, MAX, lawyer; b. Bklyn., Mar. 9, 1925; s. Joseph and Rebecca (Nadelman) Z.; m. Bernice Nelson, June 26, 1948; children—Stuart, Andrew. Student Bklyn. Coll., 1942-47; LL.B. cum laude, 1950; postgrad. NYU Grad. Sch. Labor Law, 1950-52. Bar: N.Y. 1950, U.S. Dist. Ct. (so. and ea. dists.) N.Y. 1951, U.S. Ct. Appeals (2d cir.) 1955, U.S. Supreme Ct. 1962; U.S. Ct. Appeals (D.C. cir.) 1968, U.S. Ct. Appeals (4th cir.) 1969, U.S. Ct. Appeals (9th cir.) 1975, U.S. Ct. Appeals (8th cir.) 1980, U.S. Dist. Ct. (no. dist.) N.Y. 1983, U.S. Ct. Appeals (6th cir.) 1987, U.S. Ct. Appeals (7th cir.) 1988, U.S. Ct. Appeals (3d and 5th cirs.) 1991. Mem. Zimny & Goldberg, N.Y.C., 1950-52; asst. gen. counsel Textiles Workers Union Am., N.Y.C., 1952-58; asst. gen. counsel Internat. Ladies' Garment Workers' Union, N.Y.C., 1958-63, assoc. gen. counsel, 1963-72, gen. counsel, 1972-95, gen. coun. Union of Needletrades, Indsl. and Textile Employees, 1995—, mem. Vladeck, Elias, Vladeck, Zimny and Englehard, N.Y.C., 1976-78; lectr. NYU Sch. Law, Stetson U. Sch. Law, Indsl. Rels. Rsch. Inst., Nat. Acad. Arbitrators. Bd. dirs. Nat. Resources Ctr. for Consumers Legal Svcs., Lawyers Coord. Com. AFL-CIO; mediator, fact finder N.Y. Pub. Employment Relations Bd., 1968—; mediator, arbitrator Am. Arb. Assn., mem. nat. adv. coun., chair com. on rules and procedures, chair nat. task force on ADR in employment; mem. steering com. ctr. for Law and Econ. Policy, Columbia U. Sch. Law; chmn. Consumer Adv. Coun. City of N.Y.; adv. com. N.Y. U. and Fordham Conf. on Labor, 1985—; mem. Levittown (N.Y.) Bd. Edn.; chmn. Profls. for Histadrut, N.Y.C.; bd. dirs. Corsi Labor Mgmt. Inst. Served with U.S. Army, 1943-46. Mem. ABA (chmn. com. on arbitration 1977-81, coun. labor sect. 1989—), Bar Assn. City of N.Y. (labor com.), N.Y. State Bar Assn., Order of Coif. Club: B'nai B'rith (pres. lodge). Editor: Labor Arbitrator Development, 1983, Arbitration: A Guide for Advocates, 1990, Arbitration Casebook, 1997.

ZIMOV, BRUCE STEVEN, software engineer; b. Cin., Oct. 16, 1953; s. Sherman and Sylvia Zimov; m. Ruth Ellen Zimov, Sept. 7, 1974 (div. 1981); 1 child, Sarah Eleanor. BS in Physics, U. Cin., 1975, MA in Philosophy, 1979. Physicist Kornylak Corp., Hamilton, Ohio, 1982-83; software engr. Entek Sci. Corp., Cin., 1983-89, project mgr., 1989-95, systems mgr., 1995—. Inventor chess variants, table tennis variant. Mem. IEEE, Internat. Neural Network Soc., Tri-State Online Philosophy SIG (founder). Avocations: philosophy, chess, modem/BBS, computing, neural networks, economics. Home: Unit D 150 Gateway Dr Milford OH 45150 Office: Entek IRD Internat 1700 Edison Dr Milford OH 45150-2729

ZIMRING, FRANKLIN E., legal educator, lawyer; b. 1942. B.A., Wayne State U., 1963; J.D., U. Chgo., 1967. Bar: Calif. 1968. Asst. prof. U. Chgo., 1967-69, assoc. prof., 1969-72, assoc. dir. Center for Studies in Criminal Justice, 1971-73, prof., 1972-85, co-dir. Ctr. for Studies in Criminal Justice, 1973-75, dir., 1975-86; prof. law, dir. Earl Warren Legal Inst., Univ. Calif., Berkeley, 1985—. Author: Confronting Youth Crime, 1978; (with Newton) Firearms and Violence in American Life, 1969; (with Frase) Criminal Justice System, 1979, The Changing Legal World of Adolescence, 1982; (with Hawkins): Deterrence, 1973, Capital Punishment and the American Agenda, 1986, The Scale of Imprisonment, 1991, The Search for Rational Drug Control, 1992, Incapacitation: Penal Confinement and the Restraint of Crime, 1995, Crime is not the Problem, 1997. Mem. Am. Acad. Arts and Scis. Office: U Calif Earl Warren Legal Inst Boalt Hall Berkeley CA 94720

ZIMRING, STUART DAVID, lawyer; b. L.A., Dec. 12, 1946; s. Martin and Sylvia (Robinson) Z.; m. Eve Axelrad, Aug. 24, 1969 (div. 1981); m. Carol Grenert, May 24, 1981; children: Wendy Lynn Grenert, Joseph Noah, Matthew Kevin Grenert, Dov Shimon. BA in U.S. History, UCLA, 1968, JD, 1971. Bar: Calif. 1972, U.S. Dist. Ct. (cen. dist.) Calif. 1972, U.S. Dist. Ct. (no. dist.) Calif. 1984; U.S. Supreme Ct., 1994; cert. specialist in estate planning, probate and trust law. Assoc. Law Offices Leonard Smith, Beverly Hills, Calif., 1971-73; ptnr. Law Offices Smith & Zimring, Beverly Hills, Calif., 1973-76; assoc. Levin & Ballin, North Hollywood, Calif., 1976-77; prin. Levin, Ballin, Plotkin, Zimring & Goffin, A.P.C., North Hollywood, 1978-91, Law Offices Stuart D. Zimring, North Hollywood, 1991—; lectr. Los Angeles Valley Coll., Van Nuys, Calif., 1974-82. Author: Inter Vivos Trust Trustees Operating Manual, 1994, Lending to Inter Vivos Trusts—A Guide for Bankers and Their Counsel, 1995, Durable Powers of Attorney for Health Care—A Practical Approach to an Intimate Document, 1995, Reverse Mortgages—An Update, 1996. Bd. dirs. Bet Tzedek, Jewish Legal Svcs., L.A., 1975-88, chmn. legal svcs. com., 1978-82; bd. dirs. Brandeis-Bardin Inst., Simi Valley, Calif., 1976-80; bd. dirs. Bur. Jewish Edn., L.A., 1973-88, chmn. com. on parent and family edn., 1985-87; trustee Adat Ari El Synagogue, L.A., 1982—; bd. dirs. Orgn. for the Needs of the Elderly, 1994, 1st v.p. 1995-97, pres., 1997—. Recipient Circle award Juvenile Justice Connection Project, L.A., 1989, Wiley W. Manuel award for pro bono legal svcs., 1994, 95, 96. Mem. State Bar Calif., San Fernando Valley Bar Assn. (trustee 1979-86), Nat. Acad. Elder Law Attys. (pres. So. Calif. chpt., chair nat. tech. com.). Democrat. Avocations: music, collecting wine, travel, photography. Office: 12650 Riverside Dr North Hollywood CA 91607-3421

ZINBERG, DOROTHY SHORE, science policy educator; b. Boston, Feb. 25, 1928; m. Norman E. Zinberg, 1956 (dec.); children: Sarah, Anne. Student, U. Wis., 1945-47, U. Buffalo, 1947-48; BA, Boston U., 1949, MA, 1958; PhD, Harvard U., 1966. Teaching and research asst. in biochemistry Harvard Med. Sch., Cambridge, Mass., 1949-50, 52-57; research chemist Lever Bros., Cambridge, 1950-52; sr. research asso. Daniel Yankelovich, Inc., N.Y.C., and; Cambridge Center for Research in Behavioral Scis., 1966-68; NSF research sociologist dept. chemistry U. Coll. London, 1968-69; lectr. Harvard U., 1960—, sr. rsch. assoc., 1974—; mem. adv. com. Office Sci. Pers. NRC, Washington, 1971-74, bd. on engring. edn., 1991; spl. adviser Aspen Inst.; vis. scholar NAS, China, 1987; mem. adv. bd. Erik Erikson Inst. for Edn. and Rsch., 1996. Columnist London Times Higher Edn. Supplement, 1993—, N.Y. Times Syndication, 1994. Bd. dirs. Fine Arts Workshop, Provincetown, Mass., 1970-86, internat. sci. exchs. NAS, 1974-77, mem. com. on internat. rels., 1977-80, com. on internat. human resources; chmn. adv. coun. internat. divsn. NSF, 1978-81; mem. coun. Internat. Exch. of Scholars, 1978-81, com. internat. exch. of engrs. NAE, 1987-88, adv. panel Office Tech. Assessment Edn. and Employment of Scientists and Engrs., 1986-88; bd. dirs. on Engring. Edn., NRC, 1990-95; trustee Simon's Rock Coll., 1971-75. Fellow AAAS (com. exch. of scientists with Fed. Republic of Germany 1987, 91, com. on sci. freedom and responsibility 1972-74, com. on opportunities in sci. 1973-76, com. on sci., engring., and pub. policy 1982-88); mem. NAS (com. to evaluate Internat. Sci. and Tech. Ctr. Moscow 1995—), Fedn. Am. Scientists (coun. 1980-85), Coun. on Fgn. Rels., Internat. Sci. Policy Found. (adv. bd. 1988—). Home: 3 Acacia St Cambridge MA 02138-4818 Office: Harvard U JF Kennedy St Cambridge MA 02138

ZINDER, NEWTON DONALD, stock market analyst, consultant; b. N.Y.C., Aug. 12, 1927; s. Paul and Jennie (Feld) Z.; m. Clarice Katz, Dec. 26, 1954; children—Marla, Andrea, Pamela. B.A., NYU, 1948, M.B.A., 1957; M.A., Columbia U., 1949. Securities analyst Ira Haupt & Co., N.Y.C., 1953-60; securities analyst E.F. Hutton & Co., N.Y.C., 1960-63, stock market analyst, 1963-88; stock market analyst Shearson Lehman Bros., N.Y.C., 1988-92; investment cons., 1993—. Served with USN, 1945-46. Mem. Market Technicians Assn. Home: 1734 Roland Ave Wantagh NY 11793-2856

ZINDER, NORTON DAVID, genetics educator, university dean; b. N.Y.C., Nov. 7, 1928; s. Harry Jean and (Gottesman) Z.; m. Marilyn Estreicher, Dec. 24, 1949; children—Stephen, Michael. A.B., Columbia U., 1947; M.S., U. Wis., 1949, Ph.D., 1952. Asst. Rockefeller U., N.Y.C., 1952-56, asso., 1956-58, asso. prof. genetics, 1958-64, prof., 1964—, John D. Rockefeller Jr. prof., 1977—, dean grad. and postgrad. studies, 1993-95; cons. genetic-biology NSF, 1962-66, Office Tech. Assessment, Washington, 1979-81, Chas. Pfizer & Co., 1963-67; chmn. ad hoc com. to rev. viral cancer program Nat. Cancer Inst., 1973-74; mem. vis. com. dept. biology Harvard U., 1975-81, sect. virology Yale U., 1975-83, dept. biochemistry Princeton U., 1975-86; mem. sci. adv. bd. Carter-Wallace Inc., 1982-85, Genetic Systems Corp., 1981-86; mem.adv. com. Alliance Internat. Health Care Trust, 1984— ; trustee Cold Spring Harbor Lab., 1967-85, sec. to bd., 1980-85; chmn. com. to rev. Army chem. weapons stockpile disposal program, NAS/NRC, 1987-91; chmn. program adv. com. on human genome, NIH, 1988-91, other affiliations. Assoc. editor: Virology; sect. editor Intervirology, 1973-90. Recipient Eli Lilly award in microbiology and immunology, 1962, U.S. Steel Found. award in molecular biology, 1966, medal of excellence Columbia U., 1969, award in sci. freedom & responsibility AAAS, 1982; Am. Cancer Soc. scholar, 1955-58. Fellow Am. Acad. Arts and Scis. (coun. 1984-87); mem. NAS (mem. coun. 1988-91, exec. com. Assembly of Life Scis. 1975-78, bd. army sci. and tech. 1981), Soc. Am. Biol. Chemists, Genetics Soc. Am., Am. Soc. for Microbiology, Council Fgn. Relations, Harvey Soc., Sigma Xi. Spl. research in microbial genetics. Home: 450 E 63rd St New York NY 10021-7928 Office: Rockefeller U 1230 York Ave New York NY 10021-6307

ZINGALE, ROBERT G., surgeon; b. Bklyn., Feb. 9, 1957; s. Joseph and Theresa Zingale; m. Christine A. Smith, Oct. 4, 1986; children:Jillian, Kara, Alec. BS cum laude, Pace U., 1979; MD, SUNY, Bklyn., 1983. Diplomate Am. Bd. Surgery, Surg. Crit. Care, Nat. Bd. Med. Examiners. Resident Maimonides Med. Ctr., Bklyn., 1983-88; trauma fellow Coney Island Hosp, Bklyn., 1988-89; attending physician, dir. trauma Huntington (N.Y.) Hosp., 1989—; attending physician Nassau County Med. Ctr., East Meadow, N.Y., 1991—; clin. instr. SUNY, Stony Brook, 1991—; clin. asst. prof. surgery N.Y. Med. Coll./North Shore U. Hosp., Valhalla, 1993—; dir. surg. svcs. Dolan Health Ctr. Contbr. articles to profl. jours. Fellow ACS, Suffolk Acad. Medicine; mem. AMA, Soc. Laparoendoscopic Surgeons, Am. Soc. Gen. Surgeons, N.Y. Met. Breast Cancer Grop, Med. Soc. N.Y., Suffolk County Med. Soc. Office: Huntington Med Group 180 E Pulaski Rd Huntington Station NY 11746-1915

ZINGG, PAUL JOSEPH, university provost; b. Newark, July 22, 1947; s. Carl William Zingg and Dolores Lucking Dulebohn; m. Candace A. Slater, Aug. 9, 1980. BA, Belmont Abbey Coll., Belmont, N.C., 1968; MA, U. Richmond, Va., 1969; PhD, U. Ga., 1974. Prof. St. Bernard's Coll., Cullman, Ala., 1975-77; exec. dean Daniel Hale Williams U., Chgo., 1977-78; vice dean arts and scis. U. Pa., Phila., 1978-83, asst. to pres., 1983-86; cons. U. Calif., Berkeley, 1986; dean liberal arts St. Mary's Coll., Moraga, Calif., 1986-93; dean liberal arts Calif. Poly. State U., San Luis Obispo, 1993-95, provost and acad. v.p., 1995—; vis. instr. history Ga. Coll., Milledgeville, 1971; cons., contbr. on exhibits Oakland Mus., 1992-94; cons., contbr. to PBS-TV documentary film Baseball, 1991-93; editorial cons. U. Nebr. Press, 1994—, others. Author: Pride of the Palestra, 1987, Harry Hooper, 1887-1974: An American Baseball Life, 1993, Runs, Hits and Era: The Pacific Coast League, 1903-1958, 1995, others; editor, co-author: The Academic Penn, 1986; editor: Contemporary Topics in Applied Ethics, 1984; contbr. numerous articles to profl. jours. Mem. commn. on human resources and social change Nat. Assn. State Univs. and Land-Grant Colls., 1994—; mem. bd. advisors Oakland (Calif.) Mus., 1994—; mem. Ctrl. Coast Performing Arts Ctr. Commn., San Luis Obispo, 1993—; mem. bd. advisors Artemis Theater co., 1993—; bd. dirs. Hearst Art Gallery, Moraga, Calif., 1988-90; NEH summer fellow, 1975, Ctr. for Internat. Study and Rsch. fellow, 1980-82, Am. Coun. on Edn. fellow, 1983-84; granteee St. Mary's Coll., 1987. 90, 91, 93, NIH, 1987, others. Mem. Orgn. Am. Historians, Soc. for History Edn., N.Am. Soc. for Study of Sport, Am. Studies Assn., Soc. for Am. Baseball Rsch., Am. Coun. on Edn., Assn. Am. Colls. and Univs., Merion Golf Club, U. Calif. Golf Club, Phi Alpha Theta, Phi Beta Delta. Avocations: golf, Labrador retrievers, baseball, hiking. Office: Calif Poly State U Off of Provost San Luis Obispo CA 93407

ZINGMAN, EDGAR ALAN, lawyer; b. N.Y.C., Dec. 26, 1923; s. Louis M. and Sarah (Steinberg) S.; m. Barbara Gold, Dec. 17, 1950; children: Aileen Dale, Margaret Lee, Jonathan Alan. BS, CCNY, 1947; LLB, Yale U., 1950. Bar: N.Y. 1950, Ky. 1950, U.S. Dist. Ct. (ea. and we. dists.) Ky. 1951, U.S. Ct. Appeals (6th cir.) 1952, U.S. Supreme Ct. 1965. Assoc. Wyatt, Grafton & Sloss, Louisville, Ky., 1950-57; ptnr. Wyatt, Tarrant & Combs and predecessor firms, Louisville, 1957—. Bd. dirs. ACLU, N.Y., 1965-70; chmn. bd. dirs. Ky. Civil Liberties Union, 1958-70. Recipient Disting. Svc. award Ky. Hosp. Assn., Louisville, 1978, Am. Hosp. Assn., 1988. Mem. Ky. Assn. Hosp. Attys. (bd. dirs., pres.), Am. Acad. Hosp. Attys. (bd. dirs. 1980-87, pres. 1985), Jefferson Club. Avocations: music, theater, sports, travel, reading. Office: Wyatt Tarrant & Combs 2600 Citizen's Plz Louisville KY 40202

ZINK, CHARLES TALBOTT, lawyer; b. Long Beach, Calif., Oct. 27, 1937; s. William Talbott and Nellie Grace (Hoskins) Z.; m. Deborah Sidney Burks, Nov. 26, 1983. AB, Princeton U., 1959; LLB, U. Va., 1965. Bar: Va. 1965, Ga. 1965. Mng. ptnr. Hansell & Post, Atlanta, 1965-89; ptnr. Jones, Day, Reavis & Poque, Atlanta, 1989-93, Long, Aldridge & Norman, Atlanta, 1993—; lectr. N.W. Ctr. for Profl. Edn., Washington, Atlanta and Tampa, Fla., 1983—; mem. faculty Atlanta Coll. Trial Advocacy, 1985, mem. exec. com., 1984—, pres., 1985, 86. Bd. dirs. Atlanta Humane Soc., 1983—. Lt. (j.g.) USN, 1959-62. Mem. Lawyers Club Atlanta, Atlanta Tax Forum, Capital City Club. Republican. Episcopalian. Office: Long Aldridge & Norman 5300 One Peachtree Ctr Atlanta GA 30308

ZINK, LEE B., academic administrator, economist, educator; b. Salem, Ind., June 7, 1930; s. Otto C. and Lera (Berkey) Z.; m. Patricia Louise Patton, Aug. 16, 1964; children: Kevin Patrick, Barry Lee. BA in Econs. magna cum laude, Ind. U., 1959; PhD in Econs., Okla. State U., 1967. Field rep. GM Acceptance Corp., Louisville, Ky., 1953-54; asst. mgr. Dougherty Motor Sales, Salem, 1954-56; asst. prof. econs. Southeastern State Coll., Durant, Okla., 1964-67, spl. asst. to dir. Tech. Use Studies Ctr., 1964-65, dir., 1965-68, assoc. prof. of Econs., 1967-68; dir., prin. rsch. economist, bur.

bus. and econ. rsch. U. N.Mex., Albuquerque, 1968-77; prof. bus. adminstrn. N.Mex. Highlands U., Kirtland, 1974-81; dir. Inst. Applied Rsch. Svcs. U. N.Mex., Albuquerque, 1975—, dir. Nat. Energy Info. Ctr. affiliate/U.S. Dept. Energy, 1978-87, assoc. v.p. rsch., bus. and govt. rels., 1988—; mem. Gov.'s adv. com. statis. standards for Okla., 1964-66, sci. and industry Okla., 1965-66, statewide planning com. implemenation of Tech. Svcs. Act, Okla., 1965-66; cons. majority leader U.S. Ho. Reps., 1964-68, So. Okla. Devel. Assn., 1965-68, Gov. Okla., 1965-68, Kiamichi Econ. Devel. Dist., Okla., 1967-68, N.Mex. Corp. Commn., 1969-74, N.Mex. State Planning Office, 1971, Ohio State U. Evaluation Ctr., 1972, others; mem. Gov.'s adv. com. N.Mex. Dept. Devel., 1971; adv. panel spl. tech. assistance program Office Econ. Opportunity, 1972-74; mem. Albuquerque adv. coun. U.S. Small Bus. Adminstrn., 1974-81, chmn. 1977-79; chmn. Gov.'s Coun. Econ. Advisors, 1975-78; sec. econ. devel. Gov.'s Cabinet, 1975-76, policy advisor, 1976-78; econ. devel. task force We. Interstate Commn. Higher Edn., 1979. Mem. edit. review bd. Review of Regional Economics and Business, 1976-85; bd. edit. contbrs. The Albuquerque Tribune, 1979-82; mem. edit. adv. bd. The Southwest Review of Management and Economics, 1981-85; contbr. articles to profl. jours. Organizing pres. Kiamichi Econ. Devel. Dist., Okla., 1966-67; active Monte Vista Christian Ch., 1968—; exec. dir. N.Mex. Coun. Econ. Edn., 1969-75, chmn. operating com., 1976-86; pres. East Holiday Park Neighborhood Assn., 1978-94; adv. coun. city growth and devel. Greater Albuquerque Leadership Devel. Program, 1980-82; adv. bd. U.S. Armed Svcs., 1980-87; adv. bd. econ. devel. City of Albuquerque, 1980-84; community advisor NCAA Vols. for Youth, 1981-85; mem. Bernalillo county Human Svcs. Coalition, 1982-85; apptd. by Gov.-elect Anaya N.Mex. Jobs Task Force, 1982-83; apptd. chmn. by mayor Better Albuquerque Bond Coms., 1983-87, 93-95; trustee U. Albuquerque, 1983-86; bd. dirs. Nat. Tng. Inst. Cmty. Econ. Devel., 1979-82, Inst. Study Cmty. Econ. Devel., 1980-82, Albuquerque Conv. and Vis. Bur., 1984-87, Consumer Credit Counseling Svc. N.Mex., 1985-94, pres. 1989-90, Better Bus. Bur. N.Mex., 1992—; pres. adv. coun. UNICEF, Albuquerque, 1985-95; mem. employment and tng. needs task force City of Albuquerque, 1987-88; evaluation team Congressman Lujan's South Valley task force, 1987; apptd. chmn. by Mayor Saavedra and city coun. pub. forum com. recycling, 1991. 2d lt. U.S. Army, 1951-53, Germany; lt. col. USAR, 1953-71. Fellow Nat. Defense Edn. Act, 1959-62; grantee Nat. Aeronautics and Space Administrn., 1964-68, N.Mex. Dept. Devel., 1968-80, HEW, 1968-76, 1971-72, Bank N. Mex., 1969-77, The Albuquerque Model Cities Agy., 1969-70, Four Corners Regional Commn., 1969-80, U.S. Forest Svc., 1974-77, U.S. Dept. Commerce, 1975-79, 1976—, N.Mex. Energy Resources Bd., 1976-77, The Navajo Nation, 1976-78, U.S. Army Corps. Engrs., 1976-78, U.S. Dept. Energy, 1978-87. Mem. Am. Assembly Collegiate Schs. Bus. (rsch., statis., publs. com. 1976-77, small bus. adminstrn. liasion com. 1976-78), Am. Soc. Info. Sci. (frontier chpt. exec. com. 1972-73, chmn.-elect 1972, chmn. 1973), Assn. Univ. Bus. and Econ. Rsch. (exec. com. 1971-78, v.p. 1975-76, pres. 1976-77), Mid continent Rsch. and Devel. Coun. (bd. dirs. 1965-69), Fedn. Rocky Mountain States (chmn. bus. rsch. com. 1969-75), Rocky Mountain Coun. Burs. Bus. and Econ. Rsch. (chmn. 1969-77), N.Mex. coun. Econ. Edn. (bd. dirs. 1969-90), Am. Guild Organists (dean Albuquerque chpt. 1996—), Greater Albuquerque C. of C. (end. com. 1968-73, bd. dirs. 1970-76, 78-82, chmn. growth com. 1972, v.p. 1973-74, pres. 1981), Phi Kappa Phi, Phi Beta Kappa (alpha chpt. exec. com., sec. 1973-75), Golden Key (hon.). Democrat. Avocation: pipe organs. Home: 3741 Mount Rainier Dr NE Albuquerque NM 87111-4399 Office: U NMex Inst Applied Rsch Svcs 1920 Lomas Blvd NE Albuquerque NM 87106-2744

ZINKHAM, W. ROBERT, lawyer; b. Balt., May 30, 1955; s. William H. and Claire A. (Rafferty) Z.; m. Theresa McGeehan, July 7, 1985; children: Natalie Anne, Elizabeth Claire. BA, Johns Hopkins U., 1977; JD, U. Md., Balt., 1980. Law clerk to chief judge Md. Ct. Appeals, Balt., 1980-81; assoc. Venable, Baetjer and Howard, Balt., 1981-88, ptnr., 1989—; bd. dirs. Greater Balt. Med. Ctr. Found., 1992—. Editor Md. Law Rev., 1979. Chmn. Johns Hopkins Hosp. Psychiat. Day Hosp., Balt., 1982-92; pres. Mt. Washington Hills Assn., Balt., 1984-87. Mem. ABA, Am. Acad. Hosp. Attys., Nat. Health Lawyers Assn., Md. Bar Assn., Balt. Bar Assn. Republican. Office: Venable Baetjer & Howard 2 Hopkins Plz Baltimore MD 21201-2930

ZINKHAN, GEORGE MARTIN, III, marketing educator; b. Balt., Feb. 17, 1952; s. George Martin Jr. and Mary Elizabeth (Stoner) Z.; children: George M. IV, Lydia F., Sam S. BA in English Lit., Swarthmore Coll., 1974; MBA in Ops. Rsch., U. Mich., 1979, PhD in Bus. Adminstrn., 1981. Stats. lab. counselor U. Mich., Ann Arbor, 1978-79, teaching fellow, 1979-81; asst. prof. U. Houston, 1981-86, Conn prof. mktg., 1989-93; Coca-Cola prof. mktg. U. Ga., Athens, 1994—; vis. assoc. prof. U. Pitts., 1987-88; mem. exec. com. Faculty Senate, U. Houston, 1991-92; cons. FTC, Washington, 1992-93, San Francisco, 1994-96. Editor: Enhancing Knowledge Developments in Marketing, 1995; editor Jour. Advt., Richmond, Va., 1991-95, (spl. issue) Jour. Bus. Rsch., 1996; book rev. editor, mem. rev. bd. Jour. of Mktg., College Station, Tex., 1991—; mem. rev. bd. Jour. Current Issues, 1991—, Jour. Bus. Rsch., 1994—. Mem. Am. Mktg. Assn. (track chair 1991-96, v.p. for rsch. 1996—, pres. advt. spl. interest group 1996—), Am. Acad. Advt. (named one of Top 12 Contbrs. to Advt. 1990), Acad. Mktg. Sci. (track chair, promotion mgmt. 1994), Assn. Consumer Rsch. (session chair 1990, Judge Peabody awards). Democrat. United Ch. of Christ. Avocations: soccer, basketball, swimming, tennis, chess. Home: 195 S Finley St Athens GA 30605-1113 Office: Univ Ga Dept Mktg Brooks Hall Athens GA 30602-6258

ZINMAN, DAVID JOEL, conductor; b. N.Y.C., July 9, 1936; s. Samuel and Rachel Ilo (Samuels) Z.; m. Leslie Heyman (dec.); children: Paul Pierre, Rachel Linda; m. Mary Ingham, May 19, 1974; 1 child, Raphael. B.Mus., Oberlin (Ohio) Conservatory, 1958; M.A., U. Minn., 1961. Asst. to Pierre Monteux, 1961-64; guest condr. U.S. and Europe; music dir. Netherlands Chamber Orch., 1964-77, Rochester (N.Y.) Philharm. Orch., 1974-85; prin. guest condr. Rotterdam Philharm. Orch., 1977-79, chief condr., 1979-82; prin. guest condr., music dir. designate Balt. Symphony Orch., 1983-85, music dir., 1985—; music dir. Tonhalle Orch., Zurich, Switzerland, 1995; music dir. designate Aspen Music Festival and Sch., 1997, music dir., 1998—; adj. prof. Eastman Sch. Music, Rochester. Rec. artist Phillips, Nonesuch, Decca/London, Decca/Argo, Angel/EMI, Telarc, Sony Classical. Recipient Grand Prix du Disque, 1967, 82, Edison award, 1967, 3 Grammy awards, 1990, Grammophone best selling record award, 1993, Grammophone award, 1994, Deutschen Schallplatten prize. Office: Balt Symphony Orch 1212 Cathedral St Baltimore MD 21201-5517

ZINMAN, JACQUES, former insurance agency executive; b. Phila., Nov. 7, 1922; BS, U. Va., 1943; postgrad. U. Pa., 1945. Chmn., The Zinman Group, Ins. Agy., 1950-82. Mem. exec. com. Pa. state Rep. fin. com.; mem. Presdl. Electoral Coll. from Pa., 1972; bd. dirs. Pop Warner Nat. Football League; pres. Lake Agy. of Fla., 1990—. Ensign USNR, 1943-44. Recipient Outstanding Young Man Phila. award Jewish Nat. Fund, 1961. Mem. Variety Club, Theta Delta Chi. Lodge: Masons. Contbr. articles to profl. jours. Office: Lakes Agy of Fla 627 E Atlantic Blvd Pompano Beach FL 33060-6343

ZINN, BEN T., engineer, educator, consultant; b. Tel Aviv, Apr. 21, 1937; came to U.S., 1957; s. Samuel and Fridah (Gelbfish) Cynowicz; children: Edward R., Leslie H. B.S. in Mech. Engring. cum laude, NYU, 1961; M.S. in Mech. Engring., Stanford U., 1962; M.S. in Aerospace Engring., Princeton U., 1963, Ph.D. in Aerospace Engring. and Mech. Scis., 1965. Asst. research Princeton U., 1964-65; asst. prof. Ga. Inst. Tech., Atlanta, 1965-67, assoc. prof., 1967-70, prof., 1970-73, Regents prof., 1973—, joint prof. Schs. Aerospace Engring. and Mech. Engring., 1996—, Disting. prof., 1990, Davis S. Lewis, Jr. chair Sch. Aerospace Engring., 1992—; research scientist research div. Am. Standard Co., New Brunswick, N.J., summer 1976; cons. Brasilian Space Research Inst., Sao Jose dos Campos, Brazil, Aetna Casualty & Sr. Co., Atlanta. Recipient David Orr Mech. Engring. prize NYU, 1961; recipient Founder's Day NYU, 1961, Cert. of Recognition NASA, 1974; Ford fellow, 1962-63. Fellow AIAA (assoc. editor jour. 1982—), ASME, Combustion Inst. (past. pres. Eastern sect.), Nat. Fire Acad. (bd. visitors 1979-82), Am. Tech. Soc. (v.p. Atlanta chpt. 1980-84, pres. 1984-86); mem. Nat. Acad. Engring., Sigma Xi (rsch. award 1969, sustained rsch. award 1976), Tau Beta Pi, Pi Tau Sigma. Office: Ga Inst Tech Aerospace Engring Atlanta GA 30332

ZINN, GROVER ALFONSO, JR., religion educator; b. El Dorado, Ark., June 18, 1937; s. Grover Alfonso and Cora Edith (Saucke) Z.; m. Mary Mel Farris, July 28, 1962; children: Jennifer Anne, Andrew Grover. BA, Rice U., 1959; BD, Duke U., 1962, PhD, 1969; spl. student, U. Glasgow, Scotland, 1962-63. Asst. minister The Barony Ch., Glasgow, 1962-63; instr. in religion Oberlin (Ohio) Coll., 1966-68, asst. prof., 1968-74, assoc. prof., 1974-79, prof., 1979—, Danforth prof. religion, 1986—, chmn. dept. religion, 1980-84, 85-86, 1993-94. Translator: Richard of St. Victor: The Twelve Patriarchs, The Mystical Ark, and Book Three of the Trinity, 1979; co-editor: Medieval France: An Encyclopedia, 1995; mem. editl. bd. Dictionary of Biblical Interpretation; contbr. articles on medieval Christian mysticism, theology, and iconography. H.H. Powers Travel grantee Oberlin Coll., 1969, 85; Dempster fellow United Meth. Ch., 1965-66, NEH Younger Humanist fellow, 1972-73, Research Status fellow Oberlin Coll., 1972-73, 97—, Faculty Devel. fellow Oberlin Coll. 1985, Lilly Endowment fellow U. Pa., 1981-82; recipient ACLS Travel award, 1982. Mem. Medieval Acad. Am. (councillor 1983-86), Am. Soc. Ch. History (coun. mem. 1989-92, 95—), Ecclesiastical History Soc. Democrat. Methodist. Avocations: photography, electronics. Home: 61 Glenhurst Dr Oberlin OH 44074-1423 Office: Oberlin Coll Rice Hall Oberlin OH 44074

ZINN, MARCIE LYNN, music educator, pianist; b. Canton, Ill., May 6, 1951; d. Leo G. May and Betty J. (Fanning) Hayes. BS in Piano cum laude, Ill. State U., 1986, MS in Exptl. Psychology, 1990; studied piano with Donald Walker, 1984-86; postgrad., Ill. Inst. Tech. Nat. cert. tchr. of piano, piano pedagogy and theory, Music Tchrs. Nat. Assn. Mgr. Lewistown (Ill.) Plumbing, 1974-80; owner, operator The Musician's Stress Mgmt. Ctr., St. Charles, Ill. Author: (book) Healthy Piano Playing, 1995; contbr. articles to musical edn. jours; columnist: Monthly Music Edn. column in L.A. Family Mag; author newsletter for pianists Awareness. Mem. APA, Assn. Applied Psychology and Biofeedback, Performing Arts Med. Assn. (assoc.), Mensa, Golden Key, Phi Kappa Lambda. Home: PO Box 682 Saint Charles IL 60174-0682

ZINN, ROBERT JAMES, astronomer, educator; b. Chgo., Aug. 4, 1946; s. Walter Henry and Jean Ann (Smith) A.; m. Graziella Anna di Tullio; children: Gabriele, Annalisa, Giovanni. BS, Case Inst. Tech., 1968; PhD, Yale U., 1974. Carnegie fellow Hale Obs., Pasadena, Calif., 1974-76, Las Campanas fellow, 1976-79; asst. prof. Yale U., New Haven, 1979-82, assoc. prof., 1982-87; prof., 1987—. Mem. Am. Astron. Soc., Internat. Astron. Union. Office: Yale U Dept Astronomy PO Box 208101 New Haven CT 06520-8101

ZINN, WILLIAM, violinist, composer, business executive; b. N.Y.C., Nov. 19, 1924; s. Philip and Anna (Miller) Z.; m. Sophia Kalish, July 11, 1948; children: Karen Louise Heau, David Benjamin. Student, SUNY, 1952-54. Violinist Balt. Symphony, 1944-45, Indpls. Symphony, 1945-46, Ft. Wayne Philharm., 1946-47, Pitts. Symphony, 1947-49, Mpls. Symphony, 1950-51; concertmaster New Britain (Conn.) Symphony, 1968-90, Queens Symphony, 1969-71, Ridgefield (Conn.) Symphony, 1973-76, Chappaqua (N.Y.) Symphony, 1976; soloist with orchs. on records, on radio and in recitals; founder Masterwork Piano Trio, Masterwork Piano Quartet, Classical String Quartet, Zinn's Ragtime String Quartet, Excelsior String Quartet, Queens Festival Orch., Bayside, N.Y., 1965, Assn. Musical William Zinn, Caracas, Venezuela, 1968, Vitametrics of Am., 1976, Internat. Symphony for World Peace, 1978, Big Apple Chamber Pops, 1983, Excelsior Composer's Festival Competition, 1984; tchr. mech. drafting Mondell Inst., 1956; coach ensembles for Chamber Music Assocs., 1973-78; engr. N.Y.C. Bd. Edn. 1951-57, Bodin-Zinn Corp., 1957-58, Chem. Constrn. Corp., 1958-59; pres. Zinn Originals, Inc., 1959-68, Sparx, Inc., Trademark Hall of Fame, Inc., Nice Realty Corp., MFW Restaurant Corp.; co-founder Excelsior Music Pub. Co., Visionary Music Pub. Co., Nat. Music Promotion Agy., Telecommunication Services, 1982, Assoc. Sci. Publs., 1985, Barclay House Pubs., 1985, Excelsior Typographers and Engravers Unltd., 1985, Empco Recs. Internat., 1985, Imperial Editions, 1986, Missing Link Publs., 1986, Krazy Klassics Kompany, 1986, New Age Publs., 1987, Krazy Klassics Komix, 1988, Zinn Pub. Group, 1989, Zinn Communications, 1989, 94, Decca Books, 1993, Arlington House, 1993, Zinn Labs, Inc.; sec.-treas. Spark Industries, Inc., Music Clearing House, 1989, Innovation Records, 1991, Krazy Klassics Records, 1991, Hanover House, 1991; pres. Zinn Labs, Inc., 1994, Caramoor Press Internat. Corp., 1996, Dunhill Pub. Co., 1996, ZinnPrint Internat., Inc., 1996; adj. prof. NYU, 1987—. Author: (with Edward Gordon) Themography, 1947, (with George S. Grosser) Vitametrics I, The Human Formula for Self-Evaluation, 1976, Vitametrics II, The Human Formula for Self-Improvement, 1978, (with George S. Grosser) The Lost Chord, 1981, To Whom It May Concern, 1995, 2001 Original Wise Sayings of William Zinn, 1996; composer: (perpetual movement for woodwinds, strings and percussion) Chromatique, 1946, Piccolo Concerto, 1948, Violin Concerto, 1950, String Quartet, 1963, (piano solo) Chopinesque, 1965, (ballet) Night Creatures, 1966, Andante for Strings, 1967, Concerto for Octahorn, 1976, The International Anthem For World Peace, 1977, String Symphony, 1977, Romance for French Horn or Viola and Piano, 1981, Concerto for Violin/Viola/Cello/Double Bass and Orch., 1985, Kol Nidrei Meml. for String Quartet or String Orchestra, 1985, six concert duos for violin and viola, 1988, also songs including Mia, 1989, Aloha Hawaii, 1989, The Willows, 1990 (winner Hawaiian Nat. Song Contest 1990), Our Song of Love, 1990, Symphony in Ragtime, 1990, In Old Hawaii, 1991, Christmas in Hawaii, 1991, A Tribute to the Masters for string quartet or string orch. (14 original works in the style of Bach, Vivaldi, Mozart, Beethoven, Brahms, Rossini, Chopin, Schubert, J. Strauss, Jr., Tschaikowksy, Dvorak, Debussy, Mendelssohn, Sousa), 1991, A Stroll in a Japanese Garden for violin, cello, harp trio in 24 movements, 1996; arranger numerous operatic arias for string quartet or string orch.; originator Musiphonics, 1981, 24 Paganini caprices for string quartet, 1992, 10 Sousa marches for string quartet, 1992, The Merry Widow Waltz for string quartet or string orch., 1992, Paganini perpetual motion for string quartet, 1992, Mozart Symphony # 40, 1992; arranger 21 Henry Mancini songs for string quartet/string orchestra, 1992, 16 Duke Ellington songs for string quartet/string orchestra, 1993, Gold and Silver Waltz, Skater's Waltz for string quartet and string orchestra, 1993, 7 arias from Porgy & Bess for string quartet/string orchestra, 1994, A Tribute to Fritz Kreisler for violin and piano, 1994, 15 arrangements of Fritz Kreisler works for String Quartet String Orch., 1994, 12 classic Jewish Favorites for String Quartet/String Orch., 1995, 12 Jewish Songs for String Quartet/String Orch., 1995, 6 Duets for Violin & Viola, vol. II, 1996; pioneer multi-styles of music for string quartet and string orch.; composer over 500 works; developer numerous products for home, personal, automobile and novelty use. Chmn. bd. dirs. Let Us Remember to Remember, 1984. Recipient 41st Hawaiian Nat. Song Contest award, 1990. Mem. ASCAP, Internat. Platform Assn., Nat. Council Women of U.S., Am. Fedn. Musicians, N.Y. Humanist Assn. Home: 35-19 215th Pl Bayside NY 11361-1725

ZINNEN, ROBERT OLIVER, general management executive; b. Racine, Wis., June 28, 1929; s. Aloys Henry and Mabel Helen (Holy) Z.; m. Darlene Mary Weyers, Aug. 25, 1956; children: Claudia Jane, Robert O. B.B.A., U. Wis., 1951, J.D., 1956. Bar: Wis. 1956, Ill. 1959, Mass. 1982; CPA, Ill. Tax accountant Price Waterhouse, Chgo., 1956-59; mem. firm Tenney & Bentley, Chgo., 1959-64; assoc. dir. taxes Allstate Cos., Skokie, Ill., 1964-65; v.p. fin. Do-All Co., Des Plaines, Ill., 1965-67; dir. taxes Quaker Oats Co., Chgo., 1967-71; internat. atty. Am. Hosp. Supply Corp., 1971-75; fin. cons. Alexander Proudfoot Co., Chgo., 1975-76; v.p. fin. Milton Bradley Co., Springfield, Mass., 1976-82; co-owner, exec. v.p. Roadmaster Corp., Olney, Ill., 1982-88, cons., 1988—. Mem. Housing and Traffic Commns., Highland Park, Ill., 1963-66; chmn. Congl. Action Com., Springfield; bd. dirs. Assoc. Industries, Mass. Served with U.S. Army, 1951-53. Mem. Toy Mfrs. Am. (bd. dirs. 1984-88), Quail Creek Country Club, Longmeadow Country Club. Republican. Roman Catholic.

ZINNER, MICHAEL JEFFREY, surgeon, educator; b. Miami, Fla., Apr. 2, 1945; s. Doran D. and Eve (Wernicoff) Z.; children: Darren, Daniel. BEE, Johns Hopkins U., 1967; MD, U. Fla., 1971; postgrad., NIH Found. for Edn. in the Scis., Bethesda, Md., 1973-74. Diplomate Am. Bd. Surgery (bd. dirs. 1988—). Intern The Johns Hopkins Hosp., Balt., 1971-72, jr. asst. resident in surgery, 1972-73, sr. asst. resident, 1976-79, asst. chief of svc. in surgery, 1979-80; registrar thoracic surgery Frenchay Hosp., Bristol, Eng., 1977; instr. The Johns Hopkins U. Sch. Medicine, Balt., 1978-80; asst. prof. surgery Downstate Med. Ctr., Bklyn., 1980-83, assoc. prof., 1983-85; assoc. dir. surg. residency program, coord. residency program The Johns Hopkins Med. Instns., Balt., 1985-88, assoc. prof., vice chmn. dept. surgery, 1985-88, prof., 1988; prof., chmn. dept. surgery UCLA Sch. Medicine, 1988-94; mem. staff Kings County Hosp., Bklyn., 1980-85, chief gen. surgery and oncology, 1983-85; mem. staff Balt. VA Hosp., 1985-88, Johns Hopkins Hosp., 1985-88, Wadsworth VA Hosp., L.A., 1988-94; chief of surgery UCLA Med. Ctr., 1988-94; surgeon-in-chief Brigham and Womens Hosp., Boston, 1994—; prof. Harvard Med. Sch., 1994—; ednl. cons. Cath. Med. Ctr., 1981-84; mem. Clin. Rsch. Ctr. Subcom. on Sci. Rev. Protocols, SUNY, Downstate, 1982-84. Contbr. over 100 articles to profl. jours.; lectr. in field. Maj. M.C., U.S. Army, 1973-76. Rsch. grantee NIH, 1982-86, 88—; merit rev. grantee VA, 1988; grantee numerous univers., founds., pharm. cos., 1978—. Fellow ACS (com. on rsch. and edn. 1988); mem. IEEE, NIH (ad hoc, study sect., surgery and biomed. engring. 1986), Am. Fedn. Clin. Rsch., Assn. Acad. Surgery (com. on issues 1980-82, recorder 1982-84, exec. coun. 1982—, pres. 1985-86), Am. Physiol. Soc., Am. Gastroenterol. Assn., Am. Pancreatic Assn., Soc. Univ. Surgeons (com. on publs. 1984-86, com. on edn., 1986-87, exec. coun. 1986—, pres. 1987-88), Soc. Critical Care Medicine, N.Y. Surg. Soc., Gastroenterology Rsch. Group, Surg. Biology Club, Collegium Internationale Chirugiac Digestival, Conjoint Coun. Surg. Rsch., Soc. Surgery of Alimentary Tract, Soc. Clin. Surgery, Alpha Omega Alpha. Avocations: fishing, boating. Office: Brigham and Womens Hosp Dept Surgery 75 Francis St Boston MA 02115-6110

ZINSER, ELISABETH ANN, academic administrator; b. Meadville, Pa., Feb. 20, 1940; d. Merle and Fae Zinser. BS, Stanford U., 1964; MS, U. Calif., San Francisco, 1966, MIT, 1982; PhD, U. Calif., Berkeley, 1972. Nurse VA Hosp., Palo Alto, Calif., 1964-65, San Francisco, 1969-70; instr. Sch. Nursing U. Calif., San Francisco, 1966-69; pre-doctoral fellow Nat. Inst. Health, Edn. and Welfare, 1971-72; adminstr. Sch. Medicine U. Wash., Seattle, 1972-75, Coun. Higher Edn., State of Ky., 1975-77; prof., dean. Coll. Nursing U. N.D., Grand Forks, 1977-83; vice chancellor acad. affairs U. N.C., Greensboro, 1983-89; pres. Gallaudet U., Washington, 1988, U. Idaho, Moscow, 1989-95; chancellor U. Ky., Lexington, 1995—; bd. dirs. Am. Coun. Edn., Washington; cons. Boeing Aircraft Co., Seattle; chmn. commn. on outreach and tech. transfer; bd. dirs. Nat. Assn. State Univs. and Land Grant Colls. Primary author: (with others) Contemporary Issues in Higher Education, 1985, Higher Education Research, 1988. Bd. dirs. Humana Hosp., Greensboro, 1986-88; v.p., bd. dirs. Ea. Music Festival, Greensboro, 1987-89; trustee N.C. Coun. Econ. Edn., 1985-89, Greensboro Day Sch., 1987-89. Leadership fellow Bush Found., 1981-82. Mem. Am. Assn. Higher Edn., Assn. Am. Colls. (Coun. Liberal Learning), Am. Assn. Univ. Adminstrs., AAUP, AAUW, Pi Lambda Theta, Sigma Theta Tau. Office: U Ky 111 Adminstrn Bldg Lexington KY 40506-0032*

ZINSSER, WILLIAM KNOWLTON, editor, writer, educator; b. N.Y.C., Oct. 7, 1922; s. William Herman and Joyce (Knowlton) Z.; m. Caroline Fraser, Oct. 10, 1954; children: Amy Fraser, John William. A.B., Princeton U., 1944; L.H.D., Rollins Coll., 1984; Litt.D., Ind. State U., 1985, Wesleyan U., 1988. Feature writer N.Y. Herald Tribune, 1946-49, drama editor, 1949-54, film critic, 1955-58, editorial writer, 1958-59; free-lance writer, 1959—; commentator on NBC-TV Sunday program, 1964-65; columnist Look mag, 1967, Life mag, 1968-72, N.Y. Times, 1977; faculty Yale U., 1971-79, master Branford Coll., 1973-79; gen. editor, Book-of-the-Month Club, 1979-86 . Author: Any Old Place With You, 1957, Seen Any Good Movies Lately?, 1958, Search and Research, 1961, The City Dwellers, 1962, Weekend Guests, 1963, The Haircurl Papers, 1964, Pop Goes America, 1966, The Paradise Bit, 1967, The Lunacy Boom, 1970, On Writing Well, 1976, Writing with a Word Processor, 1983, Willie and Dwike, 1984, Writing to Learn, 1988, Spring Training, 1989, American Places, 1992, Speaking of Journalism, 1994; co-author: Five Boyhoods, 1962; editor Extraordinary Lives, 1986, Inventing the Truth, 1987, Spiritual Quests, 1988, Paths of Resistance, 1989, Worlds of Childhood, 1990, They Went, 1991. Bd. dirs. Bklyn. Mus., 1967-72. Served with AUS, 1943-45, MTO. Clubs: Century Assn, Coffee House. Home: 45 E 62nd St New York NY 10021-8025

ZIOCK, KLAUS OTTO HEINRICH, retired physics educator; b. Herchen, Germany, Feb. 4, 1925; came to U.S., 1958, naturalized, 1966; s. Samuel and Elisabeth (Bauer) Z.; m. Ursula E. A. Thierbach, May 31, 1952; children—Hans-Joachim, Klaus-Peter, Robert, Michael. Diplom Physiker, U. Bonn, Fed. Republic Germany, 1949, Dr. rer.nat., 1956. Rsch. physicist E. Leybold's Nachfolger, Cologne, Germany, 1950-54; rsch. assoc. U. Bonn, Germany, 1956-58; rsch. assoc. Yale U., New Haven, 1958-60, asst. prof. physics, 1960-62; assoc. prof. physics U. Va., Charlottesville, 1962-72, prof., 1972-95, prof. emeritus, 1995—. Author: Basic Quantum Mechanics, 1969; contbr. numerous articles to profl. jours.; patentee in field. Recipient Humboldt prize Alexander von Humboldt Stiftung, 1978. Mem. Am. Phys. Soc.

ZIOLKOWSKI, JAN MICHAEL, medievalist educator; b. New Haven, Nov. 17, 1956; s. Theodore J. and Yetta (Goldstein) Z.; m. Elizabeth Ann Hillenius; children: Saskia Elizabeth, Ada Margaret, Yetta Joy. AB summa cum laude, Princeton U., 1977; PhD, U. Cambridge, Eng., 1982; MA (hon.), Harvard U., 1987. Asst. prof. Harvard U., Cambridge, Mass., 1981-84, John L. Loeb assoc. prof. of the humanities, 1984-87, prof. medieval Latin and comparative lit., 1987—. Editor Comparative Literature Studies. Fellow Guggenheim Found., 1987-88, ACLS, 1986, Rome Prize fellow, Am. Acad. in Rome, 1980-81; Marshall scholar, 1977-80. Mem. Medieval Acad. Am. (councillor 1991-94), Dante Soc. Am., Am. Philol. Assn., Phi Beta Kappa. Home: 930 Centre St Newton MA 02159-1266 Office: Harvard Univ Dept. Medieval Latin/Liter Cambridge MA 02138

ZIOLKOWSKI, THEODORE JOSEPH, comparative literature educator; b. Birmingham, Ala., Sept. 30, 1932; s. Miecislaw and Cecilia (Jankowski) Z.; m. Yetta Bart Goldstein, Mar. 26, 1951; children: Margaret Cecilia, Jan Michael, Eric Josef. AB, Duke U., 1951, AM, 1952; student, U. Innsbruck, Austria, 1952-53; PhD, Yale U., 1957. Instr., then asst. prof. Yale U., New Haven, 1956-62; assoc. prof. Columbia U., N.Y.C., 1962-64; prof. Germanic langs. and lit. Princeton (N.J.) U., 1964-69, chmn., 1973-79, Class of 1900 prof. modern langs., 1969—, prof. comparative lit., 1975—, dean Grad. Sch., 1979-92; vis. prof. Rutgers U., 1966, Yale U., 1967, 75, CUNY, 1971, Bristol U., 1987, U. Munich, 1992; vis. scholar U. Ctr. in Va., 1971, Piedmont U. Ctr., N.C., 1971; Dancy Meml. lectr. U. Montevallo, 1973; Christopher Longest lectr. U. Miss., 1979; Patten Found. lectr. Ind. U., 1980; vis. lectr. Österreichische Akademie der Wissenschaften, 1992; vis. lectr. Korean Ministry of Edn., 1996; chmn. N.Y. State Doctoral Evaluation Program in German, 1975-80; nat. rev. panel for U.S. Nat. Grad. Fellows Program, 1985-87, 91—; chmn. overseers vis. com. on German Harvard U., 1982-88; mem. selection com. for Bennett award, 1988; with German-Am. Acad. Coun., 1993—; chmn. N.Y. State Humanities Screening Com., 1996; forum assembly spkr. Brigham Young U. Author: Hermann Broch, 1964, The Novels of Hermann Hesse, 1965, Hermann Hesse, 1966, Dimensions of the Modern Novel, 1969, Fictional Transfigurations of Jesus, 1972 (James Russell Lowell prize for criticism), Disenchanted Images, 1977, Der Schriftsteller Hermann Hesse, 1979, The Classical German Elegy, 1980, Varieties of Literary Thematics, 1983, German Romanticism and Its Institutions, 1990, Virgil and the Moderns, 1993, The Mirror of Justice, 1997, also articles and revs.; editor: Hermann Hesse, Autobiographical Writing, 1972, Hermann Hesse, Stories of Five Decades, 1972, Hesse: A Collection of Critical Essays, 1972, Hermann Hesse, My Belief: Selected Essays, 1974, Hermann Hesse, Tales of Student Life, 1976, Hermann Hesse, Pictor's Metamorphoses and Other Fantasies, 1982, Hermann Hesse, Soul of the Age: Selected Letters, 1891-1962, 1991, Jahrbuch fur Internationale Germanistik, 1997—; mem. editl. bd. Germanic Rev., 1962-95, Publs. MLA, 1971-75, Arbitrium, 1983—, 17th Century Studies, 1985—, Germanistik, 1987—; mem. editl. bd. Priceton U. Press, 1972-75, trustee, 1982-95; translator (with Yetta Ziolkowski): The Poetics of Quotation (Herman Meyer) 1968, Herman Hesse: A Pictorial Biography, 1975. Chmn. N.Y. State Humanities Screening Com., 1996. Recipient Howard T. Behrman award for disting. achievement in humanities, 1978, Wilbur Lucius Cross medal Yale U., 1982, Goethe Inst. gold medal, 1987, Henry Allen Moe prize in humanities, 1988; Fulbright rsch. grantee, 1958-59, grantee Am. Philos. Soc., 1959, NEH grantee, 1978, Guggenheim fellow, 1964-65, Am. Coun. Learned Socs. fellow, 1972, 76; resident fellow Bellagio Study Ctr., 1993. Mem. MLA (exec. coun. 1976-77, pres. 1985), Acad. Lit. Studies, Am. Comparative Lit. Assn., Am. Acad. Arts and Scis., Assn. Lit. Scholars and Critics, Authors Guild, Am. Assn. Tchrs. German (hon. life), Yale Grad. Sch. Assn. (pres. 1974-76), Assn. Grad. Schs. (v.p. 1989-90, pres. 1990-91), Heinrich von Kleist Gesellschaft, Goethe-Gesellschaft, Novalis-Gesellschaft, Internat. Vereinigung für Germanistik (exec. coun. 1985-95, treas. 1990-95), Am. Philos. Soc. (councillor 1991—), Göttingen Akademie der Wissenschaften, Austrian Akademie der Wissenschaften, Phi Beta Kappa. Home: 36 Bainbridge St Princeton NJ 08540-3902 Office: Princeton U 230 E Pyne Bldg Princeton NJ 08544

ZIOMEK, JONATHAN S., journalist, educator; b. Newport News, Va., July 28, 1947; s. Stanley Walter and Joy Carmen (Schmidt) Z.; m. Rosalie Ziomek, Aug. 14, 1977; children: Joseph, Jennifer; 1 stepchild, Daniel. BA in Sociology, U. Ill., 1970, MS in Journalism, 1982. Reporter, feature writer, Sun. fin. editor Chgo. Sun-Times, 1970-78; press sec. Robert Ash Wallace for U.S. Senate campaign, Chgo., 1979-80; asst. prof. Medill Sch. Journalism, Northwestern U., Evanston, Ill., 1983-88; dir. grad. editl. programs Medill Sch. Journalism/Northwestern U., Evanston, Ill., 1988—, asst. dean, assoc. prof., 1994—; presenter writing workshops; corp. writing cons. Contbr. articles to various mags.; editor: Chgo. Journalist Newsletter, 1991-93. Participant Internat. Visitors Ctr., Chgo., 1988—; fact-finder USIA, Bulgaria and Yugoslavia, 1990. Mem. Assn. for Edn. in Journalism and Mass Communications, Soc. Profl. Journalists, Nat. Assn. Sci. Writers, Headline Club. Home: 2149 Hartrey Ave Evanston IL 60201-2571 Office: Northwestern Univ Medill Sch Journalism Evanston IL 60208

ZION, ROGER H., consulting firm executive, former congressman; b. Escanba, Mich., Sept. 17, 1921; s. Herschel G. and Helen (Hutchinson) Z.; m. Marjorie Knauss, Feb. 20, 1945; children—Gayle, Scott, Randy. B.A., U. Wis., 1943; postgrad., Grad. Sch. Bus. Adminstrn., Harvard, 1944-45. With Mead Johnson & Co., 1946-66, dir. tng. and profl. relations, 1965-66; internat. marketing mgmt. cons., 1966; mem. 90th-93d congresses from 8th Dist. Ind.; chmn. Republican Task Force on Energy and Resources; pres. Resources Devel., Inc. (cons.), Washington, 1975—. Author: Keys to Human Relations in Selling, 1963, The Hallowed Howls of Congress, 1994, The Republican Challenge, 1995. Vice pres. Buffalo Trace council Boy Scouts Am., 1961; Bd. dirs., chmn. Evansville (Ind.) chpt. ARC, 1960-65. Served to lt. USNR, 1943-46, PTO. Named Toastmaster Evansville Press Gridiron dinner, 1963; recipient Citizen of Month award New Image Com. of Evansville's Future, 1962. Mem. VFW, Am. Legion, Nat. Sales and Marketing Execs. Assn. (pres. Evansville 1962), Wabash Valley Assn., AMVETS (life), Rotary (dir. Evansville club 1964), Evansville Country Club (dir. 1960-65), Alpha Delta Phi (pres. Wis. chpt. 1941-43). Republican. Congregationalist. Home: 834 Plaza Dr Evansville IN 47715-6936 Office: 412 1st St SE Washington DC 20003-1804

ZIPERSKI, JAMES RICHARD, trucking company executive, lawyer; b. Milw., May 27, 1932; s. George Felix and Louise (Medema) Z.; m. Patricia Jean Hoag, June 28, 1958; children: Jean Marie, David Carrington, James Patrick. BS, Marquette U., 1953, JD, 1957. Bar: Wis. 1957, U.S. Supreme Ct., 1967, U.S. Ct. Appeals, 1978. Resident counsel Schwerman Trucking Co., Milw., 1957—, sec., 1962—, exec. v.p. corp., 1977-80, exec. v.p., 1980-86; exec. v.p., corp. and sec. Tankstar USA, Inc. (parent co. Schwerman Trucking Co.), Milw., 1987—, also bd. dirs. Served with AUS, 1953-55. Mem. Transp. Lawyers Assn., Westmoor Country Club, Kiwanis, Alpha Kappa Psi, Phi Delta Phi. Home: 2110 N Swan Blvd Milwaukee WI 53226-2644 Office: Tankstar USA Inc PO Box 736 611 S 28th St Milwaukee WI 53215-1201

ZIPES, DOUGLAS PETER, cardiologist, researcher; b. White Plains, N.Y., Feb. 27, 1939; s. Robert Samuel and Josephine Helen (Weber) Z.; m. Marilyn Joan Jacobus, Feb. 18, 1961; children: Debra, Jeffrey, David. B.A. cum laude, Dartmouth Coll., 1961, B.Med. Sci., 1962; M.D. cum laude, Harvard Med. Sch., 1964. Diplomate Am. Bd. Internal Medicine (mem. subsplty. bd. cardiovascular disease 1989—, chmn., 1995—, chmn. com. cert. in clin. cardiac electrophysiology 1989-96). Intern, resident, fellow in cardiology Duke U. Med. Ctr., Durham, N.C., 1964-68; vis. scientist Masonic Med. Research Lab., Utica, N.Y., 1970-71; asst. prof. medicine Ind. U. Sch. Medicine, Indpls., 1970-73, assoc. prof., 1973-76, prof., 1976-94, prof. pharmacology and toxicology, 1993—, disting. prof. medicine, 1994—; dir. Divsn. of Cardiology Krannert Inst. Cardiology, Ind. U. Sch. Medicine, 1995—; cons.; mem. cardiology adv. com. NIH, 1991-94. Author: Comprehensive Cardiac Care, 7th edit., 1991; editor: Slow Inward Current, 1980, Cardiac Electrophysiology and Arrhythmias, 1985, Nonpharmacological Therapy of Tachyarrhythmias, 1987, Cardiac Electrophysiology From Cell to Bedside, 1990, 2d edit., 1994; co-editor: Treatment of Heart Diseases, 1992, Ablation of Cardiac Arrhythmias, 1994, Antiarrhythmic Therapy: A Pathophysiologic Approach, 1994; mem. editl. bd. Circulation, 1974-78, 83—, Am. Jour. Cardiology, 1979-82, 88—, Am. Jour. Medicine, 1979-90, Jour. Am. Coll. Cardiology, 1983, Am. Heart Jour., 1977—, PACE, 1977—, Circulation Rsch., 1983-90, Am. Jour. Noninvasive Cardiology, 1985-89, Jour. Electrophysiology, 1987-89, Cardiovascular Drugs and Therapy, 1986-93, Japanese Heart Jour., 1989—, Jour. Cardiovascular Pharmacology and Therapeutics, 1994—, Jour. Cardiovascular Pharmacology, 1995—, Cardiovascular Therapeutics, 1995, Current Clin. Trials, 1995, Jour. Interventional Cardiac Electrophysiology, 1996—; editor-in-chief: Progress in Cardiology, 1988-92, Jour. Cardiovascular Electrophysiology, 1990—, Cardiology in Rev., 1992—, Contemporary Treatments of Cardiovascular Disease, 1996—; contbr. numerous articles to med. pubs.; patentee cardioverter, elec. prevention of arrhythmia, discrimination of atrial fibrillation and fixation of implantable devices. Pres., bd. dirs. Indpls. Opera Co., 1983-85; mem. study sect. NIH, Washington, 1977-81; mem. nat. merit rev. bd. VA, 1982-85, Cardiology Adv. Com. NHLBI, 1991-94, chmn. steering com. AVID; chmn. Data and Safety Monitoring Bd. AFFIRM, 1996—. Recipient Disting. Achievement award Am. Heart Assn., 1989. Fellow ACP, Am. Coll. Cardiology (chmn. ACC/AHA subcom. to assess EP studies, chmn. young investigators award com. 1988-94, trustee 1992-97, mem. nominating com. 1993-95, Disting. Scientist award 1996, chmn. devel. com. 1996—, sci. sessions program com. 1996—), Am. Heart Assn. (exec. com. 1980-88, sci. sessions program 1983-86, chmn. various coms., chmn. 1995, bd. dirs. Internat. Cardiology Found. 1993—, bd. dirs. 1994-96, chmn. emergency cardiac care com. 1995-96); mem. Am. Soc. Clin. Investigation, Assn. Univ. Cardiologists (v.p. 1994, pres. 1995), Assn. Am. Physicians, Am. Physiol. Soc., Cardiac Electrophysiology Soc. (pres. 1985-86), N.Am. Soc. Pacing and Electrophysiology (pres. 1988-90, trustee 1990—, Disting. Scientist award 1995), InterAm. Soc. Cardiology (1st v.p. 1995—), Ind. Cardiac Electrophysiology Soc. (founder). Home: 10614 Winterwood Carmel IN 46032-9688 Office: Ind U Sch Medicine 1100 W Michigan St Indianapolis IN 46202-5208

ZIPF, ROBERT EUGENE, JR., legal medicine consultant, pathologist; b. Dayton, Ohio, Sept. 18, 1940; s. Robert Eugene and Meriam (Murr) Z.; m. Nancy J. Gaskell, Sept. 11, 1965; children: Karin Lorene, Marjorie Kristine. BA, DePauw U., 1962; MD, Ohio State U., 1966. Diplomate Am. Bd. Pathology. Intern, Miami Valley Hosp., Dayton, Ohio, 1966-67; dir. forensic pathology Duke U. Med. Ctr., Durham, N.C., 1967-72; dir. radioisotope pathology Riverside Meth. Hosp., Columbus, 1974-78; dep. coroner, forensic pathologist Franklin County, Columbus, 1974-78; regional forensic pathologist State of N.C., Rocky Mount, 1978—; chmn. pathology Nash Gen. Hosp., Rocky Mount, 1978—; clin. asst. prof. East Caroline U. Med. Sch., Greenville, N.C., 1979—; adj. prof. Atlantic Christian Coll., Wilson, N.C., 1980-89, dir. Sch. Med. Tech., 1983-89; cons. in field. Contbr. articles to profl. jours. Trustee, United Fund, 1979-84; mem. Mayor's Com. on Drug and Substance Abuse, 1987—. Maj. USAF, 1972-74. Fellow Am. Soc. Clin. Pathologist, Am. Acad. Forensic Scientists; mem. Assn. Clin. Scientists, Am. Coll. Nuclear Medicine, N.C. Med. Soc., N.Y. Acad. Scis. (pres. Lab. Users Group 1988-90, 92), SMS (clin. adv. bd. 1988-91, lab. advisors bd. 1989-91), Nash County Med. Soc. (pres. 1995). Home: 120 Newby Ct Rocky Mount NC 27804-3322 Office: Nash Gen Hosp Pathology Lab Rocky Mount NC 27804

ZIPP, JOEL FREDERICK, lawyer; b. Shaker Heights, Ohio, Feb. 12, 1948; s. Jack David and Eleanor Adele Z.; m. Elizabeth Ann Frieden, Dec. 4, 1976; 1 child, Carlyn Leigh. BS, U. Wis., 1970, MS, 1972; JD, Case Western Res. U., 1975. Bar: Ohio 1975, D.C. 1976, U.S. Ct. Claims, 1976, U.S. Ct. Appeals (D.C. cir.) 1976, U.S. Ct. Appeals (5th cir.) 1979, U.S. Ct. Appeals (11th cir.) 1983, U.S. Supreme Ct. 1983. Trial atty. Fed. Energy Regulation Com., Washington, 1975-79, asst. dir. office of enforcement, 1979; assoc. Morley & Caskin, Washington, 1979-80; ptnr. Morley, Caskin & Generelly, Washington, 1981—; gen. counsel, sec. Portland Natural Gas Transmission Sys., 1993—. Notes editor Energy Law Jour., 1990—; contbr. articles to profl. jours. Bd. dirs. Westmoreland Children's Ctr., Washington, 1986-88. Smithsonian fellow, 1969. Mem ABA, Fed. Energy Bar Assn. (bd. dirs. 1993-96, past com. chair 1992, 93 ann. meetings). Jewish. Avocations: skiing, running, bicycling. Home: 9216 Burning Tree Rd Bethesda MD 20817-2251 Office: Morley Caskin 1225 I St NW Washington DC 20005-3914

ZIPPIN, CALVIN, epidemiologist, educator; b. Albany, N.Y., July 17, 1926; s. Samuel and Jennie (Perkel) Z.; m. Patricia Jayne Schubert, Feb. 9, 1964; children: David Benjamin, Jennifer Dorothy. AB magna cum laude, SUNY, Albany, 1947; ScD, Johns Hopkins U., Balt., 1953. Rsch. asst. Sterling-Winthrop Rsch. Inst., Rensselaer, N.Y., 1947-50; instr. biostats. Sch. Pub. Health, U. Calif., Berkeley, 1953-55; asst. to full rsch. biostatistician Sch. Medicine U. Calif., San Francisco, 1955-67, asst. prof. preventive medicine, 1958-60, prof. epidemiology, 1967-91, prof. emeritus, 1991—; vis. assoc. prof. stats. Stanford U., 1962; adv. WHO, 1969—; vis research worker Middlesex Hosp. Med. Sch., London, 1975; various coms. Am. Cancer Soc. and Nat. Cancer Inst., 1956—; faculty adviser Regional Cancer Centre, Trivandrum, India, 1983—; cons., lectr., vis. prof. in field. Co-author book, book chpts.; author or co-author papers primarily on biometry and epidemiology of cancer; editorial advisor Jour. Stats. in Medicine, Boston, 1981-86. Mem., alt. mem. Dem. Ctrl. Com., Marin County, Calif., 1987-96. Recipient Disting. Alumnus award SUNY, Albany, 1969, also awards, fellowships and grants for work in cancer biometry and epidemiology. Fellow Am. Statis. Assn., Am. Coll. Epidemiology, Royal Statis. Soc. Gt. Britain; mem. Biometric Soc. (mem. internat. coun. 1978-81, pres. Western N.Am. region 1979-80), Calif. Cancer Registrars Assn. (hon.), Internat. Assn. Cancer Registries (hon.), B'nai B'rith (pres. Golden Gate lodge 1970-71, pres. Greater San Francisco Bay area coun. 1974-75), Phi Beta Kappa, Sigma Xi, Delta Omega. Office: Univ Calif Dept Epidemiology/Biostats San Francisco CA 94143-0746

ZIPPRODT, PATRICIA, costume designer. B.A., Wellesley Coll.; student, Art Inst. Chgo., Art Students League N.Y., Fashion Inst. Tech. Asst. to various theatre designers; lectr., condr. master classes Yale U., Harvard U., others; vis. lectr. theatre arts NYU; prof. theatre arts Brandeis U., 1985-93; founding mem. Nat. Theater for the Deaf. Designer: (Broadway mus.) Fiddler on the Roof, 1964 (Tony award 1964), Cabaret, 1966 (Tony award 1966), Zorba, 1968 (Drama Desk award 1968), 1776, 1969 (Drama Desk award 1969, Joseph P. Maharam award 1970), Pippin, 1972 (Drama Desk award 1973), Mack and Mable, 1974, Chicago, 1975, King of Hearts, 1978, Alice in Wonderland, 1982 (Joseph P. Maharam award 1983), Sweet Charity, 1985 (Tony award 1986), Big Deal, 1986, Shogun: The Musical, 1990 (Drama Desk award 1990, Joseph P. Maharam award 1990), My Favorite Year, 1992, My Fair Lady, 1993; (Broadway plays) A Period of Adjustment, 1962, Little Foxes, 1967, Plaza Suite, 1968, Scratch, 1971, All God's Chillun' Got Wings, 1975, Poor Murderer, 1976, Kingdoms, 1981, Fools, 1981, Brighton Beach Memoirs, 1983, The Glass Menagerie, 1983, Smile, 1983, The Accidental Death of an Anarchist, 1984, Macbeth, 1988, Cat on a Hot Tin Roof, 1989; (off-Broadway plays) Our Town, 1960, The Balcony, 1960, Camino Real, 1961, Oh Dad Poor Dad Etc., 1962, A Man's a Man, 1963, The Blacks, 1962; (Guthrie Theatre) Waiting for Godot, 1973, Don Juan, 1982 (Joseph P. Maharam award 1983), The Bacchae, 1987; (Nat. Actors Theatre) The Crucible, 1991-92, Hotel Paradiso, 1991-92, The Master Builder, 1991-92, Little Hotel On The Side, 1992, School for Scandal, 1994, Picasso At The Lapin Agile, 1995; (Boston Opera) Madam Butterfly, 1962, Hippolyte E Aricie, 1966, The Rise and Fall of the City of Mahagonny, 1972; (New York City Opera) Katerina Ismailova, 1967, The Flaming Angel, 1968, Naughty Marietta, 1978; (Guggenheim Mus., N.Y.C.) The Mother of Us All, 1972; (Julliard Opera) Lord Byron, 1973; (Met. Opera) Tannhaüser, 1977, The Barber of Seville, 1982; (Am. Repertory Theatre, Cambridge, Mass.) The Fall of the House of Usher, 1988; (Am. Ballet Theatre) Les Noces, 1969, The Leaves are Fading, 1975, Estuary, 1983, Coppélia, 1990; (New York City Ballet) Watermill, 1972, Dybbuk Variations, 1974, The Sleeping Beauty, 1991; (Houston Ballet) Beads of Memory, 1985; (Ballet Hispanico) Cada Noche Tango Jnez de Castro Tres Cantos, 1988; (films) The Graduate, 1967; (television spls.) Anne Bancroft Spl., CBS, 1970, June Moon, WNET, 1973, The Glass Menagerie, ABC, 1973, Alice in Wonderland, WNET, 1983, Chrysler Skating, 1992; (nat. tours) Bette Midler, 1976, Ben Vereen, 1983; designer, advisor: The Seagull (St. Petersburg, Russia), Anna Christie (Beijing, China); exhibitor design sketches Wright-Hepburn, London, 1966, Capicorn Gallery, N.Y.C., 1968, Mus. City N.Y., 1972, U. Calif.-San Diego, 1974, Toneelmuseum, Amsterdam, The Netherlands, 1975, U.S. Internat. Theatre Inst. traveling exhibit, 1974-78, N.Y. City Ballet, 1994. Recipient award for spl. costumes NATAS, 1970, spl. award New Eng. Conf., 1973, Ritter award Fashion Inst. Tech., 1977, Disting. Career award S.E. Theatre Conf., 1985; inductee Theater Hal of Fame, 1992. Mem. United Scenic Artists, Costume Designers Guild, Motion Picture Acad. Arts and Scis. Address: 29 King St New York NY 10014-4966

ZIRAKZADEH, CYRUS ERNESTO, political science educator; b. Stillwater, Okla., Nov. 11, 1951; s. Aboulghassem and Refugio (Flores) Z.; m. Barbara Louise Macy, June 8, 1973; children: Vanessa Marie, Daniel Ernesto Winchester. BA high distinction and highest honors, U. Mich., 1974; MA, Stanford U., 1975; PhD, U. Calif., Berkeley, 1985. Vis. lectr. U. Calif., Davis, 1983, Washington U., St. Louis, 1984-85; asst. prof. polit. sci. U. Conn., Storrs, 1985-91, assoc. prof., 1991—, dir. honor programs, 1993—. Author: A Rebellious People: Basques, Protests, and Politics, 1991, Social Movements in Politics: A Comparative Study, 1997; co-author: Direct Democracy and International Politics: Deciding International Issues through Referendums, 1992; contbr. articles to profl. jours. Fellow Danforth Found., 1980. Fellow Soc. for Values in Higher Edn.; mem. Am. Polit. Sci. Assn., New Eng. Polit. Sci. Assn. (exec. coun. 1988-92, John C. Donovan prize 1988), Northeastern Polit. Sci. Assn. (exec. coun. 1989-91), Phi Beta Kappa, Phi Kappa Phi. Home: 60 Timber Dr Storrs Mansfield CT 06268-1227 Office: U Conn Polit Sci Dept U-24 Storrs CT 06269-1024

ZIRBES, MARY KENNETH, social justice ministry coordinator; b. Melrose, Minn., Sept. 4, 1926; d. Joseph Louis and Clara Bernadine (Petermeier) Z. BA in History and Edn., Coll. St. Catherine, 1960; MA in Applied Theology, Sch. Applied Theology, Berkeley, Calif., 1976. Joined Order of St. Francis, Roman Cath. Ch., 1945. Tchr. Pub. Grade Sch., St. Nicholas, Minn., 1947-52; prin. Holy Spirit Grade Sch., St. Cloud, Minn., 1953-59, St. Mary's Jr. High Sch., Morris, Minn., 1960-62; coord. Franciscan Mission Team, Peru, South America, 1962-67, Franciscan Missions, Little Falls, Minn., 1967-70; dir. St. Richard's Social Ministry, Richfield, Minn., 1971-80, Parish Community Devel., St. Paul, Mpls., Minn., 1980-85; councillor gen. Franciscan Sisters of Little Falls, 1960-62, 67-70; asst. dir. Renew-Archdiocese of St. Paul-Mpls., 1986-89; coord. Parish Social Justice Ministry-Archdiocese of St. Paul-Mpls., 1990-93; minister Franciscan Assocs., 1993—; leader of team on evangelical life Franciscan Sisters of Little Falls, 1994-96; co-developer Assn. of Pastoral Ministers, Mpls., St. Paul, 1979-81, Compañeros/Sister Parishes-Minn. and Nicaragua, 1984-89, Minn. Interfaith Ecology Coalition, 1989-92. Author: Parish Social Ministry, 1985, (manual) Acting for Justice, 1992. Organizer Twin Cities Orgn., Mpls., 1979-80; bd. dirs. Franciscan Sisters Health Care, Inc., Little Falls, 1990-93, Rice-Marion Residents Assn., St. Paul, 1991-92. Named Outstanding chair Assn. Pastoral Ministers, 1981; recipient Five Yrs. of Outstanding Svc. award Companeros, 1989. Mem. Assn. Pastoral Ministers (chair 1979), Amnesty Internat., Voices for Justice-Legis. Lobby, Audubon Soc., Network, Minn. Interfaith Ecology Coalition, Franciscan Sisters of Little Falls. Avocations: water color painting, birding, golf, reading history and biography. Office: Franciscan Sisters 116 8th Ave SE Little Falls MN 56345

ZIRILLI, FRANCESCO, mechanical engineer, engineering educator; b. Buenos Aires, Apr. 23, 1956; s. Giuseppe and Giuseppa (Nucifora) Z.; m. Joanne A. Long, July 8, 1994; 3 stepchildren: Jim Long, Kristen Long, Lisa Long. BSME, Clarkson U., Potsdam, N.Y., 1977, MSME, 1979, PhD in Mech. Enging., 1985. Assoc. engr. GE Co., Schenectady, N.Y., 1978-80; cons. engr. Stress Tech., Inc., Rochester, N.Y., 1983-84; project mgr. Xerox Corp., Rochester, 1984—; sr. lectr. U. Rochester, 1986—. Contbr. articles to profl. jours. Mem. ASME, TAPPI, Pi Tau Sigma. Achievements include 2 patents. Avocations: stamp collecting, woodworking, travel, reading. Office: Xerox Corporation 800 Phillips Rd # 207-05C Webster NY 14580-9720

ZIRIN, HAROLD, astronomer, educator; b. Boston, Oct. 7, 1929; s. Jack and Anna (Buchwalter) Z.; m. Mary Noble Fleming, Apr. 20, 1957; children: Daniel Meyer, Dana Mary. A.B., Harvard U., 1950, A.M., 1951, Ph.D., 1952. Asst. phys. scientist RAND Corp., 1952-53; lectr. Harvard, 1953-55; research staff High Altitude Obs., Boulder, Colo., 1955-64; prof. astrophysics Calif. Inst. Tech., 1964—; staff mem. Hale Obs., 1964-80; chief astronomer Big Bear Solar Obs., 1969-80, dir., 1980-96; Disting. Rsch. Prof. N.J. Inst. Tech., 1996—; U.S.- USSR exchange scientist, 1960-61; vis. prof. Coll. de France, 1986, Japan Soc. P. Sci., 1992. Author: The Solar Atmosphere, 1966, Astrophysics of the Sun, 1987; co-translator: Five Billion Vodka Bottles to the Moon, 1991; adv. editor: Soviet Astronomy, 1965-69; editor Magnetic and Velocity Fields of Solar Active Regions. Trustee Polique Canyon Assn., 1977-90. Agassiz fellow, 1951-52; Sloan fellow, 1958-60; Guggenheim fellow, 1960-61. Mem. Am. Astron. Soc., Internat. Astron. Union, AURA (dir. 1977-83). Home: 1178 Sonoma Dr Altadena CA 91001-3150 Office: Calif Inst Tech Big Bear Solar Observatory Calif Inst Tech 264-33 Pasadena CA 91125

ZIRIN, JAMES DAVID, lawyer; b. N.Y.C., Jan. 10, 1940; s. Morris and Kate (Sapir) Z.; m. Marlene Hess, May 18, 1990. AB with honors, Princeton U., 1961; JD with honors, U. Mich., 1964. Bar: N.Y. 1965, U.S. Supreme Ct. 1978. Asst. U.S. atty. U.S. Dist. Ct. (so. dist.) N.Y., N.Y.C., 1967-70; assoc. Breed, Abbott & Morgan, N.Y.C., 1965-67, 70-72, ptnr., 1972-93; ptnr. Brown & Wood, N.Y.C., 1993—. Contbr. articles to London Times, Forbes, Barron's, N.Y., Newsday, N.Y. Law Jour. Bd. dirs. Legal Aid Soc., N.Y.C., 1984-89, exec. com., 1986-89; trustee N.Y. Law Sch., 1996—. Lt. USNR, 1965-70. Fellow Am. Coll. Trial Lawyers; mem. Fed. Bar Coun. (v.p. 1982-84), Assn. of Bar of City of N.Y., University Club, The Brook. Office: Brown & Wood One World Trade Ctr New York NY 10048

ZIRINSKY, BRUCE R., lawyer; b. N.Y.C., Sept. 6, 1947. BS, Cornell U., 1969; JD, NYU, 1972. Bar: N.Y. 1973, U.S. Dist. Ct. (so. and ea. dists.) N.Y. 1973, U.S. Ct. Appeals (2d cir.) 1974, U.S. Ct. Appeals (1st cir.) 1980, U.S. Ct. Appeals (11th cir.) 1981, U.S. Ct. Appeals (5th cir.) 1986, U.S. Supreme Ct. 1991, U.S. Ct. Appeals (6th cir.), 1995. Mem. Weil, Gotshal & Manges, N.Y.C. Mem. ABA (sect. corp., banking and bus. law), N.Y. State Bar Assn. (mem. com. bankruptcy laws banking and bus. law sects. 1979—). Office: Weil Gotshal & Manges 767 5th Ave New York NY 10153-0001

ZIRINSKY, DANIEL, real estate investor and photographer; b. Bklyn., Mar. 14, 1927; s. David and Gertrude (Coleman) Z.; m. Ellen Reiss Snyder, Apr. 7, 1957 (div. Aug. 1977); children: Steven George, Mark Allen, Laura Reiss; m. Gilda Schiff, Oct. 12, 1980. BS, Syracuse U., 1949. Pres. Bus. Bldgs. of Am., Inc., Great Neck, N.Y., 1969—; real estate developer and owner/investor Great Neck, N.Y., 1950—, photographer, 1950—; judge, lectr. and tchr. photographer. One-man photography shows from 1953-87 include Great Neck House, 1987, Lincoln Savs. Bank, 1987, Gould Electronics, 1987, Bryant Libr., 1986, others; group exhbns. include Great Neck Libr., 1990, 91, 92, 93, Ind. Art Soc., 1990, Long Beach Art League, 1990, Chelsea Mansion, 1989-90, others. Treas. N. Shore Sci. Mus., Port Washington, N.Y., 1970-78; founder N.Y. Inst. Tech., Old Westbury, 1958; v.p., trustee The Advanced Ctr Psychotherapy, 1987—, Advanced Inst. Analytic Psychotherapy, 1987—. Recipient Photographic Fed. L.I. Color Print of Yr. award, 1992, 1st pl. North Shore Univ. Hosp., 1992, 93. Mem. Photographic Soc. Am. (life, 59 medals, 74 hon. mentions in U.S., Eng., Australia, Japan, Can., Mex., France, Yugoslavia, Germany), Photographic Soc. Hong Kong (assoc.), Leica Hist. Soc. Am., Am. Photographic Hist. Soc., Great Neck Color Camera Club (1991-92 Print of Yr. award, 1990-91 Color Print of Yr. award, 1989-90 Color Print of Yr. award, 28 awards, 42 hon. mentions), Artists Network Great Neck, Real Estate Bd. N.Y. Jewish. Avocations: computer, ham radio, yachting, skiing, cycling. Home: 7 Beech Dr Kings Point NY 11024-1230 Office: 60 Cuttermill Rd Great Neck NY 11021-3104

ZIRKEL, DON, public information official; b. Ozone Park, N.Y., Aug. 13, 1927; s. George Henry and Frances Anna (Neumann) Z.; m. Marie Margaret Greene, June 28, 1952; children: Jeanne Zirkel O'Connell, Barbara Zirkel Dempsey, Joseph, Thomas, Mary Zirkel Pacifico, Anne Zirkel-Hagopian, John, Paul, Timothy. Student, Fordham U., 1948-50; B.A., St. John's U., 1955. Mem. editorial staff Cath. newspaper The Tablet, Bklyn., 1948-85; editor Cath. newspaper The Tablet, 1968-85; exec. staff N.Y. State Div. Human Rights, 1985-92; dir. pub. info. Ctr. for Devel. Disabilities, Woodbury, N.Y., 1992—; lectr. in field. Contbr. articles to Cath. newspapers, mags. Rsch. asst. to Congressman James J. Delaney, 1961-63, Congressman Hugh L. Carey, 1963-65; bd. dirs. Citizens for Ednl. Freedom, Cath. Interracial Coun. Intercommunity Ctr. for Justice and Peace. With AUS, 1950-52. Recipient Best News Story award Cath. Press Assn., 1957, Americanism award Cath. War Vets., 1961, Worldmission award U.S. Mission Secretariat, 1963. Roman Catholic (lector 1966—, Eucharistic minister 1973—, ordained deacon 1979). Club: K.C. (State award 1973). Home: 150 Sunry Ln Bethpage NY 11714 Office: Ctr Devel Disabilities 72 S Woods Rd Woodbury NY 11797-1024

ZIRKEL, GENE, computer science and mathematics educator; b. N.Y.C., Dec. 2, 1931; s. George Henry and Frances Anna (Neumann) Z.; m. Patricia Lou McCormick, Apr. 15, 1968; 1 child, George Stephen. BS, St. John's Coll., Bklyn., 1953; MA, St. John's U., Queens, N.Y., 1960; MS, N.Y. Inst. Tech., 1984. Tchr. Mt. St. Michael's H.S., Bronx, N.Y., 1955-56, Cardinal Hayes H.S., Bronx, 1956-60; chair math. Marist H.S., Bayonne, N.J., 1960-62, prin., 1966-67; tchr. Aquinas H.S., Augusta, Ga., 1962; chair theology Archbishop Molloy H.S., Queens, 1962-66; prof. Nassau C.C., Garden City, N.Y., 1967-97; lectr. Marist Coll., Poughkeepsie, N.Y., 1959-66, Adelphi U., Garden City, 1973-74; com. create nat. exam Math Assn. Am.; founder New Horizon Learning Ctr. Author: Happiness Is My Decision, 1997; co-author: Understanding Statistics, 1972, Beginning Statistics, 1976, Program CSI, 1990, Understanding Fortran 77 & 90, 1994; contbr. articles to profl. jours.; columnist Standard Deviations. Union rep. Labor and Religion Coalition, L.I., N.Y., 1980s; Cath. chaplain Nassau C.C., vol. parish outreach poor, homeless and hungry; vol. Habitat for Humanity. Recipient Best Articles of 1976 award Matyc Jour. (Math. & Computer Edn.); NSF scholar, 1960. Fellow Dozenal Soc. (chmn. bd. dirs. 1991-92, pres. 1977-88, v.p. 1988-90, 96—); mem. Nat. Coun. Tchr. Math. (life). Democrat. Avocation: swimming. Home: 6 Brancatelli Ct West Islip NY 11795-2502 Office: Nassau Community Coll 1 Education Dr Garden City NY 11530-6719

ZIRKIND, RALPH, physicist, educator; b. N.Y.C., Oct. 20, 1918; s. Isaac and Zicel (Lifshitz) Z.; m. Ann Goldman, Nov. 22, 1940; children: Sheila Zirkind Knopf, Elaine Zirkind Gorman, Edward I. B.S., CCNY, 1940; M.S., Ill. Inst. Tech., 1945; postgrad., George Washington U., 1946-47; Ph.D., U. Md., 1950; D.Sc., U. R.I., 1968. Physicist Navy Dept., 1945-50, chief physicist, 1951-60; physicist Oak Ridge Nat. Lab., 1950-51, Advanced Research Project Agy., Washington, 1960-63; prof. Poly. Inst. Bklyn., 1963-70; prof. U. R.I., Kingston, 1970-72, adj. prof., 1972—; physicist Advanced Research Projects Agy., Arlington, Va., 1972-74; cons. Advanced Rsch. Projects Agy., Arlington, Va., 1974—; lectr. U. Md., 1948-50, George Washington U., 1952-53, U. Mich., 1966; cons. ACDA, Jet Propulsion Lab., Calif. Inst. Tech.; cons. to industry, 1974—. Contbg. author: Jet Propulsion Series, 1952, FAR Infrared Properties of Materials, 1968; editor: Electromagnetic Sensing of Earth, 1967; mem. editorial bd.: Infrared Physics, 1963—; contbr. articles profl. jours. Recipient Meritorious Civilian Svc. award Navy Dept., 1957, Meritorious Civilian Svc. award Dept. Def., 1970, Outstanding Educator of Am. medal, 1972, Maj. Contbn. award BMDO/AIAA, 1994. Mem. Am. Phys. Soc., N.Y. Acad. Scis., Sigma Xi, Sigma Pi Sigma, Eta Kappa Nu. Home: 820 Hillsboro Dr Silver Spring MD 20902-3202 Office: 4001 Fairfax Dr Ste 700 Arlington VA 22203-1618

ZIRKLE, LEWIS GREER, physician, executive; b. Pittsfield, Mass., July 23, 1940; s. Lewis Greer and Vivian (Shaw) Z.; m. Sara K. Zirkle, Aug. 24, 1963; children: Elizabeth, Molly, Julie. BS, Davidson Coll., 1962; MD, Duke U., 1966. Intern Duke U. Hosp., 1966-67, resident, 1968-73; resident U.S. Army, Shriner's Hosp., 1967-68; pvt. practice Richland, Wash., 1973—; bd. dirs. Orthopedics Overseas, chmn. program in Vietnam, 1992—. Contbr. articles to profl. jours. Maj. U.S. Army, 1968-73. Presbyterian. Avocations: reading, sports. Home: 2548 Harris Ave Richland WA 99352-1638 Office: NW Orthopedics 875 Swift Blvd Richland WA 99352-3513

ZIRKLE, WILLIAM VERNON, philanthropist; b. Berlin, Germany, Feb. 5, 1959; (parents Am. citizens); s. Michael Neale and Nancy (Behrend) Z. AAS in Electronics, Northern Va. C.C., 1980; BA in Humanities, U. Va., 1984. Cons. designer audio system Uno's Pizzeria, Washington, 1989; cons. crises mgmt. APC, Merrifield, Va., 1993; cons. tech. WESCO, Falls Church, Va., 1977—; proprietor Circle Enterprises, Arlington, Va., 1984—. Canvass Children's Defense Fund, Washington, 1991, 92; specializer Md. Sherriff's Youth Ranch, 1991; chair Adult Religious Edn., Falls Church, 1986. Named to Outstanding Young Men of Am., 1992, 96. Mem. Cath. Alumni Club (v.p. 1991), Cath. Young Adults Club (religion com. 1988-89, parlimentarian 1987-88), U. Va. Alumni Club. Independent. Avocations: travel, camping, computers, the arts. Home: 2932 Patrick Henry Dr Falls Church VA 22044

ZIRSCHKY, JOHN H., federal government official; b. Fullerton, Calif., July 6, 1957; m. Natalie Ziegler; 2 children. BS in Civil Engring., U. Tenn.; MS in Engring., Utah State U.; PhD, Clemson U. Registered profl. engr., S.C. Rsch. asst. Utah Water Rsch. Lab. Utah State U., Logan, 1978-80; engr. Ecology & Environment, Inc., Kansas City, Kans., 1980-82, ERM-Southeast, Inc., Atlanta, 0984-89, Dames and Moore, Atlanta, 1989-90; rsch. engr. Clemson U., 1982-84; legis. asst. Office Sen. James M. Jeffords, Washington, 1990-93; profl. staff mem. Senate Com. Environment and Pub. Works, Washington, 1993-94; acting asst. sec., prin. dep. asst. sec. Dept. of Army, Washington, 1994—. Contbr. more than 50 articles to profl. pubs. Mem. ASCE, Water Environment Fedn., Sigma Xi, Tau Beta Pi, Chi Epsilon. Office: Dept of the Army Civil Works The Pentagon Washington DC 20310-0103

ZISCHKE, DOUGLAS ARTHUR, foreign service officer; b. Sioux Falls, S.D., May 24, 1929; s. Arthur Gustav and Alice Minetta (Wedeking) Z.; m. Janice Mae Kuehnemann, June 8, 1957; children: Mark Douglas, Deborah Jan, Todd Lincoln. B.S. in Journalism, U. Wis., 1951, M.S. cum laude, 1952. Joined U.S. Fgn. Svc., 1957; tech. editor Forest Svc., Madison, 1955-57; asst. info. officer USIS, Montevideo, Uruguay, 1957-58, La Paz, Bolivia, 1958-59; asst. cultural affairs officer, br. pub. affairs officer Mexico, 1960-65; info. specialist Washington, 1965-67; pub. affairs officer Tegucigalpa, Honduras, 1967-69; dep. pub. affairs officer Buenos Aires, Argentina, 1969-71; pub. affairs officer Guatemala, Guatemala, 1971-74; assigned to U.S. Army War Coll., 1974-75; dep. pub. affairs officer Am. embassy Tehran, Iran, 1975-78; cultural coord. USICA, Washington, 1979-80; internat. cons., 1980-86; fgn. affairs advisor State Dept., 1986—. Author monograph. Bd. dirs. Boy Scouts Am; dir. Lutheran Ch. 1973-74. Served with Signal Corps, AUS, 1953-55.

ZISKIN, LAURA, film producer. Co-founder Frogwood Films; pres. Fox 2000, Beverly Hills, Calif. Films include: (assoc. prodr.) Eyes of Laura Mars, 1978; (prodr.) Murphy's Romance, 1985, No Way Out, 1987, D.O.A., 1988, Everybody's An American, 1988, The Rescue, 1988, What About Bob?, 1991, The Doctor, 1991, Hero, 1992; (exec. prodr.) Pretty Woman, 1990; producer: To Die For, 1995. Office: Fox 2000 10201 W Pico Blvd Los Angeles CA 90064-2606*

ZISMAN, BARRY STUART, lawyer; b. N.Y.C., Sept. 18, 1937; s. Harry and Florence Rita (Tucker) Z.; m. Maureen Frances Brumond, Dec. 30, 1979; children: Michael Glenn, Marlene Ann. AB, Columbia U., 1958, JD, 1961. Bar: D.C. 1962, N.Y. 1965, Tex. 1986, U.S. Dist. Ct. (ea. and so. dists.) N.Y. 1967, U.S. Ct. Appeals (D.C. cir.) 1967, U.S. Dist. Ct. (no. and so. dists.) Tex. 1986, U.S. Ct. Appeals (5th cir.) 1988, U.S. Supreme Ct. 1967. With U.S. Govt., 1962-66; pvt. practice Syosset, N.Y., 1966-71; sr. counsel CBS Inc., N.Y.C., 1972-75; asst. gen. counsel, asst. sec. M. Lowenstein & Sons, N.Y.C., 1975-79; gen. counsel Grumman Allied Indsl. Inc., Bethpage, N.Y., 1979-83; asst. gen. counsel Grumman Corp., Bethpage, 1982-83; sr. atty. FDIC, Dallas, 1984-87; of counsel Arter & Hadden, Dallas, 1987-88, ptnr., 1988; ptnr. Winstead, McGuire, Sechrest & Minick, Dallas, 1988-90, Arter & Hadden, Dallas and Washington, 1990-91, Rubinstein & Perry, Dallas, 1991-94, The Zisman Law Firm, P.C., Dallas, 1994—; advisor in field; vice-chmn. Assn. of Bank and Thrift Receivership Coun. Editor and author: Banks and Thrifts: Government Enforcement and Receivership Law, 1991. With U.S. Army, 1961-62. Home: 905 Murl Dr Irving TX 75062-4441 Office: 2626 Cole Ave Ste 400 Dallas TX 75204-1073

ZISMAN, LAWRENCE S., internist; b. 1959. MD, Albert Einstein Coll. Medicine, 1987. Postdoctoral fellow U. Colo. Health Sci. Ctr., asst. prof. of Cardiology. Recipient Clinician Scientist award Am. Heart Assn., 1995-96. Office: U Colo 5483 E Utah Pl Denver CO 80222-3948*

ZISSMAN, LORIN, marketing research, consulting company executive; b. Phila., July 13, 1930; s. Charles Louis and Sarah (Axelman) Z.; m. Beverly Ann Zissman, June 23, 1957 (div. Sept. 1987); children: Nancy Zissman Peters, Jonathan, Eric, Amy; m. Carole Winokur, Oct. 16, 1988. BA, Temple U., 1951. Rsch. analyst Benson & Benson, Princeton, N.J., 1955-56; pres. Opinion Rsch. Corp., ORC Caravan Surveys, Princeton, 1956-69; v.p. Response Analysis Corp., Princeton, 1969-70; pres. Total Rsch., Inc., Princeton, 1970-75; pres. Total Rsch. Corp., Princeton, 1975-86, pres., chief exec. officer, 1986-93, chmn., chief exec. officer, 1993—. Mem. Am. Mktg. Assn. (chmn. standards and practices com. 1973-74), Coun. Am. Survey Rsch. Orgns., Am. Assn. Pub. Opinion Rsch., Am. Contract Bridge League, Princeton Community Players, Villagers Barn Theatre. Jewish. Avocations: theatre, softball, tennis, ping pong, bridge. Home: 7F Marten Rd Princeton NJ 08540-1634 Office: Total Rsch Corp Princeton Corp Ctr 5 Independence Way Princeton NJ 08540-6627

ZITO, JAMES ANTHONY, retired railroad company executive; b. Oak Park, Ill., Feb. 5, 1931; s. Bruno and Concetta (Kalasardo) Z.; m. Mary B. De Stasio, July 9, 1983; children: Antony, Antonia. Student, Elmhurst Coll., 1956-57; sr. exec. program, Stanford U., 1981. Sr. v.p. ops. Chgo. & North Western Transp. Co., 1976-90, also bd. dirs.; former chmn. A.A.R. Op. Transp. Co.; pres. Z&B Inc., Campbell St. R.E. Corp. With USCG, 1951-53. Mem. St. Charles Country Club, KC. Home: 1655 Persimmon Dr Saint Charles IL 60174-1328

ZITRIN, ARTHUR, physician; b. Bklyn., Apr. 10, 1918; s. William and Lillian (Elbaum) Z.; m. Charlotte Marker, Oct. 4, 1942; children—Richard Alan, Elizabeth Ann. B.S., City Coll. N.Y., 1938; M.S., N.Y. U., 1941, M.D., 1945; certificate psychoanalytic medicine, Columbia, 1955. Diplomate: Am. Bd. Psychiatry and Neurology. Research fellow animal behavior Am. Museum Natural History, 1939-42; intern King County Hosp., 1945-46; resident psychiatry Bellevue Hosp., 1948-51; instr. physiology Hunter Coll., N.Y.C., 1948-49; mem. faculty N.Y.U. Sch. Medicine, 1949—, professor psychiatry, 1967—; mem. staff Bellevue Hosp., N.Y.C., 1951—; dir. psychiatry Bellevue Hosp., 1955-68, N.Y.C. Dept. Hosps., 1962- 64; pvt. practice, 1949—; attending psychiatrist Univ. Hosp., N.Y.C.; cons. psychiatrist Manhattan Va Hosp. Author papers in field. Served to capt., M.C. AUS, 1946- 48. Fellow Am. Psychiat. Assn (life), N.Y. Acad. Medicine; mem. AMA, N.Y. Soc. Clin. Psychiatry (pres. 1966- 67), Am. Psychoanalytic Assn. (life), Sigma Xi, Alpha Omega Alpha. Home: 56 Ruxton Rd Great Neck NY 11023-1529 Office: 550 1st Ave New York NY 10016-6481

ZIVARI, BASHIR, architect, industrial designer; b. Bklyn., Aug. 13, 1961; s. Farajollah and Ingeborg Elfriede (Brügmann) Z.; m. Pamela Lorraine Ray, Feb. 17, 1990. M Indsl. Design with distinction, Pratt Inst., 1991, BArch, 1984. Registered architect, N.Y.. With Russo & Sonder Architects, N.Y.C., 1984-88; pvt. practice architecture, N.Y.C., 1988; asst. designer Lee Harris Pomeroy Architects, N.Y.C., 1988-91; project mgr. The Phillips Janson Group Architects, N.Y.C., 1991—. Designs in permanent collections of Mus. Modern Art, N.Y.C., Cooper-Hewitt Mus., N.Y.C.; patentee for modular stool. Recipient 2d place Shaw-Walker furniture competition, 1987; Roscoe awards for outstanding achievement in product design Interior Design mag., 1993, best of category award for children's furniture, 1993; gold award for consumer product Businessweek mag. and Indsl. Design Soc. Am., 1994. Mem. Baha'i Faith. Avocation: squash. Home: 309 Carroll St Brooklyn NY 11231-4901

ZIVELONGHI, KURT DANIEL, artist, painter; b. Barstow, Calif., Oct. 3, 1960; s. Vincent Otto and Beverly Dean (Schwind) Z. Student, Pasadena (Calif.) City Coll., 1984-85, Art Students League, N.Y.C., 1988-89; BFA, Art Ctr. Coll. of Design, 1993. Mgr. Foothill Airplane Washing Svc., Claremont, Calif., 1980-82; sales rep. Valley Group Fin. Svc., Claremont, 1986-88; loan rep. Pacific Group Funding, Claremont, 1989-90; self employed fine artist Alhambra, Calif., 1990—. One man show at Coll. of Design Art Ctr., Pasadena, Calif., 1993, two man show at Flux Gallery, Eagle Rock, Calif., 1993, group show at Art Students League, N.Y.C., 1989. Mem. Ctr. for the Study of Popular Culture, Century City, Calif., 1994. Mem. Am. Soc. Portrait Artists. Avocations: pianist, weight lifter, theatre, cinema. Office: Local Colors Rep 16624 Marquez Ave Pacific Palisades CA 90272-3233 Representative: The Print Merchants Pacific Design Ctr 8687 Melrose Ave West Hollywood CA 90069

ZIVITZ, STEPHEN CHARLES, lawyer; b. Huntington Station, N.Y., Nov. 9, 1943; s. Emanuel and Anna (Fromer) Z.; m. Jean Graudens, July 31, 1966; children: Andrew, Jeremy. BS in Econs., U. Pa., 1965, JD, 1968; LLM, Temple U., 1972. Bar: Fla. 1969, Pa. 1969. Ptnr. White and Williams, Phila., 1969—. Capt. U.S. Army, 1969-71, Korea. Home: 1331 Centennial Rd Penn Valley PA 19072-1207 Office: White and Williams 1650 Market St Fl 18 Philadelphia PA 19103-7301

ZIZIC, THOMAS MICHAEL, physician, educator; b. Milw., Dec. 9, 1939; s. Michael Mitchell Zizic and Dorothy (Batas) Ciric; m. Karen Owens, June 15, 1962 (div. Sept. 1967); m. Martha Ann Ardos, Nov. 22, 1967; children: Lara Ann, Kristine Michelle. BS, U. Wis., 1961; MD, Johns Hopkins U., 1965. Intern Johns Hopkins Hosp., Balt., 1965-66, asst. resident, 1966-67, fellow in internal medicine, 1969-71, instr. dept. medicine, 1971-73, asst. prof. medicine, 1971-81, assoc. prof. medicine, 1981—; pvt. practice, Balt., 1988—; co-dir. Chesapeake Osteoporosis Ctr., Balt., 1988—; dir. med. affairs Murray Electronics, 1993—; v.p. med. quality care Physicians Quality Care, 1995—; pres. U.S. Osteoporosis Network, Inc., 1996—; co-founder, dir. Creative Environ. Solutions, Inc., 1996—; cons. in field. Contbr. numerous articles and abstracts to profl. jours. V.p. Md. chpt. Arthritis Found., Balt., 1976-77; chmn. Md. Commn. on Arthritis and Related Diseases, 1986-90. Fellow Am. Coll. Rheumatology, 1986; Md. Soc. Rheumatic Diseases (pres. 1975-76), D.C. Rheumatism Assn., Balt. City Med. Soc., Johns Hopkins Hosp. Med. Soc., Arthritis Found. (fellow 1971-73, v.p. 1976-77, med. and sci. com. 1977-79, chmn. profl. edn. com. 1977-78, govtl. affairs com. 1979-83), Phi Beta Kappa, Phi Kappa Phi, Phi Eta Sigma. Avocations: skiing, tennis. Office: 5601 Loch Raven Blvd Baltimore MD 21239-2905 *Give 100% today. We have only the present. Plan for the future but don't live inthe future. The future never comes. We have only today.*

ZIZZA, SALVATORE J., diversified company executive; b. Francofonte, Italy, Nov. 19, 1945; came to U.S., 1956; s. Carmelo and Gregoria (Mazzarino) Z.; m. Deborah Ann Bright, Sept. 24, 1983; children: Robert Carl, Gregory Thomas, Christopher John. B.A. in Polit. Sci., St. John's U., 1967, M.B.A., 1972. Asst. mgr. Chem. Bank, N.Y.C., 1967-71; asst. sec. Am. Bank & Trust Co., N.Y.C., 1972-73; pres. Mortgagee Affiliates, N.Y.C., 1973-78; owner, pres. Zizza & Co. Ltd., N.Y.C., 1978—; pres., chief operating officer, dir. Nico, Inc., N.Y.C., 1978—, Lehigh Group Inc., N.Y.C., 1985—; chmn. Initial Acquisition Corp., 1993, The Bethlehem Corp., 1995; dir. Gabelli, Equity-Growth-Asset Funds, Multimedia and Convertible Securities. Bd. govs. Columbus Citizens Com., N.Y.C., 1980; bd. dirs. Nat. Italian Am. Found., Washington, 1986. Mem. Young Mortgage Bankers Assn., Real Estate Bd. of N.Y., Young Pres. Orgn. Roman Catholic. Avocations: skiing; tennis; reading.

ZIZZO, ALICIA, concert pianist; b. N.Y.C., Apr. 2, 1945; d. Spiro and Christine (Corda) Theodoratos; m. Thomas Edward Zizzo; children: Peter, Claudia. BA, Hofstra U., 1965; postgrad., C.W. Post U., 1975, L.I. U., 1976, Mannes Coll. Music. performed Eastern Europe; lectr. in field. Debut as concert pianist N.Y.C.; performed in major concert halls throughout Europe, named as one of the great Am. pianists in the world; one of few Am. artists invited to perform by Ea. Bloc countries Europe; discovered lost manuscripts of George Gershwin's classical music; first pianist to record George Gershwin's Rhapsody in Blue and Concerto in "F" from origninal manuscripts; recorded reconstructed fragments of lost George Gershwin manuscipts of Lullaby and original piano score of his opera Blue Monday; created first authentic version of Preludes and Rhapsody in Blue, Warner Bros. Publs., 1995, Gershwin/21220 Edits.; feature artist Vienna and other major internat. concert series and symphony orchs.; recordings for Pro-Arte Records, Fanfare Records, Mastersound Records; music publ. by Warner Bros. Publs.; recordings include Virtuoso Piano Fantasies-Works by Chopin, The Gershwin Manuscripts, Picwick Internat. Records, London, Debussy, et. al. Address: care Jeffrey James Arts Cons 316 Pacific St Massapequa Park NY 11762 Office: Jeffrey James Arts Consulting 316 Pacific St Massapequa Park NY 11762-1807 also: c/o Allegro Imports 12630 NE Marx St Portland OR 97230-1059*

ZLATKIS, ALBERT, chemistry educator; b. Pomorzany, Poland, Mar. 27, 1924; came to Can. 1927, U.S., 1949, naturalized, 1959; s. Louis and Zisel (Nable) Z.; m. Esther Shessel, June 15, 1947; children: Debra, Lori, Robert. B.A.Sc., U. Toronto, 1947, M.A.Sc., 1948; Ph.D., Wayne State U., 1952. Rsch. chemist Shell Oil Co., Houston, 1953-55; asst. prof. chemistry U. Houston, 1955-58, assoc. prof., 1958-63, chmn. chemistry dept., 1958-62, prof. chemistry, 1963—; adj. prof. chemistry Baylor Coll. Medicine, 1975—; tour speaker Am. Chem. Soc., 1961, 63, 66, South Africa Chem. Inst., 1971, USSR Acad. Scis., 1973, Polish Acad. Scis., 1977; chmn. Internat. Symposium on Advances in Chromatography, 1963—; chmn. Expochem Analytical Symposium, 1979-81. Author: Practice of Gas Chromatography, 1967, Preparative Gas Chromatography, 1971, Advances in Chromatography, 25 vols., 1963-88, A Concise Introduction to Organic Chemistry, 1973, High Performance Thin-Layer Chromatography, 1977, 75 Years of Chromatography—A Historical Dialogue, 1979, Instrumental HPTLC, 1980, Electron Capture—Theory and Practice in Chromatography, 1981; contbr. articles to profl. jours.; mem. editorial bd. Jour. High Resolution Chromatography, Jour. Chromatograpic Science, Chromatographia, Jour. Chromatography. Recipient Analyst of Yr. award Dallas Soc. Analytical Chemistry, 1977, Tswett Meml. medal USSR Acad. Scis., 1980, Tswett Chromatography medal, 1983, NASA Tech. award, 1975, 80, NASA Patent award, 1978, Disting. Tex. Scientist award Tex. Acad. Sci., 1985, James L. Waters Pioneers in Devel. Analytical Instrumentation award, 1990; grantee USPHS, 1966, NASA, 1964-76, Welch Found., 1969, AEC, 1967, NSF, 1978, EPA, 1979, U.S. Army Rsch. Office, 1982, Gulf Coast Hazardous Substance Rsch. Ctr., 1989, Tex. Advanced Rsch. Program, 1991. Mem. Am. Chem. Soc. (chmn. S.E. Tex. sect. 1964, award in chromatography 1973, S.W. regional award 1988), Groupement pour l'Avancement des Méthodes Spectrographiques (France), Sigma Xi, Phi Lambda Upsilon. Home: 3350 McCue Rd Apt 603 Houston TX 77056-7113

ZLATOFF-MIRSKY, EVERETT IGOR, violinist; b. Evanston, Ill., Dec. 29, 1937; s. Alexander Igor and Evelyn Ola (Hill) Z.-M.; m. Janet Dalbey, Jan. 28, 1976; children from previous marriage—Tania, Laura. B.Mus., Chgo. Mus. Coll., Roosevelt U., 1960; M.Mus., Roosevelt U., 1961. Mem. faculty dept. music Roosevelt U., Chgo., 1961-66; founding mem., violinist, violist Music of the Baroque, 1971—. Violinist orch. Lyric Opera of Chgo., 1974—; concert master, pers. mgr., 1974—, violinist, violist, Contemporary Chamber Players U. Chog., 1964-82, solo violinist, Bach Soc., 1966-83; violist, violinist, Lexington String Quartet, 1966-81; rec. artist numerous recs., radio-TV and films; solo violinist appearing throughout U.S. Recipient Olive Ditson award Franklin Honor Soc., 1961. Mem. Nat. Acad. Rec. Arts and Scis. Republican. Roman Catholic. Home: 41w743 Hughes Rd Elburn IL 60119-9776 Office: Lyric Opera Chgo 20 N Wacker Dr Chicago IL 60606-2806

ZLOCH, WILLIAM J., federal judge; b. 1944. Judge U.S. Dist. Ct. (so. dist.) Fla., Ft. Lauderdale, 1985—. Office: US Dist Ct 299 E Broward Blvd Fort Lauderdale FL 33301-1944

ZLOWE, FLORENCE MARKOWITZ, artist; b. Allentown, Pa.; d. Morris and Anna (Mandel) Markowitz; m. Irwin Zlowe, May 1, 1936. Student, Pa. Mus. Coll. Art, Phila., 1929-33; fine arts courses, NYU, 1950-53. One woman show, Charles Z. Mann Gallery, N.Y.C., 1968, Community Gallery, N.Y.C., 1978; exhibited in group shows, Nat. Acad., Riverside Mus., N.Y., Nat. Arts Club, Pen and Brush Club, Lever House, Jersey City Mus., Norfolk (Va.) Mus., Fort Lauderdale (Fla.) Mus., Joe and Emily Lowe Mus., Fla.; represented in permanent collections, Norfolk Mus., Fort Lauderdale Mus., Joe and Emily Lowe Mus., Wilson Pub. Co., N.Y.C., Phila. Mus. Art, Butler Inst. Am. Art, Minn. Mus. Art, St. Paul, Cooper-Hewitt Mus. Design, Smithsonian Instn., N.Y.C., Tweed Mus., Duluth, Minn., Evansville (Ind.) Mus., Lakeview (Ill.) Center Arts and Scis., Ga. Mus. Art, Athens, Slater Meml. Mus., Norwich, Conn. Mem. Am. Soc. Contemporary Artists (dir., treas.), N.J. Soc. Painters and Sculptors, Nat. Assn. Women Artists (1st prize ann. 1958, 12 additional awards for oils 1958-84), League Present Day Artists, Artists Equity Assn. N.Y. Home: 440 E 57th St New York NY 10022-3045 Studio: 41 Union Sq W New York NY 10003-3208

ZOBEL, DONALD BRUCE, botany educator; b. Salinas, Calif., July 17, 1942; s. Bruce John and Barbara June (Lemon) Z.; m. Priscilla Fay Matthews, July 9, 1966; children: Cheryl, Gregory. BS, N.C. State U., 1964; MA, Duke U., 1966, PhD, 1968. Asst. prof. Oreg. State U., Corvallis, 1968-74, assoc. prof., 1974-82, prof., 1982—; vis. rschr. Taiwan Forestry Rsch. Inst., Taipei, 1976-77, Kumaun U., NainiTal, India, 1994, 95; Fulbright lectr. Tribhuvan U., Kathmandu, Nepal, 1984-85; Indo-Am. fellow, Kumaun U., NainiTal, India, 1991. Author: Ecology, Pathology and Management of Port-Orford-cedar (Chamaecyparis lawsoniana), 1985, A Practical Manual for Ecology, 1987; contbr. articles to profl. jours. Grantee NSF, 1974-77, 80-84, 94-98. Mem. AAAS, Ecol. Soc. Am., NW Sci. Assn. (trustee 1980-83), Internat. Assn. for Ecology, Brit. Ecol. Soc. Republican. Mem. Christian Ch. Home: 2310 NE Seavy Cir Corvallis OR 97330-4231 Office: Oreg State U Dept Botany & Plant Pathol 2082 Cordley Hall Corvallis OR 97331-8530

ZOBEL, HILLER BELLIN, judge; b. N.Y.C., Feb. 23, 1932; s. Hiller and Harriet Selma (Bellin) Z.; m. Deborah Bethell, June 21, 1958; children—John H., David H., Elizabeth T., Sarah B.; m. Rya S. Weickert, Nov. 23, 1973. B.A. cum laude, Harvard U., 1953, LL.B., 1959; postgrad., Oxford U., 1956. Bar: Mass. 1959, U.S. Ct. Appeals 1960, U.S. Dist. Ct. 1960, U.S. Supreme Ct. 1966. Assoc. firm Bingham, Dana & Gould, Boston, 1959-67; research assoc. Harvard U., 1962-63; assoc. prof. Boston Coll. Law Sch., 1967-69, prof., 1969-79; assoc., counsel firm Hill & Barlow, Boston, 1971-72; partner, counsel firm Brown, Rudnick, Freed & Gesmer, Boston, 1972-79; assoc. justice Mass. Superior Ct., 1979—; reporter Mass. Advisory Com. on Rules of Civil Procedure; spl. asst. atty. gen. Commonwealth of Mass.; spl. counsel Mass. Dept. Pub. Utilities. Author: The Boston Massacre, 1970, 96, (with J.W. Smith) Massachusetts Rules Practice, 1974-81, (with S.N. Rous) Doctors and the Law, 1993; editor: (with L.K. Wroth) Legal Papers of John Adams, 1965; contbr. articles to profl. jours. Served with U.S. Navy, 1953-55. Recipient Am. Hist. Assn. Littleton-Griswold prize, 1966. Fellow Soc. Am. Historians; mem. Am. Law Inst., Mass. Hist. Soc., Colonial Soc. Mass., Am. Antiquarian Soc., Mass. Bar Assn., Boston Bar Assn., Maritime Law Assn. U.S., Am. Soc. Legal History (v.p. 1970-71), Nat. Conf. State Trial Judges (exec. com. 1990-93). Democrat. Jewish. Office: Superior Ct Pemberton Sq Boston MA 02108

ZOBEL, LOUISE PURWIN, author, educator, lecturer, writing consultant; b. Laredo, Tex., Jan. 10, 1922; d. Leo Max and Ethel Catherine (Levy) Purwin; m. Jerome Fremont Zobel, Nov. 14, 1943; children: Lenore Zobel Harris, Janice A., Robert E., Audrey Zobel Dollinger. BA cum laude, Stanford U., 1943, MA, 1976. Cert. adult edn. and community coll. tchr., Calif. Freelance mag. writer and author Palo Alto, Calif., 1942—; writer, editor, broadcastor UP Bur., San Francisco, 1943; lectr. on writing, history, travel No. Calif., 1964—; lectr., educator U. Calif. campuses, other colls. and univs., 1969—; writing cons. to pvt. clients, 1969—; editorial asst. Assn. Coll. Unions Internat., Palo Alto, 1972-73; acting asst. prof. journalism San Jose State U., 1976; keynote speaker, seminar leader, prin. speaker at nat. confs.; cruise/shipboard enrichment lectr. and presenter of travel slide programs; coord. TV shows; TV personality. Author: (books) The Travel Writer's Handbook, 1980, (paperback), 1982, 83, 84, 85, rev. edits., 1992, 94, 97; author, narrator (90 minute cassette) Let's Have Fun in Japan, 1982; contbr. articles to anthologies, nat. mags. and newspapers; writer advertorials. Bd. dirs., publicity chair Friends of Palo Alto Libr., 1985—; officer Santa Clara County Med. Aux., Esther Clark Aux., others; past pres. PTA. Recipient award for excellence in journalism Sigma Delta Chi, 1943, awards Writers Digest, 1967-95, Armed Forces Writers League, 1972, Nat. Writers Club, 1976, All Nippon Airways and Japanese Nat. Tourist Orgn., 1997. Mem. Am. Soc. Journalists and Authors, Travel Journalists Guild, Internat. Food, Wine and Travel Writers Assn., Pacific Asia Travel Assn., Calif. Writers Club (v.p. 1988-89), AAUW (v.p. 1955-57, Nat. writing award 1969), Stanford Alumni Assn., Phi Beta Kappa. Avocations: travel, reading, writing, photography. Home and Office: 23350 Sereno Ct Unit 30 Cupertino CA 95014-6543

ZOBEL, ROBERT LEONARD, state government official; b. Reedsburg, Wis., July 28, 1935; s. Leonard Walter and Kathryn Jennifer (Cleveland) Z.; m. Faith Minnie Weatherwax, Aug. 5, 1961; children: Karl, Paul, Mary. BS in Fin., U. N.D., 1961. Investment banker Loewi & Co., Milw., 1961-65; bank examiner State of Wis., Madison, 1965-68, dir. investment bd., 1968—; mem. adv. bd. Merrill Lynch Capital, N.Y.C., Zell/Chillmack, Chgo., Hancock Internat., Boston, Horizon Ptnrs., Milw.; mem. stockholder rep. bd. Burdick, Milton/Madison, A.C. Equipment, Milw.; bd. dirs. Trak Internat., Cmty. Connection, Port Washington, Pan Vera, Madison; mem. adv. bd. U. Wis. Bus. Sch. Venture Capital; presenter nat. and internat. profl. assns., seminars, others. Mem. owners' com. Olympia Resort, Oconomowoc, Wis.; coach youth soccer, Baseball and basketball orgns.; lay min. area United Meth. Ch.; participant mission projects, including ch. bldg., Vulcain, Costa Rica, Rio Claro, Costa Rica, Prince Town, Trinidad, Portsmouth, Dominica, hosp. and sch. rehab., Bo, Sierra Leone, Maua, Kenya, Santa Cruz, Bolivia, Cochabamba, Bolivia, Gomay, St. Vincent, Cork Hill, Montserat; vol. Salvation Army; adv. bd. U. Wis.- Ventures Program. With USN, 1956-58. Mem. Elks. Avocations: mission work, golf, tennis, reading, public speaking. Home: 5312 Healy Ln Monona WI 53716-2519 Office: Wis Investment Bd 121 E Wilson St Madison WI 53703-3455

ZOBEL, RYA WEICKERT, federal judge; b. Germany, Dec. 18, 1931. A.B., Radcliffe Coll., 1953; LL.B., Harvard U., 1956. Bar: Mass. 1956, U.S. Dist. Ct., Mass., 1956, U.S. Ct. Appeals (1st cir.) 1967. Assoc. Hill & Barlow, Boston, 1967-73; assoc. Goodwin, Procter & Hoar, Boston, 1973-76, ptnr., 1976-79; U.S. dist. judge of Mass. Boston, 1979—; dir. Fed. Jud. Ctr., Washington, 1994—. Mem. ABA, Boston Bar Assn., Am. Bar Found., Mass. Bar Assn., Am. Law Inst. Office: Fed Judicial Ctr Thurgood Marshall Fed Bldg One Columbus Cir NE Washington DC 20002

ZOBRIST, BENEDICT KARL, library director, historian; b. Moline, Ill., Aug. 21, 1921; s. Benedict and Lila Agnas (Colson) Z.; m. Donna Mae Anderson, Oct. 23, 1948; children: Benedict Karl II, Markham Lee, Erik Christian. AB, Augustana Coll., Rock Island, Ill., 1946; postgrad., Stanford U., 1946-47; MA, Northwestern U., 1948, PhD, 1953; postgrad., U. Ill., 1961, Tunghai U., Taiwan, 1962, Columbia U., 1962-63, Fed. Exec. Inst., Charlottesville, Va., 1974, Hebrew U., Israel, 1978; LHD, Avila Coll., 1995. Manuscript specialist in recent Am. history Library of Congress, Washington, 1952-53; asst. reference librarian Newberry Library, Chgo., 1953-54; command historian Ordnance Weapons Command, Rock Island Arsenal, 1954-60; prof. history, chmn. dept. Augustana Coll., 1960-69, asst. dean faculty, 1964-69, asso. dean, dir. grad. studies, 1969; asst. dir. Harry S. Truman Libr., Independence, Mo., 1969-71; dir. Harry S. Truman Libr., 1971-94; exec. sec. Harry S. Truman Libr. Inst., Independence, 1971-94; mem. steering com. Harry S. Truman Statue Com., Independence, 1973-76; dir., regent Harry S. Truman Good Neighbor Award Found., 1974—; mem. Independence Truman Award Commn., 1975-94, Mo. Hist. Records Adv. Bd., 1978—; adj. prof. history U. Mo.-Kansas City, 1975—, Ottawa U., Kansas City, 1977-94, U. Mo. St. Louis, 1987-94; chmn. Independence Commn. Bicentennial of U.S. Constitution, 1987, Uptown Independence, Inc., 1989-94; mem. adv. coun. Truman Little White House State Historic Site, Key West, Fla., 1987-94. Contbr. articles, revs. to profl. jours. Trustee Heritage League of Greater Kansas City, 1981—, Liberty Meml. Assn., Kansas City, Mo., 1990—, Black Archives Mid-Am., Inc., Kansas City, 1992-94; mem. Truman Nat. Centennial Com., 1982-84. Served with AUS, 1942-46. Recipient Outstanding Alumni Achievement award Augustana Coll., 1975, Bronze Good Citizenship medal Kans. SAR, 1986, People's Choice award Independence (Mo.) Neighborhood Councils, 1987, Mid-Am.

Regional Council award for contbns. to met. community, 1987, Citizen Achievement award Black Archives of Mid-Am., 1988, Silver Good Citizenship medal Mo. SAR, 1988, Special Recognition award City of Independence, 1988, Outstanding Civic Leader in Independence, 1989, Gold Medal of Honor DAR, 1990, Spl. Commendation award Nat. Park Svc., 1993; named World Citizen of Yr. by Kans. City Mayor's UN Day Com., 1994. Mem. AAUP, Am. Hist. Assn., Jackson County (Mo.) Hist. Soc. (v.p. 1972-82, 93-95), Orgn. Am. Historians, Assn. Asian Studies, Am. Assn. State, Local History, Soc. Am. Archivists, U.S. Power Squadron, Am. Legion, La Societe des 40 Hommes et 8 Chevaux, VFW. Home: 71B T St Lake Lotawana MO 64086-9728

ZOBRIST, GEORGE WINSTON, computer scientist, educator; b. Highland, Ill., Feb. 13, 1934; s. George H. and Lillie C. (Augustin) Z.; m. Freida Groverlyn Rich, Mar. 29, 1955; children: Barbara Jayne, George William, Jean Anne. B.S., U. Mo., 1958, Ph.D., 1965; M.S., Wichita State U., 1961. Registered profl. engr., Mo., Fla. Electronic scientist U.S. Naval Ordnance Test Sta., China Lake, Calif., 1958-59; rsch. engr. Boeing Co., Wichita, 1959-60; instr. Wichita State U., 1960-61; assoc. prof. U. Mo., Columbia, 1961-69, U. So. Fla., Tampa, 1969-70; chmn. elec. engring. dept. U. Miami, Coral Gables, Fla., 1970-71; prof. U. South Fla., Tampa, 1971-72, 73-76; prof., chmn. dept. elec. engring. U. Toledo, 1976-79; dir. computer sci. and engring. Samborn, Steketee, Otis, Evans, Inc., Toledo, 1979-82; prof. computer sci. Grad. Engring. Ctr. U. Mo., St. Louis, 1982-85; prof. computer sci. U. Mo., Rolla, 1985—, chmn. dept., 1994—; rsch. prof. U. Edinburgh, Scotland, 1972-73; lectr. U. Western Cape, South Africa, 1995 summer; cons. Wilcox Electric Co., Bendix Corp., both Kansas City, Mo., 1966-68, ICC, Miami, 1970-71, Def. Comm. Agy., Washington, 1971, 72, U.S. Naval Rsch. Labs., Washington, 1971, Med. Svc. Bur., Miami, 1970-71, NASA, Kennedy Space Ctr., Fla., 1973-76, 88, 89, 93, 94, Prestolite Corp., Toledo, 1977-79, IBM, Lexington, Ky., 1983-86, Wright-Patterson AFB, Ohio, 1986, PAFB, Fla., 1987, McDonnell Douglas, Mo., 1989, Digital Systems Cons., Mo., 1989, Oak Ridge Nat. Labs., 1992. Author: Network Computer Analysis, 1969, Progress in Computer Aided VLSI Design, 1988-90; editor: Internat. Jour. Computer Aided VLSI Design, 1989-91, Object Oriented Simulation IEEE Press, 1996, Computer Sci. and Computer Engring. Monograph series, 1989-91, Internat. Jour. Computer Simulation, 1990-96, VLSI Design, 1992—; contbr. articles to profl. jours. Served with USAF, 1951-55. Named Young Engr. of Yr. ctrl. chpt. Mo. Soc. Profl. Engrs., 1967; NSF summer fellow, 1962, 64; NASA, IBM, DOE, UES/AFOSR, McDonnell Douglas rsch. grantee, 1967-88. Mem. IEEE (sr.), Soc. Computer Simulation, Am. Legion, Rotary, Sigma Xi, Tau Beta Pi, Phi Eta Sigma, Eta Kappa Nu, Pi Mu Epsilon, Upsilon Pi Epsilon. Home: 12030 Country Club Dr Rolla MO 65401-7469 Office: U Mo Dept Computer Sci Rolla MO 65409

ZOCHOLL, STANLEY ERNEST, electronics executive; b. Phila., July 23, 1929; s. Hugo Ernest and Elsa Elizabeth (Peterson) Z.; m. Edith Ruth Wolf, Aug. 23, 1952; children: Susan Louise, Joanne Edith, Carol Lynn. BSEE, Drexel U., 1958, MSEE, 1973. Various positions ITE Cir. Breaker Co., Phila., 1955-69; sr. devel. engr. Gould-Brown Boveri, Phila., 1969-81; protection engr. BBC Brown Boveri, Horsham and Allentown, Pa., 1981-87; dir. tech. Westinghouse ABB Power T&D Co. (name changed to ABB Power T&D Co., Inc. 1989), Allentown, 1987-91; disting. engr. Schweitzer Engring. Labs., 1991—. Patentee in field. Fellow IEEE (power system relay com. 1985—, instr. seminars 1988-89, Best Paper award Trans. 1988). Home and Office: 71 E Rambler Dr Southampton PA 18966-2034

ZODHIATES, SPIROS GEORGE, association executive; b. Cyprus, Mar. 13, 1922; came to U.S., 1946, naturalized, 1949; s. George and Mary (Toumazou) Z.; m. Joan Carol Wassel, Jan. 10, 1948; children: Priscilla Zodhiates Barnes, Lois Zodhiates Jenks, Philip, Mary. Student, Am. U., Cairo, 1941-45; B.Th., Shelton Coll., 1947; M.A., N.Y. U., 1951; Th.D., Luther Rice Sem., 1978. Ordained to ministry Gen. Assn. Regular Baptist Chs., 1947; gen. sec., now pres. Am. Mission to Greeks (name changed to AMG Internat. 1974), Chattanooga, N.J., 1946—; pres. Am. Mission to Greeks (name changed to AMG Internat. 1974), 1965—. Author: numerous Bible-study books and booklets including Behavior of Belief, 1959, the Pursuit of Happiness, 1966, To Love is to Live, 1967, Getting the Most Out of Life, 1976, Life After Death, 1977, Hebrew Greek Key Study Bible, 1984, Complete Word Study New Testament, 1991 (Gold Medallion 1993), Complete Word Study Dictionary: New Testament, 1992, Complete Word Study Old Testament, 1994; editor in chief: (Greek) Voice of the Gospel, 1946, Pulpit and Bible Study Helps, 1975—; spkr. New Testament Light radio program. Recipient Gold Cross Greek Red Cross, 1951; decorated Order Brit. Empire. Home: 9001 Oak Haven Dr Chattanooga TN 37421 Office: AMG Internat 6815 Shallowford Rd Chattanooga TN 37421-1755

ZOELLER, DONALD J., lawyer; b. Queens Village, N.Y., Mar. 18, 1930; s. Henry Adolph and Marion Elizabeth (Brodie) Z.; m. Susan Josephine Campisi, Sept. 3, 1955; children—Paul Joseph, Jean Marie, Diane Marie. A.B., Fordham Coll., 1951; LL.B., Fordham Sch. Law, N.Y.C., 1958. Bar: N.Y. 1959, D.C. 1967. Law clk. to judge U.S. Dist. Ct. (so. dist.) N.Y., N.Y.C., 1958-59; assoc. Mudge Rose Guthrie Alexander & Perdon, N.Y.C., 1959-68, ptnr., 1968-95, exec. ptnr., 1991-95, chmn. exec. com., 1995; counsel Carter, Ledyard & Milburn, N.Y.C., 1995-96, ptnr., 1997—; adj. prof. law Fordham U. Law Sch., 1989—; lectr. in field. Contbr. articles to legal publs. 1st lt. U.S. Army, 1951-53, Korea. Mem. ABA, N.Y. State Bar Assn., Bar Assn. City of N.Y., Nassau County Bar Assn., Inst. Jud. Adminstrn., Am. Judicature Soc., Fed. Bar Coun. Republican. Roman Catholic. Avocations: skiing; swimming; tennis; reading. Office: Carter Ledyard & Milburn 2 Wall St New York NY 10005-2001 *Notable cases include: Matsushita Electric Indsl. Co. Ltd. et al vs. Zenith Radio Corp. et al, 475 U.S. 574, 89 L. edit. 2d 538, 106, s.ct. 1438.*

ZOELLER, FUZZY, professional golfer; b. New Albany, Ind., 1952. Professional golfer, 1973—; PGA tour victories include San Diego Open, 1979, Masters, 1979, Colonial Nat., 1981, Heritage Classic, 1983, U.S. Open, 1984, Bay Hill Classic, 1985, AT&T Pro Am., 1986, Heritage Classic, 1986, Anheuser-Busch Classic, 1986. Office: care PGA Tour 112 Tpc Blvd Ponte Vedra Beach FL 32082-3046*

ZOELLER, JACK CARL, financial executive; b. Buffalo, Feb. 26, 1949; s. Ronald Carl and Margaret Lillian (Wademan) Z.; m. Kathryn Louise Helmke, Apr. 25, 1981; children: Andrew, Alexander, Charles (dec.). BS, U.S. Mil. Acad., 1970; M of Pub. Policy, Harvard U., 1972; M of Letters, Oxford (Eng.) U., 1974. Program budget officer Army Chief of Staff's Office, Pentagon, Washington, 1978-80; v.p. E.F. Hutton & Co., Inc., N.Y.C., 1982; pres. E.F. Hutton Indemnity Group, N.Y.C., 1983-85, Capital Risk Mgmt., Iselin, N.J., 1985-87; exec. v.p., bd. dirs. Comfed Mortgage Co., Lowell, Mass., 1987-88, pres., 1988-91; pres. ComFed Savs. Bank, Lowell, 1990-91; chmn. chief exec. officer ComFed Bancorp., Cambridge, Mass., 1990-95; pres. The Zoeller Group, Washington, 1993-95; bd. dirs. N.Am. Health Plans, Inc., Amherst, N.Y., 1995—; pres. N.Am. Fin. Corp., 1995—, N.Am. Health & Life Ins., Barbados, 1996—. Mem. exec. com. Lowell Devel. and Fin. Corp., 1989-91, class gift com. U.S. Mil. Acad., 1990-95; youth sports coach, 1990-96. Served to Capt. U.S. Army, 1970-80. Decorated Meritorious Svc. medals; Rhodes scholar Oxford U., 1972. Mem. West Point Soc. N.Y. (bd. govs. 1985-87), West Point Soc. D.C., Fed. Nat. Mortgage Assn. (N.E. regional adv. bd. 1990-91), New Eng. Hist. Geneal. Soc., Soc. Mayflower Descs. Home: 2810 31st St NW Washington DC 20008-3523 Office: North Am Fin Corp 1919 Gallows Rd Ste 900 Vienna VA 22182-3964

ZOELLICK, ROBERT BRUCE, corporate executive, lawyer; b. Evergreen Park, Ill., July 25, 1953; s. William T. and Gladys Zoellick; m. Sherry Lynn Ferguson, June 28, 1980. BA with honors, Swarthmore Coll., 1975; M Pub. Policy, JD magna cum laude, Harvard U., 1981. Bar: D.C. 1981. Spl. asst. to asst. atty. gen. criminal div. U.S. Dept. Justice, Washington, 1978-79; pvt. practice law, 1981-82; law clk. to Judge Patricia M. Wald, U.S. Ct. Appeals for D.C. Cir., Washington, 1982-83; v.p., asst. to chmn. and chief exec. officer of bd. Fannie Mae, Washington, 1983-85; from spl. asst. to Dep. Sec., Dep. Asst. Sec. for Fin. Instns. Policy, to counselor to sec. and exec. sec. U.S. Treasury Dept., Washington, 1985-88; counselor of Dept. with rank under sec. U.S. Dept. State, Washington, 1989-92, under sec. for econ. and agrl. affairs, 1991-92; dep. chief of staff, asst. to Pres. White House, Washington, 1992-93; exec. v.p. housing and law Fannie Mae, Washington, 1993—; bd. dirs. Alliance Capital, Junes Intercable, Said Holdings. Decorated Knight Comdr.'s Cross (for work on German unification, Germany); recipient Alexander Hamilton award U.S. Treasury Dept., 1988, Disting. Svc. award U.S. State Dept, 1992; fellow Luce Found., Hong Kong, 1980. Mem. D.C. Bar Assn., Phi Beta Kappa.

ZOELLNER, ROBERT WILLIAM, chemistry educator; b. Marshfield, Wis., May 30, 1956; s. Willard Rudolph and Marie Martha (Prihoda) Z.; m. Barbara Moore, Feb. 5, 1983; children: Joan Moore, Thaddeus Barak. BS, St. Norbert Coll., De Pere, Wis., 1978; PhD, Kans. State U., 1983. Postdoctoral assoc. Cornell U., Ithaca, N.Y., 1983-84; vis. scientist U. Aix-Marseille (France) III, 1984-85; asst. prof. No. Ariz. U., Flagstaff, 1986-92, assoc. prof., 1992—; sabbatical assoc. Istituto per lo Studio della Stereochimica Consiglio Nazionale delle Ricerche, 1994-95. Mem. Am. Chem. Soc., Internat. Coun. on Main Group Chemistry, N.Y. Acad. Scis., Wis. Acad. Sci., Arts and Letters, Sigma Xi, Alpha Chi Sigma, Phi Lambda Upsilon. Office: No Ariz U Dept Chemistry PO Box 5698 Flagstaff AZ 86011-5698

ZOFFER, H. JEROME, business educator, university dean; b. Pitts., July 23, 1930; s. William and Sarah Leah (Fisher) Z.; m. Maye Rattner, July 19, 1959; children: Gayle Risa, William Michael. BBA, U. Pitts., 1952, MA, 1953, PhD, 1956; CPCU, Am. Inst., Phila., 1954. Sales and mgmt. cons., 1952-60; instr. Sch. Bus. Adminstrn., U. Pitts., 1953-56; asst. prof. Sch. Bus. Adminstrn. U. Pitts., 1956-59, assoc. prof. Joseph M. Katz Grad. Sch. Bus., 1959-66, prof. Sch. Bus. Adminstrn., Grad. Sch. Bus., 1966—, chmn. dept. real estate and ins., 1958-60, dir. spl. studies, 1960-62, asst. dean for acad. affairs, 1962-65, assoc. dean for adminstrn., 1965-68, dean Grad. Sch. Bus., 1968-96; bd. dirs. Pennwood Savs. Bank, Homestate Pa. Growth Fund, The Enterprise Corp.; Ford Found. fellow in applied math. U. Pa., Phila., 1961-62; mem. visitation com. Am. Assembly Collegiate Schs. of Bus., 1972—, mem. standards com., 1974-78, mem. exec. com., 1975-87, chmn. accreditation rsch. com., 1974-84, v.p. bd. dirs., 1984-85, pres., 1985-86, chmn. Mid. State Evaluation Accrediting Teams, 1967-85. Author: The History of Automobile Liability Insurance Rating: 1900-1958, 1959; also monographs.; contbr. articles to profl. jours. Bd. dirs., v.p. Leadership Inst. for Community Devel., 1968-73, Allegheny chpt. Epilepsy Found. Am., 1971-77; bd. dirs. Pitts. Dist. Export Coun., 1974-77; bd. govs. Internat. Ins. Seminars, Inc., 1968-77; pres. Temple Sinai Congregation, 1979-81; mem. festival bd. Three Rivers Art Festival, 1988-93; mem. steering com. Leadership Pitts., 1986-91; sec. Am. Jewish Com., 1993-95; bd. dirs. Student Cons. Project, U. Pitts., 1970-96, Consortium for Coop. and Competitiveness, 1986-96, Moral Force in the Workplace, 1986-96; investment com. United Jewish Fedn., 1992-95. Named Man of Yr. in Edn., Vectors Pitts., 1986, Disting. Alumnus, 1989, U. Pitts. Alumni Assn. Mem. Soc. Psychol. Study Social Issues, Mid. Atlantic Assn. Colls. Bus. Adminstrn. (pres. 1972-73), Am. Assn. Univ. Adminstrs. (exec. com. 1971-79, pres. 1975-77, dir. 1980-83, pres. found. 1983-95), Univ. Club (bd. dirs. 1988-94, sec. 1990-91, v.p. 1991-92, pres. 1992-93), Omicron Delta Gamma, Beta Gamma Sigma (pres. Beta chpt. 1964-68). Home: 5620 Aylesboro Ave Pittsburgh PA 15217-1402 Office: U Pitts Pitts Campus Katz Grad Sch Bus Pittsburgh PA 15260

ZOGHBY, GUY ANTHONY, lawyer; b. Mobile, Ala., Sept. 30, 1934; s. Herbert Michael and Laurice (Haik) Z.; m. Verna Madelyn Antoine, Mar. 2, 1957 (dissolved); children: Guy Anthony II, Madelyn A., Gregory M.; m. Judy-ann EcKberg, Jan. 2, 1976. AB in English, Spring Hill Coll., 1955; JD, U. Cin., 1963; cert., U.S. Army JAG Sch., 1964. Bar: Ohio 1963, Ala. 1965, Calif. 1978, Pa. 1988. Commd. 2d lt. U.S. Army, 1955, advanced through grades to capt., 1963, various assignments, 1955-63; dep. staff JAG 11th Air Assault Div., Ft. Benning, Ga., 1963-64, 1st Cav. Div., 1964-65; atty. office of v.p. and gen. counsel IBM, Armonk, N.Y., 1965-67, staff atty., 1967-69, sr. atty., 1969-71; regional counsel IBM, Bethesda, Md., 1972-73; corp. staff counsel IBM, London, 1973-77; div. counsel IBM, Armonk, N.Y., 1977-80, mng. atty., 1980-83, group counsel, from 1983; v.p., gen. counsel PPG Industries Inc., Pitts., 1987-93; now sr. v.p., gen. counsel PPG Industries Inc., Pitts., 1994—; lectr. profl. seminars. Editor U. Cin. Law Rev., 1962-63. Bd. dirs. Allegheny ARC, 1989—, Am. Judicature Soc., 1988—, pres., 1993-95; bd. dirs. Pitts. Civic Light Opera, 1992—, Am. Arbitration Assn., 1996—; mem. Am. Law Inst., 1992—, The Duquesne Club, 1988; bd. visitors U. Cin. Coll. Law, 1986—; exec. com. Ctr. for Pub. Resource, 1994—. Decorated Commendation medal with one oak leaf cluster; recipient Lawrence Maxwell prize U. Cin. Mem. Am. Corp. Counsel Assn. (cir. 1982—, exec. com. 1982-88, chmn. 1987—), Assn. Gen. Counsel, Order of Coif. Roman Catholic. Office: PPG Industries Inc 1 Ppg Pl Pittsburgh PA 15272-0001

ZOHN, HARRY, author, educator; b. Vienna, Austria, Nov. 21, 1923; came to U.S., 1940, naturalized, 1945; s. Abraham Leon and Adele (Awin) Z.; m. Judith Ann Gorfinkle, Sept. 3, 1962; children: Steven David, Marjorie Eve. BA, Suffolk U., Boston, 1946; MA in Edn., Clark U., 1947; AM, Harvard U., 1949, PhD, 1952; LittD (hon.), Suffolk U., 1976. Credit investigator Credit Bur. Greater Boston, 1941-46; tchg. fellow in German Harvard U., 1947-51; mem. faculty Brandeis U., 1951-96, prof. German, 1967-96, chmn. dept. Germanic and Slavic langs., 1967-77, 87-90, chmn. Sch. Humanities coun., 1978-79, chmn. grad. program in lit. studies, 1981-84, prof. German emeritus, 1996—; exec. dir. Goethe Soc. New England, 1963-68. Author: Wiener Juden in der deutschen Literatur, 1964, Karl Kraus, 1971, German edit., 1990, Jüdisches Erbe in der österreichischen Literatur, 1986, Amerikanische "Thirty-Eighters" aus Wien als doppelte Kulturträger, 1994, Austriaca and Judaica, 1995, Karl Kraus and the Critics, 1997, Schüttelreime, 1997; editor: Liber Amicorum Friderike Zweig, 1952, Wie sie es sehen, 1952, Schachnovelle, 1960, Men of Dialogue, 1969, Der farbenvolle Untergang, 1970, Greatness Revisited, 1971, Deutschland, Deutschland über alles, 1972, The Saints of Qumran, 1977, Germany?, Germany!, 1990, Aus dem Tagebuch eines Emigranten, 1992, A Peter Fabrizius Reader, 1994, Die Stimme des Wortes, 1997; transl. books by Theodor Herzl, Kurt Tucholsky, Karl Kraus, Jacob Burckhardt, Walter Benjamin, Gershom Scholem, Alex Bein, André Kaminski, Fritz Molden, Manès Sperber, Hermann Langbein, others; mem. editl. bd. Modern Austrian Lit., Cross Currents; gen. editor (series) Austrian Culture. Mem. adv. com. fgn. langs. Commonwealth Mass., 1961-64; trustee Suffolk U., 1978-81, 83—. Decorated officer's cross Order Merit (Fed. Republic Germany) 1960; Cross of Honor for Sci. and Art (Republic of Austria) 1984; Gold Medal of Honor, City of Vienna, 1994; recipient Art prize Wolfgang Altendorf Cultural Found., 1991. Mem. Am. Assn. Tchrs. German (pres. Mass. chpt. 1954-59), Am. PEN Ctr., Austro-Am. Assn. Boston (chmn. bd. dirs. 1965—), Internat. Stefan Zweig Soc. (v.p. 1957-90), Internat. Arthur Schnitzler Assn. (v.p. 1978—), Austrian PEN Club, Internat. Franz Werfel Soc. (chmn. bd. dirs. 1995—), PEN Ctr. German-Speaking Writers Abroad, New Eng. MLA (past sec.-treas., chmn. Mass. chpt., bd. dirs.). Home: 48 Davis Ave Newton MA 02165-1924

ZOHN, MARTIN STEVEN, lawyer; b. Denver, Oct. 22, 1947; s. William and Alice (Lewis) Z.; m. Carol Falender, June 6, 1980; children: David Joseph, Daniel Robert. BA, Ind. U., 1969; JD, Harvard U., 1972. Bar: Calif. 1972, Ind. 1973, U.S. Ct. Claims 1980, U.S. Supreme Ct. 1980, U.S. Ct. Appeals (9th cir.) 1981. Assoc. Cadick, Burns, Duck & Neighbors, Indpls., 1972-77, ptnr., 1977-80; ptnr. Pacht, Ross, Warne, Bernhard & Sears, Inc., L.A., 1980-86, Shea & Gould, L.A., 1986-89, Proskauer Rose Goetz & Mendelsohn, L.A., 1989—; pres. Indpls. Settlements, Inc., 1977-79. Mem. Fin. Lawyers Conf., L.A. County Bar Assn. (exec. com. prejudgment remedies sect. 1985-92), Beverly Hills Bar Assn. (exec. com. bus. law sect. 1985-92), Phi Beta Kappa.

ZOIS, CONSTANTINE NICHOLAS ATHANASIOS, meteorology educator; b. Newark, Feb. 21, 1938; s. Athanasios Konstantinos and Asimina (Speros-Blekas) Z.; m. Elyse Stein, Dec. 26, 1971; children: Jennifer, Jonathan. BA, Rutgers U., 1961; MS, Fla. State U., 1965; PhD, Rutgers U., 1980. Draftsman Babcock and Wilcox Corp., Newark, 1956; designer Foster Wheeler Corp., Carteret, N.J., 1956; instr. Rutgers U., New Brunswick, N.J., 1961-62; grad. asst. Fla. State U., Tallahassee, 1962-65; rsch. meteorologist Nat. Weather Svc., Garden City, L.I., N.Y., 1965-67; prof. Kean Coll. N.J., Union, 1967—; founder meteorology program Kean Coll., N.J.; cons. Connell, Foley and Geiser, Roseland, N.J., 1986-88; chmn. Kean Coll. All-Coll. Promotion com., 1991-93. Author, editor: Papers in Marine Science, 1971; author: Observation of the Newark N.J. Nocturnal Heat Island and Its Consideration in Terms of a Physical Model, 1980, Dynamical and Physical Oceanography, 1988, Atmospheric Dynamics: Exercises and Problems, 1988, Climatology Workbook, 1988, Weather Map Folio, 1989; contbg. author: Outcomes Assessment at Kean College of N.J., 1992, Synoptic Meterology-Exercises and Readings, Vols. 1-3, 1995. Mem. AAAS, Nat. Weather Assn., Am. Meteorol. Soc. (pres. N.J. chpt. 1980-81), N.Y. Acad. Scis. (vice chmn. atmospheric scis. sect. 1986-87, chmn. 1987-88, adv. com. atmospheric sci. sect., 1988—), N.J. Marine Scis. Consortium, Phi Beta Kappa. Republican. Greek Orthodox. Avocations: guitar, banjo, fishing, baseball, snorkeling. Home: 2798 Carol Rd Union NJ 07083-4831 Office: Kean Coll of NJ Dept Meterology Morris Ave Union NJ 07083-7117 *It is water that consecrates the atmosphere as a cathedral of wonderment, as it is water that incarnates the sea as an oasis of life.*

ZOLA, GARY PHILLIP, religious educational administrator, rabbi,; b. Chgo., Feb. 17, 1952; m. Stefani Paula Rothberg; children: Amanda Roi, Jorin Benjamin, Jeremy Micah, Samantha Leigh. BA in Am. History with distinction, U. Mich., 1973; MA in Counseling Psychology, Northwestern U., 1976; PhD in Am. Jewish History, Hebrew Union Coll., Cin., 1991. Ordained rabbi, 1982. Dir. informal edn. and youth activities Temple Israel, Mpls., 1973-74; regional youth dir., asst. camp dir. Olin-Sang-Ruby Union Inst., UAHC, Chgo., 1974-77; student pulpit B'nai Israel Congregation, Williamson, W.Va., 1978-79; mem. student pulpit Anshe Sholom Congregation, Olympia Fields, Ill., 1979-80, Columbus Hebrew Congregation, Columbus, Ind., 1981-82; rabbi for high holy days Chgo. Jewish Experience, Chgo., 1982—; nat. dir. admissions Hebrew Union Coll.-Jewish Inst. Religion, Cin., 1982-89, nat. dean admissions and student affairs, 1989-91, nat. dean admissions, student affairs and alumni rels., 1991—; del. Emerging Leaders Conf., Am. Coun. for Internat. Leadership, 1989, 91; bd. dirs. Am. Jewish Com., Cin., 1982—, mem. exec. com., 1984—; bd. dirs. Hillel U. Cin., 1991—, Jewish Fedn., Cin., 1993—; pres. Greater Cin. Bd. Rabbis, 1993—, Jewish Cmty. Rels. Coun., (bd. dir.,1994—); founding mem. Kehillah of Cin., Jewish Think Tank. Author: Isaac Harby of Charleston, 1994; editor: Hebrew Union College--Jewish Institute of Religion--A Centennial History, 1875-1975, (Michael A. Meyer), 1992, Women Rabbis: Exploration and Celebration, 1996; contbr. numerous scholarly articles to profl. jours.; mem. editl. bd. Reform Judaism. bd. dirs. ethics com. Jewish Hosp., Cin.; life mem. N.Am. Fedn. Temple Youth; active NCCJ. Mem. Ctrl. Conf. Am. Rabbis, Orgn. Am. Historians, Assn. Jewish Studies, So. Jewish Hist. Soc., Am. Jewish Hist. Soc., N.Am. Fedn. Temple Youth (life). Office: Hebrew Union Coll Jewish Inst Religion 3101 Clifton Ave Cincinnati OH 45220-2404

ZOLL, MIRIAM HANNAH, activist, writer, communication specialist; b. Boston, Oct. 1, 1962; d. Nathan Hyman and Jacqueline Harper (Bonney) Z. BS in Journalism and Psychology, U. Mass., 1984. Dep. dir. comm. Earth Day, N.Y.C., 1990; spl. projects cons. Gay Men's Health Crisis, 1990-93; co-prodr., dir. comm. Take Our Daughters to Work, Ms. Found. for Women, 1992-94; nat. program cons. Mentors in Violence Prevention, 1994-97; media cons. Internat. Women's Conf., 1995; nat. project cons. Girls Inc., 1995-97; program dir. Youth Vote '96 Harvard Univ. Conf., 1996; internat. cons. Haiti Food Security program Grasroots Internat., 1996-97; mem. advance team Nat. Dem. Conv., 1992, Clinton-Gore Inaugural Com., 1993; logistician Nat. Dem. Inst., Malawi, Ctrl. Africa, 1994; media cons. Internat. Women's Health Coalition, Barbados, 1991; nat. advisor God Bless the Child Films, Boston, 1995-97; adv. bd. mem. Girls Re-Cast TV, N.Y.C., 1995-97; lectr. Inst. Politics, Kennedy Sch. Govt., Harvard U., 1996; trainer Ctr. Study Sport in Soc., Northeastern U. Contbr. articles to profl. jours. Advisor Mentors in Violence Prevention (MVP) Project, 1994-97. Avocations: writing, traveling, hiking, camping, swimming. Home: PO Box 1014 Brookline Village MA 02147

ZOLLAR, CAROLYN CATHERINE, lawyer; b. Evanston, Ill., July 5, 1947; d. Maurice Adam and Alice S. (Kelm) Z. BA, Smith Coll., Northampton, Mass., 1969; MA, Columbia U., 1970; JD, Am. U., Washington, 1976. Bar: D.C., Va. Legis. asst. Congressman William Anderson U.S. Ho. of Reps., Washington, 1970-72; planning cons. Nat. Inst. Edn., Washington, 1972, legal asst., 1973, asst. for govt. and external rels., 1973-75; assoc. Joe W. Fleming II, P.C., Washington, 1975-82; gen. counsel Nat. Assn. Rehab. Facilities, Washington, 1982-86, gen. counsel, dir. med. rehab., 1986-94; gen. counsel, v.p. policy Am. Rehab. Assn., Washington, 1994—; sec. Am. Rehab. Svcs., Inc., Washington, 1988-94; bd. adv. Ind. Living Mag., N.Y.C., 1988—; mem. Joint Commn. Accreditation Health Care Orgns. Task Force on Rehab. Svcs., 1988. Mem. editl. bd. BNA Managed Care Reporter, 1996—; contbr. articles to profl. jours. Sec. bd. dirs. Rock Creek Found., Silver Spring, Md., 1983-90, Affiliated Sante Group, 1993—; chair Nat. Rehab. Caucus, 1991—. Recipient legis. achievement award Nat. Assn. Rehab. Facilities, 1981, legis. advocacy award U. Buffalo, 1993, pub. svc. award Am. Acad. Phys. Medicine and Rehab., 1994. Mem. Am. Soc. Assn. Execs., Nat. Health Lawyers Assn., Va. Bar Assn., D.C. Bar, Women in Govt. Rels. Episcopalian. Avocations: skiing, golf, singing. Office: Am Rehab Assn 1910 Association Dr Reston VA 20191-1502

ZOLLAR, JAWOLE WILLA JO, art association administrator; b. Kansas City, Kans., Dec. 21, 1950; d. Alfred Jr. and Dorothy Delores Zollar; 1 child, Elizabeth Herron. BA in Dance, U. Mo., Kansas City, 1975; MFA in Dance, Fla. State U., 1979. Faculty Fla. State U., Tallahassee, 1977-80; artistic dir. Urban Bush Women, N.Y.C., 1984—; prof. dance Fla. State U., 1996—. Recipient N.Y. Dance and Performance award, 1992; named Outstanding Alumni U. Mo.-Kansas City, 1993; Mankato State U. Worlds of Thought Resident scholar, 1994; Nat. Endowment of Arts Choreography fellow, 1992, 93, 94. Mem. Dance U.S.A., Assn. of Am. Cultures, Internat. Assn. of Blacks in Dance. Office: Urban Bush Women 225 Lafayette St Rm 201 New York NY 10012-4015 also: care IMG Artists 22 E 71st St New York NY 10021-4911

ZOLLER, MICHAEL, otolaryngologist, head and neck surgeon, educator; b. New Orleans, July 21, 1947; s. Harry and Mildred (Daitch) Z.; m. Linda Kramer, Dec. 21, 1974; children: Rebecca, Jonathan. BS, U. New Orleans, 1968; MD, Tulane U., 1972. Resident in gen. surgery Jewish Hosp., St. Louis, 1972-74, Washington U. Sch. Medicine; resident in otolaryngology Mass. Eye and Ear Infirmary, Harvard U., Boston, 1974-77; pres. Ear, Nose and Throat Assocs., Savannah, Ga., 1977-96; chmn. Eye, Ear, Nose & Throat Dept. Candler Hosp., 1996—; asst. clin. prof. surgery Med. Coll. Ga., Augusta, 1982-96; assoc. clin. prof. surgery, 1996—; otology dir. otoneurology dept. St. Joseph's Hosp., Savannah, 1994—. Chmn. med. divsn. United Way, Savannah, 1990, chmn. profl. divsn., 1991, 94, 95, 96, 97; bd. dirs. Am. Cancer Soc., Savannah, 1993—, pres. Chatham County Unit, 1996; bd. dirs. Savannah Country Day Sch., 1993-97, chmn. ann. campaign, 1995-96; pres. Savannah Jewish Fedn., 1991-93; active Savannah Jewish Fedn. Endowment Bd., 1995—; mem. med. adv. bd. South Coll., 1996. Recipient Young Leadership award Savannah Jewish Fedn., 1985, Boss of Yr. award Savannah Jaycees, 1993, Celebrate Savannah award for outstanding contbns. to Savannah, Ga. Guardian, 1996; Harvard U. Med. Sch. fellow, 1976-77. Fellow ACS; mem. AMA, Am. Acad. Otolaryngology and Head and Neck Surgery (mem. sleep disorders com. 1996—, mem. tonsils & adenoids com. 1996—), Am. Acad. Head and Neck Soc., Am. Neurotology Soc., Ga. Med. Soc. (v.p. endowment fund 1996, sec. endowment fund 1992, pres. 1992, John B. Rabun Cmty. Svc. award 1995), 1st Dist. Med. Assn. (pres. 1987-88), Med. Assn. Ga. (bd. dirs., mem. ho. dels., Ga. Cup award 1993, Ayest-Wyeth Cmty. Svc. award 1996), So. Med. Assn., Ga. Soc. Otolaryngology (sec.-treas. 1995-96, pres.-elect 1996-97), Savannah C. of C. Office: Ear Nose and Throat Ctr 5201 Frederick St Savannah GA 31405-4501

ZOLNO, MARK S., lawyer. BA Polit. Sci., No. Ill. Univ., 1965; JD, John Marshall Law Sch., 1978; MA cum laude Internat. Rels., Universidad de las Américas, Mexico, 1974. Bar: Ill. 1978, U.S. Dist. Ct. (no. dist.) Ill. 1979, U.S. Ct. Internat. Trade 1979, U.S. Ct. Appeals (fed. cir.) 1979. With U.S. Customs Svc., Dept. Commerce, U.S. Trade Rep's. Office, Internat. Trade Commn., Fed. Trade Commn., FDA; ptnr. Katten Muchin & Zavis, Chgo., 1988—; past chmn. Chgo. Bar Assn. Customs and U.S. Trade Law Com.; lectr. in field. Contbr. articles to profl. jours. Office: Katten Muchin & Zavis 525 W Monroe St Ste 1600 Chicago IL 60661-3629

ZOLOMIJ, ROBERT WILLIAM, landscape architect, consultant; b. Phila., Oct. 13, 1942; s. William and Anna (Sikacz) Z.; m. Joanne M. Volk, Oct. 2, 1965; children: Nancy Lyn, Christopher John; m. Nancy S. Helfferich, Nov. 21, 1992. BS in Landscape Architecture, Pa. State U., 1965; M Landscape Architecture, U. Ill., 1971. Lic. landscape arch., Ill. Site planner Bucks County Planning Commn., Doylestown, Pa., 1965-67; assoc. prof. U. Ill., Urbana, 1968-78; sr. landscape arch. Skidmore Owings & Merrill, Chgo., 1978-79; sr. assoc. Barton-Aschman Assocs., Evanston, Ill., 1979-84; v.p. Harland Bartholomew Assocs., Northbrook, Ill., 1984-86, Land Design Collaborative, Inc., Evanston, 1986—. Co-author: Time Saver Standards for Landscape Architects, 1988. Univ. fellow U. Ill., 1967. Fellow Am. Soc. Landscape Archs. (chpt. treas. 1986-88, v.p. 1988-90, pres. 1990-92). Avocations: golf, travel, reading, woodworking. Home: 3429 Harrison St Evanston IL 60201-4953 Office: Land Design Collaborative 1563 Sherman Ave Evanston IL 60201-4421

ZOLOTO, JERROLD ALBERT, psychologist, consultant; b. Chgo., Jan. 1, 1944; s. Ben and Marian Idele (Cohen) Z.; m. Angela Nijole Yurkus, Sept. 27, 1981; children: Jill, Lydia, Alexandra. BS, U. Ill., 1966; MS, Wayne State U., 1972, PhD, 1979. Dir. DuPage Mental Health, Wheaton, Ill., 1973-81; dir. dept. psychiatry St. Joseph's Hosp., Chgo., 1981-82; cons. Rohrer, Hibler, Replogle, Chgo., 1982-84; v.p. Vici Internat., San Francisco, 1984-85; pres. Anova, Inc., Chgo., 1985—; adj. faculty Coll. of DuPage, Glen Ellyn, Ill., 1974-80; faculty Police Tng. Inst., Lisle, Ill., 1974-78; internship supr. numerous students at univs., 1983—; spkr. numerous orgns., 1973—; faculty mem. MBA program Coll. St. Francis, Joilet, Ill., 1997—. Author, inventor: (software) Listen: The Leadership Information System, 1990, Automated System for Individual and Organizational Assessment, Development and Performance Management. Pres., bd. dirs. Mental Health Assn., Ill., 1987-89, Du Page County, 1983-86; v.p. Breckenridge Homeowners Assn., Naperville, Ill., 1994-95; mem., bd. dirs. Girl Scouts USA, Lisle, 1984-86. Avocations: gardening, swimming, hiking. Office: Anova Inc 3 First National Plz 70 W Madison St Ste 1400 Chicago IL 60602-4267

ZOLOTOW, CHARLOTTE SHAPIRO, author, editor; b. Norfolk, Va., June 26, 1915; d. Louis J. and Ella F. (Bernstein) Shapiro; m. Maurice Zolotow, Apr. 14, 1938 (div. 1969); children: Stephen, Ellen. Student, U. Wis., 1933-36. Editor children's book dept. Harper & Row, N.Y.C., 1938-44; sr. editor Harper & Row, 1962-70; v.p., assoc. pub. Harper Jr. Books, 1976-81; editorial cons., editorial dir. Charlotte Zolotow Books, 1982-90; pub. emerita, advisor Harper Collins Children's Books, 1991—; tchr. U. Colo. Writers Conf. on Children's Books, U. Ind. Writers Conf.; also lectr. children's books. Author: The Park Book, 1944, Big Brother, 1960, The Sky Was Blue, 1963, The Magic Words, 1952, Indian Indian, 1952, The Bunny Who Found Easter, 1959, In My Garden, 1960, But Not Billy, 1947, 2d edit, 1983, Not a Little Monkey, 1957, 2d edit., 1989, The Man With The Purple Eyes, 1961, Mr. Rabbit and the Lovely Present, 1962, The White Marble, 1963, A Rose, A Bridge and A Wild Black Horse, 1964, 2d edit., 1987, Someday, 1965, When I Have a Little Girl, 1965, If It Weren't for You, 1966, 2d edit., 1987, Big Sister, Little Sister, 1966, All That Sunlight, 1967, When I Have A Son, 1967, My Friend John, 1968, Summer Is, 1968, Some Things Go Together, 1969, The Hating Book, 1969, The New Friend, 1969, River Winding, 1970, 79, Lateef and His World, 1970, Yani and His World, 1970, You and Me, 1971, Wake Up and Goodnight, 1971, William's Doll, 1972, Hold My Hand, 1972, 2d edit., 1987, The Beautiful Christmas Tree, 1972, Janie, 1973, My Grandson Lew, 1974, The Summer Night, 1974, 3d edit. 1991, The Unfriendly Book, 1975, It's Not Fair, 1976, 2d edit., 1987, Someone New, 1978, Say It, 1980, If You Listen, 1980, 2d edit. 1987, The New Friend, 1981, One Step, Two ..., 1981, The Song, 1982, I Know a Lady, 1984, Timothy Too!, 1986, Everything Glistens, Everything Sings, 1987, I Like to be Little, 1987, The Poodle Who Barked at the Wind, 1987, The Quiet Mother and the Noisy Little Boy, 1988, Something's Going to Happen, 1988, This Quiet Lady, 1992, The Seashore Book, 1992, Snippets, 1992, The Moon was the Best, 1993, Peter and the Pigeons, 1993, The Old Dog, 1995, When the Wind Stops, 1995, others; compiler An Overpraised Season, Early Sorrow. Recipient Harper Gold award for editorial excellence, 1974, Kerlan award U. Minn., 1986, Corp. award for children's books Lit. Market Pl., 1990, Silver medallion U. So. Miss., 1990, Tribute for Far Reaching Contbn. to Children's Lit., ALA, 1991, Nobel award in Econs., 1996. Mem. PEN, Authors League. Home: 29 Elm Pl Hastings Hudson NY 10706-1703 Office: 10 E 53d St New York NY 10022-5244

ZOLOTOW, ELLEN **See DRAGONWAGON, CRESCENT**

ZONANA, VICTOR, lawyer, educator; b. Zagazig, Egypt, Aug. 28, 1940; s. Isaac A. and Fortunee (Cohen Beyda) Z.; m. Mary Linda Haynie, Aug. 22, 1964; children: David A., Nancy B. BS in Econs., Hofstra U., 1961; LLB, NYU, 1964, LLM, 1966. Assoc. Kaye, Scholer, Fierman, Hays & Handler, N.Y.C., 1966-69; prof. NYU, 1969-80, adj. prof., 1981—, Charles S. Lyon vis. prof., 1994; dep. tax legis. counsel U.S. Dept. Treasury, 1975-76; cons. to asst. commr. IRS, 1975, office of chief counsel, 1994; counsel, ptnr. Kaye, Scholer, Fierman, Hays and Handler, N.Y.C., 1980-87, Arnold & Porter, N.Y.C., 1988—; prof. Bklyn. Law Sch., 1996—. Mem., chmn. adv. bd. NYU Tax Inst. Fellow Am. Coll. Tax Counsel; mem. ABA, N.Y. State Bar Assn. (co-chmn. com. on fgn. activities of U.S. taxpayers, chmn. com. on depreciation and investment credit, co-chmn, com. tax acctg. matters, com. tax policy). Office: Arnold & Porter 399 Park Ave New York NY 10022 also: Bklyn Law Sch 250 Joralemon St Brooklyn NY 11201

ZONDLER, JOYCE EVELYN, kindergarten educator; b. Jersey City, N.J., June 28, 1952; d. Vincent Roger and Marta (Gruber) Hohmann; m. Kenneth P. Zondler, June 20, 1976 (div.). BA, Jersey City State Coll., 1974, MA, 1981. Cert. elem., early childhood tchr., N.J. Kindergarten tchr. Robert Fulton Sch., North Bergen, N.J., 1974—; mem. curriculum rev. coms. for math. and sci. North Bergen Schs., 1993—, for lang. arts, 1992-93, mem. report card rev. com. Mem. exec. bd. Fulton Sch. PTA, 1976-86, sec., 1978-80, v.p. 1980-82, treas. 1982-86. Recipient Gov.'s Recognition award, 1991. Mem. North Bergen Edn. Assn. (sec. 1989-91, v.p. 1991-93, pres. 1993—). Democrat. Roman Catholic. Office: Robert Fulton Sch 7407 Hudson Ave North Bergen NJ 07047-5607

ZONIS, MARVIN, political scientist, educator; b. Boston, Sept. 18, 1936; s. Leonard and Clara (Barenberg) Z.; m. Lucy Salenger, Jan. 3, 1976; children by previous marriage-Nadia E. Leah; 1 stepdaughter, Brix E. Smith. A.B., Yale U., 1958; postgrad., Harvard Grad. Sch. Bus., 1958-59; Ph.D., M.I.T., 1968; candidate, Inst. for Psychoanalysis, Chgo., 1977-85. Mem. faculty U. Chgo., 1966—, assoc. prof. and prof. behavioral scis., 1973-89—, prof. Grad. Sch. Bus., 1989—; dir. U. Chgo. (Center for Middle Eastern Studies), 1976-79; pres. Marvin Zonis and Assocs., Internat. Cons., 1991—; cons. in field; chmn. com. on Middle East Am. Coun. Learned Socs.-Social Sci. Rsch. Coun., 1970-76; pres. Am. Inst. Iranian Studies, 1969-71; bd. dirs. CNA Fin. Corp. Author: The Political Elite of Iran, 1971, Khomeini, The Islamic Republic of Iran, and the Arab World, 1987, Majestic Failure: The Fall of the Shah, 1991, The East European Opportunity: The Complete Business Guide and Source Book, 1992; contbr. articles to profl. jours. Served with USAF, 1959-60. Recipient Quantrell award for excellence in teaching U. Chgo., 1979. Office: U Chicago 5828 S University Ave Chicago IL 60637-1515 *Psychoanalytic approaches to the study of political phenomena open new vistas to understanding as well as facilitating the design of U.S. policy.*

ZONSZEIN, JOEL, endocrinologist; b. Mexico City, Mex., Mar. 15, 1945; came to U.S., 1970; s. Szepsel and Elena (Sheinberg) Z.; m. Anat Arad Zonszein, Aug. 24, 1976; children: Yonatan, Mairav. MD, U. Nacional Autonoma de Mex., 1969. Intern Maimonides Med. Ctr., Bklyn., 1970-71, resident, 1971-72; resident Bronx Mcpl. Hosp., 1972-73; endocrine fellow Northwestern U., Chgo., 1973-74, Georgetown U., Washington, 1974-75; chief endocrinology Bronx (N.Y.) Lebanon Hosp., 1980-93; assoc. prof. medicine Albert Einstein Coll. Medicine, Bronx, 1986—, clin. co-dir. Diabetes Treatment Ctr., 1993—. Contbr. articles to profl. jours. Fellow ACP; mem. Am. Diabetes Assn. (chmn. Hispanic com. 1987—), N.Y. Acad. Scis., Endocrine Soc. Office: 1199 Park Ave Apt 1H New York NY 10128-1713

ZOOGMAN, NICHOLAS JAY, lawyer; b. N.Y.C., Apr. 2, 1947; s. Morris William and Hannah (Stern) Z.; m. Carla Ganz, June 7, 1970; children: Sarah Elizabeth, Peter William. BA, NYU, 1967; MA, Harvard U., 1969, JD, 1973. Bar: N.Y. 1974, U.S. Dist. Ct. (so. and ea. dists.) N.Y. 1974, U.S. Ct. Appeals (2d cir.) 1975, U.S. Supreme Ct. 1979, U.S. Dist. Ct. (ea. dist.) Mich. 1988, U.S. Ct. Appeals (D.C. cir.) 1990, U.S. Ct. Appeals (6th cir.) 1993. Assoc. Donovan Leisure Newton & Irvine, N.Y.C., 1973-75; ptnr. Anderson Kill & Olick, N.Y.C., 1976—. Mem. ABA, N.Y. State Bar Assn., Assn. Bar City N.Y., Phi Beta Kappa, Pi Sigma Alpha. Office: Anderson Kill & Olick 1251 Avenue Of The Americas New York NY 10020-1104

ZOOK, BILL, lawyer; b. Oak Park, Ill., Mar. 16, 1946; s. William E. and Betty L. (Kane) Z.; m. Sharon Oakley, Sept. 1, 1973; children: Aaron, Justin, Sean. BS in Engrin., U.S. Mil. Acad., 1969; JD, U. Tex., 1976. Bar: Tex. 1977, U.S. Dist. Ct. (we. dist.) Tex. 1979, U.S. Ct. Appeals (5th and 11th cirs.) 1981, U.S. Dist. Ct. (ea. dist.) Tex. 1989; cert. in personal injury trial law and civil trial law Tex. Bd. Legal Specialization. Atty. J. Howard Hayden, PC, Austin, Tex., 1976-77, Law Offices Bob Gibbins, Austin, 1977-81; pvt. practice Austin, 1981-89; atty. McLaughlin, Hutchison & Hunt, Paris, Tex., 1989-91, Ted B. Lyon & Assocs., Mesquite, Tex., 1991—. Capt. U.S. Army, 1969-74. Avocations: sports. Home: 301 Red Bird Ln Highland Village TX 75067 Office: Ted B Lyon & Assocs Ste 525 18601 Lyndon B Johnson Fwy Mesquite TX 75150-5614

ZOOK, ELVIN GLENN, plastic surgeon, educator; b. Huntington County, Ind., Mar. 21, 1937; s. Glenn Hardman and Ruth (Barton) Z.; m. Sharon Kay Neher, Dec. 11, 1960; children—Tara E., Leigh A., Nicole L. B.A., Manchester Coll., 1959; M.D., Ind. U., 1963. Diplomate Am. Bd. Surgery, Am. Bd. Thoracic Surgery, Am. Bd. Plastic Surgery. Intern Meth. Hosp., Indpls., 1963-64; resident in gen. and thoracic surgery Ind. U. Med. Center, Indpls., 1964-69; resident in plastic surgery Ind. U. Hosp., Indpls., 1969-71; asst. prof. plastic surgery Ind. U. Hosp., 1971-73; asso. prof. surgery So. Ill. U., Springfield, 1973-75; prof. So. Ill. U., 1975—, chmn. div. plastic surgery, 1973—; mem. staff Meml. Med. Center, St. Johns Hosp., Springfield. Contbr. articles to med. jours. Mem. AMA, Assn. Acad. Surgery, Am. Soc. Plastic and Reconstructive Surgery (sec. 1988-91, v.p. 1991-92, pres.-elect 1992-93, pres. 1993-94), Midwestern Soc. Plastic and Reconstructive Surgery (pres. 1986-87), ACS, Sangamon County Med. Soc. (pres. 1987), Am. Cleft Palate Assn., Am. Assn. Plastic Surgery (trustee 1987-90), Plastic Surgery Rsch. Coun. (chmn. 1981), Am. Burn Assn., Ill. Surg. Soc., Am. Soc. Surgery Hand (coun.), Am. Bd. of Plastic Surgery (sec.-treas. 1988-91, chmn. 1991-92), Am. Soc. Aesthetic Plastic Surgery, Am. Soc. Surgery of Trauma, Assn. Acad. Chmn. Plastic Surgery (pes. 1986-87), Am. Surg. Assn., RRC for Plastic Surgery, Sangamo Club, Springfield Med. Club, Island Bay Yacht Club. Presbyterian. Clubs: Sangamo, Springfield Med, Island Bay Yacht. Home: 42 Hazel Dell Springfield IL 62707-9507 Office: 800 N Rutledge St Springfield IL 62702-4911 *Do the best possible in all that is possible.*

ZOOK, MERLIN WAYNE, meteorologist; b. Connellsville, Pa., July 2, 1937; s. Ellrose Durr and Frances Adeline (Loucks) Z.; m. Maxine Beatrice Hartzler, May 1, 1965; children: Kevin Ray, Kathleen Joy. BA, Goshen (Ind.) Coll., 1959; MS, Pa. State U., 1961. Cert. consulting meteorologist, environ. profl. Rsch. assoc. U. Mich., Ann Arbor, 1958; grad. asst. Pa. State U., University Park, 1960-61; audio-visual asst., staff meteorologist Mennonite Cen. Com., Akron, Pa., 1961-63; air quality program specialist Pa. Dept. Environ. Protection, Harrisburg, 1963—; book reviewer Sci. Edn. Dept. Boston U., 1990-92, Nat. Weather Assn., Temple Hills, Md., 1983-88, book rev. editor, 1988-92; scientist, participant AAAS-Bell Atlantic Found., Washington, 1989-90. Author, contbr.: (chpt.) Behind the Dim Unknown, 1966. Guest lectr. Millersville (Pa.) State U., 1988, 90, Boy Scouts Am., Camp Hill, Pa., 1990, Pa. State U., Middletown, 1990, 91—, Cub Scouts Am., Camp Hill, 1991—. Mem. Am. Meteorol. Soc., Union of Concerned Scientists. Achievements include development of models for the daily prediction of the Pollutant Standards Index in Pa.; of collection of cloud type photographs with classifications for study of cloud charasteristics/physics; research in meso-scale meteorology and localized forecasting, on the relationship between solar radiation and formation of ozone in urban areas in Pa., research and development of mathematical models for the prediction of ozone episodes in urban areas; on migratory patterns of local birds influenced by meteorological conditions. Home: 105 June Dr Camp Hill PA 17011-5069 Office: Pa Bur Air Quality Dept Environ Protection 400 Market St Harrisburg PA 17101-2301

ZOOK, THERESA FUETTERER, gemologist, consultant; b. Barberton, Ohio, Mar. 12, 1919; d. Charles Theodore and Ethel May (Knisely) Fuetterer; m. Donovan Quay Zook, June 21, 1941; children: Theodore Alan, Jacqueline Deborah Zook Cochran. AB, Ohio U., 1941; MA in Pub. Adminstrn., Am. U., 1946. Adminstrv. intern Nat. Inst. Pub. Affairs, Washington, 1941-42; mgmt. intern U.S. Dept. Agr., Washington, 1941-42; adminstrv. analyst Office Emergency Mgmt., Washington, 1942-43, Office Price Adminstrn., Washington, 1943-45; founder Zook and Zook Cons., Arlington, Va., 1945-47; tchr. ancient history and U.S. govt. Fairfax County (Va.) Pub. Schs., 1963-64; founder, pres. Associated Gem Consulting Lab., Alexandria, 1974—, Alpha Gate Crafts Ltd., Alexandria, 1977—; color cons. Internat. Com. on Color in Gems, Bangkok, Thailand, 1983. Author: Directory of Selected Color Resources Annotated Guide, 1982, Reunion of Descendants of David and Magdalena (Blough) Zook, 1983, Basic Machine Knitting, 1979; contbr. articles to profl. jours. Bd. dirs. Am. Embassy Com. on Edn., Montevideo, Uruguay, 1962; co-founder Workshop of Arts, Santiago, Chile, 1958; mem. Nat. Trust for Hist. Preservation, Nat. Mus. Women in Arts, Nat. Mus. Am. Indian, Am. Horticulture Soc., Textile Mus. Fellow Gemmological Assn. of Gt. Britain (diplomate); mem. AAUW, DAR, Nat. Geneal. Soc., Inter-Soc. Color Coun. (chmn. com. color in gemstones 1982-84, Appreciation cert. 1984), Accredited Gemological Assn. (co-founder, v.p.), Phi Beta Kappa, Tau Kappa Alpha. Avocations: garden design, knitting, fabric creation, genealogy, music. Home: PO Box 6310 Alexandria VA 22306-0310

ZOON, KATHRYN EGLOFF, biochemist; b. Yonkers, N.Y., Nov. 6, 1948; d. August R. and Violet T. (Pollock) Egloff; BS, Rensselaer Poly. Inst., 1970; PhD Johns Hopkins U., 1975; m. Robert A. Zoon, Aug. 22, 1970; children: Christine K, Jennifer R. Interferon rsch. fellow NIH, Bethesda, Md., 1975-77, staff fellow, 1977-79, sr. staff fellow, 1979-80; sr. staff fellow div. biochem. biophysics Bur. Biologics, FDA, Bethesda, 1980-83; rsch. chemist divsn. biochem. biophysics, 1983-84, rsch. chemist divsn. virology, 1984-88, rsch. chemist div. cytokine biology, Ctr. for Biologics Evaluation and Rsch., FDA, 1988—, div. dir., 1989-92; dir. Ctr. for Biologics Evaluation and Rsch., 1992—; lectr. NIH, 1994, Reigelman Lecturship, 1994. N.Y. State Regents fellow, 1970, Rensselaer Alumni Assn. Fellows award, 1997; Person of the Yr. award Biopharm, 1992, Pub. Svc. award Genetic Engrng. News, 1995; Presdl. Meritorious Exec. Rank award, 1994, Grateful Patient award Nat. Assn. of Cancer Patients, 1997. Mem. Am. Soc. Biochemistry and Molecular Biology, Internat. Soc. Interferon Rsch., Internat. Soc. Cytokine Rsch. Roman Catholic. Contbr. numerous articles on research in biol. chemistry to sci. jours.; sect. editor Jour. Interferon and Cytokine Research, 1980—. Office: CBER 1401 Rockville Pike Rockville MD 20852-1428

ZOPF, PAUL EDWARD, JR., sociologist; b. Bridgeport, Conn., July 9, 1931; s. Paul Edward and Hilda Ernestine (Russell) Z.; m. Evelyn Lanoel Montgomery, Aug. 5, 1956; 1 child, Eric Paul. B.S., U. Conn., 1953; M.S., U. Fla., 1955, Ph.D., 1966. Asst. prof. sociology Guilford Coll., Greensboro, N.C., 1959-66, assoc. prof., 1966-70, prof., 1970-72, Dana prof. sociology, 1972-93; Dana prof. sociology emeritus, 1993—, chief. coll. marshal, 1997—; cons. local govt. agys. Author: North Carolina: A Demographic Profile, 1967, Demography: Principles and Methods, 1970, 76, Principles of Inductive Rural Sociology, 1970, Profile of Women in Greensboro: 1990, 1977, Sociocultural Systems, 1978, Cultural Accumulation in Latin America, 1980, Population: An Introduction to Social Demography, 1984, Income and Poverty Status of Women in Greensboro, 1985, America's Older Population, 1986, American Women in Poverty, 1989, Mortality Patterns and Trends in the United States, 1992; editor Guilford Coll. Self-Study Accreditation Report; contbr. articles to profl. jours. Recipient Teaching Excellence award Guilford Coll., 1978; grantee Kenan Found., 1970-79, Guilford Coll., 1979—. Mem. Am. Acad. Polit. and Social Sci., Am. Sociol. Assn., Internat. Union Sci. Study Population, So. Sociol. Soc., Rural Sociol. Soc., Population Reference Bur. Quaker. Home: 815 George White Rd Greensboro NC 27410-3317 Office: Guilford Coll Dept Sociology Greensboro NC 27410 *In my role as professor, researcher and author, I have oriented my activities to the service of students, my institution, my professional discipline, and various community agencies. I have found that pursuing various professional processes that I enjoy and can handle adequately, is the real reward. Honors, if they come, are a by-product of that pursuit; they would be elusive and perpetually inadequate if they were the principal reason for my efforts.*

ZORE, EDWARD JOHN, insurance company investment executive; b. Milw., July 5, 1945; s. Joseph F. and Marie A. Z.; m. Diane Widemshek, Aug. 19, 1967; children: Annemarie, Kathryn. B.S., U. Wis.-Milw., 1968, M.S., 1970. Exec. v.p., CFO, chief investment officer Northwestern Mut. Life Ins. Co., Milw., 1969—. Republican. Roman Catholic. Home: 129 W Miller Dr Mequon WI 53092-6189 Office: Northwestern Mutual Life Ins Co 720 E Wisconsin Ave Milwaukee WI 53202-4703

ZORIO, JOHN WILLIAM, financial services executive; b. Fayetteville, W.Va., Nov. 17, 1946; s. Nelson and Zelma (Simpson) Z.; m. Mary Ann Helen Dombrowski, Aug. 13, 1966; children: Jennifer Susan, Jonathan David. BSBA in Econs., Concord Coll., 1968. CLU, ChFC. Field underwriter N.Y. Life Ins. Co., McLean, Va., 1971-73, asst. gen. mgr., 1974-79; gen. mgr. N.Y. Life Ins. Co., Cin., 1980-83; v.p. N.Y. Life Ins. Co., N.Y.C., 1984-85; gen. mgr. N.Y. Life Ins. Co., Cleve., 1986-89; sr. v.p. N.Y. Life Ins. Co., Chgo., 1989-95; mng. ptnr. N.Y. Life Ins. Co., Rosemont, Ill., 1995—. Sgt. U.S. Army, 1969-71. Republican. Roman Catholic. Avocations: woodworking, reading, sports. Home: 540 Turicum Rd Lake Forest IL 60045-3366 Office: NY Life Ins Co 5600 N River Rd Ste 800 Rosemont IL 60018-5166

ZORITCH, GEORGE, dance educator, choreographer; b. Moscow, June 6, 1917; came to U.S., 1935; s. Serge and Helen (Grunke) Z. Diploma Lady Deterding's Russian Sch., Paris, 1933. Mem. Ida Rubinstein Ballet Co., Paris, 1933-34, Pavlova's Co., West Indies, Australia, India, Egypt and Eng., 1934-35, Col. de Basil's Ballet Russe de Monte-Carlo, U.S.A., S. Am., Europe, 1936-38; soloist Denham Ballet Russe de Monte-Carlo, U.S.A., Can., S. Am., Europe, 1938-42; prof., mem. dance faculty com. fine arts U. Ariz., 1973-87; actor, dancer plays, musicals, concert tours, Broadway and throughout U.S., S. Am., Europe, 1943-50: actor 17 movies in Hollywood, Calif. and Rome; premier danseur noble Grand Ballet du Marquis de Cuevas, Europe, Africa, S.Am., 1951-57, Denham Ballet Russe de Monte Carlo, U.S.A., 1957-62; founder George Zoritch Sch. Classical Ballet, West Hollywood, Calif., 1963-73; fine arts prof., mem. com. on dance, U. Ariz., Tucson, 1973-87, ret.; freelance engagements, 1973—. Editor records: George Zoritch for Classical Ballet, 1962-65. Recipient Key to Jacksonville (Fla.) Mayor Hans G. Tantzler Jr., 1968, The Bolshoi Theatre Medallion of Merit award IV Internat. Ballet Competition-Moscow, 1981, Ariz. Dance Treasures award Ariz. Dance Arts Alliance and Ariz. State U. Dept. Dance, 1992, Merit award Acad. of Choreographic Sch. A. Vaganova, 1993, Vaslav Nijinsky Medallion of Merit award The Consulate Gen. of Republic of Poland, 1994, Diaghilev House Silver Medallion of Merit award Sixth Dance Competition of Paris, 1994; named Amb. San Antonio World Hemisphere, 1968. Mem. Ariz. Dance Arts Alliance (hon. life mem.), Phoenix Ballet Guild (hon. mem.), Nat. Soc. Arts and Letters (Medallion of Merit award Valley of Sun chpt. 1990).

ZORKO, MARK A., financial executive; b. Cleve., Mar. 11, 1952; s. Frank A. and Dorothy E. (Bever) Z.; m. Sue A. Langdon, Sept. 6, 1975; children: Jennifer, Andrew. BS in Acctg., Ohio State U., 1976; MBA in Mgmt. Info Systems, U. Minn., 1977. CPA; cert. practicioner in inventory mgmt. Sr. staff cons. Arthur Andersen & Co., Mpls., 1978-80; fin. mgr. Honeywell, Inc., Mpls. and Brussels, 1980-87; corp. contr. Zenith Data Systems Corp., St. Joseph, Mich., 1987-91; CFO Inverness Castings Group, Inc., Bangor, Mich., 1991-93; v.p. fin., sec., CFO Comptronix Corp., Guntersville, Ala., 1993-94; v.p., CFO Network Svcs. Co., Mt. Prospect, Ill., 1995—; bd. dirs. Intellimedia Corp. Treas., bd. dirs. United Way, St. Joseph, 1988-93. Sgt. USMC, 1970-73. Mem. AICPA, Fin. Execs. Inst., Nat. Assn. Corp. Treas., Am. Prodn. and Inventory Control Soc., Minn. Soc. CPAs. Methodist. Avocations: sailing, skiing, golf, hockey, soccer. Home: 9301 Grist Mill Ct Brentwood TN 37027-5312 Office: Network Svcs Co 1550 Bishop Ct Mount Prospect IL 60056-6039

ZORN, ERIC JOHN, newspaper columnist; b. New Haven, Jan. 6, 1958; s. Jens Christian and Frances (Barnhart) Z.; m. Johanna Wolken, Nov. 2, 1985; 1 child, Alexander. BA, U. Mich., 1980. With Chgo. Tribune, 1980—, met. reporter, 1985-86, columnist, 1986—; instr. Northwestern U. Medill Sch. Journalism, Evanston, Ill., 1985-89. Co-author: Murder of Innocence, 1990. Avocation: old-time square dance caller. Office: Chgo Tribune PO Box 25340 435 N Michigan Ave Chicago IL 60611-4001

ZORNES, MILFORD, artist; b. Camargo, Okla., Jan. 25, 1908; s. James Francis and Clara Delphine (Lindsay) Z.; m. Gloria Codd, 1935; 1 son, Franz Milford; m. Patricia Mary Palmer, Nov. 8, 1942; 1 dau., Maria Patricia. Student, Otis Art Inst., Los Angeles, 1929, Pomona Coll., 1930-34. Instr. art Pomona Coll., 1946-50; art dir. Vortox and Padua Hills Theatre, Claremont, 1954-66. Exhibited, Calif. Watercolor Soc., Met. Mus., Am. Watercolor Soc., Corcoran Gallery, Bklyn. Mus., Denver Mus., Cleve. Mus., L.A. Mus., Brooks Gallery, London, Bombay Art Assn., Chgo. Art Inst., Butler Mus., Gallery Modern Masters, Washington, Santa Barbara (Calif.) Mus., Cin. Mus., Laguna (Calif.) Art Gallery, Oklahoma City Mus., Springville (Utah) Mus.; represented in permanent collections at L.A. Mus., White House Collection, Met. Mus., Pentagon Bldg., Butler Mus., UCLA, Nat. Acad., San Diego Mus., L.A. County Fair, Home Savs. and Loan Assn., L.A., Corcoran Gallery, Washington; mem. art com., Nat. Orange Show, San Bernardino, Calif., 1963-65; author: A Journey to Nicaragua, 1977, The California Style: California Watercolor Artists, 1925-1955, 1985; subject of book by Gordon McClelland: Milford Zornes, Hillcrest Press, 1991. Served with U.S. Army, 1943-45, CBI. RecipientPaul Prescott Barrow award Pomona Coll., 1987, David Prescott Burrows award, 1991, A Most Disting. Citizen award So. Utah State Coll., 1988, Am. Artist Achievement award Am. Artist Mag., 1994. Mem. NAD, Am. Watercolor Soc., Southwestern Watercolor Soc., Watercolor West, Nat. Watercolor Soc., Utah Watercolor Soc. Address: PO Box 176 Orderville UT 84758-0176 *It has been my effort in life to have awareness: not to have all knowledge because no one can encompass all knowledge; not to have only wealth or only success, because there is no dimension of completeness of wealth or success; not to achieve complete goodness, because goodness and right are relative; not to enjoy the epitomy in taste because taste is a gratification of self alone; but rather to seek and achieve understanding of relative values and a concept of the completeness of life. With this as my effort and my inner goal, I find success within the areas of my limited abilities, my meager knowledge, and my frail grasp of the infinite.*

ZORNOW, DAVID M., lawyer; b. N.Y.C., Mar. 31, 1955; s. Jack and Marion (Gilden) Z.; m. Martha Malkin, July 21, 1985; children: Samuel Morris, Hannah Jane, Ethan Lewis. AB summa cum laude, Harvard U., 1976; JD, Yale U., 1980. Bar: N.Y. 1981, U.S. Ct. Appeals (3d cir.) 1982, U.S. Dist. Ct. (so. dist.) N.Y. 1983, U.S. Ct. Appeals (2d cir.) 1984, U.S. Dist. Ct. D.C. 1989, U.S. Ct. Appeals (D.C. cir.) 1989, U.S. Dist. Ct. Ariz. 1990, U.S. Dist. Ct. (ea. dist.) N.Y. 1993. Law clerk to Judge Herbert J. Stern U.S. Dist. Ct. N.J., Newark, 1980-82; assoc. Kramer Levin Kamin Nessen & Frankel, N.Y.C., 1982-83; asst. U.S. atty. so. dist. N.Y. U.S. Atty.'s Office, N.Y.C., 1983-87; assoc. counsel Office Ind. Counsel-Iran/Contra Investigation, Washington, 1987-89; ptnr. Skadden Arps Slate Meagher & Flom, L.L.P., N.Y.C., 1989—; chmn. N.Y.C. Civilian Complaint Rev. Bd., 1994-96; vis. faculty Trial Advocacy Workshop Harvard Law Sch., Cambridge, Mass., 1988. Mem. ABA (com. on white collar crime), Fed. Bar Coun., Assn. of Bar of City of N.Y., N.Y. Coun. Def. Lawyers. Office: Skadden Arps Slate Meagher & Flom 919 3rd Ave New York NY 10022

ZORNOW, WILLIAM FRANK, historian, educator; b. Cleve., Aug. 13, 1920; s. William Frederick Emil and Viola (Schulz) Z. A.B., Western Res. U., 1942, A.M., 1944, Ph.D., 1952. Vice pres., treas. Glenville Coal & Supply Co., Real Value Coal Corp., Zornow Coal Corp., 1941-45; dep. clk. Probate Ct., Cuyahoga County, Ohio, 1941-43; prodn. planning engr. Hickok Elec. Instrument Co., Cleve., 1943-46; teaching asst. Western Res. U., 1944-47; instr. U. Akron, 1946-47, Case Inst. Tech., 1947-50, Washburn U., 1950-51; lectr. Cleve. Coll., 1948-49; asst. prof. Kans. State U., 1951-58; asst. prof. history Kent (Ohio) State U., 1958-61, asso. prof., 1961-66, prof. history, 1966—; perpetual hon. fellow Harry S. Truman Libr. Inst., Independence, Mo.; collection corr. Berkshire Loan and Fin. Co., Painesville (Ohio) Security Credit Acceptance Corp., Mentor, Ohio, 1951-60; cons. Karl E. Mundt

Library, Dakota State Coll., Madison, S.D.; presenter 1st coll. arts and scis. faculty lecture series Kent State U., 1962. Author: Lincoln and the Party Divided, 1954, rev. edit., 1972, Kansas: A History of the Jayhawk State, 1957, America at Mid-Century, 1959; author: (with others) Abraham Lincoln: A New Portrait, 1959, Kansas: The First Century, 1956; contbr. articles to encys. and profl. jours.; editor: Shawnee County (Kans.) Hist. Bull, 1950-51; abstractor: America: History and Life: Historical Abstracts, 1964—. Mem. Dir.'s Circle Cleve. Mus. Art, 1989—, Cleve. Clin. Found., 1992—, Soc. Fellows. Faculty rsch. grantee Kans. State U., 1955-57, Kent State U., 1960-64. Mem. AAAS, AAUP, Soc. Fellow of Cleve. Clinic Found., Am. Acad. Polit. and Social Sci., Am. Assn. State and Local History (award of merit 1958), Am. Hist. Assn., Orgn. Am. historians, Ohio Acad. History (chmn. awards com.), Ohio Hist. Soc. (libr. adv. com. 1969—), Ohio Soc. N.Y., Ctr. Study of Presidency, Acad. Polit. Sci., Lincoln Fellowship of Wis., Sierra Club San Francisco, Delta Tau Delta (4-star coun. 1992—), Pi Gamma Mu, Phi Alpha Theta, Phi Delta Kappa. Home: 7893 Middlesex Rd Mentor OH 44060-7617 Office: Kent State U 305 Bowman Dr Kent OH 44240-4507

ZOROWSKI, CARL FRANK, engineering educator, university administrator; b. Pitts., July 14, 1930; s. Stanley and Mary Josephine (Kozuch) Z.; m. Sarah Jane Crossley, Aug. 7, 1954 (dec. 1983); children: Kathleen Ann, Karl Alan, Kristine Alaine; m. Louise Parrish Lockwood, Apr. 13, 1985. BSME, Carnegie Inst. Tech., 1952, MSME, 1953, PhD, 1956. Instr. Carnegie Inst. Tech., Pitts., 1952-56, asst. prof., 1956-61, assoc. prof., 1961-62; prof. mech. and aero. engrng. dept. N.C. State U., Raleigh, 1964-66, R.J. Reynolds Industries prof., 1966—, assoc. dept. head, 1964-72, dept. head, 1972-79, assoc. dean acad. affairs Sch. Engrng., 1979-85, dir. Integrated Mfg. Systems Inst., 1986-92, dept. head, 1992-93; dir. Succeed/NSF Coalition, 1993—, assoc. dean acad. affairs, 1993-94. Served to 2d lt. USAR, 1952-58. Recipient research award Sigma Xi, 1967. Fellow ASME (Richards Meml. award 1975); mem. Am. Soc. Engrng. Edn. (Western Electric award 1968), Fiber Soc. (Achievement award 1970). Contbr. pubs. to profl. jours.; patentee in field. Home: 103 Windyrush Ln Cary NC 27511-9758 Office: NC State U PO Box 7901 Raleigh NC 27695

ZORTHIAN, BARRY, communications executive; b. Kutahia, Turkey, Oct. 8, 1920; naturalized 1930; s. Herbert Peter and Annaly (Markarian) Z.; m. Margaret Aylaian, June 6, 1948; children: Gregory Jannig, Stephen Arnak. BA, Yale U., 1941; LLB, N.Y. U., 1953; LLD (hon.), Ind. Inst. Tech., 1970. Bar: N.Y. 1953. Newspaper reporter, 1936-42, newspaper and radio reporter, 1947-48; news and policy editor USIA, 1948-56, program mgr. Voice of Am., 1956-61; dep. pub. affairs. officer USIS, India, 1961-64; min.-counselor for info. Am. Embassy, Vietnam, 1964-68; v.p. Time, Inc., 1969-79, v.p. govt. affairs, 1974-79; pres. Time-Life Broadcast, 1969-73, Washington/Balt. Regional Assn., 1979-81; sr. v.p. Gray and Co., Washington, 1981-84; ptnr. Alcalde & Fay, Arlington, Va., 1984—. Bd. dirs. Am. U. of Armenia, Armenian Gen. Benevolent Union; pres. Pub. Diplomacy Found. With USMCR, 1942-46; col. Res. ret. Mem. Coun. on Fgn. Rels., Am. Fgn. Svc. Assn., Bus.-Govt. Rels. Coun., Marine Corps Res. Officers Assn. Conglist., Century Assn. (N.Y.C.) Club, Congl. Country (Washington) Club, Burning Tree (Washington) Club, Met. (Washington) Club. Home: 4201 Cathedral Ave NW Apt 405E Washington DC 20016-4914 Office: Alcalde & Fay 2111 Wilson Blvd Ste 850 Arlington VA 22201-3001

ZOSIKE, JOANIE FRITZ, theater director, actor; b. Bklyn., July 6, 1949; d. Nathan and Gloria S. (Greenberg) Hieger; m. Godson E. Zosike, Dec. 12, 1995. BA in Theatre, NYU, 1980. Co-founder, actor, devel. dir. Protean Forms Collective, N.Y.C., 1986-88; mng. dir., actor Living Theatre, N.Y.C., 1990—; co-dir. DADAnewyorkDADA; bd. dirs. Gathering of Tribes; writer-in-residence Women's Theatre Project at ATA, N.Y. Author: (stage prodns.) You Told Me That the Carousel Was Crystal, Frames, Inside, 12 Steps to Murder; author: (with Hanon Reznikov) ...And Then The Heavens Closed; actress (stage prodns.) Not in My Name, Anarchia, Mysteries and Smaller Pieces, Utopia, Rules of Civility, Humanity, Body of God, I and I, The Tablets, Poland 1931, Midsummer Night's Dream, Mother! I'm Pregnant!, Visions of Paradise, 12 Steps to Murder, No Nukes at Liberty, Mother Courage, Daily Activity of Slaves, Greetings from the Abyss, (solo performances) All Right So I AM the Earth, Harpies Complex, Ereshkigal's Peg, Fritzgabriel Cabaret, Alen Mak Festival (Bulgaria), Festival des Politisches Liedes (Germany), (films) Mass and Masses, Human Flesh, (TV) The Gong Show; vocalist (radio show) Women on the Edge of Time; contbr. Between Ourselves: Letters Between Mothers and Daughters (edited by Karen Payne), Women in American Theatre (edited by Helen Krich Chinoy and Linda Walsh Jenkins); contbr. poetry and articles to artistic jours. Vol. N.Y.C. War Tax Resistance, N.Y.C. Peoples Life Fund. Action-Vista grantee; recipient Artists Residency award Edward Albee Found., 1982. Mem. War Resisters League. Office: The Living Theatre 800 W End Ave Ste 5-a New York NY 10025-5467

ZOSS, ABRAHAM OSCAR, chemical company executive; b. South Bend, Ind., Feb. 17, 1917; s. Harry and Fannie (Friedman) Z.; B.S. in Chem. Engrng., U. Notre Dame, 1938, M.S., 1939, Ph.D., 1941; m. Betty Jane Hurwich, Dec. 24, 1939; children: Roger, Joel, Hope Zoss Schladen; m. 2d, Magda Szanto, May 26, 1978. With Gen. Aniline & Film Corp., Easton, Pa., 1941-47, tech. mgr., Linden, N.J., 1947-55, plant mgr., 1955-57; mgr. mfg. adminstrn., chem. div. Minn. Mining & Mfg. Co., St. Paul, 1957-58, prodn. mgr. chem. div., 1958-60; v.p. Photek Inc., West Kingston, R.I., 1960-62; asst. corp. tech. dir. Celanese Corp., N.Y.C., 1962-65, corp. tech. dir., 1965-66, corp. dir. comml. devel., 1966-69; v.p. corp. devel. Tenneco Chems., Inc., N.Y.C., 1969-71, Universal Oil Products Co., Des Plaines, Ill., 1971-72; group v.p. Engelhard Industries div. Engelhard Minerals & Chem. Corp., Murray Hill, N.J., 1972-74, v.p. bus. devel., 1974-77; v.p. corp. devel. CPS Chem. Co., Inc., Old Bridge, N.J., 1977, dir., v.p., chief adminstrv. officer, 1978-84; pres. Bus. Devel. Internat., N.Y.C., 1984—; mem. field info. agy. Office Tech. Svc., Commerce Dept., Europe, 1946; teaching asst. U. Notre Dame, 1939-41. Mem. Met. Mus. Art, N.Y.C.. Recipient Centennial Sci. award U. Notre Dame, 1965, accredited Profl. Chemist, 1980. Fellow Am. Inst. Chemists, AAAS; mem. Am. Chem. Soc., Am. Inst. Chem. Engrng., N.Y. Acad. Scis., Comml. Devel Assn., Colloqium Cons. Strategy, Soc. Chem. Industry, Tech. Transfer Soc., Soc. Plastics Engrs., Societe de Chimie Industrielle (pres. Am. sect.), Chemists Club (N.Y.C.). Contbr. articles to profl. pubs. Patentee in field. Home and Office: 45 East End Ave Ste 11D New York NY 10028

ZOTALEY, BYRON LEO, lawyer; b. Mpls., Mar. 18, 1944; s. Leo John and Tula (Koupis) Z.; m. Theresa L. Cassady, Sept. 7, 1969; children: Nicole, Jason, Krisanthy. BA in Psychology, U. Minn., 1966; MATC, U. St. Thomas, St. Paul, 1968; JD, William Mitchell Coll. of Law, 1970. Bar: Minn. 1970, U.S. Dist. Ct. Minn. 1971, U.S. Ct. Appeals (8th cir.) 1972, U.S. Supreme Ct. 1975. Pres. LeVander, Zotaley & Vander Linden, Mpls., 1970—; arbitrator Minn. No Fault Panel, 1974—; cons. Marthe Properties, Mpls., 1980-90, Theron Properties, Mpls., 1985—. Bd. dirs. Minn. Consumer Alliance, 1994-95; mem. adv. bd. Beniloe-St. Margarets Jr. H.S., 1993-95; mem. bd. trustees St. Mary's Greek Orthodox Ch. Mpls., 1997—. Mem. ABA, ATLA, Minn. Bar Assn., Hennepin County Bar Assn., Minn. Trial Lawyers Assn. (chmn. Amicus Curiae com. 1980-87, bd. govs. 1982-93, mem. exec. com. 1987-89, emeritus, 1994—). Home: 5504 Parkwood Ln Minneapolis MN 55436-1728 Office: LeVander Zotaley & Vander Linden 720 Northstar W Minneapolis MN 55402

ZOX, LARRY, artist; b. Des Moines, May 31, 1937; s. Oscar and Mildred (Friedman) Z.; m. Jean Marilyn Glover, July 19, 1965; children: Melinda, Alexander Cassidy. Student, Okla. U., 1955-56, Drake U., 1957, Des Moines Art Center, 1955-57. vis. critic Cornell U., summer 1967; faculty (Sch. Visual Arts), 1967-68, 69-70, 70-76, Yale, summer, 1972, Kent State U., summer 1974. Exhibited one man shows at Am. Gallery, N.Y.C., 1962, Kornblee Gallery, N.Y.C., 1964-66, 68, 69, 70, 71, Andre Emmerich Gallery, 1973, 75, 76, Whitney Mus. Am. Art, 1973, Galerie Rocke, Cologne, Germany, 1968, Janie C. Lee Gallery, Houston, 1974, Hokin Gallery, Bay Harbor Islands, Fla., 1981, Meridith Long & Co., Houston, 1981, Hokin Gallery, Palm Beach, 1981, Salander-O'Reilly Galleries, N.Y., 1982, Rubiner Gallery, West Bloomfield, Mich., 1985, 90, Images Gallery, Toledo, 1986, 90, 91, Percival Gallery, Des Moines, 1987, 89, 91, Marsh Gallery U. Richmond, Va., 1992, Robert Strin-St. Louis, Mo., 1992, C.S. Schulte Gallery, Millburn, N.J., 1993-94, Gallery One Toronto, Can., others; exhibited group shows at Am. Gallery, 1963, Am. Fedn. Art, 1963-65, Mus. Modern Art, N.Y.C., 1964, Albright-Knox Art Gallery, Buffalo, 1964, Washington Gallery Modern Art, 1964, Gallery Modern Art, N.Y.C., 1965, Tibor de Nagy, N.Y.C., 1965, ann., Whitney Mus., N.Y.C., 1965-70, one-man retrospective, 1973, Art Inst. Chgo., 1965, Kornblee Gallery, 1966, Guggenheim Mus., N.Y.C., 1966, Expo Am. Pavilion, 1967, Palm Springs Desert Mus., 1973, Daniel Templon Gallery, Paris, 1975, Andre Emmerich Gallery, 1975, Andre Emmerich Gallery, N.Y., 1975, Edmonton (Alta., Can.) Art Gallery, 1977, Old Vanderbilt Mansion, Old Brookville, N.Y., 1979, Allen Rubiner Gallery, Royal Oak, Mich., 1980, Meredith Long & Co., N.Y., 1980, Md. Inst. Coll. Art, Balt., 1980, Meredith Long & Co., Houston, 1980, Mus. Fine Arts, Boston, 1981, Solomion R. Guggenheim Mus., N.Y., 1981, Salander-O'Reilly Gallery, N.Y., 1981, St. Lawrence U., 1985, Rubiner Gallery, West Bloomfield, 1986, Percival Gallery, Des Moines, 1987, Gallery of Art, 1988, Charles H. MacNider Mus., 1988, Sioux City Art Ctr., 1988, Des Moines Art Ctr., 1988, Blanden Meml. Art Mus., 1988, Muscatine Art Ctr., 1988, C.S. Shulte Gallery, N.Y. and N.J., 1991, others; represented in permanent collections Am. Republic Ins. Corp., Des Moines, J. & L. Hudson Co., Detroit, Joseph H. Hirshhorn Mus., U.S. Steel Corp., Mus. Modern Art, N.Y.C., Philip Johnson Collection, Dallas Mus. Fine Arts, Des Moines Art Center, Met. Mus. Art, N.Y.C., Indpls. Mus., Whitney Mus.; artist in residence, Juniata Coll., Huntingdon, Pa., 1964, U. N.C., 1967. Recipient Nat. Council Arts award, 1969; Guggenheim fellow, 1967. *

ZRAKET, CHARLES ANTHONY, systems research and engineering company executive; b. Lawrence, Mass., Jan. 9, 1924; s. Habib and Martha (Beshara) Z.; m. Shirley Ann Camus, Oct. 13, 1961; children: David C., Suzanne M., Elizabeth A., Caroline A. BSEE, Northeastern U., Boston, 1951; SMEE, MIT, 1953; PhD in Engring. (hon.), Northeastern U., 1988. Mem. rsch. staff digital computer lab. MIT, 1951-53, group leader digital computer lab., Lincoln Lab., 1953-58; tech. dir., then sr. v.p. MITRE Corp., Bedford, Mass. and McLean, Va., 1958-78, exec. v.p., chief oper. officer, 1978-86, pres., chief exec. officer, 1986-90; trustee MITRE, 1978-96; scholar-in-residence Kennedy Sch. Govt. Harvard U., 1990-94; bd. dirs. Alpha Industries, eNTR, Inc., Concept Five Technologies. Contbr. articles to Science, Daedalus, IEEE Jours; co-editor: Managing Nuclear Operations. Trustee Northeastern U., Hudson Inst., Computer Mus., Mitretek Systems. With AUS, 1943-46. Decorated Bronze Star, Purple Heart with oak leaf cluster, Combat Inf. badge; named Disting. Corp. Leader MIT, 1985, Dept. Def. Medal for Disting. Pub. Svc., 1990. Fellow AAAS, IEEE, AIAA (Reed Aeros. award 1993), Am. Acad. Arts and Scis.; mem. NAE, Sigma Xi, Tau Beta Pi, Eta Kappa Nu. Home: 71 Sylvan Ln Weston MA 02193-1027

ZRULL, JOEL PETER, psychiatry educator; b. Detroit, Jan. 10, 1932; s. Arthur Benjamin and Mildred (Bazy) Z.; m. Nancy Jane Eichenlaub, June 19, 1954; children: Mark Christian, Lisa Carol. BA with honors, U. Mich., 1953, MD, 1957. Diplomate Am. Bd. Psychiatry, Am. Bd. Child Psychiatry. From instr. to assoc. prof. psychiatry U. Mich. Med. Sch., Ann Arbor, 1962-73; prof., chief child psychiatry Med. Coll. Ohio, Toledo, 1973-75, prof., chmn. dept. psychiatry, 1975-97; cons. Monroe (mich.) County Intermediate Sch. Dist., 1961—; pres. Associated Physicians MCO, Inc., Toledo, 1983-84, 87-90; chief of staff Med. Coll. Hosps., Toledo, 1984-86; mem. com. on cert. in child psychiatry Am. Bd. Psychiatry and Neurology, 1986-91, chmn. 1990-91. Editor: Adult Psychiatry: New Directions in Therapy, 1983; contbr. articles to profl. jours. Grantee NIMH, 1974-76, Ohio Dept. Mental Health, 1978-86. Fellow Am. Psychiat. Assn. (life), Am. Acad. Child and Adolescent Psychiatry (chmn. com. tng. 1984-87, chmn. comm. memls. and awards 1992-95), Am. Coll. Psychiatrists, Am. Ortho-Psychiat. Assn.; mem. AMA, Soc. Profs. of Child and Adolescent Psychiatry (sec. treas. 1989-92, pres.-elect 1992-94, pres. 1994-96). Roman Catholic. Avocations: tennis, bridge, golfing. Home: 6133 W Wyandotte Rd Maumee OH 43537-1334 Office: Med Coll Ohio PO Box 10008 Toledo OH 43699

ZSCHAU, MARILYN, singer; b. Chgo., Feb. 9, 1944; d. Edwin Arthur Eugene and Helen Elizabeth (Kelly) Z. BA in Radio, T.V., Motion Pictures, U. N.C.; ed. Juilliard Sch. Music, opera theatre with Christopher West, voice with Florence Page Kimball, also studied with John Lester. Toured with Met. Nat. Co., 1965-66; debut, Vienna Volksoper, in Die Tote Stadt, 1967, Vienna Staatsoper, in Ariadne auf Naxos, 1971; with N.Y.C. Opera from 1978; debut Met. Opera, in La Boheme, 1985, La Scala, in Die Frau ohne Schatten, 1986, Royal Opera, Covent Garden; has toured and sung in many countries. Office: 6647 Saroni Dr Oakland CA 94611-2342*

ZSIGMOND, VILMOS, cinematographer, director; b. Szeged, Hungary, June 16, 1930; came to U.S., 1957, naturalized, 1962; s. Vilmos and Bozena (Illichmann) Z.; children: Julia, Susi. MA, U. Film and Theater Arts, Budapest, Hungary, 1955. Free-lance cinematographer for numerous comls., also edni., documentary and low-budget feature films, 1965-71; now dir., cinematographer on comls. (winner several nat. and internat. awards); feature films, 1971—; films include McCabe and Mrs. Miller, 1971; Images, 1972, Deliverance, 1972, The Long Goodbye, 1973, Scarecrow, 1973, Cinderella Liberty, 1973, The Sugarland Express, 1974, Obsession, 1976, Close Encounters of the Third Kind, 1977 (Acad. award 1977), The Last Waltz, 1978, The Rose, 1978, The Deerhunter, 1978 (Acad. award nomination and Brit. Acad. award), Heavens Gate, 1979, The Border, 1980, Blow Out, 1980, Jinxed, 1981, Table for Five, 1982, The River, 1983 (Acad. award nomination), No Small Affair, 1984, Real Genius, 1985, Witches of Eastwick, 1986, Journey to Spirit Island, 1988, Fatman and Little Boy, 1989, Two Jakes, 1989, Bonfire of the Vanities, 1990, Stalin, 1991 (CableAce award, Direction of Photography and/or Lighting Direction in a Dramatic/Theatrical Special/Movie or Miniseries, ASC award, Emmy award), Sliver, 1992; dir. The Long Shadow, 1992, Intersection, 1993, Maverick, 1993, The Crossing Guard, 1994, Assassins, 1995, The Ghost and the Darkness, 1996. Mem. Acad. Motion Picture Arts and Scis., Dirs. Guild, Am. Soc. Cinematographers. Office: Feinstein & Shorr 16133 Ventura Blvd Ste 800 Encino CA 91436-2409

ZUBAL, JOHN THOMAS, book exchange executive, publisher, bibliographer; b. Cleve., Nov. 5, 1939; s. Thomas A. Zubal and Anna R. Kukurudza; m. Marilyn C. Capozzoli, June 17, 1961; children: Victoria, Michael, Jean Marie, Thomas. BS, Fordham U., 1961; MA, John Carroll U., 1962; DLitt (hon.), Hay (Wales) Inst., 1981. Pres. John T. Zubal, Inc., Cleve., 1962—, U.S. Book Exch., Cleve., 1990—; ptnr. Zubal & Dole Pubs., Cleve., 1980—; assoc. prof. Cuyahoga C.C., Cleve., 1963-75. Office: US Book Exch 2969 W 25th St Cleveland OH 44113-5332

ZUBE, ERVIN HERBERT, landscape architect, geographer, educator; b. Milw., Apr. 24, 1931; s. Ervin Louis and Germaine Emma (Petersen) Z.; m. Margaret Jean Pew, June 19, 1954; 1 child, Eric Carl. BS, U. Wis.-Madison, 1954; MLA in Landscape Architecture, Harvard u., 1959; postgrad., FAAR, Am. Acad., Rome, 1961; PhD in Geography, Clark U., 1973. Asst. to dean of men U. Wis., Madison, 1953-54, Asst. prof., 1961-64; asst. prof. U. Calif., Berkeley, 1964-65; prin. Zube and Dega Assocs. Landscape Architects, Madison, Wis., 1961-64; pres. Rsch., Planning and Design Assocs., Amherst, 1966-70; prof., dept. head U. Mass., Amherst, 1965-72, dir. environ. research inst., 1972-77; dir. sch. Renewable Natural Resources U. Ariz., Tucson, 1977-83, prof. landscape architecture, 1983-84, 87-96, chmn. landscape resources divsn., 1984-87; adj. prof. geography, regional devel. U. Ariz., 1985-96, prof. emeritus, 1996; sr. Fulbright Hays Disting. prof. U. Ljubljana, Yugoslavia, 1979; Lansdowne vis. geography scholar U. Victoria, 1986; mem. Nat. Commn. on Rsch. and Resources Mgmt. Policy, Nat. Pk. Sys., 1988-89; lectr. in field; mem. exec. bd. Ency. on Environ., 1991-94; chairperson GAP analysis peer rev. panel U.S. Fish and Wildlife Svcs., Nat. Biol. Survey, 1993. Author, editor 11 books; editorial bd. Landscape Rsch., 1974—, Landscape Jour., 1981—, Jour. Archtl. and Planning Rsch., 1983—, Landscape Ecology, 1987-92, New Eng. Landscape, 1987-91, Landscape and Urban Planning, 1988—, Environ. Psychology, 1990—, Jour. Planning Lit., 1990—, Society and Natural Resources, 1991-93; contbr. articles to profl. jours., chpts. to books. Trustee Hubbard Ednl. Trust, 1969—; bd. dirs. Tucson Bot. Garden, 1981-83, 85-87, Ariz. Sonora Desert Mus., Tucson, 1981-85, 86-89, pres., 1987-88, mem. adv. coun., 1985-86, Rsch. Ranch Found., Elgin, Ariz., 1981-93, v.p., 1989-90, pres., 1990-92; active U.S. MAB program, Project 13, 1977-88, chair, 1980-86, mem. U.S. Nat. Com., 1980-83. Fellow NATO, Eng., 1977, NEA, 1983-84, Udall Ctr. for Studies in Pub. Policy fellow, 1992-93; scholar Harvard U., 1983-84. Fellow Am. Soc. Landscape Archs. (chmn. coun. edn. 1973-75, dir. profl. practice inst. 1982-87, chmn. 1986-87, Bradford Williams medal 1981, rsch. honor award 1982, ASLA medal 1995); mem. Nat. Archtl. Accrediting Bd. (dir. 1978-80), Internat. Coun. for Exch. Scholars (mem. adv. com. in arch. and city planning chairperson 1979-82), Eisenhower Consortium Western Environ. Forestry Rsch. (v.p. rsch. 1979-82), Environ. Design Rsch. Assn. (dir. 1982-85, chmn. 1984-85), Assn. Am. Geographers, S.W. Pks. and Monuments Assn. (bd. dirs. 1985-94, 95—, v.p. 1986-89, pres. 1989-92), Landscape Arch. Found. (bd. dirs. 1989-91, Alfred Lagasse medal 1992), Rincon Inst. (bd. advisors 1990—, chairperson 1994—), Nat. Pks. and Conservation Assn. (sci. adv. com. 1991-95, coun. advisors 1993-95), Conf. of Nat. Pk. Coop. Assocs. (bd. dirs. 1993—, v.p. 1994-96, pres. 1995-96). Office: U Ariz 325 Bio Sci E Tucson AZ 85721

ZUBILLAGA, JOSE GUSTAVO, education specialist; b. N.Y.C., Jan. 31, 1945. BA, U. Md., 1974; BS, SUNY, Albany, 1994; MEd, Boston U., 1977; MPA, Brenau Coll., 1985; EdD, U. S.C., 1997. Commd. 2d lt. U.S. Army, 1970, advanced through grades to 1st lt.; procurement officer U.S. Army, Vietnam, 1971-72, Heidelberg, Fed. Republic of Germany, 1972-75; edn. svcs. officer Army Continuing Edn. System, Muenster, Fed. Republic of Germany, 1975-80, Bayreuth, Fed. Republic of Germany, 1980-82; edn. specialist U.S. Army Signal Sch., Ft. Gordon, Ga., 1982-90; tng. coord. Westinghouse Savannah River Co., Aiken, S.C., 1990-92, sr. tng. specialist, lead instr., 1992—; mgr. Hispanic employment program 7th Army Tng. Command, Bayreuth, 1980-82, U.S. Army Signal Sch., Ft. Gordon, Ga., 1983-87. Mem. NRA, Nat. Arbor Day Found., Nat. Image Inc. (founder local chpt., pres. 1987-88), Am. Legion, Internat. Platform Assn., Webb Lodge 166 (master mason), Lions Club. Republican. Roman Catholic. Avocations: woodworking, target shooting, camping, hunting, fishing. Home: PO Box 207 Johnston SC 29832-0207 Office: Westinghouse Savannah River PO Box 616 Aiken SC 29802-0616

ZUBKOFF, MICHAEL, medical educator; b. N.Y.C., June 2, 1944; s. Harry and Catherine (O'Brien) Z.; children: Steven, Joel, Lisa; m. Leslee Ann Michaels, 1991. BA, Am. Internat. Coll., 1965, LLD (hon.), 1981; MA, Columbia U., 1966, cert. Internat. Fellow program, 1966, PhD, 1968; MA (hon.), Dartmouth Coll., 1980. Research assoc. conservation human resources Columbia U., N.Y.C., 1966-67; assoc. prof. econs. Fisk U., Nashville, 1967-70; assoc. prof. health econs., assoc. chmn. dept. family and community health Meharry Med. Coll., Nashville, 1967-75; assoc. prof. econs. Vanderbilt U., Nashville, 1970-75; prof. econs. and mgmt. Amos Tuck Sch. Bus., chmn. dept. community and family medicine Med. Sch. Dartmouth Coll., Hanover, N.H., 1975—; mem. inst. medicine Nat. Acad. Scis., 1982—, mem. assembly engrs. inst. med. com. on tech. and health care, 1977-79, grad. med. ednl. nat. adv. com., 1977-81., com. on grad.-med. edn. programs for mil. services Nat. Acad. Scis., 1980-82., nat. research council commn. on human resources Nat. Acad. Scis., 1980-84, com. on aging soc. Nat. Acad. Scis., 1984-89; corr. com. human rights Nat. Acad. Scis., 1983—, nat. rsch. coun. com. computer tech. and svc. sector productivity Nat. Acad. Scis., 1991-94; instr. econs. Harvard U., Yale U., and Columbia U., 1967-68. Co-author: Urban Health Services: The Case of New York, 1971, Consumer Incentives for Health Care, 1974, Health: A Victim of Cause of Inflation, 1976, Framework for Government Intervention in the Health Sector, 1978, Hospital Cost Containment: Selected Notes for Public Policy, 1980, Problem Based Learning of Social Science & Humanities by Fourth Year Medical Students, 1986, The Medical Outcomes Study: An Application of Methods for Monitoring the Results of Medical Care, 1989, Measuring Functional Status & Well Being: The Medical Outcomes Study Approach, 1992, Health Society & The Physician: Problem Based Learning of Social Sciences & Humanities, 1993; contbr. numerous articles to profl. jours. del., health spokesmen White House Summit on Inflation, 1974. Fellow Woodrow Wilson Found., 1964-66, Fulbright Found., 1967-68, USPHS, 1966-67. Mem. Am. Econ. Assn., Am. Pub. Health Assn. Home: RR 1 Fairlee VT 05045-9801 Office: Dartmouth Med Sch Dept of Community & Family Med Strasenburgh Hall 2nd Fl Rm 203 Hanover NH 03755*

ZUBROFF, LEONARD SAUL, surgeon; b. Minersville, Pa., Mar. 27, 1925; s. Abe and Fannie (Freedline) Z.; BA, Wayne State U., 1945, MD, 1949. Diplomate Am. Bd. Surgery. Intern Garfield Hosp., Washington, 1949-50, resident in surgery, 1951-55, chief resident surgery, 1954-55; pvt. practice medicine specializing in surgery, 1958-76; med. dir. Chevrolet Gear and Axle Plant, Chevrolet Forge Plant, GM, Detroit, 1977-78, divisional med. dir. Detroit Diesel Allison div., 1978-87, regional med. dir. GM, 1987-89; ret., 1989; bd. trustees LeVine Found.; mem. staff Hutzel Hosp., Detroit Meml. Hosp.; chief of surgery, chief profl. svcs. N.E. Air Command, Pepperell AFB, Newfoundland. With USAF, 1956-58. Fellow ACS; mem. Acad. Surgery Detroit, Coll. Occupational and Environ. Medicine, Mich. Occupational Med. Assn. (pres. 1990-91), Detroit Occupational Physicians Assn. (former pres.), Masons (33 degree), Phi Lambda Kappa. Home and Office: 22511 S Bellwood Dr Southfield MI 48034-2116

ZUCARO, ALDO CHARLES, insurance company executive; b. Grenoble, France, Apr. 2, 1939; s. Louis and Lucy Zucaro; m. Gloria J. Ward, Oct. 12, 1963; children: Lucy, Louis, Faye. BS in Acctg, Queens Coll., N.Y.C., 1962. C.P.A., N.Y., Ill. Ptnr. Coopers & Lybrand (and predecessor), Chgo. and N.Y.C., 1962-76; exec. v.p., chief fin. officer Old Republic Internat. Corp., Chgo., 1976-81, pres., 1981—, chief exec. officer, 1990—, also chmn. bd. dirs., 1993—, chmn. of the bd., 1993—; pres., bd. dirs. Old Republic Life Ins. Co., Old Republic Life of N.Y., Old Republic Ins. Co., Internat. Bus. and Merc. Reassurance Co., Republic Mortgage Ins. Co., Old Republic Nat. Title Ins. Co., Home Owners Life Ins. Co. Editor: Financial Accounting Practices of the Insurance Industry, 1975, 76. Mem. AICPAs. Roman Catholic. Office: Old Republic Internat Corp 307 N Michigan Ave Chicago IL 60601

ZUCCO, RONDA KAY, health facility administrator; b. Peoria, Ill., Apr. 3, 1960; d. Richard Leon Zucco. BA, So. Ill. U., 1981. Cert. addictions profl.; internat. cert. alcohol and drug counselor. Counselor Spl. Supportive Svcs., So. Ill. U., Carbondale, 1981-83; substance abuse counselor Interventions, Chgo., 1984-86; addictions counselor Parkside at BroMenn, Bloomington, Ill., 1986-89; dir. continuing care/sr. counselor Fla. Hosp. (formerly Parkside), Orlando, Fla., 1989-95, cmty. rels. rep. Ctr. for Psychiatry, 1995; addictions program mgr. Charter Behavioral Health Sys., Kissimmee, Fla., 1995-97; coord. outpatient svcs. Heart of Fla. Behavioral Ctr., Lakeland, Fla., 1997—; tng. instr. for group facilitation Parkside/Fla. Hosp., 1989-95; presenter seminars in field, bd. dirs. Ill. Cert. Bd. Addiction Profls., Bloomington, 1986-89. Vol. ARC, Cardondale, 1978-81, crisis hotline Jackson County Cmty. Mental Health Ctr., Cardondale, 1981, Alliance for the Mentally Ill Greater Orlando, 1995—, Coalition for the Homeless, Orlando, 1995—; active AIDS Spkr.'s Bur., BroMenn Healthcare, Bloomington, Ill., 1986-89. State of Ill. Gen. Assembly scholar, 1977-81. Mem. Am. Mktg. Assn., Am. Assn. for Counseling and Devel., Am. Mental Health Counselors Assn., Fla. Alcohol and Drug Abuse Assn., Fla. Prevention Assn., Nat. Businesswomen's Leadership Assn., C. of C. Greater Orlando, Kappa Delta Pi, Chi Sigma Iota. Avocations: reading, running, swimming and diving, tennis, theater. Home: 1100 Oakbridge Pkwy Apt 296 Lakeland FL 33803

ZUCK, ALFRED CHRISTIAN, consulting mechanical engineer; b. Ridgefield, N.J., Dec. 16, 1924; s. Frederick William and Margaret Christine (Umland) Z.; m. Vilma Hudson, May 6, 1951; children: Allyson, Jon, Randall. M.E., Poly. Inst. Bklyn., 1960. Registered profl. engr., 21 states including N.Y.; nat. council engrng. examiners; lic. profl. planner, N.J. From designer to sr. v.p. Syska & Hennessy, Inc., N.Y.C., 1946-78; prin. Edwards & Zuck (P.C.), N.Y.C., 1978-91, ret., 1991; mem. nat. panel Am. Arbitration Assn, Nat. Council Engrng. Examiners. Served with AUS, 1943-46; to 1st lt. USAF, 1951-52; to capt. N.J. Air N.G., 1947-56. Decorated Bronze Star (2). Fellow Am. Cons. Engrs. Council (past mem. Nat. Ethical Practices Com.); mem. NSPE, N.Y. State Soc. Profl. Engrs. (past chmn. profl. engrs. in pvt. practice program), Am. Soc. Mil. Engrs., Nat. Council Engrng. Examiners, N.Y. Assn. Cons. Engrs. (past v.p., bd. dirs.), ASHRAE, N.Y. Bldg. Congress (bd. govs.). Lutheran. Club: N.Y. Athletic. Home: 217 Rio Vista Cir Atlantis FL 33462-1123 Office: Edwards & Zuck PC 330 W 42nd St New York NY 10036-6902

ZUCK, ALFRED MILLER, association executive; b. East Petersburg, Pa., Aug. 27, 1934; s. Walter Newton and Mary (Miller) Z.; m. Geraldine Connelly, July 21, 1957; children: Susan, David. BA, Franklin and Marshall

Coll., 1957; MPA, Syracuse U., 1958. Dir. fed. program Presdl. Commn. on Youth Opportunities, Washington, 1967-68; dir evaluation Employment and Tng. Adminstrn., Dept. Labor, Washington, 1968-70, dir adminstrn. and mgmt., 1970-75; comptroller U.S. Dept. Labor, Washington, 1975-77; exec. dir. Commn. on Exec., Legis. and Jud. Salaries, Washington, 1980; asst. sec. Dept. Labor, Washington, 1977-83, acting sec., 1981; asst. adminstr. EPA, Washington, 1983; exec. dir. Nat. Assn. Schs. of Pub. Affairs and Adminstrn., Washington, 1983—; pres. Internat. Inst. Adminstrv. Scis., Brussels, 1989-92, Am. Consortium for Internat. Pub. Adminstrn., Washington, 1984-89; bd. dirs. Pub./Pvt. Venture, Inc., Phila., 1984-90. Recipient Presdl. Disting. Exec. award Pres. of U.S., 1980; Disting. Alumni award Franklin and Marshall Coll., 1980. Fellow Nat. Acad. Pub. Admisntrn. (trustee 1989—, chmn. bd. trustees 1993—); mem. Phi Beta Kappa.

ZUCKER, ALEXANDER, physicist, administrator; b. Zagreb, Yugoslavia, Aug. 1, 1924; came to U.S., 1939; s. William and Bertha (Klopfer) Z.; m. Joan-Ellen Jamieson, Nov. 28, 1953; children: Rebecca, Claire, Susannah. B.A., U. Vt., Burlington, 1947; M.S., Yale U., New Haven, 1948, Ph.D., 1950. Physicist Oak Ridge Nat. Lab., Tenn., 1950-60, assoc. dir. electro-nuclear div., 1972-75, dir. heavy ion project, 1988, assoc. dir. phys. scis., 1973-88, acting lab. dir., 1988; assoc. dir. for nuclear techs. Oak Ridge Nat. Lab., 1989-93; exec. dir., environ. studies bd. NAS-NAE, Washington, 1970-72; mem. U.S. del. to USSR on Peaceful Uses of Atomic Energy, 1963; Ford prof. physics U. Tenn., Knoxville, 1968-73; U.S. del. to Pugwash Conf., 1971; research coordination council Gas Research Inst., Chgo., 1978-85; com. Army manpower Nat. Research Council, Washington, 1982-83; adv. panel on technologies to reduce U.S. materials import vulnerability Office of Technology Assessment, Washington, 1982-85; council on energy engring. research Dept. of Energy, Washington, 1983—; industry, nat. lab. steel initiative White House, Washington, 1984. Editor Internat. Jour. Nuclear Sci. Applications, 1980—; cons. editor Ency. and Yearbook of Sci. and Tech. McGraw-Hill Pub. Co., 1989; mem. editorial bd. Science, 1981-82; contbr. articles to profl. jours. Guggenheim fellow, 1966-67; Fulbright-Hays Research scholar, 1966-67. Fellow Am. Phys. Soc., AAAS, Sigma Xi; mem. ASME, Nat. Acad. Scis. (nuclear physics del. to People's Republic of China 1979), Internat. Union Pure and Applied Physics (mem.-at-large U.S. nat. com. 1976-78). Research in nuclear physics with heavy ions and protons; accelerators, especially cyclotrons; materials research programs, especially high-temperature materials and surfaces; nuclear power reactors, especially gas-cooled reactors; research reactor with ultra high neutron flux. Office: Oak Ridge Nat Lab PO Box 2008 Oak Ridge TN 37831-2008

ZUCKER, ALFRED JOHN, English educator, academic adminstrator; b. Hartford, Sept. 25, 1940; s. Samuel and Rose (Zucker) Z.; AA, L.A. Valley Coll., 1960; AB in English, UCLA, 1962, AB in Speech, MA in English, 1962, MA in Speech, 1963, PhD, 1966, postgrad., UCLA, U. So. Calif., Harvard U.; m. Sallie Lea Friedheim, Dec. 25, 1966; children—Mary Anne, John James, Jr., James Patrick, Patrick Jonathan, Anne-Marie Kathleen, Kathleen Mary. Lectr. English, Los Angeles City Coll., 1963-68; prof. English, philosophy, chmn. div. humanities Los Angeles Southwest Coll., 1968-72, chmn. English dept., 1972-74, asst. dean instruction, 1974—; prof. English El Camino Coll., 1985—; prof. English L.A. Valley Coll., 1989—. Mem. Los Angeles Coll. Dist. Senate, 1969—. Mem. Los Angeles Coll. Tchrs. Assn. (dir.), Calif. Jr. Coll. Assn., Calif. Tchrs. Assn., AAUP, World Affairs Coun., Mensa, Phi Beta Kappa, Phi Delta Kappa (pres. U. Calif. at Los Angeles chpt. 1966-67, v.p. 1967-68), Tau Alpha Epsilon. Lodge: KC. Contbr. articles to profl. jours. Office: 5800 Fulton Ave Van Nuys CA 91401-4062

ZUCKER, ARNOLD HARRIS, psychiatrist; b. Bklyn., July 29, 1930; s. Charles Israel and Bertha (Leff) Z.; m. Marilyn Pistreich, June 10, 1962; children: Harvey, Deborah, Shoshanna, David. BA, Bklyn. Coll., 1950; MD, SUNY, Bklyn., 1954; cert. psychoanalysis, Columbia U. Psychoanalytic Ctr, 1971. Diplomate Am. Bd. Psychiatry and Neurology. Intern USPHS, Staten Island, N.Y., 1954-55; resident Kings County Hosp., Bklyn., 1955-56, Southwestern Med. Sch., Dallas, 1958-59, Albert Einstein Coll. Medicine, Bronx, N.Y., 1959-60; asst. clin. prof. psychiatry Albert Einstein Coll. Medicine, 1960-72; pvt. practice Mt. Vernon, N.Y., 1960—; assoc. attending psychiatrist, Mt. Vernon Hosp.; assoc. prof. pastoral counseling, Iona Coll., New Rochelle, N.Y., 1968—. Contbr. articles to profl. jours. Surgeon, USPHS, 1956-58. Fellow Am. Psychiat. Assn. (life), Am. Acad. Psychoanalysis (life); mem. Am. Psychoanalytic Assn., Assn. Psychoanalytic Medicine, AMA, Westchester Psychoanalytic Soc., Phi Beta Kappa. Democrat. Jewish. Avocation: religious studies. Office: 120 E Prospect Ave Mount Vernon NY 10550-2205

ZUCKER, DAVID, director; b. Milw., Oct. 16, 1947. co-founder (with Jerry Zucker and Jim Abrahams) Kentucky Fried Theatre, Madison, WI, 1969, then Los Angeles, CA, 1972. Co-screenwriter: Kentucky Fried Movie, 1977; co-screenwriter, co-dir.: Airplane!, 1980; co-exec. prodr, co-dir., co-screenwriter: Top Secret, 1984, The Naked Gun, 1988, The Naked Gun 2 1/2: The Smell of Fear, 1991, The Naked Gun 33 1/3: The Final Insult, 1994; co-dir.: Ruthless People, 1986; co-exec. prodr.: Brain Donors, 1992; TV series: Police Squad!, 1982; TV spls.: Our Planet Tonight, 1987. Office: Zucker Bros Prodns Sony Studios 10202 Washington Blvd Culver City CA 90232-3119*

ZUCKER, HOWARD ALAN, pediatric cardiologist, intensivist, anesthesiologist; b. N.Y.C., Sept. 6, 1959; s. Saul and Phyllis (Goldblatt) Z.. BS, McGill U., Montreal, Quebec, Can., 1979; MD, George Washington U., 1982. Diplomate Am. Bd. Pediatrics, subspecialties in pediatric critical care, pediatric cardiology, Am. Bd. Anesthesiology, subspecialty in anesthesia critical care. Pediatric intern Johns Hopkins Hosp., Balt., 1982-83, pediatric resident, 1983-85; anesthesiology resident Hosp. of U. Pa., Phila., 1985-87; pediatric critical care fellow Children's Hosp. of Phila., 1987-88; asst. prof. anesthesiology and pediatrics Yale U. Sch. Medicine, New Haven, Conn., 1988-90; pediatric cardiology fellow Children's Hosp., Harvard Med. Sch., Boston, 1990-92; asst. prof. pediatrics and anesthesiology Columbia U. Coll. Physicians and Surgeons, N.Y.C., 1992—; pediat. dir. ICU, dir. pediatric transport Columbia Presbyn. Med. Ctr. Babies & Children's Hosp. N.Y., N.Y.C., 1992—; involved with crew tng. of NASA Space Shuttle STS-1 Mission, 1978-80; rsch. affiliate, Man-vehicle Lab, MIT; chmn. bd. dirs. Terre Verte Found., Inc. Chmn. bd. Terre Verte Found., Inc. Named Person of Week ABC World News Tonight, 1993, one of Best Doctors in Am., Woodward & White, 1996. Fellow Am. Acad. Pediatrics, Am. Coll. Cardiology, Am. Coll. Chest Physicians; mem. AMA, Am. Soc. Anesthesiologists, Am. Heart Assn., Soc. Critical Care Medicine. Jewish. Achievements include research in adaptation to zero gravity, cardiac critical care. Home: 100 Winston Dr Apt 12G Cliffside Park NJ 07010-3240 Office: Columbia Presbyn Med Ctr Babies & Childrens Hosp NY 3959 Broadway New York NY 10032-1537

ZUCKER, JEAN MAXSON, nurse; b. Dunmore, Pa., Aug. 9, 1925; d. Earl L. and Florence M. (Cromwell) Maxson; R.N., Kings County Hosp. Center, 1948; cert. gerontol. nurse; children—Lawrence F., Pamela J., Diane K. Pvt. duty nurse various locations, N.Y., N.J., 1959-64; indsl. nurse Bendix Corp., Eatontown, N.J., 1955; asst. head nurse Point Pleasant Hosp., N.J., 1964-66; head nurse intensive and coronary care unit VA Hosp., Ft. Howard, Md., 1974-78; clin. nurse USPHS Hosp., Balt., 1978-81; nursing supr. VA Hosp. Center, Ft. Howard, 1981-94; clin. nurse VAMC, Ft. Howard, 1994—; tchr. in field. Mem. Am., Md. nurses assns., Am. Assn. Critical Care Nurses, NOW. Democrat. Methodist.

ZUCKER, JERRY, producer, director; b. Milw., Mar. 11, 1950. Student, U. Wis. co-founder Ky. Fried Theatre. Films include: Kentucky Fried Movie, 1977 (co-screenwriter, actor), Rock 'n' Roll High School, 1979 (2nd unit dir.), Airplane!, 1980 (co-dir., co-screenwriter), Top Secret, 1984 (co-dir., co-screenwriter), Ruthless People, 1986 (co-dir.), The Naked Gun, 1988 (exec. prodr., co-screenwriter), Ghost, 1990 (dir.), The Naked Gun 2 1/2: The Smell of Fear, 1991 (exec. co-prodr.), Brain Donors, 1992 (co-exec. prodr.), My Life, 1993 (co-prodr.), The Naked Gun 33 1/3: The Final Insult, 1994 (co-exec. prodr.), First Knight, 1995 (dir.). Address: Zucker Bros Prodns Sony Studios 10202 W Washington Blvd Culver City CA 90232*

ZUCKER, JERRY, energy systems manufacturing executive; b. Tel-Aviv, Israel, Aug. 24, 1949; came to U.S., 1952, naturalized, 1958; s. Leon and Zipora (Shlifkovitz) Z.; m. Anita Goldberg, June 21, 1970; children: Jonathan Michael, Andrea Michelle, Jeffrey Mark. BS, U. Fla., 1968, MEE, 1970. Electronics design engr. Vital Industries, Inc., Gainesville, Fla., 1968-71; devel. engring. group dir. Cons. Engrs., Inc., Gainesville, 1971-73; supt. process engring. and tech. services Hudson Pulp & Paper Corp. (now Ga. Pacific), Palatka, Fla., 1973-78; dir. mfg. and tech. services Raybestos Manhattan, Inc., North Charleston, S.C., 1978-82; chmn. bd., chief exec. officer InterTech Group, Inc.; bd. dirs. High Tech. Coatings Corp., Advanced Chem. Techs., Inc., Tighitco, Inc., Ecosys, Inc., Polymer Group, Inc., FiberTech Group, Inc., ConX Inc., Tycon Inc., Worthington Products Inc., Aerospace Def. Inc., Technetics Group, Inc., Thantex, Inc., Global Golf, Inc., Fabrene, Inc., Polymer Group, Inc., Daramic, Inc., RemGrit Corp.; cons. phosphate mining, pulp and paper and sugar industries. Bd. dirs. Roper Hosp., Trident United Way, Charleston Jewish Fedn., pres., Hotline Inc. (crisis intervention), Hebrew Benevolent Soc., Hebrew Orphan Soc., Orgn. Rehab. Tng., S.C. Aquarium; pres. Synagogue Emanuel. Mem. TAPPI (mem. nat. elec. engring. com. 1977-95), IEEE, Am. Chem. Soc. Jewish. Numerous patents in electrochem., mech., chem. fields. Contbr. articles to tech. jours. Home: 16 Buckingham Dr Charleston SC 29407-3455 Office: The InterTech Group Inc PO Box 5205 4838 Jenkins Ave North Charleston SC 29405

ZUCKER, NORMAN LIVINGSTON, political scientist, educator, author; b. N.Y.C., Aug. 1, 1933; s. George Meyer and Beatrice Lillian (Livingston) Z.; m. Naomi Judith Flink, June 25, 1961; children: Sara, George. B.A., Rutgers U., 1954, M.A., 1956, Ph.D., 1960. Asst. prof. polit. sci. Tufts U., Medford, Mass., 1962-66; asso. prof. polit. sci. U. R.I., Kingston, 1966-69; prof. U. R.I., 1969—; cons. Select Commn. on Immigration and Refugee Policy, 1980; manuscript cons. to pubs. Author: George W. Norris: Gentle Knight of American Democracy, 1966, The American Party Process, 1968, The Coming Crisis in Israel: Private Faith and Public Policy, 1973, The Guarded Gate: The Reality of American Refugee Policy, 1987, Desperate Crossings: Seeking Refuge in America, 1996; cons. editor World Affairs, 1975-84; assoc. editor Jour. Refugee Studies, 1987-90; contbr. articles and revs. to profl. jours., chpts. to books. Wurzweiler Found. grantee, 1963; Am. Philos. Soc. grantee, 1964; Rockefeller Found. fellow in human rights, 1980. Mem. Internat. Polit. Sci. Assn., Am. Polit. Sci. Assn., New Eng. Polit. Sci. Assn., AAUP. Office: U RI Dept Polit Sci Kingston RI 02881

ZUCKER, ROBERT A(LPERT), psychologist; b. N.Y.C., Dec. 9, 1935; s. Morris and Sophie (Alpert) Z.; m. Martine Latil; children: Lisa, Alex, Eleanor; m. Kristine Ellen Freeark, Mar. 10, 1979; 1 child, Katherine. B.C.E., CCNY, 1956; postgrad., UCLA, 1956-58; Ph.D., Harvard U., 1966. Lic. psychologist, Mich. From instr. to asst. prof. psychology Rutgers U., 1963-68; from asst. prof. to assoc. prof. to prof. Mich. State U., 1968-94; prof. psychology in psychiatry and psychology U. Mich., 1994—, dir. Alcohol Rsch. Ctr., 1994—, dir. substance abuse divsn. dept. psychiatry, 1994—; vis. prof. U. Tex., Austin, 1975; vis. rsch. prof. psychology in psychiatry U. Mich., 1990-91; vis. scholar Nat. Inst. Alcohol Abuse and Alcoholism, 1980; dir. clin. tng. Mich. State U., 1982-94; lectr. Nebr. Symposium on Motivation, 1986; cons. in field. Editor: Further Explorations in Personality, 1981, Personality and the Prediction of Behavior, 1984, The Emergence of Personality, 1987, Studying Persons and Lives, 1990, Personality Structure in the Life Course, 1992, The Development of Alcohol Problems: Exploring the Biopsychosocial Matrix of Risk, 1994, Alcohol Problems Among Adolescents: Current Directions in Prevention Research, 1995; contbr. chpts. and articles to profl. publs. Bd. dirs. Nat. Coun. on Alcoholism-Mich., 1978-82; mem. Psychosocial Initial Rev. Group, Nat. Inst. Alcohol Abuse and Alcoholism, 1989-92. Fellow AAAS, APA (pres. addictions divsn. 50 1997—), APS, Am. Orthopsychiat. Assn.; mem. Midwestern Psychol. Assn., Soc. Personology, Soc. Life History Rsch. in Psychopathology. Office: Univ Mich 400 E Eisenhower Pkwy Ann Arbor MI 48108-3308

ZUCKER, STEFAN, tenor, writer, editor, radio broadcaster; b. N.Y.C. BS, Columbia U., 1967; postgrad., NYU, 1967-72. Freelance tenor concerts and operas in U.S. and Europe, 1965—; tenor RCA Records, N.Y.C., 1972-77; guest singer radio and TV programs, U.S. and Europe, 1975—; radio producer, host WKCR-FM, N.Y.C., 1980-94; opera critic N.Y. Tribune, 1983-84; philosophy lectr. Coll. Ins., N.Y.C., 1972. Record producer including Rossini's Rivals: Music By Then-Famous, Now-Obscure, Italian Composers, 1984; restorer films of opera singers, 1987—; singer, producer, stage dir., adminstr. various operas, 1967—; editor Opera Fanatic mag., 1986—; commentator and singer (TV series) Belcanto: Tenors of the 78 rpm Era, 1996-97; contbr. articles to Internat. Dictionary of Opera, Opera News, The Opera Quar., Am. Record Guide, Opera Fanatic, News World, Professione Musica, others. Pres. Bel Canto Soc., Inc., 1985—; Named Worlds Highest Tenor by Guinness Book of World Records, 1979—; subject of record Stefan Zucker: The World's Highest Tenor, 1981. Mem. NYU Philosophy Assn. (pres. 1969-72, v.p. 1968), Music Critics Assn., Assn. Furtherment Bel Canto (pres. 1967-80). Office: Bel Canto Soc Inc 11 Riverside Dr New York NY 10023-2504

ZUCKER, WILLIAM, retired business educator; b. Bridgeport, Conn., July 21, 1917; s. Meyer and Ida Lena (Elovitz) Z.; m. Kathlyn Saltman, Jan. 16, 1944; children—Peter Bayard, Alison Beth, Jeremy Michael, David Laurence. A.B., Johns Hopkins U., 1938; AM, Harvard U., 1940, PhD, 1951. Sec. Commerce and Industry Assn. of N.Y., N.Y.C., 1944-59; v.p. Downtown Lower Manhattan Assn., N.Y.C., 1959-64; pres. Southeastern Pa. Econ. Devel. Corp., Phila., 1964-73; adj. prof. Wharton Sch. U. Pa., Phila., 1972-83, assoc. dir. Entrepreneurial Ctr., Wharton Sch., 1973-83, dir. exec. edn. Wharton Sch., 1977-83, dir. Wharton Real Estate Ctr., 1983-88, Meshulam Riklis prof. creative mgmt. Wharton Sch., 1983-88; prof. emeritus U. Pa., 1988—; pres. Adviserv Co., Phila., 1993-94; lectr. CCNY, 1956-58; vis. prof. Grad. Sch. Bus. Columbia U., 1988-91. Author: Local Development Corporations, 1980, REITS, 1975; editor Real Estate Fin. Jour., 1985—; contbr. articles to profl. jours. Mem. New Canaan Bd. Edn., Conn., 1961-64, New Canaan Bd. Fin., 1958-61. Democrat. Jewish. Home: Cathedral Village 600 E Cathedral Rd # L105 Philadelphia PA 19128-1933 Office: U Pa 2000 Steinberg Dietrich Hal Philadelphia PA 19104

ZUCKERBERG, DAVID ALAN, pharmaceutical company executive; b. Bklyn., Sept. 11, 1946; s. Murray and Selma (Gold) Z.; m. Doris Tavel, May 23, 1971; children: Stephen A., Jonathan P. BS ChemE, Poly. Inst. Bklyn., 1968; MS in Biochemistry, Fairleigh Dickinson U., 1975. Process devel. engr. Procter & Gamble, Cin., 1968-70; with research and devel. Beecham, Clifton, N.J., 1970-77; with research and devel. Block Drug Co., Jersey City, 1977-86, v.p. quality assurance, quality control, 1986-91, v.p. tech. svcs., 1991—; lectr. in chemistry St. Thomas Aquinas Coll., Sparkill, N.Y., 1978-88. Contbr. articles to profl. jours. Mem. New City Jewish Ctr. Mem. Am. Chem. Soc., Am. Inst. Chem. Engrs., Internat. Assn. Dental Rsch., Nonprescription Drug Mfrs. Assn. (mfg. controls com. 1986-90). Republican. Home: 32 Roslyn Ln New City NY 10956-3643 Office: Block Drug Co Inc 257 Cornelison Ave Jersey City NJ 07302-3113

ZUCKERBERG, ROY J., investment banking executive; b. N.Y.C., July 21, 1936; s. Sam and Gertrude R. (Rabstein) Z.; m. Barbara Hope Schwam, June 21, 1959; children: Lloyd P., Dina R. B.S., Lowell Tech. Inst., 1958. Vice pres. The Zuckerberg Co., Copiague, N.Y., 1959-67; with Goldman, Sachs & Co., N.Y.C., 1967—, v.p. securities sales, 1972, gen. ptnr., 1977, co-head securities sales div., 1988-89, co-head equities div., mem. exec. com., 1990-96, head of equities divsn., vice chmn., 1997—. Trustee L.I. Jewish Med. Ctr., 1981-89, vice chmn., 1989—; trustee Brandeis Sch., 1979-86, ARC Greater N.Y., 1992—; bd. dirs. The Brookdale Found., 1985—, Am. Jewish Joint Distbn. Com. Inc., 1992—; trustee The Bklyn. Mus., 1987-94; mem. bd. overseer Albert Einstein Coll. Medicine Yeshiva U., 1989—. Mem. Harmonie Club, Woodmere Club, River Club. also: 435 E 52nd St New York NY 10022-6445 Office: Goldman Sachs & Co One New York Plaza fl 50 New York NY 10004

ZUCKER-FRANKLIN, DOROTHEA, medical scientist, educator; b. Berlin, Aug. 9, 1930; came to U.S., 1949; d. Julian and Gertrude (Feige) Zucker; m. Edward C. Franklin, May 15, 1956 (dec. 1982); 1 child, Deborah Julie. BA, Hunter Coll., 1952; MD, N.Y. Med. Coll., 1956; D (hon.), CUNY, 1997. Diplomate Am. Bd. Internal Medicine. Intern Phila. Gen. Hosp., 1956-57; resident in internal medicine Montefiore Hosp., N.Y.C., 1957-59, postdoctoral fellow in hematology, 1959-61; with Med. Sch. NYU, N.Y.C., 1962—, prof. Med. Sch., 1974—, dir. lab., 1966—; asst. attending physician Montefiore Hosp., 1961-65; assoc. attending physician Univ. Hosp., 1968-74, attending physician, 1974—; assoc. attending physician Bellevue Hosp., 1968-74, attending physician, 1974—; cons. physician Manhattan (N.Y.) VA Hosp., 1970—, PHS Agy. for Healthcare Policy and Rsch., 1992—; sci. adv. bd., rev. panel Israel Cancer Rsch. Fund, 1982—; mem. U.S.-Israel Binat. Sci. Found., 1980—; bd. dirs. Henry M. and Lillian Stratton Found., Inc., 1987—; AID related Rsch. Rev. Com. NIHLB, 1986-90; mem. allergy immunol. com. NIH, 1974-80, pathological tng. com. NIH, 1971-74, Health Resource Coun., N.Y.C., 1971-74, blood products com. FDA, 1981-87. Mem. editl. bd. Blood, 1973-76, 80-86, Jour. Reticuloendothelial Soc., 1964-74, 80—, Am. Jour. Pathology, 1979—, Blood Cells, 1980—, Ultrastructural Pathology, 1979, Am. Jour. Medicine, 1981—, Hematology Oncology, 1982—, Jour. Immunology, 1986—; author: (with others) The Physiology and Pathology of Leukocytes, 1962, Atlas of Blood Cells, Function and Pathology, 1981, 2d edit., 1989, Amyloidosis, 1990; contbr. 250 articles to sci. publs., and 10 chpts. to med. textbooks. Recipient Career Devel. award NIH, 1965-70; NIH rsch. grantee, 1970—; postdoctoral fellow in electromicroscopy NYU, 1962-63; named Woman of Yr., Assn. of Women in Sci., 1996. Fellow AAAS, N.Y. Acad. Scis.; mem. Inst. Medicine NAS, Am. Fedn. Clin. Rsch., Am. Soc. Clin. Investigation, Am. Assn. Physicians, Am. Soc. Hematology (pres. 1995, chairperson subcom. on leukocyte physiology 1977, chairperson subcom. on immunohematology 1984, exec. coun. 1985—, advanced learning resources com. 1987—, chairperson adv. bd. 1997), Soc. Exptl. Biology and Medicine, Am. Soc. Exptl. Biology, Am. Soc. Immunologists, Am. Soc. Cell Biology, Reticuloendothelial Soc. (pres. program and nominating coms. 1984-85), N.Y. Soc. Electron Microscopists (pres. 1962, 84-85), N.Y. Soc. for Study of Blood. Office: NYU Med Ctr 550 1st Ave New York NY 10016-6481

ZUCKERKANDL, EMILE, molecular evolutionary biologist, scientific institute executive; b. Vienna, Austria, July 4, 1922; came to U.S., 1975; s. Frederic and Gertrude (Stekel) Z.; m. Jane Gammon Metz, June 2, 1950. M.S., U. Ill., 1947; Ph.D., Sorbonne, Paris, 1959. Postdoctoral research fellow Calif. Inst. Tech., Pasadena, 1959-64; research dir. CNRS, Montpellier, France, 1967-80, dir. Ctr. Macromolecular Biochemistry, 1965-75; pres. Linus Pauling Inst., Palo Alto, Calif., 1980-92, Inst. Molecular Med. Scis., Palo Alto, Calif., 1992—; cons. in genetics Stanford U., 1963, vis. prof., 1964; vis. prof. U. Del., 1976. Contbg. author: Evolving Genes and Proteins, 1965; co-author: Genetique des Populations, 1976; editor Jour. Molecular Evolution, 1971—. Decorated Order of Merit (France). Fellow AAAS; mem. Societe de Chimie Biologique, N.Y. Acad. Scis., Internat. Soc. Study Origin of Life. Home: 565 Arastradero Rd Ph A Palo Alto CA 94306-4323 Office: Inst Molecular Med Scis 460 Page Mill Rd Palo Alto CA 94306-2025

ZUCKERMAN, MARTIN HARVEY, personnel director; b. N.Y.C., Feb. 20, 1942; s. Merwin and Helen (Weinstein) Z.; m. Joyce S. Harris, July 26, 1969; children: Lyle, Evan. BA, NYU, 1963; JD, St. John's U., 1965; LLM, NYU, 1966. Bar: N.Y. 1966. Field atty. Nat. Labor Relations Bd., N.Y.C., 1966-70; sr. atty. Simpson, Thatcher & Bartlett, N.Y.C., 1970-80; v.p. compensation and benefits Chemical Banking Corp. (formerly Mfrs. Hanover Trust Co.), N.Y.C., 1980-1983, sr. v.p., asst. personnel dir., 1983-85, exec. v.p., personnel dir., 1985-92; exec. v.p., pers. dir. Chem. Banking Corp. (formerly Mfrs. Hanover Trust Co.), 1992-96; mem. mgmt. com. Chem. Banking Corp., 1994-96; mem. adv. coun. on human resources mgmt. The Conf. Bd., 1992—. Trustee Drs. Hosp., 1984-92, Beth Israel Hosp., 1987-96, Employee Benefit Rsch. Inst., 1989—; treas. Puerto Rican Legal Def. and Edn. Fund, Inc., mem. exec. com., 1985—. Mem. N.Y. State Bar Assn., N.Y. County Lawyers Assn.

ZUCKERMAN, MORTIMER BENJAMIN, publisher, editor, real estate developer; b. Montreal, Que., Can., June 4, 1937; came to U.S., 1961, naturalized, 1977; s. Abraham and Esther Z. B.A. in Econs. and Polit. Theory with 1st class honors, McGill U., Montreal, 1957, LL.B. with honors, 1961; M.B.A. with distinction, U. Pa., 1962; LL.M., Harvard U., 1962. Sr. v.p. Cabot, Cabot & Forbes, Boston, 1965-69; chmn. bd. Boston Properties Co., 1970—; pres., chmn. bd. Atlantic Monthly Co., Boston, 1980—; chmn., editor-in-chief U.S. News & World Report; chmn., co-pub. N.Y. Daily News; dir., exec. com. Stride Rite Corp., 1970-83; dir. Property Capital Trust Co., 1979-80, RET Income Found., 1976-79; public interest dir. Fed. Home Loan Bank of Boston, 1972-73; lectr., then assoc. prof. Harvard U. Grad. Sch. Design, 1966-74; vis. lectr. city and regional planning Yale U., 1967-69. Pres. bd. trustees Sidney Farber Cancer Inst., Boston, 1980; trustee Mus. Sci., 1980, Beth Israel Hosp., 1975, Ford Hall Forum, 1979-83, Urban Inst., Russell Sage Found., 1985-86; chmn. bd. visitors Boston U. Sch. Medicine, 1978-79; adv. bd. Ctr. Strategic and Internat. Studies; adv. bd. Wharton Sch.; bd. dirs. Wolf Trap Found., Tennis Hall of Fame. Mem. Coun. on Fgn. Rels., Internat. Inst. Strategic Studies. Clubs: Harvard (Boston and N.Y.C.); Harmonie (N.Y.C.). Office: New York Daily News 450 W 33rd St New York NY 10001 Office: US News & World Report 2400 N St NW Washington DC 20037-1153*

ZUCKERMAN, RICHARD ENGLE, lawyer, law educator; b. Yonkers, N.Y., Aug. 2, 1945; s. Julius and Roslyn (Ehrlich) Z.; m. Denise Ellen Spoon, July 14, 1968; children: Julie Ann, Lindsay Beth. BA, U. Mich., 1967; JD cum laude, Southwestern U., 1974. Bar: Calif. 1974, Mich. 1976, Nev. 1986, U.S. Dist. Ct. (ea. and we. dists.) Mich. 1977, U.S. Ct. Appeals (6th cir.) 1977, U.S. Ct. Appeals (9th cir.) 1982, U.S. Ct. Appeals 2d and 7th cirs.) 1994, U.S. Tax Ct. 1980, U.S. Supreme Ct. 1985. Spl. atty. organized crime and racketeering sect. U.S. Dept. Justice, Detroit, 1974-77; sr. ptnr. Raymond, Rupp, Wienberg, Stone & Zuckerman, P.C., Troy, Mich., 1977-87; sr. ptnr. Honigman, Miller, Schwartz & Cohn, Detroit, 1987—, chair litigation dept., 1996—; adj. prof. Detroit Coll. Law, 1978—; mem. Mich. Atty. Grievance Commn. (Mich. supreme ct. nominee), 1995—. Served to lt. USN, 1967-71, Vietnam. Mem. ABA (grand jury com. criminal justice sect.), Fed. Bar Assn. (chmn. criminal law sect. Detroit chpt. 1985-90, bd. dirs. 1985-94, co-chair criminal def. atty. com. 1990-95), Knollwood Country Club (West Bloomfield, Mich.), Std. Club, Am. Inns Ct. (master of bench 1995—). Republican. Jewish. Office: Honigman Miller Schwartz & Cohn 2290 First National Bldg Detroit MI 48226

ZUCKERMAN, SIDNEY, retired allergist, immunologist; b. N.Y.C., May 2, 1918; s. Max and Rose (Katz) Z.; m. Irene Elinor Cohen, Oct. 27, 1945; children: Elaine, Laurie, Jed, Amy. BA, Columbia Coll., 1939; MD, N.Y. Med. Coll., 1943. Diplomate Am. Bd. Internal Medicine, Am. Bd. Allergy and Immunology. Chief medicine 72d Sta. Hosp. US Army Med. Corps., Sendai, Japan, 1945-47; med. dir. Ford Instrument Co. divsn. Sperry Corp., N.Y.C., 1947-60; pvt. practice N.Y.C., 1947-91; med. dir. Sperry Rand Corp., Great Neck, N.Y., 1960-90. Capt. U.S. Army Med. Corps., 1945-47, Japan. Fellow ACP, Am. Coll. Allergy, Asthma and Immunology, Am. Acad. Allergy, Asthma and Immunology, Am. Coll. Occupational Medicine, Am. Assn. Cert. Allergists; mem. Masons (jr. warden). Avocations: woodworking, golf. Home: 4140 Bocaire Blvd Boca Raton FL 33487-1148

ZUCKERMAN, STUART, psychiatrist, educator; b. Syracuse, N.Y., Feb. 18, 1933; s. George and Cassie (Kolsan) Z. Student, U. Kans., 1950-51; BS, U. Ala., 1954; DO, Phila. Coll. Osteo. Medicine, 1958. Diplomate Am. Osteo. Bd. Neurology and Psychiatry, Am. Nat. Bd. Psychiatry, Am. Coll. Forensic Medicine, Bd. Forensic Medicine, Bd. Forensic Examiner; cert. correctional health profl. Rotating intern Hosps. Phila. Coll. Osteo. Medicine, 1958-59; psychiat. fellow, resident Phila. Mental Health Clinic, 1959-62, Psychoanalytic Studies Inst., Phila., 1959-62; chief resident, 1962; chief div. neuropsychiatry Grandview Hosp., Dayton, Ohio, 1962-65; asst. med. dir., chief children's and adolescent's unit N.J. State Hosp., Ancora, 1967-70; chief outpatient dept. Atlantic City, 1970-72; practice specializing in neuropsychiatry Atlantic City, 1965—; founding prof. psychiatry, chmn. dept. Ohio U. Coll. Osteo. Medicine, Athens, 1976-77; clin. prof. Ohio U. Coll. Osteo. Medicine, 1977—; mem. faculty U. Pa. Sch. Medicine, Phila. Coll. Osteo. Medicine, 1972-76; lectr. U. Pa., 1977-79; prof. dept. psychiatry, charter faculty Sch. Medicine, Marshall U., 1977-78, clin. prof., 1979-80; clin. prof. N.Y. Coll. Osteo. Medicine, 1979—; chief mental hygiene VA Hosp., Huntington, W.Va., 1978-79; liaison psychiatrist, acting chief VA Med. Center, Perry Point, Md., 1979-80; med. dir. Mental Health Clinic of Ocean County, Toms River, N.J., 1980-85, Ventnor Mental Health Ctr., Atlantic City; chief psychiatrist N.J. Dept. Corrections So. State Correctional

Facility, 1985-96; physician Atlantic City (N.J.) Beach Patrol; attending psychiatrist Atlantic City, Shore Meml., Kessler Meml., Washington Meml., Atlantic County Mental hosps., 1965-76; attending psychiatrist, asst. dir. dept. psychiatry Phila. Gen. Hosp., 1972-76; med. dir. Shawnee Mental Health Center, (Adams, Lawrence, Scioto counties), Portsmouth, Ohio, 1977-78; cons. psychiatrist Athens Mental Health and Mental Retardation Ctr., 1976-77, Scioto Meml., So. Hills, Mercy hosps., Portsmouth, 1977-78, Lansdowne Cmty. Mental Health Center, (Greenup, Carter counties), Ashland, Ky., 1977-78, Atlantic City Med. Ctr., 1984-97, Cmty. Meml. Hosp., Toms River, N.J., 1984-91, So. Ocean County Hosp., Manahawkin, N.J., 1984-91, Paul-Kimball Med Ctr., Lakewood, N.J., 1984-97, Obleness Meml. Hosp., Clin. Services of Athens, Vinton, Hocking Counties, Hudson Health Ctr., Ohio U., 1976077; cons. Bayside State Prison, Leesburg, N.J., 1989-96, Atlantic County Justice System, Mays Landing, N.J., 1992-93, child study spl. svcs. S. Jersey sch. systems; chmn. profl. adv. com. Atlantic County Mental Health Bd., 1969-71; mem. nominating com. Mental Health Assn., Atlantic County, 1972-75; exam. psychiatrist Jersey Police and Fire depts.; mem. Atlantic County Mental Health Bd.; mem. profl. adv. com. N.J. Dept. Corrections; cons. N.J. Dept. Pub. Advocate. Mem. adv. bd. Osteo. Physician, 1975—; assoc. editor Bull. Am. Coll. Neuropsychiatrists, 1963-70, Jour. Corr. Health Editl. Bd.; contbr. articles to profl. jours. Bd. dirs. Atlantic County Family Svcs. Assn., 1968-74, Cape May County Drug Abuse Coun., 1973-76, Nat. Comm. Correctional Health Care, 1988-97; mem. Ventnor City Beautification Com.; house physician Friends of the Pops Ocean City (N.J.) Music Pier. Fellow Am. Coll. Forensic Psychiatry, Am. Coll. Neuropsychiatrists (bd. reps.), Am. Acad. Disability Evaluating Physicians (charter), Acad. Medicine N.J., Phila. Coll. Physicians; mem. AMA (Physicians Recognition award 1985—), AAUP, Am. Bd. Forensic Examiners (cert. 1994), Am. Coll. Forensic Medicine (bd. cert. 1996), World Psychiat. Assn., Am. Psychiat. Assn., N.J. (confidentiality, pub. psychiatry com., gen. hosp. psychiatry com., law com., mkgt. benefits com.) Psychiat. Assn., Am. Assn. Psychiatrists in Alcohol and Addictions (founder), Am., N.J. pub. health assns., Am. Osteo. Assn. (hosp. inspection team 1971-75, bd. reps.), Am. Assn. CMHC Psychiatrists, Am. Assn. Psychiatrists in Pvt. Practice, Internat. Assn. Med. Specialists, Am. Soc. Law and Medicine, Am. Acad. Clin. Psychiatrists, Corp. Advancement Psychiatry, Am. Med. Writers Assn., Nat. Council Community Mental Health Ctrs., Met. Coll. Mental Health Assn., Am. Soc. Criminology., South Jersey Neuropsychiat. Soc., Psychiat. Outpatients Ctrs. Am., Am. Coll. Legal Medicine, Acad. Psychiatry and Law (pub. info. com., edn. com., internat. affairs com.), Am. Acad. Forensic Scis., Am. Assn. Acad. Psychiatry, Am. Coll. Emergency Physicians, Am. Acad. Psychotherapists, Am. Assn. Mental Deficiency, Am. Assn. Psychiat. Services for Children, Acad. Psychosomatic Medicine, N.J. (chmn. com. on confidentiality), Fla. assns. osteo. physicians and surgeons, N.J. Hosp. Assn., Am. Vocat. Assn., Am. Assn. Group Therapy, Am. Soc. Clin. Psychopharmacology, Assn. Mil. Surgeons U.S., Nat. Assn. VA Physicians, Am. Assn. Psychiat. Adminstrs., Am. Assn. Adolescent Psychiatry, World Med. Assn., Am. Assn. Mental Health Adminstrs., Am. Assn. Gen. Hosp. Psychiatrists, Human Factors Soc., Orthopsychiat. Assn., Am. Physicians Fellowship, Assn. for Research Nervous and Mental Diseases, Atlantic County Osteo. Med. Soc. (pres. 1970-72), N.J. Assn. Mil. Surgeons U.S. (v.p.), Am. Assn. Correctional Health Care, Am. Coll. Forensic Psychiatry (diplomate 1984), charter mem. Soc. of Correctional Physicians. Home: 6700 Atlantic Ave Ventnor City NJ 08406-2618

ZUCKERT, DONALD MACK, marketing executive; b. N.Y.C., Apr. 3, 1934; s. Sidney L. and Doris (Mack) Z.; m. Susan Liefter; children: Andrew, Timothy. AB in Govt. with honors, Bowdoin Coll., 1956; LLB, NYU, 1959. Bar: N.Y., Conn. 1960. With Ted Bates Worldwide, Inc., N.Y.C., 1960-87; pres. Ted Bates U.S. Affiliate Group, N.Y.C., 1974-83, Ted Bates Advt./N.Y., N.Y.C., 1983-86; chmn., chief exec. officer Ted Bates Worldwide, Inc., 1986-87; pres. Backer Spielvogel Bates Worldwide Inc., N.Y.C., 1987; chmn., chief exec. officer Arcature Corp., Stamford, Conn., 1989-95; vice chmn. Draft Direct Worldwide, N.Y.C., 1996—; bd. dirs. Calif. & Wash. Co., San Bruno, Calif., Suanti Ltd., Manchester, N.H., Rattlesnake Holdings, Inc., Wilmington, Del. Trustee Bowdoin Coll., Brunswick, Maine; nat. overseer Strawbery Banke Mus., Portsmouth, N.H. Served to capt. AUS, 1956-57. Mem. Innis Arden Golf Club (Old Greenwich, Conn.), Wentworth by the Sea Country Club (New Castle, N.H.), New Castle Yacht Club, River Club (N.Y.C.), Adm.'s Cove Golf Club (Jupiter, Fla.), Alpha Tau Omega. Office: DraftDirect Worldwide 633 3rd Ave New York NY 10017-6706

ZUCKMAN, HARVEY LYLE, law educator; b. Mpls., Apr. 14, 1934; s. George and Elizabeth (Polinsky) Z.; m. Charlotte Anne Snyder, Jan. 27, 1962; children: Jill Belinda, Beth Nancy, Michael Scott. A.B., U. So. Calif., 1956; LL.B., NYU, 1959. Bar: Calif. 1960, D.C. 1973, U.S. Supreme Ct. 1963. Atty. civil div. appellate sect. U.S. Dept. Justice, Washington, 1963-67; prof. law St. Louis U., 1967-70, Columbus Sch. Law of Cath. U. Am., 1970—; dir. Inst. for Communications Law Studies Columbus Sch. Law, Cath. U. Am., 1981—; adj. prof. communications Am. U., 1976-81; cons. Bur. Nat. Affairs., 1974-81. Producer: Am. Law Inst.-ABA Legal Edn. TV series, 1973-74; co-author: Mass Communications Law, 1977, 4th edit., 1994; editor ABA newsletter Comm. Lawyer, 1981-86. Served with U.S. Army Judge Adv. Gen., 1960-63. Mem. ABA (forum com. on comm. law, co-chmn. nat. celebration of 200th anniversary of 1st amendment 1991), D.C. Bar Assn. (chairperson com. on continuing legal edn. 1975-83), Fed. Comm. Bar Assn., Am. Law Inst., Assn. Am. Law Schs. (sects. family law and mass comm.). Democrat. Office: Cath U Am Columbus Sch Law 3600 John McCormick Rd NE Washington DC 20064

ZUEHLKE, RICHARD WILLIAM, technical communications consultant, writer; b. Milw., June 17, 1933; s. Harold Babcock and Phoebe Blanche (Frykman) Z.; m. Carol Sue Yates, Dec. 26, 1955; children: Kenneth Richard, William Woodfill, Deanne Elizabeth. B.S., Lawrence Coll., 1955; Ph.D., U. Minn., 1960. Instr. chemistry Lawrence U., 1958-62, asst. prof., 1962-68; Eliphalet Remington prof. chemistry U. Bridgeport, 1968-79, chmn. dept., 1968-73; vis. prof. U. R.I., 1976-77, 79-80, assoc. marine scientist, 1980-85; owner, pres. The Right Connection, Inc., 1983-91; pres. TetraR Cons., Inc., 1985-88; cons. Kimberly-Clark Corp., 1960-62, United Illuminating Co., 1969-75, Chem. Specialties Corp., 1979-81, Sperry Remington Corp., 1976-79; NSF Sci. Faculty fellow U. Pitts., 1966-67; asst. to dir. Gordon Rsch. Confs., 1990-94; cons., writer in field. Fellow Am. Inst. Chemists; mem. Am. Chem. Soc., AAAS, Sigma Xi, Sigma Phi Epsilon. Congregationalist. Lodge: Rotary. Home: PO Box 784 New London NH 03257-0784 Office: PO Box 784 New London NH 03257-0784

ZUERLEIN, DAMIAN JOSEPH, priest; b. Norfolk, Neb., May 28, 1955; s. Victor Damian and Elizabeth P. (Wegener) Z. BA, U. St. Thomas, St. Paul, 1977; MDiv, St. Paul Sem., 1981. Ordained priest Roman Cath. Ch., 1981. Tchr. Norfolk Cath. High Sch., 1981-85; asst. pastor Sacred Heart/St. Mary's Parish, Norfolk, 1981-85; assoc. pastor St. Pius X Cath. Ch., Omaha, 1985-88, Mary Our Queen Cath. Ch., Omaha, 1988-90; pastor Our Lady of Guadalupe Parish, Omaha, 1990—; cons. Archdiocesan Vocations Office, Omaha, 1985-95; bd. dirs. Juan Diego Ctr., Omaha, 1990—; chmn., co-founder Omaha Together One Cmty., 1991-95; co-founder Weaving, Women's Advocacy Group, Omaha, 1988—. Presenter (video) Loving Your Marriage, 1990, El Matrimonio: Una Jornada Para Todo Una Vida, 1995; co-author: (manual) Hispanic Pastoral Plan, 1991. Bd. dirs. United Cath. Social Svcs., Omaha, 1990-96, Chicano Awareness Ctr., Omaha, 1991—, Vis. Nurse Assn., 1996—; bd. dirs. Omaha 100 Inc., 1991-96, chair, 1991-93; advisor Mayor P.J. Morgan, Omaha, 1991-95; mem. Gov. Nelson's Urban Adv. Task Force, 1994; mem. Douglas County Commn. on Domestic Violence, 1996—. Mem. Pax Cristi, Amnesty Internat., Fontenelle Forest Assn., Priests for Equality, Greater Omaha Clergy Assn. (pres. 1987-88), South Omaha Neighborhood Assn. (bd. dirs. 1992, pres. 1994—). Avocations: canoeing the BWCA, skiing, travel, hiking. Home and Office: 2310 O St Omaha NE 68107-2837

ZUETEL, KENNETH ROY, JR., lawyer; b. L.A., Apr. 5, 1954; s. Kenneth Roy Sr. and Adelle Francis (Avant) Z.; m. Cheryl Kay Morse, May 29, 1976; children: Bryan, Jarid, Christopher, Lauren. BA, San Diego State U., 1974; JD, U. San Diego, 1978. Bar: Calif. 1978 U.S. Ct. Appeals (9th cir.) 1979, U.S. Dist. Ct. (ctrl. dist.) Calif. 1979, U.S. Dist. Ct. (so. and no. dists.) Calif. 1980, U.S. Dist. Ct. (ea. dist.) 1981. Clk. to fed. Judge Martin Pence U.S. Dist. Ct. Hawaii, Honolulu, 1978-79; assoc. litigation Buchalter, Nemer, L.A., 1979-83, Thelen, Marrin, L.A., 1983-88; ptnr. Zuetel & Cahill, Pasadena, Calif., 1988—; superior ct. arbitrator L.A. Superior Ct., 1982-90, superior ct. settlement officer, 1988-93; judge pro temp L.A. Mcpl. Ct., 1983—, L.A. Superior Ct., 1989—; guest lectr. Loyola U. Sch. Law, 1986—; CEB lectr. Author: Civil Procedure Before Trial, 1992; cons. editor: Cal. Civ. Proc., 1992; contbr. articles to profl. jours. Recipient Recognition award L.A. (Calif.) Bd. Suprs., 1988. Mem. State Bar Calif. (mem. adv. com. continuing edn. 1985-88, trial practice subcom. 1985-88, disciplinary examiner 1986), Los Angeles County Bar Assn. (chair trial atty. project 1982-83, mem. L.A. del. conf. of dels. 1986—, chair L.A. del. conf. of dels. 1995, exec. com. barristers 1984-88, superior ct. com. 1985-88, civil practice com. 1992-94, exec. com. litigation sect. 1989-90), Pasadena Bar Assn., Inns of Ct. (barrister L.A. chpt. 1991-92), Phi Beta Kappa, Phi Kappa Phi, Phi Alpha Theta, Pi Sigma Alpha. Republican. Presbyterian. Home: 567 Willow Springs Ln Glendora CA 91741-2974 Office: Zuetel & Cahill 180 S Lake Ave Ste 540 Pasadena CA 91101-2666

ZUFRYDEN, FRED S., academic administrator, marketing educator, researcher; b. Grenoble, France, June 13, 1943; came to U.S., 1956; s. Henri and Cecile (Frymer) Z.; m. Toby Marlene Levin, Dec. 24, 1967; 1 child, Ryan. B.A. in Math., UCLA, 1965, M.B.A., 1966, Ph.D. in Bus. Adminstrn., 1971. Rsch. engr. mil. ops. and systems analysis group N.Am. Aviation, Inc., L.A., 1966-67; rsch. assoc. resources rsch. dept. Planning Rsch. Corp., L.A., 1967-68; ops. rsch. specialist data systems div. Litton Systems, Inc., L.A., 1968-70; asst. prof. dept. mgmt. scis. Sch. Bus. and Econs., U. Calif., Northridge, 1970-71; asst. prof. dept. mktg. Grad. Sch. Bus. U. So. Calif., L.A., 1971-75; assoc. prof. U. So. Calif., 1975-82, prof., 1982—, Ernst Hahn prof. mktg., 1991—, chmn. mktg. dept., 1987-90, rsch. dir. internat. bus. econs. and rsch. Grad. Sch. Bus., 1983—. Mem. editorial bd. Jour. Advt. Rsch., 1981—, Mktg. Sci., 1979—, Jour. Mktg., 1978—; mem. cons. and planning com. Mktg. Sci. Jour., 1979; referee Jour. Mktg. Rsch., Mgmt. Sci., Decision Sci., Jour. Internat. Rsch. in Mktg.; mem. abstract writing staff International Abstracts in Operations Rsch./Mgmt. Sci., 1973; contbr. articles to profl. jours. including Jour. Mktg. Rsch., Mktg. Sci., Jour. Operational Rsch. Soc., Mgmt. Sci., Decision Scis., Jour. Mktg., Jour. Advt. Rsch., Jour. Internat. Rsch. in Mktg., Jour. Royal Statis. Soc., Interfaces, Rsch. in Mktg., Jour. of Mktg. Rsch. Soc., Jour. of Bus., others. Rsch. grantee U. So. Calif., 1973, 75, 76, 77, 78, A.C. Nielsen Co., 1988-90. Mem. Am. Mktg. Assn. (cert. recognition 1974), Ops. Rsch. Soc. Am., Inst. Mgmt. Sci., Omega Rho, Beta Gamma Sigma.

ZUHDI, NAZIH, surgeon, administrator; b. Beirut, May 19, 1925; came to U.S., 1950; s. Omar and Lutfiye (Atef) Z.; children by previous marriage: Omar, Nabil; m. Annette McMichael; children: Adam, Leyla, Zachariah. BA, Am. U., Beirut, 1946, MD, 1950. Diplomate Am. Bd. Surgery, Am. Bd. Thoracic Surgery. Intern St. Vincent's Hosp., S.I., N.Y., 1950-51, Presbyn.-Columbia Med. Ctr., N.Y.C., 1951-52; resident Kings County SUNY Med. Ctr., N.Y.C., 1952-56; fellow SUNY Downstate Med. Ctr., Bklyn., 1953-54; resident Univ. Hosp., Mpls., 1956; resident Univ. Hosp., Oklahoma City, 1957-58, practice surgery specializing in cardiovascular and thoracic, 1958-87, practice in heart transplantation, lung transplantation and heart-lung transplantation, 1985—; founder, dir. Transplantation Inst. Bapt. Med. Ctr., 1984—, chmn. dept. transplantation, 1994—; transplantation surgeon in chief Bapt. Hosp., Oklahoma City, 1984—; founder, chmn. Okla. Cardiovascular Inst., Oklahoma City, 1983-84, Okla. Heart Ctr., Oklahoma City, 1984-85. Contbg. author Cardiac Surgery, 1967, 2d edit., 1972; contbr. articles to profl. jours.; developer numerous med. devices, techniques, rsch. and publs. on cardiopulmonary bypass, internal hypothermia, assisted circulation, heart surgery and transplantation of thoracic organs; developer heart-lung machines; designer, use of exptl. plastic bypass hearts; originator use of banked citrated blood for cardiopulmonary bypass for open heart surgery, of clin. non-hemic primes of heart-lung machines producing intentional hemodilution, at present, the universally accepted principle of cardiopulmonary bypass for partial and total body perfusion; researcher in cardiovascular studies. Founder Islamic Ctr., Inc., Oklahoma City. Inducted into Okla. Hall of Fame, 1994. Fellow ACS; mem. AMA, NCCJ (Humanitarian award 1996), Am. Thoracic Soc., Okla. Thoracic Soc., So. Med. Assn., Okla. Med. Assn., Internat. Coll. Angiology, Am. Coll. Chest Physicians, Oklahoma City C. of C., Oklahoma County Med. Soc., Oklahoma City Clin. Soc., Okla. Surg. Assn., Oklahoma City Surg. Soc., Southwestern Surg. Congress, Am. Coll. Cardiology, Am. Soc. Artificial Internal Organs, Soc. Thoracic Surgeons (founding mem.), Am. Assn. for Thoracic Surgery, Internat. Cardiovasc. Soc., Okla. State Heart Assn., Osler Soc., So. Thoracic Surg. Assn., Lillehei Surg. Soc., Internat. Soc. Heart Transplantation, Dwight Harken's Founder's Group Cardiac Surgery, Internat. Soc. Cardiothoracic Surgery (Japan, founding mem.), Am. Soc. Transplant Surgeons, Milestones of Cardiology of Am. Coll. Cardiology, Okla. City Golf and Country Club, Okla. Hall of Fame. Achievements include originator use of banked citrated blood for cardiopulmonary bypass for open heart surgery; invention of clinical non-hemic primes of heart-lung machines producing intentional hemodilution. Home: 7305 Lancet Ct Oklahoma City OK 73120-1430

ZUHLKE, MARYBETH, elementary school curriculum consultant, educator; b. Kenosha, Wis., Jan. 16, 1946; d. Charles Casmir and Elizabeth (Mulich) Safransky; m. Lee VanLunduyt, Aug. 24, 1968 (div. 1985); children: Kyle, Ravi; m. Tom Zuhlke, Sept. 9, 1990. Student, U. Dallas, 1965-67; BS, U. Wis., Whitewater, 1968; MS, U. Wis., Milw., 1973, postgrad., 1988-89; postgrad., Marquette U., 1978-81. Cert. elem. tchr., prin., coord. instruction, Wis. Tchr. second grade Kenosha Unified Sch. Dist., 1968-70, community liaison tchr., 1974-79, dissemination specialist, 1979-82, curriculum cons., 1982—; cons. Conn. Facilitator, North Haven, 1984-86, South Ocean Internat. Sch., Datong, China, 1995-96; prin. McKinley Elem. Sch., Kenosha, 1988-89. Co-author: Kenosha Model Kindergarten Manual, 1985, Kenosha Model Math. Manual, 1986; editor: Kenosha Model Language Experience, 1979. Mem. Racine (Wis.) Arts Coun., 1980—. Mem. ASCD, Internat. Reading Assn., Parent Edn. and Childhood Assn. (exec. bd. 1976-83), Inst. of World Affairs, Wis. State and Fed. Specialists (newsletter editor 1986-87), Assn. Wis. Sch. Adminstrs., (Co-Chmn.), Exhibits Team, Imaginarium Children's Museum, 1996, Phi Delta Kappa. Avocations: reading, cross-country skiing, nature. Home: 1419 Crabapple Dr Racine WI 53405-1703 Office: Regional Staff Devel Ctr UW Parkside Kenosha WI 53144

ZUICHES, JAMES JOSEPH, academic administrator; b. Eau Claire, Wis., Mar. 24, 1943; s. William Homer and Bronnie Monica (Stich) Z.; m. Carol Ann Kurilo, Aug. 19, 1967; children:; James Daniel, Joseph Kurilo. BA in Philosophy, U. Portland, 1967; MS in Sociology, U. Wis., 1969, PhD in Sociology, 1973. Instr., asst. prof., assoc. prof. sociology Mich. State U., East Lansing, 1971-82, prof., 1982; assoc. program dir. in sociology NSF, Washington, 1979-80, program dir. in sociology, 1980-82; assoc. dir. rsch. Cornell U., Ithaca, N.Y., 1982-86; assoc. dean Coll. Agr. and Home Econs., Wash. State U., Pullman, 1986-94, dir. Agrl. Rsch. Ctr., 1986-94; program dir. food sys. and rural devel. W.K. Kellogg Found., Battle Creek, Mich., 1994-95; dean Coll. Agr. and Home Econs. Wash. State U., Pullman, 1995—; mem. adv. subcom. NSF, 1977-79; sci. adv. com. USDA Nat. Rsch. Initiative, Washington, 1992-93; com. on future land grant univ. bd. on agr., NRC, Washington, 1994-96; pub. Wash. Land and People Mag., 1987-92. Co-editor: The Demography of Rural Life, 1993; contbr. articles to profl. jours. Pres., bd. dirs. Edgewood Village Children's Ctr., East Lansing, 1978-79. Recipient sustained superior performance award NSF, 1981; rsch. grantee NIMH, 1973, ERDA, 1978. Fellow AAAS; mem. Rural Sociol. Soc. (pres. 1992-93, editor 50th Anniversary Rsch. Series, 5 vols. 1988-93), Am. Sociol. Assn., Population Assn. Am. Roman Catholic. Avocations: skiing, swimming, hiking, reading.

ZUICK, DIANE MARTINA, elementary education educator; b. Gary, Ind., May 19, 1951; d. Arnold and Matilda (Chaimovitz) Herskovic; m. Norman Robert Zuick, Aug. 12, 1973; children: Scott, Amy. BS in Edn., Ind. U., 1972, MS in Edn., 1974. Tchr. 5th grade George L. Myers Sch., Portage, Ind., 1972-73, tchr. 3d grade, 1973-83, tchr. 1st grade, 1983-90, tchr. 2d grade, 1990—; mem. prime time com. Portage Twp. Schs., 1991—, mem. reading curriculum com., 1987-88, mem. devel. com., 1983-85; mem. adv. K'ton Ton Pre-Sch., Highland, Ind., 1984-86. Chair sch. bd. Congregation Beth Israel, Hammond, Ind., 1993-95, mem. sch. bd., 1992-95, mem. exec. bd., 1994—; mem. B'nai B'rith, Hammond, 1993—, mem. dist. bd. govs., 1995—. Recipient Ind. Dept. Instrn. Prime Time award, 1988, 89; Portage Twp. Schs. grantee, 1993, 94. Mem. NEA, Ind. State Tchrs. Assn., Portage Assn. Tchrs., Tchrs. Applying Whole Langs., Internat. Reading Assn., Ind. U. Alumni Assn. Avocations: reading, travel, piano, nature, music. Home: 58 Cedar Ln Schererville IN 46375-1107 Office: Portage Twp Schs 6240 Us Highway 6 Portage IN 46368-5057

ZUIDEMA, GEORGE DALE, surgeon; b. Holland, Mich., Mar. 8, 1928; s. Jacob and Reka (Dalman) Z.; m. Joan K. Houtman, June 2, 1953; children: Karen Sue, David Jay, Nancy Ruth, Sarah Kay. A.B., Hope Coll., 1949, D.Sc. (hon.), 1969; M.D., Johns Hopkins U., 1953. Diplomate: Am. Bd. Surgery. Intern Mass. Gen. Hosp., 1953-54, asst. resident surgeon, then chief resident surgeon, 1954, 57, 58, 59; asst. prof. surgery, then assoc. prof. U. Mich. Sch. Medicine, 1960-64; prof. surgery, dir. dept. Johns Hopkins Sch. Medicine; also surgeon in chief Johns Hopkins Hosp., 1964-84; prof. surgery, vice provost med. affairs U. Mich., 1984-94; Cons. Walter Reed Army Med. Center, Sinai Hosp., Balt., Balt. City Hosp., Clin. Center of NIH; chmn. Study on Surg. Services for U.S., 1970-75. Editor: (with O.H. Gauer) Gravitational Stress in Aerospace Medicine, 1961; (with G.L. Nardi) Surgery-A Concise Guide to Clinical Practice, 1961, 4th edit., 1982; (with R.D. Judge and F. Fitzgerald) Physical Diagnosis, 1963, 6th edit., 1997; (with W.F. Ballinger and R.B. Rutherford) Management of Trauma, 1968, 4th edit., 1985; (with L. Schlossberg) Atlas of Human Functional Anatomy, 1977, 4th edit., 1997, Shackelford's Surgery of the Alimentary Tract, 4th edit., 1996; editor Jour. Surg. Rsch., 1966-72, assoc. editor, mem. editl. bd., 1972—; mem. editl. bd. Surgery Ann., 1968—, Surgery, 1970—, co-editor in chief, 1975—. Bd. dirs. Md. divsn. Am. Cancer Soc., 1964-68; trustee William Beaumont Hosp., Royal Oak, Mich., 1984-94, Hope Coll., Holland, Mich, 1987—. Capt. M.C., USAF, 1954-56. John and Mary R. Markle scholar academic medicine, 1961-66; recipient Henry Russell award U. Mich., 1963. Fellow ACS, Royal Coll. Surgeons Ireland (hon.); mem. Assn. Am. Med. Colls., Ctrl. Soc. Clin. Rsch., Soc. Univ. Surgeons, Am. Surg. Assn., So. Surg. Assn., Soc. Clin. Surgery, Soc. Vascular Surgery, Internat. Cardiovascular Surgery, Halsted Soc., Nat. Inst. Medicine, Assn. Acad. Surgeons (pres. 1967-69), Allen O. Whipple Soc., Coun. on Grad. Med. Edn., Phi Beta Kappa, Tri Beta, Alpha Omega Alpha. Home: 956 Meadowlark Ct Holland MI 49424 Office: U Mich M4100 Med Sci I Ann Arbor MI 48109-0608

ZUIDERVAART, LAMBERT PAUL, philosophy educator; b. Modesto, Calif., Aug. 1, 1950; s. Martin and Tena (Beuving) Z.; m. Joyce Alene Recker, Jan. 8, 1977. BA, Dordt Coll., 1972; MPhil, Inst. Christian Studies, Toronto, Ont., Can., 1975; postgrad., Free U. Berlin, 1977-80; PhD, Free U. Amsterdam, The Netherlands, 1981. Asst. prof. philosophy The King's Coll., Edmonton, Alta., Can., 1981-85, chmn., divsn. humanities, 1982-85; assoc. prof. philosophy Calvin Coll., Grand Rapids, Mich., 1985-89, prof. philosophy, 1989—, chairperson, dept. philosophy, 1991-97; vis. prof. Inst. for Christian Studies, Toronto, Ont., Can., 1991, mem. senate, 1993—; treas. bd. dirs. The King's Coll. Found., U.S., Grand Rapids, Mich., 1989-95; pres., bd. dirs. Urban Inst. for Contemporary Arts, Grand Rapids, 1994—; conf. dir. Calvin Coll., 1995; pub. lectr. Kendall Coll. Art and Design, 1993. Author: Adorno's Aesthetic Theory, 1991; co-author: Dancing in the Dark, 1991; co-editor: Pledges of the Jubilee, 1995, The Semblance of Subjectivity, 1997; contrib. articles to profl. jours. Pres. bd. dirs. Inn Roads Housing Coop., Edmonton, Alta., Can., 1982-85; mem. Politics Meaning Discussion Group, Grand Rapids, 1994—; mem. Internat. Critical Theory Seminar, 1995; workshop leader Leadership Grand Rapids, Mich., 1993, 94. Grantee STEP Prov. Alberta., Can., 1984, 85, Travel grant Am. Coun. Learned Socs., 1988, Rsch. Visit grant German Acad. Exch. Svc., 1994; NEH Summer Seminar grantee, 1997; Calvin Coll. Rsch. fellow, 1990, 93, 94, 96. mem. Am. Philosophical Assn., Am. Soc. Aesthetics, Can. Philosophical Assn., Can. Soc. Aesthetics, Internat. Assn. Aesthetics, Soc. Phenomenology and Existential Philosophy. Democrat. Avocations: international travel, music, film, hiking. Office: Calvin College Department of Philosophy Grand Rapids MI 49546

ZUK, JUDITH, botanic garden administrator; b. Canandaigua, N.Y., Sept. 11, 1951. BA, Rutgers U., 1973; MS, U. Del., 1976. Ceo and pres. Bklyn Botanic Garden, Brooklyn, N.Y., 1980—. Mem. Phi Beta Kappa. Office: Brooklyn Botanic Garden 1000 Washington Ave Brooklyn NY 11225-1008

ZUKERMAN, MICHAEL, lawyer; b. Bklyn., Oct. 3, 1940; s. Charles Morris and Gertrude Ethel Zukerman; m. Claire J. Goldsmith, June 25, 1961 (div. 1986); children: Steven, Amy; m. Elaine DeMasi, Nov. 21, 1986; children: Jaclyn, Laura. BS, U. Fla., 1961; LLB, St. John's U., 1964; LLM, NYU, 1966. Bar: N.Y. 1965, Pa. 1983, U.S. Tax Ct. 1984. Credit analyst, loan officer Franklin Nat. Bank, 1964-66; assoc. Jaffin, Schneider, Kimmel & Galpeer, N.Y.C., 1966-67; ptnr. Zukerman, Licht & Friedman and predecessors, N.Y.C., 1967-79, Baskin & Sears, P.C., N.Y.C., 1979-85, Graubard, Moskowitz, Dannett, Horowitz & Mollen, 1985-86, Gersten, Savage, Kaplowitz & Zukerman, 1986-89; of counsel Olshan, Grundman, Frome & Rosenzweig, 1990-95; of counsel Graham & James, 1995—; pres. First Ptnrs. Credit Corp., N.Y.C., 1988-93, exec. v.p. Brookhill Group, 1986-88, Real Mark Adv. Corp., 1993—; mem. bd. dirs. Interjurist LTD, internat. law firm, 1986—. Contbg. editor Real Estate Taxation and Acctg., 1988-93; lectr. on various subjects, 1986—. Contbr. articles to profl. jours. Trustee Temple Beth Torah, Melville, N.Y., 1972-80; bd. dirs. Dayton Mgmt. Corp., 1974—, Suffolk Jewish Community Planning Bd., Hauppague, N.Y., 1982-85, WATSCO, Inc., Am. Vending Assocs., 1983-86, Dames Moore/Brookhill LLC, 1996—; trustee, treas. YMHA Suffolk County, Hauppague, 1980-85; co-chmn. bus. adv. coun. Town of Greenburgh, 1992; bd. dirs. Congregation Bnai Elohim, 1994, 2d v.p., 1995. Mem. ABA. Home: 6 Thomas St Scarsdale NY 10583-1031 Office: Graham & James 885 3rd Ave Fl 24 New York NY 10022-4834

ZUKERMAN, PINCHAS, concert violinist, violist, conductor; b. Tel Aviv, July 16, 1948; came to U.S., 1962; s. Yehuda and Miriam (Lieberman) Z.; m. Eugenia Rich, May 26, 1968 (div.); children: Natalia, Arianna; m. Tuesday Weld, 1985. Student, Juilliard Sch. Music, 1965-68; MusD (hon.), Brown U., 1989. Ind. concert violinist, 1968—. With impresario, Sol Hurok, 1967-76; condr., soloist English Chamber Orch., 1974, Mostly Mozart Festival, N.Y.C., 1975; guest condr., soloist Los Angeles Philharm., Boston Symphony, Phila. Orch., N.Y. Philharm.; music dir. South Bank Festival, London, 1978-80, St. Paul Chamber Orch., 1980-87; prin. festival condr. Dallas Internat. Summer Music Festival, 1990—; prin. guest condr. Dallas Symphony, 1993—; toured with Isaac Stern; mem. trio with Daniel Barenboim and Jacqueline du Pre; (rec. artist) CBS, EMI, Philips Classics labels, RCA Victor Red Seal, BMG Classics. Winner Internat. Levintritt Competition, 1967. Office: care Shirley Kirshbaum & Assoc 711 W End Ave Apt 5 Kn New York NY 10025-6843*

ZUKIN, PAUL, retired health research educator; b. L.A., Dec. 26, 1919; s. Ernest Zukin and Lena Victoria Rosenkranz; m. Mary Jane Goldbloom, July 3, 1942; children: Barbara, James Henry, Donald Demetrius. BA in Psychology, UCLA, 1941; MD, U. Calif., San Francisco, 1944; MPH in Med. Care Orgn., UCLA, 1966; postgrad., Harvard U., 1972, Mass. Gen. Hosp.-Harvard U., 1979, Hammersmith Hosp.-U. London, 1980. Diplomate Am. Bd. Internal Medicine. Intern L.A. County Gen. Hosp., 1944-45; resident in internal medicine L.A. County Harbor Gen. Hosp. & Wadsworth VA Hosp., 1947-50; pvt. practice specializing in internal medicine Beverly Hills, Calif., 1950-66; dir. health and human factors Litton Internat. Devel. Corp., Greece and Turkey, 1967-69; dir. health svcs. rsch. and tng. Divsn. Comty. Health Svcs., L.A. County, 1970-74; prof. medicine, preventive medicine and pub. health UCLA, 1970-74; v.p., med. dir. Kaiser Found. Internat., Oakland, Calif., 1974-80; pres. Health Mgmt. Corp., Piemont, Calif., 1980-93; clin. prof. dept. health rsch. and policy Stanford (Calif.) U. Sch. Medicine, 1993—; cons. WHO Health Svcs., Turkey, 1973, Nepal, 1973, Burma, 1973; dir. feasibility study for prepaid health program USAID, South Korea, 1977; med. programmer Dr. Torres Hosp. Devel. Project, Saipan, 1980; dir. Health Comms. Project, Pacific Basin, 1982-91; evaluator rural health improvement project USAID, Niger, 1981;cons. Water Resource Devel. Project, Kitui Province, Kenya, 1982; cons. Taabo Dam Hosp., Ivory Coast, 1975-79; planner, cons. rural primary health care project PAHO/USAID, Brazil, 1972; cons. cost containment, revenue generation and health svcs. improvement, Am. Samoa, 1981-84, numerous other health-related projects for internat. orgns., nat. govts. and pvt. sector. Contbr. numerous articles to profl. jours. and internat. presentations. Capt. U.S. Army M.C., 1945-47. Fellow ACP, APHA, Am. Coll. Preventive Medicine; mem. AMA, Calif. Med. Assn., Greek Med. Assn., Alameda-Contra Costa County Med.

Assn., Soc. for Internat. Devel. (pres. No. Calif. chpt. 1977, 78), Delta Omega.

ZUKOSKI, CHARLES FREDERICK, surgeon, educator; b. St. Louis, Jan. 26, 1926; s. Charles F. Jr. and Bernadine (Edom) Z.; m. Elizabeth Paull Jacob, May 9, 1953; children: Helen, Charles, Robin, Ann. BS, U. N.C., 1947; MD, Harvard U., 1951. Diplomate Am. Bd. Surgery. Intern Roosevelt Hosp., N.Y.C., 1951-52; resident Univ. Hosp., Birmingham, Ala., 1955-58; asst. chief VA Hosp., Birmingham, 1958-59; rschr. Med. Coll. Va., Richmond, 1959-61; asst. prof. Vanderbilt U. Med. Ctr., Nashville, 1961-68; assoc. prof. Coll. Medicine U. N.C., Chapel Hill, 1968-69; prof. surgery Coll. Medicine U. Ariz., Tucson, 1969-95, prof. emeritus dept. surgery Coll. Medicine, 1995—; chief surg. svc. VA Hosp., Tucson, 1990-95. Contbr. 85 articles to profl. publs. Capt. USAF, 1953-55. Fellow NIH, 1959-61, 66-67, Josia Macy Found., 1976-77. Fellow ACS, Am. Surg. Assn.; mem. Soc. Univ. Surgeons, So. Surg. Assn. Achievements include research on immunosuppressive drugs. Home: 1901 E Miraval Cuarto Tucson AZ 85718

ZUKOWSKI, BARBARA WANDA, clinical social work psychotherapist; b. Queens, N.Y., Apr. 30, 1957; d. Stanley F. and Domicille K. (Trzebuchowska) Z. BS in Psychology, Bklyn. Coll., 1984; MSW, NYU, 1986; student, Bklyn. Coll. Conservatory Mus., 1982-84; student classical guitar, Am. Inst. Guitar, N.Y.C., 1982-84, 90—. Lic. social worker, N.Y. Clin. social worker on-site program Staten Island (N.Y.) Children's Community Mental Health Soc., 1986-87; clin. social worker Cath. Charities Diocese of Bklyn., 1984-85, 87-89, N.Y.C. Health & Hosps. Corp., Bklyn., 1989-92; child therapist Program for Devel. Human Potential Office of Cath. Edn., Diocese of Bklyn., 1992—; pvt. practice as dream analyst and psychotherapist, Bklyn., 1989—; developer children's creative arts therapy groups for social work use Cath. Charities Diocese of Bklyn., 1988-89. Singer/songwriter, guitarist, rec. artist, Cosmic Shindig, 1994, Emily, 1996. Music minister Pax Christi Met. N.Y., 1990-94. Mem. NASW, NARAS, BMI. Avocations: singing, songwriting, recording artist, guitarist, cycling. Home: 144 Driggs Ave Apt 3 Brooklyn NY 11222-4202

ZUKOWSKI, WALTER HENRY, administrative science educator; b. Worcester, Mass., Sept. 28, 1914; s. Frank B. and Helen (Jankowska) Z.; m. Lucille Kathryn Pinette, Dec. 26, 1955; 1 dau., Mary L.A. B.B.A., Clark U., 1948, A.M., 1949, Ph.D., 1956. Instr. Worcester Poly. Inst., 1949-50, Clark U., 1951-52; mem. faculty Colby Coll., Waterville, Maine, 1952—; prof. adminstrv. sci. Colby Coll., 1965-73, Wadsworth prof. adminstrv. sci., 1973-82; emeritus Wadsworth prof. adminstrv. sci., 1982—; chmn. dept. adminstrv. sci. Colby Coll., 1958-80; asst. prof. La. State U. (C.Z. br.), summers 1952-54; vis. prof. Rockefeller Found. grantee Al-Hikma U., Baghdad, Iraq, 1958-59, Robert Coll., Istanbul, Turkey, 1965-66; vis. prof., cons. ednl. policy Iranzamin Coll., Tehran, Iran, 1972-73; cons. in field. Mem. platform com. Maine Republican Party, 1964. Served with USAAF, 1942-46. Mem. Am. Finance Assn., Am. Econ. Assn., Am. Accounting Assn. Home: PO Box 402 Waterville ME 04903-0402

ZUKOWSKY, JOHN ROBERT, curator; b. N.Y.C., Apr. 21, 1948; s. John and Mary (Charchan) Z. BA, Hunter Coll., 1971; MA, SUNY, Binghamton, 1974, PhD, 1977. Archtl. archivist Hudson River Mus., Yonkers, N.Y., 1974-76; archtl. archivist Art Inst. Chgo., 1978-81, architecture curator, 1981—; mem. Historic Sites Adv. Council, Springfield, Ill., 1982-83, Landmarks Preservation Council, Chgo., 1982-83; jury mem. Honor awards AIA, Washington, 1987. Co-author: Hudson River Villas, 1985, The Sky's the Limit Chicago Skyscrapers, 1990, Austrian Architecture and Design, 1991; co-author, editor: Mies Reconsidered, 1986, Chicago Architecture: 1872-1922, 1987, Chicago Architecture and Design, 1923-93, 1993, The Many Faces of Modern Architecture, 1994, Karl Friedrich Schinkel, 1781-1841: The Drama of Architecture, 1994, Building for Air Travel: Architecture and Design for Commercial Aviation, 1996; editor: A System of Architectural Ornament (Louis H. Sullivan), 1990; contbr. articles to profl. jours. Decorated Chevalier des arts and lettres (France), Ritter Kreuz 2d class, Austria; recipient Honig award Chgo. chpt. Am. Soc. Appraisers, 1989; postdoctoral rsch. fellow NEH, 1977-78, Rsch. fellow, NEA, 1991. Mem. AIA (hon., Disting. Svc. award Chgo. chpt. 1986), Arts Club Chgo. Office: Art Inst Chgo Dept Architecture 111 S Michigan Ave Chicago IL 60603-6110

ZUKOWSKY, RONALD JAMES, environmental regulator; b. Toronto, Ont., Canada, Dec. 3, 1952; s. James and Lena (Fedirchuk) Z.; m. Donna Lynne Schaefer, June 29, 1985; 1 child, Matthew. BA, York U., 1975; MA, Queens U., 1981, M in Urban and Regional Planning, 1985. Intergovtl. affairs officer Dept. Intergovtl. Affairs, Regina, SK, Canada, 1981-83; constitutional rels. officer Dept. Justice, Regina, 1983-85; social policy analyst Social Policy Secretariat, Regina, 1985-87; dir. policy & legis. svcs. Saskatchewan Consumer & Comml. Affairs, Regina, 1987-90; exec. dir. environ. assessment br. Saskatchewan Environ. & Resource Mgmt., Regina, 1990—. Avocation: skiing. Office: SK Environ & Resource Mgmt Environ Assess Br, 3211 Albert St Rm 142, Regina, SK Canada S4S 5W6

ZULCH, JOAN CAROLYN, retired medical publishing company executive, consultant; b. Great Neck, N.Y., Apr. 10, 1931; d. Walter Howard and Edna Ruth (Howard) Z. B.S. in Biology, Allegheny Coll., 1952; postgrad., Hunter Coll., 1954. Med. sec. E.R. Squibb & Sons, N.Y.C., 1952; with Macmillan Pub. Co., N.Y.C., 1952-88, editorial asst. med. dept., 1952-56, asst. editor med. dept., 1956-58, editor med. dept., 1958-61, med. editor coll. and profl. div., 1961-75, sr. editor medicine, coll. and profl. div., 1975-78, exec. editor med. books, profl. books div., 1978-79, editor-in-chief, 1979-80, asst. v.p., editor-in-chief profl. books div., 1980-82; v.p., pub. med., nursing, health sci. dept. Macmillan Pub. Co., 1982-85, v.p., pub. med. books, sci., tech., med. dept., 1985-88, cons. med. pub., 1989—. Recipient Best Illustrated Med. Book award Assn. Med. Illustrators, 1977, Outstanding Book in Health Sci. award Assn. Am. Pubs., 1982. Mem. AAAS, AAUW, Post Libr. Assn., L.I.U. (rec. sec. 1990-93, exec. coun. 1990—), Friends of Locust Valley Libr. (pres. 1991-93, 94-96, treas. 1993-94, 96—), Alpha Gamma Delta, Delta Sigma Rho. Republican. Home and Office: 36 Wood Ln Lattingtown PO Box 547 Locust Valley NY 11560-0547

ZULKER, CHARLES BATES, broadcasting company executive; b. Pleasantville, N.J., Dec. 20, 1926; s. William John and Virginia (Carr) Z.; m. Virginia Wright, June 24, 1949; children: Connie Lee, Timothy Scott Charles. Adminstrv. officer Princeton (N.J.) U., 1950-60; asst. mgr. Sta. WPEL, Montrose, Pa., 1960-65; gen. mgr. Sta. WCHR, Trenton, N.J., 1965—. Trustee Princeton Evang. Fellowship, 1973-83; bd. council Word of Life Internat., Schroon Lake, N.Y., 1974-82; mem. exec. bd. Upper Makefield Community Assn., 1972-79. With U.S. Army, 1945-46. Mem. Wooden Canoe Heritage Assn. of Am., Nat. Religious Broadcasters, Nat. Assn. of Broadcasters. Office: Woodside Rd Yardley PA 19067

ZUMBRUN, ALVIN JOHN THOMAS, law and criminology educator; b. Balt., Aug. 9, 1926; s. Orrell Sylvester Tilton and Mary Kathryn (Sprinkle) Z.; m. Marianne Jane Nolan, Aug. 26, 1950; children: Mary Susan, Alvin J.T. Jr., Steven M., Diane, MaryAnn, Mary Kathleen. BA, U. Md., 1952, MA, 1956; MEd in Spl. Edn., Coppin State U., 1972, MEd in Adminstrn., 1974; JD, U. Balt., 1970. Probation officer Supreme Bench of Balt., 1950-52; budget and program dir. Cmty. Chest, Balt., 1953-55; mng. dir. Criminal Justice Commn., Balt., 1956-59; exec. dir., criminologist Md. Crime Investigating Com., Balt., 1960-96; dept. chmn., prof. criminal justice Catonsville (Md.) C.C., 1968-94; dept. chmn., dir. grad. program, prof. criminal justice U. Balt., 1974-76; adj. prof. criminal justice U. Md., Hood Coll., Coppin State U., Md. State Police Acad., Balt. County Police Acad., 1969—; mem. adv. bd. U. Balt. Criminal Justice Program, 1976-94; cons. Am. Edn. Assn., Washington, 1980—; mem. senate Catonsville C.C., 1970-83; mem. Nat. Disaster Med. System, 1993—. Author: Maryland Crime Report, 5 vols., 1959-94, Directory of Criminal Justice Agencies, 22 vols., 1962-94, Civil Disturbance Riots of 1968, 69, also rsch. in field. Mem. scholarship com. Md. Troopers Assn., Pikesville, 1990-93; mem. adv. bd. articulation com. U. Md., College Park, 1977-94; lay pres., mem. coun. Salem Luth. Ch., Catonsville, 1956-59, 65-68; pres. Maplewoods Home Owners Assn., 1996-97. Lt. (j.g.) USN, 1943-50. Recipient Superior Pub. Svc. award Afro Am. Newspaper, 1962, Excellence in Teaching award Md. State Bd. C.C.s, 1987, Superior Ednl. Svcs. award Balt. County Police Chief, 1994, Gov.'s citation for ednl. achievements Gov. of Md., 1994, Hon. Trooper 25 Yrs. Acad. Teaching Md. State Police, 1995. Mem. VFW (life), Md. Acad. Criminal Justice Profs. (pres. 1971-94), Internat. Soc. Criminology, Nat. Dist. Attys. Assn., Internat. Assn. Chiefs of Police, Maplewoods Homeowners Assn. (pres. 1995-96). Avocations: walking, biking, family activities, world travel. Home: 438 Maple Forest Rd # 9349 Catonsville MD 21228-0349

ZUMBRUNNEN, DAVID ARNOLD, mechanical engineering educator, consultant; b. Salt Lake City, Sept. 3, 1955; s. Lynn David and Anne Cecilia Z.; m. Elizabeth Buck. B in Mech. Engring., U. Minn., 1977; MS in Mech. Engring., Purdue U., 1984, PhD in Mech. Engring., 1988. Registered profl. engr., Ind., S.C. Rsch. asst. Purdue U., West Lafayette, Ind., 1982-83, rsch. fellow, asst., 1985-88; staff engr. MPR and Assocs., Washington, 1983-85; assoc. prof. Clemson (S.C.) U., 1988-97, prof., 1997—. Lt. USN, 1977-82. Presdl. Faculty fellow The White House/NSF, 1992—. Mem. ASME, AIAA, Soc. of Mfg. engrs., Soc. of Plastics engrs. Avocations: rowing, tennis, jogging, bicycling. Office: Clemson U Dept Mech Engring Clemson SC 29634-0921

ZUMETA, BERTRAM WILLIAM, retired economist; b. Rutherford, N.J., Jan. 18, 1919; s. Arthur H. and Bertha A. (Cook) Z.; m. Ruth Spencer Astbury, Apr. 1, 1943; children: William Mark, David Cook. A.B., Franklin and Marshall Coll., 1940; postgrad., U. Pa., 1946-50, 52-53. Lectr., instr. econs. and stats. Wharton Sch. U. Pa., 1945-51, 53-63; economist Fed. Res. Bank of Phila., 1959-66, Phila. Electric Co., 1966-70; sr. v.p., economist 1st Pa. Bank, 1970-72, asst. to pres., 1972; v.p., economist First Pa. Corp., 1973-74, sr. v.p., economist, 1974-78; exec. v.p., economist First Pa. Bank and First Pa. Corp., Phila., 1978-80; sr. lectr. mgmt. Wharton Sch., U. Pa., 1980-81; bd. govs. Pa. Economy League, 1979-83; mem. U.S. Sec. of Commerce's Econ. Adv. Bd., 1967-68, Pa. Gov.'s Econ. Adv. Coun., 1967-70, 74-76. Served to comdr. USNR, 1942-45, 51-53. Home: 511 Foulkeways Gwynedd PA 19436

ZUMPE, DORIS, ethologist, researcher, educator; b. Berlin, May 18, 1940; came to U.S., 1972; d. Herman Frank and Eva (Wagner) Z. BSc, U. London, 1961, PhD, 1970. Asst. to K.Z. Lorenz, Max-Planck-Inst. für Verhaltensphysiologie, Seewiesen, Fed. Republic Germany, 1961-64; rsch. asst. and assoc., lectr. Inst. Psychiatry, U. London, 1965-72; rsch. assoc. Emory U. Sch. Medicine, Atlanta, 1972-74, asst. prof. psychiatry (ethology), 1974-77, assoc. prof., 1977-87, prof., 1987—; reviewer NSF, 7 sci. jours. Contbr. over 150 articles to profl. jours. NIMH grantee, 1971—. Mem. AAAS, Internat. Soc. Psychoneuroendocrinology, Internat. Primatological Soc., Internat. Soc. for Human Ethology, Soc. for Study of Reprodn., Am. Soc. Primatologists, Soc. Behavioral Neuroendocrinology, N.Y. Acad. Scis., Earl Music Am., Viola da Gamba Soc. Am. Avocation: music. Office: Emory U Sch Medicine Dept Psychiatry Atlanta GA 30322

ZUMWALT, ELMO RUSSELL, JR., retired naval officer; b. San Francisco, Nov. 29, 1920; s. Elmo Russell and Frances Z.; m. Mouza Coutelais-du-Roche; children: Elmo Russell, James Gregory, Ann F., Mouzetta C. B.S. with distinction, U.S. Naval Acad., 1942; student, Naval War Coll., 1952-53, Nat. War Coll., 1961-62; LL.D., Villanova U., 1972, U. N.C., 1975, Nat. U., 1979; L.H.D., U.S. Internat. U., 1973; Dr. Pub. Service, Central Mich. U., 1974; D.Sc., Mich. Tech. U., 1979. Commd. ensign U.S. Navy, 1942, advanced through grades to adm., 1970; served with U.S.S. Phelps, 1942-43, U.S.S. Robinson, San Francisco and South Pacific, 1943-44; exec. officer U.S.S. Saufley, 1945-46; exec. officer, navigator U.S.S. Zellars, 1946-48; asst. prof. naval sci. U. N.C., Chapel Hill, 1948-50; comdg. officer U.S.S. Tills, 1950-51; navigator U.S.S. Wisconsin, Korea, 1951-52; head shore and overseas bases sect. Navy Dept., Washington, 1953-55; comdr. destroyer U.S.S. Isbell, 1955-57; lt. detailer Navy Dept., Washington, 1957; spl. asst. for naval personnel to Asst. Sec. Navy, Washington, 1957-58; exec. asst., sr. aide Office Asst. Sec. Navy, 1958-59; comdr. Frigate U.S.S. Dewey, 1959-61; desk officer for France, Spain and Portugal Office Sec. Def., 1962-63, dir. arms control and contingency planning for Cuba, 1963; exec. asst., sr. aide Sec. of Navy, 1963-65; comdr. Cruiser Destroyer Flotilla, 1965-66; dir. chief naval ops. systems analysis group Washington Office Chief Naval Ops.; dep. sci. officer Center Naval Analyses, 1966-68; comdr. U.S. Naval Forces Vietnam, chief naval adv. group Vietnam, 1968-70; chief naval ops. Washington, 1970-74; pub. gov. Am. Stock Exchange, 1979-85; dir. Transway Internat., Inc., 1976-85, RMI, Inc., 1983-86, Am. Bldg. Maintenance Industries, 1995, Navistar Internat. Corp., Gifford-Hill & Co., Inc., 1979-86, Unicorp Am. Corp., 1994; pres., chief exec. officer, dir. Am. Med. Bldgs., Inc., Milw., 1977-79; vice chmn. bd. Am. Med. Bldgs., Inc., 1980-83, chmn., chief exec. officer, 1983-85, chmn., 1985—; pres. Admiral Zumwalt & Cons., Inc., 1979-86, Admiral Zumwalt & Cons. Inc., 1980—; bd. dirs. NL Industries, Inc. Dallas Semiconductor; vis. prof. Vanderbilt U., 1974-75, U. Nebr., 1975, Whittier Coll., 1975; mem. bd. govs. Am. Stock Exch., 1978-84; chmn. Phelpe-Stokes Fund, 1985-93. Author: On Watch, 1976, My Father My Son, 1986. Dem. candidate for U.S. Senate, 1976; chmn. Nat. Marrow Donor Program, 1988-94, Ethics and Pub. Policy Ctr., 1988—. Decorated D.S.M. with Gold Star, Legion of Merit with Gold Star, Bronze Star with combat V, Navy Commendation medal with combat V; Philippine Republic Presdl. citation; Vietnamese Chuong My medal 1st Class; Nat. Order Vietnam 3d class; Vietnamese Navy Disting. Service Order 1st class. Address: 1000 Wilson Blvd Ste 3105 Arlington VA 22209-3901

ZUMWALT, RICHARD DOWLING, flour mill executive; b. Amarillo, Tex., Dec. 1, 1912; s. Richard Dowling and Cora Bell (Pate) Z.; m. Florine Anita Nelson, Oct. 23, 1938; 1 dau., Alexandra Anita (Mrs. Klaus Schwabe). Extension student, Tex. Tech. Coll., 1931, Dallas Coll., 1949. With J. C. Crouch Grain Co., 1931-44; with Burrus Mills, Inc., Dallas, 1944-83, exec. v.p., 1956-64, pres., 1964-83; sec.-treas. Zumwalt Inc., 1973—; ret. gen. mgr. Burrus milling dept. Cargill, Inc.; past pres. Bulgur Assos., Washington, Dallas Grain Exchange. Mem. Millers Nat. Fedn., Tex. Mfrs. Assn. (past dir.). Home: 7353 Blairview Dr Dallas TX 75230-5416

ZUMWALT, ROGER CARL, hospital administrator; b. Eugene, Oreg., Oct. 26, 1943; s. Robert Walter and Jean Elaine (Adams) Z.; m. Sharon Marlene Ryan, Aug. 22, 1970; children: Kathryn Nicole, Timothy Robert. Student, Boise State U., 1963-65; BA, Western Oreg. State Coll., 1969; postgrad., U. Iowa, 1969-71; MA cum laude, Oreg. State U., 1973. Adminstr. Coulee Cmty. Hosp., Grand Coulee, Wash., 1973-75, Eastmoreland Hosp., Portland, Oreg., 1975-81; hosp. surveyor Am. Osteo. Assn., Chgo., 1977—; exec. dir. Cmty. Hosp., Grand Junction, Colo., 1981—; speaker numerous local and nat. presentations, subjects including healthcare, hosp. mktg./success/costs, 1981—; CEO Cmty. Med. Plz., 1984—, Cmty. Health Care Providers Orgn., 1986—, Cmty. Hosp. Found., 1988—; guest lectr. Mesa Stae Coll., 1993—, Colo. Christian Coll., 1996—. Newspaper columnist, 1973-75; contbr. articles, presentations to profl. publs. Commr. Multnomah County Health Care Commn., Portland, 1978-81; health cons. Grant County Housing Auth., Grand Coulee, 1974-75; mem. pk. bd. City of Tigard, Oreg., 1976-78; caucus rep. Mesa County Rep. Party, Grand Junction, 1988; mem. adv. com., pres.'s office Mesa State Coll., Grand Junction, 1989; bd. dirs. Hospice of Grand Valley, Grand Junction, 1992—, mem. devel. com., 1993—, vice chmn. bd. dirs., 1994—; bd. dirs. Grand Valley Hospice, 1992-96. Fellow Coll. Osteo. Healthcare Execs. (bd. dirs. 1985-88, pres. 1987, examiner 1989—, Disting. Svc. award 1989); mem. Am. Osteo. Healthcare Assn. (bd. dirs. 1987—, treas. 1992-93, 1st v.p. 1994-95, 2d v.p. 1993-94, vice chairperson 1994-95, chmn. 1996-97), Am. Osteo. Assn. (ex-officio mem. bd. dirs.), Bur. Healthcare Facilities Accreditation (v.p. 1994, advisor 1995—), Joint Commn. on Am. Healthcare Orgn. (task force on small and rural accreditation 1994—), Colo. Hosp. Assn. (bd. dirs. 1987-92), Mountain States Vol. Hosp. Assn. (bd. dirs. 1984—, exec. com. 1991—, v.p. 1993, vice chmn. bd. dirs. 1992—), Western Coll. Ind. Practice Assn. (Medicine Mauls Measles com., fin. com. 1991-92), Western Colo. Health Care Alliance (bd. dirs. 1989-94, v.p. 1992, chmn. bd. dirs. 1993, past chmn. bd. dirs. 1994), Mesa County Mental Health Assn. (bd. dirs. 1988-89, 91-92), Grand Junction C. of C. (bd. dirs. 1991-93), Rotary, Masons, Shriners (pres. Grand Junction club 1989, bd. dirs. El Jebel 1986-90, 1st v.p. Western Colo. club 1989). Republican. Methodist. Avocations: golf, camping, fishing, hunting. Home: 892 Quail Run Dr Grand Junction CO 81505 Office: Community Hosp 2021 N 12th St Grand Junction CO 81501-2980

ZUMWALT, ROSS EUGENE, forensic pathologist, educator; b. Goodrich, Mich., July 18, 1943; s. Paul Lawrence and Lila Ann (Birky) Z.; m. Theresa Ann Schar, Sept. 12, 1970 (div. Apr. 1988); children: Christopher Todd, Tenley Ann; m. Cheryl Lynn Willman, Sept. 4, 1988; 1 child, David Willman Zumwalt. BA, Wabash Coll., 1967; MD, U. Ill., 1971. Diplomate in anat. and forensic pathology Am. Bd. Pathology. Intern, resident in pathology Mary Bassett Hosp., Cooperstown, N.Y., 1971-73; resident in anat. and forensic pathology Southwestern Med. Sch., Dallas, 1973-76; asst. med. examiner Dallas County, Dallas, 1974-76; staff pathologist, dir. labs. Naval Regional Med. Ctr., Camp Lejeune, N.C., 1976-78; dep. coroner Cuyahoga County, Cleve., 1978-80, Hamilton County, Cin., 1980-86; assoc. prof. pathology U. Cin. Sch. Medicine, 1980-86; prof. pathology U. N.Mex. Sch. Medicine, Albuquerque, 1987—; chief med. investigator Office of Med. Investigator, Albuquerque, 1991—; trustee Am. Bd. Pathology, Tampa, Fla., 1993—. Lt. comdr. USN, 1976-78. Fellow Am. Acad. Forensic Scis., Coll. Am. Pathologists; mem. AMA, Nat. Assn. Med. Examiners (bd. dirs. 1984—, pres. 1995-96), Am. Soc. Clin. Pathologists, Am. and Can. Acad. Pathologists. Avocation: golf. Office: Office of Med Investigator 700 Camino de Salud Albuquerque NM 87131 Also: 819 El Alhambra Cir NW Albuquerque NM 87107-6301

ZUNDE, PRANAS, information science educator, researcher; b. Kaunas, Lithuania, Nov. 26, 1923; came to U.S., 1960, naturalized, 1964; s. Pranas and Elzbieta (Lisajevic) Z.; m. Alge R. Bizauskas, May 29, 1945; children: Alge R., Audronis K., Aurelia R., Aidis L., Gytis J. Dipl. Ing., Hannover Inst. Tech., 1947; MS, George Washington U., 1965; PhD, Ga. Inst. Tech., 1968. Dir. project Documentation Inc., Bethesda, Md., 1961-64; mgr. mgmt. info. system Documentation Inc., Bethesda, 1964-65; sr. research scientist Ga. Inst. Tech., Atlanta, 1965-68, assoc. prof., 1968-72, prof. dept. computer sci., 1973-91, prof. emeritus, 1991—; cons. UNESCO, Caracas, Venezuela, 1970-72, Esquela Polit. Nacional, Quito, Ecuador, 1974-75, State of Ga., Atlanta, 1976-78, Royal Sch. Librarianship, Copenhagen, 1985-87, Clemson (N.C.) U., 1987—, N.Y. State Dept. Edn., 1993; vis. prof. Simon Bolivar U., Caracas, 1976, J. Kepler U., Austria, 1981; vis. scientist Riso Nat. Lab., Roskilde, Denmark, 1983, Lithuanian Acad. Scis., Vilnius, 1988-89. Author: Agriculture in Soviet Lithuania, 1962, National Science Information Systems in Eastern Europe, 1972; editor: Procs. Info. Utilities, 1974, Procs. Founds. of Info. and Software Sci., 1983-90; contbr. articles to tech. and sci. jours. Mem. senate Vitoldus Magnus U., Kaunas, Lithuania, 1990—. NSF grantee; Fulbright prof. NAS, 1975. Mem. Am. Soc. Info. Sci., Semiotic Soc. Am., Soc. Sigma Xi. Roman Catholic. Office: Ga Inst Tech Coll Computing North Ave Atlanta GA 30332

ZUNG, THOMAS TSE-KWAI, architect; b. Shanghai, China, Feb. 8, 1933; came to U.S., 1937, naturalized, 1954; 1 child, Thomas Bates. Student Drew U., 1950-51, (Rose scholar) Va. Poly. Inst., 1951-53, Columbia U., 1955-57; BArch, U. Mich., 1960; MS in Design Sci. (student R. Buckminster Fuller), Internat. Coll., 1982. Project architect Edward Durell Stone, architect, N.Y.C., 1958, 60-65; architect, Cleve., 1967—; pres. Buckminster Fuller, Sadao and Zung, architects, 1979—; prin. archtl. works include City Cleve. Pub. Utilities Bldg., Cleve. State U. Sports Center Dome, Mayfran, Inc., Sawmill Creek Lodge, U. Akron Guzzetta Hall, music, speech and theater arts center, Alumni Center Bowling Green State U., U. Akron Master Plan-West, City of East Cleveland, Superior Euclid beautification plan, student recreation ctr. at Bowling Green State U., Glenville Public Libr., campus bldg. Tex. Wesleyan Coll., recreation, health and phys. edn. bldg. Wittenberg U., Medina Res. Park Office, arena, health, phys. edn. complex U. Akron, Dyke Coll., Lima State Prison, Cleve. Children's Christian Home, State of Ohio Pre-Release Ctr. Cleve., Lorain-Grafton State Prison, Mayfield High Sch., Asian Village Project, Cleve. Metroparks Tropical Rainforest Bldg., Student Union Wittenberg U., YWCA Salem Ohio, China Internat. Trade Ctr. People's Rep. China, additions to Cleve. Hopkins Internat. Airport, Ohio State U. Coll. of Dentistry-Postle Hall and Hist. Costume and Textile Mus., Columbus, Western Res. Psychiat. Hosp., Ohio, Trumbull State Prison; patentee in field. Task force chmn. Greater Cleve. Growth Assn., 1970; mem. Coun. Human Rels., 1972, Leadership Cleve. Class '77; cubmaster local Boy Scouts Am., 1977-79; bd. dirs. Buckminster Fuller Inst., 1983—, Pearl S. Buck Found., 1989—, hist. house com. Pearl S. Buck House, cons. architect; trustee Pace Assn., 1970-73, Karamu House, 1974-80, Cleve. Inst. Music, 1979—, Ohio Arts Coun., 1982-84, Chinese Cultural Assn., 1980-84; vestryman St. Christopher-by-River, 1980-83. Served with Signal Corps, U.S. Army, 1953-55. Decorated 4 medals; recipient Design award Cleve. chpt. AIA, 1972, Korean Inst. Constrn. Tech., 1984; Anicka Design award U. Mich., 1959, Sr. design prize, 1960; Pub. Works award State of Ohio, 1971, Ohio Valley ABC Design Excellence award Wittenberg U. Student Union, 1989, others. Mem. AIA (dir. Cleve. chpt. 1980, design award 1989), Am. Soc. Planning Ofcls., English Speaking Union (trustee 1972-75), Ohio Soc. Architects, Ohio Assn. Minority Architects and Engrs. (trustee 1982—), Hermit Club, City Club (dir. 1972-74, v.p. 1974), Rotary. Office: Buckminster Fuller Sadao & Zung 13000 Shaker Blvd Cleveland OH 44120-2063

ZUNICH, JANICE, pediatrician, geneticist, educator, administrator; b. New Kensington, Pa., Sept. 2, 1953; d. Nick and Mary (Zivkovich) Z.; m. Milan Katic, June 20, 1981; children: Nikola Ilija, Milana. BS, Ohio State U., 1974, MD, 1978. Diplomate Am. Bd. Pediatrics, Nat. Bd. Med. Examiners, Am. Bd. Med. Genetics (clin. genetics, clin. cytogenetics). Lab. technician Community Hosp., Lorain, Ohio, summer 1974, Ohio State U. Hosp., Columbus, 1974-75; intern then resident in pediatrics Columbus (Ohio) Children's Hosp., 1978-81; genetics fellow Luth. Gen. Hosp., Park Ridge, Ill., 1981-83; asst. prof. pediats. W.Va. U. Med. Ctr., Morgantown, 1983-85, assoc. dir. cytogenetics, 1984-85; clin. assoc. prof. med. genetics, dir. Genetics Ctr. N.W. Ctr. Med. Edn., Ind. U. Sch. Medicine, Gary, 1985—; genetics cons. Community Hosp., Munster, Ind., Porter Meml. Hosp., Valparaiso, Ind., St. Anthony Med. Ctr., Crown Point, Ind., Meth. Hosp., Gary and Merrillville, Ind., St. Margaret Hosp., Hammond, Ind. Contbr. articles to profl. jours. Mem. med. com. Planned Parenthood, N.W.-N.E. Ind., Merrillville, 1987—; mem. adv. com. N.W. Ind. Sickle Cell Found., Gary, 1987—; mem. med. adv. com. Svcs. for Children with Spl. Health Care Needs, Indpls., 1989-92; mem. adv. bd. Parent Edn. Ctr., Whiting, Ind., 1988—. Named Person of Yr., Down Syndrome Assn. N.W. Ind., Highland, 1988; Charles F. Whitten fellow Sickle Cell Found. N.W. Ind., 1990. Fellow Am. Acad. Pediatrics; mem. Am. Soc. Human Genetics, Ind. State Med. Assn., Lake County Med. Soc., Great Lakes Regional Genetics Group (financing. genetics svcs. sub-com. 1988—), Phi Beta Kappa, Alpha Epsilon Delta. Eastern Orthodox. Avocations: piano, folk dancing, choral singing, travel. Office: NW Ctr for Med Edn 3400 Broadway Gary IN 46408-1101

ZUNIGA, FRANCISCO, sculptor, graphic artist; b. San Jose, Costa Rica, Dec. 27, 1912. prof. sculpture and art La Emeralda, Mexico City, 1938-70. Works exhibited at Internat. Art Fair, Basel, Switzerland, 1951, Gallery Modern Art, Scottsdale, Ariz., 1966, Mus. Modern Art, Mexico City, 1969, Phoenix Art Mus., 1972, 74, Nat. Mus. Art, Tokyo, 1974-75, Oakland (Calif.) Mus., 1977; commd. monument State Govt. Morelita, Mex., 1960, monument Adolpho Lopez Mates, Mex., 1960, Allegory to Youth fountain Dept. Pub. Works, Mex., 1964; represented in permanent collections Hirschorn Mus. Sculpture Garden, Washington, Met. Mus., N.Y.C., Mus. Modern Art, N.Y.C., Inst. Nat. Bellas Artes, Mex., Nat. Mus. Modern Art, Kyoto, Japan. Recipient First prize Ann Salon Sculpture, Mex., 1957, first prize sculpture Diego Rivera-2, Internat. Biennial Patinging, 1960. Office: c/o Brewster Gallery 41 W 57th St New York NY 10019-3409*

ZUNKER, RICHARD E., insurance company executive; b. 1938. BS, U. Wis., 1964. With Employers Ins. Wausau, Wis., 1964-69, Northwestern Nat. Investors Life, 1969-75; with Safeco Life Ins. Co., Seattle, 1975—, pres., also bd. dirs. With U.S. Army, 1956-58. Office: Safeco Life Ins Co PO Box 34690 Seattle WA 98124-1690*

ZUNZ, OLIVIER JEAN, history educator; b. Paris, July 19, 1946; s. Jean R. and Monique M. (Blin) Z.; m. Christine M. Crommen, July 3, 1970; children: Emmanuel, Sophie. Licence in history and geography, U. Paris X, 1968, M in History, 1969; Doctorat-ès-Lettres, U. Paris I, Panthéon-Sorbonne, 1982. Scientist Ctr. Nat. de la Recherche Scientifique, Paris, 1976-78; asst. prof. dept. history U. Va., Charlottesville, 1978-83, assoc. prof., 1983-88, prof., 1988—; vis. prof. Ecole des Hautes Etudes en Scis. Sociales, Paris, 1985—, Coll. France, 1997; dir. seminar for Coll. Tchrs. NEH, 1989, 92. Author: The Changing Face of Inequality: Urbanization, Industrial Development, and Immigrants in Detroit, 1980-1920, 1982, Making America Corporate, 1870-1920, 1990; editor, co-author: Reliving the

Past: The Worlds of Social History, 1985; co-editor: (with David Ward) The Landscape of Modernity: Essays on New York City, 1900-1940, 1992; mem. editorial bd. Revs. in Am. History, 1990—; contbr. articles, book revs. to profl. jours. Jr. fellow Mich. Soc. Fellows, 1973-76, John Simon Guggenheim Meml. Found. fellow, 1986-87; grantee U. Mich.-Ford Found. Population Devel. Fund, 1974-76, NSF, 1976-78, NEH, 1979-81, 84-87; also recipient numerous rsch. grants. Mem. Am. Hist. Assn., Orgn. Am. Historians. Home: 1368 Hilltop Rd Charlottesville VA 22903-1225 Office: U Va Dept History Randall Hall Charlottesville VA 22903-3284

ZUPCOFSKA, PETER F., lawyer; b. Boston, Feb. 18, 1952; s. Patrick P. and Josephine M. (Gnoza) Z. BA magna cum laude, Boston Coll., 1973, JD, 1976. Bar: Mass. 1977, U.S. Supreme Ct. 1994. Asst. register Norfolk divsn. Probate and Family Ct., Dedham, Mass., 1976-83; assoc. Burns & Levinson, Boston, 1983-88, ptnr., 1989; of counsel Bingham, Dana & Gould, Boston, 1989-92, ptnr., 1992—; mem. Commonwealth Mass. Dept. Social Svcs. No. Code adv. com., 1986-89; lectr. in field; faculty Flaschner Judicial Inst. Bench Bar Conf., Apr. 1997. Co-author: Motions and Cases in Family Law Trial Advocacy, Family Law Trial Inst.: Problems and Cases, 1992; author: Drafting Documents to Support a Divorce Action, 1994; contbr. chpt. to Massachusetts Family Law Manual, rev. edit., 1996; contbr. articles to profl. jours. Mem. Law and Child Devel. Project Boston Coll., 1974-76; apptd. to Probate and Family Ct. pretrial subcom., 1995—; participant Probate and Family Ct. Lawyer for the Day Project, 1990-96; bd. dirs. Boston Coll. Alumni, 1993-95; mem. Boston Coll. Law Sch. Alumni Coun., 1991-95, Pres. Cir., 1991—, Dean's Coun., 1986—, Leadership Gifts Com., 1987-90, chmn. Alumni Assn. Law Day, 1989, co-chmn. Class 1976 5th Yr., 10th Yr., 15th Yr. Reunion com.; vol. Hole in the Wall Gang Camp, Ashford, Conn., 1991, benefit com., 1992-94; co-chmn. Boston Benefit, 1995, 96. Fellow Mass. Bar Found. (life); mem. ABA (family law sect. 1978—, exec. mem. adoption com. 1982-83, vice-chmn. 1980-82, Merit cert. 1981-83), Mass. Bar Assn. (family law sect. 1983—, co-chmn. Norfolk probate and family ct. bench bar com. 1988-89, Cert Appreciation 1988-89, mem. family law coun. sect., editor News, co-chmn. bench, bar 1996—), Boston Bar Assn. (family law sect. 1989—), Boston Estate Planning Coun., Mass. Continuing Legal Edn. (curriculum adv. com., family law 1990-93, 95-97, chmn. 1997—). Home: 85 Dartmouth St Boston MA 02116-6009 Office: Bingham Dana & Gould LLP 150 Federal St Boston MA 02110

ZUPKO, ARTHUR GEORGE, consultant to drug industry, retired college administrator; b. Yonkers, N.Y., Nov. 22, 1916; s. George and Julia (Tutko) Z.; m. Lillian Belle Cosner, Dec. 20, 1947; 1 child, Arthur Maynard. Student, N.Y. U., 1936-38; B.S., U. Fla., 1942; M.S., Purdue U., 1948, Ph.D., 1949; D.Sc. (hon.), L.I. U., 1979. Research asst. Burroughs Wellcome Co., Tuckahoe, N.Y., 1936-38; asst. prof., assoc. prof., prof. St. Louis Coll. Pharmacy, 1949-55, assoc. dean, 1955, dean, 1956-60; provost Bklyn. Coll. Pharmacy, L.I. U., 1960-73, pres., 1973-76; pres. Arnold and Marie Schwartz Coll. Pharmacy and Health Scis., 1976-79, pres. emeritus, 1979—; bd. dirs. MedPhone, Inc., U.S. Adapted Names, Biofine Pharm.; mem. bd. pharmacy cons. Chas. Pfizer & Co. Author: (with Otto Ruhmer) Contributions of Jews to Pharmacy, 1959, Drug Interactions, 1979; Contbr. articles to profl. jours. Chmn. spl. gifts Bklyn. chpt. Am. Cancer Soc., 1963; solicitor ARC, 1962-63; merit badge counselor Hutchinson-Bronx River council Boy Scouts Am., 1963-64; solicitor United Fund, 1961-65; mem. Narcotic Addiction Centers Com., 1960-65; bd. dirs. Korean-Am. Found., Tb and Respiratory Assn., Bklyn.; mem. spl. com. Cooley's Anemia Found. Served with U.S. Army, 1934-36; Served with USNR, 1942-46. Decorated Bronze Star medal. Fellow Am. Found. Pharm. Edn.; mem. Am. Pharm. Assn. (hon. chmn. bd. trustees 1988), Am. Coll. Apothecaries, N.Y. State Pharm. Soc. (hon. pres.), Kings County Pharm. Soc., N.Y. Acad. Pharmacy, AAAS, N.Y. Acad. Sci., Sigma Xi, Rho Chi, Phi Kappa Phi, Phi Lambda Upsilon, Delta Sigma Theta, Alpha Zeta Omega. Home: 402 Santa Helena Ln Fort Myers FL 33903-1507

ZUPKO, RAMON, composer, music professor; b. Pitts., Nov. 14, 1932; s. Michael E. and Frances E. (Bartek) Z.; m. Vonette Sarche, Sept. 14, 1969; 1 child, Mischa. BS in Music, Juilliard, 1956, MS in Music, 1957. Asst. prof. music Chgo. (Ill.) Musical Coll., 1967-71; prof. music Western Mich. Univ., Sch. Music, Kalamazoo, 1971-97. Recipient composition fellowship Guggenheim Found., 1982, Composers awards Am. Acad. and Inst. of Arts and Letters, N.Y., 1982, Disting. Faculty award Mich. Assn. Governing Bds., Lansing, 1984, Composers awards NEA, Washington, 1978-80, 85, Koussevitzky Found. award 1981, Disting. Faculty scholar award Western Mich. U., 1983, Kennedy-Friedheim award, Washington, 1980. Mem. Am. Composers Alliance, Phi Kappa Phi. Avocations: biking, photography. Home: RR 1 Kalamazoo MI 49009-9801

ZUPSIC, MATTHEW MICHAEL, insurance company executive; b. Pitts., Aug. 30, 1950; s. Joseph Matthew and Antoinette (Birsic) Z.; m. Vicki Jean Quinn, Oct. 8, 1982; children: Tina Elizabeth, Matthew Quay. BA, Marietta Coll., 1972. Mktg. rep. Hartford Ins., Pitts., 1972-76; ins. agt. Githens Ins. Ctr., Belle Vernon, Pa., 1976-77; v.p., ptnr. Burchill Ins. Agy., Inc., Pitts., Pa., 1977-88; pres. Harte, Hawke & Zupsic Ins. Agy., Pitts., Pa., 1989—. Mem. Pa. Assn. Ind. Ins. Agts. (bd. dirs. 1980-88), Ind. Ins. Agts. Pitts. (treas. 1983, 1st v.p. 1984-86, pres. 1986-88), B&S Investment Club (pres 1985-87). Democrat. Roman Catholic. Avocations: sailing, skiing, boating, gardening.

ZURAWSKI, JEANETTE, rehabilitation services professional; b. June 30, 1951. Student, U. Wis., 1969-70, Portland C.C., 1974-78; BS in Chemistry, Portland State U., 1981; MD, Oreg. Health Scis. U., 1985. Diplomate Am. Bd. Phys. Medicine and Rehab. Resident U. Kans. Med. Ctr., Kansas City, 1985-89; med. dir. rehab. svcs. North Miss Med. Ctr., Tupelo, 1989-97; pvt. practice Tupelo, Miss.; mem. adv. com. Medicare Carrier; presenter in field. Past chair pers. com. Big Brothers/Big Sisters, Lee County, Miss., mem. exec. bd., current co-chair fundraising com. Mem. AMA, Am. Acad. Phys. Medicine and Rehab. (chairperson edn. com., mem. exec. coun. resident physician sect.), Am. Med. Women's Assn., Am. Bus. Women's Assn. (chair membership com., treas., recipient Woman of the Year), Miss. State Med. Assn., Assn. Acad. Physiatrists, Iota Sigma Pi. Office: 502 W Eason Blvd Ste E Tupelo MS 38801-6506

ZURHEIDE, CHARLES HENRY, consulting electrical engineer; b. St. Louis, May 9, 1923; s. Charles Henry and Ollie C. (Kirk) Z.; m. Ruth M. Plueck, June 25, 1949; children—Barbara Anne, Pamela S. B.S. in Elec. Engring, U. Mo., Columbia, 1944. Registered profl. engr., Mo. Distbn. engr. Laclede Power & Light Co., St. Louis, 1944-45; sub-sta. engr., then indsl. engr. Union Electric Co., St. Louis, 1945-51; chief elec. engr. Fruin-Colnon Contracting Co., St. Louis, 1951-54; a founder, treas., v.p. Smith-Zurheide, Inc., St. Louis, 1954-65; pres. Zurheide-Herrmann, Inc., St. Louis, 1965—, chmn. bd., 1988—; chmn. Elec. Code Rev. Commn., St. Louis, 1965-96, Mo. Bd. Profl. Engrs., 1977-82, St. Louis Indsl. Devel. Commn., 1965-67; mem. adv. panel region 6 GSA, 1977—; plan commn., City of Ferguson, Mo., 1968-73; tech. adv. com. St. Louis C. of C., 1977. Recipient Distinguished Service in Engring. award U. Mo., 1976. Fellow Am. Cons. Engrs. Council; mem. Mo. Soc. Profl. Engrs. (Engr. of Year award 1970), Cons. Engrs. Council Mo., IEEE, Illuminating Engring. Soc., Engrs. Club St. Louis, Tau Alpha Pi. Clubs: Norwood Hills Country, Mo. Athletic. Home: 25 Lake Pembroke Dr Saint Louis MO 63135-1210 Office: Zurheide-Herrmann Inc 4333 Clayton Ave Saint Louis MO 63110-1621

ZURICK, JACK, electrical engineer; b. Bklyn., May 28, 1952; s. Joseph and Edelgard (Wendland) Z.; m. Nenita Cardinal, Apr. 28, 1990. Pre-engring student, Queensborough Community Coll., 1969-71, AAS, 1971-73. Cert. Assoc. Engring. Technician. Elec. designer Ebasco Svcs., Inc., N.Y.C., 1973-76; design engr. Gibbs & Cox, Inc., N.Y.C., 1976-78; elec. designer Sci. Design Co., Inc., N.Y.C., 1978-85; design engr. Vikonics, Inc., Secaucus, N.J., 1985-87; sr. elec. designer H-R Internat., Inc., Edison, N.J., 1988-93; sr. elec. engr. Kleinknecht Elec. Co. of N.J., Maplewood, N.J., 1993-94; cons. Rotator Svcs., Inc., East Brunswick, N.J., 1994-95; elec. design engr. ICF Kaiser Engrs., Inc., Iselin, N.J., 1995-97; sr. elec. designer Fluor Daniel, Inc., Marlton, N.J., 1997—; cons. Sherman Svcs., Inc., Somerset, N.J., 1988, Gen. Indsl. Techs., Inc., Valleystream, N.Y., 1987-88. Mem. Nat. Inst. for Cert. Engring. Technols. (assoc. engring. technician), Tau Alpha Pi (v.p. 1972-73). Avocations: music, guitar, electronics, scuba diving, golf. Home: 59 Pheasant Run Freehold NJ 07728-7767 Office: Fluor Daniel Inc 301 Lippincott Dr Marlton NJ 08053-4151

ZURIER, ROBERT BURTON, medical educator, clinical investigator; b. Passaic, N.J., Feb. 19, 1934; s. Milton and Lillian (Matzner) Z.; m. Catherine Elizabeth Miers, June 3, 1962; 1 child, Adam Wheaton. BS, Rutgers U., 1955; MD, U. Tex. Southwestern Med. Ctr., Dallas, 1962; MA (hon.), U. Pa., 1981. Intern, then resident in medicine Boston City Hosp., 1962-64; fellow in medicine St. Lukes Hosp., N.Y.C., 1964-66; fellow in rheumatology NYU, 1970-73; pvt. practice internal medicine Holden, Mass., 1967-70; asst. prof. medicine U. Conn., Farmington, 1973-76, assoc. prof., 1976-80; prof., chief. rheumatology U. Pa., Phila., 1980-91; prof. medicine, dir. rheumatology div. U. Mass. Med. Ctr., Worcester, 1991—. Served to capt. USAR, 1956-68. Guggenheim Found. fellow, 1986. Mem. AAAS, Am. Coll. Rheumatology, Am. Soc. Clin. Investigation, Interurban Clin. Club (pres. 1989-90). Office: U Mass Med Ctr 55 Lake Ave N Worcester MA 01655-0002

ZURKOWSKI, PAUL GEORGE, information company executive; b. Milw., Nov. 8, 1932; s. Stanley Frank and Martha (Bednarz) Z.; m. Margaret Ann Becker, July 9, 1960; children: Paul Coleman, Pamela Carol, Patricia Christine, Peggy Catherine, Paula Claire, Peter Christopher. B.A., U. Wis., Whitewater, 1954; LL.B., U. Wis., Madison, 1957. Bar: Wis. 1957, U.S. Supreme Ct. 1961. Publisher Our Ads (shopping guide), Palmyra, Wis., 1950-55; investigator legal firm Swingen & Stern, Madison, 1955-58; atty. HHFA, Washington, 1958; examiner ICC, 1958-59; congl. legis. asst., 1959-61, 64-69; individual legal practice, also congl. home sec. Madison, 1961; exec. dir. Info. Industry Assn., Washington, 1969; pres. Info. Industry Assn., 1972-89, Ventures in Info., Chevy Chase, Md., 1989—; bd. dirs. Herner & Co. Pub. Holy Redeemer News, 1984-87, Today's Parish, 1987-90, Our Parish Times, 1990—, Family Beach Times, 1995—, Interparish Community Guide and Business Directory, 1997; editor Chatter, Rock Creek Coun., KC, 1993—. Pres. Parish Cmty. Svcs. Inc., Md., 1991—; founder, lifetime mem. Cath. Bus. Network, 1993, past pres., 1993-94, sec., 1994-96, edn. v.p., 1996—. Served with AUS, 1957, officer USAR, 1961-64. Decorated Army Commendation medal; recipient Disting. Alumni Svc. award U. Wis., Whitewater, 1974, Outstanding Svc. award, CNB, 1994; named to Info. Industry Hall of Fame, 1988. Office: 8027 Ellingson Dr Chevy Chase MD 20815-3029

ZUSPAN, FREDERICK PAUL, obstetrician, gynecologist, educator; b. Richwood, Ohio, Jan. 20, 1922; s. Irl Goff and Kathryn (Speyer) Z.; m. Mary Jane Cox, Nov. 23, 1943; children: Mark Frederick, Kathryn Jane, Bethany Anne. BA, Ohio State U., 1947, MD, 1951. Intern Univ. Hosps., Columbus, Ohio, 1951-52; resident Univ. Hosps., 1952-54; resident Western Res. U., Cleve., 1954-56, Oblebay fellow, 1958-60, asst. prof., 1958-60; chmn. dept. bo-gyn. McDowell (Ky.) Meml. Hosp., 1956-58, chief clin. svcs., 1957-58; prof., chmn. dept. ob-gyn. Med. Coll. Ga., Augusta, 1960-66; Joseph Boliver DeLee prof. ob-gyn., chmn. dept. U. Chgo., 1966-75; obstetrician, gynecologist in chief Chgo. Lying-In Hosp., 1966-75; prof., chmn. dept. ob-gyn. Ohio State U., Columbus, 1975-87, R.L. Meiling prof. ob-gyn. Sch. Medicine, 1984-90, prof. emeritus, 1991—. Founding editor Lying In, Jour. Reproductive Medicine; editor-in-chief Am. Jour. Ob-Gyn. and Ob-Gyn. Reports, (with Lindheimer and Katz) Hypertension in Pregnancy, 1976, Current Developments in Perinatology, 1977, (with Quilligan) Operative Obstetrics, 1981, 89, Manual of Practical Obstetrics, 1981, 90, Clin. and Exptl. Hypertension in Pregnancy, 1979-86, (with Rayburn) Drug Therapy in Ob-Gyn., 1981, 3rd edit., 1992; editor: (with Christian) Controversies in Obstetrics and Gynecology; contbr. articles to med. jours., chpts. to books. Pres. Barren Found., 1974-76. With USNR, 1942-43; 1st lt. USMCR, 1943-45. Decorated DFC, Air medal wth 10 oak leaf clusters. Mem. Soc. Gynecol. Investigation, Chgo. Gynecol. Soc., Am. Assn. Ob-Gyn., Columbus Ob-Gyn. Soc. (pres. 1984-85), Am. Acad. Reproductive Medicine (pres.), Am. Coll. Obstetricians and Gynecologists, Assn. Profs. of Gynecology and Obstetrics (pres. 1972), South Atlantic Assn. Obstetricians and Gynecologists (Found. prize for rsch. 1962), Ctrl. Assn. Ob-Gyn. (cert. of merit, rsch. prize 1970), Am. Soc. Clin. Exptl. Hypnosis (exec. sec. 1968, v.p. 1970), Soc. Gynecol. Investigation, Internat. Soc. Study of Hypertension in Pregnancy (pres. 1981-83), Am. Gynecology and Obstetrics Soc. (pres. 1986-87), Soc. Perinatal Obstetrics, Perinatal Rsch. Soc., Sigma Xi, Alpha Omega Alpha, Alpha Kappa Kappa. Home: Upper Arlington 4280 Llansfair Ct Columbus OH 43221 *The strength of our nation rests in the quality of our offspring. Every fetus has the privilege of being wellborn.*

ZUSY, CATHERINE, curator; b. Washington, May 4, 1958; d. Frederick John and Mary Jane (Lloyd) Z.; m. Samuel Conant Kendall, Sept. 6, 1992. BA, Bucknell U., 1981; MA in History Mus. Studies, SUNY, Oneonta, 1984. Curator of edn. Deland (Fla.) Mus., 1981-82; asst. curator State Capital Pub. Mus., Guthrie, Okla., 1982-83; rsch. asst., dept. Am. decorative arts Mus. Fine Arts, Boston, 1985-87; curator decorative arts The Bennington (Vt.) Mus., 1988-91; chief curator N.H. Hist. Soc., Concord, N.H., 1991-95; lectr. L.A. County Mus. Arts, M. H. de Young Mus., San Francisco, Mus. Fine Arts, Boston, others. Prin. author: Highlights from the Bennington Museum, 1989; author: Norton Stoneware and American Redware: The Bennington Museum Collection, 1992; contbr. author to catalogues; contbr. articles to profl. jours. Sec. N.H. Visual Arts Coalition, 1992-94; mem. steering com. N.H. Save Outdoor Sculpture, 1992-94; mem. selection com. N.H. % for Art Program, 1994-95. Hist. Deerfield Summer fellow, 1981, Nat. Mus. Act and Norse Found. fellow, 1983-84, Louise du Pont Crowninshield Rsch. fellow Winterthur Mus., 1990; grantee Am. Ceramic Cir., 1993-95; recipient Charles F. Montgomery award Decorative Arts Soc., 1993.

ŽUŽUL, MIOMIR, government official, psychologist, educator; b. Split, Croatia, Yugoslavia, June 19, 1955; s. Ivan and Agata Ž.; m. Tatjana Bradvica, Oct. 8, 1978; children: Ivana, Tiona, Mihovil, Andrija. BA, U. Zagreb, Yugoslavia, 1979, MA, 1983, PhD, 1987. Sch. psychologist Imotski High Sch., Yugoslavia, 1978-79; asst. U. Zagreb, 1979-82, research asst. dept. psychology, 1983-87, asst. prof., 1987—; ambassador to UN Republic of Croatia, 1994—. Yugoslavian rep. Psychologists for Peace, 1986—. Mem. European Assn. for Personality Psychology, Am. Psychol. Assn. (affiliated). Home: Lea Rukavine 12, Zagreb Yugoslavia 41000 Office: Embassy of Republic of Croatia 2343 Massachusetts Ave NW Washington DC 20008-2853

ZVETINA, JAMES RAYMOND, pulmonary physician; b. Chgo., Oct. 14, 1913; s. John and Jennie (Albrecht) Z.; m. Florence Courtney, Feb. 4, 1944. BS, Loyola U., 1940; MD, U. Ill., 1943. Intern West Suburban Hosp., Oak Park, Ill., 1944, resident physician, 1944-45; asst. ward med. officer USNH, NOB, Norfolk, Va., 1945; staff physician Pulmonary TB Svc. VA Med. Hosp., Hines, Ill., 1946-54; asst. chief Pulmonary Svc. VA Med. Hosp., Hines, Ill., 1954-68, sect. chief, 1968-88, attending physician, 1988-91, cons., 1992—; clin. prof. medicine Coll. Medicine, U. Ill., Chgo., 1978—; mem. adv. bd. Coll. Medicine, U. Ill., 1985—; rep. Rsch. Conf. in Pulmonary Disease, VA Armed Forces, 1946-74. Contbr. articles to profl. jours. V.p. Chgo. Cath. Physicians, 1979, pres., 1978. Comdr. USNR, 1945-46, med. officer USNR, ret. Recipient Svc. award 40 Yrs. VA Adminstrn., 1985, Svc. award 30 Yrs. U. Ill. Med. Sch., 1978. Fellow Am. Coll. Chest Physicians; mem. AMA, Ill. State Med. Soc. (Fifty Yr. club), Chgo. Med. Soc., Third Order of St. Dominic. Roman Catholic. Achievements include research in area of pulmonary infections. Home: 96 Forest Ave Riverside IL 60546-1977 Office: VA Hines Hines IL 60141

ZWAHLEN, FRED CASPER, JR., journalism educator; b. Portland, Oreg., Nov. 11, 1924; s. Fred and Katherine (Meyer) Z.; m. Grace Eleanor DeMoss, June 24, 1959; children: Molly, Skip. BA, Oreg. State U., 1949; MA, Stanford U., 1952. Reporter San Francisco News, 1949-50; acting editor Stanford Alumni Rev., Palo Alto, Calif., 1950; successively instr. journalism, news bur. asst., prof. journalism, chmn. journalism dept. Oreg. State U., Corvallis, 1950-91, prof. emeritus, 1991—; Swiss tour guide, 1991—; corres. Portland Oregonian, 1950-67. Author: (with others) Handbook of Photography, 1984. Coord. E.E. Wilson Scholarship Fund, 1964—; active budget com. Corvallis Sch. Dist., 1979. Recipient Achievement award Sch. Journalism U. Oregon, 1988. Mem. Assn. for Edn. in Journalism and Mass Communications (conv. chmn. 1983, pres.' award 1988), Oreg. Newspaper Pubs. Assn. (bd. dirs. 1980-85, student loan fund named in his honor 1988), Soc. Profl. Journalists (nat. svc. citation 1988), Corvallis Country Club, Shriners, Masons, Elks, Moose, Eagles, Delta Tau Delta. Republican. Presbyterian. Avocations: photography, sightseeing, travel. Home: 240 SW 7th St Corvallis OR 97333-4551 Office: Oreg State U Dept Student Activities Corvallis OR 97331

ZWAIN, ISMAIL HASSAN, molecular endocrinologist; b. Kufa, Iraq, July 1, 1951; arrived in U.S., 1988; s. Hassan and Amona (Hussein) Z. DVM, U. Baghdad, Iraq, 1973; MSc, U. Bordeaux, France, 1980; PhD, U. Caen, France, 1983, DSc, 1988. Reproductive endocrinologist U. Baghdad, 1973-78; post doctoral fellow U. Caen, 1983-87; reproductive biologist The Population Coun., N.Y.C., 1988-94; molecular endocrinologist reproductive medicine Sch. of Medicine U. Calif., San Diego, 1994—. Contbr. articles to profl. jours. Mem. AAAS, Am. Soc. Andrology, Endocrine Soc., Am. Fertility Soc., Soc. for Study of Reproduction, Am. Soc. Cell Biology. Office: U Calif-San Diego Reproductive Medicine-Sch Medicine 9500 Gilman Dr La Jolla CA 92093-5003

ZWANGER, JEROME, physician; b. N.Y.C., Apr. 4, 1923; s. Benjamin and Evelyn Z.; m. Bernice E. Lomazov, May 22, 1955; children: Susan, Roberta, Melissa, Betsy. AB, U. Pa., 1943; MD, Chgo. Med. Sch., 1947. Diplomate Am. Bd. Radiology. Intern Wyckoff Heights Hosp., Bklyn., 1947-49; resident L.I. Coll. Hosp., Bklyn., 1949-52; practice medicine specializing in radiology; asst. dir. dept. radiology L.I. Coll. Hosp., N.Y., 1953-54; radiologist L.I. Jewish Hosp., 1955-60; dir. radiology Cen. Gen. Hosp., Plainview, N.Y., 1961—, also bd. dirs.; asst. prof. clin. radiology SUNY, Stony Brook, 1974-80. Bd. dirs. Nassau Physicians Rev. Orgn., 1975-78; governing bd. Nassau-Suffolk Health Systems Agy.; mem. N.Y. State Bd. Medicine. Mem. vis. com. Met. Mus. Art, Phila. Art Mus.; bd. overseers Sch. Arts and Scis., U. Pa. Fellow Am. Coll. Radiology (councilor 1975—), Nassau Acad. Medicine (founder); mem. AMA, Med. Soc. N.Y., Nassau County Med. Soc. (pres.), Radiol. Soc. N.Am., N.Y. State Radiol. Soc. (pres. 1986-87), L.I. Radiol. Soc. (past pres.), U. Pa. Alumni Assn. (trustee 1977—). Office: 126 Hicksville Rd Massapequa NY 11758-5822

ZWASS, VLADIMIR, computer scientist, educator; b. Lvov, USSR, Feb. 3, 1946; came to U.S., 1970, naturalized, 1979; s. Adam and Friderike (Getzler) Z.; m. Alicia Kogut, Apr. 24, 1977; 1 child, Joshua Jonathan. MS, Moscow Inst. Energetics, 1969; MPhil, Columbia U., 1974, PhD, 1975. Mem. profl. staff IAEA, Vienna, Austria, 1970; asst. prof. computer sci. Fairleigh Dickinson U., Teaneck, N.J., 1975-79, assoc. prof., 1979-84, prof., 1984—, prof. computer sci. and mgmt. info. sys., 1990—, chmn. com. computer sci., 1976—; cons. U.S. Govt., Met. Life Ins. Co., Citibank, Diebold Group; seminar assoc. Columbia U., 1986—; speaker nat. and internat. meetings. Author: Introduction to Computer Science, 1981, Programming in Fortran, 1981, Programming in Pascal, 1985, Programming in Basic, 1986, Management Information Systems, 1992; editor-in-chief Jour. Mgmt. Info. Sys., 1983—, Internat. Jour. Electronic Commerce, 1996—; contbr. articles to profl. jours. and publs., Ency. Britannica, N.Y. Times, chpts. to books. Columbia U. fellow, 1970-71; Helena Rubinstein Found. scholar, 1971-75; grantee USN, other agys. Mem. IEEE, Assn. Computer Machinery, Assn. for Info. Sys., Sigma Xi, Eta Kappa Nu. Home: 19 Warewoods Rd Saddle River NJ 07458 Office: Sch Computer Sci and Info Sys Fairleigh Dickinson U Teaneck NJ 07666

ZWEBEN, MURRAY, lawyer, consultant; b. Elizabeth, N.J., May 9, 1930; s. Jacob and Anna (Katz) Z.; m. Elaine Tinkelman, Nov. 22, 1950 (div. Apr. 1974); children: M. Lisa, Marc Samuel, John Eric, Harry T.; m. Anne Waggoner, Apr. 23, 1974; 1 child, Suzanne Grady. BS, Albany (N.Y.) State U., 1952, MS, 1953; LLB, George Washington U., 1959. Sec. to parliamentarian U.S. Senate, Washington, 1956-59, asst. parliamentarian, 1963-75, parliamentarian, 1975-81, parliamentarian emeritus, 1983—; law clk. U.S. Claims Ct., Washington, 1959-60; atty. Columbia Gas Systems, N.Y.C., 1960-63; pvt. practice, Washington, 1981-84; cons. atty. Nossaman, Guthmar, Knox & Elliott, Washington, 1984-86, of counsel, 1986-, Elliott, Zweben & Steelman, Washington, 1986-90, Elliott & Zweben, Washington, 1990-96. Lt. USN, 1953-56. Avocation: tennis. Home: 4010 Highwood Ct NW Washington DC 20007-2131 Office: The Homer Bldg #370 S 601 13th St NW Washington DC 20005-3807

ZWEBEN, STUART HARVEY, information scientist, educator; b. Bronx, N.Y., Apr. 21, 1948; s. Max D. and Ruth (Schwartz) Z.; m. Rochelle T. Small, June 13, 1971; 1 child, Naomi. BS, CUNY, 1968; MS, Purdue U., 1971, PhD, 1974. Systems analyst IBM Corp., Kingston, N.Y., 1969-70; asst. prof. Ohio State U., Columbus, 1974-80, from vice chmn. to acting chmn. computer sci. dept., 1982-84, assoc. prof., 1980-92, prof., 1992—; chmn. Ohio State U., 1994—; pres. Computing Scis. Accreditation Bd., Stamford, Conn., 1989-91, v.p. 1987-89, sec.-treas. 1986-87; sec.-treas. Fedn. on Computing in the U.S., Washington, 1992. Contbr. articles to profl. jours. Rsch. grantee NSF, 1981-83, 88-90, 91-93, 93-97, Army Rsch. Office, 1980-83, Dept. Edn., 1983-85, Applied Info. Tech. Rsch. Ctr., 1990-91; equipment grantee AT&T Bell Labs, 1984, 86-88. Mem. AAUP, IEEE Computer Soc. (assoc. editor 1990—), Assn. for Computing Machinery (pres. 1994-96, v.p. 1992-94, coun. mem. 1982-88, chpt. bd. chmn. 1982-85, publications bd. 1988-92, fin. com. 1990-92, constn. and bylaws chmn. 1988-92, Recognition of Svc. award 1980, 85, 87, 88), Computing Rsch. Assn. (bd. dirs. 1997—). Avocations: sports, philately. Office: Ohio State U Computer Scis 2015 Neil Ave Columbus OH 43210-1210

ZWECK, RUTH EDNA FEENEY, human services administrator, psychiatric nurse; b. N.Y.C., Apr. 22, 1935; d. Archibald Thomas and Edna Marie (Kaht) Collins; married; children: Donald C., Diane C., Scott C., Michael C., Thomas C. BSN, Columbia U., 1957; MS in Mental Health Counseling, L.I. Univ., 1984. RN, N.Y., N.J., Nev.; cert. psychiat. and mental health nursing, ANA. Psychiat. nurse St. Dominic's Home, Blauvelt, N.Y., 1975-76; sch. nurse, tchr. Bergen County (N.J.) Sch. Systems, 1974-78; night supr. Rockland Children's Psychiat. Ctr., Orangeburg, N.Y., 1978-79; admission and referral coord. Rockland Children's Psychiat. Ctr., Orangeburg, 1979-85; treatment team leader Rockland Psychiat. Ctr., Orangeburg, 1985-91, treatment plan coord., 1991-92; clin. nurse coord. partial hospitalization program Montevista Hosp., Las Vegas, 1993-95; nurse clinician Mojave Mental Health Svcs., Las Vegas, 1995—; mem. adv. bd. Dominican Coll. Sch. Nursing, Blauvelt, 1986-92. Mem. Honor Soc. of Nursing (exec. bd. 1987-89), Sigma Theta Tau Internat. Avocations: tennis, hiking, sewing, cooking.

ZWECKER, WILLIAM RENE, JR. (BILL ZWECKER), newspaper columnist, television reporter; b. Chgo., Dec. 25, 1949; s. William Rene and Margaret Rishel (Bushee) Z.; m. Deborah Heidrich Bunn Alley, Sept. 1, 1973 (div. July 1977); 1 child, Brayton. AB in History cum laude, Princeton U., 1971. Legis. asst. U.S. Senator Charles Percy, Washington, 1971-73; asst. officer First Nat. Bank of Chgo., 1973-75; adminstrv. v.p. Krancer & Frank, Inc., Chgo., 1975-77; pres. Animal Accents, Inc., Chgo., 1977-83; mgr. Saks Fifth Ave, Chgo. and Oak Brook, Ill., 1983-86; regional v.p. BMW (N) Holding Corp., Chgo., 1986-87; assoc. editor, columnist Lerner Newspapers, Chgo., 1987-92; columnist Chgo. Sun-Times, 1992—; corr. The Joan Rivers Show, N.Y.C., 1990-94; host, producer Cast of Characters, Group W Cable TV, Chgo., 1988-90; entertainer reporter, film critic WMAQ-TV, NBC, Chgo., 1994—, WPNT-FM Radio, Chgo., 1993-95. Author numerous articles on lifestyle, fashion, travel in Chgo. Daily News, Crain's Chgo. Bus., Town and Country, Chgo., others. Bd. dirs. Greater N. Michigan Ave Assn., Chgo., 1980-85, Mental Health Assn. Greater Chgo., 1983-88; founding bd. dirs. Aux. bd. Lincoln Park Zoo, Chgo., 1979-89. Recipient Tradition of Excellence alumni awrd Oak Park-River Forest H.S., 1995, Peter Lisagor award in journalism, 1991. Mem. Sco. Profl. Journalists (bd. dirs. 1992-94), North Dearborn Assn. (bd. dirs. 1993—), Rotary Club of Chgo. Episcopalian. Office: Chgo Sun-Times 401 N Wabash Ave Chicago IL 60611-5642

ZWEIBEL, JOEL BURTON, lawyer; b. N.Y.C., Feb. 7, 1935; s. Jacob and Ruth (Fleischner) Z.; m. Lynn Herzog (dec. Nov. 1984); children: Jane, Emily; m. Chrystine Marie Trichter. BBA, CCNY, 1955; LLB, Yale U., 1958. Bar: N.Y. 1959. Ptnr. Kaye, Scholer, Fierman, Hays & Handler, N.Y.C., 1969-79, Gelberg & Kronovet, N.Y.C., 1979-81, Kramer, Levin, Nessen, Kamin & Frankel, N.Y.C., 1981-90, O'Melveny & Myers, N.Y.C., 1990—; lectr. 2d Ann. Uniform Comml. Code Law Inst., 1968. Author:

Creditors' Rights Handbook, 1980; co-author: Herzog's Bankruptcy, 6th edit., 1980; contbr. articles to profl. jours. Recipient award Bankruptcy and Reorgn. div. Fedn. United Jewish Appeal, 1989. Mem. ABA, Assn. of Bar of City of N.Y. (chmn. com. on bankruptcy and corp. reorgn. 1981-84), Nat. Bankruptcy Conf. (chmn. com. on avoiding powers 1983—, mem. exec. com., treas. 1991—), Am. Coll. Bankruptcy (dir., regent 2d cir.), Beta Gamma Sigma. Avocations: art, theatre, music, photography, tin whistle. Office: O'Melveny & Myers 153 E 53rd St New York NY 10022-4611

ZWEIFEL, DAVID ALAN, newspaper editor; b. Monroe, Wis., May 19, 1940; s. Cloyence John and Uva Lorraine (Skinner) Z.; m. Sandra Louise Holz, Sept. 7, 1968; children: Daniel Mark, Kristin Lynn. BJ, U. Wis., 1962. Reporter The Capital Times, Madison, Wis., 1962-71, city editor, 1971-78, mng. editor, 1978-83, editor, 1983—. V.p. Alliance for Children and Youth, Madison, 1983—; bd. dirs. United Cerebral Palsy Dane County, Madison, 1984-91. Lt. U.S. Army, 1963-65; col. USNG, ret. Named Investigative Reporter of Yr. Madison Press Club, 1972. Mem. Am. Soc. Newspaper Editors (com. freedom info.), Wis. AP (pres. 1987-88), Wis. Freedom Info. Coun. (pres. 1986—), Soc. Profl. Journalists (spl. achievement award 1992), Wis. N.G. Assn. (trustee 1975-81), U. Wis. Alumni Assn., Elks. Avocations: running, bowling, book collecting. Home: 5714 Tecumseh Ave Monona WI 53716-2964 Office: The Capital Times PO Box 8060 Madison WI 53708-8060

ZWEIFEL, DONALD EDWIN, civic affairs volunteer, consultant; b. L.A., Nov. 30, 1940; s. Robert Fredrick and Eugenia Bedford (White) Z.; m. Donna Jean Croslin; 1 son, Phillip Matthew. Student, Orange Coast Coll., 1963-67, 90-92, U. Calif., Irvine, 1968-70, Western State U. Coll. Law, 1973, Irvine U. Coll. Law, 1974-75, Rancho Santiago Jr. Coll., 1988, Chapman U., 1989, 93—; grad., Aviation Ground Sch., 1990; student, USAF Air U., 1994-95. Cert. Student Pilot, 1989. Devel. tech. Hughes Aircraft, Newport Beach, Calif., 1963-64; co-founder Sta. KUCI-FM, Irvine, Calif., 1970; owner, mgr. Zweifel Jaguar Car Sales and Svc., Santa Ana, Calif., 1975-76; pres. Zweifel & Assocs. Inc., Santa Ana, 1977-86; pres. Zweifel South Coast Exotic Cars, Orange, Calif., 1987-96, ret., 1996. Co-author: Challenge 2000, Regaining the America's Cup, 1996; editor: (coll. textbook) The Dream Is Alive, Space Flight and Operations In Earth Orbit. Vol. emergency coord. emergency mgmt. div. Orange County Fire Dept., 1985-87, Navy Relief Soc., 1993, CAP Squadron, 1993-95, sr. programs officer, 1993-94, asst. transp. officer Calif. Wing Hdqrs., 1994-95, Group VII Facilities officer, 1994-95, squadron pers. officer, 1993-95, Calif. wing rep. to Orange County Vol. Orgns. Active in Disaster, ARC, 1994-95, Calif. wing vol. Office Emergency Svcs., Calif., 1994-96, grad. Squadron Leadership Sch., 1993, Wing Supply Officers Sch., 1995; program coord. Young Astronaut Coun., 1989-90; cadet CAP, USAF auxiliary, Long Beach, Calif., 1953-60; mem. Orange County Homeless Issues Taskforce, 1994-95, 1997—, Orange County Homeless Svc. Providers for the Reuse of Marine Corps Air Sta., Tustin, Calif., 1994-95; mem. restoration adv. bd., chmn. operable unit # 1 subcom. Marine Corps Air Sta., El Toro, Calif., 1994—; apptd. to CalEPA DTSC Adv. Group Mil. Base Closure, 1995—, CalEPA Dept. Toxics & Substances Control Adv. Group rep. Orange County Citizen's Adv. Commn. and El Toro Local Redevel. Authority, 1996—; vol. mediator Victim-Offender Reconciliation program, 1995—; mem. So. Calif. Vol. Orgns. Active in Disaster, restoration adv. bd. MCAS Tustin, 1994—. With Army N.G., 1958-59. Recipient 6 certs. achievement Fed. Emergency Mgmt. Agy., 1989-96, 2 certs. appreciation CAP, 2 certs commendation, 1994. Mem. Air Force Assn. (vice-chmn. civilian recruitment Calif. state membership com. 1988-89, 90-91, v.p. membership, Gen. Doolittle chpt. bd. dirs. 1987-89, 90-92, Exceptional Svc. award Gen. Jimmy Doolittle chpt. 1988, 91, Calif. Meritorious Svc. award 1988), Calif. Assn. for Aerospace Edn. (fellow), Marine Corps Hist. Found. (life), Aerospace Edn. Found. (Gen. Jimmy Doolittle fellow 1988, Gen. Ira Eaker fellow 1989, Pres.'s award 1988), U.S. Naval Inst., AIAA (Cert. of Appreciation 1989, L.A. chpt. hist. com. 1989), Marine Corps Assn. (assoc.), Navy League, Gulf & Vietnam Vet. Hist. and Strategic Studies Assn. (cons., co-founder, trustee 1983—, exec. dir.), Am. Def. Preparedness Assn., Exptl. Aircraft Assn., Assn. of Old Crows, U.S. Marine Corps Combat Correspondents Assn. (affiliate), Confederate Air Force (col. 1989, adj. 1st Composite Group detachment 1989), Aircraft Owners and Pilots Assn., World Affairs Coun. Orange County, Free and Accepted Masons Orange Grove Lodge. Avocations: sailing, bicycle racing, traveling, flying. Home and Office: Gulf & Vietnam Vets and Strategic Studies Hist Assn 2110 W Larkspur Dr Orange CA 92868-3423

ZWEIFEL, RICHARD GEORGE, curator; b. L.A., Nov. 5, 1926; s. Harold Charles and Kathleen Marguerite (Garland) Z.; m. Frances Ann Wimsatt, July 30, 1956; children: Matthew Karl, Kenneth Paul, Ellen Katrina. B.A., UCLA, 1950; Ph.D., U. Calif. at Berkeley, 1954. Mem. staff Am. Mus. Natural History, N.Y.C., 1954-89, chmn. curator dept. herpetology, 1968-80, curator emeritus, 1989—; sci. attaché Gondwana, 1974-75. Served with AUS, 1945-46. Mem. Soc. Study Evolution, Am. Soc. Ichthyologists and Herpetologists. Home: PO Box 354 Portal AZ 85632-0354

ZWEIG, GEORGE, physicist, neurobiologist; b. Moscow, May 20, 1937; came to U.S., 1938; s. Alfred and Rachael (Frölich) Z. BS in Math., U. Mich., 1959; PhD in Physics, Calif. Inst. Tech., 1963. NAS-NRC fellow European Orgn. for Nuclear Rsch., Geneva, 1963-64; asst. prof. physics Calif. Inst. Tech., Pasadena, 1964-66, assoc. prof., 1966-67, prof., 1967-83; staff mem. Los Alamos (N.Mex.) Nat. Lab., 1981-85, fellow, 1985—; founder, pres. Signition, Inc., Los Alamos, 1985—; vis. prof. physics U. Wis., Madison, 1967-68; mem. Jason div. Inst. for Def. Analysis, Arlington, Va., 1965-72. Recipient MacArthur prize MacArthur Found., 1981, Disting. Alumnus award Calif. Inst. Tech., 1984; Alfred P. Sloan Found. fellow in physics, 1966-74, in neurobiology, 1974-78. Mem. IEEE, AAAS, NAS, Am. Math. Soc., Am. Phys. Soc., Assn. for Rsch. in Otolaryngology. Discoverer quarks, 1963; creator continuous wavelet transform for signal processing, 1975, active model of cochlear mechanics, 1987. Office: LANL MS B276 PO Box 1663 Los Alamos NM 87544-0600

ZWEIGENTHAL, GAIL, magazine editor; b. N.Y.C., Feb. 27, 1944; d. Joseph and Bessie (Lang) Z. B.A., Tufts U., 1965. Editorial asst. Gourmet mag., N.Y.C., then assoc. editor, sr. editor, mng. editor, exec. editor, now editor in chief. Office: Gourmet Mag 560 Lexington Ave New York NY 10022-6828

ZWEIMAN, BURTON, physician, scientist, educator; b. N.Y.C., June 7, 1931; s. Charles and Gertrude (Levine) Z.; m. Claire Traig, Dec. 30, 1962; children: Amy Beth, Diane Susan. AB, U. Pa., 1952, MD, 1956. Diplomate Am. Bd. Internal Medicine, Am. Bd. Allergy & Immunology. Intern Mt. Sinai Hosp., N.Y.C.; Hosp. U. Pa., Bellevue Hosp. Ctr. Hosp. U. Pa., Bellevue Hosp. Center, 1957-60; fellow NYU Sch. Medicine, 1960-61; mem. faculty dept. medicine U. Pa. Sch. Medicine, Phila., 1963—; prof. medicine, chief allergy and immunology divsn. U. Pa. Sch. Medicine, 1975—; cons. U.S. Army, NIH; co-chmn. Am. Bd. Allergy and Immunology, 1979-81. Editor Jour. Allergy Clin. Immunology, 1988-93; contbr. articles to med. jours. Served with M.C., USNR, 1961-63. Allergy Found. Am. fellow, 1959-61. Fellow ACP, Am. Acad. Allergy, Asthma and Immunology (past pres.); mem. Am. Assn. Immunologists, Am. Fedn. Clin. Rsch., Phi Beta Kappa, Alpha Omega Alpha. Office: U Pa Sch Medicine 512 Johnson Pavilion 36th and Hamilton Walk Philadelphia PA 19104

ZWERDLING, ALEX, English educator; b. Breslau, Germany, June 21, 1932; came to U.S., 1941, naturalized, 1946; s. Norbert and Fanni (Alt) Z.; m. Florence Goldberg, Mar. 23, 1969; 1 son, Antony Daniel. B.A., Cornell U., 1953; postgrad. (Fulbright scholar), U. Munich, Germany, 1953-54; M.A., Princeton U., 1956, Ph.D., 1960. Instr. English Swarthmore Coll., 1957-61; asst. prof. English U. Calif., Berkeley, 1961-67; asso. prof. U. Calif., 1967-73, prof., 1973-86; prof. English U. Calif., Berkeley, 1988—; chmn. grad. studies U. Calif., 1985-86; univ. prof. George Washington U., 1986-88; vis. prof. Northwestern U., 1977; dir. edn. abroad program U. Calif., London, 1996—; mem. advanced placement exam. com. Ednl. Testing Svc., 1975-79; mem. fellowship panel Nat. Endowment for Humanities, 1977-82, 84-87, Nat. Humanities Ctr., 1989-90; fellow Ctr. for Advanced Study in Behavioral Scis., 1964-65. Author: Yeats and the Heroic Ideal, 1965, Orwell and the Left, 1974, Virginia Woolf and the Real World, 1986; mem. adv. com. PMLA, 1978-82. Am. Coun. Learned Socs. fellow, 1964-65; NEH fellow, 1973-74; Guggenheim fellow, 1977-78; Woodrow Wilson Ctr. fellow, 1991-92, fellow Nat. Humanities Ctr., 1992-93. Mem. MLA (chmn. 20th Century Brit. lit. div. 1969-70, 85-86). Office: U Calif Dept English Berkeley CA 94720

ZWERDLING, DAVID MARK, psychiatrist; b. Detroit, Jan. 13, 1944; s. Joseph and Alice (Granoff) Z.; m. Martha A. Teitelbaum, May 29, 1977; children: Celia T., Maury T. (dec.), JoLillian T. BA, Harvard U., 1965; JD, U. Chgo., 1969; MD, Yale U., 1975. Bd. cert. psychiatry and child/adolscent psychiatry. Asst. clin. prof. psychiatry George Washington U., Washington, 1980—; assoc. staff Childrens Nat. Med. Ctr., Washington, 1980—; psychiatrist child, adolscent and adult pvr. ptactice, Silver Spring, Md., 1980—; staff psychiatrist Cmty. Psychiat. Clinic, Inc., Montgomery County, Md., 1980-88, med. dir. Wheaton office, 1988-93, med. dir., 1993—; mem. adv. bd. Ctr. for Divorcing Families, Inc., Rockville, Md., 1990-93. Author: (with others) Psychiatric House Calls, 1988. Pres. Forest Glen Park Citizens Assn., Silver Spring, 1983, 84; mem. Zwerdling Meml. Program Social Justice com. Temple Sinai, Washington. Mem. Am. Psychiat. Assn., Am. Acad. Child/Adolscent Psychiatry. Office: CPC Health Corp 2424 Reedie Dr Silver Spring MD 20902-4652

ZWERLING, GARY LESLIE, investment bank executive; b. N.Y.C., Aug. 6, 1949; s. Seymour Joseph and Evelyn Rhoda (Posner) Z.; m. Marierose Miraglia, Aug. 25, 1974; children: Cara Marisa, Craig Harris. BEngring., SUNY, Stony Brook, 1970; MBA, SUNY, Albany, 1972. V.p. Chase Manhattan Bank, N.Y.C., 1972-78; ptnr. Goldman, Sachs & Co., N.Y.C., 1978—. Mem. N.Y. One to One Sponsoring Group; bd. overseers, mem. Heritage Soc. of A Living Meml. to the Holocaust-Mus. Jewish Heritage; trustee Jewish Fedn. North Jersey. Mem. Thoroughbred Owners and Breeders Assn. Jewish. Avocation: skiing. Office: Goldman Sachs & Co 85 Broad St New York NY 10004-2434

ZWERLING, LEONARD JOSEPH, physician, educator; b. Bklyn., May 15, 1944; s. David Louis and Ray (Mooney) Z.; m. Holly Gail Margolin, June 4, 1972; children: Jared, Margo. BA, Columbia Coll., 1965; MD cum laude, Boston U., 1969. Diplomate Am. Bd. Internal Medicine, Am. Bd. Cardiovascular Disease. Intern Mt. Sinai Hosp., N.Y.C., 1969-70, resident, 1970-72; fellow cardiology Beth Israel Hosp., Boston, 1972-73, Mass. Gen. Hosp., Boston, 1975-76; pvt. practice Cardiovasc. Medicine Assocs., P.A., Miami, Fla., 1976—; clinical fellow medicine Harvard, 1972-76; staff assoc. medicine MIT Arteriosclerosis Ctr., 1975-76; clin. asst. prof. medicine U. Miami Med. Sch., 1976-83, clin. assoc. prof., 1983-91, clin. prof., 1991—; active staff, bd. dirs., pres. med. staff, chief of medicine, chmn. cardiology echocardiography coms., chmn. instl. rev. bd., mem. intensive care, emergency and ethics coms., med. dir. home health care svcs. South Miami Hosp.; co-chmn., med. leadership coun. Bapt. Health Sys.; mem. Miami Vasc. Inst.; active Staff Bapt. Hosp.; cons. HealthSouth Larkin and Doctors Hosp. Author: (chpt.) Recent Advances in Studies on Cardiac Structure and metabolism, Vol. 5, Basic Functions of Cations in Mycardial Activity, 1975, The Care of the Post MI Patient, 1986. Lt. USNR, 1973-75. Recipient Boston Women's Club award, 1969, Maimonides award Boston Medical Soc., 1969; Univ. Hosp. Award Begg HoverSoc. Fellow ACP, Am. Coll. Cardiology, Am. Heart Assn. (coun. clin. cardiology); mem. Alpha Omega Alpha. Home: 8300 Cheryl Ave Miami FL 33143 Office: Cardiovasc Medicine Assoc PA 6200 SW 73rd St # 210 South Miami FL 33143-4955

ZWERVER, PETER JOHN, linguistics educator; b. Grouw, Friesland, The Netherlands, Sept. 3, 1942; came to U.S., 1959; m. Margot Anne Otters, July 16, 1978. AA in Fgn. Langs., Cerritos Coll., 1963; BA in German and English, Calif. State U., Long Beach, 1963; MA in Edn., Azusa Pacific U., 1971; PhD in Edn., Pacific Western U., 1980; PhD in Linguistics, Clayton U., 1988; BS in Liberal Studies, SUNY, Albany, 1989; BA in Archtl. Arts, Clayton U., 1995. Cert. standard elem., jr. high sch. and gen. secondary tchr., Calif.; cert. in standard supervision and adminstrv. svcs. grades kindergarten through 12, Calif. Tchr. math. and woodworking Monrovia (Calif.) Unified Sch. Dist., 1966—; assoc. prof. applied linguistics Pacific Western U., L.A., 1984-92, prof., 1992—; v.p. adminstrv. svcs. Am. M & N U., Metairie, La., 1993—; fellow in community arts and architecture Am. Coastline U., New Orleans, 1989; mem. acad. adv. coun. Pacific Western U., 1984—; chmn. acad. coun. Am. Coastline U., 1988—. Editor jour. Internat. Inst. for Ind. Scholarship, Pacific Western U., 1983-87; contbg. author: Poetic Voices of America, 1993; columnist Foothill Inter-City Newspapers, 1983-86. Pres. Monroe Sch. PTA, 1975, Santa Anita Family Svc., Monrovia, 1982, Arcadian Christian Sch., Arcadia, Calif., 1974. Recipient Hon. Svc. award Nat. Congress of Parents and Tchrs., 1976. Mem. NEA, Nat. Assn. Scholars, Calif. Tchrs. Assn., Monrovia Tchrs. Assn., Doctorate Assn. N.Y. Educators, Phi Beta Kappa, Phi Delta Kappa (rsch. rep. U. So. Calif. chpt. 1990-91, Rsch. award 1987, Intrnat. Svc. Key, 1993). Avocations: woodworking, attending concerts, museums, architecture, reading.

ZWICK, BARRY STANLEY, newspaper editor, speechwriter; b. Cleve., July 21, 1942; s. Alvin Albert and Selma Davidovna (Makofsky) Z.; m. Roberta Joan Yaffe, Mar. 11, 1972; children: Natasha Yvette, Alexander Anatol. BA in Journalism, Ohio State U., 1963; MS in Journalism, Columbia U., 1965. Copy editor Phila. Inquirer, 1964; night news editor Detroit Free Press, 1965-67; West Coast editor L.A. Times/Washington Post News Svc, 1967-77; makeup editor L.A. Times, 1978—; adj. prof. U. So. Calif., L.A., 1975-77. Author: Hollywood Tanning Secrets, 1980. NEH profl. journalism fellow Stanford U., 1977-78. Jewish. Avocations: photography, jet skiing, snowmobiling. Office: LA Times Times Mirror Sq Los Angeles CA 90012

ZWICK, EDWARD M., director, producer, scriptwriter; b. Chgo., Oct. 8, 1952; s. Allen and Ruth Ellen (Reich) Z.; m. Lynn Liberty Godshall, Oct. 24, 1982. BA, Harvard U., 1974; MFA, Am. Film Inst., 1976. Editor, feature writer The New Republic, Rolling Stone, 1972-74; co-founder The Bedford Falls Co. Writer, prodr., dir.: (TV series) Family, 1976-80 (Humanitas prize 1980), (TV spl.) Spl. Bull., 1983 (Emmy award for outstanding drama spl. 1983, Dir. Guild award 1983, Writers Guild award 1983, Humanitas prize 1983); dir.: (TV movies) Paper Dolls, 1982, Having It All, 1982, Extreme Close-Up, 1990, (films) About Last Night, 1986, Glory, 1989, Leaving Normal, 1992, Legends of the Fall, 1994, Courage Under Fire, 1995; co-creator, exec. prodr.: (with Marshall Herskovitz) Thirtysomething, 1987-91 (Emmy award for outstanding drama series 1988), Dream Street, 1989, My So-Called Life, 1994-95, Relativity, 1996-97; author: Literature and Liberalism, 1975. Office: ICM 8942 Wilshire Blvd Beverly Hills CA 90211-1934

ZWIEP, DONALD NELSON, mechanical engineering educator, administrator; b. Hull, Iowa, Mar. 18, 1924; s. Daniel and Nellie (De Stigter) Z.; m. Marcia J. Hubers, Sept. 3, 1948; children: Donna J., Mary N., Joan L., Helen D. BSME, Iowa State Coll., 1948, MSME, 1951; DEng (hon.), Worcester Polytech. Inst., 1965. Registered profl. engr., Mass. Design engr. Boeing Airplane Co., 1948-50, sr. tool engr., summer 1953, summer faculty asso., 1955; asst. prof. Colo. State U., 1951-56, assoc. prof., 1956-57; cons. engr. aviation div. Forney Mfg. Co., 1956-57; prof., head dept. mech. engring. Worcester Polytech. Inst., 1957-88, acting head mgmt. engring., 1974-76, chmn. Mfg. Engring. Application Ctr., 1981-88, acting provost, v.p. acad. affairs, 1988-90, prof., dept. head emeritus, 1990—; constrn. engr. U.S. C.E., summer 1954; cons. engr., acting chief engr. J.J. Maier, Inc., summer 1956. Chmn. bd. trustees James F. Lincoln Arc Welding Found., 1976—. Served as pilot USAAF, World War II, CBI; lt. col. USAFR; cons. and ednl. specialist. Fellow ASME (life, v.p. edn. 1972-74, pres. 1979-80); mem. Am. Soc. Engring. Edn. (life, pres. Colo. State U. chpt. 1954-55, treas. Rocky Mountain sect. 1955, nat. bd. dirs. 1974-75), Am. Assn. Engring. Socs. (chair coun. pre-coll. edn.), Am. Welding Soc., Soc. Mfg. Engrs., Torch Club, Sigma Xi, Omicron Delta Kappa, Tau Beta Pi, Sigma Tau, Pi Tau Sigma. Methodist. Home: 47 Birchwood Dr Holden MA 01520-1937 Office: Worcester Poly Inst 100 Institute Rd Worcester MA 01609-2247

ZWILICH, ELLEN TAAFFE, composer; b. Miami, Fla., Apr. 30, 1939; d. Edward Porter and Ruth (Howard) Taaffe; m. Joseph Zwilich, June 22, 1969 (dec. June 1979). MusB, Fla. State U., 1960, MusM, 1962; D Mus. Arts, Juilliard Sch., 1975; studies with Roger Sessions and Elliott Carter; MusD (hon.), Oberlin Coll., 1987, Converse Coll., 1994; LHD (hon.), Manhattanville Coll., 1991, Marymount Manhattan Coll., 1994, N.Y. New Sch., Mannes, 1995. Composer in residence Santa Fe Chamber Music Festival, 1990, Am. Acad. Rome, 1990; first Composer's Chair, Carnegie Hall, 1995. Premiere, Symposium for Orch., Pierre Boulez, N.Y.C., 1975, Chamber Symphony and Passages, Boston Musica Viva, Richard Pittman, 1979, 82. Symphony 1, Gunther Schuller, Am. Composers Orch., 1982; violinist Am. Symphony, N.Y.C., 1965-73; composer: Sonata in Three Movements, 1973-74; String Quartet, 1974; Clarino Quartet, 1977; Chamber Symphony, 1979; Passages (for Soprano and Chamber Ensemble), 1981; String Trio, 1982; Symphony 1:3 Movements for Orch., 1982 (Grammy nomination New World Records, 1987); Divertimento, 1983; Einsame Nacht, 1971; Emlekezet, 1978; Im Nebel, 1972; Passages for Soprano and Orch., 1982; Trompeten, 1974; Fantasy for Harpsichord, 1983; Intrada, 1983; Prologue and Variations, 1983; Double Quartet for Strings, Chamber Music Soc. of Lincoln Ctr., 1984; Celebration for Orch., Indpls. Symphony, John Nelson, 1984; Symphony #2 (Cello Symphony) San Francisco Symphony, Edo De Waart, 1985, Symphony #2 Louisville Orch. recording, L.L. Smith (Grammy nomination 1991); Concerto Grosso 1985, Handel Festival Orch., Steven Simon, 1986; Concerto for Piano and Orch., Detroit Symphony, Gunther Herbig, Marc-André Hamelin, 1986; Images for 2 Pianos and Orch., Nat. Symphony Orch., F. Machetti, 1987; Tanzspiel, Peter Martins N.Y.C. Ballet, 1987; Praeludium Boston chpt. AGO, 1987; Trio for piano, violin and cello; Kalichstein, Laredo, Robinson trio, 1987; Symbolon, Zubin Mehta and the N.Y. Philharm., Leningrad and Moscow (USSR), N.Y.C. (Koussevitsky Internat. Rec. award nominee 1990), 1988; concerto for trombone and orch. J. Friedman, Sir Georg Solti, Chgo. Symphony, 1989, concerto for trombone and orch. Christian Lindberg, James De Priest, Malmö Symphony, concerto for flute and orch. D.A. Dwyer, Seija Ozawa, Boston Symphony, 1990, quintet for clarinet and string quartet David Schiffrin, Chamber Music N.W., 1990; concerto for oboe and orch. John Mack, Christoph von Dohnanyi, Cleve. Orch., 1991; concerto for bass trombone strings, timpani and cymbals Chgo. Symphony Orch. Ch. Vernon, Daniel Barenboim, 1991; concerto for violin, violoncello and orch. Jaime Laredo, Sharon Robinson, Louisville Orch., L. Smith, 1991; Immigrant Voices Peter Leonard, St. Lukes Orch., N.Y. Internat. Festival ot the Arts Chorus, Ellis Island, 1991, concerto for flute and orch, D.A. Dwyer, J. Sedares, London Symphony Orch., 1992, Symphony # 3 (Grammy nominee 1993), J. Ling, N.Y. Philharmonic, 1993, concerto for bassoon and orch., Nancy Goeres, Lorin Maazel, Pitts. Symphony, 1993, concerto for horn and string Orch., David Jolley, Rochester Philharm., L.L. Smith., 1993, Fantasy for Orch., JoAnn Falletta, Long Beach Symphony Orch., 1994, American Concerto Doc Severinsen, J. Falletta San Diego Symphony, 1994, A Simple Magnificat, 1994, Triple Concerto Kauchstein, Laredo, Robinson Trio Zdenek Macal, Minn. Orch., 1996; New World Records: Music By Ellen Taaffe Zwilich; N.Y. Philharm. conducted by Zubin Mehta. Recipient Elizabeth Sprague Coolidge Chamber Music prize, 1974, Gold medal G.B. Viotti, Vercelli, Italy, 1975, citation Ernst von Dohnanyi, 1981, Pulitzer prize, 1983, Composers award Lancaster Symphony Orch., Arturo Toscanini Music Critics award, 1987, Alfred I. DuPont award, 1991; Martha Baird Rockefeller Fund rec. grantee, 1977, 79, 82, Guggenheim fellow, 1981. Mem. AAAL (Acad. award 1984), Am. Fedn. Musicians (hon. life), Am. Music Ctr. (bd. dirs., v.p. 1982-84), BMI Found., MacDowell Colony (bd. dirs.), Fla. Artists Hall of Fame, Carnegie Hall Composer's Chair. Home: 600 W 246th St Bronx NY 10471-3611 Office: care Music Assocs Am 224 King St Englewood NJ 07631-3026

ZWINGE, RANDALL JAMES HAMILTON See RANDI, JAMES

ZWISLOCKI, JOZEF JOHN, neuroscience educator, researcher; b. Lwow, Poland, Mar. 19, 1922; came to U.S., 1951; s. Tadeusz and Helena (Moscicki) Z.; m. Ruth Gerber, Oct. 29, 1945 (div. May 1954); m. Sylvia Claire Goldman, July 11, 1954 (dec. July 17, 1992); m. Jadwiga M. Morrison, Dec. 2, 1993. Diploma, Fed. Tech. Inst., Zurich, Switzerland, 1944, Sc.D., 1948; D. honoris causa, U. Adam Mickiewicz, Poznán, Poland, 1991. Head electroacoustic lab. dept. otolaryngology U. Basel, Switzerland, 1945-51; research fellow psychoacoustic lab. Harvard U., Cambridge, Mass., 1951-57; dir. Bioacoustic Lab. Syracuse U., N.Y., 1958-63, founder, dir. Lab. of Sensory Communication, 1963-73, founder dir. Inst. for Sensory Research, 1973-84, prof. neurosci., 1984-88, Disting. prof. neurosci., 1988-92; Disting. rsch. prof. Inst. for Sensory Rsch. Syracuse U., 1992, prof. communicative disorders dept. spl. edn. Sch. Edn., 1982-92; research prof. SUNY Health Sci. Ctr. at Syracuse, 1967—; affiliate prof. bioengring. L.C. Smith Coll. Engring., Syracuse U., 1986-92; Carhart Meml. lectr. Am. Auditory Soc., 1992; mem. exec. coun. Com. Hearing, Bioacoustics and Biomechanics, NRC, Washington, 1965-68, chmn., 1967-68; mem. rev. panel on communicative scis. NIH, Bethesda, Md., 1966-70, chmn., 1969-70; mem. Communicative Disorders Program Project rev. com. NIH, Bethesda, 1971-75; chmn. Bd. Sci. Advs. Ctr. Health Scis., U. Wis., Madison, 1975-78. Inventor acoustic ear simulator, acoustic bridge, several types of ear defenders; contbr. articles to profl. jours. Recipient Faculty Research award Syracuse chpt. Sigma Xi, 1973, Internat. Ctr. Ricerche e Studi Amplifon prize, 1976, Chancellor's citation, Syracuse U., 1980, Javits Neurosci. Investigator award NIH, 1984, Kwiek medal Acoustics Inst., A. Mickiewicz U., Poland, 1991, medal Acoustical Soc. Poland, 1991, Hugh Knowles prize Northwestern U., 1992. Fellow Acoustical Soc. Am. (chmn. tech. com. on psychol. and physiol. acoustics 1962, 63, exec. coun. 1982-85, recipient 1st Bekesy medal 1985, chmn. long-range planning com. 1983-86, nominating com. 1986-87, mem. com. on tutorials 1988-91, com. on meetings 1988-91, chmn. spring meeting, 1989), Am. Speech and Hearing Assn., The Polish Inst. of Arts and Scis. of Am.; mem. NAS, Internat. Soc. Audiology (v.p. 1967-72), Internat. Union of Physiol. Scis. (commn. on auditory physiology 1982-89), Internat. Union Pure and Applied Physics (Commn. on Acoustics 1982-89), Collegium Oto Rhino Laryngologicum Amicitiae Sacrum, Assn. for Research in Otolaryngology (award of merit 1988), Hearing Research (edit. bd.), Drumlins Tennis Club. Avocations: skiing, tennis, trout fishing, inventions.

ZWOYER, EUGENE MILTON, consulting engineering executive; b. Plainfield, N.J., Sept. 8, 1926; s. Paul Ellsworth and Marie Susan (Britt) Z.; m. Dorothy Lucille Seward, Feb. 23, 1946; children: Gregory, Jeffrey, Douglas. Student, U. Notre Dame, 1944, Mo. Valley Coll., 1944-45; BS, U. N.Mex., 1947; MS, Ill. Inst. Tech., 1949; PhD, U. Ill., 1953. Mem. faculty U. N.Mex., Albuquerque, 1948-71, prof. civil engring., dir. Eric Wang Civil Engring. Rsch. Facility, 1961-70; rsch. assoc. U. Ill., Urbana, 1951-53; owner, cons. engr. Eugene Zwoyer & Assocs., Albuquerque, 1954-72; exec. dir., sec. ASCE, N.Y.C., 1972-82; pres. Am. Assn. Engring. Socs., N.Y.C., 1982-84; exec. v.p. T.Y. Lin Internat., San Francisco, 1984-86, pres., 1986-89; owner Eugene Zwoyer Cons. Engr., 1989—; chief oper. officer, treas. Polar Molecular Corp., Saginaw, Mich., 1990, exec. v.p., 1991-92. Trustee Small Bus. Research Corp., 1976-80; trustee Engring. Info., Inc., 1981-84; internat. trustee People-to-People Internat. 1974-86; v.p. World Fedn. Engring. Orgns., 1982-85. Served to lt. (j.g.) USN, 1944-46. Named Outstanding Engr. of Yr. Albuquerque chpt. N.Mex Soc. Profl. Engrs., 1969, One Who Served the Best Interests of the Constrn. Industry, Engring. News Record, 1980; recipient Disting. Alumnus award the Civil Engring. Alumni Assn. at U. Ill., 1979, Disting. Alumnus award Engring. Coll. Alumni Assn., U. N.Mex., 1982, Can.-Am. Civil Engring. Amity award Am. Soc. Civil Engrs., 1988, Award for Outstanding Profl. Contbns. and Leadership Coll. Engring. U. N.Mex., 1989. Mem. AAAS, ASCE (dist. bd. dirs. 1968-71), NSPE, Am. Soc. Engring. Edn., Am. Concrete Inst., Nat. Acad. Code Adminstrn. (trustee, mem. exec. com. 1973-79), Engrs. Joint Coun. (bd. dirs. 1978-79), Engring. Soc. Commn. on Energy (bd. dirs. 1977-82), Sigma Xi, Sigma Tau, Chi Epsilon. Home: 6363 Christie Ave Apt 1326 Emeryville CA 94608-1940 Office: 1172 San Pablo Ave Ste 200C Berkeley CA 94706-2258

ZYCHICK, JOEL DAVID, lawyer; b. Cleve., June 23, 1954; s. Eugene K. and Myra (Rotblatt) Z.; m. Evelyn Blake. BBA, George Washington U., 1976; JD, Case Western Res. U., 1979; LLM in Taxation, NYU, 1979. Bar: Ohio 1979, N.Y. 1985, D.C. 1985, U.S. Tax Ct. 1980, U.S. Ct. Claims 1980, U.S. Ct. Appeals (fed. cir.) 1982. Assoc. Jones, Day, Reavis & Pogue, Cleve., 1980-83, Milbank, Tweed, Hadley & McCloy, N.Y.C., 1983-85; counsel Hertzog, Calamari & Gleason, N.Y.C., 1986—; pres., CEO Getko Group, Inc., N.Y.C.; sec. InnoTech, Inc., Va.; gen. counsel RF Internat. Ltd., N.Y.C.; participating dir. mgmt. decision lab. NYU; dir. Northside Ctr. for Child Devel., Inc.; contbg. author and spkr. on tax topics. Dir. Northside Ctr. for Child Devel., N.Y.C. Mem. ABA (mem. tax sect., nominating com., former chmn. sales and fin. transactions com., vice-chmn. regulations com. govt. submissions), N.Y. State Bar Assn. Avocations: hiking, music, traveling. Home: 233 E 86th St New York NY 10028-3087 Office: Hertzog Calamari & Gleason 100 Park Ave New York NY 10017-5516

ZYLIS-GARA, TERESA GERARDA, soprano; b. Landwarow, Poland, Jan. 23, 1935; married; 1 child. Student conservatories. singing-master Maurice Ravel's Music Acad., St. Jean - de Luz, France, 1990—. Debut, Cracow, Glyndebourne (Eng.) Opera, 1965, Paris Opera, 1966, San Francisco Opera, Met. Opera, 1968, Salzburg (Austria) Festival, leading soprano, Deutsche Opera am Rhein, appearances with, Vienna Staatsopera, Royal Opera House-Covent Garden, London, Munich (W.Ger.) Staatsoper, Hamburg (W.Ger.) Staatsoper, La Scala, Milan, Italy, also opera houses of Berlin, Brussels, Paris, San Francisco and Chgo., Teatro Colon, Buenos Aires, Bolshoi-Moscow, soprano soloist with, Boston Symphony Orch., N.Y. Philharm. Orch., Los Angeles Philharm., Cleve. Orch., guest artist on radio and TV in, Europe and U.S.; rec. artist: Angel, Deutsche Grammophon and, Seraphim records; prin. roles in: Il Trovatore; Un Ballo in: Maschera; Desdemona in: Otello; Marschallin in: Der Rosenkavalier; also title role in: Tosca. Winner contest Assn. German Broadcasters, Internat. Singing Competition, Munich, 1960; recipient Prime Minister's prize, 1979, Mozart gold medal, Mexico City, Polish Nat. award. Fellow Kosciuszko Found., Frederic Chopin Found. Address: 16A Blvd de Belgigue, Monaco Monaco *L'artiste face a l'oeuvre est comme le roseau dans le vent: c'est lui qui doit plier. La musique est l'expression universelle de l'ame d'un peuple.*

ZYLSTRA, STANLEY JAMES, farmer, food company executive; b. Hull, Iowa, Dec. 18, 1943; s. Jerald S. and Dora (Te Slaa) Z.; m. Ruth Eileen Van Batavia, Jan. 3, 1964; children: Rachel Ann, Carl Dean. BA, Northwestern Coll., 1965; MA, Univ. S.D., 1969. Math tchr., counselor Boyden-Hull Sch., 1965-73; farmer Hull, 1970—; dir. Land O'Lakes, Mpls., 1985—, chmn. bd. dirs., 1988—. Mem. Kiwanis (pres. 1974-75). Republican. Mem. Reformed Church in America. Home: 2974 Ibex Ave Hull IA 51239-9801 Office: Land O'Lakes Inc 4001 Lexington Ave N Saint Paul MN 55126-2934

ZYROFF, ELLEN SLOTOROFF, information scientist, classicist, educator; b. Atlantic City, N.J., Aug. 1, 1946; d. Joseph George and Sylvia Beverly (Roth) Slotoroff; m. Jack Zyroff, June 21, 1970; children: Dena Rachel, David Aaron. AB, Barnard Coll., 1968; MA, The Johns Hopkins U., 1969, PhD, 1971; MS, Columbia U., 1973. Instr. The Johns Hopkins U., Balt., 1970-71, Yeshiva U., N.Y.C., 1971-72; Bklyn Coll., 1971-72; libr. instr. U. Calif., 1979, 81, 91, San Diego State U., 1981-85, 94; prof. San Diego Mesa Coll., 1981—; dir. The Reference Desk Rsch. Svcs., La Jolla, Calif., 1983—; prin. libr. San Diego County Libr., 1985—; v.p. Archaeol. Soc. Am., Balt., 1970-71. Author: The Author's Apostrophe in Epic from Homer Through Lucan, 1971, Cooperative Library Instruction for Maximum Benefit, 1989; contbr. articles to profl. jours. Pres. Women's Am. ORT, San Diego, 1979-81. Mem. ALA (chair divsn. coms. 1982—), Am. Philol. Assn., Calif. Libr. Assn. (elected to assembly 1993-95, 96—), Am. Soc. Info. Sci., Am. Classical League, Libr. Congress Cataloging in Publ. Adv. Group, Toastmasters, Beta Phi Mu. Office: PO Box 12122 La Jolla CA 92039-2122

ZYTKOW, JAN MIKOLAJ, computer science educator; b. Warsaw, Sept. 9, 1944; came to U.S., 1982; s. Swiatozar Mikolaj and Maria (Szeruda) Z.; m. Malgorzata Krzywińska, Oct. 14, 1972; children: Nikola, Ania, Andrzej, Michael. MS in Theoretical Physics, U. Warsaw, 1967, MA in Philosophy, 1970, PhD in Philosophy Sci., 1972, habilitation docent, 1979. Asst. prof. U. Warsaw, 1972-80, assoc. prof., 1981-82; vis. prof. Carnegie-Mellon U., Pitts., 1982-84; assoc. prof. Wichita (Kans.) State U., 1984-87, prof., 1987—, computer sci. chmn., 1996—. Author: (with others) Scientific Discovery, 1987; contbr. articles to profl. jours. Mem. Am. Assn. Artificial Intelligence, Philosophy Sci. Assn. Lutheran. Home: 3636 Armstrong St Wichita KS 67204-3922 Office: Wichita State U. Computer Sci Dept Wichita KS 67260

ZYWICKI, ROBERT ALBERT, electrical distribution company executive; b. Chgo., Sept. 23, 1930; s. Martin Albert and Margaret Irene (Mackowski) Z.; m. Barbara Joan Hagerty; children: Robert, Cheryl, Cindy, Carrie. B in Commerce, Northwestern U., 1966. Teller Chgo. Title and Trust Bank, Chgo., 1949-50; painter Getz Molding Co., Chgo., 1950-51; purchasing agt. Woodworker's Tool Works, Chgo., 1953-54; serviceman Addressograph Multigraph, Chgo., 1954-55; mem. Chgo. Fire Dept., 1955-62; v.p. Anixter Bros. Inc., Skokie, Ill., 1955-87; co-owner A-Z Industries, Northbrook, Ill., 1987-92, 1992—. Served as cpl. U.S. Army, 1951-53. Mem. Am. Legion (comdr.). Republican. Roman Catholic. Avocations: thoroughbred horse racing, classical music, baseball card collecting, tennis. Home: 1330 Sprucewood Ln Deerfield IL 60015-4771 *Love your family, respect your friends and co-workers, value your customers and suppliers. Always keep each in its proper perspective. Most of all, remember - love, value and respect are all two-way streets.*